A PATRISTIC GREEK LEXICON

EDITED BY

G. W. H. LAMPE, D.D.

ELY PROFESSOR OF DIVINITY
IN THE UNIVERSITY OF CAMBRIDGE

OXFORD
AT THE CLARENDON PRESS

Oxford University Press, Walton Street, Oxford OX2 6DP

OXFORD LONDON GLASGOW
NEW YORK TORONTO MELBOURNE WELLINGTON
KUALA LUMPUR SINGAPORE JAKARTA HONG KONG TOKYO
DELHI BOMBAY CALCUTTA MADRAS KARACHI
IBADAN NAIROBI DAR ES SALAAM CAPE TOWN

ISBN 0 19 864213 X

First published 1961
Fifth impression 1978

Printed in Great Britain
at the University Press, Oxford
by Vivian Ridler
Printer to the University

PREFACE

I

THE project for a Lexicon of Patristic Greek was originally suggested by the Central Society for Sacred Study in the year 1906, when its Warden was Dr. H. B. Swete, then Regius Professor of Divinity at Cambridge. Within three years some eighty clergymen and others interested in patristic study, led by Canon Herbert Moore, then Rector of Acton, Cheshire, had been invited to read the appropriate volumes of Migne's *Patrologia Graeca* and certain other texts and to assemble material for the work. Canon Moore himself continued, until his death in 1942, to devote his leisure to the collection and transcription of great quantities of slips, and there can be little doubt that but for his energy and perseverance the idea conceived by Dr. Swete would never have been carried out. At about the same time a 'Committee of Direction' was formed, consisting of Dr. Swete himself with Dr. A. J. Mason and Dr. J. H. Srawley at Cambridge, and Dr. T. B. Strong, Dr. William Sanday, and Dr. C. H. Turner at Oxford. It was not, however, until 1915 that the Committee found it possible to appoint an editor, Dr. Darwell Stone, Principal of Pusey House, Oxford, who continued to direct the work until his death in 1941.

In the meantime plans for a new edition of Liddell and Scott had begun to take shape, and its editor, Sir Henry Stuart Jones, had decided to exclude all post-biblical Christian writers from the scope of the work. It thus became clear that, although the aim and methods of the Patristic Lexicon had not yet been precisely determined, it would certainly have to form a supplement, or companion, to the ninth edition of Liddell and Scott, and on that basis the interest of the Delegates of the Oxford University Press was attracted to the project. Thus in the year 1925 Sir Henry Stuart Jones in his Preface explained the relation between the two works:

> Liddell and Scott . . . admitted a number of words from Ecclesiastical and Byzantine writers, for many of which no reference was given except the symbols 'Eccl.' and 'Byz.'. After due consideration it has been decided to exclude both Patristic and Byzantine literature from the purview of the present edition. It would have manifestly been impossible to include more than a small and haphazard selection of words and quotations from these literatures, which would therefore have had to be treated quite differently from the remains of Classical Greek. . . . There is, moreover, in preparation a Lexicon of Patristic Greek (including Christian poetry and inscriptions) under the editorship of Dr. Darwell Stone, which will, it is hoped, be printed when the publication of the present work is concluded.

The fulfilment of this hope has been long delayed. For many years Dr. Darwell Stone worked almost single-handed (though assisted for a time by the Rev. G. L. Marriott and the Rev. F. P. Long as successive sub-editors) at the task of reading texts, receiving and sorting slips sent by Canon Moore and other readers, and writing preliminary drafts of articles on the basis of such material as had by that time been collected. Progress could not, therefore, but be slow. Moreover, since the scope of the work had not been finally determined, it was not clear whether the main concern of the Lexicon was to be linguistic on the one hand, or theological and ecclesiastical on the other, with the natural consequence that whereas most of the readers had been careful to take note of rare words and usages, some of them had omitted to excerpt common theological terms in passages of great importance for the history of patristic thought.

This difficulty had not been fully resolved when, after Dr. Stone's death, the Committee, then under the chairmanship of Dr. N. P. Williams, appointed as Editor Dr. F. L. Cross, then Librarian of Pusey House and subsequently the successor of Dr. Williams in the Lady Margaret Chair of Divinity at Oxford. It had become clear that the primary value of the material so far assembled lay in its interest to students of the development of Christian theological vocabulary and of the ideas which it expressed. A number of published studies, based upon the Lexicon slips, afforded positive evidence that this was the case.[1] The Committee accordingly decided

[1] These include studies by Dr. G. L. Prestige, who spent several years in making a special study of certain doctrinal words for the Lexicon: 'ἀγέν(ν)ητος and γεν(ν)ητός and kindred words, in Eusebius and the early Arians', *JTS* xxiv (1923), pp. 486–96; 'Hades in the Greek Fathers', ibid., pp. 476–85; 'περιχωρέω and περιχώρησις in the Fathers', *JTS* xxix (1928), pp. 242–52; 'Clement of Alexandria, *Stromata* 2. 18, and the meaning of "Hypostasis" ', *JTS* xxx

that the work should be more than a mere supplement to Liddell and Scott. It was, however, plainly impossible to consider the production of an encyclopedic theological dictionary, on the lines of Kittel's *Theologisches Wörterbuch zum Neuen Testament,* to cover the vast range of patristic literature. The object of the work was therefore defined as the provision of as full treatment as possible of all words of special theological or ecclesiastical significance, and, at the same time, the listing of all words occurring in the Fathers which were either not contained in Liddell Scott–Jones or but poorly attested there (such as those cited only from glossaries). With this object in view, new readers were recruited for the study of those texts, particularly the more recently published critical editions, which had not yet been excerpted, a provisional word-list was prepared by Miss H. C. Graef, and a preliminary draft of the list of authors was compiled by the Rev. B. J. Wigan, who had been appointed to assist Dr. Cross. In 1946 the writing of articles was begun by Miss Graef, Miss M. Grosvenor, and the present Editor who succeeded Dr. Cross in 1948.

Dr. R. H. Lightfoot had become Chairman of an enlarged Committee on the death of Dr. Williams in 1943, and he now devoted much labour to the raising of funds, including many increased contributions from those academic and ecclesiastical bodies and private friends who had supported the work since its early days, in order to make possible the engagement of a larger staff of whole-time assistants. The authorities of the Bodleian Library gave much help to the project in several ways, including the provision of accommodation for the work itself and for the working library which had been built up with the aid of many friends of the Lexicon who lent texts for this purpose. Much reading remained to be done, and the existing material had to be extensively supplemented even when the work of putting it into shape was well advanced. The Editor and his staff have thus found themselves compelled, paradoxically, to work against time in the actual writing of a book whose publication must seem to the general public to have been long delayed. They would have preferred to spend much more time in remedying the deficiencies and imperfections of the Lexicon as it now stands. On the other hand, it seemed their duty rather to bring it forward for publication with the least possible delay, remembering that it is a pioneer work in its particular field (its nearest predecessor is J. C. Suicer's *Thesaurus Ecclesiasticus*, second edition, 1728), and that there is good hope that, like the rude beginnings of other large dictionaries, this Lexicon may be supplemented and corrected by the expert hands of future revisers and editors.

Many helpers have contributed to the writing of articles. Among those who have spent a considerable amount of time on the work have been Mrs. S. Argyle, Dom G. Bainbridge, O.S.B., Dr. J. E. Bickersteth, Mr. J. Bowman, Miss B. Burns, Miss N. Butler-Wright, Miss M. J. Cunningham, Mr. D. Grensted, Miss T. A. Hart, Miss J. M. Hawkins, the Rev. (now Bishop) Basil Krivocheine, Mr. W. Mitchell, Mr. (now Professor) A. Paap, the Rev. (now Professor) K. J. Woollcombe, together with the Editor's original colleagues Miss Graef and Miss Grosvenor.

It is impossible, for reasons of space, for the Editor to express his thanks to all those individuals who have contributed to the work. There have been very many valuable helpers at every stage: those who read texts and sent in slips, particularly the late Mr. E. A. Parker, who devoted most of his time to this work during the last years of his life, those who lent books to the working library, in particular the authorities of Cuddesdon Theological College and Pusey House, the sorters of slips, especially parties of theological students from Wycliffe Hall led by Mr. (now Professor) N. Q. King, and the Editor's helpers in the final stages of the revision of the manuscript and the reading of proofs, particularly Miss Janet Roseveare. Special gratitude is

(1929), pp. 270–2; '*ἀγέν(ν)ητος* and cognate words in Athanasius', *JTS* xxxiv (1933), pp. 258–65; and the detailed account of the theological language of the Fathers embodied in his book, *God and Patristic Thought* (Heinemann, 1936). Other articles of the same kind were published by Dr. Stone: '*Ἀδάμ*', *JTS* xxiv (1923), pp. 473–5; Dr. C. H. Turner: '*χειροτονία, χειροθεσία, ἐπίθεσις χειρῶν*', ibid., pp. 496–504; the Rev. E. C. E. Owen: 'St. Gregory of Nyssa: (1) Vocabulary; (2) Style', *JTS* xxvi (1925), pp. 64–71; '*ἀποτυμπανίζω*, &c.', *JTS* xxx (1929), pp. 259–66; '*δαίμων* and cognate words', *JTS* xxxii (1931), pp. 133–53; '*δόξα* and cognate words', *JTS* xxxiii (1932), pp. 132–50; '*ἐπινοέω, ἐπίνοια*, and allied words', *JTS* xxxv (1934), pp. 368–76; '*ἐπιούσιος*', ibid., pp. 376–80; '*αἰών* and *αἰώνιος*', *JTS* xxxvii (1936), pp. 265–83 and 390–404. The present Editor subsequently published '*βασιλεία τοῦ θεοῦ, βασιλεία Χριστοῦ* in the Greek Fathers', *JTS* xlix (1948), pp. 58–73, and embodied much of the material for *βάπτισμα, σφραγίς*, and related words in *The Seal of the Spirit* (Longmans, 1951).

due to Miss Gvenor for her devoted work, first as a writer and reviser of articles and subsequently as ress reader. Although no 'Sub-Editor' has been officially appointed since the early years oe Lexicon, she has in fact done as much as, or more than, an editor could reasonably ect of a colleague with that title.

The Editorcords his grateful appreciation of the kindness and encouragement which he has received, sommes in circumstances of much difficulty, from the successive Chairmen of the Committee w whom he has had the good fortune to work, Dr. R. H. Lightfoot, Dr. Leonard Hodgson, anDr. E. R. Dodds, and the members of the Committee themselves.

It is, of cose, due to the interest shown in this project, and the wise guidance given to it, by the Secrey to the Delegates and other authorities of the Clarendon Press that it has been brought succsfully to the point of publication. The manuscript of the Lexicon has presented the composi's and readers with quite exceptional difficulties: a very large work consisting in the main of eek citations and written in longhand by different hands of various nationalities, repeatedly rised and corrected by yet other hands, confronted the printer with what might seem to be almost impossible task. The skill and care with which these difficulties have been overcome h been matched by the extraordinary vigilance and accuracy of the Press reader of the page prfs, who has eliminated a great number of minor errors and inconsistencies.

It is notossible to enumerate the many benefactors who have financed this project, or to thank themdividually. From the outset regular subscriptions and single donations have been generouslyiven by Oxford and Cambridge Colleges, Cathedral Chapters, and private individuals. uring the years 1948 to 1955, when a relatively large paid staff had to be maintained, annual gras to the Lexicon were made by Oxford University. Since that time the completion of the worhas been made possible by generous help from the British Academy. Much assistance has een given at various stages by the trustees of the Denyer and Johnson Fund, the Revision Srplus Fund, the Pringle Stewart Fund, and the Hort Memorial Fund, the Jowett Copyrightrustees, the Eric Vincent Educational Trust, and the Committee of Hymns Ancient and Model, to all of whom, as to the Delegates of the Oxford University Press for undertaking the expens of publication, the Committee of the Lexicon and the Editor are deeply grateful.

II

The obct of this work is primarily to interpret the theological and ecclesiastical vocabulary of the Grek Christian authors from Clement of Rome to Theodore of Studium.

These mits are necessarily somewhat arbitrary. They have been drawn with the object of confiningthe Lexicon, as far as possible, to the formative period of the history of Christian thought nd institutions, beginning in the sub-apostolic age (but excluding any works of that period wich are contained in the canon of the New Testament) and embracing the whole era of the Ceeds, the Councils down to the Second Council of Nicaea, and the great doctrinal disputeslown to the Iconoclastic Controversy. The limits are not absolutely rigid. Some works of uncerain date which may be substantially pre-Christian are included, such as the *Confession of Asenth* and the *Testaments of the XII Patriarchs*, and also the *Psalms of Solomon* which admittelly belong to the Judaism of the first century B.C., but which, having been read, it seemed undesirable to exclude, especially since no existing Greek lexicon treats them fully. At the other end of the period some spurious works attributed to such authors as John of Damascus and Theodore of Studium have been included although they are strictly too late in date, as has also the medieval *Christus patiens* traditionally included among the poems of Gregory of Nazianzus.

All words illustrating the development of Christian thought and institutions have been treated as fully as possible, with extensive citations of the more important relevant passages. Thus the articles on such words as φύσις or πρόσωπον are intended to explain the history of the terminology of Trinitarian doctrine and Christology; the organization of the Church and its Ministry is illustrated by the articles on such words as ἀπόστολος, ἐπίσκοπος, and πρεσβύτερος; patristic 'spirituality' by those on θεωρία or εὐχή; worship by the entries dealing with liturgical terms;

and so on. Many common words, of no theological importance in themsel, have been included because they occur in typological or allegorical interpretations of bi:al texts and so may serve to illustrate patristic methods of biblical exegesis; among man thers are such commonplace words as ἵππος, ποταμός, and πούς. A few proper names ha been included because of their importance in theology (e.g. Ἀδάμ) or exegesis (e.g. Βαβυλώι

This method of treatment has the obvious disadvantage that the history oe use of words (lexicography in the proper sense) has to be combined with the history of ological ideas, liturgy, institutions, canon law, and other matters. It should, however, be bo in mind that this method has been deliberately adopted in order to make the project feale. The ideal policy would probably involve the production of two entirely distinct works, lexicon of the language used by the Greek Christian writers on the one hand, and a very lar encyclopedic dictionary of patristic theology on the other. Not only would the latter pably require many volumes, but it is the history of Christian doctrine, worship, and institutis which alone justifies the grouping of the authors with whom the Lexicon is concerned int single class labelled 'patristic'. The authors did not use one peculiar form of the Greek lauage, and it might well be argued that their exclusion from Liddell Scott–Jones was somhat illogical, since the ground for it was their religion rather than their vocabulary. Thus Sysius failed to find a place in Liddell Scott–Jones alongside the other Neoplatonist writers of the riod because he ended his career as a Christian bishop. The Christian authors, judged by the nd of Greek that they wrote, do not form a single homogeneous group. The 'classical' language the Cappadocian Fathers is very different from the vocabulary and style of Malalas or the pular Greek of much of the monastic literature. There is too great a difference between th *Didache* or Clement of Rome, with their strongly 'biblical' language, and such an authos Cyril of Alexandria, to warrant their classification under a single literary label. It is tir place in Christian history which holds them together, and consequently this Lexicon, wch studies their vocabulary in order to interpret their theology and its broad social and ethal implications, is primarily a theological dictionary of the Greek Fathers. It is in that sene that the original title given to this work by Dr. Swete, 'A Lexicon of Patristic Greek' shouldn the first instance, be understood. It is, perhaps, a first step towards the ultimate goal of full-scale theological dictionary of the Fathers in the manner of Kittel's *Theologisches Wörbuch zum Neuen Testament*.

This is to look far ahead. So far as the present work is concerned it must be made ear to the reader that he must not expect to find a *thesaurus* of patristic language or a conrdance to the Greek Fathers. The size of this Lexicon was determined by agreement betweerthe Committee and the Clarendon Press at an early stage in its history. The Press has subequently allowed those limits to be considerably exceeded; but considerations of space have aways had to determine editorial policy, and there could be no question of trying to produce work in which a reader could expect to find every instance of the use by a particular autbr of an important theological term, or information about the use in patristic exegesis of every iportant scriptural text. All that can here be offered is samples of patristic thought and specimes of the way in which biblical words and phrases were interpreted in the homilies and commenaries of the period.

A secondary object of the Lexicon is to give information about all words, whethe of any theological importance or not, which are used by these writers but not included in Liddel Scott–Jones. A very large number of such words are listed here, distinguished in each cas by an asterisk. Words that are only poorly attested in Liddell Scott–Jones or which are ısed by the Fathers with different meanings, or with differences of grammatical usage, also appear, whether or not they are relevant to patristic theology.

The dual object of the Lexicon necessitated the adoption of a format similar to that of Liddell and Scott, to which it is in part a companion. This is not ideally suited to a dictionary whose primary interest is theological, for it usually involves separate treatment for cognate words which, in a purely theological dictionary, would normally be discussed under one heading. The reader must therefore be warned that if, for example, he wishes to study the thought of the

Fathers about the subject of apostleship he will have to turn to the separate articles on ἀποστέλλω, ἀποστολή, ἀποστολικός, and ἀπόστολος. The disadvantages of this method have been mitigated as far as possible by the provision of cross-references between the various articles concerned with a single main subject, and occasionally, where no difference in the actual meaning of the associated words occurs, they are treated together in one article (e.g. εὐχή and προσευχή).

Those articles which trace the history of an idea or an institution are arranged according to the logic of their subject-matter rather than strictly lexicographically. Thus the divisions of such an article correspond to the use of the word in Trinitarian doctrine, Christology, ecclesiology, anthropology, and so on, rather than to the use of the word (if a verb) in the active, middle, and passive voices, transitively or intransitively, &c. Grammatical usage, especially if it is markedly different from that of classical Greek, is illustrated in such articles by the citations rather than by section headings. In the case of 'non-theological' entries the arrangement is more often determined by linguistic considerations.

The relation of this work to Liddell Scott–Jones demands special attention. No word which is well attested in the latter and has no particular interest for the reader of the Fathers is included in this book. The absence of a word must on no account be understood as an indication that it is not used by the patristic authors. In order, too, to make more space available for articles of major interest, the common meanings of any word, already noted by Liddell Scott–Jones, are not repeated here unless they are of significance for patristic study. Thus a common word to which Liddell Scott–Jones devote a long article may appear in this Lexicon with only one, and that an unusual, meaning. It must again on no account be supposed that the ordinary senses of such a word are absent from these authors and have been replaced by another. In all such articles the corresponding entry in Liddell and Scott is, as it were, taken as read and this Lexicon merely adds certain new information to it. The user of this work is, in fact, assumed to have Liddell and Scott by its side.

Limitations of time and space have prevented this Lexicon from taking account of biblical words or usage, except in so far as the writers of the patristic period may illuminate them by their own comments. A word treated here may have already had an interesting history in the Septuagint and the New Testament, but this cannot be described here and the reader must refer to a biblical dictionary for the scriptural antecedents of our subject-matter. Nor can this Lexicon find room for the contribution which contemporary pagan authors, especially in the field of philosophy, would sometimes make to the study of Christian thought, or for reference to the writings of Philo, of which the Fathers, particularly at Alexandria, made so much use. It has had to leave many such studies, and the light which they can throw upon the thought of the Fathers, to other existing and projected dictionaries and encyclopedias, and to confine itself strictly to the field of the Greek Fathers themselves, together with such material from Christian papyri and inscriptions as can help to illustrate their language and ideas. Those writings of the Greek Christian authors which survive only in non-Greek languages have been, for the most part, excluded, although when an article on the use of an important theological term would be seriously incomplete without reference to some work or works of a Greek author which exist only in translation, citations are given from these, preceded by 'cf.'. Such writings include those works of Origen that have come down to us only in the Latin of Rufinus or Jerome, the Latin or other versions of the *Apostolic Tradition* of Hippolytus (cited either in Latin or in English translation from the oriental versions), and Nestorius' *Book of Heraclides* (cited from F. Nau's French translation of the Syriac text).

The List of Authors and Works is not intended as a patrology, but as an indication of those works to which reference is actually made in the Lexicon, and the editions which have been used. Migne's *Patrologia Graeca* has been used in all cases where there is no critical text available, except in the case of certain authors, such as Chrysostom, Cyril of Alexandria, and Theodoret, where older editions, used by Migne, furnish a more accurate text and their book, chapter, and section numbers (where they exist), together with their page numbers, are reproduced by Migne, so that the reader who uses Migne has no difficulty in finding the references.

Many critical editions are scarce even among good libraries; for the convenie of the ordinary reader of the Fathers, therefore, Migne references have been given in additionthose to modern editions. In some cases, where the Migne enumeration of chapters or sectioriffers from that of the critical text, the Migne number has been given within the bracket thatntains the page and line of the edition and the Migne volume and column: e.g. Or. *Jo.* 1. 38 (.p. 49. 8; M. 14. 100A), where 42 is the chapter number in Migne, p. 49. 8 indicates the paand line of the critical edition (in which the same chapter is numbered 38) and the volurand column of Migne follow.

Works are usually cited by books, chapters or sections, where these exist,cording to the critical text, if any, rather than Migne, unless the contrary is expressly stat Critical texts are usually cited by page and line of the edition, except in the case of verse or wre the sections of the work are very short. In a few cases, where the sections are short and ıy easily found either in a modern edition or in Migne, no reference at all is given in additio:o the book (if any), chapter and section (e.g. *1 Clem.* 42. 4). Sometimes, as in the case of Ireeus or Cosmas Indicopleustes, the Migne reference suffices for finding a passage in the criticadition. In all such cases the Migne reference alone appears, though the critical text is, obourse, always followed.

Where numbers are attached to works, such as homilies with identical titl by the same author, which are not numbered in the editions, these numbers have no beaıg on chronological order but are introduced merely for convenience of reference. If chapte and sections are numbered concurrently in the editions, the sections alone are cited. The ezetical works of each author are listed in biblical order under the heading 'Exegetica'. Theare normally cited by the enumeration of the edition, but if this is lacking they are cited by blical chapter and verse. All biblical references are given with a colon between chapter and vse.

Alternative forms of a key-word are combined in one entry if they are rt materially different and would be adjacent in alphabetical order. In any quotation or ference the form of the key-word first printed is to be assumed unless otherwise specified;ut common variants such as -εια -ια, -ιον ιν, and -σσω -ττω are not separately noted.

Lower-case is the rule for nouns generally but a capital has been substituted ı particular instances: resurrection (general) but Resurrection (of Christ); the gospel but, irthe liturgy, the Gospel; and in lieu of the addition of 'the' in such cases as apostle (generally)ut Apostle (=S. Paul); creation (created world or any act of creation) but Creation (of ıe world); Cross for the cross of Christ and as denoting the Christian religion; church (buding) but Church (universal); and so for Fall, Law, Temple, Incarnation, etc.

It is the misfortune of the Editor of such a work as this at the present time tat critical editions of the Fathers are appearing in large numbers and with great frequency. Since the manuscript was completed several important works which had to be cited from ol editions reproduced by Migne have been edited, too late for the purposes of this book. It hs been no part of the duty of the writers of this Lexicon to edit the texts which they used, althugh some particularly dubious readings have been prefaced by 's.v.l.' (*si vera lectio*) or in a fe cases an obvious correction has been indicated. There can be no doubt, however, that the rogress of the work of critically editing the Fathers will necessitate many corrections to this Leicon and the deletion of certain entries. The opinions of patristic scholars about the authoship and dating of texts are also liable to rapid change. In the List of Authors and Works the fidings of B. Altaner in his *Patrology* (Freiburg i. Br., 1950) and of O. Bardenhewer in his *Gescichte der altkirchlichen Literatur* (Freiburg i. Br., 1902–32) have guided the attribution of works tc authors and the marking of works as dubious or spurious.

I. AUTHORS AND WORKS

ABERCIUS HIEROPOLITANUS — saec. ii
(Aberc.)
epitaph. — *epitaphium Abercii*, W. Lüdtke and T. Nissen *Teub.* 1910, M.115.1245

ABRAHAM EPHESINUS — saec. vi
(Abr. Eph.)
annunt. — *oratio in annuntiationem deiparae*, M. Jugie *PO* 16 (1922) p. 442
occurs. — *oratio in occursum domini*, *ib.* p. 448

ACACIUS BEROEENSIS — ob. 438
(Acac. B.)
ep. Alex. — *epistula ad Alexandrum Hierapolitanum*, *ACO* 1.1.7 p. 146
ep. Cyr. — *epistula ad Cyrillum Alexandrinum*, *ACO* 1.1.1 p. 99, M.77.100
ep. Maxm. — *epistula ad Maximianum Constantinopolitanum*, *ACO* 1.1.7 p. 161

ACACIUS CAESARIENSIS — ob. 366
(Acac. Caes.)
fr. Marcell. — *fragmenta contra Marcellum*, ap. Epiph. *haer.* 72. 6–10
fr. Rom. — *fragmenta in Rom.*, Staab p. 53

ACACIUS CONSTANTINOPOLITANUS — ob. 489
(Acac. CP)
‡*ep.* — *epistula ad Petrum Fullonem*, *ACO* 3 p. 18, H.2.841

ACACIUS ET PAULUS — saec. iv
(Acac. et Paul.)
ep. — *epistula ad Epiphanium*, K. Holl *Epiphanius* 1, *GCS* 1915 p. 153, M.41.156

ACACIUS MELITENUS — saec. v
(Acac. Mel.)
hom. — *homilia Ephesina*, *ACO* 1.1.2 p. 90, M.77.1468

ACTA APOSTOLORUM APOCRYPHA
M. R. James *Apocrypha Anecdota*, *TS* 2^3 (1893) and 5^1 (1897)
LB = R. A. Lipsius and M. Bonnet *Acta Apostolorum Apocrypha* 1, 2 Leipzig 1891–1903
A. Andr. A, B — *Acta Andreae*, LB 2^1 p. 46, p. 58
A. Andr. fr. — *fragmenta ex Actis Andreae*, LB 2^1 p. 38
A. (Pass.) Andr. — *Passio Andreae*, LB 2^1 p. 1; two recensions, the 2nd also in M.2.1217
A. Andr. et Mt. — *Acta Andreae et Matthaei*, LB 2^1 p. 65
A. Barn. — *Acta Barnabae*, LB 2^2 p. 292
A. Barth. — *Acta Bartholomaei*, LB 2^1 p. 128
A. Jo. — *Acta Joannis*, LB 2^1 p. 151
A. Mt. — *Acta Matthaei*, LB 2^1 p. 217
A. Paul. — *Acta Pauli*, W. Schubart and C. Schmidt Hamburg 1936, cited by page and line of the Hamburg Papyrus, partly in LB 1 p. 104
A. Paul. et Thecl. — *Acta Pauli et Theclae*, LB 1 p. 235
A. Petr. c. Sim. — *Acta Petri cum Simone*, LB 1 p. 78
A. Petr. et Andr. — *Acta Petri et Andreae*, LB 2^1 p. 117
A. Petr. et Paul. — *Acta Petri et Pauli*, LB 1 p. 178
A. (Pass.) Petr. et Paul. — *Passio Petri et Pauli*, LB 1 p. 118
A. Phil. — *Acta Philippi*, LB 2^2 p. 1
A. Phil. epit. — *Actorum Philippi epitome*, LB 2^2 p. 91
A. Thadd. — *Acta Thaddaei*, LB 1 p. 273
A. Thom. A — *Acta Thomae*, LB 2^2 p. 99
A. Thom. B — *Acta Thomae*, *TS* 5^1 p. 28
A. Thom. (consumm.) — *Actorum Thomae consummatio*, LB 2^2 p. 289
A. Tim. fr. — *Actorum Timothei fragmentum*, *AS* 2 p. 217
A. Tit. — *Acta Titi*, M. R. James *JTS* 6 (1904–5) p. 549
Tr. Phil. — *Translatio Philippi*, *TS* 2^3 p. 161

ACTA JOANNIS BAPTISTAE — saec. v
A. Jo. Bapt. — *Martyrium Joannis Baptistae*, A. Nau *PO* 4 (1908) p. 526

ACTA PILATI — saec. iv
A. Pil. A, B — C. Tischendorf *Evangelia Apocrypha* Leipzig 1876 p. 210

ACTA XANTHIPPAE ET POLYXENAE — saec. iii
A. Xanthipp. — M. R. James *TS* 2^3 (1893) p. 58

ADAMANTIUS — saec. iv
(Adam.)
dial. — *dialogus de recta in deum fide*, W. H. van Sande Bakhuyzen *GCS* 1901, M.11.1713

AENEAS GAZAEUS — ob. 518
(Aen.)
dial. — *Theophrastus* sive *dialogus*, M.85.872
ep. 1–25 — *epistulae*, *EG* p. 24

AËTIUS ANTIOCHENUS — ob. 366
(Aët.)
fr. — *fragmenta*, ap. *Doct. Patr.* 41 pp. 311–12; ap. Anast. S. *monoph.*, M.89.1181; ap. Bas. *Spir.* 4
synt. — *syntagmation*, ap. Epiph. *haer.* 76. 11–12

AFRICANUS, SEXTUS JULIUS — ob. post 240
(Afric.)
chron. — *chronicon*, M.10.64
ep. Arist. — *epistula ad Aristidem*, W. Reichardt *TU* 34^3 (1909) p. 53, M.10.52
ep. Or. — *epistula ad Origenem de historia Susannae*, *TU* 34^3 p. 78, M.11.41
‡*Pers.* — *narratio de rebus Persicis*, M.10.97; see *Pers.*

AGAPETUS CONSTANTINOPOLITANUS, DIACONUS — saec. vi
(Agap.)
cap. — *capita admonitoria*, M.86.1164

AGAPETUS PAPA — ob. 536
(Agap. Papa)
ep. syn. — *epistula synodica*, *ACO* 3 p. 152, M.*PL.* 66.47

AGATHANGELUS — saec. v
(Agath.)
v. Gr. Ill. — *vita Gregorii Illuminatoris*, P. A. de Lagarde *AGWG* 35 (1889) p. 4

AGATHO DIACONUS — saec. vii–viii
(Agath. Diac.)
epilog. — *epilogus*, H.3.1833

AGATHO PAPA — ob. 681
(Agath. Papa)
ep. imp. — *epistula ad imperatores*, M.*PL.*87.1162
ep. syn. — *epistula synodica*, *ib.* 1215

AGRAPHA
Agraph. — A. Resch, *TU* $30^{3,4}$, 1906

ALEXANDER ALEXANDRINUS — ob. 328
(Alex. Al.)
depos. — *de Arii depositione*, Opitz 3 p. 6, M.18.581
ep. Aegl. — *fragmenta epistulae ad Aeglonem*, M.18.584
ep. Alex. — *epistula ad Alexandrum Constantinopolitanum*, Opitz 3 p. 19, M.18.548
ep. encycl. — *epistula encyclica*, Opitz 3 p. 6, M.18.572

ALEXANDER HIEROSOLYMITANUS — ob. 250
(Alex. H.)
fr. — *fragmenta epistolarum*, ap. Eus. *h.e.* 6, M.10.204

ALEXANDER LYCOPOLITANUS — saec. iv
(Alex. Lyc.)
Man. — *de placitis Manichaeorum*, A. Brinkmann *Teub.* 1895, M.18.412

ALEXANDER SALAMINUS — saec. v
(Alex. Sal.)
Barn. — *laudatio in apostolum Barnabam*, *ASS* Jun. 11 p. 436
cruc. — *de inventione crucis*, M.87.4016
†*cruc. epit.* — *epitome encomii crucis*, M.87.4077; ∾ Alex. Sal. *cruc.* 4057C–4064D and 4069D–4076

ALEXANDER THESSALONICENSIS — saec. iv
(Alex. Thess.)
ep. Ath. — *epistula ad Athanasium*, ap. Ath. *apol. sec.* 66
ep. Dion. — *epistula ad Dionysium comitem*, *ib.* 80

ALYPIUS CONSTANTINOPOLITANUS saec. v
(Alyp.)
ep. *epistula ad Cyrillum Alexandrinum*, int. opp. Cyr. *ep.* 29, *ACO* 1.1.3 p. 74, M.77. 145

AMBROSIUS MEDIOLANENSIS ob. 397
(Ambr.)
fr. *fragmenta varia*, ap. Thdt. *eran.* 2 (S.4. 139); *ib.* 3 (S.4.243); ap. *Doct. Patr.*; ap. Leont. H. *monoph.*, M.86.1828; *SS* 1 p. 360; ap. C Eph. (431) *act.* 1, *ACO* 1.1.2 p. 42, H.1.1405; ap. C Chalc. *act.* 2, *ACO* 2.1.1 pp. 22–23, H.2.301–4; ap. C Later. *act.* 2, H.3.744–8; *ib.* 5, H.3.857–60, 865, 877; ap. CCP (681) *act.* 8, H.3. 1184–5; *ib.* 10, H.3.1204

AMMONAS saec. iv
ep. 1–7 *epistulae*, F. Nau *PO* 11 (1916) p. 432
fr. 1, 2 *fragmenta*, *ib.* p. 484
opusc. 1–4 *opuscula*, *ib.* p. 455

AMMONIUS AEGYPTIUS saec. iv
(Ammon. Aeg.)
ep. *epistula ad Theophilum de Pachomio et Theodoro*, F. Halkin *SH* 19 (1932) p. 97

AMMONIUS ALEXANDRINUS saec. v
(Ammon.)
exegetica
Ps. *fragmenta in Pss.*, M.85.1361
Dan. *fragmenta in Dan.*, M.85.1364, 1824
‡*Mt.* *fragmenta in Mt.*, M.85.1381
Jo. *fragmenta in Jo.*, M.85.1392
Ac. *fragmenta in Ac.*, M.85.1524
1 Petr. 3:19–20 *homilia in illud*, His qui in carcere erant, M.85.1608

AMPHILOCHIUS ICONIENSIS ob. post 394
(Amph.)
‡*circ.* *homilia in circumcisionem*, F. Combefis *Amphilochii, Methodii, et Andreae Cretensis opera* Paris 1544 p. 10
ep. syn. *epistula synodica*, M.39.93
exegeticum
hom. in Mt. 26: 39 *homilia in illud*, Pater, si possibile, K. Holl *Amphilochius von Ikonium* Tübingen 1904 p. 91, partly in M.61.751
exerc. *adversus exercitationem falsam*, G. Ficker *Amphilochiana* 1 Leipzig 1906 p. 23
fr. *fragmenta varia*, G. Ficker op. cit. p. 4, K. Holl op. cit. p. 55, M.39.97; ap. *Doct. Patr.*
hom. 1–5 *homiliae*, M.39.36
mesopent. *oratio in mesopentecosten*, M.39.120
‡*non desp.* *homilia de non desperando*, P. Possinus *Thesaurus Asceticus* Paris 1684 p. 255. (*Note*: pp. 255–64 = ‡*poenit.* pp. 100–12)
‡*poenit.* *homilia de poenitentia*, F. Combefis op. cit. p. 91 (see note above)
Seleuc. *iambi ad Seleucum*, int. opp. Gr. Naz. *carm.* 2. 2 (poem.) 8, M.37.1577
‡*v. Bas.* *vita Basilii Caesariensis*, F. Combefis op. cit. p. 155

AMPHILOCHIUS SIDENSIS saec. v
(Amph. Sid.)
ep. *epistulae fragmentum*, M.77.1516

ANAPHORA PILATI see EVANGELIA APOCRYPHA

ANASTASIANA incertae originis saec. vi f.
(Anast.)
fid. *concisa et perspicua fidei nostrae notitia*, *Mon.* 2 p. 271
liturg. *de liturgiis in quadragesimo die pro defunctis*, *Mon.* 2 p. 277
mort. *canticum in mortuorum exsequiis*, *AS* 1 p. 242 (partly in *Mon.* 2 p. 286)
narr. *narratio sacra de Romano papa Gregorio*, *Mon.* 2 p. 276
poenit. *canon pro poenitentibus*, *Mon.* 2 p. 281
temp. *doctrina de temporibus*, *Mon.* 2 p. 278

ANASTASIUS ANTIOCHENUS ob. 599
(Anast. Ant.)
ep. Serg. *epistulae ad Sergium fragmenta*, M.89.1405
fid. *explicatio brevis fidei orthodoxae*, M.89.1400
fr. *fragmenta varia*, M.89.1281, 1283, 1285; ap. *Doct. Patr.*
redit. *sermo de reditu*, *Mon.* 2 p. 251
sabb. *fragmentum de sabbato*, M.89.1405
sac. *de sacerdotio*, *Mon.* 2 p. 276
serm. 1–3 *sermones*, M.89.1361
‡*serm.* 4 *sermo de tribus quadragesimis*, M.89.1389
vit. exced. *sermo de iis qui vita excedunt*, *SVC* 1 (1825) p. 371

ANASTASIUS APOCRISIARIUS ob. 666
(Anast. Ap.)
a. Max. 1, 2 *acta Maximi Confessoris*, M.90.109, 136
fr. *fragmenta*, ap. *Doct. Patr.*

ANASTASIUS SINAITA ob. post 700
(Anast. S.)
blasph. *de blasphemia*, *AHS* 1 p. 400
defunct. *sermo in defunctis*, M.89.1192
exegeticum
Ps. 6 *oratio in Ps. 6*, two recensions, M.89.1077, 1116
fr. *fragmenta*, M.89.1283, 1285, 1287
haer. *de haeresibus*, *Mon.* 2 p. 257
hex. 12 *anagogicarum contemplationum in hexaëmeron liber duodecimus*, M.89.1052
hex. fr. *fragmenta in hexaëmeron*, M.89.937, 942, 961, 963, 966, 968
hod. *hodegus* sive *viae dux*, M.89.36
interr. *interrogatio cur feria iv et vi observetur*, *Mon.* 2 p. 274
‡*Jud. al.* *adversus Judaeos dialogus alius*, M.89.1273
‡*Jud. disp.* 1–3 *adversus Judaeos disputationes*, M.89.1204
‡*Jud. parv.* *adversus Judaeos dialogus parvus*, M.89. 1272. (*Note*: the above three works, prob. saec. ix, contain much similar to *Dial. Christ. et Jud.* q.v.)
monoph. *contra monophysitas testimonia*, M.89.1180
qu. al. 1–6 *quaestiones aliae*, *SVC* 1 (1825) p. 373
qu. et resp. 1–154 *quaestiones et responsiones*, M.89.312
†*relat.* 1–59 *relationes de patribus Sinai*, F. Nau; *relat.* 1–41 *OC* 2 (1912) p. 60; *relat.* 42–59 *OC* 3 (1903) p. 61; *relat.* 6, 7, 32, 34 also in M.88.608–9
‡*serm. imag.* *sermo in hominem in imaginem dei factum*, M.89.1143. (*Note*: M.89.1144–8D = ‡Gr. Nyss. *imag.*, M.44.1329B–1332C, 1333B–36A q.v.; M.89.1148D–9C = M.89. 1161C–4B)
serm. imag. 3 *sermo in hominem in imaginem dei factum*, M.89.1152
synax. *oratio de sacra synaxi*, M.89.825
vit. term. *de vitae termino*, *SVC* 1 (1825) p. 369

ANATOLIUS CONSTANTINOPOLITANUS saec. v
(Anat. CP)
ep. 1 *epistula ad Leonem Papam*, int. opp. Leo. Mag. *ep.* 53, *ACO* 2.4 p. xlv, M.*PL.* 54.854
ep. 2 *epistula ad Leonem Papam*, int. opp. Leo. Mag. *ep.* 101, *ACO* 2.1.2 p. 52, M.*PL.* 54.976

ANATOLIUS LAODICENUS saec. iii
(Anat. Laod.)
arith. *fragmenta ex libris arithmeticorum*, M.10. 232
can. pasch. *fragmentum ex canone paschali*, M.10.212; ap. Eus. *h.e.* 7.32.14–19
decad. περὶ δεκάδος, J. Heiburg *Annales internationales d'histoire* (*Congrès de Paris 1900*) 5th section Paris 1901

ANDREAS CAESARIENSIS CAPPADOCIAE saec. vi–vii
(Andr. Caes.)
Apoc. *commentarius in Apoc.*, M.106.216
therap. fr. *libri therapeutici secundi fragmenta*, *AP* p. 165

ANDREAS CRETENSIS (sive HIEROSOLYMITANUS) ob. 740
(Andr. Cr.)
Agath. *iambi in Agathonem*, A. Heisenburg *BZ* 10 (1901) p. 508 (the lines are confused in M.97.1437)
can. Ann. *canon in Annae conceptionem*, M.97.1305
can. BMV *canon in BMV nativitatem*, M.97.1316
can. Laz. *canon in Lazarum*, M.97.1385
can. mag. *canon magnus*, M.97.1329, partly in *AGC* p. 147
can. mesopent. *canon in medium pentecosten*, M.97.1421
†*can. Petr.* *canon in catenis Petri*, *AGC* p. 157
†*cycl.* *de cyclo solari et lunari*, M.19.1329
Geo. *oratio in Georgium*, *ASS* Apr. 23 p. xx
idiomel. *idiomela varia*, M.97.1433, partly in *AGC* p. 97

imag. *de sanctarum imaginum veneratione*, M.97.1301
Jacob. *homilia in Jacobum fratrem domini*, *AHS* 1 p. 1
or. 1–17, 19–21 *orationes*, M.97.805
†*or.* 18 *oratio in Nicolaum Myrensem*, G. Anrich *Hagios Nikolaus* 1 Leipzig 1913 p. 419, M.97.1192
triod. *triodia majoris hebdomadae*, M.97.1400

ANDREAS SAMOSATENUS saec. v
(Andr. Sam.)
fr. *fragmenta varia*, ap. Cyr. *apol. orient.*; ap. Anast. S. *hod.* 22 (M.89.292C)

ANTEON ARSINOENSIS saec. v
(Anteon)
‡*ep.* *epistula ad Petrum Fullonem*, *ACO* 3 p. 6, H.2.845

ANTHIMUS CONSTANTINOPOLITANUS saec. vi
(Anth. CP)
fr. *fragmenta contra Justinianum* ap. CCP (681) *act.* 10, H.3.1240D,E

ANTHIMUS NICOMEDIENSIS ob. 302
(Anth.)
†*eccl. fr.* *de sancta ecclesia fragmentum*, G. Mercati *ST* 5 (1901) p. 95; attributed to Marcell. by Richard *Mélanges de Science Religieuse* 1949 pp. 5 ff.

ANTIOCHUS EPARCHES saec. v
(Ant. Ep.)
ep. *epistula ad Nestorium*, *ACO* 1.1.7 p. 71

ANTIOCHUS MONACHUS ob. post 619
(Ant. Mon.)
conf. *confessio*, M.89.1849
ep. Eust. *epistula ad Eustathium*, M.89.1421
hom. 1–130 *pandecta scripturae sacrae*, M.89.1428

ANTIOCHUS PTOLEMAIEUS saec. iv–v
(Ant. Ptol.)
Adam *homilia in Adam*, Savile 5 p. 648, partly in M.86.2044
fr. *fragmenta varia*, ap. Cyr. *Arcad.*, *ACO* 1.1.5 p. 66. 32, A.5^2(3).49E; ap. Phot. *cod.* 229, M.103.973C; ap. Leont. B. *Nest. et Eut.* 1 (M.86.1315A)
nativ. *homilia de nativitate*, C. Martin *Mus.* 54 (1941) p. 56

ANTIPATER BOSTRENSIS ob. post 451
(Antip. Bost.)
annunt. *homilia in annuntiationem deiparae*, M.85.1776
fr. *fragmenta varia*, M.85.1792; *AS* 5 p. 63; ap. Leont. et Jo. *sacr.* 2, M.86.2045; ap. Jo. D. *parall.*, M.96.468, 488, 501
Jo. Bapt. *homilia in Joannem Baptistam*, M.85.1764

ANTIPATER CAPPADOX saec. iv
(Antip. Cap.)
ep. *epistula ad Basilium*, int. opp. Bas. *ep.* 187, M.32.664

ANTONIUS ABBAS ob. 356
(Anton.)
‡*ep.* *epistula*, G. Garitte *Mus.* 55 (1942) p. 99

ANTONIUS HAGIOGRAPHICUS saec. v
(Anton. Hag.)
v. Sym. Styl. *vita Symeonis Stylitis*, H. Lietzmann *TU* 32^4 (1908) p. 20

APOCALYPSES APOCRYPHAE
T = C. Tischendorf, *Apocalypses Apocryphae*, Leipzig 1866
M. R. James, *Apocrypha Anecdota*, *TS* 2^3 (1893) and 5^1 (1897)
Apoc. Adam *Apocalypsis Adam fragmenta*, *TS* 2^3 p. 139
Apoc. Bar. *Apocalypsis Baruch*, *TS* 5^1 p. 84
Apoc. Bar. rel. *Reliquiae Apocalypsis Baruch*, J. Rendel Harris *The Rest of the Words of Baruch* London 1889 p. 47
Apoc. BMV *Apocalypsis Mariae*, *TS* 2 p. 115 (later version, Vassiliev p. 125)
Apoc. Dan. A, B, C *Apocalypsis Danielis* A, Vassiliev p. 33, B, Vassiliev p. 38, C, E. Klostermann *Analecta zur Septuaginta, Hexapla und Patristik* Leipzig 1895 p. 115
Apoc. En. 1–32, 89 *Apocalypsis Enoch*, J. Flemming and L. Radermacher *GCS* 1901
Apoc. En. 97–104, 106–7 *Apocalypsis Enoch*, C. Bonner *StD* 8 (1937) p. 33
Apoc. Esd. *Apocalypsis Esdrae*, T p. 24
1 Apoc. Jo. *Apocalypsis Joannis*, T p. 70
2 Apoc. Jo. *Apocalypsis Joannis*, F. Nau *RB* 11 (1914) p. 215
3 Apoc. Jo. *Apocalypsis Joannis*, Vassiliev p. 317
Apoc. Mos. *Apocalypsis Mosis* T p. 1
Apoc. Paul. *Apocalypsis Pauli*, T p. 34
Apoc. Petr. A, B *Apocalypsis Petri*, E. Preuschen *Antilegomena* 2nd ed. Giessen 1905, pp. 84, 87
Apoc. Sedr. *Apocalypsis Sedrach*, *TS* 2^3 p. 130
Ascens. Is. A *Ascensio Isaiae*, R. H. Charles London 1900 p. 83
Ascens. Is. B *Ascensio Isaiae*, O. von Gebhardt *ZWT* 21 (1878) p. 341

APOLLINARIUS LAODICENUS ob. c. 390
(Apoll.)
anac. *anacephalaeosis*, Lietzmann p. 242, M.28.1265
corp. et div. *de unione corporis et divinitatis in Christo*, Lietzmann p. 185, int. opp. Jul. Papae, M.*PL*.8.873
†*ep. Bas.* 1–2 *epistulae ad Basilium*, int. opp. Bas. *epp.* 362, 364, M.32.1101, 1105
ep. Diocaes. *epistula ad Diocaesarienses*, Lietzmann p. 255, ap. Leont. B. *Apoll.*, M.86.1969
ep. Dion. *epistula ad Dionysium*, Lietzmann p. 256, int. opp. Jul. Papae, M.*PL*.8.929
ep. Jov. *epistula ad Jovianum*, Lietzmann p. 250, M.28.25
exegetica
Gen. *fragmenta in Gen.*, R. Devreesse *RB* 45 (1936) p. 214
†*met. Ps.* *metaphrases in Ps.*, A. Ludwich *Teub.* 1912, M.33.1313, 1627
Pr. *fragmenta in Pr.*, *NBP* 7^2 p. 76
Is. *fragmenta in Is.*, *NBP* 7^2 p. 128
Ezech. *fragmenta in Ezech.*, *NBP* 7^2 p. 82
Rom. *fragmenta in Rom.*, Staab p. 57
fid. inc. 3–7 *de fide et incarnatione fragmentum*, Lietzmann p. 194, int. opp. Jul. Papae, M.*PL*.8.876
fid. sec. pt. *fides secundum partem*, Lietzmann p. 167, int. opp. Gr. Thaum., M.10.1104
fr. 1–171 *fragmenta*, Lietzmann p. 185
inc. *de incarnatione dei verbi*, Lietzmann p. 303, M.28.89
quod un. Chr. *quod unus sit Christus*, Lietzmann p. 294, M.28.121
tom. syn. *tomus synodalis*, Lietzmann p. 262, ap. Leont. B. *Apoll.*, M.86.1952

APOLLINARIUS LAODICENUS SYRUS saec. iv
(Apoll. S.) ap. Soz. *h.e.* 2. 17. 2–3

APOLLONIUS saec. iii
(Apollon.)
fragmenta adversus Cataphrygas, ap. Eus. *h.e.* 5. 18

APOPHTHEGMATA
Apophth. Mac. Aeg. *Apophthegmata Macarii Aegyptii*, M.34.208, 221
Apophth. Patr. *Apophthegmata Patrum*, M.65.72; the following passages are in F. Nau *PO* 11 (1906) p. 403; M.65.84C; 120–4; 317B; 333C; 345A
Apophth. Patr. al. *Apophthegmata Patrum alia*, P. Possinus *Thesaurus Asceticus* Paris 1684 pp. 228–54 (pp. 243–7 in M.34.232–36)

ARCADIUS CONSTANTIENSIS saec. vii
(Arc. C.)
v. Sym. *fragmenta ex vita Simeonis Stylitis junioris*, A. Papadopoulos-Kerameus *Βυζαντίνα Χρονικά* 1 (1894) pp. 145–8, 603–4, 606–12; M. Delehaye *SH* 14 (1923) p. 238; ap. Jo. D. *imag.* 3, M.94.1393; ap. C Nic. (787) *act.* 4, H.4.217

ARETHAS CAESARIENSIS CAPPADOCIAE saec. ix–x
(Areth.)
Apoc. *commentarius in Apoc.* (incorporating earlier material), M.106.493

ARISTIDES saec. ii
(Arist.)
apol. *apologia*, Goodspeed p. 3, ap. †Jo. D.

B. J. 26–27 (passages not in Goodspeed cited from J. A. Robinson TS^{1} (1891) p. 100); fr. in *PLond.* 2486, ed. H. J. M. Milne *JTS* (1924) p. 75

ARISTO PELLAEUS — saec. ii
(Aristo)
fragmentum, ap. Eus. *h.e.* 4. 6. 3

ARIUS — ob. 336
(Ar.)
ep. Alex. — *epistula ad Alexandrum Alexandrinum*, Opitz 3 p. 12, ap. Ath. *syn.* 16
ep. Const. — *epistula ad Constantinum*, Opitz 3 p. 64, ap. Soz. *h.e.* 2. 27. 6
ep. Eus. — *epistula ad Eusebium Nicomediensem*, Opitz 3 p. 1, ap. Epiph. *haer.* 69. 6
Thal. fr. 1–17 — *de Thalia fragmenta ex Athanasio*, G. Bardy *S. Lucien d'Antioche* Paris 1936 p. 252; cited according to Bardy's enumeration from the text in which the fragments occur

ARSENIUS EREMITES — ob. 445
(Arsen.)
doct. — *doctrina et exhortatio*, M.66.1617
tent. — *in nomicum tentatorem*, M.66.1621

ARSENIUS HYPSELITES — saec. iv
(Arsen. Hyps.)
ep. — *epistula ad Athanasium*, ap. Ath. *apol. sec.* 69

ASCENSIO ISAIAE see APOCALYPSES APOCRYPHAE

ASCLEPIADES TRALLENSIS — saec. v
(Asclep.)
‡*ep.* — *epistula ad Petrum Fullonem*, *ACO* 3 p. 10, H.2.852

ASENATH, CONFESSIO
Asen. — *Confessio Asenath*, M. R. James in P. Batiffol *Studia Patristica* 2 Paris 1890 p. 39

ASTERIUS AMASENUS — ob. 410
(Ast. Am.)
hom. 1–14 — *homiliae*, M.40.164
[‡*hom.* 15–21 — *homiliae*, M.40.389 = Ast. Soph. *hom. 1–5 in Ps. 5*; *Ps. 6*; *Ps. 7*]
phar. — *homilia de pharisaeo et publicano*, A. Bretz *TU* 40^{1} (1914) p. 116
prod. — *homilia in filium prodigum*, *ib.* p. 107

ASTERIUS SOPHISTA — ob. post 341
(Ast. Soph.)
exegetica
Ps. 4 — *homilia in Ps. 4*, M.55.539
hom. 1–5 in Ps. 5 — *homiliae in Ps. 5*, int. opp. Ast. Am. M.40.389
Ps. 6 — *homilia in Ps. 6*, *ib.* M.40.444
Ps. 7 — *homilia in Ps. 7*, *ib.* M.40.460
fr. Ps. — *fragmenta in Pss.*, G. Bardy *S. Lucien d'Antioche* Paris 1936 p. 356
fr. 1–36 — *ex Athanasio et Marcello Ancyrano fragmenta*, *ib.* p. 341

ATHANASIUS ALEXANDRINUS — ob. 373
(Ath.)
apol. Const. — *apologia ad Constantium*, M.25.596, chapters 1–3 in Opitz 2 p. 279
apol. sec. — *apologia (secunda) contra Arianos*, Opitz 2 p. 87, M.25.248
Ar. 1–3 — *orationes tres adversus Arianos*, M.26.12
decr. — *de decretis Nicaenae synodi*, Opitz 2 p. 1, M.25.416
Dion. — *de sententia Dionysii*, Opitz 2 p. 46, M.25.480
ep. Adelph. — *epistula ad Adelphium*, M.26.1072
ep. Aeg. Lib. — *epistula ad episcopos Aegypti et Libyae*, M.25.537
ep. Afr. — *epistula ad Afros episcopos*, M.26.1029
ep. Amun. — *epistula ad Amunem*, M.26.1169
ep. Drac. — *epistula ad Dracontium*, M.25.524
ep. encycl. — *epistula encyclica*, Opitz p. 169, M.25.221
ep. Epict. — *epistula ad Epictetum*, M.26.1049; G. Ludwig Jena 1911
ep. fest. — *epistularum festivalium fragmenta*, ap. Cosm. Ind. *top.* 10 init., M.26.1367, 1379, 1389, 1432 ff.
ep. fest. 39 — *epistula festivalis trecesima nona*, T. Zahn *Grundriss der Geschichte des Neutestamentlichen Kanons* 2nd ed. Leipzig 1904 p. 87, M.26.1436 and 1176
ep. Jo. et Ant. — *epistula ad Joannem et Antiochum*, M.26.1165
ep. Jov. — *epistula ad Jovianum*, M.26.813; ap. Thdt. *h.e.* 4. 3
ep. Marcell. — *epistula ad Marcellinum*, M.27.12
ep. Max. — *epistula ad Maximum*, M.26.1085
ep. mon. — *epistula ad monachos*, M.26.1185
ep. mort. Ar. — *epistula ad Serapionem de morte Arii*, Opitz 2 p. 178, M.25.685
ep. Ors. 1–2 — *epistulae ad Orsisium*, M.26.977
ep. Pall. — *epistula ad Palladium*, M.26.1168
ep. Rufin. — *epistula ad Rufinianum*, M.26.1180
ep. Serap. 1–4 — *epistulae ad Serapionem*, M.26.529
exegetica
fr. Job — *fragmenta in Job*, M.27.1344; *AS* 5 p. 22
exp. Ps. — *expositio in Pss.*, M.27.56
fr. Pss. comm. — *fragmenta commentarii in Pss.*, M.27.548; *AS* 5 p. 3
fr. Cant. — *fragmenta in Cant.*, M.27.1348
hom. in Mt. 11:27 — *homilia in illud*, Omnia mihi tradita sunt, M.25.208
†*fr. Mt.* — *fragmenta in Mt.*, M.27.1364
fr. Lc. — *fragmenta in Lc.*, M.27.1392; *NBP* 2 (1844) p. 567
†*exp. fid.* — *expositio fidei*, M.25.200
†*fr.* — *fragmenta varia*, M.26.1217, 1233, 1252, 1293, 1320
fug. — *apologia de fuga sua*, Opitz 2 p. 68, M.25.644
gent. — *contra gentes*, M.25.4
h. Ar. — *historia Arianorum ad monachos*, Opitz 2 p. 183, M.25.696
h. Ar. ep. — *ad historiam Arianorum ad monachos epistula*, Opitz 2 p. 181, M.25.692
inc. — *de incarnatione*, F. L. Cross London 1939, M.25.96
inc. et c. Ar. — *de incarnatione et contra Arianos*, M.26.984
narr. fug. — *narratio ad Ammonium episcopum de fuga sua*, M.26.980
syn. — *epistula de synodis Arimini et Seleuciae*, Opitz 2 p. 231, M.26.681
tom. — *tomus ad Antiochenos*, M.26.796
v. Anton. — *vita Antonii*, M.26.837
virg. — *de virginitate*, E. von der Goltz *TU* 29^{2} (1905) p. 35, M.28.252
‡*annunt.* — *homilia in annuntiationem deiparae*, M.28.917
‡*Apoll.* 1–2 — *de incarnatione contra Apollinarem*, M.26.1093
‡*Ar.* 4 — *oratio quarta contra Arianos*, A. Stegmann Tübingen 1917, M.26.468
[‡*ascens.* — *homilia in assumptionem domini*, M.28.1092; see Bas. Sel.]
‡*azym.* — *de azymis*, M.26.1328, partly = ‡Jo. D. *azym.*, M.95.388
[‡*caec.* — *homilia in caecum a nativitate*, M.28.1001; see Tim. Ant.]
‡*comm. essent.* — *de communi essentia Patris et Filii et Spiritus sancti*, M.28.29
[‡*confut.* — *confutatio quarundam propositionum*, M.28.1337; see Euther.]
‡*corp.* — *de corpore et anima*, M.28.1432
‡*def.* — *liber de definitionibus*, M.28.533
[‡*descr. BMV* — *homilia de descriptione deiparae*, M.28.944; see Tim. Ant.]
‡*diab.* — *homilia in diabolum*, R. P. Casey *JTS* 36, 1935, p. 4
‡*dial. Trin.* 1–5 — *de Trinitate dialogi*, M.28.1116
‡*disp.* — *disputatio cum Ario in synodo*, M.28.440
‡*doct. Ant.* — *doctrina ad Antiochum ducem*, M.28.556
‡*doct. mon.* — *doctrina ad monachos*, M.28.1421
‡*ep. Cast.* 1–2 — *epistulae ad Castorem*, M.28.849 composed of extracts from Cassianus *de institutis coenobiorum*
‡*ep. cath.* — *epistula catholica*, M.28.81
‡*ep. Lib.* — *epistula ad Liberium*, M.28.1443
‡*ep. Pers.* — *epistula ad episcopum Persarum*, M.28.1565
exegetica
‡*fr. Ps.* — *fragmenta in Pss.*, V. Jagic *Denkschriften der Kaiserliche Akademie der Wissenschaften: philosophisch-historische Klasse* 52– Vienna 1906; also in M.27.61 ff.
‡*hom. in Mt. 21:2* — *homilia in illud*, Profecti in pagum, M.28.169

‡*hom. in Mt. 21:9* — *homilia in illud*, Ite in castellum, M.28.1024
‡*hom. in Lc. 19:36* — *homilia in illud*, Eunte autem illo, M.28.1033
‡*fr. in 1 Cor. 7:1* — *fragmentum in illud*, Illud bonum est, M.27.1404
‡*fr. in 2 Cor. 12:2* — *fragmentum in illud*, Novi hujus modi hominem, M.27.1404
‡*fr. in 2 Cor. 12:7* — *fragmentum in illud*, Datus est mihi, M.27.1405
‡*exhort.* — *sermo exhortatorius*, M.28.1108
‡*haer.* — *sermo contra omnes haereses*, M.28.501
‡*imag.* — *fragmentum sermonis de sacris imaginibus*, M.28.709
‡*imag. Beryt.* — *sermo in imaginem Berytensem*, two recensions, M.28.797, 805
‡*inst. mon.* — *vitae monasticae institutio*, M.28.845
‡*interpr.* — *interpretatio symboli*, *ACO* 1.1.7 p. 66, M.26.1232
‡*Jov.* — *ad imperatorem Jovianum*, M.28.532
‡*Lat.* — *sermo contra Latinos*, M.28.824
‡*Maced. dial.* 1–2 — *contra Macedonianos dialogi*, M.28.1289
‡*Melch.* — *historia de Melchisedech*, M.28.525
‡*nativ. Chr.* — *homilia in nativitate Christi*, M.28.960
[‡*nativ. Jo. Bapt.* — *homilia in nativitate praecursoris*, M.28.905; see Tim. Ant.]
‡*Novat.* — *contra Novatianos fragmenta*, M.26.1316
‡*occurs.* — *homilia in occursum Domini*, M.28.973. (*Note*: by Georgius Nicomedensis saec. ix according to the oldest MSS)
‡*palm.* — *homilia in ramos palmarum*, M.26.1309
[‡*parasc.* — *sermo in passionem domini in parasceve*, M.28.1053; see Bas. Sel.]
[‡*pasch.* 1–2 — *sermones in pascha*, M.28.1073; see Bas. Sel.]
‡*pass.* — *homilia de passione et cruce domini*, M.28.185
‡*pat.* — *sermo de patientia*, M.26.1297
‡*poenit. can.* — *canones poenitentiales*, *SS* 4 p. 457
‡*polit.* — *syntagma ad quemdam politicum*, M.28.1396
[‡*prod. Jud.* — *homilia in proditionem Judae*, M.28.1048; see Bas. Sel.]
‡*proph.* — *homilia in patres et prophetas*, M.28.1061
‡*qu. al.* 1–20 — *quaestiones aliae*, M.28.773
‡*qu. Ant.* 1–137 — *quaestiones ad Antiochum*, M.28.597
‡*qu. ev.* 1–36 — *quaestiones in evangelia*, M.28.700
‡*qu. script.* 1–130 — *quaestiones in scripturas*, M.28.712
‡*ref.* — *refutatio hypocrisis Meletii et Eusebii*, M.28.85
‡*renunt.* — *sermo pro iis qui saeculo renuntiarunt*, M.28.1409
‡*sabb.* — *de sabbatis et circumcisione*, M.28.133
‡*Sabell.* — *contra Sabellianos*, M.28.96
‡*sem.* — *homilia de semente*, M.28.144
‡*serm. Ant.* — *sermo ad Antiochum ducem*, M.28.589
‡*serm. fid.* — *sermo major de fide*, E. Schwartz *SBBAW* 1924 (6), M.26.1264
‡*symb.* — *symbolum 'Quicumque' seu Athanasianum dictum*, versiones variae, M.28.1581; C. P. Caspari *Quellen zur Geschichte des Taufsymbols und Glaubensregel* 3 Christiania 1875
‡*synops.* — *synopsis sacrae scripturae*, M.28.284
‡*syntag.* — *syntagma doctrinae ad monachos*, P. Batiffol *Studia Patristica* 2 Paris 1890 p. 121, M.28.836 and 1639 ∽ *Didasc. patr.*
‡*templ.* — *commentarius de templo Athenarum*, M.28.1428; A. Delatte *Musée Belge* 27 Liège 1923 p. 107; a later recension A. von Premerstein *Εἰς μνήμην Σ. Λάμπρου* 1932 p. 177
‡*theopasch.* — *contra theopaschitas*, H. G. Opitz *Untersuchungen zur Überlieferung der Schriften des Athanasius* Berlin 1935 p. 211
‡*Trin.* — *de Trinitate*, M.28.1604
‡*v. Syncl.* — *vita Syncleticae*, M.28.1488

ATHANASIUS ALEXANDRINUS PRESBYTER — saec. v
(Ath. Presb.)
libell. — *libellus contra Dioscorum*, ap. C Chalc. *act.* 3, *ACO* 2.1.2 p. 20, H.2.332

ATHANASIUS SCHOLASTICUS — saec. vi
(Ath. Scholast.)
coll. — *collectio novellarum constitutionum*, G. E. Heimbach *Anecdota* 1 Leipzig 1838 p. 1

ATHENAGORAS ATHENIENSIS — ob. c. 177
(Athenag.)
leg. — *legatio* sive *supplicatio* sive *deprecatio pro Christianis*, Goodspeed p. 315, M.6.889
res. — *de resurrectione mortuorum*, E. Schwartz *TU* 4^{2} (1888) p. 48, M.6.973

ATHENODORUS — ob. 264
(Athenod.)
fr. — *fragmenta*, K. Holl *TU* 20^{2} (1899) p. 161 ap. Jo. D. *parall.*, M.95.1085A

ATTICUS CONSTANTINOPOLITANUS — ob. 425
(Attic.)
ep. Afr. — *epistula ad episcopos Africanos*, ap. *Cod. Afr.*, H.1.945
ep. Call. — *epistula ad Calliopium*, ap. Socr. *h.e.* 7. 25. 5–8
ep. Cyr. — *epistula ad Cyrillum*, E. Schwartz *ABAW* 32^{6} (1927) p. 23, int. opp. Cyr. *ep.* 75, M.77.348
ep. Eups. fr. — *fragmentum epistulae ad Eupsychium*, *ACO* 2.1.3 p. 115, ap. Thdt. *eran.* 2 (S.4.167)
ep. Petr. et Aides. — *epistula ad Petrum et Aidesium*, E. Schwartz *ABAW* 32^{6} (1927) p. 24, ap. Nicephorum Callistum *hist.* 14. 26, M.146.1141C
Trin. fr. — *fragmentum in Trinitatem*, ap. *Doct. Patr.* 42 p. 317

AUGUSTINUS HIPPONENSIS — ob. 430
(Aug.)
fr. — *fragmenta varia*, *ACO* 2.1.1 p. 23, ap. Thdt. *eran.* 2 (S.4.165); ap. C Later. *act.* 2, H.3.748; *ib.* 5, H.3.860, 865–9; ap. Leont. H. *monoph.*, M.86.1837D

BARNABAE EPISTULA — saec. ii
Barn. — Bihlmeyer p. 10

BARSANUPHIUS ET JOHANNES, MONACHI — saec. vi
(Bars.)
resp. — *responsiones*, ed. Nicodemos Venice 1816; fragments in M.86.892, 88.1812

BARTHOLOMAEUS EDESSENUS — saec. viii seu ix
(Barth. Edess.)
Agar. — *confutatio Agareni*, M.104.1384
‡*Muham.* — *confutatio Muhammedis*, M.104.1448

BASILISCUS IMPERATOR — ob. 476
(Basilisc.)
antencycl. — *antencyclica*, E. Schwartz *ABAW* 32^{6} (1927) p. 52, ap. Evagr. *h.e.* 3. 7, M.86.2609
encycl. — *encyclica*, E. Schwartz op. cit. p. 49, ap. Evagr. *h.e.* 3. 4, M.86.2600

BASILIUS ANCYRANUS — ob. post 363
(Bas. Anc.)
†*virg.* — *liber de vera virginitate*, int. opp. Bas., M.30.669

BASILIUS ANCYRANUS ALIUS — saec. viii
(Bas. Anc. al.)
libell. — *libellus*, ap. C Nic (787) *act.* 1, H.4.40

BASILIUS CAESARIENSIS CAPPADOCIAE — ob. 379
(Bas.)
G. = J. Garnier and P. Maran, *Basilii opera omnia* 1–3, Paris, 2nd ed., Gaume, 1739
‡*aegr.* — *consolatoria ad aegrotum*, G.2 p. 1070, M.31.1713
[‡*arbitr.* — *sermo de libero arbitrio*, G.2.613 = Mac. Aeg. *hom.* 25 q.v.]
ascet. 1–2 — *sermones ascetici*, G.2.318, M.31.869
ascet. disc. — *sermo de ascetica disciplina*, G.2.211, M.31.648
†*bapt.* — *de baptismo*, G.2.624, M.31.1513
†*calumn. Trin.* — *adversus calumniatores Trinitatis*, G.2.609, M.31.1487
†*Chr. generat.* — *in Christi generationem*, G.2.595, M.31.1457
‡*const.* — *constitutiones asceticae*, G.2.533, M.31.1321
†*contub.* — *sermo de contubernalibus*, M.30.812
ep. 1–366 notes — *epistulae*, G.3.69, M.32.220
[‡*ep.* 8 — see Evagr. Pont.]
[‡*ep.* 10 — = Gr. Nyss. *ep.* 21]

Basilius Caesariensis Cappadociae (*cont.*)

[‡*ep.* 16 — = Gr. Nyss. *Eun.* 10 (2 p. 226. 14, M.45.828) q.v.]
[‡*ep.* 38 — = Gr. Nyss. *diff. ess.* q.v.]
†*ep.* 41 — *epistula ad Julianum*, I. Bidez and F. Cumont *Iuliani Imperatoris epistulae et leges* Paris and London 1922 p. 284
†*ep.* 42 — *epistula ad Chilonem* also attributed to Ph. Carp.
[‡*ep.* 47 — = Gr. Naz. *ep.* 42]
[*ep.* 117 — see Firminus]
[‡*ep.* 166–7 — = Gr. Naz. *ep.* 65, 66]
[‡*ep.* 189 — = Gr. Nyss. *Trin.* q.v.]
ep. 217 — *can.* 56–74 = †CCP (381) *can.* 1–17, 19–20
[‡*ep.* 321 — = Gr. Naz. *ep.* 57 q.v.]
[‡*ep.* 335–59 — = Libanius et Basilius *epp.* 1–25, *LS*]
save for
[‡*ep.* 342 — = Gr. Nyss. *ep.* 28 q.v.]
[‡*ep.* 348 — = Gr. Nyss. *ep.* 27 q.v.]
†*ep.* 360 — *epistula ad Julianum*
†*ep.* 361, 363 — *epistulae ad Apollinarem*
†*ep.* 365 — *epistula ad Theodosium*
epit. can. — *epitimia in canonicas*, G.2.530, M.31.1313
Eun. 1–3 — *adversus Eunomium libri tres*, G.1.207, M.29.497
[‡*Eun.* 4–5 — *adversus Eunomium libri duo*, G.1.279, M.29.672; see Didym.]

exegetica
hom. in Ps. — *homiliae in Pss.*, G.1.90 and 352–7, M.29.209
†*hom. in Ps.* — *homiliae in Pss.*, G.1.358, M.30.72
†*hom. in Pr.* 6:4 — *homilia in illud*, Ne dederis somnum, G.2.617, M.31.1497
†*Is.* — *commentarius in Is.* 1–16, G.1.378, M.30.117

†*exorc.* 1–2 — *orationes* sive *exorcismi*, M.31.1677
‡*exp. fid. Nic.* — *expositio fidei Nicaenae*, Hahn p. 308
fid. — *de fide*, G.2.223, M.31.676
fr. — *fragmenta*, ap. *Doct. Patr.* 2 p. 12, *ib.* 8 p. 55
‡*h. myst.* — *historia mystagogica*, F. E. Brightman *JTS* 9 (1908) pp. 257, 387
hex. 1–9 — *homiliae in hexaëmeron*, G.1.1, M.29.4
hom. 1–21, 23–24 — *homiliae variae*, G.2.1, M.31.164
[*hom.* 22 — see *leg. lib. gent.*]
†*hom. Spir.* — *homilia de Spiritu sancto*, G.2.583, M.31.1429
‡*inc.* — *homilia de incarnatione*, D. Amand *Revue Bénédictine* 58 Maredsous Belgium 1948 p. 233
†*inform.* — *sermo de informatione ascetica*, G.2.623, M.31.1509
inst. ascet. — *praevia institutio ascetica*, G.2.199, M.31.620
†*jej.* — *de jejunio oratio tertia*, G.2.621, M.31.1507
jud. — *de judicio dei*, G.2.213, M.31.653
‡*Lac.* — *homilia dicta in Lacizis*, G.2.587, M.31.1437
leg. lib. gent. — *ad adolescentes de legendis libris gentilium*, F. Boulenger Paris 1935, G.2.173, M.31.564
†*miser.* — *de misericordia et judicio*, G.2 p. 1067, M.31.1705
mor. 1–24 — *sermones de moribus ex diversis operibus Basilii collecti*, G.3.469, M.32.1116
moral. — *moralia*, G.2.230, M.31.692
†*parad.* — *homilia de paradiso*, G.1.347, M.30.61
[*perf.* — *de perfectione vitae monachorum*, G.2 p. 1065 = *ep.* 22]
‡*poen. mon.* — *poenae in monachos delinquentes*, G.2.526, M.31.1305
†*poenit.* — *de poenitentia*, G.2.603, M.31.1476
‡*poenit. can.* — *canones poenitentiales*, *SS* 4 p. 460
‡*prec.* 1–2 — *precationes*, M.31.1681
reg. br. — *regulae brevius tractatae*, G.2.414, M.31.1052
reg. fus. — *regulae fusius tractatae*, G.2.327, M.31.889
renunt. — *sermo de renuntiatione saeculi*, G.2.202, M.31.625
‡*sac. instr.* — *sermo ob sacerdotum instructionem*, M.31.1685
†*schol. Gr. Naz.* — *scholia in Gregorii Nazianzeni orationes*, M.36.904
Spir. — *liber de Spiritu sancto*, C. F. H. Johnston Oxford 1892, G.3.1, M.32.68
‡*struct. hom.* 1–2 — *homiliae de hominis structura*, G.1.324, M.30.9 (∾ ‡Gr. Nyss. *or.* 1–2 *in Gen.* 1:26)

Basilius Seleucensis (Bas. Sel.) — ob. post 458

ascens. — *homilia in assumptionem domini*, M.28.1092
enc. in Andr. — *encomium in Andream*, M.28.1101
or. 1–37, 40 — *orationes*, M.85.28
‡*or.* 38 — *oratio contra Judaeos de salvatoris adventu*, M.85.400
[‡*or.* 39 — *oratio in deiparae annuntiationem*, M.85.425 = Procl. CP *annunt.* q.v.]
†*or.* 41 — *laudatio in Stephanum*, M.85.461
parasc. — *sermo in passionem domini in parasceve*, M.28.1053
pasch. 1–2 — *sermones in pascha*, M.28.1073
pent. — *sermo in pentecosten*, M.52.809, M.64.417
prod. Jud. — *homilia in feriam quintam et proditionem Judae*, M.28.1048
v. Thecl. — *de vita ac miraculis Theclae*, M.85.477

Bassianus Ephesinus (Bassn.) — saec. v

supplic. — *supplicatio*, ap. C Chalc. *act.* 11, *ACO* 2.1.3 p. 45, H.2.548

Caelestinus Papa (Cael.) — ob. 432

ep. CP 1 — *epistula ad Constantinopolitanos*, *ACO* 1.1.1 p. 83, M.*PL*.50.486
ep. CP 2 — *epistula ad Constantinopolitanos*, *ACO* 1.1.7 p. 131
ep. Cyr. — *epistula ad Cyrillum*, *ACO* 1.1.1 p. 75, int. opp. Cyr. *ep.* 12, M.77.89
ep. episc. — *epistula ad episcopos*, *ACO* 1.1.7 p. 125
ep. Flav. — *epistula ad Flavianum*, *ACO* 1.1.7 p. 142
ep. Jo. Ant. — *epistula ad Joannem Antiochenum*, *ACO* 1.1.1 p. 90, M.*PL*.50.466
ep. Nest. — *epistula ad Nestorium*, *ACO* 1.1.1 p. 77, M.*PL*.50.470
ep. syn. — *epistula ad synodum Ephesinam*, *ACO* 1.1.3 p. 55, M.*PL*.50.506
ep. Thds. — *epistula ad Theodosium*, *ACO* 1.1.7 p. 129

Caesarius Nazianzenus (Caes. Naz.) — [saec. iv]

‡*dial.* — *dialogi*, M.38.852 — post saec. vii

Caius Romanus (Caius R.) — ob. 217

fragmenta, ap. Eus. *h.e.* 2. 25 and 3. 28, 31

Callinicus Monachus (Call.) — saec. v

v. Hyp. — *vita Hypatii*, Seminarii Philologorum Bonnensis Sodales *Teub.* 1895

Canones Apostolorum — saec. iv

Can. App. — ap. *Const. App.* 8. 47

Capreolus Carthaginiensis (Capr.) — ob. 437

ep. Eph. — *epistula ad synodum Ephesinam*, *ACO* 1.1.2 p. 52, M.*PL*.53.844

Catechesis

Catech. Stud. — *catechesis chronica monasterii Studii*, int. opp. Thdr. Stud., M.99.1693

Catenae in Sacras Scripturas

Note: words are cited from catenae only if they have not been traced to the works in which they were originally written

cat. Gen.–Reg. — *Nicephori Catena in Octateucham et libros Regum*, Leipzig 1872–3
cat. Job — *Catena in Job collectore Niceta*, P. Junius London 1637
cat. Ps. — *Expositio Patrum Graecorum in Psalmos*, B. Corderius Antwerp 1643
cat. Jer. — *Catena in Jeremiam*, M. Ghisler Lyons 1623
cat. Dan. — *Catena in Danielem*, *SVC* 1^2 (1825) p. 161
cat. Mt. — *Catenae in evangelia Matthaei et Marci*, J. A. Cramer Oxford 1840 p. 4
cat. (*symb.*) *Mt.* — *Symbolarum in Matthaeum* 1; *Catena Graecorum Patrum*, P. Possinus Toulouse 1646

cat. Lc., Jo. *Catenae in evangelia Lucae et Joannis*, J. A. Cramer Oxford 1841; see also Tit. Bost. *fr. Lc.*

cat. Ac. *Catena in Acta Apostolorum*, J. A. Cramer Oxford, 1838,

cat. Rom. *Catena in epistolam ad Romanos*, J. A. Cramer Oxford 1844

cat. Cor. *Catenae in epistulas ad Corinthios*, J. A. Cramer Oxford 1844

cat. Gal.–Thess. *Catenae in epistulas ad Galatas, Ephesios, Philippenses, Colossenses, Thessalonicenses*, J. A. Cramer Oxford 1842

cat. Tim.–Heb. *Catenae in epistulas ad Timotheum, Titum, Philemona, Hebraeos*, J. A. Cramer Oxford 1843

cat. Jac.–Apoc. *Catenae in epistolas catholicas, accesserunt commentarii in Apocalypsim*, J. A. Cramer Oxford 1840

CELSUS saec. ii
(Cels.) cit. ap. Or. *Cels.*

CHARISIUS PHILADELPHENUS saec. v
(Char.)
libell. *libellus*, ap. C Eph. (431) *act.* 6, *ACO* 1.1.7 p. 96, H.1.1513

CHRISTUS SACERDOS
Chr. Sac. A, B *quomodo Christus sacerdos factus sit*, Vassiliev p. 58

CHRONICON PASCHALE saec. vii
Chron. Pasch. M.92.69; L. Dindorf *CB* 1832

CHRYSIPPUS HIEROSOLYMITANUS ob. 479
(Chrysipp.)
enc. in BMV *encomium in Mariam deiparam*, M. Jugie *PO* 19 (1925) p. 336
enc. in Jo. Bapt. *encomium in Joannem Baptistam*, A. Sigalas *Texte und Forschungen zur Byzantinisch-Neugriechische Philologie* 20 Athens 1937 p. 29
enc. in Mich. *encomium in Michaelem archangelum*, A. Sigalas *Ἐπετηρὶς τῆς ἑταιρείας Βυζαντινῶν σπουδῶν* 3 Athens 1926 p. 88
enc. in Thdr. *encomium in Theodorum*, A. Sigalas *Byzantinisches Archiv* 7 Leipzig 1921 p. 50

CHRYSOSTOMUS, JOANNES ob. 407
(Chrys.)
G. 1–13 = B. de Montfaucon, *Joannis Chrysostomi opera omnia*, 1–13, 2nd ed. (Gaume), Paris 1834–9 (cited by page number in central column which is reproduced in M. and Field)
Field *Mt.* = F. Field, *Joannis Chrysostomi homiliae in Matthaeum*, Cambridge 1839
Field 1–7 = F. Field, *Joannis Chrysostomi interpretatio omnium epistularum Paulinarum* 1–7, Oxford 1845–62

a. exil. 1, 2 *homiliae ante ejus exilium*, G.3.415, M.52.427
Anna 1–5 *sermones de Anna*, G.4.699, M.54.631
anom. 7–12 *contra Anomoeos*, G.1.501, M.48.755
ascens. *de ascensione domini*, G.2.447, M.50.441
bapt. *de baptismo Christi*, G.2.367, M.49.363
carit. *de perfecta caritate*, G.6.287, M.56.279
catech. 1 *catechesis*, G.2.225, M.49.223
catech. 2–4 *catecheses*, A. Papadopoulos-Kerameus *ZP* 95 (1909) p. 154
catech. 5 *catechesis*, G.2.234, M.49.231
coemet. *de coemeterio et cruce*, G.2.397, M.49.393
comp. *comparatio regis et monachi*, G.1.116, M.47.387
compunct. 1 *de compunctione ad Demetrium*, G.1.122, M.47.393
compunct. 2 *de compunctione ad Stelechium*, G.1.140, M.47.411
contin. *fragmentum de continentia*, G.6.299, M.56.291
cruc. 1–2 *de cruce et latrone*, G.2.403, M.49.399
David 1–3 *de David et Saul*, G.4.748, M.54.675
delic. *de futurae vitae deliciis*, G.3.337, M.51.347
diab. 1–3 *de diabolo tentatore* sive *daemones non gubernare mundum*, G.2.246, M.49.241
dimiss. Chan. *in dimissionem Chananaeae*, G.3.432, M.52.449
Diod. *laus Diodori*, G.3.747, M.52.761
ecl. 1–48 *eclogae ex diversis homiliis*, G.12.432, M.63.567
educ. lib. *de educandis liberis*, F. Combefis Paris 1656
El. et vid. *in Eliam et viduam*, G.3.328, M.51.337
eleem. *de eleemosyna*, G.3.248, M.51.261
ep. 1–236, 242 *epistulae*, G.3.527, M.52.549
ep. carc. *epistula ad episcopos et presbyteros in carcere*, G.3.526, M.52.541
ep. Eud. *epistula ad Eudoxiam imperatricem*, M.64.493
ep. Innoc. 1 *epistula ad Innocentium papam*, G.3.515, M.52.529, ap. Pall. *v. Chrys.* 2
ep. Innoc. 2 *epistula ad Innocentium papam*, G.3.521, M.52.535
Eutrop. 1–2 *in Eutropium eunuchum*, G.3.381, M.52.391

exegetica
hom. 1–67 in Gen. *homiliae in Gen.*, G.4.1, M.53.23
serm. 1–9 in Gen. *sermones in Gen.*, G.4.645, M.54.581
fr. Reg. *fragmentum in Reg.*, M.64.50
exp. in Job *specimen expositionis in Job*, M.64.504
fr. Job *fragmenta in Job*, M.64.505
exp. in Ps. *expositiones in Psalmos quosdam*, G.5.1, M.55.35
hom. 1–2 in Ps. 48:17 *homiliae in illud*, Ne timueris, G.5.504, M.55.499
hom. in Ps. 115:1–3 *homilia in illud*, Credidi propter quod, S. Haidacher *ZKT* 31 (1907) p. 351
hom. in Ps. 145:2 *homilia in illud*, Lauda, anima mea, G.5.525, M.55.519
fr. in Pr. *fragmenta in Pr.*, M.64.660
Is. interp. *interpretatio in Is.* 1–8, G.6.1, M.56.11
hom. 1–6 in Is. 6:1 *homiliae in illud*, Vidi dominum, G.6.95, M.56.97
hom. in Is. 45:7 *homilia in illud*, Ego dominus feci lumen, G.6.145, M.56.141
fr. in Jer. *fragmenta in Jer.*, M.64.739
hom. in Jer. 10:23 *homilia in illud*, Domine, non est in homine, G.6.157, M.56.153
Dan. *interpretatio in Dan.*, G.6.200, M.56.193
hom. 1–90 in Mt. *homiliae in Mt.*, Field *Mt.*, G.7.1, M.57.58
hom. in Mt. 7:14 *homilia in illud*, Angusta est porta, *et de oratione domini*, G.3.25, M.51.41
hom. in Mt. 18:23 *homilia in parabolam debitoris*, G.3.1, M.51.17
hom. in Mt. 26:39 *homilia in illud*, Pater, si possibile, G.3.15, M.51.31
hom. 1–88 in Jo. *homiliae in Jo.*, G.8.1, M.59.23
hom. in Jo. 5:19 *homilia in illud*, Filius ex se ipso nihil facit, G.6.255, M.56.247
hom. 1–55 in Ac. *homiliae in Ac.*, G.9.1, M.60.13
hom. 1–4 in Ac. princ. *homiliae in principium Actorum Apostolorum*, G.3.50, M.51.65
hom. 1–4 in Ac. 9:1 *homiliae in mutatione nominum in illud*, Saulus autem adhuc spirans, G.3.98, M.51.113
hom. 1–32 in Rom. *homiliae in Rom.*, Field 1, G.9.421, M.60.391
hom. in Rom. 5:3 *homilia de gloria in tribulationibus*, G.3.140, M.51.155
hom. in Rom. 8:28 *homilia in illud*, Scimus quoniam diligentibus, G.3.150, M.51.165
hom. in Rom. 12:20 *homilia in illud*, Si esurierit inimicus, G.3.157, M.51.171
hom. 1–2 in Rom. 16:3 *homiliae in illud*, Salutate Priscillam, G.3.172, M.51.187
hom. 1–44 in 1 Cor. *homiliae in 1 Cor.*, Field 2, G.10.1, M.61.9
hom. in 1 Cor. 7:2 *homilia in illud*, Propter fornicationes, G.3.193, M.51.207
hom. in 1 Cor. 7:39 *homilia in illud*, Mulier alligata est, G.3.203, M.51.217
hom. in 1 Cor. 10:1 *homilia in illud*, Nolo vos ignorare, G.3.228, M.51.241
hom. in 1 Cor. 11:19 *homilia in illud*, Oportet haereses esse, G.3.240, M.51.251
hom. in 1 Cor. 15:28 *homilia in illud*, Cum autem subjecta, S. Haidacher *ZKT* 31 (1907) p. 150
hom. 1–30 in 2 Cor. *homiliae in 2 Cor.*, Field 3, G.10.417, M.61.381

CHRYSOSTOMUS, JOANNES (*cont.*)

hom. 1–3 in 2 Cor. 4:13	*homiliae in illud,* Habentes eundem Spiritum, G.3.260, M.51.271
hom. in 2 Cor. 11:1	*homilia in illud,* Utinam sustineretis, G.3.291, M.51.301
comm. in Gal.	*commentarium in Gal.,* Field 4 p. 1, G.10.657, M.61.611
hom. in Gal. 2:11	*homilia in illud,* In faciem ei restiti, G.3.362, M.51.371
hom. 1–24 in Eph.	*homiliae in Eph.,* Field 4 p. 104, G.11.1, M.62.9
hom. 1–15 in Phil.	*homiliae in Phil.,* Field 5 p. 1, G.11.189, M.62.177
hom. in Phil. 1:18	*homilia in illud,* Sive per occasionem, G.3.300, M.51.311
hom. 1–12 in Col.	*homiliae in Col.,* Field 5 p. 172, G.11.322, M.62.299
hom. 1–11 in 1 Thess.	*homiliae in 1 Thess.,* Field 5 p. 313, G.11.425, M.62.391
hom. 1–5 in 2 Thess.	*homiliae in 2 Thess.,* Field 5 p. 443, G.11.510, M.62.467
hom. 1–18 in 1 Tim.	*homiliae in 1 Tim.,* Field 6 p. 1, G.11.547, M.62.501
hom. in 1 Tim. 5:9	*homilia in illud,* Vidua eligatur, G.3.311, M.51.321
hom. 1–10 in 2 Tim.	*homiliae in 2 Tim.,* Field 6 p. 162, G.11.658, M.62.599
hom. in 2 Tim. 3:1	*homilia in illud,* Hoc autem scitote, G.6.278, M.56.271
hom. 1–6 in Tit.	*homiliae in Tit.,* Field 6, p. 264, G.11.729, M.62.663
hom. 1–3 in Philm.	*homiliae in Philm.,* Field 6, p. 325, G.11.772, M.62.701
hom. 1–34 in Heb.	*homiliae in Heb.,* Field 7, G.12.1, M.63.9
fr. in Jac.	*fragmentum in Jac.,* M.64.1040
fr. in Petr.	*fragmenta in Petr.,* M.64.1053
fr. in 1 Jo.	*fragmenta in 1 Jo.,* M.64.1060
fem. reg.	*quod regulares feminae viris cohabitare non debeant,* G.1.248, M.47.513
grat.	*non esse ad gratiam concionandum,* G.2.658, M.50.653
hom. div.	*homiliae diversae,* G.12.323, M.63.461
†*hom. prec.* 1, 2	*homiliae de precatione,* G.3.778, M.50.775
hom. suppl. 2	*homilia in poenitentiam Ninivitarum,* M.64.424
[*hom. suppl.* 4	*homilia in decem millia talenta,* M.64.444, from 444c to end = *hom. 17 in Gen.*]
incomprehens. 1–5	*de incomprehensibili dei natura* seu *contra Anomoeos,* G.1.444, M.48.701
Jud. 1–8	*adversus Judaeos,* G.1.587, M.48.843
†*Jud. et gent.*	*contra Judaeos et gentiles quod Christus sit deus,* G.1.558, M.48.813
kal.	*in kalendas,* G.1.697, M.48.953
laed.	*quod nemo laedatur nisi a seipso,* G.3.444, M.52.459
laud. Max.	*de laude Maximi et quales ducendae uxores,* G.3.211, M.51.225
laud. Paul. 1–7	*de laudibus Pauli,* G.2.476, M.50.473
Laz. 1–7	*in Lazarum,* G.1.707, M.48.963
nativ.	*in diem natalem Christi,* G.2.354, M.49.351
†*nativ.*	*in nativitatem Christi,* G.6.392, M.56.385
non desp.	*de non esse desperandum,* G.3.354, M.51.363
oppugn. 1–3	*adversus oppugnatores vitae monasticae,* G.1.44, M.47.319
ordin.	*homilia cum presbyter ordinatus fuit,* G.1.436, M.48.693
p. redit. 1	*homilia post reditum ab exilio,* G.3.424
p. redit. 2	*homilia post reditum ab exilio,* G.3.427, M.52.443
pan. Aeg.	*laudatio martyrum Aegyptiorum,* G.3.699, M.50.693
pan. Bab. 1	*panegyricum in Babylam martyrem,* G.2.531, M.50.527
†*pan. Bab.* 2	*panegyricum in Babylam martyrem et contra Julianum et gentes,* G.2.536, M.50.533
pan. Barl.	*laudatio Barlaam martyris,* G.2.681, M.50.675
pan. Bern.	*panegyricum in Bernicen et Prosdocen martyres et de quatriduano Lazaro,* G.2.634, M.50.629
pan. Dros.	*laudatio Drosidis martyris,* G.2.688, M.50.683
pan. Eust. Ant.	*panegyricum in Eustathium Antiochiae episcopum,* G.2.603, M.50.597
pan. Ign.	*panegyricum in Ignatium martyrem,* G.2.592, M.50.587
pan. Juln.	*panegyricum in Julianum martyrem,* G.2.671, M.50.665
pan. Juv.	*panegyricum in Juventinum et Maximinum martyres,* G.2.578, M.50.571
pan. Laz.	*panegyricum in quatriduanum Lazarum,* G.2.646, M.50.641
pan. Lucn.	*panegyricum in Lucianum martyrem,* G.2.524, M.50.519
pan. Macc. 1–2	*panegyrica in Maccabaeos,* G.2.622, M.50.617
pan. Macc. fr.	*fragmentum panegyrici in Maccabaeos,* G.2.633, M.50.627
pan. mart. 1–3	*panegyrica in martyres,* G.2.650, M.50.645; G.2.667, M.50.661; G.2.711, M.50.705
pan. Melet.	*panegyricum in Meletium,* G.2.518, M.50.515
pan. Pelag. Ant.	*panegyricum in Pelagiam Antiochenam martyrem,* G.2.585, M.50.679
pan. Phoc.	*panegyricum in Phocam martyrem,* G.2.704, M.50.699
pan. Polyc.	*fragmenta ex panegyrico in Polycarpum,* A. Hilgenfeld *ZWT* 45 (1920) p. 569
pan. Rom. 1–2	*panegyrica in Romanum martyrem,* G.2.611, M.50.605
paralyt.	*homilia in paralyticum demissum per tectum,* G.3.32, M.51.47
pasch.	*homilia in pascha,* G.3.750, M.52.765
pecc.	*de non evulgandis fratrum peccatis,* G.3.344, M.51.353
pent. 1–2	*homiliae de pentecoste,* G.2.457, M.50.453
Philogon.	*de beato Philogonio,* seu *contra Anomoeos* 6, G.1.492, M.48.747
poenit. 1–9	*homiliae de poenitentia,* G.2.279, M.49.277
prod. Jud. 1–2	*de proditione Judae,* G.2.376, M.49.373
prod. Jud. 3	*de proditione Judae,* G.2.721, M.50.715
proph. obscurit. 1–2	*de prophetarum obscuritate,* G.6.168, M.56.163
res. Chr.	*de resurrectione Christi et contra ebriosos,* G.2.437, M.50.433
res. mort.	*de resurrectione mortuorum,* G.2.422, M.50.417
sac. 1–6	*de sacerdotio,* J. A. Nairn Cambridge 1906, G.1.362, M.48.623
Saturn.	*homilia praedicata cum Saturninus et Aurelianus in exsilium acti essent,* G.3.405, M.52.413
scand.	*ad eos qui scandalizati sunt,* G.3.465, M.52.479
Stag. 1–3	*adhortationes ad Stagyrium a daemone vexatum,* G.1.154, M.47.423
stat. 1–21	*ad populum Antiochenum de statuis,* G.2.1, M.49.95
subintr.	*contra eos qui subintroductas habent,* G.1.228, M.47.495
†*synops.*	*synopsis sacrae scripturae,* G.6.314, M.56.313
temp.	*de temperantia,* S. Haidacher *ZKT* 30 (1906) p. 575
terr. mot.	*de terrae motu,* G.2.717, M.50.713
Thdr. 1–2	*adhortationes ad Theodorum lapsum,* G.1.1, M.47.277
theatr.	*contra ludos et theatra,* G.6.272, M.56.263
vid. 1–2	*ad viduam juniorem,* G.1.338, M.48.599
virg.	*de virginitate,* G.1.268, M.48.533
‡*Abr.*	*in Abraham,* G.2.741, M.50.737
‡*admon.*	*admonitiones spirituales,* G.11.815, M.62.741
‡*ador.* 1, 2	*de adoratione crucis,* G.3.819, M.52.835; G.11.820, M.62.747. (*Note*: *ador.* 1 contains some passages identical with *hom. 54, 55 in Mt.*)
‡*advent.*	*in secundum domini adventum,* G.8^{2}.142, M.59.619
‡*anim.*	*de salute animae,* G.9.819, M.60.735
‡*annunt.*	*in annuntiationem,* G.9.841, M.60.755
[‡*annunt.*	*in annuntiationem,* G.2.797, M.50.791 = ‡Gr. Thaum. *annunt.* 3]
‡*annunt. et Ar.*	*in annuntiationem et contra Arianos,* G.11.838, M.62.763
‡*apost.*	*in duodecim apostolos,* G.8^{2}.11, M.59.495
‡*ascens.* 1–5	*in ascensionem,* G.3.777, M.52.791

‡*ascens. Ac.*	*de ascensione et in principium Actuum*, G.3.758, M.52.773
‡*ascet. facet.*	*ascetam facetiis uti non debere*, G.1.808, M.48.1055
‡*assumpt. Chr.* 1, 2	*in assumptionem domini*, G.10.763, M.61.711; G.11.800, M.12.727
‡*Bass.*	*in Bassum martyrem*, G.2.724, M.50.719
‡*BMV*	*contra haereticos et in virginem deiparam*, G.8^{2}.238, M.59.709
‡*caec.*	*de caeco nato*, G.8^{2}.61, M.59.543
‡*caec. Zacch.*	*de caeco et in Zacchaeum*, G.8^{2}.120, M.59.599
‡*carit.* 1, 2	*de caritate*, G.10.731, M.61.681; G.11.845, M.62.769
‡*catech.*	*in catechumenos*, G.9.823, M.60.739
‡*catech. pasch.*	*sermo catecheticus in pascha*, G.8.250, M.59.721
‡*cent.*	*in centurionem*, G.10.824, M.61.769
‡*Chan.*	*in Chananaeam et in Pharaonem*, G.8^{2}.177, M.59.653
‡*circ.*	*de circo*, G.8^{2}.87, M.59.567
‡*concept. Jo. Bapt.*	*in conceptionem Joannis Baptistae*, G.2.793, M.50.787
‡*cruc.*	*in venerabilem crucem*, G.2.820, M.50.815
‡*cruc. venerand.*	*in venerandam crucem*, G.8^{2}.200, M.59.675
‡*decoll.*	*in decollationem Joannis Baptistae*, G.8^{1}.1, M.59.485
‡*disc. benign.*	*Christi discipulum benignum esse debere*, G.1.813, M.47.1069
‡*El.*	*in Eliam prophetam*, G.6.600, M.56.583
‡*eleem.* 1–4	*de eleemosyna*, G.1.817, M.48.1059; G.9.789, M.60.707; G.9.832, M.60.747; G.11.843, M.62.769
‡*ep. Caes.*	*fragmenta epistulae ad Caesarium*, G.3.742, M.52.755, M.64.496
‡*ep. mon.*	*epistula ad monachos*, G.9.837, M.60.751
‡*exalt.*	*in exaltationem crucis*, G.8.204, M.59.679
exegetica	
‡*hom. 1–3 in Gen.*	*homiliae in Gen.*, G.6.532, M.56.519
[‡*hom. in Gen.* 24:2	*homilia in illud*, Pone manum tuum, G.6.569, M.56.553 = Sever. *Abr.*, q.v.]
‡*hom. 1–4 in Job*	*homiliae in Job*, G.6.579, M.56.563
‡*Ps. arg.*	*argumentum Psalmorum*, G.5.542, M.56.533
‡*hom. in Ps.* 6	*homilia in Ps. 6*, G.5.551, M.55.543; ∾ Anast. S. *Ps.* 6, M.89.1080B–1101B
‡*hom. in Ps.* 13	*homilia in Ps. 13*, G.8.557, M.55.549
‡*hom. in Ps.* 38:7	*homilia in illud*, Verumtamen ... frustra conturbatur, G.5.566, M.55.559
‡*hom. 1–3 in Ps.* 50	*homilae in Ps. 50*, G.5.535, M.55.527
‡*hom. in Ps.* 51	*homilia in Ps. 51*, G.5.597, M.55.589; a longer recension of Eus. *Ps.* 51, M.23.441 q.v.
‡*hom. in Ps.* 75:12	*homilia in illud*, Precamini, G.5.602, M.55.593
‡*hom. in Ps.* 76:4	*homilia in illud*, Memor fui dei, G.10.739, M.61.689
‡*hom. in Ps.* 83	*homilia de turture* seu *de ecclesia*, G.5.606, M.55.599
‡*hom. in Ps.* 92:3	*homilia in illud*, Elevaverunt flumina, G.5.620, M.55.611
‡*hom. in Ps.* 94:1	*homilia in illud*, Venite exultemus, G.5.624, M.55.615
‡*hom. in Ps.* 95:1	*homilia in illud*, Cantate domino, G.5.628, M.55.619
‡*hom. in Ps.* 96:1	*homilia in illud*, Dominus regnavit, G.5.610, M.55.603
‡*hom. in Ps.* 77–107	*homiliae in Pss.* 77–107, G.5.723, M.55.711; G.5.637, M.55.629
‡*hom. 1–3 in Ps.* 118	*stationes in Ps.* 118, G.5.685, M.55.675
‡*hom. in Ps.* 139:1	*homilia in illud*, Eripe me, G.5.719, M.55.707
‡*fr. in Mt.* 1:17	*fragmentum de generatione Christi*, G.7.846, M.58.793
‡*hom. in Mt.* 4:6	*homilia in illud*, Si filius dei es, G.10.733, M.61.683. (*Note*: much of this is identical with Nest. *hom. tent.* q.v.)
‡*hom. in Mt.* 6:1	*homilia in illud*, Attendite ne justitiam, G.8^{2}.90, M.59.571
‡*hom. in Mt.* 12:14	*homilia in illud*, Exeuntes Pharisaei, G.10.758, M.66.705
‡*Mt.* 20:1	*oratio catechetica in illud*, Simile est regnum coelorum homini patrifamilias, G.8^{2}.98, M.59.577
[‡*hom. in Mt.* 21:23	*homilia in illud*, In qua potestate, G.6.417, M.56.411; see Sever.]
‡*hom. in Mt.* 26:39	*homilia in illud*, Pater, si possibile, G.10.806, M.61.751; partly identical with Amph. *hom. in Mt.* 26:39 q.v.
‡*hom. in Lc.* 2:1	*homilia in illud*, Exit edictum, G.2.800, M.50.795
‡*hom. in Lc.* 8:5	*homilia in illud*, Exiit qui seminat, G.10.828, M.61.771
‡*hom. in Lc.* 12:49	*homilia in illud*, Ignem veni, G.11.812, M.62.739
‡*hom. in Lc.* 15:11	*homilia in illud*, Homo quidam, G.10.838, M.61.781
‡*hom. in Jo.* 1:1	*homilia in illud*, In principio erat verbum, G.12.415, M.63.543
‡*hom. in Jo.* 7:14	*homilia in illud*, Ascendit dominus, G.10.792, M.61.739. (*Note*: G.10.794C–end = Eust. *Melch.* q.v.)
‡*hom. in Jo.* 7:15	*homilia in illud*, Quomodo scit literas, G.8^{2}.167, M.59.643
‡*hom. in Jo.* 7:20	*homilia de non judicante proximo*, G.9.849, M.60.763
‡*hom. in Jo.* 11:47	*homilia in illud*, Colligerunt Judaei, G.8^{2}.43, M.59.525
‡*hom. in Rom.* 7:19	*homilia in illud*, Non quod volo, G.8^{2}.188, M.59.663
‡*hom. in 2 Cor.* 12:9	*homilia in illud*, Sufficit tibi, G.8^{2}.24, M.59.507
‡*fid.*	*de fide et lege naturae et Sancto Spiritu*, G.1.825, M.48.1081
‡*fil. vid.*	*in filium viduae*, G.10.848, M.61.789
‡*fug. spec.*	*de fugienda simulata specie*, G.1.815, M.48.1073
‡*haer.*	*contra haereticos*, G.9.829, M.60.745
‡*hebd. jej.*	*homilia in mediam hebdomadam jejuniorum*, G.8^{2}.229, M.59.701
‡*Herod.*	*de poenitentia et in Herodem*, G.8.287, M.59.757
‡*hom.* 1–8, 10, 11, 13	*homiliae quaedam spuriae*, G.13.201, M.64.11
‡*hom.* 9	*homilia in illud*, Hic est filius, Mt. 17:5, G.13.232, M.64.33 ∾ Gr. Ant. *bapt.* 2 q.v.
‡*hom. jej.* 1–7	*homiliae in praedicationem jejunii*, G.9.793, M.60.711
‡*hom. suppl.* 3	*homilia de eleemosyna*, M.64.433; compilation from ‡*eleem.* 4 and Eus. Al. *serm.* 21
‡*hom. suppl.* 5	*homilia ad eos qui magni aestimant opes*, M.64.453
‡*hom. suppl.* 6	*homilia de precatione*, M.64.461
‡*hom. suppl.* 8	*homilia de virtute animi*, M.64.473
‡*inc.*	*in incarnationem*, G.8^{2}.213, M.59.687
‡*indict.* 1, 2	*in principium indictionis*, G.8^{2}.94, M.59.575; G.8^{2}.198, M.59.673
‡*infant.*	*in Herodem et infantes*, G.10.750, M.61.699
‡*ingr. jej.* 1, 2	*in ingressu jejuniorum*, G.11.799, M.62.727; G.11.817, M.62.745
‡*jej.*	*de jejunio dominica quinta jejuniorum praedicata*, G.11.803, M.62.731
‡*Jord.*	*in Jordanem fluvium*, G.10.778, M.61.725
‡*Joseph*	*de Joseph et de castitate*, G.6.604, M.56.587
‡*Jo. theol.* 1–3	*in Joannem theologum*, G.8^{2}.130, M.59.609; G.10.771, 772; M.61.719
‡*Jud.*	*contra Judaeos, gentiles et haereticos*, G.1.820, M.48.1075
‡*Jud. serp.*	*contra Judaeos et in serpentem aeneum*, G.10.851, M.61.793
‡*latr.*	*in latronem et in proditorem*, G.8^{2}.247, M.59.719
‡*Laz.* 1, 3	*in Lazarum*, G.11.846, M.62.771; G.11.852, M.62.777
[‡*Laz.* 2	*in Lazarum*, G.11.850, M.62.775; see †Hipp.]
‡*Laz. et div.*	*de Lazaro et divite*, G.8^{2}.113, M.59.591
‡*leg.*	*de legislatore*, G.6.403, M.56.397
‡*mans.*	*de mansuetudine*, G.12.422, M.63.549
‡*mart.*	*in memoriam martyrum*, G.3.811, M.52.827
‡*Marth.*	*in Martham, Mariam et Lazarum*, G.10.753, M.61.701
‡*meretr.* 1–3	*in meretricem et pharisaeum*, G.8^{2}.49, M.59.531; G.10.762, M.61.709; G.10.780, M.61.727

CHRYSOSTOMUS, JOANNES (*cont.*)

‡*mesopent.*	*in mediam pentecosten*, G.10.795, M.61.741
‡*nat. Chr.* 1, 2	*in natale Christi*, G.10.790, M.61.737; G.10.819, M.61.763
‡*nat. Jo. Bapt.*	*in natale Joannis Baptistae*, G.10.812, M.61.757
‡*neg.*	*de negatione Petri et de Joseph*, G.8^{2}.136, M.59.613
‡*occurs.*	*de occursu Christi*, G.2.812, M.50.807
‡*or.*	*de oratione*, G.11.810, M.62.737
‡*or. dom.*	*interpretatio orationis dominicae*, G.8^{2}.149, M.59.627
‡*palm.* 1, 2	*in ramos palmarum*, G.8^{2}.231, M.59.703; G.10.767, M.61.715 (‡*palm.* 1 = ‡Meth. *palm.*)
‡*pan. Macc.* 3	*panegyricum in Maccabaeos*, G.2.631, M.50.625
‡*pasch.* 1–5, 7	*in pascha*, G.8^{2}.251, M.59.723
‡*pasch.* 6	*in pascha*, P. Nautin *SC* 27 (1950), G.8^{2}.264, M.59.735
‡*pat.* 1, 2	*de patientia*, G.9.806, M.60.723
‡*pat. et consumm.*	*de patientia et in consummatione saeculi*, G.12.817, M.63.937
‡*pent.* 1, 2	*in pentecosten*, G.3.787, M.52.803
‡*pent.* 4	*in pentecosten*, G.12.812, M.63.933
‡*Petr. et El.*	*in Petrum et Eliam*, G.2.730, M.50.725
‡*Petr. et Paul.*	*in Petrum et Paulum*, G.8^{2}.7, M.59.491
‡*phar.*	*de pharisaeo Simone*, G.8^{2}.110, M.59.589
‡*poenit.* 1–4	*de poenitentia*, G.9.761, M.60.681; G.9.780, M.60.699; G.9.786, M.60.705; G.9.852, M.60.765
‡*poenit. can.*	*canones poenitentiales*, *SS* 4 p. 461; cf. ‡Ath. *poenit. can.*
‡*praecurs.* 1, 2	*in praecursorem Christi*, G.2.805, M.50.801; G.8^{2}.5, M.59.489
‡*prec.*	*precationes variae*, G.12.799, M.63.923; ap. *Euchol.* p. 581, M.64.1061
‡*prod. Jud.*	*in proditionem Judae*, G.10.738, M.61.687
‡*prod. serv.*	*in proditionem servatoris*, G.8^{2}.242, M.59.713
‡*prodig.* 1, 2	*in parabolam de filio prodigo*, G.8^{2}.33, M.59.515; G.8^{2}.150, M.59.627
‡*prov.* 1–6	*de fato et providentia*, G.2.752, M.50.749
‡*pseud.*	*de pseudoprophetis*, G.8^{2}.72, M.59.553
‡*publ.* 1, 2	*de publicano et pharisaeo*, G.8^{2}.116, M.59.595; G.11.796, M.62.723
‡*puer.*	*de tribus pueris*, G.6.612, M.56.593
‡*Rach.*	*in Rachelem et infantes*, G.10.749, M.61.697
‡*remiss.*	*de remissione peccatorum*, G.9.845, M.60.759
‡*res.*	*in resurrectionem Christi*, G.11.827, M.62.753
‡*sac.* 7	*de sacerdotio liber septimus*, G.1.805, M.48.1067 = Ephr. 3. 1
‡*sacrif.*	*de sacrificio Cain et de fato*, G.11.792, M.62.719
‡*salt. Herodiad.*	*in saltationem Herodiadis*, G.8^{2}.39, M.59.521
‡*Samarit.* 1, 2	*in Samaritanam*, G.8^{2}.53, M.59.535; G.10.797, M.61.743
‡*Samarit. parab.* 1, 2	*in parabolam Samaritani*, G.10.810, M.61.755; G.11.829, M.62.755
‡*serm. ascens.* 1, 2	*sermones in ascensionem*, *Traditio* 9 New York 1953 pp. 116–22
‡*serm. jej.* 1–4	*sermones de jejunio*, G.10.846, M.61.787; G.11.804, M.62.731; G.11.831, M.62.757; G.11.833, M.62.759
‡*serm. pasch.*	*sermo in pascha*, *Traditio* 9 New York 1953 p. 108
‡*sicc.*	*de siccitate*, G.10.775, M.61.723
‡*Spir.*	*de Sancto Spiritu*, G.3.797, M.52.813
‡*Steph.* 1–3	*in Stephanum protomartyrem*, G.12.809, M.63.929
‡*Steph. protomart.* 1, 2	*in Stephanum protomartyrem*, G.8^{2}.17, M.59.501; G.8^{2}.227, M.59.699
‡*Sus.*	*de Susanna*, G.6.607, M.56.589
‡*synax.*	*in synaxin archangelorum*, G.8^{2}.285, M.59.755
‡*theatr.*	*quod non sit accedendum ad theatrum et de Abraham*, G.6.557, M.56.541
‡*Thecl.*	*laudatio Theclae martyris*, G.2.749, M.50.745
‡*theoph.* 1, 2	*in sancta theophania*, G.2.809, M.50.805; G.10.817, M.61.761
‡*Thom.* 1, 2	*in Thomam apostolum*, G.8^{2}.14, M.59.497; G.8^{2}.207, M.59.681
‡*Thom.* 3	*in novam dominicam et in Thomam apostolum*, G.12.804, M.63.927
‡*transfig.*	*in transfigurationem*, G.10.774, M.61.721
‡*transfig.*	*in transfigurationem*, Savile 7 p. 339
‡*trid.*	*in triduanam resurrectionem Christi*, G.2.824, M.50.821
‡*Trin.*	*de Trinitate*, G.1.832, M.48.1087
‡*villic.*	*in parabolam villici iniquitatis*, G.10.843, M.61.785
‡*virg. corrupt.*	*contra virginum corruptores*, G.9.826, M.60.741
‡*virg. parab.*	*in parabolam virginum et de eleemosyna*, G.8^{2}.45, M.59.527
‡*virt. carit.*	*de virtute caritatis*, G.9.861, M.60.773
‡*virt. fid.*	*de virtute fidei*, G.9.854, M.60.767
‡*virt. spei*	*de virtute spei*, G.9.858, M.60.771
‡*Zacch.* 1, 2	*in Zacchaeum publicanum*, G.8^{2}.120, M.59.599; G.10.823, M.61.767
‡*Zach.*	*de oraculo Zachariae reddito*, G.2.790, M.50.785

CLAUDIUS APOLLINARIUS saec. ii
(Claud.)

fr. pasch.	*fragmenta de paschate*, M.5.1297

CLEMENS ALEXANDRINUS ob. ante 215
(Clem.)

ecl.	*eclogae ex scripturis propheticis*, O. Stählin *GCS* 3 (1909) p. 137, M.9.697
exc. Thdot.	*excerpta Theodoti*, *GCS* 3 p. 105, M.9.653
fr. 1–74	*fragmenta*, *GCS* 3 p. 195, partly in M.9.740
paed.	*paedagogus*, *GCS* 1 (1905) p. 89, M.8.247
paed. hymn.	*hymnus*, ap. Clem. *paed.* ad fin., *GCS* 1 p. 291, M.8.681
prot.	*protrepticus* sive *cohortatio ad gentes*, *GCS* 1 p. 1, M.8.49
q.d.s.	*quis dives salvetur*, *GCS* 3 p. 159, M.9.604
str.	*stromateis* 1–6, *GCS* 2 (1906) p. 3, M.8.685, M.9.9; *str.* 7–8, *GCS* 3 p. 3, M.9.401

CLEMENS ROMANUS saec. i

1 Clem.	*epistula Clementis ad Corinthios*, Bihlmeyer p. 35, M.1.201
2 Clem.	*homilia* sive *epistula secunda Clementis ad Corinthios*, Bihlmeyer p. 71, M.1.329 [spurious]

CLEMENTINA

Basically early third-century material, in its present form probably early fourth century

Clem. contest.	*contestatio pro iis qui librum accipiunt*, M.2.28
Clem. ep.	*epistula Clementis ad Jacobum*, M.2.32
Clem. ep. Petr.	*epistula Petri ad Jacobum*, M.2.25
Clem. epit. A	*epitome de gestis Petri*, M.2.469
Clem. epit. B	*epitome de gestis Petri*, A. R. M. Dressel *Clementinorum epitomae duae* Leipzig 1859 p. 122
Clem. recogn. suppl. 1–4	*supplementum ad recognitiones Clementinas*, M.1.1456
Clem. recogn. suppl. 5	ap. Or. *philoc.* 23. 22, M.1.1472
Hom. Clem. 1–20	*homiliae Clementinae*, M.2.57

CODEX CANONUM ECCLESIAE AFRICANAE saec. v–vii?

Cod. Afr.	H.1.861

CODEX THEODOSIANUS

Cod. Thds.	see Thds. Imp. *cod.*

COLLUTHUS saec. vi
(Coll.)

fr.	*fragmenta varia*, ap. *Doct. Patr.* 41 p. 313; ap C Later. *act.* 5, H.3.896–7

COLUMBUS AFRICANUS saec. vii
(Columb.)

ep.	*epistula ad Theodorum Papam*, int. opp. Thdr. Papae, M.*PL*.87.82

CONCILIA

The numbering of the *actiones* in H. is followed. Only the page and column on which the *actiones* begin are given below, not the pages and columns on which they continue after interruption.

Epistles, *libelli*, *supplicationes*, etc., addressed to a council and signed by a

	body of people, are not listed below. They are cited thus, e.g. *Libell.* ap. C Chalc. *act.* 1.
	Creeds promulgated by Councils are listed under *Symbola.*
C Alex.	Concilium Alexandrinum anno 338
ep.	*epistula*, ap. Ath. *apol. sec.* 3–19
C Anc. (314)	Concilium Ancyranum anno 314
can. 1–25	*canones*, Lauchert p. 29
C Anc. (358)	Concilium Ancyranum anno 358
anath. 1–19	*anathemata*, ap. Epiph. *haer.* 73. 10–11
ep. syn.	*epistula synodica*, ap. Epiph. *haer.* 73. 2–9
C Ant. (341)	Concilium Antiochenum anno 341
can. 1–25	*canones*, Lauchert p. 43. Prob. belonging to a somewhat earlier orthodox council; see Ballerini *Leonis opera* 3 pp. xxv f.; W. Telfer *HTR* 43 (Jan. 1950), p. 55
ep.	*epistula*, H.1.589
C Ant. (363)	Concilium Antiochenum anno 363
ep.	*epistula*, ap. Socr. *h.e.* 3. 25. 10–18
C Ant. (445)	Concilium Antiochenum anno 445
act.	*actio* ap. C Chalc. *act.* 14, *ACO* 2.1.3 p. 69, H.2.580
C Ant. (448)	Concilium Antiochenum anno 448
act.	*actio*, ap. C Chalc. *act.* 10, *ACO* 2.1.3 p. 21, H.2.513
C Arim.	Concilium Ariminense anno 359
decr.	*decretum*, ap. Ath. *syn.* 11
ep. Const. 1	*epistula ad Constantium*, ap. Ath. *syn.* 10
ep. Const. 2	*epistula ad Constantium*, ap. Ath. *syn.* 55. 4–7
C Beryt.	Concilium Berytense anno 449
act.	*actio*, ap. C Chalc. *act.* 10, *ACO* 2.1.3 p. 19, H.2.512
C Carth.	Concilium Carthaginense anno 256
act.	*actio*, H.1.159. For later C Carth, see *Cod. Afr.*
C Chalc.	Concilium Chalcedonense anno 451, oecumenicum quartum
act.	*actiones*, *ACO* 2.1.1 p. 55, H.2.53. (*Note*: *act.* 14 suppl., *ACO* 2.1.3 p. 83, int. opp. Leo. Mag., M.*PL*.54.1250)
act. Caros.	*actio de Caroso et Dorotheo*, *ACO* 2.1.3 p. 99, H.2.432
act. Phot.	*actio de Photio Tyrio*, *ACO* 2.1.3 p. 101, H.2.436
can. 1–27	*canones*, *ACO* 2.1.2 p. 158, Lauchert p. 89
can. 28	*ACO* 2.1.3 p. 88, Lauchert p. 96
can. 29–30	Lauchert p. 97
ep.	*epistulae variae*, *ACO* 2, H.2
CCP (360)	Concilium Constantinopolitanum anno 360
ep.	*epistula*, ap. Thdt. *h.e.* 2. 28
CCP (381)	Concilium Constantinopolitanum anno 381, oecumenicum secundum
can. 1–6	*canones*, Lauchert p. 84
‡*can.* 7	*canon septimus*, Lauchert p. 86
†*can.* 1–21	*canones*, C. H. Turner *JTS* 15 1913–14 p. 164. (*Note*: †*can.* 1–17, 19–20 = Bas. *ep.* 217 *can.* 56–74)
ep.	*epistula*, ap. Thdt. *h.e.* 5. 9
CCP (394)	Concilium Constantinopolitanum anno 394
act.	*actio*, M.119.821
CCP (448)	Concilium Constantinopolitanum anno 448
act.	*actio*, ap. C Chalc. *act.* 1, *ACO* 2.1.1 p. 100, H.2.110
ep. Eut. 1	*epistula ad Eutychem*, ap. C Chalc. *act.* 1, *ACO* 2.1.1 p. 126, H.2.144
ep. Eut. 2	*epistula ad Eutychem*, ap. C Chalc. *act.* 1, *ACO* 2.1.1 p. 129, H.2.148
CCP (449)	Concilium Constantinopolitanum anno 449
act.	*actio*, *ACO* 2.1.1 p. 148, H.2.172
CCP (518)	Concilium Constantinopolitanum anno 518
act.	*actio*, ap. CCP (536) *act.* 5, *ACO* 3 p. 67, H.2.1333
ep.	*epistula*, *ib.*, *ACO* 3 p. 62, H.2.1321
CCP (536)	Concilium Constantinopolitanum anno 536 sub Mena
act.	*actiones*, *ACO* 3 p. 25, H.2.1185
CCP (543)	Concilium Constantinopolitanum anno 543
anath. 1–15	*anathemata*, Hahn p. 227, H.3.284
CCP (553)	Concilium Constantinopolitanum anno 553, oecumenicum quintum
act. 3	*actionis tertiae fragmentum*, ap. C Later. *act.* 5, H.3.856
act. 8	*actionis octavae fragmentum*, ap. Evagr. *h.e.* 4. 38 p. 188, M.86.2776–7
anath. 1–14	*anathemata*, Hahn p. 168, more fully in H.3.193; ∾ Justn. *conf. anath.* q.v.
CCP (638)	Concilium Constantinopolitanum anno 638
act.	*actio*, ap. C Later. *act.* 3, H.3.797
CCP (639)	Concilium Constantinopolitanum anno 639
act.	*actio*, ap. C Later. *act.* 3, H.3.780
CCP (681)	Concilium Constantinopolitanum annis 680 et 681, oecumenicum sextum
act.	*actiones*, H.3.1056
ep. Agath.	*epistula ad Agathonem Papam*, M.*PL*.87.1247
or. imp.	*oratio ad imperatorem*, H.3.1416
CCP (754)	Concilium Constantinopolitanum anno 754 iconoclastum dictum
decr.	*decreta*, ap. C Nic. (787) *act.* 6, H.4.328
C Eph. (431)	Concilium Ephesinum anno 431, oecumenicum tertium
act.	*actiones*, *ACO* 1.1.2 p. 3, H.1.1354
can. 1–6	*canones*, *ACO* 1.1.3 p. 27, Lauchert p. 87
ep.	*epistulae variae*, *ACO* 1.1.2, 3, 5, 7, H.1.1434
C Eph. Orient.	Concilium orientalium Ephesi habitum anno 431
act.	*actiones*, *ACO* 1.1.5 p. 119, H.1.1449
ep.	*epistulae variae*, *ACO* 1.1.3, 5, H.1.1533, 1545–8; see also Jo. Ant.
C Eph. (449)	Concilium Ephesinum anno 449, latrocinium dictum
act.	*actio*, ap. C Chalc. *act.* 1, *ACO* 2.1.1 p. 77, H.2.84
C Gangr.	Concilium Gangrense anno 342
can. 1–21	*canones*, Lauchert p. 80
ep.	*epistula*, H.1.529
C Hier. (335)	Concilium Hierosolymitanum anno 335
ep.	*epistula*, ap. Ath. *syn.* 21
C Hier. (350)	Concilium Hierosolymitanum anno 350
ep.	*epistula*, ap. Ath. *apol. sec.* 57
C Hier. (536)	Concilium Hierosolymitanum anno 536
act.	*actio*, *ACO* 3 pp. 123–5, pp. 185–9, H.2.1409
C Illyr.	Concilium Illyricum anno 374
ep.	*epistula*, ap. Thdt. *h.e.* 4. 9
C Laod.	Concilium Laodicenum anno incerto inter 343 et 381 habitum
can. 1–60	*canones*, Lauchert p. 72
C Later.	Concilium Lateranense anno 649
act.	*actiones*, H.3.688
can. 1–20	*canones*, H.3.921
C Neocaes.	Concilium Neocaesariense anno incerto inter 311 et 325 habitum
can. 1–15	*canones*, Lauchert p. 35
C Nic. (325)	Concilium Nicaenum anno 325, oecumenicum primum
can. 1–20	*canones*, Lauchert p. 37
ep.	*epistula*, Opitz 3 p. 47 ap. Socr. *h.e.* 1. 9
C Nic. (787)	Concilium Nicaenum anno 787, oecumenicum septimum
act.	*actiones*, H.4.28
can. 1–22	*canones*, Lauchert p. 139
ep.	*epistula*, H.4.477
refut.	*refutationes decretorum synodi iconoclastae*, H.4.325 (ap. *act.* 6)
C Querc.	Concilium ad Quercum anno 403, cit. ap. Phot. *cod.* 59
C Sard.	Concilium Sardicense anno circa 343
can. 1–20	*canones*, Lauchert p. 51
ep. Alex.	*epistula ad Alexandrinos*, ap. Ath. *apol. sec.* 37–40
ep. cath.	*epistula catholica*, first part *ib.* 42–47, second part ap. Thdt. *h.e.* 2. 8. 37–52
C Sel.	Concilium Seleucense anno 359
ep.	*epistula*, ap. Epiph. *haer.* 73. 25–26 (incorporating *Symb. Sel.* q.v.)
C Syr.	Concilium Syrium annis 518–19
act.	*actio*, ap. CCP (536) *act.* 5, *ACO* 3 p. 92, H.2.1365
ep.	*epistula*, *ib.*, *ACO* 3 p. 90, H.2.1361

CONCILIA (*cont.*)

C Trull. — Concilium in Trullo anno 692, quinisextum dictum
can. 1–102 — *canones*, Lauchert p. 97
or. imp. — *oratio ad imperatorem*, H.3.1652

C Tyr. (518) — Concilium Tyrium anno 518
act. — *actio*, ap. CCP (536) *act.* 5, *ACO* 3 p. 85, H.2.1353

CONSTANS II IMPERATOR (Constans) — ob. 668
typ. — *typus*, ap. C Later. *act.* 4, H.3.824

CONSTANTINUS DIACONUS (Const. Diac.) — saec. vi?
laud. — *laudatio omnium martyrum*, M.88.480

CONSTANTINUS I IMPERATOR (Const.) — ob. 337
ep. — *epistulae variae*, cited from Athanasius and ecclesiastical historians
or. s.c. — *oratio ad sanctorum coetum*, int. opp. Eus., *GCS* 1 p. 154, M.20.1233

CONSTANTINUS II IMPERATOR (Const. II Imp.) — ob. 340
ep. — *epistula ad Alexandrinos* ap. Thdt. *h.e.* 2. 2

CONSTANTINUS IV IMPERATOR POGONATUS (Const. Pogon.) — ob. 685
edict. — *edictum*, ap. CCP (681) *act.* 18, H.3.1445
sacr. 1 — *epistula sacra*, M.*PL*.87.1147
sacr. 2 — *epistula sacra*, ap. CCP (681), H.3.1049
sacr. 3 — *epistula sacra*, M.*PL*.96.387
sacr. 4 — *epistula sacra*, M.*PL*.96.394

CONSTANTINUS VI IMPERATOR (Const. VI Imp.) — ob. 797
sacr. — *epistula sacra*, ap. C Nic. (787) *act.* 1, H.4.36

CONSTANTIUS ANTIOCHENUS (Constantius Ant.) — saec. iv–v
ep. 1–5 — *epistulae*, int. opp. Chrys. *ep.* 237–41, M.52. 741

CONSTANTIUS I IMPERATOR (Constantius Imp.) — ob. 361
cit. ap. Ath., Socr., Soz., Thdt.

CONSTITUTIONES
Const. App. — *constitutiones apostolorum*, Funk 1 p. 3 saec. iv
Const. App. epit. — *epitome constitutionum apostolorum* 8, Funk 2 p. 72
Const. Cap. — *ex constitutionibus apostolorum capitula*, Funk 2 p. 137
Const. Stud. — *constitutiones Studitanae*, int. opp. Thdr. Stud., M.99.1704

CONTRADICTIO DIABOLI JESU CHRISTO
Contrad. 1, 2 — Vassiliev p. 4

CORNELIUS PAPA (Corn.) — ob. 253
fragmenta ex epistula ad Fabium, ap. Eus. *h.e.* 6. 43. 5–20

COSMAS HIEROSOLYMITANUS MELODUS (Cosm. Mel.) — saec. viii
can. dorm. — *canon in dormitionem BMV*, *AGC* p. 180
hymn. 1–7, 9–13 — *hymni*, M.98.460–85, 489–513; *AGC* pp. 161–80, pp. 183–204
hymn. 8 — *hymnus in sabbato sancto*, *AHS* 2 p. 165, partly in M.98.485
ind. — *index historiarum in carminibus Gregorii Nazianzeni*, M.38.669
od. 1–11 — *odae*, M.98.513
schol. — *scholia in Gregorii Nazianzeni carmina*, M.38.341

COSMAS INDICOPLEUSTES (Cosm. Ind.) — saec. vi
top. — *topographia christiana*, E. O. Winstedt Cambridge 1909, M.88.49

CYPRIANUS CARTHAGINIENSIS (Cypr.) — ob. 258
ep. — *epistula septuagesima*, H.1.154
fr. 1 — *fragmentum ex epistula ad Fidonem*, K. Holl *TU* 20^2 (1899) p. 145, ap. Jo. D. *parall.*, M.96.516
fr. 2 — *fragmentum de eleemosyna*, ap. C Eph. (431) *act.* 1, *ACO* 1.1.2 p. 42, H.1.1404

CYRIACUS (Cyriac.) — saec. vi
Laz. — *hymnus in Lazarum*, K. Krumbacher *SBBAW* 1901 p. 726, *AS* 1 p. 284

CYRILLUS ALEXANDRINUS (Cyr.) — ob. 444

A. = J. Aubert *Cyrilli Opera* 1–6 Paris 1638. This edition is used where possible in preference to M., which reproduces the Aubert pages in thick type
Pusey 1, 2 = P. E. Pusey, *Cyrilli in XII Prophetas* 1, 2, Oxford 1868
Pusey 3–5 = id., *Cyrilli in Joannis Evangelium accedunt fragmenta varia* 1–3, Oxford 1872
Pusey 6 = id., *Cyrilli epistulae tres, libri contra Nestorium, etc.*, Oxford 1875
Pusey 7 = id., *Cyrilli de recta fide, etc.*, Oxford, 1877
Note: Pusey's text is used only for works not in *ACO*. It is cited where possible by the Aubert page in the margin

ador. — *de adoratione in spiritu et veritate*, A.1^1.1, M.68.133
apol. orient. — *duodecim capitum defensio adversus orientales episcopos*, *ACO* 1.1.7 p. 33, A.6^1. 157, M.76.316
apol. Thds. — *apologeticus ad imperatorem Theodosium*, *ACO* 1.1.3 p. 75, A.6^1.241, M.76.453
apol. Thdt. — *apologeticus contra Theodoretum*, *ACO* 1.1.6 p. 108, A.6^1.203, M.76.392
Arcad. — *de recta fide ad Arcadiam et Marinam*, *ACO* 1.1.5 p. 62, A.$5^{2(3)}$.42, M.76.1201
Chr. un. — *quod unus sit Christus*, Pusey 7 p. 334, A.5^1.714, M.75.1253
†*coll. VT* — *collectio exegetica in Vetus Testamentum ex operibus Cyrilli, Maximi, et patrum aliorum*, A.6^4.1, M.77.1176
defunct. — *adversus negantes offerendum esse pro defunctis, fragmenta*, Pusey 5 p. 541, M.76. 1423
deip. BMV — *quod BMV sit deipara*, *ACO* 1.1.7 p. 19, M.76.256
dial. Nest. — *dialogus cum Nestorio*, M.76.249
dial. Trin. 1–7 — *de Trinitate dialogi*, A.5^1.385 (sic), M.75. 657
Diod. — *fragmenta contra Diodorum Tarsensem*, Pusey 5 p. 493, partly in M.76.1452C
dogm. — *de dogmatum solutione*, Pusey 5 p. 549, A.6^2.366, M.76.1077. (*Note*: in M. and A. the chapters are confused with those of *resp.* below)
ep. — *epistulae*, A.$5^{2(2)}$.1, M.77.9

Note: those extant in Greek are listed below with the editions from which they are cited; *epp.* 1–85 are numbered in M. but not in *ACO*, *ABAW*, or Aubert, the M reference is therefore not listed below save where the epistle is omitted in Aubert

ep. 1 — *ACO* 1.1.1 p. 10, A.5^2.1
ep. 2 — ,, p. 23, A.5^2.19
ep. 4 — ,, p. 25, A.5^2.22
ep. 8 — ,, p. 109, A.$5^{2(2)}$.30
ep. 9 — ,, p. 108, A.5^2.31
ep. 10 — ,, p. 110, A.5^2.32
ep. 11 — *ACO* 1.1.5 p. 10, A.5^2.36
ep. 11a — *commonitorium Posidonio datum*, *ACO* 1.1.7 p. 171, M.77.85
ep. 13 — *ACO* 1.1.1 p. 92, A.$5^{2(2)}$.42
ep. 14 — ,, p. 98, A.$5^{2(2)}$.44
ep. 16 — ,, p. 96, A.$5^{2(2)}$.65
ep. 17 — ,, p. 33, A.$5^{2(2)}$.67
ep. 18 — ,, p. 113, A.$5^{2(2)}$.78
ep. 19 — *ACO* 1.1.5 p. 12, A.$5^{2(2)}$.80
ep. 20 — *ACO* 1.1.1 p. 116, A.$5^{2(2)}$.81
ep. 21 — ,, p. 117, A.$5^{2(2)}$.82
ep. 23 — *ACO* 1.1.2 p. 66, A.$5^{2(2)}$.84
ep. 24 — *ACO* 1.1.1 p. 117, A.$5^{2(2)}$.87
ep. 25 — ,, p. 118, A.$5^{2(2)}$.88
ep. 26 — *ACO* 1.1.2 p. 69, A.$5^{2(2)}$.89
ep. 27 — *ACO* 1.1.3 p. 45, A.$5^{2(2)}$.90
ep. 28 — ,, p. 50, A.$5^{2(2)}$.91
ep. 31 — ,, p. 72, A.$5^{2(2)}$.95

ep. 32	*ACO* 1.1.7 p. 137
ep. 33	,, p. 147
ep. 37	,, p. 154, A.$5^{2(2)}$.152
ep. 39	*ACO* 1.1.4 p. 15, A.$5^{2(2)}$.104
ep. 40	,, p. 20, A.$5^{2(2)}$.109
ep. 41	,, p. 40, A.$5^{2(2)}$.121
ep. 42	E. Schwartz *ABAW* 32^6 (1927) p. 19, M.77.221
ep. 43	,, ,, ,, p. 19, M.77.221
ep. 44	*ACO* 1.1.4 p. 35, A.$5^{2(2)}$.132
ep. 45	*ACO* 1.1.6 p. 151, A.$5^{2(2)}$.135
ep. 46	,, p. 157, A.$5^{2(2)}$.141. (*Note*: the second part of *ep.* 46, A.$5^{2(2)}$.146–51, is *ep.* 40, A.$5^{2(2)}$.115–20)
ep. 48	*ACO* 1.1.4 p. 31, A.$5^{2(2)}$.155
ep. 49	,, p. 34, A.$5^{2(2)}$.157
ep. 50	*ACO* 1.1.3 p. 90, A.$5^{2(2)}$.158
ep. 53	M.77.285, fragment only
ep. 54	*ACO* 1.1.7 p. 164, M.77.288
ep. 55	*ACO* 1.1.4 p. 49, A.$5^{2(2)}$.174
ep. 56	*ABAW* 32^6 p. 17, A.$5^{2(2)}$.191
ep. 57	,, p. 21, A.$5^{2(2)}$.192
ep. 58	,, p. 20, M.77.321
ep. 63	,, p. 15, M.77.328
ep. 67	*ACO* 1.1.4 p. 37, A.$5^{2(2)}$.194
ep. 69	*ABAW* 32^6 p. 15, A.$5^{2(2)}$.197
ep. 70	,, p. 16, A.$5^{2(2)}$.198
ep. 72	,, p. 17, A.$5^{2(2)}$.199
ep. 76	,, p. 25, A.$5^{2(2)}$.204
ep. 77	*ACO* 2.1.3 p. 66, A.$5^{2(2)}$.208
ep. 78	A.$5^{2(2)}$.209
ep. 79	,, 211
[‡*ep.* 80	M.77.365 = Bas. *ep.* 260. 1–6 q.v.]
ep. 81	ap. Justn. *Or.*, *ACO* 3 p. 201. 22, M.77.372
ep. 82	*ABAW* 32^6 p. 20, M.77.376
ep. 85	A.$5^{2(2)}$.212
ep. 89	*ACO* 1.1.7 p. 140
ep. 90	,, p. 153
ep. 91	,, p. 153
ep. 92	,, p. 162
ep. Calos.	*epistula ad Calosyrium*, Pusey 5 p. 603, A.6^2.363, M.76.1065
ep. Euopt.	*epistula ad Euoptium*, *ACO* 1.1.6 p. 110, A.6^1.200, M.76.385
exegetica	
glaph. Gen.–Dt.	*glaphyra in Pentateuchum*, A.1^2, M.69.13, 1273–6
fr. Num.	*fragmenta in Numeros*, M.69.641
fr. Reg.	*fragmenta commentarii in libros Regum*, M.69.681, 1276
Ps.	*explanatio in Pss.*, M.69.717
Pr. 8:22	*fragmentum in illud*, Dominus creavit me, M.69.1277
fr. Cant.	*fragmenta in Cant.*, M.69.1277
Is.	*commentarius in Is.*, A.2, M.70
fr. Jer.	*fragmenta in Jer.*, M.70.1452
fr. Bar.	*fragmentum in Bar.*, M.70.1457
fr. Ezech.	*fragmenta in Ezech.* M.70.1457
fr. Dan.	*fragmenta in Dan.*, M.70.1461
Os.–Mal.	*commentarius in duodecim prophetas*, Pusey 1, 2, A.3, M.71, 72
fr. Mt.	*fragmenta in Mt.* M.72.365, some frr. also in *Doct. Patr.*
Lc.	*fragmenta commentarii in Lc.*, M.72.476; J. Sickenberger *TU* 34^1 (1910) p. 76; Pusey 5 pp. 470–4
Jo.	*commentarius in Jo.*, Pusey 3–5, A.4, M.73, 74
fr. Ac.	*fragmenta commentarii in Ac.*, Pusey 5 p. 441, M.74.757
Rom.	*explanatio in Rom.*, Pusey 5 p. 174, M.74.773
1 Cor.	*explanatio in 1 Cor.*, Pusey 5 p. 249, M.74.856
2 Cor.	*explanatio in 2 Cor.*, Pusey 5 p. 320, M.74.916
fr. Gal.	*fragmenta in Gal.*, M.74.952
Col. 4:6	*fragmentum in illud*, Sermo vester, M.74.952
Heb.	*fragmenta explanationum in Heb.*, Pusey 5 pp. 362–423, pp. 461–8, M.74.953
fr. Jac.	*fragmenta in Jac.*, Pusey 5 p. 445, M.74.1008

fr. 1 Petr.	*fragmenta in 1 Petr.*, Pusey 5 p. 447, M.74.1012
fr. 2 Petr.	*fragmenta in 2 Petr.*, Pusey 5 p. 449, M.74.1017
fr. 1 Jo.	*fragmenta in 1 Jo.*, Pusey 5 p. 450, M.74.1021
fr. Judae	*fragmentum in epistulam Judae*, Pusey 5 p. 451, M.74.1024
expl. xii cap.	*explicatio duodecim capitum*, *ACO* 1.1.5 p. 15, A.6^1.145, M.76.293
fr.	*fragmenta varia*, Pusey 5 pp. 452–8; M.76.1453; ap. *Doct. Patr.*
hom. div.	*homiliae diversae*, A.$5^{2(1)}$.350, M.77.981; numbered in M. but not in *ACO* or Aubert; the M. reference is therefore not listed below save where the homily is omitted in Aubert
hom. div. 1	*Ephesi praedicata*, *ACO* 1.1.2 p. 96, A.$5^{2(1)}$.350
hom. div. 2	*Ephesi praedicata in die Joannis evangelistae*, *ACO* 1.1.2 p. 94, A.$5^{2(1)}$.352
hom. div. 3	*de Paulo Emeseno*, *ACO* 1.1.4 p. 14, A.$5^{2(1)}$.354
hom. div. 4	*de Maria deipara in Nestorium*, *ACO* 1.1.2 p. 102, A.$5^{2(1)}$.355
hom. div. 5	*Ephesi praedicata deposito Nestorio*, *ACO* 1.1.2 p. 92, A.$5^{2(1)}$.358
hom. div. 6	*in Joannem Antiochenum*, *ACO* 1.1.2 p. 98, A.$5^{2(1)}$.361
hom. div. 7	*Ephesi praedicata priusquam a comite comprehenderetur*, *ACO* 1.1.2 p. 100, A.$5^{2(1)}$.364
hom. div. 9	*in transfigurationem*, A.$5^{2(1)}$.366, properly part of the lost commentary on Lc.
†*hom. div.* 10	*in mysticam coenam*, A.$5^{2(1)}$.370 (ascribed by M. Richard, *Revue d'histoire ecclésiastique* 33, Louvain 1937, p. 46 to Thphl. Al.)
†*hom. div.* 11	*in Mariam deiparam*, A.$5^{2(1)}$.379 a later expanded version of *hom. div.* 4
hom. div. 12	*in occursum et circumcisionem*, A.$5^{2(1)}$.385, properly part of the lost commentary on Lc., cf. *Lc.* 2. 22–34, M.72.1496–1505 above
[‡*hom. div.* 13	*in ramos palmarum*, A.$5^{2(1)}$.391 = Eulog. *palm.* q.v.]
†*hom. div.* 14	*de exitu animi*, A.$5^{2(1)}$.404, perhaps by Thphl. Al., cf. *Apophth. Patr.*, M.65.200
hom. div. 15	*de incarnatione*, E. Schwartz *ABAW* 32^6 (1927) p. 13, M.77.1089
hom. div. 16	*de concordia ecclesiarum*, *ACO* 1.1.7 p. 173, M.77.1096
hom. div. 17	*in parabolam vineae*, M.77.1096
hom. div. 18	*fragmenta de translatione reliquiarum martyrum Cyri et Joannis*, M.77.1100
hom. div. 19	*contra eunuchos*, M.77.1105
hom. div. 20	*in deum incarnatum*, Pusey 5 p. 459, M.77.1109
hom. div. 21	*de fide fragmenta*, Pusey 5 p. 538, M.77.1112
hom. div. 22	*ad Alexandrinos*, Pusey 5 p. 460, M.77.1116
hom. pasch. 1, 2, 4–30	*homiliae paschales*, A.$5^{2(1)}$.1, M.77.401
†*inc.*	*de incarnatione*, *ACO* 1.1.5 p. 3, A.5^1.801, M.75.1413
[‡*inc.*	*de incarnatione*, M.75.1420; see Thdt.]
inc. unigen.	*de incarnatione unigeniti dialogus*, Pusey 7 p. 11, A.5^1.678, M.75.1189; very similar to *Thds.* below
Juln.	*contra Julianum*, A.6^2.1, M.76.504
Juln. 11–19 *fr.*	*fragmenta librorum contra Julianum*, M.76.1057
libell.	*libellus* ap. C Eph. (431) *act.* 4, *ACO* 1.1.3 p. 16, H.1.1486; written jointly with Memnon
Nest.	*contra Nestorium*, *ACO* 1.1.6 p. 13, A.6^1.1, M.76.9
‡*obit.*	*fragmenta de obitu sanctorum trium puerorum et Danielis*, M.77.1117
Pulch.	*de recta fide ad Pulcheriam et Eudociam*, *ACO* 1.1.5 p. 26, A.$5^{2(3)}$.128, M.76.1336
resp.	*responsio ad Tiberium*, Pusey 5 p. 576, A.6^2.366, M.76.1077. (*Note*: in A. and M. the chapters are confused with those of *dogm.* above)

CYRILLUS ALEXANDRINUS (*cont.*)

schol. inc. — *scholia de incarnatione*, *ACO* 1.5.1 pp. 219–31, A.5^1.779, M.75.1369
†*Spir.* — *argumentorum de Sancto Spiritu capita*, A.5^1.661, M.75.1124, a working over of *Thds.* below
syn. def. — *de synagogae defectu*, M.76.1421
synous. — *contra Synousiastas*, Pusey 5 p. 476
Thdr. Mops. — *fragmenta contra Theodorum Mopsuestenum*, Pusey 5 p. 511
Thds. — *de recta fide ad Theodosium*, *ACO* 1.1.1 p. 42, A.5$^{2(3)}$.1, M.76.1133
thes. — *thesaurus de Trinitate*, A.5^1.1, M.75.9
thes. fr. — *fragmenta ex thesauro*, *AS* 5 p. 38
‡*Trin.* — *de Trinitate*, A.6^3.1, M.77.1120 saec. vii

CYRILLUS HIEROSOLYMITANUS — ob. 386
(Cyr. H.)

catech. 1–18 — *catecheses illuminandorum* 1–11, W. K. Reischl *Cyrilli opera* 1 Munich 1848 p. 29, M.33.369; *catech.* 12–18, J. Rupp *Cyrilli opera* 2 Munich 1860 p. 3, M.33.725
catech. 19–23 — *catecheses mystagogicae*, J. Rupp op. cit. p. 345, M.33.1065 (ascribed in some MSS to Joannes II Hierosolymitanus; ob. 417)
ep. Const. — *epistula ad Constantium de visione crucis*, J. Rupp op. cit. p. 434, M.33.1165
‡*ep. Jul.* — *epistula ad Julium papam*, M.33.1208
fr. 1–5 — *fragmenta*, M.33.1181; *fr.* 1, ap. *Doct. Patr.* 15 p. 92; *fr.* 2, *ib.* p. 93; *fr.* 3, *AP* p. 10; *fr.* 4, ap. *Doct. Patr.* 2 p. 20; *fr.* 5, *ib.* 15 p. 104
hom. — *homilia in paralyticum ad piscinam jacentem*, J. Rupp op. cit. p. 406, M.33.1132
‡*occurs.* — *in occursum domini*, M.33.1188
procatech. — *procatechesis*, W. K. Reischl op. cit. p. 3, M.33.332

CYRILLUS SCYTHOPOLITANUS — ob. c. 558
(Cyr. S.)

v. Abr. — *vita Abraami*, E. Schwartz *TU* 49^2 (1939) p. 243
v. Cyriac. — *vita Cyriaci*, *ib.* p. 222
v. Euthym. — *vita Euthymii*, *ib.* p. 3
v. Jo. Hes. — *vita Joannis Hesychastis*, *ib.* p. 201
v. Sab. — *vita Sabae*, *ib.* p. 85
v. Thds. — *vita Theodosii*, *ib.* p. 235
v. Thgn. — *vita Theognii*, *ib.* p. 241

CYRUS ALEXANDRINUS — ob. 643
(Cyrus Al.)

cap. 1–9 — *capita*, ap. CCP (681) *act.* 13, H.3.1340
ep. 1–3 — *epistulae ad Sergium Constantinopolitanum*, *ep.* 1 ap. C Later. *act.* 3, H.3.804; *ep.* 2, 3 ap. CCP (681) *act.* 13, H.3.1337, 1340

CYRUS TYANENSIS
(Cyrus T.)

fr. — *fragmentum epistulae ad Julianum et Severum*, ap. *Doct. Patr.* 41 p. 313

DALMATIUS ARCHIMANDRITA — ob. 436
(Dalmat.)

apol. — *apologia*, *ACO* 1.1.2 p. 68; M.85.1801
ep. Eph. 1 — *epistula ad synodum Ephesinam*, *ACO* 1.1.7 p. x, M.85.1797
ep. Eph. 2 — *epistula ad synodum Ephesinam*, *ACO* 1.1.3 p. 14, M.85.1800

DAMASUS — saec. vii
(Dam.)

troph. — *trophaea*, G. Bardy *PO* 15 (1920) p. 189

DAMASUS PAPA — ob. 384
(Dam. Papa)

anath. — *anathemata*, ap. Thdt. *h.e.* 5. 11
ep. Illyr. — *epistula ad Illyricos*, ap. Thdt. *h.e.* 2. 22. 2–12
ep. orient. — *epistula ad episcopos orientales*, ap. Thdt. *h.e.* 5. 10

DANIEL RAITHENUS — saec. vii ?
(Dan. Raith.)

v. Jo. Clim. — *vita Joannis Climaci*, M.88.596

DEMETRIUS ALEXANDRINUS — saec. iii
(Dem.)

fr. — *fragmentum ex oratione de terrae motu*, *AS* 2 p. 345

DIADOCHUS PHOTICENSIS — saec. v
(Diad.)

†*Ar.* — *sermo contra Arianos*, M.65.1149
ascens. — *homilia de ascensione Domini*, M.65.1141
perf. — *de perfectione spirituali*, J. E. Weis-Liebersdorf *Teub.* 1912

DIALOGI

Dial. Ath. et Zacch. — *dialogus Athanasii et Zacchaei*, F. C. Conybeare Oxford 1898 p. 1 c. 300
Dial. Christ. et Jud. — *dialogus Christiani et Judaei* (*Papisci et Philonis*), A. C. McGiffert Marburg 1889 c. 700
Dial. Christ. et Jud. fr. — *dialogi Christiani et Judaei fragmentum*, ap. C Nic. (787) *act.* 5, H.4.293
Dial. Mont. et Orth. — *dialogus Montanistae et Orthodoxi*, G. Ficker *ZKG* 26 (1905) p. 447 saec. iv
Dial. Tim. et Aquil. — *dialogus Timothei et Aquilae*, Conybeare op. cit. p. 65

DIDACHE XII APOSTOLORUM — saec. ii

Did. — Bihlmeyer p. 1

DIDASCALIA

Didasc. Jac. 1 — *Didascalia Jacobi*, F. Nau *PO* 8 (1912) p. 745 saec. vii
Didasc. Jac. 2–5 — *Didascalia Jacobi*, G. N. Bonwetsch *AGWG* 12^3 (1910) p. 43
Didasc. patr. — *Didascalia cccxviii patrum*, P. Batiffol Paris 1887 ∞ ‡Ath. *syntag.*

DIDYMUS ALEXANDRINUS — ob. 398
(Didym.)

Eun. 4, 5 — *contra Eunomium libri* 4, 5, int. opp. Bas., G.1.279, M.29.672

exegetica

Gen. — *fragmenta in Gen.*, M.39.1112
Ex. — *fragmenta in Ex.*, M.39.1113
2 Reg. — *fragmenta in 2 Reg.*, M.39.1116
Job — *fragmenta in Job*, M.39.1120
fr. Ps. — *fragmenta in Pss.*, M.39.1617
Ps. — *expositio in Pss.*, M.39.1156
Pr. — *fragmenta in Pr.*, M.39.1621
Jo. — *fragmenta in Jo.*, M.39.1645
Ac. — *fragmenta in Ac.*, M.39.1653
Rom. — *fragmentum in Rom.*, Staab p. 1
1 Cor. — *fragmenta in 1 Cor.*, Staab p. 6
2 Cor. — *fragmenta in 2 Cor.*, Staab p. 14, M.39.1680
Heb. — *fragmenta in Heb.*, Staab p. 44
†*Jac.*, †*1 Petr.*, †*1–3 Jo.*, †*Judae* — *fragmenta in epistulas catholicas*, M.39.1749

fr. — *fragmenta dogmatica*, M.39.1109
Man. — *contra Manichaeos*, M.39.1085
Trin. — *de Trinitate*, M.39.269

DIODORUS TARSENSIS — ob. ante 394
(Diod.)

exegetica

Gen. — *fragmenta in Gen.*, M.33.1561
Ex. — *fragmenta in Ex.*, M.33.1579
Dt. — *fragmenta in Dt.*, M.33.1585
Jud. — *fragmentum in Jud.*, M.33.1587
1 Reg. — *fragmenta in 1 Reg.*, M.33.1587
Ps. — *fragmenta in Pss.*, M.33.1587
proem. Pss. — *proemium in Pss.*, L. Mariés *Recherches de Science Religieuse* 9 Paris 1919 p. 82
proem. Ps. 118 — *proemium in Ps. 118*, *ib.* p. 90
Rom. — *fragmenta in Rom.*, Staab p. 83

fat. — *excerpta de opere contra fatum*, ap. Phot. cod. 223
synous. — *fragmenta ex libris contra Synousiastas*, M.33.1560

DIOGNETUM, EPISTULA AD — saec. ii

Diogn. 1–10, ‡*Diogn.* 11–12 — Bihlmeyer, p. 141, M.2.1168 (the last two sections date from a later period)

DIONYSIUS ALEXANDRINUS — ob. c. 264
(Dion. Al.)

ep. can. — *epistula canonica*, C. L. Feltoe *The Letters and other Remains of Dionysius of Alexandria* Cambridge 1904 p. 94, M.10.1272
‡*ep. Paul. Sam.* — *epistula ad Paulum Samosatenum*, E. Schwartz *SBBAW* 1927^3 p. 3
fr. — *fragmenta*, cited from Feltoe except those

in Eus. and Ath., which are cited from these authors

fragmenta exegetica maiora

fr. Gen. — *fragmenta in Gen.*, Feltoe p. 199
†*fr. 1–4 in Job* — *fragmenta in Job, ib.* p. 201
†*fr. Cant.* — *fragmentum in Cant., ib.* p. 228
†*fr. Eccl.* — *fragmenta in Eccl., ib.* p. 210, M.10.1577
‡*fr. in Lc. 22* — *fragmenta in Lc. 22, ib.* p. 231, M.10.1589, 1597

Pseudo-Dionysius Areopagita (Dion. Ar.) — saec. v

c.h. — *de caelesti hierarchia*, M.3.120
d.n. — *de divinis nominibus*, M.3.585
e.h. — *de ecclesiastica hierarchia*, M.3.369
ep. 1–10 — *epistulae*, M.3.1065
myst. — *de mystica theologia*, M.3.997

Dionysius Comes (A) (Dion. Com. A) — saec. iv

cit. ap. Ath. *apol. sec.* 81

Dionysius Comes (B) (Dion. Com. B) — saec. v

ep. cler. — *epistula ad clericos Constantiae*, ap. C Eph. *act.* 7, *ACO* 1.1.7 p. 120
ep. Thdr. — *epistula ad Theodorum, ib.*

Dionysius Corinthius (Dion. Cor.) — saec. ii

cit. ap. Eus. *h.e.* 2. 25. 8, 4. 23. 10–12

Dionysius Romanus (Dion. R.) — ob. 268

cit. ap. Ath. *decr.* 26

Disputatio — anno 527

Disp. Phot. — *disputatio Photini Manichaei cum Paulo Persa*, M.88.529

Doctrina Patrum — saec. vii

Doct. Patr. — *doctrina patrum de incarnatione verbi*, F. Diekamp Münster 1907

Dogmata Orthodoxa — saec. viii ?

Dogm. Orth. — M.98.1229

Domitius (Domit.) — saec. vi ?

Jo. Bapt. — *carmen de Joanne Baptista, AS* 1 p. 320

Dormitio Mariae

Dorm. BMV — C. Tischendorf *Apocalypses Apocryphae* Leipzig 1866 p. 95

Dorotheus Abbas (Dor.) — ob. post 535

doct. 1–20, 22, 23 — *doctrinae diversae*, M.88.1617
ep. 1–8 — *epistulae*, M.88.1837

Dorotheus Tyrius (Dor. Tyr.) — [saec. iii–iv]

‡*disc. Dom.* — *de lxx discipulis domini et xii apostolis*, T. Schermann *Prophetarum Vitae, Teub.* 1907 p. 132, M.92.1060 — post 600

Elias Philosophus (El.) — saec. vi

fr. — *fragmenta*, ap. *Doct. Patr.*

Elias Hierosolymitanus (El. H.) — saec. vi seu viii

cant. 1, 2 — *cantica, AS* 1 p. 289
[‡*cant.* 3 — *canticum* 3, *ib.* p. 293 = *Hymn., KlT* 52–53 (1931) p. 21 q.v.]
[‡*cant.* 4 — *canticum* 4, *AS* 1 p. 296, is by Rom. Mel. q.v.]

Elias Syncellus (El. Sync.) — saec. viii

anacr. — *carmen anacreonticum, AGC* p. 47
thren. — *threneticon*, P. Matranga *Anecdota Graeca* 2 (1850) p. 645

Ephraem Antiochenus (Ephr. Ant.) — saec. vi

fr. — *fragmenta*, M.86.2104; ap. C Later. *act.* 5, H.3.885

Ephraem Chersonensis (Ephr. Chers.)

mir. Clem. — *de miraculo Clementis*, M.2.633

Ephraem Syrus (Ephr.) — ob. 373

J. S. Assemani, *Opera omnia* 1–3 Rome 1732–46. Works which occur only in Assemani are cited without title by his volume, page, and letter. Many of these are thought to be spurious

Abr. et Is. — *sermo in Abraham et Isaac*, S. J. Mercati *Ephraem Syri Opera* 1 Rome 1915 p. 43, M.56.537, Assemani 2.312
‡*Abr.* — *sermo in Abraham*, Mercati *op. cit.* p. 99
El. — *sermo in Eliam prophetam*, Mercati op. cit. p. 201, Assemani 3.240
enc. Bas. — *encomium in Basilium Magnum*, Mercati op. cit. p. 143; Assemani 2.289
†*nativ.* — *homilia in Christi nativitatem*, Mercati *Biblica* 1 Rome 1920 p. 84
non. rid. — *non esse ridendum*, W. Heffening *OC* 11 (1936) p. 62, Assemani 1.254
‡*poenit. can.* — *canones poenitentiales, SS* 4 p. 458

Epiphanes Catensis (Epiph. Cat.) — saec. viii

serm. syn. — *sermo laudatorius in synodo Nicaea habitus*, M.98.1313

Epiphanes Gnosticus (Epiph. Gn.) — saec. ii

fragmenta, ap. Clem. *str.* 3. 2

Epiphanius Constantiensis (Epiph.) — ob. 403

K. Holl *GCS* 1–3 1915, 1922, 1933

anac. — *anacephalaioses* seu *recapitulatio brevis panarii, GCS* 1 pp. 162, 234; 2, pp. 1, 211; 3 pp. 1, 230, 415; M.41.165, 281, 577, 845; M.42.9, 336, 640
anc. — *ancoratus, GCS* 1 p. 5, M.43.17
‡*anc. synops.* — *ancorati synopsis, GCS* 1 p. 1, M.43.12
ep. Arab. — *epistula ad Arabes*, ap. *haer.* 78. 2–24
ep. fr. — *epistula*, K. Holl *Gesammelte Aufsätze zu Kirchengeschichte* 2 Tübingen 1927 p. 205
‡*epit. haer.* — *haereseum 1–34 epitome*, G. Dindorf *Epiphanii opera* vol. 1 Leipzig 1859 p. 341
exp. fid. — *expositio fidei, GCS* 3 p. 496, M.42.773
fr. — *fragmenta*, ap. *Doct. Patr.* 40, 42 (pp. 299, 317), *AP* p. 227, *AS* 5 p. 72
gemm. — *epitomae duae ex opere de xii gemmis summi sacerdotis ad Diodorum*, M.43.293, M.89.588–9 (ap. Anast. S. *hod.* 40)
gemm. fr. — *fragmentum ex opere de duodecim gemmis ad Diodorum*, M.89.596–7 (ap. Anast. S. *hod.* 45)
haer. — *panarion* seu *adversus lxxx haereses, GCS* 1 p. 169–3 p. 496, M.41.173–42.882
‡*hom.* 1–6 — *homiliae*, M.43.428
inc. 1–4 — *de incarnatione Christi domini*, ap. *haer.* 20, *GCS* 1 pp. 227–33, M.41.273–80
interpr. — *de lxx interpretibus*, M.43.373
mens. — *de mensuris et ponderibus*, M.43.237
†*num. myst.* — *de numerorum mysteriis*, M.43.508
‡*patr.* — *de praegressionibus patriarcharum*, H. Gelzer *ABAW* 21 (1901) p. 531, M.86.788 — saec. vii
‡*phys.* — *ad physiologum*, M.43.517; ∞ *Phys.* B q.v.
rescr. — *rescriptum ad Acacium et Paulum, GCS* 1 p. 155, M.41.157–165c
‡*v. proph.* — *de vitis prophetarum*, C. C. Torrey *Journal of Biblical Literature, Monograph Series* 1 Philadelphia 1946, two recensions, M.43.393, 416

Epiphanius Constantinopolitanus (Epiph. CP) — saec. vi

sent. — *sententiae contra Severum et Petrum*, ap. CCP (536) *act.* 5, *ACO* 3 pp. 110–11, M.86.782

Epiphanius Tyrius (Epiph. Tyr.) — saec. vi

ep. — *epistula ad synodum Constantinopolitanam*, ap. CCP (518) *act.*, *ACO* 3 p. 80, H.2.1345

Epistulae Apocryphae

Ep. Abg. — *epistula Abgari ad Christum*, R. A. Lipsius and M. Bonnet *Acta Apostolorum Apocrypha* 1, 2 Leipzig 1891–1903 p. 279
Ep. Chr. — *epistula Christi ad Abgarum, ib.* pp. 280–1
Ep. Chr. dom. — *epistula Christi in die dominica*, Vassiliev p. 23
Ep. Chr. suppl. — *supplementum ad epistulam Christi ad Abgarum*, ap. Eus. *h.e.* 1. 13. 11–22

EPISTULAE APOCRYPHAE (*cont.*)

Ep. Her. — *epistula Herodis ad Pilatum*, J. A. Robinson *TS* 5^1 (1897) p. 68

Ep. Mar. — *epistula Mariae ad Ignatium*, Lightfoot 2^2 p. 719, M.5.873

Ep. Pil. — *epistula Pilati ad Herodem*, *TS* 5^1 p. 66

Ep. Tib. — *epistula Tiberii ad Pilatum*, *ib.* p. 76

EPISTULAE VARIAE

Ep. Aeg. — *epistula episcoporum Aegypti ad synodum Tyriam*, ap. Ath. *apol. sec.* 77

Ep. Alex. — *epistula clericorum Alexandrinorum ad Theodosium, Ursacium et Valentem*, ap. Ath. *apol. sec.* 73

Ep. Cyr. — *epistula monachorum ad Cyrillum*, Pusey 5, p. 547

Ep. Dion. 1, 2 — *epistulae episcoporum Aegypti ad Dionysium comitem*, ap. Ath. *apol. sec.* 78, 79

Ep. Dor. — *epistula ad monachum ad Dor. doct. praemissa*, M.88.1613

Ep. Lugd. — *epistula ecclesiarum Lugdunensium et Viennensium ad ecclesias Asiae et Phrygiae*, ap. Eus. *h.e.* 5. 1. 3–63, *ib.* 5. 2. 2–7; *ib.* 5. 4. 2

Ep. Mareot. 1 — *epistula clericorum Mareoticorum ad synodum Tyriam*, ap. Ath. *apol. sec.* 74–75

Ep. Mareot. 2 — *epistula clericorum Mareoticorum ad praefectum Aegypti*, ap. Ath. *apol. sec.* 76

ERECTHIUS ANTIOCHENUS PISIDA — saec. v
(Erecth.)

theoph. — *fragmentum ex homilia in theophaniam*, E. Schwartz *ABAW* 32^6 (1927) p. 28, M.86.3321

ESAIAS ABBAS — ob. 488
(Esaias)

cap. spir. — *capitula de exercitatione spirituali*, M.40.1205

fr. — *fragmenta*, M.40.1212

or. 1–29 — *orationes*, Augustinos Jerusalem 1911; Lat., save *or.* 20, M.40.1105

EUBULUS LYSTRENSIS — saec. vii
(Eub.)

fr. — *fragmenta*, ap. *Doct. Patr.* 22 p. 141

EUCHOLOGION

Euchol. — J. Goar 2nd ed. Venice 1730

EUDOCIA AUGUSTA — ob. 460
(Eudoc.)

Cypr. 1, 2 — *carmen de Cypriano*, A. Ludwich *Teub.* 1897 p. 24, M.85.832

EUDOXIUS CONSTANTINOPOLITANUS — ob. 370
(Eudox.)

exp. fid. — *expositio fidei*, ap. *Doct. Patr.* 9 p. 64

EUGENIUS DIACONUS — saec. iv
(Eugen.)

exp. fid. — *expositio fidei ad Athanasium pro causa Marcelli Ancyrani*, M.18.1301

EULOGIUS ALEXANDRINUS — ob. 607
(Eulog.)

duab. nat. — *de duabus naturis*, M.86.2937

fr. dogm. — *fragmenta dogmatica*, M.86.2944

fr. Novat. — *fragmenta adversus Novatianos*, ap. Phot. *cod.* 280

fr. Trin. — *fragmenta ex opere de Trinitate et incarnatione*, O. Bardenhewer *TQ* 78 (1896) p. 363, M.86.2940

palm. — *sermo in ramos palmarum*, M.86.2913

EUNOMIUS BERRHOEENSIS — saec. iv
(Eun. Berrh.)

fr. — *fragmenta*, Lietzmann p. 276, ap. *Doct. Patr.* 41 pp. 309, 312

EUNOMIUS CYZICENUS — ob. 393
(Eun.)

apol. — *apologeticus*, M.30.836

exp. fid. — *expositio fidei*, J. A. Fabricius *Bibliotheca Graeca* 8 Hamburg 1717 p. 253

EUNOMIUS NICOMEDENSIS — saec. v
(Eun. Nic.)

supplic. — *supplicatio*, ap. C Chalc. *act.* 13, *ACO* 2.1.3 p. 58, H.2.564

EUPREPIUS ET CYRILLUS, THRACES — saec. v
(Euprep.)

libell. — *libellus*, ap. C Eph. (431) *act.* 7, *ACO* 1.1.7 p. 122

EUSEBIUS ALEXANDRINUS — saec. v
(Eus. Al.)

fr. — *fragmenta*, K. Holl *TU* 20^2 (1899) p. 214, ap. Jo. D. *parall.* (Most of these are variant excerpts from the *sermones*)

serm. 1–12, 15, 21–22 — *sermones*, M.86.313. (*Note*: there is another version of *serm.* 5 in M.61.783)

serm. 13, 14 — *sermones*, int. opp. Eus. Em., M.86.509

serm. 16 — *sermo de die dominica*, M.86.413. Two other recensions, one in part, F. Nau *ROC* 13 (1908) p. 414; the other in full, *ib.* p. 415

serm. 17 — *sermo in parasceve*, M.62.721

serm. 18 — *sermo in resurrectionem*, M.61.733

serm. 19 — *sermo in ascensionem*, M.64.45

serm. 20 — *sermo in secundum adventum*, M.61.775

EUSEBIUS CAESARIENSIS — ob. 339
(Eus.)

‡*ant. mart. coll.* — *fragmenta ex antiquorum martyrum collectione*, M.20.1520

d.e. — *demonstratio evangelica*, I. A. Heikel *GCS* 6 (1913), M.22.13

e. th. — *de ecclesiastica theologia*, E. Klostermann *GCS* 4 (1906) p. 61, M.24.825

ecl. — *eclogae propheticae*, M.22.1021

ep. Alex. Al. — *fragmenta epistulae ad Alexandrum Alexandrinum*, Opitz 3 p. 14, ap. C Nic. (787) *act.* 6, H.4.408

ep. Caes. — *epistula ad Caesarienses*, Opitz 3 p. 42, M.20.1536

ep. Carp. — *epistula ad Carpianum ad canones evangeliorum praemissa*, M.22.1276

ep. Constant. — *epistula ad Constantiam*, M.20.1545

ep. Euphrat. — *fragmenta epistulae ad Euphrationem*, Opitz 3 p. 4, partly ap. C Nic. (787) *act.* 5, H.4.301

ep. Flacc. — *epistula ad Flaccum ad ecclesiasticam theologiam praemissa*, *GCS* 4 p. 60, M.24.824

exegetica

Ps. — *commentarius in Pss.*, *Pss.* 1–118, M.23.66; *Pss.* 119–150, M.24.76; *AS* 3 p. 369

fr. Pr. — *fragmenta in Pr.*, M.24.76

†*Cant.* — *in Cant. interpretatio*, *AS* 3 p. 530

Is. — *commentarius in Is.*, M.24.89

Is. fr. 1–53 — *fragmenta alia in Is.*, R. Devreesse *RB* 42 (1933) p. 545

fr. Dan. — *fragmenta in Dan.*, M.24.525

fr. Lc. — *fragmenta in Lc.*, M.24.529

fr. Heb. — *fragmentum in Heb.*, M.24.605

fr. — *fragmenta ex generali elementaria introductione*, K. Holl *TU* 20^2 (1899) p. 213, M.22.1272

h.e. — *historia ecclesiastica*, E. Schwartz *GCS* 2 (1903–8), M.20.45

Hierocl. — *contra Hieroclem*, T. Gaisford Oxford 1852 (cited by page of Paris (1628) edition), M.22.796

l.C. — *de laudibus Constantini*, I. A. Heikel *GCS* 1 (1902) p. 195, M.20.1316

Marcell. — *contra Marcellum*, E. Klostermann *GCS* 4 (1906) p. 1, M.24.708

m.P. — *de martyribus Palestinae*, *GCS* 2 p. 907, M.20.1457, 1441

onomast. — *onomasticon*, *GCS* 3^1 (1904) p. 2

pasch. — *de solemnitate paschali*, M.24.693

p.e. — *preparatio evangelica*, E. H. Gifford Oxford 1903 (cited by page of Paris (1628) edition), M.21.21

proph. — *de vitis prophetarum*, M.22.1261

qu. Marin. — *quaestiones evangelicae ad Marinum*, M.22.937

qu. Marin. suppl. 1, 2 — *supplementa ad quaestiones ad Marinum*, M.22.984

qu. Steph. — *quaestiones evangelicae ad Stephanum*, M.22.880

qu. Steph. suppl. — *supplementa ad quaestiones ad Stephanum*, M.22.957

theoph. fr. — *fragmenta ex opere de theophania*, H. Gressmann *GCS* 3^2 (1904) p. 3*, M.24.609

v.C. — *de vita Constantini*, *GCS* 1, M.20.905

EUSEBIUS DORYLAEENSIS — saec. v
(Eus. Dor.)

contest. — *contestatio*, *ACO* 1.1.1 p. 101 partly ap. Anast. S. *hod.* 20, M.89.277

ep. Chalc. *epistula ad synodum Chalcedonensem*, ap. C Chalc. *act.* 2, *ACO* 2.1.2 p. 8, H.2.312

ep. imp. *epistula ad imperatores*, *ACO* 2.1.1 p. 66, ap. Evagr. *h.e.* 2. 18, M.86.2549–52A

libell. *libellus contra Eutychen*, ap. CCP (448) *act.*, *ACO* 2.1.1 p. 100, H.2.110

EUSEBIUS EMESENUS ob. c. 359
(Eus. Em.)

fr. dogm. *fragmenta duo de Jesu Christi persona*, M.86.536

fragmenta exegetica

fr. Gen. *fragmenta in Gen.*, M.86.556

fr. Lev. *fragmentum in Lev.*, M.86.557

fr. Jo. *fragmenta in Jo.*, M.86.549

fr. Ac. *fragmenta in Ac.*, M.86.557, 561

fr. Rom. *fragmenta in Rom.*, Staab p. 46, M.86.561

†*fr. 1 Cor.* *fragmentum in 1 Cor.*, Staab p. 52, M.86.561

fr. Gal. *fragmenta in Gal.*, Staab p. 46

fr. 2 Petr. *fragmentum in 2 Petr.*, M.86.560

EUSEBIUS NICOMEDIENSIS ob. c. 341
(Eus. Nic.)

ep. Ar. *fragmenta epistulae ad Arium*, ap. Ath. *syn.* 17

ep. Paulin. *epistula ad Paulinum Tyrium*, Opitz 3 p. 15, M.82.913

libell. *libellus poenitentiae*, Opitz 3 p. 65, M.67.112A (written jointly with Theognis)

EUSTATHIUS ANTIOCHENUS ob. ante 337
(Eust.)

‡*alloc.* *allocutio in Constantinum imperatorem*, M.18.673

engast. *de engastrimytho contra Origenem*, E. Klostermann *KlT* 83 (1912) p. 16, M.18.613

exegetica

fr. *fragmenta*, F. Cavallera *S. Eustathii Antiocheni in Lazarum* etc. Paris 1905 pp. 65–67, 73–85; M.18.685, 696

fr. in Ps. *fragmenta in Pss. xv et xcii*, Cavallera op. cit. pp. 68–72, M.18.685–8

fr. in Pr. 8:22 *fragmenta in illud*, Dominus creavit me; primum ap. Thdt. *h.e.* 1. 8. 1–5, M.18.676; cetera, M.18.677–84

fr. *fragmenta varia*, Cavallera op. cit. pp. 87–99, M.18.689–96

‡*hex.* *commentarius in hexaëmeron*, M.18.708

‡*Laz.* *homilia in Lazarum*, Cavallera op. cit. p. 26

Melch. *fragmenta homiliae in Melchisedech*, B. Altaner *BZ* 40 (1940) p. 34; pp. 36–37 in M.61.740

EUSTATHIUS MONACHUS saec. vi
(Eust. Mon.)

ep. *epistula de duabus naturis adversus Severum*, M.86.901

EUSTATHIUS SEBASTENUS ob. 380
(Eust. Seb.)

ep. *epistula ad Liberium Papam*, ap. Socr. *h.e.* 4. 12. 10–20

EUSTRATIUS CONSTANTINOPOLITANUS ob. post 582
(Eustrat.)

stat. anim. *de statu animarum post mortem*, L. Allatius *De utriusque ecclesiae . . . de purgatorio consensione* Rome 1655 p. 336

v. Eutych. *vita Eutychii*, M.86.2273

EUTHALIUS DIACONUS saec. iv
(Euthal. Diac.)

exegetica

Ac. *editio Actuum Apostolorum*, M.85.628; another recension of M.85.652–61, M.10.1549

epp. Paul. *editio epistularum Pauli*, M.85.693

epp. cath. *editio catholicarum epistularum*, M.85.665

EUTHALIUS SULCANUS saec. vii
(Euthal. Sulc.)

fid. *confessio de fide orthodoxa*, H. von Soden *Die Schrifte des NT* 1^1 Berlin 1902 p. 638

EUTHERIUS TYANENSIS ob. post 434
(Euther.)

confut. *confutationes quarundam propositionum*, M.28.1337; additional fragments G. Ficker Leipzig 1908 p. 18

EUTYCHES saec. v
(Eut.)

conf. *libellus confessionis*, ap. C Eph. (449) *act.*, *ACO* 2.1.1 p. 40, H.2.97

ep. Thds. *epistula ad Theodosium et Valentinianum*, *ib.* p. 152, H.2.177

supplic. *supplicatio*, *ib.* p. 177, H.2.212

EUTYCHIUS CONSTANTINOPOLITANUS ob. 582
(Eutych.)

ep. Vigil. *epistula ad Vigilium papam*, M.86.2401

pasch. *sermo de paschate et de eucharistia*, M.86.2392

EVAGRIUS PONTICUS ob. 399
(Evagr. Pont.)

cap. 1–33 *capitula per gradus quosdam disposita consequentiae*, M.40.1264

cap. pract. A, B *capita practica ad Anatolium*, M.40.1220, 1244

ep. *epistula*, int. opp. Bas. *ep.* 8, M.32.245

fr. 1–67 *fragmenta*, J. Muyldermans *Mus.* 44 (1931) p. 51

Gnost. *fragmentum ex libro 'Gnosticus' inscripto*, ap. Socr. *h.e.* 4. 23. 61–71; partly in M.40.1285

or. *de oratione*, int. opp. Nil., M.79.1165

rer. mon. *rerum monachalium rationes*, M.40.1252

schol. *scholion in πιτι*, P. A. de Lagarde *Onomastica Sacra* 1 Göttingen 1870 p. 205

sent. 1–25 *sententiae spirituales per alphabetum dispositae*, M.40.1268

sent. al. 1–26 *sententiae aliae*, M.40.1269

sent. mon. *sententiae ad monachos*, H. Gressmann *TU* 39^4 (1913) p. 153

sent. virg. *sententiae ad virgines*, *ib.* p. 146

vit. cog. *de octo vitiosis cogitationibus*, M.40.1272

EVAGRIUS SCHOLASTICUS ob. c. 600
(Evagr.)

h.e. *historia ecclesiastica*, J. Bidez and L. Parmentier London 1898, M.86.2416

EVANGELIA APOCRYPHA

Anaph. Pil. A, B *anaphora Pilati*, C. Tischendorf *Evangelia Apocrypha* Leipzig 1876 pp. 435, 443

Ev. Barth. *evangelium Bartholomaei*, Vassiliev p. 10; fragments, A. Wilmart and E. Tisserant *RB* 10 (1913) pp. 185, 321

Ev. Ebion. *fragmenta ex evangelio Ebionitum*, ap. Epiph. *haer.* 30. 13, 14, 16, 17, 22

Ev. Petr. *evangelium Petri*, H. B. Swete Cambridge 1893, L. Vaganay *Études bibliques* Paris 1930 p. 202 (cited by chapter of Swete and page of Vaganay) saec. ii

Ev. Thom. A, B *evangelium Thomae*, Tischendorf op. cit. pp. 140, 158; another recension of A, A. Delatte *Anecdota Atheniensia* 1 (Liège 1927) p. 264

Keryg. Petr. *kerygma Petri*, cited from Clem.

Narr. Jos. *narratio Josephi Arimathiensis*, Tischendorf op. cit. p. 459

Protev. *protevangelium Jacobi*, *ib.* p. 1 saec. ii

EXORCISMI ET INCANTATIONES

Exorc. Vassiliev, p. 332

FAUSTUS saec. v
(Faust.)

‡*ep.* *epistula ad Petrum Fullonem*, *ACO* 3 p. 8, H.2.848

FELIX I PAPA ob. 274

fr. *fragmentum epistulae*, ap. Cyr. *apol. orient.* *ACO* 1.1.7 p. 45, A.6^1.174

FELIX III PAPA ob. 492

‡*ep. Petr.* 1, 2 *epistulae ad Petrum Fullonem*, *ACO* 3 pp. 19, 13, H.2.817, 824

‡*ep. Zen. imp.* *epistula ad Zenonem imperatorem*, *ACO* 3 p. 23, H.2.828

FIRMINUS saec. iv

ep. Bas. *epistula ad Basilium*, int. opp. Bas. *ep.* 117, M.32.533

FIRMUS CAESARIENSIS ob. 439
(Firm.)

ep. 1–45 *epistulae*, M.77.1481

FLAVIANUS ANTIOCHENUS ob. 404
(Flav. Ant.)
anath. *de non anathematizandis vivis vel defunctis*, int. opp. Chrys., M.48.945
fr. 1–11 *fragmenta e Theodoreto et Leontio*, F. Cavallera *S. Eustathii Antiocheni in Lazarum homilia* Paris 1905 p. 105

FLAVIANUS CONSTANTINOPOLITANUS ob. 449
(Flav. CP)
ep. Leon. 1, 2 *epistulae ad Leonem*, int. opp. Leo. Mag. *ep.* 22, 26, *ACO* 2.1.1 pp. 36, 38, M.*PL*.54.724, 744
ep. Thds. *epistula ad Theodosium imperatorem*, *ACO* 2.1.1 p. 35, M.65.889

FLAVIUS HIMERIUS ec. v
(Flavius)
ep. *epistula ad exactorem Mareotae*, ap. Ath. *apol. sec.* 85

FLORILEGIA CHRISTOLOGICA
Flor. *AP* p. 225

FRAGMENTA HISTORICA
Fr. hist. M.85.1808

GALLA PLACIDIA ob. post 449
(Gall. Plac.)
ep. Pulch. *epistula ad Pulcheriam*, *ACO* 2.1.1 p. 49, int. opp. Leo. Mag. *ep.* 58, M.*PL*.54.864
ep. Thds. *epistula ad Theodosium Imperatorem*, *ACO* 2.1.1 p. 5, int. opp. Leo. Mag. *ep.* 56, M.*PL*.54.860

GALLUS CAESAR ob. 354
(Gall.)
‡*ep.* *epistula ad Julianum imperatorem*, J. Bidez and F. Cumont *Juliani Imperatoris Epistulae et Leges* Paris 1922 p. 287

GELASIUS CAESARIENSIS ob. 395
(Gel. Caes.)
fr. *fragmenta*, *AP* p. 44

GELASIUS CYZICENUS ob. post 477
(Gel. Cyz.)
h.e. *historia ecclesiastica* (*historia Concilii Nicaeni*), G. Loeschke and M. Heinemann *GCS* 1918, M.85.1192

GELASIUS I PAPA ob. 496
(Gel. Papa)
‡*ep.* *epistula ad episcopos Syrios*, *ACO* 3 p. 218

GENNADIUS I CONSTANTINOPOLITANUS ob. 471
(Gennad.)
encycl. *epistula encyclica*, *AP* p. 79, M.85.1613
fr. *fragmenta* 2, 3, 4^b–7, 9, *AP* p. 77
fragmenta exegetica
fr. Gen. *fragmenta in Gen.*, M.85.1624
fr. Ex. *fragmentum in Ex.*, M.85.1664
fr. Ps. 1 *fragmenta in Ps. 1*, M.85.1665
fr. Rom. *fragmenta in Rom.*, Staab p. 352, M.85.1669
fr. 1 Cor. *fragmenta in 1 Cor.*, Staab p. 418, M.85.1728
fr. 2 Cor. *fragmentum in 2 Cor.*, Staab p. 419, M.85.1729
fr. Gal. *fragmenta in Gal.*, Staab p. 419, M.85.1729
fr. 2 Thess. *fragmentum in 2 Thess.*, Staab p. 420
fr. Heb. *fragmenta in Heb.*, Staab p. 420, M.85.1732

GEORGIUS ALEXANDRINUS saec. vii–viii
(Geo. Al.)
v. Chrys. *vita Joannis Chrysostomi*, Savile 8 p. 157

GEORGIUS LAODICENUS ob. c. 360
(Geo. Laod.)
ep. dogm. *epistula dogmatica*, ap. Epiph. *haer.* 73.12–22
ep. Maced. *epistula ad Macedonium et alios*, ap. Soz. *h.e.* 4. 13. 2–3

GEORGIUS PISIDA POETA saec. vii
(Geo. Pis.)
bell. Avar. *bellum Avaricum*, M.92.1263
carm. vit. *carmen de vita humana*, L. Sternbach *Analecta Graeco-Latina* Cracow 1893 p. 51
carm. 1–108 *carmina inedita*, L. Sternbach *Wiener Studien* 13 Vienna 1891 p. 1, *ib.* 14 (1892) p. 51
eracl. 1, 2 *Heraclias*, M.92.1297
hex. *hexaëmeron*, R. Hercher *Aeliani de animalium natura* 2 *Teub.* 1866 p. 603, M.92.1425
Pers. 1–3 *de expeditione Heraclii Persica*, M.92.1197
res. *in sanctam resurrectionem*, M.92.1373
senar. *senariorum fragmenta*, M.92.1732
Sev. *contra Severum monophysitam*, M.92.1621
van. *de vanitate vitae*, M.92.1581

GERMANUS I CONSTANTINOPOLITANUS ob. 733
(Germ. CP)
‡*contempl.* *rerum ecclesiasticarum contemplatio*, M.98.384 (saec. x–xi)
ep. dogm. 2–4 *epistulae dogmaticae*, M.98.156
hymn. BMV *hymnus in dei genetricem*, M.98.453
or. 1–9 *orationes*, M.98.221
syn. haer. *de synodis et haeresibus*, M.98.40
vit. term. *de vitae termino dialogus*, M.98.89

GREGENTIUS TAPHARENSIS saec. vi
(Gregent.)
†*disp.* *disputatio cum Herbano Judaeo*, M.86.621
†*leg. Hom.* *leges Homeritarum*, M.86.568

GREGORIUS AGRIGENTINUS ob. 592
(Gr. Agr.)
Eccl. *explanatio supra Eccl.*, M.98.741

GREGORIUS ANTIOCHENUS ob. 593
(Gr. Ant.)
bapt. 1 *de baptismo Christi*, int. opp. Gr. Thaum., M.10.1177
bapt. 2 *de baptismo Christi*, M.88.1872
exerc. *oratio ad exercitum*, M.88.1884, ap. Evagr. *h.e.* 6. 12
mul. ung. *in mulieres unguentiferas*, M.88.1848

GREGORIUS NAZIANZENUS ob. c. 390
(Gr. Naz.)
‡*astron.* *fragmentum ex oratione contra astronomos*, M.36.675
carm. *carminum libri duo*, M.37.397, 38.11
carm. 2.2 (poem.) *carmina quae spectant ad alios*, M.37.1451
carm. 2.2 (epitaph.) *epitaphia*, M.38.11
carm. 2.2 (epigr.) *epigrammata*, M.38.87
‡*Chr. pat.* *Christus patiens*, J. G. Brambs *Teub.* 1885, M.38.133 prob. saec. xi
ep. 1–242, 244 *epistulae*, M.37.21
fr. *fragmentum*, ap. *Doct. Patr.* 33 p. 257
or. 1–26, 32–45 *orationes*, M.35.396, 36.173
or. 27–31 *orationes theologicae*, A. J. Mason Cambridge 1899, M.36.12
‡*sign. in Ezech.* *significatio in Ezech.*, M.36.605
test. *testamentum*, M.37.389

GREGORIUS NYSSENUS ob. 394
(Gr. Nyss.)
‡*Abr.* *sermo in Abraham et Isaac*, S. J. Mercati *Ephraem Syri opera* 1, Rome 1915 p. 107
[‡*anim.* *de anima*, M.45.188 mainly = Nemes. *nat. hom.* 2–3 q.v.]
anim. et res. *de anima et resurrectione*, M.46.12
Apoll. *adversus Apollinarem*, M.45.1124
‡*Ar. et Sab.* *contra Arium et Sabellium*, M.45.1281
ascens. *in Christi ascensionem*, M.46.689
bapt. Chr. *in baptismum Christi*, M.46.577
bapt. diff. *adversus eos qui baptismum differunt*, M.46.416
beat. 1–8 *orationes de beatitudinibus*, M.44.1193
castig. *adversus eos qui castigationes aegre ferunt*, M.46.308
comm. not. *adversus Graecos ex communibus notionibus*, M.45.176
deit. *de deitate Filii et Spiritus sancti*, M.46.553
diff. ess. *de differentia essentiae et hypostaseos*, int. opp. Bas. *ep.* 38, M.32.325
engast. *de engastrimytho*, E. Klostermann *KlT* 83 (1912) p. 63, M.45.108
ep. 1–25 *epistulae*, G. Pasquali Berlin 1925, M.46.1000 (Pasquali reproduces Migne's column in the margin)
[‡*ep.* 26 Pasquali p. 80, by Stagirius the Sophist; ∞ Bas. *ep.* 347 q.v.]
[‡*ep.* 26 M.46.1100 = †Gr. Thaum. *ep. Philagr.* q.v.]
ep. 27 *epistula ad Stagirium*, Pasquali p. 81, int. opp. Bas. *ep.* 348, M.32.1092

ep. 28 — *epistula ad quemdam*, Pasquali p. 82, partly = ‡Bas. *ep.* 342, M.32.1088
ep. 29 — *epistula ad Petrum Sebastenum*, Pasquali p. 84, M.45.237
ep. can. — *epistula canonica*, M.45.221
Eun. — *contra Eunomium*, W. Jaeger *Gregorii Nysseni opera* 1, 2 Berlin 1921, M.45.244
exegetica
‡*or. 1, 2 in Gen. 1:26* — *orationes in Gen. 1:26*, M.44.257 ∾ ‡Bas. *struct. hom.*
Pss. titt. A, B — *Psalmorum tituli*, M.44.432, 488
Ps. 6 — *homilia in Ps. 6*, M.44.608
hom. 1–8 in Eccl. — *homiliae in Eccl.*, M.44.616
hom. 1–15 in Cant. — *homiliae in Cant.*, M.44.756
‡*hom. 1–10 in Jo.* — *homiliae in Jo.*, K. Hansmann *Forschungen zur christlichen Literatur- und Dogmen-Geschichte* 16⁴⁻⁵ Paderborn 1930 saec. vi–vii
hom. in 1 Cor. 6:18 — *homilia in illud*, Omne peccatum, M.46.489, 1108
hom. in 1 Cor. 15:28 — *homilia in illud*, Quando sibi subjecerit, M.44.1304
fat. — *contra fatum*, M.45.145
fid. — *de fide ad Simplicium*, M.45.136
fr. — *fragmenta*, ap. *Doct. Patr.* 40 p. 298, *AP* p. 14, M.46.1112
hex. — *apologia in hexaëmeron*, G. H. Forbes *Opera Gregorii Nysseni* 1 Burntisland 1855 p. 4, M.44.61
hom. opif. — *de hominis opificio*, *ib.* p. 102, M.44.125
‡*imag.* — *quid sit, ad imaginem dei*, M.44.1328
infant. — *de infantibus qui praemature abripiuntur*, M.46.161
instit. — *de instituto Christiano*, W. Jaeger, J. P. Cavarnos, and V. W. Callahan *Gregorii Nysseni opera ascetica* Leiden 1952 p. 40, M.46.288 (fragments only). The second half of this work (pp. 66–89) is incorporated in Mac. Aeg. *ep.*, M.34.420C–442 q.v.
laud. Bas. — *in laudem Basilii fratris*, M.46.788
Maced. — *de Spiritu sancto contra Macedonianos*, M.45.1301
mart. 1–3 — *in xl martyres*, M.46.749, 757, 773
Melet. — *laudatio Meletii episcopi*, M.46.852
mort. — *de mortuis*, M.46.497
nativ. — *in diem natalem Christi*, M.46.1128
‡*occurs.* — *in occursum domini*, M.46.1152
or. catech. — *oratio catechetica*, J. H. Srawley Cambridge 1903, M.45.9
or. dom. 1–5 — *homiliae in orationem dominicam*, J. C. Krabinger Landshut 1840, M.44.1120
ordin. — *in suam ordinationem*, M.46.544
paup. 1, 2 — *de pauperibus amandis*, M.46.453
perf. — *de perfectione et qualem oporteat esse Christianum*, Jaeger *ascet.* p. 173, M.46.252
Placill. — *oratio funebris de Placilla*, M.46.877
prof. Chr. — *de professione Christiana*, Jaeger *ascet.* p. 129, M.46.237
Pulch. — *oratio funebris de Pulcheria*, M.46.864
res. 1, 3–5 — *in Christi resurrectionem*, M.46.600
[‡*res. 2* — *in Christi resurrectionem*, M.46.628; see Sev. Ant.]
Spir. — *de Spiritu sancto*, M.46.696
Steph. 1, 2 — *encomia in Stephanum*, M.46.701
†*test.* — *testimonia adversus Judaeos*, M.46.193
Thdr. — *de Theodoro martyre*, M.46.736
Thphl. — *adversus Apollinarem ad Theophilum*, M.45.1269
tres dii — *quod non sint tres dii*, M.45.116
Trin. — *ad Eustathium de Trinitate*, G. Mercati *ST* 11 (1903) p. 71, §§ 1–8 int. opp. Bas. *ep.* 189, M.32.684
usur. — *contra usurarios*, M.46.433
v. Ephr. — *de vita Ephraemi Syri*, M.46.820
v. Gr. Thaum. — *de vita Gregorii Thaumaturgi*, M.46.893
v. Macr. — *de vita Macrinae*, Jaeger *ascet.* p. 370, M.46.960
v. Mos. — *de vita Mosis*, M.44.297; incomplete in Forbes op. cit. p. 322
virg. — *de virginitate*, Jaeger *ascet.* p. 247, M.46.317

GREGORIUS I PAPA (MAGNUS) ob. 604
(Gr. Mag.)
dial. 1, 3, 4 — *dialogi de vita et miraculis patrum Italicorum*, tr. Zacharias Papa (ob. 752), M.*PL*.77.150
dial. 2 — *dialogus de vita Benedicti*, tr. Zach., M.*PL*.66.125

GREGORIUS II PAPA ob. 731
(Gr. II Papa)
conf. — *confessio fidei Latinorum*, M.91.1017
ep. Germ. — *epistula ad Germanum I Constantinopolitanum*, M.98.148
†*ep. Leon. 1, 2* — *epistulae ad Leonem Isaurum imperatorem*, H.4.3, 13

GREGORIUS PRESBYTER saec. vii
(Gr. Presb.)
v. Gr. Naz. — *vita Gregorii Nazianzeni*, M.35.244

GREGORIUS QUIDAM
(Gr. quidam)
ep. — *epistula ad coenobitas*, G. Mercati *ST* 11 (1903) p. 89

GREGORIUS SYCEOTES saec. vii
(Gr. Syc.)
v. Thdr. Syc. — *vita Theodori Syceotis*, Theophilus Joannes *μνημεῖα ἁγιολογικά* Venice 1884 p. 361

GREGORIUS THAUMATURGUS NEOCAESARENSIS ob. c. 270
(Gr. Thaum.)
†*anim.* — *ad Tatianum de anima*, M.10.1137
‡*annunt.* 1–3 — *homiliae in annuntiationem BMV*, M.10.1145
ep. can. — *epistula canonica*, M.10.1020
†*ep. Philagr.* — *epistula ad Philagrium*, M.46.1101
exegetica
Eccl. — *metaphrasis in Eccl.*, M.10.986
fr. Mt. 6:22–23 — *fragmentum in Mt. 6:22–23*, M.10.1189
fid. cap. 1–12 — *de fide capitula xii*, *ACO* 1.1.6 p. 146, M.10.1128
fr. — *fragmenta*, ap. *Doct. Patr.* 33 p. 251, *AS* 3 p. 589
pan. Or. — *in Origenem oratio panegyrica*, P. Koetschau *SAQ* 9 1894, M.10.1052
†*sanct.* — *in omnes sanctos*, M.10.1197
symb. — *symbolum*, *ACO* 3 p. 3, M.10.984
[‡*theoph.* — *homilia in sancta theophania*, M.10.1177 = Gr. Ant. *bapt.* 1 q.v.]

GULOSUS AFRICANUS saec. vii
(Gul.)
ep. — *epistula ad Paulum Constantinopolitanum*, ap. C Later. *act.* 2, H.3.737

HADRIANUS MONACHUS saec. v
(Hadr.)
introd. — *introductio in sacras scripturas*, F. Goessling Berlin 1887, M.98.1273

HADRIANUS PAPA ob. 795
(Hadr. Papa)
ep. Const. — *epistula ad Constantinum*, M.*PL*.96.1215
ep. Taras. — *epistula ad Tarasium*, M.*PL*.96.1234

HEGEMONIUS saec. iv
(Hegem.)
Arch. — *acta disputationis Archelai et Manetis*, C. H. Beeson *GCS* 1906, M.10.1429

HEGESIPPUS saec. ii
(Heges.)
fragmenta ex libris commentariorum actuum ecclesiasticorum, M.5.1308, cit. ap. Eus. *h.e.*

HERACLEON saec. ii
(Heracleon)
cit. ap. Or. *Jo.*, Clem. *ecl.* 25, id. *str.* 4. 9

HERACLIANUS CHALCEDONENSIS saec. vi
(Heraclian.)
fr. — *fragmenta*, ap. *Doct. Patr.*

HERACLIUS IMPERATOR ob. 641
(Heracl.)
ecth. — *ecthesis*, ap. C Later. *act.* 3, H.3.792
ep. — *epistulae*, ap. *Chron. Pasch.* pp. 386–8, 398–402
method. — *methodus qua invenitur cujusque mensis quaecumque dies*, M.92.1124
nov. 22–25 — *novellae constitutiones*, C. E. Zacharias von Lingenthal *Collectio juris Graeco-Romani* 3 (1857) p. 33

Hermas saec. ii
(Herm.)
mand. *mandata pastoris*, J. B. Lightfoot *Apostolic Fathers* London 1898 p. 318
sim. *similitudines pastoris, ib.* p. 341; cap. 2. 8–9. 5, C. Bonner *A Papyrus Codex of the Shepherd of Hermas* Michigan 1934
vis. *visiones pastoris*, Lightfoot op. cit. p. 297

Hermias Philosophus saec. iii?
(Hermias)
irris. *irrisio gentilium philosophorum*, M.6.1169

Hesychius Hierosolymitanus ob. post 450
(Hesych. H.)
exegetica
fr. Ps. *fragmenta in Psalmos*, M.93.1180
Ps. tit. *de titulis Psalmorum*, M.27.649
Is. *epitome Isaiae prophetae*, M.93.1369
fr. Dan. *fragmentum in Dan.*, M.93.1388
proem. proph. *proemium in epitomen xii prophetarum*, M.93.1340
Os.–Mal. *epitome xii prophetarum*, M.93.1345
fr. Ac. *fragmenta in Ac.*, M.93.1388
fr. Jac. *fragmenta in Jac.*, M.93.1389
fr. 1 Petr. *fragmentum in 1 Petr.* M.93.1389
fr. Judae *fragmentum in epistulam Judae*, M.93.1392
‡*laud. Procop.* *laudes Procopii Persae*, H. Delehaye, *AB* 24 (1905) p. 475
‡*m. Long.* *martyrium Longini centurionis*, M.93.1545
qu. ev. *quaestiones ex concordia evangelica*, M.93.1392
[‡*serm.* 1 *sermo*, M.93.1449 = Hesych. M. *fr.* q.v.]
serm. 2, 4–8 *sermones*, M.93.1449

Hesychius Milesius saec. vi
(Hesych. M.)
fr. *fragmentum ex historia in Christi natalem*, M.93.1449

Hesychius Sinaiticus saec. vi–vii
(Hesych. S.)
temp. *de temperantia et virtute centuriae ad Theodulum*, M.93.1480

Hieronymus Hierosolymitanus saec. viii
(Hier. H.)
bapt. *dialogus de effectu baptismi*, M.40.860
cruc. *dialogus de cruce*, M.40.865
Trin. *dialogus de Trinitate*, M.40.848

Hieronymus Stridonensis ob. c. 419
(Hier.)
v. Paul. A, B *vitae Pauli eremitae Thebaidis* recensiones duae, J. Bidez *Université de Gand Recueil de Travaux* 25 Ghent and Brussels 1900
vir. ill. *de viris illustribus*, tr. Sophr. Pal., O. von Gebhardt *TU* 14^{1b} (1896) p. 1, M.*PL*.23.602

Hilarius Pictaviensis ob. 367
(Hil. Pict.)
fr. 1–3 *fragmenta Graeca*, *ACO* 2.1.1 p. 20, ap. Thdt. *eran.* 2, S.4.162

Hilarus Papa ob. 468
(Hil.)
ep. Pulch. *epistula ad Pulcheriam*, int. opp. Leo. Mag. *ep.* 46, *ACO* 2.1.1 p. 48, M.*PL*.54.838

Hippolytus Romanus ob. 235
(Hipp.)
antichr. *demonstratio de Christo et antichristo*, G. N. Bonwetsch and H. Achelis *GCS* 1^2 (1897) p. 3, M.10.725
‡*apost.* *de xii apostolis*, M.10.952
†*Artem.* *contra Artemonem* seu *parvus labyrinthus*, ap. Eus. *h.e.* 5. 28
Bal. *de benedictione Balaam*, *GCS* 1^2 p. 82, M.10.605
ben. Jac. *de benedictione Jacobi*, *TU* 38^1 (1911) p. 11
‡*Ber. Hel.* *contra Beronem et Heliconem*, ap. *Doct. Patr.* 44 p. 321, M.10.829 prob. saec. vi
‡*can.* *canones Hippolyti*, H. Achelis *TU* 6^4 1891; Latin with Greek fragments
can. pasch. *canon paschalis*, M.10.875
cant. Mos. *canticum Mosis*, *GCS* 1^2 p. 83, M.10.609
‡*consumm.* *de consummatione mundi*, *GCS* 1^2 p. 289, M.10.904
‡*disc.* *de lxx discipulis*, M.10.953
‡*engast.* *fragmentum de engastrimytho*, *GCS* 1^2 p. 123, M.10.605
ep. reg. *fragmenta epistulae ad reginam*, *GCS* 1^2 p. 253, M.10.869
exegetica
fr. 1–52 in Gen. *fragmenta in Gen.*, *GCS* 1^2 p. 51, M.10.584
‡*fr. 53–81 in Gen.* *fragmenta in Gen.*, *GCS* 1^2 p. 51, M.10.584
fr. in Ruth *fragmentum in Ruth*, *GCS* 1^2 p. 120
fr. in 1 Reg. *fragmenta in 1 Reg.*, *GCS* 1^2 p. 121, M.10.864
fr. 1, 18–20, 37 in Pss. *fragmenta in Pss.*, *GCS* 1^2 p. 130, M.10.608, 712
‡*fr. 2–17, 21–36, 38 in Pss.* *fragmenta in Pss.*, *GCS* 1^2 p. 130, M.10.608, 712
fr. 1–29, 54 in Pr. *fragmenta in Pr.*, *GCS* 1^2 p. 157, M.10.616
†*fr. 30, 31 in Pr.* *fragmenta in Pr.*, *GCS* 1^2 p. 157, M.10.616
‡*fr. 32–53 in Pr.* *fragmenta in Pr.*, *GCS* 1^2 p. 157, M.10.616
fr. in Eccl. *fragmenta in Eccl.*, *GCS* 1^2 p. 179
‡*fr. in Eccl.* *fragmenta in Eccl.*, *GCS* 1^2 p. 179
fr. Cant. *fragmentum in Cant.*, *GCS* 1^1 p. 343, M.10.628
fr. in Is. *fragmentum in Is.*, *GCS* 1^2 p. 180, M.10.632
fr. in Ezech. *fragmentum in Ezech.*, M.10.632
Dan. *commentarium in Dan.*, *GCS* 1^1 p. 2; for fragments not in *GCS*, M. Lefèvre *SC* 14 (1947); fragments in M.10.637, 669
‡*fr. in Mt. 6:11* *fragmentum in Mt. 6:11*, *GCS* 1^2 p. 208, M.10.700
fr. in Mt. 25:24 *fragmentum in Mt. 25:24*, *GCS* 1^2 p. 209, M.10.868
fr. 1–3 in Jo. 19:33–34 *fragmenta in Jo. 19:33–34*, *GCS* 1^2 p. 211, M.10.868
fr. *fragmentum*, ap. *Doct. Patr.* 40, p. 300
†*fr.* *fragmenta*, K. Holl *TU* 20^2 (1899) p. 137, M.10.861D, 868D
fr. res. *fragmentum de resurrectione et incorruptione*, *GCS* 1^2 p. 254, M.10.861C
Graec. *adversus Graecos*, M.10.796
haer. *refutatio omnium haeresium* sive *philosophoumena*, P. Wendland *GCS* 3 1916, int. opp. Or., M.16.3017
Jud. *demonstratio adversus Judaeos*, E. Schwartz *SBBAW* 1936^3 p. 19, M.10.788
†*Laz.* *homilia in quatriduanum Lazarum*, *GCS* 1^2 p. 215, M.62.775
†*narr.* *narratio de virgine Corinthiaca*, *GCS* 1^2 p. 275, M.10.872, ap. Pall. *h. Laus.* 65
Noët. *contra haeresin Noëti*, P. Nautin Paris 1949, M.10.804
pasch. *fragmenta ex libro de paschate*, *GCS* 1^2 p. 267, M.10.700, 864, 869
†*theoph.* *de theophania*, *GCS* 1^2 p. 257, M.10.852
[*trad. ap.* *traditio apostolica*, G. Dix *The Treatise on the Apostolic Tradition* 1 London 1937]

Hippolytus Thebanus saec. viii
(Hipp. Th.)
fr. 1–6 *fragmenta*, F. Diekamp *Hippolytus von Theben* Münster 1898, M.117.1028
†*fr.* 7–9 *fragmenta*, F. Diekamp *Hippolytus von Theben* Münster 1898, M.117.1028
‡*fr.* 10–21 *fragmenta*, F. Diekamp *Hippolytus von Theben* Münster 1898, M.117.1028

Homiliae Clementinae see **Clementina**

Honorius Papa ob. 638
(Honor.)
ep. Serg. 1 *epistula ad Sergium*, ap. CCP (681) *act.* 12, H.3.1320
ep. Serg. 2 *fragmentum epistolae ad Sergium*, *ib.* H.3.1352

Hormisdas Papa ob. 523
(Horm.)
ep. cler. *epistula ad clerum Syrum*, *ACO* 3 p. 52, M.*PL*.63.415
ep. Epiph. *epistula ad Epiphanium*, *ACO* 3 p. 56, M.*PL*.63.516

Hosius Cordubensis ob. c. 357
(Hos.)
ep. *epistula ad Constantium imperatorem* ap. Ath. *h. Ar.* 44

Hymenaeus et Alii saec. iii
(Hymen.)
ep. *epistula ad Paulum Samosatenum*, F. Loofs *TU* 44^5 (1924) p. 324

Hymni Anonymi
Hymn. — P. Maas *Hymni anonymi saec. v–vi*; *KlT* 52–53 (1931); *AGC*; *AS* I pp. 447–661

Hypatius Ephesinus — saec. vi
(Hypat.)
fr. — *fragmenta*, *AP* p. 126
fragmenta exegetica
fr. in Ps. 77 — *fragmentum in Ps. 77*, *AP* p. 129
fr. Os.–Zach. — *fragmenta in xii prophetas*, *ib.* p. 130
fr. Lc. — *fragmenta in Lc.*, *ib.* p. 151

Hyperechius — saec. vi
(Hyper.)
mon. — *adhortatio ad monachos*, M.79.1473

Ibas Edessenus — ob. 457
(Ibas)
ep. — *epistula*, ap. C Chalc. *act.* 10, *ACO* 2.1.3 p. 32, H.2.528

Ignatius Antiochenus — ob. c. 110
(Ign.)
Eph. — *epistula ad Ephesios*, Bihlmeyer p. 82, M.5.644
Magn. — *epistula ad Magnesios*, Bihlmeyer p. 88, M.5.661
Philad. — *epistula ad Philadelphios*, Bihlmeyer p. 102, M.5.697
Polyc. — *epistula ad Polycarpum*, Bihlmeyer p. 110, M.5.718
Rom. — *epistula ad Romanos*, Bihlmeyer p. 96, M.5.685
Smyrn. — *epistula ad Smyrnaeos*, Bihlmeyer p. 105, M.5.708
Trall. — *epistula ad Trallianos*, Bihlmeyer p. 92, M.5.673
spuria et interpolata — saec. iv
‡*Ant.* — *epistula ad Antiochenses*, Lightfoot p. 817, M.5.897
‡*Eph.* — *epistulae ad Ephesios recensio longior*, Lightfoot p. 834, M.5.729
‡*fr.* — *fragmenta*, ap. Jo. D. *parall.*, see K. Holl *TU* 20^2 (1899) pp. 28–31
‡*Her.* — *epistula ad Heronem*, Lightfoot p. 827, M.5.909
‡*Magn.* — *epistulae ad Magnesios recensio longior*, Lightfoot p. 748, M.5.757
‡*Mar.* — *epistula ad Mariam*, Lightfoot p. 729, M.5.881
‡*Phil.* — *epistula ad Philippenses*, Lightfoot p. 772, M.5.920
‡*Philad.* — *epistulae ad Philadelphios recensio longior*, Lightfoot p. 787, M.5.817
‡*Polyc.* — *epistulae ad Polycarpum recensio longior*, Lightfoot p. 812, M.5.857
‡*Rom.* — *epistulae ad Romanos recensio longior*, Lightfoot p. 850, M.5.801
‡*Smyrn.* — *epistulae ad Smyrnaeos recensio longior*, Lightfoot p. 802, M.5.831
‡*Tars.* — *epistula ad Tarsenses*, Lightfoot p. 763, M.5.888
‡*Trall.* — *epistulae ad Trallianos recensio longior*, Lightfoot p. 733, M.5.777

Innocentius I Papa — ob. 417
(Innoc.)
ep. Chrys. — *epistula ad Joannem Chrysostomum*, M.52.537
ep. cler. — *epistula ad clerum et populum Constantinopolitanum*, M.52.537
fr. ep. — *fragmentum epistulae ad Theophilum*, ap. Pall. *v. Chrys.* 3 p. 17, M.47.12

Interrogatio Tertulli — saec. v
Interr. Tertull. — F. de Cavalieri, *ST* 8 (1902) p. 10

Irenaeus Harpasianus — saec. v
(Iren. Harp.)
fr. — *fragmentum*, ap. *Doct. Patr.* 41, p. 312

Irenaeus Lugdunensis — ob. c. 202
(Iren.)
ep. Flor. — *epistula ad Florinum*, ap. Eus. *h.e.* 5. 20. 4–8
ep. Vict. — *epistula ad Victorem*, ap. Eus. *h.e.* 5. 24. 12–17
fr. 1, 4–34, 39–47 — *fragmenta*, W. W. Harvey *Irenaeus* 2 Cambridge 1857 p. 470, M.7.1225
haer. — *adversus haereses* (Lat. with Greek fr.), Harvey vol. 1, M.7.437; some frr. in *AHS* I pp. 387–8 and ap. Or. *Apoc. TU* 38 (1912) pp. 41–44

Irenaeus Tyrius, Comes — ob. c. 450
(Iren. Tyr.)
ep. — *epistula ad orientales*, ap. C Eph. Orient. *act.*, *ACO* 1.1.5 p. 135, H.1.1548

Isaac Syrus — saec. vii
(Isaac)
cog. — *de cogitationibus*, M.86.885
ep. — *epistulae ad Symeonem*, capitula 8–15, *NBP* 8^3 (1871) p. 162
serm. 1–82 — *sermones*, A. Spetsieri Athens 1882

Ischyras Aegyptius — saec. iv
(Ischyras)
ep. — *epistula ad Athanasium*, ap. Ath. *apol. sec.* 64

Ischyrionus Diaconus — saec. v
(Isch.)
libell. — *libellus contra Dioscurum*, ap. C Chalc. *act.* 3, *ACO* 2.1.2 p. 17, H.2.325

Isidorus Hispalensis — ob. 636
(Isid. H.)
etym. — *etymologiarum libri* (Lat.), W. M. Lindsay *Scriptorum Classicorum Bibliotheca Oxoniensis* 1911

Isidorus Pelusiota — ob. c. 435
(Isid. Pel.)
epp. — *epistularum libri quinque*, M.78.77

Joannes I Antiochenus — ob. 441
(Jo. Ant.)
ep. cler. CP — *epistula ad clerum Constantinopolitanum*, *ACO* 1.1.5 p. 127. 13, int. opp. Thdt. *ep.* 155, M.83.1448
ep. Cyr. 1–4 — *epistulae ad Cyrillum*: 1, *ACO* 1.1.1 p. 119, int. opp. Cyr. *ep.* 22, M.77.132; 2, *ACO* 1.1.4 p. 7, int. opp. Cyr. *ep.* 38, M.77.169; 3, *ACO* 1.1.7 p. 151; 4, *ACO* 1.1.7 p. 155, int. opp. Cyr. *ep.* 47, M.77.248
ep. episc. — *epistula ad episcopos orientales*, *ACO* 1.1.7 p. 156
ep. excomm. — *epistula ad episcopos excommunicatos*, *ACO* 1.1.5 p. 124, H.1.1457
ep. Maxm. — *epistula ad Maximianum*, *ACO* 1.1.7 p. 160
ep. Nest. — *epistula ad Nestorium*, *ACO* 1.1.1 p. 93, M.77.1449
ep. pop. CP — *epistula ad populum Constantinopolitanum*, *ACO* 1.1.5 p. 128, int. opp. Thdt. *ep.* 156, M.83.1448
ep. praef. — *epistula ad praefectum et magistrum*, *ACO* 1.1.5 p. 132, int. opp. Thdt. *ep.* 159, M.83.1456
ep. praepos. — *epistula ad praepositum et scholasticum*, *ACO* 1.1.5 p. 133, int. opp. Thdt. *ep.* 160, M.83.1457
ep. Ruf. — *epistula ad Rufum*, *ACO* 1.1.3 p. 39, int. opp. Thdt. *ep.* 170, M.83.1476
ep. senat. CP — *epistula ad senatum Constantinopolitanum*, *ACO* 1.1.5 p. 127, int. opp. Thdt. *ep.* 154, M.83.1445
ep. Xyst. — *epistula ad Xystum*, *ACO* 1.1.7 p. 158
ep. Xyst. et Cyr. — *epistula ad Xystum, Cyrillum et Maximianum*, *ACO* 1.1.4 p. 33, int. opp. Cyr. *ep.* 35, M.77.164
hom. — *homilia*, *ACO* 1.1.7 p. 84
propos. — *propositio Acacio Beroeensi oblata et ad Cyrillum missa*, *ACO* 1.1.7 p. 146
relat. imp. 1–6 — *relationes ad imperatorem seu imperatores seu imperatrices*: 1, *ACO* 1.1.5 p. 124, M.83.1440; 2, *ACO* 1.1.5 p. 131, M.83.1441; 3, *ACO* 1.1.5 p. 129, M.83.1452; 4, *ACO* 1.1.5 p. 131, M.83.1453; 5, *ACO* 1.1.5 p. 125, M.83.1457; 6, *ACO* 1.1.7 p. 157
sent. — *sententia*, ap. C Eph. Orient. *act.*, *ACO* 1.1.5 p. 122, H.1.1453

Joannes Caesariensis — saec. vi
(Jo. Caes.)
fr — *fragmenta*, ap. *Doct. Patr.* 24, p. 166

Joannes Carpathius — saec. vii
(Jo. Carp.)
cap. — *capitula adhortatoria*, M.85.1837

Joannes Climacus — ob. 649
(Jo. Clim.)
ep. — *epistula ad Joannem Raithenum*, M.88.625
past. — *liber ad pastorem*, M.88.1165
scal. — *scala paradisi*, M.88.632

Joannes Comes — saec. v
(Jo. Com.)
relat. — *sacrarum largitionum relatio*, *ACO* 1.1.7 p. 67

Joannes II Constantinopolitanus — ob. 520
(Jo. II CP)
ep. Epiph. — *epistula ad Epiphanium Tyrium*, ap. CCP (536) *act.* 5, *ACO* 3 p. 77, H.2.1341
ep. Jo. H. — *epistula ad Joannem III Hierosolymitanum*, *ib.*, *ACO* 3 p. 76, H.2.1341

Joannes IV Constantinopolitanus, Jejunator — ob. 595
(Jo. Jej.)
‡*can.* — *syntagma canonum*, G. A. Rhalli and M. Potli Athens 1854 p. 432
canonar. 1–3 — *canonarium* 1, L. Morinus *De disciplina poenitentiae* Paris 1651 appendix p. 101; *canonaria* 2, 3, *SS* 4 p. 438
doct. — *doctrina monialium*, *Mon.* 2 p. 226
‡*exc. poenit.* — *excerpta ex poenitentiali*, M.88.1932
liturg. — *de sacra liturgia*, *SS* 4, p. 440
†*paraen.* — *paraenesis*, *Mon.* 2 p. 235
†*poenit.* — *poenitentiale*, M.88.1889
poenit. cont. virg. — *de poenitentia continentia et virginitate*, M.88.1937 (mostly extracts from Chrys.)
pseud. — *de pseudoprophetis*, M.59.553
†*serm.* — *sermo de poenitentia*, M.88.1920 (partly = †*poenit.*)

Joannes VI Constantinopolitanus — ob. 715
(Jo. VI CP)
ep. — *epistula ad Constantinum papam*, M.96.1416

Joannes Damascenus — ob. 749
(Jo. D.)
anacr. — *oratio versibus anacreonticis*, M.96.853
‡*Artem.* — *passio Artemii*, M.96.1252, fragments int. opp. Philost., *GCS* pp. 151–65 and 7–110
‡*azym.* — *de azymis*, M.95.388
†*B.J.* — *vita Barlaam et Joasaph*, M.96.860 (capp. 26–27 = Arist. *apol.* q.v.)
carm. anast. — *carmen in anastasin*, *AGC* p. 232
‡*carm. annunt.* — *carmen in annuntiationem*, *ib.* p. 240, M.96.852; by Theophanes Graptus saec. ix–x
carm. antipasch. — *carmen in dominicam antipaschatis*, *ib.* p. 221
carm. assumpt. Chr. — *carmen in assumptionem domini*, *ib.* p. 226, M.96.843
carm. dorm. BMV — *carmen in dormitionem BMV*, *AGC* p. 229, M.96.1364
carm. pasch. — *carmen in pascha*, *AGC* p. 218, M.96.840
carm. pent. — *carmen in pentecosten*, *AGC* p. 213, M.96.832
carm. theog. — *carmen in theogoniam*, *AGC* p. 205, M.96.817
carm. theoph. — *carmen in theophaniam*, *AGC* p. 209, M.96.825
carm. transfig. — *carmen in transfigurationem domini*, M.96.848
‡*conf.* — *epistula de confessione*, ed. K. Holl *Enthusiasmus und Bussgewalt beim griechischen Mönchtum* Leipzig 1898, M.95.284
‡*Const.* — *adversus Constantinum Cabalinum, de sacris imaginibus*, M.95.309; ascribed in some MSS to Jo. Sync.
‡*corp.* — *de corpore et sanguine Christi*, M.95.401
†*creat.* 1–7 — *homiliae de creatione mundi*, C. J. Diobouniotis *Ἐκκλησιαστικὸς Φάρος* 13 Alexandria 1914 pp. 58, 119
dialect. — *dialectica*, M.94.521
disp. — *disputatio Christiani et Saraceni*, M.96.1336 (another recension, Latin with Greek fragments, M.94.1585)
drac. — *de draconibus et strygibus*, M.94.1600
ep. — *epistulae fragmentum: quid est homo?* M.95.244
‡*ep. Thphl.* — *epistula ad Theophilum imperatorem de sacris imaginibus*, M.95.345
exegetica
fr. Mt. — *fragmenta in Mt.*, M.96.1408
Rom.–Philm. — *ex interpretatione Chrysostomi loci selecti in epistulas Pauli*, M.95.441
‡*fid. dorm.* — *de iis qui in fide dormierunt*, M.95.248
fid. Nest. — *de fide contra Nestorianos*, F. Diekamp *TQ* 83 (1901) p. 560
f.o. — *de fide orthodoxa libri quattuor*, M.94.789
fr. — *fragmenta*, M.95.225, 96.816
†*fr.* — *fragmenta*, M.95.412
haer. — *liber de haeresibus*, M.94.677
haer. Nest. — *adversus Nestorianorum haeresim*, M.95.188
hom. 1–4, 8–12 — *homiliae*, M.96.545, 700
‡*hom.* 5, 6 — *homiliae*, M.96.648
[‡*hom.* 7 — *homilia in nativitatem BMV*, M.96.680 = Thdr. Stud. *nativ. BMV* q.v.]
hymn. exod. — *hymnus ad exodiasticum*, M.96.1368
‡*hymn. Tryph.* — *hymnus de Tryphone martyre*, *AS* 1 p. 435
[‡*icon.* — *adversus iconoclastas*, M.96.1348; see Jo. V H.]
imag. 1–3 — *de sacris imaginibus orationes*, M.94.1232
inst. el. — *institutio elementaris ad dogmata*, M.95.100
Jacob. — *contra Jacobitas*, M.94.1436
jej. — *de sacris jejuniis*, M.95.64
Man. 1, 2 — *dialogi contra Manichaeos*, M.94.1505, 96.1320
nat. — *de natura composita contra acephalos*, M.95.112
parall. — *sacra parallela*, M.95.1040–96.441
poem. 1–6 — *poemata*, *AGC* p. 117
prec. 1–3 — *precationes*, M.96.816
rect. sent. — *de recta sententia*, M.94.1421
spir. neq. — *de octo spiritibus nequitiae*, M.95.80
†*Trin.* — *de sancta Trinitate*, M.95.9
trisag. — *de hymno trisagio ad Jordanem*, M.95.21
virt. — *de virtutibus et vitiis*, M.95.85 = Ephr. 3.425
volunt. — *de duabus in Christo voluntatibus*, M.95.128

Joannes Diacrinomenos — saec. vi
(Jo. Diacr.)
fr. h.e. — *fragmentum historiae ecclesiasticae*, ap. C Nic. (787) *act.* 5, H.4.305; E. Müller *RA* 26 (1873) p. 401

Joannes Eleemosinarius — ob. 617
(Jo. Eleem.)
v. Tych. — *vita Tychonis*, H. Usener *Der heilige Tychon* Leipzig and Berlin 1907 p. 111

Joannes Epiphanii Discipulus
(Jo. Disc.)
v. Epiph. 1–38 — *vita Epiphanii* (1–38), M.41.24

Joannes Euboeensis — saec. viii
(Jo. Eub.)
concept. BMV — *sermo in conceptionem BMV*, M.96.1460
innoc. — *sermo in sanctos innocentes*, M.96.1501

Joannes Gabalensis — saec. vi–viii?
(Jo. Gab.)
fr. — *fragmentum ex vita Severi Antiocheni*, ap. C Nic. (787) *act.* 5, H.4.308

Joannes III Hierosolymitanus — ob. 524
(Jo. III H.)
ep. — *epistula ad Joannem Constantinopolitanum*, ap. CCP (536) *act.* 5, *ACO* 3 p. 77, H.2.1341

Joannes V Hierosolymitanus — saec. viii
(Jo. V H.)
icon. — *opusculum contra iconoclastas*, int. opp. Jo. D., M.96.1348

Joannes VI Hierosolymitanus — saec. x
(Jo. VI H.)
v. Jo. D. — *vita Joannis Damasceni*, M.94.429

Joannes Jejunator see Joannes IV Constantinopolitanus

Joannes Malalas — saec. vi
(Jo. Mal.) — (possibly identical with Jo. Scholast.)
chron. — *chronographia*, M.97.65, cited also by page of L. Dindorf *CB* 1831. Books 9–12, A. Schenk Graf von Stauffenberg *Die römische Kaisergeschichte bei Malalas*, Stuttgart 1931 (the *CB* page appears in the margin)

JOANNES MONACHUS — saec. viii–ix ?
(Jo. Mon.)
hymn. Bas. — *hymnus in Basilium*, M.96.1372
hymn. Blas. — *hymnus in Blasium*, M.96.1401
hymn. Chrys. — *hymnus in Joannem Chrysostomum*, M.96.1377
hymn. Geo. — *hymnus in Georgium*, M.96.1393
hymn. Nic. Myr. — *hymnus in Nicolaum Myrensem*, M.96.1384
hymn. Petr. — *hymnus in Petrum*, M.96.1389

JOANNES MOSCHUS — ob. 619
(Jo. Mosch.)
prat. — *pratum spirituale*, M.87.2852
prol. prat. — *prologus in pratum spirituale*, H. Usener *Der heilige Tychon* Leipzig and Berlin 1907 p. 91

JOANNES NICAENUS — saec. ix–x ?
(Jo. Nic.)
‡*fr.* — *fragmentum*, ap. ‡Tim. CP *haer. suppl.*, M.86.72D–73A
nativ. — *de festo die natali domini*, M.96.1436

JOANNES NOTARIUS — saec. v
(Jo. Not.)
v. Eus. — *vita Eusebii Alexandrini*, M.86.297

JOANNES PHILOPONUS — ob. c. 570
(Jo. Philop.)
arb. — *fragmenta operis de arbitrio*, ap. *Doct. Patr.* 36, p. 272
arith. — *arithmetica*, *SR* 2 (1839) p. 392
opif. — *de opificio mundi*, W. Reichardt *Teub.* 1897
pasch. — *de paschate*, C. Walter *Commentationes philologae Jenenses* 6^2 Leipzig 1899 p. 209
Procl. — *de aeternitate mundi contra Proclum*, H. Rabe, *Teub.* 1899

JOANNES RAITHENUS — saec. vii
(Jo. Raith.)
ep. — *epistula ad Joannem Climacum*, M.88.624

JOANNES SCHOLASTICUS — ob. 577
(Jo. Scholast.) — (possibly identical with Jo. Mal.)
coll. cap. — *collectio 87 capitulorum*, *Mon.* 2 p. 385
nomoc. — *collectio canonum L titularum*, V. Beneševič *ABAW* 14 (1937) pp. 3, 32
suppl. — *supplementum 22 capitulorum*, *Mon.* 2 p. 406

JOANNES SCYTHOPOLITANUS — saec. vi
(Jo. Scyth.)
fr. — *fragmentum operis contra Severum*, ap. *Doct. Patr.* 13 p. 85 (slightly longer version, ap. CCP (681) *act.* 10, H.3.1237)

JOANNES SYNCELLUS HIEROSOLYMITANUS — saec. viii
(Jo. Sync.)
narr. — *narratio de imaginibus*, ap. C Nic. (787) *act.* 5, H.4.320; see also ‡Jo. D. *Const.*

JOANNES THESSALONICENSIS — ob. c. 630
(Jo. Thess.)
dorm. BMV A, B — *orationis in dormitionem BMV* duae recensiones, M. Jugie *PO* 19 (1925) p. 375
fr. — *fragmentum de imaginibus*, ap. C Nic. (787) *act.* 5, H.4.292
mir. Dem. — *Demetrii martyris miracula*, M.116.1204, 1324
mul. ung. — *homilia in mulieres unguentiferas*, M.59.635
mul. ung. proem. — F. Combefis, *Patrum Bibliothecae Novum Auctarium* 1 Paris 1648 p. 792

JOBIUS EPISCOPUS — saec. iv seu v
(Job. Ep.)
symb. — *symbolum*, Lietzmann p. 286, M.86.3320

JOBIUS MONACHUS — saec. vi
(Job. Mon.)
inc. — *quaestio quare Filius incarnatus sit, non autem Pater et Spiritus sanctus*, M.86.3313

JOVIANUS IMPERATOR — ob. 364
(Jov.)
ep. — *epistula ad Athanasium Alexandrinum*, M.26.813

JULIANUS APOLLINARISTA — saec. iv
(Juln. Apoll.)
ep. — *epistulae fragmentum ad Polemonem*, Lietzmann p. 277

JULIANUS HALICARNASSENSIS — saec. vi
(Juln. Hal.)
fr. — *fragmenta*, *SR* 10 (1844) p. 206, ap. *Doct. Patr.* 41 p. 313

JULIANUS IMPERATOR — ob. 363
(Juln. Imp.) — (cited when of theological or ecclesiastical interest)
ep. 1–157 — *epistulae*, J. Bidez and F. Cumont Paris 1922 p. 1 (*ep.* 32 p. 39, int. opp. Bas. *ep.* 39, M.32.340)
†*ep.* 180–205 — *epistulae*, *ib.* p. 229 (†*ep.* 205 p. 282, int. opp. Bas. *ep.* 40, M.32.341)
[*Galil.* — *adversus Galilaeos*, cit. ap. Cyr. *Juln.* q.v.]

JULIANUS SERDICENSIS — saec. v
(Juln. Serd.)
poenit. — *libellus poenitentiae*, *ACO* 1.1.7 p. 139

JULIUS I PAPA — ob. 352
(Jul. Papa)
[‡*corp. et div.* — *de unione corporis et divinitatis in Christo*, M.*PL*.8.873; see Apoll.]
ep. Alex. — *epistula ad Alexandrinos*, ap. Ath. *apol. sec.* 52–53
ep. Dian. — *epistula ad Dianium et Flacillum*, *ib.* 21–35
‡*ep. encycl.* — *epistula encyclica*, Lietzmann p. 292
fr. — *fragmentum de homoousio*, M.*PL*.8.962

JUSTICINUS SICILIENSIS — saec. v
(Justic.)
‡*ep.* — *epistula ad Petrum Fullonem*, E. Schwartz *ACO* 3 p. 12, H.2.840

JUSTINIANUS IMPERATOR — ob. 565
(Justn.)
bull. aur. — *decretum (bulla aurea) ad abbatem Montis Sinai*, M.86.1149
cod. — *codex Justinianus*, P. Krueger *Corpus Juris Civilis* 2 Berlin 1877
conf. — *confessio rectae fidei adversus tria capitula*, E. Schwartz *ABAW* 18 (1939) p. 72, M.86.993
conf. anath. 1–13 — *anathemata*, ap. *conf.*, *ABAW* 18 p. 90, M.86.1013
ep. CP — *epistula ad synodum Constantinopolitanam de Origene*, M.86.989
ep. Thdr. Mops. — *epistula adversus Theodorum Mopsuestenum*, *ABAW* 18 p. 47, M.86.1041
ep. Zoïl. — *fragmentum epistulae ad Zoïlum Alexandrinum*, M.86.1145
fr. edict. — *fragmentum edicti*, ap. *Doct. Patr.* 21 p. 134
monoph. — *tractatus contra monophysitas*, *ABAW* 18 p. 7, M.86.1104
nov. — *novellae constitutiones*, R. Schoell and W. Kroll *Corpus Juris Civilis* 3 Berlin 1895
Or. — *liber adversus Origenem*, *ACO* 3 p. 189, M.86.945
Sev. — *constitutio sacra contra Severianos*, *ACO* 3 p. 119, M.86.1095
trop. — *troparium*, *AGC* p. 52
typ. Thdr. Mops. — *typus adversus Theodorum Mopsuestenum*, M.86.1035B

JUSTINUS GNOSTICUS — saec. ii
(Just. Gn.) — cit. ap. Hipp. *haer.* 5. 24–27

JUSTINUS II IMPERATOR — ob. 578
(Just. Imp.)
edict. — *edictum*, ap. Evagr. *h.e.* 5. 4 q.v.

JUSTINUS MARTYR, PHILOSOPHUS — ob. c. 165
(Just.)
1, 2 apol. — *apologiae*, Goodspeed p. 26, M.6.328
‡*c. Gr.* — *contra Graecos*, M.6.1457
‡*coh. Gr.* — *cohortatio ad Graecos*, M.6.241
‡*confut.* — *confutatio quorundam Aristotelis dogmatum*, M.6.1492
dial. — *dialogus cum Tryphone Judaeo*, Goodspeed p. 90, M.6.472
‡*ep. Zen. et Ser.* — *epistula ad Zenam et Serenum*, M.6.1184
†*fr.* — *fragmenta*, K. Holl *TU* 20^2 (1899) p. 49 } Some of these fragments and some others appear in M.6.1592
‡*fr.* — *fragmenta*, *ib.* p. 53 }
†*fr. res.* — *fragmentum in resurrectionem*, *ib.* p. 36, M.6.1572

JUSTINUS MARTYR, PHILOSOPHUS (*cont.*)

‡*monarch.*	*liber de monarchia dei*, M.6.312	
‡*or. Gr.*	*oratio ad Graecos*, M.6.229	
‡*qu. Chr.*	*quaestiones Christianae ad Graecos*, M.6.1401	saec. iv
‡*qu. Gr.*	*quaestiones Graecae ad Christianos*, M.6.1464	saec. iv
‡*qu. et resp.*	*quaestiones et responsiones ad orthodoxos*, M.6.1249	saec. iv

KERYGMA PETRI see EVANGELIA APOCRYPHA

LEO I IMPERATOR (Leo I Imp.) ob. 474
ep. *epistula ad Anatolium Constantinopolitanum*, ap. Evagr. *h.e.* 2. 9 p. 59, M.86. 2528

LEO III ISAURUS ET CONSTANTINUS V COPRONYMUS (Leo III Imp.) saec. viii
ecl. *ecloga legum*, G. E. Zacharias von Lingenthal *Collectio juris Graeco-Romani* Leipzig 1852 p. 9

LEO I PAPA (Leo Mag.) ob. 461

ep.	*epistulae variae*, M.*PL*.54.714 ff.
ep. 20	*ACO* 2.1.2 p. 45
23	,, ,, p. 46
28	,, 2.1.1 p. 10 (The Tome)
29	,, ,, p. 45
30	,, ,, p. 45
32	,, ,, p. 42
33	,, ,, p. 43
35	,, ,, p. 40
43	,, ,, p. 3
44	,, ,, p. 25
45	,, ,, p. 47
50	,, ,, p. 50
51	,, ,, p. 51
72	,, ,, p. 37
93	,, ,, p. 31
104	,, 2.1.2 p. 58
106	,, ,, p. 56
114	,, ,, p. 61
115	,, ,, p. 62
139	,, ,, p. 63
165	E. Schwartz *ABAW* 32^6 (1927) p. 56

LEO II PAPA ob. 683
ep. *epistula ad Constantinum IV Imperatorem*, ap. CCP (681) *act.* 18, H.3.1469, M.*PL*. 96.399

LEONTIUS ABBAS (Leont. Abb.) saec. vii
v. Gr. Agr. *vita Gregorii Agrigentini*, M.98.549

LEONTIUS BYZANTINUS (Leont. B.) ob. c. 543

Apoll.	*adversus fraudes Apollinaristarum*, M.86. 1948
arg. Sev.	*adversus argumenta Severi*, M.86.1916
cap. Sev.	*capita triginta contra Severum*, M.86.1901
fr.	*fragmenta varia*, M.86.2004
fr. def.	*fragmenta* (*definitiones*), ap. *Doct. Patr.* 33 pp. 251–2
mesopent.	*sermo in mediam pentecosten*, M.86.1976
Nest. et Eut.	*contra Nestorianos et Eutychianos*, M.86. 1268
parasc.	*sermo in sanctam parascevam*, M.86.1993
†*sect.*	*de sectis*, M.86.1193

LEONTIUS HIEROSOLYMITANUS (Leont. H.) saec. vi

monoph.	*contra monophysitas*, M.86.1769
Nest.	*adversus Nestorianos*, M.86.1400

LEONTIUS ET JOANNES (Leont. et Jo.)
sacr. *rerum sacrarum liber* seu *collectanea de rebus sacris*, M.86.2017

LEONTIUS NEAPOLITANUS (Leont. N.) ob. post 668

†*laud. Barn.*	*fragmentum Barnabae encomii*, F. de Cavalieri *ST* (1920) p. 144
serm. 1–3	*sermones*, M.93.1565
v. Jo. Eleem.	*vita Joannis Eleemosynarii*, H. Gelzer *SAQ* 5 (1893)
v. Sym.	*vita Symeonis Sali*, M.93.1669

LIBERIUS PAPA (Liber.) ob. 366

‡*ep. Ath.*	*epistula ad Athanasium*, M.28.1441
ep. Maced.	*epistula ad Macedonianos*, ap. Socr. *h.e.* 4. 12

LICINIA EUDOXIA AUGUSTA (Licin.) saec. v
ep. *epistula ad Theodosium*, int. opp. Leo. Mag. *ep.* 57, *ACO* 2.1.1 p. 6, M.*PL*.54.862

LITURGIAE ET RITUALIA (Lit.) (Rit.)

Lit. ap. *Const. App.* 8. 5–15	*Liturgy in the Apostolic Constitutions*
Lit. Bas.	*Liturgy of S. Basil*, F. E. Brightman *Liturgies Eastern and Western* Oxford 1896 p. 309; also cited from Brightman p. 400 and from the variant of the Coptic rite in M.31.1629
Lit. Chrys.	*Liturgy of S. John Chrysostom*, Brightman p. 309; also cited from Brightman p. 353 and M.63.901
Lit. Gr. Naz.	*Liturgy of S. Gregory of Nazianzus*, a variant of the Coptic rite, M.36.700
Lit. Jac.	*Liturgy of S. James*, B.-Ch. Mercier *PO* 26 (1946) p. 160; also cited from G. Cozza-luzi *NBP* 10^2 (1905) p. 37
Lit. Marc.	*Liturgy of S. Mark*, *P Dêr-Baliz.* (= Bodleian Library MS Gr. Liturg. c.3 (P.), saec. iv) ed. C. H. Roberts and B. Capelle *An Early Euchologion: The Dêr-Balizeh Papyrus enlarged and re-edited* Louvain 1949; *PStrasb.* (= Strasbourg University P. Gr. 254, saec. iv–v) ed. M. Andrieu and P. Collomp *Revue des sciences religieuses* 8 Strasbourg 1928 p. 500; *PRyl.* 465 (saec. vi); also cited from Brightman p. 113
Lit. Praesanct.	*Liturgy of the Presanctified*, Brightman p. 345
Rit. Bapt.	*Baptismal rite*, F. C. Conybeare *Rituale Armenorum* Oxford 1905 pp. 389, 438
Rit. Epiph.	*Epiphany rite of the blessing of the waters*, Conybeare p. 415
Rit. Sacr.	*Prayers for animal sacrifices*, Conybeare p. 413, p. 436
Rit. Tons.	*Rite of the Tonsure*, Conybeare p. 408

LUCIANUS ANTIOCHENUS (Lucn.) ob. 312
fr. *fragmentum*, ap. *Chron. Pasch.*, M.92.689B

LUCIUS ALEXANDRINUS (Luc. Al.) saec. iv
fr. pasch. *fragmentum sermonis in pascha*, ap. *Doct. Patr.* 9 p. 65

MACARIUS AEGYPTIUS (MAGNUS) (Mac. Aeg.) ob. c. 390

Note: all works attributed to Macarius of Egypt are generally held to be spurious

carit.	*de caritate*, M.34.908
cust. cor.	*de custodia cordis*, M.34.821
elev.	*de elevatione mentis*, M.34.889
ep.	*epistula*, M.34.409–420B; [420C–442 = Gr. Nyss. *instit.* q.v.]
hom. 1–50	*homiliae spirituales*, M.34.449 (saec. v–vi)
hom. 51–58	*homiliae*, G. L. Marriott *Macarii Anecdota HTS* 5 (1918); *hom.* 54 consists of extracts from Pall. *h. Laus.*
libert. ment.	*de libertate mentis*, M.34.936
or.	*de oratione*, M.34.853
pat.	*de patientia et discretione*, M.34.865
perf.	*de perfectione in spiritu*, M.34.841
prec.	*preces*, M.34.445

MACARIUS ALEXANDRINUS (Mac. Al.) ob. c. 393
‡*serm.* *sermo de animae exitu*, M.34.385

MACARIUS ANTIOCHENUS (Mac. Ant.) ob. 685

fr.	*fragmentum sermonis*, ap. CCP (681) *act.* 11, H.3.1300E
symb.	*symbolum*, *ib.* 8, H.3.1167

MACARIUS MAGNES (Mac. Mgn.) saec. iv–v
apocr. *apocriticus ad Graecos*, C. Blondel Paris 1876

‡fr. — *fragmenta varia in Gen.*, *AS* 5 p. 32, M.10.1389

Malchio Antiochenus (Malch.) — saec. iii

ep. — *fragmentum epistulae*, ap. Eus. *h.e.* 7. 30
fr. — *fragmenta disputationis contra Paulum Samosatenum*, F. Loofs *Paulus von Samosata TU* 44^5 (1924) pp. 335 ff.

Malchus Rhetor (Malchus) — saec. iv

exc. gent. — *excerpta de legationibus gentium ad Romanos*, C. de Boor *Excerpta historica iussu imperatoris Constantini Porphyrogeniti confecta* 1 Berlin 1903 p. 568, M.113.780
exc. Rom. — *excerpta de legationibus Romanorum ad gentes*, *ib.* p. 155, M.113.756

Manes (Man.) — ob. 275

ep. Add. — *fragmentum epistulae ad Addam*, ap. Eust. Mon. *ep.*, M.86.904A
ep. Cond. — *fragmentum epistulae ad Condarum*, ap. *Doct. Patr.* 9 p. 64
ep. Scyth. — *fragmentum epistulae ad Scythianum*, ap. Eust. Mon. *ep.*, M.86.903B
ep. Zeb. — *fragmentum epistulae ad Zebinam*, ap. *Doct. Patr.* 41, p. 306

Marcellus Ancyranus (Marcell.) — saec. iv

ep. — *epistula ad Julium papam*, ap. Epiph. *haer.* 72. 2. 3
fr. 1–115 — *fragmenta*, int. opp. Eus. *GCS* 4 p. 185; *frr.* 1–85, 87–115, ap. Eus.; *fr.* 86, ap. Epiph. *haer.* 72. 6

Marcianus Imperator (Marcian. Imp.) — ob. 457

adloc. — *adlocutio ad synodum Chalcedonensem*, ap. C Chalc. *act.* 6, *ACO* 2.1.2 p. 139, H.2.452
const. Chalc. — *constitutio de confirmatione gestorum Chalcedonensis synodi*, *ACO* 2.1.3 p. 119, H.2.661
const. Eut. — *constitutio de Eutyche*, *ACO* 2.1.3 p. 122, H.2.676
const. Flav. — *constitutio de Flaviano*, *ACO* 2.1.3 p. 121, H.2.676
decr. — *decretum*, ap. C Chalc. *act.* 5, *ACO* 2.1.2 p. 124, H.2.449
edict. — *edictum*, *ACO* 2.1.3 p. 120, H.2.660
ep. Al. — *epistula ad monachos Alexandrinos*, *ACO* 2.1.3 p. 129, partly in H.2.664
ep. Chalc. — *epistula ad synodum Chalcedonensem*, ap. C Chalc. *act.* 11, *ACO* 2.1.3 p. 44, H.2.545
ep. episc. — *epistula ad episcopos omnes*, *ACO* 2.1.1 p. 27, H.2.45
ep. Hier. — *epistula ad archimandritas Hierosolymitanos*, *ACO* 2.1.3 p. 124, H.2.668
ep. Leo. 1–4 — *epistulae ad Leonem*: 1, int. opp. Leo. Mag. *ep.* 73, *ACO* 2.1.1 p. 10, M.*PL.* 54.900; 2, int. opp. Leo. *ep.* 76, *ACO* 2.1.1 p. 8, M.*PL.*54.904; 3, int. opp. Leo. *ep.* 100, *ACO* 2.1.2 p. 55, M.*PL.*54.972; 4, int. opp. Leo. *ep.* 110, *ACO* 2.1.2 p. 61, M.*PL.*54.1018
ep. Mac. — *epistula ad Macarium*, *ACO* 2.1.3 p. 131, H.2.665
ep. Nic. 1, 2 — *epistulae ad synodum Nicaenam*, *ACO* 2.1.1 pp. 28, 30, H.2.49, 52
ep. Pal. — *epistula ad synodum Palestinam*, *ACO* 2.1.3 p. 133, H.2.684

Marcus Diaconus (Marc. Diac.) — ob. post 420

v. Porph. — *vita Porphyrii Gazensis*, H. Grégoire and M. A. Kugener Paris 1930. (*Note*: this recension dates from the seventh century)

Marcus Eremita (Marc. Er.) — ob. post 430

fr. — *fragmentum*, ap. *Doct. Patr.* 33 p. 250
Nest. — *adversus Nestorianos*, J. Kunze Leipzig 1895
opusc. 1–5, 7–10 — *opuscula*, M.65.905
†temp. — *capitula de temperantia*, M.65.1053 (= *opusc.* 6)

Maro Edessenus (Maro) — saec. vi seu vii

cit. ap. Anast. S. *hod.* 22, M.89.293D–6B

Martinus Papa (Martin.) — ob. 649

ep. 1, 3–13 — *epistulae*, M.*PL.*87.119

Martyrius Antiochenus (Mart. Ant.) — saec. v

pan. — *panegyricus Joannis Chrysostomi*, M.47.xliii

Martyrum Acta

O. von Gebhardt *Acta martyrum selecta*, Leipzig 1902
R. Knopf and G. Krüger *Ausgewählte Märtyrerakten*, Tübingen 1929 (*SAQ* 3)
T. Ruinart *Acta martyrum*, Ratisbon 1859

M. Acac. — *martyrium Acacii*, *ASS* Maii 8 p. 762
M. Agap. — *martyrium Agapae, Irenae etc.*, Knopf p. 95
M. Apollon. — *martyrium Apollonii*, Knopf p. 30
M. Areth. — *martyrium Arethae*, J. Boissonade *Anecdota Graeca* 5 Paris 1833 p. 1
M. Ariadn. — *martyrium Ariadnis*, F. de Cavalieri *ST* 6 (1901) p. 123
M. Ariadn. interr. — *martyris Ariadnis interrogatio*, F. de Cavalieri *ST* 8 (1902) p. 18
M. Artem. — int. opp. Philost. *GCS* p. 166
M. Bas. Presb. — *martyrium Basilii presbyteri*, *ASS* Martii 22 p. 15*
M. Bon. — *martyrium Bonifacii*, Ruinart p. 325
M. Carp. — *martyrium Carpi, Papyri et Agathonicae*, Knopf p. 11
M. Con. — *martyrium Cononis*, Knopf p. 64
M. Cosm. et Dam. (*Rom.*) — *martyrium Cosmae et Damiani Romanum*, L. Deubner *Kosmas und Damian* Leipzig 1907 p. 208
M. Cosm. et Dam. (*Arab.* 1) — *martyrium Cosmae et Damiani Arabum primum*, L. Deubner op. cit. p. 218
M. Cosm. et Dam. (*Arab.* 2) — *martyrium Cosmae et Damiani Arabum secundum*, L. Deubner op. cit. p. 220
M. Cyriac. — *martyrium Cyriaci et Hippolyti*, M.10.552
M. Das. — *martyrium Dasii*, Knopf p. 91
M. Eleuth. — *martyrium Eleutherii*, F. de Cavalieri, *ST* 6 (1901) p. 149
M. Esp. — *martyrium Esperi et Zoae*, F. de Cavalieri *ST* 49 (1928) p. 71
M. Eupl. — *martyrium Eupli*, Knopf p. 100
M. Eust. — *martyrium Eustathii*, M.105.376
M. Glyc. — *martyrium Glyceriae*, *ASS* Maii 13 p. 12
M. Ign. Ant. — *martyrium Ignatii Antiochenum*, Lightfoot p. 473, M.5.981
M. Ign. Rom. — *martyrium Ignatii Romanum*, Lightfoot p. 492
M. Jan. — *martyrium Januarii*, F. de Cavalieri *ST* 24 (1912) p. 105
M. Just. — *martyrium Justini*, Knopf p. 15, M.6.1565
M. Marcell. — *martyrium Marcelli tribuni et Petri militis*, F. de Cavalieri *ST* 65 (1935) p. 327
M. Ner. et Ach. — *martyrium Nerei et Achillei*, H. Achelis *TU* 11^2 (1893) p. 1
M. Nest. — *martyrium Nestorii episcopi Pergae Pamphyliae*, F. de Cavalieri *ST* 22 (1909) p. 115
M. Niceph. — *martyrium Nicephori*, Ruinart p. 283
M. Pancr. — *martyrium Pancrati*, F. de Cavalieri *ST* 19 (1908) p. 109
M. Pelag. Tars. — *martyrium Pelagiae Tarsensis*, H. Usener *Legenden der Pelagia* Bonn 1897 pp. 17–28
M. Perp. — *martyrium Perpetuae et Felicitatis*, J. A. Robinson *TS* 1^2 1891
M. Pers. — *martyrum Persarum acta*, H. Delehaye *PO* 2 (1905) p. 421
M. Petr. Al. — *martyrium Petri Alexandrini*, J. Viteau Paris 1897 p. 69
M. Pion. — *martyrium Pionii*, Knopf p. 45
M. Polyc. — *martyrium Polycarpi*, Bihlmeyer p. 120
M. Proc. — *fragmentum ex martyrio Procopii*, ap. C Nic. (787) *act.* 4, H.4.229
M. Sab. — *martyrium Sabae*, Knopf p. 119
M. Scill. — *martyrum Scillitanorum acta*, Gebhardt p. 22

Martyrum Acta (*cont.*)
M. Seb. — *martyrum XL Sebastae martyrium*, Gebhardt p. 171
M. Seb. test. — *martyrum XL Sebastae testamentum*, Knopf p. 116
M. Sirae — *martyrium Sirae*, *ASS* Maii 18 p. 172
M. Tar. — *martyrium Tarachi, Probi et Andronici*, Ruinart p. 452
M. Thdot. 1, 2 — *martyrium Theodoti*, F. de Cavalieri *ST* 6 (1901) pp. 61, 85
M. Thdot. 3 — *martyrium Theodoti*, F. de Cavalieri *ST* 33 (1920) p. 132
M. Tim. fr. — *martyrii Timothei fragmentum*, F. de Cavalieri *ST* 33 (1920) p. 144
M. Troph. — *martyrium Trophimi*, G. Mercati *ST* 5 (1901) p. 223
M. Tryph. — *martyrium Tryphonis*, F. de Cavalieri *ST* 19 (1908) p. 45

Matidius, Tarsinus, et Alii — saec. iv
(Mat.)
ep. — *epistula ad Epiphanium*, int. opp. Epiph. *GCS* 1 p. 2, M.43.13

Maurus Ravennas — saec. vii
(Maur.)
ep. — *epistula ad Martinum*, M.*PL*.87.103

Maximianus Constantinopolitanus — ob. 434
(Maxm.)
ep. Cyr. — *epistula ad Cyrillum Alexandrinum*, int. opp. Cyr. *ep.* 30, *ACO* 1.1.3 p. 71, M.77.148
ep. syn. — *epistula synodica*, *ACO* 1.1.3 p. 70, H.1.1669
ep. Tened. — *epistula ad Tenedios*, *ACO* 1.1.7 p. 137

Maximus Confessor — ob. 662
(Max.)
ambig. — *ambiguorum liber*, M.91.1032
anim. — *opuscula de anima*, M.91.353
ascet. — *liber asceticus*, M.90.912
cap. 1–5 — *capitum quinque centuriae*, M. 90.1177 (a compilation from other works by Max., esp. *qu. Thal.*)
‡*cap. al.* 1–243 — *capita alia*, M.90.1401; by Elias Ecdicus saec. xii
cap. theol. — *capitum theologicorum et oeconomicorum duae centuriae*, M.90.1084
carit. 1–4 — *capitum de caritate quattuor centuriae*, M.90.960
comput. — *computus ecclesiasticus*, M.19.1218
ep. 1–45 — *epistulae*, M.91.364
ep. Anast. — *epistula ad Anastasium monachum*, M.90.132
exp. Ps. 59 — *expositio in Psalmum lix*, M.90.856
fr. — *fragmenta*, ap. *Doct. Patr.*, M.90.1461
†*hymn.* 1–3 — *hymni*, M.91.1417
[†*loc. comm.* — *loci communes* sive *capita theologica*, M.91.721 (a florilegium of Classical, Biblical, and Christian authors)]
myst. — *mystagogia*, M.91.657
opusc. — *opuscula theologica et polemica*, M.91.9
or. dom. — *expositio orationis dominicae*, M.90.872
prol. Dion. — *prologus in opera pseudo-Dionysii Areopagitici*, M.4.16
Pyrr. — *disputatio cum Pyrrho*, M.91.288
qu. dub. — *quaestiones et dubia*, M.90.785
qu. Thal. — *quaestiones ad Thalassium de scriptura*, M.90.244
qu. Theop. — *quaestiones ad Theopemptum*, M.90.1393
schol. c.h. — *scholia* in Dion. Ar. *c.h.*, M.4.29
schol. d.n. — *scholia* in Dion. Ar. *d.n.*, M.4.185
schol. e.h. — *scholia* in Dion. Ar. *e.h.*, M.4.116
schol. epp. Dion. Ar. — *scholia* in Dion. Ar. *epistulas*, M.4.528
schol. myst. — *scholia* in Dion. Ar. *myst.*, M.4.416

Maximi Confessoris Invectiva
Max. invect. — *invectiva adversus Constantinopolitanos pro Maximo a quodam monacho conscripta*, M.90.201

Maximi Confessoris Officia
Max. offic. 1, 2 — M.90.205

Meletius Monachus — saec. ix?
(Melet.)
nat. hom. — *de natura hominis*, M.64.1076

Melitius Antiochenus — saec. iv
(Melit. Ant.)
hom. — *homilia*, ap. Epiph. *haer.* 73. 29–33

Melito Sardensis — ob. c. 190
(Mel.)
bapt. — *de baptismo*, Goodspeed p. 310
fr. — *fragmenta*, ap. Eus. *h.e.* 4. 26, Goodspeed p. 307, M.5.1213, 1221
†*fr.* — *fragmentum*, Goodspeed p. 313; ∞ M.5.1220
fr. Gen. — *fragmenta in Gen.*, Goodspeed p. 312, M.5.1216
pass. — *homilia in passionem Christi*, C. Bonner *StD* 12 (1940) (cited by section and papyrus page and line)

Memnon Ephesinus — saec. v
(Memn.)
ep. — *epistula ad clerum Constantinopolitanum*, *ACO* 1.1.3 p. 46, M.77.1464; see also Cyr. *libell.*

Menander Protector — saec. vi
(Men.)
exc. gent. — *excerpta de legationibus gentium ad Romanos*, C. de Boor *Excerpta historica iussu imperatoris Constantini Porphyrogeniti confecta* 1 Berlin 1903 p. 442, M.113.791
exc. Rom. — *excerpta de legationibus Romanorum ad gentes*, *ib.* p. 170, M.113.849

Menas Constantinopolitanus — ob. 552
(Menas)
ep. Anthim. — *epistula ad Anthimum*, ap. CCP (536) *act.* 4, *ACO* 3 p. 176, H.2.1253
ep. Petr. — *epistula ad Petrum Hierosolymitanum*, ap. C Hier. (536) *act.*, *ACO* 3 p. 124, H.2.1413

Methodius Olympius — ob. 311
(Meth.)
arbitr. — *de libero arbitrio*, G. N. Bonwetsch *GCS* 1917 p. 145, M.18.240
creat. — *de creatis*, *GCS* p. 493, M.18.332
fr. — *fragmenta*, *GCS* p. 520, M.18.408
fr. 1–25 *in Job* — *fragmenta in Job*, *GCS* p. 511, M.18.404
fr. mart. — *fragmentum ex sermone de martyribus*, *GCS* p. 520, M.18.345
lepr. — *de lepra*, *GCS* p. 451
‡*palm.* — *sermo in ramos palmarum*, M.18.384 = ‡Chrys. *palm.* 1
Porph. — *contra Porphyrium de cruce*, *GCS* p. 503, M.18.345, 397
res. — *de resurrectione mortuorum*, *GCS* p. 219, M.18.265, et ap. Epiph. *haer.* 64. 12–62
‡*Sym. et Ann.* — *sermo de Symeone et Anna*, M.18.348 saec. ix
symp. — *symposium* seu *convivium virginum*, *GCS* p. 3, M.18.28

Miracula
Mir. Anast. Pers. — *miracula Anastasii Persae*, H. Usener *Acta Anastasii Persae* Bonn 1894 p. 14
Mir. Artem. — *miracula Artemii*, A. Papadopoulos-Kerameus *ZP* 95 (1909) p. 1' saec. vii
Mir. Cosm. Dam. — *miracula Cosmae et Damiani*, L. Deubner *Kosmas und Damian* Leipzig 1907 p. 97
Mir. Geo. — *miracula Georgii*, J. B. Aufhauser *Teub.* 1913
Mir. Mich. — *miraculum Michaelis*, F. Nau *PO* 4 (1907) p. 547 saec. viii

Modestus Hierosolymitanus — ob. 634
(Mod.)
dorm. — *in dormitionem BMV*, M.86.3277
mul. ung. — *fragmentum homiliae in unguentiferas mulieres*, M.86.3273
occurs. — *fragmentum homiliae in occursum domini*, M.86.3276

Montanus et Montanistae — saec. ii
(Mont.)
fr. — *fragmenta*, ap. Eus. *h.e.* 5. 16. 17; Epiph. *haer.* 48. 2, 4, 10–13; *ib.* 49. 1; Didym. *Trin.* 3. 41
†*fr.* — *fragmentum*, ap. Or. *Cels.* 7. 9
‡*fr.* — *fragmentum*, ap. *Doct. Patr.* 41, p. 306

Narratio de Joanne Baptista
Narr. Jo. Bapt. — *narratio de praeciso Joannis Baptistae capite*, Vassiliev p. 1

NARRATIO JOSEPHI see EVANGELIA APOCRYPHA

NECTARIUS CONSTANTINOPOLITANUS — ob. 397
(Nect.)
Thdr. — *de festo Theodori*, M.39.1821

NEMESIUS EMESENUS — saec. iv
(Nemes.)
nat. hom. — *de natura hominis*, M.40.504

NESTORIUS CONSTANTINOPOLITANUS — ob. c. 451
(Nest.)
ep. Ant. — *epistula ad Antiochum praefectum*, *ACO* 1.1.7 p. 71
ep. Cyr. 1, 2 — *epistulae ad Cyrillum*, *ACO* 1.1.1 pp. 25, 29, int. opp. Cyr. *epp.* 3, 5, M.77.44, 99
ep. Thds. — *epistula ad Theodosium*, *ACO* 1.1.5 p. 13, H.1.1437
exegeticum
hom. in Heb. 3:1 — *homilia in Heb. 3:1*, F. Loofs *Nestoriana* Halle 1905 p. 230, M.64.480
fr. — *fragmenta*, Loofs op. cit. p. 165
[*Heracl.* — *liber Heraclidis*, F. Nau Paris 1910 p. 1] (French translation from Syriac)
hom. tent. 1–3 — *homiliae in tentationes*, *ib.* p. 338; fragments in M.61.683

NICEPHORUS URANUS — saec. x
(Niceph. Ur.)
v. Sym. — *vita Symeonis junioris*, M.86.2987 (cited by section). A working over of Arc. C. *v. Sym.* q.v.

NICOLAUS MONACHUS — saec. v
(Nicol.)
ep. — *epistula ad Marcum Eremitam*, int. opp. Marc. Er., M.65.1052

NILUS ANCYRANUS — ob. c. 430
(Nil.)
Alb. — *oratio in Albianum*, M.79.696
‡*Epict.* — *Epicteti enchiridion interpolatum*, M.79.1285
epp. — *epistularum libri quattuor*, M.79.81
Eulog. — *tractatus ad Eulogium monachum*, M.79.1093
exerc. — *de monastica exercitatione*, M.79.720
‡*fr. ascens.* 1–3 — *fragmenta de ascensione*, M.79.1497, prob. by Procl. CP (J. G. Davies *HTR* 49 (July 1956) pp. 179–81)
‡*fr. pasch.* 1, 2 — *fragmenta ex orationibus de pascha*, M.79.1489
inst. — *institutio ad monachos*, M.79.1236
magistr. — *de magistris et discipulis*, P. van den Ven *Mélanges Godefroid Kurth* 2 Liège 1908 p. 76
Magn. — *ad Magnam de voluntaria paupertate*, M.79.968
†*mal. cog.* — *de malignis cogitationibus*, M.79.1200
‡*narr.* 1–7 — *narrationes*, M.79.589
paraen. — *capita paraenetica*, M.79.1249
‡*perist.* 1–12 — *peristeria* seu *de virtute colenda et vitio fugiendo*, M.79.812
praest. — *de monachorum praestantia*, M.79.1061
sent. — *sententiae*, M.79.1240
serm. — *sermo in Lc. 22:36*, M.79.1264
spir. mal. — *de octo spiritibus malitiae*, M.79.1145
‡*tract.* — *tractatus moralis*, M.79.1280
†*vit.* — *de vitiis quae opposita sunt virtutibus*, M.79.1140
‡*vit. cog.* — *de octo vitiosis cogitationibus*, M.79.1436

NOMOCANON
Nomoc. — J. B. Cotelerius, *Ecclesiae Graecae Monumenta* 1 Paris 1677 p. 68

NONNUS ABBAS — saec. vi
(Nonn. Abb.)
hist. Bas. — *collectio . . . historiarum quarum meminit Gregorius in laudatione funebri Basilii*, M.36.1057
hist. Juln. — *collectio . . . historiarum quarum meminit Gregorius in invectiva adversus Julianum*, M.36.985
hist. lum. — *interpretatio historiarum quarum meminit Gregorius in oratione de sacris luminibus*, M.36.1065

NONNUS PANOPOLITANUS — saec. v
(Nonn.)
par. Jo. — *paraphrasis in Joannis evangelium*, A. Scheindler *Teub.* 1881, M.43.749 (cited by biblical reference)

OECUMENIUS — saec. v–vi
(Oecum.)
Rom.–Heb. — *fragmenta in epistulas Pauli*, Staab p. 423
Apoc. — *commentarius in Apocalypsin*, H. C. Hoskier *University of Michigan Studies* 23 Michigan 1928

OLYMPIODORUS ALEXANDRINUS — saec. vi
(Olymp.)
exegetica
Job — *fragmenta ex commentariis in Job*, M.93.13
‡*fr. Pr.* — *fragmenta in Pr.*, M.93.472, 475
Eccl. — *commentarii in Eccl.*, M.93.477
fr. Jer. — *fragmenta in Jer.*, M.93.628
fr. Lam. — *fragmenta in Lam.*, M.93.725
fr. Bar. — *fragmenta in Bar.*, M.93.761
fr. Ep. Jer. — *fragmenta in Ep. Jer.*, M.93.773
‡*Lc. 6:23* — *fragmentum in illud*, Gaudete in illa die, M.93.780
fr. Sev. Ant. — *fragmenta contra Severum Antiochenum*, ap. Anast. S. *monoph.*, M.89.1189

ORACULA SIBYLLINA — saec. ii–iii
Orac. Sib. 1–8, 11–14 — J. Geffcken *GCS* 1902 p. 1. (*Note*: the proem. is prob. saec. vi)
Orac. Sib. fr. 1–8 — *fragmenta*, *ib.* p. 227

ORDO ECCLESIASTICUS APOSTOLORUM — saec. iii–iv
Ordo Eccl. App. — A. Harnack *TU* 2^2 (1884) p. 225

ORIGENES — ob. c. 254
(Or.)
Note: the Latin translations of some works by Origen have been used and are listed below
Cels. — *contra Celsum* 1–4, P. Koetschau *GCS* 1 (1899) p. 51, M.11.641; *Cels.* 5–8, *GCS* 2 p. 1, M.11.1181
dial. — *dialogus cum Heraclide*, J. Scherer *Publications de la société Fouad I de Papyrologie, Textes et Documents* 9, Cairo 1949
engast. — *de engastrimytho* (1 Reg. 28:3–25), E. Klostermann *GCS* 3 (1901) p. 283, M.12.1012
ep. 1 — *epistula ad Africanum*, M.11.48
ep. 2 — *epistula ad Gregorium Thaumaturgum*, ap. *philoc.* 13, M.11.88
exegetica
hom. 1–16 in Gen. — *homiliae in Gen.* (Lat.), W. A. Baehrens *GCS* 6 (1920) p. 1, M.12.145; Greek fr. of *hom. 2 in Gen.*, *GCS* 6 p. 23, M.12.161, ap. Proc. G. *Gen.* 5:14, 15, M.87.273
comm. in Gen. — *fragmenta ex commentariis in Gen.*, M.12.45. (*Note*: *comm. in Gen.* 1, ap. Eus. *p.e.* 7. 20; *comm. in Gen.* 2. 1–11, *ib.* 6. 11; *comm. in Gen.* 3. 12, 13, ap. *philoc.* 23. 19, 20)
sel. in Gen. — *selecta in Gen.*, M.12.92
adnot. in Gen. — *adnotationes in Gen.*, M.17.12
hom. 1–13 in Ex. — *homiliae in Ex.* (Lat.), *GCS* 6 p. 145, M.12.297. (*Note*: Greek fr., *GCS* p. 217, M.12.353, 354)
comm. in Ex. — *fragmentum ex commentariis in Ex.*, ap. *philoc.* 27, M.12.264
sel. in Ex. — *selecta in Ex.*, M.12.281
adnot. in Ex. — *adnotationes in Ex.*, M.17.16
hom. 1–16 in Lev. — *homiliae in Lev.* (Lat.), *GCS* 6 p. 280, M.12.405. (*Note*: Greek fr. of *hom. 5 in Lev.*, *GCS* 6 p. 332, M.12.421B; of *hom. 8 in Lev.*, *GCS* 6 p. 394, M.12.493; ap. Proc. G. *Lev.* 13, M.87.733–40)
sel. in Lev. — *selecta in Lev.*, M.12.397
adnot. in Lev. — *adnotationes in Lev.*, M.17.17
hom. 1–28 in Num. — *homiliae in Num.* (Lat.), W. A. Baehrens *GCS* 7 (1921) p. 3, M.12.585
sel. in Num. — *selecta in Num.*, M.12.576
adnot. in Num. — *adnotationes in Num.*, M.17.21
sel. in Dt. — *selecta in Dt.*, M.12.805
adnot. in Dt. — *adnotationes in Dt.*, M.17.24
hom. 1–26 in Jos. — *homiliae in Jos.* (Lat.), *GCS* 7 p. 287, M.12.825; Greek fr., *GCS* 7 p. 290, M.12.917; ap. Proc. G. *Jos.*
sel. in Jos. — *selecta in Jos.*, M.12.820
adnot. in Jos. — *adnotationes in Jos.*, M.17.36

ORIGENES (*cont.*)

hom. 1–9 in Jud. — *homiliae in Jud.* (Lat.), *GCS* 7 p. 464, M.12.951
sel. in Jud. — *selecta in Jud.*, M.12.949
adnot. in Jud. — *adnotationes in Jud.*, M.17.37
fr. in Ruth — *fragmentum in Ruth*, M.12.989
hom. in 1 Reg. — *homilia in 1 Reg.* (Lat.), W. A. Baehrens *GCS* 8 (1925) p. 1, M.12.995
fr. 1–22 in Reg. — *fragmenta in Reg.*, *GCS* 3 p. 295, M.12.992, M.17.40
sel. in Job — *selecta in Job*, M.12.1032
enarr. in Job — *enarrationes in Job*, M.17.57
Ps. — *fragmenta in Pss. 1–25*, *AS* 2 p. 444; *in Pss. 26–150*, *AS* 3 p. 1
sel. in Ps. — *selecta in Pss.*, M.12.1053
exc. in Ps. — *excerpta in Pss.*, M.17.105
fr. in Ps. — *fragmenta in Pss.*, R. Cadiou *Commentaires inédits sur les Psaumes* Paris 1936
comm. in Pr. — *fragmenta ex commentariis in Pr.*, M.13.17
exp. in Pr. — *exposita in Pr.*, M.17.161
fr. in Pr. — *fragmenta in Pr.*, M.17.149, *AS* 3 p. 524
Cant. — *commentarius in Cant.* (Lat.), *GCS* 8 p. 61, M.13.61. (Note: Greek fr., *GCS* 8 p. 90, M.13.112, M.17.253, 369; ap. Proc. G. *Cant.*)
hom. 1, 2 in Cant. — *homiliae in Cant.* (Lat.), *GCS* 8 p. 27, M.13.37
schol. in Cant. — *scholia in Cant.*, M.17.253 (cited as such for fr. not in *Cant.* above)
comm. min. in Cant. — *fragmentum ex commentario minore in Cant.*, M.13.36
hom. 1–9 in Is. — *homiliae in Is.* (Lat.), *GCS* 8 p. 242, M.13.219
fr. in Is. — *fragmentum in Is.*, *AS* 3 p. 538. (*Note*: the first of the two fr. is *fr. 22 in Reg.* above)
hom. 1–20 in Jer. — *homiliae in Jer.*, *GCS* 3 p. 1, M.13.256
fr. hom. 21 in Jer. — *fragmenta ex homiliis in Jer.*, *GCS* 3 p. 195, M.14.1310
fr. hom. 39 in Jer. — *fragmenta ex homiliis in Jer.*, *GCS* 3 p. 196, M.13.541
fr. incert. in Jer. — *fragmentum incertum in Jer.*, *GCS* 3 p. 195, M.14.1309
fr. 1–71 in Jer. — *fragmenta in Jer.*, *GCS* 3 p. 199, M.13.544
sel. in Jer. — *selecta in Jer.*, M.13.544 (cited as such for fr. not in *GCS* 3); *AS* 3 p. 539
fr. 1–118 in Lam. — *fragmenta in Lam.*, *GCS* 3 p. 235, M.13.605
fr. in Lam. — *fragmentum in Lam.*, *GCS* 3 p. 279, M.13.613
hom. 1–14 in Ezech. — *homiliae in Ezech.* (Lat.), *GCS* 8 p. 319, M.13.665; Greek fr., *GCS* 8 pp. 319 ff., M.13.665 ff., 768, 769
sel. in Ezech. — *selecta in Ezech.*, M.13.768 (cited as such for fr. not in *GCS* 8)
fr. comm. in Ezech. — *fragmenta ex commentariis in Ezech.*, M.13.664
fr. in Ezech. — *fragmenta in Ezech.*, M.17.288, *AS* 3 p. 541
fr. in Dan. — *fragmenta in Dan.*, *AS* 3 p. 550
comm. in Os. — *fragmentum ex commentariis in Os.*, ap. *philoc.* 8, M.13.825
comm. in Mt. 1, 2 — *fragmenta ex commentariis in Mt.*, E. Klostermann and E. Benz *GCS* 12 (1941) pp. 3–5, M.13.829
comm. in Mt. 10–17 — *commentariorum in Mt. libri 10–17*, E. Klostermann *GCS* 10 (1935) p. 1, M.13.836
fr. in Mt. — *fragmenta in Mt.*, *GCS* 12 p. 13, E. Klostermann and E. Benz *TU* 47^{3} (1932), partly in M.17.289
comm. ser. 1–145 in Mt. — *commentariorum series in Mt.* (Lat.), E. Klostermann and E. Benz *GCS* 11 (1933) p. 1, M.13.1599; Greek fr. in *GCS* 11 pp. 21 ff.
hom. 1–39 in Lc. — *homiliae in Lc.* (Lat.), M. Rauer *GCS* 9 (1930) p. 3, M.13.1801; Greek fr. in *GCS* 9, M.17.312
fr. 1–112 in Lc. — *fragmenta in Lc.*, *GCS* 9 p. 232
schol. in Lc. — *scholia in Lc.*, M.17.312 (cited as such for fr. not in *GCS* 9)
Jo. — *commentarii in Jo.*, E. Preuschen *GCS* 4 (1903) p. 3, M.14.21
fr. 1–140 in Jo. — *fragmenta in Jo.*, *GCS* 4 p. 485
fr. in Ac. — *fragmentum ex homiliis in Ac.*, ap. *philoc.* 7. 2, M.14.829
comm. in Rom. — *commentarii in Rom.* (Lat.), M.14.833; Greek fr., ap. *philoc.* 25, M.14.841; ap. *philoc.* 9, M.14.1076; H. Ramsbotham *JTS* 13 (1912) pp. 210, 357; *JTS* 14 (1912) p. 10
comm. in 1 Cor. — *fragmenta ex commentariis in 1 Cor.*, C. Jenkins *JTS* 9 (1908) pp. 232, 353, 500, *JTS* 10 (1908) p. 29
comm. in Eph. — *fragmenta ex commentariis in Eph.*, J. A. F. Gregg *JTS* 3 (1902) pp. 234, 398, 554
fr. in Heb. — *fragmenta in Heb.*, M.14.1308, ap. Eus. *h.e.* 6. 25. 11–14
Apoc. 1–27 — *scholia 1–27 in Apoc.*, C. J. Diobouniotis and A. Harnack *TU* 38^{3} (1911) p. 21
Apoc. 28–38 — *scholia 28–38 in Apoc.*, C. H. Turner *JTS* 25 (1923) p. 1
fr. ep. 1 — *epistulae de Ambrosio fragmentum*, ap. Georgii Cedreni *historiarum compendium*, M.121.485B, C
fr. ep. 2 — *epistulae fragmentum*, ap. Eus. *h.e.* 6. 19. 12–14
mart. — *exhortatio ad martyrium*, *GCS* 1 p. 3, M.11.564
or. — *de oratione*, *GCS* 2 p. 297, M.11.416
philoc. — *philocalia* seu *ecloga de operibus Origenis a Basilio et Gregorio Nazianzeno facta*, J. A. Robinson Cambridge 1893
princ. — *de principiis* (Lat. with Greek fr.), P. Koetschau *GCS* 5 (1913), M.11.115
res. — *fragmenta de resurrectione*, M.11.96, ap. Meth. *res.* 3 (*GCS* p. 413.18), *ib.* 2 (*GCS* p. 302. 7–10)

PACHOMIUS TABENNENSIS — ob. 346
(Pach.)
†poen. — *poenae monachorum*, L. T. Lefort *Mus.* 40 (1927) p. 60
reg. A, B — *excerpta e regula*, translated from Coptic, L. T. Lefort *Mus.* 37 (1924) p. 9; recension B, M.40.948

PALLADIUS MONACHUS — ob. ante 431
(Pall.)
C. Butler, *The Lausiac History of Palladius*, *TS* 6^{2} 1904
ep. Laus. — *epistula ad Lausum*, Butler p. 6, M.34.1001
‡gent. Ind. — *de gentibus Indiae et de Bragmantibus*, E. Bysshe London 1665
h. Laus. — *historia Lausiaca*, Butler p. 9, M.34.1001
‡h. mon. — *historia monachorum in Aegypto*, E. Preuschen *Palladius und Rufinus*, Giessen 1897 (reconstruction of Gk. text of *historia monachorum*) pp. 1–97 (partly interpolated into *h. Laus.*, partly printed as *h. mon.* (*paradisus*) in M.65.441)
‡proem. — *proemium ad h. Laus.*, Butler p. 3, M.34.995
v. Chrys. — *dialogus de vita Joannis Chrysostomi*, P. R. Coleman-Norton Cambridge 1928, M.47.5

PALLADIUS SUEDRENUS — saec. iv
(Pall. Sued.)
ep. — *epistula ad Epiphanium*, int. opp. Epiph. *GCS* 1 p. 3, M.43.13

PAMPHILUS ABYDENSIS — saec. v
(Pamph. Abyd.)
ep. Jo. — *fragmentum epistulae ad Joannem Antiochenum*, ap. *Doct. Patr.* 7 p. 48 (see footnote)
‡ep. Petr. — *epistula ad Petrum episcopum Antiochiae*, *ACO* 3 p. 9, H.2.849

PAMPHILUS HIEROSOLYMITANUS — ob. post 540
(Pamph. H.)
can. 1–9 — *canones ex apostolorum in Antiochia synodo*, Funk 2 p. 144
panopl. — *panoplia dogmatica*, *NBP* 2 (1844) p. 597

PAMPHILUS MONACHUS — saec. v ?
(Pamph. Mon.)
Soter. — *encomium Soteridis*, F. de Cavalieri *ST* 19 (1908) p. 113

PAPIAS HIEROPOLITANUS — ob. c. 130
(Papias)
fr. 1–20 — *fragmenta*, Bihlmeyer p. 134

PAPYRI see List IV

PAPYRI CHRISTIANI
Pap. Chr. C. Wessely *Les plus anciens monuments de Christianisme écrits sur papyrus PO* 18 (1924) p. 356

PAULINUS NOLANUS ob. 431
(Paulin.)
v. Ambr. *vita Ambrosii*, Graece reddita saec. vii–ix, *AHS* 1 p. 27

PAULINUS TYRIUS ob. 329
(Paulin. T.)
ep. *fragmentum epistulae*, Opitz 3 p. 17, ap. Eus. *Marcell.* 1. 4
symb. *symbolum*, ap. Epiph. *haer.* 77. 21

PAULUS II CONSTANTINOPOLITANUS ob. 654
(Paul. CP)
ep. Thdr. *epistula ad Theodorum papam*, ap. C Later. *act.* 4, M.*PL*.87.91
fr. ep. Jac. *fragmentum ex epistula ad Jacobum*, ap. CCP (681) *act.* 10, H.3.1245
fr. ep. Thdr. Pharan. *fragmentum ex epistula ad Theodorum Pharanitam*, *ib.*, H.3.1247

PAULUS ELEUSENSIS saec. vi
(Paul. El.)
v. Thgn. *vita Theognii*, J. van den Gheyn *AB* 10 (1891) p. 78

PAULUS EMESENUS ob. post 432
(Paul. Em.)
ep. *epistula*, int. opp. Cyr. *ep.* 36, *ACO* 1.1.7 p. 6, M.77.165
hom. 1–3 *homiliae*, *ACO* 1.1.4 pp. 9, 11, *ACO* 1.1.7 p. 173, M.77.1433

PAULUS PERSA saec. vii
(Paul. Pers.)
judic. fr. *fragmentum sermonis de judicio*, ap. C Later. *act.* 5, H.3.896D; see also DISP. PHOT.

PAULUS SAMOSATENUS saec. iii
(Paul. Sam.)
fr. *fragmenta*, ap. Malch. *ep.* etc., F. Loofs *TU* 44^5 (1924), pp. 331–8 partly ap. Leont. B. *Nest. et Eut.* 3 suppl., M.86.1392–3
‡*fr.* 1–5 *fragmenta ad Sabinum*, F. Loofs p. 339

PAULUS SILENTIARIUS ob. post 563
(Paul. Sil.)
ambo. *descriptio ambonis*, P. Friedländer *Johannes von Gaza und Paulus Silentiarius* Leipzig and Berlin 1912 p. 257, M.86. 2251
Soph. *descriptio Sanctae Sophiae*, *ib.* p. 227, M.86.2119
‡*therm. Pyth.* *in thermas Pythicas*, M.86.2263

PECTORII EPITAPHIUM saec. ii–iii
Pect. epitaph. K. M. Kaufmann *Handbuch der altchristlichen Epigraphik* Freiburg 1917 = *IG* 2525

PERSICA CAPTIVITAS saec. vii–viii ?
Pers. capt. *de Persica captivitate*, M.86.3236

PERSICIS, NARRATIO DE REBUS saec. v seu vi
Pers. E. Bratke *TU* 19^3 (1899), M.10.97

PETITIONES ARIANORUM saec. iv
Pet. Ar. 1–4 int. opp. Ath., M.26.820–4

PETRUS I ALEXANDRINUS ob. 311
(Petr. I Al.)
ep. can. *epistula canonica*, M.18.468
fr. *fragmenta varia*, M.18.509 ff.; ap. C Eph. (431) *act.* 1, *ACO* 1.1.2 p. 39; ap. Justn. *Or.*, *ACO* 3 p. 197, M.86.981; ap. Jo. D. *parall.*, K. Holl *TU* 20^2 (1899) p. 234
‡*phys.* *physiologus*, A. Karnejev *BZ* 3 (1894) p. 32

PETRUS II ALEXANDRINUS ob. 381
(Petr. II Al.)
encycl. *fragmentum epistulae encyclicae*, M.33. 1276, ap. Thdt. *h.e.* 4. 22

PETRUS ANTIOCHENUS FULLO ob. 488
(Petr. Full.)
ep. Acac. *epistula ad Acacium Constantinopolitanum*, ap. Evagr. *h.e.* 3. 17

PETRUS LAODICENUS ob. 650
(Petr. Laod.)
fr. in Mt. Mc. Lc. *fragmenta in evangelia*, M.86.3324
or. dom. *expositio in orationem dominicam*, C. F. Heinrici *Beiträge zur Geschichte und Erklärung des Neuen Testamentes* 3^2 Leipzig 1905 p. 109, M.86.3329

PETRUS MYRENSIS saec. v
(Petr. Myr.)
Apoll. *fragmentum orationis contra Apollinarem Laodicenum*, *AP* p. 50

PETRUS PATRICIUS saec. vi
(Petr. Patr.)
exc. gent. *excerpta de legationibus gentium ad Romanos*, C. de Boor *Excerpta historica iussu imperatoris Constantini Porphyrogeniti confecta* Berlin 1903–5 p. 390, M.113.664
exc. Rom. *excerpta de legationibus Romanorum ad gentes*, *ib.* p. 3, M.113.673

PETRUS RAVENNENSIS saec. v
(Petr. Rav.)
ep. *epistula ad Eutychen*, *ACO* 2.1.2 p. 45, M.*PL*.54.740, int. opp. Leo. Mag. *ep.* 25

PETRUS SEBASTENUS saec. iv
(Petr. Seb.)
ep. *epistula ad Gregorium Nyssenum fratrem*, G. Pasquali *Gregorii Nysseni epistulae* Berlin 1925 p. 86, M.45.241

PETRUS TRAJANOPOLITANUS saec. v
(Petr. Traj.)
poenit. *libellus poenitentiae*, *ACO* 1.1.7 p. 139

PHILEAS THMUITANUS ob. 307
(Phil. Thm.)
ep. *epistula ad Thmuitas*, M.10.1561, ap. Eus. *h.e.* 8. 10

PHILIPPUS SIDETES saec. v
(Phil. Sid.)
fr. *fragmenta Christianae historiae*, C. de Boor *TU* 5^2 (1888) p. 169

PHILO CARPASIANUS saec. v
(Ph. Carp.)
Cant. *enarratio in Cant.*, M.40.28
†*ep.* *epistula ad Eucarpium*, *AHS* 1 p. 293, also int. opp. Bas. *ep.* 42, M.32.348

PHILOSTORGIUS ob. post 433
(Philost.)
fr. *fragmenta*, M.65.629
h.e. *historia ecclesiastica*, J. Bidez *GCS* 1913, M.65.460. Not the original work but fragments from a working over in later authors

PHILOTHEUS MONACHUS saec. vii
(Philoth.)
fr. ascet. *fragmenta ascetica*, M.98.1369

PHILOXENUS ob. c. 523
(Philox.)
ep. *epistula*, *NBP* 8^3 (1871) p. 157. (*Note*: sections 8–15 are by Isaac Syrus q.v.)

PHOTINUS ET ALII saec. iv
(Photinus et al.)
ep. *epistula*, cit. ap. Epiph. *haer.* 72. 11–12

PHOTINUS PRESBYTER saec. vi–vii
(Photinus)
fr. *fragmentum vitae Joannis Jejunatoris*, ap. C Nic. (787) *act.* 4

PHOTIUS CONSTANTINOPOLITANUS ob. 891
(Phot.)
Cited when incorporating material from earlier writers
cod. 1–280 *bibliothecae codices*, M.103, 104
nomoc. *nomocanon*, *Mon.* 2 p. 458, M.104.980; also cited from syntagma canonum, M.104. 441

PHOTIUS TYRIUS ob. ante 457
(Phot. Tyr.)
libell. *libellus*, ap. C Chalc. *act.* 9, *ACO* 2.1.3 p. 14, H.2.504
supplic. *supplicatio*, ap. C Chalc. *act. Phot.*, *ACO* 2.1.3 p. 104, H.2.436

PHYSIOLOGUS GRAECUS recension A c. saec. ii
recension B saec. v–vi
Phys. A, B F. Sbordone *Physiologus* Rome 1936, cf. ‡Epiph. *phys.*

PIERIUS ALEXANDRINUS saec. iii
(Pier.)
fr. *fragmenta*, C. de Boor *TU* 5^2 (1888) p. 165, M.10.244

PINNES saec. iv
ep. *epistula*, ap. Ath. *apol. sec.* 67

PIONIUS [saec. iii]
(Pion.)
‡*v. Polyc.* *vita Polycarpi*, Lightfoot p. 1015
fin. saec. iv

PLOTINUS THESSALONICENSIS init. saec. vii
(Plot.)
v. Dem. *vita Demetrii*, T. Joannes Μνημεῖα ἁγιολογικά Venice 1884 p. 40

POENAE APOSTOLORUM
Poen. App. 1, 2 Funk 2 p. 150

POLEMON (POLEMIUS) APOLLINARISTES fin. saec. iv
(Polem.)
fr. *fragmenta varia*, Lietzmann p. 273, ap. Max. *opusc*, M.91.169, 172; ap. *Doct. Patr.* 9 p. 60, 41 p. 308

POLYBIUS RHINOCOLURENSIS saec. v
(Polyb.)
†*ep.* *epistula ad Sabinum*, M.41.112
†*v. Epiph.* 39–67 *vita Epiphanii* (39–67), M.41.73

POLYCARPUS SMYRNENSIS ob. 156
(Polyc.)
ep. *epistula ad Philippenses*, Bihlmeyer p. 114, M.5.1005

POLYCHRONIUS APAMEENSIS ob. c. 430
(Polychr.)
fr. Job *fragmenta in Job*, ap. *cat. Job* q.v.
fr. Ezech. *fragmenta in Ezech.*, *NBP* 72 (1854) p. 92
fr. Dan. *fragmenta in Dan.* *SS* 1 p. 352

POLYCHRONIUS MONACHUS saec. vii
(Polychr. Mon.)
exp. fid. *expositio fidei*, ap. CCP (681) *act.* 15, H.3.1376

POLYCRATES EPHESINUS fin. saec. ii
(Polycr.)
ap. Eus. *h.e.* 5. 24. 2–8

PRECATIO JOSEPHI
Prec. Josephi cit. ap. Or. *Jo.* 2. 31 (25); *comm. in Gen.* 3. 9

PROCHORUS DIACONUS init. saec. v
(Proch.)
a. Jo. *acta Joannis*, T. Zahn Erlangen 1885

PROCLUS CONSTANTINOPOLITANUS ob. 446
(Procl. CP)
annunt. *oratio in Deiparae annuntiationem*, int. opp. Bas. Sel., M.85.425
Arm. *tomus ad Armenios*, *ACO* 4.2 p. 187, M.65.856
ep. *epistula tertia decima*, *ACO* 2.1.3 p. 67, M.65.881
fr. *fragmenta*, ap. *Doct. Patr.* 7 pp. 48 ff., M.65.885
†*fr.* *fragmenta anonyma*, C. Martin *Mus.* 54 (1941) pp. 52–56
hom. 1, 2 *homiliae*, M.65.833
hom. 3, 4 *homiliae*, C. Martin *Mus.* 54 (1941) pp. 40, 44
or. 2–19 *orationes*, M.65.692
or. laud. BMV *oratio de laudibus Mariae*, *ACO* 1.1.1 p. 103, M.65.680
‡*tract.* *tractatus de traditione divinae missae*, M.65.849

PROCOPIUS GAZAEUS ob. 538
(Proc. G.)
Anast. *panegyricus in imperatorem Anastasium*, K. Kempen Bonn 1918, M.87.2793
ep. 1–163 *epistulae*, *EG* pp. 533–98, M.87.2717
ep. *epistulae*, N. Festa *Bessarione* 8 (1900–1) pp. 36–37

exegetica
Gen.–Jud. *commentarii* seu *catenae in Octateuchum*, M.87.21
Reg.–Par. *commentarii* seu *catenae in Reg. et Par.*, M.87.1080
‡*Pr.* *commentarii in Pr.*, M.87.1221
Cant. *commentarius* seu *catena in Cant.*, M.87.1545
fr. Cant. *fragmentum in Cant.*, M.87.1756
Is. *commentarius* seu *catena in Is.*, M.87.1817
horol. *horologium*, H. Diels *Abhandlungen der königlichen preussischen Akademie der Wissenschaften: philosophisch-historische Klasse* 1917 Berlin
imag. *descriptio imaginis*, P. Friedländer *ST* 89 (1939) p. 5
‡*monod.* *monodia in Sanctam Sophiam*, M.87.2840 (by Michael Psellus, saec. xi)
†*Procl.* *fragmentum contra Proclum*, M.87.2792^c

PROTEVANGELIUM JACOBI see EVANGELIA APOCRYPHA, *Protev.*

PSALMI SALOMONIS saec. i a.C.
Pss. Sal. *The Psalms of Solomon*, H. E. Ryle and M. R. James Cambridge 1891

PSALMUS NAASSENUS saec. ii
Ps. Naas. cit. ap. Hipp. *haer.* 5. 10

PTOLEMAEUS GNOSTICUS saec. ii
(Ptol.)
ep. *epistula ad Floram*, ap. Epiph. *haer.* 33. 3–7

PULCHERIA AUGUSTA ob. 453
(Pulch.)
ep. Bass. *epistula ad Bassam*, *ACO* 2.1.3 p. 135, H.2.680
ep. Hier. *epistula ad monachos Hierosolymitanos*, *ACO* 2.1.3 p. 128, H.2.681
ep. Leon. *epistula ad Leonem*, int. opp. Leo. Mag. *ep.* 77, *ACO* 2.1.1 p. 9, M.*PL*.54.906
ep. Strat. *epistula ad Strategium Bithyniae*, *ACO* 2.1.1 p. 29, H.2.48

PYRRHUS I CONSTANTINOPOLITANUS ob. 655
(Pyrr.)
ep. *epistula ad Joannem Papam*, ap. CCP (681) *act.* 13, H.3.1353D
serm. fr. *fragmentum sermonis de voluntate et operatione*, *ib.*, H.3.1345C

QUADRATUS ATHENIENSIS ob. post 124
(Quad.)
fragmentum ex apologia, M.5.1265, ap. Eus. *h.e.* 4. 3

QUAESTIONES BARTHOLOMAEI see EVANGELIA APOCRYPHA, *Ev. Barth.*

QUINTIANUS ASCULANUS saec. v
(Quint.)
‡*ep.* *epistula ad Petrum Fullonem*, *ACO* 3 p. 15, M.85.1733

RHEGINUS CONSTANTIENSIS saec. v
(Rheg.)
libell. *libellus*, ap. C Eph. (431) *act.* 7, *ACO* 1.1.7 p. 118
serm. *sermo Ephesi habitus*, *ib. act.* 1, *ACO* 1.1.2 p. 70, H.1.1444E

RHODO fin. saec. ii
(Rhod.)
ap. Eus. *h.e.* 5. 13

RITUALE
Rit. see LITURGIAE ET RITUALIA

ROMANUS MELODUS ob. 556
(Rom. Mel.)
cited by page from the following editions:
K. Krumbacher, *SBBAW* 1898^2, 1899^2, 1901, 1903, *ABAW* 24^3 (1909)
P. Maas, *BZ* 15 (1906) [spurious], 24 (1923), *OC* 2 (1912) [spurious], *KIT* 52–53 (1931) p. 8
G. Cammelli, *Romano il Melode*, Florence 1930
J. B. Pitra, *AS* 1 1876 [pp. 202–41 are spurious]; *Sanctus Romanus*, Rome 1888

SABINIANUS PERRHANUS saec. v
(Sabinian.)
supplic. 1, 2 *supplicationes*, ap. C Chalc. *act.* 14, *ACO* 2.1.3 p. 64, H.2.572

SABINUS CONSTANTIENSIS saec. v
(Sabin.)
†*ep.* *epistula ad Polybium episcopum de obitu et funere Epiphanii*, *SVC* 7 (1833) p. 178

SCHOLIA ANONYMA
Schol. Clem. paed. — *scholia in Clementis paedagogum*, O. Stählin, *Clemens Alexandrinus*, *GCS* 1 p. 319, M.9.787
Schol. Clem. prot. — *scholia in Clementis protrepticum*, *ib.*, *GCS* 1 p. 295, M.9.777

SENTENTIAE APOSTOLORUM
Sent. App. — *Mon.* 1 p. 77

SERAPION ANTIOCHENUS — init. saec. ii
(Serap. Ant.)
ap. Eus. *h.e.* 5. 19; 6. 12

SERAPION THMUITANUS — ob. 362
(Serap.)
ep. Eudox. — *epistula ad Eudoxium*, M.40.924
ep. mon. — *epistula ad monachos*, M.40.925
euch. — *euchologium*, Funk 2 p. 158
Man. — *liber adversus Manichaeos*, R. P. Casey *Harvard Theological Studies* 1931, partly in M.40.900, partly in M.18.1116–32 (in confused order), 1213–56

SERGIA CONSTANTINOPOLITANA — saec. vii
(Sergia)
Olymp. — *Olympiadis translatio*, *AB* 16 (1897) p. 44

SERGIUS CONSTANTIENSIS — saec. vii
(Serg. C.)
ep. — *epistula ad Theodorum Papam*, ap. C Later. *act.* 2, H.3.728

SERGIUS CONSTANTINOPOLITANUS — ob. 638
(Serg.)
‡*acath.* — *hymnus acathistus*, *AGC* p. 140, M.92.1335
ep. 1–3 — *epistulae* ap. C Later. *act.* 2, H.3.776; CCP (681) *act.* 12, H.3.1309, 1312

SEVERIANUS GABALENSIS — ob. post 408
(Sever.)
Abr. — *in Abrahae dictum*, *Gen. 24:2*, M.56.553
appar. — *in dei apparitionem*, M.65.16
creat. 1–6 — *orationes in mundi creationem*, M.56.429
†*cruc.* — *in crucem*, Savile 5 p. 898
exegetica
hom. in Mt. 21:23 — *homilia in illud*, In qua potestate, M.56.411
hom. in Mt. 26:39 — *homilia in illud*, Pater, si possibile, C. Martin *Mus.* 48 (1935) p. 313, J. Zellinger *Severian von Gabala* Münster 1926
Rom.–Heb. — *fragmenta in Pauli epistulas*, Staab p. 213
fic. — *de ficu arefacta*, M.59.585
fr. — *fragmenta*, ap. *Doct. Patr.* 12 p. 76, *ib.* 18 p. 119, ap. C Later. *act.* 5, H.3.873
haer. — *fragmenta sermonis contra haereses*, ap. Jo. D. *parall.*, M.96.533
pac. — *de pace*, *AHS* 1 p. 15
serp. — *de serpente aeneo*, M.56.499
sigill. — *de sigillis librorum*, M.63.531

SEVERUS ANTIOCHENUS — ob. c. 539
(Sev. Ant.)
fr. — *fragmenta*, ap. Leont. H. *monoph.*; ap. C Later. *act.* 5, H.3.893, 897; ap. CCP (681) *act.* 10, H.3.1241; ap. Agath. Papam *ep. imp.*, M.*PL*.87.1202; *SR* 10 (1844) p. 202; ap. Eust. Mon. *ep.*
‡*fr.* — *fragmentum in Lc.*, M.1.775D
res. — *oratio in resurrectionem*, *PO* 16.794, int. opp. Gr. Nyss., M.46.628

SOCRATES SCHOLASTICUS — ob. post 450
(Socr.)
h.e. — *historia ecclesiastica*, R. Hussey Oxford 1853, M.67.29

SOPHRONIUS ALEXANDRINUS — saec. v
(Sophr. Al.)
libell. — *libellus contra Dioscurum*, ap. C Chalc. *act.* 3, *ACO* 2.1.2 p. 23, H.2.336

SOPHRONIUS HIEROSOLYMITANUS — ob. c. 638
(Sophr. H.)
aceph. Cyr. et Jo. — *vita acephala Cyri et Joannis*, M.87.3689
carm. 1–23 — *carmina anacreontica*, M.87.3733, nos. 9, 13, 20 in *AGC* pp. 43–47
conf. — *de peccatorum confessione*, M.87.3365
ep. syn. — *epistula synodica*, M.87.3148
epigr. 1–3 — *epigrammata*, M.87.4009
idiom. — *idiomela*, *AGC* p. 96
‡*liturg.* — *fragmentum commentarii liturgici*, M.87.3981 — saec. xii
mir. Cyr. et Jo. — *miracula Cyri et Joannis*, M.87.3424
nativ. — *sermo de nativitate*, H. Usener *Rheinisches Museum für Philologie* Frankfurt am Main 1886 p. 500
occurs. — *sermo in occursum domini*, H. Usener Bonn 1889
or. 2, 4, 5, 7–9 — *orationes variae*, M.87.3217
†*orat.* — *oratio*, M.87.4001
schol. — *scholium*, M.87.4012
‡*triod.* — *triodium*, M.87.3840 (by Joseph the Hymnographer, saec. ix)
trop. — *troparium horarum*, M.87.4005
v. Anast. — *vita Anastasii Persae martyris*, M.92.1680
v. Cyr. et Jo. — *vita Cyri et Joannis*, M.87.3380
v. Jo. Eleem. — *fragmentum vitae Joannis Eleemosynarii* [joint composition with Jo. Mosch.], H. Gelzer *SAQ* 5 (1893) p. 108, M.114.896
‡*v. m. Cyr. et Jo.* — *vita et conversatio et martyrium Cyri et Joannis*, M.87.3677
‡*v. Mar. Aeg.* — *vita Mariae Aegyptiae*, M.87.3697

SOZOMENUS SALAMINUS — ob. post 450
(Soz.)
h.e. — *historia ecclesiastica*, R. Hussey Oxford 1860, M.67.844

STEPHANUS AFRICANUS — saec. vii
(Steph. Afr.)
ep. — *epistula ad Constantinum*, ap. C Later. *act.* 2, H.3.737

STEPHANUS ALEXANDRINUS — ob. c. 618
(Steph. Al.)
fr. — *fragmenta*, ap. *Doct. Patr.*

STEPHANUS BOSTRENSIS — init. saec. viii
(Steph. Bost.)
fr. — *fragmenta*, G. M. Mercati *TQ* 77 (1895) p. 666; ap. Jo. D. *imag.* 3

STEPHANUS DIACONUS — saec. ix
(Steph. Diac.)
v. Steph. — *vita Stephani junioris*, M.100.1069

STEPHANUS DORANUS — saec. vii
(Steph. Dor.)
ep. — *epistula ad Martinum Papam*, ap. C Later. *act.* 2, H.3.712

STEPHANUS GOBARUS — ob. 578
(Steph. G.)
fr. — *fragmenta*, ap. Phot. *cod.* 232

STEPHANUS HIERAPOLITANUS — saec. vi
(Steph. Hier.)
agn. — *contra agnoëtas*, *AP* p. 154

SYLVESTER I PAPA — ob. 335
(Sylv.)
fr. — *fragmentum operis contra Judaeos*, *SVC* 8[2] (1833) p. 26

SYMBOLA
Symb. Ant. — *Symbolum Antiochenum*, partly ap. Eus. Dor. *contest.*, *ACO* 1.1.1 p. 102. 9, Hahn p. 141; partly reconstructed from Chrys. *hom. 40 in 1 Cor.*, Hahn p. 142
‡*Symb. Ant.* (269) — *Symbolum suppositum synodi Antiochenae anno 269*, *ACO* 1.1.5 p. 6, Hahn p. 182
Symb. Ant. (341) 1–4 — *Symbolum synodi Antiochenae anno 341*, ap. Ath. *syn.* 22–25
Symb. Ant. (345) — *Symbolum synodi Antiochenae anno 345 macrostichum dictum*, ap. Ath. *syn.* 26
Symb. Ant. (433) — *Symbolum Antiochenorum anno 433*, ap. Jo. Ant. *ep. Cyr.* 2, *ACO* 1.1.4 p. 8, M.77.172
Symb. App. — *Symboli apostolorum versiones variae*, Hahn pp. 30–34
Symb. Caes. — *Symbolum Caesariense*, ap. Eus. *ep. Caes.* 3
Symb. Chalc. — *Symbolum synodi Chalcedonensis anno 451*, ap. C Chalc. *act.* 5, *ACO* 2.1.2 p. 126, H.2.452
Symb. CP (360) — *Symbolum synodi Constantinopolitanae anno 360*, ap. Ath. *syn.* 30
Symb. CP (681) — *Symbolum synodi Constantinopolitanae annis 680 et 681*, ap. CCP (681) *act.* 18, H.3.1396
Symb. Hier. — *Symbolum Hierosolymitanum*, M.33.533, reconstructed from Cyr. H. *catech.* 6–18

SYMBOLA (*cont.*)

Symb. Nic. (325) — *Symbolum synodi Nicaenae anno 325*, Opitz 3 p. 51, ap. Eus. *ep. Caes.* 4, M.20.1540
Symb. Nic. (359) — *Symbolum synodi Nicenae Thracae anno 359*, ap. Thdt. *h.e.* 2. 21
Symb. Nic. (787) — *Symbolum synodi Nicaenae anno 787*, ap. C Nic. (787) *act.* 7, H.4.452
Symb. Nic.–CP — *Symbolum Nicaenum–Constantinopolitanum*, ap. C Chalc. *act.* 2, *ACO* 2.1.2 p. 80, H.2.288
Symb. Rom. — *Symbolum Romanum*, Hahn p. 23
[*Symb. Sard. Orient.* — *Symbolum synodi Sardicensis orientalium circa anno 343*, Lat., Hahn p. 190]
Symb. Sel. — *Symbolum synodi Seleucensis anno 359*, ap. Ath. *syn.* 29
Symb. Sirm. 1 — *Symbolum synodi Sirmiensis anno 351*, ap. Ath. *syn.* 27
Symb. Sirm. 1 *anath.* — *Symboli Sirmiensis anno 351 anathemata*, ap. Ath. *syn.* 27
Symb. Sirm. 2 — *Symbolum synodi Sirmiensis anno 357 blasphemum dictum*, ap. Ath. *syn.* 28
Symb. Sirm. 3 — *Symbolum synodi Sirmiensis anno 359*, ap. Ath. *syn.* 8

SYMEON STYLITES (Sym. Styl.) — ob. 460

ep. — *epistula ad Basilium Antiochenum*, H. Lietzmann *TU* 32^4 (1908) p. 194, ap. Evagr. *h.e.* 2. 10
serm. — *sermo de animae exitu*, *NBP* 8^3 (1871) p. 1

SYMEON STYLITES JUNIOR (Sym. Styl. J.) — ob. 596

ascet. 1–30 — *sermones ascetici*, *NBP* 8^3 p. 4
ep. Just. — *epistula ad Justinum juniorem*, M.86.3216
ep. Thom. — *epistula ad Thomam Hierosolymitanum*, ap. *v. Marth.* 59
imag. — *de sacris imaginibus*, M.86.3220, ap. Jo. D. *imag.* 3

SYMMACHUS PAPA (Symm. Papa) — ob. 514

‡*ep.* — *fragmentum epistulae contra Petrum Fullonem*, ap. *Doct. Patr.* 42 p. 318

SYNESIUS CYRENENSIS (Synes.) — ob. c. 414

T. = N. Terzaghi, *Synesii Cyrenensis Hymni et Opuscula*, 1, 2, Rome 1944

astrolab. — *sermo de dono astrolabii*, T.2 p. 132, M.66. 1577
calv. — *calvitii encomium*, T.2 p. 190, M.66.1168
catast. 1 — *catastasis*, T.2 p. 283, M.66.1573
catast. 2 — *catastasis in barbarorum excursione et elogium Anysii*, T.2 p. 285, M.66.1565
Dion — *Dion*, T.2 p. 233, M.66.1112
ep. 1–159 — *epistulae*, *EG* p. 638, M.66.1321
hom. 1–2 — *homiliae*, T.2 p. 279, M.66.1561
hymn. 1–9 — ***hymni*, T.1**, M.66.1588; numbered as in M.
‡*hymn.* 10 — *hymnus*, T.1 p. 64, M.66.1615
insomn. — *de insomniis*, T.2 p. 143, M.66.1281
provid. — *de providentia* (= *Aegyptii*), T.2 p. 63, M.66.1209
regn. — *oratio de regno*, T.2 p. 5, M.66.1053

TARASIUS CONSTANTINOPOLITANUS (Taras.) — ob. 806

apol. — *apologeticus ad populum*, M.98.1424, ap. Thphn. *chron.* p. 386
ep. 1–6 — *epistulae*, M.98.1428
praesent. BMV — *in sanctae deiparae praesentationem*, M.98. 1481

TATIANUS (Tat.) — ob. post 172

orat. — *oratio ad Graecos*, E. Schwartz *TU* 4^1 (1888), M.6.804

TESTAMENTA XII PATRIARCHUM — saec. ii a.C. ? *Graece reddita* c. A.D. 50 ?

R. H. Charles, *The Greek Versions of the Twelve Patriarchs*, Oxford 1908

T. Reub. — *testamentum Reuben*, p. 1
T. Sym. — *testamentum Symeonis*, p. 15
T. Lev. — *testamentum Levi*, p. 27
T. Jud. — *testamentum Judae*, p. 65
T. Isach. — *testamentum Isachar*, p. 105
T. Zab. — *testamentum Zabulon*, p. 116
T. Dan — *testamentum Dan*, p. 130
T. Neph. — *testamentum Nephthalim*, p. 143
T. Gad — *testamentum Gad*, p. 158
T. Aser — *testamentum Aser*, p. 171
T. Jos. — *testamentum Josephi*, p. 182
T. Benj. — *testamentum Benjamin*, p. 213

TESTAMENTUM ABRAHAE — saec. ii ?

T. Abr. A, B — M. R. James *TS* 2^2 (1892) pp. 77, 105

[TESTAMENTUM DOMINI — saec. iv–v

T. Dom. — J. Copper and A. J. McLean *The Testament of Our Lord* Edinburgh 1902: translated from the Syriac]

TESTAMENTUM JOB — saec. ii–iii

T. Job — M. R. James *TS* 5^1 (1897) p. 104

TESTAMENTUM SALAMONIS — init. saec. iii

T. Sal. — C. C. McCown Leipzig 1922, M.122.1316

THALASSIUS ABBAS (Thal.) — saec. vii

cent. — *centuriae de caritate ac continentia necnon de regimine mentis*, M.91.1428

THALASSIUS CONSTANTINOPOLITANUS MONACHUS ET BASILIUS DIACONUS (Thal. CP) — saec. v

Thds. — *libellus ad Theodosium*, *ACO* 1.1.5 p. 7, M.91.1472

THEMISTIUS ALEXANDRINUS DIACONUS (Them.) — saec. vi

fr. — *fragmenta*, ap. *Doct. Patr.* 41 p. 314; ap. C Later. *act.* 3, H.3.784; *ib.* 5, H.896–7; ap. CCP (681) *act.* 10, H.3.1240, 1241, 1300; ap. Max. *opusc.*, M.91.172

THEODORETUS CYRRHENSIS (Thdt.) — ob. 458

S. = J. L. Schultze and J. A. Noesselt, Halle 1769–74

affect. 1–12 — *graecarum affectionum curatio*, S.4.689, M.83.784, J. Raeder *Teub.* 1904
carit. — *oratio de divina et sancta caritate*, S.3.1296, M.82.1497
ep. 1–82, 84–147, 151, 162 — *epistulae*, S.4.1060, M.83.1173
ep. 83 — *epistula ad Dioscorum*, *ACO* 2.1.2 p. 48, S.4.1145, M.83.1265
ep. 171 — *epistula ad Joannem Antiochae episcopum*, *ACO* 1.1.7 p. 163, S.4.1354, M.83.1484
ep. Alex. — *epistula ad Alexandrum Hierapolitanum*, *ACO* 1.1.7 p. 79
eran. 1–3 — *eranistes* (*dialogus*), S.4.1, M.83.28
eran. suppl. — *demonstrationes per syllogismos*, S.4.263, M.83.317

exegetica

qu. 1–110 *in Gen.* — *quaestiones in Gen.*, S.1.3, M.80.76
qu. 1–62 *in Ex.* — *quaestiones in Ex.*, S.1.120, M.80.225
qu. 1–38 *in Lev.* — *quaestiones in Lev.*, S.1.176, M.80.297
qu. 1–51 *in Num.* — *quaestiones in Num.*, S.1.217, M.80.349
qu. 1–46 *in Dt.* — *quaestiones in Dt.*, S.1.256, M.80.401
qu. 1–20 *in Jos.* — *quaestiones in Jos.*, S.1.299, M.80.457
qu. 1–28 *in Jud.* — *quaestiones in Jud.*, S.1.321, M.80.485
qu. 1–2 *in Ruth* — *quaestiones in Ruth*, S.1.346, M.80.517
qu. 1–65 *in* 1 *Reg.* — *quaestiones in 1 Reg.*, S.1.353, M.80.528
qu. 1–45 *in* 2 *Reg.* — *quaestiones in 2 Reg.*, S.1.404, M.80.597
qu. 1–68 *in* 3 *Reg.* — *quaestiones in 3 Reg.*, S.1.455, M.80.668
qu. 1–57 *in* 4 *Reg.* — *quaestiones in 4 Reg.*, S.1.513, M.80.745
qu. in 1, 2 *Par* — *quaestiones in 1, 2 Par.*, S.1.554, M.80. 801
Ps. 1–150 — *commentarii in Pss.*, S.1.609, M.80.865
†*Ps. fr.* — *fragmentum in Ps. 17*, S.5.1234
Pss. proem. — *proemium in Pss.*, S.1.601, M.80.857
†*Pss. proem.* — *compendiosa ratio ex hypomnesticis de psalterio*, S.5.72, M.84.20
Cant. — *commentarius in Cant.*, S.2.1, M.81.28
xii proph. proem. — *proemium in xii prophetas*, S.2.1305, M.81. 1545
Os.–Mal. — *commentarii in xii prophetas*, S.2.1310, M. 81.1552

Is. *commentarius in Is.*, A. Möhle *Mitteilungen des Septuaginta-Unternehmens* 5 Berlin 1932, S.2.165, M.81.496
Jer. *commentarius in Jer.*, S.2.403, M.81.496
Bar. *commentarius in Bar.*, S.2.630, M.81.760
Lam. *commentarius in Lam.*, S.2.647, M.81.780
Ezech. *commentarius in Ezech.*, S.2.669, M.81.808
Dan. *commentarius in Dan.*, S.2.1053, M.81.1256
†*Lc.* *in Lc. 22:24*, S.5.83, M.84.32
epp. Paul. proem. *proemium in Pauli epistulas*, S.3.1, M.82.36
Rom.–Philm. *interpretationes in Pauli epistulas*, S.3.11, M.82.44
‡*fr.* *fragmentum*, S.4.1307, M.83.1433
‡*fr. bapt.* *fragmentum de baptismate apostolorum*, M.87.3372 = M.92.1075
h. rel. *historia religiosa*, S.3.1099, M.82.1284; book 26, H. Lietzmann *TU* 32^4 (1908) p. 1
haer. *haereticarum fabularum compendium*, S.4.280, M.83.336
h.e. *historia ecclesiastica*, L. Parmentier *GCS* 1911, S.3.722, M.82.881
hom. *homilia Chalcedoni habita*, *ACO* 1.1.7 p. 82
inc. *de incarnatione domini*, int. opp. Cyr., M.75.1420
‡*nativ. Jo. Bapt.* *homilia in nativitate Joannis Baptistae*, S.5.84, M.84.33
†*Nest.* *contra Nestorium ad Sporacium*, S.4.1041, M.82.1153
pental. *fragmenta pentalogi de incarnatione*, S.5.116, M.84.65
†*prop.* *adversus varias propositiones*, S.4.1054, M.83.1164
provid. 1–10 *orationes de providentia*, S.4.482, M.83.556
rect. conf. *expositio rectae confessionis*, int. opp. Just., M.6.1208
[*repr.* *reprehensio xii anathematismorum Cyrilli*, S.5.1, cit. ap. Cyr. *apol. Thdt.* q.v.]
serm. Chrys. *sermones in Joannem Chrysostomum*, S.5.98, M.84.48
Trin. *de sancta et vivifica Trinitate*, int. opp. Cyr., M.75.1148

THEODORUS ABUCARA ob. c. 820
(Thdr. Abuc.)
opusc. 1–17, 19–42 *opuscula varia*, M.97.1461
opusc. 18 M.94.1596
un. et inc. *de unione et incarnatione*, M.97.1601

THEODORUS ALEXANDRINUS DIACONUS saec. v
(Thdr. Al.)
libell. *libellus contra Dioscurum*, ap. C Chalc. *act.* 3, *ACO* 2.1.2 p. 15, H.2.321

THEODORUS CONSTANTINOPOLITANUS DIACONUS saec. vii
(Thdr. CP)
qu. Max. 1, 2 *quaestiones, quibus respondet Maximus*, M.91.216

THEODORUS HERACLEENSIS ob. 355
(Thdr. Heracl.)
Pss. *fragmenta in Pss.*, ap. *cat. Ps.*
Is. *fragmenta in Is.*, M.18.1308
fr. Mt. *fragmenta in Mt.*, ap. *cat. Mt.*
fr. Jo. *fragmenta in Jo.*, ap. *cat. Jo.*

THEODORUS HIEROSOLYMITANUS saec. viii
(Thdr. H.)
ep. syn. *epistula synodica*, ap. C Nic. (787) *act.* 3, H.4.141

THEODORUS ICONIENSIS saec. vi
(Thdr. Ic.)
v. Cyric. et Jul. *vita Cyricii et Julittae*, M.120.165

THEODORUS LECTOR saec. vi
(Thdr. Lect.)
exc. Vat. *excerpta Vatopediana*, A. Papadopoulos-Kerameus in *Journal des russischen Ministeriums für Volksaufklärung, Abteilung für klassische Philologie* 333 (1901), quoted from the citations in *AP* pp. 56 ff.
fr. *fragmenta ex historia ecclesiastica*, M.86.216; E. Miller *RA* 26 (1873) p. 396
h.e. *historia ecclesiastica*, M.86.165

THEODORUS MOPSUESTENUS ob. 428
(Thdr. Mops.)
S. = H. B. Swete, *Theodori episcopi Mopsuesteni in epistolas beati Pauli commentarii* 1, 2, Cambridge 1880
ep. Domn. *fragmenta epistulae ad Domnum*, S.2 p. 338, M.66.1012
exegetica
Gen. *fragmenta in Gen.*, M.66.636
Ex. *fragmenta in Ex.*, M.66.648
Ps. *fragmenta commentarii in Pss.*, R. Devreesse *ST* 93 (1939), M.66.648
Os.–Mal. *commentarii in xii prophetas*, M.66.124
Mt. *fragmenta in Mt.*, M.66.705
Mc. *fragmenta in Mc.*, M.66.713
Lc. *fragmenta in Lc.*, M.66.716
Jo. *fragmenta in Jo.*, R. Devreesse *ST* 141 (1948) p. 305, M.66.728
Ac. proem. *proemium in Ac.*, E. von Dobschütz *American Journal of Theology* 2 Chicago 1898 p. 359
Rom.–2 Cor. *fragmenta commentarii in Rom.–2 Cor.*, Staab p. 113, M.66.788
Gal.–Col. *commentarii in Gal.–Col.*, S.1 p. 1, M.66.897
1 Thess.–Philm. *commentarii in 1 Thess.–Philm.*, S.2 p. 1, M.66.932
Heb. *commentarius in Heb.*, Staab p. 200, M.66.952
fr. Apoll. *fragmenta contra Apollinarem*, S.2 p. 312, M.66.997
fr. inc. *de incarnatione filii dei*, S.2 p. 293, M.66.972
fr. mir. *fragmentum ex sermone de miraculis*, S.2 p. 339, M.66.1004
‡*resp. Chrys.* *responsio ad Chrysostomum*, int. opp. Chrys., M.48.1063
symb. *symbolum*, *ACO* 1.1.7 p. 97, M.66.1016

THEODORUS PETRANUS saec. vi
(Thdr. Pet.)
v. Thds. *vita Theodosii*, H. Usener *Der heilige Theodosius* Leipzig 1890 p. 3

THEODORUS PHARANITA saec. vii
(Thdr. Pharan.)
fr. *fragmenta varia*, ap. C Later. *act.* 3, H.3.765–8; ap. CCP (681) *act.* 10, H.3.1246, *act.* 13, H.3.1344, 1345

THEODORUS RAITHENUS saec. vii
(Thdr. Raith.)
praep. *de praeparatione*, *AP* p. 185, M.91.1484

THEODORUS SCYTHOPOLITANUS saec. vi
(Thdr. Scyth.)
libell. *libellus de erroribus Origenianis*, M.86.232

THEODORUS STUDITA ob. 826
(Thdr. Stud.)
antirr. 1–3 *antirrhetica adversus iconomachos*, M.99.328
ascet. *ascetica capitula iv*, M.99.1681
can. imag. *canon in erectione sanctarum imaginum*, M.99.1768
cant. 1–18 *cantica*, *AS* 1 p. 336
catech. magn. 1–111 *catecheses magnae*, *NBP* 9^2 (1888) p. 1; 10 (1905) p. 7
catech. parv. 1–134 *catecheses parvae*, *NBP* 9^1 p. 1; a fr. of *catech. parv.* 9, M.99.520; *catech. parv.* 114, M.99.656
conf. *canones de confessione et satisfactione*, M.99.1721
cruc. *canon in adoratione sanctae crucis*, M.99.1757
ep. *epistulae*, *NBP* 8^1 p. 1
ep. imag. *epistula ad Platonem de cultu sacrarum imaginum*, M.99.500
epp. *epistularum libri duo*, M.99.904. (*Note*: *epp.* 2. 221, R. Devreesse *AB* 68 (1950) p. 54)
iamb. 1–124 *iambi de variis argumentis*, M.99.1780
icon. *capita vii adversus iconomachos*, M.99.485
nativ. BMV *homilia in nativitatem BMV*, M.96.680
or. 1–13 *orationes variae*, M.99.688
or. icon. *oratio adversus iconomachos*, M.99.176
poen. 1, 2 *poenae monasteriales*, M.99.1733, 1748
praesanct. *explicatio divinae liturgiae praesanctificorum*, M.99.1688
probl. *problemata ad iconomachos*, M.99.477
ref. *refutatio poëmatum iconomachorum*, M.99.436

THEODORUS STUDITA (*cont.*)
resp. — *responsiones* (*canones*) *de quibusdam quaestionibus*, M.99.1729
schol. Bas. — *scholia in Basilii ascetica*, M.99.1685
test. — *testamentum*, M.99.1813

THEODORUS TRIMITHUNTIS — saec. vii
(Thdr. Trim.)
v. Chrys. — *de vita et exilio Joannis Chrysostomi*, M.47.li

THEODOSIUS ALEXANDRINUS — ob. 566
(Thds. Al.)
fr. — *fragmenta varia*, ap. Agath. Papam *ep. imp.*, M.*PL.* 87.1202; Cosm. Ind. *top.* 10, *Doct. Patr.* 41 p. 314, M.86.285

THEODOSIUS AMMORIANUS — saec. viii
(Thds. Am.)
libell. — *libellus*, ap. C Nic. (787) *act.* 1, H.4.4

THEODOSIUS BITHYNUS — saec. vii
(Thds. Bith.) cit. ap. Anast. Ap. *a. Max.* 2, M.90.136

THEODOSIUS II IMPERATOR — ob. 450
(Thds. Imp.)
Note: joint imperial letters are not distinguished
cod. — *codex Theodosianus* 9.45.4, *ACO* 1.1.4 p. 61; *ib.* 16.5.66, *ACO* 1.1.3 p. 68, H.1.1717
common. — *commonitorium ad Damascium*, ap. C Chalc. *act.* 10, *ACO* 2.1.3 p. 19, H.2.509
ep. Acac. — *epistula ad Acacium Berroeensem*, *ACO* 1.1.1 p. 112, M.77.1448
ep. Cyr. 1, 2 — *epistulae ad Cyrillum*, *ACO* 1.1.1 pp. 73, 114, H.1.1341, 1344
ep. Diosc. — *epistula ad Dioscurum*, *ACO* 2.1.1 p. 68, ap. C Eph. (449) *act.* 1, H.2.72
ep. Eph. — *epistula scripta ad C Eph.* (*431*) *per Palladium*, *ACO* 1.1.3 p. 9, H.1.1537
ep. Flav. — *epistula ad Flavianum*, *ACO* 1.1.7 p. 71
ep. Gall. — *epistula ad Gallam Placidiam*, int. opp. Leo. Mag. *ep.* 63, *ACO* 2.1.1 p. 7, M.*PL.* 54.878
ep. Jo. Ant. — *epistula ad Joannem Antiochenum*, *ACO* 1.1.4 p. 3, M.77.1457
ep. Licin. — *epistula ad Liciniam Eudoxiam*, int. opp. Leo. Mag. *ep.* 64, *ACO* 2.1.1 p. 8, M.*PL.* 54.878
ep. Sym. — *epistula ad Symeonem Stylitem*, *ACO* 1.1.4 p. 5, H.1.1685
ep. Val. — *epistula ad Valentinianum*, int. opp. Leo. Mag. *ep.* 62, *ACO* 2.1.1 p. 7, M.*PL.*54. 876
sacr. 1, 2 — *epistulae sacrae*, *ACO* 1.1.7 p. 142, H.1.1616, *ACO* 1.1.7 p. 146
sacr. 3–8 — *epistulae sacrae*, ap. C Eph. (449), *ACO* 2.1.1 p. 71, H.2.76
syn. — *sacra ad synodum Ephesinam* (449) *missa*, *ACO* 1.1.1 p. 120, H.1.1345

THEODOTUS ANCYRANUS — ob. ante 446
(Thdot. Anc.)
exp. symb. — *expositio symboli Nicaeni*, M.77.1313
fr. — *fragmentum*, ap. *Doct. Patr.* 20 p. 126
fr. Ac. — *fragmenta in Ac.*, M.77.1431
hom. 1–3 — *homiliae*, *ACO* 1.1.2 pp. 80, 73, 71, M.77. 1349
hom. BMV — *homilia in BMV*, M. Jugie, *PO* 19 (1925) p. 318
hom. BMV et Sym. — *homilia in BMV et Symeonem*, M.77.1389

THEODOTUS ANTIOCHENUS — saec. v
(Thdot. Ant.)
fr. — *fragmentum*, ap. *Doct. Patr.* 5, p. 34

THEODOTUS EBIONITES — saec. ii
(Thdot. Ebion.) cit. ap. Epiph. *haer.* 54

THEODULUS sive THEODORUS PERSA — ob. post 474
(Thdul.)
fr. — *fragmentum*, ap. *Doct. Patr.* 41 p. 315

THEOGNOSTUS ALEXANDRINUS — saec. iii
(Thgn.)
hypot. fr. — *fragmenta ex libris vii hypotyposeon*, A. Harnack *TU* 24^3 (1903) p. 75, M.10.240

THEOPHANES CONFESSOR — ob. c. 817
(Thphn.)
chron. — *chronographia*, C. de Boor *Theophanis Chronographia* 1 Leipzig 1883 (cited by page of Paris (1665) edition), M.108.56

THEOPHILUS ALEXANDRINUS — ob. 412
(Thphl. Al.)
Agath. — *ad Agathonem*, M.65.44
cathar. — *narratio de catharis*, M.65.44
common. — *commonitorium ad Ammonem*, M.65.36
ep. pasch. proem. — *proemium ad epistulas paschales*, M.65.48, ap. *Chron. Pasch.* pp. 15–17
fr. 1–5 — *fragmenta varia ex operibus deperditis*, M.65.65; other fragments cited from *Apophth. Patr.*, C Later. *act.* 5, *NBP* 6^1 (1853) p. 164
fr. ep. — *fragmenta ex epistulis variis*, ap. Pall. *v. Chrys.* 7; ap. Justn. *Or.*; E. Schwartz *ABAW* 32^6 (1927) p. 36
fr. ep. pasch. 1–7 — *fragmenta ex epistulis paschalibus*, M.65. 53, ap. Cosm. Ind. *top.* 10; Cyr. *Arcad.*; Thdt. *eran.* 2, 3; C Eph. (431) *act.* 1, *ACO* 1.1.2 p. 41; other fragments cited from *Doct. Patr.* 25 and from *ABAW* 32^6 p. 38
Men. — *ad Menam*, M.65.44
Or. — *fragmentum ex epistula contra Origenem*, *ABAW* 32^6 p. 37
poenit. — *fragmentum de poenitentia*, ap. *Doct. Patr.* 18, p. 120
theoph. — *prosphonesis in sancta theophania*, M.65.33

THEOPHILUS ANTIOCHENUS — ob. post 181
(Thphl. Ant.)
Autol. — *ad Autolycum*, G. Bardy *SC* 20, Paris 1948, M.6.1024
fr. — *fragmentum in Cant.*, M.6.1604

THEOPHILUS CAESARIENSIS ET ALII — fin. saec. ii
(Thphl. Caes.)
fragmentum, M.5.1369, cited without title from Eus. *h.e.* 5. 25

THEOPHYLACTUS SIMOCATTA — saec. vii
(Thphyl.)
exc. gent. — *excerpta de legationibus gentium ad Romanos*, C. de Boor *Excerpta historica iussu imperatoris Constantini Porphyrogeniti confecta* Berlin 1903–5 p. 477, M.113.937
exc. Rom. — *excerpta de legationibus Romanorum ad gentes*, *ib.* p. 221, M.113.928

THEOSTERICTUS — fin. saec. viii
(Thst.)
v. Nic. Heg. — *vita Nicetae Hegumeni Confessoris*, *ASS* Aprilis 1 p. xxii

TIMOTHEUS I ALEXANDRINUS — ob. 385
(Tim. I Al.)
resp. — *responsiones canonicae*, M.33.1296

TIMOTHEUS II ALEXANDRINUS ('AELURUS') — ob. 477
(Tim. II Al.)
fr. — *fragmenta*, ap. *Doct. Patr.* 24, p. 165, M.86. 273

TIMOTHEUS III ALEXANDRINUS — ob. 535
(Tim. III Al.)
fr. — *fragmenta*, M.86.265, ap. Cosm. Ind. *top.* 10 pp. 315–17

TIMOTHEUS ANTIOCHENUS (seu HIEROSOLYMITANUS)
(Tim. Ant.) — init. saec. vi
caec. — *in caecum a nativitate*, M.28.1001
cruc. — *in crucem et transfigurationem*, M.86.256
descr. BMV — *de descriptione deiparae*, M.28.944
nativ. Jo. Bapt. — *in nativitatem praecursoris*, M.28.905
Sym. — *oratio in Symeon*, M.86.237

TIMOTHEUS BERYTENSIS — saec. iv
(Tim. Beryt.)
ep. Homon. — *epistula ad Homonium*, Lietzmann p. 277, ap. Leont. B. *Apoll.*, M.86.1960
ep. Prosd. — *fragmentum epistulae ad Prosdocium*, Lietzmann p. 283
fr. — *fragmenta varia*, Lietzmann p. 279, int. opp. Jul. Papae, M.*PL.*8.954

TIMOTHEUS CONSTANTINOPOLITANUS PRESBYTER — saec. vi–vii
(Tim. CP)
haer. — *de receptione haereticorum*, M.86.12
‡*haer. suppl.* — *de receptione haereticorum* (*supplementum*), M.86.69

TIMOTHEUS HIEROSOLYMITANUS see TIMOTHEUS ANTIOCHENUS

Titus Bostrensis ob. 378
(Tit. Bost.)
arg. 1–4 — *argumenta in libros iv adversus Manichaeos*, M.18.1257
exegetica
fr. Dan. — *fragmenta in Dan.*, J. Sickenberger *TU* 21^1 (1901) p. 246
fr. Lc. — *fragmenta in Lc.*, *TU* 21^1 p. 143
Man. 1 — *adversus Manichaeos*, M.18.1069 (Books 1 and 3 contain Serap. *Man.* 25 ff.);
2 — M.18.1132
3 proem. — M.18.1208
fr. — *fragmenta ex libris adversus Manichaeos*, M.18.1257
‡*palm.* — *in ramos palmarum*, M.18.1264

Traditio Pilati saec. iv
Trad. Pil. — C. Tischendorf *Evangelia Apocrypha* Leipzig 1876 p. 449

Translatio Philippi see **Acta Apostolorum Apocrypha**, *Tr. Phil.*

Ursacius et Valens saec. iv
(Ursac.)
ep. Ath. — *epistula ad Athanasium*, ap. Ath. *apol. sec.* 58. 5
ep. Jul. — *epistula ad Julium Papam*, ap. Ath. *apol. sec.* 58. 2–4

Valentinianus III Imperator saec. v
(Valent. Imp.)
ep. episc. — *epistula ad episcopos Asiae et Phrygiae*, ap. Thdt. *h.e.* 4. 8
ep. Nic. 1, 2 — *epistulae ad Nicomedenses*, *ACO* 2.1.3 p. 61, H.2.568
ep. Thds. — *epistula ad Theodosium imperatorem*, int. opp. Leo. Mag. *ep.* 55, *ACO* 2.1.1 p. 57, M.*PL*.54.858

Valentinus Apollinaristes saec. iv
(Val. Apoll.)
apol. — *capita apologiae*, Lietzmann p. 287; ap. Leont. B. *Apoll.*, M.86.1953

Valentinus Gnosticus et Discipuli saec. ii
(Val. Gn.)
fragmenta, ap. Iren., Clem., etc.

Vaticinia de Rebus Byzantinis saec. viii–ix
Vaticin. 1, 2 — Vassiliev pp. 47, 50

Victor Antiochenus saec. v
(Vict.)
Mc. — *catena in Mc.*, J. A. Cramer *Catena in Matthaeum et Marcum* Oxford 1840 p. 266

Victor Carthaginiensis saec. vii
(Vict. Carth.)
ep. — *epistula ad Theodorum Papam*, int. opp. Thdr. Papae M.*PL*.87.86

Vigilius Papa saec. vi
(Vigil. Papa)
†*ep. decr.* — *epistula decretalis*, M.*PL*.69.121, H.3.213
ep. Eutych. — *epistula ad Eutychium*, M.*PL*.69.65

Vitae Sanctorum Anonymae
V. Aberc. — *vita Abercii*, T. Nissen *Teub.* 1910
V. Alex. Acoem. — *vita Alexandri Acoemetae*, E. de Stoop *PO* 6 (1911) p. 658
V. Amph. — *vita Amphilochii Iconensis*, M.39.13
V. Anast. — *vita Anastasii Persae*, H. Usener *Acta Anastasii Persae* Bonn 1894
V. Ath. — *vita Athanasii*, M.25.clxxxv
V. Chrys. — *vita Joannis Chrysostomi*, Savile 8 p. 249
V. Const. — *vita Constantini imperatoris*, H. G. Opitz *Byzantion* 9 Brussels 1934 p. 545; suppl. in 10 (1935) p. 399: partly int. opp. Philost., J. Bidez *GCS* 1913
V. Cosm. et Dam. — *vita Cosmae et Damiani*, L. Deubner, *Kosmas und Damian* Leipzig 1907 p. 87
V. Dan. — *vita Danieli*, L. Clygnet *ROC* 5 (1900) pp. 50, 254, 370
V. Ephr. — *vita Ephraem*, J. S. Assemani *Sancti Ephraem Syri opera omnia* 1 Rome 1732 p. xxix
V. Eudoc. — *vita Eudociae*, *ASS* Martii 1 p. 875
V. Euprax. — *vita Eupraxiae*, *ASS* Martii 13 p. 727
V. Glyc. — *vita Glyceriae*, *ASS* Maii 13 p. 12*
V. Gr. Ill. — *vita Gregorii Illuminatoris*, G. Garitte, *ST* 127 (1946) p. 23
V. Mac. A, B — *vita Macarii Romani*, Vassiliev p. 135
V. Marc. — *vita Marci evangelistae*, *ASS* Aprilis 3 p. xlvi
V. Marth. — *vita Marthae*, *ASS* Maii 24 p. 403
V. Max. — *vita Maximi Confessoris*, M.90.68
V. Nicol. Sion — *vita Nicolai Sion*, G. Anrich *Hagios Nicolaus* 1 Leipzig 1913 p. 3
V. Olymp. — *vita et translatio Olympiadis*, *AB* 15 (1896) p. 409
V. Pach. *Φ* — *vita Pachomii*, F. Halkin S.J. *Sancti Pachomii vitae Graecae* in *Subsidia Hagiographica* 19 Brussels 1932 pp. 1–96
Δ — *ib.*, pp. 122–65
Σ — *ib.*, pp. 166–271
Π — *ib.*, pp. 272–406
Γ — *ib.*, pp. 407–56
V. Pelag. Ant. — *vita Pelagiae Antiochae*, H. Usener *Legenden der Pelagia* Bonn 1879 p. 3
V. Thdr. fr. — *fragmenta vitae Theodori Hegumeni*, int. opp. Philost., *GCS* p. 177
V. Zos. — *vita Zosimi*, M. R. James *TS* 2^3 (1893) p. 96

Vitalis Apollinaristes ob. post 382
(Vital.)
fr. — *fragmentum de fide*, ap. Cyr. *Arcad.*, *ACO* 1.1.5 p. 67, A.5^2.51

Xystus III Papa ob. 440
(Xyst. Papa)
ep. Cyr. — *epistula ad Cyrillum*, *ACO* 1.1.7 p. 143, M.*PL*.50.588
ep. Flav. — *epistula ad Flavianum*, *ACO* 1.1.7 p. 143
tract. — *epistula tractatoria*, *ACO* 1.1.7 p. 144, M.*PL*.50.584

Zacharias Hierosolymitanus ob. 631
(Zach. H.)
ep. — *epistula*, M.86.3228

Zacharias Mitylenensis Rhetor ob. ante 553
(Zach. Mit.)
fr. — *fragmenta contra Manichaeos*, *AS* 5 p. 67
opif. — *de mundi opificio contra philosophos*, M.85.1012

Zeno Imperator ob. 491
(Zeno)
henot. — *fragmentum edicti henoticon dicti*, E. Schwartz *ABAW* 32^6 (1927) p. 52; ap. Evagr. *h.e.* 3. 14, M.86.2620

Zosimus Abbas saec. vi
(Zos.)
alloquia — *alloquia*, M.78.1681

II. ABBREVIATIONS OF BOOKS OF THE BIBLE

OLD TESTAMENT

Gen.	Genesis
Ex.	Exodus
Lev.	Leviticus
Num.	Numeri
Dt.	Deuteronomium
Jos.	Josua
Jud.	Judices
Ruth	Ruth
1–4 Reg.	1–4 Regum
1–2 Par.	1–2 Paraleipomenon
1–3 Esd.	1–3 Esdrae
Tob.	Tobias
Judith	Judith
Esth.	Esther
Job	Job
Pss.	Psalmi
Pr.	Proverbia
Eccl.	Ecclesiastes
Cant.	Canticum Canticorum
Sap.	Sapientia Salomonis
Ecclus.	Ecclesiasticus
Os.	Oseas
Am.	Amos
Mich.	Michaeas
Joel	Joel
Abd.	Abdias
Jon.	Jonas
Nah.	Nahum
Abac.	Abacuc
Soph.	Sophonias
Ag.	Aggaeus
Zach.	Zacharias
Mal.	Malachias
Is.	Isaias
Jer.	Jeremias
Bar.	Baruch
Lam.	Lamentationes
Ep. Jer.	Epistula Jeremiae
Ezech.	Ezechiel
Dan.	Daniel
1–3 Macc.	1–3 Maccabaeorum

NEW TESTAMENT

Mt.	Evangelium Matthaei
Mc.	Evangelium Marci
Lc.	Evangelium Lucae
Jo.	Evangelium Joannis
Ac.	Acta Apostolorum
Rom.	Epistula ad Romanos
1, 2 Cor.	Epistulae ad Corinthios 1, 2
Gal.	Epistula ad Galatas
Eph.	Epistula ad Ephesios
Phil.	Epistula ad Philippenses
Col.	Epistula ad Colossenses
1, 2 Thess.	Epistulae ad Thessalonicenses 1, 2
1, 2 Tim.	Epistulae ad Timotheum 1, 2
Tit.	Epistula ad Titum
Philm.	Epistula ad Philemonem
Heb.	Epistula ad Hebraeos
Jac.	Epistula Jacobi
1, 2 Petr.	Epistulae Petri 1, 2
1–3 Jo.	Epistulae Joannis 1–3
Judae	Epistula Judae
Apoc.	Apocalypsis Joannis

III. WORKS CITED BY EDITOR'S NAME ALONE

Bihlmeyer	F. X. Funk, revised by K. Bihlmeyer, *Die Apostolischen Väter*, Tübingen, 1924
Funk 1, 2	F. X. Funk, *Didascalia et Constitutiones Apostolorum*, Paderborn, 1905
Goodspeed	E. J. Goodspeed, *Die Ältesten Apologeten*, Göttingen, 1915
H. 1–4	J. Hardouin, *Acta Conciliorum*, 1–4, Paris, 1714–15
Hahn	A. Hahn, *Bibliothek der Symbole und Glaubensregeln der Alten Kirche*, Breslau, 1897
Lauchert	F. Lauchert, *Die Kanones der wichtigsten Altkirchlichen Concilien nebst den apostolischen Kanones*, Freiburg i. B. and Leipzig, 1896
Lietzmann	H. Lietzmann, *Apollinaris von Laodicea und seine Schule*, Tübingen, 1904
Lightfoot	J. B. Lightfoot, *The Apostolic Fathers*, 2², London, 1885
LS	See VI
M.	J. P. Migne, *Patrologia Graeca*, Paris 1857–66
M.*PL.*	See IV
Opitz 2, 3	H. G. Opitz, *Athanasiuswerke*, 2–3, Berlin, 1934–41
Savile 1–8	H. Savile, *S. Joannis Chrysostomi Opera*, 1–8, Eton, 1612–13
Staab	K. Staab, *Pauluskommentare aus der Griechischen Kirche*, Münster 1933 (*Neutestamentliche Abhandlungen* 15, ed. M. Meinertz)
Vassiliev	A. Vassiliev, *Anecdota Graeco-Byzantina*, 1, Moscow, 1893

IV. LIST OF PERIODICALS AND WORKS CITED BY THEIR TITLE

AB	*Analecta Bollandiana*, Brussels
ABAW	*Abhandlungen der bayerischen Akademie der Wissenschaften; philosophisch-philologische und historische Klasse*, Munich
ACO	E. Schwartz, *Acta Conciliorum Oecumenicorum*, 1–4, Berlin and Leipzig, 1924–40
AGC	W. Christ and M. Paranikas, *Anthologia Graeca Carminum Christianorum*, Leipzig, 1871
AGWG	*Abhandlungen der königlichen Gesellschaft der Wissenschaften; historisch-philologische Klasse*, Göttingen
AHS	A. Papadopoulos-Kerameus, *Ἀνάλεκτα Ἱεροσολυμιτικῆς σταχυολογίας*, St. Petersburg, vol. 1, 1891, vol. 2, 1894
AP	F. Diekamp, *Analecta Patristica* (*Orientalia Christiana Analecta*, 117), Rome, 1938
AS	J. B. Pitra, *Analecta Sacra*, 1–5, Paris, 1876–82
ASS	*Acta Sanctorum*, Brussels, 1643 (cited by month, date, and page)
BCH	*Bulletin de Correspondance Hellénique*, Athens and Paris
BZ	*Byzantinische Zeitschrift*, Leipzig
CB	*Corpus Scriptorum Historiae Byzantinae*, Bonn
CG–CI	N. A. Bees, *Corpus der Griechisch-Christlichen Inschriften von Hellas*, 1, Athens, 1941
CIG	A. Boeckh, *Corpus Inscriptionum Graecarum*, Berlin, 1828–77
CSEL	*Corpus Scriptorum Ecclesiasticorum Latinorum*, Vienna
EG	R. Hercher, *Epistolographi Graeci*, Paris, 1873
GCS	*Die Griechischen Christlichen Schriftsteller der ersten drei Jahrhunderte*, Leipzig
GNTK	T. Zahn, *Geschichte des neutestamentlichen Kanons*, Erlangen, 1888–92
Hesp.	*Hesperia, Journal of The American School of Classical Studies at Athens*, Harvard University Press, Cambridge Massachusetts
HTR	*Harvard Theological Review*, New York and Cambridge, Massachusetts
HTS	*Harvard Theological Studies*, Cambridge, Massachusetts
IG	A. Kirchhoff, *Inscriptiones Graecae*, Berlin, 1873–90
IGC Aeg.	G. Lefebvre, *Recueil des Inscriptions grecques chrétiennes d'Égypte*, Cairo, 1907
IGC As. Min.	H. Grégoire, *Recueil des Inscriptions grecques chrétiennes d'Asie Mineure*, Paris, 1922
JHS	*The Journal of Hellenic Studies*, London
JTS	*The Journal of Theological Studies*, Oxford
KlT	*Kleine Texte*, Bonn, Leipzig, and Berlin
MAMA	*Monumenta Asiae Minoris Antiquae*, 1–6, Manchester University Press, London, Longmans, Green & Co. Ltd., 1928–39
Mon.	J. B. Pitra, *Juris ecclesiastici Graecorum historia et monumenta*, 1, 2, Rome, 1864–8
M.*PL.*	J. P. Migne, *Patrologia Latina*, Paris, 1844–55
Mus.	*Le Muséon, Revue d'études orientales*, Louvain
NBP	A. Mai, *Nova Bibliotheca Patrum*, Rome
OC	*Oriens Christianus*, Rome and Leipzig
OGIS	W. Dittenberger, *Orientis Graecae Inscriptiones Selectae*, Leipzig, 1903–5
PAmh.	B. P. Grenfell and A. S. Hunt, *Amhurst Papyri*, London, 1901–2
PFlor.	D. Comparetti and G. Vitelli, *Papiri greco-egizii* 1–3, Milan, 1905–15
PLond.	F. G. Kenyon, *Greek Papyri in the British Museum*, London, 1893–4
PLond. 1912–1929	H. I. Bell, *Jews and Christians in Egypt*, London, 1924
PO	*Patrologia Orientalis*, Paris
POxy.	B. P. Grenfell, A. S. Hunt, et al., *Oxyrhynchus Papyri*, London, 1898– (sometimes cited from *Pap. Chr.*, see I)
PRyl.	A. S. Hunt et al., *Catalogue of the Greek Papyri in the John Rylands Library at Manchester*, Manchester, 1911–1954 (sometimes cited from *Pap. Chr.*, see I)
RA	*Revue Archéologique*, Paris
RB	*Revue Biblique*, Paris and Rome
ROC	*Revue de l'orient chrétien*, Paris
SAQ	*Sammlung ausgewählter kirchen- und dogmen-geschichtlicher Quellenschriften*, Freiburg, 1890–
SBBAW	*Sitzungsberichte der bayerischen Akademie der Wissenschaften; philosophisch-philologische und historische Klasse*, Munich
SC	*Sources Chrétiennes*, Paris
SEG	*Supplementum Epigraphicum Graecum*, Leyden, 1923–
SH	*Subsidia Hagiographica*, Brussels
SR	A. Mai, *Spicilegium Romanum*, Rome
SS	J. B. Pitra, *Spicilegium Sacrum*, 1–4, Paris, 1852–8
ST	*Studi e Testi*, Vatican
StD	K. Lake and S. Lake, *Studies and Documents*, London
SVC	A. Mai, *Scriptorum Veterum nova collectio*, Rome
Teub.	*Bibliotheca Scriptorum Graecorum et Romanorum Teubneriana*, Leipzig
TQ	*Theologische Quartalschrift*, Tübingen
TS	J. A. Robinson, *Texts and Studies*, Cambridge
TU	*Texte und Untersuchungen zur Geschichte der Altchristlichen Literatur*, Leipzig
ZKG	*Zeitschrift für Kirchengeschichte*, Gotha
ZKT	*Zeitschrift für Katholische Theologie*, Innsbruck
ZP	*Records of the historical–philological faculty of the University of St. Petersburg* (*Zapiski istoriko-philologicheskago faculteta St. Petersburgskago Universiteta*), St. Petersburg
ZWT	*Zeitschrift für Wissenschaftliche Theologie*, Leipzig

V. GENERAL ABBREVIATIONS

Note: this list contains:

1. Abbreviations used in the Lexicon.
2. Abbreviations used in List I without explanation, save for Biblical books, for which see List II.
3. Some single-letter abbreviations explained elsewhere but included here for convenience.

A.	*Acta*, see I
abs.	absolutely
acc.	accusative; according to
act.	active
adj.	adjective
adv.	adverb(ial)(ly)
agst.	against
al.	alibi (i.e. elsewhere in the same author)
anath.	*anathema*
Anon.	Anonymous
aor.	aorist
ap.	apud
apptly.	apparently
AQ	Aquilan version of OT
arg.	argumentum, hypothesis
ascet.	ascetical(ly)
ass.	associated (with)
astrol.	astrological(ly)
astron.	astronomical(ly)
bet.	between
BMV	Beata Maria Virgo
Byz.	Byzantine
C	Concilium, see I
c.	circa; contra; cum
can.	*canon*
cap., capp.	capitulum, -a
cat.	*catena*, see I
cent.	century
cf.	confer, compare
Christol.	Christological(ly)
cit., citt.	citatum, -a, cited
cj., conj.	conjecture
class.	classical
cod., codd.	codex, codices
cogn.	cognate
col.	column
comp.	comparative
conj., cj.	conjecture
constr.	construction
controv.	in controversy with
coss.	compounds
CP	Constantinople (-opolis, etc.)
dat.	dative
def.	defined, definition(s)
dep.	deponent
Dial.	Dialogus
dim.	diminutive
dist.	distinguish(ed)
distn.	distinction
Docet.	Docetist(s), Docetic
dub.	dubious
dub. l.	dubia lectio
dupl. acc.	double accusative
eccl.	ecclesiastical
ed.	edition, editor
Edict.	*Edictum*
e.g.	exempli gratia
El.	Elias
Eng.	English
ep., epp.	*epistula, epistulae*
epilog.	epilogus
epit.	epitome
eschatol.	eschatology, eschatological(ly)
esp.	especially
etc.	et cetera (i.e. in other authors)
etym.	etymology, etymological(ly)
eund.	eundem
euphem.	euphemism, -istically
exeg.	in exegesis (of)
f., ff.	following
fem.	feminine
fig.	figurative(ly)
fin.	sub finem
f.l.	falsa lectio
folld.	followed
foreg.	foregoing
fr.	fragment(s)
freq.	frequenter, frequently
fut.	future
gen.	general(ly); genitive
genit., gen.	genitive
Gnost.	Gnostic
Gr.	Greek
gram.	grammar, grammatical(ly)
H.	Hardouin, see III
H. Ghost	Holy Ghost
Hebr.	Hebrew
heret.	heretical(ly)
Hymn.	*Hymnus*
ib.	*ibidem*
id.	idem
i.e.	id est
imper.	imperative
imperf.	imperfect
impers.	impersonal
Inc.	Incarnation
incl.	including
ind., indic.	indicative
indecl.	indeclinable
indic., ind.	indicative
infin.	infinitive
init.	ad initium
Inscr.	*Inscriptio*
int. opp.	inter opera
intern.	internal
interprn.	interpretation(s)
interrog.	interrogative(ly)
intrans.	intransitive
iron.	ironical(ly)
irreg.	irregular(ly)
Jo. Bapt.	John the Baptist
l.	lege
Lat.	Latin, latine
l.c., ll.cc.	loco citato, locis citatis
lit.	literal(ly)
liturg.	liturgical(ly)
loc.	locum
LS	See VI
LUC	Lucianic version of OT
LXX	Septuagint
M.	Migne, see III
M.	*Martyrium, Martyr*, see I
Manich.	Manichean
masc.	masculine
math.	mathematical(ly)
med.	middle
medic.	medical(ly)
met.	metaphorical(ly)
meton.	metonymical(ly)
metr. gr.	metri gratia
monoph.	monophysite
MS, MSS	manuscript(s)
myst.	mystical(ly)
n., not.	note, footnote
nec.	necessary, necessarily
neg.	negative(ly)
neut.	neuter
no., nos.	number, numbers
nom.	nominative
not., n.	note, footnote
NT	New Testament
ob.	obiit
obj.	object(us)
om.	omits, omitted
op. cit.	opere citato
opp.	opposed to
opt.	optative
Orac.	*Oraculum*
orth.	orthodox
OT	Old Testament
P	*Papyrus*, see IV
p., pp.	page, pages
paratit.	paratitulus
partic.	particular(ly)
pass.	passive
perf.	perfect
perh.	perhaps
pers.	person
philos.	philosophical(ly), in philosophy
pluperf.	pluperfect
plur.	plural
poet.	poetical(ly)
poss.	possibly
prec.	*precatio*
prep.	preposition
pres.	present
prob.	probable, -ly
proem.	proemium, preface
Proem.	anonymous preface
pron.	pronoun
ptcpl.	participle
qu.	*quaestio*
q.v., qq.v.	quod vide, quae vide
ref.	with reference to, in respect of
reflex.	reflexive
rel.	relative, relation
rhet.	rhetorical(ly)
r°	recto
S., SS.	Sanctus, Saint(s)
s.	sub
saec.	saeculum
sc.	scilicet
Schol.	*Scholium*
sens.	sensus, sense
sg., sing.	singular
SM	Symmachan version of OT
sq., sqq.	sequens, sequentia
sts.	sometimes
subj.	subjunctive
subst.	substantive
superl.	superlative
suppl.	supplementum
s.v.	sub voce
s.v.l.	si vera lectio
Symb.	*Symbolum*
synon.	synonymous
synops.	synopsis

T.	*Testamentum*, see I
tab.	tabula
Tert.	Tertullian(us)
THDN	Theodotion's version of OT
theol.	theological(ly)
tit.	titulus
tr.	translated by, translation of
trans.	transitive
Trin.	Trinity, Trinitarian
t.t.	technical term
usu.	usually
v.	vide
v.	*vita*, see I
Valent.	Valentinian (Gnostic)
vb.	verb
v.l., vv.ll.	varia lectio, variae lectiones
v°	verso
vol.	volume
v.s.v., vv.	vide sub voce, vocibus
VT	Vetus Testamentum

VI. SIGNS, ETC.

LS	(see) H. G. Liddell and R. Scott, *A Greek–English Lexicon*, New Edition (9th) by H. Stuart Jones and R. McKenzie, Oxford, 1925–40
*	to denote words not in *LS*
[*]	to denote words in a different form in *LS*
§	to denote words which appear in *LS* but with a quite different meaning
‡	to denote spurious works
†	to denote works of doubtful authorship
=	equal *or* equivalent to, the same as
∽	approximately the same as
~	that part of the verb which preceded the hyphen at the head of the article
//	parallel with
ἀ. ἔ.	ἀνάθεμα ἔστω
κτλ.	καὶ τὰ λοιπά
[ ]	enclose (1) editorial deletions, (2) conjectures in inscriptions or papyri
⟨ ⟩	enclose (1) editorial insertions, (2) postulated forms

A

***ἀαρών** (*ἀρῶνα), (Hebr. אָרוֹן) *ark* χρήσιμοι [sc. Sap. and Ecclus.]...ἀλλ' εἰς ἀριθμὸν ῥητῶν οὐκ ἀναφέρονται. διὸ δὴ ἐν τῷ ἀαρὼν οὐκ ἀνετέθησαν, τοῦ τε [v.l. τουτέστιν] ἐν τῇ τῆς διαθήκης κιβωτῷ Epiph.*mens*.4(M.43.244C); ἀρῶνα *Dial.Tim.et Aquil*.77 r°.

***ἀβαδής**, *untrained to go, unbroken*, of a horse, Euthal.Diac.*Ac*. proem.(M.85.629A).

***ἀβαθμίδοτος**, *given without differences of rank*, of honour accorded equally to Persons of Trin. ἀ. δοξολογία Tim.Ant.*caec*.13 (M.28.1021B).

ἄβαθρος, *without foundation*, Geo.Pis.*hex*.131(M.92.1442A); *ib*. 563(1479A).

***ἀβάκτις**, **ὁ**, (Lat. *ab actis*) *registrar*, Nil.*epp*.2.207 tit.(M.79. 309B).

ἀβάκχευτος, *without wine*, Nonn.*par.Jo*.2:3(M.43.760C).

ἀβάλα, ἀβάλαι, ἀβάλε, ἆ βάλε, ἀβάλη, ἀββάλε, (cf. Hebr. אֲבָל, also Aram. חֲבַל); **1.** *oh! oh that!* ἆ βάλε πῶς τὸ πάροιθεν, ἄναξ, ἡγήσαο λαῶν †Apoll.*met.Ps*.67:8(M.33.1404D ἀββάλε); **2.** *woe! alas!* Ephr.2.15E; †Gregent.*disp*.(M.86.640D); ἀβάλα τῇ...ἐρήμῳ *V.Dan*. 2(p.51.15); ἀβάλε τῇ ἀνθρωπότητι Jo.Mosch.*prat*.19(M.87.2865D); *ib*. 78(2936A); ἀβάλαι, πόσα κλαύσομεν *ib*.110(2975B); Dam.*troph*.4.7 (p.275.6); ‡Jo.D.*fid.dorm*.33(M.95.277B); Thdr.Stud.*or*.11.27(M.99. 829C).

***ἀβάναυσος**, *liberal, generous, gentlemanly* ἔστω δὲ εὔσπλαγχνος, ἀ. [sc. ἐπίσκοπος] *Const.App*.2.3.3.

ἄβαξ, **ὁ**, part of amphitheatre (perh. *gangway steps*, leading to arena, or poss. *balustrade* surrounding it) ἡ δὲ Τρύφαινα ἐξέψυξεν ἑστῶσα παρὰ τὴν ἀρήναν ἐπὶ τοὺς ἄ. *A.Paul.et Thecl*.36(p.262.7); ἡ Τρύφαινα...λιποψυχήσασα...καταφέρεται τοῦ θεάτρου παρὰ τοὺς ἄ.· τόπος δὲ ἦν οὕτω καλούμενος, Ἄβακες Bas.Sel.*v.Thecl*.1(M.85.537D); *M.Eleuth*.11(p.160.11).

ἀβάπτιστος, **A.** *not submerged*, in comparison of Church with a ship ἀβάπτιστον τοῖς...τῆς κακοδοξίας κύμασι διαφύλασσε τὴν ὁλκάδα Bas.*ep*.161.2(3.252C; M.32.629C); fig. ἀ. καὶ παντὸς χειμῶνος ὑψηλοτέραν τὴν ψυχὴν διασώζων id.*hom*.5.4(2.37C; M.31.248A); ἀ. τὸ τῆς ἐκκλησίας διασώσαντα σκάφος Thdt.*h.e*.5.4.2(3.1019).

B. *unbaptized*; **1.** of unbaptized persons in gen., Ath.*ep.encycl*. 5(p.175.2; M.25.233C); Oecum.*Apoc*.3:16(p.65); *Didasc.Jac*.3.1 (p.52.6); ‡Jo.Jej.*can*.(p.443); Thphn.*chron*.p.14(M.108.92A); **2.** unbaptized to abstain from eucharistic worship, Cyr.*ador*.11(1.398C); to leave church after reading of Gospel and prayers which follow it, ‡Germ.CP *contempl*.(M.98.417B); **3.** unbaptized cannot enter kingdom of heaven (cf. Jo.3:5) εἰ μὴ ὅτι νόμος ἦν, μηδὲ δίκαιον ἀ. εἰς τὴν βασιλείαν τοῦ θεοῦ εἰσελθεῖν, τάχα που τῶν ἐθνῶν οἱ πεπλανημένοι διὰ σωφροσύνην μόνον σωθῆναι ἐδύναντο. διὰ τοῦτο λίαν ἀθυμῶ περὶ τῶν ἐν πλάνῃ σωφρονούντων, ὅτι ἄνευ ἐλπίδος ἀγαθῆς σωφρονεῖν ἑλόμενοι πρὸς τὸ βαπτισθῆναι ὀκνηρῶς ἔχουσιν *Hom.Clem*.13.21; εὔδηλον ὅτι οὐδεὶς ἀ. εἰς αὐτὴν εἰσελεύσεται ‡Ath.*qu.Ant*.101(M.28. 660C); *ib*.115(672A); **4.** question of future state of the unbaptized; **a.** unbaptized regarded as condemned to punishment μὴ...νομίσῃς ὅτι ἐὰν πάντων τῶν ποτε γενομένων εὐσεβῶν εὐσεβέστερος γένῃ, ἀ. δὲ ᾖς, ἐλπίδος τυχεῖν δυνήσῃ ποτέ. ταύτῃ γὰρ μᾶλλον πλείονα ὑφέξεις κόλασιν, ὅτι καλὰ ἔργα οὐκ ἐποίησας καλῶς *Hom.Clem*.11.25; *ib*. 13.21; **b.** unbaptized children not to be punished εἰς τὴν βασιλείαν εἰσέρχονται τὰ τῶν πιστῶν βεβαπτισμένα νήπια· τὰ δὲ ἀ. ... οὔτε εἰς βασιλείαν εἰσέρχονται· ἀλλ' οὔτε πάλιν εἰς κόλασιν· ἁμαρτίαν γὰρ οὐκ ἔπραξαν ‡Ath.*qu.Ant*.115(M.28.672A); ποῦ λέγομεν ἀπέρχεσθαι τὰ παιδία τὰ ἄκακα πενταετῆ, ἢ τετραετῆ, Ἰουδαίων καὶ ἀ.; ... ἐμοὶ δοκεῖ, οὐκ εἰσέρχεσθαι αὐτὰ εἰς γέενναν Anast.S.*qu.et resp*.81(M.89.709C); **5.** such a child to be baptized in emergency, if necessary by deacon, Eus.Al.*serm*.5(M.86.349A); responsibility for letting child die unbaptized rests with priest or parents, *ib*.; **6.** sexual union with unbaptized person is grave sin, †Jo.Jej.*poenit*.(M.88.1921D); **7.** those baptized in schism are equated with ἐθνικοὶ καὶ ἀ., ‡Jo. Nic.*fr*.ap.Tim.CP *haer*.(M.86.73A).

ἀβαρής, **1.** *without weight*; hence *not burdensome, inoffensive* ἑαυτὸν ἀ. φυλάττει Ath.*v.Anton*.50(M.26.916C); Bas.*Spir*.63(3.53D; M.32.185A); Pall.*v.Chrys*.17(p.107.12; M.47.60); **2.** *not weighed down*, of prayer that can rise to spiritual heights πενίαν καὶ θλῖψιν, τὰς ὕλας τῆς ἀβαροῦς προσευχῆς Evagr.Pont.*or*.131(M.79.1196A).

ἀβασάνιστος, **1.** *untried, unexamined*, of the characters of Jacob and Esau at the time of their respective election and rejection ῥοπῆς θελημάτων ἀβασανίστου τυχεῖν Cyr.*Rom*.9:14(p.227.1; M.74.833D); of texts of scripture not properly examined, Or.*Jo*.1.38(42; p.49. 23; M.14.100B); *ib*.32.22(14; p.466.2; 805C); Gr.Nyss.*tres dii*(M.45. 132C); of teaching not properly investigated, Or.*Jo*.6.6(3; p.113. 18; 209A); of virtue untried by temptation, Gr.Naz.*ep*.65(M.37. 128C); **2.** *untormented, uninjured*, Meth.*symp*.10.6(p.129.3; M.18. 204B); ἀ. ἡμῶν ὁ νοῦς διαμένει ἐν τοῖς τῆς θεολογίας κινήμασιν *Schol*. in Jo.Clim.*scal*.30(M.88.1164A).

ἀβασίλευτος, **A.** *not ruled by a king*; **1.** in gen., Eus.*d.e*.7.1 (p.306.14; M.22.501A); Bas.*Spir*.51(3.43D; M.32.161C); **2.** of the initiated in Naassene system τὸ μέλι καὶ τὸ γάλα, οὗ γευσαμένους τοὺς τελείους ἀ. γενέσθαι καὶ μετασχεῖν τοῦ πληρώματος Hipp.*haer*.5.8(p.94. 27; M.16.3147C); cf. μία...ἡ μακαρία φύσις τοῦ μακαρίου ἀνθρώπου τοῦ ἄνω...μία δὲ ἡ θνητὴ κάτω· μία δὲ ἡ ἀ. γενεὰ ἡ ἄνω γενομένη *ib*. (p.89.12; 3139B); **3.** of God ὁ θεὸς...ὁ μόνος ἀ. *Lit*.ap.*Const.App*.8.5.1.

B. *undisciplined, anarchical*, of an interpreter of scripture, with punning allusion to his teaching that Christ's βασιλεία will have an end ὡς τολμηρὸς ἐξηγητὴς σὺ καὶ λίαν ἀ. Gr.Naz.*or*.30.4(p.112. 17; M.36.108A).

ἀβάστακτος, *insupportable, intolerable* πικρίαν ἀ. *T.Abr*.A 17 (p.99.29); ἀ. ἀνάγκη Gr.Nyss.*ep.can*.(M.45.228A); Mac.Aeg.*hom*. 27.6(M.34.697A); of the glory of God, Didym.*Trin*.1.9(M.39.281A); ἡ κτίσις οὐχ ὁρᾷ τὸν θεὸν...οὕτως ὡς ἔστιν· ἑτέρᾳ γὰρ φύσει τοῦτο...ἀ. ὑπάρχει *ib*.2.16(544A).

ἄβατος, **A.** *untrodden*, Dion.Al.ap.Eus.*h.e*.7.21.4(M.20.684B); ‡Nil.*perist*.11(M.79.916B); of desert places as abode of demons, *T.Sal*.17.2.

B. *inaccessible*; **1.** of divine properties as inaccessible to created order ἄ. παντελῶς τὰ τῆς θεότητος ἴδια τῇ πεποιημένῃ κτίσει Cyr. *Jo*.3.5(4.305B); *ib*.9.1(802C); id.*thes*.13(5^1.126B); id.*fr*.ap.CLater. *act*.5(H.3.861A); but possessed by Christ as divine διὰ τοῦτο καὶ ἄ. ἔχει τὸ θεοπρεπὲς ἀξίωμα, καὶ τοῦτο οὐ μερικῶς, ἀλλ' ὁλοκλήρως id.*thes*.32(315A); **2.** of the divine light, Synes.*hymn*.3.134(p.10; M.66.1595); **3.** of knowledge of God as unattainable by the senses ἄβατον δὲ ἀκοαῖς καὶ τοῖς ὁμογενέσιν ἡ νόησις τοῦ θεοῦ Clem.*str*.5.6 (p.348.8; M.9.57B); or, since God is superessential, by anything which is πᾶσιν ἄ. ... τοῖς οὖσιν, ὡς πάντων ὑπερουσίως ἐξῃρημένη Dion.Ar.*d.n*.1.2(M.3.588C); οὐδὲ ὄνομα αὐτῆς ἐστιν, οὐδὲ λόγος, ἀλλ' ἐν ἀβάτοις ἐξῄρηται *ib*.13.3(981A); **4.** of truth which, being inaccessible to the profane, may be expressed only in symbols, id.*ep*.9.1 (M.3.1104B); **5.** esp. of persons or things as inaccessible to, hence free from, evil: of divine nature ἡ δέ γε θεία...φύσις...ἄ. ἀεὶ πονηρίας ἐστίν Cyr.*Is*.1.4(2.123A); ὁ υἱὸς ἁπάσης τε φθορᾶς ἀμείνων ὑπάρχων καὶ ῥοπῆς· μᾶλλον καὶ ἄ. ἔχων παντελῶς τοῖς τοιούτοις τὴν φύσιν id.*hom.pasch*.10(5^2.128B); of BMV, with pun on βάτος q.v.; χαῖρε, βάτε,...ἡ κατὰ στέρησιν ἄ. τῇ ἁμαρτίᾳ Jo.D.*hom*.2.7(M.96.689B); of resurrection body, inaccessible to passions, Isid.Pel.*epp*.2.43(M.78. 485C); of heaven, inaccessible to evil, Chrys.*hom.59.4 in Jo*.(8.350D); of Christian life inaccessible to sorrows, Synes.*hymn*.8.8(p.50; M.66.1612); of Christians who are to keep themselves ἄ. βλαπτούσαις συνουσίαις Isid.Pel.*epp*.3.287(961C); partic. of priests, inaccessible to evil passion, *ib*.5.472(1601A); πενίαν δ' ἄμοχθος οἴσει σοφίᾳ ...πικραῖς ἄβατος βίου μερίμναις Synes.*hymn*.1.39(p.59; M.66.1589 ἄβατον); *ib*.8.41(p.51; 1613); **6.** of heaven as inaccessible to men before Christ's Ascension, Cyr.*glaph.Lev*.(1.375D); to sinners hereafter, Gr.Nyss.*anim.et res*.(M.46.84B); Chrys.*stat*.1.5(2.7E); **7.** of way to Christ, inaccessible to sinners, typified by Jews' inability to follow Christ across sea of Galilee, Cyr.*Jo*.3.4(4.272A); **8.** of episcopal office, inaccessible to excommunicated offender, Isid. Pel.*epp*.2.127(M.78.572C); **9.** of one inaccessible to good influences, *ib*.3.80(785D).

C. τὰ ἄ. *privy*; scene of death of Arius, Epiph.*haer*.69.10(p.160. 21; M.42.217C).

ἀβαφής, *undipped*, ref. sop given to Judas οὐκ ἄρτος ἦν τὸ ψωμίον, καὶ οὐ ψωμίον ἀ., ἀλλὰ βεβαμμένον τῷ δυναμένῳ ἀποσπάσαι τῆς ψυχῆς αὐτοῦ τὴν ἀπὸ τοῦ λόγου...ἐγγινομένην βαφήν Or.*Jo*.32.22 (14; p.465.11; M.14.804D).

***ἀββαδικός**, *of* or *belonging to a monk* δύο στολὰς αὐτοῦ, τὴν δὲ ἀ. καὶ τὴν ἱερατικήν Anast.*liturg*.(p.278).

***ἀββαδόπουλος**, ὁ, *son of an abbot*, Leont.N.*v.Jo.Eleem*.43 (p.88.2).

***ἀββᾶς** (ἀββᾶ), ὁ, *father, abbot*; **1.** title of respect accorded to monks in gen., Ephr.1.320D; Leont.N.*v.Sym*.31(M.93.1709A); *ib*.32(1709C); Niceph.Ur.*v.Sym*.145(M.86.3121B); esp. to prominent ascetics and monks, and abbots of monasteries μοναχῶν πατέρα, ἀ. Πάμμων Ath.*narr.fug*.(M.26.980D); ὁ ἀ. Μακάριος *Apophth.Patr.* (M.65.257C); Pall.*h.Laus*.22(p.72.1; M.34.1081D); Cyr.S.*v.Sab*.9 (p.92.24); Jo.D.*trisag*.26(M.95.57A); hence **2.** ὁ ἀββᾶς, the *abbot*, as official designation λαλοῦντος τοῦ ἀ. λόγον τοῖς ἀδελφοῖς Evagr. Pont.*or*.108(M.79.1192A); Dor.*doct*.1.15(M.88.1637A); ‡Jo.D.*ep. Thphl*.13(M.95.361C); **3.** title of respect given to priests and bishops as spiritual fathers τοῦ ὁσιωτάτου ἀ. Θεοδώρου ἐπισκόπου *CIG* 8646.8(Egypt,577); cf. ὁ...ἀ. Στέφανος, ὁ κατὰ Ἀντιόχειαν πρεσβύτερος Cosm.Ind.*top*.6(M.88.321B); plur. ἀββάδες, Leont.N. *v.Sym*.48(M.93.1728D).

***ἀβδηρολόγος**, *speaking like an Abderite, talking foolishly* (cf. *LS* s.v. Ἀβδηρίτης) κατὰ τὸν κοινὸν λόγον ἀ. ἐστὶν ὁ ἀπὸ τῶν Ἀβδήρων ἄνθρωπος [sc. Democritus] Tat.*orat*.17(p.18.14; M.6.841B).

ἀβέβαιος, **1.** *unstable*, neut. as subst. τὸ μὲν ἀ. τῆς διανοίας γεννητικόν ἐστι διαφωνίας Clem.*str*.8.7(p.93.28; M.9.588B); τὸ ἀ. τῆς...περιουσίας Bas.*hom.in Ps*.33(1.149E; M.29.365D); **2.** *uncertain* τροπολογία δέ, ἀ. ἀπόδειξις Jo.D.*disp*.1.2(M.94.1588B); **3.** *invalid*, of sentence of death annulled by Cross, Bas.Sel.*or*.4.1(M.85.65B); **4.** of persons, *fickle*, Isid.Pel.*epp*.1.276(M.78.345B).

ἀβέβηλος, *not profane, sacred, pure*; **1.** in gen., of truths not revealed to common people, Synes.*ep*.154(M.66.1556C); id.*calv*.6 (p.202.9; M.66.1177D); **2.** in Christian sense, of God ὁ πάναγνος καὶ ἀ. Cyr.*Juln*.2(6^2.45B); of Christ as a sacrifice ἀ. ἱερεῖον *ib*.9(304E); of Christian way of life, *ib*.4(126C); id.*Ps*.35:1(M.69.913B); id.*Lc*. 9:1(M.72.640B); Ant.Mon.*hom*.34(M.89.1541D); of man's original mode of life, to which redeemed will return after death, Cyr.*Juln*. 8(280E); of the saints, id.*Zach*.66(3.745C); of the character of the righteous, id.*Soph*.5(3.583E); of pure worship, id.*Juln*.1(18E).

[*]ἀβελτηρία, ἡ, *depravity*; of man after Fall, ‡Chrys.*pasch*.7 (8.278C).

***ἀβῆνα** (ἀβῖνα), ἡ, (Lat. *habena*) *thong* ἀβίνας Leont.N.*v.Sym*. 38(M.93.1717A); Thphn.*chron*.p.306 (ἀβίνων M.108.745B).

ἀβίαστος, **A.** *unforced, unconstrained*; **1.** of God's will and purpose in creation, Bas.*Spir*.19(3.16E; M.32.101C); **2.** of Christ's freedom in relation to Passion ῥιγεδανὴν ἀ. ἑκούσιος ἤλυθον ὥρην Nonn.*par.Jo*.12:27(M.43.856A); **3.** of man's free will ἄνθρωπος δὲ... προαιρέσει κεκόσμηται...ἀ. δεικνὺς τῶν πρακτέων τὴν αἵρεσιν Bas. Sel.*or*.3.2(M.85.52A); οὐδεὶς γὰρ θέλει εἰς θεὸν ἁμαρτῆσαι, εἰ καὶ ἀ. πᾶς ἡμῶν τυγχάνει Jo.Clim.*scal*.10(M.88.845D); **4.** of virginity, †Bas.Anc. *virg*.51(M.30.772B); **5.** of freedom of movement, in respect of natural objects, Bas.*hex*.1.11(1.11B; M.29.25C); **6.** of unforced exegesis τῶν μύθων ἑρμηνείας ἀ. αὐτοῖς περιέχει τὴν ἐξήγησιν Eus.*p.e*. 4.1(131B; M.21.232A); Bas.*ep*.236.2(3.362C; M.32.880B).

B. *not to be overcome*; **1.** in gen., of passions, Isid.Pel.*epp*.3.148 (M.78.841A); *ib*.154(845B); **2.** of the purpose of God τὸ γὰρ παρὰ θεοῦ ὡρισμένον, ἀ. ‡Just.*qu.et resp*.33(M.6.1280C).

ἀβιάστως, *without constraint*; **1.** ref. interprn. of scriptures or exegesis made without violence to sense, Eus.*e.th*.3.3(p.151.20; M.24.992C); *Symb.Ant*.(345)10(p.254.11; M.26.736A); Isid.Pel.*epp*. 2.68(M.78.508A); *ib*.2.195(641C); Pyrr.ap.Max.*Pyrr*.(M.91.345C); **2.** ref. the action of Christ's divine nature upon his humanity, Apoll.*fr*.76(p.222.24)ap.Gr.Nyss.*Apoll*.40(M.45.1213C) cit. s. νοῦς; *ib*.79(p.223.29)ap.eund.41(1217C).

***ἀβῖνα**, ἡ, v. ἀβῆνα.

***ἀβλάκευτος**, *active*, ‡Hipp.Th.*fr*.17(p.50.11).

***ἀβλασφήμητος**, *free from slander* or *reproach*, Bas.*reg.fus*.15.4 (2.357C; M.31.956C); of Church's reputation preserved by excommunication of offenders, *Const.App*.2.43.4; of Christ, Gr.Nyss. *mart*.3(M.46.776A); neut. as subst., Socr.*h.e*.5.19.9(M.67.617A).

[*]ἀβλεπέω, *be without sight, not see*, Iren.*fr*.14(p.486; M.7. 1237D).

ἀβλεπτ-έω, *not see*; *overlook, disregard*, Eus.*h.e*.10.8.8(M.20. 896D); Cyr.*Ps*.93:7(M.69.1233A); ∼οῦντας πρὸς τὴν ἀλήθειαν Isid. Pel.*epp*.1.145(M.78.280B).

ἄβλεπτος, **1.** *unseen*; of resurrection life, Gr.Nyss.*anim.et res.* (M.46.88B); **2.** *blind, sightless*, Sophr.H.*mir.Cyr.et Jo*.69(M.87. 3660D); **3.** *undistinguished* τοῖς ἀ. βιωτικοῖς ἀστερόμουσος οὐρανὸς κατοπτεύεται Cosm.Mel.*schol*.(M.38.531) in Gr.Naz.*carm*.2.1.44.36.

ἀβλεψία, ἡ, *blindness, want of sight*; **1.** lit., Bas.*reg.fus*.proem. 4(2.331B; M.31.897D); Mac.Mgn.*apocr*.4.18(p.197.22); **2.** met.; **a.** spiritual, *M.Apollon*.34(p.33.27); Cyr.H.*catech*.4.1; esp. ref. Jews' failure to recognize Christ, Eust.*engast*.19(p.46.11; M.18. 652D); *Const.App*.5.16.2; **b.** of faculty by which God is myst. perceived: God, being in γνόφος, must be apprehended by ἀ., opp. natural vision ἡμεῖς γενέσθαι τὸν ὑπέρφωτον εὐχόμεθα γνόφον, καὶ δι' ἀβλεψίας καὶ ἀγνωσίας ἰδεῖν...τὸ ὑπὲρ θέαν...αὐτὸ τὸ μὴ ἰδεῖν Dion.Ar.*myst*.2(M.3.1025A); Max.*schol.myst*.2(M.4.421D); cf. Gnost. formula βασιλέα μονότροπον, δεσμὸν ἀβλεψίας, λήθην ἀπερίσκεπτον ἀσπάζομαι Or.*Cels*.6.31(p.101.1; M.11.1341B).

ἀβλής, *not hit* ἀ. σκοπός Gr.Naz.*carm*.1.2.9.123(M.37.677A).

ἀβοηθησία, ἡ, *helplessness*, Olymp.*fr.Lam*.4:3(M.93.752B).

ἀβόητος, *not noised abroad, kept silent*, Nonn.*par.Jo*.12:42 (M.43.857B).

***ἀβόλιστος**, *incapable of sinking* ἡ τῶν σωμάτων [edd. ὑδάτων] φύσις...ἄδυτος καὶ ἀ. ἐν τοῖς ὕδασι τῆς Μαρμαρικῆς Πενταπόλεως ‡Ath.*qu.Ant*.136(M.28.684A) where if ὑδάτων be read ἀ. will mean *incapable of being sounded*.

***ἀβολιτίων**, ἡ, (Lat. *abolitio*) *withdrawal of charge*, Pall.*v.Chrys*. 14(p.85.22; ἀβουλητίονα M.47.48).

***ἀβότανος**, *without grass*, ‡Chrys.*salt.Herodiad*.1(8.40B).

ἀβούλευτος, **1.** *ill-advised*, *Orac.Sib*.12.220; **2.** *without counsel*, denied of God prior to activity of Logos in Creation οὔτε γὰρ ἄλογος, οὔτε ἄσοφος οὔτε ἀδύνατος, οὔτε ἀ. ἦν Hipp.*Noët*.10(p.251.18; M.10.817A).

[*]ἀβουλησία, ἡ, *absence of volition*; **1.** in gen., Cyr.*dial.Trin*.2 (5^1.456A); ἐπὶ δὲ τῶν ἔξωθεν καὶ ὧν ἐσμεν ἐν ἐξουσίᾳ, βούλησις καὶ ἀ. κρατεῖ id.*thes*.7(5^1.58B); **2.** of God, ref. generation of Son θεὸς ἐργάζεται μὲν βουλήσει τὰ ἐκτός, ἐγέννησε δὲ ἀχρόνως τὸν υἱόν... οὐδένα τόπον ἐχούσης ἐν τούτῳ βουλήσεως καὶ ἀ. *ib*.(58C).

***ἀβουλητίων**, ἡ, v. ἀβολιτίων.

ἀβούλητος, **I.** *involuntary*;

A. in gen., of misfortunes τύχαις ἀ. περιπίπτοντα Clem.*str*.2.21 (p.182.22; M.8.1073A); *ib*.7.3(p.11.26; M.9.420B); οὐδὲν πείσεσθε λυπηρὸν οὐδὲ τῶν ἀ. Chrys.*hom.14.2 in Phil*.(11.307B); of automatic movements of the body, ‡Just.*qu.et resp*.19(M.6.1265A); of sinful actions performed involuntarily while dreaming, *ib*.21(1268A); of the cause of evil as residing in ignorance and matter, and hence outside the scope of volition, Clem.*str*.7.3(p.12.7; 420C); τὸ ἀ. dist. from τὸ ἄβουλον· τὸ μὲν γάρ [sc. τὸ ἄβουλον] ἐστιν ἄσκεπτος πρᾶξις, τὸ δὲ κατηναγκασμένον πάθος Isid.Pel.*epp*.5.203(M.78.1456A).

B. ref. will of God; **1.** that all men have not received grace does not argue God's lack of will or power, Gr.Nyss.*or.catech*.30(p.111.4; M.45.76D); **2.** ref. generation of Son; **a.** in Arian and 'Semi-Arian' doctrine, *Symb.Ant*.(345)8(p.253.23; M.26.732D) cit. s. ἀνάγκη; πῶς ...οὐκ ἀνάγκη συνομολογεῖν ὅτιπερ...ἐστι...ὁ υἱὸς...ἀ. εἰ μὴ ἐκ βουλήσεως...γέγονεν; Cyr.*thes*.7(5^1.56D); id.*dial.Trin*.2(5^1.454A); **b.** in orthodox teaching, denial of Son's generation βουλήσει does not imply that he is ἀ., Ath.*Ar*.3.66(M.26.464A).

C. ref. will of Christ; Passion was ἀ. in relation to his human will ὁρᾷς ὅπως ἀ. τῷ Χριστῷ διά τε τὴν σάρκα...ὁ θάνατος ἦν· θελητὸς δ' οὖν ὅμως Cyr.*Jo*.4.1(4.332C); *ib*.(333E); ἵνα τὸ παθεῖν ἀ. ἀποφήνῃ...ἐν σχήματι προσευχῆς ἐποιεῖτο λέγων, 'πάτερ, εἰ δυνατὸν κτλ.' id.*Chr.un*.(5^1.772D); but its purpose was not ἀ., *ib*.(772A); εἰ τὸ πάθος ἀκούσιον, ἀ. ἡ ἀνάστασις Bas.Sel.*or*.32.2(M.85.353B).

II. *unconsidered, ill-considered* οὐ...πιστεύετε, ἀλλὰ τῷ ἀ. ἑαυτῶν σκοπῷ ἀκολουθεῖτε *Pers*.(M.10.105A; ἀβούλῳ p.16.7); ἀ. ... φωνάς Cyr.*ep*.4(p.26.2; 5^2.22B).

ἀβουλήτως, *involuntarily*;

A. in gen. τοῖς ἀ. συμβαίνουσι Clem.*str*.5.5(p.346.1; M.9.53B); εἰ... ἀ. προήχθης πρὸς τὴν τῆς ἐκκλησίας προστασίαν Isid.Pel.*epp*.1.315 (M.78.364D).

B. ref. God's actions; **1.** ref. Creation οὐκ ἂν δὲ τὴν ἀρχὴν ὑπέστη τι τῶν ὄντων ἀ. ἔχοντος τοῦ θεοῦ Clem.*str*.6.17(p.512.15; M.9.388B); **2.** ref. generation of Son; **a.** in Arian teaching, denial that Son's generation is κατὰ βούλησιν must imply that Father is subject to constraint εἰ μὲν οὖν ἀ. ἐγέννησεν αὐτόν, πέπονθέ τι τῶν παρὰ γνώμην Cyr.*thes*.7(5^1.50C); id.*dial.Trin*.2(5^1.454B); **b.** orthodox answer applies the same reasoning *per absurdum* to God's goodness ὡς...τὸ εἶναι ἀγαθὸς οὐκ ἐκ βουλήσεως μὲν ἤρξατο, οὐ μὴν ἀ. ... ἐστὶν ἀγαθός· ...οὕτω καὶ τὸ εἶναι τὸν υἱόν, εἰ καὶ μὴ ἐκ βουλήσεως ἤρξατο, ἀλλ' οὐκ ἀθέλητον Ath.*Ar*.3.66(M.26.461C); Cyr.*thes*.7(5^1.53A); and denies the Arian dilemma οὐδεὶς [sc. τῶν ἁγίων] εὑρίσκεται λέγων ἀ. ἢ κατὰ βούλησιν γεγεννῆσθαι τὸν υἱόν *ib*.(51A); θελητῶς οὖν ἄρα καὶ ἀ. ὑπάρχει καὶ ὁ λόγος ἐν τῷ πατρί *ib*.(53B).

C. ref. Christ's actions; **1.** ref. beginning of his miracles εὐαφόρμως ἔρχεται λοιπὸν ἐπὶ τὴν τῶν σημείων ἀρχήν, εἰ καὶ ἀ. ἐδόκει καλεῖσθαι πρὸς αὐτήν Cyr.*Jo*.2.1(4.134E); **2.** his Passion was not willed by his human will, hence ἀ. σώζει τὴν κτίσιν ὑπὲρ ἧς, ἵνα σώσῃ, τὸ πάθος ὑπέμεινε Bas.Sel.*or*.32.2(M.85.353C); **3.** in reply to Nestorian assertion that the ἕνωσις φυσική implies involuntary kenosis κεκένωκεν ἑαυτὸν οὐκ ἀ. [sc. ὁ μονογενής] Cyr.*apol.Thdt*.3 (p.119.22; 6¹.213C).

***Ἀβραμιαῖος, 1.** *of* or *descended from Abraham*, ‡Ath.*sabb*.6 (M.28.141C); γένους...Ἀ. σωτήρ Nest.*hom.in Heb*.3:1(p.239.14; M.64. 488C); Olymp.*Job* 6:10(M.93.92A); of the 'daughter of Abraham' (Lc.13:16), Ath.*Ar*.3.40(M.26.408C); of 'Abraham's bosom' τοὺς Ἀ. κόλπους Eustrat.*v.Eutych*.102(M.86.2389A); **2.** *like* or *worthy of Abraham*, of Hosius ὁ Ἀ. γέρων Ath.*h.Ar*.45(p.209.5; M.25.748C); τὸ δὲ διὰ πειρασμῶν...ὑπομένειν ὀλίγων σφόδρα καὶ Ἀ. ἀνθρώπων ‡Bas.*const*.34.2(2.582A; M.31.1428B); ‡Chrys.*Petr.et El*.3(2.736C); ἀληθῶς Ἀ. τὸ καύχημα ‡Chrys.*concept.Jo.Bapt*.(2.794D); διδασκάλου Πατρικίου, ὃς τάξιν Ἀ. πληρῶν, ἐκ Χαλδαίων παραγεγονώς Cosm.Ind. *top*.2(M.88.73A).

***Ἄβραμος,** = foreg., of 'Abraham's bosom' as abode of departed Ἀ. κόλποις ἀναπαύε[τ]ε *MAMA* 1 p.xxvi(Phrygia).

***Ἀβράξας (Ἀβρασάξ, Ἀβρασάξ, Ἀβρασάκξ), ὁ,** *Abraxas*; name given by Basilideans to ἄρχων of the 365 heavens, explained numerically, cf. *trecentorum autem sexaginta quinque coelorum locales positiones distribuunt similiter ut Mathematici...esse autem principem illorum* ἀβράξας *et propter hoc ccclxv numeros habere in se*, Iren.*haer*.1.24.7(M.7.680A); τὸν μέγαν ἄρχοντα αὐτῶν εἶναι τὸν Ἀβρασὰξ διὰ τὸ περιέχειν τὸ ὄνομα αὐτοῦ ψῆφον τξέ, ὡς δὴ τοῦ ὀνόματος τὴν ψῆφον περιέχειν πάντα, καὶ διὰ τοῦτο τὸν ἐνιαυτὸν τοσαύταις ἡμέραις συνεστάναι Hipp.*haer*.7.26(p.205.4; M.16.3315C); Epiph.*haer*.24.7(p.264.1; M.41.316B); Thdt.*haer*.4.1(4.293); held to be creator and first cause, Epiph.*haer*.24.8(p.264.26; 317A); invoked in prayer χαῖραι Ἀβρασάκξ *POxy*.1566; cf. explanation, *sanctum nomen commendabat, quod est* ἀβρασάξ *cujus nominis literae...eundem numerum complent. sunt enim septem, α et β et ρ et α et σ et α et ξ, id est unum et duo et centum et unum et ducenta et unum et sexaginta*, Aug.*haer*.4(M.*PL*.42.26); hence perh. word = ἅγιον ὄνομα (an ineffable name) which has same numerical value.

***ἀβροδιαιτέω,** *live luxuriously*, Thdr.Stud.*epp*.1.11(M.99.945A).

ἀβρομία, ἡ, ?*absence of smell*, of future state of redeemed ἀφθαρσίας καὶ...ἀθανασίας καὶ ἀ. Anast.S.*hod*.14(M.89.253D), but prob. error for ἀβρωσίας.

ἄβρομος, *without smell*, Cosm.Ind.*top*.11(M.88.445B).

***ἀβροσαρκία, ἡ,** *physical softness*, Geo.Pis.*carm*.1.100.

[*]ἀβρότονος, ἡ, *aromatic plant*, prob. *southernwood* (*artemisia abrotonum*); with scent disliked by serpents, Epiph.*haer*.51.1 (p.249.2; M.41.889A).

ἀβρωσία, ἡ, *state of not needing food*, v. ἀβρομία.

***ἀβυσσικός,** *of the abyss*, in Peratic formula ἐγώ...ἡ δύναμις τοῦ ἀ. θολοῦ Hipp.*haer*.5.14(p.108.16; M.16.3167A).

ἄβυσσος, ἡ, *abyss, deep, depth*;

A. of the primeval deep (Gen.1:2) ἀ. δὲ πλῆθος ὑδάτων, δυσέφικτον ἔχον τὸ πέρας ἐπὶ τὰ κάτω Proc.G.*Gen*.1:2(M.87.45A); ἄπειρος γὰρ ἦν τῶν ὑδάτων ἡ χύσις, ὡς τὴν τῶν ἄλλων στοιχείων ἀναλογίαν ἐκβαίνειν· ὅθεν καὶ ἀ. εἴρηται *ib*.1:6(72B); from which world was marked out at Creation, Cyr.*Is*.4.3(2.618C); subject to God's power, *T.Lev*.4.9; *1Clem*.20.5; *Diogn*.7.2; Mel.*pass*.82 p.13. 31; *A.Jo*.23(p.163.26); cf. ὁ καθήμενος ἐπὶ θρόνου...καὶ ἐπιβλέπων ἀβύσσους *Lit.Bas*.(p.402.15); created by God, Gr.Nyss.*hex*.21(M.44. 84A); *Lit*.ap.*Const.App*.8.12.13; as one of four elements οὐρανοῦ καὶ γῆς καὶ ἀ. καὶ ὕδατος Eus.*e.th*.3.2(p.143.31; M.24.980B); hence not to be interpreted dualistically as representing evil powers opp. God, Bas.*hex*.2.4(1.16A; M.29.37B); Gr.Nyss.*hex*.21(M.44.81D); εἰ δὲ καλὰ ὅσα ἐποίησεν ὁ θεός, ἡ δὲ ἀ. καὶ τὰ περὶ αὐτὴν οὐκ ἔξω τῶν παρὰ τοῦ θεοῦ γεγονότων ἐστίν· ἄρα καλὰ καὶ ταῦτα τῷ ἰδίῳ λόγῳ, κἂν ἀ. ᾖ *ib*.(84A); ἐτόλμησαν δέ τινες εἰπεῖν ὅτι σκότος ὁ διάβολός ἐστιν, ἀ. οἱ δαίμονες Proc.G.*Gen*.1:2(45B); cf. μετὰ τὸν οὐρανόν, καὶ τὴν γῆν, καὶ τὴν ἀ., καὶ τὸ νοητὸν σκότος τὸν διάβολον, ὁ θεὸς λόγος Diod.*Gen*.1:2(M.33.1563B); allegorized as undifferentiated matter ἀ. γὰρ τὸ ἀπεράτωτον κατὰ τὴν ἰδίαν ὑπόστασιν, περαιούμενον δὲ τῇ δυνάμει τοῦ θεοῦ. αἱ τοίνυν οὐσίαι ὑλικαὶ ἀφ' ὧν τὰ ἐπὶ μέρους γένη καὶ τὰ τούτων εἴδη γίνεται, ἄβυσσοι εἴρηνται· ἐπεὶ μόνον τὸ ὕδωρ οὐκ ἂν εἶπεν ἀ. καίτοι καὶ ὕδωρ ἀ. ἡ ὕλη ἀλληγορεῖται Clem.*ecl*.2(p.137.17; M.9.700B); conceived as located in underworld, *Apoc.En*.17.7,8; *ib*.21.7.

B. hence as equivalent to hell or Hades; **1.** as abode of devils, *A.Phil*.111(p.43.20); ἐγώ εἰμι ὁ τὴν ἀ. τοῦ ταρτάρου οἰκῶν καὶ κατέχων *A.Thom*.A 32(p.149.18); cf. *quae est abyssus illa, nimirum, in qua erit diabolus et angeli ejus*, Or.*hom.1.1 in Gen*.(p.2.3; M.12. 146C); cf. *aqua, quae subtus est, id est aqua abyssi, in qua...princeps hujus mundi et adversarius draco et angeli ejus habitant*, *ib.1.2* (p.4.2; 148A); cf.id.*hom.8.7 in Jos*.(p.343.6; M.12.869A); ἀ. δὲ πολλαχῇ τῆς γραφῆς τὸ τῶν δαιμόνων ἐνδιαίτημα μεμαθήκαμεν Gr.Nyss.*Pss. titt*.A 8(M.44.476A); allegorized, cf. *aquis abyssi, qui sunt daemonum sensus*, Or.*hom.1.2 in Gen*.(p.5.18; 149A); **2.** as pit into which devils are cast by divine power (cf. Lc. 8:31), *A.Andr*.A 12(p.53.9); ὦ Βελία,...Χριστὸς ταπεινώσει σε εἰς τὴν ἀ. *A.Andr.et Mt*.24(p.100.15); Or.*Jo*.28.15(13; p.409.9; M.14.713C); **3.** connected with Red Sea, as deep into which Pharaoh (typifying Satan) was overthrown, cf. Or.*hom.3.3 in Ex*.(p.171.2; M.12.316D); cf. *Aegyptii vero post te insequentes demergentur in abyssum, etiamsi videntur rogare Jesum, ne eos...mittat in abyssum*, *ib.5.5*(p.190.19; 331A); cf.*ib.6.1*(p.192.1; 331D); Eus.*Ps*.105:9(M.23.1313C); **4.** as place of punishment for sinners, *A.Andr.et Mt*.26(p.103.13); *ib*.31(p.113.2); temporarily, *ib*. 33(p.116.4); *A.Phil*.24(p.13.16); ἀπελθε λοιπὸν κάτω ὅλος εἰς τὴν ἀ., *ib*.28(p.15.13); *ib*.133(p.64.7); *ib*.141(p.76.6); **5.** equivalent to ᾅδης; of abode of the dead, Or.*engast*.7(p.291.24; M.12.1024D); into which Christ descended, id.*hom.6 in Lc*.(p.42.15); ὁ κύριος...καταβέβηκεν εἰς τὴν ἀ. καὶ καταβὰς οὐ κεκράτηται Meth.*fr.11 in Job*(p.514.6); Christ's triumph over the abyss connected with the walking on the sea εἰς ἀ. πολλοὶ καταβεβήκασιν· καταβεβήκασι δέ, ὥστε δέσμιοι εἶναι, οὐχ ὥστε περιπατεῖν ἐν αὐτῇ. Ἰησοῦς μόνος ἐν ἀβύσσῳ περιεπάτησεν ὡς ἐλεύθερος...ἵνα τοὺς ὑποκειμένους θανάτῳ λυτρώσηται *ib.21*(p.517.6; M.18.405C); τὰ τοῦ ᾅδου χωρία κεκληκέναι ἀ. Eus. *e.th*.3.3(p.148.22; M.24.988A); Cyr.*Jo*.11.2(4.933C); v. ᾅδης; **6.** in interpretation of name Phiton (Pithom), cf. *Phiton quae in nostra lingua significat...os abyssi...quia abyssus perditionis et interitus ejus est locus*, Or.*hom.1.5 in Ex*.(p.152.17,22; M.12.303A,B); **7.** in interpretation of Pr.8:22–24, favourite Arian proof-text; **a.** exeg. of Marcell. τὰς ἀ. παροιμιωδῶς ὁ προφήτης τὰς τῶν ἁγίων καρδίας εἶναι λέγει τὰς ἐν τῷ ἑαυτῶν βάθει τὴν τοῦ πνεύματος ἐχούσας δωρεάν *fr*.19 ap.Eus.*Marcell*.23(p.47.19; M.24.804B); **b.** answered by Eus. οὐ συνορᾷ δὲ ὅτι αἱ τῶν ἁγίων καρδίαι...πρὸ τῆς σαρκὸς γεγόνασιν τοῦ σωτῆρος. πῶς οὖν δυνατὸν ἐπὶ τὴν σάρκα ἀναφέρειν τὸ πρὸ τοῦ τὰς ἀ. ποιῆσαι; Eus.*Marcell*.2.3(p.47.20; M.24.804C); οὐκ ἂν εὐχερῶς οὕτως ἀπεφαίνετο τὰς τῶν ἁγίων καρδίας εἶναι τὰς ἀ., ἐπιστήσας ὡς σκότος ἦν ἐπάνω τῆς ἀ. καὶ ὡς...δυσερμήνευτος ὁ περὶ αὐτῶν ἐν τῇ θείᾳ γραφῇ φέρεται λόγος id.*e.th*.3.3(p.148.16; M.24.988A).

C. exeg. Ezech.31:15 τὴν νοητὴν ἀ., τουτέστι, τὰς τῶν ἄνω πνευμάτων ἀγέλας Cyr.*Abac*.52(3.566D); exeg. Abac.3:11, as meaning the multitude of believers, *ib*.; of the whole human race, *ib*. (567E).

D. of the ocean, as distinct from primeval abyss, Eus.*l.C*.1.1 (p.197.23; M.20.1321B); id.*e.th*.3.3(p.151.23; M.24.992C).

E. met., *depth, abyss*; of God's wisdom, Thdt.*ep*.144(4.1240); goodness, id.*qu.4 in Gen*.(1.8); id.*Ps*.44:3(1.888); Jo.D.*imag*.3.29(M. 94.1349B); righteousness, Thdt.*qu.27 in Gen*.(1.42); judgements (cf. Ps.35:6), cf.Or.*hom.12.2 in Num*.(p.99.17; M.12.660C); Eus.*Ps*.35: 6,7(M.23.320B); Bas.*hom.in Ps*.32(1.136D; M.29.336B); Nil.*epp*.1.23 (M.79.89D); of the knowledge of God, Isid.Pel.*epp*.1.415(M.78. 413A); of the loving-kindness of Christ, Thdt.*Rom*.5:7(3.54); of scripture as ἀ. ζητημάτων Chrys.*hom.23.4 in Ac*.(9.191A); of the mind illuminated by wisdom, Max.*ambig*.(M.91.1412A); of the heart as ἀ. ... ἀκατάληπτος Mac.Aeg.*elev*.21(M.34.908A); of monastic humility as ἀ. εὐτελείας Jo.Clim.*scal*.25(M.88.993D); μοναχός ἐστιν ἀ. ταπεινώσεως *ib*.23(969A) = ‡Nil.*vit.cog*.(M.79.1465B); of evil, Chrys.*poenit*.1.2(2.281D); of sin, Jo.Clim.*scal*.25(1004A).

***ἀβυσσότοκος,** *born of the abyss*, Cosm.Mel.*hymn*.13(4.1,p.173; M.98.509A).

***ἀγαθαρχία, ἡ,** *source* or *principle of goodness*; of Trin., Dion. Ar.*d.n*.3.1(M.3.680B); *ib*.4.2(696C); ref. God as he is in himself ἀγαθαρχίας ἐστὶν ἐπέκεινα id.*ep*.2(M.3.1069A).

***ἀγαθαρχικός,** *being the source* or *principle of goodness* τὴν ἀ. τῆς θεαρχίας πρόνοιαν Dion.Ar.*d.n*.1.5(M.3.593D); ἀ. τριάδα *ib*.3.1 (680B).

***ἀγάθεια, ἡ,** *goodness*, Jo.Clim.*scal*.1(M.88.641B).

***ἀγαθήμερος,** *enjoying good days*, Agath.*v.Gr.Ill*.99(p.50).

***ἀγαθηφόρος,** *bringing good*, Hipp.*haer*.5.7(p.85.14; M.16.3136A).

***ἀγαθοδότις,** *giving good things*; of Trin., Didym.*Trin*.2.14(M.39. 712A); of God τὴν ἀ. ἀρχὴν ἁπάσης ἱερᾶς φωτοφανείας Dion.Ar.*d.n*. 1.3(M.3.589B); id.*e.h*.3.3.7(M.3.436C); ref. divine commandments, *ib*.7.3.6(561A); of BMV, Jo.D.*hom*.8.3(M.96.701C).

ἀγαθοδότως, *generously*, *munificently*, Dion.Ar.*c.h.*1.1(M.3.120B).

***ἀγαθοδωρία, ἡ**, *giving of good things*, Germ.CP *or.*1(M.98.228C).

***ἀγαθόδωρος**, *munificent*, *generous*, Max.*ambig.*(M.91.1289A).

ἀγαθοειδής, *having the form of goodness*, as received from goodness itself (Neoplatonist term); of the highest angelic choir, Dion.Ar.*c.h.*7.4(M.3.212B); of angels in gen., id.*d.n.*4.2(M.3.696B); *ib.*4.22(724B); of the soul, *ib.*4.30(732A); of joy, id.*c.h.*15.9(340A); τὸ δαιμόνιον φῦλον οὐκ ἔστιν ἀ. id.*d.n.*4.18(716A); ἀκριβῶς ἐπὶ τῶν ἀγγέλων τέθεικε τὸ ἀ.· ὁ μὲν γὰρ θεὸς οὐσιωδῶς αὐτὸ τὸ ἀγαθὸν ὤν, τὰ δὲ μετ' αὐτὸν ὡς ἐκ μετοχῆς καὶ ἔξωθεν ἀγαθυνόμενα τῇ περὶ αὐτὸν ἐφέσει, εἰκότως ἀ. λέγονται Max.*schol.d.n.*4.18(M.4.272D).

***ἀγαθοειδῶς**, *in good manner*, *benevolently*, esp. ref. benefits conferred on inferiors; ref. choir of archangels τοῖς ἀγγέλοις αὐτὰς [sc. θεαρχικὰς ἐλλάμψεις] ἀ. ἀγγέλλουσα Dion.Ar.*c.h.*9.2(M.3.257C); *ib.*13.3(301C); id.*e.h.*2.2.2(M.3.393B); ref. God πραγματεία...τὴν μὲν οὐσίαν ἡμῶν...ἀ. ὑποστήσασα *ib.*3.3.7(436C); *ib.*3.3.2(429B); Max.*schol.c.h.*3.10(M.4.145C); ἡ θεία ἔλλαμψις...ἀ. ἐν τοῖς μεριστοῖς ποικιλλομένη Jo.D.*f.o.*1.14(M.94.860C).

***ἀγαθοεξία, ἡ**, *good state* or *habit of mind* or *soul*, Nil.*epp.*3.262 (M.79.516B).

***ἀγαθοεργέτις**, *beneficent*, Dion.Ar.*e.h.*2.2.3(M.3.393C); *ib.*2.3.3 (397D).

ἀγαθοεργ-έω (ἀγαθουργ-έω), *do good*; **1.** in gen., Epiph.*haer.*16.4 (p.213.7; M.41.253B); Cyr.*Jo.*2.5(4.211C); Nil.*epp.*3.41(M.79.408A); **2.** of God ἀγαθὸς γὰρ ὤν, εἰ παύσεταί ποτε ~ῶν, καὶ τοῦ θεὸς εἶναι παύσεται Clem.*str.*6.16(p.504.3; M.9.369B); Cyr.*apol.Thdt.*10(p.139.2; 6[1].233C); **3.** of deified or holy men, Clem.*paed.*3.1(p.235.22; M.8.556A); id.*str.*4.22(p.309.6; M.8.1348B); Or.*exc.in Ps.*36:23(M.17.133B); *Const.App.*6.27.5.

***ἀγαθοέργημα (ἀγαθούργ-), τό**, *good deed*, Meth.*res.*2.15 (p.363.8; M.18.312A); Leont.N.*v.Jo.Eleem.*45(p.93.23); Thdr.Stud.*epp.*2.107 (M.99.1365D).

***ἀγαθοεργής**, *doing good works*, *A.Phil.*111(p.43.10).

ἀγαθοεργία (ἀγαθουργ-), ἡ, **1.** *well-doing*, Clem.*str.*4.3(p.251.16; M.8.1220B); assimilates to God, *ib.*6.14(p.486.7; M.9.329A); Hipp.*Dan.*4.31.5(M.10.652D); Epiph.*haer.*59.2(p.365.23; M.41.1020C); Jo.D.*virt.*(M.95.97B); **2.** plur., *good works* CNic.(325)*can.*12; Mac.Aeg.*libert.ment.*27(M.34.960D); Cyr.*Os.*4(3.19D).

***ἀγαθοεργικός (ἀγαθουργ-)**, *beneficent*, Dion.Ar.*d.n.*1.8(M.3.597C); *ib.*2.11(652A).

***ἀγαθοεργικῶς (ἀγαθουργ-)**, *beneficently*, Dion.Ar.*e.h.*2.3.3(M.3.400A); *ib.*4.3.12(485A); al.

***ἀγαθοεργῶς (ἀγαθουργ-)**, = foreg., Dion.Ar.*c.h.*3.11(M.3.441B); *ib.*3.12(444A).

***ἀγαθοήθως**, *out of a good heart* εὐχαριστῶν ἀ. τῷ παναγάθῳ θεῷ Nil.*epp.*2.332(M.79.364A).

ἀγαθοθέλεια, ἡ, *good will*, Nil.*epp.*1.298(M.79.192B); *Cod.Afr.* 55.

ἀγαθοθελής, *benevolent*, Agath.Papa *ep.imp.*(M.*PL.*87.1166B).

ἀγαθοποιέω, *do good*; **1.** ref. God τῆς γὰρ θείας σοφίας...τὸ ἀ. Clem.*str.*1.17(p.55.26; M.8.801A); *ib.*5.14(p.421.11; M.9.205C); *ib.*7.7 (p.32.7; 460A); Synes.*ep.*57(M.66.1384B); Dion.Ar.*d.n.*4.21(M.3.724A); **2.** ref. men; a characteristic of charity, Clem.*str.*4.18(p.298.10; M.8.1321B); *ib.*6.17(p.513.27; M.9.892B); *ib.*7.12(p.56.14; 509A); followed by peace, *2Clem.*10.2; dependent on free will, Meth.*res.*1.57(p.319.9; M.41.1153A); Jo.D.*Man.*2(M.96.1329B).

ἀγαθοποίησις, ἡ, *doing good*, Herm.*mand.*8.10; id.*sim.*5.3.4.

ἀγαθοποιία, ἡ, *well-doing*, *beneficence*, *1Clem.*2.2; *ib.*2.7; Clem.*str.*4.22(p.308.33; M.8.1348A); of God, Or.*hom.1.1 in Jer.*(p.1.1; M.13.256A).

***ἀγαθοπρεπής**, *befitting the good*, of divine gifts, emanations, etc. ἀ. δώρων Dion.Ar.*d.n.*2.1(M.3.637C); ἀ. τῆς θεαρχίας προόδους τε καὶ ἐκφάνσεις *ib.*2.4(640D); *ib.*2.6(644C); ἀ. βουλήν Gr.Agr.*Eccl.*1.14(M.98.788C); of Inc., *ib.*1.16(793A).

***ἀγαθοπρεπῶς**, *as becomes the good*, *benignly*; ref. God, Dion.Ar.*c.h.*1.2(M.3.121B); *ib.*9.2(260B); ref. Christ's appearance in the world, *ib.*4.4(181B); ref. prayer of intercession, id.*ep.*8.6(M.3.1097C).

***ἀγαθοπτικός**, *capable of seeing the good* ἀπομύσαντες [sc. devils] αὐτῶν τὰς ἀ. δυνάμεις Dion.Ar.*d.n.*4.23(M.3.725C); Max.*schol.d.n.*4.23(M.4.293A).

***ἀγαθόρρυτος**, *flowing with goodness*; of the divine 'fountain', Synes.*hymn.*1.129(p.63; M.66.1592).

ἀγαθός, *good*; etym. ἀγαθὸν λέγεται, παρὰ τὸ ἄγαν θεῖον πάντα πρὸς αὐτό· ὃ καὶ φύσει ἐστὶν ἐραστόν, καὶ ἐφετόν Jo.D.*Man.*1.64(M.94.1560B);

A. philosophical conceptions ('the good' in this section cannot always be sharply distinguished from God as 'summum bonum' in B infra); **1.** general characteristics: its unity ἓν γὰρ τὸ ἀ., πολλὰ δὲ τὰ αἰσχρά Or.*or.*21.2(p.345.19; M.11.481A); τὸ ὄντως ἀ. ἁπλοῦν καὶ μονοειδές ἐστι τῇ φύσει, πάσης διπλόης καὶ τῆς πρὸς τὸ ἐναντίον συζυγίας ἀλλότριον Gr.Nyss.*hom.opif.*20.3(M.44.200C); τὸ ἀ. ἐκ τῆς μιᾶς καὶ τῆς ὅλης αἰτίας Dion.Ar.*d.n.*4.30(M.3.729C); identity τὸ γὰρ ἀεὶ ταὐτὸν τοῦ ἀ., ἴδιον *ib.*4.23(725A); infinity, Gr.Nyss.*v.Mos.*5 (M.44.300D); id.*mort.*(M.46.504D); harmony with itself and others, Dion.Ar.*d.n.*4.21(721D); general causality and finality, *ib.*4.4 (700A); beyond definition, *ib.*1.1(588B); equated with καλόν, *ib.* 4.7(704A,B); Max.*cap.*5.83(M.90.1384B); a comprehensive summary οὐκ ἡγμένον δέ, τὸ ἀ.· πρὸ παντὸς γὰρ αἰῶνος καὶ χρόνου φύσει τὸ ἀ νοητὸν λέγει τὸ ἀ., ὅπερ δεῖ μόνον νοεῖν...ῥητὸν λέγει τὸ ἀ.· αὐτὸ γὰρ δεῖ μόνον λαλεῖσθαι...καὶ γινόμενον λέγει τὸ ἀ.· κατὰ φύσιν γὰρ ὑπάρχει ἀγέννητον...ἄφθαρτον δὲ τὸ ἀ., ὡς ἀεὶ ὄν, καὶ μή ποτε τοῦ εἶναι παυόμενον *Schol.* in Max.*qu.Thal.*55.19(M.90.564Df.); **2.** the good and being: all being contains some good τὸ γὰρ πάντῃ ἄμοιρον τοῦ ἀ. οὔτε ὄν, οὔτε ἐν τοῖς οὖσι· τὸ δὲ μικτὸν διὰ τὸ ἀ. ἐν τοῖς οὖσι, καὶ κατὰ τοῦτο ἐν τοῖς οὖσι καὶ ὄν, καθ' ὅσον τοῦ ἀ. μετέχει Dion.Ar.*d.n.*4.20(M.3.720D); διὰ δὲ τὸ ἀ. καὶ ὄν, καὶ ἀ. ὂν *ib.*(717C); τὰ ὄντα πάντα, καθόσον ἔστι, καὶ ἀ. ἐστι, καὶ ἐκ τἀγαθοῦ· καθόσον ἐστέρηται τοῦ ἀ., οὔτε ἀ., οὔτε ὄντα ἐστίν *ib.*(720B) = Jo.D.*Man.*1.47 (M.94.1549A); cf.Ath.*inc.*4.6(M.25.104C); **3.** the good and evil: good a substance, evil an accident ἀγαθόν φημι κατ' οὐσίαν εἶναι, τὸ δὲ κακὸν ἐπισυμβαῖνόν ἐστιν· τὸ ἀ. ἀσώματον, τὸ δὲ κακὸν αἰσθητόν· τῷ...ἀ. οὐκ ἐπισυμβαίνει τὸ κακόν, ἀλλὰ τῷ κατὰ θέσιν ἀ. διὰ τὸ αὐτεξούσιον Adam.*dial.*3.9(p.126.21ff.; M.11.1800B); evil a privation of the good, Dion.Ar.*d.n.*4.30(M.3.732B); εἰ οὐσία τὸ ἀ., ἀνούσιον τὸ κακὸν Jo.D.*Man.*1.52(M.94.1549C); evil exists only in virtue of the good, Dion.Ar.*d.n.*4.33(733B); πάντων, καὶ τῶν κακῶν, ἀρχὴ καὶ τέλος ἐστὶ τὸ ἀ.· τοῦ γὰρ ἀ. ἕνεκα πάντα, καὶ ὅσα ἀ., καὶ ὅσα ἐναντία Jo.D.*Man.*1.64(M.94.1560B); *ib.*(1560C); in Manicheism evil a principle opp. good, *ib.*1.2(1508B).

B. God and the good; **1.** identification of God with the 'summum bonum' τοῦ δὲ ἀ. κρεῖττον οὐδὲ ἕν, ὠφελεῖ ἄρα τὸ ἀ.· ἀ. δὲ ὁ θεὸς ὁμολογεῖται, ὠφελεῖ ἄρα ὁ θεός Clem.*paed.*1.8(p.127.12f.; M.8.325C); cf.*V.Aberc.*32(p.24.19ff.); Meth.*Porph.*3(p.506.13; M.18.401A); Ath.*inc.*3.3(M.25.101A); Bas.*hom.in Ps.*33(1.150A; M.29.368B); τὸ πρώτως καὶ κυρίως ἀ., οὗ ἡ φύσις ἀγαθότης ἐστίν, αὐτὸ τὸ θεῖον Gr.Nyss.*v.Mos.*7(M.44.301A); id.*hom.opif.*12.8(M.44.161C); id.*Eun.*9(2 p.210.23ff.; M.45.808D); for a detailed discussion of God as the good v. Dion.Ar.*d.n.*4 passim, concluding: ὕμνηται τἀγαθόν, ὡς ὄντως ἀγαστόν, ὡς ἀρχὴ καὶ πέρας πάντων, ὡς περιοχὴ τῶν ὄντων, ὡς εἰδοποιὸν τῶν οὐκ ὄντων, ὡς πάντων ἀ. αἴτιον, ὡς τῶν κακῶν ἀναίτιον, ὡς πρόνοια καὶ ἀγαθότης παντελής, καὶ ὑπερβάλλουσα τὰ ὄντα καὶ τὰ οὐκ ὄντα, καὶ τὰ κακά, καὶ τὴν ἑαυτῆς στέρησιν ἀγαθύνουσα *ib.*4.35 (M.3.736B); though, emphasizing his transcendence, the Son is also called φύσει τὸ ἀ., μᾶλλον δὲ παντὸς ἀ. ἐπέκεινα Gr.Nyss.*Eun.*8(2 p.182.5; 776A); τὸ ὑπὲρ ἔννοιαν ἀ. id.*hom.3 in Cant.*(M.44.820C); cf.Dion.Ar.*d.n.*4.4(697C); φύσει ἀ. μόνος ὁ θεὸς Max.*carit.*4.90(M.90.1069C); **2.** of Father as good in relation to Son (cf. Mt.19:16); a subordinationist interpretation τάχα καὶ ὁ υἱὸς ἀ. ἀλλ' οὐχ ὡς ἁπλῶς ἀ. καὶ ὥσπερ 'εἰκών ἐστι τοῦ θεοῦ τοῦ ἀοράτου' καὶ κατὰ τοῦτο θεός... οὕτως 'εἰκὼν τῆς ἀγαθότητος' ἀλλ' οὐχ ὡς ὁ πατὴρ ἀπαραλλάκτως ἀ. Or.*princ.*1.2.13(p.47.5ff.; M.11.143C,144A); orthodox exegesis, esp. opp. Arian use of text: as a rebuke to the scribe calling Christ good without confessing his divinity, ‡Ath.*dial.Trin.*1.11(M.28.1136B); Didym.(‡Bas.)*Eun.*4(1.291E; M.29.700C); as referring only to his humanity, Gr.Naz.*or.*30.13(p.129.9; M.36.121A); Chrys.*hom.63.1 in Mt.*(7.628B); the divinity of Christ necessarily implying his being good, Gr.Nyss.*Eun.*11(2 p.257.6; M.45.864C); *ib.*9(2 p.210.31ff.; 808D); **3.** the divine goodness diffusive of itself ὁ δὲ θεὸς τελείως ἀ. ὢν ἀϊδίως ἀγαθοποιός ἐστιν Athenag.*leg.*26.2(M.6.952A); Clem.*str.*7.7(p.32.1; M.9.457C); Or.*Jo.*1.10(11; p.15.27; M.14.41C); id.*or.*29.14(p.389.3; M.11.541A); of God's goodness showing itself in Creation εἴ τις ἀ. ὢν μὴ ἔχοι οὓς εὐεργετῆσαι δεῖ, μάτην ἀ. εἶναι δοκεῖ (τὸ γὰρ ἀ. τῶν πρὸς ἕτερον πέφυκεν εἶναι...)...εἰ δὲ πάρεισίν τινες οὓς εὐεργετεῖν δύναται, τηνικαῦτα δείκνυται μὲν αὐτοῦ πρῶτον τὸ ἀ. Meth.*arbitr.*22.5(p.203.14ff.); οὐ μὴν ἀκοινώνητόν ἐστι καθόλου ἀ. οὐδενὶ τῶν ὄντων Dion.Ar.*d.n.*1.2(M.3.588C); τὸ ἀ. ὡς οὐσιῶδες ἀ., εἰς πάντα τὰ ὄντα διατείνει τὴν ἀγαθότητα *ib.*4.1(693B); Jo.D.*f.o.*1.1(M.94.792A); **4.** of the 'good' God (ὁ ἀ.) of Marcion and his followers, i.e. the Father of Christ, opp. the 'just' God of the OT ἐδίδαξε [sc. Κέρδων] τὸν ὑπὸ τοῦ νόμου καὶ προφητῶν κεκηρυγμένο θεόν, μὴ εἶναι πατέρα τοῦ κυρίου ἡμῶν Ἰησοῦ Χριστοῦ...τὸν μὲν δίκαιον, τὸν δὲ ἀ. ὑπάρχειν Iren.*haer*.1.27.1(M.7.688A); οἱ μὲν ἀπὸ Μαρκίωνος φύσιν κακὴν...ἐκ δικαίου γενομένην δημιουργοῦ...ἀντιτασσόμενοι τῷ ποιητῇ τῷ σφῶν καὶ σπεύδοντες πρὸς τὸν κεκληκότα ἀ. Clem.*str*.3.3(p.201.2; M.8.1113B); *ib*.2.8(p.133.29ff.; 973C); Or.*or*.29.12(p.387.7; M.11.537C); id.*comm.in Ex*.(M.12.265B); cf.Hipp.*haer*.7.37(p.223.16; M.16.3343C); ὁ ἀ. as one of two, *ib*.7.29(p.210.7; 3323A), or three first principles, *ib*.10.19(p.279.22; 3435C); the redemptive work of the ἀ.: ἐλεήσας ἔπεμψε τὸν υἱὸν ὡς ⟨ἀγαθὸς⟩ ἀγαθὸν καὶ ἐρρύσατο ἡμᾶς...συνεπάθησεν οὖν ὁ ἀ. ἀλλοτρίοις...ὡς ἁμαρτωλοῖς...οὔτε ὡς ἀγαθῶν οὔτε ὡς κακῶν, ἀλλὰ σπλαγχνισθεὶς ἠλέησεν Adam.*dial*.1.3(p.6.17ff.; M.11.1720C); who does not condemn those who disobey him, *ib*.2.4(p.64.36; 1765B); but, law of demiurge being destroyed ὁ θάνατος τοῦ ἀ. σωτηρία ἀνθρώπου ἐγίνετο *ib*.2.9(p.74.26f.; 1772C); ref. Gnost. dualism in gen., Ath.*gent*.6(M.25.13C); orthodox insistence on harmony of the just with the good καθ' ἃ τὸ ἀ. ἐξετάζεται, καὶ ἡ δικαιοσύνη χαρακτηρίζεται Clem.*paed*.1.8(p.127.30; M.8.328B); *ib*.(p.131.11; 333C); Or.*Jo*.1.35(40; p.44.32ff.; M.14.92C,D); Meth.*symp*.8.16(p.107.8ff.; M.18.169C); cf. δίκαιος.

C. of the good in creation; **1.** of the good in creatures contrasted with the good in God; God being good by nature, creatures by determination of the will, Adam.*dial*.3.9(p.126.27f.; M.11.1800C); τὸ δὲ ἀ. λέγεται διχῶς· τὸ μὲν ἐν τῷ ὄντι θεῷ, τὸ δὲ ἐν γενητοῖς. καὶ τὸ μὲν ἐν τῷ ὄντι θεῷ, διχῶς νοεῖται πάλιν· τὸ μὲν φύσει, τὸ δὲ ποιήσει... τὸ δὲ ἐν γενητοῖς ἀ., τὸ μὲν φύσει, τὸ δὲ θέσει, τὸ δὲ χρησίμου ἕνεκεν· φύσει μὲν ὡς τὰ δημιουργήματα αὐτά *Disp.Phot*.(M.88.568Af.); Max.*carit*.4.90(M.90.1069C); or by participation ὁ θεὸς οὐ κατὰ μετοχὴν ἀγαθότητός ἐστιν ἀ., ἀλλ' αὐτός ἐστιν ἀγαθότης· ὁ δὲ ἄνθρωπος μετοχῇ ἀγαθότητός ἐστιν ἀ. ‡Ath.*dial.Trin*.1.12(M.28.1136B); **2.** angels καὶ οἱ ἄγγελοι οὐκ εἰσὶν ἀ. τῇ φύσει; τῇ φύσει, οὔ· μετοχῇ, ναί *ib*.(1136B); **3.** men; **a.** moral good; an effect of repentance, Herm.*sim*.8.6.6; developed by the commandments, Clem.*str*.1.6(p.23.5; M.8.729B); a matter of free will, Or.*hom.20.2 in Jer*.(p.178.16; M.13.501D); good works λέγομεν δὲ τὸν ἄνθρωπον...διὰ τὸ εὐεργετεῖν ἀ. Meth.*arbitr*.8(p.167.2); Bas.*hom.in Ps*.1(1.93A; M.29.217B); right order, Jo.D.*Man*.1.47(M.94.1548D); and fulfilment of the will of God, *ib*.1.38(1544C); its contingency τὸ ἀ. ... ἐπὶ δὲ τῶν γενητῶν ἐνέργειά τίς ἐστι περὶ τὸ ἐκτὸς γινομένη...καὶ διὰ πράξεως μὲν κατορθοῦσιν ἄνθρωποι σαρκὶ συζῶντες τὸ ἀ.· αἱ δὲ νοεραὶ δυνάμεις, διὰ θεωρίας καὶ προσευχῆς. ἐπεὶ οὖν συμβεβηκός ἐστιν τὸ ἀ. ἐπὶ τῶν γενητῶν, πάντως ἐπὶ τούτων καὶ προτερεύει τὸ εἶναι τὸ ἀ. *Disp.Phot*.(M.88.573I); **b.** true and apparent good, Clem.*str*.7.7(p.33.10; M.9.464A); πολλοὶ γὰρ τὰ μὲν ἀ., ὅταν ἐπίπονα ᾖ, κακὰ νομίζουσι· τὰ δὲ κακὰ διὰ τὴν προσοῦσαν αὐτοῖς ἡδονὴν ὡς ἀ. μεταδιώκουσι Bas.*hom.in Ps*.28(1.122C; M.29.301A,B); οὐκ ἄρα ὁ πλοῦτος ἀ. ... μάθε τίνα ἐστὶ τὰ ὄντως ἀ. ... ἀρετή, φιλανθρωπία· ταῦτα ἀ. Chrys.*hom.12.4 in 1Tim*.(11.616D,F); Jo.D.*Man*.1.36(M.94.1541D); *ib*.1.81(1580C); **c.** faith as a good, Clem.*str*.7.10(p.40.26; M.9.477C); id.*prot*.10(p.70.5; M.8.209A); esp. exeg. Rom.14:16; Chrys.*hom.26.1 in Rom*.(9.712C); ἀ. γὰρ τὴν πίστιν καλεῖ Thdt.*Rom*.14:16(3.144); **4.** devils; not wholly without good οὔτε οἱ δαίμονες φύσει κακοί· καὶ γὰρ εἰ φύσει κακοί, οὔτε ἐκ τἀγαθοῦ...οὔτε μὴν ἐξ ἀγαθῶν μετέβαλον Dion.Ar.*d.n*.4.23(M.3.724Cff.); *ib*.(725B); *ib*.4.18(716A); cf. δαίμων.

D. neut. plur. as subst.; **1.** of material good things ἐν παντὶ βρώματι καὶ πότῳ καὶ τοῖς λοιποῖς ἀ. Arist.*apol*.15.10; τῶν ἀνθρωπείων ἀ. ὧν ἔδωκεν ἡμῖν ὁ θεός Clem.*str*.7.7(p.28.4; M.9.452A); *ib*.5.10(p.367.31f.; 96A); **2.** spiritual good things of this life, Clem.*str*.7.7(p.29.28; M.9.543C); Or.*Jo*.1.10(11; p.15.18; M.14.41B); id.*Cels*.6.54(p.125.12; M.11.1381B); πίστεως, ἀγάπης, ὑπομονῆς καὶ τῶν λοιπῶν ἀ. Meth.*symp*.7.8(p.79.17; M.18.136B); τὴν μητέρα τῶν ἀ. ... ταπεινοφροσύνην Chrys.*hom.1.3 in Rom*.(9.434C); Cyr.*Is*.5.4(2.822C); id.*Mich*.70(3.469A); τὰ ὄντως ἀ., ἃ οὐδὲ ἐπὶ καρδίαν ἀνθρώπου ἀνέβη Jo.D.*Rom*.2:7(M.95.453B); **3.** eternal things in heaven, cf. Heb.9:11, 10:1 τοῖς τῆς καρδίας ὀφθαλμοῖς ἀνέβλεπον τὰ τηρούμενα τοῖς ὑπομείνασιν ἀ. *M.Polyc*.2.3; Just.*dial*.11.4(M.6.500A); Or.*Jo*.13.10(p.234.29; M.14.413C); Dion.Ar.*e.h*.3.3.11(M.3.440C).

E. ἡ κοινωνία (or μετουσία) τοῦ ἀ. as t. t. for Holy Communion, Bas.*ep*.188 *can*.4(3.272A; M.32.673B); *ib*.199 *can*.22(293C; M.724A); Gr.Nyss.*ep.can*.(M.45.229C).

F. as an epithet of grace, *Lit.Jac*.(p.166.1); of faith, *1Clem*.26.1; of works, *1Clem*.33.1; *ib*.35.4; Or.*Jo*.20.14(13; p.345.5; M.14.604C); Chrys.*Stag*.1.8(1.174A); of conscience, *1Clem*.41.1; Euthal.Diac.*epp.cath*.(M.85.685D).

G. substituted for καλόν in citation of Gen.2:17, Mel.*pass*.47 p.8.4.

H. *kind, benevolent* ἀ. προσώπῳ...ἔνευσε Gr.Mag.*dial*.(tr.Zach.) 4.13(M.*PL*.77.342A).

[*]**ἀγαθοσύνη, ἡ,** v. ἀγαθωσύνη.

ἀγαθότης, ἡ, *goodness, benignity*, most freq. of the goodness of God;

A. divine goodness in itself; **1.** in the divine nature; **a.** essential to or identical with it, Gr.Nyss.*Eun*.11(2 p.257.8; M.45.864C); οὗ ἡ φύσις ἀ. ἐστίν, αὐτὸ τὸ θεῖον id.*v.Mos*.7(M.44.301A); id.*mort*.(M.46.497C); ἡ δὲ ἄπειρος ἀ., ὁ θεός Chrys.*hom.13.6 in Mt*.(7.176A); *Disp.Phot*.(M.88.576A); Jo.D.*f.o*.1.5(M.94.801A); therefore one, Didym.*Trin*.2.6(M.39.540C) cit. s. ἀλήθεια; **b.** transcendent οὐδὲ τὸ [sc. ὄνομα] τῆς ἀ., ὡς ἐφαρμόζοντες αὐτῇ [sc. ὑπερθεότητι] προσφέρομεν, ἀλλὰ πόθῳ τοῦ ἐννοεῖν τι καὶ λέγειν περὶ τῆς ἀρρήτου φύσεως ἐκείνης, τὸ τῶν ὀνομάτων σεπτότατον αὐτῇ πρώτως ἀφιεροῦμεν Dion.Ar.*d.n*.13.3(M.3.981A); ἡ ὑπεράγαθος ἀ. *ib*.2.4(641A); *ib*.4.4(697C); also expressed by the 'via negativa' οὐδὲ θεότης, οὐδὲ ἀ. id.*myst*.5(M.3.1048A); **c.** freq. predicated of God, Iren.*haer*.4.20.5(M.7.1035C); Clem.*str*.6.17(p.511.9; M.9.385B); *A.Phil*.116(p.47.5); with epithets πατρικῆς ἀ. Dion.Ar.*c.h*.9.3(M.3.260D); θεαρχικῆς ἀ. id.*e.h*.1.5(M.3.376D); as a synonym τὴν θεαρχικὴν ὕπαρξιν, ἀ. λέγοντες id.*d.n*.4.1(M.3.693B); id.*e.h*.7.4(560A); πνεύματι ἀγαθότητος Sever.*creat*.4.6(M.56.465); **2.** in Trinitarian relationships; **a.** in gen. ἡ φυσικὴ ἀ. ... ἐκ τοῦ πατρὸς διὰ τοῦ μονογενοῦς ἐπὶ τὸ πνεῦμα διήκει Bas.*Spir*.47(3.39E; M.32.153B); ἡ οὐσία τῆς ἀ., ἡ μία τῶν ὄντων αἰτία τριάς, ἐξ ἧς καὶ τὸ εἶναι καὶ τὸ εὖ εἶναι τοῖς οὖσι δι' ἀγαθότητα Dion.Ar.*e.h*.1.3(M.3.373C); **b.** in rel. of Father to Son ὁ δὲ σωτὴρ εἰκὼν τῆς ἀ. αὐτοῦ Or.*Jo*.6.57(37; p.166.6; M.14.300B); *ib*.13.25(p.249.29; 444A); Mt.19:16 interpreted as referring only to Christ's humanity, Gr.Nyss.*Eun*.11(2 p.254.22; M.45.861B); but πῶς οὐ κοινωνεῖ τῆς ἀ. ὁ κοινωνῶν τῆς θεότητος; *ib*.(p.254.30; M.l.c.); Cyr.*thes*.13(5^{1}.133E); Nil.*epp*.2.323(M.79.357C); **3.** of Christ, freq. with sense of *loving-kindness, benignity*, Or.*fr.14 in Lc*.(p.239.21; M.17.337A); Ath.*v.Anton*.61(M.26.932B); id.*apol.Const*.17(M.25.616D); *A.Phil*.117(p.47.17); Gr.Nyss.*hom.2 in Cant*.(M.44.801A); **4.** ref. Marcionite 'good' God, opp. 'just' creator ἀγαθὴ γὰρ ἡ τοῦ θεοῦ δικαιοσύνη καὶ δικαία ἐστὶν ἡ ἀ. αὐτοῦ Clem.*str*.6.14(p.486.30; M.9.332A); *ib*.7.2(p.10.3; 416B); οἱ δὲ ἕτερον θεὸν φάσκοντες παρὰ τὸν δημιουργὸν...ἐν τῷ χωρίζειν δικαιοσύνην ἀ., καὶ οἴεσθαι ὅτι οἷόν τέ ἐστι δικαιοσύνην εἶναι ἔν τινι χωρὶς ἀ., καὶ ἀγαθότητα δίχα δικαιοσύνης Or.*comm.in Ex*.1(p.243.3f.; M.12.265B); id.*princ*.3.1.16(p.224.14; M.11.281B); iron. ὦ πολλῆς ἀ., μᾶλλον δὲ ἀθεότητος Adam.*dial*.2.7(p.70.19; M.11.1769B); cf. *Marcion praeter creatorem alium deum solius bonitatis induceret*, Tert.*praescr*.34(M.*PL*.2.47A); *quid enim tam perfectae bonitatis, quam totum hominem redigere in salutem?* id.*Marc*.1.24ff.(M.*PL*.2.274Bff.); *catholicae et summae illius bonitatis*, *ib*.2.17(304B).

B. of divine goodness in rel. to creatures; **1.** its universality τὴν ἐπὶ πάσης τῆς δημιουργίας θεωρουμένην ἀ. Athenag.*res*.12(p.62.9; M.6.997B); Gr.Naz.*or*.38.9(M.36.320C); ἡ διὰ πάντων φοιτῶσα παντελὴς ἀ. οὐ μέχρι μόνον χωρεῖ τῶν περὶ αὐτὴν παναγάθων οὐσιῶν, ἐκτείνεται δὲ ἄχρι τῶν ἐσχάτων, ταῖς μὲν ὁλικῶς παροῦσα, ταῖς δὲ ὑφειμένως, ἄλλαις δὲ ἐσχάτως Dion.Ar.*d.n*.4.20(M.3.717D); ὑπερεκτεινομένη διὰ περιουσίαν ἀγαθότητος, καὶ εἰς τὴν δαιμονίαν ζωήν *ib*.6.2(856C); ἔστι γὰρ τοῦτο τῆς...ὑπὲρ πάντα ἀ. ἴδιον, τὸ πρὸς κοινωνίαν ἑαυτῆς τὰ ὄντα καλεῖν id.*c.h*.4.1(M.3.177C); id.*e.h*.3.3.3(M.3.429A); **2.** its expression; **a.** in Creation ἀγαθότητι πάσας ἡ ὑπερούσιος θεαρχία τὰς τῶν ὄντων οὐσίας ὑποστήσασα Dion.Ar.*c.h*.4.1(M.3.177C); id.*d.n*.1.3(M.3.589C); *ib*.1.5(593D); **b.** in Inc. and Redemption διὰ τὴν αὐτοῦ ἀ. κήδεται ἡμῶν μήτε μορίων ὄντων αὐτοῦ μήτε φύσει τέκνων. καὶ δὴ ἡ μεγίστη τῆς τοῦ θεοῦ ἀ. ἔνδειξις...ὅτι...ἡμῶν...φύσει 'ἀπηλλοτριωμένων' παντελῶς ὅμως κήδεται Clem.*str*.2.16(p.152.16f.; M.8.1013A); ἀξίως τῆς ἀ. τοῦ τῶν ὅλων θεοῦ νοήσωμεν τὸν ἀμνὸν τοῦ θεοῦ αἴροντα τὴν ἁμαρτίαν τοῦ κόσμου Or.*Jo*.6.57(37; p.166.16; M.14.300C); γνώρισμα...τῆς εἰς ἡμᾶς παρ' αὐτοῦ γενομένης ἀ., ὅτι ἡμεῖς μὲν ὑψώθημεν, διὰ τὸ ἐν ἡμῖν εἶναι τὸν ὕψιστον κύριον Ath.*Ar*.1.43(M.26.101A); Dion.Ar.*e.h*.3.3.12(M.3.444A); διὰ τὴν οἰκείαν ἀ. πάντως ποιήσει, ἅπερ ἐπαγγέλλεται Chrys.*hom.2.2 in Eph*.(11.12A); Dor.*doct*.13.1(M.88.1761C); **c.** in the goodness of creatures αὐτὸς [sc. ὁ γνωστικός] ἐργάζεται τὴν εὐποιίαν, ὄργανον γενόμενος τῆς τοῦ θεοῦ ἀ. Clem.*str*.7.13(p.58.19; M.9.513B); φιλάνθρωπος γάρ ἐστιν ὁ δεσπότης, καὶ τῆς ἀ. αὐτοῦ τὸ δῶρον γίνεται Chrys.*hom.78.4 in Mt*.(7.756A); ‡Ath.*dial.Trin*.1.12(M.28.1136B); τὸ ἐκφαίνειν ἐν ἑαυταῖς [sc. angelic hierarchies] τὴν κρυφίαν ἀ., καὶ εἶναι ἀγγέλους ὥσπερ ἐξαγγελτικὰς τῆς θείας σιγῆς Dion.Ar.*d.n*.4.2(M.3.696B); *ib*.4.22(724B).

C. as form of address: to God παρακαλοῦμεν τὴν σὴν ἀ. *Lit.Jac*.(p.164.24); to Christ, *A.Thadd*.2(p.274.8); to men, Bas.*ep*.124(3.214B; M.32.544C); Gr.Naz.*ep*.219(M.37.357B); Gr.Nyss.*ep*.17(M.46.1057C).

***ἀγαθοτρυφία, ἡ,** *holy delight,* Andr.Cr.*or*.6(M.97.929A).

***ἀγαθότυπος,** *being the exemplar of the good* τὴν ὡραιότητα τῆς ἀ. θεοειδείας Dion.Ar.*d.n*.4.22(M.3.724B) cit.ap.Max.*myst*.23(M.91.701C).

ἀγαθουργ-, v. ἀγαθοεργ-.

***ἀγαθοφιλής,** *loving good,* Dion.Ar.*ep*.8.1(M.3.1085B).

***ἀγαθοφυής,** *good by nature*; of Logos, Dion.Ar.*d.n*.2.1(M.3.637A).

ἀγαθύν-ω, 1. *make* or *render good, T.Sym*.5.2; τὸ δὲ πνεῦμα τὸ ἅγιον, ἀπροσδεές ἐστι τοῦ ~οντος, ἀγαθὸν γὰρ τῇ φύσει ἐστί Gr.Nyss.*fid*.(M.45.141C); id.*or.catech*.39(p.157.9; M.45.100D); οὐ...ἡ θεία φύσις...προσδεομένη τοῦ ~οντος id.*Eun*.1(1 p.105.10; M.45.340A); ἀγαθότης...τὴν ἑαυτῆς στέρησιν ~ουσα Dion.Ar.*d.n*.4.35(M.3.736B); *ib*.4.21(721C); *improve* ἀγαθῦναι...τὸν νοῦν εἰς ἀπάθειαν Diad.*perf*.74(p.92.19); *make kind, Dial.Tim.et Aquil*.83 v°; **2.** *do good,* esp. of God θεοῦ, οὗ μόνον τὸ ἀ. ἔργον ἐστίν Clem.*str*.6.17(p.514.1; M.9.392B); *ib*.6.12(p.484.28; 325C); Bas.*ep*.123(3.214A; M.32.544B); of men, Dion.Ar.*d.n*.4.34(M.3.736A); **3.** pass., *be made good, be good,* Tit.Bost.*Man*.2.21(M.18.1176C); Dion.Ar.*ep*.2(M.3.1069A); *ib*.8(1088A); τὸ εἶναι,...τὸ ἀ. Max.*ep*.6(M.91.428D); **4.** med., *rejoice,* Gr.Agr.*Eccl*.8.6f.(M.98.1073A); pass., *be pleased, A.Mt*.10(p.227.6).

***ἀγαθωνυμία, ἡ,** *the name of good*; as one of the divine names, Dion.Ar.*d.n*.3.1(M.3.680B); *ib*.4.1(693B).

***ἀγαθώνυμος,** *having a good name*; punning epithet of S. Agatha, *Hymn.*(*AS* 1 p.642).

ἀγαθωσύνη ([*]ἀγαθοσύνη), ἡ, *goodness, benignity*; of God, *Barn*.2.9; Thphl.Ant.*Autol*.1.3(M.6.1028C); θεὸς...ἐν ταὐτότητι τῆς ἀ. ἀπαραβάτως μένει Clem.*str*.6.12(p.484.26; M.9.325B); *ib*.7.3(p.12.2; 430B); esp. towards penitents, Hegem.*Arch*.5.4(p.7.1; M.10.1436A); *Const.App*.2.21.8; *ib*.2.22.12; of Christ, Clem.*paed*.1.9(p.140.10; M.8.352C); *A.Paul.et Thecl*.1(p.235.5); Gr.Nyss.*Eun*.1(1 p.106.2; M.45.340B); Leont.N.*serm*.2(M.93.1592B); of men τῇ δικαίᾳ ψυχῇ θεία τις ἀγαθωσύνης δύναμις Clem.*str*.6.12(p.484.15; M.9.325A); Eus.*p.e*.12.2(575A; M.21.953C); ‡Bas.*const*.4.1(2.545A; M.31.1348B); Mac.Aeg.*hom*.2.5(M.34.468A); of Judgement day μοναχὸς...ὄψεται αὐτὸν [sc. Χριστόν] ἐν ἡμέρᾳ ἀγαθοσύνης στεφανοῦντα αὐτόν Hyper.*mon*.150(M.79.1488D).

ἀγάλακτος, *never having sucked,* Nonn.*par.Jo*.9:20(M.43.828B).

ἀγαλλιάζομαι, v. ἀγαλλιάω.

ἀγαλλίαμα, τό, *exultation, rejoicing,* mostly of spiritual joy τὸ ...τῶν ψυχῶν ἀ., τὸ ἐπὶ ταῖς συνάξεσι καὶ τῇ κοινωνίᾳ τῶν πνευματικῶν χαρισμάτων ταῖς ψυχαῖς ἐγγινόμενον Bas.*ep*.243.2(3.374A; M.32.905B); τὸ σὸν ἀ., ὅτι...ἀγαπᾷς ὑπὲρ οἶνον τοὺς μαζοὺς τοῦ λόγου Gr.Nyss.*hom.1 in Cant*.(M.44.785C); id.*Spir*.(M.46.700A); σταυρὸς...τὸ τοῦ πνεύματος ἀ. Chrys.*hom.in Mt.26:39*(10.19B); of sabbath ἀ. ἑβδομάδος *Const.App*.7.36.4; of Easter day ἡμέρα... ἀγαλλιάματος *Dial.Ath.et Zacch*.68(p.40); of Christ ἀ. ἁπάντων ‡Meth.*Sym.et Ann*.6(M.18.364A); of BMV ψυχῆς ἀ. Germ.CP *or*.5(M.98.321B).

ἀγαλλίασις, ἡ, *exultation, fervent joy,* mostly spiritual ἀ. ἡμῖν παρέξετε...ὑπήκοοι γενόμενοι *1Clem*.63.2; a fruit of charity, *Barn*.1.6; of the visitation of the Lord, Clem.*paed*.1.8(p.130.32; M.8.333B); of virtue ἡ ἕξις ἡ γνωστικὴ...παρεχομένη...ἀ. καὶ νῦν καὶ εἰς ὕστερον. τὴν δὲ ἀ. εὐφροσύνην εἶναί φασιν id.*str*.6.12(p.481.28; M.9.320C); ἡ πραότης εἰρήνη ἐστὶν καὶ...ἀ. *A.Thom*.A 86(p.202.5); ἐν μεγάλῃ ἀ.... ἀποκαλύψαι ὑμῖν ἔχω τὸ ὄνομα ἐκεῖνο [sc. Ἰησοῦς] *A.Phil*.9(p.5.11); of true visions, Ath.*v.Anton*.35(M.26.896A); of Resurrection, Amph.*hom*.2.8(M.39.57C); of grace, Diad.*perf*.79(p.100.22); of conversion, Jo.Mosch.*prat*.118(M.87.2981D); of joy of saints, Leont.N.*v.Sym*.25(M.93.1701B); for exeg. Ps.44:8 v. ἔλαιον.

***ἀγαλλίασμα, τό,** s.v.l., *rejoicing, joy,* of BMV τὸ ἐκκλησιαστικὸν ἀ. Thdot.Anc.*hom.BMV et Sym*.3(M.77.1393B).

***ἀγαλλιασμός, ὁ,** *exultation,* Mac.Aeg.*hom*.17.12(M.34.632B).

ἀγαλλι-άω (usu. med.), **ἀγαλλι-άζομαι,** *exult, rejoice greatly*; **1.** of God rejoicing in his creation ὁ δημιουργὸς...ἐπὶ τοῖς ἔργοις αὐτοῦ ~ᾶται, *1Clem*.33.2; of Son sharing this joy ὁμοούσιος, ἠγαλλιώμην καὶ αὐτὸς ἐνώπιον τούτου διὰ παντός ‡Proc.G.*Pr*.8:31(M.87.1297C); rejoicing in Church ~άσεται καὶ εὐφρανθήσεται Herm.*sim*.9.18.4; of Christ ~ώμενος καὶ ὑπερευφραινόμενος Clem.*paed*.1.6(p.109.11; M.8.288C); of H. Ghost ~άσεται Herm.*mand*.5.1.2; **2.** of angels ὁ ἄγγελος ἐπὶ τούτοις [sc. men] ἠγαλλιᾶτο id.*sim*.8.1.18; **3.** of Christians ~ώμενος...ὅτι...οὐδὲν ἀγαπᾶτε, εἰ μὴ μόνον τὸν θεόν Ign.*Eph*.9.2; id.*Magn*.1.1; *M.Polyc*.19.2; Herm.*sim*.9.24.2; ~ᾶται τὸ πνεῦμα τῶν ἐν Χριστῷ παιδίων Clem.*paed*.1.5(p.103.4; M.8.276A); esp. of martyrs: ref. Thecla, *A.Paul.et Thecl*.20(p.248.11); οἱ ἅγιοι ἠγαλλιάσθησαν *M.Perp*.18(p.89.18); ~ῶν *A.Phil*.16(p.9.12); *A.Thom*.A 107(p.219.7); and of others in hour of death, Diad.*perf*.100(p.150.10); of monks, ‡Pall.*h.mon*.8.52(p.47.13; M.34.1107C); of S. Paul ~άζεται Chrys.*comm.in Gal*.6:17(10.729D); ref. virtue μακροθυμία...~ωμένη Herm.*mand*.5.2.3; at Easter τὴν κυριακὴν ἡμέραν ~ᾷν Eus.*qu.Marin*.2.2(M.22.941C).

***ἀγαλλύνομαι,** *rejoice,* ‡Proc.G.*Pr*.8:31(M.87.1297D).

ἄγαλμα, τό, *statue, image*;

A. lit.; **1.** pagan: worship refused by Christians ἡμεῖς οἱ διακρίνοντες...τὸ ἀγένητον καὶ τὸ γενητὸν...προσκυνήσομεν τὰ ἀ.; Athenag.*leg*.15.1(M.6.920A); use condemned, Arist.*apol*.3.2; *ib*.7.4; connected with demons, Athenag.*leg*.27.2(953A); ἐναπομέμακται...τὰ εἴδη τῶν ἀ. τὴν διάθεσιν τῶν δαιμόνων Clem.*prot*.4(p.44.25; M.8.156A); ὥσπερ γὰρ 'τὸ χειροποίητον ἐπικατάρατον αὐτὸ καὶ ὁ ποιήσας αὐτό', οὐχ ὅτι ἐπικατάρατον αὐτὸ τὸ ἄψυχον, ἀλλ' εἴρηται χειροποίητον τὸ προσκαθεζόμενον τῷ ἀψύχῳ ἀ. καὶ χρηματίζον ἐκείνῳ τῷ ὀνόματι Or.*hom.10.6 in Jer*.(p.77.2; M.13.365B); id.*Cels*.6.5(p.75.13; M.11.1296C); inferior to animals, Clem.*prot*.4(p.39.22; 144A); *ib*.(p.40.3; 144B); **2.** Christian: of statue of Christ, said to have been erected by the woman with the issue of blood, Soz.*h.e*.5.21.1(M.67.1280B); cf.Eus.*h.e*.7.18.1–4; in description of Jewish Temple, where 'mercy seat' takes the place of an image ναοῦ λόγος οὐδείς, ὃν οὐ στέφει ἄ. Isid.Pel.*epp*.73(M.78.1133A)cit.ap.CNic.(787)*act*.1(H.4.48D).

B. met.; **1.** of bodies τὸ σχῆμα τοῦ ἀνθρωπείου ἀ. ‡Nil.*perist*.12(M.79.840A); of integrity of Lazarus' raised body as sign of creator's power, ‡Eust.*Laz*.4(p.29.8); of Christ's body, opp. pagan images, Eus.*l.C*.14(p.241.25ff.; M.20.1409A); of his humanity τὸ δ' ἔνθεον ἄ. σοφίας ἐνθέου, ἄ. πάσης ἀρετῆς ἐμπλέων, [ἄ.] θείου λόγου οἰκητήριον *ib*.(p.242.3ff.; 1409A); *ib*.15(p.244.18; 1413B); **2.** of souls τὰς ψυχὰς ἀ. τῶν σωμάτων οὔσας Meth.*symp*.1.1(p.8.10; M.18.37B); τῆς ἱερᾶς σου...ψυχῆς ἐπὶ μέσης καρδίας ἄ. περιφέρω Synes.*ep*.123(M.66.1504A); **3.** of mental and spiritual images δημιουργοῦσιν ἐν ταῖς ψυχαῖς τὰ τῆς φιλοσοφίας ἀ. Thdt.*affect*.3(p.95.8; 4.787); of figures under which divine things are represented to men, Dion.Ar.*c.h*.2.5(M.3.145A); τὸ νοητὸν...τῶν ἀ. ἀπογυμνώσαντας id.*e.h*.3.3.3(M.3.428D); cf. ἀ. μέν φησι τὰς εἰκόνας τῶν ἀοράτων καὶ μυστικῶν Max.*schol.e.h*.3.3.3(M.4.140A); τὸ...τῆς θεοειδοῦς ἀρετῆς...ἄ. Dion.Ar.*e.h*.4.3.1(473B); **4.** *image,* hence *example* ἄ. φιλοσοφίας, τοὺς τὴν ἐπισκοπὴν λαχόντας...φαίνεσθαι χρή Isid.Pel.*epp*.3.216(M.78.896C); Ἰωσὴφ...τῆς σωφροσύνης τὸ ἄ. Thdt.*ep*.83(p.48.24; 4.1145); of Justn. ὦ εὐσεβείας...ἄ. Agap.*cap*.5(M.86.1165B).

C. of divine image in man (cf. εἰκών) τὸ θεῖον καὶ ἅγιον ἄ. ἐν τῇ δικαίᾳ ψυχῇ Clem.*str*.7.4(p.21.32; M.9.440A); ἄ. ἔμψυχον...τοῦ κυρίου λέγοιτο [sc. ὁ γνωστικός] *ib*.7.9(p.39.9; 473C); ἐν ἑκάστῳ δὲ τῶν...ἐκεῖνον [sc. Christ]...μιμησαμένων ἐστὶν ἄ. τὸ 'κατ' εἰκόνα τοῦ κτίσαντος' Or.*Cels*.8.18(p.235.23; M.11.1545A); Meth.*symp*.6.2(p.65.11; M.18.116A); ‡Ign.*Phil*.13; Ἀδὰμ...τὸ τῆς ἐμῆς ἀξίας ἔμψυχον ἄ. Bas.Sel.*or*.29.1(M.85.328C); *ib*.2.1(40A); of virgins οἷον ἄ.... θεοῦ ἐκ ψυχῆς καὶ σώματος ἡ παρθένος ἐπὶ γῆς ἐπλάσθη †Bas.Anc.*virg*.58(M.30.785C).

***ἀγαλματικός,** *like (pagan) images* ἀ. εἴδωλα τὰς σεπτὰς εἰκόνας καλέσαντες ‡Jo.D.*ep.Thphl*.14(M.95.364A).

ἀγαλματογλύφος, ὁ, *carver of (pagan) images,* Thdt.*Rom*.1:23(3.25); id.*affect*.3(p.91.5; 4.782).

ἀγαλματοποιέω, *make images*; met., *form a mental concept,* ‡Nil.*perist*.11.21(M.79.933D).

ἀγαλματοφορ-έω, *bear an image in one's mind*; **1.** of things remembered, Nil.*Magn*.54(M.79.1040C); id.*exerc*.38(M.79.768A); ‡Nil.*perist*.4.4(M.79.829A); **2.** of image of God in soul τοῖς δὲ αὐτὸν ἐν ἑαυτοῖς ~οῦσι τὸν ποιητήν Athenag.*res*.12(p.62.15; M.6.997B), cf. Philo *opif.mund*.23,47; of image of Christ in soul ὅδε Χριστὸν...ἐν τῇ...~ῶν ψυχῇ Eus.*h.e*.10.4.26(M.20.860B); ἡ τελεία καὶ κεκαθαρμένη ψυχὴ...τὸν οὐράνιον λόγον ἀ. *ib*.10.4.56(872B); id.*Hierocl*.6(516B; M.22.808A); Chrys.*fr.in Pr*.22:20(M.64.728D); **3.** of Church as temple bearing image of God (Christ) within it, Or.*Jo*.10.39(23; p.215.19; M.14.381A); **4.** of Christ bearing his body as image of humanity, Leont.B.*Nest.et Eut*.2(M.86.1353A).

ἀγαμία, ἡ, *celibacy*; **1.** as praiseworthy state ἀ. δὲ ἐν τούτῳ ἔχει τὸ σεμνόν, ἐν τῷ κεχωρίσθαι τῆς μετὰ γυναικὸς διαγωγῆς Bas.*ep*.55(3.149C; M.32.401C); τῶν ἐν ἀ. διαλαμψάντων ἁγίων Gr.Nyss.*virg*.proem.(p.248.26; M.46.320A); Chrys.*virg*.48(1.308C); τὴν ἰσάγγελον ἀ. Nil.*epp*.1.181(M.79.152C); extolled by S. Paul, Bas.Sel.*v.Thecl*.1(M.85.496B); though not prescribed by God, Chrys.*ecl*.4(12.464D); **2.** ref. eccl. legislation; monastic state implies celibacy τινὲς ἑαυτοὺς τῷ τάγματι τῶν μοναζόντων ἐγκατηρίθμησαν· οἳ...δοκοῦσι παραδεδέχθαι τὴν ἀ. Bas.*ep*.199 *can*.19(3.292C; M.32.720C); virgins not to be admitted to state of celibacy before a certain age, *ib*.18(l.c.);

3. obligatory acc. Encratite teaching, Iren.*haer*.1.28.1(M.7.690A); *Const.App*.6.10.2; *Chron.Pasch*.p.260(M.92.633C).

ἀγανάκτησις, ἡ, *censure* ψῆφον ἀγανακτήσεως CCP(394)*act*.(M. 119.824D).

ἀγαπ-άω, *be fond of*, *love* [with intern. acc. ἠγάπησεν...τὸν Ἰακώβον ἀγάπην ἀνεκδιήγητον *Didasc.Jac*.5.18(p.88.13)]; **1.** dist. from φιλέω: τὸν κύριον ἡμῶν...Χριστὸν...οὐ μόνον φιλοῦντας ἀλλὰ καὶ ἀ. Or.*hom.15.3 in Jer*.(p.127.12; M.13.432A); οἰόμεθα δὲ τὸ μὲν ἀ. θειότερον εἶναι καὶ...πνευματικόν, τὸ δὲ φιλεῖν σωματικὸν καὶ ἀνθρωπικώτερον id.*fr.11 in Lam*.1:2(p.239.24; M.13.612B); but also used interchangeably with φιλέω: ἅπαντες ἡμᾶς ἀ., καὶ...ὁ θεὸς καὶ φιλήσει Chrys.*hom.19.9 in Mt*.(7.259A); id.*hom.23.3 in Rom*.(9.690B,C); and with ἐράω, *ib.23.4*(691B); id.*hom.11.4 in 2Cor*.(10.519B); **2.** of God loving man, *Barn*.1.1; *ib*.4.1; ὡς κριτής, τοὺς μὲν δικαίους ἀ. Ath.*Ar*.1.52(M.26.121A); Chrys.*hom.4.1 in Eph*.(11.26E); of Christ, Chrys.*comm.in Gal.2*:20(10.694B); pass., of Church being loved by God, Ign.*Trall*.proem.; **3.** of man loving God and Christ, in response to God's election ἀ. τὸν...πατέρα ἡμῶν ὃς ἐκλογῆς μέρος ἡμᾶς ἐποίησεν ἑαυτῷ *1Clem*.29.1; *ib*.59.3; πῶς ∼ήσεις τὸν οὕτως προαγαπήσαντά σε; ∼ήσας δὲ μιμητὴς ἔσῃ αὐτοῦ τῆς χρηστότητος *Diogn*.10.3f.; τὸν...θεοῦ λόγον...προσκυνοῦμεν καὶ ἀ. Just.*2apol*.13.4(M.6.468A); *A.Phil*.109(p.42.7); Ath.*ep.Aeg.Lib*.10(M.25.560C); of creator being loved through his creatures, Clem.*str*.6.9(p.467.31; M.9.293A) cit. s. φιλέω; **4.** of men loving each other, Ign.*Trall*.13.2; ∼ῶμεν οὖν ἀλλήλους, ὅπως ἔλθωμεν πάντες εἰς τὴν βασιλείαν τοῦ θεοῦ *2Clem*.9.6; ἀναγκάζομαι κἀγὼ εἰς τοῦτο, ἀ. ὑμᾶς ὑπὲρ τὴν ψυχήν μου *Barn*.1.4; ὁ ἐπίσκοπος ὡς τέκνα τοὺς λαϊκοὺς ἀ. *Const.App*.2.20.2; esp. saints and martyrs, Ign.*Philad*.5.2; worship of Christ dist. from love of saints, *M.Polyc*.17.3; **5.** of loving what is bad ἀ. μάταια *Barn*.20. 2; cf.*Did*.5.2; ἀ. μεγαλοφροσύνην Or.*hom.4.4 in Jer*.(p.27.4; M.13. 289D); Dion.Ar.*d.n*.8.8(M.3.896B); **6.** ὁ ἠγαπημένος of Christ (more freq. ἀγαπητός q.v.) with or without υἱός (or παῖς) *1Clem*.59.2f.; Ign.*Smyrn*.proem.; *Const.App*.1.8.2; τὸ ἀγαπώμενον of God, Gr. Nyss.*hom.6 in Cant*.(M.44.892D); *ib*.(893C); **7.** *give the kiss of peace* ὁ διάκονος. ∼ήσωμεν ἀλλήλους *Lit.Bas*.(p.320.29).

ἀγάπη, ἡ, *love*, *charity* (denoting esp. God's or Christ's love for man, man's love for God, and fraternal charity of Christians; used in preference to ἔρως on account of latter's undesirable associations, and to φιλία, which implies equality between friends);

A. of charity in gen.; **1.** definitions and order ἀ. δὲ ὁμόνοια... τῶν κατὰ τὸν λόγον καὶ τὸν βίον καὶ τὸν τρόπον ἢ συνελόντι φάναι κοινωνία βίου ἢ ἐκτένεια φιλίας καὶ φιλοστοργίας μετὰ λόγου ὀρθοῦ Clem.*str*.2.9(p.134.19; M.8.976B); *ib*.7.11(p.49.7; M.9.493C); τοῦτο γάρ ἐστιν ἡ ἀ., ἡ πρὸς τὸ καταθύμιον ἐνδιάθετος σχέσις Gr.Nyss.*anim.et res*.(M.46.93C); χρὴ...εἰδέναι τῆς ἀ. τὴν τάξιν...δεῖ γὰρ θεὸν μὲν ἀγαπᾶν ἐξ ὅλης καρδίας τε καὶ ψυχῆς...τὸν δὲ πλησίον ὡς ἑαυτόν· τὴν δὲ γυναῖκα, εἰ μὲν καθαρωτέρας ἐστὶ ψυχῆς, ὡς ὁ Χριστὸς τὴν ἐκκλησίαν· ὁ δὲ ἐμπαθέστερος, ὡς τὸ ἴδιον σῶμα id.*hom.4 in Cant*.(M.44.845D); **2.** characteristics ἀ. σχίσμα οὐκ ἔχει, ἀ. οὐ στασιάζει *1Clem*.49.5; ἀ. δὲ πολλαχῶς νοεῖται διὰ πραότητος, διὰ χρηστότητος, δι' ὑπομονῆς, δι' ἀφθονίας καὶ ἀζηλίας, δι' ἀμισίας, δι' ἀμνησικακίας· ἀμέριστός ἐστιν ἐν πᾶσιν, ἀδιάκριτος, κοινωνική Clem.*str*.2.18(p.159.16; M.8.1028A); desirable for its own sake, *ib*.7.11(p.48.17; M.9.493A); τῇ ἀ. ἐντρυφᾷς πλέον τῶν ἄλλων τοῦ πνεύματος καρπῶν Or.*schol.in Cant*.7:6f.(M.17. 284B); κλάδους δασεῖς...τὴν ἀ. φράσας· τὸ γὰρ δασὺ κατάκαρπον ὅλον ἐστὶ καὶ πυκνόν, μηδὲν ψιλὸν...ἔχον, ἀλλὰ πάντα πεπληρωμένα...τοιοῦτον γάρ ἐστιν ἡ ἀ. Meth.*symp*.9.4(p.118.23–26; M.18.185C); ἡ ἀ. ῥίζα καὶ πηγὴ καὶ μήτηρ ἐστὶν ἁπάντων τῶν ἀγαθῶν Chrys.*pent*.2.3(2.473B); id.*hom.30.1 in 2Cor*.(10.650B); eternal, id.*ep*.108(3.653D); id.*hom.2.1 in Phil*.(11.203B); not moved by physical beauty, Clem.*str*.4.18 (p.299.14; M.8.1324B); **3.** effects: union, Gr.Nyss.*hom.8 in Eccl*. (M.44.733B); εἶδες ἀγάπης ὑπερβολήν, πῶς ἀκαταγώνιστον ποιεῖ τὸν ἕνα καὶ πολλαπλασίως Chrys.*hom.78.4 in Jo*.(8.463C); removal of sin, id.*hom.4.4 in 1Thess*.(11.456E); id.*pent*.2.3(2.473C); ἡ οὖν ἀ., τὰ τρία ἀνατρέπει· τὴν μὲν οἴησιν, ἐπειδὴ οὐ φυσιοῦται· τὸν δὲ ἔνδοθεν φθόνον, ἐπεὶ οὐ ζηλοῖ· τὸν δὲ ἔξωθεν, ἐπειδὴ μακροθυμεῖ καὶ χρηστεύεται Max.*carit*.4.61(M.90.1061B); **4.** its relation to ἔρως; no essential difference between the two, except that ἀ. is the weaker term, Gr.Nyss.*hom.13 in Cant*.(M.44.1048C) cit. s. ἔρως; ἔδοξέ τισι τῶν καθ' ἡμᾶς ἱερολόγων καὶ θειότερον εἶναι τὸ τοῦ ἔρωτος ὄνομα τοῦ τῆς ἀ. ... ἐμοὶ γὰρ δοκοῦσιν οἱ θεολόγοι κοινὸν μὲν ἡγεῖσθαι τὸ τῆς ἀ., καὶ τὸ τοῦ ἔρωτος ὄνομα Dion.Ar.*d.n*.4.12(M.3.709B); ὡς μὲν ἔρως ὑπάρχον τὸ θεῖον καὶ ἀ. κινεῖται, ὡς δὲ ἐραστὸν καὶ ἀγαπητὸν κινεῖ πρὸς ἑαυτὸ πάντα τὰ ἔρωτος καὶ ἀ. δεκτικά Max.*ambig*.(M.91.1260C); cf. ἔρως; **5.** its relation to virtue and the virtues: begets poverty, Chrys.*hom.11.1 in Ac*.(9.90C); is itself the crown of benignity and humility, ‡Bas.*const*.13(2.558C; M.31.1377A); closely connected with ἀπάθεια Max.*carit*.1.2(M.90.961A), and ἐγκράτεια *ib*.4.72(1065B); **6.** praises of charity ἀ. προφητείας χορηγός· ἀ. τεράτων παρεκτική· ἀ. ἐλλάμψεως ἄβυσσος. ἀ. πηγὴ πυρός· ὅσον ἀναβλύσει, τοσοῦτον τὸν διψῶντα καταφλέξει· ἀ. ἀγγέλων στάσις· ἀ. προσκοπὴ τῶν αἰώνων Jo.Clim.*scal*.30(M.88.1160B).

B. God's love; **1.** God as love (1Jo.4:8), hence ὁ τὴν ἀ. ἔχων, τὸν θεὸν ἔχει Bas.*ascet*.2.2(2.325D; M.31.885B); Gr.Nyss.*hom.opif*.5 (M.44.137C); Dion.Ar.*d.n*.4.14(M.3.712C); ὁ οὖν κτησάμενος τὴν ἀ., αὐτὸν τὸν θεὸν ἐκτήσατο Max.*carit*.4.100(M.90.1073A); in a Trin. invocation before baptism σοὶ δόξα ἡ τῶν σπλάγχνων ἀ. *A.Thom*. A 132(p.239.26); **2.** God's love for Son, ‡Ath.*Ar*.4.24(p.72.7; M.26.505A); for man (cf. φιλανθρωπία) ἡ ἀ. σου ἐπὶ σπέρμα Ἀβραάμ *Pss.Sal*.18.4; ὦ τῆς ὑπερβαλλούσης φιλανθρωπίας καὶ ἀ. τοῦ θεοῦ *Diogn*.9.2; Christians called τέκνα ἀγάπης *Barn*.9.7; ὁ δημιουργός, ὁ κατὰ μὲν τὴν ἀ. πατήρ Iren.*haer*.5.17.1(M.7.1169A); τῆς ἀ. ... τὸ ἀξιάγαστον, ἐν τῷ δεδόσθαι τὸν υἱὸν ὑπὲρ ἡμῶν Cyr.*Jo*.2.1(4.152E); apprehended by meditation, Chrys.*hom.7.3 in Eph*.(11.49D); its character ἄνω καὶ κάτω τὴν ἀ. τίθησιν αἰτίαν· μάλιστα δὲ ἐκείνη ἀ. ἐστίν, ὅταν εὐεργετῶνται ἄνθρωποι μηδενὸς προϋπάρξαντος παρ' αὐτῶν *ib*.(49E); 'ἐν ἀ., προορίσας ἡμᾶς'. οὐ γὰρ ἀπὸ πόνων οὐδὲ κατορθωμάτων τοῦτο γίνεται, ἀλλ' ἀπὸ ἀ., οὔτε ἀπὸ ἀ. μόνης, ἀλλὰ καὶ ἀπὸ τῆς ἡμετέρας ἀρετῆς. εἰ γὰρ δὴ ἀπὸ ἀ. μόνης, ἐχρῆν ἅπαντας σωθῆναι· εἰ δὲ ἀπὸ τῆς ἡμετέρας ἀρετῆς πάλιν μόνης, περιττὴ ἡ παρουσία αὐτοῦ...ἀλλ' οὔτε ἀπὸ ἀ. μόνης, οὔτε ἀπὸ τῆς ἡμετέρας ἀρετῆς, ἀλλ' ἐξ ἀμφοτέρων *ib*.1.2(4E,F); †Gregent.*disp*.(M.86.705A); **3.** Christ's love for man ἐν ἀ. προσελάβετο ἡμᾶς ὁ δεσπότης· διὰ τὴν ἀ., ἣν ἔσχεν πρὸς ἡμᾶς, τὸ αἷμα αὐτοῦ ἔδωκεν *1Clem*.49.6; his blood being esp. associated with his love πόμα θέλω τὸ αἷμα αὐτοῦ, ὅ ἐστιν ἀ. ἄφθαρτος Ign.*Rom*.7.3; νίψαι τοὺς πόδας τοῦ...μαθητοῦ... ἀπὸ ἀ. Or.*Jo*.32.12(7; p.445.24; M.14.773A); *A.Thom*.A 72(p.188.4); συνέστησεν ἑαυτοῦ τὴν ἀ. ὁ καλὸς ἐραστὴς τῶν ἡμετέρων ψυχῶν Gr. Nyss.*hom.13 in Cant*.(M.44.1044B); Chrys.*hom.46.3 in Jo*.(8.272E); Max.*carit*.1.71(M.90.976C); represented by the bishop παρακαλῶ οὖν ὑμᾶς, οὐκ ἐγὼ ἀλλ' ἡ ἀ. Ἰησοῦ Χριστοῦ Ign.*Trall*.6.1; Cross as sign of his love, Chrys.*hom.in Mt.26:39*(10.19C).

C. man's love for God; **1.** in gen.; **a.** def. ἀ. δὲ λέγω, τὴν ἀρραγῆ, τὴν μὴ τεμνομένην, μήτε χωριζομένην ἐν ποικίλοις πειρασμοῖς καὶ βασάνοις, τὴν θεῷ πλησιάζουσαν, καὶ τέκνα θεοῦ ἀποτεκοῦσαν Ant. Mon.*hom*.128(M.89.1833A); ἀ. μέν ἐστιν, διάθεσις ψυχῆς ἀγαθή, καθ' ἣν οὐδὲν τῶν ὄντων, τῆς τοῦ θεοῦ γνώσεως προτιμᾷ. ἀδύνατον δὲ εἰς ἕξιν ἐλθεῖν ταύτης τῆς ἀ., τὸν πρός τι τῶν ἐπιγείων ἔχοντα προσπάθειαν Max.*carit*.1.1(M.90.961A); **b.** in rel. to fear πρῶτος βαθμὸς τῆς σωτηρίας ἡ μετὰ φόβου διδασκαλία,...δεύτερος δὲ ἡ ἐλπὶς...τελειοῖ δὲ ἡ ἀ. Clem.*str*.4.7(p.272.22; M.8.1265A); *ib*.7.16(p.72.6; M.9.541A); Bas.*hom. in Ps*.32(1.137D; M.29.337B); προβήτω ὁ λόγος ἐκ τοῦ φόβου τοῦ κυρίου ἐπὶ τὴν τελείαν ἀ. αὐτοῦ Ant.Mon.*hom*.128(M.89.1833A); Max.*carit*.1.81(M.90.977D) cit. s. φόβος; **c.** rel. to doctrine οὐδὲν δὲ οὕτως ἀναφλέγει καὶ κινεῖ τὴν καρδίαν εἰς τὴν ἀ. τοῦ θεοῦ ὡς ἡ θεολογία Ant.Mon.*hom*.128(M.89.1836C); **d.** rel. to prayer, v. εὐχή; **e.** its fruits: good works, Clem.*q.d.s*.28(p.178.33; M.9.633C); Chrys.*carit*.1 (6.287 et passim); but cf. χωρὶς ἀ., κἂν γένηται τὰ προστάγματα... καὶ τὰ μέγαλα χαρίσματα...ἀνομίας ἔργα λογισθήσεται †Bas.*bapt*.1.2. 25(2.647B; M.31.1568B); peace, Chrys.*hom.30.1 in 2Cor*.(10.650B); Max.*carit*.4.36(M.90.1056B); the two juxtaposed, *1Clem*.62.2; *Barn*. 21.9; Clem.*paed*.1.12(p.149.17; M.8.369A); imperturbability, Max. *carit*.1.37(968); obedience, Chrys.*serm.7.2 in Gen*.(4.676E); **f.** love 'in Christ' ὁ ἔχων ἀ. ἐν Χριστῷ *1Clem*.49.1; Or.*Cels*.3.15(p.214.13; M.11.937C); Meth.*symp*.4.6(p.52.6; M.18.96B); *Const.App*.8.46.16; esp. in his blood, with which it is almost identified ἐν ἀ., ὅ ἐστιν αἷμα Ἰησοῦ Χριστοῦ Ign.*Trall*.8.1; id.*Smyrn*.1.1; **2.** love in mystical life; **a.** its growth; through abnegation οὐ τοῦ τυχόντος δέ ἐστιν εἰς τὸ τέλειον χωρῆσαι τῆς ἀ.,...ἀλλὰ τοῦ ἐκδυσαμένου ἤδη τὸν παλαιὸν ἄνθρωπον Bas.*hom.in Ps*.44(1.160B; M.29.392A); and prayer οὐ μικρὸς σύνδεσμος τῆς πρὸς θεὸν ἀ. ἡ εὐχή Chrys.*exp.in Ps*.4(5.8A); Max.*carit*.2.52(M.90.1001B); accompanied by temptations ὅταν ἄρχηται ὁ νοῦς εἰς τὴν ἀ. τοῦ θεοῦ προκόπτειν, τότε καὶ ὁ δαίμων τῆς βλασφημίας ἄρχεται ἐκπειράζειν αὐτόν *ib*.2.14(988B); **b.** love and union with God ἀ. κολλᾷ ἡμᾶς τῷ θεῷ *1Clem*.49.4 = Or.*hom.5.2 in Jer*.(p.33.5; M.13.300A); ἀ. ὁδὸς ἡ ἀναφέρουσα εἰς θεόν Ign.*Eph*.9.1; τῇ γνωστικῇ ἀ., δι' ἣν καὶ ἡ κληρονομία καὶ ἡ παντελὴς ἕπεται ἀποκατάστασις Clem.*str*.6.9(p.469.10; M.9.296B); διὰ τῆς ἀορίστου ἀγάπης ἥνωται τῷ πνεύματι *ib*.7.7(p.33.20; 464B); ὑψωθεῖσα δι' ἀγάπης πρὸς τὴν τοῦ ἀγαθοῦ μετουσίαν ἡ κεκαθαρμένη ψυχή Gr.Nyss.*hom.5 in Cant*. (M.44.857D); id.*anim.et res*.(M.46.65A); *ib*.(96C); ἡ μὲν εἰς θεὸν ἀ. εἰ τὴν θείαν ὁμιλίαν ἀεὶ φιλεῖ πτερῶσαι τὸν νοῦν Max.*carit*.4.40(1056D);

equated with perfection, *1Clem.*49.5; *ib.*50.1; Gr.Nyss.*hom.1 in Cant.*(M.44.765B); ἡ ἀ. πρᾶγμά ἐστιν ἀγαθῶν ἁπάντων περιεκτικώτατον...δι' ἧς ἄνθρωπος οἰκειοῦται τῷ θεῷ καὶ συνάπτεται Andr.Cr. *or.*7(M.97.941A); **c.** effects of perfect love: detachment τοῖς περιτετμημένοις τὰς τῶν παθῶν ἐπιθυμίας διὰ τὴν πρὸς μόνον τὸ θεῖον ἀ. Clem.*str.*5.4(p.339.3; M.9.37C); διὰ τῆς πληρεστάτης...ἀ. τοῦ πνεύματος τῆς ἄκρας τῶν παθῶν ἐλευθερίας ἀξιωθέντας Mac.Aeg.*perf.*6 (M.34.845D); ἐὰν τὸν θεὸν γνησίως ἀγαπήσωμεν, δι' αὐτῆς τῆς ἀ. τὰ πάθη ἀποβάλλομεν. ἡ δὲ εἰς αὐτὸν ἀ. ἐστί, τὸ προτιμᾶν αὐτὸν τοῦ κόσμου, καὶ τὴν ψυχὴν τῆς σαρκός Max.*carit.*3.50(M.90.1032B); *ib.*1. 72(976C); *ib.*2.58(1004B); 'apostolate' ἀ. γὰρ ἀληθοῦς καὶ βεβαίας ἐστὶν μὴ μόνον ἑαυτὸν θέλειν σώζεσθαι, ἀλλὰ καὶ πάντας τοὺς ἀδελφούς *M.Polyc.*1.2; ἂν τοίνυν ἔχῃς ἀ., ἀπόστολος γέγονας Chrys.*hom.2.3 in Ac.princ.*(3.66C); martyrdom, Clem.*str.*4.6(p.266.23; M.8.1252C); *ib.* 4.12(p.285.34; 1293C); Or.*mart.*2(p.4.18; M.11.565B); but martyrdom without charity avails nothing, Chrys.*pan.Rom.*1.1(2.612C); **d.** love and mystical experiences: ecstasy ὅταν τῷ ἔρωτι τῆς ἀ. πρὸς θεὸν ὁ νοῦς ἐκδημῇ, τότε οὔτε ἑαυτοῦ οὔτε τινὸς τῶν ὄντων παντάπασι ἐπαισθάνεται Max.*carit.*1.10(M.90.964A); *ib.*1.12(964B); the 'wound of love' τοσούτους τετρωμένους τῇ θείᾳ ἀ. ὁμοίως τῇ ὁμολογούσῃ τοῦτο πεπονθέναι ἐν τῷ Ἄισματι τῶν ᾀσμάτων διὰ τοῦ 'ὅτι τετρωμένη ἀγάπης ἐγώ' Or.*Jo.*1.32(36; p.41.3; M.14.85B); cf.Mac.Aeg.*hom.*25.5(M.34. 669D); ἡ διὰ τῶν θείων ἀναβάσεων ὑψωθεῖσα ψυχή, τὸ γλυκὺ τῆς ἀ. βέλος ἐν ἑαυτῇ, ᾧ ἐτρώθη...ὁμοῦ τε γὰρ τὸ τῆς ἀ. βέλος ἐδέξατο,...εἰς γαμικὴν θυμηδίαν ἡ τοξεία μετεσκευάσθη Gr.Nyss.*hom.4 in Cant.*(M. 44.852B); ἐγκάρδιον δεξαμένη τῆς ἀ. τὸ βέλος *ib.*5(860A); this wound made by Christ τὸν τῆς ἀ. τοξότην *ib.13*(1044B,C).

D. fraternal charity; **1.** grounded in love of God τὴν ἀ. ἐνδείκνυται εἰς τὸν ὅμοιον διὰ τὴν ἀ. τὴν πρὸς τὸν δημιουργόν Clem.*str.*2.18(p.159. 11; M.8.1028A); Bas.*reg.fus.*3.2(2.340E; M.31.917C); **2.** a gift of H. Ghost, id.*ep.*133(3.225B; M.32.569B); διὰ δὲ τῆς εἰς τὸν πλησίον ἀ., ἡ εἰς θεὸν ἀ. κρατύνεται Andr.Cr.*or.*7(M.97.941A); **3.** hence greatest of virtues and a distinctive mark of Christians, Or.*or.* 11.2(p.322.14; M.11.449A); Bas.*fid.*5(2.328D; M.31.688C); id.*moral.* 5.1(2.238E; M.31.709A); Chrys.*hom.40.3 in Ac.*(9.305C); Max.*carit.* 4.100(M.90.1073A); **4.** its universality τὴν ἀ. αὐτῶν, μὴ κατὰ προσκλίσεις, ἀλλὰ πᾶσιν τοῖς φοβουμένοις τὸν θεὸν...παρεχέτωσαν *1Clem.*21.7; Or.*or.*11.2(p.322.21; M.11.449B); Bas.*ep.*203(3.301B; M. 32.741A); ἡ τελεία ἀ. ... πάντας ἀνθρώπους ἐξ ἴσου ἀγαπᾷ Max. *carit.*1.71(M.90.976B); esp. present between bishops and their flocks, Ign.*Eph.*3.2; *ib.*2.1; id.*Trall.*12.3; ὁ ἐπίσκοπος...τοὺς λαϊκοὺς...θερμαίνων τῇ σπουδῇ τῆς ἀ. *Const.App.*2.20.2; **5.** its unifying role in Church τοὺς τοσούτῳ τῷ πλήθει τῶν τόπων διῃρημένους τῇ διὰ τῆς ἀ. ἑνώσει καθορᾶν εἰς μίαν μελῶν ἁρμονίαν ἐν σώματι Χριστοῦ δεδέσθαι Bas.*ep.*70(3.163E; M.32.433C); ἀ. ... τὴν συγκολλῶσαν ἡμᾶς ...καὶ τοσαύτην ἕνωσιν...παρεχομένην, ὡσανεὶ μέλη πρὸς μέλη Chrys. *hom.11.1 in Eph.*(11.80C); τοῦτο γὰρ τῆς ἀ. ... πλεονέκτημα, τὸ τὴν διάθεσιν τῶν ἁπάντων ἐργάζεσθαι μίαν...μελῶν ἑνὸς σώματος δίκην συνδεδεμένων Nil.*Magn.*59(M.79.1048B); **6.** necessity for salvation δίχα ἀ. οὐδὲν εὐάρεστόν ἐστιν τῷ θεῷ *1Clem.*49.5; *ib.*50.5; οὐδένα γὰρ ἂν ἔσωσεν ἡ ἀρετή, τῆς ἀ. μὴ οὔσης Chrys.*hom.1.2 in Eph.*(11.5A); **7.** rel. to faith and hope, cf. ἐλπίς: πίστις δὲ οὐ σοφῶν τῶν κατὰ κόσμον...τὸ σύγγραμμα αὐτῆς...ἀ. κέκληται, σύνταγμα πνευματικόν Clem.*paed.*3.11(p.279.19; M.8.656C); ἡ γὰρ ἐλπὶς μέχρι ἐκείνου κινεῖται, ἕως ἂν μὴ παρείη τῶν ἐλπιζομένων ἀπόλαυσις, καὶ ἡ πίστις ὡσαύτως ἔρεισμα τῆς τῶν ἐλπιζομένων ἀδηλίας γίνεται..., ἐπειδὰν δὲ ἔλθῃ τὸ ἐλπιζόμενον, τῶν ἄλλων εὐτηρεμόντων [? ἠρεμούντων] πάντων, ἡ κατὰ τὴν ἀ. ἐνέργεια μένει Gr.Nyss.*anim.et res.*(M.46.96B); κράτος ἀγάπης ἐλπίς, δι' αὐτῆς γὰρ τὸν τῆς ἀ. μισθὸν ἀπεκδεχόμεθα Jo.Clim.*scal.*30 (M.88.1157D); ἡ μὲν πίστις καὶ ἐλπὶς μέχρι τινός· ἡ δὲ ἀ., εἰς ἀπείρους αἰῶνας Max.*carit.*3.100(M.90.1048A); love and works necessary for faith to procure salvation, *ib.*1.39(968C).

E. *act of love* or *charity*; **1.** of alms-deeds, *Orac.Sib.*8.497; cf. Chrys.*hom.22.3 in Ac.*(9.182B); μὴ ἔχων ὅθεν ἀγοράσαι, ἔλαβε παρά τινος ἀγάπην *Apophth.Patr.*(M.65.92D); Jo.Mosch.*prat.*13(M.87. 2861B) perh. to be included under 4 infra; Leont.N.*v.Jo.Eleem.*27 (p.58.12); of good deeds in gen. ἐποίησα ἐμαυτῷ ἀ. *Apophth.Patr.* (105B); **2.** *kiss of peace* in liturgy μετὰ τὸ δοθῆναι τὴν ἀ. *Lit.Bas.* (p.321.1); **3.** ποιεῖν ἀ.; **a.** ? *make apology, seek pardon, excuse oneself, PLond.*1914.28, but v. 4 infra; **b.** as idiomatic expression, *do a favour*, hence *have the goodness to, please* ποίησον ἀ. ὑποδέξαι ἡμᾶς Ephr.2.155A; ποιήσατε ἀ., μὴ λαλεῖτε *Apophth.Patr.*(M.65.117B); Dor.*doct.*1.8(M.88.1744D); Jo.Mosch.*prat.*5(M.87.2856D); *ib.*16(2864B); *ib.*93(2952C); **4.** as t. t., a *charity*, denoting common meal of fellowship to which poor were invited or from which distribution was made to those supported by Church, connected with eucharist and acc. some ancient authorities dissociated therefrom on account of disorder (a theory based on identification of ἀ. with meal described in 1Cor.11:20ff.); prob. following or preceding eucharist, though at times ἀ. appears to include eucharist or be identified with it (cf. Judae 12); οὐκ ἐξόν ἐστιν χωρὶς τοῦ ἐπισκόπου οὔτε βαπτίζειν οὔτε ἀ. ποιεῖν Ign.*Smyrn.*8.2; cf. τράπεζαν κοινὴν παρατίθενται *Diogn.*5.7; apparently abused by the greedy εἰ δ' ἀ. τινὲς τολμῶσι καλεῖν ἀθύρῳ γλώττῃ κεχρημένοι δειπνάριά τινα κνίσης καὶ ζωμῶν ἀποπνέοντα, τὸ καλὸν καὶ σωτήριον ἔργον τοῦ λόγου, τὴν ἀ. τὴν ἡγιασμένην...καθυβρίζοντες...σφάλλονται τῆς ὑπολήψεως...τὰς τοιαύτας δὲ ἑστιάσεις ὁ κύριος ἀγάπας οὐ κέκληκεν Clem.*paed.*2.1(p.156.12; M.8.384B); practised by Carpocratians εἰς τὰ δεῖπνα ἀθροιζομένους (οὐ γὰρ ἀ. εἴποιμ' ἂν ἔγωγε τὴν συνέλευσιν αὐτῶν) id.*str.*3.2(p.200.7; M.8.1112A); imitated by martyrs in prison, *M.Perp.*17(p.87.10) cit. s. δεῖπνον; celebrated at graves of departed ἦν ἔσω ἐν τῷ μνημείῳ ἀ. πολλή...εἶχον δὲ ἄρτους πέντε καὶ λάχανα καὶ ὕδωρ *A.Paul.et Thecl.*25(p.252.11); as general observance by orthodox, cf.Tert.*apol.*39(M.*PL.*1.474A); perh. cf. Hipp.*trad.ap.*26.1,2,5; cf. *diaconus in agape absente presbytero vicem gerat presbyteri quantum pertinet ad orationem et fractionem panis quem invitatis distribuat*, ‡Hipp.*can.*180; εἴ τις καταφρονοίη τῶν ἐκ πίστεως ἀγάπας ποιούντων..., καὶ μὴ ἐθέλοι κοινωνεῖν ταῖς κλήσεσι, διὰ τὸ ἐξευτελίζειν τὸ γινόμενον, ἀ. ἔ. CGangr.*can.* 11; practice restricted οὐ δεῖ ἱερατικοὺς ἢ κληρικοὺς ἢ λαϊκοὺς καλουμένους εἰς ἀ. μέρη αἴρειν, διὰ τὸ τὴν ὕβριν τῇ τάξει προστρίβεσθαι τῇ ἐκκλησιαστικῇ CLaod.*can.*27; οὐ δεῖ ἐν τοῖς κυριακοῖς ἢ ἐν ταῖς ἐκκλησίαις τὰς λεγομένας ἀ. ποιεῖν καὶ ἐν τῷ οἴκῳ τοῦ θεοῦ ἐσθίειν καὶ ἀκούβιτα στρωννύειν *ib.*28; cf.*Cod.Afr.*42; CTrull.*can.*74; followed eucharist but this practice was abandoned, cf. κοινὰς δὲ ἐποιοῦντο τὰς τραπέζας...καὶ...μετὰ τὴν τῶν μυστηρίων κοινωνίαν ἐπὶ κοινὴν πάντες ᾔεσαν εὐωχίαν Chrys.*hom.27.1 in 1Cor.*(10.240E); cf. Thdt.*1Cor.*11:17(3.235); perh. continued in Egyptian churches, cf. μετὰ γὰρ τὸ εὐωχηθῆναι καὶ παντοίων ἐδεσμάτων ἐμφορηθῆναι, περὶ ἑσπέραν προσφέροντες, τῶν μυστηρίων μεταλαμβάνουσιν Socr. *h.e.*5.22.43(M.67.636A); cf.Soz.*h.e.*7.19.8(M.67.1477B); freq. as common meal in monastic circles ἐποίησεν δὲ καὶ ἀ. ... Ἕλλην ὢν διὰ τὸ ἁμάρτημα ὃ ἐποίησεν *PLond.*1914.28 but poss. to be included under 3 supra; apparently distributed among hermits ἄρτους ἀποφέρω, ἐπειδὴ ἀ. ἐστὶ τοῦδε τοῦ ἀδελφοῦ Pall.*h.Laus.*16(p.42.11; M. 34.1042C); γενομένης ἀ., καὶ τῶν ἀδελφῶν ἐν τῇ ἐκκλησίᾳ ἐσθιόντων *Apophth.Patr.*(M.65.181A); *ib.*(300A); *ib.*(400B); ἦλθον δοῦναι αὐτῷ τὴν ἀ. Jo.Mosch.*prat.*13(M.87.2861B) perh. to be included under 1 supra; εἰ δέ τινι καὶ διαλεχθῆναι ἀναγκαῖον, προτρέψει τὸν ἀδελφὸν ἀ. λαβεῖν· εἶτ' οὖν ἄρτον ζωῆς, καὶ φιλοθέοις αὐτὸν διηγήμασι...ἑστιατέον Niceph.Ur.*v.Sym.*35(M.86.3017C); for the departed μὴ φροντίσητε ποιεῖν ἀγάπας ὑπὲρ ἐμοῦ *Apophth.Patr.*(M.65.105B); of meal in a monastery, Thdr.Stud.*or.*12.6(M.99.853A); met. τὴν συνήθη τράπεζαν ὑμῖν παραθῶμεν, καὶ ἐκ τῶν πρόσφατον ἀναγνωσθέντων παρὰ τοῦ ...Μωυσέως ἑστιάσωμεν ὑμῶν τὴν ἀ. Chrys.*hom.30.1 in Gen.*(4.295A).

F. *association* or *community of love*, almost = *Church*, so prob. in Ign. ἀσπάζεται ὑμᾶς ἡ ἀ. Σμυρναίων καὶ Ἐφεσίων Ign.*Trall.*13.1; id.*Rom.*9.3; id.*Philad.*11.2; id.*Smyrn.*12.2; id.*Magn.*15.1; ἐκκλησίᾳ ...ἥτις καὶ προκάθηται ἐν τόπῳ χωρίου Ῥωμαίων...προκαθημένη τῆς ἀ. id.*Rom.*proem.; cf. τὴν βασιλείαν τοῦ θεοῦ...ἁγίαν συνήλυσιν ἀγάπης, οὐράνιον ἐκκλησίαν Clem.*paed.*2.1(p.157.25; M.8.388A).

G. as form of address, '*your charity*', Ursac.*ep.Ath.*(p.138.24; M.25.356A); Gr.Nyss.*ep.*19(M.46.1073A); Chrys.*hom.19.2 in Rom.* (9.645A); Sophr.H.*or.*2.8(M.87.3225D).

H. as Valent. aeon, Iren.*haer.*2.14.8(M.7.756B); Hipp.*haer.*6.30 (p.157.21; M.16.3239A); Epiph.*haer.*31.2(p.386.11; M.41.477A).

I. of evil desire (cf. 1Jo.2:15), distinction between good and bad ἀ., Max.*carit.*3.71(M.90.1037C); latter having diabolic origin, Chrys. *hom.32.7 in 1Cor.*(10.296A); ‡Nil.*vit.cog.*(M.79.1468B); of love of Devil for a woman, *A.Thom.*A 43(p.160.10); ref. immoral practices: of Carpocratians μίγνυσθαι, ὅπως ἐθέλοιεν, αἷς βούλοιντο, μελετήσαντας δὲ ἐν τοιαύτῃ ἀ. τὴν κοινωνίαν Clem.*str.*3.2(p.200.12; M.8.1112A); of Simonians, Hipp.*haer.*6.19(p.146.13; M.16.3223B); ὁ μὲν ἀνὴρ τῆς γυναικὸς ὑποχωρήσας φάσκει λέγων τῇ ἑαυτοῦ γυναικὶ ὅτι 'ἀνάστα, ποίησον τὴν ἀ. μετὰ τοῦ ἀδελφοῦ'. οἱ δὲ τάλανες μιγέντες ἀλλήλοις Epiph.*haer.*26.4(p.280.23; M.41.337C); ref. love for *virgines subintroductae*, Gr.Naz.*carm.*2.2(epigr.)10.8(M.38.87A); of love of material things, Chrys.*hom.21.2 in Rom.*(9.674B); Max.*carit.*3. 17(M.90.1021A).

ἀγάπησις, ἡ, *love, affection*, in same senses as ἀγάπη; of God's love νουθετήσει δίκαιον ὡς υἱὸν ἀγαπήσεως *Pss.Sal.*13.8; ἡ εἰς ἡμᾶς ἀ. τοῦ θεοῦ Cyr.*inc.unigen.*(5[1].686D); in Christ, Sophr.H.*ep.syn.*(M.87. 3152B); of man's love for God, Cyr.*Is.*1.1(2.23D); Dion.Ar.*c.h.*1.3

(M.3.376A); Sophr.H.*v.Anast.*(M.92.1701B); for Christ, *ib.*(1709C); of fraternal charity, Bas.*renunt.*9(2.210C; M.31.645A).

***ἀγαπητέον**, *one must love*, Clem.*str.*2.12(p.143.7; M.8.993A); id. *q.d.s.*22(p.174.18; M.9.628B).

ἀγαπητικός, **1.** *loving, charitable, friendly*, of Church, typified by BMV ἀ. δὲ ὡς μήτηρ Clem.*paed.*1.6(p.115.15; M.8.300B); *ib.*3.11 (p.280.18; 657C); γράμματα ἀ. Bas.*ep.*203.1(3.300C; M.32.740A); Gr. Nyss.*hom.1 in Cant.*(M.44.784A); ἀνὴρ...ἀγαπητικώτατος Pall.*h.Laus.* 39(p.124.14; M.34.1195C); **2.** *being a lover of, in love with* γνωστικός, τοῦ...θεοῦ ἀ. ὑπάρχων Clem.*str.*7.11(p.49.13; M.9.496A); **3.** *of love, of charity* ἡ κατὰ Χριστὸν ἀ. ἡμῶν διδασκαλία *ib.*4.18(p.298.13; M.8.1321B); *ib.*5.3(p.336.14; M.9.33A); τῆς κοινωνίας τῆς ἀ. *ib.*4.18 (p.297.21; M.8.1320C); Gr.Nyss.*hom.1 in Cant.*(M.44.777B); Max. *cap.*5.89(M.90.1388A) = *schol.d.n.*4.14(M.4.268A); **4.** *(of) loving* τὴν ἀ. δύναμιν Bas.*reg.fus.*2.1(2.337A; M.31.909B); id.*ascet.*2.2(2.325B; M.31.884D); Gr.Nyss.*hom.1 in Cant.*(M.44.769C); **5.** neut. as subst., *faculty of loving* κατεσθίει...τὸ ἀ. ἡ φιλεχθρία †Bas.*Is.*19(1.391E; M.30.149D).

ἀγαπητικῶς, **1.** *lovingly, charitably*, of Christ τὸν καθηγούμενον ἀ. ἀρίστου βίου Clem.*paed.*1.3(p.95.8; M.8.260A); *ib.*3.12(p.287.19; 673A); of martyrs suffering ἀ., id.*str.*4.9(p.282.13; M.8.1285A); Eus. *p.e.*6.6(254A; M.21.432C); ἀ. πρὸς τὸ ὁμόφυλον ἔχειν Gr.Nyss.*v.Mos.* 48(M.44.317C); †Nil.*mal.cog.*27(M.79.1232C); Leont.B.*Nest.et Eut.*2 (M.86.1328B); **2.** *by way of love, through process of love* ὁ θεὸς καὶ πατήρ, κινηθεὶς ἀχρόνως καὶ ἀ., προῆλθεν εἰς διάκρισιν ὑποστάσεων Max.*schol.d.n.*2.4(M.4.221A).

ἀγαπητός, *beloved*;

A. of Christ; **1.** ref. testimony of Father in Mc.1:11, 9:7 (cf. 12:6), interpreted explicitly in sense of *only* son (cf.*LS*: *with which one must be content*, hence of *only* children) τὸ 'ἀ.' τίς ἂν εἴη ἢ υἱὸς μονογενής; ‡Ath.*Ar.*4.24(p.71.9; M.26.504C); *ib.*4.29(p.78. 14; 513C); Bas.*hom.in Ps.*44(1.160B; M.29.392A); ἀ. and μονογενής in close conjunction, Iren.*haer.*4.5.4(M.7.986A); Eus.*e.th.*1.10(p.68.15; M.24.841B); id.*Marcell.*1.1(p.2.14; M.24.713A); *Const.App.*3.17.4; as *beloved* ὁ τοῦ ἀ. καὶ εὐλογητοῦ παιδός σου Ἰησοῦ *M.Polyc.*14.1,3; ἀ. αὐτοῦ, ἐν ᾧ ηὐδόκησεν Or.*comm.in Mt.*12.42(p.167.5; M.13.1081C); *A.Phil.*19(p.10.23); **2.** subst., as Messianic title (cf. Ps.44:1) ὁ χριόμενος ἐν πένθει ἀγαπητοῦ *T.Lev.*17.3; *Ascens.Is.*3.17; τὰ περὶ τοῦ ἀ., ὃς τὴν οἰκονομίαν τῆς σαρκώσεως ὑπὲρ ἡμῶν ἀνεδέξατο Bas.*hom.in Ps.*44(1.160A; M.29.389C); of a Messianic event ἡ δὲ παρουσία αὐτοῦ ἀγαπητή *T.Lev.*8.15; **3.** of Christ as the beloved of virgins Χριστὸν ἔχεις ἀ. Gr.Naz.*carm.*2.2(epigr.)18.3(M.38.92A).

B. of men; **1.** as beloved by God τοὺς ἀ. αὐτοῦ [sc. God] βουλόμενος μετανοίας μετασχεῖν *1Clem.*8.5; *T.Jud.*18.13; of S. Paul, *T.Benj.*11.2; **2.** as beloved by other men χειροτονῆσαί τινα ὃν ἀ. λίαν ἔχετε Ign.*Polyc.*7.2; id.*Philad.*9.2; **3.** ἀγαπητέ, ἀγαπητοί, freq. in address to Christians, *1Clem.*1.1; Ign.*Magn.*11.1; Mel.*pass.*2 p.1.4.

C. as subst.; **1.** masc., of 'spiritual brothers' of *subintroductae*, †Bas.*contub.*11(M.30.825C); οἱ δ' ἀ. μίσγουσίν τι χολῆς...δίγαμον, ἢ ἀ. Gr.Naz.*carm.*2.2(epigr.)14.5(M.38.89A); *ib.*16.15(91A); Esaias *or.*4.1 (p.25); μή τινας συνόντας ἔχειν (sc. deaconesses) ἐν τάξει...τῶν καλουμένων ἀ. Justn.*nov.*6.6(p.44.14); **2.** fem., of *virgines subintroductae* μὴ ἔχειν γυναῖκα συνείσακτον, καθάπερ τινὲς ἀγαπητὰς ἐπέθεντο αὐταῖς ὀνόματα ‡Ath.*syntag.*2.7(M.28.837C); †Bas.*contub.*2(M.30. 816A); Gr.Naz.*carm.*2.2(epigr.)10.7(M.38.87A); *ib.*15.9(89A); Epiph. *haer.*63.2(p.400.1; M.41.1064D); id.*ep.Arab.*(p.461.31; M.42.716A); cf. *agapetarum pestis*, Hier.*ep.*22.14(M.*PL*.22.402); Thdt.*Philm.*2(3. 712); Phot.*nomoc.*8.14(M.104.689A).

***ἀγαπήτρια**, ἡ, *lover*, of Eve δρακοντιαίων συρισμάτων ἀ. ‡Chrys. *hom.in Ps.*92:3(5.622E).

***ἀγαπητρίς**, ἡ, *loved one, mistress*; of *subintroductae*, †Bas. *contub.*2(M.30.813C).

***ἀγαργάλιστος**, '*untickled*', hence met., *unaffected* κενοδοξίας ἀ. ‡Chrys.*hom.in Mt.*4:6(10.737A).

***ἀγάσταχυς**, *very rich in corn*, Gr.Naz.*carm.*2.2(poem.)4.45 (M.37.1509A).

§**ἀγάστωρ**, *without food, fasting*, Gr.Naz.*carm.*2.2(poem.)5.148 (M.37.1532A).

ἀγγαρεία (-ία), ἡ, *compulsory service* οὐ δεῖ τοὺς ἐπισκόπους... ἀ. διδόναι Phot.*nomoc.*6.1(M.104.633B); ἀγγαρία Ath.Scholast.*coll.* 4.3(p.53); Jo.D.*parall.*1.39 tit.(M.95.1249A); plur., *cursus publici*, Ant.Ep.*ep.*(p.71.12).

ἀγγαρεύω, *press into service, compel to serve*, *M.Tar.*10(p.473); τὸ γὰρ ἀ. τοῦτό ἐστι, τὸ ἀδίκως ἑλκύσαι Chrys.*hom.18.3 in Mt.* (7.238A); Max.*ep.*12(M.91.508C).

ἀγγελικός, **A.** *pertaining to a messenger* ἡ μὲν κηρυκικὴ ἐπιστήμη ἤδη πως ἀ. Clem.*str.*1.1(p.5.1; M.8.692A).

B. *pertaining to angels, angelic*; **1.** in gen. τοποθεσίας...ἀ. Ign. *Trall.*5.2; Just.*1apol.*52.3(M.6.405A); ἴδιον γὰρ τοῦτο τῆς ἀ. ἐστι φύσεως, τὸ ἀπηλλάχθαι τῆς γαμικῆς συζυγίας, μηδὲ πρὸς ἄλλο τι κάλλος μετεωρίζεσθαι, ἀλλ' εἰς τὸ θεῖον πρόσωπον διηνεκῶς ἀτενίζειν Bas.*ascet.*1.2(2.320B; M.31.873B); ἀ. δυνάμεις Gr.Naz.*or.*38.9(M.36. 320C); Cyr.*Is.*1.3(2.81E); of angelic powers as typified by deacons, ‡Germ.CP *contempl.*(M.98.393C); χοροὺς ἀ. Cyr.H.*procatech.*15; neut. plur. as subst., Clem.*str.*6.8(p.465.7; M.9.288B); **2.** of hymns, *T.Job* 48(p.135.14); *Chron.Pasch.*p.22(M.92.108B); **3.** of devils πατὴρ σατανᾶ, εἰ δι' ἀ. δυνάμεως Ἀζαζὴλ 'elder' ap.Iren.*haer.*1.15.6 (M.7.628A); Olymp.*fr.Job* 1:14f.(M.93.29B); **4.** in Valent. initiations τὸ ὄνομα...Χριστοῦ ζῶντος διὰ πνεύματος ἁγίου εἰς λύτρωσιν ἀ. Iren.*haer.*1.21.3(M.7.664A); εἰς λύτρωσιν ἀ., τουτέστιν ἣν καὶ ἄγγελοι ἔχουσιν Clem.*exc.Thdot.*22(p.114.9; M.9.669A); **5.** of power responsible for Creation (Gnost.), Hipp.*haer.*10.21(p.281.6; M.16. 3438C); **6.** of spiritual men: of the 'gnostic' ἐν σαρκὶ μελετήσαντος ἀ. ὑπουργίαν Clem.*ecl.*37(p.148.15; M.9.717B); id.*paed.*2.9(p.207.28; M.8.496C); μιμουμένην διὰ τῆς ἀπαθείας τὴν ἀ. καθαρότητα Gr.Nyss. *hom.4 in Cant.*(M.44.857A); ψυχῆς...ἀ. Chrys.*hom.2.3 in Tit.*(11.740E); of Jo. Bapt. Ἰωάννου ἀ. ... βίον *A.Thadd.*1(p.273.6); ἀ. ... στόμα Leont.N.*v.Jo.Eleem.*2(p.8.12); **7.** esp. of monastic life, Bas.*ascet.*1.2 (2.320B; M.31.873B); ἀ. ... βίον Chrys.*hom.38.5 in Jo.*(8.224B); Call. *v.Hyp.*(p.45); Evagr.*h.e.*1.15(p.25.7; M.86.2464A); πολιτείαν ἀ. Jo. Mosch.*prat.*168(M.87.3036A); Leont.N.*v.Jo.Eleem.*46(p.100.1); monastic habit ἀ. σχῆμα *V.Dan.*10(p.382.12); Leont.N.*v.Sym.*12(M.93. 1685C); id.*v.Jo.Eleem.*24(p.51.10); †Anast.S.*relat.*59(p.87); *Euchol.* (p.403); monks and virgins enrolled ἐν ταῖς ἀ. βίβλοις Cyr.H.*catech.* 4.24; of the solitary life τὴν ἀ. τε καὶ ἐπουράνιον...ζωήν Gr.Nyss. *v.Macr.*(p.387.21; M.46.976B); Isaac *ep.*14(p.166); **8.** of life in heaven ἀνεστοιχειοῦτο...ψυχὴ ἐπὶ τὴν ἄφθαρτον καὶ ἀ. οὐσίαν Eus.*v.C.*3.46 (p.97.10; M.20.1105D); ἀ. καὶ ἀπροσδεῆ βίον Bas.*moral.*68(2.286C; M.31.805B); Ἰησοῦ...μεταμόρφωσον τὴν μορφὴν τοῦ σώματός μου ἐν ἀ. δόξῃ *A.Phil.*144(p.87.2); *CIG* 8654(Gerasa,496); **9.** of the πνευματικοί (Naassene): τρία γένη, ἀ., ψυχικόν, χοϊκόν...τρεῖς ἐκκλησίαι, ἀ., ψυχική, χοϊκή Hipp.*haer.*5.6(p.78.20; M.16.3125B); **10.** οἱ ἀγγελικοί, a sect, so named from theory of creation by angels, or claim to live angelic lives, or place called Angeline 'beyond Mesopotamia', Epiph.*haer.*60.1(p.379.12; M.41.1037D); Jo.D.*haer.*60(M.94.713A).

ἀγγελικῶς, *in angelic manner, like angels*, Or.*Jo.*13.7(p.231.32; M.14.409A); ἀ. ἰδεῖν τὸν θεόν id.*sel.in Jer.*16:16(M.13.564C).

***ἀγγελιότης**, ἡ, *angelic nature*, Anast.S.*hod.*2(M.89.60B) = ‡Ath.*def.*1.8 (ἀγγελότης M.28.540A).

***ἀγγελῖται**, οἱ, name of sect (cf. ἀγγελικός), Tim.CP *haer.*(M.86. 60A).

***ἀγγελοειδής**, *as of angels, angelic* θεωρία Gr.Nyss.*v.Ephr.*(M. 46.840A); Dion.Ar.*c.h.*2.5(M.3.145B); id.*d.n.*6.2(M.3.856D).

***ἀγγελοθεΐα**, ἡ, ? *movement of the angels* ἐπόπτευε τὰς ἀ. Thdr. Stud.*epp.*1.2(M.99.912B).

***ἀγγελοθεσία**, ἡ, *status of angels*, Clem.*str.*7.2(p.8.19; M.9.413A); id.*ecl.*57(p.154.13; M.9.728A).

***ἀγγελομαρτύρητος**, *witnessed by angels*, ‡Chrys.*ador.*2(11.824B).

***ἀγγελομίμητος**, *imitating angels* τῆς ἀ. ἑνώσεως πρὸς θεὸν Max. *schol.d.n.*1.5(M.4.204B); of the priestly and monastic life, Const. Pogon.*sacr.*4(M.*PL*.96.398C); †Jo.D.*B.J.*1(M.96.864B); *ib.*40(1240B); Thdr.Stud.*cant.*4.3(p.343).

***ἀγγελομιμήτως**, *in imitation of the angels, in the manner of angels*, Dion.Ar.*d.n.*1.5(M.3.593B).

***ἀγγελοπλήρωτος**, *filled with angels* θυσιαστήριον Tim.Ant.*nativ. Jo.Bapt.*1(M.28.908D).

***ἀγγελοπρεπής**, *befitting angels* πολιτείαν ‡Gr.Nyss.*occurs.*(M.46. 1156B); *ib.*(1177C); ἀ. ἑνώσεις Dion.Ar.*d.n.*1.5(M.3.593B); ἀ. συντονίας id.*c.h.*15.1(M.3.328A); ᾠδαῖς ἀ. Jo.D.*hom.*9.11(M.96.737A).

***ἀγγελοπρεπῶς**, **1.** *like a messenger* ὁ Ἰησοῦς...ὡς αὐτὸς ἀ. φησιν, ὅσα ἤκουσε παρὰ τοῦ πατρός, ἀνήγγειλεν ἡμῖν Dion.Ar.*c.h.*4.4(M.3. 181D); **2.** *like angels*, Dion.Ar.*ep.*10(M.3.1117B).

ἄγγελος, ὁ, **I.** *messenger*;

A. of prophets, Hesych.H.*proem.proph.*(M.93.1344A); esp. of Malachi (cf. Mal.1:1), Amph.*Seleuc.*282(M.37.1595A); Chrys.*hom. 14.3 in Heb.*(12.144C); of Jo. Bapt., Epiph.*haer.*62.5(p.393.25; M. 41.1056C); opinion that he was angel in human form, ref. Mal.3:1 ἐφίσταμεν μήποτε εἷς τῶν ἁγίων ἀ. τυγχάνων ἐπὶ λειτουργίᾳ καταπέμπεται τοῦ σωτῆρος ἡμῶν πρόδρομος...ἄ. ὄντα ἐν σώματι γεγονέναι ὑπὲρ τοῦ μαρτυρῆσαι τῷ φωτί Or.*Jo.*2.31(25; pp.88.11–89.19; M.14. 168C–169C); rejected, Cyr.*Jo.*1.7(4.61D); cf. comparison between him and angel of pool of Bethesda, who was πρόδρομος τοῦ ἁγίου πνεύματος· οὗτινος ἀγγέλου καθ' ὁμοιότητα Ἰωάννης...ἐν ὕδατι ἐβάπτισεν Didym.*Trin.*2.14(M.39.712A).

B. of Christ ἀ. καλεῖται, διὰ τὸ ἀγγέλλειν τοῖς ἀνθρώποις ὅσαπερ βούλεται αὐτοῖς ἀγγεῖλαι ὁ τῶν ὅλων ποιητής Just.*dial.*56.4(M.6.597B); Cels.ap.Or.*Cels.*7.25(p.176.29; M.11.1458A); ὡς γὰρ ὁ παρ' ἡμῖν λόγος ἀ. ἐστι τῶν ὑπὸ τοῦ νοῦ ὁρωμένων, οὕτως ὁ τοῦ θεοῦ λόγος, ἐγνωκὼς τὸν πατέρα Or.*Jo.*1.38(42; p.49.5; M.14.100A); *Const.App.*2.30.2; for Christ as ἀ. μεγάλης βουλῆς v. βουλή.

C. met., medic., of symptom or warning of disease, Geo.Pis.*carm.*1.25.

II. *angel*;

A. definitions and properties; **1.** etym. ἀγγέλους ἀπὸ τοῦ ἔργου αὐτῶν...καλεῖν Or.*Cels.*5.4(p.4.19; M.11.1185B); ἀ. λέγεται, ἐπειδὴ τὰ τοῦ θεοῦ τοῖς ἀνθρώποις ἀναγγέλλει Chrys.*incomprehens.*3.5(1.468B); τὸ...ἄγγελος, ὄνομα λειτουργίας ἐστὶ σημαντικόν Cyr.*Heb.*1:4(p.370.5; M.74.953A); acc. Or., scripture applies term indifferently to spiritual beings and men, *Jo.*2.23(17; p.79.7; M.14.152D); **2.** ref. nature and function: ref. Heb.1:14 ἀγγέλους φαμὲν 'λειτουργικὰ' ὄντας 'πνεύματα' καὶ 'εἰς διακονίας ἀποστελλόμενα διὰ τοὺς μέλλοντας κληρονομεῖν σωτηρίαν' Or.*Cels.*5.4(p.4.13; M.11.1185A); ἀ. ἐστι ζῷον λογικόν, ἄϋλον, ὑμνολογικόν, ἀθάνατον ‡Ath.*qu.Ant.*30(M.28.616B); ἀ. ... οὐσία νοερά, ἀεικίνητος, αὐτεξούσιος, ἀσώματος, θεῷ λειτουργοῦσα, κατὰ χάριν ἐν τῇ φύσει τὸ ἀθάνατον εἰληφυῖα Jo.D.*f.o.*2.3(M.94.865B); **3.** ever-wakeful, Clem.*paed.*2.9(p.206.2; M.8.493A); cf.Or.*hom.23.11 in Num.*(p.223.12; M.12.755C); Gr.Thaum.*pan.Or.*5(p.14.23; M.10.1068C); **4.** as light, v. φῶς; **5.** serving God ἀγγέλου...ἴδιον τὸ διακονεῖν τῇ τοῦ θεοῦ προστάξει Ath.*Ar.*3.12(M.26.348A); **6.** immortal, v. ἀθάνατος.

B. creation; **1.** angels created beings, cf. *sive angeli, sive archangeli...ab eo qui super omnes est deus, et constituta sunt, et facta per verbum ejus*, Iren.*haer.*3.8.3(M.7.367C); Clem.*str.*6.7(p.461.3; M.9.280B); τοὺς μὲν ἀ. κτίσματα, τὸ δὲ πνεῦμα τὸ ἅγιον ἡνωμένον τῷ υἱῷ καὶ τῷ πατρί Ath.*ep.Serap.*1.12(M.26.560B); id.*Ar.*2.44(M.26.241A); **2.** not from necessity, but by divine goodness, Chrys.*Stag.*1.2(1.157E); **3.** created before material world ἀ. τοῦ θεοῦ οἱ πρῶτοι κτισθέντες Herm.*vis.*3.4.1; πρὸ τῶν αἰώνων νόες ἦσαν πάντες καθαροί, καὶ οἱ δαίμονες καὶ αἱ ψυχαὶ καὶ οἱ ἀ. Or.*princ.*1.8.1(p.96.2); though exact moment of creation unknown, *ib.*proem.10(p.16.1; M.11.121A); this the prevailing view, Bas.*hex.*1.5(1.5D; M.29.13B); cf.Gr.Naz.*or.*38.9(M.36.320C); Chrys.*hom.2.2 in Gen.*(4.10A); ἐποίησεν ἀγγέλους... μετὰ δὲ τὴν τούτων δημιουργίαν ποιεῖ καὶ τὸν ἄνθρωπον id.*Stag.*1.2(1.157E); Jo.D.*f.o.*2.3(M.94.873B); **4.** created simultaneously with material world, Epiph.*haer.*65.4(p.7.9; M.42.17C); id.*mens.*22(M.43.276B); reason for this view θεὸς...καὶ ἀγγέλοις, καὶ ἀρχαγγέλοις, καὶ πάσῃ τῇ κτίσει τὸ εἶναι δεδώρηται· ποίαν δὲ καὶ λειτουργίαν εἶχον πρὸ τῆς κτίσεως ὄντες, οὐδενὸς ὄντος τοῦ τῆς τούτων ὠφελείας προσδεομένου; Thdt.*qu.4 in Gen.*(1.7); moment of their creation εἰκὸς δὲ τοὺς ἀ. σὺν οὐρανῷ δημιουργηθῆναι καὶ γῇ *ib.*(1.8); though τῷ τῆς εὐσεβείας οὐ λυμαίνεται λόγῳ, τὸ πρὸ οὐρανοῦ καὶ γῆς γεγενῆσθαι λέγειν τῶν ἀ. τοὺς δήμους *ib.*(1.9); all created at same time, id.*haer.*5.7(4.402); **5.** no decision between the two possibilities οὔτε πόθεν, οὔτε πῶς γεγόνασιν οἱ ἀ., δυνατὸν φύσει ἀνθρωπίνῃ εἰπεῖν·...τὸ δὲ πότε, οἱ μέν φασι τῇ πρώτῃ ἡμέρᾳ, οἱ δὲ πρὸ τῆς πρώτης ἡμέρας ‡Ath.*qu.Ant.*3(M.28.601A).

C. nature of angels, cf. νοερός, νοητός; **1.** incorporeal and spiritual, Eus.*d.e.*4.1(p.150.22; M.22.252B); id.*p.e.*7.15(326D, 327A; M.21.552C); νοεραὶ οὐσίαι...ἀγγέλων Mac.Aeg.*hom.*16.1(M.34.613A); Gr.Nyss.*v.Mos.*(M.44.337D); ἀ. ... τὸν ἀσώματον Chrys.*hom.22.2 in Gen.*(4.195E); id.*laud.Paul.*7(2.513C); Gr.Ant.*bapt.*1.4(M.10.1180A); manna called bread of angels ὡς ἀγγέλων τῇ τούτου δωρεᾷ διακεκονηκότων. ἡ γὰρ ἀσώματος φύσις οὐ δεῖται τροφῆς Thdt.*qu.29 in Ex.*(1.144); id.*qu.47 in Gen.*(1.58); their perfect spirituality presupposed, Dion.Ar.*c.h.*15(M.3.328–40); **2.** not altogether spiritual, but of refined corporeality οἱ ἀ. σώματά εἰσιν· ὁρῶνται γάρ Clem.*exc.Thdot.*14(p.111.18; M.9.664B); οἱ μὲν ἀ. νοερὸν πῦρ *ib.*12(p.110.26; 661C); τὸ τοιόνδε μὲν ἄνθρωπός ἐστιν, τὸ τοιόνδε δὲ ἄγγελος, καὶ τὸ τοιὸν μὲν σῶμα, καὶ ποιὸν σῶμα, ἄλλο δέ τι ἕτερον σώματος Or.*Jo.*20.28(22; p.364.37; M.14.637C); needing food, *ib.*13.33(p.259.2; 457B); though this food is spiritual, id.*or.*27.10(pp.369.28–370.6; M.11.513B,C); having in themselves fountains of living water, id.*Jo.*13.7(p.231.33; 409A); τὰ τῶν ἀ. σώματα, αἰθέρια καὶ αὐγοειδὲς φῶς id.*comm.in Mt.*17.30(p.671.20; M.13.1569A); called νοερὰ σώματα Meth.*res.*3.15(p.411.25; M.18.317A); ref. Ps.103:4 ἐκ πυρὸς εἶναι ἀ. ὁμολογῶ, καὶ οὐ τούτοις παρεῖναι θηλείας λέγω Hipp.*haer.*10.33(p.289.18; M.16.3447D); Bas.*Spir.*38(3.32C; M.32.137A); Evagr.Pont.*ep.*2(M.32.249A); Ps.103 responsible for hesitations ποιεῖν γὰρ λέγεται τοὺς ἀ. αὐτοῦ πνεύματα...πνεῦμα δὲ ἀκούει, καὶ πῦρ· τὸ μὲν ὡς νοητὴ φύσις, τὸ δὲ ὡς καθάρσιος...πλὴν ἡμῖν γε ἀσώματος ἔστω, ἢ ὅτι ἐγγύτατα Gr.Naz.*or.*28.31(p.70.5; M.36.72A); *ib.*31.15(p.164.7; 149B); described as having fiery armour, Epiph.*haer.*51.34(p.310.8; M.41.953A); incorporeal in comparison with men, not in themselves πνεύματα δέ [sc. οἱ ἀ.], καθὸ πρὸς ἡμᾶς ἀσώματοι· οὐ κληθέντες πνεύματα τοῦ θεοῦ...ἀλλ' ἀ. λειτουργοί, καὶ σώματα οὐράνια, διὰ τὸ ἀπείρως ἀπέχειν καὶ ὑφιζάνειν τοῦ ἀκτίστου πνεύματος τοῦ θεοῦ Didym.*Trin.*2.4(M.39.481B); Mac.Aeg.*hom.*4.9(M.34.480A); ‡Caes.Naz.*dial.*48(M.38.917); Jo.D.*f.o.*2.3(M.94.868A); their food, vision of God, *ib.*(872B); **3.** scriptural evidence adduced on this question; **a.** corporeal nature supposed to be confirmed by Gen.6:2, interpreted of angels, *Apoc.En.*6.2; οἱ δ' ἀ. ... γυναικῶν μίξεσιν ἡττήθησαν Just.*2apol.*5.3(M.6.452B); Athenag.*leg.*24.4f.(M.6.948B); Clem.*paed.*3.2(p.244.24; M.8.576B); id.*str.*3.7(p.223.10; M.8.1161C); Meth.*res.*1.37(p.278.8ff.; M.18.293A); *Hom.Clem.*8.12–13; but also interpreted of men ἀ. τοῦ οὐρανοῦ θυγατράσιν ἀνθρώπων συνῆλθον. ἐν ἐνίοις ἀντιγράφοις εὗρον, 'οἱ υἱοὶ τοῦ θεοῦ'. μυθεύεται δέ, ὡς οἶμαι, ἀπὸ τοῦ Σήθ Afric.*chron.*2(M.10.65B); Chrys.*hom.22.2,3 in Gen.*(4.196A,E); Cyr.*glaph.Gen.*2(1.28A); Thdt.*qu.47 in Gen.*(1.59); id.*haer.*5.7(4.402); Bas.Sel.*or.*6.2(M.85.89A); **b.** ref. apparitions of angels; corporeal form, assumed only for particular purpose, does not prejudice their spirituality, Thdt.*Ezech.*1:5(2.683); id.*Zach.*1:8ff.(2.1597); οὐδὲ οἱ ἀ. κατ' οὐσίαν φαίνονται ἐπὶ τῆς γῆς τοῖς ἀνθρώποις; οὐδαμῶς· οὔτε γὰρ δύναται φθαρτὸς ὁ ὀφθαλμὸς θεωρῆσαι οὐσίαν ἄφθαρτον ‡Ath.*qu.Ant.*29(M.28.616A); Jo.D.*f.o.*2.3(M.94.869A); **4.** their freedom and need of redemption; **a.** acc. gen. opinion angels have free will, Just.*2apol.*7.8(M.6.456B); hence they are mutable and in need of being redeemed καὶ τὰ ἐπουράνια καὶ ἡ δόξα τῶν ἀ. ... ἐὰν μὴ πιστεύσωσιν εἰς τὸ αἷμα Χριστοῦ, κἀκείνοις κρίσις ἐστίν Ign.*Smyrn.*6.1; cf.Or.*hom.31 in Lc.*(p.190.4; M.13.1881A); sharing in mutability of all created things, ‡Cyr.*Trin.*2(6^{3}.2E,3A; M.77.1121Cf.); have to pray for perseverance, Clem.*str.*7.7(p.30.10; M.9.456A); because they can sin, Or.*comm.in Mt.*15.27(p.429.29; M.13.1333A); can become demons, id.*princ.*2.8.3(p.160.10); but cf. οἱ ἀ. ... δυσμετάθετοί εἰσι πρὸς κακίαν...τὸ μόνιμον εἰς ἀρετὴν τῇ δωρεᾷ τοῦ ἁγίου πνεύματος ἔχοντες Bas.*hom.in Ps.*32(1.136B; M.29.333D); cf.id.*Spir.*49(3.41B; M.32.157A); οὐκ οἴδαμεν ὅσα καὶ ἀγγέλοις συνεχώρησεν. συγχωρεῖ γὰρ κἀκείνοις Cyr.H.*catech.*2.10; Didym.*Trin.*2.4(M.39.481B); ‡Ath.*dial.Trin.*1.24(M.28.1153B); ‡Caes.Naz.*dial.*44(M.38.313); not holy in themselves but by participation in holiness of God, Cyr.*thes.*13(5^{1}.138E); ref. Inc. ὁ...λόγος, οὐ διὰ τοὺς ἁμαρτήσαντας ἀγγέλους ἄγγελος, ἀλλὰ διὰ τοὺς ἐν ἁμαρτίᾳ ἀνθρώπους ἄνθρωπος Didym.*Trin.*2.7(M.39.589A); **b.** though some admit that at least certain categories of angels might be incapable of sin, Or.*princ.*1.7.2(p.87.9; M.11.172A); ἀ. ... ἀκινήτους πρὸς τὸ χεῖρον, ἢ δυσκινήτους Gr.Naz.*or.*28.31(p.70.12; M.36.72B); cf.*ib.*38.9(321A); *ib.*40.7(365C); only lower angelic beings liable to sin, Nemes.*nat.hom.*41(M.40.777A); τοὺς δὲ ἀ., τουτέστι τοὺς τελευταίους διακόσμους, ἐνδέχεσθαι ἴσως καὶ ἐπὶ τὸ χεῖρον τραπῆναι...αὐτοὺς γὰρ περικοσμίους Max.*schol.c.h.*11(M.4.93C); ἀγγέλων ...τὸ μὴ πίπτειν, ἴσως καὶ μὴ δυναμένων, ὥς φασί τινες Jo.Clim.*scal.*4(M.88.696D); **5.** their knowledge: angels capable of learning, Clem.*str.*6.7(p.461.3; M.9.280B); no direct knowledge, ‡Just.*qu.et resp.*76(M.6.1517C); no knowledge of future, Isid.Pel.*epp.*1.195(M.78.308B); ἀγνοοῦσι...ἀ. τὰ μέλλοντα ‡Caes.Naz.*dial.*44(M.38.913); no prior knowledge of events of Redemption, Chrys.*hom.1.2 in Jo.*(8.3B); *ib.15.2*(86A); cf.Thdt.*Eph.*3:10(3.419); Max.*schol.c.h.*4.4(M.4.57B); their knowledge of supernatural truths due to teaching of Church, cf. *prophetae quoque ipsi et apostoli omne, quod resonant, non solum hominibus, sed et angelis praedicant...invenies pluribus in locis, et maxime in psalmis, et ad angelos sermonem fieri, data homini potestate, ei tamen, qui spiritum sanctum habet, ut et angelos alloquatur*, Or.*hom.23 in Lc.*(p.156.7ff.; M.13.1862B,1863Af.); cf.Gr.Nyss.*hom.8 in Cant.*(M.44.948C); ἐν γὰρ τῷ θεῷ κέκρυπτο...ἀλλὰ πόθεν τοῖς ἀ. δῆλον γέγονε; διὰ τῆς ἐκκλησίας Chrys.*hom.7.1 in Eph.*(11.46A); exeg. Ps.23:8,10, Is.63:1; interpreted of ignorance of angelic powers about mystery of Ascension (cf.Just.*dial.*36.6(M.6.556A)); Gr.Nyss.*ascens.*(M.46.693A); Thdt.*Ps.*23:7ff.(1.754); angels enjoy superior knowledge which they communicate to men τὸ θεῖον τῆς Ἰησοῦ φιλανθρωπίας μυστήριον ἄγγελοι πρῶτον ἐμυήθησαν, εἶτα δι' αὐτῶν εἰς ἡμᾶς ἡ τῆς γνώσεως χάρις διέβαινεν Dion.Ar.*c.h.*4.4(M.3.181B); *ib.*4.2(180A,B); their knowledge derived from God and transmitted from higher orders of angelic hierarchy to lower, *ib.*7.3(209A); *ib.*7.4(212A); οἱ μὲν οὖν θρόνοι καὶ τὰ χερουβὶμ καὶ τὰ σεραφὶμ ἀμέσως παρὰ τοῦ θεοῦ μανθάνουσιν...ταῦτα δὲ διδάσκει τὰ κατώτερα τάγματα...τὸ δὲ κατώτερον πάντων τάγμα εἰσὶν οἱ ἅγιοι ἄ., οἱ καὶ τῶν ἀνθρώπων ὄντες διδάσκαλοι ‡Ath.*qu.Ant.*31(M.28.616C); **6.** in rel. to man: angel highest creature in heaven, man on earth, Clem.*str.*7.2(p.5.19; M.9.408B); wiser than man, *ib.*4.3(p.251.19; M.8.1220C); superior to man, Jo.D.*f.o.*2.3(M.94.872B); τῆς κτίσεως τῆς ὁρωμένης ταύτης εἰς ἄ. μόνος ἀντίρροπός ἐστι· μᾶλλον...πολλῷ τιμιώτερος. εἰ γὰρ ἀνθρώπου δικαίου ἄξιος οὐκ ἂν εἴη πᾶς ὁ κόσμος... πολλῷ μᾶλλον ἀγγέλου οὐκ ἂν γένοιτό ποτε ἄξιος· πολλῷ γὰρ τῶν δικαίων ἄ. μείζους Chrys.*incomprehens.*2.4(1.457D); incomprehensible to man, *ib.*3.4(466A); angels may be judged by men through men's works, ref. 1Cor.6:3, cf. *non quod ipse Paulus judicet angelos, sed quod opus Pauli...judicabit aliquos; non enim omnes, sed aliquos angelorum,* Or.*hom.11.4 in Num.*(pp.82.30–83.1; M.12.647C); their power in rel. to men is limited, id.*Cels.*5.48(pp.52.17–53.6; M.11.1256B–1257A).

D. number of angels; **1.** in rel. to men; **a.** much more numerous; 'ninety-nine times' as many (ref. parable of lost sheep), Meth. *symp.*3.6(p.32.12 ff.; M.18.68D–69A); Cyr.H.*catech.*15.24; ‡Ath.*qu. Ant.*6(M.28.601D); cf.Gr.Naz.*or.*38.14(M.36.328Af.); Gr.Nyss.*Eun.* 4(2; p.63.26ff.; M.45.636A,B); **b.** equal, ‡Ath.*qu.Ant.*6(M.28.601D); **2.** innumerable, Iren.*haer.*2.30.3(M.7.816C); Clem.*str.*7.11(p.45.20; M.9.488B); Ath.*ep.Serap.*1.27(M.26.593B); Cyr.H.*catech.*16.23; Chrys. *incomprehens.*2.4(1.457D); Cyr.*hom.pasch.*12(5^{2}.166C); Thdt.*haer.*5.7 (4.402); ἡ περὶ τῶν ἀ. παράδοσις χιλίας χιλιάδας εἶναί φησι, καὶ μυρίας μυριάδας...διὰ τούτων ἐναργῶς ἐμφαίνουσα, τὰς ἡμῖν ἀναριθμήτους τῶν οὐρανίων οὐσιῶν διατάξεις Dion.Ar.*c.h.*14(M.3.321A).

E. hierarchy (idea of angelic hierarchies suggested by different biblical terms applied to angels); **1.** angels of all hierarchies of the same nature, cf.Or.*princ*,1.8.1(p.94.16ff.; M.11.176A); ἄ. πάντες ὥσπερ προσηγορίας μιᾶς, οὕτω καὶ φύσεως πάντως τῆς αὐτῆς ἀλλήλοις τυγχάνουσιν Bas.*Eun.*3.1(1.272C; M.29.656A); subjected to one another, cf.Or.*hom.11.4 in Num.*(p.85.16; M.12.649D); Gr.Naz.*or.* 40.5(M.36.364B); Gr.Nyss.*hom.opif.*17(M.44.189B); Max.*schol.c.h.*5 (M.4.60C); **2.** diversity of their various species affirmed (agst. Or.) ἄλλο γὰρ γένος τὸ τῶν ἀ. καὶ ἄλλο τὸ τῶν ἀρχῶν καὶ ἐξουσιῶν, ὅτι μὴ τάγμα ἓν καὶ μία σύστασις καὶ φυλὴ καὶ πατριὰ τῶν ἀθανάτων, ἀλλὰ γένη καὶ φυλαὶ καὶ διαφοραί. καὶ οὔτε τὰ χερουβὶμ τῆς ἰδίας ἐξιστάμενα φύσεως εἰς τὴν τῶν ἀ. ἰδέαν μετασκευάζονται, οὔτε εἰς ἑτέραν πάλιν οἱ ἄ. Meth.*res.*1.49(p.302.14ff.; M.18.277B); Ath.*Ar.*2.19(M.26.188B); question left open, Jo.D.*f.o.*2.3(M.94.869C); **3.** number of angelic hierarchies; different combinations, based on lists of Eph.1:21 and Col.1:16, believed incomplete, Or.*princ.*1.5.1(p.69.7; M.11.157B); cf.id.*Jo.*10.49(23; p.216.18; M.14.381D); Bas.*Spir.*38(3.31D; M.32.136A); Chrys.*incomprehens.*4.2(1.473B); to these were added angels and archangels, making seven, Iren.*haer.*2.30.6(M.7.818C); eight, Gr.Naz.*or.*28.31(p.70.12; M.36.72B); Thdt.*affect.*3(p.93.7; 4.784); Procl.CP *annunt.*2(M.85.429A); nine, Cyr.H.*catech.*23.6; Chrys.*hom. 4.5 in Gen.*(4.27D); Dion.Ar.*c.h.*6.2(M.3.200D–201A); **4.** classification; arranged in three triads: seraphim, cherubim, thrones; virtues, dominations, powers; principalities, archangels, angels, Dion. Ar.*c.h.*6.2(M.3.200Dff.), acc. their proximity to God, *ib.*3.2(165A).

F. state: their place in the various regions of heaven τῶν γὰρ τὸν οὐρανὸν ἐνοικούντων πνευμάτων οἱ τὴν κατωτάτω χώραν κατοικοῦντες ἄ. *Hom.Clem.*8.12; Cyr.H.*catech.*11.11; *ib.*16.23; Jo.D.*f.o.* 2.3(M.94.872C); also elsewhere εἰ γὰρ πᾶς ὁ ἀὴρ ἀγγέλων ἐμπέπλησται, πολλῷ μᾶλλον ἡ ἐκκλησία Chrys.*ascens.*1(2.448B).

G. fallen angels; **1.** gen. called ἄ. σατανᾶ (2Cor.12:7), *Barn.* 18.1; Clem.*str.*5.14(p.412.14; M.9.189A); Or.*Cels.*8.25(p.241.30; M.11.1553C); Adam.*dial.*3.9(p.128.8; M.11.1801A); *Symb.*ap.*Const.App.*7.41.2; ἄ. ἀριστεροί Or.*mart.*18(p.17.3; M.11.585B); ἐναντίοι id.*Cels.*3.37 (p.234.5; M.11.968C); **2.** reason and condition of their fallen state, cf. *angeli quidem transgressi deciderunt in judicium,* Iren.*haer.*4.16.2(M.7.1016B); due to free will, Athenag.*leg.*24.4(M.6.948A); κατὰ δὲ ἡμᾶς δαίμονές τινες...ἀσεβεῖς πρὸς τὸ ἀληθῶς θεῖον καὶ τοὺς ἐν οὐρανῷ ἀ. γεγενημένοι καὶ πεσόντες ἐξ οὐρανοῦ Or.*Cels.*4.92(p.365.10; M.11.1169C); cf. *apud plurimos...habetur opinio, quod angelus fuerit iste diabolus, et apostata effectus quam plurimos angelorum secum declinare persuaserit, qui et nunc usque angeli ipsius nuncupantur,* id.*princ.*1.proem.6(p.13.15ff.; M.11.119A); Bas.*Spir.*38(3.32C–E; M.32.137A,B); ‡Ath.*qu.Ant.*7(M.28.604A); ἀρχὴ τῶν μὴ τηρησάντων αὐτὴν ἀ. ἐστίν, ὁ λόγος τυχόν, καθ' ὃν ἐκτίσθησαν· ἢ ἡ δοθεῖσα πρὸς ἐκθέωσιν αὐτοῖς κατὰ χάριν φυσικὴ δυναστεία· ἢ πάλιν, ἡ κατὰ τὴν ἀξίαν τῆς χάριτος τάξις τῆς στάσεως· τὸ δὲ οἰκητήριόν ἐστιν, ἢ ὁ οὐρανός, ἢ ἡ κατὰ τὴν ἕξιν τῶν ὑπὲρ ἔννοιαν ἀγαθῶν σοφία, ἣν οἰκεῖν ἐδημιουργήθησαν·...ἢ ἡ...ἐπισκοπὴ τῆς ἀχράντου θεότητος, ἣν ἀπέλιπον τυραννήσαντες· ἀΐδιοι δὲ δεσμοί εἰσιν, ἡ κατὰ γνώμην αὐτῶν παντελὴς... περὶ τὸ καλὸν ἀκινησία...ζόφος δέ ἐστιν, ἡ...τῆς θείας ἄγνοια χάριτος Max.*qu.Thal.*11(M.90.292D); ἐπὶ τὸ χεῖρον τραπεὶς...διάβολος, συναποστήσας ἑαυτῷ ἱκανοὺς τῶν ἀ., οὐ φύσει, ἀλλὰ γνώμῃ τραπέντας τῇ ὑποσπορᾷ τοῦ σφῶν ἡγουμένου ‡Caes.Naz.*dial.*44(M.38.913); **3.** activities: revealed some doctrines to women (cf. Gen.6:2), hence vestiges of truth in paganism, Clem.*str.*5.1(p.332.17; M.9.24B); instigated heresy, cf.Or.*comm.3 in Cant.*(p.181.6; M.13.152A); instigated passions, cf.id.*hom.1.6 in Jos.*(p.294.18ff.; M.12.831C); instigated magic, cf.id.*hom.13.5 in Num.*(p.114.26; M.12.672C); for tears of fallen angels v. δάκρυον; **4.** in rel. to good angels οὐ πάντες ἄ. ἄ. λέγονται εἶναι τοῦ θεοῦ ἀλλὰ μόνοι οἱ μακάριοι, οἱ δ' ἐκτραπέντες ἐπὶ τὴν κακίαν ἄ. τοῦ διαβόλου ὀνομάζονται Or.*Cels.*8.25 (p.241.30f.; M.11.1553C,D); *ib.*8.36(p.252.8f.; 1572D); ἅγιοι ἄ. ἄλλης εἰσὶ φύσεως καὶ προαιρέσεως παρὰ τοὺς...δαίμονας *ib.*3.37(p.233.23; 968B); τάχα γὰρ ἀντὶ τῆς...διπλῆς συντάξεως ἀνθρώπων ἁγίων καὶ μακαρίων ἀ. πάλιν διπλῆ γίνεται ἐπὶ τὸ αὐτὸ σύνοδος ἀνθρώπων ἀσεβῶν καὶ πονηρῶν ἀ. id.*or.*31.6(p.400.3f.; M.11.556B); ζωὴν καὶ εἰρήνην δι' ἀγγέλων χορηγεῖ τοῖς ἀξίοις ὁ τῶν ἀ. κύριος· κἀκεῖνος θυμόν, καὶ ὀργήν, καὶ θλῖψιν ἀποστέλλει διὰ τῶν ἀ. τῶν πονηρῶν Gr.Nyss.*hom. 14 in Cant.*(M.44.1081A); exeg. 1Cor.11:10 διὰ τοὺς ἀ., τοὺς θεωμένους ἡμῶν τά τε φανερὰ καὶ ἀφανῆ κινήματα...καὶ διὰ τοὺς πονηροὺς ἀ., τοὺς φυλαττομένους ἡμῶν καὶ ἕξιν καὶ αἴσθησιν καὶ διάνοιαν Max.*qu. Thal.*25(M.90.336B,C); ref. visions εἰς ἄγγελον φωτὸς...πολλάκις μετασχηματίζονται [sc. demons], καὶ ἡμᾶς προσερχομένους αὐτοῖς καθ' ὕπνους ὑπέδειξαν· διυπνισθέντας δὲ χαρᾷ, καὶ οἰήσει κατεβάπτισαν· τοῦτο δή σοι ἔσται τὸ σημεῖον πλάνης· κολάσεις καὶ κρίσεις...ὑποδεικνύουσιν ἄγγελοι...πᾶσί σοι τοῖς κόλασιν...εὐαγγελιζομένοις πίστευε μόνοις Jo.Clim.*scal.*3(M.88.672A); cf.*ib.*23(968D).

H. ministry; **1.** worship of God in heaven, Gr.Naz.*or.*28.31 (p.71.12; M.36.72C); λειτουργία δὲ τῶν ἀ. ἡ ὑμνῳδία Thdt.*haer.*5.7 (4.403); ‡Ath.*qu.Ant.*31(M.28.616B); ‡Chrys.*synax.*(8.285A); ‡Germ. CP *contempl.*(M.98.412C); expressed in their names, such as Michael, etc., Or.*Cels.*1.25(p.76.9; M.11.708A); cf.id.*hom.23.4 in Jos.*(p.445.15; M.12.938A); accompanying virgins, Meth.*symp.*7.9 (p.80.2; M.18.136C); **2.** service connected with Inc.; **a.** announcing birth of Jo. Bapt., Or.*Jo.*6.13(7; p.122.1; M.14.224A); **b.** announcing birth of Christ, Dion.Ar.*c.h.*4.4(M.3.181B); and assisting at it ὁ σωτὴρ ὤφθη κατιὼν τοῖς ἀ., διὸ καὶ εὐηγγελίσαντο αὐτόν Clem.*exc. Thdot.*18.1(p.112.19; M.9.665C); ἐπεὶ θεὸς ἦν ὁ ὑπὲρ τοὺς βοηθοῦντας ἀνθρώποις ἀγγέλους ἐνυπάρχων σωτήρ,...ἄγγελος ἠμείψατο τὴν τῶν μάγων ἐπὶ τὸ προσκυνῆσαι τὸν Ἰησοῦν εὐσέβειαν Or.*Cels.*1.60(p.111.25f.; M.11.772B); cf. αἱ ἀγγελικαὶ δυνάμεις, αἱ τῆς δεσποτικῆς παρουσίας ἐπὶ τὴν γῆν προπομπεύουσαι, καὶ τὸν βασιλέα τῆς δόξης ἐντὸς τοῦ βίου παράγουσαι Gr.Nyss.*hom.5 in Cant.*(M.44.881A); (Gnost.) cf. *hos angelos falsarii Gnostici dicunt ab ogdoade venisse, et descensionem superioris Christi manifestasse,* Iren.*haer.*3.10.4 (M.7.875B); being helped by it ὁ σωτὴρ...κάτεισιν εἰς ἀνθρώπους, καὶ τοῖς οἰκείοις ἀ. ἐπαμύνων ὑπὲρ τῆς τῶν ἀνθρώπων σωτηρίας Eus. *d.e.*4.10(p.166.12; M.22.277A); and hence rejoicing in it; ref. Lc. 2:13f., *ib.*(p.166.26ff.; 277B,C); *ib.*6.25(p.294.18; 484C); **c.** assisting at Passion, tearing Temple veil, Eus.*fr.Lc.*24:4(M.24.605C); **d.** discussion of Celsus' objection to angels of Resurrection, whose presence he thought disproved Christ's divinity, Or.*Cels.*5.57(p.61.2ff.; M.11.1272C); *ib.*5.58(p.61.10ff.; 1273Aff.); cf.*ib.*5.52(p.56.3ff.; 1261C–1264A); *ib.*5.53(p.57.4ff.; 1264B,C); **e.** angels of Ascension; ref. Ps.23:4ff. ἐν γὰρ τῇ εἰς οὐρανοὺς ἀναβάσει τοῦ υἱοῦ τοῦ θεοῦ, τοὺς διακονησαμένους αὐτῷ ἀ. τὴν εἰς ἀνθρώπους οἰκονομίαν προτρέχειν αὐτῷ εἰκός, καὶ τὰς οὐρανίους πύλας αὐτῷ παρασκευάζειν Eus.*Ps.*23:4ff.(M.23.224A); speculations on two choirs οἱ διακονοῦντες τῷ σωτῆρι ἐπὶ γῆς ἄ., ἀναλαμβανομένου αὐτοῦ, ταῖς οὐρανίαις δυνάμεσι δηλοῦσιν ἀνοίγειν τὰς πύλας...ἐρωτῶσιν αἱ ἄνω δυνάμεις, τὸ παράδοξον τῆς οἰκονομίας ἐκπληττόμεναι...μυσταγωγοῦσι τοὺς ἄνω οἱ σὺν αὐτῷ ἀνελθόντες ἄ. τὸ μυστήριον Ath.*exp.Ps.*23:7f.(M.27.141C,D); Gr.Naz.*or.*45.25(M.36.657B); Gr.Nyss.*ascens.*(M.46.693A); assisted at Ascension to console apostles and to instruct them, Chrys.*ascens.*5 (2.454C–455A); angels displayed their full power only after Ascension, because they would not assist unredeemed man, Or.*Jo.*6.57 (37; p.165.30f.; M.14.300A); **f.** angels assisting at all phases of Christ's incarnate life, Chrys.*ascens.*4(2.454B), constantly guarding his body (Ps.90:11), Eus.*Ps.*90:10ff.(M.23.1160D); **3.** service at parousia, *Orac.Sib.*2.315; cf. *unusquisque angelorum in consummatione saeculi aderit in judicio, producens secum eos, quibus praefuit,* Or.*hom.11.4 in Num.*(p.82.17ff.; M.12.647B,C); cf.*ib.*20.4 (p.197.5ff.; 735C); separating the wheat from the chaff, cf.id. *Cant.*(p.205.22; M.13.171A); παρακελευόμενος τοῖς...ἀ. ἀνοῖξαι θύρας κεκλεισμένας, καὶ παρακελεύσασθαι τοῖς ἔνδον οὖσι προϊέναι Eus.Is. 13:1f.(M.24.185B); cf.ib.21:9(241C); id.fr.Lc.21:26(M.24.596C); Ephr. 3.276Aff.; Χριστὸν...ἐξ οὐρανῶν προσδόκα...ὑπ' ἀ. δορυφορούμενον Cyr.H.catech.4.15; ib.15.22; Gr.Nyss.Eun.4(2 p.63.23; M.45.636A); Chrys.incomprehens.3.7(1.470D); esp. destroyer angel, ref. parable of the ten virgins τὸ δὲ μεσονύκτιον ἡ βασιλεία τοῦ ἀντιχρίστου, καθ' ἣν ὁ ὀλοθρευτὴς ἀ. ἐπιπορεύεται τὰς οἰκίας Meth.symp.6.4(p.68.23; M.18.120A); sparing Christians sealed with blood of Christ, ib.9.1 (p.115.20; 180B); cf.Or.princ.3.2.1(p.245.1; M.11.303C); cf.id.hom.9.5 in Num.(p.60.17; M.12.629C); **4.** service to Church continuing their ministry to Christ, id.or.11.3(p.323.1ff.; M.11.449B,C); as its guardians (Apoc.1:20,2:1), Hipp.antichr.59(p.40.4; M.10.780A); τοῖς ἀ. ... τοῖς πεπιστευμένοις τὰς ἐκκλησίας Or.hom.13 in Lc.(p.92.5); cf. id.hom.20.1 in Jos.(p.416.17f.; M.12.922B); cf. *offert ergo unusquisque angelorum primitias vel ecclesiae...suae*, id.hom.11.4 in Num. (p.84.21; M.12.649A); Eus.Ps.47:13(M.23.425D); ib.90:10ff.(1161A); Bas.ep.238(3.367A; M.32.889B); †Bas.Is.46(1.416C; M.30.208B); Gr. Naz.or.42.9(M.36.469A); ib.42.27(492B); Cyr.Jo.6.1(4.638A); at its espousals with the Lamb, Gr.Nyss.hom.11 in Cant.(M.44.997A); from its beginning, cf. ἄγγελοι πρωτόκτιστοι, who operated God's covenants with Adam, Noah, Abraham, and Moses, Clem. ecl.51(p.151.13ff.; M.9.722B); cf. *ante ergo quam tempus adesset horum* [sc. Incarnation], *in multis angelorum ministerio excolebatur sponsa*, Or.Cant.(p.157.11; M.13.134A); being with men in paradise, Gr.Nyss.Pss.titt.A 6(M.44.508C); OT activities mentioned, Or.Cels.5.30(p.32.11ff.; M.11.1228A); id.hom.1.1 in Jer.(p.1. 17; M.13.256B); being in charge of Israel before coming of Christ, Eus.d.e.7.2(p.331.3; M.22.540C); esp. their part in ministering Law, Or.hom.13.1 in Jer.(p.102.26; 400C); id.Jo.13.50(49; p.277.31; M.14.489B); Dion.Ar.c.h.4.3(M.3.181A); hence cf. *angeli, qui ante adventum Christi velut 'parvulae' adhuc sponsae tutelam procurabant*, Or.Cant.(p.158.26; M.13.135A); also through helping apostles, cf.id.hom.11.4 in Num.(p.83.3; M.12.647D); id.Jo.10.34 (p.207.32; 368B); hence also to Church in sense of all who are to be saved, Dion.Ar.c.h.9.4(M.3.261C); cf.Or.hom.13.1 in Jer. (p.102.11; 400B); ministry at liturgy εἰκός ἐστι, πλειόνων συνεληλυθότων γνησίως εἰς δόξαν Χριστοῦ, παρεμβαλεῖν τὸν ἑκάστου ἀ. τὸν 'κύκλῳ' ἑκάστου τῶν φοβουμένων μετὰ τούτου τοῦ ἀνδρός, ὃν φρουρεῖν ...πεπίστευται· ὥστ' εἶναι ἐπὶ τῶν ἁγίων συναθροιζομένων διπλῆν ἐκκλησίαν, τὴν μὲν ἀνθρώπων τὴν δὲ ἀ. Or.or.31.5(p.398.25,28; M.11. 553C); cf.id.hom.23 in Lc.(p.156.26; M.13.1863B); ὅταν ἀκούσῃς, δεηθῶμεν πάντες κοινῇ, ὅταν ἴδῃς ἀνελκόμενα τὰ ἀμφίθυρα, τότε νόμισον...κατιέναι τοὺς ἀ. Chrys.hom.3.5 in Eph.(11.23D); id.res. Chr.3(2.441A); ἀ. παρεστήκασι τῷ ἱερεῖ, καὶ οὐρανίων δυνάμεων ἅπαν τὸ βῆμα καὶ ὁ περὶ τὸ θυσιαστήριον πληροῦται τόπος id.sac.6.4(p.147. 17; 1.424C); cf.Nil.epp.2.294(M.79.345D); esp. 'angel of peace', Const.App.8.36.3; Chrys.ascens.1(2.448D); id.Jud.3.6(1.614C); mission in Church typified by masons building Solomon's Temple, Or.Jo.10.39(23; p.216.18; M.14.381D); **5.** assisting faithful in reception of sacraments; **a.** at baptism, cf. *ut descendant...ab omnibus caelis angeli ad eos, qui salvandi sunt...tu heri sub daemonio eras, hodie sub angelo...omnia angelis plena sunt; veni, angele, suscipe senem conversum ab errore pristino*, Or.hom.1.7 in Ezech.(p.331. 13ff.; M.13.674C–675A); cf. *aderant enim tunc, cum tibi sacramentum fidei tradebatur...ministeria angelorum...rectissime hoc de ministris angelis magis dicitur, secundum domini sententiam dicentis de infantibus, quod et tu fuisti infans in baptismo, quia 'angeli eorum semper vident faciem patris'*, id.hom.9.4 in Jos.(p.350.2ff.; M.12. 874A); Cyr.H.procatech.15; id.catech.23.6; Gr.Naz.or.40.4(M.36. 364A); σῶμα ὁμοῦ καὶ ψυχήν, ἀ. ὑπηρετουμένων,...πνεῦμα τοῦ θεοῦ βαπτίζει Didym.Trin.2.12(M.39.672B); **b.** at eucharist, Chrys.hom. 46.3 in Jo.(8.273B) cit. s. αἷμα; miraculously giving communion to a saint in absence of priest, Soz.h.e.6.29.11(M.67.1376C); **6.** in private prayers, Clem.str.7.12(p.56.6; M.9.508C); id.exc.Thdot.27 (p.116.1; M.9.673A); οὐ μόνος δὲ ὁ ἀρχιερεὺς τοῖς γνησίως εὐχομένοις συνεύχεται ἀλλὰ καὶ οἱ ἐν οὐρανῷ χαίροντες ἀ. Or.or.11.1 (p.321.16; M.11.448B); ib.11.5(p.324.8; 452B); taking prayers to God and re-descending with blessings, id.Cels.5.4(p.4.13; M.11.1185A); ib.8.36(p.252.1; 1572C); Evagr.Pont.or.30(M.79.1173B); ib.75(1184B); οἱ ἅγιοι ἀ. προτρέπονται ἡμᾶς εἰς προσευχήν, καὶ συμπαρίστανται ἡμῖν χαίροντες ἅμα, καὶ προσευχόμενοι ὑπὲρ ἡμῶν ib.81(1185A); **7.** in moral and spiritual life in gen.; **a.** helping souls to conversion, Or.Cels.5.57(p.61.8; M.11.1272C); ἰατροὶ δὲ ἀ. ὑπὸ τὸν μέγαν ὄντες ἰατρὸν τὸν θεὸν καὶ θεραπεῦσαι τοὺς πειθομένους ἐθέλοντες id.fr.37 in Jer.(p.217.23; M.13.601B); assisting inferior Christians, while God himself guides the perfect, Clem.str.7.13(p.58.6; M.9.513A); cf.Or. hom.24.3 in Num.(p.232.9; M.12.762D); **b.** acting as guides τὸν ἀ. λειτουργὸν ἐπιπέμψω, ἀπὸ τοῦδε ἀρξόμενον τοῦ χρόνου συνεργεῖν αὐτοῦ τῇ σωτηρίᾳ καὶ μέχρι τοῦδε συνεσόμενον Or.or.6.4(p.314.16; M.11.437C); esp. in lower stages of spiritual life, cf.id.princ.3.2.5 (p.254.13; M.11.312A); ὥσπερ τινὰς ἀγελάρχας...θείους ἀ. κατεστήσατο Eus.d.e.4.6(p.160.18; M.22.268A); Bas.ep.11(3.92D; M.32.273B); Gr.Naz.carm.1.2.36.20(M.37.519A); Gr.Nyss.hom.12 in Cant.(M.44. 1033B); Chrys.hom.3.3 in Col.(11.347C); πολλῶν...πεπλήρωται τῶν ἀρετῶν ἡ ὁδὸς ἁγίων ἀ., τῶν ἑκάστης ἀρετῆς κατ' εἶδος ἐνεργητικῶν... καὶ τῶν ἀοράτων πρὸς τὰ καλὰ συνεργούντων ἡμῖν ἀ. Max.qu.Thal. 17(M.90.305A); **c.** esp. in case of saints and monks, Mac.Aeg. hom.15.44(M.34.605C); Jo.Clim.scal.4(M.88.716B); **d.** rejoicing in men's struggles, Nil.epp.4.13(M.79.556C); cf.id.sent.16(M.79.1241B); **e.** 'cultivating' men's hearts, cf. *agri autem angelorum corda nostra sunt. unusquisque ergo eorum ex agro, quem colit, offert primitias deo*, Or.hom.11.5 in Num.(p.86.6; M.12.650B); cf.id.hom.9.8 in Lev. (p.434.15ff.; M.12.520B); **f.** helping men against demons, Or.Cels. 8.36(pp.252f.; M.11.1572D); cf.id.hom.8.6 in Jos.(p.342.2; M.12.868B); Chrys.ascens.1(2.448D); **g.** guarding men's sleep, Jo.Clim.scal. 15(M.88.896B); **8.** at time of death, M.Perp.11(p.79.19); τοῖς ἐφεστῶσι τῇ ἀνόδῳ ἀ. Clem.str.4.18(p.299.19; M.8.1325A); cf. *rapiuntur ergo ab angelis hi, qui penitus purgati et leves effecti sunt a delictis; portantur vero hi, qui aliquibus adhuc reliquiis praegravantur*, Or.hom.5.3 in Num.(p.30.16; M.12.606C); cf.ib.25.5(p.240. 21; 769B); ὁ μέλλων τὴν ἑκάστου ψυχὴν παραλαμβάνειν ἀ. κατὰ καιρὸν τοῦ θανάτου Eus.fr.Lc.12:39(M.24.564A); ref. souls of virgins, id.Ps.44:15f.(M.23.404C); ref. martyrs, Gr.Nyss.mart.3(M.46.780A); παρακατάστησον φωτεινὸν ἀ. τὸν χειραγωγοῦντά με πρὸς τὸν τόπον τῆς ἀναψύξεως id.v.Macr.(p.397.22; M.46.984D); id.Pss.titt.B 6(M. 44.509A); uncertainty whether this applies also to unbaptized, id.bapt.diff.(M.46.424B); εἰς οὐρανοὺς ἀναβαίνουσιν [sc. martyrs], ἀ. αὐτοῖς προηγουμένων...τῶν ἀθλητῶν τῆς εὐσεβείας εἰς οὐρανοὺς ἀναβάντων, συντρέχουσιν οἱ ἀ. Chrys.pan.mart.3.2(2.714C,E); id. pan.Juln.3(2.675E); ‡Just.qu.et resp.75(M.6.1317A) cit. s. παράδεισος; liturg. prayer for dead ἀ. εὐμενεῖς παράστησον αὐτῷ Const. App.8.41.5; **9.** ministry outside Church; **a.** in gen., in charge of everything in world οἱ ἅγιοι ἀ. τοῦ θεοῦ...οἷς παρέδωκεν ὁ κύριος πᾶσαν τὴν κτίσιν αὐτοῦ, αὔξειν καὶ οἰκοδομεῖν καὶ δεσπόζειν τῆς κτίσεως πάσης Herm.vis.5.4.1; τὴν μὲν τῶν ἀνθρώπων καὶ τῶν ὑπὸ τὸν οὐρανὸν πρόνοιαν ἀγγέλοις, οὓς ἐπὶ τούτοις ἔταξε, παρέδωκεν Just.2apol.5.2(M.6.452B); Athenag.leg.24.3f.(M.6.948A); Clem.str.7.1 (p.4.20; M.9.405A); together with the stars, id.ecl.55(p.152.14; M.9. 724B); and the sun, ib.56(p.153.15; 725B); because of this supposed connexion, days called angels, ib.(p.153.14; 725A); cf. connexion between seven principal angels and seven planets, id.str.6.16 (p.504.19; 369C); Eus.p.e.7.16(328B; M.21.553C); ἀ. ἐποπτεύοντας τὸν ὅλον κόσμον, καὶ τῶν τῇδε πρόνοιαν ποιουμένους Nil.epp.1.59 (M.79.109A); Jo.D.f.o.2.3(M.94.872A); inferior angels in charge of pagans, Clem.str.7.2(p.6.18; M.9.409B); cf.Epiph.haer.51.34(p.309. 11; M.41.592A); **b.** specified activities: presiding at births, Clem. ecl.50(p.151.2; M.9.721A); τημελούχοις ἀ., κἂν ἐκ μοιχείας ὦσι, τὰ ἀποτικτόμενα παραδίδοσθαι Meth.symp.2.6(p.23.13; M.18.57A); in charge of plants and of birth of animals, Or.Cels.8.57(p.274.13; M.11.1604B); cf.id.hom.14.2 in Num.(p.124.18; M.12.680B); of food, drink, water, and air, id.Cels.8.32(p.248.2; M.11.1564D); all the elements, id.hom.10.6 in Jer.(p.76.16; M.13.365A); putting souls into bodies, id.Jo.13.50(49; p.277.22; M.14.489A); **10.** guardian angels; **a.** their existence taught in scripture, cf. *adest unicuique nostrum angelus bonus, angelus domini, qui regat, qui moneat, qui gubernet, qui pro actibus nostris corrigendis et miserationibus exposcendis cotidie videat faciem patris...iterum secundum ea, quae Johannes in Apocalypsi scribit, unicuique ecclesiae generaliter angelus praeest*, Or.hom.20.3 in Num.(p.194.12ff.; M.12.733B,C); cf. ib.24.3(p.231.22; 762B); τὸ δὲ συνεῖναι ἑκάστῳ τῶν πιστῶν ἄγγελον, οἷον παιδαγωγόν τινα καὶ νομέα τὴν ζωὴν διευθύνοντα, οὐδεὶς ἀντερεῖ...(ref. Mt.18:10; Ps.33:8; Gen.48:16). ὅτι δὲ πάλιν εἰσί τινες ἀ. καὶ ὅλων ἐθνῶν προεστῶτες, Μωσῆς ἡμᾶς διδάσκει (ref. Dt.32:8) Bas.Eun.3.2(1. 272D–273A; M.29.656B–657A); Thdt.qu.3 in Gen.(1.6); cf.Gr.Thaum. pan.Or.4(p.9.21; M.10.1061B); **b.** of nations and cities ἐγώ εἰμι ὁ ἀ. ὁ παραιτούμενος τὸ γένος Ἰσραήλ T.Lev.5.6; Clem.str.6.17 (p.513.6; M.9.389B); †Bas.Is.240(1.252C; M.30.541A); Gr.Naz.carm.1. 1.17.13ff.(M.37.439f.); power restricted before advent of Christ, Or. hom.12 in Lc.(p.87.10ff.; M.13.1830A,B); Eus.d.e.4.10(p.164.23; M.22. 273D); cf.id.Ps.71:9ff.(M.23.808D); hence rejoicing in birth of Christ, Or.hom.12 in Lc.(p.85.14ff.); οἱ δέ γε τῶν ἄλλων ἐθνῶν ἐπιστάται, ἀ. καὶ ποιμένες, τοὺς μὴ οἵους τε νῷ τὸν ἀόρατον ἐποπτεύειν, *μηδ' ἀναβαίνειν τοσοῦτον δι' οἰκείαν ἀσθενείαν, τοῖς ὁρωμένοις κατ' οὐρανὸν προσέχειν ἠξίουν, ἡλίῳ καὶ σελήνῃ καὶ ἄστροις* Eus.*d.e.*4.8 (p.161.19; M.22.269B); this theory of Eus. prob. based on misunderstanding of Clem.*str.*6.14(p.487.12ff.; M.9.333A); theory condemned *ὅτι μὴ τὰς τῶν ἀ. εὐθείας ἐπιστασίας αἰτιάσασθαι χρὴ τῆς τῶν ἑτέρων ἐθνῶν ἐπὶ τοὺς οὐκ ὄντας θεοὺς ἀποπλανήσεως* Dion.Ar. *c.h.*9.3(M.3.260C); angels of nations more honourable than angels of individuals, Bas.*Eun.*3.1(1.372C; M.29.656B); **c.** of individuals; **i.** all men have guardian angel, Clem.*str.*5.14(p.386.15; M.9.136A); Or.*comm.in Mt.*13.5(p.191.2; M.13.1105A), but cf. ii infra; *τῶν ἀ. ... τινὰς δὲ ἑνὸς ἑκάστου τῶν ἀνθρώπων πεπιστεῦσθαι τὴν ἐπιμέλειαν* Thdt.*haer.*5.7(4.404); Cosm.Ind.*top.*2(M.88.132C); **ii.** esp. (or only) the faithful, Or.*or.*31.5(p.398.25; M.11.553C); id.*princ.*2.10.7(p.181.21; M.11.240A); id.*hom.1.7 in Ezech.*(p.331.21; M.13.674D); Bas. *hom.in Ps.*33(1.148C; M.29.364B); *ἕκαστος γὰρ πιστὸς ἄγγελον ἔχει* Chrys.*hom.3.3 in Col.*(11.347C); id.*hom.26.3 in Ac.*(9.211D); Cyr. *ador.*4(1.113A); ref. monks, Dor.*doct.*11.6(M.88.1741Bf.); whose angels will be judged together with them, cf.Or.*hom.24.3 in Num.* (p.231.22; M.12.762B); **iii.** only the righteous *προσεκτέον οὖν ἡμῖν μήποτε εὑρεθῇ ἐν ἡμῖν 'ἄσχημον πρᾶγμα', καὶ μὴ εὕρωμεν 'χάριν' ἐνώπιον...τοῦ τεταγμένου ἐφ' ἡμῖν ἀ.· ἐὰν γὰρ μὴ προσέχωμεν, τάχα καὶ ἡμεῖς τὸ βιβλίον τοῦ ἀποστασίου ληψόμεθα* Or.*comm.in Mt.*14.21 (p.336.11; M.13.1241A); *ἐπιστήσεις...εἰ μικρῶν μέν εἰσιν ἄγγελοι ⟨τῶν⟩ πνεύματι 'δουλείας [τῶν] εἰς φόβον' ἀγομένων...μεγάλων δὲ ὁ τῶν ἀ. μείζων κύριος* ib.13.26(p.253.20ff.; 1165A,B); id.*Cels.*8.36(p.252.8; M.11.1572D); *Apophth.Mac.Aeg.*(M.34.221B); for sin causes angel to flee, Or.*princ.*2.10.7(p.181.23; M.11.240A); Bas.*hom.in Ps.*33(1.148C; M.29.364B); Nil.*epp.*1.326(M.79.200C); **d.** two guardian angels, one good the other bad *δύο εἰσὶν ἄ. μετὰ τοῦ ἀνθρώπου, εἷς τῆς δικαιοσύνης καὶ εἷς τῆς πονηρίας* Herm.*mand.*6.2.1; cf.*Barn.*18.1; Or.*hom.35 in Lc.*(p.207.17; M.13.1889C) citing Herm. l.c.; *ἑκάστῳ τῶν ἀνθρώπων πάρεισι δύο ἄ., ὁ μὲν τῆς δικαιοσύνης, ὁ δὲ τῆς ἀδικίας, καὶ ἐὰν μὲν ἀνατείλῃ ἡμῶν ἐπὶ τὴν καρδίαν τὰ ἀγαθά, δηλονότι ὁμιλεῖ ἡμῖν ὁ ἄ. τοῦ θεοῦ· ὅταν δὲ ἀναβῇ ἡμῶν ἐπὶ τὴν καρδίαν τὰ φαῦλα, ὁμιλεῖ ἡμῖν ὁ ἄ. τοῦ διαβόλου* ib.*12*(p.86.20; 1829C,D); cf.id.*or.*31.6 (p.399.17f.; M.11.556A); *λόγος τίς ἐστιν...μὴ παριδεῖν τὸν θεὸν τὴν πτῶσιν ἡμῶν ἀπρονόητον· ἀλλ' ἄ. τινα...παρακαθιστᾶν εἰς συμμαχίαν τῇ ἑκάστου ζωῇ, ἐκ δὲ τοῦ ἐναντίου, τὸν φθορέα τῆς φύσεως ἀντιμηχανᾶσθαι τὸ ἴσον διὰ πονηροῦ τινος...δαίμονος, τῇ τοῦ ἀνθρώπου ζωῇ λυμαινόμενον* Gr.Nyss.*v.Mos.*(M.44.337D); good and bad guardian angels of nations, Or.*hom.12 in Lc.*(p.86.27ff.; 1829D); power of bad angels being broken by Christ who thus provoked their wrath, cf.id.*hom.9.3 in Gen.*(p.91.6; M.12.214A); **e.** time of assuming their office: at birth, Clem.*ecl.*41(p.141.2; M.9.717C); at baptism or at birth, Or.*comm.in Mt.*13.27(p.254.8; M.13.1165B); at baptism, *Apophth.Mac.Aeg.*(M.34.221B); **f.** number of guardian angels in rel. to human population *εἰ ἑκάστῳ ἀνθρώπῳ ἄ. παρέπεται φύλαξ...οἱ δὲ ἄνθρωποι ποτὲ μὲν αὔξησιν, ποτὲ δὲ μείωσιν...ὑπέμειναν, οἱ τῆς τῶν ἀ. αὐξήσεως καὶ μειώσεως ὄντες ἀνεπίδεκτοι, ποίαν τότε λειτουργίαν ἐπλήρουν, ἑκάστου τῶν ἀ. παρὰ θεοῦ λειτουργίαν ἐξ ἀρχῆς εἰληφότος; οἱ μὲν ἄ. πάντες ἄρχοντές τε καὶ ἀρχόμενοι, λειτουργίαν ἐκπληροῦσι...οἱ δὲ λειτουργεῖν εἰληφότες τὸ παρέπεσθαι τοῖς ἀνθρώποις φύλακες ἀεὶ μὲν αὔξονται, μειοῦνται δὲ οὐδέποτε...πρὶν ἢ δὲ ταγῶσι παρέπεσθαι τοῖς ἀνθρώποις, καὶ φυλάττειν αὐτούς, ἐν ταῖς ἄλλαις ὑπὲρ ἀνθρώπων λειτουργίαις λειτουργοῦσι τοῖς οἰκείοις ἄρχουσιν* ‡Just. *qu.et resp.*30(M.6.1277B,C); **g.** only angels of good Christians see face of Father, Or.*hom.35 in Lc.*(p.208.2ff.; M13.1889C–1890Af.); **h.** because they guard men, men are their debtors, id.*or.*28.3 (p.377.8; M.11.524B); **11.** question whether all angels can be sent on missions by God; **a.** answered affirmatively, Eus.*p.e.*7.16(328B; M.21.533C); Ath.*Ar.*3.12(M.26.348A); ‡Just.*qu.et resp.*30(M.6.1277C); Gr.Naz.*or.*29.31(p.70.5ff.; M.36.72B,C); Thdt.*haer.*5.7(4.404); **b.** only two lowest orders (archangels and angels) sent on missions into world, Dion.Ar.*c.h.*5(M.3.196B); cf.*ib.*13(300B–308B).

I. exeg.; **1.** Ex.12:12, Mel.*pass.*22 p.4.8; **2.** Jos.2:1ff., cf. *exploratores isti...possunt et angeli dei putari, sicut scriptum est: 'ecce mitto angelum meum ante faciem tuam...' quod per alios quidem invisibiliter, per Johannem vero visibiliter complebatur*, Or. *hom.3.3 in Jos.*(p.304.18ff.; M.12.839C); **3.** Ps.79:10, cf. *angeli... quos sub specie cedrorum arbitror indicatos*, id.*hom.17.4 in Num.* (p.164.2; M.12.709D); **4.** Lc.10:35; innkeeper = angel of Church, cf.id.*hom.34 in Lc.*(p.204.24; M.13.1888B); **5.** Jo.4:38 *οἱ δὲ κεκοπιακότες εἰσὶν οἱ τῆς οἰκονομίας ἄ. δι' ὧν ὡς μεσιτῶν ἐσπάρη καὶ ἀνετράφη* Heracleon ap.Or.*Jo.*13.50(49; p.279.1; M.14.492B); **6.** 1Cor. 11:10 *ἀγγέλους φησὶ τοὺς δικαίους καὶ ἐναρέτους. κατακαλυπτέσθω οὖν, ἵνα μὴ εἰς πορνείαν αὐτοὺς σκανδαλίσῃ· οἱ γὰρ...ἐν οὐρανοῖς ἄ. καὶ κατακεκαλυμμένην αὐτὴν βλέπουσιν* Clem.*fr.*1(p.195.6ff.; M.9.744Df.); **7.** angels mentioned in scripture considered as signifying human thoughts: ref. Ex.4:24f. *τὸν ἐλέγχοντα λόγον εὐθὺς ὡς ἄ. κατὰ συνείδησιν θάνατον ἀπειλοῦντα θεωρεῖ* Max.*qu.Thal.*17 (M.90.304D); *ib.*(305A); ref. 2Par.32:21 *δέχεται...πρὸς σωτηρίαν ἄγγελον· δηλονότι μείζονα σοφίας καὶ γνώσεως λόγον* ib.50(472B); ref. 1Cor.11:10 *διὰ τοὺς κατὰ συνείδησιν λογισμούς, καὶ αὐτοὺς ἀ. τροπικῶς νοουμένους* ib.25(336C).

J. cult; **1.** in gen. *ἀγγέλων στρατὸν...σεβόμεθα* Just.*1apol.*6.2 (M.6.336C); Or.*Cels.*8.57(p.274.13; M.11.1604B); Thdt.*affect.*3(p.93.7; 4.785); ref. iconoclast controversy *τιμῶμεν...εἰκόνα...ἁγίων καὶ ἀσωμάτων ἀ.* CNic.(787)*act.*4(H.4.265C); *Symb.Nic.*(787)(H.4.456A); opp. iconoclast view that angels should not be represented with bodies, Jo.Diacr.*fr.h.e.*(H.4.305D); for sanctuaries dedicated to angels cf. Didym.*Trin.*2.8(M.39.589B); **2.** exaggerations repudiated *μηδὲ κατὰ Ἰουδαίους σέβεσθε,...λατρεύοντες ἀγγέλοις Keryg.Petr.*ap. Clem.*str.*6.5(p.452.9; M.9.261A); prayer to angels *ἀ. γὰρ καλέσαι... οὐκ εὔλογον...ἀρκεῖ δὲ πρὸς τὸ ἵλεως ἡμῖν τοὺς ἁγίους ἀ. εἶναι τοῦ θεοῦ καὶ πάντα πράττειν αὐτοὺς ὑπὲρ ἡμῶν ἡ πρὸς τὸν θεὸν διάθεσις ἡμῶν, ὅση δύναμις ἀνθρωπίνῃ φύσει* Or.*Cels.*5.5(p.4.29–5.5; M.11. 1185C); Eus.*d.e.*3.3(p.113.9ff.; M.22.193D); *οὐ δεῖ Χριστιανοὺς ἐγκαταλείπειν τὴν ἐκκλησίαν τοῦ θεοῦ καὶ ἀπιέναι καὶ ἀ. ὀνομάζειν καὶ συνάξεις ποιεῖν* CLaod.*can.*35; interpreted as forbidding cult of angels altogether, Thdt.*Col.*2:18(3.490); **3.** reason for representation with wings, Chrys.*incomprehens.*3.5(1.468B) cit. s. *πτέρυξ*.

K. unorthodox applications of term to Christ; **1.** Christ's angelic aspect *οἱ πάντες ἡμῶν ἀναβαθμοὶ ὁ μονογενής ἐστιν τοῦ θεοῦ...ὁ δὲ οἷον πρῶτος κατωτέρω τὸ ἀνθρώπινον αὐτοῦ, ᾧ ἐπιβαίνοντες ὁδεύομεν...τὴν πᾶσαν ἐν τοῖς ἀναβαθμοῖς ὁδόν, ὥστε ἀναβῆναι δι' αὐτοῦ ὄντος καὶ ἀ. καὶ τῶν λοιπῶν δυνάμεων* Or.*Jo.*19.6(1; p.305.24; M.14.536D); *ὁ...σωτὴρ...γέγονεν ἀνθρώποις ἄνθρωπος καὶ ἀγγέλοις ἄγγελος, καὶ περὶ μὲν τοῦ ἄνθρωπον αὐτὸν γεγονέναι οὐδεὶς τῶν πεπιστευκότων διστάξει· περὶ δὲ τοῦ ἄ. πειθώμεθα τηροῦντες τὰς τῶν ἀ. ἐπιφανείας* ib.1.31(34; p.38.32–39.2; 81A); but cf. Didym.*Trin.*2.7 (M.39.589A); cf.Or.*hom.8.8 in Gen.*(p.83.13f.; M.12.208A); **2.** Gnost., Clem.*exc.Thdot.*35(p.118.11; M.9.676C); **3.** Arian *λέγει γὰρ* [sc. Eun.] *...τοσοῦτον εἶναι κάτω τῆς θείας φύσεως, ὅσον ἀπ' ἐκείνου πρὸς τὸ ταπεινότερον ἡ τῶν ἀ. ὑποβέβηκε φύσις...ἔχει γὰρ οὕτω τὰ γεγραμμένα· ὃς τῷ μὲν ἄγγελος ὠνομάσθαι σαφῶς ἐδίδαξε δι' ὅτου διήγγειλε τοὺς λόγους καὶ τίς ὁ ὤν, τῷ δὲ καὶ θεὸς προσειρῆσθαι τὴν ἰδίαν ἔδειξε κατὰ πάντων ὑπεροχήν. ὁ γὰρ τῶν δι' αὐτοῦ γενομένων θεὸς ἄγγελος τοῦ ἐπὶ πάντων θεοῦ.' ... πάντα* [sc. Heb.1:8ff.] *πρὸς ἔνδειξιν τοῦ μονογενοῦς θεοῦ ταῦτα τοῦ ἀποστόλου διεξιόντος, τί πάθω τὸν τῶν ἀ. κύριον ἄ. εἶναι παρὰ τοῦ χριστομάχου ἀκούων;...οὗτος εἰς ἀγγέλου τάξιν κατάγει τὸν τῶν ἀ. κύριον* Gr.Nyss.*Eun.*3(2 pp.259.12–260.19; M.45.865D–868C); *οὐκοῦν εἰ τῶν μὲν γενητῶν ἄλλος ἐστί, τῆς δὲ τοῦ πατρὸς οὐσίας μόνος ἴδιον γέννημα ὁ υἱός, μεματαίωται τοῖς Ἀρειανοῖς ἡ περὶ τοῦ γενόμενος πρόφασις· κἂν γὰρ ἐν τούτοις αἰσχυνθέντες βιάζωνται πάλιν λέγειν, συγκριτικῶς εἰρῆσθαι τὰ ῥητά, καὶ διὰ τοῦτο εἶναι τὸ συγκρινόμενα ὁμογενῆ, ὥστε τὸν υἱὸν τῆς τῶν ἀ. εἶναι φύσεως, αἰσχυνθήσονται μὲν προηγουμένως ὡς τὰ Οὐαλεντίνου καὶ Καρποκράτους φθεγγόμενοι· ὧν ὁ μὲν τοὺς ἀ. ὁμογενεῖς εἴρηκε τῷ Χριστῷ, ὁ δὲ ἀγγέλους τοῦ κόσμου δημιουργοὺς εἶναί φησιν· παρ' αὐτῶν γὰρ ἴσως μαθόντες καὶ οὗτοι, συγκρίνουσι τὸν τοῦ θεοῦ λόγον τοῖς ἀ.* Cyr. *Heb.*1:4(p.371.22ff.; M.74.956C).

L. Gnost. angelology; **1.** creation of world by angels; **a.** Basilides: 'first' angels makers of 'first heaven', cf.Iren.*haer.*1.24.3 (M.7.676A); whereas creator angels occupy lowest heaven and made world, their chief being the God of the Jews, *ib.*1.24.4(l.c.); refutation of foreg. teaching that world was created by angels without knowledge and against will of supreme God, cf.*ib.*2.2.1 (713A); refutation of theory of creation of world by angels with knowledge of supreme God, *ib.*2.2.3(7.713C–714B); *ἐκ δὲ τούτων* [sc. the 'first']*...ἀ. γεγονέναι ἀνώτερον πρῶτον οὐρανόν, καὶ ἀ. ἑτέρους ἐξ αὐτῶν γεγονέναι, τοὺς δὲ ὑπ' αὐτῶν γεγονότας ἀ. πεποιηκέναι αὖθις δεύτερον οὐρανὸν καὶ αὐτοὺς δὲ πάλιν πεποιηκέναι ἀ.* Epiph. *haer.*24.1(p.257.12ff.; M.41.309B); *ἐξ ὧν ἀ. ἕνα λέγει τὸν θεόν, ὃν διελὼν τῶν Ἰουδαίων μόνον ἔφη εἶναι, ἕνα τοῦτον καὶ συναρίθμιον ἀγγέλοις τοῖς ὑπ' αὐτοῦ κατὰ μιμολογίαν ὀνοματοποιουμένοις τάσσων, καὶ ἐξ αὐτοῦ πεπλάσθαι τὸν ἄνθρωπον. καὶ τούτους ἅμα αὐτῷ μεμερικέναι τὸν κόσμον κατὰ διαίρεσιν κλήρων τῷ πλήθει τῶν ἀ.* ib.24.2 (pp.258.12–259.1; 309Cf.); **b.** Saturninus: man made by angels *τὸν ἄνθρωπον δὲ ἀγγέλων εἶναι ποίημα, ἄνωθεν ἀπὸ τῆς αὐθεντίας φωτεινῆς εἰκόνος ἐπιφανείσης, ἣν κατασχεῖν μὴ δυνηθέντες διὰ τὸ παράχρημα, φησίν, ἀναδραμεῖν ἄνω[θεν], ἐκέλευσαν ἑαυτοῖς λέγοντες· 'ποιήσωμεν ἄνθρωπον κατ' εἰκόνα'...οὗ γενομένου, φησίν, καὶ ⟨μὴ⟩ δυναμένου* ἀνορθοῦσθαι τοῦ πλάσματος διὰ τὸ ἀδρανὲς τῶν ἀ. ... οἰκτείρασα αὐτὸν ἡ ἄνω δύναμις διὰ τὸ ἐν ὁμοιώματι αὐτῆς γεγονέναι, ἔπεμψε σπινθῆρα ζωῆς Iren.*haer*.1.24.1 ap.Hipp.*haer*.7.28(p.208.13ff.; M.16.3322A,B); cf.Epiph.*haer*.23.1(p.248.6ff.; M.41.297Cff.); cf.Thdt.*haer*.1.3(4.290); refutation, cf. *non indigente patre angelis, uti...formaret hominem*, Iren.*haer*.4.7.4(M.7.992C); *non ergo angeli fecerunt nos...nec angeli potuerunt imaginem facere dei*, *ib*.4.20.1(1032B); εἰ γὰρ οἱ ἄ. ⟨τὸν ἄνθρωπον⟩ πεποιήκασιν, ἄ. δὲ πάλιν ἀπὸ τῆς ἄνωθεν δυνάμεως τὸ αἴτιον ἐσχήκασι τοῦ εἶναι, ἄρα οὐκ αὐτοὶ αἴτιοι τοῦ πλάσματος τοῦ ἀνθρώπου, ἀλλὰ ἡ ἄνωθεν δύναμις ἡ τοὺς ἀ. ποιήσασα, ἐξ ὧν καὶ ἡ πλάσις τοῦ ἀνθρώπου συνέστηκε Epiph.*haer*.23.3(p.251.9ff.; M.41.301A,B); *ib*.(p.251.19ff.; 301B,C); discussion of supreme God's attitude to angels creating man, *ib*.23.4(p.252.1–253.6; 301C–304B); God of Jews an angel, cf.Iren.*haer*.1.24.2 ap.Hipp.*haer*.7.28 (p.209.6; 3322B); Epiph.*haer*.23.2(p.250.7; 300C); Satan an angel τὰς δὲ προφητείας, ἃς μὲν ἀπὸ τῶν κοσμοποιῶν ἀ. λελαλῆσθαι, ἃς δὲ ἀπὸ τοῦ σατανᾶ, ὃν καὶ αὐτὸν ἄ. ἀντιπράττοντα τοῖς κοσμοποιοῖς ὑπέθεντο, μάλιστα δὲ τὸν τῶν Ἰουδαίων θεόν Iren.*haer*.1.24.2 ap.Hipp.*haer*.7.28 (p.210.1f.; 3323A κοσμικοῖς); Epiph.*haer*.23.2(p.251.5; 301A); world made by seven angels acc. Saturninus and Basilides, Iren.*haer*.1.24.1 ap.Hipp.*haer*.7.28(p.208.12; 3322A); Epiph.*haer*.23.1(p.248.4ff.; 297C); **c.** Valentinus: τὸν δημιουργὸν...ἄ. θεῷ ἐοικότα Iren.*haer*.1.5.2(M.7.496A); theory that created things are images of angels of Pleroma refuted, *ib*.2.7.4(M.7.730Af.); cf.Clem.*exc.Thdot*.25 (p.115.10; M.9.672B); **d.** Carpocrates τὸν μὲν κόσμον καὶ τὰ ἐν αὐτῷ ὑπὸ ἀ. πολὺ ὑποβεβηκότων τοῦ ἀγενήτου πατρὸς γεγενῆσθαι λέγει Iren.*haer*.1.25.1 ap.Hipp.*haer*.7.32(p.218.1; M.16.3338A); refutation of this teaching, Epiph.*haer*.27.7(p.311.18ff.; M.41.376Bff.); *ib*.(p.312.20; 377A); **e.** creation of cosmos by angels also taught by Menander, Iren.*haer*.1.23.5(M.7.673B); Hipp.*haer*.7.4(p.190.2; M.16.3294A); cf.Epiph.*haer*.22.1(p.246.10; M.41.296C); Thdt.*haer*.1.2(4.289); **f.** origin of this heresy attributed to Simon Magus, acc. whom angels created world, but ruled it badly, Iren.*haer*.1.23.3 ap.Hipp.*haer*.6.19(p.147.1; M.16.3223B); Epiph.*haer*.21.6(p.245.3ff.; M.41.293C); Thdt.*haer*.1.1(4.288); **g.** theory condemned as making angels homogeneous with Christ, Ath.*Ar*.1.56(M.26.129C); οὐδὲ ἄ. δημιουργεῖν δυνήσονται, κτίσματα ὄντες καὶ αὐτοί, κἂν Οὐαλεντῖνος καὶ Μαρκίων καὶ Βασιλείδης τοιαῦτα φρονῶσι, καὶ ὑμεῖς [sc. Arians] ἐκείνων ζηλωταὶ τυγχάνητε *ib*.2.21(192A); Jo.D.*f.o*.2.3(M.94.873B); **2.** their place in the system of aeons; accompanying aeon Soter, Iren.*haer*.1.2.6(M.7.465A); *ib*.1.4.5(488A); *ib*.(489A); cf.*ib*.2.19.5(773C); cf.*ib*.2.19.1(771B,C); **3.** their relation to OT; **a.** acc. Simon Magus τοὺς δὲ προφήτας ἀπὸ τῶν κοσμοποιῶν ἀ. ἐμπνευσθέντας εἰρηκέναι τὰς προφητείας...ἔθεντο γάρ, φησίν, οἱ ἄ. οἱ τὸν κόσμον ποιήσαντες ὅσα ἐβούλοντο, διὰ τῶν τοιούτων λόγων δουλοῦν νομίζοντες τοὺς αὐτῶν ἀκούοντας Iren.*haer*.1.23.3 ap.Hipp.*haer*.6.19(p.147.9,14; M.16.3223Cf.); cf.Thdt.*haer*.1.1(4.288); **b.** acc. Apelles εἶναί τινα θεὸν ἀγαθόν...τὸν δὲ πάντα κτίσαντα εἶναι δίκαιον, ὃς τὰ γενόμενα ἐδημιούργησε, καὶ τρίτον τὸν Μωσεῖ λαλήσαντα—πυρινὸν δὲ τοῦτον εἶναι—εἶναι δὲ καὶ τέταρτον ἕτερον, κακῶν αἴτιον· τούτους δὲ ἀ. ὀνομάζει Hipp.*haer*.7.38(p.224.5; M.16.3346A); cf.*ib*.10.20(p.280.22; 3438B); **c.** Justinus' system of good and evil angels described in rel. to OT and Greek mythology, *ib*.5.26(p.127.10ff.; 3194Dff.); **d.** acc. Cerinthus τὸν νόμον καὶ τοὺς προφήτας ὑπὸ ἀ. δεδόσθαι, καὶ τὸν δεδωκότα νόμον ἕνα εἶναι τῶν ἀ. τῶν τὸν κόσμον πεποιηκότων Epiph.*haer*.28.1(p.313.16f.; M.41.377D); **4.** angels not sexless, Clem.*ecl*.53(p.124.21; M.9.684C); cf. C.2 supra; **5.** apostles = angels, Heracleon ap.Or.*Jo*.13.49(48; p.276.34; M.14.488C); *ib*.13.50(49; p.279.1; 492B); **6.** angels can change their orders ἔθετο τοὺς [τε] πρωτοκτίστους ἀ. εἰς τὸ μηκέτι κατὰ τὴν πρόνοιαν τῷ ὡρισμένῳ λειτουργεῖν, ἀλλ' εἶναι ἐν ἀναπαύσει... οἱ δὲ προσεχέστεροι τούτοις προκόψουσιν εἰς ἣν ἐκεῖνοι ἀπολελοίπασι τάξιν, καὶ οὕτως οἱ ὑποβεβηκότες ἀναλόγως Clem.*ecl*.56(p.153.20; M.9.725B); **7.** angels can be baptized on behalf of men, id.*exc.Thdot*.22(p.113.29; M.9.669A); *ib*.(p.114.6; M.l.c.); **8.** angels cannot enter Pleroma without men, *ib*.35(p.118.12ff.; 676C); **9.** refutation of Basilides' ideas on angels' fear of pre-existent man, id.*str*.2.8 (p.133.14; M.8.973B); **10.** refutation of Valent. teaching that angels did not know supreme God, cf.Iren.*haer*.2.6.1–3(M.7.724B–725C); **11.** Elchezaite measurements of angels, Hipp.*haer*.9.13(p.251.14; M.16.3387B).

M. H. Ghost as an angel (Macedonian), exeg. 1Tim.5:21 ἐκεῖνοι δὲ φάσκουσιν, ἐπειδὴ τὸν θεὸν καὶ τὸν Χριστὸν ὠνόμασεν, εἶτα τοὺς ἀ., ἀνάγκη τοῖς ἀ. συναριθμεῖσθαι τὸ πνεῦμα τῆς τε αὐτῶν εἶναι συστοιχίας καὶ αὐτό, καὶ ἄ. εἶναι μείζονα τῶν ἄλλων. πρῶτον μὲν οὖν τῆς ἀσεβείας ἐστὶν Οὐαλεντίνου τοῦτο τὸ εὕρημα...ἐκεῖνος γὰρ ἔφησεν, ὅτι, πεμφθέντος τοῦ παρακλήτου, συναπεστάλησαν αὐτῷ οἱ ἡλικιῶται αὐτοῦ ἄ.· ἔπειτα δὲ τὸ πνεῦμα κατάγοντες εἰς τοὺς ἀ. εἰς τὴν τριάδα συντάσσοντες. εἰ γὰρ μετὰ πατέρα καὶ υἱὸν κατ' αὐτοὺς οἱ ἄ., δηλονότι τῆς τριάδος εἰσὶν οἱ ἄ. Ath.*ep.Serap*.1.10(M.26.556C–557A).

N. theory that men can turn into angels οἱ γὰρ ἐξ ἀνθρώπων εἰς ἀ. μεταστάντες χίλια ἔτη μαθητεύονται ὑπὸ τῶν ἀ. ... εἶτα οἱ μὲν διδάξαντες μετατίθενται εἰς ἀρχαγγελικὴν ἐξουσίαν, οἱ μαθόντες δὲ τοὺς ἐξ ἀνθρώπων αὖθις μεθισταμένους εἰς ἀ. μαθητεύουσιν, ἔπειτα οὕτως περιόδοις ῥηταῖς ἀποκαθίστανται τῇ οἰκείᾳ τοῦ σώματος ἀγγελοθεσίᾳ Clem.*ecl*.57(p.154.8ff.; M.9.725C–728A); cf. mystic transformation of apostles into angels, Or.*Jo*.10.30(18; p.203.21; M.14.361A); men changed into angels through resurrection, cf.id.*hom.9.11 in Lev*.(p.439.7; M.12.524A).

O. ascetic life as 'life of angels', Bas.*ascet*.1.2(2.320B; M.31.873B); esp. of virginal life, Meth.*symp*.8.2(p.83.8; M.18.141A); Petr.II Al. *encycl*.1(M.33.1277A); οἱ τὴν παρθενίαν ἀσκοῦντες ἄ. εἰσιν †Bas.Anc. *virg*.51(M.30.772B); Gr.Naz.*or*.37.10(M.36.296A); Jo.Clim.*scal*.15(M.88.896C); in respect of detachment, Gr.Nyss.*v.Macr*.(p.382.6; M.46.969C); Jo.Clim.*scal*.29(M.88.1148C); imitating angels: in superiority οἴδαμεν...τοὺς ἀ. οὕτως εἶναι ἀνθρώπων κρείττονας, ὥστε τοὺς ἀνθρώπους τελειωθέντας ἰσαγγέλους γίνεσθαι Or.*Cels*.4.29(p.298.12; M.11.1069B); in stability, Gr.Nyss.*hom.4 in Cant*.(M.44.856C); in ἀφθαρσία, Clem.*paed*.2.10(p.217.20; M.8.517B); myst. γίνονται ὥσπερ ἄ. ἀσώματοι, ἐν τοσαύτῃ κουφότητι ὄντες μετὰ τοῦ σώματος Mac.Aeg.*hom*.18.7(M.34.640B).

P. met., of Christians in gen. ἐξ ἀνθρώπων ἀγγέλους ποιῶν [sc. S. Paul], μᾶλλον δὲ ἀπὸ δαιμόνων ἀ. τοὺς ἀνθρώπους Chrys.*laud.Paul*.1 (2.477E).

***ἀγγελότης, ἡ,** v. ἀγγελιότης.

***ἀγγελοφάνεια, ἡ,** *appearance of angels*, Leont.B.*Nest.et Eut*.3(M.86.1369D).

***ἀγγελοχαρμόσυνος,** *joyful with angels* ἀ. τελετή Thdr.Stud. *epp*.2.88(M.99.1333C).

***ἀγγελτήρ, ὁ, 1.** *announcer, messenger* ἐπίσκοποι...οἱ δοχεῖς τοῦ λόγου καὶ ἀ. *Const.App*.2.25.7; **2.** *angel*, *Orac.Sib*.2.242; *ib*.2.214.

***ἀγγελτρία, ἡ,** *announcer* σάλπιγξ πολέμων ἀ. *Orac.Sib*.8.117.

ἄγειος, *unearthly*, Mac.Mgn.*apocr*.3.14(p.90.11).

ἀγείρω, *collect by begging*, hence *be a beggar* or *charlatan* οἱ μὲν ἐνθουσιῶντες οἱ δὲ ἀ. φασιν ἥκειν ἄνωθεν υἱὸν θεοῦ Cels.ap.Or.*Cels*.1.50(p.101.21; M.11.753C); *ib*.51(p.102.5; 756A).

ἀγελάζ-ω, 1. *be a shepherd, keep a flock* θεσπίσας Ἰάκωβον ∼ειν †Apoll.*met.Ps*.77:71(M.33.1429B); **2.** pass., *be gregarious, flock*, Chrys.*hom.3.1 in Ac.princ*.(3.71B); id.*hom.13.1 in Mt*.(7.168D).

***ἀγελαιοκόμος, ὁ,** *keeper of the flock, pastor*, Pall.*v.Chrys*.4 (p.24.27; ἀγελοκόμων M.47.16).

ἀγελάρχης, ὁ, *leader of a flock*; of spiritual leaders: Christ, Mac. Mgn.*apocr*.4.18(p.195.31); angels, Eus.*d.e*.4.6(p.160.17; M.22.268A); bishops, Gr.Ant.*bapt*.2.10(M.88.1884A) = ‡Chrys.*hom*.9(13.237E); ‡Jo.D.*Artem*.25(M.96.1273C).

ἀγελαρχία, ἡ, *leadership of a flock*, Dion.Ar.*c.h*.2.2(M.3.153A).

ἀγέλη, ἡ, *herd, flock*; met. **1.** of mankind, esp. ref. Redemption πρόκειται...τῷ θεῷ τῶν ἀνθρώπων ἀ. σώζειν Clem.*prot*.11(p.81.32; M.8.236A); id.*paed*.2.2(p.171.18; M.8.420A); Eus.*l.C*.13(p.240.29; M.20.1408A); *ib*.16(p.253.1; 1425C); of partic. nations ἄνδρες ἐξ ἀ. Ἑλληνικῆς Cyr.*Is*.5.5(2.864D); id.*Jon*.1(3.364B); **2.** of the flock of Christ, i.e. Church, Adam.*dial*.2.22(p.114.19; M.11.1792B); Chrys. *bapt.Chr*.4(2.375A); id.*hom.5.2 in 1Tim*.(11.576F); Χριστοῦ λογικαῖς ἀ. Pall.*v.Chrys*.4(p.24.24; M.47.16); ἀ. ἀπέφηνε μίαν, τούς τε ἐν οὐρανῷ, καὶ τοὺς ἐπὶ γῆς Cyr.*Lc*.2:7ff.(M.72.496A); ‡Jo.D.*Artem*.25(M.96.1273C); **3.** of partic. groups: a convent of nuns, Max.*ep*.31(M.91.625B); heret. sects, Rhod.ap.Eus.*h.e*.5.13.2(M.20.460B); **4.** of a band of demons, Cyr.*Lc*.4:22(M.72.544A).

***ἀγεληματος,** *belonging to the herd, vulgar*, Mac.Aeg.*hom*.15.45 (M.34.605D); *ib*.17.3(625B).

ἀγελικός, *belonging to a flock, gregarious*, Bas.*hex*.8.3(1.73B; M.29.172A).

***ἀγελοκομική, ἡ,** sc. τέχνη, *art of breeding cattle*, Clem.*str*.1.7 (p.24.28; M.8.732C).

***ἀγελοκόμος, ὁ,** v. ἀγελαιοκόμος.

ἀγενεαλόγητος, *without genealogy*; of Melchizedek as a type of Christ, ‡Ath.*Melch*.(M.28.529B); Marc.Er.*opusc*.10.4(M.65.1121B); hence of Christ himself τὸ κατὰ Ἰωάννην, τὸν γενεαλογούμενον εἶπον καὶ ἀπὸ τοῦ ἀ. ἀρχόμενον Or.*Jo*.1.4(6; p.8.2; M.14.29C); cf.*cat.Jo*.1:1(p.179.9); ἡ δὲ κατὰ τὴν θεότητα αὐτοῦ [sc. Χριστοῦ] γέννησίς ἐστιν ἀ. ‡Just.*qu.et resp*.67(M.6.1309A); Sev.Ant.ap.*cat.Ac*.8:33(p.145.24); Max.*ambig*.(M.91.1141D).

***ἀγενεσία**, ἡ, *ingenerateness*, ‡Ath.*dial.Trin.*2.29(M.28.1201A); ‡Just.*qu.Chr.*4.1(M.6.1445C); *ib.*4.5(1453B).

ἀγενησία, ἡ, for ἀγεννησία, ‡Hipp.*Ber.Hel.*6(M.10.837B; ἀγεννησία p.325.2).

ἀγένητος, *uncreated, unoriginated* (in pre-Nicene authors and in MSS and edd. freq. confused with ἀγέννητος q.v.);

A. gen. implications: eternal pre-existence, Clem.*str.*5.11(p.371.16; M.9.104A); unity ἓν τὸ ἀ. Meth.*arbitr.*5(p.157.10; M.18.249B); immortality, Adam.*dial.*3.6(p.122.20; M.11.1797B); causation ἀρχὴ τῶν ὅλων, ἀ. Hipp.*haer.*8.12(p.232.8; M.16.3358B ἀγέννητον).

B. non-Christian usage discussed; **1.** in Gr. philos., whence it entered Christian terminology, applied not only to the divinity, but to matter, and to the soul, and used in other non-theol. senses, Hipp.*haer.*1.19(p.20.3; M.16.3041B); *ib.*8.17(p.236.13; 3363C); these uses repudiated, Athenag.*leg.*10.1(M.6.908B); τὸ μὲν γὰρ θεῖον ἀ. εἶναι καὶ ἀΐδιον...τὴν δὲ ὕλην γενητήν *ib.*4.1(897B); ἀ. equated with ἀΐδιον, *ib.*19.1(929A); Ath.*inc.*2.3(M.25.100A); ἡ ὕλη ἀεὶ μὲν φθαρτὴ ἢ γενητή, ἄφθαρτος δὲ καὶ ἀ. οὐδέποτε ‡Just.*confut.*7(M.6.1509C); by way of privation only is matter termed ἀ. (i.e. it cannot create), *ib.*(1509D); *ib.*(1509C); cf. ὕλη; soul not ἀ., though ἄφθαρτος, ‡Just.*qu.Gr.*9(M.6.1476A); ἀφθαρσίαν μὲν διὰ χρειώδη τινὰ δύναταί τις ἔχειν, ἀγεννησίαν δὲ οὐκέτι· τὸ γὰρ ἀ., χωρὶς πάσης χρειώδους αἰτίας, δεῖ ὑπάρχειν ἀ. *ib.*(1476B); Ath.*decr.*28(p.24.23; M.25.468B); for a strict line of division runs between the uncreated and the created, Clem.*str.*4.24(p.316.12; M.8.1361B); **2.** of uncreated principle of evil in Gnost. and Manich. dualistic systems, sts. equated with Devil ἀ. ἄρα ὁ διάβολος, καὶ εἰ ἀ., καὶ ἀπαθής ...τῷ γὰρ ἀ. ... ταῦτα ὑπάρχειν δεῖ. ὁ δὲ διάβολος...κολάζεται. τὸ δὲ κολαζόμενον...πάσχει, ἀπαθὲς δὲ τὸ ἀγένητον. οὐκ ἄρα ἀ. ...ὁ διάβολος Meth.*res.*1.36(p.276.12ff.; M.41.1101Bf.); τὸν δὲ διάβολον καὶ τοὺς...δαίμονας, κατὰ Μαρκίωνος, καὶ Κέρδωνος, καὶ τοὺς Μάνεντος μύθους, οὐκ ἀ. εἶναί φαμεν Thdt.*haer.*5.8(4.406); acc. Manicheans ἔστιν ἄρα ἀρχὴ ἀ. καὶ κακή *Disp.Phot.*(M.88.556C); an assertion subversive of monotheism, Jo.D.*Man.*2(M.96.1325B).

C. in Christian theology; **1.** of divine nature αὐτογενὴς ἀ. ἅπαντα κρατῶν διὰ παντὸς *Orac.Sib.fr.*1.17; Clem.*prot.*6(p.52.5; M.8.173A); τῇ ἀ. καὶ ἀϊδίῳ αὐτοῦ ζωῇ Or.*Jo.*1.29(32; p.37.10; M.14.77D); θεός ἐστιν ὁ παντοκράτωρ, ὁ. ἀ. id.*dial.*1(p.120.8); εἰ δύναται θεός, ἀ. ὤν, ἑαυτὸν ποιῆσαι γενητόν Mac.Mgn.*apocr.*4.30(p.225.4); ἀ. οὐχ ὡς μήπω γενόμενον,...ἀλλ' ὥσπερ παναγένητον, καὶ ἀπολύτως ἀ. Dion.Ar.*d.n.*9.4(M.3.912C); contrasted with creatures κατὰ ἀντιδιαστολὴν τοῦ ἀ. θεοῦ, τὰ γενητὰ ἀπολλύμενα ἐκάλεσεν Cosm.Ind.*top.*7(M.88.369B); **2.** of Father τῆς τοῦ πατρὸς ἀ. φύσεως Eus.*d.e.*5.1(p.213.11; M.22.353C ἀγενν.); ref. status of Son μέσος τε ἑστὼς θεοῦ τοῦ ἀ. καὶ τῶν μετ' αὐτὸν γενητῶν *ib.*4.10(p.167.35; 280B ἀγενν.); Serap.*euch.*4.1; **3.** of Son; **a.** pre-Nicene τὸν ἀ. ... πρωτότοκον Or.*Cels.*6.17(p.88.21; M.11.1317A); in his humanity, both ἀ. καὶ γενητός Hipp.*haer.*9.10(p.244.16; M.16.3378A ἀγένν.); ὁ σωτὴρ...τῆς ἀ. θεότητος μετασχὼν θεός Eus.*d.e.*9.9(p.427.8; M.22.688D ἀγενν.); **b.** in Arian controversy; ἀ. suspect to orthodox as being of pagan origin τὸ μὲν ἀ. παρ' Ἑλλήνων εὕρηται τῶν μὴ γινωσκόντων τὸν υἱόν Ath.*decr.*31(p.27.16; M.25.473B); Greeks use it in several senses ἀ. τὸ μήπω μὲν γενόμενον, δυνάμενον δὲ γενέσθαι· καὶ πάλιν τὸ μήτε ὑπάρχον, μήτε δυνάμενον εἰς τὸ εἶναι γενέσθαι· καὶ τρίτον...τὸ ὑπάρχον μέν, μήτε δὲ γενητόν, μήτε ἀρχὴν ἐσχηκὸς εἰς τὸ εἶναι *ib.*28(p.25.27; 469A); third sense being denied to Son by Arians, *ib.*(p.25.23; 469B); cf.id.*Ar.*1.30(M.26.73A–76A); who confuse created and uncreated ἐπεὶ εἰ ὅμοιον τὸ γενητὸν τῷ ἀ. θέλουσιν...οὐ μακρὰν εἰσιν εἰπεῖν, ὅτι καὶ τὸ ἀ. καὶ κτισμάτων ἐστὶν εἰκών *ib.*31(76C), and contend that Son was created as an intermediary because μὴ ἐδύνατο τὰ λοιπὰ κτίσματα τῆς ἀκράτου χειρὸς τοῦ ἀ. τὴν ἐργασίαν βαστάξαι id.*decr.*8(p.7.18; M.25.'437'(429)A); thus serving two Lords ἑνὶ μὲν ἀ., τῷ δὲ ἑτέρῳ γενητῷ id.*Ar.*3.16(M.26.353C); ἀΐδιον, τοῦτ' ἔστιν ἀ., εἶναί φησιν [sc. Marcell.] τὸν λόγον Eus.*e.th.*2.3(p.102.4; M.24.904C ἀγενν.); ἀγενν. *ib.*2 tit.3(p.98.17; 897); **c.** post-Nicene, the being ἀ. of Son held to be necessarily implied in the being ἀ. of Father πατὴρ...ἀ., πῶς...ὁ ἐξ αὐτοῦ καρπὸς ἔσται γενητός; Cyr.*thes.*32(5¹.304D); ‡Ath.*dial.Trin.*1.18(M.28.1145A); and in his activity in Church ἀ. μὲν υἱός· ἁγιάζει γάρ· γενητοὶ δὲ ἡμεῖς· ἁγιαζόμεθα γάρ †Diad.*Ar.*7(M.65.1161C); def. of ἀ.: τὸ ἀ. διὰ ἑνὸς ν γραφόμενον, τὸ ἄκτιστον, ἤτοι τὸ μὴ γενόμενον σημαίνει...τὸ...σημαινόμενον διαφέρει οὐσία οὐσίας· ἄλλη γὰρ οὐσία ἄκτιστος, ἤτοι ἀ. δι' ἑνὸς ν, καὶ ἄλλη γενητή Jo.D.*f.o.*1.8(M.94.817A,B); **4.** of H. Ghost ἁγίῳ πνεύματι...ἅτε ἀ. Didym.*Trin.*2.3(M.39.477A); **5.** of Trin. πατέρα, καὶ υἱόν, καὶ ἅγιον πνεῦμα ἀ. λέγω ‡Ath.*dial.Trin.*1.19(M.28.1145B); **6.** of created things, in very restricted sense; e.g. of darkness, of which God did not say γενηθήτω σκότος, hence ἀ. μὲν οὐχ ὡς οὐ γενόμενον, ἀλλ' ὡς τὸ γένεσιν ἐν ὑπάρξει μὴ λαβόν Proc.G.*Gen.*1:5(M.87.57B).

ἀγενήτως, *eternally*, ref. matter συνεῖναί φημι ἀ. τῇ ὕλῃ δὴ τὰς ποιότητας Meth.*arbitr.*10(p.172.9; M.18.257C); Adam.*dial.*4.8(p.156.4; M.11.1817C); ref. Son οὐκ ἀ. συνυπάρχει τῷ πατρί Eus.*d.e.*5.1(p.213.20; M.22.353C ἀγεννήτως); ref. divine wisdom ἀ. συνυπάρχειν τῷ θεῷ Ath.*Ar.*2.40(M.26.232C); ref. power of God, *ib.*1.32(77B).

ἀγεννησία, ἡ, *ingenerateness*; **1.** philos., as realm of eternal principles, e.g. acc. Empedocles ἔσονται [sc. νεῖκος καὶ φιλία] ἀεὶ διὰ τὴν ἀ. φθορὰν ὑπομεῖναι μὴ δυνάμενα Hipp.*haer.*7.29(p.211.26; M.16.3326C), to which belongs the universe as being image of ingenerate demiurge, an idea rejected as self-contradictory ἐν ἀ. γὰρ ἀδύνατον τῷ κόσμῳ σώζειν τῆς εἰκόνος τὸ ὄνομα ‡Just.*qu.Chr.*4.3(M.6.1449B); **2.** these ideas reproduced by Gnostics: e.g. Peratics, whose first world principle was ἀπὸ τῆς ἀ., Hipp.*haer.*5.12(p.104.26; M.16.3162B); out of which Christ came, *ib.*(p.105.12; 3162C); *ib.*10.10(p.269.11; 3422A); by Manicheans in assertion of two ingenerate principles; idea refuted ἀγεννησίας δὲ ποίαν τις ἂν εὕροι διαφοράν, ἢ ποῦ γε ἐναντιότητα; Tit.Bost.*Man.*1.10(M.18.1081C); and of creation from ἀ.: εἰ περὶ κτίσεως ᾔδεισαν φιλοσοφεῖν Μανιχαῖοι καλῶς, οὐκ ἂν τὴν ἐξ οὐκ ὄντων...τοῖς τῆς ἀ. πρεσβείοις ἐτίμησαν Chrys.*serm.*1.1 *in Gen.*(4.645E); **3.** ἀ. held to have been borrowed from Egyptian mythology, Gr.Nyss.*Eun.*12(2 p.289.31; M.45.901D); became a key word in Arian controversy ἡ περὶ τὸ ῥῆμα τῆς ἀ. σκιαμαχία *ib.*9(2 p.222.7; 821B), used by Arians as denoting essence and prerogative of divinity of Father ἔστιν οὐδὲν ἕτερον ἢ ἀ. ἡ φύσις [sc. τοῦ θεοῦ] *ib.*12(1 p.223.14; 917C); which they denied to Son ἀξίωμα μέν ἐστιν ἡ ἀ., ὡς Εὐνομίῳ δοκεῖ Bas.*Eun.*2.31(1.268C; M.29.645A); Didym.*Trin.*1.26(M.39.385D); ἡ πολυθρύλητος ἀ. ἡ μόνη κατά σε [i.e. Eun.] τὴν οὐσίαν [sc. πατρός] χαρακτηρίζουσα Gr.Nyss.*Eun.*12(1 p.367.11; 1092B); *ib.*(p.221.18; 916B); contradictorily opp. γέννησις as characteristic of Son τὰς δύο φωνὰς τὴν ἀ. τε καὶ τὴν γέννησιν ἀντιφατικῶς ἐναντιουμένας ἀλλήλαις *ib.*(p.222.3; 916C); and itself made a divinity, *ib.*(p.369.9; 1093C); Aët.*synt.*20(p.356.9; M.42.540C); orthodox reply: ἀ. a non-scriptural word, Bas.*Eun.*2.29(1.265E; M.29.640A); ἀ. does not constitute essence of Father, Gr.Naz.*or.*39.12(M.36.348C); οὐ τὴν ἀ. εἶναι θεόν Gr.Nyss.*Eun.*12(1 p.264.14; M.45.968D); *ib.*10(2 p.235.14; 837A); οὐ σημαίνει [sc. ἀ.] οὐσίας διαφοράν, οὐδὲ ἀξίωμα, ἀλλὰ τρόπον ὑπάρξεως ‡Cyr.*Trin.*8(6³.11D; M.77.1136D); ἡ γὰρ ἀ. τῆς γεννήσεως, κατὰ μόνην διαφέρει τὴν σημασίαν Thal.*cent.*4.89(M.91.1468B); Son, therefore, though lacking ἀ., does not differ substantially from Father πάντα ὅσα ὁ πατὴρ τοῦ υἱοῦ, πλὴν τῆς ἀ. Gr.Naz.*or.*41.9(M.36.441C); Leont.H.*Nest.*2.30(M.86.1589B); Jo.D.*f.o.*1.8(M.94.816C); **4.** Trin.; ἀ. contrasted with γέννησις and ἐκπόρευσις: ἴδιον δὲ πατρὸς μέν, ἡ ἀ.· υἱοῦ δέ, ἡ γέννησις· πνεύματος δέ, ἡ ἔκπεμψις Gr.Naz.*or.*25.16(M.35.1221B); πᾶσα ἑνότης καὶ ταὐτότης ἐν τριάδι, πλὴν ἀ. καὶ γεννήσεως καὶ ἐκπορεύσεως ‡Caes.Naz.*dial.*3(M.38.861); Jo.D.*f.o.*1.8(M.94.829B); σαρκωθεῖσα ἡ τοῦ υἱοῦ ὑπόστασις, οὐ συνεσάρκωσεν ἑαυτῇ τὴν ἀ. τοῦ πατρὸς Anast.S.*hod.*17(M.89.264C); ταὐτό ἐστιν ὁ πατὴρ ὅπερ ὁ υἱὸς καὶ τὸ...πνεῦμα...τοῦτο μόνον ἔχων ἕτερον παρ' ἐκεῖνα, τὴν πατρότητα καὶ τὴν ἀ. Anast.*fid.*(p.272).

***ἀγεννητογενής**, *ungenerated-created*; sarcastic Arian term for Son acc. orthodox teaching, Ar.*ep.Eus.*(p.2.2; M.42.212A).

ἀγέννητος, *ungenerated*; **1.** as attribute of Godhead in gen., sts. used by early writers in same sense as ἀγένητος q.v. with which it is freq. confused in MSS and edd. μόνος γὰρ ἀ. καὶ ἄφθαρτος ὁ θεὸς καὶ διὰ τοῦτο θεός ἐστι Just.*dial.*5.4(M.6.488B); τοῦ δημιουργοῦ, ὅς ἐστιν ἀ. μόνος θεός Or.*princ.*4.1(8; p.308.1; M.11.357C); Hymen.*ep.*2(p.324.15) cit. s. ἄναρχος; *Symb.*ap.*Const.App.*7.41.4; of Christ in his divinity σαρκικός τε καὶ πνευματικός, γεννητὸς καὶ ἀ. Ign.*Eph.*7.2; usage unorthodox by later doctrinal standards, this phrase being quoted as γεννητὸς καὶ ἀγένητος in Ath.*syn.*47(p.271.29; M.26.776C); but cf. τὰ δεξιὰ...τῆς ἀ. θεότητος Eus.*p.e.*11.14(532B; M.21.884A); and ἓν...εἶναι τὸ ἀ. (v.l. for ἀγένητον) *ib.*11.9(524B; M.868D); id.*e.th.*2.6(p.103.10; M.24.905C); confusion increased through its being contrasted with γενητός or parts of γίνομαι: τῷ μὲν θεῷ... ἀ. ... τὰ δὲ γεγονότα Iren.*haer.*4.28.1(M.7.1105A); τῷ δὲ μὴ βουλομένῳ τὸ ἅγιον πνεῦμα διὰ τοῦ Χριστοῦ γεγονέναι ἕπεται τὸ ἀ. αὐτὸ λέγειν Or.*Jo.*2.10(6; p.65.8; M.14.125D); Hipp.*haer.*6.29(p.155.22; M.16.3235C); *ib.*(p.157.1; 3238B); and through its implying same divine prerogatives as ἀγένητος: eternal pre-existence τοῦ δὲ ἀ. οὐδὲν προϋπάρχει Clem.*str.*5.12(p.381.6; M.9.124A); unity, Just.*dial.*

5.6(M.6.489A); creative power, Or.*princ*.4.1(8; p.308.1; M.11.357C); **2.** yet even pre-Nicene writers tend to dist. ἀ. from ἀγένητος: θεῷ δὲ μόνῳ τῷ ἀ. διὰ τοῦ υἱοῦ ἑπόμεθα Just.1*apol*.14.1(M.6.348B); ἓν μὲν τὸ ἀ. ὁ παντοκράτωρ θεός, ἓν δὲ καὶ τὸ προγεννηθέν Clem.*str*.6.7 (p.461.6; M.9.280B); Or.*Jo*.1.27(p.34.26; M.14.73C ἀγένητον); **3.** need for clear distn. bet. two terms emerged in controversy with Arians, who held essence of divine nature to be ἀ., cf.Eus.*d.e*.5I(p.211.20; M.22.349C), so that Son's being γεννητός would involve inferiority, *ib*.(p.213.28; 353D); ambiguity of ἀ., so freq. identified with ἀγένητος, exploited by Arians who, like orthodox, reserved ἀ. to Father only, Ar.*Thal.fr*.2(p.242.11; M.26.705D); Arians equating ἀ. with ἀγένητος, accused orthodox of introducing δύο ἀ. ἀρχάς, Ath.*syn*.16(p.244.12; 709C); Arians used ἀ. to express essence of divinity which they denied to Son ὁ υἱὸς οὐκ ἔστιν ἀ. ... καὶ πρὶν γεννηθῇ ἤτοι κτισθῇ...οὐκ ἦν· ἀ. γὰρ οὐκ ἦν Ar.*ep.Eus*.(p.2.10; M.42.212B); ἓν μὲν τὸ ἀ., ἓν δὲ τὸ...τῆς φύσεως τῆς ἀ. μὴ μετέχον Eus.Nic.*ep.Paulin*.(p.16.1; M.82.913B); Ast.Soph.*fr*.2a ap.Ath.*Ar*.2.37 (M.26.225C); Eun.*apol*.9(M.30.844B); rejected by Homoiousians as unscriptural, Geo.Laod.*ep.dogm*.(p.291.29; M.42.437B); absurdity of ἀ. for expressing Godhead τὸ ἀ. ὄνομα οὐ μόνον ἐπὶ τοῦ ἄνευ αἰτίας ὑφεστῶτος λέγεται, ἀλλὰ καὶ πρὸς τὸ ἀνύπαρκτον ἔχει τὴν οἰκειότητα. ἀ. λέγεται καὶ ὁ σκινδαψός, ἀ. καὶ τὸ βλίτυρι, ἀ. ὁ Μινώταυρος, ὁ Κύκλωψ κτλ. Gr.Nyss.*Eun*.7(2 p.166.13ff.; M.45.756D); τὸ μὴ ἀ. θεὸς οὐκ ἔστι *ib*.(p.163.22; 753A); in orthodox view ἀ. denoted not essence of divinity, but relation of first to second Person of Trin. πατὴρ ἀ. (ἀ. γάρ ἐστιν ὁ πατέρα μὴ ἔχων) Cyr.H.*catech*.11.13; ἐγὼ δὲ τὴν μὲν οὐσίαν τοῦ θεοῦ ἀ. εἶναι...φαίην· οὐ μὴν τὸ ἀ. τὴν οὐσίαν Bas.*Eun*.1.11(1.223D; M.29.537A); Gr.Naz.*or*.29.12(p.90.14ff.; M.36.89B); Gr.Nyss.*tres dii*(M.45.133D); ἡ ἀ. ... οὐκ ἔστιν οὐσία, ἀλλ᾽ οὐσίας σημαντική ‡Ath.*disp*.23(M.28.465C); Thdt.*rect.conf*.3(M.6.1209B); *ib*.(1212A); though occasional hesitations still occur in fifth century, Christ's divinity being called ἀ. οὐσία, Bas.Sel.*or*.25.4(M.85.297B); freq. affirmation that Son is not ἀ.: ἀγένητον μὲν λέγω καὶ τὸν υἱόν, οὐκ ἀ. δέ ‡Ath.*dial.Trin*.1.18(M.28.1145A); μὴ ἀ. ὑποπτεύσῃ τις τὸν υἱόν Chrys.*hom.5.2 in Jo*.(8.37D); Jo.D.*haer*.epilog.(M.94.780A); **4.** of H. Ghost, cf. *non jam manifeste discernitur utrum natus aut innatus* [*factus sit an infectus* cit.Hier.*ep*.124(M.PL.22.1061)], *vel filius etiam ipse dei habendus sit*, Or.*princ*.1 proem.4(p.11.5; M.11.117C); **5.** def. of τὸ ἀγένητον and τὸ ἀ, ‡Cyr.*Trin*.8(6³.11E; M.77.1137A); **6.** in purely privative sense; **a.** of Adam: as type of Father τοῦ...ἀ. Ἀδὰμ τύπον...ἔχοντος...θεοῦ καὶ πατρός Meth.*fr*.3(p.521.5)ap.‡Gr.Nyss.*imag*.(M.44.1329C) = ‡Anast.S.*serm.imag*.1(M.89.1145B); and as example of fact that ἀ. and γεννητός necessitate no difference of substance ὁ μὴ γεννηθεὶς [sc. Adam] ἀ. λέγεται· οὐδὲν δὲ ἐκώλυσε τὸν Ἀδὰμ τὸ μὴ γεννηθῆναι πρὸς τὸ ἄνθρωπον εἶναι Gr.Nyss.*fid*.(M.45.141A); ‡Chrys.*hom.in Jo.1:1*(12.470D); ὁ Ἀδὰμ ἀ. ὢν...καὶ ὁ Σὴθ γεννητὸς...οὐ φύσει διαφέρουσιν ἀλλήλων Jo.D.*f.o*.1.8(M.94.817A); **b.** in gen. ἐν ἀ. χάρτῃ ταῦτα, i.e. parchment made from skin of unborn animal, *T.Sal*.C 1.3(p.8.11); **7.** of created things, implying eternity and self-subsistence; **a.** pagan: esp. of universe, Just.*dial*.5.1(M.6.485D); Παρμενίδης ἓν μὲν τὸ πᾶν ὑποτίθεται...ἀ. Hipp.*haer*.1.11 (p.16.10; M.16.3036D); ‡Just.*qu.Chr*.3.5(M.6.1441D); refuted by Christians, *ib*.3.4(1440A); of soul ἀ. ... ἐστι κατά τινας...Πλατωνικούς Just.*dial*.5.1(M.6.485C); Ath.*v.Anton*.74(M.26.948A); Eust.*fr*.47(p.88)ap.Leont.etJo.*sacr*.(M.86.2040B); of matter, Iren.*fr*.32 (M.7.1248A); **b.** Gnost.: of aeons, Epiph.*haer*.33.1(p.449.2; M.41.556D); *ib*.34.4(p.11.12; 592A); of matter as principle of evil, esp. Manich. δύο θεούς, καὶ δύο πηγὰς ἀγαθοῦ τε καὶ κακοῦ, καὶ ταύτας ἀ. Cyr.H.*catech*.6.13; ὁ Μανιχαῖος...τὴν ὑλικὴν αἰτίαν καὶ τὸ ἀ. ἀντιπαρεξάγει τῇ ἀγαθῇ φύσει Gr.Nyss.*hom.opif*.23.4(M.44.212B); Chrys.*serm.1.2 in Gen*.(4.648A); id.*hom.59.2f.in Mt*.(7.596C,D); **c.** as aeon in system of Epiphanes, Iren.*haer*.1.11.5(M.7.569A).

ἀγεννήτως, *without generation, ingenerately*, also *ingenerably*; **1.** ref. divine nature εἶναι δὲ τὴν θείαν φύσιν...ἀ. Gr.Nyss.*Eun*.12 (1 p.261.5; M.45.964D); ἀ. τὸν θεὸν ὑφεστάναι οὐ τὴν ἀγεννησίαν εἶναι θεόν *ib*.(p.264.13; 968D); τὸ μὲν τὴν ἀρχὴν μὴ ἔχειν, ἀ. εἶναι λέγειν *ib*.(p.358.8; 1080D); but existence ἀ. not necessarily to be predicated of τὸ ἀτελεύτητόν τε καὶ ἄφθαρτον *ib*.(p.367.18; 1092B); **2.** ref. Father δύναμις ἀ. καὶ ἀνάρχως ὑφεστῶσα Gr.Nyss.*diff.ess*.4(M.32.329B); **3.** ref. Son, summary of teaching of Alex. Al. by Ar. συνυπάρχει ὁ υἱὸς ἀ. τῷ θεῷ ἀειγεννής *ep.Eus*.(p.2.1; M.42.212A); this orthodox doctrine denied by Arians μηδενὸς τῶν ἔργων [incl. Son] ἀ. γίγνεσθαι δυναμένου Eun.*apol*.23(M.30.860A); Acac.Caes.*fr.Marcell*.(p.261.22; M.42.392A); ἐπεὶ μὴ ἀ. ἔχει [sc. ζωήν], μηδὲ συνθέτως, ἔχει ὁμοίως πάντα κατ᾽ οὐσίαν CAnc.(358)*ep.syn*.(p.279.6; M.42.417C); **4.** of Adam ἀ. τὸν Ἀδὰμ ὑποστῆναι Gr.Nyss.*Eun*.3(1 p.26.29; M.45.592C); **5.** in Gr. philos., of universe ὁ ἀγέννητος ἀ. ἀγέννητα ποιεῖ ‡Just.*qu.Chr*.3.5(M.6.1440D).

***ἀγεντισηρίβους, οἱ,** (Lat. *agentes in rebus*) *government agents*; often official spies, secret police, Ath.*apol.Const*.10(M.25.608B).

***ἀγερωχέω,** *be exalted, proud*, Jo.VI H.*v.Jo.D*.4(M.94.433C).

***ἀγέστον, τό,** (Lat. *aggestum, agger*) *mound* erected in besieging a town, Evagr.*h.e*.4.27(p.175.1; M.86.2748C).

***ἀγευστέω,** *not taste, be without tasting* ζωῆς τὸν ἄνθρωπον ἀγευστήσαντα Meth.*res*.1.39 ap.Epiph.*haer*.64.31(p.45.25); conj. ἄγευστον *GCS* Meth.p.281.1; M.41.1108B).

ἀγεωργησία, ἡ, *bad husbandry*, Or.*Jo*.20.5(p.332.21; M.14.584B).

ἀγεώργητος, *untilled, uncultivated*; hence **1.** *produced without natural labour*, i.e. miraculous or supernatural; **a.** ref. Christ ὁ ἀ. ἄρτος καὶ λόγος Gr.Nyss.*v.Mos*.(M.44.368C); of wine at Cana, ‡Meth.*palm*.3(M.18.389A); ‡Eust.*Laz*.4(p.29.1); of feeding of the five thousand τραπέζαν ἀ. Gr.Ant.*mul.ung*.3(M.88.1852C); id.*bapt*.2.6(M.88.1877C); **b.** ref. virginal conception ἐξ ἀ. προῆλθε γαστρός †Chrys.*nativ*.1(6.393A); ἀ. καρπός Gr.Ant.*bapt*.1(M.10.1188C); Sophr.H.*or*.2.43(M.87.3276A); typified by Aaron's rod ἀ. καρπὸν ἐξανθήσασα ‡Meth.*Sym.et Ann*.9(M.18.369B); **2.** met., *neglected* (spiritually) ἀ. ψυχήν †Bas.*Is*.147(1.483B; M.30.360B); of heathen ἀ. ἔθνος Thdt.*h.e*.1.23.9(3.805).

***ἀγεωργήτως,** *without husbandry*, *Hymn*.(*KlT* p.22).

***ἀγεωργία, ἡ,** *uncultivated condition, state of neglect*, Eus.*d.e*.7.1 (p.315.8; M.22.516A).

***ἀγηηνία, ἡ,** ? *attack* τὴν καλουμένην ἐν τοῖς πολέμοις μιμησάμενοι ἀ. Ast.Am.*hom*.12(M.40.348A); perh. = ⟨ἁγηνία⟩, ⟨σαγηνία⟩, cf. σαγηνεύω.

ἀγήρατος, *not growing old, ageless*; of primary Gnostic aeon, Hipp.*haer*.5.14(p.110.9; M.16.3170B); ὁ αὐτοπάτωρ...ὃν καλοῦσί τινες αἰῶνα ἀ. Val.Gn.ap.Epiph.*haer*.31.5(p.390.12; M.41.481B); of Valent. aeon, Iren.*haer*.1.1.2(M.7.449A); Val.Gn.ap.Epiph.*haer*.31.5(p.392.14; 484B).

ἀγήρως, *ageless, immortal, eternal*; of God, Clem.*str*.5.11(p.371.18; M.9.104B); κάλλος...ἀ. Meth.*symp*.6.1(p.64.15; M.18.113B); of Trin., Basilisc.*encycl*.(p.49; M.86.2600A); of heaven and eternal life, Eus.*v.C*.4.67(p.145.28; M.20.1224A); id.*l.C*.6(p.206.15; M.20.1340C); Thdt.*h.e*.2.26.6(3.893); of angels, *Hom.Clem*.20.7; of souls, ‡Jo.D.*Artem*.30(p.161.25; M.96.1280A); of men, Pall.*v.Chrys*.20(p.137.24; M.47.77); of messianic kingdom, Eus.*Marcell*.2.1(p.34.2; M.24.781A); neut. as subst., *immortal part* of man, Meth.*symp*.2.7(p.24.13; M.18.57C).

ἁγιάζ-ω, *sanctify, hallow, consecrate*;

A. in gen.; **1.** agents and means of sanctifying; **a.** God gen. ὁ θεὸς...ἁ. ἡμῶν τὸ σῶμα *Lit*.ap.*Const.App*.8.13.10; ‡Ath.*dial.Trin*.3.24(M.28.1240D); Eus.Al.*serm*.5(M.86.344B); Cyr.*thes*.32(5¹.284A); Sophr.H.*mir.Cyr.et Jo*.36(M.87.3553C); Trin. τριάδι τῇ...∼ούσῃ ἡμᾶς δι᾽ ἑαυτῆς *Lit.Jac*.(p.160.7); Father τελείως μὲν οἱ παρὰ πατρὸς ἁγιασθήσονται Cyr.*Jo*.1.3(4.22B); Serap.*euch*.13.18; *Lit.Jac*.(p.166.1); by whom flesh of Christ was sanctified, Cyr.*Jo*.7(4.671E); Christ, Or.*Jo*.1.34(39; p.44.2,4; M.14:89D); Ath.*Ar*.1.46(M.26.108B); *Const.App*.7.39.4; Cyr.*thes*.13(5¹.139A); ὁ δὲ ἑαυτὸν ἁ. δυνάμενος, καὶ μὴ παρ᾽ ἑτέρου τοῦτο ζητῶν, κύριος τοῦ ἁ. ἐστίν...ἵνα ἡμεῖς ἁγιασθῶμεν ἐν αὐτῷ *ib*.20(197E–198A); as ἡ σοφία sanctifying BMV, *Dial.Ath.et Zacch*.21(p.17); **b.** esp. H. Ghost ὁ Χριστὸς...τοῦ πνεύματος τῇ καθόδῳ ∼εται Clem.*paed*.1.6(p.105.17; M.8.280D); this later denied κτίσματα ∼εται παρὰ τοῦ ἁγίου πνεύματος· ὁ δὲ υἱὸς οὐχ ∼όμενος παρὰ τοῦ πνεύματος Ath.*Ar*.2.18(M.26.184B); cf.id.*ep.Serap*.1.23(M.26.584B); τοῦτ᾽ ἂν εἴη ἔργον αὐτοῦ [sc. πνεύματος], τὸ πάντας ἁ. Eus.*e.th*.3.6(p.163.32; M.24.1013B); ἡ κτίσις ∼εται, τὸ πνεῦμά ἐστι τὸ ∼ον Bas.*ep*.159(3.248C; M.32.621A); Didym.*Trin*.2.1 (M.39.449B); οὐσιωδῶς διῆκον παρὰ πατρὸς τὸ πνεῦμα, δι᾽ οὗ πάντα... ∼εται Cyr.*thes*.34(5¹.340A); *ib*.(352D); in creeds τὸ πνεῦμα τὸ ἅγιον ...δι᾽ οὗ καὶ ἁγιασθήσονται *Symb.Ant*.(345)1(p.252.3; M.26.728C); *Symb.Sirm*.1(p.254.30; M.26.736C); *Symb.Sel*.(p.257.27; M.26.745B); **c.** sacraments: baptism ἁγιασθῆναι δεῖ διὰ τοῦ λουτροῦ παλιγγενεσίας Or.*fr.36 in Jo*.(p.512.11); *ib*.79(p.547.10); Cyr.*Is*.1.1(2.18C); eucharist ἄρτους ἐσθίομεν, σῶμα γενομένους διὰ τὴν εὐχὴν ἅγιόν τι καὶ ∼ον τοὺς μετὰ ὑγιοῦς προθέσεως αὐτῷ χρωμένους Or.*Cels*.8.33(p.249.8; M.11.1565C); τυχὼν τῶν θείων μυστηρίων ἀπελθεῖν ἡγιασμένος Bas.Sel.*v.Thecl*.2.18(M.85.596C); blood of OT sacrifices foreshadowing sacraments, Chrys.*hom.46.3 in Jo*.(8.273C); oil with which dead are anointed, Dion.Ar.*e.h*.7.3.9(M.3.565B); **d.** virtues ἡ δικαιοσύνη... ∼ουσα Clem.*paed*.3.11(p.278.19; M.8.653B); id.*str*.6.7(p.462.6; M.9.281B); right doctrine, Chrys.*hom.82.1 in Jo*.(8.483E); **2.** recipients of sanctification; **a.** angels θεϊκοῦ πνεύματος ἁγιάσαντος καὶ ὑμᾶς Didym.*Trin*.2.7(M.39.588C); Cyr.*inc.unigen*.(5^1.700C); rational beings in gen., ‡Ath.*disp*.38(M.28.489A); **b.** human beings, in gen. κλητοῖς, ἡγιασμένοις ἐν θελήματι θεοῦ *1Clem*.proem.; *Barn*.15.7; Clem.*paed*.3.12(p.290.6; M.8.677C); id.*str*.3.6(p.217.25; M.8.1149C); τῇ σκιᾷ [sc. τῶν ἀποστόλων] γοῦν ἁγιασθῆναι μόνῃ Gr.Naz.*or*.21.27 (M.35.1113B); **c.** of partic. persons, *set aside* for a vocation; of Christ in his humanity Ἰησοῦν...ἀνθρωποπρεπῶς ∼όμενον Dion.Ar. *e.h*.4.3.10(M.3.484A,bis); *ib*.4.3.12(485A); of Jeremiah, Or.*hom.1.11 in Jer*.(p.10.2; M.13.268B); cf. (ref. Jer.1:5) ἐν πάσῃ τῇ μήτρᾳ γυναικός, ἡ σοφία...∼ει τοὺς ἀνθρώπους *Dial.Ath.et Zacch*.22(p.18); ref. BMV, Ath.*inc*.17.5(M.25.125C); of S. Paul, Ign.*Eph*.12.2; of monks and virgins, Gr.Naz.*ep*.238(M.37.380C); **d.** of things ∼ομένη σὰρξ οὐράνιος Clem.*paed*.1.6(p.116.3; M.8.301B); ἀγάπην τὴν ἡγιασμένην *ib*.2.1(p.156.14; 384B); τὸ βρῶμα καὶ τὸ πόμα ἡγιασμένον Ath.*virg*.14 (p.49.4; M.28.268C); ἡγίασε τὸ βάπτισμα ὁ Ἰησοῦς Cyr.H.*catech*. 3.11; ὁ τόπος ἅπας ἡγιάζετο διὰ τῆς ὑμνῳδίας τῶν ἁγίων Chrys. *hom.in Rom.8:28*(3.153D).

B. *consecrate*, in technical sense; **1.** *set apart*, for a certain office or use ἁ. αὐτούς, οἱονεὶ τὸ 'ἀφόρισον αὐτοὺς τῷ λόγῳ καὶ τῷ κηρύγματι' Chrys.*hom.82.1 in Jo*.(8.484A); λέγεται...∼εσθαι, τὸ ἀνατιθέμενον τῷ θεῷ Cyr.*Jo*.7(4.671C); id.*Is*.1.6(2.178B); **2.** persons τὸν ἐπίσκοπον Serap.*euch*.11.1; *ib*.11.2,3; Dion.Ar.*e.h*.5.2(M.3.509B); **3.** objects; **a.** most freq. of eucharist ὁ ἄρτος καὶ τὸ ἔλαιον ἁ. τῇ δυνάμει τοῦ ὀνόματος τοῦ θεοῦ Clem.*exc.Thdot*.82(p.132.10; M.9. 696C); ἁγιάσας μετέδωκεν αὐτοῖς τῶν ἁγίων...μυστηρίων *A.Thom*.B 28(p.34.18); *Lit*.ap.*Const.App*.8.12.37; τὸν τῷ λόγῳ τοῦ θεοῦ ∼όμενον ἄρτον εἰς σῶμα τοῦ θεοῦ λόγου μεταποιεῖσθαι Gr.Nyss.*or.catech*. 37(p.149.3; M.45.96D); Eus.Al.*serm*.5(M.86.349A); Leont.N.*v.Jo. Eleem*.39(p.77.22); Jo.D.*fr.Mt*.26:27(M.96.1409C); effected through H. Ghost, *Lit.Jac*.(p.194.15); **b.** objects set apart for liturgical use: vestments of OT priests, Clem.*str*.5.6(p.353.8; M.9.65B); *ib*. (p.354.1; 68A); sacred vessels, *Can.App*.73; baptismal oil, *Const. App*.7.42.3; Dion.Ar.*e.h*.4.3.10(M.3.484A); and water, *Const.App*. 7.43.5; at Epiphany, Thdr.Stud.*epp*.2.203(M.99.1617C); oil burning before relics of saints, Sophr.H.*mir.Cyr.et Jo*.36(M.87.3553C); a sacred building τὸν ναὸν...ἐν τῷ ὀνόματι...Ἰησοῦ Χριστοῦ ἁ. *A. Barth*.6(p.143.24); site of church, Marc.Diac.*v.Porph*.66; church, *ib*.94; *ib*.103.

C. *glorify*, sc. God (cf. Mt.6:9), Clem.*str*.4.23(p.313.28; M.8. 1357B); *Hom.Clem*.13.4; of seraphim, Serap.*euch*.13.9; Sophr.H.*or*. 2.3(M.87.3220C); of virtuous men, Cyr.*Am*.18(3.268D).

D. exeg.; **1.** of 'Our Father', Gr.Nyss.*or.dom*.3(p.56.7; M.44. 1156A); ἁγιασθήτω, τοῦτ' ἔστι, δοξασθήτω Chrys.*hom.19.4 in Mt*. (7.250C); Thdt.*Is*.49:7(p.195.12; 2.349); ‡Germ.CP *contempl*.(M.98. 441C); **2.** Jo.17:19 τί ἐστιν, ∼ω ἐμαυτόν; προσφέρω σοι θυσίαν Chrys. *hom.82.1 in Jo*.(8.484B); Cyr.*ador*.10(1.350B); another interprn. ἡμῶν χάριν ἑαυτὸν ∼ει, καὶ τοῦτο ποιεῖ, ὅτε γέγονεν ἄνθρωπος Ath.*Ar*. 1.47(M.26.108C); cf.*ib*.1.46(108B); **3.** 1Cor.7:14 ἡγίασται ἐν τῇ γυναικί. τοῦτο δὲ εἶπεν, οὐχ ἵνα δείξῃ ἐκεῖνον ἅγιον, ἀλλ' ἵνα ἐκ περιουσίας τὸν φόβον ἐξέλῃ τῆς γυναικός, κἀκεῖνον εἰς ἐπιθυμίαν ἀγάγῃ τῆς ἀληθείας Chrys.*hom.19.3 in 1Cor*.(10.162E); Cyr.*1Cor*.7:8ff.(M.74.876B).

E. *regard as holy* ∼ων τὸν ἀριθμὸν...Ἕρμιππος Clem.*str*.6.16(p.506. 9; M.9.376A); ∼έσθω, τοῦτ' ἔστιν, ἅγιος ἡγείσθω, ἤτουν ὁμολογείσθω Cyr.*Is*.4.4(2.666A).

F. *officiate as priest*, *Chr.sac*.B(p.71).

ἁγίασμα, τό, 1. *holy place, sanctuary* (cf.Ex.15:17); of Temple, Or.*Cels*.2.78(p.200.20; M.11.917C); id.*hom.18.5 in Jer*.(p.155.34; M. 13.472A); Eus.*d.e*.6.18(p.274.35; M.22.452C); ref. its met. interprn. in Is.8:12, id.*Is*.8:12(M.24.144D–145B); *Lit*.ap.*Const.App*.8.5.4; of a church χάριν...ἣν ἐν αὐτῷ τῷ ἁ. λαβεῖν ἐζήτεις Eustrat.*v.Eutych*. 13(M.86.2289B); of altar in a church, Eus.*h.e*.7.15.4(M.20.677A); of heaven ἐκείνων [sc. martyrs] ἐστὶν τὰ δεξιὰ μέρη τοῦ ἁ. Herm.*vis*. 3.2.1; Clem.*str*.4.4(p.255.28; M.8.1229A); *ib*.4.6(p.261.13; 1241A); **2.** *sacred object*; of oil, at anointing of Israelite kings, Thdt.*qu.38 in 4Reg*.(1.535); burning in lamps at martyrs' tombs, believed to have healing powers ἀλειφομένη...ἐκ τοῦ ἁ. τῆς τοῦ...Εὐθυμίου θήκης Cyr.S.*v.Euthym*.52(p.76.2); *ib*.54(p.76.20); of other holy oil, Eustrat. *v.Eutych*.54(M.86.2336B); cf.*ib*.53(2336A); Dor.*doct*.11.6(M.88.1741A); of holy water, †Jo.Jej.*poenit*.(M.88.1913A); ‡Jo.Jej.*can*.(p.440); *Nomoc*.400; *ib*.127; of relics of martyrs, Gr.Nyss.*mart*.2(M.46.784B); **3.** *sacrament, sacrifice*; **a.** sacrifice; in OT, *Const.App*.2.28.7; eucharistic ἐάν τις πρεσβύτερος...ἁ. τῷ θεῷ προσενέγκῃ *Cod.Afr*.11; **b.** Holy Communion τοῦ ἁ. ἀξιούμενος Bas.*ep*.217 *can*.73(3.328B; M. 32.804A); ἁ. τοῦ κυριακοῦ σώματος καὶ αἵματος *Cod.Afr*.37; more freq. plur. μέθεξις τῶν ἁ. Gr.Thaum.*ep.can*.11(M.10.1048B); Bas. *ep*.217 *can*.56(3.326B; M.32.797A); Gr.Nyss.*ep.can*.1,2(M.45.225C); *ib*. 4(229A); *Schol*. in CTrull.*can*.26(*Mon*.2 p.651); Jo.D.*haer*.95(M.94. 760A); **4.** *a making sacred, consecration, holiness*, of baptismal water οὐδὲν παρ' ἑαυτοῦ πρὸς τὸν ἁγιασμὸν εἰσφερόμενον, εἰ μὴ μεταποιηθείη διὰ τοῦ ἁ. Gr.Nyss.*Maced*.19(M.45.1325A); Christ called ἁ. γνώσεως Clem.*paed*.3.13(p.289.29; M.8.677A); of BMV στακτὴν ἁγιάσματος Thdr.Stud.*nativ.BMV* 7(M.96.692D).

ἁγιασμός, ὁ, A. *sanctity*; **1.** as divine quality; of Trin., Bas. *Eun*.3.3(1.274D; M.29.660D); of Christ, Gr.Nyss.*hom.11 in Cant*. (M.44.1008C); **2.** as a human quality ἁ. δέ ἐστι τὸ ἀνακεῖσθαι τῷ ἁγίῳ θεῷ ἐξ ὁλοκλήρου Bas.*reg.br*.53(2.433B; M.31.1117C); without which no man can see God, id.*ep*.54(3.148C; M.32.400B); ἁ. ἐστιν ἡ θεοῦ συνουσία Gr.Naz.*carm*.1.2.34.171(M.37.956A); Chrys.*hom.63.4 in Jo*.(8.380A); Cyr.*dial.Trin*.6(5^1.595D); **3.** divine name, Dion.Ar. *d.n*.1.6(M.3.596B); σὺ εἶ ὁ ἁ. ἡμῶν, θεός *Lit.Jac*.(p.234.25).

B. *sanctification*, def. ὁ ἁ., τουτέστιν, ἡ ἐν πνεύματι μέθεξις τοῦ υἱοῦ Cyr.*dial.Trin*.6(5^1.595A); **1.** agents and means; **a.** God, Cyr. *thes*.13(5^1.138E); *Lit.Jac*.(p.176.8); Trin. ἕνα εἶναι τὸν ἁ. τὸν ἐκ πατρὸς δι' υἱοῦ ἐν πνεύματι ἁγίῳ γινόμενον Ath.*ep.Serap*.1.20(M.26. 577C); Christ αὐτὸ μὲν γὰρ ἁ., ὅθεν οἱ ἅγιοι ἁγιάζονται, ἡμῖν ὁ Ἰησοῦς ἁγιάζεται Or.*Jo*.1.34(39; p.44.2; M.14.89D); id.*hom.8.2 in Jer*.(p.57. 2; M.13.337C); Gr.Naz.*or*.30.20(p.141.6; M.36.129C); Mac.Aeg.*ep*. (M.34.409C); οὐχ ἑαυτῷ δεχομένου τὸν ἁ. (αὐτὸς γὰρ ἦν ὁ ἁγιάζων), ἀλλ' ἵνα τοῦτον τῇ φύσει δι' ἑαυτοῦ προξενίσῃ Cyr.*thes*.20(5^1.197C); H. Ghost πηγὴ ἁγιασμοῦ Bas.*Eun*.3.2(1.273E, 274C; M.29.660A,C); id.*Spir*.22(3.19C; M.32.108B); τὸ στερεοῦν τὸ πνεῦμα· τί δ' ἂν ἄλλο εἴη στερέωσις ἢ ἡ κατὰ τὸν ἁ. τελείωσις;...ἁ. δὲ οὐκ ἄνευ πνεύματος *ib*.38(32B; M.136C); Didym.*Trin*.2.1(M.39.449B); Cyr.*thes*.34(5^1. 349E); id.*Jo*.1.3(4.22B); Son and H. Ghost together, Evagr.Pont. *ep*.2(M.32.249B); **b.** sacrifice, sacraments, and sacramentals; OT ὁ ἁ. ἦν ἐν τῷ προβάτῳ Chrys.*hom.72.1 in Jo*.(8.484B); baptism, Didym.(‡Bas.)*Eun*.5(1.317E; M.29.761B); τί δέ ἐστιν ὁ ἁ.; τὸ λουτρόν Chrys.*hom.1.1 in 1Cor*.(10.4B); Cyr.*Is*.2.4(2.283B); chrism used in baptism, *A.Thom*.A 121(p.230.23); eucharist, *Lit.Jac*.(p.240.13); sacraments in gen., Gr.Nyss.*Eun*.11(2 p.272.2; M.45.881B); priestly blessing, CTrull.*can*.26; **c.** virtuous living, *1Clem*.30.1; *A.Phil*.119 (p.48.13); contemplation, Max.*ambig*.(M.91.1065D); **2.** recipients; **a.** angelic powers, Bas.*Eun*.3.2(1.274A; M.29.660B); ὁ...ἁ., ἔξωθεν ὢν τῆς οὐσίας, τὴν τελείωσιν αὐτοῖς ἐπάγει διὰ τῆς κοινωνίας τοῦ πνεύματος id.*Spir*.38(3.32D; M.32.137A); **b.** men, Ath.*Ar*.1.47(M.26. 108C); both body and soul, Clem.*str*.4.26(p.320.27; M.8.1373A); *Lit.Jac*.(p.234.24); esp. inner man, Mac.Aeg.*ep*.(M.34.413B); soul, Gr.Nyss.*hom.11 in Cant*.(M.44.1008C); **c.** objects: baptismal water, Clem.*exc.Thdot*.82(p.132.14; M.9.696C); baptismal rite, Gr.Nyss. *or.catech*.34(p.126.7; M.45.85A).

C. *ascription* or *acclamation of holiness* τὸν ἡμέτερον ἁ. λεγόντων· 'ἅγιος ἅγιος ἅγιος' κτλ. Serap.*euch*.13.10; οὐδαμοῦ τις...ἀπήγγειλεν ἡμῖν...τὸν πρῶτον ἁ. κυριολογοῦντα, τὸν δὲ δεύτερον ὑποτάσσοντα, καὶ τὸν τρίτον κατώτερον τιθέντα Ath.*hom.in Mt.11:27*(M.25.217D); Gr. Naz.*or*.38.8(M.36.320B); ‡Bas.*h.myst*.60(p.394.17); Sophr.H.*or*.2.3 (M.87.3220B); of Severus' addition to Trisagion σταυρὸν ἀσεβῶς τοῖς τρισὶν ἁ. ἐπιφέρουσιν *ib*.2.5(3224A); Max.*myst*.19(M.91.696C).

D. *consecration*; **1.** of eucharist τὸν μυστικὸν τῆς ἀμπέλου καρπὸν μετὰ τὸν ἁ. αἷμα δεσποτικὸν ὀνομάζομεν Thdt.*eran*.1(4.25); *ib*.2(126); Anast.Ap.*A.Max*.1(M.90.117B); **2.** of consecrated elements οὐκέτι μέχρι τοῦ νῦν τοῦ ἁ. τούτου τετύχηκα ‡Sophr.H.*v.Mar.Aeg*.32(M.87. 3720C); **3.** of baptismal water ἀκολουθία τοῦ μεγάλου ἁ. τῶν ἁγίων θεοφανείων *Euchol*.(p.366); *Const.Stud*.37(M.99.1717D).

ἁγιαστεία (-ία), **ἡ, 1.** *holiness*, of Christ as God and man μιᾶς οὔσης ἁ. Epiph.*haer*.69.64(p.213.12; M.42.305D); *ib*.26.15(p.295.18; M.41.356D); Ἰησοῦς...πάσης ἡμᾶς ἁ. ἀποπληροῖ Dion.Ar.*e.h*.4.3. 12(M.3.485A); of ascetic life, Bas.Sel.*v.Thecl*.2.30(M.85.617B); of a church, Cyr.S.*v.Euthym*.8(p.15.22); hence *ascription* or *proclamation of holiness*; of threefold sanctus, Epiph.*anc*.10(p.18.6; M.43.36A); **2.** = ἁγιστεία *sacred rite* or *office*; of priestly office of sacrifice, Chrys.*sac*.3.4(p.53.3; 1.382E); id.*Jud*.6.5(1.656E); Ἰησοῦς...ἡ πάσης ...ἁ. τε καὶ θεουργίας ἀρχή Dion.Ar.*e.h*.1.1(M.3.372A); Zach.Mit.*opif*. (M.85.1020A).

ἁγιαστήριον, τό, *sanctuary*, †Bas.*Is*.7(1.383B; M.30.129C); Thphn. *chron*.p.98(M.108.289A).

***ἁγιαστής, ὁ,** *hallower*, *POxy*.2068.3 [saec. iv].

***ἁγιαστικός, 1.** *sanctifying*; **a.** special attribute of H. Ghost, called ἡ ἁ. ... ἐνέργεια Ath.*ep.Serap*.1.20(M.26.580A); ἁ. δύναμις Bas.*ep*.214.4(3.322E; M.32.789B); id.*Eun*.3.2(1.273D; M.29.660A); τὸ πνεῦμα...τὸ πάσης τῆς κτίσεως...ἁ. Gr.Nyss.*Eun*.2(2 p.301.2; M.45. 472B); Cyr.H.*catech*.4.16; Apoll.*fid.sec.pt*.27(p.176.22; M.10.1116B);

Didym.(‡Bas.)*Eun.*5(M.29.732B); Cyr.*thes.*34(5^1.352B); Jo.D.*f.o.*1.13(M.94.856C); Eunomian view *θεότητος μὲν καὶ δημιουργικῆς δυνάμεως ἀπολειπόμενον, ἁ. δὲ καὶ διδασκαλικῆς πεπληρωμένον* Eun.*apol.*25(M.30.861D); refuted *δύο γὰρ λεγομένων πραγμάτων, θεότητός τε καὶ κτίσεως...καὶ ἁ. δυνάμεως, καὶ τῆς ἁγιαζομένης...ἐν ποίᾳ μερίδι τὸ πνεῦμα τάξομεν; ἐν τοῖς ἁγιαζομένοις; ἀλλ' αὐτό ἐστιν ἁγιασμός* Bas.*Eun.*3.2(1.273D; M.29.660A); *τὸ πνεῦμα τὸ ἅγιον βλασφημοῦσι...ἁ. αὐτὸ δύναμιν φάσκοντες εἶναι μόνον* Epiph.*anac.*74(p.231.8; M.42.337A); *ἁ. εἶναι, φασί, τὸ πνεῦμα...οὐκ αὐτὸ καθ' ἑαυτὸ φύσει τοιοῦτον ὑπάρχον* Cyr.*thes.*34(5^1.349D); Agath.*v.Gr.Ill.*103; **b.** of other agents or means of sanctification: Trin., Gr.Nyss.*Trin.*7(p.78.12; M.32.693B); Areth.ap.*cat.Apoc.*8:3ff.(p.300.26); baptism, Didym.(‡Bas.)*Eun.*5(M.29.737C); eucharist, ‡Chrys.*pasch.*2(8.256A); 'oil of gladness', ref. Ps.45:8, Mac.Aeg.*hom.*17.1(M.34.624D); **2.** *ascribing sanctity to, calling holy*, liturg. *ἁ. δοξολογία* Max.*myst.*24(M.91.704C); cf.*ib.*13(692C); Areth.*Apoc.*8(M.106.553B).

***ἁγιόβατος**, *trodden by saints*, ‡Jo.D.*hom.*5(M.96.660C).

***ἁγιόβλαστος**, *with holy shoots*; of Aaron's rod as type of BMV, Ephr.3.529F; ‡Jo.D.*hom.*5(M.96.649B).

***ἁγιόγραφος**, **1.** *written by inspiration, scriptural*, Dion.Ar.*e.h.*1.4(M.3.376B); *ib.*3.2(425C); **2.** neut. plur. as subst., title of historical books of OT, Epiph.*mens.*4(M.43.244B); Jo.D.*f.o.*4.17(M.94.1180B).

***ἁγιοδρόμος**, ὁ, *runner in the holy race*, Ant.Mon.*hom.*1(M.89.1432B).

***ἁγιοκατήγορος**, ὁ, *accuser of saints*, CNic.(787)*act.*4(H.4.188E).

***ἁγιολεκτέω**, *greet as ἁγιόλεκτος*; salutation of abbot, Thdr.Stud.*epp.*2.219(M.99.1664D).

***ἁγιόλεκτος**, *elect in holiness*, Thdr.Stud.*cant.*16.6(p.372); ‡Sophr.H.*triod.*(M.87.3880D).

***ἁγιοπαράδοτος**, *handed down by the saints*, Thdr.Stud.*epp.*1.8(M.99.937A).

ἁγιοποιέω, *sanctify*, Leont.H.*Nest.*3.12(M.86.1648B); *ib.*4.48(1720D).

***ἁγιοποιός**, *sanctifying*; of Godhead, ‡Ath.*disp.*38(M.28.489A); of H. Ghost, Cyr.H.*catech.*16.14; of baptism, ‡Jo.D.*hom.*5(M.96.656D).

***ἁγιόπρακτος**, *done as a holy act*, Thdr.Stud.*epp.*1.34(M.99.1024B).

***ἁγιοπρεπής**, **1.** *hallowed, sacred*, *1Clem.*13.3; Polyc.*ep.*1.1; Dion.Ar.*c.h.*5(M.3.196D); *ib.*12.2(293A); **2.** *befitting saints, holy*, Or.*adnot. in Dt.*23:14(M.17.32C); Cyr.*Ps.*9:36(M.69.788B); id.*ador.*1(1.28A).

***ἁγιοπρεπῶς**, **1.** *as befits saints*, Cyr.*Is.*3.4(2.507D); id.*Lc.*9:52–54(p.93.11); **2.** *as befits holy things*, Dion.Ar.*c.h.*2.4(M.3.144B); id.*e.h.*3.3.7(M.3.436C).

***ἁγιόριζος**, *of holy root* or *source μαζὸς ἁ.* Tim.Ant.*descr.BMV* 1(M.28.944B).

ἅγιος, *separated, holy*;

A. ref. God as essence and source of holiness, in sense of separation from created things and also of excellence, and ref. Christ in his twofold nature; **1.** of God, gen. as subst. masc., *Orac. Sib.*3.709; *ἅ. ἐστι φύσει τὸ τοῦ θεοῦ ὄνομα* Cyr.H.*catech.*5.12; Bas.*ep.*11(3.92E; M.32.273C); *ὁ θεὸς ἅ. λέγεται, ἀλλ' οὐχ ὡς ἡμεῖς* Chrys.*hom. 14.2 in Jo.*(8.80C); Cyr.*dial.Trin.*6(5^1.595A); *ἅ. ἁγίων* as divine name, Dion.Ar.*d.n.*1.6(M.3.596B); *ib.*12.1(969A); of Trin., Clem.*str.*5.14(p.395.15; M.9.156B); Or.*fr.36 in Jo.3*:5(p.512.23); ‡Chrys.*Trin.*1(1.832A,C); Leont.H.*Nest.*2.1(M.86.1533D); Cosm.Ind.*top.*5(M.88.221B); of Father (cf. Jo.17:11), *Did.*10.2; *ἁ. πατρὸς ἀγενήτου* Or.*Jo.*20.22(10; p.355.24; M.14.621C); of Son in his divinity *ἅ. θεὸς 'Ιησοῦς, ὁ...λόγος* Clem.*paed.*1.7(p.123.5; M.8.316B); id.*str.*7.2(p.5.20; M.9.408B); *ἅ. ὁ τοῦ πατρὸς λόγος* Ath.*gent.*42(M.25.84B); *εἷς ἅ. ...Χριστός. ἀληθῶς γὰρ εἷς ἅ., φύσει ἅ.* Cyr.H.*catech.*23.19; Cyr.*Is.*4.4(2.666B); *Lit.Jac.*(p.180.7); of H. Ghost, *1Clem.*13.1; Arist.*apol.*15.1 et freq.; **2.** ref. Christ, in his humanity, Just.*dial.*116.1(M.6.744B); Clem.*paed.*1.7(p.123.5; M.8.316A); *ὁ ἅ. τῶν ἁ. Χριστὸς παρεγένετο* Ath.*inc.*40.1(M.25.165A); *κρύψας γὰρ τὸ ἄγκιστρον τῆς αὐτοῦ θεότητος ἔνδον τῆς ψυχῆς τοῦ ἁ. αὐτοῦ σώματος* ‡Acac.CP *ep.*(p.18.34; H.2.844C); of Inc. *τὴν ἁ. σάρκωσιν* Leont.H.*Nest.*2.1(M.86.1533B); of hypostasis of Christ, *ib.*2.2(1536D).

B. ref. Church, and its worship and scriptures; **1.** of Church; **a.** distinctive note, v. *ἐκκλησία*; **b.** of local churches, Ign.*Trall.* proem.; *Ep.*ap.CCP(536)*act.*1(p.131.18; H.2.1193C); cf. *διακόνου τῆς ἁγίας Χριστοῦ...ἀναστάσεως ib.*(p.156.9; 1229C); **c.** of a church building *συναχθῆναι εἰς τὴν ἁ. ἐκκλησίαν* Marc.Diac.*v.Porph.*20; **2.** ref. sacraments; **a.** baptism, Ath.*Ar.*2.41(M.26.233B); Cyr.*Is.*3.3(2.460B); Jo.D.*Eph.*5:26(M.95.849B); †Jo.D.*B.J.*30(M.96.1140D); baptismal water, Cosm.Ind.*top.*7(M.88.352A); Jo.D.*Eph.*5:26(M.95.849B); oil, Dion.Ar.*e.h.*2.2.7(M.3.396C); robe *τὸ ἅ. σχῆμα* Marc.Diac.*v.Porph.*101; **b.** eucharist *τῆς ἁγιωτάτης εὐχαριστίας* Dion.Ar.*e.h.*6.3.5(M.3.536C); *τῆς ἁγιωτάτης συνάξεως ib.*4.1.1(472D); *Lit.Jac.*(p.160.2); *ἅ. σύμβολα* Dion.Ar.*e.h.*3.3.10(M.3.437D; 440B); *κοινωνίαν* Ph.Carp.ap.Cosm.Ind.*top.*10(M.88.433C); of eucharistic wine *τὸ ἁγιώτατον αἷμα* Pall.*v.Chrys.*2(p.13.11; M.47.11); bread, Max.*schol.e.h.*3.10(M.4.148B); as subst. *τὰ ἅ., τῇ μετοχῇ τῶν ἁ. προσιέναι* Dion.Al.ap.Eus.*h.e.*7.9.4(M.20.656B); Ath.*apol.sec.*14(p.98.12; M.25.272B); Bas.*ep.*217 *can.*57(3.326C; M.32.797B) cf. †CCP(381)*can.*2(p.164 *τὸ ἁγίασμα*); CLaod.*can.*14; *Const.App.*7.40.1; Pall.*v.Chrys.*2(p.13.10; M.47.11); liturg. *τὰ ἅ. τοῖς ἁ.· ἅ. τὰ προκείμενα, ἐπιφοίτησιν δεξάμενα ἁγίου πνεύματος* Cyr.H.*catech.*23.19; *Lit.Jac.*(p.228.4) etc.; **3.** of sacramentals and other things connected with worship of Church; **a.** of liturg. objects and actions: kiss of peace *ἁ. εἰρήνην* Dion.Ar.*e.h.*3.2(M.3.425C); priestly vestments, id.*c.h.*8.2(M.3.241C); *ἁ. τράπεζα* ‡Germ.CP *contempl.*(M.98.420C); hour of celebration of liturgy, *Lit.Jac.*(p.182.9); **b.** of feasts and seasons: Easter, Const.ap.Eus.*v.C.*3.19(p.87.5; M.20.1077C); Gr.Naz.*or.*18.28(M.35.1017D); Pentecost, *Lit.Jac.*(p.206.3); Holy Week *τῆς ἑβδομάδος τῆς ξηροφαγίας καὶ πάσχα καλουμένης ἁ.* Epiph.*haer.*70.12(p.245.25; M.42.365A); a Sunday, Cyr.S.*v. Euthym.*28(p.48.6); **4.** threefold sanctus of liturgy, freq. cited, e.g. *M.Perp.*12(p.81.15); *1Apoc.Jo.*17; used in liturgy, Serap.*euch.*13.10; v. *ἁγιασμός, τρισάγιον*; Trin. interprn. *ἅ., ἅ., ἅ., δηλοῦσι γὰρ διὰ τούτων μίαν καὶ ἴσην δοξολογίαν πατρὸς καὶ υἱοῦ καὶ ἁ. πνεύματος* ‡Chrys.*Trin.*1(1.833A); Sophr.H.*or.*2.3(M.87.3220Bf.); **5.** of canonical scriptures *ὁ ἅ. λόγος 1Clem.*13.3; Or.*Jo.*6.42(25; p.151.14; M.14.273A); Ath.*gent.*1(M.25.4A); *δειξάτω τοιαύτην ἐκ τῶν ἁ. φωνήν* Gr.Nyss.*Eun.*10(2 p.242.13; M.45.845A).

C. of worshippers of true God, def. *ἁγίους...διὰ τῆς τοῦ πνεύματος δόσεως καὶ τῶν ὀρθῶν δογμάτων* Chrys.*hom.82.1 in Jo.*(8.483D); **1.** in heaven; **a.** angels, etym. def. *ἁ. αὐτοὺς ὀνομάζομεν, ὡς γήινον οὐδὲν ἔχοντας, ἀλλὰ τῶν περιγείων παθημάτων ἀπηλλαγμένους* Thdt.*affect.*3(p.94.15; 4.786); Herm.*vis.*3.4.1; Dion.Ar.*c.h.*6.2(M.3.200D) et freq.; holy by participation in grace of H. Ghost, Bas.*Spir.*38(3.31C; M.32.136A); Chrys.*hom.14.2 in Jo.*(8.80D); **b.** faithful departed, Or.*or.*11.1(p.321.18; M.11.448B); *γενομένους δὲ ἁ. οὐ διαδέξεται νύξ* Ath.*exp.Ps.*118:97(M.27.497D); freq. *ὁ ἐν ἁγίοις* Gr.Nyss.*anim.et res.*(M.46.12A); Eustrat.*v.Eutych.*19(M.86.2297A); Max.*Pyrr.*(M.91.329A); for whom it is salutary to offer prayers, Cyr.H.*catech.*23.9; **2.** on earth; **a.** in gen., of the faithful, Ign.*Smyrn.*1.2; Just.*dial.*139.4(M.6.796C); Didym.(‡Bas.)*Eun.*5(1.317D; M.29.761A); *οἱ ἅ., ἐν οἷς οἰκεῖ...ἁγιότης...διὰ τὸν ἕνα τοῦ βαπτίσματος ἁγιασμόν ib.*(317E; M.761B); id.*Trin.*3.24(M.39.937B); *πᾶς γὰρ πιστὸς ἅ., καθὸ πιστός ἐστι· κἂν κοσμικὸς ᾖ τις, ἅ. ἐστιν* Chrys.*hom.10.4 in Heb.*(12.108B); holiness a prerequisite of reception of eucharist, *Did.*10.6; so also of Manicheans *Μανιχαῖος...καὶ οἱ σὺν ἐμοὶ πάντες ἅ.* Hegem.*Arch.*5(p.5.23; M.10.1433A); **b.** of presbyters, Ign.*Magn.*3.1; bishops, freq., superl., Eugen.*exp.fid.*(M.18.1301A); Synes.*ep.*9(M.66.1345C); Thdt.*ep.*113(4.1189); Eustrat.*v.Eutych.*19(M.86.2296D); **c.** of councils, CNic.(325)*can.*8; Eus.*Marcell.*2.4(p.58.7; M.24.821D); Anast.S.*hod.*7(M.89.116B); Bas.*ep.*51.2(3.144B; M.32.389C).

D. of men of outstanding virtue; **1.** def. and characteristics: comprehensive picture of saints traced by Or.: submission to will of God *παντὸς μὲν ἁ. ὑπὸ θεοῦ βασιλευομένου καὶ πνευματικοῖς νόμοις τοῦ θεοῦ πειθομένου* Or.*or.*25.1(p.357.3; M.11.496C); charity, *ib.*20.1(p.344.1; 480A); prayer, *ib.*2.5(p.303.4; 421D); its efficacy *δυνάμεως πεπληρωμένους νομίζω τοὺς λόγους τῆς τῶν ἁ. εὐχῆς ib.*12.1(p.324.14ff.; 452A); their power to give spiritual food not only to men but even to angels, *ib.*27.11(p.370.15; 513C); sanctity crowned by desire for martyrdom, id.*mart.*28(p.24.9; M.11.596C); *ἅ. ... ὁ... τὸν ἔσω τέλεον διακαθαρθεὶς ἄνθρωπον* Mac.Aeg.*elev.*20(M.34.905C); *οἱ ἅ. ... τῆς οἰκουμένης ἁπάσης ὑπεριδόντες...πρὸς τὴν ἐν τοῖς οὐρανοῖς πόλιν ἔβλεπον* Chrys.*Anna* 4.4(4.735E); *τοὺς ἁ. ... τοὺς τὰ τοῦ θεοῦ προστάγματα πληροῦντας, τοὺς ἀβάτους ἁμαρτήμασι* id.*exp.in Ps.*144(5.472A); nurtured by Church, Cyr.*Is.*5.2(2.757E); *τοὺς ἀληθῶς ἁ. ἀπὸ τῶν ἔργων διάκρινε* Nil.*paraen.*84(M.79.1256C); **2.** ref. means of sanctity; **a.** asceticism *ἅ. ... οὐ φύσει, ἀλλὰ μετοχῇ, καὶ ἀσκήσει, καὶ εὐχῇ* Cyr.H.*catech.*23.19; Cyr.*ador.*16(1.561C); *οἶμαι μὴ λέγεσθαί τινα τὸ παράπαν ἅ. φερωνύμως, εἰ μὴ πρότερον τὴν γῆν ταύτην* [sc. the body] *εἰς ἁγιασμὸν μεταποιήσῃ εἴπερ καὶ ἔνεστι μεταμορφῶσαι* Jo.Clim.*scal.*15(M.88.889C); hence ascetics called saints, Thdt.*h.rel.*16(3.1222); Bas.Sel.*v.Thecl.*2.21(M.85.605A); poverty, Nil.*Magn.*29(M.79.1004D); **b.** suffering *κακοπαθοῦσι καὶ ἅ. ... εἰς κάθαρσιν καὶ τῆς μικρᾶς ἰλύος* Gr.Naz.*or.*18.28(M.35.1017C); *εἰς τὸ μετριάζειν καὶ ταπεινοφρονεῖν, καὶ τὸ μὴ φυσᾶσθαι ἐκ τῶν σημείων...*

συμβάλλεται τοῖς ἁ. ἡ κάκωσις Chrys.*stat*.1.6(2.9C); Cyr.*Is*.3.3(2.452B); **3.** their relation to God οὐδενὶ γὰρ οὕτως ὡς τοῖς ἁ. τὸ θεῖον ἐναναπαύεται Gr.Naz.*or*.31.22(p.172.19; M.36.156B); Dor.*doct*.1.9 (M.88.1628C); ὁ θεὸς...ἐν ἁ. ἀναπαυόμενος, ὡς τῇ ἁ. θεοτόκῳ, καὶ πᾶσι τοῖς ἁ. Jo.D.*imag*.3.33(M.94.1352A); **4.** their relation to men; **a.** on earth, for man's imitation, Bas.*moral*.27(2.257B; M.31.745C); id.*ep*.2.3(3.73C; M.32.229B); esp. in their humility, Chrys.*hom.in 2Cor.11:1*(3.294E); and for man's salvation, id.*stat*.16.4(2.164E); id.*Is.interp*.proem.(6.1B); Cyr.*glaph.Gen*.5(1.157C); because God is manifested through them, Nil.*paraen*.83(M.79.1256C); id.*exerc*. 43(M.79.772D); **b.** in heaven, concerned with men's needs πείθομαι τὰς τῶν ἁ. ψυχὰς τῶν ἡμετέρων αἰσθάνεσθαι Gr.Naz.*ep*.223(M.37. 368A); Chrys.*hom.in Ps.145:2*(5.527C); cf.Thdt.*affect*.8(p.212; 4. 916); assisting by their prayers, Bas.*hom*.19.8(2.156B; M.31.524C); Dion.Ar.*e.h*.7.3.6(M.3.561B); πιστεύοντες...τοῖς ἁ. ... ὡς οὖσι καὶ ζῶσι παρὰ τῷ θεῷ, καὶ τῶν πνευμάτων αὐτῶν ἁ. ὄντων καὶ δυνάμει θεοῦ βοηθούντων τοῖς ἀξίοις ὡς δεομένοις αὐτῶν Sym.Styl.J.*imag*.(M.86. 3220A); Dor.*doct*.15.4(M.88.1793C); Max.*ep*.12(M.91.509B); **c.** power of saints τοσαύτη ἡ τῶν ἁ. ἰσχύς· οὕτως ἄμαχος καὶ φοβερά, καὶ βασιλεῦσι, καὶ δαίμοσι, καὶ αὐτῷ τῷ τῶν δαιμόνων ἀρχηγῷ †Chrys. *pan.Bab*.2.23(2.577D); even of their bodies, *Const.App*.6.30.5; physical features τῶν γὰρ ἁ. οὐχὶ τὰ ῥήματα μόνον, ἀλλὰ καὶ αὐτὰ τὰ πρόσωπα πνευματικῆς γέμει χάριτος Chrys.*stat*.3.1(2.36B); id.*pan. Melet*.2(2.521C); and relics ἔγκειταί τις δύναμις τῷ τῶν ἁ. σώματι, διὰ τὴν ἐν τοσούτοις ἔτεσιν ἐνοικήσασαν ἐν αὐτῷ δικαίαν ψυχήν Cyr.H. *catech*.18.16; πηγὰς ἡμῖν σωτηρίους...τὰ τῶν ἁγίων...λείψανα, πολυτρόπως τὰς εὐεργεσίας πηγάζοντα Jo.D.*f.o*.4.15(M.94.1165A); v. λείψανον; **5.** men's relations to saints; **a.** prayers for their intercession τὴν τῶν ἁ. πρεσβείαν ἐπεκαλέσατο Gr.Nyss.*mart*.3(M.46. 784C); ὅταν ἴδῃς τὸν θεόν σε κολάζοντα...καταφύγῃς...πρὸς τοὺς φίλους αὐτοῦ, τοὺς μάρτυρας, τοὺς ἁ. Chrys.*Jud*.8.6(1.683B); id.*hom. 44.2 in Gen*.(4.449C); τοὺς ἁ. προσκυνῶ καὶ σέβομαι, καὶ δέομαι αὐτῶν τῆς πρεσβείας, καὶ ἱκεσίας. διὰ γὰρ τῶν πρεσβειῶν αὐτῶν σωζόμεθα πάντες ‡Jo.D.*Const*.3(M.95.312C); **b.** forms of devotion ἄλλοι μὲν ἄλλως τοὺς ἁ. τιμάτωσαν...οἱ μὲν ναῶν ὑψηλῶν ἀναστήμασιν, οἱ δὲ ποικίλων μαρμάρων κοσμήσεσιν, ἄλλοι δὲ χρυσαυγῶν ψηφίδων συνθέσεσιν, ἕτεροι φαιδροῖς ζωγράφων τεχνάσμασιν Sophr.H.*v.Cyr. et Jo*.7(M.87.3388B); Jo.D.*f.o*.4.15(M.94.1168A); liturg. commemoration, Bas.*ep*.93(3.186E; M.32.484B); feast of all saints, sc. first Sunday after Pentecost, Thdr.Stud.*catech.parv*.10(p.24); **6.** prominent individual saints and categories of saints; **a.** BMV, Epiph. *ep.Arab*.(p.471.28; M.42.733A); θεοτόκου, τῶν χερουβὶμ καὶ σεραφὶμ ἁγιωτέρας Mod.*dorm*.1(M.86.3280A) et freq.; **b.** scriptural personages: prophets, Ign.*Philad*.5.2; David, Just.*dial*.55.2(M.6.596B) et freq.; apostles, Chrys.*hom.38.5 in Jo*.(8.224B); S. Paul, †Nil.*mal. cog*.6(M.79.1208B) et freq.; **c.** martyrs, *Ep.Lugd*.ap.Eus.*h.e*.5.1.16 (M.20.413C); Or.*Jo*.6.54(36; p.163.13; M.14.293D); Cyr.H.*catech*.18.27; **d.** ascetics, hermits, etc., Thdt.*h.rel*.16(3.1222D).

E. ἅγια ἁγίων, τά, lit., inner shrine of Temple, *Holy of Holies*, Or. *Jo*.19.6(1; p.305.18; M.14.536C); Gr.Nyss.*beat*.7(M.44.1277B); myst. interprn. δικαιώματα πνεύματος, ὡς...τὰ ἅ. τῶν ἁ. ῥυθμίζουσα ἐν εὐαγγελικοῖς Epiph.*anc*.73(p.92.13; M.43.153C); εἰς τὰ ἅ. τῶν ἁ., τουτέστιν, εἰς τὴν βασιλείαν τῶν οὐρανῶν Cosm.Ind.*top*.10(M.88. 417B); εἰς τὰ ἅ. τῶν ἁ. γενόμενον· τουτέστι, τὴν ἅπασαν τῶν αἰσθητῶν τε καὶ νοητῶν παρελθόντα φύσιν, καὶ πάσης τῆς κατὰ γένεσιν ἰδιότητος γενόμενον καθαρόν, ἀνείμονι καὶ γυμνῇ τῇ διανοίᾳ προσβάλλειν ταῖς περὶ θεοῦ φαντασίαις Max.*cap.theol*.1.83(M.90.1117B); met. ὁ ἀρχιερεὺς [sc. Christ] ὁ πεπιστευμένος τὰ ἅ. τῶν ἁ. Ign.*Philad*.9.1; ὅρα ὅπως οὐκ ἐξορχήσῃ τὰ ἅ. τῶν ἁ. ... καὶ τὰ τοῦ κρυφίου θεοῦ...τιμήσεις Dion.Ar.*e.h*.1.1(M.3.372A); applied to holy sepulchre, Eus.*v.C*.3.28 (p.91.2; M.20.1088D); Valent. τὰ μὲν τῆς πρώτης τετράδος ὀνόματα ἅγια ἁγίων νοούμενα Iren.*haer*.1.15.1(M.7.613A).

ἁγιότης, ἡ, *holiness, sanctity*; **1.** of God; **a.** in gen. ὑπεράνω πάσης ἁ. *T.Lev*.3.4; living in ἀπροσίτῳ ἁ. Clem.*str*.6.7(p.461.2; M.9. 280B); Or.*Jo*.28.22(17; p.416.29; M.14.728A); Dion.Ar.*d.n*.12.3(M.3. 969C); Cyr.*thes*.13(5[1].138E); *ib*.32(284A); **b.** of three Persons of Trin., Didym.(‡Bas.)*Eun*.5(1.317E; M.29.761B); as expressed in Is.6:3 συναγόντων τὰς τρεῖς ἁ. εἰς μίαν κυριότητα Gr.Naz.*or*.34.13 (M.36.253A); therefore one, Didym.*Trin*.2.6(M.39.540C); **c.** but esp. ascribed to H. Ghost τῷ δὲ πνεύματι συμπληρωτικὴ τῆς φύσεώς ἐστιν ἡ ἁ. Bas.*Spir*.48(3.40D; M.32.156B); id.*ep*.159(3.248C; M.32.621B); οὗ καὶ πᾶσα νοητὴ φύσις χρείαν ἔχει τῆς ἁ. Cyr.H. *catech*.4.16; Didym.(‡Bas.)*Eun*.5(1.303A; M.29.725C); **2.** of Church εἰς τὴν καθολικὴν ἐκκλησίαν ἔλθετε καὶ τῇ ταύτης ἁ. κοινωνεῖτε Const.ap.Eus.*v.C*.3.65(p.112.18; M.20.1141B); **3.** of creatures; **a.** in gen., their sanctity accidental, Evagr.Pont.*ep*.2(M.32.249B); *ib*. 10(261C); **b.** of saints; joy and stability signs of sanctity, Ath.*v.Anton*.36(M.26.896C); sanctity extends to relics τούτων [sc. martyrs] οὐ τὰ ῥήματα μόνον καὶ τὰ ἔργα, ἀλλὰ καὶ αὐτὰ τὰ αἵματα καὶ τὰ ὀστᾶ πάσης ἁ. πλήρη ὑπάρχουσι †Jo.D.*B.J*.12(M.96.964B); **4.** of holy places and objects: shrine at Mamre, Const.ap.Eus. *v.C*.3.53(p.100.5; p.101.8; M.20.1116A,C); Holy of Holies, Gr.Nyss. *hom.1 in Cant*.(M.44.773B); id.*beat*.7(M.44.1277B); of a church, Socr. *h.e*.4.18.1(M.67.504A); of feasts; ref. Easter controversy οὐδὲ γὰρ πρέπει ἐν τοσαύτῃ ἁ. [sc. of Easter] εἶναί τινα διαφοράν Const.ap. Eus.*v.C*.3.19(p.87.6; M.20.1077C); **5.** as complimentary address, *PLond*.1925.20; as title of bishops, CEph.(431)*act*.7(*ACO* 1.1.3 p.27. 23; H.1.1621D); Thdt.*ep*.11(4.1069); Sophr.H.*ep.syn*.(M.87.3196B).

***ἁγιοτρισσολογέω,** *acclaim with the thrice holy*, Didym.*Trin*.2.7 (M.39.593A).

***ἁγιότροπος,** *living a holy life*, Agath.*v.Gr.Ill*.62(p.32).

***ἁγιοφανής,** *saintly*, Eust.*engast*.4(p.21.26; M.18.621A).

***ἁγιοφόρος,** *bearing holy things*; met., of Christians, Ign.*Eph*. 9.2; ἐκκλησίᾳ...ἁ. id.*Smyrn*.proem.

***ἁγιοχορεία, ἡ,** *choir of saints*, Thdr.Stud.*epp*.1.2(M.99.912B).

ἁγιστεία (-ία), ἡ, 1. *ritual, cult*; pagan, Or.*Cels*.7.48(p.199.22; M.11.1492A); Jewish, *ib*.4.22(p.291.28; 1056B); Eus.*d.e*.8.2(p.373.4; M.22.605B); Chrys.*hom.8.1 in 1Tim*.(11.589E); Christian, Isid.Pel. *epp*.3.245(M.78.924B); identified with ordination ἁ. ἤτοι χειροτονίαν Max.*schol.e.h*.5.5(M.4.164C) but cf. Dion.Ar.*e.h*.5.3.5(M.3.512B), ἁγιαστεία; **2.** *glory, holiness* τὴν ἱερωσύνης ἁ. Isid.Pel.*epp*.3.326 (M.78.985D); of God τριφεγγὲς τῆς ἁ. σέβας Geo.Pis.*hex*.181(M.92. 1447A); *ib*.1769(1571A); τριτταῖς παμφαῶς ἁ. Jo.D.*carm.theoph*.107 (p.212; M.96.832A); human piety, ‡Jo.D.*Artem*.18(p.157.13; M.96. 1268C); of BMV, ‡Meth.*Sym.et Ann*.14(M.18.381A); of God as δοτὴρ πάσης ἁ. *Lit.Jac*.(*NBP* p.106); as title of respect, of a deacon, Max.*opusc*.(M.91.89A).

***ἁγιώνυμος,** *of holy name*; of BMV, Andr.Cr.*or*.13(M.97.1073A).

ἁγίως, *holily, piously*, Clem.*paed*.3.11(p.267.1; M.8.628A); id. *paed.hymn*.7(p.291; M.8.681B); ἐποπτεύει τὸν θεὸν ἅγιον ἁ. id.*str*. 4.23(p.316.2; M.8.1361A); Or.*Jo*.19.4(1; p.302.31; M.14.532B).

ἁγιωσύνη, ἡ, *holiness* (v. ἅγιος, ἁγιότης), def. κυρίως...ἁ. λέγεται ἡ σωφροσύνη κατ' ἐξοχήν Chrys.*hom.4.3 in 1Thess*.(11.456A); **1.** degrees: Jewish, Christian, angelic, and divine τῆς ἁ. τὸν τρόπον εἴ τις καταμάθοι, τίς μὲν οὗτος, τίς δὲ ἐκεῖνος, πολλὴν ὄψεται πάλιν κἀνταῦθα τὴν διαφοράν. ἐκεῖνοι [sc. the Jews] μὲν γὰρ ἡνίκα μὴ εἰδωλολάτρουν...τοῦτο ἐκαλοῦντο τὸ ὄνομα· ἡμεῖς δέ, οὐκ ἐν τῇ τούτων ἀποχῇ μόνον, ἀλλὰ καὶ ἐν τῇ τῶν μειζόνων κτήσει γινόμεθα ἅγιοι... ἀλλὰ πρὸς τὴν ἁ. ἡμεῖς τὴν ἄνω κρινόμενοι, ἀκάθαρτοί ἐσμεν, ἅγιοι καὶ οἱ ἄγγελοι...ἀλλὰ καὶ ταύτης τῆς ἁ. ἑτέρα πάλιν διαφορὰ καὶ πρὸς ἡμᾶς καὶ πρὸς τὰς ὑπερεχούσας δυνάμεις Chrys.*hom.14.2 in Jo*. (8.80A–D); **2.** divine τῆς ἁ. αὐτοῦ οὐκ ἔστι πέρας Gr.Nyss.*hom.6 in Cant*.(M.44.893A); special characteristic of H. Ghost τὸ τῆς ἁ. ὄνομα...ἡ τοῦ πνεύματος προσηγορία Bas.*Eun*.3.3(1.274D; M.29. 661A); πνεῦμα ἁγιωσύνης *T.Lev*.18.11; Chrys.*hom.1.2 in Jo*.(8.4A); **3.** angelic; received from H. Ghost, Bas.*ep*.159(3.248C; M.32.621B); id.*Eun*.3.2(1.274B; M.29.660B); **4.** human; given by God, *Lit.Jac*. (p.200.8); may be lost but recovered by repentance, *M.Ner.et Ach*.5(p.4.14); obtained through struggle, *A.Thom*.A 85(p.201.14) and simplicity of life, Clem.*paed*.2.12(p.233.18; M.8.552B); perfected in love of Christ, †Bas.*bapt*.2.7(2.660E; M.31.1600A); leading to eternal life, *A.Thom*.A 85(p.201.5); τὴν ἁ. ἀσκοῦντας ἰδεῖν τὸν Χριστόν Chrys.*hom.63.4 in Jo*.(8.381C); ἡ ἁ. ναός ἐστιν τοῦ Χριστοῦ *A.Thom*.A 86(p.202.8); Nil.*Eulog*.33(M.79.1137C); **5.** *chastity*; as a particular form of holiness, *A.Thom*.A 97(p.210.10); coupled with ἁγνεία, *ib*.104(p.217.15); **6.** as title of bishop, Thdt.*ep*.82(4.1142); Petr.Full.*ep.Acac*.ap.Evagr.*h.e*.3.17(p.115.14; M.86.2629B); Max.*ep*. 7 (M.91.433A); of monk, Philox.*ep*.42(p.187); **7.** = ἁγίασμα, *sanctuary* τὸ καταπέτασμα τῆς ἁ. Cyr.H.*catech*.2.17.

ἀγκάζομαι, *enfold in an embrace*, Paul.Sil.*Soph*.375(M.86. 2134A).

ἀγκάλη, ἡ, 1. *bent arm*, hence met. ἀγκάλαις...ἀσμενίζομεν we receive *cordially*, Sophr.H.*ep.syn*.(M.87.3188B); met., of domestic seclusion ἡ παρθένος...ἐξ ἁ. γε, οὐκ ἐκ παλαίστρας ἐξῆλθε Chrys. *hom.12.4 in Col*.(11.418F); **2.** *woman's breast*, Synes.*ep*.4(M.66. 1340D); **3.** what is held in the arms, *bundle, sheaf*, met., of Christ ἡ ἁ. ἡ ἐναγκαλισθεῖσα ἐν θεῷ Epiph.*haer*.51.31(p.305.5).

ἀγκαλίζομαι, *hold in one's arms, embrace*, Philost.*h.e*.11.6(M.65. 600B); met., *embrace, cherish*, *Const.App*.2.20.2; Epiph.*haer*.51.31 (p.305.5; M.41.945A); εὐθέως ἁ. αὐτὸν [sc. an excommunicated person] ὁ σατανᾶς Eus.Al.*serm*.5(M.86.348B).

ἀγκιστρεύ-ω, *angle for, hook*; **1.** lit., Didym.*Trin*.2.10(M.39.645C);

2. met.; **a.** *ensnare*, Meth.*Porph*.1(p.503.17; M.18.397D); Nil.*epp*.2.62(M.79.228D); of heretics ~οντες πρὸς τὴν ἑαυτῶν νόσον Adam.*dial*.5.28(p.236.13; M.11.1881C); Isid.Pel.*epp*.1.102(M.78.252C); of evil women ~ουσιν τοὺς ἀθλίους Clem.*paed*.3.5(p.254.26; M.8.601A); Nil.*exerc*.67(M.79.801A); of sinful pleasures, id.*epp*.2.140(M.79.260C); id.*praest*.22(M.79.1088A); of Christ ensnaring Devil by assuming human nature, ‡Chrys.*hom.in Mt.26:39*(10.808E); Pamph.H.*panopl*.3.2(p.608); **b.** *attract* ~ει γάρ σε Ἰησοῦς,...ἵνα θανατώσας ζωοποιήσῃ Cyr.H.*procatech*.5; ‡Chrys.*transfig*.(Savile 7 p.340.23).

ἀγκιστροειδής, *hook-shaped, barbed*, met. τὰ ἀ. τῶν ὀδόντων αὐτῆς [sc. αἱρέσεως] φάρμακα Epiph.*haer*.48.15(p.241.6; M.41.880A).

***ἀγκιστροθηρευτής, ὁ,** *angler*, Thdt.*Is*.19:8(p.84.16; 2.282).

ἄγκιστρον, τό, *fish-hook, hook*; met. **1.** in bad sense; *snare*, Sophr.H.*v.Anast*.(M.92.1709D); of heresy τὰ ἄ. τῆς κενοδοξίας Ign.*Magn*.11; Thdt.*h.e*.5.13.2(3.1041); of deceitful pleasures, riches, etc., Bas.*hom*.21.1(2.164B; M.31.541D); χρυσὸς...τὸ τοῦ θανάτου ἄ. *ib*.7.7(59B; M.297B); Gr.Nyss.*or.dom*.3(p.114.21; M.44.1192C); Nil.*epp*.2.167(M.79.284A); of temptation of Eve δελέατος δίκην τῷ τῆς κακίας ἀ. τῆς τοῦ καλοῦ φαντασίας περιπλασθείσης Gr.Nyss.*or.catech*.21(p.84.5; M.45.60C); **2.** in good sense; of a lower motive, used as a hook to draw man to a higher purpose δέχομαι τὸ δέλεαρ τοῦ ἀ., καὶ καταδέχομαί σε, κακῇ προαιρέσει μὲν ἐλθόντα, ἐλπίδι δὲ ἀγαθῇ σωθησόμενον Cyr.H.*procatech*.5; of S. Paul's words on matrimony, designed to attract souls to virginity, Chrys.*virg*.28(1.288C); of the vision on road to Damascus as the hook by which Christ drew S. Paul, ‡Chrys.*ascens.Ac*.3(3.101Aff.); of the hook by which Christ drew Devil (cf. Job 40:20), Ath.*v.Anton*.24(M.26.880A); interpreted as his humanity, which deceived Satan ἐπειδὴ...φύσιν οὐκ εἶχεν ἡ ἐναντία δύναμις ἀκράτῳ προσμῖξαι τῇ τοῦ θεοῦ παρουσίᾳ...τῷ προκαλύμματι τῆς φύσεως ἡμῶν ἐνεκρύφθη τὸ θεῖον, ἵνα τῷ δελέατι τῆς σαρκὸς συγκατασπασθῇ τὸ ἄ. τῆς θεότητος Gr.Nyss.*or.catech*.24(p.93.3; M.45.65A); τὸν διάβολον, ἐν ἀνθρωπίνῳ ἀ. περιήγαγες ἐν τῷ τροπαίῳ τοῦ σταυροῦ ‡Ath.*pass*.31(M.28.240B); metaphor elaborated ὥσπερ γὰρ ὁ ἁλιεὺς...οὐ γυμνὸν τὸ ἄ. βάλλει εἰς τὴν θάλασσαν, ἀλλ' ἐνδύει ἔξωθεν σκώληκα δόλῳ τὸ ἄ. ... οὕτω καὶ ὁ Χριστὸς...οὐ γυμνῇ τῇ θεότητι αὐτοῦ τῷ διαβόλῳ προσέφερε, ἀλλὰ δόλῳ τὸν σκώληκα τὴν παναγίαν αὐτοῦ σάρκα...ἐκάλυψε τὸ ἱερώτατον ἄ. τὸν κοσμοσωτήριον αὐτοῦ σταυρόν. ... ἡ μὲν θεότης εἰς τύπον τοῦ ἀ. ἐστίν, ἡ δὲ ἀνθρωπότης εἰς τύπον τοῦ σκώληκος. θεωρήσας οὖν ὁ διάβολος ἔξωθεν τὸ ἀνθρώπινον ...ἐπλανήθη, καὶ προσελθὼν τῇ ἀνθρωπότητι, ἐκρατήθη ὑπὸ τοῦ...ἀ. τῆς θεότητος ‡Ath.*qu.al*.20(M.28.793C); περιέθηκα τῷ ἀ. μου τῆς θεότητος τὸν σκώληκα τοῦ σώματος ‡Chrys.*hom.in Mt.26:39*(10.808E); ‡Acac.CP *ep*.(p.18.34; H.2.844C); Olymp.*Job* 40:20(M.93.432D); Jo.D.*f.o*.3.27(M.94.1096C); id.*hom*.1.10(M.96.561C).

[*]**ἄγκιστρος, ἡ,** = foreg., ‡Gr.Nyss.*or.1 in Gen.1:26*(M.44.265C).

***ἀγκτικός, 1.** *of* or *connected with hanging* τοῦ Ἰούδα τὰ ἀ. ἀργύρια Thdr.Stud.*epp*.2.153(M.99.1477B); **2.** *able to raise, uplifting* τὸ ἀ. τε καὶ πρὸς τὸ κρεῖττον ῥυθμιστικόν Areth.*Apoc*.27(M.106.632C).

***ἀγκυλογνώμων,** *of crooked mind*, Olymp.*Job* 5:13(M.93.84B).

ἀγκυλοκοπέω, *hamstring*, Thphn.*chron*.p.136(M.108.373B).

***ἀγκυλόρινος,** *hook-nosed*, Jo.Mal.*chron*.5 p.106(M.97.196B).

[*]**ἀγκυλόχειλος,** = ἀγκυλοχείλης, *with curved beak*, Gr.Naz.*carm*.1.2.2.625(M.37.627A); Dion.Ar.*c.h*.2.1(M.3.137A).

ἄγκυρα, ἡ, *anchor*; met. of reason and time as anchors of human life, Clem.*paed*.2.2(p.169.21; M.8.413C); of God καθάπερ οὖν οἱ ἐν θαλάττῃ ἀπὸ ἀ. τονούμενοι ἕλκουσι μὲν τὴν ἄ., οὐκ ἐκείνην δὲ ἐπισπῶνται, ἀλλ' ἑαυτοὺς ἐπὶ τὴν ἄ., οὕτως οἱ κατὰ τὸν γνωστικὸν βίον ἐπισπώμενοι τὸν θεὸν ἑαυτοὺς ἔλαθον προσαγόμενοι πρὸς τὸν θεόν id.*str*.4.23(p.315.27ff.; M.8.1361A); of faith, Ath.*Ar*.3.58(M.26.445A); Epiph.*haer*.69.27(p.177.8; M.42.245C); of hope ταύτην κατέχομεν τὴν ἐλπίδα, καθάπερ ἄ. ἱεράν. καὶ γὰρ ἄ. ἐν τῷ βυθῷ κεκρυμμένη, οὐκ ἐᾷ κλονεῖσθαι τὰς ἡμετέρας ψυχάς Thdt.*Heb*.6:19(3.582); cf.Chrys.*hom.11.2 in Heb*.(12.113D); of words of Christ, id.*hom.33.7 in Mt*.(7.388A); of conscience, id.*Laz*.4.5(1.759A); of prayer, Antip.Bost.*Jo.Bapt*.3(M.85.1765C).

ἀγκυρωτός, *anchored, like an anchor* (i.e. holding fast), title of a book ἐν τῷ μεγάλῳ περὶ πίστεως λόγῳ,...ᾧ...ἐπεθέμεθα ὄνομα Ἀγκυρωτόν Epiph.*haer*.69.27(p.177.6; M.42.245B); cf.id.*anc*.proem.(p.1.5; M.43.12A); *Chron.Pasch*.p.25(M.92.116A).

ἀγκωνίσκος, ὁ, ? strengthening *band* on a door οἱ δὲ ἀ. εἰσὶν δύο ξύλα χρυσέμπαστα, καὶ καθηλωμένα εἰς ἑκάστην σανίδα, στρεφόμενα καὶ ἀντιπίπτοντα ἀλλήλοις, ἵνα συνδεσμεύωσιν πάσας τὰς σανίδας Cosm.Ind.*top*.5(M.88.504B).

ἀγλαϊστός, *splendid, glorious*, ‡Chrys.*hom.in Ps.76:4*(10.745C).

ἀγλαόπαις, *having splendid children*, met., *splendid* ἀ. ... ἀοιδήν Paul.Sil.*ambo*.112(M.86.2256A).

***ἀγλαότευκτος,** *splendidly built*, *Orac.Sib*.14.130.

***ἀγλαοφανής,** *shining*, Gr.Nyss.*v.Ephr*.(M.46.833C).

***ἀγλαοφανῶς,** *brilliantly*, Gr.Nyss.*v.Ephr*.(M.46.829C).

***ἀγλαοφαρής,** *in splendid robes*, *Orac.Sib*.3.454.

ἀγλαοφεγγής, *shining gloriously, splendid*, *Orac.Sib*.13.65; Euthal.Diac.*Ac*.(M.85.628A).

ἀγλαόφωνος, *with a glorious voice*, *Orac.Sib*.12.173; Gr.Naz.*carm*.2.2.7(poem.)64(M.37.1556A).

***ἀγλάτια, τά,** *garlic*, Cosm.Ind.*top*.tab.(M.88.469).

***ἄγληνος,** *without eye-balls, blind*, Nonn.*par.Jo*.9:6(M.43.824C).

***ἀγλωσσοχαρίτως,** *without flattering, sincerely*, Germ.CP *or*.7(M.98.357C).

***ἀγνατικός,** (Lat. *agnaticius*) *pertaining to a kinsman* on the father's side only; τὰ ἀ. *the rights of kinsmen* on the father's side, Ath.Scholast.*coll*. 3.4(p.49).

ἁγνεία, ἡ, A. (moral) *purity*, in gen. ἔδει γὰρ τὸν εἰληφότα ἄφεσιν ἁμαρτιῶν μηκέτι ἁμαρτάνειν, ἀλλ' ἐν ἁ. κατοικεῖν Herm.*mand*.4.3.2; id.*sim*.9.16.7; def., positive ἁ. γὰρ...τελεία ἡ τοῦ νοῦ καὶ τῶν ἔργων καὶ τῶν διανοημάτων, πρὸς δὲ καὶ τῶν λόγων εἰλικρίνεια καὶ τελευταία ἡ κατὰ τὰ ἐνύπνια ἀναμαρτησία Clem.*str*.4.22(p.311.10; M.8.1352C); negative ἡ ἁ. οὐκ ἄλλη τίς ἐστιν πλὴν ἡ τῶν ἁμαρτημάτων ἀποχή *ib*.7.4(p.20.8; M.9.436A); obtained by obedience to law of God, *ib*.4.25(p.318.27; M.8.1368B); and fear of the Lord, Didym.*2Cor*.6:3(p.30.17; M.39.1708D); as complimentary form of address, *CIG* 8662.1(Pamphylia, saec. vi–vii).

B. *chastity*; **1.** three kinds τρεῖς γὰρ τρόπους εἰσηγησάμενος [sc. Polyc.] ἁγνείας πιστοῖς, ἐφυγάδευσε...πορνείαν. ... ὁ δὲ δεύτερος τρόπος τῆς ἁ. ἐστὶν ὁ τῆς χηρείας ἐπαναβεβηκὼς τὸν προειρημένον...ὁ δὲ τρίτος τῆς πανάθλου ἁγνείας ἀσκητικὸς τρόπος τίνας οὐκ ἔχει ὑπερβολάς; ‡Pion.*v.Polyc*.15,16; **a.** in gen. τὸ ἀξιαγάπητον τῆς ἁ. ἦθος ἐνδειξάσθωσαν [sc. αἱ γυναῖκες] *1Clem*.21.7; Polyc.*ep*.4.2; of Susanna as martyr of chastity, Clem.*str*.4.19(p.301.4; M.8.1329A); in men, Ign.*Eph*.10.3; νεώτεροι...πρὸ παντὸς προνοοῦντες ἁ. Polyc.*ep*.5.3; **b.** conjugal, Herm.*mand*.4.1.1; abstinence of married people from legitimate intercourse τοσαύτης γὰρ ἁ. μετὰ τὴν κλῆσιν ὁ νομοθέτης ἐφρόντισεν, ὅτι καὶ τὴν Σεπφώραν κατέλιπεν εἰς Αἴγυπτον εἰσιών Thdt.*qu.22 in Num*.(1.235); of a bishop τὴν ἁ. ἔπεισε τῆς κοινωνίας προτιμῆσαι τὴν νύμφην id.*h.e*.4.13.2(3.969); ἔν τε ταῖς ἡμέραις τοῦ πάσχα, ὅτε παρ' ἡμῖν χαμευνίαι, ἁ., κακοπάθειαι, κτλ. Epiph.*haer*.75.3(p.335.18; M.42.508B); **c.** of consecrated virgins and widows ἁ. δὲ καὶ παντελῆ παρθενίαν γυναῖκες ἱερωσύνῃ θεοῦ καθιερωμέναι μετῆλθον Eus.*v.C*.4.26(p.127.9; M.20.1173C); id.*l.C*.17(p.255.16; M.20.1432C); Lit.ap.*Const.App*.8.12.44; *ib*.8.15.5; **d.** of BMV ἀρδεύουσα...τῆς ἁ. ἀρώματα Thdr.Stud.*nativ.BMV* 7(M.96.691D); **2.** chastity as a state of life; **a.** dist. from marriage τινες... ἀσκοῦσι τὴν ἁ. καὶ τὴν καθαρότητα, καὶ ἄλλοι...τὴν μονογαμίαν Or.*hom.20.4 in Jer*.(p.182.21ff.; M.13.508C); Eus.*h.e*.4.23.6(M.20.385B); preferable to marriage, Thdt.*haer*.5.25(4.467); but marriage not to be despised καὶ σὺ ὁ τὴν ἁ. ἔχων, ἆρα οὐκ ἐκ τῶν γεγαμηκότων ἐγεννήθης; μὴ γὰρ ὅτι χρυσίου κτῆσιν ἔχεις, τὸ ἀργύριον ἀποδοκίμαζε Cyr.H.*catech*.4.25; **b.** concerning both soul and body, Clem.*str*.4.25(p.319.15; M.8.1369A); *ib*.4.6(p.260.3; 1240A); Bas.Sel.*v.Thecl*.1(M.85.484D); **c.** reason for it: Inc. ἐν ἁ. μένειν εἰς τιμὴν τῆς σαρκὸς τοῦ κυρίου Ign.*Polyc*.5.2; hence it is made possible by Christ, Clem.*str*.3.8(p.224.25; M.8.1165A); through custody of the eyes δοκεῖ δὲ ὑπὲρ πάντα τῆς τῶν γυναικῶν ὄψεως ἀπεστράφθαι...πρὸς συγκεφαλαίωσιν ἁγνείας id.*paed*.3.11(p.382.6; M.8.661B); but rare and hard to practise, Meth.*symp*.1.1(p.7.16; M.18.37A); *ib*.3.13(p.43.3; 84A); best guarded by love towards God, *ib*.4.6(p.52.6; 96B); and other virtues αὐτὰς ὥσπερ τὰς ἀρετὰς πυλωροὺς ἔχων τοῦ τῆς ἁ. πολίσματος Diad.*perf*.57(p.64.6); **d.** effects: frees from corruption, *ib*.52(p.58.5); ἡγνίσθη γὰρ [sc. τὸ σῶμα] καὶ τρόπον τινὰ ἠφθαρτοποιήθη διὰ φλογὸς ἁγνείας διακοψάσης φλόγα Jo.Clim.*scal*.30(M.88.1157B); unites to God (cf.Mt.5:8); αὐτῇ τῇ ἁ. ὁ θεὸς ὁμιλεῖ *A.Phil*.3(p.2.30); ἡ ἁ. ὁρᾷ τὸν θεὸν *ib*.37(p.18.16); *ib*.46(p.21.1); ἁ. ... τὴν σάρκα πρὸς ὕψος αἴρουσα Meth.*symp*.8.4(p.85.5; 144B); ἁ. θεοῦ οἰκείωσις καὶ ὁμοίωσις κατὰ τὸ δυνατὸν ἀνθρώποις...μήτηρ δὲ ἁγνείας ἡσυχία σὺν ὑπακοῇ Jo.Clim.*scal*.15(888B); enlightens the mind ἁ. μαθητὴν θεολόγον εἰργάσατο δι' ἑαυτοῦ κρατύναντα τῆς τριάδος τῶν τριῶν τὰ δόγματα *ib*.30(1157C); and introduces into the incorruptible kingdom, Meth.*symp*.4.2(p.47.12; 89A); ἔλεγεν [sc. Polyc.] τὴν ἁ. πρόδρομον εἶναι τῆς μελλούσης ἀφθάρτου βασιλείας ‡Pion.*v.Polyc*.14; **e.** its praises τῶν χαρισμάτων τὸ καλλιφεγγὲς ἄστρον καὶ τιμαλφέστατον τοῦ Χριστοῦ, τὴν ἁ. Meth.*symp*.4.1(p.46.6; M.18.88B); *ib*.4.6(p.52.11; 96B); Bas.*ep*.45(3.134C; M.32.368B); gold as its symbol, Meth.*symp*.5.8(p.63.6; 112B).

C. (ritual) *purification*, pagan Αἰγύπτιοι ἐν ταῖς κατ' αὐτοὺς ἁ. Clem.*str*.7.6(p.26.8; M.9.448B); Jewish 'ἔλεγον, ὅτι δεῖ περιτέμνεσθαι καὶ' τὰς ἄλλας ἁγνείας 'παραφυλάττειν' *Const.App*.6.12.3; βαπτίσματα, ῥαντισμούς, ἁγνείας τοιάσδε *ib*.6.20.9.

ἁγνευτήριον, τό, *place of purification*, of a monastery ἁ. τε καὶ παρθενῶνας Gr.Naz.*or*.4.111(M.35.648C); of a church, id.*carm*.1.2.34.224(M.37.961A); of inner court of Temple, *POxy*.v.840.8,13 [saec. iv–v].

ἁγνεύ-ω, *be pure*, in baptismal formula of Elchezaites βαπτισάσθω ...καθαρισάτω καὶ ~σάτω Hipp.*haer*.9.15(p.253.16; M.16.3391A); esp. *live in chastity*, Clem.*q.d.s*.40(p.187.1; M.9.645B); *A.Phil*.3 (p.2.32); Meth.*symp*.9.4(p.119.17; M.18.188B); *ib*.7.2(p.73.8; 128B); ~ω σοι καὶ λάμπαδας φαεσφόρους κρατοῦσα, νυμφίε, ὑπαντάνω σοι *ib*.11(p.131.17; 208C); Ath.*inc*.48.2(M.25.181B).

ἁγνίζ-ω, 1. *cleanse, purify*; by remission of sins through blood of Christ, *Barn*.5.1; in baptism, Just.*dial*.86.6(M.6.681C); *A.Thom.* A 98(p.210.20); hence *baptize*, Meth.*symp*.8.9(p.91.20; M.18.152B); of moral and spiritual purification ἡγνισμένος καὶ λόγῳ καὶ βίῳ Clem.*str*.5.6(p.353.19; M.9.65C); διὰ...τῆς ἐνεργείας τοῦ φόβου ~ομένη...ὥσπερ ἡ ψυχὴ εἰς ἀγάπην ἐνεργουμένην ἔρχεται Diad.*perf*. 16(p.18.18); **2.** med., *offer oneself as expiatory sacrifice for* ~ομαι ὑμῶν Ἐφεσίων ἐκκλησίας Ign.*Eph*.8.1; id.*Trall*.13.3.

***ἁγνικῶς,** *reverently*, Jo.D.*virt*.(M.95.96A); cf.Ephr.3.430D, πνευματικῶς.

ἄγνινος, *of the branches of the chaste-tree*, Meth.*symp*.9.4(p.119.4; M.18.185D).

ἁγνισμός, ὁ, *purification*; **1.** closely connected with baptism οἱ εὐαγγελισάμενοι ἡμῖν τὴν ἄφεσιν τῶν ἁμαρτιῶν καὶ τὸν ἁ. τῆς καρδίας *Barn*.8.3; Epiph.*haer*.17.2(p.214.19; M.41.256B); almost = *baptism* τῷ Χριστῷ ἐπὶ τὸν ἁ. ἥκοντι τοῦ ὕδατος Meth.*symp*.8.9(p.91.6; M.18.152A); of Christians ἐπὶ τὸ ὕδωρ ἐλθεῖν τοῦ ἁ. id.*res*.1.41(p.287.2; M.18.269B ἁγιασμοῦ); **2.** by chastisement, exeg. Jer.12:3 τὰς κολάσεις ἁ. λέγει τῶν κολαζομένων Or.*hom.10.5 in Jer*.(p.76.4; M.13.364C); by blood of Christ ὁ δὲ ἀληθὴς ἁ. οὐ πρὸ τοῦ πάσχα ἦν ἀλλ' ἐν τῷ πάσχα, ὅτε Ἰησοῦς ἀπέθανεν ὑπὲρ τῶν ἁγνιζομένων ὡς ἀμνὸς θεοῦ id. *Jo*.28.25(20; p.423.8; M.14.737A); iron., of external purifications of Pharisees, Chrys.*hom.65.2 in Jo*.(8.390D); **3.** *purity, sanctity* ἁ. ἐστιν ἡ θεοῦ συνουσία Gr.Naz.*carm*.1.2.34.171(M.37.937A); *ib*.227 (962A); *chastity*, Diad.*perf*.35(p.40.15).

***ἀγνοηταί, *ἀγνοῖται, οἱ,** members of monophysite sect, followers of Themistius, who denied that human soul of Christ knew all things οἱ δὲ ἀ. ... λέγουσιν...τὸ ἀνθρώπινον τοῦ Χριστοῦ ...ἀγνοεῖν †Leont.B.*sect*.10.3(M.86.1261D); *ib*.5.6(1232D); ἀ. οἱ λέγοντες ἄλλα τέ τινα τὸν κύριον ἀγνοῆσαι κατὰ τὸ ἀνθρώπινον, καὶ τὴν ἡμέραν τῆς συντελείας Tim.CP *haer*.(M.86.41B); *ib*.(57B); Jo.D. *haer*.8.5(M.94.756A); also said to have denied omniscience to Christ in his divinity, cf.Isid.H.*etym*.8.5.68; inconsistency of their being monophysites and at same time distinguishing between Christ's divine knowledge and human ignorance pointed out, cf. *quisquis Nestorianus non est, Agnoïta esse nullatenus potest*, Gr. Mag.*epp*.10.39(M.*PL*.77.1098A).

***ἀγνοήτως,** *ignorantly, foolishly*, Thdt.*Trin*.23(M.75.1181B).

ἄγνοια, ἡ, *ignorance*;

A. as a state of man; **1.** esp. of fallen man (cf. *Eph*.4:18) μὴ... τέκνα...ἀγνοίας μένωμεν Just.*1apol*.61.10(M.6.421A); ἀρχαία πρὸς οὐρανὸν ἀνθρώποις κοινωνία, ἀγνοίᾳ μὲν ἐσκοτισμένη Clem.*prot*.2 (p.19.1; M.8.93B); id.*str*.7.16(p.71.3ff.; M.9.540A); *ib*.5.3(p.377.5; 33C–36A); *Hom.Clem*.13.11; yet never complete οὐδέ ἐστιν ὅλως ἄ. περὶ θεοῦ ‡Just.*qu.Chr*.1(M.6.1404A); and of men living in the flesh, Gr.Nyss.*infant*.(M.46.177C); which obscures truth of Christ, Or.*fr.10 in Jo*.(p.493.8); **2.** healed by Christ, Clem.*str*.1.28(p.109.23; M.8.924C); *Const.App*.7.30.1 al.; esp. by baptism, Gr.Nyss. *hom.11 in Cant*.(M.44.1001B); id.*laud.Bas*.(M.46.793C); **3.** state of soul opp. γνῶσις: φωτισμὸς...ἡ γνῶσίς ἐστιν, ὁ ἐξαφανίζων τὴν ἄ. ... ἃ γὰρ ἡ ἄ. συνέδησεν κακῶς, ταῦτα διὰ τῆς ἐπιγνώσεως ἀναλύεται καλῶς Clem.*paed*.1.6(p.107.31f.; M.8.285B); id.*str*.7.12(p.52.9; M.9.500C); τὸν καθειργμένον μὲν τῷ ζόφῳ τῆς ἀ. ἰδεῖν δὲ τὸ φῶς τῆς ἀπλανοῦς γνώσεως κωλυόμενον,...τὰ τῆς ἀ. διαρρήξας δεσμά, ἐπὶ τὸ φῶς προαγάγοι ἂν τῆς κατὰ Χριστὸν ἐλευθερίας Andr.Cr.*or*.7(M.97.944B).

B. ignorance and sin; **1.** ignorance a form of sin (cf. Lev.5:18) linked with παράβασις, Tat.*orat*.7(p.7.34; M.6.821A); and κακία, Or. *fr.13 in Jo*.(p.495.10); id.*Jo*.6.30(15; p.140.16; M.14.253A); *Const. App*.7.18.1; esp. an intellectual sin νοῦς ἐστι καθαρός, ὁ ἀγνοίας χωρισθεὶς Max.*carit*.1.33(M.90.968A); may lead to eternal damnation, *Hom.Clem*.2.40; *ib*.3.5; τῆς δὲ ἀ. πρὸς τὴν θείαν κατανόησιν ἐμποδιζούσης ἐκπεσεῖν τῆς ζωῆς τὴν ψυχὴν τὴν τοῦ θεοῦ μὴ μετέχουσαν Gr.Nyss.*infant*.(M.46.176A); ἔστι καὶ ἀγνοίας δοῦναι δίκην, ὅταν ἡ ἀ. ἀσύγγνωστος ᾖ Chrys.*hom.26.3 in Rom*.(9.715C); of culpable ignorance of scripture, id.*Laz*.3.3(1.740E); ἄ. γὰρ κακὸν μέν, ἀλλ' ἧσσον κακόν Gr.Naz.*carm*.2.1.12.331(M.37.1190A); **2.** a cause of sin δύο εἰσὶν ἀρχαὶ πάσης ἁμαρτίας, ἄ. καὶ ἀσθένεια Clem.*str*.7.16(p.71.24; M.9.540C); id.*paed*.1.6(p.107.28; M.8.285B); *Hom.Clem*.11.20; ἀ. αὐτὸν ἀναπεπλησμένον εἰσάγων, οὐχὶ καὶ ἁμαρτίας; ἐξ ἐκείνης γὰρ αὕτη, ὡς ἀπὸ πηγῆς ποταμὸς προχέεται Leont.B.*Nest.et Eut*.3(M.86.1373B); **3.** but usu. the consequence of sin, Ign.*Eph*.19.3; *Const.App*.8.2.2; Dion.Ar.*d.n*.7.4(M.3.872D); Stoic notion refuted ἀργία δέ, κακουργίας ἀρχή. μηδεὶς ἄ. προφασιζέσθω Bas.*hex*.7.5(1.67D; M.29.157D); **4.** ref. sins committed in ignorance; **a.** fully culpable, hence needing forgiveness, Herm.*sim*.5.7.3; *Hom.Clem*.3.6; and not without punishment, Bas.*jud*.6(2.219B; M.31.665C); hence οὔτε... τὸ κατὰ ἄ. ἁμαρτάνειν ἀκίνδυνον id.*moral*.9.4(2.243B; M.31.717C); **b.** but freq. ignorance excuses sin, Herm.*mand*.4.1.5; συγγνώμην τῆς πλάνης ἔχει τὴν ἄ. Clem.*prot*.10(p.72.21; M.8.213C); Or.*Jo*.2.15 (9; p.71.33; M.14.140C); *A.Thom*.A 38(p.156.7, v.l. ἀγνωσία).

C. in Christ; denied ἄ. ... οὐχ ἅπτεται τοῦ υἱοῦ Clem.*str*.7.2(p.7.8; M.9.412A); included in humiliation of Inc., Didym.*Ps*.68:6(M.39.1453A); to be attributed to his humanity, not to his divinity, Gr. Naz.*or*.30.15(p.133.3; M.36.124B).

D. Gnost., attributed to God by Basilides and Valentinus θεὸν...ἐν ἀ. γενόμενον Clem.*str*.2.8(p.133.2; M.8.973A); cf. γενομένης οὖν ἐντὸς πληρώματος ἀ. κατὰ τὴν Σοφίαν Hipp.*haer*.6.31(p.158.15; M.16.3239B); a feature of last days ἐπάξει...ὁ θεὸς ἐπὶ τὸν κόσμον ὅλον τὴν μεγάλην ἄ., ἵνα μένῃ πάντα κατὰ φύσιν καὶ μηδὲν μηδενὸς τῶν παρὰ φύσιν ἐπιθυμήσῃ *ib*.7.27(p.206.3; 3318B); which ignorance will fall also upon the higher aeons, *ib*.(p.206.17; 3318C).

***ἁγνοποιός,** *cleansing, making pure* or *holy* τὸν τοῦ θεοῦ φόβον...ἁ. Cyr.*Is*.5.2(2.776B); id.*Soph*.35(3.612D); id.*ador*.16(1.584D); Proc.G. *Is*.55:1ff.(M.87.2553B); Olymp.*Job* 37:15f.(M.93.389C).

ἁγνός, A. *chaste*, def. ἁ. ἐστιν ὁ ἔρωτι ἔρωτα διακρουσάμενος, καὶ πῦρ πυρὶ ἀΰλῳ ἀποσβέσας Jo.Clim.*scal*.15(M.88.880D); **1.** in gen.; **a.** of Christ, Clem.*prot*.12(p.84.9; M.8.240B); ὁ λόγος κυρίου ὁ ἐκ κυρίου ἁ. διαμένων εἰς αἰῶνα αἰῶνος Jo.Clim.*scal*.30(M.88.1157C); **b.** of Christians in gen. τηρήσατε τὴν σάρκα ἁ. *2Clem*.8.6; esp. martyrs, *A.Andr.fr*.7(p.41.15); ἁ. ... μείνατε, καὶ ζήσεσθε *A.Phil*.71(p.28.29); **2.** necessity of being chaste for union with God ἐν ἁγναῖς ξενοδοχοῦμεν ταῖς ψυχαῖς τὸν θεόν Clem.*prot*.9(p.63.32; M.8.196C); id.*paed*.3.11(p.280.6; M.8.657A); id.*paed.hymn*.26(M.8.681C) cit. s. ἰχθύς; ἐὰν...τηρήσητε τὰς ψυχὰς ὑμῶν ἁ. τῷ θεῷ...ἔσεσθε ἀμέριμνοι... προσδοκῶντες ἀπολήψεσθαι ἐκεῖνον τὸν γάμον τὸν ἄφθορον *A.Thom.* A 12(p.118.4); cf. 2Cor.11:2; Gr.Nyss.*hom.1 in Cant*.(M.44.772A); ref. danger of pride ὁ ἁ. ἐν τῇ σαρκὶ...μὴ ἀλαζονευέσθω, γινώσκων, ὅτι ἕτερός ἐστιν ὁ ἐπιχορηγῶν αὐτῷ τὴν ἐγκράτειαν *1Clem*.38.2; **3.** ref. life of consecrated chastity τὰς παρθένους ἐν...ἁ. συνειδήσει περιπατεῖν Polyc.*ep*.5.3; γυναῖκες...ἁ. καὶ παναγίῳ βίῳ ψυχῆς καὶ σώματος σφᾶς αὐτὰς καθιερώσασαι Eus.*v.C*.4.26(p.127.10; M.20.1173C); Ath.*ep.Amun*.(M.26.1173C); ref. consecrated widow ὀφθαλμὸς αὐτῆς ἁ. *Const.App*.3.7.6; **4.** of Church whose purity = orthodoxy ἐκκλησίαν, ἣν ἁ. εἶναι δεῖ τῶν τε ἔνδον ἐννοιῶν τῶν ἐναντίων τῇ ἀληθείᾳ τῶν τε ἔξωθεν πειραζόντων, τουτέστι τῶν τὰς αἱρέσεις μετιόντων καὶ πορνεύειν ἀπὸ τοῦ ἑνὸς ἀνδρὸς ἀναπειθόντων, τοῦ παντοκράτορος θεοῦ Clem.*str*.3.12(p.232.12; M.8.1180B); νύμφην λέγων τὴν ὅλην ἐκκλησίαν, τυγχάνουσαν ἁ. παρθένον διὰ τὴν τῶν δογμάτων καὶ ἠθῶν ὀρθότητα Or.*fr.45 in Jo*.(p.520.16); **5.** of abstracts; **a.** fear, *Lit*.ap.*Const.App*.8.6.5; ὁ φόβος κυρίου ἁ. ὢν Didym. *2Cor*.6:2–6(p.30.17; M.39.1708D); διττός ἐστιν ὁ φόβος· ὁ μὲν ἁ.· ὁ δὲ οὐχ ἁ. ὁ μὲν γὰρ ἐπὶ πλημμελήμασι κατ' ἐκδοχὴν κολάσεως συνιστάμενος φόβος, αἰτίαν ἔχων...τὴν ἁμαρτίαν, οὐχ ἁ. ... ὁ δὲ δίχα τῆς ἐπὶ πλημμελήμασι λύπης ἀεὶ συνεστώς, οὗτος φόβος ἁ. Max.*cap*.1.69(M.90.1208Af.); **b.** love μαθέτωσαν...τί ἀγάπη ἁ. παρὰ τῷ θεῷ δύναται *1Clem*.21.8; *ib*.48.1; ὁ δι' ἀγάπην τὴν ἁ. προσβλέπων τὸ κάλλος οὐ τὴν σάρκα ἡγεῖται, ἀλλὰ τὴν ψυχὴν καλὴν Clem.*str*.4.18(p.299.15; M.8.1324B); **c.** faith, truth, etc. πίστις Clem.*str*.5.1(p.334.13; M.9.28B); doctrine of the Lord, Or.*Jo*.19.9(2; p.309.10; M.14.544A); βούλομαι δὴ πρότερον ἁ. πόματι ὥσπερ ἁλμυρὸν ἀποκλύσασθαι στόμα· τὸ δ' ἁ. πόμα χεῖται διὰ πηγῆς ἀενάου τῶν ἀρετῶν τοῦ ὑμνουμένου πρὸς ἡμῶν θεοῦ Const.*or.s.c*.5(p.158.11f.; M.20.1244A); θεωρία Dion. Ar.*c.h*.2.4(M.3.144A).

B. *pure* τηρήσωμεν τὸ βάπτισμα ἁ. καὶ ἀμίαντον *2Clem*.6.9; of good works, Herm.*vis*.3.8.7; δεῖ...ἁ. εἰδώλων τὸν τοῦ ζῶντος οἶκον εἶναι θεοῦ Clem.*paed*.2.10(p.210.29; M.8.504A); μεταλάμβανε τὸν ἄρτον σου ἐν λαχάνῳ ἀναπεποιημένῳ ἐλαίῳ· πάντα ἁ. ὅσα ἄψυχα Ath.*virg*.8

(p.43.4; M.28.261B); of eucharist εὐχαριστίας θυσία...ἁ. μὲν αἵματος ἁ. δὲ πάσης βίας Const.or.s.c.12(p.171.21; M.20.1272B).

ἄγνος, ἡ, *chaste-tree, vitex agnus-castus*; associated with chastity on account of its name, hence virgins assemble under it, Meth. *symp*.proem.(p.6.10; M.18.33B); as symbol of chastity, *ib*.9.4 (p.119.25; 188B); *ib*.10.3(p.124.18ff.; 196Cff.); supposed not to be burnt by fire, cf. τί οὖν βούλεται τὸ παράδοξον;...ἵνα γινώσκωμεν ἐνδηλότερον ὅτι πάντων πυρὶ καταβασίῳ κατομβρουμένων τὰ ἐν ἁγνείᾳ σώματα διατρίψαντα καὶ δικαιοσύνῃ καθάπερ ψυχρῷ ὕδατι τῷ πυρί, οὐδὲν ἀλγυνόμενα πρὸς αὐτοῦ ἐπιβήσονται id.*res*.2.23(p.377.13; M.18. 285D).

ἁγνότης, ἡ, *purity*, gen. moral, of pagans θέλοντες βαπτισθῆναι... εἶτα ὅταν αὐτοῖς ἔλθῃ εἰς μνείαν ἡ ἁ. τῆς ἀληθείας, μετανοοῦσιν Herm. *vis*.3.7.3; *ib*.4.4.4; baptism entailing purity, *A.Thom.(consumm.)* (p.291.6); Or.*mart*.43(p.40.13; M.11.620B); of monks ἡ...τάξις ἡ τῶν μοναχῶν...τῶν οἰκείων ἐνεργειῶν ἁ. Dion.Ar.*e.h*.6.1.3(M.3.532D); of angels, as participating in divine purity, id.*c.h*.13.4(M.3.305B); *ib*. 3.3(168A); exeg. 2Cor.6:6 ἁ. δὲ ἐνταῦθα ἢ σωφροσύνην πάλιν, ἢ τὴν ἐν ἅπασι καθαρότητα, ἢ τὸ ἀδωροδόκητον, ἢ καὶ τὸ δωρεὰν τὸ εὐαγγέλιον κηρύττειν Chrys.*hom.12.2 in 2Cor*.(10.523A); ἁ. δὲ καλεῖ τὴν τῶν χρημάτων ὑπεροψίαν· οὐδὲ γὰρ τὰς ἀναγκαίας χρείας παρὰ Κορινθίων ἐδέξατο Thdt.*2Cor*.6:6(3.319).

***ἁγνοτόκος,** *producing purification*, of waters of baptism ῥοθίων ἁ. κάρτος ἀείδω Sophr.H.*carm*.5.98(M.87.3760A).

ἀγνωμόνως, *ungratefully*, Gr.Nyss.*v.Macr*.(p.394.4; M.46.981A); ‡Bas.*inc*.12(p.235.10).

***ἄγνωμος,** *inconsiderate*, *Mir.Geo*.6(p.65.21).

ἀγνωμοσύνη, ἡ, *want of sense* or *feeling*; hence **1.** *ingratitude*, in gen. τὴν Ἀκακίου πρὸς τοὺς...διδασκάλους ἀ. Ath.*decr*.3(p.3.23; M.25.'429'(421)A); of men towards God ἐν οἷς ὁ θεὸς...ἀνηγορεύετο, μεγάλως πρὸς τὴν τῶν ἀνθρώπων ἀ. ἐξίσταμαι Cyr.H.*catech*.7.12; ‡Nil.*fr.ascens*.3(M.79.1501C); of Jewish and heret. wilful lack of understanding ἅπερ [sc. Messianic texts] ἐπ' ἄνθρωπον ἀναφέρειν, πάσης ἀ. ... μεστόν Cyr.H.*catech*.7.2; of Jewish rejection of Christ διὰ τὴν ἔντυφον ἀ. Ast.Am.*hom*.7(M.40.257D); Chrys.*hom.6.4 in Rom*. (9.478A); id.*hom.69.1 in Mt*.(7.678C); id.*dimiss.Chan*.8(3.439E); **2.** *sinfulness* in gen., *Hom.Clem*.18.12; Cyr.*Ps*.50:7(M.69.1089D); **3.** *wilful misunderstanding*, ref. Arian exegesis τὰ τῆς ἀ. ῥήματα, τὸ 'θεός μου κτλ.' Gr.Naz.*or*.29.18(p.100.10; M.36.97A).

ἀγνώμων, *ungrateful*, esp. of men towards God, gen. οὐδέποτε γὰρ ἂν ἀ. περὶ τὴν ὀφειλομένην γενοίμην χάριν Const.ap.Eus.*v.C*.2.29 (p.53.15; M.20.1005C); of sinners, *Hom.Clem*.10.4; *ib*.19.23; of Adam, Chrys.*hom.61.1 in Mt*.(7.612C); of Jews ἀ. καὶ...ἀχάριστοι Arist. *apol*.14(p.110.1); ‡Ath.*Ar*.4.34(p.83.9; M.26.520C); Chrys.*hom.43.1 in Mt*.(7.458E); ἀ. λαὸς τῆς τοῦ δεσπότου καταφρονῶν ἀγαθότητος Bas.Sel.*or*.11.1(M.85.149B); Jo.D.*hom*.1.15(M.96.568D).

***ἀγνώρισμα, τό,** *ignorance*, Areth.ap.*cat.Apoc*.8:3(p.299.25).

ἀγνωσία, ἡ, *ignorance* (cf. ἄγνοια); **1.** ordinary state of man in this life ἐν νυκτὶ γάρ ἐσμεν παρὰ τὸν καιρὸν τῆς ἀ. οἱ ἄνθρωποι Bas. *hom.in Ps*.45(1.174A; M.29.424C); Jo.Clim.*scal*.29(M.88.1148B); but οὐκ ἀφῆκε...ἡμᾶς ὁ θεὸς ἐν παντελεῖ ἀ. Jo.D.*f.o*.1.1(M.94.789B); **2.** special feature of paganism δι' οὗ [sc. Christ] ἐκάλεσεν ἡμᾶς... ἀπὸ ἀ. εἰς ἐπίγνωσιν δόξης ὀνόματος αὐτοῦ *1Clem*.59.2; = paganism ταύτην τὴν δύναμιν ἡ ἀ. ἐκάλεσε Κρόνον Hipp.*haer*.5.14(p.108.23; M.16.3167A); Eus.*d.e*.1.1(p.5.3; M.22.17D); and heresy, denial of Christ's divinity being τῆς ἀληθείας ἀ., Ath.*decr*.17(p.14.7; M.25. '452'(444)B); **3.** as moral evil εἰ ἡ ζωὴ τὴν γνῶσιν σημαίνει...ἡ ὀργὴ τὴν ἀ. δηλοῖ Or.*sel.in Ps*.29:6(M.12.1293C); caused by sin, Gel. Cyz.*h.e*.2.7.35(M.85.1240D); liable to punishment, *Hom.Clem*.18.18; healed by Christ, Arsen.*tent*.(M.66.1624C); destroyed by H. Ghost, Cyr.H.*catech*.16.17; **4.** ignorance and contemplation διὰ γνώσεως ὁ θεὸς γινώσκεται, καὶ διὰ ἀ. ... καί ἐστιν αὖθις ἡ θειοτάτη τοῦ θεοῦ γνῶσις ἡ δι' ἀ. γινωσκομένη Dion.Ar.*d.n*.7.3(M.3.872A); supra-rational, mystical, knowledge of God, if compared with rational knowledge, being an 'unknowing' ἡ κατὰ τὸ κρεῖττον παντελὴς ἀ. γνῶσίς ἐστι τοῦ ὑπὲρ πάντα τὰ γινωσκόμενα id.*ep*.1(M.3.1065A); δι' ἀβλεψίας καὶ ἀ. ἰδεῖν id.*myst*.2(M.3.1025A); Max.*schol.myst*.2(M.4. 421D); id.*schol.d.n*.7.3(M.4.352D); **5.** Gnost., of men's ignorance of supreme God τὴν τοῦ ἀοράτου Βυθοῦ ἀ. Iren.*haer*.1.19.1(M.7.652A); as punishment of Devil ὁ δὲ βουληθεὶς αἰὼν τὸ ὑπὲρ τὴν γνῶσιν λαβεῖν ἐν ἀ. ... ἐγένετο Clem.*exc.Thdot*.31(p.117.10; M.9.676A); attributed to demiurge (cf. Mt.11:27); *Hom.Clem*.18.13.

***ἀγνωστέον,** *one must ignore*, Didym.*Ps*.4:7(M.39.1168B).

ἄγνωστος, A. *unknown*; **1.** of God εἰ μὴ κόσμου γένεσιν ἐποίησεν ὁ θεὸς...ἄ. ἦν Meth.*arbitr*.22(p.205.5); in degree; to higher angels he manifests himself more clearly than to lower ὡς αὐτῆς ἑκάστη κατὰ τὸ θεοειδὲς διέστηκεν, οὕτω τὴν φανὴν αὐτῆς ἔλλαμψιν συνάγει πρὸς τὸ τῆς οἰκείας κρυφιότητος ἑνιαῖον ἄ. Dion.Ar.*c.h*.13.4(M.3.305B); **2.** of Christ in his divinity Χριστὸν...κατὰ τὴν...γένεσιν...τὴν ἐξ αὐτοῦ τοῦ θεοῦ...πρὸ πάντων αἰώνων ἄ. τοῖς πᾶσιν Eus.*e.th*.1.2(p.63. 21; M.24.832B); ref. signification of his name Χριστὸς μὲν κατὰ τὸ κεχρῖσθαι καὶ κοσμῆσαι τὰ πάντα δι' αὐτοῦ τὸν θεὸν λέγεται, ὄνομα καὶ αὐτὸ περιέχον ἄ. σημασίαν Just.*2apol*.6.3(M.6.453B); **3.** Gnost.; of supreme God, called ἄ. θεός in all Gnost. systems; **a.** dist. from demiurge ἀναγκαῖον ἡγησάμην προσθεῖναι τούτοις καὶ ὅσα περὶ τοῦ προπάτορος αὐτῶν, ὃς ἄ. ἦν τοῖς πᾶσι πρὸ τῆς τοῦ Χριστοῦ παρουσίας, ἐκλέγοντες ἐκ τῶν γραφῶν πείθειν ἐπιχειροῦσιν, ἵν' ἐπιδείξωσι τὸν κύριον ἡμῶν ἄλλον καταγγέλλοντα πατέρα, παρὰ τὸν ποιητὴν τοῦδε τοῦ παντός Iren.*haer*.1.19.1(M.7.649B); *ib*.1.20.2(653B); arguing from Mt.11:27 ἐν τούτοις διαρρήδην φασὶ [sc. Gnostics] δεδειχέναι αὐτόν, ὡς τὸν ὑπ' αὐτὸν παρεξευρημένον πατέρα ἀληθείας, πρὸ τῆς παρουσίας αὐτοῦ μηδενὸς πώποτε ἐγνωκότος· καὶ κατασκευάζειν θέλουσιν, ὡς τοῦ ποιητοῦ καὶ κτίστου ἀεὶ ὑπὸ πάντων ἐγνωσμένου καὶ ταῦτα τὸν κύριον εἰρηκέναι περὶ τοῦ ἀ. τοῖς πᾶσι πατρός, ὃν αὐτοὶ καταγγέλλουσι *ib*.1.20.3(657A); cf.Chrys.*hom.38.2 in Mt*.(7.427D); refutation, cf. *debent autem in semetipsos audire: quemadmodum enim incognitus, qui ab ipsis cognoscitur? quodcunque enim vel a paucis cognoscitur, non est incognitum. dominus autem non in totum non posse cognosci et patrem et filium dixit: caeterum supervacuus fuisset adventus ejus. quid enim huc veniebat? an uti diceret nobis: nolite quaerere deum, incognitus est enim?* Iren.*haer*.4.6.4(988Bf.); Σατορνεῖλος...λέγει δὲ ἕνα πατέρα ἄ. τοῖς πᾶσιν ὑπάρχειν Hipp.*haer*. 7.28(p.208.10; M.16.1322A); Σίμων...ἕτοιμός ἐστιν...ἀποδεικνύειν, μὴ τοῦτον εἶναι θεὸν ἀνώτατον, ὃς οὐρανὸν ἔκτισε καὶ γῆν, ἀλλὰ ἄλλον τινὰ ἄ. καὶ ἀνώτατον *Hom.Clem*.3.2; *ib*.18.1; Epiph.*haer*.23.1(p.248.2; M.41.297C); *ib*.27.2(p.301.6; 364C); Thdt.*haer*.1.2(4.289); in Gnost. baptismal formula εἰς ὄνομα ἀγνώστου πατρὸς Iren.*haer*.1.21.3(661A); **b.** as father of Christ, Clem.*exc.Thdot*.7(p.108.1; M.9.657A) cit. s. αἰών; τὸν δὲ τοῦ Χριστοῦ πατέρα εἶναι ἄ. Hipp.*haer*.7.37(p.223.15; M.16.3343C); Adam.*dial*.1.22(p.42.31; M.11.1749C); and preached by Christ, Hipp.*haer*.7.33(p.221.4; 3342A); *ib*.10.21(p.281.13; 3438D); τὸν μὲν ἐκάλεσεν ἀγαθόν τε καὶ ἄ., ὃν καὶ πατέρα προσηγόρευσεν ὁ κύριος Thdt.*haer*.1.24(4.315); **c.** of Christ in Gnost. teaching φάσκει ...ὁ δὲ Χριστὸς...ὁ πᾶσιν ἄ. Adam.*dial*.2.14(p.84.22; M.11.1781B); **4.** of substance of soul, ‡Gr.Nyss.*imag*.(M.44.1332B); τὸ γὰρ τῆς οὐσίας αὐτῆς [sc. ψυχῆς] παρ' ἡμῖν ἄ. Melet.*nat.hom*.31(M.64. 1289B).

B. *unknowable* (not always clearly distinguishable from A supra), *ineffable*; **1.** of God ἄ. τὸ θεῖον Philost.*h.e*.1.2(M.65.461B); πάτερ ἄ. ... ἄγνωστε νόῳ Synes.*hymn*.4.227,229(p.32; M.66.1607); cf.*ib*.6.7 (p.40; 1609); τὸ ἕν, τὸ ἄ. Dion.Ar.*d.n*.1.5(M.3.593B); of divine substance ἄρρητον...καὶ ἄ. *ib*.5.1(816B); ἄ. γάρ ἐστιν ὁ θεὸς οὐ διὰ ποικιλίαν συλλογισμῶν ἀγνοουμένην ἡμῖν, ἀλλὰ κατὰ ἑνιαίαν τινὰ πρὸς τὰ καθ' ἡμᾶς, καθ' ἓν καὶ καθάπαξ ἀκατάληπτον ἀθανασίαν (Pachymeres emends to ἀγνωσίαν) Max.*schol.c.h*.13.4(M.4.101A); v. ἄλεκτος; **2.** of divine mysteries: generation of Son, Eus.*d.e*.5.1(p.214. 32; M.22.356D); Inc. Ἰησοῦ θεοπλαστία...ἄ. νῷ παντί Dion.Ar.*d.n*. 2.9(M.3.648A); id.*ep*.3(M.3.1069B); union of soul with God δι' ἑνώσεως ἀ. id.*d.n*.4.11(708D); *ib*.11.1(949B).

C. *unintelligible*, of Apoc. τινὲς...ἠθέτησαν...τὸ βιβλίον,...ἄ. τε καὶ ἀσυλλόγιστον ἀποφαίνοντες Dion.Al.ap.Eus.*h.e*.7.25.1(M.20.697A); of terms expressing essence of Trin., Thal.*cent*.4.90(M.91.1468C); superl. τὴν ἐν Ἀριμήνῳ δὲ σύνοδον καὶ τὴν ἐν Κωνσταντινουπόλει τὰ αὐτὰ δοξάζειν, ἥτις τὴν τοῦ μονογενοῦς γέννησιν ἀγνωστοτάτην πᾶσιν ἀπέφηνεν Philost.*h.e*.10.2(M.65.585A).

D. *ignorant* τὴν πρὸς τὴν θείαν διδασκαλίαν ἄ. ψυχήν Or.*fr.17 in Jo*.1:23(p.497.2); τὸ τῆς συνέσεως ἄ. Procl.CP *annunt*.2(M.85.429C).

ἀγνώστως, 1. *without the knowledge of others, secretly* τοῖς δεομένοις ὁ γνωστικὸς...διὰ τῆς εὐχῆς ἀ. ... παρέχεται Clem.*str*.7.13 (p.58.13; M.9.513A); **2.** *in a marvellous manner* τοὺς θεῷ προσοικειωθέντας ταῦτα πάντα [sc. the demons] ἀ. προτιμᾷ *Hom.Clem*. 9.20; **3.** myst., *without using the normal means to knowledge*, i.e. *without discursive reasoning* ἀπόλειπε...πάντα αἰσθητὰ καὶ νοητὰ... καὶ πρὸς τὴν ἕνωσιν...ἀ. ἀνατάθητι Dion.Ar.*myst*.1.1(M.3.998B); id. *d.n*.1.1(M.3.585B); ‡Proc.G.*Pr*.2:3(M.87.1236A).

***ἀγνώτης,** *ignorant*, Max.*opusc*.(M.91.57B).

***ἀγογγυσία, ἡ,** *absence of complaining, endurance*, Jo.Clim. *scal*.2(M.88.675A).

ἀγόγγυστος, *not complaining*, †Cyr.*hom.div*.14(5^2.415C); Eus. Al.*serm*.8(M.86.361D); Ant.Mon.*hom*.28(M.89.1528A).

ἀγογγύστως, *without complaining*, Nil.*epp*.2.157(M.79.273D); *ib*.4.46(572C); Jo.Clim.*past*.14(M.88.1200D).

ἀγοήτευτος, 1. *not subject to magic*, Synes.*insomn*.3(p.148.11; M.66.1285C); **2.** *not to be beguiled* τῆς ἀ. πενίας Cyr.*Jo*.6.1(4.604E).

***ἀγόμφωτος,** *not fitted together*, ‡Chrys.*Marth*.(10.757E).

ἀγόνατος, *not bending the knee, inflexible*, Socr.*h.e*.6.15.9(M.67.709A) = Geo.Al.*v.Chrys*.45(p.220.22); *ib*.6.19.4(724A) = *ib*.71(p.253.28).

***ἀγονοποιός,** *making barren* or *unfruitful*, Didym.*Trin*.2.14 (M.39.700A).

ἄγονος, 1. *without issue*, asserted by Paul. Sam. of Father, denied by orthodox ἀεὶ τὸν Χριστὸν εἶναι...οὐ γὰρ δὴ τούτων ἄ. ὢν ὁ θεός, εἶτα ἐπαιδοποιήσατο Dion.Al.ap.Ath.*Dion*.15(p.57.2; M.25.501C); ὁ πατὴρ οὐκ ἦν ποτε ἄ. *ib*.19(p.60.15; 508B); εἰ ἄ., καὶ ἀνενέργητος ὁ θεός ‡Ath.*Ar*.4.4(p.49.2; M.26.473B); ἔχων [sc. Paul. Sam.] δὲ αὐτὸν τὸν πατέρα ἕνα θεὸν ἄ. υἱοῦ Epiph.*haer*.65.3(p.5.13ff.; M.42.16A); **2.** met., *sterile, barren* εὐνοῦχος...ὁ ἄ. ἀληθείας Clem.*str*.3.15(p.241.21; M.8.1200A); *ib*.(p.241.31; 1200A); id.*q.d.s*.37(p.184.18; M.9.644A); Or.*schol.in Cant*.6:4f.(M.17.277B); ἄ. ... ψυχαί id.*or*.18.3(p.327.6; M.11.456A); ἄ. ... τῶν...παθῶν Meth.*symp*.4.5(p.50.22; M.18.93A); ἄ. ... φθορᾶς *ib*.8.11(p.93.14; 153D); Chrys.*oppugn*.3.6 (1.85A); τὸ ἄ. τῆς ψυχῆς...αἰνίττεται. ἀλλοτρία γὰρ θεοῦ ἡ τῶν ἀγαθῶν ἀκαρπία Thdt.*qu.25 in Dt*.(1.277); οὐκ ἄ. ... τὴν εὐχήν Niceph.Ur. *v.Sym*.130(M.86.3108A); of numbers τὸν ἑπτὰ ἀριθμὸν ἀμήτορα καὶ ἄ. λογίζονται Clem.*str*.6.16(p.503.3; M.9.365B).

***ἀγονυκλίτης, ὁ,** member of a sect whose members refused to pray kneeling, Jo.D.*haer*.91(M.94.757B).

ἀγορά, ἡ, *market-place*; δικαστικὴ ἀ. *law-court*, Chrysipp.*enc.in Thdr*.(p.66.6).

ἀγοράζ-ω, *buy, purchase*; **1.** *redeem, ransom* ἀ. δὲ ἡμᾶς κύριος τιμίῳ αἵματι Clem.*ecl*.20(p.142.10; M.9.708A); ὁ...σωτὴρ...τῷ...τιμίῳ αὐτοῦ αἵματι ἀγοράσας αὐτήν [sc. ἐκκλησίαν] Const.ap.Gel.Cyz.*h.e*.3.18.13; δοῦλος τοῦ Χριστοῦ ἠγορασμένος Gr.Nyss.*instit*.(p.67.14; M.46.297C); **2.** *purchase* ἀντὶ ἀγρῶν οὖν ~ετε ψυχὰς θλιβομένας Herm.*sim*.1.8; μὴ φείσῃ κινδύνων...ἵνα ἐνταῦθα βασιλείαν οὐράνιον ἀγοράσῃς Clem.*q.d.s*.32(p.181.10; M.9.637C); Chrys.*hom.6.4 in 2 Tim*.(11.698C); of Devil ὁ ἀμνὸς...ὠνούμενος τῷ ἑαυτοῦ αἵματι ἀπὸ τοῦ ταῖς ἁμαρτίαις ἡμᾶς πιπρασκομένους ἀγοράσαντος Or.*Jo*.6.53(35; p.162.8; M.14.292D).

ἀγορασμός, ὁ, 1. *purchase*, *Orac.Sib*.2.328; **2.** *redemption* χρήματα διατάσσετε διακονοῦντες εἰς τοὺς ἀ. τῶν ἁγίων *Const.App*.4.9.2; ἀ. τῶν πενήτων Anast.S.*qu.et resp*.12(M.89.452A); **3.** *day appointed for purchasing*, Epiph.*haer*.70.12(p.245.18; M.42.364C).

***ἀγόρευμα, τό,** *saying*, Thdr.Stud.*epp*.2.193(M.99.1585C).

ἀγόρευσις, ἡ, *speech, pronouncement*, Ast.Am.*hom*.8(M.40.297C); Sophr.H.*or*.7.20(M.87.3353B); ‡Caes.Naz.*dial*.30(M.38.892).

***ἀγορευτός,** *utterable, explicable*, Just.*dial*.4.1(M.6.484A).

ἄγος, τό, *pollution, guilt, crime*; **1.** gen., of fornication, murder, etc., Just.*1apol*.27.1(M.6.372A); Athenag.*leg*.35.2(M.6.969A); Gr. Nyss.*v.Mos*.(M.44.321B); id.*fat*.(M.45.169B); ἥ τε κενοδοξία καὶ ἡ ἀπόνοια, παντὸς ἄ. ... τὰς τῶν ἀνθρώπων μολύνουσι ψυχάς Chrys.*vid*. 1.6(1.346B); **2.** of the crimes of the Jews: against Christ ἄ. γὰρ ἔπραξαν τὸ πάντων ἀνοσιώτατον, τῷ σωτῆρι...ἐπιβουλεύσαντες Or. *Cels*.4.22(p.292.6; M.11.1056C); *ib*.8.42(p.257.17; 1580C); Eus.*theoph*. 12(7; p.26*.25; M.24.644A); against S. James the Just, id.*h.e*.2.23.19(M.20.204A); **3.** of heresy, Thdt.*h.e*.4.15.3(3.972).

ἀγράμματος, *unlettered, unlearned*; ref. apostles and evangelists, Or.*Cels*.8.47(p.262.17; M.11.1588A); Ammon.*Ac*.23:7f.(M.85.1589B); Pope Zephyrinus, Hipp.*haer*.9.11(p.245.14; M.16.3378C); being unlearned does not necessarily disqualify for bishop's office, *Const. App*.2.1.2; εἰ δὲ ἀ., πραῢς ὑπάρχων...μή ποτε περί τινος ἐλεγχθεὶς ἐπίσκοπος ἀπὸ τῶν πολλῶν γενηθείη *Sent.App*.2(p.82); in gen. ἀγράμματοι κρατοῦσι ῥητόρων Isid.Pel.*epp*.1.428(M.78.420A).

ἄγραπτος, 1. *unwritten, unscriptural*, of description of Father as ἀγένητος: τοῦτο...ἄ. καὶ ὕποπτον Ath.*Ar*.1.34(M.26.81B); cf. ἄγραφος, ἔγγραφος; **2.** *not able to be depicted*, of Christ εἰπὲ κατὰ ποίαν [sc. φύσιν] ἄ.; τὴν λαβοῦσαν, ἢ τὴν ληφθεῖσαν; καὶ εἰ κατὰ τὴν πρώτην, ἔσται κατὰ τὴν δευτέραν γραπτός Thdr.Stud.*probl*.1(M.99.477B); *ib*.6 (480C); τῶν ἄ. σῶμα λεγόντων ἔχοντα τὸν κύριον id.*ref*.4(M.99.445C).

***ἀγράρεα, ἡ,** ? *market-place*, Thphn.*chron*.p.249(M.108.625A vv.ll. ἀγοράν, ἀγραραίαν).

***ἀγράριον, τό,** a kind of *boat*, Thphn.*chron*.p.333(M.108.801A).

[*]**ἀγραυλίζομαι,** *camp out*, Thphyl.*exc.gent*.5(p.481.13; M.113.941A).

***ἀγραφία, ἡ,** *impossibility of being depicted*, Thdr.Stud.*epp*.2.33 (M.99.1205C).

ἄγραφος, A. *unwritten*; **1.** in gen.; of a thought, Nil.*epp*.3.283 (M.79.524C); τὸν ἄ. τοῦ θεοῦ νόμον ἐν ταῖς ἀκταῖς θεωρουμένη [sc. ἡ θάλασσα] Thdt.*affect*.4(p.116.22; 4.810); **2.** of religious traditions; **a.** Jewish ἄ. παράδοσις Eus.*h.e*.4.22.8(M.20.384A); Thdt.*2 Tim*.3:8 (3.689); **b.** of oral teaching of Christ, Nonn.*par.Jo*.5:47(M.43.793A); and apostles ἡ ἄ. τοῦ θείου κηρύγματος διδασκαλία Eus.*h.e*.2.15.1 (M.20.172B); id.*d.e*.1.8(p.39.10; M.22.76B); **c.** of oral tradition of Church καθολικῆς τοῦ θεοῦ ἐκκλησίας τὰς ἀπὸ τῶν θείων γραφῶν μαρτυρίας ἐξ ἀ. παραδόσεως ἐπισφραγιζομένης Eus.*Marcell*.1.1(p.8.24; M.24.728C); λόγος...κατὰ τὴν ἄ. μνήμην ἐν τῇ ἐκκλησίᾳ διασῳζόμενος †Bas.*Is*.141(1.478B; M.30.348C) ∞ Nil.*epp*.1.2(M.79.84A); ἄ. δέ ἐστιν ἡ παράδοσις αὕτη τῶν ἀποστόλων Jo.D.*f.o*.4.12(M.94.1136B); ἔστι δὲ ἄ. ἡ παράδοσις, ὥσπερ...τὸ προσκυνεῖν τὸν σταυρόν, καὶ ἕτερα ...ὅμοια *ib*.4.16(1172C).

B. *unscriptural, not in scripture*; **1.** of heret. doctrines drawn from non-scriptural sources: Gnost. τῆς ὑποθέσεως αὐτῶν...ἣν οὔτε προφῆται ἐκήρυξαν, οὔτε ὁ κύριος ἐδίδαξεν...ἐξ ἀγράφων ἀναγινώσκοντες Iren.*haer*.1.8.1(M.7.520B); acc. Simon Magus εἰ ἄ. ἐστι τὸ ζητούμενον...εἰσί τινες ὁδοὶ ἱκαναί, δυνάμεναι οὐχ ἧττον γραφῶν δεῖξαι τὰ ζητούμενα *Hom.Clem*.19.3; ref. Pneumatomachoi μὴ ἀ. διαστροφῇ τὰς...περὶ τοῦ πνεύματος τοῦ θεοῦ ἐγγράφους...ἀποδείξεις ...βιαζέσθωσαν Didym.*Trin*.2.19(M.39.736B); use of unscriptural terms rejected τὸν ἀναθεματισμὸν [sc. of Nicaea]...ἄλυπον εἶναι ἡγησάμεθα, διὰ τὸ ἀπείργειν ἀ. χρῆσθαι φωναῖς Eus.*ep.Caes*.8(p.46.11; M.20.1544A); οὐδὲ τὸ 'ἦν ποτε ὅτε οὐκ ἦν' ἐξ ἀγράφων ἐπισφαλῶς λέγοντας *Symb.Ant*.(345)3(p.252.14; M.26.729A); **2.** orthodox use of non-scriptural phrases; **a.** rejected by Arians ἔφασκον δὲ μὴ χρῆναι δυοῖν ἕνεκα λέξεων [sc. οὐσία et ὁμοούσιος], καὶ τούτων ἀ., διασπασθῆναι τῆς ἐκκλησίας τὸ σῶμα Thdt.*h.e*.2.18.2(15; 3.872); *ib*.2.3.7(2; 3.827); who also opposed orthodox teaching on H. Ghost τί δ' ἂν εἴποις, φασί, περὶ τοῦ ἁγίου πνεύματος; πόθεν ἡμῖν ἐπεισάγεις ξένον θεὸν καὶ ἄ.; Gr.Naz.*or*.31.1(p.145.6; M.36.133B); objecting to Basil's teaching on H. Ghost, Bas.*Spir*.25(3.21C; M.32.112C) cit. s. ἔγγραφος; **b.** vindicated by orthodox ἄλλοτε ἄλλαις [sc. φωναῖς], ὡς ἂν χρεία τῶν νοσούντων κατηνάγκασε, καὶ ταύταις πολλάκις ἀ. μέν, ὅμως δ' οὖν οὐκ ἀπεξενωμέναις τῆς κατὰ τὴν γραφὴν εὐσεβοῦς διανοίας id. *fid*.1(2.224B; M.31.677B); εἰ γὰρ ἐπιχειρήσαιμεν τὰ ἄ. τῶν ἐθῶν... παραιτεῖσθαι, λάθοιμεν ἂν εἰς αὐτὰ τὰ καίρια ζημιοῦντες τὸ εὐαγγέλιον id.*Spir*.66(3.54D; M.32.188A); **3.** orthodox and heretics blaming each other for use of unscriptural terms: Arian διὰ τί οἱ ἐν Νικαίᾳ συνελθόντες ἔγραψαν ἀ. λέξεις, τὸ 'ἐκ τῆς οὐσίας' καὶ τὸ 'ὁμοούσιον'; Ath.*decr*.1(p.1.11; M.25.416A); Athanasius' counter-accusation διὰ τί τοίνυν, ἀ. αὐτοὶ λέξεις πρὸς ἀσέβειαν ἐφευρόντες, αἰτιῶνται τοὺς ἀ. λέξεσιν εὐσεβοῦντας; *ib*.18(p.15.26; '456'(448)B); ὁ γογγυσμὸς αὐτῶν [sc. Arians], ὅτι ἄ. εἰσιν αἱ λέξεις, ἐλέγχεται παρ' αὐτῶν μάταιος, ἐξ ἀγράφων ἀσεβήσαντες id.*ep.Afr*.6(M.26.1040B); id.*syn*.36(p.263.13; M.26.757Af.); id.*tom*.5(M.26.801A); ἐπειδὴ κακουργήσαντες τὸ τῆς οὐσίας ὄνομα ἐν χρήσει τοῖς πατράσιν ὑπάρχον ὡς ἄ. ὂν δεξόμεθα Geo. Laod.*ep.dogm*.ap.Epiph.*haer*.73.19(p.291.28f.; M.42.437B); **4.** liturg. use of non-scriptural terms adduced to prove authenticity of unwritten tradition τὰ τῆς ἐπικλήσεως ῥήματα...τίς τῶν ἁγίων ἐγγράφως ἡμῖν καταλέλοιπεν;...ἀλλὰ καὶ προλέγομεν καὶ ἐπιλέγομεν ἕτερα ...ἐκ τῆς ἀ. διδασκαλίας παραλαβόντες Bas.*Spir*.66(3.55A; M.32.188B).

C. *not written on, blank*, Evagr.*h.e*.2.4(p.44.22; M.86.2500D).

D. *unsupported by (OT) scripture*, of a passage in S. Paul ἄ. τίθησιν Chrys.*hom.8.2 in Rom*.(9.499D); ἄ. ἐγγράφῳ συνάπτει id.*hom. 29.1 in 2Cor*.(10.639E).

E. *not to be painted*, i.e. *surpassing art*, of Christ εἰκὼν ἄ. ἀγράφου μορφώματος ‡Gr.Naz.*Chr.pat*.923(M.38.211A).

F. *not committed to writing, unspecified* δωρεᾷ τινι ἀ. Men.*exc. Rom*.3(p.179.19; M.113.864C).

ἀγράφως, 1. *without writing, orally*; in gen., Clem.*str*.1.1(p.10.25; M.8.704A); ὁ...νόμος διὰ Μωυσέως ἑβδομήκοντα σοφοῖς ἀνδράσιν ἀ. ἐδόθη παραδεδόσθαι *Hom.Clem*.3.47; ref. legacy without written will, Eus.*v.C*.4.26(p.127.25; M.20.1176A); **2.** *orally*, i.e. not in scripture, ref. tradition of Church ἦν γάρ τινα ἀ. παραδιδόμενα Clem. *str*.5.10(p.368.2; M.9.96B); *ib*.6.7(p.462.29; 284A); Eus.*h.e*.1.1.1(M.20.48B); ἐγγράφως τε καὶ ἀ. ἐδίδασκεν...ὁ θεός Epiph.*haer*.75.8(p.340.5; M.42.516A); ref. S. Paul's teaching ἀ. πολλὰ παρεδίδου Chrys.*hom. 26.1 in 1Cor*.(10.228D); id.*hom.4.2 in 2Thess*.(11.532B); *Chron. Pasch*.p.9(M.92.85A); τινὰς παραδόσεις καὶ ἀ. παρέλαβεν ἡ ἐκκλησία Anast.S.*hod*.1(M.89.40C); Jo.D.*f.o*.4.12(M.94.1136B); **3.** *unscripturally*, *Hom.Clem*.3.38 (perh. read ἄγραφος); ἀ. καὶ ἐγγράφως ἀποδεῖξαι δύναμαι *ib*.17.15; *ib*.17.16.

***ἀγρευτήριον, τό,** *snare*, ‡Proc.G.*Pr*.6:5(M.87.1269E); Thdr.Stud. *epp*.1.19(M.99.968B).

ἀγρεύ-ω, *take by hunting* or *fishing, catch*; met., *snatch, ensnare*; **1.** for evil τὸν ἄνθρωπον ὁ διάβολος ἤγρευσε Meth.*symp*.10.5(p.126.25; M.18.200B); Chrys.*subintr*.7(1.238E); of heretics τοῖς ὑπ' αὐτοῦ [sc. Simon Magus] ~θεῖσιν εἰς τὴν...πλάνην Epiph.*haer*.21.2(p.239.17; M.41.288A); of pagan tribes ensnaring Israelites in idolatry, Thdt.*qu.26 in Dt*.(1.277); of emperor Julian πρὸς τὸν τῆς ἀσεβείας ὄλεθρον τοὺς ἐξαπατωμένους ~οντα Thdt.*h.e*.3.15.1(3.929); **2.** for good, exeg. Lc.5:10 οἱ δὲ...ἐκ σκότους ἀγνοίας μεταβαλόντες ἐπὶ ζωὴν ἔνθεον ~θήσονται Eus.*theoph.fr*.6(p.19*.29; M.24.628B); τοὺς ὑπὸ τῶν ἀποστόλων ~ομένους ἀνθρώπους ‡Just.*qu.et resp*.20(M.6.1265C); of God τοὺς μὲν γὰρ δι' ἀνθρώπων ~ει Thdt.*qu.50 in 1Reg*.(1.386); προσηλύτους καλεῖ...ἐκ τῶν ἐθνῶν ~ομένους id.*Is*.54:15(p.217.3; 2.362); id.*h.e*.5.8.1(3.1025).

ἀγριέλαιος, *of a wild olive*, fem. as subst., met. of paganism or heresy (cf. Rom.11:17,24) ἡ ἀ. ἐγκεντρισθεῖσα τῷ ὄντως καλῷ καὶ ἐλεήμονι λόγῳ...καλλιέλαιος γίνεται Clem.*str*.6.15(p.491.15; M.9.341B); Cyr.H.*catech*.20.3; Gr.Naz.*or*.7.3(M.35.757C); *ib*.18.11(997B); Thdt.*Trin*.1(M.75.1149A).

***ἀγρηνός,** *wild*, *Orac.Sib*.7.79.

***ἀγριόβους, ὁ,** *wild ox, yak* or *bos grunniens*, Cosm.Ind.*top*.11 (M.88.444A).

***ἀγριογνώμων,** *wild of disposition*, Agath.*v.Gr.Ill*.151(p.77).

***ἀγριοειδής,** *of savage appearance*, *Apoc.Dan*.C 45(p.117).

ἀγριολάχανον, τό, *wild vegetable*, Pall.*h.Laus*.26(p.81.15, v.l. ἄγρια λάχανα M.34.1091C).

***ἀγριόμωρος,** *savage and foolish*; of Jews likened to savage bear and foolish dove, Cyr.*Is*.5.4(2.834C).

***ἀγριοφαγίτης, ὁ,** *eater of the flesh of wild beasts*, Isid.H.*etym*. 11.3.16.

***ἀγριόφρων,** *of savage mind*, Cyr.*Juln*.9(6².297D).

ἀγριώδης, *wild, ferocious*, Cyr.H.*catech*.2.17.

***ἀγριώνυμος,** *of savage name*, *M.Seb*.3(p.173.19).

ἀγροδίαιτος, *living in the country, rustic*, Synes.*regn*.24(p.53.14; M.66.1100D).

ἀγροικίζ-ω, *be rude, boorish* ~οντα τὸν λόγον τῆς ἀληθείας Gr. Nyss.*Eun*.12(1 p.217.16; M.45.909C); οἱ ῥήτορες ~ουσι Sophr.H. *v.Cyr.et Jo*.12(M.87.3393B).

ἀγροικικός, *rustic*, dist. from ἐγχώριος: ἀ. ... τὰς ἐπὶ τῶν ἐσχατιῶν ἱδρυμένας [sc. παροικίας]...ἐγχωρίους δὲ τὰς ἐν μέσοις ἀγροῖς ἢ κωμαῖς *Schol*. in CChalc.*can*.17(*Mon*.2 p.645).

***ἀγροικίς, 1.** *uncouth*, Chrys.*hom.15.3 in Heb*.(12.154C); **2.** subst., *peasant woman*, Thphn.*chron*.p.44(M.108.168A).

***ἀγροικιστί,** *in rustic* or *rude fashion*, Jo.VI H.*v.Jo.D*.3(M.94.433B).

***ἀγροικοπρεπῶς,** *in rustic fashion*, Cyr.*glaph.Gen*.1(1.15A).

***ἀγροικοστομέω,** *speak rudely*, Gr.Naz.*carm*.2.1.12.295(M.37.1187A).

ἀγρολέτειρα, ἡ, *waster of land*; of the locust, Cyr.*ador*.1(1.42C).

ἀγρός, ὁ, 1. *field, farm*; *landed property*, Herm.*sim*.1.1; *ib*.1.4; κατ' ἀγροὺς μὲν Σατύρους καὶ Πᾶνας Clem.*prot*.4(p.45.28; M.8.158A); id.*paed*.2.12(p.229.25; M.8.544B); Or.*hom.12.8 in Jer*.(p.14.26; M.13.389B); ἀ. ἐκκλησιαστικός Thdt.*ep*.10(4.1068); Philost.*h.e*.9.4(M.65.569B); *ib*.9.8(573C); symbolizing Church, exeg. Lam.4:9 ἀ. δὲ ὁ εὐλογημένος ἀπὸ κυρίου...δηλοῖ Χριστοῦ τὴν ἐκκλησίαν Or.*fr.104 in Lam*.(p.273.1; M.13.653D); **2.** *country*; esp. opp. town, Herm.*vis*. 2.1.4; *ib*.3.1.2; κατὰ πόλεις ἢ ἀ. Just.*1apol*.67.3(M.6.429B); Clem. *paed*.3.11(p.269.22; M.8.632C); **3.** eccl. *district* τὸν ἀ. ἐκεῖνον ὑποκείμενον τῇ Μηστείᾳ...κέλευσον Οὐασόδοις ὑποτελεῖν Bas.*ep*.188 *can*. 10(3.274D; M.32.680A).

ἀγρυπν-έω, A. *be awake, pass sleepless nights*; *keep vigil*; **1.** as ascetical practice of individuals: of a spiritual guide οὗτος ὑπὲρ σοῦ πολλὰς νύκτας ~ησάτω Clem.*q.d.s*.41(p.187.18; M.9.648); of a widow καθημένη ἐν τῇ οἰκίᾳ αὐτῆς ψάλλουσα...~οῦσα *Const.App*. 3.7.7; Pall.*v.Chrys*.9(p.56.16; M.47.33); discussion of practice of keeping vigil περιττὸν δὲ ἡγοῦμαι τὸ ~εῖν Nil.*epp*.1.26(M.79.92C); its spiritual usefulness pointed out πολλῶν ἀγαθῶν αἰωνίων πρόξενος τοῖς ~οῦσι καθίσταται *ib*.(93B); *ib*.1.29(97A); Jo.D.*spir.neq*.10 (M.95.84A); description of true watching πῶς δὲ ὁ φίλος ἐπέμενεν ἀωρὶ τῶν νυκτῶν παραμένων, ἕως ὅτου ἐγερθῆναι παρεσκεύασε;... τοῦτό ἐστιν ~εῖν Chrys.*hom.24.3 in Eph*.(11.183E); exeg. Ps.127:1 ~εῖν εἰς τὸ φρουρεῖν ἡμῶν τὴν ἐν τῇ ψυχῇ πόλιν Or.*princ*.3.1.18(p.231.4; M.11.289A); Cant.5:2 ὁ βαπτισθεὶς τῷ ὕπνῳ, ~οῦσαν ἔχειν τὴν καρδίαν οὐ δύναται Nil.ap.Proc.G.*Cant*.5:2(M.87.1673B); of Christ ~εῖ δὲ ἡ καρδία, καθὸ ὡς θεὸς τὸν ᾅδην ἐσκύλευσεν Cyr.*ib*.(M.87.1673C); **2.** ref. a Friday vigil ~ούντων ἡμῶν ἐν κυριακῷ...σύναξις γὰρ ἔμελλε τῇ παρασκευῇ γίνεσθαι Ath.*h.Ar*.81(M.25.793B); paschal vigil, *Const.App*.5.19.3 cit. s. γρηγορέω; ἐσόμεθα γὰρ ~οῦντες ἡμέρας τρεῖς καὶ νύκτας τρεῖς *V.Zos*.12(p.104.27); ἔν τισι δὲ τόποις τὴν μετὰ τὴν πέμπτην ~οῦσιν ἐπιφώσκουσαν εἰς τὸ προσάββατον καὶ τὴν κυριακὴν μόνας Epiph.*exp.fid*.22(p.523.25; M.42.828C); Jo.D. *hom*.3.10(M.96.600D).

B. *be watchful, vigilant*, *Did*.5.2; *Barn*.20.2; *Const.App*.7.18.2.

ἀγρυπνητέον, *one must watch, needful to watch* ἐν τῷ βίῳ τούτῳ ἀ. ἐστίν Or.*fr.62 in Lc*.(p.263.1); Eus.*fr.Lc*.12:39(M.24.564A); Isid. Pel.*epp*.2.164(M.78.617B).

ἀγρυπνία, ἡ, A. *watching, vigil*; **1.** as ascetical exercise of individuals τῇ ἀ. καὶ ἐγκρατείᾳ *A.Xanthipp*.2(p.59.20); *ib*.16(p.69.20); Mac.Aeg.*cust.cor*.12(M.34.832C); ἀ. καὶ προσευχαί Bas.*ep*.207.3(3.311D; M.32.764B); Gr.Naz.*or*.18.9(M.35.996B); Marc.Diac.*v.Porph*.10; Isid. Pel.*epp*.1.283(M.78.349A); to be modified for children εἴ σοι καὶ παιδία ἐστί...ἂν δὲ ἁπαλὰ ᾖ, καὶ μὴ φέρῃ τὴν ἀ., μέχρι μιᾶς εὐχῆς καὶ δευτέρας, καὶ κατάπαυσον Chrys.*hom.26.4 in Ac*.(9.213D); **2.** spiritual advantages ψυχὴ...κἂν ἀγρυπνίαις τὸ σῶμα καταδαπανήσῃ Mac.Aeg. *hom*.10.4(M.34.544A); εἰ βούλῃ τὸ ὠφέλιμον γνῶναι τῆς ἀ. ... πρῶτον μὲν γὰρ τὰ...ἡμῖν συμβεβηκότα πταίσματα...τῷ θεῷ ἐκκαλύπτοντες, κουφιζόμεθα τῆς ἀχθηδόνος αὐτῶν...καὶ τῷ πυρὶ τῆς ἀ. τεφροῦμεν... διόπερ δυσφορεῖ λοιπὸν ὁ διάβολος, καὶ καθ' ἡμῶν βρυχᾶται, ὅταν βλέπει ἡμᾶς τῇ ἀ. σχολάζοντας,...ἔπειτα δὲ καὶ ἡμεῖς ὀκνηρότεροι τοῦ λοιποῦ περὶ τὸ πταίειν γινόμεθα, τῆς ἀ. ἡμῖν λογισμοὺς φιλοθείας ἐναπαλασσομένης...ἡ γὰρ κατὰ θεὸν ἀ. ἐρήμους ἡμᾶς νύκτωρ παραλαβοῦσα...ὡς μήτηρ φιλόστοργος...ἀνοίγνυσι τοὺς ἑαυτῆς θησαυροὺς τῆς σοφίας Nil.*epp*.1.26(M.79.93Aff.); ἀ. πυρώσεων θραῦσις Jo.Clim.*scal*. 20(M.88.940D); ἀ. δὲ μνήμην ἐκκαθαίρει *ib*.(941A); ἀ. μέγα ὅπλον καὶ καλὸν ἡμῖν παρὰ θεοῦ δεδώρηται κατὰ τοῦ διαβόλου Ant.Mon.*hom*. 104(M.89.1748B); but vigil of a sinner is ἀνόνητος ἀ., Pall.*v.Chrys*. 20(p.133.21; M.47.74); **3.** of Sunday vigil ἀναστῶμεν εἰς τὴν ἀ. τῆς ἁγίας κυριακῆς Marc.Diac.*v.Porph*.7; *ib*.15; of Easter vigil τὰς ἓξ ἡμέρας τὰς πρὸ τοῦ πάσχα...ἐν ἀ. διατελοῦσι Epiph.*exp.fid*.22(p.523.23; M.42.828C); ἡ δὲ ἑορτὴ τῆς ἀναστάσεως τοῦ κυρίου ἐν πολλῇ ἀ. ἐκτελεῖται· ἐσόμεθα γὰρ ἀγρυπνοῦντες ἡμέρας τρεῖς καὶ νύκτας τρεῖς *V.Zos*.12(p.104.26); ἔν τε ταῖς ἡμέραις τοῦ πάσχα, ὅτε παρ' ἡμῖν... εὐχαί, ἀ. τε καὶ νηστεῖαι Epiph.*haer*.75.3(p.335.18; M.42.508B); εἴχοντο τῆς ἀ. ... ὡς εἰκὸς διὰ τὸ πάσχα Pall.*v.Chrys*.9(p.56.21; M.47.33); of Audians φάσκουσι γὰρ τὴν ἀ. φέρειν μεσαζόντων τῶν ἀζύμων Epiph. *haer*.70.10(p.243.21; M.42.357B); **4.** name of monastic *night office*, Dor.*doct*.9.2(M.88.1720A); *ib*.9.3(1720C); *ib*.11.5(1740C).

B. *watchfulness, vigilance* ἡ ἀ. εἴς τι ἀγαθόν *Barn*.21.7; χρεία ἡμῖν πολλῆς τῆς ἀ., ἐπειδὴ καὶ διηνεκὴς ἡμῖν ἐστιν ὁ πόλεμος Chrys. *hom.3.5 in Gen*.(4.19E); ἡ ἀ. καὶ τὰ δύσκολα εὔκολα ἡμῖν ἀπεργάζεται *ib.14.3*(110A).

ἄγρυπνος, *sleepless, wakeful, keeping vigil*, Nonn.*par.Jo*.1:19 (M.43.752C); esp. in prayer τὸν...παμπόνηρον θῆρα [sc. Devil]...ἡ ἄ. χαλινοῖ...εὐχή Nil.*epp*.1.26(M.79.93C); ἄ. ὄμμα ἥγνισεν νοῦν Jo.Clim. *scal*.20(M.88.940D); μοναχὸς ἄ., ἁλιευτὴς λογισμῶν *ib*.

ἀγρύπνως, *sleeplessly*, Or.*princ*.1.6.2(p.80.15; M.11.166C); *cat.Lc*. 12:37(p.103.21).

ἀγύμναστος, 1. *untrained, unexercised, unprepared*; of men in pre-Christian state ἀ. πρὸς τὴν τελείαν ἀγωγήν Iren.*haer*.4.38.1(M.7.1105B); of gentiles typified by the ass on which Christ entered Jerusalem ὁ νέος καὶ ἀ. τῶν ἐθνῶν λαός ‡Epiph.*hom*.6(M.43.504C); of those unprepared for martyrdom and other sufferings, *Ep.Lugd*. ap.Eus.*h.e*.5.1.11(M.20.413A); Chrys.*res.mort*.3(2.427B); of Jacob, Cyr.*Os*.137(3.169B); of those untrained in virtue, Bas.*ep*.261.3 (3.402E; M.32.972B); Cyr.*Jo*.3.6(4.314A); untrained in spiritual matters, ref. 1Cor.3:2; Iren.*haer*.4.38.2(M.7.1107A) cit. s. αἰσθητήριον; ὁ...σάρκινος ἄνθρωπος, ἀ. ἔχων πρὸς θεωρίαν τὸν νοῦν Bas.*Spir*. 53(3.46A; M.32.168A); id.*hex*.6.1(1.50A; M.29.117B); Synes.*ep*.154(M. 66.1556B); τὰ αἰσθητήρια πρὸς τὰ θεῖα λόγια ἐχόντων ἀ. Flav.CP *ep. Leon*.1(p.36.24; M.*PL*.54.724B); **2.** c. genit., *unaccustomed to*, of Israel leaving Egypt τῶν τοιούτων θαυμάτων ἀ. Gr.Nyss.*v.Mos*.31 (M.44.309B); **3.** *unexamined, undiscussed* οὐκ ἀ. ἐατέον καὶ τὸν περὶ τῆς κακίας λόγον Or.*Jo*.2.15(9; p.71.12; M.14.140B); ἀ. ... ἡ ὑπόθεσις Bas.*ep*.129.3(3.221C; M.32.561A); Gr.Nyss.*hom.6 in Cant*.(M. 44.901B); Jo.Clim.*scal*.27(M.88.1097A).

ἀγύναιος, *without a wife*, of candidate for episcopal office καλὸν μὲν εἶναι ἀ., εἰ δὲ μή, ἀπὸ μιᾶς γυναικός *Ordo Eccl.App*.16.

ἀγύρτης, *beggarly, false* ἀ. λόγος Epiph.*haer*.44.6(p.198.5; M.41.832A).

***ἀγυρτώδης,** *characteristic of a beggar* or *impostor, false*, Epiph. *haer*.26.3(p.279.17; M.41.336C); *ib*.30.21(p.361.18; 440D); Cyr.*Juln*. 2(6².52C).

***ἀγυρτωδῶς,** *in the manner of an impostor, falsely*, Epiph.*haer*. 73.1(p.268.9; M.42.401A).

***ἀγχιθανής,** *near to death*, Nonn.*par.Jo*.19:30(M.43.904C).

ἀγχίθεος, *near to God*, of an angel νεανίας...ὢν ἀ. Sophr.H.

v.Anast.(M.92.1708C); ἀ. καὶ θεοφίλους ἀθανασίας Euthal.Diac.*Ac.*(M.85.628A); of persons and objects near to Christ *μαθηταί* Nonn.*par.Jo.*1:40(M.43.756C); *ib.*2:12(761D); ἀγχιθέου στόμα πηγῆς *ib.*4:30(780A).

***ἀγχίθρονος**, *sitting near*, Nonn.*par.Jo.*7:39(M.43.812B); met., *near at hand*, of time, Cyr.*hom.pasch.*24(5^2.287E).

ἀγχίθυρος, *at the door*, Nonn.*par.Jo.*18:33(M.43.896B); met., *very near* ἀ. ... φασὶ...τὰς κακίας εἶναι ταῖς ἀρεταῖς †Bas.Anc.*virg.*(M.30.741C); Gr.Naz.*carm.*1.1.27.14(M.37.499A); Isid.Pel.*epp.*2.241(M.78.684A); μετὰ βραχὺ παρεσόμενον, μᾶλλον δὲ καὶ ἀ. ... τὸν λυτρωτὴν διαδείκνυσιν Cyr.*Is.*3.4(2.508E); ἀ. ὁ παρὰ θεοῦ λόγος id.*Os.*49(3.192C); τὰ...τῆς κτίσεως...ἀ. ἔχοντα τὴν παραφθοράν id.*inc.unigen.*(5^1.683D); of followers of heretics τῶν τούτοις [sc. Valentinus and Bardesanes] ἀ. Thdt.*eran.*proem.(4.3); *ib.*2(81); τὸ ἀ. *neighbourhood*, Men.*exc.Rom.*19(p.218.15; M.113.921D).

ἀγχιμαχητής, ὁ, *one who grapples at close quarters, fierce fighter*, *Orac.Sib.*11.22; *ib.*14.27; *ib.*14.164.

***ἀγχινοέω**, *apply the mind, be attentive*, Isid.Pel.*epp.*1.60(M.78.221C).

***ἀγχίπαλος**, *fighting hand to hand*, *Orac.Sib.*12.119.

ἀγχιστεία, ἡ, *kinship*; **1.** lit. ἡ γειτνίασις ἀγχιστείας τῶν υἱῶν Ἰωσὴφ πρὸς τὸν σωτῆρα ἐν ἀδελφῶν τάξει κέκληται, μᾶλλον δὲ καὶ ἐλογίσθη Epiph.*ep.Arab.*ap.*haer.*78.7(p.458.7; M.42.709B); of S. James πῶς τοίνυν αὐτὸν νοήσομεν ἀδελφόν; πότερον τῇ τῆς θεότητος, ἢ τῇ τῆς ἀνθρωπότητος ἀ.; Thdt.*eran.*3(4.224); between Father and incarnate Son τῆς μὲν θείας δυνάμεως τὴν πρὸς τὸν ὕψιστον ἀ. ... οἰκειουμένης Gr.Nyss.*Apoll.*6(M.45.1136C); **2.** met., *affinity, relationship*, between Christ and soul συνάπτει τῶν ὀνομάτων τούτων [sc. ἀδελφή et νύμφη] ἑκάτερον τὴν ψυχὴν τῷ νυμφίῳ...τῆς δὲ [sc. ἀδελφῆς] περὶ τὰ θελήματα σπουδῆς εἰς ἀδελφικὴν ἀ. προαγούσης id.*hom.9 in Cant.*(M.44.968A); between God and man, id.*or.dom.*2(p.36.10; M.44.1141D); of things offered in sacrifice πάντα, ὅσα διὰ πυρὸς εἶχε τὴν ἀ. id.*hom.9 in Cant.*(957A); between the just and sinners, exeg. Lc.16:26 διεστήκασιν...δικαίων ἀνδρῶν πολλῷ μέτρῳ οἱ οὐ δίκαιοι, οὐδὲν ἐκ φιλανθρωπίας ὠφελεῖσθαι δυνάμενοι τῷ μακρὰν κεχωρίσθαι τοῖς τρόποις τῆς πρὸς τὸ φιλάνθρωπον ἀ. ‡Nil.*perist.*12.10(M.79.960B); between Abraham and the faithful ὁ Παῦλος, δεικνὺς ὅτι τὴν πρὸς ἐκεῖνον [sc. Abraham] ἀ. μάλιστα ἡ πίστις ἐργάζεται Chrys.*comm.in Gal.*3:6(10.698B).

***ἀγχίστερος**, *neighbouring*, Cyr.*Mal.*25(3.842B).

ἀγχιστευτής, ὁ, *companion, friend* πανάγιε σταυρέ...Χριστιανῶν ἀ. ‡Chrys.*ador.*2(11.826C).

***ἀγχιστής, ὁ,** *kinsman*, Ath.Scholast.*coll.*2.2(p.31).

***ἀγχιτέλεστος**, *almost fulfilled*; of time, Nonn.*par.Jo.*16:4(M.43.877C); *ib.*16:25(881B).

ἀγχόνη, ἡ, 1. *means of strangling, halter* ποιῆσαι ἀ. διὰ σχοινίου τοῦ κρεμασθῆναι *A.Pil.*B 1.4(p.290); met. χρυσός, τῶν ψυχῶν ἡ ἀ. Bas.*hom.*7.7(2.59A; M.31.297B); Chrys.*virg.*76(1.329A); ἡ...σῴζουσα ἡμᾶς γνώμη γίνεται ἀ. τοῦ ἀντικειμένου Cyr.*Ps.*7:1(M.69.748D); **2.** *choking* (= *death*), ref. bread from heathen altars ἄρτον ἀγχόνης opp. ἄρτον εὐλογημένον ζωῆς *Asen.*8(p.49.7).

ἀγχονιμαῖος, *due to strangling* ἀ. μόρῳ Bardesanes ap.Eus.*p.e.*6.10(277D; M.21.472D).

ἄγχ-ω, *squeeze, strangle*; hence met. **1.** *distress, trouble* μή μου τὴν ψυχὴν ∼ε *A.Thom.*A 115(p.225.16); Chrys.*hom.11.4 in Mt.*(7.153C); *ib.66.4*(658E); **2.** *constrain, compel* εἰς πάντα τὰ τῆς ἀρετῆς ἐπιτηδεύματα βιάζεται ἑαυτὸν καὶ ἄ. Mac.Aeg.*hom.*19.7(M.34.648C); ∼ωμεν ἑαυτοὺς εἰς τὴν ταπεινοφροσύνην *ib.*19.8(648D); φήμη μαθητοῦ τοῦ σωτῆρος...∼ει καὶ λέξεων καὶ νοῦ κορεσθῆναι Acac.et Paul.*ep.*(p.153.19; M.41.156B); *ib.*(p.154.12; 156D); Chrys.*hom.28.3 in 2Cor.*(10.638B); id.*hom.31.3 in Heb.*(12.289C); Call.*v.Hyp.*(p.65); **3.** *restrain*, Gr.Naz.*or.*27.5(p.8.1; M.36.17A); τὴν βολὴν τοῦ ὄμματος...∼ων ἐφ' ἕτερον μέρος προνοίᾳ πολλῇ ‡Nil.*perist.*4.14(M.79.841B).

***ἀγχωμαλέω**, *fight a doubtful battle*, Gr.Naz.*carm.*1.2.10.459(M.37.713A).

ἄγω, *lead*; hence theol., *move, affect*, in Nestorian controversy (cf. ἐργάζομαι, ἐνεργέω) ref. incarnate Word: Nestorian argument πᾶν ὁτιοῦν ἑτέρῳ συντιθέμενον ἢ ἄγει τὸ ᾧ συντίθεται ὥσπερ ἡ ψυχὴ τὸ σῶμα· ἢ ἄγεται ὑπ' αὐτοῦ ὥσπερ τὸ σῶμα ὑπὸ τῆς ψυχῆς· ἢ οὔτε ἄγει οὔτε ἄγεται ὥσπερ τὰ μέρη τῆς οἰκίας...εἰ τοίνυν συνετέθη ὁ θεὸς λόγος τῷ ἐξ ἡμῶν ἀνθρώπῳ, ἢ ἄγει ἢ ἄγεται ἢ οὐδὲ τοῦτο οὐδὲ ἐκεῖνο, καὶ εἰ μὲν ἄγει...εἰ δὲ ἄγεται...εἰ δὲ οὐδὲ ἄγει...μηδὲ πάλιν ἄγεται...· reply: πᾶν ὁτιοῦν μὴ συντιθέμενον ἑτέρῳ ἢ ἄγει τὸ ᾧ οὐ σύγκειται ὥσπερ ὁ κύβερνος τὴν ναῦν ἢ ἄγεται ὑπ' αὐτοῦ ὥσπερ ἡ ναῦς ὑπὸ τοῦ κυβέρνου ἢ οὔτε ἄγει οὔτε ἄγεται ὥσπερ τὸ Σινᾶ ὄρος ὑπὸ τῆς θαλάσσης ...εἰ τοίνυν οὐ συνετέθη ὁ λόγος τῷ ἐξ ἡμῶν ἀνθρώπῳ, ἢ ἄγει ἢ ἄγεται ἢ οὐδὲ τοῦτο οὐδὲ ἐκεῖνο, καὶ εἰ μὲν ἄγει...εἰ δὲ ἄγεται...δεδώκατε γὰρ τοῦτο ὥσπερ τεκμήριον λογικοῦ τὸ μὴ ἄγεσθαι ἁπλῶς, μὴ προσθέντες δεόντως τὸ μὴ κατὰ πάντα ἀνεξουσίως ἄγεσθαι Leont.H.*Nest.*1.16(M.86.1460–4).

ἀγωγή, ἡ, *carrying away, movement*; hence **1.** *conduct, way of life*; **a.** in gen., of Christian life τῆς ἐν Χριστῷ ἀ. *1Clem.*47.6; ἐπὶ τὴν σεμνὴν τῆς φιλαδελφίας ἡμῶν ἁγνὴν ἀ. *ib.*48.1; of the Christian as the perfect mode of life, Iren.*haer.*4.38.1(M.7.1105B); ref. catechumens τοὺς βίους καὶ τὰς ἀ. τῶν προσιόντων Or.*Cels.*3.51(p.247.14; M.11.988B); compared with Jewish mode of life ἐπὶ τοιᾷδε βίου ἀ. δικαιοῦσθαι...ἄλλον μὲν τὸν νομικόν, ἄλλον δὲ τὸν εὐαγγελικόν id.*Jo.*13.49(47; p.276.14; M.14.488A); ἐπίπονος δι' ἐγκρατείας πρὸς τὸ ἀγαθὸν ἀ. ‡Proc.G.*Pr.*6:24(M.87.1276D); **b.** partic. of the persecuted, Ath.*fug.*11(p.76.14; M.25.660A); *ib.*17(p.80.15; 665C); λαμβάνουσιν ἀ., ἣν ἔχουσιν ἄγγελοι Mac.Mgn.*apocr.*4.27(p.214.8); εἰς πνευματικὴν ἀ. Nil.*Magn.*48(M.79.1032B); of saints and ascetics βλέποντες αὐτοῦ τὴν ἀ., πολλοὶ τῆς πολιτείας αὐτοῦ ἐσπουδάζοντο ζηλωταὶ γενέσθαι Ath.*v.Anton.*46(M.26.912B); κατ' ἴχνος ἰέναι τῆς ἐκείνων [sc. τῶν ἁγίων] ἀ. Cyr.*Ps.*10:1(M.69.789C); Niceph.Ur.*v.Sym.*249(M.86.3213C); leading to union with God, Dor.*doct.*1.9(M.88.1628C); **c.** of Christ's human mode of life τί οὖν ἄτοπον τὸν ἅπαξ ἐνανθρωπήσαντα καὶ κατ' ἀνθρωπίνην ἀ. οἰκονομεῖσθαι πρὸς τὸ ἐκκλίνειν κινδύνους; Or.*Cels.*1.66(p.120.9; M.11.784C); **d.** *discipline* τὰ χαρακτηριστικὰ τῆς ἐκκλησιαστικῆς ἀ. Eus.*h.e.*2.17.14(M.20.180B); Ph.Carp.*Cant.*238(M.40.148D); **2.** *condition* ψυχῶν Eus.*m.P.*1(p.931.25; M.20.1441A); of the condition of minds acc. Origenist teaching εἴ τις λέγει, ὅτι ἡ ἀ. τῶν νόων ἡ αὐτὴ ἔσται τῇ προτέρᾳ, ὅτε οὔπω ὑποβεβήκεσαν...ἀ. ἔ. CCP(543)*anath.*15.

***ἀγώγημα, τό,** *burden*, †Gregent.*leg.Hom.*51(M.86.608B).

ἀγωγός, ὁ, *aqueduct* τὸν ἀ. τοῦ ὕδατος *A.Thom.*A 18(p.127.10); Thdt.*ep.*81(4.1141); *Chron.Pasch.*p.327(M.92.869B).

ἀγωγός, *leading on, attractive, enticing* ἀ. ... τὸ ἐραστὸν πρὸς τὴν ἑαυτοῦ θεωρίαν Clem.*str.*7.2(p.9.9; M.9.413C); πλάσαι...πράγματα δυνάμενα ἀφ' ἑαυτῶν ἔχειν τὸ πρὸς πίστιν...ἀ. Or.*Cels.*3.39(p.236.1; M.11.972A); id.*princ.*4.2.9(15; p.321.8; M.11.373B).

ἀγών, ὁ, *contest, struggle*; **1.** of martyrdom οἳ καὶ μετὰ πάσης προθυμίας ἀνεπλήρουν τὴν ὁμολογίαν τῆς μαρτυρίας, ἐφαίνοντο δὲ καὶ οἱ ἀνέτοιμοι...ἀ. μεγάλου τόνον ἐνέγκειν μὴ δυνάμενοι *Ep.Lugd.*ap.Eus.*h.e.*5.1.11(M.20.413A); παρ' ὅλον τὸν ἐνεστηκότα ἀ. μεμνημένους τοῦ ἀποκειμένου πολλοῦ ἐν οὐρανοῖς μισθοῦ τοῖς διωχθεῖσι Or.*mart.*4(p.5.12; M.11.568A); *ib.*18(p.17.1; 585B); *ib.*(p.17.6; 588A); τοὺς ὑπὲρ εὐσεβείας ἀ. οἱ θεοφιλεῖς διῆλθον μάρτυρες Eus.*v.C.*1.15(p.15.18; M.20.929C); ὑποστάντες ἀ. τοῦ μαρτυρίου *ib.*2.35(p.56.12; 1012B); ὁ τελευταῖος ἀ. τοῦ μαρτυρίου *M.Thdot.1* 1(p.62.1); *M.Eupl.*2.2; Hier.*v.Paul.*B(p.5.7); **2.** of spiritual struggle; **a.** of Christian life in gen. ὁ αὐτὸς ἡμῖν ἀ. ἐπίκειται *1Clem.*7.1; ἀ. τὸν ἄφθαρτον *2Clem.*7.3; *ib.*7.5; Hipp.*haer.*9.17(p.255.26; M.16.3394C); Or.*mart.*5(p.6.15; M.11.568D); εἰσῆλθες εἰς ἀ. Cyr.H.*procatech.*6; ἡ τοῦ ἐλαίου χρῖσις ἐπὶ τοὺς ἱεροὺς ἀ. ἐκάλει τὸν τελούμενον Dion.Ar.*e.h.*7.3.8(M.3.565A); πρὸς τὸ τοῦ θανάτου πέρας ἴασιν, ὡς ἐπὶ τέλος ἱερῶν ἀ. *ib.*7.1.1(553A); *ib.*(553B); οἱ ἀ. τῶν πιστῶν ἐντολαί εἰσιν Marc.Er.*opusc.*4(M.65.989D); **b.** of struggle for salvation of others: of intercession ἀ. ἦν ὑμῖν ἡμέρας τε καὶ νυκτὸς ὑπὲρ πάσης τῆς ἀδελφότητος, εἰς τὸ σῴζεσθαι μετ' ἐλέους καὶ συνειδήσεως τὸν ἀριθμὸν τῶν ἐκλεκτῶν αὐτοῦ *1Clem.*2.4; Just.*dial.*142.2(M.6.800C); οἱ δὲ ἱερεῖς ὑπ' αὐτῷ [sc. ἱεράρχῃ] τελοῦσι τὴν τῆς χρίσεως ἱερουργίαν, ἐπὶ τοὺς ἱεροὺς ἐν τύπῳ τὸν τελούμενον ἀ. ἐκκαλούμενοι Dion.Ar.*c.h.*2.6(M.3.401D); *ib.*(404A); **c.** of struggle for perfection τὸ χάρισμα τοῦ πνεύματος τοῦ ἁγίου, ὅπερ ἡ πιστὴ ψυχὴ λαμβάνειν καταξιοῦται, μετὰ πολλοῦ ἀ. Mac.Aeg.*hom.*9.7(M.34.536B); ὁ βουλόμενος εὐαρεστῆσαι θεῷ ἐξ ἀληθείας... πρὸς δύο ἀ. ἔχει τὴν πάλην· ἔν τε τοῖς φαινομένοις τοῦ βίου τούτου πράγμασι...καὶ ἐν τοῖς κρυπτοῖς, πρὸς αὐτὰ τὰ τῆς πονηρίας ἀπομαχόμενος πνεύματα *ib.*21.1(656B); Nil.*Eulog.*2(M.79.1096B); οἱ πνευματικοὶ ἀ. Niceph.Ur.*v.Sym.*249(M.86.3213C); ἐζεύξαμεν τῇ ὑπομονῇ τὸν ἀ. ὅτι κατὰ παντὸς πάθους διαβολικοῦ τὴν νίκην ἀποφέρονται Ant.Mon.*hom.*79(M.89.1669A); Jo.Clim.*scal.*1(M.88.636C); οὐκ ὀλίγος δὲ ἀ. τὸν ἔσω ἄνθρωπον ποιῆσαι μοναχόν Max.*carit.*4.50(M.90.1060B); Thdr.Stud.*or.*12.6(M.99.853C); **d.** of Christ's temptations, Or.*Jo.*10.1(p.171.15; M.14.308A); agony, *ib.*32.23(15; p.466.13; 805C); fight with death, Eus.*l.C.*15(p.245.9; M.20.1416A).

ἀγωνιάω, *be anxious* or *in agony*; c. infin. ἀ. ... εἰπεῖν Or.*dial.*15(p.152.17).

ἀγωνίζ-ομαι, *contend for a prize*; *fight, struggle, strive*; **1.** ref. persecution; **a.** of those persecuted, esp. martyrs ∼ομένοις καὶ ἐπὶ τὸ μαρτύριον καλουμένοις Or.*mart.*18(p.16.24; M.11.585A); τὸν μέγαν ἀγῶνα *ib.*(p.17.26; 588B); id.*Cels.*1.62(p.115.2; M.11.777A);

Ath.*v.Anton.*46(M.26.909C); *M.Thdot.1* 36(p.84.25); and others, Or.*mart.*2(p.4.14; 565B); τὸν ὑπὲρ τῶν ἀποστολικῶν ἠγωνισμένον δογμάτων Thdt.*h.e.*5.4.6(3.1020); **b.** of persecutors ὑμῶν [sc. Jews] ... ἀρνεῖσθαι ἡμᾶς τὸ ὄνομα τοῦ Χριστοῦ ~ομένων Just.*dial.*96.2(M.6.704B); and adversaries of Christ, *ib.*104.1(720B); of Caiaphas κατὰ τοῦ Ἰησοῦ Or.*Jo.*28.14(12; p.408.2; M.14.712B); *ib.*28.18(14; p.412.10; 720A); of Devil ~όμενος καταβαλεῖν διὰ τοῦ ἀξιοῦν προσκυνῆσαι αὐτόν Just.*dial.*125.4(M.6.768A); δαίμονες...~ονται γὰρ ἔχειν ὑμᾶς δούλους id.*1apol.*14.1(M.6.348B); παντὶ δὲ τρόπῳ πρὸς πάντας ~ονται, ἵνα ἀπὸ τοῦ θεοῦ οἱ δείλαιοι τοὺς ἀνθρώπους χωρίσωσι Max.*carit.*2.90(M.90.1013B); **2.** of spiritual struggle ~εται γὰρ ἡ σοφία τοῦ θεοῦ πρὸς τὴν σοφίαν τοῦ κόσμου Or.*hom.8.9 in Jer.*(p.62.23; M.13.345C); in Christian life gen., *1Clem.*35.4; ἡμεῖς οὖν ἀγωνισώμεθα, ἵνα πάντες στεφανωθῶμεν *2Clem.*7.2; *Barn.*4.11; ποῖος καιρός ἐστιν, ἐν ᾧ ὡς μὴ ~όμενος περὶ τοῦ μὴ ἁμαρτήσεσθαι καταπεφρόνηκε; Or.*or.*29.5(p.383.31; M.11.533B); οἱ ἐν βίῳ ~όμενοι id.*or.*11.2(p.322.16; M.11.449A); ὀφείλουσιν οὖν οἱ Χριστιανοὶ εἰς πάντα ~εσθαι Mac.Aeg.*hom.*15.8(M.34.580D); *ib.*5.12(516D); Marc.Er.*opusc.*4(M.65.989C); in ascetic life γένοιτο δέ, ἵνα οὕτω τις ~όμενος...ἐν ὑπακοῇ...τὸ σκότος τῶν πονηρῶν δαιμόνων ἀποφυγεῖν δυνηθῇ Mac.Aeg.*hom.*9.11(537D); τοῖς ~ομένοις ὑπὲρ τῆς ἀφθαρσίας καὶ πνευματικῶς ἀθλοῦσιν Nil.*epp.*3.222(M.79.485B); id.*Magn.*59(M.79.1048B); Thdt.*h.rel.*11(3.1200); Diad.*perf.*26(p.28.7); *ib.*48(p.50.5); ἐπὰν γὰρ ἀγωνίσηταί τις πρὸς τὴν κατ' ἐνέργειαν ἁμαρτίαν...~εται, καὶ διὰ τῆς θλίψεως τῶν ἀγώνων ...καθαίρεται καὶ ἐπανέρχεται εἰς τὸ κατὰ φύσιν...ἐὰν γὰρ μὴ πειρασθῇ τις,...οὔτε ~εταί ποτε καθαρθῆναι Dor.*doct.*13.7(M.88.1768C,D); εἰ δὲ ἐν ἡσυχαστικωτέροις τρόποις ~ῃ, μή σου κυριεύσῃ τὸ τῆς κενοδοξίας γέννημα Jo.Clim.*scal.*21(M.88.945B); Max.*carit.*2.90(M.90.1013B); οἱ μὲν τῶν ~ομένων ἀποκρούονται μόνον τοὺς ἐμπαθεῖς λογισμούς· οἱ δὲ καὶ αὐτὰ τὰ πάθη περικόπτουσι *ib.*4.48(1057C); ἔμεινεν ~όμενος ἐν κυρίῳ Thdr.Stud.*or.*12.6(M.99.853C); esp. in prayer, Or.*Cels.*8.73(p.291.4; M.11.1628B); Evagr.Pont.*or.*11(M.79.1169C); v. ἀγωνοθέτης.

ἀγώνισμα, τό, *contest, conflict* (cf. ἀγών); **1.** of martyrdom, *Ep.Lugd.*ap.Eus.*h.e.*5.1.55(M.20.429B); **2.** gen. of Christian life κέκληται μὲν οὖν ἐπὶ τὸ ἀ. τὸ θέατρον Clem.*str.*7.3(p.15.4; M.9.425A); ἐστὶν ἡμῖν τὰ ἀ., τοῦ πειράζεσθαι οὐκ ἀπηλλάγμεθα Or.*or.*29.2(p.382.22; M.11.532C); ἀγώνων καιρός, οὐ τῶν ἀ. ἀντίδοσις Bas.Sel.*or.*28.2(M.85.321B); **3.** of ascetic life, Ath.*v.Anton.*10(M.26.860A); of novices ἐπιπόνοις ἀ. πεῖραν...λαμβάνοντας Bas.*reg.fus.*10.2(2.352E; M.31.945B); Nil.*Eulog.*2(M.79.1096B); id.*Alb.*(M.79.701C); **4.** in Origenist teaching ταῦτα δὲ ὑπὸ τῶν ψυχῶν εἴρηται τῶν εἰς παγίδα τὸ σῶμα, ὡς εἰς ἀ., κατενεχθεισῶν ἐκ τοῦ τρίτου οὐρανοῦ Meth.*res.*1.54(p.312.17; M.41.1148A).

ἀγωνιστήριον, τό, 1. *place of contest, palaestra* ὁ τῶν ἀνθρώπων βίος ἀρετῆς ἀ. πρόκειται Bas.Sel.*or.*1.1(M.85.28A); **2.** *proving-ground* τὸ πρῶτον ἀ. τῆς ἐν τοῖς λόγοις ἀνδραγαθίας τοῦ μάρτυρος Chrysipp.*enc.in Thdr.*(p.52.23).

ἀγωνιστής, ὁ, *one who struggles, combatant, champion*; esp. **1.** of Christ ὁ μέγας ἀ. Ἰησοῦς Clem.*exc.Thdot.*58(p.126.11; M.9.688A); Or.*Cels.*1.69(p.123.14; M.11.789A); **2.** of martyrs Μάτουρον, νεοφώτιστον μέν, ἀλλὰ γενναῖον ἀ. *Ep.Lugd.*ap.Eus.*h.e.*5.1.17(M.20.416A); ὡς εἰ τὸ τοιοῦτον ἐλέγομεν γίνεσθαι ἐπί τινων νομιζομένων παραδόξων ἀ. Or.*mart.*18(p.16.26; M.11.585B); *M.Thdot.1* 27(p.77.32); *ib.1* 3(p.63.7); Thdt.*h.e.*1.2.8(3.725); *ib.*2.17.1(870); **3.** of defenders of true faith against heretics οἱ τῆς ἀληθείας ἀ. *ib.*2.22.1(881); Ἀθανάσιος...ὁ πένταθλος τῆς ἀληθείας ἀ. *ib.*3.9.1(921); iron., of heretics ὁρᾶτε τὸν σφοδρὸν τῆς ἀληθείας ἀ. Gr.Nyss.*Eun.*1(1 p.41.24; M.45.269A); *ib.*12(1 p.255.9; 957B); **4.** in gen., of Christians struggling in this life, Or.*Cels.*6.72(p.142.8; M.11.1408B); **5.** of ascetics τῶν τῆς εὐσεβείας ἀ. Diad.*perf.*32(p.36.8); *ib.*47(p.52.21); ἐν ἀσκητικῇ γὰρ παλαίστρᾳ...ὤφθη γενναῖος ἀ. Thdt.*h.e.*5.35.2(3.1076); ὁ τῆς εὐσεβείας ἀ. Σάβας Cyr.S.*v.Sab.*47(p.137.22); monks called μοναχικῆς φιλοσοφίας ἀ. Justn.*nov.*5.3(p.31.24); ἦν τις ἔγκλειστος εἰς τὸ ὄρος τῶν Ἐλαιῶν, ἀ. πάνυ Jo.Mosch.*prat.*45(M.87.2900B); χρὴ δὲ τὸν ἀ. καὶ ἐκτήκειν τὸν ἀντίπαλον ἐν τῇ ἑαυτοῦ σαρκί Ant.Mon.*hom.*79(M.89.1669C).

ἀγωνιστικῶς, 1. *contentiously, controversially*, Meth.*symp.*8.17(p.111.15; M.18.173C); τοῦτο...οὐ δογματικῶς εἴρηται ἀλλ' ἀ. Bas.*ep.*210.5(3.316D; M.32.776A); Gr.Nyss.*or.catech.*38(p.153.7; M.45.97C); comp. τοῖς καθ' ἡμᾶς δόγμασιν ἀ. πρεσβεύσασιν Eus.*p.e.*1.3(7A; M.21.32B); Bas.*fid.*2(2.225C; M.31.680D); Chrys.*exp.in Ps.*8:10(5.90E); **2.** *valiantly* μέχρι θανάτου ἀντικαθίστασθαι πρὸς τὴν ἁμαρτίαν ἀ. Evagr.Pont.*or.*136(M.79.1196C).

***ἀγωνίστρια, ἡ,** *combatant*; of a woman martyr, *Ep.Lugd.*ap.Eus.*h.e.*5.1.18(M.20.416A).

ἀγωνοθετ-έω, *act as president* or *as judge in a contest*, *M.Ariadn.*5(p.127.4); met., of God presiding over the Christian warfare ἀγωνιζόμεθα...~οῦντος...τοῦ δεσπότου τῶν ὅλων Clem.*prot.*10(p.70.22; M.8.209B); of Satan presiding over strife between drunkards, Bas.*hom.*14.6(2.128A; M.31.457A); τίς ~ήσει...ἀγωνιζομένῳ τῷ Ἀπολιναρίῳ πρὸς τὸν Εὐνόμιον; Gr.Nyss.*Apoll.*44(M.45.1229A); of peace controlling inner strife, Thdt.*Col.*3:15(3.495).

ἀγωνοθέτης, ὁ, *president* or *judge in a contest*; met. **1.** of God or Christ, as influencing spiritual warfare of Christians or bestowing rewards; **a.** in gen. ὅ τε γὰρ ἀ. ὁ παντοκράτωρ θεός Clem.*str.*7.3(p.14.25; M.9.424C); ἀ. τῷ Χριστῷ id.*q.d.s.*3(p.162.1; 608B); Isid.Pel.*epp.*3.207(M.78.889C); Thdt.*Phil.*3:15(3.464); of God as ἀ. of Abraham, Bas.Sel.*or.*7.1(M.85.101B); ref. Mt.18:1 τί με νῦν ἀ. πρὸ τῶν ἀγώνων γενέσθαι βιάζεσθε; *ib.*28.2(321B); **b.** of martyrs Φίλιππος...ἐστεφάνωται τὸν τῆς ἀφθαρσίας στέφανον ὑπὸ τοῦ ἀ. Ἰησοῦ Χριστοῦ *A.Phil.*146(p.88.3); παρεκάλει αὐτοὺς ὁ ἀ. τῶν τῆς εὐσεβείας ἀθλητῶν Or.*mart.*23(p.21.20; M.11.593A); *M.Thdot.3*(p.136.27); ὁ γὰρ ἀ. τῇ φιλοτιμίᾳ τῶν ἀντιδόσεων ὑπερβαίνει τοὺς ἄθλους Thdt.*h.rel.*18(3.1229); ὁ ἀ. Χριστὸς ἐν τῷ πνευματικῷ σταδίῳ οὐ μόνον ἄνδρας ἀθλοῦντας, ἀλλὰ καὶ γυναῖκας ἀγωνιζομένας...στεφανοῖ *M.Glyc.*7(p.13*F); exeg. Ac.7:56 ὁ μόνος μετὰ πάσης συναγωγῆς ἀγωνιζόμενος, ὁ τὸν ἀ. πρὸς τὴν θέαν ἐξαναστήσας...πάσης γὰρ τῆς θείας γραφῆς καθήμενον λεγούσης, οὗτος ἑστῶτα εἶδεν· ἡ γὰρ σφοδρότης τοῦ ἀγῶνος ἐπὶ τὴν θέαν τὸν ἀ. ἐξανέστησεν Cosm.Ind.*top.*5(M.88.297B); Jo.D.*hom.*12.3(M.96.785B); **c.** of ascetics νίκας...μόνῳ τῷ ἀ. θεῷ...γινωσκομένας Nil.*praest.*1(M.79.1061B); οὐράνιον ἐπανῄρησαι πολιτείαν, ἀγωνίζου τὸν καλὸν ἀγῶνα τῆς πίστεως ἐν τῷ ἀγῶνι ὁρῶσα τὴν νίκην, ἐν τῇ νίκῃ τὸν στέφανον, τὸν ἀ. Ἰησοῦν Jo.Jej.*poenit.cont.virg.*(M.88.1972C); **2.** of the superior of a monastery μετὰ δὲ τὴν ἐν τῷ σταδίῳ λοιπὸν τῆς εὐσεβείας, καὶ ὑποταγῆς εἴσοδον, μηκέτι τὸν καλὸν ἡμῶν ἀ. ... ἀνακρίνωμεν Jo.Clim.*scal.*4(M.88.680D); **3.** of Christ and Satan presiding over a disputation ἀ. ἔνθεν μὲν Χριστὸς...ἐκεῖθεν δὲ δεινὸς τύραννος Gr.Naz.*or.*7.12(M.35.769B); of Devil ὁ τῆς μοιχείας ἀ. Bas.Sel.*or.*8.2(M.85.124A).

***ἀδαήπονος,** *ignorant of labour*; of a horse, *not broken in*, Sophr.H.*carm.*7.25(M.87.3765C).

ἀδαής, *ignorant*, hence *innocent*; of Adam, *Orac.Sib.*1.43; *untamed*; of foals, Clem.*paed.*3.12(p.291.17; M.8.681A); *virgin* κόρην ἀ. Jo.Mal.*chron.*2 p.37(M.97.108B); *ib.*8 p.203(317B).

[*]**ἀδαιμονέω,** = ἀδημονέω, *be sad*, Eus.Al.*serm.*21.16(M.86.441C).

ἀδαίτρευτος, *uncarved*, perh. = *for which nothing has been killed* ἰχθυόεν...δεῖπνον ἀδαιτρεύτοιο τραπέζης Nonn.*par.Jo.*21:15(M.43.917B); cf. *LS*.

***ἀδάκνως,** *without bite* or *sting*, hence *without trouble* ἀ. καὶ ἀπόνως ‡Caes.Naz.*dial.*109(M.38.981).

***Ἀδάμ, ὁ,** *Adam*;

A. derivations of name; **1.** *man* καθ' Ἑλλάδα φωνὴν ὁ Ἀ. ἄνθρωπός ἐστι, καὶ ἐν τοῖς δοκοῦσι περὶ τοῦ Ἀ. εἶναι φυσιολογεῖ Μωϋσῆς τὰ περὶ τῆς τοῦ ἀνθρώπου φύσεως Or.*Cels.*4.40(p.313.17; M.11.1093A); *ib.*7.50(p.201.15; 1493C); cf.Mac.Aeg.*hom.*15.36(M.34.600D); Ἀ. μόνον κληθείς, τὸ ἑρμηνευόμενον ἄνθρωπος Epiph.*haer.*1(p.172.11; M.41.180A); **2.** *earth*, *Barn.*6.9 cit. s. ἄνθρωπος; ὁ πρῶτος οὖν ἄνθρωπος Ἀ. ἐλέγετο· οὗτος ἐκ τῆς γῆς ἐπλάσθη. ἡ δὲ γῆ ἡ μήτηρ αὐτοῦ, ἐξ ἧς ἐγένετο, παρθένος ὑπῆρχεν, ὅτι οὔτε ἐξ αἵματος ἀνθρώπου ἦν μιανθεῖσα (comparison with Christ) *A.Barth.*5(p.137.21); τὸν Ἀ. ... τὸν γηγενῆ δηλοῦν Eus.*p.e.*7.8(307C; M.21.521A); Gr.Nyss.*hom.opif.*22(M.44.204D); cf.*ib.*16(185B); ἐπειδὴ οὖν ἀπὸ τῆς Ἐδὲμ τῆς παρθένου γῆς ἐπλάσθη ἄνθρωπος, ἐκλήθη Ἀ. συνωνύμως τῇ μητρί...ὁ θεὸς τὸν πλασθέντα ἄνθρωπον ἀπὸ τῆς γῆς εἰς ὄνομα τῆς μητρὸς ἐκάλεσεν Ἀ. ἐκείνη Ἐδέμ, οὗτος Ἀ. Chrys.*hom.2.3 in Ac.*9:1(3.113C); *ib.*(112E); id.*serm.9.5 in Gen.*(4.696C); Ἀ. γὰρ ἐκλήθη ἀπὸ τοῦ ὀνόματος τῆς μητρός, ἵνα μὴ μεῖζον φρονῇ τῆς οἰκείας δυνάμεως id.*hom.2.4 in Ac.*9:1(114D); Proc.G.*Gen.*1:27(M.87.129C); **3.** *red*; because of red earth of Eden, confused with Edom Ἀ. ἐκ τοῦ ἀπὸ τῆς γῆς ἐν Ἐδὲμ γεγενῆσθαι προσηγορεύθη. Ἐδὼμ γὰρ τὸ πυρρόν Diod.*Gen.*2:8(M.33.1566A); foreshadowing Passion, Thdt.*Heb.*13:12(3.634); **4.** signifying fire and the four quarters of the earth, the term of comparison being their universality ὁ ἄνθρωπος τῇ Ἑβραΐδι διαλέκτῳ πῦρ λέγεται. τοῦτο τὸ ὄνομα οὐκ ἐδόθη τῷ Ἀδὰμ ἀργῶς· ἀλλὰ τέσσαρά ἐστι στοιχεῖα ἐν τῷ κόσμῳ...γῆ, ὕδωρ, ἀήρ, πῦρ. τῶν ἄλλων στοιχείων ἕκαστον ὡς ἔστι μένει...τὸ δὲ πῦρ οὐ μένει οἷόν ἐστι. μικρὸς ἅπτεται λύχνος, καὶ μυρίας ἐξ αὐτοῦ ἀνάπτεις λαμπάδας...ἐπεὶ οὖν προῄδει θεός, ὅτι ἀπὸ ἑνὸς ἀνθρωπείου σώματος πληροῦται τῆς οἰκουμένης τὰ πέρατα...ἔθηκεν ὄνομα ἄξιον τοῦ πράγματος. διὰ τοῦτο καὶ αὐτὸ τοῦ Ἀδὰμ τὸ ὄνομα ἀρραβὼν ἦν τῆς οἰκουμένης. ἐπειδὴ γὰρ ἔμελλε τὰ τέσσαρα κλίματα ἐξ αὐτοῦ πληροῦσθαι, τίθησι τὸ ὄνομα τοῦ Ἀδάμ.

ἄλφα ἀνατολή, δέλτα δύσις, ἄλφα ἄρκτος, μῦ μεσημβρία. καὶ τὸ ὄνομα καὶ τὰ γράμματα μαρτυρεῖ τῷ ἀνθρώπῳ μέλλοντι πληροῦν τὴν οἰκουμένην Sever.*creat*.5.3(M.56.473f.); cf. *Hebraicum Adam in Latina interpretat 'terra caro facta', eo quod ex quattuor cardinibus orbis terrarum pugno comprehendit...oportuit illum ex his quattuor cardinibus orbis terrae nomen in se portare Adam: invenimus in scripturis, per singulos cardines orbis terrae esse a conditore mundi quattuor stellas constitutas in singulis cardinibus. prima stella orientalis dicitur anatole, secunda occidentalis dysis, tertia stella aquilonis arctos, quarta stella meridiana dicitur mesembrion. ex nominibus stellarum numero quattuor de singulis stellarum nominibus tolle singulas litteras principales, de stella anatole* α, *de stella dysis* δ, *de stella arctos* α, *de stella mesembrion* μ: *in his quattuor litteris cardinalibus habes nomen* ἀδαμ. *nam et in numero certo per quattuor litteras Graecas nomen designatur* ἀδαμ, ‡Cypr.*de montibus Sina et Sion* 4(M.*PL*.4.992Bf.).

B. his creation: reason; cf. *initio non quasi indigens deus hominis, plasmavit A., sed ut haberet in quem collocaret sua beneficia*, Iren.*haer*.4.14.1(M.7.1010A); difference of origin between Adam and his descendants does not imply a difference of nature Ἀ. μόνος ὑπὸ μόνου τοῦ θεοῦ διὰ τοῦ λόγου γέγονεν. ἀλλ' οὐκ ἐν τῷ πάλιν τὸν Ἀ. πλέον τι τῶν πάντων ἀνθρώπων ἔχειν ἢ διαφέρειν τῶν μετ' αὐτὸν ἄν τις φήσειεν, εἰ μόνος μὲν αὐτὸς ὑπὸ μόνου τοῦ θεοῦ πεποίηται καὶ πέπλασται, ἡμεῖς δὲ πάντες ἐκ τοῦ Ἀ. γεννώμεθα Ath. *decr*.8(p.8.10ff.; M.25.429C); Gr.Naz.*or*.39.12(M.36.348C); οὐδὲ γὰρ Ἄβελ, ὁ ἐκ συνδυασμοῦ γεννηθείς, ἕτερος παρὰ τὸν Ἀ., τοῦ Ἀδὰμ μὴ γεννηθέντος ἀλλὰ πλασθέντος Didym.(‡Bas.)*Eun*.4(1.282B; M.29. 680A); Adam, not being generated, is type of God the Father, ‡Gr.Nyss.*imag*.(M.44.1329Cf.); created from virgin soil, Proc.G. *Is*.15:1ff.(M.87.2101B); ἀμητρογενὴς μόνος ὁ Ἀ. Leont.H.*Nest*.4.36 (M.86.1708A); v. Ant.Ptol.*Adam* passim.

C. perfection before Fall; **1.** nearness to God τὸ πλάσμα, ὃ ἔπλασεν ὁ θεὸς τὸν Ἀ., οἶκος ἐγένετο τοῦ ἐμφυσήματος τοῦ παρὰ τοῦ θεοῦ Just.*dial*.40.1(M.6.561C); Ἀ. ... λέγουσιν αἱ ἱεραὶ γραφαὶ κατὰ τὴν ἀρχὴν ἀνεπαισχύντῳ παρρησίᾳ τὸν νοῦν ἐσχηκέναι πρὸς τὸν θεόν, καὶ συνδιαιτᾶσθαι τοῖς ἁγίοις ἐν τῇ τῶν νοητῶν θεωρίᾳ, ἣν εἶχεν ἐν ἐκείνῳ τῷ τόπῳ [sc. παραδείσῳ] Ath.*gent*.2(M.25.8B); ἦν ποτε ὁ Ἀ. ἄνω, οὐ τόπῳ, ἀλλὰ τῇ προαιρέσει, ὅτε ἄρτι ψυχωθεὶς καὶ ἀναβλέψας πρὸς οὐρανόν, περιχαρὴς τοῖς ὁρωμένοις γενόμενος, ὑπεραγαπῶν τὸν εὐεργέτην, ζωῆς μὲν αἰωνίου ἀπόλαυσιν χαρισάμενον, τρυφαῖς δὲ παραδείσου ἐναναπαύσαντα, ἀρχὴν δὲ δόντα κατὰ τὴν τῶν ἀγγέλων, καὶ ἀρχαγγέλοις αὐτὸν ποιήσαντα ὁμοδίαιτον, καὶ φωνῆς θείας ἀκροατήν Bas.*hom*.9.7(2.79B; M.31.344C); εἰς τὸν Ἀ. ὅτε ἤθελε τὸ πνεῦμα σὺν αὐτῷ ἦν, καὶ ἐδίδασκε καὶ ὑπετίθετο...πάντα γὰρ ἦν ὁ λόγος αὐτῷ, καὶ ἕως ὅτε ἐνέμενε τῇ ἐντολῇ, φίλος ἦν θεοῦ Mac.Aeg.*hom*.12.8 (M.34.561A); being, as a prophet, a worshipper of Trin., Epiph. *haer*.2(p.174.21; M.41.181B); endowed with grace from the beginning, Ath.*decr*.6(p.6.18; M.25.'436'(428)A); id.*Ar*.2.68(M.26.292C); his flesh being exempt from sin, ‡Ath.*Apoll*.1.7(M.26.1104C); **2.** gifts of wisdom and knowledge ὁ δὲ Ἀ. σοφίας πολλῆς ἐπεπλήρωτο, καὶ διαγνωστικὸς ἑκατέρων τούτων ἦν Chrys.*serm*.*6.1 in Gen*.(4.672A); ὁ προπάτωρ Ἀ. οὐκ ἐν χρόνῳ, καθάπερ ἡμεῖς, τὸ εἶναι σοφὸς ἀποκερδάνας ὁρᾶται, ἀλλ' ἐκ πρώτων εὐθὺς τῶν τῆς γενέσεως χρόνων τέλειος ἐν συνέσει φαίνεται, τὸν δοθέντα τῇ φύσει παρὰ θεοῦ φωτισμόν Cyr.*Jo*.1.9(4.75B); had knowledge of good, or of good and evil, even before Fall, ‡Ath.*Apoll*.1.15(M.26.1120B) cit. s. παρακοή; οὐ τὴν γνῶσιν ἐκώλυσεν ὁ θεὸς τοῦ καλοῦ· εἶχε γὰρ αὐτὴν ὁ Ἀ. καὶ πρὸ τοῦ φαγεῖν Sever.*creat*.6.3(M.56.487); καὶ πρὸ τῆς βρώσεως ταύτην εἶχε τὴν διάγνωσιν. εἰ γὰρ μὴ ᾔδει τί μὲν καλόν, τί δὲ πονηρόν, καὶ αὐτῶν τῶν ἀλόγων ἀλογώτερος ἦν, καὶ τῶν δούλων ὁ δεσπότης ἀνοητότερος Chrys.*serm*.*6.1 in Gen*.(4.671D); ᾔδει μὲν γὰρ καὶ πρὸ τούτου ὁ Ἀ., ὅτι καλὸν μὲν ἡ ὑπακοή, πονηρὸν δὲ ἡ παρακοή· ἔμαθε δὲ ὕστερον σαφέστερον δι' αὐτῆς τῶν πραγμάτων τῆς πείρας *ib*.*7.2*(677A); shown in naming the animals ὁ Ἀ. πρὸ τῆς παραβάσεως ἐπεπλήρωτο σοφίας καὶ συνέσεως καὶ προφητείας. ἐννόησον ὅσην εἶχε σοφίαν, ὅτι ἐπήρκεσεν ἄνθρωπος εἷς, διδάσκαλον μὴ λαβών, παρὰ μηδενὸς ἀνθρώπου διδαχθείς, θεῖναι ὀνόματα ὅλοις τοῖς πετεινοῖς, καὶ τοῖς ζώοις...καὶ πᾶσιν ἁπλῶς Sever.*creat*.6.2 (M.56.486); Chrys.*hom*.*14.5 in Gen*.(4.112C); **3.** gift of prophecy 'καὶ εἶπεν Ἀ., τοῦτο νῦν ὀστοῦν ἐκ τῶν ὀστέων μου, κτλ.' θέα μοι ἐνταῦθα...πῶς...προφητικῆς ἠξίωτο χάριτος. διὰ γὰρ τοῦτο...ἐδίδαξεν ἡμᾶς ὁ μακάριος προφήτης, ὅτι μετὰ τοῦ ὕπνου καὶ ἔκστασις αὐτὸν ἔλαβεν, ἵνα...πεισθῇς ἀκριβῶς, ὅτι προφητικῇ χάριτι ταῦτα φθέγγεται, καὶ ἐνηχούμενος ὑπὸ τῆς τοῦ ἁγίου πνεύματος διδασκαλίας Chrys. *hom*.*15.3 in Gen*.(4.119C,D); οὐ γὰρ ἔρημον προφητικοῦ πνεύματος εὑρήσομεν τὸν Ἀ., οὔπω τὴν θείαν ἐντολὴν παραβεβηκότα Cyr.*Joel*.35 (3.227E); v. προφήτης; **4.** dominion over other creatures τὸν Ἀ. μηδέπω ἁμαρτήσαντα, καὶ τὰ θηρία...ὑπήκοα ἔχοντα, καὶ ὡς δούλοις αὐτοῖς καλοῦντα ὀνόματα Chrys.*exp.in Ps*.3:1(5.3E); πᾶν γάρ, φησίν, ὃ ἐκάλεσεν αὐτὸ Ἀ., τοῦτο ὄνομα αὐτῷ. εἶδες ἐξουσίαν ἀπηρτισμένην; εἶδες δεσποτείας αὐθεντίαν; λογίζου μετὰ τῶν ἄλλων καὶ τοῦτο, ὅτι καὶ λέοντες, καὶ παρδάλεις...καθάπερ πρὸς δεσπότην μετὰ πάσης ὑποταγῆς παραγεγονότα τὰς προσηγορίας ἐδέξαντο, καὶ οὐδὲν τῶν θηρίων τούτων ἐδεδοίκει ὁ Ἀ. id.*hom*.*14.5 in Gen*.(4.112E–113A); Thdt.*qu*.*18 in Gen*.(1.20); Sophr.H.*carm*.1.23(M.87.3733B); **5.** happiness πρὸ γὰρ τοῦ παραβῆναι τὸν Ἀ. οὔτε λύπη, οὔτε δειλία, οὐ κόπος, οὐ λιμός, οὐ θάνατος ἦν ‡Ath.*serm.fid*.24(p.21; M.26.1277D); ὁ Ἀ. ἦν...ἐν παραδείσῳ, καὶ ἐν ταῖς ἀνωτάτω τρυφαῖς, πνευματικαῖς δηλονότι καὶ δόξῃ τῇ παρὰ θεῷ Cyr.*Jo*.9(4.731B); οὐκ ἦν ἐν τῷ Ἀ. πρὸ τῆς παραβάσεως δάκρυον Jo.Clim.*scal*.7(M.88.809C); γυμνὸς ἦν ποτε ὁ Ἀ. καὶ ἡ Εὔα, καὶ οὐκ ᾐσχύνοντο· γυμνὸς τῇ ἁπλότητι, καὶ ἀτέχνῳ ζωῇ. οὐκ ἦσαν αὐτοῖς τέχναι καὶ βιωτικαὶ μέριμναι Jo.D.*hom*.2.3(M.96.580D); id.*f.o*.2.11(M.94.913B); **6.** perfection not absolute Ἀ. τέλειον μὲν ὡς πρὸς τὴν πλάσιν γεγονέναι φαμέν· οὐδὲν γὰρ τῶν χαρακτηριζόντων τὴν ἀνθρώπου ἰδέαν τε καὶ μορφὴν ἐνεδέησεν αὐτῷ Clem.*str*.4.23(p.315.6; M.8.1360B); τέλειος κατὰ τὴν κατασκευὴν οὐκ ἐγένετο, πρὸς δὲ τὸ ἀναδέξασθαι τὴν ἀρετὴν ἐπιτήδειος *ib*.6.12(p.480.7; M.9.317B); **7.** question whether state before Fall was state of childhood οὐ γὰρ ὡς οἴονταί τινες, θάνατον εἶχε τὸ ξύλον, ἀλλ' ἡ παρακοή. οὐ γάρ τι ἕτερον ἦν ἐν τῷ καρπῷ ἢ μόνον γνῶσις· ἡ δὲ γνῶσις καλή, ἐπὰν αὐτῇ οἰκείως τις χρήσηται. τῇ δὲ οὔσῃ ἡλικίᾳ ὁ Ἀ. ἔτι νήπιος ἦν, διὸ οὔπω ἠδύνατο τὴν γνῶσιν κατ' ἀξίαν χωρεῖν Thphl.Ant.*Autol*.2.25(M.6.1092A); cf. *non intellectum habebant filiorum generationis; oportebat enim illos primo adolescere dehinc sic multiplicari*, Iren.*haer*.3.22.4(M.7.359A); cf. ὁ θεὸς αὐτὸς μὲν οἷός τε ἦν παρασχεῖν ἀπ' ἀρχῆς τῷ ἀνθρώπῳ τὸ τέλειον, ὁ δὲ ἄνθρωπος ἀδύνατος λαβεῖν αὐτό· νήπιος γὰρ ἦν *ib*.4.38.1(1105C); cf.Clem.*str*. 3.17(p.243.19; M.8.1205B).

D. Fall; **1.** gravity of his sin, more serious than that of Eve ὁ δὲ Ἀ. οὐδὲν ὅλως μαχεσάμενος, ἢ ἀντιλέξας, τοῦ καρποῦ μετειλήφει δοθέντος παρὰ τῆς γυναικός· ὅπερ ἀσθενείας παντελοῦς καὶ νοὸς ἀνάνδρου ἐστὶν ἀπόδειξις. ἡ μὲν γὰρ γυνὴ ὑπὸ δαίμονος καταπαλαισθεῖσα, συγγνωστὴ ὑπάρχει· ὁ δὲ Ἀ., ὡς ὑπὸ γυναικὸς ἡττηθεὶς ἀσύγγνωστος ἔσται, ὡς αὐτοπροσώπως τὴν ἐντολὴν αὐτὸς ὑπὸ θεοῦ κομισάμενος Iren.*fr*.14(M.7.1237B); ἐπεὶ τί τὸν Ἀ. ὠφέλησεν ἡ τοσαύτη αὐτοῦ εὐγένεια;...τὰ μὲν αἰσχρὰ οὗτος προθύμως εἵλετο ἑπόμενος τῇ γυναικί, τῶν δὲ ἀληθῶν καὶ καλῶν ἠμέλησεν Clem.*str*. 2.19(p.166.20; M.8.1041A); though not so grave as that of Cain Or.*hom*.*16.4 in Jer*.(p.136.21; M.13.444C); **2.** committed by his own free will; this stressed against Manicheans ὅτε τὸν Ἀ. ἀρχῆθεν ἔπλασεν ὁ θεός, μήτιγε σύμφυτον αὐτῷ δέδωκε τὴν ἁμαρτίαν; τίς οὖν ἔτι χρεία ἦν τῆς ἐντολῆς; πῶς δὲ αὐτὸν κατεδίκασεν ἁμαρτήσαντα; πῶς δὲ καὶ πρὸ τῆς παρακοῆς οὐκ ἐγίνωσκε καλὸν καὶ πονηρὸν ὁ Ἀ.; ὃν ἔπλασεν ὁ θεὸς ἐπὶ ἀφθαρσίᾳ καὶ εἰκόνι τῆς ἰδίας ἀϊδιότητος, ἐποίησεν αὐτὸν φύσιν ἀναμάρτητον, καὶ θέλησιν αὐτεξούσιον· 'φθόνῳ δὲ διαβόλου θάνατος εἰσῆλθεν εἰς τὸν κόσμον', εὑραμένου τῆς παραβάσεως τὴν ἐπίνοιαν. καὶ οὕτως ἐκ παρακοῆς ἐντολῆς θεοῦ γέγονεν ὁ ἄνθρωπος δεκτικὸς τῆς ἐπισπορᾶς τοῦ ἐχθροῦ ‡Ath.*Apoll*.1.15(M.26.1120B); cf.*ib*.2.6(1140D); Mac.Aeg.*hom*.12.8(M.34.561B); Ἀδὰμ...οὐκ ἐξ ἀνάγκης κακός, ἀλλ' ἐξ ἀβουλίας γενόμενος Bas.*hom*.9.7(2.79Bf.; M.31. 344Cf.); cf.Epiph.*haer*.42.12(p.158.2; M.41.776D) cit. s. ἁμαρτία; Chrys.*serm*.*8.2 in Gen*.(4.686A); **3.** occasioned by Eve τῷ μὲν Ἀ. ἡ δοθεῖσα κατ' αὐτὸν βοηθός...ἀντὶ συνεργοῦ πολεμία κατέστη, καὶ οὐχ ὁμόζυγος, ἀλλ' ἀντίθετος Gr.Naz.*or*.18.8(M.35.993B); *ib*.36.5(M.36. 269C); πολλοὶ γὰρ ἐνόμισαν, ὅτι ἀγνοῶν ὁ Ἀ. ἔλαβε παρὰ τῆς γυναικός, οὐκ εἰδὼς πόθεν ἤγαγε τὸν καρπόν. ἀλλ' οὐκ ἔχει ἀπολογίαν· ὁ γὰρ θεὸς ἐλέγχει, λέγων αὐτῷ· 'ὅτι ἤκουσας τῆς φωνῆς τῆς γυναικός σου...' τὸ ἔγκλημα τοῦ ἀνδρός, οὐχ ὅτι ἠπατήθη, ἀλλ' ὅτι ἐδελεάσθη Sever. *creat*.6.5(M.56.490); and through her by Devil, ‡Ath.*serm.fid*.13 (p.9; M.26.1269B); Cyr.*Jo*.6(4.561D); **4.** discussion whether God was responsible, Chrys.*Stag*.1.5(1.166B); foreseen by God and remedied by Christ, Cyr.*Is*.3.5(2.524D).

E. consequences; **1.** loss of the 'image' and of grace ἔστι πρεσβύτερον ὥσπερ ἐν τῷ Ἀ. ἐκεῖνο ὃ οἱ πολλοὶ νοοῦσι τὸ κατ' εἰκόνα τοῦ προσειλημμένου αὐτῷ, ὅτε ἐφόρεσε διὰ τὴν ἁμαρτίαν τὴν εἰκόνα τοῦ χοϊκοῦ Or.*hom*.*2.1 in Jer*.(p.17.11; M.13.277C); ὁ Ἀ. τὴν ἐντολὴν παραβάς, κατὰ δύο τρόπους ἀπώλετο· ἕνα μέν, ὅτι ἀπώλεσε τὸ κτῆμα τὸ καθαρὸν τῆς φύσεως αὐτοῦ, τὸ ὡραῖον, τὸ κατ' εἰκόνα καὶ ὁμοίωσιν θεοῦ· ἕτερον δέ, ὅτι ἀπώλεσεν αὐτὴν τὴν εἰκόνα, ἐν ᾗ ἀπέκειτο αὐτῷ κατ' ἐπαγγελίαν ἡ ἐπουράνιος πᾶσα κληρονομία Mac.Aeg.*hom*.12.1 (M.34.557A); ὁ προπάτωρ Ἀ. οὐ διέσωσε τὴν τοῦ πνεύματος χάριν παρατραπεὶς ἐξ ἀπάτης εἰς παρακοὴν καὶ ἁμαρτίαν, ὅλη τε οὕτως ἐν αὐτῷ ἐζημιοῦτο λοιπὸν ἡ φύσις τὸ θεόσδοτον ἀγαθόν Cyr.*Jo.*5.2(4.472E); id.*Joel.*35(3.228B); Thdt.*Ps.*29:8(1.789); Devil becoming master of the soul (peculiar Messalian teaching), Mac.Aeg.*hom.* 15.35(600A); **2.** death and loss of heaven *εἴπερ οὖν ἡ πᾶσα γῆ αὐτῇ ἐπικατάρατος ἐν τοῖς ἔργοις ἐστὶ τοῦ Ἀ. καὶ τῶν ἐν αὐτῷ ἀποθανόντων, δῆλον ὅτι καὶ πάντα τὰ μόρια αὐτῆς μετέχει τῆς ἀρᾶς* Or.*Cels.*7.29(p.180.5; M.11.1461B); *ὁ θεὸς...τοὺς δερματίνους χιτῶνας διὰ τοῦτο κατεσκεύασεν, οἱονεὶ νεκρότητι ⟨τινὶ⟩ περιβαλὼν αὐτόν, ὅπως διὰ τῆς λύσεως τοῦ σώματος πᾶν τὸ ἐν αὐτῷ γεννηθὲν κακὸν ἀποθάνῃ* Meth.*res.*1.38(p.281.11ff.; M.18.293B); *ἑαυτῷ τὸν θάνατον ὁ Ἀ. διὰ τῆς ἀναχωρήσεως τοῦ θεοῦ κατεσκεύασε...οὕτως οὐχὶ θεὸς ἔκτισε θάνατον, ἀλλ' ἡμεῖς ἑαυτοῖς ἐκ πονηρᾶς γνώμης ἐπεσπασάμεθα* Bas.*hom.*9.7(2.79C; M.31.345A); Cyr.H.*catech.*13.2; Thdt.*eran.*3(4.198); cf. *τοὺς οὐρανούς, οὓς ὁ Ἀ. ἔκλεισεν ἑαυτῷ τε καὶ τοῖς μετ' αὐτόν* Gr.Naz.*or.*39.16(M.36.353B); v. *ἀθανασία*; Pelagian view, that Adam would have been subject to physical death even if he had not sinned, condemned, *Cod.Afr.*109; **3.** partial loss of knowledge and dominion over creatures *πρώτη τέχνη τοῦ Ἀ. ῥαπτική. πρὸ πάσης τέχνης ἔλαβε τὰ φύλλα τῆς συκῆς, καὶ ἔρραψε. τίς ὁ διδάξας; τίς ὁ παιδεύσας; ἔλαβεν ἅπαξ παρὰ θεοῦ σύνεσιν, εἰκὼν ἦν θεοῦ, καὶ ἀμφιβάλλεις περὶ τὴν γνῶσιν;* Sever.*creat.*6.6(M.56.492); *ὁ μὲν γὰρ Ἀ. πᾶσαν ἀνέτρεψε τὴν ἐντολήν, καὶ παρέβη τὸν νόμον· ὁ δὲ θεὸς οὐ πᾶσαν ἔλυσε τὴν τιμήν, οὐδὲ πάσης ἐξέβαλεν αὐτὸν τῆς ἐξουσίας· ἀλλ' ἐκεῖνα μόνα ἔξω τῆς ἀρχῆς ἀφῆκεν εἶναι τὰ ζῶα, ἃ μὴ σφόδρα αὐτῷ συντελεῖ πρὸς τὴν τῆς ζωῆς χρείαν. τὰ δὲ ἀναγκαῖα... εἰς τὴν ζωὴν τὴν ἡμετέραν, ταῦτα εἴασε μένειν ἐν τῇ δουλείᾳ* Chrys.*serm.3.2 in Gen.*(4.657D); **4.** but punishment designed to lead Adam to repentance, cf.Iren.*haer.*3.23.5(M.7.963A); *παρήκουσεν Ἀ. ... ἆρ' οὐκ ἐδύνατο τὸν θάνατον εὐθὺς ἐπαγαγεῖν; ἀλλ' ὅρα τί ποιεῖ ὁ φιλανθρωπότατος κύριος. ἐκβάλλει μὲν αὐτὸν τοῦ παραδείσου (τῆς γὰρ ἐκεῖ διατριβῆς ἀνάξιος ἦν διὰ τὴν ἁμαρτίαν), κατοικίζει δὲ τοῦ παραδείσου κατέναντι· ἵνα βλέπων ὅθεν ἐξέπεσε...λοιπὸν ἐκ μετανοίας σωθῇ* Cyr.H.*catech.*2.6; and to put an end to sin, Meth.*res.*1.40 (p.284.12ff.; M.41.1108C).

F. salvation; **1.** denied by Tatian and Marcion, cf.Iren.*haer.*1.28.1(M.7.691A); *τὸν δὲ Ἀ. φάσκει* [sc. Marcion] *μὴ σῴζεσθαι διὰ τὸ ἀρχηγὸν παρακοῆς γεγονέναι. καὶ ταῦτα μὲν Τατιανός* Hipp.*haer.*8.16(p.236.10; M.16.3363B); Epiph.*haer.*46.2(p.205.4; M.41.840B); **2.** affirmed, cf. *cum autem salvetur homo, oportet salvari eum qui prior formatus est homo. quoniam nimis irrationabile est, illum quidem, qui vehementer ab inimico laesus est, et prior captivitatem passus est, dicere non eripi ab eo qui vicerit inimicum*, Iren.*haer.*3.23.2 (M.7.961A); *ib.*3.23.7(964C); cf. *hi, qui contradicunt saluti Adae, nihil proficiunt, nisi hoc, quod semetipsos haereticos et apostatas faciunt veritatis*, *ib.*3.23.8(965B); cf.Or.*comm.ser.126 in Mt.*(p.265.7; M.13.1777C); *εἰ ὁ Ἀ. οὐ σῴζεται, τὸ φύραμα, οὐδέ τι ⟨τῶν ἀπὸ⟩ τοῦ φυράματος σῴζεται. εἰ γὰρ ὁ πρωτόπλαστος καὶ ἐξ ἀθίκτου γῆς γενόμενος σωτηρίας οὐ μεθέξει, πῶς τὰ ἐξ αὐτοῦ γεγεννημένα ἕξει σωτηρίαν;* Epiph.*haer.*46.2(p.206.12; M.41.841A); *ib.*46.3(p.207.8; 841C); proved by parable of good Samaritan, man who fell among thieves signifying Adam, *ib.*46.4(p.208.10; 844B); **3.** delivered by Christ in his descent to Hades, cf. *extendens dominus manum suam fecit signum crucis super A. ... et tenens dexteram Adae ascendit ab inferis*, *A.Pil.*B 2.8(p.403); cf.Hipp.*cant.Mos.*(p.83.8; M.10.612A)ap. Thdt.*eran.*2(4.131); †Gr.Thaum.*sanct.*(M.10.1201B); Mac.Aeg.*hom.* 11.10(M.34.552B); *ὁ δὲ Ἐμμανουὴλ...τὸν εἰς τὸν ᾅδην κείμενον Ἀ. εἰς τοὺς οὐρανοὺς ἀνεβίβασε* Thdt.*Is.*7:14(p.38.8; 2.218); cf. *ᾅδης*; **4.** of Adam as signifying human race, Gr.Naz.*carm.*1.2.38.158ff.(M.37.534A–535A); Proc.G.*Is.*7:10ff.(M.87.1965B); id.*Gen.*1:27(M.87.133B).

G. burial on Golgotha *περὶ τοῦ κρανίου τόπου ἦλθεν εἰς ἐμέ, ὅτι Ἑβραῖοι παραδιδόασι τὸ σῶμα τοῦ Ἀ. ἐκεῖ τετάφθαι, ἵν' ἐπεὶ ἐν τῷ Ἀ. πάντες ἀποθνήσκομεν, ἀναστῇ μὲν ὁ Ἀ., ἐν Χριστῷ δὲ πάντες ζῳοποιηθῶμεν* Or.*comm.ser.126 in Mt.*(p.265.5ff.; M.13.1777C); *ὁ Χριστὸς...οὐδὲ εἰς ἄλλον τόπον σταυροῦται, ἢ εἰς τὸν κρανίου τόπον, ὃν Ἑβραίων οἱ διδάσκαλοί φασι τοῦ Ἀ. εἶναι τάφον...ἔδει γὰρ τὸν κύριον, ἀνανεῶσαι θέλοντα τὸν πρῶτον Ἀ., ἐν ἐκείνῳ τῷ τόπῳ παθεῖν, ἵνα, ἐκείνου λύων τὴν ἁμαρτίαν, ἀπὸ παντὸς αὐτὴν ἄρῃ τοῦ γένους* ‡Ath.*pass.*12(M.28.208A); ‡Ath.*qu.Ant.*47(M.28.628B); †Bas.*Is.*141 (1.478Bf.; M.30.348C); Epiph.*haer.*46.5(p.208.17; M.41.844C); Chrys.*hom.85.1 in Jo.*(8.504A); Nonn.*par.Jo.*19:17(M.43.901B); ‡Bas.Sel.*or.*38.3(M.85.409A); ‡Germ.CP *contempl.*(M.98.396C).

H. comparison with other persons; **1.** good thief *εἴσοδον ἐν τῷ παραδείσῳ, ἐξ οὗ ἐκβέβληται Ἀ., εἰς ὃν πάλιν εἰσῆλθε διὰ τοῦ λῃστοῦ* †Ath.*exp.fid.*1(M.25.201B); Cyr.H.*catech.*13.31; *τὸν δὲ λῃστήν, καὶ σὺν αὐτῷ τὸν Ἀ. ... ὁ υἱὸς εἰσήγαγεν* Didym.*Trin.*1.16(M.39.336C); v. *λῃστής*; **2.** heretics *Ἀ. παραβὰς ῥάπτειν ἔμαθεν· αἱρετικοὶ ἐκτραπέντες σχίζειν ἔμαθον* Sever.*creat.*6.6(M.56.493); **3.** God, in comparison of Church with Eve, Anast.S.*hex.*12(M.89.1072B) cit. s. *πλευρά*.

I. first and second Adam; **1.** in gen.; Christ the second Adam, cf. *a Paulo 'typus futuri' dictus est ipse Adam; quoniam futuram circa filium dei humani generis dispositionem in semetipsum fabricator omnium verbum praeformaverat, praeformante deo primum animalem hominem, videlicet ut a spirituali salvaretur*, Iren.*haer.*3.22.3(M.7.958A); *οὐ μόνον πρωτότοκός ἐστιν* [sc. *Χριστός*] *πάσης κτίσεως, ἀλλὰ καὶ Ἀ. ... ὅτι δὲ Ἀ. ἐστι φησὶν ὁ Παῦλος* Or.*Jo.* 1.18(20; p.23.7; M.14.56A); which name proves his true humanity, ‡Ath.*serm.fid.*15(p.10; M.26.1269D); *ib.*25(p.21; 1277D); *ὁ γὰρ τῶν ὅλων δημιουργὸς λόγος ὤφθη υἱὸς ἀνθρώπου, οὐχ ἕτερός τις γενόμενος, ἀλλὰ δεύτερος Ἀ.· ἵνα καὶ ἐκ τοῦ ὀνόματος γινώσκωμεν τὴν ἀλήθειαν* ‡Ath.*Apoll.*1.8(M.26.1105B); *ψυχὴν καὶ σῶμα καὶ ὅλον τὸν πρῶτον μεμαθήκαμεν ἔχειν τὸν δεύτερον Ἀ.* *ib.*2.10(1149A); Bas.*Spir.*14(3.26A; M.32.121C); **2.** Adam as type of Christ; **a.** in coming into existence without human father, cf. *quemadmodum protoplastus ille Adam de rudi terra, et de adhuc virgine...habuit substantiam... ita recapitulans in se Adam, ipse verbum exsistens ex Maria, quae adhuc erat virgo, recte accipiebat generationem Adae recapitulationis*, *εἰ τοίνυν ὁ πρῶτος Ἀ. ἔσχε πατέρα ἄνθρωπον, καὶ ἐξ ἀνδρὸς σπέρματος ἐγεννήθη, εἰκὸς ἦν καὶ τὸν δεύτερον Ἀ. λέγειν ἐξ Ἰωσὴφ γεγεννῆσθαι* Iren.*haer.*3.21.10(M.7.954C–955A); Proc.G.*Is.*7:10ff.(M.87.1964D); Max.*qu.Thal.*21(M.90.312B); **b.** in sleep *γεγράφηκάς μοι λέγων,...περιττὸν...τὸ ἀγρυπνεῖν, ἐπειδὴ τὸν ὕπνον τῷ Ἀ. ὁ θεὸς ἐπέβαλεν...τὸ μὲν τῷ Ἀ. κατ' ἀρχὰς γενόμενον αἰσθητῶς, μυστήριον νοητὸν ὑπηνίττετο, ἐσήμανε γὰρ τὸν δεύτερον Ἀ., τουτέστιν τὸν... Χριστόν, μέλλειν ὑπνοῦν τὸν ἀνθρώπινον θάνατον ἐν τῷ σταυρῷ* Nil.*epp.*1.26(M.79.92C); cf. *ἔκστασις*; **c.** in fatherhood *πᾶσα γὰρ ἀρχὴ πατριῶν τῶν ὡς πρὸς τὸν τῶν ὅλων θεὸν κατωτέρω ἀπὸ Χριστοῦ ἤρξατο τοῦ μετὰ τὸν τῶν ὅλων θεὸν καὶ πατέρα οὕτω πατρὸς ὄντος πάσης ψυχῆς, ὡς ὁ Ἀ. πατήρ ἐστι πάντων τῶν ἀνθρώπων* Or.*princ.* 4.3.7(p.333.23; M.11.388A); **d.** Adam himself assumed by Christ *φέρε γὰρ ἡμεῖς ἐπισκεψώμεθα, πῶς ὀρθοδόξως ἀνήγαγε τὸν Ἀ. εἰς τὸν Χριστόν, οὐ μόνον αὐτὸν τύπον ἡγούμενος εἶναι καὶ εἰκόνα, ἀλλὰ καὶ αὐτὸ τοῦτο Χριστὸν καὶ αὐτὸν γεγονέναι διὰ τὸ τὸν πρὸ αἰώνων εἰς αὐτὸν ἐγκατασκῆψαι λόγον. ἥρμοζε γὰρ τὸ πρωτόγονον τοῦ θεοῦ... τὴν σοφίαν τῷ πρωτοπλάστῳ...ἀνθρώπῳ κερασθεῖσαν ἐνηνθρωπηκέναι. τοῦτο γὰρ εἶναι τὸν Χριστὸν...ἦν γὰρ πρεπωδέστατον τὸν πρεσβύτατον τῶν αἰώνων καὶ πρῶτον τῆς ἀνθρωπότητος ἄνθρωπον εἰσοικισθῆναι τὸν Ἀ.* Meth.*symp.*3.4(p.30.17ff.; M.18.65A–68A); similar view held by some Ebionites *τινὲς γὰρ ἐξ αὐτῶν καὶ Ἀ. τὸν Χριστὸν εἶναι λέγουσιν, τὸν πρῶτόν τε πλασθέντα καὶ ἐμφυσηθέντα ἀπὸ τῆς τοῦ θεοῦ ἐπιπνοίας...ἔρχεσθαι δὲ ἐνταῦθα ὅτε βούλεται, ὡς καὶ ἐν τῷ Ἀ. ἦλθε...ὁ αὐτὸς ἐπ' ἐσχάτων τῶν ἡμερῶν ἦλθεν καὶ αὐτὸ τὸ σῶμα τοῦ Ἀ. ἐνεδύσατο καὶ ὤφθη ἀνθρώποις καὶ ἐσταυρώθη καὶ ἀνέστη καὶ ἀνῆλθεν* Epiph.*haer.*30.3(p.336.5–337.5; M.41.409A,B); **e.** time Adam spent in paradise compared with Christ's temptation in wilderness ‡Caes.Naz.*dial.*122(M.38.1009); **3.** Adam as type of Christ by contrast; **a.** difference of origin; ‡Ath.*serm.fid.*25(p.22; M.26.1280A,B); *γένηται δεύτερος Ἀ., οὐκ ἀπὸ γῆς, ἀλλ' ἐξ οὐρανοῦ, καὶ ἀρχὴ γένηται τῇ ἀνθρώπου φύσει παντὸς ἀγαθοῦ* Cyr.*Jo.*2(4.114B); **b.** different outcome of temptation, *A.Barth.*5(12; p.139.22); *πεῖραν προσάγει* [sc. Devil] *τῷ ἀπειράστῳ (ἐπειδὴ δεύτερον Ἀ. εἶδε τοῦ θεοῦ φαινόμενον)* Gr.Naz.*or.*24.9(M.35.1180B); *ib.*39.2(M.36.336B); *ib.*41.4 (433A); **c.** obedience and disobedience, cf. *in illa die mortem sustinuit dominus, obediens patri, in qua mortuus est Adam inobediens deo*, Iren.*haer.*5.23.2(M.7.1185C); Cyr.*Jo.*11.10(4.991D,E); *ib.*10.1(854A); *ib.*12(1045A); **d.** Adam bringing death and damnation, Christ life and salvation, ‡Ath.*Apoll.*1.7(M.26.1105A); *τύπος ἐστὶ τοῦ Χριστοῦ ὁ Ἀ. ... ὅτι, ὥσπερ ἐκεῖνος τοῖς ἐξ αὐτοῦ, καίτοιγε μὴ φαγοῦσιν ἀπὸ τοῦ ξύλου, γέγονεν αἴτιος θανάτου τοῦ διὰ τὴν βρῶσιν εἰσαχθέντος, οὕτω καὶ ὁ Χριστὸς τοῖς ἐξ αὐτοῦ, καίτοιγε οὐ δικαιοπραγήσασι, γέγονε πρόξενος δικαιοσύνης, ἣν διὰ τοῦ σταυροῦ πᾶσιν ἡμῖν ἐχαρίσατο* Chrys.*hom.10.1 in Rom.*(9.520C); Cyr.*dogm.*6(p.560.10ff.; 6².375D–376B); id.*Jo.*5.2(4.473C); *ὡς γὰρ τοῦ Ἀ. ἡ καθ' ἡδονὴν ζωή, θανάτου καὶ φθορᾶς γέγονε μήτηρ· οὕτω καὶ ὁ διὰ τὸν Ἀ. τοῦ κυρίου θάνατος, ὑπάρχων τῆς ἐκ τοῦ Ἀ. ἐλεύθερος ἡδονῆς, ἀϊδίου γεννήτωρ γίνεται ζωῆς* Max.*qu.Thal.*61(M.90.632D); **e.** detailed descriptions comparing Fall of first with Passion of second Adam *ξύλον κατὰ τοῦ ξύλου, καὶ κατὰ τῆς χειρὸς χεῖρες, τῆς ἀκρατῶς ἐκταθείσης αἱ γενναίως ταθεῖσαι· τῆς ἀνειμένης αἱ τοῖς ἥλοις δεθεῖσαι· τῆς ἐκβαλούσης Ἀ. αἱ τὰ πέρατα οἰκειούμεναι. διὰ τοῦτο ὕψος κατὰ τοῦ πτώματος...ταῦτα πάντα παιδαγωγία τις ἦν περὶ ἡμᾶς τοῦ θεοῦ, καὶ τῆς ἀσθενείας ἰατρεία τῆς ἡμετέρας, τὸν παλαιὸν Ἀ. ὅθεν ἐξέπεσεν ἐπανάγουσα, καὶ τῷ ξύλῳ τῆς ζωῆς προσάγουσα, οὗ τὸ ξύλον ἡμᾶς τῆς* γνώσεως...ἠλλοτρίωσε Gr.Naz.*or.*2.25(M.35.433C–436A); ὁ δεύτερος Ἀ. τὸν πρῶτον...ἀπεκάθηρε. παρήκουσε τοῦ θεοῦ ὁ πρῶτος καὶ πᾶσι θάνατον προεξένησεν. ὑπήκουσεν ὁ Χριστὸς τῷ ἰδίῳ πατρὶ...καὶ τὴν παρακοὴν...ἐθεράπευσεν...διὰ τοῦτο ὁ Ἰησοῦς ἀκάνθαις ἐστεφανώθη, ἵνα συντρίψῃ ἐκείνας τὰς ἀκάνθας τῆς ἁμαρτίας...ἐκεῖνος τῇ ἕκτῃ ὥρᾳ ἐν τῷ παραδείσῳ ἐπὶ τὸ ξύλον ἐξέτεινε τὴν χεῖρα κακῶς· ὁ Χριστὸς τῇ ἕκτῃ ὥρᾳ τῆς ἕκτης ἡμέρας ἐν τῷ κήπῳ τοῦ Γολγοθᾶ ἐξέτεινεν ἐν τῷ ξύλῳ τὰς χεῖρας καλῶς Eulog.*fr.Trin.*3.5ff.(pp.367ff.).

J. Gnost.; **1.** created by demiurge τὸν Ἀ. ὁ δημιουργὸς Ἐννοίᾳ προσχὼν ἐπὶ τέλει τῆς δημιουργίας αὐτὸν προήγαγεν Clem.*exc.Thdot.*41(p.119.30; M.9.680A); acc. Manicheans by ἄρχοντες, Hegem.*Arch.*12(p.19.13ff.; M.10.1445cf.); causing fear to his creators, Val.Gn. ap.Clem.*str.*2.8(p.132.14; M.8.972B); created with four natures τοῖς τρισὶν ἀσωμάτοις [sc. ἡ ἄλογος, ἡ λογικὴ καὶ δικαία, ἡ πνευματική] ἐπὶ τοῦ Ἀ. τέταρτον ἐπενδύεται ὁ χοϊκὸς τοὺς δερματίνους χιτῶνας. οὔτ' οὖν ἀπὸ τοῦ πνεύματος οὔτ' οὖν ἀπὸ τοῦ ἐμφυσήματος σπείρει ὁ Ἀ.· θεῖα γὰρ ἄμφω, καὶ δι' αὐτοῦ μέν, οὐχ ὑπ' αὐτοῦ δέ, προβάλλεται ἄμφω· τὸ δὲ ὑλικὸν αὐτοῦ ἐνεργὸν εἰς σπέρμα καὶ γένεσιν,...κατὰ τοῦτο πατὴρ ἡμῶν ὁ Ἀ. Clem.*exc.Thdot.*55f.(p.125.8ff.; M.9.685B); receiving spiritual seed from Sophia, *ib.*53(p.124.26; 685A); **2.** alleged blindness, acc. 'Simon Magus' ὁ καθ' ὁμοίωσιν αὐτοῦ [sc. δημιουργοῦ] γεγονὼς Ἀ. καὶ τυφλὸς κτίζεται καὶ γνῶσιν ἀγαθοῦ ἢ κακοῦ οὐκ ἔχων παραδέδοται, καὶ παραβάτης εὑρίσκεται *Hom.Clem.*3.39; 'Peter's' reply οὐκ ἦν. οὐ γὰρ ἂν τυφλῷ ἐντελλόμενος ἐδείκνυε λέγων· 'ἀπὸ δὲ τοῦ ξύλου...μὴ γεύσεσθε.' καὶ ὁ Σίμων· τυφλὸν ἔλεγε τὸν νοῦν αὐτοῦ. καὶ ὁ Πέτρος· πῶς καὶ τὸν νοῦν τυφλὸς εἶναι ἐδύνατο, ὁ πρὸ τοῦ γεύσασθαι τοῦ φυτοῦ συμφώνως τῷ κτίσαντι αὐτὸν οἰκεῖα πᾶσι τοῖς ζῴοις ἐπιθεὶς ὀνόματα; *ib.*3.42; τυφλοὶ δὲ οὐκ ἦσαν· ἔβλεπον γάρ· εἰ μὴ γὰρ ἔβλεπον, πῶς εἶδον τὸ ξύλον, ὅτι 'καλὸν εἰς βρῶσιν καὶ ὡραῖον τοῦ κατανοῆσαι'; Epiph.*anc.*20(p.28.26; M.43.53A); **3.** grovelling on all fours, cf.*A.Phil.*140(p.74.5); *A.Petr.et Sim.*9(p.9.4.6); **4.** in Gnost. astrology τὸν ἐν γόνασί φασιν εἶναι τὸν Ἀ., κατὰ πρόσταγμα, φησίν, τοῦ θεοῦ, καθὼς εἶπε Μωσῆς, φυλάσσοντα τὴν κεφαλὴν τοῦ Δράκοντος Hipp.*haer.*4.47(p.70.7; M.16.3111D); εἰ οὖν, φησίν [sc. ὁ Ἄρατος], ἐξομολογούμενος ὁ Ἀ. καὶ τὴν κεφαλὴν φυλάσσων τοῦ θηρίου κατὰ τὸ πρόσταγμα τοῦ θεοῦ ἐκμιμήσεται τὴν λύραν, τουτέστι κατακολουθήσει τῷ ⟨λόγῳ⟩ τοῦ θεοῦ, τοῦτ' ἔστι πειθόμενος τῷ νόμῳ, παρακείμενον αὐτῷ τὸν στέφανον λήψεται. ἐὰν δὲ ἀμελήσῃ, συγκατενεχθήσεται τῷ ὑποκειμένῳ θηρίῳ...πρώτη γάρ, φησίν, κτίσις ἡ κατὰ τὸν Ἀ. ἐν πόνοις, ⟨ὅ ἐστιν⟩ ὁ ἐν γόνασιν ὁρώμενος· δευτέρα δὲ κτίσις ἐστὶν ἡ κατὰ Χριστόν, δι' ἧς ἀναγεννώμεθα *ib.*4.48(p.71.3ff.; 3114Bff.); *ib.*4.49(p.73.16; 3118A); **5.** identified with first man in Samothracian mysteries, Hipp.*haer.*5.8(p.90.25; 3142B).

***Ἀδαμά, ἡ,** (Hebr. אֲדָמָה) *earth*, †Bas.*Is.*300(1.606E; M.30.644C).

ἀδάμας (A), ὁ, *adamant*; hard metal, met. of strength: of Christ, exeg. Am.7:8, Cyr.*Am.*68(3.326B); id.*Jo.*4.7(4.435E); of strength men receive from him λόγος...ἄνθρωπον...εἰς ἀ. τρέψας Hipp.*cant. Mos.*(p.83.13; M.10.612A)ap.Thdt.*eran.*2(4.132); Or.*sel.in Jer.*50:23 (M.13.597B); of strong souls, Eus.*l.C.*17(p.257.5; M.20.1436A); of S. Paul ὁ πνευματικὸς ἀ. Chrys.*hom.2.4 in Rom.*(9.441D); id.*hom.28.4 in Heb.*(12.261A); of Job, id.*hom.15.5 in Mt.*(7.192C); of a hard nature, Bas.*ep.*5.1(3.77C; M.32.237C).

***Ἀδάμας (B), ὁ,** *Adamas*, Gnost. name of archetypal man, heavenly counterpart of Adam ἄνθρωπον τέλειον καὶ ἀληθῆ ὃν καὶ Ἀ. καλοῦσι Iren.*haer.*1.29.3(M.7.693C); ἄνθρωπος...ἀρσενόθηλυς, καλεῖται δὲ Ἀ. Hipp.*haer.*5.6(p.78.7; M.16.3126A); ἀρχανθρώπου ἄνωθεν Ἀ. *ib.*5.7(p.88.1; 3138B); τὰ νοερά, καὶ ψυχικά, καὶ χοϊκὰ [sc. of Adamas] κεχώρηκε...εἰς ἕνα ἄνθρωπον ὁμοῦ, Ἰησοῦν *ib.*5.6(p.78.16f.; 3126B).

ἀδάμαστος, 1. *not broken to the yoke, untamed*; met., of novices, Isid.Pel.*epp.*1.258(M.78.337B); hence **2.** *innocent* τοὺς ἀ. πονηρίᾳ Clem.*paed.*1.5(p.98.26; M.8.265B); **3.** *untameable*, hence *indestructible, immortal, eternal*; of angels and souls, Meth.*res.*1.47(p.297.9; M.41.1117C); of time, Nonn.*par.Jo.*10:18(M.43.836A); of Lazarus ἀ. ... νεκρόν *ib.*11:44(845C).

***Ἀδαμιαῖος,** *belonging to Adam*, hence *human*, ‡Sophr.H.*liturg.* 16(M.87.3996D); †Jo.D.*B.J.*12(M.96.976C); οἱ Ἀ. *the race of Adam*, ‡Meth.*Sym.et Ann.*8(M.18.368C).

***Ἀδαμιανοί, οἱ,** *Adamites*; sect claiming primitive innocence and discarding clothes in religious assemblies, Epiph.*haer.*52 tit. (p.311.9; M.41.953Cff.); Jo.D.*haer.*52(M.94.709A).

***Ἀδαμῖται, οἱ,** = foreg., Thdt.*haer.*1.6(4.295f.), where origin ascribed to Prodicus; cf.Clem.*str.*3.4(p.209.30; M.8.1136A).

***ἀδαπανήτως,** *without being exhausted*, Niceph.Ur.*v.Sym.*243 (M.86.3209A).

***ἀδβοκᾶτος, ὁ,** (Lat. *advocatus*) *advocate*, Gr.Mag.*dial.*(tr.Zach.) 4.26(M.*PL.*77.359A).

[*]ἀδδηφαγία, ἡ, = ἀδηφαγία, *gluttony*, Nil.*epp.*3.106(M.79.433C); Thdt.*h.rel.*13(3.1210).

[*]ἀδδηφάγος, = ἀδηφάγος, *gluttonous*, Synes.*ep.*132(M.66.1517B; ἀδηφάγος *EG*).

ἄδεια, ἡ, *absence of fear*; hence **1.** *freedom* ἄ. τοῦ εἰσιέναι Thdr. Mops.*Joel* 1:13ff.(M.66.217A); Thdt.*provid.*2(4.502); Philost.*h.e.*7.1 (M.65.537A); **2.** *licentiousness*, Just.*dial.*1.5(M.6.476A); Athenag.*leg.* 3.1(M.6.896C); ψευδοπροφήτης...ᾧ ἕπεται ἄ. Anon.ap.Eus.*h.e.*5.17.2 (M.20.473A).

***ἀδείλανδρος,** *without fear of man, undaunted*, *A.(Pass.)Andr.* 7(p.17.20; M.2.1229B); Ephr.1.204A.

***ἀδείλαντος,** *fearless*, Thdr.Stud.*epp.*2.100(M.99.1353C).

***ἀδειλία, ἡ,** *freedom from fear, courage*; of martyrs, Pall.*v.Chrys.* 18(p.118.19; M.47.66); id.*ep.Laus.*(p.7.12; M.34.1002); Jo.Clim.*past.* 13(M.88.1192D).

***ἀδειλίατος,** *free from fear*, ref. Mt.26:38 ἀπαθὲς...τὸ θεῖον καὶ... ἀ. Sever.ap.Max.*opusc.*(M.91.165B).

ἄδειλος, *fearless* πέπειρόν τε καὶ ἄ. *Clem.ep.*13(*GCS* p.16.1); ἀ. τῇ παρρησίᾳ Pall.*v.Chrys.*9(p.56.12; M.47.33).

ἀδεισιδαίμων, *not superstitious* γνωστικὸς...καὶ ἀ. Clem.*str.*7.4 (p.16.12; M.9.428B).

ἀδέκαστος, *unbribed, impartial, just*; esp. of divine judgement, Gr.Nyss.*v.Mos.*(M.44.412B); Chrys.*hom.20.6 in Mt.*(7.267E); ἀ. βήματι τοῦ Χριστοῦ Dor.*doct.*20(M.88.1812B); neut. as subst., *impartiality, integrity* ἐπιρρώσει τῷ ἀ. τὸ συνειδὸς Men.*exc.Rom.*5 (p.190.11; M.113.880D); τῆς μελλούσης θείας κρίσεως τὸ ἀ. ‡Caes. Naz.*dial.*71(M.38.940).

ἄδεκτος, *not received, unacceptable* ἡ κακία...ἄ. τῷ θεῷ Or.*exp. in Pr.*4(M.17.172B); of Cain's offering, Bas.Sel.*or.*4.3(M.85.69A); hence *excommunicate*, Bas.*ep.*217 *can.*81(3.329D; M.32.805B); πίστιν τὴν ὀρθὴν...ἧς ἐκτὸς λέγειν ἄδεκτον Rom.Mel.(*AS* 1 p.198).

ἀδελφή, ἡ, *sister*; **1.** in gen., of Christian women (cf. ἀδελφός), Ign.*Polyc.*5.1; *Const.App.*2.58.1; **2.** of nuns, Bas.*reg.br.*104(2.452A; M.31.1153C); *ib.*108(453A; 1156C); Max.*ep.*11(M.91.457A); **3.** of BMV; in proof of reality of Inc. τῆς θεοτόκου, ἀ. τε ἡμῶν οὔσης κατὰ τὴν φύσιν Leont.B.*Nest.et Eut.*2(M.86.1325C); χαῖρε, ἀ., ἡ τοῦ καλοῦ ἀδελφοῦ παρώνυμος Thdr.Stud.*nativ.BMV* 7(M.96.693A); **4.** ref. chaste relations of a woman with a man; **a.** of a wife τῇ συμβίῳ σου τῇ μελλούσῃ σου ἀ. Herm.*vis.*2.2.3; Clem.*str.*6.12(p.482.7; M.9. 321A); of wives of apostles, *ib.*3.6(p.220.21; M.8.1157A); exeg. 1Cor. 9:5 ἀ. μὲν εἶπεν, ἵνα τὴν ἁγνείαν ἐμφανίσῃ Isid.Pel.*epp.*3.176(M.78. 863B); λέγει ὁ ἀνὴρ τῇ γυναικί· 'ἀ.' Jo.Mosch.*prat.*185(M.87.3060B); **b.** of any woman, Herm.*vis.*1.1.1; *ib.*1.1.7; **c.** of *virgines subintroductae* τὰς...συνερχομένας παρθένους τισὶν ὡς ἀ. ἐκωλύσαμεν CAnc.(314)*can.*19; **d.** of 'sisters' falsely so called, living together with men, Iren.*haer.*1.6.3(M.7.509A); **5.** met. εἰρήνη καὶ ἀγάπη... ἀδελφαί Clem.*paed.*1.12(p.149.17; M.8.369A); of Wisdom (Pr.7:4) ἀ. ἡμῶν σοφία ἐστί, διότι ὁ ποιήσας τὴν ἀσώματον φύσιν πατήρ, καὶ ταύτην πεποίηκεν Or.*exp.in Pr.*7:4(M.17.180D); of prayer and fasting τὴν ἀ. τῆς νηστείας...τὴν εὐχήν Chrys.*poenit.*5.1(2.309E); Σιὼν εἶναί φαμεν τὴν νοητὴν ἐπὶ γῆς ἐκκλησίαν, ἣ καὶ ἀ. τῆς ἄνω νοεῖται Cyr.*Ps.*9:12(M.69.768C); myst., of the soul πρὸς τὴν ἐπὶ τὰ μείζω τε καὶ ὑψηλότερα τῆς καρδίας ἀνάβασιν, οἷον ἀ. καὶ νύμφη τοῦ λόγου κατονομάζεται Gr.Nyss.*hom.9 in Cant.*(M.44.968A); ἀ. μὲν ἡμετέρα [sc. ἀγγέλων] διὰ τὴν τῆς ἀπαθείας συγγένειαν *ib.8*(948B); which must become Christ's sister, in order to be united to him εἰ γὰρ βούλει ...ἐπαρθῆναι τῆς ψυχῆς σου τὰς πύλας, ἵνα εἰσέλθῃ ὁ βασιλεὺς τῆς δόξης, χρή σε ἀ. μου γενέσθαι *ib.11*(1001D); ref. question why 'bride' is called ἀ.: ἀ. καὶ νύμφην αὐτὴν ὀνομάζει, ἵνα δείξῃ, ὅτι οὐκ ἔστιν ὁ θάλαμος ἐπαδόμενος σαρκός· ὅταν μὲν γὰρ ὀνομάζει αὐτὴν νύμφην, διὰ τὸν λόγον, τὸν μνηστευθέντα τὴν ψυχήν...ὅταν δὲ καὶ ἀ. αὐτὴν ὀνομάζει, διὰ τὴν σάρκα ἣν ἐφόρεσε Ath.*fr.6 in Cant.*(M.27. 1357C).

***Ἀδελφιανοί, οἱ,** *Adelphians*; sect identical with Messalians (Euchites) called after one of its leaders, Adelphius, Tim.CP *haer.* (M.86.48A); cf.Thdt.*h.e.*4.11.2(3.965).

ἀδελφιδέος (-οῦς, -ός), ὁ, 1. lit., *nephew*, of Christ ὅς ἐστιν ἡμῶν καὶ ἀ. ὡς ἐξ ἀδελφῆς...δεσποίνης γεγεννημένος Cyr.*Joel.*7(3.205A); ἐπειδὴ...ἀδελφαί...ἥ τε Ἰουδαίων πληθύς, καὶ ἡ ἐξ ἐθνῶν ἐκκλησία, ἐκείνης δὲ υἱὸς ὁ Χριστὸς τὸ κατὰ σάρκα· εἰκότως αὐτὸν ἀ. ἡ νύμφη καλεῖ Thdt.*Cant.*1:12(2.49); **2.** met., = *beloved one, friend* ἡ γὰρ πρότερον δούλη ψυχὴ νῦν [sc. in baptism] ἀ. ... τὸν δεσπότην ἐπεγράψατο Cyr.H.*catech.*3.16; Χριστὸς...ἀ. τῆς ποθούσης κατωνομάσθη Gr. Nyss.*hom.4 in Cant.*(M.44.836B).

ἀδελφικῶς, *in brotherly manner*, Gr.Naz.*or.*6.11(M.35.736A); Chrys.*hom.44.4 in 1Cor.*(10.413C); Isid.Pel.*epp.*1.10(M.78.185B).

ἀδελφίς, ἡ, *sister*; of Christian women, *A.Thom.*A 88(p.203.6); of nuns, Ephr.2.394E.

***ἀδελφογαμέω**, *marry one's sister*; of Zeus, *Clem.epit.*A 51.

***ἀδελφογαμία**, ἡ, **1.** *marriage of brother and sister*; ref. first generations of men, Diod.*Gen.*5:4ff.(M.33.1569C); **2.** *incest of brother and sister*, Gr.Nyss.*fat.*(M.45.169B).

***ἀδελφοζωΐα**, ἡ, *living together as brother and sister*; ref. *sub-introductae*, Pall.*v.Chrys.*5(p.31.18; M.47.20).

***ἀδελφοθεΐα**, ἡ, *fraternal relationship in the Godhead*, ref. futile questionings about Trin. ἆρα ἂν ἀ. ... ἐν τῇ τριάδι; ‡Gr.Nyss.*imag.*(M.44.1340D); ἀ. ἔχουσιν ὁ υἱὸς καὶ τὸ πνεῦμα Anast.S.*hod.*22(M.89.288B).

***ἀδελφόθεος**, ὁ, *brother of God* (i.e. of Christ); esp. of S. James, ‡Hipp.*disc.*1(M.10.953C); Cyr.*Ps.*68:28(M.69.1173C); Dion.Ar.*d.n.*3.2(M.3.681D); τὸ τοῦ ἀ. δι' ἐννόμου διαδοχῆς ἐπέχοντες [sc. patriarchs of Jerusalem] πρόσωπον Thdr.Stud.*epp.*2.121(M.99.1396C); of other brethren of Christ, Sophr.H.*or.*9(M.87.3364C); Hipp.Th.*fr.*6.6(p.32.7).

***ἀδελφοκοιτία**, ἡ, *incest of brother and sister*; ref. Zeus, Thphl. Ant.*Autol.*1.9(M.6.1037B); said to have been advocated by Epicurus and Stoics, *ib.*3.6(1129A).

ἀδελφοκτονέω, *murder a brother* or *sister*; of Cain, Thphl.Ant. *Autol.*2.30(M.6.1100B); of Devil inciting to fratricide, Pall.*h.Laus.*6 (p.22.15; M.34.1018B).

ἀδελφοκτονία, ἡ, *murder of a brother* or *sister*; esp. ref. Cain, *1Clem.*4.7; Epiph.*haer.*1(p.172.19; M.41.180A); *ib.*38.5(p.68.15; 661A).

ἀδελφοκτόνος, *murdering a brother* or *sister*; esp. of Cain, *Lit.*ap.*Const.App.*8.12.21; Chrys.*hom.7.6 in Rom.*(9.491E).

***ἀδελφομητρότεκνον**, τό, *daughter who is a* spiritual *sister and mother* (as an abbess), Thdr.Stud.*epp.*2.113(M.99.1380C).

***ἀδελφόμιξ**, *incestuous with brother* or *sister*, ‡Caes.Naz.*dial.*177 (M.38.1145).

ἀδελφομιξία, ἡ, *marriage of brother and sister*; ref. first generations of mankind, Meth.*symp.*1.2(p.10.19; M.18.41A); Diod.*Gen.*5:4 (M.33.1569C); severely punished by Church ἀ. τὸν τοῦ φονέως χρόνον ἐξομολογηθήσεται Bas.*ep.*217 *can.*67(3.327C; M.32.800B).

***ἀδελφοπάτηρ**, ὁ, = sq., Thdr.Stud.*epp.*2.61(M.99.1277C).

***ἀδελφοπάτωρ**, ὁ, *both brother and priest*; met., of an archbishop, Thdr.Stud.*epp.*1.37(M.99.1040A).

***ἀδελφοποι-έω**, *adopt as a brother* or *sister*, ‡Chrys.*Zacch.*1.4 (8.126C); met. χρὴ ~ῆσαι τὸν Χριστόν *ib.*(126E); ~εῖν ἀλλήλοις ἡμᾶς εἰδὼς τὴν ἀγάπησιν Sophr.H.*or.*8.4(M.87.3360C).

***ἀδελφοποίησις**, ἡ, *adoption as brother* or *sister*; met., of men by Christ, Ath.*Ar.*2.62(M.26.280A).

***ἀδελφοποιΐα**, ἡ, *concluding of* spiritual *brotherhood*; forbidden to monks, Thdr.Stud.*test.*(M.99.1820B).

ἀδελφοποιός, *producing brothers*, Melet.*nat.hom.*synops.(M.64. 1085A).

ἀδελφός, ὁ, *brother*; **1.** of one's fellow Christian; **a.** in address, *1Clem.*1.1; Clem.*paed.*3.12(p.287.19; M.8.673A); et freq.; so used by Const. when addressing Christians, Const.ap.Eus.*v.C.*2.46(p.60.26; M.20.1024A); Eus.*v.C.*3.24(p.89.8; 1085A); **b.** normal designation of baptized members of Church μετὰ τὸ οὕτως λοῦσαι [i.e. being baptized] τὸν πεπεισμένον...ἐπὶ τοὺς λεγομένους ἀ. ἄγομεν Just.*1apol.*65.1(M.6.428A); Clem.*str.*2.9(p.134.22; M.8.976C); and only of these ὁ μὲν κατηχούμενος, κἂν μοναχὸς ᾖ, οὐκ ἀ.· ὁ δὲ πιστός, κἂν κοσμικὸς ᾖ, ἀ. ἐστιν Chrys.*hom.25.3 in Heb.*(12.233B); ἀ. γὰρ τὸ βάπτισμα ἐργάζεται, καὶ ἡ τῶν θείων μυστηρίων κοινωνία id.*hom.79.1 in Mt.*(7.759C); of Christians as Christ's spiritual brethren through baptism μάθετε οὖν...διὰ τῆς ἐν ἐμοὶ ἀναγεννήσεως...ἵνα χρηματίσητε υἱοὶ θεοῦ, ἀ. δὲ ἐμοῦ Or.*or.*15.4(p.335.27; M.11.467B); Gr.Nyss.*Eun.*2(2 p.327.24; M.45.501C); **c.** also applied to those fallen into heresy, *Chron.Pasch.*p.272(M.92.673A); **2.** in wider sense, including all men ὑπὲρ τῶν ἄλλων δὲ ἀνθρώπων...προσεύχεσθε ...ἀ. αὐτῶν εὑρεθῶμεν τῇ ἐπιεικείᾳ Ign.*Eph.*10.3; both Jews and gentiles, Just.*dial.*96.2(M.6.704A); as being possible future converts, Clem.*str.*7.14(p.61.19; M.9.520B); and believers in one God, *ib.*5.14(p.390.19; 145A); **3.** partic. of members of a religious community, *PLond.*1914.4; Bas.*reg.br.*104(2.452A; M.31.1153C); Thdt. *h.rel.*25(3.1264); οἱ ἀ. ὀφείλουσιν ἐν ἀγάπῃ πολλῇ συνεῖναι ἀλλήλοις Mac.Aeg.*hom.*3.1(M.34.468C); **4.** of Christ; **a.** as men's brother through Inc. ὁ ὑπὸ ἀνθρώπων ἁμαρτωλῶν φωνούμενος ὡς ἀ. *A. Xanthipp.*3(p.59.31); διὰ τὴν πρὸς τὰ κτίσματα συγκατάβασιν τοῦ λόγου, καθ' ἣν καὶ πολλῶν γέγονεν ἀ. ὁ γάρ τοι μονογενής, οὐκ ὄντων ἄλλων ἀ., μονογενής ἐστιν· ὁ δὲ πρωτότοκος διὰ τοὺς ἄλλους ἀ. πρωτότοκος λέγεται Ath.*Ar.*2.62(M.26.277C); Chrys.*hom.46.3 in Jo.*(8. 373A); id.*hom.3.2 in Col.*(11.344A); ‡Chrys.*Zacch.*1.4(8.126C); Mac. Aeg.*hom.*16.8(M.34.620A); **b.** as brother of Father (Arian *reductio ad absurdum* of homoousion) εἰ...ἀΐδιός ἐστιν ὁ υἱός, καὶ συνυπάρχει τῷ πατρί, οὐκέτι υἱόν, ἀλλ' ἀ. εἶναι τοῦ πατρὸς λέγετε αὐτόν Ath.*Ar.*1.14(M.26.40C); *ib.*(41A), et passim; **5.** the 'brethren of the Lord' (Mt.12:46f.; Ac.1:14; Gal.1:19, etc.), gen. interpreted as sons of Joseph from a former marriage ἀ. μὲν οὐκ εἶχεν φύσει οὔτε τῆς παρθένου τεκούσης ἕτερον, οὐδ' αὐτὸς ἐκ τοῦ Ἰωσὴφ τυγχάνων. νόμῳ τοιγαροῦν ἐχρημάτισαν αὐτοῦ ἀ. υἱοὶ Ἰωσὴφ ὄντες ἐκ προτεθνηκυίας γυναικός Or.*fr.31 in Jo.*2:11(p.506.21); id.*Cels.*1.47(p.97.11; M.11. 748A); Epiph.*ep.Arab.*ap.*haer.*78.9(p.459.29; M.42.712C); of S. James ἀ. δὲ τοῦ κυρίου οὗτος καλεῖται διὰ τὸ ὁμότροφον, οὐχὶ κατὰ φύσιν, ἀλλὰ κατὰ χάριν *ib.*78.7(p.458.4; 709A); Chrys.*hom.5.3 in Mt.*(7.77C); Cyr.*glaph.Gen.*7(1.221E); Sev.Ant.*res.*(p.846.8ff.; M.46. 648A); Hipp.Th.*fr.*1.6(p.7.5; M.117.1040B); **6.** of a brother-sister (i.e. chaste) relationship μεθ' ἡμῶν...κοιμηθήσῃ ὡς ἀ. καὶ οὐχ ὡς ἀνήρ Herm.*sim.*9.11.3; of men in their relations to consecrated virgins ἀ. ἐν Χριστῷ παρόντων, ἑαυτὴν [sc. παρθένος] καὶ χιτῶνι... κοσμήσει †Bas.Anc.*virg.*35(M.30.740B); of men having *virgines sub-introductae* ἀ. οἱ συνοικοῦντες Chrys.*subintr.*9(1.241D); **7.** *colleague, associate* Παῦλε...ἀ. Πέτρου *A.Petr.et Paul.*5(p.180.14); *ib.*21(p.188. 2); *A.Barth.*2(p.132.27); used by kings when addressing each other, Const.ap.Eus.*v.C.*4.11(p.122.11; M.20.1160B); *Chron.Pasch.*p.333(M. 92.864C); Heracl.*ep.*(M.92.1025B).

ἀδελφός, adj. **1.** *as a brother* or *sister*, of Christ's relations to creation πρωτότοκος...ἐστι τῆς κτίσεως οὐχ ὡς ἀ. ἔχων τὴν κτίσιν ἀλλ' ὡς πρὸ πάσης κτίσεως γεννηθείς· πῶς γὰρ οἷον...ἀ. εἶναι τῆς κτίσεως καὶ δημιουργόν; εἰ γὰρ...κτίσμα ἐστίν, ἀ. ἔχει τὴν κτίσιν· οὐχ οἷον...ἀ. εἶναι καὶ δημιουργόν·...εἰ δὲ δημιουργός, οὐκ ἄρα καὶ ἀ.· εἰ δὲ οὐκ ἀ., οὐ κτίσμα Thdt.*Col.*1:15(3.477); to men by virtue of his humanity, Gr.Nyss.*Eun.*12(2 p.275.2; M.45.885B); **2.** *cognate*, Serap.*Man.*50(p.71; M.18.1245B); Chrys.*hom.3.2 in Col.*(11.344B).

ἀδελφοσύνη, ἡ, *adoption as brother* or *sister*, *Nomoc.*512.

***ἀδελφότεκνον**, τό, *cousin*, Hipp.Th.*fr.*2.6(p.14.12).

ἀδελφότης, ἡ, **A.** *brotherhood*; **1.** *fraternal relationship, brotherly feeling* or *love* ἀ. συντηρεῖν Herm.*mand.*8.10; Gr.Naz.*carm.*1.1.32. 24(M.37.513A); ἀγάπης καὶ ἀ. χάριτι *Cod.Afr.*85; Nil.*exerc.*43(M.79. 772D); **2.** *the Christian brotherhood, Church* (cf. 1Pet.2:17,5:9); **a.** in gen., *1Clem.*2.4; Iren.*haer.*2.31.2(M.7.825A); Serap.Ant.ap.Eus. *h.e.*5.19.2(M.20.481A); τοὺς ἑνὶ τῷ τῆς υἱοθεσίας πνεύματι κεκλημένους εἰς ἀ. Cyr.*Os.*10(3.31B); esp. as community of baptized τί...τὸ ποιοῦν τὴν ἀ.; τὸ λουτρὸν τῆς παλιγγενεσίας Chrys.*hom.25.3 in Heb.*(12.233B); **b.** local *church* τὴν Ῥωμαίων ἀ. Eus.*h.e.*6.45.1 (v.l. ἐκκλησίαν M.20.633B); Ath.*ep.encycl.*7(p.177.11; M.25.240A); Thphl.Al.*fr.*5(p.121.15; M.65.62C); **3.** of religious communities, Bas.*ascet.*3(2.320E; M.31.876A); τῇ εὐλαβεστάτῃ...ἐν Χριστῷ ἀ. Gr. Naz.*ep.*238(M.37.380C); Pall.*h.Laus.*43.2(p.130.10; M.34.1210C); Marc. Er.*opusc.*5.2(M.65.1032B); τοὺς ἐξηγουμένους τῆς ἀ. Mac.Aeg.*perf.*9 (M.34.848B), etc.; of communities of men and women living together, Gr.Nyss.*virg.*23(p.338.6; M.46.409B) cit. s. συμβίωσις; **4.** of Christians with Christ, in Church ὅπου...ἐκκλησία Χριστοῦ, ἐκεῖ ἀ. Χριστοῦ Tit.Bost.*fr.Lc.*8:19ff.(pp.174.9,175.1); through his humanity τὸ διὰ τῆς ἀφῆς γνωριζόμενον καὶ...τοῖς ἀνθρώποις διὰ τῆς ἀ. οἰκειούμενον Gr.Nyss.*Eun.*12(1 p.274.20; M.45.885B); Amph.*hom.*1.5(M.39.41Bf.); established by faith, Chrys.*hom.1.2 in Tit.*(11. 733D); given to the poor and ignorant, id.*hom.79.1 in Mt.*(7.759B); men being Christ's brethren by adoption, Cyr.*thes.*32(5^1.331A); **5.** Trin., in Arian *reductio ad absurdum* of orthodox position εἰ εἰς πατέρα καὶ υἱὸν ἡμῶν ἐστιν ἡ πίστις, ποία ἀ. ἐν τούτοις ἐστίν; Ath.*Ar.*1.14(M.26.41A); **6.** as form of address, collectively of members of Councils πιστεύω, ὅτι πάσῃ τῇ ἀ. ἤρεσεν *Cod.Afr.*85; of the hierarchy πᾶσαν τὴν σύν σοι ἐν Χριστῷ ἀ. προσαγορεύω Gennad.*encycl.*(p.81.20; M.85.1618D); of other groups of bishops and clergy, Synes.*ep.*72 (M.66.1436A); Nest.*ep.Cyr.*1(p.25.16; M.77.44B); *ib.*2(p.32.22; 57B); Cyr.*ep.*4(p.28.26; 5^2.25B); secular, Men.*exc.Rom.*1(p.176.24; M.113. 860B); τὴν ἀ. ὑμῶν τοῦ βασιλέως τῶν Ῥωμαίων Heracl.*ep.*ap.*Chron. Pasch.*p.402(M.92.1028A).

B. *kinship, affinity* ἀ. παθῶν Cyr.*glaph.Num.*(1.391D).

***ἀδελφοτρόπως**, *in brotherly fashion*, El.H.*cant.*1.5(p.290).

***ἀδελφοφθορέω**, *corrupt a sister*; of Zeus, *Hom.Clem.*4.16; ‡Caes. Naz.*dial.*109(M.38.980).

ἀδέσποτος, *without a master*, hence *free, self-determined*, of God ἀγέννητος καὶ ἀ. *Const.App.*7.44.2; ‡Just.*qu.Chr.*3.3(M.6.1436C); Gr. Nyss.*fat.*(M.45.149B); of nature of Father only, Eun.*apol.*20(M.30. 856A); of nature of Christ, Bas.Sel.*or.*32(M.85.353B); of human nature, Gr.Nyss.*or.catech.*5(p.28.9; M.45.25A); of Jews Ἀβραὰμ...

αἷμα φέροντες τὸ ἀ. Nonn.*par.Jo*.8:33(M.43.817B); neut. as subst., *freedom* τὸ ἀ. καὶ αὐτεξούσιον χάριτος Gr.Nyss.*or.catech*.5(p.26.8; 24C).

ἄδετος, **1.** *unbound, loose*; of hair, Gr.Naz.*carm*.1.2.29.7(M.37.884A); of a ship, *ib*.1.2.17.54(785A); **2.** *free*; of God, *ib*.1.2.1.413 (553A); of BMV, *ib*.1.2.1.198(537A); of original life, *ib*.1.2.1.726 (577A); of eremitical life, Jo.Clim.*scal*.27(M.88.1116B).

***ἀδεφένδευτος**, *undefended*, Ath.Scholast.*coll*.4.13(p.57); *ib*. paratit.6(p.78).

ἀδεῶς, *freely, without restraint*, *M.Polyc*.7.2; *Ep.Lugd*.ap.Eus. *h.e*.5.1.5(M.20.409A).

ἀδηλία, ἡ, **1.** *obscurity*, Clem.*prot*.4(p.43.12; M.8.152B); ἀναχωρεῖ ἐν σπηλαίῳ μόνος, γλιχόμενος ἀ. Pall.*v.Chrys*.5(p.28.21; M.47.18); of the mysteries of nature τὰ μακρὰ τῆς ἀ. βάθη Geo.Pis.*hex*.130 (M.92.1442A); **2.** *uncertainty*; esp. of time of death, Gr.Nyss.*virg*. 3(p.258.24; M.46.328C); id.*bapt.diff*.(M.46.420A); Chrys.*hom.9.1 in 1Thess*.(11.486E); Max.*ep*.5(M.91.424A); of future in gen., Chrys. *hom.19.3 in 1Cor*.(10.163C); *ib.39.2*(365B); in matters of faith, Vict.*Mc*.1:23(p.275.16).

***ἀδήλωτος**, *invisible*, *Mir.Artem*.38(p.63.23).

ἀδημιούργητος, *uncreated*; of Trin., Epiph.*haer*.76.50(p.405.9; M.42.621D); in refutation of pagan arguments τὸ λέγειν δημιουργὸν μὲν τὸν θεόν, ἀ. δὲ τὸν κόσμον· τὸ γὰρ ἀ. ἴσον δύναται τῷ ἀγεννήτῳ... καὶ τὸ λέγειν, ὁ ἀ. θεὸς ἀ. ποιεῖ, ὃ ἴσον ἐστὶ τῷ τὸν ἀγέννητον θεὸν ἀγεννήτως ἀγέννητα ποιεῖν ‡Just.*qu.Chr*.5(M.6.1456B); *ib*.4(1449C); Proc.G.*Gen*.proem.(M.87.32B).

***ἀδημιουργήτως**, *without being created* εἰ μὴ προῆν ἀ. ὁ ποιητὴς καὶ προνοητής, οὐκ ἂν ὑπῆν δημιουργικῶς τὰ ποιητὰ καὶ προνοούμενα Didym.*Trin*.3.5(M.39.841B).

***ἀδημόνως**, *in trouble, distressfully*, Rom.Mel.(*SBBAW* 1901 p.742; *AS* 1 p.95).

***ἀδημοσίευτος**, **1.** *not made public, kept secret*, of oral tradition of Church ἐκ τῆς ἀ. ... διδασκαλίας, ἣν ἐν ἀπολυπραγμονήτῳ...σιγῇ οἱ πατέρες ἡμῶν ἐφύλαξαν Bas.*Spir*.66(3.55B; M.32.188C ἀδημοσιεύτου); ἀ. ποιῆσαι τὸ δικαστήριον Chrys.*hom.60.1 in Mt*.(7.606C); of private examination of conscience, id.*hom.28.1 in 1Cor*.(10.250E); **2.** *hidden, withdrawn* from the world τὸ ἀ. ... τῆς ἀρετῆς Nil.ap.Proc.G.*Cant*.3:9f.(M.87.1632D); ὁ μοναχὸς...ἀ. Ant.Mon.*hom*. 102(M.89.1741B); of religious life, Jo.Clim.*scal*.3(M.88.664B).

***ἀδημοσιεύτως**, *secretly*, Jo.Clim.*scal*.10(M.88.848C).

ᾅδης, ὁ, *Hades, underworld*, etym. ᾅ. ... παρὰ τὸ ἀειδές, διὰ τὸ μὴ ὁρᾶσθαι, καθάπερ ἐλέχθη καὶ Ὠριγένει Meth.*res*.2.28(p.385.21; M.18. 316B);

A. pagan, Arist.*apol*.11.3; Hipp.*haer*.1.19(p.21.13; M.16.3044B); Or.*Cels*.2.16(p.145.19; M.11.828B).

B. Jewish, *Sheol*; *1Clem*.4.12; βυθός (Ps.68:1), τουτέστιν, ὁ ᾅ. Hipp.*Jud*.3(p.20.7; M.10.789B); Or.*Jo*.19.21(5; p.323.10; M.14.565D); sts. identified with the 'abyss', id.*engast*.7(p.291.24; M.12.1024D); Eus.*e.th*.3.3(p.148.22; M.24.988A); as freq. in apocryphal Acts, *A.Andr.et Mt*.31(p.113.4); *A.Phil*.133(p.64.3); cf. ἄβυσσος.

C. Christian conceptions; **1.** intermediate state and dwelling-place of souls of pre-Christian people (cf. Ps.15:10); **a.** all the souls οὐκ οἶδας ὅτι οἱ ἀπὸ Ἀδὰμ καὶ Εὔας πάντες ἀπέθανον;... πάντες ἐν τῷ ᾅ. κατηλλάξαντο *T.Abr*.A 8(p.85.30); ἡμεῖς οὖν ἦμεν ἐν τῷ ᾅ. μετὰ πάντων τῶν ἀπ' αἰῶνος κεκοιμημένων *A.Pil*.B 18(p.324); Ath. *Ar*.1.43(M.26.101B); κατελθόντι τῷ Ἀδὰμ εἰς τὸν ᾅ. ἠκολούθησαν οἱ μετασχόντες τῆς φύσεως Thdt.*eran*.3(4.199); **b.** only souls of wicked οἱ ἐν ᾅ. καταταγέντες καὶ εἰς ἀπώλειαν ἑαυτοὺς ἐκδεδωκότες... τίς ἂν εὖ φρονῶν ἐν μιᾷ καταδίκῃ καὶ τὰς τῶν δικαίων καὶ τὰς τῶν ἁμαρτωλῶν ὑπολάβοι εἶναι ψυχάς; Clem.*str*.6.6(p.454.9; M.9.268A); Or.*hom.18.2 in Jer*.(p.152.30; M.13.465C) cit. s. καταχθόνιος; cf.id. *engast*.3(p.285.7ff.; M.12.1016Bff.); this view attacked ἐδεινοποίει δὲ δημαγωγῶν ὅτι φάσκουσι [sc. the orthodox]...ὡς εἴη φρικῶδες ὑπολαβεῖν ἐν ᾅ. γεγονέναι τὸν εὐκλεῆ Σαμουὴλ Eust.*engast*.17(p.43. 29; M.18.649B); **2.** ref. descent of Christ (cf. 1Pet.3:19f.); **a.** Christol. implications ὁ μονογενὴς εἰσῆλθεν ὡς ψυχὴ μετὰ ψυχῶν, θεὸς λόγος ἔμψυχος· τὸ γὰρ σῶμα ἔκειτο ἐν μνημείῳ, οὐχὶ κενωθὲν τῆς θεότητος· ἀλλ' ὥσπερ ἐν τῷ ᾅ. ὤν, τῇ οὐσίᾳ ἦν πρὸς τὸν πατέρα, οὕτως ἦν καὶ ἐν τῷ σώματι καὶ ἐν τῷ ᾅ. ... θέλων ἐχωρήθη ἐν σώματι ἐμψύχῳ, ἵνα μετὰ τῆς ἰδίας ψυχῆς πορευθῇ εἰς τὸν ᾅ., καὶ μὴ γυμνῇ τῇ θεότητι Hipp.*fr.pasch*.3(p.268.23ff.; M.10.701Af.); ὥσπερ τὸ σῶμα οὐχ οἷόν τε ἦν εἰς ᾅ. καταβῆναι κἂν τοῦτο λέγωσιν οἱ πνευματικὸν λέγοντες τὸ σῶμα τοῦ Ἰησοῦ, οὕτως οὐδὲ τὸ πνεῦμα οἷόν τε ἦν καταβῆναι εἰς ᾅ., διὸ παρακαταθήκην ἔδωκεν ἕως ἀνέστη ἐκ νεκρῶν τὸ πνεῦμα τῷ πατρί Or.*dial*.8(p.138.13); his Godhead not separated from his soul even in Hades, ‡Ath.*Apoll*.2.14(M.26. 1156C); typified by Jonah's sojourn in the fish, Cyr.H.*catech*.14. 20; **b.** preaching in Hades ὁ κύριος δι' οὐδὲν ἕτερον εἰς ᾅ. κατῆλθεν ἢ διὰ τὸ εὐαγγελίσασθαι Clem.*str*.6.6(p.454.31; M.9.268C); δεχόμενοι κατὰ τὸν ᾅ. ὄντες τῆς θεογνωσίας τὸ κήρυγμα...κατελθόντος εἰς ᾅ. σωτῆρος Max.*qu.Thal*.7(M.90.284B,C); **c.** other aspects: being preceded by Jo. Bapt., Hipp.*antichr*.45(p.29.5; M.10.764B); Ἰωάννης...εἰς ᾅ. καταβέβηκε προκηρύσσων μου τὸν κύριον, ἵνα προείπῃ αὐτὸν κατελευσόμενον Or.*engast*.7(p.290.20; M.12.1024A); *A.Pil*.B 18 (pp.324f.); Gr.Naz.*or*.43.75(M.36.597A); and the OT prophets, Or. *engast*.6(p.289.27; 1021C); ‡Chrys.*hom*.11(13.247A); and followed by apostles, Clem.*str*.6.6(p.454.18; M.9.268A); bringing up the dead ὁ κατελθὼν εἰς ᾅ. μετὰ πολλῆς δυνάμεως...καὶ ἀνῆλθες μετὰ πολλῆς δόξης, καὶ συναγαγὼν πάντας τοὺς εἰς σὲ καταφεύγοντας *A.Thom*.A 156(p.265.3); κατέβη εἰς τὸν ᾅ., καὶ διέσχισε φραγμὸν τὸν ἐξ αἰῶνος μὴ σχισθέντα, καὶ ἀνήγειρεν νεκροὺς καὶ κατέβη μόνος, ἀνέβη δὲ μετὰ πολλοῦ ὄχλου πρὸς τὸν πατέρα αὐτοῦ *Ep.Chr.suppl*. ap.Eus.*h.e*.1.13.20(M.20.128C); Ath.*Ar*.3.56(M.26.441A); ‡Ath.*Apoll*. 1.5(M.26.1101A); Bas.*hom.in Ps*.48(1.186A; M.29.453A); ‡Epiph. *hom*.2(M.43.440A); commanding their release κελεύω σοι, ᾅ. καὶ σκότος,...ἔκβαλε τὰς ἐγκεκλεισμένας ψυχὰς τοῦ Ἀδάμ Mac.Aeg.*hom*. 11.10(M.34.552C); Cyr.*Nest*.5.5(p.102.13; 6[1].136D); σκυλεύσας τὸν ᾅ. τὰς αὐτόθι καθειργμένας ἐλευθερώσῃ ψυχάς id.*ep*.45(p.155.27; 5[2].139C); frightening death, Cyr.H.*catech*.14.19; in gen. κάτεισιν εἰς ᾅ. ψυχὴ τεθεωμένη, ἵνα ὥσπερ τοῖς ἐν γῇ ὁ τῆς δικαιοσύνης ἀνέτειλεν ἥλιος, οὕτω καὶ τοῖς ὑπὸ γῆν...καθημένοις ἐπιλάμψῃ τὸ φῶς· ἵν' ὥσπερ τοῖς ἐν γῇ εὐηγγελίσατο εἰρήνην...οὕτω καὶ τοῖς ἐν ᾅ. ... καὶ οὕτω τοὺς ἀπ' αἰώνων λύσας πεπεδημένους, αὖθις ἐκ νεκρῶν ἀνεφοίτησεν Jo.D.*f.o*.3.29(M.94.1101A); *A.Pil*.B 24–27(pp.330–2); condemnation of opinion that sole reason for Christ's death was his descent and preaching, Chrys.*hom.36.3 in Mt*.(7.410D); **d.** descent in rel. to baptism πῶς οὖν κατορθοῦμεν τὴν εἰς ᾅ. κάθοδον; μιμούμενοι τὴν ταφὴν τοῦ Χριστοῦ διὰ τοῦ βαπτίσματος Bas.*Spir*.35 (3.29A; M.32.129B); Chrys.*hom.40.1 in 1Cor*.(10.379C) cit. s. κατάβασις; cf.Cyr.H.*catech*.9.9; **e.** in creeds, *Symb.App*.(p.32); cf. *Symb.Sirm*.3(p.236.1; M.26.693A); εἰς τὰ καταχθόνια κατελθόντα, ὃν αὐτὸς ὁ ᾅ. ἐτρόμασε *Symb.Nic*.(359)ap.Thdt.*h.e*.2.21.4(3.880); *Symb.CP*(360)(p.259.6; M.26.748A); **3.** intermediate place for all souls until final judgement, cf.Iren.*haer*.5.31.2(M.7.1209B); ὁ περὶ ᾅ. λόγος, ἐν ᾧ αἱ ψυχαὶ πάντων κατέχονται, ἄχρι καιροῦ ὃν ὁ θεὸς ὥρισεν, ἀνάστασιν τότε πάντων ποιησόμενος Hipp.*Graec*.2(M.10. 800A); ‡Proc.G.*Pr*.15:11(M.87.1373B); regarded not as local habitation but as spiritual state, Gr.Nyss.*anim.et res*.(M.46.68Af.); ᾅ. μὴ τόπον τινὰ οὕτως ὀνομαζόμενον οἴεσθαι, ἀλλά τινα κατάστασιν ζωῆς ἀειδῆ καὶ ἀσώματον, ἣ τὴν ψυχὴν ἐμβιοτεύειν παρὰ τῆς γραφῆς ἐκδιδασκόμεθα *ib*.(85B); BMV exempt from it οὐ κατελήλυθε γὰρ ἡ ψυχή σου εἰς τὸν ᾅ. Jo.D.*hom*.8.12(M.96.720A); **4.** = γέεννα, *hell*; **a.** place of punishment for wicked, where impenitent remain after the preaching of Christ, Clem.*str*.6.6(p.456.12; M.9.272A); ὥσπερ τῷ ἀνθρώπῳ ἡ ἀρχὴ μὲν τοῦ εἶναι ἐν τῷ παραδείσῳ ἦν, τὸ τέλος ⟨δὲ⟩ διὰ τὴν παράβασιν τάχα ἐν ᾅ. κάτω Or.*Jo*.13.37(p.263.4; M.14.464D); ᾅ. τῶν ἁμαρτωλῶν κολαστήριον id.*sel.in Ps*.9:18(M.12.1189D); including various degrees of punishment and applied also to this world which, acc. Origen, is a place of punishment for fallen spirits, id.*princ*.4.3.10(23; p.337.3ff.; M.11.393A); degrees of punishment admitted, Bas.*reg.br*.267(2.507D; M.31.1265B); ἐν ᾅ. νυνὶ ἐκπρόθεσμον μετάνοιαν μετανοοῦντας [prob. ref. Lc.16:23] ὀδύρεσθαι ‡Just.*coh.Gr*.35(M.6.304B); ὁ μὲν κακός, ἐν ᾅ. γενόμενος, ὡς ἐνταῦθα [sc. in this world] τὰ ἀγαθὰ ἀπολαβών, ἐκεῖ περὶ ὧν ἥμαρτε κολασθείς *Hom.Clem*.2.13; without rest, *ib*.11.10; ‡Ath.*qu.Ant*.19(M.28.609A); **b.** no possibility of repentance and love of God, ref. Ps.6:6 οὐκ ἔστιν ἐν ᾅ. τοῖς ἀπελθοῦσιν ἐξομολόγησις καὶ διόρθωσις Gr.Naz. *or*.16.7(M.35.944C); Chrys.*hom.18.6 in Rom*.(9.639C); id.*prod.Jud*. 1.1(2.377B); ποῖος γὰρ ἔτι τῶν νεκρῶν ὁ καρπός, ἢ πῶς ἔτι μεμνήσεταί τις θεοῦ διὰ τοῦ πληροῦν ἐντολὴν τῶν ἐν ᾅ. καταβεβηκότων; Cyr.*Jo*. 3.4(4.285A); **c.** descent thither is separation from God, caused by grave sin, †Bas.*Is*.166(1.497E; M.30.392D); involving various classes of men διαφορὰς δὲ ταγμάτων καταβαινόντων εἰς τὸν ᾅ. ὁ λόγος ἀπηριθμήσατο. πρῶτον τοὺς ἐνδόξους...εἶτα οἱ μεγάλοι, οἱ ἐν δυνάμει τινὶ καὶ ἀρχῇ τῶν πολλῶν ὑπερέχοντες· καὶ οἱ πλούσιοι, οἱ πολὺ πλῆθος χρημάτων ἄδικον περιβεβλημένοι, ἢ οἱ ἀκόρεστον τὴν ἐπιθυμίαν τοῦ πλείονος ἔχοντες· καὶ οἱ λοιμοὶ αὐτῆς, ὅσοι δίκην νόσου φθοροποιοῦ κατὰ διάδοσιν ἐπινεμομένης, τοὺς προσιόντας αὐτοῖς διαφθείροντες, ἤτοι ἐκ μοχθηρᾶς διδασκαλίας, ἢ ἐκ τοῦ κατὰ τὴν ἁμαρτίαν ἐρεθισμοῦ, λοιμοὶ δικαίως προσαγορεύονται· οἵτινες καταβαίνουσιν εἰς τὸν ᾅ. *ib*.(1.498A,B; 393A); πᾶσα γὰρ ἡ κατ' ἐνέργειαν ἁμαρτία ὑπὸ τὸν ᾅ. ἐστίν Dor.*doct*.10.5(M.88.1729D); **d.** description *οἰκεῖ μὲν ἐν τῷ ᾅ., κατεσκεύασται δὲ αὐτῷ πῦρ ἄσβεστον, γέεννα ἀτελεύτητος, βόρβορος κοχλάζων, σκώληξ ἀκοίμητος* A.*Mt.*3(p.219.17); *κοινόν τινα τόπον ἐν τῷ ἐσωτάτῳ τῆς γῆς, ἐπίσκιον πανταχόθεν, καὶ ἀλαμπῆ, τὸ τοῦ ᾅ. χωρίον εἶναι· στόμιον δέ τι ἐπὶ τὰ κοῖλα καθῆκον, δι' οὗ τὴν κάθοδον εἶναι ταῖς πρὸς τὸ χεῖρον κατεγνωσμέναις ψυχαῖς* †Bas.*Is.*166(1.497C,D; M.30.392B); Cyr.*Is.*1.3(2.89A); partic. features: darkness, *A.Pil.*B 21(p.328); *A.Thom.*A 10(p.115.5); Chrys.*coemet.*2 (2.399B); joylessness, *ib.*; cf. *ἀειδής*.

D. personification, and equation with death, *A.Pil.*B 20.1(p.326); cf.Mel.*pass.*22 p.4.9; *ib.*55 p.9.18; *ib.*102 p.17.16; *οὐχὶ θάνατος δὲ μόνον, ἀλλὰ καὶ ᾅ. ἐκαλεῖτο* Chrys.*coemet.*1(2.398A); *ᾅ. δὲ ἀπὸ τῆς κατεχούσης δόξης ὠνόμασε, τῷ θανάτῳ καὶ ταύτην ἐπιθεὶς τὴν προσηγορίαν* Thdt.*Cant.*8:6(2.157); *οὐδὲ ἔστιν ᾅ. βασίλειον ἐπὶ γῆς, ἔκτισε γὰρ εἰς τὸ εἶναι τὰ πάντα* Cyr.*hom.pasch.*14(5[2].196E).

E. met. *ποῖος ᾅ. ἠρεύξατο ὁμοούσιον εἰπεῖν τὸ ἐκ Μαρίας σῶμα τῇ τοῦ λόγου θεότητι;* Ath.*ep.Epict.*2(p.4.10; M.26.1052C); ref. Job *ὁ ᾅ. οὗτος* Olymp.*Job* 19:18(M.93.208B).

ἀδήωτος, *unravaged, unharmed*, Const.*or.s.c.*17(p.178.11; M.20.1284B); Bas.Sel.*v.Thecl.*2.11(M.85.584A).

ἀδιάβατος, *not to be passed*; met., of division between the impenitent and the good, Gr.Nyss.*anim.et res.*(M.46.84B); *τὸ ἀ. τῆς ἀνυμφεύτου λοχείας πέλαγος* Procl.CP *annunt.*5(M.85.445B).

ἀδιάβλητος, *not to be blamed, unexceptionable, innocent*; **1.** in gen., of philosophical teaching *ἀ. δόγματα* Clem.*str.*6.7(p.459.26; M.9.277B); of the varying evidence for the Resurrection *ὁ λόγος ἀκριβὴς μένει καὶ ἀ. ἐπὶ καιροῖς διαφόροις καὶ τόποις ἐναλλαττούσας τὰς ὀπτασίας εἰσάγων* Eus.*qu.Marin.suppl.*1.7(M.22.996B); *ἀ. ποιεῖσθαι τὴν κρίσιν* Cyr.*Am.*15(3.266D); *τὸν τῆς ὀρθῆς καὶ ἀ. πίστεως ὅρον ἐκτιθέμενοι* id.*expl.xii cap.*1(p.17.3; 6[1].147B); id.*Ps.*45:6(M.69.1049A); *τῆς εἰς θεὸν ἀγάπης, τὸ ἀ. κάλλος* id.*ador.*6(1.183A); *μονὰς…ἀδιαίρετος, ἀ.* Anat.Laod.*decad.*(p.29); **2.** of human affections of Christ *τοῖς φυσικοῖς τῶν ἀνθρώπων καὶ ἀ. ὑπηρετήσατο πάθεσι* ‡Dion.Al.*fr.in Lc.22:43f.*(p.242.13; M.10.1592D); Cyr.*ep.*45(p.155.22; 5[2].139B); ‡Chrys.*hom.*9(13.236B); *οὐ γὰρ ἠρνήσατο τὰ τῆς φύσεως ἡμῶν ἀ. πάθη σαρκωθεὶς ὁ θεὸς λόγος* Eulog.*palm.*8(M.86.2925C); Max.*opusc.*(M.91.60B); Jo.D.*f.o.*3.20(M.94.1081A); of the will of Christ *ἄμωμον καὶ ἀ. θέλησιν* Anast.S.*serm.imag.*3(M.89.1160A); *δύο τοῦ Χριστοῦ… ἐνεργειῶν καὶ θελημάτων ἀ.* *ib.*(1160D); **3.** of God *ὥσπερ ἀ. ὁ θεὸς ἐπὶ τῇ ἀσθενείᾳ τῆς δυνάμεως, ὅτι μὴ ποιήσας πλείους κόσμους, ἀλλὰ ποιήσας ἕνα κόσμον ἔπαυσε τὴν ποίησιν· οὕτως ἀ. ὁ θεὸς ἐπὶ τῷ ἀτελεῖ τῆς δυνάμεως, ὅτι μὴ ἅμα τῷ εἶναι αὐτὸν τὸν κόσμον ἐποίησεν, ἀλλ' ὅτε ἐβούλετο* ‡Just.*qu.Chr.*3.5(M.6.1441B).

ἀδιαβλήτως, *blamelessly, faultlessly*, Clem.*str.*3.6(p.220.23; M.8.1157A); Cyr.*ador.*5(1.160C); id.*Ps.*36:30(M.69.945B).

***ἀδιαγώγητος**, = ἀδιάγωγος, *impossible to live with*, Ast.Am.*hom.*1(M.40.176B).

***ἀδιάδεκτος**, *not to be succeeded to, perpetual*; of Christ's priesthood, Ath.*Ar.*2.9(M.26.165B); of endless course of day not succeeded by night, Tit.Bost.*Man.*2.18(M.18.1169B); of day of the Lord, †Bas.*Is.*87(1.439B; M.30.260B).

***ἀδιάδοτος**, *not to be distributed*; of the divine gift of light, *unable to penetrate* the mind on account of its resistance, Dion.Ar.*c.h.*9.3(M.3.260D); neut. as subst., of sunlight, *inability to penetrate* certain substances, *ib.*13.3(301B).

***ἀδιαδότως**, *without being able to penetrate*, Max.*schol.c.h.*9.3 (M.4.85B).

ἀδιάδοχος, **A.** lit., *without successor, sterile, not followed*; of plants, Bas.*hex.*5.7(1.46E; M.29.109C); *ἀ. τὰ τῆς βασιλείας παρειλήφατε σκῆπτρα* Jo.Ant.*relat.imp.*3(p.130.25; M.83.1453A); *ἀδιάδοχον νυκτὶ τὸ…φῶς* ‡Caes.Naz.*dial.*129(M.38.1029).

B. met., *perpetual, everlasting, eternal*; **1.** of God *τῷ πάντων ἀ. βασιλεῖ* Cyr.H.*catech.*18.4; *φῶς…ἀ. ὁ θεός* Gr.Naz.*or.*44.3(M.36.609B); *ἀ. ἡ μοναρχία* *Const.App.*7.35.9; *θεότητα…ἀ.* ‡Meth.*palm.*5 (M.18.393A); *Χριστὸς ὁ…ἀ. … βασιλεύς* Tim.Ant.*cruc.*(M.86.256B); *τὰ φυσικὰ τῆς τριάδος ἰδιώματα, τοῦτ' ἔστιν τὸ ἄναρχον…τὸ ἀ.* Anast.S.*hod.*17(M.89.264C); **2.** of spiritual things; **a.** kingdom of God, Ephr.3.391D; Didym.*Trin.*1.31(M.39.424A); Thdt.*eran.*1(4.33); *Pers.*(p.31.5); Gennad.*fr.Rom.*5:21(p.365.8; M.85.1673A); †Jo.D.*B.J.*16(M.96.1001B); **b.** grace, Bas.Sel.*or.*14.2(M.85.185A); Sophr.H.*or.*4(M.87.3304A); **c.** joy, ‡Hipp.*consumm.*45(p.307.20; M.10.945D); Thdr.Stud.*nativ.BMV* 7(M.96.696D); **d.** eternal life, *Dorm.BMV* 3 (p.96); Areth.*Apoc.*67(M.106.772B); **e.** in gen. *κράτος* Isid.Pel.*epp.*1.251(M.78.336A); *ἀρχή* ‡Bas.*struct.hom.*7(1.327E; M.30.17D); Jo.Mon.*hymn.Blas.*1(M.96.1401A); *φῶς* (of the pillar of fire) Gr.Nyss.*Pss.titt.*A 7(M.44.456D).

C. *without successor*, i.e. *final*, of NT *εὐαγγέλιον…ἀ. ἐστιν* Or.*fr.*56 *in Jo.*4:13(p.529.17); *ἀ. καινὴ διαθήκη* id.*Apoc.*14(p.27.13); Ammon.*Jo.*4:13f.(M.85.1421A).

D. *interminable* *στρατεῖαι ἀ.* Anast.*mort.*27(p.248).

***ἀδιαδόχως**, *perpetually, eternally*, Ant.Mon.*hom.*130(M.89.1841B); Max.*comput.*34(M.19.1252B); Areth.*Apoc.*1(M.106.512D).

ἀδιάδραστος, **1.** act., *not escaping, secured* *τὴν μακαρίαν παράδοσιν ἀ. φυλάττειν* Clem.*str.*1.1(p.9.11; M.8.700B); **2.** pass.; *inescapable*, of God's judgement, Eus.*h.e.*6.9.8(M.20.541A); neut. as subst., Areth.*Apoc.*18(M.106.604B).

ἀδιάθετος, *not set in order*; **1.** *disorderly, unruly*, *A.Andr.et Mt.* 20(p.92.4); of false joy, Diad.*perf.*33(p.38.4); neut. as subst. *δεικνὺς τῶν εὐχομένων τὸ ἀ.* †Bas.*Is.*35(1.408E; M.30.189B); *ἀλλήλοις ἐνεκάλουν* [sc. children in market place] *τὸ ἀσυμπαθὲς ἤγουν τὸ ἀ.* Cyr.*Lc.* 7:32(M.72.620C); **2.** *uncanonical*, opp. *ἐνδιάθετος*: *λέγουσι* [sc. *οἱ Ἄλογοι*] *τὸ κατὰ Ἰωάννην εὐαγγέλιον ἀ. εἶναι* Epiph.*haer.*51.18(p.275.23; M.41.924A); **3.** *intestate*, *Cod.Afr.*81; *ἐξ ἀ.* Ath.Scholast.*coll.*9.10 (p.104).

***ἀδιαθέτως**, *without making a will*, Ath.Scholast.*coll.*7.7(pp.87f.).

ἀδιαίρετος, *undivided, indivisible*; *undifferentiated*;

A. in gen., Hipp.*haer.*1.15(p.18.7; M.16.3040B); *ἀ. … ἄτομα προσηγόρευσεν* Thdt.*affect.*4(p.102.20; 4.795); met. *τὸ τῆς φιλίας ἔργον ἐν ἀ.* Hipp.*haer.*7.30(p.216.12; 3334B); Docetic *ἄνθρωπος οὗτος μία μονάς ἐστιν…ἀ.* *ib.*8.12(p.232.16; 3358C); of the number three (ref. Trin.) *τριὰς…ἀ., καὶ πρώτη τῶν ἐξ ἀρτίων καὶ περιττῶν ἀριθμῶν συνεσταμένων* Eus.*l.C.*6(p.210.10; M.20.1348B); *μονὰς…ἀ., ἀδιάβλητος* Anat.Laod.*decad.*(p.29); of elements of the world *ἀσύγχυτον καὶ ἀ. ἀποσῴζει* [sc. divine power] Dion.Ar.*d.n.*8.5(M.3.893A); also = *inseparable* *ἀσεβείας αὐτοῦ κοινωνὸς ἀ.* Petr.II Al.*encycl.*4(M.33.1281B)ap.Thdt.*h.e.*4.22.13.

B. of unity of Godhead; **1.** in gen., from point of view of philosophy *ὁ δὲ θεὸς…ἀ.* Athenag.*leg.*8.2(M.6.905A); *ἀ. γὰρ τὸ ἕν* Clem.*str.* 5.12(p.380.22; M.9.121B); Hipp.*haer.*4.43(p.65.15; M.16.3106B); *τὴν φυσικὴν τοῦ θεοῦ ἔννοιαν ὡς…ἀσυνθέτου καὶ ἀ.* Or.*Cels.*4.14(p.284.28; M.11.1045B); Bas.*hom.*15.1(2.131D; M.31.465C); **2.** of the divine nature opp. three Persons *ἐκκλησία…τὴν μονάδα τὴν ἀ. γνωρίζει,… τὸν ἕνα…θεόν· καὶ τὸν ἐξ αὐτοῦ…υἱόν* Eus.*e.th.*2.6(p.103.9; M.24.905C); *ib.*(p.103.23; 908A); *δύο μὲν εἶναι πατέρα καὶ υἱόν, μονάδα δὲ θεότητος ἀ.* ‡Ath.*Ar.*4.1(p.44.3; M.26.468B); *τὰς τρεῖς ὑποστάσεις περιλαμβάνειν, καὶ ἕνα θεὸν λέγειν, διὰ τὸ τῆς φύσεως…ἀ.* Gr.Nyss.*tres dii*(M.45.124D); †Gr.Thaum.*ep.Philagr.*(M.46.1105A); **3.** Sabellian, without distinction of Persons *λέγων* [sc. Sabellius] *τὸν λόγον αὐτὸν εἶναι υἱόν, αὐτὸν καὶ πατέρα ὀνόματι μὲν καλούμενον, ἓν δὲ ὂν τὸ πνεῦμα ἀ.* Hipp.*haer.*9.12(p.248.27; M.16.3383C); *εἰ δὲ λέγοι Μάρκελλος τὸν λόγον εἶναι τοῦ θεοῦ τὸν σαρκωθέντα…μονάδα δοὺς ἀ., καὶ μίαν ὑπόστασιν τοῦ θεοῦ…εἰ δὲ μονάς ἐστιν ἀ. … τίνα ἂν εἴποι τις πατέρα, τίνα δὲ υἱόν, ἑνὸς ὄντος τοῦ ὑποκειμένου;* Eus.*e.th.*2.5(p.103.3ff.; M.24.905B); *ib.*2.19(p.123.34; 944C); *Χριστός, ἀ. δύναμις τοῦ θεοῦ* Marcell.*ep.*ap.Epiph.*haer.*72.2(p.257.28; M.42.385C); v. *μονάς*.

C. Trin.; **1.** of Trin. as undivided *ἡμεῖς εἴς τε τὴν τριάδα τὴν μονάδα πλατύνομεν ἀ.* Dion.Al.ap.Ath.*Dion.*17(p.58.24; M.25.505A); *τριὰς…ἀ.* Ath.*hom.in Mt.11:27*(M.25.220A); id.*Ar.*1.18(M.26.49B); id.*ep.Epict.*9(p.14.12; M.26.1065A); Chrys.*hom.30.2 in 2Cor.*(10.652B); ‡Chrys.*Trin.*1(1.833B); *τῆς τριάδος…βασιλείαν ἀ.* Thdt.*Trin.*28(M.75.1188C); Gel.Cyz.*h.e.*2.22.6(M.85.1292B); *τριὰς…ἀδιαίρετον ἔχει διαίρεσιν* Sophr.H.*ep.syn.*(M.87.3153A); *Lit.Jac.*(p.226.15); Jo.V H.*icon.*4(M.96.1352C); **2.** of the Persons as inseparable from each other; **a.** of Father and Son *ἀ. ὢν καὶ ἀμέριστος υἱοῦ γίνεται πατήρ* Or.*princ.*4.4.1(28; p.348.7; M.11.401A); *Διονύσιος ἀληθινὸν καὶ φύσει λόγον τοῦ θεοῦ…ἴδιον καὶ ἀ. τῆς τοῦ πατρὸς οὐσίας αὐτὸν εἶναι διδάσκει* Ath.*Dion.*24(p.64.16; M.25.516B); *ἡ ἐκ τοῦ πατρὸς δὲ ἐν υἱῷ ἰδιότης καὶ θεότης δείκνυσι τὸν υἱὸν ἐν τῷ πατρί, καὶ τὸ ἀεὶ ἀ. αὐτοῦ* id.*Ar.*3.6 (M.26.333A); id.*decr.*20(p.17.16; M.25.452C); *ib.*23(p.19.14; 456D); *οὐχ ὡς ἑτεροφυὴς…χωριζόμενός ἐστι τοῦ πατρός, ἀλλ' ὡς ἐξ αὐτοῦ υἱὸς ἀ. ὑπάρχει ὡς ἔστι τὸ ἀπαύγασμα πρὸς τὸ φῶς* id.*syn.*45(p.270.10; M.26.773A); ‡Ath.*Ar.*4.9(p.53.21; M.26.480B); *ib.*4.10(p.54.10; 480C); ‡Chrys.*hom.*7(13.218E); Procl.CP *or.*15.1(M.65.800C); *Chron.Pasch.* p.282(M.92.704B); **b.** of Son and H. Ghost *ἀ. γὰρ τοῦ υἱοῦ τὸ πνεῦμα αὐτοῦ* Cyr.*Jo.*4.3(4.378B); **c.** of Father, Son, and H. Ghost *τῶν ὑπ' ἐμοῦ λεχθέντων ὀνομάτων ἕκαστον ἀχώριστόν ἐστι καὶ ἀ. τοῦ πλησίον. πατέρα εἶπον, καὶ πρὶν ἐπαγάγω τὸν υἱόν, ἐσήμανα καὶ τοῦτον ἐν τῷ πατρί· υἱὸν ἐπήγαγον, εἰ καὶ μὴ προειρήκειν τὸν πατέρα, πάντως ἂν ἐν τῷ υἱῷ προείληπτο. ἅγιον πνεῦμα προσέθηκα, ἀλλ' ἅμα καὶ πόθεν καὶ διὰ τίνος ἧκεν ἐφήρμοσα* Dion.Al.ap.Ath.*Dion.*17(p.58.15; M.25.504C); *ἅγιον πνεῦμα…ἀ. τῆς οὐσίας τοῦ υἱοῦ καὶ τοῦ πατρός* Ath.*tom.*5(M.26.801B); ‡Just.*qu.et resp.*17(M.6.1264C); cf.*ib.*139(1393A); *οὐδὲ τοῦ ἁγίου πνεύματος, καὶ τοῦ σωτῆρος, καὶ τοῦ πατρός, ἐν μέσῳ τομὴν ἢ* διαίρεσιν ἐπινοηθῆναί ποτε· διότι τῶν νοητῶν...καὶ θείων ἀ. ἡ φύσις †Gr.Thaum.*ep.Philagr.*(M.46.1105C); Epiph.*haer.*76.8(p.348.23; M.42.529A); ‡Chrys.*hom.*11(13.247C); διὰ μὲν τῶν τριῶν ὑποστάσεων, τὸ ἀσύνθετον...διὰ δὲ τοῦ ὁμοουσίου καὶ τοῦ ἐν ἀλλήλαις εἶναι τὰς ὑποστάσεις...τὸ ἀ. ‡Cyr.*Trin.*9(6^3.14E; M.77.1144B); **d.** ref. moral union of Christ with Father, ‡Paul.Sam.*fr.*3(p.339.15).

D. Christol., of union of two natures; **1.** pre-CChalc.; **a.** of Melchizedekians ὁ κύριος τὸ ἡμέτερον ἀνέλαβε σῶμα...οὐ γὰρ προϋπέστησεν αὐτό, καὶ τότε ἡνώθη, ἀλλ' ἀ. ἐκ μήτρας ἐποιήσατο τὴν ἕνωσιν Marc.Er.*opusc.*10.5(M.65.1124A); **b.** in Apollinarian controversy κατὰ φύσιν ᾗ τὸ σῶμα, καὶ ἀ. ... κατὰ φύσιν τῆς τοῦ λόγου θεότητος ‡Ath.*Apoll.*1.6(M.26.1104B); οἱ...τῆς ὁμοουσιότητος τὴν ὁμολογίαν προϋπισχνούμενοι πῶς εἰς πάθος καθέλκετε τὸ ἀ. ὄνομα; *ib.*2.12(1152B); εἰ γὰρ διττὴ ἡ φύσις, ἀλλ' οὖν ἀ. ... ἡ ἕνωσις ‡Chrys.*ep.Caes.*(3.746A); **c.** in Nestorian controversy φαμὲν οὖν ἑκατέραις κεχρημένοι ταῖς γραφικαῖς φωναῖς, ὅτι καὶ ἐγένετο σάρξ, καὶ ἔλαβε τὴν τοῦ δούλου μόρφην...διὰ μὲν γὰρ τοῦ, 'ἐγένετο', τὸ ἀ. τῆς ἄκρας ἑνώσεως ὁ εὐαγγελιστὴς ὑπαινίττεται...διὰ τοῦτο δι' ἑκατέρων καὶ τὸ ἄτρεπτον τῆς θεότητος, καὶ τὸ ἀ. τοῦ μυστηρίου, ἡ θεία ὑπεμφαίνουσα γραφὴ τὸ 'ἐγένετο' εἶπε Procl.CP*Arm.*6(p.190.6ff.; M.65.861Bf.); in Cyril's dispute with Nestorius; Nest.'s assertion ὁ Χριστὸς κατὰ τὸ Χριστὸς ἀ. οὐ γὰρ ἔχομεν δύο Χριστοὺς οὐδὲ δύο υἱούς. οὐ γάρ ἐστι παρ' ἡμῖν πρῶτος <Χριστὸς> καὶ δεύτερος...ἀλλ' αὐτὸς ὁ υἱός ἐστι διπλοῦς οὐ τῇ ἀξίᾳ, ἀλλὰ τῇ φύσει Cyr.*Nest.*2.6(p.42.3; 6^1.44D); Cyril's refutation φράζε...τί δὴ ἄρα τὴν ἀ. συνάφειαν εἶναι φής; ἆρα τὴν ἕνωσιν, δῆλον δὲ ὅτι τὴν καθ' ὑπόστασιν, ἣν ἡμεῖς πρεσβεύομεν τοῖς τῆς ἀληθείας συναθλοῦντες δόγμασιν, ἢ ταυτηνὶ τὴν κατὰ παράθεσιν καὶ τὴν πρὸς τόδε τι τοῦ δεῖνος ἐγγύτητα νοουμένην;...οὐκοῦν τῆς παρ' αὐτοῦ λεγομένης συναφείας ἡ δύναμις εἰ τὴν καθ' ἡμᾶς νοουμένην ἑνότητα δηλοῖ, φημὶ δὴ τὴν καθ' ὑπόστασιν, ἔφη ἂν εἰκότως μηδεμίαν εἶναι Χριστοῦ τὴν διαίρεσιν κατὰ τὸ εἶναι Χριστόν· οὐ γάρ ἐστιν ἕτερος καὶ ἕτερος...ἔσται γὰρ οὕτω κατά γε τὴν ἀξίαν, ὡς σὺ φής, καὶ μέντοι τὴν δυναστείαν ἀ. μᾶλλον δὲ ὁ αὐτός. εἶτα πῶς τὸν ἕνα καὶ ἀ. διπλοῦν εἶναι φὴς καὶ οὐχὶ τῇ ἀξίᾳ μᾶλλον, ἀλλὰ τῇ φύσει; *ib.*(p.42.7ff.; 44Eff.); *ib.*2.8(p.45.11; 49B); τὸ γὰρ ἀ. παρ' αὐτοῖς κατὰ τὰς Νεστορίου κενοφωνίας καθ' ἕτερον λαμβάνεται τρόπον· φασὶ γὰρ ὅτι τῇ ἰσοτιμίᾳ, τῇ ταυτοβουλίᾳ, τῇ αὐθεντίᾳ, ἀ. ἐστι τοῦ λόγου ὁ ἐν ᾧ κατῴκηκεν, ἄνθρωπος, ὥστε οὐχ ἁπλῶς τὰς λέξεις προσφέρουσιν, ἀλλὰ μετά τινος δόλου id.*ep.*46.4(p.162.19; 5^2.145E); εἷς δὲ λοιπὸν ἐξ ἀμφοῖν ὁ Χριστός, ἀ. εἰς υἱότητα καὶ εἰς δόξαν θεοπρεπῆ id.*Jo.*2.1(4.151A); for further discussion of term as used in a Nestorian and in an orthodox sense v. Cyr.*apol.orient.*4(pp.41ff.; 6^1.168ff.); **2.** post-CChalc., orthodox terminology dist. from monophysite meaning εἰ τὴν ἐν δυάδι φύσεων ἀ. ὁμολογίαν ἐπὶ τοῦ κυρίου σέβοντες, περὶ τὴν ἑτέραν διαφωνοῦμεν ὑμῖν ἐξαγγελίαν τοῦ δόγματος, ἤγουν τὴν λέγουσαν μίαν φύσιν τοῦ θεοῦ λόγου σεσαρκωμένην, καὶ μὴ μᾶλλον ὑμῶν καὶ τήνδε ἀσμενιζόμεθα, ὄντως ἂν καλῶς διεστέλλεσθε παρ' ἡμῶν Leont.H.*monoph.*(M.86.1805A); μὴ διέλητε τὴν ἀνθρωπότητα αὐτοῦ ἀπὸ τῆς θεότητος αὐτοῦ· ἀ. γὰρ αὕτη...μετὰ τὴν ἕνωσιν Gr.Ant.*bapt.*2.6(M.88.1877A) = ‡Chrys.*hom.*9(13.235A); ἀ. ... λόγου καὶ σαρκὸς δοξάζομεν ἕνωσιν, ἀ. ὑπὲρ ἕνωσιν ψυχῆς καὶ σώματος Eulog.*fr.Trin.*4.8(p.371); ἀ. τὴν μίαν Χριστοῦ ὑπόστασιν δοξάζομεν Thal.*cent.*2.97(M.91.1448A); in paraphrase of *Symb. Chalc.* (v. ἀδιαιρέτως) σύνοδον Χαλκηδόνος...ὁρίσασαν δύο φύσεις ἀ. τὸν ἕνα, καὶ μόνον Χριστὸν τὸν θεόν *Schol.* in Anast.S.*hod.*6(M.89.108C); ‡Jo.D.*icon.*7(M.96.1356A); **3.** of unity of nature (Apollinarian) ὁμολογῶ τὸν κύριον Ἰησοῦν Χριστόν...πρόσωπον ἐν ἀ. Job.Ep.*symb.*(p.286.22; M.86.3320B).

E. other theol. and spiritual applications; **1.** of union of Church and its members with Christ and with one another, exeg. Jo.15:5 τὰ δὲ κλήματα ὁμοούσια...καὶ ἀ. τῆς ἀμπέλου Ath.*Dion.*10(p.53.13; M.25.494C); Jo.17:21 ἀ. δέ ἐστιν ἡ ἐν ἡμῖν ἑνότης· οὕτως ἵνα καὶ αὐτοὶ μαθόντες ἐξ ἡμῶν τὴν ἀ. φύσιν, οὕτω καὶ τὴν πρὸς ἀλλήλους συμφωνίαν διαφυλάττωσιν id.*Ar.*3.20(M.26.365B); Mt.13:31 κόκκῳ σινάπεως τὴν οὐράνιον βασιλείαν ἀπεικάζει ὁ κύριος...διὰ...τὴν ἀ. σῴζειν ὑπόστασιν Isid.Pel.*epp.*1.199(M.78.309C); εἰρήνην δὲ δὸς ἡμῖν τὴν πρὸς σὲ ἀ. ἕνωσιν ‡Bas.*h.myst.*37(p.266.26); τὴν ἑνοειδῆ καὶ ἀ. ζωὴν ἡ τῆς εἰρήνης ἱερουργία νομοθετεῖ Dion.Ar.*e.h.*3.3.8(M.3.437A); ἀ. ἡ ἐκκλησία Socr.*h.e.*1.18.15(M.67.124D); typified by undivided paschal victim τὴν οὖν ἕνωσιν τοῦ ἱερείου τὴν ἀ. ὁ νόμος εἰς Χριστὸν προετύπου ‡Chrys.*pasch.*1(8.252D); **2.** myst. ἐὰν γὰρ μὴ ἡ αὐτοῦ [sc. ἁγίου πνεύματος] θεότης...τὰ τῆς καρδίας ἡμῶν ταμιεῖα καταυγάσῃ, οὐκ ἂν δυνησώμεθα ἐν ἀ. τῇ αἰσθήσει...γεύσασθαι τοῦ ἀγαθοῦ Diad.*perf.*29(p.32.21).

ἀδιαιρέτως, *undividedly, indivisibly, inseparably*;

A. in gen. θεὸν...ἀ. ... σέβων Or.*Cels.*8.4(p.224.1; M.11.1525A); Dion.Ar.*d.n.*11.2(M.3.949C); *ib.*(952A); id.*e.h.*3.3.9(M.3.437C) cit. s. ἕνωσις.

B. Trin. ἡ ἐκ τοῦ πατρὸς εἰς τὸν υἱὸν θεότης...ἀ. τυγχάνει †Ath.*exp.fid.*2(M.25.204B); διαιρεῖται γὰρ ἀ., ἵν' οὕτως εἴπω, καὶ συνάπτεται διῃρημένως. ἓν γὰρ ἐν τρισὶν ἡ θεότης, καὶ τὰ τρία ἕν Gr.Naz.*or.*39.11(M.36.345D) cit. ap. Just.Imp.*edict.*ap.Evagr.*h.e.*5.4(p.198.22; M.86.2796B) ∾ Sophr.H.*ep.syn.*(M.87.3156C); *Lit.Jac.*(p.162.1); of the Persons ἀ. χωριζόμενοι ταῖς ὑποστάσεσιν ‡Caes.Naz.*dial.*3(M.38.860); Jo.D.*hom.*1.1(M.96.545A).

C. Christol.; **1.** ὁ...τῆς κατ' εὐδοκίαν ἑνώσεως τρόπος ἀσυγχύτους φυλάττων τὰς φύσεις, καὶ ἀ. ἐν ἀμφοτέρων τὸ πρόσωπον δείκνυσιν Thdr.Mops.*ep.Domn.*(p.339.3; cf.M.66.1013A); in Nestorian controversy: used by Nestorians, but, according to Cyril, inconsistently with their teaching τὸ δέ, ἀ., προστεθὲν παρ' αὐτοῖς δοκεῖ μέν πως παρ' ἡμῖν ὀρθῆς εἶναι δόξης σημαντικόν Cyr.*ep.*46.4(p.162.18; 5^2.145E); v. ἀσυγχύτως; **2.** at CChalc. and after πάντα γὰρ ἄνθρωπον ἀνεθεμάτισαν...μὴ τὰ θεοπρεπῆ καὶ τὰ ἀνθρωποπρεπῆ αὐτοῦ [sc. Χριστοῦ] εἶναι λέγοντα...ἀ. CChalc.*act.*4(*ACO* 2.1.2 p.102.39; H.2.401B); *Symb.Chalc.*(p.129.31; H.2.456C); difference between orthodox and heret. use ὅσοι κατά τινα ἔννοιαν δυσσεβῆ φασι δυάδα φύσεων τῶν Χριστοῦ ἡνωμένων ἀ., καταπτυστέον· ἀποδεκτέον...πάντας δὲ τοὺς ὁμολογοῦντας δυάδα φύσεων Χριστοῦ ἡνωμένων ἀ. οὐ κατά τε τῶν περὶ τὴν οὐσίαν θεωρουμένων, ἀλλὰ κατὰ τὴν ὑπόστασιν αὐτὴν τῶν φύσεων Leont.H.*monoph.*(M.86.1812D); Jo.D.*f.o.*3.3(M.94.993B); *ib.*3.5(1000D); ἥνωνται...αἱ τοῦ κυρίου φύσεις ἀσυγχύτως καθ' ὑπόστασιν, διῄρηνται δὲ ἀ. λόγῳ...τῆς διαφορᾶς...ᾧ δὲ τρόπῳ ἀ. διῄρηνται, ἀριθμοῦνται· δύο γάρ εἰσιν αἱ φύσεις τοῦ Χριστοῦ *ib.*3.8(1013B); of union of two wills, *Symb.CP*(681)(Hahn p.173; H.3.1400C); **3.** less technical Christol. uses, of union between divinity and humanity in heaven τὴν μετὰ σαρκὸς...τοῦ κυρίου ἀνάληψιν ἐν οὐρανῷ...ὡς ἀ. λοιπὸν τῷ θεῷ λόγῳ ἡνωμένης Isid.Pel.*epp.*1.478(M.78.444B); ὁ καὶ ἐν τοῖς οὐρανοῖς ὑπάρχων ἀ., καὶ ἐν τῇ παρθενικῇ μήτρᾳ διαιτώμενος ἀμολύντως Gr.Ant.*bapt.*2.5(M.88.1876B); v. ἀσυγχύτως, ἀτρέπτως.

***ἀδιακάθαρτος**, *uncleansed*; met., *impure*, of a musical chord, Chrys.*hom.27.3 in Ac.*(9.219E).

ἀδιακρισία, ἡ, *lack of discernment*, Ephr.3.346A; Gr.Nyss.*Eun.*9(2 p.217.15; M.45.816C); Nil.*epp.*2.140(M.79.261B).

ἀδιάκριτος, A. *indistinguishable, incapable of being distinguished*, ref. resurrection of dead παρ' ἀνθρώποις ἀδιάκριτον εἶναι δοκῇ τὸ τῷ παντὶ πάλιν προσφυῶς ἡνωμένον Athenag.*res.*2(p.50.28; M.6.980A); μίξις ἀ. [sc. of elements in primeval chaos] *Hom.Clem.*6.3; Cyr.*Jon.*29(3.389B); Trin. εἰ δὲ εἴποιτε μήτε τὴν φύσιν μήτε τὴν ὑπόστασιν τὰς ἰδιότητας χωρίζειν...οὔτε τοῦ πατρὸς ὁ υἱὸς κατά τι διακρίνεται, τῇ μὲν φύσει ὄντες ταυτοί, ταῖς δὲ ἰδιότησιν ἀδιάκριτοι καὶ ἀδιάγνωστοι Leont.H.*monoph.*27(M.86.1788A).

B. *undifferentiated, uniform* ἀ. πνεῦμα, ὅς ἐστιν Ἰησοῦς Χριστός Ign.*Magn.*15; τὸ ἀ. ἡμῶν ζῆν id.*Eph.*3.2; of faith, Clem.*paed.*2.3(p.180.13; M.8.437A).

C. *undiscriminating*; **1.** *undiscerning*; **a.** met. ἀ. ... μάστιξ Gr.Nyss.*v.Mos.*(M.44.393C); πυρὸς ἀδιακρίτοις...ὁρμαῖς Cyr.*Jo.*3.4(4.270D); **b.** in bad sense ἀ. ... λογισμόν Hegem.*Arch.*5(p.6.9; M.10.1433B); Diad.*perf.*96(p.140.28); ἀ. ... ἐντεύξεις Nil.*epp.*3.114(M.79.436D); of persons ἀ. πλῆθος τῶν διδασκάλων Chrys.*hom.9.2 in 2Tim.*(11.716A); neut. as subst., *Hom.Clem.*3.5; **2.** *not making distinctions* ἀγάπη...ἀ. Clem.*str.*2.18(p.159.18; M.8.1028A); ἀ. ... ἔλεον ‡Nil.*perist.*9.6(M.79.876B); neut. as subst., Bas.*reg.br.*155(2.467C; M.31.1184C).

D. *unhesitating, unwavering* διάνοιαν...ἀ. Ign.*Trall.*1.1; πίστιν Heracl.ap.Or.*Jo.*13.10(p.235.1; M.14.413C); συγκατάθεσις Bas.*fid.*1(2.224C; M.31.677D); ἐλπίς Jo.D.*f.o.*4.10(M.94.1128A); of obedience, *V.Pach.Φ* 36(p.22.9); Dor.*doct.*1.17(M.88.1640C); Jo.Clim.*scal.*1(M.88.632C); of a servant, *V.Pach.Φ* 107(p.71.9).

E. *indissoluble* ἕνωσιν ἀ. [sc. with God] Clem.*str.*7.3(p.10.30; M.9.417B).

ἀδιακρίτως, 1. *without distinction, indiscriminately*; **a.** in gen., explained τὸ παιδίον...πάντα ἀ. ποιεῖ...τοιοῦτοί εἰσιν οἱ πᾶσιν ἁπλῶς προσέχοντες καὶ ἀ. τὰς ἀκοὰς ἐκδιδόντες ἀδοκίμοις Chrys.*hom.8.3 in Heb.*(12.88C); ἵνα μὴ ἀ. ἐπελθοῦσα ἡ ὀργὴ Eus.*fr.Lc.*17:34(M.24.585C); Ephr.3.431D; νίπτων μοναχὸς πόδας ἁμαρτωλῶν ἀ. Hyper.*mon.*82(M.79.1481B); *Disp.Phot.*(M.88.556A); **b.** ref. Christian duty ἀ. πάντας σπλαγχνιζόμενοι ἐλεᾶτε *T.Zab.*7.2; δεῖ κατὰ τὸ δυνατὸν μιμεῖσθαι θεὸν ἐν τῷ ἀ. εὐεργετεῖν Thdr.Heracl.*fr.Mt.*5:44(p.41.32); **c.** ref. Church and election σαγήνη ἐστὶν ἡ ἀποστολικὴ διδασκαλία, ἡ ἀ. συλλαμβανομένη Ἰουδαίους καὶ Ἕλληνας...πονηροὺς καὶ ἀγαθοὺς Or.*fr.in Mt.*13:44(M.17.297A); μὴ ἀ. παντὶ τῷ Ἰουδαίων ἔθνει τὴν τοῦ Χριστοῦ παρουσίαν σωτήριον ἔσεσθαι ὑπέσχετο ὁ θεὸς ἀλλ' ὀλίγοις...τοῖς εἰς τὸν σωτῆρα...πεπιστευκόσιν Eus.*d.e.*2.3(p.69.22; M.22.125C); *ib.*(p.83.21; 149A); *ib.*(p.91.18; 161B); **2.** *unhesitatingly, unquestioningly* ἡ ἀδελφότης τὰ παραγγέλματα τῆς προκαθηγουμένης ἀ. δεχέσθω Bas.*ascet.*2.2(2.326D; M.31.888C); ἁγίοις ὑπακούων ἀ. *V.Pach.Φ* 135(p.85.21); Dor.*doct.*1.17(M.88.1640B).

ἀδιάλειπτος, *unintermittent, unceasing*; of prayer and contemplation, Ign.*Polyc.*1.3; Clem.*str.*5.3(p.336.18; M.9.33A); *ib.*6.9(p.470.24; 297C); *ib.*6.12(p.481.16; 320B); Or.*Jo.*2.2(p.55.7; M.14.109B); *Lit.* ap.*Const.App.*8.10.5; μνήμην ἀ. ἡμῶν ποιοῦ...θεοτόκε ‡Meth.*Sym. et Ann.*14(M.18.381B); of virtue ἀ. ἀγάπην Clem.*str.*7.1(p.4.14; M.9.405A); of eternal life, Const.*or.s.c.*7(p.162.5; M.20.1252B); ref. God ἐν ἀ. εὐποιίαις Clem.*str.*6.12(p.484.26; M.9.325B).

ἀδιαλείπτως, *ceaselessly*; in gen., *T.Jos.*3.6; Polyc.*ep.*8.1; Herm. *sim.*9.27.2; Just.*dial.*133.6(M.6.785B); Clem.*str.*1.17(p.53.14; M.8.797A); Hipp.*haer.*5.26(p.128.31; M.16.3198A); ἀνθρώποις...μὴ δυνηθεῖσιν ἀ. φέρειν αὐτοῦ [sc. H. Ghost] τὴν δόξαν Or.*Jo.*2.11(p.67.6; M.14.132B); of prayer and contemplation ἀ. προσεύχεσθε Ign.*Eph.* 10.1; Polyc.*ep.*4.3; Herm.*sim.*9.11.7; συμπαρὼν...διὰ τῆς γνώσεως καὶ τοῦ βίου καὶ τῆς εὐχαριστίας ἀ. τῷ θεῷ Clem.*str.*7.7(p.27.22; M.9.452A); Or.*or.*25(p.358.18; M.11.497C); ref. life of solitary prayer, Serap.*euch.*11.5; Ath.*v.Anton.*3(M.26.845A); Thal.*cent.*1.50(M.91.1432D); Jo.D.*f.o.*4.13(M.94.1137A); ref. divine activity, Clem.*str.* 5.14(p.392.5; M.9.149A); *ib.*7.7(p.30.18; 456B); Thdr.Heracl.*Is.*46:1 (M.18.1344A).

***ἀδιαλήκτως**, *unceasingly, without relaxation*, Jo.Clim.*scal.*14 (M.88.865C).

[*]**ἀδιάληπτος**, for ἀδιάλειπτος; ἀδιάληπτον ἔχοντας [sc. apostles and evangelists] παρ' αὐτῷ [sc. τῷ θεῷ] τὴν γνώμην Cyr.*Is.*4.4(2.676B); εὐχάς Philox.*ep.*37(p.185).

[*]**ἀδιαλόβητος**, v. ἀδιαλώβητος.

ἀδιαλόγιστος, *unreasoning*, Marc.Er.*opusc.*8.2(M.65.1104B); Anast. S.*hod.*1(M.89.44B).

***ἀδιαλύπως**, f.l. for ἀδιαλύτως *Ev.Barth.*(Vassiliev p. 11); cf. not. *ib.*1.31(*RB* 10 p.189).

ἀδιαλώβητος (-λόβητος), *unspoiled, uninjured*; in gen., Cyr.*Is.* 1.3(2.79C); of burning bush, id.*glaph.Ex.*1(1.262E); τῆς ἑαυτῶν ψυχῆς ἀδιαλόβητον...τηροῦμεν τὸ κάλλος id.*Is.*3.1(385D); Jo.VI H. *v.Jo.D.*1(M.94.429A); ref. Inc. ὁ λόγος...τῆς ἰδίας φύσεως τὴν κατὰ πάντων ὑπεροχὴν ἀδιαλώβητον ἔχων Cyr.*Nest.*2.4(p.40.3; 6^1.41D); *ib.* 4.3(p.83.21; 107D); id.*inc.unigen.*(5^1.703C) = id.*Thds.*33(p.64.23; 5^2.30E).

***ἀδιαμάσητος**, *unchewed*; *crude*, met. ὁ ὀργιζόμενος ἀδιαμάσητα ταῦτα φθέγγεται Chrys.*hom.31.4 in Ac.*(9.246C).

ἀδιαμόρφωτος, *not fully formed*, †Marc.Er.*temp.*24(M.65.1064B).

ἀδιανέμητος, *undivided*; of Christ's robe, Cyr.*Jo.*10(4.1063D).

ἀδιανόητος, *unintelligible*, Dion.Al.ap.Eus.*p.e.*14.27(783C; M.21.1288C); Gr.Nyss.*Eun.*2(2 p.309.13; M.45.481A); Leont.H.*monoph.*61 (M.86.1804A).

ἀδιανοήτως, *unintelligibly*, Gr.Nyss.*Apoll.*29(M.45.1185C).

***ἀδιάνοικτος**, *unopened*, ‡Epiph.*hom.*2(M.43.444C,452B); ἡ τῇ παρθενίᾳ ἀ. εὐκαρπία Thdr.Stud.*nativ.BMV* 7(M.96.692C).

ἀδιάπεπτος, *undigested*, Melet.*nat.hom.*synops.(M.64.1133C).

ἀδιάπνευστος, *not blown through*; **1.** *not ventilated* μὴ σκαφεῖσα ἄμπελος ἀ. ἐστι †Bas.*Is.*21(1.394B; M.30.156C); **2.** *not escaping, abiding* ἄνθος *A.Jo.*108(p.206.8); of air in a box, Gr.Nyss.*anim.et res.* (M.46.805B); of strength in the body, id.*laud.Bas.*16(M.46.805B); of the quality in scent, id.*hom.3 in Cant.*(M.44.828C).

ἀδιάπτωτος, **1.** *infallible, unerring*; of authors of scripture, Eus. *p.e.*1.3(7C; M.21.32C); of doctrine inspired by H. Ghost, id.*d.e.*5 proem.(p.209.8; M.22.348A); τὸ διδασκάλιον τῆς ἀληθείας...ἀδιάπτωτον...κατὰ τὴν γνῶσιν Bas.*hex.*3.6(1.28C; M.29.68B); Isid.Pel.*epp.* 2.63(M.78.508A); **2.** *firm, unshakeable*, met. τὴν...ἔνστασιν...ἀδιάπτωτον τῆς ψυχῆς Meth.*symp.*11.3(p.139.27; M.18.217D); ὀρθὰ βαδίζειν καὶ ἀ., εἰ τῆς τοῦ πνεύματος ἐπιλάβοιο βοηθείας Chrys.*hom.13.6 in Rom.*(9.567B); of Christ as ἔλπις τῶν ἁγίων...ἀ. Didym.*Ps.*60:3(M.39.1421A); of God's mercy and truth, Hadr.*introd.*69(M.98.1288B).

***ἀδιάριστος**, *without a* διάριον, *without subsistence* μήτε...ἐξεῖναι ἀ. τινὰς χειροτονεῖν ἢ κατατάσσειν Jo.Scholast.*coll.cap.*20(p.395).

***ἀδίαρος**, = foreg., Ath.Scholast.*coll.*1.9(p.18).

***ἀδιάρπακτος**, *not carried off*, Bas.*hom.*23.4(2.189B; M.31.600A).

ἀδιάρρευστος, *not wasting away, everlasting* τρυφῆς ἀ. χωρίον Germ.CP *or.*1(M.98.225D).

ἀδιάρρηκτος, *untorn, unbroken*; of unity of human body, Arist. *apol.*13.5; of threefold cord of faith, hope, and love, Sophr.H.*ep.syn.* (M.87.3149D); of Christ's robe, Jo.D.*hom.*3.9(M.96.600B); of BMV, Ephr.2.266B.

ἀδιασκέπτως, *without deliberation*, Didym.*Trin.*2.7(M.39.585D).

ἀδιάσπαστος, *unbroken, inseparable*; **1.** in gen., *LS*; neut. as subst., Chrys.*hom.62.1 in Mt.*(7.621A); Cyr.*Ps.*62:9(M.69.1121D); **2.** Christol. ἀσεβὲς...τὸ διορίζειν εἰς δύο υἱοὺς...μετὰ τὴν ἀ. ἕνωσιν Cyr. *Pulch.*59(p.61.23; 5^2.180B); id.*hom.pasch.*17(5^2.233A); γέγονε σὰρξ ὁ λόγος...εἰς ἕνωσιν ἀ. id.*ep.*40(p.26.3; 5^2.115C); *ib.*45(p.153.18; 137C); id.*apol.orient.*(p.44.17; 6^1.172C); δύο φύσεων ἀ. ἑνώσεως †Jo.D.*creat.* 4.29(M.96.632B).

ἀδιασπάστως, **1.** *inseparably* ἀ. εἶχεν αὐτοῦ Chrys.*hom.10.1 in 2Tim.*(11.720E); id.*hom.11.1 in Eph.*(11.80C); id.*hom.5.3 in Col.* (11.361D); of sacramental union between Christ and believers, Didym.*Trin.*2.13(M.39.692B); Trin. ἀ. γὰρ ἔχει [sc. ἡ τριάς] πρὸς ἑαυτήν Chrys.*hom.13.8 in Rom.*(9.569D); **2.** *continuously*, Gr.Nyss. *hom.opif.*13.2(M.44.165B); id.*fat.*(M.45.153A).

***ἀδιάστακτος**, *not* merely *trickling, abundant* πίστεως ἀ. Leont. N.*v.Sym.*proem.3(M.93.1672C).

***ἀδιαστάκτως**, *abundantly*; hence met., *whole-heartedly*, *Schol.*28 in Jo.Clim.*scal.*15(M.88.913C).

ἀδιάσταλτος, *not making a distinction*, Proc.G.*Gen.*1:26(M.87.120D).

***ἀδιαστάλτως**, *without distinction* τὰ αὐτὰ [sc. λεγόμενα]...ἀ. καὶ καθ' ἑκάστης ἐναρμόττειν τῶν ὑποστάσεων Areth.*Apoc.*1(M.106.512C).

ἀδιάστατος, **1.** *without intermission, continuous*, *LS*; hence of *unperturbed* life τῆς ἀταράχου καὶ ἀ. ζωῆς Or.*exp.in Pr.*2(M.17.168A); **2.** *inseparable, undivided*; **a.** in gen. ἀδιάστατος [sc. man] τῆς τοῦ θεοῦ...ἀγάπης Clem.*str.*7.12(p.51.8; M.9.497C); ἐν τῇ μελλούσῃ διαγωγῇ ἀδιαστάτους ἡμᾶς εἶναι †Jo.D.*B.J.*18(M.96.1024A); **b.** Trin. τὴν ἀ. τριάδα Cyr.*hom.div.*4(p.104.28; 5^2.358C); Jo.D.*f.o.* 1.14(M.94.860B); of relationship between Father and Son ὃς [sc. λόγος] εἰς τὸν κόλπον τοῦ πατρὸς εἶναι λέγεται ἀ. Clem.*exc.Thdot.*8 (p.108.21; M.9.657C); Gr.Nyss.*Eun.*8(2 p.181.18; M.45.773D); ἑνότης ἀ. ... ἐν αὐτοῖς Cyr.*thes.*12(5^1.115B); συμπαρεῖναι γὰρ πεπιστεύκαμεν τῷ δι' ἡμᾶς ἐνανθρωπήσαντι υἱῷ κατὰ τὴν εὐδοκίαν, καὶ τὸν ἀδιάστατον αὐτοῦ πατέρα κατὰ τὴν θεότητα ‡Meth.*Sym.et Ann.*2(M.18.352C); of relationship between Son and H. Ghost ἀ. ... συνάφεια Gr.Nyss. *Maced.*16(M.45.1321A); **c.** Christol. σὰρξ...φέρουσα τὸν θεὸν λόγον καθ' ἕνωσιν ἀ. Max.*schol.c.h.*7.1(M.4.68A); **3.** *without extension* or *dimension*; **a.** of the soul, Gr.Nyss.*anim.et res.*(M.46.45B,C); neut. as subst., Nemes.*nat.hom.*2(M.40.540C); **b.** of divine nature ἀ. καὶ ἄποσος καὶ ἀπερίγραπτος δύναμις Gr.Nyss.*Eun.*8(2 p.199.6; M.45.796A); τὸ δὲ ἄποσον καὶ ἀ., πῶς ἄν τις ἢ μετρήσειεν ἢ διαστήσειεν; ποῖον ἐπὶ τοῦ ἀπόσου μέτρον εὑρὼν ἢ ποῖον ἐπὶ τοῦ ἀδιαστάτου διάστημα; πῶς δέ τις τὸ ἀόριστον τέλει καὶ ἀρχῇ διαλήψεται; ἀρχὴ γὰρ καὶ τέλος τῶν διαστηματικῶν περάτων ἐστὶν ὀνόματα. διαστάσεως δὲ μὴ οὔσης οὐδὲ τὸ πέρας ἔστιν. ἀλλὰ μὴν ἀ. ἡ θεία φύσις· ἀ. δὲ οὖσα, πέρας οὐκ ἔχει *ib.*9(2 p.215.4ff.; 813Bf.); *ib.*(p.206.8; 804A); **4.** *not measured by time, eternal*; of generation of Son, *ib.*(p.214.2; 812C).

ἀδιαστάτως, **1.** *continuously* ἀνακεῖσθαι τῷ ἁγίῳ θεῷ...ἀ. Bas. *reg.br.*53(2.433B; M.31.1117C); ἀ. εὐχὴν...ἀναπέμπων Diod.*Ps.*71:15 (M.33.1612C); ref. incarnate Son who as God is present κάτω καὶ ἄνω ἀ. ‡Meth.*Sym.et Ann.*6(M.18.360C); **2.** *without interval, immediately* ἡ κτίσις...ἀ. δυναμωθεῖσα τῷ προστάγματι Gr.Nyss. *hom.8 in Cant.*(M.44.948A); ἀ. τῇ ἀρχῇ συναπηρτίσθη τὸ πέρας...ἐπὶ μὲν οὖν τῆς πρώτης κτίσεως, ἀ. τῇ ἀρχῇ συνανεφάνη τὸ πέρας, καὶ ἀπὸ τῆς τελειότητος ἡ φύσις τοῦ εἶναι ἤρξατο id.*hom.15 in Cant.*(M.44.1109Af.); πᾶν ἀγαθὸν πρᾶγμα καὶ ὄνομα...διὰ τοῦ μονογενοῦς θεοῦ...ἀ. εἰς τελείωσιν ἄγεται id.*tres dii*(M.45.129B); ref. generation of Son μόνον τὸν πατέρα ὁ εὐσεβὴς λόγος τῆς ὑποστάσεως τοῦ υἱοῦ προθεωρεῖ ἀ. id.*Eun.*1(1 p.201.9; M.45.448C); *ib.*(p.127.24; 364C); *ib.*(p.131.22; 369A); *ib.*12(1 p.276.1; 984A); Didym.*Trin.*1.32(M.39.429C); Jo.D. *hom.*4.4(M.96.605A); **3.** *inseparably, indivisibly*, Trin. ἀδιαίρετον δεχώμεθα συνουσίαν συνόντων ἀλλήλοις ἀ. ‡Ath.*Sabell.*12(M.28.116C); ‡Cyr.*Trin.*7(6^3.8E; M.77.1132C) cit. s. διαιρέω; ἑνούμενοι...διαστάσει ἀ. ‡Caes.Naz.*dial.*3(M.38.860); ref. relationship between Father and Son, *Symb.Ant.*(345)9(p.253.37; M.26.733B) cit. s. ἀμεσιτεύτως; Bas.*Eun.*2.12(1.247D; M.29.593C); συνῆπται...ὁ υἱὸς τῷ πατρὶ ἀ. id. *hom.*24.4(2.193E; M.31.609B); ἀ. τε ἅμα καὶ κεχωρισμένως Cyr.*Jo.*3.5 (4.306E); between Father and H. Ghost ἐξ αὐτοῦ προϊόντος ἀμερίστως τε καὶ ἀ. *ib.*11(931C); Jo.D.*f.o.*1.13(M.94.857A).

ἀδιαστίκτως, *without distinction* συνόντος...ἀδιαστίκτως τοῦ τεκόντος αὐτῷ [sc. τῷ υἱῷ] Cyr.*glaph.Num.*(1.383A).

ἀδιαστόλως, *without discrimination*, Meth.*symp.*9.4(p.119.22; M.18.188B); Eus.*p.e.*13.19(708D; M.21.1172A).

ἀδιαστρέπτως, *without wavering*, Eus.*d.e.*3.4(p.120.8; ἀδιατρέπτως M.22.204D).

ἀδιαστρόφως, *without distortion*; ref. interpretations, Eus.*e.th.*

1 proem.(p.62.16, conj. for διαστρόφως M.24.828D); Didym.*Trin.* 3.38(M.39.972C); Cyr.*ador.*14(1.497A).

***ἀδιατίμητος**, *not subject to valuation*, Phot.*nomoc.*2.1(M.104.565C).

ἀδιάτμητος, *undivided, unbroken*; **1.** in gen. ἀ. ... ἀγκύλας *A. Andr.*B 1(p.58.14); met. ἀ. τὴν εἰρήνην Cyr.*Is.*5.3(2.811B); of consistency in teaching τὸν...ἀ. τῆς διδασκαλίας αὐτοῦ λόγον Eustrat. *v.Eutych.*81(M.86.2365C); neut. as subst., Jo.VI CP *ep.*(M.96.1432D); **2.** ref. unity of Christ prefigured by undivided birds in Gen.15:10, Cyr.*glaph.Gen.*3(1.77D); by unity of man, id.*ep.*50(p.92.20; 5².160E); of unity of Christ in two natures, id.*Chr.un.*(5¹.735D); Sophr.H. *ep.syn.*(M.87.3168B); ἀ. ἐν δυσὶν ἀδιαιρέτως γνωριζόμενος φύσεσι *ib.* (3177B); **3.** of divine nature ἡ...φύσις μία ἐστίν...καὶ ἀ. ἀκριβῶς μονάς Gr.Nyss.*tres dii*(M.45.120B).

***ἀδιατράνωτος**, *not made clear, obscure* τὸ ἀ. τῆς γλώττης Ath. *ep.mort.Ar.*5(p.180.20; M.25.689C).

ἀδιάτρεπτος, *not to be turned aside, obstinate, immovable*, Eus. *h.e.*8.6.3(M.20.752C); neut. as subst., Clem.*paed.*3.2(p.240.15; M.8. 565A); Eus.*d.e.*3.4(p.120.11; M.22.205A).

ἀδιατρέπτως, *obstinately, without wavering*, Eus.*e.th.*3.7(p.165.8; M.24.1016C).

ἀδιατύπωτος, *unshapen*, Bas.*hex.*2.2(1.13C; M.29.32A); met., *unregulated* ἡ...τῶν παθῶν...ἀ. κίνησις Max.*cap.*5.23(M.90.1357A).

***ἀδιαφθορία, ἡ**, *incorruptibility* τῆς ἀ. προϋπεχάραττεν [sc. the sabbath] εἰκονίσματα Germ.CP *or.*2(M.98.204C); ἐν τῇ διδασκαλίᾳ ἀ. Ant.Mon.*hom.*102(M.89.1744B).

ἀδιάφθορος, **1.** *uncorrupted*; of Christ's flesh, Didym.*Ac.*2:31 (M.39.1660C); **2.** met., *pure, undefiled*; of Church, Heges.ap.Eus. *h.e.*3.32.7(M.20.284B); of its teaching, Eus.*e.th.*1 proem.(p.62.20; M.24.829A).

ἀδιαφθόρως, *without corruption* ἐκ παρθένου ἀ. σεσάρκωται ‡Jo.D. *fid.dorm.*20(M.95.265C).

***ἀδιαφόρησις, ἡ**, Pall.*h.Laus.*25(M.34.1091A) for ἀδιαφορία (p.80. 13).

ἀδιαφορία, ἡ, A. *indifference*; **1.** philos., as the end of life ἀδύνατον...κυνικῷ ἀδιάφορον τὸ τέλος προεμένῳ τὸ ἀγαθὸν εἰδέναι πλὴν ἀ. Just.*2apol.*3.7(M.6.449B); τέλος οὗτος [sc. Ariston] εἶναι τὴν ἀ. ἔφη Clem.*str.*2.21(p.183.15; M.8.1076B); **2.** concerning food, etc. τῆς τῶν βρωμάτων ἀ. Eus.*d.e.*4.16(p.194.16; M.22.324B); Chrys. *hom.25.2 in Mt.*(7.308D); Dor.*doct.*15.2(M.88.1789B); **3.** of culpable indifference about conduct οἱ [sc. Gnost. heretics] τὴν ἀ. εἰσάγοντες Clem.*str.*3.8(p.224.10; M.8.1164C); Νικόλαος...ἐδίδασκεν ἀ. βίου τε καὶ βρώσεως οὗ τοὺς μαθητὰς...Ἰωάννης ἤλεγχε πορνεύοντας καὶ εἰδωλόθυτα ἐσθίοντας Hipp.*haer.*7.36(p.223.9; M.16.3343B); Bas. *reg.fus.*10.1(2.352D; M.31.945A); *ib.*28.1(372C; 989A); Gr.Nyss.*ep.*2 (M.46.1012B); CEph.(431)*can.*5(p.28.12).

B. *carelessness* εἴ τε κατὰ ἀ. ἐν τῷ λαϊκῷ βίῳ ἀπαρατηρήτως ἔγραψε Bas.*ep.*224(3.343B; M.32.837A).

C. *promiscuity*, Jo.D.*haer.*21(M.94.689B); v. ἀδιάφορος.

ἀδιάφορος, A. *not different*, Trin. τῶν φύσεων οὐσῶν ἀ., αἱ ὑποστάσεις εἰσὶν ἀ. πῶς οὖν μίαν μὲν καὶ ἀ. τῆς ἁγίας τριάδος τὴν φύσιν, διαφόρους δὲ τὰς ὑποστάσεις πιστεύομεν; ἀκόλουθον γὰρ ἔσται, ὥσπερ ὧν αἱ φύσεις διάφοροι, τούτων καὶ αἱ ὑποστάσεις λέγονται καθ' ὑμᾶς διάφοροι οὕτως καὶ ὧν αἱ φύσεις ἀ., τούτων καὶ τὰς ὑποστάσεις ἀ. λέγεσθαι...ἐπεὶ οὖν οὐ μόνον ἀ. ἀλλὰ καὶ μία τῆς ἁγίας τριάδος ἡ φύσις, ἔστω καὶ ἡ ὑπόστασις μία τε καὶ ἀ. Leont.H.*Nest.*2. 13(M.86.1564A).

B. *indifferent, neither good nor bad*, of food τόδε φάγε, τόδε μὴ φάγῃς, ἅπερ ἐστὶν ἀ. Chrys.*hom.15.2 in Heb.*(12.151B); of celibacy and marriage, Or.*comm.in 1Cor.*7:19(*JTS* 9 p.507).

C. *unimportant* ἀ. πράγματι Or.*hom.12.8 in Jer.*(p.94.19; M.13. 389A); ὁ...τοῦ θανάτου φόβος ἀ. ἦν αὐτοῖς *cat.Gal.*2:11f.(p.35.13), cf. οὐδὲν ἦν αὐτοῖς ἀ. Chrys.*comm.in Gal.*2:11f.(10.688C); ref. the Elchezaites φησὶν...ὅτι τὸ ἀρνήσασθαι ἀ. ἐστιν Or.ap.Eus.*h.e.*6.38 (M.20.600A).

D. *unrestricted*; **1.** in gen. ἐν τῇ ἀ. συνηθείᾳ ζῶντα (opp. solitary life) Bas.*reg.fus.*6.1(2.344D; M.31.925C); of communion ἀ. τοίνυν ἔτι τυγχανούσης τῆς μεταξὺ τῶν δυτικῶν τε καὶ ἀνατολικῶν κοινωνίας Socr.*h.e.*2.18.7(M.67.224B); *ib.*2.22.2(245A); *ib.*5.4.1(569B); **2.** in bad sense; of use of words, Gr.Nyss.*tres dii*(M.45.132C); id.*Eun.*4(2 p.83. 17; M.45.657D); of persons ref. sexual intercourse, *promiscuous*, Athenag.*leg.*32.1(M.6.964B); cf.Epiph.*anac.*21(p.234.6; M.41.281 ἀδιαφορίαν).

E. *undifferentiated*; plur., applied to group of Manicheans dist. from ἐκλεκτοί, Leont.B.*Nest.et Eut.*3(M.86.1364A).

F. *not making a difference* or *distinction* Σαββάτιος...ἠξίου ἅμα τοῖς Ἰουδαίοις τὴν τοῦ πάσχα ἑορτὴν ἐπιτελεῖν...λογιζόμενοι [sc. Novatianists]...ἕκαστον...ἣ ἂν αὐτῷ δοκῇ, ταύτην τὴν ἑορτὴν ἐπιτελεῖν. καὶ κανόνα ἔθεντο ὃν ἀδιάφορον ἐπωνόμασαν Soz.*h.e.*7.18.4(M.67. 1469B).

ἀδιαφόρως, *without making a distinction, indifferently*; **1.** in gen., Clem.*str.*2.20(p.173.3; M.8.1053B); Chrys.*hom.10.2 in 2Tim.* (11.723A); ἕτεροι ἀ. καὶ βασιλέα καλοῦσιν [i.e. Herod the tetrarch] Vict.*Mc.*6:14(p.324.27); **2.** morally οὐκ ἀ. βιωτέον Clem.*str.*3.5 (p.215.2; M.8.1145A); Bas.*reg.br.*293(2.518B; M.31.1288C); Dor.*doct.* 4.5(M.88.1665A); **3.** ref. sexual intercourse, *promiscuously*, Athenag. *leg.*32.1(M.6.964A); Clem.*str.*3.10(p.228.5; M.8.1172B).

***ἀδιάφυκτος**, *inescapable*, Cyr.*Ps.*44:5(M.69.1036C); id.*inc.unigen.* (5¹.689C) = id.*Thds.*(p.53.8; 5².15D); id.*Lc.*13:32(M.72.781C).

***ἀδιαφύλακτος**, for ἀδιάφυκτος q.v., *cat.Lc.*13:33(p.110.31) cf. Cyr.*Lc.*13:32(M.72.781C).

ἀδιάχυτος, **1.** *not diffused*, Gr.Nyss.*hex.*27(M.44.89A); Dion.Ar. *ep.*4(M.3.1072B); Thdr.Stud.*antirr.*2.46(M.99.385A); **2.** met., *not enervated, stable, settled*; of character, Gr.Nyss.*virg.*7(p.280.24; M.46. 352B); Chrys.*Stag.*1.10(1.178A); id.*hom.8.1 in Phil.*(11.257B).

ἀδιάψευστος, *not deceitful*, Eus.*l.C.*2(p.200.10; M.20.1328A); *Const.App.*7.35.10.

ἀδίδακτος, **1.** *untaught*; **a.** of persons περὶ τούτων...οὐκ ἀ. μεμενήκαμεν Alex.Al.*ep.encycl.*6(p.10.1; M.18.577A); Nonn.*par.Jo.* 1:31(M.43.756A); *ib.*7:15(808A); **b.** of instincts and virtues, *natural, instinctive* ἀ. καὶ φυσικὴ τῆς ἑαυτῶν [sc. τῶν ἀλόγων] ζωῆς ἐπιμέλεια Bas.*hex.*9.3(1.82C; M.29.193A); τῇ ψυχῇ ἔστι τις ἀ. ἔκκλισις τοῦ κακοῦ *ib.*9.4(83E; M.196C); ἀ. ... ἡ πρὸς τὸν θεὸν ἀγάπη id.*reg.fus.* 2.1(2.336B; M.31.908B); **c.** of God as ἡ ἀ. σοφία *Lit.*ap.*Const.App.* 8.12.7; ἀ. ... μόνος...ὁ τῶν ὅλων θεός Pall.*ep.Laus.*(p.6.3; M.34.1001); **2.** *that cannot be taught* or *learned* οὐδὲν ἀκατάληπτον τῷ υἱῷ τοῦ θεοῦ, ὅθεν οὐδὲ ἀ. Clem.*str.*6.8(p.466.32; M.9.292A).

ἀδιεξίτητος, *having no way out, impassable* ἀ. ... ἡ ὁδός Socr.*h.e.* 1.20.10(M.67.132C); met. τὸν τοῦ βίου τούτου λαβύρινθον ἀ. Gr.Nyss. *or.catech.*35(p.132.5; M.45.88B); ἀ. ... τὰ κακὰ Olymp.*Job* 19:8(M.93. 205A); neut. as subst., Gr.Nyss.*Eun.*1(1 p.129.14; M.45.365C).

ἀδιεξόδευτος, **1.** *having no outlet, inescapable* πονηρία...ἀ. Chrys. *exp.in Ps.*124(5.351A); τὴν ἀ. αὐτοῦ [sc. θανάτου] φρουράν Cyr.*Ps.* 67:21(M.69.1153B); Nil.*Magn.*26(M.79.1001D); **2.** *unable to escape* λόγοι...ἀ. κατεχόμενοι Olymp.*Job* 32:17(M.93.345B); **3.** *unlimited, infinite*, †Dion.Al.*fr.2 in Job*(p.204.7).

ἀδιερεύνητος, *uninvestigated*, Clem.*str.*1.5(p.21.4; M.8.725A).

***ἀδικαίωμα, τό**, *unrighteous act, iniquity*, Ephr.3.99C.

ἀδίκαστος, *uncondemned*, Nonn.*par.Jo.*19:12(M.43.900B).

ἀδικ-έω, **1.** *do wrong*, ref. persecution of Christians εἰ μηδὲν διά τε τὴν προσηγορίαν τοῦ ὀνόματος καὶ διὰ τὴν πολιτείαν εὑρισκόμεθα ~οῦντες, ὑμέτερον ἀγωνιᾶσαί ἐστι, μή, ἀδίκως κολάζοντες τοὺς μὴ ἐλεγχομένους τῇ δίκῃ, κόλασιν ὀφλήσετε Just.*1apol.*4.2(M.6.332C); **2.** *harm, injure*; **a.** c. dat. pers., *T.Sym.*5.4; **b.** pass. ὁ θεὸς καὶ δεσπότης...εἰσέρχεται...εἰς τοὺς οἴκους, ὅπου κατεσκήνωσεν ὁ θάνατος ...κἀκεῖθεν ῥυόμενος τὸν Ἀδὰμ οὐκ ~εῖται ὑπὸ τοῦ θανάτου Mac.Aeg. *hom.*11.13(M.34.556A).

ἀδικητής, ὁ, *wronger, injurer*, ‡Chrys.*hom.2.2 in Ps.118*(5.702A).

ἀδικητικῶς, *in the manner of one disposed to do wrong*, Or.*Cels.* 5.40(p.44.12; M.11.1245A).

ἀδικία, ἡ, *injustice, unrighteousness, wrongdoing*; **1.** in gen. ἄφες ἡμῖν...τὰς ἀ. *1Clem.*60.1; μὴ...ἀγανακτῶμεν...ὅταν τις ἡμᾶς... ἐπιστρέφῃ ἀπὸ τῆς ἀ. εἰς τὴν δικαιοσύνην *2Clem.*19.2; *Barn.*3.3; Just.*1apol.*37.8(M.6.385C); id.*dial.*15.4(M.6.508B); διὰ τὰς ἀ. ὑμῶν... εἰς σημεῖον...καὶ τὸ σάββατον ἐντέταλται ὁ θεὸς φυλάσσειν ὑμᾶς *ib.*21.1 (520B); Clem.*str.*1.27(p.106.23; M.8.920A); ἀτύχημα μὲν οὖν παράλογός ἐστιν ἁμαρτία, ἡ δὲ ἁμαρτία ἀκούσιος ἀ., ἀ. δὲ ἑκούσιος κακία *ib.*2.15(p.147.19; 1004A); Or. *hom.8.7 in Jer.*(p.61.25; M.13.344D); angel of ἀ., id.*hom.12 in Lc.*(p.86.21); Ath.*inc.*5.3f.(M.25.105B); **2.** ref. Christian resistance to and abstention from ἀ., *1Clem.*35.5; ἡμᾶς ἐγερεῖ, ἐὰν ποιῶμεν αὐτοῦ τὸ θέλημα...ἀπεχόμενοι πάσης ἀ. Polyc.*ep.* 2.2; Just.*dial.*70.2(M.6.640C); Meth.*symp.*8.16(p.105.19; M.18.169A); **3.** ref. persecutions, Just.*dial.*17.1(M.6.512B); εὐχόμενοι ἵνα ἀδίκως διώκωνται καὶ μὴ δικαίως, μὴ δι' ἀ., μὴ δι' ἁμαρτίαν Or.*hom.1.13 in Jer.*(p.11.22; M.13.269C); **4.** God has no ἀ. (cf. Jo.7:18), Just. *dial.*92.5(M.6.696C); nor cause of it, *ib.*94.1(700B); Meth.*symp.*8.16 (p.106.1; M.18.169A); hating it, Just.*1apol.*68.2(M.6.432A); Ath.*Ar.* 1.51(M.26.120A); Cross as trophy of victory over ἀ., Meth.*Porph.*1 (p.504.12; M.18.400B); God removing ἀ., Chrys.*grat.*5(2.667B).

ἀδικοδοξέω, *seek fame by unworthy means*, *Schol.Clem.paed.* (p.336.25; M.9.792C).

ἄδικος, *unjust, unrighteous, wicked*; **1.** of things, qualities, etc.; denial that anything ἄ. is contained in scripture, *1Clem.*45.3; ref.

Christ's death τὴν ἀ. ψῆφον τῆς ἁμαρτίας Thdt.*Rom*.8:3(3.81); ἔδει δὲ πρὸς ἀναίρεσιν τῆς ἀδικωτάτης ἡδονῆς...ἐπινοηθῆναι...θάνατον ἀ. ... ἀ. δέ, ὡς οὐδεμίας ἐμπαθοῦς τὸ παράπαν ζωῆς ὄντα διάδοχον· ἵνα μέσος διαληφθεὶς ἡδονῆς ἀ. καὶ πόνου καὶ θανάτου δικαιοτάτου, πόνος καὶ θάνατος ἀδικώτατος, ἀνέλῃ διόλου τὴν ἐξ ἡδονῆς ἀδικωτάτην ἀρχήν, καὶ τὸ δι' αὐτὴν διὰ θανάτου δικαιότατον τέλος τῆς φύσεως Max.*qu.Thal*.61(M.90.628D); id.*cap*.4.44(M.90.1324D); **2.** personal εἰς μετάνοιαν ἐκάλεσεν ὁ Χριστὸς...τοὺς...ἀ. Just.*1apol*.15.7(M.6.349C); of sinful Israel, id.*dial*.19.5(M.6.517A); θεὸν ἐπικαλεῖται ὁ δίκαιος, τὴν σοφίαν ἐπικαλεῖται καὶ ὁ ἀ. Or.*hom.20.7 in Jer*.(p.186.35; M.13.513D); ref. prayers of the unrighteous τὸ γὰρ λέγειν 'δός μοι μερίδα μετὰ τῶν προφητῶν', μὴ παθόντα τὰ τῶν προφητῶν...ἀ. ἐστι. τὸ λέγειν 'δός μοι μερίδα μετὰ τῶν ἀποστόλων', μὴ θέλοντα... εἰπεῖν 'ἐν κόποις περισσοτέρως, κτλ.'...πάντων ἐστὶν ἀδικώτατον *ib.14.14*(p.119.19; 421B); ἡ τοῦ ἀ. προσευχὴ θυμίαμα μέν, τοιοῦτον δὲ θυμίαμα ὥστ' ἂν λεχθῆναι περὶ αὐτοῦ καὶ τοῦ εὐχομένου ἀ., εἰς κενὸν ἐθυμίασαν *ib.18.10*(p.164.20; 484A); of heretics as ἄ., Clem.*str*.7.8(p.38.1; M.9.472B); πλέον τῶν ἀδικούντων ἀδικώτεροι Ath.*apol.sec*.82(p.161.26; M.25.396C); future punishment of the wicked, Just.*1apol*.20.4(357C); with demons, *ib*.52.3(405A); κολάζονται ἐν αἰωνίῳ πυρὶ οἱ ἄ. id.*2apol*.9.1(460A); id.*dial*.5.3(488B); of Christians in rel. to Roman law τὰς πράξεις κρίνεσθαι ἀξιοῦμεν, ἵνα ὁ ἐλεγχθεὶς ὡς ἄ. κολάζηται, ἀλλὰ μὴ ὡς Χριστιανός id.*1apol*.7.4(337B); ἀλλὰ δόξας μὲν εἶναι ἄ., κολάζεται [sc. ἐπὶ τῷ ὀνόματι] Athenag.*leg*.2.4 (M.6.896A); of Devil, *M.Polyc*.19.2; of Zeus, Clem.*prot*.2(p.27.25; M.8.116A); ref. God θεὸς γὰρ οὐδαμῇ οὐδαμῶς ἄ. *ib*.10(p.71.5; 212A).

ἀδίκως, *unjustly*, ref. persecution of Christians τῶν μισούντων ἡμᾶς ἀ. *1Clem*.60.3; Just.*1apol*.1.1(M.6.329A); *ib*.45.6(397B); v. ἀδικέω; ref. Christ's suffering ἵνα πάσχων ἀ. ἀνέλῃ τὴν ἐξ ἡδονῆς ἄδικον τυραννοῦσαν τὴν φύσιν ἀρχὴν τῆς γενέσεως Max.*qu.Thal*.61(M.90.629B).

ἀδιόδευτος, *impassable* τὸ ἀ. χάσμα [i.e. in hell] Gr.Nyss.*engast*.(p.64.19; M.45.109A); ἡ διὰ τῆς δικαιοσύνης ὁδὸς...ἀ. παντελῶς τοῖς παροργίζουσιν αὐτόν [sc. τὸν κύριον] Cyr.*Jo*.3.4(4.272B).

ἀδιοικησία, ἡ, *lack of arrangement*, Meth.*res*.2.10(p.350.4).

ἀδιόρθωτος, **1.** *incorrigible* ἐλάττωμα...ἀ. Bas.*reg.br*.57(2.434D; M.31.1121A); ἑκὼν ἔμεινεν [sc. Judas] ἀ. Chrys.*prod.Jud*.1.3(2.381C); id.*hom.72.1 in Jo*.(8.424A); of sinners, id.*hom.25.3 in Mt*.(7.310B); id.*hom.4.1 in 2Cor*.(10.454E); id.*hom.5.2 in 1Tim*.(11.577A); Nil.*epp*.3.21(M.79.380C); **2.** *irremediable*, of baptism received unworthily ἀ. τὸ πρᾶγμα Cyr.H.*procatech*.7; συντριβὴν αὐτοῖς ἀπειλεῖ ἀ. Cyr.*Ps*.2:9(M.69.724C); of Jewish hostility to Rome, Thdr.Mops.*Mich*.4:6 (M.66.368B); **3.** *uncorrected* οὐ μὴν ἀφῆκεν ἡ θεία προμήθεια τὴν ἀβουλίαν ἡμῶν ἀ. Gr.Nyss.*anim.et res*.(M.46.81B); οὔτε ἀ. εἴασε τὸ τραχὺ τοῦ λόγου Chrys.*hom.14.1 in 2Cor*.(10.538A); βιβλία Synes.*ep*.154(M.66.1556A); of persons, *unreformed*, Chrys.*hom.4.2 in 2Cor*.(457A).

ἀδιορθώτως, *incorrigibly*, ‡Just.*qu.et resp*.36(M.6.1281D); Chrys.*hom.51.2 in Mt*.(7.522E); id.*hom.17.1 in 1Tim*.(11.648D).

ἀδιόριστος, *undefined, indefinite*, Clem.*str*.5.1(p.327.24; M.9.12B); ἐπειδὴ ἀ. ἐστιν ὁ περὶ τοῦ ἁγίου πνεύματος λόγος, οὔπω τότε τῶν πνευματομάχων ἀναφανέντων Bas.*ep*.140.2(3.233D; M.32.589A); οὐχὶ τέσσαρες ποταμοὶ ἀλλὰ ἀ. ἀπὸ τῆς πηγῆς ἐκείνης [sc. Christ] ἐκχέοντες Chrys.*hom.3.1 in Ac.princ*.(3.72A); Cyr.*Juln*.8(6^2.274B).

ἀδιορίστως, *without distinction* or *qualification*, Or.*Jo*.20.9(p.337.4; M.14.592A); id.*Cels*.4.58(p.330.25; M.11.1125A); Eus.*e.th*.3.2(p.139.16; M.24.972C); ἁπλῶς καὶ ἀ. εἰπεῖν ὅτι θεὸς ἦν ὁ λόγος Gr.Nyss.*Eun*.10(2 p.241.5; M.45.844B); οὐδὲ ἀ. ἅπασι...ἐπετίμα Chrys.*hom.23.1 in Mt*.(7.285B); id.*hom.38.4 in 1Cor*.(10.355B); of answer to prayer οὐ μὴν πᾶσιν ἀ., ἀλλὰ τοῖς ἀγαπῶσι τὸν νόμον Epiph.*haer*.73.29(p.303.27; M.42.457D); ref. Christ σημεῖα...ἀ. πεποιηκέναι Isid.Pel.*epp*.2.99(M.78.541D); ref. Jo.1:1 τὸ γάρ, ἦν, ἀ. ἐκφωνηθέν Cyr.*Jo*.1.1(4.14B); ἐθέσπισε [sc. Gratian] μετὰ ἀδείας ἑκάστην τῶν θρησκειῶν ἀ. ἐν τοῖς εὐκτηρίοις συνάγεσθαι Socr.*h.e*.5.2.1(M.67.568A).

***ἀδιούτωρ, ὁ**, (Lat. *adjutor*) *helper, secretary*, Nil.*epp*.2.287(M.79.341D).

***ἀδιόχλητος**, *not troublesome*, *A.Jo*.60(p.180.24).

ἀδίστακτος, **1.** *undoubting, unwavering* πίστιν...ἀ. Nil.*epp*.1.104 (M.79.128C); πίστεως μήτηρ μόχθος καὶ εὐθὴς καρδία· ἡ μὲν γὰρ ἀδίστακτον ποιεῖ Jo.Clim.*scal*.27(M.88.1113B); Leont.N.*v.Jo.Eleem*.46(p.97.18); *ib*.(p.95.19); **2.** *not drawn in two directions* τὸ γὰρ ἀνθρώπινον τοῦ θεοῦ...ἀδίστακτον, μᾶλλον δὲ στάσιμον τὴν κατ' ὄρεξιν φυσικὴν ἤτοι θέλησιν, κίνησιν ἔσχεν Max.*opusc*.(M.91.32A); **3.** *indubitable* ἀ. γνῶσιν Hipp.*haer*.10.30(p.286.8; M.16.3443B).

ἀδιστάκτως, *without separation* ὑποστάσεσι...ἀσυγχύτως ἡνωμέναις καὶ ἀ. διαιρουμέναις Jo.D.*f.o*.1.8(M.94.809A).

***ἀδίστρατος**, *for carrying baggage*; ἵππων ἀ. *pack-horses*, Heracl.*ep*.(M.92.1021B).

***ἀδιτεύω**, *enter upon* an inheritance, Ath.Scholast.*coll*.9.1(p. 96).

***ἀδιτίων, ἡ**, (Lat. *aditio*) entry upon an inheritance, Ath.Scholast.*coll*.9.1(p.97).

***ἀδιύπνιστος**, *not to be aroused* ἡ φύσις, ἀ. πρὸς ὄρεξιν μένει Tim.Ant.*nativ.Jo.Bapt*.2(M.28.909B).

***ἀδιχοτόμητος**, *not cut in two, continuous* ἀ. ... ἀνάπαυσιν Val.Gn.ap.Epiph.*haer*.31.6(p.394.1; M.41.485A).

***ἀδίψητος**, *unthirsting, not lacking moisture*, *Orac.Sib*.1.132; *ib*.1.185; *ib*.3.403.

ἀδίωκτος, *unpersecuted*, Thdr.Stud.*epp*.2.143(M.99.1449B); *ib*.2.154(1480A); *ib*.2.179(1553D).

***ἀδνατικά, τά**, *rights of agnates*, Ath.Scholast.*coll*.9.10(p.104).

***ἀδνᾶτος, ὁ**, (Lat. *agnatus*) *kinsman* on the father's side, Ath.Scholast.*coll*.9.10(p.104).

***ἀδνούμιον, τό**, (Lat. *adnumium*) *muster, levy*, Ath.Scholast.*coll*.4.11(p.56).

***ἀδογμάτιστος**, *undogmatic, holding no dogma* αἵρεσις Thdr.Stud.*epp*.1.36(M.99.1037C).

***ἀδογματίστως**, *apart from ordinance, of one's own accord*, Marc.Er.*opusc*.7.6(M.65.1077D); *Schol*.29 in Jo.Clim.*scal*.27(M.88.1124D).

ἀδοκίμαστος, *untested*, Bas.*hom.in Ps*.33(1.146D; M.29.360A).

***ἀδοκιμάστως**, *without trial* or *testing*, Mac.Aeg.*hom*.10.5(M.34.544C); Isid.Pel.*epp*.1.44(M.78.209B); CChalc.*can*.21.

ἀδόκιμος, **1.** *spurious* ἀργύριον Or.*Jo*.10.29(18; p.203.10; M.14.360C); **2.** *worthless* ἀ. ... αἱ διαιρέσεις Clem.*str*.8.6(p.92.6; M.9.585A); **3.** of persons, *discredited, reprobate*, Ign.*Trall*.12.3; Or.*mart*.35(p.33.9; M.11.609C); comp., Meth.*symp*.11(p.139.33; M.18.217D).

ἀδολεσχ-έω, **1.** *talk, discuss*, Or.*Cels*.3.35(p.231.12; M.11.964C); Meth.*symp*.1.1(p.9.17; M.18.40B); Ammon.*Ac*.1:12(M.85.1525A); **2.** *meditate* περὶ τῶν θείων ὁμιλεῖν, ὅπερ ~ῆσαι νῦν ὠνόμασεν Or.*sel.in Gen*.24:63(M.12.120B); ἐν τοῖς λόγοις ~εῖν Evagr.Pont.*or*.56(M.79.1177D); εἰς τὸ ῥητὸν ἠδολέσχουν Jo.Mosch.*prat*.40(M.87.2893C).

ἀδολεσχητέον, *one must talk idly*, Clem.*paed*.2.7(p.192.20; M.8.461C).

ἀδολεσχία, ἡ, **1.** *prating, chattering*, *LS*; *song* of birds χελιδόνος καὶ περιστερᾶς τὴν ἀ. μιμήσομαι ὕμνους ὑφαίνων σοι Thdt.*Is*.38:13 (p.151.26; 2.325); τῆς...περιστερᾶς τὴν ἀ. ἐν τοῖς θρήνοις δεικνύντες *ib*.59:11(p.231.30; 2.376); **2.** *meditation*, Marc.Er.*opusc*.5.3(M.65.1032C); ἡ ἀ. τέρψιν ἔχει καὶ ὠφέλειαν πολλήν Nil.*Magn*.6.1(M.79.1052A); ἀ. γεννᾷ συνέχειαν Jo.Clim.*scal*.7(M.88.816A).

ἀδόλεσχος, *prating, stupid* ἀ. ... δεισιδαιμονίας Eus.*p.e*.1.9(30C; M.21.70C); ἀ. φλυαρίαν *ib*.3.13(119B; M.213B); ἀ. ... γραφήν id.*e.th*.proem.(p.60.3; M.24.824C).

***ἀδόλωτος**, *uncorrupted*, Gr.Nyss.*hom.9 in Cant*.(M.44.976D).

ἀδόνητος, *unshaken, unfaltering*, †Apoll.*met.Ps*.65:9(M.33.1401C); Cyr.*Am*.56(3.311D); Nonn.*par.Jo*.18:20(M.43.893A).

ἄδοξος, **1.** *without glory, obscure, ignoble*; of Christ as man, Just.*dial*.32.1(M.6.544A); ἄ. ἡ πρώτη παρουσία *ib*.49.7(585A); εἰσῆλθεν εἰς τὸν κόσμον ἄ. Hipp.*haer*.8.10(p.230.11; M.16.3355A); Eus.*d.e*.9.17 (p.440.4; M.22.708D); **2.** *without divine glory* ἆρ' οὖν πρῶτον αὐτὸν [sc. Son] γεννήσας ὕστερον τὴν δόξαν ἔδωκε πρότερον ἀφεὶς εἶναι ἄ.; καὶ πῶς ἂν ἔχοι λόγον; Chrys.*hom.82.2 in Jo*.(8.486A); οὐκ ἄ. μετὰ τὴν ἐνανθρώπησιν Thdt.*Ps*.92:1(1.1271).

ἀδούλωτος, *unenslaved*; spiritually, Clem.*str*.7.9(p.40.4; M.9.477A); ἀ. καὶ ἀπαρεμπόδιστον τῆς ψυχῆς...κεκτῆσθαι πτερόν ‡Pion.*v.Polyc*.9; ἀ. τοῖς πάθεσι τὴν ψυχὴν φυλάξωμεν Gr.Naz.*ep*.223(M.37.365C); ἡ προαίρεσις ἀ. τι χρῆμα...ἐν τῇ ἐλευθερίᾳ τῆς διανοίας κείμενον Gr.Nyss.*or.catech*.30(p.112.12; M.45.77A); Bas.Sel.*or*.3.2(M.85.52A); neut. as subst., Clem.*str*.7.3(p.11.23; 420A).

ἀδούπητος, *noiseless*, Nonn.*par.Jo*.11:54(M.43.849A).

***ἄδουπος**, *noiseless, gentle* διδασκαλίαν Epiph.*haer*.35.3(p.43.27; M.41.632D).

***ἄδρακτος**, neut. as subst., *unseen, private place* (cf. τὰ ἴδια) Juln.Imp.ap.Cyr.*Juln*.9(6^2.305E).

ἀδρανέω, *be enfeebled* or *weak*; of persons, Nonn.*par.Jo*.11:1,3 (M.43.840A).

***ἀδρανῶς**, *weakly, feebly*, Cyr.*Soph*.42(3.620B); Dion.Ar.*c.h*.8.1 (M.3.240A).

***ἀδρεσπόνσον, τό**, (Lat. *ad responsum*) *machinery of torture* ἔχειν δὲ...πέλεκυν καὶ ῥάβδους καὶ ἀ. Ath.Scholast.*coll*.4.4(p.54).

***ἅδρησις, ἡ**, *maturity*, Bas.*hex*.6.8(1.57D; M.29.136B).

***Ἀδριανισταί, οἱ**, members of heret. sect stemming from Simonians, Thdt.*haer*.1.1(4.288).

ἀδρομερής, *consisting of large* or *coarse particles* ἀέρι...τὸ ἀ. ὕδωρ ὑποκεῖται Areth.*Apoc*.28(M.106.637B); met. ἀ. διὰ τῆς ἀκοῆς προδεχθέντα λόγον Nil.ap.Proc.G.*Cant.*4:2(M.87.1641D); of the historical, moral, and prophetic types of writing in OT, *disposed in large blocks*, †Chrys.*synops.*(6.316D).

ἁδρομερῶς, *in a general way, summarily* οὐ κατὰ λεπτὸν ἐπιδείξαντες, ἀλλ' ἁ. ἐλέγξαντες Hipp.*haer.*proem.1(p.2.2; M.16.3017B); *ib.*6.42(p.173.14; 3259D); Chrys.*hom.1.3 in Ac.*(9.5B).

ἁδροτής, ἡ, *strength, vigour* ἐν ἡμῖν ἁ. ... ἐν Χριστῷ Ἰησοῦ Or. *hom.6.3 in Jer.*(p.51.10; M.13.329A); ref. Inc. ἐν ἁ. μελῶν ὁ ἀσώματος Cyr.*Lc.*2:40(M.72.508A).

***ἀδρυντικός**, *subject to growth* ἀ. οὐσίαν (of Logos acc. Aët.) Epiph.*haer.*76.26(p.373.26; M.42.568B).

ἀδρύν-ω, *ripen*; pass. met., *grow to maturity, grow strong* ἡδρύνθη ...ἡ τῆς...βασιλείας ἰσχύς Cyr.*Mich.*39(3.428B); πικρίαν...πρὶν ∼θῆναι id.*Lc.*11:46(M.72.660C).

***ἄδρωπος**, vox nihili (v.l. ἄνδρωπος) in suggested derivation of word ἄνθρωπος: παρὰ τὸ δρῶ τὸ βλέπω...ἄ. Melet.*nat.hom.*synops. (M.64.1084B).

***ἀδσηκρῆτις**, v. ἀσηκρῆτις.

***ἀδύναμαι**, *be weak* οἱ ἀδυνάμενοι Jo.Clim.*scal.*1(M.88.636B).

ἀδύναμος, *without strength, weak* ἂν ἀπαρθῇ τὸ φῶς ἀπὸ τοῦ σκότους, μένει τὸ σκότος...ἀ. [i.e. acc. Sethians] Hipp.*haer.*5.19 (p.117.15; M.16.3179C) = *ib.*10.11(p.271.6; 3423B); denied of God οὐ γὰρ ἦν ποτε...ἀ. Didym.(‡Bas.)*Eun.*4.3(1.287A; M.29.689B).

***ἀδυνάστευτος**, *not under absolute rule, free* δῆμον τὸν ἀ. Synes. *regn.*13(p.39.10; M.66.1085B).

ἀδύνατος, **1.** *powerless*; of the infirm, *Const.App.*3.19.1,5; of the dead, Mac.Mgn.*apocr.*3.9(p.72.26); denied of God, Hipp.*Noët.*10 (p.251.17; M.10.817A) cit. s. ἀβούλευτος; Cyr.*thes.*21(5^{1}.210D); Zach. Mit.*opif.*(M.85.1033A); **2.** *impossible* οὐδὲν γὰρ ἀ. παρὰ τῷ θεῷ εἰ μὴ τὸ ψεύσασθαι *1Clem.*27.2; cf.Ath.*Ar.*2.6(M.26.160A); δύναμις ἰσχυρὰ [sc. ὁ θεός]...ᾗ μηδὲν ἀ. Clem.*ecl.*26(p.144.20; M.9.712A).

***ἀδυπληθής**, *full of sweetness*, Meth.*symp.*11.2(p.133.30; M.18. 209C).

***ἀδυσφημήτως**, *without blasphemy*, Cyr.*thes.*15(5^{1}.155E).

ἀδυσωπήτως, **1.** *without shrinking*, Cyr.H.*catech.*15.23; **2.** *inexorably*, Eulog.*fr.dogm.*(M.86.2964A).

ἄδυτος, **A.** adj.; **1.** *not to be entered, inaccessible*; **a.** of inner parts of shrines: pagan, Eus.*v.C.*3.57(p.104.23; M.20.1124B); of Holy of Holies in Temple, ‡Chrys.*concept.Jo.Bapt.*(2.793A); Thdt.*qu.60 in Ex.*(1.162) cit. s. ἀνάκτορον; Christian τὰ ἔνδον...μόνοις ἐστὶν ἱερεῦσι βατά, τοῖς δὲ ἄλλοις ἅπασιν ἄ. Thdt.*h.e.*5.18.21(3.1050); **b.** met., of secret recesses of the mind, Eus.*l.C.*proem.(p.196.1; M. 20.1317B); myst., ref. Ex.20:21 ἀ. καὶ ἀειδεῖς περὶ τοῦ ὄντος ἐννοίας Clem.*str.*2.2(p.116.1; M.8.937A); **c.** of divine light ὁ νοητὸς ἥλιος τὸ φῶς τὸ ἄ. Or.*fr.94 in Jo.*12:46(p.558.2), or perh. in sense 2 infra; εἰς καθαρὰν οἴκησιν ἀ. φώτων Meth.*symp.*4.5(p.51.21; M.18.96A); ἀ. γέγονα λαμπαδηφόρος φώτων *ib.*6.5(p.69.22; 120C); πρὸς τὸ φῶς τὸ ἄ. ὁδοιπορήσαντες Anast.S.*defunct.*(M.89.1192A); **2.** *never setting*, of Christ ὁ ἄ. ἥλιος †Sophr.H.*orat.*(M.87.4004A); of light of Resurrection, Germ.CP *or.*1(M.98.221D); **3.** *not sinking* ἡ τῶν σωμάτων φύσις ...ἄ. ἐν τοῖς ὕδασι τῆς Μαρμαρικῆς Πενταπόλεως ‡Ath.*templ.*(p.108. 4; M.28.1428A).

B. neut. as subst.; **1.** *sanctuary* (usu. plur.); **a.** pagan ἄ. Αἰγυπτίων Clem.*prot.*2(p.11.5; M.8.69A); id.*str.*5.4(p.338.30; M.9.37C); Hipp.*haer.*9.17(p.255.11; M.16.3394B); Thdt.*h.e.*3.3.2(3.913); **b.** Holy of Holies οἷς [sc. the high priests]...τὸ ἄ. βάσιμον ἦν Clem.*str.* 5.6(p.348.18; M.9.60A); Eus.*h.e.*1.6.6(M.20.88B); Chrys.*hom.46.3 in Jo.*(8.273C); **c.** of sanctuary in Christian church, Gr.Nyss.*ep.*1 (M.46.1004A); **2.** met., anything hidden or sacred; **a.** *hidden* or *inner place*, esp. of realm of death (pagan) Ἄλκηστιν...ἀπὸ τῶν ἀ. ἀνηνεγμένην Epiph.*anc.*85(p.105.9; M.43.176A); from which Christ emerged at Resurrection ὁ Χριστὸς...ἀπὸ τῶν ἀ. προήει μετὰ πολλῆς λαμπρότητος Chrys.*hom.24.4 in 1Cor.*(10.217E); Mac.Mgn.*apocr.*2. 19(p.33.3); *ib.*3.14(p.93.11); **b.** *centre, inmost part* ἐν τῷ ἀ. τῆς ἀληθείας Clem.*str.*5.4(p.338.29; M.9.37C); εἰς τὰ ἄ. κατελθὼν τὴν μυστικὴν παρ' Αἰγυπτίων ἐκμάθοι φιλοσοφίαν *ib.*1.15(p.41.29; M.8. 768A); Procl.CP *or.*6.17(M.65.753B) cit. s. ἀναμαρτησία; of the divine secrets τίς ἱκανὸς κατατολμῆσαι τῶν ἀ.; Bas.*hex.*2.1(1.12B; M.29.28C); of Christian mysteries ἐντὸς τῶν βασιλείων γινόμενοι, καὶ εἰς τὰ ἄ. διακύψαι καταξιωθέντες Chrys.*hom.84.3 in Jo.*(8.502C); id.*hom.29.6 in 1Cor.*(10.267E); Jo.D.*hom.*4.1(M.96.601C); of spiritual sense of scripture διανοίας...κατατολμώσης τῶν ἀ. τοῦ πνεύματος Thdt.*Cant.*proem.(2.2); **c.** myst., that region of soul where dwells the divine image τὴν εἰκόνα τοῦ θεοῦ κατοικοῦσαν...τῆς ψυχῆς...τὸ ἄ. Clem.*paed.*3.2(p.238.26; M.8.561A); θεὸν...ἐν τῷ ἀ. ἡμῶν παρεῖναι Or.*Jo.*6.2(1; p.108.11; M.14.201A); id.*or.*8.2(p.317.14; M.11.441C); analogy between Holy of Holies and role of the ἄ. of the soul in mystic union εἰς τὸ ἄ. εἰσάγει προσευξόμενον τῷ θεῷ τὸν ἱερέα Gr. Nyss.*or.dom.*3(p.44.37; M.44.1148D); compared with sphere that soul enters in prayer τὸ δὲ ἄ. τοῦτο οὐκ ἄψυχόν ἐστιν, οὔτε χειρόκμητον· ἀλλὰ τὸ κρυπτὸν τῆς καρδίας ἡμῶν ταμεῖον, ἐὰν ἀληθῶς ἄ. ᾖ τῇ κακίᾳ καὶ τοῖς πονηροῖς λογισμοῖς ἀνεπίβατον *ib.*(p.48.5; 1149C); ἐντὸς τῶν θείων ἀ. μυσταγωγεῖ [sc. Cant.] τὴν διανοίαν id. *hom.1 in Cant.*(M.44.772A); ἄ. as sphere of contemplation ἡ... ὁδεύουσα πρὸς τὰ ἄνω ψυχὴ...ἐντὸς τῶν ἀ. τῆς θεογνωσίας γίνεται *ib.11*(1000D); id.*v.Mos.*(M.44.377D); in highest stages mystic enters ἐν τοῖς ὑπερουρανίοις ἀ. *ib.*(384A); ref. 2Cor.12:4 ἐν τοῖς ἀ. τῶν παραδείσου...ὁρᾶν...τὰ ἀθέατα, καὶ τῶν ἀλαλήτων ἐπακροᾶσθαι ῥημάτων id.*hom.1 in Cant.*(785A); the region ruled by Christ the ἐπουρανίων ἀ. ποιμήν Nonn.*par.Jo.*1:5(M.43.760A); **3.** *secret thing* ἄ. τοίνυν ἄθεα μὴ πολυπραγμονεῖτε Clem.*prot.*2(p.10.20; M.8.68B); **4.** *hidden recess*, ref. Pythagoras ἐν ἀ. καταγείοις ἐρημεῖν ἐποίει μανθάνοντας Hipp. *haer.*1.2(p.9.2; M.16.3028A); **5.** *secret place*; of the inner enclosure of a monastery to which novices were not admitted: dubious expression in so-called 'Rule of the Angel' of Pachomian monasticism τὸν μέντοι εἰσελθόντα συμμεῖναι αὐτοῖς ἐπὶ τριετίαν εἴσω τῶν ἀ. οὐ δέχονται Pall.*h.Laus.*32(p.91.10; M.34.1100B).

[*]**ἅδω**, *please* ἅδειν γὰρ τὸ ἀρέσκειν Oecum.*Apoc.*9:17(p.118).

ᾄδ-ω, **1.** *sing*; met. ἐν ἑνότητι ∼ητε ἐν φωνῇ μιᾷ διὰ Ἰησοῦ Χριστοῦ τῷ πατρί Ign.*Eph.*4.2; **2.** trans., *celebrate in song, praise*, id.*Magn.*1.2; *Diogn.*11.6; Thdt.*h.e.*5.4.5(3.1020); **3.** pass., *be celebrated, famous*, Or.*Cels.*8.67(p.283.14; M.11.1617B); Chrys.*hom.30.4 in Rom.*(9.744D); id.*hom.26.4 in Heb.*(12.243A).

ἀδώμητος, *unbuilt* i.e. *natural* τύμβος ἀδωμήτοιο βαθυνομένης ἀπὸ πέτρης γλυπτός Nonn.*par.Jo.*19:41(M.43.908A).

***ἀδωναΐ**, (Hebr. אֲדֹנָי) *lord, master* ὁ δὲ Ματθαῖος...ἐβόησεν· ἀ. ἐλωὶ σαβαὼθ μαρμαρὶ μαρμοῦνθ *A.Mt.*21(p.245.8); οἱ αἰπόλοι καὶ ποιμένες ἕνα ἐνόμισαν θεόν, εἴτε ὕψιστον, εἴτ' ἀ., εἴτ' οὐράνιον, εἴτε σαβαώθ, εἴτε καὶ ὅπῃ καὶ ὅπως χαίρουσιν ὀνομάζοντες τόνδε τὸν κόσμον· καὶ πλεῖον οὐδὲν ἔγνωσαν Cels.ap.Or.*Cels.*1.24(p.74.5; M.11. 701B); τοῦτο δὲ τὸ ἔγκλημα οὐδαμῶς ἅπτεται τῶν κατά τινα ἀπόρρητον λόγον τὸ σαβαὼθ τασσόντων ἐπὶ τοῦ θεοῦ ἢ τὸ ἀ. ἤ τι τῶν λοιπῶν ὀνομάτων Or.*ib.*1.25(p.76.7; 705D); αὐτὴν τὴν ἑβραϊκὴν φωνὴν μετεκόμισαν· ὡς τὸ σαβαὼθ καὶ τὸ ἀ. Bas.*Eun.*2.7(1.243C; M.29.585A).

ἀδωνάριος, neut. as subst., a kind of verse, Proc.G.*ep.*146(M.87. 2785D).

ἀδωροδόκητος, *incorruptible*; of divine judgement, ‡Hipp.*consumm.*24(p.299.7; M.10.928B); *Const.App.*7.35.10; of Christians ἔσο ...ἀ. Chrys.*hom.in 2Cor.11*:1(3.298C); neut. as subst., id.*hom.12.2 in 2Cor.*(10.523A).

ἄδωρος, *taking no gifts, incorruptible*; superl., Bas.*ep.*96(3.190E; M.32.492B).

ἀεθλεύω, *fight* ἀ. ... πιστὸν ἀγῶνα Nonn.*par.Jo.*5:29(M.43.789B).

ἀεί, **1.** *always, continually, LS*; Θεοδοσίῳ ἀεὶ βασιλεῖ Licin.*ep.* (p.6.21; M.*PL.*54.862C); **2.** *eternally* Ἀστέριος...λέγων, ἀγένητον εἶναι τὸ μὴ ποιηθέν, ἀλλ' ἀ. ὄν Ath.*Ar.*1.30(M.26.76A); ref. God θεὸς...ἦν...ἀ. τοιοῦτος *Diogn.*8.8; τὸ κατὰ τὰ αὐτὰ καὶ ὡσαύτως ἀ. ἔχον...τοῦτο δή ἐστιν ὁ θεός Just.*dial.*3.5(M.6.481B); ἀ. οὔσης οὐσίας Ath.*Ar.*2.2(M.26.152B); ἀ. ὤν ‡Cyr.*Trin.*5(6^{3}.6B; M.77.1128C); Trin. in gen., Gr.Thaum.*symb.*(p.3.13; M.10.988A) cit. s. ἄτρεπτος; εἰ γὰρ νῦν ἐν τριάδι ἡ θεολογία τελεία ἐστί...ἔδει τοῦτο οὕτως ἀ. εἶναι Ath.*Ar.*1.18(M.49A); τριὰς...ἀ. τελεία ἐστί id.*ep.Epict.*9(p.15.12; M.26.1065B); ref. Father ὁ πατὴρ ἀ. πατήρ id.*ep.Serap.*4.5(M.26. 645D); ἀλλ' ὥσπερ ἀγαθὸς ἀ. καὶ τῇ φύσει, οὕτως ἀ. γεννητικὸς τῇ φύσει ὁ πατήρ id.*Ar.*3.66(464B); Thdt.*Heb.*1:2(3.547); and Son, of his very nature ὁ υἱὸς ἀ. υἱός Ath.*ep.Serap.*4.5(645D); ἦν γὰρ ἀ. καὶ ἔστιν ἴσα θεῷ id.*Ar.*1.41(96C); Thdt.*Heb.*1:2(547); ref. his titles and perfections as God ὁ κύριος ὁ ἀ. καὶ φύσει ἄτρεπτος Ath.*Ar.* 1.51(120A); πῶς ἐλάμβανεν ὃ εἶχεν ἀ., καὶ πρὶν λαβεῖν νῦν αὐτό; *ib.* 1.41(96B); εἶχε γὰρ αὐτὰ ἀ. θεὸς ὢν ὁ λόγος *ib.*3.40(409A); ref. relationship between Father and Son, denied by Arians οὐκ ἀ. ἦν ὁ τοῦ θεοῦ λόγος ἀλλ' ἐξ οὐκ ὄντων γέγονεν Alex.Al.*ep.encycl.*3 (p.7.19; M.18.573A); λέγουσα μηδόλως εἶναι τὸν λόγον, μηδὲ τὸν πατέρα ἀ. πατέρα εἶναι Ath.*ep.Aeg.Lib.*17(M.25.580A); ‡Ath.*Ar.*4. 12(p.56.23; M.26.484B); asserted οὐ συμφωνοῦμεν αὐτῷ...λέγοντι, ἀ. θεὸς ἀ. υἱός Ar.*ep.Eus.*(p.2.1; M.42.209Df.); τὸν θεόν, ἀ. τοῦ υἱοῦ πατέρα αὐτὸν εἶναι Ath.*Ar.*1.27(68B); ὁ υἱὸς ἐκ τοῦ πατρὸς γεννᾶται... ἀ. ἐν αὐτῷ ὤν ‡Cyr.*Trin.*8(6^{3}.11B; M.77.1136B); ref. H. Ghost ἐκπόρευμα ὂν τοῦ πατρὸς ἀ. ἐστιν ἐν ταῖς χερσὶ τοῦ πέμποντος πατρὸς καὶ τοῦ φέροντος υἱοῦ †Ath.*exp.fid.*4(M.25.208A); ἀναλλοίωτον καὶ τῆς τοῦ υἱοῦ ἀτρεψίας ἐστί, μένον ἀ. σὺν αὐτῷ ἄτρεπτον Ath.*ep.Serap.*1.26 (592B); ἀ. τὸ αὐτό ἐστιν *ib.*1.27(593A); liturg., in doxologies νῦν καὶ ἀ.

καὶ εἰς τοὺς αἰῶνας τῶν αἰώνων *Lit.*ap.*Const.App.*8.15.9; *Lit.Bas.*(p.411.31); *Lit.Praesanct.*(p.352.23); **3.** translation of *Selah* παρὰ μὲν Ἀκύλα μετὰ τὸ 'θυρεὸν καὶ πόλεμον καὶ μάχαιραν' τὸ 'ἀ.' Or.*sel.in Ps.*3:3(M.12.1060B).

***ἀείβλυστος**, *ever-bubbling, ever-exuberant*; of abundance of water, Max.*opusc.*(M.91.92D); met. τῆς ἀ. ... περὶ τὸ θεῖον ἐρωτικῆς θέλξεως id.*ambig.*(M.91.1245C); *ib.*(1364D).

ἀειγενής, = sq.

***ἀειγεννής**, *ever-begotten*, Alex.Al.ap.Ar.*ep.Eus.*(p.2.1; M.42.212A) cit. s. ἀγεννήτως; σύνεστιν αὐτῷ τὸ ἀπαύγασμα ἄναρχον καὶ ἀειγενῆ Dion.Al.ap.Ath.*Dion.*15(p.57.11; M.25.501D).

ἀειδής, **1.** *obscure, insignificant* τὰ παρὰ ἀνθρώποις εὐτελῆ καὶ ἀ. καὶ εὐκαταφρόνητα *Ep.Lugd.*ap.Eus.*h.e.*5.1.7(M.20.416A); **2.** *obscure, dark* ἀ. νυκτὸς τῆς δεισιδαίμονος πλάνης Eus.*p.e.*2.5(70A; M.21.136A); ᾅδης δὲ τόπος ἡμῖν ἀ. ἤγουν ἀφανής Andr.Caes.*Apoc.*64(M.106.421C); **3.** *unsightly, ugly*, Clem.*str.*4.25(p.319.8; M.8.1368C); ἀ. καὶ φοβερόν Ath.*v.Anton.*66(M.26.937A); σώματα...χολερικά...ἐστιν ἀ. Chrys.*hom.15.2 in Eph.*(11.111B); of sin, id.*hom.10.2 in Heb.*(12.104D); of incarnate Christ πρώτην παρουσίαν...ἐν ᾗ καὶ ἄτιμος καὶ ἀ. καὶ θνητὸς φανήσεσθαι κεκηρυγμένος ἐστίν Just.*dial.*14.8(M.6.505C); *ib.*49.2(584A); τὸν ἀ. καὶ ἄτιμον φανέντα, ὡς Ἡσαΐας ἔφη *ib.*85.1(676B); ἀ. ὡς αἱ γραφαὶ ἐκήρυσσον *ib.*88.8(688B); ἄνθρωπος ἀ. *ib.*100.2(709B); ref. Ascension οἱ ἐν οὐρανῷ ἄρχοντες ἑώρων ἀ. καὶ ἄτιμον τὸ εἶδος *ib.*36.6(556A); **4.** *unfathomable*, Clem.*str.*2.2(p.116.2; M.8.937A) cit. s. ἄδυτος; **5.** *formless*, ref. Gen.1:2 γῆν ἀ. Clem.*str.*5.14(p.388.2; v.l. ἁγίαν M.9.137B); Meth.*symp.*8.3(p.84.2; M.18.141B); εἶδος ἐξ ἀ. ἀπεργαζόμενος ἐποίει Eus.*l.C.*6(p.207.10; M.20.1341C); **6.** *incorporeal, immaterial*, Clem.*str.*3.17(p.244.2; M.8.1208A) cit. s. ἄμορφος; *ib.*5.11(p.374.23; M.9.109B) cit. s. ἀόρατος; ψυχαὶ...ἐν τῷ ᾅδῃ...μέλη ἱστοροῦνται ἔχειν οὐχ ὡς σώματος ἑτέρου συνυπάρχοντος αὐταῖς ἀ. Meth.*res.*3.18(p.415.18; M.18.328A); ᾅδην...τινα κατάστασιν ζωῆς ἀ. καὶ ἀσώματον Gr.Nyss.*anim.et res.*(M.46.85B); of the νοῦς, Eus.*p.e.*3.10(106C; M.21.192D); neut. as subst.; of the soul, Gr.Nyss.*anim. et res.*(68A); *invisibility*, Meth.*res.*2.28(p.385.21; M.18.316B); **7.** of God, *without form*, both as above form and as without visible form τὴν...ἀ. [sc. φύσιν] τε καὶ ἀσχημάτιστον...τῆς...ποσότητος κεχωρισμένην πῶς ἄν τις πολυειδῆ καὶ σύνθετον ὑπολάβοι; Gr.Nyss.*Eun.*1(1 p.89.11; M.45.321A).

ἀείδιος, v. ἀΐδιος.

[*]**ἀειδιότης**, ἡ, v. ἀϊδιότης.

***ἀείδρομος**, *ever-moving*; of stars, Gr.Naz.*carm.*1.1.5.66(M.37.429A).

***ἀειζάω**, (better written *divisim*) in ptcpl. *ever-living*, Bas.Sel.*v.Thecl.*1(M.85.481A) cit. s. ἀειζώων.

ἀειζωΐα, ἡ, *eternal life* οἱ ἐσθίοντες [of the tree of life, Christ] ἀ. λήψονται Hipp.*fr.17 in Pr.*11:30(p.163.2; M.10.620D); τῆς εὐθείας ἀ. Or.*exp.in Pr.*2:19(M.17.168A); θεός...πατήρ...ἡ τῆς ἀ. πηγή †Gr.Thaum.*ep.Philagr.*(M.46.1108A).

ἀείζωος, *ever-living, everlasting* ἵνα...μὴ ᾖ κακὸν ἀθάνατον ὁ ἄνθρωπος...ᾖ ἀ. Meth.*res.*1.40(p.285.5; M.18.268C); of eternal life ἀ. ζωήν Or.*exp.in Pr.*4:10(M.17.172B); θνήσκοντες ἀ. τελέθουσι Gr.Naz.*carm.*1.2.2.529(M.37.620A); †Bas.Anc.*virg.*60(M.30.792C); Isid.Pel.*epp.*1.222(M.78.321C); θεοῦ...ἀ. Nonn.*par.Jo.*1:34(M.43.756B); of eucharist ἀ. τραπέζης *ib.*6:27(797C); of BMV ἀ. ὄρπηξ τῆς παρθενίας Jo.D.*hom.*2.5(M.96.685A).

***ἀειζωότης**, ἡ, *eternal life*, Isid.Pel.*epp.*3.149(M.78.841A).

ἀειζώων, *ever-living*; of God, Nonn.*par.Jo.*1:12(M.43.752B); of Christ νεκρὸν ἀ. *ib.*19:38(906C); *ib.*19:42(908A); τὸ ἀ. ὕδωρ τῇ ἀειζώσῃ πηγῇ Bas.Sel.*v.Thecl.*1(M.85.481A); of Christ's words, Paul.Sil.*Soph.*777(M.86.2149A).

ἀειθαλής, **1.** lit., *evergreen*; in gen., Or.*adnot.in Lev.*23:40(M.17.20C); Dion.Al.ap.Eus.*p.e.*14.25(775B; M.21.1276B); ‡Just.*coh.Gr.*28(M.6.293B); ref. crown of thorns τῆς ἀ. ἀκάνθης Clem.*paed.*2.8(p.203.1; M.8.485C); **2.** met., *unfading, everlasting* σοφία *ib.*1.5(p.102.8; 273B); of baptism τὸ ἀ. εὐφροσύνης...ἐπαλειφώμεθα χρῖσμα *ib.*1.12(p.149.5; 368B); ἀ. μαρτυρίου...στέφανον Mac.Mgn.*apocr.*4.14(p.181.25); ἀ. ... εὔκλειαν Cyr.*Os.*138(3.171D); τὴν ἱερωσύνην πρὸς τὸ ἀ. ἐν Χριστῷ προβήσεσθαι Gennad.*fr.in Ex.*26:35(M.85.1665A); of God's word, Gr.Naz.*or.*6.9(M.35.733A); Nil.*epp.*2.41(M.79.216B); Cyr.*Ps.*22:2(M.69.841A).

***ἀεικενός**, *ever-empty, insatiable* τῆς ἀ. ἐπιθυμίας ‡Nil.*perist.*9.8(M.79.880C).

ἀεικινησία, ἡ, *ceaseless motion*, of seraphim τῆς προσεχοῦς καὶ ἀνενδότου καὶ ἀκλινοῦς ἀ. Dion.Ar.*c.h.*7.1(M.3.205C); ἀκαταλήκτου καὶ ὑψιπετοῦς ἀ. *ib.*13.4(305A); of angels τὸ ἀνώλεθρον αὐτὸ τῆς ἀγγελικῆς ἀ. id.*d.n.*6.1(M.3.856B); *ib.*6.2(856C); τὴν περὶ τὸ θεῖον τῆς ψυχῆς ἀ. Max.*ep.*6(M.91.432B); τὴν περὶ τὸ γνωστὸν τὸ ὑπὲρ πᾶσαν τὴν γνῶσιν ἀκατάληκτον καὶ ἐκτικὴν ἀ. id.*myst.*5(M.91.677A).

ἀεικίνητος, *ever-moving*; **1.** in gen.; of heavenly bodies and movement of time, ‡Just.*confut.*60(M.6.1561A); Cyr.*Jo.*7(4.678B); of fire, Eustrat.*stat.anim.*7(p.366); Melet.*nat.hom.*synops.(M.64.1121A); of living water τοῦ ποταμοῦ τὸ ἀ. Gr.Nyss.*hom.9 in Cant.*(M.44.977C); τὸ μὲν ἀ. ὡς ἀ. ἄφθαρτόν ἐστι Cosm.Ind.*top.*7(M.88.340B); τὸ δὲ αὐτοκίνητον ἀ.· τὸ δὲ ἀ. ἀθάνατον Max.*opusc.*(M.91.20B); Jo.D.*Man.*1.21(M.94.1525B); of seraphim τὸ ἀ. αὐτῶν περὶ τὰ θεῖα Dion.Ar.*c.h.*7.1(M.3.205B); id.*e.h.*4.3.7(M.3.481A) cit. s. πολύπορος; **2.** partic.; of soul, Clem.*paed.*2.9(p.207.21; M.8.496C); νοῦς Bas.*ep.*233.1(3.355C; M.32.864D); Nil.*praest.*23(M.79.1088B); ἐνέργειά ἐστι φυσικὴ καὶ πρώτη ἀ. δύναμις τῆς νοερᾶς ψυχῆς· τουτέστιν ὁ ἀ. αὐτῆς λόγος Jo.D.*f.o.*2.23(M.94.949B); of emotional impulse, Melet.*nat.hom.*synops.(M.64.1108C).

***ἄεικτος**, *unyielding* τὸ ἀτενὲς καὶ ἄ. Bas.Sel.*v.Thecl.*1(M.85.512C).

***ἀεικύμαντος**, *tempestuous* τῆς...ἀ. νοητῆς θαλάσσης Thdr.Stud.*epp.*1.11(M.99.944C).

ἀείλαλος, *ever-speaking* ἀείλαλον αὐτῆς [sc. BMV] τὸ πρεσβευτικὸν ὑπὲρ τοῦ παντὸς γένους ἐξανοίγει στόμα Thdr.Stud.*or.*5.2(M.99.721B).

ἀειλαμπής, *ever-shining* φῶς...ὁ θεὸς...ἀ. Gr.Naz.*or.*44.3(M.36.609B); of Christ ἥλιον...ἀ. ‡Epiph.*hom.*3(M.43.465C); of the sun, Thdr.Stud.*or.*2(M.99.693B).

***ἀειλιβής**, *ever-flowing*, Nonn.*par.Jo.*3:34(M.43.772C).

ἀειλογέω, *be always talking about*, Cyr.*Am.*82(3.347C); τὴν τῶν πατέρων ἀ. συνήθειαν id.*Mal.*37(3.857D); id.*hom.pasch.*28(5^2.333B).

***ἀειμακάριστος**, *ever-blessed*; of Constantine, Epiph.*haer.*70.7(p.242.3; ἀεὶ μακαριστοῦ M.42.353C); of BMV, cf.*Lit.Chrys.*ap.*Euchol.*(p.62).

ἀείμνηστος, *had in everlasting remembrance*; of persons, Leont.N.*v.Jo.Eleem.*42(p.84.7); ἐν τῇ πίστει τοῦ ἀ. θεοῦ καὶ σωτῆρος ἡμῶν *PLond.*1919.19.

ἀείναος, v. ἀέναος.

***Ἀείνους**, ὁ, name of Valent. aeon, coupled with *Σύνεσις*, Iren.*haer.*1.1.3(M.7.449A); Hipp.*haer.*6.30(p.157.21; M.16.3239A); Epiph.*haer.*31.2(p.386.11; M.41.477A).

***ἀειπαγής**, *permanently established* εἰρήνην ἀ. Thphn.*chron.*p.272(M.108.673A).

***ἀείπαις**, *perpetually virgin*; in gen., of ascetics, Pall.*v.Chrys.*15(p.91.6; M.47.51); of Pulcheria, Evagr.*h.e.*2.1(p.38.19; M.86.2489B); esp. of BMV, Bas.Sel.*v.Thecl.*1(M.85.481B); ‡Epiph.*hom.*5(M.43.493B); †Gregent.*disp.*(M.86.672A); ‡Jo.D.*hom.*5(M.96.648C); ‡Caes.Naz.*dial.*20(M.38.876).

***ἀειπαρθενεύω**, *remain ever a virgin*, of BMV νῷ καὶ ψυχῇ καὶ σώματι ἀειπαρθενεύουσαν ‡Jo.D.*hom.*6.5(M.96.668C).

***ἀειπαρθενία**, ἡ, *perpetual virginity*; a gift of H. Ghost, Cyr.H.*catech.*16.22.

ἀειπάρθενος, *ever-virgin*; **1.** of persons vowed to perpetual virginity τὸν...τῶν παναγίων ἀ. χορὸν τοῦ θεοῦ Eus.*v.C.*4.28(p.128.13; M.20.1177A); id.*l.C.*17(p.255.16; M.20.1432C); μονὴν τῶν ἀ. Pach.*reg.*B(p.21.13; M.40.952D); διακόνισσαι...μονογάμοι ἐγκρατευσάμεναι ἢ χηρεύσασαι ἀπὸ μονογαμίας ἢ ἀ. οὖσαι Epiph.*exp.fid.*21(p.522.21; M.42.825A); οὐδὲ ἀειπαρθένοις, ἀλλὰ κοσμικαῖς Chrys.*hom.4.5 in Heb.*(12.46D); πρεσβυτέρους καὶ ἀ. Thphn.*chron.*p.40(M.108.156B); **2.** of BMV, Petr.I Al.*fr.*(M.18.517B); σάρκα...ἐκ Μαρίας τῆς ἀ. Ath.*Ar.*2.70(M.26.296B); θεοτόκου καὶ ἀ. id.*exp.Ps.*84:11(M.27.373A); κυριοτόκος...καὶ ἀ. id.*fr.Lc.*(M.27.1393C); Epiph.*haer.*39.10(p.79.23; M.41.676C); ἀπὸ τῆς ἀ. ... ἐτέχθη Didym.*Trin.*1.27(M.39.404C); Isid.Pel.ap.*cat.Lc.*2:1(p.19.29); Eus.Al.*serm.*21.20(M.86.448D); Proc.G.*Ex.*24:1(M.87.633A); Max.*ep.*15(M.91.553).

***ἀειπλανής**, *ever-wandering*, Gr.Naz.*carm.*2.1.43.12(M.37.1347A).

ἀειπόθητος, *ever-desired*, Thdr.Stud.*epp.*2.76(M.99.1313D).

[*]**ἀείρρυτος**, *ever-flowing* ἀ. νάματα ‡Chrys.*hom.3.1 in Gen.*(6.541B); met χρόνον...ἀ. Cyr.*ador.*6(1.205B); ἀ. φόνων Geo.Pis.*Sev.*448(M.92.1656A).

ἀείρ-ω (αἴρ-ω), *lift up, raise*; **A.** act; **1.** in gen., *LS*; of lifting up hands in worship, *1Clem.*29.1; of assumption of BMV ἤρθη πρὸς κύριον τῆς δόξης ἡ ἐνεγκαμένη αὐτὸν παμφαὴς νεφέλη Mod.*dorm.*3(M.86.3285A); met. ~ειν...πρὸς οὐρανὸν τὰς ψυχάς Meth.*symp.*8.1(p.82.3; M.18.140B); *ib.*8.4(p.85.5; 144B) cit. s. ἁγνεία; ἄνω...~εται τὸ φρόνημα τῶν ἀνακαινισθέντων *ib.*8.10(p.92.12; 153A); Chrys.*hom.14.1 in Heb.*(12.140A); id.*hom.10.5 in Mt.*(7.145E); of pride κωλύων γὰρ ἐπὶ πλέον ἀρθῆναι τὴν μεγαλαύχησιν αὐτῶν [sc. demons], ἄνθρωπος ἐγένετο Meth.*Porph.*1(p.503.18; M.18.397D); Chrys.*hom.23.4 in Heb.*(308D); **2.** *extol, magnify*, Const.ap.Eus.*v.C.*2.29(p.54.5; M.20.

1008B); ἄρωμεν τὸν θεὸν ἐν τῷ σώματι καὶ ἐν τῷ πνεύματι ἡμῶν Chrys.*hom.4.3 in 1Tim.*(11.571B); **3.** *take away, remove* οὐκ ἀρεῖς ἐπὶ σεαυτὸν δόξαν *Barn.*19.3; οὐ μὴ ἄρῃς τὴν χεῖρά σου ἀπὸ τοῦ υἱοῦ σου *Did.*4.9 = *Barn.*19.5; οὐ βούλει σου τὸ ἱμάτιον ἀρθῆναι· μηδὲ σὺ τὸ τοῦ ἑτέρου ἄρῃς *Const.App.*1.1.9; in argumen. ἀρῶ σου πᾶσαν πρόφασιν *Hom.Clem.*18.7; ~ειν τὴν πρότασιν Or.*Jo.*6.13(7; p.122.7; M.14.224A); of removal of sin ἄρατε ἐξ ὑμῶν πᾶσαν ὑπόκρισιν *Barn.* 21.4; ἆρον ἀπὸ σεαυτοῦ...ἐπιθυμίαν Herm.*mand.*12.1.1; οὗ κόσμου τὴν ἁμαρτίαν ἦρεν Ἰησοῦς Or.*Jo.*1.4(6; p.7.32; 29B); **4.** *bear, endure* οἱ...πρὸς τὸν στέφανον ὁρῶντες μυρίας ~ουσι πληγάς Chrys.*hom.17.2 in 1Tim.*(11.650E); **5.** *hold, contain*, Nonn.*par.Jo.*21:25(M.43.920C); **6.** *make away with, destroy* αἶρε τοὺς ἀθέους *M.Polyc.*3.2; *ib.*9.2; Eus.*v.C.*2.19(p.48.13; M.20.996B); ἆρον Ἄρειον Thdt.*h.e.*1.14.7(3.786); **7.** *take up a journey, set out*, Eus.*v.C.*4.43(p.135.16; M.20.1193A); ἄρας ἐκ τῆς...πόλεως ‡Jo.D.*Artem.*7(p.26.6; M.96.1257B).

B. med.; **1.** *take to oneself, receive* σοφισταί, οἱ μισθὸν ~ονται τῶν λόγων Meth.*res.*1.27(p.255.15; M.41.1133B); καρπὸν ἤραντο [sc. pagans] τὸν προσήκοντα τῇ τοιαύτῃ θρησκείᾳ Const.*or.s.c.*16(p.177.1; M.20.1281A); *gain* a victory, Eus.*v.C.*2.9(p.45.5; M.20.989A); παρὰ σοῦ τὰς νίκας ἠράμεθα (prayer of Const.'s soldiers) *ib.*4.20(p.125.8; 1168B); id.*l.C.*5(p.204.17; M.20.1336C); **2.** *raise* the hand against ἀθέους ἤραντο [sc. the Jews] κατὰ Χριστοῦ χεῖρας Eus.*d.e.*1.1(p.4.25; M.22.17D); id.*l.C.*7(p.213.26; M.20.1353C); *take up* arms, id.*v.C.*1.4 (p.9.19; M.20.916C); *ib.*2.5(p.43.4; 984B); *ib.*4.6(p.119.30; 1153C); **3.** *extol, magnify* δόξαν...ἤραντο Const.*or.s.c.*17(p.178.10; M.20. 1284B).

ἀεισέβαστος, *ever-Augustus*; imperial title, Thds.*ep.Cyr.*1(p.73.3; H.1.1341A); Basilisc.*encycl.*(p.49; M.86.2600A); Sym.Styl.J.*ep.Just.* (M.86.3216C); Justn.*cod.*1.1.6 ap.*Chron.Pasch.*p.341(M.92.892A).

***ἀεισθενής,** *ever-mighty*; of man, Gr.Naz.*carm.*2.1.17.18(M.37. 1263A).

***ἀείσοος,** *safe for ever*, Nonn.*par.Jo.*10:9(M.43.833A).

***ἀειστρεφής,** *ever-turning, restless* ψυχῆς...ἀ. Gr.Naz.*carm.*1.2.31. 26(M.37.912A).

ἀείστροφος, *ever-changing* τῆς ἀ. τύχης Geo.Pis.*van.*144(M.92. 1592A).

***ἀεισύστατος,** *stable*; of created world, Cyr.*Jo.*1.6(4.50B).

***ἀεισφαλής,** *always in error*, Geo.Pis.*Heracl.*1.60(M.92.1303A).

***ἀειτάραχος,** *ever-troubled* ἀ. παριστῶν βίον Areth.ap.*cat.Apoc.* 13:1(p.369.27; ἀτάραχον M.106.672A).

***ἀειτέλειος,** *ever-perfect* ἀ. ... τὴν ἁγίαν τριάδα Eugen.*exp.fid.*3 (M.18.1304D).

***ἀείτρεπτος,** *ever-changing*; of created world, Geo.Pis.*hex.*375 (M.92.1463A).

***ἀείφατος,** *ever-famous*, *Orac.Sib.*3.415.

ἀειφεγγής, *ever-bright*; of south wind as type of H. Ghost, Gr.Nyss.*hom.10 in Cant.*(M.44.984D).

***ἀειφεγγία, ἡ,** *eternal brightness*, ‡Proc.G.*Pr.*27:11(M.87.1496A).

***ἀείφθογγος,** *ever giving tongue*; of men, ‡Caes.Naz.*dial.*1(M. 38.856); of the swallow, *ib.*140(1072).

***ἀειφιλόκοσμος,** *ever loving ornaments*, Cyr.*Jo.*12(4.1085B).

***ἀειφλεγής,** *ever-blazing*, Gr.Naz.*carm.*1.2.29.122(M.37.893A).

ἀειφόρος, *ever-bearing*; of the widow's cruse, *Hymn.*(*KlT* p.22; *AS* 1 p.294).

***ἀειφρούρητος,** *ever on guard, ever-watchful*, Nonn.*par.Jo.*3:24 (M.43.772A); Paul.Sil.*Soph.*300(M.86.2131A).

***ἀείφωτος,** *ever-shining*; of the sun, Dion.Ar.*d.n.*4.4(M.3.697C); of Trin., ‡Caes.Naz.*dial.*3(M.38.860).

***ἀειχανής,** *ever-yawning*; of depths of the abyss, Areth.*Apoc.*27 (M.106.621B).

***ἀειχαρής,** *ever-joyful*, Thdr.Stud.*nativ.BMV* 5(M.96.688A).

***ἀειχείμαστος,** *ever-stormy*, Jo.Clim.*scal.*25(M.88.996C).

***ἀείψευστος,** *ever-false*, Ant.Mon.*hom.*42(M.89.1564B).

***ἀεναΐζω,** *cause to flow continually*, *Pers.*(p.12.14; M.10.100C ἀενναΐζει).

ἀέναος (ἀείναος, ἀέννασς), 1. *ever-flowing*; **a.** lit.; of running water for baptism, *Hom.Clem.*11.35; fig. λόγος...ἐξ ἀγαθοῦ πατρὸς ὡς ἐξ ἀ. καὶ ἀπείρου πηγῆς Eus.*l.C.*12(230.3; M.20.1388A); of tears, Isid.Pel.*epp.*2.10(M.78.465A); *ib.*2.209(649C); **b.** met.; of living water, Or.*fr.54 in Jo.*4:12(p.528.23); Chrys.*hom.32.1 in Jo.* (8.185A); ἐκκλησία...ἐξ ἧς ἀ. πηγῆς ἀποστάζει σωτήριον πόμα Const. *or.s.c.*2(p.155.23; M.20.1237A); of God πηγὴ ἀ. *ib.*5(p.158.13; 1244A); Adam.*dial.*4.12(p.168.12; M.11.1828C); of the elements πηγαὶ ἀ. Eus.*l.C.*6(p.207.14; M.20.1344A); **2.** *everlasting, eternal* ἀ. τοῦ κόσμου σύστασιν *1Clem.*60.1; of Christ ἀ. φῶς *Orac.Sib.fr.*3.34(p.231); of light of heavenly bodies, Eus.*l.C.*12(p.234.30; M.20.1396B); ἀ. ζωὴν *Orac.Sib.fr.*3.46(p.232); Const.*or.s.c.*7(p.162.5; M.20.1252B); ἀ. λίμνης γεέννης φλογός Hipp.*haer.*10.34(p.292.16; M.16.3454B); ἀ. ἐλπίδος Nil.*epp.*3.40(M.79.408A); of H. Ghost, *Hom.Clem.*3.12; of Trin., Eulog.*fr.Trin.*2.1(p.364).

***ἀενναΐζω,** v. ἀεναΐζω.

ἀέννασς, v. ἀέναος.

[*]**ἀεννάως,** *eternally, continually* ὁ ἥλιος ἀ. καθ' ἡμέραν τὸν αὐτοῦ δρόμον διατελεῖ ‡Chrys.*hom.3.2 in Gen.*(6:543C); ἀ. λέγων τὰ προφητικά Nil.*epp.*2.52(M.79.224A); χαρίσματα ἅτινα ἀ. εἰς τοὺς ἁγίους κέχυται Oecum.*Apoc.*22:1(p.248); ἡσυχάζειν ἀ. τῇ διανοίᾳ Hesych. S.*temp.*2.2(M.93.1512C); ἀ. ... σὺν τέκνοις καὶ γυναιξὶ σχολάσατε Geo. Al.*v.Chrys.*13(p.175.11); προσκαρτερῶν ἀ. τῇ ἐκκλησίᾳ *ib.*28(p.196.43); παρακαλῶν τὸν θεὸν ἀ. δοῦναι αὐτῷ δύναμιν *ib.*30(p.197.28).

ἀεργής, *not working, idle* τί ἑστήκαμεν ἀ.; *A.Thom.*A 73(p.188. 12); *ib.*78(p.193.1); Paul.Sil.*Soph.*216(M.86.2128A); ref. Christ calling on Father to act ταῦτά φησιν οὐκ ἀ. ὢν αὐτός Cyr.*Ps.*34:22 (M.69.909A).

***ἀέργητος,** = foreg. οὐδ' ἂν εἰ ἐργάσαιτό τι τυχὸν ὁ υἱὸς ἀ. ὁ πατὴρ εἴη ἂν Cyr.*dial.Trin.*6(5^1.621A).

ἀεργός, *not working*, in gen. μὴ ἀργὸν μήτε ἀ. Epiph.*haer.*80.4 (p.488.16; M.42.761B); of animals, Clem.*str.*7.6(p.25.9; M.9.445B); ἐν σαββάτῳ οὐ δεῖ ἐργάζεσθαι, ἀλλὰ πάντας ἀ. εἶναι Amph.*mesopent.*(M. 39.121A); διαφεύγει [sc. ὁ θεός]...τοὺς...ἀ. Marc.Er.*opusc.*1.47(M.65. 912B); πίστις ἀ. καὶ ἔργον ἄπιστον τὸν αὐτὸν τρόπον ἀποδοκιμασθήσονται Diad.*perf.*20(p.22.25).

***ἀερικός,** *like air, light, worthless* φιλία ἀ. †Nil.*vit.*4(M.79.1144B).

ἀέριος, 1. *of the air, aerial*, of a whirlwind ἐπαρῶ...τὸν κίονα τὸν ἀ. *T.Sal.*23.2(M.122.1356A ἀεριστήν); of the winds τῶν ἀ. πνευμάτων Euthal.Diac.*epp.Paul.*(M.85.693A); τὰς ἀ. ἀρχάς Hipp.*pasch.*(p.270. 24; M.10.864A); τῶν ἀ. δρόμος *A.Jo.*112(p.212.3); ὁ διάβολος...ἀ. τι πονηρὸν πνεῦμα Sever.*Eph.*2:2f.(p.308.5); **2.** *light as air, airy* ἵνα...αἱ [sc. ἀράχναι]...διὰ...ἀ. σχεδὸν τῶν νημάτων...τοὺς ἱστοὺς ἐξυφαίνωσι Gr.Naz.*or.*28.25(p.60.2; M.36.60C).

***ἀέριστος,** *in the air* ἀ. ... πηδήματι ‡Chrys.*synax.*(8.285B).

ἀεροβατ-έω, *tread the air*; **1.** lit.; of Christ's Ascension, Cyr.*Jo.*4 (4.375C); **2.** met., of spiritual ascent παράδεισον γεωργεῖν καὶ οὐρανὸν περιπολεῖν...κατ' ἴχνος ἐκείνης τῆς φωτεινῆς ~οῦντα νεφέλης Clem.*prot.*10(p.68.6; M.8.205A); of proud gait ὡς πάντων κρατῶν οὕτως ~εῖς Chrys.*hom.20.4 in Rom.*(9.662D); ~εῖν νομίζεις Isid.Pel. *epp.*3.224(M.78.908B).

ἀεροβάτης, ὁ, *one who walks the air*, of Gabriel ἀ. δρομέα ‡Chrys. *Zach.*(2.791B).

***ἀερόβατος,** *treading the air*; of Gabriel, Tim.Ant.*nativ.Jo.Bapt.* 2(M.28.909B).

***ἀερόβιος,** *living in the air*; of birds, ‡Caes.Naz.*dial.*140(M.38. 1073).

***ἀεροκοπία, ἡ,** *beating of the air*, Eust.*engast.*1(p.17.6; M.18.616A ἑωροκοπίαις).

***ἀεροπόλος,** *coursing through the air* νηκτὰ...καὶ ἀ. καὶ χερσαῖα ‡Eust.*hex.*(M.18.737B); τὰς ἀ. ψυχάς Areth.*Apoc.*59(M.106.748C, v.l. οὐρανοπόλους).

ἀεροπορέω, *move in the air*; of birds, ‡Bas.*struct.hom.*1.14(1.330B; M.30.24B); Cosm.Ind.*top.*5(M.88.232C); of heavenly bodies, Proc.G. *Gen.*1:11(M.87.89B); met., of a preacher expounding heavenly matters, Antip.Bost.*Jo.Bapt.*3(M.85.1765C).

***ἀερόστημος,** *woven of air*, Geo.Pis.*hex.*268(M.92.1455A).

***ἀεροτηρία, ἡ,** *retention of air*; etym. of ἀρτηρία, Melet.*nat.hom.* 10(M.64.1192B).

***ἀεροφανής,** *shining like the air, sky-blue* φιάλας ἀ. Pall.*v.Chrys.* 12(p.75.27; M.47.43); Cyr.*ador.*11(1.375C).

***ἀερόφοιτος,** *roaming in air*, Tat.*orat.*19(p.21.25; M.6.849B).

***ἀερσικάρηνος,** *high-pinnacled, lofty*, Paul.Sil.*Soph.*814(M.86. 2150A).

ἀερσίνοος, *conceited, arrogant*, Nonn.*par.Jo.*8:44(M.43.820B).

ἀερτάζω, *lift up*; met., of the voice, ?*make reach* γλῶσσαν ἀ. ὅλης ὑπὲρ ἄντυγα γαίης †Apoll.*met.Ps.*72:9(M.33.1416B ἀρτάζοντες).

ἀερώδης, *like air, airy*; of the moon, Clem.*str.*5.6(p.351.12; M.9. 64A); of the paths of the stars, *Hom.Clem.*3.35; neut. as subst., one constituent of a healthy body ἀπὸ...τοῦ ἀ. τὸ εὔπνουν καὶ ἰσοστάσιον Clem.*paed.*3.11(p.272.16; M.8.640B); of resurrection body; denied by orthodox against Origenists (cf. 1Cor.15:44) σῶμα λέγεται πνευματικόν, οὐ τὸ...ἀ. καθὼς λέγουσί τινες...ὧν ἐστιν εἷς καὶ Ὠριγένης Meth.*res.*3.16(p.413.6; M.18.888A); μήτε...τὴν σάρκα... ἀφανισθήσεσθαι λέγειν...ἀντανίστασθαι δὲ ὥσπερ ἕτερόν τι πνευματικόν, ἰσχνόν φημι καὶ ἀ. Cyr.*Rom.*8:23(p.218.9; M.74.824C); met., of womb of BMV, in twofold sense of '*light as air*' and '*like the veil*' (ἀήρ) which concealed eucharistic elements ἡ τὸ γεῶδες καὶ βρῖθον σκῆνος, κοῦφόν πως ὡς ἀ. ἔχουσα τὸν ἄρτον τῆς ζωῆς ὡς ἐν θυσιαστηρίῳ καλύπτουσα Thdr.Stud.*nativ.BMV* 7(M.96.693D).

***Ἀετιανοί, οἱ**, *followers of Aëtius* Ἀ. οἱ ἀπὸ Ἀετίου τοῦ Κίλικος, οἱ καὶ ἀνόμοιοι καλούμενοι, παρά τισι δὲ Εὐνομιανοί, δι' Εὐνόμιόν τινα μαθητὴν τοῦ Ἀετίου Epiph.*anac.*76(p.231.20; M.42.337B); οἱ τότε μὲν Ἀ. νῦν δὲ Εὐνομιανοὶ προσαγορευόμενοι Socr.*h.e.*2.35.14(M.67.300B); Thdt.*haer.*4.3(4.358).

[*]**ἀετοειδής**, v. ἀετώδης.

ἀετός, ὁ, A. *eagle*, etym. ἀ. ... κέκληται διὰ τὴν πολυετίαν αὐτοῦ *Phys.*B 3(p.191.6; M.43.524A); **1.** in gen.; as object of pagan worship, Arist.*apol.*12.7; cruelty to its young a warning to human parents ἀδικώτατος περὶ τὴν τῶν ἐκγόνων ἐκτροφὴν ὁ ἀ. ... τοιοῦτοι τῶν γονέων οἱ ἐπὶ προφάσει πενίας ἐκτιθέμενοι τὰ νήπια Bas.*hex.*8.6(1.76Bf.; M.29.177C); capacity for gazing at the sun compared with power of contemplation ἀετοῦ φυσικὸς νόμος, τὸ πρὸς τὴν ἡλιακὴν μαρμαρυγὴν ἰθυτενῶς ἀτενίζειν. ὃ μιμήσεταί τις ἀπευθύνων τὸν νοῦν εἰς τὸ θεῖον φῶς †Cyr.*coll.VT*(6[4].64D; M.77.1272B); **2.** as supernatural envoy καὶ ἄρας Βαροὺχ τὴν ἐπιστολὴν...ἔδησεν εἰς τὸν τράχηλον τοῦ ἀ. *Apoc.Bar.rel.*7.8; καὶ ἔκραξεν ὁ ἀ. λέγων· 'σοὶ λέγω Ἱερεμία ὁ ἐκλεκτὸς τοῦ θεοῦ' *ib.*7.15; καὶ κατῆλθεν ὁ ἀ. ἐπὶ τὸν τεθνηκότα καὶ ἀνέζησε *ib.*7.17; μὴ οὗτός ἐστιν ὁ θεὸς ὁ ὀφθεὶς τοῖς πατράσιν ἡμῶν ἐν τῇ ἐρήμῳ διὰ Μωϋσέως, καὶ ἐποίησεν ἑαυτὸν ἐν σχήματι ἀ. καὶ ἐφάνη ἡμῖν διὰ τοῦ μεγάλου ἀ. τούτου *ib.*7.18; cf. Ex.19:4; in visions κατῆλθον ἐκ τῶν οὐρανῶν ἀ., καὶ ἦραν τὰς ψυχὰς ἡμῶν καὶ ἀπήγαγον ἐν τῷ παραδείσῳ τῷ ἐν τῷ οὐρανῷ *A.Andr.et Mt.* 17(p.86.1); *A.Thom.*A 91(p.205.12ff.); **3.** as a figure of Christ ὁ ἀ. ... ἐστιν ὁ κύριος Ἰησοῦς Χριστός *A.Xanthipp.*18(p.70.36); εὐθέως δὲ ἀνέστη ἐκ τῶν ἀνατολικῶν μερῶν ἀ. *ib.*17(p.70.12); ὅταν ὑψιπετοῦς ἀ. δίκην γενώμεθα, μηκέτι τὰ τῆς γῆς, ἀλλὰ τὰ ἄνω φρονοῦντες...ἀ. δὲ ποῖον; ἀλλὰ ἡ πάντως τοῦ Χριστοῦ περὶ οὗ Μωσῆς...ᾐνίττετο· ὡς ἀ. σκεπάζει νοσσιὰν ἑαυτοῦ Hesych.H.*fr.Ps.*102:5(M.93.1280D); διὰ δὲ τοῦ ἀ. ὡς χορηγοῦ τοῦ ζωοποιοῦ πνεύματος τοῦ ἐπιπτάντος ἡμῖν ἄνωθεν Andr.Caes.*Apoc.*10(M.106.257B); **4.** as a figure of angelic power τὴν δὲ τοῦ ἀ., τὸ βασιλικόν, καὶ ὑψίφορον, καὶ ταχυπετές, καὶ τὸ πρὸς τὴν δυναμοποιὸν τροφὴν ὀξύ, καὶ νῆφον, καὶ ἐντρεχές, καὶ εὐμήχανον, καὶ τὸ πρὸς τὴν ἄφθονον καὶ πολύφωτον ἀκτῖνα τῆς θεαρχικῆς ἡλιοβολίας, ἐν ταῖς τῶν ὀπτικῶν δυνάμεων εὐρώστοις ἀνατάσεσιν ἀνεμποδίστως κατ' εὐθὺ καὶ ἀκλινῶς θεωρητικόν Dion.Ar. *c.h.*15.8(M.3.337A); **5.** exeg. Mt.24:28 ὅπου γὰρ τὸ κατὰ τὴν οἰκονομίαν τοῦ πάθους πτῶμα πεσόντος τοῦ Ἰησοῦ, ἵνα τοὺς πεσόντας στήσῃ, συναχθήσονται...οἱ πτεροφυοῦντες μαθηταὶ καὶ κατὰ τὸν Σολομῶντα 'κατασκευάσαντες πτέρυγας' ὡς ἀ. Or.*comm.ser.47 in Mt.* (p.98.15); cf.id.*hom.16 in Lc.*(p.111.4); ἀ. γενομένους...πρὸς αὐτὸν ἵπτασθαι τὸν οὐρανόν...ἀ. δὲ καλεῖ, δεικνὺς ὅτι καὶ ὑψηλὸν εἶναι δεῖ τὸν προσιόντα τῷ σώματι τούτῳ, καὶ μηδὲν πρὸς τὴν γῆν κοινὸν ἔχειν, μηδὲ κάτω σύρεσθαι καὶ ἕρπειν, ἀλλ' ἄνω πέτεσθαι διηνεκῶς, καὶ πρὸς τὸν ἥλιον τῆς δικαιοσύνης ἐνορᾶν, καὶ ὀξυδερκὲς τὸ ὄμμα τῆς διανοίας ἔχειν· ἀ. γὰρ οὐ κολοιῶν αὕτη ἡ τράπεζα Chrys.*hom.24.3 in 1Cor.* (10.216C); 'οἱ ἀ.'· τὸ πλῆθος τῶν ἀγγέλων, τῶν μαρτύρων, τῶν ἁγίων ἁπάντων δηλῶν id.*hom.76.3 in Mt.*(7.735D); ἀ. ἡμᾶς ὁ Χριστὸς ἐκάλεσεν...ἵνα οὐρανοβατῶμεν, ἵνα ὑψηλὰ πετώμεθα τοῖς πτεροῖς τοῦ πνεύματος κουφιζόμενοι id.*bapt.*4(2.374C); ἀ. ... τοὺς ὑψιπετεῖς, καὶ τῶν γηΐνων ἀπηλλαγμένους...καὶ τοῦ μυστικοῦ σώματος ἐφιεμένους, ἐν τοῖς...εὐαγγελίοις ὠνόμασε Thdt.*provid.*5(4.550); ὁ Χριστὸς δὲ τὸ πτῶμα, ἀ. ὑψηλοπετεῖς οἱ θεοσεβεῖς καὶ φιλόχριστοι ἄνθρωποι †Gr.II Papa *ep.Leon.*1(H.4.5B); **6.** as a figure of regeneration ἐπεὶ δὲ ὁ ἀ. τῶν ὀρνέων ἐστὶ βασιλικώτατος...μόνος δὲ ζώων ἡλίου φωτὸς μαρμαρυγαῖς ἀντωπεῖν δυνατός, καὶ ἀτενὲς ἀφορᾶν αὐτῷ, εἰκότως τὴν ἀνανέωσιν τῆς ψυχῆς, καὶ...τὸν βίον αὐτῆς τὸν ἐν ἄκρῳ φωτὶ γενησόμενον, ἀετοῦ φύσει παρέβαλε Eus.*Ps.*102:5(M.23.1265B); τοῦ θεοῦ διὰ τῆς παλιγγενεσίας ἀνακαινίζοντος ἡμῶν ὡς ἀετοῦ τὴν νεότητα, τὸ τῆς ἀναστάσεως ἡμῖν κατασημαίνει χάρισμα. ἀέτῳ δὲ τοὺς ἀνακαινουμένους παρείκασεν, ὀρνίθων ἁπάντων ὄντι ὑψηλοπετεστάτῳ καὶ βασιλικωτάτῳ καὶ ταῖς τοῦ ἡλίου μαρμαρυγαῖς μόνῳ λαμπρῶς ἐνατενίζειν δυναμένῳ Ath.*exp.Ps.*102:5(M.27.432D); φασὶ γὰρ γηράσαντα τὸν ἀ. ἀμαυροῦσθαι τὰς ὄψεις, καὶ βαρεῖσθαι αὐτοῦ τὰς πτέρυγας καὶ εἰς πηγὴν ἀφικνεῖσθαι καὶ εἰς τὸν αἰθέρα ἀνιπταμένου ὑπὸ τοῦ ἡλίου τὰς πτέρυγας καταφλέγεσθαι καὶ ἀναβλέπειν, εἶτ' εὐθὺς ἐπὶ τὴν πηγὴν καταβάντα τρίτον βαπτίζεσθαι καὶ ἀνανεοῦσθαι· διὸ καὶ τὸν ψαλμὸν φάσκειν φασίν· 'ἀνακαινισθήσεται ὡς ἀετοῦ ἡ νεότης σου' ‡Eust.*hex.*(M.18.732B); *Phys.*A 6(p.22.4ff.); **7.** other fig. uses τὸν ἀ. τὴν συνείδησιν...ὅ ἐστι πνεῦμα παρὰ Παύλου λεγόμενον τοῦ ἀνθρώπου ‡Gr.Naz.*sign.in Ezech.* (M.36.665A); cf.Or.*hom.1.16 in Ezech.*(p.340.23; M.13.681D); ἀκτήμων μοναχὸς ἀ. ὑψιπετής Nil.*spir.mal.*7(M.79.1152C); διὰ δὲ τοῦ ἀ. τὴν προφητείαν· ὑψιπετὲς γὰρ τὸ ζῶον καὶ λίαν ὀξυδερκές· τοιαύτη δὲ ἡ προφητεία ὑψηλὴν ἔχουσα τὴν θεωρίαν καὶ πόρρωθεν τὰ ἐσόμενα προορῶσα Thdt.*Ezech.*1:10(2.685); of S. Mark's gospel, Iren.*haer.* 3.11.8(M.7.888A); τοῦ δὲ ἀ. τὴν σωφροσύνην...καὶ τὸ κατὰ Μάρκον εὐαγγέλιον ὡς σύντομον καὶ ἀπὸ τοῦ προφητικοῦ πνεύματος ἀρξάμενον Andr.Caes.*Apoc.*10(M.106.257A); of S. John's gospel, ‡Ath.*synops.* 76(M.28.432D).

B. *a carpet*, on which the bishop stands, so called because on it is represented an eagle in flight above a city προσφέρεται...ὁ ὑποψήφιος ἄχρις οὐρᾶς τοῦ ἀ. εἶτα προσφέρεται...ἄχρι καὶ μέσου τοῦ ἀ. ... εἶτα προσφέρεται...ἄχρι καὶ τῆς κεφαλῆς τοῦ ἀ. *Euchol.*(pp.252–5).

ἀετοφόρος, ὁ, *standard-bearer*, as adj. ἀ. λεγεώνων *Orac.Sib.*8.78.

ἀετώδης (ἀετοειδής), *in the form of* or *like an eagle*; met., of one soaring in contemplation, Gr.Nyss.*Pss.titt.*A 8(M.44.465D); in form ἀετοειδής, of Gabriel, one of seven δαίμονες of Ophites, Or.*Cels.* 6.30(p.100.15; M.11.1341A).

***ἄζαλος**, *not stormy, calm*, ‡Chrys.*nat.Chr.*2(10.819E).

§**ἀζανίτης, ὁ**, (Hebr. חַזָּן) *attendant, minister*, in Jewish synagogue ἀ. τῶν παρ' αὐτοῖς διακόνων ἑρμηνευομένων ἢ ὑπηρετῶν Epiph.*haer.* 30.11(p.346.16; M.41.424B).

ἀζηλία, ἡ, 1. *lack of aggressiveness, forbearance*, Clem.*str.*2.18 (p.159.17; M.8.1028A) cit. s. ἀγάπη; Areth.*Apoc.*3(M.106.528D); **2.** *lack of zeal, indifference* ὀλιγότητος δεῖγμα...τεκμήριον ἀ. Pall.*v. Chrys.*9(p.59.2; M.47.34); τὴν τῶν νοητῶν ἀ. *ib.*13(p.81.24; 46); *ib.*20 (p.133.20; 74); Epiph.*haer.*30.1(p.333.13; M.41.405B conj. ἀντιζηλίας).

ἀζηλότυπος, *free from envy*, Bas.*ep.*160.3(3.250A; M.32.625A).

ἀζήμιος, *without loss*; **1.** neut. as subst., *exemption from taxation*, Eus.*v.C.*4.3(p.109.3; M.20.1152C); *indemnification*, Const.et Licinius ap.Eus.*h.e.*10.5.11(M.20.885A); **2.** *inexhaustible* ἀ. ... ἡ χάρις Jo.D. *hom.*3.1(M.96.589C).

ἀζήτητος, 1. *unsearchable, incomprehensible* οὐκ ἀ. ἡμῖν...τῆς φυγῆς [sc. of Jonah] ὁ τρόπος Cyr.*Jon.*3(3.370A); of judgements of God, id. *Ps.*35:7(M.69.920A); **2.** *unquestioning* πίστιν...ἀ. id.*Jo.*4.2(4.358E).

ἀζητήτως, *without questioning* πιστεύειν ἀ. Cyr.*hom.pasch.*12 (5[2].175B).

ἀζυγής, *unyoked, unwedded*, Gr.Naz.*carm.*1.2.1.13(M.37.523A); *ib.* 1.2.1.283(543A); met. τοὺς ἀ. κακίᾳ Clem.*paed.*1.5(p.98.26; M.8.265B).

***ἀζυγία, ἡ**, *celibacy*, Gr.Naz.*or.*43.62(M.36.576C); id.*carm.*1.2.17. 41(M.37.784A); Thdr.Stud.*epp.*2.115(M.99.1384C).

ἄζυγος, 1. *unyoked, single*; of Pythagorean first principle, Hipp. *haer.*6.29(p.156.7; M.16.3235C); Gnost., of first principle opp. syzygies of aeons οἱ μὲν γὰρ αὐτὸν [sc. Βυθόν] ἄ. λέγουσι Iren.*haer.*1.11.5(M. 7.569A); ὁ δὲ πατὴρ μόνος ἄ. ἐγέννησεν Hipp.*haer.*6.30(p.158.1; 3239A); Trin. ἥ τε μονὰς ἑνιαία ἐστὶ καὶ ἄ. Sophr.H.*ep.syn.*(M.87.3153A); superl. τὴν ἀ. ὡς οἴονται διατέμνοντες...θεότητα τριάδος Thdt.*Ps.* 57:6(1.986); met. φύλαξον ἄ. ... τὴν ψυχὴν...καὶ τὴν σάρκα καὶ τὸν λογισμόν Meth.*symp.*5.2(p.54.8; M.18.97C); **2.** *peerless* τοῦ ἀ. ἐν γεννητοῖς γυναικῶν Ἰωάννου Pall.*v.Chrys.*18(p.118.3; M.47.64).

***ἀζυγοστάτιστος**, *which cannot be weighed*, ‡Chrys.*transfig.* (p.339.8).

ἄζυμος, *unleavened*; **1.** ref. Gen.18:6, Or.*Jo.*13.33(p.259.5; M.14. 457B); of Passover bread, Just.*dial.*12.3(M.6.500C); αἱ μὲν τρεῖς ὗλαι ὁ ἀμνὸς ἦσαν, τὰ ἄ. καὶ ἡ πικραλίς ‡Ath.*azym.*(M.26.1328A); forbidden to Christians εἴ τις ἐπίσκοπος ἢ ἄλλος κληρικὸς νηστεύει μετὰ Ἰουδαίων...ἢ δέχεται αὐτῶν τὰ τῆς ἑορτῆς ξένια, οἷον ἄ. ἤ τι τοιοῦτον, καθαιρείσθω· εἰ δὲ λαϊκός, ἀφοριζέσθω *Can.App.*70; **2.** met., variously interpreted, Or.*Jo.*10.17(13; p.188.12; M.14.336C); *ib.*10.18(13; p.189. 19; 337C); esp. exeg. 1Cor.5:7f.; ἄζυμα...παρ' ἐκείνοις μὲν [sc. Ἰουδαίοις] ἄ. ἐξ ἀλεύρου, παρ' ἡμῖν δὲ καθαρότης βίου Chrys.*pan. mart.*2(2.668A); οὐ...πορνεία μόνον παλαιὰ ζύμη, ἀλλὰ καὶ πᾶσα κακία ...εἰ δὲ λέγει 'καθώς ἐστε ἄ.', οὐ τοῦτο λέγει, ὅτι πάντες ἦσαν καθαροί, ἀλλὰ καθὼς πρέπει εἶναι ὑμᾶς id.*hom.15.3 in 1Cor.*(10.128D); περιεργαστικώτερον πως 'ἡ ζύμη', ἁπλούστερον δὲ 'τὸ ἄ.' ... μὴ ἐν πονηρῷ βίῳ...ἀλλ' ἐν βίῳ μὴ ἔχοντι ἐπιμιξίαν 'τῆς παλαιᾶς ἐκείνης ζύμης'· τοῦτο γάρ ἐστιν [1Cor.5:8] Sever.*1Cor.*5:7f.(p.244.26ff.); 'ζύμην παλαιὰν' τὴν πρὸ τοῦ βαπτίσματος καλεῖ· ἧς κεχωρίσθαι παρεγγυᾷ, καὶ εἶναι ἄ. Thdt.*1Cor.*5:6f.(3.193), cf. ὀφείλομεν ἄ. ... εἶναι...ζύμην παλαιὰν καὶ...ἄ. τὰς ἀρετὰς καὶ κακίας τούτοις τοῖς ὀνόμασιν ὑποδηλῶν Phot.*1Cor.*5:6ff.(Staab p.553.16ff.); **3.** neut. plur. as subst., *feast of unleavened bread, Passover*, mostly as type of Passion and Easter τοῦτο γάρ ἐστι τὸ σύμβολον τῶν ἀ., ἵνα μὴ τὰ παλαιὰ τῆς κακῆς ζύμης ἔργα πράττητε Just.*dial.*14.2(M.6.504D); Clem.*fr.*28(p.216.30; M.9.757A); ἐὰν ἀναγινώσκῃς περὶ τῶν ἀ. ἔστιν ἀκοῦσαι κεκρυμμένως, ἔστιν ἀκοῦσαι φανερῶς τῆς ἐντολῆς ὅσοι ἐν ἡμῖν· ἐγγὺς γάρ ἐστι τὸ πάσχα, ἄ. ἄγεται, τὰ ἄ. τὰ σωματικά, οὐκ ἀκούετε τῆς λεγούσης ἐντολῆς Or.*hom.12.13 in Jer.*(p.100.2; M.13.396C); *ib.*(p.122.27ff.; 425B); τὴν τῶν ἀ. ἡμέραν εἰς...δόξαν τοῦ ἁγίου...πασχα τοῦ Χριστοῦ τυπικῶς ἐπετέλουν Ἰσραηλῖται Didym.*Trin.*2.16(M.39.721A); Epiph.*haer.*70.10(p.243.22; M.42.357B); οὐκ ἔστιν ἄ. παρ' αὐτοῖς, οὐδὲ πάσχα (καὶ γὰρ τοῦτο ἀκούω λεγόντων πολλῶν ὅτι μετὰ τοῦ ἀ. τὸ πάσχα ἐστίν) Chrys.*Jud.*3.3(1.610A); for date of observance v. πάσχα.

***ἀζυμότης**, ἡ, *unleavened state*, met. τῆς...ἀ. τῆς πονηρίας Mac.Aeg.*hom.*24.4(M.34.665A).

***ἀζυμοφαγία**, ἡ, *eating of unleavened bread*, plur. *Passover season* μετὰ τὰς ἑπτὰ ἡμέρας τῶν ἀ. Just.*dial.*14.3(M.6.505A); Gr.Nyss.*res.*1(M.46.617C).

***ἀζυμοφάγος**, *eating unleavened bread*, ‡Ath.*azym.*(M.26.1328B).

ἄζυξ, *unpaired, single*, Nonn.*par.Jo.*19:18(M.43.901B); of God, Gr.Naz.*carm.*1.2.6.5(M.37.644A); of Son, *ib.*1.2.34.194(959A); of virgins, †Bas.Anc.*virg.*21(M.30.713B).

ἀζωΐα, ἡ, *absence of life*, said to be taught by Marcell. in respect of pre-incarnate Logos τοῦ βασιλέως τοῦ μεγάλου τὴν εἰκόνα λαβὼν ⟨ἐν⟩ ἀ.·...τὴν εἰκόνα τοῦ θεοῦ ἀζωΐᾳ περιγράψας Acac.Caes.*fr. Marcell.*ap.Epiph.*haer.*72.7(p.261.11,14; M.42.390Df.).

ἄζωος, *lacking life*, of pre-existent Logos acc. Marcell. as represented by Acac. Caes. τούτων [sc. divine attributes] ἀκίνητον εἰκόνα...οἱονεὶ ἄψυχον καὶ ἄ. Acac.Caes.*fr.Marcell.*(p.261.17; M.42.392A); contradicted by Acacius οὐ γὰρ ὁ λόγος θεὸς...παρέχων ζωὴν ...αὐτὸς ἄ. *ib.*(p.264.20; 396B); ἡ δὲ ὕλη ἄ. Jo.D.*Man.*1.2(M.94.1508C).

***ἀηδιστής**, ὁ, *odious person*, Dor.*doct.*11.5(M.88.1740C).

ἀήρ, ὁ, **A.** *air*; **1.** dist. from αἰθήρ: τὰ αἰθέρια ἅτινα μέχρι σελήνης ἐστίν· ἐκεῖθεν γὰρ ἀ. αἰθέρος διακρίνεται Hipp.*haer.*7.24(p.202.4; M.16.3311B); ἀ. οὐχ ὑφ' ἑαυτοῦ ἀλλ' ὑπὸ...τοῦ αἰθέρος διακαίεται...οἱ ἄνεμοι...ἐκ τῆς πρὸς τὸν ἀ. τοῦ αἰθέρος διακαύσεως καὶ θερμότητος ἐν αὐτῷ τῷ ἀ. συνίστανται καὶ δι' αὐτοῦ πανταχοῦ πνέουσι Ath.*gent.*27(M.25.53Cff.); often equated in scripture with οὐρανός, Or.*comm. in Eph.*2:2(p.404); **2.** pagan; first principle acc. Anaximenes, Clem.*prot.*4(p.49.1; M.8.165A); ἀ. and τὰ ἐν τῷ ἀ. worshipped as gods after Fall, Ath.*gent.*9(M.25.17D); as dwelling of God, a finer concept than that of God's habitation in man-made temples, Clem.*str.*7.5(p.20.21; M.9.437A); **3.** created by God, *Diogn.*7.2; the basic element, *Hom.Clem.*20.6; **4.** ref. soul: atheistic notion that soul dissolves into air on separation from body, *ib.*15.2; Manich. ὁ κινῶν τὴν χεῖρα βλάπτει τὸν ἀ., ἐπειδὴ ὁ ἀ. ψυχή ἐστι τῶν ἀνθρώπων Hegem.*Arch.*10(p.17.10; M.10.1444C); *ib.*8(p.13.11; 1440C) cit. s. στῦλος; soul transported through air after separation from body, Ath.*v.Anton.*60(M.26.929A); **5.** ref. 1Thess.4:17 ἁρπαγησόμεθα γὰρ ἐν νεφέλαις νοηταῖς εἰς τὸν μυστικὸν ἀ., καὶ οὕτως λοιπὸν πάντοτε σὺν κυρίῳ ἐσόμεθα Nil.*epp.*3.142(M.79.449B); **6.** as sphere of demonic powers, subdued and brought under power of Christ through Crucifixion 'in the air' ἔοικεν γὰρ ὁ περικεχυμένος ἡμῖν ἀ. πεπληρῶσθαι δυνάμεων ἀντικειμένων Or.*comm.in Eph.*6:12(p.572); id.*mart.*45(p.41.17; M.11.621A); Ath.*inc.*25.5,6(M.25.140B,C) cit. s. δαίμων; τὰς χεῖρας ἐκτείνας ἐπὶ τοῦ σταυροῦ τὸν μὲν ἄρχοντα τῆς ἐξουσίας τοῦ ἀ. ...κατέβαλε, τὴν δὲ ὁδὸν ἡμῖν ἐν τοῖς οὐρανοῖς καθαρὰν ἐποίει id.*ep. Adelph.*7(M.26.1081B); id.*v.Anton.*21(M.26.876A); id.*ep.fest.*(p.295.18ff.; M.26.1433A); πολλοὶ δὲ τὰ ἐπὶ γῆς καταλιπόντες, ἐλευθέρῳ τῷ βαδίσματι τὸν ἀ. διαβαίνουσι, καὶ ἐν οὐρανῷ πολιτεύονται· οὐκέτι φοβούμενοι τὸν ἄρχοντα τοῦ ἀ. ... διὰ τοῦτο γὰρ ἐσταυρώθη εἰς τὸν ἀ. ὁ σωτήρ ‡Ath.*pass.*29(M.28.233D); Chrys.*exp.in Ps.*41(5.137D); †Jo.D.*B.J.*13(M.96.981A); **7.** ref. Ascension ὡς δι' ἐκκλησίας τοῦ ἀ. διείη, ὡς ἀ. τὸν οὐρανὸν διεπέρα ὁ τῶν οὐρανίων ποιητής Procl.CP *hom.*1.3(M.65.836C); **8.** phrases: beat the *air* σκιαμαχεῖ...καὶ τοῦτο...ἐστι τὸ εἰς ἀ. δέρειν Cyr.*Nest.*3.1(p.56.8; 6^{1}.65D); ἀ. ... καταπαίοντες Dion.Ar.*d.n.*8.6(M.3.893C); rising up into the *air*, i.e. becoming fierce τὴν περὶ τῶν...νηστειῶν στάσιν μέχρις ἀ. κορυφωθεῖσαν Jo.D.*jej.*3(M.95.68A).

B. *veil*, liturg., the third large veil covering chalice and paten together τὸ καταπέτασμα...ὁ ἀ. ἐστι καὶ λέγεται ἀντὶ τοῦ λίθου οὗ ἠσφάλισε τὸ μνημεῖον Ἰωσήφ ‡Bas.*h.myst.*54a(p.392.2) = ‡Germ.CP *contempl.*(M.98.400C); τῷ ἀνωτάτῳ πέπλῳ ὃ καὶ ἀ. οἶδεν ὁ λόγος καλεῖν *Lit.Praesanct.*(p.348.25), cf. τὸ τρίτον κάλυμμα ἤτοι τὸν ἀ. *Lit.Chrys.*(p.360.18); ὁ ἱερεὺς ἄρας τὸν ἀ. ἐπιτίθησιν ἐπὶ τῶν ὤμων *ib.*(p.378.30).

ἀήττητος, **1.** *unconquered* ἀ. [sc. ὁ γνωστικός] ἡδονῇ Clem.*str.*7.11(p.46.25; M.9.489B); of Christians ἵνα ἀ. γένῃ παντὶ αἱρετικῷ πράγματι Cyr.H.*procatech.*10; οὓς [sc. newly baptized] διαφύλαξον ἀ. ἀγωνιστὰς διαμεῖναι *Rit.Bapt.*(p.407); of Church ἐνθέῳ προγνώσει ἀ. καὶ ἀκατάπληκτον ἔσεσθαι Eus.*p.e.*1.3(7D; M.21.32D); **2.** *unconquerable*, of Christ ὅρα τὸν ἀ. βοηθὸν τὸν ὑπερασπίζοντα ἡμῶν Clem.*str.*4.7(p.269.27; M.8.1260A); ὁ ἀληθὴς ἀθλητὴς ἡμῶν καὶ ἀ. *A.Thom.* A 39(p.157.10); οὗτος γάρ ἐστιν ἀ. σύμμαχος καὶ ὑπερασπιστὴς τῶν δικαίων Const.*or.s.c.*26(p.192.30; M.20.1316B); θεὸς δὲ σαρκὶ ἑνωθεὶς ἀνθρωπείᾳ...νοῦς ἀ. ὢν τῶν ψυχικῶν καὶ σαρκικῶν παθημάτων Apoll. *fid.sec.pt.*(p.178.14; M.10.1117A); of God, Const.*or.s.c.*15(p.176.10; 1280A).

ἀθαλάμευτος, *unwedded*; of BMV, ‡Chrys.*annunt.*(9.844D).

ἀθαμβής, **1.** *unperturbed, fearless*, Clem.*str.*5.4(p.338.23: M.9.37B); **2.** *not causing surprise* ἀ. μῦθον Nonn.*par.Jo.*1:51(M.43.760A).

ἀθανασία, ἡ, *immortality*;

A. of God; **1.** as divine attribute (cf. 1Tim.6:16) ὁ δὲ θεὸς καὶ ἀ. ... καὶ ζωή Meth.*res.*1.34(p.272.3; M.41.1097C); μόνος ἔχων τὴν ἀ. λέγεται ὁ θεός, ὅτι οὐκ ἐκ θελήματος ἄλλου ταύτην ἔχει, καθάπερ οἱ λοιποὶ πάντες ἀθάνατοι, ἀλλ' ἐκ τῆς οἰκείας οὐσίας ‡Just.*qu.et resp.*61(M.6.1304A); Ath.*syn.*16(p.243.29; M.26.708D); ἀρχὴ γάρ ἐστι τῶν ὄντων... πᾶσα ἀ. Dion.Ar.*d.n.*5.7(M.3.821B); *Lit.Jac.*(p.198.23); denied of humanity of Christ οὐδενὸς τῶν παρὰ τὸν θεὸν ζώντων ἔχοντος τὴν ἄτρεπτον πάντη καὶ ἀναλλοίωτον ζωήν. καὶ τί διστάζομεν περὶ τῶν λοιπῶν, ὅτε οὐδὲ ὁ Χριστὸς ἔσχε τὴν τοῦ πατρὸς ἀ.; ἐγεύσατο γὰρ ὑπὲρ παντὸς θανάτου Or.*Jo.*2.17(11; p.75.3; M.14.145B); of Logos, ‡Ath.*Apoll.*18(M.26.1164C); **2.** heret. theories; **a.** (Arian) predicated of God with implication that it was not perfectly possessed by Son οἴδαμεν ἕνα θεὸν...μόνον ἀ. ἔχοντα Ar.*ep.Alex.*(p.12.5; M.26.708D); orthodox reply ἡμεῖς δὲ κἂν ἀκούσωμεν ὅτι μόνος ὁ θεὸς ἔχει τὴν ἀ. τὸν υἱὸν διὰ τῆς ἀ. νοοῦμεν· ἀ. γάρ ἐστιν ἡ ζωή, ἥτις ἐστὶν ὁ κύριος ὁ εἰπὼν ὅτι 'ἐγώ εἰμι ἡ ζωή' Gr.Nyss.*Eun.*2(2 p.308.8f.; M.45.480C); **b.** monophysites blamed for asserting that divine nature suffered death ὁ θεὸς...οὐ γὰρ παρ' ἑτέρου τὴν ἀ. ἔχει λαβών. τοῖς δὲ ἀγγέλοις, καὶ τοῖς ἄλλοις...αὐτὸς τὴν ἀ. δεδώρηται...πῶς αὐτῷ τὸ τοῦ θανάτου προσαρμόζετε πάθος; Thdt.*eran.*3(4.217).

B. pagan, of the soul; **1.** denied Ἀριστοτέλης τῆς ψυχῆς διαβάλλει τὴν ἀ. Tat.*orat.*25(p.27.3; M.6.860B); **2.** affirmed πάντα, ὅσα περὶ ἀ. ψυχῆς ἢ τιμωριῶν μετὰ τὸν θάνατον ἢ θεωρίας οὐρανίων ἢ τῶν ὁμοίων δογμάτων καὶ φιλόσοφοι καὶ ποιηταὶ ἔφασαν, παρὰ τῶν προφητῶν τὰς ἀφορμὰς λαβόντες καὶ νοῆσαι δεδύνηνται καὶ ἐξηγήσαντο Just.*1apol.*44.9(M.6.396A); τὰ παρ' Ἕλλησι καὶ βαρβάροις...λεγόμενα περὶ τῆς ἀ. τῆς ψυχῆς...ἢ τῆς τοῦ νοῦ ἀ. Or.*Cels.*3.80(p.271.4f.; M.11.1025A); *ib.*2.12(p.141.1; 817A); apology for using philosophers' arguments in dealing with pagans μὴ ὑπολάβῃς δέ με οὐχ ἁρμοζόντως τῷ Χριστιανῶν λόγῳ παρειληφέναι πρὸς τὸν Κέλσον τοὺς περὶ τῆς ἀ. ... τῆς ψυχῆς φιλοσοφήσαντας· πρὸς οὓς κοινά τινα ἔχοντες εὐκαιρότερον παραστήσομεν ὅτι ἡ μέλλουσα μακαρία ζωὴ μόνοις ἔσται τοῖς ⟨τὴν⟩ κατὰ τὸν Ἰησοῦν θεοσέβειαν παραδεξαμένοις *ib.*3.81(p.271.15; 1025B); πολλαὶ...εἰσι τῆς ἀ. αὐτῆς [sc. ψυχῆς] ἀποδείξεις παρά τε Πλάτωνι καὶ τοῖς ἄλλοις Nemes.*nat.hom.*2(M.40.589B).

C. in Christian doctrine, of man; **1.** as gift of God; **a.** gen. τὰ δῶρα τοῦ θεοῦ...ζωὴ ἐν ἀθανασίᾳ *1Clem.*35.2; Iren.*haer.*5.2.3(M.7.1127B); θεὸς...ἅγιον τοῦτο τῇ σαρκὶ [καὶ] ἀϊδιότητος καλλώπισμα περιθείς, τὴν ἀ. Clem.*paed.*3.1(p.237.10; M.8.557B); id.*prot.*10(p.71.21; M.8.212B); μείζων...τῆς ἀ. ὁ θεός, ὁ τῇ ἑαυτοῦ βουλήσει καὶ τὰ μὴ ὄντα ἀθάνατα ποιεῖν δυνάμενος Marcell.*fr.*107 ap.Eus.*Marcell.*2.4(p.55.14; M.24.817A); Chrys.*Stag.*1.2(1.158C); ψυχὰς...καὶ τὰ συζυγῆ σώματα, πρὸς...ἀ. ἐπήγγελται [sc. God] μεταθήσειν Dion.Ar.*d.n.*6.2(M.3.856D); dependent on keeping God's commandment to Adam, Thphl.Ant.*Autol.*27(M.6.1096A); **b.** because man was made in the image of God, v. εἰκών; and created by his own hand ὅπερ ἂν τῇ ἑαυτοῦ τεχνήσηται [sc. θεός] χειρί, ἐξ ἀνάγκης ἔσται ἀθάνατον, ἅτε ἀθανασίας ἔργον. ἀθανασίᾳ γὰρ ἀθάνατα τὰ ἀθάνατα γίγνεται Meth.*res.*1.34(p.271.11f.; M.41.1097B) ∞ Proc.G.*Gen.*2:7(M.87.157A); *ib.*(p.272.4; M.41.1097C); **c.** also given to the wicked and to demons for their punishment οὐκ ἔστιν ἀθάνατος...ἡ ψυχὴ καθ' ἑαυτήν, θνητὴ δέ· ἀλλὰ δυνατὸς ἡ αὐτὴ καὶ μὴ ἀποθνήσκειν. θνήσκει μὲν γὰρ καὶ λύεται μετὰ τοῦ σώματος μὴ γινώσκουσα τὴν ἀλήθειαν, ἀνίσταται δὲ εἰς ὕστερον ἐπὶ συντελείᾳ τοῦ κόσμου σὺν τῷ σώματι θάνατον διὰ τιμωρίας ἐν ἀ. λαμβάνουσα Tat.*orat.*13(p.14.14; M.6.833A); ὥσπερ δὲ ἡμεῖς, οἷς τὸ θνήσκειν ῥᾴδιον ἀποβαίνει νῦν, εἰσαῦθις ἢ μετὰ ἀπολαύσεως τὸ ἀθάνατον ἢ τὸ λυπηρὸν μετὰ ἀ. προσλαμβάνομεν, οὕτω καὶ οἱ δαίμονες τῇ νῦν ζωῇ πρὸς τὸ πλημμελεῖν καταχρώμενοι...εἰσαῦθις ἕξουσιν τὴν αὐτὴν ἀ. ὁμοίαν τῆς παρ' ὃν ἔζων χρόνον *ib.*14(p.15.22f.; 836C); but usu. = *eternal life*, contrasted with punishment of evil-doers οἱ μὲν εἰς κρίσιν καὶ καταδίκην τοῦ πυρὸς ἀπαύστως κολάζεσθαι πεμφθῶσιν, οἱ δὲ ἐν...ἀ. συνῶσιν Just.*dial.*45.4(M.6.573A); **2.** its loss through Adam's sin, *Const.App.*6.7.3; ἂν δὲ τὰ τῆς ψυχῆς προτιμήσῃ καλά, τῆς ἀ. ἀξιωθῇ...ἐκπεσὼν οὖν τῆς τελειώσεως, ἐξέπεσεν ὁμοίως καὶ τῆς ἀ., ἣν ὕστερον ἀναλήψεται χάριτι τοῦ ποιήσαντος αὐτόν Nemes.*nat.hom.*1(M.40.513B–516B); Proc.G.*Gen.*3:18(M.87.217A); cf. exeg. Cant.1:6, Gr.Nyss.*hom.2 in Cant.*(M.44.800C) cit. s. ἀμπελών; **3.** its restoration through Christ; **a.** in gen. εὐχαριστοῦμέν σοι, πάτερ...ὑπὲρ τῆς...ἀ., ἧς ἐγνώρισας ἡμῖν διὰ Ἰησοῦ *Did.*10.2; Clem.*prot.*12(p.85.20; M.8.244A); *ib.*(p.85.1; 241B); διδάσκαλος [sc. Christ] τῶν τῆς ἀ. μαθημάτων Or.*Cels*.3.60(p.254.26; M.11.1000B); *Const. App*.7.26.2; Cyr.*Nest*.4.6(p.88.33; 6[1].115C) cit. s. ἄμφιον; **b.** through Inc., death, and Resurrection ἔθανεν ἀθανασίαν τῷ θνητῷ ποριζόμενος Meth.*Porph*.2(p.505.22; M.18.404A); οὐχ ἵν' ὁ λόγος ὠφεληθῇ τὴν ἡμετέραν ἀνείληφεν σάρκα, ἀλλ' ἵνα ἡ σὰρξ διὰ τὴν πρὸς τὸν λόγον κοινωνίαν ἀ. τύχῃ Marcell.*fr*.104 ap.Eus.*Marcell*.2.4(p.53.20; M.24.813C); Ath.*inc*.50.5(M.25.185C) cit. s. ἀνάστασις; ὁ θάνατος αὐτοῦ, ἡμῶν ἀ. ἐστί id.*inc.et c.Ar*.5(M.26.992A); ἠθέλησε τὴν ἁγίαν αὐτοῦ σάρκα γεύσασθαι τῆς τριημέρου νεκρώσεως ὑπὲρ πάσης τῆς φύσεως, ἵνα δι' αὐτῆς τῷ νενεκρωμένῳ γένει τὴν ἀ. χαρίσηται Gr.Ant.*mul.ung*.1(M.88.1849A); **c.** through eucharist, called φάρμακον ἀθανασίας Ign.*Eph*.20.2; ἐγώ σου τροφεὺς ἄρτον ἐμαυτὸν διδοὺς...καὶ πόμα καθ' ἡμέραν ἐνδιδοὺς ἀθανασίας Clem.*q.d.s*.23(p.175.13; M.9.628D); ἐπιούσιος...ἄρτος...ἰσχὺν περιποιῶν τῇ ψυχῇ καὶ τῆς ἰδίας ἀ. (ἀθάνατος γὰρ ὁ λόγος τοῦ θεοῦ) μεταδιδοὺς τῷ ἐσθίοντι αὐτοῦ Or.*or*.27.9(p.369.21; M.11.513A); τὸ δὲ ἅγιον σῶμα τοῦ Χριστοῦ, πρὸς ἀ. ... ἀποτρέφον βρῶσις ὄντως ἀληθής Cyr.*Jo*.4.2(4.364C); **d.** mediated by BMV ζωοδόχον σῶμα αὐτῆς, τὸ πηγάσαν τὴν ἔμφυτον ἀ. ... ἐν τῇ θνητῇ ...ἡμῶν φύσει Mod.*dorm*.12(M.86.3308C); **4.** its appropriation by men; **a.** through fully Christian life ἄνθρωποι μετὰ τὴν τῆς ἀ. ἀποβολὴν θανάτῳ τῷ διὰ πίστεως τὸν θάνατον νενικήκασιν, καὶ διὰ μετανοίας κλῆσις αὐτοῖς δεδώρηται Tat.*orat*.15(p.17.5; M.6.840A); in contrast with the Jewish Law εἰ...ἱκανὸς ἦν ὁ Μωσέως νόμος ζωὴν αἰώνιον παρασχεῖν...μάτην δὲ ὁ πάσας πεποιηκὼς 'ἐκ νεότητος' τὰς νομίμους ἐντολὰς παρὰ ἄλλου αἰτεῖ...ἀ. Clem.*q.d.s*.8(p.165.2; M.9.612C); through γνῶσις, id.*str*.6.8(p.466.13; M.9.289C); *ib*.7.3(p.15.3; 425A); through obedience and other virtues, Meth.*res*.2.2(p.331.16; M.18.297C); πίστις ἀνθρώπων...ἀθανασίας καρπὸν ἀθροίζουσα Const.ap.Gel.Cyz.*h.e*.2.7.5(M.85.1233A); τῆς εἰς αὐτὸν πίστεως καὶ εὐσεβείας ἀ. ... ἐστιν ὁ καρπός Ath.*gent*.47(M.25.96B); ἀθανασίας...αἰτία...ἡ φιλανθρωπία *Hom.Clem*.12.33; ἐὰν φυλάξῃ τὴν ἐντολήν, μισθὸν ταύτης τὴν ἀ. κομίσηται *Lit*.ap.*Const.App*.8.12.19; exeg. Pr.23:13 σὺ μὲν γὰρ ῥάβδῳ πατάξεις αὐτόν, τὴν δὲ ψυχὴν ῥύσῃ ἐκ θανάτου. ἔοικε τοίνυν ἀ. ἑρμηνεύειν ἡ τοῦ 'ἐπάταξαν' λέξις Gr.Nyss.*hom.12 in Cant*.(M.44.1032A); νικήσωμεν...τὸν κόσμον, πρὸς ἀ. δράμωμεν Chrys.*hom.79.3 in Jo*.(8.468D); **b.** through martyrdom ἐὰν δὲ κληθῶμεν εἰς μαρτύριον,...χαίρωμεν ὡς ἐπὶ ἀ. σπεύδοντες *Const.App*.5.6.2; **c.** mediately, through example of saints ἀ. εὕρατο διὰ σοῦ [sc. S. George] Ἀθανάσιος, τῆς ἀ. ὁ φαιδρὸς ἐπώνυμος Jo.Mon.*hymn.Geo*.8(M.96.1397D); **d.** through thoughts of death, leading to conversion, *Hom.Clem*.1.2; **5.** ref. body ὁ...ὁριζόμενος τὴν σάρκα μὴ εἶναι ταύτην ἀθανασίας δεκτικήν...βλασφημεῖ *Meth.res*.1.40(p.284.11; M.41.1108C); τὸ σῶμα τοῦτο δύναται τῷ νόμῳ τοῦ θεοῦ 'ὑποτάσσεσθαι' καὶ τὴν ἀ. ὑποδέξασθαι *ib*.1.61(p.325.20; 1157D); **6.** practical consequences of doctrine of immortality ὅταν ἴδῃ [sc. the pagan] τρέμοντα θάνατον, πῶς δέξεται τοὺς περὶ τῆς ἀ. λόγους; Chrys.*hom.72.4 in Jo*.(8.428A); τὸ τῆς ἀναστάσεως δόγμα λυμαίνεται ἡ τοῦ βίου φαυλότης, τὸ τῆς ἀ. τῆς ψυχῆς id.*hom.48.4 in Ac*.(9.356D).

D. some problems and implications of immortality: man's conception of it proof of the existence of mind, Ath.*gent*.32(M.25.64B); objection against Aristotelian doctrine of the divinity of the sky πῶς ἐστι θεὸς ὁ οὐρανός, ὁ μὴ βουλήσει τὴν ἀ. ἐνεργῶν, ἀλλὰ τῇ κινήσει τε καὶ τῇ μεταστάσει τῶν ἑαυτῶν μερῶν; ‡Just.*confut*.52 (M.6.1545A); immortality a sign of the just order of the universe, *Hom.Clem*.19.20.

E. *continued existence, permanence*; of the human race, Clem.*str*.2.23(p.189.13; M.8.1088B); Gr.Nyss.*or.catech*.28(p.107.11; M.45.73C).

ἀθανατίζ-ω, 1. *make immortal*, Christ's body τὸ ἀθανατισθὲν ὑπὸ τοῦ θεοῦ σῶμα Gr.Nyss.*or.catech*.37(p.143.3; θανατισθὲν M.45.93B); human flesh through Inc. μεταλαμβάνει τῆς ἐμῆς σαρκὸς ἵνα...τὴν σάρκα ἀθανατίσῃ Gr.Naz.*or*.38.13(M.36.325C); βουληθεὶς ἀθανατίσαι τὴν σάρκα, περιβάλλεται σάρκα Procl.CP *annunt*.3(M.85.432C); human body through Resurrection ἀθανατισθέντος τοῖς ἀνθρώποις τοῦ σώματος διὰ τῆς ἀναστάσεως Max.*myst*.24(M.91.709B); cf. πῶς οὐκ ἔστι δυνατὸν τὸ ~εσθαι τοὺς νεκροὺς βουληθέντος τοῦ θεοῦ; ‡Just.*qu.Gr*.11.44(M.6.1489A); human beings τῷ ξύλῳ τῆς ζωῆς ἐνέκειτο ~ειν φυσικῶς τὸν ἐσθίοντα Proc.G.*Gen*.2:9(M.87.161B); cf.*ib*.3:18 (216D); through eucharist δυνάμει [sc. ἄρτος] πνεύματος ἡνωμένος ἁγίου, ἐκ μόνης γεύσεως ~ει τὸν ἄνθρωπον Mac.Mgn.*apocr*.3.23(p.106.30); as consequence of good life, Clem.*str*.1.27(p.107.17; M.8.820C); **2.** *make everlasting*, the memory of righteous man ἡ μνήμη ~εται Chrys.*fr.in Pr*.10:7(M.64.684B); Proc.G.*Gen*.25:27(M.87.409B).

***ἀθανατοποιός,** *making immortal*; of love for God, *Hom.Clem*.3.8; of baptism τῆς ἀ. σφραγῖδος Const.ap.Eus.*v.C*.4.62(p.143.8; M.20.1213A); of bread of life, Eus.*fr.Lc*.14:16(M.24.572D); c. genit. ἡ ἀ. τῶν σωμάτων ἡμῶν ἁγνεία Meth.*symp*.10.6(p.129.4; M.18.204B).

ἀθάνατος, I. *immortal, everlasting*;

A. of God; **1.** in gen., Athenag.*leg*.22.5(M.6.937C) cit. s. ἀκίνητος; δεδώρηται ἡμῖν ὁ θεός...εὐθανασίαν ἀ. τε καὶ ἀγήρως ὑπάρχων Clem.*str*.5.11(p.371.17, v.l. ἀθανασίαν M.9.104B); *Orac.Sib*.1.73; *ib*.1.45; Const.ap.Gel.Cyz.*h.e*.2.7.34(M.85.1240C); Ath.*gent*.22(M.25.44D); ἐν τῷ πατρὶ...τὸ ἀ. id.*hom.in Mt.11:27*(M.25.216B); *ib*.(216D); Gel.Cyz.*h.e*.2.22.11(M.85.1292D); κυρίως ἀ. ὁ θεός· οὐσίᾳ γὰρ ἀ., οὐ μετουσίᾳ Thdt.*eran*.3(4.217); of all that appertains to God, Dion.Ar.*d.n*.10.3(M.3.937C) cit. s. ἀναλλοίωτος; **2.** ref. Christ; **a.** in gen. τὸν ἴδιον υἱὸν ἀπέδοτο λύτρον ὑπὲρ ἡμῶν...τὸν ἀ. ὑπὲρ τῶν θνητῶν *Diogn*.9.2; *A.Thom*.A 124(p.234.2); ἠρετίσατο ὁ ἀ. σταυρωθῆναι διὰ σέ Mac.Aeg.*hom*.15.44(M.34.605C); Chrys.*hom.68.1 in Jo*.(8.404D); iron. λέγων ἀ. δεικνύει νεκρόν Cels.ap.Or.*Cels*.2.16(p.144.28; M.11.825C); **b.** in his divinity 'ὑγιαίνων'...ὁ σωτήριος εἴρηται λόγος αὐτὸς ὢν ἀλήθεια, καὶ τὸ ὑγιαῖνον ἀεὶ ἀ. μένει Clem.*str*.1.8(p.26.27; M.8.737A); θεὸς ὢν ἄνθρωπος ἐγένετο, σαρκωθεὶς ἐκ τῆς παρθένου Μαρίας, ἀ. μένων σαρκί *A.Phil*.141(p.76.9); *ib*.(p.76.27); εἰκὼν ὢν τοῦ πατρός, καὶ ἀ. ὢν ὁ λόγος Ath.*Ar*.1.41(M.26.96C); opp. humanity εἰκότως υἱὸν ἄνθρωπον ἔλεγε τὸν παραδιδόμενον· ὁ λόγος γὰρ ἀ. ... ἐστι id.*ep.Serap*.4.20(M.26.669B); οὐχ οἷόν τε δὲ ἦν τὸν λόγον ἀποθανεῖν ἀ. ὄντα...τούτου ἕνεκεν τὸ δυνάμενον ἀποθανεῖν ἑαυτῷ λαμβάνει σῶμα id.*inc*.9.1(M.25.112A); *ib*.20.6(132B); ἄνθρωπος...ἀνάγκῃ φύσεως καὶ μὴ θέλων ἀποθνήσκει· ὁ δὲ κύριος, ἀ. αὐτὸς ὤν, σάρκα δὲ θνητὴν ἔχων, ἐπ' ἐξουσίας εἶχεν, ὡς θεός, ἀπὸ τοῦ σώματος χωρισθῆναι, καὶ τοῦτο πάλιν ἀναλαβεῖν id.*Ar*.3.57(444B); τὸν Χριστὸν καταγγέλλουσιν ἔρχεσθαι αἱ θεῖαι γραφαί...κύριον καὶ θεόν, καὶ ἀ. *ib*.2.16(177C); ὁ λόγος, ἀ. ὤν, τῷ νῷ κέχρηται ὀργάνῳ ‡Ath.*dial.Trin*.4.5(M.28.1257B); ἡ ἀ. αὐτοῦ θεότης ἔμεινεν ἀ.· καὶ ἐν τῷ καιρῷ τῆς τελευτῆς τῆς σαρκός, τὸ θνητὸν αὐτοῦ σῶμα...τοῦ θανάτου τὸν ὕπνον ἐδέξατο Gr.Ant.*mul.ung*.10(M.88.1860B); **c.** of Christ's body, Eus.*Marcell*.1.1(p.6.16; M.24.724A); but, acc. Marcell., separated from the Word ποῦ δέ σοι [sc. Marcell.] τὸ σῶμα τὸ ἀ. χωρήσειεν ⟨ἂν⟩ τοῦ σωτῆρος; ἀ. γὰρ ὁμολογῶν *ib*.2.4(p.56.34f.; 820C); ὁ τοῦ θεοῦ υἱὸς ἐν τριταίῳ διαστήματι τὸ γενόμενον νεκρὸν σῶμα ἔδειξεν ἀ. Ath.*inc*.26.6(M.25.141C); but not before Resurrection πόθεν ἀ. ὁ νεκρός; μανθανέτω ὁ βουλόμενος ὅτι οὐχ ὁ νεκρὸς ἀ. ἀλλ' ὁ ἀναστὰς ἐκ νεκρῶν. οὐ μόνον οὖν οὐχ ὁ νεκρὸς ἀ., ἀλλ' οὐδ' ὁ πρὸ τοῦ νεκροῦ Ἰησοῦς ὁ σύνθετος ἀ. ἦν, ὅς γε ἔμελλε τεθνήξεσθαι. οὐδεὶς γὰρ τεθνηξόμενος ἀ. ἀλλ' ἀ., ὅτε οὐκέτι τεθνήξεται Or.*Cels*.2.16(p.146.8ff.; M.11.832B); διόπερ μάτην λέλεκται τῷ Κέλσῳ, ὡς μὴ εἰδότι τὰ τοῦ πνεύματος τοῦ θεοῦ, ὅτι ἐπείπερ πνεῦμά ἐστιν ἀπὸ τοῦ θεοῦ ὁ υἱὸς ἐν ἀνθρωπίνῳ γεγονὼς σώματι, οὐδ' ἂν αὐτὸς εἴη ἀ. ὁ τοῦ θεοῦ υἱός *ib*.6.72(p.141.32; 1408A); παύσονται...οἱ εἰπόντες μὴ εἶναι δεκτικὴν θανάτου τὴν σάρκα [sc. τοῦ λόγου], ἀλλὰ τῆς ἀ. φύσεως εἶναι ταύτην Ath.*ep.Epict*.8(p.13.11; M.26.1064B); cf. θνητὸν καὶ ἀ. τὸ τοῦ πάσχα μυστήριον...θνητὸν διὰ τὴν τοῦ κυρίου ταφήν, ἀ. διὰ τὴν ἐκ νεκρῶν ἀνάστασιν Mel.*pass*.2,3 p.1.7,14; liturg. λαβὼν τὸν ἄρτον ἐπὶ τῶν...ἀ. αὐτοῦ χειρῶν *Lit.Jac*. (p.202.4); **d.** heret.: (Arian) ἀ. γὰρ ὁμοίως ἑκάτερον εἶναι καὶ οἱ ἐχθροὶ τῆς ἀληθείας ὁμολογοῦσιν, ἀλλ' εἰς τὸ ἄνω τὴν διαφορὰν ταύτην ἐπινοοῦσιν, οὐκ ἰσοῦντες πρὸς τὸν πατέρα τοῦ υἱοῦ τὴν ζωήν Gr.Nyss.*Eun*.1(1 p.125.5; M.45.361A); against monophysites μετὰ τὴν σάρκωσιν αὐτὸν γεύσασθαι θανάτου φαμέν.—ἀλλ' ἄτρεπτον αὐτὸν... ὡμολογήσαμεν. εἰ δὲ ἀ. πρότερον ὤν, ὕστερον διὰ σαρκὸς ὑπέμεινε θάνατον Thdt.*eran*.3(4.217).

B. of angels and demons οὔτε οἱ ἄγγελοι οὔτε αἱ ψυχαὶ ἀπόλλυνται ἀ. γὰρ ταῦτα Meth.*res*.1.47(p.297.9; M.41.1117C); Dion.Ar.*d.n*.6.1 (M.3.856A); *ib*.8.4(892B); ἀ. λέγονται [sc. ἄγγελοι], καὶ οὐκ ἀ. πάλιν, ὅτι μὴ παρ' ἑαυτῶν ἔχουσι τὸ ἀ. εἶναι,...ἀλλ' ἐκ τῆς πάσης ζωῆς... αἰτίας *ib*.6.1(856B); v. αἴσθησις.

C. ref. man; **1.** of soul (pagan) οὐδὲ μὴν ἀ. χρὴ λέγειν αὐτήν [sc. ψυχήν]· ὅτι εἰ ἀ. ἐστι, καὶ ἀγέννητος δηλαδή. ἀγέννητος δὲ καὶ ἀ. ἐστι κατά τινας λεγομένους Πλατωνικούς Just.*dial*.5.1(M.6.485C); παρὰ Πυθαγόρου δὲ καὶ τὴν ψυχὴν ἀ. εἶναι Πλάτων ἔσπακεν, ὁ δὲ παρ' Αἰγυπτίων Clem.*str*.6.2(p.443.12; M.9.244A); Cels.ap.Or.*Cels*.7.28 (p.179.1; M.11.1460C); cf.Nemes.*nat.hom*.2(M.40.589B); **2.** of soul (Christian); **a.** gen. ἀ. ἡ ψυχὴ ἐν θνητῷ σκηνώματι κατοικεῖ *Diogn*.6.8; Just.*dial*.4.2(M.6.484B); καθ' αὑτὴν ὡς ἀ. οὖσα, λογικῶς κινεῖται ψυχή Athenag.*leg*.27.2(M.6.953A); ἡ τῶν ἀνθρώπων φύσις ἐκ ψυχῆς ἀ. καὶ τοῦ κατὰ τὴν γένεσιν αὐτῇ συναρμοσθέντος σώματος id.*res*.15(p.65.25; M.6.1004A); Clem.*str*.5.14(p.386.8; M.9.133A); Or.*Cels*.6.58(p.129.6; M.11.1388C); Ath.*gent*.32(M.25.64C); not needing material things, Athenag.*res*.12(p.61.30; M.6.997A); *ib*.23(p.76.31; 1020B); united to the immortal God, Max.*ambig*.(M.91.1113D); **b.** proved by rational arguments ἀνάγκη τὴν ψυχὴν ἀ. εἶναι, τῷ μὴ εἶναι κατὰ τὸ σῶμα...οὐ γὰρ ἡ ψυχή ἐστιν ἡ ἀποθνήσκουσα· ἀλλὰ διὰ τὴν ταύτης ἀναχώρησιν ἀποθνήσκει τὸ σῶμα...διὰ τοῦτο...ἀ. καὶ αἰωνία λογίζεται...ἐπειδὴ καὶ ἀ. ἐστι. καὶ ὥσπερ, τοῦ σώματος θνητοῦ τυγχάνοντος, θνητὰ καὶ αἱ τούτου θεωροῦσιν αἰσθήσεις, οὕτως ἀθάνατα θεωροῦσαν καὶ λογιζομένην τὴν ψυχήν, ἀνάγκη καὶ αὐτὴν ἀ. εἶναι Ath.*gent*.33(M.25.65B–68A); **c.** taught by scripture and tradition, Meth.*res*.1.52(p.308.7; M.41.1128A); Chrys.*hom.63.3 in Jo*.(8.379C); **d.** because made in image of God τῷ γὰρ 'κατ' εἰκόνα καὶ ὁμοίωσιν'...οὐ τὸ κατὰ σῶμα μηνύεται, οὐ γὰρ θέμις θνητὸν ἀ. ἐξομοιοῦσθαι, ἀλλ' ἢ κατὰ νοῦν καὶ λογισμόν Clem.*str*.2.19(p.169.17; M.8.1048B); of the image, remaining in the immortal soul, in contrast to pagan images in temples, Or.*Cels*.8.18(p.236.12; M.11.1545C); ἐτεκτήνατο 'κατ' εἰκόνα' τῆς εἰκόνος ἑαυτοῦ τὴν ψυχήν, διὸ καὶ λογικὴ καὶ ἀ. ἐστι Meth.*symp*.6.1(p.64.19; M.18.113B); καθὼς οὖν εἴρηται, τὸ κατ' εἰκόνα καὶ ὁμοίωσιν τοῦ θεοῦ γενέσθαι τὸν ἄνθρωπον...δηλοῖ μὴ μόνον νοερὰν καὶ λογικήν, ἀλλὰ καὶ ἀ. τὴν ψυχὴν δημιουργηθῆναι Justn.*Or*.(p.192.38; M.86.953B); **e.** as consequence of God's justice, *Hom.Clem*.2.13; **f.** souls of wicked also immortal, *ib*.11.11; Thdt.*eran*.3(4.215); **g.** soul not immortal in itself οὐκ ἔστιν ἀ. ... ἡ ψυχὴ καθ' ἑαυτήν, θνητὴ δὲ...θνήσκει μὲν γὰρ καὶ λύεται μετὰ τοῦ σώματος μὴ γινώσκουσα τὴν ἀλήθειαν Tat.*orat*.13 (p.14.10; M.6.833A); **h.** Gnost. πᾶσαι αἱ ψυχαὶ τούτου τοῦ διαστήματος, ὅσαι φύσιν ἔχουσιν ἐν τούτῳ ἀ. διαμένειν μόνῳ, μενοῦσιν οὐδὲν ἐπιστάμενοι τούτου τοῦ διαστήματος διάφορον Hipp.*haer*.7.27(p.206.5; M.16.3318B); inherent immortality denied by Heracleon, Or.*Jo*.13.60(59; p.291.32ff.; M.14.513B); **3.** of man as a whole; **a.** in gen., Tat.*orat*.7(p.7.10; M.6.820B) cit. s. μοῖρα; καλὸς ὕμνος τοῦ θεοῦ ἀ. ἄνθρωπος Clem.*prot*.10(p.76.24; M.8.224A); πᾶν δὲ τὸ ὑπὸ ἀθανασίας ἐργασθὲν ἀ. ἀ. ἄρα ὁ ἄνθρωπος Meth.*res*.1.34(p.272.4f.; M.41.1097C); *ib*.1.35(p.273.13; 1100B); Ath.*gent*.2(M.25.5D); **b.** man originally made inherently immortal ὁ ἄνθρωπος...τῆς ἐξ ἀρχῆς διακοσμήσεως ἀ. ὤν, τοῦ εἶναι ἄνθρωπος οὔποτε μεταβληθήσεται, οὔτε εἰς τὴν τῶν ἀγγέλων οὔτε εἰς τὴν τῶν ἑτέρων μορφήν Meth.*res*.1.49(p.303.3; M.18.277C); and after Fall his body had to be made mortal, lest sin should be perpetuated, id.*symp*.9.2(p.116.19; M.18.181B); ἰατροῦ θεοῦ πρὸς ἐκρίζωσιν τῆς ἁμαρτίας περιελήφθη ὁ θάνατος...ἵνα μὴ διαιώνιζον ἐν ἡμῖν εἴη τὸ κακὸν ἀ. ἅτε ἐν ἀθανάτοις ἀνατεῖλαν id. *res*.1.42(p.289.2; M.41.1112B); *ib*.1.38(p.281.12; M.18.293B); *ib*.1.40 (p.285.4ff.; M.18.268C); Gr.Naz.*or*.45.8(M.36.633A); **c.** man made immortal conditionally τοὺς ἀνθρώπους, τοὺς καὶ θεῷ ὁμοίως...ἀ., ἐὰν φυλάξωσι τὰ προστάγματα αὐτοῦ Just.*dial*.124.4(M.6.765B); ἀ. ἂν ἔμεινεν ὁ ἄνθρωπος, εἰ...ἀπὸ...τοῦ ξύλου τοῦ γινώσκειν καλὸν καὶ πονηρὸν μὴ ἤσθιεν Or.*Jo*.13.34(p.260.2; M.14.460B); δι' ἁμαρτίαν δὲ ἐκπεσὼν τοῦ ἀ. εἶναι *Hom.Clem*.19.15; cf. reproach to Christians that God was jealous of man's immortality, ref. Gen.3:22f., Juln. Imp.ap.Cyr.*Juln*.3(6^2.94A); **d.** discussion of these views θνητὸς φύσει ἐγένετο ὁ ἄνθρωπος; οὐδαμῶς. τί οὖν ἀ.; οὐδὲ τοῦτό φαμεν... οὔτε οὖν φύσει θνητὸς ἐγένετο, οὔτε ἀ. εἰ γὰρ ἀ. αὐτὸν ἀπ' ἀρχῆς ἐπεποιήκει, θεὸν αὐτὸν ἐπεποιήκει. πάλιν, εἰ θνητὸν αὐτὸν ἐπεποιήκει, ἐδόκει ἂν ὁ θεὸς αἴτιος εἶναι τοῦ θανάτου αὐτοῦ. οὔτε οὖν ἀ. αὐτὸν ἐποίησεν, οὔτε μὴν θνητόν, ἀλλὰ...δεκτικὸν ἀμφοτέρων Thphl.Ant. *Autol*.2.27(M.6.1093B); Ἑβραῖοι δὲ τὸν ἄνθρωπον ἐξ ἀρχῆς οὔτε θνητὸν ὁμολογουμένως, οὔτε ἀ. γεγενῆσθαί φασιν· ἀλλ' ἐν μεθορίοις ἑκατέρας φύσεως...εἰ γὰρ ἐξ ἀρχῆς αὐτὸν θνητὸν ἐποίησεν ὁ θεός, οὐκ ἂν ἁμαρτόντα θανάτῳ κατεδίκασε...εἰ δ' αὖ πάλιν ἀ., οὐδ' ἂν τροφῆς σωματικῆς δεῖται· οὐδ' ἂν οὕτω ῥᾳδίως μετενόησε, καὶ τὸν γενόμενον ἀ. θνητὸν εὐθέως ἐποίησεν· οὐδὲ γὰρ ἐπὶ τῶν ἁμαρτησάντων ἀγγέλων τοῦτο φαίνεται πεποιηκώς, ἀλλὰ κατὰ τὴν ἐξ ἀρχῆς φύσιν ἀ. διέμειναν, ἄλλην τῶν ἡμαρτημένων ἀπεκδεχόμενοι δίκην, ἀλλ' οὐ τὸν θάνατον. βέλτιον οὖν ἢ τοῦτον τὸν τρόπον νοεῖν τὸ προκείμενον, ἢ ὅτι θνητὸς μὲν κατεσκευάσθη, δυνάμενος δέ, ἐκ προκοπῆς τελειούμενος, ἀ. γενέσθαι, τουτέστι, δυνάμει ἀ. Nemes.*nat.hom*.1(M.40.513B); **4.** of human bodies after resurrection ἀναστήσει ἡμᾶς ὁ θεὸς διὰ τοῦ Χριστοῦ... καὶ ἀ. ποιήσει Just.*dial*.46.7(M.6.576C); ἵνα πάλιν τῶν αὐτῶν ἡ σὰρξ μερῶν, μετὰ τὸ ξηρανθῆναι καὶ ἀποθανεῖν τὸ ἁμάρτημα, δίκην ἀνακαινοποιηθέντος ναοῦ ἀ. ... ἐγερθῇ Meth.*res*.1.41(5; p.286.10; M.18.269B); restored to their former immortality by Christ, *ib*.1.49 (p.303.8; 280A); τῶν ἁγίων...μεθεξόντων τῆς τοῦ θεοῦ βασιλείας ἐν... ἀ. σώμασιν Eus.*Marcell*.2.1(p.33.27; M.24.780C); *Hom.Clem*.19.20; **5.** neut. as subst., a gift from God τὸ γὰρ ἀ. ... μόνος ὁ παντοκράτωρ ἐμφυσᾷ Meth.*symp*.2.7(p.24.12; M.18.57C); Procl.CP *or.laud.BMV* 6 (p.105.15f.; M.65.685D).

D. of spiritual things; **1.** eucharist συνεισελθόντες αὐτῷ τῆς ἀ. μεταλάβωμεν τροφῆς Ath.*ep.fest*.28(p.296.16; M.26.1433D); τὴν ἀ. κοινωνίαν τοῦ σώματος καὶ αἵματος τοῦ δεσποτικοῦ Didym.*Trin*.2.14 (M.39.716B); τῶν ἀ. μετασχεῖν μυστηρίων Chrys.*hom.17.7 in Mt*. (7.233B); τῆς ἀ. τραπέζης μετέσχομεν id.*hom.13.4 in Heb*.(12.135C); which also makes men immortal ἐσθίοντές σε ἀ. γένωνται *A.Thom.* A 133(p.240.10); **2.** baptism ἀ. πηγῆς ἀπολαυσάμενος ὑδάτεσσιν τὰς πρότερον κακίας *Orac.Sib*.8.315; **3.** light and joy of heaven, *Orac. Sib*.3.787; Chrys.*hom.58.5 in Jo*.(8.343D); id.*hom.17.11 in Mt*.(7.220D); being fruit of suffering and virtue, *2Clem*.19.3; Chrys. *hom.20.5 in Mt*.(7.267B); μικρὸν ἐνταῦθα ποιήσαντες χρόνον, κατὰ τὸν ἀγήρω καὶ ἀ. αἰῶνα τῶν ἀ. ἀπολαύσωμεν ἀγαθῶν Leont.et Jo. *sacr*.2(M.86.2060C); of Christ's eternal kingdom, Jo.Eub.*concept. BMV* 7(M.96.1472A); neut. as subst. οὐκ ἀποστραφήσῃ τὸν ἐνδεόμενον ...εἰ γὰρ ἐν τῷ ἀ. κοινωνοί ἐστε, πόσῳ μᾶλλον ἐν τοῖς θνητοῖς; *Did*.4.8; of the book of life, *Mir.Geo*.15(p.143.7); **4.** of eternal damnation πῶς ἂν τὸν ἀ. θάνατον διαφύγοιεν; Chrys.*hom.52.4 in Mt*.(7.534E); τὴν ἀ. ... κόλασιν *ib*.11.6(156D); *ib*.16.8(215C); ἐπὶ τὰ...ἀ. κατ' αὐτοῦ δικαιωτήρια μετεχώρησε Evagr.*h.e*.1.7(p.16.26; M.86.2444A); neut. as subst. οἱ δαίμονες...οὐ μεθέξουσιν ἀϊδίου ζωῆς ἀντὶ θανάτου ἐν ἀ. μεταλαμβάνοντες Tat.*orat*.14(p.15.20; M.6.836B); **5.** of various spiritual matters διὰ τούτου [sc. Χριστοῦ] ἠθέλησεν ὁ δεσπότης τῆς ἀ. γνώσεως ἡμᾶς γεύσασθαι *1Clem*.36.2; τοῦ ἀ. αὐτοῦ νόμου εἰς νοῦν ἔδωκεν ἡμῖν τὴν σεμνότητα Const.ap.Gel.Cyz.*h.e*.2.7.4(M.85.1233A); of the light of truth, *ib*.2.7.7(1233B); φυτῶν ἀ. γεωργόν, θείων ἐννοιῶν ἴσως Gr.Naz.*or*.45.8(M.36.632C); **6.** ref. pagan idols, worshipped as if they were immortal, Ath.*gent*.13(M.25.29A).

E. ref. continued existence of human race ἀ. τὸ γένος ἡμῶν, τῶν ἐπιφυομένων ἀνθρώπων ἀεὶ τὴν τῶν προαπελθόντων ἀναπληρούντων καὶ φύσιν καὶ τάξιν καὶ χρείαν Bas.Sel.*v.Thecl*.1(M.85.509B); of Rome ὀφείλομεν γὰρ τῇ ἀ. πόλει ἀπομένειν ἐν πᾶσι τὰ πρωτεῖα Gall.Plac.*ep.Pulch*.(p.50.11; M.*PL*.54.866C).

II. neut. plur. as adv., *immortally, perpetually, eternally*, ref. Adam if not cast out from paradise ἀ. ἂν διετέλεσεν ἁμαρτάνων τοῦ λοιποῦ Chrys.*Stag*.1.3(1.159B); ἀ. κολαζόμεθα id.*hom.25.5 in Rom*. (9.708D); id.*hom.4.1 in 1Tim*.(11.568B); id.*fr.in Jer*.8:6(M.64.845B); ἀ. γὰρ βασανισθήσεται Nil.*inst*.(M.79.1237D).

ἀθανάτως, *immortally, perpetually*, Meth.*symp*.9.2(p.116.13; M.18.181A); Dion.Ar.*e.h*.3.3.7(M.3.433D).

ἀθαύμαστος, *not wondered at, not wonderful* χρῆμά τι ξένον καὶ οὐκ ἀ. Cyr.*ador*.2(1.61D); οὐκ ἀ. ἔχοντας τὴν ὑπομονὴν id.*Lc*.6:12 (M.72.580C); οὐδένι τῶν ὄντων ἀ. ὅτι σῶμα μὲν ἀνεβίω τὸ τῇ φύσει φθαρτόν id.*inc.unigen*.(5^1.693B).

ἀθαυμάστως, *without wondering*, Clem.*str*.2.20(p.173.1; M.8.1053B θαυμάστως).

ἀθεάμων, *not beholding* ὀνείρων ἀθεάμονας εἶναι Synes.*insomn*.12 (p.170.14; M.66.1304D).

ἀθέατος, A. pass. sense; **1.** *not seen*; **a.** *unseen by* οὔτε διὰ παντὸς ὡρᾶτο [sc. Christ after Resurrection] τοῖς μαθηταῖς οὔτε πάντῃ ἀ. αὐτοῖς ἑαυτὸν κατέστησεν ‡Just.*qu.et resp*.48(M.6.1293B); τὸ δὲ θέαμα [sc. Const.'s vision] οὐδὲ τοῖς ἐπὶ τοῦ στρατοπέδου ἀ. ἦν, ἀλλ' ἐπιδήλως ὁρώμενον Philost.*h.e*.3.26(M.65.513A); Dion.Ar.*e.h*.4.3.2 (M.3.476B); abs., *cat.Lc*.10:30(p.88.7); **b.** *invisible* τῆς ἀ. θεϊκῆς αὐτοῦ [sc. Χριστοῦ] βασιλείας ‡Chrys.*transfig*.(Savile 7 p.339.19); ἀθέατον ἡ θεία φύσις Thdr.Mops.*Zach*.1:7(M.66.504B); πιστευόμεν γὰρ ἀ. ... τὸν...θεόν Thdt.*Trin*.11(M.75.1164A); of God, Dion.Ar. *myst*.1.3(M.3.1000D); neut. as subst. τὸ τῆς θείας οὐσίας ἀθέατον Bas. Sel.*or*.1.2(M.85.32A); freq. in plur. ἐπὶ τὰ ἀ. τῇ θεωρητικῇ δυνάμει διαδυόμενος Gr.Nyss.*tres dii*(M.45.121D); id.*hom.1 in Cant*.(M.44.785B) cit. s. ἄδυτος; Chrys.*scand*.3(3.470D); Areth.ap.*cat.Apoc*.15:5 (p.406.29); **c.** *that may not be seen by, secret to* τὸ δὲ ἔνδον [sc. of Temple]...ἀ. πᾶσι, πλὴν τοῦ ἀρχιερέως μόνου Chrys.*nativ*.3(2.359A); **2.** *not able to be contemplated by* τῆς ἀπορρήτου καὶ ἀ. τοῖς πολλοῖς ἐπιστήμης Dion.Ar.*ep*.9.1(M.3.1105C); abs. ὁ τῶν ἀπορρήτων καὶ ἀ. μυστηρίων θεὸς *Lit.Praesanct*.(p.348.31).

B. act. sense; *not seeing, not contemplating* ἀθέατοι τῶν ἐντὸς τῆς σκηνῆς θαυμάτων Gr.Nyss.*hom.2 in Cant*.(M.44.789A); οὐκ ἂν...τοῦτο ποιοῦν [sc. τὸ πνεῦμα τὸ ἅγιον] εἴπερ ἦν τῶν κρυφίων ἀθέατον id.*tres dii*(M.45.124C); τοὺς μέλλοντας τὴν Παλαιστίνην ἀπολαμβάνειν ἀ. εἶναι τῶν ἐν Αἰγύπτῳ κακῶν Chrys.*exp.in Ps*.43:5(5.148C).

***ἀθεάτριστος**, *untheatrical, modest*; neut. as subst., ‡Nil.*vit.cog*. (M.79.1460C).

ἀθεεί, *without God, without God's aid* κατά τινα μαντείας εὔστοχον φήμην οὐκ ἀ. συνδραμόντες [sc. Gr. philosophers] ἔν τισι προφητικαῖς φωναῖς τὴν ἀλήθειαν κατὰ μέρη καὶ εἴδη διαλαβόντες Clem.*str*.5.5 (p.344.27; M.9.52A); τὸ φιλάνθρωπον τοῦ λόγου οὐκ ἀ. τῷ βίῳ τῶν ἀνθρώπων ἐπιδεδημηκέναι...οὐδὲν γὰρ χρηστὸν ἐν ἀνθρώποις ἀ. γίνεται. εἰ δὲ ὁ πολλῶν σώματα θεραπεύσας...οὐκ ἀ. θεραπεύει, πόσῳ πλέον ὁ πολλῶν ψυχὰς θεραπεύσας; Or.*Cels*.1.9(p.62.13ff.; M.11.673B); *ib*.4.80 (p.350.17; 1153A); *ib*.6.2(p.72.2; 1289D); οὐδὲ ἀ. πεποίημαι τὴν φυγήν Dion.Al.ap.Eus.*h.e*.6.40.1(M.20.601B); Eus.*d.e*.3.7(p.146.2; M.22.245B); ref. Const.'s resolve to build churches, id.*v.C*.3.25(p.89.16;

M.20.1085B); id.*l.C.*11(p.224.14; M.20.1376B); οὐκ ἀ. οὐδ' ἀνθρωπίνῳ λογισμῷ ταύταις ἐπιβάλλοντος ταῖς ἐπηγορίαις [sc. of biblical books] id.*Marcell.*1.2(p.13.25; M.24.741C); Gr.Nyss.*hex.*25(M.44.85D); Mac. Aeg.*carit.*12(M.34.917D); οὐκ ἀ. ... ἀλλ' ἀφράστῳ τινὶ δυνάμει Soz. *h.e.*1.18.4(M.67.916C); Areth.*Apoc.*54(M.106.724D).

***ἀθεέω**, *be godless, blaspheme* ἀθεήσαντα εἰπεῖν ὅτι ὁ τεκὼν αὐτὸς θεὸς καὶ πατὴρ οὐ θεὸς ἡμῶν οὐδὲ συγκρίνεται τῷ υἱῷ αὐτοῦ Didym. *Trin.*1.27(M.39.397D).

***ἀθεής**, *not from God* οὐκ ἔστι γὰρ ἀ. σου ἡ νόσος αὕτη Pall.*h.Laus.* 38(p.119.21, v.l. ἀληθείᾳ M.34.1193D).

ἀθεΐα, ἡ, 1. *neglect of God*, Thdt.*Ps.*4:1(1.629); εἰ...μισούμενος λογισμὸς κρατεῖ κατ' ἐξουσίαν τὸν νοῦν [sc. after baptism]..., ὅμως τοῦτο οὐκ ἔστιν ἐγκατάλειμμα τῆς τοῦ Ἀδὰμ ἁμαρτίας, ἀλλὰ τῆς μετὰ τὸ βάπτισμα ἀθεΐας. ... ὑπὸ τῆς ἁμαρτίας κρατούμεθα ἕως ἂν...ἐξαλείψῃ [sc. God] ἡμῶν τὴν ἀθεΐας ἁμαρτίαν Marc.Er.*opusc.*4(M.65. 992C); **2.** *disbelief in God* Ἐπικούρου τὴν ἀ. Gr.Naz.*or.*27.10(p.18.5; M.36.24B); **3.** *disbelief in the true God*; **a.** of non-Christians τὴν πολύθεον αὐτῶν [sc. Ἑλλήνων] ἀ. Gr.Naz.*or.*25.15(M.35.1220A); Gr. Nyss.*Eun.*12(1 p.221.7; M.45.916A); ‡Gr.Nyss.*hom.1 in Jo.*(p.106. 26); plur. εἰδωλολατρείας τε καὶ ἀσεβείας καὶ ἀ. Epiph.*haer.*4.2(p.183. 8; M.41.201A); ἀθεΐαις δαιμόνων id.*anc.*64(p.77.12; M.43.132B); **b.** of Jews' worship of golden calf, Jo.D.*hom.*3(M.96.596D); **c.** of heretics τὴν Σαβελλίου ἀ. Gr.Naz.*or.*2.37(M.35.445A); ἡ εἰς πατέρα καὶ υἱὸν καὶ ἅγιον πνεῦμα...πίστις..., ἄρνησις ἀθεΐας καὶ ὁμολογία θεότητος *ib.*23.12(1164C); εἴ τις ἠρνήσατο τὴν εἰς Χριστὸν πίστιν, ἢ πρὸς Ἰουδαϊσμόν, ἢ πρὸς εἰδωλολατρείαν, ἢ πρὸς Μανιχαϊσμόν, ἢ πρὸς ἄλλο τι τοιοῦτον ἀθεΐας εἶδος αὐτομολήσας ἐφάνη Gr.Nyss.*ep.can.*(M.45. 225C); id.*Eun.*8(2 p.193.26; M.45.789A); id.*deit.*(M.46.560B); οἱ τῆς μιαρᾶς ἀνθρωπολατρείας μιαρώτατοι κήρυκες [sc. Thdr. Mops. and Nest.] Κῦρός τε καὶ Ἰωάννης οἱ Κίλικες, οἱ τῆς αὐτῆς ἀ. ἀθεώτατοι πρόβολοι Sophr.H.*ep.syn.*(M.87.3192A).

***ἀθελής**, *without a will*, denied of Christ's humanity εἰ δὲ ἀ. ἐστιν ἡ...τοῦ κυρίου ψυχή, πρόδηλον ὅτι ἀκουσίως δίκην ἀλόγου ὑπετάττετο τῷ θεῷ λόγῳ, ὡς Ἀπολλινάριος ληρωδεῖ Anast.S.*serm. imag.*3(M.89.1173C); εἰ δὲ ἐστέρηται ἡ τοῦ Χριστοῦ ψυχὴ τῆς λογικῆς καὶ θελητικῆς καὶ βουλευτικῆς δυνάμεως, ὄντως οὔτε κατ' εἰκόνα θεοῦ ἐστιν οὔτε μὴν ὁμοούσιος τῶν ἡμετέρων ψυχῶν ὑπάρχει, ἀλλὰ τῶν ἀ. καὶ ἀβουλεύτων, καὶ ἀσόφων, καὶ ἀδιαλογίστων ἀλόγων ψυχῶν id.*hod.*1(M.89.44B).

ἀθέλητος, A. pass., *not willed*; **1.** in gen. εἰς τὸ τῆς οἰκονομίας πρόσχημα τὸ ἔκθεσμον αὐτοῖς καταρυθμίζων καὶ ἀ. Philost.*h.e.*6.3 (M.65.536A); Jo.VI CP *ep.*(M.96.1420B); **2.** theol., ref. generation of Son; orthodox denial of Arian doctrine (of generation by Father's will) does not imply that Son is ἀ.: ἆρ' οὖν ἐπεὶ... μὴ ἐκ βουλήσεώς ἐστιν ὁ υἱός...ἀ. ἐστι τῷ πατρί...; οὐμενοῦν Ath. *Ar.*3.66(M.26.461C); τὸ εἶναι τὸν υἱόν, εἰ καὶ μὴ ἐκ βουλήσεως ἤρξατο, οὐκ ἀ. ... ἐστιν αὐτῷ *ib.*(461C); οὐκ ἀ. ἐστιν αὐτῷ, εἰ καὶ βούλησις οὐδαμοῦ τῆς γεννήσεως προδραμοῦσα φαίνεται Cyr.*thes.*7 (5^1.56D).

B. act., *without will, not possessing the faculty of will*; **1.** of animals ψυχὴν ἄλογον καὶ ἀ. ἔχουσι Anast.S.*serm.imag.*3(M.89. 1165D); **2.** of monks, the object of the coenobitic life being πᾶν θέλημα ἡμῶν ἐκκόπτειν, εὐώνιοι καὶ αὐτοὶ ἡμεῖς πως γινώμεθα καὶ ἀ. Hesych.S.*temp.*1.31(M.93.1489C); **3.** Christol., neither of the two natures in Christ is ἀ., Max.*opusc.*(M.91.96A).

ἀθελήτως, *involuntarily*; **1.** in theology of Basilides, of the οὐκ ὢν θεός who willed to create τὸ δὲ 'ἠθέλησε' λέγω...σημασίας χάριν, ἀ. καὶ ἀνοήτως καὶ ἀναισθήτως Hipp.*haer.*7.21(p.196.22; M.16.3303B); **2.** ref. generation of Son ὡς γὰρ τὸ εἶναι ἀγαθὸς οὐκ ἐκ βουλήσεως ...ἤρξατο, οὐ μὴν...ἀ. ἐστὶν ἀγαθός...οὕτω...τὸ εἶναι τὸν υἱὸν...οὐκ ἀθέλητον Ath.*Ar.*3.66(M.26.461C).

ἀθεμελίωτος, *without foundation* ἡ στάσις ἡ ἀ. Epiph.*haer.*44.4 (p.196.7; M.41.828C).

ἀθεμιστία, ἡ, *wickedness*; of incestuous marriage, Bardesanes ap. Eus.*p.e.*6.10(275D; M.21.468B).

ἀθέμιστος (ἀθέμιτος), *unlawful, wicked*; in gen. τὴν ἀ. τοῦ ζήλους ἡμῶν ὀργήν *1Clem.*63.2; ὁ κοσμοπλανής...ποιήσει ἀ. *Did.*16.4; of Jewish abstention from unclean meats, as contrary to belief in divine creation πῶς οὐκ ἀ.; *Diogn.*4.2; esp. of pagan beliefs ἀθέμιτον καὶ τὸ νοεῖν...ἀνθρώπους θεῶν εἶναι φύλακας Just.*1apol.*9.5(M.6. 340B); ἐν θεῷ δὲ λέγειν εἶναί τι ἐλλειπὲς...πέρα τῶν ἀ. ἐστί Ath.*gent.* 39(M.25.77C); of pagan cult ἀ. θυμιατηρίου...ἀ. ... εἴδωλα *M.Das.* 11.1,2; of persecuting emperors, *ib.*1.1; of Caiaphas, Nonn.*par. Jo.*11:49(M.43.848B); of heretics, Const.ap.Ath.*apol.sec.*68(p.146. 10; M.25.369B); Ath.*ib.*9(p.95.23; 265B); id.*h.Ar.*59(p.216.21; M.25. 764D); of heresies, id.*ep.Epict.*2(p.5.3; M.26.1053A); οὐ θέμις εἰπεῖν ἐπὶ πατρός, ἦν ποτε, ὅτε οὐκ ἦν· ἀ. εἰπεῖν ἐπὶ υἱοῦ id.*ep.Serap.*2.2(M. 26.609C); *Lit.*ap.*Const.App.*8.9.2.

ἀθεμίστως (ἀθεμίτως), *unlawfully, wickedly, Orac.Sib.*1.169; ἀθεμίτως Bardesanes ap.Eus.*p.e.*6.10(278A; M.21.473A); Μοντάνῳ καὶ Πρισκίλλῃ τὴν τοῦ παρακλήτου προσηγορίαν ἀθεμίτως καὶ ἀναισχύντως ἐπιφημίσαντες Bas.*ep.*188 *can.*1(3.269C; M.32.668A).

***ἀθεμιτογαμέω**, *contract an unrighteous marriage, commit incest*, Bardesanes ap.Eus.*p.e.*6.10(275C; M.21.468A).

ἀθεμιτογαμία, ἡ, *unlawful marriage*, Proc.G.*Lev.*20:17(M.87.768B).

ἀθέμιτος, v. ἀθέμιστος.

***ἀθεμιτουργ-έω**, *act wickedly* τὸ ~εῖν καὶ προσκυνεῖν τῷ εἰδώλῳ Epiph.*haer.*64.1(p.403.15; M.41.1069B); of the Sodomites, ‡Chrys. *trid.*(2.827A).

ἀθεμιτουργία, ἡ, *wicked behaviour*, Eus.*h.e.*9.5.2(M.20.808A); Ath. *exp.Ps.*52:2(M.27.248D); Pall.*v.Chrys.*8(p.48.16; M.47.28).

ἀθεμίτως, v. ἀθεμίστως.

ἄθεος, 1. *separate from God, without God* εἰ δὲ νομίζει Εὐνόμιος εὑρηκέναι τὸ τί ἐστιν ὁ θεός, ἐκ τοῦ μὴ εἶναι αὐτὸν γενητόν...λεγέτω αὐτὸν καὶ ἄ., ἐπειδὴ θεὸν οὐκ ἔχει ‡Ath.*dial.Trin.*2.5(M.28.1164C); ἦν ἀχώριστος ὁ λόγος τῆς ἰδίας σαρκὸς...οὐδαμοῦ ψιλὸν ἢ ἔρημον ἀφῶν ταύτην, ἢ ἀ. Eulog.*palm.*8(M.86.2925B); cf. οἱ μὲν ἥλιον ἐθεοποίησαν, ἵνα δύνοντος ἡλίου, κατὰ τὸν τῆς νυκτὸς καιρὸν ἄθεοι μένωσιν Cyr.H. *catech.*4.6; **2.** *ungodly, immoral* πρὸς τῇ ἀ. καὶ ἀσεβεῖ καὶ ἀκρατεῖ μίξει...τέκνῳ ἢ συγγενεῖ ἢ ἀδελφῷ μίγνυνται Just.*1apol.*27.3(M.6. 372A); αἱματεκχυσίαις ἀθεωτάταις Tat.*orat.*23(p.26.5; M.6.857C); Heracleon ap.Or.*Jo.*13.25(p.249.11; M.14.441B); **3.** *disbelieving in the existence of a divine being* ἀ. μὲν γὰρ ὁ μὴ νομίζων εἶναι θεόν Clem.*str.*7.1(p.5.11; M.9.408A); λόγοις πάντη διεφθορόσι καὶ ἀ., τὴν ἐναργῆ καὶ σχεδὸν αἰσθητὴν πρόνοιαν ἀναιροῦσι Or.*Jo.*2.3(p.57.6; M. 14.113B); Bas.*hom.*6.7(2.50A; M.31.276B); of Epicurus, Cyr.*Soph.*9 (3.589C); masc. as subst., Or.*or.*5.1(p.308.13; M.11.429A); Gr.Nyss. *or.catech.*proem.(p.3.12; M.45.12A); **4.** *without the true God, not believing in the true God*; **a.** of non-Christians, Athenag.*leg.*21.2 (M.6.933B); ἀθέους...ἀποκαλῶ τούτους, οἳ τὸν μὲν...ὄντα θεὸν ἠγνοήκασιν...θεοὺς τούτους ὀνομάζοντες τοὺς οὐκ ὄντως ὄντας, μᾶλλον δὲ οὐδὲ ὄντας Clem.*prot.*2(p.17.19; M.8.89A); τῆς ἀ. πολυθεότητος Or. *Cels.*1.1(p.56.15; M.11.653A); Ath.*gent.*14(M.25.32B); of Juln. Imp., Socr.*h.e.*3.12.1(M.67.412A); masc. as subst., Ign.*Trall.*3.2; Clem. (l.c.); neut. as subst. τῶν...μάγων καὶ Χαλδαίων τὸ ἄ. Thdt.*Dan.* 5:8(2.1162); Dion.Ar.*ep.*8.6(M.3.1097D); **b.** of Christians ἄ. κεκλήμεθα· καὶ ὁμολογοῦμεν τῶν τοιούτων νομιζομένων θεῶν ἄθεοι εἶναι, ἀλλ' οὐχὶ τοῦ ἀληθεστάτου...θεοῦ Just.*1apol.*6.1(M.6.336C); *ib.*46.3(397C); cf. κηρύσσοντας [sc. Jews] ὅτι αἵρεσίς τις ἄ. καὶ ἄνομος ἐγήγερται ἀπὸ Ἰησοῦ id.*dial.*108.2(M.6.725C); εἰ...οὐκ ἔστιν ἄ. Πλάτων, ἕνα τὸν δημιουργὸν τῶν ὅλων νοῶν ἀγένητον θεόν, οὐδὲ ἡμεῖς ἄ. ὑφ' οὗ λόγῳ δεδημιούργηται καὶ τῷ παρ' αὐτοῦ πνεύματι συνέχεται τὰ πάντα, τοῦτον εἰδότες καὶ κρατύνοντες θεόν Athenag.*leg.*6.3(M.6.401C); masc. as subst. αἶρε τοὺς ἀ. *M.Polyc.*3.2; *ib.*9.2; **c.** esp. of heretics and heresies: of Docetists, Ign.*Trall.*10; of Marcion's heresy, Hipp. *haer.*7.31(p.217.19; M.16.3335C); Ἀέτιος ὁ ἐπικληθεὶς ἄ. Ath.*syn.*6 (p.234.23; M.26.689B); ὁ διαιρῶν τὸν υἱὸν ἀπὸ τοῦ πατρός, ἢ τὸ πνεῦμα κατάγων εἰς τὰ κτίσματα, οὔτε τὸν υἱὸν ἔχει οὔτε τὸν πατέρα, ἀλλ' ἐστὶν ἄ. καὶ ἀπίστου χείρων, καὶ πάντα μᾶλλον ἢ Χριστιανός id.*ep. Serap.*1.30(M.26.597C); τοιαῦτα δὲ λογιζόμενοι [sc. confusing the Persons], ἔξω μὲν τῆς ἁγίας τριάδος ἔσονται, ἄ. δὲ κριθήσονται *ib.*4.6 (645A); ἐλέγχεται δὲ πανταχόθεν Ἄρειος ἄ., ἀρνούμενος τὸν υἱὸν καὶ τοῖς ποιήμασιν αὐτὸν συναριθμῶν id.*Ar.*1.4(M.26.20C); ref. Eph.2:12 ἀθέους ἀποκαλεῖ [sc. S. Paul] τοὺς πρὸ τούτου ἐκτὸς τοῦ υἱοῦ τὸν θεὸν καὶ πατέρα μόνον ἐγνωκότας Didym.*Trin.*1.7(M.39.272A); Sophr.H. *ep.syn.*(M.87.3192A) cit. s. ἀθεΐα; masc. as subst. τὸν Σαβέλλιον ἡ ἐκκλησία τοῦ θεοῦ ἐν ἀ. καὶ βλασφήμοις κατέλεξεν Eus.*e.th.*2.4(p.102. 35; M.24.905B); **d.** of Jewish teaching, Gr.Naz.*or.*45.15(M.36.644C).

ἀθεότης, ἡ, 1. *absence of godhead* τοῦ...βασιλέως τοῦ μεγάλου τὴν εἰκόνα [sc. Christ] λαβὼν [sc. Marcell.] ⟨ἐν⟩ ἀζωΐᾳ καὶ ἀ. Acac. Caes.*fr.Marcell.*ap.Epiph.*haer.*72.7(p.261.11; M.42.389D); **2.** *godlessness, impiety*, Just.*dial.*47.5(M.6.580A); Eus.*d.e.*8 proem.(p.350.2; M.22.569A); ὁ σωτὴρ...τὴν ἀ. εἰδώλων καθαιρῶν Ath.*inc.*31.2(M.25. 149B); οὐ δεῖ τοῖς ἔθνεσι συνεορτάζειν καὶ κοινωνεῖν τῇ ἀ. αὐτῶν CLaod.*can.*39; τοῦτο γὰρ τῆς τῶν Ἑλλήνων ἀ. τὸ ἀγνόημα θηλείαις θεαῖς ἱερείας χειροτονεῖν *Const.App.*3.9.3; μέθη ἀθεότητός ἐστιν ἀρχή, σκότωσις οὖσα τοῦ διανοητικοῦ, δι' οὗ μάλιστα ὁ θεὸς ἐπιγινώσκεσθαι πέφυκεν †Bas.*Is.*157(1.490C; M.30.376B); hence *impious doctrine* μάγους, παρ' ὧν τὴν ἀ. τῶν σεβασμίων αὐτοῖς μεμαθήκασιν ἀρχῶν Clem.*prot.*5(p.50.7; M.8.168B); **3.** *disbelief in God*, Just.*1apol.*4.9 (M.6.336A); Athenag.*res.*20(p.73.16; M.6.1013C); Ἐπικούρῳ ἀθεότητος κατάρχοντι Clem.*str.*1.1(p.3.10; M.8.688A); **4.** *disbelief in the true*

God; **a.** of non-Christians, Tat.*orat.*22(p.25.3; M.6.856B); Clem.*prot.* 2(p.17.23; M.8.89B); πολύθεον ἀ. Or.*mart.*32(p.28.2; M.11.604A πολυθεοαθεότητα); ὥσπερ γὰρ ἐλέγομεν, τὴν πολυθεότητα ἀθεότητα εἶναι Ath.*gent.*38(M.25.76C); Ἕλληνες, καίτοι θεὸν διὰ χειλέων λέγοντες, ἀθεότητος ἔχουσιν ἔγκλημα, ὅτι τὸν ὄντως ὄντα...θεὸν οὐ γινώσκουσιν, τὸν πατέρα τοῦ...Ἰησοῦ Χριστοῦ id.*Ar.*2.43(M.26.237B); **b.** of Christians τρία ἐπιφημίζουσιν ἡμῖν ἐγκλήματα, ἀ., Θυέστεια δεῖπνα, Οἰδιποδείους μίξεις Athenag.*leg.*3.1(M.6.896C); *ib.*4.2(897B); Juln. Imp.*ep.*84a(p.113.10; M.67.1261C); **c.** of heretics, Or.*hom.17.3 in Jer.*(p.145.8; M.13.457A); οἱ Ἀρειομανῖται δικαίως ἂν σχοῖεν τὸ ἔγκλημα τῆς πολυθεότητος ἢ καὶ ἀ., ὅτι ἔξωθεν τὸν υἱὸν κτίσμα, καὶ πάλιν τὸ πνεῦμα ἐκ τοῦ μὴ ὄντος βαττολογοῦσι Ath.*Ar.*3.15(M.26. 353A); τούτοις [sc. Gnostics]...σκόπος ἦν εἷς καὶ ὁ αὐτὸς ἀθεότητος, τὸν μὲν παντοκράτορα θεὸν βλασφημεῖν, ἄγνωστον δοξάζειν καὶ μὴ εἶναι πατέρα τοῦ Χριστοῦ μηδὲ τοῦ κόσμου δημιουργόν *Const.App.*6. 10.1; τοῖς δόγμασι τῆς ἀ.· ὁποία ἡ νῦν παραβλαστήσασα τῶν ἀνομοίων αἵρεσις †Bas.*Is.*232(1.555D; M.30.525B); **d.** of Jews, Just.*dial.*120.1 (M.6.753C); ref. Mc.3:22 μᾶλλον ἤθελον ἀθεότητος ἔχειν ὑπόνοιαν τὸν Βεελζεβοὺλ ὀνομάζοντες ἢ ἀρνήσασθαι τὴν ἰδίαν πονηρίαν Ath.*decr.*1 (p.2.5; M.25.417B).

***Ἀθεόφιλος**, ὁ, *no friend of God*; play on name of Thphl. Al., *V.Chrys.*88(p.344.33).

ἀθεράπευτος, **1.** *unhealed, uncured*; of a sick person, *A.Jo.*19 (p.161.15); μήπως ἐν τῇ τοῦ σώματος θεραπείᾳ τὴν ψυχὴν ἀ. καταλίπωμεν Bas.*reg.br.*140(2.463B; M.31.1176C); ref. Apollinarian Christology εἴ τις εἰς ἄνουν ἄνθρωπον ἤλπικεν, ἀνόητος ὄντως ἐστί· τὸ γὰρ ἀπρόσληπτον, ἀ. Gr.Naz.*ep.*101(M.37.181C); **2.** *not treated* οὐκ οἶδα ὅπως ἀθεράπευτον [sc. πλεονεξία] ὑπὸ τῶν πατέρων ἡμῶν περιώφθη Gr.Nyss.*ep.can.*6(M.45.232D); **3.** *not able to be healed* or *cured* ἀ. γάρ ἐστιν ἀργοῦ μῶμος *Const.App.*2.63.6.

ἀθεραπεύτως, *without hope of being cured* or *healed* ὁ πρώην ἀ. ἔχων Niceph.Ur.*v.Sym.*225(M.86.3193B).

ἀθερίζω, *despise*, Gr.Naz.*carm.*2.1.1.398(M.37.999A); Eudoc.*Cypr.* 2.447(M.85.864A).

***ἀθέριξ**, ὁ, *unripe ear of corn*, Gr.Nyss.*hom.opif.*27.7(M.44.228C).

ἀθέριστος, *unreaped*, met., of BMV οὐρανίου στάχυος ἀ. ἄρουρα ‡Chrys.*nat.Chr.*1(10.791A).

ἀθέρμαντος, *without warmth* ὁ ἀ. τάρταρος ‡Chrys.*anim.*(9.819E).

ἀθεσία, ἡ, *faithlessness*, Or.*hom.20.7 in Jer.*(p.187.5f.; M.13. 516A); ἀντὶ...'τοῦ συντελεσθῆναι ἁμαρτίαν...' [Dan.9:24] ὁ Ἀκύλας πεποίηκεν 'τοῦ συντελέσαι τὴν ἀ.' Eus.*d.e.*8.2(p.370.13; M.22.601B); Didym.ap.*cat.Ps.*11:2(1.225).

ἀθεσμία, ἡ, *lawlessness*, ‡Bas.*const.*21.3(2.568C; M.31.1397C).

ἀθέσμιος, *lawless, wicked*, Nonn.*par.Jo.*19:6(M.43.897C); Eudoc. *Cypr.*1.90(M.85.836B).

ἀθεσμόβιος, *living a lawless life*, Nonn.*par.Jo.*19:24(M.43.904A).

***ἀθεσμολογία**, ἡ, *unlawful mode of expression*; of Nestorian terminology, Leont.H.*Nest.*4.24(M.86.1689A).

***ἀθεσμοσύνη**, ἡ, *lawlessness, wickedness*, †Apoll.*met.Ps.*74:5(M. 33.1420B); *ib.*78:1(1429B); *ib.*91:8(1452A).

ἀθέσμως, *lawlessly, wrongly*, *Orac.Sib.*2.282; *ib.*8.80; Cyr.*Lc.*26:66 (M.72.92B); Jo.D.*imag.*2.2(M.94.1285B).

ἀθέσφατος, **1.** *unutterable, indescribable* εἷς θεὸς...ἀ. *Orac.Sib.* 3.11; φίλτρον ἀ. Nonn.*par.Jo.*21:16(M.43.917C); **2.** *great, tremendous*; of sabbath, *ib.*19:31(905A).

ἀθετ-έω, *set aside, reject*; **1.** *disregard*, Or.*hom.20.7 in Jer.*(p.187. 14; M.13.516B) cit. s. συνθήκη; ref. administration of baptism by women οὐ δίκαιον ~ῆσαι τὴν δημιουργίαν *Const.App.*3.9.2; ~οῦσι τὰς...ὑπογραφάς Philost.*h.e.*5.1(M.65.528C); **2.** *disobey* an order δίκης ἐντεθείσης μοι τὴν ἐντολὴν ~ήσαντι Meth.*res.*2.2(p.333.7; M.18.300C); of Adam ~ήσας τὴν ἐντολὴν...ἀπεβλήθη *Const.App.*2.57. 14; τὰς ἠθετημένας ἐντολὰς τοῦ κυρίου Nil.*exerc.*12(M.79.732C); of heretics rejecting the rule of faith, †Hipp.*Artem.*ap.Eus.*h.e.*5. 28.13(M.20.516A); **3.** *despise* God, Herm.*mand.*3.2; Clem.*str.*6.15 (p.494.20; M.9.348B); ὁ Χριστὸν μὴ δεξάμενος ὡς ~ήσας τὸν πατέρα λογισθήσεται *Clem.ep.*17; Ath.*hom.in Mt.11*:27(M.25.220B); of heretics, Cyr.H.*catech.*8.4; Chrys.*hom.39.6 in 1Cor.*(10.372B); esp. of Jews, Just.*dial.*16.4(M.6.512A); Ath.*Ar.*2.59(M.26.273A); Cyr.*Is.*1.1 (2.4A); Christ τὸν λόγον ἠθέτησαν, τὸ σῶμα τοῦ λόγου...προσηλώσαντες. θεὸς γὰρ ὁ ~ηθεὶς ‡Ath.*Apoll.*2.16(M.26.1160A); †Diad.*Ar.*9 (M.65.1165A); ‡Meth.*palm.*7(M.18.396D); H. Ghost, Bas.*ep.*243.4(3. 375B; M.32.909A); OT prophets, Or.*hom.14.14 in Jer.*(p.118.25; M. 13.420C); apostles, Proc.G.*Is.*33:1(M.87.2289C); ref. conduct of a Christian ὁ ~ούμενος...καὶ μήτε λόγῳ μήτε ἐννοίᾳ τῷ ~οῦντι φιλονεικῶν, γνῶσιν ἀληθῆ κέκτηται Marc.Er.*opusc.*2.115(M.65.948B); of rejection of divine grace, Ath.*fug.*26(p.85.19; M.25.677A); id.*ep. Adelph.*6(M.26.1080C); *ib.*8(1081B); of heretics rejecting marriage, Iren.*haer.*1.28.1(M.7.690A); Clem.*str.*3.6(p.218.9; M.8.1152A); Eus. *h.e.*3.30.1(M.20.277C); Epiph.*haer.*43.1(p.187.19; M.41.820A); *Const. App.*6.8.2; cf. οὐδαμοῦ γάμον ἠθέτησαν [sc. Pauline epistles] Clem. *str.*3.12(p.235.23; 1188A); **4.** *put away, divorce* a partner in marriage, Heracleon ap.Or.*Jo.*13.11(p.236.7; M.14.416C); Eus.*h.e.*1.11.1(M.20. 113B); οὐ γὰρ ἀνὴρ ἐνταῦθα [i.e. when a virgin breaks vow] ὁ ~ούμενος, ἀλλ' αὐτὸς ὁ Χριστός Chrys.*sac.*3.17(p.89.21; 1.398D); **5.** *reject as untrue, deny* τὸν ὅρον τῆς ἡδονῆς Ἐπικούρου...~οῦσιν Clem.*str.*2.21(p.185.2; M.8.1077B); τὴν προαιώνιον ὕπαρξιν τοῦ Χριστοῦ καὶ τὴν θεότητα...~οῦσιν Ath.*syn.*26(p.253.3; M.26.732A); Gr.Naz. *or.*22.9(M.35.1141B); of denial of Son's hypostasis, Or.*Jo.*32.16(9; p.452.12; M.14.784B); of rejection of Nicene faith, Paulin.T.*symb.* (p.435.12; M.42.672C); belief in Christ, Or.*Jo.*10.3(2; p.173.30; 312A); a partic. exegesis of scripture, *ib.*32.20(18; p.462.2; 800B); **6.** *reject*; **a.** as spurious or uncanonical, Iren.*haer.*5.30.1(M.7.1203C); Clem.*str.*2.11(p.141.20; M.8.989A); Or.*ep.*1.4(M.11.57A); *ib.*1.7(64A); id.*Jo.*5.7(p.104.25; M.14.193C); Dion.Al.ap.Eus.*h.e.*7.25.1(M.20.697A); Eus.*h.e.*3.25.4(269A); *ib.*4.29.5(401A); **b.** as invalid τὸ λουτρὸν ~οῦντι τὸ ἅγιον Dion.Al.ap.Eus.*h.e.*7.8(652B); ἔδοξε...τοῖς ἐξ ἀρχῆς τὸ μὲν [sc. βάπτισμα] τῶν αἱρετικῶν παντελῶς ~ῆσαι τὸ δὲ τῶν ἀποσχισάντων...παραδέξασθαι Bas.*ep.*188 *can.*1(3.269B; M.32.668A); **7.** *nullify, overthrow*, ref. Mt.13:25 ὁ υἱὸς...'ἐπισπαρεῖσαν' τὴν ἀθέτησιν ~ήσας ‡Ath.*Apoll.*2.6(M.26.1141C); **8.** (abs.), *rebel, break faith* ἠθέτησαν εἰς τὸν θεόν Herm.*vis.*2.2.2; Ἐζεχίας...ἠθέτησεν ἐν τῷ βασιλεῖ Ἀσσυρίων Cyr.*Is.*3.4(2.477A); **9.** (abs.), *behave despitefully* or *rebelliously*, in Elchezaite oath before baptism οὐ μισήσω, οὐκ ~ήσω Hipp.*haer.* 9.15(p.254.13; M.16.3391C); σύνοδον ~ούντων Bas.*ep.*237.2(3.365D; M.32.888A); Gr.Nyss.*Eun.*6(2 p.131.21; M.45.716B).

ἀθέτησις, ἡ, *setting aside*; **1.** *rejection, spurning*, in gen. εἰς ἀ. τῆς ...πλάνης †Bas.*bapt.*2.6.1(2.659B; M.31.1596B); Gr.Nyss.*hom.3 in Eccl.*(M.44.649C); Chrys.*hom.13.2 in Heb.*(12.131D); πρόσχες μήπω μετὰ τὴν ἀ. τῶν ἀθέσμων ἔργων εἰς τὰ αὐτὰ πάλιν ἐπιστρέψῃς Jo.Jej. *poenit.*(M.88.1892C); ‡Ath.*Apoll.*2.6(M.26.1141C) cit. s. ἀθετέω; Bas. *reg.br.*280(2.514A; M.31.1280A); id.*jud.*2(2.214C; M.31.656A); Gr. Nyss.*Pss.titt.*A 8(M.44.472A); τὴν ἀ. τοῦ...δεσπότου διὰ τῆς παρακοῆς ποιησάμενος [sc. Adam] Epiph.*haer.*42.12(p.158.2; M.41.777A); ἀ. τοῦ μονογενοῦς Chrys.*hom.72.3 in Mt.*(7.704D); id.*hom.27.1 in Rom.*(9. 719E); **2.** *rejection* as untrue, *denial*, Bas.*Eun.*2.14(1.249C; M.29. 600A) cit. s. εἰμί; μηδεὶς οἰέσθω ἀ. εἶναι τῆς ὑποστάσεως τὴν ἄρνησιν τοῦ κτίσμα εἶναι τὸ πνεῦμα *ib.*3.7(278D; 669C); ἄρνησίν τε καὶ ἀ. τῆς ἀληθινῆς θεότητος Gr.Nyss.*Eun.*8(2 p.176.27; M.45.769A); ἄρνησις...καὶ ἀ. τῆς εἰς τὸν κύριον πίστεως *ib.*10(2 p.232.30; 833C); ὁ φύσει οὐσιωδῶς ἐξ αὐτοῦ γεννηθεὶς οὐκ ἔστι κατὰ τὴν τῶν ἀνομοιουσιαστῶν ἀ. Didym.(‡Bas.)*Eun.*5(1.313B; M.29.752A); **3.** *putting away, annulment*, in gen. ἐπέλαμψε...εἰς ἀ. τῆς φθορᾶς Ath.*exp.Ps.* 102:7(M.27.433B); Epiph.*haer.*42.11(p.148.16; M.41.761B); Cyr.*Ps.* 15:4(M.69.808D); esp. of the removal of sin by Christ's action ἐλθὼν εἰς ἀ. τῆς ἁμαρτίας Ath.*decr.*5(p.4.15; M.25.'432'(424)A); id. *Ar.*3.31(M.26.388D); υἱὸν...παραγενόμενον ἐκ τῶν οὐρανῶν εἰς ἀ. ἁμαρτίας *Symb.Sirm.*3(p.235.31; M.26.693A); †Bas.*Is.*24(1.398C; M. 30.165B); ‡Gr.Nyss.*occurs.*(M.46.1157A); **4.** *rejection* as spurious ὀβελός, ἀθετήσεως σύμβολον Bas.*hex.*4.5(1.37C; M.29.89A).

***ἀθετητής**, ὁ, *one who sets aside* or *despises*, ref. Christ μὴ ἀ. εἶναι τοῦ νόμου ‡Meth.*Sym.et Ann.*3(M.18.353B); of Arians ἀ. τῆς τοῦ κυρίου...τελειότητος Epiph.*haer.*69.13(p.163.18; M.42.224A); of a sinner ἀ. τῆς χάριτός σου Ephr.1.144C; ἀρνητὴν αὐτοῦ [sc. Christ] εἶναι τὸν τῆς ἁγίας αὐτοῦ εἰκόνος ἀ. Thdr.Stud.*epp.*2.78(M.99.1317A).

***ἀθετητικῶς**, *without due consideration*, Or.*Jo.*32.5(p.434.5; M.14. 753C).

***ἀθετικῶς**, *slightingly*, Didym.*Trin.*3.31(M.39.949C).

ἀθεωρήτως, *without reflection* τοῦτο...ἀ. δοκεῖ...τεθεικέναι ὁ Μάρκελλος Eus.*Marcell.*1.2(p.11.18; M.24.737A); Gr.Nyss.*Eun.*3(2 p.10. 28; M.45.573D); *ib.*(p.15.17; 580B).

ἄθηλος, *lacking womanhood*, of eunuchs ἄ., ἄνανδροι Cyr.*hom. div.*19(M.77.1109B).

ἀθήλυντος, **1.** *not womanish, not subject to weakness like a woman*; of a woman with manly character, Clem.*str.*6.12(p.482. 14; M.9.321B); of the mind not weakened by pleasure, Diad.*perf.* 49(p.54.25); Max.*schol.e.h.*2.3.5(M.4.129D); **2.** *having no female counterpart* or *element*, of certain of the Valent. aeons ὁ πατὴρ τὸν Ὅρον...διὰ τοῦ Μονογενοῦς προβάλλεται ἐν εἰκόνι ἰδίᾳ, ἀσύζυγον ἀ. Iren.*haer.*1.2.4(M.7.457A); Ὑστερήματι βούλονται συνάπτειν...ἀμιγῆ τινα Αἰῶνα καὶ ἀ. Epiph.*haer.*31.4(p.388.6; M.41.480B); μετὰ τὴν τριακοντάδα...ἐν ὄνομα μέσον καὶ ἀ. *ib.*(p.389.9; 480C); cf.Val.Gn. *ib.*31.6(p.395.6; 485B).

***ἀθηλύντως**, *with no female consort*; ref. emission of Horus by Father (Valent.), ‡Epiph.*epit.haer*.1(p.361.14); v. ἀθήλυντος.

ἄθηλυς, *not womanish* τὴν Πυθαγόρειον ἀρχὴν...ἄζυγον ἄ. Hipp. *haer*.6.29(p.156.7; M.16.3235C).

Ἀθηναΐζω, *be like an Athenian*, ‡Just.*qu.Gr*.20(M.6.1484C).

ἀθιγής, *untouched, virgin*; of BMV and Joseph, ‡Ath.*Apoll*.1.4 (M.26.1097C); of BMV φυτὸν ἀ. Thdr.Stud.*nativ.BMV* 7(M.96.689B).

***ἀθιγῶς**, *without contact, without being affected by contact*, of Inc. (Apollinarian) θεὸν ἀ. προσεληλυθότα ‡Ath.*Apoll*.1.20(M.26. 1128A); *ib*.(1136C).

***ἄθλευμα, τό**, *contest*, *Orac.Sib*.12.90.

ἀθλέω, *contend*; of martyrs, *1Clem*.5.2; Or.*mart*.2(p.4.12; M.11. 565B); *M.Das*.12.2; c. acc. cogn. τῆς...ἀθλήσεως ἦν...᾿Ιουλίττα ἤθλησεν Bas.*hom*.5.1(2.33B; M.31.237B); †Bas.*bapt*.2.9.3(2.668A; M.31. 1616A); c. acc., *contend in* θεοῦ ζῶντος πεῖραν ἀθλοῦμεν *2Clem*.20.2.

ἄθλησις, ἡ, *contest, struggle*; of martyrdom, *M.Tar*.7(p.463); *M.Thdot*.1 12(p.69.1); *ib*.1 21(p.74.10); Bas.*hom*.5.1(2.33B; M.31. 237A); *Const.App*.5.1.5; μαρτύρων μνημονεύσωμεν, ὅπως κοινωνοὶ γενέσθαι τῆς ἀ. αὐτῶν καταξιωθῶμεν *Lit*.ap.*Const.App*.8.13.6; Pamph.Mon.*Soter*.3(p.119.12); *Mir.Artem*.40(p.67.22); of spiritual struggle, esp. ascetic life τῆς ἀ. Ἀντωνίου Ath.*v.Anton*.10(M.26. 860A); †Bas.*bapt*.2.9.3(2.668A; M.31.1616A); Chrys.*hom.25.7 in Gen*. (4.243A); id.*hom.10.3 in 1Tim*.(11.603A); Mac.Aeg.*hom*.21.5(M.34. 657D); of discipline of fasting, Dion.Al.*ep.can*.(p.102.11; M.10. 1278A).

ἀθλητής, ὁ, *combatant, champion*, of Christ ὁ ἀληθὴς ἀ. ἡμῶν *A.Thom*.A 39(p.157.10); of Job τῆς ἀρετῆς ἀ. Or.*or*.30.2(p.394.21; M.11.548C); Cyr.*Ps*.78:5(M.69.1195C); ref. a bishop πάντων τὰς νόσους βάσταζε, ὡς τέλειος ἀ. Ign.*Polyc*.1.3; νῆφε ὡς θεοῦ ἀ. *ib*.2.3; *ib*.3.1; esp. of martyrs, *1Clem*.5.1; *Ep.Lugd*.ap.Eus.*h.e*.5.1.19(M. 20.416B); Or.*mart*.1(p.3.9,11; M.11.564A); Eus.*h.e*.5 proem.4(408B); of ascetics τελειοτέροις ἀ. οὐκέτι πρὸς αἷμα καὶ σάρκα παλαίουσιν Or. *or*.29.2(p.382.18; M.11.532B); Ath.*v.Anton*.12(M.26.861A); Aët.*synt*. proem.(p.352.6; M.42.536A); cf.Dion.Ar.*e.h*.2.3.6(M.3.401D).

ἀθλητικός, *of* or *belonging to a combatant* or *champion*, ref. martyrs στεφάνους ἀ. Philost.*h.e*.4.4(M.65.520B); δρόμον...ἀ. ‡Sophr. H.*v.m.Cyr.et Jo*.11(M.87.3685A); ἀ. ἀξίας *Mir.Geo*.4 epilog.(p.40.26); ref. Christians engaged in spiritual combat ἀθλητικώτερον τὸν ἀγῶνα Clem.*str*.2.20(p.173.13; M.8.1053C); Sophr.H.*v.Anast*.(M.92. 1680A).

***ἀθλητρία, ἡ**, fem. of ἀθλητής, *combatant, champion*; of ascetics, Aët.*synt*.proem.(p.352.6; M.42.536A).

[*]ἀθληφόρος, = ἀθλοφόρος q.v.; of martyrs, Didym.*Trin*.3.1 (M.39.777A); *V.Glyc*.9(p.14*B).

ἀθλιόομαι, *be made wretched*, Geo.Pis.*Pers*.1.27(M.92.1200A); id. *van*.25(M.92.1583A).

ἄθλιπτος, *not crushed, not depressed, untroubled*, Sophr.H.*ep. syn*.(M.87.3149A); μετάνοια...ἄ. στέρησις παρακλήσεως σωματικῆς Jo.Clim.*scal*.7(M.88.801).

ἀθλίπτως, *without being crushed, without depression*, Marc.Er. *opusc*.2(M.65.944B); Dor.*doct*.2.3(M.88.1644C).

ἀθλοθεσία, ἡ, *combat, contest* ὡς θεός [sc. Χριστός] ἐστι τῆς ἀ. δημιουργός Dion.Ar.*e.h*.2.3.6(M.3.401D); *ib*.(404A).

ἀθλοθέτης, ὁ, *judge of a contest, rewarder*; of Christ, Clem. *q.d.s*.3.6(p.162.7; M.9.608B); Bas.*hom.in Ps*.114(1.200A; M.29.485B); of H. Ghost ἀ. τῶν ἀγωνιζομένων Cyr.H.*catech*.17.13.

ἆθλον, τό, **1.** *prize*, Just.*1apol*.4.9(M.6.336A); οὐ γὰρ σμικρὸν ἡμῖν τὸ ἆ. ἀθανασία πρόκειται Clem.*prot*.10(p.70.23; M.8.209C); *ib*. 11(p.79.6; 229A) cit. s. παράδεισος; ἐπλήρωσε τὴν ἐντολήν, τὸ ἆ. ἐπιζητεῖ *ib*.(p.81.30; 236A); ὧν [sc. virtues] ἆ. ἡ σωτηρία id.*q.d.s*. 18(p.171.10; M.9.621C); ἆ. ἁγνείας Meth.*symp*.11.2(p.134.11; M.18. 209D); τὰ...τῆς θεοσεβείας ἆ. Eus.*d.e*.1.6(p.27.9; M.22.56A); ref. Phil. 2:8–9 οὐ γὰρ ἆ. ἀρετῆς...ἀλλὰ τὸ αἴτιον τῆς εἰς ἡμᾶς...ὑψώσεως Ath. *Ar*.1.43(M.26.101B); **2.** *contest*, Clem.*str*.2.20(p.181.18; M.8.1072A); τὰ τοῦ Ἡρακλέους ἆ. *ib*.5.14(p.396.2; M.9.157A); τὸν σωτῆρα ὡς τηλικοῦτον ἆ. μόνον ἐνέγκειν δυνάμενον Or.*Jo*.2.11(6; p.66.33; M.14. 132A); of conflict with Devil, Ath.*v.Anton*.7(M.26.852A); of ascetic life ἀγωνιζόμενος τοῖς τῆς πίστεως ἄ. *ib*.47(912B).

***ἀθλοπάτωρ, ὁ**, *father-combatant*, i.e. *monk, ascetic*, *Hymn*. (*AS* 1 p.607).

***ἀθλοπρεπῶς**, *in a manner becoming to a combatant*, Thdr.Stud. *cant*.5.2(p.344).

ἆθλος, ὁ, *contest*; of labours of Heracles, Clem.*prot*.2(p.24.19; M.8.108B); of spiritual struggle, id.*str*.7.3(p.15.2; M.9.425A); of martyrdom, Meth.*symp*.8.17(p.112.10; M.18.176A); τὸν ἆ. τῆς παρθενίας *ib*.5.1(p.53.8; 97A); αἱ...παρθενεύσασαι τῷ Χριστῷ τὰ νικητήρια φέρονται τῶν ἄ. *ib*.8.2(p.83.11; 141A); τὸν ὑπὲρ ἀθανασίας ἆ. Const.ap. Eus.*v.C*.2.60(p.65.18; M.20.1033B); θείοις ἄθλων ἀγῶσι Eus.*ib*.1.9 (p.11.14; 921B); τοὺς ὑπὲρ εὐσεβείας ἄ. id.*l.C*.7(p.215.4; M.20.1356C); Χριστοῦ...μισθαποδότου τῶν ἄ. *Const.App*.5.6.10.

***ἀθλοφορέω**, *win the prize*, Thdr.Stud.*epp*.2.28(M.99.1197A).

***ἀθλοφόρημα, τό**, *victory*; of martyrdom, Thdr.Stud.*epp*.2.62 (M.99.1280B).

***ἀθλοφορικός**, *of victory* στεφάνων ἀ. Thdr.Stud.*epp*.2.21(M.99. 1180D); *ib*.2.27(1196A).

ἀθλοφόρος, *bearing the prize, victorious*; of martyrs, *M.Scill*.15; *MAMA* 1.171(Phrygia, saec. iv); οἶκος ἁγίων ἀ. μαρτύρων *CIG* 8609 (Syria, 367); *ib*.8625(Bostra, 511).

ἀθόλωτος ([*]ἀθώλοτος), *unsullied, pure*; of mind, Or.*Jo*.10.28 (18; p.201.14; M.14.357A); †Bas.*Is*.32(1.406B; M.30.184C); Gr.Nyss. *hom.10 in Cant*.(M.44.993C); of soul, Bas.Sel.*v.Thecl*.1(M.85.484C); of prayer, Andr.Caes.*Apoc*.72(M.106.456C); of image of God in Christ and man, Cyr.*Jo*.6.1(4.659C); Zach.Mit.*opif*.(M.85.1141A); of Adam ἀθώλοτος...τῷ θείῳ φωτὶ καταλαμπόμενος Cyr.*Ps*.6:8(M.69. 748A); angels obtaining ἀ. μονήν, Mac.Mgn.*apocr*.4.18(p.194.10); of divine illumination, Cyr.*Jo*.1.8(75B); of Christ in womb ἀ. ἐν τῇ τοσαύτῃ τῶν σαρκῶν κοινωνίᾳ Eus.*d.e*.10.8(p.481.34; M.22.776A); of BMV, ‡Eust.*Laz*.24(p.47.1).

ἄθραυστος, **1.** *unbroken, perfect*, of seal of baptism τὴν σφραγῖδα τῆς πίστεως ἄ. διαφυλάξαντες ‡Hipp.*consumm*.42(p.306.29; M.10. 945A); *Const.App*.3.16.4; *Rit.Bapt*.(p.389); of Christ the second Adam τὸν αὐτὸν...ὁ θεὸς...ἄθραυστον ἐξήγαγεν εἰς τὸν βίον Meth. *symp*.3.5(p.31.21; M.18.68B); **2.** *indomitable, steadfast* ἄ. εἰς ἀλκήν Cyr.*Joel*.35(3.229D); of a lion, id.*Os*.40(3.93C); neut. as subst., id. *Ps*.26:1(M.69.852D); **3.** *harsh, obdurate* ἀπηνῆ καὶ ἄ. νοῦν id.*Is*.5.5 (2.885A); id.*Jo*.2.5(4.190B).

***ἀθρέμβολον, τό**, **1.** ? *iron* for branding ἐθεώρουν [sc. μάρτυρες]... ἀ. πυρούμενα ἐν πυρί Ephr.3.249F; **2.** ? *lance* ἀθρεμβόλοις πέφρακτο τῶν Μακκαβαίων φάλαγξ id.3.472E.

***ἄθρησις, ἡ**, *perception, understanding* μαθημάτων Cyr.*Juln*.1 (6^2.15B); Thdr.Stud.*epp*.2.78(M.99.1317A).

***ἀθρήσκευτος**, **1.** *not offering worship*, *A.Petr.et Paul*.79(p.212. 11,17; p.213.1); **2.** *not worshipped* τι...τῶν τῆς κτίσεως μερῶν ὑπῆρχε τοῖς ἀνθρώποις ἀ. Bas.Sel.*or*.9.3(M.85.136A).

***ἀθριάμβευτος**, *uncelebrated*; of a secret, *not divulged*, Dam. *troph*.proem.3(p.191.9).

ἄθριξ, *without hair*; of effeminate men, Clem.*paed*.3.3(p.245.8; M.8.577A).

ἀθροίζ-ω, *gather together, collect*, hence *form, make* ἣν [sc. ὁδόν] ἐν τῷ κεφαλαίῳ...τῆς καθολικῆς ἐκκλησίας...ἤθροισε [sc. God] Const. ap.Gel.Cyz.*h.e*.2.7.1(M.85.1232C); πίστις ἀνθρώπων...ἀθανασίας καρπὸν ~ουσα Const.*ib*.2.7.5(1233A); pass. ἕξις ~εται Synes.*insomn*.18 (p.182.21; M.66.1316A).

***ἀθροίσιμος**, *marked by an assembly*, of a feast day ἡμέρα τῶν Ἐπιφανίων καὶ ἀ. Gr.Naz.*or*.43.52(M.36.561C).

ἄθροισις, ἡ, *gathering, meeting*; of synods, Sophr.H.*ep.syn*.(M. 87.3184C).

ἄθροισμα, τό, **1.** *gathering, assembly* τοῦ πανδήμου τῶν οὐρανίων ἀ. ‡Bas.*const*.21.5(2.569D; M.31.1401A); of the Church οὐ γὰρ νῦν τὸν τόπον, ἀλλὰ τὸ ἀ. τῶν ἐκλεκτῶν ἐκκλησίαν καλῶ Clem.*str*.7.5 (p.21.25; M.9.437C;) ἔστι γοῦν τὸ παρ᾿ ἡμῖν θυσιαστήριον ἐνταῦθα τὸ ἐπίγειον [τὸ] ἄ. τῶν ταῖς εὐχαῖς ἀνακειμένων *ib*.7.6(p.24.1; 444B); ἀγγελικῶν δυνάμεων ἐφισταμένων τοῖς ἀ. τῶν πιστευόντων Or.*or*.31.5 (p.398.16; M.11.553B); id.*comm.in Mt*.10.13(p.15.28; M.13.1548C); Eus.*h.e*.10.4.1(M.20.848C); ἄνευ γὰρ τοῦ ἁγίου πνεύματος οὐ δύναται πάνδημον καὶ μυριόγλωσσον ἄ. εἰς ἓν φρόνημα τῆς ἀληθεστάτης πίστεως ἐλθεῖν Jo.V H.*icon*.11(M.96.1357C); **2.** *collection, assemblage* θεωρημάτων ἄ. ἀλλ᾿ οὐ φύσεων σύνοδον τὸν Χριστὸν εἶναι Leont.B. *arg.Sev*.(M.86.1932B); τὴν δὲ ὑπόστασιν, σχῆμα, χρῶμα, μέγεθος, χρόνος...καὶ ὅσα τούτοις ἕπεται· ὧν τὸ ἄ., φασίν, ἐπ᾿ οὐδενὸς ἑτέρου ἀληθεύειν δύναται *ib*.(1945C).

***ἀθροισματικός**, *gregarious* τὸν ἀ. ... βίον Bas.*hex*.8.3(1.73B; M.29. 172B).

ἀθροισμός, ὁ, **1.** *gathering together*; rhet. figure, ἀ., *cum plures sensus breviter expeditos in unum locum coacervant, et cum quadam festinatione decurrit*, Isid.H.*etym*.2.21.40; **2.** *collection, assembly*, Epiph.*haer*.3(p.176.22; M.41.185B); of bishops, *Cod.Afr*.76 (Lat. *turma*); νόμος ὁ διὰ Μωϋσέως...δογμάτων ἀ. ἐστι ‡Chrys.*pasch*.6.9 (p.135.6; 8.266E).

ἀθροιστικός, *bringing together* ἀθροιστικαὶ [sc. ἑορταί] γὰρ ἀνθρώπων Gr.Nyss.*res*.3(M.46.657B).

***ἄθρονος**, *having no throne*, of heavenly powers θρόνων ἀ.

‡Epiph.*hom.*2(M.43.456C, v.l. *ἀθρόων*); Eulog.*fr.Trin.*1(p.364); ref. refusal of (bishop's) throne *ἡμῖν...συγχωρήσατ' ἀ. βίον* Gr.Naz. *carm.*2.1.11.1671(M.37.1146A).

ἀθρόος, **1.** *crowded together*; hence **a.** *all at once, immediate, sudden ἀ. ... ἀπόστασις* Eus.*h.e.*8.16.4(M.20.789B); *ἀ. νόσῳ* Soz.*h.e.* 2.29.5(M.67.1020A); *ἀ. τελευτήν* Thdt.*h.e.*4.6.1(3.952); **b.** *all inclusive, liberal μὴ...ἀκριβολογώμεθα, ἀλλ' ἀ. τῇ χειρὶ σπείρωμεν* Chrys.*hom.19.3 in 2Cor.*(10.574D); **c.** *general, universal παγκοσμίῳ καὶ ἀ. συμπτώματι* Areth.*Apoc.*55(M.106.729C); **2.** neut.; **a.** as subst., *suddenness τὸ ἀ. τῆς αἰφνιδίου μεταβολῆς* Const.*or.s.c.*20 (p.184.28; M.20.1297A); *κατὰ τὸ ἀ.* Gr.Nyss.*ep.*1(M.46.1008A); **b.** as adv.; **i.** *suddenly*, Chrys.*comm.in Gal.*1:11–12(10.672D); Cyr.*Ps.* 76:19(M.69.1193C); Philost.*h.e.*7.15(M.65.553B); **ii.** *quickly*, Hadr. *introd.*87(M.98.1293A).

ἀθρόως, *quickly*, Or.*Cels.*2.18(p.147.20; M.11.833C); Eus.*h.e.*2.3.1 (M.20.141B); *suddenly*, Jo.Mosch.*prat.*76(M.87.2929A).

ἄθρυπτος, *continent*, *A.Andr.fr.*8(p.41.25).

ἀθρῶος, neut. as adv., error for *ἀθρόον* Bas.Sel.*or.*5.2(M.85. 81B).

ἄθυμος, *without anger* or *passion θεὸς* Clem.*str.*4.23(p.315.17; M.8. 1360C); neut. as subst., Jo.D.*virt.*(M.95.85C).

***ἀθυρίδωτος**, *without door* or *window τοῖχος* Chrys.*hom.11.4 in 1Cor.*(10.92A); Pall.*h.Laus.*18(p.51.13; M.34.1059C).

ἄθυρμα, τό, **1.** *plaything, toy*; of musical instruments, Cyr.*Ps.* 32:2(M.69.872A); of jesters *παρὰ τῶν ἀ. ἀγαπηθῆναι* Pall.*v.Chrys.*13 (p.82.5; M.47.47); met. of ship *κυμάτων ἄ.* Cyr.*Am.*48(3.302A; *ἀθροίσματι* Aubert); *ἄ. δὲ ὥσπερ ποιεῖσθαι τὴν ἀπειλήν ib.*61(317C); **2.** *playing*, of immoral or frivolous conduct, ref. Os.10:9 *τὰ ἐν αὐτοῖς* [sc. *βουνοῖς*] *ἀ., καὶ αἱ ψευδολατρεῖαι* Cyr.*Os.*118(3.148E); *τὰ ὑπὸ τοῦ συνεδρίου ἐκείνου ἀ.* Eustrat.*v.Eutych.*40(M.86.2321A).

***ἀθυρματώδης**, *frivolous ἀ. τὴν ἄνευ συμπλοκῆς μάχην* ‡Nil. *perist.*10.7(M.79.897D).

ἀθυρογλωσσία, ἡ, *prating, loquacity*, Ath.*Ar.*2.43(M.26.237C); Cyr.*ador.*11(1.397A); id.*thes.*32(5[1].298A).

ἀθυρόγλωσσος, *loquacious, babbling*, Clem.*paed.*3.4(p.253.13; M.8. 596C); id.*str.*7.7(p.33.29; M.9.464C); Epiph.*haer.*26.17(p.297.20; M.41. 360B).

***ἀθυρογλωττέω**, *prate, babble, talk foolishly*, Epiph.*haer.*66.54(p.90. 14; M.42.109B); Isid.Pel.*epp.*3.360(M.78.1016B); Cyr.*ador.*1(1.35B).

***ἀθυρογλώττως**, *with foolish talk ἀ. βλασφημοῦντες* Epiph.*haer.* 26.10(p.288.16; M.41.348A).

***ἀθυροστομέω**, *prate, babble*; of Christ's adversaries, Cyr.*Nest.* 3.6(p.73.38; 6[1].92C); id.*Joel.*35(3.229A); id.*Juln.*4(6[2].137E).

ἀθυροστομία, ἡ, = *ἀθυρογλωσσία*, Nil.*epp.*2.47(M.79.217D); Cyr. *Am.*2(3.250C); Leont.H.*Nest.*4.22(M.86.1688B).

ἀθυρόστομος, = *ἀθυρόγλωσσος*; masc. as subst., Pall.*v.Chrys.*19 (p.125.1; M.47.70).

***ἀθυροστόμως**, *with foolish talk*; ref. heret. statements, Anast.S. *hod.*1(M.89.41D); Maro *ib.*(296A).

ἀθύρωτος, *having no doors* or *bars*; of a house, Diod.*Gen.*1:2(M. 33.1563B); met., of the tongue or mouth, Chrys.*res.Chr.*1(2.439A); id.*catech.*1.3(2.231C); Isid.Pel.*epp.*3.290(M.78.965B); of death, whose gates Christ unbarred, Bas.Sel.*pasch.*2(M.28.1084B).

ἄθυτος, *unaccompanied by sacrifice*, of Christian worship *ἀ. τιμαῖς ποιοῦντες ἃ βούλεται Hom.Clem.*7.3.

***ἀθύτως**, *without sacrifice τυθεὶς* [sc. Christ] *ἀ. ὡς Ἰσαὰκ* †Epiph. *num.myst.*5(M.43.516C); *ἐπὶ τῆς ἱερᾶς...τραπέζης τὸν ἀμνὸν τοῦ θεοῦ...ἀ. ὑπὸ τῶν ἱερέων θυόμενον* Gel.Cyz.*h.e.*2.31.6(M.85.1317B).

[*]**ἀθώλοτος**, v. *ἀθόλωτος*.

***ἀθωοθέω**, *escape free, evade punishment*, Nil.*epp.*2.319(M.79. 356B).

***ἀθώως**, *innocently*, Thdr.Stud.*epp.*1.28(M.99.997D).

***αἰγιόμαλλον, τό**, *outer garment of goat's hair*, Leont.N.*v.Jo. Eleem.*8(p.16.11).

αἴγλη, ἡ, *radiance*, met., of Christ's divine nature *διὰ τῶν θεοπρεπῶν...θαυμάτων ἐναστράψας αὐτοῦ τῆς βιότητος τὴν αἴ.* Or. *fr.94 in Jo.*(p.558.4); cf.*ib.*(p.557.21); of the spiritual life *τοῦ ἔσωθεν ἀνθρώπου τῆς καταστολῆς αἴ. ἀποστίλβοντος* Meth.*symp.*7.2(p.73.16; M.18.128B); of scripture, Isid.Pel.*epp.*1.138(M.78.273B); of the gospel, Thdt.*h.e.*1.23.8(3.805).

***αἰγληφόρος**, *brightening, illuminating τοῦ δεσπότου...αἰ. παρουσία* ‡Epiph.*hom.*2(M.43.456D).

***αἰγοκεράστης, ὁ**, *Capricorn*, *Orac.Sib.*5.207.

αἰγονόμος, ὁ, *goatherd*, *Orac.Sib.*8.478.

***αἰγοπίθηκος, ὁ**, *goat-ape*, Philost.*h.e.*3.11(M.65.496C).

***αἰγοσκελής**, *having goat's legs*, Philost.*h.e.*3.11(M.65.496D).

***αἰγότης, ἡ**, *'goatness', common concept of goat οὐδεὶς...οἶδεν... αἰ. ἢ ἕτερον εἶδος κοινόν* Leont.H.*Nest.*2.19(M.86.1580A).

Αἰγυπτιάζ-ω, **1.** *be like an Egyptian*; of women, in fashions, Clem. *paed.*3.2(p.238.19; M.8.560C); in religious observance, Eus.*d.e.*1.6 (p.30.35; M.22.61A); in thought, teaching, etc. *τοσαῦτα περὶ ψυχῆς ὁ Πλάτων εἰπὼν δῆλός ἐστιν ∼ων τῷ δόγματι* id.*p.e.*13.16(698D; M.21. 1152A); Gr.Nyss.*v.Mos.*(M.44.345A); Anast.S.*hod.*15(M.89.257C); in desires, hence *hanker after Egypt ∼ούσης καρδίας* ‡Chrys.*pasch.*6(8. 267B); **2.** *speak Egyptian*, Or.Cels.7.60(p.210.14; M.11.1508A).

***Αἰγυπτιάς**, *Egyptian Αἰγυπτιάδος γῆς Orac.Sib.*5.507.

Αἰγύπτιος, *Egyptian*, hence met., *luxurious ἅπαν Αἰ. νόημα τῆς ψυχῆς...καὶ σώματος* Jo.D.*hom.*11.8(M.96.769D).

αἰδέσιμος, *exciting respect, venerable οὐδὲν τοῦ θεοῦ καὶ τοῦ κανόνος αἰδεσιμώτερον* Gr.Naz.*ep.*79(M.37.153A); as title of bishop, Const.ap.Ath.*apol.sec.*54(p.135.3; M.25.348A); Gr.Nyss.*ep.*1(M.46. 1000D).

***αἴδεσις**, *chaste κούρης αἰ.* Eudoc.*Cypr.*1.54(M.85.833D).

[*]**αἴδεσμα, τό**, = *ἔδεσμα*, Tit.Bost.*Man.*2.10(M.18.1153C); *ἐσθίων κεράτια, ψυχρὸν καὶ ἄτροφον αἴ.* Ast.Am.*prod.*(p.111.32).

αἰδεστικός, *modest*, Tim.Ant.*descr.BMV* 6(M.28.952C); neut. as subst., *modesty*, Jo.Clim.*past.*6(M.88.1180A); Ephr.3.425D = Jo.D. *virt.*(M.95.85D).

***αἰδεστικῶς**, *ashamedly*; comp., Jo.Clim.*scal.*10(M.88.845C).

***ἀϊδιάζ-ω**, *be eternal Μάνης...∼ουσαν αὐτὴν* [sc. *τὴν κακίαν*] *καταγγέλλει* Epiph.*haer.*66.16(p.40.12; M.42.53A); *ib.*66.18(p.42.25; 56D).

ἀΐδιος (ἀείδιος), **1.** *eternal, everlasting*; **a.** in gen. *ἐμπαθέστερος δὲ πάντως ὁ ἐν σαρκὶ βίος ὁμολογεῖται παρὰ τὸν ἀ. καὶ ἀσώματον* Or. *princ.*1.8.4(p.103.20); Gr.Naz.*or.*38.8(M.36.320B); *ἡ δὲ...ἀ. ... φύσις οὔτ' ἐν τόπῳ ἐστὶν οὔτε ἐν χρόνῳ...οὔτε αἰῶσι παραμετρουμένη* Gr. Nyss.*Eun.*1(1 p.130.2; M.45.368A); of eternal life *τὸν ἀ. τῆς ἀφθαρσίας...στέφανον* Meth.*symp.*6.5(p.65.18; M.18.120C); *θεὸς...ἐπανάγων ...ἀπὸ θανάτου αἰωνίου εἰς ζωὴν ἀ. Const.App.*7.39.3; Gr.Nyss.*v.Mos.* (M.44.321A), etc.; of eternal punishment *τῆς ἀ. κολάσεως ἐντὸς κατέστη Const.App.*5.6.7 (v.l. *αἰωνίου*); of angels, Clem.*ecl.*57(p.154. 1; M.9.725C); of universe co-existing with God, acc. Neoplatonists *ἅμα εἶναι τὸν θεὸν καὶ τὸν κόσμον ἐξ ἀ.* Zach.Mit.*opif.*(M.85.1113A); **b.** of Trin. *εἰ γὰρ οὐκ ἀιδίως σύνεστιν ὁ λόγος τῷ πατρί, οὐκ ἔστιν ἡ τριὰς ἀ.* Ath.*Ar.*1.17(M.26.48A); ‡Ath.*symb.*(M.28.1585A); **c.** of God, Athenag.*leg.*10.2(M.6.909A) cit. s. *νοῦς*; *τοῦ θεοῦ ὑπάρχοντος ἀ.* Juln.Imp.ap.Cyr.*Juln.*4(6[2].143C); *ἄναρχος, ἀτελεύτητος, αἰώνιός τε καὶ ἀ.* Jo.D.*f.o.*1.2(M.94.792C); and divine attributes *ἀγενήτῳ καὶ ἀ. αὐτοῦ ζωῇ* Or.*Jo.*1.29(32; p.37.10; M.14.77D); *ἀπαύγασμα τοῦ ἀ. φωτὸς αὐτοῦ ib.*13.25(p.249.30; 444A); *τῇ ἀ. μακαριότητι* Gr.Nyss. *Eun.*5(2 p.104.18; M.45.684B); *ἡ θεότης...πῦρ ἀθάνατόν τε καὶ ἀ.* Gel. Cyz.*h.e.*2.22.8(M.85.1292C); and all that appertains to the divine, Dion.Ar.*d.n.*10.3(M.3.937C) cit. s. *ἀναλλοίωτος*; **d.** of Son *εἰ...οὐκ ἀ. ὁ υἱός, οὐκ ἔστιν αὕτη τοῦ πατρὸς ἀληθὴς εἰκών* Ath.*Ar.*1.21(M.26. 56A); *οἱ ἅγιοι...τὸ ἀ. εὐαγγελίζονται τοῦ υἱοῦ καὶ τὸ αἰώνιον, ἐν ᾧ καὶ αὐτὸν τὸν θεὸν σημαίνουσιν ib.*1.12(36C); *ὁ υἱὸς οὐχ ἁπλῶς ἀ. ἐστιν, ἀλλὰ τοῦ πατρὸς ἀ. ὄντος, ἀ. ἂν εἴη καὶ ὁ υἱός* id.*Dion.*16(p.58.4; M. 25.504B); *τὸ ἀ. οὐ πάντως ἄναρχον, ἕως ἂν εἰς ἀρχὴν ἀναφέρηται τὸν πατέρα* Gr.Naz.*or.*29.3(p.277.6; M.36.77B); *εἰ μὴ ἀ. θεὸς ὁ υἱός, ἐξ ἀνάγκης πρόσφατος* Didym.(‡Bas.)*Eun.*4(1.287A; M.29.689B); *οὕτως ἀ. ὡς αὐτὸς ὁ πατήρ· οὐ γὰρ ἦν ἔρημος οὐδέποτε τοῦ λόγου* Chrys. *hom.4.1 in Jo.*(8.27E); Thdt.*Heb.*1:2(3.547) cit. s. *αἰών*; acc. Arians *ἔστω ἀ. ὁ υἱός, ἀλλὰ καὶ ἀϊδίως κτισθεὶς ἔχει τὸ ἀ.* ‡Ath.*disp.*14(M.28. 452C); acc. Marcellus *τοῦτον εἶναι ἀ. καὶ ἀγέννητον ἕν τε εἶναι καὶ ταὐτὸν τῷ θεῷ, ὀνόμασιν μὲν διαφόροις πατρὸς καὶ υἱοῦ χρηματίζοντα, οὐσίᾳ δὲ καὶ ὑποστάσει ἓν ὄντα* Eus.*Marcell.*1.1(p.4.24; M.24.720A); **e.** of H. Ghost *θεοῦ καὶ υἱοῦ πνεῦμα ἀ.* Didym.(‡Bas.)*Eun.*5(1.302B; M.29.725A); **f.** neut. as subst., *everlastingness λόγος ὢν...τοῦ πατρός, ἔχει πάντα τὰ τοῦ πατρός, τὸ ἀ., τὸ ἄτρεπτον* Ath.*ep.Aeg.Lib.*17(M. 25.577A); *ἀ. ... τὸ χρόνου παντὸς καὶ αἰῶνος κατὰ τὸ εἶναι πρεσβύτερον ...ἤδη δὲ καὶ τοὺς αἰῶνας ἀξιοῦσί τινες τῆς τοῦ ἀ. προσηγορίας, ὡς ἐκ τοῦ ἀεὶ εἶναι τῆς κλήσεως ταύτης τετυχηκότας. ἡμεῖς δὲ τῆς αὐτῆς λογιζόμεθα παρανοίας...τῇ κτίσει προσμαρτυρεῖν τὸ ἀ.* Bas.*Eun.*2.17 (1.253B; M.29.608C); *τὸ...πρὸ τοῦ αἰῶνος ταὐτόν ἐστι τῷ ἀ. κατὰ τὴν ἔννοιαν* Gr.Nyss.*Eun.*2(2 p.349.20; M.45.525D); *τῆς τοῦ ἀ. σημασίας δι' ἀμφοτέρων...συμπληρουμένης, ἔκ τε τῆς ἀρχῆς καὶ ἐκ τῆς τοῦ τέλους ἀλλοτριώσεως ib.*1(1 p.211.11; 460A); *τὸ ἀ. κυρίως τῆς θείας οὐσίας ἴδιόν ἐστι* Isid.Pel.*epp.*3.149(M.78.841B); *τὸ ἀ. ἀσώματόν τε καὶ ἀσχημάτιστον καὶ ἀσύνθετον καὶ ἀνεπίγραφον* Proc.G.*Gen.*1:1(M. 87.41A); **2.** *perpetual ἀ. φυγῇ* Eus.*h.e.*2.4.1(M.20.145A); Euthal. Diac.*Ac.*(M.85.632C).

ἀϊδιότης (ἀειδιότης), ἡ, *eternity*; in gen., of tree of life *ἀ. ζωῆς τοῖς γευσαμένοις δίδωσι* Gr.Nyss.*or.catech.*5(p.24.11; M.45.24A); *ἡ* ἀ. οἷον ἀειζωότης ἐστί Isid.Pel.*epp*.3.149(M.78.841A); of Trin., Gr. Thaum.*symb*.(p.3.10; M.10.985A); ἀνάγκη...μίαν ταύτης [sc. τῆς τριάδος] τὴν ἀ. Ath.*ep.Serap*.1.30(M.26.597B); Epiph.*haer*.62.3(p.392. 4; M.41.1053B); of Father, Bas.*Eun*.2.12(1.247B; M.29.593B) cit. s. πατρότης; ὁ ἀνθρώπινος βίος οὐδέν ἐστιν, ὡς πρὸς τὴν θείαν ἀ. Cyr. *Ps*.38:6(M.69.976A); ἀείδιος ὑπάρχεις ἐν τῇ σῇ βασιλείᾳ, ὁ ὢν ἐν τῇ ἀειδιότητι καὶ ἀναρχότητι καὶ ἀκαταληψίᾳ Agath.*v.Gr.Ill*.45(p.25); shared with Son υἱὸς...οὐχ ἁπλῶς ἀΐδιος, ἀλλὰ τῇ τοῦ πατρὸς ἀ. συνὼν γινώσκεται Ath.*Ar*.3.28(M.26.384B); ᾧ [sc. τῷ λόγῳ] πᾶσα ἡ τοῦ πατρὸς ἀ. ἐγκαθορᾶται Gr.Nyss.*Apoll*.5(M.45.1133B); of Son, ref. Jo.10:30 τὴν ἀ. καὶ τὸ πρὸς τὸν πατέρα ὁμοούσιον σημαίνει Ath.*ep. Serap*.3.9(624B); τῇ ἀγεννησίᾳ τοῦ πατρὸς ἡ τοῦ μονογενοῦς ἀ. γεννητῶς συνεπινοεῖται Gr.Nyss.*Eun*.1(1 p.132.17; M.45.369C); Chrys.*hom. 3.3 in Jo*.(8.20B); a divine quality bestowed upon man τὸ δὲ ἀϊδιότητος μετειληφὸς ἐξομοιοῦσθαι φιλεῖ τῷ ἀφθάρτῳ Clem.*paed*.1.5 (p.102.5; M.8.273B); νύμφην πρὸς μετουσίαν ἀναλαβὼν τῆς ἀφθάρτου ἀ. Gr.Nyss.*hom.4 in Cant*.(M.44.852D); θείας κοινωνοὶ φύσεως καὶ τῆς αὐτοῦ ἀ. μέτοχοι Max.*cap*.1.42(M.90.1193D); cf. εἰκόνα τῆς ἰδίας ἀ. ἐποίησεν [sc. τὸν ἄνθρωπον] ‡Ath.*Apoll*.1.7(M.26.1105A); upon a martyr (in form ἀειδ-), Thdr.Stud.*cant*.16.7(p.372); ref. exchange of monastic for active life μετὰ τοσοῦτον ὡραῖον τῆς ἀ. αὐτῆς [sc. ψυχῆς] κάλλος Gr.Mag.*dial*.(tr.Zach.)1 proem.(M.*PL*.77.151A).

ἀϊδίως, *eternally, from everlasting*; **1.** in gen. τὰς γνωστικὰς ψυχὰς ...ἀ. ἀΐδιον εὐφροσύνην καρπουμένας Clem.*str*.7.3(p.10.14); ἐὰν δὲ ἀπειθήσητε, αἱ ψυχαὶ ὑμῶν...εἰς τὸν τόπον τοῦ πυρὸς βληθήσονται, ὅπου ἀ. κολαζόμεναι ἀνωφέλητα μετανοήσουσιν *Hom.Clem*.1.7; **2.** ref. Trin. εἰ μὴ ἀ. ἦν, ἔδει μηδὲ νῦν οὕτως αὐτὴν εἶναι Ath.*Ar*.1.18(M.26. 49B); **3.** ref. Father ὁ θεὸς τελείως ἀγαθὸς ὢν ἀ. ἀγαθοποιός ἐστιν Athenag.*leg*.26.2(M.6.952A); **4.** ref. Son λόγος...ἀ. ὑπάρχων ἐν τῷ θεῷ Eus.*e.th*.3.14(p.171.29; M.24.1028B); οὐδέποτε γὰρ οὐκ ἦν, ἀλλὰ ἦν ὁ λόγος ἀεί, ὑπάρχων ἀ. παρὰ τῷ πατρί Ath.*decr*.20(p.16.30; M.25. 449D); ref. Son's generation ἕνα μονογενῆ...υἱόν, ἐκ τοῦ πατρὸς ἀνάρχως καὶ ἀ. γεγεννημένον †Ath.*exp.fid*.1(M.25.201A); Gr.Nyss. *Eun*.8(2 p.180.26; M.45.773C); τὸν υἱὸν...τὸν πρὸ αἰώνων ἀ. ἐκ τοῦ πατρὸς γεννηθέντα Apoll.*ep.Jov*.(p.250.1; M.28.25A); ἐγέννησεν ἀ. τὸν μονογενῆ Epiph.*haer*.76.27(p.377.12; M.42.573B); ref. his sonship opp. man's, Cyr.H.*catech*.3.14; acc. Marcellus μόνον εἶναι λόγον...συμφυᾶ τῷ θεῷ, ἀ. αὐτῷ συνόντα καὶ ἡνωμένον, οἷος ἂν εἴη ὁ ἐν ἀνθρώπῳ λόγος Eus.*Marcell*.2.1(p.31.30; M.24.777A); **5.** ref. H. Ghost τοῦ πνεύματος ἐκ τῆς οὐσίας τοῦ πατρὸς δι' υἱοῦ ἀ. ἐκπεμφθέντος Apoll. *fid.sec.pt*.(p.180.18; M.10.1117C).

***αἰδοίη**, ἡ, *sense of shame*, *Orac.Sib*.8.184.

***αἰδουμένως**, *shamefacedly*, Thdr.Stud.*epp*.2.122(M.99.1400A).

αἰθάλη, ἡ, **1.** *thick smoke, soot* εἰκόνα...καπνῷ καὶ αἰ. ... γενομένην ἀμαυροτέραν Chrys.*pan.Barl*.4(2.687C); **2.** *vapour*, Cyr.S.*v.Sab*.22 (p.106.22); in the body τὸ ἐν ἡμῖν θερμὸν ἐκ τῆς αἰ. Nemes.*nat.hom*. 28(M.40.709B); hence *fumes* of wine, Bas.*hom*.14.4(2.126C; M.31. 453A); **3.** *ashes*, ref. Ex.8:16 κεκόλακεν Αἰγυπτίους [sc. μεταστοιχειουμένης] τῆς αἰ. εἰς σκνῖπας Cyr.*Os*.5(3.23D); Geo.Pis.*hex*.1534 (M.92.1553A).

αἰθαλ-όω, *burn to ashes* τὰ σώματα τῶν μαρτύρων...καέντα καὶ ~ωθέντα *Ep.Lugd*.ap.Eus.*h.e*.5.1.62(M.20.432B).

[*]**αἰθάλ-ω**, = foreg.; *soil with soot* or *smoke* ἀπὸ γῆς ~ομένου ἀέρος ‡Caes.Naz.*dial*.118(M.38.1004).

αἰθαλώδης, *thick, dark*; of fumes or vapour, Bas.*hom*.1.9(2.8D; M.31.180C); Nemes.*nat.hom*.24(M.40.697C).

αἰθέριος, *of the upper air*, hence *heavenly, ethereal* τὴν ποιότητα τοῦ θνητοῦ κατὰ τὸ τοῦ Ἰησοῦ σῶμα...μεταβαλεῖν εἰς αἰ. καὶ θείαν ποιότητα Or.*Cels*.3.41(p.237.17; M.11.975B); τὸ τοῦ κυρίου ἐξ ἀναστάσεως σῶμα αἰ. τε καὶ σφαιροειδὲς τῷ σχήματι CCP(543)*anath*.10; cf. *tunc* [i.e. at the end of the world]...*substantia corporalis...in aetherium statum permutata*, Or.*princ*.2.3.7(p.125.11; M.11.197C).

***αἰθεροδρομέω**, *speed through the air*; of angels, Mod.*dorm*.2 (M.86.3281C).

αἰθεροειδής, *like ether*, ‡Just.*qu.Chr*.2.5(M.6.1421D); neut. as subst., Gr.Nyss.*hex*.36(p.52; M.44.96C).

***αἰθεροτρόμος**, *reverberating through the air* αἰ. βοῇ ‡Gr.Naz. *Chr.pat*.171(M.38.150A; αἰθεροδρόμῳ p. 38, cf. *LS*).

***αἰθεροφόρος**, *borne through the air*; of the seraphim, Eus.*Is*.6:2 (M.24.125A).

αἰθερώδης, *like ether* τινὰς μὲν εἰρηκέναι καὶ αὐτὸν [sc. θεόν] σωματικῆς φύσεως λεπτομεροῦς καὶ αἰ., τινὰς δὲ ἀσώματον Or.*Jo*. 13.21(p.244.21; M.14.432C).

***Αἰθιοπικῶς**, *in the manner of the Ethiopians*, Or.*Cels*.5.37(p.41. 10; M.11.1237C).

Αἰθίοψ, *Ethiopian*; of demons thought to be black, †Cyr.*hom. div*.14(5².405D); *ib*.(407A); τὰ μέλανα πρόσωπα τῶν νοητῶν Αἰ. Hesych. S.*temp*.1.23(M.93.1488B); Anast.S.*Ps*.6(M.89.1113B).

[*]**αἴθμη**, ἡ, *vapour*, Epiph.*haer*.52.2(p.312.30, v.l. ἔθμη M.41. 956C).

αἰθρία, ἡ, *clear sky*, met., of spiritual life ἐν τῇ τῆς ψυχῆς αἰ. γενόμενος, ἐνατενίζει τῷ ἡλίῳ τῆς δικαιοσύνης Jo.D.*hom*.1.10(M.96.561A).

αἰθριάζ-ω, *expose to the air* τὰ σώματα τῶν μαρτύρων...αἰθριασθέντα *Ep.Lugd*.ap.Eus.*h.e*.5.1.62(M.20.432B); intrans., *come into the open* μάρτυρες ~ουσι καὶ...τοῖς βήμασι συγκαλοῦσι λαὸν φιλόχριστον Gr.Naz.*or*.44.12(M.36.620C).

***αἰθριοποιός**, *making clear*, Diad.*perf*.75(p.92.24).

αἴθριος, **1.** *clear, bright*; of thunder *from a clear sky*, Nonn.*par. Jo*.12:29(M.43.856A); **2.** *open to the air*, Eus.*v.C*.4.59(p.141.20; M. 20.1209B); *in the open air, out of doors* γυμνότης καὶ ἀρρωστία καὶ τὸ αἴ. πλανᾶσθαι Chrys.*hom.80.2 in Mt*.(7.760D); ἀγάλματα...ἐν αἰ. ...ἑστηκότα id.*hom.10.2 in Eph*.(11.77D); Soz.*h.e*.6.2(M.67.1296C).

***αἴκισις**, ἡ, *torture, torment*, Jo.Jej.*poenit.cont.virg*.(M.88.1977C).

αἴλουρος, ὁ, ἡ, *cat*; as a nickname of Tim. I Al., Thdr.Lect.*h.e*. 1.8(M.86.169B); Evagr.*h.e*.2.8(p.56.2; M.86.2521A).

αἷμα, τό, **ὗμα** *PRyl*.3.465.15; **αἷμαν** *Mir.Geo*.6(p.70.13);

I. *blood*;

A. in gen.; **1.** sacredness and power of blood, as instanced by blood of Abel μετέσχηκεν τοῦ λόγου τὸ αἷ. τὸ ἀνθρώπινον καὶ τῆς χάριτος κοινωνεῖ τῷ πνεύματι, κἂν ἀδικήσῃ τις αὐτό, οὐ λήσεται. ἔξεστιν αὐτῷ καὶ γυμνῷ τοῦ σχήματος πρὸς τὸν κύριον λαλεῖν Clem. *paed*.3.3(p.251.7; M.8.592A); and by blood of circumcision which broke the power of the angel after Zipporah had circumcised her son (Ex.4:24–26); Or.*Cels*.5.48(p.53.1f.; M.11.1257A); **2.** speculation about blood lost on earth in rel. to resurrection bodies ἀποκρινάσθω ὁποῖον αἷ. συνανίσταται τῷ ἀνθρώπῳ, τὸ ἐν ταῖς φλεβοτομίαις, ἀλλὰ τὸ ἐν ταῖς αἱμορραγίαις...λεγέτω οὖν μοι ποῖον αἷ. συνανίσταται τῷ ἀνθρώπῳ Adam.*dial*.5.17(pp.208.15,210.3; M.11.1856B); **3.** blood as substance of soul: cf.Empedocles ap.Stobaeum *ecl*.1.41. 53; view repudiated πρωτόγονον γὰρ τὸ αἷ. εὑρίσκεται ἐν ἀνθρώπῳ, ὃ δή τινες οὐσίαν εἰπεῖν ψυχῆς τετολμήκασιν Clem.*paed*.1.6(p.113.14; M.8.296C); discussed, ref. Lev.17:11, etc.: Or.*dial*.11(p.144.15); ἐπεὶ ἔχεις ταῦτα πάντα τοῦ αἰσθητοῦ σώματος περὶ τὸν ἔσω ἄνθρωπον, μηκέτι δίσταζε καὶ περὶ τοῦ αἷ. ὅτι ὁμωνύμως τῷ αἰσθητῷ αἷ., ὡς καὶ τὰ ἄλλα μέλη τοῦ σώματος, ἐστὶν κατὰ τὸν ἔσω ἄνθρωπον. ἐκεῖνο τὸ αἷ. ψυχῆς ἁμαρτωλοῦ ἐκχεῖται *ib*.22(p.164.7ff.); Phil.1:23 cited to prove blood not = soul οὐ γὰρ σὺν Χριστῷ ἐστιν ἅμα τῷ ἀναλῦσαι, εἰ ἡ ψυχὴ αἷ. *ib*.23(p.166.2); πρὸς τοὺς δοξάζοντας, αἷ. ἢ πνεῦμα εἶναι τὴν ψυχήν, ἐπειδὴ τοῦ αἷ. ἢ τοῦ πνεύματος χωριζομένου νεκροῦται τὸ ζῶον, οὐκ ἐκεῖνο ῥητέον, ὅπερ τινὲς τῶν οἰομένων εἶναί τι γεγραφήκασι, λέγοντες· οὐκοῦν, ὅταν μέρος ἀπορρυῇ τοῦ αἷ., μέρος ἀπερρύη τῆς ψυχῆς·...ἐπὶ γὰρ τῶν ὁμοιομερῶν καὶ τὸ ὑπολειπόμενον μέρος ταὐτόν ἐστι, τῷ παντί...οὕτως οὖν καὶ τὸ ὑπολειπόμενον αἷ., ὅσον ἂν ᾖ, ψυχή ἐστιν, εἴπερ ψυχὴ τὸ αἷ. Nemes.*nat.hom*.2(M.40. 541B); Chrys.*hom.27.5 in Gen*.(4.262C); **4.** representing natural (opp. spiritual) generation, cf. Jo.1:13 οἱ γὰρ ἐκ θεοῦ γεννηθέντες, τῷ πεπιστευκέναι ὅτι Ἰησοῦς ὁ Χριστός ἐστι...ἐκ τοῦ θεοῦ ἐγεννήθησαν. οὐχ ὑπόκεινται δὲ τῇ ἐξ αἱμάτων γεννήσει, τουτέστιν οὐκ ἐξ ὑλικῶν ἔχουσι τὴν γένεσιν Or.*fr.8 in Jo*.(p.489.30); and sacrifices of old, opp. new, law, exeg. Mt.16:7 ἐπίστησον εἰ δύναται κατ' ἐπιβολὴν ἄλλην υἱὸς αἱμάτων εἶναι ὁ νομίζων θεοσεβὴς καὶ υἱὸς θεοῦ εἶναι διὰ τοῦ προσάγειν τὰς κατὰ νόμον αἰσθητὰς θυσίας *ib*.(p.490.4); **5.** met., hope as the 'blood' of faith, Clem.*paed*.1.6(p.113.6; M.8.296B); blood as a symbol of Passion, *ib*.(p.119.28; 309A); as designating grave sins, †Bas.*Is*.137(1.475B; M.30.341B).

B. eating of blood forbidden, cf. Ac.15:20; **1.** used as argument against pagan accusation that Christians ate children πῶς ἂν παιδία φάγοιεν οἱ τοιοῦτοι, οἷς μηδὲ ἀλόγων ζῴων αἷ. φαγεῖν ἐξόν; *Ep.Lugd*.ap.Eus.*h.e*.5.1.26(M.20.417C); hence this probably also Iren.'s interprn. of Apostolic Decree, *uti abstineant...a fornicatione, et a sanguine*, Iren.*haer*.3.12.14(M.7.908B); **2.** reason for prohibition γράψαι τοῖς ἀπὸ τῶν ἐθνῶν πιστεύουσιν ἐπιστολήν, μόνα, ὡς ὠνόμασαν, 'ἐπάναγκες' ἀπαγορεύουσαν ἐσθίειν· ταῦτα δ' ἐστὶ τὰ ἤτοι εἰδωλόθυτα ἢ τὰ πνικτὰ ἢ τὸ αἷ. ... τὰ δὲ πνικτὰ τοῦ αἷ. μὴ ἐκκριθέντος, ὅπερ φασὶν εἶναι τροφὴν δαιμόνων, τρεφομένων ταῖς ἀπ' αὐτοῦ ἀναθυμιάσεσιν...ἐκ δὲ τῶν εἰρημένων περὶ τῶν 'πνικτῶν' σαφὲς εἶναι δύναται τὸ περὶ τῆς ἀποχῆς τοῦ 'αἷ.' Or.*Cels*.8.29,30(p.245.2ff.; M.11.1560Af.); **3.** eccl. legislation εἴ τις ἐσθίοντα κρέα χωρὶς αἷ. καὶ εἰδωλοθύτου καὶ πνικτοῦ, μετ' εὐλαβείας καὶ πίστεως, κατακρίνοι...ἀ. ἔ. CGangr. *can*.2; εἴ τις ἐπίσκοπος ἢ πρεσβύτερος ἢ διάκονος ἢ ὅλως ἐκ τοῦ καταλόγου τοῦ ἱερατικοῦ 'φαγῇ κρέας ἐν αἷ. ψυχῆς αὐτοῦ'...καθαιρείσθω, τοῦτο γὰρ ὁ νόμος ἀπεῖπεν· ἐὰν δὲ λαϊκὸς ᾖ, ἀφοριζέσθω

*Can.App.*63; εἴ τις οὖν ἀπὸ τοῦ νῦν αἱ. ζῴου ἐσθίειν ἐπιχειροίη οἱῳδήποτε τρόπῳ, εἰ μὲν κληρικὸς εἴη, καθαιρείσθω, εἰ δὲ λαϊκός, ἀφοριζέσθω CTrull.*can.*67; v. II infra.

C. of martyrdom, the 'baptism of blood' (cf. βάπτισμα); **1.** in gen., Clem.*str.*4.7(p.268.4; M.8.1256B); *ib.*2.18(p.155.26; 1020C); *ib.* 2.20(p.181.4; 1069B); Or.*mart.*39(p.37.11; M.11.616B); *M.Perp.*21 (p.93.12); Bas.*hom.*19.7(2.155A; M.31.521A); Gr.Naz.*or.*39.17(M.36. 356A); Gr.Nyss.*mart.*3(M.46.781C); Jo.D.*f.o.*4.9(M.94.1124C); **2.** in relation to blood of Christ λοιπαὶ δὲ καὶ συγγενεῖς ταύτῃ τῇ θυσίᾳ [sc. Christ] θυσίαι αἱ ἐκχύσεις εἶναί μοι φαίνονται τοῦ τῶν γενναίων μαρτύρων αἱ. Or.*Jo.*6.54(36; p.162.16; M.14.293A); λυτρούμενος γὰρ τὴν οἰκουμένην ὁ σωτὴρ...καὶ τὴν πλευρὰν νυγείς, ἐξήγαγεν αἱ. καὶ ὕδωρ· ἵνα οἱ μὲν ἐν καιροῖς εἰρήνης ἐν ὕδατι βαπτισθῶσιν, οἱ δὲ ἐν καιροῖς διωγμῶν ἐν οἰκείοις αἱ. βαπτισθῶσι Cyr.H.*catech.*3.10; Gr. Naz.*or.*45.23(M.36.656B); τοῦτο τὸ αἱ. [sc. of martyrs] ἄγγελοι μὲν ὁρῶντες ἐτέρποντο, δαίμονες ἔφριττον, καὶ αὐτὸς δὲ ὁ διάβολος ἔτρεμεν. οὐ γὰρ αἱ. ἦν ἁπλῶς τὸ ὁρώμενον, ἀλλ' αἱ. σωτήριον, αἱ. ἅγιον, αἱ. τῶν οὐρανῶν ἄξιον, αἱ. διηνεκῶς τὰ καλὰ τῆς ἐκκλησίας ἄρδον φυτά. εἶδε τὸ αἱ., καὶ ἔφριξεν ὁ διάβολος· ἀνεμνήσθη γὰρ ἑτέρου αἱ. δεσποτικοῦ· δι' ἐκεῖνο τὸ αἱ. τοῦτο ἔρρευσεν· ἐξ οὗ γὰρ ἐνύγη ἡ πλευρὰ τοῦ δεσπότου, μυρίας ὁρᾷς λοιπὸν πλευρὰς νυττομένας Chrys.*pan.mart.*3.2 (2.714A); baptism by blood compared with Christ's baptism χθὲς [sc. feast of Epiphany]...ὁ δεσπότης ἡμῶν ὕδατι ἐβαπτίσατο, σήμερον δὲ δοῦλος αἱ. βαπτίζεται...ὥσπερ οἱ βαπτιζόμενοι τοῖς ὕδασιν, οὕτως οἱ μαρτυροῦντες τῷ ἰδίῳ λούονται αἱ. id.*pan.Lucn.*2(2.526A,B).

D. blood of Christ; **1.** as part of human nature μετέσχε καὶ αὐτὸς αἱ. καὶ σαρκός Ath.*Ar.*2.9(M.26.165A); αἱ. δὲ οὐκ ἐκ τοῦ πνεύματος τῆς τοῦ λόγου θεότητος ἐκπορεύεται· ἀλλ' ἐξ οὗ ἐφόρεσεν ἀνθρώπου ‡Ath.*serm.fid.*13(p.9; M.26.1269C); ὁ κύριος τῇ μὲν προβολῇ τοῦ αἱ. τὴν βεβαιότητα τῆς σαρκὸς ἐπεδείκνυτο ‡Ath.*Apoll.*1.18(M.26.1125B); *ib.*2.14(1156B); hence special characteristic of Son δυνάμει θεοῦ πατρὸς καὶ αἱ. θεοῦ παιδὸς καὶ δρόσῳ πνεύματος ἁγίου Clem.*q.d.s.*34 (p.182.22; M.9.640C); **2.** OT types; **a.** blood of Passover lamb, smeared on doorposts of Israelites in Egypt τὸ μυστήριον οὖν τοῦ προβάτου, ὃ τὸ πάσχα θύειν ἐντέταλται ὁ θεός, τύπος ἦν τοῦ Χριστοῦ, οὗ τῷ αἱ. κατὰ τὸν λόγον τῆς εἰς αὐτὸν πίστεως χρίονται τοὺς οἴκους ἑαυτῶν, τοῦτ' ἔστιν ἑαυτούς, οἱ πιστεύοντες εἰς αὐτόν Just.*dial.*40.1 (M.6.561B); *ib.*111.3(732C); ὅτε ὁ ὀλοθρευτὴς εἰσέρχεται εἰς πᾶσαν οἰκίαν τῆς ἐν κόσμῳ Αἰγύπτου, ἔνθα μὴ κέχρισται ἡ φλιὰ τῶν θυρῶν τῷ τοῦ Χριστοῦ αἱ. Or.*fr.48 in Lc.*(p.255.8); Cyr.H.*catech.*19.3 cit. s. ἀμνός; Χριστὸς γὰρ τὸ ἀληθινὸν...ἀρνίον ἐσφάγη, καὶ τὸ αἱ. αὐτοῦ ἐχρίσθη ἐπὶ τῶν φλιῶν τῆς καρδίας, ὅπως γένηται τὸ ἐκχυθὲν ἐπὶ τοῦ σταυροῦ αἱ. τοῦ Χριστοῦ, τῇ μὲν ψυχῇ εἰς ζωὴν καὶ ἀπολύτρωσιν· τοῖς δὲ Αἰγυπτίοις δαίμοσιν εἰς πένθος καὶ θάνατον Mac.Aeg.*hom.*47.8 (M.34.801A); Cyr.*hom.pasch.*10(5².132B); **b.** blood of the covenant (Ex.24:8), Cyr.*Zach.*59(3.738Cff.); **c.** Rahab's scarlet thread, Just. *dial.*111.4(M.6.733A); τοῦ δὲ τιμίου αἱ. διὰ τὸ χρῶμα τὸ ⟨κόκκινον⟩ σύμβολον. τοιοῦτον καὶ τὸ 'δεθὲν' ἐν τῇ γενέσει τοῦ Φαρὲς καὶ τὸ δειχθὲν ἀπὸ 'Ραὰβ τῆς πόρνης τοῖς κατασκόποις 'σημεῖον' Or.*hom.8.10 in Lev.*(p.410.25); **d.** other types and symbols: wine, exeg. Gen. 49:10, Just.*1apol.*32.11(M.6.380Bf.) cit. s. ἄμπελος; cf.id.*dial.*54.2 (M.6.593Df.); τὸν κόσμον ὅλον αἱ. πληρώσας ἀμπέλου, πότον ἀληθείας, τὸ κρᾶμα τοῦ νόμου τοῦ παλαιοῦ καὶ τοῦ λόγου τοῦ νέου...μυστικὸν ἄρα σύμβολον ἡ γραφὴ αἱ. ἁγίου οἶνον ὠνόμασεν Clem.*paed.*2.2(p.174.3,6; M.8.424B); house 'painted with vermilion' (Jer.22:14), Or.*fr.13 in Jer.*(p.204.11; M.13.569A); **3.** its redeeming qualities διὰ τοῦ αἱ. τοῦ κυρίου λύτρωσις ἔσται πᾶσιν τοῖς πιστεύουσιν...ἐπὶ τὸν θεόν *1Clem.* 12.7; *ib.*21.6; μιμηταὶ ὄντες θεοῦ, ἀναζωπυρήσαντες ἐν αἱ. θεοῦ Ign. *Eph.*1.1; *Barn.*5.1; Iren.*haer.*5.1.1(M.7.1121C); *ib.*5.2.1(1124A); cf. *si autem non salvetur haec* [sc. *caro*] *videlicet nec dominus sanguine suo redemit nos; neque calix eucharistiae communicatio sanguinis ejus*, *ib.*5.2.2(1124B); Clem.*paed.*1.5(p.104.1; M.8.277B); *A.Thom.* A 72(p.188.5); Ath.*Ar.*2.7(M.26.161C); *ib.*2.65(285A); ‡Ath.*Apoll.*1. 16(M.26.1121C); opp. blood of circumcision, Just.*dial.*24.1(M.6. 528B); **4.** universal efficacy ἀτενίσωμεν εἰς τὸ αἱ. τοῦ Χριστοῦ καὶ γνῶμεν ὡς ἔστιν τίμιον τῷ πατρὶ αὐτοῦ, ὅτι διὰ τὴν ἡμετέραν σωτηρίαν ἐκχυθὲν παντὶ τῷ κόσμῳ μετανοίας χάριν ὑπήνεγκεν *1Clem.*7.4; ἀντὶ δὲ τῶν τῆς ἁμαρτίας αἱ. τῷ ἰδίῳ αἱ. τὴν γῆν καὶ τοὺς πάντας καθαρίσῃ ‡Ath.*pass.*16(M.28.213C); *ib.*20(221A); ῥανίδες αἵματος ὀλίγαι κόσμον ὅλον ἀναπλάττουσαι, καὶ γίνονται καθάπερ ὀπὸς γάλακτι πᾶσιν ἀνθρώποις, εἰς ἓν ἡμᾶς συνδέουσαι καὶ συνάγουσαι Gr.Naz.*or.*45.29(M.36. 664A); Chrys.*hom.*1.3 *in Eph.*(11.7A,B); αἱ. ἐστιν, αἱ., ὃ τὸ χειρόγραφον τῶν ἁμαρτιῶν ἀπήλειψεν· αἱ., ὃ τὴν ψυχήν σου ἐκάθηρεν, ὃ τὴν κηλῖδα ἀπέπλυνεν, ὃ τὰς ἀρχὰς καὶ τὰς ἐξουσίας ἐθριάμβευσεν id.*cruc.* 1.3(2.404A); id.*stat.*2.9(2.34C); id.*prod.Jud.*2.6(2.395A); Cyr.*glaph. Gen.*(1.153B); its superiority to blood of martyrs εἰ καὶ μυρίους θανάτους ὑπὲρ Χριστοῦ ὑπομείνωμεν, οὐδὲ οὕτως τὸ δέον ἀνεπληρώσαμεν· ἄλλο γὰρ αἱ. θεοῦ, καὶ ἕτερον αἱ. δούλων, κατὰ τὸ ἀξίωμα, καὶ οὐ κατὰ τὴν οὐσίαν Jo.Clim.*scal.*23(M.88.968D); **5.** necessity of faith in it δι' αἱ. καθαίρων τοὺς πιστεύοντας αὐτῷ Just.*1apol.*32.7 (M.6.380B); even for angels, Ign.*Smyrn.*6.1 cit. s. ἄγγελος; opp. Docetic heresies εἰ διὰ τοῦ...αἱ. Χριστοῦ τὴν σωτηρίαν τῶν ἀνθρώπων καταγγέλλουσιν αἱ γραφαί, οὗτοι δὲ αἱ. καὶ σάρκα ἀρνοῦνται ἔχειν αὐτόν, οὔτε ἀπέθανεν ἐκείνοις κατ' ἀλήθειαν, οὔτε ἐτάφη...οὔτε γὰρ αἱ. ἐσχήκει,...οὐδὲ ἡμεῖς οὖν κατ' ἀλήθειαν ἐσώθημεν Adam.*dial.* 5.6(p.186.24; M.11.1841B); since it will be required from unbelievers, Polyc.*ep.*2.1; **6.** discussion of opinion that it was given as ransom to Devil ὁ ἀμνὸς σφαγεὶς...ὠνούμενος τῷ ἑαυτοῦ αἱ. ἀπὸ τοῦ ταῖς ἁμαρτίαις ἡμᾶς πιπρασκομένους ἀγοράσαντος Or.*Jo.*6.53 (35; p.162.8; M.14.292D); εἰκὸς δὲ ὅτι κατά σε ἐπρίατο, δοὺς ἑαυτοῦ τὸ αἱ.· πῶς οὖν καὶ ἐκ νεκρῶν ἠγείρετο; εἰ γὰρ ὁ λαβὼν τὴν τιμὴν τῶν ἀνθρώπων τὸ αἱ. ἀπέδωκεν, οὐκέτι ἐπώλησεν· εἰ δὲ μὴ ἀπέδωκε, πῶς ἀνέστη Χριστός;...ὁ γοῦν διάβολος κατέχει τὸ αἱ. τοῦ Χριστοῦ ἀντὶ τῆς τιμῆς τῶν ἀνθρώπων. πολλὴ βλάσφημος ἄνοια Adam.*dial.*1.27 (p.54.7ff.; M.11.1757B); τίνι γὰρ τὸ ὑπὲρ ἡμῶν αἱ., καὶ περὶ τίνος ἐχύθη, τὸ μέγα καὶ περιβόητον τοῦ θεοῦ, καὶ ἀρχιερέως, καὶ θύματος; κατεχόμεθα μὲν γὰρ ὑπὸ τοῦ πονηροῦ...εἰ δὲ τὸ λύτρον οὐκ ἄλλου τινός, ἢ τοῦ κατέχοντος γίνεται, ζητῶ τίνι τοῦτο εἰσηνέχθη, καὶ δι' ἥντινα τὴν αἰτίαν; εἰ μὲν τῷ πονηρῷ, φεῦ τῆς ὕβρεως· εἰ μὴ παρὰ τοῦ θεοῦ μόνον, ἀλλὰ καὶ τὸν θεὸν αὐτὸν λύτρον ὁ λῃστὴς λαμβάνει... εἰ δὲ τῷ πατρί, πρῶτον μὲν πῶς; οὐχ ὑπ' ἐκείνου γὰρ ἐκρατούμεθα. δεύτερον δέ, τίς ὁ λόγος, μονογενοῦς αἱ. τέρπειν πατέρα;...ἢ δῆλον, ὅτι λαμβάνει μὲν ὁ πατήρ, οὐκ αἰτήσας, οὐδὲ δεηθείς, ἀλλὰ διὰ τὴν οἰκονομίαν, καὶ τὸ χρῆναι ἁγιασθῆναι τῷ ἀνθρωπίνῳ τοῦ θεοῦ τὸν ἄνθρωπον Gr.Naz.*or.*45.22(M.36.653A,B); **7.** blood of Christ ridiculed by pagans παίζων γοῦν τὸ ἐπὶ τῷ σταυρῷ προχυθὲν αἱ. τοῦ Ἰησοῦ φησιν ὅτι οὐκ ἦν ἰχώρ, οἷός πέρ τε ῥέει μακάρεσσι θεοῖσιν Or.*Cels.*1.66 (p.119.15; M.11.784A); contention that it was not revenged on Jerusalem, refuted, *ib.*8.42(p.257.15; 1580C); cf.Cyr.*Os.*4(3.22A); **8.** its place in spiritual life ὁ ἀμνὸς σφαγιάζεται, καὶ σφραγίζονται τῷ τιμίῳ αἱ. πρᾶξις καὶ λόγος, εἴτουν ἕξις καὶ ἐνέργεια, αἱ τῶν ἡμετέρων θυρῶν παραστάτιδες, λέγω δὴ τῶν τοῦ νοῦ κινημάτων τε καὶ δογμάτων, καλῶς ἀνοιγομένων καὶ κλειομένων ἐκ θεωρίας Gr.Naz.*or.*45.15(M.36. 644B); ὁ Χριστὸς ἐτύθη, καὶ τὸ αἱ. αὐτοῦ ῥαντίσαν ἡμᾶς πτεροφυῆσαι ἐποίησεν, ἔδωκε γὰρ ἡμῖν πτέρυγας ἁγίου πνεύματος, πρὸς τὸ ἵπτασθαι ἀκωλύτως εἰς τὸν ἀέρα τῆς θεότητος Mac.Aeg.*hom.*47.2(M.34.797B); **9.** in formulae of greeting and various other contexts, Ign.*Philad.* proem. cit. s. αἰώνιος; ἀσπάζομαι τὸν ἀξιόθεον ἐπίσκοπον...ἐν ὀνόματι Ἰησοῦ Χριστοῦ, καὶ τῇ σαρκὶ αὐτοῦ καὶ τῷ αἱ. id.*Smyrn.* 12.2; identified with ἀγάπη, *ib.*1.1; id.*Trall.*8.1; id.*Rom.*7.3; in connexion with Christ's teaching Χριστὸς...συνήγαγε...τὸ στρατιωτικὸν τὸ ἀναίμακτον αἱ. καὶ λόγῳ Clem.*prot.*11(p.82.7; M.8.236B); **10.** interprn. of the blood and water flowing from the side of Christ, Claud.*fr.pasch.*(M.5.1300A); ἀρχὴ σημείων ἐπὶ Μωσέως αἱ. καὶ ὕδωρ, καὶ τὸ τελευταῖον πάντων τῶν σημείων Ἰησοῦ τὸ αὐτό. πρῶτον Μωσῆς τὸν ποταμὸν μετέβαλεν εἰς αἱ. καὶ ὁ Ἰησοῦς, τὸ τέλος, ὕδωρ ἐξήνεγκεν ἐκ πλευρᾶς μετὰ αἱ. διὰ τὰς δύο φωνὰς ἴσως, τοῦ τε κρίνοντος, καὶ τῶν ἐπιβοώντων...ὁ μὲν Πιλᾶτος ἔλεγεν· ἀθῷός εἰμι, καὶ ὕδατι ἀπενίπτετο τὰς χεῖρας· οἱ δὲ ἐπιβοῶντες ἔλεγον· τὸ αἱ. αὐτοῦ ἐφ' ἡμᾶς. ἦν οὖν τὰ δύο ἐκ τῆς πλευρᾶς· τὸ ὕδωρ ἴσως τῷ κρίνοντι, τοῖς δὲ ἐπιβοῶσι τὸ αἱ. καὶ πάλιν ἄλλως νοητέον· Ἰουδαίοις μὲν τὸ αἱ., Χριστιανοῖς δὲ τὸ ὕδωρ· ἐκείνοις...ἡ ἐκ τοῦ αἱ. καταδίκη Cyr.H. *catech.*13.21; αἱ. καὶ ὕδωρ τῆς πλευρᾶς χεόμενον· τὸ μέν, ὡς ἀνθρώπου, τὸ δέ, ὡς ὑπὲρ ἄνθρωπον Gr.Naz.*or.*45.29(M.36.661D); ‡Ath.*pass.*25 (M.28.228D–229A) cit. s. πλευρά; *ib.*21(224A).

E. eucharistic; **1.** in gen., Ign.*Philad.*4.1 cit. s. εὐχαριστία; Ἰησοῦ ὁ καταξιώσας ἡμᾶς τῆς εὐχαριστίας τοῦ σώματός σου...καὶ τοῦ αἱ. κοινωνῆσαι *A.Thom.*A 49(p.166.3); *A.(Pass.)Andr.*6(p.13.18) cit. s. ἀμνός; διττὸν δὲ τὸ αἱ. τοῦ κυρίου· τὸ μέν ἐστιν αὐτοῦ σαρκικόν, ᾧ τῆς φθορᾶς λελυτρώμεθα, τὸ δὲ πνευματικόν, τοῦτ' ἔστιν ᾧ κεχρίσμεθα. καὶ τοῦτ' ἔστι πιεῖν τὸ αἱ. τοῦ Ἰησοῦ, τῆς κυριακῆς μεταλαβεῖν ἀφθαρσίας· ἰσχὺς δὲ τοῦ λόγου τὸ πνεῦμα, ὡς αἱ. σαρκός Clem.*paed.* 2.2(pp.167.28–168.3; M.8.409B); **2.** OT types: Noah's vine, *Apoc. Bar.*4(p.87.30); OT sacrifices, Chrys.*hom.*46.4 *in Jo.*(8.274A); ὁ Μωϋσῆς φησιν· θύσατε ἀμνὸν προβάτων ἄμωμον, καὶ τὸ αἱ. αὐτοῦ ἐπιχρίσατε ἐπὶ ταῖς θύραις. τί λέγεις; αἱ. ἀλόγου σῴζειν ἀνθρώπους λογικοὺς οἶδεν; ναί, φησί...τὸ αἱ. ἐκεῖνο τὸ ἀναίσθητον καὶ ἄψυχον, τοὺς ψυχὰς ἔχοντας ἀνθρώπους ἔσωσεν· οὐκ ἐπειδὴ αἱ. ἦν, ἀλλ' ἐπειδὴ τοῦ αἱ. τούτου τύπος ἦν. ὅτε εἶδεν ὁ ὀλοθρεύων ταῖς θύραις ἐπικεχρισμένον τὸ αἱ., καὶ οὐκ ἐτόλμησεν ἐπιπηδῆσαι. νῦν ἂν ἴδῃ σε ὁ διάβολος, οὐχὶ ταῖς θύραις ἐπικεχρισμένον τὸ αἱ. τοῦ σώματος, ἀλλὰ τῷ στόματι τῶν πιστῶν ἐπικεχρισμένον τὸ αἱ. τῆς ἀληθείας τὸ αἱ.

τοῦ ναοῦ τοῦ Χριστοφόρου, οὐ πολλῷ μᾶλλον καθέξει; Chrys.ap.Jo.D. *parall.*(M.96.17Af.); **3.** its reality ὁ φαινόμενος οἶνος, οὐκ οἶνός ἐστιν, εἰ καὶ ἡ γεῦσις τοῦτο βούλεται, ἀλλὰ αἷ. Χριστοῦ Cyr.H.*catech.*22.9 (M.33.1104B), cf. s. οἶνος; but cf. σωτὴρ...ἐνήλλαξε τὰ ὀνόματα... ἄμπελον ἑαυτὸν ὀνομάσας, αἷ. τὸ σύμβολον προσηγόρευσεν...τὰ ὁρώμενα σύμβολα τῇ τοῦ σώματος καὶ αἷ. προσηγορίᾳ τετίμηκεν, οὐ τὴν φύσιν μεταβαλών, ἀλλὰ τὴν χάριν τῇ φύσει προστεθεικώς Thdt. *eran.*1(4.26); *ib.*(4.25) cit. s. ἄμπελος; truly food ὃν τρόπον διὰ λόγου θεοῦ...Χριστὸς...σάρκα καὶ αἷ. ὑπὲρ σωτηρίας ἡμῶν ἔσχεν, οὕτως καὶ τὴν δι' εὐχῆς λόγου τοῦ παρ' αὐτοῦ εὐχαριστηθεῖσαν τροφήν, ἐξ ἧς αἷμα καὶ σάρκες κατὰ μεταβολὴν τρέφονται ἡμῶν, ἐκείνου τοῦ σαρκοποιηθέντος Ἰησοῦ καὶ σάρκα καὶ αἷ. ἐδιδάχθημεν εἶναι Just. *1apol.*66.2(M.6.428Cff.); τὴν σάρκα...τὴν ἀπὸ τοῦ σώματος τοῦ κυρίου, καὶ τοῦ αἷ. αὐτοῦ τρεφομένην Iren.*haer.*4.18.5(M.7.1028A); *ib.*5.2.3 (1126B); φέρει γὰρ οἶνον ἡ ἄμπελος, ὡς αἷ. ὁ λόγος, ἄμφω δὲ ἀνθρώποις πότον εἰς σωτηρίαν, ὁ μὲν οἶνος τῷ σώματι, τὸ δὲ αἷ. τῷ πνεύματι Clem.*paed.*1.5(p.99.12f.; M.8.268B); Chrys.*hom.82.5 in Mt.*(7.788C); id.*laud.Max.*3(3.215C); **4.** purifying man and restoring him to innocence, *A.Thom.*A 158(p.268.3); ἐκεῖνός ἐστιν ὁ ἀληθινὸς βότρυς,...οὗ τὸ αἷ. τοῖς σῳζομένοις τε καὶ εὐφραινομένοις, πότιμόν τε καὶ σωτήριον γίνεται Gr.Nyss.*hom.3 in Cant.*(M.44.829C); τὸ τίμιον αἷ. τοῦ Χριστοῦ, εἰ μετὰ παρρησίας ληφθείη, πᾶσαν γὰρ νόσον σβέσαι δυνήσεται τοῦτο Chrys.*hom.4.9 in Mt.*(7.64A); τοῦτο τὸ αἷ. τὴν εἰκόνα ἡμῖν ἀνθηρὰν ἐργάζεται τὴν βασιλικήν, τοῦτο κάλλος ἀμήχανον τίκτει...τὸ μὲν γὰρ ἀπὸ τῶν σιτίων ἡμῖν αἷ. γινόμενον, οὐκ εὐθέως τοῦτο γίνεται, ἀλλ' ἕτερόν τι· τοῦτο δὲ οὐχ οὕτως, ἀλλ' εὐθέως τὴν ψυχὴν ἀρδεύει, καὶ μεγάλην τινὰ δύναμιν ἐμποιεῖ. τοῦτο τὸ αἷ. ἀξίως λαμβανόμενον ἐλαύνει μὲν δαίμονας καὶ πόρρωθεν ἡμῶν ποιεῖ, καλεῖ δὲ ἀγγέλους πρὸς ἡμᾶς, καὶ τὸν δεσπότην τῶν ἀγγέλων· ὅπου γὰρ ἂν ἴδωσι τὸ αἷ. τὸ δεσποτικόν, φεύγουσι μὲν δαίμονες, συντρέχουσι δὲ ἄγγελοι. τοῦτο τὸ αἷ. ἐκχυθὲν πᾶσαν τὴν οἰκουμένην ἐξέπλυνε id. *hom.46.3 in Jo.*(8.273A,B); id.*poenit.*9(2.349E); **5.** representing the Word, Clem.*paed.*1.6(p.115.30ff.; M.8.301B); interpretation proved from Abel's blood ὅτι δὲ τὸ αἷ. ὁ λόγος ἐστίν, μαρτυρεῖ τοῦ Ἄβελ... τὸ αἷ. ἐντυγχάνον τῷ θεῷ· οὐ γὰρ τὸ αἷ. ἄν ποτε προήσεται φωνήν, μὴ οὐχὶ ὁ λόγος νοούμενος τὸ αἷ.· τύπος γὰρ ὁ δίκαιος ὁ παλαιὸς τοῦ νέου δικαίου καὶ τὸ αἷ. τὸ ἐντυγχάνον τὸ παλαιὸν ὑπερεντυγχάνει τοῦ αἷ. τοῦ νέου. φθέγγεται δὲ πρὸς τὸν θεὸν τὸ αἷ., ὁ λόγος, ἐπεὶ λόγον ἐμήνυεν τοῦ νέου *ib.*(p.118.18ff.; 305C); **6.** reason for drinking Christ's blood τικτόμενον βρέφος...ἂν μὴ φάγῃ τὴν σάρκα καὶ πίῃ τὸ αἷ. τῆς μητρός, οὐκ ἔχει ζωὴν...καὶ μὴ θελήσῃς εἰπεῖν, ὡς οὐχ αἷ. τοῦτο, ἀλλὰ γάλα τυγχάνει. αἷ. γὰρ φύσει κατ' ἀλήθειαν ἐκ φύσεως ζωτικόν...εἶτα μεταβαλόμενον εἰς λευκότητα γάλακτος...εἴ γε οὖν ὁ Χριστὸς ὅσοι ἔλαβον αὐτὸν ἔδωκεν αὐτοῖς ἐξουσίαν τέκνα θεοῦ γενέσθαι ...πόθεν, ἀφήγησαι, τὰ τέκνα τοῦ θεοῦ ἄρτι τικτόμενα ζήσεται καὶ τραφήσεται; ἢ πάντως τῶν μυστικῶν σαρκῶν ἀπογευόμενα καὶ πίοντα τοῦ μυστικοῦ τῆς τικτούσης αἷ.; Mac.Mgn.*apocr.*3.23(p.103.14ff.); **7.** to be administered only by duly ordained priests, Ath.*apol.sec.* 11(p.96.32; M.25.268C); Chrys.*hom.45.3 in Mt.*(7.749B).

F. plur., of the virginal blood from which Christ was formed ἀγνοοῦμεν δὲ ὅπως ἐκ παρθενικῶν αἷ. ἑτέρῳ παρὰ τὴν φύσιν θεσμῷ διεπλάττετο Dion.Ar.*d.n.*2.9(M.3.648A); ἡ τοῦ σώματος σύμπηξις ἐκ πανάγνων αἷ. παρθενικῶν ‡Cyr.*Trin.*14(6³.20D; M.77.1152A); Jo.D. *f.o.*4.13(M.94.1140C) cit. s. ἀμώμητος.

II. plur., *shedding of blood, slaughter* ἐχώρει δὲ δι' αἱμάτων [sc. ἀνήρ] σκηπτοῦ δίκην Eus.*v.C.*1.7(p.10.15; M.20.920A); *ib.*1.57(p.34. 10; 972A); εἰς αἵματα ἐμαυτὸν ἀποδιδόναι Ath.*apol.Const.*34(M.25. 641B); Gr.Naz.*or.*33.3(M.36.217A); Germ.CP *or.*2(M.98.249D,252A).

αἱμασιά, ἡ, **1.** *wall of dry stones*, Thdt.*Is.*1:8(p.5.31; 2.173); **2.** *hedge of thorns*, Chrys.*virg.*52(1.314C); Thdt.*h.e.*2.9.3(3.850).

αἱμάσσω, intrans., *bleed*; acc. Apollinarius ἡ θεότης...αἱ. Gr. Nyss.*Apoll.*24(M.45.1176A); Jo.Mal.*chron.*2 p.32(M.97.101A).

αἱματεκχυσία, ἡ, *shedding of blood*, of gladiatorial contests αἱ. ἀθεωτάταις Tat.*orat.*23(p.26.5; M.6.857C); Epiph.*haer.*39.9(p.79.2; M.41.676A); met. τὸ ἐκκόψαι τὸ ἴδιον θέλημα αἱ. ἐστί Ant.Mon. *hom.*39(M.89.1556B).

αἱμάτινος, *of blood*; met. τὸ ζῆν τὸ αἱ. *physical* life, Pall.*v.Chrys.* 17(p.117.21; M.47.65).

***αἱματολουσία**, ἡ, *washing away of blood*, Leont.B.*mesopent.* (M.86.1985B).

***αἱματοχυσία**, ἡ, *shedding of blood*, Zach.H.*ep.*(M.86.3232C).

***αἱμοβορία**, ἡ, *bloodthirstiness*, Thphn.*chron.*p.253(M.108.633B).

αἱμοβόρος, *bloodthirsty* αἱ. θῆρες *M.Thdot.*3(p.134.29); met. ἡ ἀγριότης τῶν αἱ. καὶ πολεμίων ἐχθρῶν Const.ap.Ath.*apol.sec.*87(p.166. 15; M.25.405B); Ναβουχοδονόσορ...αἱ., ἀγριώδης Cyr.H.*catech.*2.17; Epiph.*anc.*103(p.123.20; M.43.201B); Thphn.*chron.*p.306(M.108.745A).

***αἱμοθυσία**, ἡ, *bloody sacrifice*, Thphn.*chron.*p.346(M.108.833C, v.l. αἱμοχυσία).

***αἱμολάπτις**, *blood-sucking*, Gr.Naz.*carm.*1.2.8.79(M.37.655A).

***αἱμομιξία**, ἡ, *incest*, †Jo.Jej.*serm.*(M.88.1921D); †Jo.Jej.*poenit.* (M.88.1893D); †Gregent.*leg.Hom.*2(M.86.584A).

αἱμόρροια, ἡ, *discharge of blood*; hence used of a serpent whose bite makes blood flow from all parts of the body, Epiph.*haer.*48. 15(p.241.8; M.41.880A).

***αἱμοχυσία**, ἡ, *bloodshed*, Thphn.*chron.*p.276 (v.l. αἱματο- M.108. 684A).

αἱμωδιασμός, ὁ, *having the teeth set on edge*, Or.*sel.in Ezech.*18 (M.13.816C).

αἴνεσις, ἡ, **1.** *praise*, *A.Barn.*9(p.295.19); for θυσία αἰνέσεως, v. θυσία; **2.** *song of praise, psalm* ὡς ἡ αἴ. λέγει τοῦ Δαβίδ Ath.*Ar.* 3.67(M.26.465C).

***αἰνετέον**, *one must praise*, Or.*sel.in Ps.*150:1(M.12.1684A); Thdr. Stud.*epp.*2.77(M.99.1316C).

αἰνετός, *laudatory* ὕμνον αἰ. ἀνυμνήσατε ‡Rom.Mel.(*AS* 1 p.234).

αἴνιγμα, τό, **1.** *dark saying, riddle*; ref. Moses' forbidding murder, etc., οὐ δι' αἰ. but γυμνῇ τῇ κεφαλῇ, Clem.*paed.*2.10(p.211. 10; M.8.504B); τὸ μέγεθος τῶν αἰ. τῆς γραφῆς Meth.*symp.*8.9(p.92.1; M.18.152C); opp. μυστήριον θεῖον, ref. Jo.1:1, Ath.*Ar.*1.41(M.26. 96B); Chrys.*fr.in Jer.*7:31(M.64.841C); hence = *hidden meaning, mystery* τὰ αἰ. τῶν ἡμερῶν τούτων [sc. fast days] Clem.*str.*7.12(p.54. 5; M.9.504B); of pagan gods, Cels.ap.Or.*Cels.*6.42(p.110.21; M.11. 1360B); Chrys.*hom.15.1 in Heb.*(12.150A); **2.** *figure, type*; earthly of heavenly things, so 1Cor.13:12 ἐν αἰ. ... μερικωτάτην τὴν παροῦσαν γνῶσιν...εἰ ταῦτα [i.e. S. Paul's revelations]...αἰ., λογίζου ...ἐντεῦθεν τὸ πρόσωπον ἡλίκον ἐστίν Chrys.*hom.34.2 in 1Cor.*(10. 311C,E); τοὺς...ἀγγέλους δι' αἰ. τὰ θεῖα μυστικῶς προάγοντας ὁρῶμεν Dion.Ar.*ep.*9.1(M.3.1108A); OT of NT τοῦτο ἦν ὃ ἠνίσσετο ἡ Ζαχαρίου σιωπή...ἵνα τῆς ἀληθείας τὸ φῶς, ὁ λόγος, τῶν προφητικῶν αἰ. τὴν μυστικὴν ἀπολύσηται σιωπήν Clem.*prot.*2(p.10.7; M.8.65C); τὴν τελευταίαν τοῦ σωτῆρος εἰς ἡμᾶς ἐνέργειαν...ἐπικρυπτομένην τῷ τῆς προφητείας αἰ. id.*str.*5.8(p.363.22; M.9.85C); ἐν τῷ χριστιανισμῷ... διήγησις τῶν ἐν τοῖς προφήταις αἰ. Or.*Cels.*1.9(p.61.25; M.11.673A); ref. Pr.8:22, Ath.*Ar.*2.77(M.26.312B); law as pedagogue guiding men to understanding δι' αἰ., Gr.Nyss.*anim.et res.*(M.46.132B); ‡Chrys.*pasch.*6.2(8².267A); Cyr.*glaph.Gen.*5(1.170C); of remaining in tents on sabbath αἰ. ἦν τοῦτο τοῦ, ὅτι ἐν ταῖς ἄνω μοναῖς διηνεκῶς ἀναμενοῦσιν οἱ ἅγιοι id.*Ps.*22:6(M.69.844A); Gennad.*fr.Gen.*17:10 (M.85.1645D); of scriptural imagery in gen. τοῖς μυστικοῖς λογίοις ἐστὶ πρεπωδέστατον, τὸ δι' ἀπορρήτων...αἰ. ἀποκρύπτεσθαι...τὴν ἱερὰν...τῶν ὑπερκοσμίων νόων ἀλήθειαν Dion.Ar.*c.h.*2.2(M.3.140B); id.*ep.*9.1(M.3.1104B); **3.** *symbol, sign*; of milk as a scriptural αἰ. of mercy of Word, Clem.*paed.*1.6(p.121.2; M.8.312A); ref. S. John's gospel, treating of πράγματα ὧν αἰ. ἦσαν αἱ πράξεις αὐτοῦ [sc. Christ] Or.*Jo.*1.7(9; p.12.16; M.14.36D); τὰ κρίνα τοῦ λαμπροῦ...τῆς διανοίας αἰ. γίνεται Gr.Nyss.*hom.15 in Cant.*(M.44.1093B); ἀθανασίας αἰ. ... ἡ πρὸς τὸν θεὸν ὁμιλία, τὸ ἀταλαίπωρον τῆς ζωῆς κτλ. Chrys. *hom.17.3 in 1Cor.*(10.149E); gifts of Magi τῶν μυστηρίων εἰσὶν αἰ. Amph.ap.CEph.(431)*act.*1(*ACO* 1.1.7 p.94.27; M.39.100C); sacramental: baptism ἀξιοθέου θεωρίας αἰ. φυσικοῖς...ἐσόπτροις εἰκονιζόμενα Dion.Ar.*e.h.*2.3.1(M.3.397A); eucharist ὦ θειοτάτη...τελετή, τὰ περικείμενά σοι συμβολικῶς ἀμφιέσματα τῶν αἰ. ἀποκαλυψαμένη *ib.*3.3.2(428C); *ib.*3.3.3(429B); ref. sacramental oils, *ib.*4.3.2 (476C).

***αἰνιγματίζω**, *show in figure*, Job.Mon.*inc.*4(M.86.3320A); Chrysipp.*enc.in Jo.Bapt.*(p.36.5).

αἰνιγματιστής, ὁ, *one who is fond of riddles*, Gr.Naz.*or.*20.21 (p.106.9; M.36.101C); Gr.Nyss.*Eun.*1(1 p.207.16; M.45.456A).

αἰνιγματώδης, *obscure, riddling, enigmatic* ὁ τρόπος τῆς παρ' αὐτοῖς [sc. τοῖς παρ' Ἕλλησι σοφοῖς] φιλοσοφίας, ὡς Ἑβραϊκὸς καὶ αἰ. Clem.*str.*1.14(p.38.12; M.8.760A); Αἰγύπτιοι πρὸ τῶν ἱερῶν τὰς σφίγγας ἱδρύονται, ὡς αἰ. τοῦ περὶ θεοῦ λόγου καὶ ἀσαφοῦς ὄντος *ib.*5.5(p.346.22; M.9.56A); σαφὲς εἶναι τὸ ἐνύπνιον ἔφη καὶ μηδὲν αἰ. μηδὲ ἀμφίβολον ἔχειν Thdt.*h.e.*5.6.2(3.1023).

αἰνιγματωδῶς, *darkly, in riddles, in a figure* μυρία...ὑπό τε φιλοσόφων ὑπό τε ποιητῶν αἰ. εἰρημένα Clem.*str.*5.8(p.360.23; M.9. 80B); τυπικῶς...καὶ αἰ. ἀναφερόμενα εἰς τὸν Χριστὸν τῶν ἀναγεγραμμένων ἐν τῷ νόμῳ πλεῖστα Or.*Jo.*13.26(p.251.6; M.14.445A); ὁ Χριστὸς διὰ τοῦ ῥεύσαντος ἀπ' αὐτοῦ ὕδατος καὶ αἵματος...αἰ. ἔδειξε τὴν ἡμῶν σωτηρίαν Epiph.*haer.*46.5(p.209.15; M.41.845A); τοῦτο... νόμος ἡμῖν ἱερὸς αἰ. ὑπετύπου Cyr.*ador.*14(1.480D); ref. Gen.1:26 αἰ. καὶ τὸ ταὐτὸν τῆς οὐσίας καὶ τὸν τῶν προσώπων παρεδήλωσεν ἀριθμόν Thdt.*qu.19 in Gen.*(1.23).

αἴνιξις, ἡ, = αἴνιγμα, *dark saying*, Epiph.*haer*.46.5(p.209.25; M.41.845B).

αἰνίσσομαι, *hint, signify obscurely*, Just.*dial*.76.1(M.6.652C); τοιαῦτα καὶ οἱ Πυθαγόρειοι ᾐνίσσοντο Clem.*str*.5.8(p.360.20; M.9.80B); ἡ θεία γραφή...αἰ. Or.*ep*.2.3(p.66.3; M.11.89B); Synes.*ep*.146(M.66.1541A); Max.*ambig*.(M.91.1085D).

*__αἰνομανῶς__, *with terrible raving*, Anast.S.*haer*.(p.262).

*__αἰνοσίθρησκος__, ? *reverencing fables*, Eudoc.*Cypr*.1.320(M.85.844C).

*__αἰνοσοφιστής__, ὁ, ? *dread deceiver*, Eudoc.*Cypr*.1.92(M.85.836C).

αἰνοτόκος, *born for ill* or *unhappiness* σπόρον †Apoll.*met.Ps*.20:11(M.33.1337C).

*__αἰολόδερμος__, *with dappled skin*, Gr.Naz.*carm*.1.2.15.11(M.37.766A).

αἰολόδωρος, *bestowing various gifts*, Gr.Naz.*carm*.1.1.3.5(M.37.408A).

αἰόλος, *quick-moving, changeful*, hence *various* αἰ. φῦλα Nonn.*par.Jo*.3:22(M.43.769C).

*__αἰολοσκόπος__, *shifty-eyed, crafty*; of the serpent, ‡Gr.Naz.*Chr.pat*.1647(M.38.268A).

[*]**αἰπόλος**, ὁ, = ἀείπολος, *ever-turning*, name of Phrygian god identified with Peratic Adam ὁ ἀεὶ πολῶν καὶ στρέφων...τὸν κόσμον Hipp.*haer*.5.8(p.95.10; M.16.3150); *ib*.5.9(p.99.21; 3155A).

αἱρεσιαρχ-έω, *found* or *lead a heresy, be a heresiarch* ἀντὶ τοῦ ὀνόματος τῶν Χριστιανῶν, ἀφ' ἑνός τινος τῶν ~ησάντων, ἑαυτοὺς ὀνομάζοντας, Μαρκίωνος ἢ Οὐαλεντίνου Bas.*hom.in Ps*.48(1.184D; M.29.449A); *Pers*.(p.33.17); Leont.H.*monoph*.(M.86.1816D).

αἱρεσιάρχης, ὁ, *founder* or *leader of a heresy, heresiarch*, Hipp.*haer*.5.6(p.77.23; M.16.3123B); Σίμων ὁ Μάγος...καὶ ἄλλοι τινὲς τῶν ἀθέων αἱ. Cyr.H.*catech*.15.5; Chrys.*hom.46.1 in Mt*.(7.481C).

*__αἱρεσίαρχος__, ὁ, = foreg., †Leont.B.*sect*.5.6(M.86.1232D).

*__αἱρεσιλατρεία__, ἡ, *following of heresy, attachment to heresy*, Didym.ap.*cat.Ac*.18:18(p.307.25).

*__αἱρεσιομαχέω__, *fight for a heresy*, Didym.*Trin*.3.16(M.39.865A).

αἱρεσιομάχος, ὁ, *fighter for a heresy* αἱ. οὐ μετέχουσι τοῦ θεϊκοῦ πνεύματος Didym.*Trin*.2.21(M.39.741C); *ib*.3.20(897A).

*__αἱρεσιούργημα__, τό, *work of heresy, heretical behaviour*, Const.Pogon.*sacr*.3(M.*PL*.96.391D).

*__αἱρεσιουργός__, ὁ, *promoter of heresies*, Anast.S.*haer*.(p.258).

αἵρεσις, ἡ, **1.** *way of thought*, of the Christian faith ἀνάγκη...δι' αὐτῶν τῶν γραφῶν ἐκμανθάνειν ἀποδεικτικῶς, ὅπως μὲν ἀπεσφάλησαν αἱ αἱ., ὅπως δὲ ἐν μόνῃ τῇ ἀληθείᾳ καὶ τῇ ἀρχαίᾳ ἐκκλησίᾳ ἥ τε ἀκριβεστάτη γνῶσις καὶ ἡ τῷ ὄντι ἀρίστη αἵ. Clem.*str*.7.15(p.65.21; M.9.528B); φαύλως καὶ ἐνδιαστρόφως τινὲς περὶ τῆς...αἱ. τῆς καθολικῆς ἀποδιίστασθαι ἤρξαντο Const.ap.Eus.*h.e*.10.5.21(M.20.888C); οἱ Χριστιανοί, οἵτινες τῶν γονέων τῶν ἑαυτῶν καταλελοίπασιν τὴν αἵ. Maxm.*ib*.8.17.6(793A); δέδωκα πεῖραν τῆς ἐμαυτοῦ περὶ τὸν θεὸν αἱ. Bas.*ep*.81.1(3.165B; M.32.437B); **2.** *system of thought* or *those who profess* such a *system, school, sect*; **a.** Jewish or pagan τοὺς Σαδδουκαίους ἢ τὰς ὁμοίας αἱ. Just.*dial*.80.4(M.6.665A); παρ' ὑμῖν τοῖς Ἰουδαίοις καὶ παρὰ τοῖς δοκιμωτάτοις τῶν παρ' Ἕλλησι φιλοσόφων πάμπολλαι γεγόνασιν αἱ., καὶ οὐ δήπου φατὲ δεῖν ὀκνεῖν ἤτοι φιλοσοφεῖν ἢ Ἰουδαΐζειν τῆς διαφωνίας ἕνεκα τῆς πρὸς ἀλλήλας τῶν παρ' ὑμῖν αἱ. Clem.*str*.7.15(p.63.28; M.9.524B); αἱ. φιλοσοφουμένων ἐν τοῖς Βραχμάναις Hipp.*haer*.1.24(p.27.24; M.16.3052A); προτραπεὶς ἐπὶ φιλοσοφίαν καὶ ἀποκληρωτικῶς ἐπί τινα αἱ. ἑαυτὸν φιλοσόφων ῥίψας...τῷ πιστεύειν τὴν αἱ. ἐκείνην κρείττονα εἶναι Or.*Cels*.1.10(p.62.28; M.11.673C); Eus.*h.e*.3.33.6(M.20.284B); Gr.Nyss.*or.catech*.3(p.17.1; M.45.17D); **b.** Christian, acc. Jews or pagans αἵ. τις ἄθεος καὶ ἄνομος ἐγήγερται ἀπὸ Ἰησοῦ τινος Γαλιλαίου πλάνου Just.*dial*.108.2(M.6.725C); τοὺς οὔτε Ἕλληνας οὔτε Ἰουδαίους, ἀλλὰ τῆς Γαλιλαίων ὄντας αἱ. Juln.Imp.ap.Cyr.*Juln*.2(6².43A); **c.** *faction, party*, ref. 1Cor.11:19, Chrys.*hom.27.2 in 1Cor*.(10.242B) cit. s. σχίσμα; Thdt.*1Cor*.11:19(3.236); **d.** *body of people holding false doctrine*; **i.** significance of names τῶν δὲ αἱ. αἱ μὲν ἀπὸ ὀνόματος προσαγορεύονται...αἱ δὲ ἀπὸ τόπου...αἱ δὲ ἀπὸ ἔθνους...αἱ δὲ ἀπὸ ἐνεργείας...αἱ δὲ ἀπὸ δογμάτων ἰδιαζόντων...αἱ δὲ ἀπὸ ὑποθέσεων ὧν τετιμήκασιν...αἱ δὲ ἀφ' ὧν παρανόμως ἐπετήδευσάν τε καὶ ἐτόλμησαν Clem.*str*.7.17(p.76.20; M.9.552B); **ii.** dist. from schism, etc. τὰς μὲν αἱ. ὠνόμασαν, τὰ δὲ σχίσματα, τὰς δὲ παρασυναγωγάς. αἱ. μέν, τοὺς παντελῶς ἀπερρηγμένους, καὶ κατ' αὐτὴν τὴν πίστιν ἀπηλλοτριωμένους· σχίσματα δέ, τοὺς δι' αἰτίας τινὰς ἐκκλησιαστικὰς καὶ ζητήματα ἰάσιμα πρὸς ἀλλήλους διενεχθέντας· παρασυναγωγὰς δὲ τὰς συνάξεις τὰς παρὰ τῶν ἀνυποτάκτων πρεσβυτέρων ἢ ἐπισκόπων καὶ παρὰ τῶν ἀπαιδεύτων λαῶν γινομένας Bas.*ep*.188 *can*.1(3.268D; M.32.665A); **iii.** in gen. Δοσίθεός τις...διαδέχεται τὴν αἱ. *Hom.Clem*.2.24; τὰς μὲν αἱ. ὡς μικροτέρας ἑαυτῶν ἀδελφὰς συνεχώρουν βλασφημεῖν εἰς τὸν κύριον, μόνοις δὲ τοῖς Χριστιανοῖς ἐπεβούλευον οὐ φέροντες ἀκούειν περὶ Χριστοῦ λόγων εὐσεβῶν Ath.*h.Ar*.31(p.200.13; M.25.728D); *ib*.19(p.192.32; 716B); *Const.App*.2.58.1; **3.** *heresy, false teaching* purporting to be Christian ἐν ὑμῖν οὐδεμία αἵ. κατοικεῖ· ἀλλ' οὐδὲ ἀκούετέ τινος πλέον εἴπερ Ἰησοῦ Χριστοῦ λαλοῦντος ἐν ἀληθείᾳ Ign.*Eph*.6.2; μόνῃ τῇ Χριστιανῇ τροφῇ χρῆσθε, ἀλλοτρίας δὲ βοτάνης ἀπέχεσθε, ἥτις ἐστὶν αἵ. id.*Trall*.6.1; ὁ εἰς αἱ. ὑποπεσὼν 'διέρχεται δι' ἐρημίας ἀνύδρου' Clem.*str*.1.19(p.61.23; M.8.812C); αἱ. ἀθέων Or.*Cels*.2.3(p.130.14; M.11.800C); εὐαγγέλιον ἀληθὲς κρύφα διαπεμφθῆναι εἰς ἐπανόρθωσιν τῶν ἐσομένων αἱ. *Hom.Clem*.2.17; τὸ τῆς αἱ. ἰοβόλον Cyr.H.*catech*.4.4; τῆς αἱ. βασιλεὺς Κωνστάντιος Ath.*h.Ar*.45(p.209.18; M.25.748D); τὰς μὲν αἱ. ἀναθέματι ἀναθεματίσωμεν id.*syn*.9(p.236.26; M.26.696A); id.*Ar*.1.7(M.26.25B); ὡς ζιζάνιον γέγονεν ἡ κακοῦργος αἵ. τῶν χριστομάχων *ib*.2.34(220B); *ib*.1.53(121C); caused by Devil or demons ἐγὼ Ἀπάτη· ἀπάτην πλέκω καὶ κακίστας αἱ. ἐνθυμίζω *T.Sal*.8.5(p.32.8; M.122.1328C); of Devil ὁ πατὴρ τῆς Ἀρειανῆς αἱ. Ath.*Ar*.2.73(M.26.301C); ὁ διάβολος...ἐπεγείρας ὑμῖν ...αἱ. *Const.App*.6.55; caused by over-curious speculation, Gr.Nyss.*hom.11 in Cant*.(M.44.1013C); exeg. Ps.1:1 σοφοῦ...ἀνδρὸς... 'καθέδραν λοιμῶν' τὰς αἱ. ἐκλαμβάνοντος Clem.*str*.2.15(p.149.7; M.8.1005B); Jo.16:33 ἐγὼ νενίκηκα τὸν κόσμον· ἀντὶ τοῦ, πᾶσαν πεπλανημένην αἵ. ἤλεγξα Ammon.*Jo*.1:5(M.85.1393D); ref. parables of dragnet and tares καὶ γὰρ ἐκεῖ οἱ μὲν σῴζονται, οἱ δὲ ἀπόλλυνται· ἀλλ' ἐκεῖ διὰ πονηρῶν δογμάτων αἵ. ... οὗτοι δὲ διὰ βίου πονηρίαν Chrys.*hom.47.2 in Mt*.(7.490A); of Christ's teaching, acc. Jews, *A.Phil*.15(p.8.14).

αἱρεσιώτης, ὁ, *heretic*, Just.*dial*.80.4(M.6.664C); Eus.*e.th*.1.1(p.63.13; M.24.832A); πονηροῖς ἀνθρώποις, μᾶλλον δὲ...θηρίοις ἀνθρωποειδέσιν, ἐθνικοῖς καὶ Ἰουδαϊσταῖς καὶ αἱ. ἀθέοις *Const.App*.2.21.2.

αἱρετίζ-ω, [fut. -ήσω, Jo.Mosch.*prat*.144(M.87.3005D)]; **1.** *choose* ᾑρετίσατο τὴν ἀνθρωπίνην ἐνδύσασθαι σάρκα θεὸς ὢν Meth.*symp*.1.4(p.13.7; M.18.45A); ᾑρετίσατο ὁ ἀθάνατος σταυρωθῆναι διὰ σέ Mac.Aeg.*hom*.15.44(M.34.605C); Marc.Er.*opusc*.10.10(M.65.1136C); **2.** *hold* doctrines, of a sect ταῦτα...οἱ Σαδδουκαῖοι ~ουσιν Hipp.*haer*.9.29(p.263.2; M.16.3410A); **3.** intrans., *belong to a sect, be a heretic*, Max.*prol.Dion*.(M.4.20A); οὐ δέχεσθε τὰς τῶν πατέρων χρήσεις ἀλλ' ᾑρετίσασθε Anast.S.*hod*.10(M.89.180A).

αἱρετικός, **1.** adj., *heretical* βάπτισμα...αἱ. Clem.*str*.1.19(p.62.4; M.8.813A); comp. ἕτεροι...αἱ. τὴν φύσιν, Φρύγες τὸ γένος Hipp.*haer*.8.19(p.238.4; M.16.3366C); ἐν αἱ. συναγωγῇ Or.*sel.in Ex*.(M.12.285D); μηδαμοῦ γῆς αἱ. συστήματος μηδὲ σχισματικοῦ λειπομένου Eus.*v.C*.3.66(p.113.26; M.20.1144B); τὴν αἱ. πίστιν Gr.Nyss.*Eun*.1(1 p.52.18; M.45.281A); **2.** as subst., *heretic*, Iren.*haer*.3.3.4(M.7.852B); τοῖς πανσόφοις Ἑλλήνων μεριμνηταῖς, οἷς εὔχονται μαθητεύειν οἱ αἱ. Hipp.*haer*.4.15(p.49.9; M.16.3083A); μόνον γὰρ αἱ. τινες ἀναβαπτίζονται, ἐπειδὴ τὸ πρότερον οὐκ ἦν βάπτισμα Cyr.H.*procatech*.7; Juln.Imp.ap.Cyr.*Juln*.6(6².206A); τρώγλας δὲ οἶμαι καὶ κοίτας ἀσπίδων... τὰς τῶν ἀνοσίων αἱ. οἷον οἰκίας τε καὶ καταδύσεις, ἵνα μὴ λέγωμεν ἐκκλησίας Cyr.*Is*.2.1(2.201B).

αἱρετικῶς, *heretically* αἱ. πυνθάνεσθαι, πῶς οὖν δύναται ἀϊδίως εἶναι ὁ υἱός; Ath.*Ar*.2.32(M.26.216C).

*__αἱρετισμός__, ὁ, *heresy*, Geo.Laod.*ep.dogm*.ap.Epiph.*haer*.73.12(p.285.5; M.42.428A ἐρωτισμῷ); *ib*.73.14(p.287.11; 432A).

αἱρετιστής, ὁ, **1.** *member of a sect*; Jewish, Hipp.*haer*.9.18(p.256.8; M.16.3395A); ref. Greek philosophers τοὺς ἰδίους μόνον αἱ. ἔπεισαν Clem.*str*.6.18(p.518.4; M.9.400B); **2.** *partisan* ἀπέστειλέ με κύριος... τῆς ἐπαγγελίας αἱ. μηνυτὴν ἑρμηνευτήν Mont.ap.Epiph.*haer*.48.13(p.237.11; M.41.876B).

αἱρετός, *to be chosen, desirable* οὐαὶ τοῖς ἀκούσασιν τὰ ῥήματα ταῦτα καὶ παρακούσασιν· αἱρετώτερον ἦν αὐτοῖς τὸ μὴ γεννηθῆναι Herm.*vis*.4.2.6; ἡ ἀγάπη αὐτὴ δι' αὑτὴν αἱ. Clem.*str*.7.11(p.48.18; M.9.493A); ref. Jo.15:14 τί οὖν οὐχ αἱ. παθεῖν ὑπὲρ ταύτης τῆς φιλίας; Chrys.*hom.23.3 in Heb*.(12.215C).

*__αἱρετῶς__, *voluntarily, from choice* ἀρετὴ γὰρ θελητή, διὰ τὸ αἱ. καὶ αὐτοθελῶς τὸ ἀγαθὸν ποιεῖν ἡμᾶς, οὐχὶ ἀβουλήτως καὶ ἀναγκαστικῶς Ephr.3.432F = Jo.D.*virt*.(M.95.96D).

αἱρ-έω, **A.** act.; **1.** *captivate* με ᾕρει σφόδρα ἡ τῶν ἀσωμάτων νόησις Just.*dial*.2.6(M.6.477C); Chrys.*hom.21.3 in Eph*.(11.162C); id.*hom.15.6 in Phil*.(11.319D); **2.** *befit* εὐσεβῶς κατὰ τὸν ~οῦντα Χριστιανισμῷ λόγον διεξάγων Eus.*m.P*.4.3(p.912.15; M.20.1473A).

B. med.; **1.** *undertake*, of S. Paul πόλεμον ἄσπονδον πρὸς Ἰουδαίους ἑλόμενος Chrys.*comm.in Gal*.1:1ff.(10.659D); **2.** *choose*, Herm.*sim*.5.6.6; Just.*1apol*.28.3(M.6.372C); ἡ δὲ τοῦ λόγου δύναμις ἔχουσα παρ' ἑαυτῇ τὸ προγνωστικὸν τὸ μέλλον ἀποβαίνειν οὐ καθ' εἱμαρμένην τῇ δὲ τῶν ~ουμένων αὐτεξουσίῳ γνώμῃ Tat.*orat*.7(p.7.21;

M.6.820C); ∼ούμεθα μὲν τὸ καλόν, ἐκκλίνομεν δὲ τὸ αἰσχρόν Or.*princ.* 3.1.3(p.197.14; M.11.252A).

C. pass., *be overcome* ὁ ὠμοτύραννος ἄρχων τῆς ἀκρασίας ᾑρέθη Meth.*symp.*10.1(p.122.14; M.18.193A).

αἴρω, v. ἀείρω.

αἴσθησις, ἡ, A. *sense perception, sensation*; **1.** def. ἔστι δὲ ἡ αἴ. οὐκ ἀλλοίωσις, ἀλλὰ διάγνωσις ἀλλοιώσεως. ἀλλοιοῦται μὲν γὰρ τὰ αἰσθητήρια, διακρίνει δὲ τὴν ἀλλοίωσιν ἡ αἴ. καλεῖται δὲ πολλάκις αἴ. καὶ τὰ αἰσθητήρια. ἔστι δὲ αἴ. ἀντίληψις τῶν αἰσθητῶν. δοκεῖ δὲ οὗτος ὁ ὅρος οὐκ αὐτῆς εἶναι τῆς αἰ., ἀλλὰ τῶν ἔργων αὐτῆς. διὸ καὶ οὕτως ὁρίζονται τὴν αἴ. πνεῦμα νοερὸν ἀπὸ τοῦ ἡγεμονικοῦ ἐπὶ τὰ ὄργανα τεταμένον...Πλάτων δὲ τὴν αἴ. λέγει ψυχῆς καὶ σώματος κοινωνίαν πρὸς τὰ ἐκτός Nemes.*nat.hom.*6(M.40.636B–637A); dist. from five senses ἔστι δὲ αἰσθητήρια μὲν πέντε· αἴ. δὲ μία, ἡ ψυχική, ἡ γνωρίζουσα διὰ τῶν αἰσθητηρίων τὰ ἐν αὐτοῖς γινόμενα πάθη *ib.* (636A); **2.** in induction κατὰ τὴν αἴ. δὲ ἐκ τοῦ καθ' ἕκαστα κεφαλαιοῦται τὸ καθόλου. ἀρχὴ γὰρ τῆς ἐπαγωγῆς ἡ αἴ. Clem.*str.*8.6(p.90.25f.; M.9.584A); **3.** rel. to νοῦς, ψυχή, etc. τῆς ἡμετέρας ψυχῆς οὐδὲν τοῦ σώματος ἔρημον, ἀλλ' ὅπου αἴ. ἐκεῖ καὶ ψυχή, καὶ ἐπὶ πᾶν φθάνει τὸ σῶμα Or.*fr.18 in Jer.*23:24(p.206.27; M.13.572D); νοῦς...καὶ αἴ., οὕτως ἀπ' ἀλλήλων διακριθέντα, τῶν ἰδίων ὅρων ἐντὸς εἱστήκεισαν Gr. Naz.*or.*45.7(M.36.629D); αἴ. δὲ πένταθλον αὐτῷ χαρισάμενος [sc. God] καὶ νοῦν τὸν τῆς ψυχῆς ἡνίοχον ταῖς αἰ. ἐπιστήσας *Const.App.*7.34. 6; Lit.*ib.*8.12.17; τὴν...νοερὰν οὐσίαν δεκτικὴν τοῦ πνεύματος...θεὸς ἐδημιούργησεν· τὴν δὲ αἴ. καὶ τὰ αἰσθητά, εἰς χρῆσιν αὐτῆς παρήγαγεν Thal.*cent.*4.13(M.91.1460B); ἡ μὲν αἴ. ἀντιλαμβάνεται τῶν ὄντων κατὰ ἀθρόαν μόρφωσιν· ὁ δὲ νοῦς ἐφάπτεται, τουτέστιν ἀντιλαμβάνεται τῶν ὄντων ἑτέρῳ τρόπῳ, καὶ οὐχ οἵῳ ἡ αἴ. περὶ μὲν οὖν τὸ σωματικὸν ἢ τὸ πνευματικόν, ἢ ἐν τῷ τὰς αἰ. εἶναι καὶ πρώην ἔφημεν, τὸ παθητικὸν καὶ μορφωτικόν ἐστι κίνημα, τὸ δὲ κριτικὸν καὶ ἀντιληπτικόν, τῇ ψυχῇ καὶ τῷ νῷ δοτέον Max.*schol.d.n.*1.5(M.4.201B); **4.** in souls after death εἰ εἰς ἀναισθησίαν ἐχώρει, ἕρμαιον ἂν ἦν τοῖς ἀδίκοις πᾶσιν. ἀλλ'...αἴ. πᾶσι γενομένοις μένει καὶ κόλασις αἰωνία ἀπόκειται Just. *1apol.*18.2(M.6.356A); νεκρομαντεῖαι...καὶ πάρεδροι καὶ τὰ γινόμενα ὑπὸ τῶν ταῦτα εἰδότων πεισάτωσαν ὑμᾶς, ὅτι καὶ μετὰ θάνατον ἐν αἰ. εἰσὶν αἱ ψυχαί *ib.*18.3(356A); *ib.*20.4(357C); τὰ σώματα...ἀδίκων ἐν αἰ. αἰωνίᾳ μετὰ τῶν...δαιμόνων εἰς τὸ αἰώνιον πῦρ πέμψει *ib.*52.3(405A); τὸ γὰρ κολαζόμενον...ἐν αἰ. ὃν ζῇ, κἂν πάσχειν λέγηται Clem.*str.*5.14 (p.386.9; M.9.133B); **5.** in angels and demons τοὺς ἀγγέλους εἰδέναι... τὰ ἐπὶ τῆς γῆς, οὐ κατ' αἰ. αὐτὰ γινώσκοντας, αἰσθητά γε ὄντα, κατ' οἰκείαν δὲ τοῦ θεοειδοῦς νοῦ δύναμιν Dion.Ar.*d.n.*7.2(M.3.869C); πάσας τὰς τῶν ἀλόγων ζῴων αἰ. τε καὶ πολυμερείας εἰς τὰς ἀΰλους τῶν οὐρανίων οὐσιῶν νοήσεις...ἀνάγοντες id.*c.h.*15.8(M.3.337B); δαίμονες οὐκ ἀθάνατοι οὐδὲ μὴν θνητοί (οὐδὲ γὰρ αἰ., ἵνα καὶ θανάτου, μετειλήφασιν) Clem.*prot.*10(p.74.13; M.8.220A); **6.** in rel. to God and doctrines of faith; **a.** sense perception as basis of faith (Aristotelian influence) Θεόφραστος δὲ τὴν αἴ. ἀρχὴν εἶναι πίστεώς φησιν Clem. *str.*2.2(p.118.2; M.8.940B); ἡ μὲν αἴ. ἐπιβάθρα τῆς ἐπιστήμης, ἡ πίστις δὲ διὰ τῶν αἰσθητῶν ὁδεύσασα ἀπολείπει τὴν ὑπόληψιν, πρὸς δὲ τὰ ἀψευδῆ σπεύδει καὶ εἰς τὴν ἀλήθειαν καταμένει *ib.*2.4(p.119.24; 944C); sensations echoes of divine wisdom, Dion.Ar.*d.n.*7.2(M.3. 868C); **b.** theol. truths beyond sense perception, Ath.*decr.*24(p.19. 32; M.25.457B); τὸ ὁμοούσιον ἀκούοντες ὑπερβαίνειν ὀφείλομεν πᾶσαν αἴ. id.*syn.*42(p.268.2; M.26.768A); ἀποτιθέντας...πάσας ἁπλῶς τὰς αἰ. ἀνιέναι ἐπὶ τὸν πατέρα *ib.*51(p.275.24; 785B); τὸ μὴ δεῖν τὸν εὐφρονοῦντα τῷ προφανεῖ τῆς αἰ. λόγῳ συμμάχῳ χρῆσθαι κατὰ τῆς πάντων ἀφανοῦς αἰτίας Dion.Ar.*d.n.*6.2(M.3.857A); hence it has no place in worship, Clem.*str.*5.5(p.344.13; M.9.49B); nor in spiritual life εἴ τις πρὸς τὴν αἴ. βλέποι...ἄγευστος τῆς θείας εὐφροσύνης διαβιώσεται...διὰ τοῦτο ἡ ψυχή, ὅταν μόνῃ τῇ θεωρίᾳ τοῦ ὄντος εὐφραίνηται, πρὸς οὐδὲν ἐγρήγορε τῶν ἐνεργουμένων καθ' ἡδονὴν δι' αἰ. Gr.Nyss.*hom.10 in Cant.*(M.44.993Cf.); **7.** met. ψυχὴ γὰρ αὐτοῦ [sc. ἐπισκόπου] καὶ αἴ. εἶναι ὀφείλετε [sc. deacons] *Const.App.*3.19.7.

B. *organ of sense perception, one of the senses*; **1.** place of the senses in human life; **a.** before Fall ἦν [sc. ἄνθρωπος] ἐν τρυφῇ τοῦ παραδείσου...ἔχων σώας τὰς αἰ. Dor.*doct.*1.1(M.88.1617B); **b.** after Fall; closely related to sin, Clem.*paed.*2.8(p.197.20; M.8.473B) cit. s. ψυχή; πύλαι δὲ ψυχῆς αἱ αἰ., αἵτινες ἁμαρτανούσης κατακλύζονταί τε πάθεσι καὶ γίνονται γήϊναι Or.*fr.52 in Lam.*2:9(p.257.26; M.13.636B); Meth.*res.*2.7(p.342.5; M.41.1173B); ὑπὸ τῶν αἰ. ... τὰ πάθη κινοῦνται Thal.*cent.*3.34(M.91.1452A); though they are not the only source of sin, Clem.*str.*2.11(p.139.18; M.8.985B); **c.** hence they must be dominated by νοῦς and ψυχή, Ath.*gent.*31(M.25.61C) cit. s. νοῦς; τῶν αἰ. ἐν τῷ σώματι ὡς λύρας ἡρμοσμένων, ὅταν ὁ ἐπιστήμων νοῦς αὐτῶν ἡγεμονεύῃ· τότε διακρίνει ἡ ψυχή, καὶ οἶδεν ὃ ποιεῖ *ib.*(64A); ἀθορύβου γὰρ οὔσης τῆς ψυχῆς, ἀταράχους εἶχε καὶ τὰς ἔξωθεν αἰ. id. *v.Anton.*67(M.26.940A); κρατῶν τῆς αἰ. ἀσφαλίζου καὶ τὴν μνήμην· αἱ γὰρ διὰ τῆς αἰ. προλήψεις διὰ τῆς μνήμης ἀνακινοῦσι τὰ πάθη Thal. *cent.*4.16(M.91.1460C); and calmed by ἡσυχία, *ib.*3.38(1452B); μοναχός ἐστιν...φυλακὴ αἰσθήσεων ἀνελλιπής Jo.Clim.*scal.*1(M.88.633C); **2.** in allegorical exegesis: five senses represented by five husbands of Samaritan woman (Jo.4:17f.), Or.*Jo.*13.9(p.233.20; M.14.412C); by the wise virgins ἡ γὰρ πεντάφωτος ἡμῶν ὡς ἀληθῶς λαμπὰς ἡ σάρξ ἐστιν, ἣν ἡ ψυχὴ βαστάζουσα...παρίσταται Χριστῷ τῇ ἡμέρᾳ τῆς ἀναστάσεως, παραφαίνουσα διὰ πασῶν τῶν αἰ. ... λαμπρὰν τὴν πίστιν Meth.*symp.*6.3(p.67.14; M.18.117Af.); **3.** spiritual senses of soul ἡ ἀπὸ τῶν αἰσθητῶν ἐπὶ τὰς καλουμένας θείας αἰ. ἄνοδος Or.*Jo.*10.40 (24; p.218.7; M.14.385C); ὥσπερ γὰρ ἐπὶ τοῦ σώματος διάφοροι αἰ. εἰσίν...οὕτως κατὰ τὰς λεγομένας ὑπὸ τοῦ Σολομῶνος θείας αἰ. (cf.Sap. 7.22ff.) ἄλλη μέν τις ἂν εἴη ⟨ἡ⟩ ὁρατικὴ τῆς ψυχῆς δύναμις καὶ θεωρητική, ἄλλη δὲ ἡ γευστικὴ καὶ ἀντιληπτικὴ τῆς ποιότητος τῶν νοητῶν τροφῶν *ib.*20.43(33; p.386.24f.; 676B); id.*Cels.*7.39(p.190.2ff.; M.11. 1476C); cf. ἡ θεία αἴ., καθὼς ὁ Σολομὼν ὀνομάζει, τῶν σωματικῶν ἀρωμάτων τοῦ νόμου, προστίθησι τὴν ἄϋλον...εὐωδίαν Gr.Nyss.*hom.9 in Cant.*(M.44.957C); Max.*ambig.*(M.91.1248B); vitiated by sin, Meth. *symp.*4.2(p.47.5; M.18.88C); employed in praising God τῷ τῆς θρησκείας θεῷ διὰ τῶν ἐντὸς αἰ. τῆς ἑκάστου δι' ἐκφωνητηρίων... ὑμνούντων Const.*or.s.c.*1(p.154.8; M.20.1233A); likened to the ten virgins αἱ γὰρ πέντε τῆς ψυχῆς αἰ., σύνεσις, γνῶσις, διάκρισις, ὑπομονή, ἔλεος, ἂν τὴν ἄνωθεν χάριν καὶ τὸν ἁγιασμὸν τοῦ πνεύματος δέξωνται, καὶ φρόνιμοι τῇ ἀληθείᾳ παρθένοι ἔσονται· εἰ δὲ τῇ φύσει ἑαυτῶν ἐγκαταλειφθεῖεν, μωραὶ τῷ ὄντι εὑρίσκονται Mac.Aeg.*elev.*4 (M.34.893A); in ecstasy ἤκουσε τῇ τῆς καρδίας αἰ. Nil.*Magn.*27(M. 79.1004B); **4.** senses in rel. to God; **a.** God above and outside sense, Clem.*str.*7.7(p.28.29; M.9.453A); οἰκεῖον...θεότητος, αἱ νοεραὶ φύσεις...ξένον δὲ παντάπασιν, ὅσαι ὑπὸ τὴν αἴ. Gr.Naz.*or.*45.6(M.36. 629C); being πάσης αἰ. ὑπεριδρυμένος Dion.Ar.*d.n.*7.2(M.3.868D); therefore τῇ περὶ τὰ μυστικὰ θεάματα συντόνῳ διατριβῇ καὶ τὰς αἰ. ἀπόλειπε id.*myst.*1(M.3.997B); **b.** assuming senses in Inc. χωρὶς γάρ τοι γάμου σύλληψις...καὶ αἰωνίου φύσεως ἀρχὴ χρόνιος καὶ νοητῆς οὐσίας αἴσθησις Const.*or.s.c.*11(p.168.26; M.20.1265A); ὁ τοῦ θεοῦ λόγος λαμβάνει ἑαυτῷ σῶμα...καὶ τὰς αἰ. πάντων ἀνθρώπων προσλαμβάνει Ath.*inc.*15.2(M.25.121D); *ib.*16.1(124B); **5.** *sense world,* which Christ entered, Clem.*str.*5.6(p.353.30; M.9.68A).

C. *intellectual perception, understanding*; esp. of understanding what is good or divine, *Ep.Lugd.*ap.Eus.*h.e.*5.1.48(M.20.428A) cit. s. νυμφικός; ἄφρων δὲ ἢ ἀκόλαστος ἄνθρωπος οὔτ' ἂν αἴσθησιν ἀγαθοῦ σχοίη οὔτ' ἂν κτήσεως τύχοι Clem.*paed.*3.6(p.257.20; M.8. 605C); ἡ ἀκοὴ ἐν ἡμῖν...οὐ διὰ τῆς σωματικῆς δυνάμεως ἔχει τὴν ἀντίληψιν, ἀλλὰ διά τινος ψυχικῆς αἰ. id.*str.*7.7(p.28.26; M.9.453A); ὁ δὲ καθαρὰν ἔχων τὴν διαπνοήν, καὶ διὰ τῆς αἰ. τοῦ θείου λόγου δυνάμενος ὀπίσω αὐτοῦ εἰς ὀσμὴν μύρων αὐτοῦ δραμεῖν Or.*schol. in Cant.*7:5(M.17.281D); Const.ap.Eus.*v.C.*2.48(p.61.25; M.20.1025B); Mac.Aeg.*hom.*14.2(M.34.572A); εὐξώμεθα...ἐν πληροφορίᾳ καὶ αἰ. μεταλαβεῖν τοῦ ἁγίου πνεύματος *ib.*37.7(753D); Chrys.*stat.*4.2(2.52C); βίος ἡσυχαζόντων...κατὰ συνείδησιν καὶ αἴ. γινέσθω Jo.Clim.*scal.*27 (M.88.1113A); spiritual opp. philos. understanding, exeg. Pr.2:3ff. πρὸς ἀντιδιαστολὴν τῆς κατὰ φιλοσοφίαν αἰ. εἴρηκεν ὁ προφήτης, ἣν... ἐξερευνᾶν διδάσκει εἰς τὴν ἐπὶ τὴν θεοσέβειαν προκοπήν, ἀντέθηκεν οὖν αὐτῇ τὴν ἐν θεοσεβείᾳ αἴ. Clem.*str.*1.4(p.17.24,26; M.8.717B).

D. *right reason, good sense* ἆρα οὐδεμία ἐστὶν αἴ. οὐδὲ κατὰ χάριν τῆς κοινῆς ἁπάντων φύσεως, εἴ γε τῶν τοῦ νόμου προσταγμάτων ἠμελήσαμεν; Const.ap.Ath.*apol.sec.*61(p.141.19; M.25.360C); τῶν κἂν βραχεῖαν αἴ. ἐχόντων id.ap.Ath.*decr.*16(p.13.18; M.25.'449'(441)C); τίς...ὀλίγην αἴ. ἔχων ἀνέξεται τούτων; id.ap.Ath.*syn.*32(p.260.12; M.26.749B).

E. *sense* of scripture κατ' αἴ. πνευματικήν Or.*Cant.*1(p.90.30; M.13.85D); τοιούτους ὄνους, οὓς γράφειν οἶδε τὸ πνεῦμα τὸ ἅγιον· οὐχ οὓς σωματικὴ περιγράφειν πέφυκεν αἴ., ἀλλ' οὓς ὑποδέχεται νοῦς καθαρός Max.*qu.Thal.*55(M.90.557D); id.*cap.*4.76(M.90.1337B).

αἰσθητήριον, τό, 1. *organ of sense* (usu. plur.); role in Christian life πάντα τὰ ὑπάρχοντα αὐτῷ αἰ. δοὺς τῷ θεῷ, ῥύσεται ἑαυτὸν ἐκ τῶν ἡτοιμασμένων τῷ διαβόλῳ...τιμωριῶν Or.*exp.in Pr.*6:30(M.17.180D); περὶ τὴν ἄσκησιν τῆς ἁγνείας...τὰ αἰ. τηρεῖν ἑαυτοῦ καθαρά Meth. *symp.*11(p.130.23; M.18.208A); οὐκοῦν ἀνάγκη τὰ αἰ., ὡς πύλας ἀνοίγειν τῆς πόλεως. ἀνάγκη δὲ μὴ συγχωρεῖν ἐν τῇ τῶν ἀναγκαίων ἀνοίξει, συνεισέρχεσθαι τὰ τοὺς πολεμίους θέλοντα ‡Max.*cap.al.*230 (M.90.1456C); to be closed to external things in prayer εἰσέρχεται εἰς τὸ ἑαυτοῦ 'ταμεῖον',...'τὴν θύραν' τῶν αἰ. ἀποκλείσας, ἵνα μὴ ἕλκηται ὑπὸ τῶν αἰσθήσεων Or.*or.*20.2(p.344.23; M.20.480B); senses hallowed by post-baptismal chrismation, Cyr.H.*catech.*21.3; **2.** *intellectual faculty*; enabling man esp. to distinguish between truth and error, good and evil, Clem.*str*.7.16(p.66.4; M.9.529A); developed by Christian life διὰ τὴν ἕξιν τὰ αἰ. γυμνάσαντα πρὸς διάκρισιν καλοῦ καὶ κακοῦ Or.*Cels*.4.50(p.323.10; M.11.1109B); τὸ κριτικὸν αἰ. Thdr.Heracl.*Is*.46:12(M.18.1345B); Cyr.H.*catech*.4.3; †Bas.*Is*.172(1.503B; M.30.405A); εἰς ὑπόμνησιν ἐλθὼν τῆς αἰσχρᾶς... πράξεως, τῷ ἐρρῶσθαι αὐτῷ τὸ τῆς ψυχῆς αἰ. †Bas.*hom.in Ps*.37 (1.367A; M.30.93C); ἔχωμεν τὰ αἰ. τῆς ψυχῆς γεγυμνασμένα πρὸς διάκρισιν καλοῦ τε καὶ κακοῦ, πῶς δὲ γεγυμνασμένα...τὰ αἰ.; ἀπὸ τῆς συνεχοῦς ἀκροάσεως, ἀπὸ τῆς τῶν γραφῶν ἐμπειρίας Chrys.*hom.8.4 in Heb*.(12.88E–89A); also capable of distinguishing between true and false doctrine, Alex.Al.*ep.Alex*.12(p.27.20; M.18.865C); **3.** myst., *spiritual organ* of the soul, though not always clearly dist. from 2 supra, development of 'spiritual senses' implying an advanced state of Christian life; exeg. 1Cor.3:2 ὡς οὖν ὁ ἀπόστολος δυνατὸς ἦν διδόναι τὸ βρῶμα...ἐκεῖνοι δὲ ἠδυνάτουν λαβεῖν αὐτό, διὰ τὸ ἀσθενῆ ἔτι καὶ ἀγύμναστα ἔχειν τὰ τῆς ψυχῆς αἰ. τῆς πρὸς θεὸν γυμνασίας Iren.*haer*.4.38.2(M.7.1107A); ὑγιαίνοντος κατὰ τὰ θεῖα αἰ. Or.*dial*.19(p.158.21); needing purification καταтρυφᾶν δὲ τοῦ κυρίου δυνήσεται ὁ τῆς ψυχῆς τὰ αἰ. κεκαθαρισμένος, ὡς δύνασθαι ἐσθίειν τὸν ζῶντα ἄρτον...πίνειν τε τὸ σωτήριον αὐτοῦ αἷμα Eus.*Ps*.36:2ff.(M.23.325C); may be atrophied by unbelief, Gr.Nyss.*Pss.titt*.B 13(M.44.565D); but 'sweetened' and developed by the 'fruit' of the Cross, id.*hom.4 in Cant*.(M.44.844A); by practice of virtue τὸ μέλι ποιούμενος, ὅταν ἐν τῷ ἰδίῳ καιρῷ ὁ καρπὸς τῆς ἀρετῆς καταγλυκαίνῃ τὰ τῆς ψυχῆς αἰ. *ib.10*(988D); ἀμπελών ἐστιν...ἡ πρὸς τὸ θεῖον ὁμοίωσις ...καρπὸς ἡ καθαρότης...καταγλυκαίνων ἐν ἁγνείᾳ τὰ τῆς ψυχῆς αἰ. *ib.2*(800C).

αἰσθητικός, **A.** *of sense perception, sensitive, sentient*; **1.** def. ἄλλο αἰσθητόν, καὶ ἄλλο αἰ. ... αἰσθητὸν δὲ τὸ αἰσθήσει ὑποπίπτον· αἰ. δὲ αὐτὸ τὸ αἰσθανόμενον ζῷον...αἰσθητὸν δὲ ὁ λίθος...αἰ. δὲ ὁ Στέφανος Melet.*nat.hom*.synops.(M.64.1144D–1145B); **2.** in def. of ζῷον and ἄνθρωπος: ἔστι...τὸ ζῷον οὐσία ἔμψυχος αἰ. ... εἰ τοίνυν ἔμψυχον τὸ ζῷον, ἡ ψυχὴ δὲ φύσις αἰ., δῆλον ὡς αἰ. ἤδη τὸ ἔμψυχον Clem.*str*.8.4(p.86.15ff.; M.9.573B); τρίτη δὲ οὐσία ἔμψυχος αἰ., τὸ ζῷον, ὁ ἵππος· τετάρτη δὲ οὐσία ἔμψυχος αἰ. λογική, ὁ ἄνθρωπος id.*fr*.38(p.219.28f.; M.9.769C); **3.** opp. λογικός: τῆς αἰ. ἢ τῆς λογικῆς...κρίσεως Athenag.*res*.15(p.66.3; M.6.1004B); Or.*Jo*.1.25(24; p.31.2; M.14.68B); ref. Christ's body λογικῆς δυνάμεως αἰ. οἰκητήριον Eus.*l.C*.14(p.241.30; M.20.1409A); τὰ λογικὰ τῶν αἰ. ὑπερέχει Max.*schol.d.n*.6.3(M.4.340A); Dion.Ar.*d.n*.5.3(M.3.817B); *ib*.6.3(857B); opp. νοητικός, Or.*fr.13 in Jo*.1:18(p.494.25); Dion.Ar.*d.n*.5.1(816B); **4.** sinners disciplined through sentient faculty, Clem.*str*.7.2(p.6.10; M.9.409A).

B. *perceptible* to the senses; of glory in the face of Moses, compared with interior glory of S. Stephen, Chrys.*hom.7.5 in 2Cor*.(10.487C).

C. *perceptive* (intellectually) φιλόσοφοι οἱ εἰς τὴν οἰκείαν συναίσθησιν πνεύματι αἰ. συνασκηθέντες Clem.*str*.6.17(p.511.4; M.9.385A).

D. *intelligible* ὁ βασιλεὺς ὁ ἅγιος...οὗ τὸ ὄνομα ἔφθασεν εἰς τὰ θηρία τῆς ἐρήμου καὶ ἡσύχασαν καὶ αἰ. φωνῇ ᾔνεσάν σε *A.Phil*.132 (p.64.1).

αἰσθητικῶς, **1. a.** *by means of the senses* οἷον αἰ. καταλαμβανόμενον Clem.*paed*.1.10(p.143.6; M.8.357A); αἰ. τὰ αἰσθητὰ γινώσκειν id.*fr*.48(p.224.18f.)ap.Max.*ambig*.(M.91.1085B); opp. γνωστικῶς, Dion.Ar.*d.n*.1.5(M.3.593D); *ib*.4.4(700B); **b.** *perceptibly* (i.e. to the senses) κατάβασίν...τινος καὶ αἰ. ἔστιν ἰδεῖν, ὅτε σῶμα τυγχάνει Or.*fr.20 in Jo*.(p.500.22); comp., Chrys.*hom.7.5 in 2Cor*.(10.487B); **2.** *with feeling* ὢ πόσον κινεῖ πάθος ἐν τοῖς αἰ. ἐπαΐουσιν 'ἀμπελῶνα ἐμὸν οὐκ ἐφύλαξα' Gr.Nyss.*hom.2 in Cant*.(M.44.800B).

αἰσθητός, *sensible, perceived by the senses*, def. ὁ Πλάτων... διδάσκει, τὸ δὲ οὐκ ὄν, τὸ αἰ., [γενητὸν] ἀρχόμενον εἶναι καὶ παυόμενον Athenag.*leg*.19.1(M.6.929A); cf. κάτεισιν ἡμῶν ὁ νοῦς ἐκ τῶν μεριστῶν, τουτέστι τῶν αἰ. Max.*schol.d.n*.7.2(M.4.345A);

A. in gen., Or.*hom.5.14 in Jer*.(p.43.19; M.13.316A); *ib*.6.2(p.48.15; 324C); αἰ. κόσμος Meth.*symp*.7.2(p.73.6; M.18.128B); ἀρχαὶ πάσης αἰ. οὐσίας Ath.*gent*.42(M.25.84C); γάμοι αἰ. Chrys.*catech*.2.2 (2.237C); id.*hom.26.1 in Jo*.(8.150A); αἰ. εὐωδίαι Dion.Ar.*c.h*.1.3 (M.3.121D).

B. opp. mental and spiritual; **1.** in gen., opp. νοητός, q.v., Athenag.*leg*.19.1(M.6.929A); βοήθειαν καὶ νοητὴν καὶ αἰ. Clem.*str*.3.1(p.196.10; M.8.1101A); μὴ τοῖς αἰ. προσανέχωμεν, ἐπὶ δὲ τὰ νοητὰ μετίωμεν [acc. teaching of Moses and Pythagoras] *ib*.5.5(p.344.10; M.9.49 B); *ib*.6.16(p.501.6; 361A); δυνατὸν δὲ λαβεῖν εἰκονικὸν φῶς τὸ αἰ.... ἀληθινὸν δὲ φῶς τὸ νοητὸν Or.*fr.6 in Jo*.(p.488.16); Cyr.H.*catech*.1.4; θεόν...τὸν βασιλέα πάσης αἰ. καὶ νοητῆς φύσεως *Const.App*.7.42.3; *Lit.ib*.8.12.7 al.; Dion.Ar.*c.h*.15.5(M.3.333C); id.*e.h*.1.1.2(M.3.373B); as title of one of his prob. fictitious treatises περὶ νοητῶν τε καὶ αἰ. *ib*.2.3.2(397C); opp. νοερός, id.*c.h*.2.4(144C); ref. Plato's 'ideas' ὁ Πλάτων ζῴων ἰδέας ἐν τῷ νοητῷ ἀπολείπειν κόσμῳ καὶ τὰ εἴδη τὰ αἰ. κατὰ τὰ γένη δημιουργεῖν τὰ νοητά Clem.*str*.5.14 (p.388.8; 140A); τὰ αἰ. πάντα, εἰκόνες εἰσὶ...τῶν θείων ἰδεῶν Max.*schol.d.n*.7.3(M.4.352A); **2.** ref. OT, opp. spiritual realities of NT; sacrifices αἰ. θυσίαι Or.*Jo*.10.24(16; p.196.8; M.14.349A); id.*fr.8 in Jo*.(p.490.5); μίμημα τῆς ἐκκλησίας ἐκελεύοντο δαιδάλλειν Ἑβραῖοι τὴν σκηνήν, ἵν' ἔχοιεν διὰ τῶν αἰ. τὴν εἰκόνα τῶν θείων...πραγμάτων Meth.*symp*.5.7(p.62.1; M.18.109B); μέγα ἐδόκει εἶναι [sc. δόξα Μωυσέως], ἐπειδὴ αἰ. ἦν δόξα...ἡ δὲ τῆς καινῆς νοητή Chrys.*hom.7.1 in 2Cor*.(10.479E); **3.** ref. exeg., lit. sense dist. from spiritual αἰ. εὐαγγέλιον νοητοῦ καὶ πνευματικοῦ τῇ ἐπινοίᾳ διακρίνοντες...πρόκειται τὸ αἰ. εὐαγγέλιον μεταλαβεῖν εἰς πνευματικόν· τίς γὰρ ἡ διήγησις τοῦ αἰ., εἰ μὴ μεταλαμβάνοιτο εἰς πνευματικόν; Or.*Jo*.1.8(10; p.13.12ff.; M.14.37C); exeg. Jo.13:30 συμβολικῶς τότε ἡ αἰ. νὺξ ἦν *ib*.32.24(16; p.468.27; 809C); αἱ ἐπαγγελίαι νοηταί εἰσι δι' αἰ. ἐπαγγελλόμεναι id.*princ*.4.3.6(21; p.333.7; M.11.388A); κατὰ τὸ αἰ. *literally* μὴ ὑπολάβῃ τις ἡμᾶς...λέγειν...ὅτι τὰ περὶ τοῦ σωτῆρος γεγραμμένα κατὰ τὸ αἰ. οὐκ ἀληθεύεται *ib*.4.3.4(p.329.5; 384A); id.*hom.5.14 in Jer*.(p.43.20; M.13.316A); τὴν Σαμαρεῖτιν ἀφέλκων ὁ κύριος ἀπὸ τῶν αἰ. ... πνευματικῶς διανοεῖσθαι περὶ τοῦ θεοῦ Ath.*ep.Serap*.4.19(M.26.668A); ἔτι τοῖς αἰ. ἐνδιατρίβει ῥήμασι, διὰ τὸ μηδέπω δύνασθαι χωρῆσαι τῶν πνευματικῶν τὴν ἀκρίβειαν Chrys.*hom.32.2 in Jo*.(8.186B); αἰ. μὲν τὰ ῥήματα, πνευματικὰ δὲ τὰ νοήματα *ib.34.2*(197C); *ib.32.1*(185A); ἀκούσασα ὕδωρ ζῶν, ἐνόμισε περὶ αἰ. τοῦτο λέγεσθαι. ὕστερον δὲ μαθοῦσα ὅτι πνευματικὰ ἦν τὰ λεγόμενα *ib.32.2*(185D); **4.** in moral and religious spheres; **a.** ref. turning from sensible things to those of the mind, (Pythagorean) δοκεῖς κατόψεσθαί τι τῶν εἰς εὐδαιμονίαν συντελούντων, εἰ μὴ ταῦτα πρῶτον διδαχθείης, ἃ τὴν ψυχὴν ἀπὸ τῶν αἰ. περισπάσει; Just.*dial*.2.4(M.6.477B); ref. astronomy ἐπὶ τὰ νοητὰ μετατίθησιν ἀπὸ τῶν αἰ. Clem.*str*.6.11(p.477.19; M.9.312B); ἡ πρὸς τὰ νοητὰ οἰκείωσις...περιαγωγὴ τῷ γνωστικῷ ἀπὸ τῶν αἰ. *ib*.4.23(p.313.26; M.8.1357A); θείας ἐπινοίας κατασκευαζόμεναι...ἐκ τῶν αἰ. εἰς τὰ νοητά, μᾶλλον δὲ ἐκ τῶνδε εἰς τὰ ἅγια καὶ ἁγίων τὰ ἅγια μεταγούσης ἡμᾶς *ib*.6.11(p.474.24; M.9.308B); γυμνὸν αἰσθητῶν πνευματικόν Or.*Jo*.13.40(p.265.29; M.14.469A); ἡ δὲ αὔξησις ἡμῶν οὐκ ἄλλη τίς ἐστιν ἢ τὸ ἀφίστασθαι μὲν τῶν αἰ., εἰς αὐτὸν δὲ τὸν λόγον γενέσθαι Ath.*Ar*.3.52(M.26.432C); **b.** ref. things of sense leading to spiritual things ἡ πίστις δὲ διὰ τῶν αἰ. ὁδεύσασα ἀπολείπει τὴν ὑπόληψιν...καὶ εἰς τὴν ἀλήθειαν καταμένει Clem.*str*.2.4(p.119.25; M.8.944C); οἶμαι πᾶσαν τὴν εἰσαγομένην ψυχὴν εἰς τὴν διὰ τῶν γραφῶν ἐν Χριστῷ θεοσέβειαν ἀπὸ τῶν αἰ. ... ἀρχομένην...μετὰ τὸ ὡμιληκέναι τοῖς αἰ. ἀνακῦψαί τις...ἐπὶ τὰ νοητά Or.*Jo*.13.9(p.233.19,21; M.14.412C); *ib*.10.40(24; p.218.6; 385C) cit. s. αἴσθησις; id.*Cant*.3(p.220.31; M.13.181D); *ib*.3(p.230.27; 189D); Dion.Ar.*c.h*.1.3(M.3.124A) cit. s. ἀνάγω; ἡμεῖς δὲ αἰ. εἰκόσιν ἐπὶ τὰς θείας...ἀναγόμεθα θεωρίας id.*e.h*.1.1.2 (M.3.373B); φιλανθρωπίας αἰσθητοῖς τὰ νοητὰ...περιτιθείσης id.*d.n*.1.4 (M.3.592B); *ib*.4.11(708D) cit. s. νοῦς; **c.** esp. through liturgy and sacraments καὶ τὸ βάπτισμα οὖν διπλοῦν ἀναλόγως, τὸ μὲν αἰ. δι' ὕδατος, τοῦ αἰ. πυρὸς σβεστήριον, τὸ δὲ νοητὸν διὰ πνεύματος Clem.*exc.Thdot*.81.2(p.132.3ff.; M.9.696B); rejected by Ascodrutae οἱ τὰ αἰ. πάντῃ ἀναιροῦντες καὶ μήτε βαπτίσματι μήτε εὐχαριστίᾳ χρώμενοι Or.*or*.5.1(p.308.19; M.11.429B); Thdt.*haer*.1.10 (4.302); τῇ μὲν [sc. ἱεραρχίᾳ] κοινωνοῦσα ταῖς νοεραῖς θεωρίαις, τῇ δὲ ὅτι καὶ συμβόλοις αἰ. ποικίλλεται Dion.Ar.*e.h*.5.1.2(M.3.501D); θεώμεθα...αὐτὰ [sc. divine mysteries] διὰ τῶν...αἰ. συμβόλων id.*ep*.9.1(M.3.1104B).

C. ref. God and Christ; **1.** God without qualities perceptible to senses, Clem.*prot*.4(p.40.10f.; M.8.145A); ἡ πάντων αἰτία...οὔτε ἐπαφὴν αἰ. ἔχει...οὔτε αἰ. ἐστιν...οὔτε...αἰ. ὑποκειμένη συμπτώμασιν... οὔτε ἄλλο τι τῶν αἰ. οὔτε ἐστίν, οὔτε ἔχει Dion.Ar.*myst*.4(M.3.1040D); **2.** of Christ's human birth γενέσει αὐτοῦ τῇ αἰ. Clem.*str*.6.15(p.493.9; M.9.345A); γεγέννηται τὸ αἰ. αὐτοῦ σαρκίον *ib*.(p.496.6; 352A); **3.** of incarnate body opp. body of Church ὥσπερ δὲ ἐκεῖνο τὸ αἰ. τοῦ Ἰησοῦ σῶμα ἐσταύρωται...οὕτως τὸ ὅλον τῶν ἁγίων Χριστοῦ σῶμα Χριστῷ συνεσταύρωται καὶ νῦν οὐκέτι ζῇ Or.*Jo*.10.35(20; p.210.1; M.14.372B).

αἰσθητῶς, **1.** *with the senses, sensibly* αἰ. τὰ πάντα καταλήψεσθαι Clem.*str*.5.1(p.330.5; M.9.17A); οὐ γὰρ θεμιτὸν νομίζειν αἰ. ὁρᾶσθαι τὸ πνεῦμα Or.*fr.20 in Jo*.1:31(p.500.6); id.*princ*.4.2.1(8; p.306.4; M.11.357A); opp. νοητῶς, id.*hom.16.9 in Jer*.(p.141.13; M.13.449C); **2.** *in a literal sense, literally* οὐκ αἰ. βεβοηκότα Or.*Jo*.6.18(10; p.127.18; M.14.232C); οὐκ ἔστιν τι παράδοξον γενόμενον ἐν τῇ γραφῇ, ὃ μὴ ἔστι σημεῖον...ἑτέρου παρὰ τὸ αἰ. γεγενημένον *ib*.13.64(60; p.296.31; 521C); Meth.*symp*.3.1(p.27.16; M.18.61B); Eus.*d.e*.7.1(p.317.16; M.22.520A); **3.** *as accommodated to sense, so as to be grasped by the* senses αἰ. εἰπεῖν Dion.Ar.*c.h.*7.4(M.3.212B); id.*e.h.*4.3.5(M.3.480C); τὰ μὲν αἰ. ἱερὰ τῶν νοητῶν ἀπεικονίσματα *ib.*2.3.2(397C); liturg. διαγράφει γὰρ ἐν τούτοις αἰ., ὑπ' ὄψιν ἄγων Ἰησοῦν τὸν Χριστόν, τὴν νοητὴν ἡμῶν ὡς ἐν εἰκόσι ζωήν *ib.*3.3.12(444C).

αἴσιος, *auspicious*, hence *fitting*, *meet* ἄξιος εἶ ἐν πᾶσι καιροῖς ὑμνεῖσθαι φωναῖς αἰ. *Hymn.*10(*AGC* p.40.10, v.l. ὁσίαις).

***αἰσχημοσύνη**, ἡ, *indecency*, Clem.*paed.*2.6(M.8.453B; ἀσχ- p.188.15); Sophr.H.*v.Anast.*(M.92.1684B).

***αἰσχραίνω**, s.v.l., *defile* ἵνα μὴ αἰ. τὸ σῶμα *T.Aser* 4.4 (v.l. χράνῃ).

***αἰσχρόβιος**, *living shamefully*, *shameful*, *Orac.Sib.*3.189; *Hom. Clem.*11.13.

***αἰσχρογενής**, *basely born*; of Nest., †Cyr.*hom.div.*11(5^2.383A).

[*]**αἰσχροεργία**, ἡ, = αἰσχρουργία, *shameless conduct*, †Jo.Jej. *poenit.*(M.88.1904B).

αἰσχροκερδής, *sordidly greedy of gain* αἰ. ἐστιν οὐχ...ὁ καὶ τῶν μικρῶν κερδῶν ἐφιέμενος· ἀλλ' ὁ ἐκ πραγμάτων αἰσχρῶν καὶ λίαν ἀτόπων κέρδη συλλέγειν ἀνεχόμενος Thdt.*1Tim.*3:8(3.656).

***αἰσχροπάθεια**, ἡ, *submission to obscenity*, Pall.*h.Laus.*47(p.139.5; M.34.1201C); Nil.*epp.*2.167(M.79.281B).

***αἰσχροπραγία**, ἡ, *foul conduct*, Nil.*epp.*1.69(M.79.112C).

***αἰσχροπράγος**, *acting basely*, *foul* δαίμων Nil.*epp.*3.34(M.79.401C).

αἰσχρότης, ἡ, *disgraceful conduct*, Nil.*epp.*1.129(M.79.137C); of shameful thoughts ἐὰν αἰ. σπαρῇ ἐν τῇ καρδίᾳ σου καθημένου ἐν τῷ κελλίῳ σου Esaias *or.*6.7(p.24; cf.M.40.1116C).

***αἰσχρούργημα**, τό, *obscene action*; of Gnostics, Epiph.*haer.* 26.4(p.281.2; M.41.337C); *ib.*26.15(p.295.25; 357A); in Eleusinian mysteries, id.*exp.fid.*10(p.510.14; M.42.800B).

αἰτ-έω, **1.** *ask*, *beg*; of petitionary prayer, exeg. Mt.7:8 ἀλη-θεύεται τό, πᾶς ὁ ~ῶν λαμβάνει, μὴ ἀριθμουμένων εἰς πάντας τοὺς ~ουμένους τῶν κακῶς ~ούντων (ὁ γὰρ κακῶς ~ῶν οὐκ ~εῖται) Didym.*Ac.*2:21(M.39.1656C); **2.** *inquire* ~οῦμαι...πόθεν ἥκεν; *T. Abr.*A 2(p.78.26).

αἴτημα, τό, *thing demanded*, *prey* δαιμόνων αἰτήματα ἐγένεσθε *Hom.Clem.*10.6.

αἴτησις, ἡ, *request*, *demand*, of petitionary prayer following praise, thanksgiving, and confession τὴν περὶ τῶν μεγάλων καὶ ἐπουρανίων αἰ., ἰδίων τε καὶ καθολικῶν, καὶ περί τε οἰκείων καὶ φιλτά-των Or.*or.*33.1(p.401.23; M.11.560A); in def. of prayer, v. εὐχή.

αἰτία, ἡ, **A.** *guilt*, *blame*, physical *taint*, of blisters caused by a magician but healed by baptism εὑρέθη τὰ σώματα αὐτῶν ὁλόκληρα ἐκ πάσης αἰ. *Pers.*(p.25.1).

B. *cause*; **1.** God; **a.** Father ὅταν δὲ [sc. ἀκούσωμεν ὅτι] ὁ θεὸς πατήρ, ἐπὶ τὴν ἀπαθῆ αἰ. τοῖς λογισμοῖς ἀνατρέχομεν Bas.*Eun.*2.23 (1.258D; M.29.621B); ἐφίεται μὲν πᾶσα λογικὴ φύσις θεοῦ καὶ τῆς πρώτης αἰ. Gr.Naz.*or.*28.13(p.43.7; M.36.44A); πάντων...αἰ. Dion. Ar.*d.n.*1.3(M.3.589B); of Father as first cause, opp. Son and H. Ghost διὰ τοῦ υἱοῦ δημιουργεῖν τὸν πατέρα...ὥστε ἡ 'δι' οὗ' φωνὴ ὁμολογίαν τῆς προκαταρκτικῆς αἰ. ἔχει, οὐκ ἐπὶ κατηγορίᾳ τοῦ ποιητικοῦ αἰτίου παραλαμβάνεται Bas.*Spir.*21(3.18D; M.32.105C); ἐν δὲ τούτων κτίσει ἐννόησόν μοι τὴν προκαταρκτικὴν αἰ. τῶν γινομένων, τὸν πατέρα· τὴν δημιουργικήν, τὸν υἱόν· τὴν τελειωτικήν, τὸ πνεῦμα *ib.*38(31D; M. 136B); τὸ ἄνευ αἰ. εἶναι, μόνου τοῦ πατρὸς ὄν, τῷ υἱῷ καὶ τῷ πνεύματι ἐφαρμοσθῆναι οὐ δύναται·...τὸ ἐξ αἰ. εἶναι...ἴδιόν ἐστιν τοῦ υἱοῦ καὶ τοῦ πνεύματος Gr.Nyss.*or.dom.*3(p.64.3; M.46.1109B); αἰ. ἐστὶν ἡ τοῦ θεοῦ φύσις καὶ τοῦ υἱοῦ καὶ τοῦ ἁγίου πνεύματος καὶ τῆς κτίσεως πάσης· ἀλλὰ τοῦ μὲν υἱοῦ ὡς λόγου, τοῦ δὲ πνεύματος ὡς πνοῆς...τῆς δὲ κτί-σεως ὡς ποιήματος ‡Ath.*dial.Trin.*2.23(M.28.1193A); **b.** Son ἀρχὴν τῆς κτίσεως...οὐχ ὡς κτίσμα πρῶτον κτίσεως ἀρχὴ ἐστιν αὐτῆς, ἀλλ' ὡς αἰ. τοῦ ὑπάρχειν αὐτὴν οἷα δημιουργός Or.*Apoc.*22(p.30.12); ref. Col.1:15 τὸ δὲ 'πρωτότοκος' συμπεπλεγμένην ἔχει...τὴν τῆς κτίσεως αἰ. Ath.*Ar.*2.62(M.26.280B); **c.** H. Ghost ἓν πνεῦμα ἅγιον...ζωὴ ζώντων αἰτία Gr.Thaum.*symb.*(p.3.8; M.10.985A); **2.** Satan, exeg. 2Reg.24:1 ἀδίκως...κολάσει ἡ αἰ. τῆς ἁμαρτίας τὸν ἡμαρτηκότα Or. *Apoc.*30(p.6); **3.** in gen., *that which makes a thing what it is*, hence *essence* οὐ δύναται τὸ πεφυκὸς γλυκαίνειν τῷ γλυκὺ τυγχάνειν πικράζειν παρὰ τὴν αὐτοῦ μόνην αἰ. Or.*Cels.*3.70(p.262.30; M.11. 1012D); id.*or.*29.13(p.388.1; M.11.540A) al.; ἡ τῶν μυστηρίων μετά-δοσις...ὁμοίους τῷ κατ' αἰ. ἀγαθῷ...ἀποφαίνουσα τοὺς ἀξίως μετα-λαμβάνοντας ‡Bas.*h.myst.*62(p.397.19).

C. *question*, *dispute* διά τινας αἰ. (Lat. *quaestiones*) τοῦ πάσχα Hier. *vir.ill.*(tr.Sophr.Pal.)17(p.20.3; M.*PL.*23.636B); *ib.*35(p.27.16; 650A).

αἰτίαμα, τό, *ground of accusation*, *fault*, Cyr.*Ps.*94:1(M.69.1240C).

αἰτιατέον, *one must regard as responsible*, Synes.*ep.*122(M.66. 1501C).

***αἰτιατέος**, *to be held responsible* οὐδὲ οἱ πονηροὶ ἄρα, κατὰ τὴν οἰκείαν φύσιν ζῶντες, αἰ. παρὰ δικαίῳ κριτῇ Meth.*symp.*8.16(p.110. 9; M.18.173A).

αἰτιατικός, *accusatory*, Gennad.*fr.Rom.*11:30ff.(p.402.11f.; M.85. 1720A).

αἰτιατικῶς, *causatively*, Dion.Ar.*d.n.*11.6(M.3.956A).

αἰτιατός, *produced by a cause*; of Son, Const.*or.s.c.*11.8(p.168.18; M.20.1264C); αἴτιός ἐστι μόνος ὁ πατήρ· τὰ δὲ αἰ. δύο, ὁ υἱὸς καὶ τὸ πνεῦμα ‡Ath.*qu.al.*11(M.28.784C).

***αἰτιολόγημα**, τό, *thing which can be accounted for*, Bas.*hom.* 23.4(2.188C; M.31.597B).

αἰτιολογικός, *assignable to a cause*, *explicable*, Dion.Ar.*d.n.*2.3 (M.3.640B).

αἴτιος, **A.** *causing*, subst., *cause*; **1.** God; **a.** as first cause v. εἰμί; Just.*dial.*3.5(M.6.481B); Clem.*str.*6.9(p.470.26; M.9.297C); οὐσία θεία...τῶν ὄντων αἰ. id.*fr.*37(p.219.17; M.9.749D); Or.*Jo.*2.2(p.54.17; M.14.108B); Gr.Nyss.*Eun.*12(1 p.255.4; M.45.957A); ἔξεστι γὰρ ἀντὶ τοῦ εἰπεῖν ἀγέννητον, πρῶτον αἰ. αὐτὸν προσειπεῖν *ib.*7(2 p.169.22; 760D); Max.*schol.d.n.*5.8(M.4.325B); πάντων αἰτιώτατον Thdt.*rect. conf.*2(M.6.1208B); **b.** of Father as causative principle of Son τὸ αἰ. ὡς οὐ πάντως πρεσβύτερον τῶν ὧν αἰ. οὐδὲ γὰρ τοῦ φωτὸς ἥλιος Gr.Naz.*or.*29.3(p.77.8; M.36.77B); Chrys.*hom.2.2 in Heb.*(12.15D); exeg. 1Cor.11:3 ὁ δὲ Χριστὸς τοῦ θεοῦ, ὡς αὐτὸν αἰ. ἔχων κατὰ τὸ πατέρα εἶναι id.*hom.10.2 in 1Cor.*(10.82E); Thdt.*1Cor.*11:3(3.233); αἰ. μὲν φυσικόν, ὁ πατήρ· αἰτιατὸν δέ, ὁ υἱός Jo.D.*imag.*1.9(M.94. 1204C); id.*f.o.*1.8(M.94.820B); of Son and H. Ghost τῆς πρώτης γεννήσεως τοῦ υἱοῦ καὶ τῆς πρώτης τοῦ πνεύματος ἐκπορεύσεως, ὁ πατὴρ μόνος αἰ. ... τῆς δὲ ἄλλης γεννήσεως τῆς ὑπὸ χρόνον, καὶ τῆς ἄλλης προχύσεως τῆς μεταδοτικῆς, οὐ μόνος αἰ. ὁ πατήρ, ἀλλὰ καὶ ὁ υἱὸς καὶ τὸ πνεῦμα ‡Ath.*Lat.*3(M.28.832B); of H. Ghost τὸ πνεῦμα... πατέρα οὐκ ἔχει...αἰ. δὲ ἔχει τὸν θεὸν...παρ' οὗ ἐκπορεύεται ‡Ath.*dial. Trin.*1.19(M.28.1145C); *ib.*2.28(1200B); **c.** of Logos as cause of union of natures in Inc., Leont.H.*Nest.*1.11(M.86.1445D); **d.** of Logos as creative cause αἰ. ὁ λόγος, ὁ Χριστός, καὶ τοῦ εἶναι...ἡμᾶς ...καὶ τοῦ εὖ εἶναι...ἁπάντων ἡμῖν αἰ. ἀγαθῶν Clem.*prot.*1(p.17.17; M.8.61B); τὸν δεύτερον μετὰ τὸν πατέρα τῶν ὅλων αἰ. Eus.*h.e.*1.2.3 (M.20.56A); as cause of gifts of H. Ghost, Gr.Nyss.*diff.ess.*4(M.32. 329B); **e.** refutation of Platonic theory that God is not cause of matter, Ath.*inc.*2.4(M.25.100B); **f.** denial that God is cause of evil, ref. problem of hardening of Pharaoh's heart, Or.*princ.*3.1.7(p.204. 16; M.11.260A); Meth.*arbitr.*11(p.173.3); a view implicit in astro-logical theory of destiny, id.*symp.*8.16(p.105.14; M.18.168D); **2.** angels not a cause of creative activity, belonging to created order of which οὐδὲν...ποιητικὸν αἰ. ἐστιν Ath.*Ar.*3.14(M.26.349C).

B. *blameworthy* αἰ. οὐδὲν ἐν ἀνέρι...δοκεύω Nonn.*par.Jo.*18:38 (M.43.897A).

***αἰφνιδιάζω**, *attack suddenly*; met., of abolishing idolatry, Marc. Diac.*v.Porph.*41.

αἰχμάζω, *fight with a spear*; met., *conquer* κόρον Gr.Naz.*carm.* 1.2.17.63(M.37.786A); χόλον *ib.*2.1.17.83(1268A); γλῶσσαν *ib.*2.1.34.46 (1310A).

αἰχμαλωσία, ἡ, **1.** *captivity*, met. Ἰησοῦ, ὃν...ὁ κλαυθμὸς τῶν ἐν αἰ. ἐπὶ γῆς σε ἐλθεῖν ἐποίησεν *A.Xanthipp.*24(p.75.17); αἰ. ... ἐστιν ἡ ἀπὸ τῆς προηγουμένης ζωῆς κατάπτωσις †Bas.*Is.*166(1.497E; M.30. 392C); **2.** *body of captives*, met. καὶ τὴν αἰ. λήψεται ἀπὸ τοῦ Βελιάρ [τὰς ψυχὰς τῶν ἁγίων] *T.Dan* 5.11; ref. Ps.23:9 τῆς δόξης ὁ βασι-λεὺς...ἐλεύσεται τὴν ἄπειρον ἀπαγόμενος τοῦ ᾅδου αἰ. Germ.CP *or.*2 (M.95.281A); **3.** s.v.l., *being led away* τὰς ἐν ταῖς εὐχαῖς ἀμελείας καὶ τὰς αἰ. τὰς ἐν ταῖς ψαλμῳδίαις *Apophth.Patr.*(M.65.197A).

***αἰχμάλωσις**, ἡ, ‡Epiph.*v.proph.Azariae* A(M.43.396B) for αἰχμα-λωσίαν (p.31).

***αἰχμαλώτευμα**, τό, *prize of war*, ‡Bas.*Lac.*7(2.592D; M.31. 1449C).

αἰχμαλωτεύ-ω, = αἰχμαλωτίζω, *take prisoner*, Clem.*paed.*3.2 (p.243.19; M.8.573A); met. οἱ δαίμονες τέχνῃ τοὺς ἀνθρώπους ~ουσι Tat.*orat.*18(p.20.15; M.6.848A); Χριστέ...ὁ ~σας τὸν θάνατον καὶ σκυλεύσας τὸν ᾅδην *M.Thdot.*3(p.135.12).

αἰχμαλωτίζ-ω, *take prisoner*, *capture*; met., of women ~ουσιν [sc. τοὺς ἄνδρας] *T.Reub.*5.3; of false teachers ~ουσιν ἀπὸ τῆς ἀληθείας τοὺς μὴ ἑδραίαν τὴν πίστιν...διαφυλάσσοντας Iren.*haer.*1.3.6 (M.7.477B); for good ἐπὶ σωτηρίᾳ αἰχμαλωτισθέντος ὑπὸ Χριστοῦ Or. *Jo.*2.7(4; p.61.11; M.14.120D); of Satan ~οντι τὰς ψυχάς id.*hom.1.4 in Jer.*(p.3.11; M.13.257C); Ath.*v.Anton.*42(M.26.905B); ‡Ath.*Apoll.* 2.6(M.26.1141A); τοῦ νοῦ...~ομένου Chrys.*hom.20.3 in Mt.*(7.264A); of insincere Christians ἑτέρους ~ουσι προσάγοντες τῷ πονηρῷ *Const. App.*3.6.5.

αἰχμαλωτισμός, ὁ, = αἰχμαλωσία q.v., Mac.Aeg.*hom.*11.1(M.34.545A); met. οἱ πονηρὰ βουλευόμενοι ἐν ταῖς καρδίαις αὐτῶν...αἰ. ἑαυτοῖς ἐπισπῶνται Herm.*vis.*1.1.8.

αἰχμαλωτιστής, ὁ, *captor*; ref. Ps.136:3, Meth.*symp.*4.4(p.49.24; M.18.92B).

αἰχμάλωτος, ὁ, **1.** *one taken by the spear, prisoner,* met. οἱ Βραχμᾶνες...πάντας ἀνθρώπους λέγουσιν αἰ. εἶναι τῶν ἰδίων συγγενῶν πολεμίων, γαστρὸς...χαρᾶς λύπης...καὶ τῶν ὁμοίων Hipp.*haer.*1.24(p.29.9; M.16.3052C); Ναασσηνοὶ...φάσκουσι...τρεῖς εἶναι ἐκκλησίας, ἀγγελικήν, ψυχικήν, χοϊκήν· ὀνόματα δὲ αὐταῖς ἐκλεκτή, κλητή, αἰ. *ib.*10.9(p.268.21; 3419B); βάπτισμα αἰ. λύτρον Cyr.H.*procatech.*16; **2.** *exile,* of Judas παραδείσου αἰ. καὶ γεέννης κληρονόμος Eus.Al.*serm.*14(M.86.533A).

***αἰῶλος**, ? f.l. for αἰόλος, *shifty, slippery,* or ἕωλος, *stale, out-of-date* αἰ. ... σοφιστείας Didym.*Trin.*2.6(M.39.521A).

αἰών, ὁ, *age, aeon, eternity,* def. αἰ. γὰρ οὔτε χρόνος, οὔτε χρόνου τι μέρος...ἀλλ' ὅπερ ἡμῖν ὁ χρόνος...τοῦτο τοῖς ἀϊδίοις αἰ., τὸ συμπαρεκτεινόμενον τοῖς οὖσιν Gr.Naz.*or.*38.8(M.36.320B); αἰ. ... ἐστιν οὐ φύσις ἐν ὑποστάσει γνωριζομένη ἀλλὰ διάστημα, ὅπως ποτὲ ἐπινοούμενον χρόνου εἴτε μικρὸν εἴτε μέγα Thdr.Mops.*Gal.*1:4(p.5.18; M.66.897D); ὁ αἰ. ... ἀνυπόστατον χρῆμα, συμπαρομαρτοῦν τοῖς γενητὴν ἔχουσι φύσιν Thdt.*Heb.*1:2(3.546); ὁ αἰ. ... διάστημά τι χρόνου δηλωτικόν, ποτὲ μὲν ἀπείρου, ὅταν περὶ θεοῦ λέγηται, ποτὲ δὲ τῇ κτίσει συμμέτρου, ἄλλοτε δὲ τῇ ἀνθρωπίνῃ ζωῇ id.*haer.*5.6(4.399); τὸ τοῦ αἰ. ὄνομα πολύσημόν ἐστι...αἰ. γὰρ λέγεται...ἡ ἑκάστου τῶν ἀνθρώπων ζωή·...πάλιν...ὁ χιλίων ἐτῶν χρόνος· πάλιν...ὅλος ὁ παρὼν βίος, καὶ αἰ. ὁ μέλλων, ὁ μετὰ τὴν ἀνάστασιν ἀτελεύτητος...πάλιν...οὐ χρόνος, οὐδὲ χρόνου τι μέρος...ἀλλὰ τὸ συμπαρεκτεινόμενον τοῖς ἀϊδίοις...ὅπερ γὰρ τοῖς ὑπὸ χρόνον ὁ χρόνος, τοῦτο τοῖς ἀϊδίοις ἐστὶν αἰ. Jo.D.*f.o.*2.1(M.94.861B).

A. *lifetime, LS*; of duration of existence of angel οὐδὲ τοῖς αἰ. εἰσιν ἀπερίληπτοι· 'ὁ ποιῶν' γάρ φησι 'τοὺς ἀγγέλους αὐτοῦ πνεύματα' Didym.*Trin.*2.4(M.39.481C).

B. *time* ὑμεῖς [sc. Ἕλληνες] οὐ γινώσκετε παρατρέχοντας μὲν ὑμᾶς, ἑστῶτα δὲ τὸν αἰ. μέχρις ἂν αὐτὸν ὁ ποιήσας εἶναι θελήσῃ Tat.*orat.*26(p.27.27; M.6.861B); ἔοικεν οἷόν τι μέτρον καὶ ὅρος τῆς τῶν ἀνθρωπίνων λογισμῶν κινήσεως καὶ ἐνεργείας ὁ αἰ. καὶ τὰ ἐντὸς τούτων εἶναι, τὰ δὲ ὑπερκείμενα τούτων ἄληπτα...λογισμοῖς μένει Gr.Nyss.*Eun.*1(1 p.129.16; M.45.365C); ἡ κτίσις πᾶσα...τῷ τῶν αἰ. διαστήματι παραμετρεῖται *ib.*(p.128.1; 364D); τί ποτέ ἐστιν αἰ.;... χρόνος ἐν ἡμέραις καὶ ὥραις Chrys.*comm.in Gal.*1:4(10.663D); οὐδὲν τῶν κτισμάτων προγενεστέραν τοῦ αἰ. ἔχει τὴν γένεσιν, ἀλλ' ἐν χρόνῳ πεποίηται Cyr.*thes.*32(5^1.290A); λέγουσι [sc. οἱ Ὠριγενισταί]...ὅτι τὸ τοῦ αἰ. ὄνομα ἐπὶ ὡρισμένου χρόνου λαμβάνεται, καὶ ὅταν εἴπῃ ἡ γραφὴ ὅτι αἰωνία ἐστὶν ἡ κόλασις, οὐ λέγει εἰ μὴ ἐπὶ ὡρισμένου χρόνου †Leont.B.*sect.*10.6(M.86.1265D).

C. a long but definite period, *age, era, epoch*; **1.** a thousand years, one of the seven ages of the world τοὺς ἑπτὰ αἰ. ἐγὼ [sc. θάνατος] λυμαίνω τὸν κόσμον *T.Abr.*A 19(p.101.18); τὸ σῶμά σου μενεῖ ἐπὶ τῆς γῆς ἕως ἂν πληρωθῶσιν ἑπτακισχίλιοι αἰ. *ib.*B 7(p.112.3); ἑβδόμῃ ἡμέρᾳ λέγεται ὁ αἰ. οὗτος πληροῦσθαι ‡Bas.*struct.hom.*2.8(1.342C; M.30.49D); †Andr.Cr.*cycl.*(M.19.1329C); λέγονται...ἑπτὰ αἰ. τοῦ κόσμου τούτου...ἀπὸ τῆς οὐρανοῦ καὶ γῆς κτίσεως μέχρι τῆς κοινῆς τῶν ἀνθρώπων συντελείας τε καὶ ἀναστάσεως Jo.D.*f.o.*2.1(M.94.861C); **2.** with idea of dispensation; **a.** from Creation to final judgement μέχρις ἡμέρας τελειώσεως...ἐν ᾗ ὁ αἰὼν ὁ μέγας τελεσθήσεται *Apoc.En.*16.1; **b.** from Creation to Inc. ὁ μακρὸς αἰ. τοῦ βίου πρὸ τῆς τοῦ σωτῆρος θεοφανείας Eus.*theoph.fr.*6(p.20*.3; M.24.628B); id.*d.e.*2.3(p.92.7; M.22.161D); Proc.G.*Jos.*6:4(M.87.1013B); **c.** the present *world* or *age*; **i.** in gen. αἰ. ἐστιν ὅλος τὸ μικρὸν τοῦ θεοῦ Or.*hom.12.10 in Jer.*(p.97.3; M.13.392D); οἱ αἰ. οἱ ἐν τῷδε τῷ κόσμῳ ἐκ τῆς περιόδου τῆς ἡμέρας καὶ τῆς νυκτὸς τὴν σύστασιν ἔχουσι, τὸ δὲ προϋπάρξαι τῆς ἡμέρας καὶ τῆς νυκτὸς προϋπάρξαι ἐστὶ τοῦ αἰ. τούτου Gel.Cyz.*h.e.*2.17.28(M.85.1272A); πολλάκις τὰ ἀρχαιότατα τῇ τοῦ αἰ. ἐπωνυμίᾳ χαρακτηρίζει καὶ τὴν ὅλην...τοῦ καθ' ἡμᾶς χρόνου παράτασιν αἰ. προσαγορεύει Dion.Ar.*d.n.*10.3(M.3.937C); with prepositions τῇ [sc. ἐκκλησίᾳ] προωρισμένῃ πρὸ αἰώνων εἶναι...εἰς δόξαν Ign.*Eph.*proem.; from *the beginning of the world* ἡ γῆ...ποιήσει ἀθέμιτα, ἃ οὐδέποτε γέγονεν ἐξ αἰῶνος *Did.*16.4; τὴν κληρονομίαν τῶν πατέρων αὐτῶν τὴν ἀπ' αἰ. *Apoc.En.*99.14; τὰ ἀπ' αἰ. ἐν κρυπτῷ ἀξίοις παραδιδόμενα κηρύσσων *Hom.Clem.*3.19; ἀναστήσει ἡμᾶς σὺν πᾶσι τοῖς ἀπ' αἰ. κοιμηθεῖσιν *Const.App.*5.7.1; φθορὰ...ὅσην οὐδεὶς χρόνος ἐξ αἰ. ἔγνω Philost.*h.e.*11.7(M.65.601A); **ii.** = the human race Μωϋσῆς...ὁ παντὶ τῷ αἰ. τὸν τοῦ θεοῦ νόμον προφητεύσας *Hom.Clem.*2.52; **iii.** with idea of imperfection and conflict οὐδέν με ὠφελήσει τὰ πέρατα τοῦ κόσμου, οὐδὲ αἱ βασιλεῖαι τοῦ αἰ. τούτου Ign.*Rom.*6.1; ὁ αἰ. οὗτος τοῖς δικαίοις χειμών ἐστι Herm.*sim.*3.2; ὁ πᾶς ἐνεστηκὼς αἰ. νὺξ ὀνομάζεται κατὰ τὴν ἐπίνοιαν, ὡς δηλοῖ ἡ παραβολὴ τῶν ι' παρθένων Or.*Apoc.*9(p.24); ὁ τὸν παρόντα αἰ. στάδιον δικαιοσύνης ἐνστησάμενος *Const.App.*7.33.3; exeg. Gal.1:4 ὅταν ἀκούσῃς πονηρὸν αἰ., τὰς πράξεις νόει τὰς πονηρὰς Chrys.*comm.in Gal.*1:4(10.664B); **iv.** ruled by Devil τοῦ ἄρχοντος τοῦ αἰῶνος τούτου Ign.*Eph.*17.1; ὁ νομισθεὶς εἶναι θεὸς τοῦ αἰ. τούτου καὶ τῆς ἀνωτάτω δόξης κλοπεὺς Cyr.*Juln.*1(6^2.6B); and by evil powers τῶν ἀρχόντων τούτου τοῦ αἰ. Or.*Jo.*13.59(58; p.290.27; M.14.512B); acc. Ebionites τὸν μὲν Χριστὸν...τοῦ μέλλοντος αἰ. εἰληφέναι τὸν κλῆρον, τὸν δὲ διάβολον τοῦτον πεπιστεῦσθαι τὸν αἰ. Epiph.*haer.*30.16(p.353.14; M.41.432C); Manich. 'ὁ θεὸς τοῦ αἰ. τούτου'...τὸν διάβολον ἐνταῦθα λέγεσθαι Chrys.*hom.8.2 in 2Cor.*(10.493D); **v.** of the end of the world 'ἕως τῆς σήμερον ἡμέρας' ὅπερ ἐν τῇ γραφῇ μέχρι τῆς συντελείας τοῦ παρόντος αἰ. δηλοῖ Or.*hom.21.1 in Jos.*(p.428.23; M.87.1033A); ἡ ἀνάστασις, τοῦ μέλλοντος μὲν ἀρχὴ αἰ. ὑπάρχουσα, τούτου δὲ τέλος Meth.*res.*2.25(p.382.9; M.18.329B); *Symb.Ant.*(341)4 ap.Ath.*syn.*25(p.251.9; M.26.725C) cit. s. συντέλεια; τοῦτο...ἔστω νόμιμον αἰώνιον ἕως τῆς συντελείας τοῦ αἰ., μέχρις ἂν ἔλθῃ ὁ κύριος *Const.App.*5.19.7; **d.** the *world* or *age* to come; **i.** in gen. τὴν ἐκκλησίαν...πολίτας τῶν μακαρίων ἐκείνων αἰ. ἐργάζεσθαι Meth.*symp.*8.6(p.88.16; M.18.148B); τὸν ἐσόμενον ἀΐδιον αἰ. *Hom.Clem.*15.7; ζωὴν τοῦ μέλλοντος αἰ. *Symb.*ap.*Const.App.*7.41.8; *Symb.Nic.–CP*(p.80.16; H.2.288B); Didym.*Trin.*3.20(M.39.296B); ὁ μέλλων αἰ., ἐν ᾧ μετὰ ψυχῶν συγκλειόμεθα καὶ σωμάτων Max.*ambig.*(M.91.1368D); **ii.** opp. present age ὁ δίκαιος καὶ ἐν τούτῳ τῷ κόσμῳ περιπατεῖ καὶ τὸν ἅγιον αἰ. ἐκδέχεται *Barn.*10.11; ὁ...αἰ. ὁ ἐρχόμενος θέρος ἐστὶ τοῖς δικαίοις, τοῖς δὲ ἁμαρτωλοῖς χειμών Herm.*sim.*4.2; παραδοθησόμεθα...ἀγγέλοις...μεταβιβάζουσιν ἡμᾶς ἀπὸ τοῦ αἰ. τούτου ἐπὶ τὸν μέλλοντα Or.*hom.10.7 in Jer.*(p.78.24; M.13.368B); ὁ θεὸς...δύο αἰῶνας συνεστήσατο, κρίνας τῷ πονηρῷ δεδόσθαι τὸν παρόντα κόσμον...τῷ δὲ ἀγαθῷ δώσειν ὑπέσχετο τὸν μέλλοντα αἰ. *Hom.Clem.*20.2; ἐπὶ...τοῦ μέλλοντος αἰ. οὐδὲ διατάξεως χρεία ἡμῖν τινος, ἐπείπερ ἔξω πάσης ἁμαρτίας...φυλαττόμεθα Thdr.Mops.*Gal.*1:4(p.7.28; M.66.900B); **e.** of worlds beyond heaven, Tat.*orat.*20(p.22.21; M.6.852B); one of several future ages through which the soul passes in the course of its purification, Or.*princ.*3.1.2(p.241.2; M.11.300A).

D. *period* of indefinite duration; **1.** in gen. ὁ θεὸς τῶν αἰ. Ἰησοῦ Χριστέ *A.Jo.*82(p.191.25); Or.*fr.79 in Lc.*19:22(p.272); ὁ θεὸς οἱονεὶ ἐνιαυτούς τινας...οἰκονομεῖ ὅλους τοὺς αἰῶνας id.*Cels.*4.69(p.339.14; M.11.1137D); Meth.*res.*1.37(p.279.15; M.41.1104C); τοῦτον [sc. τὸν θεόν] αἰ. ἄχρονοι πρὸ οὐρανοῦ τοῦδε καὶ πρὸ κόσμου ἄλλοι τε... ἄπειροι αἰ. αἰώνων πρὸ πάσης τῆς τῶν ὁρατῶν ὑποστάσεως...κύριον ἐπιγράφονται Eus.*l.C.*1.5(p.198.19; M.20.1324A); *Hom.Clem.*17.10; **2.** opp. χρόνος: ὅπερ ἐν τοῖς αἰσθητοῖς ὁ χρόνος, τοῦτο ἐν τοῖς ὑπερκοσμίοις ἡ τοῦ αἰ. φύσις ἐστίν Bas.*Eun.*2.13(1.248A; M.29.596B); opp. τὸ ἀΐδιον, *ib.*2.17(253B; M.608C) cit. s. ἀΐδιος; τοῖς λογίοις...ἔσθ' ὅτε καὶ ἔγχρονος αἰ. δοξάζεται, καὶ αἰώνιος χρόνος Dion.Ar.*d.n.*10.3(M.3.937D); **3.** ref. eternity of Son; **a.** in gen. ὁ παντοκράτωρ θεὸς λόγος, ὁ πρὸ πάντων αἰ. ὑποστάς *A.Andr.*A 12(p.53.14); ἐξ ἀπείρων καὶ ἀνάρχων αἰ. ἦν ὁ υἱός Eus.*d.e.*5.1(p.212.13; M.22.352D); τὸν πρὸ πάντων τῶν αἰ. ἐκ τοῦ πατρὸς γεννηθέντα *Symb.Ant.*(341)4(p.251.3; M.26.725B); *Symb.Sirm.*1(p.254.19; M.26.736A); πᾶν διάστημα ἐν τοῖς αἰ. μετρεῖται, πάντων δὲ τῶν αἰ. βασιλεύς ἐστι καὶ ποιητὴς ὁ λόγος Ath.*Ar.*1.12(M.26.37B); αἰ. πάντες κάτω που τῆς γενέσεως τοῦ μονογενοῦς νοοῦνται Bas.*Eun.*2.17(1.252E; M.29.608B); Gr.Nyss.*Eun.*2(2 p.349.20; M.45.525D) cit. s. ἀΐδιος; *Symb.Nic.–CP*(p.80.5; H.2.288B); παρὰ τίνος ἔχεις μαθεῖν [sc. πῶς γεγέννηται]; ἀλλὰ παρὰ αἰώνων; πρὸ αἰ. ὁ μονογενής Gel.Cyz.*h.e.*2.19.14(M.85.1277D); **b.** exeg. Jo.1:1 πρὸ παντὸς χρόνου καὶ αἰ. 'ἐν ἀρχῇ ἦν ὁ λόγος' Or.*Jo.*2.1(p.53.23; M.14.105C); Jo.1:3 πᾶς αἰ. καὶ χρόνος καὶ διαστήματα καὶ τὸ ποτέ, ἐν οἷς τὸ 'οὐκ ἦν' εὑρίσκεται, δι' αὐτοῦ ἐγένετο Alex.Al.*ep.Alex.*6(p.23.15; M.18.556C); πάντα δι' αὐτοῦ ἐγένετο τοῖς πᾶσι δηλονότι ἐμπεριειλημμένων καὶ τῶν αἰ. Bas.*Eun.*2.13(1.247E; M.29.596A); Ac.2:36 οὐδὲ ἡ τοῦ ἀποστόλου διάνοια τὴν πρὸ αἰ. ὑπόστασιν τοῦ μονογενοῦς ἡμῖν παρίστησι *ib.*2.3(239E; M.576D); Heb.1:2 εἴπερ ἀληθὲς πάντας αἰ. καὶ πᾶν διάστημα χρονικὸν μετὰ τὸν υἱὸν καὶ διὰ τοῦ υἱοῦ γεγενῆσθαι λέγειν Gr.Nyss.*Eun.*1(1 p.122.18; M.45.357C); Cyr.*thes.*4(5^1.20A); τῶν αἰ. ... ποιητὴν εἴρηκε τὸν υἱόν, ἀΐδιον αὐτὸν εἶναι διδάσκων, καὶ παιδεύων ἡμᾶς, ὡς ἀεὶ ἦν παντὸς οὐτινοσοῦν ὑπερκείμενος χρονικοῦ διαστήματος Thdt.*Heb.*1:2(3.546); Heb.11:3 ἀλλ' οὐδὲν κοινὸν τῷ λόγῳ πρὸς τοὺς αἰ.· αὐτὸς γάρ ἐστιν ὁ προϋπάρχων πρὸ τῶν αἰ., δι' οὗ καὶ οἱ αἰ. γεγόνασιν Ath.*decr.*18(p.15.18; M.25.448A); ἀνάγκη προϋπάρχειν αὐτὸν καὶ τῶν αἰ. ὁμολογεῖν. ὧν γάρ... πρότερον αὐτὸς τοὺς οὐκ ὄντας αἰ. ποτε πρὸς τὸ εἶναι παράγει Cyr.*thes.*32(5^1.293C); **c.** denied by Paul. Sam. πρὸ αἰ. μὲν προορισθέντα, ἐκ δὲ *Μαρίας τὴν ἀρχὴν τῆς ὑπάρξεως ἐσχηκότα* ‡Ath.*Apoll*.1.20(M.26.1128A); by Marcell. of Son, opp. impersonal Logos, ref. Pr.8:23 '*πρὸ τοῦ αἰ.*', *ἑνὸς…αἰ. ἐνταῦθα μέμνηται…καίτοι πολλῶν παρεληλυθότων αἰ.* Marcell.*fr*.14 ap.Eus.*Marcell*.2.3(p.46.32; M.24.804A); *υἱὸν …ἐξ αὐτοῦ πρὸ τῶν αἰώνων γεννηθέντα Symb.Sirm*.2(p.256.29; M.26.741A) shows that '*πρὸ τῶν αἰ.*' does not properly mean 'from all eternity'; **4.** of life hereafter *εὐφροσύνην ἀκόρεστον καρπουμένας* [sc. *ψυχάς*] *εἰς τοὺς ἀτελευτήτους αἰ.* Clem.*str*.7.3(p.10.15; M.9.416C); ref. Is.9:6 *ὁ Χριστός, ὁ 'πατὴρ τοῦ μέλλοντος αἰ.' ᾧ ἐποικοδομεῖται ἡ τῶν ἀτελευτήτων αἰ. ζωή* Gr.Nyss.*Eun*.3(2 p.20.16; M.45.585A); *ἀπέραντοι…τῆς ἀναπαύσεώς σοι αἰ.* Hyper.*mon*.(M.79.1477B); **5.** of purgatorial punishment *ὡς τῆς ἐμμιχθείσης αὐτοῖς κακίας ἀποτακείσης μακροῖς ὕστερον αἰ. καθαρὰν ἀποσωθῆναι τῷ θεῷ τὴν φύσιν* Gr.Nyss.*or.catech*.35(p.139.2; M.45.92C).

E. *eternity*; **1.** in gen. *ὁ γοῦν αἰ. τοῦ χρόνου τὸ μέλλον καὶ τὸ ἐνεστός, ἀτὰρ δὴ καὶ τὸ παρῳχηκὸς ἀκαριαίως συνίστησι* Clem.*str*.1.13(p.36.14; M.8.756A); *ὅταν…περάσωμεν εἰς τὸν αἰ. καὶ φθάσωμεν εἰς ἀπάθειαν* †Cyr.*coll.VT*(6^4.38D; M.77.1232D); Max.*ambig*.(M.91.1164B) cit. s. *χρόνος*; **2.** of eternal life *τοῦ…αἰ. ἐστιν ἀρχὴ τὸ ἡμέτερον τέλος* Clem.*paed*.1.13(p.151.17; M.8.373B); *ψυχὴν…μακαρίου αἰ. ἀθανασίᾳ τετιμημένην Eus.v.C*.1.2(p.8.4; M.20.913A); Dion.Ar.*d.n*.10.3(M.3.937D); of eternal punishment *ἐν πυρὶ ἀσβέστῳ ῥιφθείσας* [sc. *τὰς ψυχάς*] *τὸν αἰ. κολασθήσεσθαι Hom.Clem*.1.7; **3.** name for or description of God *ὁ θεὸς βασιλεὺς λέγεται τῶν αἰ. … αὐτὸς…ἐστιν ὁ αἰ. τῶν αἰ.* Dion.Ar.*d.n*.5.4(817D); **4.** in phrase *from everlasting to everlasting ὁ μέν* [sc. *θεός*] *ἐστιν κύριος ἀπὸ αἰ. καὶ εἰς τοὺς αἰ. ὁ δὲ* [sc. *διάβολος*] *ἄρχων καιροῦ τοῦ νῦν τῆς ἀνομίας Barn*.18.2; *θεὸς ἐξ αἰ. εἰς αἰ. σῴζων διὰ υἱοῦ* Clem.*str*.7.2(p.9.25; M.9.416A).

F. with prepositions, *for ever*, phrase not strictly confined to things which are eternal *πληθυνθήσονται ἅγιοι ἐξ ἐμοῦ ἕως αἰῶνας αἰώνων T.Sym*.6.2 (v.l. *αἰῶνος αἰώνων*); *ἡ ζωὴ τῶν δικαίων εἰς τὸν αἰ. Pss.Sal*.13.9; *εἰς τοὺς σύμπαντας αἰ. τῶν αἰ.* Serap.*euch*.1.4 al.; *ἔχει… τὴν ἐλπίδα οὐκ ἐφ' ἕνα αἰ. ἀλλ' εἰς τὸν αἰ. τοῦ αἰ.* Diod.*Ps*.51:10(M.33.1590B); *οὐ μὴ ἀπόλωνται…εἰς πάσας τὰς γενεὰς τῶν αἰ. Apoc.En*.103.4; *ἔσται…ἡ χάρις τοῦ κυρίου ἡμῶν…εἰς τὸν αἰ. χρόνον μεθ' ὑμῶν A.Mt*.28(p.259.14); *τοῦ σώματος…ἀδυνατοῦντος ἀτρέπτου δι' αἰ. μένειν* Meth.*res*.1.25(p.251.4; M.41.1096C).

G. *aeon* (Gnost.); **1.** derived from Greek mysteries and Phrygian cult *ἐν τῷ οἰκητηρίῳ, οὗ ἡ ῥίζα τῶν ὅλων τεθεμελίωται,…αἰ., δυνάμεων* Hipp.*haer*.5.9(p.98.19; M.16.3154B); **2.** in system of Simon Magus *τρεῖς…ἑστῶτας αἰ. ib*.6.17(p.143.3; 3219A); **3.** of Menander *ἑαυτὸν…ὡς…εἴη λέγων ὁ σωτὴρ ἐπὶ τῇ τῶν ἀνθρώπων ἄνωθέν ποθεν ἐξ ἀοράτων αἰ. ἀπεσταλμένος σωτηρίᾳ* Eus.*h.e*.3.26.2(M.20.272B); **4.** Nicolaitan *μετὰ πάντας τούτους προβεβλῆσθαί τινα αἰσχρὸν αἰ. … καὶ ἐκ τούτου…καὶ τῆς Μήτρας γεγονέναι θεούς τε καὶ ἀγγέλους* Epiph.*haer*.25.5(p.273.5; M.41.328B); **5.** Valent., *divine entity* or *emanation λέγουσι…τινα εἶναι ἐν ἀοράτοις…ὑψώμασι τέλειον αἰ. προόντα· τοῦτον δὲ…προπάτορα καὶ Βυθὸν καλοῦσιν* Iren.*haer*.1.1.1(M.7.445A); *οὗτοί εἰσιν οἱ τριάκοντα αἰ. … τοῦτο τὸ…πλήρωμα, τριχῇ διεσταμένον εἰς ὀγδοάδα, καὶ δεκάδα, καὶ δωδεκάδα ib*.1.1.3(449B); *ὅποσον ἐλάττων ἡ εἰκὼν τοῦ ζῶντος προσώπου, τοσοῦτον ἥσσων ὁ κόσμος τοῦ ζῶντος αἰ.* Val.Gn.ap.Clem.*str*.4.13(p.287.23; M.8.1297A); *ἄγνωστος…ὁ πατὴρ ὢν ἠθέλησεν γνωσθῆναι τοῖς αἰ.* Clem.*exc.Thdot*.7(p.108.1; M.9.657A); *τὴν περὶ τῶν αἰ. μυθοποιΐαν ἀρρένων καὶ θηλειῶν* Or.*comm.in Mt*.17.33(p.692.24; M.13.1589A); *Βαλεντῖνος, καὶ Σεκουνδῖνος, καὶ Μάρκος, καὶ οἱ ἐκείνων διάδοχοι παμπόλλους αἰ. πρεσβυτέρους τοῦ δημιουργοῦ φασιν εἶναι* Thdt.*haer*.5.6(4.399); of the aeon Christ, Iren.*haer*.1.8.2(524A); cf. *Ἀδάμ*; Epiph.*haer*.31.4(p.388.5; M.41.480B); **6.** Marcosian *τοὺς…φθόγγους ὑπάρχειν τοὺς μορφοῦντας τὸν ἀνούσιον καὶ ἀγέννητον αἰ.* Iren.*haer*.1.14.1(M.7.597A); *τὰ ὀνόματα τῶν στοιχείων τὰ ῥητὰ καὶ κοινὰ αἰ. καὶ λόγους, καὶ ῥίζας, καὶ σπέρματα, καὶ πληρώματα, καὶ καρποὺς ὠνόμασε ib*.1.14.2(597B); *οὕτω…διὰ τῶν δέκα ὀνομάτων* [sc. *φῶς, ἡμέρα κτλ.*] *τοὺς δέκα αἰ. μεμηνυκέναι* [sc. *Μωϋσέα*] *ib*.1.18.1(644A); *τοῖς τέσσαρσι καὶ εἴκοσι στοιχείοις τοὺς αἰ. ἀπείκασε καὶ τοὺς μὲν ἀφώνους, τοὺς δὲ ἡμιφώνους, τοὺς δὲ φωνηέντας προσηγόρευσεν* Thdt.*haer*.1.9(4.301); **7.** Naassene '*ἀπὸ σοῦ* [sc. *Ἀδάμας*] *πατήρ, καὶ διὰ σὲ μητὴρ…αἰώνων γονεῖς… μεγαλώνυμε ἄνθρωπε*' Hipp.*haer*.5.6(p.78.10; M.16.3126B); ref. Is.7:14 *ἡ παρθένος ἡ…τίκτουσα υἱόν, οὐ ψυχικόν, οὐ σωματικόν, ἀλλὰ μακάριον αἰ. αἰώνων ib*.5.8(p.97.19; 3151C); cf. *ταύτῃ τῇ ὥρᾳ σήμερον ἡ κόρη (τουτέστιν ἡ παρθένος) ἐγέννησε τὸν αἰ.* Epiph.*haer*.51.22(p.286.7); **8.** 'Docetist' *τρεῖς γεγόνασιν αἰ. ἀπὸ τῆς πρώτης ἀρχῆς τῶν ὅλων ἀρχαί·…μένει ὁ θεὸς αὐτὸς καθ' ἑαυτὸν πολὺ τῶν τριῶν αἰ. κεχωρισμένος·…ἴσων…γεγονότων ἀριθμῷ καὶ τελειότητι τῶν αἰ. … τριάκοντα γεγόνασιν αἰ.* Hipp.*haer*.8.8(p.226.21; M.16.3350B); **9.** Tatian *ἀποστὰς τῆς ἐκκλησίας…ἴδιον χαρακτῆρα διδασκαλείου συνεστήσατο, αἰ. τινας ἀοράτους ὁμοίως τοῖς ἀπὸ Οὐαλεντίνου μυθολογήσας* Iren.*haer*.1.28.1(M.7.690C); **10.** Manich. *τῆς…σελήνης μεταδιδούσης τὸν γόμον τῶν ψυχῶν τοῖς αἰ. τοῦ πατρός* Hegem.*Arch*.8(p.13.10; M.10.1440C); **11.** gen. *οἱ μὲν πλείους εἶναι θεοὺς λέγουσιν, οἱ δὲ τρεῖς ἀνάρχους, οἱ δὲ δύο ἀγεννήτους, οἱ δὲ αἰ. ἀπείρους Const. App*.6.10.2.

H. hence = *πλήρωμα*, *totality of aeons* or *whole invisible spiritual world*, acc. Ophites *φασὶ…τὸν…Χριστὸν…σὺν τῇ μητρὶ εἰς τὸν ἄφθαρτον ἀνασπασθῆναι αἰ., ἣν καὶ ἀληθινὴν ἐκκλησίαν καλοῦσι* Iren.*haer*.1.30.1(M.7.695D); *εἶναι…ἐν ἀκατονομάστῳ τινὶ ἀνωτάτῳ τε οὐρανῷ καὶ αἰ. ἀγαθόν τινα θεόν* Epiph.*haer*.45.1(p.199.17; M.41.833A); acc. Heracleon, ref. Jo.4:22 '*ἡμεῖς προσκυνοῦμεν*' *ὁ Ἡρακλέων οἴεται 'εἶναι ὁ ἐν αἰ. καὶ οἱ σὺν αὐτῷ ἐλθόντες'* Or.*Jo*.13.19(p.243.13; M.14.429D); ref. Jo.1:3 '*οὐ τὸν αἰ. ἢ τὰ ἐν τῷ αἰ. γεγονέναι διὰ τοῦ λόγου*' *ἅτινα οἴεται πρὸ τοῦ λόγου γεγονέναι ib*.2.14(8; p.70.8; 137B).

I. plur., name of supernatural beings; evil *ἐπειδὴ κατέλιπες τὴν ἐντολήν μου…κατασχεθήσῃ ἐν τοῖς αἰ. ἐπὶ τεσσαράκοντα ἡμέρας A.Phil*.137(p.69.23); good *θρόνων τε καὶ ἐξουσιῶν παραλλαγάς, αἰ. τε μεγαλειότητας, τῶν τε χερουβεὶμ καὶ σεραφεὶμ τὰς ὑπεροχάς* ‡Ign.*Trall*.5; *τὰ σεραφίμ, αἰ. τε καὶ στρατιάς, δυνάμεις τε καὶ ἐξουσίας Lit*.ap.*Const.App*.8.12.8; hence *power* of such beings (Naassene) *σὺ…ἔβδομε γεγονὼς κρατεῖν Ἰαλδαβαώθ, ἄρχων…ἣν ἔκλεισας αἰ. σῷ πύλην κόσμῳ ἀνοίξας* Or.*Cels*.6.31(p.101.9; M.11.1341C).

αἰωνίζω, *be eternal*, *A.Barth*.5(p.139.31).

αἰώνιος, *eternal*;

A. in full sense, *without beginning or end*; **1.** of the divine nature, Gr.Naz.*or*.38.8(M.36.320A); **2.** of Trin., Or.*Jo*.10.39(23; p.216.31; M.14.384A); **3.** of God, Serap.*euch*.30.1 cit. s. *ἀναλλοίωτος*; *θεὸς… αἰ. αἰωνίους ποιῶν Hom.Clem*.2.45; *θεὸς εἷς ἐστιν…οὐσία ἄναρχος, ἀτελεύτητος, αἰ. τε καὶ προαιώνιος* ‡Cyr.*Trin*.1(6^3.1A; M.77.1120A); *λέγεται ὁ θεὸς αἰ., ἀλλὰ καὶ προαιώνιος· καὶ αὐτὸν γὰρ τὸν αἰῶνα ἐποίησε* Jo.D.*f.o*.2.1(M.94.864A); *ib*.1.2(792C) cit. s. *ἀΐδιος*; **4.** of Son *σε δοξάζω διὰ τοῦ αἰ. καὶ ἐπουρανίου ἀρχιερέως Ἰησοῦ Χριστοῦ M.Polyc*.14.3; *ὁ θεὸς αἰ. ἐστι φῶς, οὔτε ἀρξάμενον, οὔτε λῆξόν ποτε. οὐκοῦν αἰώνιον…σύνεστιν αὐτῷ τὸ ἀπαύγασμα* Dion.Al.ap.Ath.*Dion*.15(p.57.10; M.25.501D); ref. Inc. *αἰωνίου φύσεως ἀρχὴ χρόνιος* Const.*or.s.c*.11(p.168.25, v.l. *αἰωνίας* M.20.1265A); *οἱ ἅγιοι… τὸ ἀΐδιον εὐαγγελίζονται τοῦ υἱοῦ καὶ τὸ αἰ., ἐν ᾧ καὶ αὐτὸν θεὸν σημαίνουσιν* Ath.*Ar*.1.12(M.26.36C); Gr.Nyss.*Eun*.10(2 p.232.13; M.45.833B) cit. s. *ζωή*; **5.** of things eternal and spiritual, opp. temporal and material *ἀνάγομαι…πρὸς τὸν…θεόν μου Ἰησοῦν Χριστόν, …πρὸς ἐκεῖνον τὸν…ἀνάξαντά με εἰς μεγαλωσύνην αἰ. A.Thom*.A 159(p.270.19); *τὸ ἀπέραντον καὶ αἰ. καὶ ἀόριστον καὶ ἄχρονον* Hipp.*haer*.6.54(p.188.17; M.16.3290B); *οἱ…ἄνθρωποι ἀποστραφέντες τὰ αἰ., καὶ συμβουλίᾳ τοῦ διαβόλου εἰς τὰ τῆς φθορᾶς ἐπιστραφέντες* Ath.*inc.et c.Ar*.5(M.25.104D); *τὴν ἐν ἡμῖν ἀναφθεῖσαν αὐτοῦ* [sc. H. Ghost] *αἰ. χάριν* Didym.*Trin*.2.10(M.39.640C); *πῶς…οὐ πολέμιος θεοῦ ὁ περὶ τὰ πρόσκαιρα μὲν…σπουδάζων, τῶν δὲ αἰ. ἀμελῶν; Const.App*.2.60.1; *ἴσμεν…κυριώτερον τὰ ὄντα τῷ αἰῶνι, καὶ τὰ ἐν γενέσει τῷ χρόνῳ, καὶ λεγόμενα καὶ δηλούμενα. χρὴ τοιγαροῦν οὐχ ἁπλῶς συναΐδια θεῷ τῷ πρὸ αἰῶνος οἴεσθαι τὰ αἰ. λεγόμενα* Dion.Ar.*d.n*.10.3(M.3.940A); **6.** of natural or revealed law *τὰς αἰ. καὶ φύσει δικαιοπραξίας καὶ εὐσεβείας* Just.*dial*.47.2(M.6.577A); of the law given by God to Adam *νόμον αἰ. ὥρισεν Hom.Clem*.8.10; **7.** acc. pagans or heretics; **a.** Heracleitus *ἐστὶ παῖς τὸ πᾶν καὶ δι' αἰῶνος αἰ. βασιλεὺς τῶν ὅλων* Hipp.*haer*.9.9(p.242.4; M.16.3374A); of the original divine principle *τὰ πάντα οἰακίζει κεραυνός…κεραυνὸν τὸ πῦρ λέγων τὸ αἰ. ib*.9.10(p.243.25; 3375B); **b.** Epicureans *τίνα…τρόπον…τὰ μέν ἐστι…αἰ. σώματα, ἢ μακραίωνά γε…φαινόμενά τε καὶ ἀφανῆ· φαινόμενα μὲν ἥλιος…γῆ τε καὶ ὕδωρ, ἀφανῆ δὲ θεοί τε καὶ δαίμονες καὶ ψυχαί;* Dion.Al.ap.Eus.*p.e*.14.25(775A; M.21.1276A); **c.** Gnost., of supreme Gnost. deity *ἔρχονται* [sc. *τὰ πνευματικά*], *αἰῶνες νοεροὶ γενόμενα, εἰς τοὺς νοεροὺς καὶ αἰ. γάμους τῆς συζυγίας* Clem.*exc.Thdot*.64(p.128.19; M.9.689C); *τὰ πάσης κακίας ἀπηλλαγμένα αἰ. χωρία* Hipp.*haer*.5.7(p.88.8; M.16.3138C); **d.** acc. Docetists *τοῖς τοῦ φωτὸς αἰ. χαρακτῆρσι ib*.8.10(p.229.11; 3354B); *ὁ μονογενὴς παῖς ἄνωθεν αἰ. ib*.(p.230.8; 3354D); *τὸ…τῶν αἰ. φῶς…καταβὰν…ἄνωθεν ἰδεῶν αἰ. ἀπεμάξατο κάτω ⟨εἰς⟩ τὸ χάος τὰς μορφάς ib*.10.16(p.277.28; 3434B).

B. *eternal* in the future, *immortal*; **1.** of spiritual beings; **a.** of angels *ὑμεῖς…ὑπήρχετε πνεύματα ζῶντα αἰ., καὶ οὐκ ἀποθνήσκοντα εἰς πάσας τὰς γενεὰς τοῦ αἰῶνος Apoc.En*.15.4; of the blessed in heaven *παραμενοῦσιν τῇ εὐωχίᾳ, ἧς οἱ αἰ. καταξιοῦνται A.Thom*.A 7(p.110.12) **b.** of Gnost. aeons *ἡ τῶν ὑπερκοσμίων…καὶ αἰ. … μακαρία φύσις* Hipp.*haer*.5.7(p.82.2; M.16.3131A); **2.** of the world hereafter; **a.** in gen., Just.*dial*.81.4(M.6.669A) cit. s. *ἀνάστασις*; *τί…ἀποβλέπεις* *εἰς ταύτην τὴν πρόσκαιρον ζωὴν καὶ περὶ τῆς αἰ. οὐδὲν ἐνθυμεῖσαι;* *A.Thom.*A 78(p.193.19); *ἐν ᾧ ὁ τοῦ θεοῦ υἱός, ὁ πρώην ποιήσας τὸν ἄνθρωπον, ζωὴν τὴν αἰ., ἣν ἀπώλεσαν διὰ τοῦ Ἀδὰμ οἱ ἄνθρωποι, ἑτοιμίσῃ* *A.Andr.*A 5(p.12.8); **b.** ref. immortality of the body, affirmed by Jews *ὁ Ἰουδαῖος...λέγει...ἐλπίζομεν...ἀναστήσεσθαι ἐν σώματι καὶ βιοτὴν ἕξειν αἰ.* Cels.ap.Or.*Cels.*2.77(p.199.13; M.11.916C); denied by Celsus *σάρκα...μεστὴν ὧν οὐδὲ εἰπεῖν καλόν, αἰ. ἀποφῆναι παραλόγως οὔτε βουλήσεται ὁ θεὸς οὔτε δυνήσεται* *ib.*5.14(p.15.22; 1201C); affirmed by Or. ref. 1Cor.15:42 *μὴ βουλέσθω οὖν ὁ θεὸς παραλόγως αἰ. ἀποφῆναι...μηδὲ τὸ σπειρόμενον 'ἐν φθορᾷ' ἀλλὰ τὸ ἀπ' αὐτοῦ ἐγειρόμενον 'ἐν ἀφθαρσίᾳ'* *ib.*5.24(p.25.20; 1217C); *ἄτοπον...τὸ οἴεσθαι τὸ σῶμα...μὴ συνέσεσθαι τῇ ψυχῇ διὰ τὸ δεσμὸν αὐτὸ...εἶναι, ἵνα μὴ αἰ. γινώμεθα...δεσμῶται κατ' αὐτοὺς φθορᾶς* Meth.*res.*1.32 (p.269.13; M.18.268B); exeg. 1Thess.4:17, ref. Am.9:11 *αἰ. ἡμῶν τὰς σκηνάς, τουτέστι τὰ σώματα...ἀπειλήφαμεν* *ib.*2.21(p.376.4; 316A); **c.** of happiness hereafter; **i.** in gen. *δώσει τοῖς ἐπικαλουμένοις αὐτὸν εἰρήνην αἰ.* *T.Dan* 5.11; Ign.*Eph.*18.1 cit. s. *ζωή*; *ἣν ἀσπάζομαι ἐν αἵματι Ἰησοῦ Χριστοῦ, ἥτις ἐστὶν χαρὰ αἰ. καὶ παράμονος* id.*Philad.* proem.; *2Clem.*5.5 cit. s. *ἀνάπαυσις*; *τοῦ...αἰ. καὶ καθαροῦ βίου ἐπιθυμοῦντες τῆς μετὰ θεοῦ...διαγωγῆς ἀντιποιούμεθα* Just.*1apol.*8.2 (M.6.337B); *ἀναμένοντες τὰς...αἰ. ἐπαγγελίας 'τοῦ κυρίου...Ἰησοῦ Χριστοῦ'* Serap.*euch.*25; **ii.** compared with prosperity in this world *ὁ μὲν* [sc. *Μωϋσῆς*]...*πρόσκαιρον ἔδωκεν αὐτοῖς τὴν κληρονομίαν,...ὁ δὲ* [sc. *Χριστός*] *μετὰ τὴν ἁγίαν ἀνάστασιν αἰ. ἡμῖν τὴν κατάσχεσιν δώσει* Just.*dial.*113.4(M.6.736D); Or.*fr.39 in Jo.*(p.515.15) cit. s. *ζωή*; *χήρα...κλέος ἔχουσα...παρὰ ἀνθρώποις ἐπὶ γῆς καὶ παρὰ θεῷ ἐν οὐρανοῖς τὸν αἰ. ἔπαινον* *Const.App.*3.1.5; Gr.Nyss.*or.catech.*40(p.164.7; M.45.105B) cit. s. *ἀντίδοσις*; *ζωὴν...νοοῦμεν αἰ., οὐ τὴν μακροημέρευσιν, ἧς πάντες μέλλουσιν ἀπολαύειν...καλοί τε καὶ κακοί, ἀλλὰ τὸ ἐν εὐθυμίᾳ διάγειν* Cyr.*Jo.*7(4.666A); contrasted with adversity in this world *οὐ σκοπεῖ τῶν κινδύνων τὸ πρόσκαιρον ἀλλὰ τὸ τῶν ἐπάθλων αἰ.* Bas.*hom.*17.1(2.139B; M.31.484B); **iii.** in creeds *εἰς...σαρκὸς ἀνάστασιν, ζωὴν αἰ.* *Symb.Rom.*(p.23); *Symb.Hier.*(M.33.533B); *πιστεύομεν καὶ περὶ σαρκὸς ἀναστάσεως καὶ ζωῆς αἰ.* *Symb.Ant.*(341) 1(p.249.8; M.26.721B); *εἰς ἀνάστασιν νεκρῶν καὶ κρίσιν δικαίαν ψυχῶν καὶ σωμάτων, καὶ εἰς βασιλείαν οὐρανῶν, καὶ εἰς ζωὴν αἰ.* *Symb.*ap. Epiph.*anc.*119(120; p.149.4; M.43 236B).

C. 1. lasting for an indefinitely long period, but not fully eternal *οὐ τὰ πάντα καὶ ἀπολύτως ἀγένητα καὶ ὄντως ἀΐδια πανταχοῦ φησιν* [sc. *τὰ λόγια*] *αἰ. ... ὡς ὅταν λέγῃ τὸ 'ἐπάρθητε, πύλαι αἰ.'* Dion.Ar.*d.n.*10.3(M.3.937C); *τοῖς λογίοις δὲ ἔσθ' ὅτε καὶ ἔγχρονος αἰὼν δοξάζεται, καὶ αἰ. χρόνος* *ib.*(937D); *αἰ. μὲν καὶ ἔγχρονα...μέσα δὲ ὄντων καὶ γιγνομένων, ὅσα πῇ μὲν αἰῶνος, πῇ δὲ χρόνου μετέχει* *ib.*(940A); **2.** *immortal*; **a.** of praise, blame, memory, etc. *ἵνα δοξασθῆτε αἰ. ἔργῳ* Ign.*Polyc.*8.1; *πολλοὶ...ἐπαισχυνόμενοι τὸ Χριστοῦ εὐγενῶς ὄνομα φέρειν εἰς αἰσχύνην αἰ. καταπεπτώκασιν* Or.*or.*29 (p.385.2; M.11.536A); *διαδέχεται...τόνδε τὸν βίον μνήμη διαρκὴς καὶ αἰ. δόξα* Const.*or.s.c.*12(p.171.14; M.20.1272A); *τὸν...μακαρίας μνήμης καὶ αἰ. Κώνσταντα τὸν ἀδελφόν σου* Ath.*apol.Const.*2(p.280.2; M.25. 597A); **b.** as a complimentary title of the emperor and empress *'αἰ.' αὐτὸν 'βασιλέα' εἰρήκασιν οἱ τὸν υἱὸν ἀΐδιον ἀρνούμενοι* id.*syn.*3 (p.232.32; M.26.685A); *ἐξετέθη ἡ πίστις...ἐπὶ παρουσίᾳ τοῦ δεσπότου ἡμῶν τοῦ...βασιλέως Κωνσταντίου Αὐγούστου, τοῦ αἰ., σεβαστοῦ* *ib.*8(p.235.22; 692B); *Θεοδοσίῳ...ἀεὶ βασιλεῖ υἱῷ Γάλλα Πλακιδία... αἰ. βασιλὶς καὶ μήτηρ* Gall.Plac.*ep.Thds.*(p.5.31; M.*PL.*54.860C); **3.** *lasting, permanent* *δότε αὐτὰ τοῖς τέκνοις...εἰς κατάσχεσιν αἰ.* *T.Ben.*10.4; *ὕπνωσεν ὕπνον αἰ.* *T.Isach.*7.9; *τοσαῦται...ἐγένοντο σφαγαὶ ὅσαι, εἰ κατὰ βαρβάρων ἐγένοντο, ἱκανὰς εἶναι πρὸς αἰ. εἰρήνην* Const.*or.s.c.*25(p.191.24; M.20.1312B); *ὑμῖν ἔστω νόμιμον αἰ. ἕως τῆς συντελείας τοῦ αἰῶνος* *Const.App.*5.19.7; *to the end of the world* *ὁ κόσμος ὄργανόν ἐστι...ἵνα τῷ ἐσομένῳ ἄρρενι αἰωνίως ἡ θήλεια τίκτῃ δικαίους αἰ. υἱούς* *Hom.Clem.*19.23; *αἰ.* [sc. *τοῦ διαβόλου*] *ἡ ἀρχή· τουτέστι, τῷ παρόντι αἰῶνι συγκαταλυομένη* Chrys.*hom.*4.1 *in Eph.* (11.26B).

αἰωνιότης, ἡ, 1. *eternity* [sc. *τὸ πνεῦμα*] *ἁγιότης καὶ αἰ. τὸ πᾶν ὑπάρχει* Didym.*Trin.*2.6(M.39.517B); *ἡ γὰρ εἰκὼν πρὸς καιρόν, ἡ δὲ ἀλήθεια εἰς αἰ. κρίνεται* *ib.*2.14(708A); **2.** as imperial title *ἡ ἡμετέρα ἔγνω αἰ. ὅ τι ὁ...Λέων παρὰ τῆς σῆς ἤτησεν αἰ.* Thds.Imp.*ep.Gall.* (p.7.27; M.*PL.*54.878B).

αἰωνίως, A. *eternally, for ever*; **1.** without beginning or end *πρόσεστιν...τῷ θεῷ...τὸ ζῆν, καὶ τὸ ζῆν αἰ.* *Hom.Clem.*19.11; *τὰ γενητὰ ...καὶ φθαρτὰ αἰ. οὐ ζῶσι* ‡Just.*confut.*52(M.6.1545B); **2.** without end *τὸ...αὐθεντικὸν βάπτισμα...ἀπὸ πάσης ἁμαρτίας αἰ. ἐλευθεροῖ* Didym. *Trin.*2.14(M.39.708B); ref. future life *αὐτῷ ζωῇ...ὄντι ζησόμενοι αἰ.* Eus.*e.th.*3.15(p.173.2; M.24.1029C); *ἀναπαυόμενοι διὰ Ἰησοῦ Χριστοῦ ...αἰ.* *Const.App.*6.30.7; Anast.S.*qu.et resp.*21(M.89.533A); ref. future punishment, *Hom.Clem.*15.11; *αἰ. τὴν τῶν συκοφαντῶν ὑπομεῖναι τιμωρίαν* Ath.*apol.sec.*88(p.167.10; M.25.408B); Jo.D.*Man.* 1.41(M.94.1545A).

B. *always* *τοῦ θεοῦ τὸ ἁμάρτημα λύσαντος θανάτῳ, ἵνα μὴ ἀθανάτως ἁμαρτωλὸς ὁ ἄνθρωπος ὢν...αἰ. κατάκριτος γενηθῇ* Meth.*symp.*9.2 (p.116.14; M.18.181A); *Hom.Clem.*19.23 cit. s. *αἰώνιος*.

αἰωνόβιος, *immortal*, Synes.*hymn.*3.163(p.11; M.66.1596).

***αἰωνοθαλής,** *eternally fresh*, Eus.*v.C.*1.2(p.8.3; M.20.912C).

***αἰωνοτόκος, ὁ,** *parent of eternity, creator of ages*, Synes.*hymn.* 3.162(p.11; M.66.1596); *ib.*7.12(p.48; 1612).

***αἰωνοχαρής,** *rejoicing in eternity*; of Son, Clem.*paed.*3.12(p.291. 16; M.8.681B).

αἰωρέω, *raise, suspend*; pass., of Christ on the Cross, ‡Gr.Naz. *Chr.pat.*607(M.38.185A).

ἀκαθαίρετος, 1. *not brought down*; *free from destruction*; *unsubdued*, Or.*Cels.*7.26(p.177.5; M.11.1457B); †Bas.*Is.*145(1.481C; M. 30.356A); of a bishop *not deposed*, Pall.*v.Chrys.*13(p.82.33; M.47.47); **2.** *not to be put down, indestructible*, Bas.*ep.*236.3(3.363B; M.32.881B); Jo.D.*hom.*11.14(M.96.776C).

***ἀκαθαιρέτως,** *without being debased, without degradation*, Jo.D. *imag.*1.4(M.94.1236B).

***ἀκαθάριτος,** ? for *ἀκάθαρτος*, Ephr.3.4F.

***ἀκαθάρσιος,** morally *unclean, impure*, *T.Abr.*A 17(p.99.16).

ἀκάθαρτος, *unclean, impure*; morally, *Barn.*10.8; Or.*or.*29.7 (p.384.26; M.11.533D); ceremonially, Just.*dial.*20.3(M.6.520A); *Hom. Clem.*8.19; Hipp.*haer.*5.19(p.120.19; M.16.3183C); of spirits, Just. *dial.*7.3(492C); Clem.*prot.*4(p.43.26; M.8.152C); Or.*Jo.*20.36(29; p.376.2; M.14.657B).

***ἀκαθαρτοφαγία, ἡ,** *eating of unclean things*, Areth.*Apoc.*5(M. 106.536D).

***ἀκαθηκόντως,** *in unseemly fashion, indecently*, Or.*Cels.*3.25 (p.221.12; M.11.949A); Geo.Al.*v.Chrys.*64(p.241.44).

***ἀκαθήκων,** *unseemly*, Ath.*h.Ar.*49(p.211.23; M.25.753B); *ib.*50 (p.212.1; l.c.).

***ἀκαθισία, ἡ,** *restlessness*, Ephr.2.151A.

***ἀκάθιστος, 1.** *unsettled, roving* *ἰδοὺ μετέβησαν πάλιν οἱ ἀ.* *Apophth.Patr.*(M.65.112A); of demon of *ἀκηδία*: *ῥεμβοὺς καὶ ἀ. ἡμᾶς ἀποτελεῖ* Ant.Mon.*hom.*26(M.89.1517A); **2.** *without sitting*; **a.** in gen. *ξηροφαγίαν ἀ. ἐπιτιμάσθω* Thdr.Stud.*poen.*1.4(M.99.1733C); **b.** esp. *ὁ ἀ. ὕμνος*, hymn in honour of BMV, sung on Saturday of the fifth week in Lent to commemorate saving of Constantinople in A.D. 626; so called probably because first sung by priest and people *standing up* all night; for text v. ‡Serg.*acath.*(*AGC* p.140; M.92.1335A).

ἀκαθοσίωτος, 1. *uncleansed, dirty*, Mac.Mgn.*apocr.*3.12(p.88.19); **2.** *impious*, Epiph.*haer.*59.3(p.366.23; M.41.1021C); *Cod.Afr.*55; *evil*, Mac.Mgn.*apocr.*3.39(p.136.9); neut. as subst., *impiety, profanity*, CEph.Orient.*ep.*(*ACO* 1.1.5; H.1.1545A).

***ἀκαθοσιώτως,** *impiously*, Ammon.*Ac.*18:17(M.85.1569B); Sophr. Al.*libell.*(p.23.33; H.2.336E).

***ἀκαινίστως,** *not in a novel way* *τῆς μὲν σαρκὸς...ἀ. ἐχούσης κατά τε φύσεως καὶ ὑποστάσεως λόγον* Leont.H.*Nest.*5.30(M.86.1749D).

***ἀκαινοτομήτως,** *without innovation, in no novel way*, Martin. *ep.*13(M.*PL.*87.194C); CLater.*act.*5(H.3.920D).

ἀκαιρέω, pass.; **1.** *be without opportunity* or *leisure, be busy*, Herm.*sim.*9.10.5; **2.** *misuse one's time*, Bas.*hex.*8.8(1.79D; M.29. 185C).

ἀκαίριος, s.v.l., *διασῴζειν ἀκαίριον* Proc.G.*Gen.*1:6(M.87.72C), prob. for *ἀκέραιον*.

***ἀκαιροβόας, ὁ,** *untimely brawler*, Clem.*paed.*2.7(p.192.22; M.8. 464A).

***ἀκαιροεπόπτης, ὁ,** *untimely spectator* *οὐκ ἔσῃ...ἀ. τῶν κακῶς ζώντων* *Const.App.*1.4.1.

ἀκαιρολογία, ἡ, *unseasonable talk*, Bas.*ascet.*1.2(2.319E; M.31. 873A); Chrys.*ecl.*48(12.774A).

***ἀκαιροπεριπάτητος,** *given to roaming about at unseasonable times, gad-about*, *Const.App.*1.5.1; *ib.*4.14.3 (vv.ll. -*περίπατος*, -*πάτιτος*).

***ἀκαιροπερίσπαστος,** v. *ἀκερο-*.

***ἀκαιρορρήμων, ὁ,** *unseasonable talker*, Or.*Cels.*7.36(p.187.15; M.11.1472C).

***ἀκαιροσπουδαστής, ὁ,** *inordinate admirer*, Hier.*ep.*85.4(M.*PL.* 22.753).

***ἀκαιροφάγος,** *eating at unseasonable times*, Epiph.*haer.*80.4 (p.488.16; M.42.761B).

***ἀκαιροφωνία, ἡ,** *untimely remark*, Mac.Mgn.*apocr.*3.7(p.62.9).

ἀκαίρως, 1. *unseasonably, unsuitably*, f.l. for *ἀκάκως* ap.Iren.

haer.5.30.1(M.7.1204A); Or.Jo.2.31(25; p.88.7; M.14.168B); **2.** *unexpectedly*, Const.App.1.3.6.

ἀκακέμφατος, *not ill-reputed*, Meth.symp.5.2(p.54.14; M.18.100A).

ἀκακία, ἡ, 1. *guilelessness, innocence*; as of children, Herm.vis. 3.8.7; Clem.paed.1.5(p.98.9; M.8.265A); ‡Chrys.hom.in Ps.100:2 (5.639B); of Job ὡς ἀκακίας ἐχόμενος ἐδικαιοῦτο Dion.Ar.ep.8.1 (M.3.1085B); Max.schol.c.h.2.5(M.4.48D); **2.** *simplicity*; as of unlearned, Bas.hom.in Ps.7(1.103A; M.29.241A); **3.** ascet. ἀ. ἐστὶν ἱλαρὰ ψυχῆς κατάστασις ἐπινοίας πάσης ἀπηλλαγμένη Jo.Clim.scal. 24(M.88.981B); καλὸς τρίδομος καὶ τρίστυλος θεμέλιος ἀ., νηστεία, σωφροσύνη ib.1(636D); ib.24(984D).

***ἀκακοποιός**, *innocent*, ‡Chrys.pasch.2(8.255C).

ἄκακος, 1. *guileless, innocent*, Herm.mand.2.1; Cyr.H.catech.4.1; Dor.doct.1.13(M.88.1633D); of Christ, Diogn.9.2; **2.** *simple, slow-witted*, Didym.Job 8:19(M.39.1141C).

ἀκακούργητος, *guileless, simple*, Schol.92 in Jo.Clim.scal.4(M.88. 760C).

***ἀκακουργήτως**, *without guile, simply*, Epiph.anc.56(p.65.16; M.43.116A).

***ἀκάκουργος (ἀκακουργί)**, *without guile, innocent*, Cyr.Am.71 (3.329A, v.l. ἀκακουργί); id.Soph.5(3.583E); id.ador.6(1.215C).

ἀκαλλής, 1. *without beauty*, of God πάνσχημος, πανείδεος, ἄμορφος, ἀ., ἀρχὰς καὶ μέσα καὶ τέλη τῶν ὄντων...ἐν ἑαυτῷ προειληφώς Dion.Ar.d.n.5.8(M.3.824B); **2.** *unlovely, devoid of charm, unattractive*; **a.** of things visible, Clem.paed.3.2(p.242.20; M.8.572A); Gr. Nyss.Eun.3(2 p.10.12; M.45.573C); Cyr.ador.1(1.5D); of Christ on the Cross, Jo.D.hom.4.24(M.96.621D); neut. as subst., ? *deformity*, Cyr.Joel.36(3.230C); **b.** of abstracts, id.Jo.11.9(4.984B); ib.12(4. 1040A); neut. as subst., *want of beauty* (sc. in language), Pall. h.Laus.proem.(p.10.25; M.34.1001); στέρησις...ἐστὶ τὸ κακὸν...καὶ ἀ. Dion.Ar.d.n.4.32(M.3.732D); **3.** *unseemly*, Cyr.Os.3(3.14E); id.Jo.1.4 (4.38D); id.Nest.1(6^1.2C); neut. as subst., *unseemliness, moral turpitude*; of idolatry, id.Ps.9:15(M.69.773A); of heresy, id.inc.unigen. (5^1.685E).

ἀκαλλιέρητος, *ill-omened*, Dion.Al.ap.Eus.h.e.7.10.4(M.20.660A); Eus.h.e.9.3(804B).

ἀκαλλώπιστος, 1. *unadorned*, Hipp.haer.10.5(p.265.15; M.16. 3414B); Gr.Naz.ep.51(M.37.105B); of language, Thphyl.exc.gent.5 (p.482.5; M.113.941C); neut. as subst., *disregard of one's personal appearance*, Jo.D.virt.(M.95.88A); **2.** *ill-favoured*; of an undernourished boy, T.Sal.D 2.2.

ἀκαμάτως, 1. *without tiring*, Just.dial.59.1(M.6.612A); **2.** *without trouble, easily*, Bas.renunt.6(2.208A; M.31.640B); Mac.Aeg.hom.6.4 (M.34.520D).

ἀκαμπής, 1. *unbent, rigid*, Nonn.par.Jo.11:44(M.43.845C); ib. 19:18(901B); *unmoved*, ib.11:32(844B); **2.** met., *inflexible*; **a.** in bad sense, *pitiless*, Cyr.ador.1(1.44C); Gennad.Rom.1:29(p.360.18; M.85. 1669C); *unbending, obdurate*, Pall.v.Chrys.20(p.142.28; M.47.79); Isid.Pel.epp.1.314(M.78.364C); Cyr.Is.1.5(2.137D); **b.** in good sense, *unflinching, steadfast*, Nonn.par.Jo.3:36(M.43.773A); neut. as subst., *constancy*, Clem.str.7.11(p.48.31; M.9.493B); A.Andr.B 6(p.61.23); Chrys.hom.56.2 in Mt.(7.567D); **3.** *inevitable*, Nonn.par.Jo.12:27 (M.43.856A).

ἄκανθα, ἡ, *thorny plant, thorn, thistle*, Barn.7.11; Or.princ.3.1.10 (p.211.4; M.11.265B); Const.App.7.40.2; met., of temporal affairs, Clem.q.d.s.11(p.166.29; M.9.616A); ἡ ὑπερηφανία...ῥίζαν πάσης τῆς κατὰ τὴν ἁμαρτίαν ἀ. Gr.Nyss.virg.4(p.268.23; M.46.340A); of sin, Gr. Nyss.nativ.(M.46.1136C); Thdt.Ps.31:4(1.802); of heresy, id.2Tim. 2:9(3.682); id.h.e.4.18.14(3.979).

[*]ἀκανθαῖα, ἡ, = ἀκανθέα, *Spanish broom (spartium junceum)*, V.Dan.(p.374.3).

ἀκανθεών, ὁ, *thorny brake*, Gr.Naz.ep.4(M.37.25C).

***ἀκανθηφόρητος,** = *ἀκανθόρος, *yielding thorns*, Ephr.2.12E.

[*]ἀκανθηφόρος, = ἀκανθο-, *bearing thorns*, Hyper.mon.112(M. 79.1484C); met., of temptations, Gr.Nyss.hom.4 in Cant.(M.44.841C).

***ἀκανθοκόπος,** *for cutting thorns*, Gr.Mag.dial.(tr.Zach.)2.6 (M.PL.66.143D).

***ἀκανθολόγημα, τό,** *thorny saying*, Jo.Clim.scal.4(M.88.701B).

***ἀκανθόρος,** *producing* or *yielding thorns*, Or.Jo.6.58(37; p.166. 29; M.14.301A); Cyr.H.catech.2.4; Gr.Naz.carm.2.2(poem.)5.121(M. 37.1530A); met., of life, ib.2.1.87.2(1433A); of sensuality, Isid.Pel. epp.1.220(M.78.321A).

***ἀκανθοτόκος,** *productive of thorns*, Cyr.glaph.Ex.1(1.263C); id. Os.13(3.34D); ib.103(137A).

ἀκανθοφορέω, *bear thorns*, Or.princ.3.1.10(p.211.1; M.11.265B); met., of souls before Christian era, †Bas.Is.205(1.532E; M.30.473A).

***ἀκανθοφορία, ἡ,** *wearing of thorns*, Gr.Nyss.Apoll.24(M.45. 1173C).

ἀκανθοφόρος, *thorn-producing, yielding thorns*, Sophr.H.or.2.22 (M.87.3241C); met. ἀ. φιλοπάθειαν Isid.Pel.epp.1.220(M.78.321A).

ἀκανθόχοιρος, ὁ, *hedgehog*, ‡Proc.G.Pr.30:26(M.87.1532A).

ἀκανθώδης, *thorny*; met., *anxious, uneasy*, Rom.Mel.(BZ 24 p.6).

***ἀκανόνιστος, 1.** *not canonical, not in the canon* of scripture CLaod.can.59; Ammon.Ac.28:23(M.85.1605C); **2.** of practices, *uncanonical, contrary to canon law*, †Hipp.theoph.4(p.259.19; M.10. 856B); Apophth.Patr.(M.65.149D); Cyr.ep.27(p.45.6; 5^2.90B); of opinions, *unorthodox, irregular*, Memn.ep.(p.47.2; M.77.1465C).

***ἀκανονίστως,** *uncanonically, contrary to canon law*, Bas.ep.188 can.10(3.275A; M.32.681A); CEph.(431)can.5; Tim.CP haer.(M.86. 45A); Thphn.chron.p.78(M.108.240C).

ἀκαπήλευτος, 1. *free from tricks of trade, from huckstering; without corruption*, Gr.Nyss.usur.(M.46.440B); Gennad.encycl.(p.80. 29; M.85.1617A); **2.** met., *unadulterated, genuine, sincere*, Synes. epp.49,130(M.66.1377A,1516B); Isid.Pel.epp.5.97(M.78.1381D); Cyr.Is. 1.1(2.25D).

***ἀκαπηλεύτως,** *disinterestedly*, Bas.fid.1(2.223E; M.31.677A); id. reg.fus.25.2(2.370D; M.31.985A).

ἀκάπνιστος, *unsmoked*; of honey (i.e. taken without smoking out the bees), Leont.N.v.Jo.Eleem.12(p.23.23).

ἀκάρδιος, 1. *without a heart*; denied of Christ, Gr.Nyss.Apoll.27 (M.45.1181B); **2.** met.; **a.** *without intelligence, senseless*, Or.exp.in Pr.17:16(M.17.200D); Cyr.ador.15(1.549D); id.Is.4.2(2.588E); **b.** *without feeling*; of Absalom, Chrys.exp.in Ps.3(5.5C); of Israel, Cyr. Lc.17:12(M.72.837B); **c.** *without courage, cowardly*, ‡Chrys.hom.8 (13.227B).

ἀκαρπία, ἡ, *unfruitfulness, barrenness*, Orac.Sib.4.73 ἀκαρπίη; Cyr.Jo.4.4(4.387E); *bad season*, Clem.ecl.55(p.152.17; M.9.724B); Hom.Clem.6.10; met., spiritual *unfruitfulness*, Sever.ap.cat.Ac.10:6 (p.173.11); Isid.Pel.epp.1.16,195(M.78.189C,308C); Vict.Mc.11:13 (p.392.18).

ἀκαρτέρητος, 1. pass., *intolerable, unbearable*, Chrys.hom.66.4 in Mt.(7.659A); ib.69.2(682A); ‡Meth.Sym.et Ann.14(M.18.381B); **2.** act., *impatient, unable to endure*; **a.** in bad sense, *wanting in endurance, lacking self-control*, Chrys.Jud.4.6(1.624D); id.hom.28.2 in 1Cor.(10.252C); Isid.Pel.epp.1.192(M.78.305C); **b.** in good sense, *eager*, Chrys.comm.in Gal.4:20(10.708D); id.hom.3.2 in 1Thess.(11. 443D); ib.4.3(455D).

ἀκαρτερήτως, *without power of endurance*, Chrys.hom.21.2 in Heb.(12.196C).

***ἀκαρύκευτος, 1.** *not carefully seasoned, plain*, of manna and quails ἀταλαίπωρον, καὶ ἀ. τράπεζαν ‡Nil.perist.11.9(M.79.916C); ‡Nil.narr.3(M.79.616A) prob. f.l. for καρύκευτος; **2.** *carefully seasoned, elaborate* ἀ. περιεργίας ἐλευθέραν τῶν ἐδωδίμων τηροῦντες τὴν μέθεξιν Cyr.hom.pasch.10(5^2.129A).

***ἀκαστορητής,** prob. for ἀνιστόρητον, *not to be investigated*, †Epiph.num.myst.1(M.43.508C).

***ἀκαταβίαστος,** *unforced, free* ἀ. γνώμῃ διαβιοῦν ἐπὶ γῆς τὸν ἄνθρωπον ἐφῆκε θεός Cyr.Juln.8(6^2.285D); id.ador.1(1.17C).

ἀκατάβλητος, *not to be thrown down, invincible* ἀ. ... διάνοιαν Bas. ascet.1.1(2.319A; M.31.872A); Rom.Mel.(AS 1 p.115; ἀτελεύτητος SBBAW 1898^2 p.131).

***ἀκατάγαυστος,** prob. for ἀκαταύγαστος, *not illuminated*, Ephr. 3.184D.

***ἀκαταγέλαστος,** *not laughed at, not subject to ridicule* ἀ. μου τὴν ἐνταῦθα εἴσοδον διαφύλαξον A.Jo.22(p.163.10).

ἀκατάγνωστος, 1. *not open to condemnation, blameless* ταύτην ἐὰν τηρήσωμεν τὴν πίστιν, ἀ. ἐσόμεθα Cyr.H.catech.5.7; Const.App. 8.22.4; ἀ. τέκνα Isid.Pel.epp.1.195(M.78.308B); neut. as subst., *freedom from condemnation*, Bas.reg.br.306(2.524A; M.31.1300D); **2.** *uncondemned*, Ath.decr.32(p.28.12; M.25.476B).

ἀκαταγνώστως, *in a manner not open to condemnation, blamelessly*, Const.App.8.25.2; Epiph.haer.80.4(p.489.24; M.42.764A).

ἀκαταγώνιστος, *invincible*; in spiritual combat, of God τῇ...ἀ. χειρὶ τοῦ θεοῦ Bas.Sel.or.23(M.85.277B); of Christ ἀ. ἀθλητὴν Χριστὸν Ep.Lugd.ap.Eus.h.e.5.1.42(M.20.421C); ἡ ἀ. τοῦ κυρίου φύσις †Bas.hom.in Ps.37(1.361A; M.30.80B); Cyr.Abac.41(3.557A); of Devil δράκων μέγας ἀνθρώποις ἀ. Cyr.H.catech.15.15; of men ἵνα ἀ. γένῃ τοῖς δαίμοσιν Chrys.hom.in Rom.12:20(3.161D); Cyr.Ps.17:33(M.69. 824D); Niceph.Ur.v.Sym.183(M.86.3156A); neut. as subst., *invincibility*; ref. those who trust in God, Chrys.Is.interp.2.2(6.21B); of love, id.hom.76.3 in Jo.(8.449B); of the light, exeg. Jo.1:5, ib.5.3 (40A).

*ἀκατάδεκτος, intolerable, Jo.Clim.scal.5(M.88.773B).

*ἀκατάδευστος, not wet δρόσον, ἢ...ἀφίησιν οὐδὲν...ἀκατάδευστον Cyr.Joel.15 (v.l. ἀκατάρδευτον 3.214E).

ἀκαταδίκαστος, uncondemned ὅπερ Ἀδὰμ ἀναμάρτητον καὶ ἀ. εἰς φθορὰν καὶ καταδίκην θανάτου κατενήνοχε, Χριστὸς τοῦτο ἄφθαρτον καὶ λυτήριον θανάτου ἀνέδειξεν ‡Ath.Apoll.1.7(M.26.1105A); ib.1.14 (1117C); Jo.Clim.scal.25(M.88.993A).

*ἀκαταζήτητος, not sought after, not required, Epiph.haer.64. 67(p.510.5).

*ἀκαταζητήτως, in a manner which precludes the need for search, plainly, Epiph.haer.69.42(p.190.18; M.42.268C).

*ἀκαταθοησία, ἡ, perh. error for *ἀκατανοησία, failure to comprehend μεγαλύνεται καὶ σμικρύνεται ὅμως διὰ τῆς ἀ. [sc. ἡ πίστις] Thdr.Stud.catech.parv.29(p.71).

*ἀκαταίσχυντος, that cannot be put to shame, confident, not made ashamed ἐλπίδα Chrys.hom.in 1Cor.11:19(3.247E); ἵνα...τὴν ἀ. πρὸς θεὸν εὕρῃ παρρησίαν Ph.Carp.Cant.83(M.40.81B); of S. Barbara πρέσβυς ἀ. πρὸς τὸν...Χριστόν Jo.D.hom.12.23(M.96.813C); of BMV ἀ. πρέσβιν καὶ μεσιτείαν εὐμενῆ Jo.Mon.hymn.Bas.10(M.96.1377B); neut. as subst., impossibility of being put to shame τὸ ἐκείνων [sc. δεσποτικῶν λογίων] ἀ. καὶ σεβασμιώτατον Philost.h.e.7.9(M.65.548A).

*ἀκαταισχύντως, without shame, of BMV ἐπὶ δὲ τοῦ θρόνου τῆς κρίσεως ἀ. προσάγουσα [sc. ἡμᾶς] Procl.CP or.39.6(M.85.452A).

*ἀκαταίτιος, not to be accused, blameless πίστις ὀρθὴ καὶ ἀ. Cyr.ep.19(p.13.17; 5².81A).

ἀκατακάλυπτος, uncovered; hence with uncovered head, exeg. 1Cor.11:5ff., Bas.moral.56.6(2.277C; M.31.788A); Chrys.hom.15.4 in Eph.(11.114C); met., undisguised, plain γυμνῇ καὶ ἀ. φωνῇ Eus.p.e. 13.1(640C; M.21.1061D).

*ἀκατακαλύπτως, with head uncovered, Jo.D.1Cor.11:2ff.(M.95. 653D).

*ἀκατάκλειστος, not shut up πύλη ἐστὶ κεκλεισμένη, τὰ μυστήρια τοῦ θεοῦ τὰ ἀ. Or.fr.in Ezech.44:1(M.17.288C).

*ἀκατάκλυστος, not swept by waves, Gr.Nyss.anim.et res.(M.46. 84C).

*ἀκατακρισία, ἡ, refusal to condemn, Jo.Clim.scal.7(M.88.804A).

ἀκατάκριτος, not liable to condemnation, free from condemnation, Ammon.Ac.23:12(M.85.1592A); Apophth.Patr.(M.65.332C); Anast.S.qu.et resp.133(M.89.785B).

*ἀκατακρίτως, without being liable to condemnation, blamelessly, Marc.Er.opusc.1.73(M.65.913C); Dion.Ar.e.h.6.3.2(M.3.533D); ἀξίωσόν με ἀ. μεταλαβεῖν τῶν θείων...μυστηρίων Jo.D.prec.1(M.96.816D).

*ἀκατακυρίευτος, not ruled, not under dominion μετὰ τὸ ἀ. ἡμᾶς εἶναι Niceph.Ur.v.Sym.34(M.86.3017B).

*ἀκατάλειπτος, never deficient, of Dives ἦν ἐν ἐσθῆτι πολυτελεστάτῃ καὶ ἀ. τρυφαῖς cat.Lc.16:19(p.124.22).

*ἀκατάλεκτος, that cannot be reckoned, incalculable τοῦ ἁγίου πνεύματος ἀ. σοφίαν Didym.Trin.2.5(M.39.505C) or perh. for ἀκατάληκτος unceasing.

ἀκατάληπτος, A. that cannot be grasped or contained; immeasurable, infinite, def. τὸ μὲν γὰρ ἀ. λέγεται, ὅταν ἐρευνηθὲν καὶ ζητηθὲν μὴ καταληφθῇ παρὰ τῶν ζητούντων αὐτό·...οἷον ἀ. λέγεται πέλαγος, εἰς ὃ καθιέντες ἑαυτοὺς οἱ κολυμβηταί, καὶ πρὸς πολὺ καταφερόμενοι βάθος, τὸ πέρας ἀδυνατοῦσιν εὑρεῖν Chrys.incomprehens.3.2(1.464E); 1. in gen. ἄγνοια Hermias irris.10(M.6.1180B); ἔρημον Cyr.Os.156 (3.189A); ἀ. τῶν πεπιστευκότων πληθύς id.Abac.52(3.566D); unattainable τὸ ἄκρον ἀ. Nil.Alb.(M.79.705C); 2. of God ἀ. καὶ ἀχώρητον, νῷ μόνῳ καὶ λόγῳ καταλαμβανόμενον Athenag.leg.10.1(M.6.908B); of Christ ἡ ἀ. πηγὴ ἡ ζωὴν βλαστάνουσα πᾶσιν ἀνθρώποις...ὑπὸ πενιχρῶν καὶ προσκαίρων ὑδάτων ἐκαλύπτετο †Hipp.theoph.2(p.258.5; M.10. 853A).

B. that cannot be grasped by the mind, incomprehensible, def. τῶν...αἰτίων...τὰ δὲ ἀ., τὰ κατὰ μηδένα τρόπον ὑπὸ κατάληψιν πεσεῖν δυνάμενα, ἃ δὴ καὶ ἄδηλα ἐν τῷ καθάπαξ λέγεται Clem.str.8.9(p.101. 11; M.9.600C); 1. in gen. βεβαιοῖ γὰρ ὁ τοιοῦτος εἶναί τινα ἀ. ὁ γνωστικὸς δὲ...τὰ δοκοῦντα ἀ. εἶναι τοῖς ἄλλοις αὐτὸς καταλαμβάνει, πιστεύσας ὅτι οὐδὲν ἀ. τῷ υἱῷ τοῦ θεοῦ ib.6.8(p.466.29; 292A); αὕτη δὲ ἡ ταπείνωσις, θεϊκή ἐστι καὶ ἀ. Dor.doct.2.8(M.88.1649C); of creation, Hier.H.Trin.(M.40.857B); neut. as subst., incomprehensibility; of wisdom, Bas.fid.3(2.226E; M.31.684C) al.; 2. theol. (often including sense A); a. of God ἀόρατον καὶ ἀ. A.Petr.et Paul.58(p.204. 7) = A.(Pass.)Petr.et Paul.37(p.150.17); Ath.decr.22.1(p.18.24; M. 25.453D) al.; Gr.Nyss.hom.1 in Cant.(M.44.781D); τὸ τοῦ θεοῦ ἀ. οὐχ οὕτως ἡμεῖς ἴσμεν ὡς ἐκεῖναι [sc. heavenly powers] Chrys.incomprehens.3.3(1.466A); Nil.inst.(M.79.1237C); φύγωμεν...τὴν Εὐνομίου τόλμαν, περικλείουσαν τῇ γνώσει τὴν ἀ. φύσιν Procl.CP Arm.13(p.193. 25; M.65.869B); τὸν πᾶσι παρόντα καὶ ἐκ πάντων εὑρισκόμενον, ἀ., καὶ ἀνεξιχνίαστον Dion.Ar.d.n.7.1(M.3.865C); Jo.D.f.o.1.1(M.94.789A); b. heret., acc. Arians ἀγνωστόν τε τὸν θεὸν καὶ ἀ. πανταχοῦ καὶ ἀνεννόητον ἐξηγεῖται· καὶ οὐκ ἀνθρώποις μόνοις...ἀλλὰ καὶ αὐτῷ τῷ μονογενεῖ υἱῷ τοῦ θεοῦ Philost.h.e.2.3(M.65.468A); ib.1.2(461B); ref. those who deny Christ's hypostatic presence in heaven during Inc. καταληπτὴν αὐτὴν [sc. οὐσίαν] εἶναί φασι καὶ πεπερατωμένην, καὶ οὐκ ἔτι μὲν ἀπεριόριστον οὐδὲ ἀ. Cyr.resp.(p.577.15; 6².385E); c. of Father, Cyr.H.catech.11.20; Lit.Bas.(p.322.23); ‡Caes.Naz.dial.17 (M.38.873A); d. of Son ὁ ἀ. ἀγγέλοις †Hipp.theoph.2(p.258.8; M.10. 853A); of divine glory revealed in Christ ἡ δόξα ἐκείνη ἀ., ἥτις δι' ἀνθρώπου τοῖς ἀνθρώποις συνελθεῖν κατηξίωσεν A.(Pass.)Petr.et Paul. 22(p.138.8); τοῖς ἁγίοις ἀγγέλοις ἀ. ὁ νυμφίος τὴν οὐσίαν ἐστί Thdt. Cant.3:4(2.79); ἠτοιμάσθη τὸ λογικὸν καταγώγιον τοῦ ἀ. Thdr.Stud. nativ.BMV 4(M.96.684B); e. of H. Ghost, Chron.Pasch.p.304(M.92. 772A); f. Trin. ὁ γὰρ τοῦ ἀκτίστου καὶ τοῦ ἀ. λόγος, εἷς καὶ ὁ αὐτὸς ἐπί τε τοῦ πατρὸς καὶ τοῦ υἱοῦ καὶ τοῦ ἁγίου πνεύματός ἐστιν. οὐ γὰρ τὸ μὲν μᾶλλον ἀ. τε καὶ ἄκτιστον, τὸ δὲ ἧττον Gr.Nyss.diff.ess.3(M. 32.328D); πατὴρ οὖν ἀεὶ ἀγέννητος καὶ ἄκτιστος καὶ ἀ., υἱὸς δὲ γεννητός, ἀλλ' ἄκτιστος καὶ ἀ. Epiph.haer.74.12(p.330.19; M.42.497D); ‡Ath. symb.(M.28.1587A); Hier.H.Trin.(M.40.852B); g. of unapproachability of God's presence τοῦ φαινομένου τε καὶ καταλαμβανομένου παντὸς ἔξω καταλειφθέντος, μόνον ὑπολείπεται τῇ θεωρίᾳ τῆς ψυχῆς τὸ ἀόρατόν τε καὶ ἀ. ἐν ᾧ ἐστιν ὁ θεός Gr.Nyss.hom.11 in Cant.(M. 44.1001A); φοβεροῦ καὶ ἀ. ὑπάρχοντος τοῦ περὶ θεὸν μυστηρίου Hier.H. Trin.(M.40.848A); h. of divine attributes τῇ ἀ. αὐτοῦ συνέσει 1Clem. 33.3; μεγαλειότητα καὶ δόξαν, καὶ λόγῳ ἀπερίληπτον οὖσαν, καὶ νῷ ἀ. Bas.fid.2(2.225C; M.31.681A); τῶν τοῦ θεοῦ κριμάτων τὸ ἀ. Gr.Naz. or.28.21(p.54.2; M.36.53C); βουλὴ ἀ. τοῖς γενητοῖς Didym.ap.cat.Ac. 20:26(p.336.7); providence, Chrys.hom.75.5 in Mt.(7.731C); wisdom, Isid.Pel.epp.2.5(M.78.464A); knowledge, Proc.G.Is.40:26ff.(M.87. 2344B); i. of generation of Son and procession of H. Ghost, Eus. e.th.1.8(p.66.22; M.24.837C); Cyr.Jo.1.1(4.14B); †Diad.Ar.2(M.65. 1153B); Jo.D.f.o.1.8(M.94.813B); Jo.V H.icon.4(M.96.1352D); 3. Valent. name of aeon of ogdoad, Hipp.haer.6.38(p.169.7; M.16.3255A); of the second aeon, ib.8.8(p.227.14; 3350C); 4. of primal number of Pythagoras ἀριθμὸς γέγονε πρῶτος ἀρχή, ὅπερ ἐστὶν [ἓν] ἀόριστον ἀ. ib.1.2(p.5.21; 3024B).

ἀκαταλήπτως, 1. incomprehensibly; of Son's generation, Symb. Ant.(345)(p.252.19; M.26.729B); Cyr.H.catech.4.7; Epiph.haer.69.15 (p.165.1; M.42.225A); Justn.conf.(p.76.16; M.86.999A); Jo.D.f.o.1.8 (M.94.816A); 2. ἀ. ἔχειν be unable to comprehend ἀ. ἔχειν τῶν σημείων Or.comm.in Gen.ap.philoc.23.19(p.208.6; M.12.81B).

ἀκαταληψία, ἡ, 1. immensity, infinity; of God, Gr.Nyss.Eun.1 (1 p.209.5; M.45.457A); of BMV ref. Bar.3:24ff., ‡Meth.Sym.et Ann. 10(M.18.373B); 2. incomprehensibility; a. in gen., Hipp.haer.1.22 (p.27.15; M.16.3049D); τῶν γραφῶν παννυχίας καὶ ἀ. Anast.S.hex.12 (M.89.1076C); ib.(1069A); b. of God εἴδησις...τῆς θείας οὐσίας ἡ αἴσθησις αὐτοῦ τῆς ἀ. Bas.ep.234.2(3.358A; M.32.869C); οἷόν τινι γνόφῳ τῇ ἀ. πανταχόθεν διειλημμένον Gr.Nyss.v.Mos.(M.44.377A); Epiph.haer.70.5(p.237.5; M.42.345C); ib.76.54(p.412.23; 636B); τοῦτο μόνον αὐτοῦ καταληπτόν, ἡ ἀπειρία καὶ ἡ ἀ. Jo.D.f.o.1.4(M.94.800B) = ‡Cyr.Trin.3(6³.4D; M.77.1125B); of Son, Agath.v.Gr.Ill.45(p.25); ‡Meth.Sym.et Ann.5(M.18.360A); of divine judgements, Ath.exp. Ps.72 proem.(M.27.328A); 3. ? inability to comprehend τὴν ἀγνωσίαν διὰ τῆς ἀ. κεκτημένοι Epiph.haer.76.54(p.413.18; M.42.636D) (or in sense 2 supra).

*ἀκατάληψις, ἡ, inability to comprehend, insensibility, Dor.doct. 6.1(M.88.1685C).

*ἀκαταλίπτως, for ἀκαταλήπτως, of fire ἀ. ἀφιπτάμενον Dion. Ar.c.h.15.2(M.3.329C).

ἀκατάλυτος, indissoluble, everlasting τὸ τῶν ἁγίων ἀ. καὶ αἰώνιον βασίλειον Hipp.Dan.4.10.2; of baptism σφραγὶς ἁγία ἀ. Cyr.H. procatech.16; of the gospel, Epiph.haer.42.11(p.152.7; M.41.768D); μονὴ ἀ. παρὰ τῷ πατρί Bas.ascet.disc.2(2.213C; M.31.652C); of Christ, Cyr.ap.cat.Lc.23:31(p.166.27) cit. s. ἀμάραντος; and his kingdom, Cosm.Ind.top.2(M.88.112B).

*ἀκαταλύτως, indestructibly, everlastingly, exeg. Rom.6:10 τουτέστιν, ἀ. [sc. ζῇ], ὡς μηκέτι κρατεῖσθαι ὑπὸ τοῦ θανάτου Chrys.hom. 11.2 in Rom.(9.532C); Marc.Er.opusc.5.8(M.65.1041B).

*ἀκατάμαχος, unconquerable, Eus.d.e.9.3(p.410.18; M.22.661B).

ἀκατανάγκαστος, 1. not compelling, not compulsory; of Law, ref. Ex.20:25, Const.App.6.20.2; ref. Mt.16:24 ἀ. ποιεῖ τὸν λόγον Chrys.hom.55.1 in Mt.(7.555D); neut. as subst., absence of compulsion, id.hom.17.1 in 2Cor.(10.558C); 2. not subject to compulsion, free εἰ γὰρ δὴ ἀβίαστον καὶ ἀ. ... τὸ θεῖον Eus.p.e.5.9(196D; M.21.

340B); *voluntary* πρότερον μέντοι θελῆσαι δεῖ, καὶ τότε εἰσακοῦσαι, ἵνα τὸ ἐφ' ἡμῖν ἀ. ᾖ †Bas.*Is*.45(1.415D; M.30.205B); neut. as subst., *freedom*; exeg. Apoc.22:11, ref. God οὐχ ὡς εἰς ἀδικίαν...προτρέπων ...ἀλλ' ὡς τὸ τῆς γνώμης φυλάττων ἀ. Andr.Caes.*Apoc*.71(M.106. 448D).

*ἀκαταναγκάστως, *without compulsion*, ‡Chrys.*ador*.1.1(3.820C); cf.Chrys.*hom.55.1 in Mt*.(7.555D ἀκατανάγκαστον).

*ἀκατανίκητος, *unconquerable*, ‡Ath.*qu.al*.20(M.28.793C).

ἀκατανόητος, 1. *inconceivable, incomprehensible*, of God ἀ. πάσῃ γενητῇ ὑποστάσει Serap.*euch*.13.1; Gr.Nyss.*or.catech*.14(p.62.11; M. 45.45D); Max.*schol.d.n*.5.5(M.4.317D); of Son's generation, †Diad. *Ar*.2(M.65.1153B); Max.*ambig*.(M.91.1080A); Christ's birth, Jo. Mon.*hymn.Nic*.4(M.96.1385A); God's works in the heavens, *Ascens. Is*.A 2.4; 2. *not known*, of divine wisdom οὐδὲ τοῖς μὴ ὁμολογοῦσιν ἀ. Clem.*str*.5.1(p.329.23; M.9.16B); 3. *uncomprehending* ἀ. διάνοιαι *Cod.Afr*.86.

*ἀκατάνυκτος, *not pricked, insensitive* καρδία Jo.Clim.*scal*.27 (M.88.1108D); Anast.S.*qu.et resp*.105(M.89.757D).

ἀκατάπαυστος, *incessant*, hence *not to be ended, eternal*; of hell fire, Clem.*paed*.3.11(p.282.13; M.8.661C); Const.*or.s.c*.13(p.173.4); of kingdom of Christ, *Symb.Ant*.(341)4(p.254.26; M.26.736B); τοῦ Χριστοῦ...τὴν ἀ. ἐξουσίαν Cyr.H.*catech*.15.31; τῶν τοῦ μέλλοντος αἰῶνος ἀγαθῶν τῶν ἀ. Ammon.*Jo*.1:4(M.85.1393C); ἀ. ... δικαιοσύνης μνήμην κέκτηται Leont.N.*v.Jo.Eleem*.45(p.93.22).

ἀκαταπαύστως, *ceaselessly, eternally* ὁ μὲν γὰρ θεὸς...γεννᾷ... ἀτελευτήτως καὶ ἀ., διά τε τὸ ἄναρχον καὶ ἄχρονον, καὶ ἀτελεύτητον, καὶ ἀεὶ ὡσαύτως ἔχον ‡Cyr.*Trin*.7(6^3.10D; M.77.1136A).

*ἀκαταπολέμητος, *invincible* τί...πολεμεῖς τὸν ἀ.; [sc. H. Ghost] Epiph.*anc*.14(p.23.7; M.43.41C).

*ἀκαταπρόδοτος, *not betrayed*; neut. as subst., *non-betrayal*, Germ.CP *or*.2(M.98.265D).

ἀκατάπτωτος, *unthrown*, in wrestling, Gr.Nyss.*Eun*.2(2 p.387. 17; M.45.569B); met., *safe* ἵνα διὰ τῆς σεπτῆς ἑπτάδος τῶν νηστειῶν ἀσφαλῆ τε καὶ ἀ. τὴν διέξοδον ὑποπτευσώμεν Joannes Atheniensis ap.Jo.D.*jej*.suppl.(M.95.76A).

*ἀκατάργητος, *not to be abolished, indestructible* νοῦς ἀ. τοῖς ἀ. χαίρειν Val.Gn.ap.Epiph.*haer*.31.5(p.390.6; M.41.481A); *T.Sal*.15.5 (M.122.1337B).

*ἀκαταργήτως, *indestructibly*, Mac.Aeg.*libert.ment*.21(M.34.956C).

*ἀκατάρδευτος, *not watered* with dew, Cyr.*Joel*.15(3.214E, v.l. ἀκατάδευστος).

*ἀκατάρτιστος, *imperfect*; neut. as subst., *imperfection*, Iren. *haer*.4.38.2(M.7.1106C).

ἀκατάσβεστος, *unquenchable*; of hell fire, Heracl.*ep*.(M.92.1020B); neut. plur. as adv., †Jo.D.*B.J*.24(M.96.1084B).

[*]ἀκατάσειρος, for ἀκατάσειστος, *unshakeable* ἀ. ἀνδρείαν Dion. Ar.ap.*cat.Rom*.8:39(p.295.10); cf.id.*c.h*.8.1(M.3.237D).

ἀκατάσειστος, *unshakeable*, of Church τὸν ἀ. οἶκον Didym.*Trin*. 2.6(M.39.519C); ἀ. καταλελοιπότες πόλιν, τὴν ἐγκράτειαν Cyr.*ador*.1 (1.19E); of God ἱδρυμένην ἔχων καὶ ἀ. φύσιν id.*Zach*.59(3.739C); ἡ θεοῦ φύσις...ἀ. ἔχει τὴν ἐφ' οἷς ἐστι διαμονήν id.*inc.unigen*.(5^1.683B); παλαιῶν ἀνδρῶν...ἀ. ἐν καρτερίᾳ φιλοσοφίαν Dion.Ar.*e.h*.3.3.4(M.3. 429C); of Christ πύργον ἀ. εἰς ἐπικουρίαν Cyr.*Is*.3.3(2.471B).

*ἀκατασείστως, *unshakeably, immovably*, Cyr.*glaph.Gen*.3(1. 106A); Dion.Ar.*c.h*.7.1(M.3.205D).

*ἀκατάσκεπτος, 1. *unconsidered, wild* ἀ., κομιδῇ τῶν τῆς ἐκκλησίας δογμάτων ποιεῖται τὴν κατάρρησιν Cyr.*Nest*.2.7(p.43.35, v.l. ἀκατάσκοπον 6^1.47B); id.*glaph.Gen*.7(1.218E); id.*glaph.Ex*.3(1.333D); 2. ? *not to be examined, beyond criticism*; neut. as subst., *faultlessness* κεκτήσεται μὲν γὰρ τὸ ἀ. παντελῶς οὐδείς, τετήρηται δὲ μόνῳ... τῷ Ἐμμανουήλ id.*ador*.16(1.585A) perh. for ἀκατάσκωπτος q.v.

*ἀκατασκέπτως, *without consideration, thoughtlessly*, Cyr.*glaph. Num*.(1.409A); id.*Juln*.4(6^2.131E); id.*Nest*.1.8(p.30.7; 6^1.26E).

ἀκατασκεύαστος, 1. *unwrought, unformed, chaotic* οὐσίαν...ἀ. Hipp.*haer*.6.30(p.158.10; M.16.3239B); Bas.*hex*.2.2(1.13B; M.29.29C); *Const.App*.7.34.1, etc.; λυθήσονται οἱ οὐρανοὶ καὶ ἔσται ὁ ἀὴρ ἀ. *1 Apoc.Jo*.19(p.87); 2. *not manufactured* σοφία καὶ δύναμις...ἀχειροποίητοι...καὶ ἀ. ‡Gr.Nyss.*Ar.et Sab*.9(M.45.1293C); met., *unpremeditated* γέγονε τοῦτο, οὐ προθεμένης μοι τῆς γνώμης ἀλλ' ἀ. οὕτω παρελθόν Synes.*ep*.137(M.66.1525C); 3. *not artificial, plain*, met. ἁπλῷ καὶ ἀ. διηγήματι Gr.Nyss.*fat*.(M.45.148A); 4. *unequipped*; of a ship, Chrys.*hom.19.3 in Eph*.(11.138C).

ἀκατασκευάστως, *roughly, without finish*; ref. an argument, *without support* of evidence, Or.*Cels*.4.58(p.330.24; M.11.1125A).

ἀκατάσκευος, 1. *not fitted out*; a. *plain, without addition*, †Bas. *Is*.29(1.402A; M.30.173C); b. *unadorned, simple*; of the faith, Gr. Nyss.*hom.opif*.26.13(M.44.224A); τὴν ἁπλῆν τε καὶ ἀκατάσκευον...τῆς θείας γραφῆς διάνοιαν id.*Apoll*.29(M.45.1185D); *naked* ἡ ἑκάστου ψυχὴ...λιτή τις καὶ ἀ. ἐπιχωριάζει τοῖς κάτω id.*ep*.1.14(M.46.1004C); neut. as subst., *simplicity* τὸ ἁπλοῦν καὶ ἀ. τῶν πνευματικῶν λόγων Bas.*hex*.3.8(1.30D; M.29.73B); c. in argument, *unsupported* by evidence ψιλὴν καὶ ἀ. τὴν βλασφημίαν προβάλλεται, οὐδενὶ λογισμῷ κατασκευάζων τὴν ἀτοπίαν Gr.Nyss.*Trin*.7(p.79.6; M.32.693C); id. *Eun*.4(2 p.79.4; M.45.653A); *ib*.(p.79.29; 653C); 2. *unformed*; of the earth at Creation, Cyr.*Is*.4.3(2.618C).

ἀκατασκεύως, 1. *without preparation* or *elaboration*, Gr.Nyss. *hom.7 in Cant*.(M.44.925C); 2. *without artifice, bluntly*, id.*Eun*.12 (1 p.231.23; M.45.928C).

*ἀκατασκίαστος, *free from shadows, clear* γυμνὸν καὶ ἀ. βλέπων τῆς ἀληθείας τὸ κάλλος Cyr.*hom.pasch*.20(5^2.261C, v.l. ἀκατασκεύαστον).

*ἀκατάσκιος, = foreg. ἐμφανῆ τε καὶ ἀ. ἐπιτηδεύειν τὴν πλημμέλειαν Cyr.*ador*.14(1.504E).

*ἀκατασκόπητος, *not to be gazed on*, Gr.Naz.*carm*.1.1.30.32(M. 37.510A).

ἀκατάσκοπος, 1. *not gazed at, unobserved*, Clem.*paed*.3.11(p.280. 9; M.8.657B); ἐν ἀ. βαπτίσαι *Hom.Clem*.14.1; 2. s.v.l., ?*faultless* δικαιοσύνην...ἄμωμόν τε καὶ ἀ. Cyr.*Is*.5.6(2.889B), cf. ἀκατάσκεπτος; 3. prob. for ἀκατάσκεπτος, *unconsidered*, id.*Nest*.2.7(6^1.47B; ἀκατάσκεπτος p.43.35).

*ἀκατάσκωπτος, *not liable to derision, blameless* ἀδιάβλητον... καὶ ἀ. προθυμίαν Cyr.*ador*.12(1.419B); ἀ. ζωήν id.*Os*.58(3.90A).

ἀκαταστασία, ἡ, 1. *anarchy, confusion*; in Church, Eus.*ep.Caes*. (p.46.11; M.20.1544A); Jul.Papa *ep.Dian*.ap.Ath.*apol.sec*.35(p.112. 32; M.25.305C); Bas.*ep*.70(3.164A; M.32.436A); Epiph.*anc*.82(p.102. 26; M.43.172A); 2. *unsettledness, instability*; mental or moral, Herm. *sim*.6.3.4; τοῦ ἤθους ἀ. Ath.*v.Anton*.36(M.26.896B); ἀ. τῶν λογισμῶν Mac.Aeg.*hom*.5.4(M.34.497C).

ἀκατάσχετος, *not to be checked, uncontrollable*; in good sense, *unrestrained, irrepressible* ἡ τοῦ ἁγίου πνεύματος ἔκχυσις...ἡ ἀ. καὶ ἄφθονος ἐπιφοίτησις αὐτοῦ Didym.*Trin*.2.6(M.39.533A); τὴν καῦσιν καὶ τὸν ἔρωτα πρὸς τὸν θεὸν ἀ. Mac.Aeg.*hom*.15.37(M.34.601B); ref. Christ δι' ὑπερβολὴν ἀγαθότητος καὶ ἀ. ἔρωτα σταυρωθείς *Lit.Jac*. (p.164.9).

ἀκατάτακτος, *not ranged with, independent*, Dion.Ar.*e.h*.2.3.5 (M.3.401A).

ἀκατάτριπτος, *not wasted away, whole* μόνη ἡ γλῶττα ἀ. ὑπῆρχε Pall.*h.Laus*.21(p.64.16; M.34.1073B).

*ἀκατάφλεκτος, *not burnt up, not consumed by fire*; of burning bush, Sev.Ant.ap.*cat.Ac*.2:3(p.21.10); met., of BMV βάτε ἀ. Ephr. 3.529D; οὐρανὸν καινὸν καὶ θρόνον ἀ. Jo.Eub.*concept.BMV* 16(M.96. 1485B); Jo.Mon.*hymn.Chrys*.6(M.96.1381C).

*ἀκατάφλευκτος, for ἀκατάφλεκτος, *not burnt up*, of BMV ὦ βάτε ἀκατάφλευκτε Ephr.3.545F.

*ἀκατάψεκτος, 1. *blameless*, Cyr.*ador*.16(1.582A); id.*Juln*.6(6^2. 210B); 2. *unblamed* οὐκ ἀ. ἐᾷ τὴν τοῦ σῴζοντος ἡμερότητα *ib*.(207A); neut. as subst., *freedom from blame* οὐ πᾶσα πάντως εἰρήνη τὸ ἀ. ἔχει id.*Lc*.12:51(M.72.756D).

*ἀκαταψέκτως, 1. *blamelessly*, Cyr.*Lc*.16:10(M.72.816C); 2. *without being blamed*, id.*Juln*.10(6^2.326B).

ἀκατέργαστος, *not worked over, not elaborately finished*, Synes. *regn*.17(p.41.14; M.66.1088C); *imperfect*, ref. Ps.138:16 τὸ μὴ [ed. μὲν] ἀ. μου ἔγνωσαν οἱ ὀφθαλμοί σου Jo.D.*anacr*.(M.96.854A).

ἀκατεύναστος, *not put to bed*; hence *sleepless, ever-watchful*; of the eye of God, Cyr.*Am*.89(3.343A); κεχειροτόνηκεν αὐτῇ [sc. Church] φύλακας σοφούς...ἀ. ἔχοντας ἐπ' αὐτῇ τὴν φροντίδα id.*Is*. 5.5(2.872D); neut. as subst., *nightly vigil* τοὺς διημερινοὺς...ἱδρῶτας καὶ τὸ τῆς θεολογίας ἀ. Sophr.H.*v.Anast*.(M.92.1708B); met., *ceaseless, perpetual* ἀ. τὴν ὑμνῳδίαν Cyr.*Ps*.46:7(M.69.1056A); of hell fire, id.*Soph*.45(3.623C); of the flame of anger, id.ap.Jo.D.*parall*. 15(M.96.273A).

ἀκατηγόρητος, *unaccused*; *blameless*; hence *innocent of sin* τὰ αὐτῆς [sc. σαρκός] οἰκειούμενος ἀ. πάθη Cyr.*thes*.28(5^1.252C); neut. as adv., *blamelessly* νῦν μὲν γὰρ ὡς ἄνθρωπος ἀ. προσκυνεῖ id.*Jo*.2.5 (v.l. ἀκατηγορήτως 4.190B).

*ἀκατηγορήτως, v.l. for ἀκατηγόρητον Cyr.*Jo*.2.5(4.190B).

ἀκατήχητος, *uninstructed, ignorant of the faith* ἀνθρώπων αἱρετικῶν ἀ. Ar.*ep.Eus*.(p.2.7; M.42.212A); τῶν ἔτι ἀ. πόλεων Bas. Sel.*v.Thecl*.1(M.85.556A); c. genit., *uninstructed in*, Gr.Nyss.*Eun*.1 (1 p.70.15; M.45.300B); Max.*schol.e.h*.3.3.6(M.4.141B).

ἀκατονόμαστος ([*]ἀκατωνόμαστος), *not to be named, unnameable*; 1. of God τῆς ἀρρήτου καὶ ἀ. ... ὑποστάσεως τοῦ πατρός Or.

*princ.*4.4.1(p.349.20); Gr.Naz.*or.*30.17(p.134.19; M.36.125B); Gr.Nyss. *tres dii*(M.45.121A); exeg. Cant.5:7 ἐκάλουν αὐτὸν ἐξ ὀνόματος, ὡς ἦν μοι δυνατὸν ἐξευρεῖν ἐπὶ τοῦ ἀ. ὀνόματος id.*hom.6 in Cant.*(M.44.892D); ref. Mt.28:19 τί οὖν σημαίνει τὸ ἀ. ὄνομα, περὶ οὗ εἰπὼν ὁ κύριος ὅτι βαπτίζοντες αὐτοὺς εἰς τὸ ὄνομα, οὐ προσέθηκεν αὐτὴν τὴν σημαντικὴν φωνὴν τὴν ὑπὸ τοῦ ὀνόματος δηλουμένην; id.*Eun.*2(2 p.301.28; M.45.472D); Isid.Pel.*epp.*1.143(M.78.432B); Dion.Ar.*d.n.*1.8 (M.3.597C); **2.** of generation of Son γεγεννημένος, ἀρρήτῳ λόγῳ καὶ δυνάμει ἀ. Eus.*l.C.*12(p.230.11; M.20.1388B); ἀκατωνόμαστον αὐτοῦ γένεσίν τε καὶ οὐσίωσιν id.*d.e.*5.1(p.211.28; -ονόμαστον M.22.352B); of union of Christ's natures εἰσὶ δὲ οἳ καὶ εὐλάβειαν περιττὴν ἢ ἔχοντες ἢ ὑποκρινόμενοι...ἄρρητον...αὐτὴν [sc. ἕνωσιν] καὶ ἀ. γεγενῆσθαι ἀπεφήναντο Leont.B.*Nest.et Eut.*1(M.86.1297D); **3.** of God as unknowable, acc. Gnostics τὸν μὲν παντοκράτορα θεὸν βλασφημεῖν, ἄγνωστον δοξάζειν...ἄλεκτον, ἄρρητον, ἀ. *Const.App.*6.10.1; Epiph. *haer.*31.2(p.386.7; M.41.477A); Jo.D.*haer.*44(M.94.704B).

ἀκατόπτευτος, 1. *not to be looked on* τὸ φῶς τὸ θεῖον ἀπροσπέλαστον καὶ ἀ. Max.*schol.d.n.*7.1.3(M.4.341A); Chrysipp.*enc.in Jo.Bapt.*(p.30.13); **2.** *unobserved* μὴ νόμιζε...τὸ σφάλμα ἀ. Rom.Mel.(*SBBAW* 1898[2] p.143).

***ἀκατόρθωτος, 1.** *not to be set right, irremediable* εἰς μεγάλην ἐξέτασιν [sc. baptism] ἔρχῃ...κατὰ τὴν μίαν ὥραν· ἣν ἐὰν ἀπολέσῃς, ἀ. σοι τὸ κακόν Cyr.H.*catech.*17.36; κακοπιστία ἀ. Epiph.*anc.*9(p.16.8; M.43.32B); ὦ τῆς τῶν ἀνθρώπων πολλῆς φρενοβλαβείας καὶ ἀ. λογισμοῦ id.*haer.*57.3(p.347.21; M.41.1000A) or perh. *not rightly directed, erring*; **2.** *not to be brought to a successful issue, impossible to fulfil* or *attain* νομίζουσιν ἀ. εἶναι τὴν ἀρετήν Or.*exp.in Pr.*19(M.17.205D); ἐπιτάγματα δυσχερῆ, ἀλλὰ μὴν οὐκ ἀ. Ammon.*Ac.*15:10 (M.85.1552A); neut. as subst., *impossibility of performance*; of the Law, *ib.*13:39(1541C); **3.** *not fulfilled* τὴν ἐντολὴν τῆς ἀγάπης ἀ. εἶναι Bas.*reg.fus.*25.2(2.370E; M.31.985B).

***ἀκατόχως,** *without being held*, of Christ τοῖς σπαργάνοις ἐγκατεχόμενον ἀ. ‡Meth.*Sym.et Ann.*3(M.18.353A).

[*]**ἀκατωνόμαστος,** v. ἀκατονόμαστος.

ἄκαυστος, 1. *without the quality of burning* ἀλαμπὲς μὲν εἶναι τὸ πῦρ τῆς κολάσεως, ἄ. δὲ τὸ φῶς τῆς ἀναπαύσεως Bas.*hom.in Ps.*28 (1.121B; M.29.297C); **2.** *unkindled*, exeg. Job 20:25 τοῦτο τὸ πῦρ τὸ παρ' ἡμῖν ὑλικὸν οὐκ ἔστιν ἄ. πῦρ· βλεπόμενον γὰρ αὐτό. ἐκεῖνο δὲ ἀόρατόν ἐστι τὸ πῦρ, τὸ ἐπὶ τοὺς ἁμαρτωλοὺς ἐρχόμενον, ὃ ἔνδον αὐτοὺς καίει Or.*enarr.in Job* 20:25(M.17.76A); κατὰ μὲν τὸ πρόχειρον, τὸ μὴ ἐκ προνοίας ἀναφθέν, ἀλλ' αὐτομάτως κατενεχθέν,...κατὰ δὲ τὸ κρυπτόμενον, ἄ. πῦρ ἐστιν, ἤτοι τὸ κατὰ συνείδησιν,...ἢ καὶ τὸ ἀποκείμενον ἐν τοῖς μέλλουσι δικαιωτηρίοις Olymp.*Job* 20:25(M.93.217D).

***ἀκαυχησία, ἡ,** *absence of boasting, humility*, Ign.*Polyc.*5.2.

ἀκέαστος, *unbroken, undivided*; of the divine nature, Gr.Naz. *carm.*1.1.2.35(M.37.404A); *ib.*1.1.3.73(414A).

***ἀκέδουκτος, ὁ,** *aqueduct*, Thphn.*chron.*p.424(M.108.1004A).

***ἀκεκρυμμένως,** *without concealment, openly*, Gr.Nyss.*hom.15 in Cant.*(M.44.1116B).

ἀκενοδοξία, ἡ, *absence of vainglory, modesty*, Chrys.*hom.8.1 in 1Tim.*(11.589D); †Nil.*vit.*4(M.79.1144D); *ib.*1(1141D); Jo.Clim.*scal.*4 (M.88.725B).

ἀκενόδοξος, *free from vain conceit, modest, humble*; in gen., exeg. Mt.8:4 διὰ μὲν τοῦ λεπροῦ τούτου ἀτύφους ἡμᾶς παρασκευάζων [sc. ὁ Χριστός] καὶ ἀ. Chrys.*hom.25.2 in Mt.*(7.309A); ἀ. μελέτη τῶν λογίων τοῦ θεοῦ Diad.*perf.*9(p.12.6); Jo.D.*dialect.*1(M.94.532C); neut. as subst., *freedom from pride, humility*, Ammon.*Ac.*14:17 (M.85.1545C); exeg. Mt.6:6 οὐ τοίνυν εἰς τὸν τόπον περιώρισε τὴν εὐχήν, ἀλλ' ἐν μόνον ἐπέταξε τὸ ἀ. Chrys.*hom.8.1 in 1Tim.*(11.589E); of Christ ὑποστέλλει μὴ δημοσιεύεσθαι, ὡς ἐπιεικὴς καὶ ἀ. Or.*fr.in Mt.*12:15(p.117.13; M.17.293D); Ammon.*Jo.*11:42(M.85.1469A); Leont. H.*Nest.*5.22(M.86.1744C).

ἀκενοδόξως, *without vain conceit*, Ephr.3.68C.

ἄκεντρος, 1. *stingless, harmless*, met. ὀφείλομεν...πρόνοιαν ποιεῖσθαι τοῦ τε λόγου, ἵν' ἄ. καὶ ὠφέλιμος ᾖ Or.*or.*28.2(p.376.19; M.11.524A); οὐ γὰρ ἄ. παντελῶς τῶν ἁγίων ἡ ἀρετή Cyr.*Joel.*64(3.244C); **2.** *not responding to the spur*, met. *dull, stupid* τούτων αὐτάρκων ὄντων τοῖς μὴ ἀ. Or.*princ.*4.3.7(p.333.10; M.11.388A).

***ἀκένωτος, 1.** *not emptied*; in gen., †Apoll.*met.Ps.*74:9(M.33.1420C); Christol. ref. *kenosis* of Logos in Inc. ὁ...λόγος κενοῦται, ἀ. τὴν φύσιν ὑπάρχων Attic.ap.Cyr.*Arcad.*(p.66.25; 5[2].49C); εἰς τοσαύτην ἑαυτὸν καθῆκεν ὁ ἀ. κένωσιν Sophr.H.*or.*2.42(M.87.3273C); **2.** *inexhaustible*, Amph.*hom.*4.9(M.39.84D); Isid.Pel.*epp.*3.129(M.78.829B); ‡Chrys.*hom.*5(13.211E).

ἀκέραιος, 1. *pure, without admixture*, of man at resurrection ἀ. καὶ πάσης τῆς κατὰ κακίαν ἐπιμιξίας ἀλλότριον ἀναστοιχειωθῆναι Gr. Nyss.*or.catech.*35(p.133.11; M.45.89A); met., *sincere* τὸ ἀ. τῆς πραΰτητος αὐτῶν βούλημα *1Clem.*21.7; of faith, Const.ap.Gel.Cyz.*h.e.*2.7.9 (M.85.1233C); *complete in itself* ἀ. δὲ καὶ τέλειός ἐστιν ὁ ἀριθμὸς τῆς τριάδος *Symb.Sirm.*2(p.257.25; M.26.744A); **2.** *unharmed, intact* ἀ. καὶ ὁλόκληρον ἀναστῆναι τὴν σάρκα †Just.*fr.res.*4(p.40; M.6.1577D); *virgin*, Isid.Pel.*epp.*2.53(M.78.497A); met., *pure, inviolate* τοὺς...τῶν πατέρων ὅρους ἀ. φυλάξωσιν Ath.*syn.*13(p.240.19; M.26.704B); hence ἐν ἀ. *in full*, Gr.Mag.*dial.*(tr.Zach.)3.37(M.*PL.*77.307C); *unprejudiced* τὸ ἥμισυ τῆς ἀκροάσεως ἀ. διασῴζειν πρὸς ἀπολογίαν τῷ μὴ παρόντι Bas.*ep.*94(3.188E; M.32.489A); **3.** of persons, *innocent; simple*, opp. subtle or learned, Or.*princ.*4.3.3(p.327.8; M.11.381A); Ath.*Ar.*1.8 (M.26.25D); Cyr.*Jo.*10.2(4.917D).

ἀκεραιοσύνη, ἡ, *guilelessness, innocence, simplicity*, *Barn.*3.6; *ib.*10.4.

ἀκεραιότης, ἡ, 1. *soundness, safety* τὴν τοῦ σώματος ἀ. Isid.Pel. *epp.*1.83(M.78.240C); **2.** *guilelessness, simplicity, innocence*, Or.*hom.17.2 in Jer.*(p.144.18; M.13.456B); ἡ σοφία δεινότητός τε καὶ ἀ. τὸ μέσον ἔχει Gr.Nyss.*v.Mos.*(M.44.420B); exeg. Cant.2:13 περιστερὰ διὰ τὴν ἀ. Ph.Carp.*Cant.*61(M.40.72A); of simplicity of speech τῶν ἐν ἀ. φθεγγομένων Nil.*epp.*2.291(M.79.345A).

ἀκεραίως, *sincerely, honestly* τοῖς μὲν ἀ. δικάζουσιν ἀπειλοῦντες *Ep.Aeg.*(p.156.34; M.25.388B).

***ἀκεροπερίσπαστος,** prob. for *ἀκαιροπερίσπαστος, *distracted in an untimely way*, ‡Ath.*syntag.*1.9(M.28.837A).

ἀκέστωρ, ὁ, *healer*, Paul.Sil.*Soph.*799(M.86.2149B).

ἀκέφαλος, 1. *headless*, astron. ὁ ἀ. πρὸς τῶν μαθηματικῶν καλούμενος ὁ πρὸ τοῦ ἀστέρος τοῦ πλανωμένου καταριθμούμενος Clem.*paed.*2.2(p.177.3; M.8.429C); **2.** *senseless*, Anast.S.*hod.*12(M.89.200B); **3.** plur., name of monoph. party; def. *Acephali dicti, id est sine capite quem sequuntur haeretici. nullus enim eorum reperitur auctor, a quo exorti sunt. hi trium Chalcedonensium capitulorum impugnatores duarum in Christo substantiarum proprietatem negant, et unam in ejus persona naturam praedicant*, Isid.H.*etym.*8.5.66; being those who separated themselves from Peter Mongus ἀποσχίζονταί τινες ἀπὸ Πέτρου διότι δεξάμενος τὸ Ἑνωτικόν, οὐ φανερῶς ἀνεθεμάτιζε τὴν σύνοδον. καὶ ἐλέγοντο οἱ τοιοῦτοι Ἀ., διότι τῷ πατριάρχῃ αὐτῶν μὴ ἀκολουθήσαντες καθ' ἑαυτοὺς ἐκοινώνουν †Leont. B.*sect.*5.2(M.86.1229B); Ἀ.· οἱ μὴ δεξάμενοι τὸ Ἑνωτικὸν Ζήνωνος, διὰ τὸ μὴ ἀναθεματισθῆναι ἐν αὐτῷ τὴν ἐν Χαλκηδόνι ἁγίαν σύνοδον Tim.CP *haer.*(M.86.56C); and as rejecting the true headship of Christ, Eust.Mon.*ep.*(M.86.940A); in gen. τούτῳ [sc. Tim. II Al.] καὶ τοῖς ἀπ' αὐτοῦ μέχρι τῆς σήμερον οὐ κοινωνοῦσιν οἱ Σευήρου, ἀ. αὐτοὺς προσαγορεύοντες *ib.*(904C); τοῖς Ἀπολιναρίου πονηροῖς ἀκολουθοῦντες δόγμασιν οἱ Ἀ., οὐχ ὁμολογοῦσιν ἐν δύο οὐσίαις εἶναι καὶ γνωρίζεσθαι τὸν Χριστόν, ἀλλ' ἐν μιᾷ Justn.*monoph.*(p.39.24; M.86.1140D); Εὐτυχιανισταί, καὶ ὁ τούτων κοινωνὸς Διόσκορος, Σευῆρος, Ἰάκωβος, καὶ οἱ λοιποὶ Ἀ. Tim.CP *haer.*(72A); Σεβῆρος καὶ Πέτρος ὁ Κναφεὺς καὶ Φιλόξενος καὶ πᾶσα ἡ ἀμφ' αὐτοῖς πολυκέφαλος ὕδρα καὶ ἀ. CNic.(787)*refut.*(H.4.409C); of their teaching ἀ. τερθρείας ἀντίπαλοι Sophr.H.*or.*2.7(M.87.3225A); οὐ μὴ περιπέσῃ τῇ ἐχθραινούσῃ θεῷ ἀ. ὑπερηφανίᾳ Jo.Clim.*scal.*22(M.88.957A); **4.** *without a head* or *superior*; of cleric not under episcopal jurisdiction, cf. *duo sunt autem genera clericorum: unum ecclesiasticorum sub regimine episcopali degentium, alterum acephalorum, id est, sine capite, quem sequantur, ignorantium*, Isid.H.*de ecclesiasticis officiis* 2.3(M.*PL.*83.779A).

ἀκήδεια, ἡ, = ἀκηδία, *weariness*, Cyr.*hom.pasch.*18(5[2].244E); Nil. *epp.*3.142(M.79.449A); ‡Nil.*perist.*11.4(M.79.909B).

***ἀκηδεμόνευτος,** *uncared for* οὐδὲν τῶν ὄντων ἀ. Cyr.*Ps.*66:4 (M.69.1141A); Thdt.*qu.83 in Gen.*(1.93); id.*Ps.*66:4(1.1052).

ἀκηδία, ἡ, A. in gen.; **1.** (physical) *fatigue, exhaustion* νυσταγμὸς...καὶ ἀ., καὶ ὁ ἐκ τῆς ὁδοῦ κόπος ἐπιτείνων τὴν ἀ. Gr.Nyss.*ep.*1 (M.46.1001D); **2.** *weariness, inertia* ὑμεῖς μαλακισθέντες ἀπὸ τῶν βιωτικῶν πραγμάτων παρεδώκατε ἑαυτοὺς εἰς τὰς ἀ. Herm.*vis.*3.11.3; κρίσις δὲ πηγῆς τῶν νοὸς βουλευμάτων· ῥίψιν δὲ τούτων οἶδα τὴν ἀ. Gr.Naz.*carm.*1.2.34.70(M.37.950A); **3.** *anxiety* ἐπειδὴ εἰς τὴν καταδυναστείαν...τῶν δαιμόνων ἀφορῶν, ἀ. πεπλήρωμαι Ath.*exp.Ps.*60:2f.(M.27.272D); στενωθεῖσα ὑπὸ τῆς ἀ. Pall.*v.Chrys.*17(p.109.2; M.47.60); **4.** *loss of hope, despair* συνέθραυσε δὲ [sc. Sennacherib] οὕτως εἰς ἀ. τοὺς ἐν τοῖς Ἱεροσολύμοις Cyr.*Am.*75(3.336D); id.*Jon.*16(3.379C); caused by attacks of concupiscence ἡμᾶς καταπυρούσης τῆς ἐπιθυμίας, καταβοῶμεν ἐξ ἀ. πολλάκις id.*Jo.*3.6(4.314A); **5.** *sadness* λυπεῖ σφόδρα καὶ εἰς ἐσχάτην ἀ. καταφέρει Cyr.*ep.*76(M.77.364B); exeg. Is.61:3 ἀντὶ πνεύματος ἀ., τουτέστιν, ἀντὶ τῆς πάλαι μικροψυχίας id.*Is.*5.5(2.862B).

B. *listlessness, torpor, boredom, 'accidie'*, t.t. for a special temptation of monks and hermits; **1.** def. ἀ. ἐστὶν ἀτονία ψυχῆς, ἀτονία δὲ ψυχῆς οὐκ ἔχουσα τὸ κατὰ φύσιν, οὐδὲ πρὸς πειρασμοὺς ἵσταται γενναίως Nil.*spir.mal.*13(M.79.1157C); cf.‡Nil.*vit.cog.*(M.79.1457B); ἀ., φιλία ἀερική, βημάτων περιαγωγός, φιλεργίας μῖσος, ἡσυχίας μάχη, ψαλμῳδίας ζάλη, εὐχῆς ὄκνος, ἀσκήσεως χαύνωσις †Nil.*vit.*4(M.79.1144B); ἀ. ἐστὶ πάρεσις ψυχῆς, καὶ νοὸς ἔκλυσις, ὀλιγωρία ἀσκήσεως, μῖσος τοῦ ἐπαγγέλματος, κοσμικῶν μακαρίστρια, θεοῦ διαβλήτωρ, ὡς ἀσπλάγχνου καὶ ἀφιλανθρώπου Jo.Clim.*scal.*13(M.88.860A); ἀ. ἐστὶν ἀσκήσεως μῖσος τοῦ μοναχικοῦ ἐπαγγέλματος, κοσμικῶν μακαρίστρια, θεοῦ διαβλήτωρ, ὡς ἀσπλάγχνου καὶ ἀφιλανθρώπου, ἀτονία ψαλμῳδίας ἐν προσευχαῖς ἀσθενοῦσα· ὁρίζομεν δὲ καὶ ταύτην μ' ἡμέρας μετανοεῖν· ἑβδομάδας τρεῖς οἴνου μὴ μεταλαμβάνειν καὶ ἐλαίου· μετανοίας ποιεῖν καθ' ἡμέραν σν'· ὅτι εἰς βυθὸν ᾅδου δύναται κατάγειν τὸ πάθος τῆς ἀ. Thdr.Stud.*conf.*6(M.99.1724C); **2.** special temptation of hermits τοῖς ἐν ἡσυχίᾳ, μάλιστα πολεμεῖ τὸ πάθος τῆς ἀ. ‡Nil.*vit.cog.*(M.79.1460A); *Apophth.Patr.*(M.65.76A); Jo.Clim.*scal.*27(M.88.1109A, 1113C); ὁ διάβολος...ὑπέβαλλεν αὐτοῖς...ἀ. πρὸς τὴν ἄσκησιν, ὥστε διαφόρως ἐπιζητεῖν αὐτοὺς ὑποστρέφειν εἰς τὸ μοναστήριον ἀπὸ τῆς ἐρήμου Leont.N.*v.Sym.*21(M.93.1697A); also of others devoted to life of prayer, Sophr.H.*mir.Cyr.et Jo.*13(M.87.3464C); **3.** causes; **a.** natural, such as sadness ἡ λύπη...πᾶσαν τὴν ψυχὴν θλίβουσα, πικρίας αὐτὴν καὶ ἀ. πληροῖ ‡Ath.*ep.Cast.*2.5(M.28.897A); τὸ πνεῦμα τῆς ἀ. τῷ πνεύματι τῆς λύπης ἀκολουθεῖ ‡Nil.*vit.cog.*(M.79.1456D); laziness and loquaciousness, ‡Ath.*ep.Cast.*2.6(900A); ἡ δὲ πολυλογία τίκτει τὴν ἀ. Ammonas *opusc.*4(p.476.11); bad thoughts οὐ δεῖ ἡμᾶς τοὺς πονηροὺς παραδέχεσθαι λογισμοὺς...ἀ. ὑποσπείροντας Cyr.S.*v.Euthym.*19(p.30.19); absorption in emotions ἡδονῇ ἢ λύπῃ ἐγχρονίζων ὁ νοῦς, τῷ τῆς ἀ. πάθει τάχιστα περιπίπτει Thal.*cent.* 1.90(M.91.1436C); **b.** preternatural; ἀ. attributed to a particular demon, most active about midday, suggested by Ps.90:6 τὸν γὰρ μεσημβρινὸν δαίμονά φησιν εἶναι τῆς ἀ. Ath.*exp.Ps.*90:6(M.27.401B); δαιμόνιον δὲ μεσημβρινὸν ὀνομάζει τὴν ἀ. ... ἀλλὰ καὶ τότε σώζει θεός, ἀπαλλάττει γὰρ ἀπὸ συμπτώματος καὶ ἐξ ἀ., τουτέστι δαιμονίου μεσημβρινοῦ Cyr.*Ps.*90:6(M.69.1220A,B); descriptions of his activities ὁ τῆς ἀ. δαίμων, ὃς καὶ μεσημβρινὸς καλεῖται, πάντων τῶν δαιμόνων ἐστὶ βαρύτερος· καὶ ἐφίσταται μὲν τῷ μοναχῷ περὶ ὥραν τετάρτην, κυκλοῖ δὲ τὴν ψυχὴν αὐτοῦ μέχρι ὥρας ὀγδόης. καὶ πρῶτον μὲν τὸν ἥλιον καθορᾶσθαι ποιεῖ δυσκίνητον ἢ ἀκίνητον, πεντηκοντάωρον τὴν ἡμέραν δεικνύς· ἔπειτα δὲ συνεχῶς ἀφορᾶν πρὸς τὰς θυρίδας, καὶ τῆς κέλλης ἐκπηδᾶν ἐκβιάζεται, τῷ τε ἡλίῳ ἐνατενίζειν, πόσον τῆς ἐννάτης ἀφέστηκε Evagr.Pont.*vit.cog.*7(M.40.1273A,B); id. *cap.pract.*A 19(M.40.1225D); τὸ πνεῦμα τῆς ἀ. ... δεινὸς...τοῖς μοναχοῖς ἀεὶ πολεμῶν· ὃς ἕκτην ὥραν ἐπιτίθεται μάλιστα· διὸ καὶ μεσημβρινὸς καλεῖται· φρίκην ἐμποιῶν καὶ ἀτονίαν, καὶ μῖσος πρὸς αὐτόν τε τὸν τόπον, καὶ τοὺς συνδιατρίβοντας ἀδελφούς, καὶ ῥαθυμίαν εἰς εὐχὴν καὶ ἀνάγνωσιν· ὑποβάλλει δὲ λογισμοὺς μεταβάσεως...προσήκει δὲ διὰ προσευχῆς αὐτὸν ἀνατρέπειν, καὶ ἀναγνώσεως, καὶ ὑπομονῆς, καὶ καρτερίας, καὶ ἀποχῆς ἀργολογίας, καὶ διὰ τοῦ ἔργου τῶν χειρῶν ‡Nil.*vit.cog.*(M.79.1456D–1457B) ∾ Leont.et Jo.*sacr.*(M.86.2065C); δεινὸς...ὁ τῆς ἀ. δαίμων...βαρύτατος ὅστις περὶ ὥραν ἕκτην ἐμπίπτει τῷ μοναχῷ, ἀγωνίαν αὐτῷ ἐμποιῶν, καὶ ἀπεχθῶς ἔχειν πρὸς τὸν τόπον, μᾶλλον δὲ καὶ πρὸς τοὺς συνδιατρίβοντας ἀδελφούς, καὶ πρὸς πᾶν ἔργον Ant.Mon.*hom.*26(M.89.1513D); **4.** effects: causes monks to leave monasteries, Nil.*spir.mal.*13(M.79.1157D); Pall.*h.Laus.*21(p.63.20; M.34.1068D); οὗτος ὁ τῆς ἀ. δαίμων ὑποβάλλει αὐτῷ [sc. μοναχῷ] καὶ λογισμοὺς μετὰ ὑποβάσεως, καὶ ὡς εἰ μὴ μεταστήσῃ ἑαυτὸν πρὸς τόπους ἑτέρους, πᾶς ὁ χρόνος καὶ ὁ πόνος μάταιος αὐτῷ γενήσεται Ant.Mon.*hom.*26(M.89.1516B); or to leave their cells unnecessarily, ‡Bas.*const.*7.2(2.553D; M.31.1368A); excites the passions, Max.*carit.* 1.67(M.90.973D) ∾ ‡Nil.*vit.cog.*(M.79.1460A) ∾ Ammon.*Mt.*24:13(M.85.1385B); ἔγνων τὸν ἀ. δαίμονα προποιοῦντα...τὸν τῆς πορνείας Jo.Clim.*scal.*27(M.88.1109C); prevents prayer under pretext of good works, *ib.*13(860B); and brings about spiritual death 'τὸ πνεῦμα μὴ σβέννυτε.' ὑπὸ μὲν γὰρ ἀ. ... σβέννυται Chrys.*hom.1.2 in 2Tim.*(11.661C); ἀ. δὲ τῷ μοναχῷ περιεκτικὸς θάνατος· ἀνδρεία ψυχὴ νοῦν ἀποθανόντα ἀνέστησεν· ἀ. δὲ καὶ ὀκνηρία ὅλον τὸν πλοῦτον ἐσκόρπισεν Jo.Clim.*scal.*13(M.88.860C); **5.** remedies: prayer and work, Pall.*h.Laus.*5(p.21.18; M.34.1017D); ἀ. θεραπεύει καρτερία, καὶ τὸ πάντα ποιεῖν μετὰ πολλῆς προσεδρείας καὶ φόβου θεοῦ· τάξον μέτρον σεαυτῷ ἐν παντὶ ἔργῳ, καὶ μὴ πρότερον ἀποστῇς, πρὶν τελέσῃς αὐτό, καὶ προσεύχου συνετῶς καὶ εὐτόνως, καὶ πνεῦμα ἀ. φεύξεται ἀπὸ σοῦ Nil.*spir.mal.*14(M.79.1160C); καθεσθέντος γάρ μου...ἐν τῇ ἐρήμῳ, ὠχλήθην ὑπὸ ἀ., καὶ παραβαλὼν αὐτῷ [sc. Abbas Moses], λέγω πρὸς αὐτόν, ὅτι δεινῶς ὀχληθεὶς ὑπὸ τῆς ἀ. ... οὐ πρότερον ἀπηλλάγην αὐτῆς, εἰ μὴ ἀπῆλθον, καὶ παρέβαλον τῷ ἀββᾷ Παύλῳ. ἀπεκρίνατο δέ μοι...γίνωσκε τοίνυν, ὅτι βαρυτέρως σε ὡς λειποτάκτην καταπολεμήσει· εἰ μὴ τοῦ λοιποῦ δι' ὑπομονῆς καὶ προσευχῆς καὶ τοῦ ἔργου τῶν χειρῶν, ταύτην καταπαλαῖσαι σπουδάσῃς ‡Ath.*ep.Cast.*2.6(M.28.900D) = Leont.et Jo.*sacr.*(M.86.2069B); cf.Cassian.*instit.*10.1ff.; Ant.Mon.*hom.*26(M.89; 1516C); Jo.D.*spir.neq.*8(M.95.81C); knowledge of the nature of the temptation ἡ ἀ. στήκει ἐπὶ πάσῃ ἀρχῇ, καὶ οὐκ ἔστι χεῖρον αὐτῆς πάθος· ἀλλ' ἐὰν γνωρίσῃ αὐτὴν ὁ ἄνθρωπος, ὅτι αὕτη ἐστίν, ἀναπαύεται *Apophth.Patr.*(M.65.360A); remembrance of death, ‡Nil.*vit.cog.*(M.79.1457D); patience, Pall.*v.Chrys.*20(p.133.29; M.47.75); ‡Ath.*ep.Cast.*2.6(M.28.900C); †Nil.*vit.*4(M.79.1144C); community life κοινόβιον ἀ. ἀντίπαλον· ἀνδρὶ δὲ ἡσυχαστῇ σύζυγος αἰώνιος Jo.Clim.*scal.*13(M.88.860A).

***ἀκηδιασμός, ὁ,** *neglect* ἀ. τῆς ψαλμῳδίας Bas.*ascet.*1.5(2.323D; M.31.881A).

ἀκηδιαστής, *subject to boredom* (ἀκηδία), *negligent, weary*, esp. of monks and hermits; characteristics of one who is ἀ.: restlessness ὀφθαλμὸς ἀκηδιαστοῦ ταῖς θυρίσιν ἐνατενίζει...καὶ ἡ διάνοια αὐτοῦ τοὺς ἐπισκεπτομένους φαντάζεται Nil.*spir.mal.*14(M.79.1160A); ἀ. μοναχῷ οὐκ ἀρκέσει μία κέλλα *ib.*13(1160A); cf.‡Nil.*vit.cog.*(M.79.1457B); indulging his own fancies ἀσθενούντων ἐπισκέψεις προβάλλεται ὁ ἀ., πληροφορεῖ δὲ τὸν ἴδιον σκόπον. ἀ. μοναχός, πρὸς διακονίαν ὀξύς, καὶ ἐντολὴν λογίζεται τὴν ἑαυτοῦ πληροφορίαν Nil.*spir.mal.*13(1157D); cf.‡Nil.*vit.cog.*(1457C); negligence in reading and prayer ἀναγινώσκων ἀ. χασμᾶται πολλά, καὶ πρὸς ὕπνον καταφέρεται εὐχερῶς Nil.*spir.mal.*14(1160B); ἀ. μοναχός, ὀκνηρὸς εἰς προσευχήν *ib.*(1160B); laziness, Ant.Mon.*hom.*26(M.89.1516C); greed οὐδενὸς ἄλλου φροντίζειν, εἰ μὴ ποῦ ἄριστα, ποῦ πότοι γίνονται· οὐδὲν γὰρ ἄλλο ἡ διάνοια τοῦ ἀ. φαντάζεται, ἢ τοὺς ἐκ τούτων μετεωρισμούς Leont.et Jo.*sacr.*(M.86.2068A); despair of salvation, Thdr.Stud.*conf.*6(M.99.1724C); ἀ. νοῦς as a state (aridity) of spiritual life ὅταν μηκέτι τῶν τῆς γῆς ὡραίων ἄρξηται ἡμῶν ἐπιθυμεῖν ἡ ψυχή, τότε ἀ. τις τὰ πολλὰ νοῦς αὐτῇ ὑπεισέρχεται, μήτε τῇ διανοίᾳ τοῦ λόγου συγχωρῶν αὐτὴν ἡδέως ὑπηρετεῖν μήτε μὴν τρανὴν ἐπιθυμίαν τῶν μελλόντων αὐτῇ καταλιμπάνων ἀγαθῶν Diad.*perf.*58(p.64.12); as term of abuse ἄνανδρε, ἀ. ‡Ath.*doct.Ant.*21(M.28.585D).

ἀκηδι-άω, 1. *be discouraged, lose heart* ἧς ἀναγινωσκομένης καὶ μὴ νοουμένης [sc. scripture] ἐνίοτε ~ᾷ καὶ ἐκκακεῖ ὁ ἀκροάτης Or.*hom.20.2 in Jos.*(p.418.33; M.12.920C); Ath.*v.Anton.*17(M.26.869A); id.*ep.Marcell.*20(M.27.32D); id.*exp.Ps.*85:5(M.27.376A) al.; μὴ ~ῶμεν πρὸς τὰ παρόντα Bas.*ep.*139.2(3.231C; M.32.584B); Gr.Nyss.*ep.*22(M.46.1088B); Chrys.*hom.2.1 in Col.*(11.334B); Cyr.*Jon.*16(3.379C); Cyr.S.*v.Sab.*41(p.131.21); **2.** *lose patience, grow bored*, Chrys.*hom.58.5 in Jo.*(8.344A); μή τις τῶν ἀκουόντων τὸν λόγον τοῦ θεοῦ ἠκηδίασεν ‡Chrys.*hom.*13(13.251C); ταῖς συμβαινούσαις θλίψεσιν ~ῶν †Cyr.*hom.div.*14(5^2.413C); *Apophth.Patr.*(M.65.185C); Tim.Ant.*descr.BMV* 1(M.28.944B); **3.** *be careless* or *lazy* ~ῶσι πολλοὶ εὐχόμενοι Chrys.*hom.10.2 in Col.*(11.398E); Esaias *cap.spir.*7(M.40.1208B); Nil.*epp.*3.254(M.79.509A); ~ῶντες ἀπὸ τοῦ ἔργου ‡Ath.*ep.Cast.*2.6(M.28.900B); ~άσῃ πρὸς τὰ τῆς εὐσεβείας ἔργα Cyr.*Ps.*90:6(M.69.1220A); id.*ep.*37(p.154.26; 5^2.152E); **4.** *neglect* ἐὰν μὴ ~άσωσι τοὺς πόνους τῆς μετανοίας Nil.*epp.*1.67(M.79.112B); ~ῶμεν τὴν προσευχήν *ib.*3.319(537C); **5.** *be sated, disgusted* ἐὰν γὰρ θελήσωμεν ἐσθίοντες κορεσθῆναι, ταχέως ~άσαντες ἐφ' ἑτέραν τραπησόμεθα ἐπιθυμίαν Marc.Er.*opusc.*9.1(M.65.1112A); **6.** in religious life; **a.** *be neglectful* or *weary (of)* ἐχώμεθα ...τῆς ἀσκήσεως, καὶ μὴ ~ῶμεν Ath.*v.Anton.*19(M.26.872A); χρησιμεύειν δὲ λογίζομαι τὴν ἐν ταῖς προσευχαῖς...ποικιλίαν...ὅτι ἐν μὲν τῇ ὁμαλότητι πολλάκις που καὶ ~ᾷ ἡ ψυχή Bas.*reg.fus.*37.5(2.384C; M.31.1016C); Bas.*ascet.disc.*2(2.212E; M.31.652A); μοναχὸς...τὴν συχνὴν ἐρημίαν ~άσας Niceph.Ur.*v.Sym.*182(M.86.3153B); **b.** *be in a state of* ἀκηδία q.v. ~ῶν οὖν καθ' ἑαυτὸν καὶ μήτε εἰς συνοδίαν βουλόμενος εἰσελθεῖν Pall.*h.Laus.*21(p.64.12; M.34.1073B); *ib.*16(p.40.22; 1041D); Marc.Er.*opusc.*2.36(M.65.936C); πόθεν ~ῶ καθήμενος ἐν τῷ κελλίῳ μου; Dor.*doct.*12.2(M.88.1749C); ~άσας ἐξῆλθεν τοῦ κοινοβίου Cyr.S.*v.Euthym.*19(p.31.1); θέλω ἀναχωρῆσαι ἐκ τοῦ τόπου οὗ κάθημαι, ὅτι πάνυ ~ῶ Jo.Mosch.*prat.*142(M.87.3004C).

ἀκηλίδωτος, *undefiled, pure*, of Christ οὗτος ἡμῖν εἰκὼν ἡ ἀ. Clem.*paed.*1.2(p.91.25; M.8.252C); πάσχει μὲν ὁ νεώς, ἡ δὲ ἀ. οὐσία ἄχραντος τὴν ἀξίαν καθέστηκεν Eust.*fr.in Pr.8:22*(M.18.684C); Alex.Al.*ep.Alex.*9(p.26.2; M.18.561C); BMV, ‡Cyr.*Trin.*14(6^2.20D; M.77.1152A); Church ἡ ἀ. παρθένος ‡Ath.*proph.*8(M.28.1072A); clergy τοὺς ἐν μηδενὶ σχίσματι εὑρεθέντας, ἀλλὰ ἀ. ἐν τῇ ἐκκλησίᾳ ὄντας CNic.(325)*ep.*(p.49.11; M.67.81A); divine inspiration, Gr.Naz.*carm.*2.1.12.755(M.37.1221A).

***ἀκηλιδώτως,** *purely, spotlessly* ηὐδόκησεν ὁ θεὸς λόγος τὴν κτιστὴν σάρκα τὴν ἐξ ἡμῶν ἀ. ἑνῶσαι ἑαυτῷ ‡Chrys.*Trin.*4(1.839E); ἀ. προσέρχεσθαι τοῖς...μυστηρίοις Call.*v.Hyp.*(p.87).

***ἀκήμωτος**, *unmuzzled*, *Const.App.*2.25.5; of S. Paul τὸ στόμα ἀ. ... βοᾷ Chrys.*hom.21.4 in 1Cor.*(10.184A); βοῦς ἀ. τῶν ἀποστόλων Mac.Mgn.*apocr.*3.40(p.140.17).

***ἄκηπος**, *not* fit to be called *a garden* τοὺς ἀ. κήπους Gr.Naz.*ep.*5 (M.37.29A).

ἀκηρασία, ἡ, *purity*, †Apoll.*met.Ps.*14:2(M.33.1328B); *ib.*17:25 (1333A).

ἀκήρατος, **1.** *uncompounded*, *uncontaminated*; of Trin., Gr.Naz. *or.*28.3(p.25.2; M.36.29A); of divine nature, Synes.*regn.*9(p.19.7; M.66.1068A); Cyr.*Is.*3.2(2.414B); Thdt.*eran.*2(4.116); **2.** *intact*, i.e. *unfading*, Hipp.*Dan.*4.60.2; ἀγαθῶν ἀ. κάλλεσιν Eus.*l.C.*6(p.211.17; M.20.1349B); στεφάνοις ἀ. Isid.Pel.*epp.*1.414(M.78.412D); of fetters, *unyielding*, Meth.*res.*2.21(p.375.12; M.18.285D); Gr.Nyss.*hom.3 in Cant.*(M.44.808D).

ἀκίνητος, **1.** *unmoved*, of God τὸ...θεῖον καὶ ἀθάνατον καὶ ἀ. καὶ ἀναλλοίωτον Athenag.*leg.*22.5(M.6.937C); of Father, Hipp.*haer.*5.17 (p.116.3; M.16.3178C); of Son ἀ. μένων παρὰ τῷ πατρί Ath.*gent.*42 (M.25.85A); Bas.*Spir.*15(3.12E; M.32.93A); of each Person ἡ ἰδιότης ἀ. ‡Cyr.*Trin.*10(6^2.16D; M.77.1144D); **2.** *unmoved* to evil; of soul of Christ, *ib.*16(22E; M.1153D); of angels, Gr.Naz.*or.*28.31(p.70.15; M.36.72B); δυσκίνητοι πρὸς τὸ κακόν, καὶ οὐκ ἀ.· νῦν δὲ καὶ ἀ., οὐ φύσει, ἀλλὰ χάριτι Jo.D.*f.o.*2.3(M.94.872B); **3.** as name of Valent. aeon, Iren.*haer.*1.1.3(M.7.449A).

ἀκίς, ἡ, *weapon*, ‡Eust.*hex.*(M.18.713D); Gr.Nyss.*Steph.*1(M.46. 708D).

***ἄκκεπτα**, τά, (Lat. *accepta*) *money placed to the credit of a soldier* and paid out to him on discharge, met. τὰ δεπόσιτα ὑμῶν τὰ ἔργα ὑμῶν, ἵνα τὰ ἀ. ὑμῶν ἄξια κομίσησθε Ign.*Polyc.*6.2.

ἀκκίζομαι, *affect indifference*, Chrys.*hom.*7.3 *in 1Tim.*(11.587D); id.*hom.1.2 in Tit.*(11.732B); Max.*or.dom.*(M.90.896A).

***ἀκ(κ)ούβιτον**, τό, **1.** *dining couch*, *A.Xanthipp.*13(p.66.7); οὐ δεῖ ἐν τῷ οἴκῳ τοῦ θεοῦ ἐσθίειν καὶ ἀ. στρωννύειν CLaod.*can.*28 = CTrull. *can.*74; Thphn.*chron.*p.335(M.108.809B); ἀκούβιτα [v.l. -ητα] *ib.*p.196 (508B); **2.** *dining room*, ‡Ath.*imag.Beryt.*2(M.28.805D).

***ἀκλάδευτος**, *without branches*, Gr.Thaum.*pan.Or.*7(p.19.12; M. 10.1073C).

§**ἀκλήϊστος**, *without name*, Gr.Naz.*carm.*1.1.29.14(M.37.508A).

***ἀκλήματος**, *not produced by the vine* γάνυσμα Gr.Naz.*carm.*2.1. 88.128(M.37.1440A).

ἀκληρονόμητος, *without share in inheritance*, Ephr.3.xxvE; οὔτε ἡ σὰρξ ἀ. ἐστι τῶν ἐπουρανίων Epiph.*haer.*42.12(p.158.8; M.41.777A); Gr.Mag.*dial.*(tr.Zach.)3.21(M.*PL.*77.271C).

ἄκλιτος, *stubborn*, Jo.Clim.*scal.*4(M.88.705B).

ἀκλόνητος, *unmoved*; of Christ, Or.*sel.in Ex.*(M.12.289B); οὐ δυνατὸν εἰρῆσθαι ἔχειν ἐκ δεξιῶν αὐτοῦ τὸν πατέρα, ὅπως ἀ. διαμείνῃ. ἄτρεπτος γὰρ ὁ θεὸς λόγος, οὐδὲ κατὰ ποσὸν κλόνον ὑφιστάμενος Didym.*Ps.*15:8(M.39.1232B); of man, Cyr.*Ps.*37:3(M.69.956A); Jo.D. *imag.*1(M.94.1284A); in gen. ἐπὶ τὴν ἀ. κατ' ἀρετὴν τελειότητα ἱδρυνθείς Or.*Ps.*39:3(p.34); Ast.Am.*hom.*14(M.40.372D); ἡ πίστις ἡ ἀκλινὴς καὶ ἀ. Jo.D.*hom.*1.6(M.96.556A).

***ἀκλονήτως**, *without being shaken*, Cyr.*Zach.*32(3.701A); ‡Jo.D. *ep.Thphl.*11(M.95.357C).

ἄκλοπος, **1.** *not stolen*; of BMV's virginity, ‡Bas.*inc.*(p.241.27); hence **2.** *honest* τάλαντον Gr.Naz.*carm.*2.2(poem.)2.7(M.37.1479A); **3.** *not liable to be stolen*, hence *secure* λόγος...κτέαρ ἄ. *ib.*2.2(poem.) 5.159(1533A); φρένας ἄκλοπος *ib.*2.1.34.9(1307A).

***ἀκλόπως**, *without theft*, *Didasc.Jac.*5.20(p.90.10).

ἀκλυδώνιστος, *not tossed by waves*; met., *peaceful* τὴν σταθηρὰν καὶ ἀ. ζωήν Gr.Nyss.*Pss.titt.*A 8(M.44.473C); of Church, *Lit.*ap.*Const. App.*8.10.4; Chrys.*p.redit.*2.5(3.431C).

***ἀκλυδωνίστως**, *without being tossed by waves*, met., Isid.Pel. *epp.*1.91(M.78.245B).

ἄκλωστος, *unspun*, hence *tortuous*, *complicated* τὰ τῶν μοιρῶν ἄ. νήματα Sophr.H.*mir.Cyr.et Jo.*28(M.87.3505A).

ἀκοίμητος, *sleepless*; οἱ Ἀ. a monastic community near Constantinople, Thdt.*ep.*141(4.1235); Evagr.*h.e.*3.18(p.117.8; M.86. 2636A); Alex.Sal.*Barn.*32(p.447B).

ἀκοινωνησία, ἡ, *excommunication*, *Libell.*ap.CChalc.*act.*3(p.29.8; H.2.345B); †Leont.B.*sect.*6.2(M.86.1236A); Thdr.Lect.*h.e.*2.41(M.86. 205A); Gr.Mag.*dial.*(tr.Zach.)2.23(M.*PL.*66.177C).

ἀκοινώνητος, **1.** *excommunicate*, CNic.(325)*can.*5; ἐδείχθη ὅτι παρὰ τοῦ σωτῆρος ἀ. γέγονεν ἡ Ἀρειανὴ μανία καὶ ὧδε καὶ ἐν τῇ πρωτοτόκων ἐν οὐρανοῖς ἐκκλησίᾳ Ath.*ep.Aeg.Lib.*19(M.25.584A); Tim.I Al. *resp.*(M.33.1301C); **2.** *not having received communion*, *Libell.*ap.CCP (518)*act.*(p.71.37; H.2.1333C).

ἀκοινωνία, ἡ, *excommunication*, Thdr.Lect.*h.e.*2.12(M.86.189A).

***ἀκολαστέω**, *be licentious*, Clem.*paed.*2.10(p.215.14, v.l. ἀκολαστευτέον M.8.512C); Or.*comm.in Gen.*(M.12.68A).

ἀκόλλητος, *not united* μὴ τοῖς φθοροποιοῖς πάθεσι κατανεκρωθέντες ἀνάρμοστοι καὶ ἀ. γενώμεθα πρὸς θεῖα μέλη Dion.Ar.*e.h.*3.3.12(M.3. 444B).

ἀκολουθία, ἡ, [[*]**ἀκολούθεια**, Cyr.*Is.*3.1(2.372D)], **1.** *sequence*, *succession*, *order*, in a book μικρὸν μετὰ τὴν ἀ. Gr.Nyss.*Eun.*11(2 p.262.20; M.45.869D); of the course of nature τὴν ἀ. τῆς φύσεως id. *hom.13 in Cant.*(M.44.1053B); τῆς γὰρ φύσεως ἡμῶν διὰ τῆς ἰδίας ἀ. ...κινηθείσης id.*or.catech.*16(p.70.16; M.45.52B); τὴν ἀναγκαίαν τῆς φύσεως ἀ. *ib.*(p.72.10; 52D); ἡ τῆς φύσεως ἀ., θείῳ βουλήματι καὶ νόμῳ διαταχθεῖσα *ib.*28(p.105.18; 73A); ὁδῷ προιοῦσαν ἐν τάξει τινὶ καὶ ἀ. τὴν σύνθετον φύσιν id.*Eun.*6(2 p.137.5; M.45.721C); id.*mort.*(M.46. 517A) al.; of the continuity from Adam of human sin ἡ τοῦ ἁμαρτάνειν ἀ. id.*virg.*12(p.299.17; M.46.372B); δι' ἧς τοίνυν ἀ. ἔξω τοῦ παραδείσου γεγόναμεν *ib.*(p.302.17; 373D); of the progress of man's salvation and deification or the economy of redemption, id.*hom.5 in Cant.*(864C); οὐ μετὰ τῆς αὐτῆς ἀ. ... κτίζεται τὰ ὄντα καὶ ἀνακτίζεται *ib.15*(1109A); τοῦ μυστηρίου τὴν ἀ. id.*or.catech.*24(p.93.9; 65A); ἀ. καὶ ἀρχὴν δοῦναι πάσῃ τῇ ἀνθρωπίνῃ φύσει τῆς ἐκ νεκρῶν ἀναστάσεως id.*Eun.*2(2 p.368.1; 548C); πάντα χρὴ τάξει τινὶ καὶ ἀ. ... τῇ θείᾳ προσοικειωθῆναι φύσει id.*anim.et res.*(M.46.105A); of the sequence of scripture and its teaching τὴν ἀ. τῆς θείας διδασκαλίας θηρωμένοις Clem.*str.*1.28(p.110.10; M.8.925B); Gr.Nyss.*hex.*6(M.44. 68C); *ib.*66(116A); τὴν ἀ. τῆς κατ' ἀρετὴν ἐπιδόσεως, ἣν ὑποδείκνυσιν ὁ λόγος, τῷ εἱρμῷ τῶν ἱστορικῶν αἰνιγμάτων ἀκολούθως ἑπόμενος id.*v.Mos.*(M.44.337A); id.*Pss.titt.*A 1(M.44.433C) al.; of eccl. canons, Thphn.*chron.*p.86(M.108.260B); **2.** *course* of life, Gr.Nyss.*Eun.* 1(1 p.32.8; M.45.260B); **3.** *consequence* ἔκλειψιν ἢ ἑτέραν τινὰ ἀ. φυσικήν Chrys.*hom.88.1 in Mt.*(7.825B); **4.** *procedure* κατὰ τὸν τῆς ἐκκλησιαστικῆς ἀ. τύπον ἐξενεχθήσεται ἡ κατ' αὐτοῦ ψῆφος *Dial.*ap.Thdt.*h.e.*2.16.2(3.864); οὐκ ἀνθρωπίνῃ ἀ., ἢ δυνάμει Polychr. *fr.Dan.*(p.352.10); **5.** *good order* ποιοῦσιν ὃ βούλονται, οὐκ ἀ. χρώμενοι *M.Thdot.*3(p.134.13); πολλὰ παρὰ πᾶσαν ἀ. ἡμεῖς πεπόνθαμεν Eus.Dor.*ep.imp.*(p.66.30)ap.Evagr.*h.e.*2.4(M.86.2497C); **6.** *rite* τὰ πρὸς τὴν ἀ. ἐπὶ τῶν μελλόντων βαπτίζεσθαι Jo.Mosch.*prat.*207(M. 87.3100B); Gr.Mag.*dial.*(tr.Zach.)3.30(M.*PL.*77.290A); ‡Sophr.H. *liturg.*1(M.87.3981C); †Anast.S.*relat.*49(*OC* 3 p.70.16); hence *formula* of a partic. rite, *office* of a feast, *Euchol.*(p.39) et passim; *daily office*, *Nomoc.*120; **7.** *order* of ministry αὐτὸς ὁ παράκλητος ταύτην διετάξατο τὴν ἀ. [sc. ἱερωσύνην] Chrys.*sac.*3.4(p.51.5; 1.382B); **8.** *precedence* τὴν τάξιν τῆς ἀ. τῶν προεστώτων Ephr.3. 339A.

ἀκόλουθος, **1.** *fitting*, *suitable*, *M.Polyc.*18.2; *Hom.Clem.*6.19; Proterius Myrensis ap.CChalc.*act.*3(*ACO* 2.1.2 p.28.2; H.2.344C); c. infin., Alex.Al.*ep.encycl.*1(p.6.4; M.18.572A); Didym.*Ps.*6:1(M.39. 1176B); Cyr.*Jo.*4.1(4.337A); as subst. τὸ δὲ ἀ. τῆς ἑρμηνείας Or.*hom. 14.16 in Jer.*(p.123.1; M.13.425B); **2.** *progressive* δι' ἀ. τινὸς ἀναβάσεως πρὸς τὰ ὑψηλότερα τῆς ἀρετῆς Gr.Nyss.*v.Mos.*(M.44.372C); **3.** masc. as subst., *acolyte* (a minor order), Corn.ap.Eus.*h.e.*6.43.11 (M.20.621A); Eus.*v.C.*3.8(p.81.4; M.20.1064A); esp. *candle bearer*, cf. *acolythi Graece, Latine ceroferarii dicuntur, a deportandis cereis, quando legendum est evangelium, aut sacrificium offerendum*, Isid.H. *etym.*7.12.29; **4.** neut. as subst., *pursuit*, *way of life* τὸ τοῦ μονήρους βίου ἀ. *Apophth.Patr.*(M.65.185D).

ἀκολούθως, *in order*, *Hom.Clem.*15.9.

ἀκόμιστος, *uncared for*, *unheeded* ἀ. ἔπος Nonn.*par.Jo.*14:24 (M.43.872A).

ἄκομψος, *without honour* or *distinction* ἀρχὴ...οὐκ ἀ. Thphyl. *exc.Rom.*1(p.221.18; M.113.928B).

ἀκον-άω, *whet*, *sharpen* τὴν γλῶσσαν Eulog.*fr.Novat.*(M.104.349C); hence *refine* διὰ τοῦτο εἰς τὴν ἔρημόν σε ἔπεμψα...ἵνα, ἔνυλος ὤν, ~ηθῇς ὡς ἄυλος Chrysipp.*enc.in Jo.Bapt.*(p.39.13).

ἀκόνη, ἡ, *acuteness*, Serap.*Man.*20(p.38; M.40.917A).

Ἀκονῖται** (Ἀκουανῖται**), οἱ, alternative name of Manicheans Ἀκουανῖται λεγόμενοι διά τινα Οὐέτρανον ἀπὸ τῆς μέσης τῶν ποταμῶν ἐλθόντα, Ἀκούαν οὕτω καλούμενον Epiph.*haer.*66.1(p.13.21; M.42. 29A); Jo.D.*haer.*66(M.94.717A).

***ἀκοντίασις**, ἡ, *shooting forth*; of poison by a venomous reptile, Epiph.*haer.*61.8(p.389.1; M.41.1049D).

ἀκοντίζω, [aor. ἠκόντησεν, Jo.Mosch.*prat.*36(M.87.2885C)]; **1.** *thrust away*, Dion.Ar.*d.n.*3.1(M.3.680D); *V.Zos.*18(p.106.32); **2.** *drain*, *empty*; a cask, *Mir.Geo.*5(p.59.4).

***ἀκοπιαστί**, *without causing trouble*, Socr.*h.e.*6.11.9(M.67.697B).

***ἀκορεστία**, ἡ, *insatiable desire*, Epiph.*anc.*104(p.126.8; M.43. 208A).

ἀκόρεστος, *not satisfying*, Or.*sel.in Num.*24:1(M.12.580D).

ἀκορέστως, *insatiably*, *V.Pach.Λ* 22(p.149.9).

ἀκόρητος, *unswept*; hence *unpolished* of style, Gr.Naz.*ep.*51(M. 37.105B).

ἀκόσμητος, **1.** *disorderly*, †Bas.*ep.*41.1(p.285.4; 3.124C; M.32. 345B); **2.** *unadorned* of style, Gr.Naz.*ep.*51(M.37.105B), etc.

ἀκοσμία, ἡ, *lack of ornament*, Isid.Pel.*epp.*2.53(M.78.497A).

ἄκοσμος, *lacking ornament* τῶν ἀ. φιλοκόσμων Clem.*paed.*2.10 (p.219.26; M.8.521B); comp., *less distinguished*, *ib.*3.11(p.268.26; 629B); neut. as subst., *that which lacks ornament*, Dion.Ar.*e.h.* 2.3.8(M.3.404C).

ἀκόσμως, *unbecomingly*, Gr.Naz.*carm.*1.1.8.36(M.37.449A).

***Ἀκουανῖται, οἱ**, v. *Ἀκονῖται.

***ἀκούβιτον**, v. ἀκκούβιτον.

***ἀκουμβίζω**, (Lat. *accubo*) *recline at table*, in form ἠκούμβησεν Gr.Mag.*dial.*(tr.Zach.)3.1(M.*PL.*77.219B).

ἀκούσιος, **1.** of persons, *acting involuntarily*, Or.*hom.19.15 in Jer.* (p.175.13; M.13.497C); **2.** of spiritual benefits, *acquired unsought*, Jo.Clim.*scal.*24(M.88.984D).

ἄκουσμα, τό, **1.** *utterance, talk*, Or.*Jo.*2.15(9; p.72.7; M.14.141A); **2.** *saying*, Cyr.*Mich.*71(3.471A); id.*Ps.*36:8(M.69.928D).

ἀκουστός, *audible* ὑποκαταβὰς εἰς πέτραν, ἀφ᾽ ἧς ἦν ἀ. Malchus *exc.Rom.*1(p.160.27; M.113.765A).

ἀκουτίζομαι, *listen attentively* ἔθος τῇ γραφῇ τὸ ἀ. λέγειν ἐπὶ τοῦ μὴ παρέργως τὸν ἐπί γε τοῖς ἀναγκαίοις πράγμασι δέχεσθαι λόγον, νηφαλέως δὲ μᾶλλον Cyr.*Is.*4.1(2.555C).

ἀκούω, **1.** *hear*; hence **a.** *receive instruction, be taught*, Herm. *mand.*4.3.1; *Barn.*7.3; Cyr.H.*catech.*19.2; **b.** *be a disciple*, Herm. *mand.*12.3.2; Or.*hom.18.2 in Jer.*(p.152.6; M.13.465A); **c.** *give heed to, hear inwardly*, *Did.*11.2; *ib.*11.12; Or.*hom.12.7 in Jer.*(p.93.24; 388C); **2.** t.t. *be asked for* a loan, Chrys.*hom.15.8 in Mt.*(7.199C).

ἄκρα, ἡ, *highest* or *farthest point*; of the tip of the tongue, Mac. Aeg.*carit.*5(M.34.912B); of time, *earliest moment* ἄνθρωπος γέγονεν ἐξ αὐτῆς ἄ. τῆς...συλλήψεως Sophr.H.*ep.syn.*(M.87.3161A); met., *height of excellence*, Eus.*l.C.*11(p.227.20; M.20.1381B).

ἀκράδαντος, **1.** *unshaken, firm* Χριστὸς κρηπὶς ἀ. Cyr.*Mich.*68 (3.464B); Anast.S.*hod.*1(M.89.48C); Χριστός...δι᾽ οὗ...γῆ...μενεῖ ἀ. Jo.D.*hom.*1.6(M.96.556B); *unaffected*, of the body by wine, Clem. *paed.*2.2(p.169.26; M.8.413C); **2.** met., *not to be changed, fixed*, Cyr. *Is.*1.3(2.70D); ἀ. εἰς εὐσέβειαν ἕξει τὸν νοῦν id.*Os.*26(3.49D); ἀνεπικούρητον ἔχων παρ᾽ ἑτέρου τὸ ἀ. εἰς ἁγιασμόν id.*Pulch.*43(p.51.3; 5[2].165A); **3.** *unchangeable* ἀ. ... ἡ τοῦ θεοῦ λόγου φύσις id.*Nest.*5.4 (p.99.34; 6[1].132E).

[*]**ἀκραίμων, ὁ**, v. ἀκρεμών.

ἀκραιφνής, *unmixed*, hence *pure*; **1.** in gen.; **a.** lit. τὰ ἀκράτητα καὶ ἀ. φῶτα τῶν σεραφίμ Meth.*res.*1.49(p.303.12; M.18.280A); Dion. Ar.*d.n.*4.22(M.3.724B) cit. s. εἰκών; neut. as subst., *purity, perfection* τὸ ἀ. τῆς τοῦ πατρὸς θεωρίας Cyr.H.*catech.*7.11; **b.** met., ref. Jo.1:4 ἡ ἀ. ζωή Or.*Jo.*2.18(12; p.76.6; M.14.148B); ἀ. καὶ καθαρᾷ διανοίᾳ Eus.*v.C.*4.9(p.121.25; M.20.1157C); τῆς ἀ. καὶ τελειοτάτης γνώσεως μεταδοῦναι [sc. νηπίοις] οὐ δυνάμενος Isid.Pel.*epp.*1.4.45(M.78.428A); of faith, Thdt.*affect.*2(p.64.18; 4.756); **2.** theol., Trin. ἀ. καὶ ἀκριβῆ τὴν ἀπ᾽ ἀλλήλων ἰδικῶς ὑφισταμένην ἔχει διάκρισιν Dion.Ar.*d.n.*2.4(M. 3.641A); of God τῆς ἀγενήτου καὶ ἀ. οὐσίας τοῦ θεοῦ Ath.*Ar.*2.26(M. 26.201B); Gr.Naz.*or.*28.3(p.26.2; M.36.29B); ἔστιν...νοῦς ὁ ὑπερτάτω τε καὶ ἀκραιφνέστατος Cyr.*Is.*3.4(2.511B); ref. Logos τὸ ἀ. τῆς πρὸς τὸν πατέρα αὐτοῦ ὁμοουσιότητος Didym.*Trin.*3.7(M.39.849A); Christol. ἑκατέρα φύσις μεμένηκεν ἀ. Thdt.*affect.*6(p.176.19; 4.878); ἡ δὲ τοῦ κυρίου σὰρξ τὰς θείας ἐνεργείας ἐπλούτησε, διὰ τὴν πρὸς τὸν λόγον ἀ. ἕνωσιν Jo.D.*f.o.*3.17(M.94.1069B).

ἀκραιφνῶς, *without adulteration, utterly, completely* τὴν ἀ. λογικὴν καὶ θείαν διοίκησιν Clem.*str.*1.24(p.100.3; M.8.905B); Thdt.*affect.*1 (p.32.18; 4.723); ἀ. εὐσεβεῖν Leont.H.*monoph.*(M.86.1880A).

[*]**ἀκράτειστος**, f.l. for ἀκράτητος, *uncontrollable, that cannot be limited*, *A.Jo.*104(p.202.25).

ἀκράτητος, **1.** *which cannot be grasped, intangible* ἀ. ... καὶ ἀόρατοι [sc. Gnostics] ταῖς ἄνω ἀρχαῖς Iren.*haer.*1.21.5(M.7.668A); σχῆμα τῶν ἀγγέλων ἀ. Adam.*dial.*5.6(p.184.6; M.11.1840A); by the mind, *incomprehensible* κτίστης ἀ. *Orac.Sib.fr.*5.1; πίστις μόνη κρατεῖ τὸν ἀ. ‡Chrys.*hom.*9(13.233D); ὁ λόγος...ἀ. ... κρατούμενος τῆς ἀκοῆς Melet.*nat.hom.*synops.(M.64.1105A); **2.** *invincible*, of God, acc. Noëtus ἀ. καὶ κρατητός Hipp.*haer.*9.10(p.244.16; M.16.3378A); of Christ οὐκ ἐνεδέχετο [acc. Valent.] παθεῖν, ἀ. ... ὑπάρχοντα Iren.*haer.* 1.7.2(M.7.513B); θεὸς γὰρ σαρκωθεὶς...νοῦς ἀήττητος ὢν τῶν...παθημάτων...καὶ οὐ μόνον ἀ. θανάτῳ ἀλλὰ καὶ λύων θάνατον Apoll.*fid. sec.pt.*30(p.178.17; M.10.1117A); ἀπέθανεν...ἀθάνατος...καὶ ἀ. τῷ θανάτῳ διαμείνας διὰ τὴν θεότητα id.*ep.Jov.*(p.252.9; M.28.28C); of his baptism Ἰησοῦν...καταδυόμενον αὐτῇ τῇ θείᾳ καὶ ἀ. καθόδῳ Dion. Ar.*e.h.*4.3.10(M.3.484B); of his risen body, ‡Ath.*Apoll.*1.17(M.26. 1124C); τὸ κεκρατημένον ἀ. Epiph.*haer.*64.64(p.504.15; M.41.1181B); ἡ θεότης ἀκοίμητος...ἀ. *ib.*64.67(p.511.16; 1188B); **3.** *unconquered*, Bas.*hom.in Ps.*7(1.99C; M.29.232D); **4.** *unrestrained, unhindered* ἡ τῶν θυρῶν κεκλεισμένων ἀ. εἴσοδος Sophr.H.*ep.syn.*(M.87.3176B); ἀ. χώρησιν [i.e. of angels] Dion.Ar.*c.h.*15.6(M.3.336A); **5.** *uncorrupted* ἐξ ἀ. ἱερέως Thdr.Stud.*epp.*2.215(M.99.1652B) perh. f.l. for ἀχράντου.

ἀκρατήτως, *so as not to be mastered, incomprehensibly*, Iren.*haer.* 1.7.1(M.7.512B); Dion.Ar.*c.h.*8.1(M.3.240A).

ἄκρατος, **1.** *unmixed, pure*; of Transfiguration, Chrys.*hom.56.4 in Mt.*(7.570D) cit. s. μεταμόρφωσις; of scripture, *free from obscurities* μὴ πάντῃ ὑπὸ τῆς λέξεως ἑλκόμενοι τὸ ἀγωγὸν ἄ. ἐχούσης Or.*princ.*4.2.9(p.321.9; M.11.375B); οὐδὲ...πάντῃ ἄ. τὴν ἱστορίαν *ib.* (p.322.15; 376B); **2.** *untempered, unmitigated* ἄ. πρός τι χρηστότερον ἡ πονηρία id.*Jo.*33.19(12; p.458.18; M.14.793C); τὰς κολάσεις ὠνόμασεν ...οἶνον ἄ., ὃν πίνουσιν οἱ ἀ. οἴνου τουτέστιν ἀ. κολάσεως ἄξιοι id.*hom. 12.2 in Jer.*(p.87.19; M.13.380B); ref. Is.19:14 οὐκ ἄ. δέδωκεν ὁ θεὸς τὸ πνεῦμα τῆς πλανήσεως *ib.20.3*(p.182.18; 508B); **3.** *perfect, absolute*, of Christ ἄνθρωπον ἀ. θεότητι καὶ τελείᾳ πεπληρωμένον Meth. *symp.*3.4(p.31.1; M.18.68A); ὁ ἄνθρωπος συγκερασθεὶς τῇ σοφίᾳ... γέγονεν...αὐτὸ τὸ εἰς αὐτὸν ἐγκατασκῆψαν ἄ. φῶς *ib.*3.8(p.35.9; 72D); Gr.Nyss.*or.catech.*24(p.92.17; M.45.64D); hence of the power of God (acc. Arians) *immediate* ὅτι μὴ ἐδύνατο τὰ λοιπὰ κτίσματα τῆς ἀ. χειρὸς τοῦ ἀγενήτου τὴν ἐργασίαν βαστάξαι Ath.*decr.*8(p.7.18, v.l. ἀκηράτου M.25.429A); id.*Ar.*2.24(M.26.200A); **4.** *intemperate*, Meth.*symp.*3.11(p.39.12; M.18.77B); ὅπου...τὸ ἥττημα διὰ τὴν ἄ. γεῦσιν ἐγένετο, ἐκεῖ καὶ ἡ νίκη διὰ νηστείας καὶ ἐγκρατείας Isid.Pel. *epp.*1.282(M.78.349A); Cyr.*Os.*130(3.163B).

ἀκράτως, *perfectly, fully* οὐδεὶς γὰρ [sc. of the synoptists] ἀ. ἐφανέρωσεν τὴν θεότητα ὡς Ἰωάννης Or.*Jo.*1.4(6; p.8.9; M.14.29D).

ἀκρεμών, ἀκρέμων, [*]**ἀκραίμων, ὁ**, *shoot, twig, branch*, esp. *topmost branch*; **1.** lit., Gr.Nyss.*hom.5 in Cant.*(M.44.869C); as food of Jo. Bapt., to be imitated by ascetics, Isid.Pel.*epp.*1.5(M.78.184A), ἀκρίδες being interpreted as οὐ ζῷα...ἀλλ᾽ ἀκρεμόνες βοτανῶν ἢ φυτῶν *ib.*1.132(269C); in simile of soul καρπὸς δὲ ἡμῶν ἡ προαίρεσις γίνεται, ἡ τῷ δρεπομένῳ ἡμᾶς θεῷ δι᾽ ἑαυτῆς ὡς διά τινος ἀκρεμόνος τὴν ψυχὴν ἐγχειρίζουσα Gr.Nyss.*hom.10 in Cant.*(985D); **2.** met., *eminent person*, Epiph.*haer.*68.1(p.141.21; M.42.185B); ἀκραίμονες καὶ τὰ πρωτεῖα ἀποφερόμενοι ἔν τε εὐσεβείᾳ καὶ ἐν βίῳ *ib.*68.5(p.145.16; 192B); *ib.*68.8(p.148.18; 196D); *ib.*77.20(p.434.14; 669D); παρὰ τοῖς ἀκρέμοσι φυλάσσεται τὸ μὴ ὀμνύναι ὅλως id.*exp. fid.*24(p.525.19; M.42.832A); ἀ. καὶ ἐξάρχους Anast.S.*hod.*10(M.89. 180C).

***ἄκρηνος**, *not* fit to be called *a spring* κρήνας εὗρον ἀ. Gr.Naz. *carm.*2.2(epigr.)2.3(M.38.83A).

ἀκριβάζομαι, *be exacting*, Dor.*doct.*17.1(M.88.1800C).

ἀκρίβασμα, τό, **1.** *exact principle* or *ordering, exactitude*, Epiph. *haer.*9.2(p.198.24; M.41.225B); τὸ τῆς ἀληθείας ἀ. *ib.*23.5(p.253.13; 304C); *ib.*69.18(p.167.16; M.42.229A); *ib.*70.12(p.245.7; 364B); **2.** *strictness* οὐκ ἔγνωσαν...τίνι ἀφώρισε τὸ ἀ. τοῦτο τῆς διγαμίας *ib.*59.7 (p.372.21; M.41.1029A); **3.** *commandment* τὰ προστάγματα αὐτοῦ, ἀ. αὐτοῦ, καὶ τὰ κρίματα αὐτοῦ Thdt.*qu.3 in 3Reg.*(1.457); Areth. *Apoc.*29(M.106.648A).

ἀκρίβεια, ἡ, **1.** *accurate account* τὴν ἀ. τῶν χρόνων τῆς γεγενημένης αἰχμαλωσίας Hipp.*Dan.*1.1.1(M.10.637A); τὴν τῶν ἀποστολικῶν δογμάτων ἀ. Gel.Cyz.*h.e.*2.19.22(M.85.1280C); **2.** *exact sense* of a word, ref. Mt.23:8 οὐκ ἔσονται οὗτοι διδάσκαλοι ὅσον ἐπὶ τῇ ἀ. τῆς τοῦ εὐαγγελίου φωνῆς Or.*Jo.*1.3(5; p.7.22; M.14.29A); ἡ τῶν ὀνομάτων ἀ. Meth.*res.*1.62(p.327.4; M.41.1160C); **3.** *taking care* ἐν τῇ περὶ τὸν κύριον μου...ἀ. ἠμέληκα †Jo.D.*B.J.*22(M.96.1057D); hence of the Christian life, *scrupulousness, exact conformity* with virtue ἀ. δὲ δεῖ πολλῆς, ὥσπερ τοῖς μακρᾷ νόσῳ πεπονηκόσι σώμασι διαίτης χρεία Clem.*q.d.s.*40(p.186.19; M.9.645B); Bas.*reg.fus.*proem.1(2.328A; M.31.892B); τὴν ἀ. τῆς πολιτείας *ib.*25.1(2.370A; 984C); Chrys.*hom. 38.5 in 1Cor.*(10.358C); id.*Stag.*1.6(1.170B); τὴν ἀρετῆς ἀ. Tit.Bost. *arg.*2.2(M.18.1136A); **4.** c. prep. in adv. sense, *tightly* τῶν ῥιζῶν μετ᾽ ἀ. τῷ βάθει τῆς γῆς περισφιγγομένων Chrys.*incomprehens.*5.7 (1.491A).

ἀκριβεύομαι, *be careful, exact* ἀ. οὖν ὀφείλομεν...περὶ τῆς σωτηρίας ἡμῶν *Barn.*2.10; Bas.*reg.br.*285(2.516A; M.31.1284A); hence *be a precisian*, Thdr.Stud.*epp.*1.30(M.99.1005D).

ἀκριβής, **1.** of ascetic life, *scrupulous*, Gr.Nyss.*ep.*2(M.46.1012A); **2.** neut. as subst., *exact nature* τὸ ἀ. τῆς πίστεως Ammon.*Ac.*18:25 (M.85.1572D); αὐτὸς γὰρ μόνος ὁ μονογενὴς τοῦ θεοῦ υἱὸς τὸ ἀ. οἶδε τῆς ἑαυτοῦ δι' ἡμᾶς ἐνανθρωπήσεως Gel.Cyz.*h.e.*2.24.16(M.85.1301C); plur., *exact details* τὰ ἀ.... τοῦ κηρύγματος Epiph.*haer.*59.6(p.372.20; M.41.1029A); **3.** c. prep. in adv. sense, *accurately* ἐπ' ἀ. ἐξετάζειν Tat.*orat.*31(p.32.17; M.6.872A); **4.** of dawn, *first showing* ὄρθρου βαθέος ὄντος, τουτέστιν ἀ. καὶ ἄρτι πρῶτον ἀρξαμένου Sev.Ant.*res.* (p.828.8, v.l. -ῶς M.46.640C).

***ἀκριβογραφής**, ὁ, *accurate delineator*, Agath.*v.Gr.Ill.*59(p.31).

ἀκριβοδίκαιος, **1.** *scrupulously righteous* μηδὲ ἐπὶ μικροῖς καταδικάζων, ὡς ἀ. αὐτὸς ὑπάρχων Bas.*hom.*20.7(2.162B; M.31.537C); Nil. *epp.*3.153(M.79.453D); μὴ ἀκριβάζου δὲ μηδὲ τὰ μικρὰ σφάλματα, ὡς ἀ. αὐτός Dor.*doct.*17.1(M.88.1800C); **2.** *severe in judgement* μὴ γίνου ἀ., ἀλλ' ὑπέρβαινε τοῦτο τῇ ἀγαθότητι Isid.Pel.*epp.*3.320(M.78. 984A).

***ἀκριβόλεκτος**, *accurately expressed*, Ammon.*Ac.*23:7f.(M.85. 1589B).

ἀκριβολογ-έομαι, **1.** *be exact* or *precise* in language, investigation, etc.; hence *inquire closely* μηδὲν ∼ώμεθα εἴτε διὰ ῥᾳδίας...εἴτε διὰ χαλεπῆς...ὁδοῦ βαδίζειν κελεύοι Chrys.*paralyt.*2(3.35B); *state expressly*, ref. Mt.23:30 δείκνυσι γὰρ αὐτοὺς μείζονα τολμῶντας...καὶ ταῦτα ∼ουμένους ὡς οὐκ ἄν ποτε τοῖς αὐτοῖς περιέπεσον id.*hom.74.1 in Mt.*(7.716A); esp. of religious observance, ref. Jo.19:31 οἱ Ἰουδαῖοι...τηλικοῦτον ἐργασάμενοι τόλμημα, περὶ τῆς ἡμέρας ἀ. id. *hom.85.3 in Jo.*(8.507C); περὶ τὰ βρώματα ἀ. Thdr.Mops.*Tit.*1:15 (p.245.25; M.66.948D); **2.** c. acc., *discuss in detail*, *Hom.Clem.*5.30; Const.ap.Socr.*h.e.*1.7.14(M.67.60A); Chrys.*hom.42.1 in Jo.*(8.249A); act., Isid.Pel.*epp.*2.72(M.78.516A); **3.** *speak severely, critically* μὴ ἀ. σφόδρα περὶ τοὺς μεταγινώσκοντας Cyr.*ep.*57(p.21.25; 5².192D).

ἀκριβολογία, ἡ, *strictness of practice*, Bas.*ep.*188 *can.*9(3.273E; M.32.677B).

ἀκριβῶς, **1.** *accurately, exactly* Μάρκος...ἀ. ἔγραψεν, οὐ μέντοι τάξει, τὰ ὑπὸ Χριστοῦ ἢ λεχθέντα ἢ πραχθέντα Papias *fr.*3.15; ἀ. ἄθεον τὸ πολύθεον Eus.*l.C.*3(p.201.27; M.20.1332A); *carefully* προσέχετε ἀ. *Barn.*7.4; **2.** *without distortion* or *modification*, hence *perfectly, completely*, Clem.*str.*7.3(p.10.12; M.9.416C); ὁ προαμαρτήσας, ἀ. δὲ μετανοήσας Or.*hom.5.10 in Jer.*(p.39.16; M.13.308C); μονογενῆ υἱόν, ἀ. ὄντα καὶ ζῶντα καὶ ὑφεστῶτα Eus.*e.th.*2.6(p.103.11; M.24.905C); **3.** in ascetic life, *scrupulously* τὴν ἐξέτασιν τοῦ πῶς ἀ. βιωτέον Clem. *str.*7.15(p.64.22; M.9.525C); πάσας...τὰς ἀρετὰς κατώρθωσεν ἀ. Alex. Sal.*Barn.*2(p.437A).

***ἀκριδοφαγέω**, *eat locusts*; of Jo. Bapt., †Bas.*ep.*42.5(3.129E; M.32.357B).

ἀκρίζ-ω, *go to extremes* ∼ουσα νηστεία καὶ πλήρωσις σιτήσεως ἐπίμεμπτα Ephr.3.404D.

ἀκρίς, ἡ, *locust*; **1.** in gen., Ath.*syn.*18(p.245.25; M.26.713B); Thdr.Mops.*Os.*13:1–3(M.66.201A); **2.** in demonic apparition θηρίον ...καὶ ἐκ τοῦ στόματος αὐτοῦ ἀ. πύριναι ἐξεπορεύοντο Herm.*vis.* 4.1.6; **3.** as food of Jo. Bapt. Ματθαῖος μὲν...σπερμάτων...ἄνευ κρεῶν μετελάμβανεν, Ἰωάννης δὲ ὑπερτείνας τὴν ἐγκράτειαν, ἀ. ... ἤσθιεν (Mt.3:4) Clem.*paed.*2.1(p.165.16; M.8.404A); μέλι ἤσθιεν καὶ ἀ., γλυκεῖαν καὶ πνευματικὴν τροφὴν *ib.*2.10(p.224.15; 532B); text of Mt.3:4 altered in *Ev. Ebion.* in order to present Jo. Bapt. as vegetarian 'καὶ τὸ βρῶμα αὐτοῦ', φησί, 'μέλι ἄγριον, οὗ ἡ γεῦσις ἡ τοῦ μάννα, ὡς ἐγκρὶς ἐν ἐλαίῳ'· ἵνα δῆθεν μεταστρέψωσι τὸν τῆς ἀληθείας λόγον εἰς ψεῦδος καὶ ἀντὶ ἀ. ποιήσωσιν ἐγκρίδα ἐν μέλιτι Epiph.*haer.*30.13(p.350.7; M.41.428D); ἀ. interpreted as name of vegetable by ascetic writers ὅτι βοτανή τίς ἐστιν ἀ. λεγομένη, ὁ Σολομὼν ἡμᾶς διδάσκει λέγων, ἀνθήσει τὸ ἀμύγδαλον, καὶ παχυνθήσεται ἡ ἀ. †Ath.*fr.Mt.*3:4(M.27.1365D); Isid.Pel.*epp.*1.132(M.78. 269C) cit. s. ἀκρεμών; ἀ. βοτανῶν ἤσθιεν ‡Chrys.*Zach.*(2.791C); ‡Chrys.*Herod.*3(8.292C); ἤσθιεν δὲ ἀ. τουτέστιν φοίνικας *Narr.Jo. Bapt.*(p.2).

ἀκρισία, ἡ, *injustice* οὐδὲ κρίσις ἐν ταῖς ὁδοῖς αὐτῶν, ἀ. δὲ πᾶσα καὶ ἀδικία Proc.G.*Is.*59:8(M.87.2604D).

***ἄκρισις**, ἡ, *lack of differentiation*; but prob. for ἀνάκρισις q.v., †Jo.Jej.*poenit.*(M.88.1913A).

ἀκριτόβουλος, *headstrong*, *Orac.Sib.*1.110; ἀ. ... καὶ πρόχειρον εἰς ὀργὴν τὸ πλῆθός ἐστι Cyr.*Jo.*4.5(4.418C).

ἄκριτος, *confused, undecided*; neut. as subst., *irregularity* τὸ ἄ. ...τῆς τῶν ἀρχιερέων καταστάσεως Eus.*d.e.*8.2(p.385.18; M.22.624B).

ἀκρίτως, **1.** *indistinguishably, continuously* βαθοῦ ἀεὶ ῥέοντος καὶ ἀ. φερομένου *Hom.Clem.*6.4; **2.** *without trial, unjustly* οὐδὲ κρίσιν ἔχων, ἀλλ' ἀ. πράττων Or.*hom.17.2 in Jer.*(p.145.1; M.13.156B); οὐκ ἀ. ἀλλ' εὖ μάλα ἐν δίκῃ Eus.*d.e.*7.1(p.313.2; M.22.512B); **3.** *without judgement, irrationally* εἰ μετὰ ἐπικρίσεως [sc. ποιεῖ ὁ θεός], τίνος ἐνδείᾳ ἐπικρίσεως δεῖται; εἰ δὲ ἀ., ποίῳ τῷ λόγῳ; ‡Just.*qu.Gr.*8(M.6. 1473C).

ἀκρόαμα, τό, *anything heard*; hence in theatre, *play* ἀπειρήσθων ...τὰ ἀ. βωμολοχίας...γέμοντα Clem.*paed.*3.11(p.278.31; M.8.656A); μετασχεῖν ἀ. ἀπρεπῶν *Const.App.*2.61.2; *tidings* τοιούτου γὰρ ἐρῶμεν ὑπὲρ ὑμῶν ἀ. Synes.*ep.*8(M.66.1345C).

***ἀκροάμων**, ὁ, *hearer*, Andr.Cr.*or.*19(M.97.1208B).

ἀκρο-άομαι, **1.** *be a hearer*; **a.** in class of penitents so called περὶ τῶν...δειπνησάντων εἰς τὰ εἴδωλα, ὅσοι...μετέσχον τοῦ...δείπνου ἀδιαφόρως, ἔδοξεν ἐνιαυτὸν ∼ᾶσθαι, ὑποπεσεῖν δὲ τρία ἔτη, εὐχῆς δὲ μόνης κοινωνῆσαι ἔτη δύο, καὶ τότε ἐλθεῖν ἐπὶ τὸ τέλειον CAnc.(314)*can.*4; CNeocaes.*can.*5; CNic.(325)*can.*11; *ib.*14; μὴ δεῖν τὰς χειροτονίας ἐπὶ παρουσίᾳ ∼ωμένων γίνεσθαι CLaod.*can.*5; Bas.*ep.*217 *can.*57 (3.326C; M.32.797B); **b.** as a catechumen κατηχοῦμεν αὐτοὺς καὶ ποιοῦμεν χρονίζειν ἐν τῇ ἐκκλησίᾳ καὶ ἀ. τῶν γραφῶν, καὶ τότε βαπτίζομεν ‡CCP(381)*can.*7 = CTrull.*can.*95; **c.** in first or elementary class of catechumens (perh. in practice assimilated to 1.a; cf.CNic.(325)*can.*14) καὶ πληρώσαντος αὐτοῦ τὸν τῆς διδασκαλίας λόγον...ὁ διάκονος κηρυττέτω· μήτις τῶν ∼ωμένων, μήτις τῶν ἀπίστων *Lit.*ap.*Const.App.*8.6.2; *ib.*8.12.2; **2.** *hear* a dispute or suit μηκέτι κατὰ τοὺς τῆς ἐκκλησίας ἀλλὰ κατὰ τοὺς δημοσίους νόμους, αὐτόν με δι' ἐμαυτοῦ τῶν πραγμάτων ∼ασάμενον (? l. ∼ασόμενον) Const.ap.Ath.*apol.sec.*68(p.147.5; M.25.372A).

ἀκρόασις, ἡ, **1.** *hearing*; **a.** by pupils, hence *instruction* μετὰ εἴκοσιν ἔτη τῆς παρ' αὐτῷ [sc. Πλάτωνι] ἀ. ἀποφοιτήσαντα τὸν Ἀριστοτέλη Or.*Cels.*2.12(p.140.30; M.11.817A); *ib.*3.54(p.250.1; 992B); Eus.*h.e.*6.15(M.20.553B); **b.** esp. of scripture ἄνθρωπος ἐντεθραμμένος τῇ νομικῇ κατηχήσει καὶ τῇ ἀ. τῶν προφητικῶν λόγων Or.*or.*2 (p.302.19; M.11.421C); δι' ἀναγνώσεως καὶ δι' ἀ. καὶ διαλέξεως πνευματικῆς Chrys.*hom.10.8 in Gen.*(4.82A); *V.Pach.A* 1(p.123.7); *ib.*19 (p.144.1); **c.** quasi-judicial *hearing* of bishops by emperor, Ath. *apol.sec.*87(p.166.7; M.25.405B); **d.** *session* of a council ἀναγιγνωσκέσθωσαν οἱ δεδομένοι τόποι ἐν ταῖς προλαβούσαις ἀ. CChalc.*act.*4(p.92. 10; H.2.384C); **2.** *thing heard*; division of a poem, Geo.Pis.*Pers.*tit. (M.92.1198); **3.** *ear* τὰς ἀ. αὐτῶν ὑπέχουσιν ἀκοῦσαι *A.Thom.*A 48 (p.165.4); **4.** = οἱ ἀκροώμενοι, the *second class of penitents* ἐπιλαβομένους ὅτι ἦσαν...Χριστιανοί, ἐκβαρβαρωθέντας δὲ ὡς καὶ φονεύειν τοὺς ὁμοφύλους...τῆς ἀ. ἀπεῖρξαι δεῖ Gr.Thaum.*ep.can.*7 (p.565; M.10.1040D); CNic.(325)*can.*12; μετὰ [sc. πρόσκλαυσιν] ἄλλην τριετίαν εἰς ἀ. μόνην παραδεχθήτω, καὶ ἀκούων τῶν γραφῶν καὶ τῆς διδασκαλίας ἐκβαλλέσθω Bas.*ep.*217 *can.*75(3.328D; M.32.804B); ἐν τῇ ἀ. παραμεῖναι, μόνης τῶν διδασκάλων καὶ τῆς τῶν γραφῶν ἀ. ... ἀξιούμενον Gr.Nyss.*ep.can.*5(M.45.232A); the *station of the second class of penitents* ἡ ἀ. ἔνδοθι τῆς πύλης ἐν τῷ νάρθηκι, ἔνθα ἑστάναι χρὴ τὸν ἡμαρτηκότα Gr.Thaum.*ep.can.*11(p.566; M.10.1048A).

ἀκροατήριον, τό, **1.** *place of audience, hall, meeting-room*; of a theatre, Tat.*orat.*22(p.25.11; M.6.857A); a church ἀ. θεῖον Chrys. *hom.58.4 in Jo.*(8.342B); **2.** *audience* τὸ ἀ. τερπόμενον Or.*hom.20.6 in Jer.*(p.186.11; M.13.513B); Meth.*arbitr.*1(p.147.18; M.18.241C); Eus. *h.e.*10.4.4(M.20.849B); **3.** *platform* or *pulpit* for public speaking, Eus.*v.C.*4.55(p.140.10; M.20.1205B); ὁ τόπος ἐν ᾧ ἐπιδείκνυνται οἱ λέγοντες, τοῦτό ἐστιν ὁ ἄμβων, ἤτοι τὸ ἀ. Bas.Sel.*v.Thecl.*2.27(M.85. 613A).

ἀκροατής, ὁ, *hearer*, **1.** in gen., Athenag.*leg.*2.4(M.6.896B); *Hom. Clem.*18.12; **2.** esp. of worshippers in church or participants in mysteries οὐδεὶς τούτων τῶν μυστηρίων ἀ. γέγονεν, εἰ μὴ μόνοι οἱ γνωστικοὶ τέλειοι Hipp.*haer.*5.8(p.94.23; M.16.3147C); κἂν παραβολαὶ...ἀναγινώσκωνται καὶ ὁ ἀ. ᾖ τῶν ἔξω Or.*hom.12.13 in Jer.* (p.100.22; M.13.397A); **3.** *pupil* γενοῦ ἀ. καὶ ἄκουε τὰς δόξας τοῦ θεοῦ Herm.*vis.*1.3.3; βουλόμενος ἀ. αὐτοῦ καὶ συνουσιαστὴς γενέσθαι Just.*dial.*2.4(M.6.477B); Or.*hom.14.3 in Jer.*(p.108.13; M.13.408A); **4.** *member of a council*, Aitherichus ap.CChalc.*act.*1(*ACO* 2.1.1 p.118. 29; H.2.133C); **5.** *referee, arbitrator* [sc. Φωτεινός] ἠξίωσε Κωνστάντιον...ὅπως ἀκροατὰς λάβοι αὖθις, τοῦ ἀποδεῖξαι ἑαυτὸν μάτην καθῃρημένον...ὁ μὲν βασιλεὺς...ἐξέπεμψε κριτὰς καὶ ἀ. Epiph.*haer.*71.1 (p.250.9; M.42.376A).

***ἀκροβάμων**, *going on tip-toe*, Gr.Naz.*ep.*2(M.37.24A).

ἀκροβολ-έω, **1.** *throw, fling*, met. προφάσεις Nil.*Eulog.*17(M.79. 1116B); **2.** *attack from a distance*, met. ἕως ὅτε ∼εῖ τὰ πάθη ἐκκρουέσθω ἵνα μὴ εἰσοικισθέντα...δυσαπάλλακτα γένηται Thdr.Stud. *epp.*2.8(M.99.1137B).

[*]**ἀκροβολιάζομαι**, = ἀκροβολίζομαι, *skirmish*, ‡Nil.*perist.*10.7 (M.79.900B).

ἀκροβολίζ-ομαι, *shoot from afar, skirmish*, met. διὰ τῶν ὀφθαλμῶν μοιχεύειν...∼ομένης τῆς ἐπιθυμίας δι' αὐτῶν Clem.*paed.*3.11 (p.274.27; M.8.645A); Chrys.*hom.12.1 in Heb.*(12.120C); id.*hom.10.1 in 1Cor.*(10.80D); Thdt.*provid.*10(4.665).

ἀκροβολισμός, ὁ, *skirmish*; fig., of rebellion, Synes.*regn.*19(p.44.

10; M.66.1089D); of temptation, Nil.*epp*.3.153(M.79.456A); Isid.Pel. *epp*.5.39(M.78.1349D).

***ἀκροβύστης**, *uncircumcised* Ἀδὰμ...ἀ. μὲν τῇ σαρκί, οὐκ εἰδωλολάτρης δὲ ἦν Epiph.*haer*.2(p.175.1; M.41.181C).

ἀκροβυστία, ἡ, 1. *foreskin*, Just.*dial*.27.5(M.6.533C); **2.** *state of uncircumcision* Ἀβραάμ, τοῦ ἐν ἀ. ἐπὶ τῇ πίστει μαρτυρηθέντος ὑπὸ τοῦ θεοῦ *ib*.11.6(500A) al.; θύραν ὁ κύριος ἑαυτὸν προσηγόρευσε...ὁδὸν καὶ ὑπέρθυρον περιτομὴν καὶ ἀ. Tim.Ant.*caec*.14(M.28.1021C); ref. Jo.12:21 τὴν δὲ ἐν σαρκὶ ἀ. ἐν πνεύματι ἔχουσαν μείζονα περιτομήν, θεωροῦσαν Χριστόν Epiph.*haer*.30.27(p.371.6; M.41.453B) al.; δύο οἶδεν ἀ., τὴν μὲν ἐκ φύσεως, τὴν δὲ ἐκ προαιρέσεως Chrys.*hom.6.3 in Rom*.(9.476B) al.; **3.** *uncircumcised people*, Hipp.*haer*.5.26(p.131.5; M.16.3202A) et freq.

ἀκρόβυστος, *uncircumcised*, **1.** lit. εἰ γὰρ [sc. ἡ περιτομή] ἦν ἀναγκαία...οὐκ ἂν ἀ. ὁ θεὸς ἔπλασε τὸν Ἀδάμ Just.*dial*.19.3(M.6.516C); ἀπὸ περιτομῆς ἀ. γίνονται τέχνῃ τινὶ ἰατρικῇ Epiph.*mens*.16 (M.43.264C); **2.** fig. ἔστι γάρ τι τῆς φιλοσόφου γονῆς ἐν μαθήμασι σαρκωδές τε καὶ ἀ. Gr.Nyss.*v.Mos*.(M.44.337A) al.; **3.** met. ἀ. μὲν οὐκ ἔτι...περιτετμημένος δὲ μᾶλλον, ὡς τῆς ψυχῆς τὴν κακίαν περιτεμών Thdt.*Rom*.2:26(3.35) al.; **4.** hence = *gentile* ἄμεινον γάρ ἐστιν παρὰ ἀνδρὸς περιτομὴν ἔχοντος χριστιανισμὸν ἀκούειν ἢ παρὰ ἀ. ἰουδαϊσμόν Ign.*Philad*.6.1; ref. Ac.21:28 ἄνδρας ἀ. εἰσήνεγκε μεθ' ἑαυτοῦ Epiph.*haer*.28.4(p.316.14; M.41.381C); ἵνα μὴ ἐξῇ [sc. Ἰουδαίοις] λέγειν ὅτι καταλιπὼν ἡμᾶς πρὸς τοὺς ἀ. ἀπῆλθε [sc. ὁ Χριστός] Chrys.*hom.31.2 in Jo*.(8.177A) al.; v. περιτομή.

ἀκρογωνιαῖος (λίθος), *(stone) as topmost angle* or *point* of pyramid, obelisk, etc., which being cut before being set in position, and being last laid, would not fit if construction were not true; hence called 'stone of testing' (Is.28:16); **1.** lit. ἦν λίθος ἀ. μέγας ὃν ἐβουλόμην θεῖναι εἰς κεφαλὴν γωνίας τῆς πληρώσεως τοῦ ναοῦ *T.Sal*.22.7; **2.** met., of Christ, Just.*dial*.114.4(M.6.740B); typified by Jacob's stone, ‡Eust.*Laz*.19(p.42.7); Gr.Naz.*or*.22.4(M.35.1136A); κατέπιε τὸν λίθον τὸν ἀ. [i.e. death] Chrys.*non.desp*.3(3.357C); interpreted as *corner-stone* joining Israel and gentiles in spiritual union, Cyr.*Is*.3.2(2.397E); Jo.D.*hom*.4.30(M.96.632C).

***ἀκρόγωνος**, = foreg.; of Christ, Gr.Naz.*carm*.2.1.14.15(M.37.1246A); Geo.Pis.*hex*.1870(M.92.1577A).

ἀκροδίκαιος, 1. *exactly correct* οἱ...ἀ. τῇ πίστει Μελητιανοί Epiph. *haer*.68.6(p.146.15; M.42.193B); **2.** *superlatively just* τοῖς γὰρ ἀτόνοις ...τὸ μέτριον ὑπέρτονον δοκεῖ, καὶ τοῖς ἀδίκοις ἀ. τὸ ἐπιβάλλον Clem. *str*.2.20(p.180.7; M.8.1068C).

***ἀκροδικαιοσύνη, ἡ**, *exact correctness, perfectly correct form*; of the truth, Epiph.*haer*.68.6(p.146.9; M.42.193A).

ἀκρόδρυον, τό, *ripe fruit* ὅπερ γάρ ἐστιν ἐν φυτοῖς τὸ ἀ. ἤτοι καρπὸς ὡραῖος, τοῦτο καὶ ἐν ψυχαῖς ἁγίων ἀρετή Cyr.*Is*.5.4(2.823A).

***ἀκροέλικτος**, *twisted at the end*, Paul.Sil.*ambo*.207(M.86.2259B).

***ἀκροθήνιος**, v. *ἀκροθίνιος.

ἀκροθιγῶς, *lightly, cursorily* ἀ. διεξήλθομεν Eus.*d.e*.10.8(p.492.14; M.22.789D); Epiph.*haer*.5.1(p.184.8; M.41.201C); ‡Pall.*proem*.(p.4.7; M.34.995); *slightly*, *Mir.Artem*.39(p.64.27).

ἀκροθίνιον, τό, *topmost* or *best of heap*; hence **1.** *choicest* of the spoils, Gr.Nyss.*hom.7 in Cant*.(M.44.929D); **2.** *first-fruits*, fig. σωφροσύνης δὲ τοὺς καρποὺς γεώργησον ἐμφρόνως, καὶ σεαυτὸν ἀ. ἀνάστησον τῷ θεῷ Clem.*prot*.11(p.83.4; M.8.237B); met., of Constantine μέγα δῶρον ἀνατιθεὶς αὐτὸς ἑαυτόν, οὗ πεπίστευται κόσμου τὸ ἀ. Eus. *l.C*.2(p.200.14; M.20.1328B); Στέφανος, τὸ τῶν μαρτύρων ἀ. Cyr.H. *catech*.17.24; Μωϋσῆς...ὁ τῶν ἐν νόμῳ τὸ ἀ. νεκρῶν Bas.Sel.*or*.25.3 (M.85.292C); **3.** *fruits, reward*, Tat.*orat*.34(p.36.1; M.6.876C); **4.** *highest rank* τῶν τοῦ θεοῦ λειτουργῶν τὰ ἀ. Eus.*v.C*.3.7(p.80.10; M.20.1061A); **5.** *supreme example*, in bad sense τελώνης καὶ βλάσφημος, τὰ ἀ. τῆς πονηρίας Chrys.*dimiss.Chan*.2(3.434B).

***ἀκροθίνιος**, *foremost, leading*, Gel.Cyz.*h.e*.3.12.2; ἀκροθήνιος, Anast.S.*qu.et resp*.20(M.89.525A).

ἀκροκελαινιάω, *be dark*, Paul.Sil.*Soph*.667(M.86.2145A).

***ἀκροκρινοχρυσόμορφος**, *with capitals in the form of golden lilies*, Sophr.H.*carm*.20.21(p.46; M.87.3817B).

ἄκρον, τό, 1. *highest* or *farthest point*; **a.** of time ἄκρα τε πολέμου γράφει καὶ τέλος Eust.*engast*.27(p.59.14; M.18.669C); Gr.Nyss.*ep*.3 (p.23.19; M.46.1021C); **b.** εἰς ἄκρον or ἐπ' ἄκρον, *extreme, complete* τὴν ἐπ' ἄ. δικαιοσύνην *Clem.ep*.16(M.2.52C); τὰ τῆς ἀνθρωπότητος ἴδια διὰ τὴν εἰς ἄ. ἕνωσιν εἰς ἑαυτὸν ἀναλαβών Cyr.*hom.pasch*.17.3(5^2.230B); id.*Nest*.1.3(p.22.10; 6^1.15C); **2.** *individual term*, ref. person of Christ in Inc. ὁμοουσιότητι μὲν τῶν ἄ., ἑτεροουσιότητι δὲ τῶν μερῶν Leont. B.*arg.Sev*.(M.86.1917D); κοινότησι μὲν τῶν μερῶν κατὰ φύσιν τοῖς ἄ. ἑνούμενος, ἰδιότησι δὲ τῶν αὐτῶν, δηλαδὴ μερῶν, καθ' ὑπόστασιν ταυτότητι τῶν οἰκείων μερῶν, πρὸς ἑαυτὸν δεικνὺς σῳζομένην τὴν τῶν ἄ. διαφοράν· ἐν δὲ τῇ τῶν μερῶν κατ' οὐσίαν ἑτερότητι, τὴν πρὸς τὰ μέρη τῶν ἄ. ταυτότητα φυσικὴν ἐπιφερόμενος Max.*ep*.15(M.91.557B); *ib*. (560D); τὴν ἐν τοῖς μέρεσι τελείαν ἔχων ταυτότητα, καὶ τὴν πρὸς τὰ ἄ. προσωπικήν, ὡς εἷς καὶ μόνος, κέκτηται διαφοράν id.*opusc*.(M.91.73C).

ἀκροπαγής, *fastened at the end, lightly fixed*, ‡Ath.*v.Syncl*.52(M.28.1520A); of knees, *jointed*, Nonn.*par.Jo*.4:23(M.43.777C).

***ἀκροπέτηλος**, *of the tips of shrubs*, Eudoc.*Cypr*.2.39(M.85.848A).

ἀκρόπολις, ἡ, *citadel*, met.; **1.** of places Θρᾴκην...τῶν συγχύσεων τὴν ἀ. Isid.Pel.*epp*.1.462(M.78.436D); Αἴγυπτον...τὴν τῆς ἀσεβείας ἀ. Bas.Sel.*or*.37.4(M.85.397C); Σιὼν τῶν ἐκκλησιῶν ἀ. Jo.D.*f.o*.4.11 (M.94.1132A); **2.** of things ἡ ἀ. τῆς κακίας ἡ φιλαργυρία Clem.*paed*. 2.3(p.181.4; M.8.437C); Adam's sin as ἀ. τῶν κακῶν Chrys.*hom. 15.2 in Mt*.(7.186C); ἀγάπη as 'citadel' of virtues, ‡Caes.Naz.*dial*. 194(M.38.1184); Easter as πασῶν τῶν ἑορτῶν κορυφὴ καὶ ἀ. ‡Epiph. *hom*.3(M.43.468A); **3.** of persons ἦν...ἀ. δὲ ἀνδρείας, μητρόπολις δὲ δικαιοσύνης Isid.Pel.*epp*.2.151(M.78.605A); S. Peter and Elijah αἱ δύο ἀ. ‡Chrys.*Petr.et El*.4(2.738C).

***ἀκροπορία, ἡ**, *lofty flight*, ‡Caes.Naz.*dial*.107(M.38.976).

***ἀκρόρριζος**, *with shallow roots, roots near the surface*, Bas.*hex*.5.7 (1.46C; M.29.109B).

ἄκρος, *highest, outermost*, hence *supreme*; **1.** theol., *consummate* διὰ τὴν ἄ. ἕνωσιν Apoll.*fr*.141(p.241.17)ap.Leont.B.*Apoll*.(M.86.1965D); ἀπηκρίβωται γὰρ εἰς ἄ. συνάφειαν, οὐκ εἰς ἀποθέωσιν Nest.ap. Cyr.*Nest*.2.7(p.44.15; 6^1.48A); Max.*ep*.12(M.91.480C); **2.** of persons, *chief* τὸν πρώτης καθέδρας ἐπίσκοπον μὴ λέγεσθαι...ἄ. ἱερέα *Cod.Afr*. 39.

ἄκροσσος, *without fringes* or *tassels*, Ath.*virg*.11(p.44.24; M.28.264B).

***ἀκρόστεγος**, *covered at the top*, Geo.Pis.*hex*.718(M.92.1490A).

ἀκροστιχίς, ἡ, (***ἀκροστίχιον, τό**), **1.** *initial letter*, *Orac.Sib*.11.17; Epiph.*haer*.70.12(p.245.32; M.42.365B); **2.** *acrostic*; **a.** poem in which the first letters of the verses form a word or series of words οὗτος ὁ νῦν προγραφεὶς ἐν ἀκροστιχίοις θεὸς ἡμῶν σωτὴρ ἀθάνατος βασιλεύς, ὁ παθὼν ἕνεχ' ἡμῶν *Orac.Sib*.8.249; cf. the acrostic Ἰησοῦς Χρειστὸς θεοῦ υἱὸς σωτὴρ σταυρός *ib*.8.217–50 cit.ap.Const.*or.s.c*.18 (p.179.17; M.20.1288A); **b.** formed of initial letters of strophae in odes of a canon οὗ ἡ ἀ. Γεωργίου μάρτυρος ὑμνῶ τοὺς ἄθλους· αἶνος Ἰωάννου Jo.Mon.*hymn.Geo*.(M.96.1393C); **3.** *responsive refrain* ἕτερός τις τοὺς τοῦ Δαυὶδ ψαλλέτω ὕμνους, καὶ ὁ λαὸς τὰ ἀ. ὑποψαλλέτω *Const.App*.2.57.6.

ἀκροτελεύτιον, τό, *burden, chorus*, Soz.*h.e*.8.8.1(M.67.1536B) cit. s. ἀντίφωνος.

[*]**ἀκροτηριάζω**, v. ἀκρωτηριάζω.

ἀκρότης, ἡ, 1. *extreme*, opp. μεσότης: ἀ. ἀμαθίας ἀθεότης καὶ δεισιδαιμονία Clem.*prot*.2(p.18.22; M.8.93A); δύο...ἀ., τὴν μὲν τοῦ καλοῦ, τὴν δὲ τοῦ ἐναντίου, ἐν ἀνθρώποις Or.*Cels*.6.45(p.116.11; M.11.1368C); αἱ οὖν ἀ., θεὸν δέ φημι καὶ κόσμον, ἀλλήλων καὶ τῆς μεσότητος, λέγω δὲ τὴν φύσιν, ἀπάγειν τὸν ἄνθρωπον εἰώθασιν Max. *ep*.9(M.91.445D); **2.** *excellence* οἱ δὲ ἄγγελοι ἐκτὸς ὄντες σαρκὸς ἐν μακαριότητος ἀ. ... καὶ δόξης εἰσίν Meth.*res*.1.49(p.302.8; M.18.277A); of S. Paul δικαιότατον...δι' ἀ. ... φιλοσοφίας τε καὶ θεοσεβείας Eus.*h.e*.2.23.2(M.20.196C); συνανῆλθόν σοι, λόγε...ἡ τῶν ἀποστόλων ἀ. ἐπὶ τοῦ ὄρους Θαβώρ Jo.D.*carm.transfig*.(M.96.848B).

ἀκρότομος, *sharp, flinty*, ref. Jos.5:2 τῇ ἀ. πέτρᾳ ὑπὸ Ἰησοῦ οἱ υἱοὶ Ἰσραὴλ...περιτέμνονται Or.*Jo*.6.45(26; p.154.16; M.14.277C); ref. Dt.8:15 λέγει ὁ Ἰησοῦς, διψῶ, ὁ ἐξαγαγὼν αὐτοῖς ἐξ ἀ. τὰ ὕδατα πέτρας Cyr.H.*catech*.13.29; ‡Meth.*Sym.et Ann*.9(M.18.369B); met. ἵνα τὴν καρδίαν ἀ. οὖσαν εἰς λίμνας ὑδάτων μεταβάλῃς Hyper.*mon*.74 (M.79.1480D).

ἀκροφανής, 1. *showing at the edge, just visible*, Nonn.*par.Jo*.1:44 (M.43.757B); *ib*.2:7(761A); *ib*.11:2(810A); **2.** *shining on high, shining forth*; of torchlight, *ib*.18:3(889B).

***ἀκροφιλόσοφος**, *consummate philosopher*, Leont.B.*Nest.et Eut*.1 (M.86.1273B).

ἀκροφυής, *highly endowed by nature*, Synes.*Dion* 17(p.275.9; M.66.1160C); ἵππον ἀ. εἰς ἅπασαν ἀρετὴν ἵππῳ προσήκουσαν id.*ep*.40 (M.66.1364C).

***ἀκροφυῶς**, *to the utmost that nature permits, perfectly*, Olymp. *Eccl*.5:8(M.93.544B); τὰ τοῦ θεοῦ ποιήματα, τὰ ἀ. συντεταγμένα *ib*. 12:10(624B).

***ἄκρυος**, *without cold, summery*, *Mir.Artem*.28(p.41.20).

ἀκρῶνυξ, *toe-nail*, *Apoc.Esd*.(p.31.18).

ἀκρώρεια, ἡ, 1. lit., *mountain ridge*; *height* of heaven, *Hom.Clem*. 6.6; **2.** met., *height, supreme excellence*, acc. Basilides ἡ δύναμις τῆς κρίσεως ἀπὸ τῆς ἀ. ἄνωθεν διὰ τοῦ δημιουργοῦ μέχρι τῆς κτίσεως, ὅ ἐστι τοῦ υἱοῦ Hipp.*haer*.7.26(p.205.18; M.16.3318A); τὴν ἀνωτάτω πάντων μακαριότητα καὶ...ἀ. τῶν ἀγαθῶν Or.*Cels*.6.44(p.115.7; M.11.1365D); ἀ. τῆς ἀρετῆς Serap.*Man*.14(p.35; M.40.912B).

ἄκρως, *utterly, supremely* ὁ θεὸς ἀ. ἀγαθός Meth.*res*.1.39(p.284.4; M.41.1108B); *perfectly* οἱ ἀκρότατον βιοῦντες Jo.D.*haer*.15(M.94.685C).

ἀκρωτηριάζ-ω ([*]ἀκροτ-), **1.** *cut off extremities, mutilate* ἠκρωτηριασμένοι [sc. lepers] τοῖς πλείστοις τοῦ σώματος μέρεσι Gr.Naz.*or*.14.10(M.35.869A); met., of demons τῷ κατὰ Χριστὸν γενομένῳ βαπτίσματι ~ονται Nil.*epp*.3.16(M.79.208A); ref. circumcision, Or.*comm.in Gen*.(M.12.76B); Gr.Nyss.*hom.5 in Cant*.(M.44.877C); ref. castration, *Can.App*.22; Chrys.*hom.4.3 in Rom*.(9.457E); hence **2.** *mutilate, diminish*; writings, Meth.*res*.1.58(p.320.12; M.41.1153D); Eus.*Marcell*.1.4(p.30.30; M.24.773C); of Ebionite gospel τῷ εὐαγγελίῳ κατὰ Ματθαῖον...ἠκρωτηριασμένῳ Epiph.*haer*.30.13(p.349.3; M.41.428C); of number of apostles ἵνα μὴ ἠκρωτηριασμένος ὁ χορὸς εἴη Chrys.*hom.3.2 in Ac*.(9.25B); of moon ἦν οὖν πανσέληνος, οὐ γὰρ εὐθὺς ἠκρωτηρίαστο Proc.G.*Gen*.1:15(M.87.87C); ref. effects of Fall ἡ παράβασις ἐκείνου ἀ. τὴν δεδομένην ἐξουσίαν Chrys.*hom.35.5 in Gen*.(4.238B); ‡Caes.Naz.*dial*.160(M.38.1121); ref. Arianism ἀνόσιον...τὸν λόγον ἠκρωτηριάσθαι Alex.Al.*ep.Alex*.7(p.24.2; M.18.557B); τὸν τῆς ἐξανθρωπήσεως ἀ. λόγον Thdt.*haer*.4.1(4.350); ref. Apollinarianism τῶν ἀνθρώπων καταδεέστερον δείκνυσιν, ἠκρωτηριασμένον τῷ κρείττονι Gr.Nyss.*Apoll*.34(M.45.1197B).

ἀκρωτηριασμός, ὁ, *mutilation*; **1.** lit., Eus.*l.C*.7(p.214.3; M.20.1353D); Bas.*hom*.7.1(2.52C; M.31.281B); Thdr.Stud.*epp*.1.27(M.99.996D); of castration, Chrys.*hom.4.3 in Rom*.(9.458A); **2.** met., *curtailment*, id.*virg*.46(1.306A).

*__ἀκτάομαι__, *lose property*, Olymp.*Job* 1:3(M.93.20C).

ἀκτέανος, *without possessions, poor*; esp. of monks, Gr.Naz.*carm*.1.2.17.43(M.37.784A); *ib*.2.2(poem.)5.147(1532A); †Apoll.*met.Ps*.48:3(M.33.1380A).

ἀκτερής, = ἀκτερέϊστος, *unhallowed by funeral rites, Orac.Sib*.3.481.

*__ἀκτημον-έω__, *live in* (voluntary) *poverty* ~οῦσι Χριστιανοί...διὰ τὴν τοῦ πνεύματος ἐπαγγελίαν Cyr.H.*catech*.16.19; Thdr.Stud.*epp*.2.132(M.99.1425B).

ἀκτημοσύνη, ἡ, *poverty* (usu. self-chosen state of poverty opp. πτωχεία, ἔνδεια);

A. in pagan philosophy ὁ τὴν εὐτέλειαν ἀγαπήσας φιλόσοφος Ἑλλήνων καὶ παράδειγμα ἐκθεὶς εὐδαίμονος βίου, ὡς οὐ κωλυόμενος εὐδαιμονεῖν ἀπὸ τῆς παντελοῦς ἀ. Or.*Cels*.6.28(p.98.28; M.11.1337A); Κράτης...Κυνικός, ἔλεγεν ἐλευθερίαν εἶναι τὴν ἀ. Epiph.*exp.fid*.9(p.507.30; M.12.796A); Ἑλλήνων δὲ φιλόσοφοι οὐκ ὀλίγοι τοσαύτην ἐπεδείξαντο ἀ. ... ὅπως αὐτοῖς ἡ τῶν ματαίων θεωρία τὴν κατάληψιν ἔχειν δοκῇ ἀκραιφνῆ μὴ ἐνοχλουμένοις ποθὲν φροντίσι πραγματικαῖς Nil.*Magn*.39(M.79.1017B).

B. Christian: 'holy poverty'; **1.** def. οὐ γὰρ τὴν ἀκούσιον πενίαν νῦν ἀ. φαμέν, ἥτις ἐξ ἀνάγκης συμβαίνουσα θλίβει τὴν γνώμην...ἀλλὰ τῆς προαιρέσεως τὸ περὶ τὴν ὀλιγαρκίαν αὐθαίρετον Nil.*Magn*.2(M.79.969D); but ὁ μὲν...τινὸς τῶν πολυτελῶν κειμηλίων πένης τε καὶ ἀκτήμων...εὑρισκόμενος, ἄθλιος τῆς πενίας καὶ ἐλεεινὸς τῆς τῶν τιμίων ἀ. ὁ δὲ πάντων τῶν κατὰ κακίαν νοουμένων ἑκουσίως πτωχεύων...οὗτος ἐν τῇ μακαριζομένῃ πτωχείᾳ Gr.Nyss.*beat*.1(M.44.1200B); as temperate use of possessions τῆς ἀ. τὸ εὐαγγελικὸν ἐκπληροῖ μέτρον ὁ περὶ χρήματα ἐγκρατῶς διακείμενος Bas.*reg.fus*.16.3(2.359C; M.31.960C); ἀ. ἐστὶν νοητή, ἡ παντελὴς ἀπάθεια, καθ' ἣν γενόμενος ὁ νοῦς ἀναχωρεῖ τῶν ἐνταῦθα Thal.*cent*.2.90(M.91.1445C); **2.** different degrees τριττῆς οὔσης ἐν τῷ βίῳ ἀγωγῆς τῆς ἄκρας ἀ. καὶ τῆς μέσης, καὶ τῆς ἐνύλου, καὶ πολυκτήμονος· μία γὰρ ἦν ἐξ ἀρχῆς, καὶ θεσπισθεῖσα παρὰ τοῦ δημιουργοῦ, καὶ πολιτευομένη πᾶσιν ὁμοίως, ἀμέριμνος, καὶ παντάπασιν ἄϋλος, ἣν ἔτεμον ὕστερον εἰς τὰς διαφορὰς ταύτας αἱ ποικίλως...σχισθεῖσαι γνῶμαι τῶν ἀνθρώπων Nil.*Magn*.13(M.79.985B); **3.** its sources: H. Ghost ἀ. ... δίδωσι...τὸ πνεῦμα τὸ ἅγιον Cyr.H.*catech*.16.22; Nil.*epp*.2.204(M.79.308B); Christ its teacher, Cyr.H.*catech*.13.5; charity εἰπὲ δή μοι, ἡ ἀγάπη τὴν ἀ. ἔτεκεν, ἢ ἡ ἀ. τὴν ἀγάπην; ἐμοὶ δοκεῖ ἡ ἀγάπη τὴν ἀ., ἢ καὶ ἐπέσφιγγεν αὐτὴν μᾶλλον Chrys.*hom.11.1 in Ac*.(9.90C); **4.** prototypes: Elijah, Chrys.*hom.12.3 in Phil*.(11.294D); Noah, *Apophth.Patr*.(M.65.336C); **5.** poverty as essential virtue of monastic or ascetic life, cf. Clem.*q.d.s*.20(p.173.5; M.9.625A) for poverty as necessary for salvation; οἱ καὶ εἰς ἄκρον ἐλάσαντες ἀκτημοσύνης διὰ τὴν κατὰ θεὸν φιλοσοφίαν Eus.*fr.Lc*.6:20(M.24.533C); δεῖ τὸν προσερχόμενον θεῷ, ἀ. ἀσπάζεσθαι κατὰ πάντα Bas.*ep*.22.3(3.101B; M.32.293A); Diad.*perf*.85(p.116.9); προσήνεγκαν οἱ πατέρες τῷ θεῷ, πρὸς ταῖς ἄλλαις ἀρεταῖς, δῶρα τὴν παρθενίαν καὶ τὴν ἀ. Dor.*doct*.1.11(M.88.1629C); ἡ ἀ. εἰλικρινῆ τὴν πολιτείαν τοῦ μοναχοῦ ἀποδείκνυσιν Ant.Mon.*hom*.89(M.89.1705C); **6.** combined with other monastic virtues and exercises ἀ. καὶ ἡ ψαλμῳδία Mac.Aeg.*cust.cor*.12(M.34.832C); τὸ τῆς ἀ. κατόρθωμα, καὶ τὸ τῆς ἡσυχίας κτλ. Bas.*ascet*.2.2(2.326B; M.31.888A); with νηστεία, Chrys.*hom.1.5 in Mt*.(7.10B); παρθενία, id.*hom.12.7 in Rom*.(9.547C); ‡Proc.G.*Pr*.13:13(M.87.1352C); ταπείνωσις, *Apophth.Patr*.(M.65.172C); as one of three principal monastic virtues with πραότης, and ἐγκράτεια, *ib*.(185A); with eremitical life, Epiph.*haer*.64.4(p.410.1; M.41.1076C); **7.** partic. characteristics and effects φαίη οὖν ἄν τις, ἀγαθὸν κειμήλιον τὴν ἀ. τῷ ἀνδρείῳ φρονήματι· καὶ γὰρ τῶν πρακτικῶν ἁμαρτημάτων χαλινὸς τυγχάνει ‡Ath.*v.Syncl*.30(M.28.1505C); [sc. Βασίλειος]...διὰ τῆς τελείας ἀ. ἀνεμπόδιστον ἑαυτῷ τὸν εἰς ἀρετὴν βίον παρασκευάζοντα Gr.Nyss.*v.Macr*.(p.377.18; M.46.965C); ἰσχυρὸν γὰρ ὅπλον ἀ. Chrys.*stat*.2.9(2.34B); ἀκτημοσύνῃ τὸ τῆς φιλοχρηματίας ἰασώμεθα πάθος Nil.*exerc*.72(M.79.805B); frees soul for contemplation, Marc.Er.*opusc*.2.137(M.65.952A); leads to heaven, Ant.Mon.*hom*.8(M.89.1460A); διὰ γὰρ τῆς ἀ. τοῖς ἀγγέλοις συναμιλλᾶται, καὶ τοῖς δικαίοις συγχορεύει *ib*.89(1705D); **8.** praise of poverty τὸ τέλειον ἀγαθόν, ἡ ἀ. ‡Ath.*v.Syncl*.72(M.28.1529B); Gr.Naz.*or*.34.4(M.36.244C); ἀ. φιλαργυρίας ἐκρίζωμα, ἀφιλαργυρίας δὲ ῥίζωμα, καρπὸς ἀγάπης καὶ σταυρὸς ζωῆς, ἀνώδυνος βίος, ἀνεπίφθονος θησαυρός, ἀμέριμνος οὐρανός...εὐαγγελίων πρᾶξις, ἄλυτος κόσμος, ὀξύδρομος ἀγωνιστής †Nil.*vit*.3(M.79.1141D); καλαὶ μὲν αἱ πράξεις, ἀλλὰ μείζων πάντων ἡ ἀ. ἐστί *Apophth.Patr*.(M.65.188A); ἀ. ἐστὶ φροντίδων ἀπόθεσις, ἀμεριμνία βίου, ὁδοιπόρος ἀνεμπόδιστος Jo.Clim.*scal*.17(M.88.928B); superior to almsgiving οὐκ ἐνδέχεται γάρ τινα ταύτης τῆς ἀρετῆς, λέγω δὴ τῆς ἀγάπης, ἐφικέσθαι, εἰ μὴ ἐκ τῆς ἀ. ... οὐ διαβάλλουσα τὸν ἔλεον ταῦτα λέγω· ἀλλὰ τῆς ἀ. τὸ καθαρὸν δεικνύουσα ‡Ath.*v.Syncl*.72,74(1329C,D); **9.** heret. [Ἀποστολικοί]...σεμνύνονται δὲ δῆθεν ἀ., σχίζουσι...ἐκκλησίαν Epiph.*haer*.61.1(p.380.16; M.41.1040C); opp. balanced view of Church ἡ ἐκκλησία...ἔχει ἀ., ἀλλ' οὐ κατεπαίρεται τῶν ἐν κτήσει δικαιοσύνης ὑπαρχόντων καὶ ἐκ τῶν ἰδίων γονέων ἐχόντων, ὅπερ ἑαυτοῖς τε καὶ τοῖς ἐπιδεομένοις ἐπαρκέσειεν *ib*.61.3(p.382.19; 1041C).

ἀκτήμων, **A.** *poor, without possessions*; **1.** in gen. ἀπέχεται...ὁ ἀ. πλεονεξίας Marc.Er.*opusc*.2.24(M.65.933C); ὁ ἀ. ἐπὶ γῆς μὲν πολιτεύεται, τὴν δὲ διατριβὴν ἐν οὐρανοῖς κέκτηται Ant.Mon.*hom*.89(M.89.1705D); ἀ. ἐργάτης...τὰ προσόντα αὐτῷ ὡς μὴ ὄντα λογιζόμενος, ἀναχωρήσεως καταλαβούσης ἡγήσατο πάντα σκύβαλα Jo.Clim.*scal*.17(M.88.928C); ἀ. ἐστὶν ὁ ἀποταξάμενος πᾶσι τοῖς ὑπάρχουσιν αὐτῷ, καὶ μηδὲν τὸ σύνολον ἐπὶ γῆς κεκτημένος πλὴν τοῦ σώματος· καὶ τὴν πρὸς αὐτὸ δὲ σχέσιν διαρρήξας, τῷ θεῷ καὶ τοῖς εὐσεβέσι τὴν ἑαυτοῦ κατεπίστευσεν οἰκονομίαν Max.*carit*.2.88(M.90.1013A); **2.** partic.: OT prophets Ἠλίας ὁ ἀ. ὡς μηδὲ ἄρτον ἔχειν παρ' ἑαυτῷ φαγεῖν Or.*sel.in Ps*.4:6(M.12.1156C); τῶν...προφητῶν τὸν ἀ. βίον ἡ ἱστορία διδάσκει Thdt.*qu.19 in 4Reg*.(1.522); Jo. Bapt., Cyr.H.*catech*.3.6; apostles, *ib*.16.10; Epiph.*haer*.61.3(p.383.21; M.41.1044B); τί γὰρ τελώνου καπηλικώτερον; ἀλλ' ὅμως γέγονεν ἀ. ὁ ἄνθρωπος, ἐκ τοῦ πείθεσθαι τοῖς τοῦ ἰατροῦ νόμοις Chrys.*hom.74.5 in Mt*.(7.722A); Titus, Thdt.*Tit*.3:13(3.709); early Christians ἀντὶ δὲ τῶν φιλτάτων, γυναικὸς λέγω καὶ παίδων καὶ παντὸς γένους, τὸν ἀ. τρόπον ἑλομένων Eus.*d.e*.3.4(p.117.7; M.22.200C); ascetics, Eus.*m.P*.11(p.934.25; M.10.1540A); Bas.*inst.ascet*.2(2.200A; M.31.621B); Thdt.*h.e*.5.35.3(3.1076); *Apophth.Patr*.(M.65.152B); Messalians ἀκώλυτοι δέ εἰσι καὶ ἐκτείνουσι χεῖρας μεταιτεῖν ὡς ἀβίωτοι καὶ ἀ. Epiph.*haer*.80.3(p.487.15; M.42.760D); **3.** ref. spiritual advantages of the poor life ἐν ἀ. καὶ ἐλευθερίῳ ζῶντα βίῳ Gr.Nyss.*fat*.(M.45.149A); οἱ...τὸν ἀ. καὶ φροντίδων ἐλεύθερον ἀσπαζόμενοι βίον, ὅλους ἑαυτοὺς ἀφιεροῦσι...θεῷ Thdt.*qu.1 in Lev*.(1.178); οὐ θλίβει τοὺς ἀ. ἐπιθυμία τῶν παρόντων, σκιρτᾶν δὲ παρασκευάζει, καὶ γάννυσθαι Nil.*Magn*.1(M.79.969C); id.*spir.mal*.7(M.79.1152C) cit. s. ἀετός; Ant.Mon.*hom*.89(M.89.1705C); ἀ. μοναχὸς δεσπότης κόσμου...ἀ. ἀνὴρ ἐν προσευχῇ καθαρός, ὁ δὲ φιλοκτήμων εἰκόνας ὕλης προσεύχεται Jo.Clim.*scal*.17(M.88.928B); but voluntary poverty not in itself perfection ὁ ἀ. φυσᾶται πολλάκις διὰ τοῦτο Chrys.*hom.32.6 in 1Cor*.(10.293E); οὐδὲ εἶπε [sc. Christ]· γίνεσθε ἀ., ὡς ὁ πατὴρ ὑμῶν ὁ οὐράνιος ἀ. ἐστίν Dor.*doct*.14.6(M.88.1784B); Jo.Clim.*scal*.17(M.88.928D); hence not required from everyone οὐ δύνασαι γενέσθαι ἀ.; δὸς ἐκ τῶν ὄντων Chrys.*hom.45.2 in Mt*.(7.478C); 'ἀφιλάργυρον', οὐκ εἶπεν ἀ. Thdt.*1Tim*.3:3(3.654); **4.** *spiritually poor, detached* μακάριός ἐστιν ὁ νοῦς, ὁ κατὰ τὸν καιρὸν τῆς προσευχῆς ἄϋλος καὶ ἀ. γίνεται Evagr.Pont.*or*.119(M.79.1193B); **5.** of God (Marcionite), denied by orthodox θεὸν...οὐ νόθον...καὶ ξένον καὶ ἀ. Adam.*dial*.5.28(p.240.7; M.11.1884A).

B. *not possessing, deprived of* τῶν ἀλλοφύλων κειμηλίων ἀ. Gr.Nyss.*v.Mos*.(M.44.360A); Bas.Sel.*or*.24(M.85.280C).

*__ἀκτησία__, ἡ, *poverty* (voluntary); esp. of monks and other ascetics, Gr.Naz.*or*.43.60(M.36.573C); ‡Bas.*const*.20.4(2.566D; M.31.1393C); Niceph.Ur.*v.Sym*.32(M.86.3016B); ‡Jo.D.*fid.dorm*.13(M.95.

257C); bringing freedom and joy, Gr.Naz.*carm*.1.2.10.267(M.37. 699A); †Jo.D.*B.J*.18(M.96.1024C); opp. *κτῆσις*, Max.*ep*.1(M.91.369D); of Rechabites *Ἰωναδὰβ δὲ παισὶν εἰσάγων ποτὲ ἀ. τε καὶ τὸν ὑψηλὸν βίον* Gr.Naz.*carm*.1.2.10.509(717A); of a Cynic philosopher, Cosm. Mel.*schol*.(M.38.557) in Gr.Naz.*carm*.1.2.10.206.

***ἀκτῖνα**, ἡ, = *ἀκτίς*, *ray*, Chrys.*a.exil*.1.3(3.417C).

ἀκτινοειδής, *raylike*, *shining*, Cyr.H.*catech*.15.20; Socr.*h.e*.3.20.14 (M.67.432A).

***ἀκτινόεις**, *furnished with rays*, *Orac.Sib*.8.191; *ib*.14.270.

***ἀκτινολαμπέω**, *shine*, Thdr.Stud.*or*.5.2(M.99.721B).

***ἀκτινοφανής**, *radiant*, Max.*opusc*.(M.91.72A).

***ἀκτινοφανῶς**, *radiantly*, Max.*ambig*.(M.91.1128A).

ἀκτίς, ἡ, *ray*, *beam*; **1.** lit., of sun's rays, Chrys.*hom.79.3 in Mt.* (7.762D); *διὰ τῆς ἀ. ἣν ἀπήστραψεν ἐν τῷ σταυρῷ* *ib.16.2*(205A); **2.** met.; **a.** of Son *τὸν υἱὸν ἐγέννα ὥσπερ τινὸς φωτὸς ἀ. καὶ ζωῆς πηγήν* Eus.*e.th*.1.8(p.66.30; M.24.837C); *ὁ σωτὴρ ὁ ἡμέτερος, καὶ τὸ πνεῦμα τὸ ἅγιον, ἡ δίδυμος τοῦ πατρὸς ἀ.* †Gr.Thaum.*ep.Philagr*.(M. 46.1105D); ref. Mal.4:2 *δικαιοσύνης ἀ. σοφίας τε αὐγαῖς τὰς παμμακαρίας καταλάμπειν δυνάμεις* Eus.*l.C*.6(p.211.27; M.20.1349C); ref. Jo.8:12 *τὰς ἡλιακὰς Χριστοῦ ἀ.* Or.*Jo*.1.25(24; p.31.26; M.14.69A); acc. Gnostics *ἀναστείλας τὴν ἐπελθοῦσαν ἀ. τῆς δυνάμεως, ὁ σωτὴρ ἀπώλεσε μὲν τὸν θάνατον* Clem.*exc.Thdot*.61(p.127.21; M.9.688D); *υἱοῦ ἀ. ἀμυδραί...συγκρατοῦσι τὴν μεταβολήν, τὴν γένεσιν* Hipp.*haer*.8.13 (p.233.10; M.16.3359B); **b.** in gen. *ψυχαὶ θεοσεβείας...ἀπλανοῦς ἀκτῖσι πεφωτισμέναι* Eus.*l.C*.8(p.217.21; M.20.1361B); *θερμὸς περὶ τὸν θεὸν ἔρως...τὸν νοῦν...ταῖς ἀ. νύττων* Thdt.*h.rel*.30(3.1292); *ταῖς δὲ τῆς διδασκαλίας ἀ. καταυγασθέντες* id.*h.e*.4.21.12(3.986); exeg. Cant.2:3 *φυγεῖν τὰς τῆς κακίας ἀ. ... ἵνα μὴ πάλιν γένηται μέλαινα* id.ad loc. (2.55); *ἀνδρί, τὰς ἀποστολικὰς ἀφιέντι ἀ.* Gel.Cyz.*h.e*.3.9.16; **3.** *midwife's instrument*, Bas.Sel.*or*.2.1(M.85.40A).

***ἀκτιστῆται**, οἱ, name of a monophysite sect *λέγουσι...ἄκτιστον γεγονέναι τὸ τοῦ κυρίου σῶμα* Tim.CP *haer*.(M.86.44C).

ἄκτιστος, *uncreated*; **1.** of divine nature or being *ἡ κτιστὴ φύσις ἀπὸ τῆς ἀ. οὐσίας ἀφέστηκεν* Eus.*v.C*.5 tit.(p.152.11; M.20.1230C); Gr.Naz.*or*.23.11(M.35.1164A); *τῆς νοητῆς φύσεως διχῇ διῃρημένης, ἡ μὲν ἄ. ἐστι καὶ ποιητικὴ τῶν ὄντων* Gr.Nyss.*hom.6 in Cant*.(M.44. 885D); *ἡ ἄ. φύσις τῆς κινήσεως...ἀνεπίδεκτος* id.*or.catech*.6(p.34.1; M.45.28C); *ἅπαντα εἴς τε κτιστὸν καὶ ἄ. διαιρούμενα...ἡ μὲν ἄ. καὶ δεσποτικὴ καὶ πάσης ἀνάγκης ἐλευθέρα, ἡ δε κτιστὴ δουλικὴ* Thdt. *rect.conf*.4(M.6.1212C); **2.** of Trin., ‡Ath.*Apoll*.1.3(M.26.1097A); Bas. *ascet.disc*.1(2.212C; M.31.649B); Gr.Nyss.*or.catech*.39(p.156.5; M.45. 100B); *ἡ μία τριὰς εἷς ἐστι θεός...ἄ.* Epiph.*haer*.76.49(p.405.6; M.42. 621D); *τρισυπόστατον θεότητα...ἄ.* ‡Meth.*palm*.5(M.18.393A); Jo. V H.*icon*.4(M.96.1352C); **3.** of Father *ἐκέλευσε ἡμᾶς βαπτίζεσθαι... οὐδὲ εἰς ὄνομα ἀκτίστου καὶ κτίσματος, ἀλλ' εἰς ὄνομα πατρὸς καὶ υἱοῦ καὶ ἁγίου πνεύματος* Ath.*decr*.31.3(p.27.24; M.25.473C); *εἰ κτίσμα καὶ οὐ γέννημα ὁ υἱός...μάτην ἀγέννητος ὁ πατὴρ λέγεται, οὐκ ὄντος ὅλως γεννήματος πρὸς ὃ καλεῖται ἀγέννητος. δικαιότερον οὖν ἄ. ἢ ἀγέννητος λέγοιτο ἄν* Didym.(‡Bas.)*Eun*.4(1.283E; M.29.681C); Cyr.*Heb*.1:8 (p.462.13; M.74.960B); Thdt.*qu.3 in Gen*.(1.6); Jo.D.*f.o*.1.2(M.94. 792C); **4.** of Son; **a.** in gen. *οἱ μὲν τὸ ὂν μὲν μήτε δὲ γεννηθὲν μήτε ὅλως ἔχον τὸν αἴτιον λέγουσιν τὸ ἀγέννητον, οἱ δὲ τὸ ἄ.* Ath.*syn*.46 (p.271.19; M.26.776B); ‡Cyr.H.*occurs*.8(M.33.1196B); opp. angels, Didym.ap.*cat.Heb*.1:7(p.131.28); *ἡ ὠδὶς τὴν ἄ. φύσιν οὐκ ἠλλοίωσεν* Procl.CP *or*.2.2(M.65.693B); *γέγονε* [sc. *Ἀδάμ*] *κατ' εἰκόνα* · [*Χριστὸς*] *εἰκὼν ἄ.* *ib*.2.3(696C); **b.** esp. agst. Arianism *τὸν υἱὸν καὶ τὸ πνεῦμα... τῆς ἀ. φύσεως* Gr.Nyss.*Eun*.1(1 p.85.16; M.45.317A); Didym.(‡Bas.) *Eun*.4(1.287A; M.29.689B) cit. s. *συναΐδιος*; Epiph.*haer*.69.56(p.204.4; M.42.292A); *ἵνα...ἡ ἁγία ἔνσαρκος οἰκονομία...συνενωθῇ ἄνω τῷ ἀ. λογῷ* *ib*.69.42(p.190.12; 268C); Chrys.*hom.2.3 in Jo*.(8.22A); Cyr.*thes*. 32(5[1].312A); ref. Pr.8:22 *κτιζομένου τοῦ σώματος, ἑαυτὸν κτίζεσθαι λέγει, καίτοι τὴν οὐσίαν ἄ. ὢν* *ib*.15(167B); *ὁ ἐμὸς πατὴρ...εὐδόκησε κτιστὸν σαρκί με γενέσθαι τὸν ἄ.* ‡Proc.G.*Pr*.8:22(M.87.1296B); acc. Eunomius *υἱὸς...κτίσμα τοῦ ἀ., οὐχ ὡς ἓν τῶν κτισμάτων* Eun.*apol*. 28(M.30.868B); **c.** of Christ's divine opp. human nature *τὸ δὲ τῷ ἀ. κοινωνῆσαν ἢ ἑνωθέν, ἴδιον μὲν τοῦ ἀ. λέγεται, οὐ μὲν αὐτὸ ἄ.* ‡Ath. *Apoll*.1.4(M.26.1100A); *εἰ ὁ ἄ. ἄ. σῶμα ἀνελάβετο...ἀπόλωλεν ὁ ἀρχέτυπος Ἀδάμ* *ib*.(1100B); *ἄ. τὸν ἐν ἀρχῇ ὄντα λόγον...κτιστὸν δὲ τὸν σάρκα γενόμενον καὶ ἐν ἡμῖν σκηνώσαντα* Gr.Nyss.*hom.13 in Cant*. (M.44.1045C); Thdt.ap.Cyr.*apol.Thdt*.(p.109.21; 6[1].204E); *οὐ μὴν τῷ ἀ. τὸ κτίσμα κατ' οὐσίαν συμπλέκεται...ἄ. ὁ υἱὸς ναὸν ἔχει τὸ κτίσμα* Bas.Sel.*or*.25(M.85.297B); Justn.*conf*.(p.80.38; M.86.1003D); *ἡ παρθένος τὸν ἄ. ἐν γαστρὶ κτιζόμενον φέρουσα* Sophr.H.*or*.7.12(M.87. 3341C); *οὔ φαμεν σάρκα ἢ ἀνθρωπότητα ἄ.* ‡Cyr.*Trin*.9(6[3].13C; M.77. 1172C); Leont.H.*monoph*.12(M.86.1777B); CLater.*can*.4; ref. monothelites *οὐ γὰρ οἷόν τε τὴν αὐτὴν καὶ μίαν ἐνέργειαν ἢ θέλησιν... θείαν ἐν ταὐτῷ καὶ ἀνθρωπίνην ὑπάρχειν, ἢ ἄ. καὶ κτιστόν* Max.*opusc*. (M.91.117A); ref. followers of Paul of Samosata, acc. Apollinarius *ἄλλον μὲν τὸν ἐξ οὐρανοῦ λέγουσι,...ἄλλον δὲ τὸν ἐκ γῆς...τὸν μὲν ἄ. τὸν δὲ κτιστόν* Apoll.*ep.Dion*.1(p.256.3; M.*PL*.8.929A); acc. Apollinarius *οὐ διατέμνεται...ὅτε πλαστὸς ὁ ἄ. ὀνομάζεται τῇ συναφείᾳ τῇ... πρὸς τὸ πλασσόμενον σῶμα· ὁμολογεῖται δὲ ἐν αὐτῷ τὸ μὲν εἶναι κτιστὸν ἐν ἑνότητι τοῦ ἀ., τὸ δὲ ἄ. ἐν συγκράσει τοῦ κτιστοῦ, φύσεως μιᾶς ἐξ ἑκατέρου μέρους συνισταμένης* id.*corp.et div*.4f.(p.187.4; M.*PL*.8.873C); *τὸ σῶμα...ἥνωται τῷ ἀ. καὶ θεὸς ὢν κατὰ τὴν τοῦ θεοῦ ἕνωσιν, ἄ. ἐστιν ᾗ θεός* id.*fr*.148(p.247.4)ap.Leont.B.*Apoll*. (M.86.1965B); [sc. *ἡ σάρξ*] *ὡς λόγος οὕτως καὶ ἄ., οὐχ ὅτι μὴ ἔκτισται, ἀλλ' ὅτι λόγος ἐκ τῆς ἑνώσεως ἀπεφάνθη* id.*fr*.145(p.242.10)ap.eund. (1968C); *ἀνάθεμα οὖν ὁ μὴ λέγων ἐκ τῆς Μαρίας τὴν σάρκα καὶ τῆς ἀ. φύσεως λέγων αὐτὴν καὶ ὁμοούσιον τῷ θεῷ* id.*tom.syn*.(p.263.12; M. 86.1952B); **5.** of H. Ghost *πιστεύομεν εἰς τὸ πνεῦμα τὸ ἅγιον...τὸ ἄ., τὸ τέλειον* ‡Ath.*interpr*.(p.66.24; M.26.1232B); Gr.Nyss.*fid*.(M.45. 141C); Didym.(‡Bas.)*Eun*.5(1.309E; M.29.744A); Epiph.*haer*.69.56 (p.204.4; M.42.292A); *πνεῦμα θεοῦ...ἄ., ἐκ τοῦ πατρός* *Symb*.ap.eund. *anc*.119(p.148.30; M.43.236B); *εἰ γὰρ ἦν κτίσμα τὸ πνεῦμα τὸ ἅγιον, οὐκ ἂν συνηριθμήθη αὐτὸ τοῖς ἀ., ἵνα σὺν αὐτοῖς προσκυνῆται* †Leont. B.*sect*.4.1(M.86.1220C); Jo.D.*disp*.(M.96.1341D).

***ἀκτιστοσυμπλαστουργοσύνθρονος**, *uncreated fellow worker sharing the throne*; of H. Ghost, Jo.D.*carm.pent*.119(p.217; *ἄκτιστον, συμπλάστουργον, σύνθρονον* M.96.873C).

***ἀκτίστως**, *without being created*, *as uncreated*, ref. Trin. *κατὰ δὲ τὸ...ἀ. εἶναι καὶ μηδενὶ τόπῳ περιειλῆφθαι* Gr.Nyss.*diff.ess*.4(M.32. 332A); *ἀ. ἀεὶ ἡ τριὰς φανερουμένη* Epiph.*haer*.76.47(p.401.19; M.42. 616C); ref. God *ἀ. ἐκ τῆς αὐτοῦ οὐσίας...τὸ ἄφθαρτον ἔχει· ὁ δὲ οὐρανὸς κτιστῶς ἐκ τῆς τοῦ θεοῦ βουλήσεως ἔχει τὸ ἄφθαρτον* ‡Just.*qu.Chr*.5.2 (M.6.1457B); ref. Son *πῶς οὖν ἀπέθανεν ὁ κύριος, εἰ ὁ ἄκτιστος ἀ. ἐπεδήμησεν ἐπὶ γῆς;* ‡Ath.*Apoll*.1.6(M.26.1101B); *τὸν ἐξ ἀρχῆς ἀ. ἐκ τοῦ πατρὸς ὄντα κύριον καὶ Χριστόν* Gr.Nyss.*Eun*.5(2 p.126.12; M.45.708D); Leont.H.*Nest*.1.39(M.86.1500B); ref. H. Ghost *ἀ. ἐκ θεοῦ. τὸ πνεῦμα τὸ ἅγιον, διὸ καὶ αἰώνιον καλεῖται* Thdt.*Trin*.27(M.75. 1188A).

***ἀκτός**, (Lat. *actus*) **1.** *directed*, hence *governed from outside* *ὁ μὲν* [sc. *κόσμος*] *ἀ. ὁ δὲ* [sc. *ἄνθρωπος*] *αὐτεξούσιος* Melet.*nat.hom*.31(M. 64.1301A); **2.** neut. as subst., *transaction* by officials, law courts, councils, etc., Just.*1apol*.35.9(M.6.384C); Epiph.*haer*.50.1(p.245.7; M.41.885A); CCP(536)*act*.1(p.152.8; H.2.1224E).

[*]**ἀκτουάριος**, ὁ, (Lat. *actuarius*) *accountant*, *paymaster*, *IGC As.Min*.211.

***ἀκτυπησία**, ἡ, *quiet*, Nil.*epp*.1.281(M.79.185B).

***ἀκυβερνησία**, ἡ, *lack of guidance*, Ephr.1.78C.

ἀκύμαντος, *waveless*, met., *calm* *οἱ λογισμοὶ* [sc. *τῆς ψυχῆς*] *ἀτάραχοι καὶ ἀ.* Ath.*v.Anton*.35(M.26.896A); *ἀ., τὴν δι' ἀρετῆς ζωήν* Gr.Nyss.*hom.3 in Cant*.(M.44.817A); Chrys.*hom.34.5 in Mt*.(7.396B); neut. as subst. *τὸ τῆς ἀταραξίας πεπηγὸς καὶ ἀ.* ‡Bas.*const*.2.1(2.541C; M.31.1340B).

***ἀκυμάντως**, *without waves*, *calmly*; met., without disturbance, Clem.*paed*.3.12(p.291.5; M.8.680C); †Jo.D.*B.J*.16(M.96.1004A).

***ἀκυμαστοθειοισόκριτος**, *chosen as unshaken to bear God*; of the Cross, ‡Chrys.*ador*.2(11.824B).

***ἀκυρίευτος**, *not to be ruled*, *overmastering* *ὀδύνη* †Gregent.*disp*. (M.86.720A); *free* *ἡ αὐτεξουσιότης...ἐστιν ἡ ἀ., πρὸς τὸ καταθύμιον ἀνεμπόδιστος κυρίευσις* Anast.S.*hod*.2(M.89.77D); ‡Sophr.H.*triod*.(M. 87.3957D).

ἄκυρος, **1.** *without authority*, *powerless*, Trin. *κακῶς ἐποίησε μόνην τὴν τοῦ πατρὸς οὐσίαν κυριωτάτην εἰπὼν...κατασκευάζων κατὰ τὸ σιωπώμενον ἄ. ... εἶναι τοῦ υἱοῦ καὶ τοῦ πνεύματος τὴν οὐσίαν* Gr.Nyss.*Eun*.1 tit.15(1 p.2.24, v.l. *ἀκύρως* M.45.245); *τὸ γὰρ ἄ. τῷ ἀνυπάρκτῳ ταὐτόν ἐστιν* *ib*.1(1 p.75.8; 305B); **2.** *without force*, *null*, *invalid*; esp. of ordination, CNic.(325)*can*.16; CAlex.*ep*.ap.Ath. *apol.sec*.12(p.97.10; M.25.269A); CAnt.(341)*can*.22; CChalc.*can*.6.

ἀκυρωσία, ἡ, *cancelling*, *annulling*, Max.*opusc*.(M.91.109B).

***ἀκυρωτέον**, *one must cancel*, Clem.*paed*.2.10(p.211.13; M.8. 504B).

ἀκωκή, ἡ, *point* of a sword, met. *διατάγματα λύθρων μιαιφόνοις ὡς εἰπεῖν ἀ. συνέταττε* Const.ap.Eus.*v.C*.2.51(p.62.29; M.20.1028C).

***ἀκωνίτης**, ὁ, *javelin-thrower*, *MAMA* 3.414.

***ἀλαβανδηνόν**, τό, a product of India, perh. species of ruby *καβήρ, βάλλουσα τὸ ἀ.* Cosm.Ind.*top*.11(M.88.448B).

[*]**ἀλαβαστρινός**, *of alabaster*, *A.Andr.et Mt*.29(p.109.10); *ib*.30 (p.111.14).

[*]**ἀλαβαστροθήκη**, ἡ, *box containing alabaster vessel*, Amph.*hom*. 4.11(M.39.88B).

ἀλαζονεία, ἡ, *arrogance, boastfulness* Χριστὸς...οὐκ ἦλθεν ἐν κόμπῳ ἀλαζονείας *1Clem.*16.2; τὴν τῆς περιτομῆς ἀ. *Diogn.*4.1; μετεώρους ἀπὸ τῆς ἀληθείας ἀ. ... ποιεῖ Clem.*paed.*2.10(p.219.8. M.8.520C); ὑπὸ ἀ. ... ἀγόμενοι τοὺς εὐτελεστέρους ὑπερορώμεθα Or.*Jo.*13.28(p.252.10; M.14.448A); μὴ γίνου κενόδοξος, μηδὲ μετέωρος, μηδὲ ὑψηλόφρων, ἐκ γὰρ τούτων...ἀ. γεννῶνται *Const.App.*7.6.6; ἀ. γὰρ δεινή, τὸ μηδενὸς οἴεσθαι χρῄζειν ἀλλ' ἑαυτῷ προσέχειν ὡς μόνῳ τὰ κράτιστα βουλεύσασθαι δυναμένῳ †Bas.*Is.*57(1.422C; M.30.221B); ὅτι γὰρ οὐδὲν εἶναι νομίζει πάντας ἀνθρώπους πρὸς ἑαυτόν, αὐτὸς ἀποφαίνεται· τοῦτο γὰρ ἀ. Chrys.*hom.65.5 in Mt.*(7.651A); id.*hom.7.1 in 2Tim.*(11.700C); ἀ. δὲ τοῦ βίου...τὴν τῶν ἀξιωμάτων ὑπεροχήν Cyr.*hom.pasch.*27.2(5².321A); ref. demons as teachers of ἀ., Thdt.*Ps.*88:11(1.1233).

ἀλαζόνευμα, τό, *boasting*, Bas.*Eun.*1.4(1.211E; M.29.509A).

ἀλαζονεύ-ομαι, 1. *make false claims, pretend, Diogn.*4.4; Aen. *dial.*(M.85.901C); **2.** *boast, be arrogant, 1Clem.*38.2 cit. s. ἁγνός; φαρισαϊκῶς ∼ομένους ἐν ἑαυτοῖς ἐπὶ τῷ Ἀβραὰμ ὡς πατρί Or.*Jo.*6.22 (13; p.132.16; M.14.240B); πρὸς πάντας ἠλαζονεύοντο Ath.*h.Ar.*59 (p.216.11; M.25.764C); Chrys.*hom.6.4 in Heb.*(12.49B); Thdt.*Ps.*2:1 (1.618).

ἀλαζονικός, *arrogant* οὐχὶ ἀλαβάστροις πίνειν κεκωλύκαμεν· ἀλλὰ τὸ ἐπιτηδεύειν ἐν τούτοις μόνον πίνειν ὡς ἀ. περικόπτομεν Clem.*paed.*2.2(p.176.28; M.8.429B); ταπεινὸς δὲ ἄνθρωπος...ὁ...τὸ ἀ. ἀποθέμενος φρόνημα †Bas.*Is.*86(1.438D; M.30.260A); ἀ. λέγομεν, ὅταν πλέον ἀπαιτῇ τῶν ὀφειλομένων αὐτῷ παρὰ τοῦ πλησίου· ὅταν τις ἑαυτὸν μὲν ἐν πάσῃ καθιστᾷ τιμῇ, ἕτερον δὲ ἀτιμάζῃ Chrys.*exp.in Ps.*4(5.7C); id.*hom. 17.2 in 2Cor.*(10.561E).

ἀλαζονικῶς, *arrogantly* πλούτου...μεταδοτέον φιλανθρώπως, οὐ βαναύσως οὐδὲ ἀ. Clem.*paed.*3.6(p.256.2; M.8.604B); ref. Lc.18:10ff. τὸν Φαρισαῖον εἰς τὸ ἱερὸν ἀναβαίνοντα ἀ. Or.*hom.4.4 in Jer.*(p.26.26; M.13.289C); Gel.Cyz.*h.e.*2.13.5(M.85.1253A).

ἀλαζών, ὁ, as subst. and adj.; **1.** *boaster* or *boastful* ἀ. καυχώμενοι ἔχειν ἃ μὴ ἔχουσιν...τετυφωμένοι μεγάλα φρονοῦντες ἐπὶ τοῖς μὴ προσοῦσι· διαφέρει δὲ τοῦ ἀ. τῷ τὸν μὲν τετυφωμένον ἀπὸ τῆς γνώμης λέγειν, ἀ. δὲ τὸν ἐπὶ ῥήματι καυχώμενον Thdr.Mops.*2Tim.*3:2(p.213.18; M.66.945C); ἀ., τοὺς οὐδεμίαν μὲν ἔχοντας πρόφασιν εἰς φρονήματος ὄγκον, μάτην δὲ φυσιωμένους Thdt.*Rom.*2:30(3.28); Gennad.*Rom.* 1:29(p.360.10; M.85.1669C,D); **2.** *arrogant* τὴν ἀ. καὶ ὑπερήφανον τῆς γλώσσης ὑμῶν αὐθάδειαν *1Clem.*57.2; Chrys.*hom.15.3 in Mt.*(7.188E); ὁ μὲν οὖν ἀ. πάντων βούλεται εἶναι μείζων, καὶ οὐδένα ἄξιον αὐτοῦ εἶναί φησι, καὶ ὅσης ἂν τύχῃ τιμῆς, πλείονος ἐρᾷ καὶ ἀντέχεται, καὶ οὐδεμιᾶς τετυχηκέναι νομίζει, καὶ διαπτύει τοὺς ἀνθρώπους, καὶ τῆς παρ' αὐτῶν ἐφίεται τιμῆς *ib.*65.5(650D); **3.** *magnificent, grand* τῇ Ῥωμαίων φωνῇ, καταπληκτικῇ μὲν καὶ ἀ., καὶ συσχηματιζομένῃ ⟨πάσῃ⟩ τῇ ἐξουσίᾳ τῇ βασιλικῇ Gr.Thaum.*pan.Or.*1(p.3.3; M.10.1053A).

ἀλάθητος, 1. *whose notice nothing escapes, all-seeing, inescapable*; of God, Didym.*Trin.*2.14(M.39.697B); Marc.Er.*opusc.*1.91(M.65.916D); τούτου ἐρᾶν ὡς ἀ. γνωστοῦ καὶ ἐσχάτου ὀρεκτοῦ ‡Proc.G.*Pr.*27:8(M.87.1493B); of God's eye, Mac.Aeg.*prec.*(M.34.448A); justice, Marc. Er.*opusc.*1.55(916D); of Christ σύμμαχον...ἀνίκητον καὶ ἀ. *ib.*8.5 (1109A); of truth, Max.*myst.*5(M.91.673D); neut. as subst.; of God, Ath.*exp.in Ps.*10:5(M.27.93B); Cyr.*Ps.*10:4(M.69.793B); of God's knowledge, ‡Cyr.*Trin.*12(6³.18B; M.77.1148A); of the eagle, Areth. *Apoc.*25(M.106.620C); **2.** *not escaping notice, unforgotten* ὁ δὲ ἀγαπῶν τὸν κύριον...καὶ ἔχων τὴν αὐτοῦ μνήμην ἀ. ‡Chrys.*poenit.*1.2(9.764B).

ἀλαλαί, exclamation of woe οὐαὶ καὶ ἀ. τῷ γένει ἡμῶν Bars.*resp.* (M.86.893C).

ἀλάλητος, 1. *unspeakable, unutterable*; ref. 2Cor.12:4, Gr.Nyss. *hom.1 in Cant.*(M.44.785B) cit. s. ἄδυτος; of BMV φανερώσασα τὸ κρυπτὸν μυστήριον καὶ ἀ. ‡Meth.*Sym.et Ann.*14(M.18.381B); **2.** *unuttered* τοῦ θεοῦ τῆς ἀ. κραυγῆς ἐπαΐοντος Gr.Nyss.*v.Mos.*31(M.44.310C); **3.** *not speaking, wordless* τῶν οὐρανῶν...ταῖς ἀ. φωναῖς τὴν δόξαν τοῦ θεοῦ διηγουμένων id.*anim.et res.*(M.46.25A); †Jo.D.*B.J.*17 (M.96.1012A).

ἀλαλήτως, *unutterably* λαλήσωμεν ἀ. Euther.*confut.*7(M.28.1357B); Amph.*hom.*4.6(M.39.76D).

ἄλαλος, 1. *speechless, A.Thom.*A 108(p.219.21); *A.Mt.*13(p.232.14); Leont.N.*v.Jo.Eleem.*22(p.46.17); **2.** *ineffable* ἀ. χρίσματι Hipp. *haer.*5.7(p.83.8; M.16.3131C); *ib.*5.9(p.102.15; 3159A); τελειῶν τοὺς μύστας τὰ ἄ. μυστήρια *ib.*5.24(p.126.2; 3191D).

***ἀλάλως,** *ineffably*, Hipp.*haer.*5.8(p.90.13; M.16.3142A); ἐκτυποῦται δὲ ὁ μὲν υἱὸς ἀπὸ τοῦ πατρὸς ἀρρήτως καὶ ἀ. *ib.*5.17(p.114.24; 3175C).

ἀλαμπής, 1. *without light, dark*; met., ref. Heb.1:3, Gr.Nyss. *fid.*(M.45.140B) cit. s. ἀπαύγασμα; exeg. Lc.12:35 ὁ διδασκαλικὸς λύχνος ψυχούσθω...ἵνα μὴ σκοτεινὸς εἴη καὶ ἀ. Isid.Pel.*epp.*4.217(M.78.1309A); **2.** *unenlightened*; of pagan writers, Gr.Naz.*carm.*2.2 (poem.)7.250(M.37.1570A); σκοτεινὴν καὶ ἀ. τὴν διάνοιαν Cyr.*Ps.*73:14 (M.69.1188A); c. genit., *without the light of, unenlightened by* ἵνα μηδὲν ἀ. ᾖ τοῦ τρισσοῦ φωτός Gr.Naz.*or.*33.11(M.36.228C); *blind* τοὺς ἀ. ὀφθαλμοὺς τῇ ἀσεβείᾳ πηρωθέντας διάνοιξον Const.Diac.*laud.* 36(M.88.521A).

***ἀλάξευτος,** *unhewn* λίθος ἀχειρότμητος [sc. Christ] ὄρους ἐξ ἀλαξεύτου [sc. BMV] ‡Sophr.H.*triod.*tit.(M.87.3856D).

ἄλας, τό, v. ἅλς.

ἀλάστωρ, ὁ, 1. *avenging spirit* δαίμονες καὶ πνεύματα καὶ ἀ. ὑποτάσσονται *A.Thom.*A 43(p.161.6); **2.** *destroyer*; of Devil, Eus.*d.e.* 4.10(p.167.3; M.22.277C); ὁ τῆς ἀνθρωπείας φύσεως ἀ. Thdt.*Ezech.* 13:16(2.760); Jo.Carp.*cap.*24(M.85.1842); of antichrist, Ephr.2. 226A; κοινοῦ τῶν ἀνθρώπων ἀ. Thdt.*Dan.*11:45(2.1293); of heathen deities as demons, id.*qu.58 in 3Reg.*(1.503); **3.** *wicked man* ὡς ἀ. τε καὶ παραβάτην τιμωρεῖσθαι Meth.*symp.*2.4(p.20.21; M.18.53B); of Simon Magus, *M.Eleuth.*4(p.152.15); of Nestorius, Evagr.*h.e.* 1.8(p.16.27; M.86.2444B); **4.** as adj., *destroying, pernicious*; of demons, Chrys.*hom.33.3 in Mt.*(7.381A); μάχης τῶν μοναχῶν, τῆς πρὸς τοὺς ἀ. δαίμονας Nil.*epp.*1.287(M.79.188A); Procl.CP *annunt.*6 (M.85.449A).

ἁλάτινος, *of salt*, Clem.*str.*2.14(p.146.14; M.8.1000B).

***ἀλατόμητος,** *unhewn*, met.; **1.** of the righteous who died before baptism συνηρμόσθησαν εἰς τὴν οἰκοδομὴν τοῦ πύργου, καὶ ἀ. συνῳκοδομήθησαν· ἐν δικαιοσύνῃ γὰρ ἐκοιμήθησαν Herm.*sim.*9.16.7; **2.** of Christ, ref. Dan.2:34 τὴν ἀ. πέτραν ἐν τῇ παρθενικῇ ἀράχνῃ ὑπερφυῶς φερομένην Procl.CP *or.*4.1(M.65.709B); **3.** of BMV ἀ. ἡ πέτρα ‡Chrys.*annunt.*(9.844D); τὸ ἀ. ὄρος ‡Sophr.H.*triod.*(M.87.3852A); *ib.* (3861C); ὄρος τὸ ἀ. ... ἐξ οὗ λίθος χειρῶν ἄνευ τμηθεὶς τὴν οἰκουμένην ἐπλήρωσεν Jo.D.*hom.*10.2(M.96.756B).

[*]ἄλατος, f.l. for ἄτλατος (ἄτλητος *LS*), *intolerable*, Ephr.2.372C.

***ἀλάτρευτος,** *without worship* τὴν ὀγδόην ἡμέραν τὴν ἀ. ... τὴν μέλλουσαν, ὅτε οὐκέτι θυσία ἢ λατρεία ὑπὲρ ἁμαρτιῶν προσφέρεται τῷ θεῷ Chrys.ap.Anast.S.*qu.et resp.*5(M.89.368C).

***ἀλάχανος,** *without vegetables*, Gr.Naz.*ep.*5(M.37.29A).

ἀλαῶπις, = ἀλαωπός 1, Nonn.*par.Jo.*9:2(M.43.824B).

ἀλαωπός, 1. *blind*, Nonn.*par.Jo.*9:24(M.43.828D); **2.** *dark* ἀ. μερίμναις Synes.*hymn.*1.97(p.62; M.66.1589); Nonn.*par.Jo.*9:14(825C).

***ἀλάωσις, ἡ,** *blinding*, Eudoc.*Cypr.*1.305(M.85.844B).

***ἀλαώψ,** *blind*, Synes.*hymn.*3.583(p.23; M.66.1602).

ἀλγεινῶς, *in pain, with suffering*, Gr.Nyss.*or.catech.*8(p.42.3; M. 45.33A).

ἀλγ-έω, 1. physically, *feel pain, suffer* ἐδέξατο ἐπὶ τῶν...χειρῶν καὶ ποδῶν ἥλους, καὶ ἤλγησε Cyr.H.*catech.*20.5; **2.** mentally; **a.** *grieve*, over sin οὐ πάντων δὲ ἡ ἁμαρτία ὑπὸ τοῦ ἀμνοῦ αἴρεται, μὴ ∼ούντων Or.*Jo.*6.58(37; p.166.20; M.14.300C); **b.** *feel bitter* μὴ τοίνυν πρὸς ἑτέρους ∼ῶμεν Chrys.*hom.79.5 in Mt.*(7.765A); of one who envies another's good fortune πρὸς τοῦτον ∼εῖς...τὸν οὐδὲν ἠδικηκότα, πολλῷ δὲ μᾶλλον πρὸς τὸν Χριστόν id.*hom.11.4 in Col.*(11.411B).

***ἀλγή, ἡ,** *sorrow*, Ast.Am.*hom.*1(M.40.172A).

ἀλδαίνω, intrans., *grow*, Const.*or.s.c.*20(p.185.1; M.20.1297A).

[*]ἀλδίσκω, = ἀλδήσκω, *increase*; intrans., *Schol.Clem.paed.* (p.338.15; M.9.794A).

ἁλεία, ἡ, = ἁλιεία, *fishing*; met., Gr.Naz.*carm.*1.2.10.556(M.37. 720A); Gr.Nyss.*hom.5 in Cant.*(M.44.881B); Chrys.*hom.3.5 in 1Cor.* (10.22D).

[*]ἁλειάς, ἡ, = ἁλιάς, *fishing-boat*, Gr.Naz.*carm.*1.2.10.555(M.37. 720A).

ἄλειμμα, τό, 1. *unguent, oil*, Clem.*paed.*2.8(p.196.29; M.8.472B); *ib.*(p.197.3; 472B); **2.** *anointing*; in baptism, Serap.*euch.*22.1ff.; met., of preparing for athletic contests, *training, exercise* αἱ ἐπιβουλαὶ τῶν ἐχθρῶν ἄ. γίνονται τῆς καρτερίας τῆς ὑμετέρας Chrys.*ep.* 5.1(3.577E).

ἀλείπτης, ὁ, *anointer*, hence *trainer* of athletes; met., exeg. Gen.32:24ff. ὁ λόγος ἦν ὁ ἀ. ἅμα τῷ Ἰακὼβ καὶ παιδαγωγὸς τῆς ἀνθρωπότητος Clem.*paed.*1.7(p.123.30; M.8.317C).

ἀλειπτικός, *of anointing* χρῖσμα ἀ. εὐωδέστατον...ὡς ἂν χρίοιντο τούτῳ οἱ τῶν κοινῶν δημοσίᾳ προστήσεσθαι μέλλοντες Eus.*d.e.*4.15 (p.174.12; M.22.289D).

ἀλείπτως, *without defect, rightly* τὸ παρασχεῖν, καὶ ἡμῖν ἀ. εἰπεῖν, καὶ ὑμῖν ἐν συνέσει ἀκούειν Cyr.H.*catech.*16.2 (v.l. ἀλήπτως).

ἀλειτουργησία, ἡ, *immunity*, of clergy from curial obligations τὴν ἀ., ἣν εἶχον οἱ αὐτοῦ κληρικοί, τοὺς αὐτοὺς πάλιν τὴν αὐτὴν θέλομεν ἔχειν Constantius Imp.*ep.Nest.*ap.Ath.*apol.sec.*56(p.136.16,18; M.25.349C); Ath.*h.Ar.*78(p.226.29; M.25.788B); οἱ ἐπίσκοποι καὶ πρεσβύτεροι καὶ διάκονοι καὶ ὑποδιάκονοι καὶ μοναχοί, κἂν μὴ ἔχωσι χειροτονίαν, ἀ. ἔχουσι πάσης ἐπιτροπῆς καὶ κουρατωρείας, σχολάζοντες μέντοι ταῖς ἐκκλησίαις καὶ τοῖς μοναστηρίοις αὐτῶν Phot.*nomoc.*8.13

(M.104.685A); cf. *immunitatem ipso jure omnes habere tutelae...et non solum tutelae esse eos expertes, sed etiam curae, non solum pupillorum et adultorum, sed et furiosi et muti et surdi et aliarum personarum,* Justn.*cod.*1.3.51(p.34).

ἀλειτούργητος, 1. *immune,* of clergy from curial obligations κληρικοὺς...ἀπὸ πάντων ἅπαξ ἁπλῶς τῶν λειτουργιῶν βούλομαι ἀ. διαφυλαχθῆναι Const.ap.Eus.*h.e.*10.7.2(M.20.893B); Ath.*h.Ar.*78.3 (p.227.5; M.25.788C); cf.*Cod.Thds.*16.2.1,2,7; in gen., from taxation τὴν μικρὰν κτῆσιν τῶν πενήτων ἀ. καταστῆσαι Bas.*ep.*142(3. 235C; M.32.592C); met., *excused from service* (of God) εἶπες τὴν τῶν ἔξωθεν μελῶν δοξολογίαν. τί οὖν; τὰ ἔσωθεν ἀ. μένει; Bas.Sel.*or.*10.1 (M.85.142A); **2.** *not served by ministers, without ministry* ὁ τὸ ἁγίασμά σου ἀ. μὴ ἐγκαταλιπών *Lit.*ap.*Const.App.*8.5.4; ἵνα μὴ τὸ εὐκτήριον ἀ. καταλείψειεν ‡Sophr.H.*v.Mar.Aeg.*1.7(M.87.3704A); **3.** *without the liturgy;* cf. *ex antiquorum Graecorum canonum praecepto missae sacrificium offerre, nisi sabbato et dominica et sancto annuntiationis die, toto quadragesimae spatio non licet... unde dies quadragesimales merito ἀ. vocantur,* N. Nilles *Kalendarium Manuale* (Innsbruck, 1897, vol.2 pp.251ff.); cf.CLaod.*can.*49; CTrull.*can.*52 cit. s. τεσσαρακοστή; εἴ τις ἱερεὺς οὐ λειτουργήσῃ, ἀλλὰ φάγῃ τὰς προσφορὰς ἀ. *Nomoc.*111; cf. *aquam illam benedictam in theophaniis, majori in pretio habent, quae inter missarum solemnia juxta altare residebat, quam quae sacrificio praesens non fuit: prior enim illa est* ἁγιασμὸς λειτουργηθεὶς...*aliam vero licet precibus iisdem benedictam ut* ἀ. ... *et ideo minus sanctam, minus existimant, Euchol.*(p.132).

ἀλείφ-ω, *anoint;*

A. lit.; **1.** as sign of rejoicing ~εσθαι κελεύσας [Mt.6:17], οὐχ ἵνα ~ώμεθα πάντως...ἀλλ' ἐπειδὴ τοῖς παλαιοῖς ἔθος ~εσθαι συνεχῶς ἦν εὐφραινομένοις καὶ χαίρουσι Chrys.*hom.20.1 in Mt.*(7.260A); **2.** in athletics, met. ref. Christian life οὐδεὶς...ἀλειψάμενος ἄνεσιν ἐπιζητεῖ id.*hom.8.3 in 2Tim.*(11.709F); **3.** of anointing of Christ's feet, allegorized ἡ γυνὴ τοὺς πόδας ἤλειφεν τοῦ κυρίου...μύρῳ γὰρ εὐώδει ~όμενοι οἱ πόδες θεϊκὴν αἰνίττονται διδασκαλίαν ἐπὶ τὰ πέρατα τῆς γῆς ...ὁδεύουσαν Clem.*paed.*2.8(p.194.2ff.; M.8.465B); Ph.Carp.*Cant.*3 (M.40.40A); **4.** of 'anointing' of Messiah ἐλαίῳ...τῷ ἐνθέῳ τῆς ἀγαλλιάσεως ἠλειμμένον Eus.*h.e.*1.3.15(M.20.73B); 'Ιουδαίους τοὺς τὸν ἠλειμμένον προσδοκῶντας ἀπατῶντα Cyr.H.*catech.*15.11; ‡Bas.Sel. *or.*38.5(M.85.425B); Cosm.Ind.*top.*6(M.88.333A); τὸν ἠλειμμένον ὃν ἐκδέχεσθε ὑμεῖς οἱ 'Ιουδαῖοι τί μέλλει εἶναι; ‡Anast.S.*Jud.disp.*3 (M.89.1240A); *ib.*(1241B); of which Christians partake ὁ ἀλειψάμενος ἐχρίσατο...χρῖσαι τὴν κεφαλὴν χρίσματι ἁγίῳ, ἵνα μέτοχος γένῃ Χριστοῦ Bas.*hom.*1.2(2.2C; M.31.165A); anointing of Christ typified by anointing of Jacob's stone, Dem.*fr.*(p.346); **5.** of anointing in connexion with baptism; **a.** in pre-baptismal unction; **i.** as sacramental rite for bestowal of H. Ghost λαβὼν δὲ ὁ ἀπόστολος τὸ ἔλαιον καὶ καταχέας ἐπὶ τῆς κεφαλῆς αὐτῶν καὶ ἀ. καὶ χρίσας αὐτοὺς ἤρξατο λέγειν· 'ἐλθὲ τὸ ἅγιον ὄνομα τοῦ Χριστοῦ...ἐλθὲ τὸ ἅγιον πνεῦμα' *A.Thom.* A 27(p.142.12ff.); for remission of sins, averting of Devil, and salvation of soul, *ib.*157(p.267.16); *Const.App.*3.16.2(cf.*ib.*7.42.3); with purpose unstated ἀ. ἐλαίῳ καθῆκεν εἰς τὴν θάλασσαν εἰς ὄνομα πατρὸς κτλ. *A.Mt.*27(p.257.5); **ii.** as rite of exorcism ἐλαίῳ ἠλείφεσθε ἐπορκιστῷ, ἀπ' ἄκρων τριχῶν κορυφῆς ἕως τῶν κάτω· καὶ κοινωνοὶ ἐγίνεσθε τῆς καλλιελαίου, 'Ιησοῦ Χριστοῦ Cyr.H.*catech.*20.3; ἀ. τῷ ἀλείμματι τούτῳ τοὺς προσιόντας τῇ θείᾳ ταύτῃ ἀναγεννήσει Serap.*euch.*22.1; Proc.G.*Jos.*3:2(M.87.1004C); **b.** in post-baptismal unction with chrism μύρον, ὃ ἁγιασθέντες ~όμεθα ὑπὸ τοῦ ἱερέως Didym.*Trin.*2.6(M.39.557C); **6.** in unction of sick (v. χρίω), Vict. *Mc.*6:13(p.324.11); **7.** Jacob's anointing of stone interpreted as symbolical of offering to God, and compared with anointing by faithful of sacred objects, relics, etc., Thdt.*qu.84 in Gen.*(1.94); v. ἔλαιον; **8.** met. μὴ ~εσθε δυσωδίαν τῆς διδασκαλίας τοῦ ἄρχοντος τοῦ αἰῶνος τούτου Ign.*Eph.*17.1.

B. met. (from anointing of athletes); **1.** *train, encourage* ὁ ἄνθρωπος...ὁ ἀ. κατὰ τοῦ πονηροῦ τὸν ἀσκητὴν 'Ιακὼβ Clem.*paed.*1.7 (p.123.29; M.8.317C); ὁ θεῖος νόμος ~ει...τὸν ἄνθρωπον ἐπὶ τὴν ἐγκράτειαν id.*str.*2.20(p.170.17; M.8.1049A); ἄφοβον οὖν καὶ...πεποιθότα ἐπὶ κύριον ἡ ἀγάπη ~ουσα...κατασκευάζει τὸν ἴδιον ἀθλητήν *ib.*7.11(p.48.21; M.9.493B); λῃστὴς κατ' ἀνθρώπων ~ων τοὺς ἑπομένους Or.*Cels.*1.30(p.81.24; M.11.717A); καλὸν παρακαλεῖν ἀλλήλους ἐν τῇ πίστει, καὶ ~ειν ἐν τοῖς λόγοις Ath.*v.Anton.*16(M.26.868A); ὁ σωτὴρ...ἡμᾶς πρὸς τὴν ὑπομονὴν ἀλείψῃ †Bas.*ep.*42.5(3.130C; M.32. 360A); Gr.Naz.*ep.*166(M.37.276B); Didym.ap.*cat.Ac.*18:11(p.304.24); Chrys.*hom.2.4 in 2Cor.*(10.434B); ~ων αὐτοὺς...γενναίους εἶναι *ib.16.2* (554B); τὸν ἔνδον αὐτὸν ~οντα θεόν id.*hom.in 2Cor.11:1*(3.296D); Pall.*v.Chrys.*1(p.6.8; M.47.7); τούτοις γὰρ ~ειν πέφυκε [sc. Devil] τὰ πάθη Nil.*praest.*20(M.79.1084C); hence *practise* τὸ δὲ πῶς, μόνος ὁ...ἐπὶ τοῦτο ~όμενος μανθάνει Clem.*str.*2.4(p.120.25; M.8.945C); **2.** *induce, suborn, encourage* (in bad sense), Pall.*v.Chrys.*2(p.9.30; M.47.9); λιπαρήσας τινὰ νεανίσκον ὑποσχέσεσι πολλαῖς, ἤλειψεν εἰς κατηγορίαν *ib.*6(p.36.22; M.47.22); *ib.*7(p.38.18; M.47.23).

C. *overlay* οὐ χρυσῷ τὸν ὄροφον ἤλειφεν Chrys.*stat.*2.5(2.27D); id. *hom.1.1 in Jo.*(8.2D); Cyr.*ador.*9(1.305D); Thdt.*h.e.*3.11.4(3.924).

D. *paint* ὀφθαλμοῖς μέλασιν ὡς ἠλειμμένοις Hipp.*haer.*4.17(p.50.19; M.16.3083D); Chrys.*hom.68.1 in Jo.*(8.404B).

E. *moisten* θεὸς ἀντέσχεν ἀντίπαλον τῷ πυρὶ τὸ ὕδωρ, ἵνα ἔχῃ ἀρκοῦσαν τὴν διαμονὴν διὰ τῶν ἄνωθεν ~όντων ὑδάτων †Jo.D.*creat.*2(p.63).

***ἀλείψανος,** *without relic,* Gr.Naz.*carm.*1.2.10.749(M.37.734A).

ἄλειψις, ἡ, *anointing;* of the sick, Serap.*euch.*17.2; at baptism, *ib.*22.2.

ἀλεκτόρειος, *of a fowl,* Synes.*ep.*4(M.66.1340B).

ἀλεκτοροφωνία, ἡ, *cock-crow,* as a time-indication, as end of paschal fast τινὰς μὲν γὰρ τῶν ἀδελφῶν λέγειν φῄς, ὅτι χρὴ τοῦτο ποιεῖν πρὸς τὴν ἀ.· τινὰς δέ, ὅτι ἀφ' ἑσπέρας χρή Dion.Al.*ep.can.* (p.94.6; M.10.1273A); *Const.App.*5.18.2 cit. s. νηστεύω; *ib.*5.19.2,3; as one of the six hours of prayer, *ib.*8.34.1.

ἄλεκτος, 1. *that cannot be conveyed in,* i.e. *too great for, words, surpassing description,* of God ἡ δ' ἔνθεος διδασκαλία τὸ τῶν ἀγαθῶν ἀνώτατον αὐτὸ δὴ τὸ πάντων αἴτιόν...φησιν...ἄρρητον καὶ ἄ. καὶ ἀνωνόμαστον...εἶναι Eus.*l.C.*12(p.229.21; M.20.1385B); φῶς [sc. ὁ Χριστός] καὶ γέννημα νοερὸν φωτὸς ἀ. *ib.*(p.232.4; 1389C); God's power ὁ...πατὴρ...ὀξὺ ὁρῶν καὶ ὀξὺ ἀκούων...δυνάμει ἀ. Just.*dial.* 127.2(M.6.772B); the Son τῆς ἀρχῆθεν θεότητος αὐτοῦ καὶ παρὰ τῷ πατρὶ δόξης ἀ. Alex.Al.*ep.Alex.*1(p.20.10; M.18.549A); ἀ. καὶ ἀρρήτοις...λόγοις...γεγεννημένον Eus.*e.th.*1.8(p.66.21; M.24.837B); ref. Phil.3:21 ἄ. τινα καὶ ἄρρητον...ὑποταγὴν ποιησόμενος *ib.*3.15(p.174.2; 1032B); **2.** *that cannot be conveyed in words, about which nothing can be predicated,* denied of God οὐκ ἄγνωστον ἢ ἄ., ἀλλὰ διὰ νόμου καὶ προφητῶν κηρυσσόμενον *Const.App.*6.11.1; asserted τῷ υἱῷ ὁ θεὸς ἄρρητος ὑπάρχει· ἔστι γὰρ ἑαυτῷ ὅ ἐστι τοῦτ' ἔστιν ἄ., ὥστε οὐδὲν τῶν λεγομένων κατά τε κατάληψιν συνίει ἐξειπεῖν ὁ υἱός Ar.*Thal.fr.* 2.34 ap.Ath.*syn.*15(p.243.15; M.26.708B); τὸν μὲν παντοκράτορα θεὸν βλασφημεῖν, ἄγνωστον δοξάζειν καὶ μὴ εἶναι πατέρα τοῦ Χριστοῦ μηδὲ τοῦ κόσμου δημιουργόν, ἀλλ' ἄ. *Const.App.*6.10.1.

***ἀλεκτρυοφώνιον, τό,** = ἀλεκτοροφωνία q.v., Didym.*Trin.*3.22 (M.39.920A).

***ἀλέκτως,** *indescribably* ἀ. ἡνωμένας...τὰς ὑποστάσεις Didym. *Trin.*2.6(M.39.520D).

ἀλέξησις, ἡ, *warding off,* Epiph.*haer.*19.2(p.219.20; M.41.264B).

ἀλεξητήρ, ὁ, *protector,* of God τοῦ ἀ. ἡμῶν ἀληθῶς καὶ ἰατροῦ Meth.*res.*1.42(p.288.13; M.41.1112B).

ἀλεξητήριος ([*]**ἀλεξιτήριος**), *able to keep off* or *defend* from βάπτισμα...ἀ. ὂν πυρός Clem.*ecl.*8(p.139.1; M.9.701B); τὴν παρὰ 'Ιησοῦ τροφήν, ἀ. οὖσαν τῶν προκαταλαβόντων κακῶν Didym.*Ps.*21:30(M.39. 1288C); neut. as subst., *protection from* δαιμόνων ἀλεξιτήριον Jo.D. *hom.*9(M.96.745B).

[*]**ἀλεξιτικός,** = ἀλεξητικός, *able to defend* from καρπὸν...ἀ. νόσων Diod.*Ps.*51:10(M.33.1590A).

ἀλεξίμορος, *warding off death;* of Christ, Nonn.*par.Jo.*12:11 (M.43.852B); *ib.*5:25(789A).

[*]**ἀλεξιτήριος,** v. ἀλεξητήριος.

ἀλεσμός, ὁ, *grinding, crushing,* Ign.*Rom.*5.3.

ἀλευρόμαντις, ὁ, *one who divines from flour,* Clem.*prot.*2(p.11.3; M.8.69A); Chrys.*fr.in Jer.*proem.(M.64.741A).

ἄλευρον, τό, usu. plur., *meal, flour;* met., of Christ ἄρτον οὐ μύλῃ καὶ χερσί, καὶ πυρὶ δημιουργηθέντα, ἀλλ' ἀρρήτως ἐξ ἀ. παρθενικῶν γεγενημένον Thdt.*pental.*(5.117).

***ἀλέω,** *salt, T.Lev.*suppl.37(p.251).

***Ἀλεώμ,** Arabian month corresponding to January, Epiph. *haer.*51.24(p.293.5; M.41.932B).

ἀληθάργητος, 1. *unforgetful,* Mac.Aeg.*hom.*19.2(M.34.644B); **2.** *free rom torpor, strenuous,* Marc.Er.*opusc.*7.16(M.65.1093D); **3.** *not to be forgotten, IGC As.Min.*9 [saec. iv]; Heracl.*ep.*ap.*Chron.Pasch.* p.388(M.92.996A).

ἀλήθεια, ἡ, *truth;*

A. in gen.; **1.** nature of truth ἡ κτίσις οὐδὲν ἔχει προσαγορευθὲν ἀ., διὰ τὸ μίαν εἶναι θεϊκὴν ἀ., ὡς μία ἐστὶν ἡ ἁγιότης, καὶ ἡ ἀγαθότης, ἀφ' ἧς ἑκάστοις ἡμῖν ταῦτα ἐφήκειν ὁμολογοῦμεν Didym.*Trin.*2.6 (M.39.540C); dist. from Christ as absolute truth, exeg. Jo.1:17, 14:6 πῶς ἡ ἀ. διὰ 'Ιησοῦ Χριστοῦ γίνεται; αὐτὸς γάρ τις δι' ἑαυτοῦ οὐ γίνεται. ἀλλὰ νοητέον ὅτι ἡ αὐτοαλήθεια ἡ οὐσιώδης καὶ...πρωτότυπος τῆς ἐν ταῖς λογικαῖς ψυχαῖς ἀ., ἀφ' ἧς ἀ. οἱονεὶ εἰκόνες ἐκείνης ἐντετύπωνται τοῖς φρονοῦσι τὴν ἀ., οὐχὶ διὰ 'Ιησοῦ Χριστοῦ ἐγένετο οὐδ' ὅλως διά τινος, ἀλλ' ὑπὸ θεοῦ ἐγένετο. ἡ δὲ παρ' ἀνθρώποις ἀ. διὰ Ἰησοῦ Χριστοῦ ἐγένετο· οἷον ἡ ἐν Παύλῳ ἀ. καὶ τοῖς ἀποστόλοις διὰ Ἰησοῦ Χριστοῦ ἐγένετο. καὶ οὐ θαυμαστὸν μιᾶς οὔσης ἀ. οἱονεὶ πολλὰς ἀπ' ἐκείνης λέγειν ἐρρυηκέναι...οὐ γὰρ τὴν μίαν ἐκζητεῖ ἀ. ὁ πατὴρ αὐτῆς, ἀλλὰ τὰς πολλάς, δι' ἃς σῴζονται οἱ ἔχοντες αὐτάς Or.*Jo.*6.6 (3; p.114.20ff.; M.14.209Df.); exeg. Jo.18:37 ἵνα μαρτυρήσῃ τῇ ἀ., τουτέστιν, ἵνα τοῦ κόσμου τὸ ψεῦδος ἐξελὼν καὶ τὸν ἐξ ἀπάτης τυραννήσαντα καταστρέψας δαίμονα, βασιλεύουσαν τῶν ὅλων ἐπιδείξῃ τὴν ἀ., τουτέστι, τὴν ἀληθῶς τε καὶ φυσικῶς βασιλίδα φύσιν Cyr.*Jo.*12 (4.1039C); realized only in heaven, exeg. Ps.38:7, Ath.*fr.Pss.comm.* 38:7(M.27.557D) = Cyr.*Ps.*38:7(M.69.976B) cit. s. εἰκών; transcended by Logos ὑπὲρ τύπον καὶ ἀ., τῷ μηδὲν ἔχειν ἀντικείμενον συνθεωρούμενον. ἀντίκειται δὲ τῇ ἀ. τὸ ψεῦδος. ὑπὲρ ἀ. ἄρα ὁ πρὸς ὃν τὰ πάντα συνάγεται λόγος Max.*ambig.*(M.91.1296C); indicated but not clearly revealed in inspired writings, *ib.*(1252D); **2.** as object of contemplation, Meth.*symp.*9.4(p.118.14; M.18.185B); τὸ ὕψος ἐκεῖνο, ἐν ᾧ τὸ φῶς τῆς ἀ. ὁρᾶται Gr.Nyss.*v.Mos.*(M.44.333A); νῦν δὲ... οἰκείοις μὲν εἰς τὰ θεῖα συμβόλοις χρώμεθα, κἀκ τούτων αὖθις ἐπὶ τὴν ἁπλῆν καὶ ἡνωμένην τῶν νοητῶν θεαμάτων ἀ. ἀναλόγως ἀνατεινόμεθα Dion.Ar.*d.n.*1.4(M.3.592C); Max.*myst.*5(M.91.676C); **3.** of reality reflected or foreshadowed in τύποι and εἰκόνες of scripture ὁ... 'νόμος' τῆς εἰκόνος ἐστὶ τύπος καὶ σκιά, τουτέστι τοῦ εὐαγγελίου, ἡ δὲ εἰκών, τὸ εὐαγγέλιον, αὐτῆς τῆς ἀ. Meth.*symp.*9.2(p.115.28; M. 18.180C); Ἰουδαῖοι μὲν τὴν 'σκιὰν' τῆς εἰκόνος τρίτην ἀπὸ τῆς ἀ. κατηγγέλκασιν, ἡμεῖς δὲ τὴν εἰκόνα τῆς κατ' οὐρανὸν διοικήσεως ἐναργῶς ἐκθειάζομεν *ib.*5.8(p.62.9; 109C); μετὰ τὰς εἰκόνας [i.e. of eucharist]...ἐπὶ τὴν θεοειδῆ τῶν ἀρχετύπων ἀ. Dion.Ar.*e.h.*3.3.1(M. 3.428A); ἀπὸ τῶν ἀτελεστέρων εἰς τὰ τελειότερα· οἷον, ἀπὸ τῶν τύπων ἐπὶ τὴν εἰκόνα· καὶ ἀπὸ ταύτης ἐπὶ τὴν ἀ. σκιὰ γὰρ τὰ τῆς παλαιᾶς· εἰκὼν δὲ τὰ τῆς νέας διαθήκης· ἀ. δὲ ἡ τῶν μελλόντων κατάστασις Max.*schol.e.h.*3.3.2(M.4.137D).

B. of divine Persons; **1.** of Trin., Ath.*Ar.*1.18(M.26.49A); **2.** of God; as truth, Gr.Nyss.*v.Mos.*(M.44.332C); Cyr.*Jo.*6(4.566A); ἡ ὄντως ἀ. ὁ θεός ἐστιν. χρὴ οὖν πάντα ἄνθρωπον ἐρωτῶντα τὰ τῆς ἀ. πρῶτον εὔξασθαι τοῦ ἐπιγνῶναι τὴν ὄντως ἀ. Ant.Mon.*hom.*66 (M.89.1628B); as father of the truth, *2Clem.*3.1; θρησκεύομεν οὖν τὸν πατέρα τῆς ἀ. καὶ τὸν υἱὸν τὴν ἀ. Or.*Cels.*8.12(p.229.32; M.11. 1533B); as source of truth, Athenag.*leg.*23.4(M.6.944B); as measure of truth, Clem.*prot.*6(p.52.23; M.8.173B); exeg. Rom.1:25 ἀ. δὲ τοῦ θεοῦ καλεῖ τὸ 'θεὸς' ὄνομα· ψεῦδος δὲ τὸ χειροποίητον εἴδωλον Thdt. *Rom.*1:25(3.26); a divine attribute ἡ γὰρ ἀ. οὐ φιλανθρωπίαν μόνην, ἀλλὰ καὶ τιμωρίαν ἔχει δικαίαν id.*Nah.*1:3(2.1520); **3.** of Christ; **a.** in gen., Papias ap.Eus.*h.e.*3.39.3(M.20.297A); Clem.*str.*4.25(p.317.23; M. 8.1365A); Or.*Jo.*32.31(19; p.478.29; M.14.825C); Meth.*Porph.*1(p.504. 7; M.18.400A); Eus.*e.th.*2.14(p.118.18; M.24.933B); τὸ εἶναι ἐξ ἀληθινοῦ ἀ. Ath.*syn.*49(p.273.27; M.26.781A); εἰκών ἐστι...τοῦ πατρὸς...καὶ ἀ., ...εἰ γὰρ οὐκ ἦν ὁ υἱὸς πρὶν γεννηθῇ, οὐκ ἦν ἀεὶ ἐν τῷ θεῷ ἡ ἀ.· ἀλλὰ τοῦτο λέγειν οὐ θέμις id.*Ar.*1.20(M.26.53B); συγκατέβαινεν μὲν ἡ ἀ. τῷ ὑπὲρ ἡμῶν ἀποθανόντι Ἰησοῦ εἰς τὴν καρδίαν τῆς γῆς· ἵνα τοὺς ὑπὸ τοῦ ψεύδους ἀπατηθέντας, αὐτὸς ἀ. ὤν, ἐλευθερώσῃ ‡Ath.*serm.fid.*35 (p.29; M.26.1288C); εἰ δὲ ἀ. ὁ κύριος ἡμῶν ἐστιν, ἐντετυπωμένην... τῇ ἑαυτοῦ καρδίᾳ ταύτην τὴν ἀ. ἕκαστος ἔχωμεν Bas.*hom.in Ps.*14 (1.354D; M.29.256C); Gr.Nyss.*Eun.*10(2 p.246.15; M.45.849B); Cyr. *Jo.*11.9(4.984C); id.*Zach.*48(3.724E) cit. s. I.3; ὁ λόγος ἐστὶν ἡ ἁπλῆ καὶ ὄντως οὖσα ἀ. Dion.Ar.*d.n.*7.4(M.3.872C); Ant.Mon.*hom.*66(M. 89.1628C) cit. s. I.3; αὐτοουσιώδης ἀ. Andr.Caes.*Apoc.*8(M.106.245B); leading men to knowledge of God, Or.*Jo.*19.6(1; p.305.15; M.14.536C); eschatological signs of Christ's advent being σημεῖα τῆς ἀ., *Did.* 16.6; **b.** Christ being, acc. Or., truth in relation to men, but not to God [cf. *filium, qui sit imago invisibilis patris, comparatum patri, non esse veritatem; apud nos autem qui dei omnipotentis non possumus recipere veritatem, imaginariam veritatem videri; ut majestas ac magnitudo majoris, quodammodo circumscripta sentiatur in filio*, Hier.*ep.*124.2(M.*PL.*22.1060); cf. *in quibus* [sc. Περὶ Ἀρχῶν]...*quod filius nobis comparatus, sit veritas, patri conlatus, mendacium*, Thphl. Al.*epistula synodica* ap.Hier.*ep.*92.2(M.*PL.*22.762); φασὶν αὐτὸν [sc. Origen] παραγγέλλειν...ὅτι ἡ εἰκὼν τοῦ θεοῦ ὡς πρὸς ἐκεῖνον οὐκ ἔστιν εἰκών, καθ' ὃ εἰκών, οὐκ ἔστιν ἀ. Phot.*cod.*117(M.103.396B)]; γενόμενοι τοίνυν ἡμεῖς κατ' εἰκόνα, τὸν υἱὸν πρωτότυπον ὡς ἀ. ἔχομεν τῶν ἐν ἡμῖν καλῶν τύπων. αὐτὸς δὲ ὁ υἱός, ὅπερ ἡμεῖς ἐσμεν πρὸς αὐτόν, τοιοῦτός ἐστι πρὸς τὸν πατέρα Or.*princ.*1.2.6(p.36.11; M.11.135B); **c.** exeg. Jo.14:6, Or.*Jo.*1.27(29; p.34.19; M.14.73B); ἀ. δέ, ὡς ἕν, οὐ πολλὰ τῇ φύσει· τὸ μὲν γὰρ ἀληθὲς ἕν, τὸ δὲ ψεῦδος πολυσχιδές· καὶ χαρακτὴρ ἀψευδέστατος Gr.Naz.*or.*30.20(p.139.17; M.36.129B); ἀ. δὲ διὰ τὴν ἀψευδίαν, ὅτι πάντως ταῦτα ἔσται, and also ὡς ἀληθὴς τῆς πίστεως ὅρος Ammon.*Jo.*14:6(M.85.1488A,B); Chrys.*hom.*73.2 *in Jo.*(8.432A); Cyr.*Jo.*9(4.768B); **d.** as reality replacing types and shadows, exeg. Jo.1:14 αὐτὸς ὢν ἡ ἀ. ... εἰ γὰρ...τῆς σκιᾶς τι μὲν ἔπαυεν ἕτερον δέ τι αὐτῆς οὐχί, οὐκ ἦν πλήρης ἀληθείας. ἀλλὰ μὴν πᾶσαν σκιὰν καὶ εἰκόνα περιέγραψεν Or.*fr.*9 *in Jo.*1:14(p.491.18); Meth.*symp.*9.2 (p.116.3; M.18.180D); Tit.Bost.*fr.Lc.*22:14(p.241); Cyr.*Jo.*1.4(4.32D); exeg. Jo.8:32 τὰ ἐν τύποις ἀφέντας καὶ αἰνίγμασιν, ἐπ' αὐτὴν ἰέναι γοργῶς τὴν ἀ., τουτέστι, Χριστὸν τὸν τῆς ἀληθοῦς ἐλευθερίας δοτῆρα καὶ λυτρωτὴν *ib.*5.5(535D); ἐκεῖνος γὰρ [sc. Melchizedek] τούτου τύπος, οὗτος δὲ τοῦ τύπου ἡ ἀ. Thdt.*Heb.*7:3(3.585); Vict.*Mc.*2:23 (p.292.7); **4.** of H. Ghost, as truth ἀ. προηγόρευται, καθὰ ὁ πατὴρ καὶ ὁ υἱός· ἐπειδὴ τῆς αὐτῆς μιᾶς ἐστι θεότητος Didym.*Trin.*2.6(M. 39.541A); exeg. Jo.17:19 ἵνα...ἡμεῖς ὦμεν ἡγιασμένοι ἐν ἀ., τουτέστιν, ἐν ἁγίῳ πνεύματι Cyr.*Jo.*11.10(4.993D); as Spirit of truth ἔδει γάρ σε...πονηρὰν συνείδησιν μετὰ τοῦ πνεύματος τῆς ἀ. μὴ κατοικεῖν Herm.*mand.*3.4; ὁ παιδαγωγὸς οὐχὶ τοῖς ἐν τῷ κόσμῳ τῷδε καταπνέουσιν ἀνέμοις ὑπείκει ποτέ, οὐδὲ ἐπιτρέπει αὐτοῖς τὸ παιδίον, ὥσπερ σκάφος...μόνῳ δὲ ἄρα τῷ ἀληθείας πνεύματι ἔπουρος ἀρθεὶς ἀντέχεται ...τῶν οἰάκων τοῦ παιδός Clem.*paed.*1.7(p.122.21; M.8.313C); νικώμενος ὑπὸ τοῦ τῆς ἀ. πνεύματος ἀνέγραψε Or.*Cels.*8.62(p.278.10; M.11. 1609C); together with Son as mediator of truth, Eus.*e.th.*3.5(p.161. 26; M.24.1009B); Ath.*ep.Serap.*1.25(M.26.589B); *ib.*1.4(537A); ὡς γὰρ ὁ παράκλητος τὸ πνεῦμα τῆς ἀ., διδάσκει ἡμᾶς τὴν ἀ., ἥτις ἐστὶν ὁ υἱός...οὕτω καὶ ὁ υἱός, ὅς ἐστιν ἀ., τὸν ἀληθινὸν θεόν...ἡμᾶς εὐσεβῶς εἰδέναι διδάξει Geo.Laod.*ep.dogm.*ap.Epiph.*haer.*73.16(p.289.8; M. 42.433B); ‡Gr.Nyss.*hom.*5.31 *in Jo.*(p.183.21,32) cit. s. αὐτοαλήθεια; that H. Ghost is Spirit of truth adduced as argument for full divinity, Gr.Nyss.*Eun.*2(2 p.371.22; M.45.552D), cf.Cyr.*Jo.*2.1(4. 126B); *ib.*10.2(925C); credal πιστεύομεν...εἰς τὸν παράκλητον τὸ πνεῦμα τῆς ἀ. Eun.ap.Gr.Nyss.*Eun.*2(2 p.369.11; 549B).

C. *reality* opp. type (cf. B.3.d); **1.** in gen. παραστήσας [sc. ὁ Χριστός]...τίς ἡ ἀ. τῶν ἐν ταῖς ἱστορίαις πραγμάτων, ἅτινα τυπικῶς συνέβαινεν ἐκείνοις; Or.*Jo.*1.6(8; p.11.12; M.14.36A); ‡Ath.*Ar.*4.34 (p.83.8; M.26.520C); Cyr.H.*catech.*19.3; Ammon.*Jo.*4:23(M.85.1424A); οἱ τύποι ἐν τῷ νόμῳ ἦσαν, ἡ δὲ ἀ. ἐν τῷ εὐαγγελίῳ Epiph.*haer.*8.6 (p.192.17; M.41.213C); τότε μὲν μέχρι τῆς γνώμης τοῦ πατρὸς ἔστη τὸ πρᾶγμα (τύπος γὰρ ἦν)· νῦν δὲ καὶ ἐπὶ τῶν ἔργων ἐξῆλθεν· ἀ. γὰρ ἦν Chrys.*hom.*85.1 *in Jo.*(8.504A); τὴν δὲ ἀ. σαφεστέραν εἰσόμεθα, ἂν τοὺς τύπους καταμάθωμεν *ib.*14.3(8.82C); Cyr.*Is.*5.2(2.775C,E); Thdt. *Abac.*3:18(2.1559); of OT and NT ἐκείνη μὲν ἐν εἰκόσι τὴν ἀ. ἔγραψεν, αὕτη δὲ παροῦσαν ὑπέδειξε Dion.Ar.*e.h.*3.3.5(M.3.432B); **2.** exeg. Jo.4:23, Or.*Jo.*13.18(p.242.23; M.14.429B); ὅταν τὸ πνεῦμα διδάξῃ ὑμᾶς, τότε δυνήσεσθε νομικῶν ἀποστῆναι τύπων, καὶ τὴν ἐν πνεύματι καὶ ἀ. ποιῆσαι λατρείαν Ammon.*Jo.*16:13(M.85.1497C).

D. of spiritual opp. literal sense of scripture, Thdt.*qu.*2 *in Ruth* (1.352).

E. revealed through Christ and gospel πορευόμενοι κατὰ τὴν ἀ. τοῦ κυρίου Polyc.*ep.*5.2; τὸν περὶ ἀληθείας λόγον *ib.*3.2; δι' οὗ [sc. Χριστοῦ] καὶ ἐφανέρωσεν ἡμῖν τὴν ἀ. καὶ τὴν ἐπουράνιον ζωήν *2Clem.* 20.5; known by apostles in that they knew Christ and in him the Father (Jo.14:9), Iren.*haer.*3.13.2(M.7.911B); ψυχικὸν ἄνθρωπον τὸν ἀπηλγηκότα πρὸς τὴν ἀ. ἀτενίσαι καὶ τὸν φωτισμὸν τοῦ μυστηρίου Meth.*res.*1.58(p.321.22); exeg. Jo.1:17 ἡ δὲ ἀ., χάρις οὖσα τοῦ πατρός, ἔργον ἐστὶ τοῦ λόγου αἰώνιον καὶ οὐκέτι δίδοσθαι λέγεται, ἀλλὰ διὰ Ἰησοῦ γίνεσθαι Clem.*paed.*1.7(p.125.23; M.8.321C); τὸν ὄντως πατέρα καὶ διδάσκαλον τῆς ἀληθείας [sc. τὸν Χριστόν] id.*str.*7.16(p.66. 15; M.9.529B); μόνη δὲ ἡ κυρία αὕτη ἡ ἀ. ἀπαρεγχείρητος, ἣν παρὰ τῷ υἱῷ τοῦ θεοῦ παιδευόμεθα *ib.*1.20(p.62.23; M.8.816A); τεκμήριον ἄρα τοῦ παρ' ἡμῖν εἶναι τὴν ἀ. τὸ αὐτὸν διδάξαι τὸν υἱὸν τοῦ θεοῦ· εἰ γὰρ περὶ πᾶν ζήτημα καθολικὰ ταῦτα εὑρίσκεται πρόσωπόν τε καὶ πρᾶγμα, ἡ ὄντως ἀ. παρ' ἡμῖν δείκνυται μόνοις. ἐπεὶ πρόσωπον μὲν τῆς δεικνυμένης ἀ. ὁ υἱὸς τοῦ θεοῦ, τὸ πρᾶγμα δὲ ἡ δύναμις τῆς πίστεως *ib.*6.15 (p.493.12; M.9.345B).

F. expressed in Christian doctrine ἰσχυροὶ...ἐν τῇ πίστει τοῦ κυρίου ἐνδεδυμένοι τὴν ἀ. Herm.*mand.*11.4; τῶν τῆς ἀ. δογμάτων Athenag.*res.*14(p.64.8; M.6.1000D); Clem.*str.*1.20(p.64.3; M.8.817B); *ib.*6.11(p.477.24; M.9.312C); τῶν διδαχθέντων τὸν λόγον τῆς ἀ. *V.Aberc.* 7(p.7.7); μηδὲν ἔξωθεν τῆς ἀ. ὁμολογεῖ [sc. Marcellus]· οὕτως γὰρ εὐσεβῶς περὶ τοῦ...Χριστοῦ ὡμολόγησε φρονεῖν, ὥσπερ καὶ ἡ καθολικὴ ἐκκλησία φρονεῖ Jul.Papa *ep.Dian.*(p.110.23; M.25.301A); Gr.Nyss. *Eun.*12(2 p.282.12; M.45.893C); ταύτην ἡμᾶς τὴν τῶν δογμάτων ὀρθότητα καὶ ἀ. ἐδίδαξεν ἡ τῶν ἁγίων πατέρων σύνεσις Cyr.*Jo.*9.1(4.784B); Thdt.*ep.*135(4.1226); opp. Jewish and pagan beliefs, Arist.*apol.*2.1; Or.*comm.in Eph.*4:25(p.419); διὰ μέσου τῶν δύο ὑπολήψεων χωρεῖν τὴν ἀ. Gr.Nyss.*or.catech.*3(p.16.10; M.45.17D); Chrys.*hom.*3.1 *in Rom.*(9.448E); and heresy, Clem.*str.*7.15(p.64.23; M.9.525C); Ath. *apol.sec.*59(p.140.1; M.25.357A); Cyr.*Am.*57(3.313E); Thdt.*ep.*135(4.

1225); subject to attack, Clem.*str*.1.20(p.64.1; M.8.817B); Thdt.*h.e.* 1.6.9(3.754); yet invincible, Just.*1apol*.12.6(M.6.344A); Chrys.*laud. Paul*.4(2.499C); Thdt.*haer*.3 proem.(4.339); breach of *disciplina arcani* is betrayal of truth, Ant.Mon.*hom*.64(M.89.1624B).

G. revealed in scripture ἀξιόπιστοι μάρτυρες [sc. prophets] τῆς ἀ. Just.*dial*.7.2(M.6.492B); *ib*.90.2(689B); Iren.*haer*.3.21.2(M.7.948A); Clem.*str*.7.16(p.66.23; M.9.529B); τῷ φωτίζοντι πνεύματι...τοὺς διακόνους τῆς ἀ., προφήτας καὶ ἀποστόλους Or.*princ*.4.2.7(p.318.10; M.11.372A); Eus.*p.e*.1.3(8D; M.21.33C); αὐτάρκεις...αἱ...γραφαὶ πρὸς τὴν τῆς ἀ. ἀπαγγελίαν Ath.*gent*.1(M.25.4A); *ib*.41(84B); Dion.Ar.*d.n*.4.21 (M.3.721C); Andr.Caes.*Apoc*.2(M.106.228D); as source and criterion of doctrinal truth, Clem.*str*.7.16(p.68.16; 533B); κριτήριον ἀσφαλὲς τῆς ἀ. ἐπὶ παντὸς δόγματος ἡ θεόπνευστός ἐστι μαρτυρία Gr.Nyss. *Eun*.1(1 p.107.23; M.45.341B); Cyr.*Am*.57(3.313D).

H. in Church, v. ἐκκλησία.

I. revealed in Christians; **1.** in gen., Or.*Jo*.6.6(3) cit. s. A.1; id.*Cels*.8.1(p.221.9; M.11.1521A); ὥς ἐστιν ἀ. ἐν τῷ Ἰησοῦ, οὕτως ἔσται καὶ ἐν ὑμῖν μαθοῦσι τὸν Χριστόν id.*comm.in Eph*.4:20–22 (p.418); Bas.*hom.in Ps*.14(1.354B; M.29.256B); Didym.*Trin*.2.6(M.39.533B); ὅ τε γὰρ παράκλητος μισεῖ πᾶν ψεῦδος, ὅ τε διάβολος πᾶσαν ἀ. *Const.App*.6.27.4; **2.** issuing in action ἔδει γάρ σε ὡς θεοῦ δοῦλον ἐν ἀ. πορεύεσθαι Herm.*mand*.3.4; Clem.*prot*.11(p.77.30; M.8.225B); exeg. 2Cor.13:8 ἀ. γὰρ νῦν τὴν εὐσέβειαν καλεῖ, ὡς νόθου ὄντος τοῦ δυσσεβοῦς βίου *cat.2Cor*.13:8(p.442.16); cf.Thdt.*2Cor*.13:8 (3.355); **3.** and in word πᾶσα ἀ. ἐκ τοῦ στόματός σου ἐκπορευέσθω, ἵνα τὸ πνεῦμα, ὃ ὁ θεὸς κατῴκισεν ἐν τῇ σαρκὶ ταύτῃ, ἀληθὲς εὑρεθῇ... καὶ οὕτως δοξασθήσεται ὁ κύριος ὁ ἐν σοὶ κατοικῶν Herm.*mand*.3.1; exeg. Zach.8:16 εἰ γὰρ δὴ προσήκοι...λαλεῖν τὴν ἀ., τὰ Χριστοῦ πάντως διαλεξόμεθα· Χριστὸς γάρ ἐστιν ἡ ἀ. Cyr.*Zach*.48(3.724E); πῶς γὰρ ἂν ἀληθεύσειεν ὁ μὴ ἐν θεῷ λαλῶν ὅς ἐστιν ἀ.; id.*Mich*.34 (3.420C); ὁ λαλῶν τὴν ἀ. ἁγιάζεται τὴν ψυχήν, καὶ τὸ σῶμα, καὶ πάντα τὰ μέλη· ἡ γὰρ ἀ. ὁ Χριστός ἐστιν Ant.Mon.*hom*.66(M.89.1628C); v. φυλάσσω.

J. as apprehended outside Christian revelation; **1.** through reason and conscience, exeg. Rom.1:18 τὴν περὶ αὐτοῦ γνῶσιν ἐξ ἀρχῆς τοῖς ἀνθρώποις ἐνέθηκεν ὁ θεός, ἀλλὰ ταύτην τὴν γνῶσιν οἱ Ἕλληνες ξύλοις περιθέντες καὶ λίθοις, ἠδίκησαν τὴν ἀ., τό γε αὐτῶν μέρος Chrys.*hom.3.2 in Rom*.(9.449D); **2.** in philosophy παρὰ πᾶσι [sc. philosophers and poets] σπέρματα ἀληθείας δοκεῖ εἶναι Just. *1apol*.44.10(M.6.396B); περιέξουσι δὲ οἱ Στρωματεῖς ἀναμεμιγμένην τὴν ἀ. τοῖς φιλοσοφίας δόγμασι, μᾶλλον δὲ ἐγκεκαλυμμένην καὶ ἐπικεκρυμμένην...· ἁρμόζει γάρ, οἶμαι, τῆς ἀ. τὰ σπέρματα μόνοις φυλάσσεσθαι τοῖς τῆς πίστεως γεωργοῖς Clem.*str*.1.1(p.13.1; M.8.708A); τὴν φιλοσοφίαν...ἀληθείας οὖσαν εἰκόνα ἐναργῆ, θείαν δωρεὰν Ἕλλησι δεδομένην *ib*.1.2(p.13.30; 709B); *ib*.1.20(p.63.2; 816B); εἰ... τὰ τῆς ἀ. ... λαβόντες σπέρματα οὐκ ἐξέθρεψαν...τούτων οὐχ ὁ διδάσκαλος αἴτιος, ἀλλ' οἱ παρακούειν προῃρημένοι *ib*.6.7(p.461.23; M.9.281A).

K. *reality, fact* δηλῶν, ὅτι ἀληθείᾳ ὑπεύθυνοι ὀργῇ τυγχάνουσιν οἱ ἁμαρτάνοντες Didym.*Man*.3(M.39.1089C); dat., *by nature, in actual fact* opp. by grace παραστῆσαι θέλων μὴ εἶναι αὐτὸ αὐτοῦ πνεῦμα τῇ ἀ., ἀλλὰ τῇ χάριτι ‡Ath.*Maced.dial*.1.6(M.28.1300A); esp. opp. semblance or fiction, Meth.*res*.2.8(p.344.19; M.41.1176C); οὐ θέσει δὲ ταῦτα ἐγίνετο...ἀλλ' ὄντως ἀ. ἀνθρώπου γενομένου τοῦ σωτῆρος Ath. *ep.Epict*.7(p.11.7; M.26.1061A); Epiph.*haer*.69.51(p.196.26; M.42.280D); Cyr.*hom.div*.15.3(p.14.17; M.77.1093A); οὗτος [sc. Eutyches] ...Χριστὸν...φάσκων...τινὰ τυγχάνειν τοῦ ἡμετέρου σώματος εἰκόνα καὶ μὴ ἀ. Leo Mag.*ep*.30(p.46.10; M.*PL*.54.788B); Max.*ambig*.(M.91.1320C); opp. image οὐ γὰρ τύπος σώματος οὐδὲ τύπος αἵματος...ὥς τινες ἐρραψῴδησαν...ἀλλὰ κατὰ ἀ. σῶμα καὶ αἷμα Χριστοῦ Mac.Mgn. *apocr*.3.23(p.106.3).

L. as a virtue τοὺς καταδεξαμένους τὰ λόγια αὐτοῦ ἐν φόβῳ καὶ ἀ. *1Clem*.19.1; γυναῖκας...στεργούσας τοὺς ἑαυτῶν ἄνδρας ἐν πάσῃ ἀ. Polyc.*ep*.4.2; at end of list of virtues ἀνδρεία, γνῶσις, ἀ. *M.Ner.et Ach*.6(p.5.4).

M. *confidence, security* ἀ. τῶν δικαίων παρὰ θεοῦ σωτῆρος αὐτῶν *Pss.Sal*.3.7.

N. as Valent. aeon, Iren.*haer*.1.1.1(M.7.448A); Clem.*exc.Thdot*.6 (p.107.23; M.9.657A); Hipp.*haer*.4.51(p.76.1; M.16.3122A); acc. Heracleon, Epiph.*haer*.36.2(p.45.15; M.41.633D).

[*]**ἀληθεινός**, = ἀληθινός, *Lit.Marc*.(*PStrasb*.r° 9); Is.25:1 cit. ap.Procl.CP *hom*.2.1(M.65.837D).

***ἀλήθευμα, τό**, *truth, established fact*, Meth.*res*.1.33(p.270.4; M.41.1145A).

ἀληθεύ-ω, **1.** *be true*; as characteristic of God, Epiph.*anc*.56 (p.65.17; M.43.116A); ‡Nil.*perist*.10.4(M.79.893A); exeg. Jo.3:33 τοῦ ~ειν ἡ ψῆφος εἰς θεὸν ἀνατείνεται πιστευομένου Χριστοῦ Cyr.*Jo*.2.3 (4.166E); of Christ κατεδίκασας τὸν Ἰησοῦν...ὡς οὐκ ~οντα Or.*hom. 14.8 in Jer*.(p.113.16; M.13.413B); Epiph.*haer*.76.34(p.383.16; M.42.585A); **2.** *speak truth*; **a.** of man in dependence on God πῶς γὰρ ἂν ἀληθεύσειεν ὁ μὴ ἐν θεῷ λαλῶν ὅς ἐστιν ἀλήθεια; Cyr.*Mich*.34 (3.420B); of prophets, Epiph.*anc*.53(p.62.11; M.43.109B); **b.** ref. truthfulness as human virtue pleasing to God, Just.*2apol*.4.4(M.6.452A); αἰδούμενος [sc. the 'gnostic'] μὴ ~ειν ἀνάξιόν τε αὐτοῦ τὸ ψεύδεσθαι γινώσκων Clem.*str*.7.8(p.38.23; M.9.473A); *ib*.7.11(p.48.23; 493B); ποιεῖν γὰρ δίκαια, καὶ ~ειν, ἀρεστὰ παρὰ τῷ θεῷ μᾶλλον ἢ θυσιῶν αἷμα Ant.Mon.*hom*.66(M.89.1629A); **c.** with distn. between spiritual and literal truth προέκειτο γὰρ αὐτοῖς [sc. evangelists] ὅπου μὲν ἐνεχώρει ~ειν πνευματικῶς ἅμα καὶ σωματικῶς Or.*Jo*.10.5(4; p.175.16; M.14.313C); of Jacob, ref. Gen.27:19 κατὰ μὲν τὸ πνευματικὸν ἠλήθευσε *ib*.(p.175.22; 313C); **3.** *think and speak truly, be right*, Clem.*exc. Thdot*.78(p.131.16; M.9.693D) cit. s. εἱμαρμένη; πῶς γὰρ ἂν ἀληθεύσῃ περὶ τοῦ πατρὸς ὁ τὸν υἱὸν ἀρνούμενος, τὸν ἀποκαλύπτοντα περὶ αὐτοῦ; Ath.*Ar*.1.8(M.26.28A); pass., *be proved true, be fulfilled* (of scripture, etc.) πολλῷ γὰρ πλειόνά ἐστι τὰ κατὰ τὴν ἱστορίαν ~όμενα τῶν προσυφανθέντων γυμνῶν πνευματικῶν Or.*princ*.4.3.4 (19; p.329.12; M.11.384B); ~εται τό [Mt.7:8], μὴ ἀριθμουμένων εἰς πάντας τοὺς αἰτουμένους τῶν κακῶς αἰτούντων Didym.*Ac*.2:21(M.39.1656C).

ἀληθής, **A.** *true*; in gen., Or.*Jo*.10.5(4; p.175.30; M.14.313D); ὁ λόγος ἀ. ὑπάρχει καὶ οὐκ ἀλληγορεῖται οὔτε τροπικῶς λέγεται Epiph. *haer*.69.51(p.198.6; M.42.281A); Dion.Ar.*c.h*.2.3(M.3.141A) cit. s. ἀπόφασις (A); of scripture, v. γραφή, *1Clem*.45.2; Or.*Jo*.20.36(29; p.377.10; 660B); τὰς ἀ. προφητείας...ἴσμεν γὰρ αὐτὰς κατ' ἐπίπνοιαν θεοῦ ἐν τοῖς ὁσίοις ἐνεργεῖσθαι *Const.App*.8.2.7; Dion.Ar.*e.h*.7.3.3(M.3.557D); Cosm.Ind.*top*.proem.1(M.88.53C); neut. plur. as subst., *truth* (i.e. Christianity), Just.*1apol*.65.1(M.6.428A).

B. *real, genuine*, of God εἰ μὲν γάρ τις ⟨τὸν⟩ ἀ. σέβει θεόν Meth. *arbitr*.15(p.185.2); τὸν παρ' ἡμῶν...κηρυττόμενον τοῦτον μόνον εἶναι θεὸν ἀ. Ath.*gent*.40(M.25.80C); τὴν ἀ. καὶ μόνην θεαρχίαν Dion.Ar. *c.h*.9.3(M.3.261A); of Son ὁ ἡμέτερος κύριος, ὁ τοῦ θεοῦ ἀληθὴς λόγος Ath.*inc*.53.1(M.25.189C); θεὸν κατὰ φύσιν τέλειον...καὶ ἀ. *Symb.Ant*. (345)4 ap.eund.*syn*.26(p.252.32; M.26.729C); of Son's generation τὴν ἀ. καὶ φύσει γέννησιν Ath.*Ar*.1.28(M.26.69C); of Inc. ἀ. σὰρξ ἦν ἐν τῷ λόγῳ...ἐκ δὲ τῶν τῆς σαρκὸς παθῶν ἐδείκνυεν, ὅτι ἀ. ἐφόρει σῶμα, καὶ ἴδιον ἦν αὐτοῦ τοῦτο *ib*.3.41(412A); in gen., Clem.*str*.7.17(p.76.5; M.9.552A) cit. s. ἐκκλησία; ἡ ἀ. καὶ μόνη θεοσέβεια Ath.*Ar*.1.18(49A); ἡ ἀ. πίστις *Const.App*.3.12.2.

C. *true, perfect*; **1.** opp. what is non-Christian τὸν ἀ. βίον Clem. *str*.1.10(p.32.1; M.8.745B); νοῦ ἀ. τοῦ δοθέντος τοῖς λέγουσιν [1Cor. 2:16b] Or.*Jo*.10.28(18; p.201.11; M.14.357A); ἀ. γνώσεως Cosm.Ind. *top*.1(M.88.57B); **2.** opp. types and images ἀληθῶν σκιαί [sc. exploits of Joshua] Or.*Jo*.4.4(2; p.111.8; M.14.205A); οἱ ἀ. προσκυνηταί...προσάγουσι...τὰς πνευματικὰς θυσίας Ammon.*Jo*.4:23(M.85.1424A); σαββατισμὸς οὖν νοητὸς καὶ ἀ., ὁ τῆς τοῦ σωτῆρος...ἐπιδημίας καιρὸς Cyr.*ador*.10(1.346C); of Cross opp. type in Ezech.9:4 ἀ. σημεῖον Thdt.*Ps*.59:6(1.1002); id.*Os*.13:14(2.1375); τὸ μὲν γὰρ μυστήριον οὐ ἦν τύπος ὁ γάμος, γεγένηται καὶ ἀ. ἐστιν Sever.*Eph*. 5:32f.(p.312.16); **3.** opp. what is earthly ἡ γὰρ ἀ. ζωὴ κατὰ τὸν μέλλοντα αἰῶνά ἐστιν Ath.*fr.Pss.comm*.38:7(M.27.557D) = Cyr.*Ps*. 38:7(M.69.976B); εἰ γὰρ κατὰ τὸν παρόντα βίον τὸν μακαρισμὸν ἔχουσιν...ἀλλ' οὖν ἀληθέστερον αὐτὸν δέξονται Thdt.*Ps*.2:13(1.625); ἀμυδραῖς τῶν ἀ. εἰκόσι Dion.Ar.*e.h*.5.1.2(M.3.501B); εἰκόνας τῶν ἀ. τὰ νῦν τελούμενα ἐν τῇ συνάξει Max.*schol.e.h*.3.3.1(M.4.137A); exeg. Jo.6:55 ἢ τοῦτο βούλεται εἰπεῖν, ὅτι ἀ. βρῶσις αὕτη ἐστὶν ἡ ψυχὴν σῴζουσα· ἢ πιστώσασθαι αὐτοὺς...ὥστε μὴ νομίζειν αἴνιγμα εἶναι τὸ εἰρημένον καὶ παραβολήν Chrys.*hom.47.1 in Jo*.(8.275D); Cyr.*Jo*.4.2 (4.364C) cit. s. ἀθανασία.

D. *true, faithful*, implying also *truthful*; of God, *Diogn*.8.8; Meth.*symp*.8.16(p.105.17; M.18.169A); οὐκ ἀ. γὰρ ἦν ὁ θεός, εἰ, εἰπόντος αὐτοῦ ἀποθνήσκειν ἡμᾶς, μὴ ἀπέθνησκεν ὁ ἄνθρωπος Ath.*inc*. 6.3(M.25.108A); Mac.Aeg.*hom*.29.4(M.34.717C); exeg. Jo.3:33 καταμαρτυρήσει γὰρ πάντως ὁ τὴν πίστιν ἀποκρουόμενος, ὅτι θεὸς οὐκ ἔστιν ἀ. Cyr.*Jo*.2.3(4.166B); of God's promises, Dion.Ar.*e.h*.7.1.1 (M.3.553A); of Christ ὁ...ἀ. ἐπιμαρτυρούμενος Cyr.*Jo*.2.3(4.166D); *ib*.9(767E); ὁ ἀ. τῆς πίστεως ὅρος *ib*.(768B); of H. Ghost πᾶσα ἀλήθεια ἐκ τοῦ στόματός σου ἐκπορευέσθω, ἵνα τὸ πνεῦμα, ὃ ὁ θεὸς κατῴκισεν ἐν τῇ σαρκὶ ταύτῃ, ἀ. εὑρεθῇ Herm.*mand*.3.1; of men ἐπισκόπους καὶ διακόνους ἀξίους τοῦ κυρίου, ἄνδρας...ἀ. *Did*.15.1; of the 'gnostic' ἀ. ἐν λόγῳ Clem.*str*.7.9(p.40.4; M.9.477A).

E. *sincere* ἡ καθ' ἕξιν ἀ. ἐπὶ τὰ θεῖα προσέλευσις Dion.Ar.*e.h*.3.3.1 (M.3.428B).

***ἀληθινολάλος**, *speaking truth, truthful*, Ant.Mon.*hom*.42(M.89.1564A).

ἀληθινός, **A.** of persons, *true, faithful*, implying also *truthful*; of God ἀψευδὴς καὶ ἀ. *M.Polyc*.14.2; κύριος γὰρ...πιστὸς καὶ ἀ. Or.*Jo*.2.6(4; p.60.15; M.14.120A); *Const.App*.7.26.3; of Christ ἀ. ἐν παντὶ ῥήματι Herm.*mand*.3.1; exeg. Apoc.3:7 ἀ. ὁ σωτὴρ ὑπάρχει διὰ τὸ βέβαιον κατ' οὐσίαν εἶναι· ἀ. γὰρ ὁ αὐτὸς ἐπ' αὐτοῦ διὰ τὸ ἀλήθειαν καὶ ἀ. εἶναι Or.*Apoc*.22(p.30); ἀ. ὡς...αὐτοουσιώδης ἀλήθεια Andr.Caes.*Apoc*.8(M.106.215B); of men, e.g. Job, Ant.Mon.*hom*.66(M.89.1629A). **B.** *real, genuine* opp. false or apparent; **1.** in gen., Ign.*Eph*. proem. cit. s. πάθος; θεοῦ τέκνα ἀ. καλούμεθα καὶ ἐσμέν Just.*dial*.123.9(M.6.764C); τῷ ἀ. βαπτίσματι τῷ τῆς ἐκκλησίας Bas.*ep*.188 *can*.1(3.270B; M.32.669A); αἱ δὲ ἀ. χῆραί εἰσιν αἱ μόνανδροι ὑπάρξασαι *Const.App*.3.3.1; τὸν Χριστὸν ἐνδεδυμένος...εἰ ὡς ἀ. ἄνθρωπος Ant.Mon.*hom*.66(M.89.1629C); **2.** of God, *1Clem*.43.6; Didym.(‡Bas.)*Eun*.4(1.294C; M.29.705C); τῆς τῶν ὄντων ὑπάρξεως αἰτίαν ἀ. Dion.Ar.*c.h*.2.3(M.3.140C); **3.** of Son as true God θεὸν ἀ. ἐκ θεοῦ ἀ. *Symb.Nic*. ap.Eus.*ep.Caes*.4(p.51; M.20.1540B); υἱὸς ἀ. φύσει καὶ γνήσιός ἐστι τοῦ πατρός Ath.*Ar*.1.9(M.26.28D); Cyr.*hom.div*.15.2(p.13.24; M.77.1092B); Gel.Cyz.*h.e*.2.15.3(M.85.1257C); ‡Meth.*Sym.et Ann*.14(M.18.381C); denied by Arians, Ar.*Thal.fr*.10(p.267; M.26.21D); μὴ ἴδιον καὶ ἀ. λόγον εἶναι τοῦ...θεοῦ τὸν υἱόν Marcell.*ep*.ap.Epiph.*haer*.72.2(p.257.10; M.42.385A); **4.** ref. Inc. ἔλαβέ γε ἀ. σάρκα Ath.*Ar*.2.70(M.26.296C); τὸ δὲ ὁμοιούσιον σημαίνει οὐκ ἀ. ἄνθρωπον, ἀλλ' ὁμοίωμα υἱοῦ ἀνθρώπου Cyr.*hom.div*.15.3(p.14.32; M.77.1093B); hence **5.** *essential*, Clem.*prot*.10(p.71.27; M.8.213A) cit. s. εἰκών; *true*, i.e. *properly so called* ἀ. οὖν θεὸς ὁ θεός, οἱ δὲ κατ' ἐκεῖνον μορφούμενοι θεοὶ ὡς εἰκόνες πρωτοτύπου Or.*Jo*.2.2(p.55.3; M.14.109B); *literal, factual* opp. allegorical, Epiph.*anc*.53(p.61.25; M.43.108C); **6.** *real, perfect*; of Christian knowledge derived from scripture, Cyr.*Am*.57(3.314A); esp. of spiritual realities opp. types and images, Just.*dial*.41.4(M.6.364D) cit. s. περιτομή; τὸν ἀ. ἄρτον τοῦ πνεύματος Clem.*exc.Thdot*.13(p.111.7; M.9.664A); Or.*Jo*.1.6(8; p.11.11; M.14.36A); δόξα τοῖς ἀ. ... πρεσβυτέροις αἱ κοσμοῦσαι αὐτοὺς νοηταὶ πολιαί *ib*.20.10(p.340.4; 596C); ref. heavenly Logos ἀ. γὰρ πρὸς ἀντιδιαστολὴν σκιᾶς καὶ τύπου καὶ εἰκόνος, ἐπεὶ τοιοῦτος ὁ ἐν τῷ ἀνεῳγότι οὐρανῷ λόγος· ὁ γὰρ ἐπὶ γῆς οὐ τοιοῦτος ὁποῖος ὁ ἐν οὐρανῷ, ἅτε γενόμενος σὰρξ καὶ διὰ σκιᾶς καὶ τύπων...λαλούμενος. τὰ δὲ πλήθη τῶν πεπιστευκέναι νομιζομένων τῇ σκιᾷ τοῦ λόγου καὶ οὐχὶ τῷ ἀ. λόγῳ θεοῦ...μαθητεύεται *ib*.2.6(4; p.60.15; 120A); Meth.*Porph*.1(p.504.23); οὐ τὴν ἀ. νῦν ζῶμεν ζωήν, ἀλλὰ τὴν ὡς ἐν εἰκόνι Ath.*fr.Pss.comm*.38:7(M.27.557D) = Cyr.*Ps*.38:7(M.69.976B); Ath.*ep.Serap*.1.33(M.26.608A); Bas.*hom*.1.1(2.2A; M.31.164A); ὁ βωμὸς αὐτῶν [sc. Jews] ...τὸ ἀ. [sc. θυσιαστήριον] προετύπου Thdt.*qu.19 in Jos*.(1.317); of Christ as true light φῶς ἀ. πρὸς ἀντιδιαστολὴν αἰσθητοῦ, οὐδενὸς αἰσθητοῦ ὄντος ἀ. ἀλλ' οὐχὶ ἐπεὶ οὐκ ἀ. τὸ αἰσθητόν, ψεῦδος τὸ αἰσθητόν Or.*Jo*.1.26(24; p.31.29; 69A); †Cyr.*hom.div*.11(M.77.1033B); life, Ign.*Eph*.7.2; bread, Clem.*paed*.3.7(p.260.1; M.8.612A); vine, Or.*Cels*.5.12(p.13.7; M.11.1197D).

ἀληθινῶς, *really, truly*; **1.** *sincerely* ἀ. τε καὶ ἐμφόβως...πιστεύομεν Ath.*syn*.23(p.250.3; M.26.724B); **2.** *literally* opp. allegorically τὴν μὲν ἀ. ὁμολογουμένην, τὴν δὲ ἀλληγορουμένην Epiph.*haer*.69.51(p.198.5; M.42.281A); **3.** *in actual fact* opp. in appearance προῆλθεν τέλειος ἄνθρωπος...ἀ. καὶ οὐ δοκήσει καὶ φαντασίᾳ Cyr.*hom.div*.15.3(p.14.8; M.77.1092C); ‡Ath.*interpr*.(p.66.18; M.26.1232A); ἡνώθη τῷ ἀνθρωπίνῳ σώματι, ἀσυγχύτως, ἀ., ἀδιαιρέτως· ἀ. μέν, ὅτι μία ὑπόστασις ἐκ τοῦ θεοῦ λόγου καὶ τοῦ ἀνθρωπίνου σώματος ἀπετελέσθη †Leont.B.*sect*.1.3(M.86.1197B); **4.** *truly, perfectly*, Or.*Cels*.8.22(p.239.16; M.11.1549D) cit. s. τέλειος.

***ἀληθογνωσία, ἡ**, *knowledge of the truth*, Dion.Ar.*d.n*.7.4(M.3.873A); τῷ εὐαγγελίῳ μὲν ὁδηγῷ...πρὸς τὴν ἀ. τὴν προφητικήν ‡Amph.*circ*.(p.16D); ἀπόδειξιν τῆς αὐτῶν περὶ τοῦ παντὸς σωτῆρος ἀ. Χριστοῦ Max.*opusc*.(M.91.169A).

ἀλήθ-ω, *grind* σῖτός εἰμι θεοῦ, καὶ δι' ὀδόντων θηρίων ~ομαι, ἵνα καθαρὸς ἄρτος εὑρεθῶ Ign.*Rom*.4.1; exeg. Dt.24:6 ἐπεὶ οὖν καὶ Ἰουδαῖοι μίαν διαθήκην ἔχουσιν· ὁμοίως δὲ καὶ πᾶσα αἵρεσις δοκοῦσα ταύτην τὴν καινὴν μόνην ἔχειν, οὐκ ~ουσι ἐν τῷ μυλῶνι τούτῳ, ἵνα γεύσωνται τοῦ ἐπουρανίου ἄρτου Or.*sel.in Dt* (M.12.813D); exeg. Eccl.12:3 αἱ ~ουσαι ἀργοῦσιν, οἱ ὀδόντες οἱ καταλεαίνοντες τὴν τροφήν Olymp.*Eccl*.12:2ff.(M.93.613D); ~ούσας δὲ τοὺς Ἰουδαίους ἐκληπτέον, τοὺς τὸν βαρὺν καὶ ἐπίμοχθον ζυγὸν ἕλκοντας τοῦ νόμου. ὀλιγοῦνται δέ, διὰ τὸ πάντας, πλὴν ὀλίγων, δεδραμηκέναι τῇ πίστει τοῦ Χριστοῦ *ib*.(616B); τῷ ἀρχισιτοποιῷ ᾅδῃ, ὃς ταῖς σαῖς πανδαμάτορσι μύλαις τὰς τῶν ἀνθρώπων πανσπερμίας ~ων, τρέφεις τὴν μισανθρωπίαν τοῦ κοσμοκράτορος Germ.CP *or*.2(M.98.280B).

ἀληθῶς, **1.** *truly, in accordance with fact* ἀ. μαρτυρήσαντα ἐν τῷ εἰρηκέναι [Jo.13:21] Or.*Jo*.32.19(12; p.460.8; M.14.796D); **2.** *seriously, in earnest* ταῦτα οὐκ ἀ. ὁ προφήτης ἔφη, ἀλλὰ...τὴν ἐκείνων [sc. false prophets] ἐλέγχων ψευδολογίαν Thdt.*Jer*.4:10(2.432); **3.** *in reality* ἀ. οὐκ ὀργίζεται...σὺ δὲ πείσῃ τὰ τῆς ὀργῆς Or.*hom.18.6 in Jer*.(p.160.21; M.13.477C); πατρός, ἀ. πατρὸς ὄντος, υἱοῦ δὲ ἀ. υἱοῦ ὄντος, τοῦ δὲ ἁγίου πνεύματος ἀ. ἁγίου πνεύματος ὄντος *Symb.Ant*.(341)2 ap. Ath.*syn*.23(p.249.30; M.26.724A); Cyr.*Jo*.12(4.1039C) cit. s. ἀλήθεια; ref. Inc., Ign.*Trall*.9.1; ἀ. ἄνθρωπος ὢν Dion.Ar.*ep*.4(M.3.1072A); Max.*ambig*.(M.91.1320D); **4.** *truly, perfectly* ἀ. κριτὴς ὁ θεός ἐστιν Thdt.*Ps*.81:1(1.1187); opp. τυπικῶς, id.*Ps*.39:9(1.861).

***ἀλήϊστος**, *not plundered*, Gr.Naz.*carm*.2.2(poem.)5.159(M.37.1533A).

[*]ἀληκτικός, Synes.*insomn*.10(M.66.1300A) f.l. for ἄληκτος (p.164.2).

ἄληκτος, **1.** *without end, everlasting* ἐξ ἀ. καὶ ἀνάρχου θεότητος Eus.*l.C*.1(p.198.30, vv.ll. ἀλήπτου, ἀλήστου; M.20.1324B); Bas.*Spir*.66(3.56C; M.32.192B); τὴν ἄ. καὶ ἀπέραντον...βασιλείαν Isid.Pel.*epp*.1.376(M.78.396A); neut. as adv. τὸ πῦρ ἄληκτα...εἰς αἰῶνας κατακαίει †Jo.D.*B.J*.24(M.96.1084B); **2.** *ceaseless, assiduous*, Thdr.Stud.*epp*.1.54(M.99.1108B).

ἄληπτος, **1.** *not to be laid hold of, not to be grasped*; met.; **a.** *unattainable* τὸ ζητούμενον ἄ. ὁ λόγος ὑπέδειξεν Gr.Nyss.*v.Mos*.9(M.44.301B); **b.** *not to be caught* or *overcome*, Meth.*res*.1.57(p.318.4; M.41.1152C) cit. s. ἁμαρτία; ἵνα...ἀ. τὰς ἀκοὰς ἀπὸ τῆς πονηρίας διαφυλάξωσιν Tit.Bost.*Man*.3.20(M.18.1256C); Chrys.*hom.62.2 in Jo*.(8.370D); ἀ. πᾶσι τοῖς ἐναντίοις Thdr.Mops.*Zach*.10:8ff.(M.66.568A); **c.** *not affording a handle* for blame ἄ. παρέχειν τῷ μώμῳ τὸν βίον Gr.Nyss.*v.Mos*.(M.44.421C); hence *irreproachable* τὸ ἄ. εἶναι καὶ μηδεμίαν παρέχειν λαβὴν ἐν τοῖς κατὰ θεὸν πράγμασιν Chrys.*hom.31.2 in Rom*.(9.748B); of God ἄ. ἡ ψῆφος αὐτοῦ, καθαρὰ ἡ κρίσις id.*hom.12.4 in 1Cor*.(10.102C); of apostles βίον...ἄ. Isid.Pel.*epp*.2.251(M.78.688D); **2.** *not to be apprehended*; **a.** in gen. ἄ. δ' ὁ τόπος, καὶ ἡ ὕλη ‡Just.*confut*.27(M.6.1524C); ἀσθενεῖν τὴν ἀνθρωπίνην φύσιν πρὸς τὴν τῶν ἀ. περίνοιαν Gr.Nyss.*Eun*.10(2 p.226.5; M.45.825); ἄ. τοῖς αἰσθητοῖς ἐστι τὰ νοητά Dion.Ar.*d.n*.1.1(M.3.588B); **b.** of God ἀ. τε καὶ ἀχωρήτου τοῖς πᾶσιν Eus.*e.th*.2.17(p.121.16; M.24.940A); φύσις ἄ. τε καὶ ἀπερίληπτος Gr.Naz.*or*.28.5(p.28.10; M.36.32B); **c.** of Son πρωτουργὸς κινήσεως δύναμις, ἄ. αἰσθήσει Clem.*str*.7.2(p.8.6; M.9.412C); τὸ τῆς φύσεως ἄ. Gr.Naz.*or*.31.21(p.142.4; M.36.132B); ὅσῳ γὰρ θεὸς ἀνθρώπου δυστεκμαρτότερος, τοσούτῳ καὶ τῆς σῆς γεννήσεως ἀληπτοτέρα ἡ ἄνω γέννησις *ib*.29.8(p.84.6; 84B); of Christ's birth θεοπρεπῆ ...καὶ ἄ. Isid.Pel.*epp*.1.18(M.78.193A); **d.** of H. Ghost ἄλλος τρόπος ὑπάρξεως οὗτος, ἄ. τε καὶ ἄγνωστος ‡Cyr.*Trin*.8(6^3.11D); Jo.D.*hom*.4.4(M.96.605A); **e.** of profundity of Christian doctrine ἄ. τοῖς μὴ ἔχουσι πνεῦμα Or.*Cels*.6.17(p.88.13; M.11.1316D).

***ἀλήπτως**, **1.** c. ἔχειν *be impregnable*, Cyr.*Nah*.31(3.509D); **2.** *accurately, rightly*, Or.*Jo*.20.14(13; p.345.18; M.14.605A); Gr.Nyss.*Eun*.2(2 p.352.2; M.45.529B); *irreproachably* ἀ. διακονήσει τοῖς πράγμασιν Chrys.*hom.14.1 in 1Cor*.(10.117D).

***ἀλήρητος**, *without foolishness*, i.e. *unmistaken, certain* ἀ. ... γνῶσιν Thdr.Heracl.*Is*.48:16(M.18.1348D).

***ἀλησμονέω**, *be not forgetful*, Jo.Carp.*cap*.43(M.85.1845).

ἄληστος, **1.** *not to be forgotten, enduring, immortal* ἄ. καὶ διαιωνίζουσαν παρεῖχε τὴν βασιλέως ἀρχήν Eus.*v.C*.4.2(p.118.25; M.20.1152B); Gr.Naz.*carm*.1.2.9.132(M.37.678A); ταῖς προσηγορίαις τῶν τόπων ἄ. ... τὴν μνήμην ἐναποτίθεται Chrys.*hom.60.2 in Gen*.(4.579B); for ἄ. γνῶσις v. γνῶσις; **2.** *unforgetting*, ref. God τὴν πάντα περιέχουσαν τοῦ θεοῦ γνῶσιν, καὶ τὴν ἄ. μνήμην Cyr.*Ps*.119:16(M.69.1273A); ‡Caes.Naz.*dial*.30(M.38.892).

[*]ἀλητήριος, v. ἀλιτήριος.

ἀλήτης, ὁ, as adj., *wandering, erring*, Nonn.*par.Jo*.1:12(M.43.752A); *ib*.8:21(816B); *ib*.12:40(857A).

ἀλῆτις, ἡ, *wanderer*; as adj., *wandering*, Or.*Cant*.2(p.142.29; M.17.257A); ἄοικος...καὶ ἀ. ἡ ψυχὴ πεπλανήσεται Gr.Nyss.*anim.et res*.(M.46.117B); Synes.*hymn*.6.26(p.41; M.66.1609).

***ἀλητοβόρος**, *eating meal*, Gr.Naz.*carm*.1.2.15.94(M.37.773A).

ἁλιδινής, *sea-tossed*, Nonn.*par.Jo*.21:4(M.43.916A).

ἁλίδρομος, *running over the sea*, Gr.Naz.*carm*.1.2.12.11(M.37.754A); Nonn.*par.Jo*.6:17(M.43.796B).

ἁλιεύς, ὁ, *fisher*; met., ref. Mt.4:19 ἁλιεῦ μερόπων τῶν σῳζομένων πελάγους κακίας Clem.*paed*.3.12(p.291; M.8.681C); of men οὐ μόνον τότε ἀλλὰ καὶ νῦν ὁ σωτὴρ ἡμῶν πέμπει ἁλιεῖς ἀνθρώπων Or.*hom.16.1 in Jer*.(p.132.10; M.13.437D); Nil.*epp*.2.49(M.79.220D); of S. Peter ὁ τῆς οἰκουμένης ἁ. Chrys.*hom.in Mt.18:23*(3.4E).

ἁλιευτής, ὁ, = foreg., Thdt.*affect*.6(p.149.7; 4.846); met., of apostles ἁ. ψυχῶν ἀνθρωπίνων Eus.*fr.Lc*.(M.24.544B).

ἁλιευτικός, *of fishers*, ref. apostles τοὺς ἁ. σολοικισμοὺς τοὺς Ἀττικοὺς καταλελυκότας ξυλλογισμούς Thdt.*affect*.5(p.142.2; 4.838); τῇ ἁ. ἁπλότητι id.*Is*.11:6(p.60.30; 2.252).

***ἁλιευτικῶς**, *in the manner of a fisherman*, i.e. of apostles ταῦτα... πεφιλοσόφηται πρὸς ὑμᾶς δογματικῶς, ἀλλ' οὐκ ἀντιλογικῶς· ἁ., ἀλλ' οὐκ Ἀριστοτελικῶς Gr.Naz.*or*.23.12(M.35.1164C).

ἁλιεύ-ω, **1.** *fish*; met., of S. Paul ὁ τῷ δρόμῳ τὴν ξηρὰν ~ων *A.Xanthipp*.8(p.63.20); **2.** *fish for, catch*; met., ref. Mt.4:19 ἐν ἁμαρτίαις ποτὲ γεγόνασι καὶ ἀπὸ ἁμαρτίων τῶν ἐν τῇ θαλάσσῃ ἡλιεύθησαν Or.*hom.16.4 in Jer*.(p.137.2; M.13.444C); of Christ Παῦλον μετὰ τὴν ἀνάστασιν ἡλίευσεν Chrys.*hom.30.1 in Mt*.(7.347B); ἴδωμεν νηὸς ποντοπορούσης ἀθεώρητον πορείαν, τῆς βυθισάσης μὲν τὸν ἀρχέκακον, ἁλιευσάσης δὲ τὸν πρωτόπλαστον Procl.CP *or*.4.1(M.65.709B).

ἁλίζ-ω, *salt, season*; met., ref. Mt.5:13 ἁλίσθητε ἐν αὐτῷ [sc. τῷ Χριστῷ] Ign.*Magn*.10.2; Chrys.*hom.15.6 in Mt*.(7.194A); τοὺς μὲν ~ων τῇ σωφροσύνῃ, τοὺς δὲ φωτίζων τῇ διδασκαλίᾳ Pall.*v.Chrys*.5 (p.29.14; M.47.19).

§**ἁλίη**, ἡ, *catch of fish*, Gr.Naz.*carm*.2.2(epitaph.)1.4(M.38.11A).

***ἁλίκμητος**, *wrought*, i.e. *caused, by the sea* ἁ. μερίμνης Paul.Sil. *ambo*.228(M.86.2260A).

ἁλικρήπις, *at the sea's edge*, Nonn.*par.Jo*.7:1(M.43.804C); *ib*.7:41 (812B).

[*]**ἀλίκτως**, = ἀλήκτως, *ceaselessly*, Euthal.Diac.*Ac*.proem.(M. 85.633B).

[*]**ἄλιμμα**, τό, = ἄλειμμα, *T.Job* 32(p.124.1).

ἄλιμος, *without starvation* ἡ ἄ. αὐτοῦ [sc. Christ]...νηστεία Leont. H.*Nest*.2.20(M.86.1580D).

ἀλιπαρής, *cheerless*, ref. Gen.21:14 ἐκπέμπεται...ἡ τῶν Ἰουδαίων συναγωγή, στυγνὸν καὶ ἀ. ἐφόδιον ἔχουσα, ἄρτον τε καὶ ὕδωρ Cyr.*glaph. Gen*.3(1.81E).

ἁλιπλανής, *sea-wandering*, Nonn.*par.Jo*.6:64(M.43.804A).

ἀλισγ-έω, *pollute* ἵνα ἐγὼ τῶν ἀσεβεστάτων θυσιῶν ~ηθῶ *M.Tar*. 9(p.473); ‡Jo.D.*ep.Thphl*.15(M.95.365B).

ἁλίσκω, [aor. ptcpl. ἁλῶν *Pers*.(p.8.9)]; act., *catch*, Chrys.*hom. 11.1 in 1Thess*.(11.503B); Evagr.*h.e*.3.24(p.122.3; M.86.2648B).

***ἀλιτάρχης**, ὁ, s.v.l., *master of impiety*, Alex.Sal.*cruc*.(M.87. 4049B).

***ἀλιτηριόνοος**, *of sinful mind*, *Schol*.40 in Jo.Clim.*scal*.27(M.88. 1228A).

ἀλιτήριος ([*]ἀλητ-), *wicked, sinful*, of Devil ὁ ἀλήτηριος Cyr. *Is*.1.4(2.103D); Thdt.*2Thess*.2:8(3.535); Olymp.*Job* 2 proem.(M.93. 33D); ἀλητηρίῳ...διαβόλῳ Oecum.*Apoc*.14:7(p.162, v.l. ἀλιτ-); of demons, Dion.Al.ap.Eus.*h.e*.7.10.4(M.20.660A); Eus.*d.e*.4.10(p.167. 1; M.22.277C); Cyr.*Os*.14(3.36C); of men, Isid.Pel.*epp*.2.114(M.78. 556A); Cyr.*Os*.proem.(3.4D); Thdt.*h.e*.3.17.4(3.933).

ἀλίτης, ὁ, = ἀλείτης, *sinner*; of Devil, Eudoc.*Cypr*.2.217(M.85. 853B).

***ἀλίτιμος**, ? *wickedly honoured*, of Ephesian Artemis ἡ ἁμαρτωλός, ἡ ἀ. ‡Chrys.*Jo.theol*.3(10.773B), or perh. f.l. for ἀλιτήμων, *sinful*.

ἀλιτρόβιος, *living wickedly*, Gr.Naz.*carm*.2.1.28.12(M.37.1288A); Nonn.*par.Jo*.15:19(M.43.876B).

***ἀλιτροδίκης**, *of unrighteous judgement*, Meth.symp.5.4(p.58.3; M.18.104B).

***ἀλκλαρία**, ἡ, for *ἀρκλαρία.

[*]**ἀλλαγίη**, ἡ, = ἀλλαγή, *change*, *Orac.Sib*.2.157.

***ἀλλάκτης**, ὁ, *dealer* γαστὴρ ἀ. ἐστὶν ἀπιστότατος ‡Chrys.*cruc. venerand*.1(8.201A).

ἀλλαχόσε, **1.** *elsewhither*, Philost.*h.e*.5.1(M.65.528C); **2.** *elsewhere*, Just.*dial*.46.2(M.6.573B); Eus.*d.e*.1.6(p.28.10; M.22.57A); Isid.Pel. *epp*.4.112(M.78.1180A).

ἀλλεπαλλήλως, *successively*, Epiph.*ep.Arab*.ap.*haer*.78.4(p.455.6; M.42.705A).

ἀλληγορ-έω, **1.** *speak allegorically, use an allegory*; **a.** abs. ~ῶν ὁ Παῦλος καὶ γάλα αὐτὸν ὀνομάζων 'ἐπότισα' ἐπιφέρει Clem.*paed*.1.6 (p.117.6; M.8.304B); ἐρεῖ μοί τις· ξένον μοι φέρεις, λόγον λέγων υἱόν. Ἰωάννης μὲν γὰρ λέγει λόγον, ἀλλ' ἄλλως ~εῖ [i.e. allegory of ἵππος λευκός]. οὕτως γὰρ δεικνύων τὸν λόγον...τοῦτον ὄντα ἀπ' ἀρχῆς καὶ νῦν ἀπεσταλμένον, ὑποβὰς ἐν τῇ Ἀποκαλύψει ἔφη [Apoc.19:11–13] Hipp. *Noët*.15(p.257.21; M.10.824A); καὶ πανταχοῦ τῆς γραφῆς οὗτος ὁ νόμος, ἐπειδὰν ~ῇ, λέγειν καὶ ἀλληγορίας τὴν ἑρμηνείαν Chrys.*Is.5 interp*.(6.55A); **b.** *convey by means of an allegory* οὐ τὴν ἀναγέννησιν ἐνταῦθα ~ῶν Clem.*paed*.1.5(p.97.8; M.8.264A); *ib*.1.8(p.129.8; 329C); id.*str*.5.11(p.371.20; M.9.104B); *ib*.7.6(p.24.22; 445A) cit. s. θυσία; hence **c.** *allegorize, say allegorically*, id.*prot*.1(p.5.21; M.8.57B); id.*paed*.1.6(p.113.2; M.8.296B); σάρκα ἡμῖν τὸ πνεῦμα τὸ ἅγιον ~εῖ, καὶ γὰρ ὑπ' αὐτοῦ δεδημιούργηται ἡ σάρξ *ib*.(p.115.31; 301B); ὄφις ~εῖται ἡδονὴ ἐπὶ γαστέρα ἕρπουσα id.*prot*.11(p.78.27; 228C); καρδία γὰρ ἡ ψυχὴ ~εῖται ἡ τὴν ζωὴν χορηγήσασα, ὅτι δι' υἱοῦ ὁ πατὴρ γνωρίζεται id.*str*.5.1(p.334.7; M.9.28A); εἴη δ' ἂν τῷ ψαλμῳδῷ κιθάρα ~ουμένη κατὰ μὲν τὸ πρῶτον σημαινόμενον ὁ κύριος, κατὰ δὲ τὸ δεύτερον οἱ προσεχῶς κρούοντες τὰς ψυχὰς ὑπὸ μουσηγέτῃ τῷ κυρίῳ *ib*.6.11(p.476.5; 309B); *ib*.6.15(p.498.8; 356B) cit. s. πίστις; *ib*.2.5 (p.123.13; M.8.952C); τὰ πάθη τὰ κατὰ τὴν Αἴγυπτον, ἅτινα, φησίν, ἐστὶ τῆς κτίσεως ~ούμενα σύμβολα Hipp.*haer*.8.14(p.234.2; M.16. 3359C); ἡ δεκάλογος ~οῦσα τὰ θεῖα τῶν λόγων μυστήρια *ib*. (p.234.9; 3362A); Or.*Jo*.20.10(p.339.15; M.14.596A); ὁ δὲ βουλόμενος λαβεῖν τὴν πρὸς Γαλάτας ἐπιστολὴν εἴσεται, τίνα τρόπον ἠλληγόρηται τὰ κατὰ τοὺς γάμους καὶ τὰς μίξεις τῶν θεραπαινίδων id.*Cels*.4.44(p.317. 18; M.11.1100D); τῶν τε μύθων τὰς ~ουμένας φυσιολογίας Eus.*p.e*. 10.1(460D; M.21.768A); Epiph.*haer*.64.65(p.506.1; M.41.1184B); πᾶν δὲ τὸ παροιμιαζόμενον οὐ ταὐτόν ἐστι τῇ δυνάμει ἀλλὰ ἄλλῃ μὲν ῥήσει διηγεῖται, ἄλλῃ δὲ δυνάμει ~εῖται *ib*.69.21(p.171.9; M.42.236A); ~ούμενα εἶπεν ὁ θεῖος ἀπόστολος, ἀντὶ τοῦ, καὶ ἑτέρως νοούμενα. οὐ γὰρ τὴν ἱστορίαν ἀνεῖλεν, ἀλλὰ τὰ ἐν τῇ ἱστορίᾳ προτυπωθέντα διδάσκει Thdt.*Gal*.4:24(3.385); **d.** *use in an allegorical sense* εὐχαριστῶν ἀεὶ τῷ θεῷ καθάπερ τὰ ζῷα τὰ δοξολόγα τὰ διὰ Ἡσαΐου ~ούμενα Clem.*str*. 7.12(p.57.19; M.9.512A); **2.** *interpret, explain allegorically*, Tat.*orat*. 21(p.23.23; M.6.853B); Hipp.*haer*.4.46(p.68.19; M.16.3110C); Cels.ap. Or.*Cels*.4.38(p.308.28; M.11.1088A); κατηγορῶν [sc. ὁ Κέλσος] τῆς Μωϋσέως ἱστορίας αἰτιᾶται τοὺς τροπολογοῦντας καὶ ~οῦντας αὐτήν Or.*Cels*.1.17(p.69.7; 692A); μαθητῶν δύο· τοῦ τ' ἐπὶ τὴν θεραπείαν τῆς ψυχῆς ἀνάγοντος τὰ γεγραμμένα καὶ ἐπ' αὐτὴν αὐτὰ ~οῦντος, καὶ τοῦ τὰ μέλλοντα ἀγαθὰ καὶ ἀληθινὰ διὰ τῶν ἐν τῇ σκιᾷ κειμένων παρίσταντος id.*Jo*.10.28(18; p.201.27; M.14.357C); δεῖ πᾶσαν τὴν κατὰ τὸν Ἀβραὰμ ~οῦντα ἱστορίαν ἕκαστον πνευματικῶς ποιῆσαι τῶν πεπραγμένων ὑπ' αὐτοῦ *ib*.20.10(p.337.31; 592C); οἱ ἑτερόδοξοι ἀ. θέλουσιν τὴν τῶν ἀνθρώπων ἀνάστασιν· ~ήτωσαν καὶ τὴν τοῦ σωτῆρος id.*comm.in 1Cor*.15:12(*JTS* 10 p.44); ὁ μὲν οὖν τις ~ῶν τὸν οὐρανὸν καὶ φάσκων αὐτὸν εἶναι τὸν Χριστόν id.*or*.26(p.360.23; M.11.501A); Meth.*symp*.3.1(p.27.9; M.18.61A); Ὠριγένης...πάσας ~ῆσαι τὰς γραφὰς ἐγχειρίσας Eust.*engast*.21(p.48.2; M.18.656A); Eus.*d.e*.7.3 (p.343.19; M.22.560C); id.*p.e*.2 proem.(44B; M.21.92C); πάλιν τε ἀκούοντες [Pr.9:1] τὸν μὲν οἶκον ~εῖτε, τὸ δέ, ἔκτισεν, οὕτω λαμβάνοντες μεταποιεῖτε αὐτὸ εἰς κτίσμα Ath.*Ar*.2.46(M.26.245C); id. *v.Anton*.76(M.26.949A); Gr.Naz.*or*.4.119(M.35.657D); ἀμέλει καὶ τὰ τυπικὰ τῶν Ἰουδαίων ~ῶν καὶ παραβάλλων ταῦτα πρὸς τὴν ἀλήθειαν Mac.Aeg.*or*.13(M.34.864A); Epiph.*haer*.69.51(p.198.1; M.42.280D); ἐντεῦθεν...ἕτερον μανθάνομεν...τὸ πότε καὶ τίνα ~εῖν χρὴ τῶν γραφῶν· καὶ ὡς οὐκ ἐσμὲν κύριοι τῶν νόμων τούτων αὐτοί, ἀλλὰ δεῖ αὐτῇ τῇ διανοίᾳ τῆς γραφῆς ἑπομένους, οὕτω τῷ τῆς ἀλληγορίας κεχρῆσθαι τρόπῳ...ἡ γραφὴ...οὐκ ἀφῆκε κύριον γενέσθαι τὸν ἀκροατὴν ἁρμόσαι τὰ εἰρημένα οἷς ἐβούλετο πράγμασιν, ἢ προσώποις, ἀλλὰ προϊοῦσα ἑαυτὴν ἡρμήνευσεν Chrys.*Is.5 interp*.(6.54D); Synes.*ep*.146(M.66. 1541A); Cyr.*Ps*.23:2(M.69.845A); Proc.G.*Gen*.17:19(M.87.361C); Anast.S.*qu.et resp*.32(M.89.569B); **3.** abs. *use allegorical interpretation* τῶν ~εῖν βουλομένων Chrys.*Is.5 interp*.(6.55B); id.*hom.52.1 in Mt*.(7.529E); Isid.Pel.*epp*.4.117(M.78.1192B); Proc.G.*Gen*.3:21(M.87. 221A); cf. *allegorizantes Babylonem diximus negotia esse terrena*, Or. *hom.20.4 in Jer*.(p.314.3; M.13.532D); *dicitur mihi: noli allegorizari, noli per figuram exponere*, id.*hom.6.8 in Ezech*.(p.386.11; M.13. 716A); **4.** *be discrepant with* χρήσεις...εἰς οὐδὲν ~ούσας τοῖς ἁγίοις καὶ ἐκκρίτοις πατράσι CCP(681)*act*.8(H.3.1157B).

***ἀλληγορητέον**, *one must explain allegorically*, Or.*fr.27 in Lam*. (p.248.8; M.13.624A).

***ἀλληγορητέος**, *to be explained allegorically*, Clem.*str*.5.9(p.365. 23; M.9.92A).

ἀλληγορητής, ὁ, *allegorical expounder*, Thdt.*qu.39 in Gen*.(1.52); Proc.G.*Gen*.3:21(M.87.220A).

ἀλληγορία, ἡ, *allegory*; **1.** in gen. Μητρόδωρος...ἐν τῷ περὶ Ὁμήρου λίαν εὐήθως διείλεκται, πάντα εἰς ἀ. μετάγων Tat.*orat*.21 (p.24.7; M.6.853B); ‡Hipp.*fr.46 in Pr*.24:13(p.174.7); Meth.*res*.1.24 (p.248.18; M.41.1093C); *ib*.1.39(p.282.15; M.18.268B); ref. Vergil *ecl*. 4.8 συνίεμεν...ἀποκρύφως δι' ἀλληγοριῶν τα⟨ῦτα⟩ λεχθέντα Const.*or. s.c*.19(p.182.16; M.20.1292C); Eus.*d.e*.4.15(p.181.35; M.22.304A); τὴν ἐπὶ τῆς ἐκκλησίας αὐτοῦ στάσιν τε καὶ βεβαίωσιν, ἣν ὄρος ἐλαιῶν ἐπὶ τοῦ παρόντος κατὰ τρόπον ἀλληγορίας ὀνομάζει *ib*.6.18(p.277.18; 456C); Bas.*Eun*.1.14(1.226D; M.29.544C); οἶδα νόμους ἀλληγορίας, εἰ καὶ μὴ παρ' ἐμαυτοῦ ἐξευρὼν ἀλλὰ τοῖς παρ' ἑτέρων πεπονημένοις περιτυχὼν id.*hex*.9.1(1.80B; M.29.188B); Gr.Nyss.*hom.in Cant*.proem. (M.44.757A) cit. s. ἀναγωγή; opp. τὰ ἀληθινά, Epiph.*anc*.53(p.61. 25; M.43.108cf.); id.*haer*.66.56(p.93.7; M.42.113B) cit. s. ἀναγωγή; Proc.G.*Gen*.1:24(M.87.105D); ἀ. ἐστὶν ἡ ἐπ' ἀψύχων· οἷον ὀρέων, βουνῶν...τροπολογία δέ ἐστιν, ἡ ἐπὶ τῶν ἡμετέρων μελῶν, οἷον κεφαλῆς, ὀφθαλμῶν Max.*qu.dub.*8(M.90.792A); Cosm.Ind.*top.*5(M.88.249B); **2.** in Alexandrine usage ἀ. is a method of exegesis which (*a*) is contrasted with literal interpretation and (*b*) is discernible from the *content* of the text ἐκείνη γὰρ ἡ λεγομένη κατάβασις ἐπὶ τὸ ὄρος θεοῦ ἐπίφασίς ἐστι θείας δυνάμεως ἐπὶ πάντα τὸν κόσμον διηκούσης καὶ κηρυττούσης τὸ φῶς τὸ ἀπρόσιτον. τοιαύτη γὰρ ἡ κατὰ τὴν γραφὴν ἀ. Clem.*str.*6.3(p.447.12; M.9.249C); Or.*Cels.*4.48(p.320.25; M.11.1105B); πῶς τὴν...κοσμογένειαν σαυτῷ διά τινος, ὡς φῄς, τυπώδους ἀ. λαμβάνεις; Cels.*ib.*6.29(p.99.9; M.11.1337B); οὐκ οἶδα δὲ πῶς οἱ φεύγοντες τὴν ἐν τούτοις ἀ., καὶ τὴν λέξιν δι' ἑαυτὴν ἀναγεγράφθαι νομίζοντες, παραστήσονται τῷ βουλήματι τοῦ ἁγίου πνεύματος πράγματα ἀναγραφῆς ἀξιώσαντος Or.*sel.in Ps.*50:1(M.12.1453B); Μωσῆς ἑώρα τῷ νοΐ τὴν ἀλήθειαν τοῦ νόμου καὶ τὰς κατὰ ἀναγωγὴν ἀ. τῶν ἀναγεγραμμένων παρ' αὐτῷ ἱστοριῶν id.*Jo.*6.4(2; p.111.7; M.14.205A); *ib.* 13.9(p.233.23; 412C); *ib.*13.17(p.240.32; 424B); μετὰ δὲ τὴν ὡς πρὸς τὸ ῥητὸν σαφήνειαν τὰ πρὸς ἀλληγορίαν ῥητέον id. *fr.27 in Jo.*1:50(p.504.10); id.*princ.*4.2.6(13; p.316.14; M.11.369A); cf. *quis ita brutus invenietur, qui non horrescens sonum litterae ad allegoriae dulcedinem ipsa necessitate confugiat?* id.*hom.16.9 in Num.*(p.151.21; M.12.701A); in Antiochene usage ἀ. is (*a*) a mode of literal expression, which is (*b*) indicated only by the *form* of the text ἡ θεία γραφὴ τῆς ἀ. τὸ μὲν ὄνομα οἶδε, τὸ δὲ πρᾶγμα οὐκ οἶδεν Diod.*proem.Ps.118*(p.90.7); Ἕλληνες μὲν γὰρ ἀ. ὀνομάζουσι πρᾶγμα ἄλλως μὲν νοούμενον, ἄλλως δὲ ἀγορευόμενον *ib.*(p.90.11); ἀλλ' οἱ καινοτόμοι τῆς θείας γραφῆς, καὶ οἰησίσοφοι, περὶ τὴν ἱστορίαν ἢ ἀτονήσαντες ἢ κακουργήσαντες, ἐπεισήνεγκαν τὴν ἀ., οὐ κατὰ τὸν νοῦν τὸν ἀποστολικόν, ἀλλὰ πρὸς τὴν αὐτῶν κενοδοξίαν ἕτερα ἀνθ' ἑτέρων ποιοῦντες νοεῖν τοὺς ἀναγινώσκοντας id.*proem.Pss.*(p.88.12); Chrys.*Is.5 interp.*(6.55B); *ib.*(54E); id. *hom.85.1 in Jo.*(8.505C); ref. Gal.4:24 καταχρηστικῶς τὸν τύπον ἀ. ἐκάλεσεν. ὃ δὲ λέγει, τοῦτό ἐστιν· ἡ μὲν ἱστορία αὕτη οὐ τοῦτο μόνον παραδηλοῖ, ὅπερ φαίνεται, ἀλλὰ καὶ ἄλλα τινὰ ἀναγορεύει· διὸ καὶ ἀ. κέκληται id.*comm.in Gal.*4:24(10.710B); Sever.*creat.*4.2(M.56.459); νῦν τῷ ὀνόματι κατεχρήσατο οὐ τῇ δυνάμει τῆς ἀ. ἡ γὰρ ἀ. οὐ στοιχεῖ τοῖς ῥητοῖς, ἄλλα δέ τινα ἐμφαινόμενα ἀπὸ τῆς κατὰ τὴν ὑφὴν τῶν νοημάτων ἀκολουθίας εἰσάγει id.*Gal.*4:24(p.302.17); ἀ. ἐκάλεσε τὴν ἐκ παραθέσεως τῶν ἤδη γεγονότων πρὸς τὰ παρόντα σύγκρισιν Thdr.Mops.*Gal.*4:24(p.79.18; M.66.908C); v. ἀναγωγή, θεωρία, μυστικός, τύπος.

ἀλληγορικός, *figurative, allegorical* εἰ δὲ ἀ. [sc. αἱ ἱστορίαι], μῦθοί εἰσι καὶ οὐκ ἄλλο τι Arist.*apol.*13.7; Eus.*d.e.*7.3(p.343.26; M.22.560C); id.*p.e.*8.8(370A; M.21.624C); τοῦ ἀ. τὸ ἱστορικὸν πλεῖστον ὅσον προτιμῶμεν Diod.*Gen.*39:11(M.33.1580A).

ἀλληγορικῶς, *figuratively, allegorically*, Clem.*paed.*3.7(p.259.4; M.8.609A); τούτου τοῦ παραδείσου ἀ. οἱ ἄγγελοι κέκληνται ξύλα, καὶ ἔστι τὸ ξύλον τῆς ζωῆς...Βαρούχ Hipp.*haer.*5.24(p.127.22; M.16.3195A); Or.*Jo.*13.40(p.267.4; M.14.472B); εἰ δεῖ...ἀλλάξαντα τὴν φωνὴν ἀ. τὸν νοῦν τῆς ἱστορίας κατανοῆσαι, μενούσης δηλαδὴ καὶ τῆς ἱστορικῆς ἀληθείας Gr.Nyss.*Eun.*12(1 p.240.27; M.45.940A); ref. eucharist οὐ γὰρ μόνοις τοῖς μαθηταῖς ἐδίδου τὴν σάρκα φαγεῖν...ἀλλὰ πᾶσιν ὁμοίως ὁσίοις ἀνδράσι καὶ προφητικοῖς ὁμοῦ ταύτην ἀ. τὴν σιταρχίαν ἔδωκεν Mac.Mgn.*apocr.*3.23(p.105.15); comp., Or.*or.*23 (p.353.2; M.11.489D); Eus.*Ps.*145:9(M.24.65A); Didym.ap.*cat.Ac.* 20:26(p.336.3).

***ἀλληγοριστής, ὁ,** *allegorical expounder*, Eus.*h.e.*7.24.2(M.20.693); cf.Thdr.Mops.*Gal.*4:30(p.86.5).

***ἀλληγορουμένως**, *allegorically*, Hipp.*haer.*10.17(p.279.9; M.16.3435B).

***ἀλληλαίτιοι**, *causing one another* ἀ. ἄρα ὁ μὲν θεὸς τοῦ κόσμου, ὁ δὲ κόσμος τοῦ θεοῦ ‡Just.*qu.Chr.*3.5(M.6.1441A); πῶς οὐκ ἀ. ἔσται ἀντικείμενα; *Disp.Phot.*3(M.88.557C); Max.*Pyrr.*(M.91.349C).

***ἀλληλένδετος**, *bound one in another, intertwined*, ‡Chrys.*palm.* 1.1(8.231A) = ‡Meth.*palm.*1(M.18.384A); met., of Persons of Trin. ὡς ἀπεριόριστοι φεραλλήλους καὶ ἀ. καὶ τὰς οἰκείας προσηγορίας ἔχουσιν ‡Gr.Nyss.*imag.*(M.44.1341D); *ib.*(1344A).

ἀλληλίζω, *have reciprocal intercourse*, Clem.*paed.*2.10(p.209.35; M.8.501A).

***ἀλληλοβασία, ἡ,** *reciprocal intercourse*, Clem.*paed.*2.10(p.211.8; M.8.504B).

***ἀλληλογονία, ἡ,** *mutual generation, procreation*, Nemes.*nat.hom.*2(M.40.573B).

***ἀλληλοεσώτερος**, *one within the other*; hence *concentric*, of two porticoes, Marc.Diac.*v.Porph.*75.

***ἀλληλομαχέω**, *fight one another*, *Apoc.Dan.*C(p.119).

***ἀλληλομητρότεκνος**, *each parent of the other* ἀναισθησία καὶ λήθη ἀ. γεννεά *Schol.*2 in Jo.Clim.*scal.*18(M.88.936A).

***ἀλληλούια,** (Hebr. הַלְלוּיָהּ) *alleluia*; **1.** interpretations λέγεται ἑβραϊστὶ θεβὲλ μαρημαθά, λαλιὰ τῷ θεῷ τῷ θεμελιοῦντι τὰ πάντα, δοξάσωμεν αὐτὸν ἐπὶ τὸ αὐτό. ὥστε πᾶς ὁ ψάλλων τὸ ἀ. θεὸν δοξάζει *Apoc.Paul.*30(p.56); ἔστι δὲ τό, ἀ., αἶνος τῷ ἀοράτῳ. λέγεται δὲ τοὺς ἀγγέλους ταύτῃ τῇ φωνῇ αἰνεῖν τὸν θεόν, ὥσπερ τὰ χερουβὶμ τό· ἅγιος, ἅγιος, ἅγιος...διαιρεῖται δὲ τὸ ἀ. οὕτως, ἄλ, θεός, ἤλ, ἰσχυρός, οὔια, κραταιός Ath.*exp.Ps.*104 proem.(M.27.441C); τὸ γάρ, ἀλληλού, ἑρμηνεύεται, αἰνεῖτε, τὸ δέ, ἴα, τὸν κύριον *ib.*134:1(525A); ἑρμηνεία ἐστὶ τοῦ μὲν ἀ. τὸ ὑμνήσατε μετὰ μέλους τὸ ὄν ‡Just.*qu.et resp.*50 (M.6.1296A); Ἀγγαῖος...ἔψαλλεν...πρῶτος ἀ., ὃ ἑρμηνεύεται, αἰνέσωμεν τῷ ζῶντι θεῷ ‡Epiph.*v.proph.Ag.*A 20(M.43.412B); τῇ γὰρ ἑβραΐδι διαλέκτῳ ἐστὶ τὸ ἄλ ἔρχεται καὶ ἐφάνη, τὸ δὲ ἤλ ὁ θεός, τὸ δὲ οὔια αἰνεῖτε ὑμνεῖτε τὸν ζῶντα θεόν ‡Bas.*h.myst.*41(p.387.14); various interpretations, ‡Germ.CP*contempl.*(M.98.412B,C); **2.** use: in gen., at end of each line in hymn of praise, *A.Xanthipp.*19(p.71.26ff.); as beginning of a doxology, *Tr.Phil.*2(p.162.13); after some verses from Psalms πάντες ἐκέκραξαν ἀ. *A.Mt.*25(p.254.2); liturg., before Gospel during censing, *Apoc.Paul.*29(p.56); ψάλλετε τὸ ἀ. καὶ ἀνάγνωτε τὸ εὐαγγέλιον καὶ προσενέγκατε προσφορὰν ἄρτον ἅγιον *A.Mt.*25(p.252.9); ‡Bas.*h.myst.*49(p.391.7); at Rome ἑκάστου ἔτους ἅπαξ...τὸ ἀ. ψάλλουσι, κατὰ τὴν πρώτην ἡμέραν τῆς πασχαλίου ἑορτῆς, ὡς πολλοῖς Ῥωμαίων ὅρκον εἶναι, τοῦτον τὸν ὕμνον ἀξιωθῆναι ἀκοῦσαί τε καὶ ψᾶλαι Soz.*h.e.*7.19.4(M.67.1476B); cf. *quod* [sc. *alleluia*] *nobis cantare certo tempore solemniter moris est, secundum ecclesiae antiquam traditionem: neque enim et hoc sine sacramento certis diebus cantamus. alleluia certis quidem diebus cantamus, sed omni die cogitamus*, Aug. *enarratio in Psalmum 106*(M.*PL.*37.1419); sung in heaven, being led by David, *Apoc.Paul.*29(p.55); θεωροῦμεν... Ἰσαὰκ καὶ Ἰακὼβ καὶ τὸν Δαυὶδ ψάλλοντα τὸ ἀ. *Dorm.BMV*44(p.109); *Tr.Phil.*3(p.162.30).

ἀλληλουχία, ἡ, *association, mutual relationship* τῆς τῶν ὁμοφυῶν ἀ. ‡Proc.G.*Pr.*30:14(M.87.1327A); Max.*schol.d.n.*1.4(M.4.196B); *solidarity* κοινωνίαν καὶ ἀ. Andr.Caes.*Apoc.*67(M.106.437C); of relationship of H. Ghost to other Persons of Trin., *reciprocity* τὴν πρὸς τὸν πατέρα καὶ τὸν υἱὸν ἀ. Didym.*Trin.*2.6(M.39.532C).

ἀλληλοῦχος, *holding together, interconnected* τῶν ἀ. γενικῶν ἀρετῶν Max.*or.dom.*(M.90.889A); id.*qu.Thal.*39(M.90.393A).

***ἀλληλούχως**, *in conjunction*, Thdr.Stud.*antirr.*2.28(M.99.372C).

ἀλληλοφαγέω, *eat one another*, Gr.Nyss.*hex.*30(M.44.92B); Isid. Pel.*epp.*4.57(M.78.1108C).

***ἀλληλοφθορέω**, *corrupt one another*, Eus.*d.e.*4.9(p.163.26; M.22.273A); id.*h.e.*1.2.19(M.20.64A).

ἀλληλοφθορία, ἡ, *corruption of one another*, Eus.*d.e.*1.6(p.31.28; M.22.61D).

ἀλληλοφθόρος, *destroying one another*, Geo.Pis.*hex.*573(M.92.1479A); id.*Pers.*1.33(M.92.1200A); οὕτω ἀντικείμενα ἀ. ῥήματα Martin.ap.CLater.*act.*4(H.3.809C).

***ἀλληλοφονέω**, *kill one another*, Meth.*Porph.*2(p.506.1; M.18.404B).

***ἀλληλοφόνται, οἱ,** *killers of one another*, Just.*1apol.*39.3(M.6.388B).

***ἀλληλοφυῶς**, *in partaking of one another's nature* ἀ. καὶ συμφυῶς, καὶ φεραλλήλως τὸ μυστήριον τῆς τριάδος καθέστηκεν Anast.S.*hod.*16 (M.89.261C).

***ἀλληλόχρεοι**, *indebted to one another*; of marriage and virginity, Amph.*hom.*2.1(M.39.45B).

***ἀλληλοχωρία, ἡ,** *interpenetration* (cf. περιχώρησις), Christol. ἐνδιδοῦντος ἑαυτὸν τῷ ἑτέρῳ καὶ μίαν ὑπόστασιν ἐξ ἑνώσεως τῶν δύο διὰ τῆς ἀ. δεικνύντος Leont.H.*Nest.*1.48(M.86.1509D).

ἀλληνάλλως, **1.** *in this way and that, variously*, Mac.Mgn.*apocr.* 4.16(p.190.10); Leont.H.*monoph.*(M.86.1884C); **2.** *confusedly* ἵνα τί ...ἀ. ἐλάλησας; †Jo.D.*B.J.*22(M.96.1061D).

***ἀλλογένεθλος**, *of differing nativity* (astrol.) ἐν...πολέμῳ πλεόνεσσιν ὁμὸς μόρος ἀ. Gr.Naz.*carm.*1.1.5.22(M.37.425A).

ἀλλογενής, **1.** *of another race, foreign*; of non-Jews, Just.*dial.* 10.3(M.6.496D); Or.*fr.53 in Jo.*(p.527.2); Eus.*p.e.*1.2(5D; M.21.29A); of non-Levites, forbidden to officiate in OT cult, *Const.App.*2.27.1; **2.** *of another kind*, Clem.*str.*6.1(p.423.1; M.9.209A); of various pseudepigraphical books of Sethian Gnostics, dist. from those ascribed to Seth himself (perh. also with connotation of *strange, exotic*), Epiph.*haer.*39.5(p.75.11; M.41.669C); of flesh opp. spirit, Nonn.*par.Jo.*6:63(M.43.804A); πῶς οὖν ἔσται τῆς δόξης κύριος ὁ υἱός, εἴπερ ὄντως τέ ἐστι ἀ., καὶ τῆς τοῦ πατρὸς οὐσίας ἀλλότριος; Cyr.*thes.*32(5^1.300C); ref. Jo.20:17 τῶν ἀμφοτέρων τούτων ὀνομασιῶν πρὸς τὰ ἀ. ὀνόματα μὴ δυναμένων ἐξισοῦσθαι Epiph.*haer.*76.34(p.383.8; M.42.584D).

ἀλλόγλωσσος, **1.** *using a strange tongue,* Gr.Nyss.*virg.*23(p.334. 18; M.46.405D); **2.** *using different tongues* οὐδὲ ἀ. εἶναι ἐθέλησεν [sc. ἡμᾶς ὁ θεός] Chrys.*hom.34.4 in 1Cor.*(10.315D).

ἀλλοδαπός, *belonging to another land, foreign;* fem. as subst., *foreign country,* Eus.*h.e.*4.23.1(M.20.384B); Chrys.*hom.in Mt.7:14* (3.26B); *foreign journey* πάσης αὐτοῦ [sc. Παύλου] τῆς ἀ. ἀκόλουθος Hier.*vir.ill.*(tr.Sophr.Pal.)7(p.11.30; M.*PL*.23.620B).

***ἀλλοδίκης,** *having strange notions of justice, Orac.Sib.*3.390; *ib.*11. 216(conj. for ἀντὶ δίκης).

ἀλλοδοξία, ἡ, *heterodoxy;* of Arianism, Ath.*ep.Serap.*1.1(M.26. 532B); id.*Ar.*3.22(M.26.369A).

ἀλλόδοξος, *heterodox,* Geo.Pis.*Sev.*89(M.92.1628B); neut. as subst., Ath.*Ar.*1.17(M.26.45D).

[*]**ἀλλόδοχος,** prob. for foreg., Geo.Pis.*Sev.*461(M.92.1656B).

[*]**ἀλλόεθνος,** = ἀλλοεθνής, *of a foreign nation,* Epiph.*haer.*30.11 (p.347.17, v.l. ἄλλου ἔθνους M.41.425A).

***ἀλλοιοτροπία, ἡ,** *variation, change,* Epiph.*haer.*66.12(p.34.4; M. 42.48B).

***ἀλλοιοφωνία, ἡ,** *variety of speech,* Epiph.*haer.*8.9(p.196.23; M.41. 221D).

ἀλλοι-όω, A. act. trans., *change, alter,* for better or worse; **1.** of redemptive activity of God, *change, convert* ὁ θεὸς...ὁ ~ῶν καὶ μεταβάλλων...τὰ κτίσματά σου Serap.*euch.*30.1; τὸν υἱὸν...~οῦντα τὰ ἄλλα καὶ μὴ ~ούμενον αὐτὸν διδάσκει [i.e. Ps.101:28] Ath.*Ar.*1.36 (M.26.85D); ἵνα πρὸς τὸ κρεῖττον ἀ. καὶ μεταβαλὼν ἐκ τοῦ χείρονος τὴν...κακίαν ἐξαφανίσῃ ἀπὸ τῆς φύσεως ἐν ἑαυτῷ τὸ κακὸν δαπανήσας Gr.Nyss.*Eun.*5(2 p.119.26; M.45.700D); ὁ πνευματικὸς λόγος...διαφυλάττει τὴν διάνοιαν ὡς ~ῶν αὐτὴν ὅλην εἰς ἀγάπην τοῦ θεοῦ Diad. *perf.*11(p.12.20); ἠλλοίωσέ με ἡ ἀγάπη σου Jo.D.*hom.*2.7(M.96.588C); ἀ. τὰ φρονήματα ἡμῶν πρὸς εὐσέβειαν *Lit.Jac.*(p.166.1); **2.** reflex. (cf. B) [sc. ὕλη] ~οῦσα...αὐτὴν ἀεὶ ἄρξεται ἀπ' ἀρχῆς Alex.Lyc.*Man.*7 (p.12.3; M.18.421A); **3.** of action of demons καρδίας ἀ. *T.Sal.*18. 30(M.122.1345B).

B. pass., *become different; suffer change;* **1.** metaphysical, corporeal things σῶμα...~ούμενον καὶ φθίνον καὶ γινόμενον Just. *dial.*5.2(M.6.488A); ὁ...διάβολος...κολάζεται· τὸ δὲ κολαζόμενον ~οῦται καὶ πάσχει, ἀπαθὲς δὲ τὸ ἀγένητον Meth.*res.*1.36(p.276.15; M.41. 1101C); denied of essences of intelligible things, Nemes.*nat.hom.* 3(M.40.596A); hence denied of soul in its union with body, *ib.*l.c.; **2.** met., *change* one's attitude towards, Ath.*h.Ar.*30(p.199.17; M. 25.728B); ? *be disturbed* in mind, ref. S. Peter in prison οὕτως ἔχαιρε καὶ οὐκ ἠλλοιοῦτο Chrys.*hom.8.2 in Eph.*(11.55C; ἤλγει Gaume); **3.** moral, *change* for the better, *be converted* ἔσχεν τὴν καρδίαν ~ωθεῖσαν *T.Job* 49(p.135.18); v. ἀλλοίωσις; *turn* to evil πρὸς τὸ χεῖρον...~ωθήσεται [sc. human soul which has come into a body] Or.*princ.*1.8.4(p.104.3).

C. philos. and theol., pass., *be subject to change;* **1.** characteristic of created things opp. God τὰ στοιχεῖα...οὐκ εἰσὶ θεοί, ἀλλὰ φθαρτὰ καὶ ~ούμενα ἐκ τοῦ μὴ ὄντος παραχθέντα Arist.*apol.*4.1; *ib.* 5.1; and of corporeal things τὸ σῶμα...~οῦται...πῶς οὖν δύναται τὸ ~ούμενον τῷ ἀναλλοιώτῳ ἐοικέναι; ‡Bas.*struct.hom.*1.6(1.326E; M.30.16C); **2.** certain pagan notions of deity accused of implying change [sc. Ζεύς] εἰ μὲν ἀήρ...~οῦται, εἰ δὲ καιρός, τρέπεται Athenag.*leg.*22.5(M.6.940A); denounced as an impiety in connexion with God, [acc. Origen] εἰ...ἦν χρόνος ὅτε οὐκ ἦν τὰ ποιήματα, ἐπεὶ τῶν ποιημάτων μὴ ὄντων οὐδὲ ποιητής ἐστιν...καὶ ~οῦσθαι καὶ μεταβάλλειν τὸν ἄτρεπτον καὶ ἀναλλοίωτον συμβήσεται θεόν Meth.*creat.*2 (p.494.25; M.18.33C); *ib.*4 passim(p.496; 336C,337A); τὸ προκριτέον ἐν πατρὶ καὶ υἱῷ καὶ ἁγίῳ πνεύματι μένον ἐν ταυτότητι καὶ μὴ ~ούμενον Epiph.*haer.*76.10(p.365.22; M.42.553B); τὸ...~οῦσθαι τῆς θείας φύσεως παντελῶς ἀλλότριον Cyr.*Jo.*1.4(4.36D); or with generation of Son ὁ πατὴρ ἐγέννα τὸν υἱόν. οὐ γάρ τι προϊέμενος οὐδ' ~ούμενος οὐδέ γε παθητικῶς κινούμενος...**ὑφίστη** αὐτόν Eus.*e.th.*1.12(p.72.16; M. 24.849A); or with Son οὐ...θέμις εἰπεῖν ἐκ τῆς οὐσίας τῆς ἀτρέπτου τρεπτὸν γεννᾶσθαι λόγον καὶ ~ουμένην σοφίαν. πῶς γὰρ ἔτι...σοφία τὸ ~ούμενον; Ath.*Ar.*1.36(M.26.88A); where ref. is to God it is to be understood virtually, never absolutely (or as in appearance only and not in reality), Epiph.*haer.*76.37(p.389.10; M.42.593D) poss. ref. Ps.76:11, v. ἀλλοίωσις; **3.** change having no place in Inc. either as touching divine nature γενόμενος ἄνθρωπος οὐκ ἠλλοίωται Alex.Al.*ep.encycl.*4(p.9.11; M.18.576B); αὐτὸς ἄτρεπτος μένων, καὶ μὴ ~ούμενος ἐν τῇ ἀνθρωπίνῃ οἰκονομίᾳ Ath.*Ar.*2.6(M.26.160B); *ib.*1.36(85C); ὁ θεὸς λόγος, οὐδὲν αὐτὸς ἀπὸ τῆς κοινωνίας τῆς περὶ τὸ σῶμα καὶ τὴν ψυχὴν ~ούμενος Nemes.*nat.hom.*3(M.40.601A); or the human nature οὔτε οὖν ὁ λόγος εἰς σῶμα...οὔτε εἰς λόγον τὸ σῶμα ἠλλοίωται Leo Mag.*ep.*35.2(p.41.25; M.*PL*.54.808A); Anast.Ant.*fr.* ap.*Doct.Patr.*20(p.126.18; M.89.1286B) cit. s. ἀνάκρασις; or as touching virginity of BMV οὐκ ἠλλοιώθη ἡ παρθένος καὶ μήτηρ ἐγένετο· οὐδὲ ~ωθείσης παρθενίας τόκος ἐγένετο Thdot.Anc.*exp.symb.*14(M. 77.1333A); not involved in Redemption, Ath.*Ar.*1.36(M.26.85D) cit. s. A.1; οὐδὲ εἰς τροπὴν ἠλλοιώθη τὸ τρεπτὸν τῆς ψυχῆς ἡμῶν ἰασαμένη [sc. ἡ θεότης] Gr.Nyss.*ep.*3(M.46.1020C); Epiph.*inc.*1 (p.227.24; M.41.273C); **4.** heret.; in accusation levelled against Apollinarius ὁ σκόπος πρὸς τοῦτο βλέπει...τὴν ἀπαθῆ καὶ ἀναλλοίωτον φύσιν πρὸς πάθους μετουσίαν ~ωθῆναι Gr.Nyss.*Apoll.*5(M.45. 1132B); change denied by Eunomius but for different reason οὐ [sc. φησί] τὸν ἄτρεπτόν τε καὶ ἄκτιστον τῷ διὰ κτίσεως γεγονότι, καὶ διὰ τοῦτο πρὸς κακίαν ~ωθέντι, καταμιχθῆναι· ἀλλὰ καὶ αὐτὸν κτιστὸν ὄντα πρὸς τὸ συγγενὲς ἐλθεῖν ἑαυτῷ καὶ ὁμόφυλον...ὅπερ ἦν, τοῦτο γενόμενον Eun.ap.Gr.Nyss.*Eun.*5(2 p.120.3; M.45.701A); implicit in monothelite position μίαν...ἐπὶ Χριστοῦ...ἐνέργειαν λέγειν οὐ θέμις ...ἐπεὶ καὶ τρεπτῆς ὑπάρχων δειχθήσεται φύσεως, καὶ τὴν οὐσίαν τῆς σαρκὸς εἰς ὅπερ οὐκ ἦν ~ώσας Max.*ambig.*(M.91.1057C).

D. for exeg. Pss.44:1,76:11 v. ἀλλοίωσις.

ἀλλοίωμα, τό, *alteration,* Meth.*res.*1.43(p.290.10; M.18.272B); φθόνος [sc. ἐστίν]...ὀφθαλμῶν ἀ. †Nil.*vit.*4(M.79.1144D).

ἀλλοίωσις, ἡ, freq. ass. with τροπή q.v.; **1.** *difference, alteration, variation, modification* οὐσία ἐστὶν αὐτῆς [sc. ὕλης] ἡ ἀ. Alex. Lyc.*Man.*7(p.12.6; M.18.421B); παθητὴν...αὐτὴν καὶ τρεπτὴν ὑπάρχουσαν εἴκειν ταῖς θεοποιήτοις ἀ. Dion.Al.ap.Eus.*p.e.*7.19(333D; M. 21.564A); superimposed upon substance οὐσία ἐστὶν...ἢ τὸ πάσας δεχόμενον τὰς μεταβολάς τε καὶ ἀ., αὐτὸ δὲ ἀναλλοίωτον κατὰ τὸν ἴδιον λόγον ἢ τὸ ὑπόμενον πᾶσαν ἀ. καὶ μεταβολήν Or.*or.*27(p.368. 6f.; M.11.512B); characterizes all that is corporeal τὰ...σώματα... εἰ θερμαίνεται...κατὰ πάθος θερμαίνεται· εἰ δὲ κατὰ πάθος...καὶ κατ' ἀ. εἰ δὲ κατ' ἀ.... καὶ κατὰ μεταβολήν ‡Just.*qu.Chr.*5(M.6.1460C); and the union of corporeal things ἐπὶ μὲν γὰρ τῶν σωμάτων ἡ ἕνωσις ἀ. τῶν συνιόντων πάντως ἐργάζεται, ἐπειδήπερ εἰς ἄλλα σώματα μεταβάλλεται Nemes.*nat.hom.*3(M.40.593B); Leont.B.*Nest.et Eut.*2(M.86. 1304D); of physical changes involved in decomposition, Meth.*res.* 3.6(p.396.9; M.18.521A); and digestion, Thdt.*carit.*(3.1297); other variations of bodily state, Evagr.Pont.*or.*63(M.79.1180D); of change involved by resurrection, Bas.*hex.*8.8(1.78E; M.29.184D); *variation* in force or quantity ἀσθένεια δὲ τί ἕτερόν ἐστιν ἢ τῆς καθ' ἕξιν δυνάμεως ἀ. καὶ μεταβολή; Leont.B.*Nest.et Eut.*2(1344C); **2.** theol. (here ἀ. appears to keep within metaphysical sphere, whereas τροπή freq. bears a moral connotation); **a.** absent from Father in begetting Son οὐδὲ ἡ οὐσία τοῦ πατρὸς ἀ. ὑπέμεινεν, εἰκόνα ἑαυτῆς ἔχουσα τὸν υἱόν Thgn.*hypot.fr.*2(p.76)ap.Ath.*decr.*25(M.25.460C); Cyr. *thes.*10(5^{1}.78D); and in procession of H. Ghost οὔτε κατά τινα τομὴν ἢ ἀπόρροιαν τὸ εἶναι ἐξ αὐτοῦ τὸν μονογενῆ καὶ τὸ ἅγιον πνεῦμα ἀ. τῆς φύσεως ἐξειργάσατο Epiph.*haer.*76.19(p.365.25; M.42. 553C); **b.** not applicable to Inc. τίς οὕτως ἐμβρόντητος...ὡς...οἴεσθαι ...μεταχωρῆσαι τὴν σάρκα κατά γε τὸν τῆς ἀ. τρόπον εἰς τὴν αὐτοῦ τοῦ λόγου; Cyr.*Chr.un.*(5^{1}.735E); σάρκα γεγονότα καὶ ἄνθρωπον...ἄνευ σωματικῆς ἀ. Sophr.H.*or.*2.36(M.87.3265A); **3.** moral (while τροπή almost invariably, though not necessarily, denotes a change for the worse, ἀ. is more commonly used of moral renewal or conversion); **a.** *change, conversion* ὁ κύριος...τὴν τῶν πραγμάτων ἀ. πρὸς οὐράνιον πολιτείαν μεθήρμοσε Isid.Pel.*epp.*1.428(M.78.420B); διὰ τὸ θειοτέρας αὐτὸν [sc. S. Paul] τυχεῖν ἀ. Cyr.*Ps.*67:28(M.69. 1156), v. 4; **b.** of effects of Fall τὴν ἀ. τὴν ἐκ τῆς παρακοῆς προσγεγενημένην ταῖς ἐνσάρκοις ἡμῶν σκηναῖς Meth.*Porph.*1(p.503.9; M. 18.397C); **4.** exeg. Pss.44:1, 76:11, interpreted as ref. **a.** Inc. ὁ... ἑαυτὸν κενώσας...ἀ.... ἔδοξεν ὑπομένειν, ἀναλλοίωτος ὢν...ὡς θεός· οἵ τε δι' αὐτοῦ...λυτρωθέντες...τὴν καλλίστην ἀληθῶς αὐτοὶ ἀ. ὑπομεμενήκασι...λαοί...ἐξομολογούμενοι τῷ θεῷ, τῆς αὐτῆς ἠξιώθησαν ἀ. ...οἱ γὰρ ἀλλοιωθέντες...ἄνθη νεαρὰ τῆς ἐκκλησίας Eus.*Ps.*44:1(M.23. 392B,C); cf.Or.*sel.in Ps.*76:11(M.12.1540B); οὔτε ἡ δεξιὰ κατὰ τὸν λόγον τῆς φύσεως ἐκείνου παρήλλακται, οὗ ἐστι δεξιά, οὔτε ἀ. αὐτῆς ἄλλη τις παρὰ τὴν τῆς σαρκὸς οἰκονομίαν λέγεσθαι δύναται...ἐν ᾧ δὲ περιείχετο τῷ τῆς σαρκὸς προσκαλύμματι κατὰ τὸ βλεπόμενον, ἄλλοιος παρ' ὃ τῇ φύσει ἦν θεωρούμενος...διὰ τοῦτο...λέγει τὸν πρὸς μόνον τὸ ἀλλοιωθὲν ἀτενίζοντα ὅτι 'βλέπε διὰ τοῦ ἀλλοιωθέντος τὸ ἀναλλοίωτον ...ὁ γὰρ ἑωρακὼς ἐμέ, οὐ τὸν ἐν τῇ ἀ. φαινόμενον, ἀλλὰ τὸν ἀληθῶς ἐμὲ τὸν ἐν τῷ πατρὶ ὄντα, αὐτὸν ἐκεῖνον ἑωρακὼς ἔσται τὸν ἐν ᾧ εἰμι' Gr. Nyss.*Eun.*6(2 p.135.31ff.; M.45.720D); Cyr.*Ps.*76:11(M.69.1192B); **b.** effects of Redemption upon mankind ἀ. λέγει ἐνταῦθα τὴν ἀπὸ κακίας καὶ ἀγνωσίας ἐπ' ἀρετὴν καὶ γνῶσιν ἐπάνοδον Or.*sel.in Ps.* 76:11(M.12.1540B); Eus.*d.e.*4.15(p.181.8ff.; M.22.301B); id.*Ps.*44:1 (M.23.392B); Chrys.*exp.in Ps.*44:1(5.160D); ὁ Χριστὸς καθ' ἡμᾶς γέγονε καὶ εἰς τὸ κρεῖττον ἠλλοίωσεν...αὕτη ἡ ἀ. ἣν ἡ δεξιὰ τοῦ ὑψίστου χαρίζεται, τὸ ἀεὶ διὰ τῶν γυμνασίων τῆς εὐσεβείας ἐπὶ τὸ μεῖζον προκόπτειν· ὁ γὰρ προκόπτων εἰς ἀρετήν, οὐκ ἔστιν ὅτε οὐκ ἀλλοιοῦται Cyr.*Ps*.76:11(M.69.1192B); ἕως ἂν...ὁ ἀγαπητὸς υἱὸς κατὰ σάρκα βλαστήσῃ καὶ τὴν καινὴν ἀ. τοῖς ἔθνεσι πραγματεύσηται...οὗτος τὴν διὰ τοῦ ἁγίου βαπτίσματος ἀ. τοῖς ἔθνεσιν ἐδωρήσατο...τοὺς δὲ ἀλλοιωθησομένους ὁ μὲν Σύμμαχος ἄνθη κέκληκεν...ἔαρ...πνευματικόν, τοῦ σωτῆρος ἡ παρουσία...περὶ τούτων ἡ παροῦσα προφητεία προαγορεύει...ὑποδεικνῦσα...τὸν ἀλλοιώσαντα καὶ ἀποφήναντα καρποφόρον Thdt.*Ps*.44:1(1.886f.); **c.** God's dealings with mankind πάλαι μὲν γὰρ αὕτη κατειργάζετο πολλά...θαύματα...νυνὶ δὲ ἀ. γεγένηται τῆς δεξιᾶς τοῦ ὑψίστου Eus.*Ps*.76:11(M.23.893B); *ib*.76:12f.(893C); ἀ. γὰρ τῆς τοῦ θεοῦ δεξιᾶς τιμωρίαν ἐκάλεσεν, ὡς τῆς δεξιᾶς τοῦ ὑψίστου εἰωθυίας τὰ ἀγαθὰ χορηγεῖν Thdt.*Ps*.76:11(1.1146); **5.** f.l. for ἀλύσεως [Chrys.*hom*.20.3 *in Mt*.(7.263B)], *cat.Mt*.6:19(p.47.23).

ἀλλοιωτικός, *digestive* τοῦ θρεπτικοῦ φυσικαὶ δυνάμεις εἰσὶ τέσσαρες, ἑλκτική, καθεκτική, ἀ., ἀποκριτική Nemes.*nat.hom*.23(M.40.693A); cf.Leont.B.*Nest.et Eut*.1(M.86.1296D); ἡ ἀ. δύναμις τῆς γαστρὸς [sc. of the fish] ἐνεργεῖν ἐκωλύετο Thdt.*Jon*.2:2(2.1467).

ἀλλοιωτός, *subject to change, mutable*; in theol. contexts nearly always ass. with τρεπτός q.v.; neut. as subst., *mutability, cat. Apoc*.4:6(p.244.23).

***ἀλλόκτιστος**, *strangely* or *inappropriately built*; of tabernacles proposed by S. Peter at Transfiguration, ‡Chrys.*transfig*.(Savile 7 p.340.30).

***ἀλλοούσιος**, *of another substance* υἱὸς...ὁμοούσιός μοι, οὐκ ἀ. Gr.Ant.*bapt*.2(M.88.1873A).

***ἀλλόπιστος**, *not of the true faith, unbelieving* καὶ ἀλλοπίστοις πολλάκις παρέχει ὁ θεὸς χαρίσματα Anast.S.*qu.et resp*.128(M.89.780A).

***ἄλλοπτος**, *of differing appearance*, ‡Caes.Naz.*dial*.140(M.38. 1052).

[*]**ἀλλοτριεπίσκοπος**, v. ἀλλοτριοεπίσκοπος.

***ἀλλοτριόγαμος**, s.v.l., *adulterous* ἀ. λῃστήν Thdt.*Ps*.50:9 (1.939, v.l. ἀλλοτρίων γάμων).

ἀλλοτριοεπίσκοπος ([*]**ἀλλοτριεπ-**), ὁ, *busybody in other men's affairs*, exeg. 1Cor.2:10 διὰ ποίαν αἰτίαν [sc. ἐρευνᾷ τὰ βάθη τοῦ θεοῦ τὸ πνεῦμα];...ὡς ἀλλοτριεπίσκοπον;...μὴ γένοιτο Epiph.*anc*.12(p.20. 22; M.43.37C); id.*haer*.66.85 (conj. p.128.7 for ἀλλότριος ἐπίσκοπος M.42.165B); of those usurping the functions of others ἐκκήρυκτος τῇ θεολογίᾳ πᾶς ὁ ἀ. Dion.Ar.*ep*.8.1(M.3.1089C).

***ἀλλοτριοκάματος**, *toiling for others*, Ant.Mon.*hom*.13(M.89. 1469A).

***ἀλλοτριόνοος**, *of strange sense, of obscure meaning* ἀ. πρὸ δυνάμεως πνευματικῆς, μὴ μετέρχου λόγους Jo.Clim.*scal*.27(M.88. 1116D); cf. ἤτοι ἀναγωγικοὺς τοὺς ἄλλο μὲν ἔχοντας τὸ φαινόμενον, ἄλλο δὲ τὸ νοούμενον *Schol*.40 in Jo.Clim.*scal*.27(M.88.1128A); also interpreted as *of another opinion*, i.e. *heretical* ἀλιτηριονόους, ἢ πλανολόγους· οἱοί εἰσι τῶν αἱρεσιωτῶν *ib*.

***ἀλλοτριοούσιος**, *alien in essence*, Ath.*Ar*.1.20(M.26.53A); οὐκ ἀ. ἐστι τοῦ πατρός, ἀλλ' ὁμοούσιος id.*syn*.51(p.274.28; M.26.784B); id. *tom*.5(M.26.801A).

ἀλλότριος, *of* or *belonging to another, alien*;

A. in gen.; **1.** *alien*; **a.** in gen. τὸ ἁμαρτῆσαι ἀ. παριστᾶσα ἡ γραφή Clem.*str*.7.13(p.58.26; τοῦ ἁμαρτῆσαι ἀ. [sc. τὸν γνωστικόν] M.9.513B); of apostates and heretics, Ath.*ep.Aeg.Lib*.21(M.25. 588A); of what is contrary to Christian faith τοῖς τὰς ἀ. ἐντολὰς μνημονεύουσιν Papias ap.Eus.*h.e*.3.39.3(M.20.297A); οὐκέτι...κατακολουθοῦντες τοῖς ἀ. Bas.*Spir*.6(3.6B; M.32.77B); hence esp. of heretics and heresies εἴ τις ἐν ἀ. γνώμῃ περιπατεῖ Ign.*Philad*.3.3; τοὺς δὲ λέγοντας ἐξ οὐκ ὄντων τὸν υἱόν...ἀ. οἶδεν ἡ...ἐκκλησία *Symb. Ant*.(341)4 ap.Ath.*syn*.25(p.251.16; M.26.728A); ἀ. καὶ μὴ ἐκ πατέρων εἶναι τὴν αἵρεσιν ταύτην Ath.*Ar*.1.8(M.26.28B); **b.** of Devil τοῦ ἀ. πνεύματος *Lit*.ap.*Const.App*.8.7.8; Lit.*ib*.8.6.6; ὁ ἀ. Gr.Naz.*or*.14.27 (M.35.896A); *Mir.Mich*.4(p.551.9); of demons τῶν ἀ., τοῦτ' ἔστιν ἀπὸ τῶν πονηρῶν καὶ πλάνων πνευμάτων Just.*dial*.30.2(M.6.540A); **2.** *alien* from, *without a share* in; **a.** in gen., of Gentiles ἀ. τοῦ θεοῦ ὄντες *1Clem*.7.7; ἀ. τῶν ἐπαγγελιῶν Cyr.*Is*.3.1(2.364B); *ib*.3.3(455E); ἀ. γὰρ θεοῦ ἡ τῶν ἀγαθῶν ἀκαρπία Thdt.*qu*.25 *in Dt*.(1.277); denied of Jews, ‡Chrys.*pasch*.5.1(8.261A) cit. s. οἰκείωσις; **b.** from Church, implying *excommunicated* τὸν Σαμοσατέα...τῆς ἐκκλησίας τοῦ θεοῦ ἀ. ἀπέφηναν οἱ ἐκκλησιαστικοὶ πατέρες Eus.*e.th*.1.14(p.74. 19; M.24.853B); Νοουάτον ἅμα τοῖς σὺν αὐτῷ συνεπαρθεῖσιν...ἐν ἀλλοτρίοις τῆς ἐκκλησίας ἡγεῖσθαι id.*h.e*.6.43.2(M.20.616C); id.*Marcell*.2.1(p.33.17; M.24.780B); **c.** from office, *degraded* ἀ. αὐτοὺς ἡγούμεθα τῆς ἐπισκοπικῆς ἀξίας CCP(359)*ep*.ap.Thdt.*h.e*.2.28.7(3.901); ἀ. εἶναι τοὺς ἐπισκόπους τῆς ἐπισκοπῆς καὶ τοὺς κληρικοὺς τοῦ κλήρου *Symb.Chalc*.(p.130.10; H.2.456E).

B. theol., *alien* i.e. not of the nature of, opp. ἴδιος τῆς οὐσίας: ταῦτα...δείκνυσι...μὴ εἶναι τὸν υἱὸν ἀ., ἀλλ' ἴδιον τῆς τοῦ πατρὸς οὐσίας Ath.*Ar*.2.82(M.26.320B); *ib*.3.17(360A); **1.** inapplicable to mutual relation of Persons in Trin., Thgn.*hypot.fr*.2(p.76; M.10. 240A) cit. s. ἀπόρροια; τριὰς τοίνυν ἁγία καὶ τελεία ἐστίν, ἐν πατρὶ καὶ υἱῷ καὶ ἁγίῳ πνεύματι θεολογουμένη, οὐδὲν ἀ. ἢ ἔξωθεν ἐπιμιγνύμενον Ath.*ep.Serap*.1.28(M.26.596A); *ib*.3.6(636A); id.*syn*.52 (p.276.12; M.26.788A); ὥσπερ...τὸ πνεῦμα τοῦ ἀνθρώπου τῆς ἀνθρωπότητος αὐτοῦ καὶ τῆς οὐσίας οὐ κεχώρισται, οὕτω καὶ τὸ πνεῦμα τοῦ θεοῦ τῆς θεότητος αὐτοῦ καὶ τῆς οὐσίας οὐκ ἔστιν ἀ. id.*inc.et c.Ar*.13 (M.26.1005B); πιστεύομεν εἰς τὸ πνεῦμα τὸ ἅγιον, τὸ οὐκ ἀ. πατρὸς καὶ υἱοῦ ἀλλ' ὁμοούσιον ‡Ath.*interpr*.(p.66.22; M.26.1232B); ἐπὶ δὲ τῆς θείας φύσεως τὸ μὲν εἶναι πνεῦμα θεοῦ εὐσεβὲς ἐνομίσθη...οὐ μὴν ἀ. τι καθ' ὁμοιότητα τοῦ ἡμετέρου πνεύματος ἔξωθεν ἐπιρρεῖν τῷ θεῷ... θεοπρεπές ἐστιν οἴεσθαι Gr.Nyss.*or.catech*.2(p.14.6; M.45.17B); οὐχ οἷόν τε τὸν ὑπὸ τοῦ θείου πνεύματος ἐνεργούμενον, ἀ. τῆς θείας φύσεως τὸν Χριστὸν ἀποφῆναι Thdt.*1Cor*.12:3(3.242); **2.** of creatures in rel. to divine essence, Ath.*Ar*.3.8(M.26.337B); and equally therefore to Son ἀ. μὲν ὢν κατ' οὐσίαν τῶν γενητῶν, ἴδιος δὲ τοῦ πατρὸς λόγος id.*ep.Serap*.2.5(M.26.616B); ὁ μὲν γὰρ λόγος, ὡς ἴδιος, ἐν τῷ πατρί ἐστι· τὰ δὲ γενητά, ἔξωθεν ὄντα, πρόσκειται, ὡς τῇ μὲν φύσει ἀ., τῇ δὲ προαιρέσει προσκείμενα ‡Ath.*Ar*.4.5(p.49.13; M.26.473D); hence acc. Arius and Eunomius characterizing relations of Son and H. Ghost to Father, Ar.*Thal.fr*.10(p.267; M.26.24A); Ath.*Ar*.1.6(M.26.24B) cit. s. ἀνόμοιος; Alex.Al.*ep.encycl*.3(p.8.3; M.18.573B); Ath.*Dion*.23 (p.62.29; M.25.513A); Bas.*Eun*.2.6(1.242C; M.29.581C) cit. s. ξένος; θεὸν μὲν τὸν υἱὸν ὁμολογοῦντες, κτιστὸν δὲ ἀποκαλοῦντες, καὶ τῆς θείας οὐσίας ἀ. Thdt.*qu*.37 *in Ex*.(1.149); and so by them imported into essence of Trin. ἀνόμοιος ἑαυτῆς ἡ τριὰς εὑρίσκεται, ξέναις καὶ ἀ. φύσεσί τε καὶ ταῖς οὐσίαις συνισταμένη Ath.*Ar*.1.17(48B); *ib*.2.43 (240B); διαιροῦντες ἀπὸ τοῦ λόγου τὸ πνεῦμα...σχίζοντες αὐτὴν [sc. τὴν τριάδα] καὶ ἐπιμίσγοντες αὐτῇ ἀ. καὶ ἑτεροειδῆ φύσιν id.*ep.Serap*.1.2 (M.26.533A); *ib*.1.17(569C); Gr.Naz.*or*.20.5(M.35.1072A); **3.** of certain predicables e.g. λύσις...ἀλλότριον πάντη θεοῦ καὶ τῆς πρώτης φύσεως Gr.Naz.*or*.28.7(p.32.2; M.36.33C); but not of divine attributes ἔστιν ἐν τῷ πατρὶ τὸ ἀΐδιον, τὸ αἰώνιον, τὸ ἀθάνατον· ἔστι δὲ ἐν αὐτῷ οὐχ ὡς ἀ. αὐτοῦ, ἀλλ' ὡς ἐν πηγῇ ἐστιν ἐν αὐτῷ ἀναπαυόμενα, καὶ ἐν τῷ υἱῷ Ath.*hom.in Mt.11*:27 (M.25.216B); **4.** Christol., of what is predicated of Christ's human nature in rel. to divinity, Ath. *Ar*.3.41(M.26.409C); cf.‡Ath.*Apoll*.1.16(M.26.1121B); but not of Christ's human body in rel. to his Person οὐ γὰρ ἦν ἀ. αὐτοῦ τὸ ἐνωθὲν αὐτῷ σῶμα Cyr.*expl.xii cap*.3(p.19.11; 6[1].149E); nor of his human nature in rel. to humanity in gen. οὐ τὸ σῶμα ἐν ὁμοιώσει τῇ καθ' ἡμᾶς μόνῃ, ἀ. δὲ σαρκὸς ἀνθρωπίνης ‡Ath.*Apoll*.1.12(1116A); **5.** of Marcion's 'good' God, Cels.ap.Or.*Cels*.6.53(p.124.15; M.11. 1380C); of his elect, Cels.*ib*.(p.124.9).

ἀλλοτριότης, ἡ, **1.** *alienation, separation*, of Trin. οὐδὲ τὴν μίαν καὶ ἀπρόσιτον φύσιν ἀποξενοῦμεν ἑαυτῆς, ἐκφύλοις ἀ. Gr.Naz.*or*.43.30 (M.36.537A); **2.** qualitative *difference*, of Trin. acc. Eunomius πολλὰς οὐσίας ὀνομάζει ὡς ἑκάστης ἰδιάζουσαν ἐχούσης τινὰ τὴν πρὸς τὰς ἄλλας ἀ. Gr.Nyss.*Eun*.1(1 p.88.13; M.45.320C).

***ἀλλοτριοτρόπως**, *in a strange manner, abnormally*, Anon.ap. Eus.*h.e*.5.16.9(M.20.468B).

***ἀλλοτριόφρων**, *abnormal in thought* ἀ. ἑτεροδιδασκαλίας ‡Amph. *circ*.(p.18B).

ἀλλοτρι-όω, *alienate*; **1.** *dissociate, separate* from; *remove* from, pass. ψυχὴ πάσης ταραχῆς ~ουμένη Or.*Jo*.6.1(p.106.11; M.14.197A); Eus.*v.C*.1.12(p.13.15; M.20.925B); Gr.Nyss.*v.Mos*.(M.44.333B); perf. ptcpl. pass. neut. as subst., opp. τὸ ἐπιρρεπές, Chrys.*hom*.47.1 *in Mt*.(7.488B); pass., of possessions, *be alienated, fall into other hands*, Bas.*hom*.7.2(2.53A; M.31.284B); in thought, *dissociate, regard as foreign* ἡμεῖς δὲ μόνα τῆς φύσεως ~οῦμεν ἐκεῖνα ὅσα ἐπίκτητα γίνεταί τισι καὶ ἀπόκτητα Gr.Nyss.*Eun*.12(1 p.341.25; M.45.1060D); Μαρκίωνος καὶ Μανιχαίου...τῶν τὴν κτίσιν ~ούντων αὐτοῦ Chrys.*hom*.49.2 *in Mt*.(7.506B); Cyr.*expl.xii cap*.3(p.19.14; 6[1].150A); Trin. οὗτος [sc. Eunomius]...~ῶν τοῦ πατρὸς τὸν μονογενῆ Bas.*Eun*.1.18(1.230B; M.29.553A); Gr.Naz.*or*.29.16(p.98.12; M.36.96A) cit. s. συνεισάγω; Christol. τὸν κύριον συκοφαντήσωσι, καὶ τῆς ἡμετέρας αὐτὸν ἀ. φύσεως Leont.B.*Nest.et Eut*.1(M.86.1297A); εἰ ὑποστατικὴν [sc. τὴν ἐνέργειαν], ~ώσομεν αὐτὸν τοῦ πατρὸς καὶ τοῦ πνεύματος κατὰ τὴν ἐνέργειαν Max.*opusc*.(M.91.108D); med., in rel. to oneself, opp. οἰκειοῦμαι, Chrys.*hom*.11.4 *in Col*.(11.410B); **2.** *exclude, deprive* τῆς ...ἐν Χριστῷ γνώσεώς τε καὶ χάριτος ἠλλοτριωμένος Eus.*Marcell*.1.1 (p.4.28; M.24.720A); Gr.Nyss.*Eun*.2(2 p.366.11; M.45.545C); Cyr. *Ps*.2:12(M.69.725A); Thdt.*Dan*.3:33(2.1116); Λέων...αὐτὸν [sc. Dioscorus]...πάσης ἱερατικῆς ἠλλοτρίωσεν ἀξίας *Libell*.ap.CChalc.*act*.3

(*ACO* 2.1.2 p.29.18; H.2.345C); med., *deprive oneself* ῥᾳστώνης... ἁπάσης καὶ τρυφηλῆς διαίτης ~ούμενος Eus.*v.C.*2.14(p.47.4; M.20.992D); **3.** *estrange, make hostile* τάξιν θεολογίας...μήτε ἀθρόως ἐκφαίνοντας, μήτε εἰς τέλος κρύπτοντας...τὸ μὲν τοὺς ἀλλοτρίους πλῆξαι δυνάμενον, τὸ δὲ ἀ. τοὺς ἡμετέρους Gr.Naz.*or.*31.27(p.180.4; M.36.164B); Nil.*epp.*1.43(M.79.101D).

ἀλλοτρίωσις, ἡ, 1. *separation* involving *diversity*; **a.** in gen., ref. blessings under old dispensation and new μή...ἀπὸ τῆς τῶν ὀνομάτων κοινωνίας, ταυτότητα πραγμάτων νομίσῃς, ἀλλὰ μηδὲ ἀ. Chrys. *hom.14.2 in Jo.*(8.79D); **b.** theol. οὐχὶ ἀ. τῆς φύσεως, ἀλλ' οἰκείωσιν πρὸς τὸν πατέρα καὶ υἱὸν ἡ κοινωνία τῶν ὀνομάτων παρίστησι Bas.*Eun.* 3.3(1.274E; M.29.661A); Gr.Naz.*or.*33.16(M.36.233D); μὴ φοβηθῇς τὴν πρόοδον...φοβήθητι δὲ τὴν ἀ. *ib.*25.17(M.35.1224A); **2.** from things, *separation, cutting* oneself *off* τῇ ἀναχωρήσει τῶν μεριμνῶν...καὶ τῇ ...ἀ. τῶν περισπασμῶν Bas.*reg.fus.*5(2.341E; M.31.920C); ἡ πρὸς τὸ θεῖον συνάφεια, καὶ ἡ τῶν κακῶν ἀ. Gr.Nyss.*hom.1 in Cant.*(M.44.776B); Nil.*Magn.*1(M.79.969B); from good things τὴν ἀπὸ τῆς ζωῆς ἀ. Bas.*Eun.*2.19(1.254E; M.29.612C); *alienation* τῆς κατὰ φύσιν μορφῆς ἀ. καὶ παραλλαγὴ τῶν γνωριστικῶν σημείων τῆς ἀνθρωπότητος, ὅταν μὴ συμπαραληφθῇ τῇ πίστει τὸ πνεῦμα Gr.Nyss.*Maced.*15 (M.45.1320C); **3.** from persons, *estrangement, alienation*, partic. from God ὑβρίζει...ὁ ἐπίορκος διὰ τῆς ἀπὸ θεοῦ ἀ. †Bas.*Is.*267(1.583B; M.30.589B); ἁμαρτία...ἐστιν ἡ τοῦ θεοῦ ἀ. Gr.Nyss.*Eun.*2 (2 p.366.8; M.45.545B); Marc.Er.*opusc.*4(M.65.1017C); as man's condition before Inc., Cyr.*Is.*4.1(2.558E); Proc.G.*Is.*43:1(M.87.2385B).

ἀλλοφροσύνη, ἡ, *change of mind*, †Apoll.*met.Ps.*76:11(M.33.1421C).

ἀλλοφυής, *of a different nature* φῶς...ὁ μονογενής, φωτὸς δὲ ἡ κτίσις μέτοχος, καὶ διὰ τοῦτο ἀ. Cyr.*Jo.*1.8(4.70B); *ib.*(72B).

ἀλλόφυλος, *of another tribe, foreign*; hence **1.** of Philistines (as LXX) ἀ. δὲ ἰδίως οἱ Φυλιστιαῖοι λέγονται, οὓς Παλαιστινοὺς Ἕλληνες ὀνομάζουσιν †Bas.*Is.*286(1.597A; M.30.621B); Isid.H.*etym.*9.2.20; **2.** of gentiles, Mel.*pass.*29 p.12.27; ὑπὸ Ἰουδαίων ὡς ἀ. πολεμοῦνται [sc. Χριστιανοί] *Diogn.*5.17; Hipp.*Dan.*2.38.3(M.10.680C); ὁ ἀ. τε καὶ ἀπερίτμητος ἔτι Cyr.*ador.*14(1.514B); **3.** met., *alien* ἡ γὰρ [sc. ψυχή] ἐκ φωτὸς οὖσα, τὴν ἀ. τοῦ πυρὸς φλόγα μὴ φέρουσα *Hom.Clem.*9.9; τὴν δὲ καθ' ὑπόστασιν ἕνωσιν...ἀγνοοῦμεν ὡς ξένην καὶ ἀ. τῶν θείων γραφῶν Thdt.ap.Cyr.*apol.Thdt.*(p.114.12; 6^{1}.208B); Geo.Pis.*hex.*1444 (M.92.1544A).

ἄλλυδις, used as if for various cases of ἄλλος, *another* καὶ τότε θρηνήσουσιν ἐπ' ἄ. ἄλλος ἄπωθεν *Orac.Sib.*2.297; *ib.*2.301; *ib.*1.181.

ἁλμ-άω, *be salt*, Gr.Nyss.*fat.*(M.45.153A); id.*infant.*(M.46.185B); τὸν ~ῶντα τοῦτον καὶ αὐχμηρὸν τόπον id.*hom.2 in Eccl.*(M.44.611B).

***Ἀλμενιχιακά, τά,** *astronomical indexes, almanacs* τοὺς λεγομένους κραταιοὺς ἡγεμόνας, ὧν καὶ τὰ ὀνόματα ἐν τοῖς Ἀ. φέρεται Porphyry ap.Eus.*p.e.*3.4(92C; M.21.169C).

ἅλμη, ἡ, *brine*; met., *bitterness*, Pall.*v.Chrys.*5(p.29.10; M.47.19).

***ἁλμυρόβρυτος,** *teeming with salt, salty*, Jo.Mon.*hymn.Chrys.*3 (M.96.1380B).

***ἁλμυρονάματος,** *with salt floods*, ‡Chrys.*hom.in Ps.76:4*(10.745A).

***ἁλμυροφόρος,** *salt-producing, salty*, Chrys.*hom.in Ps.115:1–3* (p.357.13); Sever.*fic.*(M.59.590).

§ **ἀλογεύομαι,** *have carnal relations with animals*, CAnc.(314) *can.*16,17; *Poen.App.*2.22.

ἀλογέω, 1. *be out of one's senses, rave*, Max.*opusc.*(M.91.252A); pass. ἠλογημένος, *devoid of reason*, Dion.Ar.*d.n.*7.2(M.3.868C); Thal. *cent.*3.67(M.91.1453D); **2.** *deprive of arguments, make at a loss*, Just. *dial.*93.5(M.6.700A).

ἀλογία, ἡ, 1. *folly*, Eus.*p.e.*10.8(482C; M.21.804A); τῆς Ἰουδαϊκῆς ...ἀ. Isid.Pel.*epp.*1.346(M.78.381A); **2.** *irrationality*, esp. as characteristic of beasts, hence *brutishness* εἰς γὰρ τὴν τῶν παθῶν καὶ ἡδονῶν ἀ. πεσόντες οἱ ἄνθρωποι Ath.*gent.*19(M.25.40A); of edict of Juln. Imp. against Christian teachers of literature ἵνα...προκηρύξῃ τὴν ἀ. ἐν ἀρχῇ τῆς βασιλείας, τυραννήσας πρὸ τῶν ἄλλων τοὺς λόγους Gr.Naz.*or.*4.6(M.35.537A); τίθεται δὲ [sc. ὁ Χριστός] ἐπὶ φάτνης τῆς τῶν ἀλόγων τραπέζης, καὶ τῆς τῶν ἀνθρώπων ἀ. κατηγορῶν,...ἀλλὰ νῦν τῆς ἀνθρωπείας φύσεως τὴν ἀ. ἀποβαλούσης, καὶ τὸ λογικὸν ἀναλαβούσης, ἡ μυστικὴ αὐτὴν ὑποδέχεται τράπεζα Thdt.*provid.*10(4.663); **3.** *absence of reason*, implying also *absence of the Logos*, Eus.*Marcell.* 2.4(p.57.4; M.24.820C); Ath.*Ar.*1.14(M.26.41C); Leont.H.*Nest.*1.30 (M.86.1496C).

ἀλογίζω, 1. *take no account of, disregard*, Cyr.*hom.pasch.*17(5^{2}.231B); **2.** med., *suppose foolishly*, *V.Zos.*11(p.104.1).

***ἀλόγιοι, οἱ,** = ἄλογοι (v. ἄλογος), Isid.H.*etym.*8.5.26.

***ἀλογισταίνω,** *reason foolishly*, Just.*1apol.*46.1(M.6.397B).

ἀλογίστευτος, *not guided by reason, foolish* ἀ. ἔχοντες τὸν βίον Ast.Am.*hom.*2(M.40.188C).

ἀλογιστία, ἡ, *want of judgement, irrationality* ἀνανήφων ἀπὸ τῆς ὑπ' ἐκείνοις [i.e. demons] ἀ. ἐπ' ὀλίγον τι βλέπειν τοῦ ἀληθοῦς Or.*Cels.* 8.63(p.279.12; M.11.1612B); Isid.Pel.*epp.*3.154(M.78.848A).

ἀλογοθέτητος, *immune from rendering an account*, Isid.Pel.*epp.* 2.127(M.78.569C); of power, *absolute* ἡ ἐπισκοπή...οἰκονομικὴ προστασία, οὐκ ἀ. ἐξουσία *ib.*3.216(900A).

ἀλογόομαι, *become like an irrational creature, become brutalized* ἡ ψυχὴ...ὑπὸ τῆς πονηρίας ἀποθηριοῦται...καὶ αἱρεῖται πρὸς τὸ ἀλογωθῆναι Or.*princ.*1.8.4(p.104.11; M.11.180C); of men before Inc., Ath.*inc.*13.1(M.25.117C); ἐπὶ πώλῳ ἐκάθισεν [sc. ὁ Χριστός], ἵνα τὴν ἀλογωθεῖσαν...ψυχὴν καὶ ὁμοιωθεῖσαν τοῖς κτήνεσι τοῖς ἀνοήτοις ἐπιστρέψῃ ὡς λόγον τοῦ θεοῦ Dor.*doct.*15.4(M.88.1793A).

ἄλογος, A. *without reason*; **1.** *devoid of reason, irrational*; **a.** in gen. ἀ. τύχῃ ἄγεσθαι Athenag.*leg.*25.3(M.6.949C); ζώων ἐμψύχων λογικῶν τε καὶ ἀ. Eus.*p.e.*7.3(301D; M.21.512C); Thdt.*eran.*1(4.7); neut. plur. as subst., *animals LS*; sing., *beast of burden*, Cyr.S.*v. Sab.*36(p.123.13); †Gregent.*leg.Hom.*33(M.86.600A); Leont.N.*v.Jo. Eleem.*22(p.41.12); Jo.Mosch.*prat.*33(M.87.2881C); **b.** of *irrational* or *animal* parts of human nature ἐκ λογικοῦ καὶ ἀ. συγκείμενος, ψυχῆς καὶ σώματος Clem.*str.*4.3(p.252.13; M.8.1221B); τὰ ἐν ἡμῖν ἄ. Or.*Jo.*1.37(42; p.48.28; M.14.97D); πόρρω γὰρ ἐπιθυμίας ἀ. καὶ ἁμαρτίας ἐσκήνωνται τὰ πνευματικά Meth.*res.*2.2(p.332.16; M.18.300B); τὰ κατὰ φύσιν ἄ. ἐκ τῆς αἰσθήσεως γινόμενα Proc.G.*Lev.*proem.(M.87.692A); **2.** *not according to*, or *unsupported by, reason* ἰδιωτικῆς καὶ ἀ. δόξης Just.*2apol.*3.3(M.6.449A); ἵνα...μήτε ἄ. τὴν εἰς Χριστὸν πίστιν ὑπολάβῃ Ath.*gent.*1(M.25.4B); **3.** *contrary to reason*, ‡Just.*qu.et resp.*46(M.6.1292C); *unreasonable, unsuitable* οὐκ ἄ. δοκεῖ ἐπιδεῖξαι Hipp.*haer.*10.31(p.287.3; M.16.3446A); *unfair* ἄ. ἡγούμενος ἐν τοσαύτῃ συγχύσει καταλεῖψαι τοὺς λαούς Ath.*fug.*24(p.84.15; M.25.676A); ἀ. νίκης Pall.*v.Chrys.*13(p.83.1; M.47.47).

B. *without reason*, implying also *without the Logos*; **1.** denied of God, even by non-Christians πᾶς Ἰουδαίων...ὁμολογήσειεν ἂν...τὸν θεὸν...μὴ εἶναι ἄ. Eus.*e.th.*1.20(p.97.15; M.24.893D); Gr.Nyss.*or. catech.*1(p.7.5; M.45.13A); **2.** denied of Father; **a.** ref. generation of Logos ὁ λόγος προελθὼν ἐκ τῆς τοῦ πατρὸς δυνάμεως οὐκ ἄ. πεποίηκε τὸν γεγεννηκότα Tat.*orat.*5(p.6.3; M.6.817A); **b.** ref. co-equality of Logos, exeg. Jo.1:1 εἰ γὰρ ἐλλιπὴς ἦν ἐν τῷ ἰδίῳ μεγέθει ὁ λόγος, ὥστε μὴ δύνασθαι πρὸς ὅλον τὸν θεὸν εἶναι, ἀνάγκη πᾶσα ἄ. εἶναι τοῦ θεοῦ νομίζειν τὸ ὑπερπῖπτον τοῦ λόγου Gr.Nyss.*fid.*(M.45.141A); **c.** ref. co-eternity of Logos, Hipp.*Noët.*10(p.251.17; M.10.817A) cit. s. ἀβούλευτος; exeg. Jo.1:1 οὐκ ἦν γάρ, ὅτε ἡ ἀρχὴ ἄ. ἦν Or.*Jo.*2.19(13; p.76.12; M.14.148B); Gr.Nyss.*fid.*(M.45.140D); Jo.D.*f.o.*1.6(M.94.801C); **d.** freq. in reply to Arians, Alex.Al.*ep.encycl.*4(p.9.6; M.18.576B) cit. s. ἄσοφος; Ath.*Ar.*3.63(M.26.456C); id.*ep.Serap.*2.2(M.26.609B); Cyr.*thes.*5(5^{1}.54B); **e.** in reply to Marcellus τὸν πατέρα καὶ τὸν υἱὸν ἐπὶ τὸ αὐτὸ συνάγει, τὴν μὲν οὐσίαν καλῶν τὸν πατέρα, τὸν δ' ἐν αὐτῷ λόγον τὸν υἱόν·...θεὸν ἄ. παραδεχόμενος, ἔχοντα μὲν λόγον ὡς συμβεβηκότα ἐν αὐτῷ οὐ μὴν αὐτὸν ὄντα λόγον Eus.*e.th.*2.14(p.115.13; M.24.928C); implication of Marcellus's teaching τῆς ζωοποιοῦ σαρκὸς ἐρήμου καὶ ἀ. καταλειφθησομένης id.*Marcell.*2.4(p.58.2; M.24.821C); **3.** of human reason, as dist. from Logos νομιζομένων μὲν λόγων οὐκ ὄντων δὲ ἀληθῶς λόγων ἀλλ', ἵν' οὕτως εἴπω, ὅλον τοῦτο ἀ. λόγων Or.*Jo.*2.3(p.56.3; M.14.112A); **4.** οἱ ἄ., name of sect opposing Logos theology and Johannine writings ἐπεὶ οὖν τὸν λόγον οὐ δέχονται τὸν παρὰ Ἰωάννου κεκηρυγμένον, ἄ. κληθήσονται Epiph. *haer.*51.3(p.250.21; M.41.892A); Jo.D.*haer.*51(M.94.709A); cf. τῆς...ἀ. αἱρέσεως Epiph.*haer.*54.1(p.317.5; M.41.961B).

***ἀλογοτροφεῖον, τό,** *stable* ἄνω ὁ πατρῷος...κόλπος, καὶ κάτω ἀ. μικρόν, καὶ φάτνιον Tim.Ant.*descr.BMV* 2(M.28.945B).

***ἀλογοφάνειρος,** *seemingly absurd*, ‡Ath.*doct.mon.*(M.28.1421A).

ἀλόγως, 1. *without reasoning*, i.e. without critical examination ὁμολογοῦμεν διδάσκειν πιστεύειν καὶ ἀ. τοὺς μὴ δυναμένους πάντα καταλιπεῖν καὶ ἀκολουθεῖν ἐξετάσει λόγου Or.*Cels.*1.10(p.62.25; M.11.673C); μὴ ἀ., μετὰ κρίσεως δέ Eus.*h.e.*4.8.5(M.20.324B); ἀ. πιστεύσω; καὶ μὴ ἐξετάσω τί δυνατόν, ἢ συμφέρον; Euther.*confut.*16(M.28.1388B); **2.** *without reasoning power, irrationally*, Chrys.*serm.1.2 in Gen*(4.646E); **3.** *without reason, unjustly* ἀ. πάσχομεν Athenag.*leg.* 4.2(M.6.900A).

ἀλοητός, ὁ, *threshing*, Gr.Nyss.*virg.*3(p.256.8; M.46.325A); Nil. *exerc.*19(M.79.745A).

ἀλοιδόρητος, 1. *unreviled*, ‡Bas.*const.*6.1(2.551B; M.31.1361A) **2.** *irreproachable, beyond reproach*, *Const.App.*1.10.4; of doctrin of Trin. τὴν ἀ. πίστιν Cyr.*Jo.*9.1(4.784C); *ib.*(802D).

***ἀλοιδορήτως,** *irreproachably*, Cyr.*Jo.*10.2(4.888D).

ἀλοίδορος, *not reviling*, Ant.Mon.*hom*.28(M.89.1528A).

ἀλουργίς, ἡ, *purple robe*, esp. as garment of rich or emperors; hence **1.** fig., of S. Paul, whose blindness is compared to the mordant applied to wool before it is dyed purple τριημέρῳ προεστύφθη πηρώσει, ἀ. θεοῦ [καὶ] γενόμενος, καὶ πάντας ἀνθρώπους γενέσθαι προτρεπόμενος Isid.Pel.*epp*.1.346 (M.78.381A); ref. Mt.25:40 τὰ ῥάκη διαπτύων ἔξωθεν ἀπρεπῶς περικείμενα, καὶ τὴν κεκρυμμένην ἀ. οὐ βλέπων τὸν ἔνδον βασιλέα σημαίνουσαν ‡Nil.*perist*.9.5(M.79.872A); **2.** met.; **a.** of the empire τὸν Γάλλον ἀφελέσθαι μὲν τῆς ἀ. Philost.*h.e*.4.1(M.65.517A); *ib*.11.4(597C); τυράννου...ἀναξίου τῆς Χριστιανικωτάτης ἀ. ‡Jo.D.*ep.Thphl*.14(M.95.364B); **b.** of an altar-cloth τοῦ σεπτοῦ θυσιαστηρίου τὴν ἀ. *Ep*.ap.CCP(536)*act*.5(p.95.26; H.2.1369D); **c.** of humanity of Christ συμπροσκυνῶ τῷ βασιλεῖ καὶ θεῷ, τὴν ἀ. τοῦ σώματος, οὐχ ὡς ἱμάτιον...ἀλλ' ὡς ὁμόθεον χρηματίσασαν Jo.D.*imag*.1.4(M.94.1236B); cf. ὁ Χριστός, καθάπερ ἀ. βασιλικὴν τὸ ἴδιον φόρημα περικείμενος...τὸ ἀνθρώπινον σῶμα Cyr.*Jo*.3.5(4.301A).

***ἀλουργοβαφής**, *purple-dyed*, Clem.*paed*.2.10(p.222.18; M.8.528A).

***ἀλουργοϋφής**, *purple-woven*, Epiph.*haer*.15.1(p.209.16; M.41.245A).

***ἀλουργοφορέω**, *wear purple*, Isid.Pel.*epp*.1.214(M.78.317B).

ἀλουσία, ἡ, *abstinence from washing*; as ascetic practice, Chrys.*res.Chr*.1(2.438A); Eus.Al.*serm*.21.14(M.86.440D); Eustrat.*v.Eutych*.14(M.86.2292A); Ephr.3.425F = Jo.D.*virt*.(M.95.88A).

ἀλουτέω, *abstain from washing*; as ascetic practice, Nil.*epp*.3.153 (M.79.453D); Pall.*v.Chrys*.17(p.109.16, v.l. ἀλουτῇ; M.47.61).

ἀλόχευτος, 1. *ingenerate*; of God, Synes.*hymn*.1.54(p.59; M.66.1589); **2.** *unborn*; of Christ in his divinity, Gr.Naz.*carm*.2.2(poem.)7.254(M.37.1571A); Mac.Mgn.*apocr*.2.8(p.9.12); of S. John as 'son' of BMV, Nonn.*par.Jo*.19:27(M.43.904B); **3.** *without travail*; of Christ's birth, Thdt.*qu.42 in Dt*.(1.290); Procl.CP *or*.3.3(M.65.705C); CTrull. *can*.79; of BMV, Thdr.Stud.*nativ.BMV* 7(M.96.696A).

ἅλς, ὁ; ἅλας, τό, *salt*;

A. lit.; **1.** in gen.; as sterilizing soil, Thdt.*qu.18 in Jud*.(1.335); as preservative, Mac.Aeg.*hom*.1.5(M.34.453D); applied by nurses to new-born infants, Thdt.*Cant*.proem.(2.11); eaten with bread as sole diet in fasting, *A.Thom*.A 20(p.131.7); *ib*.104(p.217.8); in pre-Easter fast μόνῳ χρώμενοι ἄρτῳ καὶ ἁ. καὶ λαχάνοις *Const.App*.5.18.1; **2.** used in magic βῶλον τῶν λεγομένων ὀρυκτῶν ἁ. κηρῷ Τυρρηνικῷ περισκεπάσας καὶ αὐτὸν δὲ τὸν λιβάνου βῶλον διχοτομήσας ἐντίθησι τοῦ ἁ. χόνδρον καὶ πάλιν συγκολλήσας ἐπ' ἀνθράκων καιομένων τιθεὶς ἐᾷ· τοῦ δὲ συγκαέντος οἱ ἅλες ἀναπηδῶντες φαντασίαν ἀπεργάζονται ὥσπερ ξένου θεάματος γινομένου Hipp.*haer*.4.28(p.56.28; M.16.3094A); **3.** religious uses; **a.** in OT sacrifices (Lev.2:13), allegorically interpreted, cf. *anima, nisi tentationibus assiduis quodammodo saliatur, continuo resolvitur ac relaxatur. unde constat propter hoc dictum esse quod omne sacrificium sale salietur*, Or.*hom*.27.12 *in Num*.(p.274.20; M.12.795C); κατεπάττετο δὲ ἁλσὶν ἡ θυσία, τοῦ τύπου σημαίνοντος τὸ ἐμφρόνως χρῆναι καθιεροῦσθαι θεῷ Cyr.*ador*.12(1.449A); δεῖ γὰρ...τῷ θείῳ φόβῳ, καθάπερ ἁλὶ καταπάττεσθαι τὴν διάνοιαν τῶν ἱερουργούντων θεῷ id.*hom.pasch*.1(5^2.22D); τὸ διακριτικὸν τῆς ψυχῆς διὰ τούτων σημαίνων. τούτου ἐστέρητο ἡ τοῦ Κάϊν θυσία Thdt.*qu.1 in Lev*.(1.181); id.*Cant*.proem.(2.11) cit. s. διαστύφω; μήνυμα δὲ οἱ ἁ. λογισμοῦ, καὶ διακρίσεως, καὶ φρονήματος εὐσεβοῦς id.*Ezech*.43:18–27(2.1032); cf.Proc.G.*Lev*.2:13(M.87.704B); in interprn. of 'covenant of salt' (Num.18:19); **i.** identified with law of Lev.2:13, Cyr.*ador*.12(1.448E); **ii.** other exegesis διαθήκην δὲ ἁλὸς τὴν κοινωνίαν ἐκάλεσεν, ἐπειδὴ...οἱ τῷ θυσιαστηρίῳ προσεδρεύοντες τῷ θυσιαστηρίῳ συμμερίζονται. τινὲς δέ φασιν ἐπειδὴ ταῖς θυσίαις ἐπιβάλλεσθαι τοὺς ἁ. προσέταξεν ὁ θεός, διαθήκην ἁλὸς τὰ ἀφιερωμένα τοῖς ἱερεῦσιν ὠνόμασεν Thdt.*qu.34 in Num*.(1.242); **b.** in eucharist τὸν ἄρτον καὶ τὸ ἁ. ἐν τῇ κλάσει τοῦ ἄρτου *A.Phil*.94 (p.36.30); τὸν ἄρτον ἐπ' εὐχαριστίᾳ κλάσας καὶ ἐπιθεὶς ἅλας *Hom.Clem*.14.1; Λατίνους...ἐχθίστους...χωρὶς ἁ. ... ἡμεῖς δέ, ἀνατρέποντες τὴν κακότροπον αὐτῶν γνώμην, τοῦ ἁ. ἐκ τοῦ ὕδατος γενομένου, καὶ εἰς τὸ ὕδωρ βληθέν· εἰ δύνασαι συνάξαι ἐκ τοῦ ὕδατος· εἰ δὲ μή, φλυαρείτω *Nomoc*.426; salt in eucharist signifies νοῦς of Christ, as leaven does his ψυχή, ‡Jo.D.*azym*.1(M.95.392A); **c.** invoked in Gnost. formulae; **i.** at baptism (Elchezaite), Hipp.*haer*.9.15(pp.253.19,254.11; M.16.3391A,C); **ii.** at eucharist δοξάζομέν σου τὸν σπόρον, τὸν λόγον, τὴν χάριν, τὴν πίστιν, τὸ ἁ. *A.Jo*.109(p.207.14); **4.** sharing of salt as token of friendship, ref. Judas πολλοὶ κοινωνήσαντες ἁ. καὶ τραπέζης ἐπεβούλευσαν τοῖς συνεστίοις Or.*Cels*.2.21(p.151.22; M.11.840C); πρὸς δὲ τὴν αὐτῆς [sc. ἀγάπης] εἴσοδον μία τίς ἐστιν ἱκανὴ πρόφασις, ἡ κοινὴ τῶν ἁ. μετάληψις *Clem.ep*.9(M.2.44B); λησταί, κοινωνήσαντες ἁλῶν, ἐπιλανθάνονται τοῦ τρόπου Chrys.*hom.32.7 in Mt*.(7.375C); *ib*.48.6(501D); hence 'covenant of salt' (2Par.13:5) τὸ βέβαιον τῆς βασιλείας ἐκάλεσεν. ἐπειδὴ καὶ βάρβαροι πολλάκις συνεσθίοντες πολεμίοις βεβαίαν εἰρήνην φυλάττουσι, τῶν ἁ. μεμνημένοι Thdt.*qu.1 in 2Par*.(1.573); in admission to communion with orthodox Church μετανοίᾳ δὲ ἀξιολόγῳ ἑκατέρους παραδεκτέον κοινωνῆσαι αὐτοῖς ἁλῶν τε, καὶ προσευχῶν [v.l. ἄλλων τε προσευχῶν] καὶ σφραγῖδος Thdr.Stud.*epp*.2.215 *qu*.9(M.99.1649D); **5.** ref. Lot's wife, *1Clem*.11.2; cf. *quod autem fit staticulum salis, insipientiae ejus indicium videtur expositum. sal enim prudentiae loco ponitur, quae ei defuit*, Or.*hom*.5.2 *in Gen*.(p.60.8; M.12.190B).

B. met.; **1.** salt as met. for *savour*, cf. *expositionis ordinem persequentes speramus quod dominus...tradat in manus nostras venationem, quam...rationabilis verbi salibus condientes benedictiones mereamur consequi a spiritali patre*, Or.*Cant*.3(p.216.30; M.13.179A); exeg. Mc.9:49, Col.4:6 διδαχθήσεται οἰκονομεῖν τοὺς λόγους εἰς οἰκοδομὴν τῆς πίστεως Bas.*reg.br*.266(2.506D; M.31.1264B); cf.Cyr. *hom.pasch*.1(5^2.21E); ἅ. δὲ τῶν παραινετικῶν λόγων ἢ τῶν θείων λογίων μαρτυρία...οὐ μόνον τοῖς εὐστομάχοις, ἀλλὰ καὶ τοῖς κακοσίτοις πρόσφορον...τροφὴν ὀρέγοντες Isid.Pel.*epp*.4.49(M.78.1100B); εἰ βρωθήσεται ἄρτος ἄνευ ἁ. ... οὕτω καὶ οἱ λόγοι...οὐκ ἔχοντες τὸ πιθανόν, ἢ τὸ εὔλογον, πείθειν οὐ δύνανται τοὺς ἀκούοντας Olymp.*Job* 6:6(M.93.89Af.); **2.** = *wisdom*, cf.Or.*hom*.5.2 *in Gen*.(p.60.8; M.12.190B); ἕως γὰρ ἂν μὴ τῷ θείῳ τῆς γραφῆς ἁ. τὸν περὶ μυστηρίου λόγον ἐπαρτύων προφέρῃ τὸ μεμωραμμένον τῆς ἔξω σοφίας ἁ. πατεῖσθαι παρὰ τῶν πιστῶν καταλείψωμεν Gr.Nyss.*Apoll*.34(M.45.1197D); Cyr. *hom.pasch*.1(5^2.21D); Thdt.*Cant*.proem.(2.11); id.*Ezech*.43:18–27(2.1032); **3.** = *doctrine*, *ib*.16:4(775); *ib*.16:8(777); **4.** Christians as 'salt of the earth' εἰ γὰρ φῶς ἐσμεν...καὶ ἅ. ... δεῖ σφίγγειν, οὐ παραλύειν Chrys.*hom*.25.2 *in 1Cor*.(10.222D); of an apostate Ἐκηβόλιος... πατήσατέ με, ἐβόα, τὸ ἅ. τὸ ἀναίσθητον Socr.*h.e*.3.13.6(M.67.413B); **5.** apostles in partic. as 'salt', Chrys.*hom.15.6 in Mt*.(7.193C); ἅ. αὐτοὶ ὑπάρχοντες ἤρτυον καὶ ἥλιζον πᾶσαν ψυχήν Mac.Aeg.*hom*.1.5 (M.34.453D); **6.** = grace of H. Ghost τὸ ἐπουράνιον ἅ. τοῦ πνεύματος *ib*.; οἱ ἠρτυμένοι τῷ ἁ. τῷ ἐπουρανίῳ φαίνονται, καὶ οἱ ἐκ τῶν θησαυρῶν τοῦ πνεύματος λαλοῦντες *ib*.15.52(612C).

ἀλσοκόμος, ὁ, *woodman, forester*, Thdt.*Ps*.103:16(1.1336); id. *affect*.8(p.196.7; 4.899).

***ἀλτάριον, τό,** (Lat. *altarium*) *altar*, Anton.Hag.*v.Sym.Styl*.29 (p.70.2).

***ἀλύγιστος,** ? *not mastered* or *overthrown*, *steadfast* ἄσκησιν ἀ. ‡Chrys.*hom*.13(13.253B).

ἀλύκη, ἡ, *distress* of mind, *Max.invect*.(M.90.204B).

ἀλυκός, προσώπῳ...†ἀλυκῷ Hipp.*haer*.4.22(p.52.13; M.16.3087A) f.l. for ? λευκῷ, ? ἀλύπῳ.

[*]**ἄλυκτος,** f.l. for ἄλληκτος, *unceasing*, †Apoll.*met.Ps*.138:45 (M.33.1524A).

ἀλύπητος, *free from sorrow* or *pain* τὸν ἀ. αἰῶνα *2Clem*.19.4; Just.*dial*.69.7(M.6.640A).

ἀλυπήτως, *without feeling pain* or *grief*, Clem.*str*.7.12(p.51.7; M.9.497C).

ἀλυπία, ἡ, *freedom from pain* or *grief*; in future life, Just.*dial*. 45.4(M.6.573A).

ἄλυπος, 1. *free from pain* or *sorrow*; esp. of future life, Just.*dial*. 117.3(M.6.748A); ἐν τῇ καινῇ καὶ ἀ. κτίσει Meth.*symp*.9.1(p.114.9; M.18.177A ἀλύτῳ); *Hom.Clem*.11.17; and life in Eden, Ath.*inc*.3.4 (M.25.101C); **2.** *untroubled, undisturbed*, Eus.*v.C*.1.6(p.10.5; M.20.917B); τὰ τῆς εἰς θεὸν εὐσεβείας ἄ. τοῖς οἰκείοις ἐβράβευεν *ib*.1.13 (928B); **3.** *causing no pain, harmless, inoffensive*, id.*ep.Caes*.8(p.46.10; M.20.1544A).

ἀλυσίδετος, *bound with chains*, Ephr.3.445B.

ἀλυσιτελής, *unprofitable, useless, worthless*, of Arian baptism ἀ. ἔχουσι καὶ τὸ παρ' αὐτῶν διδόμενον ὕδωρ, λειπόμενον εὐσεβείᾳ Ath.*Ar*. 2.43(M.26.237B); ἀ. γὰρ ἡ πρὸς τοὺς ἑτεροφρόνας εἰρήνη Cyr.*Lc*.12:51 (M.72.757A); Gennad.*fr.Gen*.6:3(M.85.1641B); morally, Nil.*Magn*.38 (M.79.1016C).

ἀλυταρχέω, *hold office of* ἀλυτάρχης i.e. *chief of police* at Olympic games, Jo.Mal.*chron*.12 p.311(M.97.468C).

***ἀλυταρχικός,** *pertaining to the* ἀλυτάρχης, Jo.Mal.*chron*.12 p.312 (M.97.468C).

ἄλυτος, A. *not to be loosed* or *broken*; hence **1.** *indissoluble* or *indestructible* αἰωνίῳ καὶ ἀ. βασιλείᾳ Just.*dial*.117.3(M.6.748A); Tat. *orat*.25(p.27.6; M.6.861A); Synes.*hymn*.4.168(p.31; M.66.1606); φυσικῇ γεννήσει καὶ ἀ. ἑνώσει ‡Ath.*Apoll*.2.2(M.26.1133C); *irremediable*; of misfortunes, Isid.Pel.*epp*.5.314(M.78.1517D); **2.** *not to be resolved* (sc. into simpler elements) τὰ μὲν γὰρ πρὸς αἴσθησιν συμβάντα ἐστὶν ἁπλᾶ τε καὶ ἄ. Clem.*str*.8.3(p.83.26; M.9.568A); **3.** *irrefutable*, *ib*.5.1(p.329.4; 16A); *insoluble*, Diod.*Gen*.11:32(M.33.1573A).

B. *undissolved*, hence *unimpaired*; of the body by illness, Eus.*v.C.*4.53(p.139.15; M.20.1204B).

C. ? for ἀπόλυτος, *unhampered* ὃς μὲν γυμνὸς ἀποδυσάμενος εἰσῆλθεν ἐν τοῖς ὕδασιν...διὰ τὸ ἄ. αὐτὸν εἶναι, ἠδυνήθη διεξελθεῖν τὴν...θάλασσαν Mac.Aeg.*hom.*5.6(M.34.508A).

ἀλύτρωτος, *not redeemed*, Cyr.*Ps.*49:16(M.69.1084A).

ἄλφα, τό, *alpha*, first letter of the alphabet; ref. Gen.17:5 διὰ τί μὲν ἓν ἄ. πρώτῳ προσετέθη τῷ Ἀβραὰμ ὀνόματι θεολογεῖς Just.*dial.*113.2(M.6.736B); προσλαμβάνει τὸ ἄ., τὴν γνῶσιν τοῦ ἑνὸς καὶ μόνου θεοῦ, καὶ λέγεται Ἀβραάμ, ἀντὶ φυσιολόγου σοφὸς καὶ φιλόθεος γενόμενος Clem.*str.*5.1(p.331.7; M.9.20A); ἡμεῖς μὲν ἐχρησάμεθα τῷ ἄ. ἕως τοῦ ω [i.e. *all possible means*] Valent.Imp.*ep.episc.*ap.Thdt.*h.e.*4.8.4(3.957).

ἀλφάβητος, ὁ, ἡ, *alphabet* ἀρίστη πᾶσιν ἀ. αὕτη. Α ὑπακοή, Β νηστεία, Γ σάκκος, κτλ. Jo.Clim.*scal.*26(M.88.1017A); met., *first elements, rudiments*, *Apophth.Patr.*(M.65.89A).

***ἀλφ-έω,** = ἀλφαίνω, *seek*, in comparison of meaning of ἄλφα with that of Hebr. אֱלֶף which Epiph. derives from אָלַף (= *learn*) παρ' Ἕλλησι τὸ ~εῖν ζητεῖν συμβέβηκε καλεῖσθαι Epiph.*mens.*24(M.43.280D).

***ἀλφηστήρ, ὁ,** = ἀλφηστής, *one who is energetic, toiler*, *Orac.Sib.*1.98; *ib.*13.13.

***ἀλφιτουργέω,** *knead barley-bread*, Cyr.*hom.pasch.*6.10(5^2.75C).

ἀλώβητος, 1. *undamaged*; **a.** *unharmed* τὸ ποίημα τὸ ἐν ὑμῖν καὶ τὸ πλάσμα σῶον καὶ ἀ. διατηρήσαντας Eus.*Is.*42:25(M.24.396A); Isid.Pel.*epp.*1.135(M.78.272B); ἐκ...σατανικῆς ἐνεργείας ἀ. †Jo.D.*B.J.*25(M.96.1088B); fig. ἐν τῷ δοχείῳ τῆς ψυχῆς τὸ θέλημα τελεσφορήσαντες ἀ. τοῦ λόγου Meth.*symp.*3.8(p.37.15; M.18.76A); **b.** *unravished*, Thdt.*qu.63 in Gen.*tit.(1.75); **c.** *undefiled* ἀ. ψυχαί Meth.*symp.*4.3(p.48.8; M.18.89B); **d.** *intact*; of virginity of BMV, Sophr.H.*ep.syn.*(M.87.3176A); Jo.D.*hom.*8.10(M.96.716B); ref. union of natures in Christ τῆς θείας τοῦ σαρκωθέντος λόγου φύσεως ἀλώβητον, τό τε φυσικὸν θέλημα, καὶ τὴν οὐσιωδῶς προσοῦσαν ἐνέργειαν συντηρήσομεν Max.*opusc.*(M.91.76B); *ib.*(108B); ‡Caes.Naz.*dial.*133(M.38.1036); Jo.D.*f.o.*3.17(M.94.1069B) cit. s. ἀσύμφυρτος; **e.** *flawless* ὡς θυσίαν θεοῦ ἄμωμον καὶ ἀ. Bas.*moral.*80.6(2.314B; M.31.861C); ἔσοπτρον...ἀ. Dion.Ar.*d.n.*4.22(M.3.724B); *sound* ἀ. ... διδασκαλίας Nil.*epp.*3.279(M.79.521D); **2.** *not to be injured, free from possibility of harm*; of God, Zach.Mit.*opif.*(M.85.1048B); of Trin., ‡Caes.Naz.*dial.*3(M.38.860); of future life, Cyr.*ador.*15(1.546C); neut. as subst., *immunity*, Gr.Nyss.*fat.*(M.45.169C).

***ἀλωβήτως,** *without injury*, Cyr.*ador.*8(1.264C); τὴν πίστιν τηρήσαντας ἀ. Geo.Al.*v.Chrys.*41(p.216.17); καθ' ἕνωσιν ἀδιάσπαστον ἀ. ‡Meth.*Sym.et Ann.*4(M.18.356C).

[*]**ἀλώη, ἡ,** = ἀλόη, *bitter aloes*, Sophr.H.*mir.Cyr.et Jo.*67(M.87.3656C).

[*]**ἀλωητής, ὁ,** = ἀλοητής, *thresher*, exeg. Dt.25:4 μόσχος...ἀ. ὁ Χριστός· δι' αὐτοῦ γὰρ ἡ κάθαρσις καὶ ἡ τῶν περιττῶν πραγμάτων ἀπόθεσις Cyr.*ador.*3(1.99E).

ἀλωνίζω, *thresh* θερίσας καὶ ἀλωνίσας *Ev.Thom.*A 12(p.151).

ἅλως (ἅλων), ἡ, *threshing-floor*; met., of Christ ἡ ἀπαρχὴ τῆς ἅ. Epiph.*haer.*51.31(p.305.5; M.41.945A); exeg. Mt.3:12 ἅ., τὴν πάνδημον τῆς οἰκουμένης ἐκκλησίαν προσαγορεύει Isid.Pel.*epp.*1.65(M.78.225A).

***ἀλωσία, ἡ,** s.v.l., *captivity*, †Gregent.*disp.*(M.86.736D).

ἅλωσις, ἡ, *capture, conquest*; *destruction* τὴν τῶν πρωτοτόκων ἅ. Mel.*pass.*26 p.4.31.

ἀλώφητος, *unceasing, everlasting*, Nonn.*par.Jo.*10:10(M.43.833A); *ib.*12:25(853C); *ib.*15:9(873C).

***ἀμαγγάνευτος,** *not tricked out, unadorned* τὸ ἁπλοῦν καὶ ἀ. τῆς ὀρθοδόξου πίστεως κάλλος Procl.CP *Arm.*15(p.195.8; M.65.873A).

***ἀμάγευτος,** *unbewitched*, *Hom.Clem.*20.12.

***ἀμαθήτευτος,** *untaught*, of Christ ref. Jo.7:15 ἡ γραμμάτων ἀ. εἴδησις Sophr.H.*ep.syn.*(M.87.3176A).

***ἀμαθητεύτως,** *without instruction*, Nil.*exerc.*22(M.79.748D).

ἀμαίευτος, *without aid of midwife*, Nonn.*par.Jo.*3:6(M.43.768A).

ἀμάλακτος, *that cannot be softened*, hence *harsh, unyielding*; of people, Olymp.*Eccl.*7:18(M.93.568D); neut. as subst. ἀρεταὶ...τὸ πρὸς κακίαν ἀ. ἐν τοῖς πειρασμοῖς διασώζουσαι Gr.Nyss.*hom.4 in Cant.*(M.44.837B).

ἀμάλθακτος, 1. *unmitigated, unalleviated* ἀ. ... ἀπομεμένηκε φλεγμονή Cyr.*Nah.*40(3.515C); **2.** *unsoftened, stubborn* τὴν γνώμην ἀ. Ast.Am.*hom.*12(M.40.344C); of sinners, Cyr.*Mich.*53(3.444E); *unyielding* χρὴ...ἀρρενωπῶς ἀ. εἶναι Dion.Ar.*e.h.*2.3.5(M.3.401C).

ἄμαλλος, *without hair* or *nap* κουκούλια...ἄ. ὡς παιδίοις Pall.*h.Laus.*32(p.90.1; M.34.1100A).

***ἀμαντεύτως,** *without power of divination*, Didym.*Trin.*2.11(M.39.665C).

***ἁμαξηγέω,** *drive a wagon*, *T.Abr.*A 10(p.87.22).

[*]**ἁμαξητός, ἡ,** = ἁμαξιτός, *carriage-road, highway*, Cyr.*Is.*4.3(2.651D).

ἁμαξόβιος, *wagon-dwelling*; name of a Scythian people, Just.*dial.*117.5(M.6.748B); Chrys.*hom.15.3 in 2Cor.*(10.547A); Thdt.*Ps.*48:3(1.914).

***ἁμαούσιος,** *of one identical* or *coincident essence* οὐ γὰρ εἴπομεν ἁ., ἀλλ' ὁμοούσιον Epiph.*haer.*73.36(p.310.22; M.42.469A).

ἀμάρα, ἡ, *drain, sewer*, Chrys.*hom.29.4 in Heb.*(12.276C); †Jo.D.*B.J.*16(M.96.1001A); met., of Gnostics εἰς ἕνα βυθὸν ἀμάρας συνάγονται Hipp.*haer.*5.23(p.125.22; M.16.3191C); τὴν ἀ. ταύτην τῆς λοιδορίας Gr.Nyss.*Eun.*12(1 p.302.24; M.45.1013C); Chrys.*hom.13.4 in 1Tim.*(11.623E).

ἀμαράντινος, *unfading*, *A.Mt.*24(p.251.1).

ἀμάραντος, 1. *unfading*, *Apoc.Petr.*A 15; **2.** met., *imperishable, everlasting*, ref. 1Pet.5:4 τῆς ἁγνείας ἀ. ἐστι στέφανος Cyr.H.*catech.*5.4; τῇ ἀ. ἀγάπῃ Nil.*epp.*2.41(M.79.216A); ἡ τῶν ἔργων φαιδρότης ἀ. ἀποτίκτει...εὔκλειαν Cyr.*Jo.*4.1(4.344D); ἀ. τῆς εἰς Χριστὸν εὐσεβείας τὸ κάλλος id.*Pulch.*(p.26.13; 5^2.129A); of Christ τὴν ἐν τῷ σώματι αὐτοῦ θεῖαν ζωὴν τὴν ἀ. καὶ ἀκατάλυτον id.ap.*cat.Lc.*23:31(p.166.27), cf.Cyr.*Lc.*23:27(M.72.936C); neut. as subst. τὸ ἀ. τῆς ἐλπίδος Or.*adnot.in Lev.*23:49(M.17.20C); **3.** met., of persons, *not growing feeble, unfailing* ὁ γὰρ ταύτην [sc. τὴν ἀλήθειαν] ἔχων...ἀγήρως ἐστὶ καὶ ἀ. Pall.*v.Chrys.*20(p.137.24; M.47.77); **4.** τὸ ἀ. *never-fading flower, amaranth*, ref. 1Pet.5:4 ὁ γὰρ καλὸς τοῦ ἀ. στέφανος ἀπόκειται τῷ καλῶς πεπολιτευμένῳ Clem.*paed.*2.8(p.202.6; M.8.485A).

ἀμάρευμα, τό, *foul water carried off by drain*, met., of language, *filth*, Gr.Naz.*or.*36.1(M.36.265C); id.*carm.*2.2(poem.)7.111(M.37.1559A); Leont.B.*Nest.et Eut.*3(M.86.1376D).

ἁμαρτάν-ω, *sin* (v. ἁμαρτία); **1.** def. and gen. characteristics οἱ ἄνθρωποι...διχῶς ~ουσιν, ὑποβαίνοντες τὰς ἐντολὰς ἢ ὑπερβαίνοντες Or.*comm.in 1Cor.*7:1–4(*JTS* 9 p.500.2); πᾶς γὰρ ὁ ἀνομῶν ~ει οὐ παντὸς ~οντος ἀνομοῦντος Ath.*exp.Ps.*50:4f.(M.27.270B); τὸ ~ειν ἴσως ἀνθρώπινον Chrys.*Thdr.*1.15(1.26A); a matter not of necessity, but of free will and human weakness, ‡Just.*qu.et resp.*103(M.6.1348C–1349B); of choice ἐφ' ἡμῖν τὸ κατορθώσασθαι καὶ ἁμαρτῆσαι Meth.*res.*1.57(p.319.9; ἁμαρτήσασθαι M.41.1153A); classification οἶμαι κατὰ τέσσαρας τρόπους ~ειν τὸν ἄνθρωπον· κατὰ συναρπαγήν, κατὰ ἀπάτην, κατὰ ἄγνοιαν, κατὰ διάθεσιν· καὶ αἱ μὲν πρῶται τρεῖς, εὐχερῶς εἰς ἐπίγνωσιν καὶ μετάνοιαν ἔρχονται· ὁ δὲ ἐκ διαθέσεως ~ων, καὶ μήτε τῇ πείρᾳ μήτε τῷ χρόνῳ εἰς μετάνοιαν ἐρχόμενος, ἀνήκεστον ἔχει τὴν κόλασιν Max.*qu.dub.*5(M.90.789A); **2.** causes: absence of fear of God, Bas.*ep.*174(3.262B; M.32.652A); demons, Jo.Clim.*scal.*10(M.88.848C); the body, v. ψυχή; ignorance, Bas.*moral.*9.4(2.243B; M.31.717C); **3.** ref. difference in gravity of sins τῶν ~ομένων τὰ μὲν ἀκούσιά ἐστι, τὰ δὲ ἀπὸ γνώμης πονηρᾶς ~εται, καὶ ὁ τοῦ δικαίου ὅρος οὐχ ὁ αὐτὸς ἐπὶ τούτοις Bas.*hom.*12.9(2.107E; M.31.404A); †Bas.*Is.*18(1.389D,E; M.30.145B); τελεία...κακία, τὸ καὶ γνώμῃ καὶ πράξεσιν ~ειν *ib.*115(1.459A; M.30.304C); Thdr.Mops.*Rom.*7:5(p.125.18; M.66.808B); involuntary sin, *1Clem.*2.3; hence difference in punishment οὐ...ἀτιμώρητος ὁ κατὰ διάνοιαν ~ων, ἀλλ' ὅσον ἐλλείπει τοῦ κακοῦ, τοσοῦτον αὐτῷ τῶν πόνων ὑφαιρεθήσεται †Bas.*Is.*115(1.459B; M.30.304D); **4.** effects of sinning: estrangement from God, Herm.*mand.*9.1 ὁ ~ων...μακρύνων ἑαυτὸν τοῦ κυρίου †Bas.*Is.*17(1.389B; M.30.144D); *Const.App.*1.3.3; deterioration, Or.*Cels.*4.99(p.373.11; M.11.1180B); psychological effects, Clem.*str.*2.15(p.146.28; M.8.1000C); Or.*hom.16.10 in Jer.*(p.142.5ff.; M.13.452Bf.); **5.** ref. forgiveness of sin; conditional on repentance ἀφίενται αὐτοῖς αἱ ἁμαρτίαι πᾶσαι ἃς πρότερον ἥμαρτον, καὶ πᾶσιν τοῖς ἁγίοις τοῖς ἁμαρτήσασιν μέχρι ταύτης τῆς ἡμέρας, ἐὰν ἐξ ὅλης τῆς καρδίας μετανοήσωσιν Herm.*vis.*2.2.4; obstacles to forgiveness ἐὰν δέ τις ἐξ παρατάξεως ἁ. ... ἄφεσιν οὐχ ἕξει *Const.App.*2.23.2; refusal to become a Christian, Chrys.*hom.53.1 in Jo.*(8.311A); lack of repentance, id.*hom.60.2 in Mt.*(7.608E); †Cyr.*hom.div.*14(5^2.414A); **6.** ref. post-baptismal sin οὐδεὶς πίστιν ἐπαγγελλόμενος ~ει Ign.*Eph.*14.2; forgiveness possible once, Herm.*mand.*4.3.1–6 (v. ἁμαρτία); its punishment in next world εἰ δὲ μετὰ τὴν ἄφεσιν τῶν ἁμαρτημάτων καὶ τὴν οἰκονομίαν τοῦ λουτροῦ τῆς παλιγγενεσίας ~οιμεν, ὥσπερ ἡμεῖς οἱ πολλοὶ οἱ μὴ τελειωθέντες...μετὰ τὸ ~ειν δὲ καὶ σὺν τῷ ~ειν τινὰ δεόντως πράττοιμεν, τί ἡμᾶς περιμένει, κατανοητέον. ἆρα ἐὰν ἐξέλθωμεν τὸν βίον ἔχοντες ἁμαρτήματα, ἔχοντες δὲ καὶ ἀνδραγαθήματα, σωθησόμεθα μὲν διὰ τὰ ἀνδραγαθήματα, ἀπολυθησόμεθα δὲ περὶ τῶν ἐν γνώσει ἡμαρτημένων;...πρῶτον ἀποληψόμεθα τὰ κακά, καὶ μετὰ ταῦτα τὰ ἀγαθά Or.*hom.16.5 in Jer.*(p.137.5ff.; M.13.445Bff.); cf.

*ib.*1.5(p.84.7; 376B); ὁ δὲ ἁμαρτήσας μετὰ τὸ βάπτισμα, οὗτος, ἐὰν μὴ μεταγνῷ καὶ παύσηται τοῦ πλημμελεῖν, εἰς γέενναν κατακριθήσεται *Const.App.*2.7.2; **7.** prevention of sin by baptism οὐκ ἐκτὸς δὲ λουτροῦ δύναται πληροῦν τὸ οὐχ ~ειν Epiph.*haer.*61.4(p.384.28; M.41.1045A); **8.** ref. Christian attitude to sin and sinners δεῖ παραδεχθῆναι τὸν ἡμαρτηκότα καὶ μετανοοῦντα Herm.*mand.*4.1.8; id.*sim.* 8.6.5 cit. s. μετανοέω; οὐ δεῖ ἀδιαφορεῖν ἐπὶ τοῖς ~ουσιν, ἢ ἐφησυχάζειν αὐτοῖς. ὅτι δεῖ τὸν ἐλέγχοντα, μετὰ πάσης εὐσπλαγχνίας...καὶ σκοπῷ τοῦ ἐπιστρέψαι τὸν ~οντα, ἐλέγχειν Bas.*ep.*22.3(3.100C; M.32.292B); ὅταν ἴδῃς ἐπὶ μετανοίᾳ τῶν ἡμαρτημένων τὸν ἀδελφὸν ὀδυρόμενον, σύγκλαυσον τῷ τοιούτῳ id.*hom.*5.9(2.42C; M.31.257D); ἐπίπλησσε τοῖς ~ουσιν...τοὺς μετανοοῦντας προσδέχου, ὅτι κύριος ὁ θεὸς ...ἐπηγγείλατο ἄφεσιν παρασχεῖν τοῖς μετανοοῦσιν ἐφ' οἷς ἥμαρτον *Const.App.*2.12.1; [sc. ἐπίσκοπος] ἐξουσίαν ἔχων κρίνειν τοὺς ἡμαρτηκότας *ib.*2.11.2; εἰ...καταγινώσκεις τοῦ ἡμαρτηκότος, τίνος ἕνεκεν καὶ αὐτὸς ~εις; Chrys.*hom.*51.3 *in Jo.*(8.303A); μὴ τῷ πταίοντι, ἀλλὰ τῷ ὑποβάλλοντι δαίμονι τὴν μέμψιν ἐπιγραφέτω· οὐδεὶς γὰρ θέλει εἰς θεὸν ἁμαρτῆσαι εἰ καὶ ἀβίαστος πᾶς ἡμῶν τυγχάνει Jo.Clim.*scal.*10 (M.88.845D).

ἁμαρτάς, 1. fem. subst., *sin*, Or.*Cels.*7.5(p.156.29; M.11.1425D); Ath.*exp.Ps.*88:47(M.27.393C); Thdt.*Ps.*31:1(1.800); **2.** masc. subst., *sinner*, Epiph.*haer.*47.1(p.216.13; M.41.852B); **3.** adj. κακοήθη καὶ ἁ. σαρκικῆς ἐπιθυμίας ἐργασίαν *Lit.Marc.*(Brightman p.142.19).

ἁμάρτημα, τό, v. ἁμαρτία.

***ἁμαρτής,** *sinful* παρέδωκαν...ἀπόστολοι...ἁ. εἶναι τὸ μετὰ τὸ ὁρίσαι παρθενίαν, εἰς γάμον τρέπεσθαι Epiph.*haer.*61.6(p.386.23; M.41.1048C ἐφάμαρτον); διὰ τὸ ἁ. *ib.*61.4(p.385.5, v.l. ἀβαρές 1045B); *ib.*69.52 (p.199.4; M.42.281D).

***ἁμάρτησις, ἡ,** *sinning*, Herm.*vis.*2.2.5.

ἁμαρτητικός, *prone, subject, to sin*; *sinful*; **1.** in gen. αἱ δὲ φιλήδονοι καὶ ἁ. [sc. πράξεις] τῷ ἥττονι τῷ ἁ. [sc. πνεύματι] περιτίθενται Clem.*str.*4.26(p.321.23f.; M.8.1376A); *ib.*4.12(p.285.14,19; 1293A); Eus.*e.th.*1.12(p.72.32; M.24.849B); Cyr.H.*catech.*3.7; †Bas.*Is.*34(1.407E; M.30.188B); **2.** of soul and mind; **a.** in gen. θάνατος...ἡ ἐν σώματι κοινωνία τῆς ψυχῆς ἁ. οὔσης Clem.*str.*4.3(p.253.18; M.8.1224C); *ib.*4.22(p.309.11; 1348B); νοῦς...ἁ. Gr.Naz.*ep.*101(M.37.185C); **b.** sinful states of soul ὁ γὰρ ἐν ἀγνοίᾳ [opp. γνῶσις] ὢν ἁ. Clem.*str.*4.26 (p.323.7; M.8.1377A); **3.** of human actions, words, thoughts πᾶσα πρᾶξις...τοῦ ἐθνικοῦ ἁ. *ib.*6.14(p.487.29; M.9.336A); χεὶρ ἁμαρτωλοῦ, ἡ ἁ. πρᾶξις Or.*Ps.*70:4(p.90); εἰπεῖν λόγον ἁ. id.*hom.*20.8 *in Jer.* (p.190.19; M.13.520C); ἁ. λογισμούς ‡Ath.*Apoll.*2.6(M.26.1140C); *ib.* (1141A); **4.** origin of sinfulness τῶν...παρὰ φύσιν, ἔνθα τὸ ἁ. φύεται Clem.*str.*2.20(p.172.22; M.8.1053B); διάβολος δέ, οὐκ ἐκ φύσεως ἐπάναγκες τὸ ἁ. λαβών...ἀλλ' ἀγαθὸς κατασκευασθείς, διάβολος γέγονεν ἐξ οἰκείας προαιρέσεως Cyr.H.*catech.*2.4; God not cause of sinful thoughts, ‡Ath.*Apoll.*2.6(M.26.1140C); **5.** of sinful spirits, Epiph.*anc.*72(p.90.20; M.43.152B); **6.** of Christ; **a.** orthodox σάρκα τὴν αὐτὴν ἡμῖν ἔχοντα παθητήν τε καὶ ἁ. Gennad.*fr.Rom.*8:3f.(p.375.17, v.l. ἁμαρτεῖν ἐπιδεχομένην); in Apollinarian controversy Ἀπολινάριος...ἔλεγε γάρ, ὅτι ὁ νοῦς ἁ. τί ἐστιν. ἄτοπον δὲ...ὑπονοῆσαι περὶ τοῦ λόγου τοῦ θεοῦ, ὅτι συνήφθη τινὶ ἁ. ἡμεῖς δὲ λέγομεν, ὅτι τοὐναντίον τῷ ἁ. δεῖ μᾶλλον αὐτὸν ὑπονοῆσαι συναφθῆναι, τῷ καὶ σωτηρίας δεομένῳ †Leont.B.*sect.*4.2(M.86.1220Cf.); **b.** Basilidean ἄνθρωπον ἁ. τολμήσας [sc. Basilides] εἰπεῖν τὸν κύριον Clem.*str.*4.12(p.285.20; M.8.1293B).

***ἁμαρτητικῶς,** *sinfully* σαρκικῶς ἰδὼν καὶ ἁ. Clem.*str.*4.18(p.299.14; M.8.1324B); opp. τελείως, *ib.*6.6(p.454.22; M.9.268B); τὰ ἁ. πραττόμενα †Bas.*Is.*186(1.517A; M.30.436B); οὐ κακὸν τὸ σῶμα τῇ φύσει, κἂν κακὸν αὐτὸ ποιεῖ ὁ ἁμαρτωλός, ἁ. αὐτῷ χρώμενος Didym.*Man.*5 (M.39.1092D); *ib.*8(1096C); ref. Christ ὑπομένων δὲ τὰ σαρκὸς...πάθη οὐκ ἐξ αὐτῶν ἁ. ἐκινεῖτο...οὐχ ἁ. ... ἄνθρωπος, ἀλλ' ὁμοίως...ἐνεργείᾳ ὡς ἄνθρωπος...ὥσπερ...οὐχ ἁ. ἀλλ' ὁμοίως τοῖς ἐν σαρκὶ ἐκινεῖτο CAnc.(358)*ep.syn.*ap.Epiph.*haer.*73.9(pp.279.27–280.6; M.42.420A,B).

ἁμαρτία, ἡ; ἁμάρτημα, τό, I. non-theol. meanings;

A. *slip, fall* (ἁμαρτία), Clem.*paed.*3.8(p.261.32; M.8.616A).

B. *slip, error*; **1.** of the pen γραφικὸν...ἁ. Or.*hom.*15.5 *in Jer.* (p.129.13; M.13.433D); **2.** of interprn. βουλόμενος [sc. Origen] μηδὲν τῶν θείων γραφῶν ἐᾶσαι ἀνερμήνευτον, εἰς ἐπαγωγὴν ἑαυτὸν περιέβαλεν ἁμαρτίας καὶ θανάσιμα ἐξηγήσατο ῥήματα Epiph.*haer.*64.3(p.409.5; M.41.1076A); οὐδὲ γὰρ δεῖ τὰ ῥήματα γυμνὰ ἐξετάζειν, ἐπεὶ πολλὰ ἕψεται τὰ ἁ. Chrys.*comm.in Gal.*1:17(10.675A); λέξεώς τε κίνδυνον μηδένα εἶναι, ἣν μὴ περὶ ἔννοιαν ἡ ἁ. γένηται Soz.*h.e.*3.18.4(M.67.1096C); **3.** doctrinal ὅσης δὲ τόλμης ἐστὶ τοῦτο τὸ ἁ. εἰκὸς μηδὲ ἐκείνους ἀγνοεῖν †Hipp.*Artem.*ap.Eus.*h.e.*5.28.18(M.20.517A); τὸ ἁ. ...διηγούμενος Philost.*h.e.*1.2(M.65.461B); **4.** of a faulty product of nature οἱ μὲν πόρναις διδόντες, οἱ δὲ...μωροῖς καὶ νάννοις· καὶ γὰρ τὰ τῆς φύσεως ἁ. ταῦτα φέρουσιν εἰς τέρψιν Chrys.*hom.*3.3 *in 1Tim.* (11.565E).

C. *failure to attain, lack* οὐκ ἔστι τοῦτο ἔφεσις, ἀλλὰ τῆς ὄντως ἐφέσεως ἁμαρτία Dion.Ar.*d.n.*4.34(M.3.733D); *ib.*4.35(736A).

II. *sin* (the two forms are gen. used interchangeably, though ἁμαρτία emphasizes sin in the abstract, ἁμάρτημα the individual act) τὸ ἁμαρτίας ὄνομα, οὐκ οὐσίαν ὑφεστῶσαν δηλοῖ, ἀλλὰ τρόπον καὶ βίον τοῦ διημαρτηκέναι τινὰ τοῦ κατὰ λόγον...ὥσπερ γὰρ γενικώτατόν ἐστιν ὄνομα ἡ ἁ., κατὰ πολλῶν καὶ διαφόρων πραγμάτων κατηγορουμένη. πᾶν δὲ ἁμάρτημα οὔτε λόγῳ, οὔτε νόμῳ προστατικῷ γίνεται· εἰ γὰρ κατὰ νόμον καὶ λόγον ἐγίνετο ὀρθόν, οὐκ ἔτι ἂν ἦν ἁμάρτημα...ἐπειδὴ ὁ θεῖος ἀπόστολος οὐχ ἁπλῶς ἁμαρτημάτων ἀλλ' ἁμαρτίας γενικωτάτης ἐχούσης φρόνημα...μνημονεύει, οὐκ ἄλλον τινὰ γενικωτάτως ἁμαρτίαν ὀνομάζει, ἀλλ' ἢ αὐτὸν τὸν τῶν ἁμαρτημάτων... πατέρα διάβολον, ὅτου χάριν καὶ βασιλεύειν τῶν ἁμαρτημάτων αὐτὸν ὁ ἀπόστολος ἀπεφήνατο...τὸν διάβολον ὡς πρώτως ἐφευρέτην γενόμενον τῆς ἁ., ἁμαρτίαν καλεῖ Diod.ap.*cat.Rom.*7:18(p.110.7ff.).

A. nature of sin; **1.** def.; **a.** moral; death of soul, Clem.*prot.*11 (p.81.18; M.8.233B); id.*paed.*1.2(p.92.12; M.8.253B); id.*str.*3.9(p.225.19; M.8.1165C); Or.*Jo.*19.14 (3; p.313.21; M.14.549C); Bas.*hom.*5.9(2.42D; M.31.260A); Gr.Naz.*or.*18.42(M.35.1041A); estrangement from God, Gr.Naz.*carm.*1.2.8.184(M.37.662A); Gr.Nyss.*Eun.*2(2 p.366.7; M.45.545B); ‡Proc.G.*Pr.*12:28(M.87.1348A); evil life, Clem.*str.*2.15(p.146.19; 1000C); a falling away from the good, or a transgression of the law ἡ δὲ ἁ. ἐστὶ τοῦ καλοῦ παρεκτροπή, ὃ μὴ φύσις τε καὶ νόμος χαρίζεται Gr.Naz.*carm.*1.2.34.179(958A); πτῶσις δέ ἐστιν ἡ ἁ. Gr.Nyss.*ep.can.*(M.45.221B); κατὰ παράβασιν νόμου τὴν ἁ. συνίστασθαι...ἡ ἔκκλισις, ἁ. ἐστίν, ἀποτυχία οὖσα τῆς εὐθείας ὁδοῦ Diod.*Ps.*52:4(M.33.1590D–1591A); ‡Caes.Naz.*dial.*123(M.38.1016); equated with pride, †Bas.*Is.*267(1.583B; M.30.589B); and folly, †Bas.*hom.in Ps.*37(1.366D; M.30.92D); with the flesh, Gr.Nyss.*nativ.* (M.46.1136C); **b.** metaphysical, as negation of being οὐδὲν γὰρ ἡ ἔχθρα οὐδ' ἡ ἁ. ἄνευ τοῦ ἐχθροῦ καὶ τοῦ ἁμαρτάνοντος Clem.*str.*4.18 (p.289.25; M.8.1301A); ἁ. ἀπότευγμα φύσεώς ἐστιν, οὐκ ἰδίωμα Gr.Nyss.*ep.*3(M.46.1020D); μὴ νόμιζε...ζῶόν τι λογικὸν τὴν ἁ. ὑπάρχειν Nil.*epp.*2.309(M.79.352B); νόθον ἡ ἁ. καὶ παρὰ φύσιν ‡Cyr.*Trin.*15 (6^3.21B; M.77.1152C); *ib.*(22D; M.1153C); **2.** conditions constituting an action a sin, distinguishing it from πάθος q.v.; **a.** possession of reason; exeg. Jo.15:22, with play on Logos and logos οὐκ ἄλλο νοητέον ἢ ὅτι ὁ λόγος φησίν, οἷς οὐδέπω συμπεπλήρωται μὴ εἶναι ἁ., τούτους δὲ ἐνόχους αὐτῆς τυγχάνειν...πῶς δὲ ἀληθὲς τὸ μὴ ἔχειν ἁ. τούτους, οἷς οὐκ ἐλήλυθε [sc. Christ]; πάντες γὰρ οἱ πρὸ τῆς ἐπιδημίας τοῦ σωτῆρος ἔσονται ἁ. πάσης ἀπολελυμένοι, ἐπεὶ οὐκ ἐλήλυθει...Ἰησοῦς. ἀλλὰ καὶ πάντες, οἷς οὐδαμῶς ἀνηγγέλη περὶ αὐτοῦ, οὐχ ἕξουσιν ἁ., καὶ δῆλον ὅτι οἱ μὴ ἔχοντες ἁ. κρίσει οὐχ ὑπόκεινται. λόγος δὲ...διχῶς λέγεται, ἤτοι κατὰ τὴν συμπλήρωσιν τῶν ἐννοιῶν... ἢ κατὰ τὴν ἀκρότητα...κατὰ...τὸ πρότερον τὸ 'εἰ μὴ ἦλθον καὶ ἐλάλησα αὐτοῖς, ἁμαρτίαν οὐκ εἴχοσαν'...τὰ ῥητὰ ἐκδεκτέον Or.*Jo.*1.37(42; p.48.8ff.; M.14.97Bf.); οὐχ ἡ πρᾶξις ἁμάρτημα ἁπλῶς, ἀλλὰ τὸ εἰδότα ὧν ἀπέχεσθαι προσήκει, ποιεῖν τι παρὰ τὰ ἐγνωσμένα καλῶς ἔχειν Thdr.Mops.*Rom.*7:8(p.127.36; M.66.812B); **b.** presence of the law νόμος...ὑπαγορεύει τὰ ποιητέα εἴργει τε ἕκαστον τῶν ἁμαρτημάτων Clem.*str.*1.27 (p.106.26; M.8.920A); exeg. Rom.7:8f. διδάσκων περὶ τῆς ἁ. ὡς μηδεμίαν ἐνέργειαν αὐτῆς ἐχούσης πρὶν νόμου καὶ ἐντολῆς ...οὐκ ἂν εἴη ἁ. μὴ ὄντος νόμου...καὶ πάλιν οὐκ ἂν εἴη ἁ. μὴ ὄντος λόγου...πᾶσα γὰρ πρόφασις ἀφαιρεῖται τοῦ βουλομένου ἐπὶ τῇ ἁ. ἀπολογήσασθαι, ἐπὰν ἐνυπάρχοντος λόγου...μὴ πείθηταί τις αὐτῷ Or.*Jo.*2.15(9; p.71.9ff.; 140B,C); Meth.*res.*2.2(p.331.7; M.18.297B); **3.** universality of sin πάντες ὀφειλέται ἐσμὲν ἁμαρτίας Polyc.*ep.* 6.1; θυσίαν περὶ ἁ. λέγουσιν ἀναφέρεσθαι καὶ περὶ τῶν ἄρτι γεγενημένων ὡς οὐ καθαρῶν ἀπὸ ἁ. Or.*Cels.*7.50(p.200.24; M.11.1493A); calling for universality of redemption ἄτοπον ὑπὲρ ἀνθρωπίνων μὲν αὐτὸν φάσκειν ἁμαρτημάτων γεγεῦσθαι θανάτου, οὐκ ἔτι δὲ καὶ ὑπὲρ ἄλλου τινὸς παρὰ τὸν ἄνθρωπον ἐν ἁμαρτήμασι γεγενημένων, οἷον ὑπὲρ ἄστρων οὐδὲ τῶν ἄστρων πάντως καθαρῶν ὄντων ἐνώπιον τοῦ θεοῦ id. *Jo.*1.35(40; p.45.25ff.; M.14.93B); ἐγράφησαν αἱ ἁ. τῶν ἁγίων, ἵνα ἀλήθεια γνωσθῇ Serap.*Man.*25(p.41; M.40.921B); εὐπερίστατον γὰρ ἡ ἁ., πάντοθεν ἱσταμένη, ἔμπροσθεν, ὄπισθεν, καὶ οὕτως ἡμᾶς καταβάλλουσα Chrys.*hom.*2.7 *in 2Cor.*(10.438C).

B. origin of sin; **1.** of original sin; **a.** caused by Devil, who is therefore called ἀρχηγὸς ἁμαρτίας, Cyr.H.*catech.*2.4; τῷ σπορεῖ τῆς ἁ. ... διαβόλῳ Max.*qu.Thal.*61(M.90.633B) = *cap.*4.47(M.90.1325C); and equated with sin ἁ. ἔθος καλεῖν τῇ γραφῇ τὸν διάβολον. διὰ τί; ἐπειδὴ ἐγένετο διδάσκαλος καὶ εἰσηγητής...ἁμαρτίας ‡Chrys.*hom.in Rom.*7:19(8.190C); **b.** due to Eve τὴν Εὔαν...ἀρχηγὸν ἁμαρτίας γεγονέναι Thphl.Ant.*Autol.*2.28(M.6.1096A); ἤρξατο ἡ ἁ. ἀπὸ τῆς γυναικός Or.*hom.8 in Lc.*(p.55.1); *A.Phil.*142(p.81.8); Ath.*exp.Ps.* 50:7(M.27.240D); *ἐξ ἀρχῆς τῆς φύσεως ἡ ἁ. κεκράτηκε. προῦλαβε γὰρ τῆς Εὔας τὴν σύλληψιν τῆς ἐντολῆς ἡ παράβασις. μετὰ γὰρ τὴν παράβασιν...ἔγνω Ἀδὰμ Εὔαν...καὶ...ἔτεκε τὸν Κάϊν. τοῦτο τοίνυν εἰπεῖν βούλεται, ὅτι τῶν ἡμετέρων προγόνων κρατήσασα ἡ ἁ., ὁδόν τινα...διὰ τοῦ γένους εἰργάσατο* Thdt.*Ps.*50:7(1.936); **c.** to Adam *Ἀδὰμ κακῶς φαγών, τὴν ἁ. παρέπεμψεν* Bas.*hom.*7.7(2.70D; M.31.324C); *ἥμαρτεν ὁ Ἀδὰμ τὴν ἁ. ἐκείνην τὴν χαλεπήν, καὶ τὸ...ἀνθρώπων κατεδίκασε γένος* Chrys.*ep.*3.3(3.554C); *ἐντεῦθεν ἡ ἁ. πάροδον ἔσχεν, τῆς μὲν ἐντολῆς ἐπεχούσης τὴν βρῶσιν, τοῦ δὲ Ἀδὰμ οὐ πρὸς τὴν ἀξιοπιστίαν τῆς ἐντολῆς βουληθέντος ἰδεῖν* Thdr.Mops.*Rom.*7:8(p.127.6; M.66. 809C); **2.** actual sin; **a.** originating in men's free will *ἅπερ πάντα κακία καὶ ἁ. ψυχῆς ἐστιν. αἰτία δὲ τούτων οὐδεμία, ἀλλ' ἡ τῶν κρειττόνων ἀποστροφή* Ath.*gent.*5(M.25.12B); *οὐκ ἄρα τὰ μέλη τῆς ἁ. αἴτια· ἀλλ' οἱ χρώμενοι τοῖς μέλεσι κακῶς* Cyr.H.*catech.*9.15; *ψυχὴ... δεκτικὴ ἁμαρτίας ἐξ ἀβουλίας ἐγένετο* Gr.Nyss.*Eun.*2(2 p.366.23; M.45.545D); *ἀρχὴ γὰρ ἁμαρτίας...ἡ προαίρεσις* Nemes.*nat.hom.*40 (M.40.769B); *Ἀδὰμ...ἔχων τὸ αὐτεξούσιον προαιρέσει ἰδίᾳ ἀφ' ἑαυτοῦ τὴν ἁμαρτίαν εἰς ἑαυτὸν διανοηθεὶς ἔπραξε* Epiph.*haer.*42.12(p.158.2; M.41.776D); *ἡ ἁ. οὐκ ἔστι τῆς φύσεως, ἀλλὰ τῆς κακῆς προαιρέσεως* Thdt.*eran.*1(4.13); Max.*qu.Thal.*61(M.90.629C); **b.** through ignorance and weakness (v. *ἄγνοια*), Clem.*str.*7.16(p.71.24; M.9.540C); *πᾶσα ἁ. τὴν ἀρχὴν ἐξ ἀφροσύνης ἔχει* Chrys.*hom.41.3 in Jo.*(8.247A); Leont.B.*Nest.et Eut.*3(M.86.1373B); **c.** through pride and disobedience *ἁμάρτημα...ἀπὸ ὕβρεως* Chrys.*hom.2.3 in Eph.*(11.13B); *παρακοῆς ἔργον ἐστὶν ἡ ἁ.* Max.*cap.theol.*2.7(M.90.1128B); **d.** through addiction to material pleasures *φιληδονία, φιλοδοξία καὶ φιλαργυρία, ἐξ ὧν συνίσταται πᾶσα ἁ.* Dor.*doct.*13.8(M.88.1769C); and neglect of prayer, Gr.Nyss.*or.dom.*1(p.4.30; M.44.1121B) cit. s. *εὐχή*; **e.** through human and diabolic interaction *ὁ δὲ κατατυραννούμενος ὑπὸ τοῦ ἄρχοντος τούτου τοῦ αἰῶνος τῷ ἑκουσίῳ τῆς ἁ. καὶ βασιλεύεται ὑπὸ τῆς ἁ.* Or.*or.*24.1(p.357.20; M.11.497A); *ἐκ τῶν ὑποκειμένων ἐν τῇ ψυχῇ παθῶν λαμβάνουσιν οἱ δαίμονες τὰς ἀφορμὰς τοῦ κινεῖν ἐν ἡμῖν τοὺς ἐμπαθεῖς λογισμούς. εἶτα διὰ τούτων πολεμοῦντες τὸν νοῦν, ἐκβιάζονται αὐτὸν εἰς συγκατάθεσιν ἐλθεῖν τῆς ἁ. ἡττηθέντος δὲ αὐτοῦ, ἄγουσιν εἰς τὴν κατὰ διάνοιαν ἁ. καὶ ταύτης ἀποτελεσθείσης, φέρουσιν αὐτὸν λοιπὸν αἰχμάλωτον εἰς τὴν πρᾶξιν. μετὰ δὲ ταύτην...ὑποχωροῦσι. μένει δὲ μόνον ἐν τῷ νῷ τὸ εἴδωλον τῆς ἁ.* Max.*carit.*2.31(M.90.993C); **f.** but never caused by God, Meth.*symp.*8.16(p.109.13; M.18.172C); **3.** pagan and unorthodox views on origin of sin; **a.** pagan: related to stars, Meth.*symp.*8.13(p.99.3; M.18.161A) cit. s. *ἀστήρ*; **b.** Origen: pre-natal sin, Or.*princ.*1.8.1(p.97.1) cit. s. *ψυχή*; *τὴν ψυχὴν...λέγει* [sc. Origen] *προϋπάρχειν, ἀγγέλους δὲ ταύτας* [sc. *ψυχάς*] *εἶναι...ἐν ἁμαρτίαις δὲ ἀμπλακησάσας καὶ τούτου ἕνεκεν εἰς τιμωρίαν εἰς τοῦτο τὸ σῶμα κατακεκλεισμένας* Epiph.*haer.*64.4(p.411.3; M.41. 1076D); **c.** but Methodius holds that sin is impossible for a being without a body *ἄληπτος γὰρ καθ' ἑαυτὴν ἡ ψυχὴ...τῇ ἁ.* Meth.*res.* 1.57(p.318.4; M.41.1152C); *τὸ σῶμα...βλασφημιῶν καὶ παντοίων αἴτιον ἁμαρτημάτων, διὰ τὸ μὴ δύνασθαι καθ' ἑαυτὴν δίχα σώματος ὅλως ἁμαρτῆσαι ψυχήν* *ib.*1.29(p.258.16; M.41.1136D); *πόρρω...ἁμαρτίας ἐσκήνωται τὰ πνευματικά* *ib.*2.2(p.332.16; M.18.300B); id.*lepr.*9(p.463. 13); **d.** Manich. *ἔστιν ἁ. σύνοικος ἐξ ἀνάγκης καὶ βίας, κατὰ τὰ Μανιχαϊκὰ δόγματα, οὖσα ἐν τῇ ψυχῇ ἀγαθῇ οὔσῃ* *Disp.Phot.*3(M.88.549A); **e.** Apollinarian argument *ὅπου γὰρ τέλειος ἄνθρωπος, ἐκεῖ καὶ ἁ. καὶ ὅτι δύο τέλεια ἓν γενέσθαι οὐ δύναται· ἐπεὶ ἔσται καὶ ἐν Χριστῷ ἡ ἐν ἡμῖν μάχη τῆς ἁ.· καὶ ἔσται αὐτῷ χρεία τοῦ καθ' ἡμᾶς καθαρισμοῦ, εἰ τὸ φρονοῦν καὶ τὸ ἄγον ἐν ἡμῖν τὴν σάρκα Χριστὸς ἐν ἑαυτῷ ἐπιδέδεικται γενόμενος ἄνθρωπος. ἀλλὰ ἔλαβε, φασί, τὸ ἀνόητον, ἵν' αὐτὸς ᾖ νοῦς ἐν αὐτῷ, καὶ ἄγευστος...τῆς ἁ. ... οὔτε γὰρ ἁμάρτοι ἂν ἡ σὰρξ τοῦ ἄγοντος τὴν σάρκα, τουτέστι τοῦ φρονοῦντος, μὴ προενθυμηθέντος τὴν πρᾶξιν τῆς ἁ., καὶ ἐνεργήσαντος διὰ τοῦ σώματος εἰς ἐκπλήρωσιν τῆς ἁ. ὅθεν σαρκὸς μὲν καινότητα Χριστὸς ἐπιδέδεικται καθ' ὁμοίωσιν ...οὕτως νοεῖται Χριστὸς χωρὶς ἁ.* ‡Ath.*Apoll.*1.2(M.26.1096B,C); orthodox counter-argument *τὸν διάβολον καὶ νόμον ἁμαρτίας καταστήσασθαι ἐν τῇ φύσει τοῦ ἀνθρώπου...ἐν τῇ λογικῇ καὶ νοερᾷ φύσει τοῦ ἀνθρώπου ἐπισπείρας εἰργάσατο διάβολος τὴν ἁ. ... διὰ τοῦτο δι' ἑαυτοῦ ἦλθεν ὁ υἱὸς τοῦ θεοῦ ταύτην* [sc. *σάρκα*] *ἐν τῇ ἰδίᾳ φύσει καταστήσασθαι ...εἰ δὲ μὴ ἐν τῇ ἁμαρτησάσῃ φύσει ἡ ἀναμαρτησία ὤφθη, πῶς κατεκρίθη ἡ ἁ. ἐν τῇ σαρκί...;...δι' ἧς φύσεως ἡ προχώρησις τῆς ἁ. γέγονε δι' αὐτῆς καὶ ἡ ἐπίδειξις τῆς δικαιοσύνης γένηται· καὶ οὕτω λυθῇ τὰ ἔργα τοῦ διαβόλου, ἐλευθερωθείσης τῆς ἀνθρώπου φύσεως ἀπὸ τῆς ἁ.* *ib.*2.6(1141A–D); for if the body itself is sinful, as Marcion and Gnostics hold, *ib.*1.12(1116A), no true Inc. is possible, *ib.*1.14 (1120A,B); but *ὅτε τὸν Ἀδὰμ ἀρχῆθεν ἔπλασεν ὁ θεός, μήτιγε σύμφυτον αὐτῷ δέδωκε τὴν ἁ.* *ib.*1.15(1120B).

C. kinds and gravity of sins; **1.** classification *δοκεῖ...τριῶν ἀποχὴν ἁμαρτίας τρόπων διδάσκειν ὁ νομοθέτης* [sc. Moses], *τῶν μὲν ἐν λόγῳ...τῶν δὲ ἐν ἔργῳ...καὶ χρὴ μηδὲ τὴν συνείδησιν ἔχειν μεμολυσμένην* Clem.*str.*2.15(p.149.17; M.8.1008A); *οὐκ εἰσὶ μόνον τρία μέρη τῆς ἁ. ... ἀλλὰ μυρία* Mac.Aeg.*hom.*3.4(M.34.469D); *παρὰ φύσιν ἐστὶν ἡ Σοδόμων ἁ. καὶ ἡ πρὸς ἄλογα, παράνομον δὲ μοιχεία καὶ πορνεία, ὧν τὰ μὲν ἀσεβήματα, τὰ δὲ ἀδικία καὶ τὸ τελευταῖον ἁμάρτημα* *Const.App.*6.28.2; **2.** various kinds: e.g. **a.** sins not subject to Law, Clem.*str.*4.17(p.295.19; M.8.1313C); **b.** sins that are against reason, id.*paed.*1.2(p.92.19; M.8.253B); **c.** heresy and schism, Chrys.*hom. 11.5 in Eph.*(11.88A); **d.** (peculiar to Origen) prayer to Son *ἐὰν οἱ μὲν τῷ πατρὶ οἱ δὲ τῷ υἱῷ εὐχώμεθα, ἰδιωτικὴν ἁ. κατὰ πολλὴν ἀκεραιότητα διὰ τὸ ἀβασάνιστον...ἁμαρτανόντων τῶν προσευχομένων τῷ υἱῷ, εἴτε μετὰ τοῦ πατρὸς εἴτε χωρὶς τοῦ πατρός* Or.*or.*16.1(p.336. 8; M.11.468C); **e.** sins of omission *ἐὰν γὰρ ἐγκρατεύσῃ τὸ ἀγαθὸν μὴ ποιεῖν, ἁ. μεγάλην ἐργάζῃ* Herm.*mand.*8.2; **3.** gen. statements on gravity of sin *κακὸν ἔσχατον ἡ ἁ.* Chrys.*exp.in Ps.*12(5.125D); *οὐδὲν γὰρ οὕτως ἀλόγιστον, ὡς ἁ., οὐδὲν οὕτως ἀνόητον καὶ μωρὸν καὶ ῥαγδαῖον· πάντα ἀνατρέπει καὶ συγχεῖ καὶ ἀπόλλυσι ἔνθα ἂν εἰσπηδήσῃ· ἀηδὴς ἰδεῖν, φορτικὴ καὶ ἐπαχθής. καὶ εἴ τις αὐτὴν ἀνέπλαττε ζωγράφος, οὐκ ἄν μοι δοκεῖ ἁμαρτεῖν οὕτως αὐτὴν ἀναπλάττων, γυναῖκά τινα θηριόμορφον, βάρβαρον, πῦρ πνέουσαν, ἀτερπῆ, μέλαιναν* id.*hom.9.4 in 1Cor.*(10.78C); id.*hom.41.4 in Ac.*(9.313D); **4.** on differences in gravity: in gen., Clem.*str.*2.15(p.148.20; M.8.1004B); *κατὰ τὴν διαφέρουσαν μερίδα τῷ κυρίῳ γινομένας ἁ., πρότερον μὲν ἀνεκτὰς... ὕστερον δὲ πλείονας μὲν ἀλλ' ἔτι ἀνεκτὰς* Or.*Cels.*5.31(p.33.3; M.11. 1228B); id.*hom.2.2 in Jer.*(p.18.26ff.; M.13.280C); Chrys.*hom.61.1 in Mt.*(7.611D); **5.** various individual sins considered greater than others; **a.** sin of the Jews *ἐπὶ Ῥωμαίων τὴν μεγίστην ποιήσαντες ἁ. ἐν τῷ ἀποκτεῖναι τὸν Ἰησοῦν* Or.*Cels.*4.32(p.303.15; M.11.1077C); reenacted by Christians returning to sins after baptism, id.*Jo.*20.12 (p.342.1; M.14.600A); **b.** idolatry, id.*mart.*32(p.28.11; M.11.604B); *μείζων εἰδωλολατρείας οὐκ ἔστιν ἁ., εἰς θεὸν γάρ ἐστιν δυσσέβεια* *Const.App.*2.23.1; **c.** sins against fraternal charity, ‡Ath.*qu.Ant.* 76(M.28.645B); **d.** unworthy Communion, †Jo.Jej.*poenit.*(M.88. 1905A); **6.** sins aggravated by accompanying circumstances: sin of unbelief greater after seeing miracles, Or.*princ.*3.1.17(p.229.6; M. 11.285C); other sins increased by judging others, Chrys.*hom.2.5 in Rom.16:3*(3.189D); id.*hom.23.2 in Mt.*(7.287A); *οὐχ εἷς λόγος τῶν τὴν αὐτὴν ἁ. κατ' ἐνέργειαν ἁμαρτανόντων ἐστίν, ἀλλὰ διάφοροι. οἷον, ἄλλο ἐστὶ τὸ ἀπὸ ἕξεως ἁμαρτάνειν, καὶ ἄλλο τὸ κατὰ συναρπαγήν· ὅς, οὔτε πρὸ τῆς ἁ. εἶχε τὴν ἐνθύμησιν, οὔτε μετὰ τὴν ἁ.· ἀλλὰ καὶ σφόδρα ἐπὶ τῷ γεγονότι ὀδυνᾶται. ὁ δὲ ἀπὸ ἕξεως, ἐκ τοῦ ἐναντίου· καὶ πρῶτον γὰρ κατὰ διάνοιαν οὐκ ἐπαύετο ἁμαρτάνων, καὶ μετὰ τὸ πρᾶξαι, τῆς αὐτῆς ἐστι διαθέσεως* Max.*carit.*3.74(M.90.1040C); by refusing obedience to priests, Chrys.*David* 3.1(4.769C); by asking for punishment of sins of others, id.*exp.in Ps.*4(5.12A); **7.** lightened through being committed inadvertently *ἡ ἐν τῇ ἀγνοίᾳ ἁ. συγχωρεῖται* Cyr.H.*catech.*3.8; though not exempt from punishment, ‡Cyr.*Trin.*15(6[3].21D; M.77.1152D); or through immediate repentance, as was sin of Adam, Or.*hom.16.4 in Jer.*(p.136.22; M.13. 444C); **8.** 'sin unto death' (1Jo.5:16), v. *θάνατος*; **9.** sin against H. Ghost (Mt.12:31f.) *πάντα προφήτην λαλοῦντα ἐν πνεύματι οὐ πειράσετε οὐδὲ διακρινεῖτε· πᾶσα γὰρ ἁ. ἀφεθήσεται, αὕτη δὲ ἡ ἁ. οὐκ ἀφεθήσεται* *Did.*11.7; *οὐ...διὰ τὸ τιμιώτερον εἶναι τὸ πνεῦμα τὸ ἅγιον τοῦ Χριστοῦ οὐ γίνεται ἄφεσις τῷ εἰς αὐτὸν ἡμαρτηκότι, ἀλλὰ διὰ τὸ Χριστοῦ μὲν πάντα μετέχειν τὰ λογικά, οἷς δίδοται συγγνώμη μεταβαλλομένοις ἀπὸ τῶν ἁμαρτημάτων, τοῦ δὲ ἁγίου πνεύματος τοὺς κατηξιωμένους μηδεμιᾶς εὔλογον εἶναι συγγνώμης τυχεῖν μετὰ τηλικαύτης...συμπνοίας τῆς εἰς τὸ καλόν* Or.*Jo.*2.11(6; p.66.13; M.14. 129C); interpreted of those who deny equality of H. Ghost with Son, Amph.*ep.syn.*(M.39.97B); but unforgivable only if unrepented *οὐκ εἶπεν ὁ Χριστός· τῷ βλασφημήσαντι καὶ μετανοήσαντι οὐκ ἀφεθήσεται· ἀλλὰ τῷ βλασφημοῦντι, εἴτ' οὖν, τῷ ἐν τῇ βλασφημίᾳ ἐπιμένοντι· ἐπειδήπερ οὐκ ἔστιν ἁ. ἀσυγχώρητος παρὰ τῷ θεῷ τοῖς γνησίως καὶ κατ' ἀξίαν μετανοοῦσιν* ‡Ath.*comm.essent.*49(M.28.77A); cf. *ἐν ἁ. τελευτήσαντι μετάνοια οὐκ ἔστιν* *Const.App.*2.13.2; **10.** other sins which, acc. individual opinions, cannot be forgiven *οὐκ οἶδ' ὅπως ἑαυτοῖς τινες ἐπιτρέψαντες τὰ ὑπὲρ τὴν ἱερατικὴν ἀξίαν, τάχα μηδὲ ἀκριβοῦντες τὴν ἱερατικὴν ἐπιστήμην, αὐχοῦσιν ὡς δυνάμενοι καὶ εἰδωλολατρείας συγχωρεῖν μοιχείας τε καὶ πορνείας ἀφιέναι, ὡς διὰ τῆς εὐχῆς αὐτῶν περὶ τῶν ταῦτα τετολμηκότων λυομένης καὶ τῆς πρὸς θάνατον ἁ.* Or.*or.*28.10(p.381.16; M.11.529B); but, acc. Or. *οἶδα δέ τινας οὐ μόνον ἐν τῷ αἰῶνι τούτῳ, ἀλλὰ καὶ ἐν τῷ μέλλοντι κρατουμένους ὑπὸ τῆς ἰδίας ἁ. ... οὐ μέντοιγε εἰ μὴ ἐν τῷ μέλλοντι αἰῶνι, ἤδη οὐδὲ ἐν τοῖς αἰῶσιν τοῖς ἐπερχομένοις* id.*Jo.*19.14(3; p.314.9; M.14.552A).

D. consequences of sin; **1.** of original sin (though not always clearly distinguishable from those of actual sin); **a.** vitiating of man's relationship with God, Or.*Cels.*7.39(p.190.4; M.11.1476D); Cyr.H.*catech.*13.33; **b.** and of his human nature ἐκ παρακοῆς ἐντολῆς θεοῦ γέγονεν ὁ ἄνθρωπος δεκτικὸς τῆς ἐπισπορᾶς τοῦ ἐχθροῦ. καὶ ἐνήργει λοιπὸν ἡ ἁ. ἐν τῇ φύσει τοῦ ἀνθρώπου πρὸς πᾶσαν ἐπιθυμίαν ‡Ath.*Apoll.*1.15(M.26.1120C); Chrys.*hom.15.4 in Gen.*(4.120D) cit. s. παράβασις; Cyr.*ep.*17.9(p.39.9; 5^2.74C); διὰ τὴν παράβασιν ἡ ἁ., διὰ δὲ τὴν ἁ. τὸ παθητὸν κατὰ τὴν γέννησιν τῇ φύσει τῶν ἀνθρώπων ἐπεισῆλθε, καὶ συνήκμαζεν ἀεὶ τῷ παθητῷ τῆς γεννήσεως διὰ τῆς ἁ. ἡ πρώτη παράβασις Max.*qu.Thal.*21(M.90.313A); propagation through generation being a punishment of sin, *ib.*(312C); **c.** inequality among men τὸν ἀδελφὸν...ἐπεισελθοῦσα ἡ ἁ. δοῦλον εἰργάσατο ...ἐπειδὴ δὲ εἰσῆλθεν ἡ ἁ., ἐλυμήνατο τὴν ἐλευθερίαν, καὶ διέφθειρε τὴν ἀπὸ τῆς φύσεως δεδομένην ἀξίαν Chrys.*hom.29.6 in Gen.*(4.289Df.); **2.** of actual sin; **a.** objective effects in society: premature deaths, id.*hom.in 1Cor.7*:2(3.196E); lowering of moral standards ἁ. γὰρ ἀνεξέλεγκτος ἑαυτῆς χείρων γίνεται καὶ εἰς ἄλλους τὴν διανομὴν λαμβάνει *Const.App.*2.17.4; Bas.*hom.in Ps.*1(1.96E; M.29.225C); **b.** physical effects on individual τὸ οὖν εἶναί τινας παραλελυμένους...καὶ ἀσθενοῦντας, τοῦτο ἐκ τῆς ἁ. προσεγένετο Mac.Aeg.*hom.*16.4(M.34.616C); πάντα ...τὰ νοσήματα ἐξ ἁμαρτημάτων; οὐ πάντα μέν, ἀλλὰ τὰ πλείονα Chrys.*hom.38.1 in Jo.*(8.217A); πᾶν ὃ ἐὰν πάθωμεν, ἐκ τῶν ἁ. ἡμῶν πάσχομεν Dor.*doct.*7.4(M.88.1701D); this view repudiated τὸ...πυρετὸν νομίζειν διὰ τὰς ἁ. γίνεσθαι ἀπαιδεύτων εἰς ὑπερβολήν ἐστι δόγμα, πολλάκις τῶν αἰτίων τῆς τοιᾶσδε νόσου προδήλων ὄντων Or.*sel.in Ps.*4 (M.12.1157C); **c.** psychological effects τὸ αἴτιον τοῦ φόβου, τὴν ἁ. Clem.*str.*4.3(p.252.22; M.8.1224A); οὐδὲν γὰρ οὕτω βαρεῖ ψυχήν, οὐδὲν οὕτω πηροῖ διάνοιαν καὶ πιέζει κάτω, ὡς ἁμαρτίας συνειδός Chrys.*hom.38.3 in Mt.*(7.429C); ἡ γὰρ ἁ., ἕως μὲν ἂν ὠδίνηται, ἔχει τινὰ αἰσχύνην· ἐπειδὰν δὲ τελεσθῇ, ἀναισχυντοτέρους ποιεῖ τοὺς ἐργαζομένους αὐτήν id.*hom.10.1 in Ac.*(9.80C); comprehensive description of these effects, Or.*hom.16.10 in Jer.*(p.142.5ff.; M.13.452Bf.); cf. ἡ ἁ. τῇ ψυχῇ μεμιγμένη ἐστίν, ἐχούσης ἑκάστης ἰδίαν φύσιν Mac.Aeg.*hom.*2.2(M.34.464D); *ib.*15.28(593D); **d.** spiritual effects: alienation from God, Chrys.*stat.*6.6(2.81D); loss of God's promises, *Barn.*14.1, and salvation, Cyr.H.*catech.*18.20; Gr.Nyss.*ep.can.*(M.45.221C); loss of freedom, Clem.*prot.*11(p.78.30; M.8.228C); Diod.*Ps.*52:7(M.33.1591B); †Bas.*Is.*170(1.501A; M.30.400C); Chrys.*serm.4.2 in Gen.*(4.660C); blinding of spiritual perception, Clem.*paed.*1.6(p.106.22; M.8.284A); †Bas.*Is.*109(455A; M.296A); engendering of more sins, *ib.*230(553E; M.521A); Chrys.*hom.86.3 in Mt.*(7.815A); **3.** punishment; **a.** proportionate to gravity of sins ὁ νόμος οὐ παντὸς ἁμαρτήματος τὴν αὐτὴν ἐποιεῖτο τιμωρίαν, ἀλλὰ ἄλλως μὲν τὰ εἰς θεὸν καὶ εἰς ἱερέα καὶ εἰς ἱερὸν καὶ εἰς ἱερεῖον, ἑτέρως δὲ τὰ εἰς βασιλέα καὶ ἄρχοντα... οὐκοῦν καὶ ὑμεῖς τῶν διαφόρων ἁμαρτημάτων διαφόρους ποιεῖσθε καὶ τὰς τιμωρίας *Const.App.*2.48.2,3; αἱ συγγενεῖς γὰρ ἁ. ὁμοιοτρόπως κολάζονται †Bas.*Is.*88(1.440D; M.30.264A); μελλούσης αὐτῶν κολάσεως καθ' ὁμοίωσιν τῶν πάλαι ἁμαρτημάτων Euthal.Diac.*epp.cath.*(M.85.689C); τοῦ θεοῦ φιλανθρωπία...πολλῷ τῆς ἁ. ἐλάττονα τὴν τιμωρίαν ἐπάγουσα Chrys.*Is.interp.*1(6.8D); id.*Laz.*6.3(1.775D); **b.** effected by God, Clem.*prot.*10(p.75.6; M.8.220C); **c.** through Devil τοῦ δράκοντος τοῦ κολάζοντος πᾶσαν ψυχὴν τὴν ἐν ἁμαρτίαις οὖσαν *A.Phil.*140(p.76.3); **d.** martyrdom conceived as punishment for sins committed in former life (Basilides), Clem.*str.*4.12(p.286.32; M.8.1296B).

E. healing of sin (v. ἄφεσις); **1.** through divine agency; **a.** God the source of forgiveness, *A.Jo.*54(p.178.13); τὸ γὰρ ἀφεῖναι ἁμαρτίας, οὐδενὸς ἑτέρου ἐστί Chrys.*hom.54.1 in Jo.*(8.316C); God's action dist. from human co-operation τὸ ἐκριζῶσαι τὴν ἁ. ... τῇ θείᾳ δυνάμει μόνον δυνατόν ἐστι...οὐκ ἔξεστι γὰρ οὔτε δυνατὸν ἀνθρώπῳ ἐξ ἰδίας δυνάμεως ἐκριζῶσαι τὴν ἁ.· τὸ ἀντιπαλαῖσαι, τὸ ἀντιμαχεσθῆναι...σόν ἐστιν· ἐκριζῶσαι δέ, θεοῦ ἐστιν Mac.Aeg.*hom.*3.4(M.34.469C); **b.** Christ, Clem.*str.*2.15(p.148.14; M.8.1004B); ὁ κύριος...τὰ μὲν ἁ. ὡς θεὸς ἀφιείς, εἰς δὲ τὸ μὴ ἐξαμαρτάνειν παραπαιδαγωγῶν ὡς ἄνθρωπος id.*paed.*1.3(p.94.7; M.8.257A); *ib.*1.6(p.120.22; 309C); *A.Thom.*A 58(p.174.19); Or.*Jo.*1.4(6; p.7.32; M.14.29B); id.*Cels.*2.67(p.189.18; M.11.901B); Ath.*decr.*5(p.4.15; M.25.'432'(424)A); id. *Ar.*3.31(M.26.388D); εἷς μόνος ἀναμάρτητος, ὁ τὰς ἁ. ἡμῶν καθαρίζων Ἰησοῦς Cyr.H.*catech.*2.10; exeg. Is.53:7, Gal.5:18 οὐκ...ὅλον κατάραν καὶ ἁ. αὐτὸν νοοῦμεν γεγενῆσθαι...τὰς δὲ ἁ. ἡμῶν...ἐβάστασεν Ath.*Ar.*2.47(M.26.248A); through Inc. θεὸς ὢν ἄνθρωπος ἐγένετο... ἀνελὼν τὸ κέντρον τῆς ἁ. *A.Phil.*141(p.77.2); ἑαυτοῦ παρουσίαν διὰ σαρκός...καθ' ἣν...ἀφέσεως ἁμαρτημάτων Meth.*symp.*7.6(p.77.12; M.18.133A); Ath.*inc.*14.2(M.25.120C); Max.*qu.Thal.*61(M.90.633A); being himself sinless, Or.*Cels.*1.69(p.123.16; M.11.789A); †Bas.*Is.*67(1.428B; M.30.236A); Max.*qu.Thal.*21(312B); through Passion and death, Or.*Cels.*1.55(p.106.17; 761C); id.*hom.17 in Lc.*(p.118.12); Ath.*Ar.*1.45(105A); Cyr.H.*catech.*13.33; Thdr.Mops.*Jo.*1:29(p.316.12; M.66.733D–736A) cit. s. ἀμνός; Max.*qu.Thal.*61(M.90.633D); which, though salvation for us, became occasion of sin to Jews, Clem.*paed.*2.8(p.195.18; M.8.468C); through his blood τῇ ἀφέσει τῶν ἁ. ἁγνισθῶμεν, ὅ ἐστιν ἐν τῷ αἵματι τοῦ ῥαντίσματος αὐτοῦ *Barn.*5.1; τοῦ αἵματος τοῦ Χριστοῦ, δι' οὗ...ἄδικοι...σώζονται, ἄφεσιν ἁμαρτιῶν λαβόντες Just.*dial.*111.4(M.6.733A); ὁ τὸ τίμιον αἷμα ὑπὲρ ἡμῶν ἐκχέας, αὐτὸς ἡμᾶς ῥύσεται τῆς ἁ. Cyr.H.*catech.*2.5; Chrys.*hom.1.3 in Eph.*(11.7B); v. αἷμα; through Cross, Clem.*paed.*3.12(p.283.9; M.8.664B); combined with baptism, Just.*dial.*86.6(681C); through baptism καταβαίνομεν εἰς τὸ ὕδωρ γέμοντες ἁμαρτιῶν,...καὶ ἀναβαίνομεν καρποφοροῦντες ἐν τῇ καρδίᾳ *Barn.*11.11; τὸ βάπτισμα...ἁμαρτιῶν ἐστιν ἄφεσις *A.Thom.*A 132(p.239.9); which, however, wipes out only original, not actual, sin ἡ τοῦ Ἀδὰμ ἁ. διελθοῦσα εἰς τὸ ἔθνος... Χριστοῦ οὖν συγχωρήσαντος ταύτην διὰ τοῦ λουτροῦ τῆς ἀφέσεως, ἐκαθαρίσθη μὲν ἡ προπατορικὴ ἁ., ἕκαστος δὲ τῶν οἰκείων ἁμαρτημάτων ὑπέχει λόγον Olymp.*fr.Jer.*31:30(M.93.689Cf.); ‡Ath.*qu.Ant.*67 (M.28.636A); v. βάπτισμα; through eucharist, *A.Thom.*A 50(p.166.20); τὸ ποτήριον τοῦτο αἷμα τοῦ Χριστοῦ σου...ἵνα οἱ μεταλαβόντες αὐτοῦ...ἀφέσεως ἁμαρτημάτων τύχωσιν *Lit.*ap.*Const.App.*8.12.39; ἀξίους εἶναι πάντοτε πρὸς τὴν τῶν οὐρανίων μυστηρίων ὑποδοχήν, ἐπεὶ καὶ ἀφέσεως ἁμαρτιῶν οὕτω καταξιούμεθα ‡Pall.*h.mon.*8(p.48.20; M.34.1148B); *Lit.Jac.*(p.236.3); forgiveness to be found only in New Covenant αὕτη δὲ καινή, καὶ ἄφεσιν ἁμαρτιῶν ἔχουσα Chrys.*hom.19.1 in Heb.*(12.180B); Thdt.*Ps.*50:21(1.944); Law being powerless, ‡Bas.Sel.*or.*38.2(M.85.405B); in Church καθολικὴ [sc. ἐκκλησία] ...καλεῖται διὰ τὸ κατὰ πάσης εἶναι τῆς οἰκουμένης...καὶ διὰ τὸ καθολικῶς...θεραπεύειν ἅπαν τὸ τῶν ἁμαρτιῶν εἶδος, τῶν διὰ ψυχῆς καὶ σώματος ἐπιτελουμένων Cyr.H.*catech.*18.23; **2.** with human co-operation, good will being essential, cf.Cyr.H.*procatech.*8; Chrys.*hom.1.2 in Philm.*(11.777C,D); **a.** through repentance and confession, Herm.*vis.*2.2.4; μετάνοια, δι' ἣν ἄφεσις ἁμαρτιῶν Clem.*str.*2.3(p.118.31; M.8.941C); *ib.*4.6(p.260.13,15; 1240B); μετάνοια τότε ἁμαρτήματος παντὸς γίνεται ἀπαλειπτική, ὅταν ἐπὶ τῷ γινομένῳ ψυχῆς σφάλματι ἀναβολὴν μὴ δέξηται Meth.*Porph.*4(p.507.8); δεινὸν... κακὸν...ἡ ἁ.· ἀλλ' οὐκ ἀθεράπευτον· δεινὸν τῷ κατέχοντι, εὐΐατον δὲ τῷ διὰ μετανοίας ἀποτιθεμένῳ Cyr.H.*catech.*2.1; †Bas.*Is.*278 (1.591E; M.30.609A); ἐξομολογήσει καὶ μετανοίᾳ...ἀποσμηξαμένους τὴν...ἁ. Chrys.*David* 3.2(4.770C); Chrys.*poenit.*3.4(2.300Bf.); esp. sacramental confession εἰδὼς...θεὸς ὅτι νέοι βαπτιζόμενοι καὶ προβαίνοντες ἐν ἡλικίᾳ μολύνομεν διὰ τὰς ἁ. τὸν ἐξ ὕδατος καὶ πνεύματος ἐξυφανθέντα ἡμῖν χιτῶνα τῆς ἀφθαρσίας, δέδωκεν ἡμῖν...δι' ἐξομολογήσεως καὶ μετανοίας καθαίρειν τοῦτον †Jo.Jej.*serm.*(M.88.1921A); cf. †Jo.Jej.*poenit.*(M.88.1889A,B) et passim; though, acc. one opinion, confession does not make worthy immediately ἐξομολογησώμεθα περὶ ἁμαρτημάτων πρὸ πεντεκαίδεκα ἐτῶν γεγενημένων, τῷ μηκέτι ἁμαρτίαν ἔχειν μετ' ἐκεῖνα ἐπὶ πεντεκαίδεκα ἔτη. εἰ δὲ χθὲς ἡμάρτομεν, οὔπω ἀξιόπιστοί ἐσμεν ἐξομολογούμενοι περὶ τῶν ἁμαρτημάτων ἡμῶν· οὐδὲ χώραν ἔχει ἀπαλειφ⟨θ⟩ῆναι τὰ ἁ. ἡμῶν ταῦτα Or.*hom.5.10 in Jer.*(p.39.21ff.; M.13.309A); but cf. ἡ ὁμολογία τῆς ἁ. λύσις ἐστὶ τῆς ἁ. Chrys.*exp.in Ps.*140(5.438B); ‡Chrys.*hom.1 in Ps.50*(5.537D); **b.** by almsgiving and other good works, *2Clem.*16.4; Chrys.*hom.1.3 in Philm.*(11.778D); Dor.*doct.*14.6(M.88.1784B); through which even original sin may be removed δὸς ὀλίγα, καὶ πολλὰ κτῆσαι· λῦσον τὴν πρωτότυπον ἁ. τῇ τῆς τροφῆς μεταδόσει Bas.*hom.*7.7(2.70D; M.31.324C); manual work, *Barn.*19.10 ∞ *Did.*4.6; keeping commandments, *1Clem.*50.5; Just.*dial.*95.3(M.6.701D); refraining from judging others, ‡Ath.*qu.Ant.*77(M.28.645C) and forgiving one's enemies, Chrys.*David* 3.9(4.783C); suffering and martyrdom, Herm.*sim.*9.28.3; Or.*mart.*39(p.37.12; M.11.616B); Chrys.*stat.*5.4(2.66B); summary, id.*hom.8.2 in Jo.*(8.47Bf.); **3.** question of post-baptismal sin: one repentance granted, Herm.*mand.*4.3.1–6 cit. s. μετάνοια; Clem.*str.*2.13(p.143.15ff.; M.8.993B); ὁ...ἐξ ἐθνῶν...ἐπὶ τὴν πίστιν ὁρμήσας ἅπαξ ἔτυχεν ἀφέσεως ἁμαρτιῶν. ὁ δὲ καὶ μετὰ ταῦτα ἁμαρτήσας, εἶτα μετανοῶν, κἂν συγγνώμης τυγχάνῃ, αἰδεῖσθαι ὀφείλει *ib.*(p.144.13; 996C); but repeated forgiveness of post-baptismal sin accepted from end of third cent., Meth.*res.*1.41(pp.286.12–287.5; M.18.269Bf.); Chrys.*hom.19.5 in Mt.*(7.252C); ἂν ἔχῃς ἁμαρτήματα, μὴ ἀπογνῷς·...κἂν καθ' ἡμέραν ἁμαρτάνῃς, καθ' ἡμέραν μετανόει...ἐπαλαιώθης σήμερον ἀπὸ τῆς ἁ.; ἀνακαίνισον σεαυτὸν ἀπὸ τῆς μετανοίας ...πάντα τὸν βίον ἐν ἁμαρτίαις διέτριψα, καὶ ἐὰν μετανοήσω σώσομαι; πάνυ id.*poenit.*8.1(2.341B); v. βάπτισμα; **4.** eccl. legislation concerning forgiveness of sins; **a.** exclusion from communion διὰ μολυσμὸν ἁμαρτιῶν Cyr.H.*catech.*23.23; **b.** degradation of clerics οἱ τὴν πρὸς θάνατον ἁ. ἁμαρτάνοντες κληρικοί, τοῦ βαθμοῦ κατάγονται, τῆς κοινωνίας δὲ τῶν λαϊκῶν οὐκ ἐξείργονται Bas.*ep.*199 *can.*32(3.295A; M.32.728A); **c.** penance to be imposed acc. gravity of sin, *Const. App.*2.16.2; **d.** Novatianist ὁ Ἀσκληπιάδης, ἐκτός, ἔφη, τοῦ ἐπιθῦσαι, καὶ ἄλλαι πολλαὶ κατὰ τὰς γραφάς εἰσιν ἁ. πρὸς θάνατον, δι' ἃς...ἡμεῖς ...τοὺς λαϊκοὺς ἀποκλείομεν, θεῷ μόνῳ τὴν συγχώρησιν αὐτῶν ἐπιτρέποντες Socr.*h.e.*7.25.19(M.67.796D); *ib.*1.10.3(101A); **5.** preventatives of sin; **a.** charity, Polyc.*ep.*3.3; Chrys.*hom.44.3 in 1Cor.*(10.410C); Max.*carit.*2.81(M.90.1009B); **b.** salutary fear and other remedies, Clem.*paed.*1.9(p.139.1; M.8.349B); δύο τῷ γένει καὶ παιδεῖαι παραδίδονται πρόσφοροι ἑκατέρᾳ τῶν ἁ., τῇ μὲν ἡ γνῶσίς τε καὶ ἡ τῆς ἐκ τῶν γραφῶν μαρτυρίας ἐναργὴς ἀπόδειξις, τῇ δὲ ἡ κατὰ λόγον ἄσκησις ἐκ πίστεώς τε καὶ φόβου παιδαγωγουμένη id.*str.*7.16(p.72.4; M.9.541A); τὸ δὲ μετὰ τὸ βάπτισμα μεῖναι νεκροὺς τῇ ἁ., τῆς ἡμετέρας δεῖ γενέσθαι ἔργον σπουδῆς, εἰ καὶ...τὸν θεὸν ὁρῶμεν βοηθοῦντα ἡμῖν Chrys.*hom.11.1 in Rom.*(9.530C); daily examination of minor faults, id.*hom.60.4 in Gen.*(4.582A); μὴ τοίνυν ὦμεν ῥάθυμοι τοῖς μικροῖς ἁ., ἀλλὰ μετὰ πολλῆς αὐτὰ ἀναστέλλωμεν τῆς σφοδρότητος id.*exp.in Ps.*6 (5.49C); *ib.*(48D); **6.** healing of sin through death τὸν θάνατον ὁ θεὸς πρὸς ἀναίρεσιν τῆς ἁ. ὑπὲρ ἡμῶν ἀνεύρατο Meth.*res.*2.6(p.339.18; M.18.304B); ἐδύνατο ζῆν εἰς τὸν αἰῶνα τὸ σῶμα...ἐκωλύθη δέ, ὅπως ἡ μὲν ἁ. συναποκτανθεῖσα τῷ σώματι θάνῃ, τὸ δὲ σῶμα ἀναστῇ τῆς ἁ. ἀπολομένης *ib.*1.40(p.285.2; M.41.1108D–1109A); τοῦ θεοῦ τὸ ἁ. λύσαντος θανάτῳ, ἵνα μὴ ἀθανάτως ἁμάρτωλος ὁ ἄνθρωπος ὤν, ζώσης ἐν αὐτῷ τῆς ἁ., αἰωνίως κατάκριτος γενηθῇ id.*symp.*9.2(p.116.12,14; M.18.181A); ἀνάστασις τοῦτό ἐστι, ψυχῆς καθαρμός, καὶ ἁμαρτιῶν ἀπαλλαγή Chrys.*hom.66.3 in Jo.*(8.398B).

F. sin and spiritual life; **1.** prevents communion with God, *T.Reub.*4.6; ὅταν ᾖ ἁ. ἐν τῷ ἀνθρώπῳ, οὐ δύναται...θεωρεῖν τὸν θεόν Thphl.Ant.*Autol.*1.2(M.6.1028A); Cyr.*Ps.*50:17(M.69.1101B); hence is greatest hindrance to prayer, †Bas.*Is.*177(1.509A; M.30.417C); freedom from sin being necessary for prayer, Clem.*str.*7.12(p.52.23; M.9.501A); Or.*or.*2.2(p.300.15; M.11.420A); *ib.*13.5(p.330.5; 460A); v. εὐχή; **2.** freedom from sin characteristic of the perfect man, Clem. *str.*2.11(p.139.18; M.8.985B); *ib.*6.12(p.480.31ff.; M.9.320A); id.*paed.* 1.6(p.121.20f.; M.8.312C) cit. s. τελείωσις; Or.*or.*22.3(p.348.9; M.11. 485A); id.*Jo.*20.26(21; p.362.21; M.14.633C); δεῖ ὡς ἀληθῶς σωθησόμενον, μὴ μόνον τῇ προαιρέσει νεκρῶσαι τὴν ἁ., ἀλλὰ καὶ αὐτὴν τὴν προαίρεσιν τῇ ἁ. ... ἵνα νεκρὰ νεκρᾶς, ὅλη ὅλης τῆς ἁ. διαιρεθεῖσα μὴ αἰσθάνηται...ὁ γὰρ νεκρώσας τῇ ἁ. τὴν προαίρεσιν, σύμφυτος γέγονε τῷ ὁμοιώματι τοῦ θανάτου τοῦ Χριστοῦ Max.*cap.*4.23(M.90.1313B); full human co-operation essential to complete destruction of sin, id.*qu.Thal.*61(M.90.636D–637A).

***ἁμαρτικός,** *sinful, liable to sin* χεὶρ ἁμαρτωλοῦ, ἡ ἁ. ἐστι πρᾶξις Diod.*Ps.*70:4(M.33.1608C), cf. ἁμαρτητικός; of soul, Gr.Nyss.*Apoll.* 23(M.45.1172A); Cyr.*Ps.*16:8(M.69.813B); of BMV ξύλον ἄσηπτον, ἡ φθορᾶς ἁ. μὴ προσηκαμένη σκώληκα Thdr.Stud.*nativ.BMV* 7(M.96. 693C).

ἁμαρτίνοος, *erring in mind* (with moral connotation); of Pharisees, Nonn.*par.Jo.*1:24(M.43.753B); *ib.*7:32(809B); of the disciples, *ib.*6:61(801B).

***ἁμαρτοέπεια, ἡ,** *false speech* τίς...τοῖς πεφλυαρηκόσιν ἡ τῆς ἁ. πρόφασις; Cyr.*Mal.*40(3.861D; ἁμαρτίας Aubert).

ἁμαρτοεπής, *false-speaking*, Cyr.*glaph.Gen.*7(1.224D); id.*Nah.*13 (3.491A); id.*ador.*6(1.185A).

ἀμαρτύρητος, *without proof, unproved*, Cyr.*Jo.*2.1(4.153C).

ἀμάρτυρος, 1. act., *not bearing witness*, Meth.*res.*1.42(p.287.13; M. 41.1109D); c. genit. ἵνα μὴ ἁ. ἑαυτὸν ποιήσῃ [sc. ὁ κύριος] τῆς θείας χάριτος Mac.Aeg.*hom.*15.29(M.34.596A); **2.** pass., *unattested, not sanctioned* ὥστε μὴ ἁ. εἶναι τὴν οἰκονομίαν τῆς ἐκκλησίας CChalc.*can.*26

ἀμαρτύρως, *without being a martyr*, of Marcionites οἳ δὴ αὐτοὺς παραδιδόναι σπεύδουσι τῇ πρὸς τὸν δημιουργὸν ἀπεχθείᾳ...τούτους ἐξάγειν ἑαυτοὺς ἁ. λέγομεν Clem.*str.*4.4(p.256.14; M.8.1229C).

***ἁμαρτωλοποιός,** *making a sinner* (i.e. *convicting of sin*), Leont. B.*mesopent.*(M.86.1981A).

ἁμαρτωλός, *sinful*; as subst., *sinner*; def. φίλον τῇ θείᾳ γραφῇ καλεῖν...ἁ. ... τοὺς παρανομίᾳ συζῆν προαιρουμένους, καὶ βίον διεφθαρμένον ἀσπαζομένους Thdt.*Ps.*1:1(1.612);

A. adj.; of souls, Clem.*str.*7.6(p.27.6; M.9.449B); Or.*Jo.*28.15(13; p.408.14; M.14.712C); τῆς συνηθείας τῆς ἁ. Clem.*str.*3.16(p.242.21; M.8.1201A); ἔθνος ἁ. Or.*Cels.*5.15(p.16.21; M.11.1204A); τοῦ ἁμαρτωλοτέρους γενέσθαι id.*Jo.*28.23(18; p.418.2; M.14.729A); τοῦ ἁμαρτωλοτάτου καὶ εἰς τὸ ἅγιον πνεῦμα δυσφημήσαντος id.*or.*27.15(p.374.15; M.11.520C); of S. Paul τὸν πάντων ἁμαρτωλότερον Chrys.*hom.4.2 in 1Tim.*(11.569D).

B. subst.; **1.** ref. God's relation to sinners; **a.** gen. ὁ ἁ. ἀγνοεῖται ὑπὸ τοῦ θεοῦ Or.*hom.1.8 in Jer.*(p.7.17; M.13.264D); [sc. θεός]... παραμυθεῖται τὸν ἁ., ἵνα διεγείρῃ Chrys.*poenit.*7.3(2.330A); ὅ ἐστιν ἐν τῷ κόσμῳ πένης, τοῦτο τῷ θεῷ ἁ. *ib.*; ὁ θεὸς [λέγεται] ἀγνοεῖν τοὺς ἁ., καθὸ μακρύνουσιν ἑαυτοὺς ἀπ' αὐτοῦ Dor.*doct.*23.3(M.88.1833D); **b.** in Christ προσφορὰ ἦν [sc. Christ] ὑπὲρ πάντων τῶν μετανοεῖν βουλομένων ἁ. Just.*dial.*40.4(M.6.564A); Clem.*paed.*1.9(p.139.8; M.8. 349B); ἐπέμφθη οὖν θεὸς λόγος καθὸ μὲν ἰατρὸς τοῖς ἁ. Or.*Cels.*3.62 (p.256.9; M.11.1001B); σαφῶς ὑπὲρ ἁμαρτωλῶν λέγεται πάντα ἀναδεδέχθαι ὁ Ἰησοῦς *ib.*4.19(p.289.18; 1052D); *ib.*4.28(p.297.25; 1069A); τοῦ λόγου γενομένου ἀνθρώπου...οἱ ἄνθρωποι οὐκέτι...μένουσιν ἁ. Ath.*Ar.*3.33(M.26.393B); μέγα...καὶ τὸ ἁ. ὄντα ὑπὲρ ὁτουοῦν ἀποθανεῖν· ὅταν δὲ καὶ δίκαιος ὁ τούτων πάσχων ᾖ, καὶ ὑπὲρ ἁ. ἀποθάνῃ... ποῖος ταῦτα παραστῆσαι δυνήσεται νοῦς; τὸν γὰρ δίκαιον, φησίν, ἐποίησεν ἁ., ἵνα τοὺς ἁ. ποιήσῃ δικαίους Chrys.*hom.11.3 in 2Cor.* (10.518A,B); ἁμαρτίας γὰρ ἐλεύθερος ὢν τὸν τῶν ἁ. ὑπέμεινε θάνατον Thdt.*2Cor.*5:21(3.318); **2.** their spiritual condition; **a.** in gen. τίς ὁ νεκρός; ὁ ἁ. Or.*hom.9.3 in Jer.*(p.67.25; M.13.353A); ζημία τῷ ἁ. τοῦ ἀληθινοῦ φωτὸς στερηθῆναι Bas.*hex.*6.1(1.50E; M.29.120B); τοῦ δὲ ἁ. ... ἡ ψυχὴ οἷον ἐν βορβόρῳ τοῖς πάθεσι τῆς σαρκὸς ἐγκεκύλισται id. *hom.in Ps.*7(1.100C; M.29.236A); though not altogether deprived of good, Chrys.*Laz.*6.9(1.787C); **b.** their spiritual limitations ἐπιτυγχάνειν τινὰς καὶ τῶν ἁ. κατὰ τὰς αἰτήσεις, σπανίως μὲν τοῦτο διὰ τὴν τοῦ θεοῦ δικαίαν ἀγαθότητα Clem.*str.*7.12(p.52.28; M.9.501A); πῶς δέ, εἰ ἁ. οὐκ ἤκουσεν ὁ θεός, ἐδιδάσκοντο οἱ ἁ. λέγειν· 'ἄφες ἡμῖν τὰ παραπτώματα ἡμῶν'...τίνων οὖν ἀκούει θεός; τῶν νευόντων εἰς μετάνοιαν, κἂν μήπω ἐπαύσαντο τοῦ εἶναι ἁ. εἰ μὴ ἤκουεν ὁ θεὸς ἁμαρτωλῶν οὐκ ἂν μετὰ τελωνῶν καὶ ἁ. ὁ σωτὴρ ἡμῶν ἤσθιεν καὶ ἔπινεν Or.*fr.70 in Jo.*9:31(p.538.15ff.); but οὔτε γὰρ τὸ σημεῖα ποιεῖν ἁμαρτωλοῦ (οὐ γὰρ δύναται ἁ. σημεῖα ποιεῖν), οὔτε τὸ παρὰ θεῷ εἶναι...ἁμαρτωλοῦ Chrys.*hom.78.2 in Jo.*(8.460A); **c.** their relations with demons τὰς ἐνεργείας οὖν τὰς τοῖς δαιμονίοις καταλλήλους ἐπιτελεῖν φησι [sc. *Barn.*16.7–9] τοὺς ἁ. Clem.*str.*2.20(p.176.12; M.8.1060C); τὰ πνεύματα τὰ ἀκάθαρτα εἰς τὴν τοῦ ἁ. ψυχὴν ἐπισπείρειν *ib.*(p.176.5; 1060B); **d.** yet they should not despair, Chrys.*poenit.*8.1(2.341A); κἂν ἁ. ὑπάρχῃς, βλέπε πρὸς τὸν τελώνην τὸν μὴ ἀποτυχόντα id.*non desp.*7 (3.360C); *ib.*8(360E); for they can be saved by repentance, *Hom. Clem.*3.6; ἁ. μὲν μετανοοῦσι χαρίζεται τὰ ἁμαρτήματα *ib.*18.2; **3.** attitude of Christians to sinners; **a.** in private, defended against Celsus ἐπεὶ δέ φησι καὶ τό· τίς οὖν αὕτη ποτὲ ἡ τῶν ἁ. προτίμησις;... ἀποκρινούμεθα ὅτι καθάπαξ μὲν ἁ. οὐ προτιμᾶται τοῦ μὴ ἁ.· ἔστι δ' ὅτε ἁ. συναισθόμενος τῆς ἰδίας ἁμαρτίας καὶ...ταπεινὸς προτιμᾶται τοῦ ἔλαττον μὲν νομιζομένου εἶναι ἁ., οὐκ οἰομένου δ' αὐτὸν ἁ. ἀλλ' ἐπαιρομένου ἐπί τισιν, οἷς δοκεῖ συνειδέναι ἑαυτῷ κρείττοσι Or.*Cels.*3.64 (p.258.1ff.; M.11.1004C); to sinners in authority τοῦ ἐπισκόπου ὑμῶν ἀκούετε,...ὅτι καὶ Μωυσέως καθέδραν τιμᾶν ἐκελεύσθητε, κἂν οἱ προκαθεζόμενοι ἁ. νομίζωνται *Hom.Clem.*3.70; **b.** at public worship τὸν βασιλέα τῶν ὅλων παρακελευσάμενος ἀνυμνεῖν, οὐδαμοῦ τὸν ἁ. ἐκάλεσεν, ἀλλὰ καὶ ἐνταῦθα αὐτῷ τὰς θύρας ἀπέκλεισε Chrys.*ordin.*1 (1.438E); ‡Chrys.*Petr.et El.*1(2.730A); **4.** ultimate fate of those who perish in sins ἁ. καυθήσονται, ὅτι ἥμαρτον καὶ οὐ μετενόησαν Herm. *sim.*4.4; Clem.*paed.*1.10(p.144.14; M.8.360B); ἁ. ... ἀπορρήτου κολάσεως τεύξωνται τὸν αἰῶνα *Clem.ep.*10; Ath.*inc.*57.3(M.25.197A); τὰς βασάνους τὰς αἰωνίους, ἐν αἷς οἱ ἁ. κολάζονται id.*virg.*17(p.52.18; M. 28.272D); Cyr.H.*catech.*4.5; **5.** sinners distinguishable from righteous in this world, Herm.*sim.*3.2; *ib.*3.3; **6.** Christians regarded as sinners by pagans καὶ μηδὲν ἀδικοῦντες ὡς ἁ. ἀναιρούμεθα Just. *1apol.*24.1(M.6.364B); Christ regarded as sinner by Jews, Chrys.*hom. 78.2 in Jo.*(8.459E); **7.** as self-depreciating style of address τῷ δεσπότῃ μου...ὁ ἁ. ... Συμεώνης Sym.Styl.*ep.*(p.194.22; M.86.2533A); †Polyb.*ep.*(M.41.112D); Cosm.Ind.*top.*prec.(M.88.52A).

***ἀματάρα, ἡ,** (Hebr. מַטָּרָה) *target*, alternatively rendered *trench*, Thdt.*qu.51 in 1Reg.*(1.387).

[*]**ἀματίζω,** = ἁμματίζω, *bandage, tie up*, Ephr.1.309A.

ἀμαυρόω, 1. *make dim, obscure*; *quench* (fire), Const.*or.s.c.*22 (p.188.19; M.20.1304C) etc.; met., *weaken, impair*; *destroy*, Meth. *lepr.*6(p.459.4); Bas.*hom.*1.6(2.5D; M.31.172D); Bas.Sel.*or.*23.1(M.85. 272A); **2.** *fall away from* εἰ δὲ ἀμαυρώσειεν ὁ νοῦς ταύτης τῆς χάριτος Ephr.1.273B.

***ἀμαχία, ἡ,** *freedom from strife*, Pall.*h.Laus.*30(p.86.6; M.34. 1098C).

ἄμαχος, *not quarrelsome* ὡς ἀγγέλους εἶναι ἁ. καὶ ἀδικασίμους τοὺς ἀνθρώπους Leont.N.*v.Jo.Eleem.*6(p.13.1).

ἀμβιτεύω, (Lat. *ambio*) *solicit*; *intrigue for* μὴ ἀμβιτεύσας τὸ πρᾶγμα Pall.*v.Chrys.*10(p.61.9; ἀμφιβατεύσας M.47.35).

***ἀμβιτίων,** (Lat. *ambitio*) *ambition*; *vanity*, Cyr.*ep.*10(p.111.29; Ἀμφιτίωνος 5².35A).

ἀμβλίσκ-ω (ἀμβλώσκω), *miscarry*, Chrys.*fr.Job* 39:1(M.64.649D);

Synes.*Dion* 13(p.268.9; -ώσκειν M.66.1152B); Thdt.*affect*.5(p.138.2; -ώσκω 4.834); pass., *be abortive*, met. οὐ πάντες...πρὶν εἰς τὸ φῶς ἐλθεῖν τῆς θεογνωσίας, ~ονται; Gr.Nyss.*v.Mos*.(M.44.330B).

***ἀμβλύττω**, *be dim-sighted, blind*, ‡Caes.Naz.*dial*.130(M.38.1032).

***ἀμβλυωπαθής**, *dimmed, darkened* ἐκ τῆς ἀ. ... ἐννοίας Thdr. Stud.*epp*.1.8(M.99.936A).

ἀμβλυωπέω, *be dim-sighted*; met., *be blind, obtuse*, *1Clem*.3.4; Clem.*paed*.1.6(p.107.29; M.8.285B); Eus.*d.e*.3.1(p.95.5; ἀναβλέπουσι M.22.165B); πρὸς τὰς ἐπαγγελίας ἀ. τῶν προφητῶν Ast.Am.*hom*.13 (M.40.352D).

***ἀμβλυώπτω**, prob. for ἀμβλυώττω (*LS*), *be dim-sighted*, Gr.Naz. *or*.35.2(M.36.257D).

ἀμβλωθρίδιος, **1.** *causing abortion* αἱ τοίνυν τὰ ἀ. διδοῦσαι φάρμακα, φονεύτριαί εἰσι Bas.*ep*.188 *can*.8(3.273D; M.32.677A); Thdt. *affect*.9(p.235.9; 4.942); CTrull.*can*.91; neut. as subst., *drug causing abortion* τὰς τοῖς ἀ. χρωμένας ἀνδροφονεῖν...φαμέν Athenag.*leg*.35.2 (M.6.969A); **2.** *abortive*, Thdt.*1Cor*.15:8(3.266); Thdr.Stud.*epp*.2.36 (M.99.1221A); met., of Eunomius's book ἀ. τε καὶ ἀτελεσφόρητον γέννημα Gr.Nyss.*Eun*.1(1 p.22.9; M.45.249C); of Jews γεννήματα τοῦ Ἀβραὰμ ἀ. Ast.Am.*hom*.14(M.40.385C); ἀνέχομαι καὶ δευτέρων ὠδίνων...ἀ. ὑμῶν γενομένων Thdt.*Gal*.4:19(3.385); neut. as subst. ἔτι τεκνία καλῶ τὰ ἀ., τὰ ἐκτρώματα Chrys.*comm.in Gal*.4:19(10.708C).

***ἀμβλωθρίζω**, *cause abortion*, ‡Jo.Jej.*can*.4(p.443).

ἄμβλωμα, τό, **1.** *abortion*; met., ref. the faithful liberated from hell ὅσοι δηλαδὴ τὸ τῆς ἀπιστίας οὐκ ἔπαθον ἀ. Germ.CP *or*.2(M.98. 285C); **2.** *abortive child*, met., exeg. Apoc.12:2 διὰ τὸ ἀ. εἶναι τοὺς ἐκ τοῦ ἀληθινοῦ φωτὸς Χριστοῦ ἐκπίπτοντας Andr.Caes.*Apoc*.33(M. 106.321A).

ἀμβλώσκω, v. ἀμβλίσκω.

ἀμβροσία, ἡ, *elixir of life, immortality* ὁ βασιλεύς, τρέφων τῇ ἑαυτοῦ ἀ. τοὺς ἐπ' αὐτὸν ἱδρυμένους *A.Thom*.A 6(p.109.5).

ἀμβρόσιος, *immortal, divine* γυνὴ...τῷ σωφροσύνης ἀ. χρίσματι συναλειφέσθω Clem.*paed*.2.8(p.197.1; M.8.471B); ref. eucharist τὴν ἀ. βρῶσιν *A.Thom*.A 7(p.110.17).

ἀμβροσιώδης, *immortal* κύριε Ἰησοῦ...πότισον...αὐτοὺς ἀπὸ τῆς ἀ. σου πηγῆς *A.Thom*.A 25(p.140.13); τῆς ἀ. τροφῆς καὶ τοῦ ποτοῦ τῆς ἀμπέλου τῆς ἀληθινῆς *ib*.36(p.154.2).

***ἀμβροσίως**, *immortally*, *Orac.Sib*.2.225.

ἄμβροτος, *immortal, divine*; of God, Synes.*hymn*.6.3(p.39; M.66. 1609); of Christ, *ib*.7.2(p.48; 1612); ἄ. εἶδος Nonn.*par.Jo*.21:1(M.43. 913C).

ἄμβων, ὁ, *pulpit*, usu. in middle of church; described by Paul. Sil.*ambo*.(M.86.2251); τοῦ δεικτηρίου· λέγεται δὲ οὕτως ὁ τόπος ἐν ᾧ ἐπιδείκνυνται οἱ λέγοντες, τουτό ἐστι ὁ ἄ., ἤτοι τὸ ἀκροατήριον Bas.Sel. *v.Thecl*.2.27(M.85.613A); place for reader of gospel and epistle and for cantor περὶ τοῦ μὴ δεῖν λαϊκοὺς ἀνιέναι ἐν τῷ ἄ., πλὴν τῶν τεταγμένων ἀναγινώσκειν ἢ ψάλλειν ἐν ταῖς διφθέραις Gel.Cyz.*h.e*.2.31. 4(M.85.1316D); also for preacher, Socr.*h.e*.6.5.5(M.67.673B); whence edicts were read, Thdr.Lect.*h.e*.2.31(M.86.200B), and notices, *Chron.Pasch*.p.391(M.92.1004C); where priests were ordained, ‡Jo. D.*ep.Thphl*.13(M.95.361C); myst. interprn. ὁ ἄ. ἐκφαίνει τὸ σχῆμα τοῦ λίθου, ὃν κυλίσας ὁ ἄγγελος ἐκάθητο ἐπάνω αὐτοῦ· αἱ βαθμίδες τοῦ ἄ. δηλοῦσι τὴν τοῦ Ἰακὼβ κλίμακα ‡Sophr.H.*liturg*.4(M.87.3985A).

ἀμεγέθης, *without magnitude, inexpressible in terms of magnitude*; of soul, Nemes.*nat.hom*.3(M.40.600B); of God, in gen. τοῦ ἀ. τε καὶ ἀορίστου Gr.Nyss.*hex*.7(p.14; M.44.69B); ὁ θεός, ἁπλοῦς, ἀ. ‡Bas. *struct.hom*.1.4(1.326B; M.30.16A); Cyr.*dogm*.1(p.549.18; 6².366D); Jo. D.*imag*.1.8(M.94.1240A); ref. relative 'greatness' of Father and Son, exeg. Jo.14:28 τὰ δὲ ἀπερίληπτα τῷ μεγέθει, μᾶλλον δὲ ἀ. καὶ ἄποσα παντελῶς, τίς ἂν ἀλλήλοις παραμετρήσειεν; Bas.*Eun*.1.25(1. 236A; M.29.568A); ἀλλ' οὐδὲ ἐν ποσῷ τῷ κατὰ μέγεθος ἐλάττων [sc. ὁ υἱός] αὐτοῦ· ἀ. γὰρ...ἡ θεία...φύσις Cyr.*Jo*.1.3(4.25D); of Son, Jo.V H.*icon*.6(M.96.1353D); neut. as subst., *infinitude*, exeg. Jo.16:14 ἀπὸ τῆς αὐτοῦ [sc. H. Ghost] ἀφάτου μεγαλειότητος ἐπιδείξει καὶ τῆς ἐμῆς θεότητος τὸ ἀ. Didym.*Trin*.3.40(M.39.981B).

ἀμέθεκτος, act., *having no share, incapable of participation*; c. genit., Dion.Ar.*c.h*.11.1(M.3.284C); neut. as subst. ἀρεταὶ τὸ πρὸς κακίαν ἀ. [ἀμάλακτον Gr.Nyss.*hom.4 in Cant*.(M.44.837B)] ἐν τοῖς πειρασμοῖς διασώζουσαι Gr.Nyss.ap.Proc.G.*Cant*.1:16(M.87.1573B).

ἀμεθεξία, ἡ, *inability to be shared* ἡ τῆς παναιτίου θεότητος ἀ. Dion.Ar.*d.n*.2.5(M.3.644B).

ἀμεθόδευτος, ? *cleared, not liable to proceedings* οἱ γὰρ ἐνταῦθα τὰς εὐθύνας ὑπέχοντες...ἀ. δοκοῦσί μοι ἔσεσθαι [i.e. in future life] ὑπὲρ ὧν ἀπολελόγηνται ‡Caes.Naz.*dial*.44(M.38.913).

***ἀμειαγώγητος**, *unweighed in the sacrificial scale*, Synes.*ep*.5 (M.66.1344B).

ἀμείβω, *requite, repay, reward* διὰ τὴν ἄκραν...πρὸς θεὸν ἀγάπην ἄκροις δώροις ἀμειφθήσονται Ephr.3.337C; med., Chrys.*hom.58.2 in Mt*.(7.586D); of man's response to God ἀ. δι' ἀγάπης τὴν εὐποιίαν Clem.*str*.7.3(p.15.17; M.9.425B); τὸν...εὐεργετήσαντα εὐχαρίστῳ ἀ. φωνῇ *Hom.Clem*.11.8.

***ἀμειδήεις**, = ἀμειδής, *gloomy*, Eudoc.*Cypr*.2.89(M.85.848D).

***ἀμειπτέος**, *to be changed*, Horm.*ep.Epiph*.(p.58.13; ἀνταμειπτέα M.*PL*.63.520B).

ἀμείρ-ω, **1.** *be wanting, fail* τὴν ὡς θεῷ φυσικὴν παροῦσαν αὐτῷ δικαιοσύνην ἐνήργησε διὰ σαρκός, φυσικῆς ἐνεργείας οὐκ ~ούσης *Schol*. 10 in Max.*qu.Thal*.53(M.90.508C); **2.** pass., *be wasted away, dwindle*, †Apoll.*met.Ps*.67:3(M.33.1404C).

ἀμείωτος, **1.** *undiminished*; in gen., Gr.Nyss.*Eun*.8(2 p.185.28; M.45.780B); Sophr.H.*v.Anast*.(M.92.1716B); Jo.D.*haer.Nest*.2(M.95. 189C); of Trin. τὴν τριάδα ἀ. εἰς τὴν μονάδα συγκεφαλαιούμεθα Ath.*Dion*.17(p.58.25; M.25.505A); of natures of Christ ἡ ἕνωσις μενόντων ἀμειώτων Sev.Ant.*fr*.ap.Leont.H.*monoph*.1(M.86.1848A); **2.** *inviolate* παρθένον ‡Caes.Naz.*dial*.177(M.38.1145).

ἀμειώτως, *without diminution*, Dion.Ar.*e.h*.3.3.3(M.3.429B); Max. *opusc*.(M.91.97A).

ἀμέλγ-ω, *milk*; met., *drain out*, Clem.*paed*.3.4(p.251.29; M.8. 593A); *drink* τοῖς ~ουσι τὸν λόγον τῶν οὐρανῶν *ib*.1.6(p.117.20; 304C); Nonn.*par.Jo*.19:38(M.43.905C).

ἀμέλεια, ἡ, **1.** *carelessness, indifference, neglect*, Herm.*mand*.10. 1.5; ἐὰν δὲ παιδίον τῇ ἀ. τοῦ πρεσβυτέρου ἀποθάνῃ ἀβάπτιστον Eus. Al.*serm*.5(M.86.349A); Jo.D.*f.o*.1.2(M.94.792B); **2.** esp. *moral indifference, lack of watchfulness* τὸν δι' ἀ. τὰ σπέρματα τῆς ἁμαρτίας κεχωρηκότα Or.*princ*.3.1.13(p.218.6; M.11.273A); ἀπὸ φιληδονίας ἀ., καὶ ἀπὸ ἀ. λήθη προσγίνεται Marc.Er.*opusc*.1.79(M.65.916A); ἐν λογισμῶν ἀ. *ib*.1.91(916D); Dor.*doct*.11.1(M.88.1736A).

ἀμελέτητος ([*]**ἀμελλέτητος**), *unexpected*, exeg. Mt.20:18ff. τοῖς μαθηταῖς...προὔλεγεν...ἵνα...μὴ ἀ. ἐπελθὸν [sc. τὸ πάθος] ταράξῃ σφόδρα αὐτούς Chrys.*hom.65.1 in Mt*.(7.644A); Bas.Sel.*or*.21.2(M. 85.257A); ἀμελλ- *ib*.17.3(224A).

ἀμελετήτως ([*]**ἀμελητήτως**), *negligently*, Apoll.*fr*.134 ap.Thdt. *eran*.2(4.172; ἀμεταβλήτως p.239.31); ἀμελητήτως, Cyr.*ador*.5(1. 148A); ἀ. ἔχειν πρός c. acc., *be negligent*, Zach.Mit.*opif*.(M.85.1141C).

ἀμελέω, *be careless* or *neglectful*, of moral indifference ἀμεληθέντες [pass. in med. sense]...τινες...ἀπετράπησαν Clem.*str*.6.12 (p.480.19; M.9.317C); Chrys.*hom.9.3 in Rom*.(9.514A); οἱ ἠμελημένοι βίοι *ib*.1.1(426A); βλέπετε μὴ ἀμελήσητε ἑαυτῶν Dor.*doct*.11.1(M.88. 1736A); perf. ptcpl. pass. as subst., *careless*, ‡Dion.Al.*fr.in Lc.22* (p.250.2; M.10.1596D).

ἀμελητέον, *one must be neglectful*, Clem.*q.d.s*.27(p.177.28; M.9. 632D).

[*]**ἀμελητήτως**, v. ἀμελετήτως.

[*]**ἀμελητί**, = ἀμελλητί, *without delay* or *hesitation*, Diod.*Ex*. 4:24(M.33.1582B); Cyr.*ador*.1(1.20B); *ib*.6(177B).

***ἀμέλιστος**, *not divided into pieces, not dismembered* εἰ γὰρ μόνη θεότης ἐστὶν ὁ Χριστός, ἡ δὲ θεότης...ἐστι...ἀ., καὶ ἄβρωτος, πρόδηλός ἐστιν ὁ Τιμόθεος ἀρνούμενος...τὴν θυσίαν...τῶν ἁγίων μυστηρίων Anast.S.*hod*.13(M.89.208D).

[*]**ἀμελλέτητος**, v. ἀμελέτητος.

ἀμελῴδητος, *without song*, ‡Proc.G.*monod*.(M.87.2840C).

ἄμεμπτος, **1.** of people, *blameless, irreproachable*; in gen. διάκονοι Polyc.*ep*.5.2; Clem.*str*.7.16(p.72.2; M.9.541A); ἐπίσκοπον...ἐν πᾶσιν ἄ. *Const.App*.8.4.2; οὐδὲ αὐτὸς [sc. S. Peter] ἀναμάρτητος, οὐδὲ ἄ. Anast.S.*Ps.6*(M.89.1093C); τὴν...ψυχήν, ἣν ἐτήρησας ἄ. Jo.D.*hom*.9. 10(M.96.736C); exeg. Lc.1:6, cf. ἐπὰν γὰρ ποιῶμεν τὰς ἐντολάς, ὥστε ἐν τῷ συνειδότι ῥύπον κενοδοξίας ἢ ἀνθρωπαρεσκείας ἢ ἑτέρου τινὸς τοιούτου ἔχειν,...οὐκ ἀμέμπτως ποιοῦμεν Or.*hom.2 in Lc*.(p.19.9); exeg. Lc.1:6, Phil.3:6 ὁ μὲν γὰρ ἀναμάρτητος ἐκ παντὸς καὶ ἄ. οὐκέτι δὲ ὁ ἄ. ἐξ ἀνάγκης καὶ ἀναμάρτητός ἐστιν. ὁ γὰρ ἁμαρτάνων παρὰ τὸν νόμον συγγνωστὴν ἁμαρτίαν,...λαβὼν τὴν ἄφεσιν, γίνεται καθαρὸς καὶ ἄ. κατὰ τὴν ἐκ νόμου δικαιοσύνην ‡Just.*qu.et resp*.141(M.6.1396A); exeg. 1Thess.3:13 τοῦτό φησιν, ὅτι ἀ. ἔμπροσθεν τοῦ θεοῦ δεῖ γενέσθαι ...ἄρα ἡ ἀγάπη ἀ. ποιεῖ Chrys.*hom.4.4 in 1Thess*.(11.456C); οὐδὲ τοῖς ...ἀγγέλοις ἐμπεπίστευκε τὸ κατὰ φύσιν καὶ ἑδραίως ἄ. Olymp.*Job* 4:17f.(M.93.77B); **2.** of things, *faultless, perfect*; in gen. ὅπως ἄ. ᾖ ἡ θυσία ὑμῶν *Const.App*.7.30.2; οὐκ ἔστιν ἄ. ἡ οἰκία, τουτέστιν, ἔχει ἐλάττωμα Chrys.*hom.14.3 in Heb*.(12.145D); ἄ. ἐμὴ κρίσις Nonn.*par. Jo*.8:16(M.43.816A); of Law, exeg. Heb.8:7 τουτέστιν, εἰ οὐδὲν εἶχεν ἐλλιπές, εἰ ἄ. ἐποίει Chrys.*hom.14.2 in Heb*.(12.142D); *ib*.14.3(145C); τὸ ἄ. ἀντὶ τοῦ τελεία τέθεικε, τουτέστιν ἀποχρῶσα πρὸς τελειότητα, ἀ. τοὺς χρωμένους ἐργαζομένη Thdt.*Heb*.8:7(3.595); Jo.D.*Heb*.8:7 (M.95.968C).

ἀμέμπτως, *blamelessly*; in gen., Just.*dial*.8.3(M.6.493A); ref. service to God esp. in ministerial office τοὺς ἀ. ... προσενεγκόντας τὰ δῶρα [sc. those who exercise ἐπισκοπή] 1*Clem*.44.4; δουλεύσητε τῷ κυρίῳ ἀ. Herm.*vis*.4.2.5; διάκονος...λειτουργείτω αὐτῷ [sc. bishop] ἀ. *Const.App*.2.26.5; ref. Christian behaviour, Serap.*euch*.5.3; exeg. 1Thess.5:23, Sever.ad loc.(p.331.21); exeg. Lc.1:6, Or.*hom.2 in Lc.* (p.19.9) cit. s. ἄμεμπτος.

ἀμεμφής, *blameless, beyond reproach* πρᾶξιν, ἄρα καὶ αἵρεσιν ἀποδεκτέον οὐ τὴν ἀ., ἀλλ' ἣν οὐδεὶς εὐλόγως καταμέμψεται Clem.*str*. 1.1(p.12.21; M.8.708A); Gr.Naz.*carm*.1.2.1.209(M.37.538A); of God as giver of rewards, Clem.*str*.7.3(p.15.7; M.9.425A); of Christ, Nonn. *par.Jo*.18:12(M.43.892A).

ἀμεμφῶς, *blamelessly, irreproachably*, Clem.*str*.7.11(p.47.7; M.9. 489C).

ἀμενηνόω, *deprive of strength, weaken*, Synes.*provid*.8(p.78.5; M.66.1225A).

ἀμέρεια (ἀμερία), ἡ, *indivisibility*, of God τὴν ἁπλότητα καὶ ἑνότητα τῆς ὑπερφυοῦς ἀμερίας Dion.Ar.*d.n*.1.4(M.3.589D); of the angelic nature ἀμερείᾳ πρὸς τὸν θεῖον νοῦν ἀποτυπουμένη *ib*.7.2 (868B).

ἀμερής, *without parts, indivisible*; **1.** mathematical and scientific ἀπλατὲς μῆκος καὶ ἐπιφάνειαν ἀβαθῆ καὶ σημεῖον ἀ. Clem.*str*.6.11 (p.477.18; M.9.312B); γεωμετρίας γὰρ...σημεῖόν ἐστιν ἀρχὴ ἀμερές Hipp.*haer*.4.51(p.74.27; M.16.3119A); [sc. ζωδιακὸν κύκλον διαιροῦσιν εἰς μέρη] δώδεκα, ἕκαστον δὲ ζώδιον εἰς μοίρας τριάκοντα, ἑκάστην δὲ μοῖραν εἰς ἑξήκοντα λεπτά· οὕτω γὰρ καλοῦσι τὰ ἐλάχιστα καὶ τὰ ἀ. *ib*.5.13(p.106.14; 3163B); *ib*.6.23(p.150.9; 3227C); of atoms, Dion. Al.ap.Eus.*p.e*.14.23(773B; M.21.1272C); Meth.*res*.2.10(p.350.2); Gr. Nyss.*Eun*.12(1 p.331.6); of soul, Leont.H.*Nest*.1.1(M.86.1404C); **2.** of God ἀ. γὰρ καὶ ἄτομον τὸ θεῖον Eus.*d.e*.5.1(p.211.33; M.22.352C); ἀ. ὤν, ἀμερίστως ἐστὶ...τοῦ υἱοῦ πατήρ Ath.*decr*.11(p.10.11; M.25. '444'(436)A); πᾶν ὅπερ λέγεται τῆς τοῦ πατρὸς οὐσίας σημαντικὸν ἴσον ἐστὶ...διὰ τὸ ἀ. καὶ ἀσύνθετον Eun.*apol*.19(M.30.853D); Bas.*Eun*.1.8 (1.220A; M.29.528C); τὴν τοῦ ἁπλοῦ καὶ ἀ. ἔννοιαν *ib*.1.29(266C; M. 640B); ‡Ath.*dial.Trin*.5.29(M.28.1285A); Bas.Sel.*or*.25.4(M.85.297C); of Son λόγος...ἀ. αὐτὸς ὤν...νοῦς ἀ. Eus.*l.C*.12(p.233.5; M.20.1392C); λόγος...τοῦ πατρὸς ἐν ᾧ τὸ...ἀ. τοῦ πατρὸς νοεῖν δυνατόν Ath.*decr*.11 (p.10.16; 436B); τοῦ μονογενοῦς ἡ θεότης...ἁπλοῦς...καὶ ἀ. Gr.Nyss. *Apoll*.5(M.45.1132C).

ἀμεριμν-έω (ἀμεριμν-άω), **1.** *be free from anxiety, care-free* Ἰησοῦς Χριστὸς...~είτω ἐγκρατῶς ἡμῶν βιούντων *A.Jo*.107(p.205.7); Gr. Naz.*carm*.1.1.6.43(M.37.433A); Cyr.S.*v.Cyriac*.(p.231.31); **2.** *be complacent, feel secure* ὑψοῦνται καὶ ~οῦσι, μὴ συντριβόμεναι τὴν καρδίαν Mac.Aeg.*hom*.10.3(M.34.541C); ὁ ἔχων φόβον θεοῦ οὐκ ~εῖ· νήφει γὰρ πάντοτε Ephr.1.3A; ref. Lc.17:10 κἂν ὑπὲρ δύναμιν δόξῃ ποιεῖν τι, οὐκ ~εῖ ὡς πληρώσας τὸ μέτρον Bas.*reg.br*.121(2.457A; M.31.1164C); ref. Mt.13:25 μὴ...σοι...~οῦντι κακῶς ἐπισπείρῃ ὁ ἐχθρὸς τὰ ζιζάνια Gr.Naz.*or*.40.34(M.36.408C); **3.** *withdraw, resign* εἰ μὴ ἀμεριμνήσῃς ἀπὸ πάσης συντυχίας καὶ παντὸς πράγματος οὐ δύνασαι κοινόβιον ἐργάσασθαι *Apophth.Patr*.(M.65.360B); ὀφείλομεν...~ῆσαι ἀπὸ πάντων τῶν τοῦ κόσμου τούτου Dor.*doct*.1.12(M.88.1634A).

ἀμεριμνία, ἡ, **1.** *freedom from anxiety, tranquillity*; **a.** in gen. ἵνα ...τὴν ἀ. ὁ φιλόσοφος κτήσηται Clem.*str*.2.20(p.178.12; M.8.1065A); τὴν ἀ. καὶ τὴν ἰσχὺν τοῦ ἡμετέρου κράτους Marcian.Imp.*ep.Leo*.2(p.8. 29; M.*PL*.54.904B); exeg. 1Tim.2:2 ἡ ἐκείνων [sc. βασιλέων] σωτηρία ἡμῶν ἀ. ὑπάρχει Chrys.*hom.6.1 in 1Tim*.(11.579C); **b.** through poverty, Bas.*hom.in Ps*.14(1.110C; M.29.273A) cit. s. πένης; Chrys. *hom.32.6 in 1Cor*.(10.295A); **c.** of spiritual peace ἐν ἀ. θεοῦ Ign. *Polyc*.7.1; μείνατε...ἐν τῇ ἁγιωσύνῃ καὶ δέξασθε τὴν ἀ. *A.Thom*.A 86 (p.202.6); Mac.Aeg.*hom*.17.8(M.34.629A); ἡσυχία ἀ. ψυχῆς Ephr. 3.234F; **d.** *freedom from anxiety* ἀ. τῶν γηΐνων πραγμάτων id. 1.172E; Chrys.*prod.Jud*.3(2.721D); **2.** *carelessness, slackness*, Mac. Aeg.*hom*.10.2(M.34.541C); Ephr.3.323F; Chrys.*hom.15.2 in 1Tim*. (11.636E).

ἀμέριμνος, **1.** *free from anxiety*, Herm.*mand*.5.2.3; τὸ ἀ. τῆς σοφίας πνεῦμα Or.*mart*.4.9(p.46.12; M.11.633C); of life before Fall, Ath.*inc*.3.4(M.25.101C); τὴν ἀ., μέριμναν, λέγω δὴ τῆς ἀδιαλείπτου προσευχῆς Leont.N.*v.Sym*.23(M.93.1700A); **2.** *careless, thoughtless* οὐχ ὡς ἀ. ἐσθίει, ἀλλ' ὡς ἔχων ἐπόπτην θεόν Bas.*reg.br*.196(2.481B; M.31.1213A).

ἀμερίμνως, **1.** *without anxiety*, Constantius Imp.ap.Ath.*apol.sec*. 51(p.132.26; M.25.541C); Ath.*v.Anton*.66(M.26.937A); ‡Bas.*const*.1.2 (2.536B; M.31.1328C); **2.** *heedlessly*, Ephr.3.516B.

ἀμέριστος, **A.** *undivided*; met. ἀ. καρδίᾳ Ign.*Trall*.13.2; id.*Philad*. 6.2; κοινὴν τὴν λειτουργίαν [sc. τῶν πνευματικῶν] καὶ ἀ. Clem.*exc. Thdot*.11.4(p.110.22; M.9.661B); φυλάξαι...σεαυτὴν...ἀ. *A.Andr.fr*.8 (p.41.26); ὁ πόθος ἀ. [sc. of parents for one child] Bas.Sel.*or*.7.1 (M.85.104D).

B. *indivisible*; c. genit. *inseparable from* ἢ...κεχώρισται τῆς ὕλης ὁ θεός, ἢ αὖ πάλιν...ἀ. αὐτῆς Meth.*arbitr*.5(p.157.9; M.18.249B) = Adam.*dial*.4.5(p.146.19; v.l. M.11.1812D); **1.** divine epithet ἀσωμάτου καὶ ἀ. θεοῦ Ath.*Ar*.1.28(M.26.69C); ‡Ath.*Apoll*.2.12(M.26.1152B); also among heretics ἣν ἀ. φῂς εἶναι εἰς...ἡμιφώνους φθόγγους ἀπομερίζων Iren.*haer*.1.15.5(M.7.625B); Eun.*apol*.28(M.30.868A); but cf. Manich. view τῷ τῆς οὐσίας λόγῳ ἀ. ἐστιν ἡ θεία οὐσία, τῷ δὲ τῆς οἰκονομίας λόγῳ μεριστή *Disp.Phot*.1(M.88.536C); **2.** of Father and Son ἑνὶ τῷ θεῷ καὶ τῷ...λόγῳ υἱῷ νοουμένῳ ἀ. Athenag.*leg*.18.2(M.6. 925B); [sc. λόγος θεός] ἀδιάστατος, ἀ., εἷς θεός Clem.*exc.Thdot*.8 (p.108.21; M.9.657C); πατέρα καὶ υἱόν, ἓν ὄντας τῇ θεότητι καὶ τῷ ἐξ αὐτοῦ ἀ. ... εἶναι τὸν λόγον ἀπὸ τοῦ πατρός ‡Ath.*Ar*.4.10(p.54.9; M. 26.480C); *ib*.4.9(p.53.21; 480B); in Son's generation [sc. πατήρ] ὡς ἀδιαίρετος ὢν καὶ ἀ. υἱοῦ γίνεται πατήρ, οὐ προλαβὼν αὐτὸν Or.*princ*. 4.4.1(28; p.348.7; M.11.401A); τὸ ἀπαθὲς καὶ τὸ ἀ. τῆς ἐκ τοῦ πατρὸς γεννήσεως Ath.*syn*.41(p.267.22; M.26.765D); Bas.*Eun*.2.16(1.251D; M.29.604C); **3.** of God in three Persons ἀ. ἐν μεμερισμένοις...ἡ θεότης Gr.Naz.*or*.31.14(p.163.2; M.36.149A) cit.ap.‡Cyr.*Trin*.10(6^3.16B; M. 77.1144B) = Jo.D.*f.o*.1.8(M.94.829B); **4.** of Father and incarnate Son [Jo.10:30] ἐπιχειρήσει διαιρεῖν ἃ ἐκεῖνος ἥνωσε καὶ ἀ. τετήρηκε Ath.*Dion*.2(p.47.16; M.25.481C); ἡ ἀ. θεότης...ἀνακραθεῖσα τῷ ὑποκειμένῳ [i.e. manhood] Gr.Nyss.*ep*.3(M.46.1021C); Nonn.*par.Jo*. 10:38(M.43.837C); *ib*.14:11(868C); Procl.CP *annunt*.4(M.85.437D); τῆς θείας καὶ ἀμεταβόλου καὶ ἀ. σου σαρκώσεως ‡Meth.*palm*.6(M.18. 396B); cf. τὸ ἀ. μερισθῆναι...ἵνα ἡμεῖς...τῷ ἑνὶ τῷ δι' ἡμᾶς μερισθέντι ἀνακραθῶμεν Clem.*exc.Thdot*.36(p.118.22; M.9.677A); **5.** Christol., of Christ as one Person ἀ. ...ἑαυτὸν...φυλάττει μετὰ τὴν ἐνανθρώπησιν Cyr.*Jo*.4.3(4.375D); οὐ...διπλοῦς ὁ εἷς καὶ μόνος Χριστός, κἂν ἐκ δύο νοεῖται...εἰς ἑνότητα τὴν ἀ. συνενηνεγμένος id.*ep*.17(p.38.6; 5^2.73A); Sophr.H.*or*.2.46(M.87.3280A); in Eutychian protest against belief in two natures τὸν ἀ. μηδεὶς χωριζέτω CChalc.*act*.1(*ACO* 3 p.93.3; H.2.100E).

C. act. sense; **1.** *without distinction, making no differentiation* ἀγάπη...ἀ. ἐστιν ἐν πᾶσιν, ἀδιάκριτος, κοινωνική Clem.*str*.2.18(p.159. 18; M.8.1028A); συμφερτὴν ἀ. ... ὀπωπήν Nonn.*par.Jo*.9:1(M.43. 824B); **2.** *not dividing*, an inheritance δύο ἀδελφοὶ...ὑπῆρχον δὲ ἀμέριστοι τὴν ὑπόστασιν Ephr.3.XXVE.

ἀμερίστως, *without involving division* or *separation, inseparably*; **1.** theol. ἀναβέβηκε...πρὸς τὸν...θεὸν ὁ...ἀ. αὐτὸν σέβων διὰ τοῦ... υἱοῦ Or.*Cels*.8.4(p.224.1; M.11.1525A); ref. generation of Son ὁ θεὸς ...ἀ. ἐστὶ...πατήρ Ath.*decr*.11(p.10.11; M.25.'444'(436)A); id.*Ar*.1.28 (M.26.69A); Eun.ap.Gr.Nyss.*Eun*.4(2 p.85.20; M.45.661A) cit. s. ἀμεσίτευτος; ὡς ἕνα ἐξ ἑνός...προελθόντα ἀ. καὶ ἀδιαστάτως Cyr.*Jo*.2.1 (4.128A); Trin. μιᾶς ἀ. καὶ ἀνελλιπῶς τὰ τρία πρόσωπα πληρούσης θεότητος Sophr.H.*ep.syn*.(M.87.3157C); εἰς θεὸς ἐν τρισὶ τελείαις ταῖς ὑποστάσεσιν ἀ. δοξολογούμενος Jo.D.*hom*.4.4(M.96.608A); **2.** Christol. εἷς ὁ αὐτὸς ὁ θεάνθρωπος· μὴ διαιρούμενος εἰς θεὸν ἰδικῶς καὶ εἰς ἄνθρωπον ἰδικῶς· ἀλλ' εἷς ἀ. ὑπάρχων ‡Cyr.*Trin*.18(6^3.24E; M.77. 1157B); ‡Meth.*Sym.et Ann*.9(M.18.369D); **3.** eucharistic [sc. τὸ... σῶμα...καὶ τὸ...αἷμα τοῦ κυρίου] μερίζεται...ἀ. ἐν ἅπασι, διὰ τὴν ἔμμιξιν Eutych.*pasch*.2(M.86.2393C); τὴν ἀναίμακτον θυσίαν...ἀ. μεριζομένην Eustrat.*v.Eutych*.3(M.86.2277B).

ἀμερσίγαμος, *robbing of marriage*, Nonn.*par.Jo*.3:24(M.43.769C).

ἀμερσίνοος, *depriving of understanding, maddening*, Gr.Naz. *carm*.2.1.46.17(M.37.1379A); Nonn.*par.Jo*.6:60(M.43.801B); *ib*.16:3 (877B).

ἀμερῶς, *without division, indivisibly*, Clem.*str*.3.10(p.227.13; M.8. 1169C); ἀ. μεριζόμενον πνεῦμα κυρίου *ib*.6.16(p.502.5; M.9.364B); τὴν θρησκείαν, ἣν σέβεσθε, ἀ. τοῖς ἄμφω [sc. Father and Son] κατανοήσατε *Pers*.(p.2.17); τὸ ἀ. ὑπερτέλειον θεῖον ὅλον Leont.H.*Nest*.1.1(M.86. 1408B).

***ἀμεσίτευτος**, *immediate, without intermediary* or *intervention, direct* ἄμικτος τῷ φωτὶ καὶ ἀ. ἐστιν ἡ ἐναντίωσις Gr.Nyss.*perf*.(p.180. 10; M.46.257B); ἀ. ... ὄντος τοῦ γινομένου καὶ μόνου τὴν αἰτίαν ἔχοντος τάφανοῦς Synes.*provid*.2.1(p.110.16; M.66.1260B); theol. θεὸς...οὐ... ἀ. τὸ ἔργον, ἀνεπιβούλευτον τὸ κράτος *Const.App*.7.35.9; ἀ. ἔχουσαν τὴν γέννησιν, ἀμερίστως δὲ σῴζουσαν τὴν πρὸς τὸν γεγεννηκότα καὶ πεποιηκότα καὶ κτίσαντα σχέσιν Eun.ap.Gr.Nyss.*Eun*.4(2 p.85.19; M. 45.661A); orthodox interpretation of word, *ib*.; Didym.(‡Bas.)*Eun*.4 (1.287B; M.29.689C); τὸν ἄχρονον καὶ...ἀ. ... πρόοδον τοῦ Χριστοῦ ἀπὸ πατρός, γέννησιν καλοῦσιν αἱ γραφαί Isid.Pel.*epp*.4.142(M.78.1224A); πατὴρ καὶ υἱός, οὐ δύο ἄναρχα, ἀλλὰ ἀ. †Jo.D.*Trin*.2(M.95.12A); neut. as subst. τὸ ταὐτὸν τῆς δόξης, καὶ τὸ ἀ. τῆς δυνάμεως *Dial. Ath.et Zacch*.98(p.50).

***ἀμεσιτεύτως**, *directly, without intermediary* ἡ τῆς ἀληθοῦς σοφίας ...χύσις ἐπιγενομένη...τὴν περὶ θεοῦ καὶ ἀ. παρέχεται...ἔννοιαν Max. *ambig.*(M.91.1308B); Trin., of union of Father and Son πεπιστεύκαμεν...ἀ. αὐτοὺς καὶ ἀδιαστάτως ἀλλήλοις ἐπισυνῆφθαι *Symb.Ant.* (345)9(p.253.36; M.26.733B); freq. ref. Son's generation αὐτὸν δὲ... γεννήσας βουλήσει καὶ δυνάμει καὶ ἀγαθότητι ἀ. *Lit.*ap.*Const.App.*8. 12.7; Cyr.H.*hom.*5(M.33.1137A); ‡Chrys.*BMV* 2(8.239D); Cyr.*thes.* 18(5^1.183E); Procl.CP *or.*4.3(M.65.716A).

ἀμεσολάβητος, *unable to be gripped round the middle*; of a good wrestler, Or.*exc.in Ps.*36:24(M.17.133D); ‡Nil.*perist.*10.7(M.79.900C); neut. as subst., Nil.*Magn.*2(M.79.972B).

***ἀμεσολαβήτως**, *uninterruptedly*, ‡Bas.*struct.hom.*2.10(1.343D; M. 30.53B).

ἄμεσος, **1.** *immediate, direct, without intermediary*, Trin. οὔτε γὰρ ἡ ἄ. αὕτη συνάφεια ἐκθλίβει τὴν βούλησιν τοῦ πατρός Gr.Nyss.*Eun.* 8(2 p.181.11; M.45.773D); ἄ. ἐστι τοῦ υἱοῦ ἡ πρὸς τὸν πατέρα συνάφεια *ib.*(p.182.8; 776B); συνεῖναι δὲ τῷ υἱῷ τὸν πατέρα...διὰ τό...ἄ. αὐτοῦ πρὸς τὸ ἐξ αὐτοῦ φυσικῶς προελθόν Cyr.*Jo.*1.5(4.45D); **2.** *unimpeded* σοι...ἡ δέησις ἄ. καὶ εἰς ὦτα θεοῦ μάλιστα πίπτουσα ‡Thdt.*nativ.Jo. Bapt.*(5.97); ὁ μὲν δέχεται διὰ τοῦ πνεύματος χάρισμα τῆς τελείας καὶ ἀ. πρὸς θεὸν...ἀγάπης Max.*cap.*1.97(M.90.1220C).

ἀμέσως, **1.** *without intermediary*; **a.** in gen., Nemes.*nat.hom.*4 (M.40.608B); ἀ. πρὸς τὴν κακίαν τῆς ἀρετῆς διεστώσης Gr.Nyss.*hom.4 in Cant.*(M.44.833A); ὁ λαὸς [i.e. at Sinai] οὐκ ἐδύναντο...ἀ. ὁμιλεῖν τῇ θεωρίᾳ †Cyr.*coll.VT*(6^4.26D; M.77.1213D); **b.** Trin. τὸν κύριον πρὸς πᾶσαν θελήματος κίνησιν ἀ. τε καὶ ἀδιαστάτως συνδιατίθεσθαι τῷ πατρί Gr.Nyss.*Eun.*12(1 p.276.1; M.45.984A); ἀ. ... καὶ προσεχῶς ὁ υἱός ἐστιν ἐν τῷ...πατρί Cyr.*Jo.*1.4(4.39A); τὸ πνεῦμα τὸ ἅγιον ἐκ τοῦ υἱοῦ ἐστιν ἀ., ἀπὸ δὲ τοῦ πατρὸς μεσιτεύοντος τοῦ υἱοῦ Gr.II Papa *conf.*(M.91.1020C); **c.** Christol. ὁ λόγος...ἀνθρώπῳ τελείῳ ἀ. τε καὶ οἰκονομικῶς ἡνῶσθαι Cyr.*Mal.*32(3.850B); **2.** of time; *without interval*, Cyr.*Joel.*4(3.200B); **3.** of place; *with nothing intervening, immediately* χερουβὶμ...καὶ σεραφὶμ...ἐγγύτητα περὶ θεὸν ἀ. ἱδρύεσθαι Dion.Ar. *c.h.*6.2(M.3.201A); cf.*Lit.Chrys.*(p.357.18).

ἀμεταβάτως, *without change* ἔμψυχον κλίμακα [sc. BMV]...δι' ἧς ὁ θεὸς καταβὰς ἀ. ‡Jo.D.*hom.*6.3(M.96.665B).

ἀμετάβλητος, *unchangeable, immutable, not subject to change*; **1.** metaphysical; of ultimate reality, Clem.*str.*6.10(p.471.26; M.9. 301A); φύσεως...τινος ἀ. opp. God the giver of all good things, Tit. Bost.*Man.*2.15(M.18.1164C); **2.** moral; in evil προεγίνωσκεν αὐτοὺς ἀ. γενησομένους πονηρούς Just.*dial.*141.2(M.6.797C); τοῖς παντάπασιν ...ἀμετανοήτοις, δέρμα τε Αἰθίοπος ἀ. κεκτημένοις Petr.I Al.*ep.can.*4 (M.18.473A); in good ἀ. ἡ τοῦ ἀγαθοῦ ἐπιστημονικὴ κτῆσις Clem.*str.*7. 12(p.50.29; M.9.497B); ἐν τῇ τούτων μεταβολῇ ἀ. τηρήσει τὴν γνώμην Isid.Pel.*epp.*5.495(M.78.1613B); an effect of baptismal grace, Serap. *euch.*21; **3.** theol. (both metaphysical and moral meanings may be present together); **a.** as divine attribute; in Platonic conception of the divine πέμπτον αἰθέριόν τι καὶ ἀ. ... σῶμα ‡Just.*coh.Gr.*5 (M.6.252A); Christian στερέωμα λέγει τὸν θεὸν τὸν ἀπαθῆ καὶ ἀ. Clem.*ecl.*52(p.151.24; M.9.721C); Ath.*Ar.*3.20(M.26.365B); διὰ τὴν τέλειαν αὐτοῦ καὶ ἀ. δύναμιν ‡Just.*qu.Chr.*2(M.6.1416C); ἀ. λέγει [sc. Apoll.] τὸ θεῖον καὶ καλῶς τοῦτο λέγει Gr.Nyss.*Apoll.*56(M.45. 1260C,D); id.*or.catech.*20(p.79.20; M.45.57B); Cyr.*Ps.*41:10(M.69. 1009D); hence, of Logos τὸ ἀ. τῆς τοῦ λόγου δικαιοσύνης Ath.*Ar.*1. 51(M.26.117C); unaffected by Inc. λόγος ὢν...σὰρξ ἐγένετο, ἀ. μενούσης τῆς φύσεως †Chrys.*nativ.*1(6.392C); **b.** of properties peculiar to each Person of Trin. ἕκαστον...τὴν τοῦ προσώπου χαρακτηριστικὴν ἰδιότητα ἀ. ... λέλογχε Sophr.H.*ep.syn.*(M.87.3160A); ἑκάστης ὑποστάσεως ἰδιαζόντως οὔσης καὶ...ἀ. μενούσης ‡Caes.Naz.*dial.*3(M.38. 861); **c.** Christol. σύνοδος, θατέρου τῶν...συγκειμένων, πρὸς τὸ ἕτερον τὴν φυσικὴν ἰδιότητα ἀνόθευτόν τε καὶ ἀ. ἔχουσα καὶ ἀδιαίρετον Max. *ep.*12(M.91.484A); *ib.*17(581B); τῶν δύο φύσεων...τὴν εἰς ἀλλήλας περιχώρησιν ἀσύγχυτον καὶ ἀ. ἐχουσῶν Jo.D.*f.o.*4.18(M.94.1184C); τῆς δυάδος τηρουμένης τῶν φύσεων, διὰ...τῆς τοῦ λόγου ἀ. σαρκώσεως id.*hom.*1.2(M.96.548D).

ἀμεταβλήτως, *without change, unchangeably*, theol. ὁ υἱὸς...ἀεὶ... ἀ. ξυνὼν τῷ γεννήτορι ‡Caes.Naz.*dial.*2(M.38.860); Christol., Cyr. *ep.*45(p.153.8; 5^2.137B) cit. s. ἀτρέπτως; ὁ λόγος σεσάρκωται, καὶ ἡ σὰρξ...ἀ. τεθέωται Sophr.H.*ep.syn.*(M.87.3164C); ‡Caes.Naz.*dial.* 24(M.38.884); Jo.D.*imag.*3.6(M.94.1325A); ‡Meth.*Sym.et Ann.*13(M. 18.380C).

ἀμετάβολος, **1.** *unchangeable*, Clem.*str.*6.7(p.462.14; M.9.281C); *A.Jo.*85(p.193.8); of God, *ib.*107(p.205.2); **2.** *without change*, Christol. τῆς...ἀ. καὶ ἀμερίστου σου σαρκώσεως ‡Meth.*palm.*6(M.18. 396B); μετὰ τῆς ἀ. καὶ ἀσυγχύτου τῶν οἰκείων ἱδρύσεως Dion.Ar.*d.n.* 1.4(M.3.592B).

ἀμετάδοτος, *not to be shared, incommunicable* ἀ. γὰρ ἡ δόξα τοῦ παντοκράτορος Eun.ap.Gr.Nyss.*Eun.*2(2 p.343.9; M.45.520B).

ἀμετάθετος, **1.** *unchangeable, immutable*, in gen. ἀ. τῶν δογμάτων βάσεις Gr.Nyss.*hom.2 in Cant.*(M.44.788D); Cyr.*Jo.*4.6(4.428C); of divine attributes and activity ἀ. σωτηρίας δόσιν Clem.*str.*6.13(p.485. 20; M.9.328B); Bas.ap.*cat.Ac.*7:55(p.129.6); τῆς ἀκτίστου φύσεως τὸ ...ἀ. ἐν ἑαυτῇ κεκτημένης Gr.Nyss.*or.catech.*39(p.155.2; M.45.100A); τὸ ἀ. τῆς ὀργῆς Cyr.*Am.*61(3.317D); of a change not permitted, *M.Polyc.*11.1 cit. s. μετάνοια; hence **2.** *steadfast* Χριστιανὸς ἀ. τυγχάνω *M.Scill.*13; πίστιν...ἀ. [v.l. ἀπαράβατον] καὶ φόβον θεοῦ ἀπαράβατον [v.l. ἀμετάθετον] Hipp.*Dan.*1.10.5(M.10.669B); ἐπιθυμίαν τῆς πρὸς τὸν θεὸν εὐαρεστήσεως...ἀ. Bas.*reg.br.*157(2.467E; M. 31.1185A); **3.** *incorrigible*, Just.*dial.*120.5(M.6.756B); *A.Jo.*39(p.170. 11); *Hom.Clem.*18.19; Vict.*Mc.*15:29(p.439.1).

ἀμεταθέτως, **1.** *unchangeably* τοῦ λόγου ἀ. ἔχοντος πρός τε τὸ σῶμα, πρός τε τὴν ψυχήν ‡Ath.*Apoll.*2.17(M.26.1061B); **2.** *incorrigibly* ἕξιν τῆς ψυχῆς,...τὴν ἀνιάτως ἔχουσαν καὶ ἀ. Chrys.*hom.19.1 in Rom.* (9.643A); Niceph.Ur.*v.Sym.*224(M.86.3192D).

ἀμετακίνητος, *immutable, unchangeable, steadfast*, in gen. τὰ πάλαι διωρισμένα...ἀ. διαφυλάττειν CArim.*ep.Const.*1(p.238.7; M.26. 697C); ἵνα...ἀσφαλισθέντες τῇ σφραγῖδι ταύτῃ διαμείνωσιν...ἀ. Serap. *euch.*25.2; ἀ. ... περὶ τὸν θεὸν πόθον Thdt.*rect.conf.*4(M.6.1213B); of S. Barnabas πέτρα ἡ ἀ. Alex.Sal.*Barn.*6(438D); of divine attributes ἀγαθωσύνη...ἡ πρὸς τοὺς...πεπιστευκότας ἀ. Clem.*paed.*1.9(p.140.11; M.8.352C); judgements, id.*ecl.*60(p.154.25; M.9.728B); power, Gr. Nyss.*or.dom.*2(p.32.13; M.44.1140C); ἀ. ἵδρυσιν Max.*ambig.*(M.91. 1284A); τὸ ἀ. of God, Dion.Ar.*d.n.*9.8(M.3.916B).

ἀμετάλλακτος, *unaltered*, Eus.*ep.Constant.*2(M.20.1545A).

ἀμεταμέλητος, **1.** *not to be repented of* or *regretted*; hence **a.** *that does not bring regret* τὴν ἀ. πολιτείαν τοῦ θεοῦ *1Clem.*54.4; *ib.*58.2; **b.** *about which no change of mind can take place, irrevocable, assured*, *Hom.Clem.*3.45; ἵνα ἡ...τοῦ πνεύματος χάρις εἰς τοὺς μαθητὰς...ἀ. γένηται Ath.*Ar.*3.25(M.26.376B); *ib.*(376C) cit. s. χάρις; **c.** *unchangeable, obstinate* τὸν ἀ. τρόπον Thdt.*Ps.*54:20(1.968); **2.** *steadfast* ἀ. ἦτε ἐπὶ πάσῃ ἀγαθοποιΐᾳ *1Clem.*2.7.

ἀμεταμελήτως, **1.** *irrevocably*, exeg. Jo.17:21f. τὸ γὰρ κατὰ φύσιν... ὑπάρχον τῷ λόγῳ ἐν τῷ πατρί, τοῦτο ἡμῖν ἀ. διὰ τοῦ πνεύματος δοθῆναι βούλεται Ath.*Ar.*3.25(M.26.376B); **2.** *without regret* ὁ ποιήσας...ἀ. τὰ ὑπὸ τοῦ θεοῦ δεδομένα δικαιώματα *1Clem.*58.2.

***ἀμεταμελῶς**, *without repentance*, Didym.*Trin.*3.31(M.39.953B).

***ἀμετανάστευτος**, *not to be removed* ἀ. ἡ κατασκήνωσις *Const. App.*7.35.9.

***ἀμετανοησία**, ἡ, *impenitence*, Nil.*epp.*1.260(M.79.180A).

***ἀμετανόησις**, ἡ, = foreg., Ephr.2.204D.

ἀμετανόητος, **1.** *not to be repented of* or *regretted*, hence *fixed, assured, unwavering* πίστιν *A.Jo.*9(p.157.1); Clem.*str.*2.13(p.143. 27; M.8.996A) cit. s. μετάνοια; σώματός τε καὶ...παθῶν ἀ. χωρισμός *ib.*5.11(p.370.27; M.9.101B); *ib.*5.1(p.329.31; 16C); **2.** *unrepentant, impenitent* ἀ. τηρεῖται εἰς αἰωνίαν κόλασιν *T.Gad* 7.5; Ephr.3.517F; ἀ. καρδίας †Bas.*Is.*34(1.407B; M.30.185C); Chrys.*hom.29.4 in 2Cor.*(10. 645D); ἔστιν ἁμαρτία πρὸς θάνατον ἡ ἀ. *Schol.*66 in Jo.Clim.*scal.*26 (M.88.1052D); neut. as subst., *impenitence*, Chrys.*hom.25.2 in Gen.* (4.233B); neut. plur. as adv., *without repentance* ἀ. ἁμαρτάνοντες Ephr.3.55D; Thdr.Heracl.*Is.*26:14(M.18.1313D); Bas.*reg.br.*9(2.417B; M.31.1088A).

ἀμετανοήτως, **1.** *without repentance, impenitently*, *Const.App.* 2.41.9; **2.** *unwaveringly, steadily* ἀ. χρωμένους γνώμῃ τῇ αὐτῇ Clem.*str.*1.25(p.103.13; M.8.912B); Hipp.*haer.*6.31(M.16.3242A; conj. ἀμετακινήτως p.159.14).

ἀμετάπειστος, **1.** *not changed by persuasion, not to be dissuaded* of martyrs ἀ. τῶν καλῶν *Const.App.*5.8.2 (v.l. ἀμετάπιστος); **2.** *unalterable*, Dion.Ar.*d.n.*7.4(M.3.872C).

***ἀμετάπιστος**, ? f.l. for ἀμετάπειστος or poss. *unchangeably trustworthy* ἀ. ἡ γνώμη *Const.App.*7.35.10; v.l. for ἀμετάπειστος *ib.*5.8.2.

ἀμεταποίητος, *unchangeable*, **1.** *obstinate* ἐν ἀκαθαρσίᾳ γεγονότες ἀ. μενεῖτε; Cyr.*Os.*88(3.120A); τὸ ἀ. τῆς γνώμης *ib.*77(111C); **2.** *immutable*, of Father ὡς ἐν ἀ. φαινόμενον εἰκόνι τῷ υἱῷ id.*Jo.*1.3(4.27B); of Son ἔχει...τὴν ἐφ' ἅπασι τοῖς ἀγαθοῖς ἀ. στάσιν id.*inc.unigen.*(5^1. 691E); τὸ ἐν...ἀ. φύσει κεῖσθαι τὸν υἱόν id.*thes.*32(5^1.278B).

ἀμετάπτωτος, *unchanging, unchangeable*; of God, Dion.Ar.*d.n.* 9.3(M.3.912B); of sonship of Christ, Alex.Al.*ep.Alex.*8(p.25.2; M.18. 560C); of Christ οἱονεὶ κιχρῶντος ἡμῖν τὸ τῆς ἰδίας φύσεως ἀ. Cyr.*Jo.* 5.2(4.473B); of men's being sons of God, Or.*or.*22.2(p.346.30; M.11. 484A); in gen. ἀ. κριτηρίῳ τῇ πίστει ἐπαναπαυώμεθα Clem.*str.*2.4 (p.119.6; M.8.944A).

***ἀμετασάλευτος**, *motionless*, Clem.*paed*.2.7(p.190.21; M.8.457C).

ἀμεταστρεπτί, *without turning round*, met., *without looking back*, *steadfastly* τῆς ἀληθείας τὴν ὁδὸν...βαδίζωμεν ἀ. Clem.*str*.5.1(p.330.28; M.9.17C); Eus.*p.e*.1.10(42B; M.21.89A); οἱ ἀ. πρὸς σὲ [sc. τὸν Χριστόν] ἀτενίζοντες Proc.G.*fr.Cant*.8:13(M.87.1777C).

***ἀμεταστρόφως**, *without change*, *unalterably* ἀγγέλους ἀ. ἐν ἀφθαρσίᾳ τὰ ἄριστα πράξοντας Meth.*res*.1.47(p.301.14; M.18.277A); *ib*.1.36(p.275.15; M.41.1101A).

***ἀμετασχηματίστως**, *without change*, of God παρὼν μὲν τοῖς ὅλοις ...ἀ. Didym.*Trin*.2.4(M.39.484B).

ἀμετάτρεπτος, *not to be turned round*; hence **1.** *unchanging*, *unalterable*, Clem.*str*.4.23(p.315.23; M.8.1360C); of God, *A.Jo*.104 (p.202.24); ἡ φύσις τῆς ὕλης...ἔμεινε...ὃ ἦν ἐξ ἀρχῆς ἀ. Jo.D.*Man*.2 (M.96.1332D); **2.** *unswerving*, *steadfast* βλέπων τε πρὸς οὐρανὸν ἀ. ὄμματι Gr.Nyss.*v.Gr.Thaum*.(M.46.948B); met. τὴν ψυχὴν *A.Jo*. 23(p.164.2); **3.** *not to be converted* ἀ. πρὸς τὸ ἀγαθὸν φρόνημα τοῦ πνεύματος Mac.Aeg.*hom*.4.7(M.34.477C); neut. as subst., *unwillingness to be converted*, *obstinacy*, Or.*comm.ser*.*119 in Mt*.(p.252.15; M.17.305C).

ἀμετάτροπος, *unalterable*, Nonn.*par.Jo*.16:22(M.43.881B).

***ἀμετάφορος**, *not to be changed* ἀπείρηται...τῇ κτίσει τὸ ἀ. καὶ ἄτρεπτον Cyr.*Jo*.5.5(4.531D).

***ἀμεταχώρητος**, *unable to pass* πρὸς τὸ μὴ ὂν ἀ. Max.*ambig*. (M.91.1329B).

***ἀμετεώριστος**, *undistracted* ἀ. ... ἐπιθυμίᾳ τῆς πρὸς θεὸν εὐαρεστήσεως Bas.*reg.br*.197(2.481C; M.31.1213A); ὁ δὲ θεὸς...δῴη σοι...νοῦν ἀ. Isid.Pel.*epp*.1.129(M.78.269A); τὸ ἀ. τοῦ νοὸς ἐμφαίνει Marc. Er.*opusc*.7.4(M.65.1076D); esp. ref. wandering thoughts ἀντιψάλλουσιν ἀλλήλοις...τὸ ἀ. τῶν καρδιῶν ἑαυτοῖς διοικούμενοι Bas.*ep*.207 (3.311B; M.32.764A); of the mind in prayer, id.*reg.br*.201(2.482E; M.31.1216C); ἀ. ψαλμῳδίας τε καὶ εὐχῆς Jo.Mosch.*prat*.171(M.87.3040B); Hesych.S.*temp*.1.61(M.93.1500B).

***ἀμετεωρίστως**, *without distraction* φιλέρημος, ἐφ' ἑαυτῷ μένων ἀεὶ ἀ. †Bas.*ep*.42.3(3.127D; M.32.353A); Nil.*Magn*.11(M.79.984B); ἀνυμνήσω σε ἀ. Hesych.H.*Ps.tit*.85.23(M.27.1016C).

ἀμέτοχος, *without a share of*, *not participating in*, of unbaptized ἀ. τῆς ζωῆς Ammon.*Ac*.16:32(M.85.1561B); οὐδεὶς γάρ ἐστιν ἀ. τῆς τοῦ θεοῦ χρηστότητος Bas.*reg.br*.253(2.500D; M.31.1252C); οὐδεὶς ἀ. τῆς διὰ Χριστοῦ σωτηρίας Cyr.*Ps*.97:3(M.69.1253D); ἔχει γὰρ ἡ κτίσις οἴκοθεν τὸ εἶναι ζωή, ζωὴ δὲ ζωῆς ἀ. id.*Jo*.1.6(4.52E); τῆς ἀληθείας ἀ. *cat.Jo*.2:18(p.201.24); of God ὡς μυρία ὅσα δεδώρηται ἡμῖν ὁ θεός, ὧν αὐτὸς ἀ. Clem.*str*.5.10(p.371.16; M.9.104A); οἱ δὲ τῷ υἱῷ μόνῳ τὸν τρισάγιον ἀνατιθέντες ὕμνον, ἀ. τοῦ ὕμνου τὸν πατέρα καὶ τὸ πνεῦμα τιθέασι Jo.D.*trisag*.8(M.95.41B); of Christ οὐδέποτε τὸ σῶμα τὸ ἅγιον ἀ. τῆς θείας δόξης ὑφέστηκεν id.*hom*.1.12(M.96.564B); Trin. (Arian) ἀ. εἰσιν ἀλλήλων αἱ οὐσίαι τοῦ πατρὸς καὶ τοῦ υἱοῦ καὶ τοῦ ἁγίου πνεύματος Ath.*Ar*.1.6(M.26.24B); ἀ. κατὰ πάντα τοῦ πατρὸς τὸν υἱόν *ib*.; of H. Ghost ἀ. αὐτὸ θεότητος ἀποφαίνεται [sc. Eunomius] Bas.*Eun*.3.5(1.276C; M.29.665A).

***ἀμετραίνω**, *observe no measure*, *act without moderation*, Gennad. *fr.Rom*.7:22(p.374.18; M.85.1688A).

ἀμέτρητος, *immeasurable*, *immense*, in gen. τὴν ἀ. τῶν πεπιστευκότων πληθὺν Cyr.*Os*.31(3.57A); of number of angels, id.*Lc*.12:32(M.72.741D); *innumerable*; of ships, *Orac.Sib*.4.77; met. τὸ ἀ. μέγεθος τῆς κακίας ἀποθέμενοι *A.Mt*.6(p.223.10); of humility, Nil.*inst*.(M.79.1236B); of God ἀ. εἰς πλάτος *Hom.Clem*.17.9; περὶ θεοῦ παντοκράτορος, ἀοράτου, ἀναλλοιώτου, ἀ. ‡Pion.*v.Polyc*.13; of grace, Or.*or*.1 (p.297.3; M.11.416A); of God's φιλανθρωπία, Ammon.*Ac*.17:30(M.85.1565B); Thdt.*Rom*.11:35(3.127); of Christ ὅτε μέτρον οὐκ ἔστιν ἐν τῷ υἱῷ, ἀ. ἄρα ἐστί Cyr.*Jo*.1.3(4.22A); of his mercy, *Ep.Lugd*.ap.Eus. *h.e*.5.1.32(M.20.420C); of H. Ghost εἰ δὲ ἡ ἐνέργεια αὐτοῦ ἀ., πολλῷ μᾶλλον ἡ οὐσία Chrys.*hom*.*30.2 in Jo*.(8.172E).

ἀμετρία, ἡ, **1.** *lack of proportion*; in verse, *lack of metre*, ‡Just. *coh.Gr*.37(M.6.309A); **2.** *excess* ἡ τοσαύτη ἀπόνοια τῆς ἀ. ‡Ath.*Apoll*. 1.9(M.26.1108B); of grief, Chrys.*hom*.*78.1 in Jo*.(8.458C); τῆς ταπεινοφροσύνης τὴν ἀ. Thdt.*1Cor*.4:8(3.188); in monophysite argument οὐκ ᾤμην αὐτοὺς διαιρεῖν τὰς φύσεις μετὰ τὴν ἕνωσιν, πολλὴν δὲ εὗρον διαιρέσεως ἀ. id.*eran*.2(4.170); **3.** *want of moderation*, *intemperance* ἀ. περὶ τὰς τροφάς Clem.*paed*.2.1(p.162.11; M.8.397A); *ib*.2.10(p.225.12; 533B); ἡ ἁμαρτία...εἰς ἀ. ἐκκαλουμένη τὰ πάθη Thdt.*Rom*.5:21 (3.60); Dion.Ar.*e.h*.2.3.3(M.3.400B); **4.** *extravagance*, in doctrine, leading to heresy ἡ δὲ ἐκκλησία...τὴν ἀμφοτέρων [sc. Valentinus and Marcion] ἀ. φεύγουσα Chrys.*sac*.4.4(p.114.5; 1.409C); of Sabellians and Arians ἐξ ἀ. ἀμφότεροι τῆς ὑγιοῦς ἐξέπεσον πίστεως *ib*. (p.115.1; 409D); **5.** *countless number* τῆς ἀ. τῶν ἁμαρτανομένων Bas.*mor*.7.7(3.510B; M.32.1208C); Gr.Nyss.*or.catech*.8(p.50.16; M.45.37D); **6.** *infinitude*, *immensity*; of God, Dion.Ar.*d.n*.1.1 (M.3.588A); τῆς...εὐεξίας τοῦ θεοῦ...ἀ. id.*ep*.9.5(M.3.1112C).

ἀμετρόβιος, *immensely long-lived*; of ravens, Gr.Naz.*carm*.2.2 (poem.)7.129(M.37.1561A), perh. for *ἀμετρόβοος, *of immoderate cry*, Cosm.Mel.*schol*.ad loc.(M.38.639).

ἄμετρος, *boundless*, *immense*, *immeasurable*; *infinite* ἄ. ὁ πρὸ τῶν αἰώνων Apoll.*fid.sec.pt*.9(p.170.22; M.10.1108D); of Christ ὅθ' ὑπῆρχες τῆς κόρης ἐγγάστριος, οὐκ ἄ. εἶχες φύσιν †Ephr.*nativ*.(p.87); εἰ δὲ ἑτέρως [opp. κατά τι ποσὸν συνεχές] ἄ. ὁ λόγος, ἤγουν τῇ δυνάμει Leont.H.*Nest*.1.25(1492C); ref. Rom.2:4 τὸ ἄ. τοῦ πλούτου αὐτοῦ [sc. τοῦ θεοῦ] Just.*dial*.47.5(M.6.580A).

***ἀμετρόφωνος**, *immoderate of speech*, Anon.ap.Eus.*h.e*.5.16.12 (M.20.469A).

***ἀμετώριστος**, for ἀμετεώριστος, Ephr.1.204A.

[*]ἀμηγέπη, = ἀμῇ γέ πῃ, *somehow*, *to some extent*, Clem.*paed*.3.5 (M.8.600B; ἀμῇ γέ πῃ p.254.21); Meth.*symp*.8.4(p.85.21; M.18.144C); Thdt. *affect*.1(p.33.18; 4.724).

ἀμήν, (Hebr. אָמֵן) *amen*, *verily*, *of a truth*, *so be it*;

A. in gen., **1.** *so be it*; in response to a request εἶπεν ὁ θάνατος· ἀ. γένοιτο *T.Abr*.A 18(p.100.28); **2.** *truly*, *indeed* ἀ. δοκεῖς...λανθάνειν; *Apoc.Paul*.17(p.47).

B. in prayer; **1.** def. and comments τὸ δὲ ἀ. τῇ Ἑβραΐδι φωνῇ τὸ γένοιτο σημαίνει Just.*1apol*.65.4(M.6.428B); χορὸς ἀγγέλων...λέγων γένοιτο, γένοιτο· ἢ κατὰ τὸν Ἀκύλαν, πεπιστωμένως, πεπιστωμένως ἢ κατὰ τὸν Σύμμαχον· ἀ. καὶ ἀ. Eus.*Ps*.71:18ff.(M.23.821A); ἐπισφραγίζων διὰ τοῦ ἀ., ὃ σημαίνει, γένοιτο, τὰ ἐν τῇ...εὐχῇ Cyr.H.*catech*. 23.18; τὸ γὰρ γένοιτο, γένοιτο, ἀ. καὶ ἀ. ὁ Ἑβραῖος καλεῖ. ὅθεν καὶ τὸ ἔθος ἐν ταῖς ἐκκλησίαις μεμένηκε τῇ δοξολογίᾳ τοῦ ἱερέως διὰ τοῦ ἀ. συντίθεσθαι τὸν λαὸν...καὶ τὴν εὐλογίαν λαμβάνειν Thdt.*Ps*.105:48 (1.1365); ὁ ἱερεὺς...λέγει εὐλογημένη ἡ βασιλεία· ὁ δὲ λαὸς...ἀποκρίνεται ἀ., τουτέστι, ἀλήθεια ‡Sophr.H.*liturg*.11(M.87.3992C); **2.** liturg. as response of people after anaphora συντελέσαντος τὰς εὐχὰς καὶ τὴν εὐχαριστίαν πᾶς ὁ παρὼν λαὸς ἐπευφημεῖ λέγων· ἀ. Just.*1apol*. 65.3(M.6.428B); εὐχαριστίας γὰρ ἐπακούσαντα καὶ συνεπιφθεγξάμενον τὸ ἀ. Dion.Al.ap.Eus.*h.e*.7.9.4(M.20.656A); *Lit.Chrys*.(p.328.21); cf. Ambr.*de mysteriis* 54(M.*PL*.16.407B); after consecration of bread, *Lit.Marc*.(p.132.32); and of wine, *ib*.(p.133.15); as individual response at reception, cf. *frangens autem panem singulis partes porrigens dicat: panis caelestis in Christo Jesu. qui autem accipit respondeat: amen*, Hipp.*trad.ap*.23.6; Corn.ap.Eus.*h.e*.6.43.19(M.20.628A); Cyr.H.*catech*.23.21,22; ὁ μὲν ἐπίσκοπος διδότω τὴν προσφορὰν λέγων· σῶμα Χριστοῦ, καὶ ὁ δεχόμενος λεγέτω· ἀ.· ὁ δὲ διάκονος κατεχέτω τὸ ποτήριον καὶ ἐπιδιδοὺς λεγέτω· αἷμα Χριστοῦ, ποτήριον ζωῆς, καὶ ὁ πίνων λεγέτω· ἀ. *Lit*.ap.*Const.App*.8.13.15; cf.Tert.*de spectaculis* 25(M.*PL*.1.657A); **3.** in other rites and in private prayers; after thanksgiving before martyrdom, *M.Scill*.17; as response after each sentence of extempore hymn, *A.Jo*.94(p.197.18ff.); after blessing of oil, *Const.App*.7.27.2; at baptism, Cyr.*Jo*.7(4.683E).

C. Gnost., equals number 99 [$\alpha' = 1$, $\mu' = 40$, $\eta' = 8$, $\nu' = 50$], Iren.*haer*.1.16.1(M.7.630B); therefore represented by ϙθ', *Pap.Chr*. (p.397).

D. in NT; **1.** in gen., interpreted as form of oath, cf. ἄκουσον ὀμνύντος αὐτοῦ τοῦ κυρίου (Mt.6:2) Gr.Nyss.*instit*.(p.88.17; M.34.442A); ὁ υἱὸς ὀμνύει καθ' ἑαυτοῦ, λέγων, ἀ. ἀ. λέγω ὑμῖν Chrys.*hom*. *11.1 in Heb*.(12.112B); but cf. exeg. Is.25:1, Hier.*comm.in Is*.8(M.*PL*.24.289D); **2.** exeg. 2Cor.1:20 τὸ πάντως ἐσόμενον δηλοῖ. αἱ γὰρ ἐπαγγελίαι ἐν αὐτῷ, οὐκ ἐν ἀνθρώπῳ, τὸ γενέσθαι ἔχουσι καὶ πληρωθῆναι Chrys.*hom*.*3.4 in 2Cor*.(10.447A); ἔστι, φησί, τὸ ἀ. φωνὴ συγκαταβάσεως ἐπὶ εὐχαριστίας τῆς εἰς τὸν θεὸν γινομένης (cf. 1Cor. 14:16) Thdr.Mops.*2Cor*.1:20(M.66.893D); δι' αὐτοῦ δὴ πάντως καὶ πᾶν ἔσται πέρας εὐχῆς· καὶ τοῦτό ἐστι τὸ ἀ. Cyr.*2Cor*.1:18(p.324.14; M.64.920C); τὸ δὲ ἀ. ἐνταῦθα οὐχ ἁπλῶς προστέθεικεν· ἀλλὰ διδάσκων ὡς οὐ μόνος ὁ προσευχόμενος ἱερεὺς προσφέρει τὸν ὕμνον, ἀλλὰ καὶ ὁ τὸ ἀ. ἐπιλέγων κοινωνεῖ τῆς προσφερομένης δοξολογίας Thdt.*2Cor*. 1:20(3.295); **3.** as divine title, exeg. Apoc.3:14 ἰσοδυναμεῖ τοῦτο τῷ τάδε λέγει ὁ ἀληθινός...ἀ. γάρ ἐστιν τὸ ναί Oecum.*Apoc*.3:14(p.64); ἀ. ἐστι τὸ ναί. ναὶ οὖν ἐστιν ἐν πᾶσι τοῖς περὶ αὐτοῦ λεγομένοις, ἤτοι ἀλήθεια καὶ οὐδὲν ψεῦδος ἐν αὐτοῖς Areth.*Apoc*.9(M.106.560D).

ἀμήρυτος, *not to be wound up*, hence *endless*, *everlasting* εἰς ἀ. ... ἀποδημήσει λόγος Cyr.*Jo*.1.1(4.11A); *ib*.1.9(102A); ἡ δοθησομένη σωτηρία μακρὰ καὶ ἀ. id.*Is*.4.5(2.709E); of future life, *ib*.3.1(369B); future happiness, id.*Jo*.11.2(934E); neut. as subst. χαῖρε ῥόδον ἀμάραντον, ἡ τὸ ἀ. εὐωδιάζουσα (throughout *eternity*) Thdr.Stud. *nativ.BMV* 7(M.96.692C).

***ἀμητρογενής**, *born without a mother*; of Adam, Leont.H.*Nest*. 4.37(M.86.1708A).

ἀμήτωρ, *without a mother, motherless*; of Son, Gr.Naz.*carm*.1.1.9.4 (M.37.459A); θεότης...εἰ ἔξω νοοῖτο σαρκὸς ἀ. ἔσται Cyr.*hom.pasch*.17 (5².228C); ἀ. ἐκ...πατρός, ἀπάτωρ ἐκ σοῦ τῆς μητρός Procl.CP *annunt*. 5(M.85.444B).

ἀμηχανία, ἡ, 1. *helplessness* γενόμενος...ἄνθρωπος, διὰ τὸ ταύτης τῆς πονηρᾶς ἐξελέσθαι τὴν τῶν ἀνθρώπων φύσιν ἀ. Max.*qu.Thal*.21 (M.90.313B); 2. *perplexity, despair*, Just.*dial*.2.6(M.6.477C); Eus. *h.e*.5.5.1(M.20.441A); Chrys.*hom.24.2 in Eph*.(11.182B); 3. *impossibility, illogicality*, id.*hom.7.2 in 2Tim*.(11.702A).

ἀμήχανος, *impossible* ἀ. ὡς ὁ θεός ἐστι γενέσθαι τινὰ τέλειον Clem. *str*.7.14(p.63.12; M.9.524A); ἀ. γὰρ ἀνθρωπίνην ψυχὴν μὴ ἀποπεσεῖν πάθεσιν Or.*comm.in Rom*.7:8(*JTS* 14 p.13); Didym.*Trin*.3.3(M.39. 825B); Chrys.*hom.23.3 in Jo*.(8.136E); ἀ. ἄνθρωπον...παρακαλοῦντα τὸν θεὸν συνεχῶς, ἁμαρτεῖν ποτε id.*Anna* 4.5(4.736D).

***ἀμίαντον**, τό (-ος, ἡ), *amianthus, asbestos* τὸ ἀ. *Protev*.10 (p.21); Ath.*inc*.28.3(M.25.144C); ἡ ἀ. Adam.*dial*.5.8(p.190.16; M.11. 1843C).

ἀμίαντος, *undefiled, pure*; 1. morally ἀ. χεῖρας αἴροντες πρὸς αὐτόν *1Clem*.29.1; ἐὰν μὴ τηρήσωμεν τὸ βάπτισμα...ἀ. *2Clem*.6.9; πᾶσα γὰρ σὰρξ ἀπολήψεται μισθὸν ἡ εὑρεθεῖσα ἀ. Herm.*sim*.5.6.7 al.; of soul, Clem.*str*.7.7(p.36.27; M.9.469A); of saints, id.*q.d.s*.34(p.182. 26; M.9.640C); neut. as subst., *purity*, *Hom.Clem*.8.13; 2. of virgins, *Protev*.10(p.20); Ath.*v.Anton*.79(M.26.953B); esp. of BMV, id.*inc*. 8.8(M.25.109C); Gr.Nyss.*virg*.2(p.254.24; M.46.324B); Leont.H.*Nest*. 4.3(M.86.1657C); *ib*.4.9(1669C); 3. of God τὴν ἀφθαρσίαν, ἀπὸ τῶν ἀ. τοῦ παντοκράτορος ἀποπηδῶσαν κόλπων Meth.*symp*.1.1(p.8.3; M. 18.37A); τὴν παιδουργίαν...ταῖς ἀ. ὁ παντοκράτωρ ἐργαζόμενος χερσίν *ib*.2.2(p.17.7; 49B); of Christ τὸν...ἀ. κτίστην...πάσης τῆς οἰκουμένης *M.Thdot*.3(p.137.27).

***ἀμιάντως**, *without defilement*, ref. Christ ἐν δούλου μορφῇ...ἀ. ‡Meth.*Sym.et Ann*.14(M.18.381C).

ἀμιγής, 1. *unmixed, pure* χρὴ...τοὺς μὲν καθαιρομένους ἀ. ἀποτελεῖσθαι καθόλου Dion.Ar.*c.h*.3.3(M.3.165D); of Trin. ἀ. ... τῶν γενητῶν Ath.*Ar*.1.18(M.26.49B); of God τοῖς πολλοῖς ἀ. καὶ ἀπλήθυντος Dion.Ar.*d.n*.2.11(M.3.649D); of Logos λαμβάνει τὸ ἡμέτερον [sc. σῶμα],...καθαρὸν καὶ ὄντως ἀ. τῆς ἀνδρῶν συνουσίας Ath.*inc*. 8.3(M.25.109C); 2. *virgin* νύμφην Meth.*symp*.7.1(p.72.12; M.18.125C); ἀ. τινα αἰῶνα Epiph.*haer*.31.4(p.388.5; M.41.480B); 3. *separate* ὥσπερ οὖν ἐναντίαι αἱ προθέσεις [sc. of the good and the wicked], οὕτως ἀ. ἡ μετάστασις Isid.Pel.*epp*.1.172(M.78.296B).

ἀμιγῶς, *without mixture*, of God ἐν ἅπασιν ἀ. κατοικῶν Didym. *Trin*.2.4(M.39.484B); of Trin. κατ' αὐτὴν τὴν ἕνωσιν ἀ. ἵδρυται, καὶ ἀσυγχύτως ἑκάστη τῶν ἐναρχικῶν ὑποστάσεων Dion.Ar.*d.n*.2.5(M.3. 641D); ἡ θεαρχία...ἀ. τοῖς διοικουμένοις ἐπάρχουσα *ib*.10.1(937A).

ἄμικτος, 1. *unmingled*, of Christ οὐδαμοῦ τὴν ἀναληφθεῖσαν ἀνθρωπότητα τῆς θείας ἐνεργείας ἄ. Chrys.*pan.Laz*.(2.647C); 2. *irreconcilable* ἄ. ἦν ἡ πρὸς ἀλλήλους φιλονεικία Eus.*v.C*.3.23(p.88.30; M.20.1084B); Gr.Nyss.*or.dom*.2(p.36.33; M.44.1144A); Pall.*v.Chrys*.20 (p.141.7; M.47.78); 3. *without social intercourse, solitary*; of monastic life, Gr.Nyss.*ep*.2(M.46.1012A).

ἀμίκτως, *without admixture*, Clem.*str*.1.28(p.109.16; M.8.924B).

ἀμιλλητήρ, 1. *contending*; *contentious*, Nonn.*par.Jo*.7:41(M.43. 812B); *ib*.2:19(764B); *contending* with μῦθον...ἀ. σιωπῆς *ib*.16:17 (880C); 2. as subst., *rival*, *ib*.19:24(904A).

ἀμιξία, ἡ, *division, disagreement* κοινῆς τινος ἀ. ... τὰς...ἐκκλησίας κατεχούσης Soz.*h.e*.8.3.3(M.67.1520C).

ἀμισγής, = ἀμιγής; of Logos, Anast.S.*hex*.12(M.89.1053C).

ἀμισθί (**ἀμισθεί**), *without reward* or *payment*, exeg. Ps.2:8 διδάσκων αἰτεῖσθαι τὴν τῶν ἀνθρώπων σωτηρίαν ἀ. Clem.*str*.4.22(p.308.19; M.8.1345C); οὐκ ἀ. τὴν δικαιοσύνην ἐργάζεται Thdr.Mops.*Ps*.57:12 (p.381.3; M.66.680A); μόνον...δίψησον τοῦ πατρός, ἀμισθεὶ σοι δειχθήσεται ὁ θεός Clem.*prot*.10(p.69.6; M.8.208A).

ἄμισθος, 1. *without pay* or *reward*, exeg. 1Tim.2:15 οὐκ ἄ. ὑμῖν ἔσται ἡ παιδοτροφία Chrys.*hom.9.2 in 1Tim*.(11.596D); συμμάχους [i.e. of God] ἐνταῦθα μὲν ἀ., ἐν οὐρανῷ δὲ ἐντελομίσθους Synes.*ep*.5 (M.66.1344B); 2. *fruitless*, of prayer ἵνα μὴ ἄ. εὑρεθῇ...τὸ πρᾶγμα Cyr.*Lc*.18:10(M.72.853B).

ἀμίσθως, *without reparation*, Leont.N.*v.Jo.Eleem*.3(p.10.9).

***ἀμισθωτί**, *without payment, freely*, Just.*dial*.58.1(M.6.608A).

***ἀμισία**, ἡ, *freedom from hatred*, Clem.*str*.2.18(p.159.18; M.8. 1028A).

[*]**ἀμίσως**, *without feeling hatred*, Jo.Clim.*scal*.27(M.88.1100D).

ἀμμά ([*]**ἀμμᾶς**), ἡ, *mother*; title given to 1. head of a convent, *Apophth.Patr*.(M.65.416B); Max.*ep*.12(M.91.460B); 2. any nun αὕτη γὰρ...ἀ. ἐστιν·—οὕτως γὰρ καλοῦσι τὰς πνευματικάς Pall.*h.Laus*.34 (p.99.18; M.34.1107B); Cyr.S.*v.Sab*.54(p.147.6); Jo.Mosch.*prat*.179 (M.87.3049B); 3. a woman not a nun, Leont.N.*v.Jo.Eleem*.11(p.22. 13).

***ἀμμασρακώθ**, (Hebr. הַמִּזְרָקוֹת cf.Jer.52:18) *bowl*; esp. for use in Jewish sacrifices, *Chron.Pasch*.p.136(M.92.340C).

[*]**ἄμμη**, ἡ, v.l. for ἄμη, *shovel, spade*, ‡Jo.D.*Artem*.68(p.96.22; M.96.1316C); Cyr.S.*v.Sab*.36(p.122.25); *ib*.84(p.190.18).

ἄμμιγα, = ἀνάμιγα, *in combination* θεὸν βροτὸν ἄ. λεύσσων [sc. Devil] Gr.Naz.*carm*.1.2.2.214(M.37.595A); *in combination* with, *Orac.Sib*.3.146; ἄ. τερπνοῖς ἄλγεα Gr.Naz.*carm*.1.2.1.633(570A).

[*]**ἀμμώωσα**, = ἀμῶσα pres. ptcpl. of ἀμάω, *reap, mow down*, †Apoll.*met.Ps*.104:34(M.33.1472A).

ἀμνάς, ἡ, *ewe-lamb*, *T.Job* 44(p.133.5); Meth.*symp*.11(p.134.20; M.18.212A); Chrys.*hom.4.3 in 1Tim*.(11.572C); met. αἱ τοῦ θεοῦ θυγατέρες αἱ ἀ. αἱ καλαί Clem.*prot*.12(p.84.12; M.8.240C); ἡ μακαρία ἀ. τοῦ Χριστοῦ *M.Ariadn*.1(p.123.18); of BMV τὸν ἐκ τῆς παρθενικῆς ἀ. προελθόντα ποιμένα Procl.CP *or*.4.2(M.65.712A).

[*]**ἀμνημονεύ-ω**, = ἀμνημονέω *be unmindful, forget* ∼εις πῶς ἐγένου νοσήσας *T.Job* 35(p.125.22, v.l. ἀμνήμων εἶς); Bas.Sel.*v.Thecl*. 2.29(M.85.613D); ἀ. τῶν πλημμελημάτων †Jo.D.*B.J*.24(M.96.1085B).

***ἀμνημονία**, ἡ, *forgetfulness*, Marc.Er.*opusc*.5.2(M.65.1029D).

***ἀμνημόνως**, *in forgetfulness*, Eus.*Marcell*.1.3(p.16.6; M.24.748B).

ἀμνημοσύνη, ἡ, *forgetfulness*, *Hom.Clem*.12.4; Jo.Mon.*hymn. Bas*.4(M.96.1373B).

ἀμνησικακέω, *forgive*; of men, *A.Mt*.17(p.238.3); Clem.*str*.7.14 (p.63.6; M.9.521C); ἀ. περὶ τῶν παρελθόντων Cyr.*ep*.57(p.21.21; 5². 192C); of God ἀμνησικάκησον ἐπ' ἐμοί, κύριε *Trad.Pil*.9(p.454); Cyr.*Is*.5.2(2.759D); id.*Jo*.4.3(4.379D).

ἀμνησικακία, ἡ, *forgetfulness of injury, forgivingness*, of men ἀγάπη...νοεῖται...δι' ἀ. Clem.*str*.2.18(p.159.18; M.8.1028A); τῆς κατὰ τὸ εὐαγγέλιον ἀ. *ib*.7.14(p.61.14; M.9.520B); μέγιστόν ἐστι κατόρθωμα ἀ. Or.*or*.9.3(p.319.9; M.11.444D); of kiss of peace ἀνακίρνησι τὰς ψυχὰς ἀλλήλαις καὶ πᾶσαν ἀ. αὐταῖς μνηστεύεται Cyr.H.*catech*.23.3; of God, id.*hom*.17(M.33.1152A); δεδικαιώμεθα γὰρ...κατὰ...τὴν δωρηθεῖσαν ἡμῖν ἄνωθεν ἀ. Cyr.*Jo*.4.3(4.379D); id.*Is*.3.2(2.427B).

ἀμνησίκακος, *forgiving* ἀ. εἰς ἀλλήλους *1Clem*.2.5; ref. Mt.5:44, Clem.*str*.7.14(p.60.30; M.9.517C); Chrys.*hom.21.4 in Eph*.(11.164C); neut. as subst., exeg. Lev.5:11 τὸ...ἀ. τῶν νεοττῶν εὐπρόσδεκτον... τῷ θεῷ Clem.*paed*.1.5(p.98.14; M.8.265A); Epiph.*haer*.37.8(p.61.14; M.41.653A); of God, Herm.*mand*.9.3; Didym.*Trin*.3.19(M.39.889A); ἀ. χάριτι δικαιοῦντος θεοῦ Cyr.*Is*.5.2(2.759C); *ib*.3.4(492C); of Christ, Gr.Nyss.*hom.4 in Cant*.(M.44.849D); ἀ. εἰμι καὶ φιλάνθρωπος Gr.Ant. *mul.ung*.11(M.88.1864B); ref. Mt.5:24 διαλλάγηθι τῷ ἀδελφῷ σου καὶ ...ἀξίως μεταλαμβάνετε τῶν ἀχράντων τοῦ ἀ. Χριστοῦ μυστηρίων Leont.N.*v.Jo.Eleem*.17(p.35.17).

ἀμνησικάκως, *without remembering wrong, forgivingly*, ref. men ὁμονοοῦντας ἀ. *1Clem*.62.2; Clem.*str*.4.22(p.309.7; M.8.1348B); Or.*or*.28.6(p.378.27; M.11.525C); ref. God ἀ. αὐτοῖς [sc. τοῖς Ἰουδαίοις] ἀνέντος θεοῦ καὶ τὰ εἰς Χριστὸν ἐγκλήματα Cyr.*Joel*.37(3.231B); id.*Is*.5.2(2.765B); ref. Christ ἀ. ... ἡμᾶς ἀνιεὶς ἁμαρτίας id.*ador*.16 (1.586C).

***ἀμνησιπόνηρος**, *unmindful of evil, forgiving* πρὸς ἐχθροὺς...ἀ. Clem.*str*.7.12 (conj. p.49.30 for μεσοπόνηροι M.9.496C).

ἀμνήστευτος, *unbetrothed*, *Can.App*.67.

ἀμνηστία (**ἀμνηστεία**), ἡ, 1. *forgetfulness*; *disregard, neglect* ἀ. τῶν εἰς τὴν ἀληθῆ συντεινόντων ζωήν Clem.*paed*.2.2(p.173.2; ἀμνηστεία M.8.421B); *oblivion* πάντα τὰ ὡρισμένα...νῦν ἀμνηστίᾳ παραδοθῆναι Constantius Imp.ap.Ath.*apol.sec*.54(p.135.8; M.25.348B); Sophr.H. *v.Anast*.(M.92.1721C); 2. *forgetfulness of injury, forgiveness*; human, Clem.*str*.2.18(p.161.15; M.8.1029C); *mutual forgiveness, reconciliation*, Synes.*ep*.66(M.66.1409A); divine τῶν παρῳχημένων...αἰτήσασθαι ...ἀ. ... παρὰ πατρός Clem.*q.d.s*.40(p.186.9; M.9.645A); ἀ. γὰρ τοῖς τοιούτοις [sc. penitent] δίδωσιν ἀρετὴ...ἐκβεβληκυῖα τὴν...κακίαν Or. *Cels*.3.71(p.263.15; M.11.1013B); πάντων κακῶν ἀμνηστείαν ποιούμενος Eus.*Is*.1:18(M.24.96D); given by Christ τοῖς μὲν πάλαι αὐτὸν γινώσκουσι...ἕνεκεν δὲ σφαλμάτων ἐν ᾅδῃ κατεσχημένοις ἀ. χαρίσασθαι Epiph.*haer*.46.4(p.208.13; M.41.844C); Thdr.Mops.*Jo*.1:29(p.316.15; M.66.736A); received in baptism ἡ...ἐκκλησία...τῶν προτέρων ἀ. πορισαμένη τῷ λουτρῷ Isid.Pel.*epp*.1.417(M.78.416A); τὸ πιστεύειν εἰς αὐτὸν τῶν πλημμελημάτων ἀμνηστίᾳ τετίμηται Cyr.*inc.unigen*. (5¹.705D).

ἄμνηστος, *forgetful of*, Nonn.*par.Jo*.20:23(M.43.912B).

ἀμνός, ὁ, *lamb*; of Christ; 1. in prophecies τὸ δὲ 'ἴδε ὁ ἀ. τοῦ θεοῦ' τουτέστιν, οὗτος ἐκεῖνος περὶ οὗ προείρηκεν Ἡσαΐας Thdr. Mops.*Jo*.1:29(p.317.4; M.66.736A); Cyr.*Jo*.2 proem.(4.114A); in rel. to πρόβατον (Is.53:7): 'ὡς ἀ. ἐκάρη', καὶ 'ὡς πρόβατον ἐπὶ σφαγὴν ἤχθη', καὶ 'ὡς ἀ.' ἐσταυρώθη Mel.*fr.Gen*.(p.312; M.5.1217A);

ἐκήρυξεν αὐτὸς ὢν τὸ πάσχα, ὁ ἀ. τοῦ θεοῦ, 'ὡς πρόβατον ἐπὶ σφαγὴν' ἀγόμενος Clem.*fr.*28(p.216.27; M.9.757A); πρόβατον δέ, ὡς σφάγιον· ἀ. δέ, ὡς τέλειον Gr.Naz.*or.*30.21(p.143.7; M.36.132C); ἀ. δὲ διὰ τὸ ἄκακον καὶ τὸ δι' αὐτοῦ τὴν ἁμαρτίαν...ἠφανίσθαι ἐν τῷ αὐτὸν τῷ πατρὶ προσενηνέχθαι πρόβατον εἰς σφαγήν Epiph.*haer.*69.35(p.184.5; M.42.257A); **2.** signifying his suffering humanity ὁ κύριος ἀ., ὡς κριός, ὃν εἶδεν Ἀβραὰμ κατεχόμενον ἐν φυτῷ Σαβέκ. ἀλλὰ τὸ φυτὸν ἀπέφαινε τὸν σταυρόν...καὶ ὁ ἀ., τὸν κύριον ἐμπεπεδημένον εἰς σφαγήν Mel.*fr.Gen.*(p.312; M.5.1216B–1217A); ἐπεὶ γὰρ ἄρνας ὀνομάζει ἡ γραφὴ τοὺς παῖδας τοὺς νηπίους, τὸν θεὸν τὸν λόγον τὸν δι' ἡμᾶς ἄνθρωπον γενόμενον, κατὰ πάντα ἡμῖν ἀπεικάζεσθαι βουλόμενον, ἀ. κέκληκεν τοῦ θεοῦ, τὸν υἱὸν τοῦ θεοῦ Clem.*paed.*1.5(p.104.21; M.8. 280A); λόγος ἀ. συμβολικῶς καλούμενος ἅμα τῷ φωτίζεσθαι τὴν ψυχὴν καταπεμπόμενος (αὕτη γὰρ ἂν εἴη ἡ ἑωθινὴ τοῦ ἐνδελεχισμοῦ θυσία) καὶ πάλιν ἐπὶ τέλει τῆς τοῦ νοῦ ἐν τοῖς θειοτέροις διατριβῆς ἀναφερόμενος Or.*Jo.*6.52(33; p.161.13; M.14.292A); τὸν ἀ. οὐκ ἄλλον τοῦ ἀνθρώπου ὑποληψόμεθα...οὗτος δὴ ὁ ἀ. σφαγεὶς καθάρσιον γεγένηται κατά τινας ἀπορρήτους λόγους τοῦ ὅλου κόσμου...ὁ δὲ προσαγαγὼν τοῦτον τὸν ἀ. ἐπὶ τὴν θυσίαν ὁ ἐν τῷ ἀνθρώπῳ ἦν θεός, μέγας ἀρχιερεύς *ib.*6.53(35; pp.161.31–162.9; 292C–293A); ἀ. ἐστιν, ὡς διδόμενος ὑπὲρ ἀφέσεως ἁμαρτιῶν Ammon.*Jo.*1:29(M.85.1401C); ἀ. δὲ αὐτὸν ἐκάλεσεν τοῦ θεοῦ· ὅπερ ἦν ὄνομα τοῦ πάθους σημαντικόν· ἐπείπερ ἐν τῷ πάθει τὴν ἁμαρτίαν κατέλυσεν...ἀνεῖλε μὲν τὴν ἐν τῇ φύσει τῆς θνητότητος ἁμαρτίαν Thdr.Mops.*Jo.*1:29(p.316.10; M.66.733D); **3.** ref. Passover and OT sacrifices πέντε ζώων προσφερομένων ἐπὶ τὸ θυσιαστήριον... ἄξιόν μοι ζητεῖν φαίνεται τί δήποτε...ὁ σωτὴρ ἀ. λέγεται καὶ οὐδὲν τῶν λοιπῶν...τὸν ἀ. ἐν ταῖς θυσίαις τοῦ ἐνδελεχισμοῦ εὑρίσκομεν προσφερόμενον Or.*Jo.*6.51,52(32,33; p.160.8,31; M.14.289A,C); ἐκεῖ αἷμα ἀμνοῦ ὀλοθρευτοῦ ἦν ὑποτρόπαιον· ἐνταῦθα τοῦ ἀ. τοῦ ἀμώμου Ἰησοῦ Χριστοῦ τὸ αἷμα δαιμόνων καθέστηκε φυγαδευτήριον Cyr.H.*catech.*19.3; ἀ. δὲ αὐτὸν καλεῖ, τῆς προφητείας ἀναμιμνήσκων Ἰουδαίους τῆς Ἡσαΐου καὶ τῆς σκιᾶς τῆς κατὰ τὸν Μωϋσέα, ἵν' ἀπὸ τοῦ τύπου μᾶλλον αὐτοὺς προσαγάγηται πρὸς τὴν ἀλήθειαν· ἐκεῖνος μὲν οὖν ὁ ἀ. οὐδενὸς καθάπαξ ἁμαρτίαν ἔλαβεν· οὗτος δὲ τῆς οἰκουμένης ἁπάσης Chrys.*hom.17.1 in Jo.*(8.97E); μυρίοι μὲν γὰρ ἐσφάττοντο, κατὰ τὸν τοῦ νόμου τύπον, ἀλλ' οὐδεὶς ἀπήλειψε τὴν ἁμαρτίαν τοῦ κόσμου...ἀνήρηκε δὲ τοῦ κόσμου τὴν ἁμαρτίαν ὁ ἀ. ὁ ἄμωμος...οὐκοῦν καὶ ὡς πρόβατον λεγόιγσται μεθ' ἡμῶν Cyr.*glaph.Gen.*6(1.185C); τεθύκασι τὸν ἀ. εἰς τύπον τοῦ Χριστοῦ id.*glaph.Ex.*3(1.334C); id.*Jo.*2 proem.(4.114B–D); Procl.CP *or.*14.3 (M.65.800A); Sophr.H.*carm.*8.64(M.87.3773B); cf. αἷμα; **4.** eucharistic ἄμωμον ἀ. καθ' ἡμέραν ἐν θυσιαστηρίῳ τοῦ σταυροῦ θύω· οὗ τὰς σάρκας μετὰ τὸν πάντα τῶν πιστῶν λαὸν φαγεῖν καὶ τὸ αἷμα αὐτοῦ πιεῖν ὁ τυθεὶς ἀ. ἀκέραιος διαμένει καὶ ζῶν *A.*(*Pass.*)*Andr.*6(pp.13.16–14.10); τὸν ἀ. τοῦ θεοῦ, τὸν αἴροντα τὴν ἁμαρτίαν τοῦ κόσμου, καὶ μυστικῶς καθ' ἑκάστην ἱερουργούμενον Or.*hom.13 in Lc.*(p.93.11); Gel.Cyz.*h.e.* 2.31.6(M.85.1317B); μελίζεται καὶ διαμερίζεται ὁ ἀ. τοῦ θεοῦ...ὁ πάντοτε ἐσθιόμενος καὶ μηδέποτε δαπανώμενος cf.*Lit.Chrys.*(p.393.26); **5.** ref. triumph and marriage of Lamb πάντα τὰ θηρία ὥρμων κατ' αὐτοῦ καὶ ἐνίκησεν αὐτὰ ὁ ἀ. *T.Jos.*19.18; ὅτε γὰρ ὡς ἀ. ἐσφαγιάσθη Χριστός, τότε αὐτὴν [sc. ἐκκλησίαν] τῷ οἰκείῳ αἵματι ἐνυμφεύσατο Areth.*Apoc.*67(M.106.765B); **6.** as pictorial symbol ἔν τισι τῶν σεπτῶν εἰκόνων γραφαῖς ἀ. δακτύλῳ τοῦ προδρόμου δεικνύμενος ἐγχαράττεται, ὃς εἰς τύπον παρελήφθη τῆς χάριτος, τὸν ἀληθινὸν ἡμῖν διὰ τοῦ νόμου προϋποφαίνων ἀ. Χριστὸν τὸν θεὸν ἡμῶν·...τὸν τοῦ αἴροντος τὴν ἁμαρτίαν τοῦ κόσμου ἀ. Χριστοῦ...κατὰ τὸν ἀνθρώπινον χαρακτῆρα καὶ ἐν ταῖς εἰκόσιν ἀπὸ τοῦ νῦν ἀντὶ τοῦ παλαιοῦ ἀ. ἀναστηλοῦσθαι ὁρίζομεν, δι' αὐτοῦ τὸ τῆς ταπεινώσεως ὕψος τοῦ θεοῦ λόγου κατανοοῦντες CTrull.*can.*82.

ἀμνοφόρος, *offering a lamb*, of eucharist δεῖπνον...ἀ. Sophr.H. *carm.*8.17(M.87.3772B).

ἀμοιβάδιος, *taking turns*, Gr.Naz.*carm.*1.2.1.417(M.37.553A).

ἀμοιβαδίς, **1.** *in turn, one after another*; hence *in return, in reply* ἀγόρευεν ἀ. Nonn.*par.Jo.*7:19(M.43.808B); *ib.*10:33(837A); **2.** *mutually* εἰ ὑμᾶς αὐτοὺς ἀ. ἠγαπᾶτε Constantius Imp.ap.Ath. *apol.sec.*61.1(p.141.9; M.25.360B).

ἀμοιβαίως, **1.** *in turn*, Eus.*v.C.*2.8(p.44.15; M.20.988B); **2.** *in return*, id.*l.C.*3(p.200.22; M.20.1328B); of Father glorifying Son, id. *e.th.*1.11(p.70.17; M.24.845B).

ἀμοιβάς, **1.** *requiting, bringing retribution for* ποινὴν...ἀ. κέντορι λόγχῃ Nonn.*par.Jo.*19:37(M.43.905B); **2.** *answering* ἀ. φωνῇ *ib.*1:20 (753A); *ib.*20:27(913A); *corresponding*, *ib.*7:52(813A).

ἀμοιβή, ἡ, *return, recompense*; from God to man, *return, reward*; undeserved unless man has free will, Just.*1apol.*43.8(M.6.393B); Clem.*str.*7.10(p.42.17; M.9.481B); ref. Mt.6:2ff. οὐδεμία ἐπὶ τούτῳ ἀπὸ θεοῦ ἀ. ἡμῖν ἕπεται Or.*or.*19(p.342.9; M.11.476D); εἰ μὲν δικαίως ἐκρίνατε, δικαίων ἀ. καταξιωθήσεσθε καὶ νῦν καὶ εἰς αὖθις *Const.App.* 2.52.3; τὸ μὲν [sc. goodness] ἔχει μισθόν, τὸ δὲ [sc. gifts of prophecy, etc.] ἐστέρηται ἀ. Chrys.*hom.21.1 in Rom.*(9.664B); Isid.Pel.*epp.* 1.387(M.78.401A); προσδοκᾶν τῶν ἱδρώτων τὰς ἀ. Cyr.*Lc.*9:26(M.72. 652C); from man to God, *return* τὰ γὰρ παρὰ θεοῦ τῆς ἐν κόσμῳ δωρεᾶς ὑπερπαίει τὴν ἀ. Tat.*orat.*32(p.33.8; M.6.872B); μία δὲ ἀ. κυριωτάτη παρὰ ἀνθρώπων, ταῦτα δρᾶν ἅπερ ἀρεστὰ τῷ θεῷ Clem. *str.*7.3(p.15.18; M.9.425B); exeg. Mc.12:30 ἄλλο δὲ [sc. than love] μηδοτιοῦν ἔχοντας ἀνενδεεῖ...θεῷ πρὸς ἀ. ἐπινοῆσαι id.*q.d.s.*27(p.178. 14; M.9.633A).

***ἀμοιδρά, ἡ**, ? *obscurity* λόγῳ πρότερον πρὸς τὴν μάθησιν ἐναγόμενοι, εἶτα χειρὶ καὶ πείρᾳ τὴν ἀ. κρατύνοντες Ast.Am.*hom.*9(M.40. 301A), perh. f.l. for ἀμυδράν.

ἀμοιρ-έω, **1.** *have no lot* or *share* in, *lack* δαίμονες...σαρκός ...~οῦσι Tat.*orat.*14(p.15.14; M.6.836B); Or.*exc.in Ps.*77:31(M.17. 144C); ἡ βλασφημία...λέγουσα...~εῖν τῆς ἁπλότητος [sc. τὸν Χριστόν] Gr.Nyss.*Eun.*10(2 p.239.27; M.45.841C); ψυχὰς ~ούσας τῆς χάριτος id.*instit.*(p.47.11; M.46.289C); of Israel τῆς δι' αὐτοῦ σωτηρίας ἠμοιρηκώς Cyr.*Ps.*41:4(M.69.1004A); Jo.D.*hom.*4.12(M.96.613A); **2.** *be exempt* from, *free* from ~ήσει γὰρ οὕτω καὶ τῶν ἐκ θείας ὀργῆς ἐποισθησομένων τοῖς εἰωθόσι πλημμελεῖν Cyr.*Mal.*36(3.856C); ἰδίᾳ τοίνυν πέπονθε σαρκί, καίτοι τοῦ παθεῖν ~εῖν εἰθισμένος, ὁ ἐκ θεοῦ λόγος id.*Arcad.*(p.102.9; 5^2.102B).

***ἀμοίρησις, ἡ**, *loss* τῶν προσδοκωμένων ‡Chrys.*catech.*(9.824B).

ἄμοιρος, **1.** *without lot* or *share* in Ἀλέξανδρός τις...οὐκ ἄ. ἀποστολικοῦ χαρίσματος *Ep.Lugd.*ap.Eus.*h.e.*5.1.49(M.20.428A); οὐκ ...ἄ. ἡ σὰρξ τεχνικῆς σοφίας καὶ δυνάμεως θεοῦ Iren.*haer.*5.3.3(M.7. 1131A); ἄθλιοι, οἱ ἐναντίοι πτωχοί, θεοῦ μὲν ἄ., ἀμοιρότεροι δὲ τῆς ἀνθρωπίνης κτήσεως Clem.*q.d.s.*17(p.171.2; M.9.621B); ἆρ' οὖν...ἡ ἔνθεος διδασκαλία...ἁπλῶς ἀφῆκε τὸ τῶν ἀνθρώπων γένος ἄ. τῆς τοῦ θεοῦ γνώσεως φέρεσθαι; Ath.*gent.*46(M.25.92A); ἄ. ... τῆς...μυήσεως [i.e. baptism] Gr.Nyss.*or.catech.*35(p.138.2; M.45.92A); ἀμερὲς γὰρ τὸ θεῖον καὶ γεννητῆς ἄ. φύσεως Bas.Sel.*or.*25.4(M.85.297C); **2.** *exempt, free* from, Clem.*str.*6.2(p.435.6; M.9.229A); οὐκ ἄ. ὀργῆς Cyr.*Lc.*12:41 (M.72.752B); **3.** *shut out, excluded*, ref. life in heaven κοινοί τε βίοι καὶ πλοῦτος ἄ. οὐ γὰρ πτωχὸς ἐκεῖ, οὐ πλούσιος *Orac.Sib.*2.321; *Hom. Clem.*13.9.

ἀμοίχευτος, *free from adultery*, *A.Andr.fr.*8(p.41.24); *A.Jo.*49 (p.176.7).

***ἀμοιχεύτως**, *without adultery, chastely*, Jo.Clim.*scal.*27(M.88. 1108C).

§**ἀμολγαῖος**, ? *of twilight* ἡμερίην σκοτόεσσαν ἀ. περὶ κόσμον *Orac.Sib.*14.221.

ἀμόλυντος, *undefiled, clean*; **1.** lit., Clem.*paed.*2.1(p.163.4; M.8. 397B); id.*str.*6.15(p.492.3; M.9.344A); προσφέρειν τῷ θεῷ τὰ δῶρα ἀ. *M.Thdot.1* 7(p.65.20); **2.** morally τὴν διάνοιαν...καὶ τὴν αἴσθησιν ἀ. Meth.*symp.*11.3(p.137.17; M.18.213C); φύλασσε σεαυτὴν ἀ. Gr.Naz. *ep.*244(M.37.388A); ἀ. νοήμασι Gr.Nyss.*hom.1 in Cant.*(M.44.765A); παίδων γένεσιν τίμιον καὶ ἀ. εἶναι πιστεύομεν *Const.App.*6.11.6; exeg. 1Cor.10:3 ἡ γὰρ χάρις αὐτοῦ τοσαύτη, ὡς κατασκευάσαι μοι τὴν ψυχὴν ἀ. Chrys.*hom.25.1 in 1Cor.*(10.221C); μὴ δυνατὸν...ἀ. τὸ καθόλου ἄνθρωπον εὑρεθῆναι Nil.*epp.*1.24(M.79.92B); id.*Magn.*1(M.79.969B); ἵνα...διατηρήσας τὸν χιτῶνα ἀ., τύχῃ τῆς μακαριότητος *Rit.Bapt.* (p.395); **3.** of virginity, Meth.*symp.*4.5(p.51.10; M.18.93C); ὁ ἀ. ... εὐνουχισμός *ib.*2.7(p.25.18; 60B); τὸ ἀ. τῆς παρθενίας ἔνδυμα Procl. CP *or.*6.2(M.65.724A); of BMV παρθένος...ἀ. *A.Barth.*4(p.135.29); Sophr.H.*ep.syn.*(M.87.3161B); ἀ. ὁ τόκος καὶ καθαρσίων ἀνεύθυνος ‡Meth.*Sym.et Ann.*3(M.18.353B); **4.** of God τί καθυβρίζεις τὴν ἀ. φύσιν; Gr.Nyss.*or.dom.*2(p.36.26; M.44.1144A); of Christ, exeg. Cant.6:9 δυνήσεται δέ τις καὶ ἑτέρως τὴν νύμφην φάναι τὴν σάρκα τὴν ἀ. εἶναι τοῦ κυρίου Meth.*symp.*7.8(p.78.17; M.18.136A).

***ἀμολύντως**, *without defilement, in purity*; in gen. ἀ. ἐνεργούμενα τῆς πίστεως ἔργα Cyr.*Ps.*17:21(M.69.824C); Jo.Clim.*scal.*27(M.88. 1108C); of Christ γεννηθεὶς διὰ γεννητικῶν πόρων...ἀ. Epiph.*exp. fid.*15(p.516.9; M.42.812B); id.*haer.*69.25(p.176.4; M.42.244C); ἐν τῇ παρθενικῇ μήτρᾳ διαιτώμενος ἀ. Gr.Ant.*bapt.*2.5(M.88.1876B).

***ἀμόναχος, ὁ**, *one who is not a true monk*, Ephr.2.148D.

***ἀμονάχως**, *in a manner unbecoming to a monk*, Ephr.2.92A.

ἀμορφία, ἡ, **1.** *being without visible form* ἡ τῶν ἀσωμάτων...ἀ. Dion.Ar.*d.n.*1.1(M.3.588B); of freedom from material images μακάριος ὁ νοῦς, ὃς κατὰ τὸν καιρὸν τῆς προσευχῆς τελείαν ἀ. ἐκτήσατο Evagr.Pont.*or.*117(M.79.1193A); **2.** *formlessness, chaos*, of primal matter τὴν ἐσχάτην ἀ. Bas.*hex.*2.2(1.13C; M.29.32A); Gnost.; a quality of the sublunar world, Clem.*exc.Thdot.*31(p.117.11; M.9. 676A); τοῦτο τὸ διάστημα τὸ καθ' ἡμᾶς, ὅπου ἐστὶν ἡ ἀ. Hipp.*haer.*7.27 (p.207.17; M.16.3319B); of body of Jesus ἔπαθεν οὖν τοῦτο ὅπερ ἦν αὐτοῦ σωματικὸν μέρος, ὃ ἦν τῆς ἀ., καὶ ἀπεκατέστη εἰς τὴν ἀ. *ib.*

(p.207.20; 3319C); **3.** *unshapeliness, ugliness,* met. ἀ. δὲ καὶ αἶσχος ἀναλαβὼν τῇ ψυχῇ Eus.*l.C.*5(p.203.29; M.20.1336A); of Church οὐδὲ ἐμίσησε [sc. ὁ Χριστός] διὰ τὴν ὑπερβολὴν τῆς ἀ. Chrys.*hom.20.2 in Eph.*(11.145A); Isid.Pel.*epp.*2.135(M.78.577C) cit. s. κάτοπτρον.

ἄμορφος, 1. *without form* or *visible shape* ἀειδὴς δὲ ἐλήλυθεν καὶ ἄ., εἰς τὸ ἀειδὲς καὶ ἀσώματον τῆς θείας αἰτίας ἀποβλέπειν ἡμᾶς διδάσκων Clem.*str.*3.17(p.244.2; M.8.1208A); τῆς...ἀ. ... πατρικῆς ὑποστάσεως Didym.*Trin.*2.4(M.39.484A); Dion.Ar.*d.n.*5.8(M.3.824B) cit. s. ἀκαλλής; but cf. *Hom.Clem.*17.11 cit. s. ἀσχημάτιστος; **2.** *without form*; of a corpse, because soul has left it, ‡Ath.*Apoll.*2.1(M.26.1133A); hence *soul-less, lifeless* ὃς [sc. a bad painter] ἄ. σώματ' ἐξεργάζεται Gr.Naz.*carm.*2.1.12.743(M.37.1220A); met., of Christians οἱ τὸ πρὶν ἄ., νῦν δὲ διὰ Χριστοῦ μορφούμενοι *A.Mt.*6(p.223.14); **3.** *unsightly, ugly*; of Christ (ref. Is.53:2), Or.*Cels.*6.76(p.146.1; M.11.1413B); τὸν εὔμορφον τοῖς νοοῦσιν καὶ ἄ. τοῖς ἀγνοοῦσιν *V.Aberc.*16(p.14.6).

ἀμόρφωτος, 1. *not formed, formless* ἕως οὖν ἀ. ... ἔτι τὸ σπέρμα Clem.*exc.Thdot.*79(p.131.20; M.9.696A); Meth.*symp.*8.6(p.88.12; M.18.148B); Gr.Nyss.*res.*3(M.46.668A); **2.** *without form,* of God τὴν ὑπερούσιον καὶ ἀ. οὐσίαν Dion.Ar.*c.h.*15.2(M.3.329A); of divine nature of Christ ὁ κατ' οὐσίαν τὴν θείαν ὅσον εἰς σχῆμα καὶ εἶδος ἀ. Sophr.H.*ep.syn.*(M.87.3160D); of the intelligible world τὰ ἀσώματα ἀ. εἰσιν Max.*schol.c.h.*2.2(M.4.40B).

***ἄμπαξ**; δι' ἄ. = διαμπάξ, *thoroughly, completely,* of Trin. οὔτε ἑνιαῖον συγκεχυμένον, οὔτε τὸ τρισσὸν δι' ἄ. διαιρούμενον Jo.D.*hom.*11.3(M.96.765A).

ἀμπείρω, = ἀναπείρω, *pierce through, Orac.Sib.*1.47.

ἄμπελος, ἡ, *vine*; **1.** lit., as symbol of resurrection ὅνπερ τρόπον τὸ ξύλον τῆς ἀ., κλιθὲν εἰς τὴν γῆν τῷ ἰδίῳ καιρῷ ἐκαρποφόρησε,... οὕτως καὶ τὰ ἡμέτερα σώματα...τεθέντα εἰς τὴν γῆν...ἀναστήσεται ἐν τῷ ἰδίῳ καιρῷ Iren.*haer.*5.2,3(M.7.1127A); regarded as accursed because, having been planted in paradise by Samael or Satan, it became tree of Fall; planted on earth by Noah after flood, leads to drunkenness and sin; but also glorified, because of eucharistic use, *Apoc.Bar.*4(pp.86.34–88.9); **2.** as symbol in OT; **a.** of Israel, Or.*fr.48 in Lam.*2:6(p.256.17; M.13.633C); exeg. Is.7:23 οἱ ἐκ περιτομῆς ἦσαν αἱ χίλιαι ἄ. †Bas.*Is.*205(1.532D; M.30.472C); Thdt.*Ps.*79:9(1.1174); **b.** of other nations: Sodom, ref. Deut.32:32, Or.*Jo.*20.4(p.332.5; M.14.581C); detailed interpretations of vines of Sodom, Sibmah (Is.16:8), Egypt (Ps.77:47), †Bas.*Is.*309f.(1.612Cff.; M.30.657Aff.); Proc.G.*Is.*16(M.87.2116Bff.); **c.** of soul θεὸς μὲν καλὴν ἄ. ἐφύτευσε τὴν τοῦ ἀνθρώπου ψυχήν Or.*hom.2.1 in Jer.*(p.17.21; M.13.277C); ὥσπερ γὰρ οἱ τὴν ἄ. τέμνοντες, συνέχουσιν αὐτῆς τὴν δύναμιν..., οὕτω καὶ ψυχὴ ἐπικαμπτομένη ταῖς θλίψεσιν, οἱονεὶ συστέλλεται καὶ ταπεινοῦται λυσιτελῶς †Bas.*Is.*146(1.482B; M.30.357A); ἡ ψυχή σου, ὡς ἄ. γέμουσα ἁπάσης εὐφροσύνης Hesych.H.*Ps.tit.*127.5(M.27.1240C); Mac.Aeg.*hom.*28.6(M.34.713D); **d.** of a wife ὑπὸ τὴν ἄ. τὴν ἑαυτοῦ ἕκαστος καθεζόμενοι, τοῦτ' ἔστι μόνῃ τῇ γαμετῇ γυναικὶ ἕκαστος χρώμενοι Just.*dial.*110.3(M.6.729B); **e.** exeg. Jud.9:13: of commandment given to Noah after flood (Gen.9:1ff.), Meth.*symp.*10.2(p.123.21; M.18.196A); of change of men's hearts from fear to joy, *ib.*(p.124.8; 196B); **f.** exeg. Is.5:2 αὕτη ἡ ἄ. ἡ πάντως που ἡ θεόπνευστος γραφή, καὶ ὁ τῆς θεοσεβείας λόγος, ἢ καὶ αὐτὸς ὁ τοῦ θεοῦ λόγος Eus.*Is.*5:2(M.24.116D); **g.** exeg. Is.16:8ff. σημαίνει...διὰ τῆς... ἀ. ... τὸ τρυφερὸν καὶ ὡραῖον τῆς τῶν δηλουμένων ζωῆς *ib.*16:8(201D); **h.** exeg. Cant.2:13ff.: of Church, Gr.Nyss.*hom.5 in Cant.*(M.44.881D); Ph.Carp.*Cant.*59(M.40.72A); of members of Church, Nil.ap.Proc.G.*Cant.*2:15(M.87.1609D); Thdt.*Cant.*2:15(2.73); **i.** exeg. Cant.6:10: of Israel, Ph.Carp.*Cant.*187(120B); Nil.ap.Proc.G.*Cant.*6:10(1725B); ἔχει γὰρ ὁ βίος τινὰς μὲν ἀνθρώπους τροπικῶς ἀ. ὀνομαζομένους...οἱ δὲ καὶ οἶνον γεωργοῦσι, τῶν ληνῶν ἄξιον τῶν πατρικῶν, τῇ θεωρίᾳ προσέχειν ἐσπουδακότες Thdt.*Cant.*6:10(136); **j.** exeg. Cant.7:12 ὅπερ ἐστίν, εἰ τὸ κήρυγμα τῆς πίστεως τὴν εὐωδίαν ἐκ τῶν πιστευσάντων διέδωκεν Ph.Carp.*Cant.*213(133C); αὗται γὰρ ἄ. ... ταύτης [sc. τῆς ἐκκλησίας] αἱ ἀρεταί, αἳ διὰ μὲν τῶν θλίψεων οἶνος γενόμενοι ἀμπέλου Nil.ap.Proc.G.*Cant.*7:12(1736D); ἐπισκεψώμεθα, φησί, τοὺς ἄρτι τὸ κήρυγμα δεξαμένους Thdt.*Cant.*7:12(150); **k.** exeg. Zach.3:10: either of spiritual joy or of Church, Cyr.*Zach.*22(3.681A); **3.** as symbol in NT; **a.** exeg. Mt.21:41 ἐνταῦθα ἄ. ὁ λόγος τῆς ἀληθείας †Bas.*Is.*309(1.612E; M.30.657B); **b.** exeg. Mt.26:29 and parallels, cf. *promisit bibere de generatione vitis cum suis discipulis, utrumque ostendens, et haereditatem terrae in qua bibitur nova generatio vitis, et carnalem resurrectionem discipulorum ejus. neque autem sursum in supercoelesti loco constitutus cum suis, potest intelligi bibens vitis generationem; neque rursus sine carne sunt, qui bibunt illud: carnis enim proprium est et non spiritus, qui ex vite accipitur potus,* Iren.*haer.*5.33.1(M.7.1212B); contrast, Chrys.*hom.82.2 in Mt.*(7.784A) cit. s. ξένως; ὁ μὲν γὰρ...'Ιωάννης ἐκείνην καινὴν πόσιν τοῦ ποτηρίου φησίν, ἣν μετὰ τὴν ἐκ νεκρῶν ἀνάστασιν ἔπιεν. ... ὁ μέντοι...Γρηγόριος...φησί· καινοῦ ποτηρίου δόσιν εἶναι τὴν ἐν τῇ μελλούσῃ...βασιλείᾳ τῶν οὐρανῶν τῶν θείων νοημάτων ἐπηγγελμένων ἡμῖν ἀποκάλυψιν Sev.Ant.ap.*cat.Lc.*22:16(p.155.29ff.); cf.Gr.Naz.*or.*45.23(M.36.656A); **c.** exeg. Apoc.14:19 ἀπεναντίας αὐτῇ ἡ ἄ. τῆς ἀπ' Αἰγύπτου παρὰ τῷ θεοπάτορι μετεωρουμένης Areth.*Apoc.*44(M.106.696D); **4.** met.; **a.** of people of God, Herm.*sim.*5.5.2; Just.*dial.*110.4(M.6.729C); **b.** of Adam, whose descendants are fruitful or unfruitful branches, cf.Or.*comm.in Rom.*1.13(M.14.859C); **c.** fruit of martyr's blood, *A.Phil.*143(p.84.4); **d.** of BMV, Abr.Eph.*occurs.*9(p.454.6) cit. s. βότρυς; **5.** of Logos ἔπειτα ἡ ἄ. ἡ ἁγία τὸν βότρυν ἐβλάστησε τὸν προφητικόν Clem.*paed.*2.2(p.167.24; M.8.409A); **6.** of Christ, in OT exeg.; **a.** Gen.49:11a interpreted of gentiles bound to Christ and Jews to Law, Hipp.*fr.23 in Gen.*49:11(p.60.6; M.10.589B); of people bound to Christ, Clem.*paed.*1.5(p.99.11; M.8.268A); Cyr.*glaph.Gen.*7(1.223E); to Christ's teaching, Chrys.*hom.67.2 in Gen.*(4.638D); of apostles and disciples bound to Christ's power, Eus.*d.e.*8.1(p.365.18; M.22.593B); of mankind bound to apostles, Thdt.*qu.110 in Gen.*(1.115); **b.** Gen.49:11b ὃν τρόπον γὰρ τὸ τῆς ἀ. αἷμα οὐκ ἄνθρωπος πεποίηκεν ἀλλ' ὁ θεός, οὕτως καὶ τοῦτο ἐμηνύετο οὐκ ἐξ ἀνθρωπείου σπέρματος γενήσεσθαι τὸ αἷμα ἀλλ' ἐκ δυνάμεως θεοῦ Just.*1apol.*32.11(M.6.380B); **c.** Mich.4:4; vine interpreted of Christ, and fig tree of H. Ghost, Meth.*symp.*10.5(p.128.9; M.18.201C); **7.** exeg. Jo.15:1; **a.** as simple metaphor τοῦτον [sc. 'Ιησοῦν] καὶ ἀνάπαυσιν καλοῦμεν καὶ ἄ. *V.Aberc.*16(p.14.18); τοῖς μὲν γὰρ εὐφροσύνης χρείαν ἔχουσιν, ἄ. γίνεται Cyr.H.*catech.*10.5; ἐφυτεύθη οὖν ἐν τῇ γῇ, ἵνα ἐκριζωθῇ ἡ διὰ τὸν Ἀδὰμ γενομένη κατάρα·...ἀνέτειλεν ἐκ τῆς γῆς ἡ ἄ. ἡ ἀληθινή, ἵνα πληρωθῇ τὸ εἰρημένον [Ps.84:12] *ib.*14.11; **b.** with expansion or detailed exeg. ἄ. δὲ ὁ κύριος ἀλληγορεῖται, παρ' οὗ μετ' ἐπιμελείας καὶ τέχνης γεωργικῆς τὸν κατὰ τὸν λόγον τὸν καρπὸν τρυγητέον Clem.*str.*1.8(p.29.1; M.8.740B); id.*q.d.s.*37(p.184.19; M.9.644A); ref. Ps.103:15 ὁ τὸν εὐφραίνοντα καρδίαν ἀνθρώπου οἶνον φέρων ἄ. ἐστιν ἀληθινή· διὰ τοῦτο ἀληθινή, ἐπεὶ βότρυς ἔχει τὴν ἀλήθειαν Or.*Jo.*1.30(33; p.37.20; M.14.80A); id.*Cels.*5.12(p.13.9; M.11.1197D); Ath.*Dion.*10.5(p.53.20; M.25.496A); Bas.*Eun.*1.7(1.218D; M.29.525A); followers of Devil's teaching sever themselves from true vine, †Bas.*Is.*309(1.612E; M.30.657C); Gr.Nyss.*Eun.*3(2 p.44.8; M.45.612C); οὕτως αὐτοὺς ἡνῶσθαι δεῖ τῇ πίστει, ὡς τὸ κλῆμα τῇ ἀ. Chrys.*hom.76.1 in Jo.*(8.447A); Thdr.Mops.*Jo.*15:1(p.395.17; M.66.780A); full discussion, Cyr.*Jo.*10.2(4.857B); **c.** opp. Devil as false vine (cf. Deut.32:32ff.) ἄ. μὲν γὰρ νηφάλιος καὶ εὐφραντική, κλημάτων δίκην ἐκ τῶν μαθημάτων τοὺς βότρυς ἱλαρῶς ἀπαιωροῦσα τῶν χαρισμάτων καταστάζοντας ἀγάπην, ὁ κύριος ἡμῶν. ...ἀγρία δὲ καὶ θανατηφόρος ὁ διάβολος, λύσσαν καὶ ἰὸν καὶ ὀργὴν ἀποστάζων Meth.*symp.*5.5(p.59.3; M.18.105B); **d.** liturg., *Did.*9.2 cit. s. ποτήριον; **e.** blood of Christ as fruit of vine τὸν οἶνον, τὸ αἷμα τῆς ἀ. τῆς Δαβίδ, ἐκχέας ἡμῶν ἐπὶ τὰς τετρωμένας ψυχάς Clem.*q.d.s.*29(p.179.11; M.9.636A); id.*paed.*2.2(p.174.3; M.8.424B); *ib.*(p.176.2; 428C) cit. s. οἶνος; ἀμβροσιώδους τροφῆς καὶ τοῦ ποτοῦ τῆς ἀ. τῆς ἀληθινῆς *A.Thom.*A 36(p.154.2); ὥσπερ γὰρ ἡμεῖς τὸν μυστικὸν τῆς ἀ. καρπὸν μετὰ τὸν ἁγιασμὸν αἷμα δεσποτικὸν ὀνομάζομεν· οὕτω τῆς ἀληθινῆς ἀ. τὸ αἷμα σταφυλῆς ὠνόμασεν αἷμα Thdt.*eran.*1(4.25); **f.** in Arian argument εἰ ἄ., φασίν, ὁ σωτήρ, κλήματα δὲ ἡμεῖς, γεωργὸς δὲ ὁ πατήρ· τὰ δὲ κλήματα ὁμοφυῆ μὲν τῇ ἀ., ἡ δὲ ἄ. οὐχ ὁμοφυὴς τῷ γεωργῷ, ὁμοφυὴς μὲν ἡμῖν ὁ υἱός, καὶ μέρος ἡμεῖς αὐτοῦ, οὐχ ὁμοφυὴς δὲ ὁ υἱὸς τῷ πατρί, ἀλλὰ κατὰ πάντα ἀλλότριος. πρὸς οὓς ἐροῦμεν οὐ τῆς θεότητος αὐτοῦ ἀλλὰ τῆς σαρκὸς εἰρηκέναι ἡμᾶς κλήματα Didym.(‡Bas.)*Eun.*4(1.291B; M.29.700A); φησὶν [sc. one who denies the homoousion] ἄ. ἑαυτὸν ὀνομάζει...γεωργὸν δὲ τὸν πατέρα· ὥσπερ οὖν οὐ ταὐτὸν εἰς οὐσίαν ἄ. τε, φησί, καὶ γεωργός· τὸ μὲν γὰρ ξύλον, ὁ δέ ἐστιν ἄνθρωπος...οὕτως οὐχ ὁμοούσιος ὁ υἱὸς τῷ πατρί Cyr.*Jo.*10.2(4.860C); ἀναπεῖσαι βούλεται τοὺς ἀκροωμένους, ὅτι πάσης ἡμῖν καρποφορίας πνευματικῆς ἡ δύναμις παρ' αὐτοῦ...διὰ τοῦτο μὲν ῥίζα ὥσπερ ἀ. ὁ Χριστός, κλήματα δὲ ἡμεῖς. εἰ δὲ γεωργὸν ὠνόμασε τὸν πατέρα...ἐπιδεῖξαι θελήσας, ὅτι καὶ ῥίζα καὶ ἀρχὴ τῆς ἐν ἡμῖν καρποφορίας πνευματικῆς καὶ ζωῆς ἡ θεία γέγονε φύσις *ib.*(861E).

ἀμπελουργία, ἡ, *vine-dressing,* Gr.Nyss.*hom.15 in Cant.*(M.44.1105B); met., ref. Mt.20:1ff. τὴν θείαν ἐκείνην ἀ. Max.*myst.*proem.(M.91.661B).

ἀμπελών, ὁ, *vineyard*;

A. met.; **1.** of Israel, Or.*fr.48 in Lam.*2:6(p.256.17; M.13.633C); Cyr.*Os.*30(3.55B); v. infra, B.5; **2.** of Church ἐργάζεται τοίνυν ὁ γνωστικὸς ἐν τῷ τοῦ κυρίου ἀ. ... θεῖος ὄντως ὑπάρχων τῶν εἰς πίστιν καταπεφυτευμένων γεωργός Clem.*str.*7.12(p.53.7; M.9.501B); φιλοσοφία ἡ Ἑλληνικὴ...διακρουομένη τὰς δολερὰς κατὰ τῆς ἀληθείας ἐπιβουλὰς φραγμὸς οἰκείως εἴρηται...εἶναι τοῦ ἀ. *ib*.1.20(p.64.2; M.8.817B); θεοῦ φυτεία ἡ καθολικὴ ἐκκλησία καὶ ἀ. αὐτοῦ ἐκλεκτός,...οἱ τὴν αἰώνιον καρπούμενοι διὰ πίστεως βασιλείαν αὐτοῦ *Const.App*.inscr.(p.3.10); ref. Cant.2:12, Lc.2:24 τρυγόνος δὲ δίκην...τῆς ἑαυτοῦ καλλιφωνίας τὸν ἴδιον ἀ. πληρῶν, τουτέστιν ἡμᾶς τοὺς πιστεύσαντας εἰς αὐτόν Cyr.*Lc*.2:22(M.72.501A); τῆς πνευματικῆς ἐργασίας τοῦ πνευματικοῦ ἀ. Max.*myst*.(M.91.661B); **3.** of soul ἕκαστος ἡμῶν αὐτοῦ τε ἀ. καὶ ἐργάτης Clem.*str*.7.12(p.55.12; M.9.508A); v. infra, B.5; **4.** of BMV ὁ παρθενικὸς ἀ. Hesych.H.*serm*.6(M.93.1469B).

B. exeg. OT; **1.** Cant.1:6: neglect of vineyard signifying loss of paradise, Gr.Nyss.*hom.2 in Cant*.(M.44.797B); ἀ. ἐστιν ἡ ἀθανασία· ἀ. ἡ ἀπάθεια, καὶ ἡ πρὸς τὸ θεῖον ὁμοίωσις, καὶ ἡ παντὸς κακοῦ ἀλλοτρίωσις *ib*.(800C); οἱ ἐχθροὶ μετέστησαν αὐτὴν [sc. τὴν ψυχήν] ἐκ τῆς τοῦ παραδείσου τρυφῆς, εἰς τὸ σπουδάζειν περὶ τὸν αὐτῶν ἀ., οὗ ὁ βότρυς γεωργεῖ τὴν πικρίαν [Dt.32:32] *ib*.(797D); αὕτη [sc. Church] ὑπὸ τῶν ἀποστόλων τίθεται φυλάκισσα ἐν ἀ. τούτῳ τῆς πίστεως πολυβότρυι καρπῷ Ph.Carp.*Cant*.14(M.40.48C); τηρεῖν ἐντελλόμενοι τὴν κατὰ τὸν νόμον λατρείαν· αὕτη γὰρ ἀ. Cyr.*fr.Cant*.1:5(M.69.1280B); ἢ γὰρ τοῦτο λέγει [sc. Church], ὅτι τὸν πρότερόν μου ἀ., ὃν πρὸ τῆς πίστεως ἐγεώργουν, τὸν πατρόθεν μοι παραδοθέντα, καταλέλοιπα ἀνεπιμέλητον...ὥστε παντελῶς τὰ πρότερα ἤδη διαφθαρῆναι...· ἢ ὅτι τὸν ἐμὸν ἀ., τουτέστι τῆς ἐμῆς ψυχῆς τὴν ὠφέλειαν ἀφιεμένη, καὶ τὰ τῶν ἄλλων κέρδη τῶν οἰκείων κερδῶν προαιρουμένη Thdt.*Cant*.1:6(2.41); **2.** Cant.2:15 ὁ ἀ. ὁ ἡμέτερος, ἡ ἀνθρωπίνη φύσις, καὶ τὴν τῶν βοτρύων φορὰν διὰ τοῦ ἄνθους τῆς ἐναρέτου πολιτείας προοιμιάζεται Gr.Nyss.*hom.5 in Cant*.(M.44.881C); of heretics harming immature Christians, Ph.Carp.*Cant*.66(M.40.73C); Thdt.*Cant*.2:15(2.73); **3.** Cant.8:11: of Church, Ph.Carp.*Cant*.242(149C); Nil.ap.Proc.G.*Cant*.8:11(M.87.1748C); Cyr.*fr.Cant*.8:11(M.69.1292D); **4.** Cant.7:12: of local churches, Ph.Carp.*Cant*.212(133C); **5.** Is.1:8, referred both to Israel and to individual soul, †Bas.*Is*.20,21(1.393Aff.; M.30.153Aff.); **6.** Is.3:14 ἀ. δὲ καλεῖ τὸν λαόν Chrys.*Is.3 interp*.(6.42B); **7.** Is.5:1ff.: detailed exeg., Eus.*Is*.5:1(M.24.116Dff.); †Bas.*Is*.139ff.(1.476Eff.; M.30.345Aff.); Chrys.*Is.5 interp*.(6.52B); Cyr.*Is*.1.3(2.77Eff.); Thdt.*Is*.5:1(2.197ff.); Proc.G.*Cant*.5:1(M.87.1908Dff.).

C. exeg. NT; **1.** Mt.20:1ff.: Or.*comm.in Mt*.15.28(p.435.10ff.; M.13.1337Aff.); Chrys.*hom.64.3 in Mt*.(7.637Eff.); **2.** Mt.21:28: Or.*comm.in Mt*.17.4(p.587.21ff.; 1484Aff.); Church as first son, *Const.App*.5.16.9; Chrys.*hom.67.2 in Mt*.(7.664C); **3.** Mt.21:33, Lc.20:9: Or.*comm.in Mt*.17.6(p.591.10ff.; 1488Aff.); Eus.*fr.Lc*.(M.24.588Cff.); Chrys.*hom.68.1 in Mt*.(7.669Dff.); Cyr.*Lc*.20:9(M.72.885Aff.); ὁ ἀ., τουτέστιν, ἡ νομικὴ γεωργία καὶ λατρεία Anast.S.*qu.et resp*.139(M.89.792B); **4.** Lc.13:6; interpreted both as angel defending synagogue and as Son acting as advocate for souls of men, Cyr.*Lc*.13:7(M.72.761Dff.).

ἀμπεχόνη, ἡ, *shawl*; possibly the *tallith, praying shawl*, worn by Scribes στολάς, εἶτ' οὖν ἀ. οἱ τοιοῦτοι ἀνεβάλλοντο Epiph.*haer*.15.1(p.209.14; M.41.245A); by Pharisees, *ib*.16.1(p.211.5; 249A); id.*anac*.15(p.167.15; M.41.172B).

ἀμπέχω, med., *put on, wear*, of Christ τὴν τοῦ παθεῖν δεκτικὴν ἠμπέσχετο σάρκα Cyr.*Chr.un*.(5^{1}.766D).

ἀμπίσχω, v. ἀμφίσκω.

[*]**ἀμπώτης,** *subject to ebb and flow of tide, tidal*, Epiph.*haer*.30.34(p.382.1; M.41.472C).

ἀμπωτίζω, *suck back*, ref. crossing of Red Sea ἡ...φύσις τοῦ ὕδατος...τούτοις ἀμπωτίσασα τοῦ πελάγους...τὰ τμήματα ‡Nil.*perist*.11.9(M.79.916C).

ἀμύγδαλος, ὁ, *amygdalus, 'burster', 'breaker through'*, Phrygian name for God λέγουσι τὸν πατέρα τῶν ὅλων εἶναι ἀ., οὐχὶ δένδρον, φησίν, ἀλλὰ εἶναι ἀ. ἐκεῖνον τὸν προόντα, ὃς...διήμυξε τοὺς κόλπους αὐτοῦ, καὶ ἐγέννησε τὸν...παῖδα...ἀμύξαι γάρ ἐστιν οἱονεὶ ῥῆξαι καὶ διατεμεῖν Hipp.*haer*.5.9(p.97.24; M.16.3151C).

***ἀμυδρόνους,** *dull-witted*, Thdr.Stud.*epp*.2.1(M.99.1120A).

ἀμυδρός, *obscure, indistinct*; perh. as subst. ἀμυδρά, ἡ, *obscurity*, Ast.Am.*hom*.9(M.40.301A) conj. for ἀμοιβρά.

ἀμυδρόω, *make indistinct*, hence *make feeble* ὁ κύριος Χριστὸς...ἀμυδρώσας τῶν ἡδονῶν τὰς ἐπιβολάς Meth.*Porph*.1(p.503.11); *ib*.p.504.2).

ἀμύητος, **I.** *uninitiated*;

A. lit.; of non-Christians and catechumens, *unbaptized*; in gen., Const.ap.Thdt.*h.e*.3.3.7(3.914); ὁ γὰρ ἀ. οὐκ ἂν δύναιτο πατέρα καλεῖν τὸν θεόν Chrys.*hom.19.5 in Mt*.(7.252C); τοὺς τὸν θεῖον τοῖς ἀ. ἔτι διαπρεσβεύοντας λόγον Cyr.*Jo*.11.8(4.969B); of non-Christian life εἰ...ὁ μετὰ τὴν μύησιν βίος συμβαίνει τῷ ἀ. βίῳ Gr.Nyss.*or.catech*.40(p.160.17; M.45.101D); *uninitiated into* ἀμύητοι τῆς καθάρσεως [i.e. baptism] *ib*.35(p.139.7; 92C); ‡Bas.*h.myst*.46(p.389.18); with partic. sense of *uninstructed* ὡς μὴ ῥᾳδίαν εἶναι τῷ περιτυχόντι τῶν ἀ. τὴν τῶν ἁγίων παραδόσεων εὕρεσιν Clem.*str*.7.18(p.78.22; M.9.556C); οὐ χρὴ γὰρ τὰ μυστήρια ἀμυήτοις τραγῳδεῖν, ἵνα μὴ Ἕλληνες μὲν ἀγνοοῦντες γελῶσι, κατηχούμενοι δὲ περίεργοι γενόμενοι σκανδαλίζωνται Ath.*apol.sec*.11.2(p.96.11; M.25.268A); Bas.*Spir*.66(3.55B; M.32.189A); Isid.Pel.*epp*.2.211(M.78.652A); Cyr.*Juln*.7(6^{2}.247E); Thdt.*eran*.1(4.24) of unbaptized as being excluded from eucharist φυλαττέσθωσαν δὲ αἱ θύραι μή τις ἄπιστος εἰσέλθοι ἢ ἀ. *Const.App*.2.57.21; Chrys.*hom.23.3 in Mt*.(7.288C); and as excluded from prayer with baptized πιστὸς μετὰ κατηχουμένου μήτε κατ' οἶκον προσευχέσθω· οὐ γὰρ δίκαιον τὸν μεμυημένον μετὰ τοῦ ἀ. συμμολύνεσθαι *Const.App*.8.34.11.

B. met.; **1.** of those uninitiated into (i.e. who have no experience of) mystical contemplation ὅρα, ὅπως μηδεὶς τῶν ἀ. ἐπακούσῃ· τούτους δέ φημι τοὺς ἐν τοῖς οὖσιν ἐνισχημένους, καὶ οὐδὲν ὑπὲρ τὰ ὄντα ὑπερουσίως εἶναι φανταζομένους Dion.Ar.*myst*.1.2(M.3.1000A); ἀ. φησὶ τοὺς μὲν τῶν μυστικῶν ἀμετόχους, τοῖς δὲ αἰσθητοῖς ἐνειλουμένους, καὶ οὐδὲν ὑπὲρ τὰ ὄντα εἶναι φανταζομένους Max.*schol.myst*.1.2(M.4.417B); **2.** in gen., *uninitiated into, without knowledge* or *understanding of* ἀνδρὶ ἀ. θεοσεβείας *A.Jo*.64(p.182.15); τοὺς ἀ. τὰς ἁγίας γραφάς Hipp.*haer*.5.8(p.89.7; M.16.3139B); Meth.*symp*.8.2(p.82.9; M.18.140C); Eus.*d.e*.10 proem.(p.446.11; M.22.717B); Bas.Sel.*or*.19.1(M.85.241B); **3.** *without experience of* ἐγκρατὴς ἐν πᾶσι, γυναικὸς ἀμύητος *M.Sab*.2.2(p.120.5); Isid.Pel.*epp*.3.176(M.78.868B); τῆς ἁμαρτίας ἀ. Thdt.*qu.28 in Gen*.(1.42); τοῦ πάθους γὰρ τὸ θεῖον ἀ. id.*Ps*.109:4(1.1396); ὡς ἄνθρωπος [sc. Christ] πεῖραν τῶν ἡμετέρων ἔλαβε παθημάτων, μόνης τῆς ἁμαρτίας διαμείνας ἀ. id.*Heb*.4:14(3.571).

II. *which is not initiation*; of pagan initiations τὰς ἀ. ὄντως μυήσεις Clem.*prot*.2(p.17.2; M.8.88A).

***ἀμυήτως,** **1.** *without initiation, without instruction*, of a monk ἀ. δὲ καὶ ἀμαθῶς...ἀποκείρεσθαι, ἐπικίνδυνον καὶ ὀλεθριώτατον, καὶ τῷ κειρομένῳ καὶ τῷ κείροντι Thdr.Stud.*epp*.2.164(M.99.1521B); **2.** s.v.l., *without being taught, of one's own nature* ἀ. ... γεννηθεὶς ἐκ τοῦ θεοῦ Procl.CP *or*.4.3(M.65.716A).

ἀμύθητος ([*]**ἀμύθευτος**), *unspeakably great* or *many, untold*; hence *ineffable* πνεύματος ἁγίου δόξα ἀ. *M.Thdot.1* 21(p.74.19); λόγος †Jo.D.*Trin*.5(M.95.16C) ∞ Anast.Ant.*fid*.(M.89.1404C ἀμύθευτος).

***ἀμυκτηρίστως,** *without being mocked*, Proc.G.*fr.Cant*.8:1(M.87.1769B).

ἀμυντήρ, ὁ, *defender against*; c. genit., Epiph.*haer*.47.3(p.218.29; M.41.853D).

ἀμυντικός, **1.** *avenging, revengeful*, Or.*Cels*.8.41(p.256.5; M.11.1577C); Gr.Nyss.*hom.15 in Cant*.(M.44.1096A); Cyr.*Ps*.44:5(M.69.1036A); **2.** *taking vengeance on* οὐκ ἔστι τοῖς δαίμοσιν ἰσχὺς ἀ. τῶν ἀνηκόων ‡Just.*qu.et resp*.42(M.6.1288A).

ἀμυντικῶς, *vindictively*, Or.*Cels*.8.42(p.256.20; M.11.1577D).

ἄμυρος, ? *watery*, *Orac.Sib*.5.129, or perh. for ἀμυδρός.

ἀμύσακτος, **1.** *clean*; of animals, Mac.Mgn.*apocr*.3.11(p.78.18); **2.** *undefiled, pure*, of Church ἡ ἀ. κόρη ‡Ath.*proph*.8(M.28.1072A).

***ἀμυσταγώγητος,** *uninitiated* ἄπιστοι καὶ ἀ. Cyr.*Is*.5.4(2.848D); ἀ. ... τῶν θείων γραφῶν Gr.Agr.*Eccl*.4:4(M.98.932B); ἄλλους τοὺς ἀμυήτους λέγει καὶ ἄλλους τοὺς ἀμύστους, ἤγουν ἀ. Max.*schol.myst*.1.2(M.4.417C).

***ἄμυστος,** *uninitiated* εἰ δὲ ὑπὲρ τούτους [sc. ἀμυήτους] εἰσὶν αἱ θεῖαι μυσταγωγίαι, τί ἄν τις φαίη περὶ τῶν μᾶλλον ἀ., ὅσοι τὴν πάντων ὑπερκειμένην αἰτίαν καὶ ἐκ τῶν ἐν τοῖς οὖσιν ἐσχάτων χαρακτηρίζουσιν, καὶ οὐδὲν αὐτὴν ὑπερέχειν φασὶ τῶν πλαττομένων αὐτοῖς ἀθέων καὶ πολυειδῶν μορφωμάτων; Dion.Ar.*myst*.1.2(M.3.1000A); Max.*schol.myst*.1.2(M.4.417C) cit. s. ἀμυσταγώγητος.

ἀμυχή, ἡ, *skin-wound*; of self-laceration as sign of mourning, Olymp.*fr.Jer*.16:6(M.93.664C).

ἀμφαγαπάζ-ω, **1.** *love*; of God ἑὸν κτέαρ ~ων Gr.Naz.*carm*.2.2(poem.)5.15(M.37.1522A); of man; for God, †Apoll.*met.Ps*.17:2(M.33.1332A); Gr.Naz.*carm*.1.2.1.287(544A); *ib*.1.2.2.245(597A); **2.** *treat kindly, make welcome* ~όμενοι πᾶσι τύποις φιλίοις *ib*.2.2(poem.)1.92(1458A).

***ἀμφαιματόω,** f.l. for ἀφιματόω q.v., Adam.*dial*.4.2(M.11.1808A; ἀφιματῶσαι p.138.4).

***ἀμφαναδείκνυμι,** *display all round*, *Orac.Sib*.12.204.

***ἀμφήλιος,** *east*, *Apoc.Paul*.27(p.54).

ἀμφήριστος, **1.** *evenly matched*; *of comparable value*, ref. eternal life and earthly life μὴ γὰρ ἀ. ἐστι τὰ πράγματα; Chrys.*hom.7.4 in Ac*.(9.62D); *matched with* τὸ μὲν σχῆμα τῶν ἱματίων οὐκ ἔστιν ἄξιον ὀβολοῦ, τὸ δὲ βρῶμα ἀ. τῶν ἱματίων Pall.*h.Laus*.68(p.164.16; M.34.1219C); **2.** *connected with strife, of dispute*, ref. Num.20:13 ἀ. ὕδωρ †Apoll.*met.Ps*.105:32(M.33.1473C).

ἀμφιάζω, *clothe, put on*, met. ἡ ψυχή, ἐὰν μὴ...ἀμφιασθῇ ἐκ τῆς θεότητος ἄρρητα ἄμφια οὐρανίου κάλλους Mac.Aeg.*hom*.1.11(M.34.461A); ὁ δὲ θεὸς...ἡμᾶς...τῇ αὐτοῦ δόξῃ ἀ. Chrys.*hom.10.5 in Col.*(11.404B); περιβαλῇ τὴν στολὴν τῶν ἀρετῶν...δι' ἧς ἡ προσγινομένη σοι ἐξ ἁμαρτίας ἀμφιασθήσεται γύμνωσις Andr.Caes.*Apoc*.9(M.106.249D); of Inc. ἑαυτὸν ἀπὸ τοῦ Ἀδὰμ φυράματος σῶμα ἀμφιάσας Epiph.*haer*.42.12(p.156.11; M.41.773D); Cyr.*ep*.46.1(p.158.21; 5².142A); Abr.Eph.*annunt*.1(p.442.11).

***ἀμφιαναδύομαι**, *rise up from, emerge from* ἡ παρθενεία...μετὰ σοῦ ἐβαπτίσθη, μετὰ σοῦ τοῦ βαπτίσματος ἀμφιανεδύθη *M.Ner.et Ach*.8(p.7.3).

ἀμφίασις, ἡ, 1. *that which clothes, garment*, Or.*enarr.in Job* 22:6 (M.17.81D); Chrys.*Thdr*.1.17(1.28D); of priests, CNic.(787)*can*.16; met., of BMV τῆς ἐμῆς γυμνότητος ἡ ἀ. Ephr.3.525D; ὁ κόσμος βέλτιον σχῆμα λαβὼν καὶ ἀ. Mac.Mgn.*apocr*.4.30(p.220.27); Cyr.*fr.Mt*.7:15(M.72.388A); **2.** *act of clothing, covering* χρήματα καὶ ἱμάτια εἰς διατροφὴν καὶ ἀ. σου †Jo.D.*B.J*.18(M.96.1024A); of altar ἡ ἔκπλυσις καὶ ἡ ἀ. *Euchol*.(p.501).

ἀμφίασμα, τό, *garment*, met. τὰ περικείμενα τῇ ἱερᾷ ταύτῃ τελετῇ συμβολικῶς ἀ. τῶν αἰνιγμάτων ἀνακαλύψας τηλαυγῶς ἡμῖν ἀνάδειξον *Lit.Jac*.(p.196.6).

***ἀμφιαστικός**, *suitable for binding* books, Thdr.Stud.*poen*.1.60 (M.99.1740D).

ἀμφιβάλλ-ω, 1. *doubt*, pres. ptcpl. med., *doubtful, not certainly genuine* τὰς καθολικὰς ἀνέκαθεν ἡ ἐκκλησία ~ομένας ἔχει Cosm.Ind.*top*.7(M.88.372D); **2.** *disagree with* ἐδόκουν ἀ. τῷ Ματθαίῳ Chrys.*hom.28.2 in Mt*.(7.335E); *dispute, quarrel* ἀγγέλων μέν ἐστι τὸ μηδὲ ὅλως μάχεσθαι,...ἀνθρώπων δὲ τὸ ἀ. Leont.N.*v.Jo.Eleem*.15(p.30.17).

[*]**ἀμφιβατεύω**, v. ἀμβιτεύω.

***ἀμφιβατήρ, ὁ**, *defender, guardian*, Synes.*hymn*.3.285(p.15; M.66.1598).

***ἀμφιβίως**, *in the manner of an amphibian*, Dion.Ar.*d.n*.4.2(M.3.696C).

ἀμφιβολεύς, ὁ, *fisherman*, Eus.*theoph.fr*.6(p.19*.32; M.24.628B).

§**ἀμφιβολή, ἡ**, *dispute, quarrel*, *A.Petr.et Paul*.28(p.191.6, vv. ll. ἀμφιβολίας, ἀντιβολάς, ἀντιβολίας).

ἀμφιβολία, ἡ, *ambiguity*; *doubt*; *dispute, quarrel*, Leont.N.*v.Jo.Eleem*.6(p.13.1).

***ἀμφιβολογία, ἡ**, f.l. for foreg., *doubt*, Epiph.*anc*.35(M.43.81A; ἀμφιβολία p.45.14).

ἀμφιγενής, *of double generation*; of Christ, Anast.S.*hex*.12(M.89.1053B).

ἀμφιγηθέω, *rejoice in*, Gr.Naz.*carm*.1.2.9.39(M.37.670A).

ἀμφίγλωσσος, *skilled in both languages*, Synes.*provid*.2.3(p.120.21; M.66.1269B).

[*]**ἀμφιγύης**, *lame in both feet*; of Hephaestus, Clem.*prot*.7(p.58.6; M.8.185A); Eudoc.*Cypr*.2.332(M.85.857C).

ἀμφιδέξιος, 1. *admitting both conditions* τῶν γὰρ ἀστέρων οἱ μὲν ἀεικίνητοι...οἱ δὲ ἱστάμενοι...οὗτος δὲ [sc. star of nativity] ἀ. φαίνεται, κινούμενος καὶ ἱστάμενος ‡Caes.Naz.*dial*.107(M.38.973); **2.** *having every advantage, convenient* ἐν καθαρᾷ τε καὶ ἀ. καταγωγῇ Bas.Sel.*v.Thecl*.2.10(M.85.581A); **3.** neut. as subst., *intermediate position* οὐ γὰρ ἔχει τὸ ἀγέννητον τοῦ πατρὸς ὁ λόγος, οὔτε τὸ γεννητικὸν ...οὐδὲ τὸ ἀ. τῆς καθέδρας Anast.S.*hod*.17(M.89.264B).

ἀμφιέννυ-μι, *put round* or *on, clothe in* or *with*, met., of Inc. βαστάσαντος αὐτὸν [sc. ἄνθρωπον] τοῦ κυρίου καὶ ἀμφιεσαμένου Meth.*symp*.3.6(p.33.5; M.18.69B); θνητοῦ δίκην ἄνθρωπον ~μενος Eus.*d.e*.4.10(p.169.2; M.22.281A); ὁ ἐκ γῆς πάλαι τὸν Ἀδὰμ πλαστουργήσας, τὸ οἰκεῖον δημιούργημα ~ται Abr.Eph.*annunt*.3(p.444.19).

***ἀμφίημι**, f.l. for ἀφίημι, Bars.*resp*.(M.88.1816B).

ἀμφιθαλής, 1. *having two parents* τρόπον τινὰ καὶ ἀ. ὄντος Χριστοῦ. γέγονε γὰρ αὐτῷ μήτηρ μὲν ἐπὶ γῆς...ἦν δὲ καὶ ἔστιν ἐν οὐρανῷ πατήρ Cyr.*glaph.Gen*.2(1.61A); **2.** *flourishing, fruitful*; of marriage, Clem.*str*.2.23(p.190.18; M.8.1089B).

***ἀμφιθέαμα, τό**, *amphitheatre*, *M.Tar*.10.

***ἀμφίθεμα, τό**, *garment*, Cosm.Mel.*schol*.62(M.38.482) in Gr.Naz.*carm*.2.2(poem.)5.208.

ἀμφίθετος, 1. *spread everywhere* κακίη δὲ ἀ. Gr.Naz.*carm*.2.1.51.31 (M.37.1396A); **2.** *put on, added*, hence *artificial, false* σκηνὴν ἀ. εἴδεσι λαμπομένην *ib*.1.2.29.298(906A); of Adam γυμνὸν ἄτερ κακίης τε καὶ εἴδεος ἀ. *ib*.1.1.8.104(454A); **3.** *of double disposition, double-dealing*, *ib*.2.1.13.82(1234A); *ib*.1.2.31.24(912A).

***ἀμφιθόωκος**, *about the throne* of God, Gr.Naz.*carm*.1.1.4.88(M.37.422A).

ἀμφίθυρον, τό, *curtain for doorway, veil*; **1.** in private houses, Chrys.*hom.83.4 in Mt*.(7.796A,B); **2.** in Temple; *veil*, id.*hom.20.3 in 2Cor*(10.581B); **3.** in church, withdrawn from before altar at consecration of eucharist ὅταν ἴδῃς ἀνελκόμενα τὰ ἀ. id.*hom.3.5 in Eph*.(11.23D); ἀ. ... κεκοσμημένον χρυσίῳ Chosroes ap.Evagr.*h.e*.6.21(p.238.4; M.86.2877A); εἰς τὰς θύρας τῆς ἐκκλησίας ἀ. χρυσᾶ διάφορα *Chron.Pasch*.p.294(M.92.737B).

***ἀμφικάκως**, *evilly on either side*, of Devil ὅπερ ἐπὶ τοῦ Ἰὼβ καὶ τοῦ θεοῦ ἀ. ποιεῖ ‡Caes.Naz.*dial*.123(M.38.1017).

***ἀμφικάλλης**, *doubly glorious*, Thdr.Stud.*epp*.2.198(M.99.1597D).

***ἀμφικατέργω**, *shut in all round, hem in*, *Orac.Sib*.2.295.

***ἀμφικέλευθος**, *having two ascents* ἄμβων Paul.Sil.*ambo*.209(M.86.2259B).

ἀμφικέφαλος, *having two places for the head*, v. ἀμφικνέφαλος.

ἀμφικλινής, *leaning in both directions, wavering*, Proc.G.*Gen*.3:22 (M.87.225C).

[*]**ἀμφικνέφαλος**, *with cushions at both ends*, Synes.*ep*.3 (v.l. ἀμφικέφαλος M.66.1324C).

ἀμφικνεφής, *wrapped in darkness, wholly dark*, Synes.*insomn*.9 (p.161.12,17; M.66.1296D,1297B); *ib*.10(p.163.7; 1297D).

***ἀμφίκοχλος, ὁ**, a kind of *sea shell* ὁ μὲν γὰρ αὐτῶν [sc. ἀμεθύστων] ἐστιν ὑακίνθῳ καθαρῷ παραπλήσιος· ὁ δὲ ἀμφικόχλῳ Epiph.*gemm*.9(M.43.300C).

ἀμφίκρημνος, 1. *with a precipice on each side, precipitous* τῆς ἀληθείας ὁδός, ἀτραπός, ἀ. Amph.*Seleuc*.201(M.37.1590A); Chrys.*hom.9.4 in 1Thess*.(11.492D); Marc.Er.*opusc*.2.181(M.65.957C); **2.** met., of a question, *presenting a dilemma*, Gr.Naz.*or*.29.9(p.85.8; M.36.85A); neut. as subst., *dilemma* τὸ ἀ. τοῦτο...τῆς ἀποκρίσεως Gr.Nyss.*Eun*.12(1 p.346.6; M.45.1065C); Max.*carit*.2.29(M.90.993A).

ἀμφίκυρτος, *bent, hump-backed* οὐ γὰρ ἀ. ... γέροντα...ἀλλ' ὄρθιον Eust.*engast*.6(p.23.22; M.18.624B).

***ἀμφιλεκτέω**, *argue*, *cat.Ac*.2:22(p.42.19).

***ἀμφιμανής**, *wildly foolish, utterly crazy*, Pall.*v.Chrys*.4(p.25.13, v.l. Ἀμφιμανίστης; M.47.16).

ἄμφιον, τό, 1. *garment*; met., of soul, Mac.Aeg.*hom*.1.11(M.34.461A) cit. s. ἀμφιάζω; ref. 1Cor.15:53 ἄ. δὲ τὸ ἐξ οὐρανοῦ καὶ ἄφθαρτον καὶ ἀθανασίας ἐμποιητικὸν γέγονεν ἡμῖν ὁ Χριστός Cyr.*Nest*.4.6(p.88.32; 6¹.115C); of BMV ἀφθαρσίας τ' ἄ. ἐστολισμένη ‡Gr.Naz.*Chr.pat*.2572(M.38.336A); **2.** *covering, cloth*; for altar, *Euchol*.(p.501).

ἀμφιπαγής, *firm all round, firmly fixed*, Nonn.*par.Jo*.11:38(M.43.845A); *ib*.19:3(897B).

***ἀμφιπερικραδάω**, *quiver all round*, Gr.Naz.*carm*.1.2.29.230(M.37.901A).

***ἀμφιπεριπλάζ-ω**, *make to wander all around*, of stone carved into form of serpents' coils ἴδοις καλὴν ὀφιώδεα σύρματα πέτρην ~ουσαν Paul.Sil.*ambo*.268(M.86.2261B).

ἀμφιπεριστέφω, 1. *put round as a crown, crown*, †Apoll.*met.Ps*.8:6 (M.33.1321A); **2.** *stand round as a crown, surround* κίονας...ἥμισυ κύκλου ἀμφιπεριστέψαντας Paul.Sil.*ambo*.134(M.86.2257A).

ἀμφιπεριτρύζω, *twitter all round*, Gr.Naz.*carm*.2.2(poem.)4.10(M.37.1506A).

ἀμφιπλήξ, *beaten on both sides*; of an isthmus, Paul.Sil.*ambo*.252 (M.86.2261A).

ἀμφιπολεύω, *serve as an attendant, care for*; met., *attend on, surround*, †Apoll.*met.Ps*.45:2(M.33.1376); *ib*.48:6(1380B); *enter upon* eternal life, Nonn.*par.Jo*.17:2(M.43.884B).

ἀμφιπρόσωπος, *double-faced*; hence **1.** *deceitful*, *Orac.Sib*.2.263; **2.** *having two senses* (literal and mystical), Gr.Naz.*carm*.2.2(poem.) 7.135(M.37.1561A).

[*]**ἀμφιρεπής**, = ἀμφιρρεπής, *inclining both ways*, Gr.Naz.*carm*.1.1.9.86(M.37.463A).

***ἀμφιρρέζω**, *perform* sacrifice *at* θείην ἀ. θύος κλισίην †Apoll.*met.Ps*.26:6(M.33.1345C).

***ἀμφισβητήτως**, *argumentatively*, Chrys.ap.*cat.Mt*.9:9(p.67.23) for ἀμφισβητῶν id.*hom.30.1 in Mt*.(7.348A).

***ἀμφισκάπτω**, *dig round, dig up*, †Apoll.*met.Ps*.79:17(M.33.1432D).

ἀμφίσκ-ω, = ἀμπίσχω, ἀμπέχω, med., *put on, wear*, Cels.ap.Or.*Cels*.6.15(p.85.21; M.11.1312D); met. τῆς τῷ ἰδίῳ λόγῳ ἀποίου ὕλης, ποιότητας ~ομένης Or.*Cels*.3.41(p.237.13, v.l. ἀμπισχομένης; M.11.973A).

***ἀμφιτάλαντος, 1.** *weighing evenly on both sides*; met. of man, *wavering in the balance* θῆκέ μιν [sc. ὁ θεός] ἀ., ὅπῃ ῥέψειε δοκεύων Gr.Naz.*carm*.1.1.8.103(M.37.454A); ἐγὼ βροτός, ἀ., μεσσηγὺ ζωῆς τε καὶ ἀργαλέου θανάτοιο *ib*.1.2.9.69(672A); of a road, *sheer on both sides*, id.*ep*.4(M.37.25C); neut. as subst., *equal balance* τὸ ἀ. Πύρρωνος καὶ τὰς ἐφέξεις ἢ ἀντιθέσεις αὐτοῦ Anon.*ep*.(J. A. Cramer,

Anecdota Graeca, Oxford 1836, 3 p.169.4); **2.** *of equal weight, equivalent* ὅσσα τ' ἀρίστοις ἕσπεται ὑστατίοισιν ἐν ἤμασιν ἀμφιτάλαντα Gr. Naz.*carm*.2.1.13.172(M.37.1241A, v.l. ἀντιτάλαντα).

ἀμφιφαής, *gleaming on every side, shining all round*, Synes. *insomn*.9(p.162.18; M.66.1297C); *ib*.10(p.163.7; 1297D).

***ἀμφίφωτος**, *shining all round*, Anast.S.*hex*.12(M.89.1076C).

***ἀμφιχολόομαι**, *be angry about*, Gr.Naz.*carm*.2.2(poem.)3.59(M.37.1484A).

***ἀμφίχροος**, *of two colours*, Gr.Naz.*carm*.1.2.29.38(M.37.887A).

***ἀμφορ-άω**, *look to, have regard to* οὐ γὰρ πρὸς τοῦ θεοῦ δόξαν ∼ᾷ †Cyr.*coll.VT*(6[4].77A; M.77.1289D).

ἀμφοτερίζ-ω, *be in both ways*, hence *have a double meaning* ∼ον ...ὄνομα *Hom.Clem*.3.25.

***ἀμφοτεροδεξιότης, ἡ**, *excellence of both kinds*, Thdr.Stud.*epp*. 2.29(M.99.1197D).

***ἀμφοτερόφθαλμος**, *having two eyes*, Cyr.S.*v.Sab*.47(p.138.2).

***ἀμφύπαρκτος**, *coexistent*, Anast.S.*hod*.2(M.89.69C) ∞ ‡Ath.*def*.5 (M.28.544D αὐθύπαρκτος) cit. s. ἕνωσις.

***ἀμφυπάρκτως**, *by coexistence* ἀ. συντρέχει ἡ ψυχή, καὶ τὸ σῶμα Anast.S.*hod*.2(M.89.69D).

ἀμώμητος, **1.** *undefiled, immaculate*; of Christ χρωτὸς ἀ. Nonn. *par.Jo*.19:36(M.43.905B); of BMV, *A.(Pass.)Andr*.5(p.12.15); τὰ τῆς ἁγίας ἀειπαρθένου καθαρὰ καὶ ἀ. αἵματα Jo.D.*f.o*.4.13(M.94.1140C); of earth before Fall, *A.(Pass.)Andr*.5(p.11.26); in gen. τὸ τῆς εὐαγοῦς καὶ ἀ. ἡμῶν θρησκείας σεβάσμιον Isid.Pel.*epp*.4.144 (M.78.1225B); διὰ τῆς ἀ. μυσταγωγίας Cyr.*Is*.3.1(2.358C); of Aaron as high priest in contrast to Christ οὐδὲ γὰρ ἦν ἀ. παντελῶς id.*Jon*.1 (3.366C); ἡ τῆς ἐκκλησίας ἀποστολικὴ καὶ ἀ. πίστις Gel.Cyz.*h.e*.2.24.30 (M.85.1305A); **2.** *unblamed* οἱ δὲ καὶ ταύτας αὐτοῦ τὰς μυσταγωγίας οὐκ ἀ. ἀφέντες εὑρίσκονται Cyr.*Lc*.11:52(M.72.724A).

ἀμωμήτως, *blamelessly, rightly*, *A.Thom*.A 146(p.254.6); Cyr.*Is*. 4.1(2.573D); ‡Meth.*Sym.et Ann*.3(M.18.353B).

ἄμωμος, *unblemished, faultless*; **1.** in gen. ἀ. συνειδήσει *1Clem*. 1.3; ἐν ἀ. χαρᾷ χαίρειν Ign.*Eph*.proem.; ὁ δὲ μηδαμῶς ἁμαρτάνων, οὗτος ἂν εἴη ἄ. Or.*sel.in Ps*.118:1(M.12.1588B); ὅπως...τὰς ὑπὲρ τοῦ λαοῦ σου ἱερουργίας ἀ. ἐκτελῇ *Const.App*.8.16.5; ἄ. γάρ ἐστιν, ὁ μηδενὸς τῶν ἀγαθῶν ἐλλιπής, ὁ ἀπὸ πάσης κακίας ἀπταίστως τὸν βίον αὐτοῦ διεξάγων Chrys.*fr.Job* 1:1(M.64.512C); ἄ. δέ ἐστιν ὁ παντὸς ἄγους καὶ μύσους καὶ ῥύπου ἀπηλλαγμένος, καὶ κηλῖδος ἁπάσης ἐκτὸς καὶ ἀνομίας καὶ ἁμαρτίας ‡Chrys.*hom.1 in Ps.118* proem.(5.685A); Dion.Ar.*e.h*.3.3.7(M.3.436B); ref. qualification for bishop's office εἰ ἄ. ἐστι περὶ τὰς βιωτικὰς χρείας *Const.App*.2.3.1; of earth before Fall, *A.(Pass.)Andr*.5(p.11.15); of Devil before his fall, Or.*princ*. 3.1.12(p.216.9; M.11.272A); **2.** of God, *1Clem*.36.2; Dion.Ar.*e.h*.2.2.5 (M.3.396A); **3.** of Christ σταυρωθεὶς ὁ ἄ. ὑπὲρ τῶν κολάσεως ἀξίων *Const.App*.2.25.9; as lamb without blemish, Cyr.H.*catech*.19.3; *Const.App*.7.47.3; ταῖς ἁγίαις καὶ ἀ. αὐτοῦ χερσὶν *Lit*.ap.*Const.App*. 8.12.36; **4.** of Church, Or.*Jo*.6.42(25; p.151.25; M.14.273B); Meth. *symp*.11.2(p.136.6; M.18.212D); τῷ λαῷ τῆς ἀ. ἐκκλησίας *Const.App*. 2.20.4; **5.** of BMV, *A.(Pass.)Andr*.5(p.11.17); her soul, Jo.D.*hom*.9. 10(M.96.736C); **6.** masc. as subst.; name given to Ps. 118 (μακάριοι ἄ.), Cyr.S.*v.Cyriac*.8(p.227.6); *Const.Stud*.12(M.99.1709A); cf.‡Chrys. *hom.1 in Ps.118* proem.(5.685A).

ἀμωμότης, ἡ, *blamelessness* οὐ διὰ τὴν ἀ. μακάριος ἄνθρωπος ὀνομάζεται, ἀλλὰ διὰ τὴν γνῶσιν τὴν τοῦ θεοῦ, ἣν μέλλει κτᾶσθαι διὰ τῆς ἀ. Or.*sel.in Ps*.118:1(M.12.1588C); τοῦ προβάτου τὴν ἀ. καὶ τελειότητα ἐπενδυσάμενος ἔσῃ πρόβατον θεοῦ ‡Chrys.*pasch*.5.1(8.262D).

***ἀμώμως**, *blamelessly*, Ign.*Rom.(Inscr.)*; Ephr.3.3D; *Lit.Jac*. (*NBP* 10[2] p.38).

***ἄμων, ὁ**, *protuberance* in the body, Melet.*nat.hom*.28–29(M.64. 1260C).

***ἀναβάζω**, *draw up* water, prob. for ἀναβιβάζω, *Apophth.Mac. Aeg*.1.30(M.34.253A).

ἀναβαθμός, ὁ, *flight of steps*; **1.** met. (plur.), of steps in argument, Chrys.*hom.1.2 in Heb*.(12.8B); as title of Ebionite work, Epiph. *haer*.30.16(p.354.12; M.41.432D); **2.** of Son as ladder to Father, Or.*Jo*.19.6(1; p.305.17; M.14.536C); **3.** exeg. Pss.119ff. (ᾠδὴ τῶν ἀ.), Chrys.*exp.in Ps*.119:1(5.328E); Thdt.*Ps*.119:1(1.1481); ὅπερ ἑρμηνεύεται ἐξομολόγησις τῶν ἐρχομένων ἀπὸ τῶν ἁμαρτιῶν, ἀνιέναι εἰς τὴν τοῦ κυρίου πίστιν Hesych.H.*Ps.tit*.119.1(M.27.1219B); cf.‡Hipp. *fr.12 in Pss*.(p.142.15; M.10.717D); **4.** (plur.) *gradual psalms*; the 18th cathisma, *Lit.Praesanct*.(Brightman p.345.18); cf. N. Nilles, *Kalendarium Manuale*, Innsbruck, 1896, 1 p.lv; also *gradual antiphons*; poet. compositions on gradual psalms, divided into 3 or 4 antiphons in the eight modes, sung at festal matins after psalmody, *Hymn.(AGC* p.53).

***ἀναβαθρεύω**, prob. error for ἀναβοθρεύω q.v., Cyr.*Lc*.9:46(M. 72.660C).

ἀναβαίν-ω, **I.** *ascend, rise*;

A. lit.; **1.** of Christ; **a.** ref. Ascension Ἰησοῦς...ἀνέβη εἰς οὐρανούς *Barn*.15.9; Just.*dial*.36.5(M.6.553D); ∼ων ὡς ἄνθρωπος Ath.*Ar*.3.48 (M.26.425B); Ἰησοῦς ἀναβὰς ἀφῆκε χαρίσματα ἐπὶ τοὺς μαθητὰς ‡Chrys.*ascens*.2(3.780E); exeg. Jo.6:62 οὐ γὰρ ὑπισχνοῦμαι μόνον, ὅτι καὶ εἰς αὐτὸν ἀναβήσομαι τὸν οὐρανόν,...ἀλλ' ἐν ὀφθαλμοῖς ὑμῖν ἡ θέα στήσεται. εἰ γὰρ μὴ δύναται ζωοποιεῖν...πῶς δὲ εἰς οὐρανοὺς ἀναβήσεται; Cyr.*Jo*.4.3(4.375B,C); ἐπήρθη μὲν...ὡς ἄνθρωπος· ἀνέβη δὲ ὡς θεός Diad.*ascens*.3(M.65.1144D); *ib*.4(1145A); **b.** ref. ascending the Cross σωτῆρα...τὸν ἐπὶ τοῦ σταυροῦ ἀναβάντα Ath.*gent*.1(M.25. 5A); id.*inc*.29.2(M.25.145B); Dor.*doct*.22.5(M.88.1828D); ὁ αὐτὸς βροτός, οὔθ' ἑτέρας ἀποκριθείσης φύσεως τὸν σταυρὸν ∼οντος ‡Caes. Naz.*dial*.133(M.38.1036); **c.** ref. Transfiguration τοῖς δὲ δυναμένοις ἀκολουθῆσαι αὐτῷ ἐπὶ τὸ ὑψηλὸν ∼οντι τῆς αὐτοῦ μεταμορφώσεως ὄρος Max.*cap.theol*.2.13(M.90.1129D); **2.** from waters of baptism (with some met. connotation) ἀνάγκην...εἶχον δι' ὕδατος ἀναβῆναι, ἵνα ζωοποιηθῶσιν Herm.*sim*.9.16.2; εἰς τὸ ὕδωρ οὖν καταβαίνουσι νεκροί, καὶ ∼ουσι ζῶντες *ib*.9.16.4,6; *Barn*.11.11 cit. s. ἁμαρτία.

B. met.; **1.** in gen. ∼ω τῷ λόγῳ ἐπὶ τὰ ἀνώτερα Or.*hom.18.2 in Jer*.(p.152.9; M.13.465A); of ascending line of argument, Meth. *res*.1.49(p.303.16; M.18.280A); of blasphemies, *ib*.1.57(p.318.10); of injury ascending from man to God, †Bas.*Is*.267(1.583B; M.30. 589A); towards spiritual sense of scripture, Cyr.*glaph.Ex*.2(1.270A); **2.** Trin. ὁ τῆς ἁγίας τριάδος ἀριθμὸς εἰς μίαν καὶ τὴν αὐτὴν ∼ει θεότητα Cyr.*Jo*.1.5(4.46D); **3.** of ascension from creaturely sphere to divine φυσιολογία, μᾶλλον δὲ ἐποπτεία...∼ουσα ἐπὶ τὸ θεολογικὸν εἶδος Clem.*str*.4.1(p.249.13; M.8.1216C); ∼οντας ἀπὸ τῶν ὁρατῶν ἐπὶ τὰ νοητά Or.*Cels*.3.47(p.244.4; M.11.981C); *ib*.6.4(p.73.23; 1293A); ref. Rom.1:20 οὐχ ἵστανταί γε ἀναβάντες ἀπὸ τῶν τοῦ κόσμου κτισμάτων ἐν τοῖς ἀοράτοις τοῦ θεοῦ· ἀλλὰ γὰρ ἱκανῶς ἐκείνοις ἐγγυμνασάμενοι καὶ συνιέντες αὐτὰ ∼ουσιν ἐπὶ τὴν ἀΐδιον δύναμιν τοῦ θεοῦ *ib*.7.46(p.198.17ff.; 1489B); ἐξ ἀμυδρῶν εἰκόνων ἐπὶ τὸ πάντων αἰτίαν ἀναβάντας Dion.Ar.*d.n*.5.7(M.3.821B); **4.** from Son to Father ∼ειν ἀπὸ τῆς γνώσεως τοῦ υἱοῦ ἐπὶ τὴν γνῶσιν τοῦ πατρός Or.*Jo*.19.6(1; p.305.3; M.14.536B); ὁ θεωρῶν τὴν σοφίαν...∼ει ἀπὸ τοῦ ἐγνωκέναι τὴν σοφίαν ἐπὶ τὸν πατέρα αὐτῆς *ib*.(p.305.11; 536B); **5.** of prayer rising to God λυπηροῦ ἀνδρὸς ἡ ἔντευξις οὐκ ἔχει δύναμιν τοῦ ἀναβῆναι ἐπὶ τὸ θυσιαστήριον τοῦ θεοῦ. διατί, φημί, οὐκ ∼ει ἐπὶ τὸ θυσιαστήριον ἡ ἔντευξις τοῦ λυπουμένου; ὅτι, φησίν, ἡ λύπη μετὰ τῆς ἐντεύξεως οὐκ ἀφίησι τὴν ἔντευξιν ἀναβῆναι καθαρὰν ἐπὶ τὸ θυσιαστήριον Herm.*mand*.10.3.2,3; id.*vis*.3.9.6; **6.** of spiritual ascent of man; **a.** in gen. καθαροὺς εἰς οὐρανοὺς ἀναβῆναι δεῖ Clem. *prot*.10 (p.72.9; M.8.213B); Or.*hom.8.9 in Jer*.(p.63.9; M.13.348A); Meth. *symp*.9.5(p.120.24; M.18.189B); Ath.*gent*.34(M.25.68C); Gr.Nyss. *hom.8 in Cant*.(M.44.944B); Jo.Clim.*scal*.30(M.88.1160D); **b.** through virtue δικαιοσύνης...τὸ σχῆμα, δι' οὗ πρὸς τὸν θεὸν ∼ετε Clem.*prot*. 12(p.85.11; M.8.241C); ἐπὶ τὴν ἁψῖδα τοῦ οὐρανοῦ διὰ τὴν ἀρετὴν ∼όντων Or.*Cels*.5.2(p.3.20; M.11.1184C); *ib*.5.53(p.57.12; 1264C); through participation in divine likeness, Didym.(‡Bas.)*Eun*.5(1. 301E; M.29.724C); and γνῶσις, Gr.Nyss.*hom.8 in Cant*.(M.44.944B); **c.** ref. Moses' ascent of Sinai as type of spiritual ascent, Or.*hom. 18.2 in Jer*.(p.152.20f.; M.13.465B); **d.** constant progress τὸ πέρας τοῦ εὑρεθέντος, ἀρχὴ πρὸς τὴν τῶν ὑψηλοτέρων εὕρεσιν τοῖς ∼ουσι γίνεται Gr.Nyss.*hom.8 in Cant*.(M.44.941C); διὰ προκοπῆς ∼οντας *ib*.7(928A); **7.** angelic ascent οἱ θεῖοι νόες...ἐπὶ τὴν ἄγνωστον ∼ουσι τῶν ὑπὲρ νοῦν ἱδρυμένων συναφήν Dion.Ar.*d.n*.11.2(M.3.949C); **8.** iron., of heretics ἀφέντες τὸ εἶναι κατὰ φύσιν, ὅπερ ἐσμέν, ἐπὶ τὴν θείαν...οὐσίαν ἀναβησόμεθα; Cyr.*Jo*.1.9(4.74E); **9.** ascending from lit. to myst. sense of scripture ἀπὸ τῶν ῥητῶν ∼ειν καὶ νοητῶς νοεῖν τὰ παρατιθέμενα ἐν τούτοις τῆς ψυχῆς βρώματα Or.*Jo*. 32.4(p.431.21; M.14.749B); id.*Cels*.3.33(p.229.30; M.11.961C); τὸ τῆς ἱστορίας φεύγοντες πάχος, εἰς τροπολογίας ∼ουσιν Cyr.*Ps*.35:6(M.69. 917B).

II. other senses;

A. *transcend, surpass*; **1.** of God and Christ ὁ θεὸς...τὴν ἀνθρώπου φύσιν...ἀναβήσεται, γεννῶν ἀμερίστως Cyr.*thes*.6(5[1].43D); *ib*.(44A); τὸν υἱὸν τοῦ θεοῦ...τὴν τῶν κτισμάτων ∼οντα φύσιν id.*Jo*.1.7(4.60A); *ib*.5.5(527D); τὸ προφητικὸν ∼ει [sc. Χριστός] μέτρον *cat.Lc*.4:33(p.39. 8) for ἐκβ- Cyr.*Lc*.4:31ff.(M.72.545D); **2.** in Arian controversy, argument for inferiority of Son τὴν ἐνέργειαν τῆς ἐνεργείας ἀναβεβηκέναι Eun.ap.Gr.Nyss.*Eun*.1(1 p.68.19; M.45.297B); refuted τίνες δὲ κἀκεῖναι αὖ αἱ ἐνέργειαι αἱ τὰς ἐνεργείας ∼ουσαι; οὔτε γὰρ τὴν ἀνάβασιν ἣν ∼ει, καθώς φησιν αὐτός, ἡ ἐνέργεια τὴν ἐνέργειαν, ὅ τι ποτὲ νοεῖ διεσάφησεν *ib.*(p.116.26f.; 352B); **3.** non-theol. ἀναβῇς τὰ λεκτά ...ὑπερβῇς τὰ ἀπαγγελλόμενα Or.*exc.in Ps.*80:2(M.17.149B); πάσῃ παρθένῳ ἔξεστι γαμεῖσθαι...ἀλλ' ἀναβᾶσα τὴν ἐξουσίαν καὶ βουλομένη καθαρὰ εἶναι...παρθενεύει Or.ap.*cat.1Cor.*6:14(p.109.22), conj. ἀναβ⟨ιβάσ⟩ασα id.*comm.in 1Cor.*6:12(*JTS* 9 p.370); **4.** perf. ptcpl., *transcendent, excellent*, of angels τῶν ἀγγέλων αἱ ἀναβεβηκυῖαι δυνάμεις...ἀγγέλων...ἀναβεβηκότων κατὰ τὴν γνῶσιν, ὅσον καὶ κατὰ φύσιν Tit.Bost.*Man.*1.21(M.18.1096C); Max.*schol.c.h.*4.3(M.4.56D); of priesthood, ‡Ign.*Smyrn.*9; of bodies opp. inanimate things, Tit. Bost.*Man.*1.21(M.18.1096D); exeg. 1Cor.12:15f. οὐ ποιεῖ τὸν πόδα τῷ ὀφθαλμῷ διαλεγόμενον, ἀλλὰ τῇ ὀλίγον ἀναβεβηκυίᾳ χειρί...ἐπειδὴ γὰρ οὐ τοῖς σφόδρα ὑπερέχουσιν, ἀλλὰ τοῖς ὀλίγον ἀναβεβηκόσι φθονεῖν εἰώθαμεν Chrys.*hom.30.2 in 1Cor.*(10.272A).

B. *enter* into one's mind or heart, of sins οὐκ ~ει αὐτῶν ἐπὶ τὴν καρδίαν ὅτι ἔπραξαν πονηρά Herm.*sim.*6.3.5; id.*mand.*4.2.2; of repentance, id.*vis.*3.7.2; of good things, id.*mand.*6.2.8; Clem.*ecl.*65 (p.155.12; M.9.728D); of S. Peter's confession of faith ἐπὶ τῆς καρδίας ἀνέβη *Hom.Clem.*17.18; Ath.*ep.Aeg.Lib.*10(M.25.560B); Gr.Nyss. *hom.8 in Cant.*(M.44.941C).

C. *arise, spring up* ἄνθος ἀνέβη ἀπὸ τῆς ῥίζης Ἰεσσαί, οὗτος ὁ Χριστός Just.*1apol.*32.13(M.6.380C); νέαι βλάσται...ἁμαρτημάτων ἀναβήσονται Meth.*res.*1.40(p.285.11, v.l. ἀναβλύζωνται M.18.269A).

D. *go back*, in time εἰς προγενεστέρας ἀρχὰς ἀναβάς Andr.Caes. *Apoc.*37(M.106.677A).

ἀναβάλλ-ω, **1.** *produce* τίς...ἐποίησεν πᾶν σπέρμα τὴν γῆν ~ειν; Athenag.*leg.*13.2(M.6.916B); **2.** *throw off* ~ομένης τῆς ἐπικειμένης τῇ ψυχῇ ἀγνοίας καὶ κακίας Didym.*Ps.*17.16(M.39.1248B); **3.** *revoke* ἥ τε καταδικάζουσα ψῆφος ἀνεβλήθη Philost.*h.e.*3.27(M.65.513C); τὴν ἀπόφασιν οὐκ ἀναβαλεῖται Cyr.*Ps.*61:12(M.69.1120B); **4.** s.v.l., *recall*, CAnc.(314)*can.*15; **5.** *put back, relegate*, Eus.*p.e.*10.4(470A; M.21.781C); **6.** *drive along*; of a boat in a storm, Leont.N.*v.Jo. Eleem.*44b(p.91.20); **7.** *divide* ταύτας ~ε εἰς ζ' *Chron.Pasch.*p.216 (M.92.525C); **8.** med., ? *put one's trust in* ἀναβάλλεσθε τῇ δυνάμει τοῦ σταυροῦ καὶ τῶν ἁγίων ἀγγέλων *CIG* 8907.

ἀναβαπτίζ-ω, *rebaptize*;

A. of repetition of Christian baptism (i.e. usu. conferment of baptism where a previous baptism is not recognized as valid); **1.** for view of early African and Asiatic councils, Cyprian, Firmilian, that all heret. and schismatic baptism is invalid, and heretics or schismatics entering Church must be baptized, v. βάπτισμα; μόνον γὰρ οἱ αἱρετικοὶ ~ονται, ἐπειδὴ τὸ πρότερον οὐκ ἦν βάπτισμα Cyr.H.*procatech.*7; cf. Διονύσιος, Ἀλεξανδρείας ἐπίσκοπος...εἰς τὸ δόγμα τῆς Κυπριανοῦ καὶ τῆς Ἀφρικῆς συνόδου συναινῶν περὶ αἱρετικῶν ἀναβαπτισθησομένων Hier.*vir.ill.*(tr.Sophr. Pal.)69(p.43.12; M.*PL.*23.680A); **2.** view that heret. and schismatic baptism is valid and not to be repeated ἐπεστάλκει μὲν οὖν πρότερον καὶ περὶ Ἑλένου...ὡς οὐδὲ ἐκείνοις κοινωνήσων διὰ τὴν αὐτὴν...αἰτίαν, ἐπειδὴ τοὺς αἱρετικούς, φησίν [sc. Στέφανος], ~ουσιν Dion.Al.ap.Eus. *h.e.*7.5.4(M.20.645A); ἕτεροι...τολμῶσι παρὰ τοὺς κανόνας...ἄνευ ἐπικρίσεως συνόδου οἰκουμενικῆς ~ειν τοὺς ἐρχομένους πρὸς αὐτούς Epiph.*exp.fid.*13(p.513.24; M.42.808A); rebaptism is 'crucifying of Christ afresh', v. ἀνασταυρόω; clerics deposed for immorality not to receive penitential imposition of hands μηδὲ ἐπιτρέπεσθαι αὐτοῖς, ὥστε ~ομένοις πρὸς τὸν τοῦ κλήρου βαθμὸν προκόπτειν *Cod.Afr.*27; children baptized in play by Athanasius not rebaptized ἐδοκίμασεν [sc. Ἀλέξανδρος]...μὴ χρῆναι ἀναβαπτίσαι τοὺς ἅπαξ ἐν ἁπλότητι τῆς θείας χάριτος ἀξιωθέντας Soz.*h.e.*2.17.9(M.67.977C); **3.** heret. baptism dist. from schismatic, Bas.*ep.*188 *can.*1(3.269B; M.32.668A), (v. βάπτισμα); and heretics whose baptism is recognized dist. from those (chiefly followers of Trin. heresies) whose baptism is rejected as invalid; lists of these heresies vary from time to time περὶ τῶν Παυλιανισάντων...ὅρος ἐκτέθειται ~εσθαι αὐτούς CNic.(325)*can.*19; ἐγκρατῖται, καὶ σακκοφόροι, καὶ ἀποτακτῖται, τῷ αὐτῷ ὑπόκεινται λόγῳ, ᾧ καὶ Ναυατιανοί...ἡμεῖς μέντοι, ἑνὶ λόγῳ ~ομεν τοὺς τοιούτους Bas.*ep.*199 *can.*47(3.296D; M.32.732A); βαπτίζονται μέν (οὐ γὰρ λέγομεν ~ονται, ἐπειδὴ μὴ ἔχουσι τὸ ἀληθὲς βάπτισμα)·...Εὐνομιανοὶ μέν...Φρύγες δέ Didym.*Trin.*2.15(M.39.720A); ὅσοι...εἰς πατέρα καὶ υἱὸν καὶ ἅγιον πνεῦμα βαπτισθέντες...αὖθις ~ονται, οὗτοι ἀνασταυροῦσι τὸν Χριστόν...ὅσοι δὲ μὴ εἰς τὴν ἁγίαν τριάδα ἐβαπτίσθησαν, τούτους δεῖ ~εσθαι Jo.D.*f.o.*4.9(M.94.1120A); **4.** practice of heretics; **a.** heretics said not to rebaptize converts from other heresies, cf. Firmilian int. opp. Cypr.*ep.*75.5(M.*PL.*3.1206B); **b.** but Eunomius ~ει...τοὺς ἤδη βαπτισθέντας, οὐ μόνον τοὺς ἀπὸ ὀρθοδόξων ...ἀλλὰ καὶ τοὺς ἀπ' αὐτῶν τῶν Ἀρειανῶν Epiph.*haer.*76.54(p.414.1; M.42.637B); Jo.D.*haer.*76(M.94.725B); **c.** and heretics rebaptize converts from orthodoxy, Epiph.*haer.*76.54(p.414.1; M.42.637B); ἀνασταυροῦσι δ' αὐτὸν αἱρετικοί, οὐ μόνον οἱ κακῶς ~ειν ἐπιχειροῦντες, ἀλλὰ καὶ οἱ τολμῶντες λέγειν ὅτι...ὑπὲρ τῶν δαιμόνων ποτὲ ὁ Χριστὸς σταυρωθήσεται Nil.*epp.*1.204(M.79.160A); **d.** Eunomian method of rebaptism διεβεβαιώσαντό τινες ὅτι κατὰ κεφαλῆς τοὺς ~ομένους βαπτίζει, τοὺς πόδας ἄνω καὶ τὴν κεφαλὴν κάτω Epiph.*haer.*76.54 (p.414.9; M.42.637C); id.*anac.*6(p.232.7; M.42.873B); ~ει δὲ αὐτοὺς εἰς ὄνομα θεοῦ ἀκτίστου καὶ...υἱοῦ κεκτισμένου καὶ...πνεύματος ἁγιαστικοῦ καὶ ὑπὸ τοῦ κεκτισμένου υἱοῦ κτισθέντος id.*haer.*76.54(p.414.3; 637B); **e.** rebaptized persons excluded from imperial service, Ath. Scholast.*coll.*2.6(p.39); Justn.*nov.*37; *ib.*3.

B. of the 'second baptism' of penitence (v. βάπτισμα), Anast.S. *Ps.*6(M.89.1129C) cit. s. δάκρυον.

***ἀναβάπτισις, ἡ**, *rebaptizing, rebaptism*; forbidden, *Cod.Afr.*48.

***ἀναβάπτισμα, τό**, = foreg.; forbidden, *Cod.Afr.*48 tit.

***ἀναβαπτισμός, ὁ**, = foreg.; of baptism on entering Church of those already baptized by heretics whose baptism is deemed invalid ἡμεῖς μέντοι, ἑνὶ λόγῳ ἀναβαπτίζομεν τοὺς τοιούτους [sc. Encratites, etc.], εἰ δὲ παρ' ὑμῖν ἀπηγορεύεται τὸ τοῦ ἀ., ὥσπερ οὖν καὶ παρὰ Ῥωμαίοις, οἰκονομίας τινὸς ἕνεκα· ἀλλ' ὁ ἡμέτερος λόγος ἰσχὺν ἐχέτω Bas.*ep.*199 *can.*47(3.296D; M.32.732A); forbidden by civil law, *Cod.Thds.*16.6.6; Justn.*cod.*1.6.2.

***ἀναβάσιμος**, *capable of ascent* ὄρος...ἀ. τοῖς ἁγίοις ὁ οὐρανός Cyr.*glaph.Ex.*3(1.327C).

ἀνάβασις, ἡ, *ascension, ascent*;

A. lit.; **1.** of Christ's Ascension (usu. ἀνάληψις q.v.), Eus.*Ps.* 23:4ff.(M.23.224A); ὅταν γὰρ ὡς ἀδυνάτῳ τῇ τοῦ σωτῆρος ἀ. ἀντιλέγωσι, μνημόνευε τῶν περὶ τῆς μεταθέσεως τοῦ Ἀββακοὺμ...εἰρημένων Cyr.H.*catech.*14.25; Gr.Nyss.*ep.*2(M.45.1013B); Chrys.*hom.in Mt.26:39*(3.18A); Sever.*serp.*4(M.56.506); Evagr.*h.e.*1 proem.(p.5. 10; M.86.2420A); Jo.D.*carm.assumpt.Chr.*80(p.228; M.96.845C) cit. s. ἀνυψόω; *ib.*89(p.228; 845D); **2.** of other 'ascents' of Christ ἀ. τὴν ἐπὶ σταυροῦ Ath.*exp.Ps.*67:25(M.27.300C); of return from Hades, ‡Bas.*h.myst.*49(p.391.5) cit. s. κάθοδος.

B. met., of spiritual ascent of soul; **1.** necessity of purgation ὡς χρυσὸς ἐν πυρὶ τῇ τῶνδε κακίᾳ βασανισθέντες καὶ πάντα πράξαντες, ἵνα μηδὲν κίβδηλον πρόωνται ἐπὶ τὴν λογικὴν ἑαυτῶν φύσιν, ἄξιοι φανέντες τῆς εἰς τὰ θεῖα ἀ. ἀνιμηθῶσιν ὑπὸ τοῦ λόγου ἐπὶ τὴν ἀνωτάτω πάντων μακαριότητα Or.*Cels.*6.44(p.115.5; M.11.1365D); Μωυσῆς ἀποκαθαρθῆναι πρῶτον αὐτὸς κελεύεται, καὶ αὖθις τῶν μὴ τοιούτων ἀφορισθῆναι; καὶ μετὰ πᾶσαν ἀποκάθαρσιν...εἶτα τῶν πολλῶν ἀφορίζεται, καὶ ἐπὶ τὴν ἀκρότητα τῶν θείων ἀ. φθάνει Dion.Ar.*myst.*1.3 (M.3.1000D); **2.** several grades ὁρῶμεν...ὥσπερ ἐν βαθμῶν ἀ. χειραγωγουμένην διὰ τῶν τῆς ἀρετῆς ἀνόδων ἐπὶ τὰ ὕψη παρὰ τοῦ λόγου τὴν νύμφην Gr.Nyss.*hom.5 in Cant.*(M.44.876B); *ib.*9(968C); id.*v.Mos.*(M.44.372C) cit. s. ἀκόλουθος; **3.** spiritual ascent and virtue οὐδὲ οὗτος ὅρος τῆς εἰς τὸ ὕψος ἀ. τοῖς δι' ἀρετῆς προκόπτουσι γίνεται Gr.Nyss.*Pss.titt.*B 16(M.44.597B); οὐ γὰρ ἔστιν ἀνελθεῖν ἐπὶ τὸ ὄρος ἐκεῖνο, εἰ μὴ ταῖς ἀρεταῖς συνοδεύσειε...ταύτης τῆς ἀ. ἔπαθλόν ἐστιν ἡ εὐλογία id.*ascens.*(M.46.692D); id.*hom.8 in Cant.*(M.44.941B); οἱ τῆς θείας ἐπιβάσεως ἄξιοι διὰ τὴν τῆς ψυχῆς καθαρότητα, ὧν ἐν ταῖς καρδίαις αἱ τοῦ θεοῦ ἀ. Thdt.*Ezech.*28:16(2.916); Συμεὼν... ἀρετὴν ἐξαστράπτων, χάριτός τε θείας πληρούμενος, ἀναβάσεις ἔτι μᾶλλον ὥσπερ ἐν τῇ καρδίᾳ ἐτίθετο Niceph.Ur.*v.Sym.*42(M.86.3024D); ἐν πάσαις ταῖς ἀ. τῶν ἀποκαλύψεων τῆς γνώσεως...εἰσάγει αὐτὸν καὶ ἐξάγει ἡ θεία ἀγάπη Philox.*ep.*29(p.178); **4.** contemplation and prayer πρᾶξις γὰρ θεωρίας ἀνάβασις Or.*hom.1 in Lc.*(p.10.1); προσευχή ἐστιν ἀ. νοῦ πρὸς θεόν Evagr.Pont.*or.*35(M.79.1173D) = Jo.D. *f.o.*3.24(M.94.1089C); τὴν θείαν φανταζόμενος θεωρίαν, καὶ τὰς τοῦ θεοῦ ἀ. Thdt.*h.rel.*12(3.1202); τὸν εὐχόμενον οὐ δεῖ στῆναί ποτε τῆς ἐπὶ θεὸν ἀγούσης ὑψηλῆς ἀ. ὡς γὰρ ἀ. χρὴ νοεῖσθαι κατὰ τὴν ἐκ δυνάμεως εἰς δύναμιν, τὴν ἐν τῇ πρακτικῇ τῶν ἀρετῶν προκοπήν Max.*cap. theol.*2.18(M.90.1133A), v. εὐχή; **5.** end of spiritual ascent: vision of God, Or.*Jo.*20.10(p.338.22; M.14.593B); Gr.Nyss.*hom.6 in Cant.*(M. 44.889C); Niceph.Ur.*v.Sym.*38(M.86.3021A); apprehension of sacraments ἀ. ἱεραῖς ἐπὶ τὰς τῶν τελουμένων ἀρχὰς ἀναβλέψαντες Dion. Ar.*e.h.*2.3.2(M.3.397C); **6.** S. Paul's ascent into third heaven ἡ μέχρις ἐκείνου πρόοδος ἢ ἀ. Gr.Naz.*or.*28.20(p.51.12; M.36.52C); *ib.* 28.21(p.53.14; 53C); **7.** spiritual interpretation of lit. 'ascents': of Israelites' ascent from Egypt to Canaan διὰ τὴν ἐκ τῶν κάτω πρὸς τὰ ἄνω, καὶ τὴν ἐπὶ τῆς ἐπαγγελίας πρόοδον καὶ ἀ. Gr.Naz.*or.*45.10 (M.36.636C); of Christ's ascent towards Jerusalem, Heracleon ap. Or.*Jo.*10.33(19; p.206.28; M.14.365C) cit. s. ἄνοδος; of Ascension τῆς ἀ. πρὸς τὸν πατέρα τοῦ υἱοῦ θεοπρεπέστερον μετὰ ἁγίας τρανότητος ἡμῖν νοουμένης, ἥντινα ἀ. νοῦς μᾶλλον ἀναβαίνει σώματος Or.*or.*23.2 (p.350.30f.; M.11.488C); **8.** exeg. Ps.83:6 μακαρίζει...τὸν καὶ ἀναβάσεις ἐσχηκότα ἐν τῇ καρδίᾳ αὐτοῦ...πᾶς οὖν ὁ...ἐν τῷ θνητῷ βίῳ τῆς παρὰ τοῦ θεοῦ ἀντιλήψεως τυγχάνων, μακάριος...ὅτε μάλιστα ἀ. τοῦ θεοῦ ἐν τῇ καρδίᾳ αὐτοῦ γίνονται...ἀγαθοὺς δὲ λογισμοὺς σημαίνουσιν αἱ ἀ. Eus.*Ps.*83:6(M.23.1009B–D); Gr.Naz.*or.*31.26(p.178.15; M.36.161D); ποίας ἀ.; τὰς εἰς οὐρανὸν δηλονότι. διενθυμούμεθα γὰρ καθ' ἑαυτούς, καὶ ἐν ἐλπίσιν ἐσμὲν ὅτι εἰς τὴν ἄνω πόλιν ἀναβησόμεθα Cyr.*Ps.*83:6(M.69.1208D).

C. as name of angelic hierarchy ἐξουσίας, λαμπρότητας, ἀ., νοερὰς δυνάμεις Gr.Naz.*or.*28.31(p.70.14; M.36.72B).

***ἀναβασταγμός**, ὁ, *support*, Melet.*nat.hom.*28–29(M.64.1265C).

***ἀναβαστακτήρ**, ὁ, *supporter*, Olymp.*Job* 38:6(M.93.397D).

ἀναβάσταξις, ἡ, *support*, Melet.*nat.hom.*22(M.64.1229C).

ἀναβατικός, *concerned with ascent*; neut. as subst., *ascension*; in titles of books τὸ Ἀ. Παύλου Epiph.*haer.*38.2(p.64.22; M.41.656D); Ἀ. Ἡσαΐα *ib.*40.2(p.82.14; 680B); *ib.*67.3(p.135.24; M.42.176C).

***ἀναβεβηκότως**, *by way of exaltation*, Didym.*Trin.*2.6(M.39.525B).

ἀναβιβασμός, ὁ, *ascent*, Synes.*Dion* 4(M.66.1125A; conj. ἀναβασμός p.245.5).

ἀναβι-όω (v. ἀναβιώσκω), **A.** in gen.; **1.** *come to life again* οἱ δὲ τηνάλλως νεκροὶ οἱ τῆς ὄντως οὔσης ἀμέτοχοι ζωῆς ἀκροαταὶ μόνον γενόμενοι τοῦ ᾄσματος ἀνεβίωσαν Clem.*prot.*1(p.5.33; M.8.57C); [sc. τὴν εὐσεβείας πολιτείαν] ἀποκρυβεῖσαν...ἀναβεβιωκέναι διὰ τῆς τοῦ σωτῆρος ἡμῶν διδασκαλίας Eus.*d.e.*1.6(p.27.18; M.22.56B); id.*e.th.*1.20(p.98.10; M.24.896C); Jo.Jej.*poenit.cont.virg.*(M.88.1956C); **2.** *live anew, afresh* τὸ δὲ ~οῦν δύνασθαι χορηγεῖ τοῖς προστρέχουσιν ὁ υἱός Cyr.*Jo.*4.1(4.340D); **3.** *live, lead one's life* φάσκων ἐναντίως μὲν τοῖς ἀναγεγραμμένοις διατεθεῖσθαι αὐτοὺς καὶ ἀναβεβιωκέναι Eus.*d.e.*3.5(p.123.34; M.22.212A).

B. theol.; **1.** ref. resurrection, *live again* ὁ εὐσεβὴς...ἄνω μετὰ τῶν πατέρων ~ώσας εὐφρανθήσεται *2Clem.*19.3; ἄλλοι...ἐπὶ τῆς Ἀραβίας...ἔλεγον τὴν ἀνθρωπείαν ψυχὴν...συναποθνήσκειν τοῖς σώμασι ...αὖθις δέ ποτε κατὰ τὸν τῆς ἀναστάσεως καιρὸν σὺν αὐτοῖς ~ώσεσθαι Eus.*h.e.*6.37(M.20.597B); ἄνθρωπος ~ώσεται οὐχ ὥστε πάλιν τεθνάναι Aen.*dial.*(M.85.973A); esp. ref. the body τὰ σώματα...ὁποῖα ἦν τοιαῦτα ~ώσαντα ἐπενδύσονται Iren.*fr.*12(M.7.1236B); ἀνόητον τὸ λέγειν ἀ. μὴ δύνασθαι τὸ σῶμα Meth.*res.*1.29(p.261.9; M.41.1140A); *ib.*1.30(p.263.6; 1140C); notion that there is no resurrection for unbelievers refuted, Cyr.*Jo.*4.2(4.354C); **2.** of Christ's Resurrection μετά...τρεῖς ἡμέρας ἀνεβίω Arist.*apol.*15.2; Eus.*d.e.*3.2(p.105.25; M.22.181C); οὐ γὰρ ὥσπερ Λάζαρος ἤ τις ἄλλος τῶν ἀναβεβιωκότων ἀλλοτρίᾳ δυνάμει πρὸς τὸ ζῆν ἐπανάγεται Gr.Nyss.*Apoll.*17(M.45.1156C); μετά γε τὸ ἀ. καὶ ἀνελθεῖν εἰς τὸν οὐρανόν Cyr.*Nah.*6(3.483A); id.*Abac.*10(3.526A); id.*hom.pasch.*16.6(5^2.221E); cf.Oecum.*Apoc.*5:7(p.79); *ib.*12:16(p.147).

ἀναβίωσις, ἡ, **1.** *renewal of life*; ref. trees, Bas.*hex.*6.8(1.57D; M.29.136B); of spiritual life τὸ συγκρίνεσθαι παρὰ θεοῦ καὶ τοὺς τόπους καὶ τὰς ἀ. καὶ τὰς ἕξεις τῶν ὑπευθύνων Jo.Clim.*past.*10(M.88.1185B); **2.** *return to life* [sc. ὁ Νάρκισσος] ὥσπερ ἐξ ἀ. ἀναφανείς Eus.*h.e.*6.10(M.20.541B); id.*v.C.*1.22(p.18.24; M.20.937A); *ib.*4.71(p.147.16; 1228A); ref. miracles νεκρῶν τε ἀναβιώσεις...ἐμαρτύρησαν id.*d.e.*3.5(p.119.20; M.22.204B); ἰδὼν...παρ' ἐλπίδα ἀ. τοῦ πατρός *A.Jo.*53(p.177.32); **3.** *resurrection*; **a.** of Christ, Eus.*l.C.*15(p.244.15; M.20.1413B); id.*d.e.*1.1(p.4.8; M.22.17B); Ath.*exp.Ps.*67:25(M.27.300C); Cyr.*Ps.*9:1(M.69.761B); θάνατον...Ἰησοῦ Χριστοῦ τήν τε ἐκ νεκρῶν ἀ. id.*ep.*17.7(p.37.23; 5^2.72C) in eucharistic context, contrast θάνατον... Ἰησοῦ Χριστοῦ καὶ τὴν...ἐκ νεκρῶν ἀνάστασιν *Lit.Marc.*(Brightman p.133.25); δέχεται...τὴν ὑγιείαν τουτέστι τὴν ἀ. Proc.G.*Is.*9:7(M.87.2008D); **b.** of dead [sc. ὁ Πλάτων] περὶ τῆς τῶν τετελευτηκότων ἀ. ...ἐπιλέγει Eus.*p.e.*11.32(561A; M.21.933B); ἀ. τῶν κεκοιμημένων *Const.App.*7.32.3; Cyr.*hom.pasch.*5.1(5^2.44E); τῆς εἰσαῦθις ἀ. τῆς σαρκός id.*Jo.*2.4(4.174D); Thdt.*Is.*arg.(p.2.9; 2.166); τὴν τῶν σωμάτων ἀ. Isid.Pel.*epp.*3.295(M.78.969C); κόκκοι...τῆς τῶν νεκρῶν ἀ. ... σύμβολον ‡Nil.*fr.pasch.*1(M.79.1493A); Bas.Sel.*or.*13.3(M.85.180D); Jo.D.*hom.*1.14(M.96.565D).

ἀναβιώσκ-ω (v. ἀναβιόω), **1.** *come to life again* Διονύσου...~οντος καὶ ἀναβαίνοντος εἰς οὐρανόν Or.*Cels.*4.17(p.286.14; M.11.1048D); of the phoenix, Eus.*v.C.*4.72(p.147.20; M.20.1228A); τῆς ~ούσης θυγατρὸς τοῦ ἀρχισυναγωγοῦ Eus.*Is.*17:6(M.24.209A); of resurrection of dead ἀνάγκη δὴ καὶ τὸ ~εσθαι εἶναι ἐκ τοῦ τεθνάναι Meth.*res.*1.53(p.309.10; M.41.1128C); **2.** met., *start afresh, enter on a new life* διὰ τῆς μετανοίας ἀ. †Bas.*Is.*34(1.408A; M.30.188C); **3.** met., of revival after sleep ὑπνούντων...καὶ τρόπον τινὰ πάλιν ~όντων Athenag.*res.*16(p.68.6; M.6.1005D); **4.** *cause to come to life again* τῶν ἀναβιωσθέντων ὑπὸ κυρίου Vict.*Mc.*11:20(p.395.3).

ἀναβλέπω, **1.** *look up to* with reverence, of spiritual eyes ἀνεγειρόμενοι καὶ ἀ. τὸ φῶς καὶ τὴν ἀλήθειαν Clem.*ecl.*35(p.148.2; M.9.717A); ἢ ἐν ἄλλῃ τινὶ κωλυούσῃ ἀ. τὴν ψυχὴν κακοδαιμονίᾳ Or.*Cels.*3.38 (p.235.3; M.11.969B); Chrys.*hom.56.1 in Jo.*(8.327D); **2.** ποιέω c. infin. = διανοίγω τοὺς ὀφθαλμούς (ref. Gen.3:7): ὁ ὄφις ἀ. ἐποίησεν *Hom.Clem.*16.6.

ἀνάβλεψις, ἡ, **1.** *recovery of sight*; lit., Sophr.H.*mir.Cyr.et Jo.*69(M.87.3664B); met., Mac.Aeg.*hom.*4.25(M.34.492C); **2.** spiritual *vision* ὁ Παῦλος βούλεται τὸν μέγαν πλοῦτον, ὃν ἔγνω, ὅς ἐστιν ἡ ἐν Χριστῷ ἀ. δοθῆναι τοῖς υἱοῖς αὐτοῦ Ammonas *ep.*3(p.439.6); Chrys.*hom.32.7 in Mt.*(7.376A); ἀ. ὀφθαλμῶν γνησίως πρὸς τὸν θεὸν ἀναβλεψάντων Nil.*epp.*3.243(M.79.500D).

***ἀναβλήχομαι**, *bleat*, Cyr.*glaph.Gen.*1(1.15B).

ἀναβλύζ-ω, **1.** trans., *pour forth*; tears, Nonn.*par.Jo.*20:11(M.43.1909B); Chrys.*hom.12.2 in Col.*(11.415B); of Christ's body σωτηρίους πηγὰς ἀ. id.*hom.25.4 in 1Cor.*(10.217B); of apostles πηγὴν δογμάτων ἀ. id.*hom.1.1 in Mt.*(7.3C); of Job's body πηγὴν σκωλήκων ἀ. *ib.15.5*(192D); of the merciful πάντα ἀ. τὰ καλά Isid.Pel.*epp.*2.130(M.78.573C); ὁ τὰς τῆς δικαιοσύνης ~ων πηγάς Thdt.*Rom.*3:7(3.39); **2.** intrans., *gush forth*; of water, Just.*dial.*131.6(M.6.781B); of springs, Ath.*gent.*44(M.25.88B); of rivers, Philost.*h.e.*3.10(M.65.493B); ‡Caes.Naz.*dial.*147(M.38.1096); met. πηγὴ ὕδατος ἀνέβλυσεν ὁ Χριστός Just.*dial.*69.6(637C); ἡ τοῦ...πνεύματος ~ει πηγή Thdt.*xii proph.proem.*(2.1306); τὸ πνεῦμα...ἐξ αὐτοῦ [sc. τοῦ υἱοῦ] ἡμῖν ἀ. Gel.Cyz.*h.e.*2.23.5(M.85.1296C); of faith, Thdt.*Col.*2:7(3.485); of truth, *Hom.Clem.*17.17; of grace, Nil.*epp.*1.26(M.79.93C); of Law ἐκ τῆς Σιὼν ἀναβλύσαντα νόμον Thdt.*affect.*10(4.966); (Ophite) of light from Bythus and Ennoia, Iren.*haer.*1.30.2(cf.M.7.695B); **3.** *swill, guzzle*, Ephr.1.203F.

ἀνάβλυσις, ἡ, **1.** *gushing forth*, Ath.*gent.*36(M.25.72C); Thdt.*Ezech.*47:1(2.1039); ‡Just.*qu.et resp.*5(M.6.1256B); **2.** *source*, of BMV ἡ δαψιλὴς τῆς εὐλογίας ἀ. Jo.D.*hom.*8.10(M.96.716C).

ἀναβλυστάν-ω, **1.** = ἀναβλύζω 2 q.v.; **2.** *come up again, emerge to surface* ῥιφέντες...ἐπ' αὐτῇ [sc. τῇ Νεκρᾷ θαλάσσῃ] ζῶντες ἄνθρωποι ~ουσι ‡Eust.*hex.*(M.18.761C).

ἀναβοθρεύ-ω, *dig up*, hence *destroy utterly* βωμούς Cyr.*Juln.*7(6^2.240B); met. τῆς σωτηρίας ἡμῶν τὴν ῥίζαν id.*Chr.un.*(5^1.722C); ὁ τοῦ θεοῦ λόγος τὴν ὡς ἔμφυτον ἐπιθυμίας οὐκ ~ει κίνησιν id.*ador.*11(1.408C).

ἀναβόλαιον, τό, **1.** part of the habit of a monk (prob. = ἀνάλαβος q.v.) τὰ ⟨δὲ⟩ ἀ. εἰσι κατὰ τὰ ἀ. ἅπερ ἐφόρουν ἱμάτια [sc. οἱ θεῖοι ἀπόστολοι] ‡Bas.*h.myst.*23(p.263.4); **2.** a vestment, prob. *amice*; typifying Inc., Tim.Ant.*descr.BMV* 7(M.28.953D); cf. *anagolaium, id est amictum, Ordo Romanus* 1.6(M.*PL.*78.940B).

ἀναβολεύς, ὁ, **1.** *one who makes his way upwards* οἱ πλέοντες τὰ βορεῖα καὶ δυτικὰ μέρη ἀ. καλοῦνται Cosm.Ind.*top.*1(M.88.88D); **2.** for ἀνάλαβος (*scapular*) q.v. ἀ. ... τοὺς ὤμους καὶ τοὺς βραχίονας ἀνέχων Soz.*h.e.*3.14.8(M.67.1072A).

ἀναβράζ-ω, **1.** trans., *stir up, make boil* ὁ δαίμων...τὰ μέλη ~ει Nil.*epp.*2.167(M.79.281A); **2.** intrans. and med., *bubble, boil up*, Ephr.3.66D; with laughter, Bas.ap.*Schol.*in Jo.Clim.*scal.*7(M.88.820B).

ἀνάβρασις, ἡ, *boiling up*, Geo.Pis.*hex.*485(M.92.1473A).

ἀναβρύ-ω, **1.** trans., *pour forth* πηγὴ...ἀνέβρυε γλυκύτατον πόμα Meth.*symp.*proem.7(p.6.4; M.18.33A); met. χωρία...πλείστην...~οντα νομήν Cyr.*Mich.*70(3.468D); ἔννοιαι...νόμον...~ουσαι id.*ador.*16(1.579A); ἀ. τῆς καρδίας αὐτοῦ τὰ ἀγαθά id.*Soph.*1(3.578B); ἀ. τὸν ἐξ οὐρανοῦ λόγον id.*Ps.*97:8(M.69.1256A); τὰ ῥεῖθρα τῆς γραφῆς ἀ. Geo.Pis.*hex.*55(M.92.1430A); **2.** intrans., *gush forth, spring up* σκώληκας ~οντας *A.Thom.*A 56(p.172.9); ὕδωρ...τὸ ἐν ἡμῖν ~ον Gr.Nyss.*or.dom.*2(p.28.30; M.44.1137B); τὴν ἐκ θεοῦ...~ουσαν ζωήν id.*Jo.*2.5(4.214A); λογισμοὶ ~όμενοι Ph.Carp.*Cant.*199(M.40.125B).

ἀνάγαιος (-γειος), **1.** *upper*, Pall.*h.Laus.*30(M.34.1098C; conj. ἀνώγεῳ p.86.3); ἀνάγειος Eus.*v.C.*3.37(p.94.11; M.20.1096C); **2.** neut. as subst., *upper floor*, Pall.*h.Laus.*30(M.34.1098C; conj. ἀνώγεων p.86.7); of the Upper Room, Thphl.Al.*fr.ep.pasch.*1(M.65.53A); of kingdom of heaven ἀ. μέγα καὶ ὑπερκόσμιον Cosm.Ind.*top.*10(M.88.416B); of firmament opp. earth, *ib.*2 (conj. p.59.8 for 81C ἀνώγεων); *ib.*4(185B).

ἀναγγελία, ἡ, *announcement*, Gr.Nyss.*Eun.*3(2 p.15.11; M.45.580A).

***ἀναγεγωνέω**, *cry aloud*, Cyr.*hom.pasch.*11.1(5^2.143E).

[*]ἀνάγειος, v. ἀνάγαιος.

ἀναγενν-άω, *regenerate, bring to new birth*;

A. ref. means of spiritual regeneration; **1.** as work of God alone, Chrys.*hom.50.3 in Mt.*(7.517B); **2.** of Father by H. Ghost, Clem.*paed.*1.5(p.102.20; M.8.276A); **3.** of Christ, Just.*dial.*138.2(M.6.793B); Clem.*exc.Thdot.*80(p.131.25; M.9.696B); id.*paed.*1.6(p.119.18; M.8.308C); id.*str.*7.16(p.66.15; M.9.529B); id.*q.d.s.*23(p.175.3; M.9.628C); by his death, *M.Thdot.3*(p.134); **4.** of Trin., Proc.G.*Gen.*

2:7(M.87.156D); **5.** of H. Ghost in baptism, with which regeneration is most freq. connected; **a.** sacramentally effected τοῖς διὰ τῆς μυστικῆς ταύτης οἰκονομίας ∼ωμένοις Gr.Nyss.*or.catech*.34 (p.129.2; M.45.85C); **b.** by rite of baptism (v. βάπτισμα), Just.*1apol.* 61.3(M.6.420C); τὸ βάπτισμα...∼ᾷ τὸν νέον ἄνθρωπον *A.Thom*.A 132 (p.239.11); οἱ ∼ώμενοι διὰ τοῦ θείου βαπτίσματος Or.*sel.in Gen*.2:13 (M.12.100B); μόνος τῶν...αὐτοκρατόρων Κωνσταντῖνος Χριστοῦ μυστηρίοις ∼ώμενος ἐτελειοῦτο Eus.*v.C*.4.62(p.143.20; M.20.1216B); ἀναγεννηθέντες...διὰ τῆς ἐν τῷ βαπτίσματι χάριτος Bas.*Spir*.26 (3.21E; M.32.113A); Gr.Nyss.*Eun*.1(1 p.106.6; M.45.340C); in rel. to Christ's baptism σήμερον ἀναγεννηθεὶς ὁ Χριστός, ἤδη τέλειός ἐστιν ἤ, ὅπερ ἀτοπώτατον, ἐλλιπής;...μή τι οὖν ὁμολογήσουσιν...τὸν λόγον, τέλειον ἐκ τελείου φύντα τοῦ πατρός, κατὰ τὴν οἰκονομικὴν προδιατύπωσιν ἀναγεννηθῆναι τελείως; Clem.*paed*.1.6(p.105.7; M.8.280C); διὰ τοῦ ἰδίου βαπτίσματος τὸ ἅγιον πνεῦμα ἐπὶ τὸ ὕδωρ ἐπισπασάμενος, ὥστε πάντων τῶν πνευματικῶς ∼ωμένων πρωτότοκον αὐτὸν γενέσθαι Gr.Nyss.*Eun*.2(2 p.327.23; M.45.501C); **c.** hence regeneration is by water and Spirit (Jo.3:5) τὸν τέλειον ἄνθρωπον, τὸν ∼ώμενον ἐξ ὕδατος καὶ πνεύματος, οὐ σαρκικόν Hipp.*haer*.5.8(p.96.4; M.16.3150B); Proc.G.*Is*.55(M.87.2552A); v. ἀναγέννησις; **i.** associated sometimes more partic. with water-baptism τὸν λόγον...δι' ὃν ἡ σὰρξ τιμία ὕδατι ∼ωμένη Clem.*paed*.2.12(p.228.8; M.8.540C); εἰς ἄφεσιν ἁμαρτιῶν βαπτισθῆναι, καὶ οὕτως διὰ τῆς ἁγνοτάτης βαφῆς ἀναγεννηθῆναι θεῷ διὰ τοῦ σώζοντος ὕδατος *Hom.Clem*.7.8; πρωτογόνῳ ἀναγεννηθεὶς ὕδατι *ib*.11.24; διὰ τοῦ ἐν τῷ βαπτίσματι ὕδατος ∼ώμεθα Anast.S.*Ps.6* (M.89.1129C); cf. ἡ...∼ήσασα τιμία κολυμβήθρα Eustrat.*v.Eutych*. 14(M.86.2289B); cf. ἐν τῷ ∼ᾶσθαι...διὰ τοῦ λουτροῦ παλιγγενεσίας Ph.Carp.*Cant*.181(M.40.117B); the water being connected with water from the side of Christ, Chrys.*hom.85.3 in Jo*.(8.507E); **ii.** sometimes with action of H. Ghost in baptismal rite as a whole τὸ πνεῦμα τῆς ἀληθείας, τὸ παράκλητον, ἀφ' οὗ λαμβάνοντες εἰς ἀφθαρσίαν ∼ῶνται προσηκόντως οἱ πεφωτισμένοι Meth.*symp*.3.8(p.36.10; M.18.73C); regeneration being distinctive work of H. Ghost opp. angels, Didym.*Trin*.2.4(M.39.481C); τὸ...ἀγαγεννῆσαν ἡμᾶς ἕν ἐστι πνεῦμα Chrys.*hom.30.1 in 1Cor*.(10.270B); Cyr.*Is*.4.2(2.609B); regeneration effected by indwelling, not merely by action at baptism τὸ τοὺς ἁγίους ∼ῶν...διὰ τοῦ κατοικεῖν ἐν αὐτοῖς id.*thes*.34 (5^1.349B); associated partic. with action in 'sealing' τοῦ ἀναγεννήσαντος καὶ σφραγίσαντος ἡμᾶς ἁγίου πνεύματος Didym.*Trin*.2.12 (680A); **iii.** sometimes with baptismal formula ἐπὶ τῆς ἀναγεννήσεως ...τὰ...ῥήματα τοῦ θεοῦ, διὰ τοῦ ἱερέως λεγόμενα...ἐν τῇ κολυμβήθρᾳ τῶν ὑδάτων, καθάπερ ἐν νηδύι τινί, διαπλάττει καὶ ∼ᾷ τὸν βαπτιζόμενον Chrys.*comm.in Gal*.4:22(10.711C); cf.Proc.G.*Gen*.2:7(M.87.156D); **d.** hence freq. synonymous with βαπτίζω q.v., Clem.*ecl*.7 (p.138.28; M.9.701B); *Hom.Clem*.11.26; Chrys.*hom.54.4 in Mt*.(7.551B); Pall.*v.Chrys*.9(p.56.10; M.47.33); ὅπερ [sc. creed]...τῇ φωνῇ πάντων τῶν ∼ωμένων προφέρεται Leo Mag.*ep*.28.1(p.11.14; M.*PL*.54.758A); hence, through baptism, Church regenerates ἡ ἐκκλησία συλλαβεῖν τοὺς πιστεύοντας καὶ ἀναγεννῆσαι Meth.*symp*.3.8(p.35.24; M.18.73B); *ib*.8.6(p.88.10; 148B); and minister of baptism can be said to regenerate ὁ ἐπίσκοπος...μετὰ θεὸν πατὴρ ὑμῶν δι' ὕδατος καὶ πνεύματος ἀναγεννήσας ὑμᾶς *Const.App*.2.26.4; *ib*.2.33.2; **6.** regeneration effected by word of truth, Clem.*prot*.11(p.82.34; M.8.237A); through gospel, Proc.G.*Is*.1:20(M.87.1852B); through repentance, Clem.*str*. 2.23(p.193.25; M.8.1097A); Church regenerated ἐξ ἐπαγγελίας Or. *Cant*.2(p.131.28; M.17.256C); **7.** not effected without faith, Clem. *paed*.1.6(p.106.8; M.8.281B); αἱ δὲ ψυχαὶ διὰ τῆς πίστεως ∼ῶνται Cyr.H.*catech*.1.2; τῆς ψυχῆς διὰ τῆς πίστεως ἀναγεννηθείσης *ib*.3.4; cf.†Bas.*Is*.216(1.541C; M.30.492D); Cyr.*thes*.34(5^1.364B); by water, faith, and wood (i.e. Cross), typified by Noah's ark, Just.*dial*. 138.2(M.6.793B); **8.** (Gnost.), effected through 'door of Jesus' (Jo. 10:9), Hipp.*haer*.5.8(p.93.5; M.16.3146B).

B. characteristics and effects; **1.** believer is reborn in God, Eus.*qu.Steph.suppl*.7(M.22.965A); to God, *Hom.Clem*.7.8; into Trin., Clem.*exc.Thdot*.76(p.131.8; M.9.693C); into Christ, id.*paed*.1.6 (p.119.18; M.8.308C); εἰς τὴν ὑπὲρ πάντα δύναμιν [Marcosian] Iren. *haer*.1.21.2(M.7.657B); **2.** new man is produced, *A.Thom*.A 132 (p.239.11); cf. Ophite doctrine of regeneration through second creation κατὰ Χριστόν, Hipp.*haer*.4.48(p.71.24; M.16.3114D); and of second Adam, *ib*.5.8(p.91.4; 3142C); **3.** regeneration necessary for salvation, *ib*.(p.93.5; 3146B); Serap.*euch*.19.3; Cyr.*thes*.34(5^1.364B); **4.** and for entry into kingdom of heaven (Jo.3:5), *Hom.Clem*.11. 26; v. βασιλεία, βάπτισμα; **5.** confers royal status on believer ὅς ἀναγεννήσας με...βασιλέων ἐποίησε βασιλικώτερον *M.Thdot*.3(p.134); **6.** and immortality, Hipp.*haer*.5.8(p.95.24; M.16.3150A); Meth. *symp*.3.8(p.36.10; M.18.73C); *Hom.Clem*.11.25; cf.Gr.Nyss.*Eun*.1 (1 p.106.6; M.45.340C); and eternal life, Clem.*exc.Thdot*.80(p.131. 25; M.9.696A); id.*q.d.s*.23(p.175.3; M.9.628C); **7.** leads to ἀνάπαυσις q.v., id.*paed*.1.6(p.116.30; M.8.304A); μέγεθος καὶ κάλλος ἀρετῆς Meth.*symp*.3.8(p.37.12; M.18.76A); God's blessing, Thphl.Ant. *Autol*.2.16(M.6.1077C); knowledge of God, Clem.*paed*.1.6(p.104.28; M.8.280B); unity with God, Cyr.*thes*.34(5^1.349B); deification, cf. Didym.*Trin*.2.4(M.39.481C); v. ἀναγέννησις; **8.** confers adoptive sonship ὁ πατὴρ...ἀναγεννήσας πνεύματι εἰς υἱοθεσίαν Clem.*paed*.1.5 (p.102.20; M.8.276A); *Const.App*.2.26.4; cf.Gr.Nyss.*Eun*.2(2 p.327. 23; M.45.501C); thereby producing new race Χριστὸς...ἀρχὴ...ἄλλου γένους γέγονεν τοῦ ἀναγεννηθέντος Just.*dial*.138.2(M.6.793B); and brotherhood among Christians, Clem.*str*.2.9(p.134.23; M.8.976C); **9.** conforms man to God μόρφωσον πάντας τοὺς ∼ωμένους τὴν θείαν καὶ ἄρρητόν σου μορφήν Serap.*euch*.19.3; **10.** changes men from σαρκικοί or ψυχικοί into πνευματικοί, Hipp.*haer*.5.8(p.93.18; M.16. 3146C); *ib*.5.21(p.124.2; 3190B); ἡ ἐκκλησία...∼ῶσα τοὺς ψυχικοὺς εἰς πνευματικούς Meth.*symp*.8.6(p.88.11; M.18.148B); **11.** regenerated are delivered from Devil and carried up to God's throne (exeg. Apoc.12:4), *ib*.8.10(p.92.11; 153A); **12.** and are placed in paradise (i.e. Church), Or.*sel.in Gen*.2:13(M.12.100B); **13.** flesh is regenerated through Christ, Clem.*paed*.2.12(p.228.8; M.8.540C); **14.** regenerated are fed with milk of the word (1Cor.3:2), *ib*.1.6(p.115.1; M.8. 300A); *ib*.(p.119.19; 308C); Proc.G.*Is*.60(M.87.2633B).

ἀναγέννησις, ἡ, *regeneration*;

A. nature and effects; **1.** spiritual, Cyr.H.*catech*.1.2; ἀ. ... ἐννοίᾳ θεωρουμένην, ὀφθαλμοῖς οὐ βλεπομένην Gr.Nyss.*bapt.Chr*.(M.46.580D); Bas.*hom*.13.1(2.133D; M.31.424B); ἡ νοητὴ περὶ ὑμᾶς ἀ. Cyr.*Is*.4.2(2. 608D); χρῄζουσιν ἑτέρας ὠδῖνος πνευματικῆς καὶ ἀ. νοητῆς id.*resp*.10 (p.593.20; 6^2.370B); **2.** is in Christ, conferring spirit of adoption (Rom.8:15) διὰ τῆς ἐν ἐμοὶ ἀ. τὸ τῆς υἱοθεσίας πνεῦμα ἀπειληφότες, ἵνα χρηματίσητε υἱοὶ θεοῦ Or.*or*.15.4(p.335.25; M.11.468B); id.*Jo*.20. 17(15; p.349.2; M.14.609B); Cyr.H.*catech*.1.2; ‡Gr.Nyss.*hom.2.61 in Jo*.(p.132.8); ἀ., τῆς υἱοθεσίας περιποιοῦσα τὴν δόξαν τοῖς αὐτῆς ἀξίοις καὶ κεκλημένοις...παρὰ κυρίου Cyr.*Os*.1(3.29A); **3.** means towards attainment of heavenly and perfect man (cf. Eph.4:13), Hipp.*antichr*.3(p.6.19; M.10.732A); cf. Gnost. doctrine; **a.** of regeneration of primal man by 'last man' (Marcosian), Iren.*haer*. 1.14.6(M.7.608A); Hipp.*haer*.6.47(p.179.10; M.16.3271B); **b.** of regeneration of Adam (Naassene) περὶ...τῆς ἀνόδου αὐτοῦ, τουτέστι τῆς ἀ., ἵνα γένηται πνευματικός, οὐ σαρκικός *ib*.5.8(p.92.15; 3143C); **4.** restores divine image in man, Cyr.*resp*.10(p.593.20; 6^2.370B); grace of regeneration being conferred by Christ in place of grace which Adam lost, Didym.*Trin*.1.27(M.39.401B); **5.** results in transformation of life, Gr.Nyss.*or.catech*.40(p.159.11; M.45.101B); newly regenerate soul being free from guilt, id.*bapt.Chr*.(M.46.581A); **6.** baptismal (v. infra) regeneration necessary for attainment of resurrection, id.*or.catech*.35(p.137.9; M.45.92A); v. βάπτισμα; **7.** leads on to ἀνάπλασις q.v. and thence to ἐπίγνωσις τῆς ἀξίας τοῦ ἀναπλάσαντος Gr.Naz.*or*.31.28(p.182.1; M.36.165A); **8.** results in deification εἰ οὖν ἀθάνατος γέγονεν ὁ ἄνθρωπος, ἔσται καὶ θεός. εἰ δὲ θεὸς... μετὰ τὴν τῆς κολυμβήθρας ἀ. γίνεται, εὑρίσκεται καὶ συγκληρονόμος Χριστοῦ †Hipp.*theoph*.8(p.262.11; M.10.860A); cf.Didym.*Trin*.2.1(M. 39.453A); **9.** produces τὴν νέαν καὶ καινὴν συναγωγήν of Church, Cyr.*Ps*.8:3(M.69.757C); and establishes relation of brotherhood between Christians, Isid.Pel.*epp*.1.171(M.78.296A); **10.** is only source of grace whereby knowledge of Trin. is granted to men, Eus.*Marcell*.1.1(p.3.11; M.24.716B).

B. means of regeneration; **1.** through Christ, Or.*or*.15.4(p.335. 25; M.11.468B); Didym.*Trin*.1.27(M.39.401B); **2.** by Father, when man keeps the commandments, Or.*Jo*.20.17(15; p.349.2; M.14. 609B); **3.** as new birth, regeneration is presided over by 12 apostles, as ordinary birth by 12 signs of zodiac, Clem.*exc.Thdot*.25(p.115. 14; M.9.672B); **4.** baptismal; **a.** foreshadowed by association of Levitical ablutions with human generation, Clem.*str*.3.12(p.234.8; M.8.1184B); **b.** not conferred by John's baptism, Or.*Jo*.6.33(17; p.143.12; M.14.257B); **c.** but Christ's baptism by John an example of conferment of divine sonship upon all who are regenerated by baptism, Eus.*qu.Steph.suppl*.5(M.22.961D); Christ received adoptive sonship at baptism in respect of his humanity, Father testifying to regeneration conferred by it, Thdr.Mops.*fr.inc*.8(p.298.25; M.66.980D); **d.** through Christian baptism; **i.** as sign of regeneration τὸ βάπτισμα ἀναγεννήσεως ὑπάρχον σημεῖον Clem.*ecl*.5(p.138.15; M.9. 700D); **ii.** effecting regeneration, Just.*1apol*.61.3(M.6.420C); ἐξάρνησιν τοῦ βαπτίσματος, τῆς εἰς θεὸν ἀ. Iren.*haer*.1.21.1(M.7.657B); βάπτισμα τοίνυν ἐστὶν...ἀνακαινισμοῦ καὶ ἀ. αἰτία Gr.Nyss.*bapt.Chr*. (M.46.580D); Nil.ap.Proc.G.*Cant*.8:5(M.87.1741C); **iii.** effected by water and Spirit (cf. Jo.3:5) δι' ὕδατος καὶ πνεύματος ἡ ἀ., καθάπερ καὶ ἡ πᾶσα γένεσις. πνεῦμα γὰρ θεοῦ ἐπεφέρετο τῇ ἀβύσσῳ [Gen.1:2] Clem.*ecl*.7(p.138.26; M.9.701A); τῇ δι' ὕδατος ἀ. καὶ πνεύματος Gr. Naz.*or*.18.13(M.35.1000D); ‡Gr.Nyss.*hom.2.61 in Jo*.(p.132.8); Thdt. *Ezech*.47:1(2.1039); by prayer, epiclesis, water and faith, Gr.Nyss. *or.catech*.33(p.124.1; M.45.84B); **iv.** associated partic. with baptismal water τὸ...εἰς ἀ. λουτρόν Just.*1apol*.66.1(M.6.428B); Cyr.H. *catech*.1.2; ἀ. τὸ πρᾶγμά ἐστι, καὶ πάλιν γεννώμεθα, ὥσπερ ἀπὸ τῆς μήτρας, οὕτως ἀπὸ τῶν ὑδάτων Chrys.*hom.2.7 in 2Cor*.(10.439B); with baptismal formula united with water, Chrys.*comm.in Gal*.4:22(10. 711C) cit. s. ἀναγεννάω; with grace acting through water δημιουργεῖ δὲ τὴν ἀ. ἡ χάρις, ὡς ἐν μήτρᾳ τῇ κολυμβήθρᾳ τὸ ἐμβαλλόμενον ἀναπλάσσει Bas.Sel.*pasch*.1.5(M.28.1080D); water of regeneration being connected with water from side of Christ, Gr.Ant.*mul. ung*.2(M.88.1849D); Jo.D.*f.o*.4.9(M.94.1121A); **v.** associated partic. with action of H. Ghost, Hipp.*antichr*.3(p.6.18; M.10.732A); ἀμφότερα συνῆψεν ὁ κύριος, τό τε ἐξ ὕδατος εἰς μετάνοιαν, καὶ τὸ ἐκ πνεύματος εἰς ἀ. †Bas.*Is*.137(1.475A; M.30.341A); Gr.Naz.*or*.31.28 (p.182.1; M.36.165A); Didym.*Trin*.2.1(M.39.453A); Nil.ap.Proc.G. *Cant*.8:5(M.87.1741C); Proc.G.*Is*.60:4(M.87.2621D); **vi.** hence is ἡ διὰ τῆς πνευματικῆς μητρὸς ἀ. Jo.VI H.*v.Jo.D*.7(M.94.440B); **vii.** as synonym for βάπτισμα q.v.: ζῶν ὕδωρ, ἔνθα ἡ τῶν δικαίων γίνεται ἀ. *Clem.contest*.1; *Hom.Clem*.11.35; *Lit*.ap.*Const.App*.8.8.1; Dion. Ar.*e.h*.2.1(M.3.392A); Max.*opusc*.(M.91.104C); hence **viii.** regeneration is sacramental τὴν μυστικὴν ἀ. Eus.*Marcell*.1.1(p.8.21; M.24. 728C); v. μυστικός; **ix.** baptismal regeneration denied by Marcosians, Iren.*haer*.1.21.1(M.7.657B); **x.** regeneration effected through faith (associated with baptism), cf.Cyr.H.*catech*.1.2; **5.** object of Gnostics' γνῶσις which delivers men from power of fate, Clem.*exc. Thdot*.78(p.131.19; M.9.696A).

C. regeneration associated with milk of the word (1Cor.3:2), v. γάλα.

D. ἀ. of penance compared with baptismal παλιγγενεσία, Ast.Am. ap.Phot.*cod*.271(M.104.213B).

E. of resurrection; of Christians λυτρωσάμενος...εἰς ἀ. πνεύματος καὶ ψυχῆς καὶ σώματος· ἀπὸ φθορᾶς εἰς ἀφθαρσίαν *Pap.Chr*.(p.442); of Christ μετὰ τεσσαράκοντα ἡμέρας τῆς ἐκ νεκρῶν ἀ. (v.l. ἀναστάσεως) ‡Cyr.H.*occurs*.12(M.33.1200B); Leo Mag.*ep*.45.2(p.48.6; M.*PL*.54.836A).

F. apparently in sense of γέννησις: εἰ μηδὲν πρὸς τὴν ἀ. συντελοῦσιν οἱ ἀστέρες, οὐδὲ ἔστιν ἐκεῖθεν τὰ ἡμέτερα στοχάσασθαι, πῶς τῇ γεννήσει τοῦ Χριστοῦ ἀστὴρ ἐπανέτειλεν; ‡Caes.Naz.*dial*.107(M.38.973).

***ἀναγέραστος**, *unhonoured*, ‡Caes.Naz.*dial*.140(M.38.1048).

ἀναγής, *polluted, unclean* ἀνάθημα...ἐπὶ τοῦ...ἀ. Thdt.*Is*.13:3 (2.260; conj. ἐναγοῦς p.65.29); of women after childbirth, ‡Meth. *Sym.et Ann*.3(M.18.353B).

ἀναγι(γ)νώσκ-ω, A. *read*; **1.** ref. imperial legislation against prophetical books θάνατος ὡρίσθη κατὰ τῶν τὰς Ὑστάσπου ἢ Σιβύλλης ἢ τῶν προφητῶν βίβλους ~όντων Just.*1apol*.44.12(M.6.396C); **2.** of Christian reading; **a.** in gen. μὴ ~ε Ἑλληνικὰς βίβλους, μήτε ἱστορικά, ἢ τροπολογικά, παλαιάν τε μὴ προσψαύσῃς τὸ σύνολον. ~ε δὲ τὴν νέαν διαθήκην, μαρτυρικὰ δέ, καὶ τοὺς βίους τῶν πατέρων σὺν τὰ γεροντικά Nil.*epp*.4.1(M.79.544D); contrast encouragement of classical learning in Bas.*leg.lib.gent*. passim and Socr.*h.e*.3.16.9 (M.67.420B), v. παίδευσις; reading of apocrypha forbidden, Cyr.H. *catech*.4.33; *Const.App*.3.5.2; μὴ σήμερον ἀναγνώσῃς, καὶ αὔριον κιθαρίσῃς Ephr.3.19B; to be preceded by prayer, id.ap.Max.*cap. theol*.proem.(M.91.721A); τοῦ μὴ ~ειν πολλῷ χεῖρον τὸ καὶ περιττὸν εἶναι τὸ πρᾶγμα νομίζειν Chrys.*hom.2.5 in Mt*.(7.30A); ~ε οὖν, ἵνα γινώσκῃς. εἰ δὲ γινώσκειν οὐ βούλει, μὴ ~ε, ἵνα μὴ καταγινώσκῃ, ὡς ἀγνοῶν ἃ ~εις Isid.Pel.*epp*.1.141(M.78.277A); ἔστω σοι ἐργάτῃ ὄντι τὰ ~όμενα πρακτικά· τούτων γὰρ ἡ ἐργασία περιττὴν ποιεῖ τὴν τῶν λοιπῶν ἀνάγνωσιν Jo.Clim.*scal*.27(M.88.1116C); **b.** in public worship προσέχειν τοῖς γεγραμμένοις, ἵνα καὶ ἑαυτοὺς σώσητε καὶ τὸν ~οντα ἐν ὑμῖν *2Clem*.19.1; τὰ ἀπομνημονεύματα τῶν ἀποστόλων ἢ τὰ συγγράμματα τῶν προφητῶν ~εται, μέχρις ἐγχωρεῖ Just.*1apol*.67.3 (M.6.429B); list of books read, *Const.App*.2.57.5ff.; ἀνεγνώσθη...ἡ αἱμορροοῦσα Chrys.*hom.in Is.45*:7(6.149A); ἐξέστω...~εσθαι τὰ πάθη τῶν μαρτύρων, ἡνίκα αἱ ἐτήσιαι αὐτῶν ἡμέραι ἐπιτελοῦνται *Cod. Afr*.46; books that may be read in church (i.e. canonical opp. apocryphal), CLaod.*can*.60; *Cod.Afr*.24; cf. ὅσα μὲν ἐν ἐκκλησίαις μὴ ~εται, ταῦτα μηδὲ κατὰ σαυτὸν ~ε Cyr.H.*catech*.4.36; ref. books which may be read to catechumens, i.e. Sap. Ecclus. Esth. Judith Tob. *Did*. Herm. ἕτερα βιβλία τούτων ἔξωθεν οὐ κανονιζόμενα μέν, τετυπωμένα δὲ παρὰ τῶν πατέρων ~εσθαι τοῖς ἄρτι προσερχομένοις καὶ βουλομένοις κατηχεῖσθαι τὸν τῆς εὐσεβείας λόγον·...κἀκείνων κανονιζομένων, καὶ τούτων ~ομένων, οὐδαμοῦ τῶν ἀποκρύφων μνήμη Ath.*ep.fest*.39.11f.(p.88; M.26.1437C); ‡Ath.*synops*.2(M.28.289B).

B. *act as reader* εἰς τὸ ~ειν δεχθήσεται Bas.*ep*.217 *can*.69(3.327D; M.32.800C); *Const.App*.2.26.3; *Cod.Afr*.54; ὁ ~ων *reader*, Just. *1apol*.67.3(M.6.429B); Chrys.*hom.3.4 in 2Thess*.(11.527D); compared with Levites, Const.App.2.25.3.

C. *recite, quote*, Gr.Nyss.*Eun*.1(1 p.157.12; M.45.397C); ref. Mt. 15:4 τὸν νόμον ~ει Chrys.*hom.51.2 in Mt*.(7.522A); νόμος ἐστὶ παρὰ τοῦ θεοῦ κείμενος, διὰ Ἱερεμίου τοῦ προφήτου τοῖς Ἰουδαίοις ἀναγνωσθεὶς *ib.64.1*(635B); Thdt.*haer*.5.25(4.466).

D. *say in writing* ~ω ὑμῖν ἔντευξιν *2Clem*.19.1; Eus.Em.*fr.dogm*. (M.86.541B).

E. *study*, Jo.Mal.*chron*.14 p.352(M.97.525A).

F. *arrange for reading, divide into lessons* τήν τε τῶν Πράξεων βίβλον...ἀναγνῶναί τε κατὰ προσῳδίαν Euthal.Diac.*Ac*.proem.(M. 85.633B).

***ἀνάγιος**, *unholy*, Gr.Naz.*ep*.79(M.37.149A, v.l. ἄναγνος).

***ἀναγκαιοκτήμων**, *possessed of bare necessities*, Nil.*epp*.3.110(M. 79.436A).

ἀναγκαῖος, **1.** *necessary*; neut. plur. as subst., *genitals*, Athenag. *leg*.22.4(M.6.937C); *A.Paul.et Thecl*.35(p.262.2); Thdr.Lect.*fr*.(M.86. 221B); **2.** *valued, important* ἐν πρώτοις καὶ ἀ. φίλων τε καὶ οἰκείων Eus.*v.C*.1.16(p.16.10; M.20.932B); of bishops συνεῖναι αὐτῷ [δεῖν] τινας τῶν ἀ. ἐν θεοσεβείᾳ προμηθούμενος *ib*.4.56(p.140.27; 1208B); of *Hexapla* δέχεται αὐτὰ ὡς ἀ. ἡ καθολικὴ ἐκκλησία Leont.N.*v.Sym*.40 (M.93.1720A); **3.** *costly*, *T.Job* 40(p.130.6); Pall.*h.Laus*.6(p.23.11; M.34.1018D); Leont.N.*v.Jo.Eleem*.22(p.42.21).

***ἀναγκασμός, ὁ**, *compulsion*; *pressure* of a crowd, Steph.Diac. *v.Steph*.(M.100.1077A).

ἀναγκαστικός, **1.** *coercive*, opp. persuasive ἡ θεία χάρις προτρεπτική, οὐκ ἀ. Mac.Aeg.*libert.ment*.3(M.34.937B); id.*cust.cor*.12 (M.34.836A); οὐκ ἀ. τοῦ θεοῦ ἡ κλῆσις Chrys.*hom.80.3 in Mt*.(7. 770B); **2.** c. genit., *necessitating* ἵνα μὴ δοκῇ ἡ πρόρρησις...ἀ. τις εἶναι τῆς παρακοῆς *ib.77.3*(745A); *ib.68.1*(670D); **3.** *cogent, compelling credence*, of logical proof Ἕλληνες δὲ σοφίαν ζητοῦσι, τοὺς ἀ. καλουμένους λόγους καὶ τοὺς ἄλλους συλλογισμοὺς δηλονότι Clem.*str*.1.18 (p.57.2; M.8.804B); *ib*.6.9(p.470.32; M.9.300A).

ἀναγκαστικῶς, **1.** *by compulsion*, Gr.Nyss.*or.catech*.31(p.113.8; M.45.77B); **2.** *under compulsion, of necessity* ὁ θεὸς εἰ τῷ εἶναι ποιεῖ, ἀ. ποιεῖ ἃ ποιεῖ ‡Just.*qu.Chr*.3.2(M.6.1436A); *ib*.3.3(1436D).

ἀναγκαστῶς, = foreg. 1, Cyr.H.*catech*.4.34.

ἀνάγκη, ἡ (cf. εἱμαρμένη), *necessity*, dist. from πρόνοια and εἱμαρμένη: τῶν γινομένων..., ἢ θεόν φασιν αἴτιον εἶναι, ἢ ἀ., ἢ εἱμαρμένην...ἀλλὰ τοῦ μὲν θεοῦ ἔργον, οὐσία καὶ πρόνοια. τῆς δὲ ἀ., τῶν ἀεὶ ὡσαύτως ἐχόντων ἡ κίνησις· τῆς δὲ εἱμαρμένης, τὸ ἐξ ἀ. τὰ δι' αὐτῆς ἐπιτελεῖσθαι· καὶ γὰρ καὶ αὕτη τῆς ἀ. ἐστί Jo.D.*f.o*.2.25(M.94.957A);

A. pagan belief; **1.** its absurdity εἰ γὰρ ὁ ἐπὶ στρατείαν ὁρμῶν οὐκ ἐκ προαιρέσεως οἰκείας τοῦτ' ἔπραττεν, ἐλαυνόμενος δὲ ὑπὸ τῆς ἔξωθεν ἀ., δηλονότι καὶ ἐπὶ λῃστείαν καὶ τυμβωρυχίας...πῶς οὖν ὁ ταῦτα μὴ ἐξ αὐτοῦ ἡγούμενος ἐγχειρεῖν, ἀλλ' ὑπὸ τῆς ἔξωθεν ἀ., προσέξοι ἄν ποτε τῷ νουθετοῦντι; Eus.*p.e*.6.6(243C,D; M.21.413D); καὶ μὴν καὶ νόμους ἀνατρέποι ἂν οὗτος ὁ λόγος...τί γὰρ δεῖ προστάττειν... τοῖς ὑφ' ἑτέρας ἀ. κατεσχημένοις; *ib*.(244D; M.416C); Gr.Naz.*carm*.1.1. 5.25(M.37.426); ‡Chrys.*prov*.5(2.770E); **2.** its impiety ὁ...ἀ. τε καὶ ἄστρων φορᾶς ἀναρτῶν τὰ πάντα, τῆς τε τῶν πλημμελουμένων ἀνθρώποις ἀτοπίας, μὴ ἐξ ἡμῶν εἶναι φάσκων τὰ αἴτια, ἀλλ' ἐκ τῆς τὰ πάντα κινούσης δυνάμεως, πῶς οὐκ ἀνόσιον...λογισμὸν εἰσφέροι ἄν; Eus.*p.e*.6.6(250D; M.21.425C); *ib*.(251C; M.428A); εἴτ' οὖν αὐτὸς [sc. θεός] καθ' ἑαυτόν, εἴτ' οὖν πάλιν αὐτὸς διά τινος ἄλλης πρὸς αὐτοῦ μεμηχανημένης ἀ., τοὺς οὐκ ἐθέλοντας τοῖσδε τοῖς κακοῖς περιβάλλοι, αὐτὸς ἂν εἴη, καὶ οὐκ ἄλλος, ὁ πάντων κακῶν ποιητικός...καὶ τίς ἂν τούτου γένοιτ' ἂν ἕτερος λόγων ἀσεβέστερος; *ib*.(251D; M.428B); ὁ θεὸς λέγει· παρέθηκά σοι...τὴν ζωὴν καὶ τὸν θάνατον, οὗ ἐὰν θέλῃς ἔκτεινόν σου τὴν χεῖρα· ὁ δαίμων λέγει, ὅτι οὐκ ἔστιν ἐν σοὶ τὸ ἐκτείνειν τὴν χεῖρα, ἀλλ' ἀ. τινί ‡Chrys.*prov*.2(2.758E).

B. man not subject to it, Meth.*arbitr*.16(p.186.14; M.18.264B); this esp. proved by totally new facts of Christian dispensation, Eus.*p.e*.6.6(253D; M.21.432A); and by diversity of circumstances of children born at same time, Gr.Nyss.*fat*.(M.45.157C); οὐδεμίᾳ ἀ. τὰ ἡμέτερα ἄγεται, πάντα δὲ ἐλευθερίᾳ προαιρέσεως τετίμηται Chrys. *hom.div*.8.6(12.381B).

C. ἀ. and Christian life; **1.** Christianity liberates from it, *Barn*. 2.6; ἐπειδὴ τὴν πρώτην γένεσιν ἡμῶν ἀγνοοῦντες, κατ' ἀ. γεγενήμεθα ἐξ ὑγρᾶς σπορᾶς...καὶ ἐν ἔθεσι φαύλοις...γεγόναμεν, ὅπως μὴ ἀνάγκης τέκνα...μένωμεν...ἐπονομάζεται τῷ ἑλομένῳ ἀναγεννηθῆναι...τὸ τοῦ πατρὸς...ὄνομα Just.*1apol*.61.10(M.6.421A); **2.** virtue not a matter of ἀ., Clem.*paed*.1.9(p.141.7; M.8.353B); πραεῖς δὲ τοὺς κατὰ προαίρεσιν, οὐ κατ' ἀ. ἐπαινεῖ id.*str*.4.6(p.264.12; M.8.1248B); ἠδύνατο... ὁ...θεὸς ποιῆσαι νομιζόμενον ἀγαθὸν ἐν ἡμῖν, ἵνα ἐξ ἀ. ἐλεημοσύνας διδῶμεν καὶ ἐξ ἀ. σωφρονῶμεν, ἀλλ' οὐ βεβούληται διὸ μὴ...ἐξ ἀ. προστάσσει ἡμῖν ποιεῖν ἃ ποιοῦμεν, ἵνα ἑκούσιον ᾖ τὸ γινόμενον Or. *hom.20.2 in Jer*.(p.178.22; M.13.504A); μηδὲν τῶν εἰς ἁγιασμὸν ἀναφερομένων κατ' ἀ. γένοιτο...ἀλλὰ κατὰ πρόθεσιν αὐτεξούσιον Meth. *symp*.3.13(p.42.14; M.18.81C); virginity esp. freeing from ἀ. imposed by passions, *ib*.8.13(p.98.18; 161A); cf.*ib*.8.2(p.82.9; 140B); **3.** exeg. Mt.18:7 ὅταν δὲ ἀ. εἴπῃ, οὐ τὸ ἀδιαίρετον τῆς ἐξουσίας ἀναιρῶν, οὐδὲ τὴν ἐλευθερίαν τῆς προαιρέσεως, οὐδὲ ἀ. τινὶ πραγμάτων ὑποβάλλων τὸν βίον...ἀλλὰ τὸ πάντως ἐσόμενον προλέγει Chrys.*hom. 59.1 in Mt*.(7.594B); id.*hom.27.2 in 1Cor*.(10.242B,C).

D. in Arian controversy; **1.** ref. Son's generation; **a.** in argument agst. Ath. τοὺς οὐ βουλήσει οὐδὲ θελήσει γεγεννῆσθαι τὸν υἱὸν εἰρηκότας ἀνευλαβῶς, ἀ. δὲ...ἀβούλητον καὶ ἀπροαίρετον περιτεθεικότας τῷ θεῷ *Symb.Ant*.(345)8(p.253.23; M.26.732D); *Symb.Sirm*.1. 25(p.256.12; M.26.740B); **b.** refuted λέγοντες [sc. Arians]· εἰ μὴ βουλήσει γέγονεν, οὐκοῦν ἀνάγκῃ καὶ μὴ θέλων ἔσχεν ὁ θεὸς υἱόν. καὶ τίς ὁ τὴν ἀ. ἐπιβαλὼν αὐτῷ, πονηρότατοι...;...οἱ δὲ ἐπιλαθόμενοι, ὅτι περὶ υἱοῦ θεοῦ ἀκούουσι, τολμῶσιν ἀνθρωπίνας ἀντιθέσεις λέγειν ἐπὶ θεοῦ, ἀ. καὶ παρὰ γνώμην, ἵνα τὸ εἶναι υἱὸν ἀληθινὸν ἀρνήσωνται τοῦ θεοῦ· ἐπεὶ εἰπάτωσαν ἡμῖν αὐτοί· τὸ ἀγαθὸν εἶναι...ἐκ βουλήσεως πρόσεστιν αὐτῷ, ἢ οὐ βουλήσει; εἰ μὲν οὖν ἐκ βουλήσεως, σκοπεῖν δεῖ, ὅτι ἤρξατο μὲν εἶναι ἀγαθός, καὶ τὸ μὴ εἶναι δὲ αὐτὸν ἀγαθὸν ἐνδεχόμενόν ἐστι...εἰ δὲ διὰ τὸ ἐκ τούτων ἄτοπον οὐκ ἐκ βουλήσεως ἀγαθὸς...ἐστίν, ἀκουσάτωσαν ἅπερ εἰρήκασιν αὐτοί· οὐκοῦν ἀνάγκῃ καὶ μὴ θέλων ἐστὶν ἀγαθός. καὶ τίς ὁ τὴν ἀ. ἐπιβαλὼν αὐτῷ; εἰ δέ ἄτοπόν ἐστι λέγειν ἐπὶ θεοῦ ἀ., καὶ διὰ τοῦτο φύσει ἀγαθός ἐστιν· εἴη ἂν πολλῷ μᾶλλον...τοῦ υἱοῦ φύσει καὶ οὐκ ἐκ βουλήσεως πατήρ Ath.*Ar*.3.62(M.26.453B–456A); **2.** ref. subordination of Son ἐξ ἀ. δέ τινος τὸ ἔλαττον ἐπὶ τῆς τοῦ μονογενοῦς ὑποστάσεως νοεῖ...λέγων...'ἀ. πᾶσα τὰς ἑκάστῃ τῶν οὐσιῶν ἑπομένας ἐνεργείας ἐλάττους τε καὶ μείζους εἶναι'. τὴν... ἀ. τὴν ταῦτα ἐν τῇ θείᾳ φύσει βιαζομένην...οὔτε...συνεῖναι μέχρι τοῦ νῦν δεδυνήμεθα. τέως γὰρ παρὰ πᾶσι κρατεῖ τὸ δόγμα...ὅτι οὐδεμία τις ἀ. τῆς θείας ὑπέρκειται φύσεως Gr.Nyss.*Eun*.1(1 p.95.23ff.; M.45. 328D–329A); **3.** ref. Christ's sinlessness λέγετε [sc. Arians]· εἰ ἡ ἁμαρτήσασα φύσις ἐν θεῷ γέγονεν, ἁμαρτίαν μὴ ποιήσασα, ἀνάγκῃ τοίνυν κατέχεται· τὸ δὲ ἀνάγκῃ κατεχόμενον βίαιόν ἐστιν· εἴπατε τοίνυν· εἰ τὸ μὴ ἁμαρτάνειν κατὰ ἀ. γίνεται, τὸ ἁμαρτάνειν κατὰ φύσιν ἔσται· δώσετε οὖν τὸν τῆς φύσεως δημιουργὸν τῆς ἁμαρτίας εἶναι ἐνεργόν. εἰ δὲ βλασφημία ἐστὶ τὸ τοιοῦτον, κατὰ ἀ. δὲ τὸ ἁμαρτάνειν συμβέβηκε· πρόδηλον, ὅτι τὸ μὴ ἁμαρτάνειν κατὰ φύσιν γέγονε. διὰ τοῦτο, ἐν τῇ τοῦ λόγου θεότητι ὀφθεῖσα ἡ τοῦ δούλου μορφή, οὐκ ἀνάγκῃ ὑποκειμένη, ἀλλὰ φύσει καὶ δυνάμει, τὴν ἀναμαρτησίαν ἐπιδείκνυται, διαλύσασα τὸν τῆς ἀ. ὅρον ‡Ath.*Apoll*.9(M.26.1145C–1148A).

***ἀναγλυφάριος**, *sculptor in bas-relief*, Mac.Aeg.*hom*.16.7(M.34. 617C).

ἀναγνωρίζω, **1.** *recognize*, in world to come ὄντως ἕκαστος ἀναγνωριεῖ τὸν πλησίον αὐτοῦ οὐ τῷ τοῦ σώματος σχήματι ἀλλὰ τῷ διορατικῷ τῆς ψυχῆς ὄμματι ‡Jo.D.*fid.dorm*.29(M.95.276A); **2.** *acknowledge* ἀναγνώρισον τὸν πατέρα Clem.*prot*.10(p.72.10; M.8.213B); **3.** *meet, see again*, Herm.*vis*.1.1.1.

ἀνάγνωσις, ἡ, **A.** *reading*, of scripture; **1.** privately; **a.** in gen. εὐχῆς καὶ ἀ. ... ὁ καιρός [sc. the morning] Clem.*paed*.2.10(p.215.9; M.8.512B); followed by prayer, Bas.*ep*.2.4(3.73C; M.32.229B); ref. monks, ‡Ath.*ep.Cast*.1.5(M.28.856C); children to be trained by example to devote time to it, Chrys.*hom.21.2 in Eph*.(11.160B); **b.** benefits and effects; in gen., id.*hom.35.1 in Gen*.(4.349C); ἡ γὰρ τῶν γραφῶν ἀ. τῶν οὐρανῶν ἐστιν ἄνοιξις id.*hom.2.2 in Is.6:1* (6.108A); indispensable for salvation, id.*Laz*.3.2(1.738A); purifies soul, *ib*.(739B); defence against sin, *ib*.3.3(740E); sanctifies, id. *hom.23.3 in Jo*.(8.188D); rescues from evil thoughts, id.*hom.3.1 in Ac.princ*.(3.72E); in time of sorrow, id.*poenit*.4.1(2.302C); ἡ τῆς ἀ. τυγχάνει χρηστομαθὴς πραγματεία, ὁσημέραι πρὸς θεωρίαν τῆς τῶν καλῶν γνώσεως...τὴν ψυχὴν ἐξασκοῦσα Euthal.Diac.*Ac*.proem.(M. 85.633B); Nil.*epp*.2.198(M.79.304D); restrains wandering mind, id. *inst*.(M.79.1236A); ‡Nil.*perist*.4.1ff.(M.79.825Bff.); θαυμάζειν...ὅτι σε ὁ θεῖος ἔρως οὐκ ἔτρωσεν ἐκ τῆς συνεχοῦς ἀ. Isid.Pel.*epp*.1.27(M.78. 200B); περὶ τῆς ἀναισθησίας τῆς ψυχῆς...συνεχὴς ἀ. τῶν θείων γραφῶν συμβάλλεται Dor.*doct*.20(M.88.1812A); Jo.Clim.*scal*.26(M.88.1116C); **c.** conditions; effective even if not understood, Chrys.*Laz*.3.2(1. 739C); but faith necessary οὐδὲν ἐκαρποῦντο μέγα τι καὶ γενναῖον, ἀπὸ τῆς ἀ. σωθήσεσθαι προσδοκῶντες μόνης, πίστεως ἔρημοι id.*hom. 41.1 in Jo*.(8.243B); also prayers, psalms and vigils, Nil.*epp*.4.60 (M.79.577B); **2.** publicly; denoting sometimes act of *reading* and sometimes *passage for reading, lection*; **a.** in gen. ἥ τε ἄλλη παιδεία χρήσιμος ἥ τε τῶν γραφῶν τῶν κυριακῶν ἀ. εἰς ἀπόδειξιν τῶν λεγομένων ἀναγκαία Clem.*str*.6.11(p.477.34; M.9.313A); **b.** liturg. τὰ ῥήματα τῆς ὅλης σήμερον ἀ. Or.*hom.4.1 in Jer*.(p.23.5; M.13.286A); ἡ δὲ ἀ. ἦν ἐπιστολαὶ Παύλου πρὸς Τιμόθεον καὶ Τίτον ‡Pion.*v.Polyc*.22; ἑρμηνευταὶ ἀπὸ γλώσσης εἰς γλῶσσαν ἐν ταῖς ἀ. ἢ ἐν ταῖς προσομιλίαις Epiph.*exp.fid*.21(p.522.23; M.42.825A); τὴν ἀ. τοῦ νόμου καὶ τῶν προφητῶν, τῶν τε ἐπιστολῶν ἡμῶν καὶ τῶν Πράξεων καὶ τῶν εὐαγγελίων *Lit*.ap.*Const.App*.8.5.11; τῆς ἀ. τῆς κατὰ τὸν τελώνην καὶ τὸν Φαρισαῖον Chrys.*poenit*.2.4(2.292A); Euthal.Diac.*Ac*.(M.85.636B) cit. s. κεφάλαιος; Dion.Ar.*e.h*.3.2(M.3.425C); πρόσχωμεν τῇ ἁγίᾳ ἀ. *Lit.Jac*. (v.l. p.172.22); preparations for it, Chrys.*hom.53.3 in Jo*. (8.313E); its significance τὰς δὲ θείας τῶν πανιέρων βίβλων ἀ., τὰς θείας...τοῦ παναγίου θεοῦ βουλήσεις τε καὶ βουλὰς ὑπεμφαίνειν Max. *myst*.10(M.91.689B); **c.** at commemorations of the departed τὴν ἀ. τῶν ἱερῶν βιβλίων ποιούμενοι καὶ ψάλλοντες ὑπὲρ τῶν κεκοιμημένων μαρτύρων *Const.App*.6.30.2; **d.** arrangement of lections and psalmody περὶ τοῦ μὴ δεῖν ἐπισυνάπτειν ἐν ταῖς συνάξεσι τοὺς ψαλμούς, ἀλλὰ διὰ μέσου καθ' ἕκαστον ψαλμὸν γίνεσθαι ἀ. CLaod.*can*.17; **e.** in monasteries during meals, Ephr.2.128F; ‡Ath.*ep.Cast*.1.7(M.28. 857C).

B. in gen., *anything read*; hence **1.** *passage, verses* or *verse* ἄλλη διαστολὴ τῆς ἀ. Or.*comm.in Eph*.1:9(p.240); exeg. Ac.8:34 ἐφοβεῖτο γὰρ μή, παρὰ πρόσωπον ἐκλαβὼν τὴν ἀ. πλανηθῇ Ath.*Ar*.1.54(M.26. 124C); Epiph.*mens*.3(M.43.241B); ἐξετάσωμεν...εἴ τι σαφὲς ἢ τῶν παρακειμένων ἀ. ἔχει Gr.Nyss.*Eun*.3(2 p.11.7; M.45.576A); **2.** *writings*, of gospels κατέχεις τὰς κωλυθείσας ἀ. *M.Eupl*.2.2.

ἀνάγνωσμα, τό, *reading*; **1.** of scripture privately μηδὲ τῶν ἀ. κατολιγωρήσῃς· μάλιστα τῆς νέας διαθήκης †Bas.*ep*.42.3(3.127E; M.32.353A); ref. ideal bishop πολὺς ἐν ἀναγνώσμασιν *Const.App*. 2.5.4; **2.** *reading publicly delivered*, denoting sometimes act of *reading* and sometimes *passage for reading, lection*; **a.** in gen. δι' ἀναγνωσμάτων καὶ διὰ τῶν εἰς τὰ ἀ. διηγήσεων προτρέποντες μὲν ἐπὶ τὴν...εὐσέβειαν Or.*Cels*.3.50(p.246.17; M.11.985C); **b.** to catechumens, Cyr.H.*catech*.4.2; **c.** liturg. σάλπιγγος μεγαλοφωνότερον... τὴν προάγουσαν τῶν ἡμερῶν ἑορτὴν ὑποσημαίνει τὰ ἀ. Bas.*hom*.1.1 (1.1A; M.31.164A); δύο δὲ γενομένων ἀ. *Const.App*.2.57.6; ἐπιτελείσθω δὲ τρίτα τῶν κεκοιμημένων ἐν ψαλμοῖς καὶ ἀ. καὶ προσευχαῖς *ib*.8.42.1; εὐαγγελικῶν ἀ. Philost.*h.e*.3.5(M.65.485B); ἐφ' ἑκάστῳ ἀ. τῆς εἰρήνης ὑποφωνήσεων Max.*myst*.12(M.91.689D); significance, Anast.S.*qu.et resp*.154(M.89.813D); **d.** during vigils, Marc.Diac.*v.Porph*.20; **3.** *passage* of scripture, Ath.*Ar*.1.55(M.26.125B); Didym.*Ps*.10:1(M.39. 1208B); Cyr.*Jo*.6(4.559B); **4.** plur., *writings*; in gen., Eus.*p.e*.10.9 (487B; M.21.809D); ἀ. Ἑλληνικῶν Cyr.*Juln*.7(6[2].231E); of scripture τὰ ἅγια ἀ. Or.*princ*.4.2.1(p.306.1; M.11.357A); Eus.*v.C*.4.35(p.131.14; M.20.1184C).

ἀναγνωστέον, *one must read*; ref. interpretations of scripture, *one must understand* ἀ. τὸ ὑπερβατὸν κατὰ ἀκολουθίαν Clem.*ecl*.56 (p.152.22; M.9.724B); Diod.*Ps*.52:5(M.33.1591A); Chrys.*hom.8.2 in 2Cor*.(10.93E).

***ἀναγνωστέος**, *to be read*, hence *canonical*, *Cod.Afr*.24.

ἀναγνώστης, ὁ, *reader* (member of minor order in Church); **1.** in gen., cf.Hipp.*trad.ap*.12; Corn.ap.Eus.*h.e*.6.43.11(M.20.621A); *PLond*.1912.29; 1914.59; bishop must first have been reader, deacon and priest, CSard.*can*.10; prayers for readers, Serap. *euch*.11.4; *Lit*.ap.*Const.App*.8.10.10; Jo.D.*Man*.1.3(M.94.1509A); cf. Tert.*praescr*.41(M.*PL*.2.57A); Cypr.*ep*.29(M.*PL*.4.310A); **2.** position regarded as within eccl. order, CLaod.*can*.24; included in clergy, cf.*Const.App*.6.17.2; but οὐκ ἔστιν ἱερεὺς ὁ ἀ., ἀλλ' ὡς γραμματεὺς τοῦ λόγου Epiph.*exp.fid*.21(p.522.14; M.42.824B); μὴ δεῖ θαυμάζειν εἰ μήτε ὑποδιακόνων ἐμνήσθη, μήτε ἀναγνωστῶν. τῶν γὰρ ἐν τῇ τῆς ἐκκλησίας λειτουργίᾳ βαθμῶν ἔξωθεν μᾶλλον οὗτοί εἰσιν, διὰ τὴν χρείαν ἐπινοηθέντες ὕστερον Thdr.Mops.*1Tim*.3:15(p.132.9; M.66.941C); readership as first stage in clerical *cursus honorum*, cf.Socr.*h.e*.7. 41.1(M.67.829C); **3.** ordination and appointment; **a.** appointed by bishop who gives him book, but does not ordain him with imposition of hands, cf.Hipp.*trad.ap*.12; *Const.App.epit*.13; Thdr.Mops. *1Tim*.3:15(p.132.12; M.66.941D) cit. s. χειροτονία; CNic.(787) *can*.14; **b.** ordained by bishop, *Const.App*.3.11.3; by imposition of hands and prayer, *ib*.8.22.1; **c.** receiving tonsure, cf.Eustrat.*v.Eutych*. 13(M.86.2288D); CNic.(787)*can*.14; **4.** age qualification: not less than 18 years, Justn.*nov*.123.12(p.604); quoted as not less than 20, Phot. *nomoc*.1.28(p.476); but as 18, M.104.552C); abuse of rule, cf.CNic. (787)*can*.14; **5.** marriage regulations: to be husband of one wife and if single should be urged to marry, *Const.App*.6.17.2; cf.*Can*.

App.26; ἀναγνωστῶν τάγμα ἐξ...παρθένων καὶ μοναζόντων καὶ ἐγκρατευομένων καὶ χηρευσάντων καὶ τῶν ἔτι ἐν σεμνῷ γάμῳ· εἰ δὲ εἴη ἀνάγκη καὶ ἀπὸ τῶν μετὰ θάνατον τῆς πρώτης γυναικὸς δευτέρᾳ συναφθέντων Epiph.*exp.fid*.21(p.522.14; M.42.824B); Justn.*nov*.6.5(p.43.9); not to marry unorthodox wife, CChalc.*can*.14; ἀ. δευτερογαμῶν μὴ προκόπτετο εἰς βαθμὸν ἱερωσύνης Ath.Scholast.*coll*.1.1(p.3); **6.** gen. regulations, CLaod.*can*.23 cit. s. ὠράριον; not to enter taverns, *ib*.24 cit. s. ἐξορκιστής; ἀ., εἰ τῇ ἑαυτοῦ μνηστῇ πρὸ τοῦ γάμου συναλλάξειεν, ἐνιαυτὸν ἀργήσας, εἰς τὸ ἀναγινώσκειν δεχθήσεται, μένων ἀπρόκοπος Bas.*ep*.217 *can*.69(3.327D; M.32.800C); κἂν εἰ τυχὸν ἀ. εἴη τις, μηδὲ τοῦτον ἀπολιμπάνειν τὸ πρότερον σχῆμα καὶ εἰς ἕτερον μετατίθεσθαι βίον Justn.*nov*.6.7(p.45.18); treatment of readers who attend heret. worship, Thdr.Stud.*epp*.2.219.1(M.99.1660C); *ib*.2.219.6(1661D); **7.** duties: reading all liturg. lections, including Gospel, cf. Just.*1apol*.67.3(M.6.429B), v. ἀναγινώσκω; later confined to OT lections and NT other than liturg. Gospel which falls to deacon or presbyter, *Const.App*.2.57.7; from pulpit (ambo), *ib*.2.57.5; Chrys.*hom.19.5 in Ac*.(9.160A); id.*hom.8.4 in Heb*.(12.91B); Soz.*h.e*.9.2.11(M.67.1600C); Eus.Al.*serm*.8(M.86.361C); not to baptize, *Const.App*.3.11.1; **8.** moral and spiritual qualities defined, including that of being διηγητικός as executing function of an evangelist, *Ordo Eccl.App*.19; prayer that reader may receive Spirit of prophecy, *Const.App*.8.22.2; cf. provision for reader to receive single portion of gifts in honour of the prophets, *ib*.2.28.5; possesses πνευματικὴ χάρις sanctified by Christ (ref. Lc.4:16ff.), Eustrat.*v.Eutych*.13(M.86.2288C); **9.** numbers: in Rome in mid-third cent. ἐξορκιστὰς...καὶ ἀ. ἅμα πυλωροῖς δύο καὶ πεντήκοντα Corn.ap.Eus.*h.e*.6.43.11(M.20.621A); in Great Church at CP, 110, Justn.*nov*.3.1(p.21); 160, Heracl.*nov*.22(p.35); *ib*.(p.36); **10.** as attached to a church ἀ. τῶν ἁγίων ἀποστόλων Call.*v.Hyp*.p.59.

ἀναγνωστικός, *of* or *pertaining to a reader* βαθμῷ ‡Jo.D.*ep.Thphl*.16(M.95.368A).

ἀναγορεύ-ω, *call, name*, Christ ὃν ἥλιον δικαιοσύνης ~ουσιν αἱ γραφαί Or.*Cant*.2(p.126.31; M.13.111D); id.*hom.17 in Lc*.(p.111.24); ἀ. αὐτὸν ἐν τοῖς φιλοσοφήσασι Synes.*Dion* 2(p.238.18; M.66.1117D).

***ἀνάγραφος,** *recorded*, Areth.*Apoc*.8(M.106.552C); cf. ἀνάγραπτος id.ap.*cat.Apoc*.3:4(p.223.5).

ἀναγράφ-ω, *enter on a register* as citizen, met. εἰ δὲ σεαυτὸν ~εις τοῦ θεοῦ, οὐρανὸς μέν σοι ἡ πατρίς Clem.*prot*.10(p.77.16; M.8.225A).

***ἀναγρηγορέω,** *awaken* (intrans.), *Ep.Lugd*.ap.Eus.*h.e*.5.1.26(M.20.417B).

ἀνάγ-ω, **A.** *lead up, bring up; lift up*, in gen.; **1.** met. τοὺς ἀσθενοῦντας ἀ. περὶ τὸ ἀγαθόν *2Clem*.17.2; σὺ εἶ ὁ ἐμὸς πατὴρ ὁ σῴζω⟨ν⟩ καὶ ~ων *Pap.Chr*.(p.447); ἡμᾶς ~ων ἐκ τῆς κάτωθεν ταπεινώσεως Gr.Naz.*or*.45.11(M.36.637B); ὅπως ἂν ἡμᾶς ἀναγάγοι διὰ τῶν αἰσθητῶν ἐπὶ τὰ νοητά Dion.Ar.*c.h*.1.3(M.3.124A); of words, *raise* to a higher level, Chrys.*hom.18.1 in Rom*.(9.631D); hence ἀνηγμένος, *lofty, elevated*, Amph.*fr*.(M.39.109A); **2.** pass., *be esteemed*, Clem.*paed*.2.10(p.225.32; M.8.536A); **3.** *bring in*; a phrase, *ib*.1.6(p.120.25; 309C); id.*str*.5.14(p.404.4; M.9.173A); *bring forward* ἕτερον δὲ ἀξιάγαστον ἀ. Evagr.*h.e*.4.15(p.164.6; M.86.2729A).

B. ref. anagogical interpretation; **1.** *interpret anagogically*, Or.*Jo*.1.26(24; p.33.23; M.14.72C); *ib*.32.12(7; p.444.24; 772A); pass., *have an anagogical meaning*, *ib*.13.41(p.267.6; 472B); ἀνηγμένος, *given to anagogical interpretation* μέσην χωροῦντες ἡμεῖς τῶν τε πάντη παχυτέρων τὴν διάνοιαν, καὶ τῶν ἄγαν θεωρητικῶν τε καὶ ἀνηγμένων Gr.Naz.*or*.45.12(M.36.637C); of sense, *anagogical*, Sev.Ant.ap.*cat.Ac*.13:4(p.214.3); **2.** *refer anagogically* ἐπὶ τὴν θεραπείαν τῆς ψυχῆς ἀ. τὰ γεγραμμένα Or.*Jo*.10.28(18; p.201.26; M.14.357C); ἡ Εὔα ἐπιτέτευκται τῷ Παύλῳ εἰς τὴν ἐκκλησίαν ἀναγομένη id.*princ*.4.7.7(p.333.25; M.11.387A); ἀνήγαγε τὸν Ἀδὰμ εἰς τὸν Χριστόν Meth.*symp*.3.4(p.30.16; M.18.65A); Dion.Ar.*c.h*.15.8(M.3.337C).

C. *bring back*; hence *report*, *A.Petr.et Paul*.21(p.188.5); Jo.Mosch.*prat*.88(M.87.2945C); Jo.Mal.*chron*.10 p.230(M.97.356B).

D. impers., *concern* οὐκ ~ει μοι τοῦτο Ephr.2.84C.

ἀναγωγεύς, ὁ, *one who guides upwards*, Ign.*Eph*.9.1 cit. s. πίστις (more prob. than *windlass*, but cf. Lightfoot ad loc.).

ἀναγωγή, ἡ, *elevation, lifting up*;

A. spiritual; **1.** in gen. ἄνω τέθεισθε σαφῶς ὑψωθέντες ὑπὸ τῆς ἡμετέρας φωνῆς καὶ ἀ. Gr.Naz.*or*.39.2(M.36.336C); καὶ δῆτα τῶν ἀρετῶν ὄναιτο ἄν τις τὸ ἀπηλλάχθαι τῆς ὑλικῆς προσπαθείας· δεῖ δὲ καὶ ἀναγωγῆς· οὐ γὰρ ἀπόχρη μὴ κακὸν εἶναι, ἀλλὰ δεῖ καὶ θεὸν εἶναι Synes.*Dion* 9(p.258.8; M.66.1140B); **2.** from sense-perception and images to divine realities ἀνατείνεσθαι διὰ τῶν φαινομένων ἐπὶ τὰς ὑπερκοσμίας ἀ. Dion.Ar.*c.h*.2.5(M.3.145B); θεολογία...νοῦν ἀνασκεψαμένη, καὶ τῆς οἰκείας αὐτῷ καὶ συμφυοῦς ἀ. προνοήσασα *ib*.2.1 (137D); commented on εἰδυῖα γὰρ ἡ τοῦ θεοῦ σοφὴ συγκατάβασις τὸν ἡμέτερον νοῦν...πρὸς ὑψηλοτέραν θεωρίαν ἀνεπιτηδείως ἔχοντα, ἀ. αὐτῷ συμφυῆ πλασαμένη, οὕτω τὰς ἀρχαγγελικὰς εἰς φανερὸν ἤγαγε διακοσμήσεις, οὐχ ὅπως ἔχουσι τῇ ἀληθείᾳ διασαφήσασα, ἀλλ' ὅπως ἡμεῖς δυνάμεθα καταλαβεῖν Max.*schol.c.h*.2.1(M.4.36D); Dion.Ar.*c.h*.4.3 (180C) cit. s. θεοφάνεια; ἡ καθ' ἡμᾶς ἱεραρχία, δεομένη τῶν αἰσθητῶν εἰς τὴν ἐξ αὐτῶν ἐπὶ τὰ νοητὰ θειοτέραν ἡμῶν ἀ. id.*e.h*.1.5(M.3.377A); τὴν διὰ τῶν σεπτῶν εἰκόνων ἐπὶ τὰ πρωτότυπα ἀ. Thdr.Stud.*antirr*.1.20(M.99.349D); hence images themselves called ἀναγωγαί (*means of elevation*), Jo.D.*imag*.1.11(M.94.1241B); **3.** causes and means ἡ δὲ τῆς θεαρχικῆς ἀγαθότητος...φιλανθρωπία...ἀ. ἡμῖν ὑπερκόσμιον δείξασα Dion.Ar.*e.h*.3.3.11(M.3.441B); τῆς συνάξεως δὲ καὶ τῆς τοῦ μύρου τελετῆς, τελειωτικῆς τῶν θεουργιῶν γνώσεως καὶ ἐπιστήμης, δι' ἧς...ἡ πρὸς τὴν θεαρχίαν ἑνοποιὸς ἀ. ... τελεσιουργεῖται *ib*.5.3.3(504C); ἐπὶ τῆς ἱερᾶς θεογενεσίας ἡ τῆς ἐσθῆτος ἄμειψις ἐδήλου τὴν ἀποκαθαιρομένης ζωῆς εἰς θεωρητικὴν καὶ φωτιστικὴν ἕξιν ἀ. *ib*.6.3.4(536B); through consecration of oils, *ib*.4.3.1(473B); ὡς ἡμῖν ἐφικτὸν ὑφηγήσασθαι τὰς ἐπὶ τὸ θεοειδὲς τῆς ἐμπυρίου δυνάμεως ἀ. id.*c.h*.13.4(M.3.304D); Μελχισεδὲκ...ἄλλοις ὡς ἱεράρχης ἡγεῖτο τῆς ἐπὶ τὴν...θεαρχίαν ἀ. *ib*.9.3(261A); through Law τελετὴ μὲν ἡ πρὸς τὴν πνευματικὴν λατρείαν ἀ. id.*e.h*.5.2(501C); **4.** gradation of ascent ψυχαγωγία... συμμετροῦσα ταῖς κατὰ μέρος τάξεσιν τὴν ἐναρμόνιον ἀ. *ib*.2.3.2 (397C); αἱ ἱεραὶ πᾶσαι τάξεις μετέχουσι πρὸς τὴν οἰκείαν αὐτῶν τῆς θεώσεως ἀ. καὶ τελείωσιν *ib*.6.3.5(536C); **5.** of angels τῶν...κυριοτήτων...ὀνομασίαν οἶμαι δηλοῦν...πάσης ὑποπεζίας ὑφέσεως ἐλευθέραν ἀ. id.*c.h*.8.1(237C); *ib*.9.2(260B); **6.** of Christ (Ebionite) λέγουσι... Χριστόν, υἱὸν ⟨δὲ⟩ θεοῦ κατὰ προκοπὴν καὶ κατὰ συνάφειαν ἀ. τῆς ἄνωθεν πρὸς αὐτὸν γεγενημένης Epiph.*haer*.30.18(p.358.5; M.41.436B).

B. *anagogical sense* of scripture (v. θεωρία); **1.** def. and descriptions γραφὴ...τριμερὴς ἐκ τῆς θείας δεδώρηται χάριτος· καὶ ταύτης οἷόν τι σῶμα τὸ γράμμα...οἱονεὶ δὲ ψυχή, ἡ τροπολογία...καθάπερ δὲ πνεῦμα, ἡ τῶν μελλόντων καὶ ὑψηλοτέρων ἀ. καὶ θεωρία πέφηνεν Andr.Caes.*Apoc*.proem.(M.106.217C); οἱ κατ' ἀλήθειαν γνωστικοί, τῶν ἐν ταῖς γραφαῖς...μυστηρίων τοὺς λόγους διδάσκοντες, ὡς παραδείγμασι τοῖς καθ' ἱστορίαν κέχρηνται τύποις, πρὸς τὴν τῶν διδασκομένων ἀ., ἁρμόζοντες τῷ τῆς ἱστορίας γράμματι τὸ πνεῦμα τῆς θεωρίας· ἵνα ὅ τε τύπος διὰ τὴν αἴσθησιν, καὶ διὰ τὸν νοῦν ὁ λόγος περὶ τὸν ἄνθρωπον σῴζωνται, τὸν ἐκ ψυχῆς καὶ σώματος *Schol*.2 in Max.*qu.Thal*.55(M.90.560A); **2.** in gen., Or.*Jo*.1.1(2; p.5.6; M.14.24C); Dion.Ar.*c.h*.15.9 (M.3.337D); coupled with synonymous terms ἀ. μυστική Or.*princ*.4.3.6(p.333.6; M.11.388A); ἀ. πνευματική Meth.*symp*.7.4(p.75.4; M.18.129B); τὴν ἀ. δι' ἀλληγορίας Epiph.*haer*.66.56(p.93.6; M.42.113B); πρὸς τύπους καὶ ἀ. τῆς τελείας θεωρίας id.*exp.fid*.4(p.500.13; M.42.780C); **3.** in rel. to literal sense; **a.** simple juxtaposition, Or.*hom.15.2 in Jer*.(p.126.5; M.13.429B); ἐπὶ τῇ λέξει...εἰς δὲ ἀ. id.*fr.7 in Lam*.(p.237.10; M.13.608D); κατὰ τὸ ῥητόν...κατ' ἀ. id.*enarr.in Job* 29:12(M.17.93A); κατὰ μὲν τὴν ἱστορίαν...κατὰ δὲ τὴν ἀ. Nil.*serm*.1 (M.79.1264B); Thdt.*Ps*.13:1(1.681); **b.** necessity and superiority to lit. sense in certain cases, Or.*engast*.2(p.284.4; M.12.1013B); οὐ χρὴ ἀνεξέλεγκτον...τὴν ἀπόδειξιν τοῦ λόγου καταλεῖψαι, φέρε δὴ καὶ τὴν κατ' ἀ. αὐτῷ συζυγίαν ἀποδῶμεν ἡμεῖς βαθύτερον ἐπισκεψάμεναι τὴν γραφήν Meth.*symp*.3.2(p.29.13; M.18.64B); εἰ δέ τι μετὰ ὑποκρύψεως ἐν ὑπονοίαις τισὶ καὶ αἰνίγμασιν εἰρημένον, ἀργὸν εἰς ὠφέλειαν εἴη κατὰ τὸ πρόχειρον νόημα, τοὺς τοιούτους λόγους ἀναστρέφειν...ὧν τὴν διὰ τῆς ἀ. θεωρίαν, εἴτε τροπολογίαν, εἴτε ἀλληγορίαν, εἴτε τι ἄλλο τις ὀνομάζειν ἐθέλοι, οὐδὲν περὶ τοῦ ὀνόματος διοισόμεθα, μόνον εἰ τῶν ἐπωφελῶν ἔχοιτο νοημάτων Gr.Nyss.*hom. in Cant*.proem.(M.44.757A); Epiph.*exp.fid*.3(p.499.7; M.42.777C); ἵνα ὁ τύπος μένοι εἰς ἀ. τοῦ λόγου *ib*.7(p.503.6; 785A); δικαίως δ' ἄν τις τὸν ψαλμὸν κατὰ ἀ. μᾶλλον ἐκλάβοι, τῆς ἱστορίας ἀνώτερος γενόμενος Chrys.*exp.in Ps*.46:1(5.188B); use necessitated by inadequacy of scriptural imagery, Dion.Ar.*c.h*.2.5(M.3.145B); needed even in NT to solve apparent discrepancies in gospel narratives, Or.*Jo*.10.2(3; p.172.25; M.14.309B); *ib*.10.31(18; p.205.7; 364B); Moses himself having been aware of anagogical sense of his histories, *ib*.6.4(2; p.111.7; 205A); taught also by S. Paul, Thdt.*qu.31 in Dt*.(1.280); **c.** but exaggerations rejected οἱ προφάσει ἀναγωγῆς...εἰς ἀλληγορίας κατέφυγον Bas.*hex*.3.9(1.31B; M.29.73C); ἀλλά τινες οὐ συνιέντες τὴν ἄφατον τοῦ θεοῦ σοφίαν, κατ' ἀναγωγὴν τὸ εἰρημένον [sc. Is.1:22] ἐξέλαβον Chrys.*Is.interp*.1.7(6.14B); need for both literal and anagogical interpretation recognized, id.*hom.23.2 in Eph*.(11.176C); Gr.Agr.*Eccl*.3.2(M.98.848C); both easily harmonized, Gr.Nyss.*v.Mos*.(M.44.368A); **4.** examples; **a.** OT statements pointing to Christ ἔχομεν, ὅτι 'προεφήτευσεν ἐπὶ πάντα τὰ ἔθνη' ὡς πρὸς τὸ ῥητὸν ὅτι 'προφήτην εἰς ἔθνη τέθεικά σε' πρὸς ἐκεῖνον. ἐὰν δὲ πρὸς ἀ., ἐὰν μὲν ἐπὶ τοῦ 'Ἱερεμίου, προειρήκαμεν, ἐὰν δὲ ἐπὶ τοῦ σωτῆρος, τί δεῖ καὶ λέγειν; Or.

hom.1.12 in Jer.(p.10.14; M.13.268C); δικαιωθείημεν ἀξίως τῶν ἑορτῶν τῶν ἐπουρανίων καὶ ⟨τοῦ⟩ πάσχα τοῦ ἐκεῖ ἐπὶ τὴν ἀ. ἐν Χριστῷ Ἰησοῦ *ib.19.15*(p.176.5; 500B); κατὰ δὲ ἀναγωγήν, πρόσωπον τοῦ θεοῦ καὶ πατρὸς ὁ υἱός Cyr.*Ps.*9:4(M.69.764B) et passim; which, however, should not be taken univocally, as was done by Arians οὗτοι γὰρ πάντες ψιλῇ λέξει τὸ τῆς ἀ. ἀπὸ τοῦ μὴ εἶναι εἰς τὸ εἶναι προκεκοφότες οὐ κατ' οὐσίαν τῇ ἀληθινῇ ἵστανται ὀνομασίᾳ, ἀλλὰ ψιλῶς ⟨λέξει⟩ καὶ μετὰ χάριν Epiph.*haer.*76.25(p.373.1; M.42.565C); οὐδὲ ὁ εἷς υἱὸς τοῖς πᾶσι κατὰ ἀ. κικλησκομένοις ἴσος *ib.*76.27(p.376.14; 565C); **b.** ref. other texts ἀναγωγῆς δὲ λόγῳ καὶ ὁ διάβολος ὄρος ὠνόμασται Or.*fr.41 in Jer.*(p.219.24); κατὰ μὲν τὴν ἱστορίαν Ναβουχοδονόσορ, κατὰ δὲ τὴν ἀ. ὁ πονηρός id.*hom.19.14 in Jer.*(p.171.3; M.13.492B); πρὸς...τὸ ῥητόν, εὐγενὴς τῶν ἀφ' ἡλίου ἀνατολῶν...πρὸς δὲ ἀ., οἱ υἱοὶ τοῦ φωτός Didym.*Job* 1:3(M.39.1120C); ψαλμὸς δὲ ὕμνος ὀργάνῳ τῷ καλουμένῳ ψαλτηρίῳ...κρουόμενος. εἴη δὲ πρὸς ἀ., ᾠδὴ ἡ θεωρία τῆς ἀληθείας μόνῃ νοήσει μεμουσωμένη γενομένη id. *Ps.*4 tit.(M.39.1165A); *ib.*18:6(1269A); Ἰσραηλιτικὸν τὸν ἐνάρετον ἡ ἀ. νοεῖν ὑποτίθεται Gr.Nyss.*v.Mos.*(M.44.356A); ἔσφαξε τὰ ἑαυτῆς θύματα. θύματα τὰ θεῖα νοήματα, ἢ τὰς ἑρμηνείας τῶν γραφῶν· κρᾶμα δέ, τὸ συμμιγνύναι τῇ ἱστορίᾳ τὴν ἀ. Chrys.*fr.in Pr.*9:2(M.64.680B); Dion.Ar.*c.h.*1.3(M.3.121C); τῇ κατὰ ἀναγωγὴν θεωρίᾳ τὴν ἐκκλησίαν ἔλεγεν ἄνθρωπον εἶναι πνευματικόν, μυστικὴν δὲ ἐκκλησίαν τὸν ἄνθρωπον Max.*myst.*6(M.91.684A).

ἀναγωγία, ἡ, *lifting up* πρὸ τῆς σελήνης [sc. Church] τῆς ἀναγωγίαν ἐχούσης πρὸς τὸν νοητὸν ἥλιον [sc. Christ] Diod.*Ps.*71:8(M.33.1611C); Dion.Ar.*c.h.*2.2(M.3.140A, v.l. ἀναγωγῶν).

***ἀναγωγικός,** **1.** *bearing upward* τὰς ἀγγελικὰς δυνάμεις ὡς ἀ. τῶν ἡμετέρων προσευχῶν Areth.*Apoc.*48(M.106.705D); **2.** *elevating*; **a.** of angels; of higher angelic hierarchies elevating the lower ἑκάστη γὰρ οὐσία νοερά, τὴν δωρουμένην αὐτῇ...νόησιν προνοητικῇ δυνάμει διαιρεῖ...πρὸς τὴν τῆς καταδεεστέρας ἀ. ἀναλογίαν Dion.Ar. *c.h.*15.3(M.3.332B); *ib.*5(196C); this power symbolized by their wings, *ib.*15.3(332D); id.*e.h.*4.3.7(M.3.481A); of angelic intercession ὧν ἡ μεσιτεία, ἀ. τῶν κάτω καθέστηκε Andr.Caes.*Apoc.*59(M.106.404D); **b.** in gen., *spiritual, mystical*; of union between God and soul [sc. πατρὸς φωτοδοσίαν] ἐπὶ τὴν ἁπλῆν αὐτῆς ἀναθῶμεν ἀκτῖνα...πρὸς ἀ. δὲ καὶ ἑνοποιὸν τῶν προνοουμένων σύγκρασιν Dion.Ar.*c.h.*1.2(M.3.121B); of contemplative powers of Christian people μέση δὲ τάξις ἐστὶν ἡ θεωρητική...πρὸς τὸν θεῖον τῆς ἐπιστήμης αὐτῶν ἔρωτα ταῖς ἀ. αὐτῶν δυνάμεσιν ἀναλόγως ἀναπτερουμένη id.*e.h.*6.2(M.3.532C); τὴν ψυχὴν τοῖς ἀ. ἐπίανε λόγοις Evagr.*h.e.*1.15(p.25.6; M.86.2464A); **3.** *anagogical*, of myst. sense of scripture κατὰ τὴν τῆς ἱστορίας τάξιν τῇ ἀ. προσαρμόσαι τὸ νόημα Gr.Nyss.*v.Mos.*(M.44.373A); τὰς ἀ. ἱερογραφίας Dion.Ar.*c.h.*2.1(M.3.137B); *ib.*15.7(336C); comp., *ib.*2.2(137C); *Schol.*40 in Jo.Clim.*scal.*27(M.88.1128A).

***ἀναγωγικῶς,** **1.** *by way of elevation, so as to lift up* τὸ τῶν ὑποβεβηκότων ἀ. ... ἀφομοιωτικόν Dion.Ar.*c.h.*7.1(M.3.205C); ταῖς φανοτάταις αὐτῶν ἱερουργίαις ἀ. ἀποκεκαθαρμένης ζωῆς id.*e.h.*5.3.8(M.3.516B); **2.** *by way of ascending*, from human nature to Logos τὸν λόγον ἐκ τῶν καθ' ἡμᾶς ἀ. ἐπὶ τῆς ὑπερκειμένης ἔγνωμεν φύσεως Gr.Nyss.*or.catech.*2(p.13.6; M.45.17A ἀναλογικῶς); **3.** *anagogically*, Gr.Naz.*or.*45.16(M.36.645B); τὰς ὑπ' αὐτῶν [sc. scriptures]...ἀ. ἐκφανθείσας τῶν οὐρανίων νοῶν ἱεραρχίας Dion.Ar.*c.h.*1.2(M.3.121A); Cyr.*Ps.*9:5(M.69.764D); Cosm.Mel.*schol.*1(M.38.352) in Gr.Naz.*carm.*2.1.1.356.

ἀναγώγιος, *raising* the mind to heavenly things ἀ. ἐρώτων Synes.*hymn.*1.119(p.63; M.66.1592).

ἀναγωγός, **1.** *lifting up, elevating*; lit., Dion.Ar.*c.h.*13.3(M.3.301B); met., of spiritual elevation, Synes.*hymn.*3.377(p.18; M.66.1599); *ib.*4.260(p.33; 1608); ἀ. ἡ μετάνοια id.*insomn.*8(p.158.14; M.66.1293D); Cyr.*Ps.*93:7(M.69.1233A); ἀ. ζωή Dion.Ar.*e.h.*3.3.11(M.3.441A), cf. ἀ. δὲ ζωὴν τὴν τὰ ἄνω ζητοῦσαν καὶ πρὸς θεὸν ἐπεστραμμένην Max.*schol.*ad loc.(M.4.148D); ἔρωτα...καὶ ἀγάπην...ὡς ἀ. δύναμιν Dion.Ar.*d.n.*4.14(M.3.712C); **2.** *not attracted* or *led* by διδάσκοντες ὧν ἀπέχεσθαι προσήκει καὶ ἀ. εἶναι τὴν παρθένον Meth.*symp.*5.5(p.58.13; M.18.105A).

***ἀναγωνίζομαι,** s.v.l., *contend*, for the faith ἐὰν ἔχῃ ἀναγωνίσασθαι καὶ ποιήσῃ θαύματα †Jo.Jej.*serm.*(M.88.1932D).

ἀναδείκνυ-μι, **1.** *show, exhibit*; hence **a.** *produce, bring forth* τὸν ἐξ αὐτοῦ τὸν πάσης κτίσεως πρωτότοκον ἀναδείξαντα Gr.Nyss.*Eun.*1(1 p.183.10; M.45.428B); ἐξ αὐτῆς [sc. φυλῆς] ~μενον κατὰ σάρκα ‡Epiph. *v.proph.Os.*ap.Cosm.Ind.*top.*5(M.88.261A); of generation of aeons, Val.Gn.ap.Epiph.*haer.*31.5(p.391.6ff.; M.41.481B); in gen., Tat.*orat.*11(p.12.16; M.6.829C); σὺ δὲ εἰς ἐργασίαν ἀρετῆς ἀνεδείχθης Tit.Bost.*fr.Lc.*6:43(p.163); εὔκολον τῷ θεῷ θάψαι τὸν ἄνθρωπον τὸν παλαιόν [sc. in baptism], καὶ ἀ. τὸν νέον Chrys.*hom.*25.2 *in Jo.*(8.146C); **b.** *show forth as* οὐσίαν μὴ οὖσαν προοῖσαι, ἢ ἔμψυχον καὶ λογικὴν ἀ. Didym.*Trin.*1.15(M.39.301A); ἵνα ἀναδείξῃς αὐτὸν [sc. λαόν]... βασίλειον ἱεράτευμα *Lit.*ap.*Const.App.*8.12.44; *Lit.Praesanct.*(p.347.12); eucharistic, ***Lit.Bas.***(p.329.32) cit. s. σῶμα; **c.** *exhibit, show forth*, liturg. λαβὼν τὸν ἄρτον, εὐχαριστήσας, ἀνέδειξε καὶ ἔκλασεν... καὶ τὸ ποτήριον...ἀ. τῷ θεῷ καὶ πατρὶ εἶπε Eutych.*pasch.*2(M.86.2393B); λαβὼν τὸν ἄρτον...ἀναβλέψας εἰς τὸν οὐρανόν, καὶ ἀναδείξας σοι τῷ θεῷ καὶ πατρὶ *Lit.Jac.*(p.202.5); similarly of cup, *ib.*(p.202.14); of bread, *Lit.Bas.*(p.327.29); **2.** *proclaim* βασιλεῖς...ἀνεδείχθησαν Eus.*v.C.*1.1(p.7.19; M.20.912B); hence *announce as appointed* ἀναδειχθῆναί τινα τῆς παρ' αὐτοῖς ἐκκλησίας ἀρχιερέα Gr.Nyss.*v.Gr.Thaum.*(M.46.933C); Socr.*h.e.*2.13.6(M.67.209A); **3.** pass., *be famous*, Evagr.*h.e.*1.19(p.28.18; M.86.2473A).

***ἀναδεικτέον,** *one must show*, Clem.*paed.*3.11(p.271.30; M.8.637C).

ἀνάδειξις, ἡ, **1.** *showing forth, manifestation*; **a.** in gen. τῆς ἀ. τοῦ κηρύγματος Or.*Jo.*6.9(6; p.118.32; M.14.217B); id.*fr.56 in Jo.*(p.529.10); *ib.*90(p.553.12); Cyr.*Soph.*47(3.625A); **b.** of Inc., ‡Ath.*Ar.*4.35(p.84.14; M.26.521B) cit. s. χρίσις; *Const.App.*2.55.1; Cyr.*Juln.*8(6^2.279E); *Chron.Pasch.*p.145(M.92.357B); †Jo.D.*B.J.*8(M.96.924A); **c.** eucharistic τῇ ἀ. τοῦ ἄρτου Bas.*Spir.*66(3.54E; M.32.188B); **2.** *appointment* τῆς τῶν ἱερέων ἀ. Gr.Nyss.*Eun.*6(2 p.133.16; M.45.717B); ἡ τοῦ Ἀαρὼν ἀ. Cyr.ap.*cat.Heb.*7:1(p.527.14); of apostles, id.*Jo.*3.1(4.251D); of Constantine, *accession*, Andr.Caes.*Apoc.*36(M.106.333A).

***ἀναδενδρ-όομαι,** *climb up a tree*; of vine, Gr.Nyss.*hom.2 in Eccl.*(M.44.661C); met. τὰ τῶν ἀρετῶν...ὑψώματα πρὸς τὸ ὕψος τῶν ἀγγέλων ~ούμενα id.*hom.2 in Cant.*(M.44.800C).

***ἀναδέξιμος, ὁ, ἡ,** *person for whom responsibility has been assumed at baptism, god-child*, *Nomoc.*183.

ἀνάδεσις, ἡ, *binding up*; of hair, Clem.*paed.*3.11(p.271.13; M.8.637A).

ἀναδεσμ-έω, **1.** *tie up*; met., ref. Mt.19:19 ἐν ἑνὶ...τὸ σύμπαν ἡμῶν ~εῖται καλόν Cyr.*hom.pasch.*8(5^2.94E); **2.** *bind on*; met., of honours, id.*Is.*2.5(2.330C).

ἀναδέχ-ομαι, **1.** *take upon oneself, take responsibility for, stand as surety for*; **a.** ref. Atonement, of God ἐλεῶν αὐτὸς τὰς ἡμετέρας ἁμαρτίας ἀνεδέξατο, αὐτὸς τὸν ἴδιον υἱὸν ἀπέδοτο λύτρον ὑπὲρ ἡμῶν *Diogn.*9.2; τὸν ἑαυτοῦ Χριστὸν ὑπὲρ τῶν ἐκ παντὸς γένους ἀνθρώπων ὁ πατὴρ...τὰς πάντων κατάρας ἀναδέξασθαι ἐβουλήθη Just.*dial.*95.2(M.6.701C); of Christ ἡμᾶς ἀναδεξάμενος χρεωφειλέτην ἑαυτὸν κατέστησε Marc.Er.*opusc.*7.15(M.65.1093A); Anast.S.*qu.et resp.*18(M.89.500C); **b.** of repentance ἐγὼ [sc. μετάνοια] ἀνεδεξάμην τοὺς παρανόμους· ἐγγεγύημαι τὸ τῶν ἀνθρώπων γένος Ephr.3.180E; **c.** ref. confession ἵνα τις ἀναδέξηται ἁμαρτίας ἑτέρου, καὶ ὑπὲρ αὐτῶν ἐκεῖνος ἀναλογίζηται ‡Jo.D.*conf.*6(M.95.289D); **d.** *receive as sponsor* at baptism ἐκ τοῦ...βαπτίσματος παῖδας ἀ. CTrull.*can.*53; **2.** *hear confession of* τοὺς ~εσθαι αὐτοὺς μέλλοντας †Jo.Jej.*serm.*(M.88.1932C); ὁ ~όμενος *confessor*, *ib.*(1921C); ἀ. λογισμοὺς *hear confessions*, ‡Jo.D.*conf.*9(M.95.293B); **3.** *deal with, concern oneself with* ~εται δὲ [sc. S. Paul] αὐτοὺς καὶ περὶ τῆς διακονίας, καὶ προτρέπεται μᾶλλον αὐτὴν πλεονάζειν *cat.2Cor.*proem.(p.345.22).

***ἀναδηλόω,** *make known*, Eus.*m.P.*11(p.933.25; M.20.1445C); Gr.Naz.*or.*5.5(M.35.669C, v.l. ἐδήλωσεν).

ἀναδημιουργ-έω, *re-create* οὓς ἡ ἁμαρτία πειρᾶται ἀπολλύειν, αὕτη [sc. ἡ μετάνοια] ~εῖ εἰς τὴν τοῦ θεοῦ εὐδοξίαν Ephr.3.160B; ὑπ' αὐτῆς [sc. Church] ἀναγεννωμένων τε καὶ ~ουμένων τῷ πνεύματι Max.*myst.*1(M.91.665C).

ἀναδιδράσκω, *run back* or *away*; **1.** in gen., Socr.*h.e.*4.22(M.67.509A); of ships to sea, *put out again*, Synes.*ep.*4(M.66.1337A); met. τῶν συμφερόντων εἰς ἀνάμνησιν ἀ. Meth.*Porph.*1(p.503.6; M.18.397C); **2.** of Logos acc. Marcellus ποτὲ...προϊέναι τοῦ θεοῦ, καὶ ἄλλοτε πάλιν ἀναδραμεῖσθαι εἰς τὸν θεόν Eus.*e.th.*2.8(p.107.10; M.24.913C); cf. Sabellian teaching πεμφθέντα...τὸν υἱόν...ἀναληφθῆναι αὖθις εἰς οὐρανόν, ὥσπερ ὑπὸ ἡλίου πεμφθείσης ἀκτῖνος καὶ πάλιν εἰς τὸν ἥλιον ἀναδραμούσης Epiph.*haer.*62.1(p.390.8; M.41.1052C).

ἀναδίδωμι, **1.** *give, deliver*; hence *disclose* πάντων ἀ. τὰ ὀνόματα Hipp.*haer.*9.12(p.247.31; M.16.3382D); Ephr.1.121B; **2.** *distribute, impart*, of eucharist χριστοφόροι γινόμεθα, τοῦ σώματος αὐτοῦ καὶ τοῦ αἵματος εἰς τὰ ἡμέτερα ἀναδιδομένου μέλη Cyr.H.*catech.*22.3; οὗτος ὁ ἄρτος εἰς πᾶσαν σου τὴν σύστασιν ἀναδίδοται εἰς ὠφέλειαν σώματος καὶ ψυχῆς *ib.*23.15; **3.** *give way* to τούτων ἀκούσασα ἀνεδίδου τῇ λύπῃ *A.Thom.*A 115(p.225.11).

ἀνάδοσις, ἡ, *giving back, restoration*, Eus.*l.C.*7(p.213.14; M.20.1353B); Soz.*h.e.*5.5.4(M.67.1228A).

ἀναδοτικός, *digestive*, Gr.Naz.*or.*17.1(M.35.965A).

ἀναδοχή, ἡ, **1.** *acceptance*, ref. Christ τῆς ὑπὲρ ἡμῶν ἀ. ἐν κόσμῳ ἐνσάρκου παρουσίας Epiph.*haer.*42.8(p.104.13; M.41.708A);

2. *acceptance on behalf of another* ἀπὸ κακίας ἀ. ἀκούσιός ἐστιν... ἐξ ἀγάπης ἀ. ἐστιν, ἣν ὁ κύριος Ἰησοῦς ἡμῖν πάντως δέδωκε Marc. Er.*opusc*.7.19,20(M.65.1097C); **3.** *acceptance of responsibility for another*, ref. spiritual direction of monks ἔστιν ἀ. κυρίως, ψυχῆς δόσις ὑπὲρ ψυχῆς τοῦ πλησίον περὶ πάντα Jo.Clim.*past*.12(M.88. 1189B); for sins of others δυνατοί, ἁμαρτίαν λαοῦ ἀναδεξάμενοι... θανάτῳ ὑπὲρ τῆς ἀ. παραδίδονται Anast.S.*qu.et resp*.18(M.89.500C); **4.** *hearing* of confession ἀ. λογισμῶν ‡Jo.D.*conf*.17(M.95.304C); *confession* ὁ τὰς ἀ. δεχόμενος Sophr.H.*conf*.(M.87.3365B); **5.** *succession* τῶν βασιλέων ταχεῖαν ἀ. ‡Jo.D.*ep.Thphl*.16(M.95.368A).

ἀνάδοχος, ὁ, *one who takes responsibility for another* οἱ τὸν ἐμπιστευθέντα πλοῦτον αὐτοῖς κενώσαντες...ζητοῦσιν εἰκότως ἄνθρωπον θεοῦ ἀ. γενέσθαι τοῦ χρέους αὐτῶν, ὅπερ...γενέσθαι ἀδύνατον ἄνευ μετανοίας ‡Jo.D.*conf*.6(M.95.289D); of Christ τὸν...λυτρωτὴν τῶν ψυχῶν ἡμῶν καὶ ἀ. Marc.Er.*opusc*.7.15(M.65.1093A); esp. *sponsor* in baptism, Dion.Ar.*e.h*.2.2.7(M.3.396C); †Gregent.*disp*.(M.86.781A); Leont.Abb.*v.Gr.Agr*.2(M.98.553A); orthodoxy a necessary qualification, Thdr.Stud.*epp*.2.219 *qu*.14(M.99.1665B); sponsors and candidates registered, Dion.Ar.*e.h*.2.2.5(396A).

ἀνάδυσις, ἡ, *rising, emergence*; **1.** from waters of baptism ἐν τῇ πρώτῃ ἀ. τὴν πρώτην ἐμιμεῖσθε τοῦ Χριστοῦ ἐν τῇ γῇ ἡμέραν... ἐν δὲ τῇ ἀ. πάλιν ὡς ἐν ἡμέρᾳ ἐτυγχάνετε ὄντες Cyr.H.*catech*.20.4; ἡ κατάδυσις τὸ συναποθανεῖν, ἡ ἀ. τὸ συναναστῆναι *Const.App*.3.17.3; threefold emergence symbolizing Persons of Trin., Ammon.*Jo*. 3:5(M.85.1409A); Dion.Ar.*e.h*.2.2.7(M.3.396D); **2.** met., of rise of heretics, Epiph.*haer*.31.1(p.383.17; M.41.473C).

ἀναδύ-ω, A. intrans.; **1.** *rise, emerge* Λίβυες...Γαράμαντά φασι πρωτόγονον αὐχμηρῶν ἀναδύντα πεδίων Hipp.*haer*.5.7(p.80.1; M.16. 3127B); of bodily resurrection, Cels.ap.Or.*Cels*.5.14(p.15.5; M.11. 1201A); of emerging from baptismal water, ref. Christ ἀναδύντος... ἀπὸ τοῦ ὕδατος Just.*dial*.88.3(M.6.685B); κατεδύετε τρίτον εἰς τὸ ὕδωρ καὶ ἀνεδύετε πάλιν Cyr.H.*catech*.20.4; cf.Gr.Nyss.*or.catech*.35 (p.135.13; M.45.89C); τὸ ἴσον ἡμῖν...ἐστὶν ὕδατί τε βαπτισθῆναι καὶ ἐκ τοῦ θανάτου πάλιν ἀναδῦναι *ib*.(p.136.9; 89D); met., of emerging from state of error, Ath.*Ar*.3.67(M.26.465C); **2.** *withdraw, retire*, Gr.Naz.*ep*.59(M.37.120A); Chrys.*sac*.4.1(p.98.20; 1.402D); id.*stat*.3.2 (2.38A); met., *relapse* into sickness, Or.*princ*.3.1.13(p.218.2; M.11. 273A); **3.** *shrink, be reluctant* μέλλομεν ἔτι καὶ ~όμεθα πρὸς τὴν καλὴν ταύτην ἐπιμέλειαν Chrys.*hom.14.11 in Rom*.(9.593B); μέλλοντά τε καὶ ~όμενον πρὸς τὸ ἀνεῖναί τισι τὰς ἁμαρτίας Cyr.*ador*.15(1.527D); Jo.Mal.*chron*.18 p.455(M.97.668A).

B. trans.; **1.** *make to emerge, raise* τὸ...καταδῦσαι τὸ παιδίον ἐν τῇ κολυμβήθρᾳ τρίτον καὶ ἀναδῦσαι, τοῦτο δηλοῖ τὸν θάνατον καὶ τὴν τριήμερον ἀνάστασιν τοῦ Χριστοῦ ‡Ath.*qu.script*.92(M.28.753C); **2.** *draw back from, shun*, Clem.*prot*.1(p.9.12; M.8.64D); μὴ ~εσθαι τὴν ὁμολογίαν Or.*Jo*.28.23(18; p.417.30; M.14.728D); id.*Cels*.1.45 (p.95.19; M.11.744B); c. dat. ~ομένους τῷ θεῷ Cyr.*Jo*.5.2(4.483D); **3.** *withhold* οὔτε...ὡς μέλλοντα καὶ ~όμενον τὴν ἐπικουρίαν καταιτιᾶται τὸν...δεσπότην id.*Ps*.6:4(M.69.745B); **4.** *put on* clothes, fig. οἱ μάρτυρες...τὴν ἀσώματον τῆς ὁμολογίας δόξαν ἀνεδύσαντο Mac.Mgn. *apocr*.2.7(p.6.17); παμμεδέουσαν ἑὴν ἀνεδύσατο μορφήν Nonn.*par.Jo*. 12:16(M.43.853A); **5.** *clothe* ὁ δημιουργὸς...τὸ ὅλον εἰς ἀθανασίαν ἀναδυσάμενος Aen.*dial*.(M.85.973A).

ἀναζάω, 1. *return to life, revive*, lit. ἤξατο Ἀνδρέας καὶ πάντες ἀνέζησαν *A.Andr.et Mt*.32(p.114.8); ἐκ...τῶν σπερμάτων...τὸ ἀ. Meth.*res*.1.53(p.310.7; M.41.1129A); Nonn.*par.Jo*.5:25(M.43.789A); **2.** met., of soul ἀ. ... τῇ πίστει Clem.*str*.4.6(p.260.14; M.8.1240B); of sin, Or.*adnot.in Lev*.4:28(M.17.17C); Chrys.*hom.22.3 in Eph*.(11. 170B).

ἀναζέω, 1. *boil up, bubble up*; met., *be fervent* δεῖται...ἡ χάρις τῆς προθυμίας τῆς ἡμετέρας, ἵνα ἀεὶ ἀναζέῃ Chrys.*hom.1.2 in 2Tim*. (11.661B); **2.** *make to boil*; met., *make fervent*, Epiph.*haer*.62.1 (p.390.11; M.41.1052C).

ἀναζωγραφ-έω, 1. *paint completely, delineate*; met., in writing, *depict, describe*, Or.*Cels*.6.74(p.144.1; M.11.1409B); in the mind, *picture, imagine*, †Bas.*Is*.120(1.462D; M.30.312D); in person, *represent*, Ath.*h.Ar*.77(p.226.12; M.25.785D); **2.** *repaint*, met., *renew*, of Christ in Inc. ~ῶν τὰ ἐξ ὑπαρχῆς καὶ ἀναπλάσσων αὖθις ἐκ παρθένου καὶ πνεύματος τεκταίνεται τὸν αὐτόν [sc. Ἀδάμ] Meth.*symp*.3.4 (p.31.5; M.18.68A); τὸ ἀρχαῖον τῆς φύσεως κάλλος ἐν ἡμῖν ἀ. Cyr.*Is*. 4.5(2.711B); of H. Ghost εἰς τὸ τῆς θεότητος κάλλος τὴν ἀνθρώπου φύσιν ἀ. id.*thes*.34(5[1].359B).

ἀναζωγράφησις, ἡ, 1. *painting, representation*, †Bas.*Is*.82(1.436B; M.30.253A); Agath.Diac.*epilog*.(H.3.1837B); CNic.(787)*refut*.(H.4. 352A); *Symb.Nic*.(787)(H.4.453E), v. εἰκών; **2.** *mental picture*, Bas. *Eun*.1.6(1.217C; M.29.524A).

***ἀναζωγραφητέον,** *one must picture* in the mind, Isid.Pel.*epp*. 3.107(M.78.813A).

***ἀναζωγραφικός,** *pictorial, imaginative* δύναμιν...ἀ. [sc. τῆς ψυχῆς] Max.*schol.d.n*.5.6(M.4.321A).

***ἀναζωογον-έω,** *engender life again, make fruitful* ~ουμένη [sc. Sarah] εἰς καταβολὴν σπέρματος Epiph.*haer*.9.3(p.199.22; M.41. 228A); met. ~εῖν δὲ τὸν τοιοῦτον καὶ ἀναζέειν...διὰ τῆς τοῦ πνεύματος δυνάμεως *ib*.62.1(p.390.10; 1052C).

***ἀναζωοποιέω,** *restore to life*; **1.** lit. ἀπέστειλεν ὁ θεὸς πνεῦμα ζωῆς ἐπὶ τοὺς τελευτήσαντας, καὶ ἀνεζωοποιήθησαν *T.Abr*.18(p.100. 31); *A.Xanthipp*.41(p.85.17); of seeds, Mac.Aeg.*hom*.11.14(M.34. 556B); ‡Just.*qu.Gr*.15.28(M.6.1485B); **2.** met. ὁ κύριος...νοήματα νενεκρωμένα ἀ. Mac.Aeg.*hom*.14.5(M.34.573A); of Church μικρὰ πνέουσαν ἀναζωοποιηθῆναι Gr.Naz.*or*.21.7(M.35.1089A).

ἀναζωπυρ-έω, 1. *rekindle, revive, excite*; of dead at resurrection, Proc.G.*Is*.60:1f.(M.87.2620A); spiritually οἱ πλείους τῶν ἠρνημένων ...ἀνεζωπυροῦντο καὶ ἐμάνθανον ὁμολογεῖν *Ep.Lugd*.ap.Eus.*h.e*.5.1.46 (M.20.425B); ἀπεψυγμένους ἡμᾶς εἰς ἅπασαν ἁμαρτίαν ἀνεζωπύρησεν ὁ σωτὴρ εἰς προθυμίαν παντὸς ἀγαθοῦ Ath.*exp.Ps*.49:3(M.27.232B); ἀ. αὐτὸν βουλόμενος ἐκ τῆς κατὰ τὴν ἄρνησιν ῥαθυμίας Ammon.*Jo*. 21:17(M.85.1521B); esp. of soul ἐν...τῇ ψυχῇ τὸ ὄντως καλὸν ὑπὸ τοῦ θείου λόγου ~ούμενον Clem.*prot*.11(p.82.25; M.8.236D); ψυχὰς ἐνθέοις παιδεύμασιν ~εῖν Eus.*l.C*.17(p.258.20; M.20.1437B); μὴ σβεννύναι τὸ πνεῦμα, ἀλλ' ἀ. ἣν ἐλάβομεν χάριν Thdt.*qu*.9 *in Lev*.(1.187); **2.** intrans., *be kindled into fire*; met., of faith, *1Clem*.27.3; Ign.*Eph*.1.1 cit. s. αἷμα.

ἀναζωπύρησις, ἡ, *rekindling, revival*; of faith, Eus.*h.e*.4.23.3 (M.20.385B); τὴν τοῦ καθαρθέντος ἐπὶ τὴν θείαν ὑπακοὴν ἀ. Dion.Ar. *c.h*.13.2(M.3.300C).

ἀναζώωσις, ἡ, *renewal of life* ζωὴ δὲ ἡ μέλλουσά ἐστιν ἀ. Or.*sel.in Ps*.118:50(M.12.1597B).

ἀναθάλλω, 1. *shoot up again, sprout afresh*; met., of life after death, Clem.*paed*.2.10(p.220.5; M.8.521C); τὸ...ἀ. πρὸς ζωήν Cyr. *ador*.10(1.342D); of human nature restored by Christ, *1Clem*.36.2; ἀ. εἰς δικαιοσύνην Cyr.*Joel*.33(3.225C); pass. in act. sense, id.*ador*.10 (1.331E); **2.** *make to sprout, produce*; of the earth, Eudoc.*Cypr*.1.40 (M.85.833C).

ἀναθάλπω, *warm again*; met. pass., *be revived, come to life again*, Gr.Naz.*ep*.72(M.37.137B).

ἀναθαρρέω, *dare*, c. infin., Isid.Pel.*epp*.1.24(M.78.197A).

ἀνάθεμα, τό, *thing dedicated, separated, accursed*, gen. def. ἀ. λέγεται τὸ ἀνακείμενον καὶ ἀφωρισμένον θεῷ καὶ εἰς κοινὴν χρῆσιν μηκέτι λαμβανόμενον, ἢ τὸ ἀπηλλοτριωμένον θεοῦ διὰ κακίαν ‡Just. *qu.et resp*.121(M.6.1372A); τὸ ἀ. διπλῆν ἔχει τὴν διάνοιαν· καὶ γὰρ τὸ ἀφιερωμένον τῷ θεῷ, ἀνάθημα ὀνομάζεται, καὶ τὸ τούτου ἀλλότριον τὴν αὐτὴν ἔχει προσηγορίαν Thdt.*Rom*.9:3(3.98); τοῦ ἀ. διssῶς νοουμένου· τοῦ μέν, ὡς τοῖς πολλοῖς ἀθίκτου, θεῷ δὲ μόνῳ ἀνατιθεμένου· τοῦ δὲ ὡς πάσῃ τῇ κτίσει καὶ ταῖς ἁγίαις δυνάμεσιν ἀψαύστου, ὡς τῷ διαβόλῳ ἀνακειμένου, διὰ τὴν ἀμιγῆ τοῦ καλοῦ ἀλλοτρίωσιν Andr.Caes. *Apoc*.68(M.106.444B); **1.** *thing dedicated, devoted* to God, ref. Achan ὑφείλετό τι τῶν ἀ. Bas.*jud*.4(2.217C; M.31.661B); Cyr.*ador*.5(1.144B); Thdt.*h.rel*.13(3.1215); of men ἀ. ... ἀξιόληπτον ἀληθῶς ἐσόμεθα τῷ θεῷ Cyr.*glaph.Ex*.2(1.278A); **2.** *thing separated*, so of people officially pronounced accursed or separated from Church either in life or after death and so *devoted* to perdition; **a.** in gen. ἀ. παρὰ πάντων γεγόνασιν Ath.*ep.encycl*.1(p.169.15; M.25.224B); εἴ τις τὸν γάμον μέμφοιτο...ἀ. ἔστω CGangr.*can*.1; ἔστωσαν ἀ. παρὰ Χριστῷ CLaod.*can*.29; οἱ...ἀ. τῆς ἐκκλησίας ποιήσαντες ἄνθρωπον, εἰς παντελῆ ὄλεθρον ἀπάγουσιν ἑαυτούς, τὴν ἀξίαν τοῦ υἱοῦ ἀφαρπάζοντες. ...τὸ γὰρ ἀ. παντελῶς τοῦ Χριστοῦ ἀποκόπτει Flav.Ant.*anath*.3 (M.48.949); ἀ. ἔστω ἀπὸ τῆς ἐκκλησίας Paul.Em.*hom*.1(p.10.13; M.77.1436B); **b.** exeg. Rom.9:3, *person separated* τὸ δὲ ἀ. τὸν ἀλλότριον δηλοῖ, ἐπειδὴ τὸ ἀνατεθὲν τοῦ ἀνα[τε]θέντος ἀλλότριον Thdr. Mops.ad loc.(p.143.17; M.66.833B); from Christ, Thdt.ad loc.(3.99); from Church, Chrys.*hom.16.1 in Rom*.(9.603E); from eternal life εἴ γε ἦν χωρισθῆναι τοῦ περὶ τὸν Χριστὸν χοροῦ, καὶ ἀλλοτριωθῆναι οὐχὶ τῆς ἀγάπης αὐτοῦ...ἀλλὰ καὶ τῆς ἀπολαύσεως ἐκείνης καὶ τῆς δόξης, κατεδεξάμην ἂν *ib*.16.2(605E); ηὐχόμην ἀ. εἶναι, τουτό ἐστιν...τὴν ἐν τῇ γεέννῃ κόλασιν ἑλόμενος id.*Stag*.3.11(1.221B); cf.id.*sac*.4.6 (p.119.16; 1.411D); ἤθελον, φησίν, ἐγὼ ἐν κατακρίσει γενέσθαι Eulog. *fr.Novat*.2 ap.Phot.*cod*.280(M.104.333A); ηὔξατο ἀ. εἶναι καὶ ἐκπεσεῖν τῆς δόξης ἐκείνης ἧς λαμβάνουσιν οἱ πιστεύσαντες εἰς Χριστόν, καὶ τοῦ χοροῦ τοῦ ἀποστολικοῦ (οὐ γὰρ δὴ τῆς ἀγάπης τοῦ Χριστοῦ) Jo.D. *Rom*.9:3(M.95.513D); *devoted* to Devil ηὐχόμην...παραδοθῆναι ἀπὸ τοῦ Χριστοῦ τῷ διαβόλῳ, ὥστε μαστιγωθῆναι, καὶ τὰς ὑπὲρ τοῦ Ἰσραὴλ κολάσεις ὑπομεῖναι Max.*qu.dub*.4(M.90.788C); **c.** exeg. 1Cor.

12:3, ἀ. paraphrased as ἀλλότριον τῆς θείας φύσεως Thdt.ad loc. (3.242); **d.** exeg. 1Cor.16:22 ἤτω ἀ.,...τουτέστι· χωρίσατε αὐτὸν ἀπὸ τῆς ἐκκλησίας ‡Ath.*qu.script*.103(M.28.760D); Thdt.*1Cor*.16:21 (3.285); **3.** as curse pronounced by Church τί οὖν ἐστιν ὃ λέγεις ἀ., ἀλλ' ὅτι ἀναθέσθω οὗτος διαβόλῳ, καὶ μηκέτι χώραν σωτηρίας ἐχέτω, γενέσθω ἀλλότριος ἀπὸ τοῦ Χριστοῦ Flav.Ant.*anath*.2(M.48.948); τὸ γὰρ ἀ. ... σημαίνει...τὸν ἀπὸ τοῦ θεοῦ χωρισμόν Justn.*conf*.(p.102.8; M.86.1025C); its use τὰς μὲν αἱρέσεις ἀναθέματι ἀναθεματίσωμεν Ath.*syn*.9(p.236.26; M.26.696A); κινήσεως γενομένης εἰ δέοι τοὺς τετελευτηκότας ἀναθέμασι περιβληθῆναι Evagr.*h.e*.4.38(p.187.18; M.86.2773B); ἀ. τῷ τοιούτῳ λεχθείη, καὶ τὸ ὄνομα αὐτοῦ μηδαμῶς παρὰ τοῖς τοῦ θεοῦ ἱερεῦσιν ἀνενεχθῇ *Cod.Afr*.81; **4.** *perdition* (addressed to one who has been anathematized) ἄπελθε εἰς τὸ σκότος καὶ εἰς τὸ ἀ. Thphn.*chron*.p.372(M.108.892A).

ἀναθεματίζ-ω, **A.** *devote* to God, *put to the ban*; of Jericho, Or.*adnot.in Jos*.6:15f.(M.17.36C); τῶν Ἱεριχουντίων ἀναθεματισθέντων ἐν στόματι ξίφους Proc.G.*Lev*.27:28(M.87.793A).

B. *bind by a curse* ἀναθεματίσωμεν πάντες ἀλλήλους μὴ ἀποστρέψαι τὴν γνώμην ταύτην *Apoc.En*.6.4,5(p.24.8,10); Ammon.*Ac*.23:12(M.85.1589D) ∞ Chrys.*hom.49.1 in Ac*.(9.365C).

C. *pronounce accursed and separated from Church*; as official pronouncement; **1.** of Church; **a.** as canonical penalty εἴ τις λαϊκὸς ὑβρίσει τὸν ἱερέα, ~έσθω *Poen.App*.2.3; εἰ μὲν κληρικὸς εἴη, τοῦ οἰκείου ἐκπιπτέτω βαθμοῦ, εἰ δὲ λαϊκὸς ἢ μονάζων, ~έσθω CChalc.*can*.2; *ib*.27; **b.** pronounced on heretics; def. κοινῇ μέντοι ψήφῳ πάντες οἱ κληρικοὶ αὐτὸν [sc. Nestorius] ἀνεθεμάτισαν. οὕτω γὰρ οἱ Χριστιανοὶ καλεῖν εἰώθαμεν τὴν κατὰ τοῦ βλασφήμου ψῆφον, ὅταν αὐτὴν ὥσπερ ἐν στήλῃ ἀναστήσαντες φανερὰν τοῖς ἅπασιν καταστήσωμεν Socr.*h.e*.7.34.15(M.67.816B); ἀνεθεματίσθησαν [sc. Arians] ἀπὸ τῆς ἐκκλησίας Alex.Al.*ep.encycl*.6(p.9.26; M.18.577A); ὡς αἱρετικὸν αὐτὸν ἀναθεματισθῆναι καὶ εἶναι ἀκοινώνητον καὶ κεχωρισμένον τῆς ἐκκλησίας CGangr.*can*.proem.; Ath.*apol.sec*.23(p.104.26; M.25.285D); Bas.*ep*.125.3(3.216C; M.32.549B); ὦ ἐπίσκοπε, μὴ ~ε ἀσπλάγχνως καὶ δίωκε ἀπὸ τῆς ἐκκλησίας Nil.*epp*.2.190(M.79.300B); pronounced on the dead, Justn.*ep.Thdr.Mops*.(p.67.17; M.86.1089B); Eustrat.*v.Eutych*.22(M.86.2300C); **c.** on heret. doctrines and writings, Epiph.*haer*.68.4(p.144.22; M.42.189D); τὰ γὰρ αἱρετικὰ δόγματα ἀ. ... χρή, ...πᾶσαν δὲ φειδὼ ἀνθρώπων ποιεῖσθαι Flav.Ant.*anath*.4(M.48.950); τὸν...τόμον [sc. Λέοντος] καὶ πάντα τὰ ἐν Καλχηδόνι...εἰρημένα... θεσπίζομεν...παρὰ τῶν...ἐπισκόπων...~εσθαι Basilisc.*encycl*.(p.50.24) ap.Evagr.*h.e*.3.4(M.86.2600D); **d.** in statements of faith, *Symb.Nic*.(325)(p.45.3; M.20.1540C); *Symb.Ant*.(341)2(p.249.35; M.26.724B); Gr.Nyss.*Eun*.2(2 p.303.9; M.45.473D); τοῖς δὲ μὴ οὕτω φρονοῦσι οὐ συνέρχομαι ἀλλὰ καὶ ~ω *Lit.Jac*.(*NBP* 10^2 p.38); *ib*.(p.39); **2.** of individuals; **a.** in gen. παρὰ τοῦ τοιούτου ἀνδρὸς ~ομένην τὴν χριστομάχον αἵρεσιν Ath.*v.Anton*.70(M.26.941B); **b.** as proof of, or sign of return to, orthodoxy ἀ. τὴν Ἀρειανὴν αἵρεσιν Eugen.*exp.fid*.2(M.18.1304A); Paulin.T.*symb*.(p.435.12ff.; M.42.672Cf.); CGangr.*can*.proem.; CLaod.*can*.7; Philost.*h.e*.9.13(M.65.577B).

D. *call accursed, condemn*; **1.** in gen. τοὺς αἱρετικούς, τοὺς ~οντας τὰ κτήματα, καὶ τὰ χρήματα, καὶ τὰ σώματα Cyr.H.*catech*.8.7; τοῦ ~οντος τὴν ἀλήθειαν καὶ ἀντιμαχομένου ἡμῖν ‡Ath.*qu.Ant*.116(M.28.672B); *Dial.Tim.et Aquil*.118 v°(p.91); **2.** exeg. 1Cor.12:3 τάχα πᾶς ὁ ἁμαρτάνων, διὰ τοῦ παρανομεῖν ~ων τὸν θεῖον λόγον, διὰ τῶν ἔργων κέκραγεν 'ἀνάθεμα Ἰησοῦς' Or.*or*.22.3(p.348.5; M.11.484D).

*__ἀναθεμάτισις__, ἡ, *anathematization*, Thdr.Stud.*epp*.1.48(M.99.1073A).

ἀναθεματισμός, ὁ, **1.** *devoting* to God, *dedicating* to destruction, so to evil εἰ ἀ. μόνον ἐπὶ τῶν ἀτόπων ἡ παλαιά τε καὶ νέα διαθήκη ἐπίσταται, πῶς ὁ...Πέτρος...ἀναθεματίζειν ἤρξατο; τίς δὲ ἡ διαφορὰ ἑκατέρων, τουτέστι τοῦ ἀ. καὶ τοῦ καταθεματισμοῦ; ‡Just.*qu.et resp*.121(M.6.1369D); v. ἀνάθεμα; **2.** *binding by a curse*, ref. Ac.23:12 ἀνάγκην τινὰ ἑαυτοῖς...περιέθηκαν διὰ τοῦ ἀ. Chrys.*hom.49.2 in Ac*.(9.366D); **3.** *declaration of anathema, anathematization*; **a.** by Church τῷ δὲ ἀ. [sc. of Arius] οὐχ ὑπεγράψαμεν Eus.Nic.*libell*.(p.65.7; M.67.112B); Eus.*ep.Caes*.8(p.46.10; M.20.1544A); πᾶς αἱρετικὸς μέχρι τέλους τῇ οἰκείᾳ πλάνῃ ἐμμείνας δικαιότερον διηνεκεῖ ἀ. καὶ μετὰ θάνατον ὑποβάλλεται Justn.*conf*.(p.102.18; M.86.1025D); **b.** by individuals, as proof of return to orthodoxy, Bas.*ep*.251.3(3.388A; M.32.937B).

*__ἀναθεματιστέος__, *to be anathematized*, Leo.Mag.*ep*.28.6(p.19.11; M.*PL*.54.780A).

ἀναθερίζω, *cut again*; of reopening a wound, ‡Max.*cap.al*.243 (M.90.1460D).

*__ἀναθερισμός__, ὁ, *cutting open, piercing*; of the soul by reproof, ‡Max.*cap.al*.29(M.90.1408B).

ἀνάθεσις, ἡ, **1.** *setting up, erection*; of serpent in wilderness, Just.*dial*.91.4(M.6.693B); ἀναθέσει ἀνδριάντος τιμηθῆναι Eus.*h.e*.3.9.2(M.20.241A); **2.** *setting, placing*; of books in a library, *ib*.2.18.8 (188A); hence **3.** *stack* of books λαβυρίνθοις ἐοίκασιν ὑμῶν τῶν βιβλίων αἱ ἀ. Tat.*orat*.26(p.27.21; M.6.861B); **4.** *offering* of sacrifice τῆς ἐν εὐσεβείᾳ ζωῆς ἀ. Cyr.*ador*.16(1.574C); τὴν τοῦ δράγματος ἀ. *ib*.17(612C).

ἀναθετέον, **1.** *one must offer, dedicate*, Cyr.*Zach*.85(3.771C); **2.** *one must assign* ἀ. αὐτῷ [sc. τῷ Χριστῷ] τὴν ἀνατολὴν εἰς προσκύνησιν Jo.D.*f.o*.4.12(M.94.1133C).

ἀναθέω, *run again* to; met., *return* to, Cyr.*ador*.15(1.555D).

ἀναθεωρέω, *examine carefully*, Meth.*res*.1.25(p.250.10; M.41.1096B); Chrys.*hom.33.3 in Heb*.(12.306C).

ἀναθηλέω, *sprout afresh*, *Orac.Sib*.11.252; met., of soul at baptism, Bas.*hom*.13.5(2.117D; M.31.433A).

*__ἀναθήλησις__, ἡ, *sprouting afresh* φυτῶν Cyr.*ador*.10(1.331D).

ἀνάθημα, τό, **A.** *that which is set up*; hence *monument*, Juln. Imp.*ep*.59(p.64.13ff.).

B. *that which is dedicated, offering*; **1.** pagan; hence plur., name of a festival ὅτε τὰς ἑορτὰς τῶν Ἀ. εἶχον οἱ Φρύγες καὶ οἱ Ἕλληνες Jo.Mal.*chron*.5 p.109(M.97.201A); *ib*.p.112(204B); **2.** Christian; **a.** in gen. ἀ. γὰρ καλοῦμεν τὰ τῷ θεῷ προσφερόμενα Thdt.*Rom*.9:3(3.99); οὔτε θυσίαις οὐδὲ μὴν ἀ. ... κηλεῖται [sc. τὸ θεῖον] Clem.*str*.7.3(p.11.18; M.9.420A); τῶν σφαζομένων ζῴων...ὁ βραχίων ἦν...ἱερὸν ἀ. τῷ θεῷ Cyr.*Zach*.85(3.771B); ἀ. δὲ οὐδὲν λύτρον ἐστίν, ἀλλ' ἅγιον ἁγίων θεῷ ἕως θανάτου, καὶ ἀντὶ λυτρώσεως ἀνατίθεται Proc.G.*Lev*.27:28(M.87.793B); **b.** of spiritual offerings ἀγάλματα δὲ καὶ πρέποντα θεῷ ἀ. ... αἱ ἀρεταί Or.*Cels*.8.17(p.234.24; M.11.1544A); Meth.*symp*.5.1(p.53.6; M.18.97A); Bas.*reg.fus*.14(2.356B; M.31.952A); κόσμησον τὴν οἰκίαν ἐλεημοσύναις, εὐχαῖς, παννυχίσιν, ἱκετηρίαις. ταῦτα γὰρ τοῦ...Χριστοῦ τὰ ἀ. Chrys.*hom.83.4 in Mt*.(7.796E); προαιρέσεως γὰρ καὶ οὐκ ἀνάγκης καρποὶ τὰ εἰς θεὸν ἀ. Cyr.*ador*.16(1.589B); Bas.Sel.*or*.14.1 (M.85.184B); **c.** of offerings given to churches, Eus.*v.C*.3.40(p.94.32; M.20.1100B); τὰς ἐκκλησίας ἀναθημάτων ἐπλήρωσεν Ath.*apol.Const*.7(M.25.604D); Soz.*h.e*.2.26.3(M.67.1008C).

ἀναθλάω, *crush in pieces*, Meth.*res*.1.43(p.290.9; M.18.272B).

ἀναθολ-όω, *make turbid, muddy*, met. τὸν ~οῦντα τῷ ἰδίῳ βορβόρῳ τὸ καθαρὸν τῶν τῆς εὐσεβείας δογμάτων Gr.Nyss.*Eun*.11 (2 p.272.31; M.45.881D).

ἀναθορυβέω, *disturb*, Eus.*h.e*.4.15.1(M.20.340B).

ἀναθρέω, *look up*; to divine light, Clem.*prot*.10(p.68.13; M.8.205B); πρὸς τὸ ἀληθὲς ἀναθρήσαντας id.*paed*.2.1(p.160.4; M.8.393A ἀναθήσαντας).

ἀναθρώσκ-ω, **1.** *spring up*; *ascend*, of Christ ἀνέθορε...πρὸς τὸν πατέρα μετὰ σαρκὸς Cyr.*glaph.Ex*.2(1.302C); *come up*; of Abraham to Canaan, id.*ador*.1(1.23A); met. εἰς τὰς τοῦ πιστεύειν ἀρχὰς ~ουσιν *ib*.17(604B); id.*inc.unigen*.(5^1.702E); **2.** ? *leap over*, met. μειρακιώδη φρόνησιν...~οντες, καὶ εἰς ἀνδρὸς ἤδη τελοῦντες μέτρον id.*ador*.4(1.132B).

ἀναθυμίασις, ἡ, *rising smoke, exhalation* ἡ δὲ τῶν ἀρωμάτων ἀ. τῆς τοῦ ἁγίου πνεύματος περιπνοίας τε καὶ πληρώσεως [sc. σύμβολον] Germ.CP *ep.dogm*.4(M.98.184C); fig. ἡ ἀπ' αὐτῶν [sc. meat and wine] ἀ. θολωδεστέρα οὖσα ἐπισκοτεῖ τῇ ψυχῇ Clem.*paed*.2.1(p.161.21 M.8.396B); cf.Bas.*hom*.1.9(2.8D; M.31.180C); of Jo. Bapt. τὸν τῆς διανοίας ὀφθαλμὸν καθαρὸν ἐφύλαττεν ἐκ τῆς εὐριπίστου τῶν σαρκικῶν ὀρέξεων ἀ. Procl.CP *or*.6.4(M.65.728A); met., ref. Is.13:13 θυμὸν δὲ ὀργῆς λέγειν τῇ γραφῇ σύνηθες τὴν ἀ. †Bas.*Is*.269(1.584D; M.30.592C); θυμὸς καὶ ὀργή...ὁ μὲν παρὰ τὴν ἀ. εἴρηται· ὁ δὲ παρὰ τὸ ὀργᾶν Isid.Pel.*epp*.4.223(M.78.1317B); διὰ θυμὸν ὀργῆς κυρίου, οὕτω λεγομένης τῆς κατὰ κόλασιν ἀ. Proc.G.*Is*.13:12(M.87.2085A).

ἀναθυμι-άω, *emit like smoke*, met. τὴν εὐωδίαν τῆς ἀγάπης ~ῶσαν [sc. virginity] κυρίῳ Meth.*symp*.5.6(p.61.10; M.18.108D); med., *rise in fume* or *vapour*; met. ἐστὶν ἡ θυσία τῆς ἐκκλησίας λόγος ἀπὸ τῶν ἁγίων ψυχῶν ~ώμενος Clem.*str*.7.6(p.24.14; M.9.444C); θυμὸν δὲ ὁρίζονται ὀργὴν ~ωμένην Or.*comm.in Rom*.2:7f.(*JTS* 13 p.215); ‡Ath.*fr.Ps*.2:5(M.27.65C) cit. s. ὀργή; Isid.Pel.*epp*.2.67(M.78.512A).

*__ἀναθωπεύω__, *coax*, Epiph.*haer*.66.71(p.113.4; M.42.141D).

*__ἀναιάζω__, *bewail*, *Orac.Sib*.5.137,312,315.

ἀναιδεύ-ομαι, **1.** *lack shame*, Herm.*vis*.3.7.5; *A.Thom*.A 15(p.122.4); **2.** *behave shamelessly* αἰσχύνῃ ~ομένη *ib*.34(p.152.2); Or.*or*.31.3 (p.397.9; M.11.552C); Ath.*inc*.32.6(M.25.152C).

ἀναίδην, for ἀνέδην, *without restraint*, *Const.App*.6.10.3; Didym.*Trin*.3.41(M.39.989A); Cyr.*Is*.4.1(2.557D).

ἀναιδίζομαι, s.v.l., *act with impudence*, Sophr.H.*v.Anast*.(M.92.1721A).

ἀναιμακτί, *without bloodshed*, Eus.*v.C.*4.53(p.139.20, v.l. ἀναιμωτί M.20.1204B).

ἀναίμακτος, *bloodless*; of sacrifices; **1.** heavenly opp. earthly λογικὴ καὶ ἀ. θυσία offered by archangels, *T.Lev.*6.3; **2.** of Christian worship in gen. ἀ. θυσίαν τὴν λογικὴν προσάγειν λατρείαν Athenag. *leg.*13.2(M.6.916C); θυσίαν ἀ. ... ἀναπέμπω...τὴν δι' εὐχῶν *M.Apollon.* 8(p.31.3); θύων τὰς ἀ. ἐν ταῖς...εὐχαῖς θυσίας Or.*Cels.*8.21(p.239.6; M.11.1549C); id.*Ps.*15:4(p.469); θυσιαστήριον ἀ. ... θεοῦ τὸ ἄθροισμα τῶν ἁγνῶν Meth.*symp.*5.6(p.61.5; M.18.108C); Gr.Nyss.*instit.*(p.43.9; M.46.288B); ὅπερ δὲ ἦν τότε ὁ...μόσχος τοῦτο νῦν ἐστιν...ἡ ἀ. δέησις Ast.Am.*hom.*13(M.40.561A); Isid.Pel.*epp.*1.106(M.78.253C); **3.** esp. of eucharist προσφορὰ ἀ. Serap.*euch.*13.11; ἀ. λατρεία Cyr.H.*catech.* 23.8; v. θυσία; ὅταν ἀ. τομῇ σῶμα καὶ αἷμα τέμνῃς δεσποτικόν, φωνὴν ἔχων τὸ ξίφος Gr.Naz.*ep.*171(M.37.281A); hence σεμνήν τε καὶ ἀ. ἱερωσύνην Gr.Nyss.*or.catech.*18(p.76.1; M.45.56A).

ἄναιμος, = foreg. τὰ σεμνὰ τῆς Χριστοῦ τραπέζης θύματα, δι' ὧν ...τὰς ἀ. καὶ λογικὰς...θυσίας...προσφέρειν...δεδιδάγμεθα Eus.*d.e.*1.10 (p.48.4; M.22.92A); id.*v.C.*4.45(p.136.18; M.20.1196B); id.*l.C.*2.6(p.200. 9; M.20.1328A).

ἀναιμωτί ([*]-τεί), *without shedding blood* οὐδὲ...ἀ. προσιέναι τῷ λόγῳ ἔξεστιν Clem.*paed.*2.8(-τεί p.202.16; M.8.485A); of a military expedition ἀ. ἐγεγένητο Thdt.*Ezech.*21:14(2.843); ‡Nil.*narr.*4(M. 79.636B); Philost.*h.e.*9.5(M.65.572B).

ἀναίρεσις, ἡ, *destruction*; of beliefs and statements, *denial, negation* σκοπείτω...ποίαν τὴν τοῦ τεθέντος ἀ. ἐνδείκνυται Gr.Nyss.*Eun.*1 (1 p.203.26; M.45.452A); ref. doctrine ἐπιχειρήσαντες [sc. Arians] τὰ εἰς ἀ. τῆς τοῦ λόγου θεότητος Alex.Al.*ep.encycl.*6(p.9.24; M.18. 576D); τῇ γὰρ τῶν φυσικῶν [sc. τοῦ Χριστοῦ] ἀ. [sc. by Ar. and Apoll.] Max.*opusc.*(M.91.97B); *exclusion* ὅτε...μόνος λέγεται ὁ πατὴρ θεὸς...καλῶς λέγεται...οὐκ εἰς ἀ. δὲ τοῦ υἱοῦ λέγεται Ath.*Ar.*3.6(M. 26.353B); μήτε τὸ εἷς κύριος ἐπ' ἀναιρέσει τοῦ πατρὸς νοητέον μήτε τὸ εἷς θεὸς ἐπ' ἀ. τοῦ υἱοῦ Thdr.Mops.*Eph.*4:5ff.(p.164.21; M.66.917C).

ἀναιρέτης, ὁ, *destroyer*; of Christ acc. Jews θυσιῶν ἀ. *Const.App.* 5.14.9; of Law δαιμόνων ἀ. Gr.Naz.*carm.*1.2.34.187(M.37.959A); of Devil ὁ τῶν καλῶν ἀ. Sophr.H.*mir.Cyr.et Jo.*37(M.87.3564A).

ἀναιρετικός, **1.** *destructive*; esp. of arguments or doctrines, Clem. *str.*8.5(p.89.10; M.9.580B); ἀ. ... τοῦ εἶναι αὐτὸν θεόν Or.*Cels.*5.24(p.25. 2; M.11.1217A); ἄτοπον καὶ...τῆς τοῦ...θεοῦ προνοίας ἀ. *ib.*5.26(p.27. 22; 1221A); τὸ ἐκ τῆς οὐσίας καὶ τὸ ὁμοούσιον ἀ. τῶν τῆς ἀσεβείας λογαρίων εἰσίν Ath.*decr.*20(p.17.24; M.25.452D); **2.** neut. as subst., *poison*, Jo.Mosch.*prat.*94(M.87.2952D).

ἀναιρ-έω, *destroy*; esp. in doctrinal arguments, *do away with, remove* ~ούντων [sc. Monarchians] υἱὸν ἀπὸ πατρὸς καὶ δυνάμει ~ούντων καὶ τὸν πατέρα Or.*dial.*4(p.126.18); τῶν ἑτεροδόξων τινὲς... τὸ αὐτοεξούσιον ~οῦντες id.*princ.*3.1.8(p.207.1; M.11.261A).

ἀναισθησία, ἡ, *lack of sensation*; **1.** *lack of perception, obtuseness* (mental, moral, or spiritual), Dion.Al.ap.Eus.*h.e.*7.6(M.20.648A); Const.*or.s.c.*11(p.167.20; M.20.1261C); ἀ. ψυχῆς Chrys.*paralyt.*4 (3.40B); moral, Dor.*doct.*3.2(M.88.1656A); in list of ψυχικὰ πάθη, Jo.D.*virt.*(M.95.88B); πρὸς ἀσέβειαν...πρηνὴς καθέστηκεν ὁδός, ἡ περὶ τὴν ζημίαν τῶν ἀρετῶν ἀ. *Schol.*7 in Max.*qu.Thal.*52(M.90.500B); **2.** in good sense, *freedom from feeling, detachment* τελείαν ἀ., καὶ ἀπόνοιαν ἐν λοιδορίαις, καὶ ὕβρεσι Jo.Clim.*scal.*4(M.88.688B); = ἀπάθεια: μακάριός ἐστιν ὁ νοῦς, ὁ κατὰ τὸν καιρὸν τῆς προσευχῆς τελείαν ἀ. κτησάμενος Evagr.Pont.*or.*120(M.79.1193B).

***ἀναίσθησις, ἡ**, *detachment* ἐξομολόγησιν, καὶ συντριμμὸν ψυχῆς ἐν ἀ. Jo.Clim.*scal.*28(M.88.1132A).

ἀναισθητ-έω, *lack perception*; *be insensible* to (mentally, morally, or spiritually) μὴ οὖν ~ῶμεν τῆς χρηστότητος αὐτοῦ Ign.*Magn.*10.1; ἀ. τοῦ ὄντως θεοῦ Athenag.*leg.*15.3(M.6.920B); εἰς ἃ [sc. ῥητὰ τῶν γραφῶν]...~οῦντες, οὐχ ὁρῶσι τὸν ἐν τούτοις νοῦν Ath.*Ar.*1.52(M.26. 121A); abs., Chrys.*hom.32.2 in Mt.*(7.366D).

***ἀναισθητότης, ἡ**, *lack of sensation*, v.l. for τὰ ἀναισθητότερα Chrys.*fr.Jer.*6:11(M.64.824D).

***ἀναισχυντί**, = ἀναισχύντως, *shamelessly, impudently*, Epiph. *haer.*69.12(p.162.5; M.42.221A).

ἀναίτιος, **1.** *not being the cause, not responsible* τῇ δὲ αἰτίᾳ τοῦ μὴ τὸ βέλτιστον ἑλομένου θεὸς ἀ. Clem.*str.*1.1(p.4.27; M.8.692A); μηδ' ἀ. φύσεως ἔργον τυγχάνειν τὸ μέγα τοῦτο...τεχνούργημα Eus.*p.e.*7.10 (314D; M.21.532D); τύχη δὲ ἀρετῆς ἀ. Synes.*regn.*4(p.11.6; M.66. 1060B); **2.** *guiltless, innocent* κακοδιδασκαλοῦντες τὰς ἀ. ψυχάς *2Clem.*10.5; **3.** *without cause, self-existent, underived*; **a.** of Trin. ἀ. γοῦν ὁ πατὴρ καὶ ὁ υἱὸς καὶ τὸ ἅγιον πνεῦμα Epiph.*haer.*76.44(p.398. 31; M.42.612B); *uncaused* by ἀ. οὖσα τῆς τοιαύτης αἰτίας ἡ τριάς *ib.*(p.398.16; 609D); **b.** of Father, opp. Son and H. Ghost ἀ., γεννητόν, ἐκπορεύσιμον Gr.Naz.*carm.*1.2.10.989(M.37.751A); τῆς τε γὰρ τοῦ ἀ. δόξης μετέχοι ἂν [sc. ὁ υἱός], ὅτι ἐκ τοῦ ἀ. id.*or.*29.11(p.90.2; M.36.89A); ἀ., καὶ ἀπαθής, καὶ ἀεικίνητος...θεός Didym.*Trin.*2.8 (M.39.609A); ‡Ath.*Maced.dial.*1.20(M.28.1328B); Jo.D.*f.o.*1.8(M.94. 809B); ‡Cyr.*Trin.*9(6³.13D; M.77.1140C); Jo.Mon.*hymn.Petr.*8(M.96. 1389A); **c.** denied of Son, exeg. Heb.1:13 εἶπε, κάθου· καὶ τοῦτο δι' οὐδὲν ἕτερον, ἀλλ' ἵνα μὴ ἄναρχον αὐτὸν νομίσῃς καὶ ἀ. Chrys.*hom. 2.3 in Heb.*(12.19D); τὸν δὲ υἱὸν οὐ λέγομεν ἀ. ‡Cyr.*Trin.*10(6³.16E; M.77.1145A); **4.** *without cause* or *reason* οὐδὲν ἀ. οὐδὲν ἀπὸ ταὐτομάτου Bas.*hex.*5.8(1.47E; M.29.113A).

ἀναιτίως, **1.** *without cause*; of Father, Gr.Nyss.*tres dii*(M.45.136); of Son ἐν ἀρχῇ ἦν ἀ.· τίς γὰρ αἰτία θεοῦ; ἀλλὰ γὰρ ὕστερον γέγονε δι' αἰτίαν Gr.Naz.*or.*29.19(p.102.9; M.36.100A); *ib.*30.11(p.123.13; 116C); Jo.D.*Jacob.*79(M.94.1476C); ref. universe μηδὲν ἀ. γίνεται Clem.*str.*2.18(p.162.20; M.8.1033A); **2.** *guiltlessly*, Hegem.*Arch.*10 (p.17.2; M.10.1444B).

***ἀναιχμαλώτιστος**, *freed from captivity* of sin, ‡Ath.*Apoll.*2.11 (M.26.1149B).

***ἀνακαθαιρέω**, *destroy utterly*, Soz.*h.e.*2.4.7(M.67.945A).

ἀνακαθαίρω, **1.** *clear away, remove*; met. ὁ λόγος ἀ. τὰς ἁμαρτίας Clem.*paed.*1.6(p.120.22; M.8.309C); of suspicion, *Symb.Ant.*(345)9 (p.254.9; M.26.733C); **2.** *clean*; *cleanse* from sin ἀ. τῷ λόγῳ τὸν θεολόγον Gr.Naz.*or.*28.1(p.21.1; M.36.25C); Philost.*h.e.*1.1(M.65.461A); ἀνακάθαρον σαυτοῦ τὸν νοῦν Isid.Pel.*epp.*5.184(M.78.1433C); **3.** *explain, interpret*, Dion.Ar.*c.h.*15.9(M.3.337D).

ἀνακάθαρσις, ἡ, **1.** *clearing up*; *end of an eclipse*, Dion.Ar.*ep.* 7.2(M.3.1081B); **2.** *explanation*, id.*c.h.*15.1(M.3.328A); *ib.*15.2,7 (328C,336C); ἀ. φησὶ τὰς ἐξηγητικὰς ἑρμηνείας Max.*schol.c.h.*15.1(M.4. 104B).

ἀνακαθαρτικός, neut. as subst., *cleansing property*, Clem.*paed.*1. 11(p.147.7; M.8.365A).

ἀνακάθημαι, ptcpl. ἀνακαθήμενος, ? *sitting upright*, Jo.Mal.*chron.* 10 p.256(M.97.388C).

[*]**ἀνακαίνησις, ἡ**, v. ἀνακαίνισις.

ἀνακαινίζ-ω, *renew*;

A. in gen., fig. διὰ τούτων [sc. scriptures] τὴν ψυχὴν τὴν ἡμετέραν ...παλαιωθεῖσαν ~ομεν Chrys.*Laz.*3.2(1.738D); ἥμαρτες σήμερον; ἐπαλαίωσάς σου τὴν ψυχήν; μὴ ἀπογνῷς...ἀλλ' ἀνακαίνισον αὐτὴν μετανοίᾳ id.*hom.20.2 in Rom.*(9.659B).

B. ref. divine renewal; **1.** of mankind; **a.** through Inc. παρεγένετο [sc. ὁ Χριστός] ἐπὶ τοὺς ἡμετέρους τόπους, ἵνα τὸν κατ' αὐτὸν πεποιημένον ἄνθρωπον ἀνακαινίσῃ Ath.*inc.*14.2(M.25.120C); τοῦτον σαθρωθέντα εἰς ἑαυτὸν λαβόμενος πάλιν ἀ. διὰ τῆς βεβαίας αὐτοῦ ἀνανεώσεως ‡Ath.*Ar.*4.33(p.82.11; M.26.520A); ‡Ath.*Apoll.*1.21(M.26.1129A); Isid.Pel.*epp.*1.201(M.78.312B); Cyr.*Jo.*4.4(4.386B); πρῶτος ἐν τῇ καινῇ κτίσει τεχθείς, ἣν ἀνεκαίνισε γεννηθείς Thdt.*Trin.*10(M.75. 1160C); Proc.G.*Dt.*33:7(M.87.981A); ἀ. τὴν παλαιωθεῖσαν αὐτοῦ καὶ φθαρεῖσαν εἰκόνα Anast.Ant.*serm.*2.8(M.89.1385A); **b.** through Cross τὰς ψυχὰς...ἀ. ... διὰ τοῦ μυστηρίου τοῦ σταυροῦ *A.(Pass.)Andr.*5 (p.11.21); Philox.*ep.*20(p.172) cit. s. ἀνακαινισμός; **c.** through remission of sins, *Barn.*6.11; **d.** through bestowal of H. Ghost, Eus.*qu. Marin.suppl.*2.9(M.22.1013C); Chrys.*hom.30.4 in Mt.*(7.353A); **e.** in baptism, Meth.*symp.*3.9(p.37.18; M.18.76B); Cyr.H.*catech.*20.1; ἡμῶν ἡ φύσις...ἐκ τοῦ παλαιοῦ ἀνθρώπου ~ομένη κατ' εἰκόνα τοῦ κτίσαντος ἐν ἀρχῇ τὸ θεοειδὲς ὁμοίωμα Gr.Nyss.*Eun.*2(2 p.297.18; M.45.468C); Epiph.*haer.*59.5(p.369.23; M.41.1025C) cit. s. μετάνοια; ‡Chrys.*hom. in Jo.1:1*(12.417E); Diad.*perf.*89(p.124.7); Dion.Ar.*e.h.*4.3.10(M.3. 484B); exeg. Heb.6:6 ἀνακαινισθῆναι· τουτέστι, καινὸν γενέσθαι· τὸ γὰρ καινοὺς ποιῆσαι, τοῦ λουτροῦ μόνον ἐστίν Chrys.*hom.9.3 in Heb.*(12.96B); cf.Thdt.*Heb.*6:4ff.(3.578); **f.** of spiritual renewal in gen.; through repentance (ref. Heb.6:6), Herm.*sim.*8.6.3; τυχὼν τῶν θείων μυστηρίων ἀπελθεῖν ἡγιασμένος, καὶ ὥσπερ τις νεοτελὴς ἀνακαινισθεὶς καὶ σῶμα καὶ ψυχήν Bas.Sel.*v.Thecl.*2.18(M.85.596C); **2.** of divine gifts τὴν ἐν ἀνθρώποις ~ομένην σωτηρίαν προφητεύει, τὴν γενομένην ἐν Χριστῷ πρὸς ἡμᾶς Ath.*Ar.*2.46(M.26.245A); ἤργησε μὲν ἡ ἀνθρώπῳ δοθεῖσα χάρις, ἀνεκαινίσθη γεμὴν ἐν Χριστῷ, ὅς ἐστι δεύτερος Ἀδάμ Cyr.*Joel.*35(3.228A); **3.** of Creation ἡμεῖς αὐτοί, τὸ κεφάλαιον τῆς δημιουργίας καὶ δι' οὓς καὶ μεθ' ὧν τὰ πάντα ~εται Gennad.*fr.Rom.*8:23ff.(p.381.17; M.85.1697C); πᾶσαν τὴν κτίσιν ~εσθαι εἰς κρείττονα καὶ μακαρίαν κατάστασιν Cosm.Ind.*top.*2(M.88. 128B).

ἀνακαίνισις, ἡ, *renewal*; **1.** of men by God through Inc. τὴν ταύτης [sc. κτίσεως] ἀ. ὑπὸ τοῦ...λόγου Ath.*inc.*1.4(M.25.97C); τὴν σάρκωσιν...πρὸς ἀνακαίνισιν ἀνθρωπότητος Apoll.*fid.sec.pt.*11(p.171. 3; M.10.1109A); Vital.*fr.*(p.67.31, v.l. ἀνακαίνωσιν; 5².51C); ἀ. εἰς ἀφθαρσίαν τε καὶ ζωήν Cyr.*inc.unigen.*(5¹.692B); Cosm.Ind.*top.*2 (M.88.121A); Jo.D.*hom.*4.33(M.96.636C); **2.** through H. Ghost τὸ πνεῦμα τὸ ἅγιον εἰς ἀ. ἡμῶν ἐνεφύσησεν ‡Chrys.*pasch*.1(8.252C); **3.** in baptism ἀ. δεχόμενος τῆς ὅλης αὐτοῦ καταστάσεως Thdr. Heracl.*Is*.62:2(M.18.1368A); Chrys.*hom.82.4 in Mt*.(7.787D, vv.ll. -νωσις, -νησις); **4.** of spiritual renewal in gen. ἐπὶ δὲ τὴν ἰδίαν ἀνάπαυσιν καὶ ἀ. βίου καλέσαντι *A.Jo*.78(p.190.6); Ath.*Ar*.2.46(M.26. 245A, v.l. -νωσιν) cit. s. ἀνανέωσις; ἐν γὰρ τῇ τοῦ νοὸς ἀ. καὶ τῇ τῶν λογισμῶν εἰρήνῃ...ἡ καινὴ κτίσις τῶν Χριστιανῶν πάντων ἀνθρώπων τοῦ κόσμου διαφέρει Mac.Aeg.*hom*.5.5(M.34.497D); ἐν μετανοίᾳ...γέγονε καὶ ἠξιώθη τῆς ἀ. καὶ ἀφέσεως τῶν ἁμαρτιῶν Jo.D.*Man*.1.33(M.94. 1540C); **5.** of whole creation in future, Gr.Naz.*or*.7.21(M.35.784B).

***ἀνακαινισμός, ὁ,** *renewal, restoration*; **1.** in gen. ὁ τῶν θεοπνεύστων ἀναγνωρισμὸς καὶ ἀ. λογίων Clem.*str*.1.21(p.77.25; M.8. 853A); ἀ. τῆς πόλεως Thphn.*chron*.p.148(M.108.401B); **2.** of divine renewal; **a.** of men through Christ, Cyr.*Am*.2(3.248E); ἐν τῇ ἐνανθρωπήσει τοῦ Χριστοῦ ἐδέξατο ἡ φύσις ἡμῶν τὸν ἀ. τῆς ἐκχύσεως τοῦ αἵματος...καὶ τότε μετὰ τὸν ἀ. ἀνεκαινίσθη, καὶ ἡγιάσθη ἡ φύσις ἡμῶν Philox.*ep*.20(p.172); εἰς διόρθωσιν καὶ ἀ., ἀλλ' οὐκ εἰς συμπλήρωσιν τοῦ παντός, ἐνανθρωπήσαντος Max.*ep*.13(M.91.517B); *Chron. Pasch*.p.87(M.92.245A); **b.** through Resurrection, Cosm.Ind.*top*.3 (M.88.165D); **c.** through H. Ghost, Didym.*Trin*.2.6(M.39.533A); τὸ δὲ ἐμφύσημα ἐποίησε τὸν ἀ. τῇ ἀνθρωπότητι Ammon.*Jo*.20:23(M.85. 1517D); Cyr.*Is*.5.2(2.770D); Proc.G.*Is*.54:1ff.(M.87.2545B) cit. s. ἀνακτίζω; **d.** through baptism, Meth.*symp*.3.8(p.36.13; M.18.73C); βάπτισμα...ἀ. καὶ ἀναγεννήσεως αἰτία Gr.Nyss.*bapt.Chr*.(M.46.580D); Epiph.*haer*.59.5(p.369.27; M.41.1025C) cit. s. μετάνοια; ‡Ath.*dial. Trin*.3.18(M.28.1229D); Thdr.Mops.*Eph*.4:22ff.(p.173.24); Marc.Er. *opusc*.3.7(M.65.976D); **e.** through eucharist ἔστω σοι τοῦτο εἰς ἄφεσιν ἁμαρτιῶν καὶ ἀ. τῆς ψυχῆς σου *A.Xanthipp*.14(p.67.9); in eucharistic prayer ἀντὶ δὲ μνημείου καινοῦ καὶ ταφῆς ἀ. τῆς ψυχῆς δεξώμεθα καὶ τοῦ σώματος *A.Thom*.A 158(p.268.14); **f.** of spiritual renewal in gen. τῶν δὲ πρὸς τὸ τοῦ θεοειδοῦς παραφθαρτικὸν ἀπολισθησάντων ἀ. καὶ ἀναμόρφωσις Dion.Ar.*d.n*.1.3(M.3.589B); Ant.Mon.*hom*.27(M. 89.1524B); **g.** of whole creation ἐκπυρωθήσεται...πρὸς κάθαρσιν καὶ ἀ. ... πᾶς ὁ κόσμος Meth.*res*.1.47(p.298.1; M.41.1117D); ref. future life οὐκ ἀ. καὶ διόρθωσις μόνον τῶν παρόντων ἐκεῖνα, ἀλλὰ γὰρ καὶ τελείωσις Thdr.Mops.*Rom*.11:15(p.157.4; M.66.856B); ἄγγελοι... ἐκδέχονται τὸν ἀ. τῆς μεσότητος τοῦ ἐλευθερωθῆναι τῆς δουλείας τῆς φθορᾶς ἐν τῇ ἐλευθερίᾳ τῶν τέκνων τοῦ θεοῦ Philox.*ep*.42(p.187); Andr.Caes.*Apoc*.65(M.106.424B).

***ἀνακαινιστής, ὁ,** *one who renews, re-creator*, of Christ ἔδει...ἀ. γενέσθαι τῶν κατεφθαρμένων Cyr.*glaph.Gen*.1(1.13B); id.*resp*.8(p.590. 7; 6^2.378C); τοῦ παντὸς κτίστης...καὶ ἀ. Sev.Ant.ap.*cat.Mt*.27:38 (p.235.8); as adj. τὸν ἀ., ἵν' οὕτως εἴπω, τῆς ἀναστάσεως...καιρόν Cyr.*Jo*.4.7(4.440B).

***ἀνακαινοποι-έω,** *renew, restore*, *T.Lev*.17.10; †Just.*fr.res*.6(p.43; M.6.1581C); ref. resurrection ὅπως οἱ ~ηθέντες ἐν ἀνακαινοποιηθέντι κόσμῳ...κατοικήσωμεν Meth.*res*.1.48(p.301.7; M.18.276C); θεοῦ...~οῦντος αὖθις τὴν σάρκα *ib*.2.21(p.375.10; 285D); φάγετε ἄρτον ~οῦντα ὑμῶν τὴν φύσιν †Cyr.*hom.div*.10(5^2.374A); διὰ τοῦ βαπτίσματος ἀνακαινοποιήσει [sc. ὁ κύριος] τὴν κτίσιν Eus.Al.*serm*.10(M.86. 372B).

ἀνακαινουργέω, *renew, restore*, *A.(Pass.)Andr*.5(p.12.17).

ἀνακαιν-όω, *renew, restore* κατὰ τὸν θεόν ἐστι...ἀ. τὰ πράγματα Or.*Cels*.4.20(p.289.27; M.11.1053A); of human nature restored in Christ κενοῦται μὲν...ἡ θεότης...~οῦται δὲ τὸ ἀνθρώπινον διὰ τῆς πρὸς τὸ θεῖον ἀνακράσεως θεῖον γινόμενον Gr.Nyss.*Eun*.5(2 p.124. 25; M.45.705D); of man's renewal by aspiration towards Logos, Ath.*gent*.2(M.25.8A); by action of H. Ghost in baptism, Didym. (‡Bas.)*Eun*.5(1.303A,B; M.29.725D,728A); by baptismal illumination, Eus.*v.C*.4.62(p.143.21; M.20.1217A).

ἀνακαίνωσις, ἡ, *renewal* ἡ ἀ. τῶν πνευμάτων Herm.*vis*.3.8.9; ἐπὶ καθαιρέσει τῆς κακίας καὶ ἀ. τοῦ παντός Or.*Cels*.4.21(p.291.11; M.11. 1056A); of NT ἡ...παράδοσις...κατὰ τὴν ἀ. τοῦ βιβλίου Clem.*str*. 6.15(p.498.17; M.9.356B); through operation of H. Ghost in baptism γεννηθέντες ἄνωθεν τὸν ἔσω ἄνθρωπον ἐν τῇ ἀ. τοῦ νοός †Bas. *bapt*.1.2.22(2.645D; M.31.1564B); Didym.(‡Bas.)*Eun*.5(1.303A; M.29. 725D); *ib*.(303C,E; M.728B,729A).

***ἀνακαινωτικός,** *renewing*, of H. Ghost ἀ. αὐτὸ τῆς δημιουργίας εἰς ἀφθαρσίαν Didym.(‡Bas.)*Eun*.5(1.297D; M.29.713C).

ἀνακαλ-έω, *recall*; from error or evil, *A.Xanthipp*.29(p.79.11); Chrys.*hom.19.3 in 1Cor*.(10.162C); Hier.(tr.Sophr.Pal.)*vir.ill*.17 (p.20.6; M.*PL*.23.636B); Eulog.*fr.Trin*.1(p.263); *revoke, retract*, Eus. *Marcell*.2.4(p.55.20; M.24.817B); ~εῖται τὴν ἀπόφασιν Diod.*Gen*.49:4 (M.33.1578C); Philost.*h.e*.2.14(M.65.477A).

ἀνακαλλύν-ω, *restore to beauty* Χριστὸς...τῷ ἁγίῳ πνεύματι ~ων τὴν ἀνθρώπου φύσιν Cyr.*glaph.Dt*.(1.432D).

ἀνακαλύπτω, *uncover, reveal, unveil*, fig. φῶς δὲ νοερόν...τὸν μόνον ἀληθῆ τοῖς πᾶσιν ἀνεκάλυψε θεόν Eus.*l.C*.10(p.222.11; M.20. 1372C); met., of God, Cels.ap.Or.*Cels*.5.6(p.6.6; M.11.1188C); ἀ. τὸν νοῦν τῶν κατὰ τὸν ἀπόστολον ἐπιχειρημάτων Meth.*symp*.3.2(p.29.2; M.18.64A); of Christ ἀ. αὐτῶν τὸ συνειδός Chrys.*hom.58.2 in Mt*. (7.587B).

***ἀνακαλύπτως,** *openly*, Eus.*d.e*.8.4(p.394.30; M.22.637C).

***ἀνακάλυψις, ἡ,** *unveiling* προσφωνησάντων...μυστικὴν ἀ. τοῦ τῆς ἑορτῆς [sc. τοῦ πάσχα] λόγου Eus.*v.C*.4.34(p.130.26; M.20.1181D).

***ἀνακαμπτήριον, τό,** *promenade*, Eus.*v.C*.4.59(p.141.22; M.20. 1209B; v.l. ἀναλαμπτήριον).

ἀνακάμπτω, intrans., *return*, Ath.*v.Anton*.3(M.26.844B); *ib*.62 (932C); Thphn.*chron*.p.53(M.108.188A); *ib*.p.343(828A).

***ἀνακαταλήκτως,** = ἀκαταλήκτως, *incessantly*, Cyr.*ador*.17(1. 599B).

***ἀνακατάσειστος,** = ἀκατάσειστος, *not to be shaken*, Cyr.*ador*.3 (1.82E).

ἀνακαχλάζω, v. [*]ἀνακοχλάζω.

***ἀνάκειμα, τό,** ? *something dedicated* μὴ προσέχειν τοῖς ἐπιγείοις κἂν θεῷ ἀνάκειμα (? for ἀνακείμενα) ᾖ Thdr.Heracl.ap.*cat.Mt*.24:6 (p.196.9).

ἀνάκει-μαι, 1. *be dedicated*; to God, of souls, *Lit*.ap.*Const.App*. 8.11.12; κυρίως ἅγια τὰ τῷ θεῷ ~μενα Chrys.*hom.82.1 in Jo*.(8. 484B); of holy places, Cyr.*Jo*.4.5(4.409C); **2.** *devote oneself to, serve*, of Christ μόνῳ τῷ...θεῷ ~μενος Eus.*d.e*.3.3(p.109.23; M.22.189A); of men to God, Or.*Cels*.4.75(p.345.13; M.11.1145D); Diod.*Ps*.84:9 (M.33.1617A); to contemplation, Or.*schol.in Cant*.2:17(M.17.268C); **3.** *belong to*, Cyr.*Jo*.11.10(4.989B); **4.** *be stored up, kept* καινότητα τοῦ πνεύματος, οἰκείαν τῆς καινῆς διαθήκης τυγχάνουσαν, ἐν πάσαις ~μένην γραφαῖς Or.*Jo*.1.6(8; p.11.23; M.14.36B); Meth.*symp*.5.8 (p.63.1; M.18.112B); Eus.*d.e*.1 proem.(p.2.7; M.22.16A); **5.** *lie, recline* at table; use of this posture at Last Supper indicates it was not a Passover, which was eaten standing, Jo.Philop.*pasch*.(p.217. 29); *lie down*; in gen., Herm.*vis*.3.12.2; μετὰ τῆς πόρνης ~μένου Leont.N.*v.Jo.Eleem*.41(p.80.15).

ἀνακεκαλυμμένως, *openly*; of speech, Chrys.*hom.27.2 in Jo*.(8. 156C); id.*hom.7.3 in 2Cor*.(10.484D); ἐν...ταῖς...ἱερουργίαις ἀ. καὶ ἀνενδοιάστως ἡ ἱερουργία ἐπιτελεῖται Thdr.Stud.*praesanct*.(M.99. 1688B).

ἀνακεράννυμι, 1. *mingle, blend* (trans.); pass., *be permeated*, Gr.Nyss.*or.catech*.37(p.143.6; M.45.93C) cit. s. συναχρειόω; met., *permeate, imbue* τὴν δι' ὅλης τῆς ψυχῆς ἀνακεκραμένην κακίαν Or. *Cels*.4.13(p.283.25; M.11.1044C); ἵνα...πολλοὺς...παιδεύοντες ἀνακραθῶσι τῷ τοῦ θεοῦ λόγῳ καὶ τῷ θείῳ νόμῳ *ib*.8.75(p.292.22; 1632A); ψυχὴν ἔρωτι καὶ φόβῳ καθαρῶς ἀνακραθεῖσαν Eus.*v.C*.3.12(p.63.33; M.20.1029D); τὴν ζωτικὴν τῆς ψυχῆς ἐνέργειαν...λόγῳ τινὶ κρείττονι... ἀνακραθεῖσαν Gr.Nyss.*anim.et res*.(M.46.44C); of persons with the One, Clem.*exc.Thdot*.36(p.118.24; M.9.677A); of demons with the soul, *Hom.Clem*.9.13,15; **2.** *make one* with, *unite* ἡ γραφὴ τοὺς ἀνακεκραμένους τινὶ καὶ ἑνωθέντας γινώσκειν ἐκεῖνό φησιν, ᾧ ἀνεκράθησαν καὶ κεκοινωνήκασιν Or.*Jo*.19.4(1; p.302.18; M.14.529D,532A); of soul with body, id.*Cels*.4.18(p.288.4; M.11.1049D); morally ταῖς ψυχαῖς ἀνακραθέντας ἴδοιμι τοὺς πάντας Const.ap.Eus.*v.C*.3.12 (p.83.3; M.20.1068C); οἷον τοῖς θεοῦ λόγοις ἀνακραθέντας Thdt.*Heb*. 4:2(3.566); **3.** Christol.; until fifth cent. freely used to express relations of deity and humanity in Christ; **a.** of the divine with the human ὁ λόγος...ἥνωται...ἡμῖν τὴν ἀπαρχὴν ἡμῶν περιθέμενος καὶ ταύτῃ ἀνακραθείς ‡Ath.*Ar*.4.33(p.82.6; M.26.517C); θεὸς σαρκὶ διὰ μέσης ψυχῆς ἀνεκράθη Gr.Naz.*or*.2.23(M.35.432B); Gr.Nyss.*ep*.3 M.46.1021C); **b.** of the human with the divine τὸν ἄνθρωπον τοῦ υἱοῦ τοῦ θεοῦ τὸν τῇ θεότητι αὐτοῦ ἀνακεκραμένον Or.*Jo*.1.32(37; p.42.13; M.14.88B); ἡ σὰρξ...ἀνακραθεῖσα...πρὸς τὸ θεῖον οὐκέτι ἐν τοῖς ἑαυτῆς ὅροις τε καὶ ἰδιώμασι μένει Gr.Nyss.*Eun*.5(2 p.123.21; M.45.705B); *ib*.6(2 p.150.21; 737A) cit. s. μίξις; τὸν ἀνακραθέντα τῷ θεῷ ἄνθρωπον id.*Apoll*.27(M.45.1181B); *ib*.17(1156C); **c.** *mix, mingle* in heret. sense φάναι [sc. Demophilus] τὸ σῶμα τοῦ κυρίου, ἀνακραθὲν τῇ θεότητι, εἰς τὸ ἀδηλότατον κεχωρηκέναι, ὃν τρόπον καὶ γάλακτος ξέστης τῷ παντὶ τῆς θαλάσσης ἐπιβληθεὶς συστήματι Philost.*h.e*.9.14 (M.65.580B); ἀλλ' ἴσως ἐροῦσιν [sc. Apollinarians] οὐκ ἀποφοιτῆσαι μὲν ὁλοτρόπως τὴν σάρκα τοῦ εἶναι ὃ ἦν, ἀνακραθῆναι δὲ ὥσπερ τῷ θεῷ λόγῳ πρὸς ἑνότητα φυσικήν...πῶς ἠγνόησαν ὅτι τὰ ἀλλήλοις ἀνακιρνάμενα τῶν ὑγρῶν...ὃ μὲν ἦσάν εἰσι καθαρῶς οὐκέτι; Cyr. *synous*.10(p.485.25ff.; cf.M.76.1432Dff.); **4.** *make one* with, *unite*, as act of God; **a.** of mutual unity in Church, Cyr.H.*catech*.23.3 cit. s. ἀνακίρνημι; πῶς τὰ ἔθνη εἰσήγαγε καὶ ἀνεκέρασε τοῖς πάλαι κατωρθωκόσι; Chrys.*hom.27.1 in Rom*.(9.719D); **b.** with God, [sc. in baptism] Or.*Jo.*19.4(1; p.303.6; M.14.532B) cit. s. γινώσκω; ἡ ψυχὴ ...διὰ πίστεως πρὸς αὐτὸν ἀνακραθεῖσα Gr.Nyss.*or.catech.*37(p.141.4; M.45.93A); myst. ὁ λέγων...ἐγνωκέναι τὸν θεόν, τὸ ἀνακεκρᾶσθαι αὐτῷ καὶ μετέχειν αὐτοῦ ἑπόμενον ἀναγκαίως ἔχει τὸ τηρεῖν αὐτοῦ τὰς ἐντολάς *cat.1Jo.*1:3ff.(p.111.21); with the Word, Or.*Cels.*8.75 (p.292.22; M.11.1632A); with H. Ghost τῷ πνεύματι τῷ ἁγίῳ...ἀνεκράθητε Clem.*str.*7.14(p.62.12; M.9.521A); Didym.*Ps.*20:2f.(M.39.1273C); ὅταν...ἡ ψυχὴ...τῷ παρακλήτῳ πνεύματι...ἑνωθεῖσα καὶ ἀνακραθεῖσα Mac.Aeg.*hom.*19.10(M.34.641A); ἐν τῇ ἀναστάσει τὰ σώματα ...τῇ δόξῃ ἐκείνῃ ἀνακραθήσονται *ib.*5.11(516D); **c.** in eucharist ἵνα ταύτῃ [sc. ζύμῃ] τρεφόμενοι, καὶ τὴν προτέραν ἀποθέμενοι τὴν νεκράν, εἰς τὴν ζῶσαν καὶ ἀθάνατον διὰ τῆς τραπέζης ἀνακερασθῶμεν ταύτης Chrys.*hom.24.2 in 1Cor.*(10.214C).

***ἀνακερατίζω,** *butt with horns*, Meth.*symp.*8.13(p.98.8; M.18.160C).

ἀνακεφαλαι-όω, *sum up*; **1.** in words, Thphl.Ant.*Autol.*3.1(M.6.1121A); Iren.*haer.*1.9.2(M.7.541A); Or.*Jo.*5.6(p.103.27; M.14.192D); μετὰ τὴν ἀνάστασιν ~ωσάμενον [sc. Christ] τοῖς ἑαυτοῦ τὸ μυστήριον Eun.*exp.fid.*2(p.258); **2.** more gen.; **a.** *sum up, concentrate* under one head ὁ υἱὸς τοῦ θεοῦ εἰς τοῦτο...ἦλθεν ἵνα τὸ τέλειον τῶν ἁμαρτιῶν ~ώσῃ τοῖς διώξασιν...τοὺς προφήτας αὐτοῦ *Barn.*5.11; *balance* accounts, Or.*comm.in Eph.*1:10(p.241); πάντα ~οῦσθαι τὸν νόμον ἐν αὐτῷ [sc. virtue of ἀμνησικακία] id.*or.*9(p.319.10; M.11.445A); Eus.*p.e.*6.6(249D; M.21.424C); οὐκ εἶπε [i.e. Rom.13:9] πληροῦται ἁπλῶς, ἀλλ' ~οῦται· τουτέστι, συντόμως...τὸ πᾶν ἀπαρτίζεται τῶν ἐντολῶν τὸ ἔργον Chrys.*hom.23.3 in Rom.*(9.690C); καλῶς οὖν τὸ ~οῦται, ἀντὶ τοῦ πάντα ἐκεῖνα τὰ διὰ πολλῶν νενομοθετημένα ὥσπερ τινὰ ἀνακεφαλαίωσιν ἐν τῷ τὸν πλησίον ἀγαπᾶν περιέχεται Thdr.Mops.*Rom.*13:10(p.163.6; M.66.864D); ὅλον...~οῦται [sc. in festival of *Hypapante*] τῆς σαρκώσεως τοῦ Χριστοῦ μυστήριον Hesych.H.*serm.*6(M.93.1468B); **b.** exeg. Eph.1:10 τὸ ὄνομα τῆς ἀνακεφαλαιώσεως εἴρηται ἐπὶ τῶν τραπεζ⟨ι⟩τικῶν καὶ τῶν παραπλησίων συμψηφιζομένων λόγων καὶ εἰς ἓν κεφάλαιον συναγομένων δόσεων καὶ ἀναλωμάτων ἢ λήψεων, ὅθεν οἴομαι καὶ τὸν ἀπόστολον ἐνταῦθα κεχρῆσθαι τῇ λέξει. πολλῶν γὰρ ὄντων λόγων τῆς οἰκονομίας...πάντων...ἀνακεφαλαίωσίς ἐστιν ἐν τῷ Χριστῷ Or.*comm.in Eph.*1:10(p.241); ~ώσασθαι ...ἐστιν...συνάψαι...σπουδάσωμεν ἐγγὺς αὐτῆς γενέσθαι τῆς ἀληθείας ...ἀνακεφαλαίωσις λέγεται καὶ διὰ μακρῶν λεγόμενα εἰς βραχὺ συστεῖλαι...ἐστὶ μὲν γὰρ καὶ τοῦτο· τὰ γὰρ διὰ μακροῦ χρόνου οἰκονομούμενα ἀνεκεφαλαιώσατο ἐν ἑαυτῷ, τουτέστι συνέτεμε. λόγον γὰρ συντελῶν, καὶ συντέμνων ἐν δικαιοσύνῃ, καὶ ἐκεῖνα περιέβαλε, καὶ ἕτερα προσέθηκε. τοῦτό ἐστι ἀνακεφαλαίωσις· ἔστι καὶ...μίαν κεφαλὴν ἅπασιν ἐπέθηκε τὰ κατὰ σάρκα Χριστόν, καὶ ἀγγέλοις καὶ ἀνθρώποις Chrys.*hom.1.4 in Eph.*(11.8D); *unite* ἐπειδὴ ἔπεσεν ὁ πλασθεὶς διὰ τῆς παρακοῆς, καὶ ἀσεβησάντων τῶν ἀνθρώπων ἀπηλλοτριώθη τὰ ἐπουράνια τῶν ἐπιγείων, ἐλθὼν ὁ Χριστὸς πάντα ἀνεκεφαλαιώσατο Sever.*Eph.*1:10(p.306.3); **c.** Trin. ὁ...Παῦλος οὐ διαιρεῖ τὴν τριάδα...τὰ πάντα εἰς ἕνα θεὸν ~οῖ λέγων [1Cor.12:4ff.] Ath.*ep.Serap.*1.30(M.26.600B); μονὰς ἐν τριάδι προσκυνουμένη, καὶ τριὰς εἰς μονάδα ~ουμένη Gr.Naz.*or.*6.22(M.35.749C); Zach.Mit.*opif.*(M.85.1141B); **d.** Christol. τὸ ταυτὸν τοῦ προσώπου, διὰ τῆς...συνδρομῆς ~ούμενον Leont.B.*Nest.et Eut.*1(M.86.1293B); **3.** *recapitulate* in one's person; **a.** in gen. ~ούμενος ἐν αὐτῷ [sc. antichrist] τὴν πρὸ τοῦ κατακλυσμοῦ πᾶσαν κακίαν...καὶ τὴν ἀπὸ τοῦ κατακλυσμοῦ πᾶσαν εἰδωλολατρείαν Iren.*haer.*5.29.2(M.7.1202Af.); μήτι εἰς ἐμὲ ἀνεκεφαλαιώθη ἡ ἱστορία τοῦ Ἀδάμ; *Protev.*13.1(p.26); *V.Zos.*6(p.100.14); **b.** of Christ [crowning with thorns likened to appearance in burning bush] ὁ κύριος...~ούμενος τὴν ἀρχὴν...ὅπως...μιᾶς ἔργον τὰ πάντα δείξῃ δυνάμεως Clem.*paed.*2.8(p.203.20; M.8.488B); as second Adam ἔδει...τὸν ~ούμενον εἰς αὐτόν, ὑπὸ τοῦ θεοῦ πεπλασμένον ἄνθρωπον τὴν αὐτὴν ἐκείνῳ τῆς γεννήσεως ἔχειν ὁμοιότητα Iren.*haer.*3.21.10(M.7.955B); σαρκὸς...ἣν εἰς αὐτὸν ἀνεκεφαλαιώσατο *ib.*3.22.2(958A); ref. Gen.3:15 τὴν ἔχθραν ταύτην ὁ κύριος εἰς ἑαυτὸν ἀνεκεφαλαιώσατο *ib.*4.40.3(1114C); **c.** by restoration, at parousia τὴν ἐκ τῶν οὐρανῶν...παρουσίαν αὐτοῦ ἐπὶ τὸ ~ώσασθαι τὰ πάντα, καὶ ἀναστῆσαι πᾶσαν σάρκα πάσης ἀνθρωπότητος *ib.*1.10.1(549B); exeg. Eph.1:10 τὸ...~ούμενον ἀναλαμβάνεταί πως καὶ οἷον ἀναβιβάζεται πρὸς τὸ ἐν ἀρχαῖς Cyr.*Soph.*44(3.622E); ὁ θεὸς...~ούμενος τὰ πάντα ἐν Χριστῷ, καὶ...τῇ ἀνθρώπου πραγματευόμενος φύσει τὴν εἰς ὅπερ ἦν ἐπάνοδον ἤγουν ἀνακομιδήν id.*Pulch.*(p.38.8; 5^{2}.145D); id.*Jo.*2.1(4.135A); ἀνακεφαλαίωσιν...καλεῖ τὴν σύντομον τῶν πραγμάτων μεταβολὴν Thdt.*Eph.*1:10(3.404); ὅσον ὁ Ἀδὰμ ἁμαρτήσας ἀπεστερήθη τούτων πάντων ἀνανέωσις γέγονεν ἐν Χριστῷ Jo.D.*Eph.*1:9f.(M.95.824D).

ἀνακεφαλαίωσις, ἡ, **1.** *summary* in words; def., Chrys.*hom.1.4 in Eph.*(11.8D) cit. s. ἀνακεφαλαιόω; ἀ. λέγομεν τὸ ἐπαναλαβεῖν ἐν ὀλίγοις τὰ προλεχθέντα Max.*schol.e.h.*1.3(4.117B); ἀ. συντόμῳ...τῶν ἀναγκαίων δογμάτων Cyr.H.*catech.*4.3; Epiph.*rescr.*6(p.161.2; M.41.165A); Thdt.*Trin.*28 tit.(M.75.1188B); **2.** *totalling* of accounts, Or.*comm.in Eph.*1:10(p.241) cit. s. ἀνακεφαλαιόω; **3.** *list* ἀ. τῶν ἀναγνώσεων καὶ ὧν ἔχουσι κεφαλαίων Euthal.Diac.*epp.Paul.*(M.85.716A); **4.** *summing up, concentration* in one person ἀ. γίνεται πάσης ἀδικίας...ἵνα ἐν αὐτῷ [sc. antichrist]...συγκλεισθεῖσα πᾶσα δύναμις ἀποστατικὴ κατὰ τὴν κάμινον ὀλισθῇ τοῦ πυρός Iren.*haer.*5.29.2(M.7.1201C); **5.** *recapitulation* τὸ πέμπτον βιβλίον τοῦ νόμου ἀ. ἐστι τῶν πρὸ αὐτοῦ γραφέντων Hipp.*haer.*6.16(p.142.15; M.16.3218C); ref. baptism ὁ Χριστὸς κενώσας ἑαυτόν, ἵνα χωρηθῇ κατὰ τὴν ἀ. ... τοῦ πάθους Meth.*symp.*3.8(p.36.2; M.18.73B); of OT types recapitulated in NT antitype πάντα γὰρ ὅσα ἐν τῇ παλαιᾷ λατρείᾳ γεγένηται εἰς τὸν σωτῆρα τὴν ἀ. φέρει...πάντα εἰς αὐτὸν τὴν ἀναφορὰν ἔχει ‡Chrys.*mart.*1(3.812C); **6.** *renewal, restoration* τῆς φύσεως ἀνανέωσίν τε καὶ ἀ. ‡Chrys.*pasch.*7(8.279D); in Christ, ref. 2Cor.5:17, Cyr.*Mich.*46 (3.434D); ref. Eph.1:10, id.*glaph.Gen.*1(1.3A); ‡Hipp.*Ber.Hel.*2(M.10.833B); τὴν ἐν Χριστῷ πάντων ἀ. καὶ θέωσιν ἐν ἑαυτῷ τῶν οὐ θείων φύσεων Leont.H.*Nest.*3.1(M.86.1605A).

***ἀνακεφαλίζω,** *hold up one's head, revive*, Call.*v.Hyp.*(p.108); Thphn.*chron.*p.155(M.108.420A).

***ἀνακεχωρημένως,** *in retirement*, Eus.*Ps.*28:1f.(M.23.253D).

***ἀνακηρυκτέον,** *one must extol*, Isid.Pel.*epp.*5.386(M.78.1557C).

§**ἀνακήρυκτος,** *loudly proclaimed, extolled*, Nil.*epp.*3.43(M.79.412C); Dion.Ar.*ep.*8.1(M.3.1085A).

ἀνακήρυξις, ἡ, *proclamation*; as bishop, Gr.Nyss.*v.Gr.Thaum.*(M.46.933D); synonym for ἀνάρρησις at ordination, Max.*schol.e.h.*5.3.1(M.4.165C); of doctrine τὴν τοῦ ὁμοουσίου ἀ. Philost.*h.e.*1.4 (M.65.464A).

ἀνακηρύσσω, *extol*, Chrys.*fr.Job* 1:8(M.64.525D); *ib.*1:20(537C).

***ἀνακικλήσκ-ω,** **1.** *call* by a name τοὺς ὀνόματι 'θεοὺς' ~ομένους Eust.*engast.*10(p.29.30; M.18.632B); **2.** *call back, recall* οὐδέπω πεισθήσομαι Ἰουδαίους ~εσθαι ‡Caes.Naz.*dial.*197(M.38.1189).

***ἀνακινητικός,** *able to stir up* εἴπερ...οἱ...σεραφὶμ ἐμπρησταὶ καὶ θερμαίνοντες ὑπὸ τῆς θεολογίας ὠνομάσθησαν...[sc. it is because] τοῦ θείου μύρου...ἀ. ἔχουσι δυνάμεις Dion.Ar.*e.h.*4.3.10(M.3.481C).

***ἀνακιρν-άω** (also ἀνακίρνημι = ἀνακεράννυμι, q.v.); **1.** *mingle, blend* ποταμοὺς...θαλάττης ~ᾶσθαι Isid.Pel.*epp.*4.192(M.78.1280D); fig., of a mixed cup τὰ ἀγαθὰ τοῖς πονηροῖς ἀ. Or.*sel.in Ps.*74:9 (M.12.1536A); met., *mix together, confuse* in the mind τὴν τῶν ὁμοουσίων εἰς ἑαυτὴν ~ᾶσθαι φύσιν Cyr.*Jo.*1.4(4.37C); **2.** *unite* ἀ. ... αὐτοὺς τῇ τῆς ἀγάπης ἰσοτιμίᾳ Chrys.*hom.31.3 in Rom.*(9.749B); morally ὁ ὁμολογῶν τινα...~ᾶται καὶ ἑνοῦται τῷ ὁμολογουμένῳ Or.*mart.*10(p.10.21; M.11.576C); Christol. τῷ θεῷ τῆς ἡμετέρας γενέσεως τὴν ἔνθεον ἀ. μεγαλουργίαν Eus.*d.e.*4.10(p.169.1; M.22.281A); rejected by Cyr. as parallel of συγχέω: οὐ συγχέων ἢ ~ῶν τὰς φύσεις Cyr.*Nest.*2.6(p.42.36; 6.45E); *ib.*4.6(p.90.22; 118B) cit. s. συγχέω; οὐ συγχέουσα τὰς φύσεις, οὔτε μὴν ~ῶσα πρός γε τὸ δεῖν ἑκατέραν ἑτεροίως ἔχειν ἢ ὅπερ ἐστίν id.*apol.Thdt.*3(p.118.25; 6.212C); man with God τῆς ψυχῆς...τῷ πνεύματι ~ωμένης Mac.Aeg.*hom.*1.3 (M.34.453B); in eucharist οἱ μὴ παρέχοντες ἐπιτήδειον τὸ σῶμα πρὸς τὴν ἀνάκρασιν τοῦ σώματος αὐτοῦ ὅπερ ἡμῖν ἔδωκεν, ἵνα πρὸς αὐτὸ κιρνάμενοι, πρὸς τὸ πνεῦμα τὸ ἅγιον ~ώμεθα ‡Chrys.*pasch.*2(8.256B); [Jo.6:56] δηλῶν, ὅτι ἐν αὐτῷ ~ᾶται Chrys.*hom.47.1 in Jo.*(8.275D).

ἀνακίρνη-μι, **1.** *mingle, blend*, fig. ἐπωφελὴς...ἡ μῖξις, καθάπερ ἀνακιρναμένου τοῦ πάθους εἰς ἀφθαρσίαν· ἐξορροῦται γὰρ ὑπὸ τοῦ οἴνου τὸ γάλα καὶ σχίζεται, καὶ ὅτιπερ αὐτοῦ νόθον, τοῦτ' ἀποχετεύεται Clem.*paed.*1.6(p.120.26; M.8.312A); (Gnost.) of demons with souls, *Hom.Clem.*9.9; *ib.*9.11; **2.** Christol. [Mt.28:18] λαβόντος τοῦ κατὰ τὸν σωτῆρα ἀνθρώπου τὴν ἐξουσίαν τῶν ἐν οὐρανῷ οἷον τῶν ἐνυπαρχόντων τῷ μονογενεῖ, ἵνα αὐτῷ κοινωνῇ, ἀνακιρνάμενος ἐκείνου τῇ θεότητι καὶ ἑνούμενος αὐτῷ Or.*or.*26.4(p.362.2; M.11.504A); Gr.Nyss.*or.catech.*27(p.101.11; M.45.69C) cit. s. συνανάκρασις; συνδεδραμηκότων δὲ ὥσπερ εἰς ἑνότητα φυσικὴν καὶ οἷον ἀνακιρνάντων ἀλλήλοιν ὅπερ ἂν ὡς ἴδιον ἑκατέρῳ προσῇ Cyr.*ep.*1(p.15.32; 5^{2}.9B); ἐσκήνωσε... ἐν ἡμῖν σαρκὶ καὶ αἵματι θεοπρεπῶς...τὴν ἰδίαν φύσιν οἱονεί πως ἀνακιρνάς id.*hom.pasch.*17.2(5^{2}.228A); but condemned by Cyr. in Apollinarian sense τὰ ἀλλήλοις ἀνακιρνάμενα τῶν ὑγρῶν...ὃ μὲν ἦσάν εἰσι καθαρῶς οὐκέτι id.*synous.*10(p.486.15; M.76.1433D note 1); **3.** *unite* οἱ ἐκ πίστεως...τοῖς ἐκ νόμου...εἰς ἑνότητα τὴν πνευματικὴν ...ἀνακιρνάμενοι id.*Mich.*72(3.473B); ~σι [sc. kiss of peace] τὰς ψυχὰς ἀλλήλαις, καὶ πᾶσαν ἀμνησικακίαν αὐταῖς μνηστεύεται. σημεῖον τοίνυν ἐστὶ τὸ φίλημα, τοῦ ἀνακραθῆναι τὰς ψυχάς Cyr.H.*catech.*23.3.

***ἀνακλαστάριον, τό,** *phial* (opened by breaking the neck), *Mir.Artem.*30(p.43.6); Gr.Mag.*dial.*(tr.Zach.)2.28(M.*PL*.66.185A).

ἀνακλ-άω, **1.** *bend back* ~ῶσι...τὰς κεφαλάς Clem.*paed.*2.2(p.176.17; M.8.429A); **2.** *turn back, restore* to normal state ὁπότε τῶν ἐκτὸς αἱ πλεονεξίαι αὖθις πρὸς ἰσότητα τοῖς λογισμοῖς ~ῶνται Tit. Bost.*Man*.2.10(M.18.1153B); **3.** *reflect*, lit. and met.; sunlight, Hipp. *haer*.4.31(p.57.20; M.16.3094C); of reflection of eyes in a polished surface, compared with light of the mind reflected by scriptures, ‡Bas.*struct.hom*.1.1(1.324B; M.30.12A); of effect of body on soul ἡ ἀπὸ τῆς σαρκὸς τῇ ψυχῇ ~ωμένη συμπάθεια ‡Caes.Naz.*dial*.140(M.38.1056); **4.** *double up* with laughter, Chrys.*oppugn*.1.3(1.48B); **5.** in music, '*break up*' the metre, *syncopate* μελῳδικῶς ~ᾶν ‡Chrys. *ascet.facet*.(1.812C).

ἀνάκλησις, ἡ, A. *calling on*; **1.** *invocation*; *salutation*; at dedication of imperial statues, Soz.*h.e*.8.20.1(M.67.1568B); **2.** *summons* from earth to heaven ἤγγικεν...ἡ ἡμετέρα ἀ.· ὁρῶ γὰρ τὸν Χριστόν μου καλοῦντα ἐμέ *A.(Pass.)Petr.et Paul*.73(p.164.1); Meth.*symp*.8.2 (p.83.9; M.18.141A).

B. *calling back*; **1.** in gen.; **a.** *recall, restoration*; from exile, Philost.*h.e*.9.8(M.65.576A); from captivity, Thdt.*Ps*.14:1(1.685, v.l. ἐπανάκλησιν); from death to life ἐκ μὲν τῶν δύο τόπων [sc. Hades and the tomb] τὴν ἀ. ‡Ath.*Apoll*.1.14(M.26.1120A); Euthal.Diac.*Ac*.29 (M.85.660B); **b.** of abstracts οὔτε μὴν εἰς χρόνους μακροὺς ἀ. ἔσεσθαι τῆς ἐλπίδος Cyr.*Is*.4.5(2.704C); *revoking* ὦ μεσημβρία τῆς δειλινῆς ἐν παραδείσῳ καταδίκης ἀ. Procl.CP *or*.11.4(M.65.785C); *renewing* μετάνοιά ἐστιν ἀ. βαπτίσματος Jo.Clim.*scal*.5(M.88.764B); **2.** spiritual *restoration* or *recall*; **a.** of Jews Ἠλίας...εἰς τὴν ἀ. τοῦ Ἰσραὴλ κεῖται προφήτης Vict.*Mc*.9:2(p.354.14); ἔσται καὶ τῶν Ἰσραηλιτῶν ἐν ὑστέροις ἀ., εἰ καὶ ἐν ἀρχῇ λεῖμμα μόνον ἐγένετο Proc.G.*Is*.1:7f. (M.87.1840C); ‡Caes.Naz.*dial*.197(M.38.1188); **b.** of mankind through Christ ὑπὲρ τῆς ἀ. ἡμῶν...τὸ τοῦ σταυροῦ ξύλον...ὑπεδέξατο *A.(Pass.) Andr*.3(p.5.27); *A.Xanthipp*.19(p.71.32); Ath.*inc*.7.4(M.25.108D); opp. παρατροπή, Gr.Nyss.*or.catech*.8(p.49.17; M.45.37C) cit. s. παρατροπή; τῇ ἀ. τῶν ἀνθρώπων...ἦν διὰ τοῦ γενέσθαι ἡμῶν πρωτότοκος πάλιν εἰς τὴν ἐξ ἀρχῆς χάριν ἀνεκαλέσατο id.*Eun*.4(2 p.63.23; M.45. 636A); Cosm.Ind.*top*.2(M.88.121A); ξύλον γὰρ καὶ γυνὴ ἐγένοντο ἀφορμὴ τῆς ἐξορίας...νῦν δὲ γυνὴ καὶ ξύλον γίνεταί σοι ἀ. Jo.Eub. *concept.BMV* 21(M.96.1496B); ‡Jo.D.*Artem*.27(M.96.1276B); **c.** of individual from sin ἀνακάλεσαι με τὴν ταπεινήν, ὁ εἰς πολλῶν ἁμαρτωλῶν ἀ. ἀποσταλείς *A.Xanthipp*.29(p.79.12); πάντων ἐστὶν...ζωή· καὶ τῶν μὲν ἀποπιπτόντων αὐτῆς ἀ. τε καὶ ἀνάστασις Dion.Ar.*d.n*.1.3 (M.3.589B).

ἀνακλητικός, *fit for summoning* or *exhorting*, *A.Xanthipp*.1(p.58. 19).

ἀνάκλητος, *called back*, Eus.*m.P*.2(p.909.19; M.20.1468A).

ἀνακλίνω, *make to rest upon*, hence *give over to*, Nil.*Eulog*.8(M.79. 1104D).

ἀνακλώθω, *unravel the thread*; of life as spun by Fates, ‡Just. *qu.et resp*.146(M.6.1400C).

ἀνακμάζω, *break out afresh*; in weeping, Germ.CP *or*.2(M.98.269A).

ἀνακοίνωσις, ἡ, *communication*, Chrys.*serm.2.1 in Gen*.(4.652C).

***ἀνακολαφή, ἡ,** *embroidery*; on a deacon's tunicle, ‡Sophr.H. *liturg*.7(M.87.3988B).

***ἀνακολουθέω,** Or.*comm.ser.63 in Mt*.(M.17.304B) for ἀντανακολουθέω (p.146.4).

ἀνακόλουθος, *inconsequent*, hence *lawless, unruly* κακῇ ὥρᾳ εἰσήλθατε ὧδε, προπετεῖς, ἀ. *Pers*.(p.7.11).

ἀνακομάω, *get fresh hair*, Cyr.*ador*.16(1.582C).

ἀνακομιδή, ἡ, 1. *return*, Tat.*orat*.39(p.40.19; M.6.884A); Clem. *str*.7.11(p.46.3; M.9.488C); Philost.*h.e*.3.6(M.65.489A); τὴν ἐκ θανάτου καὶ φθορᾶς ἀ. ... εἰς ἀφθαρσίαν Cyr.*inc.unigen*.(5[1].692B); id.*Pulch*. (p.38.10; 6[2].145D) cit. s. ἀνακεφαλαιόω; **2.** *laying up, deposition*; of relics, ‡Jo.D.*Artem*.9(M.96.1260B).

ἀνακομίζω, 1. *carry* or *bring up*; hence **a.** *raise*; of Christ's flesh raised to heaven, Meth.*symp*.7.8(p.79.11; M.18.136B); met., *exalt*, Cyr.*Chr.un*.(5[1].730B); **b.** *bring, offer*; sacrifices, Meth.*symp*.5.6(p.61. 12; 109A); τῷ Χριστῷ τὴν ᾠδὴν ἀ. Cyr.*Ps*.17:1(M.69.820C); id.*ador*. 15(1.520B); **c.** *lay up, deposit*; relics, Philost.*h.e*.3.2(M.65.481A); **2.** *bring back, restore* ἀνθρωπότητος ἀνακομισθείσης εἰς ἀφθαρσίαν Cyr.*Abac*.34(3.549C); id.*Rom*.5:3(p.182.11; M.74.784A).

ἀνακοντίζω, *hurl forth, aim*, Nonn.*par.Jo*.21:8(M.43.916C); met., *refer* ὁ ἀπόστολος...εἰς Χριστὸν ἀνηκόντισε τὰ κατὰ τὸν Ἀδάμ Meth. *symp*.3.8(p.35.10; M.18.73A).

ἀνακοπή, ἡ, *checking*; of sins by law and fear, Clem.*paed*.1.11 (p.147.19; M.8.365B); id.*str*.3.12(p.237.4; M.8.1189B).

ἀνακόπτω, 1. *check, restrain*; med., *restrain oneself, refrain*, Polyc.*ep*.5.3; **2.** *castrate*, Diod.*Ex*.31:16(M.33.1585A).

ἀνακοσμέω, *adorn anew, restore*, Meth.*res*.1.43(p.291.9; M.18. 272C; v.l. ἀνακοσμοποιηθῆναι); *ib*.1.44(p.293.7; M.41.1113D).

***ἀνακοσμοποιέω,** v. foreg.

ἀνακουφίζ-ω, 1. *lift up, raise*, met. τῇ ἀρετῇ ~όμενοι εἰς τὰ ἐπουράνια Nil.*epp*.2.199(M.79.304D); Cyr.*Mich*.17(3.406D); φύσις [sc. τοῦ Χριστοῦ] ἀ. ... πρὸς τὸ ἴδιον ἀγαθὸν τὸ κάτω πίπτον ἀεί id.*Jo*.11. 12(4.1002A); **2.** *hold up, support*, ‡Nil.*perist*.11.5(M.79.909D).

[*]**ἀνακοχλάζ-ω,** = ἀνακαχλάζω *boil up, seethe* ~ειν [v.l. ἀνακογχυλιάζειν] τὸ ὕδωρ Gr.Nyss.*anim.et res*.(M.46.37A); λέβητι ~οντι Epiph.*exp.fid*.11(p.511.25, v.l. καχλάζοντι M.42.801C); of waters at Christ's baptism καταβάντων αὐτῶν ἐπὶ τὸ ὕδωρ ἀνεκόχλασαν [v.l. ἀνεκάχλασαν] τὰ ὕδατα *Chron.Pasch*.p.225(M.92.548A); ἀνακαχλάζειν Olymp.*Job* 30:27(M.93.317C).

***ἀνακράκτης, ὁ,** *clamorous person*, Bas.*renunt*.6(2.208B; M.31. 640C).

ἀνάκρασις, ἡ, *mixture, blending, union*; **1.** in gen., Isid.Pel.*epp*. 1.461(M.78.436B); of human friendship τῆς ὑπὲρ ἀδελφοὺς ἀ. Gr. Naz.*or*.10.2(M.35.829A); of interpenetration of sensible and intelligible things in creation, Gr.Nyss.*or.catech*.6(p.30.7; M.45.25C); **2.** Christol., Or.*Cels*.3.41(p.237.9; M.11.975A) cit. s. προσλαμβάνω; favourite term of Gr. Nyss. τὸν δὲ τῆς ἀ. τρόπον τοῦ θείου πρὸς τὸν ἄνθρωπον συνιδεῖν οὐ χωροῦμεν Gr.Nyss.*or.catech*.11(p.57.16; M.45. 44B); id.*Eun*.5(2 p.117.7; M.45.697B); *ib*.(p.117.22; 697C); *ib*.6(2 p.144.13; 729C) cit. s. μεταποιέω; id.*ep*.3(M.46.1020C); id.*hom.4 in Cant*.(M.44.836D); likened to ἀ. of fire and iron, Apoll.*fr*. 128(p.238.26)ap.Thdt.*eran*.2(4.171); θεότητος...καὶ ἀνθρωπότητος... ἀπερινόητος ὁ τῆς ἀ. τρόπος Cyr.*hom.pasch*.8(5[2].103A); used of Apollinarian mixture of divine and human natures in Christ σύγχυσίν τινα καὶ ἀ., καὶ τροπὴν τὴν εἰς σάρκα τοῦ θεοῦ λόγου κατηχῶν Isid. Pel.*epp*.1.496(M.78.452C); rejected by some later orthodox writers, e.g. τὴν ἕνωσιν γεγενῆσθαι λέγοντες, οὐ κατὰ...ἀ. φάσκομεν Jo.D. *Jacob*.81(M.94.1480A); Ambr.*ib*.(1496A) cit. s. συγχέω; though used by others, Leont.B.*Nest.et Eut*.2(M.86.1353B) cit. s. ἕνωσις; τὴν δὲ ἕνωσιν αὐτοῦ τοῦ λόγου οὐσιώδους ἀνακράσεως Sophr.H.*ep.syn*.(M. 87.3168A); ἡ ἕνωσις...οὐ τῶν φύσεων ἀλλοιωθεισῶν...ἀλλὰ κατὰ τὸν τῆς ἀ. ... τρόπον, καθ' ὃ ἂν εἴποι τις αὐτὸν θεὸν καὶ ἄνθρωπον Anast. Ant.*fr*.ap.*Doct.Patr*.20(p.126.18; M.89.1286B); **3.** of union of Christ with H. Ghost ὁ...σπόγγος [given to Christ on Cross]...τὴν...τοῦ ἁγίου πνεύματος ἐν αὐτῷ γενομένην ἀ. ἀνέφηνε ‡Dion.Al.*fr.in Lc*. *22:42*(p.240.12); **4.** of eucharistic union, esp. between human body and eucharistic elements τὸ δὲ σῶμα ἕτερον τρόπον [opp. soul, which is saved by faith in baptism] ἐν μετουσίᾳ τε καὶ ἀ. τοῦ σῴζοντος γίνεται Gr.Nyss.*or.catech*.37(p.142.3; M.45.93A); cf.id.*hom. 8 in Eccl*.(M.44.737D); οὐχ ἁπλῶς μίγνυμαί σοι, ἀλλὰ συμπλέκομαι... ἵνα πολλὴ ἡ ἀ. γένηται Chrys.*hom.15.4 in 1Tim*.(11.641D); ‡Chrys. *pasch*.2(8.256B) cit. s. ἀνακιρνάω; **5.** of intellectual and myst. union; Gnost. τὴν ἀ. τὴν πρὸς τὸ πλήρωμα αὐτῆς Heracleon ap. Or.*Jo*.13.11(p.235.22; M.14.416B); intellectual οὐσία τοῦ γινώσκοντος κατὰ ἀ. ἀδιάστατον γενομένη Clem.*str*.4.22(p.308.26; M.8.1345C); of spiritual affinity, Cyr.*Ps*.36:18(M.69.936A); myst. ἑπόμενος τῷ καλοῦντι...ἄξιον ἑαυτὸν παρασχὼν...κατὰ ἀ. ἔχειν τὴν δύναμιν τοῦ θεοῦ Clem.*str*.7.12(p.56.27; M.9.509B); τῆς ἀνθρωπίνης ψυχῆς ἡ πρὸς τὸ θεῖόν ἐστιν ἀ. Gr.Nyss.*hom.1 in Cant*.(M.44.772A); *ib*.4(836D); with H. Ghost ἀπὸ τῆς...ἀ. τοῦ ἁγίου πνεύματος, εἰς ἣν μόνον ἡ πιστὴ ψυχὴ ἀναπαύεσθαι δύναται Mac.Aeg.*hom*.5.7(M.34.512D).

ἀνακραυγάζω, *cry aloud*, Chrys.*hom.17.5 in Heb*.(12.171A); Gel. Cyz.*h.e*.2.22.17.

ἀνακρίνω, 1. *examine closely*; Chrys.*hom.37.1 in Ac*.(9.281A); **2.** *judge* and so *condemn*, Epiph.*haer*.55.5(p.330.10; M.41.980C); *ib*. 76.24(p.371.14; M.42.564B) citt. s. πνευματικῶς; *ib*.69.19(p.168.16; 229D) cit. s. σαρκικός; **3.** *put off, delay* ἀνακριθεὶς τοῦ λαβεῖν τὴν αἴτησίν σου Ephr.3.223D.

ἀνάκρουσις, ἡ, *striking up* ὕμνων Or.*Ps*.48:5(p.49).

***ἀνακρουστόν,** sens. dub., ref. movement of shuttle to and fro in weaving ἱμάτιον τέχνῃ τινὶ...ἀ. ὑφαινόμενον Isid.Pel.*epp*.1.74(M.78. 233B).

ἀνακρού-ω, 1. *stop, check, restrain*; by words, Clem.*paed*.2.1 (p.162.16; M.8.307A); ἀ. τοὺς ἐρεθισμοὺς Or.*princ*.3.1.5(4; p.199.12; M.11.253A); med., Epiph.*haer*.proem.3(p.172.1; M.41.177C); **2.** *strike* hands together, *clap*, Hipp.*haer*.4.46(p.68.27; M.16.3110D); in music, Chrys.*ep*.2.3(3.538D); abs., *play*, Eus.*d.e*.4.13(p.172.26; M.22.288B); Thdt.*Ps*.91:4(1.1265); **3.** *strike up* ~ειν μέλος Cyr.*Ps*.32:2(M.69. 872A); med., Chrys.*pan.Rom*.2.2(2.620B); **4.** *thrust up*, met. τῆς πλεονεξίας μνήμην...~εσθαι καὶ ἀνασκάπτεσθαι ποιεῖς διὰ τῆς οἰκίας id.*hom.10.4 in 1Thess*.(11.500C).

***ἀνάκρυπτος,** *hidden* προφητεία Eus.*e.th*.2.18(p.121.29; M.24.940C).

ἀνακτάομαι, 1. *refresh, revive*; morally and spiritually ἀνακτήσασθε ἑαυτοὺς ἐν πίστει, ὅ ἐστιν σὰρξ τοῦ κυρίου καὶ ἐν ἀγάπῃ, ὅ ἐστιν αἷμα Ign.*Trall*.8.1; Or.*exp.in Pr*.19:17(M.17.208D); intrans., *recover oneself, revive* παραπτώματι, ἐξ οὗ μηκέτι παρὸν αὐτῷ ἀ. Mac.Aeg.*elev*.10(M.34.897B); Chrys.*hom.6.4 in 2Tim*(11.691B); **2.** *restore*, Hipp.*Dan*.4.26.8.

ἀνακτέον, *one must refer*; in spiritual interpretation of scripture, Or.*fr.57 in Jo*.(p.531.1).

ἀνάκτησις, ἡ, 1. *regaining*, of men through Cross αὕτη ἡ κόλασις μυστήριόν ἐστιν τῆς ἀνθρωπίνης ἀ. *A.(Pass.)Andr*.4(p.9.21); ‡Ath. *Apoll*.1.6(M.26.1104B); **2.** *recovery* of strength; *refreshing*, Const. Diac.*laud*.41(M.88.528A); Areth.*Apoc*.66(M.106.764C); **3.** *means of recovery*, Jo.VI CP *ep*.(M.96.1432C).

ἀνακτίζ-ω, 1. *rebuild*; fig., of men as rebuilt on foundation of Christ, Ath.*Ar*.2.77(M.26.309C); Cyr.*thes*.(5^{1}.175B); **2.** *recreate, remake*; **a.** eschatol., the universe, Meth.*res*.1.48(p.301.7, v.l. ἀνακαινισθῇ M.18.276C); ‡Just.*qu.Gr*.4(M.6.1472C); **b.** the body after death, Ast.Am.*hom*.1(M.40.169C); ‡Just.*qu.Gr*.26(1485A); **c.** of redemption: of universe by Christ, Ath.*inc*.7.5(M.25.109A); εὐδόκησεν...ἀνακεφαλαιώσασθαι τὰ πάντα ἐν τῷ Χριστῷ καὶ ἀ. τὸ ποιηθὲν εἰς τὸ ἀπ' ἀρχῆς Cyr.*ador*.2(1.69C); Cosm.Ind.*top*.5(M.88.237D); of mankind, Ath.*Ar*.2.66(M.26.288A); ἀνεκτίσθημεν γὰρ ἐν Χριστῷ τῇ ἀνακαινώσει τοῦ νοὸς ἡμῶν Cyr.*Ps*.50:12(M.69.1099A); δεύτερος...Ἀδὰμ...ἀπαρχὴ τῶν ~ομένων εἰς καινότητα ζωῆς id.*Jo*.11.10(4.991B); τὴν δευτέραν [sc. δημιουργίαν] καθ' ἣν ~όμεθα διὰ τῆς ἀναστάσεως Thdr.Mops.*Eph*.2:10(p.146.23; M.66.916B); of individual soul, Clem. *str*.7.16(p.66.16; M.9.529B); **d.** through bestowal of H. Ghost (ref. Jo.20:22), Didym.*Trin*.2.7(M.39.569A); Cyr.*glaph.Dt*.(1.432D); in gen. ὁ...λαβὼν αὐτὸ ἀνακτισθήσεται Or.*Jo*.13.23(24; p.247.27; M.14. 437C); Cyr.*Jo*.11.12(4.1001E); exeg. Is.54:16 τινὲς δὲ τὸ 'ἔκτισα', ἐπὶ τοῦ 'ἀνέκτισα', παρειλήφασιν. δηλοῖ δὲ τὸν δι' ἁγίου πνεύματος ἀνακαινισμόν Proc.G.*Is*.54:1ff.(M.87.2545B); esp. in baptism πνεῦμα...τὸ ~ον διὰ βαπτίσματος, δι' ἀναστάσεως Gr.Naz.*or*.31.29(p.184.2; M.36. 165C); Didym.*Trin*.2.12(M.39.672B); Cyr.*Jo*.5.2(4.475B); ἐκ τῆς τριάδος ~όμεθα, ὑφ' ἧσπερ ἐκτίσμεθα Proc.G.*Gen*.1:9f.(M.87.77D); cf. ἡ ψυχή...διὰ τοῦ βαπτίσματος ἀνενεώθη, ὡσανεὶ ἀνακτισθεῖσα πάλιν Chrys.*comm.in Gal*.6:16(10.729A); ~όμενοι ἐντεῦθεν ἤδη...κατὰ τύπον ἐλπίδι τῶν προσδοκωμένων Thdr.Mops.*Eph*.4:22f.(p.173.20); **3.** *build* βουλόμενος ὁ Σολομῶν...ἀ. καὶ οἰκοδομῆσαι τὴν Σιών *T.Sal*. 1.1(p.6*.8); **4.** *brick up* ἐν ἄντρῳ τινὶ τοῦτον ἀ. *Ep.Tib*.(p.80.20).

***ἀνακτικός,** *leading up*, v.l. for ἀνεκτικός *enduring, patient* διδαχῆς ἀ. Euthal.Diac.*epp.Paul*.(M.85.768C).

ἀνάκτισις, ἡ, 1. *rebuilding*; of Temple, Eus.*Ps*.126(M.24.20B); Proc.G.*Is*.44:24ff.(M.87.2416C); **2.** *recreating, remaking*; **a.** lit.; eschatol., of the world, ‡Just.*qu.et resp*.30(M.6.1277C); ‡Just.*qu.Gr*. 15.10(M.6.1481A); of dead in resurrection, Thdt.*Ezech*.37:8(2.996); οἱ δὲ ἀνιστάμενοι κατὰ ἀ. ἀνίστανται ‡Just.*qu.Gr*.15.7(1480C); **b.** of redemption of universe in Christ οὐ γὰρ τὴν πρώτην λέγει κτίσιν, ἀλλὰ τὴν ἐν αὐτῷ γενομένην ἀ., καθ' ἣν τὰ πάντα διαλελυμένα εἰς συμφωνίαν ἤχθη μίαν Thdr.Mops.*Col*.1:16(M.66.928B); περὶ τῆς ἐν Χριστῷ κτίσεως καὶ ἀ. τῆς κατὰ συνάφειαν θεοῦ Euthal.Diac.*epp. Paul*.(M.85.768C); δι' οὗ γίνεται...τῆς ἀ. καὶ ἀναστάσεως ἡ ἀρχή Cosm.Ind.*top*.2(M.88.121B); *ib*.(128A); of men μετατυπωθῆναι...κατὰ τὴν ἐκ τῆς διαθήκης ἀ. τε καὶ ἀνανέωσιν Clem.*str*.4.23(p.314.17; M.8.1357C); οὗπερ τὴν ἀ. ἐν ἑαυτῷ ποιούμενος ὁ σωτήρ Gel.Cyz.*h.e*. 2.17.28(M.85.1272A); Leont.H.*Nest*.1.18(M.86.1469B) cit. s. αὐτουργικῶς; **3.** *repairing* κανδήλης ἀ. Gr.Mag.*dial*.(tr.Zach.)1.7(M.*PL*.77. 183C).

***ἀνακτόκος, ἡ,** *mother of a prince*; of BMV, Leont.H.*Nest*.4.37 (M.86.1712A) prob. for ἀνακτοτόκος.

[*]ἀνακτορεῖον (ἀνακτόριον), τό, *temple*, Hipp.*haer*.5.8(p.96.21; M. 16.3151A); ἀνακτόριον, Eudoc.*Cypr*.1.228(M.85.841A).

ἀνακτόρεος, = ἀνακτόριος, *belonging to the emperor, royal*, Paul. Sil.*Soph*.244(M.86.2129A).

ἀνακτορία, ἡ, *lordship, rule*, *Orac.Sib*.4.66.

ἀνάκτορον, τό, *royal dwelling-place*; of house of God; **1.** Jewish Temple, Isid.Pel.*epp*.1.496(M.78.452C); of Holy of Holies τὰ δὲ ἔνδον ἄψαυστα ἦν, καὶ ἄδυτα, καὶ ἀ. Thdt.*qu.60 in Ex*.(1.162); id.*qu.26 in 3Reg*.(1.468); id.*qu.in 2Par*.proem.(1.570); **2.** of a church, Paul. Sil.*Soph*.884(M.86.2152B); of sanctuary in a church, Gr.Nyss.*ep*. 1(M.46.1004A); Thdt.*h.e*.5.18.20(3.1050); met., Eus.*l.C*.proem.4 (p.196.1; M.20.1317B); **3.** of heaven ἀ. τοκῆος Synes.*hymn*.1.107 (p.62; M.66.1589).

ἀνακτοτελέστης, ὁ, *president of the mysteries*, Clem.*prot*.2(p.15.5; M.8.81A).

***ἀνακτυπέω,** *resound*, Cyr.*Is*.1.3(2.69A).

ἀνακυΐσκω, *impregnate again*, met., *make fruitful again* δι' ἐκείνων [sc. martyrs] οἱ πλείους τῶν ἠρνημένων...ἀνεκυΐσκοντο *Ep. Lugd*.ap.Eus.*h.e*.5.1.46(M.20.425B).

***ἀνακύκλημα, τό,** *revolution*; of seasons, Cyr.*ador*.6(1.207A); of the course of an argument λόγος...διὰ τῶν αὐτῶν ἀ. στρεφόμενος id.*Jo*.2.1(4.154A).

ἀνακύκλησις, ἡ, *interchange*, Trin. λόγον...μῖξίν τινα τῶν ὑποστάσεων καὶ ἀ. κατασκευάζοντα Gr.Nyss.*tres dii*(M.45.133B).

ἀνακυκλόω, = ἀνακυκλέω, *repeat*, Cyr.*ador*.13(1.463A).

***ἀνακυλινδέομαι,** *whirl round*, *T.Sal*.14.1(M.122.1336C).

***ἀνακυλισμός, ὁ,** *whirling round* Γελγέλ...καθ' Ἑβραΐδα ἀ. ... σημαίνει Dion.Ar.*c.h*.15.9(M.3.337D).

ἀνακυλί-ω, 1. *roll, revolve*, met. ἐπὶ τὸν αὐτὸν βόρβορον [sc. of heresy] ἀνεκυλίοντο Hipp.*haer*.9.7(p.241.3; M.16.3371A); ἀπὸ κακῶν εἰς κακὰ ~ομένη Or.*fr.in Pr*.5:6(M.17.157C); **2.** *roll* the eyes in astonishment, Marc.Diac.*v.Porph*.6(p.6.25); *turn over* ἱστορίας καὶ τὰ ἑκάστου ἔτους ~οντες συντάγματα Hier.(tr.Sophr.Pal.)*vir.ill*. proem.(p.1.20; M.*PL*.23.604A); in the mind, Anast.S.*qu.et resp*.133 (M.89.785C).

***ἀνακυρτόομαι,** pass., *swell up*, Meth.*arbitr*.2.3(p.148.12; M.18. 244A).

***ἀνακύφω,** = ἀνακύπτω, *raise one's head*, Epiph.*haer*.37.4(p.55. 15; M.41.645D).

***ἀνακωδίκευσις, ἡ,** *codification*; of laws, Jo.Mal.*chron*.18 p.448 (M.97.657C).

ἀνακωχή, ἡ, = ἀνοκωχή, *cessation, pause*, of a musical rest κρουμάτων ἀ. Hipp.*fr.13 in Pss*.(p.142.24); of a truce in warfare, Chrys. *sac*.6.13(p.171.15; 1.435B); Thdt.*h.e*.2.31.1(3.907); φαυλότητος...καὶ ἁμαρτίας...ἔχει ἀ. ἡ κατὰ τὸ σάββατον ἀργία Cyr.*Jo*.4.7(4.439C).

***ἀνάλαβος, ὁ,** *scapular*, Ephr.3.255A; id.3.359A; *Apophth.Patr*. (M.65.276D); cf. *gestant etiam resticulas duplices, laneo plexas subtegmine, quas Graeci* ἀναβολάς (v.l. *analaboys*) *nos vero succinctoria, seu redimicula, vel proprie rebrachiatoria possumus appellare. quae descendentia per summa cervicis et e lateribus colli divisa, utrarumque alarum sinus ambiunt...ut constringentia latitudinem vestimenti ad corpus contrahant*, Cassian.*de institutis coenobiorum* 1.6(M.*PL*.49.71A); symbolism ὁ δὲ ἀ. πάλιν ὁ σταυροειδῶς τοῖς ὤμοις αὐτῶν περιπλεκόμενος, σύμβολόν τῆς εἰς Χριστόν ἐστι πίστεως ἀναλαμβανούσης τοὺς πραεῖς, καὶ περιστελλούσης ἀεὶ τὰ κωλύοντα, καὶ τὴν ἐργασίαν ἀνεμπόδιστον αὐτοῖς παρεχούσης Evagr. Pont.*cap.pract*.A(M.40.1221A); symbol of cross borne on shoulders, Dor.*doct*.1.13(M.88.1633B); ὁ δὲ ἀ., ἐπειδὴ καὶ ἔμπρὸς καὶ ὀπίσω τὸν σταυρὸν ἔχει, σημαίνει ὅτι χρή...μὴ μόνον σταυρωθῆναι ἡμᾶς τῷ κόσμῳ, ἀλλὰ καὶ τὸν κόσμον ἡμῖν Max.*qu.dub*.67(M.90.841A); of taking up cross and wearing shield of faith, ‡Bas.*h.myst*.25(p.263. 11); cf. gloss on †Jo.D.*B.J*.18(M.96.1025C).

ἀναλακτίζω, *spurn*, Clem.*str*.7.16(p.67.12; M.9.532B).

ἀναλαμβάν-ω, I. *receive, accept*;

A. in gen., spiritual gifts, sufferings etc. ἀ. παιδείαν, ἐφ' ᾗ οὐδεὶς ὀφείλει ἀγανακτεῖν *1Clem*.56.2; ἀποτίθεται τὴν νέκρωσιν καὶ ἀ. τὴν ζωήν Herm.*sim*.9.16.3; ἀ. τὸν ζῶντα τοῦ θεοῦ λόγον Or.*mart*.15 (p.15.10; M.11.584A); παρρησίαν ἀ. πρὸς τὸ εὐεργετεῖν *ib*.37(p.35.24; 613A); *ib*.49(p.46.13; 633C); τὴν πρὸς...θεὸν ἀγάπην...ἀ. id.*Cels*.3.81 (p.271.25; M.11.645B); of man received into holiness, Clem.*str*.7.3 (p.10.30; M.9.417B); of prayers accepted by God, *PLond*.1929.7.

B. Holy Communion ἐκεῖνον, εἰ δυνατόν, ~οντας ἐν ἑαυτοῖς ἀποτίθεσθαι καὶ τὸν σωτῆρα ἐνστερνίσασθαι Clem.*paed*.1.6(p.115.27; M.8.301A); τῷ...τὸν ζῶντα ἄρτον ~οντι εἰς τὴν τήρησιν ἑαυτοῦ Or.*Cels*. 6.44(p.114.20; M.11.1365B).

C. monastic habit ἀ. τὸ σχῆμα τὸ σεμνόν Nil.*exerc*.8(M.79.728B).

II. *accept, assimilate, understand*, ref. Christian doctrine τοὺς βουλομένους Χριστιανοὺς εἶναι δεῖν μόνους τοὺς τοῦ Χριστοῦ λόγους ἀ. Clem.*fr*.68(p.229.4,12); τὰ ῥήματα τοῦ θεοῦ ἀκούει...καὶ ἐπιστήμην αὐτῶν ἀ. Or.*Jo*.20.33(27; p.371.12; M.14.649B); ὁ παραλαμβάνων σοφίας θεωρήματα ἔσθ' ὅτε ἐπὶ προτέροις, δι' ἃ ἤδη σοφός ἐστιν ~ει δεύτερα, ἐφ' οἷς οὐ πρότερον ἦν σοφός *ib*.32.15(9; p.449.29; 780B); hence '*make one's own*' πίστεως ~ούσης τοὺς πραεῖς Evagr.Pont.*cap. pract*.proem.(M.40.1221A).

III. *assume, put on, take upon oneself*;

A. ref. Christ assuming human nature; **1.** σάρξ: ὁ υἱὸς τοῦ θεοῦ... ἐκ παρθένου...σάρκα ἀνέλαβε Arist.*apol*.15.1; υἱὸν τοῦ θεοῦ...σάρκα ἀνειληφότα Clem.*str*.6.15(p.496.5; M.9.349C); *ib*.7.2(p.7.16; 412A); Adam.*dial*.3.1(p.116.7; M.11.1793A); Eus.*e.th*.2.18(p.122.6; M.24. 941A); ὁ λόγος, σὰρξ γενόμενος, τὸν ἐκ σπέρματος Δαβὶδ ἀνείληφεν id.*d.e*.7.3(p.339.27; M.22.553C); τὴν ἡμετέραν ἐκ τῆς παρθένου σάρκα ἀνείληφε *Symb.Ant*.(345)5(p.252.39; M.26.732A); Chrys.*hom.53.1 in Jo*.(8.310E); οὔτε ἡ ἀναληφθεῖσα σὰρξ ἐχώρησεν εἰς τὴν φύσιν τοῦ ἀνειληφότος Paul.Em.*hom*.2(p.12.25; M.77.1440C); eucharistic ἐδεστὴν παραθεὶς καὶ τὴν ἀναληφθεῖσαν σάρκα Cyr.*inc.unigen*.(5^{1}.707C);

2. σῶμα, and words denoting 'body': τοῦτον ἔγνωμεν ἐκ παρθένου σῶμα ἀνειληφότα Hipp.*haer*.10.33(p.291.20; M.16.3451B); ἀναλαβὼν τὸ διὰ γενέσεως σῶμα ἀνείληφεν αὐτὸ καὶ πόνων δεκτικὸν τυγχάνον..., ὥσπερ οὖν βουληθεὶς ἀνείληφε σῶμα οὐ πάντῃ ἄλλης φύσεως παρὰ τὴν ἀνθρωπίνην σάρκα, οὕτως συνανείληφε τῷ σώματι καὶ τὰ ἀλγεινὰ αὐτοῦ Or.*Cels*.2.23(p.152.21,23; M.11.841C); *ib*.1.70(p.124.13; 789C); ὁ λόγος...τὴν ἡμετέραν μορφὴν πρότερον ἀνέλαβε Meth.*symp*.1.4 (p.13.1; M.18.44D); τὴν μορφὴν τοῦ δούλου ἀνέλαβεν id.*res*.2.18 (p.370.6; M.18.284C); Adam.*dial*.4.17(p.174.21; M.11.1832B); τοῦτο δὲ ἦν τὸ ἀνθρώπειον σκῆνος, ὃ δίκην ἀμνοῦ...ἐκ τῆς ἡμετέρας ἀγέλης οἷά τις ἀρχιερεὺς ἀναλαβὼν...προσηγάγετο τῷ πατρί Eus.*d.e*.10 proem.(p.445.16; M.22.716C); *ib*.(p.446.3; 717B); Ath.*Ar*.1.38(M.26. 89C); ἐπὶ σωτηρίᾳ καὶ εὐεργεσίᾳ τῶν ἀνθρώπων ἀ. σῶμα ἀνθρώπινον id.*v.Anton*.74(M.26.945C) Cyr.*thes*.15(5[1].160B); **3.** ἄνθρωπος q.v.; **a.** in gen. ὁ θεῖος λόγος...τὸ ἀνθρώπου προσωπεῖον ἀναλαβὼν καὶ σάρκα ἀναπλασάμενος Clem.*prot*.10(p.78.16; M.8.228A); id.*ecl*.23 (p.143.7; M.9.708D); ἐν δὲ Χριστῷ πᾶσα ἡ ἄκρα νίκη διὰ τοῦ θεοῦ καὶ διὰ τοῦ ἀνθρώπου, οὗ ἀνέλαβεν ἡ δόξα ἐκείνη ἀκατάληπτος *A*. (*Pass*.)*Petr.et Paul*.22(p.138.8); οὐκ ἂν δὲ ὅλος ἄνθρωπος ἐσώθη, εἰ μὴ ὅλον τὸν ἄνθρωπον ἀνειλήφει Or.*dial*.7(p.136.17); id.*Jo*.10.6(4; p.176.25; M.14.316C); Adam.*dial*.1.2(p.4.13; M.11.1717B); πάντα γ' ἐπιτελῶν δι' οὗ ἀνείληφεν ἀνθρώπου Eus.*d.e*.4.13(p.172.4; M.22.285D); ἐκ...Μαρίας τὸν ἡμέτερον ἀ. ἄνθρωπον Ath.*exp.fid*.1(M.25.201B); Thdr.Mops.*fr.inc*.(p.303.13; M.66.985A); ὁρᾶτε πῶς φανερῶς τὸν θεὸν λόγον φησὶ παθημάτων τετελειωκέναι τὸν ἀναληφθέντα ἄνθρωπον *ib*.(p.304.13; 985C); τὸν κατ' εἰκόνα καὶ ὁμοίωσιν θεοῦ πλασθέντα ἀ. ἄνθρωπον ‡Just.*coh.Gr*.38(M.6.309B); ἀ. δὲ αὐτὸς τὰ τῆς ἀνθρωπότητος ἴδια, θεὸν ἑαυτοῦ τὸν πατέρα καλῶν Cyr.*thes*.15(5[1].160E); including soul and spirit ὅτι...αὐτὸς ἕτερος ἦν ὧν ἀνείληφεν, δῆλον ἐξ ὧν ὁμολογεῖ· ἐγὼ ἡ ζωή...τὸ δὲ πνευματικόν, ὃ ἀ., καὶ τὸ ψυχικὸν οὕτως ἐμφαίνει· τὸ δὲ παιδίον ηὔξανεν...Clem.*exc.Thdot*.61(p.127.4,6; M.9. 688B); ...εἰκὼν τοῦ υἱοῦ τοῦ θεοῦ· ἥντινα νομίζομεν εἶναι ἣν ἀνέλαβεν ψυχὴν ὁ υἱὸς τοῦ θεοῦ ἀνθρωπίνην, γενομένην διὰ τὴν ἀρετὴν τῆς εἰκόνος τοῦ θεοῦ εἰκόνα Or.*comm.in Rom*.1:1(*JTS* 13 p.211.40); θέλων σῶσαι τὸ πνεῦμα τοῦ ἀνθρώπου...ἀνέλαβεν καὶ ἀνθρώπου πνεῦμα id. *dial*.7(p.138.1); ἀνειληφὼς σῶμα καὶ ψυχὴν ἀνθρωπίνην id.*Cels*.2.31 (p.158.28; M.11.852A); **b.** in heret. formulae τὸν ἄνθρωπον, ὃν ἀνέλαβεν ὁ σωτήρ, αὐτὸν εἶναι τὸν υἱὸν λέγουσιν ‡Ath.*Ar*.4.15(p.59.19; M.26.488C); τὸν υἱὸν καὶ κύριον καὶ θεὸν ἡμῶν σάρκα ἤτοι σῶμα, τουτέστιν ἄνθρωπον, ἀνειληφέναι ἀπὸ Μαρίας...ἄνθρωπον ἀνέλαβεν ὁ Χριστὸς ἀπὸ Μαρίας...δι' οὗ πέπονθε *Symb.Sirm*.2(p.257.19,21; M.26. 744A); **c.** orthodox statements in Christol. controversies: against Eunomius τὸ ταπεινὸν τῆς ἀνθρωπίνης φύσεως ὑπερυψοῦσθαι λέγει [sc. S. Paul], δεικνύντος τοῦ λόγου τὴν τοῦ ἀναληφθέντος ἀνθρώπου πρὸς τὸ ὕψος τῆς θείας φύσεως ἐξομοίωσιν Gr.Nyss.*Eun*.6(2 p.147.23; M.45.733B); Apollinarius Χριστὸς...ὁ λόγος ἦν, τοῦτο καὶ ὁ ἐμμιχθεὶς τε καὶ ἀναληφθεὶς ἐν τῇ θεότητι γίνεται id.*Apoll*.53(M.45.1252C); Nestorius αὐτός ἐστιν ὁ τοῦ θεοῦ ἀΐδιος υἱὸς καὶ λόγος, καὶ οὐκ ἄνθρωπος ὑπὸ θεοῦ ἀναληφθείς, ἵν' ἕτερος ᾖ παρ' ἐκεῖνον. οὐδὲ γὰρ ἄνθρωπον ἀνέλαβεν ὁ τοῦ θεοῦ υἱός, ἵνα ᾖ ἕτερος παρ' αὐτόν Felix I Papa *fr*.ap.Cyr.*apol.orient*.7(p.45.29; 6[1].174B); οὐκοῦν γέγονεν ἄνθρωπος, οὐκ ἄνθρωπον ἀνέλαβεν, ὡς Νεστορίῳ δοκεῖ Cyr.*ep*.45(p.155. 19; 5[2].139B); οὐκ ἄνθρωπον ἀνειλῆφθαί φαμεν παρὰ τοῦ θεοῦ λόγου... ἄνθρωπον δὲ μᾶλλον αὐτὸν γενέσθαι διοριζόμεθα, ταύτης τε ἕνεκα τῆς αἰτίας τῶν τῆς εὐσεβείας δογμάτων ἐξεστηκέναι φαμὲν τοὺς τολμῶντας λέγειν τὸν ἀναληφθέντα ἄνθρωπον χρῆναί τε διαβεβαιουμένους αὐτὸν ὡς ἕτερον ἑτέρῳ συμπροσκυνεῖσθαι δεῖν τῷ υἱῷ τοῦ θεοῦ id.*apol. Thdt*.8(p.132.12ff.; 6.226C); εἰ...λέγειν αὐτοὶ τεθαρσήκασιν, ἄνθρωπος ἀνελήφθη παρὰ τοῦ θεοῦ, πῶς ἐπτώχευσεν ὁ ἀναληφθείς...; ἀλλ' ὧδε φρονεῖν ἀπηχές· οὐκοῦν οὐκ ἐπτώχευσεν ὁ ἀναληφθείς...ποῦ...ὀψόμεθα τῆς πτωχείας τὸ ὑφειμένον; ἆρ' ἐν τῷ τινὰ τῶν καθ' ἡμᾶς ἀναλαβεῖν καθὰ φάναι τετολμήκασιν οἱ τῆς Νεστορίου δυσσεβείας παράσιτοι; *ib*. 10(p.138.19ff.; 233Af.); **4.** Christ 'assuming' the Church Ἰησοῦς...ἐν ἑαυτῷ δυνάμει τὴν ἐκκλησίαν ἀναλαβὼν ἀνέσωσεν καὶ ἀνήνεγκεν ἅπερ ἀνέλαβεν Clem.*exc.Thdot*.58(p.126.11,14; M.9.688A); Ath.*inc.et c.Ar*. 21(M.26.1021B).

B. ref. Christ taking upon himself **1.** human birth ἐκ παρθένου τῆς Μαρίας καὶ ἁγίου πνεύματος τὴν γένεσιν ἀνείληφεν Or.*Jo*.32.16 (9; p.452.5; M.14.784B); τὴν ἐκ παρθένου...οὐ ἀνείληφεν σκήνους γένεσιν Eus.*d.e*.6.15(p.269.27; M.22.444B); **2.** man's sins and death δυνάμενος πᾶσαν τὴν ὅλου τοῦ κόσμου ἁμαρτίαν εἰς ἑαυτὸν ἀναλαβὼν λῦσαι...τῷ μηδὲν αὐτὸν ἡμαρτηκότα τὰς πάντων ἁμαρτίας ἀνειληφέναι Or.*Jo*.28.18(14; p.413.8,14; M.14.720D,721A); τοῦ κυρίου...θάνατον τὸν ὑπὲρ ἡμῶν ἀνειληφότος *ib*.2.26(21; p.83.27; 100D); id.*comm.in 1Cor*.15:20ff.(*JTS* 10 p.48.98); ‡Just.*fr*.11(M.6.1596B) cit. s. ἀποπομπή.

C. ref. man; putting on new man and his virtues τὴν πραϋπάθειαν ἀναλαβόντες Ign.*Trall*.8.1; τὸν ἐν Χριστῷ κτισθέντα καὶ ἀνακαινισθέντα νοῦν...ἀναλαβεῖν Ath.*ep.Serap*.1.9(M.26.553C); id.*Ar*.3.18(M. 26.361B); ἀναλαβόντες δὲ τὸν νέον [sc. ἄνθρωπον] τὸν κατὰ θεὸν κτισθέντα ἐν δικαιοσύνῃ ‡Ath.*Ar*.4.34(p.83.24; M.26.521A).

IV. *take up* into heaven;

A. ref. Christ, Just.*dial*.32.3(M.6.544C); αὐτοῦ...σῶμα...εἰς οὐρανοὺς ἀναληφθέν Ath.*Ar*.1.45(M.26.104C); †Ath.*exp.fid*.1(M.25.201B); *Symb.Sirm*.3(p.236.4; M.26.693B); τὸν εἰς οὐρανοὺς ἀνθρωποπρεπῶς ἀναληφθέντα Dion.Ar.*c.h*.7.3(M.3.209B).

B. OT characters; **1.** Elijah, Clem.*str*.1.21(p.73.9; M.8.841A); Or.*Jo*.6.13(7; p.122.20; M.14.224C); Meth.*res*.3.5(p.396.7; M.18.320B); Ath.*ep.Drac*.8(M.25.532C); **2.** others: Abraham, *T.Abr*.B 7(p.112); Moses τὸν Μωυσέα ~όμενον διττὸν εἶδεν Ἰησοῦς ὁ τοῦ Ναυῆ Clem. *str*.6.15(p.498.21; M.9.356C); Jeremiah τὸ φῶς...τὸ φωτίζον με, ἕως οὗ ἀναληφθῶ πρὸς σέ *Apoc.Bar.rel*.9.3.

C. ref. BMV οὐκ ἀνελήφθης εἰς οὐρανούς, ἀλλ' ἐπὶ τῆς γῆς ἱσταμένη, τὸν οὐράνιον...βασιλέα...ἐπεσπάσω πρὸς ἑαυτήν ‡Chrys.*annunt.et Ar*. (11.840B).

D. S. John, Hipp.Th.*fr*.1.5(p.7.3); cf.*ib*.2.5(p.14.1).

E. of souls of Christians Ἀμμοῦν...οὗ τὴν ψυχὴν ~ομένην εἶδεν ὁ Ἀντώνιος ‡Pall.*h.mon*.29(p.90.11; M.34.1026D); heret. βλασφημεῖν τολμῶσι...οἳ καὶ λέγουσι μὴ εἶναι νεκρῶν ἀνάστασιν, ἀλλὰ ἅμα τῷ ἀποθνήσκειν τὰς ψυχὰς αὐτῶν ~εσθαι εἰς τὸν οὐρανόν Just.*dial*.80.4 (M.6.655A).

F. in rapture; ref. S. Paul, Meth.*res*.1.55(p.314.3; M.18.296A) cit. s. παράδεισος; ἀνειλῆφθαι αὐτὸν ἐν ὁράματι εἰς τὸν οὐρανόν ‡Pall. *h.mon*.11.18(p.59.2, v.l. ἀνειληφέναι M.65.453B).

V. *recall*, *M.Perp*.20(p.91.13).

VI. *recover*, *find refreshment*, *M.Perp*.16(p.87.1); ἐκέλευσέν τε αὐτοὺς...εἰσελθεῖν καὶ ~ειν μετ' αὐτῶν *ib*.(p.87.6).

VII. *revert* μετανοίᾳ ἀναλαβεῖν εἰς μετάμελον Pamph.Mon.*Soter*.3 (p.118.27).

VIII. *raise* wings, ‡Eust.*Laz*.24(p.46.6).

***ἀναλαμπρύνω**, *make to shine again*; v.l. for ἀναλαμβάνω, Or.*fr.14 in Jer*.(p.205.2; M.13.569C).

ἀναλάμπ-ω, **1.** *shine forth*; fig., *T.Lev*.18.4; met. τὴν...ἀναλάμψασαν διὰ...Χριστοῦ θεοσέβειαν Or.*Cels*.5.33(p.35.14; M.11.1232A); Meth.*symp*.4.5(p.50.21; M.18.93A); Cyr.*Jo*.1.3(4.23E); *revive*, Clem. *str*.5.1(p.327.29; M.9.13A); εἰς εὐδόκιμον ἀληθῶς ~οντες βίον Cyr. *Pulch*.24(p.51.18; 5[2].165C); **2.** *illuminate*, Or.*Jo*.1.6(8; p.11.23; M.14. 36B).

ἀναλγησία, ἡ, **1.** *freedom from pain*, *Ep.Lugd*.ap.Eus.*h.e*.5.1.19 (M.20.416B); **2.** *insensibility*, *lethargy* τῆς ἀργίας ἵνα μὴ εἴπω τῆς ἀ. Gr.Naz.*ep*.240(M.37.384A); Chrys.*sac*.2.4(p.34.19; 1.375A); Isid.Pel. *epp*.2.94(M.78.537C).

***ἀναλγητί**, *without pain*, Meth.*res*.1.56(p.317.8; M.41.1152B).

***ἀναλδαίνω**, *make to grow up*, *produce*, Nonn.*par.Jo*.15:5(M.43. 873A).

ἀναλέγω, **1.** *pick up*, *gather together*; met., *recover*, in disaster τὴν ψυχὴν ἀναλέξασθαι Gr.Nyss.*Pulch*.(M.46.873C); **2.** *read through*, Epiph.*haer*.64.5(p.415.6; M.41.1080B).

***ἀνάλεξις, ἡ**, *collection*, Cyr.H.*catech*.12.16; Epiph.*haer*.42.13 (p.183.1; M.41.812C); Gel.Cyz.*h.e*.1.10.2(M.85.1212B).

***ἀναλήψιμος**, *of taking up*, *of Ascension* ἡ ἀ. ... ἑορτή Socr.*h.e*. 7.26.2(M.67.800A); *Const.Stud*.5(M.99.1708A); *of Assumption*, Tim. Ant.*Sym*.(M.86.245D).

ἀνάληψις, ἡ, **I.** in gen.;

A. *acquisition*; **1.** of virtue τοὺς γενναίως φιλοσοφήσαντας καὶ μὴ ἀπογνόντας τὴν τῆς ἀρετῆς ἀ. Or.*Cels*.3.66(p.259.29; M.11.1008A); *ib*. 8.10(p.228.16; 1532B); δι' ἀρετῆς καὶ σοφίας ἀ. Eus.*p.e*.5.9(196C; M.21. 340B); *ib*.11.7(523A; M.868A); ἡ φύσις [sc. τοῦ ἀνθρώπου] ἐπιτηδείως ἔχουσα πρὸς ἀνάληψιν παντὸς ἀγαθοῦ Cyr.*resp*.8(p.590.3; 6[2].378B); *ib*. (p.590.17; 378D); Proc.G.*Is*.66:5–14(M.87.2701A); **2.** of knowledge, Or.*Cels*.6.37(p.106.28; M.11.1353B); Proc.G.*Is*.3:1–11(M.87.1896C); **3.** of wives, Areth.*Apoc*.1(M.106.504C).

B. *recovery*, *restoration* ὃς [sc. Empedocles] φυσικῶς...τῆς τῶν πάντων ἀ. μέμνηται Clem.*str*.5.14(p.396.5; M.9.157A); of health, *ib*. 1.1(p.12.25; M.8.708A); Gr.Naz.*or*.32.27(M.36.205A); ἀναγκαία μὲν ἡ τοῦ λόγου σωμάτωσις, ἀ. οὖσα τῆς διαπεσούσης εἰκόνος Proc.G.*Gen*. 1:26(M.87.120C).

C. *support*, *comfort* ἦν αὐτῆς [sc. Blandina] ἀ. καὶ ἀνάπαυσις...τὸ λέγειν ὅτι Χριστιανή εἰμι *Ep.Lugd*.ap.Eus.*h.e*.5.1.19(M.20.416B); τοῖς ἀναλήψεως δεομένοις Eus.*h.e*.6.39.5(M.20.601A).

D. *handing over*, of catechumens for baptism μετὰ τὴν ἀ. εὐχὴ Serap.*euch*.23 tit. [prob. for ἄλειψιν, since preceded by a prayer εἰς τὸ ἄλειμμα]; of bodies of martyrs for burial παρεμείναμεν τῇ ἁγίᾳ ἀ. αὐτῶν, ἵνα καὶ τὸν τόπον τῶν ἁγίων λειψάνων ἀσφαλισώμεθα *M.Tar.*11 (p.476).

II. Christol., *assumption* of humanity by Christ;

A. orthodox τοῦ τε ἀνθρωπίνου διὰ τῆς ἀ. δοξαζομένου καὶ τοῦ θείου διὰ τῆς συγκαταβάσεως μὴ μολυνομένου Gr.Nyss.*Eun.*6(2 p.132. 13; M.45.716C); exeg. Ac.2:36 ἀπόστολος...ἐκεῖνο διὰ τῆς ἀ. 'πεποιῆσθαι' φησίν, ὅπερ ὁ ἀναλαβὼν κατὰ τὴν ἑαυτοῦ φύσιν ἦν *ib.*(p.133.8; 717A); *ib.*(p.150.14; 736D); τὸ γάρ, 'λόγος σὰρξ ἐγένετο', οὐ μετάπτωσιν τῆς φύσεως μηνύει, ἀλλὰ τὴν ἀ. τῆς ἡμετέρας ἀσθενείας Sever. *sigill.*6(M.63.542); νηστεύει τεσσαράκοντα ἡμέρας...εἰ δὲ περαιτέρω προέβη, πολλοῖς ἂν...ἄπιστος ἔδοξεν εἶναι ἡ τῆς σαρκὸς ἀ. Chrys.*hom. 13.2 in Mt.*(7.169B); μετὰ τὴν τῆς σαρκὸς ἐκ τῆς Μαρίας ἀ. Thdt. *h.e.*5.11.3(3.1037).

B. in controversy; **1.** with Marcellus, to whom is attributed view that Son did not exist before assumption of flesh τοῦτον δ' ἐκ τοῦ πατρὸς πρὸ ἐτῶν οὐδ' ὅλων τετρακοσίων διὰ τῆς ἀ. τῆς σαρκὸς υἱὸν θεοῦ γεγενῆσθαι...φῄς Eus.*Marcell.*2.4(p.56.27; M.24.820B); *ib.* 1.17(p.78.30; 861A); *ib.*1.20(p.81.5; 865B); **2.** with Apollinarians, Apoll.*fr.*76(p.222.23)ap.Gr.Nyss.*Apoll.*40(M.45.1213C) cit. s. ἐπιστημοσύνη; τὸ μὲν συμπέρασμα τοῦτο· τὴν δὲ τῆς ἀ. (καὶ προσλήψεως) διαφορὰν ἑρμηνευόντων οἱ ταῖς γραμματικαῖς ψυχρολογίαις ἐμμελετήσαντες...ἡμεῖς γὰρ καὶ τὸν προσειλημμένον ἀνειλῆφθαι νομίζομεν, καὶ τὸν ἀνειλημμένον προσειλῆφθαι οὐκ ἀμφιβάλλομεν, παρὰ τῆς γραφῆς τὴν τοιαύτην χρῆσιν τοῦ λόγου μεμαθηκότες...οὐκοῦν καὶ ὁ μετὰ δόξης προσληφθεὶς ἀνελήφθη...περὶ γὰρ τοῦ αὐτοῦ τὰ δύο λέγει, ὥστε τί βούλεται ὁ λέγων, οὐκ ἀ., ἀλλὰ προσλήψει τῷ μονογενεῖ τὸ κατὰ τὸν ἄνθρωπον οἰκονομεῖσθαι μυστήριον, οὐδ' ἂν αὐτὸς εἴποι τάχα Gr.Nyss. *Apoll.*39(M.45.1212Af.); **3.** heret. denials ἐτόλμησαν εἰπεῖν τινες ὅτι μῦθος ἡ τῆς σαρκὸς ἀ. Chrys.*hom.8.1 in Mt.*(7.120B); ἄνθρωπος ἀνελήφθη παρὰ τοῦ θεοῦ...δεδόξασται γάρ· ἢ εἰ μὴ τοῦτό ἐστιν ἀληθές, διαβεβλήσεται παρ' αὐτῶν ἡ ἀ. Cyr.*apol.Thdt.*(p.138.21; 6[1].233A); Thdt.*haer.*4.13(4.372).

III. *assumption* (into heaven), *ascension*;

A. pagan διὰ τῶν δώδεκα ζῳδίων ἡ ὁδὸς ταῖς ψυχαῖς γίνεται εἰς τὴν ἀ. Clem.*str.*5.14(p.395.24; M.9.157A).

B. of Christ; **1.** in gen. μεγαλυνθήσεται ἐν τῇ οἰκουμένῃ ἕως ἀναλήψεως αὐτοῦ *T.Lev.*18.3 (v.l.); μετὰ τὴν ἀ. τοῦ σωτῆρος Clem. *str.*3.4(p.207.20; M.8.1129B); *ib.*4.21(p.307.31; 1345A); *A.Pil.*A 16.3 (p.277); Or.*Cels.*7.8(p.160.26; M.11.1432D); Just.ap.Eus.*h.e.*2.13.3 (M.20.168B; Just.*1apol.*26.1 ἀνέλευσιν); Cyr.H.*catech.*14.14; *Const. App.*7.39.5; **2.** witness of scripture; foretold by Psalms: Ps.23 τὸ τελευταῖον καὶ τὴν ἀ.· τότε...βοήσεται· ἄρατε πύλας κτλ. Serap.*Man.* 40(p.59; M.18.1225A); παρακελεύεται τῇ μὲν κάτω κτίσει, ἆραι τὰς πύλας ἐν τῇ ἐνανθρωπήσει αὐτοῦ· τῇ δὲ ἄνω, ἐν τῇ ἀ. Didym.*Trin.*1.32 (M.39.428A); Cyr.*thes.*20(5[1].195E); Ps.46 τὰ τοῦ Δαυὶδ...ῥήματα, ἅπερ ἡμῖν ἀρτίως διὰ τὴν δεσποτικὴν ἀ. ἐβόα· πάντα τὰ ἔθνη κτλ. ‡Chrys. *ascens.*3(3.782E); *ib.*5(786E); Ps.17:10 ἔστι δὲ ἡμῖν περὶ...τῆς τοῦ Χριστοῦ ἀ. τὸ διήγημα. Δαυὶδ μὲν γὰρ εἴρηκε· καὶ ἔκλινεν οὐρανούς κτλ. *ib.*4(784D); witnessed by disciples, ‡Chrys.*ascens.Ac.*15(3. 772E); scriptural evidence οὔτε οὖν Ἰωάννης ὅλως, οὔτε Ματθαῖος ὅλως, οὔτε Μάρκος κατὰ πλάτος ἐμνημόνευσαν ἀναλήψεως· αὐτὸς μέντοι ὁ Λουκᾶς ἕως τῆς ἀ. διέδραμε τὸν λόγον *ib.*8(765C); **3.** in the flesh τὴν ἔνσαρκον εἰς τοὺς οὐρανοὺς ἀ. Iren.*haer.*1.10.1(M.7.549A); *ib.*3.16.8(927C); ‡Chrys.*ascens.*1(3.777A); **4.** does not imply previous separation of humanity from divinity, Sever.*serp.*4(M.56.506); **5.** significance for Church μετὰ δὲ τὴν ἀ. αὐτοῦ ἡμεῖς προσενεγκόντες κατὰ τὴν διάταξιν αὐτοῦ θυσίαν καθαρὰν καὶ ἀναίμακτον, προεχειρισάμεθα ἐπισκόπους καὶ πρεσβυτέρους καὶ διακόνους *Const.App.*8.46. 15; **6.** effects ἐκ τῆς δεσποτικῆς...ἀ. τοῦ σωτῆρος...ἐλπίδας τρυφήσαντες Bas.Sel.*ascens.*5(M.28.1100D); σήμερον ἡ ἁμαρτία διὰ τῆς ἀ. τοῦ Χριστοῦ Ἰησοῦ ὡς καπνὸς διαλέλυται ‡Epiph.*hom.*4(M.43.481C); ἐπειδὴ...ἡ ἀ. αὐτοῦ...ἐκηρύχθη, οὐκ ἀποκλείεται χρόνῳ ἡ χάρις, οὐδὲ περιγράφεται ἡμέραις ἡ θεολογία ‡Chrys.*ascens.Ac.*1(3.759B); man's spiritual ascent, *ib.*7(764A); frees earth from sorrow, Procl.CP *hom.* 1.2(M.65.833C); **7.** feast of Ascension; **a.** date and reason of celebration ἀπὸ τῆς πρώτης κυριακῆς ἀριθμήσαντες τεσσεράκοντα ἡμέρας, ἀπὸ κυριακῆς μέχρι πέμπτης ἑορτάσατε τὴν ἑορτὴν τῆς ἀ. τοῦ κυρίου, καθ' ἣν...ἀνῆλθεν πρὸς τὸν ἀποστείλαντα αὐτὸν θεόν *Const.App.*5.20.2; τὴν ἀ. ἀργείτωσαν διὰ τὸ πέρας τῆς κατὰ Χριστὸν οἰκονομίας *ib.*8.33.4; πέμπτη...ἑορτὴ ἡ ἁγία τοῦ κυρίου εἰς οὐρανοὺς ἀ.,...πέμπτη δὲ τῶν ἑορτῶν ἐστι, καθότι καὶ πέμπτῃ ἡμέρᾳ τῆς ἑβδομάδος ἐπράχθη ‡Chrys. *ascens.*4(3.784B); **b.** excellence and effects Χριστοῦ ἀ. μετὰ σαρκὸς ἑορτάζομεν, ὡς τῶν δεσποτικῶν ἑορτῶν δεικνυμένην πλήρωμα ‡Epiph. *hom.*4(M.43.477C); τῇ τῆς ἀ. ἡμέρᾳ πάντα διὰ πάντων εὐφροσύνης πεπλήρωται *ib.*(480C); ἡ τῆς δεσποτικῆς οὖν ἀ. ἡμέρα τὸν μὲν διάβολον ...θρηνεῖν παρεσκεύασε, τοὺς δὲ πιστοὺς φαιδρύνεσθαι ‡Chrys.*ascens.*3 (3.782D); **8.** buildings dedicated to Ascension: grotto built by Constantine on Mount of Olives, Eus.*v.C.*3.41(p.95.8; M.20.1101A); *ib.*3.43(p.95.22; 1101C); ἡ ἀδελφότης συνήγετο εἰς τοὺς εὐκτηρίους οἴκους, ἐν τῷ Ἐλαιῶνι εἰς τὸν τῆς ἀ. βουνὸν ὅθεν ἀνελήφθη ὁ Ἰησοῦς Pall.*h.Laus.*43(p.130.11; M.34.1210C); church built by Helena, Socr.*h.e.*1.17.11(M.67.120C); church in Jerusalem, Thdt.*Ezech.*48:35 (2.1050).

C. ref. assumption of other persons: BMV, Hipp.Th.*fr.*1.3(p.4.4; M.117.1037B); Moses ἔσχεν τρίτον ὄνομα ἐν οὐρανῷ μετὰ τὴν ἀ. Clem. *str.*1.23(p.95.10; M.8.897B); cf. *Assumption of Moses*, mentioned, Gel.Cyz.*h.e.*2.21.7(M.85.1284D); Elijah, Ath.*Ar.*3.47(M.26.424B); with which is compared death of martyrs, Sophr.H.*v.Anast.*(M.92. 1724C); *ib.*(1729A); Jeremiah, Or.*Jo.*13.58(57; p.289.24; M.14.509B); of S. Paul's ecstatic assumption into third heaven, Gr.Naz.*or.*28. 20 (p.51.13; M.36.52C); of the death of a bad person, *Pss.Sal.*4.20.

ἀναλίσκω, **1.** *destroy*; world by fire, Hegem.*Arch.*13(11; p.21.7; M.10.1448C); *remove, get rid of*; sins by shame, Or.*hom.5.5 in Jer.* (p.36.6; M.13.304B); Const.ap.Eus.*v.C.*3.60(p.108.29; M.20.1133A); **2.** *take up, absorb*, of soul reunited with body after death ὅλον [sc. σῶμα] εἰς ἑαυτὴν ἀ. καὶ γενομένη σὺν τούτῳ ἕν Gr.Naz.*or.*7.21(M.35. 784A); *ib.*25.16(1221A).

***ἀναλλάσσω**, v.l. for ἀπαλλάσσω, Or.*Jo.*6.47(28; p.156.23; M.14. 281C); prob. error for ἐναλλάσσω, Thdt.*Ps.*59:13(1.1007).

***ἀναλλοιότως**, for ἀναλλοιώτως, q.v.

***ἀναλλοίτος**, for ἀναλλοίωτος, Philox.*ep.*32(p.180).

ἀναλλοίωτος, commonly ass. with ἄτρεπτος, q.v.;

A. *unchangeable, immutable*; **1.** theol.; **a.** of God τοῦ ὄντως θεοῦ, ὅς ἐστιν ἄφθαρτός τε καὶ ἀ. καὶ ἀόρατος Arist.*apol.*4.1; Athenag.*leg.* 22.5(M.6.937C) cit. s. ἀκίνητος; ἀ. ... καθότι ἀθάνατός ἐστι Thphl.Ant. *Autol.*1.4(M.6.1029A); μὴ πάσχει θεὸς ἀ. ὢν Or.*fr.51 in Jo.*3:36 (p.526.7); Hymen.*ep.*2(p.324.15) cit. s. ἄναρχος; τὸν ἀπαθῆ καὶ ἀ. θεόν Meth.*creat.*4(p.496.14; M.18.336C); Eus.*e.th.*2.9(p.108.31; M.24. 917A) cit. s. ἄχρονος; ὁ ἀλλοιῶν...τὰ κτίσματά σου...καὶ ἀ. καὶ αἰώνιος ὢν Serap.*euch.*30.1; Ath.*Ar.*2.34(M.26.220A); ‡Pion.*v.Polyc.* 13 cit. s. ἀμέτρητος; πῶς...δύναται τὸ ἀλλοιούμενον τῷ ἀ. ἐοικέναι; ‡Bas.*struct.hom.*1.6(1.326E; M.30.16C); θεὸν...τὸν ἄναρχον, τὸν ἀ., τὸν ἀσώματον, τὸν ἄφθαρτον Chrys.*incomprehens.*2.3(1.456B); Jo.D.*f.o.* 1.4(M.94.800A) cit. s. ἄναρχος; of divine nature and essence τὰ... συνθέτου μέρη καὶ τὰ τοῦ κινουμένου κινήματα, πρὸς τὴν ἀσύνθετον καὶ ἀ. φύσιν οὐδεμίαν ἔχει κοινωνίαν ‡Ath.*Sabell.*13(M.28.117B); ὁ θεὸς... ὁ φύσει ἀ. *Lit.*ap.*Const.App.*8.15.7; Gr.Nyss.*tres dii*(M.45.133A); ἀρρεύστου καὶ ἀ. μενούσης τῆς ἁγίας οὐσίας, ὡς θεὸς θεὸν θεοπρεπῶς ἐγέννησεν †Chrys.*nativ.*2.2(6.399E); ἁπλῆ καὶ ἀ. ἡ τῆς θεότητος φύσις ὅλη ἐν τῇ οἰκείᾳ ἀεὶ ὑπάρχει οὐσίᾳ Leo Mag.*ep.*35.2(p.41.21; M.*PL.*54.808A); one of the divine names, Dion.Ar.*d.n.*1.6(M.3.596B); ref. God in relation to creation τῆς τῶν ὄντων ἀδιαλύτου μονῆς ἀ. ἵδρυσιν id.*c.h.*13.4 (M.3.304C); **b.** of divine attributes: ἀλήθεια, *Const.App.*7.35.9; δόξα, Chrys.*hom.3.4 in Rom.*(9.453A); **c.** of Trin. οἱ τρεῖς, ἓν ὑπάρχουσιν φῶς...ἄναρχον...ἀ. ‡Caes.Naz.*dial.*3(M.38.860); **d.** of Father opp. Son τὸν μὲν ἀποστείλαντα πατέρα ἐν τῷ οἰκείῳ τῆς ἀ. θεότητος ἤθει μεμενηκέναι, τὸν δὲ ἀποσταλέντα Χριστὸν τὴν τῆς ἐνανθρωπήσεως οἰκονομίαν πεπληρωκέναι *Symb.Ant.*(345)7(p.253.19; M.26.732C); **e.** of Logos ἀ. ἡ εἰκὼν τοῦ ἀτρέπτου θεοῦ ἂν εἴη Ath.*Ar.*1.36(M.26. 85B); Procl.CP *Arm.*6(p.190.12; M.65.861B); Gel.Cyz.*h.e.*2.24.7(M.85. 1300C); Dion.Ar.*d.n.*2.6(M.3.644C); of incarnate Word as divine κενώσας μὲν ἑαυτὸν κατὰ τὴν μόρφωσιν ⟨δούλου⟩, ἀκένωτος δὲ καὶ ἀ. καὶ ἀνελάττωτος κατὰ τὴν θείαν οὐσίαν Apoll.*corp.et div.*6(p.188.2; M.*PL.*8.874A); id.*ep.Jov.*(p.252.1; M.28.28B) cit. s. ἀπαθής; Gr. Nyss.*Eun.*6(2 p.136.9; M.45.720D); id.*ep.*3.13(M.46.1020A); μανία ἄρα σαφὴς ἐπὶ τῆς ἀκηράτου καὶ ἀ. φύσεως σύγχυσιν νοεῖν Thdt.*eran.*2 (4.116); Dion.Ar.*e.h.*4.3.10f.(M.3.484A,C); θεϊκῶς ὁμοῦ καὶ ἀνθρωπίνως ἐνήργησε, τέλειον κατὰ τὸν ἑκάτερον λόγον σώζων ἑαυτοῦ φυσικῶς ἀ. ‡Hipp.*Ber.Hel.*4(p.324.9; M.10.836C); v. ἀπαθής; of Christ in rel. to Trin. ἡ καθ' ἡμᾶς Ἰησοῦ...ἀ. ὕπαρξις Dion.Ar.*d.n.*2.3(M.3. 640C); **f.** of H. Ghost, Gr.Naz.*or.*41.9(M.36.441B) cit. s. ἀχώρητος; τὸ πνεῦμα τὸ ἅγιον...κατὰ τὸ ἄφθαρτόν τε καὶ ἀ. Gr.Nyss.*Maced.*22 (M.45.1328D); μία μέν ἐστι καὶ ἀ. ἡ χάρις τοῦ πνεύματος Marc.Er. *opusc.*2.108(M.65.945B); **2.** of what appertains to God τὰ βέβαια καὶ παντελῶς ἀ. ἀναστρεφόμενοι Clem.*str.*7.3(p.12.26; M.9.421B); τὰ ἀθάνατα καὶ τὰ ἀ. ... νῷ...μόνῳ καταληπτὰ...ὄντα Const.*or.s.c.*6 (p.160.22; M.20.1248C); **3.** philos., of being οὐσία ἐστὶν...τὸ πάσας δεχόμενον τὰς μεταβολάς τε καὶ ἀλλοιώσεις, αὐτὸ δὲ ἀ. κατὰ τὸν ἴδιον λόγον Or.*or.*27.8(p.368.7; M.11.512B); of the intelligible δεδειγμένου ...τούτου, ὅτι τὰ νοητὰ ἀ. κατ' οὐσίαν ἐστίν Nemes.*nat.hom.*3(M.40. 596A); ἡ φύσις δὲ τῆς ἀληθείας ἀ. μὲν ἀεὶ μένει Philox.*ep.*32(p.180).

B. *unchanged, unchanging* (that does not in fact change); where reference is to rational beings the moral force of the word is usually prominent; **1.** of supraterrestrial substances τῶν οὐρανίων ἀρχῶν...αἰτία τ' ἀγαθόν, τῆς ἀναυξοῦς καὶ ὅλως ἀ. ταύτης οὐσίας Dion.Ar.*d.n.*4.4(M.3.697B); *ib.*8.5(892D); of immortality bestowed upon them by God, *ib.*6.2(856C); of the love of pure intelligences for God, id.*c.h.*2.4(M.3.144A); and of eternity οὐ τὰ...ἀγένητα καὶ ὄντως ἀΐδια πανταχοῦ φησιν αἰώνια, καὶ τὰ ἄφθαρτα δὲ καὶ ἀθάνατα, καὶ ἀ. ... πολλάκις δὲ...καὶ τὴν ὅλην...τοῦ καθ' ἡμᾶς χρόνου παράτασιν αἰῶνα προσαγορεύει, καθ' ὅσον καὶ ἰδιότης αἰῶνός ἐστι τὸ ἀρχαῖον καὶ ἀ., καὶ τὸ καθόλου τὸ εἶναι μετρεῖν id.*d.n.*10.3(M.3.937C); neut. as subst., *changelessness* τὸ ἀ. ἴσχει τὰ νοερὰ τῆς θεοειδοῦς ἕξεως id.*e.h.*2.3.5 (M.3.401C); **2.** of man οἱ...ἀπόστολοι...ἐν ἕξει ἀσκήσεως ἀεὶ μένοντες ἀ. μετά γε τὴν τοῦ κυρίου ἀνάστασιν Clem.*str.*6.9(p.467.20; M.9.292D); of contemplative state εἰς ἕξιν θεωρίας ἀΐδιον καὶ ἀ. *ib.*6.7 (p.463.1; 284B); of mind of 'gnostic', *ib.*4.22(p.310.12; M.8.1349A); ὁ ἡμέτερος νοῦς διαμένει καὶ μετὰ θάνατον ἀπαθής τε καὶ ἀ. Gr.Nyss. *Apoll.*30(M.45.1189C); of human virtues, id.*hom.3 in Cant.*(M.44.824B); of supernatural life imparted to man in baptism, id.*or. catech.*39(p.156.6; M.45.100B); **3.** (Arian) of Logos ὁ υἱὸς...θελήματι καὶ βουλῇ ὑπέστη...πλήρης θεός, μονογενής, ἀ., καὶ πρὶν γεννηθῇ ἤτοι κτισθῇ...οὐκ ἦν Ar.*ep.Eus.*(p.3.3; M.42.212B).

***ἀναλλοιώτως,** *without change*; **1.** of Logos, esp. in connexion with Inc. as not incurring change συμβῆναι...καθ' ἕνωσιν ἀδιάσπαστον καὶ ἀ. ἔχουσαν τῇ ἰδίᾳ σαρκὶ τὸν ἐκ θεοῦ λόγον Cyr.*Nest.*1.3 (p.22.11; 6^{1}.15C); id.*ep.*55(p.54.28; 5^{2}.181D); ἀ. ἡμῖν καὶ ἀσυγχύτως κεκοινώνηκε Dion.Ar.*d.n.*2.10(M.3.648D); id.*e.h.*3.3.12f.(M.3.444A,C); Max.*ambig.*(M.91.1320C); in form -ότως of the two natures of Christ, Sophr.H.*ep.syn.*(M.87.3165D); **2.** of H. Ghost ἐκπορευτὸν ἀ. ‡Caes.Naz.*dial.*3(M.38.861); **3.** in gen., Diod.*fat.*(M.103.860D).

ἀναλογ-έω, **1.** *be proportionate*, Bas.*hex.*2.7(1.20A; M.29.48A); fig., *Hom.Clem.*9.11; ὁ δὲ τοῦ θεοῦ λόγος, κατ' οὐδένα λόγον ἢ τρόπον ~ούσας ἔχων ταῖς οἰκείαις κατὰ φύσιν ἐνεργείαις τῆς ὑπ' αὐτοῦ προσληφθείσης φύσεως τὰς δυνάμεις Max.*ep.*13(M.91.532B); **2.** *bear relation to* or *equal* ἡμῶν...τὰ χρήματα...οὐ μὴ ~ήσῃ τοὺς λίθους... τῆς βασιλείας σου *T.Job* 28(p.121.7); Mac.Aeg.*hom.*4.17(M.34.485B); **3.** *correspond*, Clem.*prot.*4(p.39.30; M.8.144B); ἀ. τῷ μὲν ἐπὶ τοῦ προσώπου Μωυσέως καλύμματι τὴν τῶν νομικῶν διδαγμάτων ἀσάφειαν Bas.*Spir.*52(3.45A; M.32.165B); Christol. ἀ. γὰρ παρ' αὐτοῖς ἡ μὲν θεότης τῇ ψυχῇ, ἡ δὲ ἀνθρωπότης τῷ σώματι †Leont.B.*sect.*8(M.86.1249B); ἐνέργειαν...~οῦσαν αὐτοῦ τῇ δυάδι τῶν φύσεων Sophr.H.*ep. syn.*(M.87.3176D); **4.** trans., *keep in proportion* or *harmony*, Epiph. *haer.*51.17(p.274.15; M.41.921C); τὸ δὲ εὔλογον συμπρεπόντως ~εῖται υἱοῦ πρὸς πατέρα *ib.*76.52(p.406.29; M.42.625B); **5.** *accord to* τὰ μὲν εἰς Χριστὸν...προσάπτων, τὰ δὲ εἰς τὸν λόγον...~ῶν *ib.*71.2(p.251.7; 377A ~ούμενα); πάθημα δὲ θανάτου οὐ πρὸ σαρκὸς εἰς τὸν λόγον ~εῖται *ib.*69.38(p.186.24; 261A); *ib.*69.50(p.197.18; 280C).

ἀναλογή, ἡ, *choice* περὶ...τῆς ἀ., ἧς ἦλθεν ὁ σωτὴρ ἀναλέξασθαι παρθενίαν Epiph.*haer.*67.6(M.42.180C; conj. ἐκλογῆς p.138.9); *selection* of scriptural texts, *ib.*42.12(p.155.26; M.41.773B).

ἀναλογία, ἡ, **1.** *proportion*; hence in gen., *amount, degree*, esp. of faith (cf. Rom.12:6); ref. eucharist κατὰ δὲ τὴν ἐπιγενομένην αὐτῷ εὐχὴν κατὰ τὴν ἀ. τῆς πίστεως ὠφέλιμον γίνεται Or.*comm.in Mt.*11.14 (p.58.5; M.13.949B); κατὰ τὴν ἀ. τῆς πίστεως, καὶ ἡ τῶν χαρισμάτων διανομὴ παραγίνεται Eustrat.*v.Eutych.*87(M.86.2373A); χρόνον ὡρισμένον κατὰ τὴν ἀ. τοῦ ἁμαρτήματος *Const.App.*2.16.4; Dion.Ar.*d.n.* 1.1(M.3.588A); **2.** *correspondence, resemblance* δύναται γὰρ ἀ. ἔχειν τὸ αἰσθητὸν πρὸς τὸ νοητόν Or.*Jo.*1.26(24; p.31.32; M.14.69A); of Jo. Bapt. σιωπωμένης τῆς ἀρχῆς τῆς ἀποστολῆς ἀ. ἐχούσης πρὸς τὴν ἀποστολὴν τοῦ Ἡσαΐου *ib.*2.29(24; p.86.15; 165A); Gr.Nyss.*hom.1 in Cant.*(M.44.768A); **3.** *mutual relation*, of φρόνησις and βούλησις ref. Pr.8:14 ὡς ἀδελφὰ ταῦτα τῇ ἀ. συνῆψεν Ath.*Ar.*3.65(M.26.460B).

[*]**ἀναλόγιον, τό,** *desk for reading*, *Ev.Thom.*A 15(p.154.1, ed. ἀναλογεῖον).

ἀναλογισμός, ὁ, *line of reasoning* by analogy; opp. ἐπιλογισμός, Clem.*str.*8.9(p.101.5; M.9.600B); Meth.*res.*2.9(p.347.22; M.18.308C).

ἀναλογιστικῶς, *analogically*, Clem.*str.*8.9(p.101.9; M.9.600C).

***ἀναλογίστως,** = ἀλογίστως, *foolishly*, Tit.Bost.*Man.*1.18(M.18.1093A).

ἀνάλογος, *proportionate*; *equivalent to, resembling*; neut. as subst., *equivalent, parallel*, Or.*Jo.*2.3(p.57.20; M.14.113C); *ib.*10.4 (3; p.174.12; 312C); as adv., *in correspondence with*, *ib.*19.8(p.307.33; 541A); Ἰωάννης...ἀνέκειτο ἐν τοῖς κόλποις τοῦ λόγου, ἀ. τῷ καὶ αὐτὸν εἶναι ἐν τοῖς κόλποις τοῦ πατρός *ib.*32.20(13; p.461.28; 800A).

ἀναλογούντως, *proportionately*, Cyr.*Jo.*1.3(4.22A).

ἀναλόγως, **1.** *proportionately*, Marc.Er.*opusc.*3.6(M.65.973D); c. dat., Eus.*e.th.*3.16(p.175.30; M.24.1036B); Ath.*ep.Aeg.Lib.*12(M.25.565C); c. genit., Isid.Pel.*epp.*1.287(M.78.352B); **2.** *conformably to, in accordance with*, Clem.*str.*7.2(p.9.30; M.9.416B); Epiph.*haer.*77.17 (p.430.28; M.42.664D); **3.** *by analogy*, Eus.*d.e.*4.8(p.161.25; M.22.269B); ἀπὸ τῆς τῶν κτισμάτων καλλονῆς...ἀ. τὸν γενεσιουργὸν κατιδεῖν Cyr.*Ps.*13:3(M.69.801C); **4.** *similarly*, Clem.*prot.*3(p.32.13; M.8.128A); c. dat., *in the same way as*, id.*paed.*1.6(p.114.1; M.8.297B).

ἄναλος, *without salt*, s.v.l.; met., of people, Hipp.*haer.*4.19(p.51.17; M.16.3086B, edd. ἄλαλοι, ἀνώμαλοι).

ἀνάλυσις, ἡ, **1.** *dissolving*; **a.** met., of Persons of Trin. into one another, Gr.Naz.*or.*33.16(M.36.233D) cit. s. κατάποσις; **b.** *resolution, analysis*, as method of reasoning by working back to first principles, opp. ἀπόδειξις, Clem.*str.*8.3(p.84.9; M.9.568B); *ib.*5.11(p.374.5; 108B); of a whole into parts, opp. σύνθεσις, Cels.ap.Or.*Cels.*7.42(p.192.32; M.11.1481A); **c.** math., *division*, Max.*comput.*1.17(M.19.1236A); **2.** *removing*, Gr.Nyss.*hom.4 in Cant.*(M.44.832B); *cancelling* θλίψεις λογίζονται ἡμῖν εἰς ἁμαρτημάτων ἀ. Chrys.*hom.in Mt.18:23* (3.9D); **3.** *tracing back*; in a genealogy, Afric.*ep.Arist.*3(p.60.14; M.10.60A); in the mind through history, Gr.Nyss.*Eun.*1(1 p.123.29; M.45.360B); τῆς τοῦ πνεύματος ἀδηλίας κατὰ ἀ. διὰ τοῦ υἱοῦ πρὸς τὸν πατέρα διαδοθείσης *ib.*(p.144.18; 384C); **4.** *return*; of dead to life, id.*or.catech.*23(p.87.5; M.45.61C); met. ἐκ πλευρᾶς ἡ πλάνη, ἐκ πλευρᾶς [sc. of Christ] ἡ ἀ. Mac.Mgn.*apocr.*2.18(p.32.14); **5.** *departure*; of death (cf. 2Tim.4:6), *1Clem.*44.5; Gr.Naz.*or.*7.21(M.35.784A); πρὸς τὸν Χριστὸν ἀ. Gr.Nyss.*Melet.*(M.46.852A); ἀ. τῆς ψυχῆς Pall.*h.Laus.* proem.(p.10.19; M.34.1002); Diad.*perf.*100(p.150.11).

ἀναλυτικῶς, *by retracing* or *tracing backwards*, Dion.Ar.*c.h.*15.1 (M.3.328A); id.*ep.*7.2(M.3.1080D).

ἀνάλυτος, *dissoluble*, Or.*Cels.*4.14(p.284.22; M.11.1045A).

ἀναλυτρ-όομαι, *redeem* ἡ ψυχὴ [sc. of Christ] τὰς ὁμογενεῖς ~οῦται ψυχάς Eust.*engast.*18(p.45.17; M.18.652B).

ἀναλύ-ω, **1.** trans., *undo*; **a.** *break up*, Clem.*paed.*1.8(p.128.9; M.8.328C); Hipp.*antichr.*49(p.32.8; M.10.768B); **b.** *destroy*, Or.*princ.* 3.1.14(p.221.1; M.11.277A); **c.** of life, *end*, Eus.*h.e.*3.32.1(M.20.281C); **d.** *dissolve* εἰς δὲ ἐκείνην [sc. the soul] ὁλόκληρος ~εται [sc. eucharist] Chrys.*hom.3.4 in Eph.*(11.22D); **e.** math., *divide*, Max.*comput.*1.17 (M.19.1233D); †Andr.Cr.*cycl.*(M.19.1329C); **f.** *resolve* ὅπου ἀνεκυρτώθη ἡ θάλασσα πάλιν ἀνελύετο εἰς ἑαυτήν Meth.*arbitr.*2(p.148.12; M.18.244A); of Logos as resolved back into Father acc. Marcell., Cyr.H.*catech.*15.27; Gr.Naz.*or.*25.16(M.35.1221A); **g.** *remit*, Gr.Nyss. *usur.*(M.46.445A); **2.** intrans.; **a.** *depart*; esp. from life, *A.Andr.fr.*8 (p.41.29); ἀ. ἐκ τοῦ βίου Meth.*res.*1.58(p.321.13); abs., *die*, ‡Pion.*v. Polyc.*5; Ath.*ep.Jov.*1(M.26.816A)ap.Thdt.*h.e.*4.3.4; **b.** *break up*; of a meeting, Eus.*v.C.*3.21(p.87.25; M.20.1080B); **c.** *return* ἀ. ἀπὸ τῶν γάμων *A.Thom.*A 63(p.179.12); of dead to life, Gr.Nyss.*hom.opif.* 25.12(M.44.221C); of man to God, id.*or.catech.*39(p.158.14; M.45.101A); **d.** *resolve* ~σάντων πρὸς ἑαυτὰ τῶν ἐν τοῖς σώμασι στοιχείων id.*anim.et res.*(M.46.44C).

ἀνάλωμα, τό, **1.** *something to be spent* or *consumed*; of money, Or.*Jo.*32.23(p.466.28; M.14.808A); Philost.*h.e.*3.4(M.65.484A,C); of food, Bas.Sel.*or.*35.2(M.85.380B); ἄρτους εἰς ἀ. Jo.Mosch.*prat.*56 (M.87.2909C); ref. prisoners about to be killed οὓς δὲ μαχαίρας εἷλκον ποιήσασθαι ἀ. Jo.VI H.*v.Jo.D.*8(M.94.440D); **2.** *wage, payment*, *V.Dan.*(p.256.27).

ἀνάλωσις, ἡ, *wasting, consumption, destruction*, by fire τῶν φθαρτῶν ἀ. διὰ πυρός Just.*1apol.*20.1(M.6.357B); Clem.*ecl.*26.3(p.144.18; M.9.712A); ἀ. ἀπωλείας, οὐ δαπάνης id.*paed.*2.12(p.229.18; M.8.544A); ἔδωκας τὸν διάβολον εἰς ἀ. τοῖς ἁγίοις Hesych.H.*Ps.tit.*73.28 (M.27.953D).

ἀναλωτικός, *consuming, destructive*; of fire, Clem.*ecl.*25.3(p.144.1; M.9.709C); Or.*Jo.*13.23(p.246.27; M.14.437A); met. τὸ δὲ πῦρ [sc. τῆς ἀσελγείας] ἀ. τοῦ [sc. τῆς δικαιοσύνης] ἱματίου Chrys.*hom.13.3 in Eph.*(11.99D); τὸ θεῖον πῦρ...τὸ ἀ. ἁπάσης ἁμαρτίας Jo.D.*hom.*12.5 (M.96.788C); of wrath, Or.*Jo.*20.24(20; p.360.1; 629B); *able to consume*; of Christ and saints likened to the hind, *able to destroy* serpents and poisonous passions, Ath.*exp.Ps.*17:34(M.27.117B–C); Gr. Nyss.*hom.5 in Cant.*(M.44.861C) = Cyr.*Ps.*17:34(M.69.825A); Gr. Nyss.*ib.*(864A); Manich., of material universe ἑαυτῆς ἀ. τις οὖσα καὶ φθαρτική Epiph.*haer.*66.17(p.40.23; M.42.53C); *ib.*66.19(p.42.30; 57A).

ἀνάλωτος, **1.** *not to be captured, unassailable*, Or.*Cant.*3(p.240.29; M.17.265B); ἀ. τοῖς ἐχθροῖς Cyr.*Os.*118(3.149B); Bas.Sel.*or.*5.2 (M.85.84A); morally, of a judge, Gr.Naz.*ep.*234(M.37.377A); spiritually, of Christians, Chrys.*hom.22.3 in Heb.*(12.209A); Nil.*exerc.*65 (M.79.797D); Cyr.*Mich.*42(3.430E); τὴν ψυχὴν ἀ. ἔμεινεν Bas.Sel.*or.*8.2(M.85.124B); **2.** *inexhaustible* ἐκείνην [sc. τὴν θυσίαν] προσφέρομεν καὶ νῦν, τὴν τότε ἐνεχθεῖσαν, τὴν ἀ. Chrys.*hom.17.3 in Heb.*(12.169A);

of spiritual riches, id.*hom.52.4 in Mt.*(7.535B); id.*hom.21.7 in 1Cor.*(10.190D); **3.** *not subject to decay*, Chrys.*hom.52.4 in Mt.*(7.535A); spiritually [sc. ἐλεημοσύνη] πῶς ἂν καὶ τὰ ὑπάρχοντα καὶ ἡ ψυχὴ καὶ τὸ σῶμα ἀ. μένοιεν δείκνυσι *ib.*; of garments given to poor τὸ σῶμα τοῦ Χριστοῦ...οὐδὲ...μόνον φυλάσσει τὰ ἱμάτια, οὐδὲ ἀ. διατηρεῖ μόνον id.*hom.59.4 in Jo.*(8.350C).

***ἀναμαγγανεύω,** *use magical incantations repeatedly*, Sophr.H. *v.Anast.*(M.92.1697A).

ἀναμανθάνω, *learn*, Clem.*str.*7.1(p.3.4; M.9.401B); *A.Thom.*A 98 (p.210.23); Cyr.*inc.unigen.*(5^1.696D).

ἀνάμαξις, ἡ, *impression*, Or.*Jo.*20.24(20; p.358.37; M.14.628C).

ἀναμαρτησία, ἡ, A. *guiltlessness, innocence*; of Christ (ref. Lc. 23:41), Cyr.H.*catech.*13.3.

B. *sinlessness*; **1.** of Christ ἵν' αὐτὸς ᾖ τῆς ἀ. ἡ ἐπίδειξις ‡Ath. *Apoll.*1.7(M.26.1104D); εἰ δὲ μὴ ἐν τῇ ἁμαρτησάσῃ φύσει ἡ ἀ. ὤφθη, πῶς κατεκρίθη ἡ ἁμαρτία ἐν τῇ σαρκί; *ib.*2.6(1141C); τοῖς τῆς ἀ. ἐπαίνοις τὴν ἀνθρώπου φύσιν στεφανουμένην ἐν αὐτῷ θεωρῆσαί τις ἂν Cyr.*resp.*(p.599.7; 6^2.394A); of sign of cross at ordination τῇ σταυροειδεῖ τῆς οἰκείας ἀ. εἰκόνι Dion.Ar.*e.h.*5.3.4(M.3.512B); τὴν δὲ ἀ. ... ἡ τοῦ λόγου συμφυὴς ἕνωσις κατειργάσατο Leont.B.*Nest.et Eut.*2(M.86.1353A); Leont.H.*Nest.*1.19(M.86.1473D); to be imitated by men, Clem.*q.d.s.*21(p.174.8; M.9.625D); Dion.Ar.*e.h.*3.3.12(M.3.444B); **2.** of man; **a.** as bestowed by God ἡ γὰρ κλῆσις ἡ διδοῦσα ἀ. ... κατὰ χάριν ἐστίν Or.ap.*cat.Mt.*22:8(p.180.7); εἰ τοσαύτη ἐκ σοῦ καὶ διὰ σὲ κατώρθωταί μοι ἀ. Eus.*Ps.*138:23(M.24.41B); exeg. Is.1:18 ὅπερ ἐστὶ συγχωρήσεως ἁμαρτιῶν, ἢ καὶ ἀναμαρτησίας σημεῖον Cyr.H. *catech.*15.21; εἰργάσατό τε τῶν νεκρῶν τὴν ἀνάστασιν, καὶ παρέσχεν ἅπασιν ἡμῖν τὸ...ἀπεκδέχεσθαι...τῆς ἀ. τὴν ἀπόλαυσιν Thdr.Mops. *Jon.*(M.66.320D); ἔδει πάλιν...ἀναμαρτησίαν καθηγήσασθαι ἀναπλάσεως καὶ τῆς ἀθανασίας. διὰ ταῦτα...ὁ θεὸς...ἄνθρωπος γίνεται Zach. Mit.*opif.*(M.85.1125B); τὴν ἐν τῷ βαπτίσματι χάριν τῆς ἀ. Max.*qu. Thal.*61(M.90.636C); †Jo.D.*B.J.*12(M.96.972C); **b.** as reached by man βραδεῖα γὰρ γνῶσις μετάνοια, γνῶσις δὲ ἡ πρώτη ἀ. Clem.*str.*2.6 (p.127.14; M.8.961B); αὕτη [sc. πενία] τῶν ἀναγκαίων, τῆς θεωρίας λέγω καὶ τῆς καθαρᾶς ἀ., ἀπασχολεῖν βιάζεται τὴν ψυχήν *ib.*4.5(p.257.24; 1233B); *ib.*4.22(p.311.12; 1352C); exeg. Apoc.2:11 τοῦ δὲ δευτέρου [sc. θανάτου] ἐκτὸς ἔσται [sc. ὁ νικῶν] διὰ ἀ. ὡς μὴ ἀδικηθῆναι ὑπ' αὐτοῦ Or.*Apoc.*11(p.25); of virginity αὕτη τὸ ἄδυτον τῆς ἀ. ἱερόν Procl.CP *or.*6.17(M.65.753B); φεῦγε, σιώπα, ἡσύχαζε· αὗται γάρ εἰσιν ῥίζαι τῆς ἀ. *Apophth.Patr.*(M.65.88C).

ἀναμάρτητος, *free from sin, sinless*; **1.** properly of God alone, Ephr.2.7C; Chrys.*hom.39.2 in 1Cor.*(10.365D); Isid.Pel.*epp.*1.435(M.78.421C); Oecum.*Apoc.*2:20(p.55); Jo.D.*parall.*(M.95.1172A); **2.** of Christ; in gen., Just.*dial.*102.7(M.6.716A); ἀ., ἀνεπίληπτος καὶ ἀπαθὴς τὴν ψυχήν...διὰ τοῦτο γὰρ καὶ μόνος κριτής, ὅτι ἀ. μόνος Clem.*paed.*1.2(p.91.22ff.; M.8.252C); Hipp.*fr.19 in Pss.*(p.147.3; M.10.609B); Or.*Jo.*2.26(21; p.83.3; M.14.160B); Apoll.*fid.sec.pt.*(p.181.12; M.10.1120A); dist. from ἄμεμπτος, ‡Just.*qu.et resp.*141(M.6.1396A) cit. s.v.; Chrys.*hom.38.2 in 1Cor.*(10.353B); τὸ ἀ. ὁ Δαβὶδ ἐν μόνῳ θεωρήσας τῷ ἐξ αὐτοῦ κατὰ σάρκα Χριστῷ Cyr.*Ps.*58:6(M.69.1112C); Vict.*Mc.*1:10(p.272.1); ἆρα μὴ τὸ ἀ. τοῦ κυριακοῦ ἀνθρώπου λέγουσι [sc. Nestorians] τεκμήριον τῆς οὐσιώδους πρὸς τὸν λόγον ἑνώσεως; Leont.H.*Nest.*1.19(M.86.1472D); ἄνθρωπον τέλειον, ἀ. Tim.III Al.*fr.*(M.86.268B); cf. οὗ δὲ ἡ ζωὴ ἀ., τούτου πάντως ἀχώριστος ἡ πρὸς τὸν θεὸν ἕνωσις Gr.Nyss.*Apoll.*54(M.45.1256D); of his flesh, Ephr.2.46E; ταύτην ἀνίστησι κατὰ φύσιν ἀ. ‡Ath.*Apoll.*1.7(M.26.1104C); Nil. *epp.*2.150(M.79.269C); σάρκα γὰρ ἀ. εἰς ἑαυτὸν παραπέμψας ὁ ᾅδης ἀδίκως Bas.Sel.*or.*4.1(M.85.65B); τὴν ἰδίαν σάρκα ἀ. κατέστησε· καὶ τοὺς ὁμοουσίους αὐτῇ ἁμαρτωλούς, ἐνθάδε τῆς ἀ. πνευματικῆς οὐσιώσεως, ἐν τῷ μέλλοντι σὺν αὐτῇ, ἠξίωσεν ἀπεράντως Leont.H.*Nest.*1.47 (M.86.1505D); cf. τοῖς ἀ. πάθεσιν ἔφησεν τὴν ἑαυτοῦ σάρκα πειθαρχεῖν Tim.III Al.*fr.*(M.86.268A); his body σῶμα καινὸν καὶ ἀ., ἕως τοῦ κυρίου οὐκ ἐφάνη ἐν τῷ κόσμῳ Mac.Aeg.*hom.*11.9(M.34.549D); mind, ref. Lc.22:42 νοῦν ἀνθρώπινον, ἀλλ' ἀ. Epiph.*haer.*69.61(p.210.10; M.42.300D); human nature τὴν ἀόρατον τῇ ὁρωμένῃ κατεκάλυψε φύσιν, καὶ τήν τε ὁρωμένην ἀ. διεφύλαξε Thdt.*affect.*6(p.175.17; 4.876); esp. ref. redemption ἐπειδὴ διὰ τῶν τῆς σαρκὸς ἁμαρτημάτων...ἡ πτῶσις ἐγίνετο...εἰκότως πάλιν δι' ἀναμαρτήτου...τὰ κατὰ τῶν ἐχθρῶν ἀνηγείρετο τρόπαια Eus.*d.e.*7.1(p.301.25; M.22.493C); οὐδὲ λύει τὴν τῶν ἀνθρώπων ἁμαρτίαν, μὴ γενόμενος ἄνθρωπος ἀ. Apoll.*fr.*93(p.228.26)ap.Gr.Nyss.*Apoll.*51(M.45.1245D); Gr.Naz.*ep.*102(M.37.196C); **3.** of man; **a.** in full sense; **i.** possibility denied παρὰ τίσιν εὕρομεν ἀ. τὴν φύσιν, ὅπου παρὰ τοῖς ἀποστόλοις οὐχ εὕρομεν; Serap.*Man.*25 (p.41; M.40.921B); ἀ. μὲν γὰρ ἀνθρώπων οὐδεὶς παρὲξ τοῦ γενομένου δι' ἡμᾶς ἀνθρώπου *Const.App.*2.18.4; τὸ παντελῶς ἀ. ὑπὲρ τὴν ἀνθρωπίνην φύσιν ἔταξεν Gr.Naz.*or.*5.33(M.35.708A); Gr.Nyss.*or. dom.*5(p.104.23; M.44.1185B); Chrys.*Laz.*6.9(1.787A); cf. ἄνθρωποι ὄντες [sc. Novatianists], ἀ. σφᾶς εἶναι νομίζουσιν Soz.*h.e.*1.22.3 (M.67.925A); τὸ κατ' αὐτὴν ἁμαρτίας κατακρατεῖν ἀβοηθήτως, φύσεώς ἐστι μόνης τῆς ἀ.· καθ' ἣν εἰ εἴημεν, θεοὶ πάλαι ἂν ὄντες ἐδείχθημεν Leont.H.*Nest.*1.47(M.86.1505B); Rom.Mel.15.22(*AS* 1 p.115); **ii.** of man before Fall, ‡Ath.*Apoll.*1.7(M.26.1104C); τὸν ἀ. Ἀδάμ Leont.B. *Nest.et Eut.*2(M.86.1348D); φύσει ἀ. ... ἀ. δέ φημι, οὐχ ὡς μὴ ἐπιδεχόμενον ἁμαρτίαν· μόνον γὰρ τὸ θεῖον ἁμαρτίας ἐστὶν ἀνεπίδεκτον· ἀλλ' οὐχ ὡς ἐν τῇ φύσει τὸ ἁμαρτάνειν ἔχοντα, ἐν τῇ προαιρέσει δὲ μᾶλλον Jo.D.*f.o.*2.12(M.94.924A); **b.** in restricted sense; **i.** of an infant ἐὰν δὲ νήπιον ἐ]ξέλθῃ ὑπερευχαριστοῦσιν ὅτι ἀ. ἀπῆλθεν Arist. *apol.*(*PLond.*2486 r°5, ed. H. J. M. Milne, *JTS* 25 (1924) p.76); **ii.** of penitent, Just.*dial.*47.5(M.6.580A); **iii.** of those who refrain from sin τὰ μὲν πάθη ἀποτιθεμένους, ἀ. δὲ γενομένους Clem.*str.*7.3 (p.11.4; M.9.417B); μηδὲ ἐν τῷ προφορικῷ λόγῳ ψεύσασθαι θέλων ποτὲ κἂν τούτῳ τὸ ἀ. πάντοτε κατορθῶν *ib.*7.9(p.40.6; 477A); *ib.*7.12 (p.57.11; 512A); Or.*Cels.*3.69(p.262.11; M.11.1012B); Gennad.*fr.Rom.*6:21f.(p.368.24; M.85.1677C); ὧν δὲ κατὰ τὴν γέννησιν, τὴν ὅλην προαίρεσιν λαβὸν τὸ πνεῦμα τὸ ἅγιον, ἀπὸ τῆς γῆς πρὸς οὐρανοὺς δι' ὅλου μετέθηκε...τούτων σαφῶς ἀ. κατὰ τὴν ἕξιν τῆς ἀρετῆς καὶ τῆς γνώσεως ἡ προαίρεσις γέγονε Max.*qu.Thal.*6(M.90.281A); hence in prayer αἰτήσασθε, εἰρηνικὴν τὴν ἡμέραν καὶ ἀ. *Lit.*ap.*Const.App.*8.6.8; **iv.** heret.; of soul in future life, only if freed from body, Meth. *res.*1.28(p.259.5; M.41.1137A); **4.** of Church βασιλίσσης, ἣν ἀνήγαγεν ὁ κύριος ἀ. ἀποτορνεύσας τῷ πατρί Meth.*symp.*7.9(p.80.5; M.18.137A).

ἀναμαρτήτως, *sinlessly*, ref. Christ ἀ. τὰ πάντα τελείως ἔχων Epiph. *exp.fid.*15(p.515.30; M.42.812A); τὴν ἐναμάρτητον φύσιν ἀ. δεξάμενον Isid.Pel.*epp.*1.193(M.78.305C); ἤσθιεν, ἔπινεν...καθάπερ ἡμεῖς· ἀλλὰ πάντῃ ἀ. ‡Cyr.*Trin.*16(6^3.23C; M.77.1156A); ref. men, Just.*dial.*44.4 (M.6.572A); ἀ. καὶ γνωστικῶς βιοῦσιν Clem.*str.*6.12(p.482.24; M.9.321C); Or.*Jo.*1.26(24; p.32.16; M.14.69C).

***ἀναμαρτοεπής,** *uttering nothing false*, Cyr.*Joel.*65(3.245C).

***ἀνάμαρτος** (perh. for ἀναμάρτητος), *sinless*; of Christ, Procl.CP *or.*13.1(M.65.789D).

ἀναμαρυκ-άομαι (ἀναμηρυκάομαι), *chew the cud, digest inwardly*; **1.** lit. ἀναμη- Mac.Aeg.*hom.*32.2(M.34.736A); **2.** met. τῶν...~ωμένων τὸν λόγον κυρίου *Barn.*10.11; Iren.*ep.Flor.*ap.Eus.*h.e.*5.20.7(M.20.485B); of Devil pondering on miracles of Christ, Mac.Mgn.*apocr.*3.9(p.70.15).

ἀναμασάομαι, *chew over again, ruminate*; met., Or.*sel.in Dt.* (M.12.812B); Cyr.*Jo.*2.5(4.192E); id.*Nest.*4(p.85.10; 6^1.110B).

ἀναμάσσ-ω, med.; **1.** *receive an impression*; hence **a.** *receive, contract* τοῦ αἴσχους ὃ ἀνεμάξατο διὰ τῆς κακίας Bas.*Spir.*23(3.20A; M.32.109A); Chrys.*hom.10.4 in Ac.*(9.86B); Mac.Mgn.*apocr.*4.19 (p.198.14); **b.** *take upon oneself, assume* τὸν σωτήριον ὄντως ἀναμαξώμεθα τοῦ σωτῆρος ἡμῶν βίον Clem.*paed.*1.12(p.149.3; M.8.368B); τὴν θείαν μορφήν...ταῖς ἑαυτῶν ~όμενοι ψυχαῖς Cyr.*Jo.*5.5(4.550E); Nil.*Magn.*44(M.79.1024C); *take form of*, Geo.Pis.*carm.vit.*18; **c.** *take* as the meaning ἀναμαξάμενοι δὲ ἀκριβῶς τὴν τοῦ νοήματος δύναμιν Cyr.*Jo.*1.10(4.107B); *ib.*6.1(4.636B); **2.** *make* an impression ἀντιπάλαμνος ἐὸν ~εται εἶδος μυστιπόλων Eudoc.*Cypr.*2.260(M.85.856B); **3.** *rub on*, Clem.*paed.*3.2(p.240.11; M.8.564B).

***ἀνάμαυρος,** *not dim, clear*, Gel.Cyz.*h.e.*2.20.1(M.85.1281A).

ἀναμέλπ-ω, *raise a strain*; *praise in song* αὐτὸν [sc. τὸν υἱόν] ~ων ῥήμασιν ὁ μελῳδός Cyr.*Jo.*2.2(4.163C); σοι ~οντας Anast.*poenit.*7 (p.284).

***ἀναμελῳδ-έω,** *raise a melody* ὁ ψαλμῳδὸς πρὸς Χριστὸν ~ῶν Cyr.*ador.*9(1.302A); id.*Abac.*53(3.569B); id.*inc.unigen.*(5^1.684A); of Christ as instrument of God διοίσει...οὐδὲν...λύρας, ἐκεῖνο φωνῶν, ὅπερ ἂν...~εῖν τῷ πλήκτρῳ κελεύηται id.*Jo.*9.1(4.789C).

ἀναμέν-ω, *suffer, undergo* οὐκ ~ει πάθος· οὐκ ἐκδέχεται φθοράν †Ephr.*nativ.*(p.89).

[*]ἀναμέρος, = ἀνὰ μέρος, *separately*, Mac.Aeg.*elev.*13(M.34.901C); Cyr.*inc.unigen.*(5^1.679E); Jo.D.*f.o.*3.10(M.94.1020A); εἰς ἀ. *asunder*, Max.*ep.*17(M.91.581B).

***ἀναμέσον,** = ἀνὰ μέσον; **1.** *between*; c. genit., Ephr.2.12A; κρινεῖ ...ἀ. ἐμοῦ καὶ Μαυρικίου Thphn.*chron.*p.233(M.108.588C); c. dat. οἱ ἀ. τούτοις τοῖς χρόνοις περιελθόντες ‡Jo.D.*ep.Thphl.*12(M.95.360D); **2.** *among, in the midst*; c. genit., Jo.Thess.*dorm.BMV* A 8(p.387.25).

ἀναμεστ-όω, *fill up, flood* τὸν διὰ Χριστοῦ φωτισμὸν...διαρκῶς ἔχοντα...~οῦν τῶν πιστευόντων τὸν νοῦν Cyr.*ador.*9(1.321A); id.*apol. orient.*proem.(p.33.17; 6^1.157E); v.l. for ἀναμετρεῖν, id.*Joel.*9(3.207E).

***ἀναμετάβλητος,** prob. for ἀμετάβλητος, Cyr.*Is.*5.6(2.905A).

ἀναμεταξύ, *between*; c. genit., Barth.Edess.*Agar.*(M.104.1392A).

ἀναμετρ-έω, 1. *calculate, reckon up* καιρὸν...~ήσας Chrys.*hom.*

51.4 *in Mt.*(7.525E); ~ήσαντες συμφοράς Cyr.*Ps.*34:3(M.69.896A); **2.** *measure* one thing by another, *fill to the measure of* ~εῖν [v.l. ἀναμεστοῦν]...σίτῳ τὰς ἀποθήκας Cyr.*Joel.*9(3.207E); **3.** *measure out, cover* a distance; met., Meth.*symp.*3.14(p.45.9; M.18.85C); of the number ten covering or representing souls of believers ὁ τῶν δέκα παρθένων ἀριθμὸς τὰς εἰς Χριστὸν...πεπιστευκυίας ~εῖσθαι [v.l. ἀριθμεῖσθαι] βούλεται ψυχάς *ib.*6.2(p.65.20; 116A); **4.** *measure* a distance *over again*, met., of returning to the faith οἱ πλείους τῶν ἠρνημένων ἀνεμετροῦντο (v.l. ἀνενεοῦντο, conj. ἀνεμητροῦντο) *Ep. Lugd.*ap.Eus.*h.e.*5.1.46(M.20.425B); ~ουμένη...τὰ τῶν παίδων ἀγωνίσματα *ib.*5.1.55(429B).

***ἀναμέτρως**, *in due proportion*, Anast.S.*hex.*12(M.89.1052C).

ἀναμηρύομαι, **1.** *sum up, summarize* ὅλον ὥσπερ ἀ. τῆς προφητείας τὸν σκοπόν Cyr.*Os.*35(3.63B); id.*Jo.*6.1(4.639D); **2.** *repeat* ἕκαστα τῶν ἤδη προειρημένων ἀ. *ib.*3.2(255D).

***ἀναμητρόω**, *conceive again*; conj. for ἀναμετρέω, *Ep.Lugd.*ap. Eus.*h.e.*5.1.46(M.20.425B).

***ἀναμίγνυμι**, [ἀναμιγνύεις, Agath.*v.Gr.Ill.*23], *mix up, mix together*, Thphn.*chron.*p.21(M.108.112B) = Alex.Sal.*cruc.*(M.87.4064B) cit. s. σαλιβάριον; pass., *be mixed with*; *be absorbed*, of Son into Father acc. Sabellians, ‡Gr.Nyss.*Ar.et Sab.*6(M.45.1289B); in Apollinarian Christology, Cyr.*synous.*10(p.486.14; cf.M.76.1433B).

***ἀνάμικτος**, *mixed*, Gr.Naz.*or.*4.87(M.35.616B).

***ἀναμίκωτος**, *sleeveless*, Thphn.*chron.*p.372(M.108.889B).

ἀναμίλλητος, *unrivalled*, Cyr.*Jo.*9(4.725C); id.*hom.pasch.*9(5². 119A).

ἀναμιμνήσκω, *recall to mind*, med. ψαλμοῦ Just.*dial.*34.1(M.6. 548A).

ἀνάμιξις, ἡ, *mingling*; sexual *intercourse*, *Pss.Sal.*2.15.

ἀνάμνησις, ἡ, **A.** *calling to mind*; **1.** (subjective) *recollection*; **a.** def. ἀ. δὲ λέγεται, ὅταν λήθη μεσολαβήσῃ τὴν μνήμην. ἔστι γὰρ ἀ. μνήμης ἐξιτήλου γενομένης ἀνάκτησις...ἑτέρα δέ ἐστιν ἀ., ἥτις οὐκ ἔστι λήθη [l. μνήμη?] τῶν ἐξ αἰσθήσεως καὶ νοήσεως, ἀλλὰ τῶν φυσικῶν ἐννοιῶν...ὡς τὸ εἶναι θεόν Nemes.*nat.hom.*13(M.40.661B,C); Jo.D.*f.o.* 2.20(M.94.940A); **b.** applications: God εἰς ἀ. αὐτοῦ καὶ γνῶσιν ὑμᾶς καλεῖ [sc. ὁ θεός] Just.*dial.*27.4(M.6.533B); id.*1apol.*44.11(M.6.396B); what is profitable, Meth.*Porph.*1(p.503.6; M.18.397C); pleasure, Clem.*str.*2.20(p.171.14; M.8.1049C); the world εἰ...χρημάτων ἢ δόξης ἀ. γένοιτο, ἐκ τοῦ πράγματος δῆλον ὅτι ὁ θλίβων ἡμᾶς ἐπιγνωσθήσεται †Nil.*mal.cog.*2(M.79.1201C); διολισθήσει [sc. ὁ νοῦς] δ' ἂν εὐκόλως τῶν ἐν κόσμῳ περισπασμῶν εἰς ἀ. Cyr.*glaph.Dt.*(1.419C); **2.** (objective) *reminding* πρὸς ἀ. οὖν ταῦτα γράφομεν *1Clem.*53.1; πρός τε ἀ. πρός τε ἐμφάνισιν ἀληθείας Clem.*str.*4.2(p.249.27; M.8.1217A); ἐμφαίνειν δὲ [sc. τὸ μυστήριον] ὅσον εἰς ἀ. τοῖς μετεσχηκόσι τῆς γνώσεως *ib.*7.14 (p.63.4; M.9.521C); ‡Just.*qu.et resp.*53(M.6.1297A); οὐχ ὡς θεοὺς ἔχομεν αὐτὰ [sc. Cherubim] ἐν τῷ ναῷ, ἀλλ' εἰς ἀ. θεοῦ καὶ δόξαν Leont.N.*serm.*3(M.93.1605D).

B. *commemorative act, commemoration* (usu. ἀ. ποιεῖν); **1.** pagan; ref. New Year οἱ μὲν ὁπλῖται Ῥωμαίων...ἀ. τε τοῦ ἔτους ποιοῦνται Gr.Nyss.*mart.*3(M.46.773A); **2.** Jewish; of Passover ἀ. τῆς κατ' Αἴγυπτον...γεγενημένης σωτηρίας ἡγούμενοι μόνην εἶναι τὸ μυστήριον τοῦ προβάτου Meth.*symp.*9.1(p.115.12; M.18.180B); ‡Chrys.*pasch.*4 (8.259D); εἰς ἀ. τῆς ἐν Αἰγύπτῳ πικροτάτης ζωῆς Thdt.*qu.12 in Ex.* (1.140); **3.** Christian; **a.** of eucharist as *recalling* of saving work of Christ in all aspects τοῦ ἄρτου τῆς εὐχαριστίας, ὃν εἰς ἀ. τοῦ πάθους... Ἰησοῦς Χριστὸς...παρέδωκε ποιεῖν Just.*dial.*41.1(M.6.564B); περὶ τοῦ ἄρτου, ὃν παρέδωκεν ἡμῖν...ποιεῖν εἰς ἀ. τοῦ τε σωματοποιήσασθαι αὐτὸν...καὶ περὶ τοῦ ποτηρίου, ὃ εἰς ἀ. τοῦ αἵματος αὐτοῦ παρέδωκεν εὐχαριστοῦντας ποιεῖν *ib.*70.4(641A); cf. ἐπ' ἀναμνήσει δὲ τῆς τροφῆς αὐτῶν ξηρᾶς τε καὶ ὑγρᾶς, ἐν ᾗ καὶ τοῦ πάθους...μέμνηται *ib.*117.3 (745C); cf. τὸ...αὐτοῦ σῶμα καὶ αἷμα, ἅπερ ἐν τῇ μυστικῇ καὶ θείᾳ τραπέζῃ καθ' ἑκάστην ἐπιτελοῦνται θυόμενα εἰς ἀ. τῆς ἀειμνήστου καὶ πρώτης ἐκείνης τραπέζης τοῦ μυστικοῦ θείου δείπνου ‡Hipp.*fr.Pr.* 9:1(Lagarde, Leipzig, 1858, p.199.12); τὰ φρικώδη μυστήρια...εὐχαριστία καλεῖται, ὅτι πολλῶν ἐστιν εὐεργετημάτων ἀ. Chrys.*hom.25.3 in Mt.*(7.310D); ἐξάγει τῶν Ἰουδαϊκῶν ἐθῶν...καθάπερ γὰρ ἐκεῖνο ἐποιεῖτε, φησίν, εἰς ἀ. τῶν ἐν Αἰγύπτῳ θαυμάτων, οὕτω καὶ τοῦτο εἰς ἐμήν *ib.82.1*(7.782E); moral attitude required, id.*hom.27.4 in 1Cor.* (10.246E); τὸ θεομίμητον δὲ πῶς ἂν ἡμῖν ἑτέρως ἐγγένοιτο, μὴ τῆς τῶν ἱερωτάτων θεουργιῶν μνήμης ἀνανεουμένης ἀεὶ ταῖς...ἱερουργίαις; τοῦτο οὖν ποιοῦμεν...εἰς τὴν αὐτῆς ἀ. Dion.Ar.*e.h.*3.3.12(M.3.441C); καθάπερ γάρ, φησί, τὸ τοῦ ἀμνοῦ ἐποιεῖτε εἰς ἀ. τῶν ἐκεῖ θαυμάτων [i.e. Passover events], οὕτω τοῦτο εἰς τὴν ἐμὴν ἀ. ἕως ἂν παραγένωμαι Petr.Laod.*fr.in Lc.*22:19(M.86.3329A); sense of this recalling προσφέρομεν μέν, ἀλλ' ἀ. ποιούμενοι τοῦ θανάτου αὐτοῦ... τοῦτο εἰς ἀ. γίνεται τοῦ τότε γενομένου...οὐκ ἄλλην θυσίαν, καθάπερ ὁ ἀρχιερεὺς τότε, ἀλλὰ τὴν αὐτὴν ἀεὶ ποιοῦμεν· μᾶλλον δὲ ἀ. ἐργαζόμεθα θυσίας Chrys.*hom.17.3 in Heb.*(12.168Dff.); **b.** liturg.; apart from Institution words, ἀ. seems to be found only in ὁ[σάκις] ἐὰν ἐσθίητε τὸν ἄρτον τοῦτον...τὴν ἐμὴν ἀνάμν[ησιν πο]ιεῖτε *Lit.Marc.* (*PDêr-Baliz.*p.2 v° 29); cf.Hipp.*trad.ap.*4.10; cf. *for as often as ye shall eat of this bread...ye do make my memorial until I come*, *Lit. of Coptic Jacobites* (Brightman p.177.33); cf. μιμνήσκω; at prothesis εἰς ἀ. τοῦ κυρίου καὶ θεοῦ καὶ σωτῆρος ἡμῶν Ἰησοῦ Χριστοῦ *Lit.Chrys.*(p.356.30); **c.** exeg. 1Cor.11:24–25 ὁ Χριστὸς καὶ ἐπὶ τοῦ ἄρτου καὶ ἐπὶ τοῦ ποτηρίου, εἰς τὴν ἐμὴν ἀ. ποιεῖτε τοῦτο, ἔφη, τὴν αἰτίαν ἐκκαλύπτων ἡμῖν τῆς τοῦ μυστηρίου δόσεως, καὶ...ταύτην εἶναι λέγων ἀρκοῦσαν ἡμῖν εἰς εὐλαβείας ὑπόθεσιν· ὅταν γὰρ ἐννοήσῃς τί πέπονθεν ὁ δεσπότης σου διὰ σέ, φιλοσοφώτερος ἔσῃ Chrys.*hom. 27.4 in 1Cor.*(10.247A,B); **d.** of baptism as similar recalling of Passion εἰς...πλῆθος αὐξανομένης καθ' ἡμέραν τῆς ἐκκλησίας διὰ τὴν σύνερξιν καὶ τὴν κοινωνίαν τοῦ λόγου συγκαταβαίνοντος ἡμῖν καὶ νῦν ἔτι καὶ ἐξισταμένου κατὰ τὴν ἀ. τοῦ πάθους Meth.*symp.*3.8(p.35. 22; M.18.73B); cf. ἀνακεφαλαίωσιν...τοῦ πάθους *ib.*(p.36.2; 73B); οἱ ἀναγεννώμενοι...νεοφώτιστοι καλοῦνται περιφραστικῶς, τὴν πνευματικὴν αὐτοῖς πανσέληνον κατὰ τὴν περίοδον τοῦ πάθους καὶ τὴν ἀ. νέαν ἀεὶ παραφαινούσης τῆς ἐκκλησίας *ib.*8.6(p.88.22; 148C); **e.** of commemoration on different days of various acts of Christ: Sunday ἀ. ... τοῦ κυρίου ἐστὶν ἡ τῆς κυριακῆς ἁγία ἡμέρα Eus.Al.*serm.*16.1 (M.86.416B); Friday τοῦ σωτηρίου πάθους τὴν ἀ. ποιούμενοι διὰ νηστείας Eus.*pasch.*12(M.24.705C); Nativity, Bas.*ep.*232(3.355B; M. 32.864A); Epiphany, *Rit.Epiph.*(p.416); **f.** of commemoration of a saint, *A.Mt.*31(p.261.11); **g.** of commemoration of dead by liturg. offerings and almsgiving παρακαλοῦμεν...ὑπὲρ πάντων τῶν κεκοιμημένων, ὧν ἐστι καὶ ἡ ἀ. Serap.*euch.*13.17; ποιήσατέ μου τὴν μνήμην. εὐεργετοῦνται γὰρ οἱ θνητοὶ ἐν προσφοραῖς ἀναμνήσεως περὶ τῶν ζώντων ἁγίων Ephr.2.239A; διδόσθω ἐκ τῶν ὑπαρχόντων αὐτοῦ πένησιν εἰς ἀ. αὐτοῦ *Const.App.*8.42.5; Chrys.*hom.27.4 in 1Cor.*(10.246E).

ἀναμονή, ἡ, **1.** *delay, waiting, pause*, in antiphonal chanting ὡρισμένη εὐχὴ ἐν τῇ ἀ. τοῦ στίχου τοῦ πλησίον Jo.Clim.*scal.*19(M.88. 937D); **2.** *waiting* upon, *expectation* τὴν πρὸς αὐτὸν...λατρείαν καὶ ἀ. Mac.Aeg.*hom.*29.4(M.34.717C).

***ἀναμορφοποιέω**, *restore to form* ἀναμορφοποιηθῆναι τὴν ὕλην Meth.*res.*1.43(p.291.9, v.l. ἀναμορφωθῆναι M.18.272C).

ἀναμορφ-όω, *form anew*; **1.** in gen., Thdt.*h.rel.*13(3.1209); of bodies in resurrection Κόνων δὲ καὶ οἱ σὺν αὐτῷ...πάλιν ~οῦσθαι τὴν αὐτὴν ὕλην λέγουσι, κρεῖττον εἶδος δεχομένην ἄφθαρτον Tim.CP *haer.* (M.86.61D); Ὠριγένην λέγοντα ὅτι ἡ αὐτὴ ὕλη ἐν τῷ μέλλοντι αἰῶνι ~οῦται *ib.*(64C); **2.** of men's transformation by Christ, through Inc. τὴν ἀνθρώπου φύσιν ~ῶν εἰς καινότητα ζωῆς Cyr.*Soph.*44(3.622D); id.*Is.*2.1(2.189B); id.*inc.unigen.*(5¹.692A) cit. s. ἀφθαρσία; ἀποστέλλει πρὸς τὴν καταφθαρεῖσαν εἰκόνα, τὸν τῆς εἰκόνος ποιητήν, ~ῶσαι ταύτην χρώμασιν ἀγαθότητος Procl.CP *annunt.*2(M.85.432B); Anast.Ant. *serm.*2.8(M.89.1385A); ἀνεμόρφωσεν ἡμᾶς εἰς ἀφθαρσίαν Anast.S.*qu. et resp.*143(M.89.796B); through baptism διὰ τῆς παλιγγενεσίας τῆς εἰκόνος ~οῖ τὸ ἀρχέτυπον *Rit.Epiph.*(p.418); in gen. διὰ Χριστοῦ ~ούμεθα, τῆς διανοίας ἡμῶν εἰς πνευματικὴν ποιότητα διαπλαττομένης Ammon.*Jo.*3:8(M.85.1409B); into image of Christ, ref. Gal.4:19 ~οῦντος ἡμᾶς...τοῦ ἁγίου πνεύματος δι' ἁγιασμοῦ πρὸς αὐτόν Cyr.*Is.* 4.2(2.591B); through faith, id.*thes.*(5¹.288B); ὁ Χριστὸς κεφαλή... τῶν δι' αὐτοῦ πρὸς αὐτὸν ~ουμένων εἰς ἀφθαρσίαν δι' ἁγιασμοῦ ἐν πνεύματι id.*Pulch.*(p.28.16; 5².131C); Proc.G.*Gen.*5:3(M.87.264A); **3.** in baptism νεοκτίστου ψυχῆς, ἣν τὸ πνεῦμα δι' ὕδατος ἀνεμόρφωσεν Gr.Naz.*or.*7.15(M.35.773C).

ἀναμόρφωσις, ἡ, *forming anew*; of spiritual re-creation through Christ, Cyr.*Jo.*2.1(4.114B); through H. Ghost, *ib.*(148A); id.*Is.*4.2 (2.610E); τῶν πρὸς τὸ τοῦ θεοειδοῦς παραφθαρτικὸν ἀπολισθησάντων... ἀ. Dion.Ar.*d.n.*1.3(M.3.589B).

ἀναμοχλεύ-ω, **1.** *raise with levers*, hence *overturn, uproot*; of turning up earth, Chrys.*hom.3.3 in 2Thess.*(11.524E); uprooting error, id.*hom.3.3 in 1Cor.*(10.18E); arousing passions, Evagr.Pont. *or.*46(M.79.1176D); *overthrow, destroy*, Cyr.*ador.*8(1.268A); *ib.*6(177B); ‡Jo.D.*Artem.*66(M.96.1316A); *remove* disease, Isid.Pel.*epp.*2.21(M. 78.472A); Thdt.*qu.12 in Ex.*(1.130); **2.** *unbar, force open*, of Christ ἀ. τὰ καθ' ᾅδου Epiph.*haer.*77.29(p.441.12; M.42.684B); met. ~οντες νοῦν Cyr.*Jo.*3.3(4.265C); **3.** *utter* words, ‡Gr.Naz.*Chr.pat.*211(M.38. 147A); **4.** *bring forward* μὴ κρατείτωσαν οἱ τύποι, μή τε μὴν ~έσθω πρός τινος ἡ σκιά Cyr.*glaph.Dt.*(1.429D).

***ἀναμοχλίζω**, *heave up*, Gr.Nyss.*hom.15 in Cant.*(M.44.1108C).

ἀναμύ-ω, **1.** *be opened*, Meth.*res.*1.41(p.287.9; M.18.269C); **2.** *have the eyes open, gaze*; lit., Cyr.*Jo.*6.1(4.603B); met. ἀ. ... πρὸς θεόν id.

*glaph.Gen.*5(1.174B); id.*Mal.*6(3.822D); ὁ νοῦς...πρὸς αὐτὸ τὸ ἀκήρατον ~ων κάλλος id.*ador.*12(1.414C).

ἀναμφήριστος, *undisputed, incontestable*, Ath.*syn.*21(p.248.16; M.26.720B); Nonn.*par.Jo.*10:34(M.43.837B); τῷ παντοδυνάμῳ προσ-τέθεικε...τὸ ἀ. Olymp.*Job* 12:14(M.93.153A).

***ἀναμφηρίστως**, *indisputably*, Clem.*str.*1.21(p.64.21; M.8.820A); Eus.*p.e.*10.9(485A; M.21.808A); Max.*ambig.*(M.91.1081D).

***ἀναμφηρίτως**, = foreg., Soz.*h.e.*6.4.6(M.67.1301C).

***ἀναμφίαστος** (-εστος), *unclothed*, Cyr.*ador.*16(1.564C); of bodiless souls, id.*Jo.*1.9(4.84D); met., *simple, plain* πολιτείαν Or.*exc. in Ps.*36:5(M.17.121D); ἀναμφίεστον...ἀλήθειαν Cyr.*hom.pasch.*22(5^{2}.273C); id.*Is.*3.3(2.433C).

***ἀναμφιβάλλω**, *have no doubt*, *cat.Apoc.*11:17(p.348.10).

***ἀναμφίβλητος**, *indisputable*, Cyr.*Juln.18 fr.*(M.76.1061D).

ἀναμφίβολος, *unambiguous, certain, plain*, Cyr.H.*catech.*10.18; Gr.Nyss.*Eun.*1(1 p.145.29; M.45.385B); of faith, Thdr.Mops.*Os.*14:1ff.(M.66.208C); neut. as subst., †Bas.*Is.*8(1.383D; M.30.132A).

ἀναμφιβόλως, *without doubting*, Gr.Nyss.*usur.*(M.46.440B).

***ἀναμφίεστος**, v. *ἀναμφίαστος.

***ἀναμφιέστως**, *without clothes*, Cyr.*Juln.*9(6^{2}.318B).

ἀναμφίλεκτος, **1.** *undisputed, undoubted*, of 1 Pet. ταύτῃ δὲ [sc. ἐπιστολῇ] καὶ οἱ πάλαι πρεσβύτεροι ὡς ἀ. ... κατακέχρηνται Eus.*h.e.* 3.3.1(M.20.216B); **2.** *indisputable*; of arguments, id.*p.e.*10.2(463D; M.21.772C); Gr.Naz.*or.*43.68(M.36.588B); *certain* ἔπαθλον Euthal. Diac.*Ac.*(M.85.632C); **3.** *undisputing, unquestioning* τῆς τῶν ἀσκη-τῶν ἀ. ὑπακοῆς ‡Bas.*const.*22.3(2.572B, v.l. ἀναμφιβόλου; M.31.1405D).

ἀναμφιλέκτως, *unhesitatingly*, Const.ap.Eus.*h.e.*10.6.3(M.20.892B).

ἀναμφίλογος, **1.** *undoubting*; of faith, Cyr.*Is.*2.1(2.189A); **2.** *unambiguous*, id.*ep.*46 ap.†Leont.B.*sect.*8.2(M.86.1253B, cf.p.161.1; 5^{2}.144B, ἀναμφίβολος).

ἀναμφιλόγως, *unhesitatingly*, Eus.*h.e.*8.4.3(M.20.749B).

ἀναμφισβήτητος, *undisputing, unquestioning*; of faith, Vict.*Mc.* 2:13(p.287.18).

ἀναμφισβητήτως, **1.** *undisputably*, Meth.*symp.*3.13(p.43.16; M.18.84B); Thdt.*eran.*1(4.9); **2.** *without doubting*, Meth.*symp.*7.1(p.70.17; M.18.121C).

ἄνανδρος, **1.** *effeminate*; of a eunuch, *not a man*, Pall.*v.Chrys.* 15(p.92.14; M.47.52); **2.** *not a husband* Ἰωσὴφ ἄ. ἀνὴρ τῆς Μαρίας προσηγόρευται ‡Epiph.*hom.*2(M.43.444A).

ἀνανεάζ-ω, **1.** *be renewed* or *re-invigorated*, of a martyr ἀνενέαξεν ἐν τῇ ὁμολογίᾳ *Ep.Lugd.*ap.Eus.*h.e.*5.1.19(M.20.416B); **2.** trans., *renew*, of the baptized ἀνανεασθέντες Meth.*symp.*8.6(p.88.19; M.18.148B); τὴν ψυχήν μου ἀ. *M.Tar.*7(p.465); φωτοχυσία...τὰς νοερὰς... ~ουσα δυνάμεις Dion.Ar.*d.n.*4.6(M.3.701A); as subst., ref. daily bread τὸ ~ον Gr.Nyss.*or.dom.*4(p.78.22; M.44.1168D).

ἀνανε-όω, *renew*, **1.** lit. κατεφθαρμένων ἡμῶν...ἀνενέωσε τὴν ζωὴν ἡμῶν Herm.*sim.*9.14.3; Gel.Cyz.*h.e.*2.17.26(M.85.452B) cit. s. παλαιόω; of bodies at resurrection, Athenag.*res.*10(p.58.20; M.6.992B); of Ezra's renewal of lost books of Bible, Clem.*str.*1.22(p.92.26; M.8.893A); τῆς διὰ Χριστοῦ καινῆς διαθήκης ἀνανεωθείσης Eus. *d.e.*1.6(p.28.24; M.22.57B); esp. *rebuild*, Const.ap.Eus.*v.C.*2.55(p.63.36; M.20.1029D); Ephr.2.113C; Evagr.*h.e.*1.22(p.32.27; M.86.2184B); **2.** met., *revive, renew*, Iren.*haer.*3.3.3(M.7.850A); Gr.Nyss.*v.Macr.* (p.380.20; M.46.969A); Cyr.*Jo.*1.9(4.81C); ref. Christ's baptism ἡμῖν δι' ἑαυτοῦ λαμβάνει τὸ πνεῦμα, καὶ ~οῖ τῇ φύσει τὸ ἀρχαῖον ἀγαθόν *ib.*2.1(123E); *repeat* κακόνοιαν...~ῶσαι Alex.Al.*ep.encycl.*1(p.7.12; M.18.572C); *refresh* τὸ γηραιὸν τῆς τοῦ πατρὸς ἡλικίας...~ούμενος Gr.Nyss.*mart.*1(M.46.752C); *repair*, Chrys.*hom.28.2 in Gen.*(4.271A); intrans., *renew one's youth*, Herm.*vis.*5.11.3; **3.** esp. of image of God renewed in man through Christ, Ath.*inc.*13.7(M.25.120B); *Lit. Jac.*(p.200.22); and of spiritual renewal: through Inc. χρεία δὲ ἦν ἄλλου τοῦ ~οῦντος...τὴν πρώτην [sc. κτίσιν] Ath.*Ar.*2.65(M.26.285B); Bas.*hom.*1.2(2.2E; M.31.165C) cit. s. παλαιόω; ἀπαρχὴ τῆς ~ουμένης φύσεως...γέγονεν ὁ...Χριστός Cyr.*Jo.*5.2(4.473E); id.*thes.*15(5^{1}.175B); through baptism τὴν ~οῦσαν γέννησιν Or.*fr.35 in Jo.*3:3(p.510.24); Cypr.*ep.*(H.1.155C); Serap.*euch.*25.2; Chrys.*comm.in Gal.*6:15f.(10.729A) cit. s. ἀνακτίζω; in gen., Herm.*vis.*3.12.3.

ἀνάνευσις, ἡ, *movement upwards* ἡ πρὸς τὸν...θεὸν ἀ. Eus.*p.e.*1.1 2B; M.21.24B); *ib.*7.16(330A; M.557A); from ignorance, *ib.*2.5(69D; M.133D); τῆς ἐν τῷ βαπτίσματι ἀ. Bas.*ep.*236.5(3.363E, v.l. ἀναδεύ-σεως; M.32.884A); prob. from sin ἐὰν ἄλλον ἴδῃ ἐν ἀ. ... συνᾴδει Ephr.1.13A; from carnal passion, †Jo.D.*B.J.*24(M.96.1084A); *gazing upwards*; of contemplation, Dion.Ar.*e.h.*2.3.4(M.3.400C); *ib.*2.3.5 (401B); ἡμᾶς...αὐτοὺς ταῖς εὐχαῖς ἀνατείνωμεν ἐπὶ τὴν τῶν θείων... ἀκτίνων ὑψηλοτέραν ἀ. id.*d.n.*3.1(M.3.680C).

ἀνανεύ-ω, **1.** *deny, refuse*, Nonn.*par.Jo.*21:5(M.43.916B); ~ει τοῦ πρὸς τὴν βασιλίδα διαβῆναι Gel.Cyz.*h.e.*3.10.5; **2.** *lift one's eyes, look up* ἀ. τῆς γῆς εἰς αἰθέρα Clem.*prot.*10(p.76.5; M.8.221B); πρὸς Χριστὸν ~οντα...μάχεσθαι Meth.*symp.*11(p.139.15; M.18.217B); to truth, Ath. *inc.*12.6(M.25.117C); ἀ. εἰς τὴν τοῦ τέλους ἡμέραν Bas.*ep.*45.2(3.134D; M.32.368D); of consciousness of sin ~ειν οὐκ ἐᾷ Cyr.*Ps.*37:7(M.69.960B); **3.** *emerge* τῆς πλάνης ἀ. Eus.*p.e.*2.2(61B; M.21.120A); from sin, Gr.Naz.*or.*36.5(M.36.272A); from water of baptism, Chrys.*hom. 25.2 in Jo.*(8.146C); **4.** *go up* ἐπὶ τὸ Εὐρώπης κλίμα ἀ. Jo.D.*haer.*2 (M.94.680A); **5.** *stand upright* ἦν γὰρ αὕτη μικρὸν τῷ μήκει ~ουσα *Pers.*(p.17.21).

***ἀνανέωμα**, τό, *renewal, reproduction* τὰ ἀρχέτυπα [e.g. Temple] ...τῆς...λογικῆς ἐν ψυχαῖς οἰκοδομῆς ἀ. Eus.*h.e.*10.4.55(M.20.872A).

ἀνανέωσις, ἡ, *renewal*; **1.** in gen.; **a.** *repetition* ἀ. ... τιμωρίας Cyr.*Jo.*1.9(4.81C); in memory, *recollection* τῇ μνήμῃ καὶ ἀ. τῆς ...θεολογίας Dion.Ar.*ep.*10(M.3.1120A); **b.** *restoration, rebuilding*, Clem.*str.*1.21(p.77.23; M.8.853A); Eus.*h.e.*10.1.3(M.20.844A); Jo.Mal. *chron.*10 p.246(M.97.376C); **2.** spiritual: through Christ θάνατος [sc. τοῦ Χριστοῦ]...τοῦ πρωτοπλάστου Ἀδὰμ ἀ. †Hipp.*Laz.*(p.218.31; M. 62.777); ‡Ath.*Ar.*4.33(p.82.12; M.26.520A) cit. s. ἀνακαινίζω; οἰκο-νομῶν εἰς ἀ. ἀνθρωπότητος Apoll.*fid.sec.pt.*36(p.181.13; M.10.1120A); γενέσθαι διὰ τῆς πρὸς αὐτὸν συνθέσεως τὴν ἡμετέραν ἀ. Leont.H.*Nest.* 1.18(M.86.1469D); Germ.CP *or.*2(M.98.243D); through coming of H. Ghost, Cyr.*Jo.*5.2(4.474A); through baptism, Meth.*symp.*3.8 (p.36.13; M.18.73C); ζωῆς ἀ. Bas.*Spir.*32(3.27A; M.32.125A); through eucharist εἰς ἀ. ψυχῶν καὶ σωμάτων *Lit.Jac.*(p.192.20); in gen. ἀ. ... τῶν πνευμάτων Herm.*vis.*3.13.2; *A.(Pass.)Andr.*4(p.10.21); Clem. *str.*4.23(p.314.17; M.8.1357C) cit. s. ἀνάκτισις; of world through Christianity, Const.*ep.*(Opitz 3 p.59.13); τὴν κατὰ θεὸν ἀ. καὶ ἀνα-καίνισιν Ath.*Ar.*2.46(M.26.245A); Chrys.*hom.13.2 in Eph.*(11.97E).

ἀνανεωτικός, *renewing, able to renew* τὸ ἐν ἰσότητι τῇ πρὸς τὸν θεὸν...ἀ. Leont.B.*Apoll.*(M.86.1964D); ἡ θεία σοφία...ἀ. Dion.Ar.*ep.* 9.4(M.3.1112B); id.*c.h.*15.2(M.3.329B).

***ἀνάνηξις**, ἡ, *swimming up*; *rising* of mind to God, Thdr.Stud. *antirr.*1.13(M.99.344D).

ἀνανήφ-ω, **1.** *become sober again, come to one's senses*; met., from sin or ignorance, Ign.*Smyrn.*9.1; Thphl.Ant.*Autol.*2.34(M.6.1108A); ἀναγεννηθέντες...ἀνανήψωμεν Clem.*paed.*3.12(p.283.10; M.8.664C); of men before Inc. ἐβαρήθημεν τῷ ψεύδει, οὐκ ἐδυνάμεθα ἀνανῆψαι ‡Ath.*diab.*10(p.10.7); from fear, *Pers.*(p.4.16); avarice, Isid.Pel. *epp.*1.434(M.78.421B); **2.** *exercise care* ~ει εἰς τὸ ἀκριβὲς τῆς προ-φητείας ὁ λόγος Cyr.*Is.*2.5(2.337D); *ib.*3.2(418A); *ib.*3.3(425A).

ἀνανήχομαι, **1.** *swim to the surface*, Cyr.*ador.*14(1.503E); id.*Juln.*9 (6^{2}.318A); met., *rise upwards* ἀ. πρὸς ἔφεσιν ἀρετῆς id.*Is.*4.2(2.613C); εἰς τὴν...ἐλευθερίαν ἀ. πως id.*Mich.*66(3.460E); id.*Juln.*9(318B); **2.** *sail upstream*, ‡Caes.Naz.*dial.*147(M.38.1097).

***ἀνάνηψις**, ἡ, *return to one's senses*, Phot.*nomoc.*13.30(M.104. 965A); *recovery*: from sleep, Epiph.*haer.*26.13(p.293.21; M.41.353B); Jo.Clim.*scal.*20(M.88.941B); error, Cyr.*Am.*58(3.327A); sin, Ant. Mon.*hom.*27(M.89.1521D).

ἀνανοέω, *call to mind* ἀνονόησον [l. ἀνα-] τὴν αἰώνιον φλόγα Ephr. 2.85C.

ἀνάντης, *uphill, steep, difficult*; met., of people ἀλαζὼν γὰρ ὁ ἀπειθής, καὶ οἱονεί πως ἀ. καὶ ἐξήνιος Cyr.*Os.*25(3.48E); of virtue, *difficult to attain*, id.*glaph.Dt.*(1.419D); neut. as subst., *difficulty*, id.*ador.*11(1.382D); of spiritual or intellectual heights πρὸς τὸ ἄ. ... ἀνατεινόμεναι Dion.Ar.*c.h.*4.2(M.3.180A); *ib.*7.1(205D).

***ἀναντιθέτως**, *without mutual contradiction*, Epiph.*haer.*69.44 (p.192.13; M.42.272B).

***ἀναντίλογος**, *not contentious*, Dan.Raith.*v.Jo.Clim.*(M.88.605A).

ἀναντίρρητος, *not to be opposed*; *incontrovertible*, of canonical books τῶν τεσσάρων εὐαγγελίων, ἃ καὶ μόνα ἀ. ἐστιν ἐν τῇ...ἐκκλησίᾳ Or.*comm.in Mt.*1(p.3.3; M.13.829A); Eus.*h.e.*3.3.7(M.20.217C); *ib.*3. 9.5(241B).

ἀναντιρρήτως, *beyond contradiction, incontrovertibly*, Or.*Jo.*19.5 (p.304.15; M.14.533C); ‡Ath.*Ar.*4.19(p.64.11; M.26.493D); †Bas.*Is.* 19(1.391A; M.30.149A).

ἄναξ, ὁ, **1.** *king*; of God, †Apoll.*met.Ps.*77:5(M.33.1424B); and Christ ἄ. υἱὸν πατρὸς ἄ. Gr.Naz.*carm.*1.1.2.25(M.37.403A); Nonn. *par.Jo.*1:20(M.43.753A); Jo.D.*carm.theog.*29(M.96.820B); ‡Gr.Naz. *Chr.pat.*1608(M.38.265A); **2.** as adj., *royal* ἄ. χορῷ Synes.*hymn.*3.722 (p.26; M.66.1603).

ἀναξαίνω, *tear open*; met. ἀ. ῥήσεις τε καὶ ἐπινοίας Epiph.*haer.* 69.73(p.221.23; M.42.321A).

ἀναξέω, *aggravate*; of grief, Amph.*hom.*3.3(M.39.64A); prob. f.l. for ἀναέξω (*increase*) μῆνιν ἀνεξήεσσαν †Apoll.*met.Ps.*77:17(M.33. 1424D; ἀνηέξησαν Teub.).

ἀναξηρασία, ἡ, *drying up*, ‡Caes.Naz.*dial*.140(M.38.1077).

***ἀναξιεπαίνως**, *without deserving praise*, *cat.Apoc*.6:11(p.275.17).

ἀναξιοπαθέω, *be indignant at, resent as an indignity* μὴ ἀναξιοπαθήσητε...παιδεύεσθαι Tat.*orat*.12(p.14.3, v.l. ἀξιοπαθήσητε M.6.833A); ἀ. πρὸς αὐτά Mac.Aeg.*pat*.11(M.34.873C); ἀ. ἐπὶ τῇ πτωχείᾳ Marc.Diac.*v.Porph*.98.

***ἀναξιότης**, ἡ, *unworthiness*, Bas.*jud*.7(2.221C; M.31.672B); Epiph.*haer*.8.7(p.193.27; M.41.216C); Jo.D.*imag*.1.1(M.94.1232A); esp. as title of humility τῇ ἐμῇ...ἀ. †Jo.Jej.*poenit*.(M.88.1896D); Leont.N.*v.Jo.Eleem*.20(p.38.2).

ἀναξίως, *unworthily*, esp. ref. 1Cor.11:27 ὁ ἀ. [τις] μεταλαμβάνων εὐχαριστίας εἰς κρίμα λήψεται Or.*fr.50 in Jer*.(p.223.21); ὁ ἐν μολυσμῷ σαρκὸς καὶ πνεύματος ἀ. προσερχόμενος τοῖς ἁγίοις †Bas.*bapt*.1.3.3(2.651B; M.31.1577A); τοὺς...ἀ. τῶν μυστηρίων μετέχοντας, ὁ θεὸς πολλάκις...παραδίδωσιν αὐτοὺς τῷ σατανᾷ Chrys.*hom.5.3 in 1Tim*.(11.577B); πῶς γὰρ οὐκ ἀ., ὁ περιορῶν πεινῶντα; id.*hom.27.4 in 1Cor*.(10.247C); id.*prod.Jud*.1.6(2.384C); πάντων...βαρύτερον ἁμάρτημα τὸ ἀ. κοινωνεῖν †Jo.Jej.*serm*.(M.88.1929B).

ἀναξυρίς, ἡ, *cutting* of the hair; plur., *Const.App*.1.3.10.

***ἀναπάλαισμα**, τό, *renewal of struggle*, Nil.*Eulog*.14(M.79.1112B).

ἀναπαλαί-ω, **1.** *retrieve* a defeat ἀ. τὸ κατὰ τὴν παρακοὴν ἧττημα Meth.*Porph*.1(p.504.13; M.18.400B); Chrys.*hom.18.6 in Rom*.(9.639D); Thdt.*h.e*.3.17.3(3.933); **2.** abs., *renew the struggle*, of second Adam ∼σας ἀνέλυσε τὴν ἀπόφασιν τὴν δι' αὐτὸν εἰς πάντας ἐξενηνεγμένην Meth.*symp*.3.6(p.33.13; M.18.69B ἀναπλασθείς); διακόνους...θύσαντας, μετὰ δὲ ταῦτα ∼σαντας CAnc.(314)*can.2*; Gel.Cyz.*h.e*.2.33.6(M.85.1337C); **3.** *secure revocation of* ἐν τῷ τὴν καταδίκην ∼σαι ἐσπούδασε Socr.*h.e*.2.20.13(M.67.257C).

[*]**ἀναπαλέω**, prob. for ἀναπαλαίω, Nil.*epp*.2.172(M.79.288B).

ἀναπάλλακτος, *irremovable, not departing*, Pall.*v.Chrys*.10(p.61.2; M.47.35); Synes.*ep*.44(M.66.1369A).

ἀναπάρτιστος, *not made perfect*, Ign.*Philad*.5.1.

ἀναπατ-έω, *walk up and down*, Jo.Mal.*chron*.5 p.130(M.97.225B); *stroll idly* ἐργάζε καὶ μὴ ἀ. Ephr.1.93C; *ib*.93E; ὁ παρὰ τὴν ὡρισμένην ἄνεσιν ∼ῶν Thdr.Stud.*poen*.1.17(M.99.1736B).

***ἀναπαύδητος**, *indefatigable*, Clem.*str*.2.20(p.178.15; M.8.1065A).

ἀνάπαυσις, ἡ, *repose, rest; refreshment*;

A. lit., Or.*Jo*.19.7(2; p.306.32; M.14.537D) cit. s. γαζοφυλάκιον; τῆς τοῦ σώματος ἡμῶν ἀ. *Hom.Clem*.4.3; αὐτὸς [sc. Χριστός] δι' ἡμᾶς ἀπετάξατο ἀναπαύσει *Const.App*.5.5.4.

B. met.; **1.** as state of Christians ἀ. τε ἡδίστη γίνεται τοῖς ἐκμελετῶσιν αὐτούς [sc. τοῦ σωτῆρος λόγους] Just.*dial*.8.2(M.6.492D); θεῷ...ἐπὶ δὲ τὴν ἰδίαν ἀ. καὶ ἀνακαίνισιν βίου καλέσαντι *A.Jo*.78(p.190.5); διὰ πίστιν εἰς ἀ. Heracleon ap.Or.*Jo*.13.41(p.267.13; M.14.472C); Or.*Jo*.13.44(p.270.32; 477C); ref. martyr's confession of Christ ἦν αὐτῆς [sc. Blandina's]...ἀ. ... τὸ λέγειν ὅτι Χριστιανή εἰμι *Ep.Lugd*.ap.Eus.*h.e*.5.1.19(M.20.416B); ref. possession of H. Ghost οἱ Χριστιανοὶ ἐνδύονται τὸ πνεῦμα τὸ ἅγιον, καὶ ἐν ἀ. εἰσίν Mac.Aeg.*hom*.26.15(M.34.684C); **2.** ascet.; **a.** result of training in practice of virtue προπαιδείαν τῆς ἐν Χριστῷ ἀ. γυμνάζειν τὸν νοῦν Clem.*str*.1.5(p.21.20; M.8.728A); ἀ. ἔξουσι, καὶ πονηρῶν λογισμῶν καθαρεύσουσιν Isid.Pel.*epp*.1.49(M.78.213A); διὰ τῆς συντριβῆς τῆς καρδίας καταδέχεταί τις τὰς ἐντολάς...κτᾶται τὰς ἀρετάς, καὶ...ἐπανέρχεται εἰς τὴν ἰδίαν ἀ. Dor.*doct*.1.9(M.88.1628C); *ib*.2.3(1644C); **b.** consisting in spiritual perfection ἡ τοῦ τελείου καὶ γνωστικοῦ...ἀ. Clem.*paed*.1.6(p.110.35; M.8.292B); *ib*.(p.111.12; 292C); συγγενεῖς...τῷ γνωστικῷ ἠρεμία καὶ ἀ. καὶ εἰρήνη id.*str*.2.11(p.141.14; M.8.989A); οἱ γὰρ καταξιωθέντες τέκνα...θεοῦ...ἐν ἀ. πνευματικῇ ὑπὸ τῆς χάριτος ἐνεργούμενοι Mac.Aeg.*hom*.19.7(M.34.648C); admitting of degrees τῷ κυρίῳ δὲ κολλωμένη...ψυχὴ...ἀπὸ ἀ. εἰς τελειοτέραν ἀ. μετατίθεται id.*carit*.28(M.34.932B); exeg. Cant.1:6 οὐδεὶς δὲ τῆς ἀ. τῆς μεσημβρινῆς ἀξιοῦται, μὴ υἱὸς φωτὸς...γενόμενος...γνώρισον οὖν μοι...τίς ἡ ὁδὸς τῆς μεσημβρινῆς ἀ. Gr.Nyss.*hom.2 in Cant*.(M.44.801C); connected with wisdom, Evagr.Pont.*cap.pract*.A 45(M.40.1232D); contrasted with physical rest, id.*rer.mon*.5(M.40.1256D); symbolized by sabbath, v. 4 infra., Max.*cap*.5.43(M.90.1365C); associated with humility, Dor.*doct*.1.7(M.88.1625A); and with obedience, *ib*.(1625B); **3.** as a state of prayer πολλάκις ἀπέρχεται εἰς προσευχὴν ὁ ἰδιώτης, καὶ κλίνει γόνυ, καὶ εἰσέρχεται ὁ νοῦς αὐτοῦ εἰς ἀ. καὶ εἰσέρχεται εἰς ὅρασιν καὶ σοφίαν Mac.Aeg.*hom*.15.14f.(M.34.585B); *ib*.26.15(685A); **4.** in myst. interprn. of sabbath, connected with myst. meaning of number 7 τῇ ἑβδόμῃ γὰρ ἡ ἀ. θρησκεύεται...ὁ χρόνος εἴη ὁ διὰ τῶν ἑπτὰ περιόδων...εἰς τὴν ἀκροτάτην ἀ. ἀποκαθιστάς Clem.*str*.4.25(p.318.23,30; M.8.1368A,B); τὸν ἑπτὰ ἀριθμὸν ἀμήτορα καὶ ἄγονον λογίζονται, τὸ σάββατον ἑρμηνεύοντες καὶ τὸ τῆς ἀ. εἶδος ἀλληγοροῦντες *ib*.6.16(p.501.24; M.9.364A); *ib*.(p.503.4; 368A); cf. ὥραν ἑβδόμην ἀφίησιν αὐτὸν ὁ πυρετός· ὁ γὰρ ἀριθμὸς ἀναπαύσεως ἦν Or.*Jo*.13.59(58; p.290.18; M.14.512A); contrasted with Sunday as day of spiritual rest ἡ...τῶν πνευματικῶν ἀ. ἐν κυριακῇ, ἐν ὀγδοάδι Clem.*exc.Thdot*.63(p.128.9; M.9.689B); cf. Gnost. baptismal formulae ἐλθὲ ἡ μήτηρ τῶν ἑπτὰ οἴκων ἵνα ἡ ἀ. σου εἰς τὸ ὄγδοον οἶκον γένηται *A.Thom*.A 27(p.142.18); ἔλθετε τὰ ὕδατα ἀπὸ τῶν ὑδάτων...ἡ ἀ. ἡ ἀπὸ τῆς ἀ. ἀποσταλεῖσα ἡμῖν *ib*.52(p.168.16f.).

C. of rest in eternity; **1.** in gen. ἀ. τῆς μελλούσης βασιλείας καὶ ζωῆς αἰωνίου *2Clem*.5.5; *ib*.6.7; ἀπελεύσοντο πρὸς τὸν θεὸν εἰς ἀ. αἰώνιον Heracleon ap.Or.*Jo*.19.19(4; p.320.17; M.14.561C); *A.Jo*.113(p.214.1); ἐπίταξον οὖν κύριέ μου ἀναλαβεῖν τὸ πνεῦμά μου ἀπ' ἐμοῦ, ἵνα λοιπὸν ἀ. τύχω *A.Andr.et Mt*.28(p.107.15); *Const.App*.1.3.7; †Jo.Jej.*serm*.(M.88.1972A); ἕως τῆς πρὸς θεὸν αὐτοῦ ἀ. Jo.Mosch.*prat*.101(M.87.2960D); **2.** as end of Christian life τέλος δέ ἐστιν θεοσεβείας ἡ ἀΐδιος ἀ. ἐν τῷ θεῷ Clem.*paed*.1.13(p.151.17; M.8.373B); οὗ δὲ ἡ πίστις, ἐνταῦθα ἡ ἐπαγγελία, τελείωσις δὲ ἐπαγγελίας ἡ ἀ. ὥστε ἡ μὲν γνῶσις ἐν τῷ φωτίσματι, τὸ δὲ πέρας τῆς γνώσεως ἡ ἀ. *ib*.1.6(p.107.24, 26; 285B); πάντες οὖν ἄνθρωποι...καλοῦνται ἐπὶ τὴν παρὰ τῷ λόγῳ τοῦ θεοῦ ἀ. Or.*Cels*.3.63(p.257.30; M.11.1004C); id.*mart*.47(p.43.12; M.11.632A); συνεορτάζω τῷ Χριστῷ τὴν χιλιονταετηρίδα τῆς ἀ. Meth.*symp*.9.5(p.120.14; M.18.189A); ref. Lc.16:20ff. χειραγωγοῦντά με πρὸς τὸν τόπον τῆς ἀναψύξεως, ὅπου τὸ ὕδωρ τῆς ἀ. Gr.Nyss.*v.Macr*.(p.398.1; M.46.984D); Const.Diac.*laud*.41(M.88.528A); πάσης θλίψεως τέλος ἐστὶν ἡ χαρά· καὶ παντὸς κόπου, ἡ ἀ. Max.*cap*.1.44(M.90.1196A); **3.** as heavenly reward τοῖς θλιβομένοις μεταδεδωκότα τῆς ἀληθοῦς ἀ. μεταλαμβάνειν Clem.*paed*.3.7(p.259.17; M.8.609B); *ib*.1.6(p.116.31; 304A); μακάριοί ἐστε οἱ πεινῶντες ἕνεκεν κυρίου, ὅτι ὑμῖν τετήρηται ἡ ἀ. *A.Thom*.A 94(p.208.3); εἰ θέλομεν μετὰ τῶν προφητῶν ἔχειν ἀ., τὰ ἔργα τῶν προφητῶν ζηλώσωμεν Or.*hom.14.14 in Jer*.(p.119.9); *ib. 15.1*(p.125.16; M.13.420A); ἐν γὰρ τῇ καινῇ...κτίσει, ὃς ἂν ἁγνείας μὴ εὑρεθῇ κλάδοις κεκοσμημένος, οὐ τεύξεται τῆς ἀ. Meth.*symp*.9.5(p.120.1; M.18.188C); ἐὰν ὁμονοήσητε, δυνήσεσθε εἰς τὸν τῆς ἀ. ἐνεχθῆναι λιμένα *Clem.ep*.13; *ib*.16; διὰ τοὺς καμάτους...εἰς ἀεὶ ἕξει τὴν ἀ. *Hom.Clem*.3.20; in rel. to grace, *A.Andr.fr*.18(p.45.15); **4.** opp. rest on earth ὁ ἔχων ἀ. ἐν τῷ κόσμῳ τὴν αἰώνιον ἀ. μὴ ἐλπιζέτω λαβεῖν Ath.*virg*.18(p.53.5; M.28.273A); and eternal punishment, Or.*hom. 20.3 in Jer*.(p.181.7; M.13.505C); ἀντὶ ἀ. αἰωνίαν κόλασιν κληρωσάμενοι *Const.App*.1.6.11; **5.** several grades within or above heavenly ἀ.: [ἐν] τῇ ἀνωτάτω ἐκκλησίᾳ, καθ' ἣν οἱ φιλόσοφοι συνάγονται τοῦ θεοῦ...οἱ μὴ καταμείναντες ἐν ἑβδομάδι ἀναπαύσεως...εἰς ὀγδοαδικῆς εὐεργεσίας κληρονομίαν ὑπερκύψαντες Clem.*str*.6.14(p.486.7; M.9.329A); ταχεῖα τοίνυν εἰς κάθαρσιν ἡ γνῶσις...ἄχρις ἂν εἰς τὸν κορυφαῖον ἀποκαταστήσῃ τῆς ἀ. τόπον *ib*.7.10(p.41.29; 480C); κατὰ τάγματα τῶν ἀνισταμένων ἔσονται ἀ. ἐν τοῖς θησαυροῖς τοῦ θεοῦ Or.*hom.8.6 in Jer*.(p.61.2; M.13.344B); **6.** typified by Passover τοῦ γὰρ πάθους τοῦ σωτῆρος τύπος ἦν, ὅτε οὐ μόνον ἀνῃρεῖτο τὸ πρόβατον, ἀλλὰ καὶ ἀ. παρεῖχεν ἐσθιόμενον, καὶ θυόμενον ⟨μὲν⟩ τὸ πάθος τοῦ σωτῆρος τὸ ἐν κόσμῳ ἐσήμαινεν, ἐσθιόμενον δὲ τὴν ἀ. τὴν ἐν γάμῳ Heracleon ap.Or.*Jo*.10.19(14; p.190.32,34; M.14.340D); **7.** obtained for men through Resurrection, *A.Thom*.A 80(p.196.5); **8.** located in paradise, Meth.*res*.1.55(p.313.8; M.41.1148B); invisible and ineffable place of eternal rest, *A.Jo*.99(p.200.24); **9.** its essence ἡ πᾶσα ἀ. αὕτη ἐστί, τὸ θεωρεῖν εἰς τὸν υἱὸν τοῦ θεοῦ Chrys.*hom.82.3 in Jo*.(8.486B); **10.** ref. prayer for dead δεόμεθά σου περὶ τῆς...ἀ. τοῦ δούλου σου Serap.*euch*.30.2; προσήκειν ὑπὲρ ἀ. τῶν τελευτώντων ἐλεημοσύνας παρέχεσθαι Justn.*ep.Thdr.Mops*.(p.68.3; M.86.1091A); εἰς ἀ. τῶν προκοιμηθέντων ψυχῶν *Lit.Jac*.(p.194.16); ὑπὲρ μνήμης καὶ ἀ. *CIG* 8857(Cilicia); *ib*.8860(Pisidia); *ib*.8867(Bethlehem) etc.

D. as state of angels, Clem.*str*.5.6(p.350.20; M.9.61C); id.*ecl*.56(p.153.22; M.9.725B).

E. of God and Christ; **1.** of God's 'rest' οὐ τοίνυν, ὥσπερ τινὲς ὑπολαμβάνουσι τὴν ἀ. τοῦ θεοῦ, πέπαυται ποιῶν ὁ θεός Clem.*str*.6.16(p.504.2; M.9.369B); **2.** of God as ἀ.: ὁ πατὴρ καὶ θεός...ἡ ἀ. *Hom.Clem*.4.72; *ib*.17.9; **3.** of Christ; **a.** of Logos resting on humanity πότε δὲ ἐνεδύσατο τὸ σῶμα τὴν ἀφθαρσίαν εἰ μὴ διὰ τῆς ἀ. τοῦ λόγου; Ath.*fr.Cant*.4(M.27.1356C); **b.** of powers of H. Ghost resting on Christ τοῦ πνεύματος δυνάμεις οὐχ ὡς ἐνδεοῦς αὐτοῦ τούτων ὄντος φησὶν ὁ λόγος ἐπεληλυθέναι ἐπ' αὐτόν, ἀλλ' ὡς ἐπ' ἐκεῖνον ἀ. μελλουσῶν ποιεῖσθαι, τοῦτ' ἔστιν ἐπ' αὐτοῦ πέρας ποιεῖσθαι Just.*dial*.87.3(M.6.684B); *ib*.87.5(684C); **c.** exeg. Jo.4:34 τοῦτο γὰρ αὐτοῦ τροφὴ καὶ ἀ. Heracleon ap.Or.*Jo*.13.38(p.263.18; M.14.465B); **d.** Christ as ἀ. τῶν τεθλιμμένων *A.Thom*.A 10(p.114.7); *ib*.19(p.130.4); *ib*.60(p.177.12).

F. *tranquillity, peace*, of Church δεόμεθα ὑπὲρ πάντων ἀρχόντων, εἰρηνικὸν τὸν βίον ἐχέτωσαν ὑπὲρ ἀ. τῆς καθολικῆς ἐκκλησίας Serap.*euch*.5.6.

G. *resting place* κατοικητήριον ἢ ἀ. τοῦ πνεύματος, ἡ ταπεινοφροσύνη ἐστί Mac.Aeg.*cust.cor.*14(M.34.840C); ἐντὸς ἐγένετο τοῦ μαρτυρίου καὶ τῆς ἀ. τῶν ἁγίων Gr.Nyss.*mart.*3(M.46.784C).

H. of rest from evil ἀ. ἐπαγγελλόμενον τὴν ἀπὸ τῶν κακῶν Meth. *symp.*10.3(p.125.11; M.18.197A); and from endeavour, hence in sense of *laziness* μισήσατε πᾶσαν σαρκικὴν ἀ. *Apophth.Patr.*(M.65.85C).

I. μετὰ ἀναπαύσεως *easily*, Dor.*doct.*11.3(M.88.1737C).

[*]**ἀναπαυστικός**, *giving rest*, Mac.Aeg.*hom.*57.3(p.47).

***ἀναπαύστως**, *quietly, at rest*, Geo.Pis.*bell.Avar.*260(M.92.1286A).

ἀναπαύ-ω, A. act.; **1.** *make to cease, terminate*, of Christ abrogating Law δεῖ...πρότερόν με αὐτὸν πάντα πληρώσαντα...αὐτὸν [sc. νόμον] ἀναπαῦσαι Chrys.*hom.12.1 in Mt.*(7.161E); *ib.*6.3(89A); τὸν βίον ἑαυτῆς ἀ. Gr.Nyss.*v.Macr.*(p.384.21; M.46.973A); **2.** *cause to rest, give rest, calm, relieve*; **a.** in gen. ἀνάπαυσον τὴν ψυχήν μου, κύριε, καὶ γνώρισόν μοι αὐτά Herm.*sim.*9.5.4; Chrys.*hom.1.3 in Mt.*(7.7B); id.*hom.21.3 in 1Cor.*(10.182C); **b.** of soul giving rest to Christ πᾶσα ψυχὴ ἡ μὴ δεξαμένη αὐτὸν ἔνδον νῦν καὶ ἀναπαύσασα...ἐν τῇ βασιλείᾳ τῶν οὐρανῶν...κληρονομίαν οὐκ ἔχει Mac.Aeg.*hom.*30.9(M.34.728C); cf.Diad.*perf.*28(p.30.21); **c.** of Christ giving rest to believers at parousia ἐν τῇ ἐνδόξῳ αὐτοῦ παρουσίᾳ...τοὺς δὲ ἰδίους ~σει Just.*dial.*121.3(M.6.757C); **d.** in death κατὰ δὲ ὑμᾶς τοὺς λέγοντας ὅτι ἡ ψυχὴ κεῖται ἐν τῷ μνημείῳ μετὰ τοῦ σώματος...οὐκ ~εται Or.*dial.*23(p.164.23); κύριε...αὐτοὺς ἀνάπαυσον ἐν χώρᾳ ζώντων *Lit.Jac.*(p.220.10); *Lit.Marc.*(p.129.11); *ib.*(*PStrasb.*v° 11); *lay to rest*; of martyrs' relics, Gr.Nyss.*mart.*3(M.46.784D); **3.** *refresh, strengthen, restore*; **a.** materially κατὰ πάντα με ἀ. σαρκί τε καὶ πνεύματι Ign.*Trall.*12.1; id.*Eph.*2.1; *Barn.*10.11; κτῆσιν...τοῖς δεομένοις κατατίθησιν...καὶ...~σαί τινα τῶν ἐχόντων αἰώνιον σκήνην Clem.*q.d.s.*31(p.180.25; M.9.637A); *A.Jo.*82(p.192.2); **b.** spiritually, *A.Phil.*57(p.24.10); [sc. θεός]...διὰ τοῦ λόγου ἑαυτοῦ τοὺς κάμνοντας ἀ. Ath.*decr.*7(p.7.1; M.25.'436'(428)C); of Christ πάσχων...ἡμᾶς ἀ. id. *hom.in Mt.11:27*(M.25.212C); τέκνα...θεοῦ...Χριστὸν ἔχοντες ἐν ἑαυτοῖς ἐλλάμποντα καὶ ~οντα αὐτούς Mac.Aeg.*hom.*19.7(M.34.640A); *ib.* 31.3(729C); ἡ ταπεινοφροσύνη...ἀ. κόλπους Diad.*perf.*65(p.78.10).

B. med. and pass.; *cease* to do something; hence **1.** *come to an end* ἡμικύκλιον...ἐπὶ ἁψῖδος ~όμενον Gr.Nyss.*ep.*25(M.46.1096B); **2.** *be at rest, satisfied*, intellectually ἑαυτοὺς οὗτοι ἀπατῶσιν ἀναπεπαῦσθαι νομίζοντες Clem.*str.*7.15(p.65.25; M.9.528C); *ib.*1.1(p.8.24; M.8.700A); μία συμφωνία...διδασκάλῳ τῷ λόγῳ ἑπομένη, ἐπ' αὐτὴν τὴν ἀλήθειαν ~ομένη id.*prot.*9(p.65.33; M.8.200C); **3.** *repose, rest*; **a.** theol., of divine attributes reposing in God, Ath.*hom.in Mt. 11:27*(M.25.216C); of Son reposing in Father λόγος...ἐν μόνῳ τῷ πατρὶ ἀνέπαυετο id.*inc.*17.4(M.25.125C); *Symb.Ant.*(345)9(M.26.733B; ἐνανα- p.253.39); of H. Ghost reposing in Son, ‡Chrys.*annunt.et Ar.*(11.842E) = ‡Cyr.*Trin.*9(6^{2}.13B; M.77.1140B); of grace reposing in Christ τοῦ κυρίου λαβόντος, καὶ ὡς εἰς αὐτὸν ~ομένης τῆς δόσεως, βεβαία ἡ χάρις διαμείνῃ Ath.*Ar.*3.38(M.26.405B); of God ἄτρεπτον ...φῶς ἐν ἀφράστοις καὶ ἀπροσίτοις ἀ. Meth.*symp.*6.1(p.64.16; M. 18.113B); **b.** spiritually, of God dwelling in man οὐκ ἄρα ἐπιθυμήσει τινὸς ἑτέρου ὁ ἔχων ~όμενον τὸν θεόν Clem.*str.*7.13(p.58. 32; M.9.516A); as in angels, id.*ecl.*57(pp.153.26–154.1; M.9.725B,C); τὴν καρδίαν...ἐν ᾗ...ὡς ἐν ναῷ κατοικοῦν ~εται πνεῦμα Meth.*symp.* 11(p.138.30; M.18.217A); Mac.Aeg.*hom.*30.9(M.34.728B); ἀ. ἡμῶν ἐν θεῷ, καὶ ~ομένου τοῦ Χριστοῦ ἐν ἡμῖν id.*cust.cor.*14(M.34.841B); ἔχει [sc. the humble man] ~όμενον ἐπ' αὐτῷ τὸν θεόν Chrys.*hom.65.6 in Mt.*(7.652A); ἅγιε ὁ ἐν ἁγίοις ~όμενος κύριε *Lit.Jac.*(p.226.21); of man reposing in God ἐν τῷ ἀσκίῳ φωτὶ ~σομαι Gr.Nyss.*hom.2 in Cant.*(M.44.801C); **c.** eschatol., in eternity, Clem.*str.*5.14(p.409.10; M.9.181B); *ib.*2.20(p.172.19; M.8.1053A); τάξεις προφητῶν μαρτύρων τε καὶ ἀποστόλων εἰς βασιλείαν Χριστοῦ ~όμεναι Hipp.*antichr.*59(p.40.9; M.10.780A); ὁ ἐν κόλποις Ἀβραὰμ πένης ~όμενος Meth.*res.* 3.17(p.414.14; M.18.325A); prefigured by resting on sabbath ἐν τῇ σκιᾷ τοῦ νόμου...προσέταξεν ὁ θεὸς ἐν τῷ σαββάτῳ ἕκαστον ~εσθαι... τοῦτο δὲ τύπος ἦν...τοῦ ἀληθινοῦ σαββάτου τοῦ διδομένου τῇ ψυχῇ ἀπὸ τοῦ κυρίου. ἡ γὰρ καταξιωθεῖσα ψυχὴ...ἀληθινὴν ἀνάπαυσιν ἀ. ...ἐλευθερουμένη ἀπὸ πάντων τῶν σκοτεινῶν ἔργων. ἐκεῖ μὲν γὰρ εἰς τὸ τυπικὸν σάββατον, εἰ καὶ σωματικῶς ἀνεπαύοντο, ἀλλ' αἱ ψυχαὶ εἰς τὰς πονηρίας...ἦσαν δεδεμέναι. τοῦτο δὲ τὸ ἀληθινὸν σάββατον, ἀνάπαυσις ἀληθινή ἐστι, ψυχῆς...~ομένης εἰς τὴν τοῦ κυρίου ἀνάπαυσιν αἰωνίαν Mac.Aeg.*hom.*35.1(M.34.748A,B); *ib.*35.2(748B); **d.** in death μετὰ τῶν πατέρων ἀ. Ath.*ep.Ors.*2(M.26.980A); id.*virg.*24(p.59.24; M.28.281A); of martyrs' relics, Gr.Nyss.*mart.*3(M.46.784B); **4.** = *die* Ἀλέξανδρος...μακαρίως ἀνεπαύσατο Dion.Al.ap.Eus.*h.e.*6.46.4(M.20. 636B); Eus.*h.e.*4.11.6(M.20.329C); ἀναπαῆναι καὶ ἀπελθεῖν πρὸς κύριον Marc.Diac.*v.Porph.*102; Jo.Mosch.*prat.*101(M.87.2960A); opp. βιόω, Eus.*Marcell.*1.4(p.18.6; M.24.752A); **5.** *be refreshed* (spiritually) ~εται εἰς τὴν εὐχήν Mac.Aeg.*hom.*26.15(M.34.684D); ἀ. γὰρ ἐν τοῖς καιροῖς τῆς ἡσυχίας Diad.*perf.*68(p.84.7).

ἀναπαφλάζω, *bubble up*, *Apoc.Petr.*B 24; ‡Caes.Naz.*dial.*146(M. 38.1096).

ἀναπεμπάζομαι, prob. for ἀναπέμπω, *utter* φθογγὴν †Apoll.*met. Ps.*113:15(M.33.1488C).

***ἀναπεμπτέον**, *one must throw back* the accent, Isid.Pel.*epp.*4. 113(M.78.1185A).

ἀναπέμπ-ω, **1.** *send up*; *lead up*, of a road, Clem.*prot.*10(p.72.19; M.8.213C); **2.** *send forth*, id.*paed.*1.8(p.131.9; M.8.333C); **3.** *offer up* prayer or praise, Just.*1apol.*65.3(M.6.428B); Or.*Jo.*28.6(5; p.395. 26; M.14.689C); Leont.N.*v.Jo.Eleem.*46(p.102.3); of sacrifice of Christ [sc. ὁ σωτήρ] ἱερεῖον ἣν ὑπὲρ τοῦ κοινοῦ γένους ~όμενον τῷ παμβασιλεῖ θεῷ Eus.*l.C.*11(p.247.26; M.20.1420B); **4.** *refer* to a higher authority: to God τῷ βουλήματι τοῦ πατρὸς ἀ. τὸ ἐκ τοῦ πάθους κατόρθωμα ‡Dion.Al.*fr.in Lc.22:44*(p.244.10; M.10.1593C); to scriptures, Or.*Jo.*5.6(4; p.103.17; M.14.192C); to an eccl. authority τοῦ λῦσαι τὴν αὐθεντίαν εἰς τὴν ἱερατικὴν καθέδραν ἀ. Synes.*ep.*67(M.66. 1425A); **5.** *send back* ἡ τοῦ Λαζάρου ψυχὴ...ἀ. ἀπὸ τοῦ χωρίου τῶν ψυχῶν Or.*Jo.*28.6(5; p.395.32; M.14.689C); **6.** *ascribe* πρὸς τὴν πρώτην αἰτίαν...τὰ τοῦ πνεύματος ~εται Gr.Naz.*or.*41.9(M.36.441B); Dion.Ar.*d.n.*13.3(M.3.980B).

***ἀνάπεμψις**, ἡ, *sending up* to a higher authority, Sophr.H. *v.Anast.*(M.92.1713A).

***ἀναπετάζω**, = ἀναπετάννυμι, Didym.*Trin.*2.1(M.39.452B); met., *lay open* to, hence *expose* to influence of ἀ. [sc. an inquirer] πρὸς τὰς τῶν ἁγίων εἰκόνων μορφάς ‡Jo.D.*Const.*10(M.95.325C).

ἀναπετάννυμι, **1.** *unfold, open*; of mind, heart, etc. to God and divine word, Meth.*symp.*5.4(p.57.21; M.18.104A); Serap.*euch.*1.1; myst. ἡ νύμφη...τὴν ψυχὴν ἀ. τῷ λόγῳ Or.*schol.in Cant.*5:6(M.17. 273C); Jo.D.*hom.*2.7(M.96.588C); **2.** *lay open, make available*, perf. ptcpl. pass. as adj., *unfolded, explained*, Cyr.*Juln.*4(6^{2}.145C).

ἀναπηγάζ-ω, **1.** *spring up*; lit., Epiph.*anc.*58(p.68.10; M.43.120B); met. ποταμούς, ἄνδρας ἁγίους δηλονότι...τοῖς διψῶσιν...~οντας Cyr. *Is.*3.5(2.530C); of knowledge of God, id.*Jo.*2.4(4.182E); of truth, id. *Juln.*4(6^{2}.115A); **2.** *make to spring up* [sc. τὸ πνεῦμα] ἐξ ἰδίας ἡμῖν ἀ. φύσεως [sc. Χριστός] Cyr.*inc.unigen.*(5^{1}.706D); μύρον θεῖον ἐκ τῆς ψυχῆς αὐτοῦ...ἀ. ‡Rom.Mel.(*AS* 1 p.205).

ἀναπηδ-άω, **1.** *leap up*; of the eye twitching, Chrys.*hom.12.3 in Eph.*(11.94C); met. ἀ. εἰς ἔννοιαν Cyr.*Ps.*32:11(M.69.876D); **2.** *leap forth*, met. τὴν ἀφθαρσίαν ἀπὸ τῶν ἀμιάντων τοῦ παντοκράτορος ~ῶσαν κόλπων Meth.*symp.*1.1(p.8.3; M.18.37A); ἐκ τῆς Διὸς κεφαλῆς...ἀ. τὴν φρόνησιν *Hom.Clem.*6.18; **3.** *rise above*; met., c. acc. τὸ προφητῶν ἀ. μέτρον Cyr.*Jo.*2 proem.(4.113A); c. genit. τῶν ἐπιγείων ἀ. πραγμάτων id.*Is.*2.5(2.344A).

ἀναπιδύω, *well up, send forth water*, Clem.*paed.*3.7(p.259.21; M.8. 609C).

ἀναπίμπρημι, met., *inflame* ἀ. τὴν ψυχήν Philost.*h.e.*7.6^{a}.

ἀναπίν-ω, *absorb*; lit., Clem.*paed.*2.2(p.169.1; M.8.413A); fig. ὡς ἄρτος...τὸν οἶνον ἁρπάζει...οὕτως καὶ ἡ σὰρξ τοῦ κυρίου, ὁ ἄρτος τῶν οὐρανῶν, ~ει τὸ αἷμα *ib.*1.6(p.118.8; 305B).

ἀνάπλασις, ἡ, **1.** *formation anew, re-making, renewal*; **a.** of man's moral nature in resurrection life τὸν ἄνθρωπον...διέλυσεν [sc. ὁ θεός] εἰς ὕλην πάλιν, ἵνα διὰ τῆς ἀ. ἐκτακῶσι καὶ ἐξαφανισθῶσι πάντα τὰ ἐν αὐτῷ μωμήματα Meth.*res.*1.43(p.291.6; M.18.272C); **b.** of resurrection of body μὴ δύνασθαι δέ φημι δίχα τῆς κατὰ τὸ λουτρὸν ἀναγεννήσεως ἐν ἀναστάσει, γενέσθαι τὸν ἄνθρωπον, οὐ πρὸς τὴν τοῦ συγκρίματος ἡμῶν ἀ. τε καὶ ἀναστοιχείωσιν βλέπων Gr.Nyss.*or. catech.*35(p.137.10; M.45.92A); **c.** spiritual: by Trin., Gr.Naz.*or.*23. 13(M.35.1165B); by goodness of God, Zach.Mit.*opif.*(M.85.1125B); by Inc., Gr.Naz.*or.*38.4(M.36.316B); χωρηθῆναι εὐδοκεῖ δι' ἀνάπλασιν τοῦ γένους ὁ ἀχώρητος Thdr.Stud.*nativ.*4(M.96.684A); by death of Christ τὴν τιμωρίαν μυστήριον οὖσαν ἀναπλάσεως τῆς ἀνθρωπότητος *A.(Pass.)Andr.*4(p.9.10); πηγάζει θεῖον αἷμα καὶ ὕδωρ, πόμα ἀθανασίας καὶ ἀναπλάσεως βάπτισμα Jo.D.*hom.*4.21(M.96.620A); ‡Sophr.H. *liturg.*(M.87.3989A); by Resurrection τὴν μεγίστην ἡμέραν ἐν ᾗ τὸ κοινὸν ἐξανέστη τοῦ γένους εἰς ἔνθεόν τε καὶ νεὰν ἀ. Geo.Pis.*Pers.*1.134 (M.92.1207A); by H. Ghost παρὰ μὲν τοῦ πνεύματος ἡμῖν ἡ ἀναγέννησις· παρὰ δὲ τῆς ἀναγεννήσεως ἡ ἀ. Gr.Naz.*or.*31.28(p.182.1; M.36. 165A); **2.** *imagining* in dreams, Gr.Naz.*or.*28.22(p.56.13; M.36.57A) cited by Melet.*nat.hom.*30(M.64.1284B); of representations of invisible realities μυστικῶν ἀ. Dion.Ar.*c.h.*4.1(M.3.177C); **3.** met., *construction* placed on a word κατὰ τὴν αὐτόνομον τοῦ λόγου φορὰν καὶ ἀ. Gr.Naz.*or.*28.8(p.33.9; 56A); *formulation* of an argument, *ib.*31.19(p.168.8; 153C).

ἀνάπλασμα, τό, *fabrication* Μάνης ὁ...τῆς ἐξουσίας τοῦ σκότους ἀ. Thdr.Raith.*praep*.(p.187.2; M.91.1485C); *fiction, imaginary representation* ἀ. μύθων Or.*Jo*.2.28(23; p.84.31; M.14.161C); αἱρετικῶν ἀνδρῶν ἀ. Eus.*h.e*.3.25.7(M.20.272A); Gr.Naz.*or*.21.35(M.35.1125A).

ἀναπλασμός, ὁ, 1. *re-formation, renewal* ἀναμορφούμεθα...οὐ σωματικὸν ὑπομένοντες τὸν ἀ. ... διὰ δὲ τοῦ μεταλαχεῖν ἁγίου πνεύματος Cyr.*inc.unigen*.(5^{1}.706A); ἀ. τῆς ἱερωσύνης id.*ador*.2(1.59E); **2.** *formation* πρὸς τὸν ἀ. τῆς θείας καὶ οὐσιώδους γνώσεως Evagr. Pont.*or*.73(M.79.1184A); **3.** *representation, imagination* τῶν ἑτεροδόξων...ἐκπιπτόντων ἐπὶ ἀναπλασμὸν ἄλλου θεοῦ Or.*sel.in Ps*.50(M. 12.1453C); Bas.*Spir*.15(3.12D; M.32.92C); τόν γε ἀνυπόστατον τῶν προσώπων ἀ. οὐδὲ ὁ Σαβέλλιος παρῃτήσατο id.*ep*.210(3.317A; M.32. 776C); id.*Eun*.2.17(1.252E; M.29.608A).

ἀναπλάσσ-ω, 1. *form anew, re-create*; **a.** in gen., *2Clem*.8.2; Meth.*res*.1.44(p.293.1; M.18.273A); τὸ Μανιχαϊκὸν αὐτοῖς δόγμα... ἀναπλασθήσεται Gr.Nyss.*Eun*.1(1 p.165.29; M.45.408C); **b.** spiritually, *Barn*.11.6; εἰς τελειότητα πνευματικὴν ἀναπλασθεὶς Meth.*symp*. 3.9(p.37.20; M.18.76B); by baptism, Serap.*euch*.22.2; in future life τὸ σκεῦος πρὸς καιρὸν διαλύεται ἵνα τῆς κακίας ἐκρυείσης ἀναπλασθῇ τὸ ἀνθρώπινον...τοῦτο γάρ ἐστιν ἡ ἀνάστασις ἡ εἰς τὸ ἀρχαῖον τῆς φύσεως ἡμῶν ἀναστοιχείωσις Gr.Nyss.*Pulch*.(M.46.877A); by work of Christ ἵν' ὅλῳ ἀνθρώπῳ τῷ αὐτῷ καὶ θεῷ ὅλος ἄνθρωπος ἀναπλασθῇ πεσὼν ὑπὸ τὴν ἁμαρτίαν Gr.Naz.*ep*.101(M.37.177C); εἰμὶ δὲ ἄρτος ζωῆς...ὅλον ἐξ ὅλου τὸ ζῷον εἰς ζωὴν ~ων τὴν αἰώνιον Cyr.*Jo*.3.6 (4.322C); re-forming Adam by Inc., Hipp.*Dan*.4.11.5(M.10.684C) cit. s. πρωτόπλαστος; **2.** *form, fashion*, *ib*.2.27.7 cit. s. ἀνατυπόω; Clem.*prot*.10(p.78.16; M.8.228A) cit. s. προσωπεῖον; νηδύϊ κόρης δέμας ἑαυτῷ ~ων *Pers*.(p.9.2); **3.** *make up* a word, Clem.*str*.1.8 (p.29.15; M.8.741A); οἱ ἀπὸ Ἑβραϊσμοῦ ἑρμηνεύσαντες, μὴ εὑρόντες τὴν λέξιν κειμένην παρ' Ἕλλησιν, ἀναπεπλακέναι...ταύτην Or.*hom. 18.6 in Jer*.(p.159.22; M.13.476D); **4.** *imagine, invent*; ref. heretics, Just.*dial*.8.4(M.6.493B); Eus.*h.e*.4.22.9(M.20.384A); ἄλλον ἑαυτοῖς ~ονται δημιουργὸν...παρὰ τὸν πατέρα Ath.*inc*.2.5(M.25.100C); Gr.Naz. *or*.29.6(p.80.12; M.36.81A); *form a mental picture*, Chrys.*hom.53.5 in Mt*.(7.545D); τί μὴ καὶ δέκα εἴκοσι καὶ τριάκοντα φύσεις ~ομεν Χριστοῦ, ἀλλὰ δύο μόνον; Leont.H.*monoph*.10(M.86.1776A).

***ἀναπλαστέω,** *give imaginary form to*, of heretics τὰ μὴ ὄντα ἀ. Leont.H.*monoph*.10(M.86.1776B).

ἀναπλαστικός, *giving imaginary form to*, Leont.H.*monoph*.10 (M.86.1776A).

***ἀναπλαστικῶς,** *in an imaginary form, as a fiction*, Leont.H. *monoph*.10(M.86.1776C).

ἀναπλέκ-ω, 1. *interweave* ἀ. ... τῇ ἀληθείᾳ τὸ ψεῦδος Cyr.*ador*.6 (1.185C); *weave* an argument, *cat.Ac*.17:23(p.291.8); **2.** med., *mingle, blend* αἰτοῦσιν...τὸν θεὸν ἀ. ... γαληνότητι τὸν θυμόν Cyr.*Is*.5.6(2. 890B); *associate one's self*, id.*Joel*.29(3.220E); **3.** pass., *be associated, linked* ἀ. ... ἡ ὕσσωπος οἰκονομικῶς τῷ αἵματι τοῦ ἀμνοῦ id.*ador*.17 (1.600E); τῆς ἁγίας τριάδος διὰ τὴν ταυτότητα τῆς οὐσίας εἰς μίαν θεότητα δι' ἑαυτῆς ~ομένης id.*thes*.32(5^{1}.311A); *be composed, compounded* ἔκ τε θεοῦ λόγου καὶ ψυχῆς τῆς λογικῆς καὶ σώματος...ἀναπεπλέχθαι διαβεβαιούμενοι τὸν Ἐμμανουήλ id.*inc.unigen*.(5^{1}.679E).

ἀναπληρ-όω, 1. *fill up*; *supply*, of Christ (Apollinarian) ~ούσης τῆς θείας ἐνεργείας τὸν τῆς ψυχῆς τόπον καὶ τοῦ ἀνθρωπίνου νοός Apoll.*fr*.2(p.204.7)ap.Anast.S.*monoph*.(M.89.1181D); τὸν λόγον... ψυχῆς...τῆς λογικῆς τε καὶ νοερᾶς ~οῦν τὸν τόπον Cyr.*inc.unigen*. (5^{1}.679D); **2.** *fill out, expand* τὰ εἰρημένα Chrys.*hom.47.1 in Mt*. (7.487E); **3.** *complete* a building, Jo.Mal.*chron*.11 p.276(M.97.417B); *ib*.13 p.321(481A); Thphn.*chron*.p.220(M.108.561B).

ἀναπληρωτικός, *filling up, supplying* a need, Jo.D.*f.o*.2.13(M.94. 929C).

ἀναπλοκή, ἡ, *braiding, fastening*; lit., Cyr.*Abac*.26(3.540C); met. τῆς ἁγίας τριάδος ταυτότητα καὶ τὴν εἰσάπαν ἀ. ἀπομιμεῖσθαι id.*Jo*. 11.11(4.997E).

ἀνάπλοος (-πλους), ὁ, *sailing up-stream*; name for lower mouth of Bosphorus, Evagr.*h.e*.3.43(p.145.27; M.86.2696C); Soz.*h.e*.8.18.6 (M.67.1564A); Jo.Mal.*chron*.16 p.403(M.97.596C).

***ἀναπλωτάζω,** *float up, rise to the surface*, Clem.*paed*.2.2(p.176. 30; M.8.429C).

ἀναπνέω, 1. *breathe, enjoy a respite*; of land, *lie fallow*, Chrys. *hom.6.4 in Phil*.(11.239A, v.l. ἀναπαῦσαι); **2.** *draw breath*; **a.** lit. εἰς δόξαν θεοῦ...ἀ. Or.*Cels*.8.32(p.248.7; M.11.1564D); trans., *inhale*, Const.ap.Eus.*v.C*.2.29(p.53.19; M.20.1008A); **b.** met., *draw inspiration* from ἡ γραφὴ [sc. Παύλου] ἐκ τῆς παλαιᾶς ἤρτηται διαθήκης, ἐκεῖθεν ἀ. καὶ λαλοῦσα Clem.*str*.4.21(p.307.32; M.8.1345A); trans. τὸν Χριστὸν ἀεὶ ἀ. Ath.*v.Anton*.91(M.26.969C); Gr.Naz.*or*.43.2(M.36. 497A); Τιμόθεος τὸν Ὠριγένην ἀ. Socr.*h.e*.7.6.4(M.67.748C); **3.** *breathe out*; lit., *expire* ἀναγκαῖόν ἐστι τὸ ἀ. τὸν θεόν Cels.ap.Or.*Cels*.6.72 (p.142.11; M.11.1408B); met., of religious life ἀ. ... τὴν εἰς τὸ θεῖον εὐλάβειαν Soz.*h.e*.1.12.7(M.67.892C).

ἀναπόβλητος, *not capable of being lost* εἰ δὲ ἐνηνθρώπησεν ἀληθῶς ...ἀ. ἔχει τὸ εἶναι θεός Cyr.*Nest*.1.3(p.22.2; 6^{1}.15B).

***ἀναποβλήτως,** *inseparably*, Cyr.*Pulch*.(p.36.7; 5^{2}.142D).

ἀναποδείκτως, *without proof*, Clem.*str*.2.3(p.118.13; M.8.941B); *ib*. 8.3(p.84.31; M.9.569A); Or.*Cels*.1.19(p.71.6; M.11.696A).

***ἀναποδέω,** *turn back* (trans.), *hinder*, Nil.*epp*.2.52(M.79.224A).

***ἀναπόδησις (-ισις), ἡ,** = ἀναποδισμός, Jo.Mal.*chron*.1 p.9(M.97. 73A).

ἀναποδίζω, *go up*, Cyr.*hom.pasch*.6(5^{2}.62E).

***ἀναπόδισις, ἡ,** v. *ἀναπόδησις.

ἀναποδισμός, ὁ, *going back*, Cosm.Ind.*top*.5(M.88.289C); as object of superstitious observance ἀνακλήσεις καὶ ἀ. Nil.*epp*.2.151(M.79. 272A).

ἀναποδιστής, ὁ, *renegade*, Nil.*epp*.1.315(M.79.196D).

***ἀναπόδιστος,** *not to be called back, inevitable*, Or.*exp.in Pr*.20:15 (M.17.213B).

ἀναπόδραστος, *inevitable*; of blasphemy against H. Ghost, *inevitable* in its consequences, Ath.*ep.Serap*.4.20(M.26.669C); Bas. *Eun*.2.33(1.270B; M.29.649A).

ἀναπόθετος, *not to be laid aside, imperishable* ἀ. ... τὴν τοῦ σωτῆρος...βασιλείαν Cyr.*ador*.11(1.389A).

ἀνάποινος, *not to be redeemed with money*, Evagr.*h.e*.3.1(p.97.21; M.86.2596A).

ἀναπολέω, *turn up* the ground *again*, hence *repeat, reconsider, recall to mind*, Meth.*symp*.8.2(p.82.15; M.18.140C); *A.Thom*.A 88 (p.203.10); Chrys.*hom.52.3 in Mt*.(7.534A); Cyr.*Is*.5.5(2.882B); intrans., *go to and fro, wander* τοῦ τελευτῶντος...ἀ. ὁ νοῦς Anast.S. *defunct*.(M.89.1200A).

ἀναπολόγητος, 1. *inexcusable, without excuse*; of persons, Clem. *str*.7.2(p.9.16; M.9.413C); *Hom.Clem*.19.10; of actions, Just.*1apol*. 3.5(M.6.332B); ‡Just.*qu.et resp*.3(M.6.1253B); of an action whose omission is inexcusable, Clem.*paed*.3.11(p.279.16; M.8.656C); neut. as subst., *absence of excuse, failure to find an excuse*, Bas.*reg.br*.16 (2.420B; M.31.1092D); Areth.ap.*cat.Apoc*.8:13(p.311.11); **2.** *undefended, without defence*, Chrys.*hom.23.5 in 1Cor*.(10.207D); of martyrs condemned without trial, *A.Jo*.12(p.158.17); of martyrs undefended before posterity because their deaths are unrecorded, ‡Jo.D.*Artem*.2(p.152.19; M.96.1253B); of one who has not made a defence εἰ...καθαρὸς τῷ θεῷ...ἀλλὰ ἡμῖν τοῖς ἀνθρώποις οὔπω καθαρός, ἕως ἀ. ᾖς Synes.*ep*.44(M.66.1373C); of man at the judgement ἀσυνηγόρητος ἀ. Bas.*hom*.7.6(2.58B; M.31.296B); **3.** of a charge, *unanswered*, Gr.Nyss.*Eun*.6(2 p.127.6; M.45.709A); of a sentence against which no defence can be made, *irrevocable*, Clem.*str*.7.15 (p.65.15; M.9.528B); Cyr.H.*catech*.16.8.

ἀναπομπή, ἡ, *sending up*; *bringing up* the dead ψυχῆς ἀ., τὴν λεγομένην νεκρομαντείαν *Hom.Clem*.1.5.

ἀναπόνιπτος, *unwashed*; met. of sin, *not washed away*, Eus.*Is*. 3:2(M.24.109C); Synes.*ep*.44(M.66.1369A); Cyr.*Is*.1.1(2.5C).

ἀναπόσπαστος, *inseparable* τὸ τῆς κυριότητος [sc. Χριστοῦ] ἀ.· Chrys.*hom.1.1 in Heb*.(12.7B); of a companion ἔχων τὸν ἐμὸν πατέρα ἀ. Cyr.S.*v.Sab*.75(p.180.8).

ἀναπόστατος, *inseparable* τὴν ἀ. πρὸς θεὸν προσοχήν Max.*schol. d.n*.4.2(M.4.241B).

***ἀναποτάκτως,** *without renouncing* the world, Thdr.Stud.*or*.11.9 (M.99.812A).

***ἀναποτνιασμός, ὁ,** *groaning*, Gr.Nyss.*hom.opif*.12.4(M.44.160A).

ἀναπότριπτος, *not to be rubbed off, ineradicable*; of sins, Cyr.*Is*.1.1 (2.6B); id.*Juln*.8(6^{2}.280D).

ἀναπτερ-όω, 1. *furnish with wings* ἡ παχυμερεστέρα [sc. υἱότης]... ἀναδραμεῖν μὲν οὐκ ἠδυνήθη...ἀ. δὲ αὐτὴν [v.l. αὑτὴν] τῷ πνεύματι τῷ ἁγίῳ Hipp.*haer*.10.14(p.275.8; M.16.3430A); Gr.Nyss.*hom.15 in Cant*.(M.44.1101B); of woman of Samaria εὐαγγελιστῶν ἔργον ποιεῖ, ὑπὸ τῆς χαρᾶς ~ωθεῖσα Chrys.*hom.34.1 in Jo*.(8.195C); in gen., *uplift* ἡ θεωρία τῶν ἰδεῶν ἀ. μοι τὴν φρόνησιν Just.*dial*.2.6(M.6.477C); Clem.*paed*.1.13(p.152.2; M.8.376B); ἀ. ἡμῶν τὴν καρδίαν εἰς πόθον Meth.*symp*.7.2(p.73.3; M.18.128A); Chrys.*ep*.193(3.708B); Χριστοῦ... ~οῦντος...εἰς θεωρίαν Cyr.*Jo*.3.6(4.320C); *cat.Lc*.23:43(p.170.11); in bad sense, *rouse* to hostility, *T.Sal*.25.5(M.122.1356C); τὴν πόλιν ἀ. κατ' αὐτῶν Chrys.*hom.1.2 in 1Thess*.(11.428C); *excite*, id.*hom. 42.3 in Mt*.(7.456B); παρθέναι...τοὺς τῶν νέων ὀφθαλμοὺς ἀ. id.*laud. Max*.7(3.222D); **2.** pass., *fly*; lit., *Apoc.Bar*.3(p.85.33); met., Or.*or*. 29(p.384.5; M.11.533B); perf. ptcpl. pass. as adj., *flighty* γυναῖκα ...ἀνεπτερωμένην id.*hom.30.5 in Mt*.(354A); ἡδονὴ...τὴν ψυχὴν... ποιεῖ...ἀνεπτερωμένην *ib*.40.5(444A).

ἀναπτερύσσομαι, *be furnished with wings*; met., *exalt oneself*; of Nestorius, †Cyr.*hom.div.*11(5^{2}.382B).

***ἀνάπτης, ὁ**, *inflamer, disturber*, Gr.Naz.*or.*42.23(M.36.485C).

ἀνάπτησις, ἡ, *upward flight*, met. τῶν ἐξ ἐθνῶν σωζομένων...εἰς οὐρανοὺς...ἀ. Eus.*Is.*60:8(M.24.493A); νοῦ πρὸς θεὸν ἀ. Max.*ep.*12 (M.91.508C).

ἀναπτοέω, *scare exceedingly*; pass., *be excited, aroused*, Cyr.*Juln.*6 (6^{2}.191A).

[*]**ἀνάπτομαι**, = ἀναπέτομαι, *rise* δέησις...ἀ. Geo.Pis.*Pers.*1.10 (M.92.1199A).

ἄναπτος, *kindled*, Nonn.*par.Jo.*18:18(M.43.892C).

***ἀναπτυκτέον**, *one must explain*, Or.*Jo.*1.24(23; p.29.33; M.14. 65B); adj. ἀναπτυκτέος, *that must be explained*, Didym.*Trin.*1.7 (M.39.276A) cit. s. βαθύνω.

ἀναπτύσσω, *ruminate*; met., *ponder* μὴ...ῥῆμα...παραδράμῃς ἁπλῶς, ἀλλ' ἀ. τῇ διανοίᾳ †Chrys.*Jud.et gent.*12(1.575A); Eust.Mon. *ep.*(86.940D).

ἀνάπτ-ω, 1. *fasten, attach*; met. εἰ μὲν ἐπ' ἄνθρωπον...ἀνῆψά μου τῆς ψυχῆς τὴν ἐλπίδα Cyr.*Ps.*70:2(M.69.1180B); med., *fasten to oneself*; met., *secure for oneself, acquire*, Eus.*p.e.*7.8(311B; M.21.525C); id.*d.e.*8.1(p.358.18; M.22.581D); pass., *have attached* or *ascribed to oneself, be invested* or *equipped with* [sc. τὸν υἱόν] τὸν ἀνημμένον πάντων τὸ κῦρος καὶ τὸ κράτος Meth.*symp.*7.1(p.71.15; M.18.121B); Cyr.*Is.*3.4(2.477A); **2.** intrans., *cling* νῷ...~οντι πρὸς τὰ σαρκικά Cyr.*ador.*10(1.361B); pass. c. genit., *cling to* ὁ τῆς ἐκ θεοῦ συμμαχίας ἀνημμένος Eus.*h.e.*9.9.3(M.20.820D) = id.*v.C.*1.37(p.24.25; M.20.952B); **3.** *hang up* in a temple, *offer up*; met., of hymns of praise, Cyr.*Ps.* 41:5(M.69.1004D); **4.** *kindle*; med., *set oneself on fire* ἀναψάμενοι τῆς ἀρχῆς τοῦ φωτὸς ἐκείνου ἐκ τοῦ πόθου τοῦ περὶ αὐτό Clem.*ecl.*33 (p.147.9; M.9.716B); *generate* smoke, Chrys.*hom.2.5 in Mt.*(7.28C).

ἀναπυρίζω, *set on fire*, Chrys.*exp.in Ps.*3:1(5.2E).

ἀναπυρσεύω, *make glaring, set ablaze*, met. τὸ θεῖον καὶ φωτιστικὸν πῦρ ἀνῆψεν καὶ ἀ. ‡Eust.*Laz.*7(p.32.1).

ἀνάργυρος, 1. *without money*; **a.** act., *not paying*, Ast.Soph.*Ps.6* (M.40.473B); **b.** pass., *not paid for*, Cyr.*Am.*9(3.261B); ‡Paul.Sil. *therm.Pyth.*(M.86.2263); Geo.Pis.*hex.*207(M.92.1449A); **2.** *taking no payment*; hence **a.** *incorruptible* τὸν...ἀ. ῥήτορα Δανιήλ ‡Ath.*proph.*2 (M.28.1065B); **b.** of healers (saints) who performed cures without taking payment τὸν ἀ. ἰατρόν Eustrat.*v.Eutych.*54(M.86.2336D); Sophr.H.*mir.Cyr.et Jo.*tit.(M.87.3424A); *ib.*21(3484D); Thphn.*chron.* p.318(M.108.769C).

***ἀνάρδευτος**, *unwatered*, Cyr.*Abac.*51(3.565E); fig., of Christ τὴν ἀ. ἄμπελον Jo.D.*hom.*9.14(M.96.741A).

***ἀνάρηγμα, τό**, *ruin*, †Apoll.*met.Ps.*109:6(M.33.1484C).

ἄναρθρος, *inarticulate*; *incoherent*, Philost.*h.e.*9.14^{a}.

***ἀνάρθρωτος**, *without limbs*; of the eucharistic body of Christ, ‡Caes.Naz.*dial.*169(M.38.1133).

***ἀναριθμήτως**, *in innumerable ways*, Aët.*synt.*(p.359.13; M.42. 544D).

***ἀναρίθμως**, = foreg., Epiph.*exp.fid.*7(p.503.3; M.42.785A).

***ἀναρμόνιος**, *out of harmony*, Meth.*symp.*3.3(p.30.10; M.18.65A).

ἀναρμοστία, ἡ, *disharmony*; met., Meth.*symp.*3.7(p.34.20; M.18. 72B) cit. s. ἀνισότης; denied of Christ, *ib.*(p.33.20; 69C); Gr.Nyss. *hom.4 in Cant.*(M.44.848A); Isid.Pel.*epp.*4.125(M.78.1201A).

ἀνάρμοστος, *unfitting, incongruous*; *unseemly*, Gr.Mag.*dial.*(tr. Zach.)3.26(M.*PL.*77.282B).

ἀναρπάζω, 1. *snatch up*; of roots drawing up nourishment, Meth.*res.*2.9(p.347.19; M.18.308C); **2.** *snatch away, carry off*; of sudden death, Chrys.*hom.78.2 in Mt.*(7.753B); id.*hom.2.4 in 2 Thess.* (11.522B); Thdt.*Rom.*12:2(3.130).

[*]**ἀνάρπαστος, 1.** of persons, *carried up* τῶν ἁγίων...τὰ σώματα ἐν τῇ ἀναστάσει...εἰς οὐρανοὺς ἀ. ποιήσει Mac.Aeg.*elev.*2(M.34.892A); **2.** *carried off* to damnation, Chrys.*hom.9.3 in 2Cor.*(10.503A); **3.** of a city, *plundered*, id.*hom.75.3 in Mt.*(7.726E).

ἀναρρήγνυμι, *make to break out* ἀναρρήξαντος αὐτοῦ τὴν μάχην Men.*exc.gent.*32(p.477.17; M.113.849A).

ἀνάρρησις, ἡ, 1. *proclamation*; **a.** in gen. λοξὰς τῶν δαιμόνων... τὰς ἀ. ποιουμένων Philost.*h.e.*9.15(M.65.580C); τῆς τοῦ θεοῦ δόξης ἔπαινοι καὶ ἀ. ἐν ἐκκλησίαις Cyr.*Mich.*54(3.446E); of reading of liturg. lessons τὰ συντετμημένα καὶ συνεσκιασμένα μᾶλλον ἐν τῇ νοερᾷ τῶν ψαλμῶν ἱερολογίᾳ διὰ πλειόνων καὶ σαφεστέρων εἰκόνων καὶ ἀ. εὐρύνεται ταῖς ἱερωτάταις τῶν ἁγιογράφων συντάξεων ἀναγνώσεσιν Dion.Ar.*e.h.*3.3.5(M.3.432B); **b.** esp. of proclamation of victor in war or games εἰ οὖν...ἀ. καὶ στηλῶν ἐπιτυχεῖν ἀξιοῖς Isid.Pel.*epp.*1.40 (M.78.208B); hence of victorious Christian τηρεῖται ὡς εὐδόκιμος ἀθλητὴς τῇ ἀ. τῆς ἀναστάσεως Ast.Am.*hom.*10(M.40.325A); στεφάνων καὶ ἀ. μεγάλων τευξόμεθα Isid.Pel.*epp.*1.4(181B); ἀναστάσεως...ἀνηρημένης, καὶ ἡ ἀ. συνανῄρηται Thdt.*1Cor.*15:18(3.268); ἀναμένει ὁ... θεὸς...ἵνα...κοινῇ πάντας τῶν ἀ. ἀξιώσῃ τοὺς νικηφόρους id.*Heb.*11:40 (3.624); οἱ τὸν μοναδικὸν ἀσπαζόμενοι βίον...οὕτω τῆς ἀ. ἀπολαύουσιν id.*h.rel.*27(3.1283); liturg. τῶν δὲ ἱερῶν πτυχῶν ἡ μετὰ τὴν εἰρήνην ἀ. ἀνακηρύττει τοὺς ὁσίως βεβιωκότας Dion.Ar.*e.h.*3.3.9(M.3.437B); at funerals τῶν λειτουργῶν ὁ πρῶτος...ἀνακηρύττει τοὺς ἤδη κεκοιμημένους, μεθ' ὧν ἀξιοῖ τὸν ἄρτι τελειωθέντα τῆς ὁμοταγοῦς ἀ. *ib.*7.2 (556C); **c.** of an emperor at accession τῆς Οὐαλεντινιανοῦ εἰς βασιλέα ἀ. Philost.*h.e.*1 proem.(M.65.460A); *ib.*12.12(620C); of a bishop τὸν Ἀθανάσιον...πρὸς βασιλέα γράψαι τὴν εἰς τὴν ἀρχιερωσύνην ἀ. αὐτοῦ *ib.*2.11(473B); **d.** at ordination or consecration, *proclamation* of candidate's name by officiating bishop, Synes.*ep.*67(M.66.1416A); ἵνα καθαρᾶς παρὰ τῶν ἀρχιερέων τῆς ἐπὶ τῶν χειροτονουμένων ἀ. γενομένης, ἄνωθεν ἡ τοῦ ἁγίου πνεύματος χάρις ἐπιφοιτᾷ Gennad. *encycl.*(p.80.30; M.85.1617A); κοινὰ μὲν ἔστι τοῖς ἱεράρχαις τε καὶ ἱερεῦσι καὶ λειτουργοῖς ἐν ταῖς ἱερατικαῖς αὐτῶν τελειώσεσιν...ἡ ἀ. Dion.Ar.*e.h.*5.3.1(M.3.509C); ἀ. οἱονεὶ κήρυξις ἐξ ὀνόματος· σφραγίζων γὰρ αὐτὸν ὁ χειροτονῶν ἀρχιερεύς, ἐξ ὀνόματος φάσκει· σφραγίζεται ὁ δεῖνα ἀπὸ πρεσβυτέρου εἰς ἐπίσκοπον ἐν ὀνόματι πατρὸς καὶ υἱοῦ καὶ ἁγίου πνεύματος· ὁμοίως καὶ ἐπὶ πρεσβυτέρου καὶ διακόνου... ἀ. ... ὅπερ νῦν καλοῦσιν ἐπικήρυξιν ἢ ἀνακήρυξιν...ἡ ἐπὶ τῶν χειροτονιῶν ἀνακήρυξις, οἷον ἐπὶ τῆς τοῦ ἐπισκόπου· ὑπὲρ τοῦ ἁγίου πατρὸς ἐπισκόπου τοῦδε· τόδε ἀ. φησιν ὅταν ἐν αὐτῷ τῷ χειροτονεῖν κηρυττῇ· τὸν χειροτονούμενον ἡ θεία χάρις προχειρίζεται τόνδε εἰς τόνδε Max. *schol.e.h.*5.7(M.4.165B); **2.** *acclamation* νικᾷ δὲ μετὰ πολλῆς ἀ. ὁ ἐμὸς μονόμαχος Jo.VI H.*v.Jo.D.*21(M.94.460D).

ἀναρριζόω, *uproot*, Gr.Nyss.*Apoll.*1(M.45.1125A).

ἀναρριπίζω, *fan*; **1.** lit., Chrys.*hom.16.8 in Mt.*(7.215A); Nonn. *par.Jo.*18:18(M.43.892C); **2.** *stir up afresh*: persecution, Eus.*v.C.* 2.1(p.40.5; M.20.980A); controversy, Soz.*h.e.*2.21.6(M.67.988B); love, Max.*ep.*22(M.91.605C); **3.** *stir up, fan*: war, Const.ap.Eus.*v.C.*2.49 (p.62.14; M.20.1028A); desire, Gr.Nyss.*hom.1 in Cant.*(M.44.768C); **4.** fig., *cause to dart hither and thither*, Chrys.*virg.*31(1.290E); **5.** *stir up, rouse*, persons; Ast.Am.*hom.*8(M.40.284A); Dion.Al.ap. Eus.*h.e.*6.41.1(M.20.605B); Synes.*Dion* 8(p.256.1; M.66.1136D); *blow about*, Chrys.*hom.11.6 in Mt.*(7.156D); **6.** *blow away*, Chrys.*stat.*8.2 (2.94A); id.*hom.7.3 in Col.*(11.375A).

***ἀναρριπισμός, ὁ**, *upward draught*, ‡Caes.Naz.*dial.*118(M.38. 1004).

ἀναρρίπτω, *stir up* war, Men.*exc.gent.*11(p.454.30; M.113.812D).

ἀναρροιβδέω ([*]**ἀναρυβδέω**), pass., *spring* or *gush up*, ‡Paul. Sil.*therm.Pyth.*(M.86.2264); ἀναρυβδέω Philost.*h.e.*3.10(M.65.496A).

ἀνάρροπος, 1. *ascending*; neut. as subst., *upward path* τὸ μὲν ἀ. τοῦ ἀγαθοῦ φεύγουσαι ‡Proc.G.*Pr.*2:15(M.87.1237C); **2.** *retrograde*; in adv. phrase εἰς ἀ. *backwards*, Geo.Pis.*Pers.*2.337(M.92.1233A).

ἀναρρυθμίζ-ω, *re-order, re-create* νέος...καιρὸς ἐν Χριστῷ...εἰς νέαν καὶ καινὴν ~ων ζωὴν διὰ τῶν εὐαγγελικῶν παιδευμάτων Cyr.*Jo.* 4.4(4.386C).

ἀνάρρυσις, ἡ, 1. *rescue, deliverance* οὐκ ἔτι [sc. at the final judgement] ἀ. ἡμῶν τῶν ἐλεεινῶν Ephr.2.201E; of Christ's miracles τὴν τῶν καταδίκων [the diseased or demon-possessed] ἀ. Gr.Nyss. *or.catech.*23(p.87.6); [sc. Christ's baptism] τὴν κατάδυσιν τοῦ κυρίου ἡμῶν εἰς ᾅδην καὶ παράδοξον ἀ. τῶν ἐν φθορᾷ κατεχομένων προϊστορῶν ‡Meth.*Sym.et Ann.*9(M.18.372B); **2.** *ransom* τοῦ ἐκπεμφθῆναι χρήματα εἰς ἀ. [sc. τῶν αἰχμαλώτων] Jo.Mal.*chron.*18 p.460(M.97.673B).

ἀναρρύω, *draw back*; med., *rescue*; hence *repair, restore* μοναστήρια Thphn.*chron.*p.383(M.108.917B).

ἀναρρώννυμι, *strengthen afresh*; of God strengthening martyrs, *Ep.Lugd.*ap Eus.*h.e.*5.1.28(M.20.420A); συνθεόντων δὲ τῶν ἔργων τοῖς ἐκ πίστεως ἀγαθοῖς, τότε δὴ τότε καὶ συνέσται θεὸς καὶ ἀ. Cyr.*Mich.* 36(3.423E); med. with act. sense τὸ ἀδύνατον τοῦ ἐν ἡμῖν φυσικοῦ ἀγαθοῦ ἐν ᾧ ἠσθένει...ὁ θεὸς ἀ. πέμψας τὸν υἱόν Meth.*res.*2.8(p.344. 18; M.18.308A).

ἀνάρρωσις, ἡ, *recovery*, Chrys.*ecl.*6(12.471B).

ἀναρτάω, *hang upon, fasten upon* πάντες γὰρ ἀ. πρὸς τὸ ὕψος τὰ πρόσωπα Rom.Mel.(*AS* 1 p.154).

***ἀναρτίζω**, *uplift* τῶν μαθητῶν ἐκ τῆς γῆς ἀνηρτίσθησαν αἱ ὄψεις [i.e. at Ascension] Procl.CP *hom.*1.3(M.65.836D).

***ἄναρτος**, *without bread*, Gr.Naz.*carm.*1.2.10.673(M.37.728A).

***ἀναρτύτως**, *without tempering* the mortar, SM Ezech.13:10 ap. Chrys.*hom.68.2 in Mt.*(7.672A).

[*]**ἀναρυβδέω**, v. ἀναρροιβδέω.

ἀναρχία, ἡ, 1. *absence of a ruler, anarchy*; **2.** *absence of a first cause*; of Christ's human nature, by implication from views of Beron, ‡Hipp.*Ber.Hel.*6(p.325.2; M.10.837B); **3.** *disbelief in a first* *cause, atheism* τρεῖς αἱ...δόξαι περὶ θεοῦ, ἀ., καὶ πολυαρχία, καὶ μοναρχία Gr.Naz.*or.*29.2(p.74.12; M.36.76A).

ἄναρχος, A. *without a ruler*; neut. as subst.; **1.** *anarchy* τὸ... ἄ., ἄτακτον· τό τε πολύαρχον, στασιῶδες, καὶ οὕτως ἄ. καὶ οὕτως ἄτακτον Gr.Naz.*or.*29.2(p.74.14; M.36.76A); id.*carm.*1.1.3.81(M.37.414A); **2.** *freedom from subjection*; of the apostles, Thdt.*Ps.*46:10 (1.907).

B. *without beginning, eternal*; **1.** of God μόνος ἄ. ὢν καὶ αὐτὸς ὑπάρχων τῶν ὅλων ἀρχή Tat.*orat.*4(p.5.1; M.6.813A); ἡμεῖς δὲ λέγομεν θεὸν εἶναι τὸν παντοκράτορα θεὸν ἄ., ἀτελεύτητον, ἐμπεριέχοντα τὰ πάντα καὶ μὴ ἐμπεριεχόμενον Heraclides ap.Or.*dial.*2(p.122.12); ὁ θεὸς ἀγέννητος, εἷς, ἄ., ἀόρατος, ἀναλλοίωτος Hymen.*ep.*2(p.324.15); εἰ περιγράφει [sc. θεός] ἑαυτόν, ἄρα οὐκ ἄ. ἑαυτῷ, ἀλλ' ἡμῖν· οὐκοῦν οὐ φύσει ἄ. Chrys.*hom.5.3 in Col.*(11.362C); of Trin., ‡Caes.Naz.*dial.*3 (M.38.860) cit. s. ἀναλλοίωτος; Jo.Mon.*hymn.Bas.*3(M.96.1372C) cit. s. συνάναρχος; of Valentinian Propator, Iren.*haer.*1.2.2(M.7.453A); of divine attributes εἰς πάντας ἐξ ἀρχῆς ἄ. ... ἡ φυσικὴ δικαιοσύνη... οὐκ ἀρξαμένη ποτέ Clem.*str.*5.14(p.421.8; M.9.205B); διὰ τῆς ἀ. προθέσεως *ib.*6.12(p.483.3; 324A); οὔ...ἄ. ἡ γνῶσις *Const.App.*7.35.9; neut. as subst., God's *eternity* τὸ ἄ. αὐτῆς ἀγέννητον ὠνομάσθη Bas. *Eun.*1.7(1.219A; M.29.525C); ἐν τῷ ἀ. τοῦ πατρὸς ὢν ἀρχὴν ἡμερῶν οὐκ ἔχει [sc. ὁ υἱός] Gr.Nyss.*Eun.*8(2 p.179.25; M.45.772D); οὐκ ἔστιν οὖν ἔμπροσθεν τοῦ υἱοῦ ὁ...πατήρ, οὐ τῷ ἀ. οὐ τῇ οὐσίᾳ...ἀλλ' ἐπ' ἴσης Didym.*Trin.*1.15(M.39.296B); Proc.G.*Gen.*proem.(M.87.32C); τὸ μὲν α, ἀρχήν, τὸ δὲ ω, τέλος δηλοῖ...διὰ μὲν τοῦ πρώτου τὸ ἄ. τοῦ θεοῦ [sc. δηλοῦν] Oecum.*Apoc.*1:8(p.38); τὸ ἀγέννητον καὶ τὸ ἄ. καὶ τὸ ἀναλλοίωτον καὶ τὸ ἄφθαρτον...οὐ τό, τί ἐστι, σημαίνει, ἀλλὰ τό, τί οὐκ ἔστι Jo.D.*f.o.*1.4(M.94.800A); **2.** of Father opp. Son, acc. Arius, v. ἀρχή; **3.** of Son, Clem.*str.*7.1(p.4.6; M.9.404C) cit. s. ἀρχή; τὸ ἀπαύγασμα ἄ. καὶ ἀειγενές Dion.Al.ap.Ath.*Dion.*15(p.57.11; M.25.501D); Ath.*Ar.*1.12(M.26.37C); ὁ υἱὸς...ἄ. μὲν τῷ ἀεὶ συνεῖναι τῷ πατρί, γεννητὸς δὲ τῷ τὸν πατέρα ἐσχηκέναι τοῦ εἶναι ‡Gr. Nyss.*Ar.et Sab.*5(M.45.1288C); σοφίας τῆς ἀκτίστου καὶ ἀ. τοῦτ' ἔστι Χριστοῦ Gel.Cyz.*h.e.*2.19.5(M.85.1276D); denied, Eun.*exp.fid.*2 (p.255); of generation of Son τὴν ἄ. παρὰ τοῦ πατρὸς γέννησιν Alex.Al.*ep.Alex.*12(p.28.2; M.18.568A); Gr.Nyss.*fr.*4(M.46.1112B); of Christ's kingdom, Ath.*apol.sec.*45(p.122.3; M.25.332C); ref. Inc. εἰ ὁ ἄ. λόγος τῆς ἐνανθρωπήσεως γέγονεν ἀρχή, σαφὲς ὅτι ὁ Χριστὸς ἄ. διὰ τὴν ἐκ μήτρας ἕνωσιν Marc.Er.*opusc.*10.4(M.65.1121D); γεγέννηται ...ἐξ αὐτῆς τῆς οὐσίας ἐνυπόστατος αὐτοῦ λόγος καὶ ἄ. ἐν χρόνῳ τὴν ὕπαρξιν ἔχει Cyr.*ep.*1(p.15.9; 5².8B); τῆς μὲν γὰρ ἀνθρωπότητος γέγονεν ἀρχή, ἡ δὲ θεότης ἔμεινεν ἄ. Procl.CP *or.*3.3(M.65.705D); ἡμεῖς, φασί, τὴν αὐτὴν [sc. φύσιν] ἄ. καὶ ἀρξαμένην...λέγομεν· ἀλλ' οὐ τὴν αὐτὴν ἐν ταὐτῷ κατὰ τὸ αὐτό Leont.H.*monoph.*40(M.86.1793B); **4.** of created things; **a.** the world; view ascribed to Origen εἰ γὰρ ἦν χρόνος ὅτε οὐκ ἦν τὰ ποιήματα...ἀλλοιοῦσθαι...ἀναλλοίωτον συμβήσεται θεόν. ... οὐκ ἄρα δυνατὸν λέγειν μὴ εἶναι ἄ. καὶ συναΐδιον τῷ θεῷ τὸ πᾶν Meth.*creat.*2(p.494.28; M.18.333C); denied, Mac.Mgn.*apocr.* 4.11(p.172.23); **b.** matter; denied, Tat.*orat.*5(p.6.12; M.6.817A); affirmed by Valentinians ἐμοὶ ἡ ὕλη ποιότητας ἄ. ἔχειν δοκεῖ...ἵνα τῶν κακῶν ὁ μὲν θεὸς ἀναίτιος ᾖ Adam.*dial.*4.7(p.152.19; M.11.1817A); and Manicheans, Mac.Aeg.*hom.*16.1(M.34.613B); **5.** of eternity ὁ λόγος...τῷ αὐτοῦ πατρὶ συμβασιλεύων ἐξ ἀ. αἰώνων εἰς ἀπείρους καὶ ἀτελευτήτους αἰῶνας διαρκεῖ Eus.*l.C.*1(p.199.5; M.20.1323A); of infinity ὅταν μὲν εἰς τὸν ἄνω βυθὸν ὁ νοῦς ἀποβλέψῃ...τὸ ἐνταῦθα ἄπειρον καὶ ἀνέκβατον ἄ. προσηγόρευσεν Gr.Naz.*or.*38.8(M.36.320A); not of time οὐκ ἄρα ἄ. ὁ χρόνος· τοῦ μὲν γὰρ ἀ. οὐκ ἔστι γένεσις, τοῦ δὲ χρόνου ἐστίν ‡Just.*confut.*19(M.6.1520C); **6.** false view of evil κακὸν ἄ. καὶ ὑλικόν Chrys.*hom.47.4 in Ac.*(9.357A); **7.** met., of Christian who denies the world εἰ δὲ ἑαυτὸν...ἀρνήσεται καὶ ἀπολέσει τὴν ψυχὴν τουτέστι τὴν κάτω ζωὴν...ἄ. ἔσται καὶ ἀτελεύτητος...χρόνου δὲ ἀνώτερος ἔσται Cyr.ap.*cat.Heb.*7:2 suppl.(p.549.28).

C. *without source*; **1.** of Trin. τριάδος, ἢ τῆς ἀ. καὶ ἀγεννήτου φύσεως ἠρτημένη τῆς τῶν γεννητῶν ἁπάντων οὐσίας...τὰς αἰτίας ἀπείληφεν Eus.*l.C.*6(p.210.15; M.20.1348B); ἡ ἄ. τῶν ὄντων ἀρχή Procl. CP *annunt.*2(M.85.429D); **2.** of God, Clem.*fr.*37(p.219.17; M.9.749D); id.*str.*4.25(p.320.16; M.8.1372B); τὸ γὰρ πρώτως κινοῦν πάντως ἀκίνητον, ὅτι καὶ ἄ. Max.*ambig.*(M.91.1177A); **3.** partic. of Father, Meth. *creat.*11(p.499.14; M.18.344A) cit. s. ἀρχή; παρ' Ἑβραίοις...μετὰ τὴν ἄ. καὶ ἀγένητον τοῦ θεοῦ τῶν ὅλων οὐσίαν...δευτέραν οὐσίαν καὶ θείαν δύναμιν...λόγον καὶ σοφίαν καὶ θεοῦ δύναμιν Eus.*p.e.*7.12 (320C; M.21.541B); δύο ὑποστάσεις...οὐδὲ ἰσοτίμους...οὐδ' ἄμφω ἀ. ... ἀλλὰ μίαν μὲν τὴν ἀγέννητον καὶ ἄ. θατέραν...ἀρχὴν τὸν πατέρα κεκτημένην id.*e.th.*2.7(p.104.15; M.24.909A); *Symb.Sirm.*1 *anath.*26 (p.256.17; M.26.740C); ἀρχὴ γὰρ υἱοῦ ἄχρονος, ἀκατάληπτος, ἄ. ὁ πατήρ Cyr.H.*catech.*11.20; Bas.*Eun.*1.15(1.227A; M.29.545B) θεὸ ... οὐκ αὐταίτιον καὶ αὐτογένεθλον...ἀλλ' ἀΐδιον καὶ ἄ. *Const.App.*6.11.1; ὁ πατὴρ ἀγέννητος καὶ ἄ. οὐ γάρ ἐστιν αὐτοῦ τι πρεσβύτερον, ἦν γὰρ ἐκεῖνος καὶ πάντως ἦν θεός· ἄ. δὲ ὅτι μὴ ἔκ τινος ἔχει τὸ εἶναι ἢ ἐξ ἑαυτοῦ *Euchol.*(p.253); as subst., *First Cause* ἄ., καὶ ἀρχὴ καὶ τὸ μετὰ τῆς ἀρχῆς εἷς θεός...οὔτε ἡ ἀρχή, τῷ ἀρχὴ εἶναι, τοῦ ἀ. διείργεται ...ὄνομα δὲ τῷ ἀ. πατήρ Gr.Naz.*or.*42.15(M.36.476A); id.*carm.*1.2.10. 988(M.37.751A); (Arian) ξένος τοῦ υἱοῦ κατ' οὐσίαν ὁ πατήρ, ὅτι ἄ. ὑπάρξει Ar.*Thal.fr.*2 ap.Ath.*syn.*15(p.242.27; M.26.708A); ὁ μὲν θεός, αἴτιος τῶν πάντων τυγχάνων, ἐστὶν ἄ. μονώτατος, ὁ δὲ υἱὸς ἀχρόνως γεννηθεὶς ὑπὸ τοῦ πατρὸς...οὐκ ἦν πρὸ τοῦ γεννηθῆναι id.*ep.Alex.* (p.13.8; M.26.709B); *Symb.Ant.*(345)3(p.252.10; M.26.740B); **4.** denied of Son οὐκ ἰδιόκτητον καὶ τοῦ πατρὸς ἀφωρισμένην οὐδ' ἄ. τινα καὶ ἀγέννητον...ἐφελκόμενον θεότητα, ἐξ αὐτῆς δὲ τῆς πατρικῆς μετουσίας Eus.*e.th.*1.2(p.63.23; M.24.832B); οὐδὲ ἄ. οὐδὲ ἰδιόκτητον εἶχε τὴν δόξαν, ἀλλὰ παρὰ τοῦ πατρὸς λαβών *ib.*1.20(p.82.28; 868D); ref. 1Cor. 11:3 εἴ τις ἀγέννητον καὶ ἄ. λέγοι τὸν υἱόν, ὡς δύο ἄ. καὶ ἀγέννητα λέγων καὶ δύο ποιῶν θεούς, ἀνάθεμα ἔστω *Symb.Sirm.*1 *anath.*26(p.256.15; M.26.740B); ref. 1Cor.15:28 ἵνα ἅπαντα εἰς αὐτὸν ἀνηρτημένα ᾖ, ἵνα μὴ δύο τις ἀρχὰς ἀ. ὑποπτεύῃ Chrys.*hom.39.6 in 1Cor.*(10.372B); id.*hom.2.3 in Heb.*(12.19D) cit. s. ἀναίτιος; this sense carefully distinguished from B.3 by orthodox υἱὸς...οὐκ ἄ., ἐκ τοῦ πατρὸς γάρ εἰ δὲ τὴν ἀπὸ χρόνου λαμβάνοις ἀρχήν, καὶ ἄ.· ποιητὴς γὰρ χρόνων, οὐχ ὑπὸ χρόνον Gr.Naz.*or.*39.12(M.36.348B); *ib.*20.7(M.35.1073B); *ib.* 25.15(1220B); ὁρᾷς ἄ. τὸν υἱόν, οὐ κατὰ τὸ μὴ ἔχειν αἴτιον...ἀλλὰ κατὰ τὸ μὴ ἔχειν ἀρχὴν ζωῆς μήτε τέλος Chrys.*hom.12.2 in Heb.*(12.122B); but confused by heretics οἱ δέ, ἐπειδὴ τὸ ἄ. τοῦ πατρὸς ἀΐδιον ὀνομάζεται, ταὐτὸν τῷ ἀ. ἀποφαίνουσι, καὶ ἐπειδὴ μὴ ἀγέννητος ὁ υἱός, οὐδὲ ἀΐδιον εἶναι ὁμολογοῦσι Bas.*Eun.*2.17(1.253A; M.29.608C); πᾶν τὸ ἄ., καὶ ἀγέννητον ἂν εἴη· πῶς ὁ υἱὸς εἰκότως ἂν προσαγορεύοιτο ἄ., οὗ καὶ τοὔνομα ἔμφασιν ἀρχῆς ἔχει; ‡Gr.Nyss.*Ar.et Sab.*2(M.45.1284A); **5.** denied of H. Ghost οὐκ ἄ. δὲ ἡ τοῦ ἀγαθοῦ κίνησις ἐκ τοῦ πνεύματος· ἀλλὰ...ὁ μονογενὴς θεὸς πάντα ποιεῖ, οὗ χωρὶς οὐδὲν εἰς γένεσιν τῶν ὄντων ἔρχεται. ἀλλὰ καὶ αὐτὴ πάλιν τῶν ἀγαθῶν ἡ πηγὴ ἐκ τοῦ πατρικοῦ βουλήματος ἀφορμᾶται Gr.Nyss.*tres dii*(M.45.129A); ref. procession, acc. Eunomians ἡ ἀγέννητον πάντως ἢ γεννητόν· καὶ εἰ μὲν ἀγέννητον, δύο τὰ ἄ. Gr.Naz.*or.*31.7(p.153.3; M.36.140C); **6.** denied of angels, Thdt.*qu.4 in Gen.*(1.7); **7.** of Persons of Trin. (Marcionite) τρεῖς ἐναντίους, ἀ., ἀεὶ συνόντας ἑαυτοῖς *Const.App.*6.8.2; εἴ τις ἐπίσκοπος ἢ πρεσβύτερος κατὰ τὴν τοῦ κυρίου διάταξιν μὴ βαπτίσῃ εἰς πατέρα καὶ υἱὸν καὶ ἅγιον πνεῦμα, ἀλλὰ εἰς τρεῖς ἀ. ... καθαιρείσθω *Can.App.*49; of Manichean good and evil principles ὁ μὲν Μάνης δύο ἀρχὰς εἰσηγεῖται ἀ. Epiph.*haer.*66.8(p.29.4; M.42.41B); τῆς τοῦ κακοῦ...ἀρχῆς ἀ. ἔτι ἐπιμενούσης καὶ παντελῶς μὴ δυναμένης ἀναιρεθῆναι *ib.*66.24(p.52.11; 69C); **8.** *without first principles*; of a faulty argument, Gr.Nyss.*Eun.*1(1 p.88.14; M.45.320C).

***ἀναρχότης, ἡ,** *absence of beginning* οὐδὲν ὑπολέλειπται τῆς θεότητος, ὃ οὐκ ἔχει τὸ ἅγιον σῶμα τοῦ Χριστοῦ, εἴτε ἀ. εἴποις, εἴτε θεότητα Marc.Er.*opusc.*10.5(M.65.1124C); of Christ ὁ ὢν ἐν τῇ...ἀ. Agath. *v.Gr.Ill.*45(p.25).

***ἀναρχοφωτόμυστος,** *hidden in eternal light*, ‡Paul.Sil.*therm. Pyth.*(M.86.2266).

ἀνάρχως, A. *without a beginning, eternally*; **1.** of generation of Son ὁ λόγος τὸ εἶναι...ἔχει...ἐν τῷ πατρὶ...ἵνα καὶ αὐτὸς ἀ. ὑπάρχῃ ἐν τῷ πατρί, γέννημα καὶ οὐ κτίσμα τυγχάνων αὐτοῦ Ath.*Ar.*2.57(M.26. 269B); Gr.Naz.*or.*30.19(p.138.10; M.36.128C); πνεῦμα οὖν ὁ θεὸς καὶ ⟨κατὰ⟩ πνεῦμα ἀ. καὶ ἀχρόνως τὸν υἱὸν ἐγέννησεν Epiph.*haer.*69.36 (p.185.2; M.42.257D); ἄναρχος ὢν θεός, ἀ. ἐστὶ καὶ πατήρ †Diad.*Ar.*2 (M.65.1152B); Jo.D.*f.o.*1.8(M.94.813B); denied by Eusebius οὐδέ γε ἀ. συνυφέστηκεν τῷ πατρί, ἐπεὶ ὁ μὲν ἀγέννητος ὁ δὲ γεννητός, καὶ ὁ μὲν πατὴρ ὁ δὲ υἱός, προϋπάρχειν δὲ καὶ προϋφεστάναι πατέρα υἱοῦ πᾶς ὅστις οὖν ⟨ἂν⟩ ὁμολογήσειεν Eus.*d.e.*5.1(p.213.27; M.22.353D), but cf. ἄναρχος B.5; eternal pre-existence of Father asserted λέγουσιν ὅτι προϋπάρχει ὁ θεὸς τοῦ υἱοῦ ἀ. Ar.*ep.Eus.*(p.2.6; M.42. 212A); orthodox view distorted by Eunomius ἤτοι γὰρ ἀ. ἀλλήλων κεχωρίσθαι τὰς οὐσίας ταύτας ὑπολαμβάνοντες, τούτων δὲ τὴν ἑτέραν εἰς υἱοῦ τάξιν διὰ γεννήσεως ἄγοντες καὶ τὸν ἀ. ὄντα ὑπὸ τοῦ ὄντος γενέσθαι διατεινόμενοι τοῖς ἰδίοις ὑπόκεισθε λοιδορήμασιν (ὃν γὰρ ἀγέννητον εἶναι φαντάζεσθε, τούτῳ τὴν παρ' ἑτέρου γέννησιν ἐπιφημίζετε) Eun.ap.Gr.Nyss.*Eun.*1(1 p.156.30; M.45.397C); **2.** of Christ's divine opp. human nature, ref. Jo.1:1,14 τῷ μὲν γὰρ λόγῳ μηδὲ καθ' οἱανοῦν ἀρχὴν γεγονέναι μαρτυρῶν ἀ. εἶναι, τὴν σάρκα γενέσθαι φησί Leont.H.*monoph.*40(M.86.1793C); **3.** of divine attributes and gifts οὐδὲ ἅπτεται τοῦ κυρίου ἀπαθοῦς ἀ. γενομένου φθόνος Clem.*str.*7.2 (p.7.4; M.9.409C); ἡ δὲ τοῦ Χριστοῦ πίστις ἀ. ἐστὶ ἐξ αὐτοῦ [sc. θεοῦ] Const.ap.Gel.Cyz.*h.e.*3.19.34(M.85.1353A); τὴν ζωὴν ἀεί τε εἶναι καὶ ἀ. εἶναι...πάντες ἂν ὁμολογήσαιεν Chrys.*hom.4.3 in Jo.*(8.30A); of plan of salvation ἀ. ταῦτα τετύπωτο ἐν τῷ Χριστῷ γενέσθαι id.*hom.* *2.1 in 2Tim.*(11.666F); **4.** question of eternity of creation γενητὸν εἶναι ἀεὶ γενέσεως ἀρχὴν οὐκ ἔχον, ὅπως ἀ. λέγοιτο κρατεῖν τοῦ τεχνάσματος ὁ τεχνίτης Meth.*creat.*7(p.498.4; M.18.340A); εἴπερ τὸ δημιουργεῖν καλὸν καὶ πρέπον, πῶς οὐκ ἀ. αὐτῷ τὸ καλὸν καὶ πρέπον παρῆν, εἴπερ ἄναρχος ὁ θεός; Gr.Nyss.*Eun.*8(2 p.195.6, v.l. ἀνάρχῳ M.45.789D); denied by orthodox πᾶσιν τὸ εἶναι αὐτὸς [sc. ὁ θεός] παρέσχεν, οὐκ οὖσιν πρότερον, οὐδὲ τὴν σύστασιν ἀ. ἔχουσιν Meth. *arbitr.*22(p.206.7); of matter (Gnost.), *ib.*9(p.169.11; M.18.257A), where Adam.*dial.*4.7(p.152.19; M.11.1817A) reads ἀνάρχους, v. ἄναρχος B.4; not of evil εἰ ἐξ ὧν ἐνεργεῖ κακὸς ὑπάρχει κακός...οὐκ ἔσται ἀ. κακός, οὐδ' ἀγένητα τὰ κακά Meth.*arbitr.*8(p.168.14; 256D) = Adam.*dial.*4.9(p.162.2; M.11.1824B); ref. Gen.1:26 ὁ θεὸς παραγαγὼν εἰς τὸ εἶναι...τὸ ἀεὶ ὂν...εἰ καὶ μὴ ἀ., ἀλλ' ἀτελευτήτως Max. *carit.*3.25(M.90.1024B,C).

B. *without a source, originally*; of power of Father, but not of creative power of H. Ghost ἐκείνης μὲν πάντα τῆς δυνάμεως ἐκ τοῦ μὴ ὄντος εἰς τὸ εἶναι παράγεται· οὐ μὴν οὐδὲ ἐξ ἐκείνης ἀ. ἀλλά τίς ἐστι δύναμις ἀγεννήτως καὶ ἀ. ὑφεστῶσα, ἥτις ἐστὶν αἰτία τῆς τῶν ὄντων αἰτίας Gr.Nyss.*diff.ess.*4(M.32.329B).

ἀνασειράζ-ω, 1. *rein in* a horse, Evagr.*h.e.*3.25(p.122.25; M.86.2649A); met., *restrain*; heresy, Ammon.*Jo.*1:10(M.85.1396D); of God δύναμις...~ουσα [sc. τὴν ἄβυσσον] Cyr.*Ps.*32:7(M.69.873B); ref. Jer. 5:1 ἀ. τὴν θεοπρεπῆ γαληνότητα διὰ τὸ τῆς ἁμαρτίας ὑπέρογκον id. *glaph.Num.*(1.386B); id.*Jo.*9(4.739D); **2.** met., *guide back* an argument to its starting-point, id.*ador.*7(1.234E); *ib.*10(351E); **3.** *draw away*; lit., Evagr.*h.e.*2.3(p.40.13; M.86.2493A); met., *draw away* from allegiance, Nonn.*par.Jo.*6:67(M.43.804B).

***ἀνασείρασις, ἡ,** *reining back, drawing away*, Areth.*Apoc.*17(M. 106.597A).

***ἀνασειστής, ὁ,** *disturber of the peace, rebel* οἱ Χριστιανοί, οἱ ἀ. Sever.ap.*cat.Ac.*11:7(p.28.14); CChalc.*act.*1(*ACO* 2.1.1 p.70.15; H.2. 73C); *Chron.Pasch.*p.339(M.92.885A).

***ἀνασείστρια, ἡ,** *woman disturbing the peace*, Pall.*v.Chrys.*4(p.25. 12; M.47.16).

ἀνασηκόω, *move up and down, shrug*, Gr.Naz.*or.*5.23(M.35.692B).

ἀνασκαλεύ-ω, 1. *rake up* embers, fig. ~ούσης τῆς χάριτος ἐν ἐμοὶ τοὺς γνώσεως ἄνθρακας Nil.*epp.*1.28(M.79.96D); Dion.Ar.*e.h.*7. 3.11(M.3.569A) cit. s. πῦρ; met., *stir up* ~σαντι τῷ πνεύματι τὸν λογισμόν Eus.Nic.*ep.Paulin.*(p.15; M.82.913B); τῶν προτέρων ἁμαρτημάτων τὴν μνήμην ἀ. Mac.Aeg.*libert.ment.*31(M.34.964C); Cyr.*Jo.* 11.12(4.1011D); παυσαμένους θορύβους ἀ. οὐκ εὐκαίρως id.*ep.*72(p.18. 31; 5².200E); **2.** *rake up, root out* weeds; lit., *A.Thom.*B 14(p.31.8); met., *uncover* obscure truths, Cyr.*Jo.*9(4.755B); id.*dial.Trin.*(5¹. 507A).

ἀνασκάλλω, *dig up, rake up*; met.; **1.** *agitate, disturb*; of a heresy, Sophr.H.*or.*2.47(M.87.2384A); **2.** *consider*, *Ep.Mar.*2.

ἀνασκάπτω, 1. *dig up*; *exhume* bones of heretics, *Libell.*ap.CCP (518)*act.*(H.2.1337C); met., *bring to light*, Chrys.*hom.10.4 in Thess.* (11.500C); **2.** *wrench out* limbs of martyrs, id.*hom.4.4 in 1Cor*(10. 29A); **3.** *curse* ἀναθεματίσαι καὶ ἀ. ... τὸν ἐν ἁγίοις Μάξιμον Anast.Ap. *a.Max.*2.33(M.90.169C); ‡Jo.D.*Const.*25(M.95.344A); Thphn.*chron.* p.195(M.108.505A).

ἀνασκαφή, ἡ, 1. *digging up, excavation*, Thphn.*chron.*p.313(M. 108.760A); **2.** *curse* ἀναθέματι καὶ ἀ. ἔβαλον αὐτὸν ὡς ἀλάστορα *ib.*p.348 (837A).

***ἀνάσκαφος,** *accursed*, *Chron.Pasch.*p.382(M.92.981A); ὁ θεομίσητος καὶ ἀ. Χοσρόης Heracl.*ep.*(M.92.1020C); Jo.Sync.*narr.*(4.320C).

***ἀνασκέπω,** *remove, take off*; clothes, Jo.Mosch.*prat.*3(M.87. 2856A).

ἀνασκευάζω, A. 1. *ravage*, Juln.Imp.*ep.*205(p.284.1; M.32.344B); **2.** *invalidate, discredit* [sc. τὴν ἀποκάλυψιν Ἰωάννου] τινες...ἠθέτωσαν καὶ ἀ. Dion.Al.ap.Eus.*h.e.*7.25.1(M.20.697A); **3.** *demolish* an argument, Epiph.*haer.*6.3(p.185.24; M.41.205A); **4.** *reverse* a decision, Ath.*ep.Epict.*1(p.4.2; M.26.1052B); CEph.(449)*act.*(*ACO* 2.1.1 p.89. 15; H.2.96C); met., *upset, disturb* ἀ. τὰς ἀκάκους τῶν ἀδελφῶν καρδίας Ath.*ep.Aeg.Lib.*10(M.25.560B).

B. 1. *put back into place*, Bas.Sel.*v.Thecl.*2.17(M.85.596A); **2.** *remodel*, Meth.*res.*1.43(p.290.5; M.18.272A); ἵνα αὖθις ἐν τῇ παλιγγενεσίᾳ ἀνασκευάσῃ τὸ ἄγγος ἐν τῇ ἀναστάσει εἰς τὴν ἀρχαίαν φαιδρότητα Epiph.*haer.*37.1(p.52.5; M.41.644A); **3.** *restore* to health, Clem. *paed.*1.8(p.128.11; M.8.328C); med., *refresh oneself*, Thdt.*qu.56 in 1Reg.*(1.391) citing 1Reg.24:3 (LXX παρασκευάσασθαι); met., *confirm* an opinion, Eust.*engast.*4(p.22.2; M.18.621A).

ἀνασκευή, ἡ, A. 1. *destruction*, i.e. *destructive effect* τὴν τῶν ἐπιβουλῶν ἀ. Clem.*str.*4.2(p.253.21; M.8.1224C); met. ὀργὴ...κατα-στάσεως ἀ. †Nil.*vit.*3(M.79.1144A); **2.** *reversal* of a decision, Dioscorus ap.CChalc.*act.*3(*ACO* 2.1.2 p.11.27; H.2.316B).

B. *remodelling* of a statue, Meth.*res.*1.43(p.290.11; M.18.272B).

ἀνασκησία, ἡ, *lack of discipline*, Clem.*str.*2.13(p.144.20; M.8. 996C); *lack of practice* in church administration; of a monk, Chrys. *sac.*6.7(p.153.25; 1.427A).

ἀνάσκητος, *untrained, undisciplined* μήτε...ἀ. καὶ ἀναγώνιστος μείνας...τῶν στεφάνων τῆς ἀφθαρσίας ἐλπιζέτω μεταλαβεῖν Clem. *q.d.s.*4(p.161.30; M.9.608B); ἀσκείτωσαν τὴν ἁγνείαν, ἵνα ἐὰν γένηταί τι ἀνθρώπινον μὴ ἀ. καταληφθέντες ἀσχημονήσωσιν Or.*comm.in 1Cor.* 7:8(*JTS* 9 p.504); ἄσκησις μοναχοῦ μελέτη γραφῶν καὶ ποίησις ἐντολῶν τοῦ θεοῦ. ἀ. δέ ἐστιν ὁ μὴ ἐν τούτοις ἀναστρεφόμενος μοναχός Ephr.2.356C = Hyper.*mon.*4(M.79.1473A).

ἀνασκινδαλεύ-ω (-δυλεύω), *impale, crucify*, Clem.*str.*2.20(p.181.2; M.8.1069B); *ib.*4.11(p.203.5; 1288B); ref. Plato *Rep.*362A οἱ γενναῖοι ...μάρτυρες...τέλος πάντα τὰ δεινὰ παθόντες, ἀνεσκινδυλεύθησαν Eus. *p.e.*12.10(p.584B; M.21.969C); Thdt.*affect.*8(p.198.23; 4.902).

ἀνασκολοπίζω, *impale, crucify*; Christ, Hipp.*haer.*7.38(p.224.15; M.16.3346B); Cels.ap.Or.*Cels.*2.36(p.161.26; M.11.857A); Chrys.*hom.* *87.1 in Mt.*(7.819B); S. Peter, Eus.*h.e.*3.1.2(M.20.216A); Chrys.*hom.* *5.2 in 2Tim.*(11.687C).

***ἀνασκολοπισμός, ὁ,** *impalement, crucifixion* δέχεται...τὸν ἐπὶ κεφαλὴν ἀ. ὁ...Πέτρος Gr.Nyss.*beat.*8(M.44.1297D).

***ἀνασοβή, ἡ,** *disturbance, sedition* μὴ θελήσητε τὴν ἡσυχίαν τοῦ κυρίου ἡμῶν Ἰησοῦ Χριστοῦ εἰς ἀ. διαβολικὴν διεγεῖραι *A.(Pass.) Andr.*7(p.16.14); Constantius Imp.ap.Ath.*apol.sec.*55(p.135.36; M. 25.349A).

ἀνάσπαστος, *dragged away*, ‡Nil.*perist.*5.1(M.79.849D).

ἀνασπάω, 1. *draw up*; **2.** *pluck up, overthrow*; fig. τὴν Παύλου τοῦ Σαμοσατέως αἵρεσιν ἀ. [sc. Παῦλος] πρόρριζον Chrys.*hom.in 1Cor10:1*(3.236C); met. νόμους ἀ. [sc. ἡ βασκανία] φύσεως id.*hom.7.6 in Rom.*(9.491B); **3.** *draw away, separate* ἡ ἀμέριστος θεότης, ἅπαξ ἀνακραθεῖσα τῷ ὑποκειμένῳ, οὔτε τοῦ σώματος οὔτε τῆς ψυχῆς ἀνεσπάσθη Gr.Nyss.*ep.*3(M.46.1021C).

ἄνασσα, ἡ, *queen, lady*; of the Church, Meth.*symp.*11(p.133.11; M.18.209B); of BMV, Nonn.*par.Jo.*19:27(M.43.904B).

ἀναστασία, ἡ, 1. *destruction* ἀ. τε πολήων *Orac.Sib.*4.69; Alex. Sal.*cruc.*(M.87.4037B); **2.** *church of Resurrection* at CP, Gr.Naz.*or.*42. 26(M.36.489B); Socr.*h.e.*5.7.1(M.67.573D); Soz.*h.e.*7.5.3(M.67.1425A).

***ἀναστάσιμος,** *of* or *pertaining to resurrection*;

A. of Christ's Resurrection; **1.** of Resurrection day, Eus.*qu. Marin.suppl.*1.9(M.22.1000B); τίς ἂν εἴη ἡ ὀγδόη, ἢ ἡ τοῦ Χριστοῦ ἀ. ἡμέρα; Ath.*exp.Ps.*6(M.27.76C); of the hour, Gr.Nyss.*res.*1(M.46. 613A); **2.** of Feast of Resurrection; **a.** in gen., Epiph.*exp.fid.*22 (p.524.4; M.42.828D); ἐπιτελοῦμεν τὴν ἀ. ἑορτὴν τοῦ πάσχα Procl. CP *or.*14.2(M.65.796C); Soz.*h.e.*2.10.1(M.67.960C); †Gregent.*disp.*(M. 86.701B); Jo.Mosch.*prat.*165(M.87.3032B); *Chron.Pasch.*p.224(M.92. 544C); **b.** dist. from Good Friday and Holy Week ποιήσαντες τὰς ἁγίας ἡμέρας τῆς πασχαλίας καὶ τὴν ἀ. Marc.Diac.*v.Porph.*52; cf. distn. between πάσχα ἀ. and πάσχα σταυρώσιμον Nilles, *Kalendarium* 2(p.253); **c.** ref. date ἡ δὲ ἰσημερία τὴν ἀ. ἑορτὴν δεξαμένη Gr.Nyss.*ep.*4(M.46.1028C); κατὰ σελήνην τεσσαρεσκαιδεκάτης κυριακῇ συνελθούσης, οὐκ ἄγομεν ταύτην κυριακὴν ἀ. ... ὅτι ἡ μὲν τεσσαρεσκαιδεκάτη πάθους ἐστίν...τὴν παρασκευὴν ἀ. οὐ γνωρίζομεν ‡Chrys.*pasch.* 7.5(8.283C,D); *ib.*(284C); ἡ ἀ. τῇ τρίτῃ γέγονε τοῦ Ἀπριλίου μηνός *Chron.Pasch.*p.281(M.92.976D); **d.** always to be celebrated on a Sunday, *Const.App.*5.17.3; *ib.*7.36.2; **e.** proper occasion for baptism ἐν...τῇ ἀ. ἡμέρᾳ τῆς ἀναστάσεως τὴν χάριν ὑποδεξώμεθα Bas. *hom.*13.1(2.114A; M.31.424D); **f.** legislation for celebration of octave of Easter ἀπὸ τῆς ἁγίας ἀ. Χριστοῦ...ἡμέρας μέχρι τῆς καινῆς κυριακῆς τὴν ὅλην ἑβδομάδα ἐν...ἐκκλησίαις σχολάζειν δεῖ ἀπαραλείπτως τοὺς πιστούς CTrull.*can.*66; **3.** *Sunday*; when Resurrection is commemorated κυριακή ἐστιν καὶ ὅτε εὔχρηστον οὐκ ἔστιν ἐν ταύτῃ τῇ ἀ. τοῦ Χριστοῦ ἐργάσασθαί τι κακόν *A.Thom.*B 33(p.35.28); ὀγδόη ἡ ἀ. τοῦ σωτῆρος ἡμέρα κυριακή Eus.*Ps.*6:1(M.23.120A); τὴν ἀ. τοῦ κυρίου ἡμέραν, τὴν κυριακήν φαμεν *Const.App.*7.30.1; *ib.*2.59.3; Cyr. *Jo.*4.7(4.432B); id.*Os.*33(3.60E); ‡Ath.*ep.Cast.*1.8(M.28.860B); as image of world to come ὀρθοὶ μὲν πληροῦμεν τὰς εὐχὰς ἐν τῇ μιᾷ τοῦ σαββάτου...οὐ γὰρ μόνον ὡς συναναστάντες Χριστῷ...ἐν τῇ ἀ. ἡμέρᾳ τῆς δεδομένης ἡμῖν χάριτος διὰ τῆς κατὰ τὴν προσευχὴν στάσεως ἑαυτοὺς ὑπομιμνήσκομεν· ἀλλ' ὅτι δοκεῖ πως τοῦ προσδοκωμένου αἰῶνος εἶναι εἰκών Bas.*Spir.*66(3.56B; M.32.192A); **4.** τὰ ἑωθινὰ ἀ. cycle of eleven Gospel readings recounting the Resurrection, read at matins on Sundays, Nilles, *Kalendarium* 2(p.291); **5.** of Paschal sacrifice (ref. Easter eucharist) λύε τῶν ἁμαρτημάτων ἡμῖν τὸ μέγεθος, τῆς ἀ. θυσίας ἁπτόμενος Gr.Naz.*ep.*171(M.37.280C); **6.** of mystery of Resurrection νυκτὸς τὸ ἀ. ἐχούσης μυστήριον Synes.*ep.*13(M.66.1349B).

B. of resurrection of men τὴν ἀ. τῆς ἐνδόξου παρουσίας αὐτοῦ... ἡμέραν Cyr.*deip.BMV* 16(p.26.7; M.76.273C); τὴν τῶν...νεκρῶν ἀ. ῥίζαν Procl.CP *hom.*1.1(M.65.833A).

ἀνάστασις, ἡ, *resurrection, raising up*;

I. of Christ;

A. as foundation of Christian faith; **1.** in gen. παραγγελίας οὖν λαβόντες καὶ πληροφορηθέντες διὰ τῆς ἀ. τοῦ κυρίου ἡμῶν *1Clem.*42.3; ἵνα 'ἄρῃ σύσσημον' εἰς τοὺς αἰῶνας διὰ τῆς ἀ. εἰς τοὺς ἁγίους καὶ πιστοὺς αὐτοῦ...ἐν ἑνὶ σώματι τῆς ἐκκλησίας αὐτοῦ Ign.*Smyrn.*1.2; Const.*or.s.c.*20(p.184.8; M.20.1296A); ἕστηκας ἐπὶ τὴν πέτραν τῆς πίστεως τῆς περὶ τῆς ἀ. Cyr.H.*catech.*14.21; **2.** in close connexion with Passion προσέχειν...τῷ εὐαγγελίῳ, ἐν ᾧ τὸ πάθος ἡμῖν δεδήλωται καὶ ἡ ἀ. τετελείωται Ign.*Smyrn.*7.2; θανάτῳ ὑπήκουσε καὶ ἀ. ἐφανέρωσεν Hipp.*haer.*10.33(p.292.3; M.16.3451C); Or.*Cels.*2.16(p.145.13; M.11.828A); Cyr.H.*catech.*13.37.

B. pre-Christian foreshadowings; **1.** in pagan myths and philosophy Ζωροάστρην...Πλάτων...ἀναβιῶναι λέγει· τάχα...τὴν ἀ. ... αἰνίσσεται Clem.*str.*5.14(p.395.23; M.9.157A); ref. multiplication of loaves and fishes φιλοσοφίαν Ἑλληνικὴν οἱ ἰχθύες ἐμήνυον...τῆς δὲ τοῦ κυρίου μεταλαβόντες εὐλογίας τὴν ἀ. τῆς θειότητος διὰ τῆς τοῦ λόγου δυνάμεως ἐνεπνεύσθησαν *ib.*6.11(p.479.10; 316A); ἐπεὶ δὲ τὸ περὶ τῆς ἀ. Ἰησοῦ Χριστοῦ χλευάζουσιν οἱ ἄπιστοι, παραθησόμεθα μὲν καὶ Πλάτωνα [sc. *Rep.*614Bff.] Or.*Cels.*2.16(p.145.16; M.11.828B); but no true resurrection in paganism τίς δὲ ἄλλος περὶ ἀθανασίας οὕτως ἐπιστώσατο τοὺς ἀνθρώπους, ὡς ὁ τοῦ Χριστοῦ σταυρός, καὶ ἡ τοῦ σώματος ἀ. αὐτοῦ; καίπερ γὰρ τὰ πάντα ψευσάμενοι Ἕλληνες, ὅμως οὐκ ἠδυνήθησαν ἀ. τῶν ἑαυτῶν εἰδώλων πλάσασθαι Ath.*inc.*50.5,6 (M.25.185C); **2.** in OT κἂν ὁ σωτὴρ λέγῃ· 'πόθεν ἰαθήσομαι' [Jer.5:18] τὴν ἀ. τὴν ἐκ νεκρῶν προφητεύει Or.*hom.14.18 in Jer.*(p.124.13; M.13.428B); ἀ. ἔδειξεν εἰς τοῦτον φθάνειν τὰ γεγραμμένα Ath.*Ar.*2.16 (M.26.180B); τὸ μυστήριον τῆς ἀ. ἤδη ἐνεργεῖσθαι εὔχεται ὁ προφήτης Bas.*hom.in Ps.*7:7(1.100D; M.29.236B).

C. the historical event; **1.** wrought in the flesh ἐγὼ γὰρ καὶ μετὰ τὴν ἀ. ἐν σαρκὶ αὐτὸν οἶδα καὶ πιστεύω ὄντα Ign.*Smyrn.*3.1; μετὰ δὲ τὴν ἀ. [καὶ] συνέφαγεν αὐτοῖς καὶ συνέπιεν ὡς σαρκικός, καίπερ πνευματικῶς ἡνωμένος τῷ πατρί *ib.*3.3; Ἰησοῦ Χριστοῦ...ἀ. σαρκικῇ τε καὶ πνευματικῇ *ib.*12.2; τί τοῦτο πρὸς τὰ περὶ τοῦ σώματος αὐτοῦ ὑφ' ἡμῶν λεγόμενα; σαφῶς δὲ φαίνεται ἰχθύος μετὰ τὴν ἀ. βεβρωκὼς Or.*Cels.*1.70(p.124.12; M.11.789C); but resurrection body different from mortal body ἦν γε κατὰ τὴν ἀ. αὐτοῦ ὥσπερεὶ ἐν μεθορίῳ τινὶ τῆς παχύτητος τῆς πρὸ τοῦ πάθους σώματος καὶ τοῦ γυμνὴν τοιούτου σώματος φαίνεσθαι ψυχήν *ib.*2.62(p.184.11; 893B); Χριστὸς...τισὶ μὲν ἐφαίνετο μετὰ τὴν ἀ., τισὶ δὲ ἄδηλος ἦν· ἀληθῶς ἀνέστη ἐκ νεκρῶν... λεπτομεριστέρας δηλονότι τῆς σαρκὸς γενομένης διὰ τὴν ἀφθαρσίαν, ὅπερ...σῶμα, ὅταν ἤθελεν, ἀπέκρυπτε, καὶ ὅταν ἤθελεν, ἐμφανὲς καθίστη Nil.*epp.*3.120(M.79.440A); μετὰ δὲ τὴν ἀ. αὐτοῦ...οὐκέτι ὑποπίπτει ταῖς τοῦ σώματος ἀσθενείαις, καὶ χρείαις ἀναγκαίαις *ib.*1.149 (144D); **2.** by his own power τὴν ἐκ νεκρῶν ἀ. πεποιημένος θεϊκῇ δυνάμει Eus.*qu.Marin.suppl.*1.1(M.22.984C); ἀπέθανε μὲν ὡς θνητόν· ἀνέζησε δὲ διὰ τὴν ἐν αὐτῷ ζωήν, καὶ τῆς ἀ. ἐστι γνώρισμα τὰ ἔργα Ath.*inc.*31.4(M.25.149D); which is proof of divinity, id.*Ar.*1.44(M.26.104A); distinguishing it from other resurrections καινός τις... ἀναστάσεως ἐδείχθη τύπος. πολλοὶ...πρὸ ἐκείνου...ἀνέστησαν νεκροί, οὕτω δὲ οὐδὲ εἷς· οἱ...ἄλλοι πάντες ἀναστάντες πάλιν εἰς τὴν γῆν ὑπέστρεφον,...τὸ δὲ σῶμα δεσποτικὸν ἀναστὰν...εἰς τοὺς οὐρανοὺς ἀνέβη Chrys.*incomprehens.*2.6(1.460C); οἱ ἀπόστολοι κηρύττοντες τὸ εὐαγγέλιον, ἔλεγον τὸν Χριστὸν ἐγηγέρθαι ὑπὸ τοῦ πατρός, διὰ τὸ τῶν ἀκουόντων ἀσθενές...ὁ δὲ ἄγγελος τὴν εὐαγγελιζομένην τὴν ἀ. ῥήξας φωνήν, γυμνὴν ἐκφαίνων τὴν θεοπρεπεστάτην ἐξουσίαν τοῦ ἀναστάντος Sev.Ant.*res.*(p.802.4; M.46.629C); this used as argument against monophysites εἰ δὲ ἄμφω μία ἦν φύσις αὐτὴ ἡ ἐνεργοῦσα καὶ τὸ ἐνεργούμενον τὴν ἀ., τίς ἡ ἐνεργουμένη καὶ τίς ἡ ἐνεργοῦσα καὶ ἐγείρουσα αὐτὴν φύσις;...εἴπερ οὖν...τὴν ἀ. αὐτοῦ δοξάζομεν, ἐξ ἑτέρας αὐτοῦ φύσεως τὴν ἑτέραν ἑαυτοῦ φύσιν ἀνιστᾶν αὐτὴν Χριστὸν ὁμολογήσομεν Leont.H.*monoph.*39(M.86.1793A); **3.** various stages ἀναστάσεως γὰρ ἦν καὶ τὸ ἐν τῇ πρώτῃ ἡμέρᾳ γενέσθαι ἐν τῷ παραδείσῳ τοῦ θεοῦ, ἀ. δὲ ὅτε φαινόμενός φησι· 'μή μου ἅπτου'...τὸ δὲ τέλειον τῆς ἀ. ἦν, ὅτε γίνεται πρὸς τὸν πατέρα Or.*Jo.*10.37(21; p.212.4ff.; M.14.376A); ἵνα ἐν αὐτῇ καὶ τὴν ὑπὲρ ἡμῶν ἁρμόσηται ἀ., ἐξ ᾅδου μὲν τὴν ψυχήν, ἐκ τάφου δὲ τὸ σῶμα ἐπιδεικνύμενος ‡Ath.*Apoll.*2.17(M.26.1161B); ἀνάγκη γάρ τινα ἐξ ᾅδου τὴν ἀρχὴν τῆς ἀ. εἰληφέναι, ἵνα τελεία ᾖ ἡ ἀ. *ib.*2.16(1160B); **4.** time: of year (April), Mac.Aeg.*hom.*5.9(M.34.513C,D); of day πρωΐ, τῆς ἀ. εὐφροσύνη Cyr.H.*catech.*14.4; 'ὀψὲ σαββάτων' Ματθαῖος βοᾷ. αὕτη τοι ἡ ὥρα τῆς ἀ. κατὰ τὴν τοῦ ἀγγέλου φωνήν...Ματθαῖος μόνος...τὸν καιρὸν δι' ἀκριβείας ἐπεσημήνατο, εἰπὼν τὴν ἑσπέραν εἶναι τοῦ σαββάτου, τὴν ὥραν τῆς ἀ. Gr.Nyss.*res.*1 (M.46.613A,B); discrepancy between Mt. and Jo. discussed τίνι γὰρ πιστευτέον; Ματθαίῳ γράφοντι τὴν ἀ. ὀψὲ γεγενῆσθαι σαββάτων, ἢ Ἰωάννῃ ταὐτὸ τοῦτο συμβεβηκέναι πρωῒ ἔτι σκοτίας οὔσης ἱστορηκότι, ἢ Λουκᾷ καὶ Μάρκῳ; τῷ μὲν ὄρθρον βαθύν, τῷ δὲ ἀνατολὴν ἡλίου τὸν αὐτὸν καιρὸν ὀνομάσαντι; Sev.Ant.*res.*(p.796.1; M.46.628C); κατ' ἐκείνην μὲν ὁμολογουμένως...τὴν θείαν νύκτα τῆς ἀ. γενομένης· μηδενὸς δὲ τὴν ὥραν ἐπισημηναμένου *ib.*(p.798.6; 629A); cf. τὴν ἐκ νεκρῶν ἀ. ... καθ' ἣν ὥραν οὐδεὶς ἔγνω, καὶ καθ' ὃν οὐδεὶς ἐπεσημήνατο τῶν εὐαγγελιστῶν καιρόν Eus.*qu.Marin.suppl.*1.1(M.22.984C); **5.** witnesses; not all men, but only apostles and certain other disciples, Or.*Cels.*2.63(p.185.3; M.11.896A); truth enforced by death in public μύθους μὲν ἂν ἔδοξε λέγειν παρὰ πᾶσιν, ἠπιστήθη δὲ πολλῷ πλέον καὶ περὶ τῆς ἀ. λέγων, οὐκ ὄντος ὅλως τοῦ μαρτυροῦντος περὶ τοῦ θανάτου αὐτοῦ. τῆς δὲ ἀ. προηγεῖσθαι δεῖ θάνατον, ἐπεὶ οὐκ ἂν εἴη ἀ. μὴ προηγουμένου θανάτου. ὅθεν εἰ κρύφα που ἐγεγόνει τοῦ σώματος ὁ θάνατος...ἀφανὴς καὶ ἀμάρτυρος καὶ ἡ τούτου ἀ. ἢ διὰ τί τὴν μὲν ἀ. ἐκήρυττεν ἀναστάς, τὸν δὲ θάνατον ἀφανῶς ἐποίει γενέσθαι;...πῶς... μαθηταὶ παρρησίαν εἶχον περὶ τοῦ τῆς ἀ. λόγου, οὐκ ἔχοντες εἰπεῖν, ὅτι πρῶτον ἀπέθανεν; ἢ πῶς ἂν ἐπιστεύθησαν λέγοντες γεγονέναι πρῶτον θάνατον, εἶτα τὴν ἀ., εἰ μὴ παρ' οἷς ἐπαρρησιάζοντο, εἶχον τούτους μάρτυρας τοῦ θανάτου; Ath.*inc.*23.1–3(M.25.136C,D); δώδεκα δὲ τῇ ἀ. τοῦ Χριστοῦ μαρτυροῦσι, καὶ ἆρα ἔτι πρὸς τὴν ἀ. ἀπιστεῖς; Cyr.H.*catech.*4.12; testimony of nature and angels, *ib.*14.22,23.

D. proof from its effects μείζονα εἰργάσατο ἡ τούτου ἀ. τῆς ἐκείνων [sc. Elijah and Elisha] ἀ. τί γὰρ τηλικοῦτον τῷ κόσμῳ ἀπὸ τῶν ἀναστάντων παιδαρίων δι' Ἡλίου καὶ Ἐλισσαίου γεγένηται, ὁποῖον διὰ τῆς κηρυσσομένης ἀ. Ἰησοῦ; Or.*Cels.*2.58(p.182.2,4; M.11.889A); id. *hom.10.3 in Jer.*(p.73.21; M.13.361A); ὁ δὲ θάνατος ἐλέγχεται καθ' ἡμέραν αὐτὸς ἐξασθενήσας, καὶ τὰ εἴδωλα καὶ οἱ δαίμονες μᾶλλον νεκροὶ τυγχάνοντες, ὡς ἐκ τούτου μηδένα διστάζειν ἔτι περὶ τῆς τοῦ σώματος ἀ. αὐτοῦ. ἔοικε δὲ ὁ περὶ τῆς ἀ. τοῦ κυριακοῦ σώματος ἀπιστῶν ἀγνοεῖν δύναμιν θεοῦ λόγου καὶ σοφίας Ath.*inc.*31.3,4(M.25.149C); μεγίστη...ἀναστάσεως ἀπόδειξις τὸ τὸν σφαγέντα Χριστὸν τοσαύτην μετὰ θάνατον ἐπιδείξασθαι δύναμιν, ὡς τοὺς ζῶντας ἀνθρώπους πεῖσαι καὶ πατρίδος, καὶ οἰκίας...καὶ αὐτῆς ὑπεριδεῖν τῆς ζωῆς...ταῦτα γὰρ οὐχὶ νεκροῦ τινος...ἀλλ' ἀναστάντος...ἦν τὰ κατορθώματα Chrys.*pan. Ign.*4(2.599B); miracles done by apostles, id.*hom.4.6 in Ac.princ.*(3.90D); *ib.4.7*(92D); S. Peter's change of heart and S. Paul's conversion, id.*hom.1.5 in Ac.*9:1(3.105A,B); id.*hom.89.1 in Mt.*(7.833A).

E. as being Christ himself (cf. Jo.11:25) Χριστὸς κύριος, ὁ τῆς ἀ. ἥλιος Clem.*prot.*8(p.63.19; M.8.196A); ὁ λόγος σὰρξ ἐγένετο...καὶ ἐγένετο ἀ. Ath.*Ar.*1.64(M.26.145B); *Symb.Ant.*(341)2(p.249.16; M.26.721C); ἀ. δέ, ὡς...ἡμᾶς ἀπανιστάς, καὶ πρὸς τὴν ζωὴν ἐπανάγων Gr.Naz.*or.*30.20(p.141.10; M.36.132A); Mod.*dorm.*12(M.86.3308A).

F. other aspects; **1.** cause of joy to Christians Ἰγνάτιος...ἐκκλησίᾳ...ἀγαλλιωμένῃ ἐν τῷ πάθει τοῦ κυρίου...καὶ ἐν τῇ ἀ. αὐτοῦ Ign.*Philad.*proem.; Cyr.H.*catech.*14.1; Gr.Nyss.*res.*5(M.46.684D); **2.** ridiculed by pagans, Or.*Cels.*6.36(p.105.30f.; M.11.1352B); **3.** Resurrection and circumcision περιτέμνεται γὰρ τὸ παιδίον τῇ ὀγδόῃ, ἐπειδὴ ἔμελλε τῇ ὀγδόῃ ἡ ἀ. ... εἴ τις οὖν μὴ πιστεύει τῇ ἀ., ἀπερίτμητός ἐστι τῇ καρδίᾳ ‡Chrys.*occurs.*(2.812B); **4.** etym. of name Eliakim ὃς ἑρμηνεύεται θεοῦ ἀ. Cyr.*Is.*2.5(2.325C).

G. feast of Resurrection; ref. bishop τίς αὐτοῖς [sc. his flock] τὴν ἡμέραν ἀναγγελεῖ τῆς ἀ., κρυπτομένου σου; Ath.*ep.Drac.*10(M.25.533B); τὴν τῆς ἀ. ἑορτήν ‡Chrys.*pasch.*7.5(8.283E); ἐκκλησία οὐ μόνον τὸ πάθος καὶ θάνατον τοῦ Χριστοῦ, ἀλλὰ καὶ τὴν ἀ. αὐτοῦ πάσχα ὀνομάζει...εἰ καὶ ἐν οἱᾳδήποτε ἡμέρᾳ τῶν ἑπτὰ ἡμερῶν τῶν μετὰ τὴν ιδ' τοῦ πρώτου μηνὸς τῆς σελήνης εὑρεθείη αὕτη, λέγω δὲ ἡ ἀ., ἑορταζομένη *Chron.Pasch.*p.228(M.92.553A).

H. dedications to Resurrection; church in Jerusalem, built by Constantine, Eus.*v.C.*3.25(p.89.14; M.20.1085A); *ib.*3.28(p.91.1; 1088D); βασιλεῖς δι' εὐσέβειαν, ἀργυρένδυτον καὶ χρυσοκόλλητον τὴν ἁγίαν ἐκκλησίαν ταύτην ἐν ᾗ πάρεσμεν, τῆς τοῦ σωτῆρος θεοῦ ἀ., ἐξειργάσαντο Cyr.H.*catech.*14.14; cf.*ib.*14.22; situated on Golgotha, *ib.*13.4; Marc.Diac.*v.Porph.*5; ὅπου ἐτάφη καὶ κατῴκησεν ὁ Ναζωραῖος τρεῖς ἡμέρας καὶ τρεῖς νύκτας· καὶ ἀνέστη ἐκεῖθεν, καὶ εὐθέως ᾠκοδομήθη ἐπάνω τοῦ τάφου ναός, καὶ προσαγορεύεται ἡ ἁγία ἀ. †Gregent.*disp.*(M.86.729C); πατριάρχης Ἠλίας ᾠκοδόμησεν μοναστήριον πλησίον τοῦ ἐπισκοπείου καὶ ἐν αὐτῷ περισυνήγαγεν τοὺς τῆς ἁγίας ἀ. σπουδαίους εἰς τοὺς περὶ τὸν πύργον τοῦ Δαυὶδ τόπους διεσπαρμένους Cyr.S.*v.Sab.*31(p.116.6); id.*v.Thds.*(p.236.13); Evagr.*h.e.*2.5 (p.52.6; M.86.2513A); cave of Resurrection, dist. from the church, Cyr.H.*catech.*18.33; cf.Alex.Sal.*cruc.*(M.87.4037B); church of Resurrection as synonym of see of Jerusalem τὴν μὲν ἁγίαν τοῦ Χριστοῦ ἀ. τὰς τρεῖς Παλαιστίνας ἔχειν CChalc.*act*.7(*ACO* 2.1.3 p.5.23;H.2. 492E).

I. heret.; acc. Gnostics, Christ conversed with disciples for 18 months after Resurrection, Iren.*haer*.1.3.2(M.7.469A); allegorized, v. ἀλληγορέω; true Resurrection denied by Manicheans, Cyr.H.*catech*.14.21.

II. of biblical characters raised from dead;

A. Lazarus ἐξῆλθεν τῆς σοροῦ, ὁ νεκρός, οἷος ἦν πρὶν ἢ παθεῖν, μελετήσας τὴν ἀ. Clem.*paed*.1.2(p.93.23; M.8.256B); τὴν τοῦ Λαζάρου ἐκ νεκρῶν ἀ. κοινὸν ἔργον γεγονέναι υἱοῦ τοῦ εὐξαμένου καὶ πατρὸς τοῦ ἐπακούσαντος Or.*Jo*.28.9(8; p.400.8; M.14.700B); Cyr.H.*catech*.18.16; as proof of doctrine of Resurrection, Gr.Nyss.*hom.opif*.25.11(M.44. 221B).

B. of others πολλοὶ νεκροὶ ἦσαν ἐν ταῖς ἡμέραις Ἰησοῦ, ἀλλὰ μόνοι ἀνέστησαν, οὓς ἔγνω ὁ λόγος ἐπιτηδείους πρὸς τὴν ἀ. Or.*Cels*.2.48 (p.170.11; M.11.872B); of widow's son at Nain, *cat.Lc*.7:12ff.(p.56. 15); raisings of dead in gospels contrasted with τελεία ἀ. of Christ, ‡Chrys.*serm.pasch*.82.

III. of men, in the body;

A. Christ the cause of resurrection; **1.** in gen. ἀ. ἡμῶν ἐν αὐτῷ ἀπόκειται Ath.*Ar*.1.43(M.26.100C); *ib*.2.63(281B); Proc.G.*Is*.66:5ff.(M. 87.2708A); Cosm.Ind.*top*.2(M.88.121B) cit. s. ἀνάκτισις; **2.** through his death and Resurrection ὁ δεσπότης ἐπιδείκνυται διηνεκῶς ἡμῖν τὴν μέλλουσαν ἀ. ἔσεσθαι, ἧς τὴν ἀπαρχὴν ἐποιήσατο τὸν κύριον *1Clem*.24.1; τὴν γενομένην ἀ. τοῦ Χριστοῦ ἀπὸ τοῦ κατὰ τὸν σταυρὸν πάθους περιέχειν μυστήριον τῆς ἀ. τοῦ παντὸς Χριστοῦ σώματος Or.*Jo*.10.35(20; p.209.31f.; M.14.372B); affirmed against allegorizing Manicheans σαφής ἐστιν ἡ τοῦ Χριστοῦ ἀ. μεθ' ἧς εἶχε σαρκὸς γεγονυῖα ἐκ τοῦ προκειμένου ῥητοῦ, οἱ δέ, οἱ ἑτερόδοξοι, ἀλληγορεῖν θέλουσιν τὴν τῶν ἀνθρώπων ἀ. ἀλληγορήτωσαν καὶ τὴν τοῦ σωτῆρος κακῶς τῷ ἑαυτῶν ἀθετοῦντες τὸ ῥητόν Or.*comm. in 1Cor*.15:12f.(*JTS* 10 pp.44f.); τούτου ἕνεκεν τὸ δυνάμενον ἀποθανεῖν ἑαυτῷ λαμβάνει σῶμα, ἵνα τοῦτο τοῦ ἐπὶ πάντων λόγου μεταλαβόν, ἀντὶ πάντων ἱκανὸν γένηται τῷ θανάτῳ, καὶ διὰ τὸν ἐνοικήσαντα λόγον ἄφθαρτον διαμείνῃ, καὶ λοιπὸν ἀπὸ πάντων ἡ φθορὰ παύσηται τῇ τῆς ἀ. χάριτι Ath.*inc*.9.1(M.25. 112A); σωτῆρος ἀποθανόντος ὑπὲρ ἡμῶν...τῆς φθορᾶς παυομένης...ἐν τῇ τῆς ἀ. χάριτι...ἵνα κρείττονος ἀ. τυχεῖν δυνηθῶμεν *ib*.24.1(132C); id.*Ar*.1.8(M.26.28A); *ib*.2.67(289A); ἡ ταφὴ αὐτοῦ, ἡμῶν ἀ. id.*inc.et c. Ar*.5(M.26.992A); θεοῦ, τοῦ μὴ μόνον ἐπαγγελλομένου ποιεῖν τῶν νεκρῶν τὴν ἀ., ἀλλὰ καὶ διὰ τῆς ἤδη ἠργμένης ἀ. τοῦ...Χριστοῦ βεβαίαν παρεσχηκότος ἡμῖν ταύτης τὴν πίστιν ‡Just.*qu.Gr*.10.1(M.6.1477C); *ib*.10.14(1481C); ἡ ἀρχὴ τῆς ἀ. δι' ἑνὸς ἐπὶ πᾶσαν διατείνει τὴν ἀνθρωπότητα Gr.Nyss.*or.catech*.16(p.71.12; M.45.52C); id.*Apoll*.55(M.45. 1260A); ἔστι σωμάτων ἀ. τοῦτο ὁ τάφος δηλοῖ ὁ ἐν Ἱεροσολύμοις Chrys.*hom.2.5 in Ac*.(9.22C); ‡Nil.*fr.pasch*.1(M.79.1489D); **3.** through H. Ghost μεγάλη τοῦ πνεύματος ἡ ἐνέργεια, τοῦ οἰκονομοῦντος ἡμῖν τὸν ἐξ ἀ. βίον Bas.*Spir*.49(3.41D; M.32.157B); Gr.Naz.*or*.31.29(p.184. 2; M.36.165C) cit. s. ἀνακτίζω.

B. def. and general statements σωμάτων ἀ. ἔσεσθαι πεπιστεύκαμεν μετὰ τὴν τῶν ὅλων συντέλειαν, οὐχ ὡς Στωϊκοὶ δογματίζουσι κατά τινας κύκλων περιόδους γινομένων ἀεί...ἅπαξ δὲ τῶν καθ' ἡμᾶς αἰώνων πεπερασμένων [καὶ] εἰς τὸ παντελὲς διὰ μόνων τῶν ἀνθρώπων τὴν σύστασιν [ἔσεσθαι] χάριν κρίσεως Tat.*orat*.6(p.6.15; M.6.817B); ἡμεῖς...σώματα ἀνίστασθαι πεπιστεύκαμεν. εἰ γὰρ καὶ φθείρεται, ἀλλ' οὐκ ἀπόλλυται· τούτων γὰρ τὰ λείψανα γῇ ὑποδεξαμένη τηρεῖ δίκην σπόρου πιαινομένου καὶ τῷ γῆς λιπαρωτέρῳ συμπλεκομένου. αὖθις ὥσπερ κόκκος γυμνὸς σπείρεται, καὶ...ἠμφιεσμένος καὶ ἔνδοξος ἐγείρεται, οὐ πρότερον εἰ μὴ ἀποθανὼν λυθῇ, καὶ γῇ συμμιγῇ· ὥστε τὴν ἀ. τοῦ σώματος οὐ μάτην πεπιστεύκαμεν Iren.*fr*.12(M.7.1236A); οὐχ ὡς οἴεται Κέλσος, τῆς μετενσωματώσεως παρακούσαντες τὰ περὶ ἀ. φαμεν ἀλλ' εἰδότες ὅτι ἡ τῇ ἑαυτῆς φύσει ἀσώματος...ψυχὴ ἐν παντὶ σωματικῷ τόπῳ τυγχάνουσα δέεται σώματος οἰκείου...ὅπερ ὅπου μὲν φορεῖ ἀπεκδυσαμένη ⟨τὸ⟩ πρότερον ἀναγκαῖον μὲν περισσὸν δὲ ὡς πρὸς τὰ δεύτερα, ὅπου δὲ ἐπενδυσαμένη ᾧ πρότερον εἶχε, δεομένη κρείττονος ἐνδύματος εἰς τοὺς καθαρωτέρους...τόπους Or.*Cels*.7.32(p.182.31; M. 11.1465B); οὐδὲ γὰρ ἄλλο τί ἐστιν ἡ ἀ., εἰ μὴ πάντως ἡ εἰς τὸ ἀρχαῖον ἀποκατάστασις Gr.Nyss.*hom.1 in Eccl*.(M.44.633C); id.*anim.et res*.(M.46.148A); id.*Pulch*.(M.46.877A) cit. s. ἀναπλάσσω; τοῦτό ἐστι τὸ μυστήριον...τῆς ἐκ νεκρῶν ἀ., τὸ διαλυθῆναι μὲν τῷ θανάτῳ τοῦ σώματος τὴν ψυχήν...εἰς ἄλληλα δὲ ἐπαναγαγεῖν διὰ τῆς ἀ., ὡς ἂν αὐτὸς γένοιτο μεθόριον ἀμφοτέρων, θανάτου τε καὶ ζωῆς id.*or.catech*.16 (p.72.8,11; M.45.52D); τί γὰρ κοινὸν ἔχει ἡ ῥικνότης καὶ πολυσαρκία... πρὸς τὴν ζωὴν ἐκείνην, ἢ τῆς ῥοώδους τε καὶ παροδικῆς τοῦ βίου διαγωγῆς ἠλλοτρίωται; ἓν ζητεῖ μόνον ὁ τῆς ἀ. λόγος, τὸ φυῆναι διὰ γενέσεως ἄνθρωπον· μᾶλλον δὲ...εἰ ἐγενήθη ἄνθρωπος εἰς τὸν κόσμον, τὸ δὲ μακρόβιον ἢ ὠκύμορον...μάταιον τῷ τῆς ἀ. λόγῳ συνεξετάζειν... οὔτε δυσκολίας, οὔτε ῥᾳστώνης ἐκ τῆς τοιαύτης διαφορᾶς περὶ τὴν ἀ. οὔσης. τὸν γὰρ τοῦ ζῆν ἀρξάμενον, ζῆσαι χρὴ πάντως, τῆς ἐν τῷ μέσῳ διὰ τοῦ θανάτου συμβάσης αὐτῷ διαλύσεως ἐν τῇ ἀ. διορθωθείσης. τὸ δὲ πῶς ἢ πότε ἡ διάλυσις γίνεται, τί τοῦτο πρὸς τὴν ἀ.; id.*anim.et res*.(M.46.149B,C); ὅτι δὲ δυνατὸν καὶ ἐξ ἀτελῶν καὶ ἐκ τελείων, τὸ αὐτὸ γενέσθαι ἀποτέλεσμα, μαρτυροῦσιν οἱ ὑπὸ Χριστοῦ καὶ τῶν ἁγίων ἀναστάντες νεκροί· τοιούτους γὰρ αὐτούς, καίτοι τελείους ὄντας κατὰ τὰ μέρη ἡ διὰ τῆς ἀ. ἕνωσις ἀπειργάσατο, ὁποίους καὶ ἐν τῇ μήτρᾳ ἡ φύσις διαπλάττουσα συνῆψε· τὸ δ' αὐτὸ καὶ ἐν τῇ προσδοκωμένῃ κοινῇ ἀ., συμβήσεσθαι πεπιστεύκαμεν· τῶν τε γὰρ προδιαλυθέντων καὶ διεφθαρμένων ἤδη σωμάτων, καὶ τῶν ἀρτιότε ζώντων...τὴν αὐτὴν ἐκ τῆς ἀ. σύστασιν γενήσεσθαι πεπιστεύκαμεν Leont.B.*arg.Sev*.(M.86. 1941D).

C. pre-Christian foreshadowings; **1.** pagan τὴν διὰ πυρὸς κάθαρσιν τῶν κακῶς βεβιωκότων, ἣν...ἐκπύρωσιν ἐκάλεσαν οἱ Στωϊκοί· καθ' ὃν καὶ τὸν ἰδίως ποιὸν ἀναστήσεσθαι δογματίζουσι, τοῦτ' ἐκεῖνο τὴν ἀ. περιέποντες Clem.*str*.5.1(p.332.3; M.9.21A); κἂν μὴ ὀνομάζωσιν οὖν τὸ τῆς ἀ. ὄνομα, τὸ πρᾶγμά γε δηλοῦσιν, ὅτι Σωκράτης...ἀναστήσεται... καὶ ἀνατραφεὶς Ἀθήνησι φιλοσοφεῖ Or.*Cels*.5.20(p.22.2; M.11.1212A); mistaken pagan ideas about it, Gr.Nyss.*anim.et res*.(M.46.108B); **2.** OT; exeg. Ps.150:3ff. τὴν ἐκκλησίαν λέγει τὴν μελετήσασαν τῆς σαρκὸς τὴν ἀ. ἐν ἠχοῦντι τῷ δέρματι Clem.*paed*.2.4(p.182.25; M.8. 441B); Or.*hom.1.16 in Jer*.(p.15.4f.; M.13.276A); Ἐνὼχ μετέθηκε καὶ τὸν Ἠλίαν ἀνήρπασεν, αἰνιττόμενος ἡμῖν τὸ περὶ τῆς ἀ. δόγμα Chrys. *res.mort*.8(2.435C); id.*exp.in Ps*.117:17(5.323C,D).

D. defence of doctrine; **1.** statement of its difficulties τὸν περὶ τῆς ἀ. λόγον (πολὺν ὄντα καὶ δυσερμήνευτον καὶ δεόμενον σοφοῦ εἴπερ τι ἄλλο τῶν δογμάτων καὶ ἐπὶ πλεῖον διαβεβηκότος...) Or.*Cels*. 7.32(p.182.20; M.11.1465A); μέγα...τὸ τῆς ἀ. καὶ δυσθεώρητον τοῖς πολλοῖς ἡμῶν μυστήριον id.*Jo*.10.36(20; p.210.14; M.14.372C); partic. objections χρὴ καὶ τοὺς περὶ τῆς ἀ. ἀπιστοῦντας...ἢ μηδεμιᾶς αἰτίας ἐξάπτειν τὴν τῶν ἀνθρώπων γένεσιν...ἢ τῷ θεῷ τὴν τῶν ὄντων ἀνατιθέντας αἰτίαν εἰς τὴν τοῦδε τοῦ δόγματος ἀποβλέπειν ὑπόθεσιν καὶ διὰ ταύτης δεικνύναι τὴν ἀ. οὐδαμόθεν ἔχουσαν τὸ πιστόν. τοῦτο δὲ ποιήσουσιν, ἐὰν δεῖξαι δυνηθῶσιν ἢ ἀδύνατον ὂν τῷ θεῷ ἢ ἀβούλητον τὰ νεκρωθέντα τῶν σωμάτων ἢ καὶ πάντῃ διαλυθέντα πάλιν ἑνῶσαι καὶ συναγαγεῖν πρὸς τὴν τῶν αὐτῶν ἀνθρώπων σύστασιν. ἐὰν δὲ τοῦτο μὴ δύνωνται, παυσάσθωσαν τῆς ἀθέου ταύτης ἀπιστίας Athenag.*res*.2 (pp.49.31–50.6; M.6.977B); difficulty caused by eating of bodies by animals eaten in turn by men, *ib*.4(p.52.24; 981C); διὰ δύο πράγματα χρὴ ἀπιστεῖν τῶν νεκρῶν τὴν ἀ. ἢ διὰ τὸ μὴ δύνασθαι τὸν θεὸν ἐγείρειν τοὺς νεκρούς, ἢ διὰ τὸ μὴ λυσιτελεῖν τοῖς ἀνισταμένοις...τούτων δὲ τὸ μὲν ἐστιν ἀσεβές, τὸ δὲ γελοῖον ‡Just.*qu.Gr*.10.3(M.6.1480A); disbelieved by some of S. Paul's Corinthian converts, Chrys.*hom.in 1Cor*.proem.(10.2D); and by some of Chrys.'s own flock, *ib.1.6*(32A); **2.** condemnation of its denial ὃς...λέγει μήτε ἀ. μήτε κρίσιν, οὗτος πρωτότοκός ἐστι τοῦ σατανᾶ Polyc.*ep*.7.1; βλασφημεῖν τολμῶσι τὸν θεὸν Ἀβραὰμ...οἳ καὶ λέγουσι μὴ εἶναι νεκρῶν ἀ. Just.*dial*.80.4(M.6. 665A); **3.** arguments in defence; **a.** from God's omnipotence εἰ, ὥσπερ ἀπίστοις ἀνθρώποις ἀδύνατον φαίνεται γενέσθαι τὴν ἀ., οὕτως ἀδύνατόν ἐστι τῷ θεῷ τὸ ποιεῖν τὴν ἀ. οὐδὲν ἄρα κατὰ τοῦτο διαφέρει θεὸς ἀνθρώπου. εἰ δὲ ἀπειράκις διαφέρει, ὥσπερ οὖν καὶ διαφέρει, πῶς οὐκ ἔστιν ἄτοπον τὸ ἀπιστεῖν θεῷ τὴν ποίησιν ὧν ἔχει τοῦ ποιεῖν τὴν δύναμιν; ‡Just.*qu.Gr*.10.35(M.6.1488B); which raised Lazarus, Gr.Nyss.*res*.3(M.46.668A); εἰ γὰρ τέκτονος ἔργον οὐ καταλαμβάνεις, πολλῷ μᾶλλον τοῦ ἀριστοτέχνου θεοῦ. μὴ ἀπίστει τοίνυν τῇ ἀ. Chrys.*hom.17.3 in 1Cor*.(10.148E); **b.** from man's nature and end δεικτέον ἀληθῆ τὸν περὶ τῆς ἀ. λόγον ἀπό τε τῆς αἰτίας αὐτῆς, καθ' ἣν καὶ δι' ἣν ὁ πρῶτος γέγονεν ἄνθρωπος οἵ τε μετ' ἐκεῖνον,... ἀπό τε τῆς κοινῆς πάντων ἀνθρώπων ὡς ἀνθρώπων φύσεως, ἔτι δὲ ἀπὸ τῆς τοῦ ποιήσαντος ἐπὶ τούτοις κρίσεως Athenag.*res*.11(p.60.24; M.6.996A); τῆς μὲν ψυχῆς οὔσης τε καὶ διαμενούσης ὁμαλῶς ἐν ᾗ γέγονεν φύσει...τοῦ δὲ σώματος κινουμένου κατὰ φύσιν πρὸς ἃ πέφυκεν καὶ τὰς ἀποκληρωθείσας αὐτῷ δεχομένου μεταβολάς, μετὰ δὲ τῶν ἄλλων τῶν κατὰ τὰς ἡλικίας ἢ κατ' εἶδος ἢ μέγεθος τὴν ἀ. εἶδος γάρ τι μεταβολῆς καὶ πάντων ὕστατον ἡ ἀ. *ib*.12(p.63.8; 1000A); εὔδηλον ὡς τῇ τῆς γενέσεως αἰτίᾳ καὶ τῇ γνώμῃ τοῦ ποιήσαντος δείκνυται σαφῶς ἡ ἀ. *ib*.13(p.63.28,30; 1000C); ἡ δὲ τῶν αὐτῶν ἀνθρώπων σύστασις ἐξ ἀνάγκης ἑπομένην δείκνυσιν τὴν τῶν νεκρωθέντων... σωμάτων ἀ. ... ἀ. γὰρ μὴ γινομένης, οὐκ ἂν ἡ τῶν ἀνθρώπων ὡς ἀνθρώπων διαμένοι φύσις *ib*.15(p.66.18,29; 1004C–1005A); **c.** from justice; judgement believed by many to be chief cause of resurrection τοῦτο...δείκνυται ψεῦδος ἐκ τοῦ πάντας μὲν ἀνίστασθαι...μὴ πάντας δὲ κρίνεσθαι...εἰ γὰρ μόνον τὸ κατὰ τὴν κρίσιν δίκαιον τῆς ἀ. ἦν αἴτιον, ἐχρῆν δήπου τοὺς μηδὲν ἡμαρτηκότας...μηδ' ἀνίστασθαι *ib*.14(p.65.5ff.; 1001C); but δεῖ...τὸ φθαρτὸν...ἐνδύσασθαι ἀφθαρσίαν, ἵνα ζωοποιηθέντων ἐξ ἀ. τῶν νεκρωθέντων καὶ πάλιν ἑνωθέντων τῶν κεχωρισμένων...ἕκαστος κομίσηται δικαίως ἃ διὰ τοῦ σώματος ἔπραξεν εἴτε ἀγαθὰ εἴτε κακά *ib*.18(p.71.17; 1012B); εἰ γὰρ οὐ γίνεται τῶν νεκρῶν ἡ ἀ., πῶς οὐκ ἔσονται ἴσοι ἀλλήλοις οἵ τε δρῶντες τοὺς μαρτυρικοὺς ἀγῶνας καὶ οἱ ὑπομένοντες; ‡Just.*qu.Gr*.10.38(M.6.1488C); Chrys.*hom.66.3 in Jo*.(8.398A,B); εἰ γὰρ μὴ ἐβούλετο τὰς θύρας ἡμῖν ἐξ ἀρχῆς τῆς ἀ. ἀνοῖξαι, οὐκ ἂν ἀφῆκε Ἄβελ...φίλον αὐτῷ [sc. θεῷ] γεγενημένον παθεῖν id.*res.mort*.8(2.435C); **d.** from natural phenomena ἴδωμεν...τὴν κατὰ καιρὸν γινομένην ἀ. ἡμέρα καὶ νὺξ ἀ. ἡμῖν δηλοῦσιν *1Clem*.24.3; ταῦτα δὲ πάντα [sc. growth of seeds in ground, etc.] ἐνεργεῖ ἡ τοῦ θεοῦ σοφία, εἰς τὸ ἐπιδεῖξαι διὰ τούτων, ὅτι δυνατός ἐστιν ὁ θεὸς ποιῆσαι τὴν καθολικὴν ἀ. ἁπάντων ἀνθρώπων. εἰ δὲ καὶ θαυμασιώτερον θέαμα θέλεις θεάσασθαι γινόμενον πρὸς ἀπόδειξιν ἀ. οὐ μόνον τῶν ἐπιγείων πραγμάτων, ἀλλὰ καὶ τῶν ἐν οὐρανῷ, κατανόησον τὴν ἀ. τῆς σελήνης τὴν κατὰ μῆνα γενομένην Thphl.Ant.*Autol*.1.13(M.6.1044A); τί φατε...ὁρῶντες πολλὰ τῶν ἀερίων τὰς μορφὰς μεταβάλλοντα; ὁποῖα καὶ περὶ τοῦ Ἰνδικοῦ σκώληκος ἱστορεῖται τοῦ κερασφόρου· ὃς εἰς κάμπην τὰ πρῶτα μεταβαλών, εἶτα προϊὼν βομβυλιὸς γίνεται, καὶ οὐδὲ ἐπὶ ταύτης ἵσταται τῆς μορφῆς...μεμνημέναι τῆς κατὰ τὸ ζῶον τοῦτο μεταβολῆς, ἐναργῆ λαμβάνετε τῆς ἀ. ἔννοιαν Bas.*hex*.8.8(1.78E–79A; M.29.184D–185A); from myth of phoenix, Cyr.H.*catech*.18.8; from phases of moon, *ib*.18.10; from plants, Chrys.*hom.66.3 in Jo*.(8.397D); **e.** other arguments εἰ δὲ ἀ. νεκρῶν οὐκ ἔστι κατά σε, διὰ τί τοὺς τυμβωρύχους καταδικάζεις; εἰ γὰρ ἀπόλωλε τὸ σῶμα, καὶ ἀνέλπιστος ἡ ἀ., διὰ τί τιμωρίαν ὑπομένει ὁ τυμβωρύχος; Cyr.H.*catech*.18.5; εἰ δυνατόν [l. ἀδύνατόν] τινι ὑπὲρ τοῦ μὴ ὄντος πράγματος τῆς ἑαυτοῦ ζωῆς προτιμῆσαι τὸν θάνατον, πῶς, εἰ καθ' ὑμᾶς οὐκ ὄντος ἀληθοῦς τοῦ περὶ τῆς ἀ. δόγματος, ὑπὲρ τούτου τῆς ἑαυτῶν ζωῆς προετίμησαν οἱ μάρτυρες τὸν ἑαυτῶν θάνατον; ποίας δὲ ἄλλης θρησκείας πολυτρόποις βασάνοις τε καὶ θανάτοις ἐβεβαιώθη τὸ δόγμα τῆς ἑαυτῶν θρησκείας, λέγω δὴ τῶν Χριστιανῶν περὶ τῆς τῶν νεκρῶν ἀ.; ‡Just.*qu.Gr*.10.12(M.6.1481B); οὐδεὶς...λέγοι ἂν ὡς ἀπολογούμενος περὶ τῶν κατὰ τὴν ἀ. τόπως αἰσθήσεσι μὴ καταλαμβανόμενοι γνώσονται τὸν θεόν; Or.*Cels*.7.37(p.187.29; M.11.1473A); **4.** nature of resurrection body; **a.** Methodius' attack on Origen; Origen's view τὴν ἀ. τῶν νεκρῶν ἀποδεχόμενοι μεταβολάς φαμεν γίνεσθαι ποιοτήτων τῶν ἐν σώμασιν Or.*Cels*.4.57(p.330.2; M.11.1124A); *reductio ad absurdum* of opinion of those who hold that resurrection body is materially same as present body ἐὰν δ' οὖν πυνθανώμεθα αὐτῶν, τίνος ἡ ἀ. γίνεται, ἀποκρίνονται ὅτι τῶν σωμάτων ὧν νῦν περικείμεθα. εἶτα προσεπερωτησάντων ἡμῶν· πότερον τῆς οὐσίας αὐτῶν ὅλης, ἢ οὐχί; κτλ. Meth.*res*.1.20(pp.242–6ff.; M.41.1088C); τοῦτο τὸ εἶδος...τὸ σωματικόν, ὃ ἐν τῇ ἀ. περιτίθεται πάλιν τῇ ψυχῇ, ἐπὶ τὸ κρεῖττον μεταβάλλον, οὐ πάντως δὲ τόδε τὸ ἐντεταγμένον τὸ κατὰ τὴν πρώτην ὑποκείμενον *ib*.1.22(p.245.10; M.41.1092A); *ib*.1.23(p.247.1; M.41.1092C); Or.'s opinions summarized ἀκριβῶς νοεῖν, εἴσεται τὴν ἀ. ἐπὶ τούτου μὴ χρῆναι παραλαμβάνεσθαι τοῦ σώματος, ἅτε ἀδυνατοῦντος ἀτρέπτου δι' αἰῶνος μένειν, ἀλλὰ ἐπὶ τοῦ πνευματικοῦ, ἐν ᾧ ὁ αὐτὸς ὁ καὶ νῦν ἐν τούτῳ διασωζόμενος χαρακτὴρ τηρηθήσεται, ἵν' ἕκαστος ἡμῶν καὶ κατὰ τὴν μορφὴν ὁ αὐτὸς ᾖ, καθάπερ ἐλέχθη καὶ Ὠριγένει, οὕτω γὰρ ἐκεῖνος ἔσεσθαι τίθεται τὴν ἀ. *ib*.1.25(p.251.3ff.; M.41.1096C); *ib*.3.3(p.391.5; M.18.317B); Meth.'s attack οὐ...ἀνεξόμεθα φληναφώντων τινῶν...τὴν γραφήν, ἵνα αὐτοῖς δὴ σαρκὸς μὴ εἶναι προχωρήσῃ ἡ ἀ., ὀστᾶ νοητὰ καὶ σάρκας ὑποτιθεμένων Meth.*res*.1.39(p.282.13; M.18.268B); exeg. Mt. 22:23 Χριστός, εἰ μὴ ἦν ἀ. σαρκός, ἀλλὰ μόνον ἐσώζετο ἡ ψυχή, συνέθετο ἂν αὐτοῖς [sc. Sadducees] ὡς...ὀρθῶς φρονοῦσι. νυνὶ δὲ ἀποκρούεται λέγων· ἐν τῇ ἀ. οὔτε γαμοῦσιν οὔτε γαμίσκονται...οὐ τῷ σάρκα μὴ ἔχειν, ἀλλὰ τῷ μὴ γαμεῖν *ib*.1.51(p.305.5ff.; 281A); *ib*.(p.306.9f.; 281C); σῶμα λέγεται πνευματικόν, οὐ τὸ λεπτομερὲς καὶ ἀερῶδες, καθὼς λέγουσί τινες ὅτι τοιοῦτον αἱ ψυχαὶ ἐν τῇ ἀ. λήψονται σῶμα, ὧν ἐστιν εἷς καὶ Ὠριγένης, ἀλλὰ πνευματικὸν λέγεται τὸ χωροῦν πᾶσαν τοῦ ἁγίου πνεύματος τὴν ἐνέργειαν καὶ κοινωνίαν *ib*.3.16(p.413.7); ἀ. can be predicated only of body, not of immortal soul ἀ. γὰρ οὐκ ἐπὶ τοῦ μὴ πεπτωκότος ἀλλ' ἐπὶ τοῦ πεπτωκότος λέγεται καὶ ἀνισταμένου *ib*.1.51(p.306.14; M.18.281C); *ib*.1.52(p.308.1,4; M.41.1128A); Chrys.*res.mort*.7(2.434C); **b.** splendour of resurrection body Μωϋσῆς...ὑπέδειξε τὸν τύπον διὰ τῆς τοῦ προσώπου αὐτοῦ ἐπικειμένης τοῦ πνεύματος δόξης...πῶς ἐν τῇ ἀ. τῶν δικαίων δοξασθήσεται τὰ σώματα τῶν ἁγίων Mac.Aeg.*hom*.5.10(M.34.516A); endowed with spiritual wings, *ib*.5.11(516C); ἐν τῇ ἀ. ὅλα τὰ μέλη ἀνίστανται ...καὶ ὅλα γίγνονται φωτοειδῆ...ἕκαστος ἐν τῇ ἰδίᾳ φύσει καὶ ὑποστάσει μένει πεπληρωμένος τοῦ πνεύματος *ib*.15.10(581C); acc. practice of virtue in earthly life, Chrys.*hom.86.6 in Jo*.(8.512D); Proc.G.*Is*.16:15ff.(M.87.2713A); **c.** its incorruptibility, Ath.*inc*.27.2(M.25.144A); ἐγὼ γὰρ ἐν τῇ ἀ. τῶν νεκρῶν ἀπολήψομαι παρὰ τοῦ σωτῆρος ἄφθαρτον αὐτό [sc. σῶμα] id.*v.Anton*.91(M.26.972B); ἐν τῇ ἀ. ἀπολαβεῖν τὴν σάρκα, μήτε ὑπόδικον θανάτῳ, μήτε ὑπεύθυνον ἁμαρτίᾳ Bas.*ep*.261.3(3.403B; M.32.972B); ἐν τῷ τέλει τοῦ παρόντος αἰῶνος ἐκ τῆς σποδιᾶς γενήσεται ἡ ἀ. τοῦ ἐφθαρμένου σώματος, καὶ ἐξαναστήσεται ὁ ἄνθρωπος ζωοποιηθείς τε καὶ ψυχωθείς, τὴν μὲν προλαβοῦσαν φθορὰν ἀποτιναξάμενος, καὶ ἐπενδυσάμενος δὲ τὴν θείαν ἀφθαρσίαν Nil.*epp*.1.111(M.79.132A); δωρουμένου [sc. κυρίου] πᾶσιν ἐν τῇ ἀ. τὸ τῆς προαιρέσεως καὶ τὸ τῆς φύσεως ἄφθαρτον· ὡς κακίας καὶ θανάτου μηκέτι ἐνεργουμένων· κἂν ἕκαστος ἀναλόγως ἀπολαμβάνῃ τοῖς πεπραγμένοις ἐν τῇ αὐτοῦ βιοτῇ ‡Proc.G.*Pr*.16:11(M.87.1384C).

E. discussion whether resurrection is universal; **1.** resurrection of wicked denied, *Did*.16.6; οἱ ἁπλούστεροι τῶν πεπιστευκότων... νομίζουσι τοὺς ἀσεβεῖς τῆς ἀ. μὴ τεύξεσθαι Meth.*res*.1.20(p.242.3; M.41.1088B); πολλοί εἰσι καὶ νῦν λέγοντες, ὅτι ἐνίων μέν ἐστιν ἀ., ἐνίων δὲ οὔ Chrys.*hom.19.1 in Heb*.(12.181C); implied, when resurrection of OT saints is discussed or admitted οἱ ζήσαντες κατὰ τὸν νόμον τὸν διαταχθέντα διὰ Μωυσέως ζήσονται ὁμοίως τῷ Ἰακὼβ καὶ τῷ Ἐνὼχ...ἐν τῇ τῶν νεκρῶν ἀ. ἢ οὔ;...ἐπεὶ οἱ τὰ...καλὰ ἐποίουν εὐάρεστοί εἰσι τῷ θεῷ, καὶ διὰ τοῦ Χριστοῦ τούτου ἐν τῇ ἀ. ... σωθήσονται Just.*dial*.45.2,4(M.6.572B,C); **2.** universal resurrection affirmed τῆς κοινῆς ἀ., ἧς καὶ ἀσεβεῖς μετέχουσιν Chrys.*hom.45.2 in Jo*.(8.264E); ἀ. ... πάντες ἀπολαύσονται...ἐν δόξῃ δὲ οὐ πάντες ἔσονται id.*hom.7.1 in 1Thess*.(11.473D); id.*hom.5.3 in Rom*.(9.464B); id.*exp.in Ps*.48:11(5.212B); **3.** double resurrection, first of righteous only (millennium), then of all men Ἰωάννης...ἐν ἀποκαλύψει γενομένῃ αὐτῷ χίλια ἔτη ποιήσειν ἐν Ἱερουσαλὴμ τοὺς τῷ ἡμετέρῳ Χριστῷ πιστεύσαντας προεφήτευσε, καὶ μετὰ ταῦτα τὴν καθολικὴν καὶ... αἰωνίαν ὁμοθυμαδὸν ἅμα πάντων ἀ. γενήσεσθαι Just.*dial*.81.4(M.6.669A); *ib*.113.4(736D); Or.*hom.2.3 in Jer*.(pp.19.21–20.1; M.13.281A,B); Meth.*symp*.9.3(p.117.19; M.18.184B).

F. doctrine in creeds and liturgy, *Symb.App*.(p.30); πιστεύομεν ...εἰς ἀ. νεκρῶν ‡Ath.*interpr*.(p.66.26; M.26.1232B); ἀναθεματίζομεν πάντας τοὺς μὴ ὁμολογοῦντας ἀ. σαρκὸς *ib*.(p.66.33; 1232C); πιστεύομεν καὶ περὶ σαρκὸς ἀναστάσεως *Symb.Ant*.(341)1(p.249.8; M.26.721B); προσδοκῶμεν ἀ. νεκρῶν *Symb*.ap.Epiph.*anc*.118(p.147.15; M.43.232D); *Symb*.ap.Epiph.*anc*.119(p.149.9; 236B); ὁμολογοῦμεν... ἀ. νεκρῶν *Symb.Nic.–CP*(p.80.15; H.2.288B); ἐν τῇ ἐσχάτῃ ἡμέρᾳ τῆς ἀ. *Symb.Sirm*.3(p.236.5; M.26.693B); *Symb.CP*(360)(p.259.9; M.26.748B); πιστεύω καὶ εἰς νεκρῶν ἀ. ἁπάντων *Lit.Jac*.(*NBP* 10² p.38).

G. other aspects; **1.** as recompense of virtue, *Barn*.21.1; οἱ τούτοις ὑπακούοντες τοῖς προστάγμασιν...τῆς ἀ. καρπὸν τρυγήσουσιν *2Clem*.19.3; ποθοῦμεν πάντα ὅσα θεὸς τοῖς δικαίοις ἐπαγγέλλεται. οὕτως...τὴν τῶν δικαίων ἀ. ποθοῦμεν Or.*Cels*.8.50(p.265.10; M.11.1589C); οὐδεὶς τῶν ὀρθῶς βεβιωκότων τῇ ἀ. διαπιστεῖ...τίνες οὖν εἰσιν οἱ τῇ ἀ. διαπιστοῦντες; οἱ βεβήλους ἔχοντες τὰς ὁδούς Chrys.*hom.45.4 in Jo*.(8.268C); τὸ τῆς ἀ. δόγμα λυμαίνεται ἡ τοῦ βίου φαυλότης id.*hom.47.4 in Ac*.(9.356D); **2.** resurrection and baptism γνώρισμα παλιγγενεσίας, τρόπαιον ἀναστάσεως Clem.*q.d.s*.42(p.190.19; M.9.649D); τῷ μυστικῷ ὕδατι διὰ τοῦ βαπτίσματος ἐνθαπτόμενοι...ἵνα τῇ μιμήσει τοῦ θανάτου ἐπακολουθήσῃ καὶ ἡ τῆς ἀ. μίμησις Gr.Nyss.*Apoll*.55(M.45.1260C); τὸ δὲ βάπτισμα δύναμίς ἐστι πρὸς τὴν ἀ. Bas.*hom*.13.1(2.114A; M.31.424D); **3.** resurrection and chastity παρέλαβεν ὁ λόγος τὴν ἁγνείαν, διδάσκων ὅσον διαπρεπὴς...ἔσται τῇ ἀ. καὶ ὅτι χωρὶς αὐτῆς οὐδεὶς τεύξεται τῶν ἐπαγγελμάτων Meth.*symp*.9.4(p.119.15; M.18.188A); εἰκών τις εἶναι τῆς ἐν τῷ μέλλοντι αἰῶνι μακαριότητος ὁ ἐν παρθενίᾳ βίος...εἶτα ὅ τι ἐξαίρετον τῶν ἐν τῇ ἀ. καλῶν, καὶ ἐν τῷ παρόντι καρποῦται βίῳ. εἰ γὰρ ἰσάγγελος ἡ ζωὴ ἡ μετὰ τὴν ἀ. παρὰ τοῦ κυρίου τοῖς δικαίοις ἐπήγγελται· τῆς δὲ ἀγγελικῆς φύσεως ἴδιον τὸ ἀπηλλάχθαι τοῦ γάμου ἐστίν... Gr.Nyss.*virg*.13(p.309.9; M.46.381A); **4.** relation between immortality of soul and resurrection of body τῶν δὲ ἀνθρώπων κατὰ μὲν τὴν ψυχὴν ἀπὸ γενέσεως ἐχόντων τὴν ἀμετάβλητον διαμονήν, κατὰ δὲ τὸ σῶμα προσλαμβανόντων ἐκ μεταβολῆς τὴν ἀφθαρσίαν· ὅπερ ὁ τῆς ἀ. βούλεται λόγος Athenag.*res*.16(p.67.22; M.6.1005C); ἀ. τῶν νεκρῶν ψυχῶν ἀπὸ τοῦ νῦν γίνεται. ἀ. δὲ τῶν σωμάτων ἐν ἐκείνῃ τῇ ἡμέρᾳ Mac.Aeg.*hom*.36.1(M.34.749A); **5.** resurrection from Hades διαρρήξῃ τὰ δεσμὰ ψυχῶν τῶν ἐν ᾅδῃ κατεχομένων, τὸν τῆς ἀ. διαπηξάμενος ὅρον ‡Ath.*Apoll*.1.14 (M.26.1117B); ἀνάγκη γάρ τινα ἐξ ᾅδου τὴν ἀρχὴν τῆς ἀ. εἰληφέναι, ἵνα τελεία ᾖ ἡ ἀ. *ib*.1.16(1160D); ᾅδης...ὁ ἀφανὴς τόπος ἐν ᾧ μετὰ διάζευξιν τὴν ἀπὸ τῶν σωμάτων διάγουσιν αἱ ψυχαὶ πρὸ τῆς ἀ. ‡Proc.G.*Pr*.15:11(M.87.1373B); **6.** compared with feast of Tabernacles ἐξεταζομένη τῇ πρώτῃ τῆς ἀ. ἡμέρᾳ εἰσφέρω τὰ προστεταγμένα, εἰ κεκόσμημαι τοῖς τῆς ἀρετῆς καρποῖς, εἰ τοῖς κλάδοις τῆς ἁγνείας κατασκιάζομαι. νόει γάρ μοι τὴν ἀ. εἶναι τὴν σκηνοπηγίαν...καὶ τὰ εἰς τὴν σύνθεσιν παραλαμβανόμενα τῆς σκηνῆς τὰς πράξεις εἶναι τῆς δικαιοσύνης Meth.

*symp.*9.3(p.116.25; M.18.181B); ἐξελθοῦσα κἀγὼ τῆς Αἰγύπτου τούτου τοῦ βίου, ἔρχομαι πρῶτον εἰς τὴν ἀ., τὴν ἀληθινὴν σκηνοπηγίαν, κἀκεῖ τοῖς καρποῖς τῆς ἀρετῆς πήξασα τὴν σκηνήν μου...τῇ πρώτῃ τῆς ἑορτῆς ἀ. ἡμέρᾳ, τῇ κρίσει, συνεορτάζω τῷ Χριστῷ τὴν χιλιονταετηρίδα...εἶτα...ἔρχομαι...εἰς τὴν γῆν τῆς ἐπαγγελίας, τοὺς οὐρανούς *ib.*9.5(p.120.11ff.; 189A); id.*res.*2.21(p.375.5; M.18.285C); *ib.*(p.376.4; 316A); **7.** effects of resurrection and belief in it on men and other creatures χάρισμα τοῦ θεοῦ ὑπερπαίει τὴν χρείαν, ὥσπερ καὶ τὸ εἶναι ἐν δόξῃ ἡλίου ἢ σελήνης...ἐν τῇ ἱερᾷ τῶν νεκρῶν ἀ. Or.*Jo.*32.9(6; p.441.5; M.14.765B); ἡ κτίσις...χαίρουσα ἐπὶ τοῖς τέκνοις τοῦ θεοῦ τῇ ἀ. Meth.*res.*1.47(p.299.1; M.18.273C); Bas.*hom. in Ps.*44:1(1.159C; M.29.389A); ῥίζα πάσης τῆς ἀγαθοεργίας, ἡ τῆς ἀ. ἐλπίς...πᾶσα ψυχὴ πιστεύουσα μὲν εἰς ἀ., φείδεται ἑαυτῆς εἰκότως· ἀπιστοῦσα δὲ τῇ ἀ., γίνεται ἔκδοτος εἰς ἀπώλειαν Cyr.H.*catech.*18.1; **8.** description of gen. resurrection ὅτε δὲ γίνεται αὕτη ἡ ἀ. τοῦ ἀληθινοῦ...Χριστοῦ σώματος, τότε τὰ μέλη τοῦ Χριστοῦ τὰ νῦν, ὡς πρὸς τὸ μέλλον, ξηρὰ ὀστᾶ συναχθήσεται, ὀστοῦν πρὸς ὀστοῦν καὶ ἁρμονία πρὸς ἁρμονίαν Or.*Jo.*10.36(p.210.31; M.14.375A); in a certain place, *Apoc.Paul.*14 (p.44); instantaneous, Gr.Nyss.*res.*3(M.46.660C); μετὰ τὴν τῶν σωμάτων ἀ. τῆς βασιλείας ἡμῖν τὴν ἀπόλαυσιν δωρεῖσθαι ὑπέσχετο, καὶ τὴν μετὰ τῶν ἁγίων διαγωγήν, καὶ τὴν ἐν διηνεκεῖ αἰῶνι ἀπόλαυσιν Chrys.*hom.*36.5 *in Gen.*(4.371A); **9.** various aspects; **a.** question whether men will know one another τοῖς μὲν δικαίοις γνωρισμὸς γίνεται, τοῖς δὲ ἁμαρτωλοῖς οὐδαμῶς, οὔτε ἐν τῇ ἀ. δύνανται γνωρίσαι ἀλλήλους *1 Apoc.Jo.*12(p.79); **b.** ref. 1Cor.15:49 ἡ δὲ εἰκὼν τοῦ ἐπουρανίου ἡ ἐκ νεκρῶν ἀ. Meth.*res.*2.18(p.369.11; M.18.284B); **c.** resurrection promises in Liturgy of Dead λειτουργοὶ τὰς ἐν τοῖς θείοις λογίοις ἐμφερομένας...ἐπαγγελίας περὶ τῆς ἱερᾶς ἡμῶν ἀ. ἀναγνόντες, ...ᾄδουσι τὰς...τῶν ψαλμικῶν λογίων ᾠδὰς Dion.Ar.*e.h.*7.2(M.3.556C); τῶν ἱερῶν ἡ θεσμοθεσία...τὸν ὅλον ἄνθρωπον ἁγιάζουσα...τὴν ἀ. ἔσεσθαι διαγγέλλουσα *ib.*7.3.9(565C); **d.** myst. interprn. of three days ἐν τρισὶν ἡ ἀ. ἐνεργεῖται ἡμέραις...τὴν τρίτην φησὶ τὴν πνευματικὴν ἡμέραν, ἐν ᾗ οἴονται δηλοῦσθαι τὴν τῆς ἐκκλησίας ἀ. ... πρώτην λέγειν εἶναι τὴν χοϊκὴν ἡμέραν καὶ τὴν δευτέραν τὴν ψυχικήν, οὐ γεγενημένης τῆς ἐκκλησίας τῆς ἀ. ἐν αὐταῖς Heracleon ap.Or.*Jo.*10.37(21; p.212.27–32; M.14.376C).

H. heret.; **1.** resurrection only of initiated (Gnost.) ἀναγεννηθέντες πνευματικοί, οὐ σαρκικοί. αὕτη, φησίν, ἐστὶν ἡ ἀ. ἡ διὰ τῆς πύλης γινομένη τῶν οὐρανῶν, δι' ἧς οἱ μὴ εἰσελθόντες, φησί, πάντες μένουσι νεκροί Hipp.*haer.*5.8(p.93.18; M.16.3146C); **2.** resurrection in earthly flesh λέγει [sc. Heraclitus]...σαρκὸς ἀ. ταύτης <τῆς> φανερᾶς ἐν ᾗ γεγενήμεθα, καὶ τὸν θεὸν οἶδε ταύτης τῆς ἀ. αἴτιον Hipp.*haer.*9.10(p.243.19f.; M.16.3375B); ἀ. δὲ νεκρῶν ὁρίζονται [sc. Severians] εἶναι τὴν τοῦ σώματος τούτου πρὸς τὴν λογικὴν ψυχὴν δευτέραν ἕνωσιν ἀδιάλυτον Tim.CP *haer.*(M.86.64A); to ordinary carnal life, taught by certain monks φασὶ γὰρ...φλέγματι πάλιν καὶ αἵματι...καὶ τροφῇ αἰσθητῇ πρὸς τὸ ζῆν συνέχεσθαι μέλλειν τὰ σώματα κατὰ τὴν ἀ., οὐδενὸς τὸ σύνολον ξένου παρὰ τὴν παροῦσαν ζωὴν διὰ τῆς ἀ. ἀναφανησομένου, πλὴν τὸ μὴ δύνασθαι πάλιν ἀποθανεῖν Max.*ep.*7(M.91.433B,C); **3.** of heretics repudiating marriage εἰ γοῦν τὴν ἀ. ἀπειλήφασιν, ὡς αὐτοὶ λέγουσι, καὶ διὰ τοῦτο ἀθετοῦσι τὸν γάμον, μηδὲ ἐσθιέτωσαν μηδὲ πινέτωσαν. καταργεῖσθαι γὰρ ἔφη τὴν κοιλίαν...ὁ ἀπόστολος ἐν τῇ ἀ. Clem.*str.*3.6(p.218.8ff.; M.8.1152A); **4.** of Origenists εὑρηκότες γὰρ οἱ Φιλοπονιακοὶ τὸν Ὠριγένην λέγοντα ὅτι ἡ αὐτὴ ὕλη ἐν τῷ μέλλοντι αἰῶνι ἀναμορφοῦται, καὶ διὰ τοῦτο τῶν αὐτῶν σωμάτων γίνεται ἡ ἀ., ἐκάλεσαν τοὺς Κονωνίτας Ὠριγενιαστάς Tim.CP *haer.*(M.86.64C); **5.** denied altogether, Just.*dial.*80.4(M.6.665A) cit. s. ἀναλαμβάνω.

IV. met., of spiritual resurrection of man; possible already on earth ἀ. ἔδειξε τοῖς διορᾶν δυναμένοις τὴν ἔτι ἐν σαρκί Clem.*str.*4.16 (p.292.20; M.8.1308A); ὁ κύριος εἰκόνα τῆς πνευματικῆς ἀ. ποιήσας τοὺς νεκροὺς οὓς ἤγειρεν, οὐκ ἀφθάρτους τὴν σάρκα, ἀλλ' ὡς αὖθις ἀποθανουμένους ἤγειρεν id.*exc.Thdot.*7(p.108.18; M.9.657C); ἡμᾶς...ἤδη εἶναι ἐν τοῖς παλιγγενεσίας καὶ ἀ. ἀγαθοῖς Or.*or.*25.3(p.359.15; M.11.500A); id.*schol.in Cant.*3:1ff.(M.17.268D); through repentance, baptism, and mortification, Ign.*Smyrn.*5.3; Gr.Nyss.*hom.12 in Cant.*(M.44.1016D); *ib.*(1017A); in myst. life ἀ. λέγων [Jo.6:40] τὴν ἀπὸ τῆς ἐνύλου γνώσεως ἐπὶ τὴν ἄυλον θεωρίαν μετάβασιν Evagr. Pont.*ep.*7(3.85E; M.32.257B).

V. *rising again* (after a fall); *restoration*, Clem.*prot.*8(p.61.19; M.8.192A); Proc.G.*Gen.*9:4(M.87.296C); Hier.*vir.ill.*(tr.Sophr.Pal.) 63(p.41.1; M.*PL*.23.676A).

VI. *uprising, insurrection*, Cyr.*thes.*34(5^1.354B).

VII. = *elevation*, prob. f.l. for ἀνάτασις: τῆς δὲ τῶν πτερῶν ἐξαπλῆς ἱεροπλαστίας τὴν ἐπὶ τὸ θεῖον...ἀ. Dion.Ar.*c.h.*13.4(M.3.304D); id.*d.n.*4.12(M.3.709C).

ἀναστατέω, *stir up, unsettle* Σίμων...ἀ. τοὺς ὄχλους *Hom.Clem.*2.25; Cyr.*Am.*50(3.304C, vv.ll. ἀναστήσας, ἀνασπάσας).

ἀναστάτωσις, ἡ, *destruction, overthrow*, *Apoc.Dan.*C(p.123).

ἀνασταυρ-όω, 1. *crucify*; of Christ τὸ θνητὸν...προσηλοῦτο ~ούμενον, ὡς ἂν τοῖς πᾶσιν ἡ τοῦ θνητοῦ γνωρισθείη φύσις Eus. *theoph.fr.*3(p.13*.22; M.24.617C); met., of Christ destroying death τὴν δύσιν εἰς ἀνατολὴν μετήγαγεν καὶ τὸν θάνατον εἰς ζωὴν ἀ. Clem. *prot.*11(p.80.26; M.8.232C); ἡττήθη τε τελέως ὁ θάνατος εἰς ἀφθαρσίας ἐκτύπωμα ~ωθείσης τῆς σαρκός Meth.*Porph.*3(p.507.6; M.18.401C); **2.** *crucify* Christ *again, afresh*; ref. Heb.6:6, Or.*Jo.*20.12(p.341.33; M.14.600A); by a second baptism, Ephr.3.202C; Chrys.*hom.9.3 in Heb.*(12.96C); Nil.*epp.*1.204(M.79.160A); Jo.D.*f.o.*4.9(M.94.1120A) citt. s. ἀναβαπτίζω.

ἀνασταχυόομαι, *rise up*, *Orac.Sib.*3.382; *ib.*11.200; *ib.*12.194.

ἀναστέλλ-ω, 1. *send up, raise*; *gird up*, fig. τὸν...διακεχυμένον ταῖς ἐπιθυμίαις καὶ χαμαὶ τοὺς λογισμοὺς ἔχοντα συρομένους ἀ. διὰ τῆς ζώνης Chrys.*hom.23.1 in Eph.*(11.175A); med., *expose* ἀ. τὰ αἰδοῖα Clem.*prot.*2(p.16.7; M.8.84A); **2.** *draw back* ὁ πατήρ, ὅταν βούληται, ...δύναμιν αὐτοῦ προπηδᾶν ποιεῖ, καὶ ὅταν βούληται, πάλιν ἀ. εἰς ἑαυτόν Just.*dial.*128.3(M.6.776B); ἀποθανόντος γὰρ τοῦ σώματος...ἀ. τὴν ἐπελθοῦσαν ἀκτῖνα τῆς δυνάμεως ὁ σωτὴρ ἀπώλεσε μὲν τὸν θάνατον, τὸ δὲ θνητὸν σῶμα ἀποβαλὼν πάθη ἀνέστησεν Clem.*exc.Thdot.*61 (p.127.21; M.9.688D); **3.** *keep back, restrain*, id.*str.*4.18(p.300.24; M.8.1329A); id.*paed.*2.8(p.197.26; M.8.473B); Chrys.*hom.9.4 in Rom.*(9.516D); φραγμὸς ὁ νόμος...τὰς πρὸς τοὺς πονηροὺς ~ων συνουσίας id.*exp.in Ps.*138:20(5.417B); id.*hom.12.4 in Mt.*(7.166B); **4.** *remove, make away with*, ref. Nah.1:5 ἡ γῆ ἀνασταλήσεται, τουτέστι, χωρήσει πρὸς τὸ μὴ ὂν Cyr.*Nah.*6(3.482B); ἀ. τὸν χρυσάργυρον καὶ τὰ κυνήγια Thphn.*chron.*p.123(M.108.344B).

***ἀναστεναγμός, ὁ,** *groaning, lamentation*, Jo.Mal.*chron.*3 p.63(M.97.141B).

ἀνάστεμα, τό, v. ἀνάστημα.

ἀναστέφ-ω, *crown, wreathe*, Clem.*paed.*2.8(p.202.26; M.8.485B); ἐπειδὴ ἐπαύσατο τῆς νομοθεσίας...ὁ κύριος μυστικῶς αὖθις ~εται ἀκάνθῃ...ὅπως ὁ διὰ βάτου τὸ πρῶτον ὀφθείς, ὁ λόγος, διὰ τῆς ἀκάνθης ὕστερον ἀναληφθεὶς μιᾶς ἔργον τὰ πάντα δείξῃ δυνάμεως *ib.*(p.203.19; 488A).

***ἀναστηλιτεύω,** *proclaim* by public notice, Eus.*h.e.*9.7.15(M.20.813D); *ib.*9.11.2(837B).

ἀνάστημα (-εμα), τό, 1. *height, majesty*; **2.** *erection, structure*; hence *work of creation* εἶπεν ὁ παντοκράτωρ...κοινὸν ἀνάστεμα δῶμεν *Orac.Sib.*8.268; ἢ γὰρ ἴδῃ [sc. Ἀβραάμ] πάντας τοὺς ἐν ἁμαρτίᾳ διάγοντας, ἀπολέσει πᾶν τὸ ἀ. *T.Abr.*A 10(p.88.19); κύριος...ἐπήγαγεν ...τὸν κατακλυσμόν, ἵνα ἐξαλείψῃ πᾶν τὸ ἀ. *A.Andr.et Mt.*20(p.92.8); **3.** *restoration* εἰ μὴ τὸ τοῦ Ἀδὰμ σύμπτωμα εἰς ἀσύγκριτον ἀ. Χριστὸς ἀνεστήσατο ‡Ath.*Apoll.*1.7(M.26.1104C).

ἀναστηρίζω, *set up firmly*, †Apoll.*met.Ps.*67:10(M.33.1404D).

ἀναστοιχει-όω, 1. *resolve into original elements* ἔστι ζητεῖν <εἴ τι> ἔστι μεταξὺ τοῦ 'ὁ λόγος σὰρξ ἐγένετο' καὶ 'θεὸς ἦν ὁ λόγος' ἐν τοῖς ἀνθρωπίνοις ἰδεῖν, οἷον ~ουμένου τοῦ λόγου ἀπὸ τοῦ γεγονέναι αὐτὸν σάρκα καὶ κατὰ βραχὺ λεπτυνομένου ἕως γένηται ὅπερ ἦν ἐν ἀρχῇ Or.*Jo.*1.37(42; p.48.32; M.14.97D); of man at death παρεληλυθότα τὴν ἐντολὴν...εἰς θάνατον ~ωθέντα Meth.*symp.*3.6(p.32.19; M.18.69A); of world at Flood, Chrys.*Laz.*6.7(1.782D); **2.** recombine elements in original form, hence *reform, restore*; **a.** lit. οὔτε γὰρ εἰς...τοιαύτην ἔτι κατάστασιν, οἵα καὶ πρὸ τῆς διακοσμήσεως ἦν, διαλυθὲν ~ωθήσεται τὸ πᾶν οὔτ' αὖ εἰς ἀπώλειαν παντελῆ καὶ φθοράν Meth.*res.*1.47(p.300.3; M.41.1120C); id.*symp.*3.2(p.29.10; M.18.64B); **b.** spiritually; by God, Or.*princ.*3.1.13(p.218.9; M.11.273A); by Christ δεύτερος Ἀδὰμ ~ῶν τὸ γένος...εἰς καινότητα ζωῆς Cyr.*ador.*17(1.600A); in resurrection ὁ τοῦ ἡμετέρου σκεύους πλάστης...διὰ τῆς ἀναστάσεως ἀναπλάσας, πρὸς τὸ ἐξ ἀρχῆς κάλλος ~ώσει τὸ σκεῦος Gr.Nyss.*or.catech.*8 (p.45.11; M.45.36B); in eucharist δεχόμεθα ἡμεῖς [sc. Χριστόν] ἐν ἑαυτοῖς διὰ τῆς ἁγίας αὐτοῦ σαρκός τε καὶ αἵματος, ἵνα πρὸς καινότητα ζωῆς ~ούμενοι δι' αὐτοῦ καὶ ἐν αὐτῷ, τὸν παλαιὸν ἄνθρωπον ἀποσκευαζώμεθα Cyr.*ador.*12(1.419D); by H. Ghost, id.*Is.*5.2(2.770D); in baptism εἰ...τὸ ἅγιον πνεῦμα διὰ τοῦ βαπτίσματος ἀ. ἡμᾶς εἰς εἰκόνα τὴν πρώτην Didym.*Trin.*3.2(M.39.801D); of Christians ταῖς εἰς τὴν ἀμείνω ῥοπαῖς ~οῦντες τρόπον τινὰ τὸν νοῦν Or.*adnot.in Dt.*23:14 (M.17.32D); **3.** *transform* Χάλεβ...ἑρμηνεύεται ὡς καρδία...ὁ πάντα προσέχων τοῖς νοήμασιν...καὶ ὅλος ~ωθεὶς εἰς ἡγεμονικόν Or.*hom.18.2 in Jos.*(p.407.21; M.87.1028B); ἀνεστοιχειοῦτο [sc. Helena] γοῦν αὐτῇ ψυχῇ ἐπὶ τὴν ἄφθαρτον καὶ ἀγγελικὴν οὐσίαν Eus.*v.C.*3.46(p.97.9; M.20.1105D); τὸ αἰσθητὸν ὕδωρ [sc. of baptism] πρὸς θείαν ~οῦται δύναμιν, καὶ ἁγιάζει τοὺς ἐν οἷς ἂν γένηται Ammon.*Jo.*3:5(M.85.1408D); cf.Cyr.*Jo.*2.1(4.147D).

ἀναστοιχείωσις, ἡ, **1.** *dissolution* τοῦ οὐρανοῦ ἅμα τῇ γῇ πάλιν ἀ. ἔσται Didym.*Ps*.101:28(M.39.1520A); **2.** *restoration*, of world τελεσθείσης τῆς τῶν ἀνθρώπων γενέσεως, τῷ τέλει ταύτης συγκαταλῆξαι τὸν χρόνον, καὶ οὕτω τὴν τοῦ παντὸς ἀ. γενέσθαι, καὶ τῇ μεταβολῇ τοῦ ὅλου συναμειφθῆναι καὶ τὸ ἀνθρώπινον, ἀπὸ τοῦ φθαρτοῦ καὶ γεώδους ἐπὶ τὸ ἀπαθὲς καὶ ἀΐδιον Gr.Nyss.*hom.opif*.22.5(M.44.205C); *ib*.25.11 (221B); id.*Pulch*.(M.46.877A) cit. s. ἀναπλάσσω.

***ἀναστολέομαι**, med., s.v.l., ‡Chrys.*pasch*.6.5(p.187.18) v. ἀναστολίζω.

ἀναστολή, ἡ, **1.** *repression, restraint*, Clem.*str*.2.23(p.193.19; M.8.1096C); Eus.*p.e*.6.6(244D; M.21.416D); †Nil.*vit*.2(M.79.1141B); **2.** *clothing*; of angels at Resurrection, Eus.*fr.Lc*.24:4(M.24.605B).

ἀναστολίζω, *put on* τὸν παλαιὸν ἄνθρωπον ἀναστολισάμενος ‡Chrys.*pasch*.6.5(8.273C; p.187.18 ἀναστολησάμενος).

***ἀναστομίζω**, *open up* ὁ προχέων τὸ ὕδωρ ἐκ τῆς πλευρᾶς, τοῦ σιδήρου τὴν φλέβα ταύτην ἀ. Or.*exc.in Ps*.77:31(M.17.141D).

ἀναστομ-όω, **1.** *furnish with a mouth* or *outlet* τὴν πέτραν ᾗ ποτε τῷ ξύλῳ ἀνεστομώθη τὸ ὕδωρ Gr.Nyss.*laud.Bas*.(M.46.809D); hence *open up*, id.*hom.2 in Cant*.(M.44.801B); cf. ἀναστομίζω; ref. Cant. 4:12 διὰ τῆς χειροτονίας...\~ωθέντος τοῦ τῆς πηγῆς ὕδατος κοινὸν γένηται κτῆμα τῆς καθόλου ἐκκλησίας ἡ ἐν ἐκείνῳ χάρις id.*ep*.17 (M.46.1065C); pass., *find an opening, burst forth*; of an underground river, Proc.G.*Gen*.2:8f.(M.87.160A); *open up again* πηγὴν ...συγκεχωσμένην ἀ. Gr.Naz.*or*.36.2(M.36.265C); **2.** *rein in, curb*, fig. and met. ἀ. ἅμα καὶ ἐπιστρέφων...πρὸς σωτηρίαν τὸν λαόν Clem.*paed*.1.9(p.135.25; M.8.344A); ἀ. ἐπεχείρει...καθάπερ χαλινῷ Gr.Nyss.*anim.et res*.(M.46.12A); **3.** *baulk* τοσαῦτα \~ωθεὶς τῆς ἐλπίδος ταύτης †Gregent.*disp*.(M.86.721B).

ἀναστράπτω, *shine forth*, of BMV πολυφάτους χάριτας ἀ. Thdr.Stud.*nativ.BMV* 7(M.96.692A).

ἀναστρεπτέον, **1.** *one must behave* πῶς περὶ τὰς τροφὰς ἀ.; Clem.*paed*.2.1(p.153.5; M.8.377A); ἀεὶ ὡς παρόντος τοῦ κυρίου κοσμίως ἀ. *ib*.2.2(p.176.35; 429C); *ib*.2.7(p.189.30; 456C); **2.** *one must pay attention* to οὐ τοίνυν περὶ τὴν λέξιν ἀλλὰ περὶ τὰ σημαινόμενα ἀ. id.*str*.6.17(p.510.3; M.9.381C).

ἀναστρέφ-ω, **1.** *turn upside down*; met., *upset*, Hipp.*haer*.6.41 (p.172.22; M.16.3259B); **2.** *turn back*; hence *repeat* αἱρετικοὶ ἀ. πολλάκις τὰ αὐτὰ ῥήματα Didym.*Trin*.2.5(M.39.492A); *turn over in* the mind, *ponder*, Chrys.*hom.53.5 in Mt*.(7.545D); **3.** *behave* Κορινθίους...πιστεύσαντας μὲν ἤδη, τῆς δὲ πίστεως \~οντες οὐκ ἀξίως Euthal.Diac.*epp.Paul*.(M.85.701B).

ἀναστροφή, ἡ, **1.** *reversal, inversion*; **2.** *dwelling*; of man with God, Just.*1apol*.10.2(M.6.341A) cit. s. ἄφθαρτος; of Christ's life on earth, Clem.*paed*.2.8(p.194.27; M.8.468A); of millennium τὴν τοῦ κυρίου ἐπὶ γῆς ἀ. Oecum.*Apoc*.20:4(p.219); **3.** *mode of life*, Hipp. *Dan*.1.1(M.10.637A); μηδὲ ἔννοιαν φόβου θεοῦ σχόντες ἀλλὰ καὶ διὰ τῆς ἀ. αὐτῶν βλασφημοῦντες τὴν ὁδόν *Ep.Lugd*.ap.Eus.*h.e*.5.1.48 (M.20.428A); διὰ τῆς διδαχῆς αὐτοῦ καὶ τῆς ἀ. ‡Pall.*h.mon*.8(p.38.7; M.34.1139C); **4.** *mode* of speech, ref. Pr.9:1 οὐχ ἑτέρως δυνατὰ νοεῖσθαι...εἰ μὴ κατὰ μόνην μεταφορὰν καὶ ἀ. τῆς λέξεως Eus.*Marcell*.1.3(p.17.11; M.24.749B).

***ἀναστυλόω**, *set up* εἰκὼν ἀνεστυλώθη Areth.*Apoc*.37(M.106.680B).

***ἀνασυνδέω**, *bind up again*, ‡Bas.*const*.18.3(2.562C; M.31.1385A).

***ἀνασυράζω**, *draw up*, Cyr.*glaph.Dt*.(1.419C).

ἀνασύρομαι, *rage, rave* οἱ Ἀρειανοὶ ἀ., τὴν οἰκίαν...ἐνέπρησαν τοῦ ἐπισκόπου Thphn.*chron*.p.60(M.108.201C).

***ἀνασφαιρίζω**, *shoot up, lift up*, Thdt.*Ps*.52:2(1.951); ψυχὴν σὺν τῇ προσευχῇ εἰς οὐρανοὺς ἀ. Gr.Mag.*dial*.(tr.Zach.)2.37(M.*PL*.66.201B).

***ἀνασφαλής**, **1.** *uncertain*, Cyr.*Ps*.67:7(M.69.1145C); neut. as subst. τὸ ἀ. τῶν ἐτῶν Didym.*Trin*.2.14(M.39.708B); Cyr.*Nest*.2.8 (p.45.4; 6.49A); **2.** *unstable* ἐπ' ἄμφω βαίνειν εἰδώς, ὁ ἀ. id.*Os*.58 (3.90E); id.*Nah*.14(3.491E).

***ἀνασφαλίζω**, *recover*; of Magi recovering themselves from past errors through the sight of Christ, ‡Caes.Naz.*dial*.107(M.38.973).

***ἀνασφάλιστος**, *unfortified, unstable*, †Polyb.*v.Epiph*.64(M.41.108D).

***ἀνασφετερίζω**, *appropriate*, Leont.B.*parasc*.(M.86.1997C).

ἀνασφίγγ-ω, *bind up tightly* τριχὸς...ποικίλως ἀνεσφιγμένης Cyr.*Is*.4.3(2.634C); met. εἰς ἕνα θεότητος λόγον ἡ ἁγία τριὰς \~εται id.*Jo*.10.2(4.911B).

***ἀνασφραγίζω**, *seal anew, rebaptize* τὸν ναύκληρον κατηχήσατε καὶ ἀ. (ἔστιν γὰρ τῆς Ἀρείου μυσαρᾶς αἱρέσεως) Marc.Diac.*v.Porph*.56; *ib*.57.

ἀνασῴζω, **1.** *recover what is lost, rescue* Ἰησοῦς...τὴν ἐκκλησίαν ἀναλαβών,...ἀ. καὶ ἀνήνεγκεν ἅπερ ἀνέλαβεν Clem.*exc.Thdot*.58(p.126.13; M.9.688A); ὁ ἐνανθρωπήσας...ἵνα ἀνασώσηται τὴν εἰκόνα καὶ ἀναπλάσῃ τὸν ἄνθρωπον Gr.Naz.*or*.7.23(M.35.785C); **2.** *preserve* ἵνα... ἀνασώσῃ πόνους τοῦ προλεχθέντος χρόνου Ephr.1.318F; **3.** *preserve in memory* ἀγαπῶντες, εἰ...ἀποστόλων τὰς διαδοχὰς κατὰ τὰς διαπρεπούσας...ἐκκλησίας ἀνασωσαίμεθα Eus.*h.e*.1.1.4(M.20.52A); **4.** *rescind* a capital sentence τὴν ἐπ' αὐτοὺς θανατηφόρον ἀνασωσάμενος ψῆφον Philost.*h.e*.9.6(M.65.573A).

ἀνάταξις, ἡ, *arrangement, pattern*, *T.Sal*.D 8.5.

ἀνατάσσω, **1.** *arrange, appoint* τὸν κύκλον τῶν φλβʹ ἐτῶν ἀ. *Chron.Pasch*.p.10(M.92.88C); med., *set forth in order, compose, compile* Εὐνομίου...ἐγκώμιον ἀ. Philost.*h.e*.3.21(M.65.509C); Andr.Caes. *Apoc*.67(M.106.773B); **2.** *lift up* [φω]νὰς ἀπὸ ψυχῆς καὶ καρδίας πρὸς σὲ ἀνατεταγμένας *Pap.Chr*.(p.431).

ἀνατατικός, *uplifting* ἡ τῶν ὁσίων θεολόγων ἀ. σοφία Dion.Ar.*c.h*.2.3(M.3.141B); neut. as subst., *means of rising* ὁ θεῖος λόγος, πάντοθεν τὸ ἀ. ἡμῖν ποριζόμενος Jo.D.*imag*.1.11(M.94.1241B).

ἀνατατικῶς, *upwards, with uplifting effect* πᾶσα πατροκινήτου φωτοφανείας πρόοδος...ἀ. ἡμᾶς ἀναπληροῖ Dion.Ar.*c.h*.1.1(M.3.120B); πάντα πρὸς τὴν μίαν ἀρχὴν ἀ. ἐπιστρέφει †Proc.G.*Procl*.(M.87.2792[h]C); Max.*ambig*.(M.91.1385B).

ἀνατείν-ω, *draw* a sword, Anast.S.*haer*.(p.270); med. and pass., *reach up* \~όμενοι ἄνω τῇ ἐννοίᾳ Clem.*paed*.1.5(p.99.31; M.8.269A); Ath.*fr.Job*(M.27.1345A); Χριστὸς...διδάσκων ἡμᾶς...θεοῦ αἰτεῖν καὶ πρὸς αὐτὸν ἀ. Jo.D.*f.o*.3.24(M.94.1089D); *direct* one's remarks, *make reference* to πολλὰ πρὸς τὸ ἀνθρώπινον \~όμενος διελέχθη Bas.*hom. in Ps*.44:7(1.165C; M.29.404B).

ἀνατειχίζω, met., *build up, edify*, Cyr.*Joel*.41(3.239D); id.*Is*.2.5 (2.342A).

***ἀνατείχισμα**, τό, *defence* Χριστοῦ μυστήριον, ὅπλον ὥσπερ τι καὶ ἀ. Cyr.*ador*.2(1.79E).

***ἀνατενιστός**, *not to be gazed on*, of the divinity of Christ ὑπὸ τῶν χερουβὶμ ἀ. *A.Xanthipp*.14(p.68.14).

ἀνατήκω, *soften again*, Meth.*res*.1.44(p.292.4; M.18.273A).

ἀνατίθημι, **A.** act.; **1.** *refer, attribute, assign* δεῖ...τῷ θεῷ τὴν κατὰ πάντων ἐξουσίαν ἀ. *M.Polyc*.2.1; Eus.*Marcell*.1.1(p.5.6; M.24.720B) cit. s. ἀνθρώπινος; ἡλίῳ καὶ σελήνῃ...τὴν τοῦ θεοῦ τιμὴν ἀ. Ath.*gent*.9(M.25.17C); πάντα ὅσα μετὰ τὸ γενέσθαι ἄνθρωπος, ἀνθρωπίνως λέγει, ταῦτα τῇ ἀνθρωπότητι δίκαιον ἀ. id.*Ar*.3.43(M.26.413B); Chrys.*hom.5.1 in 2Cor*.(10.466B); ref. Jo.7:16 ἀ. χρησίμως τῷ θεῷ καὶ πατρὶ τὴν διδασκαλίαν Cyr.*Jo*.4.5(4.413A); ὅσα ἐστὶ τοῦ πατρὸς καὶ αὐτοῦ, τῷ...πνεύματι κοινωνικῶς καὶ ἡνωμένως ἀ. Dion.Ar.*d.n*.2.1(M.3.637C); **2.** *set up* as objects of worship ἀνθρώπους καὶ ἀνθρώπων μορφὰς... εἰς θεοὺς ἀ. Ath.*gent*.9(M.25.20A); *ib*.23(48A); fig. and met., *set up* a verbal image τὴν διὰ λόγων εἰκόνα τῇ τοῦ θεοφιλοῦς ἀ. μνήμῃ Eus.*v.C*.1.10(p.11.28; M.20.921C); as an example ἀνατύπωσιν ὥσπερ εὐαγοῦς πολιτείας τὰ καθ' ἑαυτὸν ἀ. [sc. Χριστός] Cyr.*apol.Thdt*.10 (p.139.27; 6[1].234C); *set forth, publish* ταύτην ἀ. πᾶσαν τὴν ἱστορίαν Chrys.*hom.26.6 in Mt*.(7.322A); *exalt*, Dion.Ar.*c.h*.13.4(M.3.304C); **3.** *set up as votive gift*; *dedicate*, Eus.*h.e*.5.26(M.20.509A); Ath.*inc*.56.1(M.25.196A); **4.** *set apart, devote*; **a.** things to God πάντα τὸν πλοῦτον ἀ. τῷ θεῷ Or.*Jo*.19.10(2; p.309.23; M.14.544B); ref. sabbath ὁ καιρὸς...ἅγιος ἀνατεθειμένος εἰς ἑορτὴν τῷ Χριστῷ Cyr.*Jo*.4.6 (4.428D); Andr.Caes.*Apoc*.68(M.106.444B) v. ἀνάθεμα; **b.** oneself or another to God, Just.*1apol*.25.2(M.6.365B); Clem.*str*.4.5(p.257.26; M.8.1233B); Or.*schol.in Cant*.2:16(M.17.265D); δείξωμεν τοῖς ἔργοις ὅτι...οὐδενὶ ἄλλῳ ἢ αὐτῷ ἀνεθήκαμεν id.*hom.5.2 in Jer*.(p.32.27; M.13.300A); Meth.*symp*.5.1(p.53.15; M.18.97B); Ammon.*Jo*.4:24(M.85.1424B); of candidate for baptism σοὶ αὐτὸν ἀνατίθεμεν Serap. *euch*.20.1; **c.** *devote* oneself to study, Eus.*h.e*.6.3.9(M.20.529B); to spiritual life, Gr.Nyss.*ep*.2(M.46.1009B).

B. med.; **1.** *set up* a house *for oneself*, Gennad.*fr.Gen*.1:26(M.85.1632C); **2.** *set forth, communicate*, Chrys.*hom.5.2 in 2Tim*.(11.687A); Jo.Mosch.*prat*.176(M.87.3045B); Sophr.H.*ep.syn*.(M.87.3149D); intrans., *confer* (= προσανατίθεμαι); ref. Gal.1:16, Chrys.*hom.21.1 in Ac*.(9.168E); id.*comm.in Gal*.1:16(10.675E); **3.** *take back, revoke* a sentence, Chrys.*hom.4.3 in 2Thess*.(11.534A); **4.** *put back* in time, *delay, postpone*, Synes.*ep*.72(M.66.1436B); Philost.*h.e*.8.6(M.65.561A).

ἀντιμάω, med., *value*, Mel.*pass*.39 p.14.22.

ἀνατινάσσω, *shake up*; bedding, Clem.*paed*.3.10(p.264.30; M.8.621A).

ἀνατολή, ἡ, **A.** *rising*; **1.** of sun; hence *dawn* of future life, Or.*Jo*.10.18(13; p.189.15; M.14.337C); met., of Christ (cf. Zach.6:12), Just.*dial*.100.4(M.6.709C); ἀνατολαὶ ἀνατολῶν ἐπέχουσι τὸ πᾶν, καὶ ὁ...πολὺς μέγας ἐπανθεῖ Χριστὸς τοῖς ὅλοις ὑπὲρ ἥλιον ‡Chrys.*pasch*.6.1(p.117.6; 8.264D); ἣν...ἀ., τουτέστι δικαιοσύνης ἥλιος...ὅτι φῶς ἐστι τὸ ἀληθινόν...εἰς νοῦν ἀνατέλλων Cyr.*Zach*.20(3.678A); ἐκδεχομένους τὴν ἀ. τῆς φωτοφανείας τῆς δευτέρας τοῦ Χριστοῦ παρουσίας ‡Bas.*h.myst*.10(p.260.16); χαῖρε, πύλη...ἐξ ἧς ἡ τῆς ζωῆς ἀ. Thdr. Stud.*nativ.BMV* 7(M.96.639D); text applied to Zerubbabel γνώμῃ θείᾳ ἀνὴρ ἀναπέφανται, ᾧπερ ἐκ τοῦ πράγματος ὄνομα ἀ. λέγει δὲ τὸν Ζοροβάβελ Thdr.Mops.*Zach*.6:9–15(M.66.541A); ταῦτα δὲ...περὶ τοῦ Ζοροβάβελ προαγορεύει, οὐχ ὡς μηδέπω τεχθέντος, ἀλλ' ὡς μηδέπω τὴν ἡγεμονίαν παρειληφότος. ἀ. δὲ αὐτὸν ὀνομάζει, ἐπειδὴ δίκην φωτὸς τοῖς τηνικάδε τὴν Ἱερουσαλὴμ οἰκοῦσιν ἀνέτειλεν, ἀωρίᾳ κακῶν ...κατεχομένοις Thdt.*Zach*.6:12–13(2.1621); ref. Gen.38:27–30 [sc. ὁ βίος] πρῶτος [i.e. before giving of Law] διὰ τοῦ Ζαρὰ ἐδηλοῦτο, ὃς ἑρμηνεύεται ἀ.· φωτὸς γὰρ εὐσεβείας αἱ πρῶται τῆς ἀ. αὐγαί, διὰ τῶν πρώτων ἐν ἀνθρώποις εὐσεβησάντων ἐξέλαμψαν Eus.*qu.Steph*.7.5 (M.22.909A); **2.** *the east, oriental world* Παῦλος...κῆρυξ γενόμενος ἔν τε τῇ ἀ. καὶ ἐν τῇ δύσει *1Clem*.5.6; Ath.*apol.sec*.65(p.144.21; M.25.365C); ἡ ἀ. πᾶσα σχεδὸν...(λέγω δὲ ἀ. τὰ ἀπὸ τοῦ Ἰλλυρικοῦ μέχρις Αἰγύπτου) μεγάλῳ χειμῶνι...κατασείεται...ὑπὸ...Ἀρείου Bas.*ep*.70 (3.163D; M.32.433C); **3.** sing. and plur. with preps., *eastwards*; **a.** as direction of prayer and worship, v. εὐχή; ref. Zach.14:4 οἱ Ἰουδαῖοι ἐν Ἱερουσαλὴμ προσευχόμενοι κατὰ ἀνατολάς, προσεύχονται εἰς τὸ ὄρος τῶν Ἐλαιῶν...πρὸς δὲ Ἕλληνας ἐκεῖνό φαμεν, ὅτι οὐχ ὡς ἐν ἀ. περιγραφομένου τοῦ θεοῦ κατὰ ἀ. προσκυνοῦμεν· ἀλλ' ἐπειδὴ ὁ θεὸς φῶς ἀληθινόν ἐστι...πρὸς τὸ φῶς τὸ κτιστὸν ἀφορῶντες, οὐκ αὐτὸ ἀλλὰ τὸν ποιητὴν αὐτοῦ προσκυνοῦμεν ‡Ath.*qu.Ant*.37(M.28.620A); ref. Mal.4:2, ‡Bas.*h.myst*.10(p.260.9); Jo.D.*f.o*.4.12(M.94.1133Bff.); in baptismal rite ὅτε οὖν τῷ σατανᾷ ἀποτάττῃ...ἀνοίγεταί σοι ὁ παράδεισος...καὶ τούτου σύμβολον, τὸ στραφῆναί σε ἀπὸ δυσμῶν πρὸς ἀ. τοῦ φωτὸς τὸ χωρίον Cyr.H.*catech*.19.9; *Const.App*.7.45.2; **b.** ref. orientation of churches ὁ οἶκος ἔστω ἐπιμήκης, κατὰ ἀνατολὰς τετραμμένος, ἐξ ἑκατέρων τῶν μερῶν ἔχων τὰ παστοφόρια πρὸς ἀ. *Const.App*.2.57.3; οἱ...ἀπόστολοι κατὰ ἀ. τὰς τῶν Χριστιανῶν ἐκκλησίας προσέχειν ἐποίησαν, ἵνα πρὸς τὸν παράδεισον ἀφορῶμεν ‡Ath.*qu.Ant*.37(M.28.620B).

B. *growing, springing up* διδόναι...ὑετὸν ἐν ἐρήμοις εἰς ἀ. χλόης *Pss.Sal*.5.11; Nil.*exerc*.49(M.79.780B).

ἀνατολικός, *eastern*; met., ref. Gen.2:8 τῆς ἐκπτώσεως τῶν φωτεινῶν τε καὶ ἀ. τῆς μακαριότητος τόπων...τὴν μνήμην Gr.Nyss. *or.dom*.5(p.102.15; M.44.1184C); of persons or communities εἴης πρᾷος...τοῖς σοῖς ἀ. Const.ap.Eus.*v.C*.2.55(p.63.25; M.20.1029C); *Symb.Ant*.(345)10(p.254.11; M.26.736A); ὑποστάσεις οἱ ἀ. λέγουσιν, ἵνα τὰς ἰδιότητας τῶν προσώπων ὑφεστώσας καὶ ὑπαρχούσας γνωρίσωσιν Geo.Laod.*ep.dogm*.(p.288.21; M.42.432D); Ποιμήν, ἥτις ἔν τισιν ἀ. ἐκκλησίαις δημοσίᾳ ἀναγινώσκεται Hier.*vir.ill*.(tr.Sophr.Pal.)10 (p.14.1; M.*PL*.23.657A, Lat. *apud quasdam Graeciae ecclesias*).

***ἀνατολόβλεπτος**, *facing east*, of BMV ref. Ezech.44:1ff. χαῖρε, πύλη, ἡ ἀ. Thdr.Stud.*nativ.BMV* 7(M.96.689D).

***ἀνατομεύς**, ὁ, *dissector*, met. ἀ. ... τῶν προφητικῶν λόγων Or. *hom.39.2 in Jer*.(p.297.32; M.13.544C).

ἀνατομή, ἡ, **1.** *cutting up, dissection*; of martyrdom, v.l. in Ign. *Rom*.5.3; **2.** *opening up* of ground in ploughing, Cyr.*Lc*.9:61 (p.98.18).

ἀνατομικός, *relating to anatomy* ἀ. ἐγχειρήσεσιν ‡Gr.Nyss.*or.1 in Gen.1:26*(M.44.257B); ἀ. βίβλοις Melet.*nat.hom*.synops.(M.64.1081B).

ἀνατρεπτικός, **1.** *turning upside down, overthrowing*, met. νόμοι τῶν ἐξ αἰῶνος παρ' αὐτοῖς Ἕλλησιν ἐθῶν ἀ. Eus.*d.e*.3.6(p.138.11; M.22.233A); Chrys.*hom.60.3 in Mt*.(7.610A); *refuting* wrong ideas, Dion.Al.ap.Eus.*p.e*.7.19(334A; M.21.564B); Epiph.*haer*.76.13(p.360.14; M.42.545B); in bad sense, *subversive*, Or.*Cels*.2.2(p.128.31; M.11.797C); [sc. λόγια] πίστεως ἀ. *Const.App*.2.61.3; τὰ ῥήματα...ἀ. τῆς ἀναστάσεως Chrys.*hom.2.6 in Col*.(11.342B); **2.** pass., *subverted* ἁμαρτανόντων ἡμῶν ὁ λογισμὸς ἀ. τῆς ἁμαρτίας γίνεται Proc.G.*Gen*.3:13 (M.87.201B).

ἀνατρεπτικῶς, *by way of refutation* or *subversion*, Epiph.*haer*.26.7(p.283.25; M.41.341B); *ib*.76.31(p.380.32; M.42.580C); *ib*.76.51(p.405.25; 624B).

***ἀνάτρεπτος**, *unchanged*, prob. f.l. for ἀπαράτρεπτος or ἄτρεπτος, ‡Just.*qu.et resp*.46(M.6.1292C).

ἀνατρέπω, **1.** *overthrow, upset*; *root up* ἀπὸ ψυχῆς ἀ. ... συγγεννηθέντα...δόγματα Or.*Cels*.2.2(p.128.24; M.11.797B); *refute*; *subvert* ῥήματα δούλων ἀ. δυνάμενα τὸν δεσπότην Chrys.*hom.1.1 in Philm*. (11.775C); *M.Pers*.1.3(p.423.9); **2.** *turn back* εἰς φυγὴν ἀ. Meth.*res*.2.4(p.337.14; M.41.1169C); *Pers*.(p.25.5); **3.** *throw back, throw open* gates, Chrys.*hom.9.1 in Mt*.(7.130E); hence *break open* a seal, id. *hom.10.4 in 1Thess*.(11.501A); **4.** *take back* a gift, id.*hom.61.4 in Mt*.(7.616C).

ἀνατρέχω, trans., *outrun, surpass*, Cyr.*glaph.Gen*.1(1.5D); *Exorc*.28(p.341).

ἀνάτρητος, *bored through*, Synes.*ep*.52(M.66.1380C).

ἀνατροπή, ἡ, *overthrowing, subversion* τὴν περιτομὴν ἀ. τοῦ εὐαγγελίου Chrys.*comm.in Gal*.1:7(10.669B); *checking*, of death as necessary ἐν τοῖς πᾶσιν...οἷς ἡ διάνοια πρόχειρος εἰς ἁμαρτίαν, πρὸς ἀ. ταύτης Tit.Bost.*Man*.2.12(M.18.1157A).

***ἀνατροπικῶς**, *by way of refuting*, Epiph.*haer*.76.27(p.375.22; M.42.572A).

ἀνατροφή, ἡ, *nurture, nourishment*; spiritual εἰς ἀ. σωτηρίας Clem.*paed*.1.6(p.114.24; M.8.300A); διὰ τὴν ἀ. τὴν ἐκ τοῦ λόγου *ib*. (p.119.24; 308C).

***ἀναττίκιστος**, *not in Attic style, not 'highbrow'*, Isid.Pel.*epp*.5.263(M.78.1489C).

ἀνατυπ-όω, **A.** *impress*; **1.** *stamp* τὸν...Χριστοῦ χαρακτῆρα ἐν αὐτῷ [sc. τῷ νομίσματι] κατὰ τοῦ ἰδίου ἀνετυπώσατο ‡Jo.D.*ep. Thphl*.3(M.95.348C); met. of issuing coinage Νεστόριος...τὴν μὲν θεοτόκος φωνὴν...ἀπεβάλετο, τὴν δὲ χριστοτόκος παραχαράξας ἀντεχάλκευσέ τε καὶ ἀνετύπωσε Evagr.*h.e*.1.2(p.7.10; M.86.2424B); **2.** *mould, form, fashion* τὰ μὲν φαῦλα φεύγειν, ἐν δὲ τοῖς βελτίστοις ἑαυτὸν ~οῦν Ath.*Ar*.3.20(M.26.365C); Gr.Nyss.*Eun*.1(1 p.151.12; M.45.392B); ὁ τοῦ υἱοῦ τὴν οἱονεὶ μορφὴν τῇ διανοίᾳ λαβών, τῆς πατρικῆς ὑποστάσεως τὸν χαρακτῆρα ἀνετυπώσατο id.*diff.ess*.8(M.32.340B); οὐκ ἂν ὁ Χριστὸς ἐλάμβανεν ἑαυτῷ σῶμα καὶ ἔπλασε, τὴν εἰκόνα τοῦ δημιουργοῦ εἰς ἑαυτὸν ~ῶν Epiph.*haer*.44.4(p.195.15; M.41.828A); **3.** *remodel, form anew* διὰ γὰρ τὴν ἐκείνου γραφὴν καὶ αὐτὴ ἡ ὕλη ἐν ᾗ καὶ γέγραπται, οὐκ ἐκβάλλεται, ἀλλ' ἐν αὐτῇ ~οῦται Ath.*inc*.14.1(M.25.120C); Epiph.*haer*.30.1(p.333.14; M.41.405B).

B. *represent*; **1.** in gen. ἄλλῳ τινὶ [v.l. ἐπ' ἄλλου τινὸς] τὴν ἐξήγησιν ἀνετυπωσάμην *Hom.Clem*.14.10; Gr.Naz.*or*.11.2(M.35.833B); καθάπερ τι βασιλείας εἶδος ἐν αὐτοῖς καθορᾶν τὸ διὰ τῶν καθαρῶν νοημάτων ~ούμενον Gr.Nyss.*hom.1 in Cant*.(M.44.776B); τί...τούτου...αἰσχρότερον τοῦ θήλειαν ἑαυτῷ ~οῦν τὸ πνεῦμα τῆς ἀληθείας; Epiph.*haer*.66.33(p.72.24; M.42.81B); μηδὲ...διπρόσωπον ἡμῖν ~ου τὸν Ἐμμανουήλ Cyr.*inc.unigen*.(5^{1}.694E); **2.** *picture, envisage* οὐδὲ γὰρ ἤργει [sc. ὁ δημιουργός] οὐδέποτε, τῷ λογισμῷ ~ούμενος ἐν ἑαυτῷ τὸ κάλλος αὐτοῦ τῆς τεχνῆς Meth.*arbitr*.22.9 (p.205.13); τὰ ἀνυπόστατα...κατὰ δὲ ἀναζωγράφησίν τινα τῆς ἐννοίας καὶ φαντασίαν μόνην ~ούμενα Bas.*Eun*.1.6(1.217C; M.29.524A); ἀνετύπωσεν ἡ ψυχὴ τὴν ὄψιν Chrys.*hom.18.4 in Jo*.(8.109E); διὰ τῶν ὁρωμένων...τὸν ποιητὴν τούτων...ἀνετυπώσατο Max.*ambig*.(M.91.1216B); **3.** *picture again*, ‡Meth.*Sym.et Ann*.2(M.18.352B); ἀνατύπωσόν μοι καὶ ἔτι εἰκόνα τῆς ματαιότητος τοῦ κόσμου †Jo.D.*B.J*.14 (M.96.981A); **4.** *imagine* ἄνθρωποι δὲ ταύτην [sc. κακίαν] ὕστερον ἐπινοεῖν ἤρξαντο καὶ καθ' ἑαυτῶν ~οῦσθαι Ath.*gent*.2(M.25.5C); ἀνετυπώσατό τινα ὁμιλίαν οὐκ εὐπρεπῆ Bas.*hom*.3.1(2.17C; M.31.200D); τούτων μὲν οὐδὲν προσεδόκων ἀλλὰ τἀναντία ἀνετύπουν παρ' ἐμαυτῷ Chrys.*ep*.14.1(3.595E); **5.** *devise* ἡ ψυχὴ...ζητοῦσα τὸν θεὸν κατὰ πλάνην πολλοὺς θεοὺς ἀνετύπωσε Tat.*orat*.13(p.14.30; M.6.836A); εἴδωλον δέ, ὅσα ~οῦσα ψυχὴ ποιεῖ ἐξ οὐχ ὑπαρχόντων πρωτοτύπως Or.*adnot.in Ex*.20:4(M.17.16C); Ath.*inc*.11.4(M.25.116B); ἁπλῆν εἶναι καὶ πάντῃ μίαν, φησί, τούτων ἑκάστην τῶν οὐσιῶν, ἃς τῷ λόγῳ ἀνετυπώσατο Gr.Nyss.*Eun*.1(1 p.89.8; M.45.321A).

C. *typify, figure* διὰ δὲ τοῦ ὕψους τῶν ἑξήκοντα πηχῶν τοὺς ἑξήκοντα πατριάρχας, δι' ὧν τὸ κατὰ σάρκα ἡ εἰκὼν τοῦ θεοῦ ὁ λόγος ἀνετυπώθη καὶ ἀνεπλάσθη Hipp.*Dan*.2.27.7; τῶν προσφερομένων θυμάτων, ἃ μὲν ἐδήλου Χριστὸν ὡς ὑπὲρ ἡμῶν σφαζόμενον, ἃ δὲ καὶ ἡμᾶς ~οῖ, μονονουχὶ καταθυμιῶντας τῷ θεῷ τὴν...ζωήν Cyr.*ador*.15(1.520D); id.*Jon*.1(3.366C).

ἀνατύπωσις, ἡ, **1.** *formation*, lit. ὡς τὸ φύραμα...εἰς...βελτίω ἀ. κατασκευάζεται Epiph.*haer*.37.1(p.52.11; M.41.644B); of an idea διὰ τῆς ἀ. τῶν ἐννοιῶν Marc.Er.*opusc*.5.10(M.65.1045C); hence *conception*, Gr.Naz.*or*.20.9(M.35.1076B); *ib*.29.4(p.78.1; M.36.77C); **2.** *representation* διὰ τῆς ὀνειρώδους...τῶν δογμάτων ἀ. Gr.Nyss.*Eun*.1 (1 p.138.9; M.45.376D); Cyr.*apol.Thdt*.10(p.139.26; 6^{1}.234B); Max.*ep*.4(M.91.416B); ἐπὶ ταῖς εἰδωλικαῖς ἀ. Thdr.Stud.*antirr*.1.7(M.99.337A); **3.** *prefiguration* ὁ Μωσῆς εἰκόνα καὶ ἀ. τῆς ἐν Χριστῷ μεσιτείας τὰ καθ' ἑαυτὸν ἐποιεῖτο Cyr.*ador*.2(1.50E).

***ἀναυάγητος**, *not shipwrecked*; of ships, Cyr.*deip.BMV* 1(p.19.11; M.76.256B); Rom.Mel.(*AS* 1 p.46); of sailors, ‡Chrys.*Joseph* 1 (6.604A); Leont.B.*parasc*.(M.86.1993B); hence *unsubmerged*, ref. Gen.1:9 ἀ. τοῖς πελάγεσι φυλάττων τὴν ἤπειρον Bas.Sel.*or*.1.2(M.85.32B); in gen., *unharmed* οἱ τρεῖς παῖδες...τὴν ἀνθρακίαν ὡς ῥοδοπαράδεισον κατανοοῦντες, ἀ. διέμειναν Eus.Al.*serm*.1(M.86.317C).

ἀναυξάνω, *increase* ἀνηύξαντο δὲ λαοί †Apoll.*met.Ps*.106:38(M.33.1480A; ed. ἀνηέξηντο p.228).

***ἀναυσία**, ἡ, *remedy for sickness*, Jo.Clim.*past*.2(M.88.1168D).

ἀναϋτέω, *call upon, invoke*, †Apoll.*met.Ps*.41:8(M.33.1369D); *ib*. 77:34(1425C).

[*]**ἀναύχενος**, = sq., s.v.l., Cosm.Mel.*schol*.in Gr.Naz.*carm*.2.2.7 (*poem*.)104(M.38.487).

ἀναύχην, *without a neck*, Gr.Naz.*carm*.2.2(poem.)7.104(M.37. 1559A).

[*]**ἀναφαλανδός**, = ἀναφάλαντος, *forehead-bald*, *A.Petr.et Paul*.9 (p.183.2); *ib*.21(p.188.8).

[*]**ἀναφαλάς**, = foreg., Jo.Mal.*chron*.10 p.256(M.97.388C); *ib*.5 p.106(M.97.196B).

ἀναφανδόν, **1.** lit., *visibly, openly*; as indecl. adj. μίξεις ἀ. Bas. *leg.lib.gent*.2(p.45; M.31.569A); **2.** met., *clearly* ἀ., οὐ δι' αἰνιγμάτων Clem.*paed*.2.10(p.211.10; M.8.504B); Meth.*res*.1.52(p.307.8; M.41. 1125C); μονονουχὶ βοῶντος τοῦ τύπου καὶ ἀ. ἀνακεκραγότος Cyr.*Os*.34 (3.62C).

***ἀναφέρετος**, v.l. for ἀναφαίρετος, *Lit.Jac*.(p.184.18).

ἀναφέρ-ω, **A.** *bring, carry, lift up*; *bring forth*, fig. τοῦ πνεύματος [sc. in baptism]...εἰς τὰς ἡμετέρας ἐμπεσόντος ψυχάς...τὴν...εἰκόνα τοῦ ἐπουρανίου...ὡς ἀπὸ χωνευτηρίου στίλβουσαν ∼οντος Chrys.*hom. 10.2 in Jo*.(8.59E); **1.** *hunch* the shoulders, Chrys.*hom.17.7 in Mt*.(7.232A, v.l. φερομένους); **2.** *take up* to heaven τὴν ψυχὴν εἶδεν ∼ομένην ὁ γέρων Ath.*v.Anton*.60(M.26.932A); εἰς οὐρανὸν οἱ πιστοὶ ∼ονται Cosm.Ind.*top*.3(M.88.137B); esp. ref. Ascension ∼ων εἰς τὸν οὐρανὸν ἣν ἐφόρει σάρκα Ath.*Ar*.3.48(M.26.425B); ἡμεῖς...οὓς ἀνέφερεν...διὰ τοῦ ἰδίου σώματος id.*inc*.25.6(M.25.140C); πάλιν εἰς οὐρανὸν ∼όμενος...καὶ ὡς ἐν θριάμβῳ νικηφόρος ∼όμενος Cosm.Ind. *top*.2(M.88.121D) cf. ὁ...Ἰησοῦς...ἀνήνεγκεν ἅπερ ἀνέλαβεν Clem. *exc.Thdot*.58(p.126.14; M.9.688A); **3.** *raise, uplift*, spiritually ἀνήνεγκεν ἐκ τοῦ σκότους Hegem.*Arch*.7(p.10.14; M.10.1437B); ἵνα...εἰς μείζονα ἀνενεχθῶσιν Chrys.*hom.54.1 in Mt*.(7.546B, v.l. ἐνεχθῶσιν); **4.** *bear, take upon oneself*; of Christ τὰς ἁμαρτίας ἡμῶν αὐτὸς ἀνοίσει Just.*dial*.13.7(M.6.504B); Ath.*Ar*.2.62(M.26.144A); ὁ κύριος... ∼ων διὰ τοῦτο γίνεσθαι καθ' ἡμᾶς Vict.*Mc*.15:24(p.437.7); *undergo* ἐνδείας οὐ χαλεπῶς ∼ουσιν Gr.Naz.*or*.43.34(M.36.541C); **5.** *bring up, raise* a matter εἴ τινά σοι δοκεῖ μὴ καλῶς εἰρῆσθαι...∼ων λέγε Meth.*arbitr*.3(p.155.1; M.18.248B); **6.** *call to mind, recall* ὥσπερ δι' ὀνείρων ἀμαυρὸν αὐτῶν τὸ εἶδος ∼ω *Hom.Clem*.12.8; φίλου εὐεργεσίας ἀ. Chrys.*hom.1.1 in Tit*.(11.731B); ὁ νοῦς...τῶν γεγονότων ἀ. τὰς φαντασίας †Nil.*mal.cog*.2(M.79.1201C); **7.** *raise, increase* τὰς ῥόγας ἀνήνεγκεν ἕως σ' νομισμάτων Thphn.*chron*.p.289(M.108.709B).

B. *offer*; **1.** for consideration, *bring forward, present* to the mind, Just.*dial*.71.3(M.6.644A); τὰ διδάγματα [sc. τοῦ Χριστοῦ] ἀ. id. *2apol*.2.2(M.6.444A); Or.*sel.in Ps*.16:14(M.12.1224A); **2.** ref. prayer and thanksgiving; OT ἐδέοντο Μωϋσέως ἵνα...ἀνενέγκῃ δέησιν *Barn*. 12.7; Ath.*exp.Ps*.141:2f.(M.27.540B); Diod.*Ps*.58:12(M.33.1596B); Christian τὰς προσευχὰς ἡμῶν...ἀ. πρὸς τὸν θεόν *2Clem*.2.2; οἱ πόδες ἐν ἐκκλησίᾳ...εὐχαριστίαν ∼ουσιν Bas.Sel.*or*.10.1(M.85.141A); in intercessory prayer, hence of liturg. commemoration μεγίστην ὄνησιν πιστεύοντες ἔσεσθαι ταῖς ψυχαῖς, ὑπὲρ ὧν ἡ δέησις ∼εται, τῆς... προκειμένης θυσίας Cyr.H.*catech*.23.9; περιεῖλεν τὸ ὄνομα αὐτοῦ...τοῦ μὴ ∼εσθαι ἐν τῇ προσφορᾷ Call.*v.Hyp*.(p.68); οὐ κοινωνῶ αὐτῷ οὔτε ∼ω τὸ ὄνομα αὐτοῦ *ib*.(p.69); (= *recitetur*) *Cod.Afr*.81; Anast.Ap. *a.Max*.2.17(M.90.153C); **3.** *offer* sacrifice; **a.** pagan φασί τινες... θεοὺς ἐφ' οἷς αἱ εἰκόνες...τὰς θυσίας ἐπ' ἐκείνους ∼εσθαι Athenag.*leg*. 18.1(M.6.925A); Ath.*gent*.25(M.25.49B); **b.** Jewish ἐν τῇ...παρουσίᾳ μὴ...θυσίας ἀφ' αἱμάτων ἢ σπονδῶν ἐπὶ τὸ θυσιαστήριον ∼εσθαι Just. *dial*.118.2(M.6.749C); ἀποφάσκει...τὸ δεῖν [sc. ἐπὶ τοῦ θυσιαστηρίου τοῦ Χριστοῦ]...∼εσθαι κάρπωμα Cyr.*ador*.9(1.309B); θυσίαν τῷ θεῷ ἀνενέγκας...ὁ Νῶε Cosm.Ind.*top*.2(M.88.85A); **4.** of Christ's self-offering εἰ...τῆς εὐωδίας τὸ θυμίαμα...τὸν κύριον ∼ειν λέγοιεν τῷ θεῷ...τὸ τῆς ἀγάπης δεκτὸν ∼ειν τὸν κύριον Clem.*paed*.2.8(p.197.21, 23; M.8.473B); Or.*Jo*.1.35(40; p.45.18; M.14.93A) cit. s. θυσία; ὑπὲρ πάντων τὴν θυσίαν ἀνέφερεν Ath.*inc*.20.2(M.25.132A); τὰ ἡμέτερα πάθη δέχεται παρ' ἡμῶν καὶ τῷ πατρὶ ἀ. ‡Ath.*Ar*.4.6(p.50.13; M.26. 476B); **5.** eucharistic, *offer* sacrifice γινέσθω ἡ θυσία...καὶ ὅταν ἀνενεχθῇ μεταλαμβανέτω ἑκάστη τάξις...τοῦ κυριακοῦ σώματος *Const. App*.2.57.21; also abs., *consecrate the eucharist, offer the* Christian *sacrifice* ἐπιτρέψεις δὲ αὐτῷ καὶ τὴν εὐχαριστίαν ἀνοῖσαι· ἐὰν δὲ...μὴ θελήσῃ ἀνενέγκαι, κἂν τὴν εἰς τὸν λαὸν εὐλογίαν αὐτὸν ποιήσασθαι καταναγκάσεις *ib*.5.28.3; μόνον τὸν μὲν πρεσβύτερον...ἀ., βαπτίζειν, εὐλογεῖν τὸν λαόν *ib*.3.20.2; **6.** Collyridian τινὲς...γυναῖκες...ἐν ἡμέρᾳ τινὶ...ἄρτον προτιθέασι καὶ ἀ. εἰς ὄνομα τῆς Μαρίας Epiph.*haer*.79.1 (p.476.18; M.42.741A); **7.** *set* the oblation *upon the altar* τῆς ἱερατικῆς λειτουργίας, τῆς τε τοῦ ἄρτου ἢ ποτηρίου ∼ειν [sc. τοὺς διακόνους] CAnc.*can*.2.

C. *bring* or *carry back*; **1.** *refer*; **a.** trans.; of persons, i.e. *interpret ...as referring* to τὸν ς' ἀριθμὸν εἰς τὴν ὕλην...ἀ. [sc. Heracleon] Or.*Jo*.10.38(22; p.214.33; M.14.380B); τὰς ἀποστολικὰς φωνὰς [sc. Col.1:15ff.] ἐπὶ τὴν σάρκα ἀ. Eus.*Marcell*.2.3(p.44.32; M.24.800B); ref. Lc.2:52 εἰς αὐτὸν [sc. Logos] ∼ουσι τὸ λεγόμενον 'προέκοπτεν' Ath.*Ar*.3.53(M.26.433C); **b.** pass. intrans.; of things, *have reference* to [Ex.12:10]...κεχρῆσθαι ὡς ∼ομένῳ ἐπὶ τὴν περὶ τὸν σωτῆρα οἰκονομίαν Or.*Jo*.10.16(13; p.187.3; 333C); εἰς αὐτὸν ἀ. ... ἡ ἄμπελος πολλαχῶς Meth.*symp*.10.5(p.127.31; M.18.201B); **2.** *report* τὴν... κατηγορίαν...∼ουσι δὲ καὶ τῷ βασιλεῖ Ath.*apol.sec*.65(p.144.4; M.25. 365A); εἴ τις...μὴ ∼ῃ τὸ ὄνομα αὐτοῦ Sophr.H.*conf*.(M.87.3369D); **3.** pass.; of a reading, *be read, occur* ἡ λέξις εὑρίσκεται παρὰ μὲν τοῖς ἑβδομηκονταδύο κειμένους [l. -μένη] ἐν δὲ τῷ ἑβραϊκῷ μὴ ∼ομένους [l. -μένη] Epiph.*metr*.7(M.43.248B).

ἀναφής, **1.** *impalpable*; of God, Tat.*orat*.4(p.5.4; M.6.813A); Gr.Nyss.*Eun*.12(1 p.274.9; M.45.980D); ψηλαφητὴ μὲν ἡ ἀνθρωπίνη φύσις, ἀ. δὲ τὸ θεῖον *ib*.(2 p.275.11; 885C); Jo.D.*f.o*.1.2(M.94.792C); of H. Ghost, Gr.Naz.*or*.41.9(M.36.441B); Gr.Nyss.*or.catech*.6(p.29. 10; M.45.25C) cit. s. ἀνείδεος; **2.** met., *not needing a touch* οὐκοῦν οὐκ ἐν γε τῷ θύειν τὸ δουλεύειν ἐστίν, ἀλλ' ἐν τῷ βουλεύεσθαι τρυφερόν τε καὶ οἷον ἀ. τοῖς αὐτοῦ θελήμασιν ὑποφέρειν τὸν αὐχένα Cyr.*Is*.4.1 (2.575C).

***ἀνάφθας**, ὁ, = νάφθας, *naphtha*, v.l. in Hipp.*haer*.5.17(p.115.19; M.16.3178B).

ἀναφοιτ-άω, **1.** *return, go back* ἦσαν ἐν ἐλπίσι τοῦ...εἰς τὴν ἄνωθεν αὐτοῖς...εὐγένειαν ∼ήσειν Cyr.*Nah*.15(3.493C); id.*ador*.1(1.32E); of Christ τὸν ἐν εἴδει τῷ καθ' ἡμᾶς ∼ῶντα θεὸν εἰς τὴν...οὐσιωδῶς ὑπάρχουσαν δόξαν id.*Ps*.46:6(M.69.1053D); ἀποπεράνας...τὸ μυστήριον, εἰς τὴν ἐνοῦσαν αὐτῷ κατὰ φύσιν ἀ. δόξαν id.*Lc*.19:11(M.72. 869C); **2.** *go up, ascend*, id.*glaph.Ex*.3(1.327C); of Christ τὴν ἀπὸ γῆς σάρκα πρὸς τὴν τῆς θεότητος φύσιν ἀ. id.*inc.unigen*.(5^{1}.684B); εἰς τὴν τῆς θεότητος δόξαν ∼ώσης αὐτοῦ τῆς σαρκός id.*Arcad*.(p.86.3; 5^{2}.78B); Jo.D.*f.o*.1.2(M.94.793A); Jo.Mon.*hymn.Geo*.9(M.96.1400D); met. ὁ νοῦς...ἀ. πρὸς τὸ ἄμεινον Cyr.*ador*.1(1.31B); id.*Ps*.17:34(M. 69.825B); πρὸς τὸ ὄρος τῶν ἀρετῶν τὴν ἀγάπην ∼ήσωμεν Jo.D.*hom*. 1.5(M.96.553A).

***ἀναφοίτησις**, ἡ, *ascent*; of Christ into heaven, Ath.*exp.Ps*. 67:34(M.27.304D); Cyr.*Ps*.7:8(M.69.752A); id.*Lc*.24:51(p.107.3); of his Resurrection, Thdr.Abuc.*opusc*.4(M.97.1521B); met. τὴν εἰς τὰ ὄρη νοητὴν ἀ. Cyr.*Ps*.10:2(M.69.789D).

ἀναφορά, ἡ, *leading up* to something *higher*; hence

A. *reference*; **1.** in gen. ὁ ἐξ...τὴν ἀ. εἰς τὸν υἱὸν ἀνείληφε τοῦ θεοῦ Meth.*symp*.8.11(p.95.15; M.18.157A); Eus.*d.e*.proem.(p.251.10; M.22. 413A); id.*h.e*.1.3.8(M.20.72B); Synes.*ep*.57(M.66.1393C); ταῦτα...τὴν ἀ. εἰς τὸ τοῦ...πατρὸς ἔχει πρόσωπον Cyr.*Jo*.1.5(4.48E); **2.** partic. of rel. of Son to Father πᾶσα...ἡ τοῦ κυρίου ἐνέργεια ἐπὶ τὸν παντοκράτορα τὴν ἀ. ἔχει Clem.*str*.7.2(p.7.21; M.9.412B); πᾶσα γὰρ ἀσεβὴς φωνὴ εἰς τὸν υἱὸν λέγεσθαι τολμωμένη εἰς τὸν πατέρα τὴν ἀ. ἔχει Alex.Al.*ep.Alex*.9(p.26.5; M.18.564A); Ath.*Ar*.2.62(M.26.277D); Gr.Nyss.*tres dii*(M.45.128B); of men to divine will, Const.ap.Eus. *v.C*.3.20(p.87.12; M.20.1080A); of creation to God, Gr.Nyss.*hex*.25 (M.44.85D); Thdr.Mops.*symb*.(p.98.26; M.66.1017C).

B. little different from preceding, *relationship*; **1.** of Son to Father ὁ δὲ ἐξ ἐκείνου [sc. τοῦ θεοῦ] ἔχων τὴν ἀ. ὡς ἐκεῖνον ἑνοῦται πάλιν Const.*or.s.c*.3(p.156.11; M.20.1237C); cf. supra A.2; **2.** of the two natures in Christ ἑνὸς προσώπου ἐφ' ὃ ἡ ἀ. τῶν τε φύσεων καὶ τῶν φυσικῶν ἰδιωμάτων *Lit.Jac*.(*NBP* 10^{2} p.37); in Nestorian controversy ὅταν τοίνυν ἐρωτῶσιν 'ἀνθρωποτόκος ἢ θεοτόκος ἡ Μαρία;' λεγέσθω παρ' ἡμῶν 'ἀμφότερα'. τὸ μὲν γὰρ φύσει τοῦ πράγματος, τὸ δὲ τῇ ἀ. Thdr.Mops.*fr.inc*.15(p.310.14; M.66.992B); but this conception of divinity *by relation* is rejected by orthodox, Cyr.*Chr. un*.(5^{1}.73Ef.); εἴ τις λέγει...κατ'...ἀ. ... τὴν ἕνωσιν τοῦ θεοῦ λόγου πρὸς ἄνθρωπον γεγενῆσθαι...ἀνάθεμα ἔστω Justn.*conf.anath*.4(p.90. 3; M.86.1015A); εἴ τις κατὰ ἀ. ... θεοτόκον λέγει τὴν...ἀειπάρθενον Μαρίαν...ἀ. ἔ. *ib*.5(p.92.1; 1015B); Oecum.*Apoc*.3:7(p.60); Max. *opusc*.(M.91.125Cf.); **3.** of incarnate Son's manhood to Father τῶν δὲ μετὰ τὴν ἕνωσιν τρόποι εἰσὶ τρεῖς...τὰ δὲ κατ' οἰκείωσιν καὶ ἀ., ὡς τὸ 'θεέ μου, θεέ μου, ἵνα τί με ἐγκατέλιπες;'...τὸ ἡμέτερον τοίνυν οἰκειούμενος πρόσωπον καὶ μεθ' ἡμῶν τάσσων ἑαυτόν, ταῦτα ἔλεγεν Jo.D.*f.o*.4.18(M.94.1185Df.); **4.** in gen.; body to soul, Clem.*str*.4.5 (p.257.33; M.8.1233C); other faculties to the reason, *ib*.6.16(p.500. 22; M.9.360C).

C. *transference* of idea, dist. from μεταφορά in that ἀ. implies the passage to a higher plane οὐκοῦν βίαιος καὶ κατηναγκασμένη τῶν προκειμένων λέξεων ἡ ἐπὶ τὴν σάρκα τοῦ σωτῆρος ἀ. Eus.*e.th*.3.3 (p.151.2; M.24.992A); τὰ ἀλληγορικῶς παρὰ τῶν προφητῶν περὶ τοῦ θεοῦ λεχθέντα κατ' ἀ. ἐκ τῶν φύσει εἰς τὸ οὐ φύσει ‡Just.*qu.et resp.*10 (M.6.1260B).

D. eucharistic *offering*; **1.** vague ref. to this as a whole, *Can.App.* 3; *Lit.*ap.*Const.App.*8.11.11; ἀναφοραὶ μυστηρίων ἐν ταῖς φυλακαῖς ἐπετελοῦντο Pall.*v.Chrys.*10(p.59.21; M.47.34); *M.Thdot.1* 7(p.65.17); Niceph.Ur.*v.Sym.*156(M.86.3132B); Cyr.S.*v.Euthym.*28(p.45.9); its place in whole liturgy προφητῶν ἀνάγνωσις καὶ εὐαγγελίου κηρυκία καὶ θυσίας ἀ. καὶ τροφῆς ἱερᾶς δωρεά *Const.App.*2.59.4; in rel. to intercessions μικρόν ἐστι...τὸ ἐν ταῖς ἁγίαις ἀ. ἀεὶ τὸ ὄνομά σου κεῖσθαι; Chrys.*hom.18.5 in Ac.*(9.151B); fig. ἀπὸ τοῦ περὶ τῆς εἰκόνος λόγου πεποιημένοι τὴν ἀρχὴν τῆς ἀ., ὅς ἐστιν ὁ Χριστός Or.*Jo.* 6.52(34; p.161.26; M.14.292B); **2.** properly of the *canon*, *anaphora*; **a.** in gen. πρὸ...τοῦ ταύτης [sc. τῆς ἀναιμάκτου θυσίας] ἀρχὴν ποιήσηται, τοῖς πᾶσι...παραγγέλλει λέγων· ἄνω σχῶμεν τὸν νοῦν καὶ τὰς καρδίας, καὶ τὴν τοῦ λαοῦ ὑπόσχεσιν δεξάμενος θαρρεῖ προσενέγκαι τῷ θεῷ τὴν ἀ. Cyr.S.*v.Euthym.*29(p.46.18); ἀ. λέγεται διὰ τὸ πρὸς θεὸν ἀναφέρεσθαι Anast.S.*synax.*(M.89.833C); ref. deacon's invitation before ἀναφορά: στήκετε...μετ' εὐλαβείας, στήκετε μετὰ φόβου ἐν τῇ φοβερᾷ ὥρᾳ τῆς ἀ. *ib.*(833B); *ib.*(836D); cf. πρόσσχωμεν τῇ ἁγίᾳ ἀ., ἐν εἰρήνῃ τῷ θεῷ προσφέρειν *Lit.Jac.*(p.196.20); **b.** consecratory effect of reciting it, Jo.Mosch.*prat.*25(M.87.2869Df.); **c.** its order traditional, *A.Thom.*B 48(p.39.33); ἀναφορὰν σχεδιάζει ἑτέραν παρὰ τὴν πατρόθεν ταῖς ἐκκλησίαις παραδεδομένην, μήτε τὴν τῶν ἀποστόλων αἰδεσθείς, μήτε δὲ τὴν τοῦ μεγάλου Βασιλείου ἐν τῷ αὐτῷ πνεύματι συγγραφεῖσαν, λόγου τινὸς κρίνων ἀξίαν· ἐν ᾗ ἀ. βλασφημιῶν (οὐ γὰρ εὐχῶν) τελετὴν ἀπεπλήρωσεν Leont.B.*Nest.et Eut.*3(M.86.1368C).

E. *report* συνετάξαμεν τῇδε ἡμῶν τῇ ἀ. καὶ τὸ ἀντίγραφον τῆς πίστεως CAnt.(363)*ep.*ap.Socr.*h.e.*3.25.16(M.67.453B).

F. = *prosphora*, eucharistic loaf λαμβάνει τὴν ἀ. σφραγίζων αὐτὴν μετὰ τῆς λόγχης *Euchol.*(p.85); *Nomoc.*12.

ἀναφορεύς, ὁ, *bearer, bearing-pole*, of Cross ὁ ἀληθινὸς βότρυς, ὁ ἐπὶ τῶν ξυλίνων ἀ. ἑαυτὸν δείξας Gr.Nyss.*hom.3 in Cant.*(M.44.829C); in gen. of a support, Eudoc.*Cypr.*2.112(M.85.849B).

ἀναφορικός, gram., *relative* τὸ ὅς, ἀ. ἄρθρον Areth.*Apoc.*1(M.106 508D).

ἀναφράσσω, 1. *block up*, *Apophth.Patr.*(M.65.416C); *Chron.Pasch.* p.298(M.92.745C); met. τῆς δυσσεβούσης ψυχῆς ἀ. ἐπαγγέλλεται τὰς ὁδοὺς...ὁ θεός Cyr.*Jo.*3.4(4.272C); **2.** *remove barriers, open* ἀναφράξαντες τὴν θύραν εἰσεληλύθαμεν Jo.Clim.*scal.*6(M.88.797A).

***ἀναφυή, ἡ,** *sprout*, met. ῥάβδος καὶ βλάστημα μὲν αὐτός [sc. Christ], ἤγουν ἀ. καὶ ἀνατολή Cyr.*Zach.*33(3.707B; φυή A).

***ἀναφυής,** *growing upwards*, met. ἀ. γὰρ ἡ ἀρετή, καὶ πρὸς τὸ ἄνω βλέπει Gr.Nyss.*hom.4 in Cant.*(M.44.849A).

ἀναφυράω, *mix with leaven*, fig. ἀναζυμωθέντες καὶ ἀναφυραθέντες αὐτοῦ τῷ πνεύματι ‡Chrys.*pasch.*6.3(p.161.11; 8.269E); τῇ τοῦ κυρίου ...σαρκώσει ἀ. τὸν ἅπαντα κόσμον Isid.Pel.*epp.*1.201(M.78.312B).

***ἀναφυρμός, ὁ,** *disturbance*, Cyr.*ador.*14(1.504B).

***ἀνάφυρσις, ἡ,** *ferment* ἡ ἐν πόλεσι καὶ θορύβοις ἀ. Isid.Pel.*epp.*1. 220(M.78.321A).

ἀναφύρ-ω, *mingle*; in eucharist ~ει ἑαυτὸν ἡμῖν...τούτῳ ~όμεθα καὶ γεγόναμεν ἡμεῖς Χριστοῦ σῶμα ἓν καὶ σὰρξ μία Chrys.*hom.82.5 in Mt.*(7.788B,C); κεράσωμεν οὖν ἑαυτοὺς εἰς σῶμα ἕν, οὐ τὰ σώματα ἀλλήλοις ~οντες, ἀλλὰ τὰς ψυχὰς ἀλλήλαις τῷ τῆς ἀγαπῆς συνδέσμῳ συνάπτοντες id.*prod.Jud.*1.6(2.385D).

ἀναφυσητός, *domed, arched*, Marc.Diac.*v.Porph.*75.

ἀναφυτεύ-ω, *plant*, fig. ~ει τὸ ἑαυτοῦ γεώργιον ὁ ἀληθινὸς γεωργὸς ἡμᾶς τοὺς ἀνθρώπους Gr.Nyss.*hom.15 in Cant.*(M.44.1092C).

ἀναφύω, 1. *cause to spring up*, met. ὁ...νόμος ὁ τοὺς ἐμπαθεῖς ἀ.... περισπασμούς Meth.*res.*2.6(p.340.15; M.18.304C); *Hom.Clem.*6.2; **2.** intrans., *spring up*; into spiritual life, Gr.Nyss.*or.catech.*40 (p.164.1; M.45.105A); Cyr.*Mal.*43(3.866A); of Christ's generation, id.*Jo.*3.6(4.312D).

ἀναφωνέω, 1. *announce, proclaim, acclaim*; **2.** *apply a term* to τό 'κύριος Σαβαώθ', τῷ τῶν ὅλων ἀ. θεῷ Cyr.*ador.*6(1.211B).

***ἀναφωνιστής, ὁ,** *singer*, Melet.*nat.hom.*13(M.64.1205B).

***ἀναφωτίς, ἡ,** *skylight*, Epiph.*mens.*3(M.43.241); *Dial.Tim.et Aquil.*117 r° (p.91).

ἀναχαίνω, *open the mouth*; *long for* ἄρα δυνάμεθα πρὸς ταῦτα ἀ. Ephr.1.25E; *cat.Ac.*1:4(p.5.23).

ἀναχαιτίζ-ω, 1. *hold back, check*, Chrys.*hom.86.2 in Mt.*(7.814A); αὐτοὺς ἀ. τῆς ἐλπίδος *ib.*78.1(751E); σεπταῖς ἀνεξικακίαις τὸν τῶν ἁγίων μυσταγωγὸν ἀ. νοῦν Cyr.*Lc.*6:27(M.72.593D); ἀτάκτους ὁρμὰς ἀ. Nil.*epp.*1.292(M.79.189B); **2.** *draw back*, intrans. act. and pass. ἀ. τῆς ἐπὶ τὸν θάνατον ὁρμῆς Clem.*paed.*1.9(p.140.20; M.8.353A); 'Ιορδάνην...ἀ. ἐπὶ τῇ αὐτῶν παρόδῳ Thdr.Heracl.*Is.*14:27(M.18.1340A); φύσις, ὅταν ἁμαρτάνουσα μὴ ~ηται Chrys.*hom.26.1 in Gen.*(4.244D).

***ἀναχάλκευσις, ἡ,** *forming anew, restoring* to life τὴν τῶν νεκρῶν ἀ. ‡Nil.*fr.pasch.*2(M.79.1496B); Cosm.Ind.*top.*3(M.88.165C).

ἀναχαλκεύω, *forge anew, restore*; **1.** lit. ἀνδρίαντα...ἀ. Chrys. *hom.8.1 in Col.*(11.380C); **2.** met., of restoration: to health, Cyr. *Jo.*2.5(4.193E); id.*Is.*5.6(2.919A); ‡Meth.*Sym.et Ann.*1(M.18.349A); to life, Cosm.Ind.*top.*3(M.88.144C); of human nature to immortality, Cyr.*Ps.*91:9(M.69.1228B); id.*Soph.*44(3.622D); Zach.Mit.*opif.* (M.85.1125B); of men to courage, Cyr.*Jo.*10.2(914A); τὴν τῆς... διεφθαρμένης συγχύσεως ἀ. αἵρεσιν Const.Pogon.*edict.*(H.3.1448A).

ἀναχαράσσω, *engrave anew*; of divine commandments engraved again on heart after being obliterated by sin, Gr.Nyss.*v.Mos.* (M.44.372D); id.*Pss.titt.*A 7(M.44.457A).

***ἀναχειροτον-έω,** *reordain* ~ῆσαί τινας ἐτόλμησεν ὃ μέχρι σήμερον οὐδεὶς τῶν αἱρετικῶν ποιήσας φαίνεται Bas.*ep.*130.2(3.222E; M.32. 564C); ref. glorification of Christ οὐ γὰρ ὁ ὢν κύριος ~εῖται πάλιν εἰς κυριότητα, ἀλλ' ἡ τοῦ δούλου μορφὴ κύριος γίνεται Gr.Nyss.*Apoll.*53 (M.45.1252C).

***ἀναχειροτόνησις, ἡ,** *reordination*, *Cod.Afr.*48; περὶ τοῦ μὴ γίνεσθαι ἀ. Phot.*nomoc.*1.25(M.104.1008C).

ἀναχέ-ω, 1. *pour over, saturate* τῇ ἀληθείᾳ τὸν ἀνακεχυμένον ἡμῶν τρόπον Clem.*paed.*1.5(p.102.8; M.8.273B); **2.** *pour back, reabsorb* Σαβελλιανοὶ...λέγοντες προφορικὸν καὶ πάλιν ~όμενον τὸν λόγον Epiph.*anac.*16(v.l. p.213.23; M.41.849); Thdt.*haer.*1.19(4.311); πνεῦμα...δύναμιν...οὔτε πρὸς τὸ ἀνύπαρκτον ~ομένην Jo.D.*f.o.*1.7(M. 94.805B); **3.** *mingle, pour together* ἡ μίξις...~ουσα καὶ ἀναμίξασα ἀμφοτέρων τὰ σώματα Chrys.*hom.12.5 in Col.*(11.420D); Sophr.H. *ep.syn.*(M.87.3184A); **4.** *spread* καλύπτρη...ὑπὲρ ὤμου...ἀγκέχυται λαιοῖο Paul.Sil.*Soph.*775(M.86.2149A).

ἀναχλαινόω, *clothe with a mantle*, Nonn.*par.Jo.*19:2(M.43.897B).

***ἀναχλοάζω,** *become young again*, Gr.Naz.*carm.*1.2.1.592(M.37. 567A).

[*]**ἀναχονεύω,** v. ἀναχωνεύω.

ἀναχρώννυμι, 1. *smear*, Chrys.*hom.6.8 in Mt.*(7.101B); id.*hom. 4.2 in Rom.*(9.457A); met. μέλιτος τὴν ἐπιστολὴν ἀ. id.*ep.*58(3.625D); **2.** *taint, infect*, id.*hom.15.1 in Eph.*(11.110B); id.*hom.57.3 in Jo.* (8.335D); id.*fem.reg.*3(1.253B); **3.** *perfume* τὸν ἀέρα ἀ. τῆς ὀσμῆς id. *hom.2.1 in 1Thess.*(11.432D), id.*hom.54.3 in Jo.*(8.313C); id.*ep.*27 (3.610C).

ἀνάχυσις, ἡ, *confusion*; in gen., Nil.*exerc.*46(M.79.776D); Cyr. *ador.*14(1.504B); id.*Abac.*58(3.573E); denied of natures of Christ οὐδὲ...ὁμοιότης ἀ. τινα τῶν ὑποστάσεων ἐργάσεται id.*Jo.*1.2(4.16B); μὴ ἄρα τις ἀ. συμβῆναι νομισθῇ id.*Nest.*1(p.22.8; 6.15C); καὶ οὐ δήπου φαμὲν ἀ. ... ὡς μεταστῆναι μὲν τὴν τοῦ λόγου φύσιν εἰς τὴν ἀνθρώπου id.*Heb.*(p.421.16; M.74.1004C); and of Persons of Trin. εἴπερ οὕτως ἔχων ὁμοούσιός ἐστι τῷ πατρί, τὴν δὲ εἰς ἄλληλα πάντως ἀ. ἐπιδέξεται τὰ ὁμοούσια, οὐδὲν κωλύσει κατὰ τὸ εἰκὸς πατέρα νοεῖσθαι τὸν υἱόν, ὡς ὁμοούσιον πατρί, καὶ μεταχωρεῖν εἰς ἐκεῖνο δυνάμενον ...ἀλλὰ τοῦτο ἄτοπον id.*Jo.*1.4(35E); τριάδα...ἄνευ προσωπικῆς ἀ. Sophr.H.*ep.syn.*(M.87.3152D).

***ἀναχυτέον,** *one must pour out, disperse*, Clem.*paed.*3.11(p.272. 34; M.8.640C).

ἀναχώνευσις, ἡ, *melting down again, recasting*, of body at resurrection ὅπως τὰ μὲν αἴσχη...διὰ τῆς...ἀ. ἀπόληται Meth.*res.*1.43 (p.290.11; M.18.272B); ὅταν...ἴδῃς...καταρρέουσαν ἡμῶν τὴν σάρκα... τὴν ἀ. ἀνάμενε Chrys.*Laz.*5.2(1.764C).

ἀναχωνεύ-ω, *melt down again, recast*; **1.** lit., Meth.*res.*1.43(pp.290. 4,291.7; M.18.272A,C); Chrys.*hom.40.2 in 1Cor.*(10.380B); id.*hom.8.3 in Col.*(11.384F); ἀναχονεῦσαι Nil.*epp.*2.200(M.79.305B); **2.** met., in baptism [sc. τὸ πνεῦμα] χωρὶς πυρὸς ~ον καὶ ἀνακτίζον δίχα συντρίψεως Gr.Naz.*or.*40.8(M.36.368B); τὸ πνεῦμα τὸ ἅγιον ὥσπερ ἐν χωνευτηρίῳ τῷ βαπτίσματι ~ον [sc. τὴν ψυχήν] Chrys.*hom.40.2 in 1Cor.* (10.380B); id.*Eutrop.*2.11(3.396Df.); †Jo.D.*B.J.*11(M.96.956C).

ἀναχωρ-έω, 1. *withdraw, leave*; **a.** lit., of those who withdraw from celebration of eucharist before it is finished, Chrys.*prod.Jud.* 1.4(2.374E); **b.** met., *leave* a subject, Chrys.*hom.32.4 in 1Cor.*(10. 291A); **2.** *withdraw* from world to live religious life ~ῶν τῶν βιωτικῶν πραγμάτων Mac.Aeg.*hom.*14.1(M.34.569D); ~ήσαντες τοῦ κόσμου...ἐν πολλῇ προσκαρτερήσει εὐχῆς καὶ νηστείας *ib.*29.2 (716C); *ib.*32.9(740B); as monks ἐν μοναστηρίοις...~οῦντες Epiph.*haer.*70.1 (p.232.18; M.42.340A); id.*exp.fid.*23(p.524.12; M.42.829A); and more esp. as hermits παρὰ τοῖς φύσει κατὰ τὰς ἐρημίας ~οῦσι id.*haer.* 64.4(p.410.1; M.41.1076C); ~εῖ ἐν σπηλαίῳ μόνος Pall.*v.Chrys.*5(p.28. 20; M.47.18); *Apophth.Patr.*(M.65.113C); ἔκτισεν δὲ μικρὸν κελλίον εἰς τὸ ἀναχωρῆσαι Jo.Mosch.*prat.*202(M.87.3092C); hermit life being called ὁ ἀνακεχωρημένος βίος Nil.*praest.*18(M.79.1081B); **3.** *depart*, in sense of *die*, Or.*sel.in Dt.*1:9f.(M.12.805B); of soul departing from body, Tit.Bost.*Man.*2.12(M.18.1157A); **4.** in pass. sense; **a.** *be withdrawn from, be without* σχήματος ∼ήσας ὁ θεὸς λόγος Didym.*Trin.*1.16(M.39.332C); **b.** *be deprived* εἴ τις...πράξειέ τι τοιοῦτον [sc. simoniacal practices] τῶν μὲν ἐνταῦθα θυσιαστηρίων ∼ήσει Bas.*ep.*53.2(3.147E; M.32.397C); **5.** perf. ptcpl., act. and pass., *separated, remote, hidden*; **a.** lit., of a place ταμιεῖον...οἶκον...ἀνακεχωρημένον Bas.*reg.br.*277(2.513A; M.31.1277A); neut. as subst. τὰ ἀνακεχωρημένα τῶν πόλεων Chrys.*hom.22.1 in Ac.*(9.178B); **b.** met., of life withdrawn from the standards of the world ὅταν τὸν τῶν πολλῶν βίον μιμώμεθα, ὥστε μὴ εἶναι ἀνακεχωρηκότα αὐτόν Or. *hom.14.16 in Jer.*(p.122.12; M.13.424D); neut. as subst. τὸ ἀνακεχωρηκὸς τῆς φύσεως ὁ παράδεισος ἐδήλου Chrys.*hom.5.4 in Col.* (11.364B); **c.** *esoteric*, of teachings of Gnostics ἀνακεχωρηκότα, καὶ τερατώδη, καὶ βαθέα μυστήρια Iren.*haer.*1.4.3(M.7.484B); of secret traditions of Jews κατά τινας παραδόσεις...ἀνακεχωρηκυίας Or.*Jo.* 19.15(4; p.315.4; M.14.553A); ἀ. λόγοι *ib.*(p.315.8; M.l.c.); and Egyptians, id.*Cels.*1.20(p.71.16; M.11.696B); of hidden (mystical) sense of scripture τὴν...ἐκδοχὴν...ἀνακεχωρηκυῖαν καὶ πνευματικήν id.*Jo.* 5.6(4; p.103.34; M.14.193A).

ἀναχώρησις, ἡ, 1. *departure*; **a.** in gen. ἀ. τῆς ἀποτυχίας Philost. *h.e.*9.15(M.65.580C); of demons driven out by Christ ἀ. ἀνθρώπων... πράττοντα Bas.Sel.*or.*23(M.85.276C); **b.** esp. of departure of soul from body, Ath.*gent.*33(M.25.65B); hence *death* τῶν μαρτύρων... τῆς ἀ. τῆς ἐνδόξου ὑπομνήματα Const.ap.Eus.*v.C.*2.40(p.58.16; M. 20.1017A); Const.*or.s.c.*9(p.164.17; M.20.1256C); ἄφετος αὐτὸς ἀφ' ἑαυτοῦ τὴν ἐκ τοῦ σώματος ἀ. ἐποιεῖτο [sc. Christ] Eus.*theoph.fr.*3 (p.5*.2; M.24.612A); of Ascension τὸ μετὰ τὴν ἀ. ποθεινὸν ἔσεσθαι, καὶ τὸ μὴ δύνασθαι λοιπὸν αὐτὸν εὑρεῖν Chrys.*hom.50.2 in Jo.*(8.297A); **2.** *withdrawal, retirement*, also *flight*; of Christ's withdrawal from enemies (Jo.11:54) οἱ τόποι τῆς ἀ. αὐτοῦ Or.*Jo.*28.23(18; p.419.13; M.14.732A); *ib.*28.24(19; p.420.5; 732C); ὁ κύριος...δεικνὺς τὸ κατὰ τὴν ἀ. ἄφοβον Proc.G.*Num.*33:2(M.87.888B); of Athanasius' flight, Ath.*apol.Const.*34(M.25.641A); also *retired place, solitude* εἶδεν ὄρος [sc. of Transfiguration] καὶ πολλὴν τὴν ἀ. καὶ τὴν ἐρημίαν Chrys. *hom.56.2 in Mt.*(7.568C); **3.** *withdrawal* from world, *solitude*, as aid to spiritual life; **a.** in gen., of Christ τὰς ἀ. διώκειν καὶ φεύγειν τὰς κατὰ πόλεις...ὁμιλίας Eus.*d.e.*3.6(p.133.7; M.22.225A); χρησιμεύει πρὸς σωτηρίαν ἡ τῶν θορύβων τῶν ἀστικῶν ἀ. Isid.Pel.*epp.*1.77(M.78. 236B); **b.** of religious life ἡ δι' αὐτὴν [sc. ἀρετὴν] ἀ. Ath.*v.Anton.*7 (M.26.853A); *ib.*14(865A); τὴν ἀ., μελέτην θανάτου καὶ φυγὴν τοῦ σώματος οἱ πατέρες ἡμῶν ὀνομάζουσιν Evagr.Pont.*cap.pract.*33(M. 40.1229D); ἐν ἀ. τὴν σάρκα ὑπωπιάσωμεν Epiph.*haer.*64.71(p.519.8; M.41.1196C); Pall.*v.Chrys.*17(p.106.24; M.47.60); Nil.*epp.*2.137(M. 79.257A); Diad.*perf.*18(p.22.19); **c.** description of true withdrawal κόσμου δὲ ἀ., οὐ τὸ ἔξω αὐτοῦ γενέσθαι σωματικῶς, ἀλλὰ τῆς πρὸς τὸ σῶμα συμπαθείας τὴν ψυχὴν ἀπορρῆξαι Bas.*ep.*2.2(3.71E; M.32.225B); ἀ. κόσμου ἐστὶν ἑκούσιον μῖσος ἐπαινουμένης ὕλης Jo.Clim.*scal.*1(M. 88.633C); discussion of its necessity ποῦ νῦν εἰσιν οἱ λέγοντες, ὅτι οὐχ οἷόν τε ἐν μέσῃ πόλει στρεφόμενόν τινα διασῶσαι τὴν ἀρετήν, ἀλλ' ἀναχωρήσεως δεῖ;...καὶ ταῦτα λέγει, οὐ κωλύων τὴν ἀ. τὴν ἀπὸ τῶν πόλεων...ἀλλὰ δεικνὺς ὅτι τῷ βουλομένῳ νήφειν καὶ ἐγρηγορέναι οὐδὲν τούτων κώλυμα γίνεται Chrys.*hom.43.1 in Gen.*(4.435E); ἀ. ἐν ἀγάπῃ καθαίρει καρδίαν, ἀ. δὲ μετὰ μίσους ἐκταράσσει αὐτήν Evagr. Pont.*sent.mon.*8(p.153); **4.** *abandonment, forsaking, giving up*; **a.** of bad or less perfect things διὰ τῆς τῶν εἰδώλων ἀ. Eus.*d.e.* 1.6(p.24.6; M.22.49C); ἡ τῶν γάμων ἀ. *ib.*1.9(p.42.8; 81A); ἀ. τῶν κακῶν Bas.*hom.in Ps.*1:2(1.93B; M.29.217C); *ib.*(1.93C,D; M.217C, 220A); ἡ τῶν θελημάτων ἑαυτοῦ ἀ. id.*reg.fus.*6(2.344D; M.31.925C); ἡ...τῶν ἀηδῶν ἀ. Gr.Nyss.*Eun.*1(1 p.29.23; M.45.257B); Chrys.*hom. 16.1 in Eph.*(11.116C); **b.** of good things ἀ. τοῦ ἀληθινοῦ βασιλέως Bas.*jud.*2(2.215A; M.31.656C); ἡ τῆς τραπέζης τοῦ πατρὸς ἀ. Gr.Nyss. *or.dom.*5(p.98.27; M.44.1181C); ref. schismatics ἀναχωρήσεις ἐκ τῶν οἴκων τοῦ θεοῦ...ποιούμενοι CGangr.*can.*proem.; **5.** *privation*; of evil as privation of good τις ἀπὸ τοῦ καλοῦ...τῆς ψυχῆς ἀ. Gr.Nyss. *or.catech.*5(p.27.10; M.45.24D); ἡ δὲ τοῦ κρείττονος ἀ. τοῦ ἐναντίου γίνεται γένεσις *ib.*(p.28.6; 25A).

ἀναχωρητής, ὁ, *anchorite, hermit*, *PLond.*1925.24; mode of life πλούσιοι ἄνδρες τε καὶ γυναῖκες...ἐν τῇ ἐρήμῳ ἐκεῖσε ἀναχωρητὰς ἐζήτησαν, καὶ τούτων τὰ ὑστερήματα ἐπλήρωσαν ‡Just.*qu.et resp.*110 (M.6.1360A); ἀ. γὰρ ἐδόκει εἶναι, ἐν σπηλαίῳ τινὶ καθεζόμενος Epiph. *haer.*39.1(p.81.8; M.41.677C); ἀ. ἐν τοῖς σπηλαίοις τῶν πετρῶν ἑαυτοὺς ἐγκαθείρξαντες Pall.*h.Laus.*58(p.151.12; 1203B); θαυμαστὴ βίου διαγωγὴ τῶν...ἀ. τῶν ἐν τῇ ἐρήμῳ ‡Pall.*proem.*(p.3.2; M.34.995); supernatural powers and virtues οὐδεὶς δύναται θεραπεῦσαι τὴν θυγατέρα σου, εἰ μὴ οὓς οἶδα ἀ.· καὶ ἐὰν αὐτοὺς παρακαλέσῃς, οὐκ ἀνέχονται τοῦτο ποιῆσαι διὰ ταπεινοφροσύνην *Apophth.Patr.*(M.65. 153C); ἦν γὰρ ἀ. ἀπελαύνων δαίμονας· καὶ ἐξήταζεν αὐτούς· ἐν τίνι ἐξέρχεσθε;...καὶ ἔλεγον, ὅτι οὐδὲν ἡμᾶς νικᾷ, εἰ μὴ ταπεινοφροσύνη *ib.* (204A); Jo.Mosch.*prat.*84(M.87.2941A); special temptations τοῖς μὲν ἀ. οἱ δαίμονες γυμνοὶ προσπαλαίουσι Evagr.Pont.*cap.pract.*5 (M.40.1224A); ἔστι δαίμων, πλάνος λεγόμενος...ὅστις περιάγει τοῦ ἀ. τὸν νοῦν ἀπὸ πόλεως εἰς πόλιν †Nil.*mal.cog.*8(M.79.1209C); [sc. ἀκηδία] κέλλαν ἀναχωρητοῦ ἰδοῦσα ἐμειδίασε Jo.Clim.*scal.*13(M.88. 860A); wrong reasons for becoming anchorite ὁ λέγων ὅτι διὰ τοῦτο ἀ. γίνομαι, ἵνα μηδένα ἔχω τὸν εἰς ὀργήν παρακνίζοντα, οὐδὲ διαφέρει ὁ τοιοῦτος θηρίου ἀλογίστου Nil.*epp.*3.73(M.79.421D); anchorites identified with monks ὁ βίος τῶν...ἀ. ἤτοι μοναχῶν ‡Ath *syntag.*1.1(M.28.836A).

ἀναχωρητικός, *of an anchorite, eremitical* ἀ. βίου *V.Pach.Φ*136 (p.86.7); Diad.*perf.*53(p.58.19); *Apophth.Patr.*(M.65.152A); Leont. N.*v.Sym.*11(M.93.1681D); θεωρίαν...ἀ. Philox.*ep.*29(p.178); οἴκημα ἀ. *ib.*37(p.184).

***ἀναχωρητικῶς,** *eremitically, as an anchorite*, Gr.Naz.*ep.*99(M.37. 172C).

ἀναψηλαφ-άω, 1. *examine closely, search closely*, Epiph.*haer.* 76.20(p.366.12; M.42.556A); Leo.Mag.*ep.*45.2(p.48.17; M*PL.*54.836C); *ib.*104.5(p.60.32; 998A); τοιαῦτα καλῶς καὶ θεοδείκτως ἀ. Anast.S. *qu.et resp.*127(M.89.777C); Ἀδὰμ ποῦ εἶ;...ἐγὼ γὰρ σὲ ∼ῶν ἐνταῦθα παρεγενόμην Germ.CP *or.*2(M.98.257C); **2.** *retract*, Phot.*nomoc.*13.18 (M.104.932A).

***ἀναψυκτήριον, τό,** *place of refreshment*, ‡Ath.*v.Syncl.*98(M.28. 1548C).

ἀνάψυξις, ἡ, *alleviation, refreshment*, in future life ἡ τῆς ἀφθαρσίας ἀ. *A.Jo.*4(p.153.8); θάνατος...δικαίων ἀ. †Hipp.*Laz.*(p.218.28; M.62. 777); τὸ...χωρισθῆναι τοῦ σώματος...εἰς ἀ. ἐλθεῖν Meth.*res.*1.57 (p.319.15; M.41.1153B); παρακατάστησον φωτεινὸν ἄγγελον τὸν χειραγωγοῦντά με πρὸς τὸν τόπον τῆς ἀ. Gr.Nyss.*v.Macr.*(p.398.1; M.46. 984D); Isid.Pel.*epp.*1.215(M.78.317D); of spiritual refreshment in this life, *A.Jo.*22(p.163.7); Or.*schol.in Cant.*4:5(M.17.272C); φίλος πιστὸς λιμὴν ἀναψύξεως Gr.Naz.*or.*11.1(M.35.832B); *Const.App.*2. 35.1; Cyr.*Ps.*38:14(M.69.977D); Jo.Mon.*hymn.Petr.*8(M.96.1388D); σὲ διψῶ, τὴν ἀ. τῶν κεκοιμηκότων ‡Meth.*Sym.et Ann.*6(M.18.361B); of BMV as source of ἀ., *ib.*9(369B).

ἀναψύχω, 1. *cheer, refresh*; met., Ign.*Eph.*2.1; id.*Trall.*12.2; Gr. Naz.*carm.*1.2.1.589(M.37.567A); *Const.App.*3.13.1; **2.** *relieve* poverty, Dion.Cor.ap.Eus.*h.e.*4.23.10(M.20.388B); **3.** intrans., *revive, recover oneself*, *M.Perp.*8(p.75.6); *ib.*13(p.83.11); εἴ τι...ἥμαρτον...ἄνες μοι· ἵνα ἀναψύξω καὶ εὑρεθῶ ἐνώπιόν σου ἐν τῇ ἀπεκδύσει τοῦ σώματος Gr.Nyss.*v.Macr.*(p.398.13; M.46.985A); *Const.App.*3.12.4; Mac.Aeg. *hom.*11.8(M.34.549B).

ἀνδραγάθημα, τό, *brave, manly deed*; Christian *act of virtue* ἐξ ἀνδραγαθημάτων καὶ προκοπῆς τὸ τῆς υἱοθεσίας λαβόντες πνεῦμα Alex.Al.*ep.Alex.*7(p.24.23; M.18.560A); οὔτε θαρρεῖν ἀναγκαῖον ἐπὶ τῷ πλήθει τῶν ἀ., οὔτ' ἀπογινώσκειν ἐπὶ τοῖς ἐπταισμένοις Nil.*epp.* 1.230(M.79.168A); τοῖς ἐξ ἀγάπης ἀ. Cyr.*Jo.*10.2(4.866E); *goodness* διὰ τοῦτο καὶ ἄνθρωπος γέγονε Χριστός, ἐξ ἀ. τούτου τυχών Or.*princ.* 2.6.4(p.143.18; M.11.212B); *ib.*3.1.12(p.216.6; 272A).

ἀνδραγαθία, ἡ, *bravery*; plur., *acts of bravery, noble deeds*, Eus. *h.e.*4.23.5(M.20.385A); Eustrat.*v.Eutych.*7(M.86.2281B).

ἀνδραδελφή, ἡ, *husband's sister*, *MAMA* 1.315,363,364.

[*]**ἀνδραΐζομαι,** v.l. for ἀνδρίζομαι q.v.

ἀνδρεία, ἡ, *courage*; **1.** pagan; various types ἄλλη μὲν ἡ Ἐπικούρου ἀ., ὑπομένοντος πόνους διὰ φυγὴν πόνων πλειόνων, ἄλλη δ' ἡ τοῦ ἀπὸ τῆς Στοᾶς, δι' αὐτὴν αἱρουμένου πᾶσαν ἀρετήν, ἄλλη δ' ἡ ἀπὸ Πλάτωνος, τοῦ θυμικοῦ μέρους τῆς ψυχῆς φάσκοντος αὐτὴν εἶναι ἀρετήν Or.*Cels.*5.47(p.52.1; M.11.1256A); **2.** Christian; **a.** def. ἀ., ὅταν κινδύνων καὶ θανάτων κατατολμᾷ...ὑπὲρ τῶν δοκούντων τῷ θεῷ Chrys.*hom.5.3 in Phil.*(11.232E); ἀ. δὲ ἡγούμεθα, τὴν κατὰ τῶν δυσχερῶν ὑπεροψίαν, καὶ τὸ γενναίως φέρειν τὰ συμβαίνοντα Isid.Pel.*epp.* 5.465(M.78.1597A); in list of virtues, Or.*hom.12.11 in Jer.*(p.97.18; M.13.393A); τὰς θείας ἀρετὰς...καὶ τὴν πάντων τούτων [sc. ψυχῆς κινημάτων] σωτηρίαν, ἀ. Gr.Thaum.*pan.Or.*9(p.24.4; M.10.1080B); *M.Ner.et Ach.*6(p.5.4); relation to other virtues, Dor.*doct.*14.2(M. 88.1776A); esp. as one of cardinal virtues, v. ἀρετή; **b.** of Christ, ref. Mt.26:39 τί σοι δοκεῖ; συστολῆς ὑπάρχειν, ἢ ἀ.; Max.*opusc.* (M.91.65B); **c.** of individuals; as taught by example of Job, Bas. *ep.*2.3(3.73A; M.32.228C); πολὺς ὁ Ἰὼβ παιδεύων εἰς ἀ. τὸν βίον τοῖς καθ' ἑαυτὸν ὑποδείγμασι, πολὺς ὁ παροιμιαστὴς τοῖς αἰνίγμασι Gr. Nyss.*mart.*1(M.46.749B); of 'gnostic' τῷ γνωστικῷ μετὰ γνώσεως ἡ τελειότης τῆς ἀ. ἐκ τῆς τοῦ βίου συνασκήσεως αὔξεται, μελετήσαντος ἀεὶ τῶν παθῶν κρατεῖν Clem.*str.*7.11(p.48.19; ἀνδρίας M.9.493A); of martyrs τὸ ἀνδρεῖον ἐν τῇ κατὰ ἀλήθειαν λογικῇ ἀ. ἐξετάζεσθαι *παρέχονται ib.*(p.48.6; 492C); *ὑπέλαβεν ὁ ἐχθρὸς διὰ φόβον τοῦ ξίφους εἰς δειλίαν ἐμβαλεῖν τὴν ὑμετέραν ἀ., ἵνα ἀρνήσασθε Χριστόν* Ephr.3.252C; of BMV as ἀ. of martyrs, *ib.*3.551C; of a saint *ἐν ἀ. πολλῇ τῆς θεϊκῆς ἰσχύος Χριστὸν ἐπικαλούμενος* Jo.Mon.*hymn.Nic.*4(M.96.1385A); founded upon Cross as *ἀνδρείας ὑπόθεσις...ἀλλ' οὐκ αἰσχύνης* Germ.CP *or.*1(M.98.240A); **d.** in gen.; of resolution in spiritual danger, Ath.*v.Anton.*36(M.26.896C); Gr.Nyss.*virg.*18(p.318.16; M.46.389D); Proc.G.*Is.*54:1–17(M.87.2545B).

[*]**ἀνδρεΐζομαι**, v. *ἀνδρίζομαι*.

***ἀνδρειόπαις**, ὁ, *manly boy, Hymn.*(*AS* 1 p.577).

***ἀνδρειοπλαστικός**, *of human work*, Leont.H.*Nest.*2.19(M.86.1580A).

ἀνδρειόω, *fill with courage*; **1.** *play the man*, Cosm.Ind.*top.*2(M.88.104C) citing Ptolemy III Euergetes; **2.** pass., *come to manhood*, *Chron.Pasch.*p.311(v.l. *ἀνδριωθείς*; M.92.792B); *ib.*p.326(840A).

***ἀνδριαντοπλασία (-πλαστία)**, ἡ, *moulding of images*, Epiph.*haer.*3(p.177.19; M.41.188A); *ib.*25.4(p.271.17; 325A); ‡Epiph.*epit.haer.*(p.342.15); *-τίαν* Proc.G.*Gen.*11:26(M.87.317A).

***ἀνδριαντοποιητικός**, *of the making of images*, Athenag.*leg.*17.2(M.6.924A); Eus.*p.e.*1.9(29D; M.21.70A).

***ἀνδριαντουργέω**, *portray* in words, Clem.*paed.*3.11(p.277.10; M.8.649C).

ἀνδριάς, ὁ, *statue*, met. **a.** *εὖ ποιῶν καὶ πάσχων κακῶς οὐδὲν ἔπαθεν ἀνθρώπινον...οὗτός ἐστιν ὁ ἀ. ὁ ἀδαμάντινος* Chrys.*hom.43.4 in 1Cor.*(10.405B); *example*, of Job *ἀ. δὲ αὐτὸν ὑπομονῆς καὶ παρακλήσεως* Olymp.*Job* 38 proem.(M.93.393C); **b.** esp. of the body, *human shape*, Gr.Naz.*or.*26.10(M.35.1241A); ‡Nil.*fr.pasch.*2(M.79.1496B); Andr.Caes.*therap.fr.*3(p.166.21).

ἀνδρίζ-ομαι, **1.** pass., *be made man*, of Christ *ἀνδρισθείς, τουτέστιν ἐνανθρωπήσας* Jo.D.*rect.sent.*4(M.94.1429B); **2.** *come to manhood*; met., of Adam *ὁ παῖς ~όμενος ἀπειθείᾳ* Clem.*prot.*11(p.78.29; M.8.228C); **3.** *play the man*; of women showing bravery, Clem.*str.*4.7(M.8.1260C; *ἀνδρεϊζομένη* p.270.5); *τὴν ἔσω καλῶς ἀναστρεφομένην, καὶ ~ομένην τὰ γυναικός* Gr.Naz.*or.*8.9(M.35.797C); *ἐν τοῖς ἀγῶσι τῆς πίστεως ~εσθαι* Bas.Sel.*or.*2.4(M.85.44B); hence gen., *fight bravely* in spiritual warfare, Nil.*epp.*3.71(M.79.421C); Isid.Pel.*epp.*1.75(M.78.233D); Andr.Caes.*Apoc.*10(M.106.797C); **4.** *wear men's clothes*, Clem.*str.*2.18(M.8.1020C; *ἀνδρεΐζεσθαι* p.155.21); Epiph.*haer.*66.33(p.72.27, v.l. *ἀνδραΐζεσθαι* M.42.81B).

ἀνδρικός, **1.** *of a husband*, Anast.S.*qu.et resp.*20(M.89.524A); **2.** *human ἀ. τοῦ Ἰησοῦ θεουργίας* Dion.Ar.*c.h.*4.4(M.3.181B); id.*e.h.*3.3.4(M.3.429C); *θείας ὁμοῦ καὶ ἀ. ἐνεργείας* Max.*opusc.*(M.91.100C); id.*ambig.*(M.91.1056C) v. *θεανδρικός*.

ἀνδρικῶς, *in a manly way*; *as man*, of Christ, Max.*ambig.*(M.91.1056C) cit. s. *θεανδρικῶς*.

[*]**ἄνδριος**, = *ἀνδρεῖος*, *of* or *for a man*, Pall.*h.Laus.*65(p.162.3 v.l. *ἀνδρικοῖς*; M.34.1252A *ἀνδρείοις*).

ἀνδρίς, ἡ, *woman*, Cyr.*Joel.*35(3.228A); Proc.G.*Gen.*2:18(M.87.172C).

ἀνδριστέον, *one must play the man*, Synes.*ep.*44(M.66.1396C).

***ἀνδροβασία**, ἡ, *unnatural vice*, Epiph.*haer.*27.4(p.305.16; M.41.369A).

ἀνδροβατέω, *practise unnatural vice*, Just.*2apol.*12.5(M.6.465A).

ἀνδροβατής, ὁ, *one who practises unnatural vice*, Arist.*apol.*9.9.

***ἀνδρογύναιος**, *bisexual*, ‡Ath.*dial.Trin.*3.8(M.28.1213C).

ἀνδρόγυνος, neut. as adv., *men and women together ἀ. γυνὴ πιστὴ μὴ λουέσθω Const.App.*1.9.1; plur., Epiph.*haer.*30.7(p.342.20; M.41.416D); neut. as subst., *married couple*, Ephr.3.158A; Eustrat.*v.Eutych.*45(M.86.2325C); Cosm.Ind.*top.*7(M.88.380B).

***ἀνδρογύνως**, *men and women together*; ref. mixed bathing, Epiph.*haer.*30.7(p.342.25; M.41.417A).

***ἀνδροδόκος**, *admitting men*, Paul.Sil.*ambo.*217(M.86.2260A).

***ἀνδροειδής**, *in the form of a man*, Cyr.*dial.Trin.*5(5¹.559D); *like a man*, Jo.Mal.*chron.*5 p.106(M.97.196C).

***ἀνδροεικελοποιός**, ὁ, *maker of human statues*, Adam.*dial.*5.16(p.208.9; M.11.1856B).

[*]**ἀνδροείκελος**, = *ἀνδρείκελος*, *like a man*, Meth.*symp.*2.7(p.24.17; M.18.57C); Epiph.*haer.*30.17(p.356.19; M.41.433C); Nil.ap.Proc.G.*Cant.*7:11f.(M.87.1737A).

***ἀνδροηλίκος**, *as big as a man*, *V.Mac.*A(p.161).

***ἀνδροκοίτης**, ὁ, *sodomite*, Jo.Mal.*chron.*18 p.436(M.97.644B).

***ἀνδροκτονία**, ἡ, *slaughter of men*, Cyr.*Os.*147(3.180E; *ἀνδροφονίαν* A.).

ἀνδρολογέω, *enlist*, met. *νεωστὶ πρὸς τοῦ σωτῆρος ἠνδρολογημένοι* Clem.*q.d.s.*20(p.173.7; M.9.625A).

***ἀνδρολόχευτος**, *born of a man*; of Eve, Geo.Pis.*carm.vit.*53(p.53).

***ἀνδρολυσία**, ἡ, *separation from a husband*, Arc.C.*v.Sym.*(H.4.220A).

***ἀνδρομανία**, ἡ, *unnatural lust*, Gr.Naz.*or.*38.13(M.36.325A); Anast.S.*hod.*14(M.89.252C).

***ἀνδρόμηκον**, τό, *a man's height*, Cyr.S.*v.Sab.*81(p.186.21).

***ἀνδροπλάστης**, ὁ, *maker of a man*, Leont.H.*Nest.*2.19(M.86.1580A).

***ἀνδροπλαστία**, ἡ, *making of a man*, Dion.Ar.*ep.*9.1(M.3.1105A).

***ἀνδρόπλουτος**, *enriched by a husband*, Pall.*v.Chrys.*4(p.25.10; M.47.16).

***ἀνδροπρεπής**, *manly, virile*, Cyr.*ador.*6(1.195D); *ib.*8(285A); *ib.*12(418E).

***ἀνδροστάχυν**, τό, s.v.l., a product of India *Σινδοῦ, ἔνθα ὁ μόσχος καὶ τὸ κοστόριν, καὶ τὸ ἀ. γίνεται* Cosm.Ind.*top.*11(M.88.445D; MSS *ἀνδροστάχην*; conj. *ναρδοστάχυν*, *oil of spikenard*).

ἀνδροφον-έω, *slay men, murder*; in refuting charge against Christians *οἱ τὰς τοῖς ἀμβλωθριδίοις χρωμένας ~εῖν...φαμέν, κατὰ ποῖον ⟨ἂν⟩ ~οῖμεν λόγον*; Athenag.*leg.*35.2(M.6.969A).

ἀνδροφονία, ἡ, *slaying of men, murder*; as accusation against Christians, Athenag.*leg.*35.1(M.6.969A).

***ἀνδροφόρος**, *bearing man*, Eudoc.*Cypr.*1.79(M.85.836B).

ἀνδρ-όω, **1.** *make as a man, make masculine*, Clem.*paed.*2.10(p.210.25; M.8.501C); *ib.*3.3(p.247.6; 580C); id.*exc.Thdot.*79(p.131.23; M.9.696A); **2.** pass., *grow to manhood*; **a.** of Christ, Just.*1apol.*31.7(M.6.377A); met., Mod.*dorm.*3(M.86.3288B) cit. s. *νυμφεύω*; **b.** met., of Son *γέννημα μετὰ τὴν γέννησιν ἔξωθεν προσλαβὸν ὡς ἂν εἴποι τις ἠνδρώθη* Aët.*synt.*9(p.354.6; M.42.537B); *ἠνδρώθη καὶ τέλειός ἐστιν ὁ υἱός* ‡Ath.*dial.Trin.*2.16(M.28.1181C); **3.** pass., *be made man, be made human*, ref. Inc. *~ωθέντος θεοῦ* Dion.Ar.*ep.*4(M.3.1072C); CCP(681) *act.*8(H.3.1168D); *τὴν δὲ θεϊκὴν ἐνέργειαν καθ' ἕνωσιν ἄρρητον τῇ συμφυΐᾳ τῆς σαρκικῆς ἐσχηκὼς ~ωθεῖσαν* Max.*ambig.*(M.91.1056C); Jo.D.*f.o.*3.19(M.94.1080C).

ἀνδρύν-ω, = *ἀνδρόω*, *grow to manhood, mature*, Pall.*v.Chrys.*5(p.28.7; M.47.18); met. *καρδία...~θεῖσα πρὸς σύνεσιν* Cyr.*Is.*3.3(2.444C); of. passions growing stronger, Dor.*doct.*11.3(M.88.1737C).

ἀνδρωνῖτις, ἡ, **1.** *manliness, manhood*, Clem.*paed.*2.8(p.196.23; M.8.472A); *ib.*2.10(p.220.10; 521C); **2.** *male population, manhood*, Pall.*v.Chrys.*16(p.95.5; M.47.54).

***ἄνδρωπος**, *with the face of a man*, v. *ἄδρωπος*.

***ἄνδρωσις**, ἡ, **1.** *coming to manhood, maturing τῆς τοῦ σωτῆρος ἀναγωγῆς καὶ ἀ. τῆς αὐτοῦ ἡλικίας* Epiph.*haer.*51.28(p.299.5; M.41.935D); **2.** *manhood, maturity*, Ephr.2.276A.

***ἀνεβλαβής**, prob. f.l. for *ἀνευλαβής* q.v., *irreverent*, Ephr.3.66B.

ἀνεγείρω, **1.** *wake up, rouse* from sleep; **2.** *raise* from a fall, Meth.*res.*1.53(p.309.16; M.41.1128D); **3.** *raise from the dead*; **a.** of Christ's Resurrection, Just.*1apol.*31.7(M.6.377A); id.*dial.*106.1(M.6.721C); *Const.App.*5.7.12; **b.** of individuals raised by Christ, Just.*1apol.*31.7(M.6.377A); of gen. resurrection, *ib.*52.3(405A); **c.** of individuals raised through apostles, *A.Jo.*79(p.190.9); *A.Thom.*A 41(p.158.22); **4.** *erect, build, set up* houses, trophies etc.; met. *ἡ ἐκκλησία...ἀνῳκοδόμησεν...οἶκον, τουτέστιν, ἀ. καὶ ἀνώρθωσε τῇ διδαχῇ καὶ πίστει τοὺς προσιόντας αὐτῇ* Chrys.*fr.in Pr.*14:1(M.64.700A); **5.** *restore, rebuild*, Eus.*p.e.*10.14(503D; M.21.837D); id.*d.e.*6.18(p.274.34; M.22.452C).

ἀνέγερσις, ἡ, **1.** *waking* from sleep, Jo.Clim.*scal.*19(M.88.937B); **2.** *rebuilding*, *Const.App.*7.37.4; Leont.N.*v.Jo.Eleem.*20(p.37.16); **3.** *resurrection τὴν ἀ. πίστευε* †Hipp.*Laz.*(p.227.19; M.62.778); *Const.App.*5.7.16; of Christ *τὴν θείαν ἀ.* †Jo.D.*B.J.*11(M.96.960B).

***ἀνεγερτέον**, *one must rise*, Clem.*paed.*2.9(p.205.33; M.8.493A).

***ἀνεγερτικός**, *rousing, uplifting*, Epiph.*haer.*69.69(p.217.13; M.42.313A).

ἀνέγερτος, *beyond restoration, final*, ref. Mt.7:6 *ἡ...τῶν μυστηρίων μετάδοσις, ῥῆξίς ἐστιν ἀ. τοῖς καταφρονητικῶς μεταδιδοῦσιν* Isid.Pel.*epp.*1.143(M.78.280A).

***ἀνεγέρτως**, *without being raised*, Euther.*confut.*7(M.28.1357C); *without resurrection*, ‡Just.*qu.et resp.*108(M.6.1356C).

***ἀνεγκατέω**, *disembowel*, Jo.Mosch.*prat.*75(M.87.2928C).

ἀνεγκλησία, ἡ, *freedom from accusation*, Bardesanes ap.Eus.*p.e.*6.10(274D; M.21.465C).

ἀνέγκλητος, *without reproach, blameless*; def. *τὸ δὲ ἀ., ἐπίτασις τοῦ ἀμώμου· ἀ. γὰρ τότε λέγεται, ὅταν μηδὲ μέχρι καταγνώσεως μηδὲ μέχρι ἐγκλήματος ᾖ τι πεπραγμένον ἡμῖν* Chrys.*hom.*4.1 *in Col.*(11.351D); *μηδεμίαν διδοὺς ἀφορμὴν εὐλόγου κατηγορίας* Thdt.*Tit.*1:6(3.700); of Christ, Just.*dial.*35.8(M.6.553A).

***ἀνεγχείρητος**, *not to be attempted*, Isid.Pel.*epp*.1.24(M.78.197A); sens. dub. [Mt.16:19] τοῦ κλείειν καὶ ἀνοίγειν καὶ δεσμεῖν τε καὶ λύειν σε ἀ. τῶν τούτους ὑπεναντίων *cat.Apoc*.3:7(p.225.3).

ἀνεγχώρητος, *impossible* ἀδύνατον καὶ ἀ. ποιεῖν τι τὸν υἱόν, ὧν οὐ ποιεῖ ὁ πατήρ Gr.Naz.*or*.30.11(p.123.6; M.36.116C); ‡Ath.*disp*.10 (M.28.449A); Chrys.*hom.38.4 in Jo*.(8.222B).

***ἀνεθελησία, ἡ**, *absence of volition*, of God, in respect of generation of Son; orthodox answer to Arian doctrine of generation by Father's will is τῆς θελήσεως καὶ τῆς ἀ. ... προτερεύει ὅ τε γεννήσας... πατήρ, τό τε ἀπαύγασμα τῆς δόξης αὐτοῦ ὁ υἱός Didym.*Trin*.1.9 (M.39.281C); and τῶν μὲν πρακτέων ἢ μή, θέλησίς τε καὶ ἀ. κρατεῖ· γεννήσεως δέ, οὐκ ἔτι Cyr.*dial.Trin*.2(5^1.455D).

ἀνεθέλητος;

A. pass., *not willed*; **1.** in gen.; **a.** *undesired*; of accidental misfortunes which befall men when God's guidance is withdrawn, Cyr.*ador*.1(1.11C); of undesired consequences of pursuit of pleasure, *ib*.(10D); of accidental illness, *ib*.14(481A); **b.** *unacceptable, hateful* ἀ. ἔχει τὰς τῶν παρανόμων ὁδούς Or.*exc.in Ps*.36:23(M.17.133B); ἡ... συναγωγὴ...γέγονεν ἀ. Cyr.*glaph.Dt*.2(1.420E); ἀ. ποιεῖται τὴν ἱερωσύνην id.*Mal*.12(3.829C); ἐν Χριστῷ...ἐσμεν οὐκ ἀ. τῷ θεῷ id.*ador*.11 (1.756A); **2.** ref. God; **a.** of God's unwillingness to punish ἀγαθὸς... καὶ φιλοικτίρμων ὁ θεὸς...ἀ. ἔχει τὸ πλήττειν id.*Os*.6(3.166B); **b.** ref. generation of Son; Arian objection to orthodox denial of Son's generation by Father's will εἴπερ ἐστὶν ἀ. ὁ υἱὸς τῷ πατρί, τέτοκεν οὐχ ἑκών id.*dial.Trin*.2(5^1.454A); **3.** ref. Christ; of Passion as ἀ. in rel. to Christ's human will, v. θελητός.

B. act., *without volition* οὐκ ἀ. ἡ ἡμετέρα φύσις, ἐπεὶ μηδὲ ἀνθρώπου Max.*opusc*.(M.91.157B); ἆρα οὖν ἀ. ἄνθρωπός ἐστιν; οὐδαμῶς Jo.D.*volunt*.28(M.95.165C).

***ἀνεθελήτως**, **1.** *not deliberately*; **a.** in gen., ref. sins committed involuntarily, Cyr.*Ps*.24:7(M.69.848D); ref. belief that departed souls can be subject to evil spirits ἀ. ἀκολουθεῖν περιτρέπουσιν εὐκόλως οἵπερ ἂν ἕλοιντο τυχόν id.*ador*.6(1.188A); **b.** Trin.; ref. question πότερόν ποτε θελητῶς, ἤγουν ἀ. ὁ θεὸς...ἐκτέτοκε τὸν υἱόν id.*dial.Trin*.2(5^1.454A), v. θελητῶς; **c.** ref. recording by evangelists of Christ's predictions of Passion ἵνα μήτις...τῆς...δόξης κατεπαίρηται, λέγων, ὡς...βρόχοις τοῖς Ἰουδαίων ἀ. περιπεσών id.*Jo*.9 (4.720A); **2.** ref. God's reluctance to punish sinners μόνον...οὐχὶ καὶ ἀ. αὐτοὺς καταπαιδεύοντος id.*Am*.2(3.296D); **3.** *so as to be displeasing, distasteful* εἰ πράττοιτό πως ἀ. αὐτῷ [sc. God] id.*Os*.4(3.119A).

ἀνείδεος, **A.** *without form*.

B. *formless*, i.e. *without visible shape*; **1.** in gen. οὐδὲ τὰ πνευματικὰ καὶ νοερά, οὐδὲ οἱ ἀρχάγγελοι...οὐδὲ μὴν οὐδ' αὐτὸς [sc. Christ] ἄμορφος καὶ ἀ. Clem.*exc.Thdot*.10(p.109.17; M.9.660B); ἡ...νοητὴ φύσις ἀσώματόν τι χρῆμά ἐστι καὶ ἀναφὲς καὶ ἀ. Gr.Nyss.*or.catech*.6 (p.29.10; M.45.25C); **2.** of God, acc. Greek philosophers, v. ἀσώματος; acc. Christian writers, Thdt.*Is*.44:12(p.176.1; 2.341); id.*qu.60 in Ex*.(1.163) cit. s. ἀσχημάτιστος; Ammon.*Ac*.17:29(M.85.1565A); ‡Caes.Naz.*dial*.40(M.38.905); Jo.D.*imag*.1.8(M.94.1237D); partic., of Father, Gr.Nyss.*Eun*.12(1 p.274.9; M.45.980D); of Son, as of Father, Bas.*Eun*.1.23(1.234B; M.29.561C) cit. s. ἀσχημάτιστος; Gr. Naz.*or*.37.2(M.36.285A); of Christ's divinity τοῦ Ἰησοῦ θεότης... ἀ. ἐν τοῖς εἴδεσιν, ὡς ὑπὲρ εἶδος Dion.Ar.*d.n*.2.10(M.3.618C); σαρκοῦται μὲν ἀτρέπτως ὁ ἀ. Procl.CP*fr*.(M.65.888D)ap.Cyr.*ep*.55(p.60. 15; 5^2.189E); τὸν ἐν αὐτῇ κυοφορούμενον ἀ. θεόν ‡Ath.*annunt*. 10(M.28.932A); τὸν δι' ἡμᾶς ἐν ὕλῃ καὶ εἴδει καθ' ἡμᾶς...γενόμενον θεὸν λόγον, τὸν κατὰ φύσιν κυρίως ἄυλον καὶ ἀ. Max.*ambig*.(M.91. 1273C).

C. *free from* (*not bound by*) *shape*; hence **1.** *spiritual*, v. ἄυλος; **2.** *unshaped* καρδία...ἀ. τῷ θεῷ καὶ ἀδιαμόρφωτον παραστήσασα τὴν μνήμην †Marc.Er.*temp*.24(M.65.1064B).

D. *unshapely, ugly*, Dion.Ar.*e.h*.2.3.8(M.3.404C); ἀ. δὲ ἐν τοῖς οὖσι τὸ δυσειδὲς ἀπεκάλεσαν οὐχὶ τὸ εἴδους πάντη ἀμέτοχον Max.*schol*. ad loc.(M.4.133A); of persons, Ant.Mon.*hom*.47(M.89.1580D).

***ἀνειδεότης, ἡ**, *formlessness*, Didym.*Trin*.1.27(M.39.404B).

***ἀνειδέως**, *without form*, of H. Ghost παρὼν μὲν τοῖς ὅλοις ἀΰλως, ἀ. Didym.*Trin*.2.4(M.39.484B).

ἀνειδωλοποιέω, **1.** *make idols* or *images*, Eus.*Is*.46:4(M.24.421B); *make images of*, id.*p.e*.5.3(183C; M.21.317B); *make into idols* νεκρῶν ...εἰκόνας ἀ. id.*d.e*.8 proem.(p.350.22; M.22.569C); **2.** *make into an object of worship, idolize* τῶν ἐν ὑμῖν παθῶν ἀ. τύπους Clem.*prot*. 2(p.19.24; M.8.96B); *ib*.5(p.48.32; 165A); id.*str*.6.16(p.507.11; M.9. 377B).

***ἀνειδωλοποιΐα, ἡ**, *formation of image in the mind*, Clem.*str*.4.22 (p.310.3; M.8.1349A).

***ἀνείδωλος**, *free from mental images* or *dreams*, Evagr.Pont.*cap. pract*.55(M.40.1248A); Marc.Er.*opusc*.1.141,142(M.65.921D); Jo.Clim. *scal*.15(M.88.881A).

***ἀνειδώλως**, *without mental images* or *dreams*, Jo.Clim.*scal*.15 (M.88.881A).

ἀνείκαστος, *beyond conjecture* or *comparison*; **1.** in gen., *immense*; *innumerable*, Areth.*Apoc*.29(M.106.648A); *unimaginable* ἐν δόξῃ ἀ. Ephr.2.70A; **2.** of God τὸν ποιητὴν ἀ. *A.Xanthipp*.6(p.61.35); Gr.Naz.*or*.28.13(p.43.3; M.36.44A); Jo.D.*imag*.1.8(M.94.1237D); God's mercy, Anast.S.*Ps.6*(M.89.1093A); power, *Lit.Bas*.(p.310.17); glory, Gr.Nyss.*Eun*.3(2 p.37.3; M.45.604C); **3.** of Christ ἀ. ἡ κατὰ τὸ ἀνθρώπινον τοῦ κυρίου ὑπεροχή Proc.G.*Is*.2:1f.(M.87.1872B); ἰσχὺν ἀ. ‡Meth.*Sym.et Ann*.7(M.18.364B); †Jo.D.*B.J*.24(M.96.1077B).

***ἀνεικάστως**, *incomparably*, Leont.N.*v.Sym*.8(M.93.1680A).

ἀνεικόνιστος, *that cannot be portrayed* τὸ ἀ. τοῦ θεοῦ Clem.*str*.1.24 (p.102.17; M.8.909C).

ἀνειλέω, pass.; **1.** *be unrolled, develop*, Gr.Thaum.*pan.Or*.7(p.20. 18; M.10.1076B); **2.** of planets; *revolve*, Gr.Nyss.*Eun*.12(1 p.236.22, v.l. εἰλουμένων M.45.933C).

ἀνείμων, *unclad*, Eus.*v.C*.4.28(p.128.11; M.20.1177A); Cyr.*glaph. Gen*.1(1.6C); fig., id.*Is*.3.1(2.351B).

ἀνεῖπον, *announce, proclaim*; *repeal, revoke*, *V.Aberc*.66(p.47. 12).

ἀνέκβατος, **1.** *from which there is no outlet, inescapable*, Ph.Carp. *Cant*.proem.(M.40.28A); δύο ῥήσεων...μιᾶς ἀνυπερβάτου καὶ ἑτέρας ἀ. Bas.*Eun*.2.14(1.249B; M.29.600A); **2.** *not coming to pass, not coming true*; of oracular predictions, ‡Just.*qu.et resp*.146(M.6.1400B).

***ἀνεκδειματίστως**, *fearlessly*, Jo.Clim.*past*.15(M.88.1204A).

ἀνεκδιήγητος, **1.** *indescribable, ineffable*, of God καλοποιΐᾳ ἀνεκδιηγήτος Thphl.Ant.*Autol*.1.3(M.6.1028C); τὸν ἀνεξιχνίαστον καὶ ἀ. Cyr.H.*catech*.7.11; attributes and activity, Athenag.*leg*.10.1(M.6. 908B); ἀ. τοῦ θείου κάλλους αἱ ἀστραπαί Bas.*reg.fus*.2.1(2.337B; M.31. 909C); Jo.Mosch.*prat*.79(M.87.2937B); Anast.S.*Ps.6*(M.89.1093A); of Son ἀ. ὑπόστασις Alex.Al.*ep.Alex*.4(p.22.24; M.18.553C); of his generation, Gr.Nyss.*Eun*.1(1 p.108.11; M.45.311C); of Inc., ref. Is.53:8 ἀ. τὸ γένος Just.*1apol*.51.1(M.6.404B); Jo.V H.*icon*.5(M.96. 1353C); of Christ's body, Epiph.*exp.fid*.17(p.519.3; M.42.817B); of anointing of Christ, opp. that of David, ‡Ath.*sem*.10(M.28.156C); of Christ's φιλανθρωπία, Epiph.*haer*.69.69(p.218.6; M.42.313D); of H. Ghost, Or.*exp.in Pr*.18:4(M.17.204A); of pentecostal grace, Gr. Nyss.*Spir*.(M.46.697B); τὸ ἀ. τῆς ἐνεργείας Chrys.ap.*cat.Jo*.7:38 (p.269.26); cf.id.*hom.51.1 in Jo*.(8.300B ἄφατον); of supernatural gifts, *1Clem*.49.4; salvation, Mac.Aeg.*hom*.2.3(M.34.465B); heavenly joy, Ammon.*Ac*.14:21(M.85.1548A); of demoniac possession ἀ. συμφορᾷ Pall.*h.Laus*.44(p.131.22; M.34.1209D); **2.** *not recounted, unrelated* οὐδὲ ἀ. ἐᾶσαι τὰς συκοφαντίας CSard.*ep.cath*.(p.122.32; M.25. 333C).

***ἀνεκδιηγήτως**, *indescribably*, Trin. ἀ. τῆς τριάδος οὔσης ἐν ταυτότητι δοξολογίας Epiph.*haer*.74.12(p.330.15; M.42.497C); *ib*.76.46(p.400. 7; 613C); *ib*.76.47(p.401.2; 616B); of generation of Son, Alex.Al.*ep. Alex*.12(p.27.7; M.18.565B); Epiph.*haer*.62.3(p.392.13; M.41.1053C); of Inc. ἀ. συνελήφθης Hesych.H.*Ps.tit*.65.4(M.27.904D).

ἀνεκδίκητος, *unavenged, unpunished*; *not worthy of punishment*, CAlex.(338)*ep*.ap.Ath.*apol.sec*.19(p.101.19; M.25.280B).

ἀνεκλάλητος, **1.** *unutterable, ineffable*; of God, Gr.Nyss.*or.catech*. 14(p.62.11; M.45.45D); ἔχων...φῶς ἀ. *cat.2Cor*.8:9(p.402.21); of generation of Son, Gr.Naz.*or*.29.4(p.78.8; M.36.77C); of birth of Christ, Isid.Pel.*epp*.1.377(M.78.396B); of things supernatural: light of star at Nativity, Ign.*Eph*.19.2; τὰ ἀ. μυστήρια Clem.*q.d.s*.36(p.183.22; M.9.641B); ἀναπαύσεως ἀ. Mac.Aeg.*hom*.2.5(M.34.468A); joy, Ath. *v.Anton*.36(M.26.896C); good things promised by God, Thal.*cent*. 4.9(M.91.1460A); of Valent. aeons Father and Truth, Iren.*haer*.1. 14.5(M.7.604B); **2.** *not expressing itself in words* νοῦν ἀ. Gr.Naz.*ep*. 119(M.37.213C); id.*or*.43.13(M.36.512C).

***ἀνεκλαλήτως**, *ineffably*, Mac.Aeg.*hom*.4.12(M.34.481B); ‡Ath. *annunt*.6(M.28.925A).

[*]ἀνεκλειπής, v. ἀνεκλιπής.

ἀνέκλειπτος, *unfailing*, ref. Lc.12:33 σοφίας δὲ θησαυροὶ ἀ. Clem. *paed*.3.12(p.284.14; M.8.665C); of God θησαυρὸς ἀ. id.*str*.4.6(p.263. 9; M.8.1245A); ἀ. αἰτίαν, καὶ διανομὴν τῶν...δώρων Dion.Ar.*d.n*.2.1 (M.3.637C); of God's pity, *Hom.Clem*.3.29; power, Dion.Ar.*d.n*.8.5 (892C); of angelic life, *ib*.4.1(693C).

ἀνέκλεκτος, *ineffable*; of H. Ghost, Didym.*Trin*.2.4(M.39.484A).

[*]ἀνεκλιπής, = ἀνελλιπής, *unfailing*, ref. Lc.12:33 πλοῦτος ἀ. ἡ δυσθήρατός ἐστι σοφία Clem.*str*.5.4(p.340.24, v.l. ἀνεκλειπής M.9. 41B).

***ἀνεκμέτρητος**, *immeasurable*, Cyr.*Jo*.1.3(4.25E).

ἀνέκνιπτος, *not washed out*; met., of sin, Cyr.*ador*.8(1.254D).

[*]**ἀνέκπλυντος**, = ἀνέκπλυτος, *indelible*, Bas.*mor*.14.2(3.551B; M.32.1300D); cf.id.*hom.in Ps*.33(1.147C; M.29.361A).

ἀνεκποίητος, *inalienable*, Cyr.*ador*.13(1.470A); of inheritance of kingdom of heaven, id.*glaph.Gen*.6(1.204E); Proc.G.*Lev*.24:19 (M.87.784C).

***ἀνεκπόμπευτος**, *without public display, quiet, secret* ἀ. μνήσεσιν Dion.Ar.*e.h*.7.3.10(M.3.565C); id.*c.h*.15.8(M.3.336D); Max.*cap*.3.38 (M.90.1276C).

***ἀνεκπομπεύτως**, *without public display, secretly*, Dion.Ar.*c.h*. 15.6(M.3.336A); id.*e.h*.4.3.2(M.3.476C).

***ἀνεκπόρευτος**, *not proceeding*, of Father γεννητικὸς τοῦ λόγου... καὶ ἐκπορευτικὸς τοῦ πνεύματος, καὶ ἀ. Leont.H.*Nest*.1.29(M.86. 1496A).

***ἀνέκπτωτος**, *not altering*, of Christ ἑαυτοῦ καθ' ἑκάτερον [sc. nature] ἀεὶ μένων ἀ. ‡Hipp.*Ber.Hel*.4(p.324.7; M.10.536C).

ἀνέκπυστος, *not learnt, unheard*, Synes.*ep*.137(M.66.1525C).

***ἀνεκρίζωτος**, *uneradicated*, ‡Just.*qu.et resp*.1(M.6.1249A).

***ἀνεκτίθημι**, *tell of, recount* οἱ ἀπὸ δούλων ἐξευγενισθέντες οὐ κατοκνοῦσι πολλάκις τὴν δουλείαν τῶν πατέρων ἀ., ἵνα χάριν δῶσι τῷ ἐλευθερώσαντι ‡Ath.*diab*.6(p.7.27).

ἀνεκτότης, ἡ, *absence of constraint, freedom* ἀ. βίου Bas.*renunt*.1 (2.202C; M.31.625D); ἐλεύθερον περιπατεῖν ἐν ἀ. Mac.Aeg.*hom*.11.12 (M.34.553B); *V.Zos*.13(p.104.31).

***ἀνεκτρέφω**, *bring up, rear*, Ant.Mon.*hom*.83(M.89.1685B).

ἀνεκτῶς, **1.** *patiently*, Gr.Nyss.*mart*.3(M.46.781D); **2.** *without restraint, freely*, Pall.*v.Chrys*.17(p.108.4; M.47.60).

ἀνέκφαντος, *that cannot be revealed*, of God τὴν ὑπερούσιον οὐσίαν ...ἀ. Dion.Ar.*d.n*.5.1(M.3.816B).

***ἀνεκφοιτάω**, *depart*, Jo.D.*f.o*.4.20(M.94.1196C).

ἀνεκφοίτητος, *not departing* from, hence *inseparable*; **1.** Trin., Dion.Ar.*d.n*.2.4(M.3.640D) cit. s. ὑπερίδρυσις; ἀ. ... διὰ τὴν τῆς οὐσίας ταυτότητα †Proc.G.*Procl*.(M.87.2792^{h}A); †Alex.Sal.*cruc.epit*. (M.87.4088A); ἀ. δὲ αὐτάς [sc. ὑποστάσεις], καὶ ἀδιαστάτους ἀλλήλων Jo.D.*f.o*.3.5(M.94.1000B); ἀ. ἔχοντες τὴν ἐν ἀλλήλοις ἵδρυσιν id.*Jacob*. 78(M.94.1476B); **2.** of the Son in relation to Father, id.*f.o*.4.18 (M.94.1181B); ‡Meth.*Sym.et Ann*.4(M.18.356B); in Inc. πάντων τῶν ἑαυτοῦ μεταδιδοὺς τῇ σαρκί, ἀ. μεμένηκεν ἑαυτοῦ Leont.B.*Nest.et Eut*. 2(M.86.1336D); **3.** of H. Ghost ἀ. πατρὸς καὶ υἱοῦ Jo.D.*f.o*.1.8(M.94. 821C); **4.** of eternal generation of Son, Leont.H.*Nest*.4.9(M.86. 1669C); **5.** of distinctions within Godhead, Dion.Ar.*d.n*.2.11(M.3. 652A) cit. s. διάκρισις.

***ἀνεκφοιτήτως**, *without departure*; hence *without separation*, Dion.Ar.*d.n*.2.11(M.3.649B) cit. s. ἑνικῶς; Ἰησοῦς ὁ κύριος...ἀ. ταῖς ἀπὸ μονάδος προόδοις πρὸς ἑαυτὸν μοναδικῶς πάλιν ἀποκαθιστάμενος Max.*ambig*.(M.91.1400C); of Son in relation to Father, *cat.Apoc*. 12:7f.(p.359.4); Jo.D.*hom*.4.4(M.96.605A); ἀχωρίστως καὶ ἀ. γεννώμενος *ib*.1.18(572D).

ἀνέκφραστος, *inexpressible, unutterable*; **1.** of God ἀ. οὐσίας Eus.*e.th*.2.6(p.103.20; M.24.908A); Serap.*euch*.13.2; *cat.2Cor*.8:9 (p.402.20); *Lit.Chrys*.(p.322.2); of divine attributes and activity, Thphl.Ant.*Autol*.1.3(M.6.1028B); *ib*.1.5(1032A); ἀ. ἐστιν ὡς πρὸς ἄνθρωπον ἡ κατ' αὐτὸν δημιουργία *ib*.2.18(1081A); Eus.*p.e*.3.6(97B; M.21.177D); *ib*.7.15(325A; 549B); Cyr.*dial.Trin*.2(5^{1}.445D); τῆς σῆς περὶ ἡμᾶς κηδεμονίας τὸ ἀ. μέγεθος ‡Meth.*Sym.et Ann*.8(M.18.365C); **2.** of Son τὸ...ἀ. τῆς θεότητος φῶς †Hipp.*theoph*.3(p.258.31; M.10. 853C); ἡ ἀνωτάτω σοφία...θεία τις οὖσα καὶ ἀ. δύναμις Eust.*fr.Pr*. 8:22(M.18.684B); Ammon.*Jo*.1:5(M.85.1393D); θεὸς ὢν...ἀ., ἦλθες ἐπὶ τῆς γῆς *Rit.Bapt*.(p.400); of Son's generation, Eus.*ep.Caes*.6 (p.45.19; M.20.1541B)ap.Ath.*decr*.33(p.30.26); Sophr.H.*ep.syn*.(M.87. 3164A); of union of natures in Christ, ‡Ath.*Ar*.4.32(p.81.7; M.26. 517B); ἀ. συνανακράσεως Gr.Nyss.*or.catech*.16(p.70.13; M.45.52B); **3.** of H. Ghost σοφίᾳ τῇ ἀ. Clem.*paed*.3.12(p.291.6; M.8.680C); **4.** of divine mysteries ἀ. γὰρ τὰ περὶ θεοῦ Cyr.*Jo*.5(4.450E); Anast.S.*qu. et resp*.76(M.89.705A); Gnost. ὦ χάρις ἀ. ἐπὶ ὀνόματι σταυροῦ εἰρημένη *A.Petr.c.Sim*.37(p.90.20); **5.** of things pertaining to life after death, Gr.Nyss.*or.catech*.8(p.49.3; M.45.37B); τρυφὴν ἀ. Mac.Aeg. *hom*.4.12(M.34.481B); †Jo.D.*B.J*.8(M.96.921A); **6.** of human thought about God ἀ. μένει περὶ θεοῦ τὰ νοήματα Gr.Nyss.*hom.3 in Cant*. (M.44.820C).

***ἀνεκφράστως**, *inexpressibly, unutterably*; of Son's generation, †Ath.*exp.fid*.1(M.25.201B); Gel.Cyz.*h.e*.2.15.3(M.85.1257C); of Trin. μονὰς ἀ. ἐν τριάδι προσκυνουμένη Zach.Mit.*opif*.(M.85.1141B).

ἀνεκφώνητος, **1.** *inexpressible*; of the divine nature, Gr.Nyss.*deit*. (M.46.573D); id.*hom.11 in Cant*.(M.44.1013C); *ib*.*12*(1028B); **2.** *unutterable*, ref. 2Cor.12:3f., id.*Eun*.1(1 p.114.7; M.45.349A); *not to be pronounced*; of tetragrammaton, Eus.*d.e*.9.7(p.420.29; M.22.677C); Bas.*Spir*.44(3.37E; M.32.149A); Leont.H.*Nest*.5.16(M.86.1737D).

ἀνελάττωτος, *undiminished*, of God τῇ ἀ. χύσει τῶν ἀμειώτων αὐτοῦ μεταδόσεων Dion.Ar.*d.n*.2.11(M.3.649C); of Logos in Inc. ἀ. κατὰ τὴν θείαν οὐσίαν Apoll.*corp.et div*.6(p.188.2; M.*PL*.8.874A); τὴν θεϊκὴν τῆς οὐσίας αὐτοῦ πρὸς τὸν πατέρα δόξαν τε καὶ ταυτότητα διηνεκῶς μένειν ἀ. Max.*ep*.12(M.91.468D); of angelic powers τὴν ἀ. ἔφεσιν τοῦ ἀγαθοῦ Dion.Ar.*d.n*.8.4(892C).

ἀνέλεγκτος, **1.** *not proved guilty, innocent*, Just.*1apol*.7.4(M.6. 337B); **2.** *unconvicted* of sin, Or.*Jo*.6.58(38; p.167.15; M.14.301B); **3.** *irrefutable*, Just.*2apol*.13.3(M.6.465C); Synes.*ep*.148(M.66.1545B; l. ἀνεξέλεγκτα).

***ἀνελεεινός**, *unmerciful*; comp., ‡Chrys.*virg.corrupt*.(9.826D).

***ἀνελεημοσύνη**, ἡ, *unmercifulness*; of men, Chrys.*hom.11.7 in Mt*.(7.158A); ref. Mt.25:41 ἡ ἀ. οἰκήτορας τῆς γεέννης ἐποίησεν ὑμᾶς Eus.Al.*serm*.21.5(M.86.429C); of demons, Esaias *cap.spir*.13(M.40. 1209B).

ἀνελεήμων, *merciless*; *not generous, not giving alms*, Leont.N. *v.Jo.Eleem*.22(p.40.23); *ib*.(p.41.1).

ἀνελευθέριος, *unbefitting a free man*; comp., Chrys.*hom.1.3 in 2Tim*.(11.663B).

***ἀνέλευσις**, ἡ, *ascent* τὴν ἀ. τοῦ Χριστοῦ εἰς οὐρανόν Just.*1apol*. 26.1(M.6.368A); id.*dial*.39.4(M.6.560C); *ib*.87.6(684C).

***ἀνελθετέον**, *one must ascend*, met. ἀφ' ὧν [sc. τῶν γραφῶν] ἀ. πρὸς τὸν Ἰησοῦν Or.*Jo*.13.6(p.231.8; M.14.408B).

ἀνελίσσω, **1.** *unroll*; met., *retrace* τὴν αὐτὴν αὖθις ἀ. ὁδόν Cyr.*Jo*.4.3 (4.381E); **2.** *roll over, turn over*, Chrys.*laed*.6(3.452A); id.*hom.25.4 in Heb*.(12.234C); met. τοῦτον τὸν φόβον ἀεὶ παρ' ἑαυτῷ ἀνείλιττε id. *Saturn*.5(3.409C); **3.** *multiply*, Areth.*Apoc*.10(M.106.569A).

[*]**ἀνελλειπῶς**, v. ἀνελλιπῶς.

ἀνελλιπής (-ειπής), **1.** *unfailing, unceasing*; of God, *Const.App*. 7.35.9 cit. s. διαμονή; of divine grace or power ἀ. τηρῶν ἐν ἡμῖν τὸ πνεῦμα τῆς χάριτός σου *ib*.8.16.5; ἀ. γὰρ ἡ δύναμις [sc. τοῦ Χριστοῦ] πᾶσιν ἐξαρκοῦσα τοῖς δεομένοις Vict.*Mc*.7:25(p.337.29); c. genit., *unfailing in*, of Son ἀ. ... τοῦ ἐλέους καὶ τῆς ἀληθείας Or.*Ps*.60:7f. (p.69); of grace of H. Ghost τὸ ἀ. τῆς χορηγίας Chrys.*hom.51.1 in Jo*.(8.300B); of eternity, Clem.*prot*.9(p.64.4; M.8.196C) cit. s. συνεκτείνω; ἀ. ... αἰῶνας *Lit*.ap.*Const.App*.8.12.50; future life παλινζωίαν ἀ. *cat.Apoc*.2:8(p.205.8); of things spiritual and therefore abiding, *M.Seb.test*.2.1; of prayer θησαυρὸς ἀ. Chrys.*incomprehens*. 5.6(1.488B); **2.** abs., *without defect* or *deficiency, perfect*; **a.** of Trin. ἕκαστον πρόσωπον ἀμέριστον καὶ ἀ. καὶ τελείαν ἔχει θεότητα Sophr.H. *ep.syn*.(M.87.3157B); **b.** of God, ref. Creation πρὸ τοῦ ἐργάσασθαι, καὶ μετὰ τὸ ποιῆσαι, ὁμοίως ἀ. μένει Chrys.*hom.5.3 in Jo*.(8.38E); ref. goodness, wisdom, and power, Jo.D.*f.o*.1.5(M.94.801A); of Father ἀεὶ δὲ παρόντος αὐτῷ τοῦ υἱοῦ, ἀεί ἐστιν ὁ πατὴρ τέλειος, ἀ. τυγχάνων ἐν τῷ καλῷ Alex.Al.*ep.Alex*.7(p.23.30; M.18.557B); of Son τὸ ἀ. τοῦ υἱοῦ ὡς πρὸς τὸν πατέρα Gr.Nyss.*fid*.(M.45.140D); **c.** of Son, ref. perfect divinity ἀ. εἰς θεότητος ἀξίαν Cyr.H.*catech*. 4.7; and humanity, ‡Ath.*Apoll*.1.16(M.26.1124A) cit. s. τέλειος; Thdt.*eran*.2(4.84); οὐκ...τολμητέον εἰπεῖν ὡς ἡ σὰρξ οὐκ ἀ. ἦν ἐν τοῖς οἰκείοις ἰδιώμασιν Ephr.Ant.*fr*.(M.86.2105B); Max.*Pyrr*.(M.91.320C); id.*opusc*.(M.91.73C); υἱὸς τοῦ θεοῦ...ἀ. καὶ ἀδιαίρετος, ἐν τῷ σταυρῷ Anast.S.*hod*.12(M.89.197D); **d.** of divine will, Bas.*reg.br*.276(2.512E; M.31.1276C); of decalogue νόμον ἀ. *Const.App*.6.19.2; of bodies at resurrection, Gr.Nyss.*res*.3(M.46.660C); ‡Caes.Naz.*dial*.30(M.38. 892); of moral perfection, Gr.Nyss.*hom.11 in Cant*.(M.44.1001D); in gen., *complete*, id.*hex*.24(M.44.85C); Cyr.*Is*.5.1(2.742A); hence of a sentence, *unelliptical*, Areth.*Apoc*.1(M.106.509A); **3.** c. genit.; *not wanting in, not lacking*, of God ἀ. γὰρ ἀγαθοῦ παντὸς ἡ τῆς θεότητος ὡμολόγηται φύσις Gr.Nyss.*Eun*.6(2 p.135.8; M.45.720B); of men ὧν [sc. ἁμαρτιῶν] οὐδεὶς ἀ. Marc.Er.*opusc*.3.12(M.65.981D).

ἀνελλιπῶς (-ειπῶς), *without defect* or *deficiency, perfectly*; **1.** Trin. μιᾶς ἀμερίστως καὶ ἀ. τὰ τρία πρόσωπα πληρούσης θεότητος Sophr.H. *ep.syn*.(M.87.3157C); **2.** of eternity of Son διαιωνίζοντα...κατ' ἀρχὴν μέν, ἀ., κατὰ τέλος δέ, ἀδιαδόχως Areth.*Apoc*.1(M.106.512D); **3.** of perfection of divine and human natures in Christ, ‡Cyr.H.*occurs*. 4(M.33.1192A); Max.*opusc*.(M.91.73C); Jo.D.*volunt*.10(M.95.141A); **4.** in gen. ἀ. καὶ βεβαίως πᾶσαν τὴν πίστιν ἔχειν Or.*Jo*.32.16(9; p.452.14; M.14.784B); Cyr.H.*catech*.17.34; †Gregent.*leg.Hom*.53(M. 86.609A); hence *without omission* of words, *without ellipse*, Areth. *Apoc*.1(M.106.508D); c. ἔχειν, *be perfect*, *Disp.Phot*.(M.88.577A).

ἀνελπιστία, ἡ, **1.** *despair* of salvation; prevented by mercy of God, Thdr.Heracl.*Is*.28:5(M.18.1317A); πρὸς δὲ τὸν ἅπαξ εἰς ἁμαρτίαν ὀλισθήσαντα μὴ ἑαυτὸν προέσθαι διὰ τῆς ἀ. ἀγαθὴ ἡ ἐλπὶς τοῦ ἐλέους Bas.*hom.in Ps.*61:13(1.198E; M.29.489C); Chrys.*hom.10.3 in Heb.*(12.107D); by prayer ὁ εὐχόμενος, ἀπέχεται ἀνελπιστίας Marc. Er.*opusc.*2.24(M.65.933C); and confession, †Jo.Jej.*serm.*(M.88.1920A); temptation to despair as work of Devil, *cat.1Jo.*5:16f.(p.143.18); **2.** *failure to expect, want of hope* δῶρον μὲν διὰ τὴν ἀ. τῆς ἀπολήψεως Bas.*hom.in Ps.*14:5(1.112E; M.29.277C); τῶν κατὰ τὴν πίστιν νεοπαγῶν ἡ διάνοια, εἰς παντελῆ τῶν ἀγαθῶν ἀ. ἐκπίπτει Gr.Nyss. *v.Mos.*(M.44.360D); ἡ τῶν μελλόντων ἀ. Chrys.*hom.37.1 in Jo.*(8.211C); Ant.Mon.*hom.*10(M.89.1461B); in myst. life τραυματίζεται [sc. ἡ ψυχή] τῇ ἀ. τοῦ ποθουμένου Gr.Nyss.*hom.12 in Cant.*(M.44.1037B); **3.** *unexpected event* εἶτα πάλιν ἄλλη ἀ. Chrys.*hom.16.1 in Ac.*(9.128B).

[*]**ἀνεμαῖος**, prob. for ἀνεμιαῖος, *windy*; of a spider's web, Ast. Am.*hom.*1(M.40.165B).

ἀνέμβατος, *inaccessible*; met., of God, Cyr.*dial.Trin.*4(5^1.511E); ἀ. γὰρ τῇ κτίσει...τὰ μόνης καὶ ἰδικῶς τῆς ἀνωτάτω πασῶν οὐσίας id. *Juln.*2(6^2.62C); πᾶσι τοῖς γεγόνοσιν ἀ. id.*Jo.*4.1(4.348E); ἀ. γὰρ τοῖς πολλοῖς ἡ τῆς ἄγαν ὑπερτενοῦς γνώσεως χάρις id.*ador.*7(1.224E).

***ἀνεμεσί**, *without anger*, Leont.H.*Nest.*4.9(M.86.1668D).

***ἀνέμη, ἡ**, *windlass*, *Apophth.Patr.*(M.65.261B).

ἀνεμίζω, **1.** *sail with the wind*, Jo.Mosch.*prat.*174(M.87.3044A); **2.** pass., *deteriorate through exposure to air*; of wine, Esaias *or.*12.1 (p.72).

***ἀνεμοκαύσων, ὁ**, *burning wind*, Ephr.3.70A.

ἄνεμος, ὁ, *wind*; **1.** lit.; exeg. Ps.134:7, Chrys.*exp.in Ps.*134:7 (5.387Bff.); as cause of all generation (Sethian), Hipp.*haer.*5.19 (p.118.26; M.16.3182C); *ib.*(p.120.1ff.; 3183B); **2.** fig.; evil wind of sin contrasted with divine wind of H. Ghost, Mac.Aeg.*hom.*2.4 (M.34.465Aff.); τὰ ἐνδότερα αὐτῆς [sc. τῆς καρδίας] ἀνενόχλητα ταμεῖα ...ἔνθα οὐκ εἰσὶ πονηρῶν λογισμῶν ἄνεμοι...ὠθοῦντες καὶ ψυχὴν καὶ σῶμα ἐπὶ τοὺς κρημνοὺς τῆς ἡδυπαθείας Marc.Er.*opusc.*4(M.65.1016D); **3.** met.; of God ῥῦσε ἱμᾶς, κ⟨ύρι⟩ε, ἀπὸ κατεγγε⟨λιῶν⟩ φυσοῦ σὺ ἀνέμον *MAMA* 1.428; of angels; significance explained, Dion. Ar.*c.h.*15.6(M.3.333Cff.); exeg. Eph.4:14 περιφέρεται δὲ παντὶ ἀ. ὁ παραβεβλημένος, εἴτε διδασκαλίας εἴτε θυμοῦ εἴτε ἐπιθυμίας. ἄ. δὲ τέσσαρες γενικοί, ταράσσοντες τὴν ἀνθρώπου ψυχήν, ἐπιθυμία, φόβος, ἡδονή, λύπη Or.*fr.25 in Jer.*(p.210.28; M.13.593A).

ἀνεμοσκεπής, *sheltering from the wind*, Nonn.*par.Jo.*18:3(M.43.889A).

***ἀνεμοστρόβυλος, ὁ**, *whirlwind*, *Apoc.Dan.*C(p.119, v.l. ἀνέμου καὶ στροβύλου).

ἀνεμοφθορία, ἡ, *havoc made by the wind, blasting*, Gr.Naz.*or.*16.5 (M.35.940B); Cyr.*Soph.*6(3.585E).

ἀνεμόφθορος, *blasted by the wind*; **1.** fig. ἀ. τινές ἐσμεν Or. *hom.15.3 in Jer.*(p.127.29; M.13.432C); Nil.*epp.*2.49(M.79.221B); Pall. *h.Laus.*47(p.140.11; M.34.1202A) cit. s. συνιππάζω; **2.** met., *empty, false* ἀ. ... χειροτονίας id.*v.Chrys.*16(p.94.9; M.47.53); δεῖμα...ἀ. Eudoc.*Cypr.*2.157(M.85.852B).

***ἀνέμπαικτος**, *free from injury*; neut. as subst., Ephr.3.212E.

***ἀνεμπεπλόκως**, c. ἔχειν, *be unable to be united*; of mutually exclusive qualities, Ephr.1.228C.

***ἀνεμπίπτω**, *fall into*, ‡Ath.*doct.Ant.*10(M.28.568D).

***ἀνέμπλοος**, *not sailing, at rest*, Nonn.*par.Jo.*6:22(M.43.797A).

ἀνεμώδης, *like the wind*, Nonn.*par.Jo.*19:34(M.43.905A); *ib.*20:26 (913A).

ἀνενδεής, **A.** abs., *in need of nothing*; implying **1.** *self-sufficient*; **a.** of God, Just.*dial.*23.2(M.6.525C); Athenag.*leg.*13.1(M.6.916B); Clem.*prot.*4(p.44.16; M.8.153B); *Lit.*ap.*Const.App.*8.12.6; ἀ. γὰρ ὢν ἡμῶν ὁ δεσπότης, οὐδενὸς δεῖται τῶν παρ' ἡμῶν, εἰ μὴ τῶν ῥημάτων μόνον Chrys.*hom.26.5 in Gen.*(4.252E); οὐ δεῖται τῶν ὑμνούντων...ἀ. γὰρ ἔχει τὴν φύσιν Thdt.*qu.4.in Gen.*(1.7); Bas.Sel.*or.*3.2(M.85.49D); Gennad.*fr.Gen.*1:26(M.85.1633C); ἡ δανείσασα [sc. BMV] θεῷ τῷ ἀ. σάρκα ἥνπερ οὐκ εἶχεν ‡Meth.*Sym.et Ann.*10(M.18.373A); neut. as subst., Cyr.*Ps.*15:2(M.69.808B); Jo.D.*f.o.*1.14(M.94.860A); partic. of Father θεοῦ τοῦ ἀ. ἢ τοῦ υἱοῦ αὐτοῦ Or.*Cels.*7.65(p.215.6; M.11.1513A); αὐτὸς γάρ [sc. ὁ Χριστός], ἵν' οὕτως εἴπω, ἐπισκευάζεται ἀεὶ ἀπὸ τοῦ πατρὸς τοῦ μόνου ἀ. id.*Jo.*13.34(p.259.20; M.14.460A); **b.** of Son, Alex.Al.*ep.Alex.*7(p.24.11; M.18.557C); **c.** of stars, Meth. *symp.*8.16(p.104.17; M.18.168C); denied of angels, ref. Ps.77:25, Or.*Jo.*13.33(p.259.3; M.14.457B); **d.** of men, in future life ἵνα ἀεὶ ὦσι καὶ ἀπαθεῖς καὶ ἀ., τοῖς ἡμετέροις διδάγμασι προσέχειν δεῖ Just. *1apol.*57.2(M.6.413C); of risen bodies without physical needs, ‡Just.*qu.et resp.*95(M.6.1337A); in this life, in dependence on God ἀ. τυγχάνει πᾶς ὁ ταύτης [sc. ὁδοῦ i.e. Christ] ἐπιβαίνων Or.*Jo.*1.27(26; p.34.12; M.14.73A); Cyr.*Lc.*12:24(M.72.740A); ref. Is.40:31, Thdt.*eran.*3(4.192); in gen.; of members of a self-sufficient community, Pall.*h.Laus.*7(p.26.5; M.34.1020C); **e.** acc. Docetae κεκόσμητο μὲν ἀ. πᾶσα ἡ νοητὴ φύσις Hipp.*haer.*8.9(p.228.7; M.16.3351B); **2.** *complete*, ref. Christ ἀ. τελειότητος ‡Ath.*Apoll.*1.5(M.26.1101B); **3.** *unfailing* ἀ. χορηγὸν καὶ ταμίαν θεὸν ἔχοντες Bas.*hom.*8.2(2.64A; M.31.309B).

B. c. genit., *not in need of*; **1.** of God ἀ. αἱμάτων Just.*1apol.*13.1 (M.6.345B); θεότητος ἴδιον τὸ ἀ. παντὸς τοῦ κατὰ τὸ ἀγαθὸν θεωρουμένου νοήματος Gr.Nyss.*Eun.*8(2 p.200.29; M.45.797A); **2.** of men; αὐτάρκης μὲν γενόμενος [sc. 'gnostic'] ἀ. τε τῶν ἄλλων Clem.*str.*7.7 (p.33.17; M.9.464B); *not lacking in* ἀ. ... παντὸς ἀγαθοῦ Cyr.*Os.*7 (3.182E).

***ἀνενδέησις, ἡ**, *absence of need*, ‡Chrys.*mart.*2(3.813A).

***ἀνενδείκνυμι**, for ἂν ἐνδείκνυμι, Heracleon ap.Or.*Jo.*13.10(M.14.413C; ἐνδείκνυμι p.235.1).

***ἀνένδεικτος**, *that cannot be shown, of which no instance can be given* τοῖς ἀδυνάτοις καὶ ἀ. Dion.Al.ap.Eus.*p.e.*14.25(778B; M.21.1280C, perh. for ἀνένδεκτος q.v.).

ἀνένδεκτος, **1.** *that cannot be admitted, impossible* ὥσπερ ἀνάγκη τὸ θνητὸν ἀποθνήσκειν καὶ ἀ. αὐτὸ μὴ ἀποθανεῖν...οὕτως ἀνάγκη [sc. ἐλθεῖν τὰ σκάνδαλα] καὶ ἀ. μὴ ἐλθεῖν...ἀ. γάρ ἐστιν ἄνθρωπον εὑρεθῆναι πάντη ἀναμάρτητον Or.*comm.inMt.*13.23(p.242.6; M.13.1156B); ἀ. τὴν σάρκα ὑπὲρ Χριστοῦ παθοῦσαν, μὴ σὺν Χριστῷ βασιλεύειν Epiph. *haer.*42.12(p.158.29; M.41.777C); ἀ. γὰρ κτιστόν τι ἐν τριάδι λέγειν *ib.* 74.12(p.330.10; M.42.497C); neut. as subst., *incapacity* οὔτε οὖν βλαβῆναι δύναται [sc. Christian], οὔτε βλάψαι ἕτερον. τὸ δέ, οὐ δύναται, μὴ ἀδυναμίας νομίσῃς...ἀλλὰ τὸ ἀ. λέγω. ἡ γὰρ φύσις ἐκείνη οὔτε βλάβης ἐστὶ δεκτικὴ οὔτε τοῦ ἀδικεῖν ἕτερον Chrys.*hom.51.4 in Ac.*(9.385A); **2.** *not to be admitted* πολυπραγμοσύνης ἀ. Thdr.Stud. *or.*9.9(M.99.781D).

ἀνενδεῶς, **1.** *in need of nothing, without want*, Clem.*str.*7.6(p.23.2; M.9.444A); Bas.*ep.*76(3.171D; M.32.452B); c. ἔχω, *abound* in, of BMV ἀγαθοῖς ἀ. ἔχουσα Thdr.Stud.*nativ.BMV* 4(M.96.684B); **2.** *completely*, Bas.*hex.*5.8(1.47E; M.29.113A); **3.** *unfailingly* ἀ. χορηγεῖσθαι Meth.*symp.*2.4(p.20.4; M.18.52D).

ἀνενδοίαστος, *undoubting*; of faith, Cyr.H.*catech.*23.20; Cyr.*Is.* 4.2(2.609A); of hope, ‡Bas.*const.*26.1(2.576B; M.31.1416B).

ἀνενδοιάστως (-δυάστως), **1.** *indubitably; unambiguously, plainly* ἀνακεκαλυμμένως καὶ ἀ. ἡ ἱερουργία ἐπιτελεῖται Thdr.Stud.*praesanct.* (M.99.1688B); **2.** *without doubting* ἀ. φάγε τὸ σῶμα, πίε τὸ αἷμα Gr. Naz.*or.*45.19(M.36.649C); ἀ. παραδεξόμεθα τὰ διὰ θείου πνεύματος χρησμῳδούμενα Cyr.*inc.unigen.*(5^1.694A); *unhesitatingly* ἐν ὅλῳ τῷ πνεύματι ἡμῶν ἀ. ... τὸ ἅγιον πνεῦμα προσκυνεῖν Didym.*Trin.*2.10 (M.39.641B); ἀ. κηρύττομεν Jo.D.*haer.Nest.*43(M.95.221C).

ἀνένδοτος, *not giving way*; **1.** *constant, steadfast*; in martyrdom, *Ep.Lugd.*ap.Eus.*h.e.*5.1.22(M.20.417A); ἡ πρόθεσις...ἀ. πρὸς τὸ ἧττον Clem.*str.*3.12(p.231.24; M.8.1177D); ἀρεταί...ἀ. Gr.Nyss.*hom.4 in Cant.*(M.44.837B) etc.; **2.** *stubborn, obstinate*, Or.*enarr.in Job* 41:15 (M.17.105A); ἀ. γῆν Chrys.*hom.18.1 in Jo.*(8.104B); ἀ. πρὸς μετάγνωσιν Isid.Pel.*epp.*1.154(M.78.285C); neut. as subst., of Pharaoh's heart, †Bas.*Is.*187(1.517C; M.30.437A); **3.** *uninterrupted, unceasing*, Bas.*reg.fus.*12(2.354C; M.31.949A); Diad.*perf.*33(p.36.26); ἀ. ...συμπάθειαν Leont.N.*v.Jo.Eleem.*26(p.54.3).

ἀνενδότως, *without giving way*, hence *steadfastly*, *Lit.*ap.*Const. App.*8.10.5; *stubbornly*, Chrys.*Stag.*3.14(1.226B); *ceaselessly*, Sophr. H.*mir.Cyr.et Jo.*18(M.87.3476D).

***ἀνένδοχος**, *not receptive*, Or.*Jo.*1.34(39; p.43.25; M.14.89C).

[*]**ἀνενδυάστως**, v. ἀνενδοιάστως.

ἀνενεργησία, ἡ, **1.** *inactivity, quiescence* τοῦ δὲ θεοφιλῶς αἰτιασαμένου [sc. in baptism]...τὴν τῆς ἐνθέου ζωῆς ἀ. Dion.Ar.*e.h.*2.2.5 (M.3.396A); ἡ σταυροειδὴς δὲ σφραγὶς [sc. in ordination] τὴν ἁπασῶν ὁμοῦ τῶν σαρκικῶν ὀρεξέων ἀ. [sc. ἐμφαίνει] *ib.*5.3.4(512A); ἐν τῷ ἐρήμῳ καθήμενοι, τουτέστιν, ἐν τῇ τῶν κακῶν ἀ. ‡Max.*cap.al.*122 (M.90.1428C); esp. in contemplation, Dion.Ar.*myst.*1.3(M.3.1001A) cit. s. ἑνόω; τῇ τῶν νοήσεων ἀποπαύσει καὶ ἀπολύσει...ἥντινα ἀ. τῆς ἱερᾶς κινήσεως ἐν μὲν τοῖς πρὸ τούτου ἀνοησίαν ἐκάλεσεν· ἐνταῦθα δὲ σκοτεινότατον γνόφον Max.*schol.myst.*1.1(M.4.416C); **2.** *inefficacy, powerlessness*, Andr.Caes.*Apoc.*34(M.106.328B); ἀ. τῆς πολυσχεδοῦς κακίας *ib.*58(404A).

ἀνενέργητος, **1.** *inactive*; **a.** denied of Father; ref. generation of Son, Gr.Nyss.*Eun.*4(2 p.78.11; M.45.652C); at time of Inc., *ib.*12 (2 p.288.2; 900C); but implied in heret. arguments εἰ ἄγονος, καὶ ἀ. ὁ θεός· γέννημα γὰρ αὐτοῦ ὁ υἱὸς δι' οὗ ἐργάζεται ‡Ath.*Ar.*4.4(p.49.3; M.26.473B); τὸν δὲ θεόν, σιωπῶντα μὲν ἀ., λαλοῦντα δὲ ἰσχύειν αὐτὸν βούλονται [sc. Arians]· εἴγε σιωπῶν μὲν οὐκ ἠδύνατο ποιεῖν, λαλῶν δὲ κτίζειν ἤρξατο *ib.*4.11(p.55.2; 481A); *incapable of performing* εἰς βλασφημίαν...περιτραπήσεται, δι' ἔνδειαν ὕλης ἄπρακτον καὶ ἀ. τῶν οἰκείων ἔργων τὸν θεὸν κατεχόντων Bas.*hex*.2.2(1.13D; M.29.32B); **b.** denied of Logos, Gr.Nyss.*or.catech*.1(p.10.17; M.45.16A); of Logos in man αὐτὸν...ἀ. ἔχετε παρ' ἑαυτοῖς, οὐδὲν πράττοντες ἢ νοοῦντες λογικῶς Or.*fr.18 in Jo*.(p.498.4); denied of Christ between Crucifixion and Resurrection, Bas.*hom.in Ps*.44:9(1.166D; M.29.408A); **c.** denied of H. Ghost at Creation, Gr.Nyss.*Maced*.12(M.45.1316C); **d.** of Devil τῷ σταυρῷ βέβλησαι...ἀκίνητος, ἀ. Gr.Naz.*or*.45.22(M.36.653C); **e.** of Law and prophets, superseded by grace, Mac.Mgn.*apocr*.3.41(p.143.33); **f.** of men ἀ. ἐστιν [sc. ὁ ἐν ἁμαρτίαις], ὡς ὁ καθεύδων Chrys.*hom.18.1 in Eph*.(11.128B); ὁ δὲ βαπτιζόμενος ὑπαρχέτω...ἀ. πρὸς ἁμαρτίαν *Const.App*.3.18.1; σάρκας...ἀ. πρὸς ἁμαρτίαν παρασκευαζέτω Isid.Pel.*epp*.4.3(M.78.1052B); τὸ τῆς λογικῆς ψυχῆς ἡγεμονικὸν...πρὸς τὰς θείας...θεωρίας καὶ λειτουργίας...ἀ. Gr. Agr.*Eccl*.2.12(M.98.836B); of sense of hearing in contemplation, Gr.Nyss.*hom.11 in Cant*.(M.44.993B); **g.** hence of things, *unused* ἄβατον τὸ λουτρὸν...καὶ ἀ. id.*v.Gr.Thaum*.(M.46.925A); **2.** *ineffective* ἀ. ... τὸ κήρυγμα id.*Spir*.(M.46.697D); ἄφωνός τε καὶ ἀ. id.*Eun*.12(1 p.242.21; M.45.941B); οὐδὲ ἔδει τὴν ἡμετέραν κακίαν νικῆσαι, καὶ ἀ. ποιῆσαι τὴν ἀγαθότητα αὐτοῦ Jo.D.*Man*.1.72(M.94.1572B); **3.** *not made active* τὴν δὲ σάρκα χωρίζων [sc. Marcellus] τῆς τοῦ λόγου ἐνεργείας καὶ καταλιπὼν αὐτὴν...ἀ. ὑπὸ τοῦ λόγου Eus.*e.th*.3.10(p.167.13; M.24.1020C); *without* ἐνέργεια, *not having the power of action* οὐδὲ γὰρ τὴν θείαν φύσιν...ἀ. καθορῶμεν· οὔτε μὴν τὴν...ἀνθρωπίνην οὐσίαν...ἀ. ἐπιγινώσκομεν Max.*opusc*.(M.91.96A); εἰ δὲ ἀνεθέλητος ἦν καὶ ἀ., τὸ καθ' ἡμᾶς,...οὐδὲ καθ' ἡμᾶς ὅλως γέγονεν *ib*.(157C); εἰ ἐκ τῆς ἑνώσεως αὐτῷ, κατὰ τὸν ὑμέτερον λόγον, προσγέγονεν ἡ ἐνέργεια, πρὸ τῆς ἑνώσεως ἄρα ἀ. ἦν id.*Pyrr*.(M.91.340D); **4.** *deprived of functions* in Church ἀκοινώνητοι...καὶ ἀ. παρὰ τῆς οἰκουμενικῆς συνόδου γεγόνασι CEph.(431)*ep*.(*ACO* 1.1.3 p.33.8; H.1.1592D); πάσης ἐκκλησιαστικῆς κοινωνίας...ἐκβεβλημένος καὶ ἀ. ὑπάρχων CEph.(431) *can*.1.

***ἀνενθρονίαστος**, *unconsecrated*, Thdr.Stud.*epp*.2.219.15(M.99.1665B).

ἀνενθύμητος, *inconceivable*; of generation of Son, Eus.*d.e*.5.1 (p.213.5; M.22.353B).

ἀνεννόητος, **A.** *inconceivable, beyond one's conception*; **1.** of God, Mac.Aeg.*hom*.4.10(M.34.480B); Max.*schol.d.n*.1.5(M.4.201D); of God's wisdom, Meth.*symp*.8.16(p.105.11; M.18.168D); goodness in Inc., Mac.Aeg.*hom*.4.9(480A); grace, Hipp.*haer*.6.40(p.171.16; M.16.3258C); neut. as subst.; of Father, Iren.*haer*.1.15.5(M.7.625B); of union of Christ's natures, Leont.B.*fr*.(M.86.2005D); κατὰ χάριν ἔχοντες ἐν ἑαυτοῖς τὸν θεὸν ἀρρήτῳ τε λόγῳ καὶ ἀ. τῇ διανοίᾳ θεοφόροι ...λέγονται Max.*schol.c.h*.7.1(M.4.68B); **2.** of Valent. ogdoad, Iren. *haer*.1.11.5(M.7.568B); Marcosian, of Πατήρ, *ib*.1.14.1; **3.** Arian; of God as totally unknowable, Philost.*h.e*.2.3(M.65.468A).

B. *not conceived*, hence *unexpected* ἀ. παθῶν σωματικῶν *cat. Apoc*.8:6(p.302.22).

C. *without conception*, abs. τοῖς οἴκοθεν ἀ. παραστῆσαι φύσιν ἀκατονόμαστον Synes.*insomn*.19(p.184.14; M.66.1316C); c. genit. ἀνενδεὲς δὲ τὸ θεῖον, ἀ. ἄρα πονηρίας Meth.*symp*.8.16(p.104.14; M.18.168C); *ib*.(p.104.17; 168C).

D. *without thought* or *care for*, of Cain ἀνεννόητος...αὐτοῦ [sc. τοῦ θεοῦ] γεγενημένος Proc.G.*Gen*.4:16(M.87.253A).

***ἀνέννοιος**, *without thought, unmeaning*, Jo.Clim.*scal*.7(M.88.805A).

ἀνενόχλητος, *undisturbed*; esp. *unperturbed by passion* or *desire*, Marc.Er.*opusc*.4(M.65.1016D) cit. s. ἄνεμος; Arsen.*doct*.2(M.66.1620C); Cyr.*Rom*.7:8(p.198.5); Thal.*cent*.3.31(M.91.1452A); neut. as subst., *freedom from desire*, Nil.*epp*.3.43(M.79.408D).

ἀνενοχλήτως, *without disturbance* or *hindrance*; of praying *without distraction*, Max.*carit*.2.6(M.90.985B).

***ἀνένοχος**, *without guilt*, *Lit.Chrys*.(p.317.16).

***ἀνενόχως**, *guiltlessly*, *Lit.Chrys*.(p.317.24).

***ἀνεντερίζω**, *disembowel*, Jo.Mal.*chron*.5 p.115(M.97.208D).

ἀνεντρεχής, *unskilful*, Or.*Jo*.1.15(p.19.26; M.14.49A).

***ἀνεξάγγελτος**, *unconfessed*, Thdr.Stud.*poen*.1.25(M.99.1736C).

***ἀνεξαγόρευτος**, **1.** *not to be told, secret*, Hipp.*haer*.5.7(p.84.2; M.16.3134B); **2.** *unconfessed*; of sins, Jo.Clim.*scal*.4(M.88.684D); Anast.S.*qu.et resp*.6(M.89.372C); Niceph.Ur.*v.Sym*.86(M.86.3068B).

ἀνεξάκουστος, *not to be heard*, Jo.VI H.*v.Jo.D*.27(M.94.468C).

ἀνεξάλειπτος, **1.** *not to be blotted out, indelible*; fig., of seal of baptism, Cyr.H.*procatech*.17; *Rit.Bapt*.(p.406); met., of sin, Meth.*lepr*.10(p.464.13); Eus.*d.e*.10.5(p.467.5ff.; M.22.752B); met., *indestructible, imperishable*, Or.*exp.in Pr*.5:14(M.17.173C); of circumcision ἀ. μνημόσυνον ‡Just.*qu.et resp*.102(M.6.1348B); ‡Bas.*struct. hom*.1.7(1.327F; M.30.20A); Leont.B.*parasc*.(M.86.1993B); of faith of Christians, *Dial.Christ.et Jud*.10(p.62.7); **2.** *not blotted out, unabsolved*; of sin, Marc.Er.*opusc*.1.128(M.65.921A).

***ἀνεξάντλητος**, *inexhaustible*, ‡Pion.*v.Polyc*.26; ‡Chrys.*hom.jej*.4(9.799A); ‡Proc.G.*Pr*.5:15(M.87.1264D).

ἀνεξαπάτητος, **1.** *that cannot be deceived*; of God, Chrys.*comm.in Gal*.1:10(10.671E); **2.** *undeceived*, Or.*Cels*.1.42(p.92.23; M.11.737B); Proc.G.*Gen*.3:16(M.87.212A).

***ἀνεξάπτω**, *kindle again*; met., the heart, Jo.Clim.*scal*.7(M.88.816B).

***ἀνεξάρνητος**, **1.** *not denied* μενούσης μοι τῆς κατὰ θεὸν πολιτείας ἀ. Tat.*orat*.42(p.43.15; M.6.888B); *Const.App*.8.45.1; *Rit.Bapt*.(p.389); of Church by Christ, ‡Ath.*proph*.8(M.28.1072A); **2.** *undeniable*, *A.Jo*.9(p.157.1); **3.** *not denying* ἀ. ἡμᾶς...τοῦ ὀνόματος αὐτοῦ Just.*dial*.30.2(M.6.540A).

***ἀνεξαρνήτως**, *without denial*, *M.Con*.5.3.

***ἀνεξεικόνιστος**, *unformed*, Hipp.*haer*.5.7(p.84.9; M.16.3134C); Bas.*ep*.188 *can*.2(3.271A; M.32.672A); *unable to be depicted* οὐδεὶς ἄνθρωπος ὀφθείς, ἀ. Thdr.Stud.*ref*.30(M.99.472D).

***ἀνεξεισάγω**, f.l. for ἀντεξάγω q.v., Cyr.ap.*cat.Jo*.15:26(p.359.9); cf. ἀντεξάγουσι Cyr.*Jo*.10.2(4.904A).

ἀνεξέλεγκτος, *unconvicted*, *Const.App*.2.17.4; *ib*.5.14.13.

ἀνεξερεύνητος, **1.** *not to be searched out, unsearchable*; of God and divine attributes, Dion.Ar.*d.n*.1.2(M.3.588C); ref. Inc. ὁ ἀ. τε καὶ ἀνώνυμος...δι' ὀνομασίας...φανερῶς γνωρίζεται Andr.Cr.*or*.6(M.97.913C); of power of Christ, ‡Meth.*Sym.et Ann*.7(M.18.364B); neut. as subst. τὸ ἀ. τῶν ἀβύσσων τοῦ θεοῦ κριμάτων Nil.*epp*.1.23(M.79.89D); of divine mysteries: generation of Son, Eus.*e.th*.1.12(p.71.8; M.24.848A); manner of conversion of eucharistic elements, Jo.D.*f.o*.4.13(M.94.1145A); union of Christ's natures, Jo.V H.*icon*.7(M.96.1356B); **2.** *uninvestigated*, Or.*fr.hom.39 in Jer*.(p.198.6; M.13.544C).

***ἀνεξερευνήτως**, *unsearchably*, Andr.Cr.*or*.6(M.97.917D).

ἀνεξέταστος, *not enquired into* or *examined*; of conduct μηδὲν ἀ. ἔσεσθαι παρὰ τῷ θεῷ Athenag.*leg*.36.1(M.6.969C); hence *indiscriminate* ἀ. ... φόνον Gr.Nyss.*v.Mos*.(M.44.393B); *unquestioning* ὑπακοή ἐστιν ἀ. κίνησις Jo.Clim.*scal*.4(M.88.680A).

ἀνεξετάστως, *without examination* τὰς ἐντολὰς τοῦ κυρίου ἀ. δεχόμεθα Bas.*ascet*.2.2(2.326D; M.31.888B).

[*]**ἀνεξεύρητος**, = ἀνεξεύρετος, *unsearchable*, Hipp.*haer*.5.7(p.79.9; M.16.3127A); of nature of God, Geo.Pis.*hex*.81(M.92.1435A); *ib*.594(1481A).

***ἀνεξευρίσκω**, *find out* τὴν διάνοιαν ἀ. Vict.*Mc*.proem.(p.263.13).

ἀνεξήγητος, *indescribable*; of God's goodness, Iren.*haer*.4.20.5 (M.7.1035C); of eternal generation of Son, ref. Is.53:8, Cyr.*Jo*.1.1 (4.11B).

[*]**ἀνεξήτητος**, v. ἀνεξίτητος.

ἀνεξικακ-έω, *be long-suffering*; of God, Meth.*symp*.10.2(p.124.13; M.18.196C); Chrys.*hom.3.6 in Heb*.(12.37B); Thdr.Mops.*Mal*.3:5ff. (M.66.625A); ἀ. τοῖς εἰωθόσι πλημμελεῖν Cyr.*Is*.2.5(2.345B); Proc.G. *Is*.24:18(M.87.2193C); of Christ ~οῦντος γὰρ τοῦ υἱοῦ...οὐκ ἀνέξεταί φησιν ὁ πατήρ Cyr.*Jo*.6(4.571D); ἀ. μέχρι τοῦ σταυροῦ Proc.G.*Is*.33 (M.87.2296B); Justn.*conf*.(p.106.18; M.86.1029D); of men, *M.Tar*.9 (p.471); Eus.*v.C*.2.11(p.45.26; M.20.989C); *be patient, wait*, *V.Alex. Acoem*.37(p.687.6).

ἀνεξικακία, ἡ, *forbearance, long-suffering, patient endurance*; **1.** divine; of God, Clem.*paed*.1.9(p.136.16; M.8.344C); Tit.Bost. *Man*.2.28(M.18.1189B); Cyr.H.*catech*.8.4; Chrys.*hom.22.1 in Gen*. (4.193C); καλεῖ πρὸς μετάγνωσιν τὸ τῆς ἀ. μέγεθος Cyr.*Os*.61(3.94A); of Christ, Or.*Cels*.2.34(p.161.13; M.11.856C); Eust.*engast*.10(p.31.23; M.18.633B); Eus.*d.e*.1.1(p.4.4; M.22.17B); Chrys.*hom.71.2 in Jo*. (8.419C); Arsen.*tent*.(M.66.1621B); **2.** as Christian virtue, Clem. *paed*.3.12(p.286.5; M.8.669B); οὐκ ἀδίκου τῆς δικαίας ἀμύνης οὔσης, ἀλλὰ κρείττονος τῆς ἀ. *Const.App*.6.23.2; πραότης γάρ, ἀνεξικακίας μήτηρ ‡Bas.*const*.13(2.558C; M.31.1377A); μέγα...ὅπλον ἐν τοῖς πειρασμοῖς ἀ. Chrys.*hom.30.1 in Heb*.(12.280B); exeg. Rom.12:21 λαμπρὰ νίκη, ὅταν ἐν τῷ ἀγαθῷ, τουτέστι τῇ ἀ., νικήσῃς τὸ κακόν, τὴν ὀργὴν...ἐκβαλών id.*hom.in Rom.12:20*(3.167C); τῆς πρὸς ἅπαντας ἐπιεικοῦς ἀ., ἧς τύπος ἡ ἐπὶ Νῶε τοῦ θεοῦ φιλανθρωπία· ἐφ' ἡμᾶς δὲ ἡ διὰ τοῦ βαπτίσματος τοῦ Χριστοῦ συμπάθεια Euthal.Diac.*epp. cath*.(M.85.681A); Jo.D.*virt*.(M.95.85C) = Ephr.3.425D; as expressly taught by Christ (ref. Mt.18:22), Or.*fr.382 in Mt*.(p.164; M.17.300B); (ref. Mt.26:25), Chrys.*hom.81.2 in Mt*.(7.775C); περὶ ἀ. διαλεγόμενος, μέσον ἑαυτὸν προτίθησι, κελεύων ἐκεῖθεν λαμβάνειν τὰ ὑποδείγματα id.*hom.80.1 in Jo*.(8.472D); **3.** as title of address μέμνηται ἡ ὑμετέρα ἀ. Const.ap.Thdt.*h.e*.1.20.5(3.798); Bas.*ep*.82 (3.175D; M.32.460B); *Cod.Afr*.86.

ἀνεξίκακος, **1.** *forbearing, long-suffering*; **a.** of God, Cyr.*Os.*70(3.105E); Proc.G.*Is.*55:7(M.87.2557A); Leont.N.*v.Jo.Eleem.*41(p.79.24); neut. as subst., Eus.*fr.Lc.*(M.24.581B); Tit.Bost.*Man.*2.22(M.18.1177C); *Const.App.*2.20.7; **b.** of Christians, Just.*1apol.*16.1(M.6.352C); Athenag.*leg.*34.2(M.6.968C); of the 'gnostic', Clem.*str.*7.7(p.34.8; M.9.465A); as imitating God, Gr.Nyss.*or.dom.*5(p.92.27; M.44.1177B); of the ideal bishop, *Const.App.*2.57.1; Nil.*epp.*3.134(M.79.445B); of slaves, ref. 1Petr.2:18 ἀ. ὑπομονῆς Euthal. Diac.*epp.cath.*(M.85.680C); *patient* δέχου...τὴν ἀπόδειξιν, ἀ. τοῖς λόγοις ἁπλώσας τὴν ἀκοήν Cyr.*Jo.*2.1(4.122A); **2.** *averting evil* ἀ. ἄφιξιν Sophr.H.*mir.Cyr.et Jo.*8(M.87.3437D, prob. f.l. for ἀλεξι-).

ἀνεξικάκως, *forbearingly, patiently*, of God ἴδιον γὰρ ἂν εἴη θεῷ πάντα ἀ. φέρειν Eust.*engast.*10(p.31.26; M.18.633C); of Christ τοὺς ὑβρίζοντας φέρων ἀ. Thdr.Heracl.ap.*cat.Mt.*9:34(p.73.15); *cat.Lc.*22:14(p.154.7), l. ἀνεξικακῶν Cyr.*Lc.*22:14(M.72.905A); of men, Cyr.*Jo.*1.10(4.110E); Ant.Mon.*hom.*111(M.89.1776B); superl., of S. Peter, ref. Gal.2:14, Or.*Jo.*32.5(p.434.20).

ἀνεξίτηλος, *indelible*; hence met., as subst. neut., *fixedness* εἴσω δὴ οὖν καθῆσθαι πυλῶν [sc. of Jerusalem]...κεχρησμῴδηκε θεός, τὸ ἀσφαλές τε καὶ ἀ. καὶ τὸ μηδαμῇ χρῆναι παρολισθεῖν τῆς εἰς αὐτὸν γνησιότητος τοῦ τύπου σημαίνοντος Cyr.*ador.*7(1.229C), ? f.l. for ἀνεξίτητος q.v.

ἀνεξίτητος, also [*]ἀνεξήτητος; **1.** *with no outlet*, Eus.*e.th.*3.2(p.144.30; M.24.981A); hence *inescapable*, Cyr.*Is.*2.2(2.237A); ἀνεξήτητος *ib.*(224C); *ib.*2.5(345A); *ib.*4.3(620A); *insoluble, unintelligible* ἀ. δὲ ταῖς οἰκείαις ἐννοίαις τὸ τῶν μαθημάτων ὕψος εὑρών id.*Jo.*2.1(4.146D); **2.** *abiding* ἀ. ἔχουσι τὴν εὐσέβειαν id.*hom.pasch.*10(5^2.129D); **3.** ? *unfulfilled*, ref. Ex.20:5 ἔδει σκληροῖς καταπτοεῖσθαι δείμασι τοὺς ἀ. μέλλοντας ποιεῖσθαι τὴν ἐντολήν id.*ador.*6(1.174A).

ἀνεξιχνίαστος, *unsearchable*; of God, acc. Valentinus, Iren.*haer.*1.2.2(M.7.453B); Serap.*euch.*13.2; ἀνθρωπίνως ὑπέλαβον εἶναι τὸν ἀ. Cyr.H.*catech.*6.8; Didym.(‡Bas.)*Eun.*5(1.312E; M.29.740C); Gel. Cyz.*h.e.*2.22.3(M.85.1292A); Dion.Ar.*d.n.*1.2(M.3.588C); *Rit.Bapt.*(p.392); of divine attributes and activity ἀ. δημιουργίας *Diogn.*9.5; love, Ephr.3.529A; power, Bas.*hex.*2.2(1.13C; M.29.32A); judgements, Gr.Naz.*or.*28.12(p.40.2; M.36.40C); ἀ. τὸ ἔλεος τῆς ἐπαγγελίας σου *Const.App.*2.22.12; providence, Chrys.*scand.*2(3.467A); ways, Melet.*nat.hom.*30(M.64.1280C); of Son: eternal generation, Eus.*e.th.*1.12(p.71.8; M.24.848A); ἡ ζωὴ...ἀ. †Diad.*Ar.*1(M.65.1149C); ref. Inc. φιλανθρωπίας ἀ. πελάγεσιν Jo.D.*hom.*8.10(M.96.716A); of mercy shown in descent to Hades, Or.*schol.in Lc.*1:46(M.17.324A).

***ἀνεξιχνιάστως**, *inscrutably*, Mac.Aeg.*hom.*29.1(M.34.716B).

ἀνεξόδευτος, *not going out of*, Max.*schol.d.n.*4.7(M.4.257A).

ἀνέξοδος, **1.** *unable to escape*, *Ps.Naas*.ap.Hipp.*haer.*5.10(p.103.10; M.16.3159B); **2.** as subst., *beggar* χηρῶν καὶ ἄλλων ἀ. λαβόντων ἐλεημοσύνην Ath.*h.Ar.*13(p.189.25; M.25.708C); *ib.*60(p.217.2; 765B).

***ἀνεξομολόγητος**, *without having confessed*, ‡Chrys.*serm.jej.*4(11.834D).

***ἀνεξουσίως**, *without power of self-determination*, Leont.H.*Nest.*1.16(M.86.1464C).

***ἀνέξωστος**, of a wrestler, *not to be thrown*, ‡Nil.*perist.*10.6(M.79.900C).

ἀνέορτος, *without festive joy*, Gr.Naz.*or.*27.2(p.3.8; M.36.13A); μαρτύρων δὲ μὴ ὄντων...ἡμῶν ὁ βίος ἐγίνετο...ἀ. Ast.Am.*hom.*10(M.40.316A).

***ἀνεπαίρω**, *lift up*, Jo.Clim.*scal.*20(M.88.941C).

ἀνεπαίσχυντος, *having no cause for shame*, of Adam ἀ. παρρησίᾳ ...πρὸς τὸν θεόν Ath.*gent.*2(M.25.8B); Bas.*reg.fus.*51(2.306A; M.31.1041A); of the ideal bishop, *Const.App.*2.4.1.

***ἀνεπαισχύντως**, **1.** *without cause for shame*, i.e. *rightly, duly* εἰ τὰς ἐσχάτας ὑπηρεσίας τοῖς ἁγίοις ἀ. ἐξετέλεσεν Clem.*fr.*18(p.201.2; M.9.748C); Hipp.*haer.*1 proem.(p.3.14; M.16.3020D); υἱὸν ἀ. ὁμολογήσωμεν Jo.D.*hom.*1.5(M.96.553A); **2.** *without disgrace, without dishonour*, of Christ γεννηθεὶς διὰ γεννητικῶν πόρων ἀ., ἀχράντως Epiph.*exp.fid.*15(p.516.8; M.42.812B); βρέφος κυηθείς, περιγράφεται ἀ. Thdr.Stud.*antirr.*3.35(M.99.405C); **3.** *without feeling ashamed* περὶ τοῦ ἁγίου πνεύματος ἀ. ... ἄγνοιαν ὁμολογεῖν Bas.*Eun.*3.6(1.277D; M.29.668B); Gr.Nyss.*hom.1 in Cant.*(M.44.772B); ἀ. τελώνην καλέσας εἰς μαθητείαν Vict.*Mc.*2:15(p.288.26).

ἀνέπακτος, *without epact*, Max.*comput.*25(M.19.1244B).

ἀνέπαφος, **1.** *untouched, unharmed*; **a.** sexually σάρκα συνουσίας ἀ. Meth.*symp.*5.4(p.56.21; M.18.101C); *virgin*; of BMV, Chrys.*hom.4.6 in Mt.*(7.58A); σῶμα ἀ. Isid.Pel.*epp.*5.46(M.78.1353B); Thdt.*Os.*3:2f.(2.1325); **b.** morally, Isid.Pel.*epp.*2.53(M.78.497A); δίκαιον καὶ ἀ. †Jo.Jej.*serm.*(M.88.1921B); of Christ's flesh untouched by sin, Gennad.*fr.Rom.*8:3(p.375.23; M.85.1689B); **c.** of abstracts, *intact* τῆς εὐσεβείας τὴν ὁμολογίαν ἀ. διαφυλάξαι Thdt.*Cant.*5:7f.(2.130); νόμον ἀ. τετηρήκατε id.*affect.*2(p.52.15; 4.743); τὴν ἀσύγχυτον ἕνωσιν νοῦς ἀνθρώπινος...ἀ. οἶδε διατηρεῖν Areth.*Apoc.*6(M.106.540B); **d.** of divine nature in Inc.; *unimpaired*, Chrys.*hom.11.2 in Jo.*(8.64B); **2.** *not to be touched*, of holy things ἀ. ... τοῖς ἔτι βεβήλοις Cyr.*ador.*9(1.323C); of evil deeds ἀπόβλητα καὶ ἀ. ποιεῖσθαι id.*hom.pasch.*24(5^2.290A); **3.** *that cannot be touched, unattainable*, id.*Jo.*9.1(4.802C); **4.** *intangible*; of God, Nemes.*nat.hom.*44(M.40.805B); ‡Bas.*struct.hom.*1.5(1.326C; M.30.16B); of Son, ref. Inc. ὁ αὐτός ἐστιν...ψηλαφητὸς καὶ ἀ. Leont.B.*arg.Sev.*(M.86.1945C); Sophr.H.*ep.syn.*(M.87.3165C); Jo.D.*Jacob.*48(M.94.1457B); κρατεῖται ὁ ἀ. ‡Jo.D.*hom.*5.4(M.96.653B); ‡Jo.D.*ep.Thphl.*3(M.95.349B); denied of Christ's risen body μήτε μὴν ἀ. σῶμα, σκιοειδές τε καὶ ἀέριον Cyr.*Jo.*12.1(4.1109A).

ἀνεπαχθής, *not burdensome, without offence*; neut. as subst., *gentleness, lenity*, Chrys.*hom.29.2 in Mt.*(7.344B); id.*hom.29.2 in Jo.*(8.166A).

***ἀνεπερείστως**, *independently*, *cat.Apoc.*12:1f.(p.351.4).

***ἀνεπεσχέτως**, *without restraint*, Ephr.3.59E.

***ἀνεπήκοος**, *not having heard* of, Eus.*p.e.*7.6(304D; M.21.516D).

***ἀνεπηρεαστικός**, = sq., *unmolested* δός μοι τὴν πρός σε ὁδὸν ἀνύβριστον καὶ ἀ. Ephr.1.257B; cf.*A.Jo.*114(p.214.13).

ἀνεπηρέαστος, *free from injury* or *insult, unmolested*; hence **1.** *immune* λειτουργημάτων ἀ. Eus.*v.C.*2.20(p.49.26; M.20.1000A); morally or spiritually *unharmed*; in temptation, Bas.*moral.*62.3(2.283C; M.31.800C); νοῦν εὐθὺν ἀβλαβῆ καὶ ἀ. φυλαττόμενον *Rit.Bapt.*(p.409); neut. as subst. λειτουργοὶ μὲν πρὸς τὸ ἀ. ... ἄγγελοι ‡Nil.*perist.*11.14(M.79.924B); **2.** *not deserving insult, blameless*, Bas.*ep.*271(3.417E; M.32.1005A); Marc.Er.*opusc.*1.16(M.65.908B) cit. s. συντριμμός.

ἀνεπηρεάστως, **1.** *without being harmed, safely*, Nil.*exerc.*46(M.79.777A); **2.** *without scoffing*, Gr.Nyss.*Eun.*8(2 p.182.11; M.45.776B).

ἀνεπίβατος, *inaccessible*; *unassailable*; lit., of Holy of Holies, Gr.Nyss.*v.Mos.*49(M.44.317C); ποίμνιον...λύκοις...ἀ. Sophr.H.*v.Anast.*(M.92.1689C); fig. or met. σοφίαν...ἀ. Clem.*str.*1.5(p.18.8; M.8.720A); Gr.Nyss.*Eun.*3(2 p.36.8; M.45.604A); of the heart πονηροῖς λογισμοῖς ἀ. id.*or.dom.*3(p.48.8; M.44.1149C); neut. as subst., ‡Nil.*perist.*12.11(M.79.961A); of Christ ἀ. δικαίως ἡ θεωθεῖσα [sc. φύσις] ...τῇ ἁμαρτίᾳ ‡Cyr.*Trin.*15(6^3.21C; M.77.1152D); ταύταις γὰρ [sc. ἡδοναῖς] ἡ θεία σὰρξ ἀ. Andr.Caes.*Apoc.*2(M.106.228C).

[*]**ἀνεπιβούλεστος**, for ἀνεπιβούλευτος, Ephr.3.257B.

ἀνεπιβούλευτος, **1.** *not plotted against, unassailed*, *A.Jo.*106(p.204.7); τότε...ἀ....τὴν περὶ αὐτοῦ [sc. τοῦ πνεύματος] διάνοιαν Bas.*ep.*125.3(3.216B; M.32.549A); **2.** *unassailable, secure*; **a.** as divine or supernatural; of God's might, *A.Jo.*77(p.189.26); χρῖσμα ἅγιον... καὶ σφραγὶς ἀ. *Rit.Bapt.*(p.405); **b.** in gen. ἀ. φυλάσσειν τὴν πίστιν Clem.*str.*1.9(p.29.11; M.8.740C); of poverty, Diad.*perf.*65(p.78.5); ‡Proc.G.*Pr.*24:30(M.87.1469C); neut. as subst., *security*, ref. Ps.126:1 οὐκ αὐτάρκη πρὸς τὸ ἀ. τὰ ὑφ᾽ ἡμῶν σπουδαζόμενα Didym.*Ps.*11:8(M.39.1216B).

ἀνεπίβουλος, neut. as subst., *freedom from attack, security*, Isid.Pel.*epp.*1.210(M.78.316C).

***ἀνεπιγνωμοσύνη**, ἡ, *lack of knowledge, ignorance*, ‡Proc.G.*Pr.*1:7(M.87.1225B); *ib.*2:6(1236C).

ἀνεπιγνώμων, *ignorant, unconscious*, Vict.*Mc.*3:28(p.299.22).

ἀνεπίγνωστος, *not distinctly known*; *not to be known* ἀ. πάντως ἡ τοῦ πνεύματος φύσις Gr.Nyss.*Eun.*1(1 p.144.8; M.45.384B); of God ἀ. ὢν κατ᾽ αὐτό, τὸ τί ἐστι καὶ καθ᾽ ὅ ἐστιν Max.*schol.d.n.*1.2(M.4.189C).

ἀνεπίγραφος, **1.** *without title*; of Ps.42, Or.*fr.in Ps.*49(p.80); Eus.*Ps.*136(M.24.36D); *ib.*142(48B); ‡Hipp.*fr.7 in Pss.*(p.137.16); **2.** *without name of author*; of Heb., Euthal.Diac.*epp.Paul.*(M.85.725B); *cat.Mt.*1:5(p.6.29); **3.** *without name of person addressed*, Bas.*ep.*155 tit.(3.244A; M.32.612B).

ἀνεπίδεικτος, **1.** *not displayed, hidden*, Gr.Naz.*carm.*1.2.10.282(M.37.700A); Diad.*perf.*46(p.52.15); **2.** *unostentatious* εἰ εὖ ποιεῖς, ἀ. ἔσο Isid.Pel.*epp.*1.84(M.78.241A); neut. as subst., *freedom from ostentation* τὸ ἀ. τῆς εὐλαβείας Gr.Naz.*or.*18.32(M.35.1028A); Vict.*Mc.*1:43f.(p.282.18).

ἀνεπίδεκτος, **A.** act.; **1.** *not receiving, not admitting*, Meth.*symp.*11.3(p.138.14; M.18.216C); ἀ. αἰσχρῶν...φαντασιῶν Cyr.*Ps.*16:3(M.69.816A); of Christ ἀ. ἁμαρτίας δεῖξαι τὴν σάρκα ἣν...ὁ Ἀδάμ... ἐκ παραβάσεως δεκτικὴν ἁμαρτίας πεποίηκε ‡Ath.*Apoll.*1.7(M.26.1104C); **2.** *not receptive, incapable of receiving* or *experiencing*; of God, Adam.*dial.*4.14(p.170.19; M.11.1829A) cit. s. πάθος; Eun. ap.Bas.*Eun.*2.30(1.266E; M.29.641E); ἡ μὲν ἄκτιστος [sc. φύσις]... κρείττων τε προσθήκης ἁπάσης καὶ τῆς ἐλαττώσεως, τῶν ἀγαθῶν ἀ. Gr.Nyss.*hom.6 in Cant.*(M.44.885D); id.*Eun.*12(1 p.383.2; M.45.

1112A); id.*or.catech*.6(p.34.2; M.45.28C); *Lit*.ap.*Const.App*.8.15.7 citt. s. *τροπή*; Chrys.*hom.38.4 in Jo*.(8.222A); ἀ. *ἡ θεία φύσις παντὸς πάθους* Procl.CP *Arm*.10(p.192.6; M.65.865C); of Father and Son *τὸ κακίας καὶ θανάτου καὶ φθορᾶς ἀ.* Gr.Nyss.*or.catech*.1(p.13.1; M.45.16D); of Son, ref. Jo.5:19 *ἀ. ἐστι τοῦ ἐναντίον τι τῷ πατρὶ ποιεῖν* Isid.Pel.*epp*.3.335(M.78.996A); *ἡ θεία τε καὶ ἀπόρρητος τοῦ λόγου φύσις πάθους καὶ ἀνάγκης ἀ.* Cyr.*apol.Thdt*.3(p.119.4; 6[1]. 212D); view ascribed to Eunomius *ἀ. εἶναι τὸν υἱὸν τῆς πρὸς* [sc. *τὸν πατέρα*] *ὁμοιότητος* Bas.*Eun*.1.22(1.234B; M.29.561C); of his divine nature *τοῦ Χριστοῦ ἐμπτυομένου...ἡ δὲ θεότης ἀ. ἦν τῶν ἐμπτυσμάτων* Jo.D.*fid.Nest*.46(p.579); of human nature of Christ, deduction from Apollinarius' view *εἰ...φύσις...ἄκτιστος...ἀ. θανάτου* ‡Ath. *Apoll*.1.6(M.26.1101B); of angels *αὐξήσεως καὶ μειώσεως ὄντες ἀ.* ‡Just.*qu.et resp*.30(M.6.1277B); *ἀ. μετανοίας ὅτι καὶ ἀσώματος* Jo.D. *f.o*.2.3(M.94.868B); of Devil *ἐὰν συγχωρηθῇ...ἀδύνατον...τὸ εἶναι οὐσίας ἑτέρας καὶ ἀ. τῶν κρειττόνων τὸν διάβολον, περὶ ἐκείνου ἀπολογησόμεθα ὡς οὐδαμοῦ αἰτίου τῆς πονηρίας* Or.*Jo*.20.24(20; p.357. 33; M.14.625C); *οὐ γὰρ ἂν ἐξέπεσεν ὁ ἑωσφόρος...εἰ φύσει ὑπῆρχε τοῦ χείρονος ἀνεπίδεκτος* Bas.*Eun*.3.2(1.274C; M.29.660C); of heavenly bodies *τὸν ἥλιον καὶ τὴν σελήνην...εἶναι θεῖα καὶ...ἀ. πάθους ἡδονῆς ὄντα καὶ λύπης* Meth.*symp*.8.16(p.105.2; M.18.168C); of soul after death *ἀ. παθῶν* id.*res*.3.18(p.415.4; M.18.525B); and in this life *ἡ νοερὰ...ἔλαφος* [sc. Christ] *φυλάττει τὸν ἑαυτῆς σύμβιον παντὸς ἰοῦ θανατηφόρου ἀνεπίδηκτον* [l. -εκτον] Jo.Clim.*scal*.25(M.88.992B); of man acc. determinists *φύσεις...ἀπολλυμένας, ἀ. τοῦ σώζεσθαι, καὶ ἑτέρας σωζομένας, ἀδυνάτως ἐχούσας πρὸς τὸ ἀπολέσθαι* Or.*princ*. 3.1.8(p.207.2; M.11.261A); *μὴ...ἀ.* [sc. *ἄνθρωπον*] *ἔσεσθαι μεταβολῆς τῆς ἐπὶ τὰ συμφέροντα* id.*or*.6(p.314.9; M.11.437B); ref. Ex.19:13 *εἰ δέ τις θηρίον ἐστί...ἀ. πάντῃ λόγων θεωρίας καὶ θεολογίας* Gr.Naz.*or*. 28.2(p.23.1; M.36.28B); *ἡ φύσις ἡ ἀνθρωπεία...οὔτε ἀ. ἐστι τῶν κακῶν, οὔτε φυσικῶς κέκτηται τὰ κακά* Isid.Pel.*epp*.1.303(M.78.357C); *τί γὰρ οὐκ ἀ. πεποίηκεν ὁ θεὸς τοῦ ἁμαρτάνειν ἡμᾶς*; *Disp.Phot*.(M.88.577C); of soul, ref. Gen.2:7 *εἰ γὰρ εἰς ψυχὴν τῷ ἀνθρώπῳ τὸ θεῖον πνεῦμα γέγονεν, ἔμεινεν ἂν ἡ ψυχὴ καὶ ὁ νοῦς ἀ. ἁμαρτίας* Cyr.*dogm*.2(p.553.18; 6[2].369A); of Christians *οἱ τὰς φύσεις δογματίζοντές φασι Παῦλον πνευματικὸν ὄντα ἀ. εἶναι κακίας* Didym.*Ac*.9:15(M.39.1672C); *τὸ οὖν 'οὐ δύναται ἁμαρτάνειν' οὐ κατὰ τὸ γενέσθαι τὴν φύσιν ἡμῶν ἀ. ἁμαρτίας...ἀλλὰ κατὰ τὸ μὴ ἀκόλουθον μηδὲ ἁρμόδιον* Sev.Ant.ap.*cat*. *1Jo*.3:9(p.124.23); of material objects *ὁδῷ οὐδὲ ἴχνη...ἐχούσῃ καὶ ἀ. διὰ τὸ στερρόν* Or.*Jo*.1.27(20; p.34.17; M.14.73B); *μὴ σκαφεῖσα ἄμπελος...τῆς ἐκ τοῦ ὕδατος ὠφελείας...ἀ.* †Bas.*Is*.21(1.394B; M.30. 156C); of opposites, *incompatible*, Bas.*hom.in Ps*.33(1.153C; M.29. 376A); Jo.D.*Man*.1.25(M.94.1529C).

B. pass.; **1.** *unacceptable* *τὸ κατὰ τοῦ πνεύματος βλάσφημον οὐκ ἀ. πάντως τὴν μετάγνωσιν ἕξει* Vict.*Mc*.3:29(p.299.21); **2.** *that cannot be received*, hence *unobtainable* *τὴν ἀ. τῶν ἱερῶν δογμάτων ἐπιστήμην* Cyr.*hom.pasch*.24(5[2].289A); **3.** *inadmissible* by the mind; hence **a.** *impossible* *τὸ παντελῶς ἀδύνατον καὶ ἀ.* Gr.Naz.*or*.30.11(p.123.2; M.36.116C); Cyr.*dial.Trin*.2(5[1].419C); **b.** *incomprehensible* *ἀ. παντὸς λόγου καὶ νοήματος τὸ θεῖόν ἐστι* Max.*ambig*.(M.91.1180D).

ἀνεπιδέκτως, c. *ἔχω*, *be incapable* *Μαρκίων καὶ Μανιχαῖος* [sc. *φασί*] *θεόν...ἀ. ἔχοντα κοινωνῆσαι φύσει ἀνθρωπίνῃ* ‡Ath.*Apoll*.2.3(M.26. 1136C).

ἀνεπίδηκτος, f.l. for *ἀνεπίδεκτος* q.v., Jo.Clim.*scal*.25(M.88.992B).

***ἀνεπιδοίαστος,** *unwavering*, Mac.Aeg.*carit*.11(M.34.917D).

***ἀνεπίδυτος,** *never-setting* *φῶς Χριστὸς τὸ ἀ.* Thdr.Stud.*nativ. BMV* 7(M.96.696C).

ἀνεπιθεώρητος, *not influenced* or *controlled*; astrol., *Clem.recogn. suppl*.5(p.211.14; M.1.1472D).

ἀνεπιθόλωτος, *untroubled, calm, clear*, Gr.Nyss.*bapt.Chr*.(M.46. 580B); *ἐκκλησία...καθάπερ τις κόρη ὀφθαλμοῦ ἀ.* Cyr.*Ps*.16:7(M.69. 816C); esp. of the mind *τὸν ἀ. νοῦν ἐπὶ τὰ φανὰ τῶν λογίων θεάματα προσαγαγόντες* Dion.Ar.*d.n*.2.7(M.3.645A); Max.*ep*.12(M.91.505D).

***ἀνεπιθολώτως,** *clearly*, Jo.VI CP *ep*.(M.96.1417C).

***ἀνεπιθυμήτως,** *without desire*, acc. Basilides ⟨*ὁ*⟩ *οὐκ ὢν θεός...ἀ. κόσμον ἠθέλησε ποιῆσαι* Hipp.*haer*.7.21(p.196.21; M.16.3303B).

ἀνεπικάλυπτος, *unveiled, clear*, Max.*schol.d.n*.3.2(M.4.236B).

ἀνεπικαλύπτως, *openly*, Eus.*Ps*.140:4(M.24.44D); id.*p.e*.3.9(102D; M.21.188A).

ἀνεπίληστος, *unforgotten* *ἔχε τὴν ταπείνωσιν τοῦ κυρίου ἀ. ἐν τῇ καρδίᾳ σου* Marc.Er.*opusc*.5.8(M.65.1041C); *ib*.5.10(1045A); *τὸ ἀ. τοῦ θεοῦ* Proc.G.*Is*.65:1f.(M.87.2685D).

ἀνεπιμέλητος, act.; *heedless, paying no attention* *πρὸς τὴν τούτων θεωρίαν ἀ.* ‡Proc.G.*Pr*.24:30(M.87.1469D); c. dat., *ib*.27:10(1493C).

ἀνεπίμυστος, *open, attentive* *τὸ νοερὸν ὄμμα ἀ.* Max.*ambig*. (M.91.1140A).

ἀνεπινόητος, *without experience of*; *not understanding*, Or.*Cels*. 4.76(p.346.7; M.11.1148B); Gr.Naz.*or*.43.34(M.36.544A).

ἀνεπίπλαστος, *unaffected, simple* *σχῆμα* Chrys.*sac*.6.3(p.143.19; 1.422D).

ἀνεπίπληκτος, *unpunished* *ὁ δεσπότης...ἀφίησι...οὐδαμῶς ἀ. ἐν ἡμῖν τὴν καταφθείρουσαν ἁμαρτίαν* Cyr.*glaph.Dt*.(1.423B).

ἀνεπιπλήκτως, *unblameably*, Cyr.*ador*.14(1.500A); id.*Os*.50(3.82A).

***ἀνεπίπλοκος,** *disentangled*, met. *ἀ. ... λέξει* Eust.*engast*.8(p.26. 14; M.18.628A).

***ἀνεπιπλόκως,** c. *ἔχω*, *be incapable of combination* *ἀ. ἔχει πρὸς ἄλληλα τὰ ἐναντία πάθη* Nil.*exerc*.75(M.79.809B).

***ἀνεπιρρώνυμι,** *strengthen anew*, Sev.Ant.ap.*cat.Mt*.27:38(p.235. 13).

ἀνεπισήμαντος, *not clear, ambiguous*, ‡Just.*qu.et resp*.104(M.6. 1349D); *ἀ., παρὰ τίνος τὸ πρόσταγμα...πρόεισιν. εἴη δ' ἂν παρὰ τῶν δικαίων* Areth.*Apoc*.55(M.106.728B).

***ἀνεπισημείωτος,** *not marked, unnoticed*, Clem.*str*.3.11(p.229.36; M.8.1176B); *ib*.7.14(p.60.12; M.9.517A).

ἀνεπίσκεπτος, *ill-considered*, Gr.Nyss.*Apoll*.3(M.45.1129B).

ἀνεπισκίαστος, *not overshadowed*, i.e. *clearly expressed, unambiguous*, Eus.*l.C*.18(p.249.31; M.20.1410B); Pall.*v.Chrys*.10(p.60.14; M.47.33); *ib*.18(p.118.4; 66).

ἀνεπισκόπητος, *unregarded*, Olymp.*Job* 24:13(M.93.260B); *cat. Apoc*.4:6(p.244.21).

ἀνεπίσκοπος, 1. *unsupervised, neglected* *τὸ ἀ. καὶ ἀπρονόητον ἐγκαταλειφθῆναι ὑπὸ τοῦ θεοῦ πάντων ὀλεθριώτατον* Dion.Al.*fr*.(p.254.1) ap.Leont.et Jo.*sacr*.(M.86.2064D); Thdr.Stud.*epp*.2.214(M.99.1645B); *unobserved*, Eus.*h.e*.8.1.8(M.20.741B); **2.** *without a shepherd* *ποίμνιον* Gr.Naz.*or*.42.2(M.36.460A); **3.** as subst., of a deposed bishop, '*nonbishop*' *τὸ παρὰ συγκαταβατῶν ἀ. σιτίζεσθαι* Thdr.Stud.*epp*.2.119 (M.99.1393A).

ἀνεπισκότητος, *not overclouded*; *unsullied* *παρθενίαν* Hyper.*mon*. 58(M.79.1480A).

ἀνεπιστάτητος, *ungoverned, without guidance*, ‡Ign.*Tars*.7, v.l. *ἀνεπίστατοι*; Eus.*d.e*.4.6(p.160.16; M.22.628A); Cyr.*ador*.6(1.200B); id.*Juln*.2(6[2].70D).

ἀνεπίστητος, *without a governor* *ἀβασίλευτοι καὶ ἀ.* Cyr.*Os*.34 (3.62D, v.l. *ἀνεπίστευτοι*).

ἀνεπίστροφος, 1. *not turning back*, ‡Caes.Naz.*dial*.196(M.38.1188); **2.** met., *resolute, inflexible*, Dion.Ar.*c.h*.2.4(M.3.144A); **3.** *stubborn, obstinate*, Sophr.H.*mir.Cyr.et Jo*.17(M.87.3473C); Jo.D.*imag*.1(M.94. 1281B).

ἀνεπιστρόφως, 1. *without turning*, Dion.Ar.*c.h*.15.9(M.3.337C); **2.** *stubbornly*, Isid.Pel.*epp*.1.17(M.78.192A); Areth.*Apoc*.4(M.106. 533B).

***ἀνεπισυμβάτως,** *not contingently*, ‡Gr.Nyss.*occurs*.(M.46.1157B).

ἀνεπισύναφος, *not in conjunction*, astrol., *Clem.recogn.suppl*.5 (p.211.15; M.1.1472D).

ἀνεπισφαλῶς, *steadfastly*, Meth.*symp*.4.5(p.51.20 v.l. *ἐπιφανῶς*; *προφανῶς* M.18.96A).

ἀνεπιτάτως, *without augmentation*, ref. Trin. *ἀ. ... γεννηθεὶς ἐκ τοῦ θεοῦ καὶ πατρός* Procl.CP *or*.4.3(M.65.716A).

***ἀνεπιφθόγγως,** prob. f.l. for *ἀντιφθόγγως* *antiphonally*, Anast.S. *hod*.15(M.89.257D).

ἀνεπιχείρητος, 1. *unassailable*, †Bas.*Is*.146(1.481E; M.30.356D); Synes.*ep*.57(M.66.1393A); ‡Jo.D.*conf*.4(M.95.285C); **2.** *not to be touched*, ‡Bas.*struct.hom*.2.15(1.346E; M.30.60C); met., *not to be tampered with* *κρίσιν* ‡Bas.*const*.19(2.563C; M.31.1388B); Gr.Naz.*or*. 23.10(M.35.1161B); **3.** *unattainable* *τὸ...τελέως ἄληπτον, ἀνέλπιστον καὶ ἀ.* Gr.Naz.*or*.38.7(M.36.317C); Max.*ambig*.(M.91.1216B); by the intellect, *beyond understanding* *υἱός ἐστιν...φύσις ἀ.* Anast.Ant.*fid*. (M.89.1404C).

***ἀνέργητος,** *inactive*, Melet.*nat.hom*.synops.(M.64.1117C).

***ἀνεργήτως,** *idly*, Mac.Aeg.*libert.ment*.11(M.34.944A).

***ἀνέρειστος** (*ἀνέρισ-), *unstable*, *ἀνέρισ-* ‡Caes.Naz.*dial*.112(M.38. 992); neut. as subst., Epiph.*haer*.66.10(p.31.18; M.42.45A).

***ἀνέρευθος,** *unblushing*, Gr.Naz.*carm*.1.2.29.209(M.37.899A).

ἀνερεύνησις, *ἡ*, *searching out, scrutiny*, Bas.*Eun*.1.15(1.227A; M.29.545B).

***ἀνέριστος,** v. *ἀνέρειστος.

ἀνερμήνευτος, 1. *unexplained*, Gr.Nyss.*Eun*.1(1 p.108.24; M.45. 344A); id.*tres dii*(M.45.133D); Epiph.*haer*.60.2(p.379.27; M.41.1040A); *μηδὲ μίαν...προφητείαν καταλιπεῖν ἀ.* Thdt.*Lam*.4:22(2.668); **2.** *beyond understanding* *τρόπον τῆς τοῦ παντὸς συστάσεως...ἀ.* Gr.Nyss. *or.catech*.11(p.58.8; M.45.44B); of God, Geo.Pis.*hex*.597(M.92.1481A); *ἀ. οὐσία καὶ φύσις* ‡Jo.D.*Artem*.28(p.160.19; M.96.1277B); of Son's eternal generation, Hier.H.*Trin.*(M.40.848C); Jo.V H.*icon.*5(M.96.1353C); ref. Inc. τὴν ἀ. λοχείαν Thdot.Anc.*hom.BMV et Sym.*4 (M.77.1393C); γαστὴρ ἀ. Tim.Ant.*descr.BMV* 1(M.28.944B); θεός ἐστιν ἀναλλοίωτος καὶ ἄνθρωπός ἐστιν ἀ. Sophr.H.*or.*2.20(M.87.3240C); ἄλλη ῥάβδος βλαστάνει...ἀ. Jo.Eub.*concept.BMV* 4(M.96.1465B).

***ἀνερμηνεύτως**, *inexplicably, ineffably*, Cyr.S.*v.Euthym.*26(p.40.16); Sophr.H.*trop.*(M.87.4005D); ‡Meth.*Sym.et Ann.*8(M.18.365B).

***ἀνερμηνεύω**, *enumerate*, ‡Caes.Naz.*dial.*102(M.38.968).

ἀνερυθρίαστος, *unblushing, shameless*, Or.*hom.6.3 in Jer.*(p.50.15; M.13.328A).

***ἀνερυθριάστως**, *without blushing*, †Cyr.*hom.div.*14(5^2.412A); ‡Proc.G.*Pr.*28:21(M.87.1509B); †Jo.Jej.*poenit.*(M.88.1909B).

ἀνέρχομαι, *go up, rise*; to church, †Leont.B.*sect.*4.4(M.86.1224A); to pagan temples, CAnc.(314)*can.*5; from baptism, Clem.*exc.Thdot.* 7.7(p.131.12; M.9.693C); Serap.*euch.*24 tit.; Gel.Cyz.*h.e.*2.31.5(M.85.1317A); to heaven: pagan, Just.*1apol.*21.2(M.6.360A); Tat.*orat.*10 (p.11.11; M.6.828B); of Ascension, Just.*1apol.*31.7(377A); *ib.*42.4 (392B); id.*dial.*34.2(M.6.548B); of spiritual ascent, Tat.*orat.*13 (p.14.24; 833B); Meth.*symp.*2.6(p.23.10; M.18.57A); Hegem.*Arch.*11 (p.19.1; M.10.1445B).

***ἀνερώτησις, ἡ,** *inquiry*, Just.*dial.*68.3(M.6.633B); Eus.*h.e.*1.8.1 (M.20.100B).

***ἀνερωτήτως**, *without investigation*, †Jo.D.*B.J.*24(M.96.1072B).

***ἀνέσπερος**, *without evening, never-setting*; of Christ τὸ φῶς τὸ ἄδυτον καὶ ἀ. Or.*fr.4 in Jo.*(p.558.2); Meth.*symp.*8.5(p.87.14; M.18.145C); ‡Epiph.*hom.*2(M.43.440D); of eternal day, Bas.*hex.*2.8(1.21C; M.29.52A); †Bas.*Is.*87(1.439B; M.30.260B); ἐν τῇ ἀ. ἡμέρᾳ τῆς βασιλείας σου Jo.D.*carm.pasch.*125(p.221; M.96.844B); id.*f.o.*2.1(M.94.864B); παρὰ γὰρ θεῷ ἀ. καὶ μία ἡμέρα πᾶς ὁ αἰών ‡Caes.Naz.*dial.*129 (M.38.1029); of Judgement day, Didym.*Trin.*3.22(M.39.917D).

ἀνεστραμμένως, *conversely*, Athenag.*res.*1(p.49.5; M.6.976B).

***ἀνέτασις, ἡ,** *examination*, Eus.*Hierocl.*20(525D; M.22.825C); Epiph.*haer.*69.3(p.155.14; M.42.208C).

***ἀνετοιμασία, ἡ,** *unpreparedness*, Epiph.*haer.*69.44(p.192.10; M.42.272C).

ἄνετος, *relaxed, free*; hence *open* ἀνέτην ἀφήκαμεν τὴν θύραν [sc. to the status of catecumen] Cyr.H.*procatech.*4; τοῖς προσαίταις ἄ. ὁ θεῖος νεώς Thdt.*h.e.*5.18.7(3.1047); *permitted* [sc. the tree of life] ἄνετος ἀθανάτων τροφή Gennad.*Gen.*3:22(M.85.1640B).

***ἀνευαγγέλιστος**, *unevangelized, without the gospel* ὁ τόπος ἐκεῖνος ἔτι τῆς χάριτος ἀ. ‡Pion.*v.Polyc.*27.

ἀνεύθετος, *unfitted*, Nil.*exerc.*6(M.79.725A); id.*Magn.*33(M.79.1009A).

***ἀνευλάβεια, ἡ,** *impiety, irreverence*, Thdr.Heracl.*Is.*50:9(M.18.1352A); Chrys.*hom.3.2 in Jo.*(8.18C); Isid.Pel.*epp.*5.89(M.78.1377B).

ἀνευλαβής, *irreverent, irreligious* ῥάθυμοι...καὶ ἀ. Chrys.*Jud.*4.5 (1.623A); id.*hom.26.3 in Mt.*(7.317B); οἱ τὴν ἀ. νοσοῦντες εὐλάβειαν Bas.Sel.*or.*9(M.85.440A); Leont.B.*Nest.et Eut.*1(M.86.1300A).

***ἀνευλόγητος**, *unblessed*, Proc.G.*Dt.*33:7(M.87.981B).

***ἀνευπαράδεκτος**, *unacceptable*, Cyr.*Is.*5.3(2.814B).

ἀνεύρεσις, ἡ, *recovery* of something lost, *A.Xanthipp.*42(p.85.31); Meth.*symp.*3.5(p.32.1; M.18.68C); †Jo.D.*B.J.*11(M.96.957C).

ἀνεύρετος, *undiscoverable* δυσεύρετα ἢ ἀ. Or.*sel.in Ps.*1(M.12.1081C); Nil.*epp.*3.24(M.79.381B).

ἀνευρύνω, *dilate*; met., *explain*, Cyr.*ador.*8(1.256C); *ib.*9(297D).

***ἀνευτρέπιστος**, *unprepared*, Ephr.3.313B; *Pers.capt.*(M.86.3264A).

ἀνευφημέω, **1.** *praise* τὸν...λόγον θεοῦ...ἀ. Eus.*p.e.*7.12(p.320; M.21.541C ἐνευ-); **2.** intrans., *applaud*, Zach.Mit.*opif.*(M.85.1117B).

***ἀνευφήμητος**, *unhonoured*, Gr.Thaum.*pan.Or.*4(p.8.24; M.10.1061A).

***ἀνεύφημος**, *inauspicious*, ‡Meth.*Sym.et Ann.*9(M.18.369A).

***ἀνεφίκτως**, *in a way beyond understanding* τὸν...πατέρα...γεγεννηκέναι ἀ. ... οἴδαμεν *Symb.Ant.*(345)3(p.252.18; M.26.729B).

ἀνέχω, **A.** act.; **1.** *hold up*; *send out* καθαρὸν φῶς ἀ. Const.ap. Eus.*v.C.*2.57(p.64.20; M.20.1032C); **2.** *hold back*; **a.** *endure* οὐκ ἤνεσχον αὐτὸν καλεῖν Ζαχαρίαν Or.*hom.9 in Lc.*(v.l. p.66.20 for ἠνέσχοντο; M.17.329B ἀνέσχον); **b.** intrans., *recover*, Meth.*symp.*4.2 (p.47.10; M.18.89A).

B. med., *hold up, bear*; **1.** *hold fast* to, *trust* in; c. genit., *M. Tar.*7(p.465); **2.** οὐκ ἀ. *refuse* to οὐδὲ ἀ. τὴν ἀρχὴν ἐπακοῦσαι Clem. *str.*7.16(p.72.28; M.9.541C); Chrys.*hom.6.3 in Mt.*(7.89B); Thdt.*Ps.* 17:2f.(1.702); **3.** abs., *hold out, refuse consent* ὁ σωτὴρ...τοὺς ἀνασχομένους ὠφέλησεν Const.*or.s.c.*15 tit.(p.152.13; M.20.1276B); Ath. *v.Anton.*58(M.26.928A).

***ἀνεῴκτης, ὁ,** *one that opens the way*; of the Cross, ‡Chrys.*ador.* 2(11.826B).

ἀνηβάσκω, *grow young again*, Gr.Naz.*ep.*235(M.37.377B); Gr. Nyss.*mart.*1(M.46.752C); Cyr.*hom.pasch.*9(5^2.109A).

***ἀνηγμένως**, *in an exalted way* θεὸς ὑπάρχων...ἀ. τε καὶ θεοπρεπῶς πρὸς τὸν ἑαυτοῦ πατέρα φησίν Cyr.*Jo.*11.7(4.962D).

***ἀνήγρετος**, *unwaking*, Nonn.*par.Jo.*11:13(M.43.841A).

***ἀνηδόνως**, *without pleasure, regardless of pleasure*, of father of family fulfilling duties ἀ. τε καὶ ἀλυπήτως Clem.*str.*7.12(p.51.7; M.9.497C).

***ἀνηκόως**, *inattentively*, v.l. Just.*dial.*137.4(M.6.792B).

***ἀνηλεόω**, *irradiate*, ‡Eust.*hex.*(M.18.745B).

***ἀνῆλιξ**, *not of full age*, Tit.Bost.ap.*cat.Lc.*15:12(p.117.29); ἀφῆλιξ id.*fr.Lc.*15:12(p.215).

[*]**ἀνηλόγως**, = ἀναλόγως, *conformably*, Gr.Naz.*carm.*2.1.47.24 (M.37.1383A).

***ἀνήλωτος**, *made without nails*, Or.*princ.*4.3.2(p.327.4; M.11.381A).

ἀνημέρως, *savagely* ὠμῶς τε καὶ ἀ. Cyr.*Nah.*4(3.479B).

ἀνήνυτος, *impossible*, Cyr.*Nah.*10(3.486E); Gel.Cyz.*h.e.*1.5.4(M.85.1204D).

***ἀνηροσίη, ἡ,** *state of being unploughed*, *Orac.Sib.*3.542.

ἀνήροτος, **1.** *not ploughed*, ref. Inc., fig. τὴν ἀ. ἄρουραν τοῦ οὐρανίου ἄρτου Jo.D.*hom.*9.14(M.96.741A); met., *not produced from seed* σάρκα προσλαβὼν ἐξ αὐτῆς τὴν ἀ. Sophr.H.*or.*2.46(M.87.3277C); and of the regenerate θεοῦ...ἀ. τέκνα τοκῆος Nonn.*par.Jo.*1:13(M.43.752B); **2.** met., *uncultivated* ἀ. τὴν ψυχήν Proc.G.*Is.*32:9ff.(M.87.2285A); *unprepared*, i.e. for the gospel, Chrys.*hom.1.1 in 2Tim.* (11.658B); *unrefined*, i.e. in mode of life, Gr.Naz.*or.*43.60(M.36.576A).

***ἀνησιφόρος**, for *ἀνονησιφόρος, *unprofitable*, Jo.Clim.*scal.*4(M.88.701B).

***ἀνησύχαστος**, *turbulent*, *Cod.Afr.*66.

***ἀνησυχία, ἡ,** *turbulence*, *Cod.Afr.*65.

ἀνήσυχος, *restless, hating quiet*, Nil.*Eulog.*12(M.79.1109B).

***ἄνηχος**, *silent*, Hipp.*haer.*6.11(p.137.29; M.16.3211A).

***ἀνθαγιάζω**, *sanctify in return*, Eustrat.*v.Eutych.*25(M.86.2304A).

***ἀνθεκόμος**, prob. f.l. for ἀνθοκόμος q.v.

ἀνθεκτικός, *clinging to, retentive* ἀ. δύναμιν Max.*Pyrr.*(M.91.297B).

ἀνθελιγμός, ὁ, *revolution in a contrary direction*; of heavenly bodies, Geo.Pis.*hex.*120(M.92.1440A).

***ἀνθελίττω**, *intertwine, move* feet *in contrary directions*; of a limping walk, Geo.Pis.*carm.*1.42.

***ἀνθέλκυσις, ἡ,** *drawing in* ἀ. τῆς πνοῆς Epiph.*haer.*40.8(p.90.4; M.41.692A).

ἀνθερίσκος, ὁ, v.l. for ἀνθέριξ, *beard* of an ear of corn, Jo.D.*f.o.* 4.27(M.94.1225C).

***ἀνθερμηνεύω**, *give an interpretation contrary* to τί...ἀ. τῷ Παύλῳ; Nest.*hom.in Heb.1:3*(p.236.12; M.64.484D).

[*]**ἀνθευτικός**, v.l. for ἀνθητικός q.v.

ἀνθέω, *flower*; *flourish*; hence *spring, be descended* from Ἰουβὰλ ἐξ αὐτῶν ἀ. Thdt.*qu.47 in Gen.*(1.61); id.*Zach.*4:11ff.(2.1615).

[*]**ἀνθηκομέω**, variant of ἀνθοκομέω q.v.

***ἀνθηκόμος**, prob. f.l. for ἀνθοκόμος q.v.

***ἀνθημερινός**, *a day old*, †Ath.*fr.Mt.*(M.27.1369A).

***ἀνθηνιοχέω**, *restrain*, Isid.Pel.*epp.*5.271(M.78.1496A).

***ἀνθηρεύω**, *captivate*, Leont.N.*v.Sym.*30(M.93.1708B).

***ἀνθηροπρόσωπος**, *florid-faced*, Jo.Mal.*chron.*10 p.257(M.97.389B).

***ἀνθηρόχειλος**, *with lips like flowers*, Jo.Mal.*chron.*5 p.106(M.97.196C).

ἀνθηρῶς, *brilliantly* (Lat. *florentissime*) ἀ. τὸν λαὸν ἐδίδαξε Hier. *vir.ill.*(tr.Sophr.Pal.)76(p.46.15; M.*PL.*23.686B); *ib.*79(p.47.19; 688A).

ἀνθητικός, *of flowering plants* ἀ. σπέρματα Clem.*str.*1.7(p.24.23, v.l. ἀνθευτικά M.8.732C).

***ἀνθικόμος**, prob. f.l. for ἀνθοκόμος q.v.

***ἄνθισμα, τό,** *bright dress*, Clem.*paed.*3.2(p.242.14; M.8.572A).

ἀνθισμός, ὁ, *bloom, flowering*, Proc.G.*fr.Cant.*7:12(M.87.1768B).

ἀνθιστ-άω, later form of ἀνθίστημι; pass., *withstand* ~ωμένοις τῷ πονηρῷ Jo.D.*Man.*1.68(M.94.1565B).

***ἀνθοβαφεύς, ὁ,** *dyer in bright colours*, Bas.*hom.*7.4(2.55C; M.31.289A).

***ἀνθοβαφικός**, *which colours flowers*, Thdr.Stud.*nativ.BMV* 7 (M.96.692D).

***ἀνθοειδής**, *flower-like* ἀ. ... αἵματος τῶν μαρτύρων Agath.*v.Gr. Ill.*115(p.58).

ἀνθοκομέω, *produce flowers*, Cyr.*Jo.*4.4(4.387A); ἀνθηκ-, ‡Chrys. *pasch.*6.3(p.147.5; 8.268B).

ἀνθοκόμος, *decked with flowers* ἀ. ... χθών †Apoll.*met.Ps.*76:19

(vv.ll. ἀνθεκόμος, ἀνθηκόμος; ἀνθικόμος M.33.1421D); ‡Chrys.*nat. Chr.*2(10.819D).

ἀνθολόγιον, τό, *gathering of flowers*, Clem.*prot.*2(p.14.1; M.8.77B).

ἀνθολόγος, ὁ, *gatherer of flowers*, Gr.Nyss.*hom.5 in Cant.*(M.44.865B).

***ἀνθόλοψ, ὁ,** *antelope*, ‡Eust.*hex.*(M.18.740C).

***ἀνθομοίωμα, τό,** *similarity, likeness*, Or.*Cant.*2(M.17.257D; ἀνθ' ὁμοιωμάτων p.162.27); of biblical types, Ephr.2.349D.

ἀνθομολογέομαι, *praise, return thanks* ἀ. τῷ κυρίῳ *T.Jud.*1.3; Thdt.*Ps.*78:13(1.1171); *cat.Lc.*2:36(p.25.10).

ἀνθομολόγησις, ἡ, 1. *acknowledgement* εὐχαριστίαν δὲ τὴν ἐπὶ τῷ τετευχέναι ἀγαθῶν ἀπὸ θεοῦ μετ' εὐχῶν ἀ. Or.*or.*14(p.331.9; M.11.461A); **2.** *confession* ἄχρι μαρτυρίου καὶ τελείας ἀ. ἐλθόντες Diad.*perf.* 90(p.128.17); **3.** *confession in place of another, alternative confession* ὁ μὲν [sc. Symeon]...προσωποποιούμενος τὸν νόμον, τὴν ἀπόλυσιν ἐξεζήτει· ἡ δὲ [sc. Anna] τῆς ἐκκλησίας προσωποποιὸς τὴν ἀ. προσεκόμιζε ‡Meth.*Sym.et Ann.*11(M.18.376A).

***ἀνθομολογητής, ὁ,** *one who acknowledges in return*; of God, ref. Mt.10:32, Andr.Cr.*or.*17(M.97.1177D).

ἀνθοπλίζω, *arm against*; met. ἀ. τὸν Μωσέα τῷ Παύλῳ Isid.Pel. *epp.*3.95(M.78.801B); Cyr.*hom.pasch.*5.2(5^{2}.45E).

***ἀνθοπλισμός, ὁ,** *counter-arming*, Thphn.*chron.*p.348(M.108.836C).

***ἀνθοποιός,** *producing flowers, flowery*, Jo.D.*carm.theog.*112 (p.208; M.96.824B).

ἀνθορίζω, *define in a contrary sense*, Gel.Cyz.*h.e.*2.11.12(M.85.1249A).

***ἀνθοροθετέω,** *destroy the boundaries*, Geo.Pis.*Pers.*2.315(M.92.1231A).

***ἀνθόρροια, ἡ,** *casting of flowers*, ‡Caes.Naz.*dial.*87(M.38.932).

***ἀνθοσμία, ἡ,** *scent of flowers*, Chrys.*hom.4.4 in 1Thess.*(11.457D); Geo.Pis.*Sev.*618(M.92.1668B).

ἀνθοφορ-έω, 1. *bear flowers*, *V.Zos.*3(p.98.9); met. ~οῦντες διὰ τῶν κρίνων τοῦ λόγου Gr.Nyss.*hom.14 in Cant.*(M.44.1068B); **2.** *be meretricious*; of music, Clem.*paed.*2.4(p.184.26; M.8.445B).

***ἀνθοφορία, ἡ,** *blossoming*, ‡Caes.Naz.*dial.*115(M.38.1000).

***ἀνθρακογραφία, ἡ,** *charcoal sketch*, Gr.Thaum.*pan.Or.*2(p.3.21; M.10.1053B).

***ἀνθρακόεις,** *made of coal*, Nonn.*par.Jo.*18:25(M.43.193B).

***ἀνθρακοποιΐα, ἡ,** *charcoal-burning*, Gr.Nyss.*v.Gr.Thaum.*(M.46.937A).

ἄνθραξ, ὁ, *coal*; exeg. Is.6:7, cf. *quis est iste unus de seraphim? dominus meus Jesus Christus: iste juxta dispensationem carnis missus est habens in manu sua carbonem et dicens: ignem veni mittere super terram...non quocumque simpliciter et fortuito propheta igne purgatur, sed eo, qui est de altari dei. si purgatus non fueris altaris igne, residet tibi ille de quo dictum est: ite a me in ignem aeternum...non est talis ignis de altari. omnes igni tradendi sunt, sed non omnes uni igni; alios de altari ignis exspectat, alios ille qui praeparatus est Zabulo et angelis ejus*, Or.*hom.4.4 in Is.*(p.262.4; M.13.233D); τοιοῦτός ἐστιν ὁ ἄ. τοῦ θυσιαστηρίου, τάχα που τοῦ φιλανθρώπου κυρίου πληροῦντος τὸ ἑαυτοῦ θυσιαστήριον τοιούτων τινῶν σωτηρίων καὶ καθαρτικῶν ἀ. ... παιδεύοντος ἡμᾶς τοῦ λόγου μὴ ἄλλως δύνασθαί τινα τυχεῖν ἀφέσεως ἁμαρτημάτων ἢ διὰ τοῦ θείου πυρός Eus.*Is.*6:6–7(M.24.128C); ἐπειδὴ δὲ ὁ ἄ. πῦρ ἐστι τῇ παχυτέρᾳ ἤδη καὶ γεωδεστέρᾳ ὕλῃ ἐναπομεῖναν...τάχα οὖν σημαίνει τὴν ἐν τῇ σαρκὶ τοῦ κυρίου ἐπιδημίαν †Bas.*Is.*183(1.513E; M.30.1429A); ἄ. ... τοῦτο ἄρα Χριστοῦ σύμβολον...ὥσπερ οὖν ὁ ἄ. ξύλον ἐστὶ τῇ φύσει, πλὴν ὅλος δι' ὅλου μεμέστωται τοῦ πυρός, καὶ τὴν αὐτοῦ δύναμίν τε καὶ ἐνέργειαν ἔχει, κατὰ τοῦτον, οἶμαι, τρόπον νόοιτ' ἂν εἰκότως καὶ αὐτὸς ὁ κύριος ἡμῶν...ἄνθρακι οὖν εὖ μάλα παρεικαστέον τὸν Ἐμμανουήλ, ὅς...πάντη τε καὶ πάντως ἀφαιρεῖ τὰς ἁμαρτίας Cyr.*Is.*1.4 (2.107B); τὸ δὲ σεραφὶμ...τὸν ἄ. ἔλαβε, καὶ τοῦτο ἐπιθὲν τῷ τοῦ προφήτου στόματι...προσδιαγράφεται...διὰ τούτων ἡ τῶν ἡμετέρων ἀγαθῶν μετουσία, ἡ διὰ τοῦ δεσποτικοῦ σώματός τε καὶ αἵματος τῶν ἁμαρτημάτων ἀπαλλαγή Thdt.*Is.*6:6(p.32.30; 2.210); Proc.G.*Is.*6:6 (M.87.1940f.); hence esp. ref. simile of coal heated in fire as Christol. illustration, in gen. of Christ ὁ διφυὴς ἄ. *Lit.Jac.*(p.162.7); ἡ τὸν θεῖον ἄ. ἔνδον φέρουσα Thdr.Stud.*nativ.BMV* 7(M.96.689C); ἡ λαβὶς τοῦ καθαρτικοῦ ἄ. ‡Meth.*Sym.et Ann.*10(M.18.372C); ref. eucharistic participation in Christ λαβεῖν τὸν πύρινον ἄ. *Lit.Jac.* (p.232.7); τοῦ θείου ἄ. ... μεταλάβωμεν, ἵνα τὸ πῦρ τοῦ ἐν ἡμῖν πόθου προσλαβὸν τὴν ἐκ τοῦ ἄ. πύρωσιν, καταφλέξῃ ἡμῶν τὰς ἁμαρτίας...ἄ. εἶδεν Ἡσαΐας· ἄ. δὲ ξύλον λιτὸν οὐκ ἔστιν, ἀλλ' ἡνωμένον πυρί· οὕτω καὶ ὁ ἄρτος τῆς κοινωνίας, οὐκ ἄρτος λιτός ἐστιν, ἀλλ' ἡνωμένος θεότητι Jo.D.*f.o.*4.13(M.94.1149B).

***ἀνθρωπαῖος, ὁ,** *inhabitant of man*, word coined as // Ναζωραῖος: οὐκ ἔτι μὲν σὰρξ ὁ λόγος...ἀνθρωποπολίτης δὲ μᾶλλον, καὶ ἣν ἀκόλουθον αὐτὸν ἀ. μᾶλλον, οὐκ ἄνθρωπον ὀνομάζεσθαι [i.e. if we are to believe Nestorius], καθάπερ...ὁ κατοικήσας τὴν Ναζαρέτ, Ναζωραῖος Cyr.*Chr.un.*(5^{1}.750A); Jo.D.*haer.Nest.*22(M.95.200B).

***ἀνθρωπαρέσκεια (-ία), ἡ,** *pleasing of men, love of popularity* or *applause*; **1.** in worldly matters, Just.*1apol.*2.3(M.6.329B); †Bas. *Is.*129(1.468E; M.30.328A); **2.** in spiritual matters, Marc.Er.*opusc.* 7.10ff.(M.65.1085–9); of ostentatious asceticism τὴν γαστριμαργίαν φεύγων, τὴν ἀ. φυλάξαι Thal.*cent.*4.30(M.91.1461B); in almsgiving, †Bas.*bapt.*2.8.8(2.665A; M.31.1609A); associated with vain-glory, †Jo.D.*B.J.*12(M.96.968B); and with hypocrisy, Bas.*moral.*72.6 (2.307D; M.31.849B); Jo.D.*virt.*(M.95.85D) = Ephr.3.425F; **3.** its effects: stultifies practice of virtue, Or.*hom.2 in Lc.*(p.19.11; M.17.316D); Pall.*h.Laus.*47(p.138.10; M.34.1201A); Eus.Al.*serm.*22.6 (M.86.460B); Max.*cap.theol.*3.68(M.90.1289D); leads to pride ἀρχὴ γοῦν τιμῆς ἀ. τὸ δὲ τέλος ταύτης ὑπερηφανία Nil.*Eulog.*3(M.79.1097C); -σκία, Cyr.*Lc.*16:15(M.72.817C); and to heresy, Anast.S. *hod.*3(M.89.92B); **4.** remedy is prayer, Bas.*reg.br.*277(2.513A; M.31.942C).

***ἀνθρωπαρεσκέω,** *please men* (rather than God) οὐ γὰρ θέλω ὑμᾶς ἀ. ἀλλὰ θεῷ ἀρέσαι Ign.*Rom.*2.1; Gr.Naz.*carm.*2.1.39.29(M.37.1351A); Marc.Er.*opusc.*7.8(M.65.1084B).

ἀνθρωπάρεσκος, *men-pleasing, sycophantic* ἀνακαλύψαι ὁ θεὸς τὰ ἔργα ἀνθρώπων ἀνθρωπαρέσκων *Pss.Sal.*4.8; *ib.*4.10; μὴ γινώμεθα ἀ. *2Clem.*13.1; τοὺς...ποιοῦντας τὸ ἀγαθὸν διδάσκει μὴ καυχᾶσθαι, ἵνα μὴ ἀ. ὦσιν Thphl.Ant.*Autol.*3.14(M.6.1140D); ὑποκριτής, ἀ. Cyr. H.*catech.*3.7; ἀ. δέ, ὁ πρὸς τὸ θέλημά τινος ἀνθρώπου εἰς ἀρέσκειαν αὐτοῦ ποιῶν, κἂν ἀτιμίας ἄξιον ᾖ τὸ γινόμενον Bas.*reg.br.*52(2.432D; M.31.1117B); Gr.Nyss.*hom.14 in Cant.*(M.44.1069B); ref. qualification for bishop μὴ ἀ. *Const.App.*2.21.1; Chrys.*hom.71.4 in Mt.*(7.700B); Thdr.Mops.*Ps.*52:5(M.66.672B).

***ἀνθρωπαρέσκως,** *in a sycophantic manner, pleasing men*, Pall.*h. Laus.*proem.(p.12.10; M.34.1003 ἀνθρωπαρεσκείας); Olymp.*Job* 22:7 (M.93.241C).

ἀνθρώπειος, *human*, esp. opp. divine; **1.** of pre-Christian teaching, opp. Christian as divinely revealed οὐκ ἔστι δὲ ἡμῶν τὰ διδάγματα κατὰ κρίσιν σώφρονα αἰσχρά, ἀλλὰ πάσης μὲν φιλοσοφίας ἀ. ὑπέρτερα Just.*2apol.*15.3(M.6.468C); μεγαλειότερα...πάσης ἀ. διδασκαλίας φαίνεται τὰ ἡμέτερα *ib.*10.1(460B); of heresy ἀ. διδασκαλίαις ἐνιστάμενοι θείᾳ παραδόσει ὑπὲρ τοῦ τὴν αἵρεσιν συστήσασθαι Clem. *str.*7.16(p.73.7; M.9.544A); **2.** of human nature in the resurrection ὁ γὰρ Χριστὸς ἧκεν οὐκ εἰς ἑτέραν μορφὴν πλασθῆναι κηρύσσων ἢ μετασκευασθῆναι τὴν ἀ. φύσιν, ἀλλὰ εἰς ὃ ἦν ἐξ ἀρχῆς πρὸ τοῦ ἐκπεσεῖν ἀθάνατος ὤν Meth.*res.*1.49(p.303.7; M.18.277C); **3.** Christol.; **a.** against view that body was spiritual, Bas.*Spir.*12(3.9E; M.32.85C) cit. s. θεοφόρος; **b.** of human, opp. divine, nature of Christ ἡνωμένη τῇ φύσει τοῦ θεοῦ λόγου ἡ φύσις ἡ ἀ. Leont.H.*Nest.*2.7(M.86.1552B); λέγοντος [sc. Ἀπολιναρίου] πάλαι μὲν ἀντὶ ψυχῆς σώματι ἀ. ἐγγενέσθαι τὴν θεότητα καὶ μίαν φύσιν ἀπαρτίσαι ἄψυχον θείαν τὸν Χριστόν id.*monoph.*(M.86.1869B); οὐ κατὰ θεὸν τὰ θεῖα δράσας, οὐ τὰ ἀ. κατὰ ἄνθρωπον Dion.Ar.*ep.*4(M.3.1072C); οὔτε...θεία φύσις εἰς τὴν ἀ. μετεβλήθη, οὔτε ἡ ἀ. φύσις εἰς τὴν θείαν ἐτράπη Just.Imp.*edict.* (p.200.4f.; M.86.2797B); neut. as subst., *human nature* κατὰ τὸ ἀ. εἴρηκεν Thdt.*Rom.*4:24(3.52); plur., id.*Heb.*1:8(3.552).

***ἀνθρωπέω,** *become man* προσκυνείσθω μὲν οὖν ὡς θεῷ. πιστευέσθω δέ, ὅτι καὶ ἠνθρώπησε Nil.*epp.*2.187(M.79.297B).

***ἀνθρώπησις, ἡ,** *becoming man, manhood* κηρύττει...τὴν θείαν ἀ. Ath.*exp.Ps.*66:1(M.27.292A); ἐν τῇ οὖν θεότητι πατὴρ καὶ υἱὸς ἕν, ἐν τῇ ἀ. υἱὸς καὶ οἱ μαθηταὶ ἕν Epiph.*haer.*69.69(p.218.4; M.42.314D); Max.*ambig.*(M.91.1084C).

***ἀνθρωπία, ἡ,** *humanity* τὸ τῆς ἀ. φάρμακον Gr.Naz.*ep.*32(M.37.69C, conj. ἀνίας); cf. τῆς πρώτης ἀνθρωπείας Eus.*d.e.*3.7(p.145.29; M.22.245B), where ἀνθρωπείας is perh. from adj. ἀνθρώπειος, or should be emended to ἀνθρωπογονίας.

ἀνθρωπίζ-ομαι, *become man*; **1.** ref. Inc., Gr.Naz.*or.*29.18(p.102.1; M.36.97C) cit. s. σύνθετος; Leont.H.*Nest.*1.52(M.86.1524B); Const. Diac.*laud.*9(M.88.489C); Jo.D.*f.o.*4.14(M.94.1160C); id.*Jacob.*83(M.94.1481D); ref. Transfiguration εἰ γὰρ θεοῦται μὲν ἄνθρωπος ἐν τῷ θεὸν ~εσθαι αὐτὸς δὲ ὁ εἷς θεός τε καὶ ἄνθρωπος δείκνυται id.*hom.* 1.3(M.96.552A); θεὸς ἀνθρωπισθεὶς Thdr.Stud.*antirr.*1.4(M.99.333A); **2.** opp. deification φασὶ γὰρ ἀλλήλων εἶναι παραδείγματα τὸν θεὸν καὶ τὸν ἄνθρωπον καὶ τοσοῦτον τῷ ἀνθρώπῳ τὸν θεὸν διὰ φιλανθρωπίαν ~εσθαι, ὅσον ὁ ἄνθρωπος ἑαυτὸν τῷ θεῷ δι' ἀγάπης δυνηθεὶς ἀπεθέωσε Max.*ambig.*(M.91.1113B).

ἀνθρωπικός, *human*; **1.** *merely human*, opp. divine οὐ γὰρ πρὸς ἀ. νόμους ὁ λόγος ἡμῖν Athenag.leg.32.2(M.6.964B); ἡ δὲ δοξαστικὴ ἀπόδειξις ἀ. τέ ἐστι...ἡ γὰρ ἀνωτάτω ἀπόδειξις...πίστιν ἐντίθησι Clem.str.2.11(p.139.3; M.8.985A); Or.Jo.13.5(p.230.6; M.14.405B); **2.** of predication of human attributes etc. to God πολλὰ εὕροις ἂν ἀ. ἐν τῇ γραφῇ, ὡς καὶ τὸ...'ἴσως ἀκούσονται'...τοῦτο οὐχ ὡς διστάζων ὁ θεὸς εἴρηκε Or.hom.18.6 in Jer.(p.160.1; M.13.477A); εἰ καὶ κλήσεσιν ἀ. οὐ καιρίως τοῦτο κατονομάζομεν Const.Diac.laud.18(M.88.501A); **3.** *concerned with what is only human* τὸν περιπατητικὸν [sc. λόγον] ὡς ἀνθρωπικώτατον Or.Cels.1.10(p.63.8; M.11.676A); **4.** ref. Inc. τῆς ἀ. αὐτοῦ θεουργίας Dion.Ar.d.n.2.6(M.3.644C); ἀ. ἐνεργείας Max.opusc.(M.91.125B); and Second Advent ὦ τῆς ἀνοίας τοῦ ἀπόδειξιν οἴεσθαι, ἀνθρωπικὴν αὐτοῦ μετὰ ταῦτα γενήσεσθαι τὴν ἐμφάνειαν Gr.Nyss.Apoll.57(M.45.1265A).

ἀνθρωπικῶς, *humanly*; **1.** *in a human sense*, i.e. without spiritual discernment ἀ. ἐκλαβὼν τὰ εἰρημένα Or.Jo.19.19(4; p.319.20; M.14.560D); **2.** *in human terms* κἂν αἱ...γραφαὶ...ἀ. περὶ αὐτοῦ διαλέγωνται Eus.Marcell.1.1(p.5.8, v.l. ἀνθρωπινώτερον M.24.720B); Gr.Nyss.Eun.9(2 p.208.23; M.45.805C); id.Apoll.57(M.45.1264B); Dion.Ar.d.n.6.3(M.3.857B); **3.** *as man*, of Christ οὐκ ἀ. ἀφορίζομεν id.ep.4(M.3.1072A); εἴ τις...ἐν αὐτῇ διαπεπλάσθαι λέγοι θεϊκῶς ἅμα καὶ ἀνθρωπικῶς· θεϊκῶς μέν, ὅτι χωρὶς ἀνδρός· ἀ. δέ, ὅτι νόμῳ κυήσεως, ὁμοίως ἄθεος Gr.Naz.ep.101(M.37.177C).

ἀνθρώπινος, **A.** *of* or *belonging to man*; **1.** in gen. προκλίσεως ἀ. 1Clem.50.2; σαρκὸς ἀ. Ign.Philad.7.2; καθ' ὃ οἷόν τέ ἐστιν ἀ. φύσει ἀναμάρτητον διεξάγειν βίον Clem.str.4.20(p.304.20; M.8.1337B); Meth.symp.8.16(p.105.9; M.18.168D); Gr.Nyss.Eun.12(1 p.336.29; M.45.1053D); Chrys.hom.5.1 in 1Tim.(11.574B); **2.** opp. divine πῶς...παραστήσεις μέγα...εἶναι τὸ 'οὐκ ἐπίσταμαι λαλεῖν' λεγόμενον ὑπὸ τοῦ σωτῆρος; τὸ λαλεῖν ἀ. ἐστι·...οὐκ ἐπίσταται λαλεῖν ἀ. ὄντος τοῦ λαλεῖν, ἀλλ' οὐκ ἐπίσταται, ἐπεί ἐστι μεῖζον ὃ ἐπίσταται τοῦ λαλεῖν Or.hom.1.8 in Jer.(p.7.22; M.13.264D); τὸ πάσχα κυρίου ἀ. καὶ Ἰουδαϊκὸν πάσχα id.Jo.10.19(14; p.190.25; M.14.340D); Gr.Thaum.pan.Or.5(p.12.27; M.10.1065C); Meth.symp.5.4(p.57.17; M.18.104A); οὐδὲν χρὴ θνητὸν οὐδὲ ἀ. τῷ...ἀνατιθέναι θεῷ Eus.Marcell.1.1(p.5.5; M.24.720B); ὁ νόμος οὐκ ὢν ἀ. id.e.th.2.14(p.116.5; M.24.929B); ref. ascription of human functions or attributes to God ἐὰν δὲ ἀκούωσιν, ὅτι κτίζει καὶ ποιεῖ, οὐκέτι τὰ ἀ. ἀντιτιθέασιν; ἔδει δὲ καὶ ἐν τῷ κτίζειν ἀνθρώπινα νοεῖν αὐτούς Ath.Ar.1.23(M.26.60B); Chrys.hom.1.1 in 1Tim.(11.549A); **3.** *human* (i.e. on human level, suited to man's understanding), Chrys.hom.26.3 in Jo.(8.152A); τὸ δέ 'μετεμελήθη' ...ἀ. δι' ἡμᾶς· πῶς γὰρ ὁ προειδὼς μεταμέλεται; Proc.G.Gen.6:5–7(M.87.269C); **4.** ref. Inc. ἡ ἀ. οἰκονομία Ath.Ar.2.12(M.26.172A); τῶν ἀ., ὧν ὑπέμεινεν ὁ σωτήρ ib.3.27(381B); of Christ's humanity; **a.** body of Christ, Or.hom.14.6 in Jer.(p.112.2; M.13.412B); admitted by Eutyches οὐκ εἶπον σῶμα ἀνθρώπου τὸ τοῦ θεοῦ σῶμα, ἀ. δὲ τὸ σῶμα Eut.ap.CCP(448)act.(ACO 2.1.1 p.142.27; H.2.165A); **b.** human soul ἀνέλαβεν ψυχὴν ὁ υἱὸς...ἀ. Or.comm.in Rom.1:1 (JTS 13 p.211); id.hom.14.6 in Jer.(p.112.9; M.13.412C); **c.** human will θέλημα κατὰ φύσιν εἶχεν ἀ. Max.opusc.(M.91.80C); ἀ. κίνησιν Jo.D.f.o.3.15(M.94.1061A); ἀ. ἐνεργείας ib.(1060C); **d.** humanity in gen. (v. infra D.1) ἵνα ὁ κατὰ τὸ ἀ. σχῆμα φαινόμενος υἱός, ἐν τῇ τοῦ πατρὸς φαίνηται δόξῃ Gr.Nyss.Apoll.57(M.45.1264D); βλασφημίαν ...τῷ ἀ. τοῦ κυρίου συγκρίματι προσαγομένην Hesych.H.qu.ev.9(M.93.1401B); Jo.D.f.o.3.15(M.94.1061A); cf. τῷ κυριακῷ ἀνθρώπῳ ὡς ἀπαρχῇ τοῦ ἀ. φυράματος Leont.H.Nest.1.18(M.86.1468B).

B. objective, *caused by man* παράγουσι φόβους ἀ. 2Clem.10.3; πειρασμοῦ διαβολικοῦ τε καὶ ἀ. Lit.Jac.(p.168.7); *relating to man* τὰς ἐν τοῖς εὐαγγελίοις φωνάς, τάς τε ἀ. καὶ...τὰς θεοπρεπεῖς, ἑνὶ προσώπῳ προσάψομεν Cyr.expl.xii cap.4(p.20.1; 6^1.150D).

C. *human*, implying *moderate, suited to weak men* μετιτέον τοὺς ἀνθρωπινωτέρους λόγους Synes.Dion 6(p.249.15; M.66.1129A); esp. exeg. 1Cor.10:13 ἀνθρώπινον λέγω. ὡσανεὶ ἔλεγεν, ἀπὸ ἀ. λογισμῶν, ἀπὸ τῶν ἐν συνηθείᾳ γινομένων· τὸ γὰρ σύμμετρον τῇ προσηγορίᾳ τοῦ ἀ. δηλοῖ· καὶ γάρ...φησί, πειρασμὸς ὑμᾶς οὐκ εἴληφεν, εἰ μὴ ἀ.· τουτέστι σύμμετρος καὶ μικρός Chrys.hom.12.1 in Rom.(9.542B,C); id.hom.24.1 in 1Cor.(10.211D); Thdt.1Cor.10:13(3.228); cf. οὐκ ηὔξατο μὴ πειρασθῆναι, ἐπειδὴ ἀνὴρ ἀπείραστος ἀδόκιμος, ἀλλ' οὕτως πειράζεσθαι ὡς φέρειν Sever.1Cor.10:13(p.258.26).

D. neut. as subst., *humanity*; **1.** in gen. οὐκ ἀρκεῖ τὸ ἀ. θέλειν πρὸς τὸ τυχεῖν τοῦ τέλους Or.princ.3.1.19(p.232.1; M.11.289B); πᾶν τὸ ἀ. τὸ θεραπεῦον τὸν θεῖον νόμον Const.ap.Eus.v.C.4.12(p.122.24; M.20.1161A); as united to God by Christ προσάγω ἅπαν τῷ θεῷ... ἐν ἐμαυτῷ τὸ ἀ. Gr.Nyss.Eun.2(2 p.328.29; M.45.504B); id.perf.(p.204.19; M.46.277C) cit. s. συνάπτω; **2.** of Christ, Or.hom.14.6 in Jer.(p.112.12; M.13.412C) cit. s. ἐπιδέχομαι; οὐ παρῃτήσατο διὰ τὸ ἀ. ἑαυτοῦ εἰπεῖν ἑαυτὸν καὶ ἐλάττονα τοῦ πνεύματος Ath.Ar.1.50 (M.26.116A); τοιαύτας λέξεις ἐπιρρίπτειν ἐπὶ τὸ ἀ. αὐτοῦ ib.2.4(153C); ib.2.12(172A); Gr.Nyss.or.catech.11(p.57.6; M.45.44A) cit. s. κατακιρνάω; id.Apoll.57(M.45.1265A); Chrys.hom.67.2 in Jo.(8.401E); κέκληται προφήτης καὶ...ἀπόστολος διὰ τὸ ἀ. Cyr.ap.cat.Heb.(suppl.) 5:4(p.476.27).

ἀνθρωπίνως, **A.** *in human fashion*; **1.** in gen. ἄνθρωπον ἀ. τιμητέον Tat.orat.4(p.4.25; M.6.813A); πέπονθας ἀ. Hom.Clem.5.4; **2.** opp. divinely Ἡράκλειτος γὰρ οὐκ ἀ. φησίν, ἀλλὰ σὺν θεῷ τὸ μέλλον Σιβύλλῃ πεφάνθαι Clem.str.1.15(p.44.13; M.8.776A); οὐδὲν ἀ. ὁ σωτήρ, ἀλλὰ πάντα θείᾳ σοφίᾳ καὶ μυστικῇ διδάσκει id.q.d.s.5 (p.163.16; M.9.609C); οἱ καθ' ἡμᾶς σοφοί, πνεύματι περισσοτέρῳ χρησάμενοι τῆς ἀνθρωπίνης φύσεως, οὐκ ἀ., θείως δὲ διδάσκονται τὰ ἀπόρρητα Or.comm.in Gen.2.12(p.208.9; M.12.81B); **3.** of Inc. θεοῦ ἀ. φανερουμένου Ign.Eph.19.3; αὐτοῦ γὰρ...λεγομένου ἀ. χρίεσθαι Ath.Ar.1.48(M.26.112D); ὁ...λόγος...ἀεί...ἐστιν αὐτὸς καὶ ὡσαύτως ἔχων, ἄτρεπτός τε καὶ ἀναλλοίωτος, ὑπομεμενηκὼς δὲ καὶ τοῦτο δι' ἡμᾶς ἀ. Cyr.Heb.2:9(p.386.9); διὰ τοῦ σώματος ἀ. ἐνεργῶν Leont.H.Nest.1.14(M.86.1457D); v. θεϊκῶς.

B. *humanly* (i.e. suitably to human understanding) esp. of sayings in scripture τοῦ ἀγαπᾶν πάλιν ἀνθρωπινώτερον ἀκουομένου Or.fr.50 in Jo.(p.524.27); and words of Christ Χριστὸς ἀνθρωπινώτερον πρὸς αὐτὸν διαλέγεται Chrys.hom.26.3 in Jo.(8.152A); ib.78.1 (458D).

C. *in human aspect, in respect of humanity* ἡ τοῦ σωτῆρος ψυχὴ ἀ. ἐταράττετο Or.fr.88 in Jo.(p.552.16); εἴ τις βούλοιτο τὰ ἀνθρωπινώτερον...εἰρημένα φέρειν ἐπὶ τὸν τῆς θεότητος αὐτοῦ λόγον Cyr.thes.10 (5^1.72D).

D. *in human fashion, in human terms*, of anthropomorphic conceptions of God Δανιὴλ...ἀνθρωπινώτερον τὴν θεοπτίαν ὑπογράφων Eus.h.e.1.2.24(M.20.65C); εἰ μὲν περὶ ἀνθρώπου...διαλογίζονται, ἀ. καὶ περὶ τοῦ λόγου αὐτοῦ...λογιζέσθωσαν· εἰ δὲ περὶ τοῦ θεοῦ... μηκέτι ἀ. Ath.Ar.2.35(M.26.221A); εἰ δὲ τὸ κτίζειν οὐκ ἀ. νοοῦμεν ἐπὶ θεοῦ, πολλῷ μᾶλλον οὐδὲ τὸ γεννᾶν ἀ. πρέπει νοεῖν id.syn.51(p.275.22; M.26.785A); Didym.(‡Bas.)Eun.5(1.303E; M.29.728C); Cyr.Jo.1.9(4.77D); Thdt.Heb.1:8(3.552); id.Ps.109:1(1.1392).

ἀνθρωποβορ-έω, *eat men, practise cannibalism* μηδ' ~εῖν Σκύθας διὰ τὸν καὶ μέχρις αὐτῶν ἐλθόντα τοῦ Χριστοῦ λόγον Eus.p.e.1.4 (11C; M.21.40A); Epiph.exp.fid.9(p.509.5; M.42.797A); Gr.Nyss.fat.(M.45.169B).

ἀνθρωποβορία, ἡ, *cannibalism*, ref. pagan charges against Christians οὓς γὰρ ἴσασιν οὐδ' ἰδεῖν κἂν δικαίως φονευόμενον ὑπομένοντας, τούτων τίς ἂν κατείποι ἢ ἀνδροφονίαν ἢ ἀ.; Athenag.leg.35.1 (M.6.969A); of pagan gods, Thphl.Ant.Autol.3.8(M.6.1133B); of Gnost. practices, Epiph.haer.26.5(p.282.10; M.41.340B).

ἀνθρωποβόρος, *man-eating*, Thphl.Ant.Autol.2.7(M.6.1057A); Eus.h.e.8.7.2(M.20.756C); id.Is.59:11f.(M.24.488A); ref. Christ λέων πάλιν καλεῖται, οὐκ ἀ. Cyr.H.catech.10.3; of Satan τὸν ἀ. λύκον Procl.CP or.13.3(M.65.793A).

***ἀνθρωπόβρωτος**, *eaten by man*, ‡Just.qu.Gr.11.15.1(M.6.1477B).

***ἀνθρωπογέννητος**, *born of humankind*, †Apoll.ep.Bas.1(M.32.1104A).

ἀνθρωπογονία, ἡ, *origin of man* πρὸ τῆς καθ' Ἕλληνας ἀ. ὁ Μωυσῆς ἠκμακέναι Clem.str.1.21(p.68.17; M.8.829B); Eus.h.e.1.2.4 (M.20.56B); ἀπὸ πρώτης ἀ. ib.1.2.6(56B); Μωσῆς...κοσμογονίαν καὶ ἀ. ὑπογράψας id.p.e.11.4(512C; M.21.829C).

***ἀνθρωποδίδακτος**, *taught by man*, Cyr.thes.32(5^1.309D).

ἀνθρωποειδής, *in human form, like a man*; **1.** of idols, Clem.str.1.15(p.45.13; M.8.777A); id.prot.5(p.50.1; M.8.168B); of a voice, Philost.h.e.3.11(M.65.497C); **2.** of God θεοειδής...ὁ ἀγαθὸς ἀνὴρ κατὰ ψυχήν, ὅ τε αὖ θεὸς ἀ. Clem.str.6.9(p.468.7; M.9.293B); not to be understood in physical sense οὐκ οὖν ἀ. ὁ θεὸς τοὔδ' ἕνεκα καὶ ἵνα ἀκούσῃ ib.7.7(p.28.28; 453A); εἰ καὶ ἀ. τὸ θεῖον, τῶν ἴσων δεήσεται τῷ ἀνθρώπῳ ib.7.5(p.21.17; 437B); heret. (Anthropomorphite) ἔφασκον γάρ, ἐπειδὴ κατ' εἰκόνα θεοῦ γενέσθαι τὸν ἄνθρωπον...λέγει γραφή, χρὴ πιστεύειν ὅτι ἀ. ἤγουν ἀνθρωπόμορφόν ἐστι τὸ θεῖον Cyr.ep.Calos. (6^2.363B); Christol. ἀ. δὲ τὴν Χριστοῦ ἕνωσιν καλεῖ [sc. Apollinarius] Leont.H.monoph.(M.86.1869A); ib.(1872C).

ἀνθρωποειδῶς, *in human fashion* ἀ. αὐτῷ [sc. Jesus in glory] παρεστηκότων ἀγγέλων Dion.Ar.ep.8.6(M.3.1100A).

***ἀνθρωπόθεος**, ὁ, *man-God* εἰ δὲ ἡμεῖς μὲν [φησιν] ἐκ τριῶν, αὐτὸς δὲ ἐκ τεσσάρων, οὐκ ἄνθρωπος ἀλλὰ ἀ. Apoll.fr.91(p.228.9) ap.Gr.Nyss.Apoll.49(M.45.1241B).

***ἀνθρωπόθηρος**, *catching men*, ‡Chrys.hom.13(13.255B).

***ἀνθρωποθνησία**, ἡ, *human mortality*, Eustrat.v.Eutych.84(M.86.2369B).

ἀνθρωποκτονέω, **1.** *offer human sacrifice*, Eus.l.C.13(p.239.3; M.20.

1401C); Gr.Naz.*or*.14.29(M.35.897A); **2.** *murder*; of Devil, Or.*Jo*.20.26(21; p.363.4; M.14.636A).

ἀνθρωποκτονία, ἡ, *murder*, Or.*Jo*.20.25(21; p.361.17; M.14.632C); of human sacrifice *ὑμῶν οἱ θεοὶ...πρὸς δὲ καὶ ἀ. ἀπολαύοντες* Clem.*prot*.3(p.31.18; M.8.125A); Gr.Naz.*or*.28.15(p.45.8; M.36.45B).

ἀνθρωποκτόνος, *man-slaying*, *murderous*; of Athena, Tat.*orat*.8(p.9.2; M.6.824B); of Cain, Or.*mart*.50(p.46.20; M.11.633D); freq. of Devil, ref. Jo.8:44 *ταῖς κεφαλαῖς αὐτοῦ ταῖς ἀ.* Meth.*symp*.8.13(p.98.14; M.18.160C); *τὸν ἀ. ὄφιν δεσμώτην Lit*.ap.*Const.App*.8.7.5; *Const.App*.2.21.3; *οὐκ εἶπεν ἁπλῶς, φονεὺς ἦν, ἀλλ' ἀ. οὐ γὰρ ἕνα ἀνεῖλεν, ἀλλὰ δι' ἐκείνου πάντα ἄνθρωπον* Sever.*creat*.6.2(M.56.486); Chrys.*hom.17.6 in Mt*.(7.231B); id.*Jud*.8.8(1.686D); of heresies *ἀ. τῶν Ἀρειανῶν αἵρεσις* Ath.*syn*.54(p.277.18; M.26.789B); id.*ep.Aeg.Lib*.3(M.25.543C).

ἀνθρωπολατρεία (-ία), ἡ, *worship of a man*; **1.** ref. Christian reply to pagan accusation *οὐ, καθάπερ οἴει, ἀ. τὸ χρῆμα·...ἄνθρωπον δὲ πεφηνότα τὸν τοῦ θεοῦ λόγον ἐπιγινώσκοντες πρόσιμεν ὡς θεῷ* Cyr.*Juln*.6(6^2.203C); *ib*.8(286D); **2.** in Nestorian controversy; **a.** claim that conjunction of 'the man' with God suffices to exclude possibility of worshipping a mere man, Nest.ap.CEph.(431)*act*.1(H.1.1413A) cit. s. *ἀνθρωπολάτρης*, cf. s.v. *ἀνθρωπολατρέω*; **b.** accusation that such worship is implied in Nestorian separation of the man Jesus from the divine Son *τὴν...ἡμῶν θρησκείαν, ἀ. ... ἀποφαίνουσι, ἀποκομίζοντες μὲν τοῦ κατ' ἀληθείαν υἱοῦ, συναφθέντα δέ τινα σχετικῶς αὐτῷ προσκυνεῖν ἀναπείθοντες* Cyr.*Chr.un*.(5^1.731C); *κἂν εἴ τις αὐτὸν ὀνομάζοι θεόν, ἀναπηδῶσιν εὐθὺς ἀ. εἶναι τὸ χρῆμα διοριζόμενοι* id.*Pulch*.47(p.60.26; 5^2.179A); *ib*.26(p.43.32; 154B); *εἰ μὲν οὖν εἰς ἄνθρωπον τῶν καθ' ἡμᾶς ἕνα πεπιστεύκαμεν, καὶ οὐχὶ δὴ μᾶλλον εἰς θεόν, ἀ. τὸ χρῆμα* id.*Nest*.3.2(p.61.28; 6^1.74A); *ἕτερον δὲ καὶ ἕτερον εἶναι λέγων, εἶτα τῷ ἐκ σπέρματος Ἀβραὰμ προσκομίζεσθαι δεῖν τὴν πίστιν διαβεβαιούμενος, ἴσθι...τῆς ἑαυτοῦ κεφαλῆς τὰ τῆς ἀ. καταχέων ἐγκλήματα ib*.3.6(p.73.20; 91E); *οἱ τῆς Νεστορίου ἀ.* Leont.B.*Nest.et Eut*.1(M.86.1273C); Justn.*ep.Thdr.Mops*.(M.86.1053C).

***ἀνθρωπολατρ-έω**, *worship a man*, ref. Nestorius *εἰ ἄνθρωπον εἶναί φασι ψιλόν, ~οῦσιν ὁμολογουμένως, προσκυνοῦντες αὐτῷ* Cyr.*Pulch*.42(p.49.33; 5^2.163B); but cf. Nest.*fr*.C 8(p.248.20) cit. s. *ἀνθρωπολάτρης*; in address to renegade Jews *Χριστιανίζειν ἤρξασθε ...ἀ. μεμαθήκατε πάντως Pers*.(p.37.25).

ἀνθρωπολάτρης, ὁ, *worshipper of a human being*; **1.** of pagans, in reply to accusation against Christians *Ἕλληνες δὲ μᾶλλον... γεγονότες ἀ.* Cyr.*Juln*.6(6^2.205E); **2.** in Trin. and Christol. controversy; **a.** against Arianism, Ath.*Ar*.2.16(M.26.181B); *ἀποδείκνυσιν, ὅτι ἡ κλῆσις ἡμῶν γέγονεν οὐ δι' ἀνθρώπου, ἀλλὰ διὰ Χριστοῦ, ὅς ἐστιν υἱὸς τοῦ θεοῦ, ἵνα καὶ ἐκ τούτου μάθωσιν, ὅτι οὐκ ἀ. γεγόνασι πιστεύσαντες τῷ Χριστῷ, ἀλλὰ ἀληθινοὶ θεοσεβεῖς* ‡Ath.*synops*.63(M.28.420A); Euthal.*epp.Paul*.(M.85.761D); **b.** in Apollinarian accusation against orthodox *ἀ. ἡμᾶς ὀνομάζετε* ‡Ath.*Apoll*.1.21(M.26.1129C); *ἀ. εἰμί σοι, σέβων ὅλον τὸν συντεθέντα μυστικῶς ἐμοὶ λόγον* Gr.Naz.*carm*.1.1.10.25(M.37.467A); **c.** in Nestorian controversy; **i.** accusation rebutted by Nestorius *ὁμολογεῖ* [sc. S. Paul] *τὸν ἄνθρωπον πρότερον καὶ τότε τῇ τοῦ θεοῦ συναφείᾳ θεολογεῖ τὸ φαινόμενον, ἵνα μηδεὶς ἀ. τὸν Χριστιανισμὸν ὑποπτεύῃ* Nest.*fr*.C 8 ap.CEph.(431)*act*.1(*ACO* 1.1.2 p.47.6; vv.ll. *ἀνθρωπολατρεῖν* Loofs p.248.20, *-είαν* H.1.1413A); id.*fr*.C 9 ap.Cyr.*Nest*.2.13(p.51.6; 6^1.58B) cit. s. *νεκρολάτρης*; **ii.** rejection of this defence, Cyr.*Nest*.3.6(p.73.21; 91E); *εἰ μὴ κατὰ φύσιν υἱὸς θεοῦ...τετράδι λατρεύομεν καὶ ἀ. ἐσμέν* Jo.D.*haer.Nest*.6(M.95.192A); **iii.** as stock epithet applied to Nestorians, CEph.(431)*ep*.(*ACO* 1.1.3 p.32.33; H.1.1592C); Leont.H.*Nest*.4.2(M.86.1656A); *Ep*.ap.CCP(536)*act*.1(*ACO* 3 p.147.37; H.2.1220A); Agath.Papa *ep.imp*.(M.*PL*.87.1202C); Max.*opusc*.(M.91.192C); Jo.D.*rect.sent*.(M.94.1432A); **d.** of Paul of Samosata, Eulog.*palm*.8(M.86.2928B).

***ἀνθρωπολογ-έω**, *speak of humanly*, *speak of as man ἕτερα ~ηθέντα* [sc. in scripture] *περὶ τοῦ ἀνεφίκτου θείου* Didym.*Trin*.3.3(M.39.816C); *τὰ ~ούμενα οἱ ἀμαθέστατοι τῇ θεότητι...προσάπτουσι* id.(‡Bas.)*Eun*.5(1.313B; M.29.752A); Christol. *τῇ γραφῇ σύνηθες τὸ ὅλον θεολογεῖν καὶ τὸ ὅλον ἀ. ... καὶ μὴ μερίζωμεν τὰ ἀμέριστα* Apoll.*ep.Dion*.10(p.260.19; M.*PL*.8.935A); *ὥσπερ γὰρ θεολογεῖται ἡ σάρξ ...οὕτω πολλάκις ~εῖται ὁ ἐν αὐτῇ θεὸς λόγος* Anast.S.*hod*.12(M.89.200D).

***ἀνθρωπολοιγός**, *hurtful to men*, ‡Gr.Naz.*Chr.pat*.939(M.38.212A).

ἀνθρωπόμιμος, *imitating men*, ‡Ign.*Ant*.6.

***ἀνθρωπομορφῆται, οἱ**, *Anthropomorphites*, *ἀ. οἵτινες λέγουσιν ἀνθρωπόμορφον εἶναι τὸ θεῖον* Tim.CP *haer*.(M.86.45A).

***ἀνθρωπομορφιανοί, οἱ**, = foreg.; of Egyptian monks who attributed human form to God, Socr.*h.e*.6.7.27(M.67.688B); *οἱ μὲν τοὺς ἀσώματον τὸν θεὸν ὁριζομένους, Ὠριγενιαστὰς ἀπεκάλουν, οἱ δέ, ἀ. τοὺς ἐναντίως φρονοῦντας* Soz.*h.e*.8.12.12(M.67.1549A).

ἀνθρωπόμορφος, *in human shape* or *form*; **1.** in gen.; of pagan images, Ammon.*Ac*.17:29(M.85.1565A); pagan gods, Clem.*str*.7.4(p.16.3; M.9.427B); Ath.*gent*.22(M.25.44B); demons, *T.Sal*.18.1(M.122.1341A); angels, ‡Chrys.*Zach*.(2.791B); Dion.Ar.*c.h*.15.3(M.3.329C); of S. Matthew's gospel ref. 'four living creatures' as emblems of evangelists *ἀ. ... τὸ εὐαγγέλιον τοῦτο* ‡Bas.*h.myst*.44(p.389.8); fig., of men acting like beasts *θηρίων...ἀ.* Ign.*Smyrn*.4; esp. of sinners, Chrys.*hom.6.3 in 2Cor*.(10.477B); enemies of monasticism, id.*oppugn*.1.2(1.47A); publicans, ‡Chrys.*publ*.1.2(8.118B); scoffers, Isid.Pel.*epp*.2.211(M.78.652A); **2.** of God; **a.** in Inc. *ἐγεννήθη θεὸς ἀ., τουτέστι θεὸς καὶ ἄνθρωπος* ‡Ath.*polit*.(M.28.1405B); **b.** denied of God against materialist interpretation of Gen.1:26, ‡Ath.*dial.Trin*.3.17(M.28.1229B); *οἱ γὰρ ἀ. αὐτὸ ἡγούμενοι, πάμπαν ἠλίθιοι, ἐπειδὴ τοῖς συγκαταβατικῶς εἰρημένοις περιπλέκονται* Isid.Pel.*epp*.3.95(M.78.800C); Gel.Cyz.*h.e*.2.14.1(M.85.1256B); against misinterpretation of doctrine of Trin., Gr.Naz.*or*.42.16(M.36.477A) cit. s. *τριπρόσωπος*; **c.** affirmed by Anthropomorphites *τούτοις ἀκολουθεῖ τὸ κατ' εἰκόνα τὸ σῶμα εἶναι καὶ τὸν θεὸν ἀ. διδόναι, ἢ τὴν μορφὴν τοῦ θεοῦ εἶναι κατὰ τοῦτο τὸ σχῆμα* Or.*dial*.12(p.146.19); Cyr.*ep.Calos*.(6^2.363B) cit. s. *ἀνθρωποειδής*; *ζήτησις κατὰ τὴν Αἴγυπτον κεκίνητο, εἰ τὸν θεὸν ἀ. δοξάζειν δεῖ* Soz.*h.e*.8.11.1(M.67.1543C); *Αὐδαῖος δέ τις, ἐκ τῆς πέραν Εὐφράτου Συρίας ὁρμώμενος, ἀ. ἔφησε τὸν θεόν* Thdt.*haer*.4.10(4.364); Tim.CP *haer*.(M.86.45A).

ἀνθρωποπάθεια, ἡ, *state of being subject to human passions*; of pagan gods, Eus.*p.e*.3.15(125C; M.21.224B); id.*l.C*.11(p.224.22; M.20.1377A).

ἀνθρωποπαθής, **1.** *having human affections*; in gen.; of pagan gods, Clem.*prot*.2(p.27.2; M.8.113B); id.*str*.5.14(p.405.3; M.9.173B); Eus.*p.e*.3.3(91D; M.21.169A); ‡Just.*monarch*.6(M.6.325A); of anthropomorphic language in scripture *τὸ ἔθος τῶν ἀ. περὶ θεοῦ καὶ Χριστοῦ λόγων* Or.*Jo*.10.34(19; p.208.32; M.14.369B); id.*Cels*.4.71(p.340.17; M.11.1140C); id.*comm.in Eph*.4:30(p.556); Cyr.*Juln*.5(6^2.173A); **2.** *involved in human suffering*, ref. Christ's advent *τὴν...προτέραν ἀνθρωποπαθεστέραν καὶ ταπεινοτέραν...τὴν δ' ἑτέραν...οὐδὲν ἐπιπεπλεγμένον τῇ θειότητι ἔχουσαν ἀνθρωποπαθές* Or.*Cels*.1.56(p.107.8; M.11.764A); Epiph.*haer*.69.61(p.209.24; M.42.300C); not applicable to generation of Son, Ath.*decr*.10(p.9.23; M.25.'441'(443)B); ref. heret. views about God *εἰ μὲν οὖν τὸν πατέρα λέγοι, ἔσται ὁ πατὴρ αὐτῷ ὁ γεννηθεὶς καὶ παθὼν καὶ πᾶν ἀ. ὑπομείνας, ὃ δὴ φθεγξάμενον τὸν Σαβέλλιον ἀσεβείας ἐγράψατο γραφήν* Eus.*e.th*.1.20(p.87.36; M.24.877B); Ath.*ep.Aeg.Lib*.16(M.25.576A); **3.** neut. as subst., *human feeling τοῦ ἀμνοῦ τὰ ἀ. παραστήσεται* Eus.*d.e*.10 proem.(p.446.14; M.22.717C); *τὰ ἀ. πάντα ἐν τῷ κυρίῳ ὁμολογεῖσθαι ἐν τῇ ἐνσάρκῳ αὐτοῦ ἀληθινῇ παρουσίᾳ* Epiph.*haer*.69.63(p.212.8; M.42.304D); *ib*.69.43(p.191.12; 269B); Nil.ap.Proc.G.*Cant*.8(M.87.1737D).

ἀνθρωποπαθῶς, **1.** *anthropomorphically*, *as of a man ὅταν λέγωνται μέλη ἢ μέρη, ἀ. μὲν λέγονται, θεοπρεπῶς δὲ νοοῦνται* ‡Ath.*dial.Trin*.1.6(M.28.1125C); Epiph.*anc*.32(p.41.7; M.43.73C); **2.** *as man Χριστός...πολλάκις ἀ. φθέγγεται* id.*haer*.65.7(p.10.28; M.42.24D); *ib*.69.64(p.213.8; 305C).

***ἀνθρωποπαραδότης, ὁ**, s.v.l., *one who hands down a man* (? to be worshipped) *ἀναθεματίζομεν Νεστόριον, ὡς ἀ.* Jo.Nic.*nativ*.(M.96.1449B), where perh. read *ἀνθρωπολάτρην*.

***ἀνθρωποπλαστέω**, *fashion* or *form men* [sc. *ἡ ποιητικὴ δύναμις τοῦ θεοῦ*] *τῇ φύσει χρωμένη ἔνδον ἡμᾶς ἀοράτως ἀ.* Meth.*symp*.2.5(p.21.8; M.18.53C); *ib*.2.2(p.17.21; 49C).

***ἀνθρωποποιέω**, *make*, *form man*, Gr.Nyss.*Apoll*.9(M.45.1141C).

***ἀνθρωποποίητος**, *made by man*, *Barn*.2.6.

ἀνθρωποποιΐα, ἡ, **1.** *creation of man*, Gr.Nyss.*anim.et res*.(M.46.57C); *πονηροῦ θεοῦ τὴν ἀ. ἔργον εἶναι νομίζουσιν* [sc. Manicheans] id.*or.catech*.7(p.39.12; M.45.32C); **2.** *human generation*, opp. baptism, *ib*.34(p.128.3; 85B).

***ἀνθρωποπολίτης, ὁ**, *dweller in man*; term used to describe Nestorian view of relation of divinity to humanity of Christ, Cyr.*Chr.un*.(5^1.750A) cit. s. *ἀνθρωπαῖος*.

ἀνθρωποπρεπής, *befitting*, or *adapted to*, *man*; **1.** in gen. *σύνεσιν* Cyr.*Jo*.1.9(4.87E); id.*Joel*.32(3.224B); *βίον* id.*Is*.2.1(2.198D); id.*Ps*.9:21(M.69.777B); **2.** of divine things adapted to human capacity; revelation given to prophets, id.*Is*.4.4(2.685E); in sacraments *αἰνίγματα φυσικοῖς καὶ ἀ. ἐσόπτροις εἰκονιζόμενα* Dion.Ar.*e.h*.2.3.1(M.3.397A); **3.** of what is predicated of Christ in respect of his human nature, Cyr.*ep*.40(p.27.23; 5^2.117B); CChalc.*act*.4(p.102.39; H.2.401B) cit. s. *ἀδιαιρέτως*; *διὰ τῆς ἀ. ἀναστροφῆς μετὰ θάνατον* Max.*ambig*.

(M.91.1309B); id.opusc.(M.91.80C); of his human subjection to angels, Dion.Ar.c.h.4.4(M.3.181C); πᾶσαν ἁπλῶς θεοπρεπῆ καὶ ἀ. ἐνέργειαν ἐκ Χριστοῦ...προϊέναι πιστεύομεν Mac.Ant.symb.(H.3.1172B); τῶν μετὰ τὴν ἀνάστασιν, τὰ μέν εἰσι θεοπρεπῆ,...τῶν ἀ. τρόποι εἰσὶ διάφοροι Jo.D.f.o.4.18(M.94.1189B); of Christ's sayings referring to his humanity, Didym.Trin.3.17(M.39.876B).

ἀνθρωποπρεπῶς, 1. *in human fashion, in a manner befitting man*; of Christ; a. as ἀρχηγός: ἀ. ὁδεύοντι ‡Proc.G.Pr.8:22(M.87.1296C); b. as suffering, Max.ep.19(M.91.593A); 2. *in human form*; ref. Ascension ἀ. ἀναληφθέντα Dion.Ar.c.h.7.3(M.3.209B); 3. *humanly, in respect of humanity* ποῖον ἂν ἔχοι λόγον τὸ ἐπαισχύνεσθαί τινα ταῖς παρ' αὐτοῦ φωναῖς, εἰ γεγόνασιν ἀ.; Cyr.ep.17(p.38.18; 5^{2}.73D) cit. ap. eund.apol.Orient.4(p.44.8; 6.172B); τὰ...ἀ. εἰρημένα id.ep.50(p.97.17; 5^{2}.167A); id.Ps.32:9(M.69.876B); id.Chr.un.(5^{1}.771A); τούτων δὲ τῶν ἀ. ἐπὶ Χριστοῦ λεγομένων, εἴτε ἐν ῥήμασιν, εἴτε ἐν πράγμασι, τρόποι εἰσὶν ἕξ...τούτων γὰρ...οὔτε ὡς θεός, οὔτε ὡς ἄνθρωπος ἔχρηζε· πλὴν ἀ. ἐσχηματίζετο, πρὸς ὅπερ ἡ χρεία...ἀπῄτει ‡Cyr.Trin.25(6^{3}.30E; M.77.1168B) = Jo.D.f.o.4.18(M.94.1185B,C); προφῆται...τὰ μὲν τῇ θεότητι αὐτοῦ διαφέροντα ῥήματα θεοπρεπῶς ἔλεγον, τὰ δὲ τῷ σώματι αὐτοῦ ἀ. Diad.ascens.5(M.65.1145B).

ἄνθρωπος, ὁ, *man*;

A. def. ἄ. γὰρ γῆ ἐστὶ πάσχουσα· ἀπὸ προσώπου γὰρ τῆς γῆς ἡ πλάσις τοῦ Ἀδὰμ ἐγένετο Barn.6.9; τί γάρ ἐστιν ὁ ἄ. ἀλλ' ἢ τὸ ἐκ ψυχῆς καὶ σώματος συνεστὸς ζῷον λογικόν; μὴ οὖν καθ' ἑαυτὴν ψυχὴ ἄ.; οὔ, ἀλλ' ἀνθρώπου σῶμα καλεῖται...κατ' ἰδίαν μὲν τούτων οὐδέτερον ἄ. ἐστιν, τὸ δὲ ἐκ τῆς ἀμφοτέρων συμπλοκῆς καλεῖται ἄ. †Just.fr.res.8(p.45; M.6.1585B); ὁ δὲ καὶ νοῦν καὶ λόγον δεξάμενος, ἔστιν ἄ., οὐ ψυχὴ καθ' ἑαυτήν Athenag.res.15(p.66.27; M.6.1004D); τὸν ὅρον τοῦ ἀ. ἀποδίδομεν, ὅς ἐστι ζῷον θνητόν, χερσαῖον, πεζόν, λογικόν Clem.str.8.6(p.91.25; M.9.584C); ref. Jo.2:25 εἰ μὲν γὰρ τὸ 'ἀνθρώπου' λαμβάνομεν ἐπὶ παντὸς τοῦ κατ' εἰκόνα θεοῦ ἢ παντὸς λογικοῦ...εἰ δὲ τὸ 'ἀ.' τηρήσαιμεν ἐπὶ τοῦ θνητοῦ λογικοῦ ζῴου μόνου Or.Jo.10.45(29; p.224.11; M.14.396D); cf. ἀ. ... οἷς μόνοις ἄνω...ὁρᾶν ἐπέτρεψεν Diogn.10.2; cf. ἄ. *quod sursum spectat*, Lact.div.inst.2.1(M.PL.6.257B); ὁ ἄ. ἐστι ζῷον λογικόν, θνητόν, νοῦ καὶ ἐπιστήμης δεκτικόν. λέγεται καὶ πάλιν τὸ ἐντελὲς ὄνομα τοῦ ἀ. ἀνορθοπεριπατητικόν. συνέκοψαν δὲ οἱ ὀνοματοθέται τὴν πολυλεξίαν, καὶ ὠνόμασαν αὐτὸν ἄ. ... ὁ δὲ ἄ. περιπατῶν βλέπει καὶ θεωρεῖ τὰ ἄνω. πάλιν ἄ. λέγεται, διὰ τὸ ἄνω ἀθρεῖν τὸν ὦπα ‡Ath.def.1.3(M.28.533C); ἀ.· νοῦς ἐνδεδεμένος προσφόρῳ καὶ πρεπούσῃ σαρκί Bas.hom.21.5(2.167A; M.31.549A); ‡Bas.struct.hom.1.16(1.330D; M.30.24D); ἄ. ... ζῷον λογικὸν θνητόν Chrys.stat.11.2(2.117A); ἄ. συνθετόν ἐστι πρᾶγμα· ἐκ ψυχῆς καὶ σώματος συνεστώς, κατ' οὐσίαν τούτων ἑνωθέντων, καὶ οὐχ ἕν ἐστι τῇ φύσει...τοῦτο γὰρ ὁ ἄ., ψυχὴ λογικὴ σώματι ὀργανικῶς συνημμένῳ κεχρημένη Pamph.H.panopl.6.1(p.614); v. λογικός.

B. *human being*; 1. in good sense, as possessing honour and dignity ἄ. εἶ, ἀνωτέρω εἶ τοῦ διαβόλου Or.hom.5.17 in Jer.(p.46.24; M.13.321B); as microcosm ὁ μικρὸς οὗτος κόσμος...ὁ ἄ. Gr.Naz.or.28.22(p.56.16; M.36.57A); cf.ib.45.7(M.36.632B) cit. s. G.3.i; Leont.B.Nest.et Eut.1(M.86.1284C); τὸν μικρὸν κόσμον, τὸν σύνδεσμον πάσης τῆς κτίσεως, τουτέστιν τὸν ἄ. Cosm.Ind.top.5(M.88.320A); hence ἄ.= *real man*, opp. irrational or savage creatures ἐσμὲν ἄ., καὶ φρόνησιν ἔχομεν καὶ λόγον ‡Clemens Romanus 'ep.9' ap.Leont.et Jo.sacr.2(M.86.2037A); ἐκεῖ παραγενόμενος ἄ. ἔσομαι Ign.Rom.6.2; ὁ μὲν ὄντως ἄ. ὁ τὰς κοινὰς φρένας κεκτημένος, ὁ δὲ ἄγριος καὶ θηριώδης Clem.str.8.3(p.82.17; M.9.564C); Chrys.hom.52.5 in Ac.(9.395A); 2. in depreciatory sense ἀσύνετος εἶ ἄ. Herm.mand.10.1.2; Isid.Pel.epp.1.461(M.78.436C); οὐ δυνάμεθα οὖν πιστεῦσαι ἀ. ὅστις πρὸς ὀλίγον ζῇ M.Pers.1.4(p.424.7); 3. as common designation of men and women ἐν ἐκείνῳ [sc. αἰῶνι]...τὰ ἔπαθλα οὐκ ἄρρενι καὶ θηλείᾳ, ἀνθρώπῳ δὲ ἀπόκειται...κοινὸν οὖν καὶ τοὔνομα ἀνδράσιν καὶ γυναιξὶν ὁ ἄ. Clem.paed.1.4(p.96.10; M.8.261A); hence ἡ ἄ. *woman*, †Hipp.narr.(p.275.10; M.10.872B) Soz.h.e.2.7.4(M.67.952A); Thdt.h.e.1.18.4(3.795): ὁ κύριος υἱὸν τοῦ ἀ., καὶ οὐχὶ τῆς ἀ. ἑαυτὸν ὀνομάζει, καὶ διὰ τοῦτο πειρῶνται οἱ ἄπιστοι δεικνύναι ὡς ἐκ γαμικῆς συναφείας ὁ δεσποτικὸς γέγονε τόκος ‡Just.qu.et resp.66(M.6.1308A); 4. *human being*, opp. divine, of BMV ἐκ τοῦ μνηστῆρος δείξῃ τὴν Μαρίαν ἀληθῶς ἄ. οὖσαν Ath.ep.Epict.5(p.9.3; M.26.1057C); ἆρα γὰρ καὶ τὴν Μαρίαν, ἄ. εἴποιτε εἶναι, ἢ οὐκ ἄ.; Leont.H.Nest.2.6(M.86.1545D); Μαρία...ἄ. ἦν· ὑπὸ ἀ. δὲ θεὸν τεχθῆναι ἀδύνατον Anastasius ap.Evagr.h.e.1.2(p.7.25; M.86.2425A); of Church καθόσον ἐφικτὸν αὐτῇ ἀ. οὔσῃ καταξιωθῆναι σὺν ταῖς ἀσωμάτοις θείαις δυνάμεσιν ‡Bas.h.myst.35(p.266.13); Christol., v. infra I; 5. for view that scripture makes no difference (ref. Mal.3:1) between appellations ἄ. and ἄγγελος, Or.Jo.2.23(17; p.79.3ff.; M.14.152Dff.); v. ἄγγελος; 6. *mankind* κατὰ πρόσωπον τῶν τότε ἀ. Polyc.ep.3.2; τὸν ἄ. ἐποίησεν Tat.orat.7(p.7.8; M.6.820B); Iren.haer.3.18.7(M.7.937B); ib.3.19.1(939A); Hom.Clem.19.21; δόξῃ...ἐστεφάνωται ὁ κοινὸς ἄ. Bas.Spir.55(3.47B; M.32.169B); Gr.Nyss.Eun.3(2 p.40.5; M.45.608A); θεὸν ἐν ἀνθρώπῳ γεγενῆσθαι id.or.catech.25(p.95.9; f.l. ἀνθρώποις M.45.65D).

C. *grown man*; opp. child, Epiph.haer.51.10(p.261.27; M.41.905D); οὐδὲ ἀ., ἀλλὰ παιδίῳ Chrys.hom.23.9 in Mt.(7.297E).

D. *man*, opp. woman, in false argument that woman was not created in divine image οὐ γὰρ εἶπε τὴν ἄ., φησίν, ἢ ἁπλῶς ἄ., ἀλλὰ τῇ τοῦ ἄρθρου προσθήκῃ τὸ ἀρρενικὸν ἐνέφηνεν ‡Bas.struct.hom.1.22(1.334F; M.30.33C); ποίαν ἕξει συγγνώμην ἄ. ταῦτα ποιῶν, ἐφ' οἷς ἡ γυνὴ...κολάζεται; Chrys.hom.9.5 in Phil.(11.271C).

E. in partic. phrases; 1. Semitisms ἄ. εἰμι...υἱὸς ἀνθρώπου ὡς εἷς ἐξ ὑμῶν A.Thom.A 66(p.183.11); πῶς ἄ. εἰρήνης Ἰούδας ἦν; Or.Jo.32.14(8; p.448.7; M.14.777A); 2. ἄνθρωπος τοῦ θεοῦ *man of God*; a. of Christians generally ὑπὸ τοῦ ἀ. Ἰησοῦ ἄ. γινόμενος θεοῦ Or.Jo.1.9(11; p.15.9; M.14.41A); δεῖ...τὸν τοῦ θεοῦ ἄ. καὶ παροικῆσαι ἐν τῷ σκηνώματι τῷ θεϊκῷ Mac.Aeg.ep.(M.34.409C); Pers.(p.25.29); Chrys.hom.17.2 in 1Tim.(11.649C); ἐὰν εὐσεβῇ τις, ἄ. θεοῦ ἐστιν· ἐὰν δὲ ἀσεβῇ τις, ἄ. τοῦ διαβόλου, οὐκ ἀπὸ τῆς φύσεως ἀλλ' ἀπὸ τῆς ἑαυτοῦ γνώμης γινόμενος ‡Ign.Magn.5; ἡ ἄ. τοῦ θεοῦ Μελανία Pall.h.Laus.9(p.29.10; M.34.1028A); b. of clergy [prob.], Dion.Al.ap.Eus.h.e.7.10.3(M.20.657B); bishops, Eus.v.C.3.15(p.84.7; M.20.1072B); Const.App.2.25.2; other clergy, ib.2.47.1; c. of confessors ὁ διωχθεὶς ἕνεκεν τῆς πίστεως καὶ μαρτυρήσας περὶ αὐτοῦ καὶ ὑπομείνας, οὗτος ἀληθῶς ἄ. θεοῦ ib.5.3.4; d. of OT writers οἱ τοῦ θεοῦ ἄ. τῷ θείῳ πνεύματι φωτισθέντες Eus.e.th.1.20(p.96.3; M.24.892C); e. of an angel εἰπέ μοι, ἄ. τοῦ θεοῦ T.Abr.B 7(p.111.3); f. in phrase ὁ σὸς ἄ. addressed to God, of Constantine, Const.ap.Gel.Cyz.h.e.3.19.18(M.85.1349A).

F. of man's nature and constitution; 1. tripartite division, *perfectus homo constat carne, anima, et spiritu*, Iren.haer.5.9.1(M.7.1144B); cf. πάντες...εἰς ζωὴν ἀναστήσονται, ἴδια ἔχοντες σώματα, καὶ ἰδίας ἔχοντες ψυχάς, καὶ ἴδια πνεύματα ib.2.33.5(834A); ὁ ἄ. συνέστηκεν ἐκ σώματος καὶ ψυχῆς καὶ πνεύματος Or.princ.4.2.4(p.313.2; M.11.365A); ἐκ τριῶν εἶναι τὸν ἄ. ... πνεύματος καὶ ψυχῆς καὶ σώματος Apoll.fr.88(p.226.25)ap.Gr.Nyss.Apoll.46(M.45.1233C) al.; based on scripture ὡς ἐν τρισὶ τούτοις τὸν ἄ. ἔχειν τὴν σύστασιν· καὶ μάρτυς ὁ Παῦλος ἐπευχόμενος Ἐφεσίοις τὴν...χάριν τοῦ σώματος καὶ τῆς ψυχῆς καὶ τοῦ πνεύματος Proc.G.Gen.1:26(M.87.117D), cf. Esaias or.23; 2. bipartite ἐποίησεν ἄ. ἐκ ψυχῆς ἀθανάτου καὶ σώματος Athenag.res.13(p.63.18; M.6.1000B); ib.15(p.65.25; 1004A); †Just.fr.res.8(p.45; M.6.1585B) cit. s. A; Iren.haer.5.6.1(M.7.1138A); ἄ. ... λέγεται κατὰ φύσιν οὔτε ψυχὴ χωρὶς σώματος οὔτ' αὖ πάλιν σῶμα χωρὶς ψυχῆς, ἀλλὰ τὸ ἐκ συστάσεως ψυχῆς καὶ σώματος εἰς μίαν μορφὴν συντεθὲν Meth.res.1.34(p.272.7ff.; M.41.1097D); contrast ἀ. ...λέγω τὰς χρωμένας ψυχὰς σώμασιν Or.princ.4.2.7(14; p.319.1; M.11.372A); ὁ δὲ ἄ. ἓν πρόσωπον...ἀπό τε πνεύματος καὶ σαρκός Apoll.inc.2(p.304.19; M.28.92C); διπλοῦς ὁ ἄ., ἐκ ψυχῆς καὶ σώματος συγκείμενος Cyr.H.catech.3.4; οὐ γὰρ τριχῇ διαιρεῖ τὸν ἄ. ἡ θεία γραφή, ἀλλ' ἐκ ψυχῆς καὶ σώματος τόδε τὸ ζῷον συνεστάναι φησίν Thdt.haer.5.10(4.422); Eulog.fr.dogm.(M.86.2953D); cf.Leont.B.cap.Sev.18(M.86.1908A) cit. s. σάρξ; 3. double nature of man, Clem.exc.Thdot.51(p.123.17; M.9.684A); διπλῆ τις φύσις ἥ τε πρὸς τὸν θεὸν ὡμοιωμένη...καὶ ἡ καθ' ἣν ἄρρεν καὶ θῆλυ γίνεται Proc.G.Gen.1:27(M.87.128C); a. 'inner man' cf. ὅπως...ἀνεπίληπτος ἑκάστου ἡμῶν ἄ. αὐτῷ γένοιτο Athenag.leg.31.2(M.6.961C); ἔστι κατὰ τὸν ἔσω ἄ. εἶναι παιδίον, κἂν ἐν γεροντικῇ τις ᾖ ἡλικίᾳ σώματος Or.hom.1.13 in Jer.(p.10.31; M.13.269A); cf. τὸ μὲν...τὸν ἀληθῆ ἄ., τὸν κατὰ ψυχὴν νενοημένον, τὸ δὲ τούτου χώραν περιβολῆς ἐπέχον· τοῦτο δὲ εἶναι τὸ σῶμα Eus.p.e.7.4(301B; M.21.513A); οὐ διακρίνοντες...τὸν ἔξωθεν ἄ. ἀπὸ τοῦ ἔνδον Hegem.Arch.5(p.6.13; M.10.1433C); οὐσία τοῦ ἀ. κατὰ μὲν τὸ ἐντός, εἰκὼν τοῦ θεοῦ· κατὰ δὲ τὸ ἐκτός, χοῦς ἀπὸ τῆς γῆς Proc.G.Gen.1:26(M.87.132B); πρὸς τὸν ἔσω ἡμῶν ἄ., ὅπου οὐκ ἔστιν ἐκτυπώματα τῶν λογισμῶν καὶ οὐδὲ θεωρία τῶν συνθέτων Philox.ep.22(p.174); v. εἴσω; b. 'outward man' ἔστι...κατὰ τὸν ἔξω ἄ. εἶναι παιδίον, κατὰ δὲ τὸν ἔσω ἄνδρα Or.hom.1.13 in Jer.(p.11.1; M.13.269A); περὶ τὸ τοῦ ἔξωθεν ἀσχολεῖν ἡμᾶς ἀ. Meth.symp.11(p.141.4; M.18.220D); cf. τὸν ὁρώμενον τοῖς πολλοῖς ἄ. Eus.v.C.1.42(p.27.20; M.20.956D); ἵνα γὰρ μὴ ἀκούων, ὅτι φθείρεται ὁ ἄ. σου ὁ ἔξω, ἀλγῇς, λέγει ὅτι, ὅταν παντελῶς τοῦτο γένηται, τότε μάλιστα χαρήσῃ, καὶ ἥξεις ἐπὶ βελτίονα λῆξιν Chrys.hom.10.1 in 2Cor.(10.505D); 4. of 'old man' opp. redeemed personality (Rom.6:6) εἰ ἡ αὐτὴ φύσις Χριστοῦ, οἷα καὶ ἡ ἡμῶν, ὁ παλαιός ἐστιν ἄ., ψυχὴ ζῶσα καὶ οὐ πνεῦμα ζωοποιοῦν Apoll.anac.23(p.244.22; M.28.1276D).

G. of man's creation; 1. in relation to other creatures πολὺ δὴ πλέον τῶν ἄλλων ἀγαπήσει τὸν ἄ., εἰκότως, τὸ κάλλιστον τῶν ὑπ' αὐτοῦ δημιουργηθέντων καὶ φιλόθεον ζῷον Clem.*paed*.1.8(p.127.8; M.8.325B); σοφώτατοι τῶν ἄλλων ζῴων ἄ. id.*prot*.3(p.32.21; M.8.128A); αἰσχρόν γε...δοκείτω καὶ τῶν ἀλόγων ζῴων τὸν ὑπὸ θεοῦ δημιουργηθέντα ἄ. ἀκρατέστερον εἶναι id.*str*.2.23(p.190.7; M.8.1089A); **2.** for creation in divine image and interpretations of it v. εἰκών; **3.** man's original state and destiny [for further references v. Ἀδάμ]; **a.** created neither mortal nor immortal, Thphl.Ant.*Autol.* 2.27(M.6.1093B) cit. s. ἀθάνατος; **b.** created mortal, but given immortality by grace of participation in Logos, Ath.*inc*.5.1(M.25.105A); possessing ἀφθαρσία q.v., Gr.Nyss.*beat*.3(M.44.1225D); **c.** endowed with freedom of will ἐλεύθερον γὰρ καὶ αὐτεξούσιον ἐποίησεν ὁ θεὸς τὸν ἄ. Thphl.Ant.*Autol*.2.27(M.6.1096A); v. ἐλεύθερος; **d.** with superior knowledge, Gr.Nyss.*beat*.3(M.44.1228C); **e.** with ἀπάθεια q.v., Gr.Nyss.*hom.opif*.5.1(M.44.137B); id.*or.catech.* 8(p.42.11; M.45.33B) etc.; **f.** capable of vision of God, Cyr.*Juln.* 3(6^2.89D); **g.** created perfect, Or.*Jo*.13.37(p.262.20; M.14.464B); ἔκτισε μὲν τὸν ἄ. ... ἀπροσδεᾶ παντὸς καλοῦ Cyr.*Juln*.3(89D); Proc.G.*Gen*.1:27(M.87.129C); his condition recapitulated in the 'new man', ‡Ath.*dial.Trin*.3.16(M.28.1228C); **h.** created as a child ἐβούλετο ἁπλοῦν καὶ ἀκέραιον διαμεῖναι τὸν ἄ. νηπιάζοντα Thphl.Ant.*Autol*.2.25(M.6.1092B); ὁ θεὸς...οἷός τε ἦν παρασχεῖν ἀπ' ἀρχῆς τῷ ἀ. τὸ τέλειον, ὁ δὲ ἄ. ἀδύνατος λαβεῖν αὐτό· νήπιος γὰρ ἦν Iren.*haer*.4.38.1(M.7.1105C); hence ἔδει...τὸν ἄ. πρῶτον γενέσθαι, καὶ γενόμενον αὐξῆσαι, καὶ αὐξήσαντα ἀνδρωθῆναι, καὶ ἀνδρωθέντα πληθυνθῆναι, καὶ πληθυνθέντα ἐνισχῦσαι, καὶ ἐνισχύσαντα δοξασθῆναι, καὶ δοξασθέντα ἰδεῖν τὸν ἑαυτοῦ δεσπότην *ib*.4.38.3(1108C); **i.** general condition ζῷον ἐν ἐξ ἀμφοτέρων, ἀοράτου τε λέγω καὶ ὁρατῆς φύσεως, δημιουργεῖ τὸν ἄ. ... οἷόν τινα κόσμον ἕτερον, ἐν μικρῷ μέγαν, ἐπὶ τῆς γῆς ἵστησιν, ἄγγελον ἄλλον, προσκυνητὴν μικτόν, ἐπόπτην τῆς ὁρατῆς κτίσεως, μύστην τῆς νοουμένης, βασιλέα τῶν ἐπὶ γῆς Gr.Naz.*or*.45.7(M.36.632B); **4.** man's fall and disobedience (v. Ἀδάμ, παράβασις, παρακοή), Iren.*haer*.1.10.3(M.7.556A); Marcell.*fr*.96 ap. Eus.*Marcell*.2.3(p.50.32; M.24.809A); ἐκ παρακοῆς ἐντολῆς θεοῦ γέγονεν ὁ ἄ. δεκτικὸς τῆς ἐπισπορᾶς τοῦ ἐχθροῦ ‡Ath.*Apoll*.1.15 (M.26.1120C); **5.** all men represented and symbolized by Adam εἰ δὲ καί ποτε τὸν κοινὸν καὶ πολὺν ἄ., καὶ τὸ γένος αὐτὸ χρεὼν διασημῆναι, πάλιν οἰκείᾳ καὶ προσφυεῖ χρωμένη προσηγορίᾳ, τὸν πάντα ἄ. τῇ τοῦ Ἀδὰμ ἐπωνυμίᾳ σημαίνειν Eus.*p.e*.7.8(307C; M.21.521A); πάντες ἄ. Ἀδὰμ ἐσμὲν εἰς ὄντες †Apoll.*ep.Bas*.1(M.32.1101D).

H. ἄ. as aeon in Gnostic systems; **1.** of Valentinus ἐκ δὲ τοῦ Λόγου καὶ τῆς Ζωῆς προβεβλῆσθαι κατὰ συζυγίαν Ἄ. καὶ Ἐκκλησίαν Iren.*haer*.1.1.1(M.7.448A); εἰς γὰρ ὄνομα Ἀνθρώπου πλασθεὶς Ἀδὰμ φόβον παρέσχεν προόντος Ἄ. Val.Gn.ap.Clem.*str*.2.8(p.132.13; M.8.972B); Hipp.*haer*.6.29(p.156.21; M.16.3238A) al.; Epiph.*haer*.31.10 (p.401.19; M.41.493A); Thdt.*haer*.1.7(4.297); **2.** of Marcus, Iren.*haer*.1.14.3(M.7.601B); τὰ δὲ φωνήεντα καὶ αὐτὰ ἑπτὰ ὄντα, τοῦ Ἄ. καὶ τῆς Ἐκκλησίας· ἐπεὶ διὰ τοῦ Ἄ. φωνὴ προελθοῦσα ἐμόρφωσε τὰ ὅλα *ib*.1.14.5(604B) = Hipp.*haer*.6.46(p.178.8; M.16.3270B) etc.; **3.** of Barbeliot Gnostics, cf. *emittit Autogenes hominem perfectum et verum, quem et Adamantem vocant*, Iren.*haer*.1.29.3(M.7.693A); Thdt.*haer*.1.13(4.305); **4.** thus, of *primal man* in Heracleon ὁ μὲν γὰρ ὑπὲρ τὸν τόπον υἱὸς ἀνθρώπου σπείρει· ὁ δὲ σωτήρ, ὢν καὶ αὐτὸς υἱὸς ἀ., θερίζει Heracleon ap.Or.*Jo*.13.49(47; p.276.32; M.14.488C); in Ophite system, Iren.*haer*.1.30.1(M.7.695A); Hipp.*haer*.5.6(p.78.6; M.16.3126A) cit. s. Ἀδάμας; Νaασσηνοὶ ἄ. καλοῦσι τὴν πρώτην τῶν ὅλων ἀρχήν, τὸν αὐτὸν καὶ υἱὸν ἀ. τοῦτον δὲ τριχῇ διαιροῦσιν· ἔστι μὲν γὰρ αὐτοῦ...τὸ μὲν νοερόν, τὸ δὲ ψυχικόν, τὸ δὲ χοϊκόν. καλοῦσι δὲ αὐτὸν Ἀδάμαν, καὶ νομίζουσι τὴν αὐτοῦ εἶναι γνῶσιν ἀρχὴν τοῦ δύνασθαι γνῶναι θεόν *ib*.10.9(p.268.12; 3419A); θῆλυ δὲ τὸ πνεῦμα καλοῦσι... ἐρασθῆναι δὲ...τὸν πρῶτον ἄ. Thdt.*haer*.1.14(4.306); **5.** in theory of Monoimus λέγει ἄ. εἶναι τὸ πᾶν, ὅ ἐστιν ἀρχὴ τῶν ὅλων, ἀγένητον, ἄφθαρτον, ἀΐδιον, καὶ υἱὸν ἀ. τοῦ προειρημένου γενητὸν καὶ παθητόν, ἀχρόνως γενόμενον, ἀβουλήτως, ἀπροορίστως Hipp.*haer*.8.12(p.232.7; M.16.3358B); *ib*.8.13(p.233.8; 3359A); **6.** Manichean ὁ πρῶτος ἄ. Hegem.*Arch*.7(p.10.6; M.10.1437B); *ib*.12(p.20.3; 1448A) cit. s. ἄρχων.

I. of human nature of Christ, or Christ as man; **1.** in gen. of Christ incarnate; as man ἐν ἀ. θεός Ign.*Eph*.7.2; υἱὸς δὲ θεοῦ, ὁ Ἰησοῦς...εἰ καὶ κοινῶς μόνον ἄ., διὰ σοφίαν ἄξιος υἱὸς θεοῦ λέγεσθαι Just.*1apol*.22.1(M.6.361A); διὰ δυνάμεως τοῦ λόγου κατὰ τὴν τοῦ πατρὸς...βουλὴν διὰ παρθένου ἄ. ἀπεκυήθη καὶ Ἰησοῦς ἐπωνομάσθη *ib*.46.5(397C); σταυρῶσαι...τὸν μόνον ἄμωμον καὶ δίκαιον ἄ. id.*dial.* 17.1(M.6.512B); γεγονὼς πάντα ὅσα ἐστὶν ἄ., ἐκτὸς ἁμαρτίας Hipp.*Noët*.17(p.261.26 v. not. ad loc.; M.10.825D); θεὸς καὶ ἄ. Heraclides ap.Or.*dial*.1(p.220.3); ἦν ὁ τοῦ θεοῦ λόγος ἐν τῷ ἀ. Ath.*inc*.17.4(M.25.125C); αὐτοῦ...ὄντος τοῦ σώματος, καὶ οὐκ ὄντος ἐκτὸς αὐτοῦ τοῦ λόγου, εἰκότως ὑψουμένου τοῦ σώματος, αὐτὸς ὡς ἄ. διὰ τὸ σῶμα ὑψοῦσθαι λέγεται...εἰ δὲ ὁ λόγος γέγονε σάρξ, ἀνάγκη ὡς περὶ ἀ. λέγεσθαι αὐτοῦ τήν τε ἀνάστασιν καὶ τὴν ὕψωσιν...ὅτι μὴ ὁ πατήρ ἐστιν ὁ γενόμενος σάρξ, ἀλλ' ὁ τούτου λόγος ἐστὶν ὁ γενόμενος ἄ. id. *Ar*.1.45(M.26.104C); ἄ. δὲ γέγονε, καὶ οὐκ εἰς ἄ. ἦλθε...εἰ...μόνον ἐν ἀ. φανεὶς ἦν, οὐδὲν ἦν παράδοξον *ib*.3.30(388A); id.*tom*.7(M.26.804B) cit. s. θεϊκῶς; τὸν Χριστὸν ἀπέστειλας εἰς ἀνθρώπους ὡς ἄ. *Const. App*.7.38.7; θεὸς ἄ. γεγονώς, οὐ τροπὴν ὑποστὰς ἀλλὰ σάρκα λαβών Epiph.*anc*.117(p.145.5; M.43.229A); γέγονε σάρξ, τουτέστιν ἄ. Cyr. *apol.Thdt*.1(p.111.23; 6.205D); ὁ...παντοδύναμος λόγος ἐλθὼν ἐσαρκώθη...καὶ ἐγένετο σάρξ...βουλόμενος δεῖξαι ὅτι κατ' ἀλήθειαν γέγονεν ἄ. Procl.CP *Arm*.5(p.189.30; M.65.860.D); doctrine denied by Manicheans ἐφαίνετο τοῖς ἀ. ὡς ἄ., μὴ ὢν ἄ. Hegem.*Arch*.8(p.12.12; M.10.1440B); **2.** of Christ assuming humanity, Clem.*prot*.10(p.78.15; M.8.228A) cit. s. ἀναλαμβάνω; ἡγοῦμαι οὖν βασιλέα μὲν λέγεσθαι τὴν προηγουμένην τοῦ πρωτοτόκου...φύσιν...τὸν δὲ ἄ., ὃν ἀνείληφεν, ὑπ' ἐκείνης μορφούμενον Or.*Jo*.1.28(30; p.36.5; M.14.76C); in Or.'s doctrine, of the pre-existent humanity or human soul of Christ τὸν ἄ. τοῦ υἱοῦ τοῦ θεοῦ τὸν τῇ θεότητι αὐτοῦ ἀνακεκραμένον πρεσβύτερον εἶναι τῆς ἐκ Μαρίας γενέσεως *ib*.1.32(37; p.42.12; 88B); Meth.*symp.* 3.5(p.33.7; M.18.69B); οὐκ ἂν δὲ πάλιν ἐθεοποιήθη κτίσματι συναφθεὶς ὁ ἄ., εἰ μὴ θεὸς ἦν ἀληθινὸς ὁ υἱός· καὶ οὐκ ἂν παρέστη τῷ πατρὶ ὁ ἄ., εἰ μὴ φύσει καὶ ἀληθινὸς ἦν αὐτοῦ λόγος Ath.*Ar*.2.70(M.26.296A); [sc. Valentinus] ἐν σχήματι λέγων τὸν κύριον γεγενῆσθαι, ἀλλ' οὐχὶ αὐτὸν τὸν ἄ. παρ' αὐτοῦ προσειλῆφθαι Bas.*ep*.261.2(3.402D; M.32.969C); ‡Just.*coh.Gr*.38(M.6.309B) cit. s. ἀναλαμβάνω; τὸν τοῦ θεοῦ λόγον κατελθεῖν καὶ ἀναλαβεῖν τὸν ἄ. ἐκ μήτρας Adam.*dial*.5.7(p.188.31; M.11.1844A); *ib*.5.8(p.190.5; 1844B); ἔλαβεν γὰρ ὁ μὲν υἱὸς τοῦ θεοῦ τὸν ἄ., ὃν ἐνεδύσατο ἀπὸ τῆς ἐκκλησίας Ph.Carp.ap.Cosm.Ind.*top*.10(M.88.433C); ἄ. in this sense denotes universal *humanity* not *a man*, cf. τὸν υἱὸν...σάρκα ἤτοι σῶμα, τουτέστιν ἄ., εἰληφέναι Ath.*syn*.28 (p.257.19; M.26.741D); Gr.Nyss.*or.catech*.32(p.116.9; M.45.80B); ἆρα γὰρ καὶ τὴν Μαρίαν ἄ. εἴποιτε εἶναι ἢ οὐκ ἄ.;...εἰ δὲ ἄ. καὶ πῶς τὸν καθόλου ἄ. αὕτη γεγέννηκε, πολλὰς μὲν ἀνθρώπων γενεὰς ἔχοντα πρὸ αὐτῆς, πολλὰς δὲ καὶ μετ' αὐτήν; Leont.H.*Nest*.2.6(M.86.1545D); *ib.* 2.8(1553A); hence ἄ. assumed by Son possesses no independent personality or hypostasis οὐδὲ δύο υἱούς, ἄλλον μὲν υἱὸν θεοῦ...ἄλλον δὲ ἐκ Μαρίας ἄ. Apoll.*ep.Jov*.(p.251.4; M.28.28A); **3.** hence ἄ. = *human nature* of Christ θεὸς καὶ ἄ. ἐφανερώθη, καὶ τὸν μὲν ἀ. αὐτοῦ εὐκόλως ἐστὶ νοεῖν ὅτι πεινᾷ Hipp.*fr.in Ps*.2:7(p.146.2; M.10.608C); cf.Or.*Jo*.1.32(37; p.42.12; M.14.88B); οὐκ ἄν χωρὶς τοῦ ἀ. χωρησάντων ἡμῶν τὴν ἀπὸ τοῦ λόγου ὠφέλειαν, μένοντος ὁποῖος ἦν τὴν ἀρχὴν πρὸς τὸν πατέρα θεόν, καὶ μὴ ἀναλαβόντος ἄ. *ib*.10.6(p.176.23; 316C); τὸν ἄ. τοῦ σωτῆρος, ὃν κατανοεῖν διδασκόμεθα, αὐτὸν εἶναι ποίημα...πῶς ἡμᾶς διδάσκει τὴν θεότητα αὐτοῦ τοῦ λόγου κατανοεῖν; ἀλλ'...Ἰησοῦν τὸν ἄ. τοῦ σωτῆρος...εἶπεν ἡμῖν κατανοεῖν ‡Ath.*serm. fid*.30(p.27; M.26.1285A); Pamph.H.*panopl*.5.2(p.613) cit. s. προδιάπλασις; **4.** of Christ regarded from human aspect *qua* man ὡς ἄ. μαρτυρούμενον ὑπὸ τοῦ θεοῦ ἔχειν τι θειότερον ἐν τῷ βλεπομένῳ ἀ. Or.*Cels*.1.66(p.120.21; M.11.785A); ἐροῦμεν ὅτι ἀδύνατον εἶναι οὕτως ἄ. ἀναμάρτητον. τοῦτο δέ φαμεν ὑπεξαιρουμένου τοῦ κατὰ τὸν Ἰησοῦν νοουμένου ἀ. *ib*.3.62(p.256.17; 1001C); λαβόντος τοῦ κατὰ τὸν σωτῆρα ἀ. τὴν ἐξουσίαν τῶν ἐν οὐρανῷ οἷον τῶν ἐνυπαρχόντων τῷ μονογενεῖ id.*or*.26(p.362.1; M.11.501D); τὸν ἀμνὸν οὐκ ἄλλον τοῦ ἀ. ὑπολημψόμεθα ...ὁ δὲ προσαγαγὼν τοῦτον τὸν ἀμνὸν ἐπὶ τὴν θυσίαν ὁ ἐν τῷ ἀ. ἦν θεός id.*Jo*.6.53(35; p.162.1; M.14.292C); θεὸν μὲν κατὰ πνεῦμα, ἄ. δὲ καθ' ὃ γεγέννηται ἐκ τῆς Μαρίας Heraclides ap.Or.*dial*.1(p.122.14); Eus. *h.e*.1.2.23(M.20.65B); εἰς τὸν κατὰ τὸν σωτῆρα νοούμενον ἄ. γεγράφθαι ‡Ath.*serm.fid*.28(p.25; M.26.1284B); 'μιμηταί μου γίνεσθε'...δηλονότι τοῦ ἀ. λέγει *ib*.31(p.27; 1285B); ὁ μὲν κατὰ Χριστὸν ἄ. ἐπὶ Καίσαρος Αὐγούστου τὴν ἀρχὴν λαμβάνει διὰ γεννήσεως Gr.Nyss.*Eun*.6(2 p.145.4; M.45.729D); *Const.App*.7.38.7; Socr.*h.e*.3.23.45(M.67.445B); **5.** esp. in phrase ὁ κυριακὸς ἄ. *the Christ-man*, i.e. Christ *qua* man, the historical Christ, Ath.*exp.Ps*.40:6(M.27.197B); εἰς οὐρανούς, ὅπου πρόδρομος εἰσῆλθεν ὑπὲρ ἡμῶν ὁ κυριακὸς ἄ., ἐν ᾧ μέλλει κρίνειν ζῶντας καὶ νεκρούς †Ath.*exp.fid*.1(M.25.204A); *ib*.4(205C); ὁ δὲ κυριακὸς ἄ. οὐκ ἄκων...ἀπέθανεν ‡Ath.*serm.fid*.4(p.6; M.26.1265C); τὸν κυριακὸν ἄ. ὃν εἶπεν ὁ Παῦλος μεσίτην θεοῦ καὶ ἀνθρώπων *ib*.26(p.23; 1280B); *ib*.31(p.28; 1285C); μὴ ἀπατάτωσαν οἱ ἄ. ... ἄ. ἄνουν δεχόμενοι τὸν κυριακόν, ὡς αὐτοὶ λέγουσι, μᾶλλον δὲ τὸν κύριον ἡμῶν καὶ θεόν Gr.Naz.*ep*.101(M.37.177B); ἐν τῷ γὰρ εἰπεῖν, γέγονεν ἐν ἀγωνίᾳ, τὸν κυριακὸν ἄ. ἀληθινὸν ἄ. ὄντα δείκνυσι Epiph.*anc*.37(p.46.29; M.43.84B); *ib*.44(p.54.20; 96C); *ib*.93(p.114.23; 188A); *ib*.(p.115.3; 188B); ἀπὸ προσώπου αὐτοῦ τοῦ κυριακοῦ ἀ., τουτέστι τῆς αὐτοῦ ἐνανθρωπήσεως id.*haer*.69.64(p.213.15; M.42.305D); ‡Chrys.*Spir*.7(3.805D); τῇ ἐνεργείᾳ τοῦ πνεύματος, καθ' ἣν καὶ ὁ κυριακὸς ἄ. (οὕτω γὰρ τοῖς πολλοῖς φίλον προσαγορεύειν τὸν Ἰησοῦν)...ἐκυήθη Ast.Am.*hom*.8(M.

40.280C); προέκοπτε σοφίᾳ...ὡς κυριακὸς ἄ. Nest.ap.Cyr.*dial.Nest.*(M.76.252B); ‡Nil.*perist.*4.9(M.79.836A); ἄγοιτο ὑπὸ τοῦ λόγου ὁ κυριακὸς ἄ. Leont.H.*Nest.*1.16(M.86.1464B); *ib.*1.18(1468B); *ib.*1.19(1473C); *ib.*2.14(1568A); οὐκ ἀνυπόστατον ὑμῖν τὸν ἄ. τὸν κυριακὸν δεῖξαι βουλόμεθα...ἀλλ' οὐκ ἰδιουπόστατον *ib.*2.10(1556A); Ἀπολινάριος ...ἀντὶ νοῦ ψυχικοῦ βουλόμενος εἶναι ἐν τῷ κυριακῷ ἀ. τὸν λόγον id.*monoph.*(M.86.1809C); ὁ κυριακὸς ἄ. ἔχει ἰδίαν φύσιν κατὰ τὸ σαρκικόν *ib.*(1872B); Pamph.H.*panopl.*4(p.611); **6.** emphasizing independent reality and completeness of Christ's manhood, and human centre of personality of the Christ-man; ἄ. denoting the man who embodied Christ ὥσπερ γὰρ ἦν ἄ., ἵνα πειρασθῇ, οὕτω καὶ λόγος, ἵνα δοξασθῇ· ἡσυχάζοντος μὲν τοῦ λόγου ἐν τῷ πειράζεσθαι...συγγινομένου δὲ τῷ ἀ. ἐν τῷ νικᾶν Iren.*haer.*3.19.3(M.7.941A); cf. *qui de substantia domini nostri, et de dispositione quam fecit propter hominem suum, falsa docent,* *ib.*3.24.1(966A); λόγος γὰρ ἦν θεοῦ πρωτότοκος ἀπ' οὐρανῶν ἐπὶ σὲ κατερχόμενος, καὶ ἄ. πρωτότοκος ἐν κοιλίᾳ πλασσόμενος, ἵν' ὁ πρωτότοκος λόγος θεοῦ πρωτοτόκῳ ἀ. συναπτόμενος δειχθῇ Hipp.*fr.1Reg.*2(p.121.11)ap.Thdt.*eran.*1(4.55); τὸν ἐκ τῆς παρθένου ἄ. ἀναλαβών *ib.*3(p.122.2)ap.eund.l.c.; ὁ δὲ ἄ. ἐκεῖνος, ᾧ σύνοικος ὁ λόγος...ἐξομοιοῦται τῷ θεῷ...καὶ γὰρ ὁ θεός ἐστιν· θεὸς δὲ ἐκεῖνος ὁ ἄ. γίνεται, ὅτι βούλεται ὁ θεός Clem.*paed.*3.1(p.236.22; M.8.556C); σοφίαν...τῷ...πρωτογόνῳ τῶν ἀ. ἀνθρώπῳ κερασθεῖσαν ἐνηνθρωπηκέναι Meth.*symp.*3.4(p.30.21; M.18.68A); οὐδαμῶς μὲν τοῦ εἶναι ὃς ἦν ἐξιστάμενος, ὁμοῦ δ' ἐν τῷ ἀ. φυλάττων τὸν θεόν Eus.*d.e.*4.10(p.168.31; M.22.281A); πάντα γ' ἐπιτελῶν δι' οὗ ἀνείληφεν ἄ. *ib.*4.13(p.172.5; 285D); *ib.*9.3(p.409.27; 661A); τὸν υἱὸν τοῦ ἀ. ὃν ἀνείληφεν id.*Marcell.*2.1(p.32.14; M.24.777B); id.*e.th.*1.6(p.65.6; M.24.836A); ἐκ γυναικὸς δὲ γέγονεν ἄ., ὁ...πνεύματι παγεὶς ἁγίῳ Eust.*fr.in Pr.8:22*(M.18.677B); ὁ ἄ. γὰρ ὁ ἀποθανὼν τριήμερος μὲν ἀνίσταται *ib.*(680C); κύριον δὲ τῆς δόξης αὐτὸν τὸν ἄ. τὸν σταυρωθέντα σαφῶς ὀνομάζει *ib.*(681A); εἰ...Παῦλος ἔφρασε, τὸν κύριον τῆς δόξης ἐσταυρῶσθαι, σαφῶς εἰς τὸν ἄ. ἀφορῶν, οὐ...δεήσει πάθος τῷ θείῳ προσάπτειν *ib.*(681C); τὸ τοῦ Χριστοῦ πρόσωπον εἰσιδών...ἄ. ... καθαρὸν...ἐποπτεύων id.*engast.*10(p.31.13; M.18.633B); τοῦτο οὐ πέπονθεν, ἀλλ' ὁ ἄ. ὃν ἐνεδύσατο, ὃν ἀνέλαβεν ἐκ Μαρίας τῆς παρθένου, τὸν ἄ. τὸν παθεῖν δυνάμενον· ὅτι ἄ. θνητός, θεὸς δὲ ἀθάνατος. πιστεύομεν ὅτι...ἀνέστη οὐχ ὁ θεὸς μὲν ἐν τῷ ἀ., ἀλλ' ὁ ἄ. ἐν τῷ θεῷ ἀνέστη CSard.*ep.cath.* ap.Thdt.*h.e.*2.8.48(3.847); Ath.*Ar.*2.70(M.26.296A) cit. s. 2; ἀνείληφεν ἄ., Χριστὸν Ἰησοῦν, ὃν...παθεῖν παρέδωκεν...ἐν ᾧ ἀ. ... ἀποθανὼν ...ἀνέστη †Ath.*exp.fid.*1(M.25.201B); ‡Ath.*serm.fid.*3(p.5; M.26.1265C); *ib.*24(p.19; 1276C); ‡Ath.*Ar.*4.35(p.84.12; M.26.521B) cit. s. χρίσις; Bas.*ep.*210.5(3.316E; M.32.776B) cit. s. συνάφεια; Gr.Nyss.*Eun.*5(2 p.117.7; M.45.697B) cit. s. δεξιός; *ib.*6(2 p.150.14; 736D); εἰ ταῦτα τιθείη ἀποδείκνυται τὸ μὴ ἑνοῦσθαι ἄ. θεῷ id.*Apoll.*45(M.45.1232B); ὁ ἐν Μαρίᾳ ἄ., ἐν ᾧ ᾠκοδόμησεν ἡ σοφία τὸν ἴδιον οἶκον id.*ep.*3(M.46.1021A); τέλειον εἰς ἑαυτὸν ἀναπλάσας ἄ. ἀπὸ Μαρίας...οὐκ ἐν ἀ. οἰκήσας, ὡς εἴωθεν ἐν προφήταις...κατοικεῖν...ἀλλ' αὐτὸς... συμπεριλαβὼν τὸ εἶναι ἄ. καὶ εἴ τί ἐστιν ἄ. ἄ. δὲ...τέλειον ⟨ἔχοντα⟩ ὅσα ἐν ἀ. καὶ οἷα ἄ. Epiph.*anc.*75(p.95.1f.; M.43.157C); ἑνώσει τοῦ...λόγου πρὸς τὸν ἐκ Μαρίας ἄ. Atticus CP *fr.*ap.Thdt.*eran.*2(4.167); τῶν... ἁγίων...Βασιλείου καὶ Γρηγορίου...καταψεύδεται· μὴ γὰρ λέγειν αὐτοὺς ἄ. γεγενῆσθαι τὸν υἱόν, ἀλλ' ἐνοικῆσαι ἀνθρώπῳ Philost.*h.e.*8.13(M.65.565B); esp. among Antiochene theologians, Diod.*synous.*(M.33.1560C) cit. s. χάρις; οὐκ εἶπεν τοῦ υἱοῦ, ἀλλὰ τοῦ υἱοῦ τῆς ἀγάπης αὐτοῦ· οὐ γὰρ κοινωνοὶ τῆς βασιλείας τοῦ θεοῦ λόγου γινόμεθα, ἀλλὰ τοῦ ἀναληφθέντος ἀ. Thdr.Mops.*Col.*1:13(p.260.8; M.66.928A); cf. *quemadmodum...fieri poterat, ut ille qui adsumptus est homo ipse sit et qui de caelo descendit?* id.*Eph.*4:10(p.168.4); ἄ. ... ἡνωμένον τῷ μονογενεῖ id.*fr.inc.*(p.298.12; M.66.980C); εἰ γὰρ οὐκ ἄ. ἐστιν... ἀναληφθεὶς ὁ γεννηθεὶς...θεὸς δὲ σαρκωθείς, πῶς ὁ γεννηθεὶς θεὸς ἐκ θεοῦ καὶ ὁμοούσιος λέγοιτο ἂν τῷ πατρί; id.*fr.Apoll.*3.1(p.313.8; M.66.993C, Lat.); τὸν δὲ ἄ. περὶ οὗ ταῦτά φησιν ὁ προφήτης σαφῶς...δηλοῖ Παῦλος τὸν ὑπὸ τοῦ μονογενοῦς εἰλημμένον ἄ. εἶναι...σαφῶς δεικνὺς ὅτι Ἰησοῦς ἄ. *ib.*4.4(p.320.34; 1001A); ὁ...θεὸς λόγος ἄ. εἴληφεν τέλειον ἐκ σπέρματος ὄντα...Δαβίδ...ἄ. τέλειον τὴν φύσιν ἐκ ψυχῆς τε νοερᾶς καὶ σαρκὸς συνεστῶτα ἀνθρωπίνης id.*symb.*(p.98.14; M.66.1017B); οὐ λόγῳ φύσεως ἀλλ' εὐδοκίας, καθ' ἣν ἡνώθη τῷ θεῷ λόγῳ ὁ κατὰ πρόγνωσιν ἐκ σπέρματος Δαβὶδ γενόμενος ἄ. id.*fr.mir.*(p.339.16; M.66.1004D); θεὸς γὰρ ἦν ὁ λόγος, ἀνθρώπῳ τε συνημμένος καὶ ἐνοικῶν αὐτῷ Nest.*fr.*C 11(p.278.3)ap.Cyr.*Nest.*1.2(p.20.2; 6^{1}.12B); οὐ σὰρξ ὁ τοῦ θεοῦ λόγος, ἀλλ' ἄ. ἀνειληφώς...ὃν δὲ ἀνέλαβεν ἄ. οὐ φύσει θεὸς ὢν διὰ τὸν ἀναλαβόντα αὐτὸν ἀληθῶς θεοῦ υἱὸν ὁμωνύμως αὐτῷ χρηματίζει *ib.*B 5(p.217.20)ap.Cyr.*Thds.*6(p.46.3; 5^{2}.5E); such language already implicitly attacked, Ath.*Ar.*3.30(M.26.388B); ἡμᾶς φησι δύο πρόσωπα λέγειν, τὸν θεὸν καὶ τὸν παρὰ τοῦ θεοῦ προσληφθέντα ἄ.· αὐτὸν δέ φησι μὴ οὕτως ἔχειν, ἀλλὰ...τὸν σαρκωθέντα...οὐχ ἕτερον παρὰ τὸν ἀσώματον, ἀλλὰ τὸν αὐτὸν καθ' ὁμοίωσιν ἡμετέρας ἐν σαρκὶ ζωῆς Apoll.*fr.*67(p.220.13)ap.Gr.Nyss.*Apoll.*35(M.45.1200B); *ib.*76(p.222.21; M.45.1212A) cit. s. ἐπιστημοσύνη; εἰ ἀ. συνήφθη ὁ θεός, τέλειος τελείῳ, δύο ἂν ἦσαν *ib.*81(p.224.14; 1212C); and protested aganst by Cyril ἄ. δὲ ἀνειλῆφθαι παρὰ τοῦ θεοῦ λόγου φασὶ...κατὰ σχέσιν δηλονότι καὶ οἰκειότητα τὴν πνευματικὴν τὴν ὡς ἐν θελήσει καὶ χάριτι Cyr.*apol.Thdt.*72(p.138.6; 6^{1}.232C); τοὺς δὲ λέγοντας ὅτι τὸν Λάζαρον...ἤγειρεν φωνήσας οὐχ ὁ ἄ., ἀλλὰ ὁ θεὸς λόγος, καὶ ὅτι οὐχ ὁ θεὸς ἐκοπίασε...ἀλλ' ὁ ἀναληφθεὶς ἄ. ... φαμὲν διημαρτηκέναι τῆς ἀληθείας id.*resp.*20(6^{2}.390B); ἄ. γεγονώς, καὶ οὐκ εἰς ἄ. ἐλθών, ἤγουν ἄ. ἑαυτῷ συνάψας id.*hom.pasch.*27(5^{2}.323B); but Cyril asserts ὁ λόγος ...γέγονεν ὑπὲρ ἡμῶν ἀρχιερεύς, ὥσπερ τινὰ ποδήρη τὸν ἐκ γυναικὸς ἄ. ἤτοι ναὸν ἀναλαβών *thes.*21(5^{1}.214B); cf. ὁ...Κύριλλος...εὔδηλον ἡμῖν ἐποίησεν...ὅτιπερ ὁ...υἱὸς...ἄ. τέλειον ἀνέλαβεν [Eudoxius Bosphorensis ap.CCP(448)]...καὶ ἐν τῷ ἀναγινώσκεσθαι Εὐστάθιος... Βηρυτοῦ εἶπεν· ἄ. οὐκ ἀνέλαβεν ἀλλ' ἄ. ἐγένετο· σάρκα δὲ ἀνέλαβεν CCP(448)*act.*(*ACO* 2.1.1 p.122.13; H.2.137D); employed by Thdt., ref. Christ as head of Church κατὰ τὸ ἀνθρώπειον ἡμῶν ἐστι κεφαλή, ὡς καὶ περὶ ἀ. καὶ ταῦτα εἰρῆσθαι, πᾶσαν ἐν αὐτῷ φέροντος τὴν θεότητα Thdt.*Col.*2:9(3.485); τέλειον ἄ. ὑπὸ τελείου θεοῦ ἀνειλῆφθαι id.*ep.*151(4.1298); θεοτόκον...οὐχ ὡς θεὸν φύσει γεννήσασαν ἀλλ' ὡς ἄ. τῷ... ἡνωμένον θεῷ id.ap.Cyr.*apol.Thdt.*1(p.109.18; 6^{1}.204E); οὔτε θεὸς ἀνθρωπείας κεχωρισμένος φύσεως οὔτε ἄ. γεγυμνωμένος θεότητος *ib.*(p.109.30; 205B); by Leont. H. θεοῦ ἀληθοῦς πρὸς ἄ. ἀληθῆ γέγονεν ἀληθῶς ἡ φυσικὴ σύνθεσις τοῦ δεσπότου ἡμῶν *Nest.*1.14(M.86.1457B); εἰ τοίνυν οὐ συνετέθη ὁ λόγος τῷ ἐξ ἡμῶν ἀ. ... ἔσται ὁ ἐξ ἡμῶν ἄ. ἄλογός τε καὶ ἄνους *ib.*1.16(1461B) echoing Nestorian argument οὐδὲ συνετέθη τῷ ἐξ ἡμῶν ἀ. [sc. ὁ λόγος] *ib.*(1461A); ἔχει τὴν ἄκτιστον ὑπόστασιν τοῦ λόγου, καὶ τῆς κτιστῆς αὐτοῦ φύσεως οὖσαν ὑπόστασιν, σὺν τῷ λόγῳ καὶ ὁ ἄ. ὁ ἐν Χριστῷ *ib.*1.39(1500C); **7.** of Christ as 'new man', v. καινός, Ἀδάμ; **8.** heret., of Christ as mere man οἱ...τὴν θεότητα αὐτοῦ περιγράψαντες, τὸν δὲ ἄ. ὡς ἅγιον καὶ δικαιότατον πάντων ἀ. ὁμολογήσαντες Or.*Jo.*10.6(4; p.176.15; M.14.316B); οἱ μὲν γὰρ τὸν ἄ. ὃν ἔλαβεν ὁ σωτήρ, αὐτὸν εἶναι τὸν υἱὸν λέγουσιν· οἱ δὲ τὸ συναμφότερον, τόν τε ἄ. καὶ τὸν λόγον, υἱὸν τότε γεγενῆσθαι, ὅτε συνήφθησαν ‡Ath.*Ar.*4.15(p.59.19; M.26.488C); Thdt.*haer.*2.1(4.328); v. ψιλός; **9.** of man's re-creation in Christ, cf. *deus hominis...plasmationem in se recapitulans, ut...vivificaret hominem,* Iren.*haer.*3.18.7(M.7.938B); Χριστὸς νέον τὸν παλαιὸν ἄ. ἀποτελῶν Hipp.*haer.*10.34(p.293.11; M.16.3454C); cf.id.*antichr.*4(p.7.2; M.10.732B); τί γὰρ ἄλλο πλὴν ὁ πᾶς ἄ. ὑπὸ τῆς θεότητος κατεπίνετο, καὶ πάλιν θεὸς ἦν ὁ θεὸς λόγος, οἷος καὶ πρὶν γενέσθαι ἄ., καὶ συναπεθέου γε τὸν ἄ. ἀπαρχὴν τῆς ἡμῶν ἐλπίδος Eus.*d.e.*4.14(p.173.13; M.22.170D); Ath.*Ar.*2.70(M.26.296A).

***ἀνθρωπόσαρκος**, *having human flesh,* Leont.H.*Nest.*6.5(M.86.1756C) cit. s. θεόσαρκος.

***ἀνθρωποσφαγία**, ἡ, *slaughter of men,* Tat.*orat.*23(p.26.4; M.6.857C ἀνθρωποφ-).

***ἀνθρωπόσχημος**, *in human guise* ἀ. τὸ θεῖον αἱ...γραφαὶ καταγγέλλουσιν ‡Ath.*disp.*29(M.28.476D).

***ἀνθρωπότερον**, *in a manner more suitable for men,* Proc.G.*Gen.*11:7(M.87.313C), prob. f.l. for ἀνθρωπινότερον.

ἀνθρωπότης, ἡ, **1.** *mankind, humanity,* in gen. ὑποτάσσεσθαι τὰ πάντα τῇ ἀ. Thphl.Ant.*Autol.*1.6(M.6.1033A); οἰκονομίαν τοῦ θεοῦ, τὴν ἐπὶ τῇ ἀ. γενομένην Iren.*haer.*1.10.3(M.7.556A); *ib.*3.11.8(889B); Clem.*prot.*11(p.80.23; M.8.232B); μία...τῆς ἀ. σωτηρία ἡ πίστις id.*paed.*1.6(p.108.10; M.8.285C); id.*str.*7.2(p.7.7; M.9.412A); θηρία διαφθείροντα τὴν ἀ. Hipp.*Dan.*4.2.2(M.10.680D); Meth.*symp.*1.2(p.10.14; M.18.41A); πρῶτον τῆς ἀ. ἄνθρωπον...Ἀδάμ *ib.*3.4(p.31.4, v.l. τῶν ἀνθρώπων M.18.68A); Ath.*exp.Ps.*15:1(M.27.100D); συναντᾷ αὐτῷ θόρυβος τῆς ἀ. Ephr.1.330E; Mac.Aeg.*hom.*3.6(M.34.472B); Bas.*hom.*1.3(2.3A; M.31.168A); ἐὰν ἐν πολιτείᾳ...ἡ ἀ. ζηλώσῃ σε Esaias *or.*5.5(p.20); Cosm.Ind.*top.*2(M.88.124B); **2.** abstract, *humanity, human nature;* **a.** opp. divine ἄνθρωπον οὐχὶ τὸν ὅμοια τοῖς ζώοις πράττοντα, ἀλλὰ τὸν πόρρω μὲν τῆς ἀ. πρὸς αὐτὸν δὲ τὸν θεὸν κεχωρηκότα Tat.*orat.*15(p.16.15; M.6.837B); **b.** in good sense εἰ...τὰς περὶ τὰ λεγόμενα θεῖα πράξεις μιμήσαιτο...ἀλλότριος...ἀνθρωπότητος λογισθείη ‡Just.*monarch.*6(M.6.325B); **c.** in gen. διαφόροις σπουδάσμασιν ἡ ἀ. γνωρίζεται Const.ap.Eus.*v.C.*2.59(p.65.6; M.20.1033A); Gr.Nyss.*Eun.*1(1 p.73.27; M.45.304B); τὰ τῇ ἀ. πρέποντα Cyr.*thes.*20(5^{1}.196D); ἀνθρωπότητος γὰρ ἴδιον τὸ μὴ εἰδέναι τὰ μέλλοντα *ib.*22(218C); τὴν κατ' εἰκόνα...κτισθεῖσαν ἀ. Leont.H.*Nest.*1.18(M.86.1472A); **3.** universal, *humanity* ἄτομόν ἐστιν, ἡ καθ' ἕκαστον ἡμῶν ὑπόστασις· ἀ. δὲ ἡ τῆς οὐσίας κοινότης ‡Ath.*dial.Trin.*1.16(M.28.1141D); ἡ ὑπόστασις Πέτρου ἄνθρωπός ἐστι, καὶ ἡ ὑπόστασις Παύλου ἄνθρωπός ἐστι· καὶ δύο εἰσὶν ὑποστάσεις, καὶ οὐ δύο ἀ. *ib.*1.17(1144C); παρ' Ἕλλησι...μία θεότης ...καὶ παρ' ἡμῖν ἀ. μία, τὸ γένος ἅπαν. ἀλλ' ὅμως θεοὶ πολλοί, καὶ οὐχ εἷς, ὡς δὴ καὶ ἄνθρωποι Gr.Naz.*or*.31.15(p.163.11; M.36.149B); **4.** of Christ's human nature, v. θεότης; *Παῦλος ἄλλον Χριστὸν οὐκ οἶδεν ἀλλ' ἢ τοῦτον...ὃν καὶ ἄνθρωπον λέγει...πανταχοῦ ἐπὶ τοῦ πάθους...καὶ τῆς ἀ. αὐτοῦ...τῷ τοῦ Χριστοῦ κέχρηται ὀνόματι* Iren.*haer*.3.18.3(M.7.933B); Clem.*paed*.1.5(p.99.6; M.8.268A) cit. s. νεολαία; δόξα τῇ θεότητί σου ἣ...εἰς ἀπεικασίαν ἀνθρώπων ὤφθη· δόξα τῇ ἀ. σου, ἥτις δι' ἡμᾶς ἀπέθανεν *A.Thom.*A 80(p.196.3); φύσει μὲν αὐτοῦ ἀρχὴ ἡ θεότης, πρὸς ἡμᾶς δέ, μὴ ἀπὸ τοῦ μεγέθους αὐτοῦ δυναμένους ἄρξασθαι τῆς περὶ αὐτοῦ ἀληθείας, ἡ ἀ. αὐτοῦ, καθ' ὃ... καταγγέλλεται Ἰησοῦς Χριστός Or.*Jo*.1.18(20; p.23.1; M.14.53D); οἱ ἀναιροῦντες αὐτοῦ τὴν ἀ., καὶ μόνην αὐτοῦ τὴν θεότητα παραδεξάμενοι *ib*.10.6(4; p.176.13; 316B); τὴν ὁμοιοπαθῆ ταύτην ἡμῖν ἀναλαβὼν ἀ. Cyr.H.*catech*.4.9; Ath.*Ar*.1.41(M.26.96C) cit. s. ὕψωσις; ὅσα...λέγει ἡ γραφή, ὅτι...ἐδοξάσθη ὁ υἱός, διὰ τὴν ἀ. αὐτοῦ λέγει, οὐ διὰ τὴν θεότητα id.*inc.et c.Ar*.4(M.26.989B); ἐγὼ...καὶ τὸ 'ἐν μορφῇ θεοῦ ὑπάρχειν' ἴσον δύνασθαι τῷ 'ἐν οὐσίᾳ θεοῦ ὑπάρχειν' φημί. ὡς γὰρ τὸ 'μορφὴν εἰληφέναι δούλου' ἐν τῇ οὐσίᾳ τῆς ἀ. τὸν κύριον γεγενῆσθαι σημαίνει· οὕτω δὲ καὶ τὸ 'ἐν μορφῇ θεοῦ ὑπάρχειν' τῆς θείας οὐσίας παρίστησι πάντως τὴν ἰδιότητα Bas.*Eun*.1.18(1.230A; M.29.552C); τίς δὲ τῆς ἀ., ἣν...ὑπέστη θεός, αἰτία; τὸ σωθῆναι...ἡμᾶς...ἐχρίσθη θεότητι. χρίσις γὰρ αὕτη τῆς ἀ. Gr.Naz.*or*.30.2(p.110.8; M.36.105B); ref. Jo. 17:5 φαίνεται οὖν τὰ τοιαῦτα κατ' οἰκονομίαν τῆς ἀ., οὐ κατ' ἔλλειψιν τῆς θεότητος εἰρηκώς Didym.(‡Bas.)*Eun*.4.3(1.292C; M.29.701B); Epiph.*haer*.65.7(p.11.1; M.42.24D); ref. Jo.7:1 εἶπεν...ἵνα δηλώσῃ ὅτι καὶ τὰ τῆς θεότητος ἐπεδείκνυτο, καὶ τὰ τῆς ἀ. Chrys.*hom.48.1 in Jo*.(8.283C); Cyr.*Is*.2.1(2.193C); τὸ τῆς ἀ. μυστήριον id.*thes*.20(5^1.195B); τὸν ἕνα κύριον Ἰησοῦν Χριστὸν...θεότητός τε καὶ ἀ., διὰ τῆς...πρὸς ἑνότητα συνδρομῆς id.*ep*.4.3(p.27.4; 5^2.23C); γεννηθέντα...ἐκ Μαρίας τῆς παρθένου κατὰ τὴν ἀ., ὁμοούσιον τῷ πατρὶ...κατὰ τὴν θεότητα καὶ ὁμοούσιον ἡμῖν κατὰ τὴν ἀ. *ib*.39.5(p.17.12; 5^2.106B); *Symb.Chalc*.(p.129.27; H.2.456C); τῆς ἀναληφθείσης ἀ. τὴν ἀποστολὴν εἶναι Thdt.*Trin*.15(M.75.1169A); μήπω δὴ θεὸν εἶναι τὸν δι' ἀνθρωπότητος φανερούμενον ἐπιστάμενος Bas.Sel.*or*.19.1(M.85.241A); θεότητα κεκρυμμένην ἐν ἀ. *ib*.25.2(289B); Leont.B.*Nest.et Eut*.1(M.86.1280C); ἡ δὲ ἀ. τοῦ Χριστοῦ πάντας τοὺς ἀνθρώπους, μάλιστα τοὺς Χριστούς, ἔχει μετόχους. διὰ τοῦτο γὰρ ὅτι παρὰ πάντας ἐχρίσθη ἡ ἀ. τοῦ Χριστοῦ, χρισθεῖσα πνεύματι ἁγίῳ Cosm.Ind.*top*.5(M.88.253C); Justn.*conf*.(p.74.1; M.86.995C); θεότης καὶ ἀ. ἡνώθη καθ' ὑπόστασιν Max.*ambig*.(M.91.1060A); ἀρχὴ δὲ καὶ τέλος ὁ Χριστός, ὡς πρῶτος διὰ τὴν θεότητα· καὶ ἔσχατος, διὰ τὴν ἀ. Andr.Caes.*Apoc*.66(M.106.425D); in exposition of nature of prophecy τὸ γὰρ προφητικὸν πνεῦμα τὸ σωματεῖόν ἐστιν τῆς προφητικῆς τάξεως ὅ ἐστιν τὸ σῶμα τῆς σαρκὸς Ἰησοῦ Χριστοῦ τὸ μιγὲν τῇ ἀ. διὰ Μαρίας *POxy*.5.14 [saec. iii–iv].

ἀνθρωποτόκος, *man-bearing, who is mother of man*, epithet of BMV; **1.** apptly. used in Antiochene theology in time of Gr.Nyss. (cf. teaching of Diod. *μὴ τῆς Μαρίας υἱὸς ὁ θεὸς λόγος ὑποπτευέσθω synous*.(M.33.1560C)) μὴ τὴν ἁγίαν παρθένον τὴν θεοτόκον ἐτόλμησέ τις ἡμῶν καὶ ἀ. εἰπεῖν, ὅπερ ἀκούομέν τινας ἐξ αὐτῶν ἀφειδῶς λέγειν; Gr.Nyss.*ep*.3(M.46.1024A); **2.** used by Thdr. Mops. in conjunction with θεοτόκος q.v.: ὅταν τοίνυν ἐρωτῶσιν, ἀ. ἢ θεοτόκος ἡ Μαρία, λεγέσθω...ἀμφότερα· τὸ μὲν γὰρ τῇ φύσει τοῦ πράγματος, τὸ δὲ τῇ ἀναφορᾷ· ἀ. μὲν γὰρ τῇ φύσει, ἐπείπερ ἄνθρωπος ἦν ὁ ἐν τῇ κοιλίᾳ τῆς Μαρίας, ὡς καὶ προῆλθεν ἐκεῖθεν· θεοτόκος δέ, ἐπείπερ θεὸς ἦν ἐν τῷ τεχθέντι ἀνθρώπῳ *fr.inc*.15(p.310.14; M.66.992B); **3.** used by Nest.; **a.** in preference to θεοτόκος: ὥσπερ οὖν ἡ γυνὴ τίκτει μὲν...σῶμα, ψυχοῖ δὲ θεός, καὶ οὐκ ἂν λέγοιτο γυνὴ ψυχοτόκος, ὅτι ἔμψυχον ἐγέννησεν, ἀ. δὲ μᾶλλον, οὕτω καὶ ἡ...παρθένος, καὶ εἰ τέτοκεν ἄνθρωπον, συμπαρελθόντος αὐτῷ τοῦ θεοῦ λόγου, ἀλλ' οὐ διὰ τοῦτο θεοτόκος Nest. *fr*.D 1(p.352.10)ap.Cyr.*Nest*.1.3(p.23.34; 6^1.17D); θεοτόκον μὲν οὐκ εἶναι λέγων τὴν ἁγίαν παρθένον, Χριστοτόκον δὲ μᾶλλον καὶ ἀ. Cyr.*Chr.un*.(5^1.716C); Χριστοτόκον, Κυριοτόκον, ἀ. ἐμάθομεν ἀπὸ τῆς γραφῆς λέγειν, θεοτόκον δὲ οὐδαμῶς ἐδιδάχθημεν λέγειν id.*dial. Nest*.(M.76.249A); id.*ep*.45(p.152.12; 5^2.136B); *Νεστόριος...ἀ. λέγων* τὴν ἁγίαν παρθένον, καὶ οὐ θεοτόκον Eulog.*fr.Trin*.(M.86.2944A); τῶν μὲν λεγόντων ἀ. δεῖν τὴν Μαρίαν ὀνομάζεσθαι· τῶν δὲ θεοτόκον Evagr. *h.e*.1.7(p.12.29; M.86.2436B); **b.** in conjunction with θεοτόκος, *ego una tecum clamo* τὸ θεοτόκος. *sed et* τὸ θεοτόκος *dico et addo et* τὸ ἀ. Nest.*fr*.C 18(p.301.17); *cum* θεοτόκον *vocas...memineris et* ἀ. *vocare*, *ib*.(p.309.8); *ib*.(p.312.26); id.*fr*.C 19(p.319.11); cf.id.*ep*.9(Loofs p.191.19); *nos enim vocem, qua dei genetrix nominatur, si cum voce ponatur illa, quae est hominis genetrix, integerrimum pietatis credimus characterem*, *ib*.(p.192.7); this conjunction guards against Arianism and Apollinarianism, and also against heresy of Paul of Samosata and Photinus, id.*fr*.C 18(p.303.15); **4.** used by other Antiochenes in conjunction with θεοτόκος: οὐ προέβη τοίνυν οὐδὲ τοῦτο τοῖς ἀπὸ τῆς Ἀνατολῆς...οἱ μὲν γὰρ αὐτῶν καταδέχονται θεοτόκον εἰπεῖν τὴν ἁγίαν παρθένον μετὰ καὶ τοῦ ἀ. Cyr.*ep*.27 (p.45.27; 5^2.91A); cf.Alexander Hierapolitanus ap.*Synodicon* 86(94) (Schultze, *Theodoreti opera* (Halle, 1769–74) 5.746); ἐπειδή...ναὸς ἦν θεὸν ἔνοικον ἔχων...οὐκ ἀ. ⟨μόνον⟩ ἀλλὰ καὶ θεοτόκον τὴν παρθένον προσαγορεύομεν Thdt.ap.Cyr.*apol.Thdt*.1.7(p.109.27; 6.205A); θεοτόκον καὶ ἀ. τὴν ἁγίαν παρθένον προσαγορεύομεν id.*ep*.151(4.1303); τίς οὕτως εὐήθης, ὡς φυγεῖν τὴν ἀ. φωνήν, μετὰ τῆς θεοτόκου τιθεμένην; *ib*.(1304); θεοτόκος καὶ ἀ. ἡ ἁγία παρθένος ὑπὸ τῶν τῆς εὐσεβείας διδασκάλων προσαγορεύεται id.*inc*.35(M.75.1477A); **5.** rejected by Cyril ἀρκεῖ...τὸ θεοτόκον λέγειν καὶ ὁμολογεῖν τὴν ἁγίαν παρθένον· τό γε μὴν προσεπάγειν ὅτι καὶ ἀ., οὐκ ἀναγκαῖον οὔτε ἐπωφελές *hom. div*.15.4(p.14.20; M.77.1093A); cf.†Cyr.*hom.div*.11(5^2.382D); περιττὸν δὲ οἶμαι τὸ δεῖν οἴεσθαι καὶ ἀ. αὐτὴν εἰπεῖν Cyr.*apol.Thdt*.1.15(p.113. 1; 5^2.206D); and by Thdot. Anc. ἡ παρθένος οὐκ ἔστιν ἀ. *exp.symb*. 18(M.77.1340C); **6.** rejected by later writers, e.g. Leont.H.*Nest*.4.1 (M.86.1652C); *ib*.4.21(1685C); and anathematized, Justn.*conf.anath*. 5(p.92.2; M.86.1015B); v. θεοτόκος.

***ἀνθρωποϋπόστατος**, *having a human hypostasis, subsisting hypostatically as man*, ‡Ath.*annunt*.6(M.28.925B) cit. s. θεοϋπόστατος.

***ἀνθρωποφανής**, *having human appearance*, Philost.*h.e*.3.11(M. 65.497B).

***ἀνθρωποφόρος**, *man-bearing*, of divinity of Christ τὸ δεῖν προσκυνεῖν μὴ σάρκα θεοφόρον, ἀλλὰ θεὸν ἀ. Gr.Naz.*ep*.102(M.37. 200C); εἴπερ ἡ στολὴ τοῦ λόγου ἐστὶν ἡ σάρξ...ἡ δὲ σὰρξ ἐστιν ὁ ἄνθρωπος, θεὸν ἀ. ἀκόλουθον μᾶλλον εἰπεῖν ἐπὶ Χριστοῦ Leont.H.*Nest*. 6.1(M.86.1753B); *ib*.6.2(1753D); προῆλθεν ἐκ τῆς μητρὸς θεὸς ἀ., τουτέστι θεὸς καὶ ἄνθρωπος ἐν μιᾷ ὑποστάσει Anast.*fid*.(p.273).

***ἀνθρωποφυϊκός**, *of human nature*, Dion.Ar.*myst*.3(M.3.1033A).

***ἀνθρωπόφυτος**, neut. as subst., *that which is born of man*, Melet.*nat.hom*.synops.(M.64.1084C).

***ἀνθρωπώνυμος**, *having a human name*, Anast.S.*fr*.5(M.89.1288A).

ἀνθυλακτέω, *bark* or *bay in answer*, ‡Bas.*Lac*.3(2.590A; M.31. 1445A); Gel.Cyz.*h.e*.3.15.1.

ἀνθυπάγω, **1.** *bring back into bondage* πάλιν ἀ. τοῖς ἁμαρτήμασιν Dion.Al.*fr*.(p.61.4); **2.** *bring under instead*, †Bas.*Is*.277(1.591B; M. 30.608B).

ἀνθυπακού-ω, *be obedient in reparation* ἐκείνου...παρακούσαντος, ~ει οὗτος μέχρι σταυροῦ ‡Caes.Naz.*dial*.122(M.38.1012).

ἀνθυπαντάω, *meet, reply* to objections, Anast.S.*hod*.15(M.89. 260B).

ἀνθυπατιανός, *of proconsular rank*, Hier.*vir.ill*.(tr.Sophr.Pal.)53 (p.34.15; ἀντ- M.*PL*.23.662C); *Cod.Afr*.proem.(H.1.861A); *ib*.(881B).

ἀνθύπατος, ὁ, *proconsul*, *M.Polyc*.4; Ath.*fug*.3(p.70.11; M.25. 648C); Pall.*h.Laus*.62(p.157.16; M.34.1233B); as imperial title *Μαξιμιανὸς...πατὴρ πατρίδος, ἀ.* Maximian ap.Eus.*h.e*.8.17.4(M.20.792A).

***ἀνθυπερβάτως**, *in inverted order, out of order*, Epiph.*haer*.57.6 (p.351.14; M.41.1004C); *ib*.70.12(p.246.3; M.42.365B).

***ἀνθυποβαίνω**, *descend to, submit to, in turn* ἀνθυπέβη γὰρ πᾶσι τοῖς τοῦ προπάτορος ἡμῶν ὀφλήμασιν ὁ Χριστός ‡Caes.Naz.*dial*.122 (M.38.1012).

***ἀνθυποδέχ-ομαι**, *receive in exchange* or *from one another*, ‡Bas.*const*.33.1(2.579C; M.31.1421C); 'χάριν...ἀντὶ χάριτος' χάριν γὰρ ἡμεῖς ὥσπερ καὶ δῶρον καλὸν προσφέροντες τὴν ἑαυτῶν τῷ θεῷ πίστιν, χάριν ~όμεθα οὐρανόθεν μεγίστην Nil.*epp*.2.314(M.79.353B).

***ἀνθυποκρούω**, *object in answer*, Gr.Nyss.*bapt.Chr*.(M.46.584C).

***ἀνθυπομνήσκω**, *recall in answer* to an objection, ‡Meth.*palm*.7 (M.18.396C).

ἀνθυποστρέφω, **1.** *turn back, return*; *turn again into* προβάτια... εἰς προβάτια ἀ. Eulog.*fr.Novat*.(M.104.344B); **2.** trans., *turn instead* πρὸς ἄκρον ὕψος ἀρθῶσι φρένες, πρὸς ἄκρον αὐτὰς ἀ. βάθος Geo.Pis. *hex*.1698(M.92.1566A); *send* or *bring back*, Gr.Mag.*dial*.(tr. Zach.) 1.10(M.*PL*.77.207B).

***ἀνθυποστρόφως**, *by transposition* of letters, Cyr.*syn.def*.(M.76. 1424A).

***ἀνθυποτρέχω**, *pass through*, Geo.Pis.*hex*.1443(M.92.1514A).

ἀνθυποφέρ-ω, **1.** *offer instead*, ‡Just.*ep.Zen.et Ser*.3(M.6.1185C); **2.** *bring upon instead*, of a change in fortune τέως μὲν ἐπράττομεν εὖ. εἶθ' ὥσπερ ῥεύματος ἀνθυπενεχθέντος, καὶ τὰ κοινὰ λυπεῖ καὶ τὰ ἴδια Synes.*ep*.89(M.66.1456C); id.*calv*.2(p.191.17; M.66.1169B); **3.** *reply*; *rejoin*; *reply to*, trans. ἀ. τὰ ὑφορμοῦντα Bas.*ep*.156.2(3.246B; M.32.616C); τὸν τῶν ὑπεναντίων ἀ. λόγον Gr.Nyss.*tres dii*(M.45. 125A); *offer in reply* διαλέκτῳ ἀκόλουθον ἐρωτᾶν τὸ πῶς ἐπαίνου ἐστί, καὶ μὴ ἀ. τὴν ψῆφον *Disp.Phot*.3(M.88.549B); Thdr.Stud.*epp*.2. 185(M.99.1569B); **4.** *raise an objection* ἀνθυπενεχθησομένην ἀνθυποφορὰν ὑπὸ τῶν μὴ παραδεχομένων τὸν λόγον Or.*Jo*.6.5(2; p.112.4; M.14.205D); Gr.Nyss.*anim.et res*.(M.46.36B); Isid.Pel.*epp*.3.95(M.78.

801B); Socr.*h.e.*3.23.28(M.67.444A); τὸ τοῦ ~οντος οὖν πρόσωπον ἀναλαβὼν ὁ Ἐκκλησιαστής Olymp.*Eccl.*2:24–25(M.93.505C); **5.** *bring a charge* οὔτε κατὰ φύσιν οὔτε κατὰ πρᾶξιν ~ειν ὑμᾶς δυνατὸν τὴν ἁμαρτίαν ἐν τῷ δημιουργῷ ‡Ath.*Apoll.*1.17(M.26.1124B); *ib.*1.21 (1129C).

ἀνθυποφορά, ἡ, *reply; objection;* in gen. ἀ. οὐκ εὐκαταφρόνητον Or.*Jo.*2.29(24; p.86.7; M.14.164D); *ib.*6.5(2; p.112.4; 205D) cit. s. ἀνθυποφέρω; Bas.*Spir.*34 tit.(3.28B; M.32.128B); Cyr.*Os.*125(3.157A); raised by speaker in order to be demolished δείκνυνται κατὰ ἀ. τὰ πρὸς τοῦ λαοῦ θρυλούμενα, ὡς ἐπιζητήματά τινα ὑπὸ τῶν ἀνθρώπων ἀναφέροντες Clem.*str.*3.4(p.213.28; M.8.1141C); Or.*Jo.*20.38(30; p.380.16; M.14.665A).

ἀνθυφαίρεσις, ἡ, **1.** *corresponding diminution,* Gr.Naz.*or.*28.30 (p.68.19; M.36.69B); **2.** *withdrawal,* Thdt.*qu.33 in 1Reg.*(1.378).

***ἀνθυψόω,** *exalt in turn,* ‡Caes.Naz.*dial.*108(M.38.977).

ἀνθώδης, prob. f.l. for ἀκανθώδης, *thorny,* Jo.D.*hom.*12.9(M.96.793C).

ἀνιάτρευτος, 1. *uncured* μήτε ἡμεῖς ἀ. καταλειφθῶμεν μὴ φανερουμένης ἡμῖν τῆς ἁμαρτίας ἡμῶν Bas.*ep.*203.2(3.301B; M.32.741A); ἀναγκαῖον πλήσσεσθαι τὴν κακίαν, ἵνα μὴ ἀ. διαμένωμεν. ἐπάταξε γὰρ κύριος τοὺς ἐχθροὺς αὐτοῦ...ἐπωφελῶς Nil.*epp.*3.185(M.79.472A); ἡ δὲ τελεία ἐγκατάλειψίς ὅτε τοῦ θεοῦ πάντα τὰ πρὸς σωτηρίαν πεποιηκότος, ἀνεπαίσθητος καὶ ἀ., μᾶλλον δὲ ἀνίατος, ἐξ οἰκείας προθέσεως διαμείνῃ ὁ ἄνθρωπος Jo.D.*f.o.*2.29(M.94.968B); **2.** *incurable;* of physical ailments, Sophr.H.*mir.Cyr.et Jo.*66(M.87.3649D); of moral evil ὦ τῆς ἀ. τῶν Ἰουδαίων κακίας ‡Chrys.*Steph.protomart.*1.1 (8.18B); neut. as subst. τὸ ἀ. ὑμῶν ἀπὸ τοῦ νόμου †Gregent.*disp.* (M.86.720D); neut. plur. as adv., *incurably* ἐνανθρωπήσας θεὸς λόγος ...οὐδὲ...ἀφῆκεν ἡμᾶς ἀ. νοσεῖν †Jo.D.*B.J.*11(M.96.956B); **3.** *ignorant of medicine* πῶς λέγεις ἰατρὸν τὸν ἑαυτοῦ διδάσκαλον, αὐτὸς ἀ. ὤν; Gr.Nyss.*laud.Bas.*(M.46.817C).

***ἀνίδιος,** *with nothing of one's own,* Bas.*ep.*2.2(3.71E; M.32.1140B); Jo.Mosch.*prat.*171(M.87.3040A).

***ἀνιδίως,** *so as not to be one's own,* Marc.Er.*opusc.*1.161(M.65.925A).

ἀνίδρυτος, *of no fixed abode, unlocalized* εἴπερ οὖν ὁ θεὸς ἱδρύεται πρὸς ἀνθρώπων, ἀ. ποτε ἦν καὶ οὐδ' ὅλως ἦν· τοῦτο γὰρ ἂν εἴη ἀ., τὸ οὐκ ὄν Clem.*str.*7.5(p.21.8; M.9.437A); στέρησίς ἐστι τὸ κακὸν...καὶ ἀ. Dion.Ar.*d.n.*4.32(M.3.732D); ὁ πάσης παντελῶς ἑνώσεως ἀποπέπτωκε...ἄπειρον καὶ ἀ. καὶ ἀόριστον *ib.*11.5(953A).

ἀνίερος, 1. *unholy, unhallowed, impious;* of demons, Eus.*l.C.* 15(p.247.32; M.20.1420B); of Jews, Ath.*fug.*2(p.69.12; M.25.645C); **2.** *not a priest* οὗτοι δὲ...ἐκ τῆς Καισαρέων ἐκκλησίας χειροτονίαν μὴ λαμβάνοντες, πῶς οὐκ εἰσὶ παντελῶς ἀ. καὶ ἀχειροτόνητοι, καὶ οἱ ἐξ αὐτῶν βαπτιζόμενοι παντελῶς ἐθνικοὶ καὶ ἀβάπτιστοι; Tim.CP *haer.* (M.86.73A); ἀ. ἢ ἱερέα παύοντα τῆς λειτουργίας οὐκ ἔξεστιν δέχεσθαι τὰς ἐξομολογήσεις *Nomoc.*44; Jo.D.*hom.*2.5(M.96.585A).

ἀνιερ-όω, *make unhallowed, profane* τεθείακεν θεὸν ὁ βασιλεὺς ὁ Ῥωμαίων...Ἀντίνοον [ὃν] ~ωσεν οὕτως ὡς Γανυμήδην ὁ Ζεὺς Clem.*prot.*4(p.38.7; M.8.140C).

***ἀνιέρως,** *profanely, sacrilegiously* ὅπως μὴ...ἀ. οἰώμεθα τοὺς... θεοειδεῖς νόας πολύποδας εἶναί τινας καὶ πολυπροσώπους Dion.Ar.*c.h.* 2.1(M.3.137A).

ἀνίημι, 1. *let go; set free;* **a.** persons ἀνεθεὶς τοῦ φόβου Chrys. *hom.35.3 in Jo.*(8.205E); τῆς αἰχμαλωσίας ἀνῆκε τὸν Ἰσραὴλ Cyr. *Nah.*1(3.475E); **b.** things, *make available* πᾶσιν ὁμοίως ἀνεῖται τὸ ἀπ' αὐτῆς [sc. τῆς σοφίας] ὠφέλιμον Bas.*hom.*12.4(2.100B; M.31.392D); **c.** places, *leave open* ἡ θάλασσα ἀνίεται πᾶσιν Clem.*ecl.*28 (p.145.17; M.9.713A); δυνάμεις ἀφανεῖς ἀμφὶ τὰ δι' ἀέρος ἀνειμένα πεδία ποτώμεναι Eus.*l.C.*1(p.198.13; M.20.1324A); hence **2.** *set at ease* ἐν τῷ θάλπει...τὰ ἐκτετριμμένα τῶν ἱματίων...ἀνίησι τὸ σῶμα Chrys.*hom.10.3 in Phil.*(11.278D); ἀ. αὐτοῦ τὴν ψυχὴν id.*hom.51.1 in Ac.*(9.379E); pass., in good sense, *have relief;* from illness, Thdr. Lect.*fr.*(M.86.225C); from weariness, Jo.Mosch.*prat.*1(M.87.2853A); in bad sense, *live at ease,* Chrys.*hom.26.3 in Heb.*(12.239A); perf. ptcpl. pass. as adj., *unconstrained* 'ηὐλίσαμεν ὑμῖν καὶ οὐκ ὠρχήσασθε'· τουτέστι, τὸν ἀνειμένον βίον ὑπέδειξα καὶ οὐκ ἐπείσθητε id. *hom.37.4 in Mt.*(7.419C); **3.** intrans., *give up, cease;* hence *refrain* οὐ γὰρ ἀνήσω μὴ οὐχὶ εἰπεῖν Clem.*prot.*2(p.16.4; M.8.84A).

***ἀνικανότης,** ἡ, *insufficiency,* Epiph.*haer.*proem.1(p.169.21; M. 41.176A).

***ἀνικάνως, 1.** c. ἔχω, *be insufficient,* Cyr.*Is.*1.1(2.16B); id.*Jo.*12 (4.1066D); id.*inc.unigen.*(5¹.701D); **2.** *unbecomingly, inadequately* to one's position ἀ. τὸν βίον διατελῶν Thphn.*chron.*p.319(M.108.772C).

ἄνικμος, *without moisture;* met., of the heart, Geo.Pis.*hex.*4(M. 92.1426A).

***ἀνίκμως,** *without moisture* Ἀαρὼν ῥάβδον ἀ. βλαστήσασαν ‡Ath. *occurs.*16(M.28.993C).

***ἀνίλεως,** *unmercifully,* *T.Gad* 5.11; Chrys.*Laz.*1.10(1.721D); Gr. Mag.*dial.*(tr.Zach.)2.30(M.*PL.*66.187B).

***ἀνίμαστος,** *unscourged,* Nonn.*par.Jo.*19:1(M.43.897B).

ἀνιμ-άω, 1. *draw up, raise;* **a.** lit. τὰ σφάλματα τοῦ ἡμιτριταίου προσετάχθην ~ᾶσθαι *T.Sal.*7.6(M.122.1325D); **b.** fig. or met., of souls by Christ ἵνα...~ηθῶσιν ὑπὸ τοῦ λόγου ἐπὶ τὴν ἀνωτάτω μακαριότητα Or.*Cels.*6.44(p.115.6; M.11.1365D); (Manich.) ὁ υἱὸς...πρὸς σωτηρίαν τῶν ψυχῶν...μηχανὴν συνεστήσατο ἔχουσαν δώδεκα κάδους, ἥ τις ὑπὸ τῆς σφαίρας στρεφομένη, ~ᾶται τῶν θνησκόντων τὰς ψυχάς Hegem. *Arch.*8(p.12.15; M.10.1440B); τῇ φύσει τῶν ἀνθρώπων...διὰ τῆς τοῦ σωτῆρος ἡμῶν ἐνανθρωπήσεως ~ηθείσῃ Thdt.*Ps.*39:4(1.857); of soul by asceticism ξηρὸν σῶμα ὑπὸ νηστείας γινόμενον ἐπὶ μοναχοῦ, ψυχὴν ἐκ βυθοῦ ~ᾶται Hyper.*mon.*89(M.79.1481C); of sinners, Eus.*d.e.* 1.6(p.27.32; M.22.56C); καθάπερ οἱ εἰς φρέαρ ἐμπεσόντες...οὕτω καὶ ὁ εἰς βάθος ἐλθὼν τῶν ἁμαρτημάτων. χαλάσωμεν οὖν σχοινία...καὶ ~ησώμεθα Chrys.*hom.8.4 in 1Cor.*(10.71A); id.*hom.57.5 in Mt.*(7.583B); of ideas, Or.*Jo.*13.3(p.228.17; M.14.404A); ἀπὸ τῆς τοῦ προφήτου διδασκαλίας...Παῦλος...~ώμενος ὡς καθαρὸν ὕδωρ ἀρδεύει... ἐκκλησίαν Epiph.*haer.*42.12(p.160.5; M.41.780B); hence **2.** *soak up, absorb,* ref. Inc. Μαρία μὲν ~ᾶται τὸν λόγον εἰς σύλληψιν, ὡς ὑετὸν ἡ γῆ Epiph.*anc.*66(p.80.12; M.43.136C); ὁ θεὸς λόγος, ὢν ἥλιος νοητός, εἰς σάρκα κατελθών, οὐδὲν μὲν ἐκ τῆς σαρκὸς ~ᾶται νόσημα Mac.Mgn. *apocr.*4.28(p.216.12); Evagr.Pont.*or.*128(M.79.1193D) cit. s. ἀντικοτέω; **3.** *draw out* with the nostrils, *smell out,* exeg. Cant.2:9,17 τὰ εἰσπεμπόμενα τῆς κακίας ἐνθυμήματα ὑπὸ τοῦ πονηροῦ ταῖς τῶν δικαίων διανοίαις...ἐλάφου δίκην ~ώμενος ὁ οὐράνιος λόγος Ph.Carp.*Cant.*49 (M.40.65C); τὰς [sc. ἐν καταχθονίῳ τόπῳ] κρατούσας δυνάμεις τῇ ὀσφρήσει καθάπερ ἔλαφος ~ησάμενος κατάργησον Nil.ap.Proc.G. *Cant.*2:17(M.87.1613D); **4.** *draw out* the moisture from, hence *dry up* ἐξῆλθεν ἐκ τῆς πυρᾶς ὡς ὁμοίωμα δράκοντος καιομένου καὶ ~ώμενου τὴν γῆν *A.Mt.*22(p.247.21).

ἀνίμησις, ἡ, *exhalation,* Dion.Al.ap.Eus.*h.e.*7.21.8(M.20.685B).

ἀνίπταμαι, *fly up,* Clem.*paed.*3.2(p.242.18; M.8.572A); fig. and met., Didym.*Trin.*2.20(M.39.737B); †Jo.D.*B.J.*1(M.96.864B).

***ἀνισομέτρως,** *in unequal measure,* Cyr.*Chr.un.*(5¹.768B).

***ἀνισονομέω,** *be out of harmony with,* *Schol.*19 in Max.*qu.Thal.*61 (M.90.645B).

***ἀνισόπλατυς,** *of unequal breadth,* Melet.*nat.hom.*20(M.64.1224C).

ἄνισος, *unequal,* of Son ἄ. γὰρ ἑαυτῷ θεὸς υἱὸν καὶ ἀνόμοιον οὐκ ἄν ποτε τίκτων γεννήσειεν Sophr.H.*or.*2.30(M.87.3253C); *uneven,* of numbers, Meth.*symp.*3.3(p.30.4; M.18.64C); *unequal,* in sense of *greater, different in kind* ἐξ ὕλης καὶ εἴδους τὸ σῶμα. ἡ μὲν οὖν ὕλη φθείρεται καὶ διαλύεται· μένει δὲ ὁ ἄ. τοῦ εἴδους ὁ λόγος Aen.*dial.* (M.85.981B).

ἀνισότης, ἡ, **1.** *inequality;* **a.** in gen. ἰσότης μὲν γάρ ἐστιν ἡ ζωή, ἀ. δὲ ἡ φθορά...οὔτε ἀναρμοστία καὶ ἀ. ὁ ἄνθρωπός ἐστιν οὔτε μὴν ἰσότης καὶ εὐαρμοστία· ἀλλ' ὅτε μὲν ἐδέξατο τὴν ἀναρμοστίαν, ὅπερ ἐστὶ...τὴν ἁμαρτίαν, γέγονεν ἀνάρμοστος καὶ ἀπρεπὴς Meth.*symp.*3.7 (p.34.3,20; M.18.72Af.); ὁ ταῖς τῶν πολλῶν κατὰ τὸ φαινόμενον ἀνισότησι κατ' αἴσθησιν ὑπαντῶν, ἐν τοῖς δίκην πυλῶν πεφυκόσιν εἰσάγειν πρὸς ψυχὴν τὰς τῶν ὁρατῶν ἐπιφανείας αἰσθητηρίοις, καὶ παρὰ τῶν ἀ. ἐμποδιζόμενος διαβῆναι κατὰ νοῦν πρὸς τὸν ἕνα τῆς τῶν ἀνθρώπων φύσεως λόγον ‡Proc.G.*Pr.*12:13(M.87.1341A); of unevenness of character τῆς ἀγάπης τὴν δύναμιν...πᾶσαν τὴν ἐν πᾶσι κατὰ τὴν γνώμην ἀ. τε καὶ διαφορὰν ἐξισοῦσάν τε καὶ ὁμαλίζουσαν· καὶ εἰς τὴν ἐπαινετὴν ἀ. δεόντως προβιβάζουσαν, ἑκάστου...τὸν πέλας... ἑαυτοῦ προτιμῶντος Max.*ep.*2(M.91.400A); **b.** ref. Son, Gr.Naz.*or.*29. 14(p.95.5; M.36.93A); εἰ τοῦτο ἀληθὲς...χωρεῖ δὲ ὁ υἱὸς τὸν πατέρα, ὥσπερ ὁ πατὴρ τὸν υἱόν, εὔδηλον ὁ τῆς ἀ. λόγος ἐκβέβληται Thdt. *Trin.*13(M.75.1165C); **2.** *inequity, injustice* ζυγὸς ἀδικίας [Os.12:7a], τουτέστιν, ἀ. καὶ πλεονεξία Cyr.*Os.*140(3.173C); *ib.*141(174B).

***ἀνισότιμος,** *of unequal value,* Gr.Naz.*or.*29.14(p.95.5; M.36.93A).

ἀνισοφυής, *of unequal nature* ἕτερον μὲν...ἀνθρωπότης, ἕτερον δὲ... θεότης...πῶς οὖν...μιᾷ προσκυνήσει τιμᾶν ἀξιοῖς τὰ οὕτως ἀλλήλοις ἀ.; Cyr.*Nest.*2.12(p.51.1; 6¹.58A); id.*dial.Trin.*1(5¹.409E); δυὰς γὰρ ἡμῖν υἱῶν ἀ. ἀναφαίνεται id.*Chr.un.*(5¹.735A); πῶς οὐ...ἐπενήνεκται δὲ τῇ ἁγίᾳ καὶ ὁμοουσίῳ τριάδι τὸ ἀ. αὐτῇ; *ib.*(732D).

ἀνίστη-μι (ἀνιστάνω, ἀνιστάω), I. trans., *make to stand up;*

A. *raise up;* **1.** in gen., plants from seed, *Const.App.*5.7.26; persons from illness, Serap.*euch.*5.10; ἀσθενῶν ἤμην καὶ οὐκ ἀνεστήσατέ με Chrys.*hom.60.4 in Jo.*(8.357B); met., *raise* spirits, *cheer* διὰ τῶν ῥημάτων αὐτοὺς ἀ. id.*hom.63.2 in Mt.*(7.631A); **2.** *raise* from the dead; **a.** of Christ's Resurrection τὴν μέλλουσαν ἀνάστασιν...ἧς τὴν ἀπαρχὴν ἐποιήσατο [sc. ὁ δεσπότης] τὸν κύριον Ἰησοῦν Χριστὸν ἐκ νεκρῶν ἀναστήσας 1Clem.24.1; ὑπὲρ ἡμῶν ἀ. [sc. ὁ Χριστός] τὸ ἑαυτοῦ σῶμα Ath.Ar.2.61(M.26.277C); **b.** of persons restored to life on earth: by Christ, Cels.ap.Or.Cels.2.48(p.169.18; M.11.869C); by apostles, Chrys.hom.25.2 in Jo.(8.145B); id.hom.3.5 in Heb.(12.35C); **c.** of resurrection of the body, Just.dial.46.7(M.6.576C) cit. s. ἀθάνατος; ib.69.7(640A); Const.App.5.7.1 cit. s. αἰών; **3.** spiritually, from sin, Clem.prot.8(p.59.12; M.8.188A); id.str.7.3(p.11.2; M.9.417B); to communion with Christ, ref. Mt.26:32 αὐτὸς γὰρ προάγει πάντα, καὶ τὴν ἀφανῶς σωζομένην ψυχὴν ἀναστήσειν ἠνίσσετο καὶ ἀποκαταστήσειν οὗ νῦν προάγει id.exc.Thdot.61(p.127.14; M.9.688C); ref. baptism ἀνιστῶν τρισσῶς καινὸν ἄνθρωπον A.Thom.A 132(p.239.14); in prayer for demon-possessed σῶσον καὶ ἀνάστησον αὐτοὺς... ἐν τῇ δυνάμει σου Lit.ap.Const.App.8.7.3.

B. *set up*; *appoint* to an office οἱ δὲ ὁμοθυμαδὸν εἶπον· Πολύκαρπός ἐστιν ἡμῶν ποίμην...ἀνέστησαν αὐτὸν πολλὰ ἱκετεύοντα καὶ παραιτεῖσθαι θέλοντα ‡Pion.v.Polyc.22; ~σιν ὁ στρατὸς Ἰωβιανὸν βασιλέα Philost.h.e.8.1(M.65.558A); *put forward* claims προϊὼν ὑψηλότερα ~σι Chrys.hom.22.2 in 2Cor.(10.591E); *put forward, postulate*, an idea, Cyr.hom.pasch.17(5^2.231D).

II. intrans., *stand up*;

A. *rise*; **1.** of plants, Or.Cels.5.22(p.23.12; M.11.1216A); **2.** *recover* from illness etc., A.Thom.A 81(p.196.18); Proc.G.Dt.34:6(M.87.992C); met., from defeat, Chrys.hom.21.2 in 2Cor.(10.585C); **3.** *rise* from the dead (v. also ἀνάστασις); **a.** of Christ, Barn.15.9 cit. s. ὄγδοος; ὁ γὰρ ἀληθῶς ἀποθανών, εἰ ἀνέστη, ἀληθῶς ἀνέστη, ὁ δὲ δοκῶν ἀποτεθνηκέναι οὐκ ἀληθῶς ἀ. Or.Cels.2.16(p.145.14; M.11.828B); acc. Celsus ἀναγκαῖόν ἐστι τὸ ἀναπεπνευκέναι τὸν θεόν. καὶ τούτῳ ἀκόλουθον τὸ μὴ δύνασθαι ἀναστῆναι μετὰ τοῦ σώματος τὸν Ἰησοῦν· οὐκ ἂν γὰρ ἀπειλήφει ὃ δέδωκε πνεῦμα ὁ θεὸς καταμεμολυσμένον τῇ τοῦ σώματος φύσει Cels.ib.6.72(p.142.12; 1408B); ref. Col.1:18 οὐ γὰρ ἐκ νεκρῶν ἀνέστη πρῶτος...Χριστός· ἀλλ' ὁ δι' Ἐλισσαίου...ἀποστὰς ἀπέστη πρότερος, καὶ Λάζαρος...καὶ ἐν τῷ καιρῷ τοῦ πάθους πολλὰ σώματα τῶν κεκοιμημένων ἀνέστησαν Marcell.fr.2 ap. Eus.Marcell.1.2(p.11.14; M.24.737A); his Resurrection compared with baptism καθάπερ γὰρ ἡμεῖς εὐκόλως βαπτιζόμεθα καὶ ἀνανεύομεν, οὕτω καὶ αὐτὸς εὐκόλως ἀποθανὼν ὅτε ἠθέλησεν ἀνέστη Chrys.hom.25.2 in Jo.(8.146E); **b.** of persons restored to life on earth, Clem.str.2.11(p.139.2; M.8.985A); ὅτι δὲ καὶ νεκροὺς ἀνίστη καὶ οὐκ ἔστι πλάσμα τῶν τὰ εὐαγγέλια γραψάντων, παρίσταται ἐκ τοῦ, εἰ μὲν πλάσμα ἦν, πολλοὺς ⟨ἂν⟩ ἀναγεγράφθαι τοὺς ἀναστάντας, καὶ τοὺς ἤδη χρόνους ἔχοντας πλείονας ἐν τοῖς μνημείοις Or.Cels.2.48(p.169.25; M.11.869D); **c.** of resurrection of body μὴ λεγέτω τις ὑμῶν, ὅτι αὕτη ἡ σὰρξ οὐ κρίνεται οὐδὲ ἀνίσταται 2Clem.9.1; οὔτε ἀγνοεῖν τὸν θεὸν δυνατὸν τῶν ἀναστησομένων σωμάτων τὴν φύσιν Athenag.res.2(p.50.25; M.6.977D); ἔτι δὲ καὶ τῶν λεγόντων μὴ ἀνίστασθαι τὴν σάρκα, οἱ μὲν ὡς ἀδύνατον ἀναστῆναι λέγουσιν, οἱ δὲ ὡς μὴ προσῆκον τῷ θεῷ ἀνιστάνειν αὐτὴν διὰ τὸ εὐτελὲς καὶ εὐκαταφρόνητον αὐτῆς †Just.fr.res.5(p.40; M.6.1577D); οἷον ὄψεται θέαμα Ῥώμη, τὸν Παῦλον ἐξαίφνης ἀνιστάμενον ἀπὸ τῆς θήκης ἐκείνης μετὰ Πέτρου, καὶ αἰρόμενον εἰς ἀπάντησιν τοῦ κυρίου Chrys.hom.32.2 in Rom.(9.757C); acc. Stoics κατὰ περίοδον ἐκπύρωσιν τοῦ παντὸς γίνεσθαι καὶ ἑξῆς αὐτῇ διακόσμησιν...κἂν μὴ ὀνομάζωσιν οὖν τὸ τῆς ἀναστάσεως ὄνομα, τὸ πρᾶγμά γε δηλοῦσιν, ὅτι Σωκράτης...ἀναστήσεται Or.Cels.5.20(p.22.3; M.11.1212A); **d.** of souls in world to come: of righteous τὰ ψυχικὰ μὲν οὖν οὕτως ἀνίσταται καὶ ἀνασώζεται, πιστεύσαντα δὲ τὰ πνευματικὰ ὑπὲρ ἐκεῖνα σῴζεται, ἐνδύματα γάμων τὰς ψυχὰς λαβόντα Clem.exc.Thdot.61(p.127.23; M.9.689A); κατὰ τάγματα τῶν ἀνισταμένων ἔσονται ἀναπαύσεις ἐν τοῖς θησαυροῖς τοῦ θεοῦ Or.hom.8.6 in Jer.(p.61.2; M.13.344B); of sinners ἀναστήσονται δὲ καὶ οἱ ἁμαρτωλοί, ἀλλ' οὐκ ἔσονται ἐν τῇ βουλῇ καὶ τῷ τάγματι τῶν δικαίων Cyr.Ps.1:5(M.69.720A); **4.** *rise* spiritually to new life: by love, Ign.Smyrn.7.1; by participation in Christ, Or.Jo.1.37(42; p.47.25; M.14.97A); by baptism, Const.App.7.45.1; δεῖ σε γὰρ ἀποθανεῖν καὶ ἀ. Cyr.H.procatech.5; ὡς...τεθνηκότας τῷ θεῷ τοὺς ὑπ' ἀσελγείας... νενικημένους ὡς νεκροὺς πενθοῦσι, καὶ ὡς ἐκ νεκρῶν ἀναστάντας, ἐὰν ἀξιόλογον ἐνδείξωνται μεταβολήν..., ὕστερόν ποτε προσίενται Or.Cels.3.51(p.248.1; M.11.988C).

B. ἀνεστηκώς, *outstanding, excellent* εἴπερ ἄνθρωποι, οἱ τοσοῦτον ἀνεστηκότες τῷ μεγαλείῳ τῆς φύσεως Gr.Nyss.mart.2(M.46.761B); Cyr.Ps.1:5(M.69.720B).

ἀνιστορ-έω, **1.** *record* τὸ ὑπὸ Μωυσέως...~ημένον Just.dial.54.1(M.6.593C); Eus.p.e.10.13(502A; M.21.836C); id.h.e.5.16.6(M.20.465B); **2.** *portray, depict*, Mir.Geo.7(p.91.25); ὀφείλομεν τὰς τῶν ἁγίων εἰκόνας ~ῆσαι ‡Jo.D.Const.2(M.95.313B); τῆς...Μαρίας τὴν τιμίαν εἰκόνα ~ησε [sc. Λουκᾶς] ib.6(321C); **3.** *record anew* ~ησα ἣν καὶ προέγραψα Just.dial.78.6(M.6.660A).

ἀνιστόρητος, **1.** *unrecorded*; neut. as subst., *lack of information*, ‡Just.qu.et resp.116(M.6.1365B); **2.** *that cannot be recorded, untold* φόνον ἀνθρώπων...ἀ. Philost.h.e.11.8(M.65.604A).

***ἀνισχύρως**, *invalidly*, Phot.nomoc.2.1(M.104.568D); ib.13.4(912A).

ἄνισχυς, *without strength*, Cyr.Ag.7(3.635E, v.l. ἀνίσχυροι A.); Melet.nat.hom.27(M.64.1256B, v.l. ἀνίσχυροι); Ant.Mon.hom.17(M.89.1481D).

***ἀνιχνευτής, ὁ**, *investigator*, Hier.vir.ill.(tr.Sophr.Pal.)81(p.48.11; M.PL.23.690A).

***ἀννάλιος**, (Lat. *annalis*) *yearly*, Justn.cod.1.3.45.13.

ἀννώνη (*ἀννόνη), **ἡ**, (Lat. *annona*); **1.** *annual donation* εἰσὶ πόλεις λαμβάνουσαι δῶρα καὶ ἀννόνας παρὰ τοῦ βασιλέως Mac.Aeg.hom.26.14(M.34.684B); ἦσαν δέ τινα μοναστήρια καὶ μαρτύρια λαμβάνοντα ἀ. παρὰ τῆς βασιλίσσης †Polyb.v.Epiph.62(M.41.104B); to a retired official, Chron.Pasch.p.292(M.92.729A); **2.** *annual tribute* ἀ. εἰσίν, ὡς ἂν εἴπῃ τις, βασιλεῖ κεχρεωστημέναι. ... μεγάλοι ἄνθρωποι... οὐ μόνον ἀ. παρέχουσι τῷ βασιλεῖ ἀλλὰ καὶ δῶρα προσφέρουσιν αὐτῷ Dor.doct.1.10(M.88.1629A); **3.** *provisions*, Ant.Ep.ep.(p.71.12).

ἀνοδία, ἡ, *path that is no path*; met., of false doctrine, Clem.str.6.10(p.472.30; M.9.304A); Μάρκελλος...τὴν εὐθεῖαν παρεκτραπεὶς ὁδὸν ἀ. ἑαυτῷ ἐπενόησεν Eus.Marcell.2.3(p.46.10; M.24.801C); διαπλανᾶται ταῖς πολυοδίαις, μᾶλλον δὲ ταῖς ἀ., ἡ βλασφημία Gr.Nyss.Eun.10(2 p.236.22; M.45.837D).

ἄνοδος, ἡ, **I.** *ascension, ascent*;

A. of Christ; **1.** in gen., Just.dial.82.1(M.6.669B); Eus.e.th.3.5(p.161.16; M.24.1009A); Ath.exp.Ps.67:25(M.27.300C); Symb.Ant.(345)1(p.252.2; M.26.728C); **2.** foreshadowed in OT; exeg. Ps.143:3, 5 and Ps.17:10f. δι' ὧν τὰ τῆς ἀ., ἣν ἀπὸ γῆς εἰς οὐρανοὺς ἐποιήσατο, θεσπίζει. ... κάθοδον χρὴ νοεῖν καὶ ἄ. τοῦ θεοῦ λόγου οὐ τοπικῶς μεταβάσεις ποιουμένου, τροπικῶς δὲ τὰς τοιάσδε οἰκονομίας αὐτοῦ τοῦτον τῆς γραφῆς ἀποκαλούσης τὸν τρόπον Eus.d.e.6.9(p.259.15f.; M.22.425D); by entrance of high priest into Holy of Holies, Bas.Sel.ascens.4(M.28.1097D); through Jacob's ladder, representing BMV, Thdr.Stud.or.5.4(M.99.725B); Gnost., of Adamas, exeg. Ps.23:7,9 περὶ δὲ τῆς ἀ. αὐτοῦ τουτέστι τῆς ἀναγεννήσεως Hipp.haer.5.8(p.92.15; M.16.3143C); **3.** function of angel explained διὰ τοῦτο ἕστηκεν ὁ ἄγγελος τὴν ἀπὸ τῆς ἀ. γινομένην λύπην διὰ τῆς ἐπανόδου πάλιν παραμυθούμενος Chrys.ascens.5(2.454D).

B. of Christians' ascent into heaven; **1.** made possible by Christ's Ascension εὐφημία τῇ ἀ. σου τῇ ἐπὶ τοὺς οὐρανούς· δι' αὐτῆς γὰρ ἡμῖν ὑπέδειξας τὴν ἄ. τοῦ ὕψους A.Thom.A 80(p.196.6f.); ὁ κύριος...ὁδοποιήσῃ ἡμῖν τὴν εἰς οὐρανοὺς ἄ. Ath.inc.25.6(M.25.140B); †Ath.exp.fid.1(M.25.201C); and descent, Ath.inc.et c.Ar.5(M.26.992B); **2.** presided over by special angels τοῖς ἐφεστῶσι τῇ ἀ. ἀγγέλοις Clem.str.4.18(p.299.19; M.8.1325A); in Celsus' opinion by various monsters, attributing Ophite ideas to orthodox οὐκ εἶδέ γε ὅτι οὐδεὶς τῶν τὸν λεοντοειδῆ...νομιζόντων εἶναι θυρωροὺς τῆς ἀ. ἕως θανάτου ἵσταται Or.Cels.7.40(p.191.11; M.11.1480A).

C. of ascent in various scriptural contexts, ref. Babel τὴν τοῦ πύργου ποίησιν...δι' ἧς οἱ τὸ τηνικαῦτα ἄνδρες τὴν εἰς οὐρανὸν ἄ. δύνασθαι κατασκευάζειν ἑαυτοῖς ᾤοντο ‡Just.coh.Gr.28(M.6.293C); exeg. Ps.46:2ff. τί ἕτερον βούλεται σημαίνειν ἡ διὰ τούτων δηλουμένη κυρίου τοῦ θεοῦ ἄ. ἢ τὴν πρὸς τῆς ἀ. κάθοδον αὐτοῦ; Eus.d.e.6.2(p.253.5; M.22.416B); of ascent of angels on Jacob's ladder, Gr.Naz.or.28.18(p.49.2; M.36.49B); Christ's ascent to Jerusalem τὴν ⟨εἰς⟩ Ἱεροσόλυμα ἀ. σημαίνειν τὴν ἀπὸ τῶν ὑλικῶν εἰς τὸν ψυχικὸν τόπον τυγχάνοντα εἰκόνα...ἀνάβασιν τοῦ κυρίου Heracleon ap.Or.Jo.10.33(19; p.206.26; M.14.365C).

D. of spiritual ascent of soul; **1.** in gen. ἀποστεροῦντας τὸν ἄνθρωπον τῆς εἰς θεὸν ἀ. Iren.haer.3.19.2(M.7.939A); Or.Jo.10.40(24; p.218.7; M.14.385C) cit. s. αἴσθησις; Synes.Dion 9(p.257.10; M.66.1137C); χειραγωγεῖ δὲ ἡμᾶς πρὸς τὴν ἄ. χάρις Μωσαϊκῆς γλώττης ἐπιβαίνουσα προφητική Bas.Sel.or.1.2(M.85.29A); Jo.Clim.scal.30(M.88.1160C); **2.** through virtue σπευδὼν πρὸς τὴν τοῦ πνεύματος ἄ., οὐκ ἀποχῇ κακῶν μόνον δικαιωθείς, πρὸς δὲ καὶ τῇ κυριακῇ τελειωθεὶς εὐποιΐᾳ Clem.str.4.6(p.261.6; M.8.1241A); ἐν τοσαύταις ἀ. ὑψωθεῖσα δι' ἀγάπης πρὸς τὴν τοῦ ἀγαθοῦ μετουσίαν ἡ κεκαθαρμένη ψυχή Gr.Nyss.hom.5 in Cant.(M.44.857D); ib.(876B) cit. s. ἀνάβασις; signified by cleansing of garments of Moses before ascent of Sinai, id.v.Mos.(M.44.373C); **3.** demons' endeavour to prevent it πνεύματα ἐχθρὰ...κωλύοντα τὴν τῆς ψυχῆς ἄ. καὶ δι' ἀρετῆς πορείαν Or.Cels.7.3(p.155.10; M.11.1424C); δαίμονες...θέλοντες ἐμποδίζειν ἡμᾶς τῆς εἰς οὐρανοὺς ἀ. Ath.v.Anton.22(M.26.876B); frustrated by Christ, id.ep.fest.22(p.295.20; M.26.1433A); **4.** several degrees ὅσην ὁρῶμεν τῆς εἰς τὸ ὕψος ἀ. τὴν προκοπὴν ἐπὶ τῆς ψυχῆς γινομένην. πρώτη ἄ., τὸ πρὸς τὴν καθαιρετικὴν τῆς Αἰγυπτίας δυνάμεως ἵππον ὁμοιωθῆναι.

δευτέρα ἄ., τὸ πλησίον αὐτὴν γενέσθαι...τρίτη τοίνυν ἄ. τὸ μηκέτι πλησίον, ἀλλ' ἀδελφὴν τοῦ δεσπότου ὀνομασθῆναι Gr.Nyss.*hom.4 in Cant.*(M.44.841B); *ib.6*(888cf.); **5.** in negative theology τὴν διὰ τῶν ἀποφάσεων ἄ. προτετιμήκασιν Dion.Ar.*d.n.*13.3(M.3.981B); κατὰ τὸ μέτρον τῆς ἀ. συστέλλεται, καὶ μετὰ πᾶσαν ἄ. ὅλος ἄφωνος ἔσται id. *myst.*3(M.3.1033C).

II. *raid, invasion* τῶν τε περὶ τὸν Γὼγ τὴν ἄ. Thdr.Mops.*Joel*.3: 1–3(M.66.233C).

***ἀνόδως**, *without method* οἱ ἀ. καὶ ἀμέτρως ἐνατενίζοντες τῷ ἡλίῳ βλάπτονται τὰς ὄψεις *cat.Rom.*7:18(p.111.23).

ἀνοησία, ἡ, 1. *want of understanding*, Adam.*dial.*1.27(p.56.5; M. 11.1757C); Epiph.*haer.*57.8(p.354.1; M.41.1008A); Dion.Ar.*e.h.*3.3.7 (M.3.433D); **2.** *state of being beyond intelligence*; **a.** of God νοῦς ἀνόητος καὶ λόγος ἄρρητος· ἀλογία καὶ ἀ. καὶ ἀνωνυμία id.*d.n.*1.1(M. 3.588B); **b.** in contemplation, beyond ratiocination, Max.*schol. myst.*1.1(M.4.417A) cit. s. ἀνενεργησία.

***ἀνοητ-έω**, *be witless*, perh. coined from Noëtus οὗτος [sc. Νόητος]...καὶ οἱ ἐξ αὐτοῦς ~οῦντες Epiph.*haer.*57.6(p.351.21; M.41. 1004D); *ib.*52.1(p.312.1, v.l. ἀνοηταίνει M.41.956A).

ἀνόητος, 1. *beyond the power of thought*; of deity ἀγνοοῦμεν δὲ τὴν ὑπερούσιον αὐτῆς καὶ ἀ. καὶ ἄρρητον ἀοριστίαν Dion.Ar.*c.h.*2.3(M.3. 141A); ἀ. φησιν οὐ τὸ ἠλίθιον ἀλλὰ τὸ μὴ νοούμενον ὑπό τινος· ἀόριστος δὲ ὁ θεός Max.*schol.*ad loc.(M.4.40D); **2.** *without a human mind*; of Christ acc. Apoll., ‡Ath.*Apoll.*1.2(M.26.1096B) cit. s. ἁμαρτία; denied πῶς δ' ἂν λέγοιτο ἄψυχον ἢ ἀ. τὸ σῶμα τοῦ Χριστοῦ; ταραχὴ γὰρ καὶ λύπη καὶ ἀδημονία οὔτε σαρκὸς ἀψύχου οὔτε ψυχῆς ἀ. οὔτε θεότητος ἀτρέπτου οὔτε δοκήσεως ἔνδειξις Gr.Thaum.*fid.cap.*2 (p.149.17; M.10.1133B); οὐ σῶμα ἄψυχον, οὐδ' ἀναίσθητον, οὐδ' ἀ. εἶχεν ὁ σωτήρ. οὐδὲ γὰρ οἷόν τε ἦν...ἀ. εἶναι τὸ σῶμα, οὐδὲ σώματος μόνου, ἀλλὰ καὶ ψυχῆς ἐν αὐτῷ τῷ λόγῳ σωτηρία γέγονεν Ath.*tom.*7 (M.26.804B); ἡ γὰρ ἀ. σὰρξ πάσης ἠλλοτρίωται κατὰ φύσιν θελήσεως, εἴπερ οὐδέν ἐστι θέλησις ἢ νοῦς περί τι κινούμενος ‡Ath.*serm.fid.*fr.2 (M.26.1292D); ref. Lc.22:15 ἐπιθυμία δὲ ἐκ θεότητος οὐ γίνεται, οὐδὲ ἐκ σαρκὸς μονωτάτης οὐδὲ ἐκ ψυχῆς ἀ., ἀλλ' ἐκ τελείας ἐνανθρωπήσεως ...παντὸς οὕτινος τοῦ ἐν ἀνθρώπῳ τυγχάνοντος Epiph.*haer.*77.27 (p.439.26; M.42.680C).

ἀνοήτως, *without intelligence*; ref. God acc. Basilides, Hipp.*haer.* 7.21(p.197.1; M.16.3303B) cit. s. ἀθελήτως.

ἀνόθευτος, *pure, genuine*; **1.** in gen. οὔπω γεγόναμεν...ἀ. εἰκὼν θεϊκή Mac.Aeg.*hom.*25.5(M.34.669D); τὴν τοῦ νόμου βούλησιν...ἀ. διερμηνεύειν Cyr.*Is.*1.1(2.26C); id.*Lc.*9:46(*TU* p.88.36; ἀνώθευτον M.72. 660D); Dion.Ar.*d.n.*13.4(M.3.984A); of human nature before Fall, ‡Caes.Naz.*dial.*123(M.38.1016); of writings, *genuine*, Areth.*Apoc.*1 (M.106.500A); **2.** of Son, ref. Jo.6:27 ἡ σφραγὶς ὡς καὶ ὁ χαρακτὴρ τὸ ὅμοιον καὶ ἀ. σημαίνει Didym.*Trin.*1.16(M.39.336B); ἐξ ἧς [sc. BMV] Χριστὸς ἀ. ἐξ ἀσπορίας στολὴν περιεβάλετο Thdr.Stud.*nativ. BMV* 7(M.96.692C).

***ἀνοθεύτως**, *without contamination*, Bas.*fid.*1(2.223E; M.31.677A); ref. translators of LXX μὴ συνδοιάσαι μετ' ἀλλήλων ἀλλ' ἀ. ἑρμηνεῦσαι Epiph.*mens.*3(M.43.241C); of Christians, *sincerely* ἀ. τρέχοντα ἐπὶ τὴν ἀρέσκειαν τοῦ δεσπότου Nil.*epp.*4.22(M.79.560D).

ἄνοια, ἡ, *folly*; *distress of mind, despair*; of Job, Didym.*Job* 1:19(M.39.1128D).

***ἀνοιγή, ἡ,** *opening, spreading out*, ‡Chrys.*hom.3.6 in Pss.77–107*(5.660E).

ἄνοιγμα, τό, *opening*, *Tr.Phil.*4(p.162.35); Proc.G.*Gen.*6:16(M.87. 276C).

ἀνοίγ-νυμι (ἀνοίγ-ω), *open*; **1.** lit.; **a.** in gen. προσευχομένου δέ μου ἠνοίγη ὁ οὐρανός Herm.*vis.*1.1.4; ἀ. ἡ γῆ τὸ στόμα *A.Phil.*26(p.14. 14); **b.** *open* a church, when after its consecration it is pronounced to be a place of prayer, Thphn.*chron.*p.193(M.108.501A); **c.** of God (Marcosian) ἠνοιχέναι τὸ στόμα...καὶ προενέγκασθαι λόγον Iren.*haer.*1.15.5(M.7.625A); of Christ οὐκ ἐδύνατο ἀ. τὸν τάφον, ἀλλ' ἐδεήθη ἄλλου ἀποκινήσαντος τὴν πέτραν Cels.ap.Or.*Cels.*5.52(p.56.12; M.11.1261D); κωφῶν τὴν ἀκοὴν ἤνοιξε...τοῦ ἐκ γενετῆς τυφλοῦ τοὺς ὀφθαλμοὺς ~οντα Ath.*inc.*18.4(M.25.128B); **2.** met. ὦτα...τοῖς πρὸς ἡδονὴν ἀνεῳγότα Clem.*str.*7.10(p.69.26; M.9.536C); Hipp.*haer.*4.24 (p.52.28; M.16.3087B); of heart ἠνεῴχθησαν ἡμῶν οἱ ὀφθαλμοὶ τῆς καρδίας *1Clem.*36.2; Herm.*vis.*4.2.4; Or.*Cels.*6.67(p.137.15; M.11.1400C); of a way for spiritual blessings τότε ἀνοίξω τὰ ταμεῖα τῆς εὐλογίας ...ἐν τῷ οὐρανῷ *Apoc.En.*11.1(p.34.13); εὐδόκησον ἀ. μοι θύραν τῆς μετανοίας Ephr.3.483B; Thdt.*Is.*64:8(p.251.5; 2.392); of heaven, Cyr.H.*catech.*19.9 cit. s. ἀνατολή; ref. Ac.10:4 τοὺς οὐρανοὺς ἀ. [sc. ἡ ἐλεημοσύνη] Chrys.*hom.50.4 in Mt.*(7.519D); of OT prophecies, *explain, open meaning of*, Hipp.*Dan.*4.33.6(M.10.656A).

ἀνοίκειος, *incongruous, inconsistent* λέγειν ὡς ἦν ποτε καιρός, ὅτε τοῖς κακοῖς ἔχαιρεν ὁ θεός...ἀ. τῆς φύσεως αὐτοῦ Meth.*arbitr.*3(p.153. 13; M.18.248A); δίκαιόν ἐστιν ἀκούοντας τὸ 'ἔκτισε' καὶ τὸ 'δοῦλος' καὶ τὸ 'πέπονθε' μὴ τῇ θεότητι λογίζεσθαι, ἀ. γάρ Ath.*decr.*14(p.12. 21; M.25.'448'(440)C); of Son acc. Eunomius, Bas.*Eun.*2.6(1.242C; M.29.584A) cit. s. ξένος; of a slanderer, as ἀ. μέλος [sc. τῇ ἐκκλησίᾳ] *Const.App.*2.43.4.

ἀνοικειότης, ἡ, *lack of intimacy*, cf. ἀνοίκειος *LS*, Synes.*ep.*53 (M.66.1380D); *ib.*84(1453C).

ἀνοικίζομαι, *migrate inland*; met., pass. c. genit., *be removed from, be above* or *beyond* νοῦ παντὸς ἀνῴκισται, πῶς παρθένος... ἔτεκεν μείνασα...παρθένος Didym.*Trin.*3.2(M.39.793C); τῶν γηΐνων πραγμάτων ἀνῴκισται λίαν Cyr.*Is.*3.1(2.353B); Dion.Ar.*c.h.*7.1(M.3. 205D); perf. ptcpl. pass. as adj., *exalted, sublime*, Cyr.*ador.*12(1. 439B); *ib.*1(8D); ἀνῳκισμένην...ζωήν, καὶ οὐ βάσιμον τοῖς πολλοῖς id. *Ps.*46:9(M.69.1057C).

ἀνοικοδομέω, *build up*; met. ἀγάλμασι καὶ σκιαγραφίαις ἀ. τὴν σκαιότητα τοῦ ἔθους Clem.*prot.*1(p.4.27; M.8.56B).

***ἀνοικοδόμημα, τό,** *building*, met. χρὴ...ἐρειπωθῆναι τὰ τῆς κακίας ἀ. Gr.Nyss.*hom.6.3 in Eccl.*(M.44.708A).

ἀνοικοδόμησις, ἡ, *rebuilding*, Leont.N.*v.Jo.Eleem.*20(p.37.16).

***ἀνοικοδόμητος,** *not built*, *Orac.Sib.*5.409.

ἀνοικονόμητος, *unprovided for*, *Hom.Clem.*2.23; *badly managed, uneconomical* ἀ. ἡ διοίκησις Ast.Am.*hom.*5(M.40.232D).

***ἀνοικονομήτως,** *without good management, uneconomically*, Chrys.*hom.48.3 in Ac.*(9.363A).

***ἀνοικτόκλειστος,** *shut but ready to open*, Geo.Pis.*hex.*1745(M.92. 1569A).

ἀνοικτός, *open*, *A.Paul.et Thecl.*23(p.251.4); of veil in liturgy, *unfolded, spread out*, cf.*Lit.Chrys.*(p.383.5).

***ἀνοινία, ἡ,** *abstinence from wine*, Eus.*l.C.*17(p.255.19; M.20. 1431C).

ἄνοιξις, ἡ, *opening* of prison, hence of resurrection, ‡Chrys.*hom. suppl.*8(M.64.480A).

***ἄνοιστρος,** *unexciting*, Gr.Naz.*carm.*2.1.88.88(M.37.1438A).

***ἀνολβίζω,** *pronounce happy*, †Apoll.*met.Ps.*143:15(M.33.1529B).

ἀνόλεθρος, *deathless*, Jo.D.*f.o.*1.8(M.94.808B).

***ἀνολιγώρως,** *not carelessly*, Dan.Raith.*v.Jo.Clim.*(M.88.600A).

***ἀνολίσθητος,** *not slipping*, Gr.Nyss.*Eun.*4(2 p.54.27, v.l. οὐκ ἂν ὀλίσθοιμεν M.45.625A).

***ἀνολισθήτως,** *without slipping*, Gr.Nyss.*hom.15 in Cant.*(M.44. 1105A).

***ἀνόλιστος,** *free from slipping*, hence *faultless*, Gr.Naz.*carm.* 1.2.2.368(M.37.607A).

***ἀνομαλέω,** *be thrown off balance, upset*, Sophr.H.*mir.Cyr.et Jo.*8 (M.87.3440B).

***ἀνομβρητικός,** *shedding forth*, Epiph.*haer.*76.25(p.372.21; M.42. 564B).

***ἀνομβρ-όω,** *gush forth*; met. ὁ θεοῦ λόγος ἄνωθεν ἐξ ἀγαθοῦ πατρὸς ὡς ἐξ ἀενάου καὶ ἀπείρου πηγῆς ~ῶν Eus.*l.C.*12(p.230.4; M.20. 1388A); pass., *be poured forth* πηγαὶ σωτηρίου λόγοι εἰσὶν εὐαγγελικοί, ἐξ ἁγίου πνεύματος ἀνωμβρωμένοι id.*Is.*12:3(M.24.184A); *be watered, refreshed*, Sophr.H.*ep.syn.*(M.87.3196C).

ἀνομ-έω, *transgress, break the law* τὸν οἰκόν σου τὸν ~ήσαντα εἰς τὸν κύριον Herm.*vis.*1.3.1; Meth.*symp.*10.2(p.123.23; M.18.196A); Marc.Er.*opusc.*3.12(M.65.984B).

ἀνόμημα, τό, *that which is unlawful*, esp. of heret. opinions κατάβαλε τὸ εὔηθες τοῦτο ἀ. ... καὶ τὰ κακὰ πρὸς ἀπιστίαν τῶν ἀνοήτων ἐξάδων Const.ap.Gel.Cyz.*h.e.*3.19.15(M.85.1348D); Σαβελλιανῶν τὸ ἀ. Sophr.H.*ep.syn.*(M.87.3153B).

ἀνομία, ἡ, 1. *lawless act, transgression* αἱ ἀ. ... τῶν δούλων τοῦ θεοῦ Herm.*sim.*5.5.3; ἀ. γὰρ ὄντως μεγάλη τὸ ἀθετεῖν τὰ λόγια τοῦ θεοῦ Cosm.Ind.*top.*2(M.88.128C); of heresy, *unlawful opinion* ὁ πονηρὸς...Ἄρειον ἡμῖν ἀνομίας ἐργαστήριον κατεστήσατο Const.ap. Gel.Cyz.*h.e.*3.19.12(M.85.1348C); οἱ πρώην ὑπολαμβάνοντες ἀ., ὅτι ὅμοιός ἐστιν [sc. ὁ Χριστός] ἡμῖν Leont.H.*Nest.*1.19(M.86.1484D); **2.** τὸ ἐν ἀνομίαις συλληφθῆναι ἀσύγκριτον ἔχει τὸ διάφορον *ib.*(1477A), f.l. for ἀνομοίοις.

ἀνομίλητος, *having no communion with others*; in pass. sense, *free from contact with*, Mac.Aeg.*libert.ment.*4(M.34.937C).

ἀνόμματος, *blind, sightless*; met. ὅταν ἡ ψυχὴ...ταῖς τοῦ ἀπροσίτου φωτὸς ἀκτῖσιν ἐπιβάλλῃ ταῖς ἀ. ἐπιβολαῖς Dion.Ar.*d.n.*4.11(M.3.708D); ψυχὴ...ἀπολαύουσα τῶν θείων μαρμαρυγῶν...ταῖς ἀ. τοῦ νοῦ καταστάσεσιν Max.*schol.*ad loc.(M.4.264B).

ἀνομογενής, *of different kind*, Leont.H.*Nest.*1.52(M.86.1521C).

***ἀνομοιητής, ὁ,** *Anomoean*, member of extreme Arian sect (Eunomians), ‡Jo.D.*Artem.*70(p.107.33; M.96.1317D).

ἀνομοιογενής, *unlike in kind*, Ath.*syn*.50(p.274.14; M.26.781C); Proc.G.*Gen*.6:16(M.87.273B).

***ἀνομοιογλωσσία**, ἡ, *dissimilarity of language*, ‡Eust.*hex*.(M.18.753C).

ἀνομοιοειδής, *heterogeneous*, Leont.H.*Nest*.1.10(M.86.1440C); *ib*. 3.4(1609D).

ἀνομοιομερής, *consisting of unlike parts, not homogeneous* *τὰ ὀνόματα ταῦτα* [sc. *ἀόρατον, ἄφθαρτον*...]...*εἰς τὴν οὐσίαν ἅπαντα φέροντες*...*οὐχὶ μόνον σύνθετον ἀλλὰ καὶ ἐξ ἀνομοιομερῶν αὐτὸν συγκείμενον ἀποδείξομεν* Bas.*Eun*.2.29(1.266C; M.29.640C); Leont.H. *Nest*.1.1(M.86.1404A); *Disp.Phot*.2(M.88.541A).

ἀνομοιοούσιος, v. *ἀνομοιούσιος*.

ἀνόμοιος, *unlike, dissimilar*;

A. in gen. *θεοὶ*...*ὅτι ἀγένητοι, οὐχ ὅμοιοι· τὰ μὲν γὰρ γενητὰ ὅμοια τοῖς παραδείγμασιν, τὰ δὲ ἀγένητα ἀ.* Athenag.*leg*.8.1(M.6.905A); *πᾶν γὰρ τὸ κτιστὸν ἀ. τυγχάνει τῷ κεκτικότι, κἄν τε κατὰ χάριν ἀφομοιοῖτο* Epiph.*haer*.76.3(p.344.1; M.42.521A).

B. theol.; **1.** of God, acc. pagans *εἰ γὰρ ἐκ μερῶν συνέστηκε, πάντως αὐτὸς ἑαυτοῦ ἀ. φανήσεται, καὶ ἐξ ἀνομοίων ἔχων τὴν συμπλήρωσιν* Ath.*gent*.28(M.25.56C); in a true sense *θεολογία τὸ ἀ. αὐτὸν εἶναι πρεσβεύει καὶ τοῖς πᾶσιν ἀσύντακτον ὡς καὶ πάντων ἕτερον*... *καίτοι οὐκ ἐναντίος ὁ λόγος τῇ πρὸς αὐτὸν ὁμοιότητι· τὰ γὰρ αὐτὰ καὶ ὅμοια θεῷ καὶ ἀ.· τὸ μὲν κατὰ τὴν ἐνδεχομένην τοῦ ἀμιμήτου μίμησιν, τὸ δὲ κατὰ τὸ ἀποδέον τῶν αἰτιατῶν τοῦ αἰτίου καὶ μέτροις ἀπείροις καὶ ἀσυγκρίτοις ἀπολιμπανόμενον* Dion.Ar.*d.n*.9.7(M.3.916A); **2.** heret., of Persons in Trin., Arian *μεμερισμέναι τῇ φύσει, καὶ ἀπεξενωμέναι, καὶ ἀπεσχοινισμέναι, καὶ ἀλλότριοι, καὶ ἀμέτοχοί εἰσιν ἀλλήλων αἱ οὐσίαι τοῦ πατρὸς καὶ τοῦ υἱοῦ, καὶ τοῦ ἁγίου πνεύματος, καὶ*...*ἀ.* ... *ἀλλήλων* Ath.*Ar*.1.6(M.26.24B); esp. of Word in rel. to Father *πάντων ξένων καὶ ἀ. ὄντων τοῦ θεοῦ κατ' οὐσίαν, οὕτω καὶ ὁ λόγος ἀλλότριος μὲν καὶ ἀ. κατὰ πάντα τῆς τοῦ πατρὸς οὐσίας καὶ ἰδιότητός ἐστι* Ar.*Thal.fr*.10.*ib*.(24A); *φασί*...*κτίσμα*... *ἐστι καὶ ποίημα ὁ λόγος καὶ ξένος καὶ ἀ. κατ' οὐσίαν τοῦ πατρός* Ath.*decr*.6(p.5.26; M.25.'433'(425A)A); asserted by Eunomius *τὴν ἀγεννησίαν οὐσίαν εἶναι τοῦ θεοῦ*·...*ἀ. εἶναι κατ' αὐτὴν τὴν οὐσίαν τὸν μονογενῆ υἱὸν τῷ πατρί* Bas.*Eun*.1.6(1.216C('D'); M.29.521A); *ἀ. βουλόμενος*...*τὸν υἱὸν*...*ἐπιδεῖξαι, τὸ μὲν τοῦ πατρὸς καὶ τοῦ υἱοῦ ὄνομα σιωπᾷ, ἁπλῶς δὲ περὶ ἀγεννήτου καὶ γεννητοῦ διαλέγεται* *ib*. 1.16(228C; M.548D); *οὐ μόνον τῇ τοῦ γεννητοῦ πρὸς τὸ ἀγέννητον διαστολῇ, ἀλλὰ καὶ τῇ τοῦ παθητοῦ πρὸς τὸ ἀπαθὲς ἀντιθέσει τὸ κατ' οὐσίαν ἀ. ἀποδεικνύειν σπουδάζουσι* Gr.Nyss.*Eun*.6(2 p.128.5; M.45.712A); asserted by Aëtius, ref. Heb.2:10 *ἀ. δὲ τῷ ἐξ οὗ τὸ δι' οὗ, ἀ. ἄρα καὶ τῷ πατρὶ ὁ υἱός* Bas.*Spir*.4(3.4C; M.32.73B); Thdt.*haer*.4.3(4.354); v. *ἀλλότριος*; teaching anathematized, CAnc.(358)*anath*.3,5(p.281.12,19; M.42.421B); apparently denied at Council of Seleucia *λέγεται καινοτομεῖσθαι ὑπό τινων τὸ ἀ. υἱοῦ πρὸς πατέρα*...*τὸ ἀ. ἀναθεματίζομεν* CSel.*ep*.(p.298.23; M.42.452A); but true position exposed *πῶς*...*γράφετε 'ἐκβάλλομεν τὸ ὁμοούσιον'*; ...*πῶς ἀναθεματίζετε τοὺς ἀ. εἶναι λέγοντας τὸν υἱόν; εἰ γὰρ οὐχ ὅμοιος κατ' οὐσίαν, πάντως ἀ. ἐστι*...*ποίᾳ μηχανῇ τὸ ἀ. ὅμοιον λέγετε καὶ τὸ ὅμοιον ἀ. φρονεῖτε;* Ath.*syn*.38(p.264.27; M.26.760C); *εἰ*... *ἕτερόν τινα τρόπον θεότητος ἔχειν τὸν υἱὸν καὶ μὴ εἰκόνα*...*τοῦ πατρὸς εἶναι*...*ἔστω ἀ.* *ib*.52(p.275.30; 785B); and finally admitted *οἱ περὶ Ἀκάκιον*...*ἀναφανδὸν λέγοντες ὅτι κατὰ πάντα ἀ. ὁ υἱὸς τῷ πατρί, οὐ μόνον κατὰ τὴν οὐσίαν ἀλλὰ δὴ καὶ κατὰ βούλησιν* Socr.*h.e*.2.45.10(M.67.360C); **3.** denied by orthodox *μία ἡ φύσις· οὐ γὰρ ἀ. τὸ γέννημα τοῦ γεννήσαντος· εἰκὼν γάρ ἐστιν αὐτοῦ* Ath.*Ar*.3.4(M.26.328C); id.*ep.Serap*.1.20(M.26.577A); *ib*.1.30(597B); ref. Gen.1:27, Bas.*hex*.9.6(1.88D; M.29.208B); *μήτε εἰς τρεῖς ἢ ξένας καὶ ἀ. οὐσίας*...*διαιρεθέντα* Gr. Naz.*or*.20.6(M.35.1072B); *εἰ ἀ. κατὰ τὴν φύσιν τῷ πατρὶ ὁ υἱός, πῶς μίαν κατασκευάζει τῶν διαφόρων φύσεων τὴν εἰκόνα;* Gr.Nyss.*hom.opif*.6.3(M.44.140B); *οὔτε ὅμοιον οὔτε ἀ. λέγομεν τὸν υἱὸν τῷ πατρί*... *ὅμοιον καὶ ἀ. κατὰ τὰς ποιότητας λέγεται· ποιότητος δὲ τὸ θεῖον ἐλεύθερον* Evagr.Pont.*ep*.3(M.32.249B); **4.** of Christ's divinity in rel. to man *τὴν ὑπὲρ αὐτοῦ δύναμιν καὶ τὸ πρὸς ἡμᾶς ἀ. τῆς φύσεως διηγεῖται ἡ γραφή* Ath.*inc*.34.3(M.25.156A); *ἡμῶν μὲν οὖν ἀ. ἐστιν ὁ λόγος, τοῦ δὲ πατρὸς ὅμοιος* id.*Ar*.3.20(M.26.365A).

C. as name of those who assert unlikeness of Son to Father, *Anomoean*, Ath.*syn*.31(p.260.20; M.26.749A); CAnt.(363)*ep*.ap.Socr. *h.e*.3.25.15(M.67.453B); *ἡ πᾶσα μαχὴ*...*τοῖς ἐκκλησιαστικοῖς πρὸς τοὺς ἀ. ἐστὶ περὶ τοῦ δεῖν ἢ κτιστὸν νοεῖν τὸν υἱὸν καὶ τὸ πνεῦμα* ...*ἢ τῆς ἀκτίστου φύσεως* Gr.Nyss.*Eun*.1(1 p.85.14; M.45.317A); Epiph.*haer*.76.1(p.340.15; M.42.516B); Philost.*h.e*.9.13(M.65.577B) etc.; neut. as subst., *doctrine of Anomoeans* *ταυτησὶ τῆς*...*ἀσεβείας, τῆς κατὰ τὸ ἀ., λέγω* Bas.*ep*.9.2(3.90C; M.32.268D); Gr.Nyss.*Eun*.3(2 p.35.21; M.45.601C); *τὴν τοῦ ἀ. δόξαν* Socr.*h.e*.2.20.9(M.67.257A).

ἀνομοιότης, ἡ, *unlikeness, dissimilarity*; **1.** in gen. *ἡμέτερον μὲν ὄντως ἐστὶ κακὸν ἡ πρὸς τὸν θεὸν ἀ. τε καὶ ἄγνοια* Meth.*Porph*.5(p.507.13); *τὸ θεοπρεπὲς κάλλος*...*ἀμιγές ἐστι καθόλου πάσης ἀ.* Dion.Ar.*c.h*.3.1(M.3.164D); **2.** of Son to Father, acc. Eunomians *εἰ γὰρ ἀσύγκριτος ὁ πατήρ, πόθεν λαβὼν τῆς ἀ. τοῦ υἱοῦ τὰς ἀποδείξεις παρέξεται;* Bas.*Eun*.1.27(1.238A; M.29.572B); *τὴν μὲν ὕπαρξιν συγχωροῦσι, καὶ ἴδιον εἶναι πρόσωπον υἱοῦ, καὶ ἴδιον πατρὸς συντίθενται· ἀ. δὲ τῆς φύσεως παρεισάγουσι* id.*hom*.24.2(2.190C; M.31.601B); *ὁ ἑτεροούσιον λέγων τὸν γεγεννημένον πρὸς τὸν γεννήσαντα, δύο καὶ οὗτος λέγει θεούς, διὰ τὴν τῆς οὐσίας ἀ. τὸ πολύθεον παρεισάγων* *ib*. 24.4(192B; M.605C); Cyr.*thes*.12(5^1.111E); hence of doctrine of Anomoeans *τὸ ἄθεον τῆς ἀ. δόγμα* Bas.*ep*.212.2(3.319B; M.32.781B); *ὁ τῆς ἀ. λόγος αὐτῶν* Gr.Nyss.*Eun*.1(1 p.202.29; M.45.449C).

***ἀνομοιουσιαστής**, ὁ, *Anomoean*, Didym.(‡Bas.)*Eun*.5(1.313B; M.29.752A).

***ἀνομοιούσιος, ἀνομοιοούσιος**, *of unlike substance* *εὐλαβητέον γὰρ μὴ τὰ τοῦ πατρὸς ἴδια μεταφέροντες ἐπὶ τὸ ἀνομοιοούσιον αὐτῷ καὶ ἐν ἀνομοιογενεῖ καὶ ἀλλοτριοουσίῳ χαρακτηρίζοντες τὴν τοῦ πατρὸς θεότητα, ξένην*...*ἄλλην εἰσάξωμεν οὐσίαν* Ath.*syn*.50(p.274.14; M.26.781C); *ἡ*...*ὀρθὴ*...*ἔννοια*...*μὴ τὸ ἀ. ἐπινοήσασα υἱοῦ πρὸς πατέρα* Epiph.*haer*.76.30(p.379.24; M.42.577C); Cyr.*thes*.10(5^1.76E); Leont. H.*Nest*.2.5(M.86.1541B).

ἀνομοίως, *differently*; ref. God, acc. implications of Marcellus' view *ὁ θεὸς ἔσται ἑαυτῷ ἀνόμοιος, πάλαι μὲν ἔχων ἐν ἑαυτῷ τὸν λόγον καὶ ἐπὶ συντελείᾳ τοῦ παντὸς ἀποληψόμενος αὐτὸν*...*ἐν δὲ τῷ μεταξὺ χρόνῳ ἀ. κείμενος* Eus.*Marcell*.2.9(p.108.26; M.24.916D); acc. Anomoeans *τὰ ἀ. προφερόμενα καὶ κατὰ τὴν φύσιν ἀ. ἔχειν* Gr.Nyss.*Eun*.7(2 p.157.1; M.45.745A).

ἀνομολογέω, *admit, acknowledge*, Clem.*ecl*.32(p.146.27; M.9.716A); id.*str*.6.15(p.493.18; M.9.345B); *συνοδικαῖς ψήφοις ἀ.* ... *ὁμοούσιον τῷ πατρὶ τὸν υἱόν* Philost.*h.e*.1.7(M.65.464C); of writings, *acknowledge as genuine*, Clem.*q.d.s*.5(p.163.14; *ὁμολογουμένως* M.9.609B); *τοῦ Κλήμεντος ἐν τῇ* [sc. *ἐπιστολῇ*] *ἀνωμολογημένῃ παρὰ πᾶσιν* Eus.*h.e*.3.38.1(M.20.293C).

ἀνομολογούμενος, **1.** *inconsistent* *τὸ τῆς κακίας* [sc. *τῶν Φαρισαίων*] *ἀ. καὶ τυφλόν*...*τῷ τοσαῦτα σημεῖα πεποιηκότι ἐπιβουλεῦσαι, ὡς μηδὲν ὑπὲρ ἑαυτοῦ ἐν τῷ ἐπιβουλεύεσθαι δυναμένῳ* Or.*Jo*.28.12(11; p.403.7; M.14.704C); **2.** *not admitted*, Clem.*str*.5.5(p.346.13; M.9.56A).

ἀνομοούσιος, *of different essence*, Ptol.*ep*.ap.Epiph.*haer*.33.7(p.457.12; M.41.568B); *πᾶσα σύνθεσις ἡ καθ' ὑπόστασιν ἐξ ἀνομοουσίων* Leont.H.*Nest*.1.26(M.86.1493A).

***ἀνομοφυής**, *of different nature*, Leont.H.*Nest*.1.26(M.86.1493A).

***ἀνομοφυΐα**, ἡ, *difference of natures* *ἐκ τῆς ἀ. καθ' ὑπόστασιν ὑποπτευτέαν εἶναι τὴν ἕνωσιν τοῦ λόγου καὶ τῆς σαρκός* Leont.H. *Nest*.1.26(M.86.1493A).

***ἀνονειδίστως**, *without reproach*, Herm.*sim*.9.24.2.

***ἀνόνη**, ἡ, = *ἀννώνη*, †Gregent.*leg.Hom*.(M.86.580A).

ἀνονοέω, f.l. for *ἀνανοέω*.

ἀνονόμαστος, v. *ἀνωνόμαστος*.

ἀνόπιν, *back, backwards* *ὀκλάσαντος ἵππου καὶ ἀ. ὥσπερ ὑφιζηκότος* Cyr.*glaph.Gen*.7(1.230A); id.*Jo*.1.1(4.11A); met., of spiritual declension *Ἰσραὴλ*...*ἀ. ὥσπερ ἰὼν*...*καὶ*...*εἰδωλολατρείας ἠγαπηκὼς τὰ ἐγκλήματα* id.*glaph.Ex*.3(1.334A); *Γαλάται πρὸς τὰς τοῦ νόμου σκιὰς ἀ. ἰόντες μετὰ τὴν πίστιν* id.*Ps*.24:10(M.69.849C); *farther back, earlier* in a book *διὰ τῶν ἀ. περὶ Κύρου* id.*Is*.4.2(2.603D).

ἀνόργανος, *without bodily parts*, Ast.Soph.*hom.1 in Ps*.5(M.40.401B).

***ἀνοργάνωτος**, *shapeless* *τροχός τις, ὃν λέγουσι χερσαῖον τέρας ἀ.* Geo.Pis.*carm*.1.98.

ἀνορεκτ-έω, *have no appetite*; met., Or.*fr.in Ps*.106:17(p.93); ~*οῦσαν πρὸς τὰ θεῖα τὴν*...*ψυχήν* Max.*ep*.36(M.91.629D); Sophr.H. *v.Anast*.(M.92.1701B).

ἀνόρεκτος, *without appetite*; met. *ἀ. παρέχειν τὰς ἀκοὰς τῷ*... *νόμῳ* Const.*or.s.c*.12(p.170.34; M.20.1269C).

ἀνορέκτως, *without appetite*, Clem.*str*.7.6(p.23.19; M.9.444A); *ἀ. ἔχων περὶ τὸ βρῶμα* ‡Pall.*h.mon*.28.13(p.89.7; M.34.1050D).

ἀνορεξία, ἡ, *want of desire* or *appetite* *ἡ τῶν ἀρετῶν προκοπή, ὅταν τὴν ἀπάθειαν καὶ τὴν ἀ. κτήσησθε* ‡Pall.*h.mon*.8.15(p.37.2; M.34.1139A); met. *ἀρχὴ ἀποστασίας*...*ἀ. λόγου, ὃν ἀεὶ πεινᾷ ἡ ψυχὴ τοῦ φιλοθέου* Pall.*ep.Laus*.(p.7.20; M.34.1002).

***ἀνορθοπεριπατητικός**, *walking upright*, ‡Ath.*def*.1.3(M.28.533C) cit. s. *ἄνθρωπος*.

ἀνορθ-όω, *restore, set straight again*; *raise up, lift up*, lit., for execution *ὁ Παπύλος προσηλωθεὶς εἰς τὸ ξύλον ἀνωρθώθη* *M.Carp*. 37; met. *τὸ ταπεινὸν τῆς ψυχῆς*...*ἐξεγείρων καὶ* ~*ῶν μαθήμασιν* Gr. Thaum.*pan.Or*.8(p.22.6; M.10.1077B); *εὐαγγέλιον*...*θεοῦ καλεῖ ἀπὸ* τῶν προοιμίων ∼ῶν τὸν ἀκροατήν Chrys.*hom.1.1 in Rom.*(9.431A); hence pass., *be erect*; acc. Satornilus not man's original position, Iren.*haer.*1.24.1(M.7.674B) cit. s. σπινθήρ; ἡ καμηλοπάρδαλις...τὸν αὐχένα...φέρει εἰς ὕψος ∼ούμενον Philost.*h.e.*3.11(M.65.496C); *be exalted* εἰσὶν ἐν τῇ ἐκκλησίᾳ πολλοί. εἰσὶν εἰς ὕψος ἀνωρθωμένοι Chrys. *hom.10.1 in Eph.*(11.75E).

***ἀνορθωτής**, ὁ, *one who raises up, restores*; of God, Ephr.2.161B.

ἀνόρμητος, *not setting itself in motion, without free will* ὁ μεμφόμενος τὸν ποιητὴν ὡς μὴ φυσικῶς κατασκευάσαντα ἡμᾶς ἀναμαρτήτους, οὐδὲν ἕτερον ἢ τὴν ἄλογον φύσιν τῆς λογικῆς προτιμᾷ, καὶ τὴν ἀκίνητον καὶ ἀ. τῆς προαιρετικῆς καὶ ἐμπράκτου Bas.*hom.*9.7 (2.79E; M.31.345B); of Christ, ref. Mt.26:39 ἀναφαίνεται...ἀ. αὐτοῦ ἡ εἰς ᾅδου...κάθοδος Didym.*Trin.*3.21(M.39.905B); ref. Jo.14:24,31 οὐκ ἀπροαίρετος ὢν οὐδὲ ἀ. ... ἀλλὰ δηλῶν τὴν οἰκείαν γνώμην ἡνωμένως καὶ ἀδιαστάτως τοῦ πατρὸς ἐχομένην Bas.*Spir.*20(3.17D; M.32. 104B).

***ἀνόρπηκος**, *without branches*, ‡Nil.*perist.*9.7(M.79.877D).

***ἀνορυκτικός**, *for digging*, Nil.*exerc.*8(M.79.728D); Proc.G.*Dt.* 23:13(M.87.933A).

ἀνόρυκτος, *not made by digging*; of Christ φρέαρ ἀ. Rom.Mel.(*AS* 1 p.1); τὴν ἀ. πηγὴν τοῦ τῆς ἀφέσεως ὕδατος Jo.D.*hom.*9.14(M.96. 740D).

ἀνορύσσ-ω, **1.** *dig up, uncover*; fig. ἡμᾶς...παραλαβὼν καὶ τέχνῃ ἑαυτοῦ τῇ γεωργικῇ...κατανοῶν οὐ τὰ πᾶσιν ὁρώμενα μόνον...∼ων δὲ καὶ τῶν ἐνδοτάτων ἀποπειρώμενος Gr.Thaum.*pan.Or.*7(p.19.18; M. 10.1073D); φιλοσόφει καὶ διατέλει τὸ ἐν ἡμῖν ἀνακεχωσμένον ὄμμα ∼ων Synes.*ep.*136(M.66.1525D); met. λογισμοὺς ἀ., δι' ὧν ἀποφαίνειν ἐσπούδακεν ὡς οὐκ ἂν εἴη τρεπτὸς ὁ τοῦ θεοῦ λόγος Cyr.*apol.Thdt.*5 (p.127.1; 6[1].220E); **2.** *root out*, lit. τίς τῶν ὀνύχων ∼ομένων γενναίως ἤνεγκε; Chrys.*hom.4.4 in 1Cor.*(10.29A); met. ∼ονται οἱ πλείους τῶν γαστριμάργων Pall.*v.Chrys.*5(p.32.6; M.47.20).

ἀνόσιος, *profane, unholy*; *monstrous, marvellous*, of the burning bush ἀ. ἀληθῶς καὶ πέρα λόγου παντὸς τὸ δρώμενον Cyr.*glaph.Ex.*1 (1.262B).

ἀνοσιότης, ἡ, *impiety, wickedness*, Cyr.*Os.*50(3.81B); id.*expl.xii cap.*proem.(p.16.4; 6[1].146A).

ἀνέστητος, *whence no one returns*, Nonn.*par.Jo.*2:22(M.43.764C); *ib.*5:25(789A); *ib.*5:28(789B).

***ἀνοστία**, ἡ, *? weakness*, Agath.*v.Gr.Ill.*30(p.18).

ἀνόστιμος, = ἀνόστητος, Nonn.*par.Jo.*20:9(M.43.909A).

ἄνοστος, *unwholesome*, met. τὸ γὰρ ἄχαρί τε καὶ ἄ. πρέποι ἂν ἥκιστα τοῖς εὐσεβεῖν ἑλομένοις Cyr.*ador.*15(1.526A).

ἀνόσφιστος, *not stolen*, i.e. *kept in trust* μετὰ προσευχῆς φυλάξαντες ἀ. τὸ ἐπάγγελμα ‡Chrys.*fug.spec.*(1.817B).

ἀνουθέτητος, *that will not be warned, stubborn, ungovernable*; of natural forces θάλασσα Cyr.*glaph.Ex.*3(1.335D); νόσῳ id.*Jo.*4.5(4. 416E); of wrath of God, *inexorable*, id.*Is.*2.2(2.221B).

ἄνους, *without reason, mindless*, in gen. οὔτε ὁ νοῦς ἄλογος, οὔτε ἄ. ὁ λόγος Dion.Al.ap.Ath.*Dion.*23(p.63.17; M.25.513C); ὁ Ἰακὼβ ἐν ἑβδομήκοντα πέντε ψυχαῖς τοῖς Αἰγυπτίοις ἐπιξενούμενος, οὐκ ἄ. οὔτε ἄσαρκος...ὑπὸ τῆς γραφῆς ἱστορεῖται Gr.Nyss.*Apoll.*10(M.45.1144C); Dion.Ar.*d.n.*4.3(M.3.697A); of Christ, acc. Apollinarius τὸν γὰρ τοῦ σώματος Ἰησοῦ ναὸν προδιέγραψεν ὁ ἄψυχος καὶ ἄ. καὶ ἀθελὴς τοῦ Σολομῶντος ναός Apoll.*fr.*2(p.204.16)ap.Anast.S.*monoph.*(M.89. 1184A); Gr.Naz.*ep.*101(M.37.177B) cit. s. ἄνθρωπος; πάλαι καὶ ἄψυχον ἐδογμάτισεν Ἀπολινάριος εἶναι τὸν κύριον, εἶτα ὡς ἐκ μεταμέλου ἄ. καὶ ἄψυχον λέγειν αὐτὸν μετέμαθε Leont.H.*monoph.*(M.86.1865C); denied οὔτε οὖν ἄπνους οὔτε ἄ. οὔτε ἀκάρδιος τῇ ἐπισκιάσει τῆς τοῦ ὑψίστου δυνάμεως, καὶ ἐπελεύσει τοῦ ἁγίου πνεύματος Gr.Nyss.*Apoll.* 27(M.45.1181B); εἴ τις εἰς ἄ. ἄνθρωπον ἤλπικεν, ἀνόητος ὄντως ἐστί Gr.Naz.*ep.*101(181C); οὔτε ἄψυχον οὔτε ἄ. ἢ ἀτελῆ τὴν τῆς σαρκὸς οἰκονομίαν CCP(381)*ep.*ap.Thdt.*h.e.*5.9.12(3.1032).

ἀνούσιος, **A.** *non-existent*; **1.** in gen. ἀγέννητον ἀ. νοοῦμεν τὸ μηδαμῇ μηδαμῶς ὄν. εἰπέ τις ἀνούσιον, ὑπόστασιν ἀνεῖλε καὶ οὐσίας ὕπαρξιν, ἀ. καὶ ἀνυπόστατον, τὴν μὴ ὑπάρχουσαν μήτε οὖσαν ὅλως φύσιν Didym.(‡Bas.)*Eun.*5(1.312D; M.29.749B); ἐν αὐτῷ [sc. τῷ ἀγαθῷ] μόνῳ καὶ τὸ ἀ. οὐσίας ὑπερβολή, καὶ τὸ ἄζωον ὑπερέχουσα ζωή Dion.Ar.*d.n.*4.3(M.3.697A); **2.** of matter εἰ...ἀ. καὶ τοῦ εἶναι τόδε τι ἐστερημένη ἡ ὕλη πρὸ τοῦ λαβεῖν τὸ εἶδος καὶ γενέσθαι οὐσία, ...πῶς ἀγένητος ὁ κόσμος; ‡Just.*confut.*50(M.6.1541D); γενητὸς ἄρα ὁ κόσμος, καὶ μεταβλητὸς ἐκ τοῦ ἀ. εἰς οὐσίαν ‡Just.*qu.Chr.*3.5 (M.6.1441C); ἡ ὕλη καὶ ἀ. λέγεται...ὡς αὐτὴ φθαρτὴ οὖσα, καὶ οὐκ ἀεὶ οὖσα Max.*schol.d.n.*4.19(M.4.277A); **3.** of evil εἰ οὐσία τὸ ἀγαθόν, ἀνούσιον τὸ κακόν Jo.D.*Man.*1.13(M.94.1517A).

B. *without independent existence, not self-subsistent* ὁ ἐν ἀνθρώποις λόγος, ἰδίως μὲν ἀ. ὢν καὶ ἀνυπόστατος Eus.*d.e.*5.5(p.228.27; M.22. 377B); ref. God ἡ πάντων αἰτία...οὔτε ἀ. Dion.Ar.*myst.*4.1(M.3. 1040D); ref. Persons of Trin. τρεῖς μὲν ὑποστάσεις ὁμολογοῦμεν, μίαν δὲ τούτων φύσιν καὶ οὐσίαν καταγγέλλομεν, οὐδ' ὁποτέραν μὲν τούτων ἀ. γινώσκοντες Leont.B.*arg.Sev.*(M.86.1920D); αἱ τρεῖς [sc. ὑποστάσεις] ἔχουσι μίαν φύσιν...καὶ οὔτε ἀ. ἐπὶ μιᾷ ἑκάστῃ αὐτῶν, οὐδὲ ἑκάστῃ ἰδίαν ἔχει οὐσίαν Jo.D.*fid.Nest.*7(p.562); id.*Jacob.*11 (M.94.1441B); of Logos, acc. Marcellus υἱὸν ἀρνούμενος, λόγον δὲ ψιλὸν ἀ. ... ὑποτιθέμενος Eus.*Marcell.*2.4(p.56.21; M.24.820B); μόνον ὄνομα εἶναι υἱόν, ἀ. δὲ...εἶναι τὸν υἱὸν τοῦ θεοῦ ‡Ath.*Ar.*4.8(p.52.17; M.26.477C); Epiph.*haer.*72.7(p.261.12; M.42.389D); in view ascribed to Homoousians by 'Semi-Arians' ἀ. ὄντος τοῦ υἱοῦ ἢ ἀνυποστάτου τοῦ ἁγίου πνεύματος Ath.*tom.*6(M.26.801C); above views denied υἱὸς...οὐχ ὡς λόγος ἀ. ..., ἀλλ' ὡς ἀληθῶς υἱὸς ὢν μονογενὴς Eus.*e.th.* 1.20(p.86.7; M.24.873C); ἡ μονὰς...ὁλόκληρος μένει, καὶ ὁ ταύτης υἱὸς οὐκ ἀ. ... ἀλλ' οὐσιώδης ἀληθῶς ‡Ath.*Ar.*4.2(p.45.26; 469C); of Christ's humanity Εὐτυχοῦς...φαντασίαν λέγοντος τὴν σάρκωσιν... καὶ...τὸ σῶμα αὐτοῦ...ἑτεροούσιον ἡμῶν, μᾶλλον δὲ καὶ ἀ. ὑπάρχον Anast.S.*hod.*7(M.89.113A); ref. monothelite teaching ἔσται...τῇ μὲν ἀναιρέσει τῶν φυσικῶν ἐνεργειῶν ὁ Χριστὸς κατὰ Σευῆρον ἀ. Max.*opusc.*(M.91.53A); μὴ ἔχειν [sc. Χριστόν]...θέλησιν ἢ ἐνέργειαν φυσικήν, ἀλλὰ ἀ. αὐτὸν καὶ ἀνύπαρκτον κατ' αὐτοὺς ὑπάρχειν Martin. *ep.*1(M.*PL.*87.122D); orthodox denial of monophysite views, interpreting ἀνούσιος as *without* φύσις: εἰ...σὰρξ ἀ., ἢ φύσεως ἐκτός, δείξατε τίς οὖσα καὶ πῶς ἔχουσα τυγχάνει αὕτη. ... εἰ γὰρ ἔστι σὰρξ ἀ., τουτέστι φύσιν οὐκ ἔχουσα, οὐκ ἔστι δὲ φύσις ἀνυπόστατος, οὐκ ἄρα ἔσται σὰρξ ἀνυπόστατος Leont.B.*Nest.et Eut.*1(M.86.1277Af.); τὸ γὰρ Χριστὸς χρῖσιν...σημαίνει περί τινα χριόμενον· ὅτι δὲ οὔτε χρῖσις ἄνευ οὐσιωμένου χρίσματος, οὔτε χριόμενος ἀ. τίς ἐστιν, οὔτε ἔτι τὸ χρῖσμα καὶ τὸ χριόμενον μία ἐστὶν οὐσία, φανερόν Leont.H. *monoph.*21(M.86.1784A); id.*Nest.*2.4(M.86.1537B); cf.Max.*opusc.*(M. 91.205B), citt. s. ἐνούσιος.

C. *unreal*, of evil τὸ δὲ κακὸν οὔτε ἐν τοῖς οὖσιν οὔτε ἐν τοῖς μὴ οὖσιν, ἀλλὰ καὶ αὐτοῦ τοῦ μὴ ὄντος μᾶλλον ἀπέχον τἀγαθοῦ, ἀλλότριον καὶ ἀνουσιώτερον Dion.Ar.*d.n.*4.19(M.3.716D); of present life πρὸς... τὴν μέλλουσαν τῆς...ζωῆς ἀρχετυπίαν, ἡ παροῦσα συγκρινομένη ζωὴ παίγνιόν ἐστι, καὶ πᾶν εἴ τι ἄλλο τούτου καθέστηκεν ἀνουσιώτερον Max.*ambig.*(M.91.1416C, MSS. ἀνοσιώτερον).

D. *immaterial*, ref. spiritual beings τὸ γενητὸν οὐκ ἀ. μέν, οὐχ ὅμοιον δὲ μορφὴν καὶ σῶμα ἔχει τοῖς ἐν τῷδε τῷ κόσμῳ σώμασιν Clem.*exc.Thdot.*10(p.109.21; M.9.660C); of soul, acc. Aristotle, Nemes.*nat.hom.*2(M.40.537A).

ἀνουσίως, *not essentially, not in reality* εἰ κατ' οὐσίαν οὐκ ἔπασχεν ὁ λόγος τῇ σαρκί, δῆλον ὅτι ἀ. ἔπασχεν· εἰ δὲ ἀ., οὐδὲ ἔπαθεν· οὐσίας γὰρ τὰ πάθη κυρίως Leont.H.*Nest.*7.9(M.86.1768[h]A).

ἀνούστατα, superl., *very foolishly*, Cyr.*Os.*94(3.125A).

ἀνοχή, ἡ, **1.** *holding up*; of the hand shading the eyes, ‡Bas. *struct.hom.*2.16(1.347A; M.30.61A); **2.** *holding back*, hence *cessation* ἀ. τῆς οἰκοδομῆς Herm.*sim.*9.5.1; *respite* ἐδίδου ἀ. ὁ μακρόθυμος θεὸς καὶ πρὸ μιᾶς ἡμέρας...τῆς αἰχμαλωσίας Or.*hom.1.3.in Jer.*(p.2.26; M.13.257B); **3.** *bearing, endurance*; ref. Christ's human nature ἀ. τοῦ πάθους ‡Ath.*Apoll.*1.3(M.26.1097B); ἐν ἀ. τῆς γεννήσεως τῆς ἐκ γυναικὸς *ib.*2.8(1145B); **4.** *forbearance* ἀ. καὶ ἐρώτησίς σοι οὐκ ἔσται περὶ...ἀδικημάτων *Apoc.En.*13.2(p.36.4); of God, Esaias *or.*12.2 (p.73; Lat. M.40.1137B); **5.** *lifting up*, hence *Ascension*, Geo.Pis. *carm.*76 tit.

ἀνοχλίζω, **1.** *lift up* τὸν τῆς διανοίας ὀφθαλμὸν ἀ. Cyr.*Jo.*2.5(4. 199B); *ib.*3.6(317B); **2.** *heave out, root out*, *ib.*1.2(14D); **3.** *hold up, support*, Paul.Sil.*ambo.*110(M.86.2256A).

ἀνταγαπάω, *love in return*, Clem.*paed.*1.3(p.95.7; M.8.260A); Or. *exp.in Pr.*8:18(M.17.183D); Gr.Nyss.*hom.1 in Cant.*(M.44.769C).

***ἀνταγώνισμα**, τό, *conflict*, Clem.*str.*7.3(p.15.1; M.9.425A).

ἀνταγώνιστος, *refractory*, Gr.Nyss.*Eun.*12(2 p.285.16 conj. ἀνανταγώνιστος; M.45.897B).

ἀντᾴδω, *sing in answer*; *speak, sing in opposition to*, Clem.*paed.* 2.12(p.229.5; M.8.541B).

ἀνταίρω, intrans., *rebel* against θεῷ *Didasc.Jac.*1.18(p.755.22); abs. Κρᾶσος ἀντῆρε Thphn.*chron.*p.5(M.108.68A).

***ἀνταίτιος**, *causing in return*, Clem.*str.*8.9(p.99.28; M.9.397C).

***ἀνταιχμαλωτεύω**, *make captive in turn*, Isid.Pel.*epp.*1.400(M.78. 405D); Nil.*Magn.*49(M.79.1032C).

***ἀνταιχμαλωτίζω**, = ἀνταιχμαλωτεύω, †Bas.*Is.*41(1.412A; M.30. 197A); ‡Caes.Naz.*dial.*20(M.38.877).

ἀντακολουθία, ἡ, *reciprocal implication*; of the virtues, Clem. *str.*4.26(p.320.28; M.8.1373A); πιστὴ τοίνυν ἡ γνῶσις, γνωστὴ δὲ ἡ πίστις θείᾳ τινὶ ἀκολουθίᾳ τε καὶ ἀ. γίνεται *ib.*2.4(p.121.8; 948A); σὺν καὶ τῇ τῶν ἔργων ἀνταποδόσει τε καὶ ἀ. *ib.*6.14(p.486.14; M.9.329B).

ἀνταλλαγή, ἡ, *exchange* ὦ τῆς γλυκείας ἀ. [sc. of Atonement] *Diogn.*9.5; Epiph.*haer.*39.5(p.76.11; M.41.672A).

ἀντάλλαγμα, τό, 1. *exchange, substitute* οὐκ ἔδωκα ὑμῖν ἀ. τοῦ κακοῦ τὸ ἀγαθόν *A.Phil.*139(p.73.4); *Ep.*ap.CSyr.(H.2.1368D); **2.** *substitute* καὶ προσελήφθη τὰ ἔθνη καὶ γεγόνασιν ἀ. τοῦ Ἰσραήλ Cyr.*Is.* 4.1(2.560A); *ib.*(561A); *representative* Χριστὸς ὀνομαζόμενος τίνα ἄλλον ἢ τὸν αὐτὸν δηλοῖ, οὗ τὸ ἀ. δηλονότι τὴν ἐκκλησίαν, ὠνείδισαν; Eus.*d.e.* 4.16(p.188.15; M.22.313C); **3.** *exchange, equivalent*; ref. Atonement τὸ τίμιον αἷμα Χριστοῦ τὸ...ἀ. ὑπὲρ τῆς τοῦ κόσμου ζωῆς Ath.*exp.Ps.* 54:20(M.27.253B); *ib.*88:51(393D); σῶμα ἀντὶ σώματος καὶ ψυχὴν ἀντὶ ψυχῆς δέδωκε καὶ τελείαν ὕπαρξιν ὑπὲρ ὅλου ἀνθρώπου· τοῦτ' ἔστι τὸ ἀ. τοῦ Χριστοῦ ‡Ath.*Apoll.*1.17(M.26.1125A); Bas.*hom.in Ps.* 48:8(1.185D; M.29.452B); λάβῃ τε ἀ. τοῦ πεπτωκότος τὸν Χριστόν Gr.Naz.*carm.*1.1.10.71(M.37.470A); δοὺς ἑαυτὸν ἀ. τοῦ σοῦ θανάτου Gr. Nyss.*Eun.*11(2 p.253.6; M.45.860B); *ib.*5(2 p.114.9; 693C); τὸν ἴδιον υἱὸν τῆς ἁπάντων ἡμῶν σωτηρίας ἀ. δέδωκεν ὁ πατήρ Cyr.*glaph.Ex.*2 (1.276C); id.*Is.*4.2(2.606A); id.*Zach.*59(3.738C); Cosm.Ind.*top.*5(M. 88.241C) cit. s. ἀντίδειξις; of ransom paid to Satan τίνος ἂν ἀντηλλάξατο τὸν κατεχόμενον, εἰ μὴ δηλαδὴ τοῦ ὑψηλοτέρου καὶ μείζονος ἀ. Gr.Nyss.*or.catech.*23(p.86.10; M.45.61B); *ib.*24(p.93.1; 64D); **4.** *change of clothes*, Thdr.Stud.*poen.*29(M.99.1736D).

***ἀντάλληλος,** *mutually contradictory*, Max.*ep.*13(M.91.524B).

***ἀνταλλήλως,** *in return*, *Hymn.*(*AS* 1 p.460).

ἄνταλλος, *corresponding*, Leont.H.*Nest.*3(M.86.1636B).

ἀνταμείβομαι, 1. *render in return* τί ἀνταμειψώμεθα; σὲ θεαρχικώτατε λόγε *Lit.Jac.*(*NBP* 10^2 p.105); **2.** *requite* τὴν τῶν Ἑβραίων ἀρρένων μιαιφονίαν ὁμοίᾳ θεὸς ἀντημείψατο ἐκδικήσει Isid.Pel.*epp.* 1.198(M.78.309B); **3.** *reward*, *cat.Lc.*12:37(p.103.17); †Jo.D.*B.J.*28 (M.96.1125C).

ἀντάμειψις, ἡ, *reward*, *A.*(*Pass.*)*Andr.*11(p.27.24); *M.Ner.et Ach.* 5(p.4.12); Eus.Al.*serm.*21.2(M.86.425A).

ἀνταμοιβός, *corresponding*, Geo.Pis.*Pers.*2.133(M.92.1220B).

***ἀνταμφιέννυμι,** med., *put on instead*, Isid.Pel.*epp.*1.126(M.78. 268A); ‡Caes.Naz.*dial.*191(M.38.1169).

***ἀνταναβαίνω, 1.** *come into the place of* τῶν ἐθνῶν ἡ πληθὺς καὶ εἰς τὸν ἐκείνων ἀντανέβη κλῆρον Cyr.*Mich.*19(3.407E); id.*Jo.*3.6(4. 327B); **2.** *be absorbed* into, *identified* with οὐ γὰρ ἐπειδήπερ ὁμοούσιος ὑπῆρχεν ὁ προπάτωρ Ἀδάμ πως τῷ ἐξ αὐτοῦ φυντὶ παιδί, διὰ τοῦτο χωρήσει μὲν ὁ πατὴρ εἰς υἱόν, ἀνταναβήσεται δὲ αὖθις ὁ υἱὸς εἰς πατέρα *ib.*1.4(35A).

***ἀντανάγνωσις, ἡ,** *reading for the purpose of comparison* ἐκ τῆς ἑκατέρων ἀ. τὴν κακουργίαν τοῦ λογογράφου φωρᾶσαι Gr.Nyss.*Eun.*12 (1 p.343.3; M.45.1061C).

ἀνταναίρεσις, ἡ, *taking away*, Or.*princ.*4.1(p.299.13; M.11.349B).

ἀνταναιρετικός, *abolishing*, Leont.B.*Nest.et Eut.*3(M.86.1369A).

ἀνταναιρέω, *recover, get back*, Geo.Pis.*carm.*2.10,19.

***ἀνταναίρω,** *rebel*, *A.Thom.*A 141(p.248.8).

ἀντανακλασμός, ὁ, *flexion*; of muscular movements, Melet. *nat.hom.*15(M.64.1212A).

***ἀντανάκρασις, ἡ,** *fusion*, Cyr.*Jo.*11(4.996D).

***ἀντανακρούω,** *resist*, Steph.Diac.*v.Steph.*(M.100.1112A).

ἀνταναπληρ-όω, *compensate for* ὁ γνωστικὸς...τὴν ἀποστολικὴν ἀπουσίαν ~οῖ βιοὺς ὀρθῶς Clem.*str.*7.12(p.55.9; M.9.505B).

***ἀντανάπτω,** *kindle in return*, Geo.Pis.*hex.*1508(M.92.1551A).

***ἀνταναστρέφω,** *rebound*, Clem.*paed.*1.13(p.151.30; M.8.376A).

***ἀντανατείνω,** *lift up against*, Cyr.*Ps.*16:13(M.69.820B).

ἀντανατέλλω, *rise instead* of, Isid.Pel.*epp.*3.127(M.78.828B).

***ἀνταναφύω,** *spring up instead*, Cyr.*Mich.*19(3.408B); id.*hom. pasch.*24(5^2.287C); id.*ep.*31(p.73.26; 5^2.97D).

***ἀνταναφωνέω,** *shout in answer*, Didym.*Trin.*2.18(M.39.545B); Cyr.*inc.unigen.*(5^1.698B).

ἀντανεμία, ἡ, *contrary wind*, Cyr.S.*v.Jo.Hes.*15(p.213.9).

***ἀντάνεμος,** *blowing against*, Nil.*Eulog.*21(M.79.1120D).

***ἀντανέρχομαι,** *return*, Geo.Pis.*Pers.*3.168(M.92.1244B); id.*hex.* 203(M.92.1449A); id.*carm.*2.35.

ἀντανισόω, *compensate, make good*, Hipp.*haer.*1.19(p.20.11; M.16. 3041C); Synes.*provid.*2.6(p.126.10; M.66.1276B).

***ἀντανιστάω,** = ἀντανίστημι, *set up in rivalry*, Const.Diac.*laud.*9 (M.88.489C).

***ἀντανίσχω, 1.** *rise in turn*, Bas.*hex.*6.3(1.53A; M.29.124D); **2.** *correspond, match*, of Rome and Constantinople κάλλει δὲ κάλλος ἀ. συζύγως Gr.Naz.*carm.*2.1.11.567(M.37.1068A); **3.** *hold up in turn* to θεῷ τὰ ἀνθρώπου καὶ ἀνθρώπῳ τὰ θεοῦ ἀ. [sc. BMV] Thdr.Stud.*nativ. BMV* 7(M.96.696B).

***ἀνταξία, ἡ,** *equivalent*, Hipp.*antichr.*49(p.33.9, v.l. τὰ ἀντάξια M.10.769B).

ἀντάξιος, 1. *worthy*, v.l. for ἄξιον Chrys.*hom.57.3 in Mt.*(7.579C); Eudoc.*Cypr.*2.223(M.85.853C); **2.** *worthy instead* τοιοῦτον θηρίον ἀνάξιον ⟨μὲν⟩ τοῦ νεώ, χηραμοῦ δὲ...ἢ βορβόρου ἀ. Clem.*paed.*3.2 (p.238.14; M.8.560C); **3.** *worth as much as* ἀ. σωτηρίας μισθόν id. *prot.*9(p.64.22; M.8.197B); id.*str.*7.5(p.21.28; M.9.440A); id.*q.d.s.*21 (p.174.3; M.9.625D); of virginity τὸ δῶρον οὗ μηδὲν ἀ. ἄλλο προσενέγκασθαι πάρεστιν ἀνθρώποις θεῷ Meth.*symp.*5.1(p.53.7; M.18.97A); Bas.*hom.*13.3(2.116C; M.31.429C); **4.** esp. of Christ, *worthy* as a ransom *for* ὑπὲρ ἡμῶν ἑκάστου κατέθηκε τὴν ψυχὴν τὴν ἀ. τῶν ὅλων Clem.*q.d.s.*37(p.184.10.; M.9.641C); τῆς ἁπάντων ζωῆς ἀ. Cyr. *Chr.un.*(5^1.766C); id.*inc.unigen.*(5^1.692D); **5.** lit., *due in return*, hence *required for the satisfaction of justice* ᾗ δ' ἂν ἡμέρᾳ κριτὴς καθεσθῶ, ἀποδώσω τῶν ἁμαρτιῶν αὐτῶν τὰ ἀ. Clem.*paed.*1.7(p.124. 20; M.8.320B); Hipp.*antichr.*49(M.10.769B; l. ἀνταξίαν p.33.9); ἔργῳ καὶ ἐνεργείᾳ τὰ ἀ. ⟨ἀσ⟩κοῦντες εὐεργετήματα *Pap.Chr.*4.15.2.28 (p.443).

ἀνταπατάω, *deceive in return*, Gr.Nyss.*or.catech.*26(p.97.16; M.45. 68B).

ἀνταποδίδωμι, 1. *repay, give in return*, Clem.*str.*7.14(p.60.25; M.9.517B); τῷ προσενέγκαντι πολυπλασίως ἀ. *Hom.Clem.*3.70; *ib.* 16.20; Thdt.*qu.in 2Par.*(1.597); **2.** *offer* or *furnish an explanation*, Or.*comm.in Eph.*3:1(*JTS* 3 p.408).

ἀνταπόδομα, τό, *requital, retribution*, *Barn.*21.1; Thdt.*qu.in 2Par.*(1.597); Marc.Er.*opusc.*4(M.65.1013B); οὐκ ἔστι μοναχὸς ποιῶν ἀ. *Apophth.Patr.*(M.65.344C).

ἀνταπόδοσις, ἡ, 1. *requital, recompense, retribution*, Clem.*paed.* 1.8(p.131.8; M.8.333C); ἀ. ἁμαρτίας θάνατον σωτηρίας *ib.*2.1(p.159.10; 392A); †Bas.*Is.*233(1.556C; M.30.528B); Gr.Nyss.*v.Mos.*(M.44.352A); ἡ ἡμέρα τῆς ἀ. Nil.*epp.*3.18(M.79.377D); μηδὲ τὴν ἡτοιμασμένην ἀ. δεδοικώς Jo.Mosch.*prat.*43(M.87.2897A); πιστεύω καὶ εἰς...ἀ. τῶν πεπραγμένων ἑκάστῳ *Lit.Jac.*(*NBP* 10^2 p.38); *ib.*(*PO* 26 p.194.19); **2.** *reward* ἀ. τινα τῆς ἐργασίας τοῦ ἀγαθοῦ ἐλπίζειν Dor.*doct.*4.3 (M.88.1661A).

***ἀνταποδότης, ὁ,** *requiter*, *Did.*4.7; Chrys.*hom.22.2 in Heb.*(12. 205A); Thal.*cent.*1.63(M.91.1433B).

ἀνταποδοτικός, 1. *retributive*, Or.*princ.*3.1.16(p.224.13; M.11. 281B); Cyr.H.*catech.*18.4; Nil.*epp.*2.279(M.79.340C); **2.** *correlative*, Proc.G.*Gen.*1:16(M.87.340C).

ἀνταποδύ-ομαι, 1. *strip for contest with*, met. γεμίσας [sc. Christ] ...τὸ πᾶν πρὸς πάσας τὰς ἀερίους ἀρχὰς γυμνὸς ἀνταπεδύσατο Hipp. *pasch.fr.*7(p.270.27; M.10.864A); Synes.*calv.*4(p.196.11; M.66.1173A); hence **2.** *struggle against, contend with*; labours, Cyr.*hom.pasch.*19 (5^2.250B); heretics, id.*ep.*67(p.38.30; 5^2.195D); **3.** *conflict with* ἥ γε τῆς πίστεως παράδοσις τοῖς...σοῖς ~εται λόγοις id.*Nest.*1.2(p.20.3; 6.12B).

ἀνταποκρίν-ω, A. act.; *answer*, *A.Barth.*2(p.132.21).

B. med. and pass., **1.** *answer back, answer in turn*, Just.*1apol.* 17.2(M.6.353C); *T.Job* 5(p.106.18); *A.Barth.*1(p.130.17); Leont.N. *v.Jo.Eleem.*35(p.68.23); *Chron.Pasch.*p.395(M.92.1012B); **2.** *answer* an objection ἀνταπορούμενοι...ὑπὸ σοῦ...~ονται Epiph.*haer.*64.67 (p.509.26); †Leont.B.*sect.*5.6(M.86.1233A); **3.** *object* in answer, Meth. *symp.*10.3(p.125.20; M.18.197B); Epiph.*haer.*30.21(p.361.27; M.41. 441A).

ἀνταπόκρισις, ἡ, *reply*; to an objection, †Cyr.*hom.div.*10(5^2. 376C); to a letter, ‡Sophr.H.*v.m.Cyr.et Jo.*3(M.87.3680A).

***ἀνταποπέμπω,** *throw back*, Gr.Naz.*carm.*1.2.15.74(M.37.771A).

ἀνταπορέω, 1. *set a problem* to someone *in turn*, †Leont.B. *sect.*10.6(M.86.1265D); **2.** *meet a counter-objection*, Epiph.*haer.*64.67 (p.509.25); Leont.H.*monoph.*1(M.86.1769A).

***ἀνταπορρίπτω,** *relegate instead*, Or.*Jo.*32.6(5; p.435.21; M.14. 756D).

[*]**ἀνταποτίννυμι,** *repay*, Cyr.*fr.1Reg.*9:7(M.69.681B); of Christ σάρκα... τὴν ἰδίαν τῆς ἁπάντων σαρκὸς ἀ. id.*inc.unigen.*(5^1.692D).

ἀνταποφαίνω, 1. act., *show on the other hand*, Cyr.*Jo.*5.2(4.482E); **2.** med., *hold a contrary opinion*, Clem.*str.*7.16(p.67.29; M.9.533A); *ib.*8.2(p.81.26; 561C); Pall.*v.Chrys.*9(p.52.15; M.47.30).

ἀνταριθμέω, *count in turn*, Geo.Pis.*Sev.*262(M.92.1641A).

ἀνταρσία, ἡ, *rebellion*, Hesych.H.*Ps.tit.*58(M.27.881D); τῆς ἀ. τοῦ ἀνοσίου Βασιλίσκου κατὰ τῆς...ἐκκλησίας Gel.Cyz.*h.e.*1 proem.9 (M.85.1193D); Leont.B.*parasc.*(M.86.1992A); Jo.Eub.*innoc.*1(M.96. 1501A).

ἄνταρσις, ἡ *insurrection, revolt* τὴν...κατὰ τοῦ θεοῦ ἄ. Alex.Lyc. *Man.*5(M.18.417B); ἡ γὰρ προνοίας ἄρσις, ἄ. θεοῦ Gr.Naz.*carm.*1.1. 6.16(M.37.431); Gr.Nyss.*fat.*(M.45.173B); Epiph.*haer.*39.9(p.79.5; M. 41.676A); Cyr.*ador.*9(1.304E).

ἀντάρτης, ὁ, *rebel*; in gen., *Cod.Afr.*53; Cyr.S.*v.Sab.*74(p.178.25);

Chron.Pasch.p.301(M.92.756B); of Christ οὐκ ἔστιν ἀ. ἀλλὰ βασιλεύς Ammon.Jo.18:37(M.85.1509C); Vict.Mc.15:1(p.434.9); of antichrist, Apoc.Esd.46(p.29); of Devil ὁ ἄνω ἀ. Ast.Soph.hom.2 in Ps.5(M.40.412A); Chrys.exp.in Ps.3:1(5.5B); ὁ ἀρχαῖος ἀ. Isid.Pel. epp.1.180(M.78.300B); Cosm.Ind.top.2(M.88.120A); ‡Jo.D.hom.5(M.96.657A).

***ἀνταρτικῶς**, *rebelliously*, Jo.D.imag.3.33(M.94.1352D).

ἀνταστράπτω, *shine over against, shine in rivalry*, Paul.Sil.Soph. 770(M.86.2148B).

ἀνταύγεια, ἡ, *effulgence*, of a precious stone ὁποίοις γὰρ ἂν ἱματίοις κατακρυβῇ, ἡ ἀ. αὐτοῦ ἔξωθεν τῆς περιβολῆς φαίνεται Epiph. gemm.4(M.43.296D); of the sun in Pythagorean theory δεχόμενον μὲν τοῦ ἐν τῷ κόσμῳ πυρὸς τὴν ἀ., διηθοῦντα δὲ πρὸς ἡμᾶς τὸ φῶς Thdt.affect.4(p.105.24; 4.798).

ἀντεγγράφω, *write instead*, Chrys.hom.11.7 in Mt.(7.158E).

ἀντεγείρ-ω, **1.** *raise in opposition*, Gr.Nyss.Eun.11(2 p.273.6; M.45.884A); ἄλλο παρά τινων ~εται ἡμῖν θυσιαστήριον id.ep.3(M.46. 1024B); id.Steph.1(M.46.705D); med., *rise in opposition*, id.Eun.3(2 p.1.15; M.45.573A); id.v.Mos.(M.44.329D); Cyr.Jo.3(4.271C); **2.** *raise opposite* ἀλλήλαιν καὶ ἀντιπροσώπως ἀντεγηγερμέναιν Cyr.ador.9(1. 318D); **3.** *raise instead*, ib.2(59D); **4.** *extol in turn, in comparison*, Gr.Naz.ep.231(M.37.373C); Cyr.glaph.Gen.7(1.221D).

***ἀντεγκομίζω**, *bring up forces against*, Cyr.ador.3(1.87D).

***ἀντεγκύκλιον, τό**, *circular letter in opposition*, Evagr.h.e.3.7 (p.106.28; M.86.2609B).

***ἀντεικονίζω**, *portray instead*, Pamph.H.can.4 cit. s. θεανδρικός.

***ἀντεικόνισμα, τό**, *likeness*, Jo.Mal.chron.2 p.36(M.97.108A).

ἀντεισάγ-ω, **1.** *introduce in turn*, Clem.str.3.6(p.216.32; M.8. 1149A); Gr.Nyss.or.catech.28(p.107.4; M.45.73C); **2.** *introduce instead*, Clem.q.d.s.19(p.172.10; M.9.624); Meth.res.1.25(p.252.5; M.41. 1129C); σοφίαν...ἥντινα καὶ δημιουργὸν ~ουσι τοῦ κόσμου Ath.Ar. 2.38(M.26.228C); Gr.Naz.or.7.15(M.35.773C); Chrys.sac.1.7(p.16.7; 1. 367D); Thdt.Ezech.1:1(2.679).

ἀντεισαγωγή, ἡ, *introduction in place of*, hence *substitution* ἀ. δὲ τοῦ ὁμοουσίου τὸ ὅμοιον κατ' οὐσίαν †Apoll.ep.Bas.2(M.32.1108A); οὐκ ἄλλην προθεσμίαν ἐν ἄλλῃ ᾔτησεν ὁ Χριστός, ἢ τὴν τοῦ προβάτου σφαγήν, ὡς ἂν τὴν ἀ. ἐπιδείξειε ‡Chrys.pasch.7.4(8.281D); Euthal. Diac.Ac.(M.85.652C); Leont.B.Nest.et Eut.2(M.86.1345C).

***ἀντεισδρομή, ἡ**, *entrance instead*, Cyr.Is.5.4(2.818D).

ἀντείσειμι, *enter instead*, Gr.Nyss.or.catech.37(p.145.11; M.45. 96A); id.v.Macr.(p.409.21; M.46.996A); Socr.h.e.5.7.11(M.67.576B).

ἀντεισενεκτέον, *one must introduce instead*, Synes.regn.25(p.56. 1; M.66.1101C).

***ἀντεισκαλέω**, *call in instead*, Cyr.glaph.Gen.3(1.100E).

***ἀντεισκομίζω**, *bring in instead*, Cyr.Jo.10.2(4.870E).

ἀντεισκρίν-ω, *introduce instead* θεοῦ ~οντος ἐν ἡμῖν τὸ θέλειν ἀγαθουργεῖν Cyr.Is.5.4(2.818E); ib.(821C); ib.4.1(561B).

***ἀντεισοικίζω**, *make to dwell instead*, Jo.D.hom.11.11(M.96. 773C).

***ἀντειστρέχω**, *enter as an enemy*, Cyr.ador.6(1.202A).

ἀντεισφέρ-ω, *introduce correspondingly* ὁ νόμος...τὴν κατ' αὐτὸν ἱερουργίαν ~ει δὲ ὥσπερ τὴν ἐν Χριστῷ λέγων Cyr.ador.17(1.629B); συνεισάγων [sc. ὁ υἱός] μὲν ἑαυτῷ τὴν περὶ τοῦ πνεύματος γνῶσιν, ~όμενος δὲ αὖθις διὰ τῆς τοῦ πατρὸς ἐπωνυμίας ὡς υἱός id.thes.32(5. 286C).

ἀντεισφορά, ἡ, *substitution*, Martin.ep.3(M.PL.87.141C); Geo. Pis.carm.4.5.

***ἀντεκήνσωρ, ὁ**, (Lat. *antecessor*) *teacher of law*, Nil.epp.1.192 tit. (M.79.156A).

***ἀντεκλογή, ἡ**, *opposing selection*, Leont.H.Nest.1.7(M.86. 1428B).

ἀντεκφέρω, *adduce in reply*, Sophr.H.v.Anast.(M.92.1704C).

ἀντεκφύω, *produce in turn*, Andr.Cr.or.14(M.97.1093C).

ἀντελλογέω, *reckon against*, Marc.Er.opusc.2.41(M.65.936D).

ἀντέμβασις, ἡ, *interpenetration*, Jo.D.dialect.65(M.94.664B).

ἀντεμβιβάζ-ω, *replace one by another, substitute* (ref. Jo.14:10) οὐ γὰρ...~όμενοι εἰς ἀλλήλους εἰσὶν...ὥσπερ ἐν ἀγγείοις κενοῖς ἐξ ἀλλήλων πληρούμενοι Ath.Ar.3.1(M.26.324B); οὐ προσήκει νοεῖν... [sc. τὸν υἱόν] ~εσθαι...τῷ πατρί, οὗτος δὲ ἐν ἐκείνῳ, κἀκεῖνος ἐν τούτῳ φαίνεται Cyr.Jo.1.3(4.28D).

***ἀντεμβιβασμός, ὁ**, *replacement of one by another, substitution*, materialistic conception of heretics εἰ καθάπερ σῶμα ἐν σώματι χωρεῖν...τὸν υἱὸν ἐν πατρί, εἰκότως ἂν...καὶ ζητεῖν ἔλοισθε τὸν εἰς ἀλλήλους ἀ. Cyr.thes.12(5^1.107A).

ἀντεμβολή, ἡ, **1.** *mutual incursion* λόγος...καὶ σοφία διὰ...τὴν εἰς ἄλληλα...ἀ. Cyr.Jo.1.5(4.47A); Jo.D.dialect.65(M.94.664B) cit. s. κρᾶσις; **2.** *substitution* πολλαῖς ἀ. λόγων...λανθάνειν πειρώμενοι Leont.H.Nest.4.3(M.86.1656D).

ἀντεμπαίζω, *trick in turn*, Pall.h.Laus.100(M.34.1204B).

ἀντεμπλοκή, ἡ, **1.** *combination*; of atoms, Bas.hex.1.2(1.3B; M.29. 8B); Gr.Nyss.Eun.12(1 p.277.25; M.45.984D); τὴν ἀ. ἔμπαλιν ἐχούσης τῆς θεολογίας τῇ οἰκονομίᾳ Leont.B.Nest.et Eut.1(M.86.1309B); **2.** *conflict* ἀ. γὰρ συγκροτεῖται καὶ μάχη τῶν σῶν ἀγώνων νῦν ὁμοῦ μεμιγμένων Geo.Pis.Heracl.1.223(M.92.1315B).

***ἀντενάγω**, *bring forward in opposition*, Cod.Afr.120; ? *prosecute in turn*, Ath.Scholast.coll.1.2(p.11).

***ἀντεναγωγή, ἡ**, *counter-charge*, Ath.Scholast.coll.5.1(p.71).

ἀντένδειξις, ἡ, *change of indication* or *description*, Leont.H.Nest. 3.8(M.86.1637D) cit. s. ἀντωνομασία.

ἀντενδύομαι, *put on instead*, Ath.inc.44.5(M.25.176A).

***ἀντένεξις, ἡ**, *holding out against*, Andr.Caes.Apoc.26(M.106. 625D).

***ἀντενθρονίζω**, *enthrone instead*, Geo.Pis.Heracl.2.177(M.92. 1329A).

ἀντεξάγ-ω, **A.** act.; **1.** *lead out against* Ἰησοῦ...Ἀμαλεκίταις τὸν στρατὸν ~οντος Gr.Nyss.v.Mos.43(M.44.313C); **2.** *adduce in opposition, set in opposition* τὸ πνεῦμα ᾧ...ἑαυτοὺς ~ουσι id.Maced.21 (M.45.1328C); ~ουσι...ταῖς τοῦ διαβόλου δυστροπίαις τὸ...ἀκατάσειστον Cyr.glaph.Dt.(1.421C); id.Abac.10(3.525D); τὴν τῶν πατέρων ὁμολογίαν...ἀ. id.apol.Thdt.1(p.112.2; 6^1.205E); **3.** intrans.; **a.** *oppose, withstand* δόγμασιν id.ador.11(1.397A); id.Is.3.3(2.455D); id.ep.40 (p.25.25; 5^2.115B); **b.** *come to meet*, Proc.G.ep.136(77; M.87.2780A); **c.** abs., *be in opposition* βλασφήμως ἀ. Didym.Trin.1.8(M.39.276C). **B.** med., *oppose*, Gr.Naz.or.25.16(M.35.1221A).

***ἀντεξαγωγή, ἡ**, **1.** *setting up in opposition*, Gr.Nyss.ep.3(M.46. 1024A); **2.** *contrast*, Cyr.Is.5.6(2.905B).

ἀντεξανίσταμαι, *rise up against*, Cyr.hom.pasch.9(5^2.118A); ib.11 (154E).

***ἀντεξαποστέλλω**, *send on in turn, forward* μίαν τῶν...ἐπιστολῶν ἀντεξαπέστειλά σοι Jo.VI H.v.Jo.D.16(M.94.456B).

***ἀντεξηγέομαι**, *interpret in a hostile sense*, Or.Cels.5.65(p.68.21; M.11.1288B).

ἀντεπάγ-ω, **1.** *introduce in turn* ἡ δὲ πίστις ἔδρασμα ἀγάπης ~ουσα τὴν εὐποιίαν Clem.str.2.6(p.129.9; M.8.965B); †Gregent.disp.(M.86. 656B); **2.** *object in turn*, Chrys.hom.32.1 in Jo.(8.184B); id.hom.13.3 in Mt.(7.171C); Cyr.thes.7(5^1.53A); **3.** med., *assume correspondingly* τῆς μὲν ἐνθέου δυνάμεως τῷ θνητῷ χορηγῶν, τῆς δ' ἐκ τοῦ θνητοῦ μετουσίας οὐκ ~όμενος Eus.d.e.4.13(p.172.22; M.22.288B); ib.7.1 (p.302.15; 496A).

***ἀντεπαγωγή, ἡ**, *counter-attack*, Cyr.Jo.11.12(4.1017D).

***ἀντεπαίρω**, *exalt against*, Gr.Nyss.Eun.12(1 p.229.29; M.45. 925C).

***ἀντεπαπορέω**, *raise a further difficulty*, Epiph.haer.64.67(p.509. 13).

***ἀντεπαρύομαι**, *partake of in return*, Eus.l.C.14(p.243.18; M.20. 1412B).

ἀντεπεισάγω, *introduce instead*, Thdr.Mops.Eph.4:22(p.173.23).

ἀντεπεξάγω, *contrast with*, Chrys.hom.8.3 in Rom.(9.502A).

ἀντεπεξέρχομαι, *retaliate*, Chrys.hom.16.2 in Eph.(11.119B).

ἀντεπερώτησις, ἡ, *counter-question*, Iren.haer.1.20.2(M.7.656A); Cyr.thes.4(5^1.29D).

ἀντεπηχέω, *resound instead*, Const.Diac.laud.27(M.88.509C).

***ἀντεπίβουλος**, *plotting against*, Jo.Clim.scal.6(M.88.797B).

***ἀντεπιζεύγνυμι**, *link up with*, Iren.haer.1.17.1(M.7.637B).

***ἀντεπίθυμος**, *lusting against*, Nil.Eulog.6(M.79.1101A).

***ἀντεπικλάω**, *break in turn*, Geo.Pis.hex.1005(M.92.1512A).

***ἀντεπίσκοπος, ὁ**, *rival bishop*, Gr.Naz.carm.2.1.11.456(M.37. 1060A).

***ἀντεπίσπαστος**, *correspondingly brought upon* ταῖς σφῶν αὐτῶν ἀπειθείαις ἀ. ἐφ' ἑαυτοῖς ἐχόντων τὴν νόσον Cyr.Jo.6.1(4.634C; αὐτ- Pusey p.204.15).

ἀντεπισπάω, *draw over*, Cyr.ador.10(1.336D).

***ἀντεπίστ-αμαι**, *rival in knowledge* πῶς γὰρ οἷόν τε ~ασθαι τῷ θεῷ; Clem.str.2.4(conj. ἀντεφ- p.121.7; ἀνεπ- M.8.948A).

***ἀντεπιστολή, ἡ**, *letter in reply*, Epiph.anc.1 tit.(v.l. ἐπιστολή p.5.1; M.43.17).

ἀντεπιστρέφω, *turn against*, Jo.Mosch.prat.110(M.87.2973C).

ἀντεπιστροφή, ἡ, *corresponding movement* οἱονεὶ γὰρ ἀ. τίς ἐστι τῆς προνοίας ἡ τοῦ γνωστικοῦ ὁσιότης Clem.str.7.7(p.31.30; M.9. 457C).

ἀντεπιφέρω, *bring* an argument *against*, Gr.Nyss.Eun.4(2 p.62. 14; M.45.633B).

ἀντεπιχείρησις, ἡ, *rebutting force*, Or.*comm.in Eph.*2:2(p.403).

***ἀντεπιχέω**, *pour in alternately*, Hipp.*haer.*6.40(p.171.15; M.16.3258C).

***ἀντεπιχωριάζω**, *be interchangeable*, Bas.*Spir.*12(3.10A; M.32.85C).

***ἀντεργάτης**, ὁ, *opponent*, Bas.*renunt.*6(2.208B; M.31.640C).

***ἀντεργάτις**, ἡ, *substitute* οὐδεὶς...τὴν χεῖρα κιχρᾷ τῶν ποδῶν ἀ. Geo.Pis.*Heracl.*1.48(M.92.1302A).

***ἀντέρεισμα**, τό, **1.** *support*, Bas.*hex.*1.9(1.9C; M.29.21C); **2.** *obstacle*, Geo.Pis.*Pers.*2.352(M.92.1234A).

***ἀντεριδαίνω**, *contend*, Nonn.*par.Jo.*7:12(M.43.805C).

ἀντερίζω, *strive against*, Geo.Pis.*Heracl.*1.137(M.92.1310A).

***ἀντερώτημα**, τό, *rebutting question*, Or.*comm.in Mt.*17.1(p.577.1; M.13.1473C).

***ἀντερωτηματως**, *by questioning in turn*, Thdr.Stud.*antirr.*3.3.11 tit.(M.99.425A).

***ἀντερώτησις**, ἡ, = ἀντερώτημα, Socr.*h.e.*6.22.7(M.67.728B); Cosm.Mel.*schol.*119(M.38.561).

***ἀντερωτητέον**, *one must ask in return*, Clem.*str.*8.4(p.85.22; M.9.572B); Anast.S.*hod.*3(M.89.88D).

***ἀντευλογέω**, *bless in return*, Cyr.*Lc.*10:4(p.103.13; M.72.668A).

***ἀντευφημέω**, *praise in turn*, Amph.*hom.*1.5(M.39.44A); Synes.*ep.*17(M.66.1353A).

***ἀντευφραίνω**, *gladden in turn*, Gr.Nyss.*mort.*(M.46.536C); Cyr.*Mich.*54(3.446D).

ἀντεφίστημι, med., *withstand*, Clem.*str.*2.4(conj. for ἀντεπ- p.121.7; ἀντεπίστασθαι M.8.948A).

***ἀντιβαδιάζ-ω**, *obstruct* ἐὰν τεχνίτην...~ῃ †Gregent.*leg.Hom.*44 (M.86.605A), perh. for ἀντιβιάζῃ or ἀντιβαδίζει.

ἀντιβάλλω, *converse, communicate*, *Hom.Clem.*1.15; *ib.*1.16; οἱ διάκονοι...τῷ ἐπισκόπῳ ἀ. *ib.*3.67; Epiph.*haer.*30.9(p.344.27; M.41.421A); *ib.*71.1(p.250.23; M.42.376C).

***ἀντιβασανίζω**, *investigate in turn*, Or.*hom.14.3 in Jer.*(p.108.19; M.13.408B).

ἀντιβιάζομαι, *force in the opposite direction*, Sophr.H.*v.Anast.*(M.92.1708D).

ἀντιβλέπω, *look in the face*; hence **1.** *withstand, oppose*, Or.*Jo.*2.14(8; p.70.35; M.14.137D); ἀ. τῷ κυρίῳ *ib.*10.30(18; p.204.21; 361D); ἀ. τῇ γραφῇ id.*engast.*3(p.284.26; M.12.1016A); id.*Cels.*1.52(p.103.13; M.11.757A); τούτοις δὲ πᾶσιν ἀ. δύνασθαι οὐδὲ τοὺς σφόδρα ἀγνωμονεστάτους ἡγοῦμαι Eus.*d.e.*3.2(p.107.19; M.22.185A); Ath.*Dion.*3 (p.47.27; M.25.484A); **2.** *face* a difficulty πρὸς...τοὺς ἀγῶνας τούτους οὐδὲ ἀ. ἴσχυσεν Chrys.*ep.*2.7(3.542E); **3.** *bear comparison* [sc. ὁ Ἰώβ] πρὸς...Παῦλον ἀ. δυνάμενος id.*ecl.*36(12.714D); cf.id.*laud.Paul.*1(2.479E παρισοῦσθαι).

ἀντιβοάω, **1.** *shout in opposition*, Gr.Nyss.*Eun.*10(2 p.242.15; M.45.845A); **2.** *cry in response*, Jo.Mosch.*prat.*110(M.87.2973C); **3.** *cry on behalf of, make supplication for*, *A.Thom.*A 139(p.246.8).

ἀντιβολέω, *meet as suppliant, entreat*, c. inf., Thdt.*Is.*25:5(p.101.35; ἀντιβουλόμενος 2.294).

ἀντιβολή, ἡ, *discussion, disputation*, Epiph.*haer.*66.10(p.30.28; M.42.44C); Marc.Er.*opusc.*7 tit.(M.65.1072A); †Jo.D.*B.J.*25(M.96.1092C).

***ἀντιβουκολέω**, *foster instead*, ‡Just.*ep.Zen.et Ser.*10(M.6.1196A).

***ἀντιβούλομαι**, *wish the reverse*, prob. f.l. for ἀντιβολέω q.v.

***ἀντιγελάω**, *turn the laugh against*, Gr.Nyss.*Eun.*1(1 p.194.16; M.45.440D).

***ἀντιγεμίζω**, *refill*, Amph.*hom.*3.5(M.39.65A).

ἀντιγεννάω, *beget in turn* ὁ λόγος ἐν ἀρχῇ γεννηθεὶς ἀντεγέννησε τὴν καθ' ἡμᾶς ποίησιν Tat.*orat.*5(p.6.8; M.6.817A); Cyr.H.*catech.*7.16; Chrys.*ecl.*27(12.636B).

***ἀντίγομφος**, *fixed in opposition*, Geo.Pis.*hex.*1691(M.92.1566A).

ἀντίγραμμα, τό, *letter in defence*, Jo.Nic.*nativ.*6(M.96.1448C).

ἀντιγραφεύς, ὁ, (Lat. *magister scriniorum*) *chief secretary of state*, *Chron.Pasch.*p.380(M.92.973B).

ἀντιγραφή, ἡ, *imperial rescript*, Eus.*h.e.*4.8.8(M.20.325B); Pall.*v.Chrys.*11(p.64.18; M.47.37).

ἀντίγραφον, τό, **1.** *copy*; of a document, Just.*1apol.*68.4(M.6.432B); †Hipp.*Artem.*ap.Eus.*h.e.*5.28.16(M.20.516B); Ath.*syn.*10 (p.237.1; M.26.696B); esp. of scriptures, Or.*hom.8.1 in Jer.*(p.55.19; M.13.336B); Bas.*reg.br.*251(2.500A; M.31.1249C); Chrys.*hom.17.1 in Jo.*(8.96D); **2.** *letter*, Chrys.*ep.*123(3.664A); **3.** *reply*, Synes.*ep.*67 (M.66.1432B); Marc.Diac.*v.Porph.*27.

***ἀντιδανείζω**, *lend in turn*, Chrys.*pan.Rom.*2.2(2.619C).

ἀντίδειξις, ἡ, *substitute, counterpart* ὁ εἰς ἀ. τῆς τριάδος γενόμενος ἄνθρωπος Leont.B.*Nest.et Eut.*3(M.86.1372C); τῆς σαρκὸς διδομένης, τὸν ἴδιον υἱὸν δίδοσθαι λέγει ἡ γραφή, ἀντάλλαγμα καὶ ἀ. οὖσαν τοῦ υἱοῦ κατὰ τὸν τύπον τοῦ...Ἰσαάκ Cosm.Ind.*top.*5(M.88.241C).

***ἀντιδειπνίζω**, *entertain in return*, Or.*Jo.*13.32(31; p.257.7; M.14.456A).

***ἀντιδέξιος**, *taking the hand of another*, Chrysipp.*enc.in Mich.* (p.91.8).

***ἀντιδέρω**, *strike back, resist*, Ephr.1.88A; *Apophth.Patr.*(M.65.336A); Dor.*doct.*5.2(M.88.1677A).

ἀντιδέχ-ομαι **1.** *receive instead* ἀντὶ τούτου τοῦ ἔθνους πάντα τὰ ἔθνη...~θήσεται παρὰ τοῦ θεοῦ Thdr.Heracl.*Is.*29:17(M.18.1320C); **2.** *take up* a refrain from others καὶ γὰρ τετράμορφα ζῷα ἀντιφωνητικῶς ἀλλήλων ~όμενα βοῶσι ‡Bas.*h.myst.*60(p.394.14).

***ἀντιδηλόω**, *state in reply*, Pall.*v.Chrys.*17(p.109.4; M.47.60); Philost.*h.e.*7.6[a](p.84.24); Jo.Mal.*chron.*13 p.328(M.97.489C).

ἀντιδημιουργ-έω, *create in rivalry* πῶς οὖν ~οῦσι τῷ θεῷ; Clem.*paed.*3.3(p.246.13; M.8.580A); Gr.Naz.*or.*8.10(M.35.800C).

***ἀντιδιάθεσις**, ἡ, *antagonism*, †Bas.*Is.*199(1.528C; M.30.462C).

***ἀντιδιαιρετικός**, *distinguishing, making a distinction*, Gr.Nyss.*Eun.*12(1 p.294.8; M.45.1004C).

ἀντιδιάκειμαι, *be logically contrasted*, Gr.Nyss.*Apoll.*37(M.45.1205D).

ἀντιδιαλέγομαι, *answer in discussion*, Clem.*paed.*2.7(p.192.5; M.8.461B).

***ἀντιδιάμετρος**, *opposed*, Jo.Mosch.*prat.*187(M.87.3065A).

***ἀντιδιασταλτέον**, *one must contrast*, Or.*Jo.*10.45(29; p.224.10; M.14.396D).

***ἀντιδιάστασις**, ἡ, *opposition*, Gr.Nyss.*Eun.*10(2 p.244.18; M.45.848B).

ἀντιδιαστέλλ-ω, *contradistinguish*, Or.*fr.in Pr.*1:3(M.17.153B); id.*Jo.*10.13(p.183.14; M.14.328B); †Bas.*Is.*119(1.461E; M.30.312A); ἀ. τῷ νόμῳ τὰ διὰ Χριστοῦ Cyr.*Ps.*24:10(M.69.849B); τῷ...μέρει τὸ...πᾶν ~εται Isid.Pel.*epp.*3.243(M.78.921C); of theol. distinctions εἰ τὸ ἀγέννητον οὐσίας ἐστὶ δηλωτικόν, εἰκότως πρὸς τὴν τοῦ γεννήματος οὐσίαν ~εται Aët.*synt.*16(p.355.8; M.42.581D); οὐκ ἔστι καθ' ὑπόστασιν εἰπεῖν τὸ μὴ ὂν ~εσθαι πρὸς τὸ ὂν Gr.Nyss.*or.catech.*6(p.33.6; M.45.28C); οὐκ οἶδ' ὅπως οὐσίαν ~ει τῷ γράμματι *ib.*7(p.152.17; 581D); Didym.(‡Bas.)*Eun.*4(1.283A; M.29.681A); *ib.*(284A; M.684A); ἐπειδὴ ~ομένη [sc. ἡ ἀνθρωπίνη ἐνέργεια] τῇ θείᾳ ἐνεργείᾳ, πάθος λέγεται κατὰ τοῦτο Max.*Pyrr.*(M.91.349C).

ἀντιδιαστολή, ἡ, **1.** *contradistinction*, Clem.*paed.*1.5(p.102.1; M.8.273B); ὁ ἀπόστολος πρὸς ἀ. γνωστικῆς τελειότητος τὴν κοινὴν πίστιν πῇ μὲν θεμέλιον λέγει id.*str.*5.4(p.342.2; M.9.45A); φῶς δὲ ἀληθινὸν οὐ πρὸς ἀ. ψεύδους, ἀλλὰ πρὸς διαφορὰν εἰκονικοῦ εἴρηται Or.*fr.6 in Jo.*1:8(p.488.13); ἀληθινὸς γὰρ πρὸς ἀ. σκιᾶς καὶ τύπου καὶ εἰκόνος id.*Jo.*2.6(4; p.60.16; M.14.120A); πρὸς γὰρ ἀ. τῶν οὐκ ἰδίων, αὐτὸν ἴδιον υἱὸν ἔφησεν εἶναι Alex.Al.*ep.Alex.*8(p.24.27; M.18.560B); κατὰ ἀντιδιαστολὴν τοῦ μὴ ὄντος ὁ ὢν ἑαυτὸν εἶναί φησιν Marcell.*fr.*58 ap.Eus.*e.th.*2.19(p.123.17; M.24.944B); τὸ πνεῦμα...πρὸς ἀ. τοῦ σωματικοῦ Ath.*ep.Serap.*4.19(M.26.665C); ἵνα τῇ πρὸς τὸ γεννητὸν ἀ. τὸν τῆς ἀνομοιότητος κακουργήσωσι τρόπον Gr.Nyss.*Eun.*1(1 p.156.2; M.45.397A); πρὸς τὰ κτίσματα...νοεῖν τὰς ἀ. δεῖ, οὐκ εἰς τὸν πατέρα καὶ τὸν υἱόν Didym.(‡Bas.)*Eun.*4(1.294B; M.29.705B); σκιὰ θανάτου καὶ ὁ φυσικὸς καὶ κοινὸς θάνατος πρὸς ἀ. τοῦ προαιρετικοῦ θανάτου, τοῦ τῆς ψυχῆς Cyr.*Ps.*22:4(M.69.841B); κατὰ ἀ. αὐτῆς [sc. BMV] ὑπ' αὐτοῦ ἐμακαρίσθησαν ἕτεροι ‡Just.*qu.et resp.*136(M.6.1388D); ἡ γὰρ καθ' ὑπόστασιν ἕνωσις, πρὸς τὴν διαίρεσιν ἔχουσα τὴν ἀ. ... τῆς μὲν ποιεῖται τελείαν ἀναίρεσιν, τῆς δὲ παγίαν ἐργάζεται τήρησιν Max.*ep.*14(M.91.536B); id.*schol.c.h.*2.4(M.4.44D); προσηγόρευσαν γὰρ αὐτὴν [sc. τὴν ἀνθρωπίνην κίνησιν] καὶ δύναμιν καὶ ἐνέργειαν...οὐ κατὰ ἀ. τῆς θείας ἀλλ' ὡς συνεκτικὴν μὲν καὶ ἀναλλοίωτον δύναμιν id.*Pyrr.*(M.91.352A); **2.** *counter-dilatation* τὴν τοῦ πνεύμονος πρὸς τὸν θώρακα ἀ. Clem.*str.*7.6(p.24.10; M.9.444B).

ἀντιδιατάσσω, *oppose*, Or.*Cels.*2.68(p.189.22; M.11.901C); †Bas.*Is.*26(1.399C; M.30.168B); Didym.(‡Bas.)*Eun.*5(1.306D; M.29.736A).

ἀντιδίδωμι, **1.** *give in exchange* ὑπὲρ σοῦ τὴν ψυχὴν ἀντιδώσω τὴν ἐμήν Clem.*q.d.s.*42(p.190.7; M.9.649C); Gr.Naz.*ep.*232(M.37.376A); Χριστὸς πάντων ἀνθρώπων ἀντιδοθεὶς Proc.G.*Num.*3:45(M.87.801A); **2.** *exchange with* τῇ ὑστεραίᾳ ἀντιδιδόασιν ἀλλήλοις, καὶ τὸ πλέον τῆς ἀθυμίας ἐκεῖνος δέχεται Chrys.*hom.5.4 in Ac.*(9.46B); **3.** *give back* προσεύχεται ὁ...υἱὸς ὅπως ὃ ἔλαβεν παρὰ τοῦ πατρὸς ἀντιδῷ καὶ αὐτὸς τῷ πατρί Leont.B.*parasc.*(M.86.1996D); **4.** *give reciprocally*, Christol., of *communicatio idiomatum* (v. ἀντίδοσις) αἱ ὑπολήψεις καὶ δόξαι τῆς κατὰ τὸν ἕνα...Χριστὸν φύσεως ἑκατέρας ἀντιδίδονται πολλάκις ἑκατέρᾳ ‡Gr.Nyss.*hom.10.33 in Jo.*(p.305.19); Leont.B.*Nest.et Eut.*1(M.86.1304C); ἥ τε γὰρ διαιρετικὴ [sc. ἕνωσις] σχετική τις οὖσα, καὶ μηδὲ τὴν ἀρχὴν τὰς φύσεις συνάπτουσα, κεχωρισμένα ἀλλήλων καταλείπει τὰ πράγματα, μηδ' ὅσα κοινά, μηδ' ὅσα ἴδια, τούτοις διδοῦσα ἢ ἀντιδιδοῦσα id.*arg.Sev.*(M.86.1940D); τῆς κατ' οὐσίαν ἑνώσεως ἀντιδιδούσης τὰ τῇ θατέρᾳ φύσει προσόντα τῇ θατέρᾳ Pamph. H.*panopl.*9.4(p.634); ‡Cyr.*Trin.*27(6^{3}.35E; M.77.1172D).

ἀντιδικαιολογέω, *plead the contrary, contradict,* Alex.Sal.*Barn.*40 (p.450E).

***ἀντιδικομαριανίτης,** ὁ, *Adversary of Mary, Antidicomarianite,* name given to 4th-cent. heretics from Arabia who denied perpetual virginity of BMV, Epiph.*haer.*78 tit.(p.452.1; M.42.700B).

***ἀντιδογματίζω,** *pronounce a doctrine contrary to,* †Bas.*Is.*172 (1.504A; M.30.408A); Gr.Nyss.*hex.*6(M.44.68B); of Eunomius ἀ. τοῖς εὐαγγελίοις id.*Eun.*1(1 p.77.13; M.45.308B).

ἀντιδοξάζ-ω, **1.** *hold a contrary opinion,* Eus.*Marcell.*1.3(p.16. 20; M.24.748C); δι' αὐτοῦ τούτου κατηγορεῖται ἡ βλασφημία ὅτι τοῖς ἁγίοις προφήταις ~ει τῷ λόγῳ Gr.Nyss.*Eun.*2(2 p.385.10; M.45. 568A); **2.** *glorify in return* ὃν οὕτω δοξάζοντα τὸν ἑαυτοῦ πατέρα ἀμοιβαίως ~ων ὁ πατήρ Eus.*e.th.*1.11(p.70.17; M.24.845B); Niceph. Ur.*v.Sym.*49(M.86.3032B); Jo.Mon.*hymn.Geo.*3(M.96.1396B); *Lit.Bas.* (p.343.23).

***ἀντιδοξία,** ἡ, *contradictory opinion,* Eus.*p.e.*14.9(739D; M.21. 1217A).

ἀντίδοσις, ἡ, **1.** *exchange* ἀ. χοϊκῶν πρὸς πνευματικά (cf. 2Cor. 8:14) Or.*Jo.*32.22(p.464.25; M.14.804B); κατ' ἀντίδοσιν πλήττειν [i.e. reciprocally] Const.ap.Ath.*apol.sec.*62(p.141.30; M.25.361A); κοινωνίαν τὸ πρᾶγμα καλεῖ δεικνὺς ἀ. γινομένην (cf. 1Cor.9:11) Chrys. *comm.in Gal.*6:6(10.725D); Christol., of reciprocal relations between natures, by which human attributes can be predicated of one who is God, and divine of one who is Man ἐπειδὴ τὸν Χριστὸν Ἰησοῦν αὐτὸν εἶναι τὸν πρὸ αἰώνων υἱὸν ἀπεφήναντο, ὅρα πῶς πάλιν τὸν πρὸ αἰώνων μονογενῆ δεικνύουσιν ἄνθρωπον γεγενημένον· ταῖς ἀ. ταύταις τῆς σωτηρίου οἰκονομίας τὴν ἕνωσιν ἐφιστῶντες Thdot.Anc. *exp.symb.*16(M.77.1336D); διὰ τῆς ἀ. τῶν ἰδίων καθορᾶται [sc. ἡ ἕνωσις] Leont.H.*monoph.*10(M.86.1776D); Max.*opusc.*(M.91.189D); *ib.*(240A); id.*Pyrr.*(M.91.296D); οὗτός ἐστιν ὁ τρόπος τῆς ἀ., ἑκατέρας φύσεως ἀντιδούσης τῇ ἑτέρᾳ τὰ ἴδια, διὰ τὴν τῆς ὑποστάσεως ταυτότητα καὶ τὴν εἰς ἄλληλα αὐτῶν περιχώρησιν. κατὰ τοῦτο δυνάμεθα εἰπεῖν περὶ Χριστοῦ, 'οὗτος ὁ θεὸς ἡμῶν ἐπὶ τῆς γῆς ὤφθη',...καί, 'ὁ ἄνθρωπος οὗτος ἄκτιστός ἐστι καὶ ἀπαθής' ‡Cyr.*Trin.*27(6^{3}.33E; M.77. 1172D); μεταδίδωσι τῇ σαρκὶ τῶν ἰδίων, κατὰ τὸν ἀντιδόσεως τρόπον, διὰ τὴν εἰς ἄλληλα τῶν μερῶν περιχώρησιν καὶ τὴν καθ' ὑπόστασιν ἕνωσιν Jo.D.*f.o.*3.3(M.94.993D); id.*Jacob.*81(M.94.1480B); ἀ. τῶν ἰδιωμάτων = Lat. *communicatio idiomatum*: υἱὸν ἀνθρώπου τὸν λόγον ὀνομάζοντες, καὶ κύριον τῆς δόξης ἐσταυρῶσθαι ὁμολογοῦντες· ἀλλ' οὐ παρὰ τοῦτο τῇ ἀ. τῶν ἰδιωμάτων ἀναιροῦμεν τὸν ἴδιον λόγον τῆς θατέρου ἐν ταυτῷ ἰδιότητος Leont.B.*Nest.et Eut.*1(M.86.1289C); οὐ...ἀ. ἂν τῶν ἰδιωμάτων ἐγίνετο, εἰ μὴ ἐν ἑκατέρῳ ἔμεινε, καὶ ἐν τῇ ἑνώσει ἡ ἰδιότης ἀκίνητος id.*arg.Sev.*(M.86.1941A); Leont.H.*monoph.*25(M. 86.1785C); **2.** *repayment, return* οἷον ἄνθρωποι τρεῖς, καὶ θεοὶ τρεῖς οὐχὶ τρία τάδε καὶ τάδε. τίς γὰρ ἡ ἀ.; τοῦτο νομοθετοῦντός ἐστι τοῖς ὀνόμασιν, οὐκ ἀληθεύοντος Gr.Naz.*or.*31.19(p.168.2; M.36.153B); ἐπὶ μὲν τοῦ θεοῦ χάρις ἦν...ἐπὶ δὲ ἡμῶν ἀ. Chrys.*hom.4.2 in 2Tim.*(11. 681E); τῶν ὕμνων αὐτῷ προσφέρειν τὰς ἀ. [i.e. thanksgivings] Thdt. *Ps.*28:1(1.779); hence *requital* κρίσις ἔσται καὶ ἀ. Chrys.*hom.31.5 in Rom.*(9.753D); ‡Just.*qu.et resp.*13(M.6.1261B); *retribution* ἄλλοι τὰς ἀμοιβὰς τῆς κακίας ἐπισκοπήσαντες θεοποιοῦσι τὰς ἀ. προσκυνοῦντες καὶ τὰς συμφοράς Clem.*prot.*2(p.19.19; M.8.96A); ἡ...τοῦ κατ' ἀξίαν ἀ. δι' ἧς ὁ ἀπατεὼν ἀνταπατᾶται, τὸ δίκαιον δείκνυσι Gr.Nyss. *or.catech.*26(p.97.16; M.45.68B); εἰς ποίαν ἀπίασι κόλασιν ἐν τῷ τοῦ τελοῦς καὶ τῆς ἀ. καιρῷ; Oecum.*Apoc.*19:11–16(p.206); but more often *compensation, reward,* Gr.Naz.*or.*40.12(M.36.373C); νῦν μὲν κατὰ τὸν βίον, μετὰ ταῦτα δὲ κατὰ τὴν αἰωνίαν ἀ. [i.e. future life] Gr. Nyss.*or.catech.*40(p.164.7; M.45.105B); ὑπερβαίνω σου τοὺς πόνους ταῖς ἀ. Chrys.*hom.76.4 in Mt.*(7.738B); Isid.Pel.*epp.*2.29(M.78.477A); Thdt.*h.e.*5.32.6(3.1072).

ἀντίδοτος, **1.** adj.; **a.** *given in lieu of* ὄξος ὀλέθρου ἀντίδοτον βασιλῆϊ μελισταγέος νιφετοῖο ἄρτου θεσπεσίοιο Nonn.*par.Jo.*19:29 (M.43.904C); **b.** *answering* οὐ Πιλάτῳ στόμα λύσας ἀ. μύθοισιν ἀμοιβαίην πόρε φωνήν *ib.*19:9(900A); **c.** *given to counteract* a malady, hence *remedial* καθάπερ ἀ. τι φάρμακον ἔδωκε τὸ λουτρόν Chrys. *hom.11.5 in Phil.*(11.289E); **2.** subst. ἀ., ἡ [ὁ Epiph.*rescr.*1(p.155. 13; M.41.157D); τό †Nil.*vit.*3(M.79.1144A) v. infra]; **a.** lit., *remedy, medicine,* Clem.*str.*2.14(p.146.1; M.8.1000A); *Hom.Clem.*11.9; †Bas. *hom.in Ps.*37:2(1.363B; M.30.85A); Germ.CP*or.*1(M.98.229C); **b.** met., Ign.*Eph.*20.2 cit. s. ἄρτος; τὰς ἀ. δὲ ἁπάσας τῆς σωτηρίας Clem. *paed.*1.12(p.150.3; M.8.369B); Eus.*Is.*28:21(M.24.293A); Epiph.*rescr.* 1(l.c.); Chrys.*exp.in Ps.*3:1(5.3B); **c.** in bad sense, *drug, poison* μὴ γενέσθω τὸ οὖς σου τῆς πικρᾶς ταύτης ἀ. Nil.*Eulog.*17(M.79.1116A); ὑπνωτικὸν ἀ. †Nil.*vit.*3(l.c.).

***ἀντιδυσωπέω,** *put to shame in turn,* Eus.*v.C.*4.33(p.130.17; M.20.1181C).

ἀντίδωρον, τό, **1.** *reward,* Men.*exc.Rom.*1(p.179.26; M.113.864D); Jo.Clim.*scal.*15(M.88.900D); **2.** *blessed bread*; distributed at close of liturgy, *Lit.Chrys.*(p.399.3); *Nomoc.*132; *Mir.Geo.*6(p.69.20), cf. εὐλογία.

***ἀντιδωροφορέω,** *present with gifts in return,* Men.*exc.Rom.*1 (p.190.29; M.113.881B).

ἀντιζεύγνυμι, *yoke together*; things contrasted or compared, ‡Meth.*Sym.et Ann.*2(M.18.349C).

ἀντιζηλόομαι, *be emulous of,* Clem.*str.*1.1(p.5.29; M.8.692C).

ἀντίζηλος, ὁ, ἡ, *rival, adversary,* *T.Jos.*7.5; ὁ δὲ ἀ. ... καὶ πονηρός, ὁ ἀντικείμενος *M.Polyc.*17.1; Epiph.*haer.*3(p.178.6; M.41. 189A); ἡ ἀ. αὐτῆς [sc. the Church] ἡ συναγωγή Ast.Soph.*hom.3 in Ps.*5(M.40.417B); ‡Nil.*perist.*12.2(M.79.941A); ὁ ἀ. τῇ τοῦ...Χριστοῦ προβησόμενος ἐνανθρωπήσει *cat.Apoc.*12:3(p.354.32).

***ἀντιζήλως,** *in jealous opposition,* *cat.Apoc.*12:3(p.354.25).

ἀντιζυγόω, *counterbalance,* Gr.Naz.*carm.*1.1.6.60(M.37.434A); *ib.* 2.1.11.795(1084A).

[*]**ἀντιζωγρ-εύω** (**-έω**), *take alive in turn* θηρεύσαντες γὰρ τὸν ἄνθρωπον εἰς θάνατον ἀντεζωγρεύθησαν Or.*Ps.*38:4(p.7); καὶ ἦλθον ἐμφανίσαι σοι ἐμαυτὸν διὰ τοῦ ἐλάφου τούτου, καὶ ~ῆσαί σε *M.Eust.* (M.105.381C).

***ἀντιζώνη,** ἡ, *opposite zone,* Or.*princ.*2.3.7(p.125 note; M.11. 197C).

***ἀντιζώννυ-μαι,** med., fig., *arm oneself against* ταῖς αὐταῖς αὖθις τὸν ἀντίπαλον ~ται λέξεσι Sophr.H.*y.Anast.*(M.92.1709C).

***ἀντίθεια,** ἡ, *hostility to God,* Didym.*Trin.*3.18(M.39.881C); Bas. Sel.*ascens.*(M.28.1093C).

ἀντίθεος, **1.** adj.; **a.** *comparable with God, godlike* ἐμοὶ δὲ καὶ οἱ ποιηταὶ τοὺς ἐκλεκτοὺς παρὰ σφίσι θεοειδέας προσαγορεύειν δοκοῦσι καὶ δίους καὶ ἀ. Clem.*str.*4.26(p.324.16; M.8.1380B); ἀ. μαθηταῖς Nonn.*par.Jo.*3:22(M.43.769C); *ib.*11:54(849A); Thdt.*affect.*3(p.82. 16; 4.773); **b.** *hostile to God,* Athenag.*leg.*24.2(M.6.945B); ἔχων σε πρόδρομον ἀ. πανουργίας Anon.ap.Iren.*haer.*1.15.6(M.7.628A); ἐσταύρωσαν οἱ Ἰουδαῖοι τὸν Χριστὸν ὡς γιγνώσκοντες αὐτὸν ἀ. ‡Just.*qu.et resp.*108(M.6.1356C); Gr.Naz.*or.*20.6(M.35.1072B); ἀ. φρόνημα Chrys. *hom.15.5 in Mt.*(7.191C); Thdt.*Is.*57:4(p.223.30; 2.368); ἐπὶ τὸν ἀ. Χριστὸν μεταφέρει τὴν προφητείαν, ὃν Ἰουδαῖοι προσμένουσιν, ὡς αὐτοί φασι id.*Zach.*11:14(2.1648); Nonn.*par.Jo.*5:43(M.43.792C); Eudoc.*Cypr.*1.90(M.85.836B); Cosm.Ind.*top.*2(M.88.128B); Jo.D.*f.o.* 3.24(M.94.1092A); **c.** *rivalling God,* of H. Ghost οὔτε ἀφ' ἑαυτοῦ λαλεῖ, ἢ ποιεῖ, ἢ ἔρχεται ὡς ἀ. Didym.*Trin.*2.15(M.39.544A); **2.** subst.; **a.** *enemy of God* ἐπειδὴ γὰρ ἀεὶ αὐτοὶ τοῦτο ἐνεκάλουν, ὅτι ἀ. τίς ἐστι, καὶ ἐχθρὸς τῷ θεῷ Chrys.*hom.74.3 in Mt.*(7.719A); id.*hom.23.2 in Jo.*(8.133D); id.*hom.3.2 in 2Thess.*(11.525C); hence **b.** *the anti-God* (i.e. Devil), Bas.*renunt.*10(2.211C; M.31.648B); ὡς ὁ Χριστὸς τῷ θεῷ καὶ πατρὶ τοὺς ὁσίους προσάγει, οὕτως ὁ ἀντίχριστος τῷ ἀ. τοὺς πειθομένους αὐτῷ Mac.Mgn.*apocr.*2.21(p.43.9); *ib.*4.15(p.184.19); **c.** *rival to God* ὡς περὶ λῃστοῦ τινος ἢ ἀ. ποιῇ τὸν λόγον Gr.Naz.*or.* 30.5(p.114.4; M.36.108C); *ib.*31.26(p.179.9; 164A); εὐχαριστεῖ ἵνα μὴ δόξῃ ἀ. εἶναι Ammon.*Jo.*6:11(M.85.1432D); hence **d.** *rival god* καὶ ἃ παρὰ τοῦ θεοῦ ἐκομίσατο δῶρα, ταῦτα τοῖς ἀ. ἐκείνοις προσήνεγκε Thdt.*Os.*2:8(2.1320); **e.** *representative of God* ἀποτίθεσθαι τὸν μονογενῆ τὴν βασιλείαν,...ὑποτάσσεσθαί τε τῷ θεῷ ὥς τινα ἀ. Didym. *Trin.*3.20(M.39.893A).

ἀντίθεσις, ἡ, **1.** *contradiction, antithesis,* (ref. Apoc.12:3) τὰ δέκα κέρατα...αἱ δέκα ἀ. ... τῆς δεκαλόγου Meth.*symp.*8.13(p.98.7; M.18.160B); ref. title of Marcion's work, cf. *antitheses..., id est contrariae oppositiones quae conantur discordiam evangelii cum lege committere,* Tert.*Marcion.*1.19(M.*PL.*2.267C); **2.** *objection, opposing argument,* Gr.Naz.*ep.*235(M.37.380A); Gr.Nyss.*anim.et res.*(M.46. 57B); Didym.(‡Bas.)*Eun.*5(1.312B; M.29.749A); Chrys.*hom.40.1 in Jo.*(8.237A); Thdt.*eran.*1(4.27).

***ἀντιθεσπίζω,** *make a counter-enactment,* Proc.G.*Is.*55:4(M.87. 2556A).

***ἀντιθετικῶς,** *in antithesis,* Gr.Nyss.*Eun.*12(2 p.281.11; M.45. 892D); *antithetically,* Max.*ambig.*(M.91.1265D).

ἀντίθετος, **1.** *opposed, hostile, contrary,* †Hipp.*Artem.*ap.Eus.*h.e.* 5.16.4(M.20.465B); ἀ. ... τὸ ἀντιτεταγμένον τῷ θελήματι τοῦ πατρός ‡Ath.*Trin.*1.16(M.28.1141C); μύθοις ἀ. σοφοὶ σκεδάοντες ἀπίστους Gr.Naz.*carm.*1.2.2.312(M.37.603A); Gr.Nyss.*Eun.*12(1 p.349.22; M. 45.1069C); αὕτη γὰρ τῶν ἀ. ἡ φύσις, ὡς τῇ τοῦ ἑνὸς ἀφαιρέσει τὴν τοῦ ἀντικειμένου θέσιν ἀντεισιέναι *ib.*(p.382.21; 1110D); Epiph.*haer.*

42.11(p.128.3; M.41.732C); οὐδὲ ἀ. ὁ Χριστὸς τῷ θεῷ τῷ δεδωκότι νόμον καὶ προφήτας *ib*.42.12(p.173.22; 800C); Jo.D.*hom*.11.11(M.96.773C); hence esp. ἐξ ἀ. *in opposition* οὐσίαν...δουλικὴν δὲ εἶναι ἐξ ἀ. τὴν τοῦ μονογενοῦς ἀποφαίνεται Bas.*Eun*.2.31(1.268A; M.29.644C); Gr.Nyss.*v.Mos*.(M.44.332A); id.*anim.et res*.(M.46.56B); **2.** of poetic parallelism, *antiphonal, antithetical* τέρψιν ἔχων ἱερῶν ἀ. μελέων Gr.Naz.*carm*.2.1.50.44(M.37.1388A); τὰ ἀ. ταῦτα [i.e. sons of Hannah] εἰς τὴν...ἐκκλησίαν...προφητεύεται Proc.G.*1Reg*.2:4(M.87.1084A); **3.** *taking the place* of ἀ. προτέρης χάριτος χάριν Nonn.*par.Jo*.1:16(M.43.752C); **4.** *in reversed position* τὴν ἀ. τοῦ Πέτρου...σταύρωσιν Sophr.H.*v.Anast*.(M.92.1720B).

***ἀντιθεωρέω**, *consider in contrast*, Gr.Nyss.*Eun*.9(2 p.220.24; M.45.820B).

***ἀντιθηρεύω**, *hunt in turn*, *M.Eust*.(M.105.380D).

***ἀντιθησαυρίζω**, *lay up treasure in exchange*, Chrysipp.*enc.in Thdr*.(p.57.10).

***ἀντιθόωκος**, *occupying a rival place*, Gr.Naz.*carm*.1.1.7.44(M.37.442A).

***ἀντίθρονος**, *enthroned as a rival* καὶ σύ, Μανιχαίοιο κακὸν σκότος, οὐ πάρος ἧες ἀκροτάτοιο φάους ἀντίθρονον Gr.Naz.*carm*.1.1.4.25(M.37.417A); of an usurper bishop, id.*or*.21.8(M.35.1089B); of ecclesiastical factions, *ib*.42.22(M.36.484B).

***ἀντιθύρετρος**, *instead of a door*, Nonn.*par.Jo*.11:39(M.43.845B).

ἀντικαθαιρέω, *depose in turn*, Socr.*h.e*.2.42.1(M.67.349C).

***ἀντικαθέζομαι**, *be set over against one another*, Gr.Naz.*carm*.2.1.45.66(M.37.1358A).

***ἀντικαθιδρύω**, *establish in the place of*, Philost.*h.e*.5.1(M.65.528C).

ἀντικακόω, *injure in return*, ‡Just.*qu.et resp*.125(M.6.1373D).

ἀντικαλέω, *name instead*, Val.Gn.ap.Epiph.*haer*.31.6(p.393.8; M.41.484C).

***ἀντικάμπτω**, *bend in return*, Geo.Pis.*hex*.1884(M.92.1578A).

ἀντικαταβάλλω, *cast down again*, of reincarnation as taught by Carpocratians καὶ ταῦτα πάντα ἐάν τις πράξῃ ἐν τῇ μιᾷ ταύτῃ παρουσίᾳ, οὐκέτι μετενσωματοῦται αὐτοῦ ἡ ψυχὴ εἰς τὸ πάλιν ἀντικαταβληθῆναι Epiph.*haer*.27.4(p.305.7; M.41.368C).

ἀντικαταλείπω, *abandon in turn*, Or.*or*.29(p.390.3; M.11.541C).

ἀντικατάλλαγμα, τό, *return, exchange* τί...ἔχομέν σοι δοῦναι, κύριε, ἀ. τῆς σῆς ψυχῆς ἧς ἔδωκας ὑπὲρ ἡμῶν; *A.Thom*.A 72(p.188.7); τὸν θάνατον τοῦ σωτῆρος, ὃς ἔσται αὐτοῖς ἀ. καρπουμένοις ἀντὶ ταφῆς καὶ θανάτου ζωὴν αἰώνιον καὶ ἄφθαρτον ἀθανασίαν Thdr.Heracl.*Is*.53:9(M.18.1357B); of a sacrificial victim ὑπὲρ οὗ προσφέρουσίν σοι τὸ ἀντίλυτρον τοῦ ἀ. ζῴου τούτου *Rit.Sacr*.(p.413).

ἀντικαταλλάσσω, act.; **1.** *receive instead*, Ath.*fug*.2(p.69.7; M.25.645B); **2.** *exchange*, Cyr.H.*catech*.4.24.

***ἀντικάταλλος**, *mutually opposite*, Leont.H.*Nest*.3.10(M.86.1644C).

***ἀντικαταμειδιάω**, *mock at*, Cyr.*Soph*.45(3.623C).

***ἀντικαταπέμπω**, *send down in return* θυμίαμα προσφέρομεν...ὁ προσδεξάμενος...ἀντικατάπεμψον ἡμῖν τὴν χάριν τοῦ ἁγίου σου πνεύματος *Lit.Marc*.(p.118.28); *Lit.Bas*.(p.319.29); cf.*Lit.Chrys*.(p.359.35); δέχου τὴν εὐχὴν ἡμῶν· ἀντικατάπεμψον δὲ τὰ ἐλέη σου ἐπὶ πάντας Andr.Cr.*triod*.(M.97.1408C).

***ἀντικαταράομαι**, *curse in turn*, Gr.Thaum.*Eccl*.7:23(M.10.1005C).

***ἀντικαταράσσω**, *confuse the issue against*, Leont.H.*monoph*.testimonia(M.86.1845A).

***ἀντικαταστρέφω**, *overthrow*, Thdr.Lect.*h.e*.2.49(M.86.209A).

***ἀντικατατάσσω**, *appoint instead*, Clem.*str*.1.14(p.38.9; M.8.760A); *ib*.6.13(p.485.8; M.9.328A).

ἀντίκει-μαι, **1.** *be adverse to, hostile to*, Clem.*str*.7.12(p.50.3; M.9.496D); ταῖς ~μέναις δουλεύειν ἡδοναῖς *ib*.(p.61.32; 500B); Ἀπελλῆς ...τὰς προφητείας ἐξ ~μένου λέγει πνεύματος Rhod.ap.Eus.*h.e*.5.13.2(M.20.460B); οὗτος [sc. Manes] δύο σέβει θεοὺς ἀγεννήτους, αὐτοφυεῖς, ἀϊδίους, ἕνα τῷ ἑνὶ ~μενον Hegem.*Arch*.7(p.9.13; M.10.1437A); hence *resist*, Clem.*paed*.3.3(p.246.14; M.8.580A); *be next to* ~ται τὸ μὲν θέρος τῷ μετοπώρῳ, ὁ δὲ χειμὼν τῷ ἔαρι Cyr.*Ps*.73:17(M.69.1188B); *be opposite* ~μένην ὄχθην Gr.Nyss.*v.Mos*.(M.44.312A); hence esp. in logic, *be opposite, contrary*, Meth.*arbitr*.12(p.176.16; M.18.261A); Ath.*inc*.7.1(M.25.108C); ‡Just.*qu.Chr*.5(M.6.1457D); **2.** pres. ptcpl. ἀντικείμενος used specially; **a.** of evil powers as *adversaries* παραδίδονται γὰρ δυνάμεις ἀ. δυνάμεσιν ἑτέραις ἀ. εἰς κόλασιν Or.*fr.25 in Jer*.(p.211.11; M.13.593A); id.*schol.in Cant*.1:7(p.145.28; M.17.257B); Meth.*symp*.6.1(p.65.3; M.18.113C); τούτῳ...τῷ σωτηρίῳ σημείῳ πάσης ἀ. καὶ πολεμίας δυνάμεως ἀμυντηρίῳ...ἐχρῆτο βασιλεύς Eus.*v.C*.1.31(p.22.16; M.20.948A); ἀ. δαίμονας Ath.*v.Anton*.51(M.26.917A); ἀ. ἐνεργείας Serap.*euch*.22.2; Cyr.H.*procatech*.10; id.*catech*.20.2; *ib*.21.4; ἀ. πνεύματα Bas.*Spir*.38(3.32E; M.32.137B); Chrys.*hom.8.2 in Jo*.(8.50C); Thdr.Mops.*Col*.2:15(p.291.14); Cosm.Ind.*top*.2(M.88.120A); **b.** of Satan, *adversary*, *M.Polyc*.17.1; τοῦ ἀ. διαβόλου Ptol.*ep*.(p.451.3; M.41.557B); Or.*fr.28 in Jer*.(p.213.20; M.13.596D); τὸν πονηρὸν δράκοντα τὸν ἀ. ἡμῖν *A.Phil*.144(p.86.8); Cyr.H.*catech*.23.18; **c.** οἱ ἀ. *the adversaries*, Clem.*exc.Thdot*.73(p.130.7; M.9.692D); **d.** ὁ ἀ. *the adversary, the Devil*, *1Clem*.51.1; *Apoc.Esd*.40(p.27); *Ep.Lugd*.ap.Eus.*h.e*.5.1.5(M.20.409A); Anon.ap.Eus.*h.e*.5.16.7(M.20.465C); Clem.*paed*.1.8(p.128.21; M.8.329A); id.*str*.2.5(p.123.25; M.8.953A); ὁ δ' Ἑβραίων διαλέκτῳ σατᾶν καὶ Ἑλληνικώτερον ὑπό τινων ὀνομασθεὶς σατανᾶς μεταλαμβανόμενος εἰς Ἑλλάδα φωνήν ἐστιν ἀ. πᾶς δὲ ὁ τὴν κακίαν ἑλόμενος...σατανᾶς ἐστι, τουτέστιν ἀ. τῷ υἱῷ τοῦ θεοῦ Or.*Cels*.6.44(p.115.10; M.11.1368A); τῶν ἐπαγομένων κακῶν ἀπὸ βορρᾶ, βορρᾶ τοῦ ἀ., ὡς πολλάκις λέλεκται id.*hom.5.16 in Jer*.(p.46.7; M.13.321A); *Const.App*.3.7.1; Cosm.Ind.*top*.2(M.88.117C); **e.** ref. antichrist ὁ κύριος γὰρ Ἰησοῦς ἀναλοῖ τῷ πνεύματι τοῦ στόματος αὐτοῦ...τὸν ἀ. λόγον καὶ ἐπαιρόμενον ἐπὶ πάντα λεγόμενον θεὸν ἢ σέβασμα Or.*Jo*.20.11(p.340.26; M.14.597A); ὁ ἀ. ... ἄγει τινὰ ἄνθρωπον μάγον, καὶ τῆς ἐν φαρμακείαις καὶ ἐπαοιδαῖς...ἐμπειρότατον Cyr.H.*catech*.15.11; ‡Hipp.*consumm*.21(p.297.14; M.10.924A); **f.** neut. as subst. (esp. plur.), in logic, *opposites, contraries* ὅταν...δύο συνημμένα λήγῃ εἰς τὰ ἀλλήλοις ἀ. Or.*Cels*.7.15(p.166.19; M.11.1441A); ὁ θεὸς ποικίλον τι χρῆμα καὶ σύνθετον ἐξ ἀ. τινῶν συγκεκροτημένος [apud Eunomium] Gr.Nyss.*Eun*.1(1 p.213.2; M.45.461A); εἰ...ἀναιρετικὸν ἦν τοῦ ἑτέρου τὸ ἕτερον κατὰ τὴν τῶν ἀ. φύσιν, ἀναγκαίως ἡ τοῦ ἑνὸς θέσις τὴν ἀναίρεσιν τοῦ λοιποῦ κατεσκεύαζεν *ib*.(p.178.2; 421C); ὡς πάλιν τὸ ἀ. δηλοῖ Didym.*Trin*.2.2(M.39.461A).

***ἀντικεράννυμι**, *give to drink in return*, ‡Chrys.*pasch*.6.5(p.179.22; 8.272C).

ἀντικηρύσσω, *preach against, declare openly against*, Eus.*d.e*.3.5(p.122.32; M.22.209B); id.*p.e*.4.1(131A; M.21.229D).

ἀντικινέω, med., *change one's position*, Philost.*h.e*.2.13(M.65.476C; l. αὐτοῦ κινεῖσθαι).

***ἀντικίρναμαι**, variant of ἀντικεράννυμι, med., *mingle*, or pass., *be mixed, interchanged*; of qualities of vinegar and copper, Leont.H.*monoph*.testimonia(M.86.1816D).

***ἀντικιχράω**, med., *borrow in return*, Cyr.*thes*.6(5[1].49B).

ἀντικλάω, pass.; **1.** *reverberate*, Gr.Naz.*carm*.2.1.11.1381(M.37.1124A); **2.** *change in turn*; of a body eaten by a fish, the fish by the fisherman etc., Geo.Pis.*hex*.1444(M.92.1544A).

ἀντίκλεις, ἡ, **1.** *false key*, Clem.*str*.7.17(p.75.4; M.9.548A); **2.** *bar, barrier*, Serap.*Man*.18(p.36; M.40.913C).

***ἀντικλέπτω**, *catch in turn*, Geo.Pis.*Pers*.2.222(M.92.1225A).

***ἀντικληρόω**, med., *receive in exchange*, Jo.VI H.*v.Jo.D*.7(M.94.440B).

ἀντικλίνω, *oppose*, ‡Nil.*perist*.1.5(M.79.816B).

ἀντικνήμη, ἡ, *blow on the shin*, Leont.N.*v.Sym*.6(M.93.1721B).

ἀντικοτ-έω, *oppose, obstruct* εἰ πνεύματι προσεύχεσθαι βούλει, μηδὲν ἀνιμήσῃ ἀπὸ σαρκὸς καὶ οὐχ ἕξεις νέφος ~οῦν σοι ἐν τῷ καιρῷ τῆς προσευχῆς Evagr.Pont.*or*.128(M.79.1193D); ὁ διάβολος ~εῖ ἵνα μὴ στεφανωθῇ ὁ ἄνθρωπος Anast.S.*qu.et resp*.134(M.89.788A).

ἀντικράζω, *cry out against*, Thdr.Lect.*h.e*.2.26(M.86.197A); Ant.Mon.*hom*.27(M.89.1521A).

***ἀντίκρουμα**, τό, *blow delivered in return*, Geo.Pis.*Pers*.1.185(M.92.1210A).

***ἀντικτάομαι**, *gain in return*, Bas.*hom*.7.1(2.52D; M.31.281C).

***ἀντικτείνομαι**, *kill in return*, Adam.*dial*.1.9(p.20.13; M.11.1752C).

***ἀντικτίζω**, *set up against*, Geo.Pis.*Pers*.3.74(M.92.1240A).

***ἀντίκτυπος**, *resounding in response*, Nonn.*par.Jo*.8:39(M.43.820A).

ἀντιλέγ-ω, **1.** *resist* ἀποπαυστέον τὸ ἔθος...καὶ πρὸς τὸ ἀ. αὐτῷ τὴν ψυχὴν γυμναστέον Clem.*str*.7.16(p.70.26; M.9.537C); Or.*Jo*.32.6(p.435.15; M.14.756C); *A.Andr*.A 5(one MS only, p.49.5a); **2.** *gainsay, contradict* ἀ. τῇ δωρεᾷ τοῦ θεοῦ Ign.*Smyrn*.7.1; δίκαιος...ὁ δημιουργὸς εἶναι οὐκ ~εται Clem.*paed*.1.8(p.132.17; M.8.337A); Meth.*res*.1.36(p.276.9); **3.** *demur*, Thdt.*Rom*.11:31(3.126); τοὺς μὲν πλείστους ἐθέλοντας, τοὺς δὲ ~οντας καὶ παρὰ γνώμην δουλεύοντας id.*affect*.10(p.256.18; 4.966); **4.** *dispute*, ref. books of doubtful authenticity τῇ...τοῦ Τωβὴτ βίβλῳ ~ουσιν οἱ ἐκ περιτομῆς ὡς μὴ ἐνδιαθήκῳ Or.*or*.14(p.332.3; M.11.461C); ἰστέον ὡς καὶ τοῦτο [sc. Herm.] πρὸς μέν τινων ἀντιλέλεκται δι' οὓς οὐκ ἐν ὁμολογουμένοις τεθείη Eus.*h.e*.3.3.6(M.20.217B); *ib*.3.24.18(268C); of a doubtful reading ἐπεὶ δὲ νομίζεις τοῦτο ~όμενον εἶναι, πληροφορήθητι καὶ ἐξ ἄλλης γραφικῆς ἀποδείξεως ‡Ath.*dial.Trin*.3.20(M.28.1233C); hence τὰ ἀ. *the disputed books*,

Eus.*h.e.*3.25.3(269A); τὰ...ἀ. τῆς παλαιᾶς ‡Ath.*synops.*74(M.28.432A); **5.** *deny* ~ουσι [sc. Encratites] τῇ τοῦ πρωτοπλάστου σωτηρίᾳ Iren. ap.Eus.*h.e.*4.29.2(M.20.400B); **6.** *refuse* οὐκ ἀντερεῖ ὁ Ἰωάννης καὶ τὸν νεκρὸν ἀναστῆσαι *A.Jo.*46(p.174.5); **7.** *answer* τί τούτοις ἀντερεοῦμεν; Cyr.*inc.unigen.*(5¹.689C).

ἀντίλεξις, ἡ, *opposition,* Cyr.*Ps.*6:11(M.69.748C).

***ἀντιλήγω,** *come to an end in turn* οὐδὲ γὰρ ἀντιλήξειεν (conj. ἄν τι λήξειεν ed.) εἰς τέλος μὴ ἀπ' ἀρχῆς ὁρμώμενον Eun.*apol.*22(M.30.857C).

ἀντιληπτέον, *one must lay hold of,* Mac.Aeg.*libert.ment.*13(M.34.945B).

ἀντιληπτικός, 1. *susceptible of* ἀληθῶς γέγονεν ἄνθρωπος ἀ. παθῶν Just.*dial.*98.1(v.l. -κῶς M.6.705B); **2.** *helping,* Cyr.*Jo.*4.1(4.346B).

ἀντιληπτικῶς, 1. *so as to be susceptible of,* Just.*dial.*98.1(M.6.705B; l. -ος); **2.** *so as to assist, Mir.Geo.*1(p.2 n.).

ἀντιλήπτωρ, ὁ, *helper*; **1.** in gen., *M.Perp.*10(p.77.16); Gr.Naz.*or.*42.26(M.36.492A); Eus.Al.*serm.*21.3(M.86.425D); Sophr.H.*mir.Cyr.et Jo.*48(M.87.3601D); **2.** of God or of Christ ὁ σωτὴρ καὶ ἀ. μου ἐν παντὶ καιρῷ ἔσωσέ με *Pss.Sal.*16.4; *A.Thom.*A 19(p.130.14); ἵνα τὸν ἀ. ἡμῶν Ἰησοῦν Χριστὸν ἐπιγνῶμεν *A.Xanthipp.*40(p.85.11); ἀ. διὰ τῆς θεότητος· μόνη γὰρ ἡμῶν ἀντιλαβέσθαι διὰ τῆς ἀπαθείας ἐδύνατο Cyr.*Ps.*17:3(M.69.821A); ‡Nil.*perist.*12.9(M.79.957A); liturg. γενοῦ ἀ. τοῦ λαοῦ σου τούτου *Lit.*ap.*Const.App.*8.11.5; *ib.*8.13.10; *Euchol.*(p.40); **3.** of BMV σὲ γὰρ τὴν πανάχραντον ἀ. κεκτήμεθα *ib.*(p.405).

ἀντίληψις, ἡ, 1. *help, succour* ἡ ἀ. ἡ παρὰ τοῦ κυρίου Hipp.*fr.38 in Gen.*49:19(p.66.1; M.10.593B); *A.Xanthipp.*24(p.75.20); *M.Perp.*1(p.63.12); Eus.*h.e.*1.1.2(M.20.49A); ὅπερ...εἰς ἀ. ἑκάστῳ διὰ τοῦ υἱοῦ γίνεται Ath.*Ar.*1.63(M.26.144B); τί ἐστιν 'ἀντιλήψεις'; ὥστε ἀντέχεσθαι τῶν ἀσθενῶν Chrys.*hom.32.2 in 1Cor.*(10.287C); φῶς τουτέστιν ἡ ἀ. ἡ θεία Thdr.Mops.*Zach.*14:5–7(M.66.592A); ὁμοίαν τῆς θλίψεως εὑρίσκει τὴν ἀ. Marc.Er.*opusc.*1.43(M.65.912A); περὶ ἀ. τοῦ ἁμαρτάνοντος ἀδελφοῦ διὰ προσευχῆς Euthal.Diac.*epp.cath.*(M.85.685D); Sophr.H.*ep.syn.*(M.87.3197B); exeg. Ps.21:1 τινὲς δὲ ἀ. ἑωθινὴν λέγουσι τὸν τῆς ἀναστάσεως τοῦ σωτῆρος καιρόν Cyr.*Ps.*21 tit.(M.69.837B); *ib.*23:1(844C); ἀ. γὰρ ἑωθινὴ τοῦ σωτῆρος ἡμῶν ἐπιφάνεια Thdt.*Ps.*21:1(1.733); **2.** *grasp, laying hold of* ἀ. κραταιοτέρα τῇ κοινωνίᾳ τῶν δακτύλων Bas.*ep.*97(3.191B; M.32.493B); διεγείρων ἡμᾶς...πρὸς τὴν ἐκείνης [sc. τῆς ἀγάπης] ἀ. Chrys.*hom.34.3 in 1Cor.*(10.313D); id.*hom.12.1 in 2Cor.*(10.521D).

***ἀντιλόγημα, τό,** *act of gainsaying, Dial.Tim.et Aquil.*99 r° (p.79).

ἀντιλογία, ἡ, 1. *legal dispute, Can.App.*37; *Const.App.*2.47.1; **2.** *offence,* Niceph.Ur.*v.Sym.*116(M.86.3093D); **3.** in phrase δι' ἀντιλογίαν *conversely,* Vict.*Mc.*4:11(p.305.21).

ἀντίλοξος, 1. *oblique, winding,* Geo.Pis.*hex.*1144(M.92.1522A); *ib.*1159(1523A); id.*carm.*2.86; **2.** *bent back,* id.*hex.*1252(1531A).

ἀντίλυτρον, τό, *ransom*; **1.** *of Christ* ἑαυτὸν παρεδίδου ὁ κύριος ὑπὲρ τῶν ἁμαρτιῶν ἡμῶν ἵνα γένηται ἀντίψυχον καὶ ἀ. ἡμῶν Eus.*Is.*53:6f.(M.24.457C); id.*d.e.*10.8(p.477.15; M.22.768B); ‡Ath.*Apoll.*1.19(M.26.1125C); Cyr.*Jo.*4.2(4.353B); ψυχήν...ψυχῆς ἀ. τῆς ἁπάντων ποιούμενος id.*inc.unigen.*(5¹.692D); **2.** *of one man for another* ἐμαυτὸν ἀ. τῶν ὑμετέρων ψυχῶν οὐκ ἂν παραιτήσωμαι δοῦναι εἴπερ... καλέσοι καιρός Max.*ep.*18(M.91.589B); **3.** ref. animal sacrifice, *Rit.Sacr.*(p.413) cit. s. ἀντικατάλλαγμα.

ἀντιμάχησις, ἡ, *conflict with,* Clem.*str.*2.20(p.178.15; M.8.1065A).

***ἀντιμαχητής, ὁ,** *antagonist, Orac.Sib.*14.164 (v.l. ἀγχιμαχητής).

ἀντίμαχος, *opposed to, in opposition,* CArim.*decr.*(p.238.38; M.26.700C); Isid.Pel.*epp.*1.164(M.78.292B).

***ἀντιμελετάω,** *practise in opposition to,* Ath.*fug.*2(p.69.8; M.25.645C).

***ἀντιμεριμνάω,** *care in turn,* Eus.*fr.Lc.*12:22(M.24.560C).

***ἀντιμεριστής, ὁ,** *partner with,* Thdr.Abuc.*opusc.*20(M.97.1545C).

ἀντιμεταβάλλ-ω, 1. *change in turn* τὰ ἡμέτερα σώματα ~ονται, καὶ ἐν...θηρίοις γίγνονται μέρη τῶν ἐκείνων σωμάτων, καὶ πάλιν ἐκεῖνα ὑπὸ ἀνθρώπων...ἐσθιόμενα ~ει καὶ γίγνεται ἀνθρώπων...σώματα Or.*sel.in Ps.*1:5(M.12.1092C); cf.Meth.*res.*1.20(p.243.7; M.41.1189A); Ath.*Ar.*2.18(M.26.185B); **2.** *change right round* ἐκτὸς εἰ μὴ ἀντιμεταβέβληται τὸ ἔργον τῆς εἰρήνης καὶ τὰ τοιαῦτα εἰρήνην ὀνομάζετε Jul.Papa *ep.Dian.*ap.Ath.*apol.sec.*30(p.110.3; M.25.300C).

ἀντιμετάγω, *transfer in turn,* Gr.Nyss.*hex.*14(M.44.77A); Sophr.H.*v.Anast.*(M.92.1728D).

***ἀντιμεταφέρω,** *bring back again,* Socr.*h.e.*2.38.24(M.67.328B).

ἀντιμετρ-έω, 1. *measure out in turn, repay* τὸ πρὸς ἀξίαν τοῖς κακούργοις ~οῦσαι Bas.*hex.*2.5(1.17A; M.29.40B); Euthal.Diac.*Ac.*(M.85.633A); Ant.Mon.*hom.*27(M.89.1521C); **2.** *measure against,* Clem.*q.d.s.*37(p.184.7; M.9.641C); οὐκ ~ησῃς σεαυτὸν ἑταίρῳ Nil.*Eulog.*4(M.79.1100A); Dion.Ar.*e.h.*2.2.2(M.3.393B).

ἀντιμέτρησις, ἡ, *recompense,* Bas.*hom.in Ps.*7:4ff.(1.99E; M.29.233B); Gr.Naz.*or.*42.7(M.36.465D); Nil.*epp.*3.5(M.79.368C).

ἀντιμιμ-έομαι, 1. *retaliate by imitating* πρὸς τὸ ἄγριον αὐτῶν ὑμεῖς ἥμεροι, μὴ σπουδάζοντες ~εῖσθαι αὐτούς Ign.*Eph.*10.2; **2.** *counterfeit* τὸ παραχαράττειν τὴν ἀλήθειαν καὶ ~εῖσθαι ἐκκλησίας τρόπου, μὴ ὄντας Χριστιανούς Epiph.*haer.*80.2(p.486.14; M.42.760A).

***ἀντιμίμημα, τό,** *counterpart,* Epiph.*haer.*42.11(p.150.7; M.41.765B).

ἀντίμιμος, ὁ, 1. subst.; **a.** *imitator, rival* οἱ ἀ. τοῦ δημιουργοῦ οἱ τῇ ἐκ μεσότητος ψυχῇ...ἐμφυσῶντες τὴν ζωὴν τὴν ἄνωθεν Clem.*str.*4.13(p.288.16; M.9.1300A); Hipp.*haer.*5.16(p.113.4; M.16.3174C); **b.** *substitute,* Meth.*symp.*5.6(p.60.7; M.18.108A); **c.** *counterpart, type* τινα σκιώδη καὶ εἰκονικὸν ἀλλ' οὐκ ἀληθῆ χριστὸν καὶ ἀρχιερέα τοῦ κατ' οὐρανὸν χριστοῦ τε καὶ ἀρχιερέως ἀ. ἀπεργαζόμενος Eus.*d.e.*4.15(p.180.23; M.22.300D); ὄφις καὶ δράκων, ἀ. τοῦ ἐκβαλόντος ἡμᾶς ἐκ παραδείσου, προσεκυνήθησαν Cyr.H.*catech.*6.10; Proc.G.*Gen.*9:4(M.87.296B); **2.** adj.; **a.** *like* ἀ. τῆς γαλήνης τὴν ὄψιν ῥυθμίζουσιν ‡Chrys.*hom.*6(13.213E); **b.** *conterfeit, imitating* [sc. ὁ διάβολος] τοὺς ...περισωθέντας...ἐκ τοῦ κατακλυσμοῦ διὰ τὴν τῆς πνευματικῆς εὐφροσύνης ἄμπελον ἀ. πόματι μεθύσας κατεχλεύασεν Meth.*symp.*10.5(p.126.28; M.18.200C); Areth.*Apoc.*39(M.106.684B).

ἀντιμίνσιον, v. ἀντιμίσιον.

ἀντιμισθία, ἡ, *recompense, reward, repayment,* Clem.*str.*4.22(p.309.7; M.8.1348B); Amph.*mesopent.*(M.39.121C); Philost.*h.e.*3.15(M.65.505A); esp. in contrast between earthly and heavenly rewards ὀνειδισμὸν ἐδεξάμην ἐπὶ τῆς γῆς, τὴν δὲ ἀμοιβὴν καὶ τὴν ἀ. δίδου μοι ἐν οὐρανοῖς *A.Thom.*A 147(p.257.9); ‡Bas.*const.*24.1(2.574D; M.31.1412C); διδόναι τῷ Χριστῷ, ἤγουν τοῖς πτωχοῖς καὶ πένησιν, ἵνα τὴν ἀ. λάβωμεν παρὰ τοῦ δικαίου μισθαποδότου θεοῦ Leont.N.*v.Jo.Eleem.*22(p.47.14); of recompense made by man to God τίνα...ἡμεῖς αὐτῷ δώσομεν ἀ.; *2Clem.*1.3; but usually vice versa προφῆται...κατηξιώθησαν τὴν ἀ. ταύτην λαβεῖν ὄργανα θεοῦ γενόμενοι Thphl.Ant.*Autol.*2.9(M.6.1064A); τὴν ἀ. τῆς σῆς ἐνεργείας δίδωσιν τὴν αἰώνιον ζωήν *A.Thom.*A 76(p.191.10); ἧς ἀ. ἐν ἑαυτοῖς ἀπελάβομεν, ζωῆς ἀιδίου θάνατον ἀνταλλαξάμενοι Thal.*cent.*3.94(M.91.1457A); of punishment καὶ γὰρ ὁ θεὸς ποιησάντων ἡμῶν εἰς αὐτὸν πολλὰ κακὰ...ἀ. ἡμῖν οὐκ ἀπέδωκεν ἀλλὰ μετανοίαν *A.Jo.*81(p.191.13); in gen., of God's gifts to men, Clem.*str.*1.1(p.7.27; M.8.696B); Thdr.Heracl.ap.*cat.Mt.*10:37(p.82.25).

ἀντιμίσιον (-μίνσιον), τό, (Lat. *mensa*), **1.** *cloth* ornamented with cross, crucifixion, or entombment, consecrated by bishop and containing relics of saints, which, no doubt used originally as a portable altar or placed on an unconsecrated altar, was later held to be essential for celebration of liturgy ἱερεὺς χωρὶς ἀ. λειτουργήσας ποιείτω μετανοίας σ' *Nomoc.*72; ἀντιμίνσια *Euchol.*(p.517); **2.** *portable altar* or *table,* the later τετραπόδιον placed before altar, *ib.*(p.389).

***ἀντιμνημονεύω,** *remember in turn*; of intercession of saints before throne of God, *Lit.Jac.*(p.218.13); Jo.VI H.*v.Jo.D.*38(M.94.489A).

***ἀντιμνηστήρ, ὁ,** *rival suitor, Schol.Clem.prot.*2.36(p.308.10; M.9.783C)..

***ἀντίμωμος,** ? *culpable* (poss. contrasted with ἄμωμος, but text is corrupt) Ναβυχοδονόσορ καὶ ἀ. εἰκόνα ποιησάμενος Hipp.*Dan.*2.27.9 (cf. *ib.*2.27.6 ἄμωμος).

***ἀντινεύω,** *nod* or *beckon in answer,* Leont.N.*v.Sym.*6(M.93.1724B).

ἀντινήχομαι, *swim against,* Geo.Pis.*hex.*1715(M.92.1567A).

ἀντινομία, ἡ, 1. *conflict of laws* πρῶτον τὸν νόμον ὑμῖν ἀναγνούς, οὕτω τὴν δοκοῦσαν ἀ. λῦσαι πειράσομαι Chrys.*hom.in 1Cor.7:39*(3.203E); **2.** *opposition to the Law* of Moses, Chrys.*hom.62.1 in Mt.*(7.620B).

ἀντινομοθετ-έω, 1. *legislate in opposition* to ἀ. ... τῷ θεῷ Ptol.*ep.* ap.Epiph.*haer.*33.4(p.453.13; M.41.561A); Eus.*d.e.*3.7(p.142.15; M.22.240B); Epiph.*haer.*61.6(p.386.7; M.41.1048A); Chrys.*virg.*16(1.280E); abs., *make contrary laws,* Or.*Cels.*7.18(p.169.19; M.11.1445D); Ath.*fug.*2(p.69.5; M.25.645B); **2.** *contravene, contradict* ἀ. τῇ τε κοινῇ χρήσει καὶ τῇ διδασκαλίᾳ τοῦ πνεύματος Bas.*Eun.*1.8(1.220A; M.29.528C); †Bas.*Is.*26(1.399C; M.30.168B); Gr.Nyss.*v.Mos.*(M.44.352D); παραχρώμενοι τῷ βίῳ, οὐ χρώμενοι, ~οῦντες τῷ Παύλῳ Ast.Am.*hom.*1(M.40.165D); τίς...οὕτως ἐμβρόντητος ὡς...Παύλου βοῶντος ἀκούων, εἷς κύριος κτλ. [Eph.4:5]...~ῆσαι τῇ διδασκαλίᾳ τοῦ πνεύματος καὶ διχῇ τὸν ἕνα τεμεῖν Thdt.*ep.*145(4.1247); **3.** *set up, determine, in opposition* τὴν τοῦ θεοῦ πορείαν...ἀφέντες, καὶ τὴν ἰδίαν ~ήσαντες Proc.G.*Lev.*18:3(M.87.752C).

[*]**ἀντιξέω,** = ἀντιξοέω, *oppose, resist,* Andr.Cr.*or.*21(M.97.1272B).

ἀντίον, τό, *beam,* forming part of a fire engine, Steph.Diac. *v.Steph.*(M.100.1176C).

ἀντιπάθεια, ἡ, 1. *antidote, Hom.Clem.*3.36; *ib.*9.18; **2.** *antidotal influence,* Bas.*hex.*9.3(1.82D; M.29.193A); Gr.Nyss.*or.catech.*37(p.142.13; M.45.93B); id.*v.Mos.*(M.44.324B); **3.** *antipathy,* in nature τῶν κατὰ τὸν Δημόκριτον συμπαθειῶν τε καὶ ἀ. Tat.*orat.*17(M.6.841B); Clem.*paed.*1.6(p.120.15; M.8.309B); Eus.*d.e.*4.5(p.156.13; M.22.261A); ζῴων τε εἶναι καὶ φυτῶν καὶ ῥιζῶν ἀ. μυρίας id.*p.e.*4.1(132A; M.21.232C); Nil.ap.Proc.G.*Cant.*2:9(M.87.1597A); Procl.CP *or.*6.16(M.65.752A); **4.** *opposition, aversion,* Didym.*Trin.*2.8(M.39.585A); Socr. *h.e.*1.6.32(M.67.52B); Dor.*doct.*4.10(M.88.1672C); Jo.D.*hom.*2.6(M.96.585C); **5.** *correspondence of feelings,* of rapprochement τάχα ἀ. ἐστι διὰ τὴν φιλανθρωπίαν τοῦ ὠφεληθέντος πρὸς τὸν ὠφελήσαντα Or.*hom.* *14.3 in Jer.*(p.108.4; M.13.408A).

ἀντιπαθέω, 1. *be an antidote,* Epiph.*gemm.*2(M.43.296B); **2.** *be opposed* to, Socr.*h.e.*7.13.5(M.67.761B).

ἀντιπαθής, 1. *antipathetic* to ἀμιάντῳ...ὃ δὴ λέγεται ἀ. εἶναι τοῦ πυρός Ath.*inc.*44.7(M.25.176B); **2.** abs., *inclined to oppose, quarrelsome* φιλόνεικον...τὸ τῶν ἀνθρώπων γένος καὶ ἀ. Chrys.*hom.7.5 in Phil.*(11.252D).

ἀντιπαίζω, *return jest for jest,* Gr.Naz.*or.*4.77(M.35.604A).

***ἀντιπάλαισμα, τό,** *method of resistance,* Gr.Nyss.*Pss.titt.*A 13 (M.44.561A).

ἀντιπαλαί-ω, *wrestle against, contend with,* Herm.*mand.*12.5.2 cit. s. καταπαλαίω; ~σαντας ἡμᾶς τῇ ἁμαρτίᾳ Or.*comm.in Gen.* (M.12.68C)ap.Eus.*p.e.*6.11(289D); id.*sel.in Ps.*6:11(M.12.1177A); ἡ... πέτρα...ἰσχυροτέρα τῶν ~ουσῶν αὐτῇ πυλῶν ᾅδου id.*comm.in Mt.* 12.11(p.89.24; M.13.1004C); Cyr.H.*catech.*15.16; †Bas.*Is.*35(1.408D; M.30.189B); τὸν ἔνδοθεν ἡμῖν ἀντιπολεμοῦντα καὶ ~οντα Gr.Naz.*or.* 2.21(M.35.429C); ἀνθρωπίνου θελήματος οὐ πάντως ἑπομένου τῷ θείῳ ἀλλ'...~οντος *ib.*30.12(p.126.4; M.36.117C); ὅστις...βούλεται τῷ κανόνι τῆς ἐκκλησίας ~σαι Dam.Papa *ep.orient.*ap.Thdt.*h.e.*5.10.6 (3.1036); οἱ δαίμονες ἀ. τοῖς ἀδελφοῖς Call.*v.Hyp.*36(p.97.9).

***ἀντιπαλαμάομαι,** *fight against,* Jo.VI H.*v.Jo.D.*3(M.94.433A).

***ἀντιπάλαμνος, ὁ,** *adversary,* Eudoc.*Cypr.*2.29(M.85.845B).

ἀντίπαλος, *rival, antagonistic*; as subst. masc., *adversary,* esp. of Devil or of demons ἐκβεβιακότες τὸν ἀ. *Ep.Lugd.*ap.Eus.*h.e.*5.1.38(M.20.424A); Tit.Bost.*fr.Lc.*8:31(p.177); ἐχθρὸς δημιουργίας θεοῦ καὶ προνοίας τῆς ἐκείνου ἀ. *Const.App.*6.14.4; Eudoc.*Cypr.*1.28(M.85.833B); καὶ ἔξω τοῦ σκάμματος ὑπερακοντίσας τὸν ἀ. τῆς ἀνθρωπίνης φύσεως Cosm.Ind.*top.*5(M.88.288C); perh. as subst. fem. (sc. τάξις), *opposing force* οὐδὲ στήσεται [sc. ὁ σατανᾶς]...ὁρῶν τὰς ἀ. παρατεταγμένας Meth.*symp.*8.12(p.97.4; M.18.157C).

***ἀντιπανουργεύ-ομαι,** *exert every effort to oppose* τί οὐκ ~η τῇ ματαιότητι; Ephr.3.187F.

ἀντιπαραβάλλω, *adduce for comparison*; *adduce in opposition* κατὰ τῶν αἱρετικῶν ἀναπλασμάτων ἀ. τὸ ὕψος τοῦ εὐαγγελικοῦ κηρύγματος Or.*Jo.*5.8(p.105.13; M.14.196B); id.*sel.inGen.*1:26(M.12.93B).

***ἀντιπαραδείκνυμι,** *exhibit side by side in opposition,* Gr.Nyss. *hom.opif.*15.1(M.44.176D); id.*Eun.*4(2 p.71.22).

ἀντιπαραδίδωμι, 1. trans., *give back again,* Philost.*h.e.*2.16(M.65.477C); **2.** intrans., *give place in turn,* Cyr.H.*catech.*9.6.

ἀντιπαράδοσις, ἡ, *mutual exchange*; of the sun and moon in their courses, ‡Caes.Naz.*dial.*104(M.38.972).

***ἀντιπαραζεύγνυ-μι,** *couple* or *join instead* of ἡ παροῦσα πανήγυρις ...τὴν ἀλήθειαν τῶν τυπικῶν συμβόλων ~σα Andr.Cr.*or.*1(M.97.809A).

ἀντιπαράθεσις, ἡ, 1. *comparison, contrast* ἡ συναφὴ τῶν δογμάτων διὰ τῆς ἀ. τὴν ἀλήθειαν μνηστεύεται Clem.*str.*1.2(p.14.4; M.8.709B); *ib.*1.18(p.57.21; 804C); Hipp.*haer.*7.14(p.191.16; M.16.3295B); Eus. *l.C.*9(p.217.33; M.20.1361C); πνεῦμα αὐτοῦ κατὰ ἀντιπαράθεσιν τοῦ ἡμετέρου πνεύματος Didym.*Trin.*2.2(M.39.457A); ἡ σοφία τοῦ πατρὸς μονοειδής ἐστι, μὴ ἔχουσα ἀ. ἄλλην Epiph.*anc.*43(p.53.18; M.43.93C); μὴ ὂν...λέγεται ἡ ὕλη κατὰ ἀ. τῆς θείας κατὰ οὐσίαν ὑπάρξεως Max. *schol.d.n.*4.19(M.4.277A); ref. *antitheses* of Marcion, Hipp.*haer.*7.30(p.215.14; 3331C); τούτου τὸ δόγμα ἐκράτυνε Μαρκιών, τάς τε ἀ. ἐπιχειρήσας *ib.*7.37(p.223.17; 3346A); **2.** *correspondence,* ref. Gnost. aeons εἶναι...τούτους ὡς ὑποτέτακται, κατὰ ἀ. ἑκάστου ἀρρενικοῦ ὀνόματος τεταγμένου ἄντικρυς τοῦ θηλυκοῦ ὀνόματος Epiph.*haer.*31.2 (p.384.29; M.41.476C).

***ἀντιπαράθετος,** *set over against, occupying corresponding position*; hence **1.** *parallel* (of Origen's *Hexapla*) τὴν Ἑβραϊκὴν γραφὴν Ἑβραϊκοῖς στοιχείοις...ἐν σελίδι μιᾷ συντεθεικώς, ἄλλην σελίδα ἀ. δι' Ἑλληνικῶν μὲν γραμμάτων, Ἑβραϊκῶν δὲ λέξεων Epiph.*mens.*7(M.43.248A); met. πνεῦμα θεοῦ, πνεῦμα Χριστοῦ...ἀ. ‡Chrys.*Trin.*3(1.838D); **2.** *comparable* ὁ πατὴρ πατὴρ καὶ οὐκ ἔχει ἀ. Epiph.*anc.*8 (p.14.24; M.43.29A); *ib.*49(p.58.26; 104A); ‡Caes.Naz.*dial.*38(M.38.904); **3.** *opposed* βεβιασμένως δὲ ὁρῶ ἀ. τὰ λεγόμενα Epiph.*anc.*43 (p.53.20; 93C).

***ἀντιπαραθεωρέω,** *view in contrast,* Gr.Nyss.*beat.*3(M.44.1228A); id.*ordin.*(M.46.545A).

ἀντιπαραλαμβάνω, *take again, recover,* Jo.Mal.*chron.*18 p.470(M.97.684C).

ἀντιπαραλλάσσω, *change from one state to another,* hence perf. ptcpl. pass., *past* μὴ...ὁμοιωθῆτε τῷ ἀντιπαρηλλαγμένῳ τύπῳ *A.Phil.* 140(p.75.1).

ἀντιπαραμένω, *stand fast against,* Meth.*Porph.*2(p.505.28; M.18.404A).

***ἀντιπαραμετρέω,** *measure out in return,* Bas.Sel.*v.Thecl.*2.12(M.85.588C).

***ἀντιπαραμυθέομαι,** *be encouraged instead,* Leont.N.*v.Jo.Eleem.* 28(p.61.25).

ἀντιπαραπέμπω, *send in return,* Serap.*Man.*12(p.34; M.40.909C).

ἀντιπαράστασις, ἡ, a figure of speech denoting *admission* of an argument *with a distinction* ἀ. δὲ ἡ δεχομένη μὲν τὸν λόγον ὡς ἀληθῆ, δεικνύουσα δέ, ὡς οὐδὲν βλάπτει πρὸς τὸ προκείμενον Jo.D.*dialect.* 65(M.94.657C).

ἀντιπαράταξις, ἡ, 1. *resistance,* Gr.Naz.*or.*21.32(M.35.1120C); Niceph.Ur.*v.Sym.*58(M.86.3040B); Anast.S.*haer.*(p.263); **2.** *opposing battle-line*; fig., of defence against devils, ‡Chrys.*poenit.*2.1(9.780A); Nil.*Eulog.*6(M.79.1101C); Gr.Agr.*Eccl.*9.2(M.98.1085D).

ἀντιπαρατάσσω, 1. act., *draw up in opposition, Ep.Lugd.*ap.Eus. *h.e.*5.1.6(M.20.409B); **2.** med. and pass., *withstand, ib.*5.1.20(416C); Meth.*res.*1.27(p.255.5; M.41.1133A); *ib.*2.4(p.337.10; 1109C); Cyr.*Jo.* 1.5(4.44C).

***ἀντιπαρατρέπω,** *direct instead,* Cyr.*dial.Trin.*5(5[1].583D).

***ἀντιπαραφυλάσσομαι,** *guard oneself in turn,* Clem.*paed.*3.8(M.8.613C; ἄν τι παρα- p.261.29).

ἀντιπαραχωρέω, f.l. for ἀντιπεριχωρέω q.v., Anast.*fid.*(p.272).

***ἀντιπαρεκδύομαι,** *strip for a contest*; hence *be compared* or *contrasted,* Synes.*regn.*16(p.35.8; M.66.1081B).

ἀντιπαρέκτασις, ἡ, 1. *interpenetration,* Hipp.*haer.*1.21 (conj. for ἀνάστασιν p.26.8; ἀνάκλασιν M.16.3049A); **2.** *comparison,* Gr.Naz. *or.*43.71(M.36.592C).

***ἀντιπαρέλκω,** *drag off in opposite direction, 2Clem.*17.3.

ἀντιπαρεξάγ-ω, 1. *bring into action as an enemy* ~ειν αὐτὸν ἐπιχειροῦσαι Eus.*d.e.*10.8(p.489.2; M.22.785B); id.*Hierocl.*21(525A; M.22.828A); **2.** *compare, contrast* ὁ Δαβὶδ ~ει ταῖς τῶν παρανόμων κολάσεσι τὰ τῶν ἁγίων γέρα Or.*exc.in Ps.*36:11(M.17.125D); Gr. Nyss.*laud.Bas.*(M.46.801B); Cyr.*Jo.*9(4.773A); **3.** *place on a par with* τῇ...τοῦ θεοῦ δυνάμει ~ουσιν αὐτῆς [sc. τῆς ὕλης] τὴν ὑπόστασιν Bas.*hex.*2.2(1.13C; M.29.32A); Zach.Mit.*opif.*(M.85.1104A).

ἀντιπαρέρχ-ομαι, 1. *pass by, neglect, disregard* ἀντιπαρελθεῖν σιγῇ τὸν λόγον Eus.*e.th.*1.1(p.62.26; ἄν τι παρελθεῖν M.24.829B); id.*l.C.*7 (p.214.21, v.l. παρελθεῖν M.20.1356B); **2.** *pass by in turn* ἀλλήλους μὲν ἐγώ τε καὶ ὁ χρόνος ὡς...νέες ἐν πελάγει ~όμεθα Gr.Naz.*carm.* 1.2.13.2(M.37.754A).

***ἀντίπασχα, τό, 1.** *Sunday next after Easter, dominica in albis,* †Jo.Jej.*poenit.*(M.88.1913C); Leont.Abb.*v.Gr.Agr.*15(M.98.576A); *ib.* 18(580C); Jo.D.*carm.antipasch.*tit.(p.221); **2.** *week following Easter week,* Anast.*temp.*(p.278).

***ἀντιπάσχ-ω, 1.** *be of opposite nature to* οἱ Φαρισαῖοι πονηροὶ ὑπάρχοντες ~ουσιν αὐτόν Ephr.2.302A; **2.** gram. ἀντιπεπονθώς *reflexive,* Or.*Cels.*6.57(p.127.31; M.11.1385B).

ἀντιπατέω, *tread on in turn,* Dor.*doct.*19(M.88.1808C); Cosm.Ind. *top.*2(M.88.132B).

***ἀντιπείθω,** *persuade on the contrary,* ‡Chrys.*prov.*2(2.759A).

ἀντιπελάργωσις, ἡ, *return of benefits,* Bas.*hex.*8.5(1.75C; M.29.176D).

ἀντιπέμπ-ω, 1. *send back,* hence *reflect* ἡ ψυχή...δέχεται ἀκτῖνα ἀπὸ τῆς δόξης τοῦ πνεύματος καὶ ταύτην ~ει Chrys.*hom.7.5 in 2Cor.* (10.486E); **2.** *throw to and fro* σφαῖραν ἀλλήλοις ἀ. Thdt.*h.e.*4.15.5 (3.972).

***ἀντιπεπονθότως,** *in a contrary sense,* Dion.Ar.*d.n.*7.1(M.3.865B).

***ἀντιπεραιόομαι,** *cross over,* Soz.*h.e.*9.15.1(M.67.1625B).

***ἀντιπεράω,** = foreg., Jo.Mal.*chron.*5 p.95(M.97.181A); Thphn. *chron.*p.270(M.108.669C).

ἀντιπεριάγω, *drive back,* Synes.*ep.*57(M.66.1392B).

***ἀντιπερίαμμα, τό,** *amulet*; used as counter-charm for evil purposes, Eus.*Ps.*69:2–4(M.23.768D).

ἀντιπεριΐστημι, 1. *compress together again*; air, Bas.*hex.*4.1(1.

33D; M.29.80C); **2.** *transfer* εἰ...δυναίμην ἀ. τοῖς κομήταις τὸ ὄνειδος Synes.*calv*.4(p.196.13; M.66.1173A); Isid.Pel.*epp*.2.236(M.78.676A).

***ἀντιπεριπίπτω,** *strike against* ἀντιπεριπεσὼν ὑφάλοις πέτραις Clem.*paed*.2.2(M.8.424A; conj. ἂν περιπεσὼν p.173.20).

ἀντιπερισπ-άω, med., *pull against* ἄλληλα ~ώμενα συμβαστάζουσι καὶ ἀκίνητα διαμένουσι Cosm.Ind.*top*.2(M.88.80D).

ἀντιπερίστασις, ἡ, 1. *mutual opposition, resistance*, ‡Just.*confut*. 49(M.6.1541B); **2.** *reconsideration*, of an argument πρὸς ταύτην...τὴν ἀπορίαν ἐνστάσει καὶ ἀ. μαχώμεθα †Leont.B.*sect*.7.1(M.86.1240C).

***ἀντιπεριτέμνω,** *circumcise again*, Epiph.*mens*.16(M.43.264B).

***ἀντιπεριτρέπω, 1.** *reverse*, †Nil.*vit*.1(M.79.1140C); Eust.Mon.*ep*. (M.86.940C); **2.** *oppose in turn*, Zach.Mit.*opif*.(M.85.1088A); **3.** pass., *revert upon* ἀντιπεριτραπείσης αὐτοῖς τῆς ἰδίας κακουργίας Leont.H. *Nest*.1.1(M.86.1405A).

***ἀντιπεριτροπή, ἡ,** *reversal of meaning*, Max.*schol.d.n*.7.1(M.4. 341C).

***ἀντιπεριφέρω,** *carry round in opposite direction*, Leont.H. *monoph*.testimonia(M.86.1812C).

ἀντιπεριχωρέω, of the *communicatio idiomatum*, *interchange*, Leont.B.*Nest.et Eut*.2(M.86.1320B); Anast.*fid*.(p.272).

***ἀντιπεριχώρησις, ἡ,** *alternation*, Max.*schol.d.n*.5.8(M.4.328A).

ἀντιπίπτ-ω, 1. *resist*; **2.** *fall into* αὐτῇ [i.e. fault] ἀ. Chrys.*hom*. *31.4 in Jo*.(8.180D); **3.** *fit into* δύο ξύλα...~οντα ἀλλήλοις Cosm.Ind. *top*.5(M.88.204B); **4.** τὸ ~ον *obstacle*, *Lit.Jac*.(p.168.9).

***ἀντιπλάσσω,** *remould*, Clem.*paed*.2.10(p.209.3; M.8.500A).

ἀντιπλέκ-ω, *weave a plot against* ἤρξατο πρὸς ἡμᾶς μίσει καὶ ἔχθρᾳ ...~ειν *A.Andr.fr*.18(p.45.20).

ἀντιπλεονεκτέω, *surpass in turn*, Isid.Pel.*epp*.5.380(M.78.1556A); *ib*.5.452(1589A).

***ἀντιπλήκτης, ὁ,** *one who strikes back*, Bas.*renunt*.6(2.208B; M.31. 640C).

***ἀντίπληξις, ἡ,** *counter-stroke*, Gr.Naz.*carm*.1.2.25.39(M.37.816A); ‡Just.*qu.et resp*.97(M.6.1340B).

ἀντιπληρόω, *fulfil in return*, Gr.Nyss.*mart*.2(M.46.757A); id. *v.Macr*.(M.46.965A; conj. ἀποπληρ- p.376.8).

***ἀντιποιητέον,** *one must trouble about, seek after*, Clem.*paed*.2.10 (p.218.16; M.8.520A).

***ἀντιποιητικός,** *striving after* τὴν δὲ κατὰ φύσιν [sc. δειλίαν] ὡς τῆς ἐνυπαρχούσης τῇ φύσει ἀντιποιητικῆς τοῦ εἶναι δυνάμεως ἐνδεικτικήν Max.*Pyrr*.(M.91.297D).

***ἀντιποιμαίνω,** *play the rival shepherd*, Gr.Naz.*or*.42.21(M.36. 484A).

ἀντιποι-οῦμαι, 1. *strive after*; **a.** in good sense εἰ...~ῃ σωτηρίας Just.*dial*.8.2(M.6.492D); τῆς βασιλείας τῶν οὐρανῶν ~ηθῆναι Or. *exp.in Pr*.5:15(M.17.173D); Ath.*inc*.47.5(M.25.181A); τοῦ...δημιουργοῦ ~ουμένου τῆς δόξης τοῦ ἰδίου πλάσματος †Bas.*bapt*.1.2.7(2.634B; M.31.1537A); Chrys.*hom.15.3 in Mt*.(7.189B); **b.** in bad sense, Ephr. 1.208E; Ammon.*Jo*.4:43(M.85.1428B); ἀ. τοῦ πολυπραγμονῆσαι id. *Ac*.16:29–30(M.85.1561A); Nil.*epp*.2.177(M.79.289D); *ib*.3.52(416D); esp. of eccl. authority ἀ. [sc. Novatian] τῆς ἐπισκοπῆς Corn.ap.Eus. *h.e*.6.43.13(M.20.621B); Chrys.*sac*.3.6(p.56.16; 1.384B); Proc.G.*Num*. 17:2(M.87.841D); hence **2.** *contend for*, Rhod.ap.Eus.*h.e*.5.13.2(M.20. 460B); **3.** *lay claim to* μήτε τῶν προσόντων τε καὶ ἰδίων ~ούμεθα †Bas.*bapt*.1.2.11(2.637C; M.31.1544C); **4.** *take the side of, uphold, defend* τῶν προσφευγόντων τῇ προστασίᾳ τῆς σῆς μεγαλονοίας ~εῖσθαι Bas.*ep*.86(3.178E; M.32.485C); Tit.Bost.*fr.Lc*.7:24(p.167.9); Chrys. *hom.20.6 in Eph*.(11.152C); Pall.*v.Chrys*.9(p.59.8; M.47.34); τοὺς Ὠριγένους ~ουμένους Justn.*Or*.(p.192.10; M.86.951C); id.*conf.anath*. 11(p.92.26; M.86.1017A); **5.** *offer instead* τὰς...πρεσβείας ἃς ἀντεποιοῦντο πολλάκις ὑπὲρ τῶν πλημμεληκότων Cyr.*Ps*.78:5(M.69.1196A).

ἀντιπορεύομαι, *go in a contrary direction*, Gr.Naz.*carm*.1.2.12.2 (M.37.753A).

***ἀντιπορθμέω,** *carry over in face of opposition*, ‡Gr.Naz.*Chr.pat*. 1642(M.38.267A).

ἀντίπορος, 1. *opposite, face to face*, Nonn.*par.Jo*.1:18(M.43.752C); hence *antiphonal*, Paul.Sil.*Soph*.432(M.86.2136A); **2.** *opposing, contrary*, Nonn.*par.Jo*.6:18(M.43.796C); *ib*.9:28(829B); *ib*.10:34(837A).

***ἀντιποτίζω,** *give to drink in return*, Isid.Pel.*epp*.1.483(M.78. 445B).

***ἀντιπράκτωρ, ὁ,** *one who counteracts*, Sophr.H.*v.Anast*.(M.92. 1709D).

ἀντίπρασις, ἡ, *barter*, *A.Jo*.33(p.168.11).

ἀντιπροβάλλομαι, 1. *put forward in opposition*, Gr.Nyss.*v.Gr. Thaum*.(M.46.916C); **2.** *cite* an authority *against* ἐπειδὴ δ' Ὅμηρον... προβάλλῃ, τὸν αὐτὸν ἀντιπροβαλοῦμαι Isid.Pel.*epp*.2.228(M.78.665A); Proc.G.*Gen*.3:1(M.87.188D).

ἀντιπροσάγω, *proffer instead* of τροφῆς εὐτελεστάτης ἀ. αὐτῷ τὴν δουλείαν Cyr.*Is*.1.2(2.58E).

***ἀντιπροστίθημι,** *add by way of objection*, Meth.*symp*.3.3(p.29.18; M.18.64B n.).

ἀντιπροσφέρω, *allege in comparison*, Gr.Nyss.*laud.Bas*.(M.46. 805B).

ἀντιπρόσωπος, 1. *facing, face to face*, Phil.Thm.*ep*.ap.Eus.*h.e*. 8.10.5(M.20.765A); Gr.Nyss.*hom.4 in Cant*.(M.44.833B); τοῖς εἰς ὄψιν ἠγμένοις δι' ἁγιασμοῦ καὶ ἀ. ἤδη γεγονόσι διὰ τῆς ἐν πίστει παρρησίας Cyr.*ador*.9(1.299E); Thdt.*Jer*.34:19(2.560); ἀ. βλέπων τῷ θεῷ Bas. Sel.*or*.35.2(M.85.377B); neut. sing. as prep., *in front of* ἀ. τῶν ἀγαλμάτων Clem.*str*.7.7(conj. p.33.2 n. for ἀπαντι- M.9.461A); ‡Nil. *perist*.9(M.79.916D); hence **2.** *confronting, in opposition* ἀ. ἡμῖν οἱ τῆς θεοπνεύστου γραφῆς λόγοι Bas.*reg.fus*.proem.(2.332A; M.31. 900C); *Const.App*.6.1.2 = Anast.S.*qu.et resp*.62(M.89.649A); Gr. Nyss.*hom.in 1Cor.6:18*(M.46.492A); **3.** *before one's face*, Clem.*str*.5.4 (p.340.1; M.9.41A); Cyr.*Jo*.5.1(4.465A); Bas.Sel.*or*.29.1(M.85.328C); **4.** *as substitute, representative* ἀπόκρυψις προσώπου εἰς ἀ. Leont.H. *Nest*.3.8(M.86.1636A); εἰ...ἀ. δέδωκεν, οὐκ ὄντως εἴρηται τάδε περὶ τῆς ἀγάπης αὐτοῦ *ib*.5.2(1725C); **5.** neut. as subst., *underside* οὐκ ἐπὶ ἀ. τῆς γῆς εἶπεν ἀλλ' ἐπὶ προσώπου Cosm.Ind.*top*.2(v.l. ἐπὶ παντὶ προσώπῳ M.88.132A).

ἀντιπροφέρω, *cite as parallel*, Gr.Nyss.*fat*.(M.45.161A).

ἀντιπτωτικός, *contradicting*, Max.*ep*.6(M.91.425A).

***ἀντιπυνθάνομαι,** *inquire in turn*, *Hom.Clem*.2.39; Thdt.*h.rel*.6 (3.1171).

ἀντιρρητικός, 1. *refuting, answering*, Gr.Naz.*or*.43.7(M.36.585A); Gr.Nyss.*Apoll*.tit.(M.45.1123); βιβλία...ἀ. οὕτω λεγόμενα Pall.*h. Laus*.38(p.121.1; M.34.1194B); ἀ. λίβελλοι *counter-plea* addressed to court by one party after other party has initiated an action, *PMasp*.(v. *LS*. p.xliv)67295; **2.** *controversial*, Dion.Ar.*d.n*.6.2(M.3. 857A).

ἀντιρρητορεύω, *raise an objection*, Ephr.1.113A; Jo.D.*hom*.8.7 (M.96.709C).

***ἀντιρρητορέω,** = foreg., ‡Ath.*palm*.(M.26.1312B).

***ἀντίρρητος,** in phrase ἐξ ἀντιρρήτου *by inverse argument* οὐ πλατὺς μὲν ὁ λόγος· οὐ γὰρ ἔστιν εἰπεῖν ἐξ ἀ. λαβόντα καὶ σαφηνίσαι Cyr.*Jo*.6(conj. 4.583E for ἀντηρίτου).

***ἀντιρριζόω,** *plant instead* ξύλον [i.e. the Cross] ξύλῳ ἀ. ‡Chrys. *pasch*.6.5(p.177.1; 8.271E).

ἀντίρροπος, *equivalent to* ἵνα μηδὲ ἡ τοῦ τόπου ἀξιοπιστία...ἀ. τῆς ἀληθείας εἶναι νομίζηται Thdr.Mops.*Gal*.1:8(p.11.18; M.66.901C); Isid.Pel.*epp*.3.373(M.78.1021D); Max.*opusc*.(M.91.113B).

***ἀντισαγηνεύω,** *catch in turn*, ‡Chrys.*hom*.13(13.252B).

ἀντισκοτέω, *obstruct*, Pall.*v.Chrys*.5(conj. p.30.11 for ἠντικότει; ἠψυχώθη M.47.19).

ἀντισοφίζομαι, 1. *use counter-devices*, Gr.Naz.*or*.2.19(M.35.428C); **2.** *make repartee*, Bas.Sel.*or*.20.2(M.85.252C).

***ἀντισοφίστευμα, τό,** *hostile device*, Tat.*orat*.12(p.14.7; M.6.833A).

ἀντισ-όω, 1. act., *regard as equal, compare* ἀ. τῷ φωτὶ ἐκείνῳ τὸ τοῦ Ἰησοῦ φῶς Ammon.*Ac*.26:13(M.85.1596D); **2.** pass., *be equal* τοῖς ἁμαρτήμασι τὰ τῆς ὕβρεως ~ώθη Gr.Naz.*ep*.143(M.37. 215A); **3.** pres. ptcpl. as subst. τὸ ἀντισοῦν *counterpoise* τὸ ἀ. τοῦ τῆς δικαιοσύνης...ζυγοῦ Clem.*paed*.1.10(M.8.360B; ἀντισηκοῦν p.144.11).

***ἀντιστάδη, ἡ,** *opposite quarter*, Geo.Pis.*Pers*.2.285(M.92.1229A).

ἀντισταθμάω, *weigh against*, hence *compare*, Bas.*hom.in Ps*.61:10 (1.197B; M.29.480A); id.*ep*.226.2(3.347D; M.32.848A); Gr.Naz.*ep*.223. 2(M.37.365A).

ἀντισταθμίζ-ω, 1. act., *weigh out in return* πάντων αὐτῷ τῶν προσόντων ἀ. Isid.Pel.*epp*.1.182(M.78.301A); Diad.*perf*.42(p.48.24); Anast.S.*Ps.6*(M.89.1125D); **2.** med., *bear comparison with* οὐκ ἔστιν ...γονεῦσιν ~όμενον κτῆμα Tim.Ant.*caec*.1(M.28.1001A).

ἀντίσταθμος, ὁ, *balancing*, Cyr.*Jo*.12.1(4.1119B).

***ἀντισταλτέον,** *one must contrast*, Isid.Pel.*epp*.3.381(M.78.1025B).

ἀντίστασις, ἡ, 1. *revolt*, Chrys.*hom.69.2 in Jo*.(8.411A); Procl. CP *ep*.(p.67.28; M.65.881B); **2.** fig., *assault*, of arguments παντὶ ἀντιστάσεως τρόπῳ κεχρημένοι οἱ Ἕλληνες ‡Just.*qu.Gr*.15.45(M.6. 1489B); †Leont.B.*sect*.7.1(M.86.1240A); **3.** *resistance* σατανᾶς...δέδιε ...τοῦ πλουτοῦντος κατ' ἀρετὴν τὴν ἀ. Cyr.*Ps*.9:30(M.69.784C); id.*Os*. 80(3.113A); id.*Nah*.25(3.503E); **4.** in music, *balance* κατὰ τὴν ἴσην ἀ. ἀλλήλαις συνηχοῦσι Ath.*gent*.38(M.25.77A).

***ἀντιστασιώδης,** *conflicting with*, Clem.*str*.2.2(p.115.4; M.8.933C).

ἀντιστατικός, *opposing, hostile*, Meth.*Porph*.1.5(p.504.2; M.18. 400A); Mac.Aeg.*hom*.15.48(M.34.609A).

***ἀντιστατικῶς,** *in opposition*, Gr.Nyss.*hom.2 in Eccl*.(M.44.645D).

***ἀντίστατος**, *counterpart*, Gr.Naz.*carm*.1.2.34.209(M.37.960A).

***ἀντιστέλλω**, *set in contrast*; pass., *differ from*, Bas.*ep*.188 *can*.15 (3.276A; M.32.684B).

ἀντιστήκω, pres. formed from perf. tense of ἀνθίστημι, *resist, withstand*, Didym.*Trin*.3.21(M.39.901A).

ἀντιστηρίζω, **1.** *strengthen in return*, Nil.*Eulog*.14(M.79.1112B); **2.** *support*, Didym.*Ps*.17:19(M.39.1249C); Cyr.*glaph.Ex*.2(1.274D); id.*glaph.Lev*.(1.364B).

***ἀντίστιχον, τό**, *line copied*, Thdr.Stud.*poen*.1.54(M.99.1740C).

ἀντιστοιχ-έω, **1.** *stand opposite in pairs*, of Gnost. aeons ἔνθεν ἀλλήλοις ~οῦντες συζυγίαν ἔχουσι Hipp.*haer*.6.18(p.144.16; M.16.3222A); hence **2.** *stand opposed to, be opposite* οὐ γὰρ μόνον ἐν τῷ πυρὶ καὶ ὕδατι θεωροῦμεν τὰς ~ούσας ποιότητας Gr.Nyss.*hex*.29 (M.44.89C,D); id.*or.dom*.4(p.68.3; M.44.1161B); **3.** *correspond, exchange places* πάρεστι...μυθήριά σοι νοεῖν ~ούντων τῶν γραμμάτων τὰ μυστήρια Clem.*prot*.2(p.12.3; M.8.73A).

***ἀντιστοίχως**, *correspondingly*, Didym.*Trin*.3.16(M.39.873A).

ἀντιστρατεύ-ω, **1.** act.; fig., *array against*, Chrys.*hom.16.11 in Mt*.(7.220B); Isid.Pel.*epp*.3.154(M.78.848D); Cyr.*thes*.11(5^1.92D); **2.** med.; **a.** lit., *take the field against*, Isid.Pel.*epp*.2.107(M.78.548D); **b.** fig. ὁ...νόμος ~όμενος...τῷ νόμῳ τοῦ θεοῦ Meth.*res*.2.6(p.340.13; M.18.304C); *ib*.2.7(p.342.10; M.41.1173C); Isid.Pel.*epp*.3.182(M.78.873A).

***ἀντιστρεπτικῶς**, *back again*, ‡Jo.D.*ep.Thphl*.28(M.95.381A).

ἀντιστρέφ-ω, **1.** trans.; **a.** *reverse, invert*, *A.Petr.et Paul*.81 (p.215.5); Bas.*Spir*.37(3.31C; M.32.133C); Chrys.*hom.22.4 in Mt*.(7.280C); id.*hom.4.2 in 2Cor*.(10.456C); **b.** *retort* in argument τί οὖν αὐτὸς ἀντιστρέψας φησί; id.*hom.41.1 in 1Cor*.(10.387B); **c.** *convert against* τὰ κυρίως ἀλλήλοις ἀντικείμενα ὅλην τὴν ἀπόφασιν καθ' ὅλης τῆς καταφάσεως ~ουσιν Leont.B.*cap.Sev*.18(M.86.1908A); **2.** intrans.; **a.** in logic, *be convertible* ~ει δὲ ἃ καὶ τοῖς τὸν ἐναντίον χειρίζουσι λόγον ἐπ' ἴσης ἔστιν εἰπεῖν, ὡς τὸ εἰ ζῷον τὸ κατὰ γαστρὸς ἢ οὐ ζῷον Clem.*str*.5.1(p.328.31; M.9.13D); Or.*fr.13 in Jo*.1:18(p.495.3); οὔτε γοῦν ὅρος οὔτε ἴδιον τὸ ἀγέννητος· οὐ γὰρ ~ει Didym.(‡Bas.)*Eun*.4(1.286B; M.29.688C); Chrys.*hom.39.2 in 1Cor*.(10.365C); οὐ...ἡ φύσις ὑπόστασις, ὅτι μηδὲ ~ει Leont.B.*Nest.et Eut*.1(M.86.1280A); of the 'Theotokos' ἀναγκαῖον τῷ καθ' αὑτὸ ὀνόματι ἢ τῷ πρὸς ἕτερον κειμένῳ, πρὸς τὸ ἀλλαχόθεν εἰλημμένον ὄνομα ~ειν Leont.H.*Nest*.4.41(M.86.1716B); id.*monoph*.(M.86.1856D); Max.*ambig*.(M.91.1225B); **b.** *be the converse*, Or.*Jo*.20.17(p.348.22; M.14.609C); **3.** impers. ~ει *the relation is reciprocal* τί ἄρα ἐστὶν ἡ προαίρεσις; ἆρα τὸ ἑκούσιον ἐπειδὴ πᾶν τὸ κατὰ προαίρεσιν καὶ ἑκούσιόν ἐστιν; ἀλλ' οὐκ ἀ. ... εἰ ταὐτὸν ἦν ἑκούσιον καὶ προαίρεσις Nemes.*nat.hom*.33(M.40.732A); **4.** med., *change sides* ~ονται πρὸς ἑκατέρους παρ' ἀλλήλων αἱ τάξεις Bas.Sel.*or*.27.1(M.85.312B).

ἀντιστροφή, ἡ, **1.** in logic; **a.** *correspondence*, Athenag.*res*.11 (p.59.16; M.6.993A); Max.*opusc*.(M.91.52B); κατὰ ἀντιστροφήν *reciprocally*, Leont.B.*cap.Sev*.17(M.86.1905C); Max.*opusc*.(M.91.52B); **b.** *obversion* τὴν ὑπὸ τῆς σῆς ἀγχινοίας νομοθετουμένην ἀ., μᾶλλον δὲ καταστροφήν [ref. Apollinarius] Thdr.Mops.*fr.Apoll*.(p.320.13; M.66.1000D); **c.** *inversion* τῷ καιρῷ τῆς ἀναστάσεως κατὰ τὴν καλῶς γενησομένην ἀ. ἐν πνεύματι ἁγίῳ...καταποθήσεται ἡ σὰρξ ὑπὸ τῆς ψυχῆς Max.*ambig*.(M.91.1252A); **d.** *converse*, Or.*comm.in Mt*.10.15 (p.18.27; M.13.872A); *conversion*, Leont.B.*cap.Sev*.11(M.86.1904C); **2.** *reversal* τὴν καλὴν ἀ. καὶ...οὕτως ἐκ τῶν λυπηρῶν ἐπανελθεῖν τὰ χρηστότερα Gr.Naz.*or*.38.4(M.36.316A); Cyr.*ador*.15(1.540E); Geo.Pis.*Pers*.1.57(M.92.1202A).

ἀντισυζυγία, ἡ, *coupling of opposites*, *Hom.Clem*.3.33.

***ἀντισυνάγ-ω**, *hold a rival assembly* τοὺς...ἀποσχίσαντας δὲ καὶ ~οντας τοῖς κανονικοῖς...ἐπισκόποις CCP(381)*can*.6.

***ἀντισύναξις, ἡ**, *rival assembly*, CCP(381)*ep*.ap.Thdt.*h.e*.5.9.7 (3.1029).

ἀντισυνάπτω, *join at opposite ends*, Cosm.Ind.*top*.1(M.88.65C).

***ἀντισύνδρομος**, *surging in conflict*; of waves, Geo.Pis.*bell.Avar*. 486(M.92.1291B).

***ἀντισύνθεσις, ἡ**, *converse*, Geo.Pis.*hex*.1687(M.92.1566A).

***ἀντισύνθετος**, *corresponding*, Geo.Pis.*hex*.1145(M.92.1522A); *ib*. 1174(1524A).

***ἀντισυνοδικά, τά**, *exchanged synodical letters*, Jo.VI CP *ep*. (M.96.1429B); Taras.*ep*.5(M.98.1476D).

***ἀντισυντάσσω**, *compose a reply*, Epiph.*haer*.72.5(p.259.25; M.42.388D).

***ἀντισυστρέφω**, *roll together in opposite direction*, Geo.Pis.*hex*. 1069(M.92.1516A).

***ἀντισύστροφος**, *turned round in the opposite direction*, Geo.Pis. *Sev*.90(M.92.1628B).

ἀντισφαιρίζω, *throw an objection*; as if playing ball (i.e. thoughtlessly), Meth.*symp*.3.4(p.30.13; M.18.65A).

ἀντισφίγγω, *bind tightly* to, Geo.Pis.*hex*.119(M.92.1440A).

***ἀντίσωμος**, *serving as substitute*, Gr.Mag.*dial*.(tr.Zach.)3.1(M. *PL*.77.218C); neut. as subst., *substitute*, Ephr.2.273A.

***ἀντιτάκτης, ὁ**, *one who sets* men *against* God, hence οἱ ἀ. a Gnostic sect, Clem.*str*.3.4(p.211.16; M.8.1137C); Thdt.*haer*.1.16 (4.309).

***ἀντιτακτικῶς**, *in opposition*, Gr.Nyss.*hom.8 in Eccl*.(M.44.744A).

***ἀντιταλάντευσις, ἡ**, *contrariness* εὐμεταμέλητον γὰρ τὸ γένος τὸ τῶν ἀνθρώπων, καὶ πρὸς ἀ. ἕτοιμον ‡Chrys.*hom*.13(13.255D).

ἀντιταλαντεύ-ω, **1.** trans.; **a.** *weigh against, balance against* ~ων τὴν ἐκείνων ὠκύτητα τῇ ἑαυτοῦ βραδύτητι Iren.*haer*.1.17.1(M.7.637B); Gr.Naz.*carm*.1.2.15.60(M.37.770A); Chrys.*fr.Job* 6:1(M.64.589D); πᾶσαν...τὴν κτίσιν ἀ. τῇ περὶ τὸν θεὸν ἀγάπῃ Thdt.*Rom*.8:39(3.96); ταύτην μου...τὴν ταπείνωσιν καὶ τὴν ταλαιπωρίαν ταῖς ἐμαῖς ~σας παρανομίαις δὸς τὴν ἄφεσιν id.*Ps*.24:18(1.762); Cosm.Ind.*top*.7 (M.88.368C); **b.** *weigh out instead* ~ουσι τοῖς εὐθυγενέσι βρέφεσιν ἄργυρον καὶ τοῦτο προσκομίζουσι τῷ θεῷ Thdt.*qu.38 in Lev*.(1.216); **c.** *apportion* αὐτοῖς ἡ δίαιτα ἀκριβέσιν ~εται ζυγοῖς Evagr.*h.e*.1.21 (p.31.23; M.86.2481B); **2.** intrans., *counterbalance* ἡ ~ουσα γνῶσις Clem.*paed*.1.9(p.142.2; M.8.356C); οὐκ ~ουσαν μόνον ἔχων τὴν ἀξίαν τῷ πλήθει τῶν ὑποδίκων Procl.CP *or.laud.BMV* 6(p.105.17; M.65.685D).

ἀντιτάλαντον, τό, *compensation, reward*, Gr.Naz.*carm*.2.2(poem.) 2.11(M.37.1478A); v.l. for ἀμφιτάλαντος q.v., *ib*.2.1.13.172(1241A).

ἀντιταράσσω, *stir up in opposition*, Nil.*Eulog*.4(M.79.1100B).

ἀντιτάσσ-ω, **1.** act., *set in opposition*, Clem.*str*.3.4(p.211.20; M.8.1140A); Thdt.*Rom*.2:27(3.35); **2.** med., *set oneself against, resist* μὴ ~εσθαι τῷ ἐπισκόπῳ Ign.*Eph*.5.3; *Diogn*.6.5; ‡Ath.*dial.Trin*.1.16 (M.28.1141C).

***ἀντιτελής**, ? *at the end of one's life*, but prob. f.l. for παντελής Or.*Ps*.14:5(p.469); cf.Eus.*Ps*.14:5(p.408).

ἀντιτεχνέω, *act craftily against*, Meth.*symp*.8.1(p.81.12; M.18.140A).

ἀντίτεχνος, **1.** *scheming against*, Clem.*paed*.3.2(p.243.1; M.8.572B); **2.** neut. as subst., *counter-scheme*, Nil.*Eulog*.14(M.79.1112B).

***ἀντίτητος**, *impregnable*, ‡Ath.*renunt*.3(M.28.1412C).

ἀντιτίθημι, **1.** *set against*; **a.** in comparison or contrast ἀ. τῷ μὲν ἀσωμάτῳ τὸ πνεῦμα Clem.*ecl*.25(p.144.4; M.9.709C); Ath.*Ar*.1.23 (M.26.60B) cit. s. ἀνθρώπινος; **b.** in opposition, Gr.Nyss.*hex*.2(M.44.64B); ὁ διάβολος...πᾶσαν αἵρεσιν ἣν ἀντέθηκεν τῷ λόγῳ τῆς ἀληθείας Thdr.Mops.*2Thess*.2:3(M.66.933B; cf. p.51.11 n.); **2.** *object, oppose*, Just.*1apol*.30.1(M.6.373B); Epiph.*haer*.70.1(p.233.7; M.42.340B).

ἀντιτιμώρησις, ἡ, *vengeance*, Or.*sel.in Ps*.2:5(M.12.1105C); Nemes.*nat.hom*.21(M.40.692A); Jo.D.*f.o*.2.16(M.94.932D).

ἀντιτιτρώσκω, *wound in turn*, Bas.*hom*.14.8(2.129C; M.31.460C).

ἀντιτονέω, *resist stoutly*, Meth.*Porph*.2.3(p.505.27, v.l. ἀντιτορήσῃ M.18.404A).

ἀντιτραχύνομαι, *be exasperated in turn*, Gr.Nyss.*Eun*.12(1 p.302.26; M.45.1013C).

***ἀντιτρέπω**, *change back*, *Hom.Clem*.20.9.

ἀντιτρέφω, *feed in return*, Or.*Jo*.13.32(31; p.257.3; M.14.456A).

***ἀντιτρέχω**, **1.** *run in rivalry*, Gr.Naz.*or*.45.24(M.36.657A); Max.*ambig*.(M.91.1381A); **2.** *rush violently*, ‡Paul.Sil.*therm.Pyth*.(M.86.2263).

***ἀντιτρυτανεύω**, *make compensation for*, ‡Caes.Naz.*dial*.122(M.38.1012).

ἀντιτυπ-έω, **1.** *resist, rebut*; **a.** lit., Bas.*hom.in Ps*.32:5(1.135A; M.29.332B); **b.** fig., Just.*1apol*.8.2(M.6.337C); ἡ...ἐναντιουμένη τῷ θείῳ βουλήματι σκληρύνεσθαι καὶ ~εῖν δίκην λίθου...τὸν λόγον Or.*sel.in Ex*.3:21(M.12.284A); οὐ μόνον ἠλίθιον πεῖσαι ἀλλὰ καὶ ἀνόητον ~ῆσαι δύνανται Adam.*dial*.4.12(p.168.6; M.11.1828C); **2.** med., *rebound* πρὸς σκληρὰν καὶ ἀπειθῆ καρδίαν λόγος...ὥσπερ ~ούμενος πρὸς ἑαυτὸν ἐπανέρχεται †Just.*fr.res*.(p.49; M.6.1600B).

ἀντιτύπησις, ἡ, *resistance*, Meth.*Porph*.2.3(p.505.24; M.18.404A).

ἀντιτυπία, ἡ, **1.** *resistance, solidity* σῶμα οὕτω στερεὸν καὶ ἀ. ἔχον Just.*dial*.5.2(M.6.488A); εἰς τίνα ἐρείσῃ; ἀ. γὰρ οὐκ ἔχων εἰς κενὸν ἐκβαθρεύεται *Hom.Clem*.17.11; Bas.*Eun*.1.6(1.217C; M.29.524A); τῆς θεότητος ἀπὸ τῆς...ἀσυνθέτου φύσεως εἰς σαρκώδη ἀ. ἀλλοιωθείσης Gr.Nyss.*Apoll*.2(M.45.1128A); id.*or.catech*.23(p.88.4; M.45.61C); εἰκότως ἀνδρίσῃ καὶ τῶν τιτρωσκόντων τὴν ψυχὴν ξιφῶν ὑπερανάσχῃς, ἀ. κτησάμενος τὴν ἀπάθειαν, ἄγγελοί σοι μετὰ τὴν πάλην διακονήσουσι Isid.Pel.*epp*.1.75(M.78.236A); of resurrection body of Christ ἀ. σώματος πληροφοροῦσα τοὺς ἁπτομένους †Ath.*fr*.(M.26.1237B); τὸ σῶμα ἐκεῖνο...πάσης ἀ. ὑπέρτερον γεγονός ‡Cyr.*Trin*.17(6^3.23E; M.77.

1156C); **2.** *figurative representation, symbolism* ἄνελε ταῦτα πάντα καὶ εἴ τι ἕτερον εἰς ἀ. θείαν Thdr.Stud.*icon*.1(M.99.489B).

ἀντίτυπος (ἀντίτυπον, τό), A. *answering*; **1.** in gen. ἀ. φάτο μῦθον Nonn.*par.Jo*.6:70(M.43.804B); *ib*.16:27(881C); hence *resounding* καὶ τὰ μὲν ἀντιτύποισιν ἐπαυχήσαντα βοείαις Paul.Sil.*Soph*.983 (M.86.2156B); **2.** *corresponding*, as stamp to die ἀ. μίμημα *Orac. Sib*.1.33; *ib*.1.333; *ib*.8.270; Nonn.*par.Jo*.3:5(M.43.765C); λίθον ...ἀ. στήριγμα χαραδραίου πυλεῶνος *ib*.20:8(909A); hence *in accordance* θεημάχος ἐστὲ γενέθλη...ἔργοις ἀ. ἐπιστώσασθε γενέθλην *ib*.8:40 (820A); **3.** *copy*; **a.** of a document τῷ ἀ. τοῦ θείου γράμματος Flavius *ep*.ap.Ath.*apol.sec*.85(p.164.8; M.25.401B); CAnc.(358)*ep. syn*.ap.Epiph.*haer*.73.2(p.270.10; M.42.405C); Liber.*ep.Maced*.ap. Socr.*h.e*.4.12.27(M.67.492A); hence *draft copy* καὶ τοῖς ταχυγράφοις τὰ ἀ. δοῦναι τῶν τότε γραφέντων ἐπέταξα Synes.*ep*.67(M.66.1432B); **b.** of an image τῇ καρδίᾳ ἐπαρθεὶς ἀ. ταύτης εἰκόνα ἐποίησεν Hipp. *Dan*.2.15.2(M.10.677B); Gel.Cyz.*h.e*.1.6 tit.(M.85.1205B); τίνος δὲ χάριν οἱ πιστοὶ ἅπαντες σταυροὺς μὲν ἀ. τοῦ σταυροῦ τοῦ Χριστοῦ ποιοῦμεν; ‡Ath.*qu.Ant*.41(M.28.624A); **4.** = τύπος *symbol* of things to come Ἀβραάμ...θύει θυσίαν ξένην καὶ τῆς μεγάλης ἀ. Gr.Naz.*or*.28. 18(p.48.17; M.36.49A); προτυπῶν [sc. Melchizedek] τῶν μυστηρίων τὰ αἰνίγματα, ἀ. τοῦ σώματος τοῦ κυρίου Epiph.*haer*.55.6(p.331.14; M.41.981A); πρόβατον ἐνιαύσιον...ὅπερ ἦν ἀ. τοῦ σωτῆρος *ib*.51.31 (p.304.10; 944B); *cat.Apoc*.16:19(p.422.2); *opposite, contrary symbol* ὁ δὲ χαλκοῦς ὄφις κρεμᾶται μὲν κατὰ τῶν δακνόντων ὄφεων, οὐχ ὡς τύπος δὲ τοῦ ὑπὲρ ἡμῶν παθόντος, ἀλλ' ὡς ἀ. Gr.Naz.*or*.45.22(M.36. 654B); **5.** *antitype*, in sense of fulfilment of type: of BMV χαίροις, ἡ ἀ. τῆς τοῦ Νῶε ἔμψυχος θήκη ‡Jo.D.*hom*.5(M.96.649B); of Cross ἡ ἀ. τοῦ ἐσταυρωμένου θεανθρώπου μορφή Germ.CP *or*.1(M.98.232A); **6.** cf. τύπος; *earthly form corresponding to a heavenly reality*, or, in this sense only, *antitype*, cf. οὐ γὰρ εἰς χειροποίητα εἰσῆλθεν ἅγια Χριστός, ἀ. τῶν ἀληθινῶν Heb.9:24; ἡ γὰρ σὰρξ αὕτη ἀ. ἐστιν τοῦ πνεύματος· οὐδεὶς οὖν τὸ ἀ. φθείρας τὸ αὐθεντικὸν μεταλήψεται *2Clem*.14.3; ἄνθρωπον ὠνόμασαν ὅτι ἦν ἀ. τοῦ προόντος ἀγεννήτου Val.Gn.*fr*.ap.Epiph.*haer*.31.5(p.391.7; M.41.481C); ὃ [sc. the offspring of Achamoth] δὴ καὶ αὐτὸ ἐκκλησίαν εἶναι λέγουσιν, ἀ. τῆς ἄνω ἐκκλησίας Iren.*haer*.1.5.6(M.7.501B); cf. *ex eorum derivatione cum alii facti essent et antitypi eis qui super eos essent*, *ib*.1.24.3(676A); τὰ ἀ. οὖν τῶν ἀληθινῶν ποιήσας Μωϋσῆς, ἔδωκεν τῷ κατὰ σάρκα Ἰσραήλ *Dial.Tim.et Aquil*.126 r°(p.96); ἐπειδὴ τοῦ κόσμου παντὸς ἀ. τὴν Μωυσέως σκηνὴν οἶδεν ὁ λόγος Gr.Naz.*or*.28.31(p.69.18; M.36. 72A); ἀ. γάρ ἐστι ταῦτα τῶν ἐπουρανίων Epiph.*haer*.66.85(p.128.13; M.42.165C); ὃν...Ἰαννὴς καὶ Ἰαμβρὴς ἐφύτευσαν ἀ. τοῦ ἀληθινοῦ παραδείσου ποιῆσαι βουλευόμενοι ‡Pall.*h.mon*.28.5(p.87.21); εἴρηται τῷ ἐν ἁγίοις Γρηγορίῳ ἐν τῷ Ἀπολογητικῷ...τὰ νῦν θεῖα μυστήρια ἀ. εἶναι μειζόνων μυστηρίων Oecum.*Heb*.10:1(p.466.18; M.119.384D); ἐν μνημείῳ καινῷ λελατομημένῳ ἐκ πέτρας, ὅπερ ἐστὶν ἀ. τοῦ ἁγίου μνήματος ἐκείνου τὸ θυσιαστήριον ‡Bas.*h.myst*.50(p.391.12); **7.** applied to sacraments, *sign*, cf. τύπος; **a.** in baptism (cf. 1Petr. 3:21) τῶν τοῦ Χριστοῦ παθημάτων ἀ. Cyr.H.*catech*.20.6; χριστοὶ δὲ γεγόνατε τοῦ ἁγίου πνεύματος τὸ ἀ. δεξάμενοι...ὑμῖν...ἐδόθη χρῖσμα, τὸ ἀ. οὗ ἐχρίσθη Χριστός *ib*.21.1; **b.** in eucharist γενόμενοι γάρ, οὐκ ἄρτου καὶ οἴνου κελεύονται γεύσασθαι ἀλλὰ ἀντιτύπου σώματος καὶ αἵματος τοῦ Χριστοῦ Cyr.H.*catech*.23.20; εἴ πού τι τῶν ἀ. τοῦ τιμίου σώματος ἢ τοῦ αἵματος ἡ χεὶρ ἐθησαύρισεν Gr.Naz.*or*.8.18(M.35.809C); ἐν τῇ ἐκκλησίᾳ προσφέρεται ἄρτος καὶ οἶνος, ἀ. τῆς σαρκὸς αὐτοῦ καὶ τοῦ αἵματος. καὶ οἱ μεταλαμβάνοντες ἐκ τοῦ φαινομένου ἄρτου, πνευματικῶς τὴν σάρκα τοῦ κυρίου ἐσθίουσι Mac.Aeg.*hom*.27.17(M.34. 705B); τὰ ἀ. μυστήρια τοῦ τιμίου σώματος *Const.App*.5.14.7; τὴν ἀ. τοῦ βασιλείου σώματος Χριστοῦ δεκτὴν εὐχαριστίαν *ib*.6.30.2; *ib*.7. 25.4; εἰ δὲ ἡ σὰρξ εἰς θεότητος μετεβλήθη φύσιν, οὗ δὴ χάριν μεταλαμβάνουσι τῶν ἀ. τοῦ σώματος; περιττὸς γὰρ ὁ τύπος ἀνῃρημένης τῆς ἀληθείας Thdt.*eran*.3(4.269); in later writers, applicable only to unconsecrated elements λαβὼν τὸν ἄρτον εὐχαριστήσας ἀνέδειξε καὶ ἔκλασεν, ἐμμίξας ἑαυτὸν τῷ ἀ. Eutych.*pasch*.2(M.86.2393B); καθὼς καὶ σφραγὶς μία, πάντα τὰ ἐκτυπώματα αὐτῆς...τοῖς μεταλαμβάνουσι μεταδίδωσι καὶ μία μένει...σῶμα καὶ αἷμα τοῦ κυρίου, τοῖς ἀ. ἐντιθέμενον διὰ τῶν ἱερουργιῶν *ib*.2,3(2393C,D); προθέντες τὰ ἀ. τοῦ ἁγίου σώματος καὶ αἵματος *Lit.Bas*.(p.329.24); cf. *tunc jam offeratur oblatio a diaconibus episcopo et gratias agat panem quidem in exemplum (quod dicit Graecus antitypum) corporis Christi; calicem vino mixtum propter antitypum (quod dicit Graecus similitudinem) sanguinis, quod effusum est pro omnibus qui crediderunt in eum*, Hipp.*trad.ap*.23.1; later writers contended against above usage, except as applied to unconsecrated elements ἐσφάλλετο διὰ ἰδιωτείαν καὶ ἔλεγεν 'οὐκ ἔστι φύσει ὁ ἄρτος ὃν λαμβάνομεν σῶμα Χριστοῦ ἀλλ' ἀ.' *Apophth.Patr*.(M.65.157A); μὴ γένοιτο ἡμᾶς εἰπεῖν ἀ. τοῦ σώματος Χριστοῦ τὴν ἁγίαν κοινωνίαν ἢ ψιλὸν ἄρτον Anast.S.*hod*.23 (M.89.297B); οὐκ εἶπεν, τοῦτό ἐστι τὸ ἀ. τοῦ σώματος καὶ τοῦ αἵματός μου *ib*.(297C); ‡Sophr.H.*liturg*.3(M.87.3984C); πρὸ μὲν τῆς τοῦ ἁγιασμοῦ τελειώσεως ἀντίτυπά τισι τῶν ἁγίων πατέρων εὐσεβῶς ἔδοξεν ὀνομάζεσθαι· ὧν ἐστιν Εὐστάθιος CNic.(787)*refut*.(H.4.369D); πρὸ τοῦ ἁγιασθῆναι ἐκλήθη ἀ., μετὰ δὲ τὸν ἁγιασμὸν σῶμα κυρίως Χριστοῦ *ib*.(372A); εἰ δὲ καί τινες ἀντίτυπα τοῦ σώματος καὶ αἵματος τοῦ κυρίου τὸν ἄρτον καὶ τὸν οἶνον ἐκάλεσαν, ὡς ὁ θεοφόρος ἔφη Βασίλειος, οὐ μετὰ τὸ ἁγιασθῆναι εἶπον ἀλλὰ πρὶν ἁγιασθῆναι Jo.D.*f.o*.4.13(M. 94.1152C); ἀ. δὲ τῶν μελλόντων λέγονται...ὅτι νῦν μὲν δι' αὐτῶν μετέχομεν τῆς Χριστοῦ θεότητος, τότε δὲ νοητῶς διὰ μόνης τῆς θέας *ib*.(1153B).

B. *resistant*; **1.** *that which obstructs, intercepts* σχεθεῖσα [sc. a ray of light] τῷ ἀ. Gr.Naz.*or*.31.32(p.189.2; M.36.169C); Sophr.H.*v. Anast*.(M.92.1709A); **2.** *firm, solid* ἐν σώματι αὐτὸν ἀ. ἐγηγέρθαι Or.*Cels*.2.61(p.183.25; M.11.893A); τὸ τῆς σωματικῆς ὕλης ἀ. Eus.*d.e*. 6.20(p.286.19; M.22.469D); Gr.Nyss.*or.catech*.37(p.151.4; M.45.97A); Chrys.*stat*.9.3(2.101D); Dion.Ar.*d.n*.2.6(M.3.644B); **3.** met., *refractory, obstinate* ἀ. πρὸς τὴν ἀλήθειαν Or.*princ*.3.1.15(p.221.16; M.11.280A); id.*hom.6.3 in Jer*.(p.50.21; M.13.328B); Cyr.*Joel*.25(3.218A); Olymp. *Job* 22:21(M.93.248C).

ἀντιτυπ-όω, *represent symbolically* τὸ ἐπουράνιον καὶ νοερὸν θυσιαστήριον ἐν ᾧ ~οῦσι τὰς νοερὰς καὶ λογικὰς ἱεραρχίας τῶν ἀΰλων καὶ ἄνω δυνάμεων καὶ οἱ ἐπίγειοι καὶ ἔνυλοι ἱερεῖς ‡Bas.*h.myst*.5(p.259.8); ἡ ἐκκλησία ἐστὶν ἐπίγειος οὐρανὸς...~οῦσα τὴν σταύρωσιν καὶ τὴν ταφὴν καὶ τὴν ἀνάστασιν Χριστοῦ *ib*.1(p.257.12).

***ἀντιτύπως**, **1.** *stubbornly, obstructively*, Gr.Nyss.*Eun*.1(1 p.48. 25; M.45.277A); id.*or.catech*.31(p.113.8; M.45.77B); **2.** *firmly*, Const. *or.s.c*.15(p.175.11).

***ἀντιφαντιαστής, ὁ,** *enemy*, Jo.Mosch.*prat*.166(M.87.3033A).

***ἀντιφαντικῶς**, *in contradiction*, Jo.D.*Jacob*.52(M.94.1460D).

ἀντιφάρμακος, *remedial*, Geo.Pis.*hex*.1588(M.92.1558A); neut. as subst.; lit., *antidote*, Clem.*paed*.2.2(p.168.28; M.8.413A); met. πρόχειρον ἔχων τῆς κατὰ τοῦ υἱοῦ βλασφημίας τὸ ἀ. Gr.Nyss.*Eun*.10 (2 p.240.27; M.45.844A); of the Cross ξύλον ἀ. ξύλου τῇ φύσει χαρίζεται Bas.Sel.*parasc*.1(M.28.1056C); ὡς ἀ. τὰ διδόμενα μετανοίας ἐπιτίμια ‡Jo.D.*conf*.5(M.95.289C).

ἀντιφέρω, 1. act.; *transfer* ἀ. εἰς τὸν ἕτερον ὦμον Hegem.*Arch*.8 (p.12.1; M.10.1440A); **2.** med. and pass.; **a.** *set oneself against, fight against*, Cyr.*Ps*.35:7(M.69.920C); id.*Os*.3(3.13C); Philost.*h.e*.4.11(M. 65.524C); **b.** of rain in the antipodes, *fall in the opposite direction*, Cosm.Ind.*top*.1(M.88.65C).

***ἀντιφθεγγία, ἡ,** *opposition*, Geo.Pis.*hex*.1093(M.92.1566A).

ἀντιφθέγγ-ομαι, *respond antiphonally* εὔχου...ἀξίους ἡμᾶς εἶναι... λαμβάνειν στόμα καὶ σοφίαν εἰς τὸ τολμᾶν ~εσθαι ὑμῖν Bas.*ep*.50(3. 143A; M.32.388A); ὁ λαὸς ~εται 'τῷ πνεύματί σου' Chrys.*hom.36.4 in 1Cor*.(10.339D); Thdt.*h.rel*.17(3.1226); καὶ ἦν ἐν Σιὼν ἰδέσθαι ὥσπερ ~όμενα καὶ ἀντασπαζόμενα ἄλληλα τὰ οὐράνια καὶ τὰ ἐπίγεια Eulog. *palm*.12(M.86.2936B).

ἀντίφθογγος, 1. *antiphonal* ὕμνον Meth.*res*.1.56(p.316.10; M.41. 1149D); id.*symp*.3.6(p.32.16; M.18.69A); **2.** *sung in contradiction* νέα ψαλτήρια καὶ ἀ. τῷ Δαβίδ [i.e. of Apollinarians] Gr.Naz.*ep*.101 (M.37.193A).

***ἀντιφιλολογέομαι**, *exchange in friendly discussion*, Leont.N. *v.Sym*.1(M.93.1677C).

ἀντιφιλοτιμέομαι, pass.; **1.** *display a rival ambition, vie eagerly, emulate*, Or.*Eph*.1:8(p.239) cit. s. συμπαρεκτείνω; Gr.Naz.*or*.4.25(M. 35.552C); Chrys.*hom.18.1 in Mt*.(7.235B); **2.** (in bad sense) *be moved by jealousy against*, hence *contend in rivalry against* ἀ. τῷ θείῳ τοῦ Ἰωάννου κηρύγματι Gr.Nyss.*Eun*.10(2 p.239.30; M.45.841C); Chrys.*hom.74.4 in Mt*.(7.721C).

***ἀντιφιλοτίμησις, ἡ,** *rivalry*, Bas.Sel.*v.Thecl*.1(M.85.557A).

ἀντιφονεύω, *execute in turn*, Ptol.*ep*.(p.454.21; M.41.564B); *A.Jo*. 49(p.175.33).

***ἀντίφορος, ὁ,** 'ante-forum', name of ornamental square in Daphne, suburb of Antioch, Evagr.*h.e*.3.28(p.124.22; M.86.2653A); Jo.Mal.*chron*.16 p.398(M.97.589A).

ἀντίφορτος, *of balancing weight*, Leont.N.*v.Jo.Eleem*.10(p.19.19).

ἀντίφραγμα, τό, *bulwark, barrier*, Geo.Pis.*hex*.510(M.92.1475); *ib*.1577(M.1557); ἀποσκίασμα γὰρ καὶ ἀ. τῆς ἀρετῆς Max.*schol.e.h*. 2.8(M.4.133A).

ἀντίφρασις, ἡ, 1. *exposition by allusion*, Cosm.Mel.*schol*.proem. (M.38.343,344); ‡Meth.*Sym.et Ann*.4(M.18.357B); **2.** *opposing argument*, Gel.Cyz.*h.e*.2.18.1(M.85.1273A).

***ἀντίφρων, ὁ,** *adversary*, Cyr.*hom.pasch*.14(5^{2}.197C).

ἀντιφυσάω, *blow in turn*, Nil.*Eulog*.21(M.79.1120D).

***ἀντιφύσησις**, ἡ, *counterblast*, Gr.Naz.*or*.5.22(M.35.689C).

ἀντιφυτεύω, *plant in turn, in rivalry*, *Orac.Sib*.2.147; Gr.Nyss. *hex*.2(M.44.64B).

***ἀντίφυτος**, *planted in opposition*, †Nil.*vit*.2(M.79.1141C).

ἀντιφων-έω, **1.** *answer* ὥσπερ οὖν ~οῦσα τῇ εὐχαριστίᾳ λέγει ἡ νύμφη Ph.Carp.*Cant*.25(M.40.53C); **2.** *go surety for, guarantee* οὐχ ἑτέρως αὐτὸν [sc. Eutyches] βούλονται ἀπολῦσαι ἵνα εἰσέλθῃ εἰς τὴν ἁγίαν ὑμῶν σύνοδον, εἰ μὴ ~ήσομεν ἀποκαθιστᾶν αὐτοῦ τὸ πρόσωπον CChalc.*act*.1(*ACO* 2.1.1 p.138.7; H.2.160B); Justn.*nov*.4.1(p.24.26); Jo.Mal.*chron*.18 p.460(M.97.673B).

ἀντιφώνησις, ἡ, **1.** *official* or *imperial reply*, Eus.*v.C*.4.34(p.130.27; M.20.1184A); *ib*.4.37(p.132.11; 1185C); **2.** *surety* ὑπὲρ οὗ τὰς ἐντολὰς ἔγραψεν ἢ τὴν ἀ. ὑπῆλθε Justn.*nov*.4.1(p.25.31); Germ.CP *or*.7 (M.98.352A).

ἀντιφωνητής, ὁ, *one who goes surety for*, Justn.*nov*.4.1(p.24.26); *ib*.99 proem.(p.482.6).

***ἀντιφωνητικῶς**, *antiphonally*, ‡Bas.*h.myst*.60(p.394.14) cit. s. ἀντιδέχομαι.

***ἀντιφωνία**, ἡ, *discord*, f.l. for διαφωνίας, Eus.*p.e*.1.8(25D; M.21.61C).

ἀντίφωνος, **1.** *sung alternately, antiphonally* ὡς μὴ...ἀντίφωνον ἀγγέλων πλάσμα σὸν ἡσυχάζειν Gr.Naz.*carm*.1.1.32.37(M.37.513A); Socr.*h.e*.6.8.2(M.67.689A); Ἰγνάτιος ὁ Ἀντιοχείας...ὀπτασίαν εἶδεν ἀγγέλων διὰ τῶν ἀ. ὕμνων τὴν ἁγίαν τριάδα ὑμνούντων, καὶ τὸν τρόπον τοῦ ὁράματος τῇ ἐν Ἀντιοχείᾳ ἐκκλησίᾳ παρέδωκεν *ib*.6.8.11(692A); cf. πρῶτοι [sc. Flavian and Diodore] διχῇ διελόντες τοὺς τῶν ψαλλόντων χορούς, ἐκ διαδοχῆς ᾄδειν τὴν Δαυιτικὴν ἐδίδαξαν μελῳδίαν, καὶ τοῦτο ἐν Ἀντιοχείᾳ πρῶτον ἀρξάμενον Thdt.*h.e*.2.24.9(3.889); **2.** neut. as subst., *antiphon*, verses of psalm followed by a short refrain: v. ἐφύμνιον, ὑπακοή, ὑπόψαλμα. This, after its introduction in Antioch, was a widely used form of psalmody συμψάλλων αὐτοῖς ἓν ἢ δεύτερον ἀ. Pall.*h.Laus*.43(p.130.17; M.34.1210D); Socr.*h.e*.6.8.3 (M.67.689A); νύκτωρ πρότερον ἐν ταῖς δημοσίαις στοαῖς συνελέγοντο, καὶ εἰς συστήματα μεριζόμενοι κατὰ τὸν τῶν ἀ. τρόπον ἔψαλλον, ἀκροτελεύτια συντιθέντες πρὸς τὴν αὐτῶν δόξαν πεποιημένα Soz.*h.e*.8.8.1 (M.67.1536B); cf. *atque ut Theodorus Mopsuestenus scribit, illam psalmodiae speciem, quas antiphonas dicimus, illi ex Syrorum lingua in Graecam transtulerunt*, Nicetas Choniata *thes*.5.30(M.139.1390C); later this was abandoned, but among other traces it left the name ἀντίφωνον as designating each of the three *subdivisions* into which each κάθισμα (q.v.) of the psalter is divided, *Lit. Praesanct*.(p.345.23); the ἀ. in its original form still exists in ἔναρξις of Liturgy, *Lit.Bas*.(pp.310.15; 311.3,21); cf.*Lit.Chrys*.(p.364.1,2,5, 22,29) etc.; ᾄδονται τοιγαροῦν...μετὰ τὴν πρώτην αἴτησιν τὰ ἀ. ‡Sophr.H.*liturg*.12(M.87.3992C); τὰ ἀ. τῆς θείας λειτουργίας εἰσὶ τῶν προφητῶν αἱ προρρήσεις προκαταγγέλλουσαι τὴν παρουσίαν τοῦ υἱοῦ τοῦ θεοῦ ‡Bas.*h.myst*.32(p.265.4).

ἀντιχαλκεύω, *forge against*, Evagr.*h.e*.1.2(p.7.10; M.86.2424B).

***ἀντιχαράσσω**, *write in answer*, Marc.Er.*opusc*.5.13(M.65.1053B).

***ἀντιχειρόγραφον**, τό, *substitute for a bond of surety*, Ephr.2.262D.

ἀντιχειροτονέω, **1.** *raise the hand against* μὴ ἀ. τῷ θεῷ Or.*or*.10.1 (p.319.26; M.11.445B); **2.** *appoint instead* ὁ Κωνστάντιος...Ἀθανάσιον ...ἐλαύνει, ἀντιχειροτονηθῆναι δὲ γνώμην ἀποφαίνει Γεώργιον Philost. *h.e*.3.3(M.65.481A).

ἀντιχορεύω, *dance in harmony*; hence *move in harmony*, of the stars, Synes.*hymn*.4.159(p.31; M.66.1606).

ἀντίχριστος, ὁ, *antichrist*, cf.*Pss.Sal*.2.1; 2.29; *T.Dan* 5.6,5.10;

A. his person; **1.** titles ὥστε τὴν μὲν τοῦ καλοῦ ἀκρότητα εἶναι ἐν τῷ κατὰ τὸν Ἰησοῦν νοουμένῳ ἀνθρώπῳ...τὴν δὲ τοῦ ἐναντίου ἐν τῷ κατὰ τὸν ὀνομαζόμενον ἀ. ... ἐχρῆν δὲ τὸν μὲν [sc. Ἰησοῦν] ἕτερον τῶν ἄκρων καὶ βέλτιστον υἱὸν ἀναγορεύεσθαι τοῦ θεοῦ διὰ τὴν ὑπεροχήν, τὸν δὲ τούτῳ κατὰ διάμετρον ἐναντίον υἱὸν τοῦ πονηροῦ δαίμονος καὶ σατανᾶ καὶ διαβόλου Or.*Cels*.6.45(p.116.20; M.11.1368D); ἐλθὼν ὁ τούτου [sc. διαβόλου] κῆρυξ ἀ. Ath.*h.Ar*.78(p.227.13; M.25.788D); ὅτι δὲ κοινωνοῦσιν ἀλλήλοις ὁ διάβολος [καὶ] ὁ ἀ., καὶ ὁ ψευδοπροφήτης, ὥσπερ ταῖς πράξεσιν, οὕτω καὶ τοῖς ὀνόμασι, δῆλον ἐξ ὧν θηρίον ἕκαστος τούτων προσαγορεύεται Andr.Caes.*Apoc*.51(M.106.412B); v. θηρίον; δράκων, **2.** names, based on numerical interpretations of Apoc.13:18 εἰδέναι τὸ τοῦ ἀ. ὄνομα...*oportet...ad verum recurrere nominis numerum...id est, sexcentorum sexaginta sex...ΕΥΑΝΘΑΣ ...nomen habet numerum de quo queritur...et ΛΑΤΕΙΝΟΣ...et ΤΕΙΤΑΝ*...ἡμεῖς...οὐκ ἀποκινδυνεύομεν περὶ τοῦ ὀνόματος τοῦ ἀ. Iren.*haer*.5.30.3(M.7.1204C–1207A); Hipp.*antichr*.50(p.33.16ff.; M.10.769C); *ΛΑΜΠΕΤΙΣ, ΤΕΙΤΑΝ,...ΛΑΤΕΙΝΟΣ,...ΒΕΝΕΔΙΚΤΟΣ,...* κακὸς ὁδηγὸς...ἀληθῶς βλαβερός, ἀμνὸς ἄδικος Andr.Caes.*Apoc*.38 tit.(M.106.340D); cf. *ΛΑΜΠΕΤΙΣ, ΤΕΙΤΑΝ,...ΛΑΤΕΙΝΟΣ,...Ὁ ΝΙΚΗΤΗΣ* Areth.*Apoc*.38(M.106.681B); v. μιαρός; **3.** appearance οἱ ὀδόντες αὐτοῦ σπιθαμιαῖοι κτλ. ... καὶ εἰς τὸ μέτωπον αὐτοῦ γραφή· ἀ. *Apoc.Esd*.(p.29); τότε φανήσεται ὁ ἀρνήτης...ὁ λεγόμενος ἀ. ... τὸ εἶδος τοῦ προσώπου αὐτοῦ ζοφῶδες *1 Apoc.Jo*.6(p.74); **4.** nature; **a.** consisting of Satan or satanic energy and a man, cf. *ille enim omnem suscipiens diaboli virtutem*, Iren.*haer*.5.25.1(M.7.1189A); cf. Cyr.H.*catech*.15.11 cit. s. ἀντίκειμαι; ἄνθρωπον ἁμαρτίας αὐτὸν [sc. τὸν ἀντίχριστον] καλεῖ·...τίς δὲ οὗτός ἐστιν; ἆρα ὁ σατανᾶς; οὐδαμῶς· ἀλλ' ἄνθρωπός τις πᾶσαν αὐτοῦ δεχόμενος τὴν ἐνέργειαν Chrys. *hom.3.2 in 2 Thess*.(11.525Bf.); ὁ ἐν τῷ ἀ. ἐνεργῶν διάβολος Andr. Caes.*Apoc*.33(M.106.324D); *ib*.36(332C); *ib*.54(380B); **b.** as Devil incarnate, cf. '*hominem*' *equidem eum* [*sc. antichristum*] *nominavit justa ratione, eo quod et homo erit, daemone in eo omnia inoperante, sicut et in illum hominem qui pro nostra salute sumptus est, deus verbo omnia perfecisse videtur*, Thdr.Mops.*2 Thess*.2:3–4(p.50.5); *ib*. 2:8(p.56.1); ἀποστασίαν αὐτὸν ἐκάλεσε τὸν ἀ. ... ἀποστῆσαι γὰρ ἅπαντας τῆς ἀληθείας πειρᾶται. ἄνθρωπον δὲ ἁμαρτίας προσηγόρευσεν, ἐπειδὴ ἄνθρωπός ἐστι τὴν φύσιν, πᾶσαν ἐν ἑαυτῷ τοῦ διαβόλου δεχόμενος τὴν ἐνέργειαν...μιμεῖται τὴν ἐνανθρώπησιν, καὶ ὥσπερ αὐτὸς [sc. ὁ σωτήρ] ἀνθρωπείαν φύσιν ἀναλαβὼν...οὕτως ἐκεῖνος [sc. ὁ σατανᾶς] ἄνθρωπον ἐκλεξάμενος...δι' αὐτοῦ πάντας ἐξαπατῆσαι τοὺς ἀνθρώπους πειράσεται Thdt.*2 Thess*.2:4(3.532f.); **5.** uniqueness καὶ γενικῶς μὲν εἷς ἀ., ὡς τὸ ψεῦδος ἕν· ἰδικῶς δὲ πολλοὶ καὶ πολλὰ ψευδῆ διδάγματα καὶ δόγματα. ὡς δὲ Χριστοῦ, ἀληθοῦς λόγου, προφῆται, καὶ ἀ. ὄντος ψευδοῦς λόγου, ψευδοπροφῆται Or.*comm.ser.47 in Mt*.(p.96.26; M.13.1668D Lat.); **6.** as Messiah whom Jews expect τῷ ἀ. καὶ δι' αὐτοῦ τῷ ἀντιθέῳ πειθόμενοι [sc. οἱ Ἰουδαῖοι] Mac.Mgn.*apocr*.2.21(p.44.23); ἄνθρωπον ἀλλότριον ἐφ' ἑαυτοῖς κεχειροτονήκασι τὸν τῆς ἀπωλείας υἱόν, τοῦτ' ἔστι, τὸν ἀ., ἔκφυλόν τε καὶ ἀλλογενῆ, καὶ οὐδ' ἐξ αἵματος Ἰσραήλ Cyr.*ador*.8(1.279B); ὃν δὲ ἐκδέχονται οὗτοι ὅτι ἔρχεται πλάνος ἐστὶ καὶ ἀ. *Dial.Christ.et Jud*.7(p.56.14); Jo.D.*f.o*.4.26(M.94.1216Af.); for adherence to whom Jews will be condemned, Cyr.*Zach*.84(3.769C); his appearance the proof of Jews' sacrilege in crucifying Christ ἐπειδὴ γὰρ Ἰουδαῖοι...ὡς ἀντίθεον τῷ σταυρῷ τὸν δεσπότην προσήλωσαν, μέγιστος αὐτῶν ἔλεγχος τῆς ἀσεβείας γενήσεται τοῦ ἀ. ἡ παρουσία Thdt.*haer*.5.23(4.456).

B. events preceding his reign; **1.** heresies are his forerunners Μάρκος δέ τις...ὡς πρόδρομος ὢν ἀληθῶς τοῦ ἀ. Iren.*haer*.1.13.1 (M.7.580A); of Arianism, Alex.Al.*ep.encycl*.1(p.7.2; M.18.572B); τὴν Ἀρειανὴν αἵρεσιν,...τοῦ ἀ. πρόδρομον Ath.*apol.sec*.90(p.168.9; M.25.409D); αἵρεσιν ἐσχάτην λέγων εἶναι ταύτην, καὶ πρόδρομον τοῦ ἀ. Ath.*v.Anton*.69(M.26.941A); †Apoll.*ep.Bas*.2(M.32.984A); Gr.Nyss. *Eun*.11(2 p.273.10; M.45.884A); πρὸ τοῦ ἀ. ἀντίχριστος Thdr.Stud. *epp*.2.75(M.99.1312C); **2.** beast of Apoc.13:1, who is the false prophet and forerunner of antichrist, likened to Simon Magus, Andr.Caes.*Apoc*.37(M.106.340A); for the similarities between antichrist myth and Simon Magus myth see esp. *Hom.Clem*.2.17; *ib*. 2.33; *A.Petr.c.Sim*.(Lat. only)28f.(pp.74f.); *A.(Pass.)Petr.et Paul*. 14(p.130.18); *ib*.22(p.138.10); **3.** the present time as his opportunity δέδοικα μὴ καπνὸς ᾖ τοῦ προσδοκωμένου πυρὸς τὰ παρόντα, μὴ τούτοις ὁ ἀ. ἐπιστῇ, καὶ καιρὸν λάβῃ τῆς ἑαυτοῦ δυναστείας Gr.Naz.*or*.22.7(M.35.1140B); Pall.*h.Laus*.118(p.147.13; M.34.1227B).

C. his reign; **1.** advent τήν τε τοῦ ἀ. παρουσίαν Hipp.*Dan*.4.7.1; ἔρχεται γὰρ ὁ ἀ. εἰς μέρος πεντηκοστῆς ὡς τὴν βασιλείαν ἅμα Χριστῷ κληρονομεῖν μέλλων *ib*.4.55.3(M.10.665D); *Hom.Clem*.2.17; contrasted with suddenness of Christ's second advent, Chrys. *hom.9.2 in 1 Thess*.(11.488C); προσεκτέον ὅτι 'ἀποκάλυψιν' τοῦ ἀ. ἐκάλεσεν τὴν φανέρωσιν Thdr.Mops.*2 Thess*.2:7(p.55.16; M.66.936A); **2.** origin; in Dan ἐκ τῆς τοῦ Δὰν φυλῆς ὁ ἀ. γεννηθήσεται Hipp. *antichr*.14(p.11.13; M.10.737B); ὁ γὰρ ἀ. ... ἐκ τῆς Γαλιλαίας ὅθεν ὁ Χριστὸς ἐξῆλθεν, ἐξέρχεται, ὥς φησιν ἡ γραφή· σκύμνος λέοντος Δὰν καὶ ἐκπηδήσει ἐκ Βασάν, αὕτη δέ ἐστιν Σκυθόπολις ‡Ath.*qu.Ant*.109 (M.28.665A); cf. Βηθσάν...αὕτη ἐστὶ Σκυθόπολις...καλεῖ δὲ αὐτὴν ἡ γραφὴ καὶ οἶκον Σάν, ὅπερ ἐστὶν οἶκος ἐχθροῦ Eus.*onomast*.(p.54.8); εἰκὸς δὲ καὶ τὸν ἀ. ἐκ τῶν ἀνατολικῶν μερῶν τῆς Περσικῆς γῆς, ἔνθα ἡ φυλὴ τοῦ Δάν, ἐκ ῥίζης Ἑβραίων ἐξερχόμενον Andr.Caes.*Apoc*.51 (M.106.368C); hence of the Neronic traits in this and kindred myths, v. infra; **3.** birth ὁ ἀ. ... ἐκ γυναικὸς ταῖς φαντασίαις γεννᾶται ἀκαθάρτου ἐκπλανήσει δὲ ἀνόμους ὡς παρθένος αὐτὸν τίκτει Rom.Mel. (*SBBAW* 1898[2] p.169); cf.Ephr.3.137E; id.2.226B; Jo.D.*f.o*.4.26(M.94.1217B); v. διάβολος; **4.** appearance at end of the Roman empire, and assumption of its power ἔρχεται...ἀ. οὗτος, ὅταν πληρωθῶσιν οἱ καιροὶ τῆς Ῥωμαίων βασιλείας...ὁ ἀ. ἐκ τῆς μαγικῆς κακοτεχνίας τὴν Ῥωμαϊκὴν ἐξουσίαν ἁρπάσας Cyr.H.*catech*.15.12; ὡς Ῥωμαίων βασιλεὺς...ἐλεύσεται [sc. ὁ ἀ.] Andr.Caes.*Apoc*.54(M.

106.384A); **5.** relations with Jews: pays them special honours ὁ ἀ. μεγαλυνεῖ τοὺς Ἰουδαίους *Apoc.Dan.*C(p.119); cf.Ephr.3.138A; Jews return homage, *ib.*138C; Rom.Mel.(*SBBAW* 1898² p.169); and are utterly deceived bv him, Cyr.H.*catech.*15.11f.; cf.‡Hipp. *consumm.*24(p.299.1; M.10.928A); **6.** deception even of elect ὅθεν εἴρηται τοὺς μὲν τῆς κλήσεως ἀνθρώπους κατὰ τὴν παρουσίαν τοῦ ἀ. πλανηθήσεσθαι Clem.*exc.Thdot.*9(p.109.5; M.9.660A); 'δώσουσι... σημεῖα καὶ τέρατα, ὥστε πλανῆσαι...καὶ τοὺς ἐκλεκτούς.' ἐνταῦθα τὸν ἀ. φησι, καὶ δείκνυσί τινας καὶ διακονησαμένους αὐτῷ Chrys.*hom.76.2 in Mt.*(7.735B); Oecum.*Apoc.*12:1(p.135); cf. βλέπετε τὴν πλάνην τοῦ ἐχθροῦ...πῶς διὰ παντὸς σκοτίσαι βούλεται τὸν νοῦν τῶν ἀνθρώπων ‡Hipp.*consumm.*29(p.301.18; M.10.933A); **7.** military operations; **a.** first sally τὸ δὲ ὅρμημα αὐτοῦ πρῶτον ἔσται ἐπὶ Τύρον καὶ Σιδῶνα, καὶ τὴν πέριξ χώραν Hipp.*antichr.*52(p.35.10; M.10.772C); **b.** subjection of three kings, or three nations κρατήσας ἐν παρατάξει πολέμου τῶν τριῶν κεράτων τῶν ἐκ τῶν δέκα κεράτων, καὶ ἐκριζώσας αὐτά, ἅπερ ἐστὶν Αἰγύπτου, καὶ Λιβύων, καὶ Αἰθιόπων, λαβὼν τὰ σκῦλα καὶ τὰ λάφυρα Hipp.*antichr.*52(p.35.4; M.10.772B,C); cf.Iren. *haer.*5.26.1 cit. s. θηρίον; **8.** rebuilding of Temple to deceive Jews ἀνέστησεν ὁ σωτὴρ καὶ ἀπέδειξε τὴν ἁγίαν σάρκα αὐτοῦ ὡς ναόν, καὶ αὐτὸς [sc. ὁ ἀ.] ἀναστήσει τὸν ἐν Ἱεροσολύμοις λίθινον ναόν Hipp. *antichr.*6(p.8.12; M.10.733C); Cyr.H.*catech.*15.15; ναὸν δὲ τότε ποιήσεται περιούσιον, τῶν Ἑβραίων τὸ σύστημα πλανῶν Rom.Mel. (*SBBAW* 1898² p.170); ‡Gr.Naz.*sign.in Ezech.*(M.36.668C); *Apoc. Dan.*C(p.119); **9.** session in Temple of Jerusalem, cf. *ea quae erunt sub antichristo ostenditur...cujus* [sc. *dei*] *jussu hoc, quod est in Hierosolymis, factum est templum...in quo adversarius sedebit,* Iren. *haer.*5.25.1f.(M.7.1188C); ὥστε αὐτὸν [sc. τὸν ἀ.] εἰς τὸν ναὸν τοῦ θεοῦ καθίσαι. ποῖον ἄρα ναόν; τὸν καταλελυμμένον τῶν Ἰουδαίων φησί· μὴ γένοιτο γὰρ τοῦτον ἐν ᾧ ἐσμεν Cyr.H.*catech.*15.15; ὁ ἀ. ἥξει γὰρ εἰς Ἱεροσόλυμα ὡς ἀνοικοδομήσων τὸν ναόν, καὶ στήσεται ἐν τῷ ἁγίῳ τόπῳ θεὸν ἑαυτὸν ἀναγορεύων Sever.*2 Thess.*2:1–4(p.333.30); Jo.D.*f.o.*4.26(M.94.1216C); Temple interpreted as Christian Church or churches καθεσθήσεται [sc. ὁ ἀ.] εἰς τὸν ναὸν τοῦ θεοῦ, οὐ τὸν ἐν Ἱεροσολύμοις μόνον, ἀλλὰ καὶ καθ' ἑκάστην ἐκκλησίαν Chrys.*hom.3.2 in 2 Thess.*(11.525C); Thdr.Mops.*2 Thess.*2:4(p.51.14); Thdt.*2 Thess.* 2:4(3.533); **10.** character; **a.** feigned similarity to Christ, cf. *he will do and speak like the beloved and he will say: 'I am God and before me there has been none.'* *Ascens.Is.*A 4.6(p.27); κατὰ πάντα γὰρ ἐξομοιοῦσθαι βούλεται ὁ πλάνος τῷ υἱῷ τοῦ θεοῦ. λέων μὲν ὁ Χριστός, καὶ λέων μὲν ὁ ἀ. ... ἀπέστειλεν ὁ κύριος τοὺς ἀποστόλους... αὐτὸς ὁμοίως πέμψει ψευδαποστόλους Hipp.*antichr.*6(p.8.3; M.10. 733B); τὰ πρῶτα μὲν ἐπιείκειαν, ὡσανεὶ λόγιός τις καὶ συνετός, σωφροσύνην τε καὶ φιλανθρωπίαν ὑποκρίνεται Cyr.H.*catech.*15.12; Jo.D.*f.o.*4.26(M.94.1217B); cf.Ephr.3.137F cit. s. παμμίαρος; **b.** real qualities, cf. *veniet* [sc. *antichristus*]*...quasi apostata et iniquus et homicida, quasi latro, diabolicam apostasiam in se recapitulans,* Iren.*haer.*5.25.1(M.7.1189A); τίς δ' ὁ ἀ.; πλῆρες ἰοῦ θηρίον, ἀνὴρ δυνάστης Gr.Naz.*carm.*1.2.34.245(M.37.963A); cf. ἐπειδὴ γὰρ ὁ κλέπτης, καὶ ἀλάστωρ καὶ ἀπηνής, πρῶτος μέλλει ἔρχεσθαι ἐν τοῖς ἰδίοις καιροῖς Ephr.2.225F; **11.** miraculous power; **a.** signs and wonders καὶ οὕτως βασιλεύσει ὁ ἀ. καὶ πράξει θαυμαστὰ καὶ παράδοξα πράγματα *Apoc.Dan.*C(p.119); cf.‡Hipp.*consumm.*29(p.301.19; M.10.933A); Rom.Mel.(*SBBAW* 1898² p.172); καὶ Βελίαρ θ' ἥξει καὶ σήματα πολλὰ ποιήσει *Orac.Sib.*2.167; cf. *and there will be the power of his miracles in every city and region,* *Ascens.Is.*A 4.10–11(p.28); *Test.Dom.*1.9; **b.** change of shape, cf. ἐκ μορφῆς εἰς ἑτέραν μορφὴν μεταβάλλεται Rom.Mel.(*SBBAW* 1898² p.170); **c.** powers inherited from Devil or apostate spirits, cf.Iren.*haer.*5.28.2(M.7.1199B); Andr.Caes.*Apoc.*36(M.106.333D); **d.** his raising of dead a phantasm τὸ εἰπεῖν τὸν ἀπόστολον περὶ τοῦ ἀ. ὅτι ἐν πᾶσι σημείοις καὶ δυνάμεσι πλάνης εὔδηλον ὅτι καὶ νεκρὸν δείκνυσιν ἐγειρόμενον οὐκ ἐν ἀληθείᾳ, ἀλλ' ἐν φαντασίᾳ ‡Ath.*qu.Ant.*110(M.28.665A); cf. ὁ γὰρ πατὴρ τοῦ ψεύδους τὰ τοῦ ψεύδους ἔργα φαντασιοσκοπεῖ ἵνα τὰ πλήθη νομίσῃ θεωρεῖν νεκρὸν ἐγειρόμενον τὸν μὴ ἐγειρόμενον Cyr.H.*catech.* 15.14.

D. last days of antichrist; **1.** the witnesses, v. Ἠλίας; their war with Satan, Cyr.H.*catech.*15.17 cit. s. αὐτοπροσώπως; **2.** his persecution of the saints, *Ascens.Is.*A 4.2–3(p.95); Iren.*haer.*5.25.4 (M.7.1191C); Hipp.*antichr.*58(p.39.3; M.10.777B); τήν τε τοῦ ἀ. ἐν αὐτοῖς φανέρωσιν καὶ τὸν τούτου πρὸς τοὺς ἁγίους πόλεμον id.*Dan.* 4.14.1; *ib.*4.50.2(M.10.665B); τοῦ ἀ. καὶ τῶν ψευδοπροφητῶν θλῖψις τότε ἔσται μεγάλη Vict.*Mc.*13:24(p.413.10); cf.Ephr.2.223F cit. s. παμμίαρος; Rom.Mel.(*SBBAW* 1898² p.172) cit. s. πάγκακος; and flight of the faithful, Ephr.3.142cf.; Andr.Caes.*Apoc.*33(M.106. 324D); cf.Rom.Mel.(*SBBAW* 1898² p.171); **3.** drought, famine and portents, Ephr.3.139F; Rom.Mel.(*SBBAW* 1898² p.171); ‡Hipp. *consumm.*27(p.300.13; M.10.929C); *Apoc.Dan.*C(p.119); fear of which is insufficient to convert the obstinate νῦν φανεῖται μὲν ὁ ἀ. μεθ' ὃν ἡ συντέλεια,...οἱ δὲ τῇ μέθῃ τῆς κακίας κατεχόμενοι οὐδὲ αἰσθήσονται τοῦ φόβου τῶν ἐσομένων Chrys.*hom.77.2 in Mt.*(7.743B); **4.** seal of antichrist, v. δράκων, θηρίον, τύραννος; consequences of bearing seal of antichrist δώσει [sc. ὁ ἀ.] αὐτοῖς χάραγμα ἐν τῇ χειρὶ τῇ δεξιᾷ καὶ ἐν τῷ μετώπῳ ἵνα μή τις τὸν τίμιον σταυρὸν ποιήσῃ ἐν τῷ μετώπῳ τῇ δεξιᾷ αὐτοῦ χειρὶ [ἀλλὰ δέδεται αὐτοῦ ἡ χείρ] καὶ ἀπὸ τότε οὐχ ἕξει ἐξουσίαν σφραγίσαι τι τῶν μελῶν αὐτοῦ, ἀλλὰ τῷ πλάνῳ προστεθήσεται καὶ αὐτῷ δουλεύσει καὶ μετάνοια ἐν αὐτῷ οὐκ ἔστιν ‡Hipp.*consumm.*28(p.300.37; M.10.932B); cf. πάντες δὲ οἱ λαβόντες τὴν σφραγίδα τοῦ ἀ. ... οὐκ ἔχουσί τινα μερίδα ἐν τῇ βασιλείᾳ τοῦ Χριστοῦ· ἀλλὰ μετὰ τοῦ δράκοντος βληθήσονται ἐν τῇ γεέννῃ Ephr. 2.228D; **5.** his days numbered, Rom.Mel.(*SBBAW* 1898² p.168); cf.*ib.*(p.175); **6.** judgement of antichrist πᾶσα φύσις ἀνθρωπίνη καὶ πᾶν πνεῦμα πονηρὸν μετὰ τοῦ ἀ., καὶ σταθήσονται ἐνώπιόν μου πάντες γυμνοὶ καὶ τετραχηλισμένοι *1 Apoc.Jo.*17(p.85); cf.Ephr.3. 143E cit. s. τύραννος; **7.** destruction οἱ τῷ ἀ. συναιρόμενοι καὶ σὺν αὐτῷ εἰς τὴν αἰώνιον κόλασιν βαλλόμενοι Hipp.*Dan.*4.56.6(M.10.687B); ὃς [sc. Χριστός] ἀνελὼν τὸν ἀ. τῷ πνεύματι τοῦ στόματος αὐτοῦ [cf. 2Thess.2:8, Is.11:4], τῷ τῆς γεέννης τοῦτον παραδώσει πυρί Cyr.H. *catech.*15.12; κἀκεῖνο δὲ ἀσόφως σοφίζου, τὸν τοῦ διαβόλου ἀ. μὴ κολασθήσεσθαι λέγων, φθαρήσεσθαι δὲ καὶ εἰς τὸ μὴ ὂν ἀναλυθήσεσθαι Leont.B.*Nest.et Eut.*3(M.86.1372A); παραδοθήσεται ὁ διάβολος καὶ οἱ δαίμονες αὐτοῦ, καὶ ὁ ἄνθρωπος αὐτοῦ, ἤγουν ὁ ἀ., καὶ οἱ ἀσεβεῖς καὶ οἱ ἁμαρτωλοὶ εἰς τὸ πῦρ αἰώνιον Jo.D.*f.o.*4.27(M.94.1228A); cf. Rom.Mel.(*SBBAW* 1898² p.178); Jo.D.*f.o.*4.26(1217C).

E. other uses of antichrist myth in exegesis: (2Thess.2:4) cf. *eos qui ab ignorantibus deum dii dicuntur significat, id est idola. etenim pater omnium deus dicitur, et est; et non super hunc extolletur antichristus; sed super eos qui dicuntur quidem, non sunt autem dii,* Iren.*haer.*3.6.5(M.7.863B); (Ps.90:13) *significans quia illud quod erigeretur et dilataretur adversus hominem peccatum, et frigidum reddebat eum, evacuaretur cum regnante morte, et conculcaretur ab eo in novissimis temporibus insiliens humano generi leo, hoc est antichristus,* *ib.*3.23.7(964C); (Dan.3:1) ὅλη γὰρ ἡ εἰκὼν ἐκείνη προτύπωσις ἦν τῆς τοῦ ἀ. παρουσίας *ib.*5.29.2(M.7.1202C); (an unknown prophet quoted in support of Jer.8:16), Hipp.*antichr.*15(p.12.3ff.; M.10. 740A); (Lc.18:2–5) ἀδιστάκτως τὸν ἀ. λέγει, ὃς υἱὸς ὢν τοῦ διαβόλου καὶ σκεῦος τοῦ σατανᾶ *ib.*57(p.37.17; 776B); (Dan.7:8) τὸ μικρὸν κέρας, ὅπερ ἐστὶν ὁ ἀ. id.*Dan.*4.5.3(M.10.681D); (Dan.11:36ff.) ταῦτα ...περὶ τοῦ ἀ., ὡς ἔσται ἀναιδὴς καὶ πολεμοτρόφος καὶ τύραννος τολμῶν ὑπὲρ πάντα θεὸν ἑαυτὸν ὑπεραίρειν *ib.*4.49.1(665A); (Jer.27:17) μὴ πάντως δὲ ἐπὶ τὸν διάβολον ἢ τὸν ἀ. ἐκλάβῃς τὸν λόγον Or.*fr.29 in Jer.*27:17(p.213.28); (Ezech.16:51) *sic est quidam justificandus ab antichristo qui ad illum comparatur et illius iniquitate ac sceleribus minor reperitur,* id.*hom.9.3 in Ezech.*(p.410.30; M.13.736A); (Mt. 25:6) τὸ δὲ μεσονύκτιον ἡ βασιλεία τοῦ ἀ., καθ' ἣν ὁ ὀλοθρευτὴς ἄγγελος ἐπιπορεύεται τὰς οἰκίας Meth.*symp.*6.4(p.68.23; M.18.120A); (Ex.17:8) Ἀμαλὴκ δὲ ἑρμηνεύεται ἀ. ὅθεν καὶ τῷ διαβόλῳ ἀφομοιώθη *Dial.Tim.et Aquil.*99 v°(p.80); (Mt.24:15) βδέλυγμα ἐρημώσεως καθολικῶς ὁ ἀ. Thdr.Heracl.ap.*cat.Mt.*24:15(p.196.34); (Dan.7:16) ἐρωτᾷ τί ποτέ ἐστι τὰ φαινόμενα· καὶ μανθάνει περὶ τοῦ ἀ. Chrys.ad loc.(6. 241B); (Jo.5:43) id.*hom.41.1 in Jo.*(8.244B); (Jo.10:1) *ib.59.2*(346D); (2Thess.2:7) Νέρωνα ἐνταῦθά φησιν ὡσανεὶ τύπον ὄντα τοῦ ἀ. ... καὶ καλῶς εἶπε τὸ μυστήριον· οὐ γὰρ φανερῶς, ὡς ἐκεῖνος, οὐδὲ ἀπηρυθριασμένως id.*hom.4.1 in 2 Thess.*(11.529E); (Zach.12:1) τὴν ἀφήγησιν...τὴν ἐπί γε τῷ ἀπείρῳ τε καὶ ὠμοτάτῳ καὶ κρεανομοῦντι τὰ πρόβατα· τοῦτον δὲ εἶναί φαμεν τὸν ἀ. Cyr.*Zach.*86(3.772B); (Apoc. 13:11) τρία...εἶδε θηρία·...τὸ μὲν γάρ ἐστιν ὁ ἀρχέκακος δράκων...τὸ δὲ τρίτον ὁ ἀ. Oecum.ad loc.(p.149); (Dan.7) Δανιὴλ περὶ Ἀντιόχου προεφήτευσεν, ὡς ἐσομένου τύπου τῆς τοῦ ἀ. ἐλεύσεως Andr.Caes. *Apoc.*33(M.106.324A).

F. poss. instances of absorption of Nero myth into antichrist myth, cf.*Ascens.Is.*A 4.2(p.95); *Orac.Sib.*3.63; *ib.*5.222; *ib.*5.361.

G. uses of word which are not referable to the myth proper: **1.** of a demon who takes the form of Christ ἐξελθὼν οὖν [sc. Valens] καὶ θεασάμενος τὴν παράταξιν τῶν λαμπαδηφόρων, ὡς ἀπὸ σταδίου δὲ τὸν ἀ., πεσὼν προσεκύνησεν Pall.*h.Laus.*25(p.80.8; M.31.1090D); **2.** of false Christs τὰ μὲν τῶν ἀ. ... σημεῖα καὶ τέρατα λέγεται εἶναι 'ψεύδους' Or.*Cels.*2.50(p.173.14; M.11.876C); **3.** relation of sin and heresy to antichrist οὗτοι...ὡς ἐγγύτεροι τοῦ ἀ. γενόμενοι Alex.Al.*ep. encycl.*6(p.9.25; M.18.576D); cf. *vas es* [sc. *Manes*] *antichristi,* Hegem.*Arch.*40(p.59.3; M.10.1487A); *ib.*(p.59.10; 1487B); τίς...ἔτι τολμᾷ λέγειν Κοστύλλιον Χριστιανόν, καὶ οὐ μᾶλλον ἀντιχρίστου τὴν εἰκόνα; Ath.*h.Ar.*74(p.224.4; M.25.781C); *ib.*77(p.226.5; 785C); ὁ τοίνυν οὐ λέγων θεὸν εἶναι ἀληθῶς τὸν Χριστόν...τὸ τοῦ ἀ. πνεῦμα ἔχων ἁλώσεται Cyr.*Arcad.*(p.97.5; 5².94E); ἀ. γὰρ οὐδὲν διενήνοχεν ὁ τῆς σαρκὸς νόμος, ἀεὶ παλαίων τῷ πνεύματι καὶ τῷ αὐτοῦ θείῳ νόμῳ ἀντιτασσόμενος Max.*ambig.*(M.91.1132A); hence heretics are antichrists ἀ. δὲ οὗτοι τυγχάνουσι ὅσοι διὰ τὴν Ἀρείου μανίαν ἔρχονται πρὸς ὑμᾶς Ath.*ep.Aeg.Lib.*9(M.25.557B); id.*h.Ar.*62(p.218.2; M.25.768C); τί ποιεῖν αὐτὴν [sc. τὴν αἵρεσιν] ἐχρῆν ἢ τἀναντία τοῦ σωτῆρος, ὡς χριστόμαχον ἡγεμόνα τῆς ἀσεβείας ἐπιγραφομένην Κωνστάντιον, ὡς αὐτὸν τὸν ἀ.; *ib.*67(p.220.5; 773B); ὁ Χριστὸς ὁ ἀναβάς, ἔρχεται πάλιν ἐξ οὐρανῶν, οὐκ ἀπὸ γῆς...ἐπειδὴ πολλοὶ μέλλουσιν ἀ. νῦν ἀπὸ γῆς ἔρχεσθαι Cyr.H.*catech.*4.15; Gr.Nyss.*Eun.*11(2 p.273.15; M.45.884A); cf. *illi sint antichristi, qui ab ecclesia salvatoris abscesserint, ut etiam praesidere videantur haeresibus*, Didym.*1Jo.*2:18(M.39.1784A); Jo.D.*f.o.*4.26(M.94.1216A); **4.** word 'antichrist' a linguistic peculiarity of Johannine writings ὁ ἔλεγχος τοῦ κόσμου, τοῦ διαβόλου, τοῦ ἀ., ἡ ἐπαγγελία τοῦ ἁγίου πνεύματος Dion.Al.ap.Eus.*h.e.*7.25.21(M.20.701C).

***ἀντίχροος,** *of answering hue*, Gr.Naz.*carm.*2.1.88.146(M.37.1441A).

ἀντιχώννυμι, *fill up again*, ‡Jo.D.*Artem.*68(p.96.23; M.96.1316C).

ἀντιψάλλω, *sing in response*, Bas.*ep.*207.3(3.311B; M.32.764A).

ἀντίψυχος, *as life for life* (cf.4Macc.6:29; *ib.*17:22); **1.** as subst.; **a.** *substitute* ἀ. ὑμῶν ἐγώ Ign.*Eph.*21.1; id.*Smyrn.*10.2; id.*Polyc.* 2.3; τῆς σφῶν ψυχῆς ἀντίψυχα προσκομίζοντες [sc. τὰ ἄλογα ζῷα] Eus.*d.e.*1.10(p.44.16; M.22.85A); δύναται πολλάκις μία κερδηθεῖσα ψυχὴ...γενέσθαι ἡμῖν ἀ. Chrys.*Jud.*8.9(1.688A); ref. the vicarious nature of Atonement, Eus.*d.e.*1.10(p.46.7; M.22.88B); τὸν μὴ γνόντα ἁμαρτίαν...ἀ. ὑπὲρ πάντων *ib.*10.1(p.449.34; 724B); id.*l.C.*15(p.247.31; M.20.1420B); ἱερεῖον ἦν ἀ. τοῦ κοίνου γένους id.*theoph.fr.*3(p.9.21; M.24.616A); ὁ λόγος...τὸν ἑαυτοῦ ναὸν καὶ τὸ σωματικὸν ὄργανον προσάγων ἀ. ὑπὲρ πάντων Ath.*inc.*9.2(M.25.112B); Proc.G.*Is.*53:1–12(M.87.2524C); **b.** *fee* for divination εἴτις δίδει ἀ. τοῖς μάντεσιν *Poen.App.*17 = Sophr.H.*conf.*(M.87.3368B); **2.** as adj., *instead of natural life* πλάττεται ἐν τῷ ὕδατι λαμβάνει δὲ ἀ. πνεῦμα Chrys.*hom. 6.4 in Col.*(11.370A).

ἀντλητήρ, ὁ, *drawer of water*, met., of prophets and gospel δύο ἀ. ἀπὸ μιᾶς πηγῆς ἀντλοῦντας Epiph.*haer.*66.85(p.128.20; M.42.165D).

ἀντλία, ἡ, *bilge-water*; met., of baptism (in comparison of Church with a ship), Hipp.*antichr.*59(p.39.19; λίνον M.10.777C).

ἀντοικ-έω, 1. *deport, exile*, Thdr.Heracl.*Is.*63:19(M.18.1369C); **2.** pres. ptcpl. pass. as subst. ἡ ~ουμένη *the southern hemisphere*, Eus.*Ps.*47:2–3(M.23.421B).

ἀντοικοδομέω, *build instead*, †Jo.D.*B.J.*33(M.96.1180A).

***ἀντολικός,** poet. for ἀνατολικός, *eastern*, Paul.Sil.*Soph.*201(M.86.2127B); *ib.*354(2133A).

***ἀντομματέω,** *treat with disdain*, *Const.App.*6.2.1.

ἀντονειδίζω, *upbraid in return*, Nil.*Eulog.*5(M.79.1100D).

ἀντονομαστικός, *pronominal*, Gr.Nyss.*Eun.*11(M.45.865C; ἀντωνυμικῆς 2 p.258.21).

***ἀντοπτεύω,** *gaze on*, prob. f.l. for κατοπτεύοντα, Cosm.Ind.*top.*3 (M.88.153A).

ἀντορχ-έομαι, lit., *dance against*, hence *appear in contrast to* ~εῖται τῇ κόρῃ τὸ σχῆμα τῆς λύπης Bas.Sel.*or.*18.2(M.85.234B).

***ἀντοφρύομαι,** *be supercilious in turn*, Geo.Pis.*van.*27(M.92.1583A).

***ἀντοψία, ἡ,** *aspect*, Pall.*h.Laus.*87(M.34.1234D; p.163 omits).

***ἄντριος,** s.v.l., *cave-like* Thdt.*eran.*2(4.115).

***ἀντυμνέω,** *sing in accompaniment*, *T.Job* 14 (v.l. for αὐταὶ ὕμνουν, p.112.3).

ἄντυξ, ἡ, *rim, orbit, circle*; an instrument of torture, *wheel*, *M. Ner.et Ach.*16(p.15.27); Ephr.3.xxix c.

***ἀντωνομασία, ἡ, 1.** *change of name* ἡ τοῦ Ἀβραὰμ ἀ. Cyr.*syn.def.* (M.76.1421A); **2.** applied to interchangeability of names of Christ εἰ...ὀνομάζουσι καὶ λόγον τὸν Χριστόν, καὶ τὸν λόγον Χριστόν, εἰς προσώπου ἀντένδειξιν ἄρα καὶ ἀ.· τῆς κλήσεως τῆς σαρκὸς καὶ τὸν λόγον αὐτὸν μεταλαβεῖν φασιν Leont.H.*Nest.*3.8(M.86.1637D).

ἀντωνυμία, ἡ, 1. *pronoun*, Or.*schol.in Cant.*7:6(M.17.284B); ref. Ex.20:1 διὰ τῆς ἀ. ἕνα εἶναι θεὸν...ἀποφαίνεται Eus.*e.th.*2.19(p.125.1; M.24.945C); Thdt.*Dan.*4:28(2.1151); ‡Just.*coh.Gr.*17(M.6.273C); Leont.H.*Nest.*2.48(M.86.1601A); **2.** either *pronoun*, or phrase acting as substitute for any of the terms associated with the category of substance, Lat. *vox indicativa* διδάξαντες τί μὲν οὐσία, τί δὲ ὑπόστασις, καὶ ὡς φύσις ταὐτόν ἐστι τῇ οὐσίᾳ, ὑπόστασίς τε τῷ προσώπῳ... τάς τε ἀ. αὐτῶν Leont.B.*Nest.et Eut.*1(M.86.1309B); τὸ ἄλλος καὶ ἄλλος ἀ. ὑποστάσεων...τὸ δὲ ἄλλο καὶ ἄλλο ἀ. φύσεων id.*cap.Sev.*12 (M.86.1904C); ἀντωνυμίων διὰ τοῦ φάσκειν, ἄλλο τὸ ἀνθρώπινον θέλημα καὶ τὸ θεῖον ἄλλο· καὶ ἄλλην, καὶ ἄλλην ἐνέργειαν CLater.*act.*5 (H.3.888E); τὰς ἐν ἀ. καὶ ἀριθμῷ δυϊκὰς σημασίας Max.*opusc.*(M.91.89A); Jo.D.*Jacob.*64(M.94.1648D).

ἀντωνυμικῶς, *like a pronoun*, Cyr.*Jo.*5.4(4.505E).

ἀντωπ-έω, 1. *look in the face*, hence *gaze at* ᾧ [sc. ἡλίῳ] μηδὲ ἀ. ἔστι ῥᾳδίως Clem.*exc.Thdot.*12(p.111.2; M.9.664A); Eus.*d.e.*4.6(p.158.27; M.22.265A); Dion.Ar.*e.h.*2(M.3.392C); ἐγὼ δὲ εὐπροσίτως ~ῆσαι αὐτῷ ἐνίσχυσα ‡Meth.*Sym.et Ann.*10(M.18.373A); met. τῇ τοῦ θεοῦ δόξῃ ἄνθρωπος θνητὸς οὐ δύναται ~ῆσαι Thphl.Ant.*Autol.*1.5(M.6.1032A); Clem.*str.*6.15(p.499.8; M.9.357B); **2.** *withstand, defy* τὰ κακὰ ...μηδὲ ~ῆσαι τῇ ψυχῇ δυνάμενα Serap.*Man.*44(p.62; M.18.1229C); hence **3.** *brazen* it *out* τί...πρὸς ταῦτα λέγειν ἢ ὅλως ~ῆσαι δύνανται; Ath.*inc.*39.3(M.25.164C); ταῖς τοῦ σωτῆρος...λέξεσι πρὸς ἃς οὐκ ἠδυνήθησαν ἀ. Epiph.*haer.*16.4(p.214.2; M.41.253D).

***ἀντωπία, ἡ,** *seeing face to face, direct vision*, ‡Meth.*Sym.et Ann.*5(M.18.357D).

***ἀντωτίς, ἡ,** *ear-cap* worn by boxers, Clem.*paed.*2.6(p.187.15,27; M.8.452B,453A).

ἀνύβριστος, 1. *uninsulted* οὐδὲν τῶν θείων καταλιμπάνει ἀ. Isid. Pel.*epp.*1.439(M.78.424C); hence *undisgraced* μήτε τὸν συκοφάντην ἀτιμώρητον ἐάσητε, μήτε μὴν τὸν ἐλεγχθέντα ἀ. *Const.App.*2.50.4; **2.** *undefiled*, Athenag.*leg.*32.3(M.6.964C); αὐτὸς...ἄλυπος θέλων μένειν, ἀ. *A.Jo.*106(p.204.7); *ib.*114(p.214.13); ἐξ ἀ. παρθένου ἐτέχθη *Pers.*(p.32.15); **3.** *incapable of being insulted*, Gr.Thaum.*pan.Or.* 2.15(p.5.5; M.10.1036B); ref. Inc. τὸ ἀ. ὕβρεως δεκτικόν ‡Ath.*Apoll.* 1.7(M.26.1104C).

ἀνυβρίστως, *free from insult*, Herm.*sim.*1.6.

***ἀνύκτερος,** *undimmed by night*, ‡Caes.Naz.*dial.*2(M.38.857).

***ἀνυλακτέω,** *bark*, Sophr.H.*v.Anast.*(M.92.1729A).

ἀνυμν-έω (-είω), 1. *raise* a cry ταύτην αὐτῷ πρῶτον ~ήσαντες τὴν φωνήν, χαῖρε φῶς Clem.*prot.*11(p.80.15; M.8.232B); εἰ μὴ τὰ δύσφημά τις ~οίη ῥήματα Dion.Al.ap.Eus.*h.e.*6.41.8(M.20.608A); **2.** *praise*, Clem.*str.*2.8(p.133.2; M.8.973A); καθαρὸς λόγος ἐκ στόματος καθαρῶν προέλθῃ καὶ ~ήσῃ...τὸν ἐπουράνιον πατέρα Hipp.*Dan.*1.10.6(M.10.669C -νῇ); ἀ. εὐχαριστίαν Bas.*hom.*4.6(2.30D; M.31.232B); ἄξιον ὡς ἀληθῶς καὶ δίκαιον πρὸ πάντων ~εῖν σε *Lit.*ap.*Const.App.*8.12.6; Nemes.*nat.hom.*42(M.40.788A); τῶν σεραφεὶμ...~ούντων εἰς τὴν θεϊκὴν τριάδα Tim.Beryt.*ep.Prosd.*(p.283.23); ποτήριον δὲ εὐλογίας ἐκάλεσεν, ἐπειδὴ αὐτὸ μετὰ χεῖρας ἔχοντες, οὕτως αὐτὸν ~οῦμεν Chrys.*hom.24.1 in 1Cor.*(10.213A); Κωνσταντῖνος τὸν πανηγεμόνα καὶ τῆς νίκης αἴτιον θεόν...αὐτοῖς ἔργοις ~ήσας Gel.Cyz.*h.e.*1.7.5(M.85.1208A); οἱ μὲν 'κύριε ἐλέησον' ἐβόων ἄλλοι δὲ ἄλλως ~ουν Jo.Mosch. *prat.*79(M.87.2937B); ‡Meth.*Sym.et Ann.*2(M.18.352C); **3.** *commend* ταῦτα οὖν ~ει [al. ~εῖν] τὸν εὑρετὴν τῶν γραμμάτων Synes.*ep.*138 (M.66.1528B); **4.** in form ἀνυμνείω, *sing in praise* ὕμνον ~είοντες ἀκήρατον Gr.Naz.*carm.*1.1.34.11(M.37.515).

***ἀνύμνησις, ἡ,** *praise*, Sophr.H.*or.*8.6(M.87.3364A).

ἀνύμφευτος, *unwedded, virgin*, Meth.*symp.*proem.(p.6.19; M.18.36A); Procl.CP *annunt.*5(M.85.445B); Gr.Ant.*bapt.*2.5(M.88.1876C); χαῖρε, νύμφη ἀ. ‡Serg.*acath.*(p.140.6; M.92.1335A).

ἀνυμφής, *virgin*, Gr.Naz.*carm.*1.1.9.68(M.37.462A).

ἀνυπαίτιος, *blameless* οἷς ὁ βίος ὡς πρὸς στάθμην τὸν θεὸν κανονίζεται ὅπως ἀ. ... γένοιτο Athenag.*leg.*31.2(M.6.961C); Meth.*symp.* 4.1(p.46.3; M.18.88A); ἡ...προκοπὴ δόκιμος...ἀνεπίληπτος μὲν πρὸς ἀνθρώπους, ἀ. δὲ συνειδήσει ‡Pion.*v.Polyc.*11; Bas.*reg.br.*231(2.493B; M.31.1237A); ὡς ἀ. παντελῶς τὴν ἐπὶ θεῷ δύνασθαι γνῶσιν ἑλεῖν Cyr.*ador.*16(1.579B); id.*Jo.*10(4.831C); προσεχρήσατο δὲ καθάπερ ὀργάνῳ τῇ μὲν ἰδίᾳ σαρκὶ...ψυχῇ δὲ αὖ τῇ ἰδίᾳ πρὸς τὰ ἀνθρώπινά τε καὶ ἀ. πάθη id.*inc.unigen.*(5¹.692C); neut. as subst. ἡ ἐν Χριστῷ δικαίωσις, δι' ὑπακοῆς εἰσβαίνουσα, καὶ τὸ ἀ. ἔχουσα παντελῶς id. *resp.*(6².393E); τὸ ἀ. ἔχουσα παρρησίας ἐφόδιον ‡Nil.*perist.*12.8(M.79.953D).

ἀνύπαρκτος, 1. *non-existent, unreal*; **a.** in gen. τὸ μὴ ἀ. οὐσίαν κατονομάζομεν Gr.Nyss.*Eun.*12(1 p.324.17; M.45.1040C); λέγομεν... μὴ εἶναι...ἀντὶ τοῦ ἀ. εἶναι Max.*ambig.*(M.91.1273A); with vb. to be, *cease to exist, perish* πολλοὶ...κρημνῶν φοβερῶν κατερχόμενοι καὶ ἀ. γινόμενοι *T.Abr.*A 19(p.101.27); ἀπολομένης γὰρ τῆς ὁδοῦ, ἀ. ἡ ἀσέβεια γίνεται Or.*Ps.*1:6(p.447); τὸ οὖν κακὸν...εἰ παντελῶς κακὸν καὶ παντελῶς φθορά, καὶ ἑαυτοῦ ἔσται ἀναιρετικὸν καὶ ἀ. Jo.D.*Man.* 1.27(M.94.1532A); **b.** Trin. καθ' ἑαυτὰ...ἀσώματα τὸν πατέρα καὶ τὸν υἱὸν καὶ τὸ πνεῦμα...καὶ μὴ διὰ τοῦτο ἀ. ‡Ath.*Sabell.*11(M.28.116A); ἐν τῷ μὴ διδόναι τὸν υἱὸν κυρίως εἶναι τὸ μηδὲ ὅλως εἶναι κατασκευάζοντες· τὸ γὰρ ἄκυρον τῷ ἀ. ταὐτόν ἐστιν Gr.Nyss.*Eun.*1(1 p.75.9; M.45.305B); εἰ...ἀνυπόστατόν τι πρᾶγμα λέγοι τὴν ἐνέργειαν ἧς ἀποτέλεσμα τὸν υἱὸν διορίζεται...εὑρεθήσεται...ἀκολουθοῦντα μὲν τῷ θεῷ τὰ ἀ., αἴτια δὲ τῶν ὄντων τὰ μὴ ὄντα, *ib.*(p.94.24; 328B); Epiph. *anac.*(*GCS* 3 p.1.5; M.42.9A) cit. s. λόγος; **c.** Christol., Martin.ap. CLater.*act.*3(H.3.785D); οὐδὲ γὰρ τὴν θείαν φύσιν καὶ ἄκτιστον ἀ. καὶ ἀθέλητον ἢ ἀνενέργητον...οὔτε μὴν τὴν κτιστὴν καθ' ἡμᾶς καὶ ἀνθρωπίνην οὐσίαν ἀ. Max.*opusc.*(M.91.96A); μίαν ἐνέργειαν λέγοντες, ὁποίαν [sc. λέγετε], θείαν ἢ ἀνθρωπίνην ἢ οὐδετέραν;...εἰ οὐδετέραν ...οὐδὲ θεὸν οὐδὲ ἄνθρωπον ἀλλ' ἀ. δογματίζετε τὸν Χριστὸν id.*Pyrr.*(M.91.340C); φυσικῆς...ἑτερότητός ἐστι μετὰ τὴν ἕνωσιν ἡ διαφορά, ἀλλ' οὐ τῆς κατὰ ποιότητα μόνην ἀνομοιότητος, χωρὶς τῶν ὑποκειμένων ταῖς ποιότησι φύσεων...ἵνα μὴ...ψευδῆ τὴν διαφορὰν εἰσάγωμεν καὶ ἀ. id.*ep.*18(M.91.588C); **d.** in sense of *imaginary, fictitious*, Eus.*h.e.* 4.4.7(M.20.317A); Bas.*renunt.*9(2.210B; M.31.645A); of casting nativities τὴν ἀ. ταύτην τέχνην id.*hex.*6.5(1.55B; M.29.129B); ref. generation of Son τὸ πρὸ τῆς γεννήσεως τοῦτο...ἀ. ἔτι παντελῶς καὶ διανοίας ἀναπλασμός id.*Eun.*2.17(1.252E; M.29.608A); of Christ's human life in alleged teaching of Apoll. ψευδὴς κατ' αὐτὸν ἡ βρῶσις, ψευδὴς ὁ ὕπνος, ἀ. πάντα τὰ κατὰ τὰς ἰάσεις θαύματα Gr.Nyss.*Apoll.*23(M.45. 1172B); neut. as subst., of false doctrine τῇ περὶ τὸ ἀ. σπουδῇ id. *hom.11 in Cant.*(M.44.996C); of an argument, *baseless, invalid*, CLater.*act.*5(H.3.905A); **e.** neut. as subst., *non-existence, nothingness*, ref. Ex.3:14 εἴ τις λέγοι θεοῦ ὅτι πρότερον μὲν ἦν νῦν δὲ οὐκ ἔστιν ἢ ὅτι νῦν μὲν ἔστι πρότερον δὲ οὐκ ἦν...κολοβοῦται...ὁ τῆς ἀϊδιότητος λόγος καθ' ἑκάτερον μέρος ὁμοίως τῷ ἀ. περισκεπόμενος Gr.Nyss.*Eun.*8(2 p.176.22; M.45.769A); κἂν λόγος θεοῦ λέγηται, οὐκ ἐν τῇ ὁρμῇ τοῦ φθεγγομένου καὶ τὴν ὑπόστασιν ἔχειν νομισθήσεται, καθ' ὁμοιότητα τοῦ ἡμετέρου μεταχωρῶν εἰς ἀ. id.*or.catech.*1(p.8.16; M. 45.13B); τῇ ἀρχῇ καὶ τῷ τέλει τὸ ἄπειρον τῆς [sc. τοῦ λόγου] ζωῆς εἰς τὸ ἀ. ἄγοντες [sc. Arians] id.*Eun.*8(2 p.200.20; 796D); πνεῦμα...δύναμιν οὐσιώδη...οὐδὲ πρὸς τὸ ἀ. ἀναχεομένην id.*or.catech.*2(p.15.5; 17C); as ultimate fate of soul if pre-existent, Justn.*Or.*(p.200.25; M.86. 967A); εἴ τις λέγει...ὅτι...πάντων ὁμοίως εἰς τὸ ἀ. χωρήσει ἡ τῶν σωμάτων φύσις, ἀνάθεμα ἔστω CCP(543)*anath.*10(p.229; H.3.285D); θεὸς...δυνάμενος τὸν Σαοὺλ ἄρδην ἀφανίσαι καὶ εἰς τὸ ἀ. καταστῆσαι Jo.D.*parall.*(M.95.1228B); **2.** *not possessing independent existence*; **a.** in gen. ἀ. τί ἐστι καθ' ἑαυτὴν ἡ κακία Gr.Nyss.*or.catech.*5(p.28.5; M.45.25A); ref. Eph.4:22 παλαιὸν ἄνθρωπον ἀ. μέν, φθειρόμενον δὲ... εἴδωλόν τι ἀπωλείας ἐκ μιαρῶν καὶ ἀσεβῶν λογισμῶν Nil.*epp.*1.131(M. 79.141B); [sc. τῆς οὐσίας] μὴ ὑπαρχούσης, ἀ. εἶναι τὴν ποιότητα Isid. Pel.*epp.*2.72(M.78.516A); τὸ σκότος κατὰ στέρησιν τοῦ φωτός· ὥστε τὸ μὲν ἐν ὑπάρξει τὸ φῶς, τὸ δ' ἀ. τὸ σκότος Olymp.*Eccl.*2:13(M.93. 500B); of shadows, Proc.G.*Gen.*1:5(M.87.57A); ἀδύνατον...καταλαβεῖν ...ἀετοῦ ἴχνη...ὄφεως ὁδούς...ἐπειδὴ ταῦτα ἀ. ‡Proc.G.*Pr.*30:18(M. 87.1529A); **b.** Trin., denied of Son εἰ μὲν δὴ λόγος ἦν ἀ., μηδαμῶς ἔξωθεν τοῦ θεοῦ ὑφεστώς, ἀλλ' ἔνδον ὢν ἐν αὐτῷ...πῶς οὗτος ἦν ἐν μορφῇ θεοῦ; Eus.*e.th.*1.20(p.91.13; M.24.884B); *Symb.Ant.*(345)5 (p.252.35; M.26.729D) cit. s. λόγος; οἱ πατέρες οἱ κρίναντες Παῦλον τὸν Σαμοσατέα...οὐσίαν εἰπεῖν καὶ τὸν υἱόν, τὴν διαφορὰν τοῦ τε καθ' ἑαυτὸν ἀ. καὶ τοῦ ὑπάρχοντος...ἐπιδεικνύντες Geo.Laod.*ep.dogm.* (p.285.7; M.42.428B); μήτε τὸν θεὸν...ποτὲ ἄλογον, μήτε τὸν υἱὸν ἀ. ποτε Ath.*Ar.*1.19(M.26.52D); Epiph.*haer.*73.31(p.306.29; M.42.464A); οὐδεὶς ἀναγκάσει λόγος ἀ. εἶναι πρὸ τῆς γενήσεως τὸ γενηθὲν Cyr. *thes.*5(5¹.33C); heret., exeg. Heb.1:3 ἀ. ὁ υἱὸς εἴπερ...ὡς χαρακτὴρ ἐν τῷ πατρί id.*dial.Trin.*5(5¹.557E); of H. Ghost, denied by orthodox τὸ πνεῦμα τὸ ἅγιον οὐκ ἀ. ἐστιν, ἀλλ' ὑπάρχει καὶ ὑφέστηκεν ἀληθῶς Ath.*ep.Serap.*1.28(M.26.596B); asserted by Sabellians ἀνυπόστατον τὸν υἱὸν...καὶ ἀ. τὸ ἅγιον πνεῦμα ‡Ath.*Apoll.*1.21(M.26.1129C); **c.** Christol. ἡ ὑπόστασις καὶ ἡ οὐσία καὶ ἡ φύσις...μὴ ὡς τὰ καθ' αὑτὰ ἀ. συμβεβηκότα...ἀλλ' ὑφ' ἑαυτῆς ἑστάναι Leont.H.*Nest.*2.1(M. 86.1532A); *ib.*2.6(1549C); πῶς...τὴν ἐν ποιότησιν ἀ. ... ἀντεισαγάγοι [sc. Severus] διαφοράν; [sc. τῆς σαρκὸς πρὸς τὸν λόγον] Max.*opusc.* (M.91.253C).

***ἀνυπάρκτως**, *without individual existence* ὑφέστηκεν ἰδικῶς, καὶ ἔστιν υἱὸς ἀληθῶς οὐκ ἀνυπόστατος χαρακτήρ, οὐδὲ ἀ. ἐπερριμμένος ἢ συμβεβηκὼς ὡς εἶδος ἐν σώματι Cyr.*dial.Trin.*5(5¹.558E); Proc.G. *Gen.*1:5(M.87.57C).

ἀνυπαρξία, ἡ, **1.** *non-existence, nothingness*; **a.** in gen.; def. ὀνόμασι μὲν διαφόροις τὴν ἀ. σημαίνομεν, ἢ μὴ γεγενῆσθαι τὴν ἀρχὴν ἢ τεθνάναι τὸ γενόμενον λέγοντες Gr.Nyss.*Eun.*9(2 p.220.16; M.45. 820B); ἡ ἀπιστία...δυνατὴν δείκνυσι τὴν...πίστιν· ἀνυπαρξίας γὰρ στέρησις οὐκ ἂν λεχθείη Clem.*str.*2.12(p.142.30, v.l. ἀνυπαρξία M.8. 992C); [sc. τοῦ χρόνου] τῆς ὑπάρξεως προηγεῖται ἡ ἀ. ‡Just.*confut.*17 (M.6.1520A); κακῆς ὑπάρξεως ἀ. αἱρετώτερον Vict.*Mc.*14:18(p.422.2); τὸ εἶναι [sc. τοῦ κακοῦ] χαρακτηρίζει ἡ ἀ. Max.*ambig.*(M.91.1332A); **b.** ref. creation out of nothing, acc. pagans ἐκ τῆς ἀ. εἰς ὕπαρξιν τὸν θεὸν καὶ τὸν κόσμον αὐτοπαράκτως παραγόμενον ‡Just.*qu.Chr.*5.1 (M.6.1456B); ἡ ἐκ τοῦ μὴ ὄντος εἰς τὸ εἶναι πάροδος ἀλλοίωσίς τίς ἐστι, τῆς ἀ. κατὰ θείαν δύναμιν εἰς οὐσίαν μεθισταμένης Gr.Nyss.*or.catech.*21 (p.81.11; M.45.57D); **c.** in sense of *annihilation*, with verbs of sending or going, *annihilate* or *be annihilated*; of world, ref. Lc.23:45 τὸ πᾶν ἀ. ἠπείλει βλέπον τὸν φέροντα τὰ πάντα ἐπὶ σταυροῦ κρεμάμενον Thdt.*Ps.*95:5(1.1290); ἥλιος μὲν οὖν ἔσται, ὅτι μηδ' εἰς ἀ. χωρήσῃ ὁ νῦν κόσμος, ἀλλ' εἰς ἀνακαινισμόν Areth.*Apoc.*28(M.106.641A); Thdr. Stud.*nativ.BMV* 4(M.96.684A); of evil γίνεται ἡ ἀληθινὴ σοφία... ἵνα...τὸ κακὸν εἰς ἀ. μεταχωρήσῃ Gr.Nyss.*res.*1(M.46.608C); ταῖς τῶν ἐναντίων νεκρώσεσι καὶ ἀ., τὸ ἀναλλοίωτον ἴσχει τὰ νοερὰ τῆς θεοειδοῦς ἕξεως Dion.Ar.*e.h.*2.3.5(M.3.401B); of body at death μή τις νομίσῃ εἰς ἀ. χωρεῖν τὸ σῶμα Olymp.*Eccl.*12:6(M.93.620C); ref. Jo.3:14 τὸν θάνατον αὐτοῦ νομίζων [sc. ὁ ἀκροατής] ἀ. εἶναι Chrys. *hom.27.2 in Jo.*(8.156C); of soul at death μὴ εἰς ἀναίρεσιν καὶ ἀ. τὴν ψυχὴν μετὰ τὴν τῶν σωμάτων διάλυσιν ἄγειν Gr.Nyss.*anim.et res.*(M.46.72C); Epiph.*haer.*75.7(p.338.29; M.42.513B); εἰ δὲ νομίζων τὸν θάνατον εἰς ἀ. παραπέμπειν, ἀδεῶς πλημμελεῖς, σεαυτὸν ἀπατῶν λανθάνεις Isid.Pel.*epp.*3.248(M.78.928B); Dion.Ar.*e.h.*2.3.7(M.3.404B) cit. s. θάνατος; ἐὰν ἀποθάνῃ ἄνθρωπος...οὐκ εἰς ἀ. χωρεῖ, ἀλλὰ ζῇ τῇ ψυχῇ, περιμένων τὴν ἀνάστασιν Olymp.*Job* 14:13(M.93.168C); of spiritual death ψυχὴ ἀποθνήσκουσα ὅλως οὐκ ἔστιν· εἰς ἀ. γάρ ἐστι τῶν ἀθανάτων ὁ θάνατος Eus.Em.*fr.dogm.*(M.86.544B); ref. 1Cor.3:15 μὴ...νομίσῃς εἰς ἀ. χωρεῖν τοὺς καιομένους Chrys.*hom.9.3 in 1Cor.* (10.77C); Proc.G.*Gen.*4:13(M.86.244C); of the demon-worshipper εἰς ἀ. ... ἐμπεπτώκει καὶ ἀπωλείας κίνδυνον Dion.Ar.*e.h.*3.3.11(441A); denied of τὰ θεῖα, *cat.Apoc.*12:8(p.359.10); **d.** Trin.; agst. Arian doctrine, exeg. Pr.8:22, ref. Am.4:13 τὸ 'κτίζων' ⟨οὐκ⟩ ἐπὶ τοῦ γεγονότος ἐξ ἀ. παρείληφεν Eus.*e.th.*3.2(p.140.22; M.24.973C); τὸν...λόγον... ἀνυποστάτῳ πράγματι...ὑποστῆναι λέγει...οἷόν τινι ἑρκίῳ τῇ ἀ. πανταχόθεν διειλημμένον Gr.Nyss.*Eun.*1(1 p.95.9; M.45.328C); ἡ τοῦ μὴ κυρίως εἶναι κατασκευὴ τῆς παντελοῦς ἀ. ἀπόδειξις γίνεται *ib.*(p.71.28; 301A); ὅταν ὁ υἱὸς μὴ εἶναι λέγηται, καὶ ἡ τοῦ πατρὸς ἀ. ... ἐκ τοῦ ἀκολούθου...κατασκευάζεται *ib.*8(2 p.192.26; M.45.788C); **e.** Christol., Epiph.*haer.*78.24(p.475.15; M.42.740A) cit. s. σύγχυσις; τὴν τῶν ἑνωθέντων πραγμάτων δογματίζων [sc. Severus] ἀ., εὕροι πρὸς ἀπολογίαν...τὴν ὡς ἐν ποιότητι φυσικῇ διαφοράν Max.*opusc.*(M.91.41A); ref. other monophysites τοῦ σαρκωθέντος λόγου...τὰ τὴν ἡμετέραν φύσιν οὐσιωδῶς χαρακτηρίζοντα...ἢ...πρὸς τὴν ἑαυτοῦ θείαν μετασκευάσαντος φύσιν...ἢ πάμπαν εἰς ἀ. μεταχωρῆσαι ποιήσαντος *ib.* (93A); denied, Jo.D.*f.o.*3.3(M.94.988B); τὸ μὴ θέλειν μηδὲ βούλεσθαι τὴν νοερὰν τοῦ κυρίου ψυχὴν ἀ. τῆς οὐσίας Anast.S.*serm.imag.*3 (M.89.1176A); **2.** *unreality* οἱ τῷ θεῷ τῷ ὄντι μὴ ἡνωμένοι κατὰ τὴν πίστιν τῇ ἀ. τοῦ ψεύδους οἰκειωθέντες Bas.*Eun.*2.19(1.254E; M.29. 612C); Gr.Agr.*Eccl.*1.5(M.98.769B); ἐν φαντασίᾳ ψιλῇ καὶ ἀ. τὸ [sc. τῆς ἐνανθρωπήσεως] κεῖσθαι μυστήριον CLater.*act.*5(H.3.913E).

***ἀνύπατος**, *without a consul*, *Chron.Pasch.*p.377(M.92.964A).

ἀνύπεικτος, *unyielding, hard*, Gr.Nyss.*infant.*(M.46.189C); id. *v.Ephr.*(M.46.832C).

ἀνυπέρβλητος, *unsurpassable*, *1Clem.*53.5; *M.Polyc.*17.3; ἡ δὲ ἀρίστη ἀγωγὴ εὐταξία ἐστίν...κατ' ἀρετὴν ἀνυπέρβλητος Clem.*paed.*3. 12(p.283.15; M.8.664C); διὰ τοῦ τῆς ἀ. εἰς ἡμᾶς χάριτος ὑπηρέτου Ἰησοῦ Χριστοῦ Or.*or.*1(p.297.4; M.11.416A); θεός, ὁ ἀ. δυνάμει τεχνίτης...πάντων Meth.*res.*2.27(p.384.8) = Adam.*dial.*5.18(p.212.2; M.11. 1857B); *Hom.Clem.*10.20; τὸν ἀ. αὐτοῦ [sc. θεοῦ] φόβον Evagr.Pont. *or.*100(M.79.1189B); neut. as subst., *invincibility* τὸ τῆς πίστεως ἀ. Hipp.*Dan.*2.22.4; Philost.*h.e.*3.23(M.65.512B).

ἀνυπερβλήτως, *unsurpassably*, Or.*Jo.*20.34(27; p.372.26; M.14. 652B).

***ἀνυπερήφανος**, *free from pride, arrogance*; of God, *A.Xanthipp.* 30(p.79.25,29); of man, Bas.*renunt.*2(2.204D; M.31.632B); Leont.N. *v.Jo.Eleem.*27(p.58.10); Jo.D.*virt.*(M.95.85C) = Ephr.3.425D.

***ἀνυπεσταλμένως**, *plainly*, ‡Ath.*proph.*2(M.28.1065C).

ἀνυπεύθυνος, *not accountable*, Meth.*res.*2.1(p.330.5; M.18.297A); Cyr.H.*catech.*23.2 cit. s. χείρ; ἵνα...πάντας ἀ. ... τῆς ἀρχαίας παραβάσεως ποιήσῃ Ath.*inc.*20.2(M.25.132A); Gr.Nyss.*or.dom.*5(p.104.24; M.44.1185B).

***ἀνυπόβλητος**, *not subject to*, ‡Just.*qu.et resp.*114(M.6.1364A).

***ἀνυπογράφω**, s.v.l., *designate*, Gr.Nyss.*anim.et res.*(M.46.56B).

ἀνυπόδητος, *unshod*, of a discalced order ἀρχιμανδρίτης μονῆς τοῦ ὁσίου Θαλασσίου, τῶν ἐπίκλην ἀ. CCP(536)*act.*5(*ACO* 3 p.68.12; H.2.1330C).

ἀνύποιστος, *irresistible* ἀ. σπουδῇ Hier.*vir.ill.*(tr.Sophr.Pal.)61 (p.40.3; M.*PL*.23.674A); perh. τὸ ἀ. καὶ ἀπερίληπτον μέγεθος [sc. τοῦ Χριστοῦ] ‡Gr.Nyss.*Ar.et Sab.*2(M.45.1284D).

ἀνυποίστως, *insupportably*, Thdr.Mops.*1Cor.*4:12(M.66.880C).

ἀνυπόκριτος, *without dissimulation, unfeigned*, Clem.*q.d.s.*41

(p.187.22; M.9.648A); Gr.Naz.*or*.23.13(M.35.1166B); Marc.Er.*opusc*. 2.45(M.65.937A).

ἀνυποκρίτως, *without dissimulation, unfeignedly, 2Clem*.12.3; Clem.*paed*.2.10(p.223.5; M.8.529A); Chrys.*hom*.6.1 *in 2Tim*.(11.693C).

***ἀνυπόλειπτος**, *complete*, ‡Caes.Naz.*dial*.127(M.38.1024).

ἀνυπόληπτος, *disreputable*, Ephr.2.79E; Cyr.*ep*.9(p.108.21; 5². 31E).

***ἀνυπομονησία**, ἡ, *lack of endurance*, Mac.Aeg.*ep*.2(M.34.436A); Nil.*epp*.1.295(M.79.189D); Gr.Mag.*dial*.(tr.Zach.)4.10(M.*PL*.77.334C).

ἀνυπομόνητος, *not enduring, impatient, A.Paul.et Thecl*.21(p.250. 2); Ephr.1.7B; Leont.N.*v.Jo.Eleem*.35(p.69.3); neut. as subst., *impatience*, Mac.Aeg.*perf*.16(M.34.852C).

ἀνυπομονήτως, *impatiently*, Mac.Aeg.*hom*.6.1(M.34.517D).

ἀνυπονοήτως, *ingenuously, candidly*, Hipp.*haer*.7.20(p.195.25; M.16.3302C); Ammonas *opusc*.2.2(p.460.5).

***ἀνυποσημειώτος**, *unnoted*, Clem.*str*.1.1(p.10.29; M.8.704B).

***ἀνυπόσκευος**, *without support*, Gr.Nyss.*ep*.25(M.46.1097B).

ἀνυπόστατος, **A.** *that cannot be withstood or endured, irresistible*; of God's wrath, *Const.App*.2.22.12; *absolute* εἰ οὐ θέμις ἀ. κυριότητι οὐσιῶσθαί τινα φύσει εἰς κύριον Leont.H.*Nest*.5.14(M.86.1736D); of a sin that cannot be tolerated [i.e. by God] ἀ. καὶ ἀδιάφευκτος ἀνομία ἡ εἰς τὸν θεὸν βλασφημία Ephr.2.243E.

B. 1. *without sure foundation*; of heretical or erroneous beliefs, Iren.*haer*.1.9.5(M.7.548A); Marc.Er.*opusc*.10.11(M.65.1140B); of an accusation, *baseless*, Gr.Nyss.*Eun*.5(2 p.116.7; M.45.696D); ref. Mt. 28:15 ἀ. φήμη Diad.*ascens*.1(M.65.1141B); of water, *unstable*, Gr. Nyss.*v.Mos*.(M.44.393A); **2.** *without substance, immaterial*, ref. creation doctrine of Docetae ὁ πυροειδὴς θεὸς...πεποίηκε τὸν κόσμον ...αὐτὸς ὢν ἀ. σκότος ἔχων τὴν οὐσίαν Hipp.*haer*.8.10(p.229.9; M.16. 3354B); ref. resurrection of body εἰ ῥευστὸν [ἦν] τὸ σῶμα, ἕτερον ἀνθ' ἑτέρου γινόμενον, ἀδύνατον ὃ ἦν εὑρεῖν τὸ σῶμα, ἀ. [ὂν] Adam.*dial*.5.16 (p.208.2; M.11.1856A); of smoke, †Bas.*Is*.289(1.598E; M.30.625B); hence fig., of the present world and human activities φθαρτὴ...ἡ ἐπ' αὐτῷ [sc. τῷ κόσμῳ] δόξα καὶ ἀ. *ib*.126(1.467C; M.30.324B); ref. 1Cor.3:15 καλαμώδη...πρᾶξιν καὶ ἀ. Cyr.H.*catech*.15.21; ref. Ps. 101:4, Chrys.*hom*.2.5 *in Mt*.(7.28B); ref. 1Cor.7:31, id.*hom*.20.2 *in Rom*.(9.658E); of fire in burning bush, ‡Meth.*Sym.et Ann*.7(M.18. 364C); **3.** *unsubstantial, without independent existence*, of accidental or secondary qualities, defined and distinguished from 4 infra ἀνούσιον καὶ ἀ. τὴν μὴ ὑπάρχουσαν μήτε οὖσαν ὅλως σημαίνει φύσιν. τὸ δὲ ἐνούσιον καὶ ἀ. λέγων τις, τὴν ἐνυπάρχουσαν οὐσίαν ἐδήλωσε Didym. (‡Bas.)*Eun*.5(1.312D; M.29.749B); τὸ ἀ. διττόν. λέγεται γὰρ ἀ. καὶ τὸ μηδαμῶς ὄν, ὡς τραγέλαφος καὶ ἱπποκένταυρος· λέγεται πάλιν... τὸ ἔχον ἐν ἑτέρῳ τὴν ὑπόστασιν, καὶ μὴ καθ' ἑαυτὸ ὑφιστάμενον· ὡς τὰ συμβεβηκότα †Leont.B.*sect*.7.2(M.86.1240D); **a.** in gen., Eus.*d.e*. 5.5(p.228.28; M.22.377B) cit. s. ἀνούσιος; ‡Just.*qu.Chr*.3.1(M.6. 1432D) cit. s. ἐνυπόστατος; εἰ κατ' οὐσίαν ὑφέστηκεν ὁ θυμὸς ἢ ὁ φόβος...ἢ τινες ἀ. κινήσεις τυγχάνουσι Gr.Nyss.*Eun*.1(1 p.117.1; M.45.352B); εἰ μήτε ψυχὴν μήτε προαίρεσιν ἔχει [sc. τὸ τυχὸν] μήτε κατ' ἰδίαν θεωρεῖται ὑπόστασιν· πῶς τοσαύτην μαρτυρεῖται παρ' ὑμῖν ἔχειν τὴν δύναμιν, ὥστε...κρατεῖν τῶν ὑφεστώτων τὸ ἀ.; id.*fat*.(M.45. 160A); ἡ ὁρμὴ τῆς θείας προαιρέσεως...πρᾶγμα γίνεται...τῆς παντοδυνάμου ἐξουσίας...μὴ ἀ. ποιούσης τὸ θέλημα· ἡ δὲ τοῦ θελήματος ὕπαρξις οὐσία ἐστί id.*anim.et res*.(M.46.124B); ref. 1Cor.15:50 δείκνυμι [sc. σάρκα ἀ.] μὴ εἰρῆσθαι τῷ Παύλῳ περὶ τῆς σαρκὸς ἧς αὐτὸς ὠνόμασας, ἀλλὰ ἀ. τι λαμβάνει κἀνταῦθα *Disp.Phot*.3(M.88. 548B); **b.** Trin., ref. Sabellian, Samosatene, and Marcellan views οὐ γὰρ ἀ. τὴν τριάδα λέγομεν· ἀλλ' ἐν ὑποστάσει αὐτὴν γινώσκομεν Eugen.*exp.fid*.2(M.18.1304B); οὐχ ὡς ψιλὸς θεοῦ λόγος, ἀ., ἓν καὶ ταὐτὸν ὑπάρχων τῷ θεῷ Eus.*Marcell*.1.1(p.7.33; M.24.725C); Ath. *syn*.41(p.267.25; M.26.768A); τὸν ἀ. τῶν προσώπων ἀναπλασμὸν οὐδὲ Σαβέλλιος παρῃτήσατο Bas.*ep*.210.5(3.317A; M.32.776C); Epiph. *haer*.65.5(p.7.29; M.42.20B); v. ἀνούσιος; against Jewish conception of monotheism ἄπρακτα πάντως καὶ ἀ. κἀκεῖνα κατασκευάζουσιν οἱ πρὸς τὴν ὁμοιότητα τοῦ παρ' ἡμῖν λόγου τὸ θεῖον κατάγοντες Gr.Nyss. *or.catech*.4(p.19.7; M.45.20C); v. ῥῆμα; against Eunomius, id.*Eun*.1 (1 p.94.20; M.45.328B) cit. s. ἀνύπαρκτος; εἰ ὁ υἱὸς ἐνέργημα, καὶ οὐ γέννημα, οὔτε ὁ ἐνεργήσας, οὔτε μὴν τὸ ἐνεργηθὲν αὐτός ἐστιν...ἀ.· οὐδεμία γὰρ ἐνέργεια · ἐνυπόστατος Didym.(‡Bas.)*Eun*.4(1.287B; M.29.689C); exeg. 1Cor.1:24, Isid.Pel.*epp*.2.143(M.78.585D) cit. s. ἐνυπόστατος; exeg. Heb.1:3 ἐπειδὴ τὸ ἀπαύγασμα ἐλάττονα δείκνυσι τὴν φύσιν παρ' ἐκεῖνο οὗ ἐστιν ἀπαύγασμα καὶ οὐκ ἐν ἰδίᾳ ὑποστάσει, ἑτέρᾳ λέξει τοῦτο παρέστησεν εἰπὼν 'καὶ χαρακτὴρ τῆς ὑποστάσεως', τὸ μὲν πρῶτον τεθεικὼς εἰς ἀπόδειξιν τοῦ ἐκ τῆς οὐσίας ἀμερῶς εἶναι, τὸ δὲ δεύτερον, ὅτι οὐκ ἀ. Sever.*Heb*.1:3(p.346.28); υἱὸς ἀληθῶς, οὐκ ἀ. χαρακτήρ, οὐδὲ ἀνυπάρκτως ἐπερριμμένος ἢ συμβεβηκὼς ὡς εἶδος ἐν σώματι Cyr.*dial.Trin*.5(5¹.558E); εἰ μὴ αὐτός ἐστιν ὁ...υἱὸς...καὶ...ὁ λόγος...λεγέτωσαν ἡμῖν πότερον...ὁ...ἐπινοούμενος λόγος ἐνυπόστατός ἐστιν ἢ οὐχί·...εἰ ἀ. ἐροῦσιν αὐτὸν...πῶς ἔσται τρίτος ἐκ πατρός; id.*Jo*.1.4(4.38C); οὐκοῦν ἐνυπόστατος ὢν ὁ υἱὸς...τῇ ἀ. βουλήσει κατ' οὐδὲν ἔσται προσεοικώς id.*thes*.7(5¹.61E); πνεῦμα...θεοῦ...οὐ...πνοὴν ἀ. Jo.D.*f.o*.1.7(M.94.805B); cf.Gr.Nyss.*or.catech*.2(p.14.17; M.45. 17B); **c.** Christol. οὐκ ἀ. ὑμῖν τὸν ἄνθρωπον τὸν κυριακὸν δεῖξαι βουλόμεθα...ἀλλ' οὐκ ἰδιοϋπόστατον, τουτέστιν ἀπὸ τοῦ λόγου χωριζόμενον Leont.H.*Nest*.2.10(M.86.1556A); Leont.B.*Nest.et Eut*.1(M. 86.1276D) cit. s. φύσις; *ib*.(1277D) cit. s. ὑπόστασις; ὃ γὰρ ὑμεῖς λέγετε ἑνωθῆναι, τοῦτο λέγομεν ἡμεῖς μετὰ τὴν ἕνωσιν. εἰ μὲν οὖν ἀ. τὰς φύσεις λέγετε ἑνωθῆναι, καὶ ἡμεῖς τοῦτο λέγομεν· εἰ δὲ ἐνυποστάτους, ἄτοπον †Leont.B.*sect*.7.1(M.86.1240B); Max.*opusc*.(M.91.261C); εἰ δὲ τῇ μὲν ἐνεργείᾳ, τὸ θέλημα· τῷ δὲ θελήματι, συναναιρεῖται τὸ πρόσωπον, ἀ. ἔσται κατὰ Σευῆρον ὁ Χριστός *ib*.(52C); οὐκ οὖν ὡς ἐπὶ τῆς θεότητος τοῦ Χριστοῦ, καὶ φύσιν αὐτῆς καὶ ὑπόστασιν ὁμολογοῦμεν, οὕτως δήπου καὶ ἐπὶ τῆς ἀνθρωπότητος αὐτοῦ, ὥσπερ φύσιν, οὕτως καὶ τὴν ἰδικὴν ταύτην ὁμολογεῖν ὑπόστασιν ἀνάγκη, ἵνα μὴ ἀ. ... τὴν φύσιν ἐκείνην λέγειν ἀναγκαζώμεθα Jo.D.*haer*.83(M.94.752B); ὥσπερ οὐκ ἔστιν ὑπόστασις ἀνούσιος...οὕτως οὐκ ἔστι φύσις ἀ., καὶ οὐκ ἀνάγκη ἐπὶ τῶν ἑνουμένων ἑκάστην φύσιν καὶ ἀνὰ μέρος ἔχειν ὑπόστασιν id. *fid.Nest*.6(p.562); **4.** *non-existent, unreal, imaginary*, of things existing only in thought; **a.** in gen., Cyr.H.*catech*.13.37; τὰ ἀ. μὲν παντελῶς, κατὰ δὲ ἀναζωγράφησίν τινα τῆς ἐννοίας καὶ φαντασίαν μόνην ἀνατυπούμενα Bas.*Eun*.1.6(1.217D; M.29.524A); τὸ μὴ ὄν, ὃ ἐν τῷ δοκεῖν εἶναι μόνον ἐστίν, ἀ. ἔχον ἐφ' ἑαυτοῦ τὴν φύσιν Gr.Nyss. *v.Mos*.(M.44.333B); ref. Ac.1:5 μὴ...ἐν ἐπαγγελίαις...μηδὲ...ἐνέργειαν ...ἀ. Chrys.*hom*.1.5 *in Ac*.(9.9E); ἐπειδὴ τὰ ἐν ἐλπίδι ἀ. εἶναι δοκεῖ, ἡ πίστις ὑπόστασιν αὐτοῖς χαρίζεται id.*hom*.21.2 *in Heb*.(12.197B); ref. Jac.5:16 μὴ...ἀργὴν...τὴν δέησιν καὶ ἀ., ἀλλ' ἐνεργὸν καὶ ζῶσαν Max.*qu.Thal*.67(M.90.589D); Anast.S.*hod*.2(M.89.61A); **b.** of negations ἀ. [sc. τὸ κενόν]. οὐσία γὰρ τοῦ κενοῦ τὸ μηδέν Alex.Lyc.*Man*. 8(p.13.16; M.18.421D); of darkness, exeg. Gen.1:2 σκότους ἄνευ ἄρθρου ἐμνήσθη, ἀβύσσου δὲ μετὰ ἄρθρου...ἐπείπερ τὸ μέν, ἀ., τὸ δέ, οὐσιῶδες Diod.*Gen*.1:2(M.33.1563A); Thdt.*qu*.7 *in Gen*.(1.12); γένεσιν πράγματος ἀ. πῶς εἶχεν εἰπεῖν ἡ γραφή; στέρησις γάρ ἐστι τοῦ φωτὸς [sc. τὸ σκότος] Proc.G.*Gen*.1:2(M.87.44B); of evil ἀ. εἶναι τὴν κακίαν (οὔτε γὰρ ἦν ἀπ' ἀρχῆς οὔτε εἰς τὸν αἰῶνα ἔσται) Or.*Jo*.2.13(7; p.68.26; M.14.133D); ἀνούσιός ἐστι καὶ ἀ. ἡ κακία, διὰ τῆς ἡμῶν ἀμελείας ἐκ τοῦ μὴ ὄντος συνισταμένη· πάλιν διὰ τῆς ἡμῶν κατορθώσεως ἀπολλυμένη Dor.*doct*.11.4(M.88.1737D); ἀ. τὸ κακόν, ἐπειδὴ μὴ μετέχει τοῦ θεοῦ Max.*schol.c.h*.4.1(M.4.53A); **c.** of pagan or heretical beliefs, Or.*mart*.7(p.8.14; M.11.572B); ἡ μυθοποιΐα...ἀ. εἰδοποιεῖ Eust.*engast*. 27(p.59.7; M.18.669B); Gr.Nyss.*hom*.16 *in Cant*.(M.44.1060C); **d.** in view of Inc. ascribed to Apollinarians σάρκα τὴν ἀ. συγκεράσας ἑαυτῷ ὁ λόγος, ἔδειξε τὸν ὄντως λογικὸν καὶ τέλειον ἄνθρωπον ‡Ath. *Apoll*.2.16(M.26.1160C); φαντάζεσθε ἀ. εἶναι τὸν Χριστόν, καὶ μόνον ἕως λόγου καὶ δοκήσεως τὴν ἐνδημίαν τῆς ἐνσάρκου παρουσίας αὐτὸν πεποιηκότα Epiph.*haer*.77.24(p.437.7; M.42.676B); in view of Inc. ascribed to Nestorians τὴν ἕνωσιν τοῦ λόγου πρὸς τὸ ἀνθρώπινον... κατὰ συνάφειαν σχετικὴν δουλοπρεποῦς καὶ ἀ. μορφῆς πρὸς ἀ. καὶ θείαν μορφήν Cyr.*apol.Thdt*.1(p.113.22; 6¹.207C); ἀ. τι καὶ ἀνάπλασμα καὶ λόγῳ μόνον ἓν πρόσωπον ἐξ ἑνώσεως φυσικῶν προσώπων εἶναι δογματίζετε Leont.H.*Nest*.2.34(M.86.1593A); **e.** neut. as subst., ref. Mt.26:24, Gr.Nyss.*infant*.(M.46.184A); **5.** *without significance* ἦχος ὀνόματος ἀ. Const.*or.s.c*.6(p.161.18; M.20.1249C).

***ἀνυποταγή**, ἡ, *disobedience, insubordination*, Ephr.1.72B; *ib*. 1.86B; *ib*.2.115E.

ἀνυποτακτέω, *be unsubmissive, not subject*, Or.*comm.in Eph*.1:22 (*JTS* 3 p.401).

ἀνυπότακτος, **1.** *insubordinate, A.Thom*.A 142(p.249.17); *Trad.Pil* 3(p.450); Bas.*ep*.188 *can*.1(3.268E; M.32.665A); neut. as subst., *insubordination, A.Thom*.A 123(p.233.1); Cyr.*Juln*.4(6².138B); **2.** ref. Inc., *not subject* ἐν τῷ ἀντιτείνειν σε πρὸς τὴν ἀρετὴν ἀ. ἑαυτὸν ὀνομάζει Evagr.Pont.*ep*.8(M.32.261A); τὸ ἐμὸν ἀ. ἑαυτοῦ ποιεῖται, ὡς κεφαλὴ τοῦ παντὸς σώματος. ἕως μὲν οὖν ἀ. ἐγὼ...ἀ. τὸ κατ' ἐμὲ καὶ Χριστὸς λέγεται Gr.Naz.*or*.30.5(p.114.7; M.36.108D); τῷ καθ' ἡμᾶς ἀ. λέγεται καὶ Χριστὸς ἕως ἂν ταύτης καὶ ἡμᾶς ἀπολύσῃ τῇ δυνάμει τῆς ἐνανθρωπήσεως Max.*opusc*.(M.91.60B); *ib*.(237B).

ἀνυποταξία, ἡ, *insubordination, disobedience*, Cyr.*Ps*.94:1(M.69. 1240B); Jo.Mosch.*prat*.109(M.87.2972D); Anast.S.*qu.et resp*.59(M.89. 628A); ref. Inc. ὑποτεταγμένος ἐδόκει τε καὶ διείληπτο τὴν ἀ. τοῦ λαοῦ ‡Gr.Nyss.*Ar.et Sab*.7(M.45.1292B); Max.*opusc*.(M.91.216B).

***ἀνυποταχθέω**, = ἀνυποτακτέω, s.v.l., Ephr.3.294D.

ἀνύπουλος, *sound, genuine* συνείδησις πίστεως ἀ. *Const.App*. 7.33.3; Mac.Mgn.*apocr*.4.18(p.194.17); Nil.*epp*.3.219(M.79.484B).

***ἀνυπούλως**, *soundly, genuinely*, Geo.Laod.*ep.dogm.*(p.288.3; M.42.432C); Chrys.*hom.6.1 in 2Tim.*(11.693C).

***ἀνυπόφορος**, *intolerable*, *T.Abr.*A 19(pp.101.15,102.7).

***ἀνύστακτος**, *vigilant, wakeful* ὀφθαλμός Gr.Nyss.*v.Ephr.*(M.46.829D); *Didasc.Jac.*1.29(p.763.9); Jo.Mon.*hymn.Nic.*9(M.96.1389B).

***ἀνυστάκτως**, *without slumbering, vigilantly*, Gr.Nyss.*Eun.*1(1 p.29.12; M.45.257A); Procl.CP *Arm.*5(p.189.15; M.65.860B).

***ἀνυστέρητος**, *not lacking*, Ign.*Smyrn.*proem.; Herm.*mand.*9.4.

***ἀνυστερήτως**, *lacking nothing*, Epiph.*haer.*77.18(p.432.7; M.42.665D).

ἀνυτής, ὁ, (Lat. *exactor*) *provincial administrator*, Eustrat. *v.Eutych.*68(M.86.2352A).

ἀνυψ-όω, **1.** *lift up*; **a.** lit. τοῦ σωτῆρος ~ωθέντος Eus.*d.e.*10.7(p.469.30; M.22.756C); ὁ ἱερεὺς...~οῖ τὸν ἄρτον τῆς ζωῆς Anast.S. *synax.*(M.89.841A); **b.** met. δεῖ τὸν νοῦν ἡμῶν...τῆς γῆς ~οῦν *cat. Mt.*6:9(p.45.4); τὴν φωνὴν ἀ. Eus.*v.C.*4.63(p.143.27; M.20.1217A); id. *Ps.*149:6(M.24.72C); **2.** *lift up again*, *V.Zos.*3(p.98.4); **3.** *erect* building etc. *in honour* of someone, Eus.*l.C.*9(p.221.24; M.20.1372A); τῆς εἰς οὐρανοὺς πορείας...τὴν μνημὴν...ἀ. id.*v.C.*3.43(p.95.32; M.20.1104A); *ib.*3.50(p.98.26; 1109C); **4.** *exalt, honour*, Hipp.*Dan.*2.27.7; Eus.*v.C.*3.1(p.76.19; 1053B); Nonn.*par.Jo.*8:28(M.43.817A); Philost. *h.e.*8.3(M.65.557B); τὸν τῇ αὐτοῦ καταβάσει καθελόντα τὸν ἀντίπαλον καὶ τῇ αὐτοῦ ἀναβάσει ἀ. τὸν ἄνθρωπον Jo.D.*carm.assumpt.Chr.*80(p.228; M.96.845C); *ib.*89(p.228; 845D).

***ἀνύψωσις, ἡ**, *exaltation*, ‡Ath.*synops.*46(M.28.377C); Gr.Nyss. *Eun.*5(2 p.116.17; M.45.697A).

ἄνω, **I.** *up, upward, above*;

A. lit. θεὸς τοὺς ἀνθρώπους ἠγάπησε...οἷς μόνοις ἄ. πρὸς οὐρανὸν ὁρᾶν ἐπέτρεψεν *Diogn.*10.2; v. ἄνθρωπος; of Christ on Cross μεγάλα ἄ. ὢν ἐπεδείξατο θαύματα...τὰς πέτρας ῥηγνύς, τοὺς τετελευτηκότας ἐγείρων Chrys.*hom.79.3 in Mt.*(7.762D).

B. met.; **1.** of Christ's divinity being located 'above' αὐτὸς γὰρ καὶ ἄ. φῶς ἦν καὶ ἐστὶ τὸ ἐπιφανὲν ἐν σαρκὶ καὶ τὸ ἐνταῦθα ὀφθὲν οὐχ ὕστερον τοῦ ἄ. Clem.*exc.Thdot.*4(p.106.17,19; M.9.656A); even while being in Hades, Or.*engast.*8(p.292.7; M.12.1025A); πανταχοῦ γὰρ τοῦ λόγου ἑαυτὸν ἁπλώσαντος, καὶ ἄ., καὶ κάτω...ἄ. μὲν εἰς τὴν κτίσιν, κάτω δὲ εἰς τὴν ἐνανθρώπησιν Ath.*inc.*16.3(M.25.124C); **2.** *above, on high, in heaven* ὁ εὐσεβὴς...ἄ. μετὰ τῶν πατέρων ἀναβιώσας *2Clem.* 19.4; τὰς ἐπαγγελίας ἄ. περιαθροῦσι, τὸν οὐράνιον διψῶσαι...τόπον Meth.*symp.*4.5(p.51.1; M.18.93B); often best translated by adj., *heavenly* οἱ ἄγγελοι ἐκεῖνοι οἱ τὸν ἄ. κλῆρον εἰληχότες κατολισθήσαντες εἰς ἡδονάς Clem.*str.*5.1(p.332.17; M.9.24B); τῆς ἄνω πατρίδος ἄξιος id.*q.d.s.*3(p.162.7; M.9.608C); τίς οὐκ ἂν εὔξαιτο μετὰ τούτων [sc. angels and saints] ἔχειν τὴν ἄ. σύνοδον; Ath.*ep.fest.*43(p.298.14; M.26.1441B); τύπος τῆς ἄ. χαρᾶς καὶ ἡ νῦν ἐστιν ἑορτή [i.e. Easter] *ib.*44(p.298.30; 1441D); heaven called ἡ ἄνω Ἱερουσαλήμ (cf. Gal. 4:26), Clem.*paed.*1.6(p.116.31; M.8.304A); Ath.*virg.*24(p.59.23; M. 28.281A); Ant.Mon.*hom.*112(M.89.1781A); **3.** esp. ref. angels as being from heaven τὴν ἄ. τῶν ἀγγέλων ζωήν Ammon.*Jo.*3:4(M.85. 1408C); hence as their epithet, *angelic* ἡ ἄ. κτίσις Didym.*Trin.*1.32(M.39.428A); αἱ ἄ. δυνάμεις Chrys.*hom.13.4 in Phil.*(11.302E); Cyr. *Jo.*3.4(4.287E); *Chron.Pasch.*p.23(M.92.108C); **4.** of spiritual realities to which men's minds are turned τοῦ μὲν [sc. πνεύματος] γάρ ἐστιν ἄ. τὸ οἰκητήριον, τῆς δὲ [sc. ψυχῆς] κάτωθέν ἐστιν ἡ γένεσις Tat.*orat.* 13(p.14.25; M.6.833B); ἀνατεινόμενοι δὲ ἄ. τῇ ἐννοίᾳ, κόσμῳ καὶ ἁμαρτίαις ἀποτεταγμένοι Clem.*paed.*1.5(p.99.31; M.8.269A); Or.*hom. 18.2 in Jer.*(p.151.32; M.13.464D); exeg. Jer.18:1 καταβαίνουσι καὶ τὴν ψυχὴν ἔχουσιν ἄ., ὑπὲρ τοῦ ἰδεῖν τὸν λόγον τὸν ἀνωτάτω περὶ τῶν κατωτάτω *ib.*(p.153.11; 468A); *ib.19.13*(p.169.11; 489A); ἄ. πρὸς ὕψος ἁρπαζομένων τῶν ἀναγεννωμένων πρὸς τὸν θρόνον τοῦ θεοῦ· ὃ δή ἐστιν, ἄ. περὶ τὴν θείαν ἕδραν...τῆς ἀληθείας αἱρεῖται τὸ φρόνημα τῶν ἀνακαινισθέντων...ἵνα μὴ ἀπατηθῇ πρὸς τοῦ δράκοντος βρίθοντος κάτω· οὐ γὰρ αὐτῷ θέμις τοὺς ἄ. νεύοντας καὶ τοὺς ἄ. βλέποντας ἀφανίσαι Meth.*symp.*8.10(p.92.10ff.; M.18.153A); esp. virgins, *ib.*8.2(p.83.8; 141A); ὅτε γὰρ οὐ συνομιλεῖ τοῖς σώμασιν ὁ νοῦς ὁ τῶν ἀνθρώπων... ἀλλ' ὅλος ἐστὶν ἄ. ἑαυτῷ συνὼν ὡς γέγονεν ἐξ ἀρχῆς· τότε δή, τὰ αἰσθητὰ...διαβάς, ἄ. μετάρσιος γίνεται Ath.*gent.*2(M.25.8A); id.*virg.* 17(p.52.12; M.28.272C) cit. s. δάκρυον; εἰς πάντα ἄ. ὀφείλομεν προσέχειν κἂν καλῶς, ἢ κακῶς ἃ πάθωμεν παρά τινος, ἄ. προσέχειν, καὶ εὐχαριστεῖν Dor.*doct.*7.4(M.88.1701C); **5.** of contemplation ἡ ἄ. τροφή Clem.*paed.*2.1(p.160.4; M.8.393A); ἀνωτάτη θεωρία Or.*Jo.*2.8(4; p.62.25; M.14.121D); τὰ ἄ. θεωρήματα Ath.*v.Anton.*13(M.26. 864A); ἡ ἄ. φιλοσοφία Nil.*Alb.*(M.79.705A); Jo.VI H.*v.Jo.D.*13(M. 94.449A); **6.** τὰ ἄ., τὰ ἀνώτερα *heavenly* or *spiritual things*, Or.*hom. 18.2 in Jer.*(p.152.9; M.13.465A) cit. s. κατώτατος; πηδᾶν ἐπὶ τὸ ἀνώτερον, ἐπὶ τὴν αἰώνιον ζωήν id.*Jo.*13.3(p.228.30; M.14.404B); Meth.*symp.*5.4(p.57.19; M.18.104A); Ath.*ep.fest.*43(p.298.7; M.26. 1441A); ἀπ' αὐτῶν γὰρ τῶν κοσμικῶν...τὰ ἄ. νοοῦμεν id.*virg.*2(p.37. 17; M.28.253D); **7.** liturg. ἄ. τὸν νοῦν, *sursum corda*, *Lit.*ap.*Const. App.*8.12.5; ἄ. σχῶμεν τὸν νοῦν *Lit.Jac.*(p.198.15) etc.; **8.** Gnost., ref. heavenly man Adamas γνωρίσασα ἡ ἄ. ψυχὴ τὸ συγγενὲς αὐτῆς Iren.*haer.*1.14.8(M.7.612A); ἡ μακαρία φύσις τοῦ μακαρίου ἀνθρώπου τοῦ ἄ., τοῦ Ἀδάμαντος Hipp.*haer.*5.8(p.89.11; M.16.3139B); Manich., of men in gen. οἱ ἄνθρωποι πάντες ῥίζας ἔχουσι κάτω συνδεθεῖσας τοῖς ἄ. ... ἐὰν δὲ τὰ ἄ. τῆς ῥίζης τόνῳ σαλεύσῃ, σεισμὸς γίγνεται Hegem.*Arch.*9(pp.14.14–15.3; M.10.1441B).

II. comp. and superl., *higher, superior to, highest*;

A. of God; **1.** as highest being εὐσέβεια...τὸ ἀνωτάτω... αἴτιον σέβειν...διδάσκουσα Clem.*str.*2.18(p.154.1; M.8.1016C); εἷς θεὸς μία φύσις ἡ ἀνωτάτω Gr.Naz.*or.*31.10(p.157.5; M.36.144B); **2.** in subordinationist theology; of Father, exeg. Ps.110:1 τὸν μὲν ἀνωτάτω θεὸν διὰ τοῦ πρώτου κυρίου, τὸν δὲ τούτου δεύτερον διὰ τῆς δευτέρας ὑποφήνας προσηγορίας Eus.*p.e.*11.14(532B; M.21.884A); ἔκ τε τῆς ἀνωτάτω...οὐσίας καὶ ἐκ τῆς δι' ἐκείνην μὲν οὔσης μετ' ἐκείνην δὲ πάντων τῶν ἄλλων πρωτευούσης Eun.ap.Gr.Nyss.*Eun.*1(1 p.67.23; M.45.297A); **3.** Gnost., ref. demiurge and highest God οὔτε θεόν, τὸν κτίσαντα τὸν κόσμον, ἀνώτατον εἶναι λέγει [sc. Simon Magus] *Hom.Clem.*2.22; μὴ τοῦτον εἶναι θεὸν ἀνώτατον, ὃς οὐρανὸν ἔκτισε καὶ γῆν...ἀλλὰ ἄλλον τινὰ ἄγνωστον καὶ ἀνώτατον, ὡς ἐν ἀπορρήτοις ὄντα θεὸν θεῶν *ib.*3.2; *ib.*18.1; Σίμων...θέλει νομίζεσθαι ἀνωτάτη τις εἶναι δύναμις καὶ αὐτοῦ τοῦ τὸν κόσμον κτίσαντος θεοῦ *ib.*2.22; **4.** of divinity as superior to creation χρόνων δὲ καὶ αἰώνων ἀνώτερος ὁ θεός Chrys.*hom.4.2 in Jo.*(8.28D); πάσης γὰρ ἀνωτέρα μεταβολῆς ἡ οὐσία αὕτη *ib.11.2*(64C); κτίσεως γὰρ ἀνωτάτω...θεός Cyr.*ador.*10(1. 369C); ἡ ἀνωτάτω πασῶν οὐσία *ib.*1(26D); exeg. Lc.8:23ff. τὸν γὰρ ὕψεως ἀνώτερον...ὕπνος κατέχειν οὐκ ἔμαθε Bas.Sel.*or.*22.1(M.85. 265B).

B. ref. men ἄνθρωπος εἶ, ἀνωτέρω εἶ τοῦ διαβόλου Or.*hom.5.17 in Jer.*(p.46.24; M.13.521B); τὸ...ὅλης ψυχῆς ἀνωτέρω, νοῦς Alex.Lyc. *Man.*23(p.33.8; M.18.441D); Chrys.*hom.23.3 in Jo.*(8.136D); Cyr. *ador.*1(1.28A).

C. *superior*, hence *valuable* ἄργυρον καὶ ἕτερα πράγματα ἀνώτερα Leont.N.*v.Jo.Eleem.*28(p.60.14).

ἀνώγεον (-ων), τό, *upper storey*, Pall.*h.Laus.*6(p.24.9, v.l. τὰ ἀνάγαια M.34.1019B); in the Attic form ἀνώγεων, of the firmament opp. earth, Cosm.Ind.*top.*2(M.88.81C; ἀνάγαιον p.59.8).

ἀνωδίνω, *be in labour, bring forth*, met., Cyr.*ador.*8(1.260A).

***ἀνωδίνως**, *without birth-pangs*, Jo.D.*f.o.*4.14(M.94.1160C).

***ἀνώδρομος**, *tending to rise*, †Jo.D.*creat.*3(p.66).

ἄνωθεν, **I.** *from above*;

A. ref. Son and H. Ghost, descending from above ὁ ἔχων τὸ πνεῦμα [τὸ θεῖον] τὸ ἄ. πραΰς ἐστι Herm.*mand.*11.8; αὐτὸς [sc. Christ] γὰρ αὐτὸ [sc. H. Ghost] ἄ. ἔπεμπεν, ὡς θεός· καὶ αὐτὸς αὐτὸ κάτω ὑπεδέχετο, ὡς ἄνθρωπος Ath.*inc.et c.Ar.*9(M.26.997C); τὸν ἐπ' ἐσχάτων τῶν ἡμερῶν κατελθόντα ἄ. καὶ γεννηθέντα ἐκ παρθένου *Symb.Ant.*(341)2(p.249.21; M.26.721C); ἀφῖκται γὰρ ἄ. καὶ παρὰ πατρὸς πρὸς ἡμᾶς ὁ λόγος Cyr.*Os.*63(3.97B); ref. generation of Logos, Ath.*inc.et c.Ar.*8(996A) cit. s. κάτωθεν.

B. ref. baptismal regeneration 'from above' ἄ. ἐξ ὕδατος καὶ πνεύματος ἀναγεννηθέντες Ath.*Ar.*3.33(M.26.396A); βαπτιζόμενος... ἀνακαινίζεται δέ, ἄ. γεννηθεὶς τῇ τοῦ πνεύματος χάριτι id.*ep.Serap.*4. 13(M.26.656B); εἰς παρθενίαν διὰ τῆς ἄ. γεννήσεως ἀνακαινισθεῖσα Gr.Nyss.*hom.9 in Cant.*(M.44.956A); [sc. φύσιν]...διατυπώσαντος [sc. Christ] ἄ. τῇ δι' ὕδατος ἀναγεννήσει καὶ πνεύματος Chrys.*hom.11.2 in Jo.*(8.65A).

C. ref. divine gifts descending from above (cf. Jac.1:17) ἡ πίστις ἄ. ἐστι παρὰ τοῦ κυρίου Herm.*mand.*9.11; Athenag.*leg.*18.2(M.6.925B); κατάγωμεν δὲ ἄ. ἐξ οὐρανῶν ἀλήθειαν Clem.*prot.*1(p.4.8; M.8.53B); ἀλήθεια οὐρανόθεν ἄ. ἐπὶ τὴν συναγωγὴν τῆς ἐκκλησίας ἀφιγμένη id.*str.*6.3(p.448.16; M.9.252C); of grace, id.*prot.*10(p.75.3; M.8.220C); τῆς ἄ. κρίσεως ἠρτῆσθαι τὴν ζωὴν καὶ τὸν θάνατον τῶν ἀνθρώπων Ath.*fug.*15(p.79.9; M.25.664C); ἡμῶν δέ, ὧν ἐστι καὶ ὁ πάσχα, ἡ κλῆσις ἄνωθέν ἐστι id.*ep.fest.*43(p.297.11; M.26.1440B); τὴν εἰρημένην σάρκα βρῶσιν ἄ. οὐράνιον...παρ' αὐτοῦ διδομένην id.*ep.Serap.* 4.19(M.26.668A); διὰ τῆς ἄ. συμβουλῆς ὁδηγεῖσθαι Gr.Nyss.*v.Mos.*31(M.44.309C); Cyr.*Os.*20(3.43D); ref. grace, id.*Jo.*proem.(4.1A); salvation, *ib.*2.1(151A).

D. exeg.; **1.** Jo.3:3 τὸ 'ἄ.', ὁτὲ μὲν 'ἐκ τῶν ἄνω' καὶ 'ὕψωθεν'... ὁτὲ δὲ τὸ 'αὖθις'...γίνεται δὲ ἡ ἄ. γέννησις, περὶ ἧς ὁ σωτὴρ διδάσκει, ἐξ ἀναλήψεως ἀρετῆς...πλὴν εἰ καὶ ἐσφαλμένως ὁ Νικόδημος ἀπήνησε τοῖς εἰρημένοις, ἀλλ' οὖν ἔχει τι ἀληθὲς τὰ ὑπ' αὐτοῦ λεχθέντα...ἀληθῶς γὰρ οὐδεὶς καταμένων ἐν τῷ ἄνθρωπος εἶναι...τὴν κατὰ πνεῦμα καὶ ἄ. γέννησιν δέξασθαι δύναται...ᾧ ἕψεται, ὡς ἄ. γεννηθέντι ἐν καινότητι ζωῆς περιπατῆσαι Or.*fr.35 in Jo.*(p.510.11ff.); cf. *Graeci ἄ. dicunt qui sermo utrumque significat, et 'denuo', et 'de superioribus'. in hoc ergo loco, quia qui baptizatur a Jesu, in Spiritu Sancto baptizatur, non ita 'denuo' dicitur, ut 'de superioribus' intelligi conveniat; nam 'denuo' dicimus, cum eadem quae gesta sunt repetuntur: hic autem non eadem nativitas repetitur vel iteratur, sed, terrena hac omissa, de superioribus suscipitur nova nativitas,* Or.*comm.in Rom.*5.8(M.14.1038B); ταῖς τοῦ Νικοδήμου ὑπολήψεσίν ἐστι τὸ γινόμενον, ὃς περὶ τοῦ δεῖν ἄ. γεννηθῆναι παρὰ τοῦ κυρίου μαθὼν διὰ τὸ μήπω χωρῆσαι τοῦ μυστηρίου τὸν λόγον ἐπὶ τὸν μητρῷον κόλπον τοῖς λογισμοῖς κατεσύρετο. ὥστε εἰ μὴ πρὸς τὴν ἄκτιστον φύσιν, ἀλλὰ πρὸς τὴν συγγενῆ καὶ ὁμόδουλον κτίσιν ἑαυτὸν ἀπάγοι, τῆς κάτωθεν, οὐ τῆς ἄ. ἐστι γεννήσεως. φησὶ δὲ τὸ εὐαγγέλιον ἄ. εἶναι τῶν σωζομένων τὴν γέννησιν Gr.Nyss.*or.catech.*39(p.158.16; M.45.101A); τὸ ἄ. ἐνταῦθα, οἱ μὲν ἐκ τοῦ οὐρανοῦ φασιν, οἱ δὲ ἐξ ἀρχῆς Chrys.*hom.24.2 in Jo.*(8.140C); Cyr.*Jo.*2.1(4.146D); ὁ τὴν ἄνω τῶν ἀγγέλων ζωήν, καὶ τὰ ὑψηλὰ δόγματα διὰ Χριστοῦ μαθών, ἄ. γεννᾶται. ὁ τὴν δευτέραν, τὴν διὰ τοῦ λουτροῦ γέννησιν ὑπομένων, οὗτος ἄ. γεννᾶται, καὶ ὁ μετέχων πνεύματος ἁγίου. τὸ ἄ. τὴν διὰ τοῦ πνεύματος ἀναγέννησιν σημαίνει, καὶ δείκνυσιν ὅτι ἐκ τῆς οὐσίας ἐστὶ τοῦ πατρὸς τὸ πνεῦμα. οὕτω γὰρ καὶ ἑαυτὸν ἄ. ὀνομάσας, ἐκ τῆς οὐσίας ὄντα τοῦ πατρὸς σημαίνει Ammon.*Jo.*3:4(M.85.1408C,D); **2.** Jo.3:31 τὸ ἄ. ἐν τούτοις οὐδὲν ἕτερον οἶμαι σημαίνειν, ἢ τὸ ἐκ τῆς ἀνωτάτω πασῶν οὐσίας Cyr.*thes.*32 (5[1].320C).

E. Gnost.; **1.** ref. highest God opp. demiurge μείζονα ἐφθέγξατο [sc. Valentinus] τῆς πλάσεως διὰ τὸν ἀοράτως ἐν αὐτῷ σπέρμα δεδωκότα τῆς ἄ. οὐσίας Clem.*str.*2.8(p.132.10; M.8.972B); *ib.*(p.133.15; 973B); **2.** in teaching on origin of soul ἡγεῖται [sc. Julius Cassian]...θείαν οὖσαν τὴν ψυχὴν ἄ. ἐπιθυμίᾳ θηλυνθεῖσαν δεῦρο ἥκειν εἰς γένεσιν καὶ φθοράν *ib.*3.13(p.239.6; M.8.1193B); Valentinian, *ib.* 4.13(p.288.18; 1300A); **3.** ref. heavenly man, Adamas ἀπὸ τοῦ μακαρίου ἄ. ἀνθρώπου ἢ ἀρχανθρώπου ἢ Ἀδάμαντος Hipp.*haer.*5.7 (p.86.7; M.16.3135B).

F. ref. God's dealings with souls, soul being likened to a horse whose rider is God ἄ. ἑαυτῷ ἐφαρμόζοι τὸν ἵππον, ὁ...ἐπιβαίνων ἐφ' ἡμᾶς τοὺς ἵππους Gr.Nyss.*hom.3 in Cant.*(M.44.820A).

G. ref. BMV λόγοις δ' ἐμοῖς ἄ. εὐμενὴς ἔσο ‡Gr.Naz.*Chr.pat.*2574 (M.38.336A).

II. *again*, ref. re-baptism ἐπίσκοπος ἢ πρεσβύτερος τὸν κατὰ ἀλήθειαν ἔχοντα βάπτισμα ἐὰν ἄ. βαπτίσῃ...καθαιρείσθω ὡς γελῶν τὸν σταυρόν *Can.App.*47; v. supra I.D.1.

[*]**ἀνώθευτος**, f.l. for ἀνόθευτος.

***ἀνωθισμός**, ὁ, *assault*, Chrys.ap.Jo.D.*parall.*(M.95.1185C).

ἀνώλεθρος, *indestructible*, of God θεὸν ἀ. καὶ ἀγένητον Clem.*prot.*6 (p.52.5; M.8.173A); Meth.*symp.*6.5(p.69.21; M.18.120C); ‡Cyr.*Trin.* 7(6[2].8A; M.77.1132A); δύναμιν...διὰ θανάτου ζωὴν δημιουργοῦσαν ἀ. Max.*ambig.*(M.91.1044C).

ἀνωμαλ-έω, **1.** *be irregular*, i.e. by excess or deficiency μία γὰρ ἐπ' ἀμφοῖν...ἡ τελειότης, οὔτε κοιλαινομένη τῷ λείποντι οὔτε ~οῦσα τῷ πλεονάζοντι Gr.Nyss.*Eun.*4(2 p.76.27; M.45.649C); id.*or.dom.*4(p.68.15; M.44.1161C); **2.** *be indisposed*, *PLond.*1929.12; ‡Chrys.*Abr.*2 (2.744B).

ἀνωμαλία, ἡ, **1.** *irregularity, unevenness*; of weather, Chrys.*hom. 54.3 in Ac.*(9.409D); id.*hom.21.4 in Eph.*(11.163E); Marc.Diac.*v. Porph.*4; of life, Athenag.*res.*17(p.68.20; M.6.1008B); of the soul τὰς τῆς ψυχῆς αὐτῶν ἀ. ἀποβάλλων Clem.*str.*7.12(p.55.11; M.9.505C); hence *disquiet* ἐν ἀ. μὲν ἀεί, ἐν ἡσυχίᾳ δὲ οὐδέποτε ὤν Chrys.*hom.40.5 in Mt.*(7.443E); *difficulty*, Jo.Ant.*ep.Cyr.*1(p.119.12; M.77.132B); **2.** *disparity, inequality* οὐ δοκεῖ σοι ἀδικωτάτη ἡ ἐν ἀνθρώποις ἀ.; ὃς μὲν γὰρ πένεται, ὃς δὲ πλουτεῖ *Hom.Clem.*19.23; Chrys.*hom. in Phil.1:18*(3.305D); Thdr.Mops.*Gal.*3:28(p.57.29; M.66.905C); **3.** *anomaly, irreconcilability* τὴν ἀ. τῶν λόγων Eun.ap.Gr.Nyss.*Eun.*1(1 p.173.20; M.45.417A); *ib.*6(2 p.134.23; 720A).

ἀνώμαλος, **1.** *irregular*, of health, *indisposed, sick* ἐμπεσεῖν...εἰς ἀ. διάθεσιν Dor.*doct.*11.1(M.88.1736A); **2.** *anomalous*, ‡Bas.*Lac.*2(2.588B; M.31.1441A): Ammon.*Ac.*15:39(M.85.1553C); Gel.Cyz.*h.e.*2.8.4 (M.85.1244C).

ἀνωμάλως, *irregularly*; ἀ. ἔχειν *be indisposed*, *A.Thom.*A 64(p.180.13); *ib.*89(p.204.11).

***ἀνωμετέωρος**, *suspended in space above*, Chrys.*fr.in Jer.*10:13 (M.64.861B).

ἀνωνόμαστος, ἀνονόμαστος, *nameless, ineffable*, of God Ἰουδαῖοι ...διδάσκουσι τὸν ἀ. θεὸν λελαληκέναι τῷ Μωσεῖ Just.*1apol.*63.1(M.6.424A); Tat.*orat.*4(p.5.13, v.l. ἀνον-; M.6.813B); Clem.*paed.*1.7(p.123.33, v.l. ἀνον- M.8.317C); cf.id.*exc.Thdot.*31(p.117.9; M.9.676A); of mysteries ἀνον. ... καὶ ἀρρήτων...μυστηρίων Epiph.*haer.*31.5(p.390.7, v.l. ἀνων-; M.41.481A); Gnost., Iren.*haer.*1.6.4(M.7.509A); δυάδα ἀνον. *ib.*1.11.1(561A); Σιγὴν ἦν τὸν ἀνον. ὀνομάζει *ib.*1.15.5(625A).

ἀνώνυμος, **1.** *nameless*, cf. ἡ κυριακὴ ἀ. vel *Dominica III Quadragesimae*, cf. Nilles 2 p.136; vel *Septuagesima Latinorum*, *ib.* p.572; **2.** *ineffable*; of Inc., Andr.Cr.*or.*6(M.97.913C) cit. s. ἀνεξερεύνητος; **3.** *not to be named, unspeakable*, *A.Phil.*1(p.1.11); *M.Das.* 1.3; Leont.N.*v.Jo.Eleem.*18(p.36.9).

ἀνωνύμως, *without mentioning names*, Chrys.*hom.27.4 in Mt.*(7.332B); Vict.*Mc.*15:41(p.442.13); *cat.Lc.*16:19(p.124.5; but -ος, Cyr. ad loc., M.72.825D).

***ἀνωρεπής**, *mounting upwards*, ‡Ath.*v.Syncl.*55(M.28.1520D).

ἀνώτατος, -τάτω, v. ἄνω II.

ἀνωτερικός, *inland*, Epiph.*haer.*26 proem.(p.235.19; M.41.282C).

ἀνώτερος, -τέρω, v. ἄνω II.

ἀνωφερής, **1.** *borne upwards, ascending* ἀφθαρσίας ἁγνεία, ἀ. τὴν σάρκα πρὸς ὕψος αἴρουσα Meth.*symp.*8.4(p.85.5; M.18.144B); ἀ. ὁ Ἠλίας ἐγένετο Gr.Nyss.*laud.Bas.*(M.46.808B); **2.** *uplifted, sublime* ἀ. τε καὶ μετέωρος ἦν αὐτῶν ἡ ζωή Gr.Nyss.*v.Macr.*(p.383.3; M.46.972A); τὰς τῆς ψυχῆς ἀ. ... διατριβάς Nil.*exerc.*15(M.79.737C); ἀπερίττος εἰ μὴ ἐκ πάντων ὁ νοῦς τῶν κατ' αἴσθησιν γένηται, ἀ. γενέσθαι οὐ δύναται ‡Max.*cap.al.*82(M.90.1417D).

***ἀνωφερῶς**, *upwards*, Max.*schol.c.h.*7.1.10(M.4.65D).

ἄξεστος, *incapable of being wrought, adamant*, *A.Jo.*29(p.167.4).

ἀξία, ἡ, **1.** *value, worth*; of God, *worthiness*, quality calling forth worship ἀμείνων ὁ νεὼς οὗτος [sc. the Church] εἰς παραδοχὴν μεγέθους ἀξίας τοῦ θεοῦ Clem.*str.*7.4(p.21.27; M.9.437C); ref. Lc.2:13 ἄνωθεν ἐπιμαρτυρούσας τῷ ὑπερφυεῖ τῆς ἀ. ... φωνάς Gr.Nyss.*or. catech.*23(p.87.1; M.45.61B); **2.** of persons, *reputation, dignity, standing*; **a.** theol., of Son κενωθεὶς...εἰς τὴν ἑαυτοῦ τελειότητα πάλιν ἀνεπληρώθη καὶ τὴν ἀ. Meth.*symp.*8.11(p.96.1; M.18.157A); Eus.*h.e.* 1.2.2(M.20.53B); acc. Marcellus, ref. Is.1:1, Os.1:1 τῆς ἴσης ἀ. τῷ μονογενεῖ υἱῷ τοῦ θεοῦ κἀκείνοις ἅπασιν [sc. τοῖς προφήταις] μετῆν Eus.*Marcell.*2.4(p.57.26; M.24.821B); acc. Eunomius οὐκ οἰκειοῦται ταύτην τὴν ἀ. [sc. ὁ μονογενής]· ἀ. γὰρ ὀνομάζει τὴν τοῦ ὄντος προσηγορίαν Gr.Nyss.*Eun.*10(1 p.247.28; M.45.852B); Christol.: in Nestorian usage, of union κατ' ἀξίαν opp. ἕνωσις φυσική, anathematized εἴ τις ἐπὶ τοῦ ἑνὸς Χριστοῦ διαιρεῖ τὰς ὑποστάσεις μετὰ τὴν ἕνωσιν, μόνῃ συνάπτων αὐτὰς συναφείᾳ τῇ κατὰ τὴν ἀ. ἢ γοῦν αὐθεντίαν καὶ οὐχὶ δὴ μᾶλλον συνόδῳ τῇ καθ' ἕνωσιν φυσικήν Cyr.*expl.xii cap.*3 (p.18.22; 6.149B); τὸ τῆς ἀ. ἀκούοντες ὄνομα δοθὲν αὐτῷ, τὴν φύσιν ἀντεισάγετε·...τοῖς λέγουσιν ἀ. ἀσύγκριτον εἶναι τὴν ἕνωσιν τῆς ἐξ ἡμῶν σαρκὸς πρὸς τὸν θεὸν λόγον, καὶ οὐ φυσικὴν σύνθεσιν, ὑμεῖς ἀντιφέρεσθε Leont.H.*Nest.*1.19(M.86.1472C); Leont.B.*Nest.et Eut.*1 (M.86.1300C); Θεόδωρος καὶ Νεστόριος...λέγουσι δύο πρόσωπα τοῦ θεοῦ λόγου καὶ τοῦ Χριστοῦ, ὃν ψιλὸν ἄνθρωπον ἀποκαλοῦσι. κατὰ σχετικὴν δὲ συνάφειαν καὶ τὴν αὐτὴν ἀ. τε καὶ τιμὴν ἓν πρόσωπον ἀναφαίνεσθαι λέγουσιν Justn.*conf.*(p.98.2; M.86.1021B); id.*ep.Thdr. Mops.*(p.59.30; M.86.1071B); id.*conf.anath.*4(p.90.29; M.86.1015A); ἐκ δύο φύσεων τελείων τὴν ἕνωσιν γεγενῆσθαι...οὐ...κατ' ἀ. ... ἢ ὁμοτιμίαν Jo.D.*Jacob.*(M.94.1480A); of H. Ghost acc. Eunomius πάντων προῦχων τῶν τοῦ υἱοῦ ποιημάτων κατὰ τὴν οὐσίαν καὶ τὴν φυσικὴν ἀ. Eun.*exp.fid.*3(p.258); οὐ χρὴ...πατρὶ καὶ υἱῷ συντετάχθαι τὸ ἅγιον πνεῦμα, διά τε τὸ τῆς φύσεως ἀλλότριον καὶ τὸ τῆς ἀ. καταδεές Bas.*Spir.*24(3.20E; M.32.112A); used in orthodox sense αὐτὸ ἐν τῇ πρώτῃ καὶ βασιλικῇ τῆς τῶν ὅλων ἀρχῆς ἀ. καὶ τιμῇ Eus.*p.e.*7.15 (325B; M.21.549B); τῆς ὑπερεχούσης πάντα νοῦν ἀ. τοῦ πνεύματος Bas.*Spir.*48(40C; M.156A); **b.** in gen.; **i.** *rank* or *title*; in army τῶν ἐν Ῥωμαϊκαῖς προκοπαῖς οὐ μικρᾶς ἐπείληπται ἀ. Eus.*m.P.*11(p.942.25; M.20.1453C, where p.942.12; M.20.1508B reads τιμῆς); of nobles and magistrates τὴν τοῦ ἐπιφανεστάτου...ἀ. Philost.*h.e.*12.12(M.65.620C); τὴν τοῦ καίσαρος ἀ. *ib.*12.13(621A); Εὐγένιόν τινα, μάγιστρον τὴν ἀ. *ib.*11.2(593C); εἰσέρχεσθαι εἰς πατρικίου ἀ. Thphn.*chron.*p.83 (M.108.252A); of angels τὴν ἀγγελικὴν ἀ. Bas.*ascet.*1.2(2.320B; M.31.873B); **ii.** *office* περιαιροῦντες τὰς ἀ. τῶν εἰδωλομανῶν καὶ τὰ ἄλλα πολιτικὰ ὀφφίκια Marc.Diac.*v.Porph.*41; τὴν τοῦ ὑπάτου ἀ. Socr.*h.e.*6.5.3(M.67.673A); τῆς τοῦ διακόνου ἀξίας...τυχὼν *ib.*6.3.10 (669A); τῇ τῆς ἐπισκοπῆς ἀ. τιμῆσαι Gel.Cyz.*h.e.*3.15.19; ref. 1Tim. 3:6 μὴ παρέχειν ταχέως ἀ. νεοφύτῳ Cosm.Ind.*top.*3(M.88.148D); hence **c.** *persons of rank* or *office, dignitaries*, Pall.*v.Chrys.*7(p.39.9; M.47.24); πᾶσαι τῶν στρατιωτῶν αἱ ἀ. *A.Petr.et Paul.*72(p.208.13); πατρίκιοι, ἰλλούστριοι καὶ πᾶσα ἀ. Marc.Diac.*v.Porph.*47; of angelic hierarchy, Bas.*hex.*2.5(1.17C; M.29.40C); **d.** outward signs of rank or dignity, *pomp*, a *train* or *escort* ἐν...ἐπιφανείᾳ πολλῆς διακονίας γιγνομένης σαλπίγγων καὶ δυνάμεων ἔμπροσθεν τῆς δεσποτικῆς ἀ. Mac.Aeg.*hom.*6.3(M.34.520A); of a pagan festival μετὰ ἀναιδοῦς καὶ ἀνεπαισχύντου ἀ. *M.Das.*1.2; Jo.Mal.*chron.*2 p.42(M.97.113C); **3.** *due, merit, desert*; of those worthy to hear the gospel, ref. 1Petr.3:19 τοὺς ἀ. μᾶλλον ἐσχηκότας ἐν δικαιοσύνῃ [sc. τῇ κατὰ νόμον καὶ κατὰ φιλοσοφίαν] Clem.*str.*6.6(p.454.24; M.9.268B); Or.*princ.*3.1.17(p.227.9; M.11.285A); of a communicant τὴν ἀ. ... τῆς προσόδου Chrys. *hom.5.3 in 1Tim.*(11.577C); κατ' ἀξίαν *duly, deservedly*; of rewards and punishments ἕκαστον ἐπ' αἰωνίαν κόλασιν ἢ σωτηρίαν κατ' ἀ. τῶν πράξεων πορεύεσθαι Just.*1apol.*12.1(M.6.341C); Or.*hom.20.2 in Jer.*(p.178.28; M.13.504A); Serap.*euch.*20.2; εἰ δή τις νοεῖ θεόν (κατ' ἀ. μὲν οὐδαμῶς, τίς γὰρ ἔννοια ἀ. θεοῦ; ἀλλ' ὡς δυνατόν ἐστι) Clem.*ecl.*21(p.142.20; M.9.708B); ὁ παντοδύναμος θεός...τοῦ ἰδίου θείου πνεύματος τὸ ἁγιώτατον κατ' ἀ. σῶμα ἐνοικεῖν τε αὐτῷ καὶ...σωτηριῶδες ...εἶναι κατηξίωσεν Const.ap.Gel.Cyz.*h.e.*2.7.21(M.85.1236D); **4.** *moral value, standard* πῶς ἑτέρως δουλωθῆναι τῇ δικαιοσύνῃ δύναται ἄνθρωπος...ἐὰν μὴ...πολιτεύσηται κατ' ἀ. τοῦ Χριστοῦ; Meth.*res.*1.60 (p.324.9).

***ἀξιαγάπητος,** *worthy of love, 1Clem.*1.1; *ib.*21.7; Ign.*Philad* 5.2.

ἀξιάγαστος, *astonishing, marvellous,* Gr.Naz.*or.*29.16(p.97.10; M.36.93C); Cyr.*Jo.*1.9(4.73C); *ib.*2.2(161B).

***ἄξιαγνος,** v.l. for ἀξιόαγνος.

***ἀξιαγωγεύς, ὁ,** *worthy leader*; of Christ, *Pap.Chr.*4.1.1.19(p.446).

ἀξιάκουστος, 1. *worth hearing,* Isid.Pel.*epp.*3.178(M.78.869B); Cyr.*Am.*73(3.332A); hence *noteworthy,* Cyr.*glaph.Gen.*1(1.23A); id. *Joel.*4(3.200E); **2.** *worthy to be heeded* τὰ...ἀ. τῆς ἐκκλησίας δόγματα Cyr.*Chr.un.*(5^1.750C).

ἀξιαφήγητος, *worth narrating,* Isid.Pel.*epp.*2.218(M.78.660C).

***ἀξιέντρεπτος,** *worthy of respect,* Clem.*ecl.*28(p.145.26; M.9.713A).

ἀξιεπαίνετος, *worthy to be praised,* superl., Cyr.*ador.*6(1.199B); id.*Is.*3.4(2.486E); comp., Andr.Cr.*or.*17(M.97.1169D); *Proem.*in Gr. Mag.*dial.*(tr.Zach.)(M.*PL.*77.147A).

***ἀξιεράστως,** *lovingly,* ‡Caes.Naz.*dial.*113(M.38.996).

ἀξινάριον, τό, *small axe,* Hipp.*haer.*9.23(p.258.12; M.16.3399B).

ἀξίνη, ἡ, *axe* Ἰησοῦς...αὐτὸς ἦν ἡ ἀ. τοῦ ἀκάρπου δένδρου Or. *hom.18.5 in Jer.*(p.156.33; M.13.472D); ἀ. ... τὸν κύριον τῆς δόξης προσαγορεύειν οὐκ ἐπαισχύνεται Bas.*Eun.*2.2(1.239D; M.29.576C); Ἰωάννης τὴν ἀναιρετικὴν τῆς κακίας δύναμιν τοῦ κυρίου τῷ τῆς ἀ. διασημαίνων ὀνόματι Gr.Nyss.*Eun.*12(1 p.313.21; M.45.1028A).

[*]**ἀξινόρυξ, ὁ,** *pickaxe,* Agath.*v.Gr.Ill.*124(p.63).

***ἀξιόαγνος,** *worthy in purity,* Ign.*Rom.*proem.(v.l. ἄξιαγνος).

***ἀξιόγραφος,** *worth recording,* Thphn.*chron.*p.370(M.108.888A).

***ἀξιόδεκτος,** *worthy of acceptance,* Thdr.Abuc.*opusc.*18(M.94.1596D).

***ἀξιόδηλος,** *worthy of being made clear,* Jo.D.*hom.*12.21(M.96.809D).

***ἀξιοδιήγητος,** *worthy of narration,* Eus.*h.e.*3.30.2(M.20.277C).

***ἀξιοεπίτευκτος,** *worthy of success,* Ign.*Rom.*proem.

ἀξιοζήλωτος, *deserving of emulation,* Or.*Ps.*36:2(M.17.120A); Cyr.*Os.*121(3.152B); id.*Juln.*7(6^2.246D).

ἀξιόθεος, *worthy of God*; of Roman church, Ign.*Rom.*proem.; of a bishop, id.*Magn.*2; id.*Smyrn.*12.2; of BMV, Procl.CP *annunt.* 5(M.85.444B); ‡Jo.D.*hom.*6.7(M.96.672B).

***ἀξιοκατάκριτος,** *worthy of condemnation,* Max.*schol.e.h.*7.3.6(M.4.180A).

ἀξιόληπτος, *worthy of acceptance,* Cyr.*ador.*1(1.46D); id.*Zach.*112 (3.811B); id.*glaph.Gen.*1(1.7C); id.*Juln.*6(6^2.202A).

***ἀξιολόγιστος,** *reasonable,* ‡Germ.CP *contempl.*(M.98.441C).

ἀξιολόγως, *reasonably* πλούτου...μεταληπτέον ἀ. Clem.*paed.*3.6 (p.256.2; M.8.604B); δεῖ ἐπερωτωμένῳ...ἀ. ἀποκρίνεσθαι Bas.*moral.* 9.4(2.243A; M.31.717B); comp., Athenag.*leg.*17.1(M.6.921C).

ἀξιομακάριστος, *worthily called blessed,* Ign.*Eph.*12.2; id.*Rom.* proem.; *ib.*10.1.

***ἀξιονόμαστος,** *deservedly famous,* Ign.*Eph.*4.1.

ἀξιοπιστία, ἡ, 1. *trustworthiness*; of God, Clem.*str.*6.9(p.470.2; M.9.297A); *credentials,* of the writer of a book, ‡Hipp.*fr.33 in Pr.* (p.170.9; M.10.616B); ref. Ac.8:36 μὴ ζήτει ἀ. τοῦ κηρύσσοντος μηδὲ τοῦ βαπτίζοντος Gr.Naz.*or.*40.26(M.36.396B); μὴ νομίσῃς ὅτι...ἦλθεν ὁ βαπτιστὴς...ἵνα τι τῷ δεσπότῃ προσθῇ εἰς ἀξιοπιστίας λόγον Chrys. *hom.6 in Jo.*(8.43C); ἡ ἀ. τῶν προφητῶν καὶ ἀποστόλων Cosm.Ind. *top.*3(M.88.168A); of statements, *credibility,* Tat.*orat.*25(p.26.26; M.6.860B); Alex.Lyc.*Man.*19(p.26.18; M.18.436C); Gr.Nyss.*hom.8 in Cant.*(M.44.949C); in bad sense, *plausibility,* Hipp.*haer.*1 proem. (p.2.10; M.16.3020A); of things, *dependability, certainty* ἡ ἀ. τῶν μισθῶν ἔλεγχος τῆς δοκιμῆς τῶν ἔργων ‡Nil.*narr.*7(M.79.692D); ‡Nil. *perist.*4.6(M.79.829D); **2.** *authority, reputation, respect due* to persons in their official capacity Ἀχὰζ οὕτως ἐδέξατο τὴν περὶ τῶν ἐσομένων προφητείαν...ὡς Φαραώ, ὡς Καιάφας τὸ τελευταῖον, οὐ διὰ τὴν τοῦ βίου ἀξίαν, ὅσον διὰ τὴν ἐκ τοῦ ἀξιώματος προσοῦσαν αὐτῷ ἀ. †Bas. *Is.*199(1.528A; M.30.461B); τὴν τοῦ προσώπου [sc. τοῦ βασιλέως] ἀ. Chrys.*hom.1.2 in Philm.*(11.776B); Socr.*h.e.*1.8.1(M.67.60C); Max. *ambig.*(M.91.1089C); *credit* in commercial transactions, Tat.*orat.*11 (p.12.6; M.6.829B); hence of the weight carried by ideas εἶχεν ἀ. τινά καθ' αὐτὴν ἡ τοῦ νόμου προσηγορία Thdr.Mops.*2Cor.*3:7(p.197.20; M.66.896A); id.*Gal.*1:6(p.10.27; M.66.901C); Cyr.*Jo.*1.7(4.62C).

ἀξιόπιστος, A. *trustworthy*; **1.** in gen. τίς ἀξιοπιστότερός σοι σύμβουλος τοῦ θεοῦ; Bas.*hom.*13.3(2.116C; M.31.429C); of Christ δογματιστὴν ἀ. Isid.Pel.*epp.*1.20(M.78.196A); of scripture, Cosm. Ind.*top.*2(M.88.73D); Jo.D.*f.o.*4.27(M.94.1224C); παρ' ἡμῖν ἀξιοπιστότερα τῶν λόγων τὰ πράγματα Hadr.*introd.*33(M.98.1281A); neut. as subst., *credibility,* Areth.*Apoc.*2(M.106.513C); *probability,* Clem. *paed.*3.4(p.252.1; M.8.593A); **2.** of persons qualified for a task, *competent,* Gr.Naz.*or.*40.26(M.36.396B); of things, *sufficient, adequate,* Bas.*Spir.*48(3.40C; M.32.156A); Chrys.*sac.*3.12(p.69.8; 1.389D); ‡Chrys.*Abr.*(2.742C); **3.** *worthy of respect* or *consideration,* ‡Nil. *perist.*5.1(M.79.852A); τοῦ ἁγιωτάτου πατριάρχου· ἑτέρων τε ἀ. προσώπων Thdr.Stud.*test.*(M.99.1816B); neut. as subst., *authority, prestige* τὸ γεραῖον τῆς ἡλικίας καὶ ἀ. οὐκ ἐπικαλυπτέον Clem.*paed.* 3.11(p.271.30; M.8.637C); Gr.Naz.*or.*6.20(M.35.748C); διὰ τοῦ ἀ. τοῦ προσώπου τὸ ὑψηλὸν τοῦτο δόγμα...συνίστησι Ammon.*Jo.*1:18(M.85.1400D); **4.** *plausible,* Ign.*Philad.*2.2; id.*Polyc.*3.1; *Diogn.*8.2.

B. *able to believe* ἵνα ἀ. αὐτοὺς ἐργάσηται Chrys.*hom.4.2 in Phil.* (11.221C).

ἀξιοπίστως, 1. *honourably,* ‡Nil.*perist.*12.6(M.79.949A); **2.** *plausibly,* Iren.*haer.*1.8.1(M.7.520B); Anon.ap.Eus.*h.e.*5.16.9(M.20.468B); **3.** *on credit,* Tat.*orat.*2(p.2.22; M.6.808A).

***ἀξιόπλοκος,** *fitly wreathed,* Ign.*Magn.*13.1.

***ἀξιοπόθητος,** *worthily beloved,* Serap.*ep.mon.*8(M.40.933D).

***ἀξιοπραγία, ἡ,** *worthy conduct,* Clem.*paed.*2.10(p.213.31; M.8.509A).

***ἀξιοπρέπεια, ἡ,** *dignity* Κωνσταντίνου...ἀ. ὄψεως Thphn.*chron.* p.15(M.108.96B); ‡Jo.D.*Artem.*52(conj. p.88.7 for ἀξιορρέπειαν M.96.1300B).

ἀξιοπρεπής, *worthy of honour,* Ign.*Rom.*proem.; superl., id. *Magn.*13.1.

***ἀξιοπρεπῶς,** *with proper dignity,* Gr.Thaum.*pan.Or.*2(p.4.10; M.10.1056A).

***ἀξιορρέπεια, ἡ,** prob. f.l. for ἀξιοπρέπεια.

ἄξιος, 1. *meet, proper*; liturg., cf.Hipp.*trad.ap.*4.3; Serap.*euch.* 13.1; *Lit.*ap.*Const.App.*8.12.5; ἄ. καὶ δίκαιον, πρέπον τε καὶ ἐποφειλόμενον σὲ αἰνεῖν *Lit.Jac.*(p.198.18); **2.** *worthy* ἀξίους τῷ [sc. θεοῦ] ...βουλεύματι Just.*1apol.*10.2(M.6.340C); esp., *worthy* of bishop's office, Bas.*ep.*230(3.353D; M.32.860C); Const.*App.*8.4.4; cry raised by people at bishop's enthronement τὸν πάντα λαόν...ἄ. ἐπιβοῆσαι καὶ...ἐπὶ τὸν θρόνον τῆς ἐπισκοπῆς...αὐτὸν ἐπιθεῖναι Eus.*h.e.*6.29.4 (M.20.588C); Socr.*h.e.*4.30.4(M.67.544B); Philost.*h.e.*9.10(M.65.576C); as subst. plur., *worthies, dignitaries* Πιλάτῳ...καὶ τοῖς ἀμφ' αὐτὸν ἀξίοις Mac.Mgn.*apocr.*2.19(p.33.9).

***ἀξιότης, ἡ,** *dignity,* Mac.Aeg.*hom.*27 tit.(M.34.693A).

ἀξιοφανής, *deservedly famous* τὸν ἀ. τῆς ἐνθέου πολιτείας σου ζῆλον Eust.*engast.*1(p.16.7; M.18.613A); Mac.Mgn.*apocr.*3.41(p.141.11); *ib.*3.43(p.150.5).

ἀξι-όω, 1. *deem worthy* ἐκ τῶν ἰδίων ἔργων ἀνάξιοι ζωῆς νῦν ὑπὸ τῆς τοῦ θεοῦ χρηστότητος ~ωθῶμεν *Diogn.*9.1; Χριστοῦ παρόντος ἐπὶ τῷ βελτιῶσαι καὶ κρείττονος ~ῶσαι παιδείας τὸν ἄνθρωπον Mac. Mgn.*apocr.*3.41(p.143.15); of baptism, Cyr.H.*catech.*19.1; ref. view of Christ ascribed to Thdr. Mops. διὰ τοῦ βαπτίσματος...υἱοθεσίας ~ωθῆναι Justn.*conf.anath.*11(p.92.29; M.86.1017A); ~ώσαντες τὸ τεχθὲν τοῦ...βαπτίσματος Eustrat.*v.Eutych.*46(M.86.2328B); of communicating, *ib.*13(2289A); **2.** *think fit,* hence *require, pray* ὃ ~οῖ ὑμᾶς οὗτος ὁ καινὸς νομοθέτης Just.*dial.*14.3(M.6.505A); ἀ. τὴν σήμερον ἑαυτῷ, τὴν δὲ αὔριον τῷ κυρίῳ Bas.*hom.*13.6(2.119E; M.31.437C); ὑπὲρ πράγματος μικροῦ ἠξίωσεν, ὑπὲρ ἑνὸς ἀνδρός Chrys.*hom. in Philm.*proem.(11.772C); c. ὥστε and infin., id.*hom.3.1 in Ac.*(9.23C); **3.** *deign* τὸν ἄνθρωπον...ἠξίωσε ταῖς ἑαυτοῦ ποιῆσαι χερσίν Meth.*res.*1.35(p.275.8; M.41.1100D); θεὸς γὰρ ὢν ἠξίωσεν ἄνθρωπος γίνεσθαι Justn.*ep.Thdr.Mops.*(p.56.18; M.86.1063C).

ἀξίωμα, τό, 1. *honour, high reputation*; **a.** of persons ὁ μὲν ἀκούων ὡς θεοῦ λογίων, τὸ μὲν ἀ. τοῦ λέγοντος τηρῶν ἀποδέχεται Or.*comm.in Ex.*(M.12.272B); γνώριζε, ὦ ἐπίσκοπε, τὸ ἀ. σου *Const. App.*2.18.3; **b.** of things and qualities τὸ ἀ. ἐνυβρίσαντες τῶν καλῶν Or.*princ.*3.1.17(p.227.1; M.11.284A); τὸ ἀ. τῆς ἀρετῆς id.*sel.in Ps.* 4:6(M.12.1160B); τὸ ἀ. τῆς παρθενίας μέγιστον παρὰ τῷ θεῷ Meth. *symp.*1.5(p.14.10; M.18.45C); τὸ ἀ. τῆς ἁγνείας *ib.*3.11(p.39.8; 77A);

Chrys.*ep*.1.4(3.533A); **2.** *worth, value*; of divine promises, Or. *princ*.4.3.7(p.333.5; M.11.388A); and commandments, Diod.*Gen*.3:8 (M.33.1568D); **3.** *dignity, high status, worthiness*; **a.** of dignity or majesty of God, Trin. οὐ δύο...θεούς, ἀλλ' ἓν ὁμολογοῦμεν τῆς θεότητος ἀ. *Symb.Ant*.(345)9(p.254.1; M.26.733B); in Eunomian teaching, of superiority of Father to Son ἡ γὰρ ἂν ἐκεῖνο πρὸ τοῦ δευτέρου τὸ τῆς θεότητος ἔσχεν ἀ. Bas.*Eun*.1.5(1.214A; M.29.516A); μία γοῦν ἡ ἀρχὴ καὶ ἐξ αὐτῆς ὁ υἱός...μία οὖσα θεότης καὶ ἓν ἀ. Epiph.*haer*.65.8(p.11.32; M.42.25D); Jo.D.*Man*.3(M.94.1509A); as synonym for God τὸ δεσποτικὸν...ἀ. Mac.Aeg.*hom*.4.23(M.34.489D); **b.** of Christ; **i.** Trin. οὔτ' οὖν καταμερίζειν χρὴ εἰς τρεῖς θεότητας τὴν ...θείαν μονάδα οὔτε ποιήσει κωλύειν τὸ ἀ. ... τοῦ κυρίου Dion.R.ap. Ath.*decr*.26(p.23.12; M.25.465A); ἐπεὶ δὲ ἐχρῆν ἡμᾶς γνῶναι καὶ ὁποίου ὑπῆρχεν ἀ., ἀναγκαίως συνῆψεν τὸ 'καὶ θεὸς ἦν ὁ λόγος' Eus.*e.th*. 2.14(p.117.3; M.24.932B); οὐδὲν γὰρ πρόσφατον ὁ Χριστὸς προσείληφεν ἀ., ἀλλ' ἄνωθεν τέλειον αὐτὸν...πεπιστεύκαμεν *Symb.Ant*.(345)6 (p.253.12; M.26.732B); Bas.*Eun*.2.31(1.268A; M.29.644C); **ii.** ref. Inc., Or.*Jo*.10.25(16; p.197.13; M.14.349D); τὸ 'κάθου ἐκ δεξιῶν μου' οὐκ ἀνθρώπου μὲν τὸ ἀ., ἀλλὰ θεοῦ. ἀλλ' ἐπειδὴ τὸ τοῦ θεοῦ ἀ. ἀνθρώπου ἀ. γέγονεν, ἵνα τὸ τοῦ ἀνθρώπου ἀ. θεοῦ ἀ. πιστευθῇ, εἴρηται ‡Ath.*Apoll*.2.15(M.26.1157B); Cyr.*Ps*.32:8(M.69.876A); οὐ καθυβρίσω τὸ ἄκτιστον ἀ., εἰ ἐνοικήσω εἰς τὸ κτισθὲν ὑπ' ἐμοῦ οἴκημα Procl.CP *or*.5.14(M.65.748C); **iii.** in gen. οὐκ οἶδα ὑμᾶς πόθεν ἐστέ· ὅπερ ἐὰν ἁπλούστερον νοῆται, παρὰ τὸ ἀ. δόξομεν τοῦ σωτῆρος ὑπολαμβάνειν Or.*Jo*.32.14(8; p.447.24; 776C); **c.** of H. Ghost πόθεν ἂν οὖν τῆς...ἀξίας τοῦ πνεύματος τὰς ἀποδείξεις λάβοιμεν, εἴπερ ἡ πατρὸς καὶ υἱοῦ κοινωνία μὴ ἀξιόπιστος αὐτοῖς πρὸς μαρτυρίαν ἀξιώματος ἐνομίσθη; Bas.*Spir*.48(3.40C; M.32.156A); **d.** of men in relation to divine grace οἷον μέγα εἶχεν ἀ. ὁ Ἰωάννης...ὁ μικρότερος τοίνυν ἐν τῇ βασιλείᾳ...μείζων αὐτοῦ ἐστιν...ὅτι...συγκρίνωμεν τὸ ἐνταῦθα ἀ. ἐκείνῃ τῇ προσδοκωμένῃ χάριτι *cat.Lc*.7:24(p.59.20); ὁ...κύριος... καθῆκεν ἑαυτὸν εἰς κένωσιν δι' ἡμᾶς, ἵνα ἡμῖν χαρίσηται τῆς πρὸς αὐτὸν ἀδελφότητος τὸ ἀ. Cyr.*Nest*.3(p.60.24; 6.72C); τοῦ τῆς υἱοθεσίας τετυχήκαμεν ἀ. Thdt.*Rom*.8:15(3.85); **4.** *rank, position*; **a.** of worldly status in gen. ἐμφαίνεται δὲ αὐτοῦ τὸ ἀ. καὶ ἐκ τοῦ ἤδη αὐτοῦ καταβαίνοντος τοὺς δούλους αὐτῷ ἀπηντηκέναι Or.*Jo*.13.58(57; p.288.20; 508C); Chrys.*hom.45.3 in Ac*.(9.341C); id.*hom.28.5 in Mt*.(7.341B); Nil.*epp*.3.303(M.79.533A); id.*exerc*.16(M.79.740B); Ammon.ap.*cat. Ac*.10:8(p.174.25); ἀ. νομοθέτου...εἶχεν ὁ Μωυσῆς Sev.Ant.*ib*.3:22 (p.68.23); **b.** of official rank; **i.** civil τῶν νομιζομένων ἀ. [sc. of senators] Just.*2apol*.1.1(M.6.441A); εἰσὶν υἱοὶ ἡγεμόνων καὶ...γένους εἰσὶ τῶν ἀπὸ κοσμικῶν ἀ. μεγάλων Or.*hom.12.8 in Jer*.(p.94.18; M.13.389A); Ἡράκλειός τις τῷ ἀ. κόμης Ath.*h.Ar*.48(p.211.12; M.25. 753A); οἱ ἐν ἀξιώμασιν, οἱ ἀπὸ βικαρίων, οἱ ἀπὸ ἡγεμόνων Chrys.*ep*. 14.3(3.598D); Pall.*v.Chrys*.11(p.65.13; M.47.37); ἄρχων, τὸ ὑπατικὸν ἔχων ἀ. Socr.*h.e*.4.30.2(M.67.544B); τὸ τῆς βασιλείας ἀ. Philost.*h.e*. 3.22(M.65.512A); Gel.Cyz.*h.e*.3.17.13; Heracl.*ep*.ap.*Chron.Pasch*. p.399(M.92.1021A); **ii.** OT τριῶν...ἀ. παρ' Ἑβραίοις διαπρεπόντων... τοῦ βασιλικοῦ...τοῦ προφητικοῦ...τοῦ ἀρχιερατικοῦ Eus.*d.e*.8 proem. (p.349.12; M.22.568B); **iii.** in Church ἀ. τῆς ἐπισκοπῆς *Can.App*. 76; τοὺς ἀξιωθέντας χαρισμάτων ἢ ἀ. *Const.App*.8.1.22; ἀποστολικὸν ἀ. Tit.Bost.*fr.Lc*.22:3(p.240.10); ref. status of BMV and other women in time of Christ οὐκ ἐπέτρεψεν αὐτῇ δοῦναι βάπτισμα...οὐ τὸ ἄρχειν...ἐκέλευσεν...οὔτινα τῶν ἐπὶ τῆς γῆς γυναικῶν τοῦτο ποιεῖν προσέταξεν τὸ ἀ. Epiph.*haer*.79.7(p.482.14; M.42.752A); πρεσβυτέρῳ μὴ ἐπιπλήξῃς. ἄρα τὸ ἀ. νῦν φησιν; οὐκ...ἀλλὰ περὶ παντὸς γεγηρακότος Chrys.*hom.5.2 in 1Tim*.(11.618F); Philost.*h.e*.3.4(M.65.484A); *ib*.4.3(520A); Mod.*dorm*.9(M.86.3300B); †Jo.Jej.*poenit*.(M.88.1889C); **iv.** as title of address, *Cod.Afr*.50; **c.** of man in order of creation, Gr.Nyss.*or.catech*.6(p.36.4; M.45.29B); Mac.Aeg.*hom*.15.22(M.34. 589D); **d.** ref. differences of status in future life μοναὶ πολλαὶ παρὰ τῷ πατρί· τουτέστιν, ἀξιωμάτων διαφοραί Bas.*Spir*.40(3.34C; M.32. 141B); **5.** *honourable person, dignitary* ἐπικατάρατος ὃς τὴν ἐλπίδα ἔχει ἐπ' ἄνθρωπον, ἅμα δὲ πρὸς τοὺς ἐλπίζοντας ἐπὶ ἀξιώμασιν Or.*hom. 15.6 in Jer*.(p.131.2; M.13.437A); ἑκάστῳ οὖν ἀ. οἱ λαϊκοὶ τὴν προσήκουσαν τιμὴν νεμέτωσαν *Const.App*.2.28.5; Pall.*v.Chrys*.13(p.79.30; M.47.45); *M.Thdot*.1 23(p.75.28); **6.** *proper quality* ἄτρεπτος δὴ διὰ τὴν γνώμην, ἀλλ' οὐ διὰ τὸ ἐν οὐσίᾳ ἀ. ‡Ath.*dial.Trin*.2.18(M.28. 1185C); ἀ. φύσεώς ἐστιν ἡ οὐσία ἀμετάβλητος *ib*.2.27(1197C); ἀ. δὲ τῆς ἀνωτάτω φύσεως, τὰ πάντα εἰδέναι Cyr.*ador*.6(1.182D); id.*Ps*.44:4 (M.69.1033B); μετέχει οὖν ἡ βασιλεία τῶν Ῥωμαίων τῶν ἀ. τῆς βασιλείας τοῦ...Χριστοῦ Cosm.Ind.*top*.2(M.88.113B).

ἀξιωματικός, *honourable, high in rank*; as subst., *dignitary, official*, civil or military πάντας πολίτας καὶ...ἀ. Gr.Naz.*ep*.141(M. 37.241B); contrasted with στρατευόμενος τίρων Mac.Aeg.*cust.cor*.11 (M.34.832B); position or title given to the empress's brother, *Chron.Pasch*.p.313(M.92.796B); ὁ δοὺξ Παλαιστίνης...καὶ...ὁ ἀ. Καισαρείας Jo.Mal.*chron*.15 p.382(M.97.568B); neut. plur., *honoraria, subventions*, Phot.*nomoc*.8.7(M.104.1088A).

ἀξίως, *worthily, fitly*; of communicants τοὺς ἀ. μεταλαμβάνοντας ‡Bas.*h.myst*.62(p.397.20).

ἀξίωσις, ἡ, *claim, request, petition*; *prayer* to God, Or.*or*.14 (p.331.8; M.11.461A); Eus.*h.e*.6.5.6(M.20.533C); Ath.*Ar*.3.25(M.26. 376A).

***ἀξιώτης**, ὁ, *petitioner*, Pall.*v.Chrys*.7(p.42.5; M.47.25).

ἄξυστος, *unpolished*, Ath.*gent*.13(M.25.28C).

ἄξων, ὁ, plur., *tablets of laws* οὐκ ἐκ τῶν Ῥωμαϊκῶν ἀ. τὸν νόμον ἀνέγνωμεν Synes.*Dion* 16(p.274.17; M.66.1160B).

***ἀοιδοσύνη**, ἡ, *singing, poetry*, Gr.Naz.*carm*.2.1.87.8(M.37.1433A).

***ἀοίκιστος**, *uninhabited*, Thdr.Stud.*or*.11.4(M.99.805D).

***ἄοικτος**, = foreg., met. ἀδιάβατον καὶ ἄοικτον καὶ ἀπρόσβλεπτον τοῖς σαρκικοῖς παρανοθεύμασι Thdot.Anc.*hom.BMV et Sym*.6(M.77. 1397C).

ἀόμματος, *sightless*, Bas.Sel.*or*.26.2(M.85.305B).

***ἀόπλως**, *without weapons* Μαρία...οἷα στρατηγέτις καταβάλλουσα ἀ. τὰς φάλαγγας τῶν ὑπεναντίων *Hymn.*(*AS* 1 p.530).

ἄοπτος, *unseen*, Cyr.*dial.Trin*.4(5^{1}.534A); id.*inc.unigen*.(5^{1}.693D); id.*hom.pasch*.25(5^{2}.301C).

ἀορασία, ἡ, **1.** *blindness*, Iren.*haer*.4.39.3(M.7.1111A); Eust.*engast*. 6(p.23.30; M.18.624B); met. καθάπερ ἀ. τινὶ τοὺς τῆς ψυχῆς ὀφθαλμοὺς πεπληγμένος Bas.*Eun*.1.26(1.236D; M.29.568D): *ib*.2.16(251B; M.604B); **2.** *invisibility* οὐχὶ τῷ διαφέρειν τοῦ ἀρχετύπου τὴν εἰκόνα κατὰ τὸν τῆς ἀ. καὶ τῆς ἀγαθότητος λόγον Gr.Nyss.*diff.ess*.8(M.32. 340B); Didym.*Trin*.3.16(M.39.868A); **3.** *condition of invisibility, darkness*, Chrys.*sac*.6.12(p.168.8; 1.433D); Mac.Mgn.*apocr*.3.41 (p.142.7).

ἀόρατος, *invisible, unseen*;

A. in gen., def. ἀόρατον, τὸ μέν, ὃ μὴ πέφυκεν ὀφθαλμοῖς σαρκὸς καθορᾶσθαι..., τὸ δέ, ὃ τῇ φύσει ὁρατὸν ὑπάρχον...ἀποκρύπτεται Bas. *hex*.2.1(1.13A; M.29.29B); of light διχῶς τὸ φῶς ὀνομάζεται, σωματικόν τε καὶ πνευματικὸν ὅπερ ἐστὶ νοητόν, καὶ ὡς μὲν αἱ γραφαὶ ἂν λέγοιεν ἀ., ὡς δ' ἂν Ἕλληνες ὀνομάσαιεν ἀσώματον Or.*Jo*.13.22(p.246. 5; M.14.436B); id.*fr.13 in Jo*.(p.494); σημαίνεται διὰ...τοῦ ἀ. τὸ νοητὸν καὶ ἀσώματον Gr.Nyss.*infant*.(M.46.172D); τῆς δὲ νοητῆς φύσεως πάσης ὄνομα μὲν κοινόν ἐστι...τὸ ἀ. id.*Eun*.1(1 p.100.7; M.45. 333B).

B. of God; **1.** in gen.; **a.** stock epithet after S. Paul e.g. *Hom. Clem*.3.36; Arist.*apol*.4.1 cit. s. ἀναλλοίωτος; Tat.*orat*.4(p.5.4; M.6. 813A); **b.** ref. Jo.1:18 τὸ ἀ. καὶ ἄρρητον κόλπον ὀνομάσας θεοῦ Clem. *str*.5.12(p.380.12; M.9.121A); ref. Rom.1:20 τὰ ἀ. αὐτοῦ, τουτέστιν ἡ δημιουργία αὐτοῦ, καὶ ἡ πρόνοια, ἡ δικαία ἐφ' ἑκάστῳ ψῆφος, καὶ αἱ παντοδαπαὶ οἰκονομίαι Thdt.ad loc.(3.24); **2.** of Father; **a.** in gen., Athenag.*leg*.10.1(M.6.908B); cf. *si invisibilem eum dicitis per naturam, neque salvatori debet esse visibilis*, Or.*princ*.2.4.3(p.13.27; M. 11.202A); ὁ μόνος ἀ. μόνῳ τῷ ἀ. τὴν φύσιν φαίνεται Ammon.*Jo*.6:46 (M.85.1437B); **b.** as invisible 'bishop' τῷ πατρὶ Χριστοῦ τῷ πάντων ἐπισκόπῳ...οὐχ ὅτι τὸν ἐπίσκοπον τοῦτον τὸν βλεπόμενον πλανᾷ τις, ἀλλὰ τὸν ἀ. παραλογίζεται Ign.*Magn*.3.2; **3.** of Son; **a.** as image of invisible Father is invisible by nature, cf. *sicut ipse* [sc. *pater*] *est invisibilis per naturam, ita imaginem quoque invisibilem genuerit*, Or.*princ*.1.2.6(p.36.3; M.11.135A); *cum invisibilis dei ipse sit imago invisibilis, participationem sui universis rationabilibus creaturis invisibiliter praebuit*, *ib*.2.6.3(p.141.28; 211B); id.*Jo*.1.31 (34; p.39.28; M.14.84A); **b.** became visible τὸν ἀ. τὸν δι' ἡμᾶς ὁρατόν Ign.*Polyc*.3.2; ὃν λόγον ἔχων ἐν ἑαυτῷ ἀ. τε ὄντα, τῷ κτιζομένῳ κόσμῳ ὁρατὸν ποιεῖ...προῆκεν τῇ κτίσει κύριον τὸν ἴδιον νοῦν ⟨ὃν⟩ αὐτῷ μόνῳ πρότερον ὁρατὸν ὑπάρχοντα· τῷ δὲ γενομένῳ κόσμῳ ἀ. ὄντα ὁρατὸν ποιεῖ Hipp.*Noët*.10(p.253.4; M.10.817B); δύναμιν...ἔχει ...ἀ. εἶναι τῇ θεότητι αὐτοῦ, παρὼν παντὶ ἀνθρώπῳ Or.*Jo*.6.30(15; p.140.11; M.14.252D); **c.** remaining same Son μή τις ὑπολάβῃ ἕτερον εἶναι τὸν ἀ. καὶ διήκοντα ἐπὶ πάντα ἄνθρωπον...παρὰ τὸν ἐνανθρωπήσαντα καὶ ἐπὶ τῆς γῆς ὀφθέντα *ib*.(p.140.18; 253A); ἐπειδὴ γὰρ ἀ. ἡ θεία φύσις, τὸ δὲ σῶμα ὁρατόν, ὡς ἐν εἰκόνι τινὶ διὰ τοῦ σώματος προσκυνεῖται Thdt.*Rom*.8:29(3.92); **d.** as Lord of unseen powers ὁ ἀόρατος οἶδε τῶν ἀσωμάτων τὰ πάθη Tit.Bost.*fr.Lc*.10:18(p.192); **e.** acc. Marcellus, could not be εἰκὼν τοῦ ἀ. θεοῦ until Inc. αἱ γὰρ εἰκόνες τούτων ὧν εἰσιν εἰκόνες...δεικτικαί εἰσιν, ὥστε καὶ τὸν ἀπόντα δι' αὐτῶν φαίνεσθαι δοκεῖν. ... πῶς εἰκὼν τοῦ ἀοράτου θεοῦ ὁ λόγος καθ' ἑαυτὸν εἶναι δύναται, καὶ αὐτὸς ἀ. ὤν; Marcell.*fr*.82 ap.Eus. *Marcell*.1.4(p.24.28; M.24.764A).

C. of man created in image of God; **1.** in gen. = rational, spiritual ἀνάγκη...τοῦ ἀ. θεοῦ ἀ. εἶναι καὶ τὴν εἰκόνα, καὶ τῆς ἀ.

εἰκόνος ἀ. τὸν κατ' εἰκόνα ἄνθρωπον ‡Ath.*dial.Trin.*3.17(M.28.1229B); cf. θεοῦ τοῦ ἀ. ἐστὲ εἰκών *Hom.Clem.*11.4; *ib.*17.7; **2.** more exactly of rational soul; an invisible essence ἀ. ἡ ψυχὴ ἐν ὁρατῷ φρουρεῖται τῷ σώματι *Diogn.*6.4; τὴν λογικὴν ψυχὴν πειρωμένους ἀποδεικνύναι... οὐσίαν ἀ. καὶ ἀσώματον Or.*Cels.*6.71(p.141.21; M.11.1405C); of νοῦς, Eus.*l.C.*12.3(p.230.6; M.20.1388A); for soul is νοερόν τι like God νοερὰ...ἑκάτερα καὶ ἀ. καὶ...ἀσώματα Or.*mart.*47(p.43.1; M.11.629B); ἀσώματος καὶ ἀ. ψυχή id.*Cels.*7.32(p.182.32; 1465B); same phrase being used of God, *ib.*7.38(p.188.12; 1473B); τῆς ψυχῆς...οὔσης ἀ. καὶ ἀσωμάτου, κατὰ γὰρ τὴν εἰκόνα γέγονε τοῦ ἀ. θεοῦ id.*fr.53 in Lc.* (p.259.29); cf. ὡς ἐνιδρυμένου τῷ δημιουργήματι ἀ. τοῦ σπέρματος τῆς ἄνωθεν οὐσίας Clem.*str.*2.8(p.133.15; M.8.973B); of soul's activities and faculties ἡ...ζήτησις ἀειδὴς καὶ ἀ. *ib.*5.11(p.374.23; M.9.109B); Or.*hom.20.1 in Jos.*(p.417.24; M.12.920).

D. the universal pattern of interpretation for Christian mystery, ὁρατός–ἀ., illustrated by characteristic examples; **1.** invisible heaven, ref. Gen.1:2 τὸ πνεῦμα...τὰ πάντα δημιουργεῖ...μετὰ τὸν ἀ. οὐρανὸν τὸν φαινόμενον ἐφαπλῶσαν, ἵνα τὰ ἄνω τοῖς τοῦ φωτὸς ἀγγέλοις οἰκηθῇ, τὰ δὲ κάτω ὑπὸ ἀνθρώπου ἅμα τοῖς δι' αὐτὸν γενομένοις πᾶσι διοικηθῇ *Hom.Clem.*11.22; **2.** in spiritual life 'gnostic' must pass beyond the visible to the invisible, τὰ ἀ. τοῦ θεοῦ (Rom.1:20), cf. Or.*Cels.*6.59(p.130.3; M.11.1380A) etc.; ὅταν ἐπιστημονικοῦ θεωρήματος κατάληψιν λάβῃ, τὸν κύριον ὁρᾶν νομίζει, τὰς ὄψεις αὐτοῦ πρὸς τὰ ἀ. χειραγωγῶν Clem.*str.*7.12(p.54.22; M.9.505A); καταφρονεῖν μὲν ὡς προσκαίρων πάντων τῶν αἰσθητῶν καὶ βλεπομένων, σπεύδειν δὲ ἐπὶ τὰ ἀ. καὶ σκοπεῖν τὰ μὴ βλεπόμενα Or.*Cels.*3.47(p.243.27; 981B); μᾶλλον...πεφίμωντο τῷ προφήτῃ Δανιὴλ οἱ ἀ. λέοντες ἤπερ οἱ αἰσθητοί id.*or.*16(p.337.25; M.11.469C); πειθόμεθα γὰρ κρεῖττονα ἔχειν ὕπαρξιν οὐ γηΐνην ἀλλ' οὐδὲ σωματικὴν ἀλλά τινα ἀ. καὶ ἀσώματον id.*mart.*44 (p.41.14; M.11.621A); **3.** heavenly powers good and bad, Ign. *Smyrn.*6.1 cit. s. ἄρχων; οὐ χωρὶς προστασίας ἀοράτων...γεωργῶν καὶ ἄλλων οἰκονόμων...τὰ ὑπὸ φύσεως λεγόμενα διοικεῖσθαι...οὐ μὴν τοὺς ἀ. φαμὲν εἶναι δαίμονας Or.*Cels.*8.31(p.246.26; M.11.1561f.); δαίμοσι καὶ ἄλλαις ἀ. δυνάμεσι *ib.*3.36(p.233.7; 968A); id.*mart.*46(p.42.13; M.11.628A); id.*Jo.*28.5(4; p.395.2; M.14.689A); **4.** invisible washing in baptism τοῦ καὶ τὰ ἀ. ἡμῶν ἁγιάζεσθαι Clem.*ecl.*7(p.138.30; M.9.701B); ἐπεὶ τὸ βάπτισμα γίνεται δι' ὕδατος καὶ πνεύματος, ἀλεξητήριον ὂν πυρὸς τοῦ δισσοῦ, τοῦ τε τῶν ἀ. ἁπτομένου καὶ τοῦ τῶν ὁρατῶν... τὸ δὲ ἐπουράνιον ὕδωρ διὰ τὸ εἶναι νοητὸν καὶ ἀ. πνεῦμα ἀλληγορεῖται ἅγιον, τῶν ἀ. καθαρτικόν *ib.*8(p.139.1,5,6; 701B,C).

E. of creation, God as creator of things invisible; God as φύσις ἀ., Or.*Jo.*20.19(16; p.351.10; M.14.613D); Bas.*Eun.*1.8(1.220A; M.29.528D); as creator of things invisible μόνος τῶν ἀ. ἐστὶ καὶ ἀνωλέθρων ποιητής Meth.*symp.*2.7(p.24.14; M.18.57C); ἀ. εἶναι τὸν θεὸν καὶ εἶναί τινα δημιουργήματα ἀ. τουτέστι νοητά Or.*Cels.*7.37(p.187.28; M.11.1473A); θεὸν τὸν ἀόρατα βλέποντα *Hom.Clem.*13.17; ἐν...τῇ μονάδι συνίστησιν οὐρανὸν ἀ. γῆν ἀειδῆ καὶ φῶς νοητόν Clem.*str.*5.14(p.388.2; M.9.137B); as creator of all things visible and invisible πιστεύομεν εἰς ἕνα θεὸν...πάντων ὁρατῶν τε καὶ ἀ. ποιητὴν *Symb.Nic.*(325)(p.51; M.20.1540B); cf. ἐν ἀρχῇ τῶν ὁρατῶν τε καὶ ἀ. κτισμάτων ἦν ὁ λόγος, πάντων αὐτῶν ὢν ἀρχή τε καὶ ποιητής Or.*fr.1 in Jo.*(p.484.18); cf. strange explanation of this, Chrys.*hom.3.2 in Col.*(11.344D).

F. Gnost.; **1.** name of an aeon in Valent. ogdoad, Epiph.*haer.* 32.7(p.446.19f.; M.41.553A,B); **2.** ἔλεγεν [sc. Marcus] ἐν αὐτῷ τὴν μεγίστην ἀπὸ τῶν ἀ. καὶ ἀκατονομάστων τόπων εἶναι δύναμιν Hipp. *haer.*6.39(p.170.13; M.16.3258A); **3.** ὁ ψυχικὸς Χριστός, ὃν ἐνεδύσατο [sc. Ἰησοῦς] ἀ. ἦν Clem.*exc.Thdot.*59(p.126.22; M.9.688B); *ib.*26 (p.115.17; 672B); **4.** of primal or essential man, *ib.*50(p.123.14; 684A); **5.** of heavenly powers governing the stars, *ib.*69,70(p.129. 16,21; 692A,B).

ἀοράτως, *invisibly*, of divine activity τῇ ποιητικῇ δυνάμει τοῦ θεοῦ, ἥτις...ἡμᾶς ἀ. ἀνθρωποπλαστεῖ Meth.*symp.*2.5(p.21.8; M.18.53C); Ath.*inc.*30.4(M.25.148A); Bas.*reg.fus.*55.2(2.398C; M.31.1045C); ὁ ἄνω τῷ πατρὶ συγκαθεζόμενος καὶ ὧδε ἡμῖν ἀ. παρών *Lit.Bas.* (p.341.9); ref. Jo.7:30 ὁρᾷς αὐτοὺς ἀ. κατεχομένους Chrys.*hom.50.2 in Jo.*(8.295C); of healing action of H. Ghost θεοῦ ἔργον ἐστὶν ἀ. ἐπιδημεῖν κατὰ τὸ ἑαυτοῦ πνεῦμα μετὰ τοῦ πνεύματος Χριστοῦ οἷς κρίνει δεῖν ἐπιδημεῖν Or.*Cels.*5.1(p.1.12; M.11.1181A).

***ἀοργετέομαι**, s.v.l., *bear without irritation*, ‡Ath.*doct.mon.*(M.28.1424A).

ἀοργησία, ἡ, *freedom from anger*; in lists of principal virtues, Ath.*v.Anton.*17(M.26.869B); Eus.Al.*serm.*22.5(M.87.457C); ὅρος τῆς ἀ.· ἐπιθυμία πολλὴ τοῦ μὴ ὀργίζεσθαι Diad.*perf.*proem.(p.5.9); linked with ἐγκρατεία, *ib.*99(p.148.1).

ἀόργητος, *free from anger*, of God ἀ. ὑπάρχει πρὸς πᾶσαν τὴν κτίσιν αὐτοῦ *1Clem.*19.3; Ign.*Philad.*1.2; *A.Jo.*107(p.205.3); Cyr. *hom.pasch.*25(5^2.297E); of true Christian, Diad.*perf.*6(p.8.15); *ib.* 35(p.40.12).

ἀοριστ-έω, *be indeterminate*; **1.** act. καταπεσοῦσα δὲ [sc. ἡ ψυχή] ἀχλυοῦται καὶ ~εῖ καὶ ψεύδεται Synes.*insomn.*10(p.163.15; M.66.1297D); **2.** med., Germ.CP *vit.term.*15(M.98.117D).

ἀοριστία, ἡ, *infinitude*, Dion.Ar.*c.h.*2.3(M.3.141A); ὑπέρκειται τῶν οὐσιῶν ἡ ὑπερούσιος ἀ. id.*d.n.*1.1(M.3.588B); Max.*ambig.*(M.91.1360D); *ib.*(1400B).

ἀόριστος, **1.** *undefined, indefinite*; of Jephthah's vow δεξάμενος ὁ διάβολος τὸ ἀ. τῆς εὐχῆς...πολλὰ γάρ ἐστιν ἄτοπα κατὰ τὴν οὕτως ἀ. εὐχὴν εὐλαβηθησόμενα ‡Just.*qu.et resp.*99(M.6.1344B); of man's life τὸ τοῦ χρόνου ἀ. *ib.*33(1280B); of evil τὰ κακὰ...ἄπειρα, καὶ ἀ. Dion.Ar.*d.n.*4.31(M.3.732B); ὅτε καθ' ἑαυτὴν ἁπλῶς φύσις λέγεται, μὴ προσκειμένου ταύτῃ ἰδικοῦ τινος προσώπου, ἀ. τι, καὶ ἀνυπόστατον δηλοῖ Justn.*conf.*(p.88.2; M.86.1011A); gram., Geo.Pis.*hex.*1666(M.92.1564A); **2.** *limitless*; in number, Meth.*symp.*1.5(p.14.17; M.18.45D); of aeons in Tatian's system, *Chron.Pasch.*p.260(M.92.636A); in size, *T.Sal.*15.5(M.122.1337B); **3.** *infinite*; **a.** of God τὸν ἀ. καὶ ἄπειρον, καὶ οὐδενὶ τέλει καταληπτὸν προσαγορεύομεν ἄφθαρτον Bas. *Eun.*1.7(1.219A; M.29.525C); θεότητος ἀρχὴν...ἀχώριστον καὶ ἀ. Gr. Naz.*or.*23.8(M.35.1160C); Gr.Nyss.*hom.8 in Cant.*(M.44.941A); id. *tres dii*(M.45.129C); πῶς γὰρ σῶμα τὸ...ἀ.; Cyr.*Trin.*3(6^3.3E; M.77.1124C); Dion.Ar.*c.h.*2.3(M.3.140D); ὁ δὲ θεὸς...ἐπιτείνειν μᾶλλον τῶν ἀπολαυόντων αὐτοῦ διὰ τῆς μετοχῆς πρὸς τὸ ἀ. τὴν ὄρεξιν πέφυκεν Max. *ambig.*(M.91.1089B); Jo.D.*f.o.*1.4(M.94.797B); *ib.*1.14(860A); **b.** of Christ's divine nature εἰ δὲ ἀνεπιδεκτός ἐστι τοῦ χείρονος ἡ θεία... φύσις,...ἀ. πάντως ἐν τῷ ἀγαθῷ θεωρεῖται, τὸ δὲ ἀ. τῷ ἀπείρῳ ταὐτόν ἐστι Gr.Nyss.*Eun.*1(1 p.73.6; M.45.301D); ὁ φανερωθεὶς ἡμῖν ἐν σαρκὶ θεὸς...ἦν καὶ ἐστιν ἀ. id.*Apoll.*18(M.45.1160A); of wisdom of Christ, id.*hom.1 in Cant.*(M.44.765D).

ἀορίστως, **1.** *indeterminately, confusedly*; of Epicurean concourse of atoms, Dion.Al.ap.Eus.*p.e.*14.24(774A); **2.** *indefinitely*; **a.** of expression ἀ. ὁμολογοῦσι τὸ κοινὸν ὄνομα τὸ θεός Or.*Cels.*1.25(p.76.25; M.11.708B); οὐ γὰρ εἶπεν 'ἐν ἀρχῇ ἦν ὁ τοῦ θεοῦ λόγος', ἀλλ' ἀ., 'ἐν ἀρχῇ ἦν ὁ λόγος' Eus.*e.th.*2.12(p.113.26; M.24.925B); Chrys.*hom.24.2 in Jo.*(8.140A); Thdt.*qu.2 in Jos.*(1.301); id.*eran.*1(4.13B); **b.** of time, Clem.*ecl.*56(p.153.1; M.9.724C); τὸ μὲν υἱὸν αὐτοῦ εἶναι ἀ. ἀπεφήνατο καὶ ἀχρόνως Meth.*symp.*8.9(p.91.8; M.18.152A).

ἀοχλησία, ἡ, *quietude, freedom from disturbance*, Clem.*str.*2.2 (p.186.22; M.8.1081C); *ib.*2.23(p.189.18; 1088B); τῆς ἀγγελικῆς ἡδονῆς καὶ τῆς ἐν ἐκείνοις ἀ. Max.*schol.c.h.*15.8(M.4.113C).

ἀόχλητος, *undisturbed*, Clem.*paed.*2.8(p.201.28; M.8.484A); Dion. Al.ap.Eus.*p.e.*14.25(777D; M.21.1280B); Bas.*hom.in Ps.*1:1(1.92C; M.29.216B).

***ἄπα, ἀπᾶ,** = ἀββᾶς, *father, abbot*, title of respect given to bishops and priests in Egypt τῷ ἀγαπητῷ ἀδελφῷ ἄπα Παιηοῦ καὶ Παταβεῖτ πρεσβυτέροις *PLond.*1914.1; *ib.*1914.34; ὁ θεοφιλέστατος ἀπᾶ Θεόδωρος ἐπίσκοπος *CIG* 8647; cf. ἀββᾶ Θεοδώρου ἐπισκόπου *ib.*8646.

ἀπαγγελία, ἡ, **1.** *declaration, statement*, Or.*sel.in Ps.*3:5(M.12.1124A) etc.; **2.** *recital*, Eus.*h.e.*6.2.8(M.20.524C); of the creed, v.l. for ἐπαγγελία q.v., Cyr.H.*catech.*5.12; of formula of baptism τὴν ἀ. τῶν μυστικῶν ῥημάτων Chrys.*hom.40.1 in 1Cor.*(10.379B, v.l. ἐπ-).

ἀπαγγέλλ-ω, **1.** *bring tidings, report*; **2.** of speakers or writers, *relate, describe*; *declare*, Just.*2apol.*2.2(M.6.444A); *profess*, Gr. Thaum.*pan.Or.*10(p.25.7; M.10.1081A); **3.** *expound* scripture, *Dial. Tim.et Aquil.*76 r°; *ib.*79 v°; **4.** *recite* μεθ' ἡμέραν τε καὶ νύκτα οἱ ἱεροὶ ~ονται νόμοι ὕμνοι τε καὶ ᾠδαί Gr.Thaum.*pan.Or.*16(p.37.23; 1100B); CLaod.*can.*46 cit. s. πίστις; of eucharist ὁ θεῖος Βασίλειος ...ἐπιτομώτερον ταύτην...~ει ‡Procl.CP *tract.*(M.65.852B); **5.** *play the part of* τὸν ἱκετεύοντα...ἀ. Evagr.*h.e.*5.18(p.213.20; M.86.2828C).

***ἀπάγγελμα, τό,** *report*, Thdr.Stud.*epp.*2.15(M.99.1161B).

ἀπαγγελτήρ, ὁ, *messenger*, *Orac.Sib.*7.83.

ἀπαγγελτικός, *declaring, expressing*, Cyr.H.*catech.*20.1; ‡Proc.G. *Pr.*2:2(M.87.1233C); of Logos ἐν ἀνθρώπῳ τῆς τοῦ πατρὸς εὐσεβείας ἀ. Eus.*d.e.*5 proem.(p.202.9; M.22.336B); *ib.*4.4(p.155.7; 260A); neut. as subst., *expression*, Or.*Jo.*1.38(42; p.49.33; M.14.100C).

ἀπαγής, *not firm, unstable*; met., *uncertain, unreliable* ἐπειδή... φθαρτὴ καὶ ἀσθενὴς ἡμῶν ἡ φύσις, διὰ τοῦτο...ἀνυπόστατος ἡ δύναμις, ἀ. ὁ λόγος Gr.Nyss.*or.catech.*1(p.8.11; M.45.13B); Nil.*epp.*4.1(M.79.545B); neut. as subst. τὸ περὶ πρόρρησιν ἀ. καὶ ἀσύστατον Gr.Nyss. *fat.*(M.45.165B); id.*Eun.*10(2 p.238.4; M.45.840C).

***ἀπαγίδευτος**, *not ensnared*, Or.*exp.in Pr.*31:11(M.17.249D).

ἀπαγκωνίζομαι, *bare the elbows*; hence met. **1.** *divest oneself* ἀπαγκωνισάμενος μὲν καὶ...ἀπορρίψας πάντας τοὺς βιωτικοὺς δεσμοὺς ‡Pion.*v.Polyc.*16; **2.** of outspoken language, *take the gloves off* κατὰ τῶν φιλοσόφων...λόγος ἐσπουδάσθη σφόδρα ἀπηγκωνισμένος καὶ οὐδὲν σχῆμα ὀκνήσας Synes.*Dion* 1(p.237.1, v.l. ἀπεικονισμένος M.66. 1116D).

ἀπαγόρευσις, ἡ, 1. of statements or arguments, *rejection, denial*, Bas.*Eun.*1.10(1.222E; M.29.536B); Chrys.*hom.10.4 in Rom.*(9.525B); **2.** *failure*, Corn.ap.Eus.*h.e.*6.43.12(M.20.621A); Tit.Bost.*Man.*1.2 (M.18.1072B).

ἀπαγορεύ-ω, 1. *reject, refuse, renounce*, Athenag.*leg.*20.2(M.6. 932A); Meth.*symp.*6.3(p.67.3; M.18.117A); Eus.*h.e.*3.33.1(M.20.285B); βίβλους Epiph.*haer.*19.5(p.222.16; M.41.263B); **2.** *give up, fail*, hence *despair of* ψυχὴ...ἐπειδὰν...~σῃ τὴν σωτηρίαν τὴν ἑαυτῆς Chrys.*Thdr.* 1.16(1.27C); id.*scand.*11(3.493D); esp. medic., *give up as hopeless* τὰ σώματα ἀ. id.*hom.5.4 in 2Tim.*(11.691B); Call.*v.Hyp.*(p.36); Marc. Diac.*v.Porph.*28; perf. ptcpl. pass., *abandoned*; of Jezebel γύναιον ...ἀπηγορευομένον Chrys.*poenit.*2.3(2.290C).

***ἀπαγροικίζομαι,** pass., *be rustic*; met., of a country church, Gr.Naz.*or.*18.16(M.35.1004C).

ἀπαγχονάω or **ἀπαγχονέω,** *strangle*, hence *kill* τοὺς δὲ...λιμὸς ἀπηγχόνησεν Const.Diac.*laud.*38(M.88.524A).

ἀπαγχονίζω, 1. *strangle*, met., Chrys.*hom.28.2 in Rom.*(9.726D); pass., *be choked*, by any strong emotion, id.*hom.42.2 in Mt.*(7. 454C); id.*hom.4.2 in 2Cor.*(10.457D); id.*hom.div.*9.2(12.384A); **2.** *practise semi-starvation* from ascetic motives; of Manicheans and other dualistic ascetics, id.*hom.55.6 in Mt.*(7.563C); id.*hom.1.4 in Tit.* (11.735C); id.*sac.*3.13(p.70.3; 1.389E).

***ἀπαγχόνισις, ἡ,** *hanging*, Thdt.Stud.*epp.*2.153(M.99.1476C).

ἀπάγ-ω, 1. *lead away, carry off*, met., of death ὅταν...ἐντεῦθεν ~ώμεθα Chrys.*hom.66.4 in Mt.*(7.658E); id.*hom.32.3 in Heb.*(12. 298A); **2.** *lead astray* ἐπιθυμίαις ~ομένους *Diogn.*9.1; **3.** *keep away, divert from*, Just.*1apol.*5.3(M.6.336B); Chrys.*hom.10.1 in 1Thess.* (11.495C); id.*grat.*2(2.660A); Eulog.*fr.Novat.*(M.104.304C); **4.** ~ε as exclamation of horror ~ε τῆς τόλμης Chrys.*sac.*1.9(p.24.15; 1.371A); Cyr.*Is.*3.5(2.518B); *far be it! certainly not!*, *cat.Lc.*2:44(p.27.1); Chrys.*hom.63.1 in Mt.*(7.628B); Thdr.Stud.*epp.*2.66(M.99.1289B).

ἀπαγωγή, ἡ, 1. lit., *leading away* after arrest; *carrying off* into captivity; of Israel, †Gregent.*disp.*(M.86.733B); **2.** met.; **a.** *carrying off* by death ποῦ μετὰ τὴν ἐντεῦθεν ἀ.; Chrys.*hom.15.5 in 1Cor.* (10.132B); **b.** *leading astray* into error ἐπὶ ἀπατῇ καὶ ἀ. τοῦ ἀνθρωπείου γένους Just.*1apol.*54.1(M.6.408C); **c.** *leading away* from evil ἀρκεῖται τοῖς ὀνόμασι μόνοις εἰς τὴν ἀ. Chrys.*hom.24.3 in 1Cor.*(10.215C); **d.** *distraction, diversion* of mind, Philost.*h.e.*5.2a(M.65.632A); Jo. Mosch.*prat.*171(M.87.3040A); **3.** (in logic) *reductio* τῇ εἰς ἄτοπον ἀ. Chrys.*hom.24.3 in 1Cor.*(10.215D); *ib.39.4*(367C); Cyr.*Jo.*1.3(4.27A); Gr.Agr.*Eccl.*3.23(M.98.893A).

ἀπᾳδόντως, *unbefittingly, discrepantly, discordantly*, Or.*Jo.*1.25 (24; p.30.30; M.14.68A); Cyr.*Os.*1(3.9B); id.*Jo.*4.5(4.414C); Zach. Mit.*opif.*(M.85.1121B).

ἀπᾴδ-ω, 1. *differ* from ὡς μηδὲν ἀ. νεβρῷ Or.*schol.in Cant.*2:8 (p.199.32; M.17.264A); ‡Caes.Naz.*dial.*138(M.38.1044); **2.** *be discrepant* with ὁ δὲ Ὀλύμπιος ὑμῶν, εἰκόνος εἰκών, πολύ τι τῆς ἀληθείας ~ων Clem.*prot.*10(p.71.24; M.8.212C); Or.*ep.*1.9(M.11.68B); Ath.*ep. Serap.*1.21(M.26.581A); **3.** *be discordant, incongruous* οὐκ εἶπε 'θεμέλιον' ὅπερ ἀπῇδεν, ἀλλὰ 'ἄγκυραν' Chrys.*hom.11.2 in Heb.*(12.113D); Dion.Ar.*c.h.*2.4(M.3.144B); Zach.Mit.*opif.*(M.85.1121A); **4.** *be displeasing* to, Cyr.*ador.*6(1.187E); id.*Am.*5(3.257E); id.*Jo.*5.5(4.521A).

ἀπαθανατίζ-ω, *make immortal*; **1.** mankind, if man had eaten of tree of life, Gr.Naz.*or.*44.4(M.36.612B); Leont.B.*Nest.et Eut.*2 (M.86.1348C); through Christ ἐγηγέρθαι κηρύττεται [sc. σὰρξ τοῦ Χριστοῦ], ἵνα ἡμᾶς ἀπαθανατίσας πρυτανεύσῃ ἡμῖν...τὴν τῆς ἀναστάσεως ἡμῶν ἐλπίδα Gel.Cyz.*h.e.*2.31.7(M.85.1317C); Germ.CP *or.*2 (M.98.256A); **2.** individuals; **a.** through Christ, exeg. Jo.8:52 δύναμαι γὰρ ~ειν, ἐπείπερ οἶδα τοῦτο ποιεῖν ἰσχύοντα τὸν ἐξ οὗπέρ εἰμι Cyr.*Jo.*6(4.581B); ref. Jo.6:48ff. ὁ ἄρτος ὁ τοὺς μετέχοντας ~ειν δυνάμενος id.*thes.*14(5^1.141D); cf.id.*Jo.*4.3(372A); **b.** esp. through baptism; ref. Ps.81:6 υἱοποιούμενοι τελειούμεθα, τελειούμενοι ~όμεθα Clem.*paed.*1.6(p.105.21; M.8.281A); id.*str.*4.25(p.319.13; M.8.1369A); πνεῦμα ἅγιον...δι' οὗ υἱοθετεῖται ἄνθρωπος, καὶ ~εται τὸ θνητόν Bas. *ep.*105(3.200B; M.32.513B); ~όμενοι διὰ τῆς τοῦ λουτροῦ παλιγγενεσίας Thdt.*Ps.*59:7(1.1003); **c.** in gen. ~εσθαι δὲ ἡμεῖς μόνους δεδιδάγμεθα τοὺς ὁσίως καὶ ἐναρέτως ἐγγὺς θεῷ βιοῦντας Just.*1apol.*21.6(M.6. 361A); τῆς πίστεως ἡ κοινωνία ἡ πνευματικὴ πρὸς τὸν παθητὸν ἄνθρωπον...εἰς ἀϊδιότητα συστέλλει τὸν ἄνθρωπον, τοῖς θείοις ~ουσα Clem. *paed.*1.6(p.120.31; M.8.312A); Enoch, Areth.*Apoc.*30(M.106.649A); **3.** the body, Tat.*orat.*25(p.26.9; M.6.861A); ref. 1Cor.15:53, Didym. (‡Bas.)*Eun.*5(1.296D; M.29.712B); Nemes.*nat.hom.*1(M.40.521A); Max.*schol.d.n.*6.2(M.4.337B); **4.** the beast and the false prophet ἐν ῥιπῇ ὀφθαλμοῦ ~όμενοι, τῷ δευτέρῳ θανάτῳ τῇ λίμνῃ τοῦ πυρὸς καταδικάζονται Andr.Caes.*Apoc.*59(M.106.405D); **5.** the world ~ειν μέλλει τόνδε τὸν κόσμον ὁ θεός, καὶ...ἀναπλάττειν ἐπὶ τὸ κάλλιον Zach.Mit.*opif.*(M.85.1120C).

ἀπαθανατισμός, ὁ, *immortalization* τῶν ψυχῶν ἀ. τε καὶ μετενσωματώσεις Epiph.*haer.*7(p.186.5; M.41.205B); ἀ. ... καὶ μεταγγισμοὺς ...ψυχῶν ‡Epiph.*epit.haer.*5(p.346.1).

***ἀπαθανατ-όω, 1.** *immortalize* (in idea) τοὺς ὄνους ἀ. Oenomaus ap.Eus.*p.e.*5.34(230B; ἀπαθάτους M.22.396A); **2.** *make immortal* (in fact) οὐδὲν...κτιστὸν οὐσιοῦν ἢ ~οῦν ἢ λογικοὺς ποιεῖν δύναται Didym. *Trin.*1.15(M.39.300B); [sc. τὸ βάπτισμα] τὸ γενόμενον ἐν ἀληθείᾳ ~οῖ καὶ ἀποθεοῖ ἡμᾶς *ib.*2.14(716A).

***ἀπαθανίζω,** s.v.l., *make immortal*, Thdr.Stud.*nativ.BMV* 7(M. 96.692B).

ἀπάθεια, ἡ, *impassibility, insensibility, freedom from emotion, freedom from sin*; these senses not always clearly distinguishable;

A. abs., *impassibility*; **1.** of God, Bas.*Eun.*2.23(1.258E; M.29. 621C); ἐν ἀ. τὸν θεὸν διαμεῖναι Gr.Nyss.*or.catech.*15(p.64.4; M.45. 48B); Epiph.*haer.*76.31(p.380.18; M.42.580B); by nature incompatible with the propensities of the flesh, Gennad.*fr.Rom.*8:7 (p.376.10; M.85.1689D); as a divine name ἐγώ εἰμι ὁ θεός, καὶ ἡ ἀ. Jo.Clim.*scal.*29(M.88.1152B); **2.** of Christ in divine nature ὁ Χριστός, καὶ θεὸς καὶ ἄνθρωπος...ἵνα τὸ διπλοῦν κήρυγμα...ἔχῃ τὴν πεισμονὴν τοῦ τε πάθους καὶ τῆς ἀ. ‡Ath.*Apoll.*1.10(M.26.1112A); Gr.Nyss.*Eun.* 12(2 p.321.21; M.45.1036D); ὁ ἀπαθὴς θεὸς λόγος παθὼν ἐν σαρκὶ... μένων δὲ ἐν ἀ. Epiph.*haer.*51.25(p.295.18; M.41.933C); ἀντιλήπτωρ διὰ τῆς θεότητος· μόνη γὰρ ἡμῶν ἀντιλαβέσθαι διὰ τῆς ἀ. ἐδύνατο Cyr.*Ps.*17:3(M.69.821A); Leont.B.*Nest.et Eut.*1(M.86.1284C); divine ἀ. adduced by Nestorians as ground of their Christology, Leont.H. *Nest.*1.17(M.86.1464D); **3.** of angels, Gr.Nyss.*hom.4 in Cant.*(M. 44.857A); cf.id.ap.Proc.G.*Cant.*2:7(M.87.1592A); Chrys.*hom.33.4 in 1Cor.*(10.304C); id.*ep.*2.7(3.543B); of the thrones τῆς θεαρχικῆς ἐπιφοιτήσεως ἐν ἀ. πάσῃ...δεκτικόν Dion.Ar.*c.h.*7.1(M.3.205D); **4.** of man in paradise ἐν ἀ. ἦμεν κατὰ τὸ πρὸ τοῦ παραπτώματος... χάρισμα Bas.*reg.fus.*55.1(2.297D; M.31.1044D); Anast.S.*hod.*14(M.89. 253D); of man after general resurrection, Just.*dial.*15.4(M.6.573A); Meth.*res.*3.5(p.396.13; M.18.320C); Mac.Mgn.*apocr.*4.16(p.187.13).

B. *insensibility*; *freedom from sin*; of Christians in general, def. φραγμός ἐστιν ἀ. ψυχῆς λογικῆς Or.*exp.in Pr.*24:31(M.17.232A); ἀ. ἐστιν ἀκινησία ψυχῆς πρὸς κακίαν· ἧς τυχεῖν ἀμήχανον ἄνευ ἐλέους Χριστοῦ Thal.*cent.*1.40(M.91.1432B); **1.** *freedom from* πάθος, *insensibility*, understood in Christian sense, as acquired with help of God, but its Stoic origin still discernible ὁμοίως Χριστῷ βιώσαντες ἐν ἀ. συγγενέσθαι τῷ θεῷ Just.*2apol.*1.2(M.6.441A); ἀ. γὰρ καρποῦται παντελὴς τῆς ἐπιθυμίας ἐκκοπή Clem.*str.*6.9(p.468.30; M.9.296A); acquired by patience, *ib.*2.20(p.169.25; M.8.1048B); but not without divine aid, id.*q.d.s.*21(p.173.16; M.9.625B); Eus.*d.e.*3.4(p.116.22; M.22.200A); **2.** *absence of sin* or *of sinful emotions*; **a.** its exact interpretation disputed, esp. in Didym. ἀπαθής ἐστιν ὁ πατήρ· εἰμί, ὡς καὶ τοὺς μετόχους μου ἀ. μεταλαμβάνειν Didym.*Trin.*1.26 (M.39.384C); ἡμᾶς συμμόρφους ποιήσας ἑαυτοῦ, εἰς ἀ. μετέστησεν *ib.* 3.12(860C); but prob. no more is meant than state of purification from sin after baptism or penance, πάθος here denoting sin rather than passion; for discussion see M.39.192–5; **b.** obtained for men by Passion of Christ, with a play on words πάθος, πάσχω etc. and ἀ.: ὁ υἱός...ὃς...τὴν σάρκα τὴν ἐμπαθῆ φύσει γενομένην ἀναλαβὼν εἰς ἕξιν ἀπαθείας ἐπαίδευσεν Clem.*str.*7.2(p.7.16; M.9.412A); τὸ γὰρ πάθος αὐτοῦ, ἡμῶν ἀ. ἐστι Ath.*inc.et c.Ar.*5(M.26.992A); id.*inc.*54.3 (M.25.192C); διὰ γὰρ τοῦ ἐμοῦ πάθους ἐβουλήθης τοῖς ἀνθρώποις τὴν ἀ. δωρήσασθαι Thdt.*Ps.*108:26f.(1.1389); Bas.Sel.*or.*31.3(M. 85.345C); Sophr.H.*ep.syn.*(M.87.3173C); Jo.D.*hom.*2.1(M.96.576C); issuing from side of Christ as Eve from side of Adam ἐκ πλευρᾶς τὸ πάθος, ἐκ πλευρᾶς ἡ ἀ. Mac.Mgn.*apocr.*2.18(p.32.15); **c.** being result of faith, Clem.*str.*7.3(p.11.7; M.9.417B); and of keeping of commandments, Or.*exp.in Pr.*28:4(M.17.244A); id.*Jo.*20.36(29; p.376. 27; M.14.657D); Thal.*cent.*2.25(M.91.1440C); produced by baptism φωτοειδεῖς ἐσθῆτας ἐκβάλλουσι τῷ τελουμένῳ· τῇ γὰρ...τῶν ἐναντίων ἀ. ... κοσμεῖται Dion.Ar.*c.h.*2.8(M.3.404C).

C. *mastery over the passions*, hence *detachment, tranquillity*, in varying degrees characteristic of the different stages of contemplative life; four degrees being given by Max. πρώτη...ἀ., ἡ παντελὴς ἀποχὴ τῶν κατ' ἐνέργειαν κακῶν...δευτέρα δέ, ἡ παντελὴς κατὰ διάνοιαν περὶ τὴν τῶν κακῶν συγκατάθεσιν ἀποβολὴ λογισμῶν... τρίτη, ἡ κατ' ἐπιθυμίαν περὶ τὰ πάθη παντελὴς ἀκινησία...τετάρτη ἀ., ἡ καὶ αὐτῆς τῆς ψιλῆς τῶν παθῶν φαντασίας παντελὴς κάθαρσις Max.*qu.Thal.*55(M.90.544C); **1.** gen., as Christian development of

Stoic ideal of *imperturbability*, an essential feature of Clem.'s 'gnostic' *οὐκ ἐγκρατὴς οὗτος ἔτι, ἀλλ' ἐν ἕξει γέγονεν ἀπαθείας* Clem. *str*.4.22(p.309.12; M.8.1348B); *ib*.6.13(p.484.29; M.9.325D); Or.*exp.in Pr*.19:17(M.17.209A); *ἀ. ἔχει ψυχή, οὐχ ἡ μὴ πάσχουσα πρὸς τὰ πράγματα, ἀλλ' ἡ καὶ πρὸς τὰς μνήμας αὐτῶν ἀτάραχος διαμένουσα* Evagr.Pont.*cap.pract*.39(M.40.1232B); *ἀ. δὲ λέγω...τὴν κατὰ διάνοιαν τοὺς ἐμπαθεῖς λογισμοὺς περικόπτουσαν* †Nil.*mal.cog*.25(M.79.1229C); ideal of old Egyptian monks, whose successors are blamed because *πολλοὶ...τῶν ἀδελφῶν...ἠστόχησαν ἀπαθείας* Pall.*h.Laus*.proem.(p.12.3; M.34.1003); many examples being given *ἐπὶ τοσοῦτον δὲ ἤλασεν ἀπαθείας ταριχευθεὶς τὸ σῶμα ὡς ἤλιον διαφαίνειν αὐτοῦ τῶν ὀστέων ib*.48(p.143.9; 1211D); *ib*.37(p.116.4; 1188B); Arsen.*doct*.2(M.66.1620C); Max.*carit*.4.54(M.90.1060C); **2.** in relation to contemplation; **a.** removing obstacles *τὸ δὲ καθαρεῦον πάσης ἐμπαθοῦς διαθέσεως, πρὸς τὸν ἀρχηγὸν τῆς ἀ. βλέπει, ὅς ἐστιν ὁ Χριστός* Gr.Nyss.*perf*.(p.212.5; M.46.284D); *ἔνδυμά ἐστι γαμικὸν ἀ. ψυχῆς λογικῆς, κοσμικὰς ἀρνησαμένης ἐπιθυμίας* Evagr.Pont.*cap.pract*.64(M.40.1237D); *ib*.36(1232A); Jo.Clim.*scal*.29(M.88.1149B); **b.** leading to it *ἀ. δὲ κτησάμενος, χρονίσει τε ἐν τῇ θεωρίᾳ* Or.*exp.in Pr*.31:21(M.17.252B); and to life of perfection, Gr.Nyss.*hom.opif*.5.1(M.44.137B); id.*or.catech*.6(p.35.6; M.45.29A); to *γνῶσις*, Hesych.S.*temp*.1.67(M.93.1501D); and to all virtues *ἡ δὲ ἀ. τὰς ἀρετὰς* [sc. *ἔχει*] *κόσμον· οὐδὲν γὰρ ἕτερόν τι ἔγωγε ἀ. ὑπείληφα εἶναι ἀλλ' ἢ ἐγκάρδιον νοὸς οὐρανόν, τὰς τῶν δαιμόνων πανουργίας ἀθύρματα λοιπὸν λογιζόμενον* Jo.Clim.*scal*.29(M.88.1148B); equated with purity, *ib*.(1148D); and chastity, Socr.*h.e*.1.11.4(M.67.1104A); Bas.Sel.*v.Thecl*.1(M.85.485A); **3.** *tranquillity*, *contemplative peace*, characteristic of higher stages of contemplative life; producing deification *εἰς δὲ τὴν ἀ. θεούμενος ἄνθρωπος...γίνεται* Clem.*str*.4.23(p.315.26; M.8.1361A); and itself produced by charity, Diad.*perf*.89(p.126.17); through indwelling of the impassible Christ, Mac.Aeg.*ep*.(M.34.409C); making man like angels [sc. *ἄνθρωπος*]...*ἰσάγγελος διὰ τῆς ἀ. γενόμενος* Gr.Nyss.*hom.1 in Cant*.(M.44.777A); *ib.4*(857A) Chrys.*hom.33.4 in 1Cor*.(10.304C); leading him to understanding of immaterial things, Gr.Nyss.*hom.8 in Cant*.(948A); being part of his spiritual nourishment, id.*hom.5 in Eccl*.(M.44.696A); and equated with kingdom of God (*ἀ.* being substituted for *εἰρήνη* of Rom.14:17), *ib*.(696B) cit. s. *βασιλεία*; *βασιλεία οὐρανῶν ἐστιν ἀ. ψυχῆς* Evagr.Pont.*cap.pract*.2(M.40.1221D); does not exclude attacks from Devil, *ib*.60(1248D); for *ἀ. ἐστιν οὐ τὸ μὴ πολεμεῖσθαι ὑπὸ τῶν δαιμόνων...ἀλλὰ τὸ πολεμουμένους ὑπ' αὐτοῦ ἀπολεμήτους μένειν* Diad.*perf*.98(p.144.21); its perfection being the possession of all virtues *ἀ. ἔχει ψυχή, ἡ οὕτως ποιωθεῖσα ταῖς ἀρεταῖς, ὡς οἱ ἐμπαθεῖς ταῖς ἡδοναῖς* Jo.Clim.*scal*.29(M.88.1149A); *ib*.(1149D); identified with *ἀγάπη* and *υἱοθεσία*, *ib*.30(1156B); its great model being S. Anthony, *ib*.28(1148D); its highest stage *σημεῖον ἄκρας ἀ., τὸ ψιλὰ τὰ νοήματα τῶν πραγμάτων ἀεὶ ἀναβαίνειν ἐπὶ τὴν καρδίαν, καὶ ἐγρηγορότος τοῦ σώματος, καὶ κατὰ τοὺς ὕπνους* Max.*carit*.1.93(M.90.981B); as a state of perfection, aimed at by some sects, e.g. Marcianists *λέγουσιν ὅτι ἡ...τριὰς...πέφυκε καθορᾶσθαι ὑπὸ τῶν εἰς τὴν...ἐρχομένων ἀ.* Tim.CP *haer*.(M.86.49A).

ἀπαθ-έω, **1.** *leave unaffected*, *make no impression upon*, of a prayer displeasing to God *~εῖ δὲ τοῦτο τῷ φιλαγαθῷ θεῷ* Cyr.*Ps*.37:20(M.69.968C); abs., of earthly glory, Bas.*hom*.23.2(2.186B; M.31.592C); **2.** *be free from suffering* *μᾶλλον...τὸν λόγον παθεῖν λέγοιτο σαρκὶ ἐν Χριστῷ ἤπερ ~εῖν* Leont.H.*Nest*.7.11(M.86.1768[1]A).

ἀπαθής, *unhurt*, *impassible*, *calm*;

A. *unhurt*, *unscathed*; **1.** lit., ref. Dan.3:27ff. *ἀπαθεῖς ἐδείκνυ* Chrys.*hom.8.9 in Eph*.(11.67C); Euthal.Diac.*Ac*.(M.85.649A); Thdt.*h.e*.2.17.2(3.870); *immune* from illness, Eus.*v.C*.4.53(p.139.15; M.20.1204B); **2.** met., of true Christian who remains unhurt by riches, Clem.*paed*.3.6(p.256.26; M.8.605A); of Esther *τὸν Ἰσραὴλ...ἀ. διεφύλαξεν* id.*str*.4.19(p.300.26; M.8.1329A).

B. *impassible*, of the Divinity, to whom this quality had already been ascribed by Stoics; i.e. being free not only from pain and emotion but also from any other form of passivity; **1.** of divine nature, Chrys.*hom.23.1 in 2Cor*.(10.595C); Cyr.*Jo*.2.1(4.127E); Jo.D.*f.o*.1.1(M.94.792A); **2.** of God *θεὸς ἀγένητος καὶ ἀ.* Athenag.*leg*.8.2(M.6.905A); Just.*1apol*.25.2(M.6.365B); Clem.*str*.2.16(p.151.13; M.8.1012A); Epiph.*haer*.42.8(p.104.14; M.41.708A); Chrys.*hom.5.2 in Heb*.(12.53B); Jo.D.*f.o*.1.8(M.94.808C); in strict sense a prerogative of Trin. only *ἔχει ἡ τριὰς τὸ ἀ. καὶ ἀπαράλλακτον, τὰ δὲ πάντα τὰ μετὰ τὴν τριάδα πάθει ὑποκείμενα, εἰ μή τι ἂν δωροῖτο ὁ ἀ. τὸ ἀ. διὰ τῆς ἀφθαρσίας* Epiph.*haer*.76.39(p.392.26ff.; M.42.601A); of God's love *ἐρῶν...ἔρωτα ἀ.* Chrys.*scand*.6(3.474A); **3.** of Father; **a.** in gen., Eus.*Marcell*.1.4(p.22.26; M.24.760C); this esp. stressed by Arians, who say of orthodox that *τὸν...ἀ. πατέρα...παθητὸν διὰ τῆς ἐνανθρωπήσεως ὑποτίθενται* *Symb.Ant*.(345)7(p.253.16; M.26.732C); Bas.*Eun*.2.23(1.258D; M.29.621B); **b.** in act of generating Son; affirmed against Arians *ὁ θεὸς...ἀ. τοῦ υἱοῦ πατήρ* Ath.*decr*.11(p.10.11; M.25.436A); id.*Ar*.1.28(M.26.69A); *τοῦ θεοῦ ἀ. ὄντος...ἐν τῷ γεννᾶν* Epiph.*haer*.69.36(p.184.29; M.42.257D); generation itself being called *ἀ.*, Ath.*Ar*.1.28(69B); *εἰ γὰρ ἡ ἐνσώματος* [sc. *γέννησις*] *ἐμπαθής, ἀ. ἡ ἀσώματος* Gr.Naz.*or*.29.4(p.77.14; M.36.77C); Chrys.*hom.5.4 in Col*.(11.364A); Thdt.*rect.conf*.9(M.6.1224A); **4.** of Christ in divine nature v. *πάσχω*; **a.** orthodox *τὸν ἀ., τὸν δι' ἡμᾶς παθητόν* Ign.*Polyc*.3.2; Clem.*str*.7.2(p.7.4; M.8.409C); *τὴν σάρκα...δι' ἧς καὶ ὑπὸ πάθος ἦλθεν, ὁ ἀ. τοῦ θεοῦ λόγος* Ath.*Ar*.3.34(M.26.396A); ref. Eph.4:10 *οὕτως ὁ ἀπόστολος τὸ ἀ. τοῦ λόγου δεῖξαι θέλων καὶ τὸ ἄτρεπτον* Adam.*dial*.5.7(p.189.34; M.11.1844B); *ib*.5.8(p.190.21; 1844C); *μὴ φεισάμενος σταυρῷ καὶ θανάτῳ...συνεχώρησεν παθεῖν τὸν τῇ φύσει ἀ. ...τὸν θεὸν λόγον* *Const.App*.2.24.3; *σταυρῷ προσηλώθη ὁ ἀ.* *Lit.ib*.8.12.33; *θεὸν λόγον...ἄτρεπτον ὄντα καὶ ἀναλλοίωτον, ἀ. ... συμπάσχοντα δὲ τῷ ἡμετέρῳ γένει...ἀναπλάσαντα ἑαυτῷ τὴν σάρκα...καὶ ψυχὴν εἰληφότα* Epiph.*inc*.1(p.227.24; M.41.273C); relations bet. impassible Godhead and passible manhood, Gr.Naz.*or*.30.5(p.115.9; M.36.109B); Epiph.*haer*.69.38(p.186.25; M.42.261A); id.*exp.fid*.17(p.517.21; M.42.813C); Procl.CP *or.laud.BMV* 4(p.104.21; M.65.684C) cit. s. *πολυπαθής*; **b.** heret.: Cerinthus *τὸν Ἰησοῦν πεπονθέναι...τὸν δὲ Χριστὸν ἀ. διαμεμενηκέναι* Hipp.*haer*.7.33(p.221.6; M.16.3342A); Epiph.*haer*.28.1(p.314.11; M.41.380A); Apollinarians refuted *ὅτι τὴν θεότητα ἐν τῷ πάσχοντι εἶναι ὁμολογοῦμεν, οὐ μὴν τὴν ἀ. φύσιν ἐμπαθῆ γενέσθαι* Gr.Nyss.*Apoll*.54(M.45.1253C); but cf. *ἀ. ... διαμείνας καὶ ἀναλλοίωτος κατὰ τὴν θεότητα* Apoll.*ep.Jov*.(p.252.1; M.28.28B); *αὐτῷ* [sc. Apoll.]...*ὁ σκοπὸς πρὸς τοῦτο βλέπει...τὴν ἀ. καὶ ἀναλλοίωτον φύσιν πρὸς πάθους μετουσίαν ἀλλοιωθῆναι* Gr.Nyss.*Apoll*.5(M.45.1132B); Nestorians *εἰ ἡ τριάς, φησίν, ὁμοούσιος, ἡ τριὰς ἀ.· ὁ δὲ θεὸς λόγος...ἀ. εἰ δὲ ὁ θεὸς λόγος ἀ., εὑρεθήσεται ὁ σταυρωθεὶς ἕτερος παρὰ τὸν θεὸν λόγον τὸν ἀ.* Procl.CP *Arm*.10(p.191.30; M.65.865B); *εἰ οὖν θεία φύσις ἦν ἐν τῷ πάσχοντι σώματι, ἄρα ἢ καὶ αὐτὴ οὐκ ἀ. μεμένηκεν, ἢ οὐδὲ ἡ σὰρξ ἀληθῶς πέπονθε* Leont.H.*Nest*.1.17(M.86.1464C); Eutychians *οὐ κατὰ φύσιν ἀ. ... τὸ σῶμα...ἀλλ' ἑνώσει πρὸς τὸν θεὸν λόγον γενόμενον* Leont.B.*Nest.et Eut*.2(M.86.1325B); *ib*.(1329C); monophysites, refuted by Thdt. in *eran*.3 against whose assertion that *διὰ τοῦ παθητοῦ τὸ ἀ. ὑπομείνῃ τὸ πάθος ib*.(4.176), he affirms orthodox doctrine *τοῦ παθητοῦ σώματος τὸ πάθος εἶναί φαμεν, τὴν ἀ. δὲ φύσιν ἐλευθέραν μεμενηκέναι τοῦ παθους ὁμολογοῦμεν ib*.(190), et passim; **5.** of sinless Christ as man *ἔοικεν ὁ παιδαγωγὸς ἡμῶν...τῷ πατρί...ἀναμάρτητος, ἀνεπίληπτος καὶ ἀ. τὴν ψυχήν* Clem.*paed*.1.2(p.91.23; M.8.252C).

C. of spiritual creatures; **1.** angels *ἰδίωμα ἀγγελικῆς φύσεως τὸ ἀ. τῆς οὐσίας...ἀ. δέ, τὸ ἀθάνατον* Anast.S.*hod*.2(M.89.64B); **2.** of Satan, acc. Manicheans *παθητὸς μὲν κατ' αὐτοὺς ὁ θεός, ἀ. δὲ ὁ σατανᾶς* Serap.*Man*.34(p.51; M.18.1129C); *ib*.30(p.46.14; 1117C); of Simon Magus *Σίμων θεὸς...ἀ. δὲ ἐκγεννητοῦ* Hipp.*haer*.6.18(p.144.7; M.16.3219D).

D. of man; **1.** *impassible*, *incapable of suffering*; **a.** in state of innocence *τοὺς ἀνθρώπους τοὺς καὶ θεῷ ὁμοίως ἀ.* Just.*dial*.124.4(M.6.765B); *ἀ. δὲ τὴν φύσιν· τοῦ γὰρ ἀ. μίμημα ἦν* Gr.Nyss.*or.catech*.6(p.36.6f.; M.45.29B); lost through Fall, *ib*.8(p.42.9; 33B); **b.** of Christ after Resurrection *πρῶτον παθητὸς καὶ τότε ἀ.* Ign.*Eph*.7.2; *μετὰ ταύτης* [sc. *σαρκός*] *ἔρχεται κρίνων τὴν οἰκουμένην, ἀ. αὐτὴν ἔχων* Chrys.*hom.11.2 in 2Cor*.(10.514E); of resurrection bodies of Christians *ἀναστήσει ἡμᾶς ὁ θεὸς...καὶ ἀ.... ποιήσει* Just.*dial*.46.7(M.6.576C); Meth.*res*.1.25(p.252.22; M.41.1129D); and of souls of blessed, Athenag.*leg*.31.3(M.6.961C); **c.** denied to men in this life *οὐ δύναται ἄρα ἀ. εἶναι ὁ ἄνθρωπος* Meth.*res*.1.47(p.297.2; M.41.1117C); Tit.Bost.*Man*.2.11(M.18.1153D); except with some qualification; so of apostles, who rejoiced in persecution *ὥσπερ ἀ. σῶμα ἐχόντων* Chrys.*hom.1.2. in 1Thess*.(11.428D); **2.** *without passion*, *calm*, *serene*, denoting a high stage of spiritual life (v. *ἀπάθεια*); **a.** as quality of certain types of Christians *τὸν γνωστικὸν σώφρονα καὶ ἀ.* Clem.*str*.7.11(p.49.4; M.9.493C); *ὁ ἅγιος...ἐν χερσὶ κυρίου μένων ἀ.* Or.*fr.30 in Jer*.27:33(p.214.17; M.13.597B); of the true philosopher, Gr.Naz.*or*.26.13(M.35.1245B); of monks *ἐν παθητοῖς σώμασι τὴν ἀ. βιοτὴν μελετῶντες* Thdt.*h.e*.4.28.1(3.1007); Evagr.*h.e*.1.21(p.31.3; M.86.2480B); of those who have to teach others, *Apophth.Patr*.(M.65.353D); **b.** acquired by following Christ *ὡς αὐτὸς ἀ. τυγχάνῃ, καὶ τοὺς δεξαμένους αὐτὸν ἀ. κατασκευάσῃ* Mac.Aeg.*ep*.(M.34.409C, 412A); Gr.Nyss.*hom.1 in Cant*.(M.44.764D); by prayer, Evagr.Pont.*or*.52(M.79.1177C); **c.** its effects: defeats demons, Just.*1apol*.58.3(M.6.416B); assimilates to God, Clem.*str*.4.23(p.313.15; M.8.1356D);

ἀπαθεὶς...προσεύξωνται καὶ ὑπὲρ τῶν ἐχθρῶν *ib.*7.14(p.60.29; M.9.517C); and procures inhabitation of Father and Son in soul, Proc. G.*Ex.*33:21(M.87.680B); ἀ. ... ὁ τὴν σάρκα μὲν ἄφθαρτον ποιήσας, τὸν δὲ νοῦν τῆς κτίσεως ἀνυψώσας Jo.Clim.*scal.*29(M.88.1148B); **d.** as epithet, of saints ὁ...ἀπαθέστατος...Γρηγόριος Pall.*h.Laus.*38(p.117.2; M.34.1188C); of θεωρία, Dion.Ar.*c.h.*2.4(M.3.144A); **e.** τὸ ἀ., of that part of soul in which contemplation takes place, Dion.Ar.*ep.*9.1(M.3.1108A); **3.** of a lower stage of spiritual life, *without sin* or *sinful passion* (cf. ἀπάθεια) ὁ δεδιὼς δὲ τὸ πτῶμα ἄφθαρτον ἑαυτὸν καὶ ἀ. εἶναι βούλεται Clem.*str.*2.8(p.134.13; M.8.976B); διὰ δὲ τῶν ἐκρυέντων ἐκ τῆς πλευρᾶς...ἀ. γενομένας τὰς οὐσίας Clem.*exc.Thdot.*61(p.127.10; M.9.688C); **4.** ? *making sinless*, of baptism ἀ. γὰρ ἡμῶν ἐστιν...τὸ χρῖσμα τοῦ Χριστοῦ καὶ ὡς σίδηρον ἐστόμωσεν τὸ ἅγιον βάπτισμα *M.Thdot.*3(p.133.16).

***ἀπαθητικός**, *making impassible* οὐ γὰρ ἁπλῶς ἀπαθὲς τὸ θεῖον ἴσμεν, ἀλλὰ καὶ ἀπαθηστικὸν [sic] τῶν οἷς προσγίνεται Leont.H.*Nest.*7.11(M.86.1768^{1}A).

***ἀπάθητος**, *impassible* ἀ. ὁ Χριστός †Ath.*fr.*(M.26.1237A).

***ἀπαθοποιός**, *making impassible*; of Christ, Leont.H.*Nest.*7.11 (M.86.1768^{1}A).

***ἀπαθρέω**, *see*, Cyr.*Jo.*10 proem.(4.826A).

***ἀπαθωόω**, *put away from one*, Anast.S.*qu.et resp.*62(M.89.649B).

ἀπαθῶς, **1.** *without injury* τὸ πῦρ ἀδύνατον ἀ. ἑνωθῆναι τῷ χόρτῳ Anast.S.*hod.*1(M.89.49C); **2.** *impassibly, without passion*; **a.** ref. God, Hipp.*haer.*7.21(p.196.21; M.16.3303B); Epiph.*haer.*76.31(p.380.3; M.42.577D); **b.** ref. generation of Son, freq.; [sc. ὁ θεός] ἀπαθὴς ὢν...ἀ. ... τοῦ υἱοῦ πατήρ ἐστι Ath.*Ar.*1.28(M.26.69A); γεγεννημένον ἀ. ἐκ τοῦ θεοῦ *Symb.Sirm.*3(p.235.27; M.26.692C); Chrys.*hom.23.2 in Eph.*(11.176A); Cyr.*thes.*4(5^{1}.25C); Sophr.H.*ep.syn.*(M.87.3152C); **c.** ref. Christ ἑνωθεὶς δὲ μᾶλλον τῇ καθ' ἡμᾶς ἀνθρωπότητι, πάθοι ἂν ἀ. σαρκὶ τῇ ἰδίᾳ τὰ ἀνθρώπινα Cyr.*Pulch.*31(p.50.9; 5^{2}.163E); heret.; acc. Basilides ἀ. ἀνεχώρησεν [sc. Christ] εἰς τὸν οὐρανόν Epiph.*haer.*24.3(p.260.15; M.41.312C); acc. monophysites ἀ. αὐτὸν πεπονθέναι φαμέν Thdt.*eran.*3(4.216); **3.** *dispassionately, calmly*, Eus.*l.C.*7 (p.214.28; M.20.1356B); ἀ. ἐπεσκόπουν τὴν τῶν ὄντων φύσιν Gr.Nyss.*or.catech.*7(p.39.15; M.45.32C); Pall.*v.Chrys.*20(p.144.18; M.47.80); of those who are perfectly detached in matter of food τὸ ἀ. ἐσθίειν Evagr.*h.e.*1.21(p.31.7; M.86.2480C).

ἀπαιδαγώγητος, **1.** *without direction* or *discipline* ἵνα μηδὲ τὸ λυποῦν ἀθεράπευτον ᾖ, μηδὲ τὸ εὐφραῖνον ἀ. Gr.Naz.*ep.*165(M.37.273C); of Israel ἡγουμένων δίχα...καὶ ἀπαιδαγώγητοι μενοῦσιν Cyr.*Os.*37(3.68D); id.*Is.*5.1(2.729D); **2.** *not calling for discipline, not to be controlled* τὸ δεῖπνον ἔστω λιτόν...οὐκ ἀ. οὐδὲ τοῦτο Clem.*paed.*2.1 (p.158.6; M.8.388B); **3.** *unrestrained, undisciplined* γνώμην ἀ. Chrys.*fr.Job* 2:5(M.64.549A) = Olymp.*Job* 2:5(M.93.41A); ἀ. ἔχοντας νοῦν Cyr.*Is.*4.3(2.649B); ὁ...Ἰωσήφ, οὐ τὸ τῆς νεότητος ἀνειμένον ἀ. ἔχων id.*ador.*14(1.516E).

***ἀπαιδαγωγήτως**, *ignorantly, without instruction*, Cyr.*Jo.*3.2(4.257C); *ib.*5(446C).

ἀπαιδοτρίβητος, *without training*, Nil.*Alb.*(M.79.701C).

ἀπαιθαλόω, *burn to ashes*, Bas.*hex.*3.7(1.29A; M.29.69A).

***ἀπαιθερόομαι**, *become ethereal*, Synes.*insomn.*6(p.155.4; M.66.1292B).

ἀπαίρω, *depart*; ref. death ἀ. ... πρὸς τὴν μακαρίαν...ζωήν Gr. Nyss.*v.Ephr.*(M.46.837C); Chrys.*sac.*6.4(p.148.9; 1.424D).

ἄπαις, *childless*; ref. Father οὐ γὰρ ἄ. ὢν πρὸ τούτου, πατὴρ γέγονεν, ὕστερον μεταβουλευσάμενος Cyr.H.*catech.*7.5.

ἀπαίτησις, ἡ, **1.** *demanding back*, hence *demand for compensation* τούτους τοῖς αὐτοῖς Χριστιανοῖς ἄνευ ἀργυρίου καὶ ἄνευ τινὸς ἀ. τῆς τιμῆς...ἀποκαταστήσωσι Eus.*h.e.*10.5.9(M.20.884A); **2.** in gen., *demand*; esp. **a.** for payment of a tax, Chrys.*hom.58.1 in Mt.* (7.585D); id.*hom.23.3 in Rom.*(9.688E); id.*stat.*3.6(2.45C); Synes.*ep.*79(M.66.1445A); **b.** moral, for almsgiving ἐνταῦθα τὰ διδόμενα ἀπαίτησίς ἐστιν, ἐκεῖ χρῆσις καὶ δάνειον καὶ ὄφλημα Chrys.*hom.66.5 in Mt.*(7.659E); **c.** logical, *demands, requirements* of a subject, Clem.*str.*4.1(p.248.4; M.8.1213C).

ἀπαιτητής, ὁ, *tax collector*, *A.Thom.*A 148(p.257.12); Bas.*ep.*85 (3.178B; M.32.465A); Gr.Nyss.*usur.*(M.46.437B).

***ἀπαιτιάομαι**, *accuse*, Cyr.*hom.pasch.*8(5^{2}.101A).

ἀπαιωρ-έω, **1.** act.; **a.** *hang...from* or *upon* σφαιρικὰ...σχήματα...τραχήλων ἀ. Clem.*paed.*3.3(p.247.1; M.8.580C); Eus.*Is.*14:24f.(M.24.196B); **b.** *hang up*, Jo.VI H.*v.Jo.D.*17(M.94.456D); **c.** (in idea) *suspend, regard as suspended* τὴν γῆν βαρυτέραν οὖσαν τοῦ ὕδατος ~οῦσι τοῦ μέσου τῶν ἐσχάτων ἀπάγοντες Bas.*hex.*3.5(1.26E; M.29.64B); **d.** fig., *keep suspended* or *in suspense*, Chrys.*hom.13.5 in 1Cor.*(10.116C); **e.** met., *make to depend upon* τὸν ἄνθρωπον τῆς γνώμης αὐτοῦ τὰ τῆς φύσεως ἀπῃώρησεν †Just.*fr.*(p.52; M.6.1596C); τὴν διάνοιαν...τῆς ἐκεῖθεν ~ει προνοίας Thdt.*Ps.*118:10(1.1440); ? for ἀφήρησας: τειρομένων ἐπίκουρον ~ησας ὀπωπήν †Apoll.*met.Ps.*9:22 (M.33.1324A); **2.** med., intrans.; *hang down from, hang*; met., *be dependent on, depend upon*, Eus.*p.e.*1.1(2B; M.21.24B); †Apoll.*met. Ps.*32:20(1356A).

***ἀπαιώρησις**, ἡ, *hanging down*, Clem.*paed.*2.10(p.225.3; M.8.533A).

ἀπακοντίζω, *hurl away* like a javelin; fig. τὸ...πνεῦμα φόβου...ἀφηκόντισεν [sc. Christ] Eus.*d.e.*10.2(p.456.5; M.22.733C).

ἀπακριβόω, **1.** *perfect, finish in detail*; a painting, Gr.Naz.*ep.*230(M.37.372D); virtue, Gennad.*fr.Rom.*7:14(p.372.3; M.85.1684B); **2.** *study minutely, ascertain precisely* Ἰώσηπος...τὰς...ἰουδαϊκὰς δευτερώσεις ἀπηκριβωκὼς Eus.*d.e.*6.18(p.281.3; M.22.461B); Geo.Pis.*hex.*544(M.92.1477B); **3.** pass.; **a.** *be fashioned exactly*, hence *correspond in detail, conform exactly* ἀπηκρίβωνται...αἱ ψυχαὶ τῷ γεννήσαντι Meth.*symp.*6.1(p.64.10; M.18.113A); **b.** perf. ptcpl. pass. with πρός: πάντα πρὸς ἐκείνην ἀπηκριβωμένον τὴν πρωτότυπον τοῦ πατρὸς καὶ μονογενῆ εἰκόνα Meth.*res.*1.35(p.274.4; M.41.1100B); ἐξουσίαν ἀ. πρὸς τὸν γεγεννηκότα Chrys.*hom.39.6 in 1Cor.*(10.371E); Cyr.*Jo.*1.2 (4.16A); *ib.*2.8(232E); **c.** perf. ptcpl. pass., *precisely determined*, hence *precise, exact*, Dion.Al.*ep.can.*(p.95.9; M.10.1273A); κατὰ τὸν ἀ. αὐτῷ χρόνον Eus.*h.e.*1.8.1(M.20.101A); Chrys.*hom.55.4 in Mt.*(7.560B) ∞ Isid.Pel.*epp.*3.166(M.78.860B); Chrys.*sac.*1.2(p.7.10; 1.364B).

***ἀπακρίβωσις**, ἡ, *accurate computation*, Max.*comput.*8(M.19.1225D).

***ἀπακροάομαι**, *hear*, *A.Thom.*A 150(p.260.1, v.l. ἠκροάσαντο, scribendum ἠκροάσατο?).

ἀπάλαιστρος, *untrained in the palaestra, unskilled in wrestling*, Iren.*haer.*5.13.2(M.7.1157A).

ἀπαλαίωτος, *not growing old*, Isid.Pel.*epp.*5.106(M.78.1388B); ‡Hesych.H.*m.Long.*15(M.93.1560A); Agap.*cap.*60(M.86.1181C).

***ἀπάλακτε**, ? f.l. for ἀπάλαλκε (ed., p. 31), Eudoc.*Cypr.*1.92(M.85.836C) or for ἀπάλλαττ' (metr. gr. for ἀπάλλαττ').

ἀπαλάομαι, *go astray, wander*, Meth.*Porph.*3(p.506.26; M.18.401B).

ἀπαλγέω, *cease to feel grief, become devoid of feeling* or *hardened*, in gen. παιδεύσεις δὲ αἱ ἀναγκαῖαι...τοὺς ἀπηλγηκότας ἐκβιάζονται μετανοεῖν Clem.*str.*7.2(p.10.5; M.9.416B); ψυχικὸν ἄνθρωπον τὸν ἀπηλγηκότα πρὸς τὴν ἀλήθειαν ἀτενίσαι Meth.*res.*1.58(p.321.22); *Const.App.*2.12.3; Chrys.*hom.40.3 in 1Cor.*(10.382B); exeg. Eph. 4:19 τὸ δὲ ἀπηλγηκότες ὥσπερ τῶν ἀπὸ πάθους τινὸς μέρη πολλάκις τοῦ σώματος νενεκρωμένων, οἷς...ἄλγος οὐδὲν ἐκεῖθεν ἐγγίνεται Thdr. Mops.ad loc.(p.172.20; M.66.920B); of a religious sect in India τῶν τε αἰσχροποιῶν, τῶν τε ἀπηλγημένων Epiph.*exp.fid.*10(p.509.28; M.42.797C).

***ἀπαλειπτικός**, *wiping away*, Meth.*Porph.*4(p.507.8; M.18.345A).

ἀπαλείφω, **1.** lit., *wipe, sponge* τοὺς ὀφθαλμοὺς καὶ τὸ πρόσωπον *M.Cyriac.*2(M.10.556A); **2.** *wipe off, expunge*; **a.** esp. from a record or register; **b.** met., sin δρόσῳ πνεύματος ἀ. τὰ προημαρτημένα Clem.*q.d.s.*40(p.186.11; M.9.645A); Hipp.*Dan.*4.32.5(M.10.652B); εἰ μὲν ἦν ἡ ἁμαρτία μου γεγραμμένη μέλανι, ἀπήλειψα ⟨ἂν⟩ αὐτήν Or.*hom.16.10 in Jer.*(p.142.10; M.13.452B); **3.** *wipe out, destroy*, Ath.*Ar.*1.10 (M.26.32B); id.*syn.*4(p.233.29; M.26.688B); θάνατον id.*inc.*10.1(M.25.112D); persons τοὺς...τῆς βάαλ προφήτας id.*fug.*20(p.82.7; M.25.669C); ἀ. τῆς γῆς τὸν ἀσθενῆ Cyr.*Am.*73(3.332C); τοῦ δημιουργοῦ μὲν ἔπλαττον χεῖρες, βασιλέως δὲ χεῖρες τοῖς ὕδασι τὴν πλάσιν ἀπήλειφον Bas.Sel.*or.*9.1(M.85.129A).

ἀπαλέξησις, ἡ, *defence against*, Clem.*paed.*2.10(p.220.24; M.8.524B).

***ἀπαλλαγ-έω**, s.v.l., *leave off, take a rest from* κυβερνᾶν ~ήσασαι τὰ σφέτερα σκάφη Meth.*symp.*4.2(p.47.4, v.l. ~εῖσαι M.18.88C).

ἀπαλλακτιάω, *wish to be rid of*, Diod.*Ps.*56:3(M.33.1594C); Cyr.*ador.*1(1.44B); id.*glaph.Ex.*2(1.302B).

ἀπαλλάσσ-ω, **1.** *turn out, make* τεχνίτης...~ων...σκεύη Ephr.1 70F; **2.** pass., *recover* from leprosy, Cyr.*Is.*5.6(2.892A).

ἀπαλλότριος, *alienated*, superl., Or.*sel.in Ezech.*8:3(M.13.796D).

ἀπαλλοτρι-όω, *estrange, alienate*; met., *disown* οἱ ἀπόστολοι ...~οῦσι τὴν τοῦ Ἐβίωνος πίστιν Epiph.*haer.*30.24(p.366.4; M.41.445D); *separate, sever*, theol.; **a.** not applicable to relation of Persons in Trin. μήτε ἀπηλλοτρίωται πατὴρ υἱοῦ ἢ πατὴρ Dion.Al. ap.Ath.*Dion.*17(p.58.19; M.25.504C); τοὺς...χωρίζοντας τὸν υἱόν, καὶ ~οῦντας τὸν λόγον ἀπὸ τοῦ πατρὸς χωρίζεσθαι τῆς καθολικῆς ἐκκλησίας προσήκει CSard.*ep.cath.*ap.Ath.*apol.sec.*47(p.123.14; M.25.336B); πᾶσαν τὴν τοῦ υἱοῦ κρίσιν τοῦ πατρικοῦ μὴ ἀπηλλοτριῶσθαι βουλήματος Gr.Nyss.*tres dii*(M.45.128B); **b.** nor to attributes common to Father and Son οὐ διακόπτοντες ἡμεῖς τῆς θεότητος τὴν κυριότητα λέγομεν οὐδ' ~οῦντες θατέρου θάτερον Apoll.*fid.sec.pt.*17(p.172.25; M.10.1112A); c. of relation of God to flesh ὅσῳ...τῆς γεώδους σαρκὸς ὁ...θεὸς...ἀπηλλοτρίωται καὶ ἀπεσχοίνισται τῇ φύσει τοσούτῳ χρὴ νοεῖν καὶ τῆς τῶν σαρκῶν γενέσεως ἀπηλλοτριῶσθαι τὸν τρόπον, καθ' ὃν ὁ πατὴρ ἐγέννα τὸν υἱόν Eus.*e.th.*1.12(p.72.13f.; M.24.848D, 849A); cf. τὴν σάρκα...~οῖς τῆς τοῦ θεοῦ δημιουργίας *Disp.Phot.* 3(M.88.545D); as result of Fall, Sever.*Eph.*1:10(p.306.3) cit. s. ἀνακεφαλαιόω.

ἀπαλλοτρίωσις, ἡ, *alienation of oneself, dissociation* οἱ μὲν διὰ τὴν οἰκείωσιν [sc. πρὸς τὰς ἐντολάς], οἱ δὲ διὰ τὴν ἀ. τὴν ἐκ προαιρέσεως Clem.*str.*4.13(p.289.24; M.8.1301A); ἡ...ἀ. τῶν πρὸς τὴν ὀλεθρίαν ἡδονὴν φερόντων Bas.*reg.fus.*19.1(2.362B; M.31.968A); Thdt.*Jer.* 13:25ff.(2.483).

ἀπαλοιφή, ἡ, *expunging,* Nil.*Eulog.*23(M.79.1124C).

***ἀπαλόστρακος,** *soft-shelled,* Nemes.*nat.hom.*1(M.40.520A); *ib.*2 (544A).

ἀπαλότης, ἡ, *softness, tenderness;* met., in good sense ἡ ἐν ἀνθρώποις ἀ. ...τῆς διανοίας Clem.*paed.*1.5(p.98.9; M.8.265A); of the heart, Or.*comm.in Ex.*(p.244.18; M.12.273B); of moral *weakness* μαλακτικὸν τῆς ψυχῆς εἰς ἀ. ‡Chrys.*pasch.*2(8².255A).

ἀπαλόφρων, *tender-hearted,* Clem.*paed.*1.5(p.101.7; M.8.272A).

ἀπαλύν-ω, *soften,* met. ὕδωρ ἔλαιον ~ει †Hipp.*theoph.*1(p.257.17; M.10.852B); Gr.Nyss.*hom.7 in Cant.*(M.44.925C); fig. ἐὰν ἡ καρδία σου ~θῃ Esaias *or.*18.2(p.112); Jo.Clim.*scal.*20(M.88.940D).

***ἀπάλωσις, ἡ,** *softening,* ‡Ath.*sem.*3(M.28.148B).

ἀπαμαυρόω, *darken, dull,* met. τοῦ νοῦ τὸ φαιδρὸν ἀ. Ephr.3.522B; τούτου τὴν διάνοιαν ἀ. ‡Sophr.H.*v.m.Cyr.et Jo.*9(M.87.3684A).

***ἀπαμφιάσκω,** *reveal,* ‡Nil.*perist.*9.9(M.79.881D).

ἀπαμφιέννυ-μι, 1. *strip off clothes,* fig. ~μεθα...ἐν τῷ...βαπτίσματι Cyr.*glaph.Dt.*(1.418C); met., *strip, deprive* ὅταν...ἀπαμφιέσω μὲν αὐτὴν τῆς...ἐπικουρίας id.*Os.*18(3.40C); σατανᾶν...τὸν ἁπάσης εὐσεβείας τὸν ἐν αὐτοῖς ~ντα νοῦν *ib.*70(106C); id.*Jo.*5.5(4.520D); κόσμου καὶ δόξης...λοιπὸν ἀπημφιεσμένους, τοὺς οὐκ ἔχοντας τὸν Ἐμμανουήλ id.*glaph.Ex.*3(1.339A); φροντίδος...καὶ φειδοῦς τῆς ἄνωθεν ~μενοι id.*ador.*1(M.68.156B; ἐπαμφιεννύμενοι 1.14E); Christol. οἱ σαρκὸς...~ντες τὸν λόγον id.*inc.unigen.*(5¹.690E); *ib.*(713D); **2.** *lay bare, reveal,* met. ἀ. τὴν ὀργήν Cyr.*glaph.Ex.*1(1.246C); pass., id. *ador.*12(1.431B); ptcpl., *undisguised* τὴν τελευτείαν φωνήν, γυμνήν τε καὶ ἀπημφιεσμένην ποιεῖσθαι *ib.*5(150A).

ἀπαμφίζω, *divest,* Jo.D.*imag.*1.21(M.94.1252C).

***ἀπαναδύομαι,** *rise again to one's feet,* ‡Nil.*perist.*1.1(M.79.812A).

ἀπαναισχυντέω, 1. *behave shamelessly, with effrontery;* in good sense, *put away shame;* of Syrophenician woman, Chrys.*hom.52.2 in Mt.*(7.531B); **2.** *render shameless* or *brazen,* Chrys.*hom.23.1 in 1Cor.*(10.200D); *ib.11.3*(90B); id.*hom.31.2 in Heb.*(12.287A).

ἀπαναχωρ-έω, *withdraw, retire completely, sever oneself from,* Or.ap.*cat.Jo.*13:10(p.338.22); τῆς ἁμαρτίας ~ῆσαι v.l. for ὑπαναχωρῆσαι *cat.Mt.*21:28(p.173.22); *come off* duty τῆς νυκτερινῆς φυλακῆς ~οῦντί μοι...ἀστὴρ...κατεφαίνετο Sophr.H.*v.Anast.*(M.92.1728B).

ἀπανδρ-όω, 1. act., *treat as mature* (ref. Gal.4:1ff.) ὡμολόγησεν εἶναι νηπίους τοὺς ὑπὸ φόβον...τοὺς δὲ ὑπὸ τὴν πίστιν...ἀπήνδρωσεν Clem.*paed.*1.6(p.110.16; M.8.289D); **2.** pass., *be brought to maturity,* met. νήπιοι...καὶ οἱ φιλόσοφοι, ἐὰν μὴ ὑπὸ τοῦ Χριστοῦ ~ωθῶσιν Clem.*str.*1.11(p.34.23; M.8.752A); **3.** pass., of females, *become male, be made male,* Clem.*exc.Thdot.*21.3(p.113.25; M.9.668C).

ἀπανθρωπία, ἡ, *inhumanity* συμβουλεύομεν τοῖς πτωχοῖς διὰ τὴν ὑμετέραν [sc. the rich] ἀ. Bas.*hom.in Ps.*14(1.112D; M.29.277B); Thdr.Mops.*1Tim.*5:10(p.161.25); Cyr.*hom.pasch.*5.6(5².55B); id.*Os.* 147(3.180C); Dion.Ar.*ep.*8.4(M.3.1093C,D); freq. with ὠμότης, Chrys. *hom.64.2 in Gen.*(4.611A) al.; Isid.Pel.*epp.*5.510(M.78.1620A) al.; Cyr. *Abac.*20(3.534C) al.; opp. φιλανθρωπία, Chrys.*hom.4.1 in Ac.princ.* (3.82A); id.*hom.in Mt.7:14*(3.27D); characteristic of pagan society εἰς κοινὸν τῶν ἐθνῶν τῆς ἀ. θέαμα *Ep.Lugd.*ap.Eus.*h.e.*5.1.37(M.20.421C) and religion μέρος εὐσεβείας αὐτοῖς ἡ ἀ. Gr.Naz.*or.*14.29(M.35.897A); τῆς...τῶν Ἑλληνικῶν θεῶν θηριώδους ἀ. ‡Just.*qu.et resp.*99 (M.6.1344A); and of certain heretical sects τὴν εἰς πτωχοὺς ἀ. εἰσάγουσι [sc. Messalians] Jo.D.*haer.*80(M.94.732C).

***ἀπανθρωπότης, ἡ,** = ἀπανθρωπία, *inhumanity,* Chrys.ap.*cat. Mt.*6:5(p.43.3) cf. ἀπανθρωπίας Chrys.*hom.19.1 in Mt.*(7.245D).

ἀπανθρώπως, *inhumanly* τὸν...φιλανθρώπως κατηχοῦντα ἀποσφάττειν ἀ. Clem.*prot.*10(p.75.2; M.8.220C); τοὺς ὠμῶς καὶ ἀ. ἡγουμένους καὶ μὴ κιρνῶντας τῇ καθαρότητι τὴν φιλανθρωπίαν Isid.Pel. *epp.*2.25(M.78.473B); Cyr.*Os.*123(3.155C).

ἀπανούργευτος, *guileless,* ‡Chrys.*hom.*13(13.253B); Const.Diac. *laud.*28(M.88.512B); Jo.Eub.*concept.BMV* 6(M.96.1468B).

ἀπανουργεύτως, for ἀπανουργήτως, CTrull.*can.*23(H.3.1669D).

***ἀπανουργήτως,** *without guile, without corruption,* CTrull.*can.*23 cit. s. χάρις.

ἀπάνουργος, *guileless;* of persons, Iren.*haer.*1.9.4(M.7.545A); Eus. *d.e.*3.5(p.128.20; M.22.217C); Cyr.*Abac.*7(3.523A); of thoughts and expression: διδασκαλία Eus.*d.e.*1.1(p.5.19; M.22.20B); λόγος *Hom. Clem.*1.11; ἁπλοῦν...τὸν λόγον τῆς ἀληθείας, τοῦτ' ἔστιν ἀ. Anast.S. *hod.*21(M.89.281D); νοῦς Cyr.*Jon.*26(3.387E); διανοίαις...ἀπανουργότερον ἐχούσαις τὸ κίνημα id.*Jo.*1(4.7B); of the quality of simplicity, Horm.*ep.Epiph.*(p.57.26; M.*PL.*63.518C).

ἀπανούργως, *guilelessly, Hom.Clem.*1.10; *cat.2Cor.*4:2(p.372.23).

***ἀπανταχόσε,** *to every place, everywhere,* Vict.*Mc.*6:7(p.322.24); Cyr.*Lc.*6:27(M.72.593C); *ib.*9:3(641C).

ἀπαντ-άω, 1. *meet, encounter,* by chance or design; **2.** with hospitality, ***entertain*** ἐὰν παραβάλλῃ σοι ὁ μοναχὸς ἢ κοσμικός, μὴ θέλε ~ᾶν αὐτῷ ὑπὲρ δύναμιν...ἀλλὰ παράθες ὃ ἐὰν ὁ κύριος εὐοδοῖ σε Ephr.1.309F; **3.** abs., *arrive,* Chrys.*ep.*13(3.593E); Hier.*v.Paul.*B (p.29.15); **4.** ἀ. πρὸς *meet* a liability, *PLond.*1915.21; **5.** of things; *present itself as an obligation, be in one's line* of duty οὐκ ~ᾷ με *I do not feel called on;* οὐ δύναμαι τόδε ποιῆσαι, βλάπτομαι· οὐκ ~ᾷ με Dor.*doct.*4.11(M.88.1673B); c. dat. οὐκ ~ᾷ τοῦτο ἡμῖν δοῦναι, οὐδὲ παρέχομεν Jo.Mosch.*prat.*85(M.87.2941C).

ἀπαντή, ἡ, *meeting, encounter,* Jo.Clim.*scal.*22(M.88.952C); of the feast of the Purification εἰς τὴν ἀ. τοῦ κυρίου Sophr.H.*carm.*4 tit. (M.87.3749B); ἐν τῇ ἀ. τοῦ Συμεὼν Anast.S.*hod.*10(M.89.176A).

ἀπάντησις, ἡ, 1. *meeting;* of the feast of the Purification τὴν ἁγίαν ἀ. τοῦ σωτῆρος ἡμῶν *Chron.Pasch.*p.11(M.92.89A); *assembly* for worship ἐὰν γένηται ἀ. ἐν σαββάτῳ ἢ ἐν κυριακῇ *Apophth.Patr.* (M.65.392C); **2.** *meeting in argument; answering a summons, appearance in court* οἱ τὴν ἐπὶ ταῖς ἀ. αἰσχύνην μὴ φέροντες Bas.*mor.*5.6(3.496D; M.32.1177C); but ἀπαιτήσεσιν id.*hom.in Ps.*14(1.112C; M.29.277B).

***ἀπαντιπρόσωπον,** *face to face with,* Clem.*str.*7.7(p.33.2; M.9.461A, cf. ἀντιπρόσωπος).

ἀπάνωθεν, *from the beginning,* Meth.*symp.*1.5(p.14.15; M.18.45D).

ἀπαξι-όω, *deem unworthy;* hence *disdain;* or simply *refuse* περὶ ὧν δαιμόνων αὐτὸς ~ῶν λέγειν τοῖς περὶ αὐτῶν εἰρηκόσιν προσέχειν ἀξιοῖ Athenag.*leg.*23.2(M.6.944A).

ἀπαράβατος, 1. *unalterable,* Hipp.*Dan.*1.10.5(M.10.669C) cit. s. ἀμετάθετος; ὅρκῳ...ἐβεβαίωσε τὰς ἐπαγγελίας διὰ τὸ ἀ., ὅτι πάντως ἔσται Or.*schol.in Lc.*1:46(M.17.324B); **2.** *inviolable, not to be transgressed* χρὴ γὰρ ἀ. μένειν ἀεὶ τὴν...παράδοσιν Bas.*Spir.*28(3.23D; M.32.117A); τεταγμένου τε καὶ ἀ. ῥυθμοῦ Gr.Nyss.*Pss.titt.*A 3(M.44.440D); Didym.*Trin.*3.2(M.39.805B); **3.** *eternal,* exeg. Heb.7:24 εἰ γὰρ ὁ ἱερεὺς ἀ. ἐστιν, πάντως καὶ ἡ σκηνὴ ἔνθα ἱερουργεῖ ἀ. ἐστιν, τουτέστιν ἀδιάδοχος Cosm.Ind.*top.*7(M.88.345A); **4.** *infallible;* of a remedy, Procl.CP *or.*6.4(M.65.728A).

ἀπαραβάτως, 1. *immutably,* Gr.Nyss.*fat.*(M.45.149B); *inevitably,* Marc.Er.*opusc.*1.118(M.65.920C); Jo.D.*imag.*1.11(M.94.1241A); **2.** *without transgressing,* Clem.*str.*2.6(p.127.22; M.8.961C); *ib.*2.21 (p.183.5; 1076A); *without mistake, correctly,* Didym.*Trin.*2.7(M.39.597C).

***ἀπαράβλαπτος,** *uninjured, unimpaired,* Leont.H.*Nest.*1.1(M.86.1408C).

ἀπαράβλητος, 1. *not to be thrown* to, ref. Mt.7:6 χοίρους...τοὺς ἀσεβείᾳ καὶ ἡδοναῖς συζῶντας, οἷς καὶ ἀ. καὶ ἀπόκρυφα τὰ...ἀποστολικὰ...κηρύγματα δεῖ εἶναι Meth.*creat.*1(p.493.10; M.18.332A); **2.** *not comparable, admitting no comparison;* of the world opp. God μὴ ἔχων τὸ ἀ. καὶ ἀνυπέρβλητον *Hom.Clem.*10.20; of things diametrically opposed ἄλλοις...μυρίοις ἀ. διενηνοχότων Leont.H.*Nest.* 4.33(M.86.1700B); **3.** *incomparable, surpassing* ὁ δὲ παράδεισος... δῆλον ὡς ἀ. ὑπεροχῇ τῆς ὑφ' ἡλίῳ πάσης ἐν πᾶσι τὸ κρεῖττον φέρει Philost.*h.e.*3.11(M.65.500B); Isid.Pel.*epp.*3.123(M.78.825A); τὴν ἀ. ὀρθοδοξίαν τοῦ...Διονυσίου Max.*schol.e.h.*4.3.10(M.4.157A); **4.** theol., in senses 2 and 3 sts. combined, of divine essence ἀγέννητον οὖν τὸ ἀληθινόν· διὸ καὶ ὡς ἀ. ὄν, ἀληθινὸν λέγεται †Diad.*Ar.*2(M.65.1152D); ὥστε κοινωνοὺς ἀνθρώπους...τῆς ἀ. ἐκείνης...γενέσθαι δύνασθαι φύσεως *ib.*6(1161A); with ἀσύγκριτος: ἀσύγκριτον...πρᾶγμα θεότητος καὶ ἀ. Cyr.*thes.*20(5¹.205C); Leont.H.*Nest.*1.10(M.86.1437D); ref. Mt.17:2 τί συγκρίνεις τὰ ὄντως ἀσύγκριτα; τί παρατιθεὶς καὶ παραβάλλεις τὰ ὄντως ἀ.; Jo.D.*hom.*1.13(M.96.565A); not applicable to relations of Father and Son οὐκ ἐξοχώτερος τοῦ υἱοῦ, οὐδὲ ἀ. πρὸς αὐτόν Didym. *Trin.*3.2(M.39.793A); of divine attributes ἵνα...τὰ ἀ. παραβολικῶς πως παραδειχθείη *ib.*1.15(308A); e.g. μεγαλειότης Or.*sel.in Ps.*4:9f.

(M.12.1168B); ἡμερότης Diod.Ps.93:7(M.33.1627A); Cyr.Is.4.3(2.643E); id.Ps.35:7(M.69.920A); ἀγάπη id.Is.4.4(2.674A); δόξα ib.4.1(568B); of Christ, id.glaph.Gen.7(1.238E); τὴν ἀ. δόξαν τοῦ πάντων ἐπέκεινα id.Lc.8:26f.(M.72.633D); id.hom.pasch.15.3(5^{2}.203C); δύναμις Proc.G.Is.64:4(M.87.2681A).

***ἀπαραβλήτως**, *incomparably, beyond compare*, Hom.Clem.2.40; λαμπρότητι...ἀ. ἀμείνων ἡλίου φύσις Cyr.ador.6(1.214A); of God ἀ. τὴν ὑπεροχὴν ἔχει Hom.Clem.10.19; τοῦ ἐν ἡμῖν βλεπτικοῦ πνεύματος ἀ. λαμπρότερος ὢν τὸ σῶμα ib.17.7.

***ἀπαράγραπτος**, *unexceptionable* τὸ...τῆς θεοειδοῦς ἀρετῆς ἀ. εὖ μεμιμημένον ἄγαλμα Dion.Ar.e.h.4.3.1(M.3.473B); of persons, Olymp.Job 42:18(M.93.468C); μάρτυρα τῆς ἀληθείας σου ἀ. ἀνέδειξας Thdr.Stud.epp.2.5(M.99.1124C); neut. as subst., *unimpeachability* τὸ...ἀ. καὶ γνήσιον τῆς ἀληθείας Jo.VI CP ep.(M.96.1428D).

***ἀπαραδέκτως**, *without receiving* or *admitting*; ἀ. ἔχειν *be unfavourably disposed* ἀ. πρὸς τὸ κήρυγμα ἔχουσι τοῦ εὐαγγελίου Isid.Pel.epp.1.139(M.78.273C); ἀ. ἔχοντα καὶ ἀπίστως Niceph.Ur.v.Sym.211(M.86.3180C).

ἀπαράθετος, **1.** *not to be compared, not comparable* τὸ τοῦ ζῴου σῶμα ἀ. συγκρίσει κρεῖττον εἶναι τοῦ ἔξωθεν αὐτῷ περικειμένου ἐνδύματος Eus.Lc.12:22(M.24.556C); Bas.Eun.1.26(1.237A; M.29.569A); **2.** *incomparable, surpassing*; of Max. ἀνὴρ...ἔχων...ἄθλησιν γενναίαν καὶ ἀ. V.Max.1(M.90.68A); **3.** of what pertains to God, perh. in both senses; of Solomon's wisdom as a type of Christ ἀσύγκριτος καὶ ἀ. Gr.Nyss.hom.1 in Cant.(M.44.765C); ref. Cant.1:3 interpreted of divine attributes τῶν οὐρανίων μύρων ἡ ὀσμὴ...ἀ. ἔχει τὴν χάριν πρὸς ταῦτα τὰ ἀρώματα τὰ παρ' ἡμῶν γινωσκόμενα ib.(781C); of divine mercy, M.Tar.11(p.475); neut. as subst. τὸ τοῦ παντοκράτορος θεοῦ ἀ. ‡Ign.Trall.5.

ἀπαράθραυστος, *that cannot be broken*; met., *indestructible, inviolate, invincible* τὴν...ἐκ θεοῦ συνεργίαν ἄμαχον εἶναι καὶ ἀ. Eus.v.C.1.27(M.20.941B; ἀήττητα p.20.12); ἡ...εἰς θεὸν ἀγάπη τὸ γνήσιον ...καὶ τὸ ἀ. Cyr.Am.73(3.334B conj. A.; l. ἀπαράφθορον); ἣν εἰ μή τις ἀκεραίαν καὶ ἀ. συντηρήσειεν...ἀπολεῖται ‡Ath.symb.2(M.28.1585A); ἔχειν...τὰς κατ' ἀρετὴν ἐν ψυχαῖς ἀπαραφθάρτους [v.l. ἀπαραθραύστους] εἰκόνας Dion.Ar.e.h.4.3.1(M.3.473B); 'εὐλογητὸς ὁ θεός' λέγων ὡς ταπεινότητος σύμβολον καὶ ἱκετηρίας ἀ. Thdr.Stud.praesanct.(M.99.1688C).

ἀπαραιτήτως, **1.** *inevitably*, Cyr.Jo.4.1(4.339A); **2.** *incontrovertibly*, Pers.(p.28.7).

***ἀπαρακλητικός**, *without comfort, comfortless* ἡ τῶν τόπων ἡμῶν ἀναχώρησις ἔστω, εἰς τὰ ἀπαρακλητικώτερα...καὶ ταπεινότερα μέρη Jo.Clim.scal.3(M.88.668B).

ἀπαράκλητος, **1.** *without consolation, comfortless*; **a.** subjectively, *unconsoled, inconsolable* καταυλισθήσῃ...ἐν ἐρήμοις...πλὴν ἀπαράκλητον οὐκ ἐᾷ παντελῶς Cyr.Mich.43(3.432B); κατὰ δύο τρόπους συλᾶν τὸν ἄνθρωπον...ἢ ἀπὸ ὀδύνης καρδίας ἀ., ἢ ἀπὸ ἐφέσεως ἀλογίστου Thdr.Stud.epp.2.153(M.99.1476B); **b.** objectively, *without consolation, not admitting consolation* ταῖς...ἀ. βαλλόμεθα συμφοραῖς Cyr.Is.4.5(2.720C); εἰ μὲν οὖν ἀ. ὑμῖν ὁ λόγος ἠπείλησε τὴν ἀποδημίαν καὶ διηνεκῆ τὴν ἀπόλειψιν Cyr.Jo.10(4.841B); Thdr.Stud.epp.2.145(M.99.1456A); **c.** of surroundings etc., *cheerless, dreary* φοβερὸς ὁ τόπος καὶ ἀ. Pall.h.Laus.39(p.124.13; M.34.1195C); σκληρᾶς...καὶ ἀ. ... βρώσεως †Jo.D.B.J.38(M.96.1221C); **2.** *not to be persuaded, inexorable*, Jo.Mosch.prat.50(M.87.2905B); **3.** s.v.l., *undisputed* ἐν ἀ. ὑπεροχαῖς πρὸς τὸν Μωυσέως νόμον ὄντα Χριστόν Cyr.ap.cat.Lc.5:12ff.(p.43.29), but prob. f.l. for ἀπαραβλήτοις id.Lc.5:14(M.72.557A).

***ἀπαρακολουθησία**, ἡ, *inability to follow*; esp. *inability to follow with the mind, stupidity* οὐχ οὕτω...χρηστέον τῇ σαρκί, ὥστε...εἰς ...ἀ. τὸν νοῦν...ἐκβιάσασθαι †Bas.Is.32(1.406D; M.30.185A); διὰ τῆς ἰδίας ἀπειρίας καὶ ἀ. Epiph.haer.59.3(p.367.1; M.41.1021C); κατὰ ἰδιωτείαν ἢ κατὰ ἀ. ib.77.18(p.432.32; παρακολουθησίαν M.42.668C).

ἀπαρακολούθητος, *unable to follow with the mind*; either through being *not in full possession of one's faculties* or through being *stupid* οὐκ ἐκστατικοῦ ἀνδρὸς οὐδὲ ἀ., ἀλλὰ ἐρρωμένην ἔχοντος τὴν διάνοιαν Epiph.haer.48.6(p.228.7; M.41.864D); ib.51.4(p.252.18; 893B).

ἀπαρακολουθήτως, *not in full possession of one's faculties* κἂν μὴ τέλεον ἐξιστώμεθα καὶ ἀ. ἔχωμεν ἑαυτοῖς, ἀλλὰ δοκῶμεν παρακολουθεῖν οἷς λέγομεν Or.Jo.28.20(15; p.414.23; M.14.724A).

***ἀπαρακόμιστος**, *not carried away*; met., *unwavering, constant* πίστιν Cyr.ep.18(p.113.30; 5^{2}.79B).

***ἀπαρακράτητα**, neut. plur. as adv., *without anyone preventing* οὕτως ἀ. διὰ τῶν κήπων ἐξῆλθεν Thphn.chron.p.268(M.108.665C, conj. for παρακράτητα).

ἀπαραλείπτως, **1.** *without intermission*; hence *without exception* καταριθμήσεις δ' ἂν ἀ. ἕκαστα τῶν ἡμᾶς μὲν λανθανόντων Eus.l.C.18(p.259.19; M.20.1440A); ὥστε...τῇ ἐκκλησίᾳ πάντα ἀ. ἀποσωθῆναι Gr.Naz.test.(M.37.389C); Jo.D.dialect.10(M.94.564A); τὰ μιᾶς οὐσίας, τὰς αὐτὰς ἀ. ἕξει διαφοράς id.Jacob.60(M.94.1468B); **2.** *flawlessly, perfectly completely*, Or.Jo.6.40(24; p.150.2; M.14.269C); τὸ μὲν ὕδωρ ἔξωθεν περιχεῖται, τὸ δὲ πνεῦμα καὶ τὴν ἔνδοθεν ψυχὴν βαπτίζει ἀ. Cyr.H.catech.17.14; ἀ. ἁγναὶ καὶ καθαραὶ ψυχῇ τε καὶ σώματι Sergia Olymp.13(p.50.28); διὰ τοῦ 'σεσαρκωμένην' εἰπεῖν τῆς καθ' ἡμᾶς οὐσίας ἐντελῶς ἐν αὐτῷ Χριστῷ...καὶ ἀ. ... σημαίνειν CLater.can.5(H.3.921E).

***ἀπαράληπτος**, **1.** *impregnable*, Jo.Mal.chron.5 p.109(M.97.200B); **2.** = ἀπαράλειπτος, *complete*, CLater.act.4(H.3.808D).

ἀπαράλλακτος, **I.** *invariable, unchanging*; of pronouncements etc., Cels.ap.Or.Cels.7.3(p.154.24; M.11.1424B); ἀποφάσεις ἀ. ... τοῦ θεοῦ Meth.symp.3.2(p.29.7; M.18.64A); id.res.1.45(p.294.11; M.41.1116B); τὴν ἀ. ... τοῦ...θεοῦ πίστιν Ephr.2.233A; ἀ. καὶ ἀμώμητον πίστιν ‡Felix III Papa ep.Zen.imp.(p.24.8; H.2.828B); essential to form τὸ ἀ. ἡ μορφὴ δείκνυσι, καθὼς ἐστι μορφή Chrys.hom.6.3 in Phil.(11.238D); of Gnostic aeon τῆς ἀγεννήτου καὶ ἀ. ... δυνάμεως Hipp.haer.6.12(p.138.19; M.16.3211C) = ib.10.12(p.273.18; 3426C); ib.6.14,17(pp.140.6,144.3; 3214D,3219C); of God θεός ἐστιν ἀΐδιος οὐσία καὶ ἀ. Jo.D.f.o.1.13(M.94.856C); of Christ ἡ τῶν ἱερῶν συμβόλων παράδοσις...ἀ. εἰδυῖα καὶ διαγραφοῦσα τὸν Χριστόν Dion.Ar.e.h.4.3.10(M.3.484A); in metaphysical sense connected with ἀπαθής, Aët.ap.Epiph.haer.76.39(p.392.14; M.42.600C); id.ib.76.52(p.406.8; M.42.624D); Epiph.haer.76.39(p.392.26; M.42.601A) cit. s. ἀπαθής; ib.(p.393.30; 601D).

II. in relation to something else, *in no way varying* or *differing*; **A.** in gen.; **1.** *precisely similar, identical* (i.e. of different things) ὡς...τὸ παρηλλαγμένον ἀνάρμοστον, οὕτω τὸ...ὁμολογεῖται τὸ εὐάρμοστον ἀ. πάντως Gr.Nyss.Eun.4(2 p.95.6; M.45.672B); εἶδες πῶς ἀ. αὐτῷ μαρτυρεῖ σπουδήν Chrys.stat.1.3(2.5B); τῆς ἐκθέσμου πολιτείας τὸ ἀ. Philost.h.e.8.4(M.65.560A); τῆς κατὰ φύσιν ταυτότητος ἐν ἀ. τοῖς ἰδιώμασιν Cyr.Jo.2.8(4.230A); esp. with εἰκών: ὁ γονεὺς υἱὸν...ἐσχηκώς, οὐκ ἔξωθεν οὐδὲ ἀλλότριον, ἀλλ' ἐξ ἑαυτοῦ καὶ ἴδιον τῆς οὐσίας καὶ ἀ. ἔσχεν εἰκόνα Ath.Ar.1.26(M.26.65B); τὴν...εἰκόνα, καθό ἐστιν εἰκὼν...ἀ. δεῖ εἶναι Chrys.hom.3.1 in Col.(11.343D); **2.** from neg. point of view, c. genit., *indistinguishable from* ἄλλος γάρ τις ἀ. Παύλου ἐν τοῖς οὖσιν οὐκ ἐστί Or.or.24(p.354.2; M.11.492B); **3.** from positive point of view ἑξῆς...διακόσμησιν πάντ' ἀ. ἔχουσαν ὡς πρὸς τὴν προτέραν διακόσμησιν Or.Cels.5.20(pp.21.24,22.16; 1212A,B); c. dat., *exactly like* ἀ. τις τῷ Σωκράτει, γαμήσων ἀ. τῇ Ξανθίππῃ καὶ κατηγορηθησόμενος ὑπὸ ἀ. Ἀνύτῳ καὶ Μελήτῳ ib.4.68(p.338.12; M.11.1137A); ib.5.20(p.22.9f.; 1212B); ib.4.12(p.282.14; 1041B); ἀ. τῷ ...γραφέντι...τὸ...χρησμῳδηθέν Didym.Trin.1.15(M.39.317B); **4.** with ὁμοιότης *exact, perfect*; of a representation, Athenag.leg.17.2(M.6.924A); ἀ. γάρ ἐστιν ἡ ἐν τῇ εἰκόνι τοῦ βασιλέως ὁμοιότης Ath.Ar.3.5(M.26.332A); **5.** also of what does not differ because it 'is' in every respect, *perfect* ἡ μορφὴ τοῦ δούλου οὐδὲν ἄλλο ἐμφαίνει ἢ ἄνθρωπον ἀ. Chrys.hom.2.2 in Heb.(12.17B).

B. Trin.; most freq. of Son in relation to Father, *in no way differing, exactly like*; **1.** to CNic.(325); Or.Jo.13.36(p.260.32; M.14.461A) cit. s. θέλημα; ὁ υἱὸς τοῦ πατρός, τὴν κατὰ πάντα ὁμοιότητα αὐτοῦ ἐκ φύσεως ἀπομαξάμενος καὶ ἀ. εἰκὼν τοῦ πατρὸς τυγχάνων Alex.Al.ep.Alex.9(p.25.25; M.18.561B); ib.12(p.27.15; 565C); originally proposed as safeguard of Trin. orthodoxy at CNic.(325), Ath.decr.20(p.16.18; M.25.449C) cit. s. ὅμοιος; τοῦ πατρὸς...εἰκόνα... ἀ. κατὰ πάντα τοῦ πατρὸς id.ep.Afr.5(M.26.1037C), but abandoned when accepted in equivocal sense by Arians, Ast.Soph.fr.21 ap.Eus.Marcell.1.4(p.25.8; M.24.764C) cit. s. εἰκών; Philost.h.e.2.15(M.65.477B); in 'Eusebian' formula, as expressing nearest permissible approximation to ὁμοούσιος, Symb.Ant.(341)2(p.249.18; M.26.721C) cit. s. εἰκών; formula ascribed to Lucian of Antioch, ‡Ath.dial.Trin.3.2(M.28.1205B); adopted by Acac. Caes. and Eudox., Acac.Caes.fr.Marcell.ap.Epiph.haer.72.6(p.260.14; M.42.389B); Ath.syn.36(p.263.25; M.26.757B); ib.37(p.264.10; 760A); adopted in emergency even by Aëtius though elsewhere he was opposed to it, Philost.h.e.4.12(528A); ib.5.1(528C); cf. Macedonian position ἀ. λέγω [sc. βούλην, δύναμιν, δόξαν], τὴν αὐτὴν οὐ λέγω ‡Ath.dial.Trin.3.2(M.28.1205A); ‡Ath.Maced.dial.1.18(M.28.1321A); **2.** in orthodox writers after CNic.(325): Arians, with (apparently) idea of material representation in mind, had not objected to expression because a representation however exact necessarily differs from the original in being a mere representation, cf. in a different connexion εἰ καὶ τὸ ἀ. καὶ πάντη ὅμοιον ἔχει ἡ εἰκὼν πρὸς τὸ ἀρχέτυπον, ἀλλ' ἡ οὐσία, φησί, διάφορος Max.schol.e.h.4.3.1(M.4.152D). But word not eschewed by orthodox on this account but freq. found, both with and without εἰκών, in writers who fully accepted ὁμοούσιος, because they maintained that ἀ. given its full force would include idea of essence, Ath.*Ar*.3.11(M.26.344A,B); εἰκὼν...οὐκ ἐν σχήματος ὁμοιότητι, ἀλλ' ἐν αὐτῇ τῇ οὐσίᾳ τὸ ἀ. ἀεὶ διασώζουσα Bas.*Eun*.1.18(1.230A; M.29.552C); id.*ep*.9.3(3.91A,B; M.32.272A) cf. ἀπαραλλάκτως fin.; Gr.Naz.*or*.30.20(p.140.5; M.36.129B); βουλὴ...βουλῆς ἀ. οὖσα ἡ αὐτή ἐστι βουλή· καὶ δύναμις δυνάμεως ἀ. οὖσα, ἡ αὐτή ἐστι δύναμις ‡Ath.*dial.Trin*.3.2(M.28.1205A); **a.** with εἰκών (2Cor.4:4, Col.1:15): ἐμφέρειάν τε καὶ εἰκόνα ἀ. ... πρὸς τὸν πατέρα Ath.*Ar*.2.33(M.26.217B); λόγος...τοῦ ἑαυτοῦ πατρὸς εἰκών ἐστιν ἀ. id.*gent*.41(M.25.81C); *ib*.46(93C); τὸ διὰ πάντων τῆς εἰκόνος ἀ. πρὸς τὸν οὗ ἐστιν εἰκὼν θεωρεῖται Gr.Nyss.*Eun*.8(2 p.179.29; M.45.772D); ὁ...υἱὸς...ἴσος διὰ τῆς ἀληθινῆς εἰκόνος καὶ ὁμοιώσεως οὐ παρηλλαγμένης, ἀλλ' ἀ. Epiph.*haer*.76.3(p.343.17; M.42.520C); ‡Ath.*dial.Trin*.1.4(M.28.1121D); πῶς ...εἰκὼν ἀ. εἴη τοῦ γεννήσαντος, μὴ πάντα ἔχων τὰ τοῦ γεννήσαντος; Thdt.ap.Cyr.*apol.Thdt*.4(p.121.21; 6.215B); ἡ...ζῶσα εἰκών, καὶ τὸ ἀ. ἔχουσα τὴν αὐτὴν ἔχει φύσιν τῷ ἀρχετύπῳ id.*Col*.1:15(3.477); ὄργανόν ἐστι παναρμόνιον ἀντὶ τοῦ εἰκὼν ἀ. *Schol.Clem.prot*.(p.298.3; M.9.778A); **b.** with χαρακτήρ (Heb.1:3): ἀ. τῆς θεότητος χαρακτῆρές εἰσιν ἐν τῷ υἱῷ Cyr.H.*catech*.11.18; τὸ ἀ. δηλοῖ οὗ ἐστι χαρακτήρ, τὸ ὅμοιον κατὰ πάντα Chrys.*hom.2.2 in Heb*.(12.16D); [sc. υἱόν] ἀ. χαρακτῆρα ἀοράτου μορφῆς ‡Chrys.*hom.in Mt.20:1*(8.140B); χαρακτὴρ ἀ. τῆς ὅλης αὐτοῦ ὑποστάσεως Gel.Cyz.*h.e*.2.16.21(M.85.1265A); **c.** with ὁμοιότης: τὸν υἱὸν ἔχοντα πάντα ὅσα ἔχει ὁ πατήρ, ἐκ τῆς ἀ. ὁμοιότητος καὶ ταυτότητος ὧν ἔχει Ath.*Ar*.3.36(M.26.400B); λόγου τὴν πρὸς τὸν θεὸν ἰδιότητα, καὶ τὴν ἀ. ὁμοιότητα τοῦ ἀπαυγάσματος πρὸς τὸ φῶς id.*decr*.24(p.19.33; M.25.457B); ὁμοούσιος...ὁ υἱὸς τῷ πατρί, καὶ ὁ πατὴρ τῷ υἱῷ· διὸ δὴ εἰς ἀ. ἀναβαίνουσιν ὁμοιότητα Cyr.*Jo*.1.2(4.15E); **d.** abs. τὸ ἀ. αὐτοῦ πρὸς τὸν πατέρα Chrys.*exp.in Ps*.8(5.92C); (exeg. Heb.1:3) ἐνταῦθα...τὸ ἀ. δεικνὺς τοῦτό φησι id.*hom.2.2 in Heb*.(12.14B); ἐν μὲν τῷ υἱὸς εἶναι, τὸ ἀ. σώζων πρὸς τὸν πατέρα Procl.CP *or.laud.BMV* 6(p.105.19; M.65.688A); ‡Meth.*Sym. et Ann*.8(M.18.365D); in respect of μορφή: μίαν ἐν τῷ θεῷ πατρὶ καὶ θεῷ μονογενεῖ τὴν οἱονεὶ μορφὴν θεωρεῖσθαι τῷ ἀ. τῆς θεότητος ἐνιζομένην Bas.*Spir*.45(3.38B; M.32.149B); φύσις: τὸ ἀ. τῆς φύσεως ὁμολογοῦντες, τὴν κατὰ τὸ αἴτιον καὶ αἰτιατὸν διαφορὰν οὐκ ἀρνούμεθα Gr.Nyss.*tres dii*(M.45.133B); ὁ υἱός, οὐχ ἕτερόν τι παρ' αὐτόν [sc. τὸν πατέρα] ἐστιν ὅσον εἰς οὐσίας ταυτότητα λέγω, καὶ φύσεως ἀ. ὁμοιότητα Cyr.*Jo*.5.5(4.525D); οὐσία: τῆς κατὰ πάντα ἀ. καὶ ὁμοίας οὐσίας αὐτῶν Didym.(‡Bas.)*Eun*.4(1.287C; M.29.692A); τῶν...ὀνομάτων τὰ μέν ἐστι κοινά, τὰ δὲ ἴδια—κοινὰ μέν, ἵνα τὸ ἀ. δείξῃ τῆς οὐσίας, ἴδια δέ, ἵνα τὴν ἰδιότητα χαρακτηρίσῃ τῶν ὑποστάσεων Chrys.*incomprehens*.5.2(1.482C); id.*hom.69.1 in Mt*.(7.679B); Ammon.*Jo*.12:45(M.85.1480A); Cyr.*Jo*.1.3(4.23D); ὡς ἐν ταυτότητι τῆς οὐσίας ἀ., καὶ τῇ κατὰ φύσιν ἑνότητί τε καὶ ὁμοιότητι *ib*.(28E); υἱός ἐστιν...ἀ. οὐσία, φύσις ἀνεπιχείρητος Anast.Ant.*fid*.(M.89.1404C); and of θεότης: τὸ ...'ποιήσωμεν' τὸ...ἀ. τῆς τοῦ πατρὸς καὶ υἱοῦ θεότητος παρίστησιν ἡ φωνή Gel.Cyz.*h.e*.2.14.6(M.85.1257A); ‡Caes.Naz.*dial*.3(M.38.860); will (exeg. Jo.5:30) τὴν...ὁμόνοιαν δηλῶν καὶ τὸ ἀ. τῆς ψήφου Chrys.*hom.39.4 in Jo*.(8.232B); honour, id.*incomprehens*.4.4(1.476B); authority ἐστὶν ἐν πατρὶ καὶ υἱῷ καὶ θεότης, καὶ τῆς αὐτῆς φύσεως ἀ. ἐξουσία τε καὶ δύναμις Cyr.*Jo*.5.2(4.293C); **3.** of H. Ghost in relation to Father (ref. Jac.1:17) ἐν τῷ θεῷ ὂν τὸ πνεῦμα τὸ ἅγιον ...ἂν εἴη...ἀ. Ath.*ep.Serap*.1.26(M.26.592A); Didym.*Trin*.2.2(M.39.460C); *ib*.2.5(504A); **4.** of Trinity of Persons ἡ...ἄκτιστος φύσις... ἐν μὲν τῇ κατὰ τὸ ἄκτιστον κοινωνίᾳ τὸ ἀ. ἔχουσα, ἐν δὲ τοῖς ἐξαιρέτοις τῶν ἰδιωμάτων ἑκάστου τὸ ἀκοινώνητον Gr.Nyss.*Eun*.1(1 p.102.3; M.45.336B); κατάρχουσιν [i.e. the Son and the H. Ghost] αὐτοφυῶς διὰ τὴν ἀ. πρὸς τὸν ἐξ οὗ προῆλθον πατέρα θεότητα Didym.*Trin*.2.11(M.39.660C); ἡ μία τριὰς πρὸς ἑαυτὴν ἀ., τὰ δὲ ἄλλα ⟨τὰ⟩ ἐξ αὐτῆς παρηλλαγμένα Epiph.*haer*.76.52(p.407.8; M.42.625C); Chrys.*hom.8.3 in 2Cor*.(10.495D); **5.** ref. divine image in man τὸ...θεοπρεπὲς κάλλος ...τελειωτικὸν...κατὰ τὴν πρὸς ἑαυτὸ τῶν τελουμένων...ἀ. μόρφωσιν Dion.Ar.*c.h*.3.1(M.3.164D).

ἀπαραλλάκτως, A. *without change*; **1.** *invariably, with complete regularity* ἔδει θέρος ὁμοῦ καὶ χειμῶνα καὶ ἔαρ καὶ μετόπωρον ἀ. καὶ κατὰ τὸ αὐτὸ συνίστασθαι Ath.*gent*.29(M.25.57C); σελήνην...φθίνουσαν καὶ πληρουμένην ἀ. *ib*.35(72A); Bas.*hom.in Ps*.48:13(1.185A; M.29.449C); **2.** *without* undergoing *change* τῆς...ἀναλλοιώτου οὐσίας, ἐφ' ἧς ...ἐπιπρέπει νοεῖν...εἶναι ἀ. ἀεὶ κατὰ τὰ αὐτὰ καὶ ὡσαύτως ἔχουσαν Eus.*e.th*.2.9(p.108.32; M.24.917A); Dion.*e.h*.4.3.3(M.3.476D) cit. s. ἰδιότης.

B. in relation to something else, *without any difference*; **1.** in gen.; **a.** *indistinguishably, identically, in exactly the same way* εὑρήσει τὸ ἐκτύπωμα τοῦ οὐρανοῦ καὶ τῆς γῆς...ἀ. ὑποκείμενον Hipp.*haer*.5.19(p.118.16; M.16.3182B); *T.Sal*.1.3(p.8.15); τοῦ γεννηθέντος οἰκείως ἔχειν ὀφείλοντος πάντως καὶ ἀ. πρὸς τὸν γεννήσαντα Bas.*Eun*.2(1.242C; M.29.581C); Cyr.*ador*.10(1.351E); *ib*.11(379D); οὐκ ἂν εἴη τῶν ἐνδεχομένων ἀ. ἐνυπάρχειν τινὶ τὴν θεῷ πρέπουσαν ἐνέργειαν... εἰ μὴ καὶ αὐτὸς κατὰ φύσιν ὑπάρχοι θεός id.*Jo*.3.1(4.253B); id.*Is*.3.5(2.516B); ἑνοῦνται τῷ θεῷ λόγῳ οὕτως ἀ. αἵ τε ἐπουράνιαι δυνάμεις...ὡς αὐτὸς ὁ νοῦς ὁ λεγόμενος παρ' αὐτῶν Χριστός CCP(543)*anath*.12(p.229; H.3.285D); εἰ τὸν αὐτὸν ἅπαντες ἔσωζον ἀ. χαρακτῆρα, πόση σύγχυσις; Melet.*nat.hom*.30(M.64.1277D); **b.** ref. words, *in precisely the same sense* 'εἰκὼν τῆς ἀγαθότητος' [sc. ὁ σωτήρ] ἀλλ' οὐχ ὡς ὁ πατὴρ ἀ. ἀγαθός Or.*princ*.1.2.13(p.47.8; M.11.144A); πολύς ἐστιν ὀνομάτων κατάλογος οἷς ἀ. ὁ μονογενὴς τῷ πατρὶ συνονομάζεται Gr.Nyss.*Eun*.7(2 p.162.24; M.45.752); Leont.H.*monoph*.(M.86.1809C); **2.** theol., with special ref. Persons in Trin., *without distinction, identically* εἰ γὰρ κατὰ τὴν οὐσίαν ἀ. ἔχει, ἀ. ἕξει καὶ κατὰ τὴν δύναμιν Bas.*Spir*.19(3.17C; M.32.104A); Didym.*Trin*.1.20(M.39.369B); *ib*.3.2(804B); τὸ ἅγιον πνεῦμα...ἔχει...τὰ...πάντα ἀ. πρὸς τὸν πατέρα καὶ τὸν υἱόν *ib*.2.25(748A); Cyr.*Jo*.2.8(4.232E); with ὅμοιος *exactly* ἀμείψασθαι... τὸν Ἀέτιον τοσοῦτον ἐνδεῖν τῷ πατρὶ τὸν υἱὸν ἀνόμοιον εἰπεῖν...ὥστε καὶ ἀ. ὅμοιον αὐτὸν κηρύττειν Philost.*h.e*.4.12(M.65.528A); qualifying formula 'ὅμοιος κατ' οὐσίαν' making it equivalent to 'ὁμοούσιος', Bas.*ep*.9.3(3.91A,B; M.32.272A) cit. s. ὅμοιος.

ἀπαραλλαξία, ἡ, *indistinguishability*; *exact likeness*; **1.** in gen., ref. analogies, *in every respect like* κατὰ ἀπαραλλαξίαν ὡς Leont.H.*Nest*.6.4(M.86.1756B); **2.** theol.; **a.** of Son in relation to Father εἰκών ἐστιν ἀπαράλλακτος, οὐ τῆς ἀ. πατέρα ποιούσης, ἀλλ' υἱὸν ἀπηκριβωμένον Acac.Caes.*fr.Marcell*.ap.Epiph.*haer*.72.10(p.264.32; M.42.396C); τὸ ἓν εἶναι πρὸς τὸν πατέρα, τὴν πρὸς αὐτὸν ἀ. δηλοῖ Chrys.*hom.3.4 in Jo*.(8.22E); μάλιστα ἰσότητα καὶ ἀ. ἐνδείξασθαι *ib.4.3*(31A); *ib.61.2*(364C); τὸ γὰρ 'οὕτω', καὶ τὸ 'ὁμοίως', καὶ τὸ 'καθὼς' ἀπαραλλαξίας ἐστίν id.*exp.in Ps*.44:3(5.165E); οὐ τοιαῦτα, ἀλλὰ τὰ αὐτά, ὃ μείζονός ἐστιν ἀ. id.*hom.56.2 in Jo*.(329A); τὰ αὐτὰ τῷ πατρὶ ποιοῦντα, ὃ μείζονός ἐστιν ἀ. Thdr.Mops.*Jo*.9:3(M.66.753C); **b.** ref. Christ as perfect God and perfect Man ἵνα...τῷ ἀνελλιπεῖ τῆς πρὸς αὐτὰ...φυσικῆς καὶ οὐσιώδους ἀ. τέλειος ᾖ τὰ ἑκάτερα Max.*opusc*.(M.91.73C); **c.** of image of God in man (ref. Gen.1:26) οὐκ οὐσίας ἀ., ἀλλ' ἀρχῆς ὁμοιότης Chrys.*serm.3.1 in Gen*.(4.656A).

ἀπαραλόγιστος, *not to be deceived, unerring*, of God ἁγίασον αὐτοὺς...ἀπαραλόγιστε *Lit*.ap.*Const.App*.8.11.6; ὁ...λόγος αὐτοῦ ἀ. Chrys.*hom.82.4 in Mt*.(7.787D); usu. in judgements ἀ. γὰρ ἡ τοῦ θεοῦ ψῆφος εἰς τὸ δικαιότατον κρῖμα Clem.*str*.7.3(p.15.3; M.9.425A); πῶς παραπείσεις τὸν ἀ. δικαστήν; Bas.*hom*.7.6(2.58B; M.31.296B); τὸν πανδερκῆ καὶ ἀ. ὀφθαλμὸν τοῦ κρίνοντος Cyr.*ador*.14(1.493B).

ἀπαραλογίστως, *without being deceived, unerringly*; of divine judgement, *Const.App*.2.25.13; Gr.Naz.*or*.43.71(M.36.592C).

***ἀπαραμίκτως,** *without admixture*, Or.*Jo*.6.19(11; p.127.30; M.14.232D).

ἀπαραμίλλητος, *unrivalled*, ‡Just.*or.Gr*.5(M.6.237B).

***ἀπαράμιλλος,** *unrivalled*, Niceph.Ur.*v.Sym*.28(M.86.3012B).

ἀπαραμύθητος, **1.** *unsupported*, of evidence οὐδένα ἀ. ἐῶντες τῶν λεγομένων ὅρων Or.*Jo*.6.20(12; p.130.6; M.14.236D); *standing alone*, of a negative ἀρκεῖ...εἰς ἀνατροπὴν ἡ ἀ. ἀπόφασις *ib*.(p.129.28; 236C); **2.** *insatiable* ἐπὶ...ἀρετῇ...καὶ πάμπαν ἀ. [sc. ὁ φθόνος] Isid.Pel.*epp*.2.224(M.78.664A).

ἀπαράμυθος, *without consolation, admitting no consolation*, Ephr.3.309C.

***ἀπαρανάγνωστος,** *unread*, Thphn.*chron*.p.87(M.108.264A).

***ἀπαράνοικτος,** *unopened, shut*, ‡Chrys.*virg.parab*.(8.47C).

ἀπαράομαι, perf. ptcpl. ἀπηρημένος, ? *prayed against*, hence *dreaded, terrible* τὰς ἀ. ἐκδειματώσεις Pall.*v.Chrys*.20(p.146.27; M.47.82).

***ἀπαραποίητος,** *unmodified*; **1.** *unchanged, identical* ἀ. τῶν πατέρων διεφύλαξαν τὴν παράδοσιν Bas.*Spir*.16(p.37.15; M.32.93C); **2.** *unadulterated, not counterfeit, genuine* τῆς...εὐσεβείας τὸ κάλλος ἀκραιφνὲς...καὶ ἀ. ἐναστράπτον ἐν αὐτοῖς ἦν Cyr.*glaph.Gen*.2(1.29D); *ib*.(35C); ἄθραυστον...καὶ ἀ. τὴν εἰς αὐτὸν τηρήσαντες πίστιν id.*hom.pasch*.8.1(5^2.94B); Leont.B.*Apoll*.(M.86.1957C); theol., of Son in relation to Father φύσεως ἀ. καρπὸν ἄτρεπτον καὶ ἀναλλοίωτον ἀγαθόν Cyr.*Jo*.1.8(4.65B); *ib*.5.5(530D); *ib*.2.6(215D); ἐστὶν ὁ μονογενὴς τῆς...πατρὸς οὐσίας ἀ. χαρακτήρ id.*hom.pasch*.12.3(5^2.170E); τὸ τῆς οὐσίας ἀπαράλλακτον καὶ τὸ ἐν τῷ χαρακτῆρι...ἀ. id.*Jo*.1.3(29B).

ἀπαραποιήτως, *genuinely, inalienably, unchangeably*, of Son in relation to Father τὸ εἶναι θεὸς ἀ. ἔχων Cyr.*Pulch*.(p.27.27; 5^2.130C); ἀ. ... ἐν ἑαυτῷ τὸν γεννήσαντα ζωγραφῶν id.*Jo*.1.2(4.16A); *ib*.1.9(74E); *ib*.6(564C,581C).

***ἀπαρασάλευτος**, *unshaken*, Chrys.*hom.18.2 in 1Tim.*(11.655D); ‡Jo.D.*fid.dorm.*3(M.95.248C); Thdr.Stud.*epp.*2.143(M.99.1449C).

***ἀπαρασαλεύτως**, *unshakeably*, Epiph.*haer.*69.40(p.188.23; M.42.264D).

ἀπαρασήμαντος, **1.** *unnoticed* μηδὲ τοῦτο...ἀ. ἐάσωμεν Or.*Jo.*2.23 (18; p.80.21; M.14.156A); Ath.*inc.*35.6(M.25.156C); Bas.*hex.*3.4(1.26C; M.29.61C); id.*Eun.*2.20(1.256D; M.29.616C); **2.** *not well-marked, indefinite* ἵνα μὴ τῷ ἀ. τῆς κλήσεως, ἀνύπαρκτον αὐτὴν ἀποφήνωσιν Martin.ap.CLater.*act.*3(H.3.785D).

ἀπαρασημείωτος, *unmarked, without indication* or *note*, Thdr.Stud.*epp.*2.31(M.99.1201C).

ἀπαράσημος, *not counterfeit, genuine* ὁ υἱὸς...ἀ. τὸ θεῖον...παρέδειξε κάλλος Cyr.*dial.Trin.*5(5^1.559E); id.*Chr.un.*(5^1.742C); id.*Juln.*1(6^2.25C).

***ἀπαράσπονδος**, *faithful to one's pledged word, trustworthy*, Jo.VI H.*v.Jo.D.*16(M.94.456B).

ἀπαράσσω, *strike* or *tear off*; met., *sweep away, destroy*, Clem.*prot.*4(p.47.15; M.8.160C).

ἀπαρατήρητος, *not observed*; **1.** *unnoticed, overlooked* μηδὲ τοῦτο...ἀ. ἐάσῃς Or.*comm.in Mt.*14.4(p.281.21; M.13.1192A); **2.** *not closely watched* ἐλευθερίαν τὸ ἀ. καὶ ἀκώλυτον λέγω Chrys.*hom.25.1 in 1Cor.*(10.221A); **3.** *indiscriminate* ὅτι ἀ. τῇ γραφῇ τῶν συλλαβῶν τούτων ἡ χρῆσις Bas.*Spir.*6 tit.(3.5E; M.32.77A).

ἀπαρατηρήτως, **1.** *heedlessly, carelessly*; *inadvertently* σφόδρα...ἀ. ὁ Ἡρακλέων οἴεται Or.*Jo.*10.34(19; p.208.23; M.14.369A); εἴ τι κατὰ ἀδιαφορίαν ἐν τῷ λαϊκῷ βίῳ ἀ. ἔγραψε Bas.*ep.*224.2(3.343B; M.32.837A); Cyr.*thes.*21(5^1.215D); **2.** *freely, without scruple* Μωσέα γνοίης ἂν...τροφῆς...τῆς Αἰγυπτίας ἀ. μετειληχότα Eus.*d.e.*1.6(p.25.9; M.22.52C); *Const.App.*6.30.7; *ib.*6.29.4; 6.30.2; τὸν...Χριστιανὸν οὐδὲν τοιοῦτο δεῖ παραφυλάττεσθαι, ἀλλὰ πάντα ἀ. ποιεῖν Eus.Al.*serm.*7(M.86.356B); *without limitation* πάσας αὐτὰς [sc. θεωνυμίας] ἀμερῶς, ἀπολύτως, ἀ., ὁλικῶς ἁπάσῃ τῇ ὁλότητι...πάσης θεότητος ἀνατίθεσθαι Dion.Ar.*d.n.*2.1(M.3.636C); cf. ἀ. ὡς ἐφ' ἑνὶ ἑκάστῳ, καὶ ἐπὶ τοῖς τρισὶ κοινῶς Pachymeres *paraphr.d.n.*2.1(M.3.657C).

ἀπαράτρεπτος, **1.** *not to be turned aside*; *undeviating, inexorable*; of times and seasons ὡρισμένας ὥρας καὶ καιροὺς εὐκαίρους καὶ τροπὰς ἀ. Dion.Al.ap.Eus.*p.e.*14.25(777B; M.21.1277D); οὐδὲ ἀ. ἀνθρώποις καιρὸς ὥρισται θανάτου Eus.*Is.*38:1ff.(M.24.356B); **2.** *not to be perverted, unswerving*, of the goodness of God τοῦ θεοῦ ἀγαθὸν ὥσπερ ἀγένητον, οὕτως καὶ ἀ. *Disp.Phot.*32(M.88.565A); neut. as subst., *incorruptibility, steadfastness* ἵνα...τὸ ἀκλινές τε καὶ ἀ. ἐν τοῖς ἀγαθοῖς κατορθώσωμεν Gr.Nyss.*hom.8 in Cant.*(M.44.945D); **3.** *unperverted, undistorted*; of truth, Eun.*apol.*6(M.30.840C).

***ἀπαράτρωτος**, *uninjured, unimpaired*, Nil.*Magn.*1(M.79.968C); Philost.*h.e.*2.15(M.65.477A); Sophr.H.*ep.syn.*(M.87.3188B).

***ἀπαρατρώτως**, *without violation*, Philost.*h.e.*3.5(M.65.485B).

***ἀπαράφθαρτος**, *uncorrupted, inviolate*, Dion.Ar.*d.n.*1.4(M.3.592A, v.l. ἀπαράθραυστα); Max.*opusc.*(M.91.88B).

***ἀπαραφθάρτως**, *incorruptibly* τὰς νοερὰς ἡμῶν δυνάμεις πρὸς τὴν ἐπὶ τὸ χεῖρον ὕφεσιν ἀ. διακειμένας Dion.Ar.*e.h.*4.3.4(M.3.477D, v.l. ἀπαραθραύστως).

ἀπαράφθορος, *uncorrupted, inviolate* ἀ. ἐν ἑαυτῷ τηρήσας τὴν πίστιν Cyr.*Os.*139(3.172E); id.*ador.*8(1.280B); *ib.*12(421D); ἡ...εἰς θεὸν ἀγάπη τὸ γνήσιον εἰς πίστιν καὶ τὸ ἀ. ἔχει id.*Am.*73(3.334B; A. conj. ἀπαράθραυστον).

***ἀπαράφορος**, *undeviating* ἀκλινῆ...καὶ ἀ. τὴν ὁμολογίαν Cyr.*hom.pasch.*8.1(5^2.94B, v.l. ἀπαράφθορον).

ἀπαραφύλακτος, *unguarded* ἄλογον...[sc. ἐστί]...τὴν...διάνοιαν περιφέρειν ἀ. Ephr.3.212E.

***ἀπαραφυλάκτως**, **1.** *without a guard* ἀ. καὶ πάσης ὑποψίας ἐκτός Thphn.*chron.*p.314(M.108.761C); **2.** *carelessly, without scruple*, Eus.*d.e.*1.6(p.25.5; M.22.52C); ἐξομνυμένους ἀ. τὴν πίστιν id.*h.e.*4.7.7(M.20.317A).

ἀπαραχάρακτος, **1.** *free from counterfeit, genuine, authentic* ἐκεῖνα...ἐθέλειν...τὸν πατέρα, ἃ τὴν θείαν αὐτοῦ δόξαν ἀ. οἶδε τηρεῖν Cyr.*Jo.*9(4.779C); Bas.Sel.*or.*28.3(M.85.324A); Const.Pogon.*sacr.*3(M.*PL.*96.390D); **2.** *inviolate* τὸν νόμον ἀ. ... ἐφύλαττε Jo.D.*hom.*8.6(M.96.709A); id.*f.o.*4.24(M.94.1208B).

***ἀπαραχαράκτως**, *without falsification, genuinely*, Or.*Jo.*5.8(4; p.105.11; M.14.196A).

ἀπαρέγκλιτος, **1.** *not bent, straight*; met., *unbending, not giving way* ἀ. ὑφέσει πάσῃ Max.*schol.e.h.*2.3.5(M.4.132A); **2.** *not turned aside, direct*; hence met., *unswerving* ἀσάλευτον...καὶ ἀ. πίστιν Isid.Pel.*epp.*2.299(M.78.725C); Dion.Ar.*e.h.*4.3.1(M.3.473C); of God, id.*d.n.*9.10(M.3.917A).

***ἀπαρείκαστος**, *not to be compared, incomparable*, Marc.Er.*opusc.*3.2(M.65.968C).

ἀπαρεμφάτως, **1.** *without specifying, indefinitely, not definitively* ταῦτα...πλαττόμενος ἀ. ἐβούλετο σημαίνειν Eust.*engast.*11(p.32.6; M.18.633C); ἀ. ... τὸ πρόσωπον ὑπέφαινε τοῦ ἁγίου πνεύματος Epiph.*haer.*69.76(p.224.27; M.42.325C); (ref. Lc.5:32) πάντας τοὺς παραβαίνοντας καλεῖ...εἰπὼν ἀ., μᾶλλον δ' ἀορίστως Mac.Mgn.*apocr.*4.18 (p.197.13); **2.** *unequivocally* τὸ μὲν τροπικῶς εἰρημένον ἀληθείᾳ φέρειν εἴωθαν, τὸ δὲ ἀληθῶς καὶ ἀ. κεκηρυγμένον εἰς ἕτερον πρόσωπον ἀλληγοροῦσιν Epiph.*haer.*69.50(p.196.24; M.42.277D).

ἀπαρενόχλητος, *undisturbed* χωριζομένη τοῦ σώματος ἡ...ψυχὴ...ἀ., καὶ φωτεινοτέρα εὑρισκομένη ‡Gr.Nyss.*imag.*(M.44.1344C); εἰς κατάστασιν ἔρημον κακίας καὶ ἀπαρενόχλητον ἐπιμιξίας φαυλότητος †Cyr.*coll.VT* (6^4.3B; M.77.1177C); Jo.Carp.*cap.*52(M.85.1848).

***ἀπαρεξόδευτος**, *from which there is no straying*, exeg. Jo.14:6 ἀγαθὴ...ὄντως ὁδός, ἀ. καὶ ἀπλανής, ὁ κύριος ἡμῶν Bas.*Spir.*18(3.16B; M.32.100C).

***ἀπαρέσκεια, ἡ**, *disgust with* or *weariness of life*, Hesych.S.*temp.*2.100(M.93.1544C).

ἀπάρεστος, *displeasing*, Or.*Cels.*1.9(p.62.21; M.11.673C); *ib.*4.53 (p.326.12; 1116C); *ib.*5.37(p.41.2; 1237C).

ἀπαρηγόρητος, **1.** *not admitting consolation*; neut. plur. as adv., *inconsolably*, Bas.*hom.*14.3(2.124D; M.31.449A); **2.** *ineffaceable* αἰσχύνην ἀ. ‡Bas.*const.*5(2.569D; M.31.1400D).

ἀπαρηγορήτως, *inconsolably*, Nil.*epp.*1.311(M.79.196B).

***ἀπαριθμισμός, ὁ**, *enumeration*, Thdr.Lect.*fr.*(M.86.228A).

ἀπαρκτέον, *one must begin*, Clem.*paed.*2.9(p.207.12; M.8.496B).

ἀπαρν-έω, **1.** act., *deny utterly, reject, repudiate* ἀσύμφορόν ἐστιν ~ῆσαι τὸν νόμον σου Herm.*sim.*1.5; usu. med.; in religious sense ὅν [sc. Χριστὸν] τινες...~οῦνται...μὴ ὁμολογῶν αὐτὸν σαρκοφόρον Ign.*Smyrn.*5.1f.; Herm.*vis.*3.6.5; id.*sim.*8.8.2; τοὺς τὴν ἰδίαν πίστιν ~ησαμένους ‡Ath.*pat.*8(M.26.1308C); **2.** med., *deny oneself* οὐκ εἶπεν, 'ἀρνησάσθω'; ἀλλ', '~ησάσθω' καὶ τῇ μικρᾷ ταύτῃ προσθήκῃ πολλὴν...ἐμφαίνων τὴν ὑπερβολήν Chrys.*hom.55.1 in Mt.*(7.557A); ἡ...περὶ θεοῦ γνῶσις, ἣν οὐκ ἂν δυνήσῃ...κτήσασθαι, εἰ μὴ [σαυτὸν] τῷ κόσμῳ ~ησάμενος ‡Pall.*h.mon.*16.15(p.74.20; M.34.1170A).

***ἀπαρνησία, ἡ**, v.l. for ἐπαρνησιθεΐα, Epiph.*haer.*61.4(p.384.16; M.41.1044D).

***ἀπαρνησιθεΐα, ἡ**, = ἐπαρνησιθεΐα, *denial of* the true *God*, Epiph.*haer.*19.3(p.219.25; M.41.264C); *ib.*24.5(p.262.5; 313B).

***ἀπαρνησίθεος**, v. ἐπαρνησίθεος.

ἀπάρνησις, ἡ, *denial*; *renunciation*; of apostasy, *M.Areth.*(p.21).

***ἀπαρνητικῶς**, *with vehement denial*, †Bas.*bapt.*1.2.25(2.647C; M.31.1568C).

ἀπαρόδευτος, **1.** *not passing away, abiding* τὰ ἀ. θεοῦ δῶρα Ephr.3.261E; **2.** *not traversible* ἀδιάβατον...ἀνάγκην, καθάπερ τι βάραθρον ἀχανές τε καὶ ἀ. Gr.Nyss.*anim.et res.*(M.46.84B).

***ἀπάροιστος**, f.l. for εὐπάροιστος, *easily carried away*, Cyr.ap.*cat.Jo.*11:8(p.315.4); cf.id.*Jo.*7(4.678B).

ἀπαρρενόω, v. ἀπαρσενόω.

ἀπαρρησίαστος, *deprived of boldness* or *liberty, unfree*;

A. in gen. ἡ πονηρία ἄμετρος...οἱ προεστῶτες ἀ. Bas.*ep.*92.2(3.184E; M.32.480C); μεταμορφώσατε...τοὺς ἀ. εἰς παρρησίαν Gr.Nyss.*res.*3(M.46.660A); ψιθυρισμὸς γάρ ἐστιν ἀ. φθέγμα Cyr.*Ps.*40:8(M.69.996C); neut. as subst. = *fear* οὐδεὶς...αὐτῶν ἐτόλμα ἅπερ ἐβούλετο...εἰπεῖν...οἱ μὲν διὰ τὸ ἀ., οἱ δὲ διὰ φιλαρχίαν Chrys.*hom.57.2 in Jo.* (8.335A).

B. as result of sin; **1.** of original sin τῶν τότε νηπίων ἔτι τυγχανόντων...καὶ ἀ., διά τε τὴν ἀρχαίαν παρακοὴν καὶ τὸ καταλεῖψαι θεὸν ζῶντα Didym.*Trin.*3.39(M.39.980A); Chrys.*hom.17.3 in 1Cor.*(10.150A); **2.** of actual sin, *Const.App.*6.27.2; Epiph.*haer.*24.5(p.262.23; M.41.313D); ἀπὸ τῆς ἐργασίας τῆς ἀρετῆς τὰς θύρας ἐστὶν εὑρεῖν ἠνεῳγμένας τῆς πρὸς αὐτὸν [sc. θεόν] παρρησίας· ὡς ὁ μὴ ἐντεῦθεν τὴν παρρησίαν κτησάμενος, ἐν τοῖς ἠτιμωμένοις καὶ ἀ. γενήσεται Chrys.*hom.66.4 in Gen.*(4.633E); οἱ δὲ ἀ., καὶ συνειδότες ἑαυτοῖς ἁμαρτήματα πολλά, μεταβαλλώμεθα id.*ascens.*5(2.456C); id.*hom.in Mt.18:23*(3.10E); id.*exp.in Ps.*140:2(5.431D); id.*Anna* 4.2(4.731E); Nil.*epp.*3.135(M.79.445C); ref. publican διὰ τὸ ἀ. τύπτοντα τὸ στῆθος *ib.*3.33 (393C); Χριστὸς...τὴν ἀνθρωπότητα...τὴν ἀ. πρώην υἱοθεσίας ἀξιώσας Cyr.*apol.orient.*12(p.62.12; 6^1.196D); ὁ γὰρ πίπτων συντρίβεται καὶ ἀ. ἐν προσευχῇ...παρίσταται Jo.Clim.*scal.*25(M.88.997A); **3.** esp. in Day of Judgement ἁμαρτωλὸς...ἀ. ἐστιν ἐπὶ τοῦ φοβεροῦ βήματος Tit.Bost.*fr.Lc.*7:39(p.170); Bas.*hom.*7.6(2.58B; M.31.296B); ὑπὸ τοῦ βορβόρου τῶν ἡδονῶν σπιλοῦται, καὶ οὕτως ἀ. ἡ ψυχὴ ἐν ἡμέρᾳ κρίσεως εὑρίσκεται Mac.Aeg.*hom.*4.5(M.34.476C).

C. esp. ref. liberty of speech, the saints not ἀπαρρησίαστοι despite their material poverty, Chrys.*hom.18.2 in Heb.*(12.177A) cit. s. πενία.

D. of not having freedom to do certain things *τίς, τὰ αὐτὰ ποιῶν τῷ ἐγκαλουμένῳ, ἀ. ... πρὸς τὸ κρίνειν τὸν ἀδελφόν;* Bas.*reg.br.*164(2. 470C; M.31.1192A) = Anast.S.*qu.et resp.*70(M.89.696B); Jo.D.*spir. neq.*4(M.95.80B).

E. *not to be divulged, secret τὸ ἐσφραγίσθαι τὸ βιβλίον τὸ ἀ. τῶν ἐν αὐτῷ γεγραμμένων δηλοῖ* Areth.*Apoc.*13(M.106.585C); hence *apocryphal*, exeg. Cant.6:7 *τὰς μὲν ἑξήκοντα βασιλίσσας τὰς ἐγκρίτους λέγομεν εἶναι βίβλους...τῆς παλαιᾶς καὶ καινῆς διαθήκης· τὰς δὲ ὀγδοήκοντα παλλακάς...τὰς λεγομένας ἀποκρύφους. παλλακαὶ δὲ ὀνομάζονται διὰ τὸ ἀ. καὶ νόθους αὐτὰς εἶναι* Ant.Mon.*hom.*proem.(M. 89.1428C).

[*]**ἀπαρσεν-όω (ἀπαρρενόω), 1.** *make masculine, make a mature man of πάντας γενέσθαι νυμφίους ἀπηρσενωμένους διὰ τοῦ παρθενικοῦ πνεύματος* Hipp.*haer.*5.8(p.97.16; M.16.3151B); **2.** met., *make manly* (ref. Is.66:7f.) *ἵνα γεννήσῃ τὸν λαὸν ἡ νοητὴ Σιὼν τὸν ἄρσενα, τὸν τῶν γυναικείων παθῶν...εἰς τὴν ἑνότητα τοῦ κυρίου καταντήσαντα καὶ ∼ωθέντα τῇ σπουδῇ* Meth.*symp.*8.7(p.90.3; M.18.149B); *ἀπηρσενωμένον ἔχουσα τὸν νοῦν* Cyr.*Jo.*2.4(4.183B); *τὸ θηλυδριῶδες αὐτῆς* [sc. *τῆς ὀργῆς*] *ἀπαρρ.* Diad.*perf.*62(p.72.3).

***ἀπάρτημα, τό,** *pendent ornament*, Gr.Nyss.*v.Mos.*(M.44.389C); *ἀπήρ- ib.*(320C,D).

ἀπαρτία, ἡ, *departure, removal*, *Hom.Clem.*15.4; Cosm.Ind.*top.*5 (M.88.205A).

ἀπαρτίζω, *complete*; **1.** perf. ptcpl. pass., *complete εὐχὰς ἐποιεῖτο ...καὶ ἀπηρτισμένην ἱερουργίας ἀκολουθίαν* ‡Sophr.H.*liturg.*(M.87. 3981C); *whole* opp. *τοὺς διαλελυμένους*, Chrys.*hom.7.2 in 1Thess.* (11.474B); **2.** *make up, complete* a sum, Thdr.Mops.*Ps.*7:10(M.66. 652C); Thdt.*Ps.*7:10(1.647); **3.** *accomplish*; **a.** *bring to perfection*, Or.*princ.*3.1.19(p.232.12; M.11.292A) cit. s. *τελείωσις*; of old Law in the new, Chrys.*hom.23.3 in Rom.*(9.690C) cit. s. *ἀνακεφαλαιόω*; Nil. *Magn.*5(M.79.976C); **b.** *perform* a rite, Cyr.H.*catech.*23.8 cit. s. *θυσία*; Gnostic, Hipp.*haer.*5.9(p.102.15; M.16.3160) cit. s. *πύλη*; **c.** *accomplish, fulfil* prophecy etc. *ἀπαρτισθησομένους καὶ...πληρωθησομένους ὥσπερ λέγονται αἱ προφητεῖαι πεπληρῶσθαι* Or.*comm.in Gen.*3.9(M.12.73B)ap.Eus.*p.e.*6.11(292C); Chrys.*hom.38.1 in Mt.*(7. 425B); **d.** perf. ptcpl. pass.; **i.** *accomplished, adept βουλαῖς ἀπηρτισμένοι* Hipp.*haer.*4.18(p.51.8; M.16.3086A); hence of the baptized *οὔπω τῶν ἀ. ἦσαν, οὐδὲ ἀδελφῶν γεγενημένων* Chrys.*hom.30.2 in Mt.*(7.349E); **ii.** in gen., *perfect, utter, absolute ἀ. ὑπακοῆς* Chrys. *hom.30.1 in Mt.*(7.348B); *ἀ. Ἕλλην* Nil.*epp.*3.8(M.79.372A); (Gnost.) *θεοῦ...γνῶσις ἀ. τελείωσις* Hipp.*haer.*5.8(p.96.8; M.16.3150B); *ib.*5.6 (p.78.15; 3126B); of wrong-doing *μοιχὸς...ἀ.* Chrys.*hom.16.3 in Mt.* (7.207A); *ib.41.4*(450E); **4.** in moral sense; **a.** *perfect ἡ προσευχὴ ὑμῶν με ἀπαρτίσει* Ign.*Philad.*5.1; id.*Eph.*3.1; Chrys.*hom.35.3 in Jo.*(8.205B); **b.** as perf. ptcpl. pass., morally *perfect οὐδὲ τέλειοί πως καὶ ἀπηρτισμένοι ἦσαν* Chrys.*hom.83.2 in Jo.*(8.491A); *ib.24.1* (137D); **5.** *ἔτι ἀπηρτισμένος τοῦ...σταυροῦ* Cyr.ap.*cat.Lc.*6:27(p.52. 13) f.l. for *ἀπηρτημένος*, cf. id. ad loc.(M.72.596A).

ἀπάρτισμα, τό, = *ἀπαρτισμός, completion, consummation τὸ... εὐαγγέλιον ἀ. ἐστιν ἀφθαρσίας* Ign.*Philad.*9.2.

***ἀπαρτισμάτιον, τό,** *perfection γνήσιοι* [sc. *μαργαρῖται*] *ἐν αὐτοῖς ἀπαρτισμάτια ἔχοντες* Ephr.2.269D; *ἀ. λέγονται, ἐπειδὴ ἀπαρτίσαντα τὴν αὔξησιν καὶ πέμψαντα τὴν οὐσίαν εἰς τὴν δύναμιν τῆς φύσεως, οὐκ αἴρονται ἀλλὰ τίκτονται ib.*2.269F.

ἀπαρχή, ἡ, *first-fruit*;

A. lit., as offered by Church; in gen., Or.*Cels.*8.34(p.249.14; M.11.1565C); to be given to prophets, *Did.*13.3; to be brought to bishop, *Const.App.*2.22.6; first-fruits for priests, tithes for the poor, *ib.*8.30.2; prayer of thanksgiving, *ib.*8.40.1; to be sent to house of bishop or priest for distribution to clergy, *Can.App.*4; except for milk and honey, *Cod.Afr.*37; cf. *εὐλογέω*; of OT first-fruits ref. alms, *Const.App.*2.26.2 cit. s. *προσφορά*; cf.Iren.*haer.* 4.17.5(M.7.1023C) cit. s. *προσφέρω*; cf. B.2 infra.

B. met., of what is first, best, or representative; **1.** of Christ; **a.** as united to and so representative of the whole of humanity *ἐκ πάσης δὲ τῆς ἀνθρωπίνης φύσεως, ᾗ κατεμίχθη τὸ θεῖον, οἷον ἀ. τις τοῦ κοινοῦ φυράματος ὁ κατὰ Χριστὸν ἄνθρωπος ὑπέστη, δι' οὗ προσεφύη τῇ θεότητι πᾶν τὸ ἀνθρώπινον* Gr.Nyss.*hom.in 1Cor.15:28* (M.44.1313B); *ib.*(1316A); *οἱ πόδες* [i.e. man] *ἐγένοντο κεφαλή, καὶ εἰς τὸν θρόνον ἀνηνέχθησαν τὸν βασιλικὸν διὰ τῆς ἀ.* Chrys.*diab.*1.2 (2.249B); Cyr.*Lc.*3:21(M.72.524C); as the second Adam *τῆς γὰρ τοῦ γένους ἡμῶν ἀ. δι' ἁμαρτίαν κατακριθείσης, δευτέρας ἔχρῃζεν ἀ. ἀναμαρτήτου* Procl.CP *annunt.*3(M.85.432D); *οὗ* [sc. *τοῦ ἀνθρωπίνου φυράματος*] *καὶ ἀ. γεγονώς, εἰς ἑαυτὸν ἀνεζύμωσεν καὶ τὸ ὅλον φύραμα* Leont.B.*Nest.et Eut.*2(M.86.1344A); Leont.H.*Nest.*1(M.86.1468B); of Christ's humanity, ‡Ath.*Ar.*4.33(p.82.5; M.26.517C) cit. s. *ἀνακεράννυμι*; *τὴν ἀ. ἡμῶν εἰς οὐρανὸν ἀνήγαγε* Chrys.*anom.*8.6(1.523A); *οἱ λέγειν τολμῶντες μὴ ἐκ τῆς φύσεως ἡμῶν παρὰ τοῦ σωτῆρος εἰλῆφθαι τὴν ἀ.* Euther.*confut.*15(M.28.1384B); *ἀναγκαῖον οὖν...τὴν πλήρωσιν τοῦ νόμου, τὴν διὰ τῆς ἀ. γενομένην, ὅλῳ λογίζεσθαι τῷ φυράματι ib.* (1385A); *τὴν τοῦ ἀνθρώπου φύσιν ὡς ἐν ἀ. τῷ Χριστῷ τῇ τοῦ ἁγίου πνεύματος χάριτι κατακεχρισμένην* Cyr.*Lc.*4:1(M.72.525B); *οὐ γὰρ ἦν ἀεὶ ἡ ἐξ ἡμῶν ληφθεῖσα ὑπὸ τοῦ θεοῦ λόγου ἀ., ἀλλὰ πρὸς τῷ τέλει αἰώνων ἐγένετό τε καὶ ἀνελήφθη ὑπὸ τοῦ θεοῦ λόγου* Thdt.*Trin.*8 (M.75.1157A); *διὰ τὴν ἐμὴν σωτηρίαν περιβέβλησαι τὴν ἐμὴν ἀ.* Gr. Ant.*bapt.*1(M.10.1180D); Germ.CP *or.*2(M.98.256A); **b.** esp. ref. Christ's Resurrection (cf. 1Cor.15:20) *ἀνάστασιν...ἧς τὴν ἀ. ἐποιήσατο τὸν κύριον 1Clem.*24.1; Eus.*l.C.*15(p.247.12; M.20.1420A); Ath.*inc.* 20.2(M.25.132A) cit. s. *ἄφθαρτος*; id.*inc.et c.Ar.*12(M.25.1004B); Cyr. *hom.pasch.*1.6(5^2.16B); Cosm.Ind.*top.*3(M.88.137A); cf. 5.b infra; **c.** as supreme in virtue *ἀνδρῶν μὲν καθαρότητος τῆς ἐν ἁγνείᾳ ἀπαρχὴν γεγονέναι τὸν Ἰησοῦν, γυναικῶν δὲ τὴν Μαρίαν* Or.*comm.in Mt.*10.17(p.22.2; M.13.877A); **2.** of elements in eucharist *τὸ γοῦν προσαγόμενον...καλεῖται...ἀ. ... ὡς πάντων τῷ θεῷ προσενηνεγμένων τυγχάνουσα ἱερωτέρα καὶ ἀνωτέρα* ‡Sophr.H.*liturg.*(M.87.3989A); cf. A supra; **3.** of people, first converts of missionaries *κατὰ... πόλεις κηρύσσοντες καθίστανον τὰς ἀ. αὐτῶν...εἰς ἐπισκόπους 1Clem.* 42.4; *δυνάστην...τὰ τοῦ θείου λόγου ὄργια μετασχόντα τῶν...πιστῶν ἀ. γενόμενον* Eus.*h.e.*2.1.13(M.20.137D); of one outstanding in virtue *ἡ τοῦ θεοῦ δούλη καὶ ἀ. τῶν καλῶν* Gr.Naz.*ep.*222(M.37.364A); of S. Peter *ἡ ἀ. τοῦ κυρίου ἡμῶν Clem.Ep.*1; of S. Stephen *ἀ. τῶν μαρτύρων* Ast.Am.*hom.*12(M.40.340B); ref. Lc.23:43 *ἐνδιαίτημα δὲ τὸ ἀρχαῖον τοῖς πιστεύουσι διδοὺς ἐν ἀ. καὶ πρώτῳ τῷ συγκεκρεμαμένῳ λῃστῇ* Cyr.*ador.*2(1.69D); *τὰς ἀ. τῆς λογικῆς φύσεως ὁ θεὸς ἔλαβεν τὸν Ἐνώχ* Proc.G.*Gen.*5:4ff.(M.87.264C); **4.** in gen.; **a.** of what is first *τῶν μελλόντων δοὺς* [sc. *ὁ δεσπότης*] *ἀπαρχὰς ἡμῖν γεύσεως Barn.*1.7; *νῦν μὲν ὡς ἐν ἀ. λαμβάνουσα τῆς υἱοθεσίας τὸν ἀρραβῶνα, καὶ τὴν τῆς ἀναστάσεως ἐλπίδα* Or.*schol.in Cant.*7:1(M.17.280D); *τούτων δὲ* [sc. *τὰ...ἀγαθά, ὅσα μέλλουσιν ἐν τῇ ἀναστάσει λαμβάνειν οἱ δίκαιοι*] *οἱ ἀρραβῶνες καὶ ἀ., ἐν ταῖς καρδίαις τῶν βεβαιοπίστων ἀπὸ τοῦ νῦν πνευματικῶς ἐνεργοῦσιν* Marc.Er.*opusc.*4(M.65.1009B); **b.** of what is best *μετὰ γὰρ τοὺς πάντας καρποὺς ἀναφέρεται ἡ ἀ., πρὸ δὲ πάντων τὸ πρωτογέννημα. τῶν τοίνυν φερομένων γραφῶν...οὐκ ἂν ἁμάρτοι τις λέγων πρωτογέννημα μὲν τὸν Μωυσέως νόμον, ἀ. δὲ τὸ εὐαγγέλιον* Or.*Jo.*1.2(p.6.8; M.14.28A); of virginity *τὸ οὖθαρ τῆς ἐκκλησίας... καὶ ἡ ἀ. αὐτῆς* Meth.*symp.*1.1(p.7.11; M.18.36C); cf. B.2 supra; **5.** exeg.; **a.** 1Cor.15:20 *εἰ δὲ ἀ., καὶ τούτους ἀναστῆναι δεῖ* Chrys. *hom.39.3 in 1Cor.*(10.366D); *ἀ. τῶν κεκοιμημένων, πρῶτος τῶν ἐπὶ τῆς γῆς πατήσας τὸν θάνατον· καθάπερ...καὶ ὁ...Ἀδὰμ πρῶτος εἰς αὐτὸν ἐμβέβηκεν, καὶ γέγονεν ἀ. τῶν ὠλισθηκότων εἰς φθοράν* Cyr. ad loc.(p.303.7; M.74.900D); *ἐγήγερται...ὡς ἀ. Χριστός, ἵνα γένηται ἐν πᾶσιν αὐτὸς πρωτεύων ib.*(p.304.14; 901B); *πρῶτος γὰρ ἔλυσε τοῦ θανάτου τὸ κράτος· τῇ ἀ. δὲ πάντως ἀκολουθήσει τὸ φύραμα* Thdt. ad loc.(3.269); **b.** Rom.8:23 *τὴν ἀ. τοῦ πνεύματος...τουτέστι, τῶν μελλόντων ἤδη γευσάμενοι. ... εἰ γὰρ ἡ ἀ. τοσαύτη, ὡς δι' αὐτῆς καὶ ἁμαρτημάτων ἀπαλλαγῆναι,...ἐννόησον τὸ ὅλον ἡλίκον* Chrys.*hom.14.6 in Rom.*(9.583D); Thdt.ad loc.(3.89); Gennad.*fr.Rom.*8:26(p.382.10; M.85.1700A); **c.** Rom.16:5, interpreted as either *first* or *best*, Chrys. *hom.31.1 in Rom.*(9.746A); as *first*, Thdt.ad loc.(3.157); cf. exeg. 1Cor. 16:15, Chrys.*hom.44.2 in 1Cor.*(10.408E); Thdt.*1Cor.*16:15(3.284).

***ἀπαρχῆς,** = *ἀπ' ἀρχῆς*; **1.** *εἰς τὸ ἀ. to the original state* or *position*, Cyr.*ador.*2(1.69C); *ib.*8(274C); **2.** *from the beginning*, *Asen.*23(p.74.10).

***ἀπαρχία, ἡ,** *inability to govern, senility τοὺς μὲν* [sc. *τῶν ἀρχόντων*]...*φιλαρχία κατεῖχε, τοὺς δὲ δειλία καὶ ἀ. cat.Jo.*9:16(p.290. 18); cf.Chrys.*hom.57.2 in Jo.*(8.334D).

ἀπάρχ-ομαι, 1. *offer a sacrifice first*; of institution of eucharist *πρῶτος αὐτὸς ∼όμενος καὶ τοῖς ἀποστόλοις τοῦτο παραδούς* Sev.Ant. ap.*cat.Lc.*22:16(p.156.10); **2.** *offer, dedicate*; met. *χειρῶν καὶ ποδῶν καὶ στόματος καὶ τῶν ἄλλων ἁπάντων ∼ώμεθα τῷ θεῷ* Chrys.*hom. 20.1 in Rom.*(9.657A); **3.** = *ἄρχομαι begin*, Meth.*symp.*3.8(p.37.10; M.18.76A); *παντὸς λόγου καὶ πράγματος ἀπ' εὐχαριστίας ἀ. τῷ θεῷ* Thdr.Mops.*Rom.*1:8(p.113.19; M.66.788A); of Christ *τοῦ ἁγιασμοῦ καὶ τῆς ἡμετέρας λυτρώσεως ∼όμενος cat.Lc.*3:23(p.32.18).

***ἀπάρψετον, τό,** name of a wind, *Ev.Barth.*(Vassiliev, p.17).

ἀπαστία, ἡ, *abstinence from food, fast*, ‡Epiph.*phys.*7(M.43. 524C); *ἀ. καὶ χαμευνίας καὶ ἐκ τριχῶν ἀμπεχόνης* Thdt.*h.rel.*10(3. 1195).

***ἀπαστισοῦν,** *everyone, anyone whatever*, Cyr.*Juln.*2(6^2.58E); id. *Jo.*2.1(4.119C); id.*apol.orient.*4(6.171B; *ἅπας τις οὖν* p.43.19).

ἄπαστος, *unable to feed oneself, suckling*; neut. as subst., fig. τὸ ἁπαλὸν ἔτι τῆς κατὰ ψυχὴν ἡλικίας καὶ ἄ. Gr.Nyss.*hom.1 in Cant.*(M.44.768B).

ἀπαστράπτ-ω, 1. *flash forth*; of Moses (ref. Ex.34:29f.) ἥλιος γίνεται...τοῦ προσώπου τὸ φῶς ~ων Gr.Nyss.*hom.12 in Cant.*(M.44.1025C); **2.** met., of truth τὰ λόγια τοῦ κυρίου ταῖς τῆς ἀληθείας ~οντα αὐγαῖς Clem.*paed.*2.10(p.225.7; M.8.533A); Thdt.*affect.*proem.(4.691; ἀστράπτ- p.2.12); τῶν προφητῶν ὁ χόρος...θεογνωσίας φῶς ~οντες Bas.Sel.*or.*34.1(M.85.368C); of moral qualities τῆς εὐσεβείας...τὸ κάλλος ~ει Cyr.*Soph.*41(3.620B); of resurrection body στήλη...τις ἔσται φῶς ~ουσα θεῖον, τὸ σῶμα τῆς ἀναστάσεως Eus.*Is.*60:19(M.24.496D); ἵνα τὸ σῶμα λοιπὸν λάβῃς ἀθάνατον, ἀφθαρσίας μαρμαρυγὰς ~ον Jo.D.*hom.*12.19(M.96.808D); of divine light φῶς δ' ἀμφ' αὐτὸν ~ον Eus.*l.C.*1(p.196.21; M.20.1320A); **3.** theol. θεὸν καὶ πατέρα, τὸ ἴδιον αὐτοῖς ἀποστεῖλαι φῶς, τουτέστι τὸν ἐκ τῆς οὐσίας αὐτοῦ... ἀπαστράψαντα λόγον Cyr.*Ps.*42:3(M.69.1013D); pass. ὁ...ἐκ πατρὸς πεφηνώς τε καὶ ἀπαστραφθεὶς λόγος id.*Jo.*2.3(4.169B).

ἀπασφαλίζομαι, *make secure, establish*, Epiph.*anc.*27(p.35.29; M.43.65B).

***ἀπασχολάζ-ω,** *be wholly occupied with* τῷ Μωσῇ...τῇ πρὸς θεὸν ὁμιλίᾳ...~οντι Gr.Nyss.*v.Mos.*(M.44.321A).

ἀπασχολ-έω, 1. *leave* one *no leisure*; pass., *be wholly employed* or *engrossed*; reflex., *absorb oneself* (ref. Lc.14:18ff.) πολλοὶ δὲ τῶν κεκλημένων...~ήσαντες ἑαυτούς †Jo.D.*B.J.*9(M.96.933D); **2.** *withdraw*; **a.** intrans. τῆς θεωρίας...~εῖν βιάζεται [sc. poverty] τὴν ψυχήν Clem.*str.*4.4(p.257.24; M.8.1233B); **b.** trans., *divert* τὰ πάτρια ὑμᾶς...τῆς ἀληθείας ~εῖ ἔθη id.*prot.*10(p.70.17; M.8.209B); Ath.*ep.Amun.*(M.26.1172A); τὸ ~ηθῆναι τὸν νοῦν ἀπὸ τῆς εἰς θεὸν θεωρίας *Apophth.Patr.*(M.65.197C); **c.** pass. intrans., *spare time for* οὐκ ἠδυνάμην...~ηθῆναι οὐδὲ εἰς τὸ ἐπιτάξαι αὐτῷ τὸ φαγεῖν μου Dor.*doct.*10.2(M.88.1725A).

***ἀπασχόλησις, ἡ,** *diversion* from occupation, *interruption*, Epiph.*haer.*42.11(p.129.13; M.41.733C).

ἀπατεών, ὁ, *cheat, rogue* κηρύττων τὴν ἀλήθειαν...τοὺς φιλοσόφους...ἀπατεῶνας συνήλεγχεν [sc. Justin Martyr] Tat.*orat.*19(p.21.6; M.6.848B); of Simon Magus, *Hom.Clem.*2.18; of witch of Endor, Eustrat.*stat.anim.*21(p.507); esp. of Devil, the *Deceiver*, Clem.*prot.* 1(p.8.11; M.8.64A); acc. Manicheans τὴν δὲ σάρκα αὐτὴν...ἔργον εἶναι καὶ πλάσιν τοῦ ἀ. Serap.*Man.*51(p.73; M.18.1249A); ὁ ἀ. ἀντ-απατᾶται Gr.Nyss.*or.catech.*26(p.97.16; M.45.68B); *ib.*(p.98.10; 68D); τοὺς ἀπατηθέντας ἐρωτᾷ, τὸν ἀ. οὐκ ἐρωτᾷ †Jo.D.*creat.*6(p.140); cf. τοὺς ἀ. ἐκάλεσε δαίμονας Thdt.*h.e.*3.1.2(3.913); as adj. ὁ μισόκαλος καὶ ἀ. διάβολος ‡Anast.Ant.*serm.*4(M.89.1389C).

ἀπάτη, ἡ, 1. *fraud, deceit, treachery*; esp. of allurements of the world τῆς ἀ. τοῦ κόσμου καὶ τῆς πλάνης *Diogn.*10.7; Clem.*str.*2.10 (p.138.2; M.8.984A); κάθαρον ἡμῶν τὸν νοῦν...ἀπὸ...κοσμικῆς ἀ. *Lit.Jac.*(p.182.11); of the flesh τῆς τρυφῆς καὶ ἀ. Herm.*sim.*6.4.4; ἐπιθυμίαι καὶ ἄλλαι ἀ. Hegem.*Arch.*11(10; p.18.2; M.10.1445A); plur., Herm.*sim.*6.2.4; *ib.*6.5.6; ταῖς ἀ. τῆς ἡδονῆς Meth.*symp.*3.6(p.33.6; M.18.69B); and of Devil, Just.*1apol.*54.1(M.6.408C); τὴν τῶν δαιμόνων ἀ. Ath.*inc.*6.6(M.25.108A); τῆς παλαιᾶς ἀ. Gr.Thaum.*pan.Or.* 16(p.35.22; M.10.1096C); contrasted with ἀ. from God, Or.*hom. 20.3 in Jer.*(p.182.5; M.13.508B); and on part of Saviour ὁ μὲν γὰρ ἐπὶ διαφθορᾷ τῆς φύσεως τὴν ἀ. ἐνήργησεν, ὁ δὲ δίκαιος...καὶ σοφὸς ἐπὶ σωτηρίᾳ...τῇ ἐπινοίᾳ τῆς ἀ. ἐχρήσατο Gr.Nyss.*or.catech.*26(p.98.15ff.; M.45.68D); **2.** (subjective) *deception, delusion, error* τῆς εἰκαιότητος καὶ ἀ. *Diogn.*4.6; ἐκ...τῆς...ἀγνοίας καὶ τὰς ἀμφισβητήσεις γίνεσθαι καὶ τὰς ἀ. συμβαίνει Clem.*str.*8.6(p.92.27; M.9.585C); τὴν τῶν υἱοπατόρων λεγομένων ἀ. Gr.Nyss.*Eun.*12(1 p.227.17; M.45.924A).

ἀπάτωρ, 1. *without father*; **a.** of Gnost. aeon, offspring of Achamoth, Iren.*haer.*1.5.1(M.7.492B); **b.** of Melchizedek ἀ. ... τουτέστιν οὐκ ἴσμεν ποτὲ τίνα πατέρα ἔσχεν Chrys.*hom.12.1 in Heb.* (12.121C); ἀ. ... καὶ ἀμήτορα καλεῖ, ὡς τῆς θείας γραφῆς γονέας αὐτοῦ μὴ διηγουμένης Thdr.Mops.*Heb.*7:3(p.207.17; M.66.961C); ἀ. λέγει ...κατὰ τὸν τῆς ἱερατείας λόγον· οὔτε γὰρ γένος ἱερατικὸν εἶχεν Sever. *Heb.*7:3(p.350.13); **c.** theol., of first Person of Trin. οὐκ ἀ. τρία ...ἀλλὰ τὸν μὲν πατέρα...ἀ. ... ὁ δὲ υἱὸς πατέρα...ἔχει ‡Ath.*dial.Trin.* 1.19(M.28.1145B); **d.** Christol., of Christ in respect of human nature ἵνα ἐν ἐκείνῳ [sc. Melchizedek] καθάπερ εἰκόνι τὸν ἀληθῶς ἀ. ... Χριστὸν ἐνοπτρισώμεθα· ἀ. γὰρ Χριστὸς ἐπὶ τῆς κατὰ σάρκα, ἀμήτωρ ἐν οὐράνοις κατὰ πνεῦμα κατὰ τὴν θεότητα Eust.*Melch.* (p.37; M.61.741); Μελχισεδέκ, ὡς ἀμήτωρ τὸ ὑπὲρ ἡμᾶς, καὶ ἀ. τὸ καθ' ἡμᾶς Gr.Naz.*or.*30.21(p.143.8; M.36.132C); ὥσπερ οὗτος [sc. Melchizedek] ἀ. τῷ μὴ γενεαλογεῖσθαι, οὕτως ὁ Χριστὸς αὐτῇ τῇ φύσει τοῦ πράγματος Chrys.*hom.12.1 in Heb.*(12.122A); ὁ Χριστὸς ἦν...ἀ. γεννήσει τῆς ἀνθρωπείας φύσεως Thdr.Mops.*Heb.*7:3(M.66. 961D); Cyr.*glaph.Gen.*2(1.62E); Thdt.*Heb.*7:3(3.585); Procl.CP *annunt.*5(M.85.444B); ἀ. ... κάτω...ἀμήτωρ...ἄνω Gr.Ant.*bapt.*2.6(M. 88.1877A); ‡Chrys.*ascens.*5(3.787A); Jo.D.*carm.transfig.*(M.96.849A); **2.** *without legal father*, Synes.*ep.*3(M.66.1328B); met. ὧν [sc. Nicene fathers] ἐκπεσόντες οὗτοι [sc. the Arians] εἰκότως ἀ. γεγόνασιν Petr. II Al.*encycl.*(M.33.1284B)ap.Thdt.*h.e.*4.22.18.

ἀπαυγάζ-ω, 1. *shine forth, radiate light*, ref. Heb.1:3 οὐ γὰρ δυνατὸν τῇ ἑαυτοῦ εἰκόνι ἀχρόνως ἀπαυγασθείσῃ τὸν θεὸν...μὴ ἐξ ἀιδίου συνεῖναι Bas.*Eun.*1.20(1.231D; M.29.556C); ὥσπερ τὸ ἐκ τοῦ λύχνου φῶς καὶ ἐκ τῆς φύσεώς ἐστι τοῦ ~οντος Gr.Nyss.*fid.*(M.45. 140B); **2.** trans., *make to shine forth* πηγὴ ὢν φωτὸς...ἐξ ἑαυτοῦ τὸ μονογενὲς φῶς τῆς ἀληθείας ἀ. Gr.Nyss.*Eun.*9(2 p.225.11, v.l. ἐπ- M.45.825A).

ἀπαύγασμα, τό, *radiance*;

A. Trin., of physical radiance as illustrating **1.** generation of Son as eternal τὸ ἀ. τῆς δόξης οὐχὶ ἅπαξ γεγέννηται καὶ οὐχὶ γεννᾶται· ἀλλὰ ὅσον ἐστὶν τὸ φῶς ποιητικὸν τοῦ ἀ., ἐπὶ τοσοῦτον γεννᾶται τὸ ἀ. τῆς δόξης τοῦ θεοῦ Or.*hom.9.4 in Jer.*(p.70.17; M.13.337A); and as mediatorial, cf. *splendor...hujus lucis est unigenitus filius et ex ipso inseparabiliter velut splendor ex luce procedens et illuminans universam creaturam...qui splendor fragilibus se et infirmis mortalium oculis...offerens...capaces eos efficit ad suscipiendam gloriam lucis, etiam in hoc velut quidam 'mediator hominum ac lucis' effectus*, id.*princ.*1.2.7(p.37.7; M.11.135Cf.); **2.** co-eternity of Persons, Dion.Al.ap.Ath.*Dion.*15(p.57.4f.; M.25.501C) cit. s. αἰώνιος; ἐκ τοῦ πατρὸς ὁ υἱός, καὶ οὐδέποτε χωρὶς τοῦ υἱοῦ ὁ πατήρ· οὐκ ἐγχώρει γὰρ ἀλαμπῆ εἶναι τὴν δόξαν, ὡς οὐκ ἐγχώρει ἄνευ ἀ. εἶναι τὸν λύχνον· δῆλον δὲ ὅτι ὥσπερ τὸ εἶναι ἀ. μαρτυρία ἐστὶ τοῦ κατὰ τὴν δόξαν εἶναι...οὕτως τὸ λέγειν μὴ εἶναί τε ἀ., ἀπόδειξίς ἐστι τοῦ μηδὲ τὴν δόξαν εἶναι, ὅτε οὐκ ἦν τὸ ἀ. Gr.Nyss.*fid.*(M.45.140B); εἰ ἀ. παντὸς φωτὸς γεννᾶται μὲν ἐκ τοῦ φωτός, οὔ ποτε δέ, ἀλλὰ ἀχρόνως καὶ συναϊδίως ἐκείνῳ (οὐ γάρ ἐστι φῶς χωρὶς ἀ.)· καὶ ὁ υἱὸς ἀ. τυγχάνων, οὔ ποτε ἔσται, ἀλλὰ συναϊδίως, φωτὸς ὄντος τοῦ θεοῦ Didym.(‡Bas.) *Eun.*4(1.280E; M.29.676B); τὸ...ἀ. καὶ ἐκ τοῦ πυρός ἐστι, καὶ σὺν τῷ πυρί ἐστι· καὶ αἴτιον μὲν ἔχει τὸ πῦρ, ἀχώριστον δέ ἐστι τοῦ πυρός. ἐξ οὗ γὰρ τὸ πῦρ, ἐξ ἐκείνου καὶ τὸ ἀ. εἰ τοίνυν ἐπὶ τῶν αἰσθητῶν δυνατὸν εἶναί τι ἔκ τινος, καὶ συνυπάρχειν τούτῳ ἐξ οὗπέρ ἐστιν· μὴ ἀμφιβάλῃς, φησίν, ὡς ὁ θεὸς λόγος...καὶ γεγέννηται ὡς υἱός, καὶ συνυπάρχει τῷ γεγεννηκότι ὡς λόγος, ὅς ἀ. δόξης Thdt.*Heb.*1:3 (3.547); **3.** consubstantiality, Thgn.*hypot.fr.*2(p.76; M.10.240A) cit. s. ἀπόρροια; τὴν λέξιν τοῦ ὁμοουσίου ἀκούοντες, μὴ εἰς τὰς ἀνθρωπίνας αἰσθήσεις πίπτοντες...ἀλλ' ὡς ἐπὶ ἀσωμάτων διανοούμενοι, τὴν ἑνότητα τῆς φύσεως καὶ τὴν ταυτότητα τοῦ φωτὸς μὴ διαιρῶμεν... πάλιν γὰρ τὸ παράδειγμα τοῦ φωτὸς καὶ τοῦ ἀ. ἀναγκαῖον εἰς τοῦτο. τίς τολμήσει λέγειν τὸ ἀ. ξένον καὶ ἀνόμοιον εἶναι τοῦ ἡλίου;...τίς μᾶλλον...οὐκ ἂν εἴποι...ὄντως τὸ φῶς καὶ τὸ ἀ. ἕν εἰσι καὶ τοῦτο ἐν ἐκείνῳ δείκνυται καὶ τὸ ἀ. ἐν τῷ ἡλίῳ τυγχάνει ὄν, ὥστε τὸν ὁρῶντα τοῦτο βλέπειν κἀκεῖνο; Ath.*decr.*24(p.20.7; M.25.457C); ὁ πατὴρ... ἐγέννησε τὸν υἱόν...καὶ οὐκ ἔκτισεν...ὡς ἀ. ἀπὸ φωτὸς †Ath.*exp.fid.*4 (M.25.208A); ζητῶν παραστῆσαι...τὸ ἐκ τῆς οὐσίας τοῦ πατρὸς γεγεννῆσθαι τὸν λόγον, τοῦ ἀ. ἐμνημόνευσεν· τὸ γὰρ ἀ. ἐκ τῆς οὐσίας ἐστὶν ἐκείνου οὗ ἐστιν ἀ., καὶ διηνεκὲς καὶ ἐξ αὐτοῦ καὶ οὐδεποτ' ἄνευ ἐκείνου ἐπινοουμένου οὗ ἐστιν ἀ. Sever.*Heb.*1:3(p.346.21); τὸ αἰσθητὸν τοῦτο πῦρ φύσις μία ὂν ἤτοι οὐσία τριάς ἐστι κατὰ τοῦτο, πῦρ ἀ. φῶς. καὶ οὐδὲν τούτων προϋπάρχον τοῦ θατέρου εὑρίσκεται...ταῦτα κατὰ νοῦν λαβὼν τὰ αἰσθητά...πρὸς τὴν ἀίδιον...τοῦ θεοῦ οὐσίαν...καὶ ἀπαντήσει σοι ἡ χάρις...δεικνύουσά σοι μίαν θεότητα, πῦρ οὖσαν ἀθάνατον καὶ ἀ. καὶ φῶς Gel.Cyz.*h.e.*2.22.16(M.85.1293A); cf.Or.*Jo.*13.25(p.249. 29; M.14.444A) cit. s. ἀπόρροια; *ib.*32.28(18; p.474.7; 820A).

B. of divine irradiations and influences ναὶ μὴν καθάπερ τῷ Μωσεῖ...ἐπίχροιά τις ἐπεκάθιζε τῷ προσώπῳ δεδοξασμένη, οὕτως καὶ τῇ δικαίᾳ ψυχῇ θεία τις ἀγαθωσύνης δύναμις...οἷον ἀ. νοεροῦ καθάπερ ἡλιακῆς ἀλέας ἐναποσημαίνεταί τι, δικαιοσύνης σφραγῖδα ἐπιφανῆ, φῶς ἡνωμένον ψυχῇ Clem.*str.*6.12(p.484.17; M.9.325B); τὸ δὲ νῦν εἶναι βραχεῖά τις ἀπορροὴ πᾶν τὸ εἰς ἡμᾶς φθάνον καὶ οἷον μεγάλου φωτὸς μικρὸν ἀ. Gr.Naz.*or.*28.17(p.48.4; M.36.48C); τὰς ἀγγελικὰς...δυνάμεις...φῶς εἰσι καὶ αὐταὶ τελείου φωτὸς ἀπαυγάσματα *ib.*6.12(M. 35.737B); of a supernatural radiance, *A.(Pass.)Andr.*14(p.33.8).

C. of demons τῆς γὰρ ὕλης καὶ πονηρίας εἰσὶν ἀ. Tat.*orat.*15(p.17.2; M.6.840A).

***ἀπαυγαστικός,** *emitting light*, Gr.Nyss.*hex.*12(M.44.73D).

ἄπαυστος, *unceasing, endless, everlasting*; esp. of things pertaining to next world: πῦρ Just.*dial.*130.2(M.6.777D); ζωή Clem. *q.d.s.*23(175.5); ἡμέρα Bas.*Spir.*66(3.56C; M.32.192B); of the Christian hope εὐφροσύνη...ἔστω σοι...ἄ. ὁ Χριστός Clem.*fr.*44(p.222.23); theol., of Persons in Trin. τῆς ἀιδίου κοινωνίας καὶ ἀ. συναφείας Bas.

*Spir.*59(50C; M.177A); of Father οὐ...ἀ. ἡ εὐσέβεια *Const.App.* 7.35.10; of H. Ghost ἡ...προαιώνιος ὕπαρξις καὶ ἀ. διαμονὴ μεθ' υἱοῦ καὶ πατρὸς θεωρουμένη Bas.*Spir.*63(53A; M.184B).

ἀπαύστως, *unceasingly, everlastingly, for ever*; of hell fire καταδίκην τοῦ πυρὸς ἀ. κολάζεσθαι Just.*dial.*45.4(M.6.573A); of God's activity, ‡Just.*qu.Chr.*2.4(M.6.1421B); of Father and Son (Anomoean) ἑκατέρας φύσεως ἀ. διαμενούσης ἐν τῷ οἰκείῳ τῆς φύσεως ἰδιώματι Aët.*synt.*4(p.353.12; M.42.536C om.).

***ἀπαφητός**, *that can be deceived*, *Orac.Sib.*7.129.

***ἀπάφρισις, ἡ**, *emission of seed*, ‡Caes.Naz.*dial.*140(M.38.1049).

ἀπεγνωσμένως, f.l. for ἀπεγνωσμένους Chrys.ap.*cat.Tit.*3:4(p.98. 19); cf.id.*hom.*5.3 *in Tit.*(11.761C).

ἀπείθανος, for ἀπίθανος, *incredible, unlikely; unconvincing*, Didym.*Trin.*1.18(M.39.341C); *ib.*3.4(828C).

ἀπείθεια, ἡ, 1. *disobedience*; **a.** in gen.; to civil authority, on the part of a martyr οὗτός σοι τῆς καλῆς ἀ. μισθός Sophr.H.*v.Anast.* (M.92.1720A); **b.** to God, Clem.*str.*7.16(p.72.15; M.9.541B); Bas.*jud.*4 (2.217B; M.31.661A); τῇ ἀ. καὶ ἀποστασίᾳ ἡμῶν id.*reg.fus.*2.4(2. 339D; M.31.916B); οἱ ἄγγελοι...ὑπείκουσιν, μήπως ἀπειθείας κριθέντες ἀπόλωνται *Hom.Clem.*5.5; *ib.*3.31; on the part of demons, Ath.*inc.* 25.5(M.25.140B); of Israel, Thdr.Mops.*Jon.*proem.(M.66.321B); plur. τὰς εἰς ἀπώλειαν φερούσας ἀ. Clem.*paed.*1.12(conj. p.150.8 for ἀπειλάς M.8.369C); personified, Herm.*sim.*9.15.3; **c.** of Jewish rejection of Christ, Sophr.H.*nativ.*(p.514.6); τῆς Ἰουδαϊκῆς ἀ. τὴν τριαδικὴν δοξολογίαν...τὰ ἔπαθλα ‡Meth.*Sym.et Ann.*12(M.18.377B); **2.** *non-compliance* οὐκ ἀνέξεται ὁ ἰατρὸς τῆς τοῦ κάμνοντος ἱκεσίας...καὶ τὴν ἀ. οὐκ ἀπανθρωπίαν, ἀλλὰ φιλανθρωπίαν ὀνομάζομεν Chrys.*hom.in Mt.*7:14(3.27D).

ἀπειθ-έω, 1. *be disobedient, disobey*; freq. having God as object ἀ. τοῖς ὑπ' αὐτοῦ δι' ἡμῶν εἰρημένοις *1Clem.*59.1; *ib.*58.1; Polyc.*ep.*2.1; Gnost. ὁ τῆς χοϊκῆς φύσεως πάντως ~εῖ θεῷ Or.*princ.*3.1.8(p.207.8; M.11.261A); **2.** *disbelieve, reject*, Ign.*Magn.*8.2; τῶν μὲν πεπιστευκότων σωτὴρ...τῶν δὲ ~ησάντων κύριος Clem.*str.*7.2(p.7.18; M.9.412A); πρὸς Ἕλληνας λεκτέον, ~οῦντας τῇ ἐκ παρθένου γενέσει τοῦ Ἰησοῦ Or.*Cels.*1.37(p.88.20; M.11.729D); ἡμᾶς τοὺς πρότερον ~οῦντας Ath.*Ar.*2.12(M.26.172C); Sev.Ant.*res.*(p.814.10; M.46.636B); ᾔδει [sc. David]...ὡς ~ήσουσιν Ἰουδαῖοι Χριστῷ Sophr.H.*nativ.*(p.514.2); **3.** *refuse* ἡ κόλασις μείζων τῷ δυναμένῳ καὶ ~ήσαντι [sc. οἰκονομεῖν τὴν ἐκκλησίαν] *Hom.Clem.*3.65; **4.** *not comply with*, hence *be incompatible with* (cf. Is.7:16) ἡ θεία φύσις...οὐσιωδῶς ~οῦσα τῇ πονηρίᾳ ...ὥσπερ ἂν εἴ τις λέγοι περὶ τοῦ φωτὸς ὅτι ~εῖ που εἶναι σκότος Cyr. *Is.*1.4(2.123B).

***ἀπείθημα, τό**, *act of disobedience*; of the Jews, *Dial.Tim.et Aquil.*99 r°.

ἀπειθής, 1. *disobedient*, of heretics ἀ. μὲν γονεῦσι γεγόνασι, διαμάχονται δὲ πρὸς οἰκουμενικὴν σύνοδον Ath.*syn.*33(p.260.30; M.26. 752A); to God φαμὲν δ' αὐτῷ ἐχθροὺς εἶναι τοὺς ἀ. καὶ μὴ κατὰ τὰς ἐντολὰς αὐτοῦ πορευομένους Clem.*str.*7.12(p.50.5; M.9.496D); Cyr. *Mich.*52(3.443E); of Jewish nation, Just.*dial.*130.3(M.6.780A); *ib.* 120.5(756A); *ib.*140.2(797A); Cyr.*Os.*5(3.25B); **2.** *unbelieving*, Chrys. *hom.*26.3 *in Jo.*(8.152C) and perh. ref. the woman of Samaria οὔτε ...εὔκολος ἡ γύνη...οὔτε ἀ. καὶ φιλόνεικος *ib.*32.2(186A); Nonn.*par. Jo.*16:9(M.43.880A).

ἀπεικασμός, ὁ, *copy, representation* ὁ κτίσας τῷ κεκτισμένῳ ἀνόμοιος ὑπάρχει...εἰ μή τι ἂν πρὸς ἀ. καὶ ἀπεικόνισμα κατὰ μίμησιν μόνον θεωρίας ἐστὶ τὸ ἐκτυπούμενον Epiph.*haer.*76.3(p.344.3; M.42. 521B); *ib.*76.5(p.346.4; 524D).

ἀπεικονίζ-ω, 1. *represent in a statue* or *picture*; **a.** in gen. οὐ γὰρ ἄν ποτε ὁ μηδὲ γλυπτὸν εἴδωλον δημιουργεῖν παραινέσας αὐτὸς ἀπηκόνιζεν τῶν ἁγίων ἄγαλμα Clem.*str.*5.6(p.351.2; M.9.61C); οὐ περιγράφεται τόπῳ θεὸς οὐδὲ ~εταί ποτε ζῴου σχήματι *ib.*7.6(p.22.6; 440B); Epiph.*anac.*3(p.163.6; M.41.168A); **b.** theol., ref. relation of Son to Father ἡ εἰκὼν τὸ τοῦ ἀπεικονισθέντος κάλλος δι' ἑαυτῆς ἑρμηνεύει Gr.Nyss.*Eun.*11(2 p.264.25; M.45.873A); **c.** pass., *be modelled* or *formed*, of man τὸ...ὑπ' αὐτοῦ καὶ πρὸς αὐτὸν [sc. θεόν] ἀπεικονισμένον Clem.*paed.*1.3(p.94.12; M.8.257A); (ref. Ps.138:16) σπαρέντα πρὶν ἀπεικονισθῆναί με ἔγνως με Epiph.*haer.*30.30(p.375.17; M.41. 460B); met., of Constantine ὁ πρὸς τὴν ἀρχέτυπον τοῦ μεγάλου βασιλέως ἀπεικονισμένος ἰδέαν Eus.*l.C.*5(p.204.18; M.20.1336C); **2.** *represent to oneself, picture mentally* πρὸς τὰς προλήψεις ἡ ἑκάστου ψυχὴ ἰδέας δαιμόνων ~ει *Hom.Clem.*9.16; pass., *be represented to the mind, described* ὁ τῆς μελλούσης κρίσεως ~εται φόβος Bas.Sel.*or.*19.2 (M.85.244A); **3.** s.v.l., *express in similes* λόγος ἐσπουδάσθη σφόδρα ἀπεικονισμένος καὶ οὐδὲν σχῆμα ὀκνήσας Synes.*Dion* 1(M.66.1116D; ἀπηγκωνισμένος p.237.1); **4.** pass., *be reflected*; **a.** ὥσπερ...ὁ ἐν τῷ καθαρῷ κατόπτρῳ...κατανοήσας, ἐναργῆ τοῦ ἀπεικονισθέντος προσώπου τὴν γνῶσιν ἔσχεν Gr.Nyss.*diff.ess.*8(M.32.340C); **b.** theol., of relation of Logos to Father ἡ τῶν ὅλων ἀρχὴ ἥτις ἀπεικόνισται ...ἐκ τοῦ θεοῦ τοῦ ἀοράτου Clem.*str.*5.6(p.353.1; M.9.65A).

ἀπεικόνισμα, τό, 1. *representation, likeness*; **a.** in art, not possible of God, Clem.*str.*6.18(p.516.7; M.9.396B); cf.Jo.D.*f.o.*4.16(M.94. 1173A); Geo.Pis.*Pers.*2.87(M.92.1218A); of idols ἀ. νεκρῶν ἀνθρώπων Thphl.Ant.*Autol.*1.10(M.6.1040A); *M.Apollon.*21; τοὺς ἑαυτῶν προπάτορας δι' ἀπεικονισμάτων τετιμηκότες *Chron.Pasch.*p.48(M.92. 173A); cf. τῶν λεγομένων ἡρώων τὰ ἀ. ... εἴδωλα...οὐχ ὑπάρχουσι Mac.Mgn.*apocr.*3.42(p.147.10); of brazen serpent of Num.21:8, Thdr.Mops.*Jon.*proem.(M.66.321B); of images of saints etc., Jo.D. *imag.*1.10(M.94.1249B); **b.** of a child παῖς, αὐτὸ...τῶν γεννησαμένων τὸ ἀ. Gr.Nyss.*virg.*3(p.261.22; M.46.332A); **c.** of man as made in image of God ἐνταῦθα...τὸ ἀ. ... τὸ θεῖον καὶ ἅγιον ἄγαλμα ἐν τῇ δικαίᾳ ψυχῇ Clem.*str.*7.5(p.21.31; M.9.440A); τὴν αἰώνιον ἀπομιμησάμενος φύσιν...ἧς καὶ χαρακτήρ ἐστιν ὁ ἄνθρωπος καὶ ἀ. Meth. *symp.*6.2(p.65.11; M.18.116A); Eus.*d.e.*3.3(p.112.27; M.22.193A); ἀ. ... τοῦ ἀρχετύπου...κάλλους Gr.Nyss.*or.catech.*6(p.36.5; M.45.29B); *ib.* (p.32.6; 28A); id.*hom.*2 *in Cant.*(M.44.793B,805D); *ib.*12(1020C); τὴν ἡμετέραν φύσιν...τῆς ἰδίας ἀγαθότητος ἀρίδηλον ἀ. ... κατέστησεν Max. *ep.*3(M.91.409A); **d.** theol., of Son οὐ τὴν ἀγεννησίαν τοῦ πατρὸς ἐν τῷ ἀ. βλέπων Gr.Nyss.*diff.ess.*8(M.32.340B); τοῦ γεννωμένου υἱοῦ πρὸς τὸν πατέρα...ἀπεικονίσματος...λοιπὸν εὑρισκομένου Epiph.*haer.* 76.3(p.343.13; M.42.520C); **2.** *copy*, (Arian) οὐκ ἐκ τῆς οὐσίας ὑπάρχων τοῦ πατρὸς ὁ υἱὸς ἀναδείκνυται, ἀλλὰ μᾶλλον ἀ. τῆς οὐσίας αὐτοῦ Cyr.*Jo.*3.5(4.301B).

***ἀπεικονισμός, ὁ**, *representation, statue*, Epiph.*anac.*1.1(p.163.11; M.41.168A).

***ἀπεικονιστέον**, *one must liken, compare*, Meth.*symp.*3.6(p.32.21; M.18.69A).

***ἀπειληφόρος**, *bringing threats, threatening*; ref. Day of Judgement ἀγγέλους ἀ. Chrys.*hom.*53.5 *in Mt.*(7.545C); ἀ. ... δυνάμεις id. *hom.*9.4 *in 2Cor.*(10.504C); id.*Laz.*6.1(1.773D).

***ἀπειλικρινέω**, *purify, purge*, Synes.*provid.*2.6(p.127.7; M.66. 1276C).

ἄπειμι (-εἶναι), *be absent*; hence **1.** *fail, be wanting*; of persons ἐπέρχονται ἡμῖν θλίβερα πράγματα, τοῦτο μὲν δι' ἀνθρώπων φθονούντων...πλανώντων, ἀπόντων Marc.Er.*opusc.*7.17(M.65.1096C); **2.** ἀπείη as interjection, *God forbid!* (cf. Lat. *absit*), Just.*1apol.*21.5(p.36. 7; M.6.360B); *Hom.Clem.*1.22; *ib.*2.43.

ἄπειμι (-ιέναι), 1. *go out to, attend* a social function (ref. 1Cor. 10:27) οὐ γὰρ...ἐνομοθέτησεν ἀπιέναι, ἀλλ' οὐδὲ ἐκώλυσεν Chrys.*hom.* 25.1 *in 1Cor.*(10.220C); a funeral εἴτε εἰς ἐκφορὰν ἀπιέναι...εἴτε εἰς ἄριστα id.*hom.*30.2 *in Heb.*(12.281D); **2.** impers., *it leads* or *approximates* to ἀπῄει...εἰς ἀφροσύνην ἐπαρθέντα φρονῆσαι τοῦτο Meth. *res.*1.35(p.275.11; M.41.1100D); **3.** ? *have just* (cf. French, *venir de*), *A.Petr.et Paul.*17,18(pp.186.14,187.3); **4.** with λαμβάνω; **a.** *come off with* πολλοὺς λαβὼν ἄπεισι μώλωπας Chrys.*hom.*23.6 *in 1Cor.* (10.210D); **b.** *take away, carry off* ὡς...αἰχμάλωτον λαβὼν αὐτὸν ὁ διάβολος ἄπεισι Chrys.*hom.*58.3 *in Mt.*(7.589A); id.*hom.*2.7 *in 2Cor.*(10.439A); τοῦ σώματος λέγω· ὃ κἂν μὴ οὗτοι ἀποκτείνουσιν ἡ φύσις λαβοῦσα ἄπεισι πάντως id.*hom.*34.2 *in Mt.*(7.392B); id.*hom.* 13.4 *in Phil.*(11.301E).

[*]**ἀπεινής**, = ἀπηνής, *harsh, cruel*, ‡Nil.*perist.*11.1(M.79.901B).

ἀπειραγαθέω, *be ignorant of what is good*, Epiph.*haer.*73.37 (p.312.13; M.42.472C).

ἀπειραγαθία, ἡ, *ignorance of the good*, hence *vain magnificence, ostentatious display*, ref. Jo.4:7 σκοπὸν...τὴν χρείαν ἐτίθετο [sc. ὁ Χριστός], οὐ τὴν ἀ. Clem.*paed.*2.3(p.180.4; M.8.437A); ref. life of Jo. Bapt. in desert ἐκτὸς πάσης κενοσπουδίας, ἀ., μικροπρεπείας *ib.*2.10 (p.224.19; 532B); of women, *ib.*2.12(p.231.24; 548A).

ἀπειράγαθος, *infinitely good* τῆς ἀ. δυνάμεως Dion.Ar.*d.n.*8.4 (M.3.892C, v.l. ἀπειροδυνάμου).

ἀπείρανδρος, *not having known man, virgin*; of BMV, Sophr.H. *or.*2.17(M.87.3236D); ‡Jo.D.*hom.*6.6(M.96.669A); Jo.Mon.*hymn.Blas.* 7(M.96.1405A).

ἀπείραστος, 1. *that cannot be tempted, incapable of being tempted*, of God μακάριος ὅστις οὐκ ἐπείρασεν ἐν σοὶ τὸν θεόν· ὁ γὰρ σὲ πειράζων τὸν ἀ. πειράζει *A.Jo.*57(p.179.28); *ib.*90(p.196.2); ‡Ign.*Phil.*11; Gr. Naz.*or.*24.9(M.35.1180B); **2.** *that has not been tempted, untried, untested*, Clem.*str.*7.12(p.51.11; M.9.500A); ὁ...Ἀντώνιος ἔλεγεν ἡμῖν ὅτι οὐδεὶς ἀ. δυνήσεται εἰσελθεῖν εἰς τὴν βασιλείαν τοῦ θεοῦ Ammonas *ep.*4(p.443.3) ∾ Dor.*ep.*5(M.88.1840D); λέγει ἡ γραφή 'ἀνὴρ ἀδόκιμος ἀ. παρὰ τῷ θεῷ' *Const.App.*2.8.2; οὐ δόκιμον τὸ ἀ.· τὸ δὲ βασανισθὲν ἐν τοῖς πράγμασι δοκιμώτερον Gr.Naz.*ep.*214(M.37.349B); ἀνὴρ ἀ., ἀδόκιμος, οὐδενὸς λόγου ἄξιος Jo.D.*f.o.*2.30(M.94.977C); **3.** *without* experience εἰ παντελῶς ἀ. αὐτῶν ἡ ἡμετέρα φύσις μεμενήκει Thdt. *provid.*5(4.560); Max.*qu.Thal.*(M.90.256A); **4.** *inexperienced, unskilled* ἀνθρώπους ἀ. γραμμάτων *A.Thom.*B 59(p.42.24).

***ἀπειράστως**, *without making trial, not captiously*, Dam.*troph.*1.1 (p.192.6).

ἀπειρία, ἡ, *infinity*; of God, Gr.Naz.*or.*38.7(M.36.317C); τὴν κρυφίαν αὐτῆς ἀ. Dion.Ar.*d.n.*1.2(M.3.588C); Max.*ambig.*(M.91. 1188A).

***ἀπεῖρξις, ἡ,** *exclusion*, Thdr.Stud.*epp.*2.32(M.99.1205A).

***ἀπειροαγαλλίατος**, *of eternal rejoicing*, Thdr.Stud.*epp.*1.2(M.99. 912C).

***ἀπειροβαθής**, *of infinite depth, unfathomable*, Synes.*hymn.*4.171 (p.31; M.66.1606).

***ἀπειρόβουλος**, *whose will is infinite*; in refutation of Severus' Christology, Max.*opusc.*(M.91.53Aff.) cit. s. ἀπειροπρόσωπος.

***ἀπειρογαμία, ἡ,** *inexperience of marriage, celibacy*, Tit.Bost. *Man.*2.33(M.18.1197D).

ἀπειρόγαμος, *without experience of marriage, virgin*; **1.** in gen., Chrys.*hom.7.5 in Phil.*(11.253C); dist. from life of professed virginity οὐδὲ παρθενία τοῦτό ἐστι τὸ ἀ. εἶναι id.*hom.7.4 in 2 Tim.*(11. 704E); παρθένον ἐνταῦθα λέγων, οὐ τὴν ἀποταξαμένην, ἀλλὰ τὴν ἀ. μόνον id.*hom.in 1Cor.7:39*(3.209B); ref. distn. between παρθένος and νεᾶνις, †Bas.*Is.*201(1.528E; M.30.464B); **2.** of BMV, Eus.*d.e.* 7.1(p.301.16; M.22.517B); *ib.*4.10(p.169.3; 281B); Procl.CP *or.*4.2 (M.65.712C); Gr.Naz.*carm.*1.1.9.46(M.37.460A); Bas.Sel.*v.Thecl.*1(M. 85.506A); Cyr.*schol.inc.*25(p.228.18; 5[1].794B Lat.); Sophr.H.*ep.syn.* (M.87.3160D); hence term λοχεία inappropriate, Gr.Nyss.*hom.13 in Cant.*(M.44.1053A); free from the pains of childbirth, Paul.Em. *hom.*1(p.10.3; M.77.1436A); λοχεία Paul.Sil.*Soph.*436(M.86.2136B); λόχος ‡Meth.*Sym.et Ann.*11(M.18.376C).

***ἀπειρογάμως**, *without experience of marriage, without sexual union*, ‡Caes.Naz.*dial.*36(M.38.901); ἡ ἀ. κυήσασα Jo.D.*carm.dorm. BMV* 4(M.96.1364C).

***ἀπειρόγνωστος**, *of infinite knowledge, omniscient* τῆς θεαρχικῆς καὶ ἀ. σοφοποιίας Dion.Ar.*c.h.*14(M.3.321A); Max.*ambig.*(M.91. 1188B).

ἀπειροδύναμος, *infinitely powerful*; of God τῆς αὐτοκρατορικῆς ἀ. ... φύσεως Didym.*Trin.*1.27(M.39.405A); as divine name ὡς ἀ., οὐ μόνον τῷ πᾶσαν δύναμιν παράγειν, ἀλλὰ καὶ τῷ ὑπὲρ πᾶσαν καὶ τὴν αὐτοδύναμιν εἶναι Dion.Ar.*d.n.*8.2(M.3.889D); Jo.D.*f.o.*1.8(M.94. 808C); *ib.*1.14(860A); αὐτὸς ὢν...ἀ. δύναμις id.*imag.*3.29(M.94.1349B); esp. in creation τὸ τῆς θείας προνοίας περὶ τὸν ἄνθρωπον καὶ τεχνικῆς οἰκονομίας ἀ. ‡Bas.*struct.hom.*2.17(1.347D; M.30.61C); ἀ. ... θελήσει τοῦ θεοῦ καὶ γέγονε πάντα, καὶ σῴζεται τὰ γενόμενα ‡Hipp.*Ber.Hel.*1 (p.321.15; M.10.829C); Max.*ambig.*(M.91.1188B); of incarnate Christ ἀ. ἅτε καὶ θεός id.*schol.e.h.*1.1.6(M.4.116B); Jo.D.*volunt.*11(M.95. 141A); his power, Max.*ep.*12(M.91.501B); id.*opusc.*(M.91.120A); goodness, Dion.Ar.*d.n.*3.2(M.3.681D); of H. Ghost, Jo.D.*f.o.*1.8(M. 94.821B).

***ἀπειρόδωρος**, *boundlessly munificent, infinitely abundant*; of God, Dion.Ar.*d.n.*5.3(M.3.817B); δωρεὰς...κατὰ ἀ. χύσιν *ib.*9.2(909C, v.l. ἀπειροδύναμον); ἀ. χύσιν ἀγαθότητος Max.*ambig.*(M.91.1288C); ἀ. χάριν τῆς ἀκηράτου θεώσεως Andr.Cr.*or.*7(M.97.933B).

***ἀπειρόζυγος**, *without experience of the yoke*, Cyr.*Is.*2.3(2.250E); of BMV ἡ ἀ. δάμαλις Sophr.H.*trop.*(M.87.4008B); ref. monastic discipline, Isid.Pel.*epp.*1.260(M.78.337D); ref. Mt.11:29 of the unbaptized, Bas.*hom.*13.1(2.114D; M.31.425C).

ἀπειροθάλαττος, *unused to the sea*, Bas.*hom.*5.8(2.41D; M.31. 256D); Isid.Pel.*epp.*5.225(M.78.1468C); Eustrat.*v.Eutych.*1(M.86. 2276B).

***ἀπειροθεΐα, ἡ,** *an infinite number of gods* εἴπερ ὁμοούσιος καὶ αὐτῇ [sc. BMV] ὁ ὁμοούσιος θεῷ· διὸ δὴ καὶ ἡμᾶς πάντας τοὺς ὁμοουσίους αὐτῇ, θεοὺς ἂν εἴποιεν εἰκότως· καὶ ἀ. εἰσάγουσι προφανέστατα Leont.H.*Nest.*3.6(M.86.1621B).

***ἀπειροθρήσκως**, *without experience of* true *religion*, *Pers.* (p.10.5).

ἀπειρόκακος, *without experience of evil, innocent*; of children, ref. 4Reg.2:24, ‡Just.*qu.et resp.*80(M.6.1321B); ref. 1Petr.2:2, †Bas. *Is.*216(1.541C; M.30.492D); hence *simple* ψευδολογίαις...τὸν ἀ. λαὸν διαχλευάζων ‡Jo.D.*ep.Thphl.*17(M.95.368C); neut. as subst., *innocence*, exeg. Ps.40:13 τὸ ἀ. τοῦ ἀμνοῦ τοῦ θεοῦ Eus.*d.e.*10.1(p.450. 6; M.22.724C).

***ἀπειρολογέομαι**, *talk interminably*, Leont.B.*Nest.et Eut.*3(M.86. 1372B).

***ἀπειρόλογος**, *inexperienced in using words*; of children, ‡Epiph. *hom.*1(M.43.537A); Eulog.*palm.*5(M.86.2921A).

ἀπειρομεγέθης, *infinitely great*, of God τῆς ἀνεκφράστου καὶ...ἀ. φύσεως Eus.*d.e.*4.6(p.158.25; M.22.264C); ἐκ τοῦ παναγάθου καταπεμφθεὶς θεοῦ λόγος, ὥσπερ τις ἀ. φωτὸς αὐγή id.*p.e.*1.1(2D; M.21. 24D); Bas.*ep.*233.2(3.356D; M.32.868A); σύγκρισιν γὰρ ὁ ἀ. οὐκ ἐπιδέχεται Hesych.H.*fr.Ps.*76:14(M.93.1245D); Hesych.S.*temp.*2.90 (M.93.1541A); of his power, Eus.*p.e.*7.15(325A; M.21.549B); neut. as subst., Proc.G.*Is.*6:1ff.(M.87.1933B).

***ἀπειρομεγέθως**, *infinitely greatly*, Epiph.*haer.*76.40(p.395.1; M. 42.605A).

***ἀπειρονίκης, ὁ,** *one who is not experienced in victory*, Dion.Ar. *d.n.*8.6(M.3.893C).

***ἀπειρόνυμφος**, *of innumerable brides*; of Christ as Spouse of virgins, Thdr.Stud.*epp.*2.150(M.99.1468).

***ἀπειροπάθεια, ἡ,** *unbounded emotion, excess of feeling*, contrasted with ἀπάθεια and μετριοπάθεια, Synes.*ep.*140(M.66.1532C).

***ἀπειροπλάσιος**, *infinitely multiplied, infinitely more*, ref. Is.40:2 and Ps.78:12 οὐκ ἀ. μέν, ἤτοι δὲ διπλάσια ἢ ἑπταπλάσια λήψονται οἱ ἡμαρτηκότες ἐκ χειρὸς κυρίου τὰ ἁμαρτήματα Or.*comm.in Mt.*13.30 (p.267.16; M.13.1177B); Gr.Nyss.*hom.1 in Cant.*(M.44.784B); Jo.D. *B.J.*33(M.96.1181C); neut. as subst., *infinite amount*, of God οὐχ ἑνὶ κόσμῳ σύμμετρον τὴν ποιητικὴν ἔχων δύναμιν, ἀλλ' εἰς τὸ ἀ. ὑπερβαίνουσαν Bas.*hex.*1.2(1.3D; M.29.8C).

ἀπειροπλασίων, *infinitely multiplied, infinitely more*; *infinitely greater*, Bas.*hex.*6.9(1.59E; M.29.141A); ἀ. εἶναι τὸν ποιητὴν πάντων τῶν μόνῳ θελήματι παραχθέντων εἰς γένεσιν Gr.Nyss.*Eun.*12(1 p.250. 23; M.45.952B); Proc.G.*Gen.*1:16(M.87.100A); neut. plur. as adv., Pall.*h.Laus.*71(p.167.18, vv.ll. ἀπειροπλασιόνως, πολυπλασίως; M.34. 1258C).

***ἀπειροπλασίως**, *in infinite measure, infinitely* ἡ θεία δύναμις ...ἀ. ὑπεραίρουσα τὴν φύσιν ἡμῶν Gr.Nyss.*Eun.*12(1 p.333.18; M.45. 1049D); Nil.*epp.*3.313(M.79.536B); ‡Caes.Naz.*dial.*68(M.38.936).

ἀπειροπληθής, *infinitely* or *immensely great* or *numerous*; of the mercy of God, Areth.*Apoc.*55(M.106.732B); neut. as subst., *vast number*; of the angels, *cat.Apoc.*19:12(p.459.32).

***ἀπειρόπλουτος**, *infinitely wealthy*; or poss. *unused to wealth* ἀπειροκάλως εὐθὺς ἀπὸ πρώτης ὁμιλίας ἀπειροπλούτου δίκην ἐνεπιδείκνυσθαι τὸ τῆς προγνώσεως πλεονέκτημα Eus.*Hierocl.*19(524B; M.22.825B).

***ἀπειρόπους**, *of an infinite number of feet* τὸ ἀ. αὐτῶν [sc. Seraphim] καὶ πολυπρόσωπον Dion.Ar.*c.h.*13.4(M.3.304D).

***ἀπειροπρόσωπος**, **1.** *of an infinite number of faces*; of seraphim, Dion.Ar.*e.h.*4.3.7(M.3.481A); **2.** *whose person is infinite*, in a refutation of Severus' Christology κατὰ δὲ τὴν πρότασιν, σαφῶς ὁ τῆς οἰκονομίας αὐτῷ νενόθευται λόγος, τὸν ἕνα Χριστὸν ἀνούσιον, ἄβουλον, ἀνυπόστατον· καὶ πάλιν τὸν αὐτὸν ἀπειρόβουλόν τε πρεσβεύοντι καὶ ἀ.; οὗ τί δυσσεβέστερον; Max.*opusc.*(M.91.53B); *ib.*(53A).

ἄπειρος, **A.** *infinite*; **1.** in gen. φαμὲν γὰρ ὅτι τὸ ἄ., πολλαχῶς λέγεται Leont.H.*Nest.*1.48(M.86.1508Bff.); **2.** of God διχῇ δὲ τοῦ ἀ. θεωρουμένου, κατά τε ἀρχὴν καὶ τέλος (τὸ γὰρ ὑπὲρ ταῦτα, καὶ μὴ ἐν τούτοις, ἄ.) Gr.Naz.*or.*38.8(M.36.320A); Gr.Nyss.*Eun.*1(1 p.73.6; M.45.301D) cit. s. ἀόριστος; ἄ. γὰρ τὸ μέσον θεοῦ τε καὶ ἀνθρώπων Procl.CP *annunt.*4(M.85.437A); opp. matter ἡ ὕλη...εἰ δὲ ἄ. ... δύο πάντως τὰ ἄ. ... θεὸς καὶ ὕλη, ὅπερ εἶναι ἀμήχανον Max.*ambig.*(M.91. 1184B); πῶς γὰρ σῶμα τὸ ἄ.; Jo.D.*f.o.*1.4(M.94.797B); **3.** of Logos εἰ δὲ οὐκ ἔστι συναΐδιος ὁ λόγος τῷ πατρί, πῶς ἄ. αὐτῷ τὴν ζωὴν ἐρεῖς; εἰ γὰρ ἀρχὴν ἄνωθεν ἔχει, κἂν ἀτελεύτητος ᾖ, ἄ. ὅμως οὐκ ἔστι. τὸ γὰρ ἄ., ἑκατέρωθεν ἄ. εἶναι χρή Chrys.*hom.4.2 in Jo.*(8.30A); μόνος γὰρ ἔχεις...τὴν ὕπαρξιν ἐπ' ἄ. Thdt.ap.*cat.Heb.*1:12 suppl.(p.372.18); ref. Inc., Gr.Nyss.*or.catech.*10(p.54.10; M.45.41B) cit. s. θεότης; ἡ γὰρ ἄ. ὂν τῇ δυνάμει καὶ πρὸς πᾶσαν ἐνέργειαν ἰσχύον δύναιτο ἂν καὶ διὰ περατῆς φύσεως...ἐνεργεῖν τὰ ἴδια πάντα Leont.H.*Nest.*1.48 (M.86.1509C); **4.** of eternity τῆς ψυχῆς...τὸν ἄ. αἰῶνα Or.*princ.*3.1.13 (p.217.7; M.11.273A); Eus.*h.e.*1.3.18(M.20.76A); οὗ ἡ βασιλεία ἀκατάλυτος οὖσα διαμένει εἰς τοὺς ἀ. αἰῶνας Ath.*syn.*25(p.251.10; M.26. 725C).

B. *unlimited, innumerable*, Hipp.*haer.*7.26(p.205.1; M.16.3315B); εἰς τὸ ἄ. τεῖναι τὰς ἐπινοίας Eus.*h.e.*4.7.4(316C); of Gnost. error πολλοὺς θεούς...ἀ. ... δοξάζουσιν *Const.App.*6.8.2; of evil ἄ. καὶ ἀόριστα καὶ ἐν ἄλλοις φερόμενα καὶ τούτοις ἀ. Dion.Ar.*d.n.*4.31 (M.3.732B).

***ἀπειροσθενής**, *of infinite might* τὸ...θεῖον...ἐστι καὶ μετὰ σαρκωσιν...ὑφεστὼς οὐσιῶδες μόνον ἀ. ἀγαθόν ‡Hipp.*Ber.Hel.*1(p.322.14; M.10.832C).

***ἀπειρόσοφος**, *infinitely wise*; of the power of Christ, Max. *myst.*1(M.91.668A).

***ἀπειροστημόριον, τό,** *infinitely small particle,* Or.*hom.8.7 in Jer.*(p.61.19; M.13.344C).

ἀπειρότοκος, *never having brought forth,* Cyr.*hom.pasch.*5(5².49A).

ἀπειρώδιν ([*]**ἀπειρώδινος**), *not knowing the pangs of child-birth* ἀπειρώδινον ἔχιδναν Epiph.*haer.*26.19 (cj. p.299.25ff. for ἀπειρώδυνον M.41.361Dff.); of BMV ἀ. ἀνάσσης Nonn.*par.Jo.*19:27(M.43.904B).

***ἀπειρώνυμος,** *of infinite names*; of God, Dion.Ar.*d.n.*12.1(M.3.969A).

ἄπειστος, *not to be persuaded* πείθειν ἀπείστους Eun.ap.Gr.Nyss.*Eun.*5(2 p.108.15; ἀπίστους M.45.688B).

ἀπεκδέχ-ομαι, 1. *await eagerly, expect*; in gen., *A.Paul.et Thecl.*3 (p.237.5); τὰ μέλλοντα ἐλπίδι ἀ. Clem.*str.*2.12(p.142.2; M.8.992A); ref. Lc.10:7 ἐλπίδι ~όμενος τὴν ἀποδοθησομένην...ἀμοιβὴν παρὰ τοῦ τὸν μισθὸν τοῖς ἐργάταις...ὑπεσχημένου *ib.*1.1(p.7.25; 696B); of men persecuting prophets οὔτε τὴν χάριν τὴν ἄνωθεν ~όμενοι, οὔτε τὴν κόλασιν ἐκτρεπόμενοι id.*prot.*10(p.75.3; M.8.220C); ref. Rom.6:22 τὸ τέλος οὐ θάνατον, ἀλλ' αἰώνιον ~όμενος σωτηρίαν Meth.*arbitr.*1(p.146.6; M.18.240B); ref. 1Cor.13:12 τὸ ἐκ μέρους νῦν εὐχαρίστως δεχόμενος, τὸ τέλειον εἰς τὸ μέλλον περιχαρῶς ~εται Bas.*fid.*2(2.225D; M.31.681A); ref. Rom.8:19 ἡ ἀποκάλυψις...τῶν υἱῶν τοῦ θεοῦ, ἣν ὑπὲρ ἡμῶν ἀεὶ καραδοκοῦσι [sc. οἱ ἄγγελοι] καὶ ~ονται Gr.Nyss.*Eun.*4(2 p.63.30; M.45.636B); of God ἐκ τούτου τὴν μετάνοιαν ὁ φιλάνθρωπος ἀπεξεδέχετο ‡Jo.D.*Const.*24(M.95.341C); **2.** *take as, understand* ἀπὸ τῶν ἡμετέρων παθῶν ἀναγόμενοι, τὸ βούλημα τοῦ ἀπαθοῦς θεοῦ ὁμοίως τοῖς ἡμεδαποῖς κινήμασιν ~όμενοι Clem.*str.*2.16(p.151.13; M.8.1012A).

***ἀπεκδιδύσκ-ομαι,** *strip off, doff,* ref. Col.3:9 ὁ δὲ βαπτιζόμενος τὸν μὲν παλαιὸν ~εται Ath.*ep.Serap.*4.13(M.26.656B); τὸν γὰρ τῇ ἕκτῃ ἀποθανόντα ~όμεθα, καὶ ἀνακαινούμεθα τῇ κυριακῇ, ὅτε ὁ παλαιὸς ἀπεκδυθείς, ἀνεγεννήθη τῇ ἀναστάσει ‡Ath.*sabb.*5(M.28.141A); *ib.*(141A).

***ἀπεκδοχή, ἡ,** *eager expectation,* Clem.*str.*7.13(p.59.7; M.9.516A); of souls awaiting resurrection ἀ. ἔχοντας τῶν μελλόντων αὐτοῖς ἀποκληροῦσθαι θείων δωρεῶν Ath.ap.‡Jo.D.*fid.dorm.*31(M.95.277A).

ἀπέκδυσις, ἡ, *stripping off, putting off*; of a garment, Gr.Nyss. *hom.13 in Cant.*(M.44.1040B); met., of the body in death, id.*v.Macr.*(p.398.15; M.46.985A); exeg. Col.2:11 τῆς γὰρ διὰ τοῦ βαπτίσματος ἀ. τύπος ἦν ἡ περιτομή †Ath.*sabb.*5(M.28.140C); Thdt.*Col.*2:11(3.487); exeg. Col.2:15 διὰ τῆς ἀ. καὶ τῆς ἀποθέσεως τῆς σαρκὸς τὰς ἐναντίας δυνάμεις καθεῖλεν Sever.*Col.*2:14f.(p.324.2).

ἀπεκδύ-ω, 1. in gen.; **a.** act., *strip, divest* ὁ...πιστῶς βαπτίζων... ~ων αὐτὸν ἀπὸ τῆς προϋπούσης αὐτῷ θρησκείας Ammon.*Ac.*19:5 (M.85.1573B); **b.** med., *strip off from oneself, put off,* Gr.Nyss.*hom. 12 in Cant.*(M.44.1029B); met. ἀ. τὰ πάθη Clem.*str.*6.14(p.486.23; M.9.332A); of Christ, acc. Docetists ψυχὴ ἐκείνη ἐν τῷ σώματι τραφεῖσα, ~σαμένη τὸ σῶμα καὶ προσηλώσασα πρὸς τὸ ξύλον Hipp.*haer.*8.10(p.230.20; M.16.3355B); the body at death, Meth.*res.*2.15 (p.363.13; M.18.312B); Const.Diac.*laud.*40(M.88.525B); ref. Col.2:11 περιτέμνου...καὶ ~ου τὸ σῶμα μετὰ Χριστόν ‡Chrys.*pasch.*5.2(8².264C); **2.** esp. ref. Col.2:15; **a.** *put off* (as 1.b), Or.*Cels.*2.64(p.186.25; M.11.897B); ~σάμενος αὐτάς, καὶ οἱονεὶ ἀπορρίψας ὃ εἴχομεν ἀπ' αὐτῶν ὑφασμένον ἡμῖν ἔνδυμα †Bas.*Is.*249(1.569E; M.30.557C); ἀπεξεδύσατο μὲν τὸ λανθάνειν, γυμνῇ δὲ τῇ κεφαλῇ ὁρᾶν τὴν θεότητα μετὰ τοῦ σώματος οὖσαν ἐδείκνυεν Sever.*Col.*2:14f.(p.324.19ff.); Max.*qu.Thal.*21(M.90.316Aff.); prob. also, Or.*comm.in Mt.*12.25(p.126.31; M.13.1040B), id.*Jo.*20.36(29; p.376.16; M.14.657C) but poss. in sense c. infra; cf.Cyr.H.*catech.*20.2; Chrys.*hom.6.3 in Col.*(11.368C); Thdr.Mops.*Col.*2:15(M.66.929C); Thdt.*Col.*2:15(3.488); Jo.D.*Col.*2:14f.(M.95.896A); **b.** *put off* the flesh, cf. *exutus carnem,* Novatianus *Trin.*21(M.*PL.*3.956B); *spolians se carne* Hil.Pict.*Trin.*10.48(M.*PL.*10.381C); *vice indumenti corpus fuisse, quo se ista exspoliavit Dominus in passione,* Ambr.*Lc.*5.107(M.*PL.*15.1665C); Aug.*ep.*149.26(M.*PL.*33.641); **c.** *despoil* ἄλλοι δὲ τὸ ~σάμενος ἀντὶ τοῦ ἐκδύσας ἐξέλαβον Sever.*Col.*2:14f.(p.324.26).

***ἀπέκθεσις, ἡ,** *stripping off, putting off,* exeg. Eph.4:22ff. ἀ. ... τοῦ σαρκός, τῶν σαρκικῶν ἡδονῶν τὴν ἀπόθεσιν διακαλῶν Cyr.*ador.*14 (1.515B).

***ἀπεκκλησιασμός, ὁ,** *secession from the Church,* of monophysites, Leont.H.*monoph.*testimonia(M.86.1881A).

***ἀπεκκλύζω,** *wash away completely,* met. οὐκέτι λοιπὸν ἀπεκκλύσασθαι τὰ πλημμελήματα συγχωρούμεθα Chrys.*virg.*84(1.335C).

***ἀπεκκρίνω,** *separate from, excrete,* in discussion of the resurrection body οἱ δὲ γενναιότεροι αὐτῶν, ἵνα μὴ ἀναγκάζωνται τὰ αὐτὰ αἵματι συναγαγεῖν τῷ λόγῳ, ἃ πολλάκις ἀπεκκριθῆναι τῶν σωμάτων ἡμῶν συνέβη, φασὶν τὸ ἐπὶ τέλει ἡμῶν ἀναστήσεσθαι σῶμα Meth.*res.*1.20(p.242.14, v.l. ἀποκρ- M.41.1088C); waste products from body, *ib.*1.22(p.244.19, v.l. ἀποκρ- 1089D); seed from the male, *ib.*2.20 (p.374.7; ἀποκρ- M.18.285B).

ἀπεκλογή, ἡ, *rejection,* ref. 1Cor.7:38 ὁ ἀπόστολος διδάσκων ἡμᾶς τὴν ἀληθῶς εὐχάριστον ἐκλογὴν οὐ κατὰ ἀ. τῶν ἑτέρων ὡς φαύλων, ἀλλ' ὡς καλῶν καλλίονα ποιεῖσθαι μεμήνυκεν Clem.*str.*4.23(p.314.6; M.8.1357B); οὐχ ἡ ἀπόφασις δὲ [sc. τοῦ θεοῦ] τὸ ἀποθανεῖν πεποίηκεν· οὐδὲ γὰρ ἀπόφασις τὸ προειπεῖν τὸ ἑπόμενον πρὸς τὴν αἵρεσιν ἢ τὴν ἀ. Proc.G.*Gen.*3:18(M.87.217B).

***ἀπεκπέμπω,** *send out,* Thphyl.*exc.gent.*5(p.481.13; M.113.941A).

***ἀπεκπροθέ-ω,** *run away ahead, extend beyond, transcend*; ref. contemplation of the divine nature ἀεὶ τοῦ ζητουμένου ~οντος καὶ μηδεμίαν στάσιν τῇ πολυπραγμοσύνῃ τῆς διανοίας ὑποδεικνύοντος Gr.Nyss.*Eun.*1(M.45.365A; conj. ὑπεκ- 1 p.128.16).

***ἀπεκτίννυ-μι,** f.l. for ἀποκτίννυμι (= ἀποκτείνω) *mortify* οἱ...τὰς ἡδυπαθεῖς τοῦ σώματος πράξεις ~ντες Areth.ap.*cat.Apoc.*20:6(p.472.11; ἀποκτιννύντες M.106.753A).

ἀπελασία, ἡ, *driving away, casting out,* Cyr.H.*catech.*17.30; of devils by Christ, ‡Meth.*palm.*3(M.18.389A).

ἀπέλασις, ἡ, *driving away, casting out* of devils, Or.*Jo.*20.36 (29; p.376.12; M.14.657B); *power of casting out,* Epiph.*haer.*51.5 (p.253.11; M.41.893D); as gift of H. Ghost, Cyr.H.*catech.*16.22; Προκόπιος...ἔσχεν δὲ καὶ τὴν κατὰ δαιμόνων ἀ. Marc.Diac.*v.Porph.*34.

***ἀπελαστέον,** *one must drive away, expel* ἀ. τὴν...ὑπόκρισιν Nil.*epp.*1.244(M.79.172D).

ἀπελαστικός, ἀπελατικός, *capable of driving away, expulsive* πολλὰ...εἴδη ῥιζῶν...τὰ μὲν ἀποκρουστικὰ καί τινων ἀπελαστικά Eus.*p.e.*4.1(131D; M.21.232B); Epiph.*haer.*51.1(p.249.4; M.41.889A); ῥῆμα ...θεοῦ...δαιμόνων...ἀ. ‡Just.*qu.et resp.*107(M.6.1356A).

ἀπελαύν-ω, 1. *drive away,* of the Jews ὁ Χριστός, ὅτε αὐτὸν ἀπήλασαν, τότε καὶ ἐκείνων [sc. τῶν ἐθνῶν] ἥπτετο Chrys.*hom.31.2 in Jo.*(8.177A); **2.** *drive away, cast out*; devils, Or.*Cels.*7.67(p.216.25; M.11.1516B), Ath.*gent.*1(M.25.5A) citt. s. δαίμων; fever ~ει γε τὸν πυρετὸν λόγῳ ὁ Χριστός Or.*Jo.*13.59(58; p.290.8; M.14.509D); **3.** *expel from office*; bishops, Evagr.*h.e.*2.5(p.52.23; M.86.2513B).

***ἀπελεγκτικός,** *convicting, exposing* διδασκαλίαν ἀ. τῆς εἰδωλολάτρου πλάνης Eus.*v.C.*2.47(p.61.13, v.l. κατά M.20.1024C); id.*p.e.*4.21(171A; M.21.297C).

***ἀπέλεγξις, ἡ,** *refutation,* Eus.*Hierocl.*1(511B; M.22.797A).

ἀπελεύθερος, ὁ, *freedman*; met., ref. 1Cor.7:22 ἐγὼ δὲ μέχρι νῦν δοῦλος· ἀλλ' ἐὰν πάθω, ἀ. Ἰησοῦ Χριστοῦ, καὶ ἀναστήσομαι ἐν αὐτῷ ἐλεύθερος Ign.*Rom.*4.3.

Ἀπελλαῖος, ὁ, Macedonian month corresponding to *December,* Eus.*m.P.*10(p.930.20; M.20.1496C); Epiph.*haer.*51.24(p.294.3; M.41.932C); Chrys.*nativ.*1.5(2.362C); but said to correspond to *August,* Epiph.*haer.*11(p.204.22; 236A).

ἀπελπίζ-ω, A. *despair*; **1.** ref. salvation; **a.** not to be despaired of ἕως ἔξεστιν, ἑαυτοὺς ἀπὸ τοῦ πτώματος ἀναλάβωμεν, μηδὲ ἀπελπίσωμεν ἑαυτῶν; ἐὰν ἀναλύσωμεν ἀπὸ τῶν κακῶν Bas.*ep.*46.6(3.139D; M.32.380C); μηδεὶς οὖν ἀπελπίσῃ τῆς ἑαυτοῦ σωτηρίας Cyr.H.*catech.*2.19; μηδένα ~ωμεν Chrys.*hom.10.4 in Heb.*(12.110B); (ref. Ps.95:7) σήμερον, εἶπεν, ὥστε μηδέποτε ~ειν αὐτούς *ib.*6.3(66C); *Const.App.*2.20.5 cit. s. παράπτωμα; in oxymoron Χριστέ, ἡ ἐλπὶς τῶν ἀπελπισμένων *M.Thdot.1* 21(p.74.9); ref. salvation of Adam, denied by Tatian πῶς δὲ οὐ σώζεται ὁ Ἀδὰμ ὁ παρὰ σοὶ ~όμενος; Epiph.*haer.*46.3(p.206.27; M.41.841C); **b.** of converts to Gnosticism who came to despair through it, Iren.*haer.*1.13.7(M.7.592A); **c.** ἐλπίδος ~ω reflex., *cut oneself off from hope*; of heretics οἱ ἑαυτοὺς τῆς μελλούσης ἐλπίδος τῶν Χριστιανῶν ἀπελπίσαντες ‡Jo.D.*ep.Thphl.*15(M.95.365A); **d.** of despairing of resurrection of body, ref. Col.3:5 ἵνα μή τινες ἀντὶ τῶν φαύλων ἔργων τὴν τοῦ σώματος πλάσιν ἀπελπίσωσιν [ἐκ] τῆς ἀναστάσεως Epiph.*haer.*66.87(p.131.8; M.42.169C); ref. 1Cor.15:53 μή πως νομίσωσι τὴν σάρκα ἀπὸ τῆς τῶν νεκρῶν ἀναστάσεως ἀπηλπίσθαι *ib.*77.27(p.440.15; 681A); **2.** ref. scriptural difficulties, Or. *fr.hom.39.1 in Jer.*(p.196.10; M.13.541D) cit. s. πρόσκομμα; οὐδ' ~ομεν ὑπὸ Χριστοῦ...βοηθούμενοι καταλαβεῖν τὰ ἐν τῇ παραβολῇ δηλούμενα Or.*comm.in Mt.*14.6(p.288.27; M.13.1197A); **3.** in gen., ref. Mt.26:51f. ἐγκαλῶν [sc. ὁ Χριστός] ὡς ἀπελπίσαντι τῆς πρὸς αὐτὸν καταφυγῆς Const.*or.s.c.*15(p.175.19; M.20.1277B); οὐ γὰρ ~ω τῆς ἐκκλησίας τὰ νεῦρα Cyr.H.*catech.*15.16; of Devil οὐδέποτε ἡμῶν ~ει τὴν ἀπώλειαν Chrys.*hom.36.6 in Mt.*(7.386B).

B. *hope* that a thing will *not* happen, *fail to expect,* with negation; of the disciples οὐκ εἰκὸς ἦν ἀπελπίσαι τὰ πάντα ὑπὲρ αὐτοῦ [sc. Χριστοῦ] πείσεσθαι Eus.*d.e.*3.5(p.121.35; M.22.208B); of Job προωρᾶτο τὸ μέλλον, καὶ πράττων καλῶς, τὴν ἀθυμίαν οὐκ ~ετο Chrys.*fr.Job* proem.(M.64.508B).

C. exeg. Lc.6:35: Fathers throw little light on meaning, but paraphrase as meaning *hope to receive back* οὐ δανείζετε παρ' ὧν ἐλπίζετε ἀπολαβεῖν Gr.Nyss.*usur.*(M.46.444A); δανείζετε γάρ, φησί, παρ' ὧν μὴ προσδοκᾶτε λήψεσθαι Chrys.*hom.15.8 in Mt.*(7.199A); δίδοτε γάρ, φησί, παρ' ὧν οὐ προσδοκᾶτε λαβεῖν *ib.*56.6(575A).

ἀπελπισμός, ὁ, *despair* ὑπομνήσει προλαβουσῶν ἁμαρτιῶν, εἰς ἀ. φερουσῶν τὸν ἄνθρωπον Mac.Aeg.*hom.*4.24(M.34.492B); Gr.Nyss. *v.Mos.*(M.44.400A); of the unrepentant ἐπὶ τὰς ἡδονὰς ῥέποντι, καὶ προφάσει ἀπελπισμοῦ φιληδονοῦντι Marc.Er.*opusc.*3.7(M.65.976C); ἡ παιδευτικὴ παραχώρησις φέρει μὲν λύπην πολλὴν...καὶ ἀ. δὲ σύμμετρον τῇ ψυχῇ Diad.*perf.*87(p.120.3).

ἀπελπιστία, [*]**ἀφελπιστία, ἡ,** *despair,* exeg. Rom.8:19f. ἁμαρτήσαντος γὰρ τοῦ ἀνθρώπου...ἐλελύπηντο οἱ ἄγγελοι, ἀ. τοῦ παντὸς ἀναλογιζόμενοι Cosm.Ind.*top.*2(M.88.120B); ἀφ. *ib.*5(v.l. ἀπ- 225D).

*__ἀπεμβάς, ὁ,__ f.l. for ἐπεμβάς, Paul.Sil.*Soph.*308(M.86.2131B).

*__ἀπεμβολή, ἡ,__ f.l. for ἀπεμπολή, Cyr.ap.*cat.Lc.*18:18(p.136.4).

ἀπεμ-πολάω (-πολέω, -πωλάω, -πωλέω), 1. *sell,* met. ὁ τὰς κρίσεις ~πωλῶν Isid.Pel.*epp.*1.177(M.78.297C); τὰς τοῦ ἁγίου πνεύματος ~πωλοῦντας δωρεάς *ib.*1.106(253C); **2.** *surrender, lose, betray* σπουδάζετε...συνέστιοι ἀλλήλων γίνεσθαι...ὅπως αὐτὴν [sc. ἀγάπην] μὴ ~πολήσετε *Clem.ep.*9; exeg. Ps.2:7 ἆρ' οὖν διὰ τοῦτο νομιοῦμεν αὐτὸν [sc. τὸν Χριστόν] τὴν τοῦ προϋπάρχειν τῶν ὅλων ~πολῆσαι δόξαν; Cyr.*hom.pasch.*17.2(5².226B); ἀπημπόληκε μὲν [sc. ἡ ἀνθρωπεία φύσις] τὸ ἄφθαρτον ἐν Ἀδάμ id.*glaph.Gen.*2(1.44A); τῇ προσλήψει τῆς τῶν ἑτεροδόξων ὁμολογίας...~πολοῦσα αὐτόν [sc. τὸν Χριστόν], εἰς ἀναίρεσιν τῆς ἐξ ἡμῶν...αὐτοῦ σαρκός Max.*opusc.*(M.91.73A); **3.** *acquire, experience* τὴν τοῦ παιδὸς ὀδύνην ἣν εἰς τὸ γύναιον ἀπημπόλησεν Epiph.*haer.*30.8(p.343.6; M.41.417B); of Manes κακίζων τὴν πᾶσαν κτίσιν...ἐκ τῶν ἐν ἡμῖν σφαλμάτων γινομένων τὰς προφάσεις ~πολήσας *ib.*66.17(p.40.8; M.42.53A).

ἀπεμπολή, ἡ, 1. *sale*; of worldly goods, Cyr.*Lc.*18:28(M.72.860B); of Christ by Judas, Jo.D.*hom.*1.7(M.96.557C); **2.** *surrender, loss,* ref. Lc.21:2f. τῶν ἄγαν εὐτελεστάτων τὴν ἀ. Cyr.*ador.*9(1.291C); of paradise, id.*Juln.*3(6².75C); of man's original nature τῆς εἰκόνος τῆς ἐν ἁγιασμῷ τὴν ἀ. id.*dial.Trin.*7(5¹.638E); **3.** *putting away, riddance* οὐ τῶν ἐν σώματι παθῶν τὴν ἀ. ἐπαγγέλλεται τὸ...βάπτισμα id.*Juln.*7(6².248C); τῶν γὰρ ἐκτόπων ἐπιθυμιῶν τε καὶ ἡδονῶν... ἀπεμπολὴν ὑπαινίττεται [sc. ἡ περιτομή] *ib.*10(353B); exeg. Is.11:6f. ὁμοῦ...τῇ πίστει, κεκερδήκασι καὶ τῆς ἀρχαίας ὠμότητος τὴν ἀ. id.*Is.* 2.1(2.199A).

ἀπεμπολητής, ὁ, *seller,* of Judas ἀ. αἰσχρός ‡Gr.Naz.*Chr.pat.* 1688(M.38.271A).

*__ἀπέμπροσθεν,__ *from before,* Epiph.*haer.*66.64(M.42.128D; ἀπ' ἔμπροσθεν p.103.23).

*__ἄπεμπτος,__ f.l. for ἄπεπτος, *undigested,* Gr.Nyss.*hom.opif.*13.4 (M.44.168B).

[*]**ἀπεμπωλάω, -έω,** v. ἀπεμπολάω.

*__ἀπεμφαινόντως,__ *incongruously, in an unlikely manner,* Or. *comm.in Ex.*10:27(p.246.1; M.12.269Bf.).

ἀπεμφαίν-ω, 1. *be incongruous, unsuitable, unseemly, absurd*; **a.** of ideas or language about God ἐὰν δέ τινι ~ον φαίνηται οὐσιῶσθαι λέγειν τὸ τοῦ θεοῦ θέλημα Or.*comm.in Eph.*1:1(*JTS* 3 p.235.14); of idea that God created evil, exeg. Jo.1:3 κἂν γὰρ σφόδρα ~ειν δοκῇ, οὐ πάνυ τι δοκεῖ μοι εὐκαταφρόνητον εἶναι id.*Jo.*2.15(9; p.71.14; M. 14.140B); exeg. Mt.6:13 ~ει...τὸν θεὸν νομίζειν εἰσάγειν τινὰ εἰς πειρασμόν id.*or.*29(p.386.19; M.11.537A); as an argument of those who oppose prayer, *ib.*5(p.311.1; 433B) cit. s. ἄτρεπτος; ref. Jo.9:3 οὐ κακὸν δὲ τὸ αἴτιον τῆς φανερώσεως τῶν ἔργων τοῦ θεοῦ, διὸ οὐδὲ ~ει εἰπεῖν ὅτι ὁ θεὸς τυφλοῖ τινα Didym.*Ac.*9:6(M.39.1672A); of σκώληξ applied to Christ, ref. Ps.21:7, Dion.Ar.*c.h.*2.5(M.3.145A); of the impression conveyed by words 'Father' and 'Son', as applied to God, acc. Eunomius τὸ ~ον τῆς ἐν τοῖς ῥήμασι τούτοις διανοίας Bas. *Eun.*2.22(1.258C; M.29.621A); **b.** of attributes and actions in relation to the nature of God τίς γὰρ οὐκ ἐρεῖ ~οντα εἶναι ἀναφερόμενα ἐπὶ θεὸν τὸ ἔχειν αὐτὸν ὀργήν; Or.*hom.20.1 in Jer.*(p.176.12; M.13. 500B); Eus.*d.e.*10.1(p.449.26; M.22.724B); ἐκ δύο γὰρ τούτων, οἱονεὶ χαρακτήρ τις ἡμῖν ἐγγίγνεται τοῦ θεοῦ, ἔκ τε τῆς τῶν ~όντων ἀρνήσεως, καὶ ἐκ τῆς τῶν ὑπαρχόντων ὁμολογίας Bas.*Eun.*1.10(1.222C; M.29. 533C); οὐδὲν τῆς ἀτρέπτου καὶ ἀναλλοιώτου φύσεως ἐν ταῖς ὑπὲρ ἡμῶν ἐνεργείαις πρὸς τὸ ~ον μεθαρμοζομένης Gr.Nyss.*ep.*3(M.46. 1020B); of God making the blind, the dumb, and the lame ὅπερ ~ει θεοῦ Proc.G.*Ex.*4:11(M.87.536A); **c.** of other things in relation to God, e.g. of certain events recorded by Evangelists οἱ...μηδὲν τῆς ἀληθείας ἐν τοῖς ~ουσι καὶ σκυθρωποῖς παραχαράξαντες Eus.*d.e.*3.5 (p.130.8; M.22.220D); exeg. Ex.4:3 μὴ ταρασσέσθω τοὺς φιλοχρίστους, ὡς ~οντι ζῴῳ προσαρμοζόντων ἡμῶν τὸν τοῦ μυστηρίου λόγον Gr.Nyss.*v.Mos.*(M.44.336A); ~ούσας εἰκονογραφίας Dion.Ar.*c.h.*2.2 (M.3.140B); *ib.*2.5(145A); ref. Temple as habitation of God, Max. *qu.Thal.*31(M.90.372A); **2.** *differ from* τὸ ζῶον οὐ πολὺ ~ον ἀετοῦ Hipp.*haer.*4.46(p.68.25; M.16.3110C); *ib.*1.5(p.10.5; 3028D); *ib.*5.11 (p.104.9; 3159C); **3.** *make clear, demonstrate* τῇ φύσει μᾶλλον ἁρμόττουσα ἀναμφιβόλως ἀπεμφάνθη ἡ ἀρετή Isid.Pel.*epp.*2.240(M.78.681B).

*__ἀπεμφανής,__ *obscure, hidden,* Thdr.Abuc.*opusc.*18(M.94.1597B).

ἀπέμφασις, ἡ, 1. *absurdity* εἰς ἀ. αὐτοῖς ὁ λόγος χωρεῖ Clem.*str.* 1.17(p.53.26; M.8.797B); *ib.*4.12(p.285.29; 1293B); **2.** *incongruity, apparent inconsistency*; with the nature of God τὴν ὁμοίαν δὲ ἔχει ἀ. ... τὰ περὶ μαρτύρων προστεταγμένα Or.*Jo.*6.54(36; p.163.7; M.14. 293C); of certain scriptural passages, id.*fr.comm.in Ezech.*(M.13. 664C); id.*or.*29(p.387.25; M.11.537D); **3.** *unlikeness, dissimilarity* τὴν ἐν τοῖς συμβόλοις τῶν θείων καὶ νοητῶν διασκοπήσας ἀ. Max.*qu. Thal.*65(M.90.749C); id.*cap.*3.55(M.90.1284C); **4.** *negative predication* τὸ μὴ γεγεννῆσθαι ἀκούσαντες, οὐ τὸ ὑποκείμενον διὰ τῆς ἀ. ἔγνωμεν, ἀλλὰ τί οὐ χρὴ περὶ τὸ ὑποκείμενον νοεῖν ὡδηγήθημεν Gr.Nyss.*Eun.* 7(2 p.171.27; M.45.761D).

ἀπέναντι, *before the face of, before,* *Pss.Sal.*17.5; ὁ Πιλᾶτος ἀπενίψατο τὰς χεῖρας αὐτοῦ ἀ. τοῦ ἡλίου *A.Pil.*A 9.4(p.244).

*__ἀπεναντίας,__ *opposite*; *contrarily,* exeg. Mt.5:6 ἢ τὴν καθόλου φησὶν ἀρετήν, ἢ τὴν μερικὴν ταύτην τὴν ἀ. τῇ πλεονεξίᾳ κειμένην Chrys.*hom.15.3 in Mt.*(7.189B); *in opposition to* ἡτοίμασας ἡμῖν πνευματικὴν τράπεζαν, ἵνα φαγόντες καὶ ἰσχύσαντες, δυνηθῶμεν ἐλθεῖν ἀ. τῶν ποτε θλιβόντων ἡμᾶς Cyr.*Ps.*22:5(M.69.841C).

ἀπεναντίως, *opposite, contrarily,* Didym.*Trin.*1.30(M.39.417B); πύλαι τῆς θυγατρὸς τῆς Σιὼν ἀ. ταῖς πύλαις τοῦ θανάτου ἔχουσαι id. *Ps.*9:15(M.39.1196B); id.ap.*cat.Ac.*4:25(p.79.26; ἀπεναντίους M.39. 1664A).

ἀπενεόομαι, *become speechless, be struck dumb,* Ath.*v.Anton.*82 (M.26.957A); Ephr.2.17C; Gel.Cyz.*h.e.*2.13.11(M.85.1253D).

ἀπεντεῦθεν, *thenceforth,* Mac.Aeg.*hom.*30.4(M.34.724C); Epiph.*ep. Arab.*ap.*haer.*78.24(p.474.31; M.42.737C); Cosm.Ind.*top.*5(M.88.313B).

*__ἀπεντρέπομαι,__ *disregard,* Or.*hom.8 in Lc.*(M.17.321A; ἵνα προτραπῶσιν p.55.4).

*__ἀπεξεργάζομαι,__ *make for oneself, invent* ὁ...Μωσῆς...ἄλλον... [sc. θεόν] οὐχ ὑπείληφε δεύτερον, οὔτε ὅμοιον, οὔτε ἀνόμοιον, καθάπερ ὑμεῖς ἀπεξείργασθε Juln.Imp.ap.Cyr.*Juln.*8(6².253C).

*__ἀπεξεσμένως,__ *in a polished manner,* hence *with finished excellence, completely,* Cyr.*ador.*12(1.411B); id.*ep.*55(p.49.28; 5².175B); Olymp.*Job* 28:27(M.93.297A).

ἀπέραντος, 1. *boundless, infinite*; *eternal*; of God ὥσπερ γὰρ ἄπειρος ὢν πανταχόθεν διὰ τοῦτο λέγεται ἀ. *Hom.Clem.*16.17; *ib.*17.10; ἐν...ζωῇ τῇ ἀ. ‡Eust.*Laz.*29(p.51.2); ἀ. βασιλείαν Isid.Pel.*epp.*1.218 (M.78.320C); τὸν σεαυτοῦ λογισμὸν πεῖσον, ὅτι τῶν ἀ. οὐκ ἐφίξεται ‡Bas.*struct.hom.*1.4(1.326B; M.30.16A); ref. opinion of Origen γίνεται κόλασις, ἀλλ' οὐκ ἀ. †Leont.B.*sect.*10.6(M.86.1265B); neut. as subst., *infinitude* τῆς ἐπιγνώσεως τοῦ θεοῦ τὸ ἀ. Bas.*mor.*15.3(3.556B; M.32. 1312B); of God, Jo.D.*f.o.*1.14(M.94.860A); **2.** *impassable* ὠκεανὸς ἀνθρώποις *1Clem.*20.8(v.l. ἀπέρατος).

ἀπεράτωτος, *unbounded, infinite*; of the divine nature, Gr.Nyss. *v.Mos.*7(M.44.301A, v.l. ἀπερατώτατος); of divine attributes τὰ περὶ αὐτὸν ἀ. id.*Eun.*3(2 p.35.6; M.45.601B); ἀ. ἡ παντελὴς ἀρετὴ νοείσθω ‡Caes.Naz.*dial.*171(M.38.1136).

ἀπεργάζ-ομαι, 1. *finish off, complete*; **2.** *make, cause*; of demons σφίσιν αὐτοῖς δουλεύειν τοὺς ἀνθρώπους ~ονται Tat.*orat.*17(p.19.8; M.6.844B); **3.** *make to be*; in contrast between 'breath of life' and H. Ghost πνοὴ ζωῆς, ἡ καὶ ψυχικὸν ~ομένη τὸν ἄνθρωπον Iren.*haer.* 5.12.2(M.7.1152A); τροφὴ...οὐδὲν δικαιοτέρους ἢ ἀδικωτέρους ~εται Clem.*ecl.*14(p.140.24; M.9.704D); *ib.*37(p.148.13; 717B); ref. miracle of Cana ὕδωρ...οἶνον ~εται Hipp.*fr.18 in Pss.*(p.146.16; M.10.609A); Meth.*symp.*3.2(p.29.1; M.18.64A); of S. Paul βοηθὸς ἀπειργάσθη καὶ νύμφη τοῦ λόγου *ib.*3.9(p.37.21; 76B); θεὸς ἀθάνατον μορφὴν...ἐχούσας αὐτὰς ἀπειργάζετο *ib.*6.1(p.64.13; 113B); βασιλέας, οὓς...προφῆται χρίοντες εἰκονικούς τινας Χριστοὺς ἀπειργάζοντο Eus.*h.e.*1.3.7(M.20. 72A); of Adam's creation πνοῆς τῆς ζωτικῆς...τὸν ἄνθρωπον ἀπεργασαμένης ζῶον λογικόν Diod.*Gen.*2:7(M.33.1565B).

*__ἀπέργης,__ s.v.l., *idle,* Leont.N.*v.Sym.*33(M.93.1712B).

*__ἀπερεγχείρητος,__ prob. f.l. for ἀπαρεγχείρητος, *inviolable,* Max. *myst.*5(M.91.680A).

ἀπερίβλεπτος, 1. *not looked at from all sides, invisible*; of God, †Jo.D.*Trin.*5(M.95.16B); **2.** *regardless, heedless,* Hipp.*haer.*4.46 (p.68.29; M.16.3110D).

*__ἀπεριβλέπτως,__ *without looking round*; hence **1.** *unostentatiously* πάντα ἀτύφως καὶ ἀ. εἰργάζετο ‡Pion.*v.Polyc.*10; **2.** *carelessly* παρήνει μηδαμῶς...ὡς ἔτυχεν ἀ. ὁρᾶν ἐπ' αὐτῷ [sc. sign of Cross] Eus.*v.C.*2.16(p.47.24, v.l. ἀπερισκέπτως M.20.993B).

***ἀπεριβόητος**, *ineffable*, *Mir.Geo.*6(p.85.11).

ἀπερίγραπτος, *uncircumscribed, infinite*; **1.** of God ἀ. δέ ἐστιν, οὗ τόπος οὐδείς [τόπος], τὸ κατὰ πάντα ἐν πᾶσιν καὶ ἐν ἑκάστῳ ὅλον καὶ ἐφ' ἑαυτοῦ τὸ αὐτό Clem.*fr.*39(p.220.9; M.9.769C); μόνος...ὁ θεὸς ἀ. Ath.*fr.Job*(M.27.1345A); μίαν δὲ τῆς τριάδος...φύσιν...ἀ. Thdt. *Trin.*28(M.75.1188C); ref. scriptural description καὶ μαρτὺς τοῦ λόγου ἡ Μωσαϊκὴ συγγραφή, παχεῖα καὶ ἀνάξια θεοῦ τοῦ ἀ. περιέχουσα ῥήματα Or.*Ps.*10:4(p.465); **2.** of Logos, Hier.H.*Trin.*(M.40.857D) cit. s. ἀσώματος; ὁ λόγος...φύσει...ἀ. Leont.B.*Nest.et Eut.*1 (M.86.1284B); **3.** esp. of divine nature of Christ περιγραπτὸν σώματι, ἀ. πνεύματι Gr.Naz.*ep.*101(M.37.177B); θεὸς...ἀ. ... ἐν ἀνθρωπίνῃ περιγραφῇ ἑωρᾶτο Gr.Nyss.*Apoll.*18(M.45.1160A); ὁ Χριστὸς περιγραπτὸς μέν ἐστι κατὰ τὸ σῶμα, ἀ. δὲ κατὰ τὴν θεότητα Pamph. H.*panopl.*6.1(p.615); οὖσα δὲ ἡ θεότης...ἡ ἀ. καὶ ἐν τῷ ἐσταυρωμένῳ αὐτῆς σώματι Eulog.*fr.Trin.*7.12(p.377); μόνος ὡς θεὸς ἀ. ... ἐν τάφῳ σωματικῶς περιγράφεται Jo.D.*hom.*4.29(M.96.632A); of BMV ἡ περιγραφὴ...τοῦ ἀ. ‡Meth.*Sym.et Ann.*10(M.18.372C).

***ἀπεριγράπτως**, *without being circumscribed* τίς εἶδε, τίς ἤκουσεν, ὅτι μήτραν ὁ θεὸς ἀ. ᾤκησε; Procl.CP *or.laud.BMV* 1(p.103.22; M. 65.681B).

ἀπερίγραφος, *without limit, incomprehensible*; **1.** of God ἀ. ἡ μεγαλειότης *Const.App.*7.35.9; θεὸς καὶ τῇ οὐσίᾳ καὶ τῇ σοφίᾳ καὶ τῇ δυνάμει τὸ ἀ. ἔχει Thdt.*qu.20 in Gen.*(1.28); of his omnipresence ἐπειδὴ δὲ καὶ ἅπασι πάρεστι τῇ φύσει καὶ κεχώρισται ὧν ἐθέλει τῇ γνώμῃ, οὐδὲν τῶν ἀναξίων ἀπὸ τοῦ παρεῖναι τὸν θεὸν ὠφελουμένων... αὐτῷ...τὸ τῆς φύσεως ἀ. διασώζεται Thdr.Mops.*fr.inc.*7(p.295.27; M.66.976A); **2.** of Son ἡ τοῦ σωτῆρος ἡμῶν ἀρχὴ...ἀ. Eus.*Is.*9:6 (M.24.152D); ἔστι δὲ ἐν οὐρανῷ, τῷ ἀ. τῆς φύσεως πᾶσι παρών Thdr. Mops.*fr.inc.*10(p.301.26; M.66.984C); ἐκ τοῦ οἰκείου ἀ. εἰς τὸ περιγεγράφθαι...ἐληλυθώς Leont.B.*Nest.et Eut.*1(M.86.1284C); **3.** of divine things ἀ. γάρ [sc. χάρις], ὡς αἰτίαν τὸν ἀναίτιον ἔχουσα λόγον Max.*opusc.*(M.91.57C); ἡ ἀληθὴς θεωρία...ἀ. id.*ambig.*(M.91.1140A); ὁ τῆς ἁγίας γραφῆς λόγος, κἂν εἰ δέχεται περιγραφὴν κατὰ τὸ γράμμα ...ἀλλὰ κατὰ τὸ πνεῦμα...μένει...ἀ. id.*qu.Thal.*50(M.90.165B).

ἀπεριγράφως, *without being circumscribed* τὸ ἅγιον πνεῦμα ταύτῃ πως μεταφυτεύεται διανενεμημένον κατὰ τὴν ἑκάστου περιγραφὴν ἀ. Clem.*str.*6.15(p.492.11; M.9.344B).

***ἀπεριγραψία, ἡ**, *incapability of circumscription*, Leont.H.*Nest.* 1.1(M.86.1408D).

***ἀπερίδρακτος**, *not to be grasped, incomprehensible*, Ath.*Dion.*20 (p.61.7; M.25.509A); τὸ...λογισμοῖς ἀ. ἴσον ἐστὶν ἐφ' ἑκάστου τῶν ἐν τῇ τριάδι πεπιστευμένων προσώπων Gr.Nyss.*ep.*24(M.46.1089C).

ἀπεριέργαστος, **1.** *not curiously* or *carefully examined*; of faith, *simple* ἀ. τε καὶ ἀπολυπραγμόνητον καταλιμπάνομεν [sc. τροφήν] Gr.Nyss.*v.Mos.*(M.44.357B); of Christ's advice to Nicodemus ἀπεριεργάστῳ λοιπὸν τῇ πίστει συμβουλεύει χρῆναι λαβεῖν ὃ νοεῖν οὐ δύναται Cyr.*Jo.*2.1(4.149C); in bad sense, of peace with heretics οὐδὲ...χρὴ πάντως οἰκονομικήν τινα καὶ ἀ. εἰρήνην ἀσπάζεσθαι, πρὸς οὓς ἐστι κρείττων ἡ μάχη id.*ep.*76(p.26.1; 5^2.205A); **2.** *not to be curiously examined*; *beyond investigation* τὰ γὰρ τῇ πίστει παραδιδόμενα ἀ. ἔχει τὴν γνῶσιν Ath.*ep.Serap.*4.5(M.26.644B); ἀ. ... τῆς θαυματουργίας οἱ τρόποι Cyr.*glaph.Ex.*2(1.287B); ref. Is.53:8 τῆς ὑποστάσεως αὐτοῦ πάσῃ τῇ γενητῇ φύσει ἀ. τυγχανούσης, καθὼς καὶ αὐτὸς ὁ πατὴρ ἀ. ἐστι Alex.Al.*ep.Alex.*12(p.27.8ff.; M.18.565B); **3.** *not curiously examining, uninquisitive* διδασκαλίας, ἣν ἀπολυπραγμονήτῳ καὶ ἀ. σιγῇ οἱ πατέρες ἡμῶν ἐφύλαξαν Bas.*Spir.*66(3.55B, v.l. ἀπεριέργῳ; M.32.188C); ὁ ξένος...δεῖται...ἀ. τῆς σωφροσύνης Chrys.*laud.Max.*7(3.224B).

ἀπεριεργάστως, *simply*, Bas.*hex.*2.5(1.17B; M.29.40B); ἐν ἁπλότητι καρδίας ἀ. πεποιθότων θεῷ †Bas.*hom.in Ps.*115:1(1.371D; M.30. 104C).

ἀπερίεργος, **1.** *not over-curious, simple*; of faith διὰ τῆς ἁπλῆς καὶ ἀ. ὁμολογίας λατρεύοντες τῷ κυρίῳ Bas.*ep.*172(3.260D; M.32.648B); πίστις τελεία καὶ ἀ. †Ath.*fr.*(M.26.1253C); ref. Is.6:3 οὐ λογοθετοῦσιν τὴν τῆς τριάδος ταυτότητα·...βίον ἔχουσι τὸν ἀ. ὕμνον Gr. Ant.*bapt.*2.3(M.88.1873B); neut. as subst., *absence of curious inquiry, simple acceptance*; of Evangelists τὸ ἀ. αὐτῶν τοῦ τῆς ἀναστάσεως θαύματος Vict.*Mc.*16:9(p.447.8); **2.** *not to be curiously examined, beyond scrutiny* ἀ. ὁ λόγος καὶ ὁ τρόπος τῆς εὐσεβείας, πίστει μόνῃ, ἀλλ' οὐκ ἐξερευνήσει γνωριζόμενος ‡Ath.*qu.Ant.*1(M.28. 597D); **3.** neut. as subst., *freedom from interference*; ref. persecution τῶν καθ' ἡμᾶς ἡσυχῇ τὸ ἀ. εἰληφότων Eus.*m.P.*13(p.947.14; M.20.1513B); **4.** *unconnected with magic*, id.*Hierocl.*35(534A; M.22. 845C).

ἀπεριέργως, **1.** *simply*; comp. ὁ μὲν [sc. ὁ Ματθαῖος] μόνην ἔφη τὴν κεφαλὴν ἀ. Thdr.Mops.*Jo.*12:3(p.370.18; M.66.765D); **2.** *without curious inquiry, uncritically, simply*, ref. 1Cor.10:25 τὰ ἐκ μακέλλου ἀ. ὠνεῖσθαι προσέταξεν Clem.*paed.*2.1(p.160.20; M.8.393B); ἐν γραφαῖς δὲ ἁγίαις τριὰς ἡμῖν καταγγέλλεται καὶ πιστεύεται ἀ. Epiph. *anc.*67(p.81.22; M.43.137B); Didym.(‡Bas.)*Eun.*5(1.306B; M.29.733B); comp., Cyr.*Am.*17(3.267C).

***ἀπερίζυγος**, *odd*, of numbers, Hipp.*haer.*4.44(p.67.7; M.16. 3107C).

ἀπεριήχητος, **1.** *undisturbed by sound, undisturbed* τὴν ἀκοὴν ἀ. ...φυλαχθῆναι Gr.Nyss.*virg.*6(p.279.3; M.46.349B); ὁ λογισμός, ἀ. μένων ἐκ τῆς αἰσθητικῆς κινήσεως id.*hom.10 in Cant.*(M.44.993C); *ib.12*(1025B); **2.** *without sound of, not told of* τὴν κρίσιν τοῦ θεοῦ... ἧς οὐδ' οἱ μακρὰν τῆς...θεοσοφίας ἀ. μεμενήκασιν Leont.B.*Nest.et Eut.*3(M.86.1368D).

***ἀπερίθετος**, *free from the wrapping of, free from*, Leont.H.*Nest.* 1.48(M.86.1509D).

***ἀπερίθραυστος**, *uncrushed, unsubdued*, of Israel γαῦρόν τε καὶ ἀ. ἔχοντα τὸν αὐχένα Cyr.*Is.*4.3(2.644A).

ἀπερικάθαρτος, *uncleansed, unpurified*, Or.*princ.*3.1.21(p.238.1; M.11.296C); οἱ γὰρ τελευτῶντες ἀ. καὶ τὴν διὰ Χριστοῦ λύτρωσιν οὐκ ἀξιωθέντες ἑλεῖν Cyr.*Is.*4.5(2.699A).

***ἀπερικακήτως**, *indefatigably*, Mac.Aeg.*hom.*5.27(M.34.493A); *ib.* 29.3(717B).

ἀπερικάλυπτος, *unveiled*, met. ταῖς ἀ. ἐλλάμψεσιν Dion.Ar.*c.h.* 15.2(M.3.329B).

ἀπερικαλύπτως, *undisguisedly, openly*, of the divine nature ὡς φῶς ἀ. καὶ νοητῶς καταυγάζον Dion.Ar.*c.h.*2.5(M.3.144D); Max. *ambig.*(M.91.1252D, conj. for εὐπερι-).

***ἀπερίκλαστος**, *unbroken, steadfast*, of Judas ὥσπερ καὶ ἀ. τόνῳ πρὸς ἐκεῖνο καὶ μόνον ὁρῶν...τῆς φιλοκερδείας νόσημα Cyr.*Jo.*9 (4.738E).

***ἀπερικράτητος**, *not held fast*, met. ἀ. ὑπὸ τοῦ θεοῦ τὸν λαόν †Bas.*Is.*77(1.433B; M.30.248A).

ἀπερικτύπητος, *undisturbed by sound, silent*, Nil.*epp.*1.26(M.79. 93D); of meditation ἐν ἀ. σχολῇ ‡Bas.*const.*2.1(2.541C; M.31.1340A).

ἀπερίληπτος, *incomprehensible*, of God τῇ...φύσει τὸ ἄπειρον ἀ. Or.*princ.*2.9.1(p.164.6; M.11.225C); ὅλον δόξα, καὶ ὅλον ἀ. ὑπὸ πάντων...κεκτισμένων Epiph.*haer.*76.41(p.395.26; M.42.605C); of divine nature, Gr.Nyss.*tres dii*(M.45.129C); τριάς Gr.Naz.*or.*6.22 (M.35.749C); λόγος *ib.*45.9(M.36.633C); περιληπτικόν, ἀ. Dion.Ar. *c.h.*5.2(M.3.329B); ref. Inc. εἰ ὅπερ ἦν ἔμεινεν, ἀπρόσιτον ἑαυτὸν φυλάττων καὶ ἀ., ὀλίγοι ἂν ἠκολούθησαν τυχόν Gr.Naz.*or.*37.3(M.36. 285B); τῇ πρὸς τὸν ἄνθρωπον ἑνώσει τοῦ θεοῦ λόγου, καθ' ἣν ἑνωθεὶς ἔμεινεν ἀσύγχυτος καὶ ἀ., οὐ κατὰ τὸν τῆς ψυχῆς τρόπον Nemes. *nat.hom.*3(M.40.601A); τὸν ἐν περιλήψει ἀ. ‡Meth.*Sym.et Ann.*6 (M.18.360C); ref. faith εἰ γὰρ μέλλοιμεν πάντα τῇ καταλήψει μετρεῖν, καὶ τὸ τοῖς λογισμοῖς ἀ. μηδὲ εἶναι τὸ παράπαν ὑπολαμβάνειν, οἰχήσεται μὲν ὁ τῆς πίστεως...μισθός Bas.*Eun.*2.24(1.260E; M.29.628A); hence *indescribable* τὴν θεοῦ...δόξαν λόγῳ ἀ. οὖσαν Bas.*fid.*2(2.225C; M.31. 681A); τὸ ἀνθρώπινον...'Ἰησοῦς ὠνομάσθη· ἡ δὲ θεία φύσις ἀ. ἐστιν ὀνόματι Gr.Nyss.*Apoll.*21(M.45.1165C).

***ἀπεριληψία, ἡ**, *incomprehensibility*, Thdr.Stud.*epp.*2.190(M.99. 1580C).

ἀπεριμερίμνως, *without due consideration, carelessly*, Synes.*Dion* 2(p.238.13; M.66.1117D); Cyr.*ador.*6(1.213A).

***ἀπερίμετρος**, *immeasurable*, Eus.*d.e.*3.2(p.101.24; M.22.176C).

ἀπερινόητος, **1.** *uncomprehending, without understanding* ψυχὴ... ἀ. ... τοῦ πατρός Athenag.*leg.*27.1(M.6.953A); **2.** *unintelligible*, ref. punctuation of Jo.1:3 'ὃ γέγονεν, ἐν αὐτῷ...' ἀλλ' οὕτως ἀ. γίνεται τὸ λεγόμενον Chrys.*hom.5.1 in Jo.*(8.35A); ref. Jo.1:15, *ib.13.3*(75D); ref. Phil.2:6 εἰ ἦν θεός, πῶς εἶχεν ἁρπάσαι; καὶ πῶς οὐκ ἀ. τοῦτο; id.*hom.6.2 in Phil.*(11.235C); ref. Ps.73:15 ὅπερ ἐν τοῖς παλαιοῖς ψαλτηρίοις κείμενον, ἔν τισι τῶν νέων ὡς ἀ. ἴσως οὐκ ἐνεγράφη Isid. Pel.*epp.*2.66(M.78.509A); **3.** *incomprehensible*; **a.** def. ἀχώρητον γὰρ κατὰ τὴν οὐσίαν, καὶ ἀ. κατὰ τὴν δύναμιν Max.*ambig.*(M.91.1184D); **b.** of God κύριε παντοκράτωρ...ὁ ἀγέννητος καὶ ἀ. *Apoc.Bar.rel.* 9.6; Clem.*ecl.*21(p.142.21; M.9.708B) cit. s. φῶς; ὁ πατὴρ...τέλειος, ἄπειρος, ἀ. ὤν Eust.*fr.in Ps.*(p.72; M.18.685B); ἀ. ἀνθρώπου φύσει... ἡ οὐσία τοῦ θεοῦ Bas.*Eun.*1.14(1.227A; M.29.545A); ὁ ἄρρητος, ὁ ἄφθαρτος, ὁ ἀ., ὁ ἀόρατος, ὁ ἀκατάληπτος Chrys.*hom.in Mt.26:39* (3.21A); Mac.Aeg.*elev.*8(M.34.896B); τὸ πνεῦμα...ἐκ τῆς ἀ. καὶ θείας οὐσίας Cyr.*thes.*34(5^1.358C); ἡ μία καὶ ἄφραστος καὶ ἀ. τοῦ θεοῦ φύσις id.*Juln.*1(6^2.24A); id.*Ps.*46:9(M.69.1056C); ‡Cyr.*Trin.*1(6^3.1B; M.77. 1120A); Gennad.*fr.Gen.*1:26(M.85.1633C); Jo.D.*f.o.*1.2(M.94.792C); **c.** of Son τὸν λόγον τὸν ἅγιον καὶ ἀ. *Diogn.*7.2; ὦ ἀ. δόξα ἡμῶν *A.Jo.* 77(p.189.19); ὁ λόγος...ἔστι τὴν φύσιν θεὸς αὐτάρκης, ἄπειρος, ἀ. Eust.*fr. in Pr.8:22*(M.18.677B); Chrys.*hom.2.2 in Mt.*(7.21B); ref.

heretical and over-literalistic exegesis εὑρίσκεται...ἀνέφικτος μὲν ὁ υἱός, ὁ δὲ πατὴρ ἐφικτός· καὶ ὁ μὲν [sc. υἱός] ἀ., ὁ δὲ πατὴρ θεατός Thdt.*Trin.*11(M.75.1161D); Gr.Agr.*Eccl.*4.5(M.98.936D); ‡Sophr.H. *triod.*(M.87.3972C); **d.** of Son's generation ὁ τρόπος ἄρρητος καὶ ἀ. Bas.*Eun.*2.24(1.260E; M.29.628A); Procl.CP *or.*15.3(M.65.801D); **e.** of Inc., Mod.*dorm.*8(M.86.3296C); **f.** of union of two natures ἀ. συνδρομῇ Cyr.*Jo.*4.2(4.361B); **g.** of manner of Christ's sacrifice, Max. *ambig.*(M.91.1277C); **h.** of divine mysteries in gen. τοῖς ἀ. ἐμβατεύειν εἰκῇ καὶ δόγμασι κρατύνειν τὰ τῆς ματαίας...οἰήσεως παρευρήματα Gr.Nyss.*Eun.*12(1 p.244.25; M.45.944C); Thdt.*Trin.*2(M.75. 1149B); **i.** of wisdom τὸ ἀνέφικτον αὐτῆς καὶ ἀ. †Dion.Al.*fr.4 in Job* (p.206.3).

ἀπερινοήτως, 1. *unintelligibly, absurdly,* v.l. for ἀνοήτως, Chrys. *hom.53.1 in Mt.*(7.538E); **2.** *incomprehensibly*; **a.** of Son's generation ἐγεννήθη δὲ ἀνεκφράστως καὶ ἀ. †Ath.*exp.fid.*1(M.25.201B); Cyr.*Jo.*6(4.579C); Gel.Cyz.*h.e.*2.15.3(M.85.1257C); **b.** of Inc. ἴδιον ἐποιήσατο τὸ ἐνωθὲν αὐτῷ σῶμα ἀφράστως, ἀ. Cyr.*apol.orient.*11 (p.60.29; 6¹.194D).

***ἀπεριόδευτος,** ? *untended,* i.e. without the care and guidance of God, exeg. Is.5:6 ἀρθῇ εἰς αὐτὸν ἁμαρτία πολλή, ὡς εἰς ἔθνος ἄνομον καὶ ἀ. †Gregent.*disp.*(M.86.689C).

ἀπερίοπτος, 1. *unregarding, heedless of*; **2.** *not to be seen, incomprehensible,* ref. Mt.11:27 and 1Cor.2:10f. εἰκὸς αὐτὴν μὲν τὴν οὐσίαν ἀ. εἶναι παντί, πλὴν εἰ τῷ μονογενεῖ καὶ τῷ ἁγίῳ πνεύματι Bas.*Eun.*1. 14(1.226C; M.29.544B).

ἀπεριόριστος, *uncircumscribed, unlimited, infinite,* of God οὐσίαν...μεγέθει ἀ. Bas.*Spir.*22(3.19C; M.32.108B); τόπῳ ἀπεριόριστος Didym.ap.*cat.Ac.*17:23(p.291.34); Cyr.*Ps.*9:22(M.69.777C); neut. as subst., *infinitude* τὸ ἐν παντὶ τῷ κατὰ τὸ ἀγαθὸν νοουμένῳ ἀ. Gr. Nyss.*Eun.*12(1 p.332.16; M.45.1037B); of divine attributes or gifts εἰρήνη †Bas.*Is.*226(1.550D; M.30.513B); φιλανθρωπία Chrys.*poenit.* 8.1(2.341D); power, Dion.Ar.*d.n.*8.2(M.3.889D); ref. Transfiguration αἴγλης θείας χύσις ἀ. Jo.D.*hom.*1.2(M.96.545B).

ἀπεριορίστως, *without limitation, indefinitely,* exeg. Num.24:7 Μωσῆς ταῦτα οὐκ ἀ. προλέγει Eus.*d.e.*3.2(p.101.23; M.22.176C); Dion. Ar.*d.n.*1.7(M.3.597A) cit. s. ἁπλῶς; *ib.*5.4(817D).

***ἀπεριουσία, ἡ,** *scarcity,* Vict.*Mc.*6:42(p.328n., one MS only).

ἀπερίπτωτος, *not fortuitous, designed,* Isid.Pel.*epp.*3.320(M.78. 984B).

ἀπεριπτώτως, *not haphazard, thoughtfully,* ref. prayer ἔστι λυσιτελὲς λαλεῖν ἀ. Gr.Thaum.*Eccl.*5:1(M.10.1000C).

ἀπερισάλπιγκτος, *unaroused by the trumpet,* hence prob. *unsummoned* to the mysteries, *uninitiated, ignorant* οἱ μὲν ἀ. καθόλου τῶν ἱερῶν τελετῶν Dion.Ar.*e.h.*3.3.6(M.3.432C).

***ἀπερισαλπίγκτως,** *without warning* ἐπέπεσεν αὐτοῖς ἀ. Thphn. *chron.*p.377(M.108.904A, v.l. -πίκτως).

***ἀπερισάλπιστος,** *not disturbed* or *roused by the trumpet* ὕπνον ἀ. Synes.*catast.*2.5(p.292.6; M.66.1572C); met., *unwarlike* τὸν ἀ. τε ἂν εἰς φιλοτιμίαν ἐγείραι id.*regn.*13(p.28.1; M.66.1076A).

ἀπερίσπαστος, 1. *undistracted*; esp. by worldly matters, exeg. Rom.2:10 ἐν εἰρήνῃ δέ ἐστι πᾶς ὁ ἀ. Or.*comm.in Rom.*2:10(*JTS* 13 p.215); of the soul, Meth.*res.*3.18(p.415.6; M.18.325B) cit. s. ἀσώματος; of monastic life, Bas.*renunt.*1(2.202C; M.31.625D); of the mind οἱ ἀ. αὐτὸν...ἔχοντες, οἱονεὶ ἐνηχοῦντα ἑαυτοῖς ἔχουσι τὸν λόγον τοῦ θεοῦ †Bas.*Is.*184(1.515A; M.30.432B); neut. as subst., *freedom from distraction* ἐπὶ τῶν πατέρων ἡμῶν περισπουδαῖον ἦν τὸ ἀ.· νυνὶ δὲ πράττει ἐπὶ ἡμῶν χύτρα καὶ χείρεργον Jo.Mosch.*prat.*130(M.87. 2996A); **2.** *undistracted, unseparated* from, exeg. 1Cor.7:35 ἀπροσπαθῆ τὸν γάμον ἀξίων εἶναι...ἀ. τῆς πρὸς τὸν κύριον ἀγάπης Clem. *str.*7.11(p.46.7; M.9.489A); τὸν νοῦν...ἀ. ἀπὸ τοῦ θεοῦ ποιῆσαι Pall. *h.Laus.*18(p.53.16; M.34.1058C); **3.** *not to be distracted, unwavering, continuous*; of prayer κατὰ τὴν ἀ. πρὸς τὸν θεὸν ἐπιστροφήν Clem. *str.*7.7(p.32.32; M.9.461A); exeg. Mt.6:24 ὧν [sc. heavenly gifts] τὴν κτῆσιν περιγίνεσθαι ἡμῖν ἀμήχανον, μὴ ἀ. ... πόθου ἄγοντος ἡμᾶς πρὸς τὴν αὐτῶν αἴτησιν Bas.*reg.fus.*8.3(2.350C; M.31.940B); neut. as subst., assiduity τὸ ἐν προσευχαῖς ἀ. Gr.Naz.*or.*19.7(M.35. 1052A).

ἀπερισπάστως, 1. *without distraction of mind, undistractedly*; in gen. θεοσεβεῖν ἀ. Eus.*d.e.*1.9(p.40.28; M.22.77D); ταῖς ὑψηλοτέραις ἀσχολίαις παρεδρεύειν ἀ. Gr.Nyss.*virg.*proem.(p.247.10; M.46.317A); of virgins πρὸς τὸ δύνασθαι ἀ. τῷ θεῷ εὐχαριστεῖν Bas.*moral.*77.1 (2.312A; M.31.857B); of monks τὰς πρὸς τὸ θεῖον ὁμιλίας ποιεῖσθαι ἀ. ‡Nil.*narr.*3(M.79.620C); of prayer, v. εὔχομαι; **2.** *without intermission, unceasingly* ἀ. δὲ βοώσης ἐννοίας ἐπακούει ὁ κύριος Marc.Er. *opusc.*2.32(M.65.936B); **3.** *inseparably, immovably* τὸ εἰς αὐτὸν καὶ τὸ δι' αὐτοῦ πιστεῦσαι μοναδικόν ἐστι γενέσθαι, ἀ. ἑνούμενον ἐν αὐτῷ Clem.*str.*4.25(p.318.6; M.8.1365B) = Or.*Apoc.*5(p.22); of the 'gnostic' ἀ. προσομιλῶν τε καὶ συνὼν τῷ κυρίῳ Clem.*str.*7.3(p.10.25; M.9. 417A); τὴν δὲ κραυγὴν...τὸ τῆς διανοίας ἔντονον καὶ ἐρηρεισμένον ἀ. πρὸς θεόν Cyr.*Ps.*27:2(M.69.853D).

ἀπερίστατος, 1. *solitary, friendless,* Or.*fr.*77 *in Jo.*(p.544.14); Eus.*v.C.*3.44(p.96.21; M.20.1105A); *Const.App.*3.3.2; neut. as subst., *solitude,* Eus.*v.C.*1.43(p.28.4; 957B); **2.** ? *not admired,* as pun on εὐπερίστατος: τροφῶν βραχέων ἀντέχου καὶ εὐκαταφρονήτων, μὴ πολλῶν καὶ εὐπεριστάτων, ἢ μᾶλλον ἀ. ‡Ath.*inst.mon.*1(M.28.845D); **3.** *destitute* of οὐσίας καὶ ὑγιείας...ἀ. ‡Chrys.*hom.*5(13.212D).

***ἀπεριστάτως,** *unaffected by circumstances, securely,* exeg. Jo. 13:4 ὅρα εἰ δύνασαι...λέγειν ὅτι ἀ. μὲν αὐτὸν εὔφρανεν τὸ...δειπνεῖν· περιστατικῶς δὲ καὶ ἀναγκαίως...ἐγείρεται Or.*Jo.*32.3(p.431.13; M.14. 749B); id.*fr.64 in Jo.*(p.535.17).

ἀπερίστροφος, *not turning round, unswerving,* Anast.S.*hex.*12 (M.89.1076A).

ἀπερίτμητος, *uncircumcised*; **1.** in gen., Hipp.*haer.*9.26(p.260.12; M.16.3403B); ‡Ath.*Novat.*(M.26.1317C); *cat.Ac.*16:3(p.263.7); **2.** of gentiles διδάσκαλον...ἐθνῶν καὶ ἐκδικητὴν τῶν ἀ. [sc. S. Paul] *A.*(*Pass.*)*Petr.et Paul.*1(p.118.6) = *A.Petr.et Paul.*22(p.188.13); **3.** of Christians καινὸν καὶ ξένον ἔθνος...ἀ. *A.Jo.*3(p.152.12); ἡμεῖς δὲ λαὸς κεκλῆσθαι ἠξιωμένοι ὁμοίως ἔθνος ἐσμὲν διὰ τὸ ἀ. εἶναι Just.*dial.* 123.1(M.6.761A); **4.** met. ἀ. καρδίᾳ ταῖς θείαις γραφαῖς ἐναντιούμενοι Didym.(‡Bas.)*Eun.*5(1.314B; M.29.753A).

ἀπερίτρεπτος, *not to be overturned, immovable, unmoved, secure,* in the spiritual life ἵνα ἀ. καὶ ἄπτωτοι διὰ πίστεως...μείνωμεν ‡Pion.*v.Polyc.*31; of future life, exeg. Ps.114:8 ἐνταῦθα πολὺς ὁ κίνδυνος τοῦ ὀλισθήματος·...ἐκεῖ δὲ...ἀ. ἡ ζωή Bas.*hom.in Ps.*114:8 (1.203A; M.29.492C); exeg. 2Cor.8:2 ἀλείφων αὐτοὺς ἐν τοῖς πειρασμοῖς γενναίους εἶναι καὶ ἀ. Chrys.*hom.16.2 in 2Cor.*(10.554B); exeg. Mt.16:18 τὸ ἀ. τὴν ἐκκλησίαν ποιῆσαι ἐν τοσαύτῃ κυμάτων ἐμβολῇ id.*hom.54.2 in Mt.*(7.548C); of S. Peter τὴν προσηγορίαν ἐντεῦθεν ἔλαβε διὰ τὸ ἀκλινὲς καὶ ἀ. τῆς πίστεως id.*comm.in Gal.*2:11(10.686E).

ἀπεριτρέπτως, *firmly, unwaveringly,* Chrys.*hom.3.4 in 2Cor.*(10. 448A); Bas.Sel.*or.*1.2(M.85.29C).

ἀπέριττος, 1. *without superfluity, plain, simple* σύντομον καὶ ἀ. τῆς τριάδος θεολογίαν Gr.Naz.*or.*31.3(p.148.11; M.36.136C); of the Lord's Prayer εὐχῆς κανόνα καὶ τύπον ἀ. Gr.Nyss.*usur.*(M.46.444A); of S. Paul, exeg. Ac.28:3 οὕτως ἦν ἀ. ... ὅτι καὶ τὴν οἴκησιν εἶχεν... ἀφ' ὧν αὐτὸς εἰργάζετο Chrys.*hom.55.2 in Ac.*(9.414C); neut. as subst., *simplicity*; *conciseness,* exeg. Mt.4:24 σκόπει τὸ ἀ. τοῦ εὐαγγελιστοῦ, πῶς οὐ καθ' ἕκαστον ἡμῖν διηγεῖται τῶν θεραπευομένων id.*hom.14.3 in Mt.*(7.181C); of Christ πανταχοῦ παιδεύει τὸ αὐτουργόν, καὶ ἀ. Ammon.*Jo.*4:6(M.85.1420B); **2.** *free from excretions* ἀ. μένοντες κάλλιον λογιζόμεθα Melet.*nat.hom.*synops.(M. 64.1129D).

ἀπεριττότης, ἡ, *simplicity,* Clem.*paed.*1.12(p.149.10; M.8.368C).

***ἀπερίφρακτος,** *not fenced round, unprotected,* exeg. Eph.2:14 οὐκ ἀ. καταλιμπάνων τὸν ἑαυτοῦ λαόν, ἀλλὰ μιᾷ περιλαμβάνων αὐλῇ †Bas. *Is.*145(1.481A; M.30.356A); met., of soul, Ephr.3.212E.

***ἀπεριφυλάκτως,** *unguardedly, thoughtlessly,* Anast.S.*fr.*(M.89. 1285A).

***ἀπεριχαρῶς,** *without joy,* Thdr.Stud.*epp.*2.100(M.99.1353B).

***ἀπέρπερος,** *free from vainglory, modest,* Pall.*h.Laus.*56(M.34. 1249A); of monastic life, Isid.Pel.*epp.*1.278(M.78.345C); Nil.*epp.*4.41 (M.79.569C) etc.

***ἀπερυθριάστως,** *shamelessly,* Nil.*epp.*2.50(M.79.221C).

ἀπερυθριάω, *be past blushing, be shameless*; *be shameless enough* to ἀ. ... τὸν θεὸν βλασφημῆσαι Hipp.*haer.*7.11(p.190.16; M.16.3294B); neut. ptcpl. as subst., *shamelessness,* Andr.Caes.*Apoc.*53(M.106. 377A).

ἀπέρχομαι, *go away*; of death, *depart,* Const.ap.Eus.*v.C.*2.36 (p.57.1; M.20.1013B); τὴν οἰκίαν [sc. τὴν ψυχήν]...ἣν καὶ λαβόντες ἀπελευσόμεθα Chrys.*hom.24.5 in 1Cor.*(10.219C); id.*hom.75.5 in Mt.* (7.730C).

***ἀπεσκληκότως,** *in a hardened manner, obdurately,* c. ἔχω *be hardened,* Synes.*ep.*139(M.66.1529B).

***ἀπεσχισμένως,** *in separation,* Bas.*reg.fus.*16.3(2.359B; M.31. 960C).

***ἀπεσχοινισμένως,** *in separation,* Cyr.*Nest.*4.2(p.80.37; 6.103C); οὐδέ τι τούτων [sc. ὑποστάσεων] ἐν Χριστῷ ἀ. ἐστὶ τοῦ ἑτέρου ὑφεστώς Leont.H.*Nest.*5.28(M.86.1748D).

ἀπευδοκ-έω, *despair,* Hipp.*haer.*6.20(p.148.10; M.16.3226B); ~εῖ οὖν ἑαυτὴν...ἡ ψυχή Mac.Aeg.*hom.*47.13(M.34.804D); *despair of* ἀ. τῆς σωτηρίας Ath.*exp.Ps.*73:9(M.27.336B).

***ἀπευδόκησις, ἡ,** *despair,* *Mir.Artem.*13(p.13.13).

***ἀπευδοκία**, ἡ, *despair*, ‡Max.*cap.al.*152(M.90.1436C).

***ἀπευδοκίμησις**, ἡ, *rejection, contempt*, of Cain θάνατον ᾐτήσατο ἐν ἀ. ζωῆς Or.*sel.in Gen.*4:13(M.12.101D).

***ἀπευθυντήρ**, ὁ, *guide*, Cyr.*Jo.*2.1(4.156A).

***ἀπευκτέος**, *to be abominated, detestable*, ‡Chrys.*Abr.*2(2.744C).

***ἀπευλογίας**, *deprived of benediction* (i.e. blessing of monks before retiring to bed), as monastic punishment γενέσθω ἀ. ‡Bas.*poen. mon.*15–20(2.528A–B; M.31.1308C–1309A).

***ἀπευτελίζω**, *disparage, abase*, Bas.Sel.*or.*28.1(M.85.317C).

***ἀπεχθέω**, *be at enmity, be hostile*, Cyr.*Is.*1.1(2.2B).

***ἀπεχθημοσύνη**, ἡ, *enmity*, Philost.*h.e.*6.4(M.65.536B).

***ἀπεχθιάζω**, *be hostile*, †Polyb.*v.Epiph.*42(M.41.104B).

***ἀπεχθίζω**, *hate*, Cyr.*ador.*1(1.18D).

ἀπέχ-ω, med.; **1.** *abstain* or *desist from*, Polyc.*ep.*6.1; Herm. *mand.*2.3; τοσούτοις ἀ. Chrys.*oppugn.*3.7(1.86C); ∼όμενος, *abstinent*, *M.Sab.*2.2; **2.** *fall away* from faith, Chrys.*hom.5.2 in 1Tim.*(11. 575F); from Christ, id.*hom.7.3 in Phil.*(11.249B).

***ἀπέωθεν**, *from the early morning*, Epiph.*haer.*75.3(M.42.503B; ἀφ' ἕωθεν p. 335.20).

***ἀπηδάλωτος**, *rudderless*, Ephr.1.90E.

ἀπηκριβωμένως, *particularly, with exactitude*, Eus.*d.e.*3.1(p.95.11; M.22.165C); Cyr.*ador.*7(1.249E); *ib.*9(298B).

ἄπηκτος, **1.** *not solid, soft*, Meth.*symp.*2.6(p.23.2; M.18.56C); **2.** *not compacted, simple*, of God οὔτι παθητός, ὅς τις πάμπαν ἄ., ἀσώματος Gr.Naz.*carm.*1.1.2.16(M.37.403A).

***ἀπηλεγής**, *ruthless*, Gr.Naz.*carm.*2.1.46.18(M.37.1379A).

***ἀπήλικος**, *without magnitude*, Dion.Ar.*d.n.*9.3(M.3.912B); of God, Jo.D.*imag.*3.8(M.94.1328D); Jo.V H.*icon.*6(M.96.1353D).

ἀπηλιώτης, ὁ, **1.** name of an *east wind*; hence *east*, Hegem.*Arch.* 8(p.13.5; M.10.1440B); Cosm.Ind.*top.*2(M.88.116B); **2.** interpreted as *south* by SM, Thdt.*Ezech.*20:48(2.838).

***ἀπηλλοτριωμένως**, *in alienation*, Epiph.*anc.*52(M.43.108A; conj. ἀπηρυθριασμένως p.61.7).

***ἄπηλος**, *free from mud, mudless*, word coined in jest, Gr.Naz. *ep.*2(M.37.21B).

***ἀπημφιεσμένως**, *without disguise, openly*, met. γυμνῶς τε καὶ ἀ. ...διδάσκει Cyr.*Ps.*44:5(M.69.1036A); id.*ador.*4(1.126B); id.*Jo.*9(4. 805B).

ἀπήνεια (-ία), ἡ, *harshness, cruelty*, Gr.Nyss.*or.dom.*1(p.16.21; M.44.1129A); Chrys.*sac.*1.5(p.6.16; 1.363E); *-ία* Thdt.*qu.37 in Gen.* (1.47); Proc.G.*Gen.*6:5(M.87.269C).

ἀπηνής, *harsh, cruel*; *obstinate* τῆς ἀ. ἀπειθείας Clem.*str.*7.16 (p.72.15; M.9.541B); Cyr.*Lc.*22:27(M.72.913A).

***ἀπήνοια**, ἡ, prob. f.l. for ἀπήνη, usu. ἅμαξα, the *Chariot* constellation, i.e. the Great Bear, Plough, or Charles' Wain, ‡Caes. Naz.*dial.*104(M.38.972).

***ἀπηνότης**, ἡ, *cruelty*, Epiph.*haer.*52.2(p.313.18; M.41.957A); *ib.* 76.1(p.341.23; M.42.517A).

ἀπήορος, *suspended on high*, Gr.Naz.*carm.*1.2.2.627(M.37.627A).

***ἀπήρτημα**, τό, v. *ἀπάρτημα.

***ἀπηρυθριασμένως**, *shamelessly* ἀ. βλασφημῶν [sc. Marcion] Iren.*haer.*1.27.2(M.7.688A); βιαζομένων ἀ. τὴν γραφήν Meth.*res.*1.39 (p.282.12; M.18.268B); exeg. 2Thess.2:6 καλῶς εἶπε τὸ μυστήριον· οὐ γὰρ φανερῶς, ὡς ἐκεῖνος [sc. Nero], οὐδ' ἀ. Chrys.*hom.4.1 in 2Thess.*(11.529F).

[*]ἀπησυχάζω, ? f.l. for ἀφησυχάζω, *settle down*; *A.Phil.*66(p.27. 17).

***ἀπηυχενισμένως**, *without restraint* ἀ. ἀναβοήσαντες Cyr.*Jo.*6.1 (4.617A).

ἀπήχημα, τό, *echo*; met., of dreams as the reflection of waking life, Bas.*hom.in Ps.*33:2(1.144D; M.29.354C); *faint echo, trace* ἀ. τινα τῆς νοερᾶς εὐπρεπείας Dion.Ar.*c.h.*2.4(M.3.144B); Jo.D.*Man.*1. 35(M.94.1541A).

ἀπηχής, **1.** *discordant, out of tune*; **2.** met.; **a.** *unpleasant, harsh* ἀ. ἀπειλάς Thdt.*Joel.*2:11(2.1393); of Jonah's prophecies, id.*xii proph.proem.*(2.1308); **b.** *unreasonable, absurd*, Cyr.*Jo.*4.5 (4.410B); of the views of Nestorius, id.*ep.*18(p.113.14; 5^2.78D); neut. as subst. καθαρίσουσι τὸ ἀ. βωμολοχίας Ἑλληνικῆς καὶ ἀπάτης δαιμονίων id.*Is.*4.2(2.617B); **c.** *unseemly, disgraceful*, exeg. Is.50:1 ἀποβέβληται γὰρ ὡς πεπορνευμένη καὶ ἐπὶ τοῖς ἄγαν ἀ. κατεγνωσμένη id.*glaph.Gen.*4(1.129E); id.*Ps.*37:17(M.69.965C).

***ἀπηχύς**, ? *cumbrous* ἀ. τε εἰκὸς καὶ βαρὺ...ξύλον Cyr.*Jo.*2.6(4. 220C).

***ἀπιδιάζω (*ἀφιδιάζω)**, **1.** *live alone* or *apart*, (ἀφ-) Bas.*reg.fus.* 6.1(2.344B; M.31.925B); of hermits, Jo.Clim.*scal.*8(M.88.832A); **2.** *remain aloof, keep to oneself* οὐκ ἀπράκτου...τοῦ πατρὸς ἐν τῷ καιρῷ τῆς οἰκονομίας ἀπιδιάσαντος Gr.Nyss.*Eun.*12(2 p.288.4; M.45. 900C).

***ἀπιδιαστικός (*ἀφιδιαστικός)**, *solitary*, of hermits ἀφ. βίος Bas. *reg.fus.*7.1(2.345E; M.31.929A); *aloof, unco-operative* ἤθη...ἀκοινώνητα, ἀπ. †Bas.*Is.*283(1.594D; M.30.616B).

***ἀπιθυντήρ**, ὁ, *guide, director*; of a hand-rail, Paul.Sil.*ambo*.78 (M.86.2255A).

ἀπίλλ-ω, ? *let slip, lose* ἐπλησιάσαμεν τῷ θανάτῳ, καὶ βλέπομεν ὅτι ∼ομεν τὸν καιρόν Dor.*doct.*11.2(M.88.1736D) poss. f.l. for ἀπόλλυμεν.

ἀπιστ-έω, **1.** *disbelieve, refuse to believe*; of Moses (cf. Num. 11:23), Just.*dial.*126.6(M.6.772A); of Jews, in Christ, *ib.*75.4(652C); Or.*hom.15.5 in Jer.*(p.129.21; M.13.436A) al.; of pagans, Just. *1apol.*55.8(M.6.413A); in life after death, *ib.*57.3(413C); of Arians disbelieving scriptures, Ath.*Ar.*2.36(M.26.224B); effects τὸ μὲν ∼εῖν τῇ ἀληθείᾳ θάνατον φέρει Clem.*str.*4.3(p.251.13; M.8.1220B); **2.** *be an unbeliever*; opp. Christians, ref. Cross σκάνδαλον τοῖς ∼οῦσιν Ign. *Eph.*18.1; Or.*Apoc.*5(p.22); Ath.*inc.*28.5(M.25.145A); effects τὸ δὲ ∼ῆσαι διστάσαι ἐστὶ καὶ...μερισθῆναι Clem.*str.*4.25(p.318.6; M.8. 1365B); exeg. Jo.3:18 αὐτὸ τὸ ∼εῖν ἀμετανόητα, κόλασίς ἐστι Chrys. *hom.28.1 in Jo.*(8.159E); cf.*ib.*(160B); **3.** *be faithless, deny the faith*, ref. Mt.24:51 τὸ ∼οῦν αὐτοῦ μέρος μετὰ τῶν ὑποκριτῶν θήσει *Hom. Clem.*3.60.

ἀπιστία, ἡ, **1.** *unbelief* ἀ. ὑπόληψις τοῦ ἀντικειμένου ἀσθενὴς ἀποφατική Clem.*str.*2.6(p.127.31; M.8.964A); ἀ., ἀπόστασις οὖσα τῆς πίστεως *ib.*2.12(p.142.29; 992C); opp. πίστις, Ign.*Eph.*8.2; *Hom. Clem.*7.7; Chrys.*hom.28.3 in Jo.*(8.162C); personified, Herm.*sim.* 9.15.3; of pagans in Christianity, Tat.*orat.*32(p.33.12; M.6.872B); Clem.*str.*2.2(p.117.8; 940A); of Greeks in Jewish law, *ib.*1.26(p.105. 30; 917B); of Jews in Christ μεθ' ὅρκου ὁ θεὸς διὰ τὴν ἀ. ὑμῶν ἀρχιερέα αὐτὸν κατὰ τὴν τάξιν Μελχισεδὲκ εἶναι ἐδήλωσε Just.*dial.*33.2 (M.6.545B); of Pharisees, Ath.*inc.*23.3(M.25.137A); ref. heresy, of Marcellus, Eus.*Marcell.*2.1(p.31.22; M.24.776A); Arianism διὰ τὴν ἀ. τῶν τολμηρῶν λέγειν ἁπλούστερον Ath.*ep.Serap.*1.20(M.26.577C); ref. followers of Paul. Sam. δι' ἀπιστίαν θεότητος ἐκπεσόντων ‡Ath.*Apoll.*2.19(M.26.1165A); *lack of faith*, as moral defect πονηρὰ πράσσοντες οὐ γινώσκομεν διὰ τὴν...ἀ. τὴν ἐνοῦσαν ἐν τοῖς στήθεσιν ἡμῶν *2Clem.*19.2; τὴν θεόθεν ἤκουσαν συνείδησιν ἀπιστίᾳ κατεμίαναν Clem.*str.*2.6(p.129.1; 965A); producing evil, id.*paed.*1.8(p.131.1; M.8.393B); in Christ, put to shame by him, id.*prot.*1(p.9.9; M.8. 64D); inexcusable since his advent, id.*str.*7.2(p.9.15; M.9.413C); **2.** *distrust* of oneself ὑπακοὴ γάρ ἐστιν ἀ. Jo.Clim.*scal.*4(M.88. 680C); **3.** *unreliability* of earthly things, Isid.Pel.*epp.*1.31(M.78. 201C).

***ἀπιστόκορος**, *filled with unbelief*, *Orac.Sib.*1.150; *ib.*1.177; *ib.*1. 329.

ἄπιστος, **1.** *incredible, not to be believed*; of pagan fables, Athenag.*leg.*30.3(M.6.960C); of Inc., Just.*1apol.*33.2(M.6.381A); hence *incredibly great* or *good*, Gr.Naz.*ep.*26(M.37.61B); id.*carm.*2. 1.13.28(M.37.1229A); **2.** *unbelieving*; of Jews, Ath.*inc.*18.2(M.25. 128A); Arians, *Pet.Ar.*4(M.26.824A); Meletians, Ath.*h.Ar.*79(p.227. 28; M.25.789B); hence *pertaining to an unbeliever* ὀνόματα αὐτῶν, ὄντα ἀ. Ign.*Smyrn.*5.3; **3.** subst., *unbeliever* opp. Christian, Ign. *Magn.*5.2; *2Clem.*17.5; opp. elect, *M.Polyc.*16.1; ὁ Ἰησοῦς...ὑπὸ μὲν τῶν ἀ. καταδικάζεται Or.*hom.14.8 in Jer.*(p.113.21; M.13.413B); εἰς μαρτύριον τοῖς ἀ. οἱ μάρτυρες μαρτυροῦσι id.*Jo.*2.34(28; p.93.21; M.14.177A); Ath.*gent.*1(M.25.5B); punishment ἀπίστοις...στεῖρα καὶ ἔρημος περιλείπεται Clem.*prot.*1(p.10.3; M.8.65C); ὑπολείπεται τοῖς ἀ. ... κρίσις καὶ καταδίκη *ib.*9(p.63.15; 196A); Chrys.*hom.28.1 in Jo.* (8.160A); opp. orthodox, of Docetists, Ign.*Trall.*10; id.*Smyrn.*2; opp. personal disciples of Christ, ‡*Diogn.*11.2.

ἀπιστόφιλος, *cherishing unbelief*, *Orac.Sib.*8.186.

ἀπίστως, *without* Christian *faith*, Didym.(‡Bas.)*Eun.*5(1.313D; M.29.752B); ἀπίστως βιούς *Hom.Clem.*15.10.

ἀπλανής, *not wandering*; **1.** astron., *fixed*, of stars opp. planets ἡ ἀ. [sc. σφαῖρα] *the firmament*, Or.*Cels.*1.58(p.109.29; M.11.768B); *ib.*8.52(p.267.19; 1593C); **2.** met.; **a.** *unerring* ἀ. παράδοσιν τοῦ ἀποστολικοῦ κηρύγματος Eus.*h.e.*4.8.2(M.20.321B); Bas.*renunt.*2(2. 204C; M.31.632B); Cyr.*ador.*4(1.135D); **b.** *without error, true* τὴν ἀ. θεοσέβειαν *Const.App.*1 proem.; δός μοι...γνῶσιν ἀ. *ib.*7.45.3; **c.** *sure, certain* τῇ ἀ. σωτηρίᾳ Hesych.H.*Ps.tit.*68:28(M.27.924D).

ἀπλάνητος, **1.** *not wandering, not going astray* ἀ. ... φυλαχθῆναι τὴν ὄψιν Gr.Nyss.*virg.*6(p.279.4; M.46.349B); τὰ ἀ. πρόβατα ‡Chrys. *hom.in Ps.83*(5.608E); **2.** *straight, direct* οὗτος [sc. τρίβος]...σαφὴς ἀ. *Orac.Sib.fr.*1.28.

***ἁπλάριος**, *simple-minded, foolish*, plur., Manichean term for orthodox Christians ἁ. προσκυνοῦσι τὴν ἐπιθυμίαν, θεὸν αὐτὴν ἡγούμενοι Manes ap.Hegem.*Arch*.11(p.19.11; M.10.1445C).

***ἄπλειστος**, prob. f.l. for ἄπληστος, *insatiable*; ἡδονὴν ἄμετρόν τε καὶ ἄ. Thdt.*h.rel*.proem.(3.1105).

ἄπλεκτος, *not entwined*, †Bas.Anc.*virg*.59(M.30.788C).

ἀπλεονέκτητος, **1.** *free from avarice*, Clem.*str*.5.5(p.345.26; M.9.53B); **2.** *insuperable, irresistible*, Cyr.*hom.pasch*.6(5^2.62D); id.*Jo*.9.12(4.1016D).

ἄπλετος, *boundless, immense*; *innumerable*, *Orac.Sib*.2.208; Epiph.*haer*.66.59(p.96.15; M.42.117D).

ἄπληγος, **1.** *unsmitten*; *unharmed* τὰς ψυχὰς ἀ. ἀνέσπα ‡Ath.*v.Syncl*.107(M.28.1553A); Geo.Pis.*hex*.399(M.92.1464A); Melet.*nat.hom*.synops.(M.64.1132C); **2.** *not inflicting a blow* ἀ. μάστιγι †Andr.Cr.*or*.18.6(p.424.15; M.97.1200B); **3.** *that is not a blow, without a blow*, as oxymoron, ref. Jo.20:25ff. εὗρον [sc. ὁ Θωμᾶς] ἄ. πληγήν, εἶδον τραῦμα καὶ φθορὰ οὐκ ἦν Ephr.3.468B.

ἀπλήθυντος, *not multiplied, without plurality*, of God τοῖς πολλοῖς ἀμιγὴς καὶ ἀ. Dion.Ar.*d.n*.2.11(M.3.649D); of Trin. τὸ ὁμοούσιον...ἀρραγὲς ἔχει...οὐ μὴν ἀλλὰ καὶ ἀ. Sophr.H.*or*.2.2(M.87.3217B); of Son, Max.*ep*.13(M.91.532A) cit. s. ἑτεροούσιος; *ib*.(524A); of H. Ghost, Didym.*Trin*.2.4(M.39.484A).

ἀπληκεύ-ω, **1.** *encamp*; act., *Chron.Pasch*.p.298(M.92.747B); Thphn.*chron*.p.314(v.l. ἀπλικεῦσαι M.108.761C); med., *Chron.Pasch*.p.318(808C); **2.** *lodge, put up* οἶκον εὐρύχωρον εἰς τὸ ~σαι αὐτὸν ἐζήτει Gr.Mag.*dial*.(tr.Zach.)3.4(M.*PL*.77.223C); CNic.(787)*act*.4(H.4.221E).

ἄπληκτον, τό, *camp*, Heracl.*ep*.(M.92.1020C).

ἄπληκτος, **1.** *unstricken*, met., *unwounded, without receiving a blow* τὸν ἄ. στεφανούμενον †Bas.Sel.*or*.41(M.85.472B); **2.** *not striking, harmless*, Gr.Nyss.*Eun*.7(2 p.157.21; M.45.745C); *ib*.12(1 p.387.4; ἐκπλήκτοις 1116C).

***ἀπλημμελής**, *free from sin, sinless* ἄρτιον καὶ ἀ. ὁμοῦ πάσης τὸ σῶμα τῆς ἀρετῆς Nil.*Magn*.8(M.79.980C); διαιρεῖν τὰς ὑποστάσεις μετὰ τὴν ἕνωσιν, οὐκ ἀ. Cyr.*apol.orient*.4(p.45.16; 6.173D); neut. as subst., *sinlessness*; **a.** of Christ καταπεπλούτηκεν γὰρ ἐν ἰδίᾳ φύσει τὸ ἀ. ὡς θεός id.*glaph.Lev*.(1.372C); ref. sacrificial heifer typifying Christ ἄμωμος δέ, διὰ τὸ ἀ. id.*glaph.Num*.(1.402D); **b.** of human nature in Christ ἐν αὐτῷ τὸ ἀ. ἡ ἀνθρώπου φύσις εὑρέθη πλουτήσασα id.*Lc*.23:46(p.475.1; M.72.940A); id.*Chr.un*.(5^1.757B).

ἀπλήξ, *unstruck, unhurt*; **1.** lit., Cyr.*glaph.Dt*.(1.428A); id.*ador*.9(1.290D); id.*Os*.54(3.84D); **2.** met., Gr.Naz.*carm*.2.1.11.732(M.37.1079A); φυλάττουσι δὲ μᾶλλον ἀ. τὸν νοῦν Cyr.*Is*.5.3(2.801A); id.*hom.pasch*.26(5^2.303C).

***ἀπληροφόρητος**, **1.** *unsatisfied* οὐ γὰρ δυνατὸν ἀνθρώπῳ ἐκκόψαι μου τὴν ἀ. λύπην *A.Xanthipp*.5(p.61.18); **2.** *lacking in confidence, uncertain*, Dor.*doct*.7.5(M.88.1704A); τὸ ἐνδοιάζειν ἐν ταῖς κρίσεσι, καὶ ἀ. ... διαμένειν Jo.Clim.*scal*.26(M.88.1060A); *uncertain in faith* ἥστινος [sc. θείας ἐλλάμψεως] ὁ μετέχων οὐκ ἀ., ἀλλὰ καὶ ἔμπεδος Hesych.S.*temp*.1.84(M.93.1505D); *without sure hope* of salvation ἄνες μοι διὰ πληροφορίας, ἵνα ἀναψύξω πρὸ τοῦ με ἀπελθεῖν ἐντεῦθεν ἀ. Jo.Clim.*scal*.5(M.88.730A).

***ἀπληροφορία, ἡ,** *uncertainty* of mind, i.e. lack of sure faith, Jo.Clim.*scal*.27(M.88.1108D).

ἀπλήρωτος, **1.** *not to be sated* or *satisfied, insatiable* τὴν ἀ. τῆς θεωρίας εὐφροσύνην Clem.*str*.6.9(p.469.5; M.9.296B); τῆς τοῦ ὄντως ὄντος ἀ. ἐμπίμπλασθαι θέας id.*paed*.2.1(p.160.5; M.8.393A); **2.** *not to be completed* or *exhausted*, hence *unending* νὺξ Mac.Mgn.*apocr*.4.11(p.173.6); *inexhaustible*, of God πλῆθος ἀμερές, ἀ. ὑπερπλῆρες Dion.Ar.*d.n*.2.11(M.3.649C); **3.** *unfilled*; **a.** lit. ἔτι γὰρ ὁ κόσμος ἀνθρώπων ἀ. ὢν Meth.*symp*.1.2(p.10.12; M.18.41A); **b.** met., *unfulfilled*, of prophecies about Christ ἀ. καὶ ἀτελεῖς ἔμενον, εἰς ὅτε ...ἐπιτέθεικεν ἅπασι τέλος Eus.*d.e*.8.2(p.372.23; M.22.605A); Chrys.*hom*.16.2 *in Mt*.(7.205E); of Law, exeg. Gal.5:3 μίαν δὲ ἐάσας ἐντολὴν ἀ. Mac.Mgn.*apocr*.3.40(p.139.1); **c.** *incomplete, imperfect* ἀ. ἔχον τὴν διάνοιαν Thdr.Mops.*Ps*.71:5(p.472.16; M.66.689C); ref. Inc. τὴν ἐξ ἡμῶν ἔμψυχον σάρκα εἰ μὴ πρὸς τὸ εἶναι υἱὸν ἀ. νομίζετε Leont.H.*Nest*.3.1(M.86.1604A).

***ἀπληρώτως**, *insatiably* ἡσυχαστὰς καὶ τὴν φλεγομένην αὐτῶν πρὸς θεὸν ἐπιθυμίαν...ἀ. πληρώσαντας Jo.Clim.*scal*.27(M.88.1098D).

ἀπληστεύομαι, *be insatiable*; *have an insatiable desire* for ἀ. ἐν κάλλει βρωμάτων Ephr.1.15F; Ant.Mon.*hom*.7(M.89.1452A); ἀ. ... μετασχεῖν ματαίων καὶ ἀπολλυμένων Thdr.Stud.*epp*.2.123(M.99.1404A); in good sense ἀ. τὰ θεάρεστα *ib*.1.7(929C).

ἀπληστία, ἡ, *insatiate desire, greediness*; **1.** *immoderation, violence*, of a ship in a storm τὴν ἀ. τῆς βιαίας φορᾶς Synes.*ep*.4 M.66.1337B); **2.** *unfailing abundance, immensity*, ref. Dan.3:6 ἀπληστίᾳ τροφῆς ταύτην [sc. κάμινον]...αὐξήσας Thdt.*provid*.8(4.627); of God, exeg. Jo.1:14 τῆς φιλανθρωπίας τὴν ἀ. id.*eran.suppl*.(4.267); ἀγαθότητος ἀ. Bas.Sel.*or*.36.2(M.85.388C).

***ἀπληστόκορος**, *insatiate*, *Orac.Sib*.14.5; *ib*.14.20.

ἄπληστος, *insatiable, greedy*; *boundless* μετ' εὐφημιῶν καὶ ἀ. χαρᾶς ὑπεδέχοντο Eus.*v.C*.1.39(p.26.9; M.20.953C); *immoderate*, of Aëtius οὐδὲ ἀσέβειαν ἄμετρον, ἀλλὰ συγγραφὴν ἄ. ἐγκαλέσαντες Gr.Naz.*or*.21.23(M.35.1108B).

ἀπλήστως, *insatiably, greedily* θεοῦ μόνου, θείων τε ἀ. ἔχειν Gr.Naz.*carm*.1.2.33.145(M.37.938A).

ἄπλητος, = ἄπλετος, *boundless, great*, Thdt.*provid*.3(4.513).

[*]**ἀπλικεύω**, v. ἀπληκεύω.

***ἁπλόη, ἡ,** *simplicity*, Synes.*ep*.148(M.66.1549B).

ἁπλοϊκῶς, *with simplicity*, Thdt.*Abac*.proem.(2.1537); id.*h.rel*.3(3.1149); comp., Bas.*fid*.2(2.225C; M.31.680D).

[*]**ἁπλόκομος**, *with straight hair* or *with cropped hair*, ‡Caes.Naz.*dial*.111(M.38.989).

ἄπλοκος, **1.** *unplaited*, hence *smooth* ἄ. ... ἄκρον ὑπήνης Nonn.*par.Jo*.18:19(M.43.893A); **2.** *not to be plaited, unable to be twined*, of combining daily life and contemplation πλέκει θαυμασίως ἀμφότερα, τὴν χρυσῆν ὄντως σειράν, καὶ τοῖς πολλοῖς ἄ. Gr.Naz.*or*.21.6(M.35.1088B).

***ἁπλοπότιον, τό,** *single* (i.e. not two-handled) *cup* κόνδυ μέν, τὸ λεγόμενον ἁ. λέγει Thdr.Mops.*Gen*.44:5(M.66.645A).

***ἁπλοσύνθετος**, *both simple and compound* μὴ λέγοντες δοξάζοιτε ἁ. μίαν φύσιν θεότητος καὶ ἀνθρωπότητος Thdr.Stud.*probl*.9(M.99.481C).

ἁπλότης, ἡ, **A.** *simplicity*, metaphysical; **1.** of God; **a.** in gen. τῶν θεουμένων θεαρχία, καὶ τῶν ἁπλουμένων ἁ. Dion.Ar.*d.n*.1.3(M.3.589C); *ib*.1.4(589D) cit. s. ἀμέρεια; κατὰ μίαν ἁπλότητος ὑπερβολὴν πᾶσαν διπλόην ἀπαναινομένη *ib*.5.9(825A); πάσης ἁ. ὁ θεῖος ὑπερήπλωται λόγος *ib*.7.4(872C) al.; Gel.Cyz.*h.e*.2.15.8(M.85.1260B); Zach.Mit.*opif*.(M.85.1069B); θεὸς...ὁ μηδέποτε τῆς οἰκείας ἀμεροῦς ἁ. ἐξιστάμενος Max.*ambig*.(M.91.1257B); implicitly denied by heretics καθ' ὑμῶν ἔσται τὰ ὑμέτερα, μηδὲ αὐτῷ τῷ θείῳ ἄνευ τῆς ἐκ μερῶν ὁλότητος, συγχωροῦντα τὴν ἁ. Leont.H.*Nest*.1.1(M.86.1408B); **b.** ref. generation of Son, Tat.*orat*.5(p.5.22; M.6.813C) cit. s. θέλημα; **c.** Trin. τίς γὰρ οὐκ οἶδεν ὅτι κατὰ τὸν ἴδιον λόγον ἡ ἁ. ἐπὶ τῆς ἁγίας τριάδος τὸ μᾶλλόν τε καὶ ἧττον οὐκ ἐπιδέχεται; Gr.Nyss.*Eun*.1(1 p.89.18; M.45.321B); **2.** of angels and souls ταῖς οὐρανίαις καὶ θεοειδέσιν ἁ. Dion.Ar.*c.h*.2.2(M.3.137C); commented θεοειδεῖς ἁ. φησι τὰς νοητὰς οὐσίας. ἄϋλοι γὰρ οὐσίαι καὶ ἀσύνθετοι πάντως εἰσίν Max.*schol.c.h*.2.2(M.4.37B); cf.Dion.Ar.*c.h*.4.1(177C) al.; ἡ ψυχή, οὐκ ἄν ποτε πρὸς τοῦ παχυμερεστέρου ὕδατος πάθοι τι δεινόν, διὰ λεπτότητα καὶ ἁ. μὴ κρατουμένη, ᾗ καὶ ἀσώματος προσαγορεύεται Clem.*str*.6.6(p.458.8; M.9.273C).

B. *simplicity, singleness*, moral and spiritual τί γὰρ ἄλλο ἐστὶν ἁ. ἀλλ' ἢ φρόνησις;...ὁδός τίς ἐστιν ἐπὶ φιλοσοφίαν ἡ ἁ. Chrys.*hom*.7.3 *in Ac*.(9.59D,E); ἁ. ἐστὶν ἕξις ψυχῆς ἀποίκιλος, πρὸς κακόνοιαν γενομένη ἀκίνητος Jo.Clim.*scal*.24(M.88.981B); **1.** of heart and mind, as an ordinary Christian virtue πορεύεσθε ἐν ἁ. καρδίας *T.Reub*.4.1; ἐν...δικαιοσύνῃ καὶ ἁ. καρδίας *1Clem*.60.2; σῴζει σε...ἡ ἁ. σου Herm.*vis*.2.3.2; τὴν ἐν ἀνθρώποις...ἁ. τῆς διανοίας, τὴν ἀκακίαν Clem.*paed*.1.5(p.98.9; M.8.265A); μυστικῶς τοῦ λόγου τὴν ἁ. τῆς ψυχῆς εἰς ἡλικίαν ὑπογραφομένου παιδικὴν *ib*.(p.98.19; 265B); ref. faith τῆς τῶν ἀνδρῶν ἁ. καὶ πίστεως Eus.*m.P*.13(p.949.29; M.20.1517C); ἡ τῆς ἁ. πίστις βελτίων ἐστὶ τῆς ἐκ περιεργίας πιθανολογίας Ath.*Ar*.3.1(M.26.324A); Gel.Cyz.*h.e*.2.26.4(M.85.1308A); coupled with ἀγνότης, Ath.*ep.fest*.39(p.87.3; M.26.1436B); *sincerity, guilelessness*, Chrys.*hom*.1.2 *in Mt*.(7.5C); id.*sac*.4.1(p.97.21; 1.402B); διὰ τὴν νηπιώδη ἁ. Diad.*perf*.65(p.78.12); ὁ Ἀδὰμ...γυμνὸς τῇ ἁ., καὶ ἀτέχνῳ ζωῇ Jo.D.*hom*.2.3(M.96.580D); opp. sin, Clem.*prot*.11(p.78.30; M.8.228C); **2.** as advanced stage of spiritual life ἴστωσαν, ὡς ἄρα στερεὰν τροφὴν τὸ βρῶμα λέγοντες καὶ σάρκα καὶ αἷμα τοῦ Ἰησοῦ ὑποφέρονται τῇ ...σοφίᾳ ἐπὶ τὴν ἁ. τὴν ἀληθῆ Clem.*paed*.1.6(p.113.14; M.8.296C); καρπὸς...εὐχῆς ἁ. ἀγάπη κτλ. Gr.Nyss.*instit*.(p.82.20; M.34.436B); Diad.*perf*.34(p.38.27); ἡμᾶς...ἐπιστρέφει πρὸς τὴν...θεοποιὸν ἁ. Dion.Ar.*c.h*.1.1(M.3.121A); ἑώρακα ἑτέρους...εἰς βαθυτάτην ἀκακίαν, καὶ ἁ. σεσοφισμένην...ἐληλακότας Jo.Clim.*scal*.4(M.88.688B); ψυχὴ πραεῖα θρόνος ἁπλότητος *ib*.24(981A); closely connected with humility, *ib*.(984B); Max.*cap.theol*.2.81(M.90.1164A); πρὸς τὴν ἁ. τῶν νοητῶν θεαμάτων τὸν νοῦν ἀναβιβάζουσαν id.*qu.Thal*.1(M.90.245A); dist. from ordinary simplicity, as being ταπεινοφροσύνης καὶ πραότητος ...πρόξενος Jo.Clim.*scal*.24(984A); S. Paul its example, *ib*.(984C); **3.** its effects φρόνιμοι γένεσθε καὶ ἀβλαβεῖς· τάχα που ὁ κύριος ἁπλότητος ὑμῖν δωρήσεται πτερόν...ἵνα δὴ τοὺς χηραμοὺς καταλείποντες οἰκήσητε τοὺς οὐρανούς Clem.*prot.*10(p.76.9; M.8.221C); ἁ. τῇ ὑπακοῇ παραδίδωσιν Gr.Nyss.*instit.*(p.77.20; M.34.432B); Diad.*perf.*22(p.24.15); ἡ ἁ. ... ἁγνίζει τὴν καρδίαν ἀπὸ τοῦ πονηροῦ *Schol.*8 in Jo.Clim.*scal.*24(M.88.985C).

C. *stupidity* τὴν καθ' ἁ. καὶ ἰδιωτισκὸν συνήθειαν Iren.*ep.Vict.* ap.Eus.*h.e.*5.24.13(M.20.504A); Hipp.*Dan.*3.20.1; ταῦτα τῆς σῆς ἁ. καθαπτόμενος ἔγραψα, ἣν οὐδ' ἄλλως πρέπουσαν Χριστιανοῖς Bas.*ep.*58(3.152C; M.32.409A); ἀφύλακτον ἡ ἁ., καὶ μετὰ σαθροῦ τὸ φιλάνθρωπον Gr.Naz.*or.*4.38(M.35.564B); Thdt.*h.e.*2.21.1(3.879); Dor.*doct.*4.10(M.88.1672A); *ib.*6.5(1689D).

D. *unity* τῆς ἐκκλησίας τὴν ἁ. μᾶλλον ζηλωσάτωσαν Apoll.*ep. Dion.*13(p.262.4; M.*PL.*8.935B).

E. *liberality,* exeg. 2Cor.8:2 εἰς πλοῦτον ἁπλότητος, τουτέστι, δαψιλείας *cat.2Cor.*8:2(p.400.18).

F. ἐν ἁ. *simply, plainly,* *Barn.*8.2; *ib.*17.1.

ἁπλοῦς, *simple, single, sincere;*

A. metaphysical; **1.** of God; **a.** in gen. ὁ θεὸς...πάντη ἕν ἐστι καὶ ἁ. Or.*Jo.*1.20(22; p.24.23; M.14.57B); ἡ πρώτη...θεοῦ δύναμις, καθ' ὃ μὲν ἁ. τις καὶ ἀσύνθετος...ἐπινοεῖται, ἁ. τῷ τοῦ ἐλαίου προσρήματι [cf. Ps.44:7] παραβέβληται Eus.*d.e.*4.15(p.176.2f.; M.22.293A); εἰ δὲ ἁ. τί ἐστιν ὁ θεός, ὥσπερ οὖν καὶ ἔστι, δηλονότι λέγοντες τὸν θεὸν καὶ ὀνομάζοντες τὸν πατέρα οὐδέν τι ὡς περὶ αὐτὸν ὀνομάζομεν, ἀλλ' αὐτὴν τὴν οὐσίαν αὐτοῦ σημαίνομεν Ath.*decr.*22(p.18.28; M.25.456A); οὐ γὰρ σύνθετος ὁ θεός...ἁ. γάρ ἐστιν οὐσία id.*ep.Afr.*8(M.26.1044B); id.*ep.Aeg.Lib.*16(M.25.576A); id.*syn.*35(p.262.10; M.26.753C); Gr. Nyss.*tres dii*(M.45.133A); Chrys.*incomprehens.*1.5(1.450A); *ib.*4.3(474E) cit. s. ἀσχημάτιστος; πῶς οὖν ὁ πατὴρ εὑρεθήσεται τῶν πάντων ἀρχή, σύνθετος ὢν καθ' ὑμᾶς καὶ οὐχ ἁ; Cyr.*thes.*13(5^1.134E); *ib.*34(359A); φύσις...θεότητι μία καὶ ἁ. id.*dial.Trin.*2(5^1.442D); cf.id. *Pulch.*(p.60.1; 5^2.177E); ἁ. τῆς εἰρηνικῆς ἑνώσεως θεωρήσωμεν φύσιν Dion.Ar.*d.n.*11.2(M.3.949C); *ib.*12.3(969C); μονὰς...ἄναρχος καὶ ἁ. Max.*cap.theol.*2.1(M.90.1125A); *ib.*2.3(1125D); **b.** ref. Logos and Inc. ἀπαθὴς [sc. θεός] ὢν καὶ ἁ., ἀπαθῶς καὶ ἀμερίστως τοῦ υἱοῦ πατήρ ἐστι Ath.*Ar.*1.28(M.26.69A); heret. views on Son destroying simplicity of God, id.*syn.*34(p.261.37; M.26.753B); λόγον ἀκούων τὸν συναφθέντα τῇ σαρκί, τὸ θεῖον ἓν καὶ ἁ. νοείτω μυστήριον ‡Ath.*Ar.*4.32(p.81.14; M.26.517B); Bas.*Eun.*1.23(1.234D; M.29.564A) cit. s. ἀσύνθετος; τὸ γὰρ ἓν καὶ ἁ. ... Ἰησοῦ...λόγου τῇ καθ' ἡμᾶς ἐνανθρωπήσει πρὸς τὸ σύνθετόν τε καὶ ὁρατὸν...ἀγαθότητι...προελήλυθε Dion.Ar.*e.h.*3.3.12(M.3.444A); id.*d.n.*1.4(M.3.592A) cit. s. συντίθημι; τὸ...θεομητρικὸν σῶμα, ἐξ οὗπερ ὁ ἁ. Ἰησοῦς συνετέθη Mod.*dorm.*13(M.86.3309A); of creative activity of Word ὁ τοῦ θεοῦ λόγος ἑνὶ καὶ ἁ. νεύματι...τόν τε ὁρατὸν κόσμον καὶ τὰς ἀοράτους δυνάμεις κινεῖ Ath. *gent.*44(M.25.88C); **c.** ref. eucharist ἡ θεία τῆς συνάξεως τελετή...ἁ. ἔχουσα...ἀρχήν, εἰς τὴν ἱερὰν ποικιλίαν τῶν συμβόλων...πληθύνηται Dion.Ar.*e.h.*3.3.3(M.3.429A); **d.** ref. H. Ghost εἰ δὲ μὴ ἁ. ἐστι τὸ πνεῦμα τὸ ἅγιον, ἐξ οὐσίας καὶ ἁγιασμοῦ συνέστηκε· τὸ δὲ τοιοῦτον, σύνθετον. καὶ τίς οὕτως ἀνόητος, ὡς σύνθετον εἰπεῖν τὸ πνεῦμα τὸ ἅγιον, καὶ μὴ ἁ., καὶ κατὰ τὸν τῆς ἁπλότητος λόγον ὁμοούσιον πατρὶ καὶ υἱῷ; Evagr.Pont.*ep.*10(M.32.264B); πῶς δὲ ἁ. ὁ θεός, εἴπερ τὸ ἐν αὐτῷ πνεῦμα κτιστὸν ὑπάρχον; Cyr.*thes.*34(5^1.359A); **e.** of various divine properties ἡ ἁ. καὶ πολυποίκιλος σοφία Dion.Ar.*c.h.*15.4(M.3.333A); divine light, *ib.*1.2(121B); divine beauty, *ib.*3.1(164D); **f.** heret., of Persons of Trin. ἑκάστης τούτων οὐσίας εἰλικρινῶς ἁ. καὶ πάντη μιᾶς οὔσης Eun.ap.Gr.Nyss.*Eun.*1(1 p.68.4; M.45.297A); **2.** of other simple beings; **a.** angels ἐπὶ τὰς ἁ. τῶν οὐρανίων ἱεραρχιῶν ἀκρότητας Dion.Ar.*c.h.*1.3(M.3.124A); τῶν ἀγγελικῶν νοῶν δυνάμεις τὰς ἁ. καὶ μακαρίας ἔχουσι νοήσεις id.*d.n.*7.2(M.3.868B); but not in sense in which it is used for the divine nature, Evagr. Pont.*ep.*2(M.32.249A); **b.** various features of simple things εἰ σύνθετα τὰ ἔργα αὐτοῦ [sc. θεοῦ], πᾶν δὲ σύνθετον ἐξ ἁπλῶν σύγκειται, καὶ ἀδύνατον ἅμα εἶναι τὰ ἁ. τοῖς συνθέτοις· πρῶτα γὰρ τὰ ἁ., ὕστερον δὲ τὰ σύνθετα ‡Just.*qu.Chr.*3.5(M.6.1441B); τῶν ἁ. ἐφ' ἑαυτῶν ἀγνώστων [sc. to men] Dion.Ar.*c.h.*2.2(M.3.137B); ἄληπτα...τοῖς ἐν πλάσει καὶ τύπῳ τὰ ἁ. id.*d.n.*1.1(M.3.588B); **c.** discussion whether matter is simple πότερον ἁ. τις ἦν ἡ ὕλη ἢ σύνθετος;...εἰ γὰρ ἁ. τις ἐτύγχανεν ἡ ὕλη καὶ μονοειδής, σύνθετος δὲ ὁ κόσμος...ἀδύνατον τοῦτον ἐξ ὕλης γεγονέναι λέγειν, τῷ τὰ σύνθετα μὴ οἷόν τε ἐξ ἑνὸς ἁ. τὴν σύστασιν ἔχειν· τὸ γὰρ σύνθετον ἁ. τινων μῖξιν μηνύει. εἰ δ' αὖ πάλιν τὴν ὕλην σύνθετον λέγειν ἐθέλοις, πάντως ἐξ ἁ. τινων συντεθεῖσθαι φήσεις. εἰ δὲ ἐξ ἁ. συνετέθη, ἦν ποτε καθ' ἑαυτὰ τὰ ἁ., ὧν συντεθέντων γέγονεν ἡ ὕλη, ἐξ οὗπερ καὶ γενητὴ οὖσα δείκνυται. εἰ γὰρ σύνθετος ἡ ὕλη, τὰ δὲ σύνθετα ἐξ ἁ. τὴν σύστασιν ἔχει, ἦν ποτε καιρὸς ὅτε ἡ ὕλη οὐκ ἦν, τουτέστι πρὶν τὰ ἁ. συνελθεῖν Meth.*arbitr.*12(pp.175.12–176.9; M.18.260C,D); nature of bodies not simple, Ath. *decr.*11(p.10.8; M.25.'444'(436)A).

B. moral and spiritual; **1.** of men; **a.** as a virtue ὁ ἁ. χρυσίον οὐ πλεονεκτεῖ *T.Isach.*4.2; πατὴρ...τὰς χάριτας αὐτοῦ ἀποδιδοῖ τοῖς προσερχομένοις αὐτῷ ἁ. διανοίᾳ *1Clem.*23.1; ἔσῃ ἁ. τῇ καρδίᾳ καὶ πλούσιος τῷ πνεύματι *Barn.*19.2; Herm.*sim.*9.24.2; ἁ. ἐστιν ὁ τῶν ἀποστολικῶν ἀνδρῶν τρόπος Ath.*ep.Aeg.Lib.*8(M.25.557A); οὐδεὶς οὕτως ἐστὶ τὴν ψυχὴν καλός, ὡς ὁ ἁ. Chrys.*hom.*7.3 *in Ac.*(9.59D,E); ἁ. γὰρ ὢν [sc. κύριος],...ἁ. τινας καὶ ἀκεραίους τὰς ἑαυτῷ προσερχομένας ψυχὰς εἶναι βούλεται Jo.Clim.*scal.*24(M.88.984B); *ib.*(984C); **b.** esp. implying childlikeness ἁ. γὰρ οἱ νήπιοι ὡς πρόβατα ἀλληγορούμενοι Clem.*paed.*1.7(p.121.31; M.8.313A); *ib.*1.5(p.99.10; 268A); *ib.* 1.6(p.109.24; 289B); **c.** *ignorant, uninstructed* εἴτε συνετῶν, εἴτε ἁπλουστέρων Or.*Cels.*3.49(p.245.14; M.11.985A); ἤκουσεν ἀπό τινων ἁ. ... καὶ μὴ εἰδότων τὸ τοῦ λόγου βούλημα *ib.*7.27(p.178.11; 1460A); νοείσθω δὲ ὁ ἄρτος καὶ τὸ ποτήριον τοῖς μὲν ἁπλουστέροις κατὰ τὴν κοινοτέραν περὶ τῆς εὐχαριστίας ἐκδοχήν, τοῖς δὲ βαθύτερον ἀκούειν μεμαθηκόσιν κατὰ τὴν θειοτέραν καὶ περὶ τοῦ τροφίμου τῆς ἀληθείας λόγου ἐπαγγελίαν id.*Jo.*32.24(16; p.468.14; M.14.809B); οἱ ἁπλούστεροι τῶν πεπιστευκότων ὁρμώμενοι νομίζουσι τοὺς ἀσεβεῖς τῆς ἀναστάσεως μὴ τεύξεσθαι id.ap.Meth.*res.*1.20(p.242.2); ἐπισκόπους τρεῖς, ἀνθρώπους ἀγροίκους καὶ ἁπλουστάτους Corn.ap.Eus.*h.e.*6.43.8(M.20.620A); Ath.*ep.Aeg.Lib.*4(M.25.545B); ἁ. ... καὶ μὴ κατηχθεὶς *ib.*(548A); Cyr. *hom.pasch.*16.5(5^2.219B); **d.** used by Gnostics of orthodox who have faith only and not γνῶσις, Clem.*str.*2.3(p.118.14; M.8.941B); Hegem.*Arch.*5(p.6.9; M.10.1433B); v. γνῶσις; **2.** of abstracts; **a.** of Christian faith and knowledge κατήχησα ὑμᾶς ἐν Χριστῷ ἁ. ... τροφῇ τῇ πνευματικῇ Clem.*paed.*1.6(p.111.5; M.8.292C); *ib.*3.12(p.285.1; 668A); τῇ τῶν ἀθέων πανουργίᾳ τὴν ἁ. τῶν θείων γραφῶν πίστιν καπηλεύοντες Eus.*h.e.*5.28.15(M.20.516B); μὴ τέχνῃ τινί...ἀλλ' ἁ. τῇ πίστει Ath.*ep.Aeg.Lib.*18(M.25.580A); τὴν ἁ. τῆς ἀληθείας γνῶσιν ἐχόντων τῶν πεπεισμένων Dion.Ar.*d.n.*7.4(M.3.872C); τὸ πασῶν αὐτὴν [sc. τὴν τῶν Χριστιανῶν ἀληθογνωσίαν] εἶναι καὶ ἁπλουστέραν καὶ θειοτέραν, μᾶλλον δὲ τὸ αὐτὴν εἶναι τὴν μόνην ἀληθῆ καὶ μίαν καὶ ἁ. θεογνωσίαν *ib.*(873A); id.*ep.*9.4(M.3.1112A); of simple rites by which simple Christians cast out demons, Or.*Cels.*7.4(p.156.15f.; M.11.1425C); **b.** of realities to which faith and knowledge lead ἡ πίστις δὲ χάρις ἐξ ἀναποδείκτων εἰς τὸ καθόλου ἀναβιβάζουσα τὸ ἁ. Clem.*str.*2.4(p.120.7; M.8.945A); τῇ διαλεκτικῇ προσχρήσεται ὁ γνωστικός...καὶ τὴν τῶν ὄντων προσήσεται διάκρισιν, μέχρις ἂν τῶν πρώτων καὶ ἁ. ἐφάψηται *ib.*6.10(p.472.1; M.9.301A); Or.*Jo.*2.4(p.58.28; M.14.116C); of Law of God, *Const.App.*1.1.7; *ib.*6.19.2; **c.** of myst. contemplation and knowledge ἐπὶ τὰς ἁ. καὶ ἡνωμένας ἀνάγεται θεωρίας Dion.Ar.*d.n.*4.9(M.3.705B); ὁ ἀξιωθεὶς ἐν τῷ θεῷ γενέσθαι, πάντας εἴσεται...λόγους, καθ' ἁ. τινα...γνῶσιν Max.*cap.theol.* 2.4(M.90.1128A); id.*opusc.*(M.91.20A); **3.** exeg., *literal* (non-mystical) κρύπτων μὲν τὸ μυστικόν, ἐμφαίνων δὲ τὸ ἁπλούστερον Or.*Jo.*13.40(p.266.12; M.14.469C); κατὰ τὴν ἁπλουστέραν ἐκδοχήν *ib.*20.41(33; p.383.19; 669B).

C. *simple, single,* opp. manifold ὁ θεὸς...οὐδὲ ἁ. τὴν περὶ ἑαυτοῦ γνῶσιν αὐτοῖς δεδωκώς, ἀλλὰ καὶ ποικίλως καὶ διὰ πολλῶν Ath.*inc.* 11.7(M.25.116D).

D. *absolute, essential, free from additional matter* ὅταν...σημαίνῃ [sc. γραφή] τὴν κατὰ σάρκα γένεσιν τοῦ λόγου, τίθησι καὶ τὴν αἰτίαν... ὅταν δὲ περὶ τῆς θεότητος αὐτοῦ...λέγῃ...πάντα ἁ. τῇ λέξει, ἀπολελυμένῃ τε τῇ διανοίᾳ Ath.*Ar.*2.53(M.26.260C).

E. *straight;* of hair, Gr.Naz.*carm.*2.1.11.754(M.37.1081A); ref. BMV ἁ. τριχώματι *Pers.*(p.17.22).

F. *level, even* εἶδον πεδίον ἁ. *Apoc.Bar.*10(p.91.18).

ἁπλουστέρως, *with more simplicity,* Jo.D.*haer.*88(M.94.757A).

***ἁπλουστικῶς,** *simply,* i.e. *without criticism,* Vict.*Mc.*16:9(p.447.7).

ἁπλ-όω, A. *spread out, unfold, extend;* **1.** of Christ on the Cross; **a.** his hands ἄνθρωπον...τὸν τῇ φθορᾷ δεδεμένον, χερσὶν ἡπλωμέναις ἔδειξε λελυμένον Clem.*prot.*11(p.79.4; M.8.228C); ὃς παλάμας ἥπλωσεν ἐπὶ ξύλου πολυκάρπου *Orac.Sib.*5.257; διὰ τοῦ σταυροειδοῦς, ὡς εἴρηται, σχήματος, τὸν τῇ φθορᾷ δεδυναστευμένον ἄνθρωπον δείξας ἐλεύθερον χερσὶν ἡπλωμέναις Meth.*Porph.*1(p.504.20; M.18.400B); Χριστὸς... ἐν αὐτῷ τῷ ἀέρι τὰς χεῖρας ἥπλωσεν Ath.*ep.fest.*22(p.295.18; M.26.1433A); πατρικὴ ἡ φωνή, ἡπλωμέναις ἀγκάλαις πρὸς ἑαυτὸν καλοῦντος τοὺς τέως ἀφηνιάζοντας...τὸν εἰρηνοποιήσαντα τὰ πάντα διὰ τοῦ σταυροῦ Bas.*hom.in Ps.*45:9(1.175B; M.29.428A); **b.** his body ἡ τῆς ζωῆς βίβλος [sc. Christ]...ἐπὶ ξύλου ἥπλωται Hipp.*Dan.*4.60.2; οἱ ἀστέρες ...τὸν πρὸ ἑωσφόρου βλέποντες ~ούμενον ‡Chrys.*pasch.*6(p.183.7; 8.272E); being himself stretched out, 'stretched' man upwards, Meth.*Porph.*3(p.506.24; M.18.401B); **c.** of beams of Cross τὸ μέν σου εἰς οὐρανοὺς ἀνατείνεται...τὸ δέ σου ἥπλωτο δεξιᾷ καὶ ἀριστερᾷ, ἵνα ...τὸν κόσμον συναγάγῃ εἰς ἓν *A.Andr.*A 14(p.54.25); **2.** hands in prayer Ἀνδρέας...ἥπλωσεν τὰς χεῖρας αὐτοῦ ἑπτάκις, καὶ εἶπεν... φοβήθητι τὸν τύπον τοῦ σταυροῦ *A.Andr.et Mt.*29(p.109.11); *A.Barth.* 7(p.144.19); Moses' hands, supported by Aaron and Hur οἱ ἐπιεικέστεροι...ἐξ Ἰσραὴλ...~οῦσι τὰς χεῖρας, τοῦτ' ἔστι, καταδέχονται τὸν σταυρόν Cyr.*ador.*3(1.90B); τὰς χεῖρας ~ώσας καὶ τὸ ὄμμα τείνας εἰς τὸν οὐρανόν Gel.Cyz.*h.e.*2.29.2(M.85.1312C); εὗρεν αὐτὸν ἐν ἐκστάσει, καὶ αἱ χεῖρες αὐτοῦ εἰς τὸν οὐρανὸν ἡπλωμέναι *Apophth.Patr.* (M.65.409A); hands in almsgiving τὴν πᾶσι τοῖς δεομένοις ἡπλωμένην χεῖρα Nil.*epp.*2.274(M.79.337D); **3.** hand of God τοῦ δημιουργοῦ...~οῦντος τὴν χεῖρα τοῖς ἐπὶ τῆς γῆς Cyr.*Os.*30(3.55A); **4.** of God in creation θεὸς...γλαυκὴν δ' ἥπλωσε θάλασσαν *Orac.Sib.*1.11; γῆν δὲ χερσαίοις πᾶσιν ἥπλωσεν ἄνετον Gr.Naz.*or.*14.25(M.35.889C); *ib.*32.8(M.36.181C); ὁ θεός, καθάπερ τι καταπέτασμα τὸ σκότος κατὰ τῆς οἰκουμένης ~ώσας Chrys.*compunct.*2.5(1.148D); id.*hom.13.6 in Mt.*(7.177B); **5.** nets, met. τί οὖν Παῦλος; ἐπὶ πλέον ~οῖ τὴν σαγήνην, καί φησιν... Chrys.*hom.33.6 in 1Cor.*(10.307B); τὸ τῆς πολυθέου πλάνης ~ώσας λίνον Cyr.*Abac.*23(3.537B); τῆς ματαιότητος δίκτυα ~ωσάσης ἁπανταχοῦ ‡Nil.*perist.*1.2(M.79.813A); **6.** a table, ref. eucharist κύριος...τὴν πνευματικὴν ἡμῖν ~ώσας τράπεζαν Cyr.*Ps.* 32:19(M.69.881C); fig. ὁ πέντε ἄρτοις πεντακισχιλίους χορτάσας... αὐτὸς καὶ ὑμῖν δι' ἡμῶν ~ώσει τῆς διδασκαλίας τὴν τράπεζαν Bas.Sel. *or.*6.1(M.85.84D); *ib.*11.1(148B); liturg. εὐχὴ...μετὰ τὸ ~ωθῆναι τὸ εἰλητὸν *Lit.Bas.*(p.316.10); **7.** ἁ. ἑαυτόν *prostrate oneself*, Jo.Mosch. *prat.*202(M.87.3092B); **8.** fig., of soul through body, Eus.*l.C.*12 (p.233.9; M.20.1393A).

B. *unfold, reveal, show forth*; **1.** in gen. θάλασσα ~οῖ δὲ γαλήνην Cyr.*Jon.*9(3.374D); ἥπλωσεν ὁ ἐχθρὸς πᾶσαν τὴν κακίαν αὐτοῦ Dor. *doct.*1.1(M.88.1620A); fig. ἀκτῖνας Chrys.*hom.4.1 in Phil.*(11.220D); **2.** theol. contexts ~ώσας δὲ ὁ λόγος τὴν ἀλήθειαν ἔδειξε τοῖς ἀνθρώποις τὸ ὕψος τῆς σωτηρίας Clem.*prot.*11(p.81.33; M.8.236A); id.*q.d.s.* 5(p.163.20; M.9.609C); λόγος...τὴν σοφίαν ~ῶν Or.*Jo.*2.4(p.58.28; M.14.116C); λόγος...θεοῦ...διὰ πάντων ἑαυτὸν ~ώσας Eus.*l.C.*11 (p.228.18; M.20.1384B); Ath.*inc.*16.3(M.25.124C) cit. s. ἄνω; *ib.*45.6 (177B); ~οῦν τὴν αὐτοῦ γνῶσιν ἐπὶ πάντα τὰ ἔθνη Epiph.*haer.*69.68 (p.216.22; M.42.312B); ἐπὶ πάντας ἥπλου τὴν αὐτοῦ εὐεργεσίαν *ib.*66.35 (p.74.21; 84C); Cyr.*Am.*68(3.326C); Dion.Ar.*e.h.*2.3.3(M.3.397D); *ib.* (400B).

C. *open*, fig. ~οῦντες τὰς ὄψεις, τὸ φῶς εἰσδέχοιντο Thdr.Stud. *epp.*2.208(M.99.1629C); met., of mind or soul ~ωσόν σου τὸ ἡγεμονικὸν τῆς ψυχῆς καὶ δέξαι τὴν γνῶσιν *A.Andr.*A 16(p.56.15); *A.Jo.*52 (p.177.9); ὁ Πολύκαρπος ἥπλωσεν ἑαυτὸν λέγων ‡Pion.*v.Polyc.*5; ταῖς καρδίαις πρὸς τὸν θεὸν ἡπλωμέναις Dion.Al.ap.Eus.*h.e.*7.24.8 (M.20.696B); ἡπλωμένῃ δὲ καὶ εἰρηναίᾳ ψυχῇ δέξασθαι τοὺς περὶ Ἄρειον CHier.(335)*ep.*(p.247.32; M.26.717C); Cyr.*ador.*8(1.257C).

D. *proclaim, publish*; **1.** in gen. ἁ. [sc. Christ] τὴν ὑπόσχεσιν ἐπὶ τὴν γῆν ἅπασαν Chrys.*hom.64.1 in Mt.*(7.636A); *ib.1.4*(9A); πᾶσι γὰρ τὸ θεῖον εὐαγγέλιον ἁ. Proc.G.*Is.*45:18ff.(M.87.2432D); **2.** decrees ἡπλοῦτο...βασιλικὸν ἁπανταχοῦ γράμμα Eus.*v.C.*1.41(p.27.10; M.20. 956B); *ib.*2.20(p.49.8; 997B); *Chron.Pasch.*p.277(M.92.688B).

E. *level, make plain* ἡ πέτρα ἐν ἡπλωμένῳ χώρῳ Eus.*theoph.fr.*3 (p.14*.13; M.24.620A); id.*v.C.*3.56(p.104.2; M.20.1121B); Ast.Am.*hom.* 13(M.40.353B); Chrys.*hom.69.3 in Mt.*(7.684A).

F. *explain*, Or.*enarr.in Job* 29:12(M.17.93A); ἐν ἀκριβείᾳ τὸν λόγον ἁ. Gr.Nyss.*or.catech.*38(p.153.6; M.45.97C); Cyr.*Ps.*33:13(M.69.889B).

G. *diffuse* grace υἱὸς...δι' οὗ...χάρις ~ουμένη ἐν ἁγίοις πληθύνεται ‡*Diogn.*11.5; Proc.G.*Is.*40:1–8(M.87.2337D).

H. *make simple* τῶν ~ουμένων ἁπλότης Dion.Ar.*d.n.*1.3(M.3. 589C).

ἄπλυτος, *unwashed*; met. ἄ. τινες καὶ κατεσπιλωμένοι τῇ τοῦ βίου περιβολῇ Gr.Nyss.*v.Mos.*(M.44.376C).

ἅπλωμα, τό, *that which is unfolded* or *spread out*; hence **1.** *table-cloth*, Gr.Naz.*carm.*2.1.88.111(M.37.1439A); *altar-cloth*, Cyr.S. *v.Cyriac.*(p.226.2); *Chron.Pasch.*p.294(M.92.737A); esp. of the second of the three cloths laid on the altar; also called τραπεζόφορον or ἐνδυτή, q.v., it lay above the κατασάρκα and beneath the εἰλητόν, q.v.; λαμβάνει τὸ ἅ., ἤτοι τὴν ἐπένδυσιν τῆς ἁγίας τραπέζης *Euchol.* p.660; *ib.*p.664; *ib.*p.665; **2.** *veil* of the Temple ἔσται τὸ ἅ. τοῦ ναοῦ σχιζόμενον (cf. Mc.15:38 etc.) *T.Benj.*9.4; ‡Epiph.*v.proph.Abac.*A (p.29; M.43.409C) = *Chron.Pasch.*p.151(M.92.372B); **3.** *covering*; of the cloud in the wilderness, ref. Num.10:34 ὡσὰν...στεγανῷ δὲ τῆς νεφέλης σκιάζοιντο τῷ ἁ. ‡Nil.*perist.*12.7(M.79.952D).

ἁπλῶς, (senses not always clearly distinguishable from each other);

A. *simply, without multiplicity*, ref. God πάντα δὲ ἁ. καὶ ἀπεριορίστως ἐν ἑαυτῇ τὰ ὄντα προείληφε [sc. ἡ πάντων αἰτία] Dion.Ar.*d.n.*1.7 (M.3.597A); *ib.*4.6(701A); in action towards man ὁ θεὸς...πᾶσιν ἁ. τὰς ἀκτῖνας ἐπιλάμπων τῆς ἀγαθότητος Max.*cap.theol.*1.12(M.90. 1088B).

B. *simply*, i.e. *essentially, absolutely, without qualification*; **1.** of being of God ὁ θεὸς οὐ πῶς ἐστιν ὤν, ἀλλ' ἁ. Dion.Ar.*d.n.*5.4(M.3. 817D); **2.** ref. names and properties of God ἔστι...ἐκ τῶν ὀνομάτων τούτων, τὸ μὲν ἁ. οὕτως ἐφ' ἑαυτοῦ μεμνημένον...ἕτερα δὲ...τὸ πρός τι χρήσιμον ἀποσημαίνει μόνον Gr.Nyss.*Eun.*1(1 p.182.17; M.45.428A); Dion.Ar.*d.n.*10.3(M.3.940A) cit. s. συναΐδιος; οὐκ ἔστιν ὁ θεὸς οὐσία, κατὰ τὴν ἁ. ἢ πῶς λεγομένην οὐσίαν...οὔτε ἐνέργεια, κατὰ τὴν ἁ. ... λεγομένην ἐνέργειαν Max.*cap.theol.*1.4(M.90.1084B); **3.** ref. relation between Father and Son ὁ υἱός, ἁ. καὶ χωρὶς συμπλοκῆς τινός ἐστιν ἐν τῷ πατρί Ath.*Ar.*3.23(M.26.372A); **4.** ref. absolute statements, in scripture and elsewhere μὴ ὡς ἐν παρρησίᾳ εἰρημένον ἁ. ἐκλαμβάνειν Ath.*Ar.*2.44(M.26.241A); ἁ. καὶ ἀπολελυμένως εἴρηκεν *ib.*3.22(369A); οὐχ ἁ. ἐπαινετὸν τὸ ἀπέχεσθαι τῶν τοῦ βίου καλῶν, οὔτε ἁ. ψεκτὸν τὸ ἀντέχεσθαι αὐτῶν ‡Just.*qu.et resp.*46(M.6.1292B); Chrys.*hom.40.1 in Jo.*(8.237A); ὅταν δὲ λέγῃ, ὅτι 'πᾶς ὅστις ἀφῆκε γυναῖκα' (Mt.19:29) οὐ τοῦτό φησιν, ὥστε ἁ. διασπᾶσθαι τοὺς γάμους id.*hom.64.2 in Mt.*(7.636E).

C. *simply*, i.e. *without additions* προφήτης πόλιν οὐχ ἁ. ἀλλὰ 'τοῦ θεοῦ' πόλιν ὠνόμασεν Eus.*d.e.*8.2(p.369.25; M.22.600D); οὐχ ἁ. ἔλεγεν, ἀλλ' ὅρκοις ἐπεσφράγιζε τοὺς λόγους Ath.*h.Ar.*22(p.195.9; M.25. 720A); *ib.*26(p.197.9; 724A); Chrys.*hom.1.1. in 2Tim.*(11.659A); id. *hom.31.4 in Jo.*(8.181A); *ib.32.1*(184C); Thdr.Mops.*fr.in Jo.*12:3ff. (p.370.5; M.66.765C).

D. *merely, only*; **1.** in gen. ἁ. ἀκούοντες 'πνεῦμα', ἐνομίσατε... κτίσμα τὸ πνεῦμα τὸ ἅγιον Ath.*ep.Serap.*1.3(M.26.536B); μὴ...ἁ. νομίσῃς [sc. λόγον]· μαχαίρας γάρ ἐστι...τομώτερος Chrys.*hom.7.1 in Heb.*(12.71C); καθάπερ χοῖροι ἐσθίοντες ἁ. λακτίζουσι id.*hom.82.2 in Mt.*(7.784B); **2.** Christol. οὐ γὰρ ἁ. ὅμοιον εἰρήκασι τὸν υἱὸν τῷ πατρί, ἵνα μὴ ἁ. ὅμοιος θεῷ, ἀλλ' ἐκ θεοῦ θεὸς ἀληθινὸς πιστεύηται Ath.*ep.Jov.*4(M.26.817C)ap.Thdt.*h.e.*4.3.13; οὐδὲ ἔξωθεν ἁ. ὅμοιος id.*decr.*23(p.19.22; M.25.457A); ‡Ath.*Ar.*4.3(p.47.9; M.26.472B); υἱὸς κατὰ Ἰωάννην θεὸς οὐχ ἁ., ἀλλ' ἀληθινὸς θεός *ib.*4.26(p.74.13; 508C); esp. opp. οὐσιώδης, *ib.*2(p.45.6; 469A); οὐ...ἁ. φωνὴ σημαντική, ἀλλ' οὐσιώδης λόγος *ib.*1(p.44.18; 468C); οὐχ ἁ. λόγον προφορικὸν ἢ ἐνδιάθετον τοῦ θεοῦ, ἀλλὰ ζῶντα θεόν *Symb.Ant.*(345)6(p.253.4; M.26. 732A); **3.** οὐχ ἁ. ... ἀλλὰ *not only...but also* οὐχ ἁ. ζῆσαι, ἀλλὰ... δοξασθῆναι Eus.*Marcell.*2.1(p.34.16; M.24.781B); Ath.*Ar.*2.42(M.26. 237A); Evagr.Pont.*or.*142(M.79.1197A); Chrys.*hom.34.2 in Mt.*(7. 391B).

E. exeg., *literally* (opp. allegorically etc.) τί ὄφελός μοι ἁ. λεχθεῖσα ἡ ἱστορία τοῦ Ἰούδα καὶ τῆς Θάμαρ; Or.*engast.*2(p.284.8; M. 12.1013C); ὁ...πολὺς ἁπλούστερον ἐκλήψεται τὰ περὶ τῶν προφητῶν εἰρημένα id.*Jo.*2.1(p.52.14; M.14.105A); ζητῆσαι...πότερον ἁπλούστερον τοῦτο ἐκδεκτέον *ib.*10.39(23; p.215.9; 380C); ἁπλούστερον τούτων ἀκούσωμεν, μηδὲν πέρα τῆς λέξεως περιεργαζόμενοι *ib.*13.21(p.244.28; 432D); Eus.*h.e.*6.8.2(M.20.536B); οὐ δεῖ τὴν πρόχειρον λέξιν ἁ. ... ἐκλαμβάνειν Ath.*Ar.*2.44(M.26.240C); πόσα ἄτοπα τίκτεται, ἐὰν ἁ. τὰ λεγόμενα ἐκδεξώμεθα; Chrys.*hom.13.7 in Rom.*(9.568A).

F. *in simplicity*, whether in sense of *sincerely* or *without questioning*; **1.** ref. prayer and the spiritual life τὰς προσευχὰς ἡμῶν ἁ. ἀναφέρειν πρὸς τὸν θεόν *2Clem.*2.2; πᾶσιν ὑστερουμένοις δίδου ἁ., μὴ διστάζων τίνι δῷς ἢ τίνι μὴ δῷς Herm.*mand.*2.4; *ib.*2.6; χήραν... ἁπλούστερον περὶ τῶν θείων φρονοῦσαν Or.*Jo.*19.8(2; p.307.33; M.14. 541A); τοὺς...ἁπλούστερον πιστεύοντας id.*Cels.*1.53(p.104.31; M.11. 760B); βουλεύεσθαι καὶ πράττειν ἁπλούστερον, ἢ ἀσφαλέστερον Gr. Naz.*ep.*40(M.37.81B); Chrys.*sac.*1.7(p.15.9; 1.367B); πάντες οἱ τὸν κύριον ἑαυτοῖς ἐπισπάσασθαι βουλόμενοι, ἁ. καὶ ἀπλάστως...ὡς διδασκάλῳ...προσέλθωμεν Jo.Clim.*scal.*24(M.88.984B); **2.** ref. simple faith οὐχ ἁ. ἡ πίστις, ἀλλ' ἡ περὶ τὴν μάθησιν πίστις Clem.*str.*1.6 (p.23.9; M.8.729B); *ib.*4.18(p.298.20; 1321C) cit. s. πιστεύω; οὐχ ἁ. ὡς οἱ λοιποί, ἀλλὰ μετὰ γνώσεως *ib.*7.14(p.61.31; M.9.520C); οὐκέτι ἁπλούστερον πιστεύοντες...ἀλλ' ἤδη καὶ διορατικώτερον κατανοοῦντες Or.*Jo.*20.33(27; p.370.21; M.14.648C); δεῖν μὴ ἁ. πιστεύειν ἀλλὰ λογισμὸν ὑπέχειν τῶν πιστευομένων id.*Cels.*6.10(p.80.1; M.11.1304C).

G. *in an ordinary, normal way* τὸ δὲ τέλος Ἀρείου, ἐπεὶ μὴ ἁ. γέγονε,...διηγήματος ἄξιον Ath.*ep.Aeg.Lib.*19(M.25.581B); Ἀαρὼν... γέγονεν ἀρχιερεύς· καὶ γέγονεν οὐχ ἁ., οὐδὲ ἐκ τῶν συνήθων ἱματίων γνωριζόμενος id.*Ar.*2.7(M.26.161B).

H. *in a common* (*mediocre*) *degree, moderately* οὐχ ἁ. εὑρήσεις διαφορὰν Or.*Jo.*19.22(5; p.323.26; M.14.568A); εἰς...ἅπαντας αὐτοὺς ὑπερβαλλόμενος τῇ πρὸς ἡμᾶς φιλίᾳ, τοσοῦτον...ὅσον ἐκεῖνοι τοὺς ἁ. πρὸς ἡμᾶς διακειμένους Chrys.*sac.*1.1(p.2.5; 1.362A); id.*hom.12.3 in 2Cor.*(10.524D).

I. *indiscriminately, without distinguishing* ὁ σπείρων οὐ διαιρεῖ τὴν ὑποκειμένην ἄρουραν, ἀλλ' ἁ. καὶ ἀδιακρίτως βάλλει τὰ σπέρματα Chrys.*hom.44.3 in Mt.*(7.471A); ref. 1Cor.10:25 ἁ. ἐσθίειν ἅπαν τὸ ἐξ ἀγορᾶς id.*hom.25.1 in 1Cor.*(10.220A).

J. (οὐχ) ἁ. (*not*) *even* μηδ' ἁ. ἀγαθὸν εἶναι μηδένα, μηδ' ἀγαθόν τι πράττειν Eus.*v.C.*1.54(p.33.3; M.20.969A); οὐδὲ ἁ. αὐτὸν ἀναμνῆσαι τῶν προτέρων ἠνέσχετο Chrys.*hom.10.5 in Rom.*(9.528A); καὶ τὸ ἁ. θυμοῦσθαι κωλύσας id.*hom.17.4 in Mt.*(7.227B).

K. *without reason* or *cause* ἐπισκοπῶμεν πότερον ἁ. καὶ μάτην γέγονεν ἄνθρωπος, ἢ τίνος ἕνεκεν Athenag.*res.*12(p.60.32; M.6.996B); εἰ γὰρ ἁ. ἔμελλον οἱ ἄνθρωποι γίνεσθαι, οὐδεὶς ἂν πρὸς οὐδένα σχέσιν ἔσχεν Chrys.*hom.10.4 in 1Thess.*(11.500A); id.*sac.*3.13(p.70.8; 1.390A); *ib.*1.7(p.14.11; 1.366E); Dion.Ar.*myst.*1.3(M.3.1000C); Thdt. *Jer.*2:21(2.416).

L. *lightly, rashly, thoughtlessly* τίς οὖν οὐ δικάζει τὸν Χριστιανὸν λόγον; τίς τῶν ἐθνῶν κἂν ἁ. οὐκ ἐξετάζει αὐτόν; Or.*hom.14.8 in Jer.* (p.113.7; M.13.413A); μὴ νομίσητε ταῦτά με λέγειν ἁ., ἀλλ' ἀπὸ πείρας καὶ ἀληθείας Ath.*v.Anton.*39(M.26.900A); id.*apol.sec.*5(p.91.27; M.25.257A); id.*gent.*13(M.25.29B); *ib.*30(60C); τί γέγονεν ἐκ τούτων οὐκέτι λοιπὸν ἁ. εἰπεῖν...οὔτε χωρὶς δακρύων id.*ep.encycl.*3(172.4; M.25.228C); *superficially* ἁ. ζῶντες καὶ εἰκῇ Chrys.*hom.68.3 in Mt.* (7.673C); opp. μετὰ ἀκριβείας, id.*hom.28.3 in Rom.*(9.729B); ref. divine punishments of Israelites οὐχ ἁ. ταῦτα γεγένηται, κατὰ τὴν ἔμπροσθεν ἐν τοῖς ἀνθρώποις οὖσαν συνήθειαν, ἀλλ' ἐκ τῆς ἄνωθεν ὀργῆς. διὰ τοῦτο οὐδὲ ἁ. ταῦτα ἥξειν φησίν, οὐδὲ ἀθρόως id.*hom.* *75.1 in Mt.*(7.724A); *ib.*4.7(58B); *ib.*23.7(294C); Thdt.*Ps.*138:13(1.1534); *casually* ἐνταῦθα μὲν γὰρ [sc. at church] καὶ ἁ. καὶ ἀφοσιούμενος παραγίνῃ· ἐκεῖ δέ [sc. at theatre], μετὰ σπουδῆς...καὶ πολλῆς τῆς προθυμίας Chrys.*hom.37.6 in Mt.*(7.422B); *anyhow* τὰ ἀμφότερα εἰς ἓν συνήγαγεν, οὐχ ἁ. οὐδὲ δοκήσει, ἀλλὰ ἐναργῶς ἐν τῷ αἵματι αὐτοῦ Epiph.*haer.*42.12(p.179.23; M.41.808D); *ib.*46.5(p.209.26; 845B).

M. ἁ. ἔδοξέν σοι; *did it seem right to you?* Jo.Mosch.*prat.*92(M.87.2949C).

***ἁπλωτής, ὁ,** *displayer*, *A.Thom.*A 121(p.230.24).

ἁπλωτικός, *making simple*, of union of soul with God τὴν ἁ. ... ἕνωσιν Dion.Ar.*c.h.*1.2(M.3.121B); of the illumination granted to highest order of angels κρυφιωτέρᾳ μὲν [sc. φωτοδοσίᾳ] ὡς νοητοτέρᾳ, καὶ μᾶλλον ἁ. καὶ ἑνοποιῷ *ib.*10.1(272D).

***ἁπλωτός,** *spread out, flat*, *Mir.Artem.*45(p.75.14).

ἄπνευστος, **1.** *not exhaled*, Melet.*nat.hom.*synops.(M.64.1133C); **2.** *without the Holy Ghost* βαπτίζειν, ἀπύροισι καὶ ἀ. λοετροῖς Nonn. *par.Jo.*1:33(M.43.756B).

ἄπνοος, ἄπνους, **1.** *without breath*; **a.** of inanimate things, Epiph.*haer.*77.17(p.431.3; M.42.665A); Nonn.*par.Jo.*1:3(M.43.749A); **b.** of men, *lifeless*, Hipp.*haer.*5.7(p.80.6; M.16.3130A); Or.*Cels.*2.16 (p.145.20; M.11.828B); *A.Xanthipp.*15(p.68.25); of Jo. Bapt. ἄ. μὲν τῆς ἐπικήρου ζωτικῆς ἐνεργείας, εὔπνουν δὲ...τῇ τῆς θείας χάριτος μυρωδίᾳ Thdr.Stud.*or.*8.8(M.99.768C); *in a coma* ἄ. ἔμεινε καὶ διὰ μέσης νυκτὸς τὴν ψυχὴν ἔδωκε Jo.Mal.*chron.*5 p.111(M.97.204A); **c.** of Christ's body between death and Resurrection, ref. Lc.23:46 ψυχὴ σὺν τῇ θεότητι ἀπὸ σώματος ἐκπορευθεῖσα, τοῦ σώματος ἀ. μείναντος Epiph.*haer.*42.11(p.153.11; M.41.769C); id.*exp.fid.*17(p.517.27; M.42.813C); Anast.S.*hod.*13(M.89.241A); **2.** *without spirit* οὔτε ...ἄ. [sc. ὁ Χριστός], οὔτε ἄνους, οὔτε ἀκάρδιος Gr.Nyss.*Apoll.*27(M.45.1181B).

ἀπό,

I. denoting position;

A. in space; *from*; **1.** ?*apart from* κοινωνεῖν...ἔνδον τοῦ θυσιαστηρίου, εἶναι δὲ ἀ. ἱερέων Pall.*v.Chrys.*15(p.90.20; M.47.51); perh. as C.1 infra; **2.** *distant*, idiomatic in the form μὴ ἐν αὐτῇ τῇ πόλει, ἀλλὰ ἀ. ἑπτὰ σταδίων ‡Just.*coh.Gr.*13(M.6.265C) al.

B. in time; **1.** *after* τῶν ἀ. μονογαμίας ἐγκρατευομένων Epiph. *haer.*48.9(p.231.14; M.41.868D); ὁ ἀ. τοῦ λουτροῦ...παραπτώμασι περιπεσών *ib.*59.2(p.365.31; 1021A); **2.** of having just come from τὸν μάρτυρα ἔτι ἐμπνέοντα μικρὸν ἀ. τοῦ ξύλου Chrys.*hom.1.4 in 2Cor.* (10.424C); ἡ ἀ. λέχους, φησίν, ἀκάθαρτος id.*hom.4.4 in Tit.*(11.748E); or escaped from τοὺς ἀ. πρώτου γάμου τελευτησάσης τῆς αὐτῶν γυναικός Epiph.*haer.*59.4(p.367.13; 1024A); ἀ. ... κινδύνων ὄντες μεγάλων Chrys.*hom.2.2 in 1Thess.*(11.434E).

C. denoting deprivation; **1.** of having lost, being *without* κενὸς ἀ. τοῦ πνεύματος τοῦ δικαίου Herm.*mand.*5.2.7; ἀποτυφλοῦται ἀ. τῆς διανοίας τῆς ἀγαθῆς *ib.*; στερηθεῖσαν ἀ. ... κοινωνίας *A.Thom.*A 88 (p.203.15); τῶν νεοφωτίστων ἀ. στιχαρίων καὶ ἀνυποδήτων ὄντων CSyr.*act.*(*ACO* 3 p.99.31; H.2.1377A); phrase ὁ ἀ. ὀμμάτων [γενόμενος] of Didymus the *Blind*, Pall.*h.Laus.*4(p.19.19,22; M.34.1012D); **2.** *without mention of* ἐὰν...σιωπήσητε ἀ. ἐμοῦ, ἐγὼ λόγος θεοῦ Ign.*Rom.*2.1; **3.** healing or saving *from* θεράπευσον ἀ. τῶν ἑλκῶν *A.Thom.*A 67(p.184.19); so in exclamations without vb. ὢ ἀ. τοῦ δολίου καὶ ἀπίστου...ὢ ἀ. τοῦ διαβόλου...τῆς πλάνης...τῆς πονηρίας *ib.*41(p.161.16ff.).

D. of change in state, status, or career; **1.** of *ex*-officials ἐνταῦθά φησιν ἀρχιερεῖς τοὺς ἀ. ἀρχιερέων Chrys.*hom.79.3 in Mt.*(7.761E); later t.t. and freq. Ἀνθημίου ἐπάρχου καὶ ἀ. ὑπάτων *Chron.Pasch.* p.308(M.92.784A); τὸν ἀ. τριβούνων *ib.*p.319(812B); Κωνσταντῖνα ἡ ἀ. βασιλισσῶν *ib.*p.380(972B); **2.** of *ex*-slaves, freedmen Κρίσπῳ ἀ. αἰχμαλωσίας Nil.*epp.*2.267 tit.(M.79.336C); ἦν...ἀ. δούλων *Apophth. Patr.*(M.65.301C); **3.** of religious converts Αὐρηλιανῷ Ἰλλουστρίῳ ἀ. Ἑλλήνων Nil.*epp.*1.54 tit.(M.79.105D) al.; **4.** of convalescents εὗρον αὐτόν πως ἀ. ἀρρωστίας Dor.*doct.*11.1(M.88.1736A).

E. *with*, clothing ἀ. χιτωνίσκου μόνου...εἰσελθών Chrys.*hom.21.3 in 2Cor.*(10.586C); weapons ἀ. σπαθίου Jo.Mal.*chron.*18p.493(M.97.713B).

II. denoting source, origin, composition;

A. 1. *consisting of* μοναστήρια ἀ. διακοσίων καὶ τριακοσίων Pall. *h.Laus.*32(p.94.5; M.34.1100D); **2.** *as a result of* ἀ. ... διψυχίας... ἀφίουσιν τὴν ὁδόν Herm.*vis.*3.7.1; *ib.*3.9.3; ἀ. τοῦ καθ' ἡμῶν... μίσους Or.*Cels.*6.27(p.97.18; M.11.1333B); cf. ψυχῇ ῥερυπωμένῃ ἀ. ἁμαρτίας Nil.*inst.*(M.79.1237A); **3.** *beginning with, in* τὸ γέννημα οὐκ ἀ. χρόνου νοεῖσθαι εὐσεβὴς χωρεῖ λόγος Epiph.*haer.*76.21(p.390.15; M.42.597A); τοὺς ἀ. τοῦ 'ἄλφα' ἔχοντας τὸ ὄνομα Jo.Mal.*chron.*7 p.179(M.97.285C); **4.** of founders of sects, schools Μαρκίωνος, ἀφ' οὗ οἱ λεγόμενοι Μαρκιωνισταί *M.Polyc.*epilog.3; Ἀριστοτέλης καὶ οἱ ἀπ' αὐτοῦ Athenag.*leg.*6.3(M.6.901C).

B. *belonging to, of* some persuasion; **1.** in gen. τοὺς ἀ. φιλοσοφίας Athenag.*leg.*2.3(M.6.896A); Ἕλλησι καὶ τοῖς ἀ. τοῦ λόγου ἡμῶν Or.*Cels.*6.2(p.72.7; M.11.1292A); παρ' ἡμῖν λόγιοι ἄνδρες καὶ τῶν ἀ. παιδείας οὐδενὸς δεύτεροι Eus.*p.e.*10.9(487A; M.21.809D); **2.** of members of the Church αἱρετισώμεθα ἀ. τῆς ἐκκλησίας τῆς ζωῆς εἶναι *2Clem.*14.1; Or.*princ.*4.2.1(p.308.5; M.11.360A).

C. *in the name* or *person of* Ἡσαΐας ἀ. τοῦ πατρὸς πρὸς υἱόν Didym. *Trin.*2.2(M.39.453C); ὡδί πως ἀ. τοῦ θεοῦ καταλέγει *ib.*2.10(644A); Ἰὼβ ἀ. πάντων ἡμῶν κέκρακεν *ib.*3.10(857C).

D. of procession of H. Ghost (more usu. ἐκ) τὸ πνεῦμα...ἀ. θεοῦ ὄν Ign.*Philad.*7.1; ἀ. πατρὸς ἐκπορευόμενον Epiph.*haer.*62.3 (p.392.1; M.41.1053B); *ib.*74.11(p.329.12; M.42.496D); opp. ἐκ of Son υἱῷ τῷ ἐξ αὐτοῦ καὶ ἁγίῳ πνεύματι τῷ ἀ. αὐτοῦ καὶ διὰ τοῦ μονογενοῦς *ib.*76.44(p.398.13; 609D).

III. *by means of*;

A. of instrument τόπος...ἀπερρηγὼς ἀ. τῶν ὑδάτων Herm.*vis.* 1.1.3; *2Clem.*17.3; Epiph.*haer.*76.22(p.393.10; M.42.601B).

B. of agent (replacing ὑπό), *1Clem.*45.3; Hegem.*Arch.*8(p.12.3; M.10.1440A); with virtual pass. ἀ. ... ἀγγέλων τὸν κόσμον γεγενῆσθαι Hipp.*haer.*7.28(p.208.12; M.16.3322A).

IV. replacing ἀνά *each, apiece* παρεῖχεν πᾶσιν...ἀ. δύο λεπτῶν Jo.Mosch.*prat.*127(M.87.2989D); πολλαὶ...ἀ. ἑνὸς παιδὸς...κατέχουσαι, ἄλλαι δὲ καὶ ἀ. δύο Jo.Eub.*innoc.*2(M.96.1504B).

V. with comp., *than*, freq. in LXX etc.; perh. *compared with* ὀλίγα ἐστὶν ἀ. τῶν πολλῶν ὧν ὁ θεὸς ἔχει *A.Thom.*A 36(p.153.5).

VI. with acc., *T.Abr.*A 8(p.85.24); ἐσθίουσιν ἀ. τὰ δύο μέρη (? cf. IV supra) †Gregent.*leg.Hom.*45(M.86.605B); ἀ. τοὺς κατηχουμένους ἐξέρχεσθαι *after*, †Jo.Jej.*poenit.*(M.88.1912D); not c. dat. ἀ. βλεφάροιιν (genit. dual) †Apoll.*met.Ps.*67:3(v.l. βλεφάροισιν M.33.1404C).

***ἀποαρκτοτρόφος, ὁ,** *ex-bear-keeper*, CChalc.*act.*4(H.2.421B; ἀπὸ ἀρκτοτρόφων *ACO* 2.1.2 p.115.2).

ἀποβάλλ-ω, **A.** in gen., *throw away, reject* ζήσονται τῷ θεῷ, ὅσοι ἂν ἀποβάλωσιν ἀφ' ἑαυτῶν τὴν λύπην Herm.*mand.*10.3.4; ref. the lapsed ἐσκανδαλισμένους ἀπὸ τῆς πίστεως μὴ ~εσθαι, ἀλλ' ἐπιστρέφειν *ib.*8.10; id.*vis.*3.5.5; ἐὰν μὴ ποιῆτε τὰς ἐντολάς μου, ἀποβαλῶ ὑμᾶς *2Clem.*4.5; of rejecting a dogma, Or.*Cels.*8.51(p.266.15; M.11.1592C); putting away thoughts, id.*Jo.*10.30(18; p.203.28; M.14.361A); *Hom.Clem.*3.8; *Const.App.*2.13.3; ἀ. [sc. at baptism] τὴν παλαιότητα τῆς ἁμαρτίας Pamph.H.*can.*2; of rejecting an opinion, Cosm. Ind.*top.*7(M.88.377D); Μανιχαῖοι καὶ Μαρκιωνισταί, τὰς σάρκας ~όμενοι *ib.*5(281A); μὴ ἀ. ἐκ τοῦ νόμου ἢ τῶν προφητῶν βίβλον *Dial. Tim.et Aquil.*76 v°; εἰ δὲ θεότητος...εἰκόνα τις τολμήσει ποιῆσαι, ὡς ψευδῆ ~όμεθα Jo.D.*imag.*2.11(M.94.1293D).

B. of exclusion from Church; **1.** *refuse admission* to catechumenate; of certain categories of persons, e.g. makers of idols, *Const.App.*8.32.8; stage-performers of all kinds, *ib.*8.32.9; **2.** *excommunicate, reject from communion* οὐδέποτε διὰ τὸ εἶδος τοῦτο [sc. different custom of observing fast before Easter] ἀπεβλήθησάν τινες, ἀλλ' αὐτοὶ μὴ τηροῦντες...τοῖς...τηροῦσιν ἔπεμπον εὐχαριστίαν

Iren.ep.Vict.ap.Eus.h.e.5.24.15(M.20.505A); †Hipp.Artem.ib.5.28.6 (513A); τοὺς ὑφ' ἑτέρων ἀποβληθέντας ὑφ' ἑτέρων μὴ προσίεσθαι CNic.(325)can.5; CAnt.(341)can.4; ἀποβεβλημένοι ἢ ἀκοινώνητοι CCP(381) can.6; **3.** *exclude* from prayers; lowest grade of penitents, Gr. Nyss.castig.(M.46.312B).

C. *thrust out* from office, *degrade* ἐὰν...τῆς ἐπισκοπῆς ἀποβάλωμεν 1Clem.44.4; οὐχ εὑρήσετε δικαίους ἀποβεβλημένους ἀπὸ ὁσίων ἀνδρῶν ib.45.3; Const.App.8.23.4.

D. *cast out* a demon, Or.Cels.2.49(p.172.8; M.11.873C).

E. *lose* by death, Meth.symp.3.12(p.40.20; M.18.80A); Const.App. 8.25.2; Chrys.pan.Melet.3(2.522C); id.hom.9.1 in 1Tim.(11.596A); ‡Nil.perist.6.2(M.79.857C).

***ἀποβαπτίζω,** *'unbaptize'* ἀποσχηματίζειν μοναχόν, ἴσον ἐστὶ τῷ ἀ. Thdr.Stud.epp.2.164(M.99.1521B).

***ἀπόβασμα, τό,** *prating*, Cyr.hom.pasch.14(5^2.196E).

***ἀποβαστάζ-ω,** *carry away*, Apophth.Patr.(M.65.172B); of Christ ἀπεδήμησεν...οὐρανόν, ~ων ὥσπερ τὰς ἁμαρτίας ἡμῶν Cyr.glaph.Lev. (1.375B).

ἀποβδελύσσω, *loathe*, ‡Amph.poenit.(p.96C).

ἀποβηματίζω, *go downstairs*, Mir.Artem.32(p.47.27); ib.38(p.63.7).

ἀποβιάζω, *fling away violently*, Ephr.1.94C.

ἀπόβλεψις, ἡ, *gazing*, Thdr.Stud.epp.1.40(M.99.1052B).

ἀπόβλητος, *to be rejected, cast out, eschewed*; **1.** in gen., Clem. str.6.17(p.510.27; M.9.384C); Or.comm.in Mt.10.7(p.9.12; M.13.853A); κἀκεῖνο δὲ μνήμης οὔ μοι δοκεῖ ἀ. εἶναι Eus.v.C.4.33(p.130.6; M.20. 1181B); μόνην τὴν ἐν κακίᾳ ζωὴν κρίνων ἀ. Gr.Nyss.v.Gr.Thaum. (M.46.940A); of Devil, Isid.Pel.epp.1.180(M.78.300B); Cyr.hom. pasch.24(5^2.290A) cit. s. ἀνέπαφος; **2.** ref. rejection by God, fig., of foreign matter eliminated in refining of gold by fire, image of divine purging away of evil, Gr.Nyss.or.catech.26(p.99.6; M.45. 69A); μηδὲν ἀ. εἴη τῆς κτίσεως...μηδὲ τῆς θείας κοινωνίας ἀπόκληρον ib.6(p.31.1; 25D); μηδένα ἡμῶν ἀ. ποιήσῃς Lit.ap.Const.App.8.12.44; ib.8.15.8; of the Jews, Cyr.Ps.34:4(M.65.896D); of Cain's sacrifice, ‡Just.qu.et resp.119(M.6.1369A); **3.** of ecclesiastical rejection of apocryphal books, ‡Ath.synops.76(M.28.432C); contrast οὐχ ὡς ἀ. τὰ τῆς παλαιᾶς βιβλία [i.e. in monastic reading] Nil.epp.4.1(M.79. 545A); of excommunicate persons τῆς ἐκκλησίας εἶεν ἂν ἀ. Eus.e.th. 1.6(p.65.10; M.24.836A); CAnt.(341)can.1; ὁ...δικαίως...ἀφορισθεὶς ...αἰωνίου ζωῆς καὶ δόξης ἀ. γέγονεν Const.App.2.47.3; ἀποβάλλομαι ὅσους...ἀ. τῆς καθολικῆς...ἐκκλησίας ἡγήσαντο Sophr.H.ep.syn. (M.87.3188A); of penitents to be excluded from prayers τοὺς ἐν πορνείᾳ μολυνθέντας ἐν τρισὶ μὲν ἔτεσι καθόλου τῆς εὐχῆς ἀ. εἶναι Gr.Nyss.ep.can.4(M.45.229A); of clergy to be degraded from office, CAnt.(341)can.16; Bas.ep.188 can.3(3.271B; M.32.672B); Gr.Nyss.ep. can.5(232B).

***ἀπόβλυσμα, τό,** *outflowing, result* πάντα...ἐγκλήματα, οἴνου ἐστὶν ἀ. Isid.Pel.epp.1.203(M.78.312D).

***ἀποβοάω,** *shout*, Pall.h.Laus.21(p.67.20; M.34.1075C).

ἀποβολή, ἡ, *throwing off, rejection*; of men by God, Hom.Clem. 3.9; Cyr.Mich.68(3.464D); τῇ ἀ. τῶν προγόνων (ref. Mt.3:9) Chrys. hom.11.4 in Mt.(7.153D); Nil.ap.Proc.G.Cant.2:10(M.87.1605B); ἀ. τοῦ Ἰσραὴλ διὰ τὴν ἀνομίαν αὐτῶν Cyr.Ps.58:6(M.69.112C).

ἀποβόλημα, τό, cf. sq.

ἀποβολιμαῖος, *worthless*, conj. for ἀποβόλημα (vox nihili), Or.ap. cat.1Cor.1:29(p.30.18).

***ἀποβουκόλημα, τό,** *thing intended to lead astray*; of betrothal of BMV, which hid fact of virgin birth, Jo.D.f.o.4.14(M.94.1160B).

***ἀποβουλλόω,** *unseal*, Leont.N.v.Jo.Eleem.12(p.24.18); *break seal*, CCP(681)act.15(H.3.1376A).

***ἀπόβουλος,** *without counsel*, Or.hom.20.5 in Jos.(p.424.22; M. 87.1032A).

***ἀπόβρασις, ἡ,** *emission*; of seed, ‡Caes.Naz.dial.139(M.38.1044).

***ἀποβροντάω,** *thunder forth*, Mac.Mgn.apocr.3.9(p.70.14).

***ἀποβρύω,** *pour forth*, Isid.Pel.epp.1.58(M.78.220B).

***ἀπόβρωσις, ἡ,** *devouring*, Eus.d.e.1.8(p.39.22; M.22.76C).

ἀποβυρσόω, *remove the hide*, Chron.Pasch.p.396(M.92.1016A).

***ἀπόβυστος,** *hidden* οὐκ ἐν ἀ. ... ἀλλ' ἐμφανῶς Thdr.Stud.epp.1. 37(M.99.1040D).

ἀποβύ-ω, *stop up, block*, Clem.prot.10(p.66.22; M.8.201B); Sev. Ant.ap.cat.Lc.18:12(p.133.31); οἱ πρὸς πάντα τὰ θεῖα...τὴν ἀκουστικὴν τῆς ψυχῆς ~σαντες δύναμιν Max.opusc.(M.91.224B).

ἀπογαιόω, v. ἀπογεόω.

ἀπογαλακτίζω, *wean*, met. ἀπογαλακτισθέντες ἀπὸ νομικοῦ γάλακτος Eus.Is.28:9(M.24.288D); ἐκκλησία τοὺς ἑαυτῆς τροφίμους... ἀπογαλακτίσασα...τῶν λόγων τῆς κατηχήσεως Bas.hom.13.1(2.114A; M.31.425A); †Bas.Is.216(1.541C; M.30.492D); Proc.G.Gen.21:8(M.87. 384B).

ἀπογαλάκτισις, ἡ, *weaning*, Thdr.Stud.or.7.3(M.99.749C).

ἀπογαλακτισμός, ὁ, = foreg., Or.comm.in Mt.12.31(p.138.13; M. 13.1053B); Proc.G.Gen.21:8(M.87.384B).

***ἀπογαλακτώδης,** *milky*, Nil.ap.Proc.G.Cant.7:7(M.87.1733A).

***ἀπογαμέω,** *defile, violate* a woman, Nomoc.211.

***ἀπογαυρόομαι,** *be elated, bear oneself arrogantly*, Cyr.ador.10 (1.340E); id.Is.3.2(2.398E).

ἀπογεμίζω, *unload*, Apophth.Patr.(M.65.281B).

ἀπογενν-άω, *beget, engender*; **a.** in gen. τῇ ὁρμῇ τῶν ~ώντων Gr.Nyss.or.catech.39(p.154.4; M.45.97D); id.v.Mos.(M.44.328B); Mac. Mgn.apocr.2.21(p.44.16); **b.** ref. generation of Son υἱόν...θεός, οἷα πατὴρ ἀγαθὸν ~ήσας καρπόν Eus.l.C.12(p.231.29; M.20.1389C); ἐκ τῆς οἰκείας οὐσίας ὁ πατὴρ τὸν υἱὸν ἀπεγέννησεν Thdt.rect.conf.2(M. 6.1209A); Cyr.thes.32(5^1.320D); **c.** met. Κάλλιστος...αἵρεσιν ἀπεγέννησεν Hipp.haer.10.27(p.283.13; M.16.3442A); διὰ τῶν σῶν [sc. God's] χειρῶν πάντα τὰ ἀγαθὰ ἔργα ~ᾶται A.Thom.A 10(p.114.14); ἀπεγεννήθη [sc. ἡ γῆ] δὲ ὁπηνίκα εἶπεν ὁ θεός Diod.Ps.89:1(M.33.1624D); νέον ἄνθρωπον ~ηθῆναι πεποίηκε [sc. Christ, by his death] Chrys. hom.79.1 in Jo.(8.466A).

ἀπογέννημα, τό, *offspring* ἓν καὶ μόνον ἀ. [sc. Son] †Apoll.ep.Bas. 1(M.32.1104D); met. οἱ πλουτοῦντες καὶ οἱ πενόμενοι τῆς αὐτῆς εἱμαρμένης ὑπάρχουσιν ἀπογεννήματα Tat.orat.8(p.8.9; M.6.821B).

***ἀπογεννήτωρ, ὁ,** *begetter*, of God τοῦ [sc. ἔρωτος καὶ ἀγάπης]... αἴτιος, καὶ ὥσπερ προβολεύς, καὶ ἀ. Dion.Ar.d.n.4.14(M.3.712C).

ἀπογεόω (-γαιόω), *turn into earth*, Gr.Nyss.hex.43(v.l. -γαιούμενον; M.44.101B); ib.53(v.l. -γαιώθησαν; 108B); -γαιόω id.hom.7 in Cant.(M.44.912C); Geo.Pis.hex.1222(v.l. -γαιοῖ M.92.1528A); met., *render earthy*; of πνεῦμα, Or.fr.53 in Lam.(p.258.11; M.13.636C); of νοῦς, Schol. in Max.qu.Thal.proem.(M.90.268A).

ἀπογινώσκω, *despair, give up hope* [sc. of salvation] τὸν ἡμῶν τῶν ἀπεγνωσμένων σωτῆρα Ἰησοῦν Eus.h.e.10.4.10(M.20.852C); ἰατρόν [sc. Christ] τῶν ἀπεγνωσμένων Ant.Mon.hom.27(M.89.1525A).

ἀπογνώμων, *able to distinguish*, Mac.Aeg.pat.13(M.34.876B).

***ἀπογνωρίζω,** *reject*, Herm.vis.2.2.8.

ἀπόγνωσις, ἡ *despair*, in gen. οὐδὲν...χεῖρον ἀπογνώσεως ‡Chrys. hom.1(13.205C); τὸ τῆς ἀ. πάθος...φέρει...τὸν ἄνθρωπον εἰς ἀπιστίαν καὶ ἀνελπιστίαν Ant.Mon.hom.27(M.89.1520B); two kinds ἔστιν ἀ. ἐκ πλήθους ἁμαρτημάτων...καὶ ἔστιν ἀ. ἐξ ὑπερηφανίας καὶ οἰήσεως ἡμῖν ἐπισυμβαίνουσα, λογιζόμενον ἑαυτὸν ὡς ἀνάξιον ὄντα τοῦ συμβεβηκότος πτώματος Jo.Clim.scal.26(M.88.1032D); caused by Devil, Nil.epp.2. 172(M.79.288B); Ant.Mon.hom.27(M.89.1525A); by demons, Or.exp. in Pr.18:8(M.17.204B); Jo.Mosch.prat.110(M.87.2973C); by human perversity, Chrys.hom.8.4 in 1Cor.(10.71B); id.sac.2.4(p.35.3; 1.375B).

***ἀπογνωστικός,** *involving final rejection*, Jo.D.fr.Mt.27:5(M.96. 1412A) cit. s. ἐγκατάλειψις.

ἀπογομόω, *unload* a cargo; of souls ferried from moon to sun acc. Manich. doctrine, Hegem.Arch.8(p.13.7; M.10.1440C); Epiph. haer.66.22(p.50.20; M.42.68B).

ἀπογραφεύς, ὁ, *informer*, Synes.provid.2.3(p.121.1; M.66.1269B).

ἀπογραφή, ἡ, **1.** *list, register*; of a family tree, Afric.ep.Arist. (p.61.18; M.10.61A); of persons liable to taxation (cf. Lc.2:2), Just. 1apol.34.2(M.6.384A); Eus.h.e.1.5.2(M.20.81A); of the baptized τῶν ἱερέων ἡ σωτηριώδης ἀ. τοῖς σωζομένοις αὐτὸν ἐγκαταλέγουσα Dion. Ar.e.h.2.3.4(M.3.400D); of saints commemorated in the liturgy τῶν ἁγίων ἀπογραφή ib.3.3.9(437C); **2.** *assessment* for taxation, Bas.ep. 36(3.114C; M.32.324A); ib.309(442C; M.1057B); Gr.Naz.ep.67(M.37. 132B).

ἀπογράφομαι, **1.** *enter in a list, enroll*; **a.** lit., at baptism ἀπογράψασθαι κελεύει τοῖς ἱερεῦσι τὸν ἄνδρα καὶ τὸν ἀνάδοχον Dion.Ar.e.h.2. 2.6(M.3.396A); **b.** met., pass., of Christians τοῖς τοῦ θεοῦ μαθηταῖς ἀπογεγραμμένοις Clem.q.d.s.33(p.182.9; M.9.640A); εἰς ταύτην [sc. τὴν ἐπουράνιον Ἱερουσαλήμ]...ἀπεγράψατο [i.e. as citizen] Marc. Diac.v.Porph.4; Dion.Ar.ep.9.5(M.3.1112D); †Gregent.disp.(M.86. 685A); **c.** *enter oneself* for a contest; of an ascetic καθάπερ ἀθλητὴς ἀπογραψάμενος εἰς τὸν ἀγῶνα τῆς εὐσεβείας ‡Nil.perist.11.21(M.79. 933B); **2.** pass., *be assessed* for taxation περισσοπρακτίαι ἀπεγράφησαν ἥ τε ἁγία Ἀνάστασις καὶ οἱ λοιποὶ σεβάσμιοι τόποι Cyr.S. v.Sab.54(p.145.28).

ἀπογυμν-όω, **A.** *strip*; met., *strip, deprive*; **1.** in gen., of disembodied souls παντὸς ~ωθεῖσαι περιβλήματος Meth.res.3.18(p.416.1; M.18.328A); οἱ πρῶτοι ἄνθρωποι...τῆς μακαριότητος...ἀπεγυμνώθησαν Gr.Nyss.or.catech.8(p.43.4; M.45.33C); ἐπειδὴ δὲ διὰ τὴν παράβασιν ἐκολάζετο...ἀπεγυμνώθη τῆς χάριτος Cyr.Jo.1.9(4.95A); theol. οὐ γάρ...ἡ...ταπείνωσις [sc. at Inc.] τοῦ κατὰ φύσιν προσόντος ἀξιώματος ~ώσει τὸν υἱόν *ib.*1.3(22C); **2.** of rank, Chrys.*hom.7.1 in Heb.*(12.73C); τὸν Γάλλον εἰς ἰδιώτην ~ωθέντα Philost.*h.e.*4.1(M.65.517A).

B. *reveal*; **1.** *disclose* what is secret ἀ. τὰ κρυπτὰ τῆς καρδίας Bas.*reg.fus.*26(2.371B; M.31.985D); τὴν καρδίαν ~ώσαντα τὴν ἐμὴν Chrys.*sac.*6.12(p.165.21, v.l. γυμνώσαντα 1.432D); **2.** *make plain* a meaning οὕτως ἀ. τοῦ ἰδίου βουλήματος τὴν διάνοιαν Gr.Nyss.*Apoll.*9(M.45.1140C); τὸ κήρυγμα Chrys.*hom.8.1 in 2Cor.*(10.493C); Cyr.*Jo.*2.1(4.143D); Thdt.*epp.Paul.proem.*(3.2); **3.** of Christ's disclosure of his divinity and humanity οὐδέπω τοῦ καιροῦ ~ῶσαι τὴν θεότητα σαφῶς Chrys.*hom.49.1 in Mt.*(7.504A, vv.ll. ἀποκρύψαι, ἀποκαλύψαι); ἵνα μὴ μειζόνως τὴν θεότητα ~ώσῃ *cat.Jo.*7:10(p.262.6); συγκαταβαίνει δὲ μᾶλλον, τὴν ἀνθρωπίνην φύσιν ~ῶν. δακρύει δέ Cyr.*Jo.*7(4.685A).

***ἀπόδειγμα, τό,** *illustration, proof, Apophth.Patr.*(M.65.77D); Cosm.Ind.*top.*2 tit.(M.88.72C).

ἀποδεικτικῶς, *demonstrably, with proof given*, Clem.*str.*7.15(p.65.19; M.9.528B); Or.*Cels.*4.89(p.361.2; M.11.1165A); Thdt.*eran.*3(4.199).

***ἀποδείπνια (ἀπόδειπνα), τά,** *after-supper service, compline*, Leont.Abb.*v.Gr.Agr.*56(M.98.645D); τῶν ἀποδείπνων Thdr.Stud.*poen.*1.20(M.99.1736B); ἐκ τότε τὰ ἀ. ὁλόκληρα ποιοῦμεν, πλὴν σαββάτου ἑσπέρας, καὶ ἑορτῆς δεσποτικῆς, καὶ μνήμης ἁγίου *Const.Stud.*3(M.99.1705C); cf. τῆς νυκτὸς ἀρχομένης, ἡ αἴτησις τοῦ ἀπρόσκοπον ἡμῖν καὶ φαντασιῶν ἐλευθέραν ὑπάρξαι τὴν ἀνάπαυσιν Bas.*reg.fus.*37.5(2.384B; M.31.1016B); cf.Chrys.*hom.14.4 in 1Tim.*(11.631C); cf. Eus.*Ps.*117:161–4(M.23.1392A).

ἀποδεκατόω, **1.** *take tithe of*, Gr.Naz.*or.*30.21(p.143.12; M.36.133A); **2.** *pay tithe of* ἀ. πάντα...τῷ κυρίῳ *T.Lev.*9.4.

***ἀποδεκάτωσις, ἡ,** *tithing* ἦν ἐκεῖ [sc. amongst the Jews] ἀ. ἀσφαλιζομένη, ἵνα μὴ λάθῃ ἡμᾶς τὸ ἰῶτα, ἡ δεκάς, τὸ πρῶτον στοιχεῖον τοῦ Ἰησοῦ ὀνόματος Epiph.*haer.*8.6(p.192.24; M.41.213D); id.*anac.*1.15(p.167.14; M.41.172A); Jo.D.*haer.*15(M.94.688A).

***ἀποδεκταῖος,** *acceptable*, Serap.*ep.mon.*1(M.40.928B).

ἀποδεκτέος, *to be praised* ἀποδεκτέοι...οἱ ἄνδρες τῆς πίστεως †Ath.*fr.Mt.*(M.27.1365B).

***ἀποδεκτικός,** *receptive*; neut. as subst., *acceptance* τὸ ἀ. [sc. by God] τῆς πρὸς αὐτὸν ἡμῶν ἐννοίας τε καὶ εὐνοίας ‡Cyr.*Trin.*12(6³.18C; M.77.1148B).

ἀποδέχομαι, *accept, welcome*: persons; of God, Chrys.*hom.15.1 in Mt.*(7.186A); situations, id.*hom.15.2 in Phil.*(11.312D); Cyr.*hom.div.*9(5².369B); Bible as authentic, Thdr.Stud.*test.*(M.99.1816A).

ἀποδ-έω, *bind, fasten*, fig. ἐξ αὐτῆς [sc. τῆς ἁγνείας] ~ήσαντες ἡμῶν τὰ σώματα πλοίων δίκην Meth.*symp.*4.2(p.47.12; M.18.89A).

ἀποδέ-ω, *fall short of*; **1.** truth, ref. terms applied to God in affirmative theology ~όντων δὲ καὶ οὕτω τῆς θεαρχικῆς πρὸς ἀλήθειαν ἐμφερείας Dion.Ar.*c.h.*2.3(M.3.140C); of lower celestial orders which fall short of superior universal knowledge of higher, although they participate in it, as being parts of same whole τῆς ὁλικῆς καὶ ὑπερκειμένης τῶν πρεσβυτέρων διακόσμων δυνάμεως ~ουσιν οἱ τελευταῖοι *ib.*12.2(292C); **2.** virtue, Chrys.*sac.*3.7(p.59.20; 1.385D); *ib.*4.1(p.101.17; 404A).

***ἀποδημαγωγέω,** *lead astray*, Clem.*str.*2.1(p.114.9; M.8.933A).

ἀποδημέω, **1.** *depart from*; c. genit., met., at death ἀ. τοῦ βίου πρὸς τὸν κύριον Clem.*str.*7.11(p.46.8; M.9.489A); of soul, Ath.*gent.*33(M.25.65D); of evil spirit from one possessed, Chrys.*hom.28.4 in Mt.*(7.339B); c. acc. χώρας ἀ. Ath.*gent.*31(64B); **2.** abs., *depart* [sc. from this life], Cyr.*ep.*72(p.18.22; 5².200C).

ἀποδημητικός, *migratory*; of fish, Bas.*hex.*7.4(1.66D; M.29.156C).

ἀποδημία, ἡ, *departure*; **1.** from home, *journey*, Chrys.*hom.6.1 in Mt.*(7.85B); id.*comm.in Gal.*1:18(10.677E); id.*hom.1.4 in Tit.*(11.736E); of exile, Ath.*ep.encycl.*2(p.171.7; M.25.225C); met., of earthly life ἀ. ὁ παρὼν βίος. μὴ γὰρ πολίτης εἶ; ὁδίτης εἶ. ἡ πόλις ἄνω ἐστίν, τὰ παρόντα ὁδός ἐστιν Chrys.*Eutrop.*2(3.390D); id.*stat.*2.5(2.8B); **2.** from life, *death*, Meth.*res.*1.29(p.258.18; M.41.1136D); Chrys.*hom.83.1 in Jo.*(8.489A); id.*hom.41.5 in 1Cor.*(10.393D); id.*stat.*2.7(2.85C).

***ἀποδιάθεσις, ἡ,** *separation, aversion* ἡ πρὸς τὴν ὑλικὴν περιουσίαν ἀ. Gr.Nyss.*infant.*(M.46.164C); τὴν ψυχῆς πρὸς αἴσθησιν λελογισμένην ἀ. Max.*qu.Thal.*68(M.90.596B); Anast.S.*qu.et resp.*32(M.89.569D).

ἀποδιαιρ-έω, *divide, separate*, Clem.*str.*8.6(p.91.8; M.9.584B); Or.*Jo.*13.55(54; p.285.33; M.14.504B); Cyr.*Jo.*11.8(4.967D); of natures of Christ ~οῦντές φασιν οὐκ εἶναι υἱὸν ἀληθινὸν τὸν ἐκ γυναικός id.*Pulch.*(p.98.1; 5².96A).

ἀποδιάκει-μαι, *be antagonistic* or *conceive a dislike* to, Clem.*paed.*2.8(p.196.23; M.8.472A); of God οὐδὲ ~ται πρὸς τὰ ἑαυτοῦ ποιήματα Thdr.Heracl.*Is.*26:16(M.18.1316A).

ἀποδιαλαμβάν-ω, *set apart* ~όμενα χωρία [sc. in the ark] Or.*hom.2 in Gen.*(p.23.24; M.12.161B).

ἀποδιαπέμπομαι, *send away, expel*, Pall.*v.Chrys.*20(p.143.3; M.47.79).

***ἀποδιασπάω,** *tear away, separate*; met., of Gnostics τῆς σαρκὸς ἀ. τὸν λόγον Hipp.*fr.in Mt.25:24*(p.209.10; M.10.868B).

ἀποδιαστέλλ-ω, **1.** *separate, distinguish*, Dion.Ar.*e.h.*5.1.1(M.3.500D); Leont.H.*monoph.*10(M.86.1776C); med. ὑπόστασις...τοῦ κοινοῦ τὸ ἴδιον ~εται Leont.B.*Nest.et Eut.*1(M.86.1280A); **2.** abs., *make a distinction*, ‡Chrys.*Trin.*2(1.836B); **3.** pass., *be cut off* τὸ τοῖς πτεροῖς ~εσθαι τὴν...θεωρίαν Dion.Ar.*c.h.*13.4(M.3.305A).

ἀποδιδάσκομαι, *learn to avoid*, Const.Diac.*laud.*33(M.88.517A).

ἀποδιδύσκ-ω, *take off*; met., of Christ ~ων αὐτοὺς [sc. τοὺς ἁμαρτωλούς] τὸν τῆς ἁμαρτίας χιτῶνα Eus.*Is.*54:12(M.24.461A).

ἀποδίδωμι, **1.** *render, pay, give back*; **a.** of God to men ὁ...πατὴρ ...τὰς χάριτας αὐτοῦ ἀ. τοῖς προσερχομένοις αὐτῷ *1Clem.*23.1; *Barn.*11.8; τὰς ἀντιμισθίας ἀ. ἑκάστῳ τῶν ἔργων αὐτοῦ *2Clem.*11.6; Just.*1apol.*43.2(M.6.393A); ὁ κύριος...ἀποδώσει κατὰ τὰ ἔργα Pall.*v.Chrys.*20(p.143.13; M.47.80); **b.** of men to God ἂν...ψυχὰς...καταθώμεθα, ἆρα τὴν ἴσην ἀποδώσομεν; οὐδαμῶς Chrys.*hom.3.4 in Philm.*(11.785A); **2.** *give up* soul at death, *V.Pach.Σ* 88(p.268.24); **3.** *offer up* prayers, Eus.Al.*serm.*5(M.86.349A).

***ἀποδιϊστάω,** = sq., Jo.D.*dialect.*66(M.94.669A); ἀ. τὴν εἰς θεὸν πίστιν τῆς τοῦ κυρίου πίστεως Areth.*Apoc.*42(M.106.692A).

ἀποδιΐστημι, c. acc. only, *differentiate*, Cyr.*Soph.*16(3.596B); *isolate* τῷ ἑνὶ Χριστῷ καὶ υἱῷ τὴν τομὴν ἐπιφέροντες ἀποδιϊστᾶσιν τὸν θεὸν λόγον id.*ep.*50(p.99.21, v.l. -ῶσιν 169D); med., *separate oneself, withdraw*, Const.ap.Eus.*h.e.*10.5.21(M.20.888C); *separate* from ἀ. τὸ φύσει τῶν κατὰ χάριν Cyr.*Jo.*1.8(4.64E); ἀ. αὐτοῦ [sc. Χριστοῦ] τὸν ἐκ θεοῦ λόγον id.*ep.*1(p.16.11, v.l. -ῶντες 5².9D).

***ἀποδιυλίζω,** *strain clear, filter*, Ign.*Rom.*proem.; Cyr.H.*catech.*13.11.

***ἀποδιυλισμός, ὁ,** *filtering*, Ign.*Philad.*3.1.

ἀποδιωθέομαι, *thrust away from oneself*, met. ἀ. τὴν ἀλήθειαν Clem.*str.*7.16(p.72.36; M.9.541D); ἁγνείαν ἀ. Meth.*symp.*9.4(p.119.8; M.18.188A).

***ἀποδογματίζω,** *lay down definitely*, Mac.Mgn.*apocr.*2.7(p.4.2).

ἀποδοκιμάζ-ω, *reject* οἵ τε τὴν μὲν καινὴν ἐγκρίνοντες, τὴν δὲ παλαιὰν ~οντες διαθήκην Or.*fr.comm.in Ezech.*(p.61.1; M.13.664B); οὐδὲ λόγον φιλόσοφον προτιμήσαντας, οὔτε αὖ ἀποδοκιμάσαντας, οὔτε Ἑλληνικὸν οὔτε βάρβαρον, πάντων δὲ ἀκούοντας Gr.Thaum.*pan.Or.*13(p.29.19; M.10.1088B); ref. formal censure by Church ἡ δ' ἁγία τοῦ θεοῦ σύνοδος ἀπεδοκίμαζε τὸ γράμμα Eus.*Marcell.*2.4(p.58.30; M.24.824B); τὸν Σαβέλλιον φθεγξάμενον ἀπεδοκίμασεν ἡ ἐκκλησία τοῦ θεοῦ id.*e.th.*1.1(p.63.12; M.24.829D); the Montanist heresy, Anon.ap. eund.*h.e.*5.16.10(M.20.468C).

ἀποδόκιμος, *unworthy*, c. genit. ἀ. ζωηροῦ χώρου ‡Meth.*Sym.et Ann.*9(M.18.368B).

ἀποδορά, ἡ, *flaying*, Const.Diac.*laud.*32(M.88.516A).

ἀπόδοσις, ἡ, **1.** *payment* of debt, ‡Bas.*struct.hom.*1(1.324A; M.30.9A); **2.** *due fulfilment*, Clem.*str.*6.11(p.478.17; M.9.313B); -δωσις Thdr.Heracl.*fr.Jo.*ap.*cat.Jo.*8:25(p.277.17); **3.** *statement*, Clem.*str.*8.6(p.93.3; 585C); Cyr.*Ps.*9:34(M.69.784C); id.*Nest.*1.8(*ACO* 1.1.6 p.29.1; 6¹.25A); **4.** *interpretation*, Or.*Jo.*1.31(34; p.40.7; M.14.84B); Eus.*e.th.*3.3(p.154.5; M.24.996D); Cyr.*Nest.*1.5(p.25.39; 20E); **5.** *pronunciation*, Epiph.*exp.fid.*10.7(p.511.2; M.42.801A).

***ἀποδότης, ὁ,** *rewarder*, Thdr.Stud.*epp.*1.56(M.99.1112C).

ἀποδρομή, ἡ, *running away, flight*, Cyr.*Nah.*9(3.486A); id.*Soph.*35(3.612D); met. τὴν ἀχάλινον ἀ.... εἰς...ἐπιθυμίας id.*ador.*5(1.156B).

ἀποδύρομαι, c. ἐπί et genit., *mourn* over, Mel.*pass.*27 p.5.2.

ἀποδυσπετ-έω, *lose patience* with, *give up in despair* ἀ. ἐπὶ τοῖς ἁμαρτήμασι τοῦ λαοῦ Clem.*str.*3.16(p.242.5; M.8.1200B); ~ήσαντας ἁγνείαν βαστάσαι Meth.*symp.*3.13(p.43.3; M.18.84A); of S. Paul οὐκ ἀπεδυσπέτει πρὸς τὴν συνέχειαν τῶν κακῶν Bas.*hom.in Ps.*33(1.143E; M.29.352C); Ast.Soph.*Ps.*6(M.40.457C); Chrys.*Anna* 2.3(4.715D); Nil.*epp.*3.13(M.79.376A).

ἀποδυσπέτησις, ἡ, *impatience, despair*, Chrys.*hom.20.4 in Heb.*(12.191D); Thdr.Mops.*Zach.*11:15(M.66.580A); Olymp.*Job* 3:20(M.93.65B); *discouraging experience*, Thdr.Mops.*Ps.*35:1(p.194.16).

***ἀποδυσφορέω,** *be indignant*, Pall.*v.Chrys.*20(p.135.12; M.47.75).

***ἀποδυσωπέω,** *importune*, *cat.Lc.*16:19(p.125.1).

ἀποδύ-ω, **A.** act., *strip*; **1.** of possessions, Chrys.*hom.3.4 in Eph.*(11.15C); id.*hom.6.5 in Phil.*(11.242C); **2.** of rank, Philost.*h.e.*3.22(M.65.512A); *ib.*12.3(609A).

B. med., *strip, undress* oneself; **1.** lit., of 'gnostic' who prays οὐ

...μόνον ἀναστὰς...ἀλλὰ καὶ...ἀμφιεννύμενός τε καὶ ~όμενος Clem.*str*.7.12(p.57.16; M.9.512A); for baptism, Pall.*v.Chrys*.2(p.13.3; M.47.11); fig., *put off*, ref. death τί...ἐστὶ θάνατος; ὥσπερ ἐστὶν ἱμάτιον ~σασθαι Chrys.*stat*.5.3(2.64D); **2.** met., *put off*; **a.** the body, of martyrs δι' εὐσέβειαν ἀ. τὰ σώματα Or.*Cels*.8.44(p.259.4; M.11.1581C); **b.** the 'old man', by baptism οἱ προσομιλοῦντες τῷ βαπτίσματι, τῆς παλαιᾶς στυγνότητος ~ονται τοὺς χιτῶνας Didym.*Trin*.2.14(M.39.700B); ref. Col.3:9, Just.*dial*.116.1(M.6.744B); †Bas.*Is*.proem.(1.378B; M.30.120B); **c.** virginity, ref. similitude of the tower and the unfaithful virgins τῶν δὲ παρθένων ἀπεδύσαντο τὴν δύναμιν Herm.*sim*.9.13.8; ref. wedding garment in parable, here understood of virginity ὅτι μὴ ἐμνημόνευσαν τὸν κόσμον ~σασθαι τὸν νυμφικόν Meth.*symp*.4.5(p.51.23; M.18.96A); **d.** of high priest, typifying Christ putting on the sensible world in Inc., and 'gnostic', in reverse order, putting it off to enter spiritual world ἄλλως δ' οἶμαι, ὁ κύριος ~εταί τε καὶ ἐνδύεται κατιὼν εἰς αἴσθησιν, ἄλλως ὁ δι' αὐτοῦ πιστεύσας ~εται τε καὶ ἐπενδύεται...τὴν ἡγιασμένην στολήν Clem.*str*.5.6(p.353.29; M.9.68A); **e.** ἀπεδύσω γὰρ τὴν τρικυμίαν [i.e. the storm of life] Pall.*v.Chrys*.20(p.143.15; M.47.80); **3.** esp. of athletes preparing for arena, met. of Christians in this world τὰ παρόντα ἀγὼν...οὐδεὶς ~σάμενος...ἄνεσιν ἐπιζητεῖ Chrys.*hom.8.3 in 2Tim*.(11.709E); esp. against Devil πρὸς γὰρ ἐκεῖνον ~εσθαι μέλλομεν μετὰ τὸ βάπτισμα id.*catech*.1.4(2.231B); id.*hom.17.11 in Mt*.(7.221A); ‡Caes.Naz.*dial*.178(M.38.1148); in polemic ~σάμενοι δ' οὖν περιφανῶς ἐν τῷ τῆς ἀληθείας σταδίῳ γνησίως ἀγωνιζώμεθα Clem.*prot*.10(p.70.20; M.8.209B); of ascetics ἀθλητικῶς ~όμενος Nil.*Eulog*.2(M.79.1096B); of apostles πρὸς μεταβολὴν τῶν τῆς οἰκουμένης ἁπάσης ἐθῶν...~σασθαι Chrys.*hom.5.3 in 1Cor*.(10.37D); id.*hom.32.2 in Mt*.(7.367B); **4.** of giving up one's own possessions τὰ ἄλλα ~σαμένους τοῦ κηρύγματος ἔχεσθαι Chrys.*hom.47.2 in Mt*.(7.489C); *ib.21.1*(270A); following example of Greek philosophers, *ib.21.4*(273E); *ib.15.8*(198B); **5.** *throw off, clear oneself of* charges, Chrys.*hom.24.5 in Eph*.(11.187D); abs., *clear oneself* καθαρῶς ἀ. id.*comm. in Gal*.5:11(10.715E).

[*]**ἀπόδωσις,** ἡ, v. ἀπόδοσις.

ἀποζάω, *live by* ταῖς χερσὶν ἀ. Pall.*h.Laus*.58(p.151.11; M.34.1203B).

ἀποζέννυμι, s.v.l., *boil out*, met. βάτραχοι...καὶ ἐμπίδες καὶ κώνωπες ἐξ αὐτῶν [sc. marshes] ἀπεζέννυντο Bas.*hex*.7.1(1.62E; M.29.148B).

ἀποζεύγν-υμι, 1. *separate* γυναῖκας ἀνδρῶν ἀ. Chrys.*hom.4.3 in Tit*.(11.752D); pass. τῷ 'Ωριγένει...τὸ εἶδος λέγοντι μετὰ τὴν τελευτὴν ~ύμενον ἀπὸ τοῦ σώματος τῇ ψυχῇ δίδοσθαι Meth.*res*.3.6(p.396.17; M.18.321A); τῆς ψυχῆς τοῦ σώματος ἀποζευχθείσης Alex.Lyc.*Man*.18(M.18.433D); **2.** pass., *be at variance with, differ in import from* οὐκ ἀπέζευκται ἐκεῖνο τὸ κεφάλαιον...τῶν λοιπῶν ‡Ath.*disp*.10(M.28.449A).

ἀποζέω, *cease boiling* or *fermenting*; met., of the passions, Gr.Nyss.*v.Mos*.(M.44.348D).

***ἀποζητέω,** *inquire for, ask for direction to*, Jo.Mosch.*prat*.53(M.87.2908C).

***ἀποζοφέω,** *be darkened*, Thdr.Stud.*epp*.1.37(M.99.1040A).

ἀπόζω, *smell of*, met., c. genit. τῆς νεκρᾶς τοῦ παλαιοῦ ἀνθρώπου δυσωδίας ἀ. Gr.Nyss.*hom.1 in Cant*.(M.44.772D); c. acc. τῆς ἀπαιδευσίας τὴν μέθην ἀ. Mac.Mgn.*apocr*.3.14(p.92.19).

ἀποζώννυμι, 1. med., *take off the girdle*, ‡Bas.*h.myst*.15(p.261.19); **2.** met., pass., *be deprived of* one's rank, *Chron.Pasch*.p.322(M.92.824A).

***ἀποθαμβέομαι,** *be astounded*, Didym.*Trin*.3.17(M.39.876B).

[*]**ἀποθανητέον,** *one must die*, Or.*Cels*.8.26(p.242.13; M.11.1556A).

***ἀποθαυμαστικῶς,** *wonderingly*, ref. Ps.21:3, Eus.*d.e*.10.8(p.479.18; M.22.772A).

ἀποθειάζ-ω, 1. *regard as divine* οἱ...'Εβραίων θεολόγοι...τὴν τρίτην καὶ ἁγίαν δύναμιν, ἅγιον πνεῦμα προσειπόντες, ~ουσιν, οὗ καὶ ἐφωτίζοντο θεοφορούμενοι Eus.*p.e*.7.15(326A; M.21.552A); **2.** *praise extravagantly*, Philost.*h.e*.1.9(M.65.465A); *ib*.8.2(557A); *ib*.10.6(588B).

ἀποθε-όω, *deify, make into a god*;

A. pagan ἀνθρώπους ~οῦν τετολμήκασι Clem.*prot*.10(p.70.27; M.8.209C); ἄνθρωποι πρότερον ἦσαν καὶ ἀπεθειώθησαν Or.*hom.5.3 in Jer*.(p.33.21; M.13.300C).

B. Christol.; **1.** of Christ in pagan writings ὁ λόγος...ὃν ὁ βάρβαρος [sc. S. John] ἀξιοῖ...θεὸν εἶναι...ἀμέλει καὶ ἀναλυθέντα πάλιν ~οῦσθαι, καὶ θεὸν εἶναι Amelius ap.Eus.*p.e*.11.19(540C; M.21.900B); also ap.Cyr.*Juln*.8(6[2].283E) and Thdt.*affect*.2(p.60.3; 4.751); **2.** orthodox, in Apollinarian controversy Ἀπολλ.: δύο οὖν ἡγεμονικὰ ἐν τῷ σώματι ἦσαν, ὁ θεὸς λόγος καὶ ὁ ἄνθρωπος νοῦς...'Ορθ.: ...ὁ νοῦς, καταλαμπόμενος καὶ ~ωθείς, ἕν ἐστιν, καὶ οὐκ ἔστι δύο ἡγεμονικά ‡Ath.*dial.Trin*.4.5(M.28.1257A); Christ not a deified man οὐκ ἄνθρωπον ~ωθέντα κηρύττομεν, ἀλλὰ θεὸν σαρκωθέντα ὁμολογοῦμεν Procl.CP *or.laud.BMV*4(p.104.23; M.65.685A); Max.*opusc*.(M.91.36A); Jo.D.*f.o*.3.2(M.94.988A); of Christ's flesh ηὐδόκησε γὰρ ὁ θεὸς λόγος τὴν κτιστὴν σάρκα...ἑνῶσαι ἑαυτῷ· προσκυνητὴ οὖν ἐστι σὺν τῷ θεῷ λόγῳ, καθὼς καὶ ἀπεθέωσεν αὐτήν ‡Chrys.*Trin*.4(1.839E); **3.** heret., denying divine nature; **a.** acc. Paul of Samosata ἐξ οὐρανοῦ ἀποτεθεῶσθαι τὸν κύριον Gr.Nyss.*Apoll*.9(M.45.1140C, but cf. not. ad loc.); **b.** Apollinarian, replying to supposed orthodox teaching of deification after resurrection πῶς δὲ καὶ πρὶν ἑνωθῆναι, καὶ ~ωθῆναι λέγει 'ἐγὼ καὶ ὁ πατὴρ ἕν ἐσμεν'; Apoll.*fr*.98(p.230.6) ap.Gr.Nyss.*Apoll*.57(M.45.1261C); **c.** Nestorian, accusing orthodox of deifying humanity ἀπεστάλησαν [sc. by heretics]...δύο χαρτία...ἓν...ἀλλόκοτον ἔχον τὴν ἐπιγραφήν, ἔχει δὲ οὕτως 'πρὸς τοὺς διὰ τὴν συνάφειαν ἢ τὴν θεότητα τοῦ μονογενοῦς νεκροῦντας (v.l. σμικροῦντας) ἢ ~οῦντας τὴν ἀνθρωπότητα' Cyr.*ep*.10(p.110.22; 5[2].33B); accused by orthodox of making divine what was not divine by nature μὴ καταδεῖσαι λέγειν ὡς ἔν τινι 'Ιησοῦ τῷ ἐκ παρθένου τεχθέντι ἐνοικήσαντα τὸν θεὸν λόγον τοῦτον ~ῶσαι...ἀποτεθεῶσθαι λέγειν τὸν ἐσχηκότα τὴν ἐνοίκησιν *ib*.50(pp.92.28,93.4; 161B,C); ἐρωτήσομεν, πῶς μετὰ τὴν ἕνωσιν ἀπεθεώθη τὸ σῶμα [sc. Χριστοῦ]; Thdt.*rect.conf*.15(M.6.1233C); **d.** monoph. τὸν 'Ιουλιανὸν [sc. τὸν Ἁλικαρνασσέα]...~ωθεῖσαν καὶ τραπεῖσαν, καὶ ὡς σταγόνα ὄξους πρὸς τὸ πέλαγος τῆς θεότητος λέγοντα ἀλλοιωθεῖσαν τὴν ἁγίαν σάρκα τοῦ Χριστοῦ Anast.S.*hod*.14(M.89.244C).

C. myst., sacramentally, through baptism βάπτισμα...τὸ γενόμενον ἐν ἀληθείᾳ ἀπαθανατοῖ καὶ ~οῖ ἡμᾶς Didym.*Trin*.2.14(M.39.716A); through power and grace of God οὗτος...διὰ τῆς δυνάμεως τοῦ πνεύματος, καὶ τῆς ἀναγεννήσεως τῆς πνευματικῆς, ἔρχεται εἰς τὰ μέτρα τοῦ πρώτου Ἀδάμ, καὶ μείζων αὐτοῦ γίγνεται. ~οῦται γὰρ ὁ ἄνθρωπος Mac.Aeg.*hom*.26.2(M.34.676C); *ib*.15.35(600B); through virtue, Mac.Mgn.*apocr*.4.16(p.186.8); εὐχαριστήσωμεν τῷ θεῷ τῷ...δόντι ἡμῖν τὸ αὐτεξούσιον· δι' οὗ ~ωθῆναι δυνάμεθα κτίζοντες ἑαυτῶν τὰς ψυχὰς διὰ τῶν ἀγαθῶν πράξεων *V.Aberc*.34(p.26.12); τοσοῦτον τῷ ἀνθρώπῳ τὸν θεὸν διὰ φιλανθρωπίαν ἀνθρωπίζεσθαι, ὅσον ὁ ἄνθρωπος ἑαυτὸν τῷ θεῷ δι' ἀγάπης δυνηθεὶς ἀπεθέωσε Max.*ambig*.(M.91.1113B); of man in next world, Or.*schol.in Lc*.14:20(M.17.365A) = id.*fr.436 in Mt*.

ἀποθεράπευσις, ἡ, *restoration* εἰ...μετὰ ἀποθεραπεύσεως [*cum satisfactione*]...τὸν αὐτὸν ἀποκαταστήσῃ κληρικόν, ὃν ἐτόλμησε χειροτονῆσαι *Cod.Afr*.54.

ἀποθεραπεύω, 1. *cure*; a person, Pall.*h.Laus*.17(p.47.17; M.34.1049D); *ib*.25(p.80.13; 1091A); *ib*.29(p.85.15; 1098B); an injury, *A.Xanthipp*.12(p.65.35); met. ἀ. τὴν τῶν...ἀδελφῶν ὑπόνοιαν Eus.*Marcell*.2.4(p.58.16; M.24.824A); **2.** *quiet, appease* ἀ. τὸν ὄχλον *Chron.Pasch*.p.391(M.92.1004B); **3.** *eradicate* ἀ. ἀπὸ ψυχῆς σώματος πνεύματος...πᾶν σημεῖον ἁμαρτίας Serap.*euch*.22.

ἀποθερίζω, [aor. ἀπέθριξα], *tonsure*, ‡Amph.*v.Bas*.(p.188C); Cyr.S.*v.Euthym*.3(p.10.20); Eustrat. *v.Eutych*.14(M.86.2289B).

ἀπόθεσις, ἡ, **1.** *putting off, laying aside*; in gen., Clem.*exc.Thdot*.27(p.115.25; M.9.672C); Cyr.*Nah*.29(3.506E); of soul's putting off the body at death, Clem.*str*.1.19(p.60.27; M.8.812A); Meth.*res*.1.29(p.261.12; M.41.1140A); Diod.*Ps*.51:20(M.33.1610C); **2.** *rejection*; of sin or evil, Chrys.*hom.39.5 in Gen*.(4.403C); Cyr.*Abac*.19(3.534B); flesh τὸ φώτισμα, σαρκὸς ἀπόθεσις, πνεύματος ἀκολούθησις Gr.Naz.*or*.40.3(M.36.361B); things of this world, Clem.*str*.4.25(p.318.27; M.8.1368B); faith, Iren.*haer*.1.21.1(M.7.657B); **3.** *laying aside, storing up*, fig. ὁ πνευματικὸς θερισμὸς...τὴν...ἀ. ... ἐν οὐρανοῖς ἔχει Ammon.*Jo*.4:36(M.85.1425D); in concrete sense, *store*, *T.Sym*.2.9; **4.** *burial*, Ath.*gent*.33(M.25.65B).

ἀποθετέον, *one must set aside* or *store*, Clem.*str*.1.6(p.22.19; M.8.728C).

ἀπόθετος, *laid by, stored up*; neut. as subst., *store*, Gr.Nyss.*v.Mos*.(M.44.345B); met. πονηρὸν ἀ. ἡ μνησικακία id.*hom.7.6 in Eccl*.(M.44.720D).

ἀποθέωσις, ἡ, *deification*; of pagan gods, Clem.*str*.1.21(p.67.19; M.8.828B); *ib*.(p.85.13; 873A) al.; Christol., Nestorian οὐκ εἰς ἀ. [sc. τῆς ἀνθρωπότητος] κατὰ τοὺς σοφοὺς τῶν δογματιστῶν τῶν νεωτέρων Nest.*fr*.C 10(p.275.13); myst. αὐτῆς τῆς ψυχῆς ἑαυτὴν ὥσπερ ἐν κατόπτρῳ ὁρᾶν μελετώσης, καὶ τὸν θεῖον νοῦν, εἰ ἀξία γένοιτο τῆς κοινωνίας τῆσδε, ἐν αὐτῇ κατοπτριζομένης, ὁδόν τε ἀπόρρητόν τινα ταύτης ἀ. ἐξιχνευομένης Gr.Thaum.*pan.Or*.11(p.27.16; M.10.1084C).

ἀποθηριόω, pass., *be enraged*; c. εἰς, *Ep.Lugd*.ap.Eus.*h.e*.5.1.15(M.20.413C); c. πρός, Or.*hom.10.8 in Jer*.(p.77.24; ἐπεθηριώθη M.13.365D); abs., id.*sel.in Gen*.49:9(M.12.145B).

ἀποθησαυρίζ-ω, *store up*, met. ~ει θεὸς τοῖς ἀνθρώποις τὰ πλημμελήματα Cyr.*Jo*.2.5(4.210E).

ἀποθησαυρισμός, ὁ, *laying by, storing up*; fig., Ammon.*Jo*.4:36 (M.85.1425D).

***ἀποθησαυριστέον**, *one must store up*, Clem.*str*.1.6(p.22.19; ἐπι- M.8.728C).

***ἀποθιγγάνω**, **1.** *touch*, Cyr.*ador*.14(1.508C,510E); *ib*.17(603C); met. ἀποθίγειν...πολέμου *ib*.5(170A); **2.** *observe* ψευδῶν σαββάτων ἀ. id. *Am*.58(3.315A).

ἀποθνήσκ-ω, **1.** *die*, met.; **a.** at baptism ἐν τῷ αὐτῷ ἀπεθνήσκετε καὶ ἐγεννᾶσθε Cyr.H.*catech*.20.4; δεῖ σε γὰρ ἀ. καὶ ἀναστῆναι id. *procatech*.5; εἰς τὸ καὶ αὐτοὶ ἀποθανεῖν ὥσπερ ἐκεῖνος· σταυρὸς γάρ ἐστι τὸ βάπτισμα Chrys.*hom.10.4 in Rom*.(9.525E); ἐπειδήπερ ἅπαξ ἀπέθανεν ἐκεῖ, νεκρὸν δεῖ μένειν διαπαντὸς τῇ ἁμαρτίᾳ *ib.11.1*(531E); **b.** of spiritual death ἀ. εἰς τὸν αἰῶνα Herm.*sim*.9.18.2; Clem.*str*. 2.23(p.193.25; M.8.1096D); Or.*or*.27(p.366.29; M.11.509C); τὴν νέκρωσιν, καθ' ἣν καὶ ζῶντες ~ομεν Chrys.*hom.11.5 in Rom*.(9.536E); **2.** c. dat., *die to*, i.e. *renounce* ἀ. τῷ κόσμῳ παραιτούμενος τὴν ἐν αὐτῷ μανίαν Tat.*orat*.11(p.12.10; M.6.829B); ἤδη τεθνήκασι τῷ θεῷ Clem.*paed*.3.11(p.280.32; M.8.660A); ἀ. ... τῇ ἁμαρτίᾳ id.*str*.4.6 (p.260.14; M.8.1240B).

***ἀποθολόω**, *obscure*; light, Mac.Mgn.*apocr*.4.28(p.216.11).

ἀποθρασύν-ομαι, **1.** *have audacity, dare*, *Hom.Clem*.18.14; Ath. *Dion*.7(p.51.2; M.25.489B); **2.** *speak audaciously, use insulting language*, Bas.*Spir*.79(3.67D; M.32.217A); ἐπειδὰν ~ηταί τι κατὰ τῆς δόξης τοῦ πνεύματος Gr.Nyss.*Maced*.20(M.45.1328A); **3.** *cause to speak audaciously*, of Christ ~εται...τοὺς ἀνόμους γραμματεῖς Cyr. *glaph.Num*.(1.382B).

ἀπόθριξ, *hairless, bald*, Cyr.*Jo*.5.1(4.465A).

***ἀπόθρονος**, prob. *rejecting a throne*, or poss. *springing from* or *occasioned by a throne* λιπεῖν...θρόνους καὶ ἀ. εὖχος Gr.Naz.*carm*. 1.2.15.115(M.37.774).

***ἀποθρυλλέω**, *say freely, designate freely*, Mac.Mgn.*apocr*.2.20 (p.41.5); παράνομον ἀ. τὸν γάμον *ib*.3.43(p.151.29); *ib*.4.18(p.197.3).

***ἀποθωρήσσω**, ? *take off as a breast-plate*, *Orac.Sib*.3.455(conj. ἀποθωΰξουσιν *shout aloud*).

ἀποιδέω, *cease swelling, settle down*, ‡Nil.*perist*.11.1(M.79.901C).

ἀποίητος, *uncreated*; **1.** in gen., ‡Just.*qu.Chr*.2.5(M.6.1424A); **2.** of God, *Keryg.Petr*.ap.Clem.*str*.6.5(p.451.11; M.9.257C); *Orac.Sib. fr*.7; Eun.*apol*.28(M.30.868B); Mac.Aeg.*hom*.4.9(M.34.480A); Epiph. *haer*.76.29(p.378.12; M.42.576B); with polemical emphasis against the orthodox doctrine of Son ὁ μὲν γάρ ἐστιν ἀγεννήτου καὶ ἀποιήτου γέννημα καὶ ποίημα Eun.*apol*.17(852C); ποίημα τοῦ ἀ., οὐχ ὡς ἓν τῶν ποιημάτων *ib*.28(868B).

ἀποιήτως, *without making*, ‡Just.*qu.Chr*.3.2(M.6.1433C); *ib*. (1436A).

ἀποικεσία, ἡ, *captivity* ἀπαχθῆναι...ἐν ἀ. *Pss.Sal*.9.1.

ἀποικίζω, **1.** act., *settle* or *make to dwell far from*, met. τοῦ κόσμου ἑαυτὸν ἀ. Gr.Nyss.*or.dom*.5(p.114.18; M.44.1192C); τῆς περὶ τὰς ἡδονὰς διαθέσεως τὸν νοῦν ἀποικίσαντες id.*or.catech*.7(p.39.15; M.45. 32C); **2.** med., *dwell far from*, id.*or.dom*.5(p.114.25; 1192C); met., *be separate* or *remote from* τὰ ἀλόγιστα πάθη...ἀπῴκισται τοῦ ἡμεδαποῦ χοροῦ Clem.*paed*.2.4(p.181.18; M.8.440B); ἡδονῆς καὶ λύπης ἀπῳκισμένον Meth.*symp*.8.1(p.81.7; M.18.137C); of God as remote from change, Cyr.*Jo*.1.9(4.96B); theol., of Son οὔτε ὁ υἱὸς ἀπῴκισται τοῦ πατρός· ἡ γὰρ 'πατήρ' προσηγορία δηλοῖ τὴν κοινωνίαν Dion. Al.ap.Ath.*Dion*.16(p.58.20; M.25.504D).

ἀποίκιλτος, *unvariegated, uniform*, Clem.*paed*.3.10(p.267.19; M.8. 628B); Dion.Ar.*c.h*.7.4(M.3.212A); *Disp.Phot*.(M.88.572A).

ἀποίμαντος, *without a shepherd, untended* τὸ τοῦ θεοῦ ποίμνιον, ἀ. ὂν Gr.Naz.*ep*.152(M.37.257B); Mac.Mgn.*apocr*.3.42(p.146.6); Zach. H.*ep*.(M.86.3228).

ἄποιος, *without quality* or *attribute*; **1.** in gen., ref. 4Reg.2:21 as type of baptism τὸ ἄ. ὕδωρ γόνιμον καὶ νόστιμον πᾶσιν γεγενῆσθαι Didym.*Trin*.2.14(M.39.700B); of false consolations proceeding from evil spirits ἡ δὲ χαρὰ ἐκείνη ἄ. ἐστι καὶ ἀδιάθετος Diad.*perf*.33(p.38.4); **2.** of formless matter, esp. primal matter at Creation; **a.** in Greek, esp. Aristotelian, philosophy τὴν...ὕλην ἄ. καὶ ἀσχημάτιστον λεγομένην Clem.*str*.5.14(p.385.8; M.9.132A); ἀσχημάτιστον γὰρ αὐτὴν οὖσαν καὶ ἄ., προσλαβοῦσαν σχήματα καὶ ποιότητας γενέσθαι σῶμα Hipp.*haer*.1.19(p.20.1; M.16.3041B); τοῖς δὲ ἐπακολουθητικὴν αὐτὴν εἶναι νομίζουσι...οὐσία ἐστὶν ἡ πρώτη τῶν ὄντων ὕλη...ἄ. τε καὶ ἀσχημάτιστος Or.*or*.27(p.368.9; M.11.512B); ἄ. καὶ ἀσχημάτιστον, τῇ δὲ τοῦ θεοῦ δυνάμει τὸν κόσμον αὐταῖς ποιότησι προσειληφέναι Eus.*p.e*.7.18(333B; M.21.561C); ἡ ὕλη...ἄ. τε καὶ ἄποσος ‡Just. *confut*.50(M.6.1544A); **b.** in Christian thought; in gen. πᾶν σῶμα ὑλικὸν ἔχει φύσιν τῷ ἰδίῳ λόγῳ ἄ. τυγχάνουσαν...καὶ ποιότητας χωροῦσαν, ἃς ἐὰν βούληται αὐτῇ περιτιθέναι ὁ δημιουργός Or.*Jo*.13.21 (p.245.6; M.14.433A); οὐκοῦν εἰ ἄ. ἐτύγχανεν ἡ ὕλη...τῶν ποιοτήτων γέγονεν ποιητὴς ὁ θεός; Meth.*arbitr*.7(p.162.9; M.18.253B); Bas.*hex*. 1.8(1.9A; M.29.21A); ref. function of Logos endowing matter with qualities, Athenag.*leg*.10.2(M.6.909A); in Peratic theory ἡ ὕλη ἄ. οὖσα καὶ ἀσχημάτιστος ἐκτυποῦται τὰς ἰδέας ἀπὸ τοῦ υἱοῦ, ἃς ὁ υἱὸς ἀπὸ τοῦ πατρὸς ἐτυπώσατο Hipp.*haer*.5.17(p.114.21; M.16.3175C); ref. Manich. theory ἔδοξέ μοι συνυπάρχειν τι αὐτῷ ᾧ τοὔνομα ὕλη, ἐξ ἧς τὰ ὄντα ἐδημιούργησε...ἐξ ἧς καὶ τὰ κακὰ εἶναι δοκεῖ. ἀ. γὰρ καὶ ἀσχηματίστου οὔσης αὐτῆς Meth.*arbitr*.3(p.154.3; M.18.248B); ἡ δὲ ὕλη ἄ. ἦν, τῶν δὲ ποιοτήτων ποιητὴν εἶπας τὸν θεὸν εἶναι, ἔσται καὶ τῶν κακῶν δημιουργὸς ὁ θεός *ib*.8(p.165.5; 257A); εἰ δὲ τούτων ἐκτὸς οὖσα ἡ ὕλη, καθ' ἑαυτὴν ἄ. ἐστι καὶ ἀνείδεος, πῶς ποιεῖ τι ἡ ὕλη, ἡ μηδὲ τὸ πάσχειν δύνασθαι καθ' ἑαυτὴν ἔχουσα; Dion.Ar.*d.n*.4.28(M.3. 729A); **c.** of body before being informed by soul ὕλη γάρ ἐστιν ἄ., καὶ οὐ σῶμα Nemes.*nat.hom*.2(M.40.564B); **3.** of God, Gr.Nyss. *beat*.3(M.44.1225B) cit. s. ἀσχημάτιστος; ἀμερὲς γὰρ πάντη τὸ θεῖόν ἐστιν, ὅτι καὶ παντελῶς ἄποσον, ἄποσον δὲ παντελῶς, ὅτι καὶ παντελῶς ἄ., ἄ. δὲ παντελῶς, ὅτι καὶ πάντη ἁπλοῦν Max.*ambig*.(M.91. 1232B); of Trin., Jo.D.*haer*.epilog.(M.94.777B); of Logos, ‡Jo.D. *ep.Thphl*.3(M.95.349B); of H. Ghost, Gr.Naz.*or*.41.9(M.36.441B) cit. s. ἀχώρητος.

ἀποκαθαίρ-ω, **1.** act.; **a.** *remove by purging* ~ουσα τὴν πλάνην ἡ ἐκκλησία Eus.*e.th*.1.8(p.64.14; M.24.837B); Gr.Nyss.*mort*.(M.46. 525A); id.*anim.et res*.(M.46.88A); **b.** *purify from* θειοτέρων οὐσιῶν τὰς ὑφειμένας ἱερὰς καὶ οὐρανίας διακοσμήσεις ἀγνοίας...ἀπάσης ~ουσῶν Dion.Ar.*e.h*.6.3.6(M.3.537B); id.*c.h*.7.3(M.3.209C); simply *purify* ~ει τοὺς ἀτελέστους id.*e.h*.5.1.3(504B); id.*c.h*.13.1(300B); **2.** med., *purify oneself from* τοὺς τῆς ψυχῆς ἀποκεκαθαρμένος σπίλους Clem.*str*.7.13 (p.59.15; M.9.516B); τῶν ~ομένων τὴν φθορὰν τῷ λουτρῷ Meth.*symp*. 8.6(p.88.6; M.18.148A); abs. οὔπω...ἀποκαθηράμενος Cyr.*Ag*.15(3. 644E); **3.** pass.; **a.** *be purified* οἱ...ἄγγελοι...τὴν οὐσίαν ἀποκεκαθαρμένοι Clem.*exc.Thdot*.12(p.110.27; M.9.664A); τὴν ~ομένης ζωῆς εἰς θεωρητικὴν καὶ φωτιστικὴν ἕξιν ἀναγωγήν Dion.Ar.*e.h*.6.3.4(M.3. 536B); *ib*.5.3.8(516B); **b.** *be set apart as pure* ὁ ἄρτος τῆς προθέσεως λέγεται ἤγουν ~όμενος ‡Bas.*h.myst*.28(p.263.21); *ib*.29(p.264.6,7).

ἀποκαθάρισμα, τό, *refuse, leavings*, plur. τὰ ἀ. τῶν λαχάνων Pall.*h.Laus*.32(p.95.1; M.34.1105).

***ἀποκαθαρισμός, ὁ**, *purification*, *Chron.Pasch*.p.40(M.92.153C).

ἀποκάθαρμα, τό, *that which is cleared off, excretion*; of menstrual discharge, Clem.*paed*.2.10(p.212.19,22; M.8.505cf.).

ἀποκάθαρσις, ἡ, **1.** *purification*; **a.** abs., Clem.*str*.7.12(p.54.14; M.9.504B); ῥαντίζει...ἡμᾶς καὶ ἐν τῷ αἵματι αὐτοῦ πρὸς ἀποκάθαρσιν Cyr.*Arcad*.(p.85.1; 5².76E); Dion.Ar.*myst*.1.3(M.3.1000C); **b.** c. genit. τῆς ἑκάστου ἀ. [sc. after death] Clem.*str*.6.14(p.486.31; M.9.332A); τὴν ἀ. τοῦ ἀλόγου μέρους τῆς ψυχῆς *ib*.7.6(p.24.24; 445A); ὁ κύριος διὰ...τὴν τῶν ἀπίστων ἀ. ἔπιεν τὸ ποτήριον *ib*.4.9(p.281.31; M.8. 1284D); **2.** *purgation* ἔοικεν...τὸ μαρτύριον ἀ. εἶναι ἁμαρτιῶν μετὰ δόξης *ib*.(p.281.26; M.8.1284C); τὸ...θεῖον πνεῦμα χρώμενον ὕδατι πρὸς τὴν τῶν ἁμαρτίας ῥύπων ἀ. Didym.(‡Bas.)*Eun*.5(1.308C; M.29. 740A); τὸ θεῖον...δεχόμενοι βάπτισμα ῥαντιζόμεθα τῷ αἵματι Χριστοῦ πρὸς ἀποκάθαρσιν ἁμαρτίας Cyr.*Zach*.106(3.787B); ἀδρανὴς ὁ νόμος πρὸς ἀποκάθαρσιν ἁμαρτίας id.*Ps*.50:8(M.69.1096A); τὴν ἁπάσης ὁμοῦ κακίας δι' ἐναρέτου καὶ θείας ζωῆς ἀ. Dion.Ar.*e.h*.2.3.1(M.3.397B); *ib*.3.3.1(428B).

ἀποκαθεύδω, *be asleep, remain asleep*, Chrys.*hom.89.2 in Mt*.(7. 834B; καθευδῆσαι Gaume); Mac.Mgn.*apocr*.4.11(p.173.7).

ἀποκάθημαι, *be menstruous*, pres. ptcpl., Thdt.*Ezech*.36:17(2. 987); Olymp.*fr.Ep.Jer*.28(M.93.776D).

***ἀποκάθισις, ἡ**, sens. dub., a kind of bodily affliction interpreted ref. spiritual life ἀ. ἐστιν ἀδυναμία λογικῆς ψυχῆς, καθ' ἣν τὰς συντελούσας ἀρετὰς πρὸς τὴν μόρφωσιν τοῦ Χριστοῦ εἴωθεν ἀποβάλλειν Evagr.Pont.*cap*.7(M.40.1265A).

***ἀποκαθίστασις, ἡ**, *putting away*; of elements after eucharist, *Lit.Bas*.(p.352.5); Thdr.Stud.*praesanct*.(M.99.1689C).

ἀποκαθιστάω, late form of sq.; **1.** *restore, give back*, Tat.*orat*.18 (p.20.18,24; M.6.848A); Clem.*fr*.44(p.223.20); Or.*Cels*.2.24(p.154.5; M.11.844C); *restore* to health, hence *heal*, Ath.*Ar*.3.40(M.26.409A); **2.** *put back*, *Chron.Pasch*.p.390(M.92.1001C).

ἀποκαθίστημι, **A.** trans.; **1.** *restore*, a text ὁ δὲ θέλων ἀποκαταστῆσαι τὰ κατὰ τὸν τόπον χωρὶς σολοικίας, σκέψαι εἰ μὴ βιάσεται οὕτως τὴν φράσιν ἀποκαταστάς Or.*comm.in Eph*.3:17–19(p.411); *ib*. 3:1–3(p.408); id.*sel.in Ps*.50(M.12.1453B); **2.** *establish* τὴν ψυχὴν... ἀποκαταστήσειν οὐ νῦν προάγει [sc. Christ] Clem.*exc.Thdot*.61(p.127. 15; M.9.688C); Εὐζώιον...ἐπίσκοπον Ἀντιοχείας ἀ. Philost.*h.e*.5.5(M.

65.532A); **3.** *accompany* πάντων τῶν Χριστιανῶν...ἀποκαταστησάντων αὐτὸν ἕως δύο μιλίων Marc.Diac.*v.Porph.*62.

B. intrans. (pass. and 2nd aor.); **1.** *be restored, return*; **a.** abs. οὐδ' ἀποκατασταθήσονται [sc. the Jews] Or.*Cels.*4.22(p.292.5; M.11.1056C); εἰ δὲ μὴ γέγονεν ἄνθρωπος, καὶ ὁ γενόμενος σὰρξ λόγος ἀναιρεθεὶς ἀποκατέστη, καὶ ἀποκαθίσταται ἕκαστος ἐπὶ τοῦτο ὅπερ ἦν πρὶν γένηται σάρξ id.*Jo.*20.11(p.341.10; M.14.597B); Meth.*res.*1.43 (p.290.15; M.18.272B); ὁ θεῖος ἔρως...ὥσπερ τις ἀΐδιος κύκλος...ἐν ἀπλανεῖ συνελίξει περιπορευόμενος καὶ ἀποκαθιστάμενος Dion.Ar. *d.n.*4.14(M.3.713A); id.*e.h.*3.3.3(M.3.429B); esp. of the sick, *Hom. Clem.*9.18; ἀποκατασταθήσεται ὑγιὴς ὡς ἡ ἄλλη [sc. χείρ] Apoll.ap. *cat.Mt.*12:10(p.91.14); **b.** to a previous position or state ἀποκατέστη ἡ τοῦ Λαζάρου ψυχὴ ἐπὶ τὸ σῶμα αὐτοῦ Or.*Jo.*28.6(p.395.31; M.14.689C); ἀποκατασταθήσονται ἀσεβεῖς τε καὶ δαίμονες εἰς τὴν προτέραν αὐτῶν τάξιν id.*princ.*2.10.8(p.183.4) cf. ἀποκατάστασις; βούλεται ὁ Ὠριγένης τὴν μὲν αὐτὴν σάρκα μὴ ἀποκαθίστασθαι τῇ ψυχῇ Meth.*res.*3.2(p.391.1; M.18.317B); μηδ' ἕτερον μὲν οὖσαν [sc. the divine essence] πρότερον εἶτα ἄλλο τι γιγνομένην καὶ πάλιν εἰς τὸ ἀρχαῖον ἀποκαθισταμένην Eus.*e.th.*2.9(p.109.2; M.24.917A); ἀποκαθιστάμενοι τῇ κοινωνίᾳ *Cod.Afr.*138(H.1.949A); **2.** *be established* εἰς τελειότητα ἀποκαθιστάμενοι Clem.*ecl.*57(p.154.9; M.9.725C); id.*exc. Thdot.*22(p.114.4; M.9.669A).

ἀποκακέω, *give up in despair, become wearied*, Petr.II Al.*encycl.* 6(M.33.1285A)ap.Thdt.*h.e.*4.22.21; Proc.G.*Gen.*12:7(M.87.328C).

ἀποκάλυμμα, τό, *revelation*, Herm.ap.Clem.*str.*1.29(p.111.2; M.8.928A), om. Herm.*vis.*3.4.3.

***ἀποκαλυπτικός, 1.** *revealing, enlightening* λόγος Clem.*paed.*1.1 (p.90.23; M.8.249C); πνεῦμα Gr.Naz.*or.*31.29(p.184.5; M.36.168A); **2.** *capable of receiving revelation* ψυχῆς...ἔτι παιδαγωγικῶς δεομένης ἐπὶ τὴν ἀ. ἕξιν τῶν θείων...ἀναδραμεῖν Max.*qu.Theop.*(M.90.1400D).

ἀποκαλύπτ-ω, 1. *uncover*, med. and pass. τὴν Αἰνείᾳ γυναῖκα... μηδὲ τῆς Τροίας ἁλισκομένης...ἀποκαλύψασθαι Clem.*paed.*2.11(p.280.14; M.8.657B); οὐδὲ αὐτὴ κατανοήσεις ἀποκεκαλυμμένη τῷ σώματι Ath.*virg.*11(p.45.12; M.28.264C); αὐτὴν ἀφ' ἑαυτῆς ἀποκαλυψαμένην τὰ παραπετάσματα Dion.Ar.*e.h.*4.3.2(M.3.476B); met., *open* ὑπὲρ τοῦ ἀποκαλυφθῆναι τοὺς ὀφθαλμοὺς ἡμῶν, ἔτι κεκαλυμμένους ὑπὸ τῆς διὰ τὴν κακίαν ἀτιμίας ἡμῶν Or.*Jo.*20.32(26; p.369.19; M.14.645D); **2.** *reveal*, in gen. ὅρα...μήποτε διχῶς ἔστιν ἰδεῖν 'ἀποκαλυπτόμενον', καθ' ἕνα μὲν τρόπον ὅτε νοεῖται, καθ' ἕτερον δὲ ἐὰν ᾖ τοῦτο προφητευόμενον, ὥστε γενέσθαι καὶ πληρωθῆναι αὐτό· τότε γὰρ ~εται, ὅτε ἐπιτελεῖται πληρούμενον *ib.*6.5(2; p.112.6; 205D); of God ἀπεκάλυψε διὰ τοῦ... παιδὸς καὶ ἐφανέρωσε τὰ ἐξ ἀρχῆς ἡτοιμασμένα *Diogn.*8.11; ἔλεγον [sc. οἱ προφῆται] ταῦτα, ἅπερ αὐτοῖς μόνοις ἦν ὑπὸ θεοῦ ἀποκεκαλυμμένα Hipp.*antichr.*2(p.5.6; M.10.729A); ἵνα θεοῦ ~οντος ἡμῖν τὰ ἑξῆς, θεωρήσωμεν Or.*Jo.*20.44(33; p.388.32; M.14.677D); ὅπερ συνέφερεν ἡμῖν γνῶναι ἀπεκάλυψεν· ὅπερ δὲ οὐκ ἐδυνάμεθα φέρειν ἀπεσιώπησε Jo.D.*f.o.*1.1(M.94.792A); of Christ ἀπεκάλυψεν...ἡμῖν πάντα ὅσα καὶ ἀπὸ τῶν γραφῶν διὰ τῆς χάριτος αὐτοῦ νενοήκαμεν Just.*dial.* 100.2(M.6.709B); ὁ τοῦ θεοῦ λόγος...~ει ὃν ἔγνω πατέρα Or.*Jo.*1.38 (42; p.49.8; 100A); ἔχοντες ἐν ἑαυτοῖς τὸν κύριον ~οντα αὐτοῖς ἐν τῷ πνεύματι ἑαυτόν τε καὶ δι' ἑαυτοῦ τὸν πατέρα Ath.*ep.Serap.*1.32 (M.26.605C); of H. Ghost ~ει...βροτοῖς ἐκείνους [sc. Father and Son] ‡Caes.Naz.*dial.*3(M.38.861); of prophets ὅσα εἶπον καὶ ἐποίησαν οἱ προφῆται...παραβολαῖς καὶ τύποις ἀπεκάλυψαν Just.*dial.*90.2 (M.6.689B); ἐν ἀρχῇ τὸν υἱὸν ἀπεκάλυψεν [sc. Moses] Chrys.*hom. 33.2 in Jo.*(8.192B); Thdt.*1Cor.*12:1(3.240); c. ὅτι: ἐὰν ὁ κύριός μοι ἀποκαλύψῃ ὅτι...πάντες...συνέρχεσθε ἐν μιᾷ πίστει Ign.*Eph.*20.2; abs. ἵνα καὶ ἡμεῖς ~οντος τοῦ υἱοῦ γνῶμεν πῶς πνεῦμά ἐστιν ὁ θεός Or.*Jo.*13.25(p.248.20; M.14.440C); τοῦ εἰς τὸ ~ειν ὡρισμένου υἱοῦ *Hom.Clem.*18.10; Ath.*v.Anton.*34(M.26.893B); med., Clem.*paed.*2.9 (p.206.29; M.8.496A); Dion.Ar.*e.h.*3.3.2(M.3.428C); impers. in pass. ἄχρις ἂν...αὐτοῖς ἀποκαλυφθῇ ἐπανελθεῖν εἰς τὴν χώραν αὐτῶν Just. *dial.*103.3(M.6.717A); ἀπεκαλύφθη δέ μοι...κοιμωμένῃ ὑπὸ νεανίσκου... λέγοντός μοι Herm.*vis.*2.4.1; pass., *have revealed*, c. acc. ἐπιτέτραπται νύττεσθαι τοὺς πρώτους ὑπὸ τῶν ἀποκαλυφθέντων Χριστοῦ τὸ μυστήριον ἐσχάτων ‡Faust.*ep.*(p.8.3; H.2.848C); **3.** *explain* οἷς ἔδει ἀποκαλυφθῆναι τὰ ὁράματα Herm.*vis.*3.4.3; Just.*dial.*94.4(M.6.701A); Chrys.*hom.25.1 in Jo.*(8.143C); abs., Herm.*vis.*3.10.2.

ἀποκάλυψις, ἡ, 1. *uncovering, laying bare*; of ground after flood, Clem.*str.*5.14(p.393.5; M.9.152A); σῶμα ἐν ἀσχήμῳ ἀ. *Const.App.* 1.6.13; met. ἡ τῶν χειρόνων ἀποβολὴ τῶν κρειττόνων ἐστὶν ἀ. Clem. *paed.*1.6(p.107.32; M.8.285B); *T.Abr.*A 6(p.83.27); τῆς συσκευῆς τὴν ἀ. Pall.*v.Chrys.*1(p.7.26; M.47.8); **2.** *explanation*, Herm.*vis.*3.10.9; **3.** *vision* κατὰ ἀποκάλυψιν φανερώσαντός μοι τοῦ μακαρίου Πολυκάρπου *M.Polyc.*22.3; ἀ. πέμπτη Herm.*vis.*5 tit.; δι' ἀποκαλύψεως τῆς γεγενημένης Ἰησοῦ τῷ τοῦ Ναυῆ [ref. Jos.5:13ff.] Just.*dial.*62.4 (M.6.620A); of S. John ἐν ἀ. γενομένῃ αὐτῷ *ib.*81.4(669A); τοῦ...τὴν ἀ. ἑωρακότος...πρὸς τῷ τέλει τῆς Δομετιανοῦ ἀρχῆς Iren.*haer.*5.30.3 (M.7.1207B); of S. Peter, ref. Ac.10:15 τοῦ Πέτρου τὴν ἀ. ἰδόντος *ib.* 3.12.7(M.7.900A); Juln.ap.Cyr.*Juln.*9(6^{2}.314D); of S. Paul, ref. 2Cor. 12:23 δύο ἀ. ... ἑωρακέναι μηνύει Meth.*res.*1.55(p.314.2; M.18.296A); **4.** *revelation*; **a.** in gen. κατὰ θείαν ἀ. ἐξῆλθεν ὁ Ἰωάννης ἔν τινι κώμῃ *A.Jo.*48(p.175.24); τοὺς ἀποστόλους, ὡς ἐν καιρῷ ἀποκαλύψεως γενομένους, εἰπεῖν ἄν· 'στήκετε καὶ κρατεῖτε τὰς παραδόσεις' Or.*Jo.* 13.48(46; p.275.2; M.14.485A); ref. 1Cor.14:6 ἀ. ἐστιν ὅταν ὁ νοῦς ἔξω γίν⟨η⟩ται τῶν γηινῶν καὶ ἀποθ⟨ῆ⟩ται πᾶσαν πρᾶξιν σαρκικὴν δυνάμει θεοῦ· ὁ τούτου τυχὼν γέγονεν ἐν ἀ. id.*comm.in 1Cor.*14:16 (*JTS* 10 p.36); ἀ. ἐστι τὸ ἐν πάσαις καρδίαις ἀνθρώπων ἀπορρήτως κείμενον κεκαλυμμένον, ἄνευ φωνῆς τῇ αὐτοῦ βουλῇ ἀποκαλυπτόμενον *Hom.Clem.*18.6; ἀ. ... ἐστιν ἡ τῶν κρυπτῶν μυστηρίων δήλωσις, καταυγαζομένου τοῦ ἡγεμονικοῦ, εἴτε διὰ θείων ὀνειράτων εἴτε καθ' ὕπαρ ἐκ θείας ἐλλάμψεως Andr.Caes.*Apoc.*1(M.106.220D); ref. Mt. 16:16 εἰ γὰρ ὁ πατὴρ ἀπεκάλυψε τῷ Πέτρῳ περὶ ὧν ὁ κύριος ἐπυνθάνετο, δῆλόν ἐστι, ὅτι διὰ τοῦ υἱοῦ γέγονεν ἡ ἀ. Ath.*Ar.*3.46(M.26.421A); Πέτρου εἰπόντος κατὰ ἀ. καὶ γνῶσιν καὶ ὁμολογίαν Thal.CP *Thds.*(p.7.15; M.91.1472B); with subjective genit. τὴν γνῶσιν αὐτοῦ [sc. S. Peter] ⟨δι'⟩ ἀποκαλύψεως τοῦ πατρὸς γεγονέναι Eus.*e.th.*1.16 (p.75.28; M.24.856C); διὰ τῆς ἀ. τοῦ πνεύματος φανερὰ τὰ τῆς καρδίας κρυπτὰ γίνεται Thdt.*Trin.*26(M.75.1185C); Cosm.Ind.*top.*arg.(M.88.56B); with objective genit. τὴν ἀ. τῶν τοῖς λοιποῖς ἀπορρήτων Bas. *fid.*2(2.226B; M.31.681C); ὁ Χριστός, ὁ τὴν οὕτως ἀπόρρητον ἀπλανῆ καὶ θείαν ἀ. τῶν ἑαυτοῦ μυστηρίων ἐναστράπτων ἑαυτῷ Cyr.*inc.unigen.* (5^{1}.699D); ἐν τῷ καιρῷ τῆς τῶν μελλόντων [ἀπορρήτων] ἀγαθῶν ἀ. ‡Bas.*h.myst.*55(p.392.6); **b.** exeg. Rom.8:19 'τὴν ἀ.,' οἷον τὴν κεκρυμμένην αὐτῶν μακαριότητα μικρὸν ὕστερον ἀποκαλυφθησομένην Diod.*Rom.*8:19(p.13.29); 'τὴν' γὰρ 'ἀ. τῶν υἱῶν τοῦ θεοῦ' λέγει τὴν ἀνάστασιν Thdr.Mops.*Rom.*8:19(p.138.32; M.66.825D); **5.** as title of book, *Apocalypse, Revelation*; **a.** NT, Hipp.*haer.*7.36(p.223.10; M.16.3343B); Or.*Jo.*2.8(4; p.63.5; M.14.124B); ἡ ἀ. φησιν Clem. *paed.*2.10(p.222.7; M.8.525C); written by S. John the evangelist, Or.*Jo.*5.3(p.101.30; M.14.189A); perh. written by John the elder, Eus.*h.e.*3.39.6(M.20.297B); perh. written by Cerinthus, Dion.Al.*ib.* 7.25.2(697A); canonicity doubted, Eus.*ib.*3.24.18(268C); Amph. *Seleuc.*316(M.37.1597A); included in list of canonical books, Ath. *ep.fest.*9(M.26.1437B); Epiph.*haer.*76.22(p.369.24; M.42.561A); Jo.D. *f.o.*4.17(M.94.1180C); omitted from such lists, *Can.App.*85; CLaod. *can.*60; Cyr.H.*catech.*4.36; Gr.Naz.*carm.*1.1.12.39(M.37.474A); †Chrys. *synops.*(6.318A); **b.** apocryphal Πέτρος ἐν τῇ ἀ. φησί Clem.*ecl.*41 (p.149.4; M.9.717C); Πέτρου...εὐαγγέλιον...καὶ τὴν καλουμένην ἀ. οὐδ' ὅλως ἐν καθολικοῖς ἴσμεν παραδεδομένα Eus.*h.e.*3.3.2(M.20.217A); τὴν καλουμένην ἀ. Πέτρου, ὡς νόθον παντελῶς πρὸς τῶν ἀρχαίων δοκιμασθεῖσαν, ἔν τισιν ἐκκλησίαις εἰσέτι νῦν ἅπαξ ἑκάστου ἔτους ἀναγινωσκομένην ἔγνωμεν, ἐν τῇ ἡμέρᾳ παρασκευῆς Soz.*h.e.*7.19.9(M. 67.1477B); τὴν δὲ νῦν ὡς ἀ. Παύλου τοῦ ἀποστόλου φερομένην, ἣν οὐδεὶς ἀρχαίων εἶδε, πλεῖστοι μοναχῶν ἐπαινοῦσιν, ἐπὶ ταύτης δὲ τῆς βασιλείας ἰσχυρίζονταί τινες ταύτην ηὑρῆσθαι τὴν βίβλον *ib.*7.19.10(M. 67.1477C); ἄλλην [sc. βίβλον]...ἐξ ὀνόματος Ἀβραάμ, ἣν καὶ ἀ. φάσκουσιν [sc. Sethians] εἶναι, πάσης κακίας ἔμπλεον· ἑτέρας δὲ ἐξ ὀνόματος τοῦ Μωυσέως, καὶ ἄλλας ἄλλων Epiph.*haer.*39.5(p.75.12; M.41.669D); ἀποκαλύψεις...τοῦ Ἀδάμ *ib.*26.8(p.284.13; M.41.341D); αἱ γραφαὶ αἱ ψευδεῖς αἱ καλούμεναι ἀ., αἱ ἐκτεθεῖσαι ὑπὸ τῶν αἱρεσιαρχῶν τῶν πεφθαρμένων αἱρέσεων ἐν τῇ φαντασίᾳ τῶν δαιμόνων Philox.*ep.*36 (p.183).

ἀποκάμπτω, error for ἀποκαλύπτω, Thdt.*qu.1 in 2Par.*(1.594).

ἀποκαραδοκ-έω, *earnestly expect*; *despair*, of despair of angels over man's Fall, dispelled by 'revelation' of men as 'sons of God' καραδοκεῖν λέγεται τὸ ἐλπίζειν, ~εῖν δὲ τὸ ἀπελπίζειν Thdr. Mops.*Rom.*8:19(p.137.9; M.66.824B).

ἀποκαραδοκία, ἡ, *earnest expectation* ἀ. γὰρ ἡ σφόδρα προσδοκία ἐστίν Chrys.*hom.14.4 in Rom.*(9.581D).

***ἀποκαρπεύομαι**, *gather fruits*, of Adam ἐν τῷ παραδείσῳ...ἀ. Meth.*symp.*8.3(p.84.12; M.18.141C); *ib.*proem.(p.5.2, v.l. καρπεύεσθαι 32A); *ib.*8.3(p.84.21; 144A).

ἀποκαρπίζω, med., *reap the fruits of, enjoy*; met., c. genit., Clem.*paed.*1.5(p.97.21; M.8.264B).

ἀποκαρπόω, med., *enjoy, indulge in*, Epiph.*haer.*26.15(p.295.8; M.41.356C); *ib.*69.17(p.167.10; M.42.228D).

***ἀπόκαρσις, ἡ,** *cutting, shaving*, of the hair, exeg. Lev.19:27 οἶμαι τὴν ἀ. τὸν νόμον ἀπαγορεύειν ‡Ath.*qu.script.*28(M.28.720A); ἡ... τῶν τριχῶν ἀ. ἐμφαίνει τὴν καθαρὰν...ζωήν Dion.Ar.*e.h.*6.3.3(M.3.536A); Proc.G.*Num.*30:3(M.87.880A).

ἀποκαρτερέω, 1. *persevere in abstaining, starve oneself*, Tat.*orat.*2

(p.3.3; M.6.808A); Pall.*h.Laus.*69(p.164.26; M.34.1241A); **2.** *stop persevering, give up,* Areth.*Apoc.*3(M.106.528B,C).

ἀποκαρτέρησις, ἡ, **1.** *abstinence,* cf. *apocarteresei probes te Marcionistam, id est repudiatorem Creatoris,* Tert.*Marc.*1.11(M.*PL.*2¹.262B); **2.** *suicide by starvation ἀποκαρτέρησιν optavit* [sc. Lycurgus], id.*apol.*46(M.*PL.*1.512A).

***ἀποκαταλείπω,** *discard, drop,* Epiph.*ep.Arab.*(p.456.15; M.42.708A).

ἀποκαταλλάσσ-ω, *reconcile completely,* of Atonement *ἐν...τῷ δευτέρῳ Ἀδὰμ ἀποκατηλλάγημεν* Iren.*haer.*5.16.2(M.7.1168C); *ἀ. ἡμᾶς πρὸς τὸν πατέρα cat.Lc.*2:14(p.20.24); *ἐν αὐτῷ τὰ πάντα ~οντος* †Bas.*Is.*250(1.570B; M.30.560A); *~οντος ἡμᾶς ἑαυτῷ καὶ ἐν ἑαυτῷ τῷ πατρί* Dion.Ar.*d.n.*11.5(M.3.953B).

ἀποκατάστασις, ἡ, **A.** *return*; **1.** in gen., Clem.*str.*1.21(p.77.27; M.8.853A); *τὴν ἀ. τοῦ λαοῦ ἀπὸ τῆς αἰχμαλωσίας* Or.*Jo.*10.42(26; p.219.29; M.14.389A); id.*princ.*3.1.19(p.233.1; M.11.292A); *Schol.*27 in Max.*qu.Thal.*(M.90.533C); **2.** of Christ to heaven, Eus.*h.e.*1.2.23 (M.20.65B); id.*d.e.*4.16(p.191.31; M.22.320B); Gr.Naz.*or.*41.11(M.36.444B); *τὴν ἀνάληψιν...καὶ εἰς οὐρανοὺς ἀ. Lit.Jac.*(*NBP* 10².p.39); **3.** astron. *φωστήρων...ἀπὸ τῶν αὐτῶν εἰς τὰ αὐτὰ περιοδικῆς ἀ.* Dion.Ar.*d.n.*4.4(M.3.697B); *ib.*8.5(892D); Max.*ambig.*(M.91.1176C).

B. *restoration, restitution, re-instatement*; **1.** in gen. *εἰς ἀ. ἀμφοτέρων τε καὶ τῶν ἐλευθέρων τέκνων καὶ τῶν ἐν αὐτοῖς δούλων Χριστὸς ἐλήλυθε* Just.*dial.*134.4(M.6.788A); Clem.*str.*3.9(p.225.27; M.8.1168A); *τὴν ἀ. τῆς ὁράσεως* Or.*princ.*3.1.15(p.223.6; M.11.280C); Chrys.*hom.37.3 in Gen.*(4.378A); *τῆς ἀ.... τῶν...εἰκόνων* Hadr.Papa *ep.Const.*(M.*PL.*96.1222D); **2.** ref. Ac.3:21 *ἐν τῇ ἀ. πάντων ὀψόμεθα οὐχ ὡς νῦν ὃ οὐκ ἔστιν, ἀλλ' ὡς πρέπει τότε, ὅ ἐστι* Or.*fr.in Lc.*14:19–20(M.17.364D); *ἐν τῇ λεγομένῃ ἀ.* id.*Jo.*1.16(p.20.12; M.14.49C); *εἰ τοίνυν ἐν τῷ καιρῷ τῆς ἀ. ἁπάντων καὶ αὐτὴν τὴν κτίσιν ἐκ τῆς δουλείας εἰς τὴν ἐλευθερίαν μεταβληθήσεσθαι ὁ Παῦλος ἔφη...πῶς ἔτι τὴν τοῦ δούλου μορφήν...συνεῖναι τῷ λόγῳ [δι' αὐτὴν] γένοιτ' ἂν δυνατόν;* Marcell.*fr.*104 ap.Eus.*Marcell.*2.4(p.54.21; M.24.816B); *'ἄχρι χρόνων ἀποκαταστάσεως'...ἡγητέον ὡς ὁ Χριστὸς...ἐλευσόμενος... ἀποκαταστάντων πάντων λοιπόν, ὧν προεθέσπιζον οἱ προφῆται* Didym.*Ac.*3:21(M.39.166B); *εἰ νῦν οἱ ἀπόστολοι καὶ οἱ μάρτυρες θαυματουργοῦσι καὶ ἐν τοσαύτῃ τιμῇ ὑπάρχουσιν, ἐν τῇ ἀ. εἰ μὴ ἴσοι γένοιντο τῷ Χριστῷ ποία ἀ. αὐτοῖς ἔστιν;* Theodorus Askidas ap.CCP(553)*act.*8 (p.189.25; M.86.2780A); *ἐν τῇ ἀ. ὅτε οἱ θεῷ φίλοι ἁρπαγήσονται...εἰς ἀπάντησιν τοῦ κυρίου εἰς ἀέρα cat.Apoc.*12:6(p.357.18); Gnost., Hipp.*haer.*6.42(p.175.4; M.16.3263A); *ib.*7.27(p.206.19; 3318C); **3.** in theory of Or. (cf. *ἀποκαθίστημι*) and his followers *περὶ δὲ τῆς ἀ. οὕτω δοξάζει* [sc. Or.]*...κολαζομένου...τοῦ σώματος κατὰ μικρὸν καθαίρεται ἡ ψυχή, καὶ οὕτως ἀποκαθίσταται εἰς τὴν ἀρχαίαν τάξιν. καὶ τοὺς δαίμονας δὲ καὶ ἀγγέλους λέγει ἀποκαθίστασθαι* †Leont.B.*sect.*10.6 (M.86.1265C); *ἐνέπεσα εἰς τὰ βιβλία τοῦ 'Ωριγένους καὶ Διδύμου καὶ εἰς τὰ γνωστικὰ Εὐαγρίου, καὶ τὰ τῶν μαθημάτων αὐτοῦ. καὶ λέγουσιν ὅτι...ἔχουσιν οἱ ἄνθρωποι καὶ οἱ ἄγγελοι καὶ οἱ δαίμονες ἐπανελθεῖν ἧς* [l. *ὡς*] *ὑπῆρχον νόες γυμνοί, ὃ λέγουσιν ἀποκατάστασιν* Bars.*resp.*(M.86.892B); *τὴν παρ' αὐτοῖς* [sc. *τοῖς τὰ 'Ωριγένους φρονοῦσιν*] *μυθευομένην τῶν νοῶν προϋπαρξιν καὶ ταύτῃ ἑπομένην τερατώδη ἀ.* Cyr.S.*v.Euthym.*26(p.39.30); *πάντων δὲ τῶν λογικῶν, ἀγγέλων, ἀνθρώπων, δαιμόνων ἀποκατάστασιν φάσκοντες* [sc. *'Ωριγένης...Δίδυμος, καὶ Εὔαγριος καὶ ὁ λοιπὸς αὐτῶν...ὅμιλος*] Sophr.H.*ep.syn.*(M.87.3184A); Anast.S.*hod.*22(M.89.289D); this theory refuted from scripture, Bars.*resp.*(M.86.893B); Justn.*Or.*(p.207.21; M.86.979B); and condemned *εἴ τις λέγει...ὅτι ἐν τῇ μυθευομένῃ ἀ. ἔσονται μόνοι γυμνοί* [sc. *οἱ λογικοί*] *...ἀ. ἔ.* CCP(543)*anath.*14(Hahn p.229; H.3.288A); *εἴ τις λέγει...ἀ. ἔσεσθαι δαιμόνων ἢ ἀσεβῶν ἀνθρώπων, ἀ. ἔ.* Justn.*Or.*anath.9(p.214.5; M.86.989C); **4.** to a former position; **a.** of things *ἀ. τῆς...τελείας εὐγενείας...εἰς τὸ πλήρωμα τοῦ θεοῦ* Clem.*str.*4.21(p.307.7; M.8.1344B); *ἀ. τῶν συγκεχυμένων εἰς τὰ οἰκεῖα* Hipp.*haer.*7.27(p.207.29; M.16.3319C); *τῆς ἀληθινῆς εὐσεβείας ἀ. πρὸς τὸν θεόν* Or.*Cels.*7.3(p.155.11; M.11.1424C); *ἡ τῆς θείας εἰκόνος εἰς τὸ ἀρχαῖον ἀ.* Gr.Nyss.*virg.*12(p.302.6; M.46.373C); **b.** of persons, c. dat. *τῇ θεωρίᾳ τῇ ἀϊδίῳ ἀποκατάστασις* Clem.*str.*7.10(p.41.23; M.9.480B); Heracleon ap.Or.*Jo.*13.46(p.272.7; M.14.480C); **c.** prep. *εἰς τὴν τελείαν υἱοθεσίαν διὰ τοῦ υἱοῦ ἀ.* Clem.*str.*2.22(p.187.8; M.8.1084A); *οὐδεὶς ἀποκαθίσταται εἴς τινα τόπον μηδαμῶς ποτε γενόμενος ἐκεῖ, ἀλλ' ἡ ἀ. ἐστιν εἰς τὰ οἰκεῖα* Or.*hom.14.18 in Jer.*(p.124.21; M.13.428B); Meth.*symp.*4.2(p.46.10; M.18.88B); †Bas.*Is.*59(1.423A; M.30.224A); Gr.Naz.*or.*40.8(M.36.368C); *ἡ εἰς τὸ ἀρχαῖον ἀ. τῶν νῦν ἐν κακίᾳ κειμένων* Gr.Nyss.*or.catech.*26 (p.100.7; M.45.69B); id.*Eun.*3(2 p.18.23; M.45.584A); *ἡ τῆς ἀναστάσεως χάρις οὐδὲν ἕτερον ἡμῖν ἐπαγγέλλεται ἢ τὴν εἰς τὸ ἀρχαῖον τῶν πεπτωκότων ἀ.* id.*hom.opif.*17.2(M.44.188C); *τὸ γὰρ ὅμοιον ἐκείνοις* [sc. *τοῖς ἀγγέλοις*] *τὸν ἄνθρωπον εἶναι πρὸ τῆς παραβάσεως, δείκνυσι ἡ εἰς ἐκεῖνο πάλιν ἀ. ib.*17.3(189B); Mac.Aeg.*libert.ment.*34(M.34.965D); *τρεῖς ἀ. οἶδεν ἡ ἐκκλησία. μίαν μέν, τῆς ἑκάστου κατὰ τὸν τῆς ἀρετῆς λόγον.... δευτέραν δέ, τὴν τῆς ὅλης φύσεως ἐν τῇ ἀναστάσει. τρίτην δέ, ᾗ καὶ μάλιστα κατακέχρηται ἐν τοῖς ἑαυτοῦ λόγοις ὁ Νύσσης Γρηγόριος, ἔστιν αὕτη, ἡ τῶν ψυχικῶν δυνάμεων τῇ ἁμαρτίᾳ ὑποπεσουσῶν, εἰς ὅπερ ἐκτίσθησαν πάλιν ἀ.* Max.*qu.dub.*13(M.90.796A,B).

C. *revolution,* astron. *ἥλιον...ἐν δεκαδύο μησὶ περιερχόμενον καὶ τερματίζοντα τὴν κυκλικὴν αὐτοῦ ἀ.* Iren.*haer.*1.17.1(M.7.640A); Hipp.*haer.*1.27(p.206.24; M.16.3319D); *τῶν ὡρῶν τὴν ἀ.* Melet.*nat.hom.*30 (M.64.1277C); *ἡ ἀρχὴ τῆς ἀ. ἤγουν περιόδου τῶν φλβ' ἐνιαυτῶν Chron. Pasch.*p.374(M.92.953C); fig. *οἱ ἐν τῇ ἄκρᾳ ἀποκαταστάσει πρωτόκτιστοι* Clem.*ecl.*57(p.153.25; M.9.725B).

D. *development σώματος...αὔξησις, ἡ ἀπὸ μικροῦ εἰς τὸ καθῆκον μέτρον ἀ.* ‡Bas.*struct.hom.*2.2(1.338E; M.30.41D).

E. *fulfilment τὴν ἐπὶ τῇ πίστει τῆς ἐπαγγελίας ἀ.* Clem.*str.*2.22 (p.188.22; M.8.1085B); *ἡ...τῆς ἐλπίδος ἀ. ὁμωνύμως ἐλπὶς εἴρηται ib.*(p.188.13; 1085A); *ib.*(p.187.16; 1084A).

ἀποκαταστατικός, **1.** *recurrent δέκα δὲ μονάδες μίαν ἀποφαίνουσι δεκάδα· δεκὰς δὲ πέρας μονάδων, ὅρος καὶ καμπτὴρ ἀ⟨πο⟩καταστατικός* Eus.*l.C.*6(p.210.32; codd. *ἀκαταστ-, καταστ-*; M.20.1348D *καταστ-*); of planets, *Clem.recogn.suppl.*5(p.211.10; M.1.1472D); *τὰς πίστεις ἀ. εἶναι περιόδοις ἀστέρων* Synes.*provid.*7(p.128.18; M.66.1277B); **2.** *bringing back* to a point *τὴν κατὰ φύσιν ὀκτωκαιεικοσαετηρίδα τοῦ ἡλίου, ἥτις...ἀ. τυγχάνουσα ἡμέρας μηνὸς ἡλιακοῦ καὶ ἡμέρας ἑβδομάδος καὶ ἔτους τετραετηρίδος βισσέξτου Chron.Pasch.*p.12(M.92.89C); **3.** *capable of restoring σοφίας...ἀ.* Clem.*str.*2.8(p.132.5; M.8.972B).

ἀποκάτωθεν, prep. c. genit., *from the bottom* of, Cosm.Ind.*top.*4 (M.88.188D).

ἀποκείρ-ω, *cut, clip off*; properly the hair, hence **1.** act. in med. sense, *have* the hair *cut,* Chrys.*hom.4.8 in Mt.*(7.61C); **2.** *tonsure σφραγισάμενος αὐτὸν* [sc. monk] *ὁ ἱερεὺς ~ει* Dion.Ar.*e.h.*6.2(M.3.533B); *εἴ τις φωραθῇ ~ων τινὰ...καθαιρείσθω· ὁ δὲ ἀποκαρεὶς...μοναστηρίῳ διδόσθω* Sophr.H.*conf.*(M.87.3369B); Jo.Clim.*scal.*4(M.88.684B); **3.** met., *cut off, eradicate τὸ φιλόδοξον πάθος ἀ.* Cyr.*Lc.*9:46 (M.72.660C); *ib.*6:37(600A); Zach.Mit.*opif.*(M.85.1085B).

***ἀποκεκληρωμένως,** *specifically,* exeg. 1Cor.1:26 *οὐ γὰρ ἀ. τοὺς ἰδιώτας ἐκάλει καὶ τοὺς σοφοὺς ἠφίει* Chrys.*hom.5.1 in 1Cor.*(10.34A).

***ἀποκεκομμένως,** *summarily, briefly,* Cyr.*Jo.*4.5(4.414B).

ἀποκεκρυμμένως, **1.** *with hidden meaning,* ref. Zach.2:10 *Ζαχαρίᾳ ...ἀ. κηρύσσοντι* Just.*dial.*115.1(M.6.741A); **2.** *covertly κἂν ἀ. υἱὸν βούλεται* [sc. Aët.] *λέγειν τὸν μονογενῆ* Epiph.*haer.*76.28(p.377.5; M.42.573B).

ἀποκέλλω, *get out of course, swerve aside εἰς ἑτεροδόξους διδασκαλίας ἀ.* Eus.*h.e.*6.12.2(M.20.545A).

ἀπόκενος, **1.** *empty,* Herm.*mand.*12.5.2; *Apoc.Bar.*15(pp.93.33, 94.1); met. *ἀποπλανᾷ* [sc. *ὀξυχολία*]*...τοὺς ἀ. καὶ διψύχους ὄντας* Herm.*mand.*5.2.1; *ib.*12.5.2,4; **2.** *barren ὥσπερ ὁ γεωργὸς ἐν τῷ ἀ. χώρᾳ λυπεῖται, οὕτως καὶ ὁ κύριος ἐν τῇ ἀ. καρδίᾳ καὶ μὴ καρποφορούσῃ λυπεῖται* Mac.Aeg.*hom.*32.11(M.34.741A).

ἀποκεν-όω, **1.** *make empty, drain*; of a sucking child, Mac.Aeg.*hom.*12.12(M.34.564C); pass. *ἡ ὑστέρα...~οῦται καθαιρομένη κυήσει* Clem.*paed.*2.10(p.213.4; M.8.508A); **2.** *hollow θάνατος...~οῖ...ὀφθαλμούς* Cyr.*Zach.*108(3.806E; Aubert *ἀποκείρει*); **3.** *drain off ἐμέτοις ~ῶσαι τὴν νοσοποιὸν ὕλην* Bas.*hom.in Ps.*51(1.196E; M.29.477B); pass., Bas.Sel.*v.Thecl.*2.8(M.85.577C).

***ἀποκεραμ-έω,** sens. dub., ?for *ἀποκαρατομέω*: *τοῦ ἀνθρώπου αὐτὸν* [sc. *ὄφιν*] *~ῆσαι ἰχνεύοντος* ‡Epiph.*phys.*15(M.43.528D).

ἀποκερδαίνω, **1.** *gain, enjoy the benefits of ἀναριθμήτων ἐγκλημάτων ἀ. τὴν ἄφεσιν* Cyr.*Is.*3.2(2.406B); *τῆς διὰ Χριστοῦ σωτηρίας ἀ. τὴν χάριν ib.*(410E); id.*ador.*6(1.215C); **2.** *avoid, escape ὧν* [sc. torments of hell] *ἵνα τὴν πεῖραν ἀποκερδάνωσιν* id.*Jo.*5.3(4.499E).

***ἀποκηρυκεύ-ομαι,** *negotiate to bring to an end ~εται πρὸς 'Ορμίσδαν τὸν πόλεμον* Thphyl.*exc.Rom.*4(p.223.29; M.113.932A).

***ἀποκηρυκτέος,** *to be banished from,* c. genit., Gr.Naz.*or.*4.11 (M.35.541A).

ἀποκήρυκτος, **1.** *disinherited from ἀποκηρύκτους* [sc. sinners] *εἶναι τῆς βασιλείας τοῦ θεοῦ* Clem.*str.*3.18(p.246.31; M.8.1212C); Gr.Nyss.*res.*1(M.46.628A); abs. *οὐκέτι* [i.e. since Inc.] *ἐν ἀποκηρύκτοις ὁ ἄνθρωπος* id.*Eun.*12(2 p.279.7; M.45.889C); **2.** *disowned* by Church, *excommunicated,* Gr.Naz.*ep.*102(M.37.200A); Isid.Pel.*epp.*2.127(M.78.572A); Gennad.*encycl.*(p.81.3; M.85.1617B).

ἀποκήρυξις, ἡ, **1.** *expulsion from τὴν ἀ. τῆς...οἰκίας* Philost.*h.e.*3.15(M.65.505A); **2.** *rejection* of sinner by God, Chrys.*hom.20.1 in Heb.*(12.186C); **3.** *excommunication,* Synes.*ep.*72(M.66.1436B); Socr.*h.e.*1.6.40(M.67.53B).

ἀποκηρύσσ-ω, **1.** *renounce publicly, reject* ~ων [sc. God]...αὐτὸν ἐν τῇ μοσχοποιΐᾳ Or.*Jo*.10.14(11; p.184.25; M.14.329C); θεὸς αὐτοὺς [sc. Jews] ἀποκηρῦξαι ἐβούλετο Chrys.*hom.4.3 in Col*.(11.355A); **2.** *denounce publicly, condemn* γράμματα...τὴν ἐκκλησίαν ~οντα CAlex. *ep*.ap.Ath.*apol.sec*.19(p.101.18; M.25.280A); οὓς λόγῳ μὲν ἀ. ... ἔργῳ δὲ προήγαγον Gr.Naz.*or*.21.23(M.35.1108B); ἀ. πορνείαν καὶ μοιχείαν Epiph.*exp.fid*.24(p.525.7; M.42.829D); ἀ. τὴν...αἵρεσιν Thdt.*ep*.140 (4.1235); ἀ. τὸ ἑτεροούσιον Philost.*h.e*.4.11(M.65.524C); **3.** *cut off publicly*; **a.** *outlaw* τοὺς πανταχοῦ διεσπαρμένους ἀ. Chrys.*hom.76.1 in Mt*.(7.733C); esp. from Church ἀπεκηρύχθησαν καὶ ἀνεθεματίσθησαν ἀπὸ τῆς ἐκκλησίας Alex.Al.*depos*.6(p.9.26; M.18.577A); τὸν δὲ... ἀπὸ τῆς ἐκκλησίας καὶ τῆς ζωῆς ~ει Epiph.*haer*.59.4(p.369.1; M.41. 1025A); **b.** *cut off from* τοῦ...τῶν ἀνθρώπων αὐτὴν [sc. τυχὴν] ~ων βίου Dion.Al.ap.Eus.*p.e*.14.27(782A; M.21.1285C); τὰς ψυχὰς αὐτῶν ἑκόντες τοῦ ἁγίου πνεύματος ἀ. Const.*or.s.c*.17(p.177.12; M.20.1281B); esp. *cut off from* religious gatherings or privileges Βίκτωρ Θεόδοτον ...ἀπεκήρυξεν τῆς κοινωνίας †Hipp.*Artem*.ap.Eus.*h.e*.5.28.6(M.20. 513A); Παύλου τοῦ Σαμοσατέως...ἀποκηρυχθέντος τῆς ἐκκλησίας Alex.Al.*ep.Alex*.9(p.25.12; M.18.561A); τοὺς δὲ παρὰ ταῦτα φρονεῖν αἱρουμένους ~ομεν τῆς ἁγίας συνόδου...καὶ τοῦ πληρώματος τῆς ἐκκλησίας Flav.CP ap.CCP(448)*act*.2(*ACO* 2.1.1 p.114.11; H.2.128E); **c.** *excommunicate* αὐτὸν ἀνεθεματίσατε καὶ ἀπεκηρύξατε Ath.*ep. encycl*.6(p.175.12; M.25.236A); μετὰ τὸ ἀποκηρῦξαι Pall.*v.Chrys*.7 (p.38.16; M.47.23); ἐπανάγειν...εἰς τὴν ἐκκλησίαν τοὺς ἀποκηρυχθέντας Socr.*h.e*.1.6.40(M.67.53B); med. τὸν Ἄρειον ἀποκηρύξασθαι Philost. *h.e*.1.7(M.65.464C); *ib*.2.7(469C).

ἀποκινδυνεύ-ω, *venture*, c. ptcpl. οὐκ ~ομεν περὶ τοῦ ὀνόματος τοῦ ἀντιχρίστου ἀποφαινόμενοι βεβαιωτικῶς Iren.*haer*.5.30.3(M.7. 1207A).

ἀποκιν-έω, **1.** *remove* clergy *from* office τοῦ βαθμοῦ αὐτὸν [sc. a bishop] ~ήσωσι CSard.*can*.5; τοῦ ἐκκλησιαστικοῦ ~ηθῶσι καθήκοντος *Cod.Afr*.25; Socr.*h.e*.6.15.7(M.67.709A); Evagr.*h.e*.3.21(p.119. 16; M.86.2640B); **2.** *remove* Φαυστίνου...ἐκ τῆς...ἐκκλησίας ~ηθέντος *Cod.Afr*.138(H.1.949D); **3.** *depose* ἐπισκόπων...~ηθέντων...παρὰ Εὐσταθίου CChalc.*act.Caros*.(*ACO* 2.1.3 p.108.19; H.2.441E).

***ἀποκίνησις**, ἡ, *moving, removal*, Eus.*qu.Marin.suppl*.1.1(M.22. 985B); Sev.Ant.*res*.(p.836.3; M.46.644A).

***ἀπόκλαυσις**, ἡ, *wailing, lamentation*, Or.*sel.in Pss*.proem.(M.12. 1072D).

ἀποκλ-άω, pass., *be broken off from* τῆς πατρικῆς διαθέσεως ~ώμενος [sc. Absalom] Chrys.*exp.in Ps*.3:1(5.5A).

ἀπόκλεισις, ἡ, **1.** *shutting, closing* τῆς τῶν θυρῶν ἀ. Chrys.*hom. 19.3 in Mt*.(7.247D); **2.** *shutting up* τὴν ἀ. τοῦ προφήτου τὴν ἐν τῷ κήτει id.*hom.5.4 in Col*.(11.363D); **3.** *shutting out* οὐ γέγονε... τὸ σάββατον εἰς ἀ., ἀλλ' εἰς ἔργον ἀγαθόν Epiph.*haer*.66.85(p.127. 18; M.42.165A); **4.** met., *parsimony*, Pall.*v.Chrys*.13(p.79.9; M.47. 45).

ἀποκλεισμός, ὁ, *exclusion* τὸν ἀ. αὐτῆς [sc. θεωρίας] ἐντὸς σιωπῆς Philox.*ep*.36(p.184).

***ἀποκλειστέον**, *one must shut*, Eus.*p.e*.6.6(252D; M.21.429B).

ἀποκλεί-ω, **1.** *shut off from* τὴν ἀκοὴν...ἀ. τοῦ ἀκούειν Ath.*gent*. 32(M.25.64D); pass., *be excluded from* οὐκ ~εται ἡ λογικὴ φύσις τῆς θεραπείας Or.*princ*.3.1.13(p.218.12; M.11.275B); Eus.*h.e*.4.7.2(M.20. 316B); δείκνυται ὁ Ἑζεκίας ~όμενος τῶν χρόνων τῆς προφητείας id. *d.e*.6.1(p.305.23; M.22.500C); **2.** c. acc. only; **a.** *shut up* ἀ. σῖτον Chrys.*hom.17.3 in 2Cor*.(10.563A); met. οὐ γὰρ ~σαι καὶ ὥσπερ σφραγίσαι τὰς προφητικὰς ὁράσεις ἐπιδεδήμηκεν ὁ σωτήρ Eus.*d.e*.8.2 (p.372.8; M.22.604D); *ib*.(p.372.18; 605A); τὴν ἀκοὴν ἀ. Ath.*Ar*.1.35 (M.26.84B); reflex., of monks γέρων τις πνευματικὸς ἀ. ἑαυτὸν *Apophth.Patr*.(M.65.216D); ἑαυτὸν ἀ. εἰς ἕνα τῶν τειχῶν τοῦ πύργου Jo.Mosch.*prat*.32(M.87.2881A); **b.** *shut off, enclose* ὁ κόσμος σφαιρικὸς ἀποτελεσθεὶς οὐρανοῦ κύκλοις ἀποκέκλεισται Athenag.*leg*.8.2(M.6. 905A); of a monk ἐν ἀνώγεῳ...ἀποκεκλεισμένος Pall.*h.Laus*.30 (p.86.3; M.34.1098C); **c.** *shut out, exclude, reject* ἀ. τὸν σαββατισμὸν καὶ νεομηνίας *A.(Pass.)Petr.et Paul*.1(p.118.9); pass. τῶν θείων ἔξω περιβόλων ἀποκλεισθείσας [sc. foolish virgins] Meth.*symp*.6.3 (p.67.3; M.18.117A); **d.** *preclude* ἑώρων...~όμενον τὸν χρόνον τῆς πρὸς σὲ γραφῆς Or.*ep*.1.15(M.11.85C); πᾶσαν δὲ φιλονεικίαν αὐτῶν ~ουσιν αἱ...γραφαί Didym.(‡Bas.)*Eun*.4(1.281E; M.29.677C); **3.** abs., *preclude further argument* διὰ τούτων τῶν δύο ῥήσεων [sc. Jo.1:1] ἀπέκλεισεν ὁ εὐαγγελιστής, μιᾶς ἀνυπερβάτου, καὶ ἑτέρας ἀνεκβάτου Bas.*Eun*.2.14(1.249B; M.29.597D); αὐτὸς περὶ ἑαυτοῦ ὁ δεσπότης αἱρετικοῖς που πάντως ~ων εἶπεν [Jo.8:58] Didym.*Trin*.1.15(M.39. 325A); **4.** med., *shut oneself off from, avoid* ἁλμυρᾶς ἀναγνώσεως τὸν ναυτιασμὸν ~σάμενος Isid.Pel.*epp*.1.143(M.78.280A).

ἀποκληρόνομος, **1.** *disinherited*, sc. from kingdom of heaven; of sinners, ‡Just.*qu.et resp*.120(M.6.1369C); Chrys.*hom.23.5 in Eph*. (11.173D); of Jews, Ast.Soph.*hom.2 in Ps*.5(M.40.408C); *ib*.5(433B); ‡Caes.Naz.*dial*.183(M.38.1161); masc. plur. as subst., *disinherited persons*, Chrys.*hom.16.1 in Heb*.(12.157C,158A); **2.** *disinherited from* μή τις ἀ. γένηται τῆς γῆς ταύτης Ephr.1.8E; **3.** masc. as subst., *one who is not an heir* ἀγαθὴ κληρονομία μοναχοῦ σωφροσύνη καὶ ἁγιασμός· ἀποκληρόνομος δὲ πατέρων γίνεται ὁ ἐκτὸς τούτων μοναχός Hyper.*mon*.3(M.79.1473A).

ἀπόκληρος, **1.** *without lot* or *share in* τὸ δὲ πνεῦμα ἀ. ... τῆς κοινωνίας τοῦ θεοῦ καὶ τοῦ Χριστοῦ αὐτοῦ Bas.*Spir*.69(3.58D; M.32.197A); ἀπόκληροι τῶν θείων ἀγαθῶν Cyr.*Jo*.5.1(4.465E); **2.** abs.; **a.** *without lot* or *portion* ἀ. μὲν τὸ Λευιτικὸν ἐποιεῖτο γένος, καὶ κλῆρον αὐτῷ τὸν ἐξαίρετον, ἑαυτὸν ἐπιδούς Cyr.*ador*.13(1.464D); **b.** *disinherited* ἀ. ὁ Ἰσραὴλ τὴν πίστιν οὐ προσηκάμενος *ib*.(471A); id.*Abac*.56(3.571A); **3.** *exclusively assigned* τὸν μόνοις ἱερεῦσί τε καὶ λειτουργοῖς ἀπόκληρον τόπον [sc. ἱερατεῖον] Max.*myst*.2(M.91.668D).

ἀποκληρ-όω, **A.** act.; **1.** *allot* to, *assign* to, *grant as a portion* to ἀ. αὐτῷ τὴν πόλιν ἐκείνην Gr.Nyss.*v.Gr.Thaum*.(M.46.909B); οὐκ ~ῶμεν μὲν πατέρι τὸν νόμον, υἱῷ δὲ τὸ εὐαγγέλιον Isid.Pel.ap.*cat. 1Cor*.9:23(p.181.22); Max.*opusc*.(M.91.193D) esp. of God, Athenag. *res*.12(p.62.17; M.6.997B); Epiph.*haer*.76.53(p.408.9; M.42.628C); τῇ πτωχείᾳ τὸν μακαρισμὸν ἀ. Nil.*epp*.1.238(M.79.169C); τὴν ἐν τῷ ἀέρι καὶ τῇ γῇ διατριβὴν αὐτοῖς [sc. fallen angels] ἀ. Thdt.*affect*.4(p.116.1; 4.809); ἡ θεία θεσμοθεσία...τὴν ἱερὰν τοῦ θυσιαστηρίου τελετουργίαν ταῖς τῶν ἐνθέων ἱεραρχῶν τελεσιουργοῖς δυνάμεσιν ἐνιαίως ἀπεκλήρωσεν Dion.Ar.*e.h*.5.1.5(M.3.505C); hence *devote* to πάντα ἀπεκλήρου τῇ ἑαυτοῦ ἀπολαύσει Ast.Am.*hom*.3(M.40.192B); τὸ πολὺ τοῦ χρόνου ἀ. τῇ προσεδρείᾳ τοῦ λόγου ‡Nil.*perist*.4.3(M.79.828C); **2.** *have as one's lot* τὰς ἀποκληρώσεις καθ' ἃς ἐνθάδε τὴν οἰκείαν ζωὴν ἀπεκλήρωσαν Dion.Ar.*e.h*.7.3.1(M.3.557A); **3.** *exclude from lot* or *portion, reject* ὁ τῶν συμβόλων δημιουργὸς ~οῖ δικαιότατα τὸν οὐχ ὁσίους αὐτῷ...τὰ ἱερὰ συνδειπνήσαντα *ib*.3.3.1(428B); ἡ διακόσμησις τὸ... ἀκόσμητον...~οῦσα *ib*.5.1.1(500D); *ib*.7.3.7(564C); **4.** reflex., *devote* oneself to τῇ θεωρίᾳ τῶν θείων...σφᾶς αὐτοὺς ἀ. Thdt.*affect*.12(p.306. 5; 4.1019); c. prep. ἑαυτὸν ~ῶσαι τὸν Ἰσραὴλ ἐπὶ τὴν τοῦ...θεοῦ θεραπείαν Dion.Ar.*c.h*.9.4(M.3.261C).

B. med.; **1.** *have allotted, have as one's lot* or *portion*, Cyr.*Jo*.3.1 (4.253C); εἰς τὸν ἀεὶ ὄντα αἰῶνα τὰς μακαριωτάτας ~ώσονται λήξεις Dion.Ar.*ep*.8.5(M.3.1097A); Philost.*h.e*.12.4(M.65.612A); **2.** *allot to oneself*, *ib*.8.8(564A).

C. pass.; **1.** *be allotted to, assigned to, destined for*, esp. by God εἰ...τὸ παρὰ τοῦ θείου βουλήματος ~οῦσθαι τοῖς ἀνθρώποις τὴν πίστιν, τῶν μὲν καλουμένων, τῶν δὲ λοιπῶν ἀμοιρούντων τῆς κλήσεως, καιρὸν εἶχεν τὸ τοιοῦτον ἔγκλημα κατὰ τοῦ μυστηρίου προφέρεσθαι Gr.Nyss.*or.catech*.30(p.111.8; M.45.76D); οὐδὲ τὰ ὀνόματα ὡς ἀποκεκληρωμένα διεῖλε, τῷ μὲν υἱῷ τὸ κύριος, τῷ δὲ πατρὶ τὸ θεός Chrys.*hom.20.3 in 1Cor*.(10.172D); οὐ...τοῦ Ἰσραὴλ εἰς ἐθνάρχην καὶ ἐθναγὸν ~ωθέντος Dion.Ar.*c.h*.9.4(M.3.261C); ὅτι τὸ βάπτισμα υἱοθεσίας ἡ ῥίζα, τῷ πνεύματι διαφερόντως ἀποκεκλήρωται Job.Mon.*inc*.2 (M.86.3316B); ἕκαστον...ἔθνος ἄγγελον ἔχει ἀποκεκληρωμένον αὐτῷ Max.*schol.c.h*.9.2(M.4.84C); abs. φύσει ἀποκεκληρωμένη Aët.*synt*.31 (p.358.13; M.42.544A); τὸν ἠναγκασμένον θάνατον μὴ ἄλλως ἢ παρ' ἐκείνης [sc. τῆς εἱμαρμένης] ~οῦσθαι Gr.Nyss.*fat*.(M.45.148D); id. *Eun*.1(2 p.22.22; M.45.249D); **2.** *have allotted to one* ὡς αὐτοῦ τούτου ἕνεκα ~ωθῆναι τοῦ βίου τὴν ἀτιμίαν Gr.Nyss.*fat*.(M.45.157D); πᾶν ὁτιοῦν ὁμοφυές, καὶ τὸν τῆς αὐτῆς οὐσίας λόγον ἀποκεκληρωμένον Cyr.*Jo*.1.3(4.25B).

***ἀποκλήρωμα**, τό, v. ἀποκλήρωσις 2.b.

***ἀποκληρωμένως**, *specifically* (cf. ἀποκεκληρωμένως), Hesych.H. *qu.ev*.15(M.93.1405C).

ἀποκλήρωσις, ἡ, **1.** *allotting*, Gr.Nyss.*Eun*.12(1 p.317.5; M.45. 1032B); Leont.H.*Nest*.2.13(M.86.1564A); **2.** *lot*; **a.** *portion*, hence *task* αὗται μὲν αἱ ἱερατικαὶ τάξεις τε καὶ ἀ. Dion.Ar.*e.h*.6.1.1(M.3. 529D); **b.** *endowment* φύσεως ἀ. ἀγεννήτου Aët.*synt*.21(p.357.3; M.42.541A); *ib*.33(p.359.4; 544C); *ib*.35(p.359.14; ἀποκληρώματα M. 42.544D); ἀ. ἰδικὴν τοῦ γεγεννημένου Cyr.*hom.pasch*.15(5^2.203E); **c.** *appointment*, exeg. Rom.1:1 ἐμοὶ...οὐ τὴν ἀ. δοκεῖ μόνον αἰνίττεσθαι, ἀλλ' ὅτι πάλαι καὶ ἄνωθεν πρὸς τοῦτο ἦν τεταγμένος Chrys. *hom.1.1 in Rom*.(9.430D); **d.** *inheritance* τὴν κοινὴν ἀ. [i.e. resurrection] Athenag.*res*.25(p.79.2; M.6.1021D); Dion.Ar.*e.h*.1.2(M.3.373B); *ib*.7.3.1(557A) cit. s. ἀποκληρόω; ἀμοιβαίαν ἔξει τὴν ἀ. ἕκαστος *ib*.7.3.6(560D); **e.** *fate, destiny* ὁ ἀγέννητος θεός, ἐλεύθερος ἀποκληρώσεως ὑπάρχων Aët.*synt*.31(p.358.14; M.42.544A); Epiph.*haer*.76.38 (p.391.12; M.42.597D); astrol., Bas.*hex*.6.5(1.54B; M.29.128A); Gr. Nyss.*Eun*.11(2 p.268.8; M.45.877A); ‡Caes.Naz.*dial*.109(M.38.980); **3.** *choice by lot*, hence *random* or *arbitrary choice*, denied as principle of God's action οἶδα τίσιν ἔδωκεν ὁ πατήρ· ὅταν δὲ ἀκούσῃς, ὅτι 'δέδωκε', μὴ ἀ. ἁπλῶς νόμιζε, ἀλλ' ἐκεῖνο πίστευε, ὅτι ὁ παρασχὼν ἑαυτὸν ἄξιον τοῦ λαβεῖν, αὐτὸς ἔλαβεν Chrys.*hom.47.3 in Jo.*(8.279A); exeg. Mt.13:11, id.*hom.45.1 in Mt.*(7.476A); exeg. Mt.19:11, *ib.62.4*(624B); esp. in phrase κατὰ ἀποκλήρωσιν: οἱ...πειθόμενοι μὴ ἄλλον εἶναι θεὸν παρὰ τὸν δημιουργὸν φρονοῦσιν ὡς ἄρα κατὰ ἀ. ὁ θεὸς ὃν θέλει ἐλέει, ὃν δὲ θέλει σκληρύνει, αἰτίαν οὐκ ἔχοντος τοῦ τόνδε μὲν ἐλεεῖσθαι τόνδε δὲ σκληρύνεσθαι ὑπ' αὐτοῦ Or.*comm.in Ex.*1 (p.242.19; M.12.265A); Tit.Bost.*fr.Lc.*10:6(p.189); κατὰ τίνα ἀ. καὶ Ἱερεμίας ἁγιάζεται, καὶ ἄλλοι ἐκ μήτρας ἀλλοτριοῦνται; Gr.Naz.*or.*37.14(M.36.300C); Gr.Nyss.*hom.6 in Cant.*(M.44.897B); **4.** *principle of choice, reason*; in phrase τίς ἡ ἀ.; *what is the reason why...? what is the reason for...?*, c. infin. τίς...ἡ ἀ. μὴ οὐχὶ...ὁμολογεῖν...; Clem.*paed.*1.6(p.114.13; M.8.297C); Or.*Cels.*1.25(p.76.3; M.11.705C); Meth.*symp.*4.1(p.46.2; M.18.88A); τίς ἡ ἀ., τοσούτων ὄντων τῶν περὶ θεοῦ λεγομένων, ἐν ἑνὶ τούτῳ μόνῳ τὴν ἀκρίβειαν ἐπιδείκνυσθαι; Bas.*Eun.*1.8(1.22D; M.29.529B); Gr.Naz.*ep.*101(M.37.192A); Gr.Nyss.*Eun.*1 (2 p.47.21; M.45.276B); c. genit. εἰ δ' ἀληθές ἐστι τὸ σκότος γεγονέναι φῶς, τίς ἡ ἀ. τοῦ μὴ πᾶν σκότος δύνασθαι γενέσθαι φῶς; Or.*Jo.*2.20 (14; p.77.12; M.14.149B); τίς ἡ ἀ. τοῦ, ἐπὶ τοῦ πατρὸς τοιῶσδε, ἐπὶ τοῦ υἱοῦ ἑτέρως; Proc.G.*Ex.*21:8(M.87.616B); Zach.Mit.*opif.*(M.85.1097A).

ἀποκληρωτικός, 1. *random, indefinite* ἀ. καὶ οὐκ ἀποδεικτικὸς ὁ λόγος Leont.B.*arg.Sev.*(M.86.1924A); id.*cap.Sev.*29(M.86.1913A); **2.** neut. as subst., *lack of discrimination*, Or.*Jo.*1.36(41; p.47.10; M.14.96C); id.*Cels.*4.91(p.364.25; M.11.1169B).

***ἀποκληρωτικῶς, 1.** *capriciously*, Or.*Jo.*10.3(2; p.173.29; M.14.312A); id.*Cels.*3.23(p.220.10; M.11.948A); Bas.*hex.*1.10(1.10B; M.29.24C); οὐ γὰρ ἀ. τῷ Ἄβραμ ὁ θεὸς κελεύει ἀποστῆναι τῆς συγγενείας αὐτοῦ Proc.G.*Gen.*12:17(M.87.320C); **2.** *without discrimination*, Leont.H.*monoph.*testimonia(M.86.1852C); **3.** *exclusively*, Eus.*Is.*13:1(M.24.184D); οὐχὶ ἀ. τῷ ἁγίῳ πνεύματι ἡ 'ἐν' συλλαβὴ διενήνοχεν, ἀλλὰ κοινὴ πατρός ἐστι καὶ υἱοῦ Bas.*Spir.*65(3.54C; M.32.185D); Max.*schol.d.n.*2.1(M.4.212B).

ἀπόκλητος, prob. f.l. for ἀπόκληρος, *disinherited*, *cat.Lc.*14:34 (p.117.6).

ἀποκλίν-ω, 1. *turn away from, avoid* ἀ. τὸν...κίνδυνον Clem.*paed.*3.8(p.261.31; M.8.616A); ἀ. τὴν συντυχίαν Ast.Am.*prod.*(p.113.8); **2.** *decline towards evening* τῆς ἡμέρας ~ούσης Eus.*v.C.*1.28(p.21.15; M.20.944B); **3.** reflex., *turn oneself aside* πρὸς δὲ τὸν ἐκείνου λόχον ἑαυτοὺς ~ωμεν Bas.*hom.*21.1(2.164B; M.32.541C); **4.** pass., *sink down* τὴν γῆν...διὰ τὴν ἴσην πάντοθεν πρὸς τὸ ἄκρον ἀπόστασιν οὐκ ἔχουσαν ὅπου μᾶλλον ἀποκλιθῇ id.*hex.*1.10(1.10B; M.29.24B); **5.** sens. dub., perh. error for ἀποφαίνω or ἀποκλείω, Or.*comm.in Rom.*4:9–12 (*JTS* 13 p.358).

ἀπόκλισις, ἡ, *inclination* τὴν ὁλικὴν ἀ. ἐπὶ τὸ ὄντως ἐφετόν Dion.Ar.*c.h.*2.4(M.3.144B).

ἀποκλιτέον, *one must incline* πρὸς τὴν εἰρήνην Gr.Naz.*or.*22.15 (M.35.1148C).

ἀποκλύζ-ω, 1. *wash away*, Clem.*paed.*2.10(p.212.21; M.8.505C); met. ὥσπερ ~ομένης τῆς αἰδοῦς αὐτοῖς κατὰ τὰ λουτρά *ib.*3.14(p.255.7; 601B); **2.** *wash clean from* τῶν ἐνδυμάτων πάσης κηλῖδος ἀποκλυσθέντων τῷ ὕδατι Gr.Naz.*v.Mos.*(M.44.373B); met. ὕδατι...τοῦ βαπτίσματος πᾶσαν κτίσιν...τοῦ αἴσχους ~οντα ‡Caes.Naz.*dial.*113 (M.38.996).

ἀπόκλυσις, ἡ, *washing away*; in the Flood, ‡Caes.Naz.*dial.*113 (M.38.996).

***ἀπόκλυσμα, τό,** *offscourings, filth*, Nil.*epp.*4.26(M.79.561C).

ἀποκναί-ω, 1. *be wearisome, tedious*, Meth.*symp.*4.1(p.45.25; M.18.88A); **2.** *be weary, become weary* τὸ ἀεὶ κατατείνειν τοῖς πόνοις ~ειν ποιεῖ Chrys.*hom.11.1 in Gen.*(4.82D); id.*hom.31.5 in Jo.*(8.182D); v. ἀποκνέω; **3.** *make to shrink from* doing, c. infin. τοῦ πλήθους...τῶν πιστῶν...αὐτὸν...~οντος ἐπὶ τὸν...ἐφορμῆσαι πόλεμον Eus.*h.e.*8.4.4(M.20.749C); **4.** *guard from* διὰ...παραπετάσματος τοὺς ὀφθαλμοὺς τῷ φωτὶ ~ουσι Bas.Sel.*or.*9.3(M.85.136C); **5.** pass., *be made wearisome, tedious* πᾶν συμπόσιον ~εσθαι φλυαρίᾳ Gr.Naz.*or.*27.2(p.3.6; M.36.13A).

***ἀποκνεύομαι,** *be indolent, unconcerned* πρὸς τὴν ἰδίαν σωτηρίαν ἀ. ‡Proc.G.*Pr.*19:15(M.87.1416D, ? error for ἀποκναιόμενον).

ἀποκνέω, *shrink from*; c. genit., Gr.Thaum.*pan.Or.*3(p.7.6; M.10.1057D); abs., c. πρός, Bas.*hom.in Ps.*1(1.93C; M.29.217C); Chrys.*hom.6.3 in 1Tim.*(11.582E; Gaume ἀποκναίει).

ἀποκνίζω, *pluck* καρπούς Cyr.*Am.*71(3.329B).

***ἀποκνισσόομαι,** *turn into fatty smoke*, †Bas.*Is.*26(1.399D; M.30.169A).

ἀποκοιμ-άομαι, 1. *fall asleep*, Or.*engast.*1(p.283.12; M.12.1013A); **2.** *sleep away from home*, hence met., *be parted from* τὴν ἀποκεκοιμημένην ἀπὸ τῆς κατ' ἀλήθειαν πίστεως διάνοιαν Anon.ap.Eus.*h.e.*5.16.9(M.20.468B); ὅταν...~ηθῶμεν ἀπὸ ἀγαθῶν ἔργων Epiph.*haer.*66.65(p.105.31; M.42.132C).

***ἀποκοινόω,** f.l. for ἀποκενόω (v. *LS* s.v.), 1Reg.24:4 cit.ap. Eus.*Ps.*141:1(M.24.45B).

***ἀποκοινωνητέος,** *to be excommunicated*, *Cod.Afr.*134(H.1.941C).

***ἀποκοινώνητος,** *excommunicated*, Cael.*ep.CP* 1.7(p.89.11; M.*PL.*50.498A).

ἀποκολλάω, pass., *be unglued*, hence *be moved*; of a statue from its place, *A.Andr.et Mt.*13(p.80.2).

***ἀποκόμβι(ο)ν, τό,** *money-bag, purse*; for alms-giving, Leont.N.*v.Jo.Eleem.*8(p.16.15,18); *ib.*26(p.54.18).

ἀποκομίζ-ω, 1. *bring*, Polyc.*ep.*13.1; **2.** *give*, *A.Petr.c.Sim.*1 (p.78.10); **3.** *carry away*, Meth.*symp.*2.5(p.20.24; M.18.53B); to next world, Hipp.*Dan.*4.51.4; Bas.*hom.*6.3(1.45E; M.31.265D); **4.** *lead away*, met. λογισμοὺς τοὺς εἰς ἐκτόπους ἡμᾶς ἐννοίας ~οντας Cyr.*Pulch.*(p.39.13; 5^2.147C); id.*apol.Thdt.*4(p.123.28; 6^1.217D); **5.** *lead away from*, met. τοῦ πράγματος...ἀ. τὸν λόγον id.*ador.*5(1.144E); id.*Is.*3.1(2.385A); **6.** *lead back* ἀ. εἰς ἐπίγνωσιν αὐτούς *ib.*(384E); abs. τὸ ἀ. ... τῷ θεῷ id.*ador.*2(1.63E); τὴν ὁδὸν τὴν ~ουσαν πρὸς τὸν πατέρα id.*Ps.*66:3(M.69.1141A).

ἀποκομιστής, ὁ, f.l. in Cyr.*ep.*24(5^2.87A; διακομ- p.117.27).

ἀποκομπάζω, *utter boastful language*, Soz.*h.e.*6.1.3(M.67.1288B).

ἀποκονίω, *shake off like dust* τὰ ἐκ τῆς αἰχμαλωσίας ἀπεκονίσατο βλάβη Cyr.*Zach.*17(3.674A).

ἀποκοπή, ἡ, *cutting off*; **1.** *amputation*, *Hom.Clem.*6.13; met. τῶν παθῶν ἀ. Clem.*str.*4.9(p.281.10; M.8.1284B); **2.** *severance* γέγονεν [sc. ὁ κόσμος]...κατὰ μερισμόν, οὐ κατὰ ἀ. Tat.*orat.*5(p.5.25; M.6.816A); of umbilical cord, Clem.*paed.*1.6(p.113.27; M.8.297B).

***ἀποκοπόομαι,** *be wearied*, Hegem.*Arch.*9(p.14.10; M.10.1441A).

***ἀποκοπτέος,** *to be cut off from* ἀποκοπτέος ἡμῶν Synes.*ep.*58(M.66.1401C).

ἀποκόπτ-ω, 1. *cut off, amputate*, Chrys.*comm.in Gal.*5:12(10.717B); met.; **a.** *excommunicate* ὡς μὴ ~οι ὅλας ἐκκλησίας θεοῦ Eus.*h.e.*5.24.11(M.20.500A); *Const.App.*2.21.4; τὸν πεπορνευκότα...ἀ. Chrys.*hom.27.3 in 1Cor.*(10.245C); **b.** *root out* πάθη Clem.*q.d.s.*40 (p.187.5; M.9.645C); πᾶσαν αἰσχρὰν ἐπιθυμίαν Esaias *or.*27.3(p.189); τὸ σεαυτοῦ ~ων θέλημα Jo.Clim.*past.*11(M.88.1188A); **2.** *cut off from* ἀνιάτως ἔχοντα τῆς ἐκκλησίας ~ε *Const.App.*2.41.9; reflex. ἵνα μὴ θεότητος ἑαυτοὺς ἀποκόψωσι Didym.(‡Bas.)*Eun.*5(1.301C; M.29.724A); pass., c. dat. οὐκ ἀποκέκοπται τέλεον αὐτοῖς ἡ κληρονομία Clem.*q.d.s.*3(p.161.14; M.9.605D); **3.** med., *cut off, exclude*, id.*str.*1.13 (p.36.20; M.8.756A); **4.** *castrate*, reflex., Ath.*fug.*26(p.85.28; M.25.677B); Chrys.*comm.in Gal.*5:12(10.717A); pass., Just.*1apol.*27.4(M.6.372A); Thphl.Ant.*Autol.*1.9(M.6.1037C).

ἀποκοσμ-έω, *strip of* ornaments etc. ~ήσαντα τὴν κεφαλὴν τοῦ διαδήματος Gr.Naz.*or.*5.17(M.35.685C); Chrys.*vid.*2.2(1.352D).

***ἀποκουκουλ-όω,** *take off the hood of* εὐχὴ εἰς τὸ ~ῶσαι παιδίον *Euchol.*(p.305).

***ἀποκουρεύ-ομαι,** *be tonsured* ὁ ~όμενος *Schol.*15 in Jo.Clim.*scal.*1(M.88.648D).

***ἀποκουροπαλάτης, ὁ,** *ex-major-domo*, Thphn.*chron.*p.144(M.108.393A).

ἀποκράζω, *cry out, call out*, Jo.Disc.*v.Epiph.*28(M.41.60B).

ἀποκρατ-έω, 1. *hold back, check*, Meth.*symp.*10.5(p.127.23; M.18.201A); **2.** *hold on to*, *A.Mt.*18(p.239.8); *grasp* ~ούντων τὰς ἀλλήλων χεῖρας *A.Jo.*94(p.197.15).

ἀποκρεμ-άννυμι, pass., *hang upon*, met. ἐμῆς γλώσσης λαὸς ~αται Gr.Naz.*carm.*2.1.50.36(M.37.1388A); *depend* πρὸς αὐτὸν τῇ ἐπιζητήσει...~άμενος Mac.Aeg.*hom.*4.27(M.34.493C); Call.*v.Hyp.*(p.66); ~αται εἰς τὴν ἐλπίδα *ib.*(p.43); Dam.*troph.*1.8(p.214.7).

ἀποκρεμ-άω, *make to depend upon* πάντας ~όωσα φίλων ἰθύφρονας ἔργων †Apoll.*met.Ps.*93:15(M.33.1453A); τῷ τῆς εὐχῆς δοτῆρι τὴν ψυχὴν ~ῶν Nil.*Eulog.*29(M.79.1132C).

***ἀπόκρεος, ὁ, ἡ,** *abstinence from meat* τὰς δύο ἑβδομάδας, τῆς τε ἀ. [i.e. second week before Lent after which abstinence from meat is required] καὶ τῆς προφωνησίμου †Jo.Jej.*poenit.*(M.88.1913C); τῇ ἕκτῃ τῆς ἀ. Thdr.Stud.*catech.parv.*49 tit.(p.118); τῇ κυριακῇ τοῦ ἀ. [i.e. second Sunday before Lent] *ib.*50 tit.(p.120).

***ἀποκρεώσιμος,** *preceding a fast* τὴν ἀ. ἑορτήν Max.*comput.*21(M.19.1240A); *ib.*3(1221C); ἡ ἀ. *Sunday before Lenten fast*, Jo.Mal.*chron.*18 p.482(M.97.700A).

ἀπόκριμα, τό, 1. *judicial sentence*, exeg. 2Cor.1:9 τί ἐστι 'τὸ ἀ. τοῦ θανάτου'; τὴν ψῆφον, τὴν κρίσιν, τὴν προσδοκίαν Chrys.*hom.2.2 in 2Cor.*(10.430E); ἀ. δὲ θανάτου, τὴν τοῦ θανάτου ψῆφον ἐκάλεσε Thdt.

*2Cor.*1:9(3.291); **2.** *that which is discharged* (cf. ἀποκρίνω), hence *semen*, ‡Caes.Naz.*dial.*139(M.38.1048).

ἀποκρίν-ω, 1. *separate, set apart*; **a.** *reject* τῶν ἀποστολικῶν ἢ πάντα ∼ειν, ἤ τινα μὲν ἐγκρίνειν, τινὰ δὲ ∼ειν Or.*fr.comm.in Ezech.*(p.61.27,28; M.13.665A); **b.** *discharge* τῆς εἰς τὸ ∼ειν ἐνεργείας Or.*comm.in Eph.*5:4(*JTS* 3 p.559); **c.** *divide* ἀποκριθείσης τῆς ἁγίας ἐκκλησίας Evagr.*h.e.*1.7(p.12.28; M.86.2436A); πάσας τὰς ἐκκλησίας εἰς ἰδίας ἀποκριθῆναι μοίρας *ib.*3.30(p.126.22; 2657A); pass. in extended sense, *go over to* τὸ πᾶν τῆς πόλεως κεφάλαιον εἰς τὴν Ἀστερίου μοῖραν ἀπεκρίθη *ib.*6.7(p.226.3; 2852B); **2.** *separate from, set apart from*; **a.** *expel from* τοὺς μερίζοντας τὸν ἕνα κύριον...∼ομεν τῆς μοίρας τῶν φιλοχρίστων Thdt.*ep.*83(p.50.14; 4.1148); ∼ονται τῆς ἁγίας κοινωνίας Evagr.*h.e.*1.5(p.10.22; M.86.2432B); τῆς Πέτρου κοινωνίας ἑαυτοὺς ἀπέκριναν *ib.*3.16(p.114.32; 2628A); **b.** *distinguish from* αὐτὸν τῶν πολλῶν ∼ομεν Gr.Nyss.*tres dii*(M.45.120A); id.*hex.*26(M.44.88C); *ib.* 12(73D); **c.** pass., *be begotten from* πρὸ τοῦ...τῆς πατρικῆς ἀποκριθῆναι ὀσφύος ‡Caes.Naz.*dial.*166(M.38.1125); met. τῶν ἀπὸ τῆς ὕλης ∼ομένων Athenag.*leg.*20.4(M.6.932C); **3.** *answer* οἱ μαθηταὶ ∼οντες καὶ φασίν Or.*Ps.*78:3–6(p.112); **4.** med.; **a.** *render account to* οἰκονόμοι δεσπόταις ∼όμενοι Mac.Mgn.*apocr.*3.11(p.77.23); **b.** *respond, make answer*, at baptism τοὺς ἀσθενοῦντας οἵτινες ὑπὲρ ἑαυτῶν ∼εσθαι οὐ δύνανται *Cod.Afr.*45; in liturgy ὁ λαὸς ∼άσθω 'καὶ μετὰ τοῦ πνεύματός σου' *Lit.*ap.*Const.App.*8.11.7; *ib.*8.5.11; *Lit.Jac.*(p.190.12); in school τοῦ διδασκάλου...φήσαντος...εἰπὲ ἄλφα, ∼ασθαι τὸ ἄλφα Iren.*haer.*1.20.1(M.7.653A).

ἀποκρισιάριος, ὁ, (Lat. *apocrisiarius*) *messenger* (cf. ἀπόκρισις), **1.** in gen., *Pers.*(p.42.5); Marc.Er.*opusc.*1.154(M.65.924C); τοῦ βασιλικοῦ ἀ. Isid.Pel.*epp.*4.144(M.78.1225A); met. πάντας ἀ. τῆς δεσποτικῆς οἰκονομίας ἡγούμενοι Mac.Aeg.*hom.*37.2(M.34.752B); ὁ τῆς καθ' ἡμᾶς ἱερωτάτης καθέδρας ἐνδημῶν ἐνταῦθα ἀ. [i.e. conscience] Jo.VI CP *ep.*(M.96.1421A); **2.** eccl., *legate* of a partic. church τοὺς τῆς ἁγίας Ἀναστάσεως ἀ. Cyr.S.*v.Sab.*86(p.192.23); ἀ. τῆς κατὰ Ῥώμην ἐκκλησίας *V.Max.*17(M.90.85D); representing bishop, Justn.*nov.*6.2(p.41.3); esp. at councils, CCP(536)*act.*1(p.127.13ff.; H.2.1189B); τοῦ πάπα Ῥώμης συμφωνήσαντος αὐτῇ καὶ συνευρεθέντος διὰ τῶν οἰκείων ἀ. *Ep.*ap.CNic.(787)*act.*3(M.98.1476C); **3.** in monasteries, *steward*, Cyr.S.*v.Abr.*(p.244.7); δεῖ δὲ ἕκαστον μοναστήριον...ἔχειν ...τοὺς λεγομένους ἀ. ... οἳ τοῖς πράγμασι καὶ ταῖς αὐτῶν ἀπησχόληνται χρείαις Justn.*nov.*133.5(p.672.22); ‡Ath.*doct.Ant.*14(M.28.576C); Dor.*doct.*7.8(M.88.1696A); Jo.Mosch.*prat.*88(M.87.2945A).

ἀπόκρισις, ἡ, 1. *response*, liturg., *M.Seb.*2(p.172.29); **2.** *message*: oral, Jo.Mal.*chron.*10 p.253(M.97.385B); Marc.Diac.*v.Porph.*43,93; *cat.Lc.*1:30(p.11.24); *Chron.Pasch.*p.338(M.92.884A); written, *ib.* p.386(992A); *ib.*p.398(1017B); **3.** *commission, business, affairs*, sg. and plur. τὰς τοῦ πατριάρχου δεξάμενος ἀ. Cyr.S.*v.Euthym.*43(p.63.4); διάκονος...πληρῶν τὰς ἀ. ... τοῦ πατριάρχου CCP(536)*act.*1(p.127.34; H.2.1189B); ἐγὼ [sc. Gabriel] λάτρις εἰμὶ θεοῦ καὶ λειτουργὸς ἀποκρίσεων Sophr.H.*or.*2.26(M.87.3249B); esp. of a monastery ἀπέστειλεν αὐτὸν εἰς ἀπόκρισιν Cyr.S.*v.Sab.*49(p.139.3); *V.Pach.A* 23(p.150.23); Dor.*doct.*9.2(M.88.1720A); conducted by an *apocrisiarius*, Justn.*nov.*123.25(p.613.21); Jo.Mosch.*prat.*145(M.87.3009A); ‡Ath.*doct.Ant.*14(M.28.576D).

ἀποκριτικός, medic., *excretory*, Gr.Nyss.*Eun.*1(1 p.134.13; M.45.372D); Nemes.*nat.hom.*23(M.40.693A); Leont.B.*Nest.et Eut.*1(M.86.1296D).

ἀπόκριτος, *rejected*; of Satan, Isid.Pel.*epp.*1.180(M.78.300B).

***ἀποκρίτως, 1.** *separately, exclusively*, Didym.*Trin.*2.8(M.39.609A); **2.** f.l. for ἀπροκρίτως q.v.

ἀπόκροτος, *hard*; hence met., *stubborn, obdurate*, Epiph.*haer.*70.2(p.234.16; M.42.341B).

ἀποκρότως, *stubbornly, obdurately*, Epiph.*haer.*70.2(p.234.8; M.42.341B).

ἀποκρουνίζ-ω, med., *gush out from* ὕδωρ...τῆς...πέτρας...∼εται Germ.CP *or.*2(M.98.248B).

ἀπόκρουσις, ἡ, 1. *waning* of moon, Clem.*str.*6.16(pp.504.27,505.4; M.9.372A); Hegem.*Arch.*8(p.13.5; M.10.1440B); **2.** *warding off* ἀ. ...κακῶν Proc.G.*Is.*52:1–6(M.87.2501B).

ἀποκρουστικός, *able to drive off*, fig. ἔννοιαν...τῆς Ἰουδαίων δυστροπίας ἀποκρουστικήν Cyr.*Jo.*2.5(4.209E).

ἀπόκρουστος, *refracted*, Gr.Naz.*carm.*1.1.7.2(M.37.439A).

ἀποκρού-ω, med., *beat off, repel*; met. **1.** *ward off, avoid* ταύτην ἀ. τὴν ὑπόνοιαν Chrys.*hom.33.5 in Mt.*(7.384D); id.*hom.14.2 in 2Cor.*(10.539D); Thdt.*2Thess.*1:4(3.529); Jo.D.*parall.*(M.95.1228B); *ward off from* πῶς αὐτῶν τὴν ὀδύνην ∼σόμεθα; Chrys.*hom.6.2 in 1Thess.*(11.468D); **2.** *reject*, Chrys.*hom.54.2 in Jo.*(8.317B); μὴ ∼σησθε αὐτὴν [sc. τὴν εὐεργεσίαν τοῦ θεοῦ] *cat.2Cor.*6:1(p.387.28); **3.** *expel* ἀπεκρούσθη παραβάς [sc. Adam] Meth.*symp.*10.3(p.125.8; M.18.197A); **4.** *refute*, *ib.*2.3(p.18.6; 52A); Anon.ap.Eus.*h.e.*5.16.4(M.20.465B); abs., *make refutation*, Meth.*res.*1.51(p.305.6, v.l. ἀποκρίνεται M.41.1124D); **5.** *hold back* ἀπειπάμεθα δὲ καὶ ἀπεκρουσάμεθα πρὸς τὰ κρυπτὰ τῆς αἰσχύνης *cat.2Cor.*4:2(p.372.19).

ἀποκρύβω, = ἀποκρύπτω, *conceal*, Mel.*fr.*6(M.5.1221A); *A.Mt.*29(p.260.15); ‡Bas.*const.*31 tit.(2.578D; M.31.1420D).

***ἀποκρυπτέον,** *one must conceal*; hence *one must omit, pass over* οὐκ ἀ. οὐδὲ τοὺς ἀμφὶ τὸν Πυθαγόραν Clem.*prot.*6(p.55.7; M.8.180A); abs., *ib.*2(p.18.7; 92A).

ἀποκρύπτ-ω, 1. *conceal* τὴν ἀόρατον θεότητα τοῦ λόγου, τὴν ἐν κόλποις πατρῴοις ἀποκεκρυμμένην ‡Ath.*serm.fid.*30(p.27; M.26.1285A); αὐτὴν [sc. σάρκα] ∼ει [sc. Christ], ἵνα μάθῃς ὅτι οὐ ψιλὸς ἄνθρωπος ἦν Chrys.*anom.*7.6(1.511C); **2.** *throw into the shade, eclipse, surpass*, met., id.*hom.48.3 in Mt.*(7.497A); id.*hom.13.4 in Eph.*(11.101E); id.*hom.13.5 in 1Cor.*(10.116D); with instrumental dat. αὐτὸν ἀ. τῇ μεγαληγορίᾳ Bas.*Eun.*1.12(1.224C; M.29.540A); τὰ θηρία...∼ων τῇ ὠμότητι Chrys.*hom.21.5 in Rom.*(9.678E); Thdt.*Cant.*proem.(2.3); **3.** *make to vanish* ἥλιος θερμὸς...τὴν δρόσον...∼ει Chrys.*hom.22.6 in Mt.*(7.283B).

ἀποκρυφή, ἡ, *concealment*, *Protev.*22(p.44); Ἄρειος δὲ σάρκα μόνον πρὸς ἀποκρυφὴν τῆς θεότητος ὁμολογεῖ ‡Ath.*Apoll.*2.3(M.26.1136C); ‡Ath.*synops.*76(M.28.432C).

ἀπόκρυφος, 1. *hidden, concealed, secret* ἐν ἀ. ... κιβωτοῖς τισιν ἢ θαλάμοις Gr.Nyss.*v.Macr.*(p.403.7; M.46.989B); ἀπόκρυφον τῆς ψυχῆς ταμεῖον ἡ καρδία προσείρηται Nil.*epp.*3.64(M.79.420B); ἐν τῷ ἀ. οἴκῳ τῆς διανοίας *ib.*3.65(420B); τοῦ Χριστοῦ τοῦ ἀ. *A.Thom.*A 39(p.156.14); esp. of divine mysteries, Hesych.S.*temp.*1.1(M.93.1481A); Anast.Ant.*serm.*3.1(M.89.1385C); Areth.*Apoc.*20(M.106.609D); neut. as subst., *hidden place* τὸ ἀ. τε καὶ ἄδυτον τοῦ ναοῦ Gr.Nyss.*anim.et res.*(M.46.133A); ἐν τοῖς ἀ. τῆς ψυχῆς ‡Ath.*ep.Cast.*2.2(M.28.877A); *hidden thing, secret*, *A.Xanthipp.*26(p.77.6); *A.Thom.*A 50(p.166.11); Hipp.*haer.*5.28(p.134.1; M.16.3203D); τὰ ἀ. τῆς πατρῴας διανοίας ‡Ath.*serm.fid.*31(p.28; M.26.1285C); Ἡσαΐαν τὸν τῶν ἀ. θεατήν †Bas.*ep.*42.5(3.130B; M.32.360A); Gnost. τὸ ἀ. τοῦ Βυθοῦ Iren.*haer.*1.20.2(M.7.656A); ἐν ἀποκρύφῳ *secretly*, Clem.*str.*3.6(p.218.20; M.8.1152B); Hipp.*haer.*6.36(p.166.3; M.16.3250C); *ib.*4.42(p.64.14; M.16.3103C); ἐν ἀποκρύφοις Or.*Jo.*13.58(57; p.288.6; M.14.508A); **2.** *private, esoteric, secret* ὁ δεχόμενος αὐτοῦ [sc. Christ] τὰ ἀ. λόγια *A.Thom.*A 39(p.156.15); Βασιλείδης...καὶ Ἰσίδωρός φησιν εἰρηκέναι Ματθίαν αὐτοῖς λόγους ἀ., οὓς ἤκουσε παρὰ τοῦ σωτῆρος κατ' ἰδίαν διδαχθείς Hipp.*haer.*7.20(p.195.20; M.16.3302B); εἰ...πάντα φανερῶς ἐδίδαξε [sc. Christ], τὰ λεγόμενα παρά τισι περὶ αὐτοῦ ἀ. οὐκ εἰσὶ δεκτά Ammon.*Jo.*18:20(M.85.1505D); ἕκαστον...τῶν περὶ Χριστοῦ δογμάτων ἀπόκρυφον ἔχει καὶ μυστικὸν λόγον *ib.*19:36(1513B); esp. of books πλῆθος ἀ. καὶ νόθων γραφῶν, ἃς αὐτοὶ ἔπλασαν, παρεισφέρουσιν [sc. Marcosians] Iren.*haer.*1.20.1(M.7.653A); βίβλους ἀ. τἀνδρὸς τοῦδε [sc. Zoroaster] οἱ τὴν Προδίκου μετιόντες αἵρεσιν αὐχοῦσι κεκτῆσθαι Clem.*str.*1.15(p.44.6; M.8.773B); Σευῆρος...βίβλους τινὰς ἀ. παρεισάγει Epiph.*anac.*45(p.4.2; M.41.581A); βίβλους ἑαυτοῖς ἐπλαστογράφησαν [sc. Archontics] τινας ἀ., ὧν τὰ ὀνόματά ἐστι ταῦτα· τὸ μὲν γὰρ Συμφωνίαν μικρὰν δῆθεν βιβλίον καλοῦσι, τὸ δὲ μεγάλην Συμφωνίαν id.*haer.*40.2(p.82.9; M.41.680B); διχῇ γὰρ τὰς ἱερὰς βίβλους μετὰ τῶν νόθων διελόντες [sc. Audians], διαφερόντως γὰρ ταύτας νομίζουσιν ἀ. καὶ μυστικάς Thdt.*haer.*4.10(4.365); of 'gnostic' traditions, Clem.*str.*1.12(p.35.31; M.8.753B); neut. as subst., *esoteric book*; of Apoc., Epiph.*haer.*51.3(p.250.26; M.41.892B); ἐν ἀποκρύφῳ *with secret meaning*, ref. scripture, Proc.G.*Dt.*27:15(M.87.941B); plur., Dion.Ar.*d.n.*5.2(M.3.816C); of books not publicly read in churches, hence *apocryphal* βιβλία ἀ. Μωσέως καὶ Ἐνὼχ καὶ Ἀδάμ, Ἡσαΐου καὶ Δαυὶδ καὶ Ἠλία καὶ τῶν τριῶν πατριάρχων, φθοροποιὰ καὶ τῆς ἀληθείας ἐχθρά *Const.App.*6.16.3; neut. as subst. αἱ παραδόσεις λέγουσι πεπρίσθαι Ἡσαΐαν...καὶ ἔν τινι ἀ. τοῦτο φέρεται Or.*ep.*1.9(M.11.65B); τῶν λεγομένων ἀ. Eus.*h.e.*4.22.9(M.20.384A); τινες ἐπεχείρησαν ἀνατάξασθαι ἑαυτοῖς τὰ λεγόμενα ἀ., καὶ ἐπιμῖξαι ταῦτα τῇ θεοπνεύστῳ γραφῇ Ath.*ep.fest.*39.2(M.26.1436B); ἐπειδὴ δὲ οὐκ εἴρηται ποῦ [sc. Enoch's destination] ἐν τοῖς δεδημοσιευμένοις βίβλοις, ἐν ἀποκρύφοις λέγεται, ὅτι ἐν τῷ παραδείσῳ Didym.*Ac.*8:39(M.39.1669C); forbidden to be read, Cyr.H.*catech.*4.35; Bas.*ascet.*1(2.212C; M.31.649B); named τὰ δὲ ἀ. ... τῆς παλαιᾶς διαθήκης ταῦτα· Ἐνώχ, Πατριάρχαι, Προσευχὴ Ἰωσήφ, Διαθήκη Μωϋσέως, Ἀνάληψις Μωϋσέως, Ἀβραάμ, Ἐλδὰδ καὶ Μωδάδ, Ἠλίου προφήτου, Σοφονίου προφήτου, Ζαχαρίου πατρὸς Ἰωάννου, Βαρούχ, Ἀμβακούμ, Ἐζεχιήλ, καὶ Δανιὴλ ψευδεπίγραφα ‡Ath.*synops.*75(M.28.432B); ἀ. τισί, μάλιστα ταῖς λεγομέναις Πράξεσιν Ἀνδρέου καὶ τῶν ἄλλων Epiph.*haer.*63.2(p.399.25; M.41.1064C); τοῦ Ἀναβατικοῦ Ἡσαΐα

...καὶ ἄλλων τινῶν ἀ. *ib.*40.2(p.82.15; 680B); of Enoch and Moses, Euthal.Diac.*epp.cath.*(M.85.672A); of Elijah, *ib.*(733B); of Jeremiah, *ib.*(737D); dist. from canonical and deutero-canonical books, Ath.*ep.fest.*39.12(M.26.1440A); ‡Ath.*synops.*74 tit.(M.28.432A); cf. *quos* [sc. deutero-canonical books] *licet Judaei inter apocrypha separant, ecclesia tamen Christi inter divinos libros...honorat,* Isid. H.*etym.*6.1.9; **3.** *underhand* βούλαις ἀ. Hipp.*haer.*4.15(p.49.20; M.16.3083B); **4.** *hidden from,* c. dat., *A.Thom.*A 34(p.152.8); Meth. *creat.*1(p.493.11; M.18.332A); ‡Pion.*v.Polyc.*12(p.1025).

ἀποκρύφως, *in veiled language*; ref. Vergil's 'Messianic Eclogue', Const.*or.s.c.*19(p.182.16; M.20.1292C).

ἀπόκρυψις, ἡ, 1. *secret meaning,* Or.*Cels.*1.29(p.80.28; M.11.716B); **2.** *disappearance,* i.e. *setting,* of stars, Olymp.*Jer.*10:2(M.93.649A); **3.** f.l. for ἀπόκρισις *disclosure* of Christ at his temptation ταῖς εὐθυβόλοις ἀ. ὑπερκόψας, ἐξέκυπτε διὰ τῶν δικτύων Nil.ap.Proc.G. *Cant.*2:9(M.87.1600D).

ἀποκτ-άομαι, *give up possession of, give up,* Tit.Bost.*Man.*2.10 (M.18.1153C); Chrys.*hom.*47.2 *in Mt.*(7.489C); Cyr.*Lc.*20:1(M.72. 896A); Diad.*perf.*66(p.80.21); μέγας...ὁ ~ώμενος εὐσεβῶς χρήματα· ἅγιος δὲ ὁ ~ώμενος τὸ ἑαυτοῦ θέλημα Jo.Clim.*scal.*17(M.88.928D); c. genit. οἱ...ἐν αἰχμαλωσίᾳ διάγοντες, καὶ μὴ θέλοντες, πολλῶν ἁμαρτιῶν ~ῶνται Zach.H.*ep.*(M.86.3232C); abs., Gr.Naz.*or.*18.20(M.35. 1008C); τὸ καλῶς ~ᾶσθαι *ib.*40.32(M.36.404C); τὸν ~ώμενον Thdt. *1Cor.*13:3(3.252).

[*]**ἀποκτέννυμι,** = ἀποκτείνω, *kill,* Meth.*res.*1.46(p.295.18; ἀποκτίννυται M.41.1116D).

***ἀποκτην-όω, 1.** *make into an animal,* by magic ~οῦν ἄνθρωπον πολλάκις δοκοῦσιν οἱ φαρμακοί Nil.*epp.*1.308(M.79.193C); in metempsychosis, pass. ἡ ψυχὴ ὑπὸ τῆς ἀνοίας ~οῦται Or.*princ.*1.8.4(p.104. 10; M.11.180B); Gr.Nyss.*anim.et res.*(M.46.112D); **2.** met., pass., *be made like an animal, become brutish,* i.e. unspiritual; of man through sin, Ath.*hom.in Mt.11*:27(M.25.209D); Gr.Nyss.*anim.et res.*(M.46. 64A); Cyr.*thes.*28(5^{1}.251A); τὸν τῶν ~ωθέντων ἐκτρέφουσι νοῦν, ἵνα καὶ εἰς σύνεσιν ἀναβῶσιν ἀνθρωποπρεπῆ id.*Joel.*32(3.224B); of the mind ὁ λόγος ~οῦται διὰ τῆς πρὸς τὸ ἄλογον ῥοπῆς Gr.Nyss.*hom.opif.* 18.3(M.44.192D); τῶν Ἰουδαίων ὁ νοῦς ἀπεκτηνώθη τρόπον τινά, καὶ νένευκεν ἀεὶ πρὸς τὸ κάτω, βλέπει δὲ τῶν οὐρανίων οὐδέν Cyr.*Jo.*5.2 (4.494D).

ἀπόκτησις, ἡ, *loss* τῆς τῶν προσόντων...ἀ. Gr.Nyss.*Eun.*11 (2 p.253.15; M.45.860D); Chrys.*hom.12.4 in 1Tim.*(11.616D).

***ἀπόκτητος,** *able to be lost* ὁ ἐκλεκτὸς...κτητά τε καὶ ἀ. εἰδὼς πάντα Clem.*str.*4.26(p.321.33; M.8.1376B); Gr.Nyss.*Eun.*12(1 p.341. 26; M.45.1060D); Chrys.*hom.10.2 in 1Thess.*(11.497E).

ἀποκτυπ-έω, pass., *be sounded* λόγον...διὰ γλώττης ~ούμενον Cyr.*thes.*4(5^{1}.31E); Proc.G.*Is.*11:3(M.87.2044D).

***ἀποκτύπησις, ἡ,** *loud sound* τῶν θείων δογμάτων ἀ. καὶ εὐηχίᾳ Cyr.*ador.*11(1.387D).

ἀποκυ-έω, 1. *bring forth, bear*; **a.** c. acc., of Gnost. aeons ἐγκύμονα γενομένην [sc. Σιγήν] ~ῆσαι Νοῦν Iren.*haer.*1.1.1(M.7.445B); ὃ ἀπεκύησε, τουτέστι τὸ πνευματικόν *ib.*1.5.1(492A); met. κηλῖδας... κακίας...ἃ ὁ ἄρχων τοῦ σκότους ἀπεκύησε Meth.*res.*1.38(p.281.9; M.41.1105B); ~ῆσαι βουλόμενος βλασφημίαν Marcell.*fr.*89 ap.Eus. *Marcell.*1.4(p.29.17; M.24.772B); ἂν πατάξεις λίθον ~εῖται πῦρ ‡Caes. Naz.*dial.*56(M.38.925); τὸ πρῶτον...μοναστήριον...τὸ καὶ ἄλλα ~ῆσαν μοναστήρια Pall.*h.Laus.*32(p.93.10; M.34.1100D); **b.** abs. πρὸς τὸ ~εῖν γενῶνται Clem.*str.*4.8(p.276.23; M.8.1273B); id.*paed.*2.10(p.213.1; M.8.508A); **2.** *conceive* ἡ βοῦς...ἀπεκύησε καὶ ἐγέννησε τέκνον Or. *enarr.in Job* 21:10(M.17.77C); met. ~ήσεις λογισμοὺς ἀγαθούς ‡Hipp. *fr.10 in Pr.*(p.160.10; M.10.617D).

***ἀποκύημα, τό,** *offspring, product, Hom.Clem.*6.4; οὐκ ἔστιν ἐξ ἀληθείας ψεύδους ἀ. †Cyr.*hom.div.*10(5^{2}.373A); of Christology of Severus τῆς νέας σοφίας τὸ καινὸν ὄντως ἀ. Leont.B.*arg.Sev.*(M.86. 1928A).

ἀποκυΐσκ-ω, *bring forth, bear,* met. φόβῳ τὸν νοῦν πληγεῖσα [sc. ἐπιθυμία], δι' ὀνείρων τὰς ἰδέας ~ει *Hom.Clem.*9.15; λόγος ὁ πρὸς αὐτῆς [sc. ψυχῆς] ~όμενος †Gr.Thaum.*ep.Philagr.*(M.46.1104C); ἡ ψυχὴ...νοημάτων ἀπείρων ~ει πλῆθος *ib.*(1105A).

***ἀποκυριεύω,** *rule over, dominate,* c. genit., Just.*dial.*83.4(M.6. 673A).

ἀποκυρ-όω, 1. *be master* ~οῦντος ἐν αὐτῷ τελείου λογισμοῦ CGangr. *can.*19; **2.** *annul* ἀπεκυρώσαμεν...τὸν τῶν αἱρετικῶν ἀσύμβατον λόγον Martin.*ep.*3(M.*PL*.87.140C).

***ἀποκύω,** *bear, bring forth,* ‡Caes.Naz.*dial.*102(M.38.968).

***ἀποκωμάζω,** *jeer at,* Mac.Mgn.*apocr.*2.8(p.9.15).

ἀποκωφόω, *deafen,* Eus.*Is.*6:10(M.24.129B); met. ἀ. τὸν νοῦν Leont.B.*Nest.et Eut.*1(M.86.1308B).

ἀπολαλέω, *rave, cry out in frenzy,* Call.*v.Hyp.*(p.60).

ἀπολαμβάν-ω, 1. *take up again, resume* παραθήκην Or.*dial.*8 (p.138.15); τὰς συνήθεις ἀ. διατριβάς Eus.*v.C.*4.33(p.130.22; M.20. 1181C); id.*l.C.*6(p.211.6; M.20.1349A); *receive back*; the body at resurrection, Just.*1apol.*18.6(M.6.356B); Meth.*symp.*6.4(p.69.11; M. 18.120B); cf. τὴν οἰκείαν ~ει [sc. τὸ σῶμα] ψυχήν Chrys.*hom.18.2 in Eph.*(11.130B); persons after absence, Gr.Thaum.*pan.Or.*5(p.13. 21; M.10.1068A); Chrys.*hom.36.5 in 1Cor.*(10.340D); hence gen., *receive, welcome,* Ign.*Eph.*2.1; Eus.*v.C.*1.1(p.7.3; 912A); ἥλιον... δικαιοσύνης...τάς τε εὐσεβείᾳ παρεσκευασμένας ψυχὰς...τοῖς αὐτοῦ κόλποις ἀπολαβόντα id.*l.C.*6(p.211.29; 1349C); **2.** *receive* as a due ᾧ ἐὰν εὐαρεστήσωμεν ἐν τῷ νῦν αἰῶνι, ἀποληψόμεθα καὶ τὸν μέλλοντα Polyc.*ep.*5.2; *2Clem.*8.6; *receive the penalty for* δεῖ ἀπολαβεῖν αὐτοὺς τὰς ἁμαρτίας αὐτῶν Or.*hom.16.5 in Jer.*(p.137.20; M.13.415A); abs., *receive one's due,* Chrys.*hom.21.3 in 2Cor.*(10.586B); id.*hom.8.4 in 2Tim.*(11.712A); ἐν τῷ κόσμῳ τούτῳ ἀπολαβεῖν ὑπὲρ τῶν ἁμαρτημάτων αὐτοῦ Anast.S.*qu.et resp.*18(M.89.501D); **3.** *take over, transfer* ταύτην τὴν γραφήν...μεταληφθεῖσαν ἐκ τῆς Ῥωμαίων φωνῆς, ἀπολαβεῖν ...τῷ παρόντι λόγῳ Eus.*v.C.*2.47(p.61.18; 1052A); **4.** ?*take support from, hang from* κώδωνες χρύσεοι καὶ ῥοΐσκοι, ἐκ παραλλήλου τὸ κάτω κράσπεδον ἀπειληφότες Gr.Nyss.*v.Mos.*(M.44.320D); **5.** *take out, select,* Eus.*v.C.*3.41(p.95.4; M.20.1101A); id.*l.C.*9(p.221.5; M.20.1369B); *take away* by death κώμοις ἀποληφθέντα καὶ μέθαις id.*v.C.*1.7(p.10. 13; 917C); *cut, separate* τὴν σύμπασαν...ἀρχὴν δυσὶ τμήμασιν ἀποληφθεῖσαν *ib.*1.49(p.30.19; 964C); **6.** *enclose* στοαὶ...μέσον...τὸ αἴθριον ~ουσαι *ib.*4.59(p.141.22; 1209B); τὸν ὑπὸ τοσαύτης δυσχερείας ἀπειλημμένον Chrys.*sac.*6.12(p.165.10; 1.432A); id.*hom.6.3 in Eph.*(11. 43C); *imprison,* id.*hom.in Heb.*proem.1(12.2C); pass., met., *be caught* τῆς θείας ἐντολῆς καὶ τῶν ὅρκων μέσος ἀποληφθείς Thdt.*qu. 13 in Jos.*(1.311); math., *contain* τριὰς...ἀρχὴν καὶ μεσότητα καὶ τελευτὴν ἴσην ἀπολαβοῦσα Eus.*l.C.*6(p.210.14; M.20.1348B).

ἀπολανθάνομαι, *forget,* c. genit., Aen.*dial.*(M.85.885B); pass., *A.Andr.fr.*8(p.41.30); v.l. for ἐπιλ-, †Apoll.*met.Ps.*43:25(M.33. 1373B).

ἀπόλαυσις, ἡ, *pleasure, enjoyment, fruition*; **1.** of material enjoyments; **a.** sinful, *2Clem.*10.3; ἡ παρὰ τὴν ὄψιν ἀ. αὐτοῖν [sc. ἄνθους and κάλλους] ὕβρις ἐστίν Clem.*paed.*2.8(p.200.13; M.8.480B); πρόσκαιρον ἔχειν ἁμαρτίας ἀ. Gr.Nyss.*hom.12 in Cant.*(M.44.1025B); **b.** legitimate, of things created for man's enjoyment πηγαὶ πρὸς ἀ. ... δημιουργηθεῖσαι *1Clem.*20.10; τροφήν τε καὶ ποτὸν ἔδωκας τοῖς ἀνθρώποις εἰς ἀ. ἵνα σοι εὐχαριστήσωσιν *Did.*10.3; εὐλογήσαντας τὸν θεὸν ἐπὶ τῇ μεταδόσει τῶν ἀ. Clem.*paed.*2.9(p.204.18; M.8.489B); id. *str.*7.7(p.28.17; M.9.452C); χρώμενος [sc. the 'gnostic']...τοῖς κτιστοῖς ...κατὰ τὴν ἐπὶ τὸν κτίσαντα εὐχαριστίαν καὶ τῆς ἀ. κύριος καθίσταται *ib.*7.11(p.44.34; 485C); opp. ὕβρις: ἡμεῖς δὲ τὸ εἰρηνικὸν γένος εἰς ἀ., οὐκ εἰς ὕβριν ἑστιώμενοι id.*paed.*2.2(p.175.27; 428B); of natural beauty, Gr.Nyss.*hom.10 in Cant.*(980B); **2.** spiritual enjoyment χάριν ὁμολογῶ τῷ θεῷ καὶ περὶ τῆς σῆς σωτηρίας καὶ περὶ τῆς ἐμῆς ἀ. *Hom.Clem.*1.22; of God and divine things πολλαχῶς ἀλληγορεῖται ὁ λόγος, καὶ βρῶμα καὶ σὰρξ καὶ τροφὴ καὶ ἄρτος καὶ αἷμα καὶ γάλα, ἃ πάντα ὁ κύριος εἰς ἀ. ἡμῶν τῶν εἰς αὐτὸν πεπιστευκότων Clem.*paed.*1.6 (p.118.12; M.8.305B); never giving satiety, Gr.Nyss.*hom.1 in Cant.* (777D); οὗ [sc. θεοῦ] ἡ ἀ. ἡ ἀεὶ γινομένη ἀφορμὴ μείζονος ἐπιθυμίας γίνεται *ib.*(777B); *ib.*(1084C); eucharistic τὴν ἀ. τοῦ σώματος αὐτοῦ καὶ τοῦ αἵματος Cyr.H.*catech.*22.2; **3.** eschatol. μετὰ ἀπολαύσεως τὸ ἀθάνατον...προσλαμβάνομεν Tat.*orat.*14(p.15.22; M.6.836C); ὁ πένης ...μαθὼν τοῦ συμπτώχου σου [sc. Lazarus] τὴν μακαρίαν ἀ. Ast.Am. *hom.*1(M.40.173A); πατρίδα ἔχεις ἐν οὐρανοῖς· πάντα ἐκεῖ μετάθες, ἵνα καὶ πρὸ τῆς ἀ. ἐνταῦθα ἀπολαύσῃς τῆς ἀμοιβῆς Chrys.*stat.*2.6(2.28E); ἀθάνατος...ἡ τῶν δικαίων ἀ. Thdt.*Is.*65:20(p.255.34; 2.396); of enjoyment of food in resurrection ὁ Παπίας...τὰς διὰ βρωμάτων εἶπεν ἐν τῇ ἀναστάσει ἀ. Max.*schol.e.h.*7.2(M.4.176C); iron., of the damned 'ἀπέλθετε ἀπ' ἐμοῦ, οἱ κατηραμένοι'...δέξασθε ἑαυτοῖς καὶ τὴν ἀ. ‡Hipp.*consumm.*45(p.307.26; M.10.948A).

***ἀπολαυστήριον, τό,** *place of enjoyment,* Thdr.Stud.*epp.*2.149(M. 99.1465D).

ἀπολαύ-ω, *enjoy, have the benefit of*; **1.** Christian teaching, Tat. *orat.*32(p.33.7; M.6.872B) cit. s. πένης; Or.*schol.in Cant.*7:4(M.17. 281C); τῶν τῆς ἀληθείας ἀ. μαθημάτων *Hom.Clem.*2.21; *ib.*13.13; **2.** God and divine things (in this life) εὐχαριστεῖν ὅσιον τῷ θεῷ τῆς αὐτοῦ χάριτος καὶ φιλανθρωπίας ἀ. Clem.*paed.*2.4(p.184.7; M.8. 444C); Christ χρήσασθαι αὐτῷ καθ' ὃ ποιμήν ἐστιν, ἵνα τις δυνηθῇ αὐτοῦ ~σαι καὶ βασιλέως Or.*Jo.*19.6(1; p.305.28; M.14.536D); Gr. Thaum.*pan.Or.*15(p.34.29; M.10.1096A); θείας δέ τινος ~ειν φωνῆς εὔχομαι...θεῖα διδασκόμενος μυστήρια Meth.*arbitr.*1(p.146.3; M.18. 240B); οἱ πρωτόπλαστοι...ἀθανασίας ~οντες id.*res.*1.33(p.270.13; M.

41.1097A); Mac.Aeg.*hom*.49.2(M.34.813B); Cyr.*Jo*.5.5(4.539E); Thdt. *qu.in 1Reg*.proem.(1.353); Dion.Ar.*d.n*.12.2(M.3.969C); of creatures other than men καὶ τὸν ἀέρα τῆς τοῦ θεοῦ ~οντα προμηθείας Thdt. *provid*.2(4.504); **3.** eternal life κατοπτεύσεις τὸν θεόν,...καὶ τῶν ἐν οὐρανοῖς ~σεις ἀποκεκρυμμένων Clem.*prot*.12(p.83.29; M.8.240A); τῆς αἰωνίου μακαριότητος ἀ. id.*fr*.44(p.223.19); ἐν τῷ παραδείσῳ τῆς τρυφῆς τοῦ θεοῦ ἀ. Or.*Jo*.32.1(p.425.17; M.14.740C); Meth.*res*.1.37 (p.278.15; M.41.1104B); id.*Porph*.1(p.504.24; M.18.400C); οἱ ἀγαθοὶ ...τῶν ἀπορρήτων ἀγαθῶν ἀιδίως ~σωσιν *Clem.ep*.10(M.2.45B); *Hom. Clem*.1.7; τὴν τοῦ ἀιδίου θεοῦ εὐαγγελίζεται βασιλείαν, ἧς ~ειν λέγει *ib*.1.6; *ib*.8.23; τῶν εἰσαεὶ ἐσομένων ἀγαθῶν ἀ. *ib*.9.8.

***ἀπολέγδην**, *by choice* or *selection* δύο τινὰς ἀ. τῶν ἁγίων ἀποστόλων Tit.Bost.ap.*cat.Lc*.22:7(p.153.22); Cyr.*ador*.4(1.109D); id. *glaph.Ex*.1(1.245B).

ἀπολελυμένως, 1. in gen., *absolutely, in itself*, exeg. Mt.18:21 εἰσί τινες τῶν βασιλέων τῆς γῆς υἱοὶ καί ⟨τινες⟩ οὐχ υἱοὶ αὐτῶν, πλὴν υἱοὶ καὶ ἀ. υἱοί Or.*comm.in Mt*.13.11(p.209.5; M.13.1121B); id.*Cels*. 1.13(p.66.1; M.11.680B); οὐδὲν ἀ. ἐστὶ μοναχὸν οὐδὲ ἁπλοῦν καὶ εἰλικρινὲς τῶν ὁρωμένων καὶ αἰσθητῶν Bas.*hex*.4.5(1.38A; M.29.89C); of ordination without title μηδένα δὲ ἀ. χειροτονεῖσθαι CChalc.*can*.6; *on one's own authority only*, Chrys.*hom.71.2 in Mt*.(7.697A); **2.** *in an absolute sense, without qualification*, opp. relatively, in gen. καθ' αὑτὴν μὲν καὶ ἀ. μὲν εἴρηται ἡ τοῦ κόσμου φωνή Or.*comm.in Mt*.13.20 (p.234.16; M.13.1148C); Ath.*Ar*.1.56(M.26.129A); τῶν ὀνομάτων τὰ μὲν ἀ. καὶ καθ' ἑαυτὰ προφερόμενα (οἷον, ἄνθρωπος)...τὰ δέ, πρὸς ἕτερα λεγόμενα, τὴν σχέσιν μόνην ἐμφαίνει τὴν πρὸς ἃ λέγεται (οἷον, υἱός) Bas.*Eun*.2.9(1.244E; M.29.588C); Cyr.*Ps*.57:4(M.69.1109B); **3.** *freely*, Or.*Jo*.28.7(6; p.398.11; M.14.696B); **4.** *unreservedly*; of a legal concession, Const.ap.Eus.*h.e*.10.5.8(M.20.881C); **5.** *without specification*, Cyr.*Jo*.6.1(4.635A).

ἀπολέμητος, *invincible, indomitable* διατί πρὸς τὴν ἀ. εἰρήνην [sc. of Christ] μελετᾶτε πόλεμον; ‡Meth.*palm*.4(M.18.389C); ‡Just.*qu. et resp*.128(M.6.1380A); ἀπάθειά ἐστιν...τὸ πολεμουμένους ὑπ' αὐτῶν [sc. δαιμόνων] ἀπολεμήτους μένειν Diad.*perf*.98(p.144.23); τὸ ἀ. ἔχουσιν *ib*.(p.146.2).

ἀπολεπτύν-ω, 1. *refine*; **a.** souls, ref. purgatorial punishment τῆς ψυχῆς ~ομένης τε καὶ ἐκτηκομένης ἐν τοῖς ὑπὲρ τῆς ἁμαρτίας ἐλεγμοῖς Gr.Nyss.*or.catech*.8(p.48.12; M.45.37A); ref. purification in this life, id.*v.Mos*.(M.44.388D); ref. divine judgement on sinners like cleansing of a wound, Cyr.*Am*.39(3.294E); **b.** words of scripture, drawing out spiritual sense τὴν τοῦ νομικοῦ παχύτητα γράμματος εἰς πνευματικὴν θεωρίαν ἀ. Cyr.*Jo*.3.2(4.257B); *ib*.5.5(521A); id.*Am*.76(3.339B); **2.** *reduce, diminish*; an army, Philost.*h.e*.8.1 (M.65.556A); τῆς διαβολικῆς ἀχλύος τὸ πάχος ἀ. Proc.G.*Gen*.17:23 (M.87.361B); **3.** *lighten, clear* τὸν τῆς διανοίας ἀ. ὀφθαλμόν Cyr.*hom. pasch*.10(5^2.129A).

ἀπολευκαίνω, *make clear*, Cyr.*Jo*.9.1(4.819E); Thdr.Stud.*epp*.1.4 (M.99.921B).

***ἀπολησμονέω**, *forget*, Steph.Diac.*v.Steph*.(M.100.1180D).

ἀπολιγωρέω, *lose heart*, Didym.*Ps*.89:12(M.39.1500A).

***ἀπολιθοποι-έω**, *turn into stone*, met. τῆς πήξεως...~ούσης τὰ κύματα Gr.Nyss.*mart*.2(M.46.765D).

ἀπολιθ-όω, *turn to stone, petrify*, met., αὕτη ἡ πέτρα ἀνθρωπίνη ἐστὶ ψυχὴ...διὰ τὴν κακίαν ~ωθεῖσα Or.*princ*.3.1.14(p.219.5; M.11. 276A); ὡς...~ωθῆναι αὐτοὺς τῷ φόβῳ Eus.*qu.Marin.suppl*.1(M.22. 984B); πῶς γὰρ οἱ τοῖς ἀψύχοις προσκυνοῦντες οὐκ ἀπελιθώθησαν τὰς ψυχάς; Ath.*exp.Ps*.134:15(M.27.525D); ref. paralysis τὸ ἥμισυ μέρος τοῦ σώματος ~ωθέν *Anaph.Pil*.A 3(p.438); τὸν [sc. Satan] τὴν ἁπαλὴν τῶν ψυχῶν φύσιν ὕδατος δίκην ~οῦντα διὰ τῆς πήξεως Gr.Nyss. *hom.10 in Cant*.(M.44.984C); ἑωρακὼς [sc. S. Paul] τὸν Ἰησοῦν... ἀπελιθώθη τὸ διορατικὸν τῆς ψυχῆς Ammon.*Ac*.9:3(M.85.1532B); *ib*.22:6(1585C); of frozen water, Leont.B.*cap.Sev*.17(M.86.1905C); ἀπελιθώθη...ἡ καρδία αὐτοῦ Olymp.*Job* 41:15(M.93.445B).

ἀπολιμπάν-ω, 1. med. or pass., *be left behind*, ref. soul at dissolution of bodily elements οὔτε ἀποφοιτησάντων...~ομένη Gr.Nyss. *anim.et res*.(M.46.45C); *lose* friends, Chrys.*hom.10.3 in 2Tim*.(11. 725A); **2.** med., *fall short, fail* μιμήσεως...τοῦ θεοφιλοῦς ἀπελιμπάνετο Eus.*v.C*.1.49(p.30.26; M.20.964C); Bas.*fid*.2(2.226A; M.31. 681B); ἀ. ... τῆς ἀρετῆς Gr.Nyss.*instit*.(p.87.11; M.34.440C); πάντα τῆς ἀξίας ~εται id.*or.catech*.27(p.105.7; M.45.72D); Cyr.*Ps*.38:5 (M.69.973A); abs., Eus.*Ps*.144:2(M.24.57C); Ath.*ep.mon*.1(p.181.12; M.25.692B); **3.** *be absent* οὐδὲ νῦν μετὰ τὴν ἀνάληψιν τῆς γῆς ~εται Didym.*Trin*.3.18(M.39.881A); τὸ θεῖον...πανταχῆ μὲν ὑπάρχειν, ~εσθαι δὲ οὐδενός Cyr.*resp*.(p.578.4; 6^2.386B); from a church council, Eus.*v.C*.3.7(p.80.14; M.20.1061A); *ib*.4.43(p.135.24; 1193B); CLaod. *can*.40; μὴ δύνασθαι τὸ τῶν ~ομένων ἀναδέξασθαι πρόσωπον Evagr. *h.e*.2.18(p.89.1; M.86.2580D); from church meetings, Chrys.*ecl*.48 (12.775B).

***Ἀπολιναριανός (-ιαστής)**, v. Ἀπολιναριστής.

***Ἀπολιναρίζω**, *be a follower of Apollinarius*, Leont.H.*Nest*.5.32 (M.86.1752B).

***Ἀπολιναριστής (-ιαστής, -ιανός), ὁ**, *a follower of Apollinarius*, Gr.Naz.*ep*.125(M.37.217C); ‡Ath.*haer*.11(M.28.520C); †Leont.B.*sect*. 8.3(M.86.1253C); Leont.H.*monoph*.(M.86.1812B); ‡Gr.Nyss.*hom.7. 152 in Jo*.(p.278.35); -ιανός Gr.Naz.*ep*.152(M.37.257C); Pall.*h.Laus*. 38(p.121.11; M.34.1194B); -ιαστής ‡Ath.*dial.Trin*.4 tit.(M.28.1250C); Justn.*ep.Thdr.Mops*.(p.48.11; M.86.1045B); Tim.CP *haer*.(M.86.72A).

ἄπολις, *city-less, lacking a country*, of soul withdrawn from the world ἄ., ἄοικον, ἀνίδιον Bas.*ep*.2.2(3.71E; M.32.225B); οὐχ οὕτως ἄ. εἰμί τις, οὐδὲ ἀνέστιος Synes.*ep*.103(M.66.1473B); of bishops without a diocese ἀνθρώπων ἐπισκοπῆς ἐχόντων ὄνομα, ὧν οἱ μέν εἰσιν ἀ., σχολάζοντες δὲ καὶ ἐκκλησίας οὐκ ἔχοντες CEph.(431)*ep*.(*ACO* 1.1.3 p.7.24; H.1.1508B); *ib*.(p.9.1; 1509C).

ἀπολισθαίν-ω, 1. *slip away* νηὸς...~ούσης τοῖς ὕδασι Gr.Nyss. *hom.12 in Cant*.(M.44.1016A, or perh. read ἐπολ-); **2.** *fall away from, lose* τῶν ἀρχαίων φρυαγμάτων ἀπολισθήσαντες Cyr.*Os*.50(3.81D); ἀπώλισθε...τῆς πρὸς θεὸν οἰκειότητος ὡς κυριόκτονος ὁ Ἰσραήλ id. *Juln*.8(6^2.288D); ἄνθρωπος πέφηνε [sc. ὁ λόγος]..., οὐκ ἀπολισθήσας τοῦ εἶναι θεός id.*expl.xii cap*.1(p.17.10; 6^1.147C).

ἀπόλλυμι, 1. *destroy, ruin*, of spiritual ruin in present life τὰ ἀπολλύντα τὴν ψυχήν *Barn*.20.1; Herm.*mand*.11.1; *Const.App*. 8.2.3; of future damnation, Herm.*sim*.9.23.4; δύναμις ἰσχυρὰ [sc. ὁ θεός],...ᾗ καὶ τὸ ἀπολέσαι δυνατόν Clem.*ecl*.26(p.144.21; M.9.712A); τοῦ θεοῦ σῴζοντος καὶ ἀπολλύντος οὓς ἐὰν αὐτὸς βούληται Or.*princ*. 3.1.7(p.206.9; M.11.260C); Chrys.*hom.64.4 in Jo*.(8.388B); **2.** *lose*, of spiritual loss ἐκεῖνοι [sc. Jews]...εἰς τέλος ἀπώλεσαν αὐτὴν [sc. τὴν διαθήκην] *Barn*.4.7; ἀ. τὴν ζωὴν αὐτοῦ Herm.*sim*.8.7.5; πιστὸς τῷ κυρίῳ διαμένειν ἀπολώλεκεν Clem.*str*.7.16(p.67.12; M.9.532B); ὑπὸ τῆς ἄγαν ἀλαζονείας καὶ τὸ ἀνθρώπους αὐτοὺς νομίζειν ἀπολωλεκότες Chrys.*oppugn*.3.9(1.92A); **3.** med., *perish, be destroyed* or *lost*; in present life τί μώρως ἀπολλύμεθα; Ign.*Eph*.17.2; id.*Polyc*.5.2; δεῖ τοὺς ἀπολλυμένους σῴζειν *2Clem*.2.5; Or.*princ*.2.8.3(p.155.16; M.11. 221B); ref. future damnation, *Did*.16.5 cit. s. δοκιμασία; δικαίως ἀπολεῖται ἄνθρωπος, ὃς...ἑαυτὸν εἰς ὁδὸν σκότους ἀποσυνέχει *Barn*. 5.4; ψυχὴν ἤδη γινώσκουσαν τὸν θεὸν οὐ δεῖ ἀπόλλυσθαι *2Clem*.17.1; μετανοῆσαι ἦν δυνατὸν...εἰ ἠβούλετο ἡ Ἰεζάβελ, οὐ φύσεως ἀπολλυμένης ἐστίν Or.*Apoc*.17(p.28); *Const.App*.2.39.6; Chrys.*hom.55.3 in Jo*.(8.325B); ptcpl. plur. as subst., *the lost*, *Lit*.ap.*Const.App*.8. 12.30; *Const.App*.5.13.4; of things, Ign.*Smyrn*.10.1; καλὸν τὸ ἁρπάζειν, ἀλλ' οὐχὶ τὰ ἀπολλύμενα, ἀλλὰ τὴν βασιλείαν τῶν οὐρανῶν Chrys.*hom.54.4 in Jo*.(320C).

ἀπολογ-έομαι, 1. *make a defence, be advocate for* [the Christian faith], of apologists ἀ. ὑπὲρ τοῦ λόγου Athenag.*leg*.2.4(M.6.896B); Clem.*str*.7.15(p.63.20; M.9.524B); Or.*Cels*.proem.(p.51.8; M.11.644A); of martyrs on trial, *M.Polyc*.10.2; τότε δὲ πᾶσι μὲν ἀπελογοῦντο, κατηγόρουν δὲ οὐδενός *Ep.Lugd*.ap.Eus.*h.e*.5.2.5(M.20.436A); Clem. *str*.4.9(p.281.14; M.8.1284B); as part of priest's duty to unbelievers, Dion.Ar.*e.h*.7.3.11(M.3.568A); **2.** *make a defence, justify* or *excuse oneself*: in controversy, Clem.*str*.4.12(p.286.30; M.8.1296B); at law, Gr.Nyss.*Eun*.1(1 p.40.21; M.45.268C); before God πῶς οὖν ~ήσεταί τις ὀλιγωρήσας ἢ ἐκστὰς τῆς ἐκκλησίας τοῦ θεοῦ; *Const.App*.2.60.5; ~ήσασθαι [i.e. in prayer] διὰ τί ἐχθροὺς ἔχεις Chrys.*hom.5.4 in 2Cor*. (10.470E); Eus.Al.*serm*.21.5(M.86.429A); of Christ on behalf of sinners αὐτὸς ~εῖται Dion.Ar.*ep*.8.1(M.3.1088A); of priest excusing unworthiness in liturgy, id.*e.h*.3.3.12(M.3.441D); usu. c. dat. of person before whom defence is made, also c. acc. τί...~οῦνται τὸν ἀπροσωπόληπτον δικαστήν; Eus.Al.*serm*.21.5(M.86.429A); **3.** *make a defence* for other persons or things, c. περί of subject of defence ~εῖσθαι πειρώμενοι...περὶ τῆς...προνοίας τοῦ θεοῦ Or.*princ*.3.1.17 (p.228.1; M.11.285B); id.*Jo*.5.8(p.105.20f.; M.14.196B); Meth.*fr.7 in Job* 25:4(p.512.13); or c. dat. δέον ~εῖσθαι ὁμοίως [sc. as in OT exeg.] τοῖς ἀπὸ τῆς καινῆς Or.*princ*.3.1.16(p.225.10; 281C); τῷ ταύτης [sc. δικαιοσύνης] ~ουμένους ἀξιώματι Diad.*perf*.71(p.88.9); **4.** *make satisfaction*, to God διὰ νηστείας ἀ. τῷ θεῷ Bas.*hom*.1.3 (2.3B; M.31.168A); Gr.Naz.*ep*.11(M.37.41C); Chrys.*hom.36.2 in Jo*. (8.209B); Thdt.*Jer*.31:6(2.543); **5.** *render an account* ὡς περὶ πλειόνων...~ούμενος περὶ πάντων φρόντιζε *Const.App*.2.18.7; **6.** *answer*, ‡Amph.*v.Bas*.(p.204C,D); **7.** pass., *be opposed, resist* ἐὰν ~ηθῇ [sc. μοναχός] τῷ ἡγουμένῳ αὐτοῦ ἐπόρνευσεν Sophr.H.*conf*.(M.87.3368B).

ἀπολογητικός, *suitable for defence, apologetic*; [sc. λόγος] *apology*, cf. *apologeticum est excusatio, in quo solent quidam accusantibus respondere, in defensione enim aut negatione sola positum est; et est* *nomen graecum*, Isid.H.*etym*.6.8.6; ἀ. δεύτερος Ath.*apol.sec*.tit. (p.87.1; M.25.247 not. 63); Gr.Naz.*or*.9 tit.(M.35.820A); ὁ...Γρηγόριος...ἐν τῷ μεγάλῳ ἀ. [sc. *or*.2] Max.*ep*.12(M.91.493D).

***ἀπολογητικῶς**, *in defence*, Thdr.Stud.*epp*.1.25(M.99.988C).

ἀπολογία, ἡ, 1. *speech in defence*, esp. of Christian faith by a martyr before judge τῆς ἀ. δεκτικός, τῆς ἀληθείας ἔκδικος ἀποτελεσθείς *A.*(*Pass.*)*Andr*.8(p.21.21; M.2.1233B); before senate, *M.Apollon*.1.5; Eus.*h.e*.5.21.4(M.20.488B); **2.** *excuse, defence, vindication* before God παρέχων ἄφεσιν ἁμαρτίων ταῖς ἡμετέραις ψυχαῖς καὶ καλὴν ἀ. *Inscr.*(*JHS* 11 p.236), Cilicia, saec. iii; at Last Day, Chrys.*hom*.45.4 *in Jo*.(8.267D); τὸν βίον ἔχει πρὸς ἀ. ἀρκοῦντα Proc.G.*ep*.142(83; M.87.2784C); καλὴν ἀ. ἐπὶ τοῦ φοβεροῦ βήματος τοῦ Χριστοῦ *Euchol*.p.32; cf.*Lit.Chrys*.(p.382.4); **3.** *explanation*, *Ev.Thom*.A 7(p.147); Or.*princ*.3.1.16(p.224.5; M.11.281A); **4.** *answer*, *A.Pil*.B 4.4(p.296).

ἀπολογισμός, ὁ, *defence, plea*, Clem.*paed*.2.12(p.228.19; M.8.541A); Eus.*p.e*.10.4(473A; M.21.785D).

ἀπόλουσις, ἡ, *washing*; of annual cleansing of an idol, *M.Thdot.1* 14(p.70.7); of baptism δέξασθαι αὐτὰ [sc. παιδία] ἐκ τῆς τιμίας ἀ. *V.Marth*.1(405A).

***ἀπολουσμός, ὁ,** *ablution*; of preparation for pagan rites, Thdt.*Is*.66:17(p.260.34; 2.401).

***ἀπολουτρ-όω**, *cleanse by baptism* ∼ουμένων v.l. for ἀπολουομένων Meth.*symp*.8.7(p.89.4; M.18.148D); f.l. *ib*.(M.18.149A; ἀπολυτρ- p.89.15).

ἀπολού-ω, med.; **1.** *wash clean*; in baptism, Or.*Jo*.6.38(p.146.34; M.14.265A); *A.Mt*.4(p.220.15); Meth.*symp*.8.7(p.89.4; M.18.148D); CAnc.(314)*can*.11; pass. τὸ...τὴν ψυχὴν...κηλίδων...καθαρὰν ∼θῆναι τοῦ κόσμου Meth.*symp*.10.1(p.121.25; 192C); **2.** *wash away*; one's sins, Chrys.*hom*.3.4 *in Phil*.(11.217C); id.*hom*.41.4 *in Mt*.(7.449E); Cyr.*dial.Trin*.4(5^1.529D); sins of others ∼όμενος [sc. Ἰησοῦς] τὰ ἡμέτερα ἁμαρτήματα ἵν' ἡμεῖς τῷ λουτρῷ αὐτοῦ καθαρισθῶμεν Or.*comm.in Mt*.16.6(p.485.21; M.13.1385A).

***ἀπολυπέω**, pass., *be overcome with grief*, Pall.*h.Laus*.33(p.97.11; M.34.1105D).

***ἀπολυπλασίαστος**, *not multiplied*, Cyr.*Lc*.12:41(M.72.752A).

ἀπολυπραγμόνητος, 1. *not to be curiously inquired into*, of God ἀ. ἐὰν τὴν θείαν οὐσίαν Gr.Nyss.*Eun*.12(1 p.243.30; M.45.944A); of his works ἀ. ... τὰ παρ' αὐτοῦ τεχνουργούμενα Cyr.*Is*.4.2(2.609A); of a mystery of faith, Gr.Nyss.*v.Mos*.(M.44.388A); τὸ πίστει παραδεκτὸν ἀ. εἶναι χρή Cyr.*Juln*.10(6^2.360C); **2.** free from curious questioning, hence *unquestioning*, Cyr.*Juln*.8(6^2.269C); πίστις δέ ἐστιν ἀ. συγκατάθεσις Jo.D.*f.o*.4.11(M.94.1128D); **3.** free from prying, *reverent* στοργὴν ἀ. Nil.*epp*.2.167(M.79.280D).

***ἀπολυπραγμόνως**, *without curious inquiry* ἡ...ἐκκλησία...πάντα [sc. τὰ θεῖα] ἀ. σέβει Jo.V H.*icon*.8(M.96.1356C).

ἀπολύσιμος, 1. *of discharge* τὴν ἀ. ἐπιστολὴν Hipp.*haer*.9.12 (p.247.33; M.16.3382D); **2.** eccl., [sc. ἡμέρα] *concluding day of an octave*, esp. of Low Sunday τοὺς νεοφωτίστους τῷ σαββάτῳ τῆς ἀ. Bas.Sel.*pasch*.2 tit.(M.28.1082A).

ἀπόλυσις, ἡ, 1. *release* τῆς ἀ. τῆς ψυχῆς Clem.*str*.4.25(p.318.27; M.8.1368B); **2.** *casting out* of a devil, Vict.*Mc*.9:28(p.362.15); **3.** *death*, Chrys.*hom*.36.4 *in Gen*.(4.368E); **4.** *end* of a performance, met. of death ἐλεύσεται...ὥρα ὅταν τὸ θέατρον τοῦ κόσμου τούτου διαλυθήσεται...οὐκ ἔστι μετὰ τὴν τοῦ θεάτρου ἀ. στεφανωθῆναι Chrys.*poenit*.9(2.350E); **5.** liturg.; **a.** *dismissal*; **i.** at end of a service, *Pet.Ar*.3(M.26.821B); Marc.Diac.*v.Porph*.67; Jo.Disc.*v.Epiph*.34 (M.41.68D); ἀπὸ...τῆς τῶν λυχνικῶν ἀ. ἕως...ὥρας ἐνάτης Cyr.S.*v.Sab*.60(p.161.10); *Const.Stud*.2(M.99.1705B); its formula, *Euchol*.(p.724); **ii.** of catechumens, Max.*myst*.14(M.91.693A); **b.** *conclusion* of Gospel, Leont.N.*v.Jo.Eleem*.42(p.83.20); Sophr.H.*v.Cyr.et Jo*.11 (M.87.3460D); **c.** *concluding* (corresponding to octave) *day* of a festival ἡ τελευταία τῆς ἑορτῆς ἡμέρα ἦν...ἀ. καλεῖν ἡμῖν ἔθος Bas.Sel.*v.Thecl*.2.18(M.85.596B).

***ἀπολυσσάω**, *recover from madness*, Isid.Pel.*epp*.1.304(M.78.360A).

***ἀπολυτής**, *loosing, disruptive*; of Semiarian heresy, Epiph.*haer*.73.27(M.42.456A; conj. ἀπατηλήν p.301.25).

***ἀπολυτίκιον, τό,** *dismissal hymn*, i.e. a short hymn sung before the ἀπόλυσις at matins and vespers καὶ ψάλλεται τὸ ἀ. τῆς ἡμέρας *Euchol*.(p.4); *ib*.(p.34); in liturgy, *Lit.Chrys*.(pp.368.34,396.20).

ἀπολυτικός, 1. *of dismissal* εὐχὴ ἀ. *Lit.Jac*.(*NBP* 10^2. p.105); neut. as subst., *Const.Stud*.2(M.99.1705B); **2.** [sc. ἐπιστολή] *letter of leave* (Lat. *dimissoriae litterae*), granted to clerics to cross the sea, *Cod.Afr*.23,56; to visit the imperial court, *ib*.106; to clergy leaving their own diocese to settle in another, CTrull.*can*.17.

ἀπολυτρ-όω, *rescue, redeem*, freq. pass. ἕκαστος...ἐκείνῳ τῷ ἁγιασμῷ ἁγιάζεται καὶ κατ' ἐκείνην τὴν ἀπολύτρωσιν ∼οῦται Or.*Jo*.1.34(39; p.44.4; M.14.89D); τὴν ἐκκλησίαν εἶναι τὴν...γεννῶσαν τοὺς ∼ουμένους Meth.*symp*.8.7(p.89.15; M.18.149A); ὥσπερ ἐκ Βαβυλῶνος τῆς κατὰ τὸν ἐνεστῶτα βίον...αἰχμαλωσίας ∼ωθέντες εἰς τὴν οὐρανόπολιν Eus.*d.e*.4.17(p.198.21; M.22.329D); med. ταύτην τὴν σωτηρίαν ...πάντα τὰ ὄντα...τῆς τῶν οἰκείων ἀγαθῶν ἀποπτώσεως ∼ουμένην Dion.Ar.*d.n*.8.8(M.3.897A).

ἀπολύτρωσις, ἡ, *ransoming, redemption*, in gen. τὴν αὐτὴν τῆς ἀ. ἡμῖν πίστιν καὶ ἐλπίδα ἔχουσιν ἀδελφοῖς *Ep.Lugd*.ap.Eus.*h.e*.5.1.3 (M.20.409A); Clem.*str*.7.10(p.41.19; M.9.480B); τὴν ἀ. ἡμῶν ἀπὸ τῆς φθορᾶς...τοῦ σώματος Meth.*res*.1.47(p.299.1; M.18.273C); ‡Ath.*Apoll*.1.5(M.26.1101A); through baptism τοῖς ἐπὶ τὰ ὕδατα τῆς ἀ. ἀφικνουμένοις Meth.*symp*.9.3(p.117.25; M.18.184B); Ath.*exp.Ps*.50:1 (M.27.237B); δὸς αὐτῷ τὴν χάριν τῆς ἀ. *Rit.Bapt*.(p.400); of Christ (ref. 1Cor.1:30) ἀ. αὐτός Or.*hom*.8.2 *in Jer*.(p.57.7; M.13.337C); ἀ. ...ὡς ἐλευθερῶν ἡμᾶς...καὶ λύτρον ἑαυτὸν ἀντιδιδοὺς ἡμῶν τῆς οἰκουμένης καθάρσιον Gr.Naz.*or*.30.20(p.141.7; M.36.132A); ἀ. διὰ τὸ σώζειν ἐκ φθορᾶς τὴν ζωὴν ἡμῶν ‡Ath.*dial.Trin*.1.18(M.28.1144D); παρὰ σοὶ ἡ ἀ. *Euchol*.(p.41); of the divine essence ἀ. αὐτὴν ὀνομάζουσιν οἱ θεόλογοι, καὶ καθ' ὅσον οὐκ ἐᾷ τὰ ὄντως ὄντα πρὸς τὸ μὴ εἶναι διαπεσεῖν Dion.Ar.*d.n*.8.9(M.3.897A); Gnost., of Marcosian second baptism, Iren.*haer*.1.13.6(M.7.588B); *ib*.1.21.1(657A); Hipp.*haer*.6.41(p.172.22; M.16.3259B); ‡Epiph.*epit.haer*.(p.368.29).

ἀπολύτως, 1. *absolutely* οὔτε ἀ. κακόν Gr.Nyss.*hom.opif*.20.3(M.45.200B); *unconditionally* ἡ ἐξουσία τοῦ ἀφιέναι οὐκ ἀ. δέδοται· ἀλλ' ἐν ὑπακοῇ τοῦ μετανοοῦντος Bas.*reg.br*.58(2.435A; M.31.1121B); opp. relatively οὐκ ἐπὶ τοῦ κυρίου φημί, ἀλλ' ἀ. Jo.D.*Jacob*.14(M.94.1444C); of number in the abstract, Leont.B.*arg.Sev*.(M.86.1920B); ref. God τὸ δὲ θεὸς ὄνομα, ἀ. καὶ ὡσαύτως κατηγορεῖται ἑκάστου τῶν προσώπων Gr.Nyss.*comm.not*.(M.45.176B); Dion.Ar.*d.n*.12.3(M.3.969C); *ib*.10.3(937C); ref. certain divine names, dist. from those which imply a relation ἐστι...ἐκ τῶν ὀνομάτων τούτων τὸ μὲν...ἀ. εἰπεῖν...ἕτερα δὲ...τὸ πρός τι χρήσιμον ἀποσημαίνει Gr.Nyss.*Eun*.1(1 p.182.17; M.45.428A); **2.** *without qualification*; of language, Or.*Jo*.2.5 (4; p.59.12; M.14.117A); Eus.*e.th*.2.14(p.114.23; M.24.928A); Thdt.*qu*. 5 *in Gen*.(1.9); Anast.S.*hod*.13(M.89.208A); **3.** *disconnected*, of style ἀ. ... τῷ μεταβατικῷ συνδέσμῳ μὴ χρησάμενος *cat.Apoc*.2:24(p.215.30); **4.** eccl., opp. ἰδικῶς, *without title* τοὺς δὲ ἀ. χειροτονουμένους ὥρισεν ἡ σύνοδος ἄκυρον ἔχειν τὴν τοιαύτην χειροθεσίαν CChalc.*can*.6.

ἀπολύ-ω, 1. *set free, release*, of death ἀ. τοῦ σώματος καὶ τῶν τούτου ἁμαρτημάτων τὴν ψυχήν Clem.*str*.5.8(p.363.18; M.9.85B); θανάτῳ ∼όμενοι πρὸς τὸν κύριον *ib*.4.11(p.283.24; M.8.1288C); Or.*Cels*.6.59 (p.129.21; M.11.1388D); Ath.*gent*.33(M.25.68A); ‡Chrys.*occurs*.(2.813D); *loose* an arrow, Or.*Cels*.4.90(p.363.3; 1168B); **2.** *allow* ἀ. τὸν μάγον...τοιαῦτα πράττειν *A.Petr.et Paul*.50(p.200.6); ἀ. τὸν μάγον ...πράξαντα κακά *A.*(*Pass.*)*Petr.et Paul*.29(p.144.1); μὴ ἀ. σοὺς ὀφθαλμοὺς ῥέμβεσθαι Ephr.1.80D; **3.** eccl.; **a.** *absolve* με θᾶττον ∼σατε, τῶν πρεσβυτέρων μοί τινα κάλεσον Dion.Al.ap.Eus.*h.e*.6.44.3(M.20.629C); **b.** *dispense* ἐάν τις ᾖ ἀσθενῶν...καὶ ἔλθῃ τὸ ἅγιον πάσχα, πάντως ὀφείλει νηστεύειν, ἢ ∼ει αὐτὸν ὁ κληρικὸς λαμβάνειν οὐ δύναται; Tim.I Al.*resp*.(M.33.1301D); **4.** *lose*; *lay aside*; **a.** act. τὰ τῶν ἀνθρώπων σώματα...τὴν...οἰκείαν οὐκ ἀ. φύσιν Thdt.*eran*.2 (4.122); **b.** med., *put away, get rid of*: sins ∼εσθαι τὰ ἁμαρτήματα χρή Chrys.*hom*.14.2 *in Eph*.(11.106A); id.*hom*.41.4 *in Mt*.(v.l. for ἀπολουομένων 7.449E); any burden, Cyr.*Is*.4.3(2.647C); id.*ador*.2(1.79E); **5.** *send away* a wife, Herm.*mand*.4.1.6; Athenag.*leg*.33.2(M.6.968A); Clem.*str*.2.23(p.193.16; M.8.1096C); *divorce* a vinculo under Mosaic law, Afric.*ep.Arist*.(p.59.15; M.10.57B); **6.** liturg.; **a.** *dismiss* congregation μετὰ τὸ ῥηθῆναι τὸν ὀρθρινὸν καὶ ∼σαι αὐτὸν τοὺς κατηχουμένους κτλ. *Const.App*.8.38.1; *Apophth.Patr*.(M.65.269B); μὴ ἐξέλθῃς τῆς ἐκκλησίας ἐὰν μὴ ∼θῇς Eus.Al.*serm*.16.2(M.86.416D); **b.** med., *depart* ὁ διάκονος ἐρεῖ '∼εσθε ἐν εἰρήνῃ' *Lit*.ap.*Const.App*.8.15.10; '∼εσθε οἱ ἐν μετανοίᾳ' *ib*.8.9.11; **7.** intrans., *finish* a service etc.; *break up*, Ephr.2.94B; Epiph.*exp.fid*.22(p.524.2; M.42.828C); μετὰ τὸ ∼σαι τὴν ἀγρυπνίαν Dor.*doct*.9.2(M.88.1720A); **8.** intrans., *die* ὁ ἁγιώτατος Κύριλλος ἀπέλυσεν ἐν κυρίῳ Jo.Not.*v.Eus*.1(M.86.301C); **9.** perf. ptcpl. pass., *absolute*; hence **a.** *detached from, independent of* εἰ δέ τις ζητεῖ τὸ ἐφ' ἡμῖν ἀ. εἶναι τοῦ παντός Or.*comm.in Gen*.ap. Eus.*p.e*.6.11(290C; M.12.69B); **b.** *dissolute*, Chrys.*hom*.4.7 *in Mt*. (7.60B).

***ἀπομαδαρ-όω**, *shave* 'οὐκ ∼ώσετε'...φησὶν ὁ νόμος, 'τοὺς πώγωνας ὑμῶν' *Const.App*.1.3.11.

***ἀπομάθησις, ἡ,** *unlearning*, Bas.*ep*.2.2(3.72A; M.32.225B).

ἀπομαίνομαι, *rave furiously*, Pall.*h.Laus*.23(p.76.18; M.34.1089A); *ib*.65(p.161.9; 1251B).

***ἀπομακρύνω**, *remove far away*; met., from sins, Chrys.*hom.14.4 in Heb.*(12.146C); from commandments of God, ‡Chrys.*hom.2.5 in Ps.118*(5.708D); from God, Thdr.Stud.*epp.*2.84(M.99.1325C).

ἀπομανθάνω, **1.** *unlearn*, Gr.Thaum.*pan.Or.*15(p.33.23; M.10.1093B); Ath.*Ar.*2.28(M.26.208A); μέχρις ἂν γυμνασίᾳ πολλῇ καὶ χρόνῳ αὐτὸν ἀπομαθεῖν τὰ πρῶτα ‡Nil.*perist.*12.6(M.79.949A); **2.** *learn thoroughly, finish learning*; habit of silence, Bas.*reg.fus.*13(2.354E; M.31.949B); Chrys.*hom.9.1 in Col.*(11.391E).

ἀπομαντεύομαι, *rave, talk wildly, irrationally*, Just.*dial.*9.1(M.6.493C); Didym.*Trin.*3.41(M.39.984B).

***ἀπομαστίζω**, *scourge severely*; met., of devil afflicting lunatic boy (Mt.17:15), Mac.Mgn.*apocr.*2.10(p.16.11).

***ἀπομαφορτίζω**, *strip off the veil*, conj. for ἀπομαφορίζω, Ath.*ep.encycl.*4(p.173.9; -φοριζόμεναι M.25.229C).

ἀπομάχομαι, *contend, disagree with*, Bas.*Spir.*52(3.43D; M.32.164A); †Bas.*Is.*172(1.504A; M.30.405C); Philost.*h.e.*5.1(M.65.528C).

ἀπόμαχος, **1.** *not engaged* in battle, *without fighting*, Synes.*insomn.*13(p.174.4; M.66.1308B); Socr.*h.e.*2.11.5(M.67.205B); **2.** *invincible* ὁ...νόμος...ἀ. μένει Gr.Nyss.*v.Mos.*(M.44.372A).

ἀπομειόω, *diminish, impair*, †Bas.*poenit.*4(2.606E; M.31.1484A); Sophr.H.*mir.Cyr.et Jo.*30(M.87.3516D); Christol. ἥτις γέννησις χρονικὴ τῆς θείας αὐτοῦ...γεννήσεως οὔτε τι ἀπεμείωσεν Leo Mag.*ep.*28.2(p.11.27; M.*PL*.54.760A); μηδὲν αὐτῶν...[sc. τὰς Χριστοῦ φύσεις] ἀ. ἢ ἐξαρνεῖσθαι Max.*opusc.*(M.91.96C); πῶς οὖν τὴν οὕτω δημιουργηθεῖσαν [sc. οὐσίαν] ὑπὸ αὐτοῦ προσληφθεῖσαν τῇ οἰκείᾳ σαρκώσει κατὰ φυσικὴν ἀπεμείωσε θέλησιν καὶ ἐνέργειαν; Martin.*ep.*3(M.*PL*.87.140D).

***ἀπομείωσις**, **ἡ**, *diminution, truncation*, ref. monophysite Christology οἱ τὴν τῶν προσόντων αὐτῷ φυσικῶς ἀ. ἀσεβῶς δογματίζοντες Max.*opusc.*(M.91.73C).

ἀπομέν-ω, **1.** *remain behind, stay*, Hipp.*haer.*6.20(p.148.17; M.16.3226B); Ath.*inc.*44.6(M.25.176A); Bas.*hex.*3.2(1.22E; M.29.53C); **2.** *continue* δικαιοσύνης ἀ. κεναί Meth.*symp.*6.2(p.65.24; M.18.116B); οἱ Ἀρειομανῖται αἱροῦνται ~ειν Ἰουδαῖοι Ath.*Ar.*2.17(M.26.181C); ἄνθρωπος γεγονὼς ὁ...λόγος ἀπομεμένηκε καὶ οὕτω θεός Cyr.*expl.xii cap.*9(p.23.20; 6^1.154E); **3.** *abide by, hold fast* to [sc. Pharisaic tradition] ἀ. τῷ γράμματι Sev.Ant.ap.*cat.Mt.*15:5(p.122.29); **4.** *desist* from, *surrender* ἀ. ἐκ τῶν μειζόνων τοῦ πνεύματος προκοπῶν Ephr.3.336E; **5.** *be left behind, be left over, A(Pass.)Andr.*8(p.20.20); οὐδὲ ἴχνος ἀ. τῆς ταραχῆς Chrys.*hom.28.2 in Mt.*(7.335B); τὴν μυστικὴν εὐλογίαν εἰ ~οι λείψανον αὐτῆς Cyr.*ep.Calos.*(6^2.365B); of payment, *be deferred, T.Job* 12(p.111.12); math., *be left* after division, Max.*comput.*17(M.19.1236A); †Andr.Cr.*cycl.*(M.19.1332C).

ἀπομεριμνάω, *become free from anxiety* ἀ. περὶ αὐτοῦ Leont.N.*v.Sym.*12(M.93.1684D); *be freed from the anxiety of* ἀ. πειρασμῶν Nil.*epp.*3.205(M.79.477B); in bad sense, *become careless*, Ephr.3.323F.

ἀπομερισμός, **ὁ**, **1.** *apportionment*, Val.Gn.ap.Epiph.*haer.*31.5(p.391.12); **2.** *division*, †Bas.*ep.*361(3.463D; M.32.1104B); **3.** *divorce* λύσις καὶ ἀ. *Chron.Pasch.*p.316(M.92.804B).

***ἀπομετεωρίζ-ω**, pass.; **1.** *be raised aloft*, ‡Bas.*struct.hom.*1.14(1.330B; M.30.24B); **2.** met., *be elevated* ὅρα...οἷον ἀπομετεωρισθεὶς κατεκρημνίσθης, τῶν οἰκείων μέτρων ἐκστάς Thdr.Stud.*epp.*2.162(M.99.1512A); **3.** met., pass., *be distracted, carried away*, Bas.*reg.fus.*32(2.375A; M.31.996A); *ib.*37.5(384C; M.1016C); ἵνα μὴ ~εσθαι πρὸς τὸ μέλος, ἀλλ' ἵνα...ὁ νοῦς...συμπεπύρωται τῇ δυνάμει τῶν λόγων Dor.*doct.*22.1(M.88.1821B).

***ἀπομήκοθεν**, *from afar*, Epiph.*haer.*69.41(M.42.265B; ἀπὸ μήκοθεν p.189.7); τὸ ἀ. as subst., *remoteness* τὸ ἀ. τῆς...χώρας Anast.S.*hod.*6(M.89.104B).

ἀπομιμνήσκω, **1.** *remind*, Chrys.*fr.Jer.*2:2(M.64.756C); **2.** pass., *be recorded, mentioned* περὶ τοῦ...ἁγίου πνεύματος ἀ. Didym.*Trin.*1.36(M.39.440B); **3.** med., *remember*, Cyr.*dial.Trin.*1(5^1.386C); Thdt.*Pss.proem.*(1.602).

ἀπομιτρόω, *divest of the mitre*, Cyr.*ador.*12(1.433A).

ἀπόμματος, *blind*, Gr.II Papa *ep.Germ.*(M.98.152B); Steph.Diac.*v.Steph.*(M.100.1160C).

***ἀπομματόω**, *blind*, Geo.Pis.*carm.*10.2.

ἀπομνημόνευμα, **το**, **1.** plur., *memoirs*; in gen., Eus.*h.e.*5.8.8(M.20.449C); of the gospels οἱ...ἀπόστολοι ἐν τοῖς γενομένοις ὑπ' αὐτῶν ἀ., ἃ καλεῖται εὐαγγέλια Just.*1apol.*66.3(M.6.429A); id.*dial.*100.4(M.6.709C) al.; Eus.*d.e.*3.6(p.132.10; M.22.224B); **2.** *recorded saying*, Clem.*str.*2.20(p.177.3; M.8.1061B); **3.** *recollection* ἤ τι...εἰρημένον ἢ πεπραγμένον φέρειν ἀ. Gr.Naz.*or.*43.77(M.36.600B).

ἀπομνημονεύ-ω, **1.** *remember* οὐδὲν ἥμαρτεν Μάρκος, οὕτως ἔνια γράψας ὡς ἀπεμνημόνευσεν Papias *fr.*2.15; of Heb. τὰ μὲν νοήματα τοῦ ἀποστόλου ἐστίν, ἡ δὲ φράσις καὶ ἡ σύνθεσις ~σαντός τινος τὰ ἀποστολικά Or.*fr.in Heb.*ap.Eus.*h.e.*6.25.13(M.14.1309A); ταῦτα...~σας τὰ ἐν τῇ συνόδῳ τότε πραχθέντα δεδήλωκα Ath.*decr.*32(p.28.15; M.25.476B); **2.** *record* ὡς οἱ ~σαντες πάντα τὰ περὶ τοῦ σωτῆρος... ἐδίδαξαν Just.*1apol.*33.5(M.6.381B); Hipp.*haer.*6.6(p.134.22; M.16.3206C); οἱ...~οντες [i.e. the Evangelists] Or.*Jo.*6.34(18; p.143.29; M.14.257D); **3.** *make mention* of ἀ. τοῦ παραλύτου Amph.*mesopent.*(M.39.124A); Thdt.*h.rel.*4(3.1155); **4.** *recite* ἀναλέγεσθαι εἰώθασι καὶ ταύτας διὰ στόματος ~ειν Eus.*d.e.*2.1(p.52.24; M.22.97B).

ἀπόμοιρα, **ἡ**, *portion*, *Orac.Sib.*3.245; ‡Proc.G.*Pr.*15:16(M.87.1376A); ref. sabbath σχολῆς ἕνεκα τῆς πρὸς θεόν, ἵνα κἂν σμικροτάτην ἀ. [sc. of life] αὐτῷ ἀπονέμωσι Jo.D.*f.o.*4.23(M.94.1204B); *offering* καλὸν ἐντάφιον...τῷ...ἀ. θεῷ εἰσοίσουσα Thdr.Stud.*epp.*2.188(M.99.1577A).

ἀπόμοιρος, *without a share in* πῶς οὖν ἡ αἵρεσις [sc. of Eunomius]...ἀ. ποιεῖ τὸν πατέρα τῆς...εὐχαριστίας; Gr.Nyss.*Eun.*12(2 p.288.7; M.45.900D).

***ἀπομόναχος**, **ὁ**, *ex-monk, apostate monk*, Ephr.2.181C.

ἀπόμοργμα, **τό**, *impression, reflection*, of a seal τὰ ἀ. τῆς μιᾶς... ἀρχετυπίας Dion.Ar.*d.n.*2.6(M.3.644B); of icons ἀμέτοχα γὰρ τῆς φύσεως εἶεν ἂν τὰ ἐκμαγεῖα τῶν ἀρχετύπων ἐν τοῖς τεχνητοῖς, μόνην ἐπιδεικνύμενα ὡς ἐν κατόπτρῳ τὴν ἐμφέρειαν τῶν ὧνπέρ εἰσιν ἀπομόργματα Thdr.Stud.*ref.*1(M.99.489A).

ἀπομορφ-όω, **1.** *change form*, Hipp.*haer.*10.11(p.272.10; M.16.3426A); **2.** pass., *? lose sight of* ὡς...τῆς τε ἀθανασίας ~ωθῆναι τὸ κάλλος αὐτοῖς Const.Diac.*laud.*2(M.88.480B); **3.** pass., *be formed* ἐκ τοῦ συγγενοῦς τῆς γῆς...σὺ ἀπεμορφώθης ‡Gr.Nyss.*or.2 in Gen.1*:26(M.44.292C); πρὸς τὴν ἱερατικὴν...~οῦσθαι ζωήν Dion.Ar.*e.h.*6.3.2(M.3.533D).

ἀπομοτικός, *denying on oath*, neut. as subst., Didym.*Ps.*109:4(M.39.1540D).

***ἀπόμοτος**, *to be forsworn, hostile* ἐκεῖνον νομίσας εἶναι θεόν... ὅνπερ ἔχειν ἀ. ὁ τῆς θείας ἐντολῆς διετάξατο λόγος Max.*qu.Thal.*1(M.90.253C).

ἀπομυζάω, *suck*, Ast.Am.*hom.*1(M.40.177B).

***ἀπομυκτηρισμός**, **ὁ**, *turning up the nose, derision*, Clem.*paed.*2.6(p.187.9; M.8.452B).

***ἀπομυρίζω**, *? anoint with holy oil*, Thdr.Stud.*epp.*2.219.8,10(M.99.1664B,C).

***ἀπομύρισμα**, **τό**, *holy oil*, with healing properties εὐχὴν δὲ ποίαν, ἢ ἀ. ποῖον δῶμεν ἁμαρτωλοὶ τυγχάνοντες; Thdr.Stud.*epp.*1.55(M.99.1109A).

***ἀπομυσάττομαι**, *despise, treat as contemptible*, Thdr.Stud.*epp.*1.28(M.99.1001B).

ἀπομύ-ω, **1.** *shut* the eyes; fig., ‡Gr.Nyss.*occurs.*(M.46.1180B); **2.** met., *shut out, seal up* sight κἂν αὐτοὶ [sc. fallen angels] μὴ ὁρῶσιν, ~σαντες αὐτῶν τὰς ἀγαθοποιητικὰς δυνάμεις Dion.Ar.*d.n.*4.23(M.3.725C); id.*myst.*1.3(M.3.1001A) cit. s. γνόφος; Max.*schol.myst.*1.3(M.4.421A); **3.** *wither*, met. ἀ. τὰς βλαστὰς διὰ τὴν ἁμαρτίαν Meth.*symp.*10.5(p.127.23; M.18.201A).

***ἀπομφακίζω**, *ripen*, †Hipp.*theoph.*1(p.257.16; M.10.852B).

***ἀπομωραίνω**, pass.; **1.** *become foolish*, Eus.*Is.*19:19(M.24.233A); Cyr.*ador.*1(1.30E); **2.** *become insipid*; of salt, ref. Mt.5:13, *ib.*(31A).

ἀποναρκ-άω, **1.** *become numb*, Bas.*hom.*6.4(2.47B; M.31.269B); **2.** met., *be torpid, sluggish* τῶν ~ᾶν πρὸς τὸ εὔχεσθαι ποιούντων Or.*or.*5(p.311.14; M.11.433C); Epiph.*exp.fid.*19(p.520.15; M.42.820C) cit. s. ἀποσικχαίνω; πεποιήκασι...τοὺς καρποφορεῖν εἰωθότας ~ῆσαι Isid.Pel.*epp.*3.325(M.78.985C); **3.** *be benumbed, struck with fear* or *awe* εἰ...ταῖς τῶν τυράννων ἀπειλαῖς τὰς ψυχάς τινες ἀπενάρκησαν Eus.*h.e.*10.4.35(M.20.864A); *Hom.Clem.*1.14; Cyr.*Jo.*2(4.115E); Vict.*Mc.*14:22ff.(p.423.22); **4.** *shrink from* τὸν ἕνα...υἱὸν ἀ. διελεῖν εἰς δύο Cyr.*hom.pasch.*8(5^2.101D); id.*Jo.*2.8(4.230D); πρὸς μόνον ἀ. τὸν...τύπον *ib.*2.5(4.189E).

ἀπονεμητέον, *one must assign*, Clem.*str.*7.16(p.71.11; M.9.540B); Chrys.*hom.26.2 in 1Cor.*(10.229C); Isid.Pel.*epp.*4.16(M.78.1064C).

ἀπόνευμα, **τό**, *slope*; met., *natural inclination, disposition* τῶν εἰς τὸ φαῦλον ἀσχέτων ἀ. Cyr.*ador.*1(1.14E).

ἀπονευρ-όω, *unnerve, enervate, weaken* ἡδονῇ...προκατεφθαρμένος ὁ νοῦς οὕτω τε ~ούμενος Cyr.*ador.*3(1.103D); κύριος, ὁ νεῦρα διδοὺς τοῖς ἠσθενηκόσι, καὶ ~ῶν τοὺς λελυπηκότας id.*Am.*23(3.274D); τὸ μυσαρὸν τῶν δαιμόνων ~ῶσαι στῖφος id.*Juln.*8(6^2.279C); id.*Mich.*71(3.470E).

ἀπόνευσις, **ἡ**, *turning from*; *turning* to ἀ. πρὸς ἀρετὴν ἢ κακίαν Or.*or.*6(p.313.1; M.11.436C); 'ἀπόκλισιν' ἀντὶ τοῦ 'ἀ.' Max.*schol.c.h.*2.4(M.4.44C); Areth.*Apoc.*51(M.106.712C).

ἀπονεύω, *turn away from* one direction *to* another; *depart, go off* ἐληλεγμένος ἀπένευσε τότε ὁ διάβολος Just.*dial.*125.4(M.6.768B); *A.Paul.et Thecl.*7(p.240.10).

ἀπόνηρος, *without malice, innocent, simple*, *Const.App.*2.49.4; ἀσφραγίστους μέν, ἀ. δέ Gr.Naz.*or.*40.23(M.36.389C); Ast.Am.*hom.*4 (M.40.220D); Leont.N.*v.Sym.*11(M.93.1684A); of Christian life οἱ μετὰ συνέσεως πρᾶοι ὄντες, καὶ ἀ., τοῦτο γάρ ἐστι βίος ἀγγελικός *cat.Mt.*19:6(p.154.14) but cf. Chrys.*hom.62.4 in Mt.*(7.624E); Cyr.*Lc.*9:46(M.72.660C); neut. as subst., Ammon.*Jo.*17:14(M.85.1504B).

***ἀπονήρως**, *innocently, guilelessly, without malice*, Cyr.*Ps.*100:2 (M.69.1261A); ἁπλῶς καὶ ἀπλάστως καὶ ἀποικίλως καὶ ἀ. Jo.Clim. *scal.*24(M.88.984B); Anast.S.*hod.*13(M.89.204C).

***ἀπονησόω**, *make an island of*, Evagr.*h.e.*5.9(p.204.17; M.86.2809A).

***ἀπονηστεύ-ω**, *break one's fast* ~σαντες ἄρξασθε τῆς ἁγίας τοῦ πάσχα ἑβδομάδος *Const.App.*5.13.4; ~σαι προσέταξεν τῇ ἑβδόμῃ ἡμέρᾳ ἀλέκτορος φωνήσαντος *ib.*5.14.20; *ib.*5.19.7.

ἀπονηστίζ-ομαι, *break one's fast*, during Lent ~εσθαι δὲ δεῖ οὗ ἂν ἐνπέσῃ κυριακή Hipp.*can.pasch.*(M.10.876); at Easter ἐπέστειλάς μοι...πυνθάνομενος καθ' ἣν ὥραν ~εσθαι δεῖ τῇ τοῦ πάσχα περιλύσει Dion.Al.*ep.can.*(p.94.4; M.10.1272B); *Const.App.*5.19.2; Eus.*qu. Marin.*2.2(M.22.941C); χρὴ τοὺς πιστοὺς περὶ μέσας τῆς περὶ τὸ μέγα σάββατον νυκτὸς ὥρας ~εσθαι CTrull.*can.*89.

***ἀπονίκησις, ἡ**, *complete victory*, Cyr.*Am.*74(3.334E).

ἀπονίπτω, **1.** *wash off* τὸν ῥύπον τῶν ποδῶν Or.*Jo.*32.8(6; p.437.29; M.14.760D); c. acc. dupl., met. πᾶσαν τὴν ῥυτίδα τῆς ἁμαρτίας ἡμᾶς ἀ. Diad.*perf.*89(p.124.10); med., from oneself, Or.*fr.63 in Jo.* 9:6(p.534.18); Ath.*gent.*24(M.25.48C); met. τὴν...ὑποψίαν οὐκ ἀ. id. *apol.fug.*26(p.86.1; M.25.677B); Chrys.*sac.*4.1(p.103.1; 1.404D); id. *hom.10.5 in Mt.*(7.146A); **2.** *wash*, Hipp.*haer.*4.33(p.59.19; M.16.3098A); med., met. ἵν'...ἀπονίψωνται τὰς ἑαυτῶν ἀσεβεῖς ἀκοάς Ath.*decr.*2(p.2.33; M.25.'428'(420)B); id.*gent.*34(M.25.68C); **3.** *have ...washed* ὡς ἂν παρετοιμαζομένους...ἀπονίψασθαι τοὺς πόδας πρὸς τοῦ κυρίου τοὺς μαθητάς Clem.*fr.*28(p.216.32; M.9.757A).

ἀπόνιψις, ἡ, **1.** *washing off* or *away* (ref. Jo.13:8) ἐνόμισεν ὁ Πέτρος ὅτι ἡ ἀ. ἐκείνη ἁμαρτιῶν ἦν ἄφεσις...ἡ δὲ οὐχ...ἀλλ' εὐλαβείας ὑπόθεσις ‡Chrys.*prod.serv.*3(8^{2}.245D); διὰ τῶν ὑδάτων ἀ. ... ἀκαθαρσίας δὲ τῆς εἰς νοῦν καὶ καρδίαν Cyr.*Lc.*11:42(M.72.712B); id.*ador.*2(1.52B); met., of baptism ἀ. καλεῖ...τῶν ῥυτίδων...ἐκείνων ἀφανισμόν Isid.Pel.*epp.*1.417(M.78.416A); **2.** *washing*, liturg. ὑποδιάκονος διδότω ἀ. χειρῶν τοῖς ἱερεῦσιν v.l. *Lit.*ap.*Const.App.*8.11.12 (l. ἀπόρρυψιν); ἡ...τοῦ ἱεράρχου...ἄχρι τῶν ἄκρων...ἀ. Dion.Ar.*e.h.* 3.3.10(M.3.440B).

ἀπονο-έω, **A.** act., *make proud* ἵνα μὴ...αὐτοὺς ~ήσῃ Chrys. *hom.64.4 in Mt.*(7.639E).

B. usu. pass.; **1.** *be desperate, abandoned*, esp. perf. ptcpl. pass. οἱ ἀκάθαρτοι καὶ πάντα ἀπονενοημένοι Just.*dial.*141.3(M.6.800A); *A. Xanthipp.*13(p.66.13); Didym.*Trin.*1.17(M.39.341A); **2.** *be desperately proud* or *vain, vaunt oneself*, Chrys.*hom.10.3 in Mt.*(7.143A); πρὸς ἐκείνους μέν, ἵνα μὴ ~ῶνται, μηδὲ ὀνειδίζωσι τοῖς περὶ τὴν ἑνδεκάτην id.*hom.64.4 in Mt.*(7.639D); **3.** *be desperate* against evil, *determined* φιλονείκου τινὸς καὶ βιαίας καὶ ἀπονενοημένης κατὰ τῶν ἐπιθυμιῶν δεῖ ψυχῆς Chrys.*virg.*27(1.287A).

ἀπόνοια, ἡ, **1.** *loss of right reason, madness*; shown in **a.** desperate, shameless wickedness καταντικρὺ τὸν τῆς διεστραμμένης ἀ. βίον ἡ κακία προὐβέβλητο Const.ap.Eus.*v.C.*2.48(p.62.1; M.20.1025B); ἀθεμίτῳ...καὶ ἀπανθρώπῳ...ἀ. *ib.*2.34(p.56.5; 1012A); ὁ διάβολος οὐδαμόθεν ἑτέρωθεν τοιοῦτος ἐγένετο, ἀλλ' ἢ ἀπὸ τοῦ πρότερον μὲν ἀπογνῶναι, ὕστερον δὲ ἐκ τῆς ἀπογνώσεως εἰς ἀ. ἐμπεσεῖν Chrys. *Thdr.*1.16(1.27C); plur., *M.Tar.*7(p.464); **b.** overweening arrogance, presumption ἡ ἀ. τῆς συμμετρίας ἐκπίπτουσα καὶ ἀπὸ τοῦ νοῦ γινομένη, διὸ καὶ ἀ. λέγεται· καὶ μωροὺς καὶ ἀλαζόνας ἐργάζεται Chrys.*hom.20.4 in Rom.*(9.662A); μετὰ πολλῆς ὁρμήσαντες τῆς ἀ., ὡς καὶ αὐτῷ γε...πολεμήσοντες τῷ θεῷ Thdr.Mops.*Nah.*proem.(M.66.400A); Cyr.*Ps.*9:5(M.69.764C); sin of fallen angels καθάπερ...ὁ διάβολος ἐξ ἀ. ἔπεσεν, οὕτω καὶ ὁ ἐνεργούμενος ὑπ' αὐτοῦ εἰς ἀ. ἀλειφόμενος Chrys.*hom.1.1 in 2Thess.*(11.512A); and of Adam ἐξ ἀ. ἥμαρτεν...προσδοκήσας ἰσοθεΐαν id.*hom.65.6 in Mt.*(7.652D); **c.** desperate folly, *1Clem.*1.1; *ib.*46.7; Clem.*prot.*9(p.63.2; M.8.193C); καταλήγει...εἰς ἀ., εἰς ἔκστασιν, εἰς μανίαν Chrys.*hom.1.6 in Col.*(11.331C); of heretics, Hipp.*haer.*6.7(p.135.5; M.16.3206D); *ib.* 7.29(p.210.9; 3323B); Gr.Naz.*ep.*125(M.37.217C); Const.ap.Gel.Cyz. *h.e.*3 suppl.2(p.200.10); **2.** *want of sense, weakness of understanding* διὰ τὴν ἀ. ... μηδέπω συνιέναι δυναμένων Chrys.*anom.*10.5(1.536A); τὴν ἐσχάτην ἀ. οὐκ εἶχον, τὸ νομίζειν ἑαυτοὺς εἶναι σοφούς id. *hom.5.1 in 1Cor.*(10.34B); **3.** *guilelessness, simplicity*, Dor.*doct.*7.1 (M.88.1697B); **4.** *detachment* τελείαν ἀναισθησίαν καὶ ἀ. ἐν λοιδορίαις καὶ ὕβρεσι Jo.Clim.*scal.*4(M.88.688B).

ἀπονοσφίζ-ω, med.; **1.** *embezzle*, Cyr.*Zach.*29(3.696C); of Ananias, id.*thes.*34(5^{1}.340D); **2.** locally, *get away from* ὄχλων ἀ. Cyr. *Jon.*5(3.371D); id.*ador.*1(1.48C); *be away, be distant*, id.*Jo.*3.4(4.291D); met., *hold aloof from* τῆς...διαφορᾶς καθ' ἣν ἀλλήλων τὰ ἔθνη πρὸς ἑτεροίως ἔχειν ~εται id.*Juln.*4(6^{2}.143E); id.*hom.pasch.*23 (5^{2}.279C); ref. Nestorian Christology ὑποστάσεσί τε καὶ γνώμῃ... ἀλλήλων ἀπενοσφίζοντο id.*Nest.*2.1(p.35.25; 6^{1}.35A).

***ἀπόνουσος**, *free from disease, in good health*, Synes.*hymn.*8.35 (p.51; M.66.1613).

ἀπονυστάζ-ω, *fall asleep* ἀπονυστάξαντες ἴδωσιν ἐν ὀνείροις Chrys. *Thdr.*1.9(1.12E); Cyr.*Jon.*5(3.371E); Leont.N.*v.Jo.Eleem.*22(p.43.3); met. ἵνα ἐγρηγόρους αὐτοὺς...καταστήσῃ...μή ποτε...ἀπονυστάξαντες ...ἐκπέσωσιν τῆς ἐπουρανίου ζωῆς Hipp.*Dan.*4.16.2; *be drowsy, sluggish* μήποτε ~ωμεν Chrys.*hom.12.13 in Heb.*(12.124B); Isid.Pel. *epp.*5.111(M.78.1389C); of Adam and Eve τῇ μέθῃ τῆς παραβάσεως τὸν ὀφθαλμὸν τῆς καρδίας ἀπονυστάξαντας...κοιμηθέντας ὕπνον εἰς θάνατον Jo.D.*hom.*9.3(M.96.728A).

***ἀπονυστακτέον**, *one must sleep*, Clem.*paed.*2.9(p.205.27; M.8.492C).

***ἀπονύχιον**, *early in the morning*, *Chron.Pasch.*p.338(M.92.880B).

***ἀποξενίζ-ω**, *dissociate, separate from* διαιρεῖν αὐτὸ [sc. τὸ πνεῦμα] τῇ φύσει, καὶ ~ειν ἀπὸ τοῦ υἱοῦ Ath.*ep.Serap.*1.9(M.26.552B).

ἀποξεν-όω, **1.** *banish* or *estrange from*; reflex. ἀπεξένωσεν ἑαυτὸν τοῦ ἐλέους τοῦ θεοῦ Dion.Al.ap.Eus.*h.e.*7.10.6(M.20.661A); ὡς μὴ ~ώσαιμεν ἑαυτοὺς...κοινωνίας βίου Bas.*reg.fus.*5.2(2.342B; M.31.921A); ‡Jo.D.*ep.Thphl.*15(M.95.365A); **2.** pass., *be in exile from*, met. ~ωθεῖσαν τοῦ θεοῦ τὴν ἡμετέραν ζωήν Gr.Nyss.*Eun.*12(2 p.278.20; M.45.889B); perf. ptcpl. pass., *foreign* τῆς ἀ. θαλάσσης Clem. *paed.*2.12(p.227.17; M.8.540A); met., *alien, outside* ἀπεδίδου τὴν λειτουργίαν, ἀ. δέ τισιν καὶ ἀλλοτρίοις τῆς τῶν ἀρχιερέων διαδοχῆς Eus.*d.e.*8.2(p.381.25; M.22.617C); οὐκ ἀ. τῆς κατὰ τὴν γραφὴν διανοίας Bas.*fid.*1(2.224B; M.31.677B); Mac.Aeg.*hom.*25.3(M.34.668D); *strange, unusual* ἀ. ... καὶ ἀσύνηθες Bas.*Spir.*16(3.13B; M.32.93B); **3.** theol.; **a.** act. and med., *separate* mentally, *regard as alien* ὁ μὲν Ἄρειος...~οῖ τὸν λόγον ἀπὸ τοῦ πατρός Ath.*Dion.*24(p.64.16; M.25.516B); ἀπεσχοίνιζον καὶ ἀπεξενοῦντο...τὴν οὐσίαν τοῦ υἱοῦ ἀπὸ τοῦ πατρός id.*syn.*45(p.271.2; M.26.773C); ~οῦντας αὐτὸ [sc. τὸ πνεῦμα] τῆς θείας...φύσεως Bas.*ep.*125.3(3.216D; M.32.549B); **b.** perf. ptcpl. pass., *alien, foreign, strange* αὐτὸς...ὤν...ἡ αὐτοῦ τοῦ πατρὸς...σοφία ...οὐκ ἔστιν...ὥσπερ τις ἀ. αὐτοῦ Gr.Thaum.*pan.Or.*4(p.8.22; M.10.1060D); μεμερισμέναι τῇ φύσει καὶ ἀ. καὶ ἀπεσχοινισμέναι καὶ ἀμέτοχοί εἰσιν ἀλλήλων αἱ οὐσίαι Ath.*Ar.*1.6(M.26.24B); ‡Ath.*Maced.dial.*1.16 (M.28.1316D); Gr.Naz.*or.*20.6(M.35.1072C); of Logos in rel. to creation, Cyr.*thes.*15(5^{1}.159A).

ἀποξένωσις, ἡ, **1.** *exile*, Gr.Naz.*or.*14.6(M.35.864C); **2.** *separation, alienation*; of Son from Father in Arianism, Max.*opusc.*(M.91.116C).

ἀπόξεσις, ἡ, *smoothing away*, Andr.Caes.*Apoc.*65(M.106.424C).

ἀποξέω, **1.** *scrape off*, Meth.*res.*1.28(p.257.8; M.41.1136A); Gr. Nyss.*infant.*(M.46.164C); met., *strip off, remove*, Chrys.*hom.10.4 in Phil.*(11.280B); of Christ λεπρῶν δὲ τὴν λέπραν ἀ. Thdt.*provid.*10 (4.665); **2.** *whittle away, carve* ξόανα προσηγορεύετο διὰ τὸ ἀπεξέσθαι τῆς ὕλης Clem.*prot.*4(p.35.17; M.8.133B ἀπάξεσθαι); *polish*, met. ὅτι μάλιστα εἰς κάλλος ἑαυτοὺς ἀ. Gr.Naz.*or.*40.22(M.36.389A); perf. ptcpl. pass., *polished, precise. exact* ῥινὸς...ἀρετῇ...τὸ εὐθεῖαν εἶναι καὶ ἀπεξεσμένην ἑκατέρωθεν Chrys.*hom.4.3 in 1Tim.*(11.572E); τῆς ...τριάδος, ὀρθὴ καὶ ἀ. δήλωσις Cyr.*glaph.Gen.*2(1.37A); of people, *scrupulous, particular* τήν τε δίαιταν τούς τε τρόπους εὐσταθής τε ὢν καὶ ἀ. Evagr.*h.e.*5.19(p.214.30; M.86.2832A); neut. as subst. τὸ τοῦ ἤθους εὐσταθές, καὶ βεβηκὸς καὶ ἀπεξεσμένον Gr.Naz.*or.*43.64 (581A).

ἀποξυλόομαι, *turn into wood*, Meth.*res.*2.9(p.347.28; M.18.309A); *become hard* like wood, ‡Eust.*hex.*(M.18.761D).

***ἀποοικονόμος, ὁ**, *ex-bursar*, CAnt.(445)*act.*(H.2.588C; ἀπὸ οἰκονόμων *ACO.*2.1.3 p.76.20).

ἀποπαιδαγωγέω, *teach*, Tit.Bost.*Man.*2.20(M.18.1176B).

ἀποπαρθενεύ-ω, *make virgin*, ref. Mt.19:12 ὁ κύριος εἰς τὴν βασιλείαν εἰσελάσαι τῶν οὐρανῶν τοὺς ~σαντας ἐκείνους σφᾶς αὐτοὺς ἐπαγγέλλεται Meth.*symp.*1.1(p.7.13; M.18.37A).

***ἀπόπασχα, τό**, *the time after Easter*, Leont.N.*v.Sym.*35(M.93.1713A).

ἀποπάτησις, ἡ, *evacuation* of the bowels, *motion*, Melet.*nat.hom.* synops.(M.64.1133D).

***ἀποπατίζ-ω**, *open the bowels* τῷ σαββάτῳ...οὐδὲ ~ουσι [sc. Essenes] Hipp.*haer.*9.25(p.259.23; M.16.3402C).

ἀπόπαυσις, ἡ, *cessation* τῶν φυσικῶν ἐννοιῶν ἀποπεράτωσις καὶ ἀ.

†Cyr.*coll.VT*(6^4.18D; M.77.1201D); Dion.Ar.*d.n.*1.5(M.3.593B); Max. *schol.d.n.*1.4(M.4.200A).

***ἀποπαυστέον**, *one must put a stop to*, Clem.*str.*7.16(p.70.26; M.9.537B).

***ἀποπείθ-ω**, *persuade* rather, *turn* someone *from* one course of action to another, Germ.CP *syn.haer.*18(M.98.57A); ~ω σε *don't suggest* it, *V.Pach.Φ*120(p.77.31).

***ἀποπεμπτέος**, *to be dismissed, banished*, Clem.*paed.*2.4(p.182.7; M.8.440C); λογισμὸς...ἀ. τῆς διανοίας Gr.Nyss.*hom.7 in Eccl.*(M.44. 724A).

ἀπόπεμπτος, **1.** *rejected, banished*, Ephr.2.432C; ἔσται τῆς πρὸς θεὸν οἰκειότητος ἀ. ὁ Ἰσραήλ Cyr.*Is.*proem.(2.****B); *ib.*3.3(2.458D); id.*Os.*34(3.62D); id.*ador.*8(1.284A); *debarred* Στέφανος, καίτοι τραπεζῶν διάκονος προχειρισάμενος, οὐκ ἀ. ἐποιεῖτο τὸ χρῆναι μυσταγωγεῖν id.*1Cor.*1:17(M.74.860B); **2.** *to be rejected* or *repudiated*, Gr.Naz. *carm.*1.2.1.627(M.37.570A); Cyr.*ador.*14(1.487B).

ἀποπενθέω, *cease from mourning*, Gr.Naz.*ep.*166(M.37.276B).

ἀποπεραίν-ω, **1.** *perform fully* τὰς...θυσίας Cyr.*Juln.*4(6^2.125E); ἀ. ... τῆς μετὰ σαρκὸς οἰκονομίας τὸ μυστήριον id.*Lc.*19:11(M.72.869C); id.*ador.*6(1.187D); **2.** *complete, satisfy, fulfil* ἀ. ... τὴν εἰς γονέας αἰδῶ *ib.*16(1.573C); τὸν νόμον *ib.*1(1.5C); ἀ. ... αὐτούς [sc. τοὺς τύπους] id.*Juln.*9(6^2.319B); ἀ. τὰ αἰτήματα id.*Ps.*4:4(M.69.737A); ~οιτο...'ἡ τῶν ὀμμάτων ἐπιθυμία' περὶ...ὕλης φαιδρότητα id.*hom.pasch.*14(5^2. 189D); **3.** ?*be on the frontiers of, bound* ἀ. τὴν χώραν *A.Barth.*1 (p.128.10).

ἀποπερατόω, *accomplish to the full* ἀ. τὰ θεῖα...τάγματα Dion. Ar.*c.h.*5(M.3.196B); ἀ. ἕνωσιν Max.*ambig.*(M.91.1305B).

ἀποπεράτωσις, ἡ, 1. *end, completion*, of movement of stars τῶν οὐρανίων ἀρχῶν καὶ ἀ. αἰτία τὸ ἀγαθόν Dion.Ar.*d.n.*4.4(M.3.697B); τὴν ἄγνωστον ἡμῖν καὶ ἀόρατον κρυφιότητα τῶν κινητικῶν ἀρχῶν καὶ ἀποπερατώσεων id.*c.h.*15.6(M.3.336A); πασῶν μὲν τῶν...γνώσεων καὶ δυνάμεων τὰς ἀ. ἅμα καὶ πάσας ὑπερουσίως ἐν ἑαυτῇ προειληφυῖαν [sc. the divine being] id.*d.n.*1.4(592D); μέχρι τῆς πάντων ἀ. τῶν αἰώνων Max.*ambig.*(M.91.1357B); **2.** *conclusion* (logical), id.*opusc.*(M.91. 20A); (arithmetical), id.*ambig.*(M.91.1400C).

***ἀποπεταλόω**, *strip off gold-leaf*; pass., Thphn.*chron.*p.191(M.108. 191C).

ἀποπέτομαι, *fly away*; from memory, Meth.*symp.*3.14(p.45.13; M.18.85C); *be wrenched out of*, Chrys.*ep.*1(3.528B).

***ἀποπετρ-όω, 1.** *harden, solidify* ἔτι γὰρ πηλουργούμενον τὸν Ἀδάμ, ὡς ἔστιν εἰπεῖν, καὶ τηκτὸν ὄντα..., καὶ μηδέπω φθάσαντα δίκην ὀστράκου τῇ ἀφθαρσίᾳ κραταιωθῆναι καὶ ~ωθῆναι Meth.*symp.*3.5 (p.31.17, v.l. ἀποπαγιωθῆναι; om. M.18.68B); **2.** *turn into stone*, met ~οῦσθαι ταῖς ἀναισθήτοις τῆς διανοίας ὁρμαῖς Const.Diac.*laud.*14 (M.88.496D).

ἀποπήγνυμι, 1. *freeze*, pass. intrans., met., with astonishment or fear, *Apophth.Patr.*(M.65.217D); Anast.Ap.*a.Max.*2.12(M.90. 145B); **2.** pass., *be stuck in*, of thorns τοὺς ἀποπαγέντας ἐν αὐτοῖς σκόλοπας Ath.ap.Socr.*h.e.*2.28.10(M.67.273A), ἐναπο- Ath.*fug.*7(p.73.2; M.25.652C).

ἀποπηδ-άω, A. *depart from, turn away from*; **1.** of sinners going astray, Meth.*symp.*proem.(p.5.17; M.18.32C); ἀ. ἡ διάνοια τῶν ἀνθρώπων ἀπὸ θεοῦ Ath.*gent.*9(M.25.17C); ἑκουσίως γὰρ εἰς θεὸν ἐπανελθεῖν δεῖ τοὺς ἑκουσίως ~ήσαντας ‡Chrys.*pasch.*5(8^2.261D); Thdr.Mops.*Jo.*1:13(M.66.732C); but cf. πρόβατα αὐτοὺς καλεῖ ἀπολωλότα οὐκ ~ήσαντα Chrys.*hom.32.4 in Mt.*(7.369D, conj. for ἀποδημήσαντα); **2.** from Church into heresy, Alex.Al.*ep.encycl.*6 (p.9.26; M.18.577A); Philost.*h.e.*2.2(M.65.465C); Gel.Cyz.*h.e.*proem. 11(M.85.1196A); ἀπὸ τῶν προγόνων παραδόσεως ἀ. Thds.Imp.*ep.Val.* (p.7.13; M.*PL.*54.876B); **3.** from heresy, Ath.*tom.*1(M.26.797A); id. *Ar.*1.2(M.26.16B); **4.** of a monk changing his state ὁ...πρὸς ἄλλον βίον ~ήσας ἱερόσυλος γέγονεν Bas.*reg.fus.*14(2.355B; M.31.949C).

B. *leap* at; met., *pounce* on ~ῶσι καὶ πρὸς τὸ λόγιον τοῦτο Didym. *Trin.*2.11(M.39.657B).

***ἀποπιεσμός, ὁ,** lit., *squeezing out* [sc. of the breath] hence *sobbing*, Melet.*nat.hom.*synops.(M.64.1136D).

ἀποπίμπλημι, 1. *fill up* τὸ μέτρον τῆς ἀνοίας Gr.Thaum.*pan.Or.* 2(p.5.16; M.10.1036C); **2.** *accomplish* πᾶσαν εἰ δυνατὸν πρόνοιαν καὶ ἐπιμέλειαν ἀ. *ib.*5(p.14.26; 1068D); *ib.*3(p.7.16; 1060A); a period of time, Eus.*h.e.*3.14.1(M.20.249A).

ἀποπίπτ-ω, 1. *fall away from* God or beatitude; **a.** of angels, ref. Gen.6:2 οἱ ἄγγελοι τοῦ θεοῦ τὸ κάλλος καταλελοιπότες διὰ κάλλος μαραινόμενον καὶ τοσοῦτον ἐξ οὐρανῶν ἀποπεσόντες χαμαί Clem.*paed.* 3.2(p.244.25; M.8.576B); id.*str.*7.2(p.8.27; M.9.413B); ὑπὸ τῷ Μιχαὴλ γενομένων, διὰ δὲ φιληδονίαν ~όντων ἐκείνου Or.*comm.in Mt.*14.21 (p.335.31; M.13.1240C); id.*Jo.*20.22(20; p.355.5; M.14.621A); Eus. *d.e.*4.9(p.162.17; M.22.272A); Dion.Ar.*d.n.*4.18(M.3.716A); οὐκ ἠλλοιώθη τὸ δοθὲν αὐτοῖς ὅλον ἀγαθόν, ἀλλ' αὐτοὶ τοῦ δοθέντος ἀποπεπτώκασιν ὅλου ἀγαθοῦ *ib.*4.23(725C); εἰ γάρ τις αὐτῶν ὑπὸ κακίας ἑάλω, τῆς μὲν οὐρανίας...ἀποπεπτώκει τῶν θείων νοῶν ἁρμονίας id. *e.h.*6.3.6(M.3.537A); **b.** of men, as fallen from first state ἀ. τῆς μακαριότητος Or.*Jo.*32.18(11; p.457.10; M.14.792B); Dion.Ar.*e.h.*3.3. 11(M.3.441A); from worship of true God, Or.*Cels.*3.73(p.265.9; M. 11.1016B); Gr.Naz.*or.*39.6(M.36.341A); αὐτοὺς ἐκείνους οἰκείαις ῥοπαῖς ἐκ τῆς ἐπὶ τὸ θεῖον εὐθείας ἀναγωγῆς ἀποπεπτωκότας Dion.Ar.*c.h.* 9.3(M.3.260C); from divine law, Or.*Cels.*7.69(p.218.13; 1517B); ἀ. ... εἰς τὰς...πλανήσεις Dion.Ar.*e.h.*7.1.2(553C); from virtue, *2Clem.* 5.7; Clem.*str.*7.7(p.34.28; M.9.465B); *ib.*7.16(p.67.6; 532A); τῶν μὲν ~όντων αὐτῆς ἀνάκλησίς τε καὶ ἀνάστασις Dion.Ar.*d.n.*1.3(M.3. 589B); abs. ἔτι ἀ. καὶ ἐκτρεπομένους τὰς τοῦ ἐνυπάρχοντος πνεύματος συμβουλίας Or.*Jo.*2.11(6; p.66.16; 129C); **c.** of the universe from God and divine order δεσμός τις...θεοῦ λόγος...συνδέων τὰ διεστῶτα καὶ μὴ μακρὰν ~ειν αὐτὰ συγχωρῶν Eus.*l.C.*12(p.231.17; M.20.1389B); ὡς ἂν μὴ παντελῶς ἡ τῶν γενητῶν ἀποπέσοι φύσις id.*d.e.*4.6(p.159. 24; M.22.265C); οὐδέν ἐστι τῶν ὄντων, ὃ πάσης παντελῶς ἑνώσεως ἀποπέπτωκε Dion.Ar.*d.n.*11.5(M.3.952D); *ib.*4.20(721A); **d.** from a position or rank, e.g. of Judas τὸ ἀπὸ τάξεως ἀποστολικῆς...ἀποπεπτωκέναι Or.*Jo.*32.18(11; p.457.1; M.14.792B); **2.** abs., *lapse, apostatize* τὸ ἀ. τινα δεδιότες *Ep.Lugd.*ap.Eus.*h.e.*5.1.12(M.20.413B); **3.** *be deposed, degraded* from eccl. rank τῆς ἐπισκοπῆς ἀποπεπτωκότος Eus.*h.e.*7.30.18(v.l. ἐκπεπτωκότος M.20.717A); εἰ μὲν ἐπίσκοποι εἶεν ἢ κληρικοί, τοῦ οἰκείου παντελῶς ~ειν βαθμοῦ CEph.(431)*can.*6 (p.28.17); **4.** *fall short, fail*; in prophesying, of a demon, Eus.*p.e.*6.6 (242C; M.21.413A); in matters of faith, of the Jews, id.*d.e.*4.1 (p.150.10; M.22.249D); **5.** *lose* a husband *by divorce* ἡ...ἀποπεσοῦσα ...ἀνδρός Or.*comm.in Mt.*14.21(p.335.17; M.13.1240C); **6.** *fail to attain* παντελῶς ἀ. τῆς ἱερατικῆς τάξεως...ὁ μὴ φωτιστικός Dion.Ar. *ep.*8.2(M.3.1092B); **7.** pass. intrans., *fall from* ἅπερ [sc. τὰ λευκώματα] τῶν ὀμμάτων...ἀποπτωθέντα Sophr.H.*mir.Cyr.et Jo.*2(M.87. 3429C).

ἀποπλέκω, *unplait*, Pall.*h.Laus.*22(p.71.15; M.34.1081C).

***ἀποπληροφορία, ἡ,** *full conviction*, Thdot.Anc.*hom.BMV et Sym.*10(M.77.1404C).

ἀποπληρ-όω, *fill*; **1.** *fill up*; pass., *be filled, absorb* αἱ λεπτότεραι ...τῶν οὐσιῶν, πρῶται τῆς...αἴγλης ἀ. Dion.Ar.*e.h.*3.3.14(M.3.445A); *be filled, feast* θείας τροφῆς ἀ. id.*c.h.*7.4(M.3.212A); *complete* a number ἀ. τὰς ἀγγελικὰς ἱεραρχίας *ib.*5(196C); **2.** *supply* a need, Tat. *orat.*41(p.42.17; M.6.885C); Ath.*ep.Rufin.*(M.26.1181B); id.*gent.*22 (M.25.45A); πατρὸς αὐτῷ τάξιν ἀ. Philost.*h.e.*9.16(M.65.581A); *serve for, fill the place of* ἵνα τὰ γράμματα τὴν τῶν μὴ παραγενομένων παρουσίαν ~ώσῃ *Ep.Mareot.*1(p.154.38; M.25.384C); **3.** *fill the measure of, render due* ἀ. τὴν ἀξίαν τῶν αὐτῷ προσηκόντων αἴνων Gr.Thaum. *pan.Or.*4(p.8.25; M.10.1061A); τὰ χαριστήρια...δι' εὐχῶν ἀ. Eus.*v.C.* 3.42(p.95.14; M.20.1101B); χάριν ἀ. τῷ εὐεργέτῃ Bas.*hom.*5.6(2.39E; M.31.252C); τὴν δοξολογίαν ἀ. id.*Eun.*2.7(1.243C; M.29.585A); *ib.*1.7 (1.219B; M.525C); **4.** *fulfil, accomplish* τὸ [sc. λουτρόν] τοῦ σώματος... διὰ...ὕδατος ~οῦται Clem.*paed.*3.9(p.264.15; M.8.620B); id.*str.*7.2(p.6. 15; M.9.409B); τὰ...τῆς...λατρείας δι' εὐχῶν ἀ. Eus.*v.C.*4.71(p.147.3; M.20.1225B); Thdt.*Abac.*3:6(2.1552); precepts, Eus.*v.C.*3.47(p.97. 28; 1108B); Chrys.*hom.64.4 in Mt.*(7.642C); period of time, Tat. *orat.*38(p.39.18; M.6.881A); *Hom.Clem.*2.23; prophecy, Eus.*l.C.*3 (p.200.33; M.20.1329A); **5.** *perform, celebrate* τριακονταετηρικὰς ἑορτὰς ἀ. Eus.*l.C.*6(p.211.11; M.20.1349B); διὰ...τοῦ οἴνου, τὴν μυστικὴν εὐλογίαν ὑποδηλοῦν, καὶ τῆς ἀναιμάκτου θυσίας τὸν τρόπον, ἣν ἐν ταῖς ἁγίαις ἐκκλησίαις ~οῦν εἰθίσμεθα Cyr.*Is.*3.1(2.353D); λειτουργίαν ἀ. Thdt.*Os.*8:8f.(2.1348); **6.** *pay* a debt, id.*provid.*10(4.666).

ἀποπλήρωσις, ἡ, 1. *plenitude*, Dion.Ar.*c.h.*1.3(M.3.121D); **2.** *satisfaction, fulfilment* ἀ. τῆς ἐκτίσεως Clem.*str.*6.14(p.486.31; M.9.332A); τῆς ἀγάπης ἡ ἀ. Gr.Nyss.*hom.4 in Cant.*(M.44.845D); τὸ ἐν Χριστῷ ...μυστήριον...τοῦ...ἐν τῷ προπάτορι παρεθέντος ἀπόδειξις καὶ ἀ. ἐστιν Max.*ambig.*(M.91.1097D); **3.** in pass. sense, *a being satisfied* πρῶτον ἐν μετουσίᾳ [sc. of the eucharist] γενέσθαι καὶ ἀ. τὸν ἱερὸν καθηγεμόνα Dion.Ar.*e.h.*3.3.14(M.3.445A); **4.** *function* τὰς ἱερατικὰς τάξεις τε καὶ ἀ. *ib.*5.1.1(500D).

***ἀποπληρωτέον**, *one must complete*, Clem.*str.*4.1(p.249.18; M.8. 1216D).

***ἀποπλήρωτος**, *incomplete*, Sophr.H.*or.*7.4(M.87.3325C).

***ἀποπλουτέω**, *give away riches*, Gr.Naz.*or.*8.5(M.35.793C); *ib.*18.8 (993C).

ἀπόπλυμα, τό, dish-*water* ἀ. τοῦ πίνακος Pall.*h.Laus.*34(p.99.21; M.34.1107B).

ἀποπλύνω, 1. *wash thoroughly*, met. ἀ. ... τοὺς πιστεύοντας αὐτῷ

Just.*dial*.54.1(M.6.593C); ἀ. τὴν ψυχὴν ἁμαρτημάτων Bas.*hom*.1.2 (2.2C; M.31.165A); med., Or.*hom.2.2 in Jer*.(p.18.2; M.13.280A); Gr. Thaum.*pan.Or*.13(p.29.25; M.10.1088C); Bas.*hom*.1.2(l.c.); **2.** *wash out* αὐτὴν τῶν ὑδάτων τὴν φύσιν ἀ. Mac.Mgn.*apocr*.3.40(p.139.28).

***ἀπόπνευστος,** *exhaled*, Gr.Naz.*carm*.1.1.8.8(M.37.447A).

ἀποπνέω, 1. *exhale*; hence, *breath one's last* ἐπὶ τοῦ σκόλοπος...ὅτ' ἀπέπνει Cels.ap.Or.*Cels*.2.55(p.178.22; M.11.884B); Chrys.*hom.26.1 in Mt*.(7.313C); **2.** *smell of*, fig. τούτου [sc. τοῦ μύρου] ἀπέπνεον οἱ ἀπόστολοι...οὐ τὸ σῶμα δὲ μόνον...ἀλλὰ καὶ τὰ ἱμάτια τοῦ μύρου τοῦ πνευματικοῦ ἀπέπνεον Chrys.*hom.2.3 in 1Tim*.(11.559F); *ib*.(560B); met., *be redolent of* γυνὴ δὲ ἀποπνείτω Χριστοῦ Clem.*paed*.2.8(p.196. 28; M.8.472B); τὸ δὲ καὶ εἰς τὸ ἑξῆς τούτου [sc. chrism] ἀποπνεῖν, τῆς ἡμῶν ἐστι σπουδῆς. διὰ τοῦτο καὶ τὸ παλαιὸν μύρῳ ἐχρίοντο οἱ ἱερεῖς, τῆς ἀρετῆς σύμβολον διδόντες, ὅτι τὸν ἱερέα καλὸν ἀ. δεῖ. τῆς ἁμαρτίας οὐδέν ἐστι δυσωδέστερον Chrys.*hom.2.3 in 1Tim*.(11. 560C).

***ἀπόπνιξις, ἡ,** *suffocation*, Thdr.Stud.*epp*.2.18(M.99.1173C).

ἀποποι-έω, A. *reject*; **1.** act., *repudiate*; persons, Cypr.*ep*.(H.1. 158A); Chrys.*hom.2.5 in 2Cor*.(10.435C); things τοῦ Χριστοῦ... ποιεῖς εἰκόνας, τῶν δὲ ἁγίων...~εῖς τὸ ἀπεικόνισμα Jo.D.*imag*.1.19 (M.94.1249B); pass., *be discarded* ἑλκομένης...διὰ ῥιζῶν τῆς τροφῆς καὶ ~ουμένης διὰ...φύλλων Gr.Nyss.*anim.et res*.(M.46.60B); reflex., *set* oneself *against*, *oppose* oneself ἀ. ἑαυτὸν...τῆς τῶν Χριστιανῶν εὐσεβείας ‡Jo.D.*Const*.20(M.95.337A); intrans., *be opposed* ἀ. γάμου Hipp.*haer*.9.28(p.261.16; M.16.3406B); **2.** med., Gr.Nyss.*or.catech*.10 (p.56.9; M.45.41D); id.*Eun*.1(1 p.210.5; M.45.457C); *disown*, *disclaim* ἀ. [sc. ὁ ἀετός] ὃν ἐγέννησεν Bas.*hex*.8.6(1.76B; M.29.177C); τὰ ἐν ἡμῖν ὄντα, ὡς ἀλλότρια τῆς φύσεως ἡμῶν ἀ. Gr.Nyss.*anim.et res*. (M.46.53B); οὐ μὴ ~ήσεται ὁ θεὸς τὸν ἄκακον Jo.Carp.*cap*.(M.85. 1845B); *deny* μὴ ~οῦ μου τὸ κρίμα, τουτέστι μὴ ἀπαρνοῦ ὅπερ ἔκρινα περὶ σοῦ Meth.*fr.22 in Job* 40:3(p.517.19).

B. *make*, *effect* ἀ. σημεῖον ‡Eust.*Laz*.10(p.35.6).

ἀποπομπαῖος, *sent away*, of the scapegoat (Lev.16:8,10) ἀ. θυέεσσι Gr.Naz.*carm*.2.1.13.60(M.37.1232A); Gr.Nyss.*Steph*.1(M.46. 709C); Thdr.Mops.*Ps*.29:12(M.66.665C); abs., *scapegoat* περὶ ἁμαρτιῶν καὶ καθαρισμοῦ καὶ ἀ. *Const.App*.2.35.1; Thdt.*ep*.83(4. 1150); interprn. τινες...οἴονται τὸν ἕνα τῶν τράγων, ἀ. τινὶ καὶ ἀκαθάρτῳ δαίμονι δεδόσθαι Cyr.*glaph.Lev*.(1.373E); rejected, *ib*. (374A); Thdt.*qu.22 in Lev*.(1.199); as type of Christ in two natures ἐγράφετο δὲ δι' ἀμφοῖν...εἷς ὁ Χριστός, καὶ ἀποθνήσκων ὑπὲρ ἡμῶν κατὰ σάρκα, καὶ θανάτου κρείττων ἀναδεικνύμενος κατά γε τὴν τῆς θεότητος φύσιν. ἐξεπέμπετο δὲ εἰς τὴν ἔρημον, ἀνατυπούσης ἐφ' ἑαυτῇ τὴν τῶν ἐθνῶν ἀκαρπίαν τῆς ἐρήμου καὶ ἀνηρότου γῆς Cyr.*Juln*.9(6[2]. 302A); id.*glaph.Lev*.(1.374D–375D); id.*ep*.41(p.43.3; 5[2].124E); Thdt. *qu.22 in Lev*.(1.200); of the two advents of Christ μιᾶς μέν, ἐν ᾗ ὡς ἀ. αὐτὸν παρεπέμψαντο...οἱ ἱερεῖς...θανατώσαντες αὐτόν, καὶ τῆς δευτέρας δὲ αὐτοῦ παρουσίας, ὅτε...ἐπιγνωσθήσεσθε αὐτόν, τὸν ἀτιμωθέντα ὑφ' ὑμῶν, καὶ προσφορὰ ἦν ὑπὲρ πάντων Just.*dial*.40.4(M. 6.564A).

ἀποπομπή, ἡ, *sending away*; **1.** of scapegoat ὁ τῆς ἀ. τράγος τὸν τύπον τοῦ τὰς τῶν ἀνθρώπων ἁμαρτίας ἀναλαμβάνοντος ἐξετέλει ‡Just. *fr*.11(M.6.1596B); Thdt.*qu.22 in Lev*.(1.200); **2.** of a divorced wife, Cyr.*Mal*.29(3.846E).

ἀποπόμπιμος, *averting*, *dispelling*, of formulae used in warding off evil λυτηρίους ᾠδὰς ἢ ἀ. φωνάς Or.*Cels*.6.39(p.108.30; M.11. 1357A).

***ἀποπόρευσις, ἡ,** *return journey*, Evagr.*h.e*.4.35(p.185.3; M.86. 2768B); *ib*.5.10(p.206.29; 2812C).

***ἀποπότε,** for ἀπὸ πότε = ἀφ' οὗ, *from what time* ζητητέον ἀ. λέγει βασιλεῦσαι τοὺς βασιλέας Proc.G.*Gen*.36:31(M.87.465A).

***ἀποπραγματεύ-ομαι,** *sell one's whole stock*, *sell out* πραγματευόμενοι, μέχρις οὗ ~σονται Cosm.Ind.*top*.2(M.88.100C).

***ἀποπρεπ-έω,** *be unsuitable* υἱὸν...οὐκ ~οῦντα πατρί Epiph.*haer*. 76.35(M.42.588D; conj. ἀπρεποῦντα p.385.20).

***ἀποπροσποίησις, ἡ,** *dissembling*, Phot.*nomoc*.9.30(M.104.788B).

***ἀπόπτησις, ἡ,** *shunning*, *avoidance*, Gr.Nyss.*hom.2 in Cant*. (M.44.796D).

ἀποπτήσσω, pass., *be alarmed*, Mac.Aeg.*hom*.23.2(M.34.661A).

ἄποπτος, 1. *not to be seen*, Cyr.*Os*.47(3.78B); **2.** *hidden*, *invisible*, of Christian truth ἐπιστήμην τὴν ἄ. καὶ γνῶσιν τὴν ἀνέλεγκτον Just. *2apol*.13.3(v.l. ἄπωπτος; M.6.465C); of God ἄ. ... ἡ ὑπὲρ πάντα νοῦν ἐστι φύσις Cyr.*ador*.9(1.295E); τῆς ὑπάρξεως τὴν ἀρχὴν ἄ. τε καὶ ἀκατάληπτον ἔχων id.*Nest*.3.3(p.64.36; 6.78E); ἄ. ... αὐτῷ παντελῶς οὐδέν id.*Os*.53(3.84A).

***ἀποπτυέλισμα, τό,** *spittle*; met., of heretics, ‡Jo.D.*ep.Thphl*.8 (M.95.356A).

***ἀποπτυστέος,** *to be rejected*, Clem.*paed*.2.1(p.154.22; M.8.380A); id.*str*.6.11(p.477.5; M.9.312A).

ἀπόπτυστος, A. *detestable*; *despicable* ἀ. καὶ εὐκαταφρόνητον Bas.*hex*.5.6(1.46A; M.29.109A); ψυχρὰ καὶ ἀ. ... λημμάτια Cyr.*Mich*. 27(3.413E).

B. as subst., *one who rejects* τῶν τῆς ὀρθῆς πίστεως ἀ. ‡Jo.D.*fid. dorm*.25(M.95.272B).

ἀποπτύ-ω, *abominate*; *let go of*, *discard* ἄληστον ἔχειν τὴν μνήμην... μηδὲ ~ειν τὰ λεγόμενα Chrys.*hom.4.1 in Heb*.(12.39A); med. τὸ... ῥᾳδίως κτηθὲν καὶ ~εσθαι τάχιστα, ὡς πάλιν ληφθῆναι δυνάμενον Gr.Naz.*or*.28.12(p.40.9; M.36.40D).

ἀπόπτωμα, τό, *falling away*, Clem.*paed*.3.2(p.244.23; M.8.576A) cit. s. παράπτωμα; οὐκέτι...τὰ ἁμαρτήματα καὶ τὰ ἀ. [sc. διὰ τοῦ λόγου γεγονέναι] Or.*Jo*.2.13(7; p.68.25; M.14.133D); τὸ μισεῖν...τὸν ἀδελφὸν αὐτοῦ τῆς κυρίως καλουμένης γνώσεώς ἐστιν ἀ. *ib*.2.25(20; p.82.25; 160A); τὸ...κακὸν ἐκ τῶν προαιρετικῶν ἀ. τὴν ἀρχὴν εἰληφός Bas.*hex*.2.5(1.16E; M.29.40B); Gr.Nyss.*ep.can*.1–2(M.45.225B).

ἀπόπτωσις, ἡ, *falling away*; **A.** of Fall; **1.** of Satan τὴν ἀπὸ τῶν κρειττόνων δι' οἰκείαν μεγαλαυχίαν...ἀ. μεμαθήκαμεν Eus.*p.e*.7.16 (329B; M.21.556C); τὴν πρὸ τῆς ἀ. αὐτοῦ δόξαν Cyr.*Is*.2.5(2.346C); and angels, Dion.Ar.*d.n*.4.23(M.3.725B); **2.** (Valent.) of supramundane fall, Didym.*Trin*.3.42(M.39.992C); **3.** (Origenist) of preexistent fall of soul παρὰ τὴν ἀ. γέγονεν ἡ νῦν λεγομένη ψυχή Or. *princ*.2.8.3(p.161.2; M.11.223A); *ib*.1.8.4(p.104.12; πτώσεως 180C); **4.** of Adam γέγονεν ἡ σωτηρία ὅτε γέγονεν ἡ ἀ. Cyr.H.*catech*.14.10; *ib*.13.19; Gr.Nyss.*hom.12 in Cant*.(M.44.1021B); τὴν...τῶν πρωτοκτίστων ἀνθρώπων...ἀ., ἥτις ἅπαν τὸ αὐτῶν ἐπενέμετο γένος Gel.Cyz. *h.e*.2.24.4(M.85.1300B); τὰ διὰ τὴν ἀ. τῶν πρωτοπλάστων λυθέντα *ib*. 2.24.20(1301D); **5.** as source of evil in soul τὸ κακόν ἐστιν οὐχὶ οὐσία...ἀλλὰ διάθεσις ἐν ψυχῇ...διὰ τὴν ἀπὸ τοῦ καλοῦ ἀ. Bas.*hex*.2.4 (1.16D; M.29.37D); τοῦτο...ἐστι καὶ νοῖς, καὶ ψυχαῖς, καὶ σώμασι κακόν, ἡ τῆς ἕξεως τῶν οἰκείων ἀγαθῶν...ἀ. Dion.Ar.*d.n*.4.27(M.3. 728D); **6.** cosmological τί ἄλλο χρὴ λέγειν αἴτιον γεγονέναι τοῦ ὑποστῆναι αὐτὸν [sc. τὸν κόσμον] ἢ τὸ ποικίλον τῆς ἀ. τῶν οὐχ ὁμοίως τῆς ἑνάδος ἀπορρεόντων; Or.*princ*.2.1.1(p.107.4; M.11.182B).

B. of actual sin τάς τε ἠθικὰς κατὰ τὸν βίον ἀ. Eus.*d.e*.6.18(p.279. 25; M.22.460B); *ib*.7.1(p.318.5; 520C); id.*h.e*.4.23.6(M.20.385B); Chrys. *hom.13.4 in Heb*.(12.135C); τὸ ἀπαλλοτριοῦσθαι τοῦ θεοῦ διὰ τῆς ἐπὶ τὸ χεῖρον ἀ. Thdt.*Is*.1:4(2.170).

***ἀποπτωτικός,** *able to fall away* οὐκ ἔστιν ἁμάρτημα ἀ. εἶναι τοῦ καλοῦ Or.*sel.in Ps*.4:5(M.12.1144A); id.*comm.in Gen*.ap.Eus.*p.e*.6. 11(295C; M.12.81A).

ἀποπωλέω, *sell off*, Eus.*d.e*.3.6(M.22.229B; ἀπεμπολήσαντες p.135. 29).

ἀπορ-έω, *be perplexed*, *confused*, *at a loss*; Gnost., of Sophia, Iren. *haer*.1.2.4(M.7.456A); Hipp.*haer*.6.32(p.161.4; M.16.3243B); trans., *perplex*, *confuse*, ref. Mt.21:23 τῇ ἀντεπερωτήσει ~ῆσαι αὐτούς Iren.*haer*.1.20.2(M.7.656A); Chrys.*hom.57.3 in Mt*.(7.579A); *ib.80.2* (768B); id.*hom.42.3 in Ac*.(9.322A); an argument, Meth.*res*.1.51 (p.305.2; M.18.281A).

ἀπόρησις, ἡ, *question*, *difficulty*, Aët.*synt*.(M.42.536A; ἐπαπ- p.352. 11).

ἀπόρθητος, *impregnable*, Isid.Pel.*epp*.3.385(M.78.1028C).

ἀπορία, ἡ, *dismay*, *disturbance*; Gnost., Iren.*haer*.1.5.3(M.7. 497A) cit. s. διάβολος; εὑρὼν αὐτὴν ἐν πάθεσι τοῖς πρώτοις τέτρασι, καὶ φόβῳ καὶ λύπῃ καὶ ἀ. καὶ δεήσει Hipp.*haer*.6.32(p.160.23; M.16. 3243A); *ib*.(p.160.29; 3243A).

[*]**ἀποριφή, ἡ,** v. ἀπορριφή.

***ἄπορνος,** *free from licentiousness*, *pure*, Geo.Pis.*Pers*.2.248(M.92. 1227A).

ἄπορος, *in doubt*, *at a loss* about, of persons ἄ. ὄντες τῆς πίστεως ‡Ath.*Apoll*.2.18(M.26.1164A); f.l. for ἄπειρον, Tat.*orat*.12(p.12.24; M.6.829C); for ἀπεριστάτων, Eus.*m.P*.22(M.20.1548B; ἀπεριστάτων p.943.5).

***ἀπορόφησις, ἡ,** *swallowing down*, *gulp*, Areth.*Apoc*.9(M.106. 564A).

***ἀπορραγάς, ἡ,** *fragment*, Hipp.*haer*.6.25(p.152.16; M.16.3231B).

***ἀπορρεπής,** *inclined* to; neut. as subst. τὸ πρὸς τὴν ὕλην...ἀ. Jo.D.*f.o*.4.23(M.94.1201B).

***ἀπορρέπω,** *have an inclination* or *tendency*, Serap.*Man*.20(p.38; M.40.917A).

ἀπόρρευσις, ἡ, *emission*, Antip.Bost.*fr*.ap.Leont.et Jo.*sacr.2*(M. 86.2049C,D).

ἀπορρ-έω, 1. *emanate*; of H. Ghost, Athenag.*leg*.10.3(M.6.909B) cit. s. ἀπόρροια; denied of Son γέννημα τέλειον...οὐκ ~εῦσαν ἐκ πατρός Melit.Ant.*hom*.ap.Epiph.*haer*.73.30(p.305.17; M.42.461A); of

Valent. aeons, Iren.*haer*.1.15.3(M.7.620B); *ib*.1.18.1(644B); **2.** *emit* ∼έουσί τε ἄνθρωποι γεννῶντες...ὁ δὲ θεὸς ἀμερὴς ὢν...οὔτε γὰρ ἀπορροὴ τοῦ ἀσωμάτου ἔστιν οὔτ' ἐπιρροή τις εἰς αὐτὸν γίνεται Ath. *decr*.11(p.10.9; M.25.'444'(436)A).

ἀπόρρηξις, ἡ, *breach, severance* of communion, Bas.*ep*.244.3 (3.378B; M.32.916A).

ἀπόρρητος, 1. *secret*; ref. *disciplina arcani* ἀδικοῦνται...οἱ τῆς ἐκκλησίας διδάσκαλοι, τῶν μαθητῶν ἐκλαλούντων τὰ τῶν δογμάτων ἀ. Proc.G.*Jos*.2:20(M.87.1001D); of sacraments ἀναγκάζοντες ἢ μὴ λέγειν σαφῶς, ἢ εἰς αὐτοὺς [sc. τοὺς ἀμυήτους] ἐκφέρειν τὰ ἀ. [sc. of baptism] Chrys.*hom*.*40.1 in 1Cor*.(10.379A); παρὰ τῶν σοφῶν [sc. μιμάδων καὶ Ἰουδαίων] τὰ ἀ. τῆς ἱερωσύνης καταπιστεύονται Pall.*v. Chrys*.15(p.91.24; M.47.52); **2.** *esoteric, mysterious*, Jewish and pre-Christian τὸ περὶ μετενσωματώσεως δόγμα...οὐκ ἀλλότριον τῆς ἐν ἀπορρήτοις διδασκαλίας αὐτῶν Or.*Jo*.6.12(7; p.121.30; M.14.221D); οὐ πᾶσι τοῖς βαπτιζομένοις ἀλλὰ τοῖς πρὸς τὸ βαπτίζεσθαι μαθητευομένοις ἐν ἀ. παρεδίδου [sc. Jo. Bapt.]·...εὐχαὶ...πνευματικαὶ... πεπληρωμέναι ἀ. δογμάτων id.*or*.2(p.303.2f.; M.11.421D); πάλαι τοῖς Ἰσραηλίταις ἀ. Proc.G.*Dt*.29:29(M.87.949A); Gnost. τὰ μεγάλα... καὶ ἀ. μυστήρια Iren.*haer*.1.1.3(M.7.452A); οὗτός ἐστιν ὁ ἀ. αὐτοῖς λόγος καὶ μυστικός Hipp.*haer*.5.7(p.83.21; M.16.3134B); Christian ταύτας [sc. παραδόσεις opp. scripture]...παρέδωκεν ὁ σωτὴρ...τοῖς ἀποστόλοις ἐν ἀ. Or.*comm.in 1Cor*.4:6(*JTS* 9 p.357); esp. of spiritual meaning of scripture ἐν ταῖς γραφαῖς ἃ μέν ἐστιν ἀπορρητότερα καὶ μυστικώτερα id.*hom*.*12.7 in Jer*.(p.94.2; M.13.388C); ἄλλοι δ' ἑρμηνείας τῶν θείων ἀναγνωσμάτων ἐποιοῦντο, τὰς ἀ. ἀποκαλύπτοντες θεωρίας Eus.*v.C*.4.45(p.136.17; M.20.1196B); Isid.Pel.*epp*.1.360(M.78. 388A); τὸν ἀ. νοῦν Cyr.*Nah*.4(3.479E); of sacrament of baptism σωτηρίου...πάθους ἀ. σύμβολα Eus.*h.e*.10.3.3(M.20.848B); id.*v.C*.4.62 (p.143.18; 1216A); Chrys.*hom*.*25.1 in Jo*.(8.144E); and of eucharist ἐμυσταγώγησε τοὺς μαθητὰς διὰ τῆς μεταλήψεως τῶν ἀ. μυστηρίων Alex.Sal.*Barn*.13(440D); **3.** *ineffable*, of God ἐν ἀ. τοῦ πατρὸς λογισμοῖς Eus.*e.th*.3.3(p.155.24; M.24.1000A); ἡ θεία...καὶ ἀ. φύσις Cyr.*Os*.39(3.70B); id.*syn.def*.(M.76.1424A) cit. s. μυστικός; ἡ τοῦ θεοῦ ἀ. σοφία Philost.*h.e*.3.9(M.65.492C); Bas.Sel.*or*.9.2(M.85.132A); of generation of Son τὴν κρύφιον καὶ τοῖς πᾶσιν ἀ. αὐτοῦ γενεσιουργίαν Eus.*p.e*.7.12(322C; M.21.545A); τὴν γέννησιν...τὴν ἑαυτοῦ τὴν ἀ. ... καὶ ἄφραστον Chrys.*hom*.*27.1 in Jo*.(8.153D); τὰ...ἀπορρητότερα καὶ φρικωδέστερα...πῶς ἐγέννησε τὸν υἱόν...καὶ τίς ἡ οὐσία id.*hom*.*2.6 in Rom*.(9.447C); of H. Ghost τὴν ἀ. χάριν [sc. τὸ πνεῦμα] id. *hom*.*86.3 in Jo*.(8.516E); of Christ's Person and work ἐπεχείρει ταῖς θαυματουργίαις...θείᾳ καὶ ἀ. δυνάμει Eus.*d.e*.3.6(p.133.23; M.22. 225B); ἰατρὸν ἑαυτὸν ἐκάλεσεν, ἐνταῦθα δὲ νυμφίον, τὰ ἀ. μυστήρια διὰ τῶν ὀνομάτων τούτων ἐκκαλύπτων Chrys.*hom*.*30.3 in Mt*.(7.352A); *ib*.*54.3*(7.549B); ἀπορρητότερος δὲ τῆς ἐν Χριστῷ μεσιτείας ὁ τρόπος Cyr.*ador*.2(1.51A); †Thdt.*Nest*.(4.1052); πῶς τὴν ἀ. ἕνωσιν θεοῦ πρὸς τὸν ἄνθρωπον λόγῳ ζητεῖς; Thdot.Anc.*exp.symb*.4(M.77.1320A); ἐκ τῆς θεοτόκου παρθένου ἀ. σαρκώσεως Gel.Cyz.*h.e*.proem.6(M.85. 1193C); of certain doctrines as beyond knowledge or as mystically revealed τὰ ἀποκεκαλυμμένα δὲ τῷ Ἰωάννῃ τίς οὐκ ἂν ἀναγνοὺς καταπλαγείη τὴν ἐπίκρυψιν ἀ. μυστηρίων καὶ τῷ μὴ νοοῦντι τὰ γεγραμμένα ἐμφαινομένων; Or.*princ*.4.2.3(10; p.310.14; M.11.361B); ref. 2Cor.12:2ff. μύρια γε καὶ ἀ. λέγειν ἔχων Eus.*h.e*.3.24.4(M.20. 264C); ἐστι...τοῖς ἀνθρώποις ἀδύνατον ἐπαξίως εἰπεῖν περὶ τῶν ἀ. Ath.*ep.Serap*.1.17(M.26.572C); ἐκστάσει...ἅπαντες ὡς εἰκὸς τῶν ἀπορρητοτέρων ἐδέχοντο τὴν γνῶσιν Thdr.Mops.*Nah*.1:1(M.66.401C); τῶν ἀ. διδάσκαλος [i.e. S. Paul] Isid.Pel.*epp*.1.139(M.78.276A); Dion. Ar.*ep*.9.1(M.3.1105D) cit. s. μυστικός; οὐδὲ πάντα ἀ., οὐδὲ πάντα ῥητά, τά τε τῆς θεολογίας, τά τε τῆς οἰκονομίας Jo.D.*f.o*.1.1(M.94. 792B).

ἀπορριζόω, *uproot, destroy utterly*; met., Gr.Nyss.*hom*.*6 in Eccl*. (M.44.705B); Cyr.*Is*.4.2(2.610C); Sophr.H.*ep.syn*.(M.87.3188A).

***ἀπόρριμμα, τό,** *thing fit to be cast away, rubbish*, Epiph.*haer*.37.1 (p.52.3 conj. for ἀπόρρυμα M.41.644A).

ἀπορρινήματα, τά, *filings, scales*, Olymp.*Job* 40:13(M.93.428B).

ἀπορριφή, ἡ, a *being cast out* οὐκ αἰσθητὴν...ἀ. λέγει, ἀλλὰ νοητὴν *cat.Mt*.9:32(p.73.2); of Satan from heaven, ἀποριφή *cat.Apoc*.12:9 (p.359.18).

ἀπορροή, ἡ, 1. *emanation* οἱ μακάριοι προφῆται τὴν θείαν αἴσθησιν εὑρόντες...καὶ ἁπτόμενοι τοῦ λόγου μετὰ πίστεως, ὥστ' ἀ. αὐτοῦ ἥκειν εἰς αὐτοὺς θεραπεύσουσαν αὐτούς Or.*Cels*.1.48(p.98.23; M.11. 749B); in prayer ἀ. γὰρ νοητοῦ τινος θειοτέρου μεταλαμβάνουσι τότε id.*or*.9(p.319.2; M.11.444C); [sc. those outside the Church] συναπολαύειν ἀ. ... καὶ μετουσίας τῶν θεόθεν ἡμῖν Eus.*h.e*.10.1.8(M.20. 845A); of generation of Son, Ath.*decr*.11(p.10.12; M.25.'444'(436)A) cit. s. ἀπορρέω; Epiph.*haer*.73.4(p.272.19; M.42.408D); of angels τοῦ πρώτου φωτὸς ἀ. τις Gr.Naz.*or*.40.5(M.36.364B); **2.** *influence* of stars, Gr.Nyss.*fat*.(M.45.153A).

ἀπόρροια, ἡ, I. *emanation, effluence*;

A. divine; in man πᾶσιν γὰρ ἁπαξαπλῶς ἀνθρώποις...ἐνέστακταί τις ἀ. θεϊκή. οὗ δὴ χάριν καὶ ἄκοντες μὲν ὁμολογοῦσιν ἕνα γε εἶναι θεόν Clem.*prot*.6(p.52.4; M.8.173A); οἱ δὲ ἀμφὶ τὸν Πλάτωνα νοῦν μὲν ἐν ψυχῇ θείας μοίρας ἀ. ὑπάρχοντα id.*str*.5.13(p.384.7; M.9. 129A); Eus.*p.e*.6.15(694D; M.21.1145A); to be understood in limited sense ἐφ' οὓς ἡ ἀ. τοῦ πρώτου καλοῦ καὶ κατὰ δεύτερον λόγον ἔφθασεν Gr.Naz.*or*.30.13(p.129.15; M.36.121A); in Creation τὸ ἀόρατον κάλλος, καὶ τὴν πηγὴν τῆς σοφίας, ἧς ἡ ἀ. τὴν τῶν ὄντων συνεστήσατο φύσιν Gr.Nyss.*hom*.*13 in Cant*.(M.44.1052A).

B. of divine essence; **1.** asserted; **a.** in H. Ghost τὸ...ἅγιον πνεῦμα ἀ. εἶναί φαμεν τοῦ θεοῦ, ἀπορρέον καὶ ἐπαναφερόμενον ὡς ἀκτῖνα ἡλίου Athenag.*leg*.10.3(M.6.909B); **b.** in Son, Clem.*fr*.23 (p.202.21)ap.Phot.*cod*.109(M.103.384B) cit. s. λόγος; cf. λόγος...οὐ συγκρίνεται...τῷ πατρί...ἐστιν...ἀπαύγασμα οὐ τοῦ θεοῦ ἀλλὰ τῆς δόξης αὐτοῦ...καὶ ἀ. εἰλικρινής Or.*Jo*.13.25(p.249.31; M.14.444A); cf. *igitur aporrhoea gloriae dei secundum hoc, quod omnipotens est... glorificata tamquam aporrhoea omnipotentiae vel gloriae*, id.*princ*. 1.2.10(p.43.25; M.11.141C); advanced to illustrate rel. of Son to Father ἀ. γὰρ νοῦ λόγος καί...ἀπὸ καρδίας διὰ στόματος ἐξοχετεύεται ἕτερος γινόμενος τοῦ ἐν καρδίᾳ λόγου...καὶ οὕτως...ἕν εἰσιν ὄντες δύο Dion.Al.ap.Ath.*Dion*.23(p.63.7; M.25.513B); οὐκ ἔξωθέν τίς ἐστιν ἐφευρεθεῖσα ἡ τοῦ υἱοῦ οὐσία...ἀλλὰ ἐκ τῆς τοῦ πατρὸς οὐσίας ἔφυ ...ὡς ὕδατος ἀτμίς...οὔτε ⟨ἡ τοῦ υἱοῦ οὐσία⟩ αὐτός ἐστιν ὁ πατὴρ οὔτε ἀλλότριος ἀλλὰ ἀ. τῆς τοῦ πατρὸς οὐσίας Thgn.*hypot.fr*.2 (p.76; M.10.240A); Eus.*d.e*.4.3(p.153.33f.; M.22.256D); limitations of material illustrations, Gr.Naz.*or*.31.32(p.188.4; M.36.169B); τὰς ...ἐξ ἀλλήλων γενέσεις τῶν ζώων ἡ φύσις οἰκοδομεῖ διὰ τῆς ἐν τοῖς σώμασιν ὑλικῆς ἀ., ἐφ' ὧν καὶ τὸ προηγούμενον μένει οἷόν ἐστι καὶ τὸ ἀπ' ἐκείνου ῥέον ἀφ' ἑαυτοῦ νοεῖται, ὡς ἐπὶ τοῦ ἡλίου καὶ τῆς ἀκτῖνος... ἢ ἐπὶ τῶν ἀρωμάτων...καὶ τῆς ἐκεῖθεν ἐκδιδομένης ποιότητος Gr.Nyss. *Eun*.8(2 p.185.24; M.45.780B); ἐπειδὴ οὐχ ἱκανὸν ἦν...συμπαραλαμβάνει καὶ ἕτερον τῆς γεννήσεως εἶδος πρὸς σημασίαν τῆς τοῦ υἱοῦ θεολογίας τὸ ἐκ τῆς ὑλικῆς ἀ., καί φησιν ἀπαύγασμα δόξης *ib*.(p.188. 22; 784A); in Christ ὁ τῇ τοῦ πατρὸς ἀ. σώζων τὰ πάντα ‡Chrys. *hom*.7(13.219A); **2.** materialistic interpretation of the metaphors condemned as Sabellian οὐ...ταῖς ἐκ διαιρέσεων ἀ. ... ἀλλ' ἀρρήτως Alex.Al.*ep.Alex*.12(p.27.6; M.18.565A); πατέρα μὲν ἐξ ἑαυτοῦ γεγεννηκότα ἄνευ ἀ. καὶ πάθους τὸν υἱόν CAnc.(358)*ep.syn*.ap.Epiph. *haer*.73.6(p.276.10; M.42.413C); Ath.*Ar*.1.21(M.26.57A); πιστεύομεν ...ἕνα...λόγον...λόγον δὲ...οὐκ ἀ. τοῦ τελείου, οὐ τμῆσιν τῆς ἀπαθοῦς φύσεως †Ath.*exp.fid*.1(M.25.201A); πατὴρ...κατὰ τὴν ἡμετέραν χρῆσιν ...πάθος...καὶ ἀ. ... καὶ τοιαῦτα ἐπιφημίζει Bas.*fid*.3(2.226D; M.31. 684B); Epiph.*haer*.76.19(p.365.24; M.42.553C); ἀ. καὶ ὅσα τοιαῦτα πάθη, νοείσθω περὶ τὰ σώματα...ὁ δὲ [sc. υἱός] τὸ εἶναι σῶμα διαφυγὼν καὶ τὰ σωμάτων διαφεύξεται πάθη Cyr.*thes*.21(5^1.212A).

C. Gnost. καθ' ὁμοίωσιν [sc. of God] δὲ τὸν ψυχικόν, ὅθεν καὶ πνεῦμα ζωῆς τὴν οὐσίαν αὐτοῦ εἰρῆσθαι, ἐκ πνευματικῆς ἀ. οὖσαν Iren.*haer*. 1.5.4(M.7.501A); Clem.*exc.Thdot*.2(p.106.2; M.9.653B) cit. s. σπέρμα; Hipp.*haer*.6.53(p.188.14; M.16.3290B); of letters of the alphabet τὰ μὲν γὰρ ἄφωνα γράμματα ἐννέα νόμισον εἶναι τοῦ πατρὸς καὶ τῆς ἀληθείας...τὰ δὲ ἡμίφωνα, ὀκτὼ ὄντα, τοῦ λόγου καὶ τῆς ζωῆς, διὰ τὸ μέσα ὥσπερ ὑπάρχειν τῶν τε ἀφώνων καὶ τῶν φωνηέντων καὶ ἀναδέχθαι τῶν μὲν ὕπερθεν τὴν ἀ., τῶν δὲ ὑπ' αὐτὰ τὴν ἀναφοράν *ib*.6.46(p.178.7; 3270B); in Valent. view accounting for origin of evil ἐμοὶ γὰρ ἡ ὕλη ποιότητος ἀνάρχως ἔχειν δοκεῖ, οὕτω γὰρ τὰ κακὰ ἐκ τῆς ἀ. αὐτῆς [sc. ὕλης] λέγω, ἵνα τῶν κακῶν ὁ μὲν θεὸς ἀναίτιος ᾖ Meth.*arbitr*.9 (p.169.12; M.18.257A) = Adam.*dial*.4.7(p.152.20; M.11.1817A).

D. of Church on earth ὑπό τινων λέγεσθαι ἐκκλησίας τινὸς ἐπουρανίου καὶ κρείττονος αἰῶνος ἀ. εἶναι τὴν ἐπὶ γῆς ἐκκλησίαν Or. *Cels*.6.35(p.104.19ff.; M.11.1349B).

E. met., of *agape* at Corinth in rel. to 'all things common' of Ac.2:44 ὥσπερ τις ἀ. τῆς κοινωνίας ἐκείνης ἐναπομείνασα Chrys. *hom*.*27.1 in 1Cor*.(10.240D).

II. *influence*, of stars; in Peratic doctrine ὡς γέγονεν ὁ κόσμος ἀπὸ τῆς ἀ. τῆς ἄνω, οὕτως τὰ ἐνθάδε ἀπὸ τῆς ἀ. τῶν ἀστέρων γένεσιν ἔχειν καὶ φθορὰν λέγουσι καὶ διοικεῖσθαι Hipp.*haer*.5.15(p.110.25; M.16.3170C); in pagan astrology, Meth.*symp*.8.14(p.101.12; M.18. 164C); Gr.Nyss.*fat*.(M.45.153B).

ἀπορροφέω, *swallow*, Synes.*Dion* 12(p.266.21; M.66.1148C); id. *ep*.120(M.66.1500A); Pall.*h.Laus*.2(p.18.10; M.34.1012A).

ἀπόρρυμα, τό, Egyptian liquid measure, Epiph.*mens*.21,24(M. 43.272C,284B); prob. f.l. for ἀπόρριμμα q.v., id.*haer*.37.1(M.41. 644A).

ἀπορρύπτω, *wash away*; met., sin, Clem.*paed*.1.6(p.105.24; M.8.281A); Gr.Nyss.*bapt.Chr*.(M.46.577C); heresy, Eus.*h.e*.4.30.3(M.20.404A).

ἀπόρρυσις, ἡ, *excrement*, Epiph.*haer*.26.11(p.289.13; M.41.348D).

ἀπόρρυτος, *flowing out*; hence *dissipated, wasted* σῶμα Bas.*hom*.14.6(2.128A; M.31.458A).

ἀπόρρυψις, ἡ, *washing*; liturg. εἷς...ὑποδιάκονος διδότω ἀ. χειρῶν τοῖς ἱερεῦσιν *Lit*.ap.*Const.App*.8.11.12.

ἀπορρώξ, ἡ, *piece broken off*, of the breath of life ἐν γὰρ ἔηκε πνεῦμα, τὸ δὴ θεότητος ἀειδέος ἐστὶν ἀ. Gr.Naz.*carm*.1.1.8.73(M.37.452); met., of BMV as David's *scion*, Paul.Sil.*Soph*.434(M.86.2136A).

***ἀπορύπωσις, ἡ,** *cleansing* ἐβαπτίσθη [sc. Christ]...οὐκ αὐτὸς ἀπορυπώσεως...χρείαν ἔχων *Const.App*.7.22.5.

ἀπορφανίζω, *orphan, bereave* τῶν...ἀδελφῶν ἀπορφανισθέντες Dion.Al.ap.Eus.*h.e*.7.11.23(M.20.672A); ἐάν τις...ἀλλοτριωθεὶς τοῦ θεοῦ οἱονεὶ ἀπορφανισθῇ τῆς προνοίας αὐτοῦ †Bas.*Is*.42(1.412C; M.30.197C); *Apophth.Patr*.(M.65.225A); met., *separate from* τῶν ἀπορφανισάντων ἑαυτοὺς ἀπὸ τοῦ θεοῦ Or.*exp.in Pr*.23:10(M.17.224A); Ephr.2.201E; †Bas.*Is*.232(1.555C; 525A); *deprive of* ἀπορφανισθέντα τῆς τοῦ θεοῦ βοηθείας Chrys.*fr.Job* 6:25–27(M.64.596C); Nil.*epp*.1.326 (M.79.200C).

ἀποσαλεύω, *shake away*; hence **1.** *loosen, draw out* τὴν ὁλκάδα τοῦ λιμένος ἀ. Gr.Nyss.*hom.12 in Cant*.(M.44.1013D); **2.** *remove* ἀ. τὴν τοῦ νομικοῦ γράμματος σκιάν Cyr.*hom.pasch*.26(5².310B).

ἀποσαρκ-όω, A. act., *endow* (mentally) *with flesh, regard as corporeal*, as implication of Apollinarius' view ∼ώσει καὶ ἐπὶ πατρὸς τὴν τῆς θεότητος φύσιν Gr.Nyss.*Apoll*.19(M.45.1161B).

B. pass.; **1.** *become corporeal* οἱ δαίμονες ἀσώματοι μέν εἰσιν... ἀλλὰ οἱονεὶ ἀπεσαρκώθησαν ταῖς τῶν ὑλικῶν ἐπιθυμίαις προστετηκότες †Bas.*Is*.97(1.447B; M.30.277B); **2.** *be changed into flesh* μία φύσις τοῦ θεοῦ λόγου σεσαρκωμένη...κατὰ τροπὴν οὐσίας [sc. ἔχει τὴν ἔννοιαν], οἱονεὶ μία φύσις...∼ωθεῖσα Leont.B.*cap.Sev*.17(M.86.1905C); cf. οἱ δοκήσει αὐτὸν φάσκοντες ἐληλυθέναι, ἢ ἐξ ἑτέρας οὐσίας σεσαρκῶσθαι Vict.*Mc*.10:46 (v.l. ἀποσεσαρκ- p.388.8); **3.** met., *become fleshly, carnally minded* ὅσα ταῖς ψυχαῖς ἡμῶν διὰ τῆς τῶν παθημάτων κοινωνίας ∼ωθείσαις Gr.Nyss.*or.catech*.8(p.48.1; M.45.36D); ∼ωθείη τῇ διανοίᾳ id.*anim.et res*.(M.46.88A); **4.** *be discarnate* οὐ γὰρ ∼οῦται [sc. Christ] εἰς τοὺς...αἰῶνας Ath.ap.*Chron.Pasch*.p.223(M.92.544A); οὐ κεκραμμένος ἐν αὐτῷ [sc. ὁ ναὸς ἐν Χριστῷ] ἢ ἀποσεσαρκωμένος, ἀλλ' ἀποσώζων...τῶν δύο φύσεων...τὴν ἰδιότητα Cyr.*hom.div*.21 (p.539.22; M.77.1113A).

***ἀποσάρκωσις, ἡ,** *abolition of flesh*, ref. Inc. οὐ κατὰ...ἀ. ἀλλὰ καθ' ἕνωσιν ἄρρητον Cyr.*hom.div*.21(p.540.18; M.77.1113A).

***ἀποσαρόομαι,** *be swept away*; met., of sins etc., Meth.*symp*.9.4 (p.118.9; M.18.185A); Gr.Nyss.*virg*.12(p.301.11; M.46.373A).

***ἀποσειριάζω,** *cast off like a chain* ἀ. ... τὴν...πλάνην Thdot.Anc.*hom.BMV et Sym*.12(M.77.1408B).

ἀποσεί-ω, *shake off*; met., *repel, refuse, repudiate*, Meth.*symp*.5.3 (p.56.5; M.18.101A); μνήμην...∼όμενος Eus.*qu.Steph.suppl*.6(M.22.964C); ∼σάμενοι τὰ μίση Const.ap.Ath.*apol.sec*.61(p.141.10; M.25.360B); τῆς...δουλείας ∼όμενοι τὸν ζυγόν Cyr.*Nah*.14(3.492A); Χριστοῦ ...∼ομένοις ἐντολάς id.*Ps*.24:10(M.69.849C); ἰατρικὴν...∼εσθαι τέχνην Thdt.*Is*.39:1(p.152.31; 2.325); id.*Ps*.5:4(1.636); μή μοι γένοιτο παρὰ θεοῦ ἀποσείσασθαί τι τῶν γραφῶν *Dial.Tim.et Aquil*.fol.77 r°(p.66); c. infin., *refuse* Χριστὸν ἀνακρίνειν ἀπεσείσατο [sc. Pilate] Nonn.*par.Jo*.18:31(M.43.896A).

***ἀποσικχαίν-ω,** *be utterly disgusted, nauseated* νοῦ...ἀπὸ πολλοῦ τῶν αἱρέσεων ἰοῦ ἀποναρκήσαντος καὶ ∼οντος Epiph.*exp.fid*.19(p.520.15; M.42.820C).

ἀποσιτίζ-ομαι, *refrain from eating* ∼εσθαι τοὺς βιωτικοὺς κρέων Thdr.Stud.*catech.parv*.50(p.120).

ἀπόσιτος, *fasting*; *without appetite*; met., *without taste of, without share in*, Cyr.5.1(4.465E).

***ἀποσκαίρω,** *leap away*, Const.Diac.*laud*.29(M.88.512C).

ἀποσκέλλω, in perf. ἀπέσκληκα with pres. sense, *dry up*; hence **1.** *be hardened, calloused* ἀ. τὰ γόνατα αὐτοῦ [sc. of S. James of Jerusalem] δίκην καμήλου Heges.ap.Eus.*h.e*.2.23.6(M.20.197A); Chrys.*34.5 in 1Cor*.(10.317B); met., in sin, *Const.App*.2.41.9; *be hard, callous* in character, Chrys.*hom.4.5 in 1Thess*.(11.458D); Cyr.*Os*.35(3.64B); *ib*.46(77A); **2.** *be hard, unyielding*; of sinews in a lash, *V.Max*.34(M.90.104C); met., of truth, Chrys.*hom.17.2 in 1Tim*.(11.650D); *be hard, austere*; of ascetic life, id.*hom.1.2 in Phil*.(11.197A).

ἀποσκεπάζω, *uncover*; the head at confession, †Jo.Jej.*poenit*. M .88.1892D); †Jo.Jej.*serm*.(M.88.1924C); a tomb, Jo.Clim.*scal*.4 (M.88.697C); Hades, *1Apoc.Jo*.19(p.87.8); met., *reveal* τὰ...'Ιουδαϊκὰ παρατηρήματα ἔτι μένει, μὴ ἀποσκεπασθέντα καὶ γνωσθέντα ἐνίοις Didym.*Trin*.2.10(M.39.637C).

***ἀποσκεπής,** *uncovered, bare*, *Orac.Sib*.1.37.

ἀποσκευάζ-ω, A. act.; **1.** *keep off, impede* τὰς ἀκτῖνας Gr.Nyss.*v.Mos*.(M.44.349B); *prevent* ἀ. ἡμῶν νόμῳ τὴν ἐπήρειαν Athenag.*leg*.2.1(M.6.893B); **2.** (= ἐπισκευάζω) *restore*, for ἐπισκευάζω (LXX), Thdt.*2Par*.29:3(1.595); *equip for* ἀνθρώπου...ἀπεσκευασμένου ἤδη... μεταναστάσεως τῆς πρὸς τὸ θεῖον Gr.Thaum.*pan.Or*.2(p.4.3; M.10.1053C).

B. med.; **1.** *get rid of* persons ἀ. τοὺς ὄχλους Chrys.*hom.49.3 in Mt*.(7.508B); Philost.*h.e*.11.3(M.65.597B); **2.** *throw off*; **a.** an attitude of mind ἀ. τὸ μάταιον βάρος τοῦ γηΐνου φρονήματος Bas.*hex*.5.6 (1.46B; M.29.109A); ἀ. ... φρόνημα τὸ κτηνοπρεπές Cyr.*Ps*.31:9 (M.69.868D); an evil habit τὴν ἀπατῶσάν σε συνήθειαν ἀ. *Diogn*.2.1; τὸ...τῶν ἁμαρτημάτων φορτίον ἀ. Chrys.*hom.7.9 in 1Cor*.(10.64D); τοῦ ὄκνου...τὸν πηλὸν...ἀ. Nil.*epp*.4.60(M.79.577B); **b.** abs., *change one's mind, abandon a policy* ἀποσκευάσασθαι δὲ παρέπεισεν αὐτὸν ὁ...ἀρχισυνάγωγος, τοὺς...ὁσίους ἄνδρας κτείνυσθαι καὶ διώκεσθαι κελεύων Dion.Al.ap.Eus.*h.e*.7.10.4(M.20.657B); **c.** *remove, dispel* from the mind of another τὴν...λύπην ἀπεσκευάζετο Cyr.*glaph.Gen*.5 (1.158E); τὸ 'ἐγώ εἰμι'...πᾶσαν φαντασίαν ∼εται Sev.Ant.ap.*cat.Mt*.14:27(p.118.22); **3.** *dispose of, demolish* a claim in argument τῶν ἐναντίων λόγων λογισμοῖς ὀρθοῖς ∼ομένη λόγον Eus.*p.e*.7.18(333C; M.21.561C); [sc. εἰ μὴ ἔστι φύσις ἀνυπόστατος] ἢ τέλεον ἀποσκευάσασθαι σαρκὸς τὴν φύσιν, ἢ δύο ὑποστάσεις διδόναι τῷ κυρίῳ Leont.B.*Nest.et Eut*.1(M.86.1277B); τῆς...ἑρμηνείας ἀποσκευάσασθαι τὸ ἄτοπον ἐπειράσθησαν Gennad.*fr.Gen*.6:3(M.85.1641D); **4.** *refute, rebut*: charges against oneself δι' ἔργων ∼ομαι τὴν κατηγορίαν Chrys.*David* 2.3(4.765A); τῶν μὲν ἐργαζομένων ἡμῶν αὐτῶν ∼ομένους τὴν διαβολήν, εἰς δὲ τὸν οὐκ ὄντα αἴτιον μετατιθέντας τὴν κατηγορίαν ‡Chrys.*prov*.3(2.762C); Cyr.*Juln*.2(6².38A); charges against another ὅπως...τὴν καθ' ἡμᾶς ἐπήρειαν ἀποσκευάσησθε Athenag.*leg*.9.2(M.6.907A); an accuser ∼όμενος τοὺς...διαβάλλοντας αὐτόν Leont.H.*monoph*.(M.86.1813B); **5.** *avert, ward off* οἱ...πλοῦτον ἔχοντες τὸν ἐπίγειον καὶ δι' αὐτοῦ πολλάκις τὰς...ἐφόδους ∼ονται Cyr.*Ps*.76:2(M.69.1189C); ἀ. τὴν ὀργήν id.*Am*.80(3.344E).

ἀποσκευή, ἡ, *household goods*, *T.Jud*.7.4; τὸ θῆλυ γένος τῶν λογισμῶν μετὰ τῆς ὑλικῆς ἀ. τῷ κάτω καταλείπεται Gr.Nyss.*hom.1 in Cant*.(M.44.773B).

ἀποσκην-όω, *remove one's habitation* μὴ ∼ώσῃς ἀφ' ἡμῶν, ὁ θεός *Pss.Sal*.7.1.

***ἀποσκίασις, ἡ,** *overshadowing, darkening*, Gr.Nyss.*Eun*.12(1 p.236.28; M.45.933C).

ἀποσκίασμα, τό, 1. *shadow, shade*, Gr.Nyss.*hex*.13(M.44.76C); Thdt.*qu.7 in Gen*.(1.11); Jo.D.*fr.Mt*.27:45(M.96.1412C); met., *overshadowing*; of Christ's conception, ref. Pr.9:1 τὸν οἶκον τῆς σοφίας οἰκοδομούσης, καὶ τῷ τῆς δυνάμεως ἀ. ... ἔνδοθεν καταμορφωθέντος [sc. Χριστοῦ] Gr.Nyss.*res*.1(M.46.616B); *shading over, obscuration*, of a corrupt life ἀ. ... καὶ ἀντίφραγμα τῆς ἀρετῆς Max.*schol.e.h*.2.3.8(M.4.133A); **2.** opp. substance, *shadowy outline, faint trace*, Jo.D.*haer*.101(M.94.769B); met. ἀ. τῆς ἀληθείας ‡Bas.*hom.struct*.1.25(1.336E; M.30.37C); Gr.Naz.*or*.30.17(p.135.13; M.36.125C); μαίνεσθαι νομίζω τοὺς οἰηθέντας...τροπῆς ἀ. περὶ τὴν θείαν τοῦ λόγου φύσιν Cyr.*ep*.39(p.19.5; 5².107E).

***ἀποσκιρ-όω (-ιρρόω),** *harden, bring hardness* σατανικοῦ φρονήματος, εἰς τὰς ἀνοσίους...ψυχὰς ∼ώσαντος Alex.Al.*ep.Alex*.10(M.18.564B); conj. ἀποσκιρτήσαντος p.26.15); ἐστι...ψυχῆς...ἦθος ποιότης τοιάδε ἀπεσκιρρωμένη Melet.*nat.hom*.synops.(M.64.1141A).

ἀποσκιρτ-άω, *leap away, shy*; met., of rebellion or sin; from truth, Clem.*str*.2.7(p.130.7; M.8.968B); from God or divine law, Or.*sel.in Ps*.2:8(M.12.1108B); Chrys.*comm.in Gal*.5:13(10.718E); of rebellious Israel, Clem.*paed*.1.9(p.134.20; M.8.341A); Cyr.*Os*.149(3.183D); ref. Christ's mission ἵνα...προσκομίσῃ θεῷ τὸ ∼ῆσαν αὐτοῦ id.*Nah*.12(3.489C); from repentance, Chrys.*hom.in Mt.26:39*(3.15B); id.*hom.4.3 in 2Cor*.(10.459D); of rushing into sin, id.*Anna* 1.3(4.703E); and error ἀ. εἰς δόξας αἱρέσεων Clem.*str*.7.16(p.67.13; M.9.532B).

ἀποσκοπεύ-ω, 1. *look* ἀ. διὰ τῶν θυρίδων εἰς τὰς πλατείας *A.Xanthipp*.7(p.62.9); met. ἀ., ὅθεν ἥξει σωτηρία αὐτοῦ *Pss.Sal*.3.6; εἰς τὴν ...αὐτοῦ κατὰ σάρκα ζωὴν ἀ. Dion.Ar.*e.h*.3.3.12(M.3.444B); **2.** *watch*, fig. ἑώρων γὰρ ∼ουσα...ὑμᾶς ἐκτρεπομένας Meth.*symp*.proem.(p.5.16; M.18.32C); met. θεόπαιδα γεννήσασαν ἀ. Thdr.Stud.*nativ.BMV* 2(M.96.681A).

***ἀποσκοπή, ἡ,** *look-out, watch*, Epiph.*haer*.61.4(M.41.1044D; ἐπισκοπῆς p.384.20).

***ἀποσκόπησις, ἡ,** *regard, consideration*, Max.*opusc*.(M.91.197C).

ἀπόσκοπος, *erring from the mark*; met., of man as erring from the way, Hesych.H.*Ps.tit.*17(M.27.708D).

ἀποσκορακισμός, ὁ, *rejection*, Eus.*Is.*66:16(M.24.520D); τὸν...ἀ. 'ἐπιτίμησιν' ἐκάλεσαν οἱ λοιποί Thdt.*Is.*66:15(p.260.19; cf.2.400).

***ἀποσκορακιστέον,** *one must reject utterly*, Clem.*paed.*2.12(p.230.3; M.8.544B); *ib.*3.11(p.276.20; 649B); τοὺς...λέγοντας τὸ μίαν φύσιν τοῦ θεοῦ λόγου σεσαρκωμένην ἀ. Leont.H.*monoph.*(M.86.1812D).

ἀποσκυβαλίζω, *throw away as vile rubbish, excrete*, Dion.Al.ap.Eus.*h.e.*7.22.10(M.20.689B); Synes.*calv.*7(p.203.19; M.66.1180C); Melet.*nat.hom.*18(M.64.1220B); met., Gr.Naz.*ep.*88(M.37.161C); λογισμὸν ...ῥυπαρὸν τῆς ψυχῆς ἀ. Mac.Aeg.*elev.*13(M.34.901A); ἀ. τὰς αἱρέσεις, ὡς ἄχυρα Procl.CP *or.*18.2(M.65.820C); *treat as worthless* εἰ...τις ὡς μικροπολῖτιν τὴν ἐκκλησίαν ἀποσκυβαλίσει Synes.*ep.*58(M.66.1401D); *cat.Apoc.*7:4(p.287.11).

ἀπόσμηξις, ἡ, *cleansing* ῥύπου παντὸς ἀ. Proc.G.*Is.*60:1ff.(M.87.2621A).

ἀποσμήχ-ω, *clean*; of spiritual purification; **1.** *purge away*; **a.** act., Meth.*symp.*1.1(p.9.9; M.18.40A); ἀ. τοῦ βίου τὴν θεοστυγίαν Eus.*h.e.*10.9.9(M.20.904C); Chrys.*hom.80.1 in Mt.*(7.765D); id.*hom.4.6 in 2Cor.*(10.463C); *ib.15.5*(10.551A) cit. s. ἐκκλησία; οὐδὲν οὕτως ἀ. τὰ ἁμαρτήματα, ὡς δάκρυα id.*hom.12.4 in Col.*(11.417D); **b.** med., Hipp.*Dan.*1.33; Chrys.*David* 3(4.770B); id.*hom.1.3 in Philm.*(11.778E); οὐ γὰρ ἦν ἑτέρως ~εσθαι τῆς τῶν πλανωμένων ψυχῆς τὴν... κηλῖδα, μὴ οὐχὶ διὰ τοῦ ἁγίου βαπτίσματος Cyr.*Is.*2.4(2.283B); of Jewish ritual washings μολυσμούς...δι' ὑδάτων καὶ λουτρῶν ἀ. Epiph.*haer.*15.1(p.209.8; M.41.244A); **2.** med., *wipe off on oneself*; met., *acquire by contact* τούτου τὴν σκληραγωγίαν τέτρασιν ἀποσμηξάμενος ἔτεσιν Jo.D.*hom.*11.8(M.96.769C); **3.** *cleanse, purify*; **a.** act., Ath.*inc.*57.3(M.25.196C); τὴν στολὴν τῆς ψυχῆς ἀ. Chrys.*hom.2.1 in Mt.*(7.19A); id.*hom.23.4 in Heb.*(12.218B); †Jo.D.*B.J.*20(M.96.1041B); **b.** med., fig. μηδενὸς...πολέμου...τὰ ὅπλα ἀ. Chrys.*hom.3.4 in 1 Thess.*(11.446A); **c.** pass., Meth.*symp.*1.1(p.8.12; M.18.37B); ψυχὰς θείῳ λουτρῷ...~θείσας Eus.*h.e.*10.4.64(M.20.876A); Max.*ep.*8(M.91.441D); **4.** *reveal, make plain*, Cyr.*hom.pasch.*6(5[2].61B).

ἀποσοβ-έω, 1. *scare away, drive off*; insects διάκονοι...~είτωσαν τὰ μικρὰ τῶν ἱπταμένων ζῴων, ὅπως ἂν μὴ ἐγχρίμπτωνται εἰς τὰ κύπελλα *Lit.*ap.*Const.App.*8.12.3; heretics from the flock of Christ, Eus.*h.e.*4.24(M.20.389B); τῆς κοινωνίας ἀ. Chrys.*grat.*2(2.660A); Satan τὸν διάβολον ἀ. id.*hom.22.6 in Mt.*(7.283D); Cyr.*Ps.*80:7(M.69.1204C); Christ οἱ Φαρισαῖοι...ἀπεσόβουν μὲν αὐτῆς [sc. τῆς συναγωγῆς] τὸν ἐξ οὐρανοῦ νυμφίον id.*Os.*35(3.66A); sins ὅταν πλεονεξίαν ~ήσωμεν τῆς ψυχῆς Chrys.*hom.19.2 in Eph.*(11.136B); Χριστὸν ἐνδεδυμένοι τὸν πᾶσαν ἔξωθεν προσβάλλουσαν ~οῦντα ἐπήρειαν Nil.*Magn.*43(M.79.1021C); **2.** *dissociate* τοῦ μὲν θεοῦ λόγου τὰς τοιάσδε φωνὰς ~εῖσθαι δεῖν Cyr.*apol.Thdt.*4(p.125.5; 6[1].218E); ref. Nestorian view ἐκβάλλετε τοῦ εἶναι θεὸν...τὸν ἐκ τῆς ἁγίας παρθένου, τὸ παθεῖν αὐτῷ προσνέμοντες μόνῳ, καὶ ~οῦντες αὐτὸν τοῦ θεοῦ λόγου id.*ep.*55(p.61.3; 5[2].190E).

ἄποσος, *without quantity*; of God, Gr.Naz.*or.*41.9(M.36.441B); ἐπὶ γὰρ τοῦ ἀ. μέτρον οὐκ ἔστιν Gr.Nyss.*v.Mos.*(M.44.405B); id.*beat.*3(M.44.1225B); Cyr.*ep.Calos.*(6[2].364A); τὸ μέγεθος τοῦτο καὶ ἄπειρόν ἐστι, καὶ ἄ. Dion.Ar.*d.n.*9.2(M.3.909C); ref. Creation πῶς τὸ ποσὸν ἐκ τοῦ ἀ.; Gr.Nyss.*hex.*7(M.44.69B); of Trin., Gr.Nyss.*Eun.*3(2 p.35.20; M.45.601C); ‡Caes.Naz.*dial.*18(M.38.873); of Logos ποσοῦται ὁ ἄ. ‡Jo.D.*hom.*5(M.96.653B); ‡Jo.D.*ep.Thphl.*3(M.95.349B); ref. false visions φυλάττου τὰς παγίδας τῶν ἐναντίων...ἵνα τὸ ἀθρόως ἐκκαλυφθέν σοι, ποσὸν τὸ θεῖον εἶναι πείσῃ. ἄποσον δὲ τὸ θεῖον Evagr.Pont.*or.*67(M.79.1181B).

***ἀποσοφίζομαι,** *argue subtly, display ingenuity*, Mac.Mgn.*apocr.*3.14(p.91.3).

ἀποσπαίρω, *quiver convulsively*, Bas.*hom.*8.3(2.65C; M.31.312C).

ἀποσπάραγμα, τό, *fragment*, Anast.S.*hod.*23(M.89.296D).

ἀποσπαργαν-όω, *take off wrappings*; pass., *be stripped* ἐσπαργανώθη μέν, ἀλλ' ~οῦται τὰ τῆς ταφῆς ἀνιστάμενος Gr.Naz.*or.*29.19(p.103.9; M.36.100B).

ἀποσπάω, *drag away*; *detach*; **1.** *pull up* a plant, Meth.*res.*1.41(p.285.15; M.18.269A); Dor.*doct.*11.2(M.88.1737A); **2.** *seduce*, Arist.*apol.*10.8; met., pass., from God, Herm.*sim.*6.2.3; and from good, Isidorus Gnost.ap.Clem.*str.*3.1(p.196.2; M.8.1101A); Eus.*d.e.*1.9(p.40.29; M.22.77D); **3.** *rescue* ἀπὸ τῶν εἰδώλων ἀ. *2Clem.*17.1; ἐξ ὧν... ἀ. ἡμᾶς Ἰησοῦς Just.*dial.*116.2(M.6.744C); Clem.*exc.Thdot.*67.4(p.129.10; M.9.692A); **4.** reflex., *withdraw* for contemplation πάντων ἑαυτοὺς ἀ. προσέχοιμεν τοῖς λεγομένοις Thdr.Mops.*Nah.*1:1(M.66.401D).

ἀποσπερμαίνω, *beget*, Dion.Al.ap.Eus.*p.e.*14.26(778D; M.21.1281B).

ἀποσπινθηρίζω, *emit in sparks* φλογμὸν ἀ. Rom.Mel.(*AS* 1 p.192).

ἀποσπογγίζ-ω, *wipe away as with a sponge*; liturg., *wipe, cleanse* τά τε ἴδια χείλη καὶ τὸ ἱερὸν ποτήριον τῷ...καλύμματι ἀ. *Lit.Chrys.*(p.359.14ff.); met., *wipe out, extinguish* ψαλμὸς...~ει τὰ πάθη Procl.CP *or.*2.1(M.65.692C); of the holy name σκιαῖς πυρετοὺς ἀ. Leont.B.*mesopent.*(M.86.1989C).

ἀποσπουδάζ-ω, 1. *despise, reject*; pass., Cyr.*Juln.*5(6[2].177B); *ib.*6(193A); **2.** *shun, be averse from* τὸ παρεῖναι [sc. ἡμᾶς] ἀ. Gr.Naz.*ep.*43(M.37.89B); τοὺς...τοῖς φαύλοις προσκεκλιμένους, ~οντας δὲ τὸ ἀγαθόν Cyr.*Mich.*30(3.417C); ~ειν κελεύει μᾶλλον δὲ ἀποστρέφεσθαι παντελῶς...τὸ θύειν εἰδώλοις id.*ador.*6(1.178B); med., id.*apol.Thdt.*3(p.120.19; 6[1].214B).

ἀποστασία, ἡ, 1. *revolt, defection*, esp. spiritual; **a.** of fallen angels ἀγγέλους...ἐν ἀ. γεγονότας Iren.*haer.*1.10.1(M.7.552A); of Devil and demons ὑπόθεσις δὲ αὐτοῖς τῆς ἀ. οἱ ἄνθρωποι γίνονται Tat.*orat.*8(p.8.4; M.6.821A); Clem.*str.*6.8(p.465.9; M.9.288B); Hermias *irris.*1(M.6.1169A); **b.** of man, by original sin, Cyr.H.*catech.*19.4; by sin in gen. ὁ κατακλυσμὸς ἐγένετο διὰ τὴν ἀ. Iren.*haer.*5.29.2(M.7.1202C); ἡ ἀπὸ τοῦ εὐαγγελίου ἀ. Clem.*str.*7.14(p.62.23; M.9.521B); ἡ τῆς ὄντως ἀγαθότητος ὀλέθριος ἀ. Dion.Ar.*e.h.*3.3.11(M.3.440C); *ib.*2.3.3(400B); from truth, †Bas.*bapt.*2.10.1 cit. s. σκάνδαλον; **2.** *apostasy*; from paganism προσνείμαντες ἑαυτοὺς τῷ τῆς ἀ. πνεύματι Juln.ap. Cyr.*Juln.*7(6[2].237D); from Judaism, an accusation against S. Paul, ‡Ath.*dial.Trin.*1.5(M.28.1124D); from Christianity, under persecution τῶν ἐν στρατείαις ἐξεταζομένων τινὲς ἠπατήθησαν εἰς ἀ. *Chron.Pasch.*p.296(M.92.744A); of Julian, *ib.*p.295(740A); ref. 2 Thess.2:3, of antichrist, Just.*dial.*110.2(M.6.729A); Iren.*haer.*5.28.2 ap.Or.*Apoc.*38(p.41); Chrys.*hom.3.2 in 2Thess.*(11.525B); from orthodoxy of Theodotus the cobbler, †Hipp.*Artem.*ap.Eus.*h.e.*5.28.6(M.20.513A); of Arians, Ath.*decr.*27(p.24.8; M.25.465D); of Eunomius, Gr.Nyss.*Eun.*2(2 p.362.6; M.45.541A); from the Church, *secession, schism* σχίσματα καὶ ἀ. ὅλων ἐκκλησιῶν γεγονέναι Dion.Al.ap.Eus.*h.e.*7.24.6(M.20.696A); ἄνδρες παράνομοι καὶ Χριστομάχοι διδάσκοντες ἀ., ἥν...ἄν τις πρόδρομον τοῦ ἀντιχρίστου...καλέσειεν Alex.Al.*ep.encycl.*1(p.7.1; M.18.572B); of Novatian, Eus.*h.e.*6.45.1(633B); of Meletians, Ath.*v.Anton.*68(M.26.940B); **3.** *divorce* τὸν περὶ τοῦ τῆς ἀ. βιβλίου νόμον Or.*comm.in Mt.*14.22(p.338.32; M.13.1214B); *A.Xanthipp.*6(p.62.8); **4.** *departure*; **a.** *removal* τὴν...ἀ. εἰς Ἱερουσαλὴμ *Dorm.BMV* 33(p.105); **b.** *defection* from a monastery, ‡Bas.*const.*34(2.581A; M.31.1425B); **5.** s.v.l., *standing aloof* (ref. Mt.11:16–19) ἔμειναν ἐπὶ τῆς αὐτῶν ἀπειθείας Chrys.*hom.37.4 in Mt.*(7.420B, v.l. ἀ.).

***ἀποστασιάζω,** *stir up in revolt*, Synes.*ep.*67(M.66.1413B); Pall.*h.Laus.*21(p.65.6; M.34.1073D).

ἀποστάσιον, τό, 1. *divorce* τὴν τοῦ ἀ. ῥῆσιν [sc. in Mt.5:32] Clem.*str.*3.6(p.219.11; M.8.1153A); βιβλίον τοῦ ἀ. Or.*comm.in Mt.*14.22(p.338.26; M.13.1214B); Chrys.*hom.17.4 in Mt.*(7.227A); also *bill of divorce*, Or.*Jo.*13.9(p.233.24; M.14.412C); **2.** legal *alienation, renunciation*, Sophr.H.*v.Anast.*(M.92.1684B).

ἀπόστασις, ἡ, 1. *departure* ἑκάτερος [sc. ὕπνος καὶ θάνατος]... δηλοῖ τὴν ἀ. τῆς ψυχῆς Clem.*str.*4.22(p.310.20; M.8.1352A); **2.** *defection, revolt*; *apostasy* φθορὰν...ἡ ἀπὸ τῆς τοῦ θεοῦ γνώσεως ἀ. παρέχει *ib.*5.10(p.369.3; M.9.97B); Gr.Naz.*carm.*1.2.34.247(M.37.963A); τῆς ἀ. τῆς ἀπὸ τοῦ θεοῦ διὰ τῆς παρακοῆς προηγήσατο [sc. Eve] Gr.Nyss.*Eun.*12(2 p.280.3; M.45.892A); Cyr.*Is.*3.2(2.420C); *defection* from a monastery, ‡Bas.*const.*34(2.581B; M.31.1425C); **3.** *giving up, renunciation* διὰ τὴν θείαν σπουδὴν ἢ τοῦ γένους ἀ. Vict.*Mc.*10:31(p.382.24); **4.** *absence* μηδὲ ἀ. σημαίνειν τοῦ χείρονος τὴν ἀφαιρετικὴν σημασίαν (e.g. in ἄφθαρτος) Gr.Nyss.*Eun.*12(2 p.382.13; 1109D); **5.** *separation, distinction* ὑπόστασις ὑποστάσει ἡνωμένη εἶναι οὐ δύναται σωζομένων ἄμφω τῶν ὑποστάσεων· εἴτουν ἀποστάσεων Leont.H.*Nest.*2.7(M.86.1552B); **6.** *divorce* ἀποστάσεως βιβλίον Or.*comm.in Mt.*14.22(p.338.22; M.13.1214A); τὴν ἀ. τῆς μισουμένης γυναικός Vict.*Mc.*10:3ff.(p.374.4).

ἀποστατ-έω, 1. *stand aloof from, fail* οὐδενὸς τῶν ὄντων ~εῖ [sc. God] Dion.Ar.*d.n.*5.5(M.3.820A); **2.** *fall away* Χριστὸς...εἰς φιλίαν εἰσάγων τὰ τῆς προσάλληλα κοινωνίας ~ήσαντα τουτέστιν, ἄνθρωπον καὶ θεόν Cyr.*thes.*32(5[1].296C); *reject* the scriptures, *Hom.Clem.*2.39; *apostatize*, Meth.*res.*1.32(p.268.15; M.41.1144C); †Bas.*Is.*269(1.584B; M.30.592B); by sin, *ib.*270(585B; M.593B); Cyr.*thes.*32(5[1].292D); ἀ. τῆς ἰδίας ποίμνης *Const.App.*2.20.5; from Christ, Or.*Jo.*28.7(6; p.397.33; M.14.696A).

ἀποστάτης, ὁ, 1. *rebel* against God; **a.** of Devil ἀ. ὁ ἄγγελος οὗτος καὶ ἐχθρός, ἀφ' ὅτε ἐζήλωσε τὸ πλάσμα τοῦ θεοῦ Iren.*haer.*4.40.3(M.7.1113C); Clem.*str.*1.17(p.55.12; M.8.800C); ὁ δράκων ὁ ἀ. Cyr.*Ps.*36:32(M.69.945D); ἐπ' ἐκείνου οὐκ ἐξ ἀρχῆς ἦν [sc. ἡ πονηρία] ἀλλὰ μετὰ ταῦτα ἐπεγένετο, διὸ καὶ ἀ. λέγεται Chrys.*diab.*2.2(2.262E); as adj. τὸν ἀ. δράκοντα Gr.Nyss.*Eun.*12(2 p.280.10; M.45.892B);

τὸν ἀ. διάβολον Oecum.*Apoc.*13:8(p.153); τὸν ἀρχέκακον καὶ ἀ. ... δαίμονα Proc.G.*Is.*16:6–14(M.87.2116A); ref. name Satan τὸ γὰρ σατὰν τῇ Ἰουδαίων καὶ Σύρων φωνῇ ἀ. ἐστί Just.*dial.*103.5(M.6.717B); Chrys.*hom.13.3 in 2Cor.*(10.533E); καλοῦσιν Ἑβραῖοι τὸν ἀντικείμενον ἀ. Proc.G.*2Reg.*22:1(M.87.1144B); of demons, *Lit.*ap.*Const.App.*8.7.2; Cyr.*Juln.*4(6^2.150A); of fallen angels, Clem.*str.*7.14(p.61.13; M.9.520B); Valent.Imp.*ep.episc.*ap.Thdt.*h.e.*4.8.3(3.957); in guise of pagan gods, Cyr.*Juln.*6(210E); **b.** of man τοῦ θείου νόμου...ἀ. Eus.*Is.*8:21(M.24.148C); ἀ. τῆς εὐσεβείας *M.Thdot.3* 4 (p.63.15); οἱ τῆς ἱερᾶς ἀ. ζωῆς Dion.Ar.*e.h.*3.3.7(M.3.436B); of Simon Magus, *A.Petr.et Paul.*35(p.194.17); *A.(Pass.)Petr.et Paul.* 14(p.132.5); **2.** *apostate*, from Judaism; S. Paul so termed by Ebionites, Eus.*h.e.*3.27.4(M.20.273B); Thdt.*haer.*2(4.328); in list of sins against Law, Cyr.*Juln.*9(6^2.304B); of Israelites, id.*Is.*3.2(2.419D); of Saul, Gr.Nyss.*Eun.*3(2 p.31.14; M.45.597A); of Uzziah, ‡Meth.*Sym.et Ann.*12(M.18.377C); from Christianity; of lapsed in gen., Herm.*sim.*8.6.4; *Const.App.*2.60.4; dist. from those who fall into sin, Or.*comm.in 1Cor.*1:2(*JTS* 9 p.232); of Julian, Gr.Naz.*or.*21.26(M.35.1112C); id.*carm.*1.2.34.247(M.37.963A); Philost.*h.e.*7.7(M.65.544C); Socr.*h.e.*3.12.1(M.67.412A); from orthodoxy; of Arians, Ath.*ep.Aeg.Lib.*23(M.25.592A); of heretics and Jews, Ephr. 2.242E.

ἀποστατικός, *rebellious* ἀ. διάνοια Gr.Nyss.*virg.*18(p.321.24; M.46.393C); of Jewish nation τοῦ ἀ. σώματος ‡Meth.*Sym.et Ann.*12 (M.18.377C); of fallen angels ἀ. πνευμάτων Iren.*haer.*5.28.2 ap.Or.*Apoc.*38(p.42; cf.M.7.1199B); ἀ. δυνάμεις *ib.*1.15.6(M.7.628A); Bas.*Spir.*51(3.43C; M.32.161C); Gr.Naz.*or.*38.9(M.36.321A); Gr.Nyss.*hom.5 in Cant.*(M.44.861D); Mac.Aeg.*ep.*(M.34.420B).

ἀποστατικῶς, *by rebellion, as a rebel* ὧν [sc. αἰώνων] δύναται εἷς ἀ. πονηρὸς γεγονέναι, καὶ λέγεσθαι αἰὼν τοῦ κόσμου τούτου Or.*comm.in Eph.*2:5(*JTS* 3 p.403).

ἀποστάτις, ἡ, fem. of ἀποστάτης, *apostate* γέγονε...ἀ. καὶ βέβηλος [sc. ἡ γῆ], καὶ ταῖς τῶν εἰδώλων προστεθεῖσα λατρείαις Cyr.*Os.*3(3.17E; Aubert ἀποστάτης); id.*Zach.*96(3.786E).

***ἀποστατρία, ἡ,** *apostate* (fem.), Thdr.Stud.*epp.*1.36(M.99.1037C).

***ἀποστεγόω,** *uncover, take off* a roof, ‡Just.*qu.et resp.*29(M.6.1277B).

***ἀποστειρ-όω,** *make sterile*, Meth.*symp.*4.3(p.49.2; M.18.89D); pass., *become sterile, barren*, Cyr.*Jo.*proem.(4.5B); γῆ...οὐκ ∼οῦται διὰ τὸ σάββατον id.*hom.pasch.*6(5^2.75A).

***ἀποστελεστικός,** error for ἀποτελεστικός q.v., Diod.*Ps.*70:4 (M.33.1608C).

ἀποστέλλ-ω, *send out, dispatch*;

I. in gen.;

A. persons, esp. messengers, *1Clem.*65.1; Ign.*Smyrn.*12.1; and those commissioned to perform a task κατάσκοπον εἰς τὴν Χαναὰν Ἰησοῦν...ἀποσταλέντα Just.*dial.*113.1(M.6.736B); εἰς πρεσβείαν... ἀποσταλείς Philost.*h.e.*2.5(M.65.468C); and to act on behalf of sender βασιλεὺς ἄρχοντας ∼ων, ἐξουσίαν εἰς δεσμωτήριον καὶ ἐμβαλεῖν καὶ ἀφιέναι δίδωσι Chrys.*hom.86.3 in Jo.*(8.516D).

B. a letter, Hegem.*Arch.*5(p.6.7; M.10.1433B).

II. of God and Christ;

A. Son by Father ἀπέστειλε λόγον, ἵνα κόσμῳ φανῇ ‡*Diogn.* 11.3; υἱός...τὴν τοῦ ἀποστείλαντος πατρὸς βούλησιν ἐκφαίνων *Hom.Clem.*1.7; Meth.*res.*1.39(p.283.17; M.41.1108B); Cyr.H.*catech.*19.3; ἀνελήφθη...εἰς τὸν οὐρανὸν πρὸς τὸν ἀποστείλαντα αὐτόν *Const.App.* 5.7.30; τοῦ ἀποστείλαντος πατρός, τοῦ ἐλθόντος Χριστοῦ, τοῦ μαρτυρήσαντος παρακλήτου *ib.*7.22.1; Chrys.*hom.55.2 in Jo.*(8.323D); sending of Son not incompatible with unity of Godhead, Cyr.*Jo.* 1.2(4.18E); εἶπεν...γενόμενον ἐκ γυναικὸς ἀπέστειλεν, ὡς εἶναι δῆλον, ὅτι τῇ ἐνανθρωπήσει πρόσφορον τὸ τῆς ἀποστολῆς ὄνομα Thdt.*Heb.* 3:2(3.562); Sabellian αὐτὸς ἔσται ὁ...ἀπεστάλθαι λέγων ὑφ' ἑαυτοῦ Eus.*e.th.*2.12(p.114.4; M.24.925C); in interpretation of Σιλωάμ (ἀπεσταλμένος): πάντα δὲ ταῦτα περὶ τὸν υἱὸν τοῦ θεοῦ στρέφεται· κατὰ γὰρ διαφόρους ἐπινοίας αὐτός ἐστι καὶ ὁ ἀπεσταλμένος Or.*fr.63 in Jo.*(p.534.26); but name explained without ref. to Christ, on ground that water from pool was *sent* to Isaiah to drink before his death, ‡Epiph.*v.proph.Is.*2(p.20; M.43.397B) = *Chron.Pasch.* p.155(M.92.381A).

B. H. Ghost, ‡Ath.*Maced.dial.*1.11(M.28.1305C); ἐξαποστελεῖς τὸ πνεῦμά σου [Ps.103:29]...οὐδήπου δὲ αὐτὸς ἑαυτὸν ∼ει· ἀποστολὴν δὲ καλεῖ τὴν πρὸς τὸ ἔργον αὐτοῦ συγκατάβασιν, οὐ τὴν ἐκ τόπου εἰς τόπον μετάβασιν Didym.(‡Bas.)*Eun.*5(1.297E; M.29.716A); cf.Thdr.Mops.*Jo.*15:26(p.398.17; M.66.780B) cit. s. ἀποστολή; ἀπέστειλεν εἰς ἡμᾶς ὁ κύριος Ἰησοῦς τὴν δωρεὰν τοῦ ἁγίου πνεύματος *Const.App.* 5.20.4; *ib.*7.41.7; of sending of ζῶν πνεῦμα (Manich.), Hegem.*Arch.* 7(p.10.12; M.10.1437B).

C. angels ἐγὼ...ὁ ἄγγελος τῆς μετανοίας...ἀπεστάλην...μεθ' ὑμῶν εἶναι τῶν μετανοούντων Herm.*mand.*12.6.1; ὁ ἀποσταλεὶς δὲ πρὸς... τὴν παρθένον...ἄγγελος Just.*1apol.*33.5(M.6.381B); διακονίαν ∼ομένων πνευμάτων Thdr.Mops.*Jo.*15:26(p.398.20; M.66.780B).

D. men; **1.** in gen., as commissioned by God δύναται κατὰ μὲν τὸ κοινότερον πᾶς ἄνθρωπος ἀπεστάλθαι ἀπὸ θεοῦ, κυρίως δὲ λέγεσθαι ἀπεστάλθαι ὑπὸ θεοῦ οὐκ ἄλλος ἢ ὁ ἐπὶ διακονίᾳ θείᾳ καὶ λειτουργίᾳ σωτηρίας γένους ἀνθρώπων ἐπιδημῶν τῷ βίῳ Or.*Jo.*2.30 (24; p.87.24; M.14.168A); **2.** OT prophets etc.: Moses, Cyr.H.*catech.*19.2; Isaiah, Or.*Jo.*2.29(24; p.86.11; 164D); οὐχ εὕρομεν γοῦν τὸ ∼εσθαι ἀπὸ θεοῦ ἐπ' ἄλλου του ἢ τῶν ἁγίων κειμένον· ἐπὶ μὲν τοῦ Ἡσαΐου...τοῦ Ἱερεμίου...τοῦ Ἰεζεκιήλ *ib.*2.30(24; p.87.30; 168A); Jo. Bapt., *ib.*2.29(24; p.86.4; 164C); Cyr.*Jo.*1.7(4.62A); **3.** of Christ's apostles, def. πέμπει μὲν τοὺς διὰ τὸ ∼εσθαι ὑπ' αὐτοῦ ἀποστόλους ὀνομαζομένους...καὶ νῦν οὖν ὃν ἐὰν ∼ῃ ὁ σωτὴρ διακονησόμενον τῇ τινων σωτηρίᾳ, ὁ ∼όμενος ἀπόστολός ἐστιν Ἰησοῦ Χριστοῦ. ἀλλ' ὁ ἀπόστολος, ὥσπερ τοῦ ἀποστείλαντός ἐστιν ἀπόστολος, οὕτως τισὶν πρὸς οὓς ἀποστέλλεται μόνοις ἐστὶν ἀπόστολος Or.*Jo.*32.17(10; p.453.7ff.; 785Bff.); sent by Christ or H. Ghost, Chrys.*comm.in Gal.*1:2 (10.660A); their sending compared with Christ's (Jo.17:18) τὸ δὲ 'καθὼς' πάλιν ἐνταῦθα οὐχ ὁμοιώσεως ἐπ' αὐτοῦ καὶ τῶν ἀποστόλων κεῖται· (πῶς γὰρ ἄλλως ἦν ἐγχωροῦν ἀνθρώποις ἀποσταλῆναι;) id.*hom.82.1 in Jo.*(8.484B); instructed by God, Cyr.*Jo.*1.7(4.62B); sent as missionaries, Just.*1apol.*39.3(M.6.388B); *Hom.Clem.*17.7; with authority to act in Christ's name, Chrys.*hom.86.3 in Jo.* (516D); v. ἀπόστολος.

E. Law ὁ θεὸς ἀπέστειλε βασιλεύσοντα νόμον Meth.*symp.*10.4 (p.126.6; M.18.197C).

III. false apostles by Devil, *Const.App.*6.8.1.

IV. of 'dismissal' to God of the departed τοὺς...πάλιν τῆς θείας χάριτος κοινωνοὺς ἀποφανθέντας, καὶ ὡς ἐλευθέρους πρὸς τὸν κύριον ἀπεσταλμένους Dion.Al.*fr.*(p.61.2).

V. intrans., *visit* ἤδη γὰρ ∼ει ὁ θεὸς ἐφ' ὑμᾶς Pall.*h.Laus.*21 (p.68.6; M.34.1075D).

ἀποστενοχωρέω, pass., *be shut up, confined*, Nil.*epp.*3.125(M.79.441B).

ἀποστεφανόω, *uncrown*, of Christ defeating Devil τοῦ ἀκανθίνου στεφάνου, ὃς τὸν νικητὴν ἡμῶν ἀπεστεφάνωσε Gr.Naz.*or.*33.14(M.36.232B).

ἀποστηθίζ-ω, *learn by heart, repeat from memory*, esp. scriptures ἀ. τὰ ἐν ταῖς γραφαῖς παραγγέλματα Ath.*v.Anton.*55(M.26.921B); Epiph.*haer.*67.1(p.133.11; M.42.172D); Pall.*h.Laus.*11(p.34.6; M.34.1034B); χάριν δὲ αὐτῷ δεδόσθαι θεόθεν ἔλεγεν ∼ειν ἔξωθεν τὰς γραφάς ‡Pall.*h.mon.*11.5(p.55.13; M.65.449C); Jo.Clim.*scal.*4(M.88.700A); εἶχεν μὲν οὖν γνῶσιν καὶ τῶν θείων γραφῶν ὁ ἐν ἁγίοις, οὐκ ἐν σοφίᾳ δὲ λόγου ταύτας ὡς ἐπὶ κενοδοξίας ∼ων, ἀλλὰ δι' αὐτῆς τῆς τῶν ἔργων πράξεως καὶ τῆς τῶν ἐντολῶν τηρήσεως Leont.N.*v.Jo.Eleem.*18(p.36.3); id.*v.Sym.*22(M.93.1697B).

***ἀποστηθισμός, ὁ,** *repetition by heart* ἀναγνώσεσι...γραφῶν ἁγίων καὶ ἀ. Epiph.*exp.fid.*23(p.525.2; M.42.829C).

***ἀποστιβάζω,** *unpack*, Herm.*mand.*11.15.

ἀποστίλβ-ω, 1. *shine brightly, be resplendent*; of gems, Gr.Nyss.*v.Mos.*(M.44.320B); ἁλουργίδα...τὸ τῆς θαλάσσης ∼ουσαν ἄνθος Bas.Sel.*or.*2.1(M.85.37A); met. τὸ τοῦ ἔσωθεν ἀνθρώπου τῆς καταστολῆς αἴγλην ∼οντες Meth.*symp.*7.2(p.73.16; M.18.128B); of Church ἤδη δὲ λαμπροτάτων δίκην φωστήρων τῶν ἀνὰ τὴν οἰκουμένην ∼ουσῶν ἐκκλησιῶν Eus.*h.e.*4.7.1(M.20.316A); *ib.*4.7.13(320B); **2.** *illuminate*, met. τῆς γνώσεως αἱ ἀκτῖνες...τὸν...∼ουσαι ἄνθρωπον Clem.*prot.*11 (p.81.24; M.8.236A); *ib.*1(p.4.10; 53B).

***ἀποστολεῖον, τό,** *shrine of an apostle, church dedicated in honour of an apostle* εἰς Δρῦν, Χαλκηδόνος...προάστειον,...ἐν ᾧ...μεγάλη ἐκκλησία ἣν αὐτὸς Ῥουφῖνος ἐπὶ τιμῇ Πέτρου καὶ Παύλου...ἐδείματο, καὶ ἀ. ἐξ αὐτῶν ὠνόμασε Soz.*h.e.*8.17.3(M.67.1560A); of basilica of S. Peter at Rome, *ib.*9.10.4(1617A); of church of S. Thomas at Scythopolis, Cyr.S.*v.Sab.*61(p.162.28); *ib.*75(p.180.19); of church of S. Thomas at CP, *Chron.Pasch.*p.320(M.92.816A); v. ἀποστόλιον.

ἀποστολεύς, ὁ, *sender*, of Father as mentioned in baptismal formula τοῦ πατρὸς ἡ μνήμη ὡς αἰτίου καὶ ἀ. *Const.App.*3.17.2.

ἀποστολή, ἡ, *sending forth, mission, apostleship*;

I. in gen., of things;

A. *casting forth, outpouring* τῆς χίονος ἡ ἀ. Olymp.*Job* 37:6 (M.93.385C); exeg. Cant.4:13 ἧς γὰρ ἐκ τοῦ στόματος ἀ. ῥοῶν εἰσι καὶ ἀρωμάτων παράδεισοι, αὕτη νῦν πηγὴ γίνεται Gr.Nyss.*hom.9 in*

Cant.(M.44.977A); met., of utterance τὰς δὲ τῶν εὐσεβούντων γλώττας εἰς τὴν συνήθη ἀ. τὰ νάματα προχεῖν Thdt.*ep.*141(4.1236).

B. *sending forth, bestowal* ἐν ἀ. τελειώσεως (translation of Aramaic formula) Epiph.*haer.*19.4(p.222.3; M.41.268A).

C. *sending of orders, dispatch* ἐξ ἀ. δὲ τοῦ...Καίσαρος Just.*1apol.* 68.3(M.6.432B, v.l. ἐπιστολῆς).

II. of persons, *sending out, mission, commission*;

A. in gen., Cyr.*Ag.*9(3.636B).

B. of Christ's mission, received from Father, variously interpreted τὸ τοίνυν ἀ. τοῦ λόγου σημαίνεσθαι ἕνωσιν δηλοῖ τὴν πρὸς τὸν ἐκ Μαρίας Ἰησοῦν...τὴν γὰρ πρὸς τὸν ἄνθρωπον ἕνωσιν, σὺν ᾧ γνωρισθῆναι ἀνθρώποις ἦν δυνατὸν τὴν ἀόρατον φύσιν διὰ τῆς ὁρωμένης, ἀ. ὠνόμασεν ‡Ath.*Ar.*4.36(p.86.3–10; M.26.524B,C); ἐπειδὴ δὲ τὸ ἐξαπόστειλον [Ps.42:3] λέγει, δῆλος ἂν εἴη λοιπόν, ἕτερον μέν τινα τὸν ἀποστέλλοντα εἰδώς, ἕτερον δὲ τὸν ἀποστελλόμενον· ὁ δὲ τῆς ἀ. τρόπος νοείσθω θεοπρεπῶς Cyr.*Jo.*1.2(4.18E); ἐν ἀρχῇ γὰρ ἦν...ὁ ἐνανθρωπήσας λόγος...καίτοι γεννηθεὶς...καὶ κεχρισμένος εἰς τὴν εἰς τονδε τὸν κόσμον ἀ. παρὰ τοῦ θεοῦ καὶ πατρός id.*inc.unigen.*(5[1].711E); Thdt. *Heb.*3:2(3.562) cit. s. ἀποστέλλω; id.*Trin.*15(M.75.1169A) cit. s. ἀνθρωπότης.

C. of sending of H. Ghost, Didym.(‡Bas.)*Eun.*5(1.297E; M.29. 716A) cit. s. ἀποστέλλω; εἰ γὰρ μὴ τὴν φυσικὴν ἐκεῖθεν πρόοδον ἔλεγεν διὰ τοῦ 'ἐκπορεύεται', ἀλλά τινα ἀ. ἔξωθεν γινομένην, ἄπορον περὶ τίνος λέγει, πολλῶν ὄντων κοινῶς τῶν κατὰ διακονίαν ἀποστελλομένων πνευμάτων Thdr.Mops.*Jo.*15:26(p.398.17; M.66.780B).

D. of sending of angels, for divine vengeance (cf. Ps.77:49) ἱκετεύει...Δαβὶδ μὴ...δι' ἀποστολῆς ἀγγέλων πονηρῶν παιδευθῆναι †Bas.*hom.in Ps.*37:2(1.363E; M.30.85C).

E. of sending by God of Moses, Cyr.*glaph.Ex.*2(1.304D); Μωσέα καὶ ὀκνοῦντα τὴν ἀ. id.*Os.*3(3.12E); id.ap.*cat.Heb.*(suppl.)7:1(p.528. 1); prophets αὐτὸν βούλεται ἑκόντα καταδέξασθαι τὴν ἀ. ὁ κύριος, καὶ ὅτι μὲν χρεία τῆς ἀ. ἔδειξε...Ἡσαΐας δὲ τὴν χρείαν διδαχθεὶς τῆς ἀ., ἑκὼν ἑαυτὸν ἐπέδωκε †Bas.*Is.*184(1.514C,D; M.30.429C,432A); Jeremiah ᾔδει προφήτην ἐσόμενον καὶ ἐπιτηδείως ἔχοντα πρὸς ἀποστολήν Cyr.*Mal.*4(3.820C); Jo. Bapt. σιωπωμένης τῆς ἀρχῆς τῆς ἀ. ἀναλογίαν ἐχούσης πρὸς τὴν ἀ. τοῦ Ἡσαΐου, ἀποστέλλεται βαπτίζειν Or.*Jo.*2.29(24; p.86.15; M.14.165A); *ib.*2.31(25; p.88.7; 168B).

F. esp. of commissioning by Christ of apostles; **1.** the Twelve ἀπέσταλμαι [sc. Ἰωάννης] οὖν ἀ. οὐκ ἀνθρωπίνην *A.Jo.*33(p.168.10); ἄξιοι φανῆναι...τῆς παρ' αὐτοῦ ἀ. Bas.*fid.*2(2.226B; M.31.681C); Gr. Naz.*carm.*1.2.34.233(M.37.962A); **2.** S. Paul, Euthal.Diac.*Ac.*(M.85. 656A); hence,

III. *apostolate, office of an apostle*; **1.** of Christ's apostles Πέτρον ...τὸν ἀπὸ ἁλιέων εἰς τὴν διακονίαν τῆς ἀ. προσκληθέντα Bas.*Eun.*2.4 (1.240E; M.29.580A); ὑπατίαν πνευματικὴν ἐκαλέσαμεν τὴν ἀ. Chrys. *hom.3.4 in Ac.princ.*(3.77B); τὰ τῆς ἀ. ἐπιτηδεύματα συνελών, οὕτως ἀποστεῖλαί φησιν αὐτοὺς καθάπερ αὐτὸν ὁ πατήρ, ἵν' εἰδεῖεν ἐντεῦθεν, ὡς καλεῖν ὀφείλουσιν ἁμαρτωλοὺς εἰς μετάνοιαν, θεραπεύειν δὲ τοὺς κακῶς ἔχοντας, σωματικῶς τε καὶ πνευματικῶς, ἐν δὲ ταῖς τῶν πραγμάτων οἰκονομίαις τὸ ἴδιον οὐχὶ πάντως θέλημα ζητεῖν, ἀλλὰ τὸ τοῦ ἀποστείλαντος, σώζειν τε καθόσον ἐνδέχεται ταῖς διδασκαλίαις τὸν κόσμον Cyr.*Jo.*12.1(4.1094D); Thdt.*1Tim.*3:1(3.652) cit. s. ἐπίσκοπος; apostolate exercised by others besides Twelve and S. Paul, e.g., Zacchaeus ὁ τελώνης κεκλημένος εἰς ἀ. Cyr.*ador.*15 (1.535D); S. Stephen τῷ διπλοῦς στεφάνους ἀναδησαμένῳ ἀ. καὶ μαρτυρίου Didym.*Trin.*2.11(M.39.597C); Thecla διὰ τοῦτο γάρ σε καὶ Χριστὸς ἐξελέξατο δι' ἐμοῦ, ἵνα σε καὶ εἰς ἀ. προσαγάγηται, καί τινάς σοι τῶν ἔτι ἀκατηχήτων πολέων ἐγχειρίσῃ Bas.Sel.*v.Thecl.*1(M.85.553D); **2.** Manich. pretensions to apostolate μὴ ποιοῦντες γὰρ ὃ ποιοῦσιν οἱ ἀπόστολοι, ἀλλὰ μαχόμενοι τῷ ὑπ' ἐκείνων γεγραμμένῳ, ψεύδονται τὴν ἀ. ψευδοπροφῆται ὄντες Serap.*Man.*48(p.68; M.18.1240D); **3.** Jewish apostolate, i.e. office of travelling emissaries of Jewish patriarch τῷ Ἰωσήπῳ τῆς ἀ. δοῦναι τὴν ἐπικαρπίαν. καὶ μετ' ἐπιστολῶν οὗτος ἀποστέλλεται εἰς τὴν Κιλίκων γῆν Epiph.*haer.*30.11(p.346.6; M.41. 424A).

IV. *sphere of apostle's mission* ὁ ἐκλεξάμενος ἡμᾶς εἰς ἀ. ἐθνῶν *A.Jo.*112(p.211.1); τὴν ἀ. τοῦ κόσμου Sever.ap.*cat.Ac.*2:3(p.22.27); Θωμᾶς μὲν τὴν Πάρθων ἀ. ὑπεδέχετο Socr.*h.e.*1.19.2(M.67.125B).

***ἀποστολικομαθής**, *learning from the apostles* οἱ...κτηνόφρονες ἄνθρωποι προφητικόγνωστοι καὶ ἀ. ... ἐγίνοντο Agath.*v.Gr.Ill.*151 (p.77).

ἀποστολικός, *having a mission, of* or *pertaining to an apostle* or *apostles, apostolic*;

I. *having a mission, being sent out* ἀ. τὸ πνεῦμά ἐστιν· ἀποστέλλεται γὰρ ‡Ath.*Maced.dial.*1.11(M.28.1305C).

II. *of* or *belonging to apostles*;

A. *consisting of apostles* ἀπὸ τάξεως ἀ. Or.*Jo.*32.18(11; p.456.22; M.14.792B); χορὸς...ἀ. Eus.*Ps.*146:7(M.24.68A) etc.; χορείας ἀ. id. *v.C.*3.7(p.80.24; M.20.1061B).

B. *belonging to Christ's apostles*; **1.** of apostles' status Παῦλος ὡς...ἐξουσίαν ἔχων ἀ. Or.*hom.8.8 in Jer.*(p.62.8; M.13.345A); τὸν Ἰούδαν ὁ θεὸς ἐξελέξατο...καὶ τὴν ἀ. ἀξίαν...ἐνεχείρισεν Chrys.*sac.*4.1 (p.101.23; 1.404B); ὁ προφήτης ἄρχων ἐστί·...ὁ ποιμὴν καὶ διδάσκαλος ἄρχων ἐστὶ πνευματικός· ἀλλὰ τούτων ἁπάντων μείζων ἐστὶν ἀρχὴ ἡ ἀ. id.*hom.3.3 in Ac.princ.*(3.75D); ἔσχεν [sc. Ἰούδας]...ἀντὶ ἐπισκοπῆς ἀ. τὸν τόπον τῆς ἀπωλείας Epiph.*haer.*38.8(p.71.12; M.41. 665B); **2.** qualities and endowments τῆς ἀ. [φωνῆς] χάριτος Clem. *paed.*2.12(p.228.12; M.8.541A); Thdt.*qu.38 in 3 Reg.*(1.380); τὸν ἀ. ... ζῆλον Chrys.*hom.8.5 in Mt.*(7.127C); συνέσεως...τῆς ἀ. id.*hom.5.3 in Rom.*(9.465B); of festival of S. Barnabas ἀ. γὰρ ἅμα καὶ μαρτυρικῆς εὐωδίας πεπλήρωται †Leont.N.*laud.Barn.*(p.144.27); **3.** their experiences πειρασμῶν τῶν ἀ. Chrys.*hom.76.1 in Mt.*(7.731E); *ib.32.5* (371C); πανταχόθεν αὐτῷ θόρυβος καὶ ταραχὴ...οὗτος ἀ. χαρακτήρ id. *hom.25.2 in 2Cor.*(10.615A); **4.** of their teaching recorded in their writings; **a.** of apostles in gen., Clem.*str.*5.14(p.417.22; M.9.197B); ἀ. λόγοις Or.*Cels.*2.65(p.187.16; M.11.900A) etc.; dist. from rest of scripture, Clem.*q.d.s.*42(p.190.25; M.9.652A); τῶν εὐαγγελικῶν γραφῶν,...τῶν ἀ. λόγων Or.*hom.5.13 in Jer.*(p.42.28; M.13.313C); cf.id. *comm.in Mt.*10.2(p.14.6; M.13.861C); id.*Jo.*5.8(p.105.7; M.14.196A); *ib.*13.52(51; p.280.17; 493C); **b.** esp. of citations from S. Paul ἡ ἀ. γραφή Clem.*prot.*1(p.5.27; M.8.57B); *ib.*(p.8.14; 64A); λέξιν ἀ. Or.*hom. 19.15 in Jer.*(p.175.24; M.13.497D); Eus.*Marcell.*1.2(p.11.27; M.24. 737B); τῇ ἀ. διηγήσει Or.*hom.14.16 in Jer.*(p.123.1; M.13.425B); ἀ. ῥητόν id.*princ.*3.1.21(p.235.10; M.11.293B); Eus.*Marcell.*1.2(p.11.22; 737B); Chrys.*hom.5.5 in Rom.*(9.468A); ἀ. προρρήσεων Ath.*ep.Aeg. Lib.*20(M.25.585A); ἀ. φωνῆς Gr.Nyss.*Eun.*12(1 p.381.24; M.45. 1109B); Chrys.*stat.*1.1(2.1A); ἀ. περὶ τοῦ Χριστοῦ θεολογίας Eus.*e.th.* 3.6(p.164.29; M.24.1016A); ἀ. ... ὅρῳ Gr.Nyss.*ep.can.*6(M.45.233A); ἀ. νόμον Chrys.*hom.55.5 in Mt.*(7.561E); **c.** hence neut. as subst.; **i.** *apostolic saying*, of quotation from gospels τὸ ἀ. 'τὸ γὰρ πτύον ἐν τῇ χειρὶ αὐτοῦ' κτλ. [Mt.3:12] Clem.*ecl.*25(p.143.23; M.9. 709B); from S. Paul κἀκεῖνο τὸ ἀ. ἅπαξ μνησθεὶς Or.*hom.5.1 in Jer.* (p.31.7; M.13.296C); τὸ ἀ., 'ἐν παντὶ τόπῳ προσεύχεσθαι' †Bas.*Is.*35 (1.408B; M.30.189A); Chrys.*hom.81.2 in Mt.*(7.776A); (plur.), Gr. Nyss.*Eun.*4(2 p.61.27; M.45.633A); **ii.** (plur.), *the epistles* as part of NT ἐκ τῶν εὐαγγελικῶν καὶ τῶν ἀ. ... ἀποδείξεις ποιεῖσθαι Iren.*haer.* 1.3.6(M.7.477A); Clem.*str.*7.14(p.60.17; M.9.517B); ὅπως συνᾴδοι τὰ προφητικὰ τοῖς ἀ. καὶ τὰ ἀ. τοῖς εὐαγγελικοῖς Epiph.*haer.*57.7(p.353.6; M.41.1005C); cf. βιβλίον ἀ. Socr.*h.e.*4.23.4(M.67.509C); **iii.** *corpus of epistles* collected into volume τῷ σῷ φάλσῳ οὐ πιστεύω ἀ. Adam. *dial.*1.5(p.10.19; M.11.1724A); esp. of Marcionite corpus of Pauline epistles προένεγκε τὸ ἀ. σου, εἰ καὶ τὰ μάλιστα περικεκομμένον ἐστί *ib.*(p.10.20; 1724A); τὸ...παρ' αὐτῷ...ἀ. καλούμενον Epiph.*haer.*42.10 (p.106.11; M.41.709A); προσέθετο δὲ ἐν τῷ ἰδίῳ ἀ. καλουμένῳ καὶ τῆς καλουμένης πρὸς Λαοδικέας *ib.*42.12(p.182.11; 812B); cf. of Pauline epistles τοῖς ῥητοῖς τοῦ ἀ. τεύχους Euthal.Diac.*epp.Paul.*(M.85. 720C); **iv.** liturg., *the Epistle* ὅταν δὲ ἀναγινώσκηται τὸ εὐαγγέλιον, ἢ ἀ. ‡Gr.Thaum.*annunt.*2(M.10.1161C); v. ἀπόστολος; **5.** of style or manner of an apostle ἀσπάζομαι...ἐν ἀ. χαρακτῆρι (i.e. in manner of S. Paul's letters) Ign.*Trall.*proem.; **6.** of times of the apostles, ‡Just.*qu.et resp.*115(M.6.1364B); ἐγγὺς τῶν ἀ. χρόνων *Chron.Pasch.* p.6(M.92.80C); *ib.*p.7(81A).

C. *of the apostles*, in gen. ὁ γνωστικὸς...τὴν ἀ. ἀπουσίαν ἀνταναπληροῖ βιοὺς ὀρθῶς Clem.*str.*7.12(p.55.9; M.9.505B).

III. *connected with*, or *partaking of character of, the apostles*; **1.** *associated with the apostles*, i.e. belonging to apostolic age σεμνύνων τοὺς κατ' αὐτὸν ἀ. ἄνδρας, ἐξ Ἑβραίων, ὡς ἔοικε, γεγονότας Eus.*h.e.*2.17.2(M.20.176A); **2.** *having the character of an apostle*, of S. Barnabas μάρτυν τὸν ἀ. Clem.*str.*2.20(p.176.6; M.8.1060B); Nicolas, *ib.*(p.177.9; 1061B); Polycarp διδάσκαλος ἀ. καὶ προφητικὸς γενόμενος *M.Polyc.*16.2; ὁ μακάριος καὶ ἀ. πρεσβύτερος Iren.*ep.Flor.* ap.Eus.*h.e.*5.20.7(M.20.485B); ἀ. ἄνδρα Eus.*h.e.*3.36.10(M.20.289B); *ib.*4.15.46(360A); Ignatius ἀνὴρ ἐν τοῖς πᾶσιν ἀ. *M.Ign.Ant.*1; Dionysius the Areopagite, Jo.VI CP *ep.*(M.96.1424A); Job ἄνδρα θαυμαστόν τινα καὶ ἀ. Olymp.*Job* proem.(M.93.13C); **3.** hence of qualities etc., *worthy of*, or *like, an apostle* τῆς μεγάλης σου...καὶ ἀ. ψυχῆς Bas.*ep.*80(3.173D; M.32.456B); Chrys.*hom.32.1 in Jo.*(8.185B); ἐν γυναικὶ ψυχὴν ἀ. id.*hom.33.3 in 1Cor.*(10.302B); id.*hom.21.2 in Heb.*(12.195B); βίον ἀ. βιούς Socr.*h.e.*4.9.3(M.67.477D); Nil.*epp.*3.26 (M.79.384C); ἐπίσκοπος...Ἰάκωβος...τῆς δὲ ἀ. χάριτος τὰς ἀκτῖνας οὗτος ἠφίει Thdt.*h.e.*2.30.2(3.905); †Jo.D.*BJ.*40(M.96.1236C).

IV. *following the apostles' example, in keeping with the apostles'* *practice*; **1.** of persons ὁ δὲ πιστὸς καὶ ἀ. ἀνὴρ...θαυμάζει τὸν ἐν σώματι κύριον [sc. in contrast with heretics] Ath.*ep.Serap*.4.15(M.26.657B); **2.** of qualities ἀ. δὲ οἶμαι, καὶ τὸ ταῖς ἀγράφοις παραδόσεσι παραμένειν Bas.*Spir*.71(3.60A; M.32.200B).

V. *derived from the apostles*;

A. of orthodox doctrine τὴν ἀ. καὶ ἐκκλησιαστικὴν σώζων ὀρθοτομίαν τῶν δογμάτων Clem.*str*.7.16(p.73.16; M.9.544A); ἑτέραν ἀντὶ τῆς ἀ. παραδεικνύντες ὁδόν Or.*adnot.in Dt*.27:18(M.17.33C); ἀ. δόξης Alex.Al.*ep.Alex*.1(p.20.6; M.18.549A); οἱ αὐχοῦντες τὴν ἀ. διδασκαλίαν τετηρηκέναι, καὶ κατὰ διαδοχὴν ἀπ' ἐκείνων τὸ κήρυγμα τοῦ εὐαγγελίου παρειληφέναι †Bas.*Is*.172(1.504B; M.30.408A); Thdt.*h.e*.2.27.5(3.895); with partic. reference to doctrinal tradition in Roman Church ἐναντιούμενος τῇ ἀ. διδαχῇ Cael. *ep.Cyr*.1(p.76.26; M.77.93A).

B. of Catholic faith, Ath.*Ar*.1.4(M.26.20A); τὴν καθολικὴν καὶ ἀ. πίστιν, ἥτις μέχρι τῆς κατὰ Νίκαιαν συνόδου ἀκεραία...διέμεινε Liber.*ep.Maced*.ap.Socr.*h.e*.4.12.25(M.67.492A); Bas.*fid*.5(2.229A; M.31.689B); of faith defined at Nicaea, Thdt.*h.e*.2.26.3(3.892); Eulog.*fr.Trin*.5.1(p.371).

C. ἀ. παράδοσις *apostolic tradition* of doctrine and practice maintained in orthodox Church, Or.*princ*.1 proem.2(p.8.28; M.11.116B); Const.ap.Eus.*v.C*.3.61(p.109.9; M.20.1136A); *Symb.Ant*.(341)2(p.249.11; M.26.721B); Thdt.*haer*.4.12(4.371); as title of work by Hippolytus, *CIG* 8613A; v. παράδοσις.

D. of Church order τὸν ἀ. κανόνα Alex.Al.*ep.Alex*.2(p.21.5; M.18.552A); Eus.*v.C*.3.61(p.109.14; M.20.1136A) where cf. CNic.(325)*can*.15; ἐν γὰρ τοῖς ἐκκλησιαστικοῖς οὐ λόγων ἐπίδειξίς ἐστιν, ἀλλὰ κανόνες ἀ. Jul.Papa *ep.Dian*.ap.Ath.*apol.sec*.21(p.103.12; M.25.284B).

E. of succession of teachers in Church, including Pantaenus and others, who taught apostolic doctrine τοὺς ἐμφανεστέρους ἧς κατείληφεν ἀ. διαδοχῆς ἐπισημηνάμενος Eus.*h.e*.5.11.2(M.20.457A); for apostolic succession of bishops, v. ἀπόστολος, ἐπίσκοπος.

F. of Church, as founded by apostles and maintaining their doctrine and practice πιστεύομεν ὡς τῇ ἀ. ἐκκλησίᾳ δοκεῖ Alex.Al.*ep.Alex*.12(p.26.30; M.18.565A); ἀναθεματίζει ἡ καθολικὴ καὶ ἀ. ἐκκλησία *Symb.Nic*.(325)*anath*.(p.52.5); Epiph.*haer*.57.4(p.349.10; om. M.41.1001A); *ib*.67.6(p.138.11; M.42.180C); Pall.*v.Chrys*.20(p.147.6; M.47.82); CCP(553)*anath*.11(p.170); *Lit.Jac*.(p.208.1); in creeds, Alex.Al.*ep.Alex*.12(p.28.11; M.18.568B = Hahn p.20); *Symb*.ap. Epiph.*anc*.118(p.147.14; M.43.232D); *Symb*.ap.Epiph.*anc*.119(p.149.8; M.43.236B); ‡Ath.*interpr*.(p.66.25; M.26.1232B, some MSS only); *Symb*.ap.*Const.App*.7.41.7; *Symb.Nic.-CP*(p.80.14; H.2.288B).

G. of sees claiming apostolic foundation ἀ. θρόνων...Ἱεροσολύμων, ...Ἀντιοχείας,...Ἀλεξανδρείας,...Ῥωμαίων Soz.*h.e*.1.17.2(M.67.912B); Jerusalem, Eus.*h.e*.7.32.29(M.20.733B); Soz.*h.e*.4.25.2(1196A); Sophr.*H.v.Anast*.(M.92.1688A); Antioch, Soz.*h.e*.1.2.2(864B); Thdt.*ep*.112(4.1184); id.*h.e*.3.19.1(3.935); *ib*.5.9.16(1033); cf.*CIG* 8799; Alexandria, Soz.*h.e*.1.17.2(912B); Thdt.*ep*.83(*ACO* 2.1.2 p.50.34; 4.1150); Rome, Ath.*h.Ar*.35(p.202.29; M.25.733C); as *the* apostolic see ὅτι τῇ ἀ. καθέδρᾳ τὴν ὀφειλομένην αἰδῶ ἡ ἀγάπη ὑμῶν ἀπονέμει Dam. Papa *ep.orient*.ap.Thdt.*h.e*.5.10.1(3.1034); *Cod.Afr*.proem.(H.1.861C); Eutych.*ep.Vigil*.(M.86.2404D); Jo.VI CP *ep*.(M.96.1420C); Cyprus (Salamis) as founded by S. Barnabas, Alex.Sal.*Barn*.37(448A).

H. of Nicene Council, as defining apostolic faith σύνοδον... καθολικὴν καὶ ἀ. Amph.*ep.syn*.(M.39.96A);

VI. of a church, *dedicated in honour of the apostles* τὴν ἀ. ἐκκλησίαν τὴν ἐν τῇ καλουμένῃ Παλαιᾷ διακειμένην Thdt.*h.e*.2.31.11(3.910).

VII. *patriarchal* τὴν ἀ. ἐνδεδυμένον στολήν Eustrat.*v.Eutych*.94(M.86.2380C); Thphn.*chron*.p.140(M.108.381B).

VIII. (plur.) name of ascetic sect otherwise called Apotactici, related to followers of Tatian, Encratites, and Cathari, Epiph.*haer*.61.1(p.380.11; M.41.1040C); τὸν γάμον τινὲς ἀπαγορεύουσι, καὶ τὸ γεννᾶν, Σατορνεῖνος καὶ οἱ ἀ. Ammon.*Jo*.1:3(M.85.1393B); ἀ., οἳ καὶ ἀποτακτικοί· καὶ οὗτοι περὶ τὴν Πισιδίαν μόνον ὁρμώμενοι, μόνον ἀποτακτικοὺς δεχόμενοι Jo.D.*haer*.61(M.94.713B).

***ἀποστολικῶς**, **1.** *in the manner of an apostle*, Or.*mart*.21(p.19.10; M.11.589B); Bas.*ep*.200(3.298B; M.32.733B); Thdt.*Dan*.7:13f.(1.1201); **2.** *by the apostle*, i.e. by evidence from S. Paul εὐαγγελικῶς τε καὶ ἀ. ... καὶ πατρικῶς παρέστησά σοι Thdr.Stud.*epp*.1.48(M.99.1080C).

ἀποστολιμαῖος, *dispatched, missive*; neut. as subst. μαθὼν παρὰ τοῦ ἀ. τὴν ἀλήθειαν Thphn.*chron*.p.269(M.108.668B).

***ἀποστόλιον, τό**, *church dedicated in honour of an apostle, in which an apostle is buried* (= ἀποστολεῖον q.v.); of church of S. John at Ephesus, CEph.Orient.*act*.(*ACO* 1.1.5 p.121.22; H.1.1449A); προσεύξασθαι...εἰς τὸ ἅγιον...ἀ. id.*ep*.(*ACO* 1.1.5 p.131.16; H.1.1548C); Jo.Ant.*relat.imp*.5(p.126.38; M.83.1461C).

***ἀποστολοευάγγελα, τά**, *readings from Epistle and Gospel*, arranged for festivals and saints' days throughout the year, *Euchol*.p.711; v. not. *ib*.p.723.

ἀπόστολος, ὁ, *emissary, apostle*;

I. in gen. ἕκαστός γε τῶν πεμπομένων ἀπό τινος, ἀ. ἐστιν τοῦ πέμψαντος Or.*Jo*.32.17(10; p.453.17; M.14.785C); ὁ ἀπόστολον ἑαυτὸν καλῶν, οὐ τὰ παρ' ἑαυτοῦ διδάσκει, ἀλλ' ἅπερ ὁ ἀποστέλλων ἐκέλευσεν. ἀποστόλου γὰρ ἀξίωμα, μηδὲν οἴκοθεν ἐπεισάγειν Chrys.*Is.interp*.1.1(6.4B); οὐδέ τις ἀνὴρ ἡγεμόνος πέμψαντος ἀ. ἐστιν ἀρείων Nonn.*par.Jo*.13:16(M.43.861C).

II. of Christ as sent forth from Father (Heb.3:1) θεοῦ υἱὸς καὶ ἀ. ὢν Ἰησοῦς Χριστός Just.*1apol*.12.9(M.6.345A); ὃς καὶ ἄγγελος καὶ ἀ. κέκληται *ib*.63.5(425A); as apostle to Hebrews, S. Paul being apostle to gentiles, Clem.*fr*.22(p.201.26; M.9.749B), citing 'ὁ πρεσβύτερος'; οὗτος ὁ ἀ. ἐκείνου ἐστίν, ἐνδείκτης τῆς ἀληθείας *A.Thom*.A 79(p.194.11); Or.*Jo*.32.17(10; p.453.25; M.14.785C); cf. τοῦ γὰρ ὑπὸ θεοῦ πρὸς σωτηρίαν κόσμου ἀπεσταλμένου ἀληθοῦς προφήτου ἀληθὴς ἐστιν ἀ. [i.e. Πέτρος] *Hom.Clem*.20.19; Ath.*Ar*.2.9(M.26.165A); αὐτός ἐστιν... ὃς ἐγένετο πιστὸς ἀ. καὶ ἀρχιερεὺς τῷ ποιήσαντι αὐτόν ‡Ath.*serm.fid*.18(p.12; M.26.1272C); ἀ. τε τῆς πίστεως ἡμῶν *Symb.Ant*.(341)2(p.249.22; M.26.721C); Chrys.*hom*.5.3 *in Heb*.(12.56C); εἴ τις τοίνυν ἀρχιερέα καὶ ἀ. ἡμῶν γεγενῆσθαί φησιν οὐκ αὐτὸν τὸν ἐκ θεοῦ λόγον, ὅτε γέγονε σὰρξ καὶ καθ' ἡμᾶς ἄνθρωπος, ἀλλ' ὡς ἕτερον παρ' αὐτὸν ἰδικῶς ἄνθρωπον ἐκ γυναικός...ἀνάθεμα ἔστω Cyr.*ep*.17(p.41.23; 5².77B); Christ's apostleship in different category from that of his followers 'καθὼς ἀπέστειλέ με, κἀγὼ ἀπέστειλα ὑμᾶς.' ὁρᾷς ὅτι οὐδὲ ἐνταῦθα τὴν αὐτὴν ἰσχὺν ἡ λέξις ἔχει; εἰ γὰρ τοῦτο οὕτως ἐκδεξόμεθα, οὐδὲν ἔσονται διεστηκότες οἱ ἀ. τοῦ Χριστοῦ Chrys.*hom*.75.2 *in Jo*.(8.441A).

III. of one sent by God or Christ to preach and act on his behalf;

A. in gen., term applicable to λειτουργικὰ πνεύματα (Heb.1:14): Isaiah (cf. Is.6:8), Jo. Bapt. (cf. Jo.1:6), Or.*Jo*.32.17(10; p.453.20; M.14.785C); prophets, Just.*dial*.75.3(M.6.652B); ‡Ath.*Ar*.4.33(p.82.15; M.26.520A); Moses καὶ Μωϋσῆς δὲ τῶν ἀ. ἐστί †Bas.*Is*.184(1.515C; M.30.432C); †Bas.*bapt*.2.4.1(2.655E; M.31.1588A); and anyone sent with divine commission, e.g. women at the sepulchre ὅτι δύναμαι καὶ γυναῖκας ἀ. χειροτονεῖν Gr.Ant.*mul.ung*.11(M.88.1864B); woman of Samaria (Jo.4:28–30), Or.*Jo*.13.28(p.252.18; M.14.448B).

B. of NT apostles, comprising **1.** the Twelve (v. F infra); **2.** other leaders of primitive Church κατὰ μίμησιν τῶν δώδεκα πλείστων ὅσων ὑπαρξάντων ἀ. Eus.*h.e*.1.12.5(M.20.120A); e.g. S. Paul (v. G infra); S. James, ‡Epiph.*v.proph*.ap.Cosm.Ind.*top*.5(M.88.264B); Jo.Mal.*chron*.10 p.258(M.97.392B); S. Stephen, Didym.*Trin*.3.41(M.39.988C); cf.*ib*.2.11(597C) cit. s. ἀποστολή; Apollos, *1Clem*.47.4; Timothy, Or.*Cels*.1.63(p.116.2; M.11.777C); Chrys.*p.redit*.1.2(3.425B); Philost.*h.e*.3.2(M.65.481A); Thdt.*Is*.11:14(p.63.3; 2.255); Titus, *ib*.; S. Luke ὥς φησιν ὁ ἀ., εἰρήνη ἐπὶ τῆς γῆς καὶ δόξα ἐν ὑψίστοις (Lc.2:14; 19:38); Clem.*exc.Thdot*.74(p.130.17; M.9.693A) [unless ὁ ἀπόστολος refers to the angel]; cf. οἱ ἀ. δὲ οὐ ξένοι τῶν πολλῶν ἐθνῶν τε καὶ πόλεων εἰς ἃς ἐμερίσθησαν...τί Παύλῳ κοινὸν πρὸς τὰ ἔθνη, Λουκᾷ πρὸς Ἀχαΐαν; Gr.Naz.*or*.33.11(M.36.228C); Epiph.*inc*.4(p.232.15; M.41.280A); S. Mark, Gr.Naz.*or*.33.11(M.36.228C); *Lit.Marc*.(Brightman, p.128.28); S. Thaddaeus Θαδδαῖον ἀ., ἕνα τῶν ἑβδομήκοντα Eus.*h.e*.1.13.11(M.20.124B); the Seventy as a whole, Or.*Cels*.2.65(pp.187–8; M.11.897C); Chrys.*hom*.38.4 *in 1Cor*.(10.355D); Thdt.*1Cor*.12:28(3.249); Clement of Rome, Clem.*str*.4.17(p.294.18; M.8.1312A); Philip 'the deacon' by confusion with Philip, one of the Twelve, Polycr.ap.Eus.*h.e*.5.24.2(M.20.493B); Clem.*str*.3.6(p.220.14; M.8.1156A); **3.** envoys commissioned by churches, e.g. Epaphroditus as ἀ. τῶν Φιλιππησίων Thdt.*1Cor*.12:28(3.249) [treated by Thdt. as an apostle in full sense of term, i.e. as commissioned by Christ].

C. of travelling missionaries, associated with prophets, *Did*.11.4,6.

D. of Thecla τῆς ἁγίας πρωτομάρτυρος καὶ ἀ. Θέκλης *A.Paul.et Thecl*.tit.(p.235n.); ‡Chrys.*Thecl*.tit.(2.749A); Bas.Sel.*v.Thecl*.1(M.85.560C).

E. of Const. ὁ ἐν βασιλεῦσι τοῦ Χριστοῦ ἀ. ‡Jo.D.*ep.Thphl*.3(M.95.348B).

F. esp. of the Twelve; **1.** as specially selected by Christ ὁ σωτὴρ ...τοὺς δώδεκα ἀ. ἀνακαλεῖται, οὓς καὶ μόνους τῶν λοιπῶν αὐτοῦ μαθητῶν κατά τι γέρας ἐξαίρετον ἀ. ὠνόμασεν Eus.*h.e*.1.10.7(M.20.

113A); **2.** list of names discussed, Chrys.*hom.32.3 in Mt.*(7.368D sqq.); doubtful whether Levi should be included, Or.*Cels.*1.62 (p.113.20; M.11.773C); **3.** number: regarded as thirteen by inclusion of S. Paul ἡμεῖς οἱ δεκατρεῖς ἀ. *Const.App.*8.46.13; but S. Paul usu. dist. from Twelve ἀ. δὲ δέκα καὶ δύο καὶ ὁ Παῦλος Ath. *Ar.*2.27(M.26.204B); appearance of Christ to Twelve (1Cor.15:6) implies appearance after Matthias' election, hence after Ascension, Chrys.*hom.38.4 in 1Cor.*(10.355B); **4.** their character, in origin sinners ὅτε δὲ τοὺς ἰδίους ἀ. ἐξελέξατο, ὄντας ὑπὲρ πᾶσαν ἁμαρτίαν ἀνομωτέρους, ἵνα δείξῃ ὅτι οὐκ ἦλθεν καλέσαι δικαίους ἀλλὰ ἁμαρτωλούς *Barn.*5.9; and illiterate, Cyr.H.*catech.*17.21; cf.Gr. Naz.*carm.*2.1.12.192(M.37.1180A); Gr.Nyss.*ep.*17(M.46.1061B); Chrys. *hom.32.3 in Mt.*(7.369B); *ib.33.1*(378C); Isid.Pel.*epp.*2.4(M.78.460C); hence despised by pagans τελώνας καὶ ναύτας πονηροτάτους λέγων ὁ Κέλσος τοὺς ἀ. Or.*Cels.*1.63(p.115.15; M.11.777A); Celsus' opinion perhaps derived from *Barn.* (v. supra), *ib.*(p.115.21; 777B); Isid.Pel.*epp.*4.27(M.78.1080C); not orators, Or.*Cels.*1.62(p.113.25; 776A); nor philosophers, *ib.*; αἴτιον τοῦ μὴ γενέσθαι τοὺς ἀ. σοφούς, οὐκ ἀσθενείᾳ τοῦ χαρίσματος, ἀλλ' ἵνα μὴ βλαβῇ τὸ κήρυγμα Chrys. *hom.3.3 in 1Cor.*(10.19D); but possessed of philosophy superior to that of pagans, id.*hom.63.3 in Jo.*(8.379Aff.); all were Jews, Cyr. H.*catech.*14.15; οἱ γὰρ ἅγιοι ἀ., σπέρμα τοῦ Ἀβραὰμ ὄντες *Dial.Ath. et Zacch.*66(p.39); οἱ ἅγιοι ἀ., φύσει Ἑβραῖοι ὄντες καὶ κατὰ σάρκα καὶ κατὰ πνεῦμα *ib.*91(p.47); hence Is.45:26 τὸ σπέρμα τῶν υἱῶν Ἰσραήλ refers to them, Cyr.*Is.*4.3(2.624E); **5.** typified in OT, e.g. by 12 wells of Ex.15:27, Marcell.*fr.*20 ap.Eus.*e.th.*3.3(p.149.11; M.24.988C); but Eus. replies that wells might equally typify tribes, patriarchs, prophets, hours of day, or months of year, *ib.*(p.149.19; 988C); by 12 bells on high priest's robe (Ex.28:29, perh. confused with Ex.28:9), Just.*dial.*42.1(M.6.565A); 12 stones on high priest's breast, Cyr.*ep.*55(p.56.8; 5².183E); 12 stones of altar (Ex. 24:4), id.*glaph.Ex.*3(1.330C); 12 loaves of shewbread, id.*Jo.*4.2 (4.356A); 6 loaves symbolizing sending out of apostles two by two, Or.*fr.in 1Reg.*9(p.298.12; M.12.993B); 12 dividers of Canaan, Cyr.H.*catech.*10.11; in NT, by 12 stars of Apoc.12:1, Oecum.ad loc.(p.137); for types of apostles in gen., v. infra J; **6.** are 12 pillars of Church, corresponding to 12 tribes of Israel, Iren. *haer.*4.21.3(M.7.1045B); **7.** (Gnost.) regarded as corresponding to 12 months of year, the 30 disciples of John Baptist, of whom Simon Magus was chief, corresponding to days of lunar month, *Hom.Clem.*2.23; as typifying Valent. dodecad of aeons, Iren.*haer.* 2.21.1(M.7.779B); as corresponding to signs of zodiac, presiding over regeneration as zodiac over birth, Clem.*exc.Thdot.*25(p.115. 12; M.9.672B); **8.** Christ's command to Twelve apostles not to take two coats signifies need to put off old man and put on new, Or.*hom.23 in Lc.*(p.152.6; M.13.1860C); **9.** S. Peter as chief of 12 apostles, cf. *Petrus...apostolorum princeps*, Or.*hom.17 in Lc.*(p.106. 5; M.13.1845B); as first to recognize Christ, he is ἀπαρχὴ τῶν ἀ. Or.*Cels.*2.65(p.187.5; M.11.897C); ὁ τῶν ἀ. πρῶτος *Clem.ep.*1; Chrys. *Jud.*8.3(1.677C); Thdt.*eran.*1(4.37); id.*haer.*5.2(4.385); id.*ep.*145(4. 1250); S. Peter as ὁ ἀ. Chrys.*hom.in Gal.2:11*(3.364E); ἐκκλησίᾳ, ἐν ᾗ ὁ ἅγιος ἀ. καθεζόμενος ἐδίδαξε Dam.Papa *ep.orient.*ap.Thdt.*h.e.* 5.10.1(3.1034).

G. of S. Paul: ὁ ἀ. ‡*Diogn.*12.5; Athenag.*res.*18(p.17.15; M.6. 1012B); Iren.*haer.*4.27.4(M.7.1060B); Clem.*prot.*2(p.17.27; M.8.89B); Apollon.ap.Eus.*h.e.*5.18.5(M.20.477A); Anon.*ib.*5.17.4(473B); Hipp. *haer.*6.35(p.164.10; M.16.3247B); id.*Dan.*3.2.4; Or.*mart.*6(p.8.10; M.11. 572A); id.*Cels.*2.50(p.173.5; M.11.876B); id.*Jo.*10.39(23; p.215.13; M.14.380D); Meth.*symp.*2.7(p.25.1; M.18.57D); Didym.*Trin.*1.15 (M.39.316B); described as μέγας, θεῖος, ἅγιος, μακάριος Clem.*prot.*9 (p.63.7; 193C); id.*paed.*3.11(p.268.20; M.8.629B); Or.*princ.*3.6.6(p.288. 26; M.11.339C); id.*fr.14 in Jer.*22:24ff.(p.205.11; M.13.569D); Eus. *Marcell.*1.1(p.3.29; M.24.717A); *ib.*(p.5.21; 721A); Cosm.Ind.*top.*2 (M.88.92A); rejected by Ebionites τὸν δὲ ἀ. ἀποστάτην καλοῦσι Thdt.*haer.*2.1(4.328); hence ὁ ἀ. *the Pauline corpus*, Or.*hom.1.7 in Jer.*(p.6.14; M.13.264A); *ib.20.3*(p.180.3; 504D); τὸν ἀ. τέλεον ἀθετεῖ [sc. the Elchezaite sect] id.ap.Eus.*h.e.*6.38(M.20.600A); Eus.*h.e.*5. 27(509B); Epiph.*haer.*42.12(p.182.8; M.41.812B); *Apophth.Patr.*(M. 65.340C); and liturg., *the Epistle*, *Lit.Jac.*(p.168.22); *Lit.Marc.*(p.118. 18); cf.*Lit.Chrys.*(p.371.13).

H. times of the apostles; **1.** commanded by Christ to remain 12 years in Jerusalem, Apollon.ap.Eus.*h.e.*5.18.14(M.20.480C); many remained in Jerusalem until its fall, *ib.*3.7.8(236A); **2.** their teaching completed in Nero's reign, Clem.*str.*7.17(p.75.12; M.9. 548A); **3.** but apostles were known to Polycarp, Iren.*ep.Vict.*ap. Eus.*h.e.*5.24.16(M.20.508A); id.*haer.*3.3.4(M.7.851B); Eus.*h.e.*3.36.1 (288B); Justin being οὔτε τῷ χρόνῳ πόρρω...τῶν ἀ. Meth.*res.*2.18 (p.370.12; M.18.313B).

I. status and functions; **1.** 'first-fruits' of Christian believers τῶν ἁγίων ἀ. ὁ χορὸς ὡς ἀπαρχὴ γεγονὼς τῶν ἡγιασμένων ἐν πνεύματι Cyr.*glaph.Gen.*4(1.126E); ὡς ἐν ἀπαρχῇ τῶν σεσωσμένων τοῖς ἁγίοις ἀ. id.*Is.*1.3(2.74D); *ib.*3.1(388A); **2.** founders and foundations of Church, cf. *ecclesia vero per universum mundum ab apostolis firmum habens initium*, Iren.*haer.*3.12.7(M.7.901B); ἀ. ὡσπερεὶ θεμελίοις τῆς καταβαλλομένης οἰκοδομῆς τοῦ Χριστιανισμοῦ Or. *Cels.*3.28(p.225.12; M.11.956A); id.*Jo.*10.39(23; p.216.11; M.14.381C); **3.** sent by Christ with particular commission, Or.*Jo.*32.17(10; p.453.28; M.14.785D) cit. s. ἀποστέλλω; representing Christ as ambassadors, Cyr.*glaph.Gen.*7(1.228E); ἀ. ἡμᾶς...πεποίηκεν...ἀντὶ τοῦ Χριστοῦ ἡμεῖς διεδεξάμεθα τὰ ἐκείνου Jo.D.*2Cor.*5:20(M.95.736C); endowed with Christ's authority, Or.*Cels.*1.62(p.114.17; M.11. 776C); *ib.*8.47(p.262.6; 1585C); Chrys.*hom.51.1 in Jo.*(8.300C); gen. regarded as directly appointed by Christ, cf. Παῦλον...διὰ φωνῆς ἰδίας ἀπ' οὐρανοῦ ἀ. ... ἐξελέξατο Epiph.*inc.*4(p.232.11; M.41.280A); hence Simon Magus claims to have been appointed in a vision, *Hom.Clem.*17.19; but S. Luke described as appointed by S. Paul, Epiph.*inc.*4(p.232.15; M.41.280A); **4.** witnesses of Christ's life, death, resurrection, ascension, Just.*1apol.*67.7(M.6.432A); τῶν ἀ. ... τῶν αὐτοπτῶν τοῦ Ἰησοῦ Or.*Cels.*3.11(p.211.3; M.11.933A); Cyr.H. *catech.*14.22; Cyr.*Am.*81(3.346D); **5.** evangelists οἱ ἀ. ἡμῖν εὐηγγελίσθησαν ἀπὸ τοῦ κυρίου Ἰησοῦ Χριστοῦ...καὶ πληροφορηθέντες διὰ τῆς ἀναστάσεως...ἐξῆλθον, εὐαγγελιζόμενοι τὴν βασιλείαν τοῦ θεοῦ μέλλειν ἔρχεσθαι *1Clem.*42.1–3; ἐκηρύχθη...ὁ υἱὸς τοῦ θεοῦ διὰ τῶν ἀ. Herm.*sim.*9.17.1; ‡*Diogn.*11.3; Just.*1apol.*45.5(M.6.397A); οἱ ἀπὸ Ἱερουσαλὴμ ἐξελθόντες ἀ. αὐτοῦ ἐμήνυσαν τὰ περὶ αὐτοῦ, καὶ τὰς προφητείας παρέδωκαν *ib.*49.5(401A); id.*dial.*42.2(M.6.565A); τῇ φωνῇ τοῦ θεοῦ, τῇ διά τε τῶν ἀ. τοῦ Χριστοῦ λαληθείσῃ *ib.*119.6(753A); Clem.*ecl.*16(p.141.13; M.9.705B); διὰ δὲ τῶν ἀ. ὁ κύριος προσεκαλέσατο πάντα τὰ ἔθνη Hipp.*Dan.*4.9.2; Or.*Cels.*3.2(p.204.14; M.11.921C); *ib.*2.30(p.158.7; 849C); id.*princ.*4.1.5(p.300.14; M.11.352A); id.*Jo.*1.8 (10; p.13.20; M.14.37C); Gr.Naz.*or.*33.11(M.36.228C); Is.52:7 interpreted of apostles as missionaries, †Chrys.*Jud.et gent.*5(1.565A); Didym.*Trin.*2.4(M.39.488A); ἐκ περάτων εἰς πέρατα τοῦ ὑπὸ οὐρανόν, ὁ τῶν ἁγίων ἀ. διαπεφοίτηκε λόγος Cyr.*Is.*2.5(2.343B); missionary task symbolized by feet-washing (Jo.13:4–17), Nil.*epp.*1.80(M.79. 117C); hence generating sons to Christ through gospel, Cyr.*Os.*(3. 25A); their preaching centred on Resurrection, containing little about Christ's birth, Chrys.*hom.3.1 in Mt.*(7.34A); apostles believed to have assembled in Jerusalem and divided spheres of their missionary work, *A.Thom.*A 1(p.99.2); Eus.*h.e.*3.1.1(M.20.213D); cf. Gr.Naz.*or.*33.11(M.36.228C); ‡Chrys.*apost.*(8.11C); Socr.*h.e.*1.19.2 (M.67.125A,B); **6.** inspired by H. Ghost, *1Clem.*42.3; Iren.*haer.*3.1.1 (M.7.844B); Or.*princ.*3.3.4(p.261.5; M.11.317C); hence associated with OT prophets, *ib.*; Eus.*e.th.*3.4(p.159.19; M.24.1005B); *ib.*3.6 (p.163.33; 1013B); inspiration bestowed by Christ (Jo.20:22) ὁ μὲν παρέχων ἦν ὁ σωτήρ, τὸ δὲ διδόμενον τὸ ἅγιον πνεῦμα, οἱ δὲ λαμβάνοντες οἱ ἀ., τὸ δ' ἐμφύσημα καθαρτικὸν...τῶν ἀ. ἢ καὶ ἐνεργητικὸν τῆς μεταδόσεως τοῦ ἁγίου πνεύματος, ἑκατέρως γὰρ νοεῖν δυνατόν *ib.*3.5 (p.160.17; 1008B); effect of Pentecost τῆς δυνάμεως τοῦ ἀγαθοῦ πνεύματος ταῖς ψυχαῖς τῶν ἀ. σκηνωσάσης, τὸ μὲν τῆς κακίας κάλυμμα εἰσάπαν αὐτῶν ἀφῃρέθη, τὰ πάθη δὲ κατηργήθη, καὶ τὰ τῆς καρδίας αὐτοῖς ἀπεκαλύφθησαν ὄμματα Mac.Aeg.*carit.*11(M.34.917C); τοὺς ἀ., οἳ καὶ πανταχοῦ ἐν ἑαυτοῖς εἶχον τὰ χαρίσματα Jo.D.*1Cor.*12:28(M.95. 673C); were 'trumpets of Spirit', Taras.*ep.*2(M.98.1437B); ascended Christ spoke in them, Or.*princ.*1 proem.1(p.8.12; M.11.115B); received Spirit for exercise of authority to forgive sins (Jo.20:23) followed by τῶν σημείων...ἐνέργεια at Pentecost, Chrys.*hom.86.3 in Jo.*(8.517A); exhibited παρρησία q.v., Chrys.*hom.10.3 in Ac.* (9.85A); were prophets προφήτας...εἶναι τοὺς ἀ. λέγοντες, εὖ ἂν εἴποιμεν, ἑνὸς καὶ τοῦ αὐτοῦ ἐνεργοῦντος διὰ πάντων ἁγίου πνεύματος Clem. *str.*5.6(p.352.11; M.9.65A); Chrys.*hom.15.5 in Mt.*(7.191E); John was apostle and prophet, Or.*Jo.*2.5(4; p.59.22; M.14.117B); hence, 'apostolic decree' (Ac.15:28) was inspired εἰ καὶ δι' ἀ. ἀνθρώπων ἦν τὸ γραφέν, ἀλλ' ἐξ ἁγίου πνεύματος...ἐστι τὸ διάταγμα Cyr.H.*catech.* 17.29; their writings (v. infra) declare oracles of God, Or.*hom. 10.1 in Jer.*(p.71.6; M.13.357B); ἀ. ... τὸ πνεῦμα ἐν τῇ διανοίᾳ περιφέροντες...βιβλία καὶ νόμοι γινόμενοι διὰ τῆς χάριτος ἔμψυχοι Chrys.*hom.1.1 in Mt.*(7.3C); **7.** performed miracles τὰ τέρατα καὶ σημεῖα τῶν ἀ. ἀπόδειξις ἦν μεγίστη τῆς ἀναστάσεως Chrys.*hom.4.7 in Ac.princ.*(3.91E); φύσει γὰρ μείζονα ἦν, ὅτι μὲν τοῦ Χριστοῦ οὐδέποτε σκιαὶ νεκροὺς ἀνέστησαν· ἐπὶ δὲ τῶν ἀ. αἱ σκιαὶ αὐτῶν πολλὰ τοιαῦτα ἐποίουν *ib.*(92B); but their acts, rather than miracles, are an example; hence title '*Acts* of the Apostles', *ib*.2.3(65E); cf.id.*hom.32.5 in Mt*.(7.372D), *compunct*.1.9(1.137C); tribulations of apostles permitted so as to prevent them from being esteemed as gods on account of miracles, id.*stat*.10.4(2.111A); **8.** corresponded in function to OT prophets (v. προφήτης); cf. *qui igitur nos per apostolos undique vocavit Dominus, hic per prophetas vocabat eos qui olim fuerunt*, Iren.*haer*.4.36.5(M.7.1095B); ἐκπέμπει ποτὲ μὲν προφήτας, ποτὲ δὲ ἀ., σωτῆρας τῶν ἀνθρώπων Clem.*ecl*.16(p.141.13; M.9.705B); τοῖς τοῦ θεοῦ προφήταις καὶ τοῖς τοῦ Ἰησοῦ ἀ. Or.*Cels*.3.58(p.253.20; M.11.997B); Pall.*v.Chrys*.12(p.76.18; M.47.43); εἰσβεβηκέναι γεμὴν ἐπὶ τοῖς τῶν ἁγίων προφητῶν τοὺς ἀ. διαβεβαιοῦται πόνοις Cyr.*Jo*.2.5(4.200E); but greater than prophets, being missionaries to whole world, Chrys.*hom.15.6 in Mt*.(7.194A); id.*hom.34.2 in Jo*.(8.197D); ἦσαν οἱ προφῆται τοῦ ἰδίου οἴκου μόνον φωστῆρες τοῦ Ἰσραήλ· οἱ δὲ ἀ. ἥλιοι ἦσαν ἐκλάμποντες τὰς ἀκτῖνας εἰς ὅλα τὰ μέρη τοῦ κόσμου Mac.Aeg.*hom*.14.5(M.34.573B); building Church on foundation laid by prophets, Chrys.*hom.2.2 in Ac.princ*.(3.62D); **9.** associated with prophets οἱ εὐαγγελισάμενοι ἡμᾶς ἀ. καὶ οἱ προφῆται οἱ προκηρύξαντες τὴν ἔλευσιν τοῦ κυρίου Polyc.*ep*.6.3; Clem.*str*.1.9(p.30.1; M.8.741B); Or.*princ*.4.2.7(p.318.11; M.11.372A); id.*Jo*.1.16(p.20.22; M.14.49D); Meth.*symp*.7.1(p.71.13; M.18.124A); Ath.*Ar*.3.10(M.26.341C); Eulog.*palm*.3(M.86.2920A); and patriarchs μακάριαι ψυχαὶ πατριαρχῶν καὶ προφητῶν καὶ ἀ. Eus.*e.th*.2.9(p.109.34; M.24.917D); Pall.*v.Chrys*.9(p.46.12; M.47.28); *Lit.Jac*.(p.212.17); with evangelists, Cyr.*Is*.3.2(2.431A); with teachers, Herm.*sim*.9.15.4; *ib*.9.16.5; *ib*.9.25.2; with ἐπίσκοποι καὶ διδάσκαλοι καὶ διάκονοι Herm.*vis*.3.5.1; **10.** governed Church εἰκότως ἄρα ὑπατίαν πνευματικὴν ἐκαλέσαμεν τὴν ἀποστολήν. ἄρχοντες γάρ εἰσιν ὑπὸ θεοῦ χειροτονηθέντες οἱ ἀ. ἄρχοντες, οὐκ ἔθνη καὶ πόλεις διαφόρους λαμβάνοντες, ἀλλὰ πάντες κοινῇ τὴν οἰκουμένην ἐμπιστευθέντες Chrys.*hom.3.4 in Ac.princ*.(3.77B); τὴν οἰκουμένην ἅπασαν ἐπέδραμον οἱ ἀ., καὶ πάντων ἀρχόντων ἄρχοντες ἐγένοντο κυριώτεροι, βασιλέων δυνατώτεροι...πάσῃ τῇ οἰκουμένῃ νόμους ἔθηκαν· καὶ οὐχὶ ζώντων αὐτῶν ἐκράτησαν μόνον, ἀλλὰ καὶ τελευτησάντων id.*exp.in Ps*.44(5.181C); τοὺς ἀ., οἵτινες ἦσαν δυνάσται, τὸ τῆς δυνάμεως ἠμφιεσμένοι πνεῦμα Pall.*v.Chrys*.18(p.117.12; M.47.65); Cyr.*Is*.3.3(2.463C); hence Gen. 49:16 interpreted of τῶν ἁγίων ἀ. χορόν· οἱ εἰς ἀρχὴν τέθεινται τῶν πεπιστευκότων, καὶ τὸ κρίνειν ἔλαχον Cyr.*glaph.Gen*.7(1.228D); Proc. G.*Gen*.49:16–18(M.87.506); **11.** believed to have legislated for future ordering of Church διαταγμάτων τῶν ἀ. Ign.*Trall*.7.1; διδαχὴ κυρίου διὰ τῶν δώδεκα ἀ. τοῖς ἔθνεσιν *Did*.tit.; cf. title of work by Hippolytus, *CIG* 8613A, s.v. ἀποστολικός; *Ordo Eccl.App.* passim; *Can.App*.tit.[some MSS]; ἅμα τοίνυν ὑπάρχοντες ἡμεῖς οἱ δεκαδύο τοῦ κυρίου ἀ. τάσδε τὰς θείας ὑμῖν ἐντελλόμεθα διατάξεις περὶ παντὸς ἐκκλησιαστικοῦ τύπου *Const.App*.8.4.1; **12.** constituted a bond of Christian unity σύνδεσμον ἀ. Ign.*Trall*.3.1; Chrys.*hom.82.2 in Jo*.(8.484E); **13.** as authors of scriptural writings; **a.** gospels, Just.*1apol*.66.3(M.6.429A) cit. s. ἀπομνημόνευμα; τῇ ἡλίου λεγομένῃ ἡμέρᾳ...τὰ ἀπομνημονεύματα τῶν ἀ., ἢ τὰ συγγράμματα τῶν προφητῶν ἀναγινώσκεται μέχρις ἐγχωρεῖ *ib*.67.3(429B); id.*dial*.100.4(M.6.709C); *ib*.102.5(713C); *ib*.103.6(717B); including apocryphal story of kindling of fire in Jordan at Christ's baptism (recorded in *Ev.Ebion*.), *ib*.88.3(685B); **b.** epistles, gen. dist. as οἱ ἀ. from gospels τοῦ εὐαγγελίου καὶ τῶν ἀ. Clem.*str*.5.5(p.346.4; M.9.53B); *ib*.6.11(p.476.11; 309C); *ib*.7.16(p.67.18; 532B); Or.*princ*.4.2.9(p.322.14; M.11.376B); οἱ προφῆται, καὶ τὰ εὐαγγέλια, καὶ οἱ ἀ. id.*Cels*.6.76(p.146.10; M.11.1413C); v. G supra; **c.** of Christian writings opp. OT *2Clem*.14.2; Or.*Cels*.5.5(p.5.4; M.11.1185C); **d.** 'Jerusalem decree' (Ac.15:28) τὴν ἐπιστολὴν τὴν καθολικὴν τῶν ἀ. Clem.*str*.4.15(p.291.8; M.8.1304B); **14.** teachers, cf.Herm.*vis*.3.5.1 cit. s. διακονέω; ἡ τῶν δώδεκα μαθητεία *Ascens.Is*.A 3.13(p.92); Just.*1apol*.50.12(M.6.404A); Chrys.*hom.15.6 in Mt*.(7.194A); and source of doctrinal tradition in Church, v. παράδοσις, παραδίδωμι; Just.*dial*.100.4(M.6.7C9C); cf. *traditionem itaque apostolorum in toto mundo manifestatam, in omni ecclesia adest respicere*, Iren.*haer*.3.3.1(M.7.848A); Hipp.*haer*.8.18(p.238.3; M.16.3366C); τοῖς πειθομένοις μὴ ἀνθρώπων εἶναι συγγράμματα τὰς ἱερὰς βίβλους, ἀλλ' ἐξ ἐπιπνοίας τοῦ ἁγίου πνεύματος...ἀναγεγράφθαι καὶ εἰς ἡμᾶς ἐληλυθέναι...ἐχομένοις τοῦ κανόνος τῆς Ἰησοῦ Χριστοῦ κατὰ διαδοχὴν τῶν ἀ. οὐρανίου ἐκκλησίας Or.*princ*.4.2.2(p.308.15; M.11.360B); *ib*.4.2.7(p.318.11; 372A); tradition originated from SS. James of Jerusalem, John, and Peter, being transmitted by them to other apostles and to the Seventy, Clem.*fr*.13(p.199.22; M.9.749A); must not be subjected to cavilling criticism, Cyr.*inc.unigen*.(5^{1}.689C); preserved by episcopal succession (v. infra), Iren.*haer*.3.2.2(M.7.847A); *ib*.3.3.1(848A); and including unwritten tradition, Chrys.*hom.4.2 in 2Thess*.(11.532B); and tradition of order and liturgical practice λόγον δὲ εἰς τοῦτο [sc. baptism] παρὰ τῶν ἀ. ἐμάθομεν τοῦτον Just.*1apol*.61.9(M.6.421A); cf.Polycr.ap.Eus.*h.e*.5.24.6(M.20.496A); Eus.*h.e*.2.17.24(184A); οὐκ εἰκῇ ταῦτα ἐνομοθετήθη ὑπὸ τῶν ἀ., τὸ ἐπὶ τῶν φρικτῶν μυστηρίων μνήμην γίνεσθαι τῶν ἀπελθόντων Chrys.*hom.3.4 in Phil*.(11.217E); apostles handed down tradition of Christ's facial appearance, to be reproduced in images, ‡Jo.D.*ep.Thphl*.3(M.95.348D); **15.** their teaching the norm of orthodoxy, Ign.*Magn*.13.1; source of rule of faith, Iren.*haer*.1.10.1(M.7.549A); though works attributed to apostles are to be rejected if evidently heretical in doctrine, Serap.Ant.ap.Eus.*h.e*.6.12.3(M.20.545A); apostolic doctrines are Christian faith, Meth.*creat*.1(p.491.13; M.18.332B); ὁρίσαι ταῦτα ἃ τῇ τῶν ἀ. παραδόσει σύμφωνα ἂν εἴη Const.ap.Eus.*v.C*.3.62(p.110.24; M.20.1137B); Ath.*v.Anton*.82(M.26.960B); ὁ γὰρ τοῖς ἀ. πιστεύων, οὐκ αὐτοῖς πιστεύει, ἀλλὰ τῷ θεῷ Chrys.*hom.69.1 in Jo*.(8.409A); cf.*Const.App*.6.11.1; Thdt.*eran*.(4.37); ἔδει μὲν πάντας...τὴν ἁπλῆν τῶν ἀ. στέργειν διδασκαλίαν id.*Trin.* proem.(M.75.1148A); Arians expected by Ath. to claim sanction of apostles for their teaching, Ath.*Dion*.7(p.51.3; M.25.489B); acc. Julian Christians departed from apostles' doctrine in calling Jesus God, Juln.ap.Cyr.*Juln*.10(6^{2}.327A); garments of apostles laid in the way (Lc.19:36) represent their words and acts which now adorn the believer, Or.*hom.37 in Lc*.(p.220.14; M.13.1896B); apostles are spiritual physicians, Cyr.*Is*.3.1(2.366B); and stewards of God's mysteries, id.*ador*.13(1.454A); and the faithful are numbered with apostles, Or.*mart*.34(p.30.13; M.11.605D); baptized Christians being their sons, Cyr.*Is*.4.2(2.582A); but Montanists regarded prophetesses as superior to apostles, Hipp.*haer*.8.19(p.238.12; M.16.3366D); **16.** apostles as priests οἱ ἀ. καὶ οἱ τοῖς ἀ. ὡμοιωμένοι, ἱερεῖς ὄντες κατὰ τὸν μέγαν ἀρχιερέα Or.*or*.28(p.381.2; M.11.529A); succeeding Jewish priesthood as spiritual leaders, Cyr.*Is*.1.1(2.30B); **17.** appointed Christian ministry; **a.** tradition that surviving apostles assembled and appointed Symeon to succeed S. James at Jerusalem, Eus.*h.e*.3.11(M.20.245B); **b.** appointed bishops and deacons *1Clem*.42.2,4 cit. s. ἐπίσκοπος; οἱ ἀ. ... ἔγνωσαν...ὅτι ἔρις ἔσται ἐπὶ τοῦ ὀνόματος τῆς ἐπισκοπῆς. διὰ ταύτην οὖν τὴν αἰτίαν πρόγνωσιν εἰληφότες τελείαν κατέστησαν τοὺς προειρημένους, καὶ μεταξὺ ἐπιμονὴν [v.l. ἐπινομὴν] δεδώκασιν ὅπως, ἐὰν κοιμηθῶσιν, διαδέξωνται ἕτεροι δεδοκιμασμένοι ἄνδρες τὴν λειτουργίαν αὐτῶν *ib*.44.1,2; bishops, cf. *habemus annumerare eos qui ab apostolis instituti sunt episcopi*, Iren.*haer*.3.3.1(M.7.848A); at Rome θεμελιώσαντες οὖν καὶ οἰκοδομήσαντες οἱ μακάριοι ἀ. τὴν ἐκκλησίαν, Λίνῳ τὴν τῆς ἐπισκοπῆς λειτουργίαν ἐνεχείρισαν *ib*.3.3.3(849A); at Smyrna Πολύκαρπος...ὑπὸ ἀ. κατασταθεὶς εἰς τὴν Ἀσίαν, ἐν τῇ ἐν Σμύρνῃ ἐκκλησίᾳ, ἐπίσκοπος *ib*.3.3.4(852A); cf.Clem.*q.d.s*.42(p.188.5; M.9.648B); Πέτρος...ἐνδιατρίψας τῇ Τύρῳ...ἐπίσκοπον αὐτοῖς καταστήσας *Hom.Clem*.7.5; *ib*.11.36; *Const.App*.8.46.9,13; list of bishops of chief sees supposedly appointed by apostles, *ib*.7.46; **18.** as examples of Christian living, *1Clem*.5.3; Polyc.*ep*.9.1; ἀ. ... γνωστικοὶ καὶ τέλειοι ὑπὲρ τῶν ἐκκλησιῶν ἃς ἔπηξαν ἔπαθον Clem.*str*.4.9(p.282.1; M.8.1284D); ἀποστόλων τῶν ἀγγελικὸν ἐπιδειξαμένων βίον Chrys.*hom.38.5 in Jo*.(8.224B); of philosophical (monastic) life, Nil.*exerc*.4(M.79.721D); of married life τὸ γαμεῖν δὲ ἐὰν ὁ λόγος αἱρῇ λέγω καὶ ὡς καθήκει· γενόμενος γὰρ τέλειος εἰκόνας ἔχει τοὺς ἀποστόλους Clem.*str*.7.12(p.51.5; M.9.497C); **19.** baptism of apostles; **a.** Christ said to have baptized S. Peter, who baptized S. Andrew, and so on, cf.Clem.*fr*.6(p.196.21; M.9.745C); **b.** received only S. John's baptism with water, completed by pentecostal baptism with H. Ghost, ‡Chrys.*ascens.Ac*.2.13(3.770A); **20.** successors of apostles; **a.** presbyters in church assembly typify apostles, as bishop typifies God, Ign.*Magn*.6.1; id.*Trall*.3.1; id.*Smyrn*.8.1; cf.id.*Philad*.5.1; οἵ τε πρεσβύτεροι εἰς τύπον ἡμῶν τῶν ἀ. ὑμῖν νενομίσθωσαν *Const.App*.2.26.7; *ib*.2.28.4; **b.** notable teachers Εἰρηναῖος ὁ τῶν ἀ. διάδοχος Thdt.*haer*.2.2(4.329); and other distinguished Christians, Ignatius, Quadratus, etc., of early second century, Eus.*h.e*.3.37.1(M.20.292D); **c.** bishops holding office in succession of appointment from apostles, Iren.*haer*.1.27.1(M.7.687B) cit. s. ἐπισκοπικός; *ib*.3.3.3(849B) cit. s. ἐπισκοπή; cf. *episcopi quibus apostoli tradiderunt ecclesias*, *ib*.5.20.1(1177A); ἀ. καὶ τοὺς τούτων διαδόχους ἐπισκόπους καὶ διδασκάλους τῶν ἐκκλησιῶν Or.*hom.34 in Lc*.(p.202.18); Firmilianus int.opp.Cypr.*ep*.75.16(M.*PL*.3.1216C); Eus.*h.e*.3.4.11(M.20.221A); *ib*.4.20(377A); Ἰακώβου...τοῦ πρώτου...τὴν ἐπισκοπὴν πρὸς τοῦ σωτῆρος καὶ τῶν ἀ. ὑποδεξαμένου *ib*.7.19(681A); Serap.*euch*.28.1 cit. s. διαδοχή; Dion.Ar.*ep*.8.4(M.3.1093C); identity in NT of ἐπίσκοποι and πρεσβύτεροι (q.v.) suggests to later writers that functions of later bishops, esp. ordination, were performed in NT times by apostles οἱ δὴ τὴν τοῦ χειροτονεῖν ἐξουσίαν ἔχοντες, οἱ νῦν ὀνομαζόμενοι ἐπίσκοποι,...τῇ τῶν ἀ. ἐκαλοῦντο προσηγορίᾳ Thdr.Mops. *1Tim.*3:8(p.121.14); id.*Tit.*1:7(p.239.16); Thdt.*1Tim.*3:1(3.652) cit. s. ἐπίσκοπος; apostle's status contrasted with martyr-bishop's οὐχ ἱκανὸν ἑαυτὸν εἰς τοῦτο ᾠήθην, ἵνα ὢν κατάκριτος ὡς ἀ. ὑμῖν διατάσσωμαι Ign.*Trall.*3.3; id.*Rom.*4.3; bishops in succession to apostles partake of their grace of H. Ghost, Hipp.*haer.*proem. (p.3.2; M.16.3020C); hence prayer that Spirit who was upon apostles may be bestowed on bishop at consecration, cf.Hipp. *trad.ap.*3.4; *Lit.*ap.*Const.App.*8.5.5; authority given to apostles to bind and loose is exercised by bishops, cf.Hipp.*trad.ap.*3.5; **d.** Church as a whole has received H. Ghost through apostles, Hipp.*haer.*proem.(p.3.2; M.16.3020C); *Const.App.*8.33.8; **21.** liturg., commemoration of apostles in Church Triumphant, *Lit.Jac.*(p.174.21); *ib.*(p.188.21); ὃν ὑμνοῦσιν...ψυχαὶ μαρτύρων καὶ ἀ. *ib.*(p.198.27); *Lit.Marc.*(p.117.20); *ib.*(p.128.25).

J. types of apostles, v. freq.; e.g. Gen.49:12, Hipp.*ben.Jac.*19 (p.35.4) cit. s. γάλα; sons of high priest, Or.*hom.7.1 in Lev.*(p.373.12; M.12.477A); id.*hom.5.1 in Num.*(p.26.24; M.12.603C); foundations of tabernacle, id.*hom.9.3 in Ex.*(p.239.15; M.12.365A); and its pillars, *ib.*(p.239.18; 365A); Proc.G.*Ex.*26:15(M.87.650); compared with Levites, id.*Num.*35:2(M.87.890); equivalent to 'heavens' (Ps.18:1), cf. *perfecti quique coelestes facti, vel coeli effecti,...apostoli, qui erant coeli...Boanerges nomen accipiunt...ut per tonitrui potestatem vere eos coelos esse credamus,* Or.*hom.1.13 in Gen.*(p.16.16; M.12.156C); typified by 'mountains of light' (cf. Jer.13:16), id.*hom.12.12 in Jer.*(p.98.12; M.13.393C); 'mountains and hills' (Pr.8:25) ὄρη καὶ βουνοὺς τοὺς ἀ. καὶ τοὺς τῶν ἀ. διαδόχους λέγει Marcell.*fr.22* ap.Eus.*Marcell.*2.3(p.48.13; M.24.805A); interpretation rejected by Eus.*e.th.*3.3(p.150.31; M.24.992A); but accepted ref. Is.30:25 by Cyr.*Is.*3.2(2.431A); apostles' law typified by the bramble (Jud. 9:15), Meth.*symp.*10.2(p.123.25; M.18.196A); apostles are princes of Nephthalim (Ps.67:28), Eus.*d.e.*9.9(p.426.2; M.22.688A); their mouths trumpets, Chrys.*exp.in Ps.*46(5.194E); they are 'sapphires' (Is.54:11), Cyr.*Is.*5.2(767B); branches of mustard-tree (Lc.13:19), Iren.*fr.*29(p.494; M.7.1245A); and feet of the Lord, Clem.*paed.*2.8(p.194.14; M.8.465C); Is.37:31–32 foretells their election, Eus.*d.e.*2.3(p.85.16; M.22.152C); they are πτέρυγες τῆς γῆς (Is.24:16) Proc.G.*Is.*24:1–23(M.87.2193A); cf.Cyr.*Is.*2.5 (2.343E).

K. festivals of apostles, *Const.App.*8.33.8; cf.Gr.Nyss.*laud.Bas.* (M.46.789A).

L. burial of apostles (Peter and Paul) by Vespasian's order, *Chron.Pasch.*p.246(M.92.592A); by Galba, Jo.Mal.*chron.*10 p.258(M.97.392B); τὰ τρόπαια τῶν ἀ. to be seen on Vatican and on Ostian way, Caius R.ap.Eus.*h.e.*2.25.8(M.20.209A).

M. churches of apostles: at Jerusalem, on site of pentecostal events, Cyr.H.*catech.*16.4; cf.Epiph.*mens.*14(M.43.261A); in Constantinople; burial-place of Constantine, Eus.*v.C.*4.70(p.146.32; M.20.1225A); Soz.*h.e.*2.34.5(M.67.1032C); cf. χαίρετε, ἀ. Gr.Naz.*or.* 42.26(M.36.489B); id.*carm.*2.1.16.59(M.37.1258A); Chrys.*p.redit.*1.2 (3.425B); Soz.*h.e.*8.10.6(1544B); *ib.*8.14.10(1553B); burial place of imperial family, *Chron.Pasch.*p.384(M.92.985A); and of patriarch, *ib.*p.381(976B); church of apostles consecrated A.D. 370, *ib.*p.302 (760B); μαρτύριον of apostles across Bosphorus, Pall.*v.Chrys.*17 (p.105.8; M.47.59).

N. pictures of apostles Peter and Paul preserved, Eus.*h.e.*7.18.4 (M.20.680C).

O. in titles of books Πράξεις τῶν ἀ. cf.Iren.*haer.*3.12.11(M.7.905A); Clem.*paed.*2.1(p.165.18; M.8.404A); Or.*Cels.*3.46(p.243.2; M.11.980D); Διδαχὴ...τῶν ἀ. Ath.*ep.fest.*39.11(M.26.1437C); Epiph.*haer.* 45.4(p.202.4; M.41.836B).

P. false apostles; Gnostic, cf.Heges.ap.Eus.*h.e.*4.22.6(M.20.381A) cit. s. ψευδαπόστολος; warnings against them, *A.Thom.*A 79 (p.194.13); sent by Devil, *Hom.Clem.*12.35; opposed the apostles, Chrys.*exp.in Ps.*7(5.58B); v. ψευδαπόστολος.

Q. of Manes, as self-styled apostle of Christ, Hegem.*Arch.*5 (p.5.22; M.10.1433A); Epiph.*haer.*66.19(p.43.6; M.42.57A).

IV. Jewish apostles, emissaries of Jewish patriarch ἀ. δὲ εἰσέτι καὶ νῦν ἔθος ἐστὶν Ἰουδαίοις ὀνομάζειν τοὺς ἐγκύκλια γράμματα παρὰ τῶν ἀρχόντων αὐτῶν ἐπικομιζομένους Eus.*Is.*18:1–2(M.24.213B); εἰσὶ δὲ οὗτοι μετὰ τὸν πατριάρχην, ἀ. καλούμενοι. προσεδρεύουσι δὲ τῷ πατριάρχῃ Epiph.*haer.*30.4(p.338.21; M.41.409D); *ib.*30.11(p.346.12; 424B); cf.*Cod.Thds.*16.8.14.

V. as adj., *apostolic* ἀ. ἔχων τιμὴν Χριστοῦ *MAMA* 1.238.

***ἀποστομαχίζομαι**, pass. ?*be disordered in the stomach*, ref. Christ's Resurrection ὁ λέων κατέπιεν τὸν ἀμνόν, καὶ ἀπεστομαχίσθη Ast.Soph.*hom.5 in Ps.5*(M.40.436A).

ἀποστομίζ-ω, **1.** *reduce to silence* τοὺς φιλοσόφους ἀπεστομίζεν ‡Pall.*h.mon.*27(M.65.448C; ἐπεστόμιζεν p.86.12); of Christ ἤρξατο ~ειν τὸν διδάσκαλον περὶ τοῦ πρώτου γράμματος *Ev.Thom.*A 6 (p.145); ἐθαύμαζον, πῶς παιδίον...~ει τοὺς πρεσβυτέρους καὶ διδασκάλους τοῦ λαοῦ *ib.*19.2(p.156); **2.** *know by heart* Ἔσδρας νομικώτατος ὤν, καὶ ~ων πᾶσαν τὴν παλαιὰν διαθήκην Or.*sel.in Jos.*6:26(M.12.824B).

ἀποστρακίζω, *bake hard*, Or.*hom.18.1 in Jer.*(p.151.25; M.13.464C).

ἀποστρατεύομαι, *be dismissed from military service*, Eus.*v.C.* 1.54 tit.(p.6.3; M.20.968B); Socr.*h.e.*3.22.2(M.67.436A).

***ἀποστρεφικός**, *preventing, deterring*, †Jo.Jej.*serm.*(M.88.1924A).

ἀποστρέφ-ω, **1.** *turn away* or *aside, pervert* ἐγὼ οὐκ ἀπέστρεψα αὐτόν, ἀλλ' ὑπέστρεψε πρὸς τὸν θεόν *A.Barth.*8(p.148.20); **2.** med. and pass., *turn away from*, c. dupl. acc. ὃν [sc. Lazarus] ἀπεστρέφετο τὰς ὄψεις αὐτοῦ [sc. Dives] Eus.Al.*serm.*21.19(M.86.445B); also c. genit. ἀ. τοῦ μηκέτι προσκόπτειν Mac.Aeg.*hom.*4.21(M.34.488D); *repudiate* persons πάντες...ὑμᾶς [sc. Arians] ~ονται πλὴν μόνου τοῦ διαβόλου Ath.*decr.*27(p.24.7; M.25.465D); ὁ...Σαοὺλ...ἐπειδὴ αὐτὸν ἀ. καὶ ἐμίσει Chrys.*stat.*7.3(2.88E); οὐδένα τῶν προστρεχόντων ~εται [sc. God] †Jo.Jej.*serm.*(M.88.1956B); things ἀ. τὴν...βλασφημίαν Alex.Al.*ep.Alex.*11(p.26.22; M.18.564C); Ath.*ep.encycl.*4(p.173.15; M.25.232A); Bas.*hom.*12.10(2.106E; M.31.408B); τὸ καὶ Ἰουδαίων... τοῦτο ἀποστραφῆναι Chrys.*hom.32.1 in Ac.*(9.249D); pass. abs., *be deflected from one's purpose, change one's mind* οὐκ ἀπεστράφη τοῖς γεγραμμένοις Philost.*h.e.*9.7(M.65.573B).

ἀποστροφή, ἡ, **1.** intrans. sense, *turning away* on the part of God, *rejection* καὶ ἐν τῇ ἀ. ηὔξετο τὸ ἔθνος Chrys.*hom.16.2 in Mt.* (7.129A); Cyr.*Am.*15(3.265E) cit. s. συνομαρτέω; id.*Abac.*14(3.529A); πεπονθότες...τὴν ἀ. διὰ τὴν ἐν Ἀδὰμ παράβασιν *ib.*37(3.553A); **2.** trans. sense, *deterrent* εἰς ἀ. τῶν ἄλλων ἀνθρώπων Just.*2apol.*13.1 (M.6.465B); **3.** *gift, contribution* ἠθέλησεν ἐλεῆσαι αὐτόν, καὶ δοῦναι μικρὰν ἀγάπην εἰς ἀ. Jo.Mosch.*prat.*193(M.87.3073A).

ἀπόστροφος, *turned away*; *remote* ἦν...ἐν τῇ νήσῳ εἰς τὰ ἀ. αὐτῆς μονάζων τις Marc.Diac.*v.Porph.*34.

ἀποσυνάγω, *assemble* τὸν σωρὸν τῶν κακῶν ἐπὶ τοῦ βαπτίσματος ἀ. Mac.Mgn.*apocr.*4.25(p.210.23).

ἀποσυνάγωγος, **1.** *cast out of the synagogue*, Chrys.*hom.61.2 in Jo.*(8.363E); **2.** *cast out of the Church, excommunicated* εἰ συμφέρει τόνδε ἀ. εἶναι κρίναντες αὐτὸ ποιοῦσιν Or.*comm.in 1Cor.*4:5(*JTS* 9 p.356); ἀ. ἔμεινε τριῶν ἐπισκόπων πολυετεῖς χρόνους Alex.Al.*ep.Alex.* 9(p.25.13; M.18.561A); CNic.(325)*can.*5; ποιήσεις οὖν αὐτὸν ἀ. ὡς φονέα ἀδελφοῦ *Const.App.*2.43.1; *ib.*4.8.3; Euthal.Diac.*epp.Paul.* (M.85.772D); **3.** *cast out from one's society* ὁ μηδέποτε διὰ λύπην ἀ. εὑρισκόμενος ‡Max.*cap.al.*35(M.90.1409A).

***ἀποσύνακτος**, **1.** *excluded from the synagogue*, Epiph.*haer.*69.81 (p.229.20; M.42.333C); Cyr.*Jo.*6.1(4.615B); **2.** *excluded from the congregation, excommunicated*, Epiph.*haer.*76.3(p.344.8; M.42.521B); **3.** as subst., *seceder*, Cyr.*ep.*11(p.11.11; 5^2.37D); *ib.*13(p.92.4; 5^2.42E).

***ἀποσυνάπτω**, *disjoin*, Thdr.Stud.*epp.*2.51(M.99.1261B).

ἀποσυνεθίζω, *wean*, met. ἀ. αὐτοὺς τῆς...ὑποθέσεως Epiph.*haer.* 66.71(p.112.21; M.42.141C).

***ἀποσυνέχω**, *keep, confine* ἑαυτὸν εἰς ὁδὸν σκότους ἀ. *Barn.*5.4.

ἀποσυνίστημι, *break up, demolish*, Sever.ap.*cat.Ac.*2:11(p.32.10).

ἀποσυντάσσομαι, *have nothing to do with*; *dismiss*, Jo.Mosch. *prat.*189(M.87.3068C).

ἀποσυρίζω, *hiss out, eject with hissing* ἵνα μὴ...δρακόντειον ἰὸν ἀποσυρίσωσιν αἱ τῶν Ἰουδαίων γλῶτται Mac.Mgn.*apocr.*2.19(p.33.7).

***ἀποσύστασις, ἡ**, *disruption, dissolution* ἡ...ἀπιστία, ἀ. οὖσα τῆς πίστεως Clem.*str.*2.12(M.8.992C; conj. ἀπόστασις p.142.29).

***ἀποσφαγή, ἡ**, *cessation of slaughter*, Jo.Mal.*chron.*12 p.285(M.95.432A).

ἀποσφαιρίζω, *turn* ἀ. [sc. adversity] σου τὸν νοῦν πρὸς τὸν δυνάμενόν σοι βοηθεῖν Bas.*ep.*45.1(3.133C; M.32.365B).

***ἀποσφενδονίζω**, *hurl, throw*, Evagr.*h.e.*4.27(p.175.22; M.86.2749B).

ἀποσχετλιάζω, *inveigh* against πάντες πρὸς ἐκείνου ἀ. Ast.Am. *hom.*5(M.40.232B).

ἀποσχηματίζω, *divest of the habit, unfrock*, *Apophth.Patr.*(M.65.249C).

ἀποσχίζ-ω, *split*; *separate*; **1.** mentally οὗτος δὲ ἀλλοτριῶν τοῦ πατρὸς τὸν μονογενῆ, καὶ παντελῶς ~ων τῆς πρὸς αὐτὸν κοινωνίας Bas.*Eun.*1.18(1.230B; M.29.553A); **2.** eccl., *cut off* from the Church ἀκοινώνητον [sc. Novatian] ἐποίησεν σὺν...τοῖς ἅμα αὐτῷ ἀποσχίσασιν ἑαυτοὺς τῆς ἐκκλησίας Corn.ap.Eus.*h.e.*6.43.20(M.20.628B); *excommunicate*, Anast.S.*hod.*10(M.89.164A); pass. ὅταν...εἰς αἵρεσιν ἐκπεσὼν ἀποσχισθῇ τοῦ σώματος τῆς ἐκκλησίας Chrys.*sac.*4.9(p.125.14; 1.414B); *be put out of the Jewish synagogue*, Chrys.*hom.*30.5 *in Mt.*(7.354A, v.l. διασχισθῆναι); **3.** intrans., act. and med. ἀποσχίσεσθαι τοῦ διαβόλου Meth.*symp.*10.4(p.126.18; M.18.200A); eccl., *separate oneself, secede from* the Church ἀπό τινος αἱρέσεως ἐνδιαστρόφου τῆς ἐκκλησίας ἀπεσχισμένον Bas.*hex.*5.7(1.47C; M.29.112B); of the Donatists, *Cod.Afr.*67; of seceders from Ephesus ἡμῶν ἀπέσχισαν CEph.(431)*ep.*(*ACO* 1.1.3 p.33.4; H.1.1592D); ∼ονταί τινες ἀπὸ τοῦ Πέτρου [sc. the Fuller] καὶ οὐκ ἐκοινώνουν αὐτῷ †Leont.B.*sect.*5.2(M.86.1229A); μονοφυσῖται οἱ προφάσει τοῦ ἐν Χαλκηδόνι συντάγματος τοῦ τόμου ἀποσχίσαντες τῆς ὀρθοδόξου ἐκκλησίας Jo.D.*haer.*83(M.94.741A); from sects συνεπόμενος τῷ... Μαρκίωνι καὶ ἀπὸ τούτου ἀποσχίσας καὶ αὐτὸς ἄθροισμα ἑαυτῷ ποιησάμενος αἱρέσεως προέστη Epiph.*haer.*43.1(p.187.5; M.41.817C); τοῦτον δή φασιν...ἀποσχίσαι μὲν τῆς ἄλλης Εὐνομιανῶν μοίρας Philost.*h.e.*12.11(M.65.620C); abs., *break away from the Church, secede* κτίστην εἶναι...τὸν θεόν, καὶ οἱ καθ' οἱανδήποτε πλάνην ἀπεσχισμένοι συντίθενται Bas.*Eun.*2.22(1.258A; M.29.620C).

ἀπόσχισμα, τό, *schism, sect* πρόσφατος τοῦ ἀ. αἵρεσις (ref. Montanists) Anon.ap.Eus.*h.e.*5.16.6(M.20.465B); Σαμαρεῖς ἀ. ὄντες Ἰουδαίων Socr.*h.e.*5.22.72(M.67.644B); *Pers.*(p.43.21).

***ἀποσχίστης, ὁ,** *schismatic* θήσω...τινος νέου ἀποσχίστου αὐτῶν πατρός Ph.Carp.ap.Cosm.Ind.*top.*10(M.88.436B); Cosm.Ind.*top.*10 (417C); as name of a heresy, οἱ ἀ. Jo.Nic.*nativ.*(M.96.1448B); of those not accepting Chalcedon, *Apophth.Patr.*(M.65.432B); τῶν...ἀ. μοναχῶν...τῶν ἀκεφάλων Cyr.S.*v.Sab.*55(p.147.14); id.*v.Euthym.*30 (p.47.7); Thdr.Lect.*h.e.*2.26(M.86.197A); of Paulicians ἀ. οἱ καὶ δοξάριοι Jo.D.*haer.*103(M.94.777A).

ἀποσχοινίζ-ω, *separate by a cord, cut off, debar*; **1.** in gen. τῆς προκειμένης ὑποθέσεως ἀπεσχοίνισται Gr.Nyss.*or.dom.*4(p.68.18; M.44.1161C); Thdt.*Dan.*proem.(2.1055); κοινωνίαν...ἀπεσχοινισμένην Pall.*v.Chrys.*6(p.35.12; M.47.22); **2.** moral, from God or good Ἕλληνες ὅσον τῆς ἀληθείας ἑαυτοὺς ἀπεσχοίνισαν Ath.*gent.*29(M.25.60B); ὁ ἀεὶ ἐν πάθει γενόμενος, τῆς πρὸς τὸ θεῖον συναφείας ∼εται Gr.Nyss.*or.dom.*5(p.94.6; M.44.1177C); ἀ. διὰ τὴν ἁμαρτίαν Cyr.*Is.*4.3(2.620A); Bas.Sel.*v.Thecl.*2.30(M.85.617A); from evil, Nil.*epp.*2.13(M.79.205D); Pall.*v.Chrys.*18(p.113.1; M.47.62); Cyr.*ador.*1(1.32A); **3.** of God; ref. transcendence, Eus.*e.th.*1.12(p.72.13; M.24.848D) cit. s. ἀπαλλοτριόω; καθ' ὅσον σκιὰ σώματος καὶ ὄναρ τῆς ἀληθείας ἀπεσχοίνισται, τοσοῦτον διέστηκε τῆς...τοῦ θεοῦ σοφίας ἡ... τοῦ κόσμου σοφία Sever.*sigill.*1(M.63.531); Cyr.*thes.*19(5¹.189A); ref. heret. divisions in Trin. ἀλλότριος καὶ ἀπεσχοινισμένος ἐστὶν ὁ λόγος τῆς τοῦ θεοῦ οὐσίας Alex.Al.*ep.encycl.*3(p.8.3; M.18.573B); Ath.*Ar.*1.6(M.26.24B) cit. s. ἀνόμοιος; Gr.Nyss.*Trin.*5(p.75.3; M.32.689A); κἂν...τῆς πρὸς τὸν πατέρα ὁμοτιμίας διὰ τὴν περὶ τὸν σταυρὸν οἰκονομίαν τὸν υἱὸν ∼ωσιν Gr.Nyss.*Eun.*5(2 p.114.5; M.45.693C); *ib.*11 (2 p.254.24; 861B).

***ἀποσχοινισμός, ὁ,** *exclusion*, Thdr.Stud.*epp.*1.28(M.99.997B).

***ἀποσχοῖνος,** *made of rushes*, Geo.Pis.*Pers.*1.217(M.92.1211B).

***ἀποσχολ-έω,** *keep busy, occupied*, Hipp.*Dan.*3.22.1; ἵνα σε ∼ήσῃ [sc. Devil], καὶ ἐμποδίσῃ σε τοῦ ἀναγνῶναι Ephr.3.232A; Chrys.*hom.*66.3 *in Jo.*(8.399C).

ἀποσώζ-ω, 1. *keep, preserve*, Iren.*haer.*1.5.2(M.7.493B); πῶς ∼εται...ἡ γραφή; [i.e. of a commandment] Meth.*lepr.*14(p.469.10); τὸ ὑπὲρ πάντων εὔλογον ἀ. πρὸς τὸν πατέρα Ath.*inc.*7.5(M.25.109A); Gr.Nyss.*or.catech.*35(p.139.3; M.45.92C); **2.** *reserve* for ἑκάστῳ τὸ δίκαιον τοῦ θεοῦ ∼οντος Marc.Er.*opusc.*2.116(M.65.948B); **3.** *support, maintain* τὸν Χριστιανισμὸν λόγον ∼ειν...ὑπειλήφασιν Eus.*p.e.*1.1 (3D; M.21.23D); **4.** *carry off*; of the veinous system, ‡Eust.*hex.*(M.18.749B); pass., *escape safely*, *LS*.

ἀποσωρεύ-ω, *heap up, store up* ἑαυτοῖς τὴν εἰς τὸ μέλλον ∼σειν ἀσφάλειαν Cyr.*hom.pasch.*7(5².82B); Areth.*Apoc.*8(M.106.556B).

ἀποταγή, ἡ, *renunciation*;

A. of Devil, in baptism μετὰ τὴν ἀ. εὐχή Serap.*euch.*21 tit.; θεμέλιον...κατεβαλόμεθα ἐν τῷ βαπτίζεσθαι, τουτέστιν ἀ. τῶν ἔργων τοῦ σατανᾶ †Ath.*fr.*(M.26.1221B); μανθανέτω τὰ περὶ τῆς ἀ. τοῦ διαβόλου *Const.App.*7.40.1; *Symb.ib.*7.41.3; τρὶς διακελεύεται τῷ σατανᾷ, καὶ προσέτι τὰ τῆς ἀ. ὁμολογῆσαι· καὶ τρὶς αὐτῷ τὴν ἀ. μαρτυρόμενος Dion.Ar.*e.h.*2.2.6(M.3.396B); *ib.*2.3.5(401B); made facing west, *ib.*5.1.6(508A); made by godparents in place of children, *ib.*7.3.11(568A); τὴν ἀ. τοῦ σατανᾶ ἣν ἀπετάξαντο ἐν τῷ βαπτίσματι Cosm.Ind.*top.*1(M.88.60B); Jo.D.*hom.*2.6(M.96.585C).

B. in ascetical (religious) life; **1.** def. ἔστιν οὖν ἡ ἀ. ... λύσις μὲν τῶν δεσμῶν τῆς ὑλικῆς ταύτης καὶ προσκαίρου ζωῆς, ἐλευθερία δὲ τῶν ἀνθρωπίνων καθηκόντων, ἐπιτηδειοτέρους κατασκευάζουσα πρὸς τὸ ἀπάρξασθαι τῆς πρὸς θεὸν ὁδοῦ Bas.*reg.fus.*8.3(2.350C; M.31.940B); διὰ τοῦτο γὰρ ὀνομάζεται ἡ ἀ., ὅτι τῶν γηΐνων ἀποτασσόμενοι, τῶν ἐπουρανίων συντασσόμεθα Ant.Mon.*hom.*112(M.89.1781A); ἀ. τινες γνωστικοὶ καλῶς ὡρίσαντο λέγοντες ταύτην ἔχθραν πρὸς σῶμα, καὶ μάχην πρὸς κοιλίαν Jo.Clim.*scal.*15(M.88.881D); **2.** essence of religious life, sts. used almost as synonym ἐν μὲν τῇ ἀρχῇ τῆς ἀ. σου ἀνδρίζου, μὴ καθελκυσθῆναι ὑπὸ τῆς προσπαθείας τῶν κατὰ σάρκα συγγενῶν Bas.*renunt.*2(2.204B; M.31.632A); ποιῆσαι τήν τε ἀ. αὐτῷ κατὰ τὸ ἀρέσκον θεῷ id.*ep.*23(3.102A; M.32.296A); μετὰ γὰρ τὸ συνθέσθαι αὐτοὺς τῷ θεῷ περὶ τῆς ἀ. ... ὑπεισελθὼν τῷ ζύγῳ τῆς ἀ. Eus.Al.*serm.*22.7(M.86.460C,D); Dor.*doct.*1.11(M.88.1632B); Leont.N.*v.Sym.*11(M.93.1684B); together with ὑποταγή chief component of monastic life οἱ...τῆς μοναχικῆς φιλοσοφίας κορυφαῖοι...τὰς προσηγορίας ἁρμοδίας τοῖς πράγμασι πρὸς νουθεσίαν ἡμῶν...ἔθεντο, ἀ. τὴν τῆς ὕλης ἀναχώρησιν, καὶ ὑποταγὴν τὴν εὐπείθειαν καλέσαντες... χρὴ τοίνυν τὴν μὲν ἀ. λήθην εἶναι προκατασχούσης γνώμης Isid.Pel.*epp.*1.1(M.78.180A); **3.** necessity ἐὰν μὴ κτήσηται ἄνθρωπος...ἀ. τῆς κατὰ πνεῦμα ὀργῆς καὶ κακίας, καὶ ἀ. τῆς ὕλης, καὶ τῶν κατὰ σάρκα συγγενῶν ἅμα καὶ ἡδονῶν· καὶ ἀ. τῷ διαβόλῳ καὶ πᾶσι τοῖς ἔργοις αὐτοῦ...οὐ δύναται τέλειος εἶναι *Apophth.Mac.Aeg.*1(M.34.233Af.); χρὴ...τὴν τῶν ὑπαρχόντων ἀ. κατορθωθῆναι τῷ πρὸς τὸν ὑψηλὸν ἀποβλέποντι βίον Bas.*ascet.*2.1(2.324A; M.31.881C); **4.** degrees and difficulties ἡ μὲν τελεία ἀ. ἐστιν ἐν τῷ τὸ ἀπροσπαθὲς κατορθῶσαι καὶ πρὸς αὐτὸ τὸ ζῆν, καὶ τὸ ἀπόκριμα τοῦ θανάτου ἔχειν, ὥστε μὴ ἐφ' ἑαυτῷ πεποιθέναι Bas.*reg.fus.*8.1(2.348E; M.31.936C); ὁ τὴν ἀ. ἀσκεῖν προῃρημένος, πίστει τειχιζέσθω, καὶ ἀγάπῃ κραταιούσθω, καὶ ἐλπίδι βεβαιούσθω...μὴ οὖν τῇ πάλῃ τῶν ἐντὸς λογισμῶν ἐνδώσῃς, ὅτι οὐκ ἐν ἀρχῇ τῆς ἀ. τὸ τέλος εὐφημεῖται Nil.*Eulog.*11(M.79.1108Bf.); φαντασιῶν ἀ., τὴν τελειοτάτην ἐμφαίνει τῶν μοναχῶν φιλοσοφίαν Dion.Ar.*e.h.*6.3.2(M.3.533D); ἐὰν ἀφῆκε γονεῖς...καὶ χρήματα ἢ κτήματα, καὶ ἕκαστον πρᾶγμα ὃ δ' ἂν ἀποτάξηταί τις, θέλῃ καὶ αὐτῇ τῇ προσπαθείᾳ αὐτοῦ ἀποτάξασθαι...καὶ αὕτη ἐστὶν ἡ τελεία ἀ. Dor.*doct.*1.13(M.88.1633C); οὐδεὶς ἐν τῷ οὐρανίῳ νυμφῶνι στεφανηφορῶν ἐλεύσεται, μὴ τὴν πρώτην, καὶ δευτέραν, καὶ τρίτην ἀ. ἀποταξάμενος· λέγω δὴ τὴν πάντων πραγμάτων, καὶ ἀνθρώπων, καὶ γονέων, καὶ τὴν ἐκκοπὴν τοῦ ἰδίου θελήματος· καὶ τρίτην ἀ. τῆς κενοδοξίας, τῆς ἐπακολουθήσης τῇ ὑπακοῇ Jo.Clim.*scal.*2(M.88.657A); ἀ. πρώτη ἡ τῶν πραγμάτων ἀπαλλαγή, δευτέρα δὲ καὶ τρίτη ἡ τῶν παθῶν καὶ τῆς ἀγνοίας Thal.*cent.*3.25(M.91.1449C); **5.** effects and rewards τῇ ἀ. τῶν γηΐνων πραγμάτων τετίμηκας σεαυτὸν παρὰ Χριστῷ Bas.*renunt.*2 (2.204C; M.31.632B); τὴν ἐκ τῆς τελείας ἀ. ἀναδέξασθαι ταπεινοφροσύνην *Apophth.Patr.*(M.65.245C); Nil.*Eulog.*2(M.79.1096C); πᾶς γὰρ ὁ τρέχων πεπληροφορημένος...καταλαμβάνει τὸν στέφανον τῆς ἀ. Ant.Mon.*hom.*112(M.89.781C).

***ἀποτακτήτης, ὁ, 1.** *one who renounces* the world, *hermit*, *M.Thdot.1* 19(p.73.21); **2.** member of Encratite sect, *Apotactite*, Tim.CP *haer.*(M.86.16C); v. ἀποτακτῖται.

ἀποτακτικός, *renunciatory, of a recluse* or *hermit* τὸ σχῆμα τὸ ἀ. Pach.*reg.*B 49(p.176.4; M.40.949A); ἀ. ... τρόπον Epiph.*haer.*75.3 (p.335.23; M.42.508B); masc. as subst. ἔδοξαν...τὸν Φίλιππον εἶναι φιλόσοφον ἐπειδὴ ἦν ὁδεύων σχήματι ἀποτακτικοῦ *A.Phil.*6(p.4.4); Pach.*reg.*B 49(p.174.10; 949A); ref. 1Cor.7 πρὸς βιωτικοὺς καὶ ἀ. τὴν διαφορὰν πεποίηται Ephr.2.164A; ἐν τῷ διδόναι ἀφειδῶς ἀ. ἐπιγνωσθήσῃ Nil.*Eulog.*10(M.79.1108A); of an Encratite sect βούλονται... ἀποτακτικοὺς ἑαυτοὺς λέγειν Epiph.*haer.*61.1(p.380.12; M.41.1040C); *ib.*61.7(p.387.14; 1049A); Jo.D.*haer.*61(M.94.713B).

***ἀποτακτικῶς,** *in isolation* τοὺς...λόγους...ἀ. εἰρῆσθαι Or.*or.*18 (p.341.3; M.11.476A).

ἀποτακτῖται, οἱ, *Apotactites*, an Encratite sect; to be baptized on submission to Church, Bas.*ep.*199 *can.*47(3.296D; M.32.729C) cit. s. ἀναβαπτίζω; Mac.Mgn.*apocr.*4.3(p.151.23); ἀνίκητος πρεσβύτερος τῶν ἀ. *MAMA* 1.173; in form ἀποτακτῆται, Tim.CP *haer.*(M.86.16C) cit. s. σακκοφόροι.

ἀποτακτός (*LS* ἀπότακτος), *fixed, defined* τόπον [v.l. τύπον] ἀ. Clem.*exc.Thdot.*48(p.123.1; M.9.681C).

ἀποταμιεύ-ομαι, *store up, reserve, keep*; med., Cyr.*ador.*13(1.453A); καιρῷ τῷ πρέποντι τὴν τῆς βασιλείας ἐκφανεστέραν ἐπίδειξιν ∼όμενος id.*Jo.*3.4(4.289B); ‡Proc.G.*Pr.*1:18(M.87.1229B); met. ἐν τῷ θέλειν τοὺς νόμους ἔθετο [sc. ὁ Χριστός]· ἐν τῇ θελήσει τὰ νομιμὰ ∼εται Serap.*Man.*27(p.42; M.18.1121C); pass. τῇ...ἀνακαινώσει τῇ διὰ τοῦ πνεύματος ἐσομένῃ..., ∼εται...ἡ τῶν ἔτι βαθυτέρων ἐξήγησις Cyr.*Jo.*10.2(4.924B).

***ἀποταμίευσις, ἡ,** *storehouse*, met. ἀ. τοῦ καθ' ἁμαρτίαν ὀλέθρου τῆς ψυχῆς ‡Proc.G.*Pr.*7:27(M.87.1288B).

***ἀποταξία, ἡ, 1.** *desertion* of God, *disobedience* τῆς ἐξ Ἀδὰμ ἀ. ἀφανίζων τὰ ἐγκλήματα Cyr.*ador*.11(1.396A); **2.** *renunciation*; of the world, on entering religious life, Bas.*renunt*.3(2.205B; M.31.633A); Epiph.*haer*.61.3(p.382.18; M.41.1041C).

ἀπόταξις, ἡ, *renunciation*; of Devil, in baptism, Cyr.H.*catech*. 19.8(M.33.1073A); εἰς νοῦν μὴ λαβόντες τὴν σύνταξιν τοῦ Χριστοῦ καὶ τὴν ἀ. τοῦ διαβόλου †Cyr.*hom.div*.14(5².412B); Leont.B.*Apoll*.(M. 86.1973A); of world, in asceticism, Epiph.*haer*.40.1(p.81.9; M.41. 677C); τὴν ἀ. τῆς οὐσίας Eus.*h.e*.2.17.5(M.20.177A); Nil.*Eulog*.10 (M.79.1108A).

ἀποτάσσ-ω, I. *take leave of, part from* ἀποταξάμενοι ἑαυτοῖς Thphl.Ant.*Autol*.2.1(M.6.1048A); *A.Jo*.31(p.167.25); τοῖς ἐν Τριπόλει τῆς Φοινίκης ἀποταξάμενος *Hom.Clem*.11.36; *ib*.12.23; Euthal.Diac. *epp.Paul*.(M.85.701C).

II. *renounce, give up*;

A. Devil, in baptism τέλος λέγεται τοῦ παλαιοῦ βίου τὸ βάπτισμα ~ομένων ἡμῶν ταῖς πονηραῖς ἀρχαῖς Clem.*exc.Thdot*.77(p.131.9; M.9.693C); ὁ γὰρ καταβαίνων μετὰ πίστεως εἰς τὸ τῆς ἀναγεννήσεως λουτρὸν ~εται τῷ πονηρῷ †Hipp.*theoph*.10(p.263.14; M.10.861A); Or. *mart*.17(p.16.20; M.11.585A); Cyr.H.*catech*.19.4; Bas.*Spir*.66(3.55B; M.32.188C); †Bas.*Is*.221(1.545E; M.30.504A); *Const.App*.3.18.1; *Symb.ib*.7.41.1,2; τί χαριέστερον τῶν ῥημάτων, δι' ὧν ~όμεθα τῷ διαβόλῳ; δι' ὧν συντασσόμεθα τῷ Χριστῷ; Chrys.*hom.1.3 in Eph*. (11.6E); id.*hom.6.4 in Col*.(11.369C); Dion.Ar.*e.h*.5.1.6(M.3.508A); ἀπεταξάμεθα διαβόλῳ, μὴ πάλιν αὐτῷ τεχνικῶς συνταξώμεθα. συνεταξάμεθα τῷ Χριστῷ, μὴ πάλιν αὐτῷ δαιμονικῶς ἀποταξώμεθα Bas.Sel. *or*.27.2(M.85.316A); Cosm.Ind.*top*.1(M.88.60B); *ib*.5(313B); Jo.D. *hom*.2.6(M.96.585C); baptismal renunciations used as ejaculatory prayer ὅταν μέλλῃς προβαίνειν τὰ πρόθυρα τοῦ πυλῶνος, τοῦτο φθέγξαι τὸ ῥῆμα πρῶτον, ~ομαί σοι, σατανᾶ...τοῦτό σοι βακτηρία ἔσται, τοῦτο ὅπλον Nil.*epp*.3.287(M.79.525B).

B. things incompatible with Christianity; **1.** in gen. ἔστιν δὲ οὗτος ὁ αἰὼν καὶ ὁ μέλλων δύο ἐχθροί· οὗτος λέγει μοιχείαν καὶ φθορὰν ...ἐκεῖνος δὲ τούτοις ~εται *2Clem*.6.4; (non-baptismal) ἀγγέλῳ τῆς πονηρίας ἀποτάξασθαι Herm.*mand*.6.2.9; πᾶσι τοῖς ἐν τῷ κόσμῳ ἀπεταξάμεθα Just.*dial*.119.6(M.6.753A); idols, id.*1apol*.49.5(M.6. 401A); Gr. philosophy, Tat.*orat*.1(p.2.9; M.6.805B); sins and worldliness, Clem.*paed*.1.5(p.99.32; M.8.269A); *ib*.1.6(p.121.19; 312C); possessions, id.*q.d.s*.14(p.169.9; M.9.617D); ἀποταξάμενοι τοῖς ἐλαττώμασιν αὐτῶν, διυλιζόμενοι βαπτίσματι id.*paed*.1.6(p.109.3; 288B); *ib*.2.4(p.184.24; 445B); ἀπεταξάμην γὰρ τοῦ ματαίου βίου τούτου *A.Thom*.B 50(p.40.14); ἀποταξώμεθα τοῖς ἔργοις τῆς νεκρότητος Or.*hom.9.3 in Jer*.(p.68.8; M.13.353B); Gr.Naz.*or*.44.6(M.36.613B); ἀπετάξατο μὲν τῶν ἐγκυκλίων μαθημάτων Pall.*h.Laus*.58(p.152.8; M. 34.1203D); ἐθέλεις ὑφ' ἓν τῶν κακιῶν ἀπαλλαγῆναι; τῇ μητρὶ τῶν κακῶν τῇ φιλαυτίᾳ ἀ. Thal.*cent*.2.1(M.91.1437B); *ib*.3.44(1452D); heresies, ‡Ath.*Maced.dial*.1.8(M.28.1301A); ἀναθεματίζω καὶ ἀ. αὐταῖς ὡς Χριστιανὸς ὀρθόδοξος *Lit.Jac*.(*NBP* 10² p.39); **2.** special obligation of bishops ἔστω [sc. ὁ ἐπίσκοπος]...ἀποτεταγμένος πᾶσιν τοῖς ἐν τῷ βίῳ πονηροῖς ἐπιτηδεύμασιν *Const.App*.2.6.3; **3.** example of Christ ἐκεῖνος [sc. Χριστός] μὲν ἀπετάξατο ἀνέσει, τρυφῇ, δόξῃ *Const. App*.5.5.3; αὐτὸς δι' ἡμᾶς ἀπετάξατο ἀναπαύσει *ib*.5.5.4; **4.** its reward ἐὰν γὰρ ταῖς ἡδυπαθείαις...ἀποταξώμεθα...μεταληψόμεθα τοῦ ἐλέους Ἰησοῦ *2Clem*.16.2; **5.** iron., ref. S. Peter at Transfiguration ἐπεὶ τὸ ὄρος τοῦτο ποθεῖς, ~ου λοιπὸν οὐρανοῖς Procl.CP *or*.8.2(M.65. 768B).

C. the world (non-technical, but implying high standard of perfection) ἐὰν ἀποτάξῃ πάντων τῶν ὑπαρχόντων σου καὶ τῆς γυναικός σου ὡς καὶ ἡμεῖς ἀπεταξάμεθα, τότε καὶ σὺ ποιήσεις σημεῖα *A.Petr. et Andr*.13(p.123.8); ἀκολουθεῖ [sc. Χριστῷ] δὲ ἀποταξάμενος τῷ κόσμῳ καὶ αἴρων τὸν σταυρόν Or.*hom.18.2 in Jer*.(p.153.4; M.13. 465D); ref. sect of Therapeutae, mentioned by Philo, interpreted by Eusebius as referring to first Christians πάσαις ἀποταξαμένους ταῖς τοῦ βίου φροντίσιν, ἔξω τειχῶν προελθόντας Eus.*h.e*.2.17.5(M.20. 177A); ὁ κόσμος σταυροῦται τῷ ἀνθρώπῳ, ὅτ' ἂν ~εται ἄνθρωπος τῷ κόσμῳ Dor.*doct*.1.11(M.88.1629C); as condition of life of prayer and contemplation, Evagr.Pont.*or*.36(M.79.1176A); nec. for attainment of γνῶσις, Thal.*cent*.3.44(M.91.1452D); of individuals Παῦλος ἀποταξάμενος τῷ κόσμῳ Epiph.*haer*.80.4(p.488.18; M.42.760D); οἱ παῖδες οἱ ἐν τῇ Βαβυλῶνι,...χρήμασι καὶ δόξῃ ἀποταξάμενοι *ib*.80.5(p.490.9; 764C).

D. as t.t. for renouncing the world for monastic or eremitical life; **1.** in gen. τῆς εὐσεβείας ἀσκητάς, ἀποταξαμένους τῷ κόσμῳ, Bas.*ep*.207.2(3.310C; M.32.761A); τινὲς ἀπετάξαντο τῷ βίῳ Epiph.*fid*. 23(p.524.29; M.42.829C); μὴ γὰρ ἀπεταξάμην; μὴ γὰρ μοναχός εἰμι; Chrys.*hom.21.6 in Gen*.(4.189E); τὸν παντελῶς ἀποτεταγμένον τοῖς ἔξω θορύβοις, καὶ τὸν...ἡσύχιον ἑλόμενον βίον Nil.*Magn*.32(M.79. 1008C); τοῦ βίου...ἀποτάξασθαι ‡Ath.*qu.Ant*.92(M.28.653C); ἀπετάξαντο πρὸς αὐτοὺς ἀδελφοὶ δύο Cyr.S.*v.Euthym*.8(p.16.10); ~ομαι, καὶ γίνομαι μοναχός Jo.Mosch.*prat*.32(M.87.2881A); Leont.N.*v.Jo. Eleem*.36(p.75.12); **2.** spiritual motives δεῖ...τὸν ἀποταξάμενον τῷ κόσμῳ τούτῳ, βεβαίως πιστεῦσαι, ὅτι χρὴ εἰς ἕτερον αἰῶνα τῷ φρονήματι ἀπὸ τοῦ νῦν διὰ τοῦ πνεύματος μεταβῆναι Mac.Aeg.*hom*. 49.2(M.34.813B); ἔρωτι πληγεὶς ἀθανασίας ἀπετάξατο τοῖς θορύβοις Pall.*h.Laus*.21(p.64.10; M.34.1073B); διὰ τὸν θεόν, ἀφ' οὗ ἀπεταξάμην *Apophth.Patr*.(M.65.369B); **3.** conditions of renunciation τῷ διαβόλῳ πρὸ πάντων ~όμεθα, καὶ τοῖς πάθεσι τῆς σαρκός...καί, τὸ τούτων ἀναγκαιότερον, αὐτὸς ἑαυτῷ ~εται ὁ ἀποδυσάμενος τὸν παλαιὸν ἄνθρωπον...,~εται δὲ καὶ πάσαις προσπαθείαις τοῦ κόσμου Bas.*reg. fus*.8.1(2.348C,D; M.31.936A,B); physical mortification, Hesych.H. *Ps.tit*.67(M.27.917C); ὁ ἱερεύς, ἐπὶ τὸν τελούμενον ἐλθών, ἐπερωτᾷ πρῶτον αὐτόν, εἰ πάσαις ~εται ταῖς διαιρεταῖς οὐ μόνον ζωαῖς, ἀλλὰ καὶ φαντασίαις Dion.Ar.*e.h*.6.2(M.3.533B); ὥσπερ ἀπεταξάμεθα τῷ κόσμῳ...οὕτως ὀφείλομεν καὶ αὐτῇ τῇ προσπαθείᾳ τῇ περὶ τὰς ὕλας ἀποτάξασθαι, καὶ εἰδέναι τί ἐστιν αὕτη ἡ ἀποταγή, καὶ διὰ τί ἤλθομεν εἰς τὸ μοναστήριον Dor.*doct*.1.11(M.88.1632B); **4.** temptations and difficulties ὅταν ἀποτάξῃ ταῖς ἔξωθεν ὕλαις ἁπάσαις, πρόσεχε τοὺς ζοφερούς λογισμούς...καὶ γὰρ ~όμενος, δι' ἐκείνους ~ῃ δι' ὧν ἄθλων ὀνειδίζῃ Nil.*Eulog*.11(M.79.1108C); ἀπέκρυψεν ὁ κύριος ἀπὸ τῶν ἐν κόσμῳ τὴν τοῦ σταδίου δυσχέρειαν...εἰ γὰρ ταύτην ἔγνωσαν, οὐκ ἂν ἀπετάσσετο πᾶσα σάρξ Jo.Clim.*scal*.1(M.88.641B); **5.** of sinners becoming monks or nuns λῃσταὶ...τέσσαρες...δοξάσαντες τὸν θεὸν κἀκεῖνοι ἀπετάξαντο Pall.*h.Laus*.19(p.60.6; M.34.1066C); ἄλλαι πόρναι ἠκολούθησαν αὐτῇ καὶ ἀπετάξαντο Leont.N.*v.Jo.Eleem*.43(p.88.24); for it ensures salvation, Pall.*h.Laus*.35(p.104.1; 1114B); **6.** obligation for persons widowed for second time to become monks or nuns, †Gregent.*leg.Hom*.49(M.86.608B); **7.** distinction between Church and heretics in these matters ἐκκλησία...ἔχει ἀποταξαμένους τῷ κόσμῳ καὶ μὴ πεφυσιωμένους [as the heretics] κατὰ τῶν ἔτι ἐν κόσμῳ ὑπαρχόντων Epiph.*haer*.61.3(p.383.19; M.41.1044A); cf. *ib*.80.3(p.487.11; M.42.760D); **8.** ptcpl. as subst., *monk* or *nun*; **a.** in gen. γένηται ἀποτεταγμένος *A.Thom*.A 100(p.213.19); *Apophth. Patr*.(M.65.245C); *Schol*.13 in Jo.Clim.*scal*.1(M.88.648B); *ib*.17(649A); fem., Leont.N.*v.Jo.Eleem*.36(p.74.26); **b.** opp. βιωτικός, Chrys.*hom. 16.5 in 1Cor*.(10.141D); μή...λεγέτω τις τὰ ψυχρὰ ῥήματα ἐκεῖνα... ἀνὴρ εἰμι βιωτικός· οὐκ ἔστιν ἐμὸν γραφὰς ἀναγινώσκειν, ἀλλ' ἐκείνων τῶν ἀποταξαμένων, τῶν τὰς κορυφὰς τῶν ὀρέων κατειληφότων Chrys. *Laz*.3.1(1.737B); **c.** their duties, Marc.Er.*opusc*.1.99(M.65.917B); ὁ ~όμενος, ὀφείλει κατὰ διάνοιαν μεθίστασθαι τῶν ὁρωμένων Ant.Mon. *hom*.112(M.89.1780C).

E. marriage, *A.Phil*.50(p.22.7); παρθένος...ἀποταξαμένη τῷ γάμῳ Bas.*ep*.199 *can*.18(3.292A; M.32.720B); of a bishop ἀποταξάμενος τῆς οἰκείας γαμετῆς πάλιν αὐτῇ συνῆλθεν Pall.*v.Chrys*.13(p.84.2; M.47. 48); but this action by individuals does not imply renunciation by Church like that practised by some heret. sects εἰ μόνον τυγχάνει ἡ ἁγία τοῦ θεοῦ ἐκκλησία τῶν τῷ γάμῳ ἀποταξαμένων, οὐκέτι ὁ γάμος ἐκ θεοῦ ὑπάρχων Epiph.*haer*.61.1(p.381.7; M.41. 1040D).

F. life for martyr's death, Ign.*Philad*.11.1; *Const.App*.5.5.4; *ib*. 5.6.1.

G. kingship, by abdication, Jo.Mal.*chron*.12 p.312(M.97.468C).

ἀποταυρ-όομαι, *rage like a bull*, Cyr.*Jo*.3.6(4.311C); of Cain εἰς ὀργὰς ~ούμενος id.*glaph.Gen*.(1.16B); of remnant of Israel οὗτοι... ἦσαν οἱ πραεῖς, οὐκ ~ούμενοι πρὸς ὀργὰς τὰς ἐπὶ Χριστῷ id.*Soph*.41 (3.619C).

***ἀπότε,** ?*from the time when*, *Chron.Pasch*.p.112(M.92.296C), conj. ἀφότε = ἀφ' οὗ.

***ἀποτεθηπώς,** *being amazed at*; perf. ptcpl. with pres. sense, cf. τέθηπα *LS*, Cyr.*Jo*.11.9(4.982D).

ἀποτείν-ομαι, 1. *direct one's speech* εἰς αὐτὸν ἀφορῶν ὁ προφήτης ~εται Eus.*p.e*.11.10(527B; M.22.873C); τινες τῶν πατέρων οὐχὶ πρὸς ζητήσεις ὑποκειμένας ~όμενοι Bas.*Eun*.1.4(1.211E; M.29.509B); ὁ Ἄρειος εἰς τὸν υἱὸν τὴν δυσφημίαν ἀπετείνετο Epiph.*haer*.74.14(p.332. 20; M.42.501C); **2.** *refer, allude* Ἰεζεκιὴλ...~όμενος πρὸς τὸν ἐχθρόν Isid.Pel.*epp*.3.78(M.79.424C); πρὸς Ἰουδαίους ὁ προφητικὸς ~εται λόγος Thdt.*Ps*.67:17(1.1064); **3.** *inveigh against*, Clem.*paed*.1.9 (p.139.15; M.8.349C); id.*str*.3.4(p.213.31; M.8.1144A); **4.** *contend against* πρὸς τὸ κατὰ Ματθαῖον ~όμενος εὐαγγέλιον Eus.*h.e*.6.17 (M.20.560A).

ἀποτελει-όω, *consecrate, initiate* εἰς ἑνοειδῆ καὶ θείαν ~ώσας [sc. Ἰησοῦς] ζωὴν...δωρεῖται τῆς θείας ἱερωσύνης τὴν δύναμιν Dion.Ar.*e.h*. 1.1(M.3.372B); *ib*.5.2(509B); ἡ θεαρχία ἀποκαθαίρει πρῶτον, εἶτα φωτίζει, καὶ φωτισθέντας ~οῖ πρὸς θεοειδῆ τελεσιουργίαν *ib.*5.1.7 (508D); ἐν ἐσχάτῃ...καὶ ἀκροτάτῃ τῶν ἱερούργων δυνάμεων ~οῖ τοὺς τῷ θείῳ φωτὶ κεκοινωνηκότας ἐν ταῖς...τελειώσεσιν *ib.*5.3.8(516C).

ἀποτέλεσμα, τό, 1. *accomplishment, fulfilment*, esp. of prophecy ταῖς τῶν παλαιῶν φωναῖς τὰ διὰ τῶν ἔργων ἀ. συντρέχειν ἐπιδεικνύμενον Eus.*p.e.*1.1(3D; M.21.25C); Diod.*Ps.*88:5(M.33.1620A); Cyr. *Abac.*36(3.551E); ‡Meth.*Sym.et Ann.*1(M.18.348A); **2.** *product*, ref. hypostatic union οἱ δὲ Θεοδοσιανοὶ...λέγουσιν, ὅτι ἡμεῖς ὁμολογοῦμεν διάφορα εἶναι τὰ μέρη, τὸ δὲ ἀ. ἕν, ὥσπερ οὖν καὶ ἐπὶ τοῦ ἀνθρώπου διάφορά εἰσι τὰ μέρη, ἥ τε ψυχὴ καὶ τὸ σῶμα, τὸ δὲ ἀ. ἕν †Leont.B. *sect.*7.6(M.86.1245C); Eust.Mon.*ep.*(M.86.912B); Sophr.H.*ep.syn.*(M. 87.3168A); **3.** *conclusion* or *import* of a sentence, Didym.*Trin.* 3.24(M.39.937B); **4.** *work, activity*; **a.** in gen. τοῦ...σωτῆρος τὰ καθ' ἡμᾶς ἀ. Eus.*l.C.*17(p.254.8; M.20.1429B); οὔτε γὰρ ἐκ θεωρίας τῆς ἐν τοῖς ἀ. τοῦ πατρὸς...ποιητής ἐστιν [sc. ὁ υἱός] Cyr.*Jo.*2.6(4.219C); id.*Ps.*7:15(M.69.756A); Ammon.*Jo.*1:15(M.85.1400B); hence **b.** *property, characteristic*, Const.*or.s.c.*13(p.172.9); τὰ τῆς ἡμετέρας φύσεως ἀ. Didym.*Trin.*1.16(M.39.332A); *ib.*2.3(480B) al.; **c.** *function* τὸ τῆς ἱεραρχίας ἀ. Max.*schol.c.h.*3.2(M.4.49D); **5.** *production* φωνῆς ὄργανον ἐξηχοῦν κατὰ ἀ. πνεύματος Melet.*nat.hom.*10(M.64.1196B); **6.** *end, remotest part* οἱ μυχοὶ τοῦ βυθοῦ καὶ τὰ ἀ. Epiph.*haer.*70.8 (p.240.13; M.42.352B); **7.** sens. dub., plur. ? *created objects* στοιχειοῦσθαι ἀ. εἰς δράκοντας *Apoc.Adam* 2(p.142); cf.*ib.*4(l.c.).

ἀποτελεσματικός, A. in gen.; **1.** *complete, perfect* τῆς τῶν... προφητειῶν ἀποτελεσματικῆς συμπληρώσεως Eus.*d.e.*1.1(p.6.3; M.20. 20D); **2.** *completing* or *effecting its purpose* ἐνέργειαν ἀ. Max.*ambig.* (M.91.1261C); **3.** *actual*, i.e. *committed*; of sin opp. ἁμαρτία κατὰ διάνοιαν, Cyr.*Ps.*18:14(M.69.833B); cf. ἀποτελεσματικῶς.

B. astrol., *concerned with effects*, sc. of stars on human destiny, *astrological* τῆς ἀστρονομίας, ὃ μέρος ἀ. καλοῦσι Soz.*h.e.*3.6.5(M.67. 1045C); neut. plur. as subst.; **1.** *astrology*, Cosm.Mel.*schol.*(M.38. 552) in Gr.Naz.*carm.*1.1.5; **2.** *effects resulting from influence of stars*, Bas.*hex.*6.6(1.55C; M.29.129C).

***ἀποτελεσματικῶς, 1.** *effectually*, Max.*ambig.*(M.91.1261C); **2.** *actually* ἐν ἑαυτῷ φυλάττει αὐτὰ...οὐδὲ πράττει ἀ. Or.*sel.in Ps.*54:5(M.12. 1465B); **3.** *in a manner denoting what actually happens*, Olymp. *Job* 5:3(M.93.81A).

***ἀποτελεστής, ὁ,** *accomplisher, performer*, Cyr.*Chr.un.*(5^{1}.749B); id.*Jo.*9.1(4.811C); *cat.Lc.*10:13(p.84.32).

ἀποτελεστικός, 1. *able to execute* or *put into effect* τῶν τοῦ νοὸς ἐνεργειῶν αἱ χεῖρες ἀ. Melet.*nat.hom.*26(M.64.1248A); **2.** *produced by* τὸ κακὸν...πρακτικῆς ἀνθρωπίνης ἐνεργείας ἀποτελεστικόν Epiph.*haer.* 66.15(p.39.7; M.42.52C); **3.** *as a product* or *creation*, cf. *mundus hic factus est apotelesticos a deo*, Iren.*haer.*2.28.3(cj. *apotelestos* M.7. 807A).

***ἀποτέλεστος,** s.v.l., *unfulfilled* Ἐνὼχ...πρῶτος τῆς τελευτῆς τὴν ἀπόφασιν δείξας ἀποτέλεστον Bas.Sel.*or.*14.1(M.85.184B ? l. ἀτέλεστον).

***ἀποτελετής, ὁ,** *fulfiller* τῶν πάλαι προειρημένων ἀ. Cyr.ap.*cat.Lc.* 7:20(p.58.21).

ἀποτελ-έω, A. act.; **1.** *make up, constitute* τῶν ~εσασῶν φύσεων [i.e. the two natures of Christ] Eust.Mon.*ep.*(M.86.913A); **2.** *convey* a meaning or interpretation, Didym.*Trin.*1.9(M.39.289A).

B. pass.; **1.** *be made* or *rendered*, eucharistic τὸ μέλλον ~εῖσθαι δεσποτικὸν αἷμα ἐν τῷ προσήκοντι πάθους καιρῷ διὰ τῆς τοῦ ζωοποιοῦ πνεύματος ἐπιφοιτήσεως ‡Sophr.H.*liturg.*10(M.87.3989D); **2.** of a priest, *be ordained*, Dion.Ar.*e.h.*5.2(M.3.509B,C); **3.** *be made perfect*; of persons, id.*ep.*8.4(M.3.1093D); of angels, id.*c.h.*8.2(M.3.240C).

ἀποτέμν-ω, 1. *cut off*; **a.** lit., c. acc. pers. Παῦλον τῆς κεφαλῆς ἀπέτεμε Gr.Nyss.*castig.*(M.46.316C); τῆς κεφαλῆς ἀπετμήθη Ast.Am. *hom.*4(M.40.224C); Philost.*h.e.*7.15(M.65.553B); hence **i.** *behead*, esp. in pass., *be beheaded* Παῦλός τε ~εται Eus.*d.e.*3.5(p.122.22; M.22. 209A); Chrys.*hom.7.1 in 2Cor.*(10.480C); *Chron.Pasch.*p.380(M.92. 973A,976A); **ii.** pass., *be castrated*, Chrys.*hom.4.3 in Rom.*(9.458A); Jo.D.*haer.*58(M.94.713A); **b.** met. ~ουσαν ⟨καὶ⟩ καίουσαν τὰς ψευδεῖς δόξας αὐτῶν Clem.*str.*7.16(p.72.34; M.9.541C); Meth.*symp.* 1.3(p.11.7; M.18.41C); **c.** from Church, *excommunicate* τὰς παροικίας ~ειν...τῆς κοινῆς ἑνώσεως Eus.*h.e.*5.24.9(M.20.497B); Chrys.*hom. 60.1 in Mt.*(7.607A); τὸν χωριζόμενον τῆς ἐκκλησίας πάντων ~ων id.*hom.16.1 in Rom.*(9.603E); **d.** med. οὐ ποταμὸς τὴν διάβασιν ~εται Bas.*hex.*7.3(1.66B; M.29.156B); **2.** *cut off*, sc. from life; *destroy*, martyrs τοῖς διὰ τὸν Ἰησοῦν ~ομένοις Or.*mart.*34(p.32.1; M.11. 609A); ἀπέτεμον δὲ τὸν...Ἰάκωβον Thdt.*Is.*57:1(p.223.2; 2.367); **3.** pass., *be severed* or *divided* ἀπετμήθης...θυγατρὸς Thdr.Stud.*epp.* 2.68(M.99.1296D); **4.** pass., of Son, *be divided* οὐ γὰρ ἐξίσταταί ποτε τῆς αὐτοῦ περιωπῆς...οὐ μεριζόμενος, οὐκ ~όμενος, οὐ μεταβαίνων ἐκ τόπου εἰς τόπον Clem.*str.*7.2(p.5.27; M.9.408C); **5.** pass., *be struck off* ἀπετμήθη [sc. ὁ Ἰούδας] τοῦ ἁγίου τῶν ἀποστόλων καταλόγου Epiph.*inc.*4(p.232.3; M.41.277D).

ἀπότεξις, ἡ, 1. *bringing to birth*; **a.** of generation of Son ὁ πρὸ παντὸς αἰῶνος καὶ χρόνου τὴν ἐκ θεοῦ τοῦ καὶ πατρὸς ἀ. ἔχων [sc. ὁ υἱός] Cyr.*hom.pasch.*17(5^{2}.226A); **b.** of spiritual birth or regeneration in baptism, Dion.Ar.*e.h.*3.3.6(M.3.432D); **2.** *product, result* τὸ ἀσθενεῖν τῶν ἐξ ὀργῆς κινημάτων ἀπότεξις ἦν Cyr.*Os.*170(v.l. ἀπότευξις 3.195D).

[*]**ἀποτέρω,** for ἀπωτέρω, *farther from*, c. genit., Bas.Sel.*v.Thecl.* 2.7(M.85.576B).

***ἀποτεταγμένως,** *exclusively, specifically* τὸ μὴ ἐπονομάζεσθαί τινι ἀ. μήτε ἱμάτιον μήτε σκεῦος Bas.*ascet.*2.1(2.324B; M.31.881C); Gr. Nyss.*ep.*24(M.46.1089B); Thdr.Stud.*epp.*2.135(M.99.1436A).

***ἀποτετευγμένως,** *unsuccessfully*, Or.*Cels.*4.51(p.324.25; M.11. 1112B).

***ἀποτετολμημένως,** *audaciously*, Or.*Cels.*6.44(p.115.21; M.11. 1368B); id.*comm.in Rom.*6:8(*JTS* 13 p.364).

***ἀπότευκτος,** *failing to hit the mark, unsuccessful*, Max.*ambig.* (M.91.1066A, conj. ἀπευκτοῖς).

***ἀποτεχνέομαι,** *fashion*, ‡Caes.Naz.*dial.*130(M.38.1032).

ἀποτηγανίζ-ω, 1. *broil, grill*; of torture, in gen., Or.*sel.in Ezech.* 4(M.13.780C); met., of Job ~ομένου πάντοθεν, ἔνδοθεν, ἔξωθεν Chrys. *hom.div.*4.2(12.342B); ref. torments of hell, of Dives ἀπετηγανίζετο ἐν τῇ φλογὶ τῆς καμίνου Bas.*hom.*1.9(2.7B; M.31.177A); Chrys.*hom. 41.3 in Mt.*(7.449D); in gen., *ib.43.4*(464B); **2.** *dry up* τὰ τῶν ὀφθαλμῶν δάκρυα ἀ. Jo.Clim.*scal.*5(M.88.765C).

ἀποτηρ-έω, 1. *watch for*; of Church, ref. Gen.3:15 σὺ καὶ μόνη τηρεῖς καὶ ~εῖς...τὴν κεφαλὴν τοῦ...δράκοντος Anast.S.*hex.*12(M.89. 1073A); **2.** *keep back, reserve* πρεσβύτερος πρὸ τῶν τριάκοντα ἐτῶν μὴ χειροτονείσθω,...ἀλλ' ~είσθω CNeocaes.*can.*11; or poss. med., *let him await* the due time.

***ἀποτήρησις, ἡ,** *keeping back, reservation* οὐκ ἐνήστευσεν [i.e. one who fasts without giving alms], ἀλλὰ ἀ. τῶν νηστειῶν...ἐποιήσατο Eus.Al.*serm.*1(M.86.316B).

ἀποτίθ-ημι, A. act. and pass.; **1.** *lay aside* ἀπέθηκε χιτῶνας Nonn. *par.Jo.*13:4(M.43.860C); **2.** pass., *be replaced* εἰς τόπον ἴδιον ἀποτεθειμένων Herm.*sim.*9.5.4; *ib.*9.9.4; **3.** pass., *be buried* ἠρίοις βασιλικοῖς ἀπετίθετο Eus.*v.C.*3.47(p.97.14; M.20.1108A).

B. med.; **1.** *put off* the body at death ἀποθέμενοι...τὸ σῶμα Hipp. *haer.*1.24(p.29.15; M.16.3052D); Cels.ap.Or.*Cels.*3.42(p.238.20; M.11. 975D); Or.*mart.*47(p.43.9; M.11.529B); τὴν γηΐνην ποιότητα...~εσθαι Meth.*res.*1.23(p.246.18; M.41.1092C); **2.** met., *renounce* τὸ σῶμα... ἀποθέσθαι κατὰ τὸν Παῦλον (cf. 1Cor.9:27) Chrys.*fem.reg.*7(1.263C); **3.** τὸν βίον ἀ. *die*, Eus.*v.C.*1.21(p.18.15; M.20.937A); τὴν τελευτὴν ἀ. τοῦ βίου *ib.*2.21(p.50.1; 1000B); τὸν τῇδε βίον ἀπέθετο Evagr.*h.e.*1.7 (p.14.2; M.86.2437B); **4.** *put away from oneself, reject, refuse* ἀποθέσθαι τὸ τηνικαῦτα Eus.*v.C.*2.28(p.57.20, v.l. ἀπέχεσθαι M.20. 1016B); **5.** *lose* λιμῷ πιεζόμενος, ὡσαύτως πᾶν τὸ ὑγρὸν ~εται Thdt. *provid.*3(4.520); **6.** *record* τὴν ἱστορίαν ~έμενος ἔνθα τῷ φιλανθρώπῳ παρασταίη θεῷ Evagr.*h.e.*1.1(p.6.35; M.86.2421C); *ib.*1.11(p.20.19; 2452D); λογίως ἀπέθετο *ib.*1.13(p.21.17; 2453C).

ἀποτίμησις, ἡ, 1. *assessment, valuation* for taxation, Bas.*ep.*313 (3.444A; M.32.1061A); **2.** *estimated value* ἀνοικοδομεῖν ἢ τὰς...ἀ. ἐκτιννύειν Soz.*h.e.*5.5.5(M.67.1228B); *ib.*5.10.9(1244C); **3.** met., *estimation* τῆς ὑπὲρ ἀξίαν μου ἀ. σου Thdr.Stud.*epp.*1.37(M.99.1037D).

ἀποτινάσσ-ω, 1. act., *strike off* τὴν κεφαλὴν *A.Paul.*(*PHamb.*p.10. 26; LB p.115.16); met., *destroy, extinguish* τὸ περὶ τῆς τῶν ἐχθρῶν δυνάμεως διεξιέναι τὴν ῥαθυμίαν ~ει Chrys.*hom.22.4 in Eph.*(11. 170C); id.*hom.1.3 in Phil.*(11.198D); **2.** med., *shake off from oneself*; **a.** things ἡμῶν ἐγερθέντων καὶ ἀποτιναξαμένων τὴν νεκρότητα τῆς σαρκός Meth.*res.*1.47(p.299.3; M.18.273D); ἀποτινάξασθαι τὸ ἁμαρτάνειν *ib.*2.4(p.336.15; 301B); of Arians οἱ τὴν ἀποστολικὴν ἀποτιναξάμενοι πίστιν Ath.*Ar.*1.4(M.26.20A); **b.** persons, *reject*, Chrys.*hom.5.6 in Rom.*(9.470A); Cyr.*Jo.*3.2(4.262A); Jo.Mosch.*prat.* 31(M.87.2880B).

ἀπότισις, ἡ, *repayment*, Bas.*reg.fus.*proem.2(2.328D; M.31.893A).

ἀπότιστος, *unwatered*, Gr.Thaum.*pan.Or.*7(p.19.12; M.10.1073C).

[*]**ἀποτίτθιος,** *taken from the breast, weaned*; met., *M.Pion.*10.3.

ἀπότιτθος, = foreg., Bas.Sel.*v.Thecl.*2.8(M.85.576D).

ἀπότμησις, ἡ, *cutting off*, plur., Tat.*orat.*8(p.8.23; M.6.824A); Eus. *h.e.*5.4.3(M.20.440A).

ἀπότολμος, *pusillanimous*, Cyr.*ador.*4(1.140C).

ἀποτομή, ἡ, 1. *cutting off, division*, in God οὐδ' ἐν μέρει καταγίνεταί ποτε οὔτε περιέχων οὔτε περιεχόμενος ἢ κατὰ ὁρισμόν τινα ἢ κατὰ ἀ. Clem.*str.*2.2(p.116.5; M.8.937A); ref. generation of Son τὴν δύναμιν ταύτην γεγεννῆσθαι ἀπὸ τοῦ πατρὸς...ἀλλ' οὐ κατὰ ἀ., ὡς ἀπομεριζομένης τῆς τοῦ πατρὸς οὐσίας Just.*dial.*128.4(M.6.776B); οὔτ' οὖν κατὰ διαίρεσιν οὔτε κατά τινα ἀ. ἐκ τοῦ πατρὸς ὑποστῆναι Eus.*ep.Caes.*7(p.44.5; M.20.1541B); **2.** *decapitation,* Andr.Cr.*or.*15 tit.(M.97.1109A); Max.*comput.*34(M.19.1252C); **3.** *castration, Hom. Clem.*6.2.

ἀπότομος, 1. *severe*; of persons, Polyc.*ep.*6.1; *Const.App.*2.21.1; Nil.*epp.*2.190(M.79.297D); of things ἀποτομωτάτην...τὴν διάνοιαν Cyr.H.*catech.*15.12; Isid.Pel.*epp.*5.165(M.78.1424A); **2.** *inadequate, crude* τὴν ἀ. ... τῶν ἀγγελικῶν ὀνομάτων σκηνήν Dion.Ar.*c.h.*2.2 (M.3.137B); ἀ. ... τὴν ξένην, καὶ οἷον τῶν συνήθων ἀποτετμημένην ὁδὸν καὶ πλάσιν Max.*schol.*ad loc.(M.4.37A).

ἀποτορνεύ-ω, 1. *round off* as by the lathe; pass., Chrys.*Dan.*1:4 (6.201D); Thdr.Stud.*or.*3.6(M.99.708B); med. τῶν μὲν [sc. ἀτόμων] ἀποτετορνευμένων αὐτομάτων εἰς ἥλιον Dion.Al.ap.Eus.*p.e.*14.25 (776D; M.21.1277B); **2.** met., *make ready, equip, prepare* βασιλίσσης ἣν ἀνήγαγεν ὁ κύριος ἀναμάρτητον ~σας τῷ πατρί Meth.*symp.*7.9 (p.80.5; M.18.137A); ἰσομεγέθη...τοῖς αἰτιάμασιν ~ων [sc. ὁ νόμος] τὴν κίνησιν Cyr.*ador.*8(1.258D); εἰς ἐννοίας ἡμᾶς ὁ λόγος ~ει λεπτάς id.*glaph.Lev.*(1.354C); τοὺς μαθητὰς...εἰς ἕκαστα τῶν τελούντων εἰς ἀρετὴν τοῖς καθήκουσιν ~σας λόγοις id.*Jo.*9.12(4.1010D).

***ἀποτραγῳδέω,** *tell in tragic* or *moving language,* Isid.Pel.*epp.*2. 240(M.78.680C).

***ἀποτρακτεύω,** *investigate, examine,* Eus.Al.*serm.*5(M.86.345A).

ἀποτρεπτέος, *to be avoided,* Eus.*d.e.*3.3(p.113.20; cod. ἀποτρεπταίας M.22.193D).

ἀποτρεπτικός, 1. *dissuasive,* abs., Clem.*paed.*1.10(p.142.21,25; M. 8.356C); c. genit. λόγους ἀ. τοῦ πορνεύειν Or.*mart.*10(p.10.16; M.11. 576C); id.*Cels.*3.44(p.240.16; M.11.977B); Eus.*p.e.*11.4(512D; M.21. 849D); c. infin., Or.*comm.in Mt.*11.9(p.49.19; M.13.932B); neut. as subst., Clem.*paed.*1.10(p.142.19; M.8.356C); **2.** *capable of repelling* φυλακτηρίοις ἀποτρεπτικοῖς δαιμόνων Or.*hom.8.3 in Ex.*(p.223.23); Isid.Pel.*epp.*4.184(M.78.1276C).

ἀποτρέχ-ω, *run away from*; met., *abandon* τί μακρὸν ~εις τῆς ἀληθείας; Bas.*hex.*2.4(1.15E; M.29.37A).

ἀποτρίβ-ω, 1. *rub away, crush* τὸ ἄνθος...εἰς ὕδωρ ἀποτριβέν Meth. *symp.*4.3(p.49.1; M.18.89D); **2.** *rub clean, cleanse* ἵνα...καὶ τῶν ἀναγνωσομένων τὰς γλώττας, καὶ τῶν ἀκουσομένων τὰς ἀκοὰς ἀποτρίψωμεν Thdt.*haer.*proem.(4.282); **3.** med.; **a.** *rub oneself clean,* Clem.*paed.*3.2(p.239.16; cod. ἀποτεινόμεναι M.8.561C); **b.** *excrete,* abs., *ib.*2.3(p.181.2; 437C); trans., ‡Just.*ep.Zen.et Ser.*11(M.6.1196B); **c.** ἀ. ... τὸ μέτωπον, *harden one's forehead,* as it were by perpetual rubbing, i.e. *be utterly hardened, dead to shame,* Epiph.*haer.*76.2 (p.342.11; M.42.517C); cf. παρατρίβω.

***ἀποτρίζω,** *creak,* Cyr.*Am.*23(3.273A); id.*Jon.*4(3.371B).

***ἀπότριμμος,** *worn* ἀ. ἱμάτιον ‡Chrys.*eleem.*4(11.843B), ? f.l. for ἀποτετριμμένον.

***ἀποτρίχω,** *shave, tonsure* head on taking monastic vows, Eustrat.*v.Eutych.*14(M.86.2289B).

***ἀποτρίχωσις, ἡ,** *shaving of the head,* Leont.H.*monoph.*testimonia(M.86.1900A).

ἀπότριψις, ἡ, *rubbing off, riddance,* Clem.*paed.*3.11(p.272.29; M.8. 640C); met., of sin, Cyr.*ador.*16(1.557A).

ἀποτρόπαιος, A. 1. *averting evil,* of Christ's death ἱερεῖον δαιμονικῆς πλάνης ἀ. Eus.*l.C.*15(p.247.28; M.20.1420B) = id.*theoph. fr.*3(p.9.23; M.24.616A); of martyrs τῶν κακῶν ἀ. Thdt.*affect.*8 (p.208.19; 4.912); prayers ἀ. ἱκετηρίας τῶν δεινῶν Philost.*h.e.*2.17 (M.65.480A); **2.** neut. as subst., *averter, prophylactic* τὰ τῶν κακῶν ἀ. Gr.Nyss.*v.Mos.*(M.44.321C); of Cross νικητικὸν τρόπαιον, δαιμόνων ἀ. Eus.*l.C.*6(p.212.6; M.20.1352A); of blood of paschal lamb, Cyr.H.*catech.*19.3, term rejected by Cyril ἀ. ... τὸν ἀποπομπαῖον ἀποκαλεῖ, καινοτομήσας ὄνομα τοῖς...ἱεροῖς νόμοις οὐκ ἐγνωσμένον Cyr.*Juln.*9(6^2.299C).

B. *to be turned away from*; hence neut. as subst., *abomination* μάστιξ δὲ ἀ. θυμῷ γὰρ ὑπηρετεῖται Synes.*ep.*57(M.66.1385A); κοινὸν ἀνάθεμα κείσθω καὶ ἀ. *V.Const.*27(p.559.26).

ἀποτροπή, ἡ, *perversion, distortion* εἰς ἀ. τῶν δεδιδαγμένων ὑφ' ἡμῶν Just.*1apol.*46.1(M.6.397B).

ἀποτροπία, ἡ, *dissuasion,* Epiph.*haer.*63.3(p.400.25; M.41.1065B).

ἀποτροπιάζω, 1. *drive away,* pass., Or.*Cels.*6.43(p.113.25; M.11. 1364D); med., *avert evil by sacrifice, procure expiation,* Thdt.*Ezech.* 16:22(2.782); **2.** med., *turn away from, avoid,* Synes.*ep.*4(M.66. 1329C); *ib.*50(1377B).

ἀποτροπίασμα, τό, *victim* or *sacrifice to avert evil,* Ath.*gent.*24 (M.25.49A).

***ἀποτρόπου,** *unreasonably,* Thphyl.*exc.Rom.*3(M.113.929C; ἀπὸ τρόπου p.223.13).

ἀποτροφή, ἡ, *nourishment, sustenance,* Max.*qu.Thal.*55(M.90. 556C).

ἀπότροφος, 1. *reared apart from; nourished,* met. ἁμαρτίαις ἀ. Isid.Pel.*epp.*1.120(M.78.261D); **2.** *without food,* superl., *V.Const.*57 (p.582.21).

ἀποτρυγ-άω, *gather grapes* or *fruit,* met. καὶ ταῦτα [sc. νοήματα], ἀντὶ δρεπάνης τῷ λόγῳ χρησάμενοι...~ήσωμεν Chrys.*Laz.*4.1(1.751E); ~ήσομεν...τοὺς τῆς ἐπιεικείας καρποὺς Cyr.*Am.*85(3.352E); ἕκαστος γὰρ...τῶν εἰς λειτουργίαν τὴν ἱερὰν ἠγμένων, τοὺς καρποὺς τῶν ἰδίων ~ήσει πόνων id.*ador.*12(1.442B); hence *cut off* or *gather* for punishment, id.*Os.*69(3.105A).

ἀποτυλ-άω, *cut off* ἀμπέλου...γέγονας κλῆμα...~ώμενος ξίφει δὲ καὶ ποσίν...ἀποθλιβείς Jo.Mon.*hymn.Blas.*1(M.96.1401B); ? f.l. for ἀποτιλλόμενος.

***ἀποτυλίσσω,** *unroll, unwrap,* Thdr.Lect.*fr.*(M.86.224A).

ἀποτυμπανίζω, 1. *beat to death,* Chrys.*hom.40.3 in Mt.*(7.440E); Nil.*epp.*1.198(M.79.157A); **2.** *beat,* Gr.Nyss.*castig.*(M.46.312A); **3.** *behead, Ep.Lugd.*ap.Eus.*h.e.*5.1.47(M.20.425B); Thdt.*qu.42 in Dt.*(1. 291); **4.** *put to death* in any cruel and violent manner, Chrys.*hom. 33.5 in Mt.*(7.384B).

ἀποτυμπανισμός, ὁ, *beheading* ἀ. λέγεται ὁ ἀποκεφαλισμός Chrys. *hom.27.2 in Heb.*(12.248C).

ἀποτυπ-όω, 1. *stamp an impression*; **a.** lit., *engrave, impress,* Clem.*prot.*4(p.46.33; M.8.160B); ἀ. τὸ σταυροειδὲς γράμμα Socr.*h.e.*5. 17.7(M.67.609A); **b.** met., *impress* on the mind τὰ τῶν αἰσθήσεων κινήματα κατά τε τὴν διάνοιαν ~οῦνται κατά τε τὴν ἀπὸ τοῦ σώματος ἐνέργειαν φανεροῦνται Clem.*str.*6.16(p.501.4; M.9.361A); **2.** *mould, model, fashion*; **a.** lit. εἴ τις βούλοιτο ἀπὸ κηροῦ ἀνδροείκελον κατασκευάσαι καὶ πρότερον μὲν βραχείᾳ ὑποστάσει ~ωσάμενος Adam.*dial.* 5.16(p.208.6; M.11.1856A); Meth.*symp.*6.2(p.65.10; M.18.116A); Gr. Nyss.*v.Mos.*(M.44.396B); **b.** fig. ἡ τοῦ πνεύματος χάρις...εἰς μίαν ἅπαντας ἔπλασε μορφήν, καὶ εἰς ἕνα ἀπετύπωσε χαρακτῆρα τὸν βασιλικόν Chrys.*hom.10.2 in Jo.*(8.59D); **c.** med. and reflex., *fashion oneself, transform oneself* ~οῦντες ἑαυτοὺς [sc. οἱ δαίμονες] εἰς σχήματα μοναχῶν Ath.*v.Anton.*25(M.26.881A); ~οῦνται κατὰ τὴν ἑκάστου τῶν ἱερῶν νόων ἀναλογίαν Dion.Ar.*c.h.*3.2(M.3.165B); *ib.*4.2(180A); **d.** *conform* πρὸς τὸν θεῖον ὑπέρσοφον καὶ νοῦν καὶ λόγον...~ουμένη [sc. ἡ νοερὰ δύναμις] διὰ τὴν θείαν σοφίαν Dion.Ar.*d.n.*7.2(M.3.868B); id.*e.h.* 2.3.3(M.3.400B); **3.** *represent,* Meth.*symp.*6.2(p.65.21; M.18.116B); σωμάτων ἰνδάλματα οὐ μὴν ἀθανάτου ψυχῆς ~οῦντα ἰδέας Eus.*v.C.* 1.3(p.8.25; M.20.916A); Dion.Ar.*c.h.*7.2(M.3.208C); id.*e.h.*4.3.6(M.3. 480D); **4.** *express* in words ὃ γὰρ αὐτῷ καθ' ἡδονὴν ἐτύγχανεν ὄν, τοῦτο τῇ συντομίᾳ τῆς φράσεως ἀπετυπώσατο Const.ap.Gel.Cyz.*h.e.* 3.19.10(M.85.1348A).

ἀποτύπωμα, τό, *impression,* such as that made by a seal; met., of BMV τοῦ ἀφθάρτου κάλλους ὁμοίωμα, τῆς ἀληθινῆς θεότητος ἀ. Gr.Nyss.*hom.2 in Cant.*(M.44.805D); μηδὲ ἀτιμάζειν αὐτὰ [i.e. τὰ ἱερὰ σύμβολα] τῶν θείων ὄντα χαρακτήρων ἔκγονα καὶ ἀ. Dion.Ar. *ep.*9.2(M.3.1108C).

ἀποτύπωσις, ἡ, *impression,* ref. Creation τῆς πρὸς τὸ ἀρχαῖον κάλλος ἀ. ἐν ταυτῷ μένοι [sc. ἄν] τὸ ἀφομοίωμα Andr.Cr.*or.*21(M.97. 1269D).

ἀποτυφλ-όω, *blind,* met. ~οῦται ἀπὸ τῆς διανοίας τῆς ἀγαθῆς Herm.*mand.*5.2.7; Clem.*q.d.s.*41(p.187.14; M.9.645D); ὁ θάνατος... θανατοῖ καὶ νεκροῖ τὴν θεωρήσασαν αὐτὸν ὄψιν καὶ ~οῖ Or.*Jo.*20.39 (31; p.382.29; M.14.668D).

ἀποτυχία, ἡ, *failure*; hence **1.** *barrenness* τῆς γῆς τὴν ἀ. Chrys. *hom.25.7 in Gen.*(4.242A); *ib.*55.5(537D); **2.** *missing* of a road ἀ. ... τῆς εὐθείας ὁδοῦ Diod.*Ps.*52:4(M.33.1591A).

***ἀποῦπατος, ὁ,** *ex-consul,* Nil.*epp.*3.62 tit.(M.79.420A).

***ἀπουρανόθεν,** *from heaven,* Rom.Mel.(*AS* 1 p.20).

ἀπουσία, ἡ, 1. *absence*; hence *vacant place* ὁ γνωστικὸς οὗτος...τὴν ἀποστολικὴν ἀ. ἀναπληροῖ Clem.*str.*7.12(p.55.9; M.9.505B); **2.** *emission of semen,* id.*paed.*2.10(p.214.13; M.8.509B).

ἀπουσιάζ-ω, *lose substance,* ref. eucharistic elements ὥσπερ κηρὸς πυρὶ προσομιλήσας, οὐδὲν ~ει, οὐδὲν περισσεύει· οὕτω καὶ ὧδε νόμιζε συναλίσκεσθαι τὰ μυστήρια τῇ τοῦ σώματος οὐσίᾳ Chrys.*poenit.*9(2. 350A).

ἀπουσι-όω, *deprive of essence,* Christol. οὐσιῶσαι καὶ μετουσιῶσαι καὶ ~ῶσαι τὰς φύσεις δύναται Leont.H.*monoph.*6(M.86.1773A).

ἀποφαίν-ω, 1. *show forth* as, *declare* to be; in eucharistic epiclesis, that elements may be shown forth as body and blood of Christ, *Lit.*ap.*Const.App.*8.12.39; **2.** of numbers, *make* δέκα δὲ μονάδες μίαν ~ουσι δεκάδα Eus.*l.C.*6(p.210.31; M.20.1348D).

***Ἀποφάνιος, ὁ,** *the Obscure* οἱ περὶ Ἐπιφάνιον, μᾶλλον δὲ Ἀποφάνιον τὸν πυρίκαον, ἀλλ' οὐ πατρίκιον *Max.invect.*(M.90.203A).

ἀποφαντικῶς, **1.** *by way of statement*, Or.*comm.in Mt.*10.14(p.16.19; M.13.868A); id.*comm.ser.in Mt.*118(p.251.8; M.17.305B); Cyr.*Is.*4.2(2.587E); **2.** *positively, categorically*, Eus.*Marcell.*2.3(p.49.17; M.24.805D); τὸ μὲν εὐαγγέλιον...ἀ. διακελεύεται πάντα ἄνθρωπον τόδε μὴ ποιεῖν Mac.Aeg.*elev.*19(M.34.905B); Thdt.*Cant.*1:1(2.26); ἀποδεικτικῶς, οὐκ ἀ., χρὴ λέγειν τῆς ἐκκλησίας τὰ δόγματα id.*eran.*3(4.199).

ἀπόφασις (A), **ἡ**, (ἀπόφημι) **1.** *denial, negation*, as only true way of speaking of attributes of God αἱ μὲν ἀ. ἐπὶ τῶν θείων ἀληθεῖς, αἱ δὲ καταφάσεις ἀνάρμοστοι Dion.Ar.*c.h.*2.3(M.3.141A); cf.Max.*ambig.*(M.91.1165B) cit. s. κατάφασις; τὰ θεῖα τιμᾶσθαι ταῖς ἀληθέσιν ἀ., καὶ ταῖς πρὸς τὰ ἔσχατα τῶν οἰκείων ἀπηχημάτων ἑτεροίαις ἀφομοιώσεσιν Dion.Ar.*c.h.*2.5(145A); τὰ ἐπὶ τῇ φιλανθρωπίᾳ τοῦ Ἰησοῦ καταφασκόμενα, δύναμιν ὑπεροχικῆς ἀ. ἔχοντα id.*ep.*4(M.3.1072B); cf.Max.*schol.* ad loc.(M.4.533B); εἰσὶ δὲ καί τινα καταφατικῶς λεγόμενα ἐπὶ θεοῦ δύναμιν ὑπεροχικῆς ἀ. ἔχοντα. οἷον, σκότος λέγοντες ἐπὶ θεοῦ, οὐ σκότος νοοῦμεν, ἀλλ' ὅτι οὐκ ἔστι φῶς, ἀλλ' ὑπὲρ τὸ φῶς· καὶ φῶς, ὅτι οὐκ ἔστι σκότος Jo.D.*f.o.*1.4(M.94.800B); **2.** *negative particle*; perh. in this sense ἡ 'οὐκ' ἀ. Or.*fr.59 in Jer.*(p.227.16; M.13.584A) but more probably = *word* (v. ἀπόφασις (B) 5).

ἀπόφασις (B), **ἡ**, (ἀποφαίνω) **1.** *decree, judgement*; of God, *M.Carp.*19; ἡ...ἀ. τοῦ θεοῦ καὶ τὸ διάταγμα τὸ ἐπὶ τῆς παιδοποιίας Meth.*symp.*2.1(p.15.13; M.18.48C); Const.*or.s.c.*13(p.173.3); **2.** *statement* opp. question, ‡Just.*qu.et resp.*38(M.6.1284B); Diod.*Ps.*52:5(M.33.1591A); Thdr.Mops.*Rom.*2:17(p.116.10; M.66.789C); **3.** *statement, declaration*; as title of work attributed to Simon Magus, Hipp.*haer.*6.11(p.137.29; M.16.3211A); **4.** *opinion*; ἰδίᾳ ἀ. *self-opinionated*, *ib.*4.17(p.51.1; M.16.3086A); ἰδίας ἀ. *ib.*(p.51.15; 3086B); **5.** *word* ἡ αὐτὴ ἀ. [sc. 'ἡμῖν'] Or.*Jo.*1.34(39; p.44.13; M.14.92A); cf. ἡ 'οὐκ' ἀ. id.*fr.59 in Jer.*(p.227.16; M.13.584A) unless = *negative particle* (v. ἀπόφασις (A) 2).

ἀποφατικός (A), (ἀπόφημι) *negative*, ref. knowledge of God by way of negation τίνες αἱ καταφατικαὶ θεολογίαι, τίνες αἱ ἀ.; Dion.Ar.*myst.*3 tit.(M.3.1032C); τῆς ἄκρας καὶ ἀ. τοῦ λόγου θεολογίας, καθ' ἣν οὔτε λέγεται, οὔτε νοεῖται Max.*ambig.*(M.91.1081B); of a negative statement, opp. a question, Clem.*str.*1.18(p.57.14; M.8.804C); of a command, *prohibitory*, Ast.Am.*hom.*1(M.40.164A).

§ἀποφατικός (B), (ἀποφαίνω) **1.** *asseverative* τῇ ἀ. ταύτῃ...φωνῇ (cf. Jo.10:38,14:10) Gr.Nyss.*Eun.*9(2 p.218.29; M.45.817B); τῇ ἀ. ἀπαγορεύσει Thdt.*Rom.*6:1(3.61); **2.** *declarative* 'λόγον' ἀποφατικὸν ὀργῆς Proc.G.*Is.*9:8–13(M.87.2013A).

ἀποφατικῶς (A), (ἀπόφημι) *negatively*; of prohibitive law-giving, Cyr.*Jo.*4.6(4.464B); of knowledge of God *by way of negation* ἀποστρέφει κατὰ τὴν τῶν ὑπὸ φύσιν καὶ χρόνον ἀφαίρεσιν, ἀ. θεολογούμενος, πρὸς τὴν πλήρη χάριτος...ὡς μονογενοῦς παρὰ πατρὸς δόξαν ‡Proc.G.*Pr.*23:5(M.87.1452A); Thal.*cent.*4.83(M.91.1468A); μέχρι τῆς πασῶν καθ' ὑπεροχὴν ἀνωτάτης φύσεώς τε καὶ τάξεως ἀ. προοδεύουσα Max.*ambig.*(M.91.1240D); τῶν θείων ὀνομάτων τὰ μὲν ἀ. λέγεται, δηλοῦντα τὸ ὑπερούσιον·...τὰ δὲ καταφατικῶς λεγόμενα, ὡς αἰτίου τῶν πάντων κατηγορεῖται Jo.D.*f.o.*1.12(M.94.845D); *ib.*(848C).

§ἀποφατικῶς (B), (ἀποφαίνω) **1.** *in the form of a statement* (opp. question), Eus.*d.e.*10.8(p.479.2; M.22.769C); **2.** *positively, dogmatically*; comp., Diod.*Rom.*5:18–19(p.84.28).

ἀποφέρ-ω, **A.** act. and pass.; **1.** *carry* or *bear away*, met. τὰ δεινὰ...εἰς ἔσχατον ~οντα κακοῦ Cyr.*Is.*4.5(2.715D); πίστις...ὁδὸς εἰς ζωὴν ~ουσα τὴν ἀμήρυτον *ib.*(717D); pass. ~έσθω τῇ διανοίᾳ Gr.Nyss.*or.catech.*40(p.163.17; M.45.105A); **2.** *remove, withdraw* ~ων ἑαυτὸν τῶν ἠδικημένων Cyr.*Ps.*9:22(M.69.777B); **3.** *turn aside* ὁ προφήτης...τῆς ἐπ' αὐτοῖς ~ων ὀργῆς [sc. τὸν θεόν] id.*Soph.*4(3.582E); **4.** ψῆφον ἀ. *deliver a judgement*, Eus.*h.e.*5.21.3(M.20.488A).

B. med.; **1.** *take away*, met. ταῖς γυναιξὶ ταῖς ~ομέναις τὴν ζωὴν αὐτῶν Herm.*sim.*9.21.4; μοχθηρῶν ἀνδρῶν, δόξαν θεῶν ἀπενεγκαμένων *Hom.Clem.*6.18; **2.** *acquire from* Μαρσύου...τὴν αὐλητικὴν ἀπηνέγκασθε Tat.*orat.*1(p.1.13; M.6.804B); **3.** *bear*, met. κακίας...δόξαν ἀ. Athenag.*leg.*36.2(M.6.969C); Gr.Thaum.*pan.Or.*3(p.7.2; M.10.1057C); Meth.*symp.*5.4(p.57.2; M.18.101C).

ἀποφθείρω, *destroy utterly*; pass. c. genit., *be removed from*, sc. by death τοῦ ζῆν καὶ τῆς ἀρχῆς...ἀπεφθάρη Philost.*h.e.*11.1(M.65.593A).

***ἀποφιλοτιμέομαι**, *display in rivalry*, Eus.*Hierocl.*14(522A; ἀντεφ- M.22.821A).

ἀποφιμόω, *silence completely*, Epiph.*haer.*66.11(p.33.4; M.42.45D).

ἀποφοιτ-άω, **1.** *depart, go away*; **a.** abs., Mac.Mgn.*apocr.*4.11(p.173.4); Isid.Pel.*epp.*2.34(M.78.477D); προστάσσει τοῦ ἔχοντος αὐτὸν [sc. πνεύματος] ~ᾶν *cat.Lc.*4:34(p.39.19); **b.** c. genit., *depart from* ὁ...σωτὴρ...οὐκ ~ᾷ τῶν δεομένων αὐτοῦ Cyr.*Lc.*5:30(M.72.569C); id.*Ps.*27:1(M.69.853C); met., from a master or doctrine, Or.*Cels.*2.12(p.140.31; M.11.817A); Cyr.*apol.Thdt.*10(p.138.4; 6^{1}.232C); id.*Nest.*3(p.62.17; 6^{1}.75B); in gen. τῆς χάριτος Gr.Nyss.*or.catech.*30(p.113.4; M.45.77B); Cyr.*hom.pasch.*23(5^{2}.279B); τὸ ἐξηρμόσθαι καὶ οἷον ~ᾶν τῆς κατὰ φύσιν ἁρμονίας id.*Ps.*37:4(956B); hence *differ* φασὶ...ἀλλήλων ~ᾶν τὰς φύσεις [sc. of Christ] id.*apol.Thdt.*3(p.118.18; 6^{1}.212A); id.*ep.*46(p.162.3; 5^{2}.145B); **2.** *shrink from* ~ήσαντα τοῦ παθεῖν id.*Lc.*9:27(M.69.653D).

ἀποφοίτησις, **ἡ**, *departure*, Cyr.*Nah.*38(3.840B); met., from this life, Meth.*res.*3.18(p.415.2; M.18.325B); τὴν ἐκ σώματος ἀ. Cyr.*Jo.*1.9(4.85C); τὴν ἐν τῷ καλῷ προκοπὴν καὶ τὴν ἐκ τοῦ καλοῦ ἀ. ‡Cyr.*Trin.*2(6^{3}.3A; M.77.1121D); cf.†Jo.D.*B.J.*17(M.96.1012A); τῶν...ἐντολῶν ἀ. Dion.Ar.*e.h.*7.3.6(M.3.561A); τῶν ἐναντίων ἢ παντελὴς καὶ ἀνεπίστροφος ἀ. *ib.*1.4(376A).

ἀποφορά, **ἡ**, **1.** *effluvium, smell*; met. τοιαύτη ἀναπεπαυμένη παρῆλθεν ὑπεράνω μου νύξ· ἦλθε γάρ μοι ἀ. τοῦ ξύλου τοῦ ἁγίου *M.Pers.*1.11(p.430.17); **2.** *leading astray, seduction* νοῦς...ἀκάθεκτος καὶ...ἕτοιμος εἰς ἀ. Cyr.*ador.*9(1.289E).

ἀποφόρητος, *carried away*; neut. plur., *presents* which guests received of the food at table *to take home*; at *agape*, Hipp.*trad.ap.*26.8.

ἀποφορτίζ-ω, **1.** *unload*, act. ἀ. τὴν ναῦν Cyr.*Jon.*4(3.371B); met. ἀ. τὸν ἐκείνων πλοῦτον ‡Ath.*hom.in Lc.19:36*(M.28.1045C); τούτων [sc. τῶν ὑπαρχόντων] ~ων αὐτόν Nil.*Magn.*52(M.79.1036D); med. τὴν περὶ τούτου γνῶσιν αὐτῶν ἀ. Alex.Al.*ep.Alex.*5(p.23.7; M.18.556B); **2.** med., *lay down, lay aside* a burden, met. ἀ. τὴν κτῆσιν Clem.*q.d.s.*12(p.167.24; M.9.616C); ἀ. τὴν ἁμαρτίαν Cyr.*Zach.*112(3.811C); id.*Mal.*1(3.816A); **3.** med., *escape from* ἀ. τὴν ἀπληστίαν τῆς βιαίας φορᾶς Synes.*ep.*4(M.66.1337B).

***ἀποφορτόω**, *unload, remove* a burden, Pall.*h.Laus.*115(M.34.1220A); sickness ἡ...τοῦ θεοῦ ἐλπὶς ταύτην ἐξ αὐτοῦ ἀπεφόρτου Marc.Diac.*v.Porph.*5.

***ἀπόφραγμα**, **τό**, *blocking up, barricade*, Cyr.*Is.*2.5(2.347D).

***ἀποφρίττ-ω**, *shrink from* εἰς τοῦτο προελθεῖν δυσσεβείας οὐκ ~οντας Cyr.*Jo.*1.3(4.20C).

***ἀποφρονέω**, *despise* οὐκ ἀ. τοῦ γένους τῶν ἀνθρώπων Hesych.H.*Ps.tit.*21(M.27.728C, v.l. οὐ κατεφρόνησε).

ἀποφρύγω, *dig up*, *Apoc.Dan.*C (p.119).

***ἀποφρυόω**, *humble, break pride*, Gr.Naz.*carm.*2.1.68.14(M.37.1410A).

ἀποφυσάω, *hiss*, of a snake, *A.Jo.*71(p.186.2).

***ἀποφυσόω**, *make to swell*, *T.Abr.*A 19(p.102.17).

ἀποφύω, *be absent* τούτων...τῶν ὀνομάτων...τὰ μὲν τῶν προσόντων τῷ θεῷ τὰ δὲ τῶν ἀποπεφυκότων ἔχει τὴν ἔμφασιν Gr.Nyss.*Eun.*12(1 p.252.19; M.45.953B).

ἀποφωνέω, *make a declaration, state dogmatically*, Max.*opusc.*(M.91.176C).

ἀποχάζομαι, *refrain from*; c. infin., Eudoc.*Cypr.*2.288(M.85.856D).

ἀποχαλκεύω, *fashion in copper* or *bronze*, Mac.Mgn.*apocr.*1.6(p.1.8).

***ἀποχαραδρόω**, *cut into channels*, †Bas.*Is.*156(1.489E; M.30.373C).

ἀποχαρακ-όω, *fence in*; as joke in reply to request for χάρακες *deprive of poles* ἡμεῖς, οἱ...δι' ἐπιστολιμαίας δυνάμεως ~ούμενοι Gr.Nyss.*ep.*27(p.82.1; M.32.1092C).

ἀποχαράσσω, *inscribe*, hence *write*, CIllyr.*ep.*ap.Thdt.*h.e.*4.9.1,5(3.960,962).

***ἀποχαρτουλάριος**, **ὁ**, *ex-keeper of archives*, Anast.S.*relat.*20(*OC* 2 p.71).

***ἀποχαυν-όομαι**, *become slack, relax* μὴ...τῆς κατὰ θεὸν πολιτείας ~ωθῆτε Leont.N.*v.Sym.*19(M.93.1693C).

ἀποχειρίζω, *cut off the hands*, *Chron.Pasch.*p.396(M.92.1013C).

[*]**ἀποχειροβιωτικός**, prob. f.l. for ἀποχειροβίοτος, *living by the work of one's hands*, Thdt.*Ps.*24:12(1.760, v.l. ἀποχειροβιότοις).

ἀποχειροτονέω, *deprive of office, degrade* from priesthood, Soz.*h.e.*3.7.8(M.67.1052A); Leo Mag.*ep.*32(p.42.32; M.*PL.*54.796A); Dion.Ar.*ep.*8.4(M.3.1096A).

***ἀποχερσόω**, *dry up*, Gr.Nyss.*v.Gr.Thaum.*(M.46.925D); Nil.*epp.*3.253(M.79.509A); Cyr.*Jo.*2.1(4.138D).

ἀποχέτευσις, **ἡ**, *conduit*, Eus.*p.e.*9.37(453B; M.21.756D).

ἀποχέ-ω, *pour forth*, met. τὸ ἀγαθὸν ἀπ' αὐτοῦ ~όμενον Athenag.*leg.*23.4(M.6.944B).

ἀποχή, **ἡ**, **1.** *renunciation*, implying rejection ἀπὸ Σατορνίνου καὶ Μαρκίωνος οἱ καλούμενοι ἐγκρατεῖς...ἐμψύχων ἀποχὴν εἰσηγήσαντο Iren.*haer.*1.28.1(M.7.690B); ἀ. οἴνου καὶ κρεῶν Clem.*str.*3.6(p.220.27; M.8.1157A); τῶν εἰδωλοθύτων ἀ. Or.*Cels.*8.31(p.246.10; M.11.1561B);

τοιωνδὶ βρωμάτων ἀ. [sc. on the part of Jews] Eus.*e.th.*2.20(p.127. 14; M.24.949C); ἀ. δαιμονικοῦ σεβάσματος Euthal.Diac.*epp.cath.* (M.85.688A); characteristic of Novatianists τὴν συνεχῆ νηστείαν... τὴν ἀ. τῶν ἐμψύχων Socr.*h.e.*7.17.4(M.67.772C); of sin νηστεύειν [sc. ἡμᾶς βούλεται ὁ σωτήρ]...ἀλλ' οὐχὶ τὴν σωματικὴν...ἀλλὰ τὴν πνευματικήν, ἐν ᾗ ἐστιν ἀ. πάντων τῶν φαύλων Ptol.*ep.*ap.Epiph. *haer.*33.5(p.455.15; M.41.564D); [Tob.12:8] νηστεῖαι...ἀποχὰς κακῶν μηνύουσιν πάντων ἁπαξαπλῶς Clem.*str.*6.12(p.483.13; M.9.324B); *ib.* 2.15(p.149.17; M.8.1008A); *ib.*3.15(p.241.23; 1200A); τὸ ἐν...ἔργον, ἡ τῆς μοιχείας ἀ., παρὰ τὰς προθέσεις τῶν ἀπεχομένων οὐ ταὐτὸν ἀλλὰ διάφορον γίνεται Or.*Cels.*7.63(p.213.25; M.11.1512A); κοινὸν...τῶν ἀψύχων καὶ τῶν ἀλόγων ἡ τῶν κακῶν ἀ. id.*Ps.*1:2(p.444); ‡Ath. *Apoll.*1.2(M.26.1096C); τὸ βάπτισμα...τῶν μιαρῶν ἀπολαύσεων ἀ. Gr.Nyss.*bapt.diff.*(M.46.425D); Marc.Er.*opusc.*2.24(M.65.933C); †Jo. Jej.*poenit.*(M.88.1912A); **2.** *abstention* (ref. Gen.2:17) διαστείλασθαι τὴν ἀ., ὥστε μὴ τούτοις περιπεσεῖν, οἷς νῦν ἑαυτὸν περιέβαλες Chrys. *hom.17.4 in Gen.*(4.139D); νόμος αὐτῷ τις περὶ ἀ. ... δοθείς Thdr. Mops.*Rom.*7:8(p.127.1; M.66.809C); Proc.G.*Gen.*2:9(M.87.165D); **3.** *abstinence*, i.e. practice of asceticism, Clem.*ecl.*14(p.140.23; M. 9.704D) cit. s. νηστεία; τροφῶν ἀποχαῖς ἀσιτίαις...πολυημέροις Eus. *l.C.*17(p.255.18; M.20.1432C); Epiph.*haer.*58.4(p.362.14; M.41.1016C); πάλην διὰ τῆς τῶν αἰσθητῶν ἀ. Marc.Er.*opusc.*2.148(M.65.953B); *ib.* 2.211(964B); ἡ πάντων τῶν περιττῶν ἀ. Jo.Mosch.*prat.*171(M.87. 3040A); not an end in itself ἡ...ἐγκράτεια οὐκ ἐν ἀ. ἀλόγων βρωμάτων ἐστίν, ἀλλ' ἐν τελείᾳ ἀναχωρήσει τῶν ἰδίων θελημάτων Bas.*reg.br.* 128(2.459C; M.31.1168C); περὶ μὲν χρημάτων ὁ Χριστὸς πολλαχοῦ διέταξεν, ὥστε φεύγειν τὴν ἐντεῦθεν λύμην· περὶ δὲ ἀ. γυναικός, οὐχ οὕτως Chrys.*hom.5.2 in Tit.*(11.758E); οὔτε...ἡ βρῶσίς ἐστί τι κατὰ ἀλήθειαν οὔτε ἡ ἀ., ἀλλὰ πίστις δι' ἀγάπης τοῖς ἔργοις παρεκτεινομένη Pall.*h.Laus.*proem.(p.13.17; M.34.1003); its dangers τὴν...πρὸς ἐπίδειξιν γινομένην ἀ. τῶν βρωμάτων †Bas.*Is.*31(1.404D; M.30.180C); ἐπὶ ἀποχῇ...μεγαλοφρονοῦντας Pall.*v.Chrys.*19(p.122.25; M.47.68); **4.** *refusal, withholding* ἀ. τῆς χάριτος Cyr.H.*catech.*6.28.

***ἀπόχορδος,** *discordant*, Clem.*str.*2.20(p.180.5; M.8.1068B).

ἀπόχρησις, ἡ, *destruction, ruin*, Or.*Jo.*32.5(p.433.27; M.14.753B).

ἀποχρί-ω, *scrape off, wipe away*, hence *unseal* ∼σαντες...τὴν θύραν [sc. τοῦ μνήματος] Pall.*h.Laus.*5(p.21.9, v.l. ἀποκρούσαντες M.34.1017C); med., met. ἡ τῶν θείων γραφῶν ἀνάγνωσις...τὸ... σφοδρὸν καὶ διακαὲς τῆς ὀδύνης ∼ομένη Chrys.*poenit.*4.1(2.302C).

ἀπόχυμα, τό, *a mode of dressing the hair* οὐκ ἔξεστίν σοι τρέφειν τὰς τρίχας...ἢ ἀ. ἢ μεριστὴν τηρεῖν *Const.App.*1.3.10.

ἀπόχυσις, ἡ, *pouring forth*; hence *fullness* of the moon, ‡Ath. *azym.*(M.26.1328A).

***ἀποχωριστικός,** *expressive of separation, separative* ἀ. ... νοήμασί τε καὶ ῥήμασιν Gr.Nyss.*Eun.*12(1 p.378.4; M.45.1105A).

***ἀποψαί,** *in the evening*, Leont.N.*v.Sym.*32(M.93.1709B).

ἀποψεύδομαι, *speak falsely*, Mac.Mgn.*apocr.*3.8(p.66.2).

***ἀποψία, ἡ,** ? *inspection, visitation*, by bishops μετὰ θεοῦ καταβάντες εἰς ἀποψίαν, εἴτουν ἔρευναν τῶν ἐκείνων λόγων CLater.*act.*4 (H.3.805C).

***ἀποψυκτικός,** *cooling* ἀ. τῶν ἐν ζέσει παθῶν ἡ τοῦ θείου λόγου δύναμις Cyr.*Jo.*3.6(4.318B).

ἀπόψυξις, ἡ, **1.** *cooling*, met. θερμοὺς καὶ ζέοντας ὁρᾶσθαι τῷ πνεύματι...οὐκ εἰς ἀ. καταφερομένους διὰ κοσμικῶν ἡδονῶν Cyr.*ador.* 12(1.437B); ref. Ex.28:42 ὑποσημαίνει...τὸ λινοῦν...ὅτι τοῖς ἁγίοις πρεπωδεστάτη τῶν τῆς σαρκὸς ἡδονῶν ἡ ἀ. *ib.*11(390B); **2.** *becoming cold, fainting*; of epileptic fits, Synes.*ep.*154(M.66.1556C); ref. end of the world συνοχή τις ἔσται δεινὴ καὶ ἀ. εἰς θάνατον Cyr.*Lc.*21:25 (M.72.897D).

ἀπραγμοσύνη, ἡ, **1.** *freedom from worldly cares, quietness of life*; in gen., Gr.Naz.*ep.*49(M.37.101A) etc.; of monastic life, Chrys. *sac.*6.7(p.153.24; 1.427A); of virgins ὅρον διδοὺς [sc. ὁ Παῦλος] τῆς παρθένου καὶ τῆς οὐ παρθένου, οὐ γάμον εἶπεν...ἀλλὰ ἀ. καὶ πολυπραγμοσύνην id.*hom.19.6 in 1Cor.*(10.167E); Isid.Pel.*epp.*2.8(M.78. 464C); τὸ...παιδίον...πολλὰς ἔχον τὰς ἀρετάς, ἀφέλειαν, ταπεινοφροσύνην, ἀ. Chrys.*hom.58.3 in Mt.*(7.588A); **2.** *inexperience of business*, Gr.Naz.*ep.*14(M.37.48A).

ἄπραγος, *inactive, idle*, Pall.*v.Chrys.*19(p.122.33; M.47.69); comp., *ib.*11(p.64.4; M.47.36); *Apophth.Patr.al.*(p.245).

ἀπρακτ-έω, *be ineffective*; *be inoperative* μετὰ τὴν ἐκ νεκρῶν ἀνάστασιν...∼ήσει τῆς ἁμαρτίας τὸ κέντρον Cyr.*Lc.*24:38(M.72.948B); id.*Rom.*5:15(p.184.29; M.74.785D); id.*Is.*1.1(2.16B); wrongly of eucharist φασὶν ∼εῖν εἰς ἁγιασμὸν τὴν μυστικὴν εὐλογίαν, εἰ ἀπομείνοι λείψανον αὐτῆς εἰς ἑτέραν ἡμέραν id.*ep.Calos.*(6^2.365B).

ἄπρακτος, *idle*; neut. plur., *holiday* κελεύει ἄπρακτα γενέσθαι ἐν τῇ πόλει *V.Dan.*3(p.61.23).

***ἀπρεπόντως,** *unfittingly, improperly*, Anast.S.*hod.*proem.(M.89. 36A).

***ἀπρεπώδης,** *unbecoming*, Epiph.*haer.*76.20(p.366.8; M.42.556A).

ἄπρηκτος, = ἄπρακτος, *free from work*, of the sabbath ἅ. ... ἠώς Nonn.*par.Jo.*9:14(M.43.825C); *ib.*5:18(788B).

***Ἀπρίλιος, ὁ,** = Ἀπρίλλιος, Chrys.*nativ.*1.5(2.362B); *Chron.Pasch.* p.9(M.92.85Aff.).

***Ἀπρίλλιος, ὁ,** *April*, *M.Agap.*7.2; Epiph.*haer.*50.1(p.246.1; M. 41.885A).

ἀπροαίρετος, **1.** *without purpose* or *choice*; ref. generation of Son, *Symb.Ant.*(345)8(p.253.23; M.26.732D) cit. s. ἀνάγκη; denied of assumption of flesh by Logos ἵνα μὴ τὴν πρὸς τὴν σάρκα τοῦ λόγου σύνοδον ἀκούσιον ποιώμεθα καὶ ἀ. Max.*ep.*13(M.91.517A); **2.** *without power to choose*, denied of Christ οὐκ ἀ. ὢν οὐδὲ ἀνόρμητος...ταῖς τοιαύταις χρῆται φωναῖς [Jo.12:49 etc.] Bas.*Spir.*20(3.17D; M.32. 104B).

ἀπροαιρέτως, *involuntarily*, ref. generation of Son οὔτε γὰρ ἡ ἄμεσος αὕτη συνάφεια ἐκβάλλει τὴν βούλησιν τοῦ πατρός, ὡς κατά τινα φύσεως ἀνάγκην ἀ. τὸν υἱὸν ἐσχηκότος Gr.Nyss.*Eun.*8(2 p.181.13; M.45.773D).

***ἀπρόβλεπτος,** *improvident*, *Chron.Pasch.*p.71(M.92.217A).

***ἀπρόβλητος,** *not to be put forward*, of the inner meaning of the Law ἀφόρητα...καὶ ἀ. Cyr.*ador.*1(1.6C, prob. f.l. for ἀπόβλητα).

***ἀπρόγνωστος,** *not possessing foreknowledge* πατὴρ ἀ. καὶ ἄγνωστος Hipp.*haer.*5.26(p.126.32; M.16.3194C); *Hom.Clem.*3.38.

***ἀπρογνώστως,** *without foreknowledge*, Hipp.*haer.*10.15(p.276.20; M.16.3431B).

ἀπρόθεσμος, *not fixed beforehand, untimely*, ‡Chrys.*virg.corrupt.* (9.826D).

ἀπροϊδής, *unseen, secret*, Nonn.*par.Jo.*12:42(M.43.857B); *ib.*8:59 (824A); ἀ. Χριστοῖο...μαθητής *ib.*19:38(905C).

ἀπρόϊτος, *not going out*, *V.Dan.*2(p.58.5); Jo.Mal.*chron.*14 p.356 (M.97.532B); τὸν υἱόν...ἀ. ἐποίησεν ἐπὶ ἡμέρας ἱκανάς Thphn.*chron.* p.392(M.108.936A); neut. as subst., Ephr.3.425F = Jo.D.*virt.*(M.95. 88A).

ἀπροκατασκεύαστος *unprepared, spontaneous* ἀ. λόγος Jo.Clim. *scal.*24(M.88.981C).

***ἀπρόκοπτος,** = ἀπρόκοπος, *making no advance, not improving*, ‡Ath.*dial.Trin.*2.3(M.28.1161C).

ἀπροκρίτως, *without discussion, immediately*, Cyr.*ep.*54(p.164.19; ἀποκρίτως M.77.288C).

ἀπρονόητος, **1.** *uncared for* παροικίαν ἀ. καὶ ἐκτὸς ἐπισκόπου Socr.*h.e.*6.23.17(M.67.736A); **2.** *destitute of God's providence*; **a.** in gen. οὐδὲν ἀ., οὐδὲν ἠμελημένον παρὰ θεοῦ Bas.*hex.*7.5(1.68A; M.29. 160B); **b.** of sublunary sphere, acc. Aristotle, Tat.*orat.*2(p.3.6; M.6.808B); Athenag.*leg.*25.2(M.6.949B); exeg. Ps.35:6 τινὲς δὲ ἀκούσαντες ὅτι 'ἡ ἀλήθειά σου ἕως τῶν νεφελῶν' καὶ ἀπατηθέντες ἐντεῦθεν ἀ. τὰ ὑπὸ σελήνην ἀπεφήναντο Cyr.*Ps.*35:6(M.69.917B); **c.** of persons, Dion.Al.*fr.*(p.254.1) cit. s. ἀνεπίσκοπος; Chrys.*hom.24.5 in Gen.*(4.223D); id.*hom.16.6 in Mt.*(7.212C).

ἀπρόοδος, *inaccessible*, prob. f.l. for ἀπρόσοδος; Chrys.*pan.Laz.* (2.649A).

ἀπροόπτως, *in an unforeseen way, unexpectedly*, Bas.*hom.*21.1 (2.163D; M.31.541A); Gr.Nyss.*Eun.*7(2 p.159.26; M.45.748D); Socr. *h.e.*7.18.10(M.67.776A).

***ἀπροορίστως,** *without previous determination*, Hipp.*haer.*8.12 (p.232.10,14; M.16.3358B,C).

***ἀπροπαράσκευος,** *unprepared, unprovided for*, of Christ τὸ αὐτοσχέδιον, καὶ ἀ. πάντη τῆς ὅλης αὐτοῦ ἐνσάρκου ζωῆς Max.*schol.* *d.n.*3(M.4.237A).

***ἀπροσάντητος,** *irresistible*, Clem.*ecl.*26(p.144.20; M.9.712A).

ἀπρόσβλεπτος, *not to be gazed upon*; of the power of God, ‡Meth. *palm.*6(M.18.393C).

ἀπρόσβλητος, **1.** *unapproachable*, Cyr.*hom.pasch.*10(5^2.139C); id. *Juln.*1(6^2.24C); of the glory of God, id.*Is.*5.1(2.742C); **2.** *not to be attacked*, hence *invincible*; of skill, cleverness, id.*hom.pasch.*11 (5^2.143A); id.*Juln.*proem.(6^2.4A).

ἀπροσδεής, **1.** *without want*, of God ἀ. ... ὁ δεσπότης τῶν ἁπάντων *1Clem.*52.1; Athenag.*res.*12(p.61.23; M.6.996D); of Son πάσης προσθήκης ἀ. ἐστιν Ath.*Ar.*1.40(M.26.96A); of H. Ghost ἀ. ... τῆς ἑτέρων χάριτος Gr.Nyss.*Maced.*10(M.45.1313B); ἀ. ... τοῦ ἀγαθύνοντος id. *fid.*(M.45.141C); **2.** abs., *self-sufficient*; of God, Clem.*str.*6.16(p.501. 22; M.9.364A); Meth.*creat.*3(p.495.1; M.18.333C); of Son, Alex.Al. *ep.Alex.*12(p.27.14; M.18.565C); of Christ's teaching, Clem.*str.*1.20 (p.63.29; M.8.817A); of life before Fall, ‡Bas.*struct.hom.*2.4(1.340C; M.30.45C); neut. as subst., Clem.*paed.*1.6(p.105.27; M.8.281A); Gr.

Nyss.*v.Mos.*(M.44.333B); Procl.CP *or.laud.BMV* 6(p.105.20; M.65.688A).

ἀπρόσδεκτος, *not received* or *admitted*, of persons ἀ. ... πρὸς πᾶσαν κοινωνίαν χρήσεως βιωτικῆς Bas.*ep.*288(3.426D; M.32.1024C); ἀ. ἔστω ταῖς ἀδελφότησιν id.*reg.fus.*36(2.381C; M.31.1009A); ἀ. ὤν, οὐκ εἰσέρχεται εἰς τὴν τῶν οὐρανῶν βασιλείαν Ammon.*Ac.*10:35(M.85.1537D).

***ἀπροσδεῶς**, *with complete self-sufficiency, without need of anything* δυναμένης μὲν ἑκάστης θείας ὑποστάσεως ἀ. πάντα ποιῆσαι τελείως Didym.*Trin.*2.1(M.39.452A).

ἀπροσδιορίστως, *without specification*; *without qualification* φαγεῖν ἐκ τῶν δειχθέντων ὁ...ἀπόστολος ἀ. κελευόμενος ‡Just.*qu.et resp.*89(M.6.1332A); Ammon.*Ac.*8:17(M.85.1532A); Hesych.H.*qu.ev.*2(M.93.1396A); ἀ. τοῦ 'θεοτόκος', ὡς τοῦ 'θεὸς' ὀνόματος πολλαχῶς λεγομένου Leont.H.*Nest.*4.1(M.86.1652A).

ἀπροσεκτ-έω, *be heedless, careless* ταῖς ~ούσαις ψυχαῖς Or.*sel.in Ps.*4:6(p.238.8; M.12.1160A); id.*Jo.*20.39(p.382.21; M.14.668C); id. *ser.63 in Mt.*(p.148.4; M.17.304C).

ἀπρόσεκτος, *unconsidered, carelessly ordered* τράπεζα ἀ. μήτηρ παρρησίας Jo.Clim.*scal.*9(M.88.841B); neut. as subst., *heedlessness, carelessness* αὐτὸ τὸ ἀ. ἁμαρτία ἐστίν, ἢ...ἁμαρτίας ἀρχή ‡Cyr.*Trin.*15(6^{3}.21D; M.77.1152D).

***ἀπροσεξέω**, *be careless*, ‡Nil.*perist.*10.2(M.79.889A).

***ἀπροσεχής**, *careless*, Ephr.3.360B.

***ἀπροσέχως**, *carelessly*, Isid.Pel.*epp.*1.79(M.78.237A).

ἀπρόσηκος, *unbecoming*, Didym.*Trin.*2.6(M.39.545B); *ib.*2.8(604A).

ἀπρόσιτος, **A.** *unapproachable, inaccessible*; **1.** of God; **a.** in gen. ὁ θεὸς...ἀ. τοῖς γενητοῖς Ath.*Ar.*1.63(M.26.144B); Bas.*Eun.*2.19(1.255B; M.29.613B); τῆς μιᾶς καὶ ἀ. θεότητος Gr.Naz.*ep.*185(M.37.305A); σὲ τὸν ὄντα θεὸν ἀγέννητον ἕνα, ἀ. μόνον *Const.App.*7.47.2; **b.** as light (cf. 1Tim.6:16) τὸ ἀ. ... τῆς θεότητος φῶς †Hipp.*theoph.*3(p.258.31; M.10.853C); Eus.*e.th.*1.20(p.82.1; M.24.868A); Dion.Ar.*d.n.*4.11(M.3.708D) cit. s. ἀνόμματος; v. φῶς; **2.** of divine attitibutes ἀ. ἁγιότητι Clem.*str.*6.7(p.461.2; M.9.280B); τὸ ἀ. τῆς θείας φύσεως κάλλος Gr.Nyss.*hom.1 in Cant.*(M.44.773D); τὸ ἀ. τε καὶ ἀχώρητον λογισμοῖς ἀνθρωπίνοις τῆς θείας δυνάμεως *ib.*(781C); **3.** of Son εἶναι μὲν ἐν τῷ πληρώματι τῆς θεότητος ἴσα θεῷ ἀ. καὶ ἀπροσπέλαστον Gr.Nyss.*Apoll.*20(M.45.1164C); **4.** of H. Ghost as φῶς νοητόν, ἀ. τῇ φύσει Bas.*Spir.*22(3.19D; M.32.108C); **5.** ref. knowledge of God Δαβὶδ...φανερῶς ὁμολογεῖ τῆς γνώσεως τὸ ἀ. Bas.*Eun.*1.12(1.224D; M.29.540B); **6.** ref. ministry to God τὸ γὰρ διακονῆσαί σοι μέγα καὶ φοβερὸν καὶ ταῖς ἐπουρανίοις δυνάμεσιν ἀ. *Lit.Jac.*(p.178.28); cf. *Lit.Bas.*(p.318.9).

B. *not approaching* τὸ παρερχόμενον οὔτε ἀ. ἐστιν οὔτε καταμένον ‡Dion.Al.*fr.in Lc.22:42*(p.232.9; M.10.1597B).

***ἀπροσκλινής**, *impartial* ἀ. ... τὸ θεῖον Cyr.*Am.*82(3.348A; Aubert ἀποκλινές); Sophr.H.*ep.syn.*(M.87.3148C); Jo.VI CP *ep.*(M.96.1425A); neut. as subst., *impartiality* τὸ τῆς ἀνωτάτω φύσεως...ἀ. Cyr.*ador.*16(1.565D).

***ἀπροσκλινῶς**, *without partiality* or *attachment, unswervingly, firmly* χρῆσθαι...αὐτοῖς [sc. God's gifts], ὡς ἄρχοντας, ἀ. Clem.*paed.*2.1(p.160.2; M.8.393A); κατ' ἴχνος ἰόντες ἀ. τῆς τῶν πατέρων ὁμολογίας Cyr.*ep.*55(p.58.22; 5^{2}.187A); *ib.*69(p.16.23; 198B).

***ἀπρόσκλιτος**, *impartial*; neut. as subst., *impartiality*, Ast.Am. *hom.*9(M.40.304B).

***ἀπροσκλίτως**, *impartially*, Bas.*reg.fus.*35.3(2.381A; M.31.1008B).

***ἀπρόσκολλος**, *disconnected, incoherent*, Gr.Nyss.*Eun.*2(2 p.377.18; M.45.557D); neut. as subst., *incoherency*, id.*Apoll.*42(M.45.1220C).

***ἀπροσκόμιστος**, *not to be offered, unfit to be offered*, Cyr.*ador.*10(1.359D).

ἀπρόσκοπος, **1.** *free from stumbling, void of offence* ὁ...πατὴρ... ἀ. ὑμῶν διατηρήσειε τὴν ζωήν Bas.*hex.*2.8(1.21E; M.29.52B); Gr.Naz.*or.*24.19(M.35.1193B); Isid.Pel.*epp.*1.145(M.78.280C); ‡Sophr.H.*v.m.Cyr.et Jo.*4(M.87.3680A); neut. as subst., *freedom from offence* χρὴ τὸ ἀ. ... φυλάττειν Bas.*reg.br.*72(2.440E; M.31.1133B); **2.** *not giving offence* ἀ. τοῖς πολίταις Clem.*str.*3.4(p.210.15; M.8.1136C); Hipp.*antichr.*67(p.46.21; M.10.788A); Max.*ambig.*(M.91.1373D).

ἀπρόσκοπτος, = foreg., *Apoc.Paul.*8(p.38); πῶς...πρὸς τὸν...δεσπότην ἔσῃ καταπειθὴς καὶ ἀ; Gr.Nyss.*or.dom.*5(M.44.1189D; ἀπρόσκοπος p.112.13).

ἀπροσκόπτως, *without stumbling*, Herm.*mand.*6.1.4; Mac.Aeg.*hom.*4.1(M.34.472D); Marc.Er.*opusc.*5.12(M.65.1048C).

ἀπροσκόπως, *without offence* ἀμέμπτως καὶ ἀ. ἐν τῇ ἐπισκοπῇ διατελείτω Serap.*euch.*28.2; Gr.Nyss.*Eun.*1(1 p.213.29; M.45.461C); †Bas.*Is.*6(1.381E; M.30.128A).

ἀπρόσκρουστος, *giving no offence*; neut. as subst., *inoffensiveness*, Bas.*reg.fus.*25.2(2.370C; M.31.985A).

***ἀπροσκρούστως**, *without giving offence, tactfully*, Gr.Nyss.*deit.*(M.46.572A).

***ἀπροσκύνητος**, *not to be worshipped*, Christol., ref. unity of Person οὐ δύο φύσεις τὸν ἕνα υἱόν, μίαν προσκυνητὴν καὶ μίαν ἀ. Apoll.*ep.Jov.*(p.251.1; M.28.29A); οὐκ ἀ. τὴν σάρκα λέγοντες Jo.D.*f.o.*3.8(M.94.1013C); ἡ σὰρξ αὐτοῦ, κατὰ μὲν τὴν ἑαυτῆς φύσιν ἀ. ἐστιν, ὡς κτιστή *ib.*4.3(1105A); in gen. ἀ. οὔσης τῆς εἰκονικῆς οὐσίας Thdr.Stud.*antirr.*3.3.2(M.99.421A).

***ἀπροσληπτικῶς**, *with nothing received in addition*, Epiph.*haer.*76.32(M.42.581D; conj. προσληπτικῶς p.382.1).

ἀπρόσληπτος, *not assumed*, ref. Apollinarius' denial of Christ's human rational soul τὸ γὰρ ἀ. ἀθεράπευτον Gr.Naz.*ep.*101(M.37.181C).

***ἀπροσμάχητος**, = ἀπρόσμαχος, *irresistible*; of BMV, Andr.Cr.*or.*14(M.97.1108B) citing †Serg.*acath.*1(p.140.4; M.92.1335A).

ἀπρόσοδος, *unable to approach, without access to*; c. genit., *cat. Apoc.*16:15(p.420.9).

***ἀπρόσοχος**, = ἀπροσεχής, Isid.Pel.*epp.*1.177(M.78.297C).

***ἀπροσπάθεια**, ἡ, *freedom from affection* or *desires* ἐκ τῆς ἀ. ... ἔρχεται εἰς τὴν ἀπάθειαν Dor.*doct.*1.14(M.88.1636D); ἀκτήμων ἐργάτης, ἀπροσπαθείας υἱός Jo.Clim.*scal.*17(M.88.928C).

ἀπροσπαθής, *unmoved by emotion, free from affection* or *desire*, of the soul ἀ. ... τῶν περὶ τὰς σωματικὰς ἡδονὰς...πλημμελημάτων Athenag.*res.*18(p.70.31; M.6.1009D); of marriage, exeg. 1Cor.7:29, Clem.*str.*7.11(p.46.7; M.9.488C) cit. s. ἀπερίσπαστος; ἡ...ἀ. καὶ ὑγιὴς περὶ αὐτὰ [sc. worldly goods] διάθεσις Bas.*reg.br.*92(2.447E; M.31.1145C); ὁ...Σεραπίων ὁ ἀ. Pall.*h.Laus.*85(M.34.1188A); neut. as subst., Clem.*paed.*2.7(p.190.29; M.8.460A); Bas.*reg.fus.*8.1(2.348E; M.31.936C) cit. s. ἀποταγή.

***ἀπροσπαθῶς**, *without being moved by emotion*, ref. Mc.10:29 τὸ ἀ. βιοῦν Clem.*str.*4.4(p.255.25; M.8.1229A); of an ascetic, Bas.*hom. in Ps.*14:1(1.353A; M.29.253A); Max.*opusc.*(M.91.224B).

***ἀπροσπάσχω**, *feel no strong affection*, Thdr.Stud.*epp.*2.132(M.99.1425B).

ἀπρόσπλοκος, *not to be interwoven*; hence *not admitting union*, exeg. Jo.2:20 τὸν [sc. ἀριθμόν] τῶν τεσσαράκοντα, ὅ τετράς ἐστι...ἡ ἀ. Heracleon ap.Or.*Jo.*10.38(22; p.214.35; M.14.380B).

***ἀπροσποίητος**, *unfeigned*, Jo.VI CP *ep.*(M.96.1417A).

ἀπροσποιήτως, *without pretence, unfeignedly*, Gr.Nyss.*castig.*(M.46.312B); ‡Pall.*h.mon.*3.2(p.27.18; M.34.1131C).

***ἀπροσπόριστος**, *not procured*, Ath.Scholast.*coll.*9.10(p.104).

***ἀπροστασία**, ἡ, *lack of a leader* or *guardian*; ref. a church without a bishop, Bas.*ep.*102(3.197E; M.32.508C).

ἀπροστάτευτος, *without a champion* or *protector, unprotected*; of Christ, Hipp.*theoph.*4(p.259.11; M.10.856A); of BMV ὡς ἀ. αὐτὴν... τῷ μαθητῇ παρατίθεται Chrys.*hom.5.3 in Mt.*(7.77B); of a church without a bishop, CAnt.(445)*act.*(p.80.14; H.2.593B); neut. as subst., *defencelessness*, Chrys.*hom.44.4 in 1Cor.*(10.413D).

***ἀπροστάτης (ἀπρόστατος)**, = foreg. ὡς ἐν ἀνόμῳ καὶ ἀ. χώρῳ Eus.*v.C.*3.55(p.103.9; M.20.1121A); id.*l.C.*8(p.217.7, v.l. ἀποστάτῃ; M.20.1360D).

***ἀπροστρόπαιος**, ? *guiltless* ἐσθῆτ' ἀ. ἐγχλαινούμενος· μόνοις δ' ἀ. οἷς πέλει χλιδή ‡Gr.Naz.*Chr.pat.*1394–5(M.38.247A; Teub.p.106 ἐσθῆτα προστρόπαιον...μόνοις δ' ἀποτρόπαιον, οἷς πέμφιξ χλιδή).

***ἀπροσχάριστος**, *impartial*, *Lit.*ap.*Const.App.*8.11.6.

***ἀπρόσχορδος**, *out of tune*, Gr.Nyss.*Eun.*4(2 p.93.27; M.45.669C).

***ἀπρόσχυτος**, *not to be poured upon*, Gr.Nyss.*or.catech.*8(M.45.36A; p.45.1 ἀπρόχυτος).

***ἀπροσωπία**, ἡ, *absence of personal existence*, hence *non-existence*, Nil.*epp.*2.42(M.79.216C).

ἀπροσωπόληπτος (-λημπτος), **A.** *without respect of persons*; **a.** of God; ref. Jews and Gentiles (cf. Ac.10:34), Clem.*str.*6.6(p.455.10; M.9.269A); in gen. ἀ. ἐστιν, ἀποδιδοὺς ἑκάστῳ τῷ ὑπακούοντι ἀγαθά *T.Job* 4(p.106.12); ref. Col.3:11, Petr.I Al.*ep.can.*7(M.18.480B); *Lit.*ap.*Const.App.*8.11.5; ref. Mt.5:45 and 1Tim.2:4, Eus.Al.*serm.*5(M.86.341D); as judge, *A.Phil.*132(p.63.5); Cyr.*Am.*88(3.342D); **b.** of persons προχειρίσασθε...ἐπισκόπους...ἀ. *Const. App.*7.31.1; Procl.CP *ep.*(p.86.9; M.65.884A); Jo.Not.*v.Eus.*1(M.86.297B); **c.** of Inc. τῆς πρὸς ἕκαστον ἀγάπης ἀ. κατὰ νόμον Euthal. Diac.*epp.cath.*(M.85.677B); neut. as subst., *impartiality*; of God, Clem.*str.*6.8(p.463.31; M.9.285B); τὸ ἑαυτοῦ εὔσπλαγχνον καὶ ἀ. ἐνδείκνυσι διὰ πάντων τῶν ἁγίων ὁ λόγος Hipp.*antichr.*3(p.6.3; M.10.729C).

B. *not to be seen face to face*; of God, Cyr.*Is.*5.1(2.742B).

ἀπροσωπολήπτως (-λήμπτως), *without respect of persons, impartially* ἀ. ... πάντα ἐποιεῖτε *1Clem.*1.3; ὁ κύριος ἀ. κρινεῖ τὸν κόσμον *Barn.*4.12; ἀ. ἑκάστῃ ἀδελφῇ τὸ οἰκεῖον ἔργον...οἰκονομοῦσα Bas.*reg.br.*153(2.466D; M.31.1184A).

***ἀπροσωποληψία, ἡ,** *impartiality*, Esaias *or.*21.6(p.126).

ἀπρόσωπος, 1. *shamefaced*, of sinner at Judgement ἀπαρρησίαστος καὶ κατηφὴς καὶ ἀ. Anast.S.*Ps.6*(M.89.1080B); *shameful, causing shame*, Nil.*epp.*3.284(M.79.524D); **2.** of a play, *without characters* ἀ. τὸ τῆς ἀπολογίας ὑπεισέρχεται δρᾶμα Bas.*Eun.*1.2 (1.209C; M.29.504B); **3.** *impersonal*; **a.** *without reference to a person, anonymous*, ref. Mt.26:21 ἀ. τὴν πρόρρησιν ἐποιήσατο Chrys. *prod.Jud.*3(2.721C); id.*hom.5.2 in 1Tim.*(11.576B); ἀ. τὴν κατηγορίαν εἰσήνεγκεν Thdt.*1Tim.*6:10(3.670); **b.** *impersonal, without* πρόσωπον; of human nature of Christ, in argument ref. unity of Person ὅταν μὲν γὰρ τὰς φύσεις διακρίνωμεν, τελείαν τὴν φύσιν τοῦ ...λόγου φαμέν, καὶ τέλειον τὸ πρόσωπον· οὐδὲ γὰρ ἀ. ἔστιν ὑπόστασιν εἰπεῖν· τελείαν δὲ καὶ τὴν τοῦ ἀνθρώπου φύσιν, καὶ τὸ πρόσωπον. ὁμοίως ὅταν...ἐπὶ τὴν συνάφειαν ἀπίδωμεν, ἓν πρόσωπόν φαμεν...ὅταν δὲ πρὸς τὴν ἕνωσιν ἀποβλέψωμεν, τότε ἓν εἶναι τὸ πρόσωπον ἄμφω τὰς φύσεις κηρύττομεν Thdr.Mops.*fr.inc.*8(p.299.21; M.66.981B); ἄνθρωπος ἄρα γέγονεν τῇ τῆς φύσεως τῆς ἀνθρωπίνης προσλήψει, εἰ καὶ ἀπροσώπῳ, ἡ αὐτὴ ὑπόστασις τοῦ λόγου Leont.H.*Nest.*2.35(M. 86.1593B); εἰ δὲ τὸ ἐν δύο ζωαῖς θεωρούμενον, ζῷόν ἐστι, καὶ τὸ δύο οὐσιῶν μετειληφός, οὐσιωμένον ἐστί τι, οὐ μὴν ἡ οὐσία, εἴτουν φύσις, ἀ. id.*monoph.*(M.86.1857B); ἤκουσά τινος αὐτῶν...οἰομένου διαλέγεσθαι ὅτι οὐκ ἔστι φύσις ἀ., ἀλλὰ παρέπεται τῇ φύσει καὶ πρόσωπον. ...εἰ γὰρ οὐκ ἔστι φύσις ἀ. ... φασὶ δὲ ἐκ δύο φύσεων τὴν...ἕνωσιν ἐν Χριστῷ γεγονέναι, ἄρα...ἀνέῳκται λοιπὸν τοῖς βλασφημοῦσι παρρησία δύο πρόσωπα λέγειν ἐν Χριστῷ, ὅπερ μανίας ἀνάμεστον Eulog.*fr. dogm.*(M.86.2948D); Eust.Mon.*ep.*(M.86.921A); πῶς λοιπὸν οὐ παύεσθε τιτθυρίζοντες μάτην, καὶ λέγοντες, οὐκ ἔστι φύσις ἀ., ἀλλὰ ταὐτόν ἐστι φύσις καὶ πρόσωπον; ἐκ ποίου τῶν πατέρων τοῦτο παρέλαβες, δεῖξον Anast.S.*hod.*9(M.89.148A); εἰ γὰρ καὶ μή ἐστι φύσις ἀνυπόστατος, ἢ οὐσία ἀ. ἐν ὑποστάσεσι γὰρ καὶ προσώποις ἥ τε οὐσία καὶ ἡ φύσις θεωρεῖται· ἀλλ' οὐκ ἀνάγκη τὰς ἀλλήλαις ἑνωθείσας φύσεις καθ' ὑπόστασιν, ἑκάστην ἰδίαν κεκτῆσθαι ὑπόστασιν Jo. D.*f.o.*3.9(M.94.1017A); id.*nat.*5(M.95.120A); id.*Jacob.*11(M.94.1441A); id.*fid.Nest.*9(p.563); *ib.*32(p.575).

ἀπροσώπως, *impersonally, anonymously*, ref. Mt.5:21 (ἐρρέθη τοῖς ἀρχαίοις), ὁ καὶ ἐκεῖνα δούς, αὐτός ἐστιν· ἀλλὰ τέως ἀ. αὐτὰ τίθησιν Chrys.*hom.16.5 in Mt.*(7.210C); id.*hom.28.2 in Jo.*(8.218A); *ib.53.2*(312B).

ἀπροφύλακτος, *incautious, unconsidered* ἐρώτησις ἀ. Const.ap. Eus.*v.C.*2.70(p.69.16; M.20.1044A).

ἀπροφυλάκτως, *without forethought, heedlessly* περὶ τοῦ μὴ ἀ. φθέγγεσθαι τοῖς ἁμαρτήσασι ‡Ath.*synops.*(M.28.380D).

***ἀπρόχυτος,** *unable to be poured out*, Gr.Nyss.*or.catech.*8(p.45.1, v.l. ἀπροσχυτον M.45.36A).

ἄπτιστος, *not pounded*, Gr.Naz.*carm.*1.2.10.691(M.37.730A).

ἀπτοεπής, *reckless in speech* ἀ. ... λαὸς Ἰουδαίων Nonn.*par.Jo.* 8:13(v.l. ἀπτοεπής M.43.813B).

***ἀπτοησία, ἡ,** *fearlessness* τοῦ χαρίσματος τῆς ἀ. Nil.*epp.*1.186 (M.79.153A); *ib.*2.204(308B); Pall.*ep.Laus.*(p.7.12; M.34.1001).

***ἀπτοητί,** = ἀπτοήτως, *fearlessly*, Bas.*renunt.*7(2.208D; M.31. 641A).

***ἀπτολίεθρος,** *cityless*, Gr.Naz.*carm.*2.1.43.11(M.37.1347A).

ἁπτός, = ἁπτικός, *of touch* τὴν ἁ. ... δύναμιν Thdt.*provid.*4(4.531).

[*]**ἀπτρήν, τό,** = ἄπτριον, *wick*, Gr.Mag.*dial.*(tr.Zach.)1.5(M.*PL.* 77.178C), s.v.l.

ἅπτ-ω, med.; **A.** *touch, affect*; **1.** Christol. οὐδὲ ~εται τοῦ κυρίου ἀπαθοῦς ἀνάρχως γενομένου φθόνος,...ἄλλος δὲ ὁ φθονῶν [sc. διάβολος], οὗ καὶ πάθος ἥψατο...ἄγνοια γὰρ οὐχ ~εται τοῦ υἱοῦ Clem.*str.*7.2 (p.7.4ff.; M.9.409C–412A); ἔπρεπε δὲ τὸν κύριον...ἀνθρωπίνην σάρκα... μετὰ τῶν ἰδίων παθῶν αὐτῆς ὅλην ἐνδύσασθαι...εἰ καὶ μὴ ἥπτετο κατὰ τὴν θεότητα αὐτοῦ Ath.*Ar.*3.32(M.26.392B); οὐχ ~εται τροπὴ τῆς τοῦ θεοῦ φύσεως Jo.D.*f.o.*1.8(M.94.812C); **2.** of men as no longer affected by consequences of original sin τοῦ λόγου γενομένου ἀνθρώπου, καὶ ἰδιοποιουμένου τὰ τῆς σαρκός, οὐκέτι ταῦτα τοῦ σώματος ~εται Ath.*Ar.*3.33(M.26.393B); *ib.*3.58(445A).

B. *assume, embrace*, ref. Inc. θελήσουσι δὲ λέγειν, ὅτι ἔδει τὸν θεὸν...νεύματι μόνῳ ποιῆσαι καὶ μὴ σώματος ἅψασθαι τὸν τούτου λόγον Ath.*inc.*44.1(M.25.173B); τί ἐπαισχύνονται τῇ ὁμολογίᾳ τοῦ θεὸν ἀνθρωπίνης ἅψασθαι φύσεως; Gr.Nyss.*or.catech.*15(p.66.7; M.45.49A); *ib.*16(p.68.6; 49C) cit. s. πάθος; *ib.*32(p.116.7; 80B).

C. *attain to*, ref. spiritual blessings οἱ θέλοντες...ἅψασθαί μου τῆς βασιλείας ὀφείλουσιν θλιβέντες...λαβεῖν με *Agraph.*68(p.89)ap.*Barn.* 7.11; τὸν οὔπω...ἡμμένον τοῦ πράγματος [sc. ἱερωσύνης] Synes.*ep.*72 (M.66.1436B); doctrine οὐδὲ τῶν συμβόλων ~εσθαι θεμιτὸν Dion.Ar. *e.h.*1.5(M.3.377A); τάχα...οἱ πρότεροι [sc. Israelites] ἥψαντο μὲν τῆς τριάδος, οὐ μὴν καθαρῶς Proc.G.*Jos.*1:12(M.87.997A).

D. *partake of* sacraments τῆς εὐχαριστίας ~ονται CNic.(325)*can.* 18; τῆς ἱερᾶς ~εσθαι θυσίας Chrys.*bapt.*4(2.373E); ~ονται τῶν ἱερῶν μυστηρίων *ib.*(374A); Synes.*ep.*57(M.66.1389B).

E. *touch*; **1.** lit., ref. ordination αἱ τῶν...ἀποστόλων χεῖρες τῆς ἱερᾶς ἥψαντο κεφαλῆς Chrys.*pan.Ign.*2(2.594A); **2.** met. τὴν ἐκκλησίαν...τὴν ~ομένην οὐρανῶν Clem.*paed.*1.9(p.139.22; M.8.352A); **3.** spiritually; ref. Lc.8:45f., Or.*dial.*19(p.160.5ff.) cit. s. ἀφή; ἀφὴ τῆς ψυχῆς, ἡ ~ομένη τοῦ λόγου Gr.Nyss.*hom.1 in Cant.*(M.44.780D); **4.** exeg. Jo.20:17 'μή μου ἅπτου.' ἐβούλετο γὰρ τὸν ~όμενον αὐτοῦ ὁλοτελοῦς ἅψασθαι, ἵνα ἁψάμενος ὁλοτελοῦς ὠφεληθῇ ἀπὸ τοῦ σώματος τὸ σῶμα, ἀπὸ τῆς ψυχῆς τὴν ψυχήν, τὸ πνεῦμα ἀπὸ τοῦ πνεύματος Or. *dial.*8(p.138.18f.); τίνος δὲ ἕνεκεν εἶπε, 'μή μου ~ου';...δοκεῖ μοι βούλεσθαι αὐτὴν ἔτι συνεῖναι αὐτῷ, ὥσπερ τότε, καὶ ἀπὸ τῆς χαρᾶς μηδὲν ἐννοῆσαι μέγα, εἰ καὶ πολλῷ βελτίων ἐγεγόνει κατὰ σάρκα. ταύτης γοῦν ἀπάγων αὐτὴν τῆς ἐννοίας, καὶ τοῦ μετὰ πολλῆς αὐτῷ ἀδείας διαλέγεσθαι...ἀνάγει αὐτῆς τὴν διάνοιαν Chrys.*hom.86.1–2 in Jo.* (8.514Dff.).

F. *be concerned with* ὁ λόγος...μὴ ~όμενος τοῦ σώματος τῆς ὥρας Meth.*symp.*7.1(p.72.18; M.18.125C); τοῦτο...τῆς κατὰ σάρκα οἰκονομίας ~εται Ath.*Ar.*2.75(M.26.305B); τὸ...προαιρέσεως ~όμενον Gr.Nyss.*or.catech.*16(p.67.7; M.45.49B).

G. *tamper with*; *take* μηδὲ τοῦ ἀλλοτρίου ἅψησθε Herm.*sim.*1.11.

***ἀπτωσία, ἡ,** *freedom from falling*; met., into sin, Max.*qu. Thal.*54(M.90.520D).

***ἄπτωσις:** δι' ἀπτώσεως error for διὰ πτώσεως Jo.D.*schol.*30 in Jo.Clim.*scal.*27(M.88.1125A).

ἄπτωτος, 1. *free from stumbling*; hence *impeccable* ὁ γνωστικὸς μηδὲ ἀποπεσεῖν τῆς ἀρετῆς αἰτήσεται, συνεργῶν πρὸς τὸ ἄπτωτος διαγενέσθαι Clem.*str.*7.7(p.35.1; M.9.465C); of original state of man ἦν ἡμῶν καὶ πρόσθεν ἄ. ἡ σκηνή Meth.*symp.*9.2(p.116.11; M.18.181A); *uninterrupted, steady* ἵνα ἡ τῶν ἀνθρώπων προκοπὴ ἄ. διὰ τὸν συνόντα λόγον διαμείνῃ Ath.*Ar.*3.53(M.26.436A); *undisturbed*; of peace in future life, *Hom.Clem.*3.62; **2.** *not liable to fall*; hence *stable, reliable* οὐδὲν ὃ ἄ. καὶ ἀχείρωτον, πλὴν μόνης τῆς θείας τριάδος ‡Caes. Naz.*dial.*164(M.38.1180); of Father πάσης θεότητος ἐπὶ τὸν πατέρα ἀναφερομένης διὰ τὸ ἄ. τῆς μονάδος Epiph.*haer.*76.52(p.406.27; M.42. 625B); of deity of Christ ἡ θεότης αὐτοῦ ἀκοίμητος, ἄ., ἀκράτητος *ib.*64.67(p.511.16; M.41.1188B); of the gospel, Gr.Naz.*or.*8.12(M.35. 804A); of Christians ἵνα ἀκλινεῖς ὄντες ἄ. διὰ πίστεως τῆς εἰς τὸν σωτῆρα μείνωμεν ‡Pion.*v.Polyc.*31; of body after resurrection ἔστ' ἂν ἀνακαινοποιηθεῖσαν ἡμῖν ἄ. ἀναλάβωμεν οἰκίαν Meth.*res.*2.15 (p.363.12; M.18.312B).

***ἀπτώχευτος,** *knowing no poverty, without poverty*; *not impoverished*, of Christ ὁ πτωχεύσας, ἐν τοῖς ἰδίοις αὐτοῦ ἀ., δι' ἡμᾶς ‡Meth.*palm.*5(M.18.392C).

***ἀπτωχεύτως,** *without poverty*; *without impoverishment*, ‡Chrys. *palm.*1.2(8².233E), cf. ἀπτώχευτος.

***ἀπύθμαντος,** *bottomless*, Jo.Clim.*scal.*6(M.88.797B).

ἄπυρος, *fireless* ὁλοκάρπωμα...ὑπὲρ ἡμῶν ἄ. θῦμα ὁ Χριστός Clem. *str.*5.11(p.373.12, v.l. ἄπορον M.9.108A); ἀ. καὶ ἀπνεύστοισι λοετροῖς Nonn.*par.Jo.*1:33(M.43.756B); abs., *uncooked food* ἐσθίουσιν ἄ. Pall.*h.Laus.*18(p.48.4; M.34.1051A).

***ἀπύρσευτος,** *not emitted by fire*, Paul.Sil.*Soph.*750(M.86.2148A).

***ἀπφώ,** v. ἀφφώ.

***ἀπῳδικός,** *out of tune*, Hipp.*haer.*6.24(p.151.14; M.16.3230C).

ἀπωθέω, *drive away, expel*, from the body οὐδὲν τῶν παρὰ φύσιν ...κἂν ἀπωσθῇ ποτε φαρμάκοις Athenag.*res.*6(p.55.4; M.6.985B); *excrete*, Gr.Nyss.*or.catech.*37(p.37.47; M.45.93D); from the Church ἤδη γέ τοι πλείους τούτων [sc. Gnostics] ἀπεώσθησαν Eus.*h.e.*2.1.12 (M.20.137C); ἵνα οἱ τῶν Ἀρειανῶν σπουδασταὶ...δικαστῶν σχήματι τοὺς ἐχθροὺς τῆς ἀσεβείας ἀπώσωνται CAlex.*ep.*ap.Ath.*apol.sec.*17 (p.99.39; M.25.276B); *Const.App.*2.42.1.

ἀπώλεια, ἡ, A. theol.; **1.** *perdition* ἠλέησεν ἡμᾶς θεασάμενος ἐν ἡμῖν πολλὴν πλάνην καὶ ἀ. *2Clem.*1.7; ὁ θάνατος ἀ. ἔχει αἰώνιον Herm.*sim.*2.4; brought about by oneself τῶν ἀπολλυμένων σπουδαζόντων ὑπὲρ τῆς ἑαυτῶν ἀ. Chrys.*hom.55.3 in Jo.*(8.325B); its cause ἀρχὴ ἀπωλείας ἀποταξία *Hom.Clem.*3.69; caused to others τῆς ἑτέρων ἀ., οὓς ἀπόλλυμεν Chrys.*hom.42.5 in Jo.*(254B); dist. from bodily death ἀ. οὔ φησι τὴν τοῦ θανάτου, ἀλλ' ἐκείνην τὴν αἰώνιον *ib.83.1*(490D); of Manicheism μακρὰν φεύγειν τήνδε τῆς θρησκείας ἀ. Didym.*Trin.*3.42(M.39.989C); of heresies in gen. τὸν ἴδιον ἰὸν τῆς ἀ. ἐπισπείραντες Ath.*Ar.*1.1(M.26.13A); **2.** equivalent to *Abaddon* ὑμῖν τοῖς τέκνοις τῆς γεέννης καὶ τῆς ἀ. *A.Thom.*A 74(p.189.10); ἑκὼν ἑαυτὸν ἐπὶ βάραθρα τῆς ἀ. φέρων Chrys.*hom.48.3 in Jo.*(8.287B); *ib.* 79.4(470E).

B. *depravity* ὑπερνηχόμενον αὐτοῦ τῆς ἀ. τῷ βάθει *M.Thdot.1* 5 (p.64.2); Chrys.*hom.4.1 in Rom.*(9.455B).

***ἄπωπτος,** v. ἄποπτος.

***ἀπωσιωμένως,** v. *ἀφωσιωμένως.

ἀπωσμός, ὁ, *driving away, expulsion,* Or.*fr.20 in Lam.*1:7(p.244. 8; M.13.617C); met., *rejection, reprobation* ἀποδοκιμασίᾳ καὶ ἀ. Chrys.*fr.in Jer.*14:19(M.64.900C).

***ἀπωστέος,** *to be thrust away, rejected,* Clem.*q.d.s.*15(p.169.27; M.9.620B).

ἀπωστικός, *driving away, repelling* Max.*ep.*4(M.91.417B).

ἄραβδος, *without staff,* of apostles ἀχάλκῳ, καὶ ἀ., καὶ μονοχίτωνι Gr.Naz.*or.*45.19(M.36.649B); id.*carm.*2.1.12.201(M.37.1180A); Max. *ambig.*(M.91.1368A).

[*]**ἀραβικός,** v. ἀρραβικός.

ἀραβών, ὁ, v. ἀρραβών.

ἀραδιούργητος, *not tampered with, inviolate;* of Easter observance, Polycr.ap.Eus.*h.e.*5.24.2(M.20.493B); of tradition and doctrine, Marc.Diac.*v.Porph.*1; ‡Nil.*perist.*9.2(M.79.865A); of a fundamental principle, Max.*ambig.*(M.91.1341D).

ἀραιῶς, of space, *here and there,* Call.*v.Hyp.*(p.8).

ἄραξ, ὁ, the *chick-pea,* Clem.*str.*1.7(p.24.23; M.8.732C); ἕνα αὔλακα σίτου...καὶ ἕτερον ἄρακος *V.Pach.Φ* 107(p.70.38).

ἀραρότως, 1. *inevitably, necessarily* τῷ θεῷ ἔγνωσται ἀ., τὸ μὴ ἀ. τόνδε τινὰ τὸν ἄνθρωπον καὶ βεβαίως βούλεσθαι τὰ κρείττονα Or.*or.*6 (p.314.7f.; M.11.437B); πάντα ὅσα βεβούλευμαι...ἀ. γενήσεται Eus. *Is.*46:8ff.(M.24.421C); τῷ μὲν ἀ., τῷ δὲ ἀμφίβολον προμηνυθῆναι τὸν θάνατον Gr.Nyss.*fat.*(M.45.164C); **2.** *definitely, certainly, without doubt,* Epiph.*haer.*76.16(p.362.16; M.42.548D); ἀ. εἰπεῖν οὐκ ἂν δύναιτό τις Cyr.*Is.*1.6(2.164E); id.*Rom.*7:15(p.204.2; M.74.809B) al.; **3.** *fixedly, unshakeably;* of trust and belief, †Bas.*bapt.*2.4.1(2.656A; M.31.1588B); Cyr.*Jo.*4.4(4.394E); Sophr.H.*ep.syn.*(M.87.3153A); of God ἀ. ὑπεριδρῦσθαι Dion.Ar.*d.n.*9.8(M.3.916B); of the divine illumination μένει...ἔνδον ἑαυτῆς ἀ. id.*c.h.*1.2(M.3.121B); **4.** *fitly, properly* οὐκ ἀ. ... ἐπὶ τῇ αἱρέσει...ἐπιμέμφεται; Didym.*Trin.*2.11 (M.39.661B); *ib.*2.13(689C); Thdt.*Am.*4:3(2.1425).

ἀράσσ-ω, *rattle,* of one whose teeth chatter from fear οὐκ ὀδόντας ~ων Andr.Cr.*Geo.*(p.xxi E).

***ἀραφός, τό,** ? *flawlessness, soundness* (cf. ἀρραφής, *LS*); of a 'watertight' argument μὴ δυνάμενοι τὸ ἀ. καὶ ἰσχυρὸν τῶν ἀποδείξεων...ἀποφυγγάνειν Zach.Mit.*opif.*(M.85.1089A).

[*]**ἀραχνεῖος (-αῖος, -ιος), 1.** *of a spider* αὐτῶν τὰ σοφὰ τοῖς ἀ. ὑφάσμασιν ἔοικεν Bas.*hex.*6.6(1.55E, v.l. -νίοις; M.29.132A); Gr.Naz. *or.*27.9(M.36.24A); **2.** met., *intricate,* of sophistic arguments ἐν ἀραχναίοισι λόγοις id.*carm.*1.2.1.434(M.37.555A).

ἀράχνη, ἡ, *cobweb;* met., of fragility and transience ὁ παρὼν βίος ...ἀ. καὶ σκιά Chrys.*hom.31.5 in Mt.*(7.364A); id.*ep.*2.3(3.538B); Germ.CP *or.*2(M.98.281D); of what is of small account, a *trifle* οὐδὲ ...ἀ. ταῦτα εἶναι ἐνόμισεν Chrys.*laud.Paul.*2(2.483E); ref. spiritual neglect εὑρήσεις τὴν ἀ. ἔνδον [i.e. one's conscience] id.*hom.63.4 in Mt.*(7.633B); ref. BMV, Procl.CP *or.*4.1(M.65.709B) cit. s. ἀλατόμητος.

***ἀραχνίδιον, τό,** dimin. of ἀράχνη, *little cobweb;* met., of intricacies of Marcionite reasoning μὴ...τὰ ἀ. διακόπτοντες ματαιοπονῶμεν Chrys.*hom.40.1 in 1Cor.*(10.378E).

ἀράχνιος, v. ἀραχνεῖος.

***ἀραχνόδοξος,** *like a spider's web,* of the unreliability of popular favour τὴν ἀ. ... βδέλλαν Dan.Raith.*v.Jo.Clim.*3(M.88.600B).

ἀραχνοϋφής, *spun as by spiders,* i.e. *fine-spun,* Nil.*exerc.*16 (M.79.741A).

[*]**ἀργεία,** = ἀργία, Thdt.*Ezech.*20:13(2.826); Jo.D.*virt.*(M.95. 88D).

***ἀργέλλιον, τό,** v. *ναργέλλιον.

***ἀργενταρία, ἡ,** (Lat. *argentaria*) *box containing silver, case of silver,* Pall.*h.Laus.*10(p.30.8; M.34.1028C).

ἀργεύομαι, *be slow moving;* of heavy ships difficult to manœuvre, Thphn.*chron.*p.331(M.108.797C).

ἀργ-έω, 1. *not to earn one's living; do nothing;* met., of man as not having earned salvation ~οῦντα ἔσωσεν Chrys.*hom.39.4 in Mt.* (7.436B); **2.** *observe the sabbath;* of Christian observance, *abstain from servile work, keep holiday* τὴν μεγάλην ἑβδομάδα πᾶσαν... ~είτωσαν οἱ δοῦλοι *Const.App.*8.33.3ff.; pass., *be observed as a holiday* τὴν κυριακὴν παρὰ πᾶσιν ~εῖσθαι Thdr.Lect.*h.e.*1.14(M.86. 173A); **3.** *abstain cease,* in gen. ~ήσωμεν ἀπὸ τῆς ἀγαθοποιΐας; 1Clem.33.1; οὐκ ~ήσεις σωματικῶν, ἵνα ἄρῃς πνευματικά; Cyr.H. *procatech.*6; *ib.*8; οὐκ ~οῦμεν τῆς ἐνεργείας ἡμῶν *V.Pach.Λ* 26(p.153. 20); abs. τῶν αἱμάτων ἤργησεν ἡ δεινὴ χύσις Geo.Pis.*carm.*3.61; **4.** *be fruitless, ineffectual* οὐ γὰρ ~εῖ χάρις προφητική Or.*engast.*9 (p.293.14; M.12.1025D); ἔστηκεν ~ῶν ὁ Ἰουδαϊσμός Chrys.*hom.6.4 in Rom.*(9.477B); id.*pan.Pelag.Ant.*1(2.586B); **5.** *become meaningless; be nullified, brought to an end,* Serap.*Man.*23(p.40; M.40.920C); ἐν... τοῖς αἰσθητοῖς...~εῖν τὸν λόγον τοῦτον...οἶμαι Gr.Nyss.*Eun.*1(1 p.151.21; M.45.392C); ~ήσει...τὸ ἕτερος καὶ ἕτερος διὰ τὴν...ἕνωσιν Cyr.*Jo.*6.1(4.632A); ἡ τῆς τιμωρίας ψῆφος ~εῖ Thdt.*Ezech.*27:34ff. (2.907); ~ούσης καὶ τῆς ἐν αὐτῷ [sc. τῷ μοναστηρίῳ] προσιούσης ὑποθήκης Ath.Scholast.*coll.*2.1(p.29); Anast.S.*defunct.*(M.89.1196A); hence *be rescinded, abrogated* προστάσσει τούτων ~εῖν τὴν ἐπικουρίαν Pall.*v.Chrys.*5(p.32.9; M.47.20); ~ούσης ἱερωσύνης Cyr.*Os.*34(3.61E); ~εῖν ἔφη τὸν νόμον ἀναφανείσης τῆς πίστεως Thdt.*Rom.*4:25(3.52); **6.** *cease to exercise one's ministry;* usu. under censure, hence *be suspended,* Bas.*ep.*55(3.150A; M.32.404B); *ib.*217 *can.*69(3.327D; M. 800C); Epiph.*haer.*27.6(p.309.8; M.41.373A); *ib.*73.37(p.312.10; M.42. 472C); Socr.*h.e.*6.18.13(M.67.721A).

ἀργία, ἡ, 1. *abstention* ἀ. τῆς πονηρίας Bas.*hom.*13.5(2.118E; M.31.436B); *neglect* ἄλλος...τῇ ἀ. τῶν ἐντολῶν τοῦ θεοῦ τὰς χεῖρας βεβλαμμένος, ἐὰν...παυσάμενος τῆς ἀ. ἐργάσηται τὸ ἀγαθόν *V.Pach. Φ* 47(p.30.16ff.); *stoppage, interruption;* of work, Zach.Mit.*opif.* (M.85.1085A); **2.** *sabbath rest, sabbath* ἀπέκλεισε τὸν σαββατισμὸν ...καὶ τὰς νομίμους ἀ. *A.(Pass.)Petr.et Paul.*1(p.118.10); μηκέτι... σαββατίζωμεν Ἰουδαϊκῶς καὶ ἀργίαις χαίροντες ‡Ign.*Magn.*9; τῆς κατὰ νόμον ἀ. Cyr.*Jo.*4.6(4.422C); also of other days besides sabbath διπλῆ ἡ ἀ. ... τοῦ σαββάτου...καὶ ἑτέρας ἑορτῆς διαδεχομένης Chrys. *hom.39.1 in Mt.*(7.431D); cf. σοι προστάσσω καθαρισμοὺς...ἀ. διαφόρους *Const.App.*6.20.9; not interpreted literally by Christians τυπικῶς τοῖς ἀρχαιοτέροις ἡ κατὰ τὸ σάββατον ἀ. νενομοθέτητο Cyr. *Jo.*3.4(4.269D); Vict.*Mc.*2:23f.(p.292.10); abstention from servile work, hence *holy day, feast* κήρυξον...μίαν ἀ. τῇ πόλει, μίαν ἀ. τοῖς ὀρθοδόξοις CTyr.(518)*act.*(p.87.17; H.2.1357A); μίαν ἀ. τῇ θεοτόκῳ *ib.* (p.88.34; 1360A) cf. Nilles, *Kalendarium* 1 p.50, 2 p.414; **3.** *abstention from duties of one's office,* (usu. under censure, hence) *suspension; degradation* οὐδὲ τὴν ἑαυτοῦ ψυχὴν διὰ τῆς ἀ. καταδικάσει Bas. *ep.*188 *can.*10(3.274D; M.32.680B); τελευτήσεις ἀργῶν, καὶ δώσεις τῷ κυρίῳ λόγον τῆς σεαυτοῦ ἀ. *ib.*55(150A; M.404B); εἰ...παρ' οὐδὲν ἡγησάμενος τὴν...ἀ. δέξηται αὐτοὺς ὡς κληρικούς *Can.App.*16; τὸ ἀργεῖν ἀφόρισμός ἐστιν, ὥστε παύσασθαι τῆς ἱερουργίας...καὶ λόγον δώσει τῆς τοιαύτης ἀ., ἀδιόρθωτος μένων *Schol.*in Bas.*epp.can.*88 (*Mon.*2 p.654).

ἀργόλας, ὁ, a kind of *snake,* employed by Jeremiah to rid Egypt of poisonous serpents τοὺς ὄφεις τοὺς λεγομένους ἀ., ὅ ἐστιν ὀφιομάχους ‡Epiph.*v.proph.Jer.*6(p.21; ἀργολαίους M.43.422), cf. ἀργῆς, *LS;* ? transliteration of חַרְגֹּל (*locust*) name applied by Egyptian Jews to *mongoose,* from rapid movements; hence חַרְגֹּל rendered ὀφιομάχης in LXX Lev.11:22; above passage reproduced with form Ἀργολάους *Chron.Pasch.*p.157(M.92.385A) and explanation οὓς ἤνεγκεν ἐκ τοῦ Ἄργους τοῦ Πελοποννησιακοῦ, ὅθεν καὶ Ἀργόλαοι καλοῦνται, τουτέστιν Ἄργους δεξιοί. λαλιὰν [l. λαιὰν] δὲ ἔχουσι...πᾶν εὐώνυμον *ib.*(385B).

***ἀργολογ-έω 1.** *talk idly, chatter,* ‡Bas.*poen.mon.*5(2.527A; M.31. 1305D); ἐν καιρῷ ψαλμῳδίας σιγᾷ ἢ τῷ πλησίον ~εῖ Ephr.1.72D; id.2.171B; Dor.*doct.*4.6(M.88.1665B); Gr.Mag.*dial.*(tr.Zach.)1.4(M. *PL.*77.171B); of written word, ‡Bas.*struct.hom.*1.19(1.332E; M.30. 29B); **2.** *account idle, make light of* ἠνιᾶτο...ὅταν ὑπό τινων ~ούντων ἐστερεῖτο...τῶν θείων λογίων Cyr.S.*v.Euthym.*4(p.12.6).

ἀργολογία, ἡ, *idle chatter,* Bas.*reg.fus.*51,53(2.395E,396D; M.31. 1041A,1044A); *Apophth.Patr.*(M.65.245B); πλῆθος δὲ λόγων μὴ τὴν πολυεπείαν νόμιζε, ἀλλὰ τὴν ἀ. Olymp.*Eccl.*5:6(M.93.541C); calling for discipline, Bas.*reg.br.*23(2.423A; M.31.1097D); plur., Ephr.1.16E; ἀργολογίας καὶ ὕθλους †Gr.II Papa *ep.Leon.*2(H.4.16A).

***ἀργότης, ἡ,** *futility,* Epiph.*haer.*72.4(p.259.10; M.42.388C).

***ἀργοτροφέω,** *be supported in idleness,* Cyr.*ep.Calos.*(p.607.9; 6². 366B).

***ἀργότροφος,** *lazy in pasturing* flocks; of idle shepherds (ref. Jer.12:10), Pall.*v.Chrys.*13(p.80.14; M.47.46).

***ἀργόφαγος,** *kept in idleness, eating without working* ἄσωτος ἢ μέθυσος ἢ ἀ. *Const.App.*2.50.1; Pall.*h.Laus.*21(M.34.1074A).

***ἀργυραμοιβ-έω,** *act as a money-changer; profiteer* οὐκ ~οῦντες οὐδὲ χρυσορυχοῦντες ‡Chrys.*ascens.*1(3.778A).

ἀργυρένδετος, *inlaid with silver, decorated with silver;* of chariots, Chrys.*hom.63.4 in Mt.*(7.633C); a bed, id.*hom.53.3 in Jo.*(8.314C);

Ephr.3.117A; †Jo.Jej.*poenit.cont.virg.*(M.88.1968C); a book, *bound in silver*, CCP(681)*act.*10(H.3.1201E,1225B).

***ἀργυρένδυτος,** *overlaid with silver*; *inlaid with silver*, of a church ἀ. καὶ χρυσοκόλλητος Cyr.H.*catech.*14.14; an altar, Thdr. of Pentapolis ap.Jo.D.*imag.*3(M.94.1404B); a book *bound in silver*, v.l. in CCP(681)*act.*10(H.3.1201E).

ἀργυρίζομαι, **1.** med., *get* or *extort money from*, *LS*; also c. εἰς: εἰς ὃν ἠργυρίσω Mel.*pass.*p.14.18; **2.** pass., *be bribed*, Taras.*ep.*3 (M.98.1441B).

ἀργυρισμός, ὁ, *silver-standard* οὐ κατὰ τὸν ἀ. Epiph.*mens.*24 (M.43.292D).

***ἀργυροδέκτης, ὁ,** *taker of money*; of Judas, ‡Gr.Naz.*Chr.pat.*140 (M.38.148A).

***ἀργυροκάπηλος,** *money-grubbing*, Cyr.*hom.pasch.*14(5[2].195A).

***ἀργυρόκρανος,** *silver-headed*; of Hadrian, *Orac.Sib.*5.47.

ἀργυρολόγος, *money-loving*, Pall.*v.Chrys.*16(p.98.13; M.47.55).

***ἄργυρον, τό,** Byzantine silver coin ἄ., τοῦτό ἐστιν ὃ οἱ Ῥωμαῖοι μιλιαρίσιον καλοῦσιν Epiph.*mens.*24(M.43.289B).

***ἀργυρονόμος, ὁ,** *money-changer* γίνεσθε οὖν ὡς ἀ. ... τὰ φαῦλα τῶν νομισμάτων ἀποκρίνουσιν, τὰ δὲ δόκιμα οἰκειοῦνται *Const.App.* 2.37.2.

***ἀργυροποίητος,** *made of silver*, Men.*exc.gent.*14(p.458.4; M.113. 817B).

[*]**ἀργυροπράκτης, ὁ,** v. ἀργυροπράτης.

***ἀργυροπρατεῖον (-ατίον, -άτιον), τό,** *banker's* (orig. silver-smith's) *shop*, *V.Dan.*(p.370.7); Thphn.*chron.*p.157(M.108.424C); -ίον Jo.Mal.*chron.*16 p.395(M.97.584B); -άτιον Jo.Mosch.*prat.*188(M.87. 3065B); *Chron.Pasch.*p.337(M.92.880A).

ἀργυροπράτης (-πράκτης), ὁ, *money-dealer*, †Polyb.*v.Epiph.* 45(M.41.81A); ἀπομιμεῖσθαι...τοὺς ἐμπειροτάτους τῶν ἀργυροπρατῶν, οἳ προσίενται μὲν τῶν νομισμάτων τὸ εὐδοκιμοῦν, ἀπόβλητον δὲ ποιεῖσθαι σπουδάζουσι τὸ παράσημον Cyr.*Nest.*proem.(p.13.25; 6.2B); Jo.Mal.*chron.*18 p.492(M.97.712A); Jo.Mosch.*prat.*185(M.87.3061A); τὸν ἀργυροπράκτην Sophr.H.*mir.Cyr.et Jo.*32(M.87.3524D).

***ἀργυροπρατίον, (-άτιον), τό,** v. *ἀργυροπρατεῖον.

***ἀργυροπωλεῖον, τό,** *silver-dealer's shop*, Soz.*h.e.*8.4.11(M.67. 1524C).

***ἀργυροπώλος, ὁ,** *silver-dealer*, Soz.*h.e.*8.4.11(M.67.1524C).

***ἀργυρότευκτος,** *made of silver*, Epiph.*haer.*3(p.177.14; M.41. 188A).

***ἀργυροτρώκτης, ὁ,** *money-grubber*, *miser*; of Judas, ‡Gr.Naz. *Chr.pat.*141(M.38.148A).

***ἀργυροφανής,** *like silver in appearance*, *bright as silver*; of steel, Cyr.*Is.*5.4(2.851E).

ἀργυροφύλαξ, ὁ, *hoarder of money*, *miser*; of Judas, ‡Gr.Naz. *Chr.pat.*141(M.38.148A).

ἀργυροχάλινος, *with silver-mounted bridle*, Bas.*hom.*3.6(2.22C; M.31.212C).

***ἀργυροχοέω,** *smelt* or *work silver*, Cyr.*Zach.*30(3.698C).

ἀργυροχόος, ὁ, *worker in silver*, Epiph.*haer.*64.71(p.518.8; M.41. 1196A).

ἀργυρόχροος, *silver-skinned*, *silver-coloured*; of sheep, *with fleece like silver*, ‡Chrys.*poenit.*4(9.854A).

***ἀργυρόχρυσος,** *of gold and silver*; of images in a temple of Juno, *Pers.*(p.13.6; M.10.101B).

ἀργώδης, *lazy*, Melet.*nat.hom.*30(M.64.1272A).

***ἄρδευμα, τό,** *irrigation*, *watering*, Eus.*l.C.*6(p.209.5; M.20. 1345B).

***Ἀρειανέω,** *be a follower of Arius*, †Leont.B.*sect.*6.5(M.86.1237C).

***Ἀρειανίζ-ω,** *Arianize*, *adopt the views of Arius*, *be an Arian* οὔτε τῷ ἑνὶ Σαβελλίζοντες κατὰ τῶν τριῶν...οὔτε τοῖς τρισὶν ~οντες κατὰ τοῦ ἑνός Gr.Naz.*or.*42.16(M.36.476C); εἰ τῆς σαρκὸς μὲν μέρος οὐκ ὁ θεὸς λόγος, τοῦ δὲ ἀνθρώπου μέρος ἦν, πῶς οὐκ ~εις; Leont.H. *Nest.*5.32(M.86.1752B); ἕνα θεόν, μίαν οὐσίαν...ὁμολογοῦμεν, ἵνα μὴ Ἀρειανίσωμεν Anast.Ant.*fid.*(M.89.1404B); in differing degrees ἔμεινε δὲ Εὐδόξιος ~ων, οὐ μέντοι γε κατὰ τὸν Ἀέτιον Epiph.*anac.*6(p.232. 1; M.42.873A); of those before Arius Ὠριγένης...ἀνέφυ, τὰ τῶν ἀμφοτέρων [sc. of Sabellius and Marcellus] κυρῶν καὶ ~ων Germ. CP *syn.haer.*9(M.98.45D).

***Ἀρειανικός,** *Arian*, *of Arius* τὴν Ἀ. ... νόσον Thdt.*Heb.*proem.(3. 541); τῆς Ἀ. φάλαγγος id.*h.e.*2.4.4(3.829); τοῦ Ἀ. σμήνους Germ.CP *syn.haer.*17(M.98.56B); *of the Arian schism* οἱ δὲ τῆς Ἀ. ἐκκλησίας Juln.Imp.*ep.*115(p.196.6).

***Ἀρειανικῶς,** *Arianwise* τρεῖς μὲν φύσεις λέγων Ἀ. ἐν τοῖς τρισὶ προσώποις τῆς ἁγίας τριάδος Anast.S.*hod.*22(M.89.292D).

***Ἀρειανισμός, ὁ,** *Arianism*, Gr.Naz.*or.*21.22(M.35.1108A).

***Ἀρειανίτης, ὁ,** *follower of Arius*, an *Arian*, Jo.Mal.*chron.*14 p.372(M.97.553B).

***Ἀρειανός,** **1.** *Arian*, *of Arius* ἡ Ἀ. αἵρεσις Ath.*Ar.*1.1(M.26.13C); id.*ep.Epict.*1(p.3.13; M.26.1052B); id.*ep.Aeg.Lib.*5(M.25.549A,B); τῆς Ἀ. μανίας Bas.*ep.*197.1(3.288B; M.32.712A); τὸ Ἀ. ... φρόνημα *ib.*244. 9(3.381E; M.924B); τὴν Ἀ. δραματουργίαν Epiph.*haer.*76.3(p.344.12; M.42.521B); **2.** as subst., *an Arian*, *follower of Arius* τῇ Ἀρειανῶν αἱρέσει Ath.*syn.*14(p.241.24; M.26.705A); ἀντὶ Χριστιανῶν λοιπὸν Ἀρειανοὺς ὀνομάζεσθαι id.*Ar.*1.2(M.26.16B); Pall.*h.Laus.*63(pp.158. 5,159.1; M.34.1235B); *Chron.Pasch.*pp.301,304(M.92.756A,769A); with schismatic 'church' κοινωνίαν Ἀρειανῶν καὶ Σαβελλιανῶν ἐρεσχελίαν Epiph.*ep.Arab.*ap.*haer.*78.24(p.475.5; M.42.740A); id.*haer.*66.20 (p.47.15; 64A); *ib.*68.6(p.146.19; 193B); and bishops, id.*anac.*6(p.231. 21; M.42.337B); fusion with Meletians, id.*haer.*68.6(p.146.19ff.; M. 42.193C); *ib.*76.1(p.340.17; 516B); their dialectic, *ib.*69.14ff.(p.163ff.; 224Bff.); identified with Eudoxians and dist. alike from Anomoeans and Semi-Arians, CCP(381)*can.*1; as including others than Arius and his immediate followers τῶν Ἀ. τῶν περὶ Ἀκάκιον Epiph.*haer.* 73.28(p.303.2; M.42.457A); *ib.*73.23(p.296.12; 445A); but contrasted with Anomoeans, *ib.*76.28(p.377.4; 573B); though sometimes in later times including Anomoeans also, Tim.CP *haer.*(M.86.37B,C); also of persons of a later period holding views in common with Arius λέγων [sc. Θεοδώρητος] ὅτι Ἀ. ἐστι Κύριλλος †Leont.B.*sect.*4.5(M. 86.1224B); **3.** their theology: God's essence is incommunicable; everything outside the monad is created, Ar.*Thal.fr.*10 ap.Ath. *Ar.*1.6(M.26.24A) cit. s. ἀνόμοιος; id.ap.Ath.*syn.*15(p.242.9ff.; M.26. 705D–708A); id.*ep.Alex.*(p.12.7ff.; M.26.709A,B); Logos created *ex nihilo* to make world, therefore before time (which pertains to creation) but not eternal, *ib.*(p.13.2ff.; 709B); id.*Thal.fr.*1 ap.Ath. *Ar.*1.5(M.26.21A); id.*ep.Eus.*(p.3.3f.; M.42.212B); Didym.(‡Bas.)*Eun.* 4(1.288C;M.29.693A); Socr.*h.e.*1.5.2(M.67.41B); a creature who exists by the will of God ὑποστήσαντα ἰδίῳ θελήματι...κτίσμα τοῦ θεοῦ τέλειον Ar.*ep.Alex.*(p.13.8; 709A); id.*ep.Eus.*(p.3.1ff.; 212B); not truly God but so-called as participating in divine grace, id.*Thal. fr.*10 ap.Ath.*Ar.*1.6(M.26.21D); ὑπόβασιν ἔλεγε τοῦ υἱοῦ, ὥσπερ ...οἱ Ἀ. †Leont.B.*sect.*10.4(M.86.1264C); denied human soul of incarnate Logos, Didym.*Trin.*3.21(M.39.904A); acknowledged one nature only μίαν φύσιν δοξάζων ὡς οἱ Ἀ. †Leont.B.*sect.*4.5(1224B); οὐδὲ γὰρ αὐτοὶ [sc. οἱ Ἀ.] τὰ τῆς σαρκὸς πάθη, τουτέστι σταυρὸν καὶ ...θάνατον, ἔλεγον τὴν θεότητα ἐπιδέχεσθαι...μετὰ τὴν ἐνανθρώπησιν Eust.Mon.*ep.*(M.86.917C).

***Ἀρειανοφρονέω,** *hold Arian views*, Thphn.*chron.*p.145(M.108. 376A).

***Ἀρειανόφρων,** *Arian-minded*, Ath.*decr.*33(p.28.28; M.20.1536D not.); Thphn.*chron.*p.25(M.108.121C).

***Ἀρειανῶς,** *like Arius*, *Arianwise* ἴσον γὰρ εἰς ἀσέβειαν, καὶ Σαβελλίως συνάψαι, καὶ Ἀ. διαστῆσαι, τὸ μὲν τῷ προσώπῳ, τὸ δὲ ταῖς φύσεσιν Gr.Naz.*or.*31.30(p.186.8; M.36.169A).

***Ἀρειοθολ-όω,** *infect with Arianism* Μακεδόνιον...~ωθέντα τὴν διάνοιαν *Chron.Pasch.*p.304(M.92.769A).

***Ἀρειομανίτης, ὁ,** *one with the Arian madness*; a name for an *Arian*, Ath.*Dion.*1(p.46.8; M.25.480A); id.*v.Anton.*68(M.26.940C); Petr.II Al.*encycl.*ap.Thdt.*h.e.*4.22.18(3.993); Nil.*epp.*1.70(M.79.113B).

***Ἀρειομανῖτις,** *Arian-mad* τὴν Ἀ. αἵρεσιν Epiph.*haer.*69.11(p.160. 32; M.42.220A); *ib.*73.1(p.268.16; 401B).

***Ἀρειοπλάνης, ὁ,** *one in Arian error*, *one led astray by Arius*, ‡Gr.Nyss.*Ar.et Sab.*6(M.45.1289A).

***ἀρειότης, ἡ,** *excellence*, Cyr.*glaph.Ex.*3(1.332C).

***ἀρέμβαστος,** v. *ἀρρέμβαστος.

***ἀρεμβάστως,** met.; **1.** *without distraction* δέησις...ἀπερισπάστως καὶ ἀ. προσφερομένη Nil.*epp.*3.153(M.79.509A); **2.** *without wavering*, *regularly* τὸ ἀ. καὶ ἀμετεωρίστως τῇ...εὐχῇ προσπαραμένειν *ib.*1.31 (97B).

***ἄρεμβος,** v. *ἄρρεμβος.

***ἄρεπτος,** *steady* ἄ. ψυχῆς ὄμμα Jo.Clim.*scal.*27(M.88.1116D conj. ἀρέμβαστον).

ἀρέσκεια, ἡ, **1.** *benignity* βασιλικὸν...ἡ τῆς εἰρήνης ἀ., ὡς καὶ τυράννων ἴδιον τὸ φιλόνεικον Thphyl.*exc.gent.*3(p.479.21; M.113. 937B); **2.** *allurement* ταῦτα ποιῶν διὰ ἀρέσκειαν ἐναντιούμενος τῷ νόμῳ *Const.App.*1.3.11; ψευδεῖς ἀρέσκειαι καὶ μάταιον κάλλος γυναικὸς μὴ ἔστω ἐν σοί *ib.*1.8.13.

ἀρετή, ἡ, *virtue*, etym. ὅθεν, ὦ ἀ., εἴτε...εἴτε διὰ τὸ αἱρεῖν καὶ μετεωρίζειν...τὰς ψυχάς Meth.*symp.*8.1(p.82.3; M.18.140B); ἀ. ... ἐκ τῶν ἀριστείων πρακτικὸν ὄνομα κέκληται ‡Nil.*tract.*3(M.79.1097B); ἀ. ... καλεῖται διὰ τὸ αἱρεῖσθαι Jo.D.*virt.*(M.95.96D).

A. of animals or things, *virtue*, *goodness*, *LS*.

B. of man; **1.** *moral virtue, excellence* of character; **a.** def. ἀ. ἐστι διάθεσις βελτίστη Gr.Naz.et Bas.ap.*Doct.Patr.*33(p.250.9); ἀ. ἐστιν ἕξις ἀρίστη ψυχῆς λογικῆς, καθ' ἣν δυσκίνητος γίνεται πρὸς κακίαν Evagr.Pont.*ib.*(p.250.10); Marc.Er.*opusc.*2.24(M.65.933C); ἀ. ὡρίσαντο τὴν πρὸς τὸν θεὸν ἀναπτεροῦσαν καὶ τὰ περὶ γῆν ἐν τάξει πηδαλιουχοῦσαν Procl.CP *Arm.*3(p.188.14; M.65.857B); **b.** made ground of Christ's sonship by Ebionites διὰ...ἀρετὴν βίου ἥκοντα εἰς τὸ καλεῖσθαι υἱὸν θεοῦ Epiph.*haer.*30.18(p.358.9; M.41.436C); and by Arius ὁ θεὸς...προλαβὼν αὐτῷ ταύτην τὴν δόξαν δέδωκεν ἣν ἄνθρωπος καὶ ἐκ τῆς ἀ. ἔσχε μετὰ ταῦτα Ar.*Thal.fr.*9 ap.Ath. *ep.Aeg.Lib.*12(M.25.564C); another interpretation of Arius πῶς... ἔτι λόγος, εἰ τρεπτός ἐστιν;...εἰ μὴ ἄρα ὡς ἐν οὐσίᾳ συμβεβηκός... ὡς ἐν ἰδιαζούσῃ τινὶ οὐσίᾳ συμβεβηκέναι τινὰ χάριν καὶ ἕξιν ἀρετῆς Ath.*Ar.*1.36(M.26.88A); contested by orthodox εἰ...μισθὸν προαιρέσεως ἔλαβεν ἃ ἔσχεν...ἐξ ἀ. ἄρα καὶ βελτιώσεως ταῦτα ἐσχηκώς... οὐκ ἐστὶν ἀληθινὸς υἱός *ib.*1.37(89A); id.*decr.*22(p.19.7; M.25.456C); ἵνα...ἄλλην οὖσαν τὴν τοῦ υἱοῦ ὁμοίωσιν...δείξωσι παρὰ τὴν ἐν ἡμῖν... μίμησιν, ἣν ἐξ ἀ. διὰ τὴν τῶν ἐντολῶν τήρησιν ἡμεῖς προσλαμβάνομεν *ib.*20(p.17.11; 452B); **c.** not ground of union of Christ's natures ἥνωσεν ἑαυτῷ σῶμα...οὐ πρότερον ὑπάρξαν, καὶ τότε κατ' ἀρετὴν ἑνωθὲν ‡Ath.*dial.Trin.*4.2(M.28.1252C); **2.** particular form of virtue, a single virtue, Just.*dial.*4.3(M.6.484C) cit. s. δικαιοσύνη; ὁ τέλειος καὶ πάσας ἔχων τὰς ἀ. ... τελείαν ἔχει τὴν σοφίαν καὶ...τὴν σωφροσύνην...καὶ τὴν εὐσέβειαν καὶ τὰς λοιπάς Or.*Jo.*32.15(9; p.450.16; M.14.780D); Gr.Naz.*or.*14.5(M.35.864B); οὐ γὰρ ἀρκεῖ μία μόνον ἀ. Chrys.*hom.4.3 in Eph.*(11.29A); Dor.*doct.*14.1(M.88.1773B); freq. of cardinal virtues, Clem.*str.*7.3(p.13.8; M.9.421C) cit. s. δικαιοσύνη; Nil.*epp.*1.223(M.79.164D); τέσσαρας γενικὰς ἀ. ‡Proc.G.*Pr.*23:2 (M.87.1449B); ψυχικὰς μὲν ἀ. λέγομεν εἶναι προηγουμένως γενικωτάτας τέσσαρας ταύτας...ἀνδρεία, φρόνησις, σωφροσύνη, καὶ δικαιοσύνη· καὶ ἐκ τούτων ἀποτίκτονται ψυχικαὶ ἀ.· πίστις, ἐλπίς, ἀγάπη, προσευχή, ταπείνωσις κτλ. Jo.D.*virt.*(M.95.85C); and of theological virtues πολλὰ μὲν ἀρετῆς εἴδη, τρία δὲ ταῦτα ἐξαίρετα ἀνεβόησεν, πίστιν, ἐλπίδα καὶ ἀγάπην· ὧν ἡ μὲν πίστις χαρίζεται τοῖς ἀνθρώποις τὰ ὑπὲρ φύσιν...ἡ δὲ ἐλπὶς οὐκ ὀνειροπολεῖν ἀξιοῖ...ἀλλὰ γενναίως κρατεῖν ἐν τοῖς παροῦσι παρασκευάζει τὰ μέλλοντα...ἡ δὲ ἀγάπη τοῦ καθ' ἡμᾶς μυστηρίου ἐστὶ τὸ κεφάλαιον...ἑκατέρα τοίνυν ἀλλήλαις συμβαίνει· ἡ μὲν γὰρ πίστις ἔσοπτρόν ἐστιν ἀγάπης, ἡ δὲ ἀγάπη βεβαίωσις ὑπάρχει πίστεως...πᾶς τοίνυν Χριστιανὸς ὁ μὴ πλουτῶν πίστει καὶ ἐλπίδι καὶ ἀγάπῃ οὐκ ἔστιν ὃ λέγεται, ἀλλ' εἰ καὶ δοκεῖ πολλάκις δουλαγωγεῖν τὸ σῶμα...τὴν ἠθικὴν μόνην ἀ. κατορθώσας, τῶν τῆς νίκης στεφάνων οὐκ ἀξιοῦται Procl.CP *Arm.*3(pp.188.16–189.3; M.65.857B–860A); τὴν μὲν τελείαν πρᾶξιν τῆς ἀ., πίστις ὀρθὴ ποιεῖ, καὶ φόβος εἰς θεὸν ἀνόθευτος· τὴν δὲ κατὰ τὴν ἀνάβασιν ἄπταιστον φυσικὴν θεωρίαν, ἐλπὶς βεβαία καὶ ἀλώβητος σύνεσις· τὴν δὲ κατὰ τὴν ἀνάληψιν θέωσιν, ἀγάπη τελεία, καὶ νοῦς τοῖς οὖσι καθ' ὑπεροχὴν πάμπαν ἑκουσίως πεπηρωμένος Max.*cap.*5.93(M.90.1388C); love as principal μία δὲ κυριωτάτη τῶν ἀ. ... ἐστὶν ἡ πρὸς τὸν πλησίον ἀγάπη Or.*or.*11(p.322.13; M.11.449A); ἀρχὴ καὶ τέλος τῆς ἀ. ἡ ἀγάπη Chrys.*hom.23.3 in Rom.*(9.690C); τὰ...κατ' εἶδος ἐπαριθμούμενα τῶν ἀ. κατορθώματα μία γενικὴ ἀ. περιέλαβεν, ἧς ἡ ἀγάπη τοὔνομα Isid.Pel.*epp.*4.15(M.78.1064B); **3.** in gen.; **a.** in rel. to nature of man οὔτε...φύσει τὴν ἀ. γεννώμεθα ἔχοντες, οὔτε γενομένοις ...φυσικῶς ὕστερον ἐπιγίνεται (ἐπεὶ οὐδ' ἂν ἦν ἔθ' ἑκούσιον οὐδὲ ἐπαινετόν) Clem.*str.*7.3(p.14.13; M.9.424B); engendered by soul, not of its own power but as bride of Christ, Or.*fr.45 in Jo.*3:29 (p.519.21); ἄνθρωπος· καλὸς μὲν...οὐσίᾳ...τὸ δὲ ἀγαθὸν τὸ διὰ μόνης ἀ. προσγινόμενον πόνῳ κτᾶται Tit.Bost.*Man.*2.3(M.18.1137D); οὐ φύσεως ἀλλὰ προαιρέσεως ἡ κακία καὶ ἡ ἀ. Chrys.*serm.9.5 in Gen.*(4.695E); ἔχει...ἡ φύσις ἐν ἑαυτῇ τῶν ἀ. ... τὸ κριτήριον...ἐπειδὴ δ' ὤκλασεν ἡ φύσις, καὶ ἠμαύρωσε τοὺς τῆς ἀ. χαρακτῆρας, ἐδόθη καὶ ὁ νόμος γραπτὸς Isid.Pel.*epp.*4.53(M.78.1104Af.); τὰ ἔμφυτα τῆς ἀ. σπέρματα...ἃ τῶν ἀρχαίων ἐπιεικέστερα [l. ἐπιεικέστεροι] ἐγεώργησαν *ib.*4.187(1277B); φυσικαί εἰσιν αἱ ἀ. ... ἡ ἄσκησις...οὐ πρὸς τὸ ἔξωθεν ...ἐπεισαγαγεῖν τὰς ἀ. ... ὅθεν τῆς κατὰ φύσιν ἀ. τὴν λαμπρότητα ἐνδείκνυται ἡ ψυχή Max.*Pyrr.*(M.91.309Bf.); presupposing intelligence ἀ. ... ἐν ἀλόγοις οὐκ ἐστίν Or.*princ.*1.8.4(p.104.3); ἐφ' ἡμῖν δέ, καὶ ὁ τῶν ἀ. λόγος, τῶν κατὰ φύσιν δυνάμεων ὑπάρχων ἐνεργούμενος νόμος Max.*opusc.*(M.91.24B); as well as free will ἀρετῆς μὲν ἐὰν ἀνέλῃς τὸ ἑκούσιον, ἀνεῖλες αὐτῆς καὶ τὴν οὐσίαν Or.*Cels.*4.3(p.276.18; M.11.1033A); οὐ γὰρ ἀδυναμία ἀκολασίας ποιεῖ σωφροσύνην...ἀλλὰ τὸ δύνασθαι μὲν πράττειν, λόγῳ δὲ ἀπέχεσθαι, τοῦτο ἡ ἀ. σωφροσύνης τε καὶ δικαιοσύνης...οὐκ ἄλλη τις εὑρεθεῖ παρὰ ἀνθρώποις ἀ. Tit.Bost. *Man.*2.2(M.18.1136Bf.); *ib.*2.5(1141C); ἡ ἀ. τοῦ θέλειν ἡμῶν μόνου χρείαν ἔχει· ἐπειδήπερ ἐν ἡμῖν ἐστι, καὶ ἐξ ἡμῶν συνίσταται Ath. *v.Anton.*20(M.26.873A); Chrys.*hom.12.2 in Jo.*(8.69A); χρῆμα... ἀδέσποτον ἡ ἀ. Cyr.*Juln.*5(6^{2}.159D); gift of God τρεῖς...ἀρετὰς παραλαβὼν ὁ προφήτης τοῦ θεοῦ, ἰσχὺν...σοφίαν...φρόνησιν Or.*hom.8.1 in Jer.*(p.55.4; M.13.336A); summed up in Christ κακία μὲν αὐτῶν οὐκέτι κυρία ἦν, ὁ λόγος δέ, καὶ ἁπαξαπλῶς ὁ κύριος, ἡ πᾶσα ἔμψυχος καὶ ζῶσα ἀ. id.*Jo.*32.11(p.444.3; M.14.769C); gained by prayer, v. εὐχή; work of H. Ghost, Nil.*epp.*2.204(M.79.308A); as θεία, v.s.v.; σκιὰν...θείων πτερύγων...τὰς ἀ. τις νοῶν οὐχ ἁμαρτήσεται Gr.Nyss. *Pss.titt.*B 14(M.44.585C); ultimate source οὐκ ἦν...ποτε, ὅτε οὐκ ἦν ἀ. ... πάσης γὰρ...ἀ., δημιουργός ἐστιν ὁ θεός Max.*cap.theol.*1.50(M.90.1101B); **b.** character fundamentally one, Clem.*str.*2.18(p.155.3; M.8.1020A) cit. s. γνωστικῶς; ἀλλήλων ἐκδέδενται πᾶσαι αἱ ἀ. Mac. Aeg.*hom.*40.1(M.34.764A); with two spheres of operation ὁ λόγος ...σὰρξ γενόμενος τὴν αὐτὴν ἀ. πρακτικὴν ἅμα καὶ θεωρητικὴν ἐπιδεικνύς Clem.*paed.*1.3(p.95.21; M.8.260B); ἀ. πρακτικὰς καὶ διανοητικάς Or.*fr.45 in Jo.*(p.519.21); Didym.*2Cor.*4:5f.(p.24.30; M.39.1700A); Isid.Pel.*epp.*4.174(M.78.1265B); τὸ τέλειον...ἐν τοῖς μαθηταῖς, ἐν ἴσῃ τῇ ξυνωρίδι, τῇ τε πραγματικῇ φημι καὶ τῇ κατὰ θεωρίαν ἀ. Cyr.*Jo.*4.2(4.357A); τῆς ἀ. πολλὰ μόρια Thdt.*Ps.*7:6(1.645); Olymp. *fr.Bar.*5:2(M.93.773A); relation to σοφία: ὑπόστασιν...σοφίας τὴν ἀ.· οὐσίαν δέ φασιν ἀρετῆς εἶναι τὴν σοφίαν *Schol.*in Max.*opusc.*(M.91.37C); and to knowledge of God προσήκει...πρότερον τῆς ἄλλης ἀ. ἐπιμεληθῆναι, εἶθ' οὕτως τῆς τῶν θείων κατατολμῆσαι γνώσεως Thdt. *Os.*10:12(2.1360); a golden mean, Hipp.*fr.8 in Pr.*4:27(p.159.12; M.10.617B); †Bas.*Is.*174(1.505D; M.30.409C); Gr.Naz.*or.*42.16(M.36.476C); mark of Christian life even before Christ, Eus.*d.e.*1.6(p.24.7; M.22.49C) cit. s. Χριστιανικῶς; τότε δυσκολωτέρα ἦν ἡ ἀ. ... γυμνὴ καθ' ἑαυτὴν ἡ φύσις ἠγωνίζετο Chrys.*hom.72.3 in Jo.*(8.420D); as wings to heaven, Gr.Nyss.*anim.et res.*(M.46.113C); id.*ascens.*(M.46.692D); id.*Pss.titt.*B 16(M.44.597B) cit. s. ἀνάβασις.

C. of angels κοινωνοῦσι...ταῖς θεουργικαῖς αὐτοῦ [sc. τοῦ Ἰησοῦ] καὶ φιλανθρώποις ἀ. Dion.Ar.*c.h.*7.2(M.3.208C); θείας ἀ. ... ἐφιέμεναι [sc. seraphic hierarchy] *ib.*13.3(301C).

D. in rel. to God; **1.** 'virtue' i.e. *attribute*; differently predicated of God and man μὴ τὴν αὐτὴν εἶναι ἀ. ἀνθρώπου καὶ θεοῦ Clem.*str.*2.22 (p.188.1; M.8.1084C); *ib.*6.14(p.489.17; M.9.337C); αἱ ἀ. σου ὑπὲρ τὰς παρ' ἡμῖν ἀ. Or.*schol.in Cant.*1:1(M.17.253B); θεὸν μὲν γὰρ οὔτε σώφρονα κλητέον...καὶ τὰ τοιαῦτα· ἐπάνω γὰρ τῆς ἀνθρωπίνης ἀ. ὑπάρχει Tit.Bost.*Man.*2.2(M.18.1136C); analogically related τῇ τῶν αἰσθητῶν συμβόλων ποικιλίᾳ...ὑφ' ὧν...ἀναγόμεθα ἐπὶ θεόν τε καὶ θείαν ἀ. Dion.Ar.*e.h.*1.2(M.3.373A); **2.** plur., *excellences, glories* λαὸς...τεταγμένος τῷ τὰς ἀ. αὐτοῦ ἐξαγγέλλειν *Const.App.*5.15.2; **3.** *manifestation of power* ἀρετῇ τε τοῦ πάντα δυνατοῦ θεοῦ καὶ παραινέσεσιν ἅμα καὶ βοηθείαις Const.ap.Eus.*v.C.*2.42(p.59.7; M.20.1017C); of Christ δι' ἐναργοῦς...ἀ. τοῦ αὐτοῦ σωτῆρος αὐτόρριζος...ὁ νεὼς ἀνετρέπετο Eus.*v.C.*3.56(p.104.9; 1124A).

E. as mode of address ἡ ὑμετέρα πάντιμος ἀ. Jo.D.*jej.*2(M.95.65C).

F. *ornament, ornamentation* κοσμήσας αὐτὸ [sc. τὸ ἱππικόν] χαλκουργήμασι καὶ πάσῃ ἀ. Jo.Mal.*chron.*13 p.320(M.97.480A); εἰς κόσμησιν τῆς...Κωνσταντινουπόλεως δι' ἀρετῆς *ib.*16 p.401(593A).

***ἀρευσία**, v. *ἀρρευσία.

[*]ἄρευστος, *without change; imperishable; indissoluble*, Gr.Naz. *carm.*1.2.9.11(M.37.668A); Sophr.H.*or.*2.18(M.87.3237B); Anast.S. *hod.*2(M.89.76A); of the Godhead, Gr.Naz.*carm.*1.1.3.88(415A); *ib.* 2.1.11.1176(1109A); of the incarnate Son, *undiminished* ἐκ παρθένου ...ἄ. Didym.*Trin.*1.15(M.39.309C).

***ἀρεύστως**, v. *ἀρρεύστως.

[*]ἀρήδηλος, for ἀρίδηλος, *clear, evident*, Didym.*Trin.*3.3(M.39.805C).

ἀρήν, ὁ, [acc. sing. ἄρνα], *young lamb*, Cyr.*ador.*10(1.359A).

***ἀρῆνα, ἡ,** (Lat. arena) *amphitheatre, arena*, *A.Paul.et Thecl.*36 (p.262.6).

ἀρητήρ, ὁ, *one who prays*; hence *priest*, of a Christian priest ἕσπετο δ' ἀ., ἱερῆς δ' ἐξῆρχε χορείης, ἀ. πολύυμνος Paul.Sil.*Soph.* 344f.(M.86.2133A); *ib.*963(2155B); ἀ. ἐσθλὸς τοῦ θεοῦ κῖτε...καὶ τοὔνομα Ἀνίκητος εἰερεὺς ὢν ἰδιοπραέων *MAMA* 1.237; *ib.*1.370.

[*]ἀρθῖτις, ἡ, for ἀρθρῖτις, *gout*, *A.Thadd.*4(MS *V* only, p.275.3).

ἀρθρέμβολος, *dislocating* the joints, †Jo.D.*B.J.*23(M.96.1069B); neut. plur. as subst., *instruments of torture*, Or.*mart.*15(p.15.15; M.11.584A); Gr.Naz.*or.*15.4(M.35.917A); Const.Diac.*laud.*6(M.88.485C).

ἄρθρωσις, ἡ, *articulation* of joints, Melet.*nat.hom.*30(M.64.1269C).

***ἀριδημία, ἡ,** Eus.*m.P.*11(M.20.1456A) f.l. for ἀποδημία (p.944.8).

[*]ἄριζος, v. ἄρριζος.

ἀριθμητής, ὁ, *calculator* τὸν μέγαν γεωμέτρην καὶ ἀ. ἥλιον Hipp. *haer.*6.28(p.154.16; M.16.3234D); of one engaged in the drawing up of contracts, Ath.Scholast.*coll.*14.3(p.150).

ἀριθμός, ὁ, *number*, def. ἀ. ὁρίζεται σωρεία μονάδων, οὐχὶ διαίρεσις μονάδων, ἀλλ᾽ οὐδὲ σύγχυσις μονάδων Anast.Ant.ap.*Doct.Patr*.33 (p.251.24); **1.** *number*, denoting how many πᾶς ἀ. τῆς ποσότητος τῶν ὑποκειμένων ἐστὶ δηλωτικός, οὐ τῆς φύσεως τῶν πραγμάτων Gr.Naz.*or*.31.18(p.166.14; M.36.152C); Max.*ep*.12(M.91.476C); *ib*. (474A); *ib*.13(513C); *numeral, particular number*; as possessing mystic significance or power, Or.*sel.in Ezech*.4:14(M.13.781B); Gr.Naz.*or*.4.19(M.35.548B); *ib*.41.2(M.36.429C); Proc.G.*Gen*.2:2(M. 87.140B); male and female, Clem.*str*.6.16(p.502.24ff.; M.9.365A); Hipp.*haer*.1.2(p.5.23ff.; M.16.3024B); the *number* 3, Or.*fr*.79 *in Jo*. 11:4(p.547.10); 4, *ib*.(p.546.24); 6, Heracleon ap.Or.*Jo*.10.38(22; p.214.33; M.14.380B); Clem.*str*.6.16(p.502.24; M.9.365A); Or.*Jo*.10.39 (23; p.216.28; 384A); *ib*.28.1(p.389.1; 680B); 7, Clem.*str*.6.16(p.503. 3f.; 365B); Or.*fr*.80 *in Jo*.11:18(p.547.21); id.*Jo*.10.39(23; p.217.5; 384B); Gr.Naz.*or*.41.3(M.36.433A); 8, Or.*fr*.80 *in Jo*.11:18(p.547. 21f.); 6, 7, and 8, id.*sel.in Ps*.118:1(M.12.1588A); cf.*ib*.118:164 (1624B,C); 10, Clem.*str*.6.11(p.473.30; 305A); Or.*Jo*.2.36(29; p.95.15; 180C); *Const.App*.6.3.1; cf.Clem.*str*.6.16(p.499.13; 357C); 66, Or. *sel.in Ps*.66:2(M.12.1504B); 666, cf.Iren.*haer*.5.30.3(M.7.1206) etc.; *item* in a series, ordinal *number*; *order* of importance πόστον ἂν ἀ. ἔχειν λέγοιτο...ἡ κυβερνητικὴ τέχνη; [i.e. compared with the part of divine providence in ensuring a safe voyage] Or.*princ*.3.1.19 (p.232.16; M.11.292A); **2.** *amount, sum*; as applied to God (ref. Dt.25:13ff.) στάθμιον καὶ μέτρον καὶ ἀριθμὸν τῶν ὅλων ὑπολαμβάνων τὸν θεόν Clem.*prot*.6(p.53.1; M.8.176A); freq. of *number* of the elect, *1Clem*.59.2; λαβεῖν με μέρος ἐν ἀ. τῶν μαρτύρων *M.Polyc*.14.2; ἐν ἀ. τῶν σωζομένων Clem.*str*.3.10(p.228.6; M.8.1172B); *Lit*.ap. *Const.App*.8.5.6; ἐν τῷ ἀ. τῶν αὐτοῦ δούλων *A.Thom*.A 136(p.243.5); abs. ἐγκαταμείγνυε αὐτοὺς τῷ σῷ ἀ. *ib*.156(p.266.1); τοῦ καταθεῖναι καὶ ἡμᾶς εἰς τὸν σὸν ἀ. *A.Xanthipp*.19(p.71.37); a *period* of time ἀ. χιλιονταετίας Caius R.ap.Eus.*h.e*.3.28.2(M.20.273D); διορισμὸν... ἀριθμῶν χρόνου Meth.*symp*.8.15(p.104.2; M.18.168A); αὗται αἱ ψυχαὶ ...ἐν ἡμέραις ἀριθμοῦ παρεδόθησαν εἰς κόλασιν *A.Thom*.A 55(p.172.1) etc.; a large *sum* of money, Attic.*ep.Call*.ap.Socr.*h.e*.7.25.6(M.67. 793B); **3.** abstract *number* ὁ ἀ. διττὸς λέγεται, ὁ μέν τις ἁπλῶς καὶ καθ᾽ ἑαυτόν, ὁ δὲ ἐν σχέσει καὶ πράγμασι θεωρούμενος, ὥσπερ λευκὸν ἥ τε λευκότης καὶ τὸ λελευκασμένον...ὁ ἀ. αὐτὸς καθ᾽ ἑαυτὸν οὔτε διαιρεῖ οὔτε συνάπτει· ἀλλ᾽ ἀμφότερα δέχεται τῇ ποιᾷ σχέσει Leont.B. *arg.Sev*.(M.86.1920A,B); Pamph.H.*panopl*.6.4(p.617); πᾶς...ἀ. τὴν διαφορὰν κέκτηται σύνοικον, καὶ πᾶσα διαφορὰ...τὸν ἀ. συνεπάγεται σύμφυτον Sophr.H.*ep.syn*.(M.87.3156B); ref. God σὺ...εἶ...ὁ πρῶτος τῇ φύσει καὶ μόνος τῷ εἶναι καὶ κρείττων παντὸς ἀ. *Lit*.ap.*Const.App*. 8.12.7; **4.** theol.; **a.** of numerical distinction of Persons in Trin. ᾤοντο ἐκ τούτων [i.e. Jo.2:19] παριστάσθαι μὴ διαφέρειν τῷ ἀ. τὸν υἱὸν τοῦ πατρός Or.*Jo*.10.37(21; p.212.14; M.14.376B); ὁ πατὴρ καὶ ἔστιν ἐν υἱῷ, καὶ υἱὸς ἐν πατρί· οὐχ ὡς ταὐτὸν δὲ ὄντες, οὐδὲ ὡς ἓν ἀ. Cyr.*thes*.7(5^1.60B); ὁ πατὴρ καὶ ὁ υἱὸς ἓν μέν εἰσι κατὰ φύσιν, δύο δὲ ἐν ἀ. *ib*.12(110A); εἴπερ οὖν εἰς ἕν τι τῷ ἀ. τὸ τῆς ἁγίας τριάδος πλάτος... συστέλλεται, καὶ...ἀναιροῦσι τὸ ὑφεστάναι καθ᾽ ἑαυτοὺς πατέρα καὶ υἱόν· τίς ὁ πρὸς τίνα λέγων ἐστὶ 'ποιήσωμεν ἄνθρωπον' κτλ.; id.*Jo*.1. 2(4.17A); **b.** ref. the unity of essence ὁ...ἀ. ἐστι τοῦ ποσοῦ· τὸ δὲ ποσὸν τῇ σωματικῇ φύσει συνέζευκται...ἡ δὲ μονὰς καὶ ἑνὰς τῆς ἁπλῆς ...οὐσίας ἐστὶ σημαντική Evagr.Pont.*ep*.2(M.32.249A); ἕνα θεόν, οὐ τῷ ἀ., ἀλλὰ τῇ φύσει ὁμολογοῦμεν *ib*.(248C); Cyr.*Jo*.1.5(46D) cit. s. ἀναβαίνω; ἄλλοι Σεβηρῖται...ἕνα θεὸν καὶ μίαν οὐσίαν καὶ φύσιν τὸν πατέρα καὶ τὸν υἱὸν καὶ τὸ ἅγιον πνεῦμα λέγουσιν, οὐκ ἀριθμῷ ἀλλὰ ...ἰσότητι Tim.CP *haer*.(M.86.61C); **c.** of Son as only-begotten ὅπως μὴ μόνον τῆς οὐσίας τοῦ πρώτου ἀλλὰ τοῦ κατὰ τὸ πόσον ἀ. τὴν ὁμοίωσιν ἐπάγοιτο Eus.*d.e*.4.3(p.153.21; M.22.256C); **d.** Christol. ὅταν οὖν λέγωμεν τὰ δύο ἐπὶ τοῦ Χριστοῦ, οὐ τῷ ἀ. λέγομεν αὐτὸν 'δύο', ἀλλ᾽ 'ἕνα' μὲν τῷ ἀ., 'δύο' δὲ τῷ εἴδει, τοῦτο ἔστιν τῇ φύσει Leont.B.*fr*.(M.86.2016Bf.); Christ's natures εἰ μὲν ὁ ἀ. φύσεσιν ἐπιφημισθῇ, οὐ τὸ πόσον αὐτῶν προηγουμένως, ἀλλὰ τὸ ἑτερογενὲς συνίστησιν id.*arg.Sev*.(M.86.1920D); Pamph.H.*panopl*.6.5(p.618); οὐκοῦν ὁ ἀ. τῶν φύσεων ἐπὶ τοῦ ἑνὸς...προσώπου, τὸ μὲν διάφορον τῶν εἰς μίαν ὑπόστασιν ἑνωθέντων παρίστησι, πραγματικὴν δὲ οὐκ εἰσάγει τομὴν ἢ διαίρεσιν *ib*.(l.c.); διδάσκει ὁ ἐν ἁγίοις Γρηγόριος, ὅτι ἐπὶ τοῦ κατὰ Χριστὸν μυστηρίου ὁ μὲν ἐπὶ τῶν προσώπων τὸν ἀ. λέγων, ὡς ἀσεβὴς κατακρίνεται· ὁ δὲ ἐπὶ τῶν φύσεων ἐξ ὧν ὁ εἷς συνετέθη Χριστός, τοῦτον παραλαμβάνων ὀρθῶς ὁμολογεῖ Justn.*conf*.(p.84.1; M.86.1007A); μίαν...φύσιν σεσαρκωμένην ὁμολογεῖν...καὶ δύο πάλιν φύσεις λέγειν...καὶ πρὸς τοῦτο καὶ μόνον τὸν ἀ. παραλαμβάνειν Max. *ep*.12(M.91.480D); use of number defended, *ib*.13(513C); *ib*.15(564); **5.** *unit of troops*; cohort, Pall.*v.Chrys*.9(p.57.7; M.47.33); τὰ 'Ρωμαίων τάγματα, ἃ νῦν ἀ. καλοῦσιν Soz.*h.e*.1.8.11(M.67.880C); Jo.Mal. *chron*.18 p.430(M.97.633B); **6.** plur., the *Book of Numbers*, Clem. *str*.3.4(p.210.23; M.8.1137A); Cyr.*ador*.8(1.275C); Cosm.Ind.*top*.2(M. 88.133D).

[*]**ἀριπρέπια, ἡ,** for ἀριπρέπεια, *beauty*; ref. Esther, Gr.Naz.*carm*. 1.2.29.292(M.37.905A).

***ἀριστάρχης, ὁ,** *best of leaders*, *Mir.Geo*.(p.153.27).

***ἀρισταρχία, ἡ,** *best administration*, Thdr.Stud.*epp*.2.187(M.99. 1573C).

§**ἀριστεροί, οἱ,** name given to themselves by *Novatian schismatics*, ‡CCP(381)*can*.7.

ἀριστερόχειρ, *left-handed*, Synes.*ep*.4(M.66.1329A).

ἀριστεύς, ὁ, met., *prince* ἀ. τῶν γραφόντων βιβλία Andr.Cr.*Agath*. (M.97.1440B).

[*]**ἀριστήριον, τό,** *refectory*, Jo.Mosch.*prat*.166(M.87.3033B); Thdr. Stud.*poen*.1.45(M.99.1737D).

***ἀριστητάριος, ὁ,** *one in charge of a refectory*, Thdr.Stud.*iamb*.13 tit.(M.99.1784D).

ἀριστητήριον, τό, *refectory* τὴν τοῦ ἀ. διακονίαν Cyr.S.*v.Euthym*.48 (p.69.17); *ib*.9(p.18.3); *ib*.43(p.64.18).

ἀριστογόνος, *having the best offspring*; of David, Nonn.*par.Jo*. 4:29(M.43.780A).

***ἀριστόδικος,** *best of judges*; of Christ, Gr.Naz.*carm*.2.1.50.114 (M.37.1393A).

***ἀριστοεπέω,** *speak excellently, rightly*, Cyr.*Mich*.34(3.420C); id. *Nest*.1.4(p.24.1; 6^1.18A); id.*hom.pasch*.16(5.213A).

***ἀριστοεπής,** *best at speaking, excellent in expression*, Cyr.*glaph*. *Ex*.2.5(1.305B); id.*Juln*.8(6^2.258E).

***ἀριστολόγημα, τό,** *excellent speech*, Amph.*hom*.2.7(M.39.53B).

***ἀριστολύρης,** *expert on the harp*; of David, Eudoc.*Cypr*.1.273 (M.85.841D).

ἄριστον, τό, 1. *morning meal*; **a.** of eucharist ἐπιτιμῶν περὶ τοῦ μὴ ἀναμένειν ἑαυτοὺς τοῖς ἀ. Chrys.*hom.9.2 in 1Cor*.(10.76C); δεῖπνον τὸ ἀ. ἐκάλεσε *ib*.27.2(243E); **b.** met., of martyrdom τὸ ἄ. τοῦτο ἐμοὶ ἡτοίμασται, δεῖ...φαγεῖν τοῦ ἐνδόξου ἀ. *M.Carp*.42; **2.** also masc. δαψιλεστάτους ἀρίστους Thphn.*chron*.p.320(M.108.776A).

ἀριστοποιΐα, ἡ, *getting one's morning meal, having breakfast* or *lunch*, Hipp.*haer*.9.21.2(p.257.15; M.16.3398B).

ἄριστος, ὁ, v. ἄριστον.

Ἀριστοτελικός, *Aristotelian* ἐξ Ἀ. ἀπηχημάτων Gr.Nyss.*Eun*.1 (1 p.35.9; M.45.261D).

ἀριστοτέχνης, ὁ, *sovereign artificer, master maker*; of God, Bas. *hom*.3.8(2.24B; M.31.216C); Chrys.*hom.30.3 in 1Cor*.(10.272D); *Rit. Tons*.(p.411).

[*]**ἀριστότεχνος, ὁ,** = foreg.; of God, ‡Caes.Naz.*dial*.154(M.38. 1108).

ἀριστοτόκος, *bearing the best children*; of places, Gr.Naz.*carm*.2.2 (poem.)1.278(M.37.1471A); Isid.Pel.*epp*.3.245(M.68.924A); met., of martyrdom, Gr.Nyss.*mart*.(M.46.769C).

***ἀριστότροφος,** *rich, very fertile*, Cyr.*glaph.Num*.(1.390A).

ἀριστώδιν, as adj., *distinguished in its fruit*; of art or craftsmanship, Paul.Sil.*Soph*.199,281(M.86.2127B,2130B).

***ἄρκα, ἡ,** (Lat.*arca*) **1.** *state treasury, public revenue*, Justn.*nov*. 128.1(p.637); **2.** any *chest* or *coffer*, Gr.Mag.*dial*.(tr.Zach.)1.4(M.*PL*. 77.175C).

***ἀρκαδική, ἡ,** v. *ἀρκαδίκιον.

ἀρκαδίκι(ο)ν, τό** (ἀρκαδική, ἡ**), kind of garment worn over the rest (cf. Eng. *Ulster, Inverness*), ref. μανδύας (1Reg.18:4) εἶδός ἐστιν ἐφεστρίδος...ἢ ἀρκαδίκιν...ἢ...μαντίον Thdt.*qu.44 in 1Reg*.(1.383); ἐξωμίδα μόνην ἣν νῦν καλοῦσιν Ἀρκαδίκιν id.*qu.1 in 1Par*.(1.562); Proc.G.*2Reg*.8:4(M.87.1133A); ἀρκαδική id.*1Reg*.18:4(M.87.1104B).

ἀρκάριος, ὁ, (Lat. *arcarius*) *treasurer* ποιεῖσθαι τοὺς λογισμοὺς πρὸς τοὺς ἀ. τῆς...ἐκκλησίας Justn.*cod*.1.2.24(p.18); id.*nov*.147.2 (p.720).

ἀρκεύθινος, *of juniper*, *M.Thdot.1* 11(p.67.30); Pall.*v.Chrys*.18 (p.117.30; M.47.63).

***ἄρκλα, ἡ,** (Lat. *arcula*) *chest* for money, Gr.Mag.*dial*.(tr.Zach.) 1.9(M.*PL*.77.194Bf.); *ib*.2.27(M.*PL*.66.183C).

***ἀρκλαρία, ἡ,** = foreg., *Pers*.214a(p.11.5, v.l. ἀλκλαρίαις M.10. 100A); *ib*.245a(p.44.6).

***ἀρκοειδής,** *in the form of a bear, bear-like*, Or.*Cels*.6.30(p.100.17, v.l. ἀρκτοειδής M.11.1341A).

[*]**ἀρκόμορφος,** *in the form of a bear, bear-like*, Jo.Mal.*chron*.5 p.120(M.97.213B).

***ἀρκοπίθηκος, ὁ,** *bear-ape*, Philost.*h.e*.3.11(M.65.496C).

ἄρκτιος, *arctic*; *northern*, Hipp.*haer*.4.47(p.69.14; M.16.3111B); Meth.*symp*.8.14(p.101.19; M.18.164C).

***ἀρκτοειδής,** v. ἀρκοειδής.

ἅρμα, τό, 1. *chariot*, met. *αἰσχυνέσθωσαν Ἄρειος, καὶ Εὐνόμιος, Μακεδόνιός τε καὶ Νεστόριος, τὸ τετράπωλον τοῦ διαβόλου ἅ.* Procl.CP *or*.2.1(M.65.693A); **2.** *shield*, †Anast.S.*relat*.51(p.72); **3.** *habit* of a monk, Pach.*reg*.A 26(32; p.178.11; *AS* p.115); *ib*.43(49; p.180.17; *AS* p.115); *ἐνδύσουσι...αὐτὸν τὸ ἅ. τὸ ἀποτακτικόν ib*.17(21; p.175.3; *AS* p.114 *ἄρμα*).

§ἄρμα, τό, 1. band of *troops* (Lat. *armati*) *ἀγανακτήσας ἐκέλευσεν ἅ. κατ' αὐτῶν ἐξελθεῖν* Jo.Mal.*chron*.12 p.314(M.97.472B); *ib*.16 p.394(584A) but v. note; *Chron.Pasch*.p.329(M.92.849B); **2.** plur. (Lat. *arma*), *arms σκυλεύσαντες τοὺς νεκροὺς ἔλαβον τὰ λωρίκια αὐτῶν...καὶ πάντα τὰ ἅ.* Thphn.*chron*.p.266(M.108.660C); *ib*.p.362 (868C); *ib*.p.390(929B); **3.** *habit* of a monk, Pach.*reg*.A 17(21; *AS* p.114; *ἄρμα* p.175.3); v. *ἅρμα*.

***ἀρμάδα, ἡ,** *naval force ἀ. ... πολλὴ καὶ δύναμις τῶν Ῥωμαίων ἔσται Apoc.Dan*.C(p.121.25).

***ἀρμαμέντον, τό, 1.** *armoury, arsenal* (Lat. *armamentarium*), Justn.*nov*.85.3(p.416); Thphn.*chron*.p.231(M.108.584C); *ib*.pp.249, 370(625A,888A); **2.** collective, *arms*, of an army *ἔχων καὶ αὐτὸς κατήνας τξ' ἀρμαμέντον τε καὶ δαπάνας ib*.p.332(801A).

***ἀρμάριον, τό,** (Lat. *armarium*) *chest, safe*, Cyr.S.*v.Euthym*.48 (p.69.14ff.); Jo.Mosch.*prat*.79(M.87.2936D); †Anast.S.*relat*.30(p.78).

***ἀρμαστατιών, ἡ,** *muster, Chron.Pasch*.p.393(M.92.1008B).

[*]ἁρματιαῖος, *belonging to a chariot*, Thdt.*affect*.4(p.106.3; 4.798).

***ἁρματοποιΐα, ἡ,** *chariot-building*, Hermias *irris*.5(M.6.1173C).

***ἀρματόω (*ἁρματόω),** *equip with arms, arm*, Thphn.*chron*.p.364 (M.108.873A); *ἁρμ-* Barth.Edess.*Agar*.(M.104.1436A).

ἀρμενίζω, *sail, T.Neph*.6.2; ‡Petr.I Al.*phys*.5(p.35); Leont.N. *v.Jo.Eleem*.10(p.19.10).

***ἀρμενογράφος, ὁ,** *writer of Armenian, MAMA* 3.293.

ἀρμενοφόρος, *sail-bearing*, Ephr.3.463C.

***ἀρμεντάριον, τό,** sens. dub., prob. *rack* for torture, *M.Cyriac*.6 (M.10.568C).

***ἁρμοδιότης, ἡ,** *fittingness*, Max.*schol.d.n*.8.9(M.4.368A).

ἁρμοδίως, *fittingly, appropriately*, Or.*princ*.3.1.11(p.214.2; M.11. 269A); Eus.*p.e*.11.9(523D; M.21.868C); Thphn.*chron*.p.295(M.108. 721C).

ἁρμόζω, 1. *belong* to *Ῥωμαίοις ἁ. τήμερον* [sc. *Σουανία*] Men. *exc.Rom*.3(p.178.28; M.113.864A); ref. estate of deceased person, Ath.Scholast.*coll*.4.22(p.65); Phot.*nomoc*.9.25(M.104.765D); **2.** of an action, *lie* against *τὸ τῆς ἱεροσυλίας καὶ κατὰ κληρονόμων ἁ.* Phot. *nomoc*.2.2(M.104.581D).

ἁρμολογ-έω, pass., *be constituted, composed οὐχ ὁ λόγος ἔφασκε... ἀλλ' αὐτὸς ὁ ἐκ παντοδαπῶν ἡρμολογημένος μελῶν ἄνθρωπος* Eust.*fr*. 23 ap.Thdt.*eran*.3(4.234); *αὕτη...ἡ πόλις ἐξ ἁγίων ~εῖται* Andr.Caes. *Apoc*.65(M.106.425A).

***ἁρμολογία, ἡ, 1.** *compactness, solidarity φυλάσσεται* [sc. *τὰ μέλη τῆς ἐκκλησίας*] *διὰ τοῦ συνδέσμου τῆς εἰρήνης πρὸς τὴν πνευματικὴν ἁ. παγίως* Bas.*ep*.29(3.109D; M.32.312C); *περὶ...ἁ. τῶν...ἀρετῶν* Dor. *doct*.14 tit.(M.88.1772D); **2.** *solidity ὀστέων ἁ. καὶ λεπτότης τριχῶν* Procl.CP *or*.2.4(M.65.697A); **3.** in music, ?*modulation*, Jo.VI H. *v.Jo.D*.9(M.94.441C).

***ἁρμονεύς, ὁ,** *director, moderator*, of Christ *ὁ πασῶν τῶν νοερῶν φύσεων σοφώτατος ἁ.* †Diad.*Ar*.9(M.65.1165B).

***ἁρμονιακός, ὁ,** *musician*, Nil.*epp*.3.242(M.79.496C).

ἁρμόνιος, 1. a. *adapted, well-fitting*; of stones, Or.*Jo*.10.39(23; p.216.26; M.14.384A); **b.** *fitted, suitable, ib*.(26; p.154.33; 280A) cit. s. *μάννα*; **c.** *agreeable, conformable τοῖς ἐκ Περιπάτου...ἁ. ἥδε ἡ δόξα* Clem.*str*.2.7(p.130.31; M.8.969A); Or.*Jo*.4.19(11; p.127.31; *ἁρμοδίου* M.14.232D); **2.** poss. = *ἁρμονικός of harmony, of the theory of music τοὺς ἀριθμητικοὺς καὶ τοὺς ἁ. ... λόγους* Athenag.*leg*.6.1(M.6. 901A).

ἁρμοστής, ὁ, *musician ὁ ἀνθρώπινος νοῦς...καθάπερ τις ἁ. ἔντεχνος, τῶν ἐμψυχῶν τούτων ὀργάνων ἁπτόμενος* Gr.Nyss.*hom.opif*.9.3(M.44. 149C).

ἁρμοστικός, *suitable*, Petr.I Al.*fr*.(M.18.513B).

ἁρμοστός, *joined*, as fem. subst., *betrothed bride*, Ephr.1.194A.

ἄρνα, v. *ἀρήν*.

ἀρν-έομαι, med. and pass.; **1.** *deny, disown, repudiate*; freq. ref. religious belief, whether error *~ηθῆναι αὐτὰ* [sc. *τὰ ἐξ ὕλης κατασκευάσματα*] *καὶ ἐλπίζειν ἐπὶ τοῦτον τὸν Χριστόν* Just.*dial*.69.4 (M.6.637B); *ἴσμεν μὲν τὰ τῶν ἀπατεώνων, ~ούμεθα δὲ αὐτά* Or.*Cels*. 6.32(p.102.14; M.11.1345B); or truth *ἀ. διὰ τῶν λόγων ἢ διὰ τῶν ἔργων τὸν Ἰησοῦν 2Clem*.17.7; *ἀ. τὴν εἰς Χριστὸν πίστιν* Ath.*inc*.27.2 (M.25.141D); *ἀ. ... τὸ ὁμοούσιον* Thdt.*h.e*.2.31.1(3.907); with pass. meaning *ὅν τινες ἀγνοοῦντες ~οῦνται, μᾶλλον δὲ ἠρνήθησαν ὑπ' αὐτοῦ* Ign.*Smyrn*.5.1; **2.** abs., *apostatize, M.Polyc*.9.2; Herm.*sim*. 9.26.5; id.*vis*.2.3.4; Or.*mart*.35(p.33.9; M.11.609C); note in this connexion the sum of the numerals *ΑΡΝΟΥΜΕ* = 666 (cf. Apoc. 13:18), ‡Hipp.*consumm*.28(p.301.8, v.l. *-οῦμαι* M.10.932C).

***ἀρνησιθεΐα (-οθεΐα), ἡ,** *denial of God*; of Judas' betrayal, Epiph. *haer*.38.5,6(pp.68.11,69.7; M.41.661A,C); *ib*.38.8(p.71.6; 665B); of heresy *ib*.71.3(p.251.19; M.42.377B); in form *ἀρνησοθεΐα Chron. Pasch*.p.22(M.92.108A).

***ἀρνησίθεος,** *God-denying, atheistic τῆς ἀ. ἀποστασίας* †Hipp. *Artem*.ap.Eus.*h.e*.5.28.6(M.20.513A); Malch.*ep*.ap.eund.7.30.5(712A); as subst., *one who denies God*, Or.*comm.in Mt*.12.12(p.91.23; M.13. 1008B); id.*fr.in Ps*.118:161(p.118); Bas.*Spir*.27(3.22D; M.32.116A); Chrys.*hom.14.1 in 1Tim*.(11.625D).

ἄρνησις, ἡ, *denial, negation*; hence **1.** *repudiation, disavowal*; **a.** of evil, esp. in baptism *βάπτισμα...ἀ. ὃν ἀθεΐας* Gr.Naz.*or*.42.16 (M.36.477A); Thdt.*Cant*.1:2(2.30); abs. *ὅταν ὁ νοῦς κρατήσῃ δι' ἀ. τὴν μονολόγιστον ἐλπίδα* Marc.Er.*opusc*.2.140(M.65.952C); **b.** of faith *ἀ. τῆς εἰς τὸν Χριστὸν πίστεως* Eus.*h.e*.2.23.1(M.20.196C); *ἀ. τοῦ σταυροῦ* ‡Ign.*Phil*.4; *τῇ...ἀ. τοῦ δεσπότου Χριστοῦ* Thdt.*Ps*.80:16 (1.1185); *τῆς περὶ τοῦ υἱοῦ ἀ.* Gel.Cyz.*h.e*.2.23.12(M.85.1297C); **c.** abs., *apostasy ἵνα διὰ τῆς...κολάσεως εἰς ἀ. αὐτοὺς τρέψῃ M.Polyc*.2.4; Dion.Al.*fr*.(p.15.4; M.10.1304C); *Const.App*.5.6.5; **2.** *refusal*; *abnegation, renunciaton ἀ. ... ἐστὶν ἑαυτοῦ ἡ παντελὴς τῶν παρελθόντων λήθη* Bas.*reg.fus*.6.1(2.344D; M.31.925C); *ἀ. ... ψυχῆς, τὸ μηδαμοῦ ζητεῖν τὸ ἑαυτοῦ θέλημα* Gr.Nyss.*instit*.(p.67.2; M.46.297B); ref. Mt. 26:39, Max.*opusc*.(M.91.68B–69A).

***ἀρνησίφαγος,** *denying that one eats*; of gluttons, Bas.*renunt*.6 (2.208B; M.31.640C).

***ἀρνησίχριστος,** *denying Christ*; as subst., *denier of Christ*, Bas. *Spir*.27(3.22D; M.32.116A); id.*ep*.210.5(3.317B; M.32.777A); of iconoclasts, Thdr.Stud.*epp*.2.204(M.99.1621A).

***ἀρνησοθεΐα, ἡ,** v. *ἀρνησιθεΐα*.

***ἀρνησοχριστεΐα, ἡ,** *denial of Christ*, Anast.S.*haer*.(p.260).

***ἀρνητής ὁ,** *denier*; of antichrist, *1Apoc.Jo*.6(p.74); of Saracens *οἱ ἀ. τοῦ Χριστοῦ* Thphn.*chron*.p.294(M.108.717D).

***ἀρνικός,** *belonging to the Lamb, befitting the Lamb* [sc. *Christ*], Areth.*Apoc*.39(M.106.685A).

ἀρνίον, τό, *lamb*; freq. of Christ, cf.Apoc.5:6 etc.; **1.** reason for title, ref. Jer.11:19 *διόπερ καὶ...ἀ. ὁρᾶται ἑστηκὸς ὡς ἐσφαγμένον* Or.*Jo*.6.53(35; p.162.4; M.14.292D); *ἀ. μὲν τὸν κύριον ἐκάλεσε διὰ τὴν ἀκακίαν καὶ τὸ ποριστικὸν* Oecum.*Apoc*.5:6(p.78); *ἀ. ὁ Χριστός, ὃ καὶ διὰ τοῦ κατὰ τοῦ νομικοῦ πάσχα θυομένου προετυποῦτο ἀμνοῦ... τὸ πάθος ἡμῖν τοῦ θεανθρώπου διατυποῦν* Areth.*Apoc*.12(M.106.580B); **2.** eucharistically and myst. *ἀγαλλίασις τῇ ψυχῇ τὸ τοῦ ἁμώμου ἀ. αἷμα* Mac.Aeg.*hom*.47.8(M.34.801A,B); *προκόπτει ἡ ψυχή, λαβοῦσα ζωὴν πνεύματος ἁγίου καὶ ἀπογευσαμένη τοῦ ἀ., καὶ χρισθεῖσα τῷ αἵματι αὐτοῦ ib*.47.11(804A); Areth.*Apoc*.39(M.106.685A).

ἀρνός, ὁ, *young lamb*, Sophr.H.*v.Anast*.(M.92.1689C).

ἀρνοφάγος, *lamb-eating*; ref. Passover, Nonn.*par.Jo*.2:23(M.43. 765A).

***ἀρνύω,** *put away, banish*, Polycr.ap.Eus.*h.e*.5.24.6(M.20.496B).

***ἀρξέτης, ὁ,** *governor διὰ τοῦ ἀ. ἤγουν τοῦ ἐπάρχου* †Gregent.*leg*. *Hom*.58(M.86.613A).

***ἀρόγευτος,** *unpaid*; of an army, Thphn.*chron*.p.405(M.108. 964C).

***ἀροῖσι,** *ἀροῖσιν ἀληθέσιν* Eudoc.*Cypr*.2(f.l. M.85.860D, cj. Ludwich *ἁρμοῖσι* (*ἁρμός, joining, union*), or ?*ἀρότοισι* (*ἄροτος, procreation of children*)).

***ἀροτρία, ἡ,** *ploughing, T.Job* 32(p.123.9).

ἀροτριασμός, ὁ, *ploughing, T.Job* 10(p.109.24); *T.Abr*.A,B 2 (pp.79.2,105.9).

ἀροτρι-άω, 1. *plough, till*, met. *ἀπόστολοι...ἠροτρίασαν τῷ σταυρῷ τὸν κόσμον* Procl.CP *or*.18.2(M.65.820C); **2.** *plough, harrow*; met., ?of brutal treatment, destruction in war *τοῦ δὲ Ἰουστινιανοῦ ...ἐπαπειλοῦντος πάλιν ἕτερον ἐκπέμπειν στόλον καὶ ~ᾶν ἅπαντας* Thphn.*chron*.p.316(M.108.765C).

***ἀρούβατον, τό,** Syriac ܥܪܘܒܬܐ *Friday, day of the preparation ὅτε τῷ ἀ. ἀπεκρεμάσθη, ὥρας ἕκτης ἡμερινῆς σκότος ἐφ' ὅλης τῆς γῆς ἐγεγόνει A.Jo*.97(p.199.12).

***ἄρουλα, ἡ,** *brazier, Pers*.(p.25.11); *ἐσχαρίδες· ἃς νῦν ἀρούλας καλοῦσιν· ἐπιτευκτικώτερον δέ, τὰ κατζία οὕτω νῦν καλούμενα λέγειν Schol.Clem.paed*.3.5(p.337.30; M.9.793A).

ἄρουρα, ἡ, 1. *tilled* or *arable land*; met., of a child-bearing woman *εὐφημεῖται Σάρρα ὡς λαῶν ἄ.* Procl.CP *or*.5.3(M.65.720B); as epithet of BMV, ‡Chrys.*nat.Chr*.1(10.791A); *ὦ ἄ., ἐν ᾗ ὁ τῆς φύσεως γεωργὸς τὸν ἄσταχυν ἀσπόρως ἐβλάστησεν* Procl.CP *or.laud*.

BMV 3(p.104.14; M.65.684B); **2.** *level surface, flooring*, Paul.Sil. *ambo*.129(M.86.2257A).

ἀρουραῖος, *measuring an aroura*, i.e. 100 sq. cubits τὸν...γρῦπά φασιν εἶναι ζῶον παμμεγεθέστατον ὡς ἀ. σκιὰν ἐκτελεῖν ‡Eust.*hex*.(M.18.744C).

***ἀρουρογονία, ἡ,** *productivity of land*, Hesych.H.*serm*.4(M.93.1453D).

ἁρπαγή, ἡ, 1. *rapture*; myst., of S. Paul (ref. 2Cor.12:2) τὸ τῆς ἁ. μυστήριον Gr.Naz.*or*.28.20(p.51.14; M.36.52C); ὅμως δύο ἁ. εἰσι δηλούμεναι, ἕως τρίτου οὐρανοῦ, καὶ ἕως εἰς τὸν παράδεισον Didym. *2Cor*.12:2(p.41.19; M.39.1725D); ἐξήρκει τὴν ἁ. εἰπόντι, σιγῆσαι Chrys.*hom*.26.1 *in 2Cor*.(10.618E); id.*hom*.3.3 *in Col*.(11.346E); Παῦλος...ἐν ἐκστάσει δὲ διὰ τὴν εἰς τρίτον οὐρανὸν ἁ. Cyr.*Ps*.67:28(M.69.1156C); as consummation of Christian prayer ἔστι...προηγουμένη τῶν τελείων προσοχὴ ἁ. τις τοῦ νοῦ Nil.*Magn*.27(M.79.1004A); τὸ δὲ ταύτης [sc. προσευχῆς] τέλειον ἁ. πρὸς κύριον Jo.Clim.*scal*.28(M.88.1132D); **2.** *robbery, plunder*, exeg. Phil.2:6, v. s. ἁρπαγμός.

ἁρπαγιμαῖος ([*]**ἁρπαγημαῖος**), **1.** *to be secured, desirable* ἐν ἐρήμῳ βότρυς...τριπόθητος καὶ ἁ. Cyr.*Juln*.3(6^2.111A); **2.** neut. plur. as subst., *allurements* τὰ ἐκείνου ἁρπαγημαῖα [v.l. -ιμαῖα] Chrys. *fr.in 1Petr*.3:10(M.64.1056B).

ἅρπαγμα, τό, 1. *booty, prey* ἑτέρου διασαλπίσας ἀλλοτρίῳ κρυφιότητα παραπτώματος, ὡς θεῖον ἀποσυλῶν...ἐξαγγελίαν τινὸς πρὸς ἕτερον ἀποκαλύπτων...ὡς ἅ. ποιούμενος τὴν...τοῦ θεοῦ ψῆφον Ephr.3.406B; **2.** *opportunity, occasion* οἷον ἅ. τι τὴν ἐπάνοδον ποιησάμενοι ...μὴ μετὰ φόβου σὺν ἡμῖν βιῷεν Const.ap.Eus.*v.C*.2.31(p.54.23; M.20.1009A); μηδὲ σὺ ἅ. πρὸς τὴν ἀσέβειαν λάβῃς τὴν τῶν προσώπων διαίρεσιν Bas.*hom*.24.3(2.191D; M.31.605A).

ἁρπαγμός, ὁ, A. in gen.; **1.** *robbery, rape*; met., *usurpation* κρῖναί ἐστιν τῆς τοῦ θεοῦ ἀξίας ἀναιδὴς ἁ. Jo.Clim.*scal*.10(M.88.848D); **2.** *prize, privilege* ὁ Πέτρος δὲ ἁ. τὸν διὰ σταυροῦ θάνατον ἐποιεῖτο διὰ τὰς σωτηρίους ἐλπίδας Eus.*fr.Lc*.6:20(M.24.537C); Thdr.Mops. *Phil*.2:6(p.215.21ff); **3.** *god-send, piece of luck*, (ref. Gen.19:3) μειζόνως κατεβιάζετο, καὶ οὐχ ἁ. τὴν παραίτησιν...ἐποιεῖτο Cyr. *ador*.1(1.25A).

B. exeg. Phil.2:6; **1.** *prize, privilege*; **a.** to be retained οἳ καὶ... μιμηταὶ Χριστοῦ ἐγένοντο [sc. the martyrs] [Phil.2:6] ὥστε ἐν τοιαύτῃ δόξῃ ὑπάρχοντες καὶ...πολλάκις μαρτυρήσαντες...οὔτ᾿ αὐτοὶ μάρτυρας ἑαυτοὺς ἀνεκήρυττον *Ep.Lugd*.ap.Eus.*h.e*.5.2.2(M.20.433A); θειοτέραν...τὴν ἀγαθότητα φαίνεσθαι τοῦ Χριστοῦ, ὅτε [Phil.2:8], ἢ εἰ 'ἁ. ἡγήσατο κτλ.', καὶ μὴ βουληθεὶς...γενέσθαι δοῦλος Or.*Jo*.1.32 (37; p.41.15; M.14.85C); cf. *in forma enim dei erat...nec rapinam ducit esse se aequalem deo...quod ipse quidem aequalis deo et unum cum patre est*, id.*Rom*.5.2(M.14.1022C); *vere Jesus 'non rapinam arbitratus est esse se aequalem deo', et non semel sed frequenter pro hominibus seipsum humiliavit*, id.*comm.ser.in Mt*.118(p.250.15; M.13.1769D); προὼν μὲν αὐτῆς [sc. τῆς οἰκονομίας]...θεότητι πατρικῆς δόξης τετιμημένος· οὐ μὴν 'ἁ.' ἡγούμενος Eus.*e.th*.1.13(p.74.3; M.24.852C); ἐν αὐτῇ τῇ βασιλείᾳ αὐτοῦ ἐγενήθη πένης [Phil.2:6], ἀλλ' ἑαυτὸν ταπεινῶν id.*ecl*.3.4(M.22.1128B); cf. ὅτε λέγει [Phil.2:5f.], οὐ χωρίσας εἶπεν, οὐ ἡ θεότης ἐν μορφῇ θεοῦ οὐχ ἁ. ἡγήσατο κτλ., καίτοι ἡ θεότης οὔτε 'Ιησοῦς ὠνόμασται πρὸ τῆς ἐκ παρθένου γεννήσεως, οὔτε τὴν ἐν ἁγίῳ πνεύματι χρίσιν ἔσχηκεν Apoll.*corp.et div*.9(p.189.6; M.*PL*.8.874B); cf. *rapere hominibus est moris illa, ex quibus aliquid adquirere sese posse existimant. dicimus enim frequenter quoniam 'rem illam rapiendam esse existimavit', hoc est, 'cum celeritate illud suscepit, quasi quia magnum illi lucrum possit conferre'. hoc ergo dicit de Christo* [Phil.2:6]; *hoc est, 'non magnam reputavit illam quae ad Deum est aequalitatem, et elatus in sua permansit dignitate; sed magis pro aliorum utilitate praeelegit humiliora sustinere negotia quam secundum se erant'*, Thdr.Mops.*Phil*.2:6 (p.215.21ff.); Cyr.*Juln*.6(6^2.195B); ἐν μορφῇ...θεοῦ ὑπῆρχε, καὶ οὐχ ἁ. ἡγήσατο κτλ. φύσει γὰρ εἶχε τὴν ἰσότητα ταύτην Thdt.*Phil*.2:11 (3.456) v. *ib*.2:6(3.454 cit. infra); ὁ λόγος...τελείως εἶχεν ἀεί· πρὸς δὲ τὸ ἐκπληρῶσαι τὴν ἰδίαν εὐδοκίαν...καθ' ἣν 'οὐχ ἁ.' ἡγούμενος κτλ. Leont.H.*Nest*.3.1(M.86.1605A); οὐχ ἁ. ἡγήσατο, τουτέστιν οὐκ ἀπηξίωσεν ὡς ἄνθρωπος ὑπακοῦσαι καὶ ἀγγέλοις Max.*schol.c.h*.4.4 (M.4.57D); **b.** to be seized, grasped eagerly τῆς...'Ιησοῦ μόνου φιλανθρωπίας ἦν...μέχρι θανάτου καταβαίνειν ὑπὲρ ἀσεβῶν, οὐχ ἁ. ἡγουμένου κτλ. ταῦτα δὲ πάντα ἐπιτελῶν μᾶλλον τὸ θέλημα τοῦ πατρὸς...ἤπερ τὸ ἑαυτοῦ...οὐκ ἀθρόως λαμβάνων ὑποπόδιον...τοὺς ἐχθροὺς Or.*Jo*.6.57(37; p.166.3; M.14.300B); *ib*.13.48(46; p.276.1; 485D); οὐ γὰρ ἄνθρωπος ὢν πρῶτον, ὕστερον θεὸς ἐσχημάτισεν· οὕτω γὰρ ἁ. ἡγήσατο, ἀλλὰ θεὸς ὢν ἀπ' ἀρχῆς, ὕστερον γέγονεν ἄνθρωπος Jo.D.*haer.Nest*.10(M.95.193A); // μέγα, θαυμάσιον κτλ. Or.*Cels*.6.15 (p.86.4; M.11.1313A); οὕτω...θαυμαστὸν...ἐστι τὸ μαρτύριον, ὅτι αὐτὸς ὁ κύριος...τιμῶν αὐτὸ ἐμαρτύρησεν 'οὐχ ἁ.' ἡγησάμενος 'τὸ εἶναι ἴσα θεῷ', ἵνα καὶ τούτῳ τὸν ἄνθρωπον τῷ χαρίσματι εἰς ὃν κατέβη στέψῃ Meth.*fr.mart*.1(p.520.4; M.18.345C)ap.Thdt.*eran*.1(4.56); θεὸς...ὤν, καὶ φύσει θεός, καὶ τὴν πρὸς τὸν πατέρα ἰσότητα ἔχων, οὐ μέγα τοῦτο ὑπέλαβε Thdt.*Phil*.2:6(3.454); **c.** in this sense text often paraphrased as οὐχ ἥρπασε (= *take, claim* as one's possession): χρισθεὶς...ὁ Δαβὶδ εἰς βασιλείαν, οὐχ ἅμα ἥρπασε τὴν βασιλείαν, ἀλλ' ἠνείχετο πολλοῖς χρόνοις...καὶ ὁ σωτὴρ ἡμῶν γεννηθεὶς βασιλεὺς...ἠνείχετο· 'οὐχ ἁ. ἡγήσατο κτλ.' ‡Ath.*sem*.9(M.28.153D); ‡Ath.*dial.Trin*.1.26(M.28.1156B); ἄλλος ὁ 'μὴ ἁ. ἡγησάμενος κτλ.' παρ' ἐκεῖνον οὐ ἴσος ὑπάρχει, ἀλλ' οὐχ ἥρπασεν τὴν πρὸς αὐτὸν ἰσότητα Thdt.*inc*.10(M.75.1432A); opp. λαμβάνω (= *receive*): υἱὸς... τοῦ πατρὸς εὐπειθής, οὐχ ἁρπάσας τοῦ κυριεύειν, ἀλλὰ παρ' αὐτοπροαιρέτου λαβὼν φυσικῶς. οὔτε γὰρ ὁ υἱὸς ἥρπασεν, οὔτε πατὴρ ἐφθόνησε τῆς μεταδόσεως Cyr.H.*catech*.10.9; // λαμβάνω (= *take*): 'οὐχ ἁ. ἡγήσατο κτλ.' ἀντὶ τοῦ, οὐχ ἥρπασεν, οὐκ ἔλαβε Didym.*Trin*. 3.17(M.39.877A); *ib*.1.26(389A); **2.** containing notion of violence; **a.** *something seized by force* (= ἐξ ἁρπαγῆς) οὐκ ἐφοβήθη καταβῆναι τοῦ ἀξιώματος. οὐ γὰρ εἶχεν ἐξ ἁρπαγῆς τὴν θεότητα...ἀλλὰ θεὸς ὢν τέλειος, ἠθέλησε καὶ ἄνθρωπος γενέσθαι ‡Ath.*qu.script*.115(M.28.764D); ὁ ἁρπάσας τι τῶν μὴ προσηκόντων κατέχει τοῦτο διηνεκῶς καὶ ἀποθέσθαι οὐκ ἂν ἕλοιτο, δεδοικὼς καὶ θαρρεῖν οὐκ ἔχων ὑπὲρ τῆς κτήσεως· ὁ δὲ ἀναφαίρετον ἔχων ἀγαθόν, κἂν ἀποκρύπτῃ τοῦτο, οὐ δέδοικεν...ἔστω τις τοῦ αὐτοῦ, ὁ μὲν οἰκέτης, ὁ δὲ υἱός...ὁ...υἱὸς οὐ παραιτήσεται ἐπιτελέσαι πᾶν ἔργον δουλικόν...ἐπειδήπερ οὐκ ἐξ ἁρπαγῆς αὐτὴν ἔχει, καθάπερ ὁ οἰκέτης, ἀλλ' ἄνωθεν καὶ ἐκ πρώτης αὐτῷ συγκληρωθεῖσαν ἡμέρας. τοῦτο οὖν καὶ ὁ Παῦλος δηλῶν περὶ τοῦ Χριστοῦ φησιν...αὐτοῦ οὐκ ἐπείσακτος ἦν [sc. ἡ δόξα], οὐδὲ κατὰ ἁρπαγὴν δοθεῖσα...ἀλλὰ φυσικὴ καὶ γνησία Chrys.*anom*.10.6 (1.537E–538B); οἱ ἐξ ἁρπαγῆς ἔχοντές τι, δεδοίκασιν ἀποθέσθαι...καὶ μὴ διαπαντὸς εἶναι ἐν ἐκείνῳ, ἐν ᾧ εἰσιν. ἀλλ' οὐχ οἱ μὴ ἐξ ἁρπαγῆς ἔχοντες· οἷον, ὁ ἄνθρωπος ἀξίωμα ἔχει τὸ εἶναι λογικός...ὁ τοῦ θεοῦ υἱὸς οὐκ ἐφοβήθη καταβῆναι ἀπὸ τοῦ ἀξιώματος· οὐ γὰρ ἁ. ἡγήσατο τὴν θεότητα, οὐκ ἐδεδοίκει μή τις αὐτὸν ἀφέληται τὴν φύσιν, ἢ τὸ ἀξίωμα. διὸ καὶ ἀπέθετο αὐτό, θαρρῶν ὅτι αὐτὸ ἀναλήψεται...ὅτι οὐχ ἁρπάσας εἶχε τὴν ἀρχήν, ἀλλὰ φυσικήν, οὐ δεδομένην, ἀλλὰ μόνιμον καὶ ἀσφαλῆ id.*hom*.7.1 *in Phil*.(11.245Bff.); ὅπερ...οὐκ ἔχει τις ἁρπάσαι σπουδάζει. οὐκοῦν οὐ καθ' ἁρπαγμὸν εἶχε τὴν κατὰ φύσιν ἰσότητα, ταύτην γὰρ...εἶχεν οὐσιωδῶς Ambrosiaster ap.CLater. *act*.2(H.3.744E); [sc. among pagan deities] ἁρπαγὰς θεότητος καὶ ἔρεις καὶ πολέμους...ταύτην...τὴν ἄγνοιαν...ὁ...διδάσκαλος διορθούμενός φησι [Phil.2:5f.] τουτέστιν, ἣν (v.l. οὐχ) ἥρπασε θεότητα... ἀλλ' ἔμφυτον ἔσχε...οὐδὲ ἀφαιρεθῆναι ὑπέλαβεν Isid.Pel.*epp*.1.139 (M.78.276A); ὁ ἐξ ἁρπαγῆς ἐλευθερίαν λαβών, οὐδὲν δουλικὸν ὑπομένει...ἐπειδὴ τῇ φύσει δεσπότης ἦν, 'οὐχ ἁ. ἡγήσατο κτλ.' τὸ γὰρ τῆς οἰκονομίας οὐδὲν ἔβλαψε τὴν θεότητα Thdot.Anc.*hom*.3.4(M.77.1389A); **b.** perh. with additional idea of good fortune εἰ ἕρμαιον ἡγήσατο τὸ εἶναι ἴσον, οὐκ ἂν ἑαυτὸν ἐταπείνωσεν, ἵνα μὴ ἡ ὑπερουσία πρόκριμα ποιήσῃ τῇ ἀξίᾳ. ἀλλ' ἐπειδὴ ἐκ φύσεως ἴσος ἦν, καὶ οὐσιώδη εἶχε τὴν εὐγένειαν...ταπεινῶσαι ἑαυτὸν οὐ παρῃτήσατο. δοῦλος μὲν γὰρ καὶ ἐλευθερωθεὶς...ἅτε ἅρπαγμα ἢ εὕρεμα τὴν ἀξίαν ἡγησάμενος, οὐκ ἂν ὑποσταίη οἰκετικὸν ἔργον ἀνῦσαι Isid.Pel.*epp*. 4.22(M.78.1072B); **c.** containing notion of injustice, *presumption, unjustified claim* ὅλος θεός ἐστιν ὁ υἱός. διὰ τοῦτο...'οὐχ ἁ. ἡγήσατο κτλ.' Ath.*Ar*.3.6(M.26.332B); πῶς δὲ οὐχ ἁ. ἡγήσατο τὸ εἶναι ἴσα θεῷ, εἰ...οὐδέποτε ἴσος; Bas.*hom*.24.3(2.191C; M.31.604C); ὁ...υἱὸς 'οὐχ ἁ. ἡγησάμενος κτλ.', πῶς ἀνόμοιος καὶ ἄνισος θεῷ; Didym. (‡Bas.)*Eun*.4(M.29.708B); Cyr.*thes*.13(5^1.126B); in controversy with Arians Chrys. denies that phrase is equivalent to οὐχ ἥρπασε, Chrys.*hom*.7.1 *in Phil*.(11.244D); *ib*.6.2(235Bf.); φύσει γὰρ ἐλάττων οὐκ ἂν δύναιτο ἁρπάσαι τὸ εἶναι ἐν τῇ μεγάλῃ· οἷον ὁ ἄνθρωπος οὐκ ἂν δύναιτο ἁρπάσαι τὸ εἶναι ἴσος ἀγγέλῳ κατὰ τὴν φύσιν...ὁ ἵππος... ἴσος ἀνθρώπῳ...εἴ τις μὴ ἔχων ἐξουσίαν πλεονεκτεῖν μένοι τὰ ἑαυτοῦ κεκτημένος, τοῦτον ἐπαινεσόμεθα ἐπὶ δικαιοσύνῃ; οὐδαμῶς *ib*.6.2f. (236B,E).

ἁρπάζ-ω, 1. *snatch, seize* [*and carry off*]; met.; **a.** *usurp* μή... τὴν τῶν ἀποστόλων ἀξίαν ἁ. ‡Jo.D.*conf*.9(M.95.293B); **b.** *seize upon, pounce on* a word or expression, Clem.*q.d.s*.21(p.173.28; M.9.625C); ‡Ath.*dial.Trin*.2.9(M.28.1169A); (ref. 1Cor.8:6) οὐ τίθησι δύο...ἵνα μή τις ἁρπάσῃ τῶν δύο τὸν ἀριθμὸν εἰς πολυθεΐαν Chrys. *hom*.7.1 *in 1Tim*.(11.586C); **c.** *catch* the eye (ref. Judith 16:9) τὸ σανδάλιον τῆς 'Ιουδὶθ ἥρπασε τὸν ὀφθαλμὸν τοῦ 'Ολοφέρνου Nil. *praest*.22(M.79.1088A); **d.** *snatch* sleep ἁ. ὀλίγου ὕπνου διὰ τὴν τῆς φύσεως ἀνάγκην *V.Pach.Α* 29(p.156.28); Dor.*doct*.10.2(M.88.1725B); **2.** *claim, take* (without idea of violence or injustice), ‡Ath.*sem*.9 (M.28.153D); for other reff. exeg. Phil.2:6 v. ἁρπαγμός; **3.** met., *claim, appropriate*, whether justly or unjustly ὅταν τι λέγῃ Χριστὸν ἀνθρωπίνως τοῦτο ἡμεῖς ~ομεν εἰς ὄνησιν ἑαυτῶν Cyr.*Ps*.34:10(M.69.900D); Thdt.*Ps*.43:1(1.878); εἰ...διέμεινεν ἐν τῇ Σιὼν ἡ Ἰουδαίων βασιλεία...εἰκότως καὶ Ἰουδαῖοι τὴν προφητείαν ~ουσι id.*Mich*.4:7 (2.1496); οἱ...ἐν Χριστῷ τὴν διὰ πίστεως ἁρπάσαντες χάριν id.*Is*.5.6 (2.904C); τὴν ἐξ ἐθνῶν ἐκκλησίαν...ἁρπάσαι διδάσκεται τὴν κοινωνίαν ...Ἰουδαίων id.*Ps*.105:4(1.1355); **4.** *overpower*; perh. *rule* ἡλίου καὶ σελήνης ὑφ' ὧν...ἡ κτίσις ~εται Hegem.*Arch*.12(p.20.12; M.10.1448B); pass., met., *be seized* or *possessed* by passions, *V.Pach.Λ* 12 (p.136.21); *ib.Φ* 15(p.10.14); *ib*.118(p.76.35); **5.** *rescue* τοῦ σοῦ κατεφρόνησας αἵματος μόνος ἐξ αἵματος ἅπαντας ἁρπάσαι θέλων Geo.Pis.*carm*.3.50(p.9); **6.** myst., *seize in rapture*; **a.** esp. ref. 2Cor.12:2, Didym.ad loc.(M.39.1725B); S. Paul's humility in speaking about it ὅρα δὲ πῶς καὶ ἐν αὐτῷ τούτῳ μετριάζει τῷ τὰ μὲν εἰπεῖν, τὰ δὲ ὁμολογεῖν ἠγνοηκέναι. ὅτι μὲν γὰρ ἡρπάγη, εἶπεν, εἴτε δὲ ἐν σώματι, εἴτε οὐκ ἐν σώματι, οὐκέτι φησὶν εἰδέναι Chrys.*hom.26.1 in 2Cor*.(10.618E); speculations on its exact nature futile τί οὖν; ὁ νοῦς ἡρπάγη καὶ ἡ ψυχή, τὸ δὲ σῶμα νεκρὸν ἔμεινεν; ἀλλὰ τὸ σῶμα ἡρπάγη; ἀλλ' οὐκ ἔστιν εἰπεῖν. εἰ γὰρ ὁ Παῦλος ἠγνόει ὁ ἁρπαγείς... πολλῷ μᾶλλον ἡμεῖς *ib*.(619A); reason for it τίνος δὲ ἕνεκεν καὶ ἡρπάγη; ὑπὲρ τοῦ δοκεῖν αὐτόν, ὡς ἔγωγε οἶμαι, ἔλαττον ἔχειν τῶν λοιπῶν ἀποστόλων. ἐπειδὴ γὰρ ἐκεῖνοι συνεγένοντο τῷ Χριστῷ, οὗτος δὲ οὐδαμῶς, διὰ τοῦτο εἰς δόξαν ἥρπασε καὶ τοῦτον εἰς τὸν παράδεισον *ib*.(619C); ‡Caes.Naz.*dial*.142(M.38.1089–1092) cit. s. παράδεισος; **b.** of other raptures: of Elijah, Didym.*2Cor*.12:2(M.39.1725B); of Ezekiel, Philox.*ep*.3(p.159); κατάστασις...προσευχῆς...ἔρωτι ἀκροτάτῳ εἰς ὕψος νοητὸν ~ουσα τὸν φιλόσοφον Evagr.Pont.*or*.52(M.79.1177C); of bodies of saints, which will be caught up into heaven by glory which is in their souls on earth, Mac.Aeg.*hom*.6.11(M.34.516C); of mind in prayer, Max.*carit*.2.6(M.90.985B) cit. s. εὐχή.

ἅρπαξ, ὁ, *committer of rape, ravisher*, Ath.Scholast.*coll*.10.9 (p.130); εἰ μὲν δούλη ἢ ἀπελευθέρα ἁρπαγῇ, ἀναιροῦνται οἱ ἅ. Phot.*nomoc*.9.30(M.104.788D).

***ἁρπαστής, ὁ,** = foreg., Tat.*orat*.10(p.11.19; M.6.828C).

***ἀρραβικός,** *of Arabia* ἐν τῇ ἀ. γῇ Just.*1apol*.62.3(p.93.12; M.6.421C ἀρα-); id.*dial*.78.10(M.6.661A).

ἀρραβών (ἀραβών), ὁ, A. in gen.; **1.** *earnest-money* in business contracts κατὰ τὴν ἀναλογίαν τῆς ποσότητος τοῦ ὅλου ἀργυρίου δίδοται ἀ. Or.*comm.in Eph*.1:14(p.243); ὁ δὲ ἀ. μέρος ἐστὶ τοῦ παντός, καὶ ὑπὲρ τοῦ παντὸς πιστός Chrys.*res.mort*.8(2.435D); id.*Eutrop*.2.12 (3.397D); id.*exp.in Ps*.44:3(5.164A); διὰ μέντοι τοῦ ἀ. ἠνίξατο τῶν δοθησομένων τὸ μέγεθος. ὁ γὰρ ἀ. μικρόν τι μέρος ἐστὶ τοῦ παντός Thdt.*2Cor*.1:22(3.295); opp. τὸ τέλειον, Bas.*Spir*.36(3.30A; M.32.132B); *ib*.40(35A; M.144A); ἀ. λέγει πνεύματος, ὀφειλέτην αὐτὸν ποιῶν τοῦ δοῦναι καὶ τὸ τέλειον *cat.2Cor*.5:5(p.381.15); cf.Chrys.*hom.10.2 in 2Cor*.(10.507E); **2.** *pledge, token* of what is present, of attachments to earthly things as *tokens*, i.e. indications, of the passions τοὺς ἀ. αὐτοῦ ἔχεις, καὶ λέγεις, διὰ τί ὀχλεῖ μοι;...δὸς αὐτοῖς τὸν ἀ. αὐτῶν, καὶ ὑπάγουσι Dor.*doct*.13.4(M.88.1765A); **3.** *betrothal* εἴ τις ἐπίσκοπος... τρίτον ἀ. δώσει, ἢ δίγαμον στεφανώσει, καθαιρείσθω ‡Ath.*poenit.can*.1 (p.457); ὥσπερ...οἱ ἐπὶ τῶν γάμων ἀ. οὓς ἀλλήλοις οἱ γαμοῦντες διδόασιν, ἐγγυῶνται τὰ μετὰ ταῦτα...οὕτως...καὶ ἡ 'ἀπαρχὴ τοῦ πνεύματος', τοῦτ' ἔστι τὸ μερικὸν τοῦ πνεύματος χάρισμα, ὅ 'ἐστιν ἀ. τῆς κληρονομίας ἡμῶν', τὴν ἐπὶ καιροῦ δοθησομένην καθόλου χάριν ἡμῖν βεβαιοῖ Gennad.*fr.Rom*.8:26(p.382.8ff.; M.85.1700A); εὐλόγησον τὸν ἀρραβῶνα τῶν δούλων σου...στήριξον τὸν ἀρραβῶνα αὐτῶν ἐν πίστει καὶ ὁμονοίᾳ *Euchol*.(p.312).

B. theol., *pledge, earnest, foretaste*; **1.** of Christ τῷ ἀ. τῆς δικαιοσύνης ἡμῶν, ὅς ἐστι Χριστὸς Ἰησοῦς Polyc.*ep*.8.1; ἀ. τῆς ἀναστάσεως...Ἰησοῦς *Const.App*.5.19.7; *ib*.5.7.12; *ib*.6.30.9; incarnate in womb of BMV ὁ ἐξ αὐτῆς τῆς ἡμετέρας φύσεως ἀ. Leont.B.*Nest.et Eut*.2(M.86.1328C); of union of natures ἔδει οὖν τὸν Χριστὸν θεοῦ καὶ ἀνθρώπων μεσίτην γενόμενον, παρ' ἀμφοτέρων ἀ. τινα εἰληφέναι, ἵνα φανῇ δύο προσώπων μεσίτης Hipp.*Bal*.(p.82.7; M.10.605B); of his human nature κατὰ τὸν ἀ. τῆς ἀφθαρσίας ἤδη ἔχειν τὴν τοῦ λόγου ἀφθαρσίαν Leont.B.*Nest.et Eut*.2(M.86.1356B); **2.** of gift of H. Ghost τὸν...τῆς ζωῆς ἀ. παρεχομένου τοῦ πνεύματος Bas.*Spir*.35 (3.29C; M.32.129C); τὸν ἀ. τοῦ πνεύματος τοῦ ἁγίου κτήσασθε διὰ τῆς πίστεως Cyr.H.*catech*.1.2; Gr.Naz.*or*.14.14(M.35.876A); ὅτι...ῥανὶς ἣν ἐδήλωσε τῷ εἰπεῖν 'ἐκχεῶ ἀπὸ τοῦ πνεύματός μου' καὶ τῷ ἀ. καλέσαι Chrys.*exp.in Ps*.44:3(5.164B); νυνὶ μὲν γὰρ διὰ πίστεως τῆς εἰς Χριστὸν ὡς ἐν ἀρραβῶνος τάξει τὴν ἀπαρχὴν τοῦ ἁγίου πνεύματος πεπλουτήκαμεν Cyr.*Zach*.106(3.801C); in rel. to perfect blessedness of heaven ὁ μετέχων ὁπωσποτε πνεύματος ἁγίου ἔχει τὸν ἀ. τῆς κληρονομίας...ὥσπερ ἐπὶ τῶν συνωνουμένων τι καὶ διδόντων ἀ. κατὰ τὴν ἀναλογίαν τῆς ποσότητος τοῦ ὅλου ἀργυρίου δίδοται ἀ., οὕτως κατὰ τὴν ἀναλογίαν τῶν ἑκάστου προεγνωσμένων ἁγίου μελλόντων ἀγαθῶν, δίδοται ἀ. τῆς κληρονομίας Or.*comm.in Eph*.1:14(p.243); ὁ ἀ. τῶν ἀϊδίων ἀγαθῶν Didym.*Trin*.2.1(M.39.452C); Chrys.*hom.11.6 in Mt*.(7.157B); id.*hom.3.4 in 2Cor*.(10.447E); Thdt.*2Cor*.1:22(3.295); Gennad.*fr.Rom*.8:26(p.382.8ff.; M.85.1700A); *cat.2Cor*.1:22(p.357.10f.); **3.** ref. sacraments as effecting union with God: baptism ταῦτα γὰρ ὁ ἀ.· τὰ δὲ τελειότερα ἐν τῷ μέλλοντι Ammon.*Jo*.3:29(M.85.1413D); ἄσυλον τὸν ἀ. διαφύλαξον καὶ ἀξίωσον αὐτοὺς εἰς τὴν ζωὴν τὴν αἰώνιον *Rit.Bapt*.(p.407); *Euchol*.(p.287); Holy Communion [sc. θεαρχικώτατε λόγε] θάνατον καταργήσας καὶ ἀνάστασιν θεσμοθετήσας δοὺς ἡμῖν ἐνταῦθα τούτων ἀραβῶνα τὴν μετουσίαν τοῦ ἀχράντου σου σώματος *Lit.Jac*.(*NBP* 10² p.106); **4.** in various spiritual matters προοίμια καὶ ἀ. τῶν ἄθλων δίδωσιν αὐτῷ [sc. τῷ Ἰώβ], χρηματίσας αὐτῷ διὰ νέφους καὶ λαίλαπος Or.*sel.in Job* 40:7(M.12.1045A); τὸ παθεῖν ὑπὲρ Χριστοῦ, τῷ φίλτρῳ προστίθησι καὶ οἷον ἀ. γίνεται τῶν ἑξῆς ἄθλων Gr.Naz.*or*.34.4(M.36.244D); of the old dispensation in rel. to the new τύποι μὲν γὰρ ἐκεῖνα τῶν γενικωτέρων, καὶ τῆς καθόλου φιλοτιμίας εἰς τὸ κατὰ μέρος ἐπίδειξις ἦν, ὡς ἐν ἀ. τοῖς προειληφόσιν Cyr.*Jo*.3.6(4.312B); ὥσπερ ἀ. τῆς ζωῆς τῆς παιδὸς ἀκουσάντων τὸν λόγον *V.Pach.Θ* 18(p.107.10); of the lesser habit ἔλαβε τὸν ἀ. τοῦ μεγάλου καὶ ἀγγελικοῦ σχήματος *Euchol*.(p.386); freq. in rel. to world to come τὰ τῆς γνώσεως...οὔτε γὰρ πᾶν κεκομίσμεθα οὔτε παντὸς ὑστεροῦμεν, ἀλλ' οἷον ἀ. τῶν αἰωνίων ἀγαθῶν Clem.*ecl*.12(p.139.30; M.9.704B); τῆς...τοῦ θεοῦ βασιλείας ἀρραβῶσιν ἐφοδιαζομένους Eus.*fr.Lc*.9:3(M.24.545A); ἐν τῷ νῦν βίῳ ἀ. τῆς τοιαύτης δωρεᾶς λαμβάνοντες Ammon.*Ac*.14:21(M.85.1548A); δὸς τὸ χρυσίον πτωχοῖς, ἀ. γὰρ ἡμῖν γέγονε σωτηρίας Pall.*h.Laus*.37(p.110.16; M.34.1185B); in rel. to Hades ὦ Κάιν...ἀ. κατὰ σεαυτοῦ τὸν ἀδελφὸν τῷ ᾅδῃ προπέμπεις; Bal.Sel.*or*.4.3(M.85.72A).

ἀρραβωνίζ-ομαι, 1. *give a pledge to, guarantee* ἤδη ἡ χάρις ἡ τοῦ θεοῦ ~εται τοὺς ἀθλητάς Or.*enarr.in Job* 40:3(M.17.97B); τὸ ἐκεῖνα λέγειν, ἅπερ αὐτοῖς τὴν αἰώνιον ἠρραβωνίζετο φλόγα Cyr.*Jo*.6(4.569C); pass., *be given a pledge, receive an earnest* οὐδὲν...ἐνδεῖ τῇ πίστει... οὐδὲ μετὰ τὴν ἐνθένδε ἀποδημίαν ἄλλα μένει τοὺς πεπιστευκότας, ἀδιακρίτως ἐνταῦθα ἠρραβωνισμένους Clem.*paed*.1.6(p.107.21; M.8.285A); ἐντεῦθεν ἀρραβωνισθέντων ἡμῶν τὰ πρόσοδα τῆς μακαρίας ζωῆς *V.Pach.Λ* 19(p.145.11); **2.** *plight, betroth* ἐπιδίδωσι πρῶτον τῷ ἀνδρὶ τὸν χρυσοῦν...λέγει...~εται ὁ δοῦλος τοῦ θεοῦ...τὴν δούλην τοῦ θεοῦ *Euchol*.(p.311); *ib*.(p.312).

***ἀρραβώνισμα, τό,** *pledge* τὸ φαιὸν ἱμάτιον, ἡ ἀκολούθησις τοῦ Χριστοῦ· ἅτινά ἐστι...ἀ. τῆς βασιλείας τῶν οὐρανῶν Thdr.Stud.*epp*.2.177(M.99.1549C).

***ἀρρᾳδιουργήτως,** *without guile, sincerely*, Ath.Scholast.*coll*.7.3 (p.84).

***ἀρρανής,** ? *unbreakable* ? from ῥαίω, *shatter, destroy* or ? f.l. for ἀρραγής, *unbroken; unbreakable* (ref. Is.31:9) πέτραν ἐν τούτοις ἡμῖν τὴν ἀ. καὶ ἄθραυστον τοῦ σωτῆρος δύναμιν ὀνομάζει Cyr.*Is*.3.3 (2.441E).

ἄρραφος, *seamless*; of Christ's robe, Nonn.*par.Jo*.19:23(M.43.904A); met., of Church, Bas.*hom*.23.4(2.188A; M.31.596C); symbolizing divine nature of Christ, ‡Ath.*pass*.21(M.28.221B).

***ἀρρέμβαστος (*ἀρέμβαστος),** met.; **1.** *not wandering, recollected, free from distraction* ἀ. νοΐ καὶ ἀμετεωρίστῳ ὄμματι Sergia *Olymp*.13(p.50.15); ἀθολώτῳ νοΐ καὶ ἀρ. λογισμῷ Ephr.3.578A; Ant.Mon.*hom*.34(M.89.1541D); esp. of prayer εὐχὴν...ἀ. Mac.Aeg.*hom*.31.2(M.34.729B); ἀρέμβαστος †Cyr.*hom.div*.14(5².415B); Andr.Caes.*Apoc*.72 (M.106.456C); **2.** *unwavering, steady* περὶ τῶν οἰκείων πταισμάτων τελείαν καὶ ἀρ. μνήμην Jo.Clim.*scal*.10(M.88.848B).

***ἄρρεμβος (*ἄρεμβος), 1.** *undistracted, recollected* ἀ. διανοίᾳ Marc.Er.*opusc*.7.5(M.65.1077A); *ib*.2.90(944B) or ? sub 2; **2.** *unwavering, constant* προσευχῆς νηφούσης καὶ ἀρ. Nil.*epp*.3.148(M.79.452D).

ἀρρεν-, v. also ἀρσεν-.

***ἀρρενιστέον,** *one must adapt to a man, make as befits a man*, Clem.*paed*.2.9(p.205.24; M.8.492C).

***ἀρρενοβασία, ἡ,** *sodomy*, Thphl.Ant.*Autol*.3.6(M.6.1129A).

ἀρρενογονία, ἡ, *bearing of male children* τῶν δὲ ζωδίων...ἐστιν... ἅπερ συνεργὸν ἔχει φύσιν πρὸς ἀ. Hipp.*haer*.5.13(p.106.17; M.16.3163B).

***ἀρρενοειδῶς,** *in male form*, (Manich.) τὸ πνεῦμα...ἀ. ὀπτάνεσθαι τοῖς ἄρχουσιν Epiph.*haer*.66.33(p.72.25; M.42.81B).

***ἀρρενοθηλυμάνης,** *mad after vice*, *Vaticin*.2(p.55).

ἀρρενόθηλυς (ἀρσενόθηλυς), 1. *hermaphrodite, masculo-feminine*; freq. of Gnost. aeons: Bythos οἱ μὲν γὰρ αὐτὸν ἄζυγον λέγουσι μήτε ἄρρενα μήτε θήλειαν...ἄλλοι δὲ ἀ.... ἑρμαφροδίτου φύσιν αὐτῷ περιάπτοντες Iren.*haer*.1.11.5(M.7.569A); Anthropos, Hipp.*haer*.5.6(p.78.7; M.16.3126A); other aeons, Iren.*haer*.1.1.1(448A); *ib*.1.30.2(695D);

ἀρσ- ἔχων τὴν θήλειαν ἐν ἑαυτῷ Simon Magus ap.Hipp.*haer*.6.18 (p.145.3; M.16.3222C); Epiph.*haer*.31.1(p.383.1; M.41.473B); Gr.Naz. *or*.31.7(p.154.3; M.36.141A); Jo.D.*haer*.31(M.94.697A); **2.** *male and female, of both sexes*, i.e. *either sex*, †Gr.Thaum.*ep.Philagr*.(M.46.1104C); ‡Just.*qu.et resp*.49(M.6.1293C); met., of two millstones, Or. *sel.in Dt*.24:6(M.12.813D); *Hom.Clem*.12.26 cit. s. φιλανθρωπία; of the number 6, †Anat.Laod.*decad*.(p.34).

***ἀρρενοκοιτία (*ἀρσενοκοιτία), ἡ,** *sodomy*, ἀρσ- Arist.*apol*.13.7; Mac.Aeg.*hom*.4.22(M.34.489B); ἀρσ- Nil.*epp*.2.282(M.79.341A); †Cyr. *hom.div*.14(5^1.414C); ἀρσ-...διαφοραὶ τρεῖς †Jo.Jej.*poenit*.(M.88.1893C).

***ἀρρενομαν-έω,** *be raving after men, be man-mad* ~ουσῶν γυναικῶν ‡Caes.Naz.*dial*.139(M.38.1044).

ἀρρενομιξία, ἡ, *sodomy*, Clem.*paed*.2.10(p.210.21; M.8.501C); Eus. *d.e*.5 proem.(p.205.24; M.22.340D); *Hom.Clem*.6.18.

ἀρρενοπρεπής, *befitting men, manly*, Cyr.*hom.div*.19(M.77.1109A).

ἀρρενοτοκία, ἡ, *bearing of male children*, Thdr.Heracl.*Is*.66:7 (M.18.1373D).

ἀρρενοτόκος, *bearing male children*, Leont.H.*Nest*.4.1(M.86.1652A,C).

ἀρρενοφανής, *masculine-looking* γυναικῶν...ἀ. Max.*schol.e.h*.3.5 (M.4.132A).

***ἀρρενοφθορέω,** *commit sodomy*, Gr.Nyss.*v.Mos*.(M.44.348A); ‡Caes.Naz.*dial*.139(M.38.1044).

***ἀρρενοφθόρος, ὁ,** *sodomite*, Bas.*ep*.188 *can*.7(3.272B; M.32.673C).

ἀρρενόω, 1. act., *make manly, fortify* ἀ. τὴν ἱεράν σου ψυχήν Synes.*ep*.146(M.66.1540D); **2.** med., *become manly, show virility*, Clem.*str*.2.18(p.155.23; M.8.1020C); Synes.*Dion* 1(p.237.19; M.66.1117B); **3.** pass. θηλειῶν τε ὡσαύτως νεανικαὶ ψυχαὶ...ἠρρενωμέναι Eus.*l.C*.7(p.214.6; M.20.1356A); id.*h.e*.8.14.14(M.20.785B).

ἀρρενωπῶς, *like a man, courageously, firmly* οὐ γὰρ ἀναχωρῆσαι χρὴ μόνον ἀπὸ κακίας ἁπάσης, ἀλλὰ καὶ ἀ. ἀμάλθακτον εἶναι Dion.Ar. *e.h*.2.3.5(M.3.401C); Leont.B.*Nest.et Eut*.1(M.86.1285A); τῶν ἐν ἡμῖν νοερῶν δυνάμεων...πρὸς θεὸν ἀ. συγχωρεῖν ἀνατείνεσθαι Max.*ep*.12 (M.91.508A); Jo.D.*hom*.4.30(M.96.632D).

***ἀρρευσία (*ἀρευσία), ἡ, 1.** *failure of excretive powers of body*, ‡Nil.*vit.cog*.(ἀρ- M.79.1468C, v.l. ἀρρ-); **2.** *absence of excretion*, as characterizing man before Fall, Anast.S.*hod*.14(ἀρ- M.89.253D, v.l. ἀρρ-); and after his restoration, Hipp.*fr.res*.(p.254.6; ἀρευσία M.10.861C).

***ἀρρευστία, ἡ,** = foreg. 1, Jo.Clim.*scal*.15(M.88.892A, v.l. ἀρευσία).

***ἀρρεύστως (*ἀρεύστ-), 1.** *without flux* or *change*, of divinity of Son ἡ ἐκ τοῦ πατρὸς εἰς τὸν υἱὸν θεότης ἀρρ. καὶ ἀδιαιρέτως τυγχάνει Ath.*exp.fid*.2(M.25.204B); ὁ δὲ...μονογενὴς θεὸς ἀτρέπτως καὶ ἀρρ. ἐγένετο Didym.*Trin*.3.4(M.39.836D); freq. of generation of Son ἀφραστῶς τε καὶ ἀ. ἐκ πατρὸς...γεννηθέντα ‡Eust.*Laz*.29(p.50.10); ὡς γὰρ ὁ ἡμέτερος λόγος ἀρ. ... γεννᾶται ἐκ τοῦ νοῦ...οὕτω καὶ ἡ γέννησις τοῦ υἱοῦ Ammon.*Jo*.1:1(M.85.1392D); ἀρ. also in Cyr.*thes*.6 tit.(5^1.43A) and Procl.CP *ep*.2.7(M.65.864A); ἀρρήτως, ἀ., ἀγάστως id.*or*.4.3(M.65.716A); θεὸς...ἀπαθῶς καὶ ἀ. γεννᾷ ‡Cyr.*Trin*.7(6^3.10C; M.77.1133D); ὁ Χριστὸς ἐκ πατρὸς ἀνάρχως, ἀ. ... γεγεννημένος Jo.D. *f.o*.4.24(M.94.1209C); id.*hom*.4.4(M.96.604C); †Jo.D.*Trin*.1(M.95.9A); **2.** met., of life-giving waters of truth proceeding *without stream, without flowing* from Council of Nicaea compared with flowing water at Jericho and elsewhere, *Hymn*.(*KlT* 52–53 p.25; *AS* 1 p.495).

ἄρρην (ἄρσην), 1. *male*; the *male* ἡ κοινωνία τοῦ ἄ. prob. tr. early Syriac rendering of *Son of Man* as ܒܪܗ ܕܓܒܪܐ *A.Thom*.A 27,50(pp.142.16,166.8); **2.** *masculine*, in character or in gender, *LS*.

***ἀρρητολεπτόπνευστος,** *inexpressibly finely* (i.e. *delicately, gently*) *inspired*, ‡Paul.Sil.*therm.Pyth*.(M.86.2266).

***ἀρρητολογία, ἡ,** *unspeakable language*, Eus.*p.e*.3.13(122A; M.21.217C); *ib*.5.32(227A; M.389A).

ἀρρητοποιέω, *practise unmentionable vice*, Thphl.Ant.*Autol*.3.3 (M.6.1125A); Eus.*d.e*.4.9(p.163.26; M.22.273A); Epiph.*anac*.63(p.213.24; M.41.849B).

ἀρρητοποιΐα, ἡ, *practice of unmentionable vice*, Eus.*h.e*.2.13.7(M.20.169B); Bas.*ep*.160.3(3.250E; M.32.625D); Thphn.*chron*.p.373(M.108.893A).

ἀρρητόρευτος, *not rhetorical in character* ἔστι μὲν οὖν ἐν ταῖς ῥητορείαις ὁ νόμος τὸ ἀ. ... ὅ τι μὴ παρὰ τὴν πειθὼ τοῦ λέγοντος ἀλλὰ παρὰ τὴν πολιτείαν ἰσχύει Synes.*Dion* 16(p.274.10; M.66.1160A).

ἄρρητος, 1. *unspoken* τοῦτο γὰρ [sc. his deity] Ἰησοῦ κέκρυπται... καὶ λεγόμενον ἄ. μένει Dion.Ar.*ep*.3(M.3.1069B); *unintelligible, inaudible* λέγουσί...τι φωνῇ ἀ. Hipp.*haer*.6.41(p.173.3; M.16.3259C); **2.** *that cannot be spoken, indescribable, immense*; esp. of divine things, *ineffable* συμπέπλεκται τῷ ῥητῷ τὸ ἄ. Dion.Ar.*ep*.9.1(M.3.1105D); οὐδὲ πάντα ἄ., οὐδὲ πάντα ῥητά Jo.D.*f.o*.1.2(M.94.792B); of God, pre-Christian ἔφρασε τρεῖς μεγίστας ὑποστάσεις εἶναι τὸ τοῦ ἀ. καὶ δημιουργοῦ ὄνομα, μίαν δὲ θεότητα εἶπε· διὸ καὶ ἐκλήθη... τρισμέγιστος Ἑρμῆς Jo.Mal.*chron*.2 p.26(M.97.93A); Christian, Just. *2apol*.12.4(M.6.464B); id.*dial*.126.2(M.6.769A); ὁ...θεὸς...ἄ. ὢν δυνάμει τῇ αὐτοῦ Clem.*str*.5.10(p.369.28; M.9.100B); τῆς ἀ. οὐσίας ἐκείνης Chrys.*hom.39.3 in Jo*.(8.230A) etc.; of Son διὰ τῆς ἐπιδημίας τοῦ ἀ. σου λόγου Serap.*euch*.19.1f.; of his eternal generation by the Father, Eus.*d.e*.5.1(p.213.5; M.24.353B); πρᾶγμα ἄ. καὶ φύσεως ἴδιον θεοῦ Ath.*Ar*.2.36(M.26.224A); Cyr.*Jo*.1(4.8D); *ib*.1.5(4.45B); id.*Lc*.19:11(M.72.869C); of Inc. εἴωθε δὲ ἡ γραφὴ τῇ λέξει τοῦ 'ὁ πέμψας' καὶ τοῦ 'ἀπεστάλη' ἐπὶ τῆς ἀ. συγκαταβάσεως προσχρῆσθαι Didym.*Trin*.3.18(M.39.881B); of union of natures in Christ (wrongly) οἱ...πεπατημένην τὴν περὶ τῆς ἑνώσεως ἔννοιαν ἔχοντες, ἄ. αὐτὴν ἔλεγον Leont.B.*Nest.et Eut*.1(M.86.1297D); of work of redemption τὴν...ἄ. θεουργίαν, ἣν δέδρακε καθ' ἡμᾶς γεγονὼς ὁ ἀναλλοίωτος Dion.Ar.*d.n*.2.6(M.3.644C); of H. Ghost πνεῦμα...ζῶσα δύναμις, καὶ θεία φύσις, ἄ. ἐξ ἀ. στόματος πεφηνυῖα, ἀρρήτως... εἰς τὸν ἄνθρωπον ἀπεσταλμένη Didym.(‡Bas.)*Eun*.5(1.303E; M.29.728D); of divine attributes: εὐεργεσία Or.*princ*.3.1.12(p.217.2; M.11.121A); γνώμη Eus.*h.e*.1.2.3(M.20.53C); βουλή *ib*.1.4.2(77A); Euthal. Diac.*epp.Paul*.(M.85.700A); δύναμις Eus.*e.th*.2.6(p.103.29; M.24.908A); Chrys.*hom.38.4 in Jo*.(8.222A); χαρίσαι ἡμῖν ἱερουργῆσαι ἀ. δυνάμει *Lit.Jac*.(p.178.14); τοὺς ἀναγεννωμένους τὴν θείαν καὶ ἄ. σου μορφήν Serap.*euch*.19.3; τοὺς ἀ. τῆς σοφίας ἑαυτοῦ καὶ τῆς δικαιοσύνης λόγους Bas.*hom*.5.5(2.38B; M.31.249A); τὴν ἄ. μορφὴν ἐμφανῆ δεῖξαι αὐτοῖς Cyr.*Lc*.20:9(M.72.885B); in matters pertaining to God τὰ περὶ τοῦ θεοῦ μυστήρια καὶ ἄ. δόγματα Or.*fr.58 in Jer*. 38:23f.(p.227.10); διηγήσασθαι τὰ ἄ. σου μυστήρια Serap.*euch*.13.6; ὁ τῶν ἀ. καὶ ἀθεάτων μυστηρίων θεός *Lit.Praesanct*.(p.348.31); Gnost., Clem.*exc.Thdot*.29(p.116.24; M.9.673B); ἐκεῖνο οὐχ ἁπλῶς ἄ., ⟨ὃ⟩ ὀνομάζεται...καὶ γὰρ τὸ οὐδ' ἄ. οὐκ ἄρρητον ὀνομάζεται ἀλλὰ ἐστὶν... ὑπεράνω παντὸς ὀνόματος ὀνομαζομένου Hipp.*haer*.7.20(p.196.1ff.; M.16.3302C); *ib*.5.7(p.84.9; 3134C); ref. 2Cor.12:3f. ταῦτά ἐστιν...τὰ ἄ. ὑπὸ πάντων λεγομένων μυστήρια *ib*.5.8(p.93.26; 3147A); θεὸν βλασφημεῖν...ἄλεκτον, ἄ. κτλ. *Const.App*.6.10.1; Arian τῷ υἱῷ ὁ πατὴρ ἄ. ὑπάρχει Ar.*Thal.fr*.2 ap.Ath.*syn*.15(p.243.14; M.26.708B); of mystical experiences ὡς τοῖς πολλοῖς ἄ. Dion.Ar.*d.n*.3.3(M.3.684A); **3.** *not to be spoken*, i.e. divulged, because sacred; plur. abs., of pagan mysteries, Hipp.*haer*.1 proem.(p.2.2; M.16.3017B).

***ἀρρητοτόκος,** *ineffable Father*, Synes.*hymn*.3.203(M.66.1596).

ἀρρητουργέω, *do unutterable things*, *Hom.Clem*.4.16.

ἀρρητουργία, ἡ, 1. *unspeakable deed, practice of abominations*, Clem.*prot*.2(p.13.6; M.8.76A); Epiph.*haer*.27.4(p.305.14; M.41.369A); *ib*.38.2(p.64.21; 656D); Philost.*h.e*.7.4(M.65.541A); **2.** *celebration of pagan mysteries* as sacred action not to be revealed, Synes.*provid*. 2.5(p.123.9; M.66.1272C).

***ἀρρητουργός, ὁ,** *doer of infamy*, Tat.*orat*.3(p.4.3; M.6.812A).

***ἀρρητοφώνως,** *with unutterable voice*; *in inexpressible words* τὸν ἀ. βροντοηχούμενον ἐξ οὐρανοῦ Chrysipp.*enc.in Jo.Bapt*.(p.33.17).

ἀρρήτως, 1. *indescribably, inexplicably*; **2.** *ineffably, inexpressibly* τριὰς ἀ. εἰς μονάδα ἀνακεφαλαιουμένη Zach.Mit.*opif*.(M.85.1141B); ref. generation of Son, Alex.Al.*ep.Alex*.12(p.27.7; M.18.565B); Epiph.*haer*.69.15(p.165.1; M.42.225A); Procl.CP *or*.4.3(M.65.716A) cit. s. ἀρρεύστως; procession of H. Ghost, ‡Ath.*dial.Trin*.1.20 (M.28.1148B); Christ's birth, Gr.Naz.*or*.40.45(M.36.424B); Inc., Isid. Pel.*epp*.1.59(M.78.221A); τὴν ἀνθρωπίνην ἐσχατιὰν ἐξ ἧς ἀ. ὁ ἁπλοῦς Ἰησοῦς συνετέθη Dion.Ar.*d.n*.1.4(M.3.592A); ref. H. Ghost ἀ. ... εἰς τὸν ἄνθρωπον ἀπεσταλμένη Didym.(‡Bas.)Eun.5(1.303E; M.29.728D).

ἄρριζος ([*]ἄριζος), 1. *without root*, of Aaron's rod, ἄρ- Gr.Nyss. *v.Mos*.(M.44.324D); id.*hom.11 in Cant*.(M.44.1001A); ἄρ- *ib.2*(793B); **2.** met., of death, *ib.12*(1021B); Bas.Sel.*pasch*.1.3(M.28.1077B); *groundless* τὴν ἄ. δυσμένειαν Gr.Nyss.*ep*.1.4(M.46.1001A); τὸ ἀπαγὲς τοῦ λόγου καὶ ἄ. id.*Eun*.10(2 p.238.4; ἄρ- M.45.840C); *not grounded* in, of 'heavenly humanity' of Christ ἕτερον ἄνθρωπον ἄ. καὶ ἀσυναφῆ πρὸς τὴν ἡμετέραν φύσιν ἀναπλάσσει τῷ λόγῳ id.*Apoll*.33(M.45.1196D).

***ἄρροπος,** *not swayed by inclination*; of a judge, *impartial*, Gr. Naz.*carm*.1.2.8.193(M.37.662A); *ib*.2.2(poem.)2.7(1478A); of thoughts, *undeviating*, Esaias *cap.spir*.18(M.40.1212B).

ἀρρυθμία (ἀρυθμία), ἡ, *want of rhythm* or *proportion*, Meth. *Porph*.1.9(p.505.5; M.18.400D); ἀρ- Melet.*nat.hom*.2(M.64.1161D).

ἀρρύπαντος, *undefiled*, Nil.*epp*.1.293(M.79.189C); †Jo.D.*B.J*.12 (M.96.964C).

[*]**ἀρρύπαρος**, = ἀρύπαρος, *undefiled*; of the flesh, Serap.*Man.* 3.17(p.74; M.18.1252B); of Christ's birth, Cyr.H.*catech.*12.32; *ib.* 17.6.

***ἀρρυπάρως** (*ἀρυπάρως), *without defilement*, ref. Christ's birth ἀρρήτως καὶ ἀρ- Gr.Naz.*or.*40.45(M.36.424B); Anast.Ant.*serm.*4(M. 89.1397B).

ἄρρυπος ([*]ἄρυπος), *unpolluted, undefiled*; of air, ἄρ- Anast.S. *qu.et resp.*96(M.89.744C); (morally) καθαρᾷ τῇ καρδίᾳ καὶ ἀρ- *Const. App.*2.53.5; βίον σεμνὸν καὶ ἄρ- *A.Phil.*A 119(p.48.13); Olymp.*Job* 25:4(M.93.268C).

ἀρρύπωτος, *undefiled, unspotted*, morally, fig. ὃν δέδωκέ μοι ἡ χάρις ἀ. χιτῶνα, ἐγὼ ῥυπάνω; *Pers.*(p.42.9); τὸ τῆς ἀφθαρσίας ἔνδυμα ...ἀ. ... διατήρησον *Rit.Bapt.*(p.406); ref. preservation of divine image in man, Jo.VI H.*v.Jo.D.*1(M.94.429A); met. τὴν εὐαγγελικὴν ...πολιτείαν,...τὸ ἀόργητον...τὸ φιληδονίας ἀ. Bas.*Spir.*35(3.29E; M. 32.132A); ref. virginity, ‡Chrys.*hom.*13(13.253B); of BMV, Jo.Thess. *dorm.BMV* B 14(p.438.11).

***ἀρρυπώτως**, *without defilement*, of Christ's birth ἀρρήτως καὶ ἀ. †Jo.D.*Trin.*1(M.95.9A).

***ἀρρύτιδος**, *unwrinkled* ἄσπιλός τε καὶ ἀ. [sc. ἐκκλησία] Thdr. Stud.*epp.*1.48(M.99.1080A), ? f.l. for ἀρρυτίδωτος.

ἀρρυτίδωτος ([*]ἀρυτίδωτος), *unwrinkled*, of Church of Gentiles ἡ νέα καὶ ἀ. ... νύμφη Cyr.*Joel.*7(3.205D); ἀρ- id.*ador.*12(1.434C).

[*]**ἀρρωγή, ἡ**, for ἀρωγή, *help, succour*, Gr.Agr.*Eccl.*7.1(M.98. 1024A).

ἀρρωστ-έω, 1. *be in ill health*; **2.** met., *be weak in* δοκεῖ δέ μοι πολὺ τὸ εὐπίθανον ~εῖν ὁ λόγος Cyr.*Is.*4.4(2.668C).

Ἀρσάκης, ὁ, name of a Persian king ἀρσάκην ὅ ἐστι βασιλέα Jo. Mal.*chron.*11 p.270(M.97.409A).

ἀρσεν-, v. also ἀρρεν-.

***ἀρσενοκοιτέω**, *commit sodomy*, Or.*Pr.*7:12(M.17.181B); Eus.*d.e.* 1.6(p.33.30; M.22.65C); Jo.Mal.*chron.*18 p.436(M.97.644A).

ἀρσενόπαις, *begetting male issue*, Nonn.*par.Jo.*4:12(M.43.776B).

[*]**ἀρσενόφρων**, *of manly spirit*, Cyr.*hom.pasch.*10(5^{2}.135A).

ἄρσις, ἡ, 1. *lifting, raising*; **2.** *uprising, rebellion* Ἄρης ἀπὸ τῆς ἄ. καὶ ἀναιρέσεως κεκλημένος Clem.*prot.*5(p.49.12; M.8.165B); hence *presumption* εἰς μανίαν ἄρσεως κατὰ τοῦ κυρίου τολμηθείσης Epiph. *haer.*76.5(p.345.35; M.42.524D); **3.** what is raised, *burden*, Or.*Jo.* 10.39(23; p.216.22,25; M.14.381D,384A); hence **4.** *removal, putting away* of leaven, Gr.Naz.*or.*41.2(M.36.432A); *transportation*, Thdt. *qu.11 in 3Reg.*(1.461); **5.** *rejection* νηπίων ἄ. τύπων Gr.Naz.*carm.*1.2. 34.197(M.37.959A); ἡ...προνοίας ἄ., ἄνταρσις θεοῦ *ib.*1.1.6.16(431A).

ἀρτάβη, ἡ, an Egyptian measure of capacity varying from 24 to 42 χοίνικες, Epiph.*mens.*21(M.43.272B); *Apophth.Patr.*(M.65.128A); Leont.N.*v.Jo.Eleem.*3(p.9.12); ref. Is.5:10 interpreted allegorically of books of NT ἐξ τοίνυν ἀ. ... τέτταρας μὲν τὰς τῆς θεηγορίας πυκτάς, πέμπτην δὲ τὴν τῶν θεσπεσίων Πράξιν· ἕκτην δὲ τὴν τοῦ ὑψηλοῦ Παύλου μονότευχον δεκατεσσάρων ἐπιστολῶν ‡Caes.Naz.*dial.*193 (M.38.1176).

[*]**ἀρτάζω**, for ἀερτάζω.

ἀρτάω, *LS*; *be in suspense*, Ath.*inc.*26.6(M.25.141B).

ἀρτεμέω, *be safe and sound*, Gr.Naz.*carm.*1.1.36.24(M.37.519A); Nonn.*par.Jo.*4:50(M.43.784A).

***ἀρτίας**, *now, just now*, Gr.Mag.*dial.*(tr.Zach.)1.12(M.*PL.*77. 214B).

***ἀρτιβαφής**, *newly-dyed*, Synes.*ep.*44(M.66.1369A).

***ἀρτιγαλακτοτροφοῦμαι**, *be weaned*, Ast.Am.*hom.*6(M.40.241A).

***ἀρτιγεύστος**, *newly-tasting*, met., of a novice ἀ. τῆς μοναδικῆς πολιτείας Thdr.Stud.*epp.*1.28(M.99.997C).

***ἀρτικός**, *prepared, ordered* ἀ. διάθεσιν Melet.*nat.hom.*10(M.64. 1193B).

ἄρτιος, *complete*; *perfect*; *suitable* ἄ. δὲ πάντως ἐκεῖνός ἐστιν, ᾧ τελείως ὁ τῆς φύσεως συμπεπλήρωται λόγος Gr.Nyss.*hom.6 in Eccl.* (M.44.704A); of Christian character and virtue, ‡Ath.*dial.Trin.*3.16 (M.28.1228B); Thdt.*affect.*3(p.68.15; 4.760); opp. τὰ ἐξαμβλωθέντα, Chrys.*Thdr.*1.13(1.20A); ref. 2Tim.3:17, Meth.*symp.*5.2(p.54.3; M. 18.97C); ἄ. ... φησὶ τόν...ἐπιτηδείως ἔχοντα πρὸς τὸ κατορθοῦν...τὴν ἀρετήν Cyr.*ador.*14(1.497A).

***ἀρτιόω**, *make sound, heal*, Jo.Mon.*hymn.Petr.*4(M.96.1392D).

ἀρτίπαις, ὁ, *growing boy*, opp. new-born child, Epiph.*anc.*40 (p.51.5; M.43.89C).

***ἀρτιποδέω**, *be sound of foot*, Cyr.H.*catech.*2.5.

***ἀρτισύστατος**, *just established, newly-planted*, Meth.*Porph.*4 (p.507.12; M.18.345A).

***ἀρτισφαγής**, *recently slaughtered*, Thdr.Stud.*epp.*1.51(M.99. 1097C).

ἀρτίτοκος, 1. *new-born*; **2.** *born sound and whole*, opp. ἔκτρωμα, Chrys.*ordin.*4(1.443A).

***ἀρτιτότε**, *just then*, Leont.B.*arg.Sev.*(M.86.1941D).

***ἀρτίτυπος**, *newly-formed*, Nonn.*par.Jo.*9:7(M.43.825A).

***ἀρτιύμνητος**, *just (being) celebrated*, Germ.CP *or.*3.1(M.98.292C).

ἀρτιφαής, 1. *newly-shining*; of Magi's star, Gr.Naz.*carm.*1.1.5.61 (M.37.429A); **2.** *newly-seeing, just endowed with sight*, Nonn.*par.Jo.* 9:17(M.43.828A).

ἀρτιφανής, *just seen, having newly appeared*, Nonn.*par.Jo.*6:17 (M.43.796C); Cyr.*Joel.*32(3.324B); id.*ador.*10(1.331D); of practices, id.*Juln.*7(6^{2}.249A); of persons, Nonn.*par.Jo.*16:21(M.43.881A); of Greek philosophers in comparison with Moses, Cyr.*Juln.*1(14B); of Nestorius δράκοντος ἀρτιφανοῦς id.*Chr.un.*(5^{1}.716B).

***ἀρτιφρονέω**, *hold sound views*, Cyr.*Abac.*32(Aubert; ἀρτίφροσιν 3.547C).

ἀρτίων, s.v.l., form of pres. ptcpl. from ἀρτίζω or ? ἀρτύω, *prepare, devise* δόλον αὐτῷ πικρὸν ἀ. Cyr.*Is.*2.1(2.195E).

ἀρτίως, 1. *just, newly*; **2.** *exactly*, hence *aptly*, Eus.*e.th.*2.25(p.136. 4; M.24.965B); Didym.(‡Bas.)*Eun.*5(1.302C; M.29.725B); *integrally* τὸ κάλλος...τὸ πνευματικὸν ἕν...ἐστιν ἐκ πολλῶν ἀρετῶν συνηγμένον εἰς τὸ ἀ. ἔχειν Cyr.*Ps.*29:8(M.69.856C).

ἀρτοθήκη, ἡ, *pantry*, Cyr.S.*v.Euthym.*17(p.27.19).

ἀρτοποιητικός, *pertaining to bread-making*; ἡ ἀ. *the baker's art, bread-making*, Chrys.*hom.52.4 in Mt.*(7.534C).

ἀρτοπωλεῖον, τό, *baker's shop*, Pall.*h.Laus.*37(p.112.2; M.34. 1186A); v.l. for μαγκίπια, *Chron.Pasch.*p.341(M.92.889A).

ἄρτος, ὁ, 1. *loaf* of bread; **2.** collective and plur., *bread*; of unleavened bread ἄζυμον ἄ. Just.*dial.*12.3(M.6.500C); Or.*Jo.*10.18 (13; p.189.20; M.14.337C); Gr.Nyss.*v.Mos.*(M.44.364B); of shewbread ἄ. προθέσεως Cyr.H.*catech.*22.5; Thdt.*qu.60 in Ex.*(1.164); diet of fast before Easter, *Const.App.*5.18.1 cit. s. ἅλς; *panes civiles, dole bread* ἐκάλεσεν τοὺς ἄ. πολιτικοὺς διὰ τὸ τῇ ἰδίᾳ πόλει τούτους δωρήσασθαι, καὶ ἠφόρισεν ἐκ τῶν ἰδίων αὐτοῦ χωρίων πρόσοδον ἀναλογοῦσαν εἰς λόγον τῶν αὐτῶν πολιτικῶν ἄ. *Chron. Pasch.*p.263(M.92.641B); *ib.*p.389(997A); **3.** *food*; **a.** in gen., *sustenance* τὸν ἄ. τοῦ ἔργου *1Clem.*34.1; πᾶσα...τροφὴ ἄ. λέγεται κατὰ τὴν γραφήν Or.*or.*27(p.365.8; M.11.508B); ἄ. ἢ τοὺς νοητοὺς τῆς φρονήσεως ἢ τοὺς αἰσθητοὺς οἷς τὸ σῶμα τρέφεται ‡Bas.*const.*34 (2.580D; M.31.1425A); ἄ. ... εἰπών, πᾶσαν τὴν σωματικὴν περιλαμβάνει χρείαν Gr.Nyss.*or.dom.*4(p.90.18; M.44.1176D); **b.** *manna* ἄ. ἀγγέλων Just.*dial.*57.2(M.6.605C); Gr.Naz.*or.*14.1(M.35.860A); ἄ. ἀγγέλων καλεῖ ὡς δι' ἀγγέλων χορηγηθέντα Thdt.*Ps.*77:25(1.1154); ἄ. ἄνωθεν id.*Ps.*104:40(1352); **c.** met., of divine wisdom ἄ. ἀγγέλων Or.*or.*27(p.369.28ff.; M.11.513B); of gift of wisdom ἄ. ἡ σοφία Gr.Nyss.*hom.5 in Eccl.*(M.44.696A); of pain ἄ. δακρύων Thdt.*Ps.* 101:10(1.1318); **4.** *pain bénit, panis benedictionis*, an offering for the clergy and virgins of Church οἱ ἄ. τῶν λειτουργῶν καὶ τῶν παρθένων Ath.*ep.encycl.*4(p.173.11; M.25.232A); Gr.Naz.*or.*18.30(M.35.1024A); ἀπὸ...τῶν ἐκκλησιῶν...κατὰ κυριακὴν δύο ἄ. τῶν εὐλογιῶν ἐλάμβανεν Socr.*h.e.*7.12.9(M.67.760B); Niceph.Ur.*v.Sym.*121(M.86.3100A); perh. also Gnost., *A.Jo.*93(p.196.24ff.); from which bread for eucharist was taken, Or.*hom.19(18).13 in Jer.*(p.169.32; M.13.489C); *A.Thom.* A 50(p.166.1); **5.** met., of Christ ὁ κύριος...θύραν ἑαυτὸν λέγων...καὶ ἄ. Bas.*Eun.*1.7(1.218C; M.29.524D); Ἰησοῦς...ὁ ἀληθινὸς ἄ. καὶ τῆς ἀληθινῆς ζωῆς αἴτιος Gr.Naz.*or.*14.1(M.35.860A); cf. *Christus enim panis noster est quia vita Christus et vitae panis*, Tert.*de oratione* 6 (M.*PL.*1.1263A); τοῦτον Ἰησοῦν καλοῦμεν...καὶ ὁδὸν καὶ ἄ. *V.Aberc.* 16(p.14.16); Isid.Pel.*epp.*1.360(M.78.388A); Thdt.*pental.*(5.117) cit. s. ἄλευρον; as bread of angels (ref. Jo.6:51) τοῦτον...τὸν ἄ. ἤσθιον μὲν πρότερον ἄγγελοι, νυνὶ δὲ καὶ ἄνθρωποι Or.*sel.in Ps.*77:25(M.12. 1541C); ὁρᾷς ὅπως καὶ ἐν οὐρανῷ ὑπάρχων ἄ. ἦν ζωῆς Eus.*e.th.*1.20 (p.86.36f.; M.24.876B); as bread from heaven, Or.*or.*27(p.364.21ff.; M.11.505D,508A); Gr.Nyss.*v.Mos.*(M.44.368C); Proc.G.*Is.*3:1(M.87. 1893C); ὁ θεὸς ἡμῶν ὁ τὸν οὐράνιον ἄ. ... τὸν κύριον ἡμῶν...ἐξαποστείλας σωτῆρα *Lit.Jac.*(p.180.15); κύριος ὁ θεὸς ἡμῶν ὁ οὐράνιος ἄ. *ib.*(p.232.17); opp. manna, Chrys.*hom.46.2 in Jo.*(8.270E,271A); ref. BMV οὐ κατὰ τὴν χρυσῆν στάμνον τὸ μάννα χωρήσασα, ἀλλὰ τὸν οὐράνιον ἄ. ἐν γαστρὶ χωρήσασα Procl.CP *annunt.*6(M.85.449B); as bread of life ἄ. ἐστὶ ζωῆς...ὡς...τὸ ζῶον εἰς ζωὴν ἀναπλάττων Ammon.*Jo.*6:35(M.85.1436B); Chrys.*hom.45.2 in Jo.*(8.264A); of BMV τὸ ἔμψυχον θυσιαστήριον τοῦ ἄ. τῆς ζωῆς ‡Meth.*Sym.et Ann.*14 (M.18.381B); of BMV in heaven κατατρυφῶσα τοῦ ζωοποιοῦ οὐρανίου ἄ. τῆς ζωῆς Mod.*dorm.*2(M.86.3285A); Gnost., *A.Jo.*98(p.200.7) cit. s. σταυρός; **6.** eucharistic (v. σῶμα); **a.** of the act ἕνα ἄ. κλῶντες, ὅς ἐστιν φάρμακον ἀθανασίας, ἀντίδοτος τοῦ μὴ ἀποθανεῖν, ἀλλὰ ζῆν Ign.*Eph.*20.2; κατὰ κυριακὴν δὲ κυρίου συναχθέντες κλάσατε ἄ. *Did.*14.1; παραγίνεται...ἐξ ἑωθινῆς εἰς τὸ μνῆμα...ὅπως ἄ. κλάσωμεν ἐκεῖ *A.Jo.*72(p.186.6); *ib.*85(p.193.2); Ath.*virg.*13(p.47.2; M.28. 265C); *Hom.Clem.*14.1; CLaod.*can.*49 cit. s. προσφέρω; for the dead, ‡Pion.*v.Polyc.*20; **b.** of element of *bread* εὐχαριστίᾳ τοῦ ἄ. Just. *dial.*117.1(M.6.745B); Iren.*haer.*4.18.5(M.7.1028B) cit. s. εὐχαριστία; *ib.*5.2.2f.(1125B); Ath.*virg.*13(p.47.5; M.28.265C); ἐπιδημησάτω...ὁ ἅγιός σου λόγος ἐπὶ τὸν ἄ. τοῦτον, ἵνα γένηται ὁ ἄ. σῶμα τοῦ λόγου Serap.*euch.*13.15; †Ath.ap.Eutych.*pasch.*8(M.86.2401B) cit. s. εὐχή; τοῦ ἄ. τῆς εὐχαριστίας Bas.*Spir.*66(3.54E; M.32.188B); ἐπικλήσεως ...γενομένης ὁ...ἄ. γίνεται σῶμα Χριστοῦ Cyr.H.*catech.*19.7; *ib.*21.3; Gr.Nyss.*bapt.Chr.*(M.46.581C); cf. *ante verba Christi quod offertur, panis dicatur; ubi Christi verba deprompta fuerint, jam non panis dicitur sed corpus appellatur,* Ambr.*de sacramentis* 5.4.24(M.*PL.*16. 471B); Mac.Mgn.*apocr.*3.23(p.106); Dion.Ar.*e.h.*3.2(M.3.425C); with salt, v. ἅλς; not consecrated in even numbers μόνη...ἡ ἁγία τριὰς ...διὰ τοῦτο οὖν ἄνισα προτίθησιν ἡ ἐκκλησία τοὺς ἄ. ... τὸ θεῖον ἐν τούτοις χαρακτηρίζουσα Max.*qu.dub.*41(M.90.820A); **c.** of consecrated bread διεχάραξεν τῷ ἄ. τὸν σταυρόν, καὶ κλάσας ἤρξατο διαδιδόναι *A.Thom.*A 50(p.166.18); τὸν ζωοποιὸν καὶ πανάγιον τοῦ μονογενοῦς σου υἱοῦ σαρκοφόρον ἄ. v.l. Ath.*virg.*13(p.47.9); Dion.Ar.*e.h.*3.3.12 (M.3.444A); λαμβάνουσι τὸν ἄ. ἤτοι τὸ δεσποτικὸν σῶμα ‡Sophr.H. *liturg.*3(M.87.3984C); *ib.*9(3989B); *Lit.Jac.*(pp.226.20,228.23); as received in Holy Communion ἄ. θεοῦ θέλω, ὅ ἐστιν σὰρξ τοῦ Χριστοῦ Ign.*Rom.*7.3; τοῦ εὐχαριστηθέντος ἄ. Just.*1apol.*65.5(M.6.428B); Ammon.*Jo.*6:52(M.85.1437C); ἐπιχώριοι πρεσβύτεροι...οὐ δύνανται... ἄ. διδόναι ἐν εὐχῇ CNeocaes.*can.*13; οὐ δεῖ ὑπηρέτας ἄ. διδόναι CLaod.*can.*25; Cyr.H.*catech.*22.5; *ib.*22.8; *Apophth.Patr.*(M.65. 157C); for discussion of ἄ. as τύπος and ἀντίτυπος v.s.vv., also εὐλογέω; **d.** in Gnost. eucharistic rite καὶ ὁ ἄ. καὶ τὸ ἔλαιον ἁγιάζεται τῇ δυνάμει τοῦ ὀνόματος θεοῦ Clem.*exc.Thdot.*82(p.132.10; M. 9.696C); heret. τῶν ἄ. καὶ ὕδατι κατὰ τὴν προσφορὰν μὴ κατὰ τὸν κανόνα τῆς ἐκκλησίας χρωμένων αἱρέσεων...εἰσὶ γὰρ οἳ καὶ ὕδωρ ψιλὸν εὐχαριστοῦσιν Clem.*str.*1.19(p.61.29; M.8.813A); ref. Manicheans οὔτε ἄ. κλῶσιν Thdt.*haer.*1.26(4.321); their rite δεξάμενος εἰς χεῖρας τὸν ἄ. ... 'ἐγώ σε οὐκ ἐποίησα', φησιν ὁ Μανιχαῖος τῷ ἄ. Cyr.H. *catech.*6.32; **7.** met., Ign.*Rom.*4.1 cit. s. ἀλήθω.

***ἀρτοτυρῖται, οἱ,** sect akin to Quintillians, offshoot of Montanists, origin of name ἀ. ... αὐτοὺς καλοῦσιν ἀπὸ τοῦ...ἐπιτιθέντας ἄρτον καὶ τυρὸν [καὶ] οὕτως ποιεῖν τὰ αὐτῶν μυστήρια Epiph.*haer.*49.2 (p.243.11; M.41.881B); cf.Jo.D.*haer.*49(M.94.708A); *artotyritae ab oblatione vocati, panem enim et caseum offerunt, dicentes primis hominibus oblationem a fructibus terrae et a fructibus ovium fuisse celebratam,* Isid.H.*etym.*8.5.22; admitted women to holy orders, Epiph.*anac.*49(p.211.11ff.; M.41.848A).

***ἀρτοφαγία, ἡ,** *eating of bread,* ‡Meth.*palm.*3(M.18.389A).

[*]**ἀρυθμία, ἡ,** v. ἀρρυθμία.

[*]**ἄρυθμος,** *ill-proportioned;* of the eye, Melet.*nat.hom.*2(M.64. 1164A,B).

***ἀρυπάρως,** v. *ἀρρυπάρως.

[*]**ἄρυπος,** v. ἄρρυπος.

[*]**ἀρύπωτος,** *undefiled,* Ephr.2.260A; id.2.276D.

ἀρύσιμος, *that may be drawn* (like water); met., Gr.Naz.*carm.* 1.2.10.165(M.37.692A).

[*]**ἀρυτίδωτος,** v. ἀρρυτίδωτος.

***ἀρύτως,** f.l. for ἀρύπως, *without defilement,* Ph.Carp.*Cant.*198 (M.40.125A).

ἀρχαγγελικός, *pertaining to archangels, archangelic,* Clem.*ecl.* 57.5(p.154.11; M.9.728A); Gr.Naz.*or.*28.3(p.26.6; M.36.29B); Dion. Ar.*c.h.*5(M.3.196B); of Satan before his fall ὁ τῆς ἀ. δόξης ἔχων τὸ ἀξίωμα Eus.Al.*serm.*3(M.86.332A).

***ἀρχαγγελικῶς,** *in the manner of an archangel* ἀ. ἐχαιρέτιζον τὴν...θεομήτορα Mod.*dorm.*9(M.86.3301A).

ἀρχάγγελος, ὁ, *archangel* (angel of second lowest hierarchy, acc. Dion.Ar.*c.h.*6.2(M.3.201A); for nature etc. v. ἄγγελος); **1.** having authority over angels, cf.Or.*princ.*1.8.1(p.94.24; M.11.176B); ἀ. λέγεται, ἐπειδὴ τῶν ἀγγέλων ἄρχει Chrys.*incomprehens.*3.5(1.468B); ἡ τῶν ἀ. ἁγία τάξις...τὰς θεαρχικὰς ἐλλάμψεις ἱεραρχικῶς διὰ τῶν πρώτων δυνάμεων ἀποδεχομένη, καὶ τοῖς ἀγγέλοις αὐτὰς ἀγαθοειδῶς ἀγγέλλουσα Dion.Ar.*c.h.*9.2(257C); **2.** individual archangels: Michael, *A.Phil.*137(p.69.10); *A.Andr.et Mt.*30(p.110.15); ‡Chrys.*synax.*(8. 285A); prayer addressed to him, *Pap.Chr.*(p.436.3); Gabriel, *Protev.* 12; Ath.*v.Anton.*37(M.26.897A); Procl.CP *or.*6.11(M.65.740Bff.); Thdt.*Cant.*proem.(2.18); id.ap.Cyr.*apol.Thdt.*9(p.133.6; 6¹.227B); Raphael, cf.‡Chrys.*synax.*(8.285B); Uriel, *T.Sal.*2.4(M.122.1319B); Azael, *ib.*7.7(1328A); Satan a fallen archangel ἀ. γὰρ ὤν, διάβολος ὕστερον ἐκλήθη Cyr.H.*catech.*2.4; ἀντὶ ἀρχαγγέλου διάβολος αἱρησάμενος εἶναι *Const.App.*5.27.6; **3.** functions; worshipping God and ministering to men (v. ἄγγελος) ὁ θεὸς...ᾧ λειτουργοῦσιν ἀρχάγγελοι ‡Pion.*v.Polyc.*32; κατ' ἔθνος καὶ κατὰ βασιλείαν ἀ. διοικοῦσιν φυλάττοντες Cosm.Ind.*top.*2(M.88.132C); *IGC As.Min.*166; δοξολογοῦσιν ἀ. Andr.Cr.*or.*7(M.97.933C); represented at earthly altar by priests, ‡Sophr.H.*liturg.*3(M.87.3984C); **4.** term applied to a Gnost. aeon (? Christ) μόνος δὲ ὁ ἀ. εἰσέρχεται πρὸς αὐτὸν [sc. τὸν Τόπον πύρινον] οὗ κατ' εἰκόνα καὶ ὁ ἀρχιερεὺς ἅπαξ τοῦ ἐνιαυτοῦ εἰς τὰ ἅγια τῶν ἁγίων εἰσῄει Clem.*exc.Thdot.*38(p.119.1; M.9.677B); **5.** as proper name; of an imperial palace at Constantinople, *Chron.Pasch.*p.383(M.92. 981A); of a church, *ib.*p.391(1001A).

ἀρχαΐζ-ω, **A. 1.** *date from beginning* of time or *from eternity* τοῦ θεοῦ λόγου τὰ λογικὰ πλάσματα ἡμεῖς, δι' ὃν ~ομεν, ὅτι 'ἐν ἀρχῇ ὁ λόγος ἦν' Clem.*prot.*1.6(p.7.13; M.8.61A); of the Faith, Epiph.*haer.* 76.15(p.361.15; M.42.548A); not of evil, *ib.*24.6(p.263.11; M.41.316A); *ib.*42.12(p.158.6; 777A); *ib.*66.59(p.96.10; M.42.117D); of Inc. προσφάτως προσφάτῳ ἐπικοινωνήσας, τῶν ~όντων μενόντων ἐν ταυτότητι *ib.*76.34(p.383.22; 585B); **2.** gen., *be ancient* φασὶ δέ τινες...μηδὲ ~ειν τὴν Ἑβραίων φωνὴν καθ' ὁμοιότητα τῶν λοιπῶν, ἀλλὰ...θαυματοποιηθῆναι Gr.Nyss.*Eun.*12(1 p.288.9; M.45.997A); **3.** *be archaic, copy the ancients* in manners or language; **4.** trans., *assign an early date to,* Clem.*prot.*4.48(p.37.20; M.8.140A); id.*str.*1.21(p.81.14; M.8.865A).

B. *hold sway, rule* ὅσοι...ἐν βασιλεῦσιν...~οντες καὶ πρωταρχοῦντες Thdr.Stud.*epp.*2.207(M.99.1628C).

[*]**ἀρχαίκακος,** v. ἀρχέκακος.

***ἀρχαιογενής,** *senior* in position or standing ἀπέστειλε...Ἰωάννην τὸν πατρίκιον...ὡς ἀ. τῆς πολιτείας καὶ πολύπειρον ὄντα Thphn.*chron.* p.295(M.108.721C); *ib.*p.321(776B).

***ἀρχαιογνώριστος,** *made known, attested, of old,* Thdr.Stud.*epp.* 2.35(M.99.1209D).

ἀρχαιογονία, ἡ, 1. *ancient origin* Ἰουδαίων συγγραφέων... πρεσβύτερον τῆς παρ' Ἕλλησιν ἀ. Μωυσέα τε καὶ τὸ Ἰουδαίων γένος ἀποδειξάντων Eus.*h.e.*6.13.7(M.20.549A); οἴει με τὴν ἀ. αὐτῆς [sc. τῆς νηστείας] ἀπὸ τοῦ νόμου τίθεσθαι Bas.*hom.*1.3(2.2E,3A; M.31.165C); εἴτε ἀρχαιογονίας [sc. ὀρέγῃ] ἔχεις τὴν Γένεσιν *Const.App.*1.6.5; **2.** *origin, descent* (racial); ref. baptism ἵνα καθαρθῇ ἐν αὐτοῖς διὰ τῆς παλιγγενεσίας ὅπερ εἵλκυσαν ἐκ τῆς ἀ. *Cod.Afr.*110; (family) τῆς ἀ. αὐτοῦ [sc. τοῦ Χριστοῦ] ζήτησις κινεῖται Petr.Rav.*ep.*(p.46.1; M.*PL.* 54.743A); Thdt.*eran.*2(4.89); **3.** *origins, ancient history* τοὺς συγγραψαμένους...ἀ. Μωυσέως καὶ τοῦ Ἰουδαϊκοῦ ἔθνους Hier.*vir.ill.*38 (p.30.2; M.*PL.*23.654B).

ἀρχαιόθεν, *from of old,* Cosm.Ind.*top.*5(M.88.197B).

ἀρχαιολόγος, *telling of ancient times* ἀ. ἱστορία Thdr.Stud.*epp.* 2.190(M.99.1580D).

ἀρχαῖον, τό, (Lat. *archivum*) plur., *archives,* Jo.Mal.*chron.*18 p.449(M.97.660C).

***ἀρχαιοπαράδοτος,** *handed down from of old* ψαλμῳδίαι ἀ. Thdr. Stud.*epp.*2.15(M.99.1164B).

ἀρχαῖος, 1. *from the beginning, original;* **a.** of things, *primeval,* Meth.*symp.*4.2(p.46.15; M.18.88C); τὴν ἀ. πλάνην id.*lepr.*10(p.464.19); **b.** of men, *ancient, of old time,* of patriarchs τῶν ἀ. ὑποδειγμάτων *1Clem.*5.1; Or.*engast.*10(p.294.21; M.12.1028D); of pre-Christian prophets, *Did.*11.11; **c.** superl., *eternal* ἀντὶ τοῦ συναΐδιος ἦν τῷ πατρί, ἐν τῇ τοῦ πατρὸς ὑπάρχων φύσει, ἔχων τόπον ἀρχαιότατον τὴν τοῦ γεννήσαντος φύσιν Ammon.*Jo.*1:2(M.85.1393A); **2.** of Christian era, *ancient, original, primitive,* i.e. belonging to the first days; **a.** of things ἡ...τῆς πίστεως ὑμῖν ῥίζα, ἐξ ἀ. καταγγελλομένη χρόνων Polyc.*ep.*1.2; τὰ ἀ. ἔθη CNic.(325)*can.*6 etc.; of Church τὴν...ἀ. Κορινθίων ἐκκλησίαν *1Clem.*47.6; τῇ ἀληθείᾳ καὶ τῇ ἀ. ἐκκλησίᾳ Clem. *str.*7.15(p.65.20; M.9.528B); πίστεως τε ἀ. κανόνα †Hipp.*Artem.*ap. Eus.*h.e.*5.28.13(M.20.516A); τὴν τῶν ἀ. παράδοσιν Meth.*res.*1.22 (p.244.15; M.41.1089C); Eus.*h.e.*5.23.1(M.20.492A); **b.** of persons, Eus.*h.e.*2.1.8(M.20.137A); Εἰρηναῖος...καὶ ὁ πᾶς τῶν ἀ. χορὸς *ib.*4.22.9 (384A); τῶν ἀ. πρεσβυτέρων *ib.*6.13.9(549A); Κλήμης...ἀνὴρ ἀρχαιότατος καὶ οὐ μακρὰν τῶν ἀποστολικῶν...χρόνων *Chron.Pasch.*p.7(M.92. 81A); **3.** *old, antiquated,* i.e. outworn; of pre-Christian times, Or.*hom.12.12 in Jer.*(13; p.101.7; M.13.397C); ἐκεῖνοι τῇ ἀ. παραδόσει παρεμεῖναν τὴν θεότητα γυμνὴν...ὑπογραψάσῃ Euther.*confut.*12 (M.28.1373D); Chrys.*hom.11.2 in 2Cor.*(10.515B); **4.** *former, existing before,* Tat.*orat.*18(p.20.24; M.6.848A); τὴν ἀ. ἐπιζητοῦμεν πατρίδα, τὸν παράδεισον Bas.*Spir.*66(3.56A; M.32.192A); *Const.App.*2.41.1; Cyr.*Jo.*2.1(4.123E) cit. s. ἀνανεόω; **5.** *original,* i.e. first of a series, of Nicaea τὴν ἀ. σύνοδον Ath.*syn.*20(p.247.1; M.26.716C); **6.** *senior* in office (or perh. in age) ἐπισκόπων, ὧν Πάλμας ὡς ἀρχαιότατος προυτέτακτο Eus.*h.e.*5.23.3(M.20.493A); **7.** *old* in years, *aged,* Pall. *h.Laus.*18(p.56.13; M.34.1065C).

***ἀρχαιότευκτος**, *made in olden times, antique*, Thphn.*chron*.p.419 (M.108.993A).

ἀρχαιότης, ἡ, 1. *antiquity, ancient date*; of the gospel, Thdt. *Rom*.14:23(3.147); id.*Col*.1:26f.(3.482) al.; **2.** *ancient history*, as title of Josephus' work τὰ Φλαυΐου Ἰωσήφου περὶ τῆς Ἰουδαίων ἀ. δύο βιβλία Or.*Cels*.4.11(p.281.30; M.11.1041A); Eus.*p.e*.10.6(476D; M.21.793A); **3.** of first days of Church, *primitiveness, early date*; ref. Quadratus τὴν καθ' ἑαυτὸν ἀ. παραφαίνει Eus.*h.e*.4.3.2(M.20.308B); of Papias, *ib*.3.39.13(300B); **4.** *original standard* or *value* γέγονεν...νόμισμα ἐξάγραμμον ἀργυροῦν, καὶ βασιλικαὶ ῥόγαι δι' αὐτοῦ γεγόνασι καὶ κατὰ τὸ ἥμισυ τῆς ἀ. *Chron.Pasch*.p.386(M.92.989C); **5.** *being from the beginning*; of Son, Alex.Al.*ep.Alex*.12(p.27.25; M.18.568A).

***ἀρχάνθρωπος, ὁ,** *primal man*, Hipp.*haer*.5.7(p.86.7; M.16.3135B); *ib*.(p.88.1; 3138B); οἱ Σαμοθρᾷκες τὸν Ἀδὰμ ἐκεῖνον παραδιδόασιν ...ἀ. *ib*.5.8(pp.90.26,91.4; 3142C); cf.Iren.*haer*.1.14.3(M.7.601B); *ib*. 1.30.1(695A).

***ἀρχαρικός,** *of novices*, conj. for ἀρχαϊκός: ἐν τῷ ἐσχάτων ἀρχαρίων κατατάττει χορῷ...ἦν ἰδεῖν πολιὰν αἰδέσιμον ἐν τῇ ἀρχαϊκῇ [? ἀρχαρικῇ] διάγουσαν τάξει Jo.Clim.*scal*.4(M.88.696C).

***ἀρχάριος, ὁ, 1.** *beginner at school, young scholar* ἀπέρχεται πρὸς τὴν σχολὴν τῶν γραμμάτων, καὶ ἔστι πάλιν ἐκεῖ ὅλων ἔσχατος, ἀ. Mac.Aeg.*hom*.15.42(M.34.604D); **2.** *novice* (monastic) ἀ. ... ταπεινῶσιν μισῶν ὅπλον οὐκ ἔχει κατὰ τοῦ ὑπεναντίου Ephr.1.79B; id.1.108A; id.318F al.; φυλάττουσι μή τις μετὰ ἄλλου, καὶ μάλιστα ἀ. ἀπολειφθῇ τῶν ἀδελφῶν ‡Ath.*ep.Cast*.1.2(M.28.852D); Cyr.S.*v.Jo.Hes*.5(p.205.7); **3.** met., *beginner* ποιεῖ τις τὸ θέλημα τοῦ θεοῦ διὰ τὸν φόβον τῶν κολάσεων...ἀ. ἐστιν Dor.*doct*.4.1(M.88.1657C).

ἀρχέγονος (ἀρχίγ-), 1. (perh. accent -γόνος) *which is the first author* or *origin* τὸ ἀ. πάσης κτίσεως ὄνομά σου *1Clem*.59.3; οἱ ἀμφὶ τὸν Ἡράκλειτον τὸ πῦρ ὡς ἀ. σέβοντες Clem.*prot*.5(p.49.17; M.8.168A); ὥς κεν ἐμ' ἀρχεγόνοιο θεὸς χειρὶ κτεατίσσῃ Gr.Naz.*carm*.1.1.2.53(M.37.405A); πάντα τελεῖ, ἅτε θεῖος ἃ μήδεται ἀ. φρήν Anon.ap. Didym.*Trin*.2.27(M.39.753B); **2.** *original, primordial*, **a.** of Gnost. aeons εἶναι ταύτην πρώτην καὶ ἀ. Πυθαγορικὴν τετρακτύν Iren.*haer*. 1.1.1(M.7.448A); of ogdoad, *ib*.1.5.2(493B); *ib*.1.9.3(544A); *ib*.1.11.5 (568B); Hipp.*haer*.5.7(p.83.18; M.16.3134A); Thdt.*haer*.4 proem.(4.349); **b.** of things; of principle of motion as common to men and animals, ‡Eust.*hex*.(M.18.737A); μηδὲ ἀ. τινα φύσιν πονηρίας φαντάζου Bas.*hex*.2.5(1.16D; M.29.40A); τὴν ἀ. ὕλην Gr.Naz.*or*.29.9(p.85.5; M.36.85A); τὸν Ἀδὰμ ἐκλυτρούμενος ἐκ τῆς ἀ. ἀρᾶς Sophr.H. *trop*.(M.87.4008A); τὸ σκότος...ἢ ἀρχίγονον ἦν, ἢ ὁ διάβολος αὐτὸ ἐποίησεν; ‡Caes.Naz.*dial*.61(M.38.928); comp., Synes.*ep*.140(M.66.1532C; l. ἀρχιγ-); **c.** as subst., of Adam (ref. genealogies of Mt. and Lc.) Χριστὸν κατάγουσιν ἀφ' αἵματος ἀ. Gr.Naz.*carm*.1.1.18.3 (M.37.481A); πρώτη ἀρχεγόνου κακίη *ib*.2.2(poem.)1.346(1476A); ‡Chrys.ap.Phot.*cod*.277(M.104.269C); **d.** of God μία...τῶν ὅλων ἀρχή, μᾶλλον...ἀρχῆς ἀνώτερον...καὶ μονάδος ἀρχεγονώτερον...ὁ εἷς καὶ μόνος θεός Eus.*d.e*.4.1(p.151.9; M.22.252C); σοφίας...τῆς ἀ., τῆς πρὸ τῶν ἄλλων...συγκαταβληθείσης τῇ κτίσει Bas.*hom*.12.3(2.99D; M.31.392B); Nonn.*par.Jo*.1:9(M.43.752A); νοείσθω...ὁ λόγος φῶς εἶναι τὸ ἀ. ὃ πρώτῃ φωνῇ τοῦ θεοῦ δι' αὐτοῦ τοῦ λόγου γεγένηται Thdt.*rect.conf*.12(M.6.1229A,B); with H. Ghost τὰς δύο λέγων ἀ. δυνάμεις εἶναι τὰς δορυφορούσας τὸν θεόν Meth.*symp*.10.6(p.128.23; M.18.201D); of H. Ghost, Nonn.*par.Jo*.14:17(M.43.869B); **3.** *ancient*; **a.** of things, ref. Is.44:3 ἀ. ... θεοῦ...μῦθος Nonn.*par.Jo*.7:38(M.43.812A); *ib*.18:39(897A); of baptism, *ib*.1:6(749B); **b.** of persons: Isaiah, *ib*.1:23(753B); David, *ib*.7:42(812B); Solomon, *ib*.10:23 (836B).

***ἀρχέδοτος (*ἀρχίδοτος),** *given at the beginning, primeval* τῆς ἀρχεδότου...στοιχείων κινήσεως Anast.S.*qu.et resp*.96(M.89.748A); νόμοι...ταῖς ἀρχιδότοις πρὸς ἄνδρας ἐξεφάνθησαν θεοτυπίαις Thdr. Stud.*or*.6.1(M.99.729C).

ἀρχέκακος, *beginning mischief, originating evil* ἀρχεκάκους μύθων ἀθέων καὶ δεισιδαιμονίας ὀλεθρίου πατέρας Clem.*prot*.2(p.12.15; M.8.73B); Meth.*lepr*.5(p.455.15); τὴν ἀ. ἁμαρτίαν Cyr.*Jo*.4.6(4.426B); esp. of Devil ἀ. δαίμων Bas.*hex*.6.1(2.50C; M.29.117C); ἀ. πνεῦμα ‡Ign.*Smyrn*.7; ἀ. ὄφις *Lit*.ap.*Const.App*.8.12.23; ἀ. δράκων Cyr.*Is*. 3.3(2.434D); as subst., *author of evil*, Or.*sel.in Ezech*.16:48(M.13.813A); Andr.Caes.*Apoc*.60(M.104.409B); Sophr.H.*mir.Cyr.et Jo*.34 (M.87.3536C); in form ἀρχαίκακος Max.*opusc*.(M.91.80B).

[*]**ἄρχεος,** variant of ἀρχαῖος, *PLond*.1913.10(p.49).

***Ἀρχεστράτειος,** *agreeing with, belonging to school of Archestratus of Gela*, Just.*2apol*.15.3(M.6.469A).

***ἀρχετυπία, ἡ,** *archetype, original*, Dion.Ar.*c.h*.2.4(M.3.144B); opp. σφραγίς, id.*d.n*.2.6(M.3.644B); ἑτοίμους ὁ λόγος...καθίστησι τῇ παραδοχῇ τῆς τῶν ἀληθῶν ἀ. ... γενέσθαι ζώσας εἰκόνας Χριστοῦ Max. *ambig*.(M.91.1253D); *ib*.(1277B).

ἀρχέτυπος, 1. *first-formed*, of the original impression or stamp ἡ ἀ. τῶν πρὸ Μωΰσεως θεοφιλῶν ἀνδρῶν εὐσέβεια Eus.*d.e*.1.6(p.29.13; M.24.57D); ὁ ἀ. Ἀδάμ ‡Ath.*Apoll*.1.4(M.26.1100B); *ib*.1.7(1104D); **2.** *original*, of a seal ὥσπερ σφραγῖδος ἐκτυπώματα πολλὰ μετέχει τῆς ἀ. σφραγῖδος Dion.Ar.*d.n*.2.5(M.3.644A); ref. a portrait, of the painter's idea ἀγαθὸς γραφεὺς τὰς ἀ. ἰδέας ἐκ τῶν πατρικῶν λογισμῶν ἀπολαμβάνων Eus.*e.th*.3.3(p.155.12; M.24.997D); Dion.Ar.*e.h*.4.3.1(M.3.473B,D); **3.** *archetypal* ἔργων ἀ. ἐν ἀπορρήτοις τοῦ πατρὸς λογισμοῖς προϋφισταμένων Eus.*e.th*.3.3(p.155.24; M.24.1000A); Gr.Naz.*carm*.1.2.31.8(M.37.911A); Gr.Nyss.*or.catech*.6(p.36.6; M.45.29B); id.*hom.2 in Cant*.(M.44.793B); τὴν ἀ. χάριν id.*mort*.(M.46.521D); τὸ πνεῦμα τὸ ἅγιον, τουτέστι, τὴν πνοὴν τῆς ζωῆς, δι' ἧς πρὸς τὸ ἀ. διεπλάττετο κάλλος Cyr.*Jo*.9.1(4.822E); Dion.Ar.*e.h*.3.3.7(M.3.436C); Χριστοῦ... τὰ παραδειχθέντα διὰ τῶν ἐνταῦθα αἰσθητῶν συμβόλων ἡμῖν ἀ. χαριζομένου μυστήρια Max.*myst*.24(M.91.705A); id.*qu.Thal*.55(M.90.536D); Thdr.Stud.*or*.11.4.22(M.99.824D); theol., of Logos φωτὸς ἀρχέτυπον φῶς Clem.*prot*.10(p.71.26; M.8.213A); Or.*Jo*.2.2(p.55.4; M.14.109B); Cyr.*1Cor*.11:3(p.282.18; M.74.881B); of Godhead of Father τὴν ἀ. θεότητα τοῦ πατρός Eus.*e.th*.2.17(p.120.32; M.24.937C); cf.*ib*.2.23(p.133.29; M.24.961B); ‡Proc.G.*Pr*.27:8(M.87.1493B); in rel. to Son ὁ μὲν υἱὸς ἐν τῷ πατρὶ ὡς τὸ ἐπὶ τῆς εἰκόνος κάλλος ἐν τῇ ἀ. μορφῇ Gr.Nyss.*Eun*.1(1 p.200.6; M.45.448A); of nature of Godhead ποῦ γὰρ ἐν εἰκόνι μιᾷ διαφορὰ τῆς ἀ. φύσεως εὑρεθήσεται; Bas.Sel.*or*.1.3(M.85.36A); hence freq. with εἰκών q.v.: πῶς...οἱ καθ' ὁμοίωσιν γεγονότες αὐτῷ, κατὰ φύσιν ἐσμὲν...πατέρες, εἰ μὴ πρόσεστι τοῦτο τῇ ἀ. εἰκόνι; Cyr.*Jo*.1.3(4.24C); τῆς αὐτεξουσίου προαιρέσεως ...οὐ θελούσης...μεταγράψαι ἀπὸ τῆς ἀ. καὶ πατρίου θεοειδοῦς εἰκόνος Thdr.Stud.*epp*.1.8(M.99.936D); **4.** *model, pattern, example* γένοιτο δ' ἂν καὶ οὗτος ἀ. εἰκών, ζῶσα καὶ ἔμψυχος, τοῖς ἐξ αὐτοῦ γεγενημένοις ὑπόδειγμα τρόπου θεοφιλοῦς παρεσχημένος Eus.*p.e*.7.8(309A; M.21.524A); Chrys.*sac*.3.14(p.72.1; 1.390D); id.*hom.15.4 in Eph*.(11.114F); ἵνα μὴ γενναίως τὴν προσβολὴν δεξάμενος καὶ ταύτην ἀποκρουσάμενος ἀνδρείας τοῖς ἄλλοις ἀρχέτυπος γένηται Thdt.*h.e*.4.19.2(3.980); **5.** neut. as subst.; **a.** *first impression, original stamp*; of the state of man's innocence, *original state* διορθώσασθαι ὑμᾶς πρὸς τὸ ἀ. Clem.*prot*.12(p.85.9; M.8.241B); Isid.Pel.*epp*.1.206(M.78.313B); **b.** *original* of a portrait etc., Ath.*gent*.25(M.25.49A); Gr.Naz.*or*.30.11(p.124.3; M.36.116D); τὸν δὲ ἀνδριάντα...ἐθεράπευον...τὸν περὶ τὸ ἀ. πόθον ἐπιδεικνύμενοι Philost.*h.e*.7.3(M.65.540B); Thdt.*affect*.12(p.306.8; 4.1019); Gennad.*fr.Gen*.1:26(M.85.1632D); **c.** *archetype* τὸ κάλλος... ἀληθινὸν ἀ. ἐστι τῶν καλῶν Clem.*prot*.4(p.38.17; M.8.141A); οὐκ ἂν εὕροι...ἐπὶ τὴν ἀληθινὴν ἥκειν ὁδόν, εἰ μή τι ἂν ἑκάστη ἀνακάμψῃ εἰς τὸ ἀ. τῆς ὁδοῦ, τουτέστιν τὴν βασιλικήν Epiph.*haer*.59.12(p.377.22; M.41.1036C); Dion.Ar.*e.h*.3.3.1(M.3.428A); usu. contrasted with εἰκών q.v.: κόσμον...τὸν μὲν ἀ., τὸν δὲ εἰκόνα Clem.*str*.5.14(p.387.22; M.9.137A); εἰκὼν μὴ παρόντος μὲν τοῦ ἀ. τὴν ἴσην ἐκείνῳ δόξαν ἀποφέρεται id.*fr*.33(p.218.3; M.100.416B); δι' εἰκόνος...ἡ γνῶσις τοῦ ἀ. γίνεται Bas.*Eun*.1.17(1.229D; M.29.552B); ἡ εἰκὼν ἀνέλθῃ πρὸς τὸ ἀ. Gr.Naz.*or*.28.17(p.47.20; M.36.48C); *ib*.30.20(p.140.2; 129B); ἡ ψυχὴ ...οἷον ἐν κατόπτρῳ καὶ εἰκόνι...πρὸς τὸ ἀ. βλέπουσα Gr.Nyss.*anim. et res*.(M.46.89C); ἄνθρωπος ὀνομάζεται οὐχ ὁ...ἐπὶ τῆς εἰκόνος δεικνύμενος, ἀλλ' ὁ κυρίως λεγόμενος...τὸ ἀ. id.*Eun*.1(1 p.74.30; M.45.305A); id.*hom.opif*.6(M.44.140C); *ib*.16(180B); ἕτερον εἶναι τὸν υἱὸν λέγοντες παρὰ τὸν πατέρα καθάπερ εἰκόνα πρὸς τὸ ἀ. Cyr.*Jo*.3.5(4.306B); ἀλλὰ καὶ οὕτω δημιουργῶν ὁ ἄνθρωπος μιμεῖται ἀμηγέπη τὸν ποιητήν, ὡς εἰκὼν τὸ ἀ.· καὶ γὰρ ἡ εἰκὼν ἔχει τὰ τοῦ ἀ. ἰνδάλματα Thdt.*qu.20 in Gen*.(1.27); ἀ. δὲ τοῦ Ἀντιόχου ὁ ἀντίχριστος, καὶ τοῦ ἀντιχρίστου εἰκὼν ὁ Ἀντίοχος id.*Dan*.11:35(2.1286); Dion.Ar.*e.h*.4.3.1(M.3.473C); id.*d.n*.4.1(M.3.693B); sometimes contrasted with πρωτότυπον q.v.: θαυμάτων δὲ θαυμασιώτερα τά τε ἀ., καὶ τούτων τὰ πρωτότυπα νοητὰ καὶ θεοπρεπῆ παραδείγματα, τὰ τῆς ἐνθέου φημὶ καὶ λογικῆς ἐν ψυχαῖς οἰκοδομῆς ἀνανεώματα Eus.*h.e*.10.4.55(M.20.872A); theol., of Father προνοίας...ἦν ὁ θεὸς αὐτὸς ἑαυτὸν ἐν τοῖς νοητοῖς στήσας ἀ., δίδωσιν εἰκόνα τῆς προνοίας Synes.*regn*.8(p.18.5; M.66.1065B); ἵνα ἐν αὐτῷ [sc. τῷ υἱῷ] τὸν πατέρα ὀψώμεθα, καὶ ὡς εἰκόνα βλέποντες...ἐννοῶμεν τὸ ἀ. Cyr.*Zach*.15(3.671B); id.*dial.Trin*.7(5^1.639B); of nature of Godhead τῆς ἑτερότητος τοῦ κατ' εἰκόνα γενομένου πρὸς τὸ ἀ. οὔσης ἐν τῷ τὸ μὲν ἄτρεπτον εἶναι τῇ φύσει...τὸ δὲ μὴ οὕτως ἔχειν Gr.Nyss.*or.catech*.21(p.82.5; M.45.60A); τὸ θεῖόν ἐστιν... τὸ δὲ ἀ. πρὸς ὃ καὶ μεμόρφωται Cyr.*thes*.13(5^1.133C); of Logos, opp. πρωτότυπον which is here used of Godhead, cf. ἀληθινὸς οὖν θεὸς ὁ θεός, οἱ δὲ κατ' ἐκεῖνον μορφούμενοι θεοὶ ὡς εἰκόνες πρωτοτύπου· ἀλλὰ πάλιν τῶν πλειόνων εἰκόνων ἡ ἀ. εἰκὼν ὁ πρὸς τὸν θεόν ἐστι λόγος Or.*Jo*.2.2(p.55.4; M.14.109B); νοεῖν δὲ εἰκόνα τοῦ θεοῦ τοῦ ἀοράτου, οὐ κατὰ τὰς τεχνητὰς ταύτας ὕστερον ἀπεργασθεῖσαν πρὸς τὸ ἀ., ἀλλὰ συνυπάρχουσαν καὶ παρυφεστηκυῖαν τῷ πρωτοτύπῳ ὑποστήσαντι, τῷ εἶναι τὸ ἀ. οὖσαν, οὐκ ἐκτυπωθεῖσαν διὰ μιμήσεως, ὥσπερ ἐν σφραγῖδί τινι τῆς ὅλης φύσεως τοῦ πατρὸς ἐναποσημανθείσης τῷ υἱῷ Bas.*Eun*.2.16(1.251E; M.29.605A); of Christ, combining archetype and image in Inc. αὐτὸς...ἐν ὑπεροχῇ μένων τῆς οἰκείας θεότητος ...τῇ εἰκόνι τὸ ἀ. μίγνυται Jo.D.*hom*.1.4(M.96.552C); as archetype of own image Χριστὸς...ὡς πάντων ἐστὶν ἀρχηγὸς σωτηρίας, εἰκόνος οἰκείας ἐστὶν ἀ. Thdr.Stud.*antirr*.3.2.6(M.99.420B); notion condemned that man is image of image of God περιττὸν οὖν ἄρα τὸ περιεργάζεσθαι καὶ ἰσχνοεπεῖν καὶ λέγειν, ὅτι οὐ τοῦ θεοῦ μᾶλλόν ἐσμεν εἰκόνες, οὐδὲ τοῦ ἀ., ἀλλὰ τῆς τοῦ θεοῦ εἰκόνος Cyr.*dogm*.(p.558.20; 6^{2}.374C); **d.** *repository of original documents, archives*, *Cod.Afr*.86; **e.** *pattern, model, example*; of Christ's earthly life, ‡Bas.*const*.4(2.547B; M.31.1353A); παιδεῦσαι πρὸς ἡσυχίαν...τῷ ἀ. τῆς σιωπῆς Gr.Naz.*or*.19.2(M.35.1045B); of S. Paul, Chrys.*laud.Paul*.2(2.486B); τὸ ἀ. τοῦ βίου αὐτὸς ἔσο, ὥσπερ εἰκὼν προκείμενος id.*hom.13.1 in 1Tim*.(11.618A); Thdt.*Tit*.2:7(3.704); id.*qu.17 in Dt*.(1.274).

***ἀρχέφωτος**, v. *ἀρχίφωτος.

ἀρχή, ἡ, I. *beginning, source, principle*, def. (cited under appropriate headings), Or.*Jo*.1.16ff.(16–21; pp.20ff.; M.14.50–56); Bas.*hex*.1.5(1.6Bf.; M.29.16A); id.*hom*.16.1(2.135Bf.; M.31.473C); Jo.D.*Man*.1.3(M.94.1509A,B).

A. *beginning*; **1.** with regard to time; **a.** in time τὸν ἐξ ἀ. παραδεδομένον ἡμῖν τῆς εἰρήνης σκοπόν *1Clem*.19.2; εἰ δὲ τὴν ἀπὸ χρόνου λαμβάνοις ἀ., καὶ ἄναρχος [sc. ὁ υἱός] Gr.Naz.*or*.39.12(M.36.348B); λέγεται ἀ. κατὰ χρόνον, ὡς λέγομεν ἀ. ἡμέρας Jo.D.*Man*.1.3(M.94.1509A); esp. ref. Gen.1:1 ἀ. ... τῆς ποιήσεως φῶς ἐστιν Thphl.Ant.*Autol*.2.11(M.6.1065B); ἐν τῇ ἐπινοουμένῃ ἀ. Or.*princ*.2.9.1(p.164.1; M.11.225C); τὰ μὲν κτίσματα ὑπὸ τὴν ἀ. πεποίηται, καὶ διαστηματικὴν ἀ. τοῦ εἶναι ἔχει Ath.*Ar*.2.57(M.26.268C); τουτέστιν, ἐν ἀ. ταύτῃ τῇ κατὰ χρόνον...μετὰ τὰ ἀόρατα...τῶν ὁρατῶν τούτων...τὴν ἀ. τῆς ὑπάρξεως διηγεῖται Bas.*hex*.1.5(1.6B; M.29.13C); and gen. of Creation, ref. Jo.1:2 δύναται...τὸ τῆς ἀ. ὄνομα λαμβάνεσθαι καὶ ἐπὶ τῆς τοῦ κόσμου ἀ. Or.*Jo*.2.4(p.58.3f.; M.14.116A); Gr.Nyss.*or.catech*.5(p.21.4; M.45.20D); Cosm.Ind.*top*.2(M.88.125D); not predicated of God, Hipp.*haer*.1.1(p.4.19; M.16.3021C); εἴ τις...ἐξ οὗ ἐγεννήθη ἐκ Μαρίας ...ἀ. εἰληφέναι τὸν θεὸν εἶναι, ἀνάθεμα ἔστω *Symb.Sirm*.1 *anath*.27 (p.256.22; M.26.740C); ἀ. βάλλω *make a beginning*; of entering novitiate, Ephr.1.305A,F; 315F; plur. ἐν ταῖς ἀ. Or.*Jo*.20.10(p.338.19; M.14.593B); Ath.*v.Anton*.3(M.26.844B); τὰς ἀ. τῆς νυκτός *Const.App*.8.37.3; abs., of one's life, Eus.*d.e*.4.11(p.169.11; M.22.281C); **b.** before time, *eternity*, ref. Jo.1:1 θεὸς ἦν ἐν ἀ. Tat.*orat*.5(p.5.16; M.6.813C); Bas.*hom*.16.1(2.135A; M.31.473B); ἐν ἀ. ... τοῦτο δὲ τοῦ ἀϊδίου δηλωτικόν Thdt.*haer*.5.2(4.385); of God ἐξ ἀ. ἀνάρχου Clem.*str*.5.14(p.421.8; M.9.205B); εἰ μὴ ἐξ ἀ. δῶμεν τὸν υἱὸν συνυπάρχειν τῷ πατρὶ ἐξ αὐτοῦ γεγεννημένον, τροπὴν τῆς τοῦ πατρὸς ὑποστάσεως παρεισάγομεν Jo.D.*f.o*.1.8(M.94.812B); **2.** *beginning* in space or movement; **a.** *start* ἡ μὲν γάρ τις ὡς μεταβάσεως, αὕτη δέ ἐστιν ἡ ὡς ὁδοῦ καὶ μήκους...[Pr.16:5] Or.*Jo*.1.16(p.20.3,6f.; M.14.49B); λέγεται μὲν οὖν ἀ. καὶ ἡ πρώτη κίνησις ὡς [Pr.16:5] Bas.*hex*.1.5(1.6B; M.29.16A); id.*hom*.16.1(2.135B; M.31.473C); ἀ. καὶ κατὰ τόπους λέγομεν, ἀ. ὁδοῦ Jo.D.*Man*.1.3(M.94.1509A); ἡ μὲν ἀ. εὐοικονόμητός ἐστιν Ign.*Rom*.1.2; ἄλλην ἰδίαν ἀ. ἐπὶ τοῖς σώμασιν ἐλάμβανεν ἡ ὕβρις αὐτῶν *Ep.Lugd*.ap.Eus.*h.e*.5.1.57(M.20.429C); Meth.*symp*.8.14(p.102.6; M.18.165A); prob. the *lower* heaven ἦν ἡ ἀ. τοῦ οὐρανοῦ τεθελιωμένη ἐπὶ τοῦ ποταμοῦ τοῦ ὠκεανοῦ *Apoc.Paul*.(p.57); plur. met. ὅροι φύσεως, ἀ., καὶ μέσα, καὶ τέλη τῆς τῶν ὅλων οὐσίας περιειληφότες Eus.*Hierocl*.6(515A; M.22.805A); ref. ἀρχὴν ὁδῶν (Pr.8:22): οὐ τὴν ἀ. τῆς θεότητος...τοῦ σωτῆρος ἡμῶν παραστῆσαι βουλόμενον...ἀλλὰ τὴν δευτέραν κατὰ σάρκα οἰκονομίαν Marcell.*fr*.9 ap.Eus.*Marcell*.2.3(p.46.11; M.24.801C); Eus.*e.th*.3.3(p.146.23; M.24.984C); **b.** *tip, end, edge*; of a spear, Eus.*v.C*.1.31(p.22.12; M.20.945B); of a thread, chain etc., Gr.Naz.*or*.28.25(p.60.4; M.36.60C); *ib*.31.8(p.154.9; 141A); Chrys.*virg*.41(1.300D); Thdt.*provid*.4(4.535); of a cloak, *Chron.Pasch*. p.331(M.92.857A); Leont.Abb.*v.Gr.Agr*.81(M.98.693A); **3.** *beginning* in order, *starting-point* ἀ. τοῦ κόσμου τὸ ὕδωρ· καὶ ἀ. τῶν εὐαγγελίων ὁ Ἰορδάνης Cyr.H.*catech*.3.5; τὸ ἰῶτα, ὅπερ ἐστὶν ἀ. ὀνόματος Ἰησοῦ *Const.App*.2.26.2; Thdt.*h.rel*.21(3.1234); ἀ. καὶ κατὰ τάξιν· ὡς πρῶτον τὸ τοῦ ἀναγνώστου ἀξίωμα, εἶτα ὑποδιάκονος Jo.D.*Man*.1.3(M.94.1509A); in logical sequence πᾶς λόγος ἐκ τῶν φανερῶν...τὰς ἀ. λαμβάνων Gr.Nyss.*Eun*.1(1 p.85.6; M.45.317A); τὴν ἀ. τοῦ λόγου πρῶτον ἐπί τινος ἀναντιρρήτου βάσεως στήσαντας *ib*.4(2 pp.77.21,78.26; 652A,D).

B. *element*; **1.** lit., constituent *element* τὰ τῶν ἀνθρώπων σώματα καὶ τὰς τούτων ἀ. Athenag.*res*.3(p.51.10,13,29; M.6.980B,981A); αὗται αἱ ἀ. τινῶν εἰσιν ἀ. ... ἀ. γὰρ τῆς γραμμῆς, τὸ σημεῖον· καὶ ἀ. τῆς ἐπιφανείας, ἡ γραμμή· καὶ ἀ. τοῦ σώματος, ἡ ἐπιφάνεια Bas.*hom*.16.1(2.135C; M.31.473Df.); λέγεται ἀ. καὶ τὸ φύσει πρότερον ὡς ἐπὶ τοῦ ἀριθμοῦ...ἀ. ... τῶν δύο τὸ ἓν λέγεται Jo.D.*Man*.1.3(M.94.1509A); id.*f.o*.1.5(M.94.801C); **2.** of *first matter* τὸ ἐξ οὗ οἷον τὸ ἐξ ὑποκειμένης ὕλης, ἀ. παρὰ τοῖς ἀγένητον αὐτὴν ἐπισταμένοις, ἀλλ' οὐ παρ' ἡμῖν τοῖς πειθομένοις Or.*Jo*.1.17(18; p.22.14; M.14.53B); from which Adam was formed (Manich.) οἱ θερισταὶ...ἐοίκασι τοῖς ἄρχουσι τοῖς ἀπ' ἀ. οὖσιν εἰς τὸ σκότος Hegem.*Arch*.10(p.15.12); (Gnost.) cf. *choicum, substantia* ἀρχῆς, Tert.*adversus Valentinianos* 25(M.*PL*.2.616A); ultimate indivisible *point*; in respect of time, *instant*, of no duration (ref. Gen.1:1) τάχα διὰ τὸ ἀκαριαῖον καὶ ἄχρονον τῆς δημιουργίας εἴρηται τὸ 'ἐν ἀρχῇ ἐποίησεν', ἐπειδὴ ἀμερές τι καὶ ἀδιάστατον ἡ ἀ. Bas.*hex*.1.6(1.6E; M.29.16C); Gr.Nyss.*hex*.8 (M.44.72A); **3.** of instruction, *elements, rudiments* ἔστιν ἀ. καὶ ὡς μαθήσεως, καθ' ὃ τὰ στοιχεῖά φαμεν ἀρχὴν εἶναι γραμματικῆς Or.*Jo*.1.18(20; p.22.27; M.14.53C); Marcell.*fr*.79 ap.Eus.*Marcell*.1.4(p.24.4; M.24.761C); τῆς...τῶν τεχνῶν ἀναλήψεως ἀ. ἐστιν ἡ στοιχείωσις Bas.*hom*.16.1(2.135B; M.31.473C).

C. *principle* ἔστι δὲ ἀ. καὶ ἡ ὡς γενέσεως...ἀ. υἱοῦ ὁ πατὴρ καὶ ἀ. δημιουργημάτων ὁ δημιουργὸς καὶ ἁπαξαπλῶς ἀ. τῶν ὄντων ὁ θεός Or.*Jo*.1.17(pp.21.3,22.10f.; M.14.52A,53A); λέγεται δὲ ἀ. καὶ ὅθεν γίγνεταί τι τοῦ ἐνυπάρχοντος αὐτῷ ἑτέρου, ὡς ἐπὶ οἰκίας θεμέλιος, καὶ...ἀ. σοφίας, φόβος κυρίου Bas.*hex*.1.5(1.6B,C; M.29.16A); hence **1.** *foundation, basis* ταύτην [sc. τὴν πίστιν] τὴν ἀ. τῆς ὑποστάσεως κέκληκε Thdt.*Heb*.3:14(3.565); opp. τέλος, Ign.*Eph*.14.1 cit. s. ζωή; id.*Magn*.13.1; Clem.*str*.7.10(p.41.3; M.9.480A); *Barn*.1.6 cit. s. ζωή; ἡ ἀρχὴ καὶ ⟨τὸ⟩ τέλος δοκεῖ κατὰ τὴν συνήθειαν ὡς ἐπὶ ἡνωμένου λέγεσθαι, οἷον ἀ. οἰκίας ὁ θεμέλιος καὶ τέλος ἡ στεφάνη Or.*Jo*.1.31 (34; p.39.31f.; M.14.84A); **2.** logical *premiss, basis* of argument; *ground* of belief, Cels.ap.Or.*Cels*.5.65(p.68.23; M.11.1288B); Or.*Cels*.3.12(p.212.15; 936A); ταύτην ἀ. ὑποστησάμενος ἀκολούθως ἐκ τῆς δοθείσης αὐτῷ ὑποστάσεως ἐπὶ τὸ καταψεύδεσθαι τῆς θεοπνεύστου γραφῆς Eus.*e.th*.1.18(p.80.10; M.24.864B); id.*d.e*.3.5(p.123.19; M.22.209C); †Bas.*Is*.152(1.486D; M.30.368A); Gr.Nyss.*Eun*.5(2 p.121.8; M.45.701D); **3.** *origin, source*; **a.** lit., of a river, *Apoc.Paul*.(p.50); **b.** of nations, families, species, *Apoc.En*.15.9(p.42.14); ἔστι γὰρ ἄνθρωπος ζῷον ἀπ' ἐκείνου τοῦ ζῴου λαμβάνον τὴν ἀ. Hipp.*haer*.7.16 (p.192.5; M.16.3295D); πᾶσα...ἀ. πατρίων...ἀπὸ Χριστοῦ ἤρξατο Or.*princ*.4.3.7(21; p.333.21; M.11.388A); id.*Cels*.3.6(p.207.16; M.11.928A); *Lit*.ap.*Const.App*.8.12.22; **c.** of literary sources, Eus.*Marcell*.1.3 (p.17.13; M.24.749B); **d.** of beliefs and practices, Hipp.*haer*.proem. 8(p.3.19; M.16.3021A); τὴν ἀ. αὐτοῦ [sc. τοῦ συνθήματος ἡμῶν] εἶναι θεὸν...διδάσκοντα τοὺς ἀνθρώπους Or.*Cels*.3.14(pp.213.29; 214.1; M.11.937A,B); **4.** *cause* ἀ. καὶ τὸ καθ' ⟨ὃ⟩ οἷον κατὰ τὸ εἶδος· εἴπερ εἰκὼν τοῦ θεοῦ...ὁ πρωτότοκος πάσης κτίσεως, ἀ. αὐτοῦ ὁ πατήρ ἐστιν. ὁμοίως δὲ καὶ Χριστὸς ἀ. τῶν κατ' εἰκόνα γενομένων θεοῦ Or.*Jo*.1.17 (19; p.22.19ff.; M.14.53B,C); *ib*.1.18(21; p.23.9f.; 56A); Bas.*hex*.1.5 (1.6Bf.; M.29.16A); πᾶσα ἀ. παραδειγματική, τελική, ποιητική, εἰδική, στοιχειώδης, καὶ ἁπλῶς πᾶσα ἀ., πᾶσα συνοχή, πᾶν πέρας Dion.Ar.*d.n*.4.10(M.3.705D); λέγεται καὶ ἀ. κατὰ τὸ αἴτιον, καὶ τοῦτο τριχῶς· ἢ γὰρ φυσικόν, ὡς ἀ. υἱοῦ, πατήρ· ἢ ποιητικόν, ὡς ἀ. κτίσεως, ὁ κτίστης· ἢ μιμητικόν, ὡς ἀ. εἰκόνος τὸ εἰκονιζόμενον Jo.D.*Man*.1.3(M.94.1509B); in gen., Clem.*str*.7.16(p.71.24; M.9.540C) cit. s. ἄγνοια; Meth.*symp*.2.1(p.16.5; M.18.48D); τοῦ κόσμου...ἀ. ἔχοντος τοῦ εἶναι...τὴν ἐκείνου θέλησιν ‡Just.*confut*.proem.(M.6.1493A); Jo.D.*f.o*.1.4(M.94.797B); **5.** *law* of nature or being ἐξ ὑποκειμένης τινὸς ἀ. κατὰ φύσιν ὁρμώμενον Athenag.*res*.1(p.48.5; M.6.973A); ἐν τοῖς ἀλόγοις...οὐκ ἄλλην ὄψεται ἀ. ἢ τὴν...ἄλογον Or.*Cels*.4.85(p.356.16; M.11.1160C); id.*Jo*.6.14(7; p.123.33; M.14.225C); Aen.*dial*.(M.85.925B); ἡ τοῦ σπέρματος ἀ. *ib*.(l.c.); of natures of Christ τὸ λέγειν ἐκ δύο φύσεων τὸν Χριστὸν...ὡς ἀπὸ τῶν ἀ. ... εἴπερ ἀρχαὶ αὐτοῦ κατὰ μὲν τὴν θεότητα, ὁ πατήρ, κατὰ δὲ τὴν ἀνθρωπότητα, ἡ μήτηρ Leont.B.*cap.Sev*.28(M.86.1912B,C); **6.** *first principle* of knowledge, reasoning etc., Clem.*str*.7.11(p.46.15; M.9.489A); ἔχομεν γὰρ τὴν ἀ. τῆς διδασκαλίας τὸν κύριον...τὴν ἀ. δ' εἴ τις ἑτέρου δεῖσθαι ὑπολάβοι, οὐκέτ' ἂν ὄντως ἀ. φυλαχθείη *ib*.7.16(p.67.16ff.,24; M.9.532B,C); ref. Jo.4:36 ἐπὶ πάσης τῆς...τέχνης καὶ ἐπιστήμης σπείρει μὲν ὁ τὰς ἀ. εὑρίσκων Or.*Jo*.13.46(p.272.20; M.14.480D); as title of work by Origen, Marcell.*fr*.78 ap.Eus.*Marcell*.1.4(p.23.25; M.24.761A); cf. Περὶ Ἀρχῶν *quod vel de Principiis vel de Principatibus dici potest*, Rufinus proem.ad.Or.*princ*.3(p.193.6; M.11.247); **7.** *fundamental principle, ultimate source, first cause* τὰς οὐσίας ἔχοντες οὐκ ἔξωθεν τοῦ θεοῦ. οὐδὲ γὰρ ἔστιν ἑτέρα τις ἀ. *Hom.Clem*.20.3; πολλαὶ...ἀ. πολλῶν πραγμάτων κατὰ τὸν βίον τοῦτον ἀλλὰ μία ἀ. ἐπὶ πάντων, ἡ ἐπέκεινα Bas.*hom*.16.1(2.135A; M.31.473C); ref. Jo.1:1 οὔτε γὰρ ἀρχῆς ἐστί τι ἐπινοῆσαι πρεσβύτερον. οὐ γὰρ ἔτι ἂν ἀ. εἴπερ ἔχοι τι ἑαυτῆς ἐξώτερον...τὸ σημαινόμενον τοῦτο τῆς ἀ. ἀπολελυμένον καὶ ἄσχετον, τὴν ἀνωτάτω φύσιν δῆλοι Bas.*Eun.*2.14(1.249C f.; M.29.600A); ἵνα μὴ τρεῖς ἀ. μεμερισμέναι πολυθέως παραδεχθῶσιν Gr.Naz.*or.*31.30(p.186.7; M.36.168C); οὐκ...ἔστιν ἐπινοῆσαι τῷ λόγῳ...οὐκ ἄλογον ἀ., οὐκ ἄπαιδα πατέρα Gr.Nyss.*Eun.*8(2 p.193.16; M.45.788D); πῶς οὖν πολυθεΐα ἔσται καὶ πολλαὶ ἀ., εἰ εἷς κύριος Ἰησοῦς Χριστός; Epiph.*haer.*56.3(p.342.14; M.41.993B); Cyr.*thes.*2(5^{1}.14C); Dion.Ar.*d.n.*4.21(M.3.721C,D); ref. Hebrew monotheism μετὰ τὴν ἄναρχον καὶ ἀγένητον τοῦ θεοῦ τῶν ὅλων οὐσίαν...δευτέραν οὐσίαν καὶ θεΐαν δύναμιν, ἀρχὴν τῶν γενητῶν ἁπάντων πρώτην τε ὑποστᾶσαν κἀκ τοῦ πρώτου αἰτίου γεγενημένην, εἰσάγουσι [sc. οἱ Ἑβραῖοι]...θεοῦ δύναμιν αὐτὴν προσαγορεύοντες Eus.*p.e.*7.12(320C; M.21.541B); Dion.Ar.*c.h.*9.3(M.3.261A); ref. pagan philosophy, Hermias *irris.*3(M.6.1172C); ἀ. φθαρτὴν εἰσάγοντος Or.*Cels.*1.21(p.72.14; M.11.697A); Max.*ep.*12(M.91.489A).

D. theol.; **1.** in rel. to creation, *First Cause, Creator*; **a.** of Trin. ἡ ἄναρχος τῶν ὄντων ἀ. Procl.CP *annunt.*2(M.85.429D); **b.** of Father, Tat.*orat.*4(p.5.2; M.6.813A) cit. s. ἄναρχος; ἀ. υἱοῦ ὁ πατὴρ καὶ ἀ. δημιουργημάτων ὁ δημιουργὸς καὶ ἁπαξαπλῶς ἀ. τῶν ὄντων ὁ θεός Or.*Jo.*1.17(p.22.10f.; M.14.53A); Eus.*d.e.*4.1(p.151.8; M.22.252C) cit. s. ἀρχέγονος; cf. διὰ δὲ τοῦ κυρίου, ὅς ἐστιν ἡ πάντων ἀ., τῆς ἐπέκεινα πάσης ἀ. ἡμῖν εὑρισκομένης, ἥτις ἐστὶν ὁ ἐπὶ πάντων θεός Gr.Nyss.*Eun.*1(1 p.172.2f.; M.45.416A); ἀ. ... τῶν ὄντων μία, δι' υἱοῦ δημιουργοῦσα καὶ τελειοῦσα ἐν πνεύματι Bas.*Spir.*38(3.31E; M.32.136B); id.*ep.*125.3(3.216D; M.32.549C); Thdt.*haer.*5.1(4.377); Dion.Ar.*d.n.*1.3(M.3.589B); **c.** more freq. of Son ἀ. πρὸ πάντων τῶν κτισμάτων ὁ θεὸς γεγέννηκε δύναμίν τινα ἐξ ἑαυτοῦ λογικήν Just.*dial.*61.1(M.6.613C); θεὸς ἦν ἐν ἀ., τὴν δὲ ἀ. λόγου δύναμιν παρειλήφαμεν...τοῦτον ἴσμεν τοῦ κόσμου τὴν ἀ. Tat.*orat.*5(p.5.16,24; M.6.813C, 816A); τὴν ἄχρονον ἄναρχον ἀ. τε καὶ ἀπαρχὴν τῶν ὄντων, τὸν υἱόν Clem.*str.*7.1(p.4.6; M.9.404C); πατρὸς μὲν καὶ ἀνάρχου καὶ ἀ. ... ὡς αἰτίου καὶ ὡς πηγῆς...υἱοῦ δέ, ἀνάρχου μὲν οὐδαμῶς, ἀ. δὲ τῶν ὅλων Gr.Naz.*or.*20.7(M.35.1073A); *ib.*29.17(p.99.6; M.36.96C); ἄναρχον, ἀ., πνεῦμα τριὰς τιμία id.*carm.*1.2.10.988(M.37.751A); in rel. to Inc., ref. Is.9:6 φέρων αὐτὸς ἐπὶ τοῦ ὤμου αὐτοῦ ταύτης αὐτοῦ τῆς κάτω γεννήσεως τὴν ἀ. τοῦτ' ἔστιν, αὐτὸς ἑαυτοῦ ἀ. τυγχάνων Didym.*Trin.*1.27(M.39.397B); exeg. Gen.1:1 ἐν ἀ. ἐποίησεν ὁ θεὸς τὸν οὐρανόν, τουτέστι διὰ τῆς ἀ. γεγενῆσθαι τὸν οὐρανόν Thphl.Ant.*Autol.*2.13(M.6.1072B); cf.*ib.*1.3(1028C); 'ἀ. τῶν ἁπάντων ἐποίησεν' μηνύων τὸν πρωτόγονον υἱὸν ὁ Πέτρος γράφει *Keryg.Petr.*ap.Clem.*str.*6.7(p.461.8; M.9.280B); Clem.*ecl.*4(p.138.5; M.9.700C); cf. *quod est omnium principium nisi dominus noster...Christus Jesus?...in hoc ergo principio, hoc est in verbo suo, Deus coelum et terram fecit,* Or. *hom.1.1 in Gen.*(p.1.2f.; M.12.145C); ἀ. μετὰ τὴν ἰδίαν ἄναρχον ἀ., τὸν πατέρα, αὐτὸς τῶν ἄλλων γίνεται, δι' ἧς ἅπαντα δημιουργεῖται Meth.*creat.*11(p.499.13; M.18.344A); cf. *aiunt quidem et Genesim in Hebraïco ita incipere 'In principio Deus fecit sibi filium'*, Tert. *adversus Praxeam* 5(M.*PL.*2.160A); *Breshith...tres significantias in se habet, id est 'in principio' et 'in capite' et 'in filio'*, Hil.Pict.*Ps.*2(M.*PL.*9.263A); *plerique existimant...in Hebraeo haberi 'in filio fecit Deus coelum et terram' quod falsum esse ipsius rei veritas comprobat,* Hier.*qu.Hebr.in Gen.*(M.*PL.*23.985–7); exeg. Apoc.3:14 ἀ. ...τῆς κτίσεως εἶπεν αὐτόν. οὐχ ὡς κτίσμα πρῶτον κτίσεως ἀ. ἐστιν αὐτῆς, ἀλλ' ὡς αἰτία...οἷα δημιουργός· ἀ. γὰρ ποιημάτων ὁ ποιητής Or.*Apoc.*22(p.30); cf.*ib.*7(p.23); cf. βούλεται...οὐδὲν ἕτερον ἢ ἄρχων τῆς κτίσεως τοῦ θεοῦ, καὶ ὁ τὴν κατὰ πάντων ἀ. ἔχων Oecum.*Apoc.*3:14(p.64); ἀντὶ τοῦ, βασιλεία· καὶ ἀ. πάντων, ὡς τῶν κτισμάτων δεσπόζουσα. ἀ. γὰρ [τῆς] κτίσεως ἡ προκαταρκτικὴ αἰτία καὶ ἄκτιστος Andr.Caes.*Apoc.*9(M.106.249A); **2.** ref. divine essence; **a.** of Godhead μίαν θεότητα, μίαν ἀ. Gr.Nyss.*Eun.*1(1 p.171.25; M.45.416A); πιστεύομεν...εἰς ἕνα θεόν, μίαν ἀ., ἄναρχον Jo.D.*f.o.*1.8(M.94.808B); **b.** of Father in relation to Son ὡς ἀ. τιμῶν τὸν πατέρα ‡Dion.Al.*fr. in Lc.22:44*(p.244.11; M.10.1593C); ὁ πατὴρ ἀ. τοῦ υἱοῦ καὶ γεννήτωρ ἐστί Ath.*Ar.*1.14(M.26.41A); οὔτε δύο εἰσὶν ἀ.· ἀλλὰ κεφαλὴ τοῦ υἱοῦ ὁ πατήρ, μία ἡ ἀ. Cyr.H.*catech.*11.14; *Symb.Ant.*(345)(p.252.20; M.26.729B); Apoll.*fid.sec.pt.*27,32(pp.176.19,180.1; M.10.1116B, 1117B); Jo.V H.*icon.*4(M.96.1353A); not in respect of time μὴ χρονικὴν ἀ. τοῦ υἱοῦ καταδέξῃ τινὸς λέγοντος, ἀλλὰ ἄχρονον ἀ. γίνωσκε τὸν πατέρα Cyr.H.*catech.*11.20; Gr.Naz.*or.*20.7(M.35.1073A); ἀ. λέγεται ὁ πατὴρ τοῦ υἱοῦ κατὰ μόνον τὸ ἐξ οὗ· τῇ γὰρ αἰτίᾳ ὁ πατὴρ τοῦ υἱοῦ προεπινοηθήσεται, οὐ μὴν τῇ ὑπάρξει προθεωρηθήσεται Ammon. *Jo.*1:1(M.85.1393A); ref. Jo.14:28 μείζονα αὐτόν φησιν ὡς ἄναρχον, ἔχων ἀ. κατὰ μόνον τὸ ἐξ οὗ Cyr.*thes.*11(5^{1}.86A); Jo.D.*Man.*1.4(M.94.1509C); manifesting unity of divine essence μιᾶς...οὔσης ἀ. τε καὶ κεφαλῆς, πῶς ἂν γένοιντο θεοὶ δύο; Eus.*e.th.*1.11(p.69.35; M.24.844D); μίαν ἀ. ὁμολογοῦσα, τὸν ἕνα καὶ ἀγέννητον καὶ ἄναρχον θεόν· καὶ... μονογενῆ υἱόν...οὐκ ἄναρχον ὄντα, ἵνα μὴ δύο ἀ. καὶ δύο θεοὺς ὑποστήσηται, ἐξ αὐτοῦ δὲ γεννηθέντα τοῦ πατρὸς καὶ ἀ. ἔχοντα τὸν γεγεννηκότα *ib.*2.6(p.103.10ff.; 905C); ὥστε δύο μὲν εἶναι πατέρα καὶ υἱόν, μονάδα δὲ θεότητος ἀδιαίρετον...λεχθείη δ' ἂν καὶ οὕτω μία ἀ. θεότητος, καὶ οὐ δύο ἀρχαί ‡Ath.*Ar.*4.1(p.44.4f.; M.26.468B); τὴν τριάδα...εἰς μίαν...ἑνότητα καὶ μίαν ἀ. τοῦ θεοῦ καὶ πατρὸς ἀναγομένην Epiph.*exp.fid.*14(p.514.21; M.42.809A); id.*haer.*65.8(p.11.21; M.42.25B); exeg. Jo.1:1 ἀ. υἱοῦ ὁ πατὴρ...παραμυθήσεται δὲ διὰ τοῦ 'ἐν ἀ. ἦν ὁ λόγος' λόγον νοῶν τὸν υἱόν, παρὰ τὸ εἶναι ἐν τῷ πατρὶ λεγόμενον εἶναι ἐν ἀ. Or.*Jo.*1.17(p.22.10; M.14.53A,B); τὴν...ἀ., ἀφ' ἧς ἀνεβλάστησεν ὁ...λόγος, τὸν πατέρα καὶ ποιητὴν τῶν ὅλων φατέον Meth.*creat.*11(p.499.9; M.18.341B); ὁ θεῖος εὐαγγελιστὴς...δοὺς αὐτῷ ἀ., δῆλον δ' ὅτι τὴν γέννησιν, τὴν ἐκ τοῦ πατρός Eus.*e.th.*2.14(p.116.26f.; M.24.929D,932A); Gr.Nyss.*Eun.*4(2 p.53.21ff.; M.45.624B); *ib.*2(2 p.305.1; 476D); ὡς ἐν ἀ. τῷ πατρὶ ἦν ὁ λόγος, ἵνα νοῇς ἅμα τε ὄντα τὸν πατέρα, καὶ τὸν ἐξ αὐτοῦ καὶ ἐν αὐτῷ λόγον Cyr.*thes.*32(5^{1}.312D); **c.** heret.; Valent., of aeon Νοῦς, Βύθος being known as προαρχή, Iren.*haer.*1.1.1(M.7.448A); *ib.*1.9.2(540B); *ib.*1.11.5(568B); cf.*ib.*3.11.1(880A); Clem.*exc.Thdot.*6(p.107.18; M.9.657A); Hipp.*haer.*6.38(p.169.6; M.16.3255A); cf.Tert.*adversus Valentinianos* 7(M.*PL.*2.586A); Marcionite Ἀπελλῆς μὲν...μίαν ἀ. ὁμολογεῖ...ἕτεροι δέ, καθὼς καὶ αὐτὸς [sc. Marcion]...δύο ἀ. εἰσηγοῦνται...ἄλλοι δὲ...τρεῖς ὑποτίθενται φύσεις Rhod.ap.Eus.*h.e.*5.13.2ff.(M.20.460B,C); Dion.R.ap.Ath.*decr.*26(p.22.13; M.25.464A) cit. s. μοναρχία; Adam.*dial.*2.1(p.60.12ff.; M.11.1761B,1764A); Epiph.*haer.*65.8(p.11.25; M.42.25C); Marcellus, ref. Jo.1:1 ἵνα...δείξῃ δυνάμει ἐν τῷ πατρὶ εἶναι τὸν λόγον. ἀ. γὰρ ἁπάντων τῶν γεγονότων ὁ θεός Marcell.*fr.*47 ap.Eus.*Marcell.*2.2(p.37.2; M.24.785C); ἀδύνατον γὰρ τρεῖς ὑποστάσεις οὔσας ἑνοῦσθαι μονάδι εἰ μὴ πρότερον ἡ τριὰς τὴν ἀ. ἀπὸ μονάδος ἔχοι *ib.*60 ap.Eus.*e.th.*3.4(p.157.33; M.24.1004A); Manich. νομίζουσιν...ἐκ δύο ῥιζῶν ἢ δύο ἀ. ἐνεργεῖσθαι τὰ πάντα Epiph.*haer.*66.2(p.18.9; M.42.32D); id.*anac.*5(p.1.12; M.42.9A); ἡ ἀγαθὴ ἀ. τῶν Χριστιανῶν ἄρχει, ἡ δὲ δημιουργικὴ τῶν Ἰουδαίων, ἡ δὲ πονηρὰ τῶν ἐθνικῶν Adam.*dial.*1.3(p.4.26; M.11.1720A); Jo.D.*Man.*1.2(M.94.1508Bff.); ref. orthodox doctrine acc. Manes μίαν ἀ. εἰσηγούμενοι, οὐ διακρίνοντες...τὸ ἀγαθὸν ἀπὸ τοῦ κακοῦ Hegem.*Arch.*6(p.6.11; M.10.1433C); Arian τοῦτον [sc. Father] ἀνυμνοῦμεν διὰ τὸν ἀ. ἔχοντα· ἀ. τὸν θεὸν ἔθηκε τῶν γενητῶν ὁ ἄναρχος Ar.*Thal.fr.*2 ap.Ath.*syn.*15(p.242.12; M.26.705D); *ib.*(p.243.22; 708C); id.*ep.Eus.*(p.3.4; M.42.212B); cf. κεφαλή ...ἐστι καὶ ἀ. πάντων ὁ υἱός. κεφαλὴ δέ ἐστι τοῦ Χριστοῦ ὁ θεός. οὕτω γὰρ εἰς μίαν ἄναρχον τῶν ὅλων ἀ. δι' υἱοῦ εὐσεβῶς τὰ πάντα ἀνάγομεν *Symb.Sirm.* 1 *anath.*26(p.256.16f.; M.26.740B).

II. *rule, authority*; in gen. ἀ. λέγονται καὶ αἱ πολιτικαὶ δυναστεῖαι Bas.*hom.*16.1(2.135B; M.31.473C); λέγεται ἀ. καὶ κατὰ τὸ ἀξίωμα καὶ ἐξουσίαν, ὡς λέγομεν ἀ. εἶναι τὸν βασιλέα τῶν ὑπηκόων Jo.D.*Man.*1.3(M.94.1509A).

A. divine; **1.** of Trin. τὸ βασιλεύειν τῶν ὄντων...τῇ τῆς φύσεως ὑπεροχῇ...τὸ μὴ εἰς διαφόρους ἀ. τῇ ἑτερότητι τῆς φύσεως διῃρημένας τὸ τῆς μοναρχίας δόγμα καταμερίζεσθαι, ἀλλὰ μίαν θεότητα, μίαν ἀ., μίαν τῶν πάντων ἐξουσίαν εἶναι πιστεύειν Gr.Nyss.*Eun.*1(1 p.171.23ff.; M.45.413D,416A); μίαν ἐνέργειαν, μίαν ἀ., μίαν ἐξουσίαν Jo.D.*f.o.*1.8(M.94.809A); faith in sovereignty of God attributed to Devil before his fall, Thdt.*Ps.*81:7(1.1188); **2.** of Logos οὗτος λέγεται ἀ., ὅτι ἄρχει καὶ κυριεύει πάντων τῶν δι' αὐτοῦ δεδημιουργημένων Thphl.Ant.*Autol.*2.10(M.6.1064C); εἰ λόγον εἴπω ἀ. αὐτοῦ λέγω· νοῦν ἐὰν εἴπω φρόνησιν αὐτοῦ λέγω *ib.*1.3(1028C); ref. Jo.1:1 τὴν ἐξουσίαν [sc. τοῦ λόγου] ἀ. εἰπών Meth.*creat.*11(p.499.13; M.18.344A); Chrys.*hom.7.1 in Phil.*(11.245D) cit. s. ἁρπαγμός.

B. of creatures; ref. Gen.1:16, cf. *utrum etiam ipsa* [sc. sun, moon and stars] *inter 'principatus' haberi conveniat pro eo quod dicuntur 'in* ἀρχάς' *(id est 'in principatum') diei facta vel noctis, an putanda sint istum solum habere 'principatum diei ac noctis' quas inluminandi officium gerunt,* Or.*princ.*1.7.2(1; p.86.28; M.11.171C); of saints judging world κἂν διδῶται ταῦτα πάντα [i.e. earthly honours], ὑπερόψεται ὑπὲρ τοῦ τῶν ἀληθινῶν ἀ. καὶ θειοτέρων ἐξουσιῶν μὴ ἀποτυχεῖν id.*or.*17(p.339.27; M.11.473A); of Satan εἰ...ὁ...πονηρὸς ἀπέστη τοῦ δίκαιος εἶναι...διὰ τί ἀρχῇ τετίμηται; *Hom.Clem.*19.16; [sc. ἡ πάντων αἰτία] τὰς ὅλας ἀ. καὶ τάξεις ἀφορίζουσα, καὶ πάσης ἀ. καὶ τάξεως ὑπεριδρυμένη Dion.Ar.*d.n.*2.10(M.3.648C); of bishops, Chrys.*hom.10.1 in 1Tim.*(11.598B) cit. s. αὐθεντία; cf. εἰς διδασκαλίαν λόγου προεχειρίσθημεν, οὐκ εἰς ἀ. οὐδὲ εἰς αὐθεντίαν id.*hom.11.5 in Eph.*(11.87F); of S. Peter μηδέπω τὴν ἀ. ἐγχειρισθείς, τὴν πρέπουσαν ἄρχοντι κηδεμονίαν ἐφύλαττε id.*hom.in Mt.18:23*(3.6A); plur., of *reign* of a king εἰς τὰς ἀ. τοῦ...βασιλέως Μαυρικίου Jo.Mosch.*prat.*155(M.87.3024B); *ib.*112(2976B); ?met., *chief place* ἔπαρον τὸν λίθον τοῦτον εἰς τὴν ἀ. τῆς γωνίας τοῦ ναοῦ *T.Sal.*23.2(p.69.7; M.122.1353D);

C. those holding office; usu. plur., *rulers, magistrates*; their authority derived from God, *M.Polyc.*10.2; met., *chief, prince,* i.e. *best* μικρὸν ἐν πετεινοῖς ἡ μέλισσα, καὶ ἀ. γλυκασμάτων ὁ καρπὸς αὐτῆς ‡Ath.*synops.*46(M.28.380A).

D. ecclesiastical *authority*; *orders* of ministry; not for the lapsed, Or.*Cels.*3.51(p.248.3; M.11.988C); ἱερατικὴν ἀ. opp. ῥωμαϊκὴν ἀ. *Can.App.*83; τὴν ἀναίμακτον...ἀ. opp. τὴν μετὰ ξίφους καὶ τελαμῶνος Gr.Naz.*ep.*224(M.37.368C); ἑτέρα ἀ. τῆς πολιτικῆς ἀ. ἀνωτέρα Chrys.*hom.15.4 in 2Cor.*(10.548B); full comparison, *ib.*(10.548B–550); Thdt.*Rom.*13:1(3.136); of episcopate τῆς ἀ. ἐκφυγεῖν τὸν ὄγκον v.l. in Chrys.*sac.*3.10(Gaume; τὴν ἀ. 1.388A); of priesthood μείζων [sc. τῆς βασιλείας] ἡ ἀ. αὕτη id.*hom.4.5 in Is.6:1*(6.127E).

E. plur., *spiritual powers*; **1.** among good angels, order of *principalities,* Hipp.*haer.*6.19(p.147.3; M.16.3223B); ἀρχαγγέλους τε καὶ θρόνους, καὶ κυριότητας, καὶ ἀ., καὶ ἐξουσίας ὑπερανίους Or.*or.*17(p.339.21; M.11.472D); id.*Cels.*4.29(p.298.18; M.11.1069C); ἄλλο ...γένος τὸ τῶν ἀγγέλων καὶ ἄλλο τὸ τῶν ἀ. καὶ ἐξουσιῶν Meth.*res.*1.49(p.302.14; M.18.277B); Sever.*serp.*1(M.56.499); κυριότητας...καὶ ἀ. καὶ ἐξουσίας τοὺς τῶν ἐθνῶν πεπιστευμένους τὴν ἐπιμέλειαν Thdt.*Col.*1:16(3.478); Dion.Ar.*c.h.*9.1f.(M.3.257–60); cf. ἐπιφημίζομέν σε τὸ τῆς μητρὸς ὄνομα, ἀπορρήτου μυστηρίου ἀ. τε καὶ ἐξουσιῶν κεκρυμμένων *A.Thom.*A 133(p.240.11); of angels in gen. τὸ μὲν στόμα αὐτῆς ἀνέλαβεν τὴν διάλεκτον τῶν ἀ., ἐδοξολόγησεν δὲ...τὸ ποίημα *T.Job* 49(p.135.20); **2.** *powers of wickedness, evil angels* ἀποτασσομένων ἡμῶν ταῖς πονηραῖς ἀ. [i.e. in baptism] Clem.*exc.Thdot.*77(p.131.9; M.9.693C); τοῖς χείροσιν ἀ. καὶ ἐξουσίαις καὶ κοσμοκράτορσι Or.*princ.*1.6.3 (p.83.5); ὁ θεὸς τὸν υἱὸν αὐτοῦ...ἀπέστειλεν...πάντα δαίμονα ἀ. τε πᾶσαν καὶ δύναμιν ὑπερήφανον ἀσθενῆ ποιῆσαι *V.Aberc.*24(p.19.15); ἀ. τινάς φησι...τῆς πονηρίας...καθάπερ καὶ ἐπὶ τῶν ἐπουρανίων...ἀ. Chrys.*hom. 22.3 in Eph.*(11.169D,170A); cf.id.*hom.6.3 in Col.*(11.368C); Oecum.*Eph.*10(M.118.1249C).

ἀρχηγέτης, ὁ, 1. *first leader, author,* esp. founder of city or family; of Adam, Cyr.*thes.*11(5^{1}.95A); of Christ τούτου [of the resurrection] παράδειγμα καὶ ἀ. τὸν πεμπόμενον ἡμῖν ἔσεσθαι Cels. ap.Or.*Cels.*2.77(p.199.14; M.11.916C); **2.** in gen., *leader,* of Christ τῆς στάσεως ἀ. id.*ib.*8.14(p.231.8; M.11.1536C); **3.** *first cause, author*; of God, id.*ib.*5.14(p.15.19; M.11.1201B); Gr.Nyss.*Eun.*12(1 p.253.16; M.45.956A).

ἀρχηγέτις, ἡ, fem. of ἀρχηγέτης; *author, origin* κενοδοξία... αἱρέσεων ἀ. †Nil.*vit.*4(M.79.1144C).

ἀρχηγικός, 1. *principal, chief*; hence *powerful* οὕτω...ἂν εὑρεθείη τὰ γήινα τῶν οὐρανίων ἀρχηγικώτερα Gr.Nyss.*fat.*(M.45.169C); *authoritative,* id.*Eun.*12(1 p.296.25; M.45.1008A); **2.** *originating* ἡ ...ἐν ταῖς πονηραῖς δυνάμεσι κακία, ἀ. τυγχάνουσα τῆς ἐν ἀνθρώποις κακίας Or.*comm.in Mt.*13.23(p.242.30; M.13.1156B); of God πάντων ὑποστάτις, ἀ. καὶ τελειωτική Dion.Ar.*d.n.*1.7(M.3.596C).

***ἀρχηγικῶς,** *in the primal, original sense* ἀπολύτως καὶ ἀ. εἶναι Dion.Ar.*d.n.*11.6(M.3.953C).

ἀρχηγός, A. adj., *originative* τὴν ἀ. τῶν κακῶν γενομένην γνώμην Hipp.*haer.*9.6(p.240.13; M.16.3370B); πῶς...δυνάμεως θείας ἐπίκλησις ἐπὶ τοῦ ὕδατος γινομένη ζωῆς ἀ. τοῖς μυηθεῖσι γίνεται; Gr. Nyss.*or.catech.*33(p.124.5; M.45.84B).

B. as subst.; **1.** *founder*; esp. of a family, *original ancestor,* of Abraham ἀ. καὶ προπάτορα...παῖδες Ἑβραίων αὐχοῦσι Eus.*h.e.*1.4.5 (M.20.77B); of Adam τοῦ ἀ. πάντων ἀνθρώπων Nil.*epp.*1.2(M.79.84A); **2.** *leader,* of Marcellus τὸν τῶν...αἱρεσιωτῶν ἀ. Eus.*e.th.*2.9 (p.109.5; M.24.917A); of Jo. Bapt. ὁδηγὸν καὶ ἀ. ἐν τοῖς κρείττοσιν ‡Thdt.*nativ.Jo.Bapt.*(5.97); of Christ, ref. Ac.5:31 τοῦ τῶν ἁγίων ἀ. Ἰησοῦ Or.*Jo.*32.18(11; p.456.8; M.14.789C); ἀ. καὶ φωστήρ Eus.*fr. Lc.*21:25(M.24.596B); τῆς ἐκκλησίας...ἀ. ... καὶ κεφαλή id.*e.th.*1.11 (p.69.33; M.24.844C) etc.; *chief minister* ὁ ἀ. τῆς εὐδοκίας τῶν δεσποτῶν τῆς οἰκουμένης *M.Ariadn.*5(p.126.29); **3.** *first cause, author*; of Adam ἀ. παρακοῆς Hipp.*haer.*8.16(p.236.10; M.16.3363B); acc. Ophites τοῦ ὄφεως ὡς ἀ. τῶν καλῶν Or.*Cels.*6.28(p.98.24; M.11.1336B); of Cain ἀ. τῶν φόνων Cyr.H.*catech.*2.7; Ammon.*Jo.*8:44 (M.85.1453A); of Satan τῷ...ἀ. τῆς ἀποστασίας διαβόλῳ Iren.*haer.*4.40.1(M.7.1112B); Cyr.H.*catech.*2.4; οὐ γὰρ ἂν ἠδυνήθημεν νικῆσαι τῆς ἁμαρτίας καὶ τοῦ θανάτου τὸν ἀ. Leo.Mag.*ep.*28(p.12.1; M.*PL.*54.760A); esp. of God ἁπάντων ἀ. ἀγαθῶν Clem.*str.*7.4(p.16.13; M.9.428B); πάντων ἀ. καὶ πατέρα Const.ap.Eus.*v.C.*4.11(p.122.12; M.20.1160B); id.*or.s.c.*23(p.189.22; M.20.1308A); τὸν ἀ. τῆς ζωῆς ἡμῶν τῆς παρούσης καὶ τῆς μελλούσης Bas.*hex.*6.1(1.50D; M.29.120A); ἀ. καὶ αἴτιον...τοῦ παντός Gr.Nyss.*Eun.*12(1 p.253.14; M.45.956A); of Trin. τὴν ἁγίαν τριάδα...ἀ. ... ποιεῖσθαι τῆς ἰδίας ζωῆς [sc. by baptism] Gr.Nyss.*or.catech.*39(p.157.3; M.45.100C); of Christ τῶν...γινομένων ἀ. καὶ σύμβουλον καὶ ἐργάτην...λόγον Hipp.*Noët.*10(p.253.2; M.10.817B); ἀ. ... δευτέρου τοῦ...τῆς καινῆς διαθήκης νόμου Eus.*d.e.*1.7 (p.37.14; M.22.72D); *ib.*(p.38.2; 73B); ἀνάγκη τὸν ἀ. καὶ ἡγεμόνα τοῦ τοιούτου κατορθώματος εἶναι θεὸν καὶ θεοῦ λόγον Ath.*gent.*1(M.25.5B); τῆς χορηγίας τῶν ἀγαθῶν τῶν διὰ τοῦ πνεύματος ἡμῖν ἐνεργουμένων ἀ. καὶ αἴτιον τὸν μονογενῆ θεὸν εἶναι Gr.Nyss.*diff.ess.*4(M.32.329B); ἀ. τῆς δευτέρας καταστάσεως Cosm.Ind.*top.*5(M.88.193B, 244D,272A); esp. in rel. to salvation and eternal life, exeg. Heb.2:10, Ac.3:15 τὸν σωτῆρα καὶ ἀ. τῆς ἀφθαρσίας *2Clem.*20.5; τὸν ἀ. τῆς ἀναστάσεως Eus.*Marcell.*2.1(p.33.28; M.24.780C); ἀπόστολον...τῆς πίστεως ἡμῶν καὶ ἀ. τῆς ζωῆς *Symb.Ant.*(341)2(p.249.22; M.26.721C); ὥσπερ ἀ. τῆς κακίας αὐτὸς ἂν εἴη ὁ τὴν κακίαν τεκών, καὶ ἀ. φόνου ὁ τὸν φόνον πρῶτος εἰσαγαγών· οὕτω καὶ ἀ. ζωῆς ὁ παρ' ἑαυτοῦ τὴν ζωὴν ἔχων Chrys.*hom.9.3 in Ac.*(9.73A); Cyr.*Is.*1.1(2.11C); Thdot.Anc.*exp.symb.*3(M.77.1317C); of H. Ghost αὐτῶν ὁ πάντων ἀ. Gr.Thaum.*pan.Or.*15(p.34.2; M.10.1093C); **4.** in gen., *cause* εἰδὼς ἀ. ὡς τὰ πολλὰ τοῦ κατὰ κακίαν βίου τὸ καθ' ὑπερηφανίαν πάθος Gr. Nyss.*v.Gr.Thaum.*(M.46.908B); **5.** *responsible agent* σὺ καθέστηκας τοῦ πράγματος ἀ. ... ἄλλος τίς ἐστι...ὑποβολεύς, ὁ διάβολος Cyr.H. *catech.*2.3.

ἀρχῆθεν, 1. *from the beginning*; **a.** in time ὁ δὲ οὐ νῦν γε πρῶτον ᾤκτειρεν ἡμᾶς...ἀλλ' ἄνωθεν ἀ. Clem.*prot.*1.7(p.8.2; M.8.61C); *ib.*(p.8.13; 64A); Eus.*h.e.*8.16.2(M.20.789A); esp. *from the time of Creation, beginning of world* οὐκ οἴδαμεν ὅ τί ποτε ἐροῦσιν οἱ τὰς πνευματικὰς ἀ. φύσεις εἰσάγοντες id.*Eph.*2:3(p.404); Or.*Jo.*2.31(25; p.88.20; M.14.168C); ζῆλος...καὶ φθόνος ἀ. ἀδελφοκτονίαν εἰργάσαντο Eus.*Marcell.*1.1(p.1.13; M.24.712A); Didym.*Trin.*2.7(M.39.573B); Jo.VI H. *v.Jo.D.*1(M.94.429A); from creation of an individual τὰ τῆς πίστεως ἡμῶν ταῖς κοιναῖς ἐννοίαις ἀ. συναγορεύοντα Or.*Cels.*3.40 (p.236.10; M.11.972B); id.*princ.*3.1.21(20; p.237.7; M.11.296B); in rel. to Church τά τε ἀ. πρὸς τῶν ἀποστόλων ἔθη παραδεδομένα Eus. *h.e.*2.17.24(M.20.184A); **b.** in eternity, of Son ὃν...νομίζομεν...ἀ. εἶναι θεὸν καὶ υἱὸν θεοῦ Or.*Cels.*3.41(p.237.5; M.11.972D); μόνου τοῦ μονογενοῦς φύσει υἱοῦ ἀ. τυγχάνοντος id.*Jo.*2.10(6; p.65.22; M.14.129A); **c.** in order, of a book ἐν τῇ πρώτῃ τῶν Παραλειπομένων ἀ. Or.*Jo.*6.41(24; p.151.5; M.14.272C); **2.** *from of old, from early days,* Hipp. *haer.*9.30(p.263.16; M.16.3410B); τὰ Ἑβραίων...ἀ. ἐπὶ τὴν Ἑλλάδα φωνὴν μεταβεβλημένα Eus.*p.e.*10.8(483A; M.21.804B); **3.** *originally* Ἰουδαίων μὲν ἀ. ἓν ἦν ἔθος Hipp.*haer.*9.18(p.255.28; M.16.3394D); Or.*Jo.*32.14(8; p.448.16; M.14.777B); *ib.*32.19(12; p.459.9; 796A); hence τὸ ἀ. *the original state,* ref. Jo.4:13 διψῆσαι πάλιν, εἰς ὅμοιον τῷ ἀ. ἀποκαταστάς *ib.*13.3(p.228.11; 401D); **4.** *essentially, by nature* οὐδεὶς ἀνθρώπων ἀ. υἱός ἐστιν θεοῦ Or.*Jo.*20.33(27; p.370.30; M.14.648D); ref. Jo.4:19, *ib.*13.12(p.236.26; 417A); *ib.*13.48(46; p.275.30; 485C).

***ἀρχήφωτος,** v. *ἀρχίφωτος.

***ἀρχιαιρεσία, ἡ,** *assembly for election of magistrates,* Const.ap. Ath.*apol.sec.*62(p.142.7, v.l. ἀρχιερεσίαν M.25.361B).

***ἀρχιαναγνώστης, ὁ,** *chief of the readers* (eccl.), CAnt.(445)*act.* (*ACO* 2.1.3 p.70.11; H.2.580C).

***ἀρχιατρικός,** *belonging to the chief physician* οὐ νικᾷ σου τὰ τραύματα τὴν ἀ. ἐμπειρίαν Cyr.H.*catech.*2.6.

ἀρχιατρός or proparoxytone ([*]**ἀρχιητρός, ἀρχιϊατρός**), **ὁ, 1.** *court physician*; **2.** *archiatrus popularis, medical officer for the community,* Bas.*epp.*151,193 titt.(3.241E,285D; M.32.605D,705A); *MAMA* 3.22; Ἰάκωβος...ἀρχιητρὸς ὢν τῆς πόλεως *Chron.Pasch.*p.322(M.92.824A); of Christ, *supreme physician* τί δὲ ἄτοπόν ἐστιν ἵνα καὶ ὁ ἀρχίατρος καταβῇ πρὸς τοὺς κακῶς ἔχοντας; ἐκεῖνοι [sc. οἱ ἰατροί] μὲν ἦσαν πολλοί, ὁ δὲ κύριός μου καὶ σωτὴρ ἀ. ἐστι Or.*engast.*6(p.289.22ff.; M.12.1021B); πέμπων τοὺς θεραπεύοντας μέχρις οὗ ἔλθῃ ὁ ἀ. ... ὁ διαφέρων ἰατρῶν ἰατρός id.*hom.18.5 in Jer.*(p.156.16; M.13.472C); τοῦ κυρίου ἡμῶν καὶ ἀρχιϊατροῦ τῶν ψυχῶν *Pap.Chr.*(p.430) saec. iii; τῷ οὐρανίῳ ἀ. Ἰησοῦ Nil.*epp.*3.327(M.79.540C).

***ἀρχιβασιλεύς, ὁ,** Lat. *rex regum, supreme king*; title of Persian king, Heracl.*ep.*ap.*Chron.Pasch.*p.387(M.92.993B).

***ἀρχιγένειος, ὁ,** *with the first beard of youth,* ref. appearance of Christ ὤφθη ἐμοὶ ὑπόψιλον ἔχων, τὸ δὲ γένειον δασὺ καταγόμενον, τῷ δὲ Ἰακώβῳ ἀ. νεανίσκος *A.Jo.*89(p.194.23); Jo.Mal.*chron.*5 p.105(M.97.196A); *ib.*12 p.283(428C); Thphn.*chron.*p.264(M.108.656B).

***ἀρχιγόης, ὁ,** *arch-impostor*; of devils, Gr.Naz.*carm.*1.1.7.79(M.37.444A).

***ἀρχιγονία, ἡ,** *root cause* ὑπεροψία,...ἀ. τῶν ἁμαρτημάτων Leo Mag.*ep.*106.1(M.*PL.*54.1004A; ἀρχαιογονία p.56.29).

[*]**ἀρχίγονος,** v. ἀρχέγονος.

ἀρχιδαίμων, ὁ, 1. *king, ruler of demons,* of God εἰ...προὔχει τῶν ὁσίων οὗτος [sc. ὁ δαίμων], ἀκόλουθον ὑπολαμβάνειν, ὅτι καὶ τούτου πάλιν αὐτὸς ὁ ἀ. Eust.*engast.*10(M.18.632B); **2.** *arch-fiend, Devil* πῶς πυνθάνεται ὁ Χριστὸς παρὰ τοῦ ἀ. λέγων· τί σοί ἐστιν ὄνομα; Adam.

dial.1.17(p.36.19; M.11.1745A); λέγει...ἄρχοντα σὺ τὸν δημιουργὸν... ἀλλ' ἀ. τινα, κακίας γεωργόν Mac.Mgn.apocr.2.20(p.37.9).

*ἀρχιδεκανός, ὁ, chief of the δεκανοί q.v., in charge of burial of dead τάφος Ὀνο[ρίου] ἀρχιδεκα[νοῦ] IGC As.Min.269.

*ἀρχιδιάβολος, ὁ, arch-devil, A.Pil.B 23(p.330).

*ἀρχιδιακονέω, hold office of archdeacon, Isid.Pel.epp.1.177(M.78.297C).

ἀρχιδιάκονος, ὁ, archdeacon;

A. references to early existence: Rome, saec.iii, Eulog.fr.Novat.(M.104.353C), but contrast Corn.ap.Eus.h.e.6.43.11(M.20.621A); Athanasius ὁ ἀ. τῆς Ἀλεξανδρέων ἐκκλησίας Gel.Cyz.h.e.2.7.44(M.85.1244A); cf. Ἀθανάσιος...τοῦ χοροῦ...τῶν διακόνων ἡγούμενος Thdt.h.e.1.26.3(3.812).

B. appointment and status; 1. is senior deacon in a church; cf. Andreas...qui non provectus a nobis, sed gradu faciente archidiaconi dignitate fuerat honoratus, Anat.CP ep.int.opp.Leo Mag.ep.132.2(M.PL.54.1083A); 2. more often, is specially appointed (without regard to seniority) by bishop; cf. πάνυ νέος μὲν ὢν [sc. Ἀθανάσιος] τὴν ἡλικίαν Thdt.h.e.1.26.3(3.812); τὸν ἀ. ... τὸν ἐμόν Pall.v.Chrys.2(p.9.25; M.47.9); Σεραπίων, ὃν ἀ. αὐτοῦ κατέστησεν [sc. Chrysostom] Soz.h.e.8.9.1(M.67.1537C); 3. must be deacon; hence promotion to presbyterate involves degradation, cf. virum catholicae fidei... archidiaconem [v. ἀρχιδιάκων] sub honoris specie degradaret et dispensationem totius causae et curae ecclesiasticae...transferret Leo Mag.ep.111.2(M.PL.54.1021B); Eulog.fr.Novat.(M.104.353C); 4. gen. secular, but an archdeacon described as living in monastery, Jo.Clim.scal.4(M.88.696B).

C. duties; 1. as senior deacon, exercise of authority over deacons, Isid.Pel.epp.1.29(M.78.200C); Jo.Clim.scal.4(M.88.696B); 2. liturg.; at Alexandria has sole right of reading Gospel, Soz.h.e.7.19.6(M.67.1477A); at Constantinople either reads himself or delegates task, Euchol.(p.225); carries the pallium, ‡Sophr.H.liturg.(M.87.4001B); leads certain post-Communion thanksgivings, Lit.Jac.(p.236.1); 3. attends upon bishop, cf. ὁ παρεστὼς τῷ ἀρχιερεῖ διάκονος Const.App.2.57.16; Pall.v.Chrys.2(p.9.25; M.47.9); †Leont.B.sect.5.4(M.86.1232A); acting as his emissary κατῆλθε πρὸς ἡμᾶς ὁ ἀ. αὐτοῦ CEph.(431)act.5(ACO 1.1.3 p.23.18; H.1.1497B); and as his deputy, representing him at councils, CChalc.act.1(ACO 2.1.1 p.57.5; H.2.56D); 4. acts as guardian of see during vacancy τὸν ἀ. καλέσας τὸν ἐμὸν ἐξ αὐθεντείας πολλῆς, ὥσπερ χηρευσάσης ἤδη τῆς ἐκκλησίας καὶ οὐκ ἐχούσης ἐπίσκοπον Pall.v.Chrys.2(p.9.25; M.47.9); cf.CChalc.ep.(ACO 2.1.2 p.42.8; H.2.377C,D); 5. acts, even more fully than other deacons, as 'bishop's eye' Λουκίῳ ἀ. ... εἰ ὀφθαλμοὶ ἐπισκόπου τυγχάνουσιν οἱ...διάκονοι, σὺ...ὅλος ὀφθαλμὸς ὀφείλεις ὑπάρχειν Isid.Pel.epp.1.29(M.78.200C); 6. acts under bishop's orders and must pay him deference, Jo.Mosch.prat.146(M.88.3009D); 7. may take prominent part in councils, CChalc.act.1(ACO 2.1.1 p.83.24,30; H.2.88E); ἀ. καὶ πριμικήριος νοταρίων ib.3(p.10.1; 313A); Evagr.h.e.2.18(p.74.7; M.86.2560A); 8. is in charge of Church business, cf. eum nunc constituisse archidiaconum...quem quia nunc ecclesiasticis negotiis praeposuit, Leo Mag.ep.112.1(M.PL.54.1023B); esp. poor-relief, cf.CCarth.4(398)can.17; 9. controls ordinations ἐπεχείρησεν αὐτὸν ἐπίσκοπον χειροτονῆσαι...καὶ κωλυθεὶς παρὰ τοῦ τηνικαῦτα ἀ. αὐτοῦ, ἠγανάκτησε CBeryt.act.(ACO 2.1.3 p.24.30; H.2.517D); and receives fees, cf. warning against covetousness, Isid.Pel.epp.1.29(M.78.200C); 10. preserves order in church, Soz.h.e.4.28.8(M.67.1204A); 11. often succeeds to episcopate, said to be rule at Rome saec.iii εἶναι δὲ τότε θεσμὸν τῇ ἐκκλησίᾳ Ῥωμαίων τὸν ἀ. τελευτῶντος τοῦ ἐπισκόπου εἰς τὸν τῆς ἐπισκοπῆς ἀντιχειροτονεῖσθαι θρόνον Eulog.fr.Novat.(M.104.353C); ib.(M.103.533A).

D. met. ὁ καλὸς τῆς ὑπομονῆς διάκονος καὶ τῆς καρτερίας ἀ. Jo.Clim.scal.4(M.88.696C).

*ἀρχιδιάκων, ὁ, = foreg., Anast.narr.(p.277); Thphn.chron.p.381 (v.l. ἀρχιδιακόνου M.108.912C); cf.Leo.Mag.ep.111.2(M.PL.54.1021B).

*ἀρχιδιδασκαλία, ἡ, primary teaching, Ath.Ar.2.12(M.26.172B).

*ἀρχιδιδάσκαλος, ὁ, chief teacher ὁ ἀρχιποίμην καὶ ἀ. καὶ ἀρχισοφιστὴς Ἰησοῦς ὁ Χριστός Pall.v.Chrys.12(p.78.22; M.47.44).

*ἀρχίδοτος, v. ἀρχέδοτος.

*ἀρχιδύναμος, having the chief power; containing the source of power, Dion.Ar.c.h.8.1(M.3.240A).

*ἀρχιεβδομαδάριος (*ἀρχιεβδομάριος), ὁ, one in charge of those responsible for weekly duties in a monastery εἴ τις ὀχλεῖ τῷ ἀρχιμανδρίτῃ...πλὴν τοῦ κελλαρίου, ἢ τοῦ ἀρχιεβδομαρίου, γενέσθω ἀπευλογίας· ἵνα ἑκάστης ἐφημερίας ὁ ἀ. καὶ ὁ φροντιστὴς περὶ πάσης χρείας φροντίζωσιν ‡Bas.poen.mon.51(2.530A; M.31.1313A); CSyr.act.(H.2.1380A; ἀρχιεβδομάριος ACO 3 p.100.40).

*ἀρχιεβδομάριος, ὁ, v. foreg.

*ἀρχιεπισκοπή, ἡ, archbishopric, Epiph.haer.68.1(p.141.13; M.42.185A).

ἀρχιεπίσκοπος, ὁ, archbishop; 1. def., archiepiscopus Graeco vocabulo quod sit summus episcoporum. tenet enim vicem apostolicam et praesidet tam metropolitanis quam episcopis ceteris...archiepiscopus princeps episcoporum Isid.H.etym.7.12.6,10; 2. title given usu. to patriarchs; a. of Alexandria, Ath.apol.sec.71(p.150.30; M.25.377A); Epiph.haer.68.1(p.141.11; M.42.185A); ἐκκλησίαι...ἐν Ἀλεξανδρείᾳ ὑπὸ ἕνα ἀ. τυγχάνουσιν οὖσαι καὶ κατ' ἰδίαν ταύταις ἐπιτεταγμένοι εἰσὶ πρεσβύτεροι ib.69.1(p.152.22; 201D); τοῦ...θεοφιλεστάτου καὶ ὁσιωτάτου ἀ. Κυρίλλου CEph.(431)act.1(ACO 1.1.2 p.16.2; H.1.1368A); and of Cyril some 65 times in CEph.(431)act.1; Paul.Em.ep.(M.77.165B; p.6.13 ἐπισκόπῳ); Isid.Pel.epp.1.323 tit.(M.78.369A); CChalc.can.30; Thdt.ep.144(4.1243) where ἐπίσκοπος is used of Damasus and Leo; b. of Rome, CEph.(431)act.1(ACO 1.1.2 p.36.9; H.1.1396B); Cyr.hom.div.4(5^2.358B); ἀ. πάσης τῆς οἰκουμένης, πατέρα τε καὶ πατριάρχην †Cyr.hom.div.11(5^2.384E); CChalc.can.30; Thdt.ep.116(4.1197); ib.118(1200); c. of Antioch, CEph.(431)act.1(ACO 1.1.5 p.120.4; H.1.1449E); Jo.Ant.relat.imp.5 ib.(p.125.23; M.83.1457D); Thdt.ep.83(p.49.17; 4.1146); ib.92(1163); d. of Constantinople, Cyr.ep.49(5^2.157E; MSS followed by p.34.4 omit); χειροτονεῖσθαι...τοὺς μητροπολίτας τῶν προειρημένων διοικήσεων παρὰ τοῦ Κωνσταντινουπόλεως ἀ. CChalc.can.28; ib.29; Evagr.h.e.2.18(p.77.24; M.86.2564C); e. of Jerusalem; i. of S. James, title being accorded him either as compliment to contemporary bishop of Jerusalem or as meaning first bishop ἀποστόλου καὶ ἀ. Thal.CP Thds.(p.7.17; M.91.1472B); Nil.epp.1.145(M.79.141D); ii. of bishops, Thds.Imp.sacr.8(p.74.20; H.2.80C); τοῦ...ἀ. καὶ πατριάρχου Πέτρου CHier.(536)(ACO 3 p.123.19; H.2.1412A); f. before A.D. 500 title usu. reserved for patriarchs, but occasionally used of bishops of metropolitan or other important sees, and later of relatively unimportant sees also; e.g., of archbishop of Cyprus, regularly after A.D. 500, CLater.act.2(H.3.728D); Ephesus, Jo.Mosch.prat.97(M.87.2956C); Caesarea in Palestine, Thds.Imp.sacr.8(p.74.21; M.2.80C); Thessalonica, CChalc.act.3(H.2.366B); Jo.Mosch.prat.43(2896D); Seleucia–Ctesiphon, Soz.h.e.2.9.1(M.67.956B); Cyzicus, Gel.Cyz.h.e.proem.2(M.85.1193A); Caesarea in Cappadocia, Rit.Epiph.(p.430); Milan, Thdt.h.e.5.18(3.1048; l. ἀρχιερέως); Smyrna, apparently made autocephalous archbishopric between A.D. 451 and 457, cf. Αἰθέριχος ἐπίσκοπος Σμύρνης CChalc.act.1(ACO 2.1.1 p.193.39; H.2.264A); and Αἰθερίχου τοῦ ἀ. ἡμῶν CIG 8618, bestowal of latter title being suggested by fact that Aethericus is one of bishops to whom Leo's encyclical is sent directly in 457 (H.2.691B); Miletus, probably made independent of Aphrodisias c. 536–8 ἐπισκοποῦντος Ὑακίνθου τοῦ ἁγιωτάτου ἡμῶν ἀ. IGC As.Min.219(Miletus, 538); cf. Ὑάκινθος...ἐπίσκοπος τῆς Μιλησίων πόλεως CCP(536)act.5(ACO 3 p.115.20; H.2.1401A); but uncertain whether last two examples indicate change of status of bishops' sees or development of more general application of term ἀ.; Meletius as archbishop in Egypt (when bishop of Lycopolis), Epiph.haer.69.3(p.154.24; M.42.208A).

*ἀρχιεράρχης, ὁ, bishop δεῖ γὰρ τὸν ἀ. ἔνθεόν τε καὶ θεῖον ἄνδρα εἶναι Ant.Mon.hom.122(M.89.1812A); V.Chrys.61(p.325.45).

ἀρχιερατεία, ἡ, high-priesthood; 1. of OT high-priesthood, Ath.Ar.2.8(M.26.161C); 2. of bishops' office ἀπόστολοι...ὧν ἡμεῖς διάδοχοι τυγχάνοντες τῆς τε αὐτῆς χάριτος μετέχοντες ἀ. τε καὶ διδασκαλίας καὶ φρουροὶ τῆς ἐκκλησίας λελογισμένοι Hipp.haer.proem.(p.3.4; M.16.3020C).

ἀρχιερατεύ-ω, hold office of high priest; 1. of Jewish high priests, A.Pil.B 1(p.288); Thdt.Dan.11:23(2.1279); 2. of bishops δὸς... ποιμαίνειν τὴν...ποίμνην καὶ ~ειν σοι Lit.ap.Const.App.8.5.6; Anon.proem.in Dor.doct.(M.88.1613A); Thphn.chron.p.342(M.108.825A); 3. met., of penitence μεγάλη ἡ μετάνοια καὶ θεῷ λίαν προσφιλεστάτη ...~ει θεῷ ἐξόχως Ephr.3.168E.

ἀρχιερατικός, high-priestly; 1. of Jewish high priests ἐνδύματος ἀ. Or.sel.in Jos.(M.12.820B); A.Phil.14(p.7.23); ib.28(p.15.14); Ath.Ar.2.8(M.26.161C); †Bas.Is.125(1.466D; M.30.321B); τὸ ἀ. ... χρῖσμα ...ἀδελφῶν συναφείᾳ παρεικάζεσθαι ἄξιον ib.130(469E; M.329A); Chrys.hom.65.1 in Jo.(8.389C); Thdt.qu.4 in 1Reg.(1.358); of lineal descent of BMV ἐκ φυλῆς βασιλικῆς καὶ ἀ. Jo.Eub.concept.BMV 18(M.96.1489B); 2. of high-priestly office of Christ ἡ ἀ. λειτουργία μετετέθη ἀπὸ Ἀαρὼν εἰς τὸν Χριστόν, οὗ τύπος ἦν ὁ Μελχισεδέκ, οὐκ ὢν ἐκ τοῦ Λευί Euthal.Diac.epp.Paul.(M.85.776A); 3. of Christians as body deriving high-priestly character from Christ ἡμεῖς, οἱ διὰ τοῦ Ἰησοῦ ὀνόματος ὡς εἷς ἄνθρωπος πιστεύσαντες...ἀ.

τὸ ἀληθινὸν γένος ἐσμὲν τοῦ θεοῦ Just.*dial.*116.3(M.6.745A); θρόνος γὰρ Δαυὶδ καὶ βασιλικὴ ἕδρα ἐστὶν ἡ ἐν τῇ ἁγίᾳ ἐκκλησίᾳ ἱερωσύνη ὅπερ ἀξίωμα βασιλικόν τε καὶ ἀ. ὁμοῦ ἐπὶ τὸ αὐτὸ συνάψας ὁ κύριος δεδώρηται τῇ ἁγίᾳ αὐτοῦ ἐκκλησίᾳ Epiph.*haer.*29.3(p.323.6; M.41.392A); **4.** of bishops ἡ...περὶ ἡμᾶς καινοτομία ἡνίκα...ὑμεῖς ὁ λαὸς βοῶντάς τε καὶ ὀδυρομένους ἐπὶ τὸν θρόνον τοῦτον ἐθήκατε, τὸν οὐκ οἶδ' εἴτε τυραννικὸν χρὴ λέγειν, εἴτε ἀ. Gr.Naz.*or.*36.2(M.36.268B); τὴν ἀ. τιμήν, ἥτις μίμησιν περιέχει τοῦ μεγάλου ἀρχιερέως Ἰησοῦ Χριστοῦ *Const.App.*8.46.4; οὐ πάντως πᾶς ὁ πιστεύσας ἤδη καὶ ἱερεὺς κατέστη ἢ ἀ. ἀξίας ἔτυχεν. μετὰ δὲ τὴν ἀνάληψιν αὐτοῦ...προεχειρισάμεθα ἐπισκόπους καὶ πρεσβυτέρους καὶ διακόνους *ib.*8.46.14; τὸν ἀ. ... θρόνον Synes.*ep.*67(M.66.1412B); τῆς ἀ. αὐτῷ χάριτος μεταδούς Thdt. *h.e.*1.23.8(3.805); id.*ep.*42(4.1100); esp., in later authors, of bishops of greater sees, e.g. Constantinople, id.*h.e.*1.3.3(3.727); Philost. *h.e.*2.10(M.65.472C); Eustrat.*v.Eutych.*25(M.86.2304A); Evagr.*h.e.*3.32(p.130.4; M.86.2664B); CNic.(787)*act.*3(H.4.129E); Alexandria, Thdt.*h.e.*4.21.1(3.984); Philost.*h.e.*2.11(M.65.476A); Ephesus, Evagr. *h.e.*3.5(p.104.26; 2604C); Milan, Thdt.*h.e.*4.6.7(3.954); of see of Patricius, catholicos of Persia ἐπὶ τοὺς...ἀ. θρόνους ἀνήχθη τῆς ὅλης Περσίδος, καθολικὸς ἐπίσκοπος αὐτόθι κατασταθείς Cosm.Ind.*top.*2 (M.88.73A); **5.** of perfected soul ἡ ψυχὴ...μεταβαίνει εἰς τὰ πνευματικά, λογικὴ τῷ ὄντι καὶ ἀ. γενομένη Clem.*exc.Thdot.*27(p.116.4; M.9.673A).

***ἀρχιερατικῶς**, *in the manner of a high priest*; **1.** of Christ (cf. Heb.4:14) υἱοπρεπῶς μὲν διὰ τὴν φύσιν, ἀ. δὲ διὰ τὴν μεσιτείαν, προσάγων εὐχαριστήρια τῷ πατρί †Diad.*Ar.*7(M.65.1161C); **2.** *episcopally* τὰς πόλεις ἀ. ἰθύνειν πεπιστευμένος Thdt.*h.e.*4.35(3.1012).

***ἀρχιερεσία, ἡ,** Const.ap.Ath.*apol.sec.*62(M.25.361B; f.l. for ἀρχιαιρεσία p.142.7).

ἀρχιερεύς, ὁ, *high priest, chief priest*;

A. Jewish; **1.** as belonging to tribe of Levi ἐντέλλομαι ὑμῖν ἀκούειν τοῦ Λευί, ὅτι αὐτὸς...θυσιάσει ὑπὲρ τοῦ Ἰσραὴλ μέχρι τελειώσεως χρόνων ἀ. χριστός *T.Reub.*6.8; ἐκ γὰρ τῆς φυλῆς τοῦ Συμεὼν ἦσαν οἱ γραμματεῖς, ἐκ δὲ τοῦ Λευί οἱ ἀ. Hipp.*ben.Jac.*14 (p.29.20); in Messianic expectation ἀναστήσει γὰρ κύριος ἐκ τοῦ Λευί ὡς ἀ. καὶ ἐκ τοῦ Ἰούδα ὡς βασιλέα *T.Sym.*7.2; **2.** life-tenure of office, and hereditary succession, prescribed by Law, altered after death of Hyrcanus into brief tenure, often of only one year, Thdt.*Dan.*9:25(2.1246); τῶν παρὰ Ἰουδαίοις ἀ. καὶ βασιλέων ἐκλειπόντων, Ἡρώδης ἀλλόφυλος βασιλεύει...καθ' ὃν τῆς τοῦ Χριστοῦ γενέσεως πλησιαζούσης ἡ ἐκ προγόνων διαδοχὴ καὶ ἀρχιερωσύνη... κατελύθη, συμπληρουμένης τῆς παρὰ Μωυσεῖ προφητείας [Gen.49:10] *Chron.Pasch.*p.189(M.92.464D); cf.Chrys.*hom.65.1 in Jo.*(8.389E); id.*hom.79.3 in Mt.*(7.761E) cit. infra B; **3.** existence of one ἀ. only at any one time a distinctive mark of Judaism, Or.*Cels.*5.44 (p.47.21; M.11.1249B); but Lc.3:1–2 interpreted as denoting illegal creation of two high priests simultaneously, Thdt.*Dan.*9:25 (2.1247); **4.** 3Reg.1:34 interpreted as demonstrating precedence of high priest over prophet, Thdt.*qu.2 in 3Reg.*1:38(1.456); **5.** high priest can remit sins, Or.*hom.10.1 in Num.*(p.68.8; M.12.635D); *ib.* (p.71.9; 638A); *ib.10.2*(p.72.26; 639A); **6.** possessed gift of prophecy by virtue of office (cf. Jo.11:51) προεφήτευσεν [sc. Caiaphas] ἀ. ὤν. ὁρᾷς πόση τῆς ἀρχιερατικῆς ἐξουσίας ἡ δύναμις; ἐπειδὴ γὰρ ὅλως ἠξίωτο τῆς ἀρχιερωσύνης, καίτοι ἀνάξιος ὢν τοῦ πράγματος, προεφήτευσεν, οὐκ εἰδὼς ἅπερ ἔλεγε Chrys.*hom.65.1 in Jo.*(8.389C); Spirit being transferred from high priests to apostles after arrest of Jesus, *ib.*(389E); cf. στόματι λαλοῦντι μόνον...πρὸς τιμὴν τῆς ἱερατείας, ἐδόθη αὐτῷ τὸ προειπεῖν (οὐ μὴν ὡς προφήτῃ) Ammon. *Jo.*11:51(M.85.1469D); contrast ὁ γοῦν Καϊάφας, ἀ. ὢν τοῦ ἐνιαυτοῦ ἐκείνου, προεφήτευσεν μὲν...οὐ μὴν καὶ προφήτης ἦν...καὶ μοχθηρὰ ψυχὴ ἐπιδέχεταί ποτε τὸ προφητεύειν. κατηγορεῖται γὰρ ἡ τοῦ Καϊάφα μοχθηρία, ὃς ἦν ἀ. τοῦ ἐνιαυτοῦ ἐκείνου ὅτε ὁ σωτὴρ...ἐπιτελεῖ οἰκονομίαν Or.*Jo.*28.13(12; pp.404.20,405.21; M.14.705D,708C); περίστασις αἰτία ποτὲ γίνεται τοῦ προφητεύειν, ὥσπερ καὶ νῦν...τὸ εἶναι αὐτὸν ἀ. τοῦ ἐνιαυτοῦ ἐκείνου...ὄντων γὰρ καὶ ἄλλων ἀ. ... οὐδεὶς προφητεύει ἢ ὁ τοῦ ἐνιαυτοῦ ᾧ ἔμελλεν πάσχειν ὁ Ἰησοῦς ἀ. *ib.*28.20 (15; p.414.33; M.14.724B); **7.** high priest's robes; **a.** symbolize cosmos, cf. *dicitur etiam in indumento pontificis mundi rationem contineri, sicut in Sapientia Salomonis invenimus, cum dicit quia in vestimento poderis erat universus mundus*, Or.*princ.*2.3.6(p.121.9; M.11.194B); cf.Gr.Nyss.*v.Mos.*(M.44.388C); **b.** symbolize virtues, Or.*hom.9.3 in Ex.*(p.240.13; M.12.365D); cf. τὸν μέντοι λόγον [sc. cosmic interpretation] οὐκ ἀποβάλλω· συντείνει γὰρ πρὸς τὴν κατ' ἀρετὴν θεωρίαν νόημα...ἡ οὖν λαμπηδὼν τῶν καλῶν ἔργων, οἱ χρυσοῖ κώδωνές εἰσι Gr.Nyss.*v.Mos.*(M.44.388C); **c.** as applied to Christ as antitype of high priest, cf. *quod si vis audire de excelsioribus indumentis ejus, accipe verba prophetica: 'amictus', inquit, 'lumen sicut vestimentum...' hic est mei magni pontificis habitus, quo indicatur profunda scientiae et sapientiae luce vestitus, quae vere sancta sunt indumenta*, Or.*hom.12.3 in Lev.*(p.459.7; M.12.538B); id.*hom.9.5 in Num.*(p.60.34; M.12.630A); **d.** investiture of high priest compared with assumption of flesh by Logos, Ath.*Ar.*2.7(M.26.161A,B); cf. Clem.*str.*5.6(p.354.2; M.9.68A); **e.** high priest's breastplate contained the stones, δήλωσις and ἀλήθεια, which were type of Christ, Cyr.*Os.*34(3.62B); **f.** robed high priest reverenced by Alexander (cf. Josephus *Antiquitates* 11.8.3–5) φασὶ καὶ τὸν Ἰουδαίων ἀ. ἐνδύντα τὴν ἱερατικὴν στολὴν προσκεκυνῆσθαι ὑπὸ τοῦ Ἀλεξάνδρου, φάσκοντος ὦφθαι αὐτῷ τούτῳ τῷ σχήματι ἑωρακέναι τινά, ἐπαγγελλόμενον αὐτῷ ...ὑποτάξειν τὴν Ἀσίαν ὅλην Or.*Cels.*5.50(p.54.23; M.11.1260B); **g.** robes are part of Jewish system which has passed away in fulfilment of prophecy, Or.*princ.*4.1.3(p.296.13; M.11.345C); **8.** of Melchizedek as high priest, *Lit.*ap.*Const.App.*8.12.23; Moses as βασιλεὺς ὁμοῦ καὶ ἀ. *Const.App.*2.29; νομοθέτης ὁμοῦ καὶ ἀ. καὶ προφήτης καὶ βασιλεύς *ib.*6.19.4; as consecrator of Aaron, *ib.*8.46.17; of Aaron as elder brother to Moses, but inferior to him as result of divine election, *Hom.Clem.*2.16; of Samuel οὔτε...παρ' οὐδὲν ἡγήσατο τὸν...Δαυίδ, καίτοι ἀμφότεροι προφῆται καὶ ὁ μὲν ἀρχιερεύς, ὁ δὲ βασιλεύς *Const.App.*8.1.14; **9.** of Zacharias as 'great high priest' and example to Christian priests, Ant.Mon.*hom.*121(M.89. 1809D); **10.** as type of Christ, v. infra; **11.** in comparison of OT with Christian ministry, *1Clem.*40.5 cit. s. λευίτης; **12.** apparent mistaken identification of ἀρχιερεύς with ἀρχισυνάγωγος, *A.Thadd.*5 (p.276.5).

B. of Jewish 'chief priests', *A.Andr.et Mt.*11(p.77.12); *ib.*13 (p.79.7); *A.(Pass.)Petr.et Paul.*20(p.136.13); perh. *A.Thadd.*5 supra; Clem.*fr.*28(p.217.4; M.9.757B); Nonn.*par.Jo.*19:6(M.43.897C); confused with 'high priest' in comment on Mt.26:3 καὶ πόσοι ἦσαν οἱ ἀ.; ὁ γὰρ νόμος ἕνα εἶναι βούλεται· ἀλλὰ τότε πολλοὶ ἦσαν...πῶς οὖν τότε πολλοὶ οἱ ἀ.; ἐνιαυσιαῖοι ὕστερον ἐγίνοντο. καὶ τοῦτο ἐδήλωσεν ὁ εὐαγγελιστής, ὅτε περὶ τοῦ Ζαχαρίου διελέγετο, εἰπὼν ἐξ ἐφημερίας αὐτὸν εἶναι Ἀβιά. αὐτοὺς οὖν ἐνταῦθά φησιν ἀρχιερεῖς τοὺς ἀπ' ἀρχιερέων Chrys.*hom.79.3 in Mt.*(7.761Df.); confused with scribes τοὺς ἀ., τοὺς καθίσαντας μὲν ἐπὶ τῆς καθέδρας Μωϋσέως Jo.D.*hom.*2.4(M.96.581D).

C. of Christ; **1.** offering himself to Father, cf. Χριστὸν ἀ. τοῦτον τὸν σταυρωθέντα Just.*dial.*116.1(M.6.744B); ὁ ἀ. θυσίαν ἑαυτὸν προσήνεγκεν Or.*mart.*30(p.27.6; M.11.601B); cf. *ipse et hostia est et pontifex. secundum spiritum namque offert hostiam patri, secundum carnem ipse in altari crucis offertur*, id.*hom.8.9 in Gen.*(p.84. 29; M.12.209A); *ovis qui immolatur in pascha ipse dicitur...et pontifex qui offert sacrificium*, *ib.14.1*(p.122.3; 236B); id.*Cant.*1 (p.98.14; M.13.91B); τὸν εἰς τὸν αἰῶνα ἀ. κατὰ τὴν τάξιν Μελχισεδέκ, καὶ τὸν ἀμνὸν τοῦ θεοῦ id.*Jo.*19.19(4; p.319.27; M.14.561A); ἀ. πάσης νοερᾶς καὶ λογικῆς κτίσεως, τὸν ἡμῖν ὁμοιοπαθῆ, οἷα πρόβατον...ἐκ τῆς ἀνθρώπων ἀφορίσας ἀγέλης, τούτῳ τε ἐπιγράψας τὰς πάντων ἡμῶν ἁμαρτίας, καὶ τὴν κατάραν γε αὐτῷ...περιάψας...τοῦτο πέπονθεν αὐτὸς...γενόμενος ὑπὲρ ἡμῶν κατάρα Eus.*d.e.*1.10(p.47.4; M.22.89A); ἀ. ὅτι προσφέρεις τὸ σῶμα Gr.Naz.*or.*37.4(M.36.288A); *Lit.*ap.*Const. App.*8.12.30; **2.** contrasted as antitype with OT high priest, cf. *pontificem legis confert pontifici repromissionis*, Or.*hom.9.2 in Lev.* (p.419.26; M.12.509C); **3.** as eternal high priest, Polyc.*ep.*12.2; Or.*hom.5.12 in Lev.*(p.358.15; M.12.466B); Thdt.*Heb.*6:20(3.583); **4.** entry through veil (Heb.10:20) interpreted of Christ's entry through veil of flesh and veil of heaven, Or.*hom.1.3 in Lev.*(p.285. 11; M.12.409B); Christ's high-priestly right to enter holy place signifies his supreme place in God's revelation, Ign.*Philad.*9.1; Atonement typified by high priest's entry, Or.*hom.9.5 in Lev.* (p.427.5; M.12.515A); **5.** wins redemption for faithful and presents them to God, Or.*hom.9.5 in Lev.*(p.427.11; M.12.515B); ἀ. δίκην τοὺς ὑπ' αὐτῷ ἱερουμένους πάντας λευχειμονας...παριστῶν αὐτῷ Eus.*e.th.* 3.16(p.175.11; M.24.1033C); πότε δὲ ἀ. τῆς ὁμολογίας ἡμῶν γέγονεν, ἢ ὅτε, προσενέγκας ἑαυτὸν ὑπὲρ ἡμῶν...καὶ νῦν αὐτὸς τοὺς προσερχομένους αὐτῷ τῇ πίστει προσάγει...τῷ πατρί; Ath.*Ar.*2.7(M.26.161A); *Const.App.*5.6.10; ἀ. δὲ εἰς τὸν αἰῶνά ἐστιν, οὐχ ὡς θυσίας προσφέρων, ἅπαξ γὰρ τὸ ἑαυτοῦ προσενήνοχε σῶμα, ἀλλ' ὡς μεσίτης προσάγων τῷ πατρὶ τοὺς πιστεύοντας Thdt.*Heb.*6:20(3.583); **6.** intercedes for men, Clem.*prot.*12(p.84.30; M.8.241A); ὁ ἀ. τοῖς γνησίως εὐχομένοις συνεύχεται Or.*or.*11(p.321.15; M.11.448B) etc.; **7.** through whom men offer prayer πᾶσαν μὲν γὰρ δέησιν καὶ προσευχὴν καὶ ἔντευξιν καὶ εὐχαριστίαν ἀναπεμπτέον τῷ ἐπὶ πᾶσι θεῷ διὰ τοῦ ἐπὶ πάντων ἀγγέλων ἀ., ἐμψύχου λόγου καὶ θεοῦ Or.*Cels.*5.4(p.4.25; M.11.1185B); ἀναπεμπόντων εὐχὰς τῷ δημιουργῷ τοῦ παντὸς...ὡς δι' ἀ. τοῦ τὴν εἰλικρινῆ θεοσέβειαν ἀνθρώποις παραστήσαντος *ib.*7.46(p.197.21; 1488C); *ib.*8.26

(p.242.27; 1556B); λείπεται τοίνυν προσεύχεσθαι μόνῳ τῷ θεῷ τῷ τῶν ὅλων πατρί, ἀλλὰ μὴ χωρὶς τοῦ ἀ. id.or.15.1(p.334.14; M.11.465B); in liturg. worship, Lit.Jac.(p.170.5); ib.(p.178.29); v. εὐχή; as high priest Christ receives 'first-fruits' of prayer, Or.hom.11.5 in Num.(p.86.10; M.12.650C); through whom praise is offered, 1Clem.61.3; M.Polyc.14.3; Or.hom.23.4 in Num.(p.217.5; M.12.751A) etc.; and the sacrifice of good living, 1Clem.36.1; ib.64; Clem.paed.2.8(p.197.21; M.8.473B); Or.hom.9.8 in Lev.(p.433.22; M.12.520A); id.hom.11.3 in Num.(p.81.12; M.12.646B); **8.** who offers incense on glowing hearts of the faithful, Or.hom.9.9 in Lev.(p.437.16; M.12.522C); **9.** who cleanses from sin, Meth.lepr.6(p.458.23); and is merciful high priest, Cyr.Heb.2:17(p.466.4; M.74.968C); **10.** who is universal high priest ἀ. πάσης νοερᾶς καὶ λογικῆς κτίσεως Eus.d.e.1.10(p.47.4; M.22.89A); ἀ. πάντων τῶν λογικῶν ταγμάτων Const.App.6.30.10; and 'high priest of high priests', Or.hom.4.6 in Lev.(p.325.9; M.12.441B); ib.6.2(p.362.4; 469A); **11.** and sole high priest Ἰησοῦς, εἷς ὁ μέγας ἀ. θεοῦ τε ἑνὸς τοῦ αὐτοῦ καὶ πατρός...ἥκετε ὡς ἐμέ, ὑφ' ἕνα ταχθησόμενοι θεὸν καὶ τὸν ἕνα λόγον τοῦ θεοῦ Clem.prot.12(p.84.30; M.8.241A); αὐτὸς ὁ ἀ. εἷς, ἑνὸς ὄντος τοῦ θεοῦ id.str.4.23(p.315.22; M.8.1360C); πάντες ὡς εἰς ἕνα ναὸν θεοῦ συντρέχετε, ὡς ἐπὶ ἓν θυσιαστήριον, ἐπὶ ἕνα Ἰησοῦν Χριστὸν τὸν ἀ. ‡Ign.Magn.7; **12.** as high priest, is present in ministrations of clergy, ‡Pion.v.Polyc.23; **13.** and is represented in the bishop, ‡Ign.Magn.4; Const.App.8.46.12; **14.** fulfils type of Aaron in 'standing between the dead and the living' (Num.16:48), Or.hom.26.3 in Jos.(p.462.28; M.12.947C Lat.); **15.** and in having a rod which budded (Num.17:8), cf. *verus pontifex...cujus virga crucis non solum germinavit sed etiam floruit*, id.hom.9.7 in Num.(p.63.18; M.12.632B); **16.** who will reveal the tabernacle on Last Day, Cosm.Ind.top.5(M.88.208D); **17.** 'sons of the high priest' are Christ's apostles, Or.hom.7.1 in Lev.(p.373.12; M.12.477A); id.hom.5.1 in Num.(p.26.24; M.12.603C); martyrs, ib.10.2(p.71.15; 638A); and doctors of Church, ib.11.7(p.89.26; 653A); **18.** Christ revealed as high priest in Transfiguration, Or.fr.22 in Lc.22(p.243.12); **19.** as being ἀ., ἀρχιπροφήτης, ἀρχάγγελος, ἀρχιπάρθενος, Christ was first to teach virginity, Meth.symp.1.4(p.12.19; M.18.44C); **20.** Christol.; **a.** Logos as high priest ὁ προὼν αὐτοῦ μονογενὴς λόγος, ὁ δὴ μέγας ἀ. τοῦ μεγάλου θεοῦ, παντὸς χρόνου...πρεσβύτατος Eus.l.C.1(p.198.23; M.20.1324B); high-priesthood one of his eternal attributes, ib.3(p.202.3; 1332B); id.e.th.1.20(p.96.28; M.24.893B); **b.** Marcellus' teaching implies denial of Christ's high-priesthood, id.Marcell.2.1(p.33.21; M.24.780B); **c.** Christ is high priest in virtue of his humanity αὐτὸς γέγονεν ἀ. κατὰ τὸ ἀνθρώπινον. καίτοι παρὰ πάντων τὰς θυσίας δεχόμενος θεϊκῶς, αὐτὸς τὸ θῦμα κατὰ τὴν σάρκα...οὐκ αὐτῇ μέντοι τῇ τοῦ λόγου φύσει, τὸ ἀ. κεκλῆσθαι...ἀλλὰ τῇ μετὰ σαρκὸς οἰκονομίᾳ Cyr.Heb.2:17(M.74.965C,D); ἀ. δὲ οὐχ ὡς θεός, ἀλλ' ὡς ἄνθρωπος κέκληται Thdt.eran.2(4.92); id.ep.145(4.1249); Proc.G.Gen.14:18(M.87.336A); **d.** high-priesthood implied in title Χριστός, Eus.h.e.1.3.5(M.20.69C); **21.** Valent. προβέβλητο ὁ κοινὸς τοῦ πληρώματος καρπός, ὁ Ἰησοῦς...ὁ ἀ. ὁ μέγας Hipp.haer.6.32(p.160.9; M.16.3242C).

D. of archangels as high priests οἱ ἀρχάγγελοι τῶν ἀγγέλων ἀ. γενόμενοι Clem.exc.Thdot.27(p.116.5; M.9.673A); archangel, as high priest, identified with Jesus, ib.38(p.119.2; 677B).

E. title applied to Christian ministers; **1.** of S. James officiating as high priest at Jerusalem αὐτὸν...ἔτι δὲ καὶ ἱερατεύσαντα αὐτὸν κατὰ τὴν παλαιὰν ἱερωσύνην ηὕρομεν. διὸ καὶ ἐφίετο αὐτῷ ἅπαξ τοῦ ἐνιαυτοῦ εἰς τὰ ἅγια τῶν ἁγίων εἰσιέναι, ὡς τοῖς ἀ. ἐκέλευσεν ὁ νόμος Epiph.haer.29.4(p.324.21; M.41.396A); cf.Heges.ap.Eus.h.e.2.23.6(M.20.197A); **2.** applied, in direct allusion to OT type; **a.** to Christian prophets δώσεις τὴν ἀπαρχὴν τοῖς προφήταις· αὐτοὶ γάρ εἰσιν οἱ ἀ. ὑμῶν Did.13.3, where identification of prophets with ἀρχιερεῖς is perh. due to Jo.11:51 but more prob. to Ex.7:1; **b.** to bishops, cf. gen. equation of high priest, priests, Levites, with Christian ministry, 1Clem.40.5 cit. s. λευίτης; ἐπισκόπων...οὗτοι γάρ εἰσιν ὑμῶν οἱ ἀ.· οἱ δὲ ἱερεῖς ὑμῶν οἱ πρεσβύτεροι καὶ οἱ λευῖται ὑμῶν οἱ νῦν διάκονοι Const.App.2.26.3; Epiph.haer.29.4(p.325.15; M.41.396A); Thdt.Ps.73:15(1.1132); **3.** used without direct allusion to OT; **a.** of bishops, †Ath.fr.(M.26.1293B); Gr.Naz.ep.167(M.37.277B); id.carm.2.2(epitaph.)60(M.38.41A); Gr.Nyss.v.Gr.Thaum.(M.46.933C); Lit.ap.Const.App.8.11.1; ib.8.12.4; Const.App.2.57.16; Thdt.qu.18 in Num.(1.233); id.ep.80(4.1138); Philost.h.e.5.1(M.65.528D); Bas.Sel.v.Thecl.2.18(M.85.596C); MAMA 1.208; ib.1.412; **b.** of patriarchs ὁ ἀ. τῆς Αἰγυπτιακῆς διοικήσεως Pall.v.Chrys.7(p.39.5; M.47.24); of Leo Mag., CChalc.act.4(H.2.401A; ἀρχιεπίσκοπον ACO 2.1.2 p.102.29); **c.** of priests, Thdt.Jer.38(40):23–26(2.558); Anast.S.fr.6(M.89.1288C); **d.** of celebrant at eucharist, usu. bishop τὴν...εἰς τὴν ἁγίαν ἐκκλησίαν τοῦ ἀ. κατὰ τὴν ἱερὰν σύναξιν εἴσοδον Max.myst.8(M.91.688C); Anast.S.synax.(M.89.840B).

F. title applied to emperor τῷ εὐσεβεῖ, τῷ ὀρθοδόξῳ...τῷ ἀ. βασιλεῖ CEph.(449)act.(ACO 2.1.1 p.138.28; H.2.160D); Sophr.H.trop.(M.87.4009A).

G. title of pagan priests Κυρίλλου τοῦ ἀ. τοῦ Διός (at Lystra) A.Barn.1(p.292.10); of Asiarchs ἐπὶ ἀ. Φιλίππου Τραλλιανοῦ M.Polyc.21.

H. met.; **1.** of Christians in gen., cf.Just.dial.116.3(M.6.745A); of advanced Christians οἱ πάντων διαφέροντες καὶ οἱονεὶ τὰ πρωτα τῆς καθ' ἑαυτοὺς γενεᾶς ἔχοντες ἀ. ἔσονται κατὰ τὴν τάξιν Ἀαρών, καὶ οὐ κατὰ τὴν τάξιν Μελχισεδέκ. ἐὰν γάρ τις ἀνθυποφέρῃ πρὸς τοῦτο, νομίζων ἡμᾶς ἀσεβεῖν τὸ τοῦ ἀ. ὄνομα τάσσοντας ἐπ' ἀνθρώπων...λεκτέον...τὸν προφήτην εἰρηκέναι περὶ Χριστοῦ· σὺ ἱερεὺς...κατὰ τὴν τάξιν Μελχισεδέκ, καὶ οὐ κατὰ τὴν τάξιν Ἀαρών Or.Jo.1.2(3; p.5.24; M.14.25B); **2.** of the soul; **a.** of enlightened reason θεραπεύων τὸν τῶν ὅλων θεὸν διὰ τοῦ ἀ. λόγου Clem.str.2.9(p.137.12; M.8.981A) (if reference here be not to Logos as high priest); **b.** of purified soul arrayed in virtues as high-priestly garments, cf. *homo noster interior Deo pontifex adornetur, ut introire possit...et in sancta sanctorum*, Or.hom.9.4 in Ex.(p.243.23; M.12.368B); receiving its robes in place of 'coats of skin' which it has put off, id.hom.6.2 in Lev.(p.362.2; M.12.468D); offering λογικαὶ θυσίαι to Christ, Jo.Clim.scal.28(M.88.1137B); **c.** of pious disposition, cf. *pontifex iste sensus pietatis et religionis...qui in nobis per orationes et obsecrationes, quas Deo fundimus, velut quodam sacerdotio fungitur*, Or.hom.2.4 in Lev.(p.294.30; M.12.416C); **d.** of heretical opinion as 'lawless high priest', compared with Ananias who smote Apostle, Or.hom.19.12 in Jer.(p.167.19; M.13.488A).

ἀρχιερεύω, *hold office of high priest*, Chron.Pasch.p.146(M.92.360B).

***ἀρχιερόπλοκος**, *wreathed by a high priest*, in address to BMV τὸ ἀ. τῆς βασιλείας διάδημα referring to Christ as high priest, Andr.Cr.or.3(M.97.1100A).

***ἀρχιεροπρεπής**, *befitting a bishop*, Taras.ep.2(M.98.1437B).

ἀρχιερωσύνη, ἡ, *high-priesthood*; **1.** Jewish; **a.** in gen., A.Pil.B proem.(p.287); Eus.Marcell.1.2(p.10.15; M.24.733B); Const.App.8.46.3; Cyr.Os.91(3.123B); Dion.Ar.ep.8.1(M.3.1085A); **b.** of hereditary succession to high-priesthood, abolished by time of Christ, Chron.Pasch.p.189(M.92.464D); **c.** of prophetic gift inherent in the office (cf. Jo.11:51), Chrys.hom.65.1 in Jo.(8.389C); v. ἀρχιερεύς; **d.** of Aaronic high-priesthood as type of Christ's, Cyr.Jon.1(3.366B); and Christ's high-priesthood as archetype of Melchizedek's, Thdt.Ps.109:4(1.1396); **e.** of OT high-priesthood transferred to bishops in Christian dispensation, Epiph.haer.29.4(p.325.15; M.41.396C); Const.App.8.46.10; **2.** of Christ's high-priesthood ἡ ἀληθὴς τοῦ σωτῆρος ἡμῶν ἀ. Or.Jo.28.12(11; p.404.6; M.14.705C); Eus.h.e.1.3.2(M.20.69A); Gr.Naz.or.30.16(M.36.124D); Thdt.Heb.5:4(3.573); κατὰ μὲν οὖν τὰ θεοπρεπῆ ταῦτα καὶ ὄντως θεῖα, τύπος ὁ Μελχισεδὲκ τοῦ δεσπότου Χριστοῦ· κατὰ δέ γε τὴν ἀ., ἥτις ἀνθρώποις μᾶλλον ἢ θεῷ προσήκει, ὁ δεσπότης Χριστὸς ἀρχιερεὺς γέγονε κατὰ τὴν τάξιν Μελχισεδέκ id.eran.2(4.92); v. ἀρχιερεύς; **3.** in Christian ministry, *office of bishop*; **a.** as typified by OT high-priesthood, Const.App.8.46.10; v. ἀρχιερεύς; **b.** without direct ref. to OT, Chrys.hom.3.5 in Ac.(9.30B); οἱ τὸν καλλιεπῆ καὶ θεόμορφον τῆς ἀ. θρόνον ἐπέχοντες †Cyr.hom.div.11(5^2.379C); Philost.h.e.1.3(M.65.461C); Thdt.h.e.1.2.9(3.725); id.h.rel.1(3.1111); of Ignatius διὰ τῆς...Πέτρου δεξιᾶς τῆς ἀ. τὴν χάριν ἐδέξατο id.eran.1(4.49); of Athanasius τὴν ἀ. ἐκόσμησε id.ep.144(4.1243); Max.ep.28(M.91.621A); Eustrat.v.Eutych.23(M.86.2300D); Lit.Marc.(p.121.17).

ἀρχιεταῖρος, ὁ, *chief friend, boon companion*, transliteration of אַרְכִּי applied to Cushi in 2Reg.15:32,16:16; cf. 15:37, Ath.exp.Ps.7(M.27.77C); Χουσὶ...υἱὸς δὲ Ἀραχὶ ἀπὸ τοῦ πατρός· ἀ. δέ, ὁ ἄρχων τῶν φίλων καὶ παλαιὸς κατὰ τὴν φιλίαν Didym.Ps.7:1(M.39.1180B); οὗτος τοῦ μακαρίου Δαβὶδ ἀ. ἐγένετο...ἀ. ... ἐλέγετο κατὰ ἕνα τῶν δύο τρόπων, ἢ ὅτι τῆς ἑταιρίας τῶν στρατηγῶν Δαβὶδ ἦρχεν ὡς ἀρχιστράτηγος, ἢ ὅτι ἄνωθεν αὐτῷ καὶ ἐξαρχῆς ἑταῖρος καὶ φίλος ἐγένετο Ast.Soph.hom.in Ps.7(M.40.460B).

ἀρχιευνοῦχος, ὁ, *chief of the eunuchs*, T.Jos.13.5; Jo.Mal.chron.13 p.340(M.97.505C).

***ἀρχιζωγράφος, ὁ**, *chief painter*, met. Ἀβραὰμ ὁ ἀ. τῆς Χριστοῦ ταφῆς καὶ τῆς ἀναστάσεως Germ.CP or.2(M.98.280A).

***ἀρχίζωος**, *life-giving*; of baptism, Dion.Ar.e.h.3.3.6(M.3.433A).

[*]**ἀρχιητρός, ὁ**, v. ἀρχιατρός.

***ἀρχίθεος**, *God from the beginning, eternally divine* ἡ ἀ. καὶ ὑπεράρχιος τοῦ υἱοῦ τοῦ θεοῦ ὑπόστασις ‡Ath.*annunt*.9(M.28.929D); δοκεῖ μὲν εἶναι...τοῦ ἑνὸς θεοῦ διάκρισις καὶ πολλαπλασιασμός, ἔστι δὲ οὐδὲν ἧττον ὁ ἀ. καὶ ὑπέρθεος ὑπερουσίως εἷς θεός Dion.Ar.*d.n*.2.11 (M.3.649C).

ἀρχίθρονος, ὁ, *occupying the chief see, presiding*, Andr.Cr.*or*.16 (M.97.1157B).

***ἀρχικουνίτης, ὁ,** ? *head of a* (monastery) *dorter* εἴ τις τῶν ἀ. εὑρίσκει τινὰ ταράσσοντα ἢ διαλεγόμενον ἐν τῷ κουνίῳ ‡Bas.*poen.mon*. 15(2.527E; M.31.1308C); *ib*.30(2.528E; M.1309C).

ἀρχικῶς, 1. *principally, primarily*, Dion.Ar.*c.h*.9.1,2(M.3.257B,C); ref. cherubim ἡ πρώτη τῶν οὐρανίων ἱεραρχιῶν...καὶ τὰς πρωτουργοὺς θεοφανείας...εἰς αὐτὴν ὡς ἐγγυτάτην ἀ. διαπορθμεύεσθαι *ib*.7.1 (205B); **2.** *in a primary sense, fundamentally* εἰς ὃν [sc. Judas] μετὰ τὸ ψωμίον εἰσῆλθεν ὁ σατανᾶς ἀρχικώτερον τοῦ Ἰούδα παραδιδοὺς αὐτόν Or.*schol.in Lc*.9:44(M.17.349A); αὐτοεῖναι, καὶ αὐτοζωήν, καὶ αὐτοθεότητά φαμεν ἀ. μὲν οὖν, θεϊκῶς καὶ αἰτιατικῶς, τὴν μίαν πάντων ...ἀρχὴν καὶ αἰτίαν Dion.Ar.*d.n*.11.6(M.3.956A); **3.** *authoritatively*, of S. Peter μετὰ κοινῆς πάντα ποιοῦντα γνώμης· οὐδὲν αὐθεντικῶς, οὐδὲ ἀ. Chrys.*hom.3.1 in Ac*.(9.23D); ὁ Κύριλλος ἐνθρονισθεὶς ἐπὶ τὴν ἐπισκοπὴν ἀρχικώτερον Θεοφίλου παρῆλθε Socr.*h.e*.7.7.4(M.67.749C).

ἀρχιμάγειρος, ὁ, רַב־טַבָּחִים or שַׂר הַטַּבָּחִים, orig. *head slaughterer, butcher* and/or *cook*, 1Reg.9:23f.; for *chief of bodyguard, captain of the guard*, Gen.37:36 al.; 4Reg.25 passim; Jer.40:1 al.; Dan.2:14 etc.; in Egypt, of Potiphar οὗτος ὁ ἀ. Φαραὼ ἐπίστευσέ μοι τὸν οἶκον αὐτοῦ *T.Jos*.2.1; *ib*.16.2 (v.l.); Or.*sel.in Gen*.37:36(M.12.129A); Chrys.*Dan*.1:9(6.204B); in Babylon (of Nabuzardan), Hipp.*Dan*.1.3.5(M.10.640C); Nil.*epp*.2.107(M.79.248B); Ναβουζαρδὰν ἀρχιστράτηγος ἦν, οὗ ἐκτὸς οὐδεὶς ἀνῃρεῖτο· διὸ καὶ ἀ. καλεῖται, ὡς ἐπὶ τῶν φόνων Olymp.*fr.Jer*.40:1(M.93.700C); *Pers*.(p.1.4).

ἀρχίμαγος (-μάγος), ὁ, *chief magician, wise man* of Persian court, Soz.*h.e*.2.10.3(M.67.960D); τὸν ἀ. ... καὶ τοὺς μάγους Thphn.*chron*.p.145(M.108.397A); ἐπ' ὄψεσι τοῦ ἀ. καὶ τοῦ ἐπισκόπου τῶν Χριστιανῶν *ib*.p.146(397A); plur., *leading wise men* of court ὁ τῶν Περσῶν βασιλεὺς ἠγανάκτησεν· ὡσαύτως δὲ καὶ οἱ ἀ. τῶν Περσῶν Jo.Mal.*chron*.18 p.444(M.97.653B); Thphn.*chron*.p.145(M.108.396C); *M.Pers*.1.4(p.423.11).

***ἀρχιμανδρίτη, ἡ,** *abbess* φώνει μοι τὴν ἀμμᾶν τὴν ἀρχιμανδρίτην *V.Dan*.7(p.68.16).

ἀρχιμανδρίτης, ὁ, *monastic superior, archimandrite*; **1.** in gen. Ἀκάκιος πρεσβύτερος καὶ Παῦλος πρεσβύτερος, ἀρχιμανδρῖται Acac.et Paul.*ep*.ap.Epiph.*haer*.(p.153.13; M.41.156B) etc.; though usu. a priest, the ἀ. is sometimes a deacon, Thal.CP *Thds*.(p.7.8; M.91.1472A); Cyr.*ep*.69(p.15.27; 5^2.197A); *ib*.70(p.16.36; 5^2.198E); Thdt.*ep*.27 tit.(4.1089); occasionally a simple monk, CChalc.*act*.1(p.147.6,25; H.2.169E,172B); **2.** ἀ. and ἡγούμενος q.v.: latter is superior of particular monastery; ἀ. may be this, but may also enjoy higher eccl. rank; **a.** ἀ. = ἡγούμενος: φυγὼν ἐκ τῆς μονῆς τοῦ ἀ. μου Pall.*h.Laus*.21(p.63.21; M.34.1068D); εἴ τις πλύνει...ἱμάτιον παρὰ γνώμην τοῦ ἀ., γενέσθω ἀπευλογίας ‡Bas.*poen.mon*.33(2.529A; M.31.1309D); **b.** superior of a group of monasteries, title of Dalmatius and his successors ἀ. τῶν μοναστηρίων Cyr.*ep*.23(p.66.10; 5^2.84A); παρὰ Μαριανοῦ μοναχοῦ καὶ ἀ. μονῆς τοῦ μακαρίου Δαλματίου, καὶ ἐξάρχου τῶν...μοναστηρίων τῆς βασιλίδος καὶ τῶν αὐτῆς ἀ. *Ep*.ap.CCP(536)*act*.1(*ACO* 3 p.131.10; H.2.1193B); Eulog.*fr.dogm*.(M.86.2944A); also in Palestine προεβλήθησαν Θεοδόσιος καὶ Σάβας ἀ. καὶ ἔξαρχοι πάντων τῶν...μοναστηρίων. ὁ μὲν ἀββᾶς Θεοδόσιος ἀρχηγὸς γέγονε καὶ ἀ. παντὸς τοῦ κοινοβιακοῦ κανόνος...ὁ δὲ πατὴρ ἡμῶν Σάβας ἄρχων κατεστάθη καὶ νομοθέτης παντὸς τοῦ ἀναχωρητικοῦ βίου Cyr.S.*v.Sab*.30(p.115.17f.); *ib*.7(p.91.20).

***ἀρχιμανδρίτησσα, ἡ,** *superior* of a convent of nuns, *abbess*, *V.Euprax*.17(730D).

***ἀρχιμάρτυς, ὁ,** *chief of martyrs, first of martyrs* ὁ Χριστὸς...ἀ. ἐστὶ καὶ πολλῶν ὄντων μαρτύρων...ἐκεῖνος ὁ ἄρχων ἐστὶ τῶν μαρτύρων Or.*comm.in 1Cor*.1:6(*JTS* 9 p.233.32); ἀ. Χριστός, πρῶτος παθών, καὶ τοῖς δούλοις τὸν ζῆλον ἀφείς Ast.Am.*hom*.10(M.40.324D).

***ἀρχιμεγιστάν, ὁ,** *chief noble* (Persian) οἱ ἀ. τοῦ βασιλέως καὶ ἕτεροι ἀρχιμάγοι πολλοί *M.Pers*.10.24(p.495.1).

***ἀρχιμηνία, ἡ,** v. *ἀρχομηνία.

ἀρχιοινοχόος, ὁ, *chief cup-bearer*, †Bas.*Is*.155(1.488E; M.30.372C); Ast.Soph.*hom.5 in Ps*.5(M.40.440B); Nil.*epp*.1.78(M.79.116C); of Nehemiah, Clem.*str*.1.21(p.77.11; M.8.852B); *Chron.Pasch*.p.163(M.92.401B).

[*]ἄρχιος, s.v.l., variant of ἀρχαῖος: τί ἀνταμιψώμεθά σε θεαρχικώτατε λόγε; ὑπὲρ ἀρχίου πατρός *Lit.Jac*.(*NBP* 10^2 p.105; ? l. ὑπεραρχίου).

ἀρχιπάρθενος, *chief of virgins*; of Christ, Meth.*symp*.1.4(p.12.20; M.18.44C); *ib*.10.3(p.124.26; 196D).

***ἀρχιπάτωρ, ὁ, 1.** *patriarch*, Chrys.ap.Jo.D.*fid.dorm*.30(M.95.276B); **2.** *first forefather*; of Adam, ‡Bas.*const*.18(2.561C; M.31.1384A); Thdr.Stud.*epp*.1.50(M.99.1092D).

***ἀρχίπεζος,** *praefectus peditum, commander of infantry*, *M.Sirae* 24(181C,182D).

ἀρχιποίμην, ὁ, 1. *chief herdsman*, *T.Jud*.8.1; **2.** met., *chief shepherd* (1Petr.5:4); **a.** of Christ, Meth.*symp*.1.5(p.13.16; M.18.45B); Pall.*v.Chrys*.12(p.78.22; M.47.44); *ib*.20(p.147.13; M.47.82); Sophr.H.*ep.syn*.(M.87.3197C); as uniting in one flock Jews and gentiles, Cyr.*Is*.2.1(2.199D); *ib*.4.4(677C); id.*Zach*.78(3.760A); **b.** of bishops: Gr. Naz., before his elevation to see of CP κατάρτισαί μοι τὸν λαὸν τῷ σῷ θρέμματι, καὶ μετὰ τοῦτο ποιμένι, νῦν δὲ ἀ. Gr.Naz.*or*.16.4 (M.35.937C); patriarch of CP, Nect.*Thdr*.11(M.39.1829C); *M.Areth*.(p.49); Thdr.Stud.*epp*.2.79(M.99.1320A); Pope, CLater.*act*.2(H.3.733A); patriarch of Alexandria, Leont.N.*v.Jo.Eleem*.27(p.60.4) al.; metropolitan of Damascus, Jo.D.*rect.sent*.proem.(M.94.1421A).

***ἀρχιππάριος, ὁ,** *commander of cavalry*, Anton.Hag.*v.Sym.Styl*. 20(p.49.4).

***ἀρχιπρεσβύτερος, ὁ,** *chief presbyter*, i.e. senior presbyter, who took place of bishop when absent, and performed administrative functions, Soz.*h.e*.8.12.3(M.67.1545C); cf. *ut episcopus gubernationem viduarum...non per seipsum, sed per archipresbyterum aut per archidiaconum agat*, CCarth.4(398)*can*.17; as successor to bishop ὑμεῖς δὲ βουλεύσασθε περὶ ἐπισκόπου, καὶ...ἐξελέξαντο τὸν ἀ. *V.Aberc*. 78(p.54.15).

***ἀρχιπρόεδρος, ὁ,** *chief president*, i.e. *presiding, chief, bishop*, of Pope ὁ κοινὸς ἡμῶν πατὴρ ὁ ἀ., ὁ τὸν ἀποστολικὸν ἔχων θρόνον Leont. Abb.*v.Gr.Agr*.41(M.98.621C).

ἀρχιπροφήτης, ὁ, *chief prophet*; *chief of prophets*; of Christ, Meth.*symp*.1.4(p.12.19; M.18.44C); *ib*.1.5(p.13.17; 45B); Eus.*h.e*.1.3.8(M.20.72B).

***ἀρχιπροφῆτις, ἡ,** *queen of prophets*; of BMV, Thdr.Stud.*or*.5.3 (M.99.724B); *ib*.9.3(773B).

***ἀρχισατράπης, ὁ,** *governor of a province* or *district*, ‡Jo.D.*ep.Thphl*.14(M.95.361D); εἷς τῶν τοῦ βασιλέως, ἀ. τὴν ἀξίαν †Jo.D.*B.J*.2(M.96.868A); of Satan, *A.Pil*.B 22.1f.(p.329).

***ἀρχισάτραψ, ὁ,** = foreg., El.H.*cant*.2.3(p.292).

***ἀρχισοφιστής, ὁ,** *chief of sages*; of Christ, Pall.*v.Chrys*.12(p.78.22; M.47.44).

ἀρχιστράτηγος, ὁ, 1. *commander-in-chief*, Or.*Cels*.1.27(p.78.33; M.11.712B); of Naaman, Ephr.3.259E; of Joab, Chrys.*exp.in Ps*.3 (5.5B); **2.** of Christ, *captain of the host* (Jos.5:14), Just.*dial*.34.2 (M.6.548B); ποτὲ...ἀ. ἑαυτὸν λέγει, ἐν ἀνθρώπου μορφῇ φανέντα τῷ τοῦ Ναυῆ Ἰησοῦ *ib*.61.1(613C); Meth.*symp*.3.6(p.32.10; M.18.68D); Eus.*p.e*.7.15(324D; M.21.549A); id.*l.C*.3(p.202.3; M.20.1332B); id.*h.e*.1.2.3(M.20.53C); *ib*.1.2.11(60A); Thdr.Stud.*or*.6.3f.(M.99.733D,736A); **3.** *prince, leader, of the* heavenly *host* ἀ. τις τῆς δυνάμεως κυρίου λέγεται ὁ Ἰησοῦ τῷ τοῦ Ναυῆ ἐπὶ τοῦ Ἰορδάνου φανερωθεὶς...ὁ τοίνυν ἀ. τῶν ἐν ταῖς λεγεῶσι κατατεταγμένων ἀγγέλων, ἄρχων ἐστὶ δηλονότι Bas.*Eun*.3(1.273B; M.29.657B); Gr.Nyss.*hom.3 in Cant*.(M.44.812A); of Michael, *T.Abr*.A 1,9 passim(pp.77.13,86.14ff.); *Apoc.Bar*.11 passim(p.92.10ff.); *Apoc.Esd*.(p.28); *Apoc.BMV* 23(p.123.2,15); of Raphael, *Apoc.Esd*.(p.24); plur. στρατιάν τε ἀγγέλων καὶ ἀ. ἐν αὐτοῖς δυνάμεων κυρίου ἀρχαγγέλους τε καὶ θρόνους Or.*or*.17(p.339.20; M.11.472C); Dion.Ar.*c.h*.2.1(M.3.137A); Thdr.Stud.*or*.6.1(M.99.729C); of Satanic hosts, Or.*or*.13(p.327.15; 456B); of S. Stephen as protomartyr ἀ. τῶν καλλινίκων μαρτύρων Στεφάνου Isid.Pel.*epp*.1.447(M.78.428D).

***ἀρχιστρατηλάτης, ὁ,** *commander-in-chief*, *A.Thom*.A 93(p.206.15).

***ἀρχισύμβολον, τό,** *chief of symbols, master symbol*; of eucharistic elements, Dion.Ar.*e.h*.3.3.1(M.3.428B).

***ἀρχισυμπότης, ὁ,** *master of the feast*, ‡Chrys.*hom.in Ps*.95:1 (5.633B).

***ἀρχισυναγωγός,** *which more than all else brings together, supremely reconciliatory* πάντα πρὸς ἑαυτὴν ἡ ἀγαθότης ἐπιστρέφει, καὶ ἀ. ἐστι τῶν ἐσκεδασμένων Dion.Ar.*d.n*.4.4(M.3.700A); τὴν θείαν καὶ ἀ. εἰρήνην...ἀνευφημήσωμεν· αὕτη γάρ ἐστιν ἡ πάντων ἑνωτική *ib*.11.1(948D); cf.id.*c.h*.1.1(M.3.120B); Max.*schol.d.n*.11.1(M.4.389C).

ἀρχισυνάγωγος, ὁ, *ruler of the synagogue*, Just.*dial*.137.2(M.6.792A); *A.(Pass.)Petr.et Paul*.10(p.128.7); φασὶ...τὸν...πατριάρχην τῶν Ἰουδαίων κατ' ἔτος ἀμείβειν, ἢ καὶ παρ' ἔτος, τοὺς ἀ. ἐπὶ συλλογῇ τοῦ ἀργυρίου Pall.*v.Chrys*.15(p.90.24; M.47.51); met., *ruler, president, of an assembly*, of Macrianus, favourite of Valerian ὁ διδάσκαλος καὶ τῶν ἀπ' Αἰγύπτου μάγων ἀ. Dion.Al.ap.Eus.*h.e.*7.10.4 (M.20.657C).

ἀρχιτεκτόνημα, τό, *thing constructed, building, work* of an artificer τὴν πρωτότοκον σοφίαν...τὸ τέλειον τελείου δημιούργημα, καὶ σοφοῦ σοφὸν ἀ. Eus.*d.e.*4.2(p.152.4; M.22.253B); ὅροι φύσεως...δι' ὧν τόδε τὸ πᾶν μηχάνημά τε καὶ ἀ. τοῦ παντὸς κόσμου τελεσιουργεῖται id.*Hierocl.*6(515B; M.22.253B).

***ἀρχιτελεία, ἡ,** liturg., *beginning and end*, of the two Advents ἀρχιτελεία τῆς σωτηρίας cf. Nilles *Kalendarium Manuale* 2(p.535); cf.*ib.*(pp.236,263 not.1).

***ἀρχιτελωνέω,** *be a chief publican, chief toll-collector*, Steph.Diac. *v.Steph.*(M.100.1125C).

***ἀρχιτέχνας,** [genit. in -ᾱ] or ***ἀρχιτέχνης, ὁ,** *chief artificer, master craftsman* ἅτε συνδημιουργὸς [sc. H. Ghost]...τοῦ ὑποστήσαντος αὐτὴν [sc. τὴν γῆν] κατ' ἀρχὰς ἀρχιτέχνα θεοῦ Didym.*Trin.* 2.7(M.39.564B); ἑαυτῷ ἀναπλασάμενος ὁ ἀ. λόγος σῶμα ἀπὸ Μαρίας Epiph.*haer.*62.5(p.394.18; M.41.1057A); ὁ...ἀρχιτέχνης λόγος πάντων ἐστὶ ποιητής id.*anc.*28(p.37.15; M.43.68C).

ἀρχιτρίκλινος, ὁ, *master of the feast* (Jo.2:8f.) συμποσίαρχοι δέ τινες...καὶ ἀρχιοινοχόοι καὶ ἀ., καὶ τάξις ἐν ἀταξίᾳ †Bas.*Is.*155(1.488E; M.30.372C); ἀ. λέγει τὸν ἐξάρχοντα τῆς ὑπηρεσίας καὶ τῆς εἰς τὸν γάμον παρασκευῆς Thdr.Mops.*fr.in Jo.*2:9(p.320.1; M.66.740C).

***ἀρχίφαντος,** *being source of light*; of God, ‡Jo.D.*hom.*6.4(M.96.665D).

***ἀρχιφάρμακος, ὁ,** *chief magician*, Thdr.Stud.*epp.*2.37(M.99.1225B).

ἀρχίφυλος, ὁ, 1. *chief of a tribe* κληροδοτεῖ...'Ιησοῦς μετὰ τῶν ἀ. τοῦ 'Ισραήλ Proc.G.*Jos.*18:4(M.87.1028A); cf.Or.*hom.18.1 in Jos.* (p.406.9; M.12.913C); ἀ. Σαρακηνῶν Jo.Mal.*chron.*18 p.460(M.97.673B); τις ἀ. ... τὸ Σαρακήνων τάγμα...ἄγων Geo.Pis.*Pers.*2.217(M.92.1224B); **2.** *founder of a tribe* δώδεκα φυλῶν παρ' 'Εβραίοις οὐσῶν,...μιᾶς τούτων προπάτωρ γέγονεν καὶ ἀ. ὁ 'Ιούδας Eus.*d.e.*7.3(p.347.4; M.22.565A); *ib.*8.1(p.355.22; 577D); ὁ δὲ 'Ιούδα τοῦ ἀ. παῖς id.*qu.Steph.*2.1 (M.22.893A); Andr.Caes.*Apoc.*67(M.106.768C).

***ἀρχίφωτος (*ἀρχέφωτος, *ἀρχήφωτος),** *source of light*; of Trin., Ephr.3.541A; of Father, Dion.Ar.*c.h.*1.2(M.3.121A); id.*d.n.*4.6(M.3.701B); Thdr.Stud.*praesanct.*(M.99.1689B); ‡Sophr.H.*triod.*(M.87.3972C); ἀρχέφωτος Jo.D.*hom.*12.11(M.96.796D); ἀρχήφωτος *Lit.Jac.* (*NBP* 10² p.107); ref. baptism πρὸς τὴν ἐκ θεογενεσίας ἀρχίζωον καὶ ἀ. καὶ μακαρίαν προσαγωγήν Dion.Ar.*e.h.*3.3.6(M.3.433A); of bishops ἔσοπτρα...δεκτικὰ τῆς ἀ. καὶ ἀρχικῆς ἀκτῖνος Ant.Mon.*hom.*122(M.89.1816C).

***ἀρχιχιλίαρχος, ὁ,** *chief of the captains of thousands* κἀγὼ 'Ισραὴλ ἀρχάγγελος δυνάμεως κυρίου καὶ ἀ. εἰμι ἐν υἱοῖς θεοῦ *Prec.Josephi* ap. Or.*Jo.*2.31(25; p.88.35; M.14.169A); ἀ. δυνάμεως κυρίου καὶ ὄνομα πάλαι κεκτημένος 'Ισραήλ *Prec.Josephi* ap.eund.*comm.in Gen.*ap. eund.*philoc.*23.19(p.208.19; M.12.81C).

***ἀρχομηνία (*ἀρχιμηνία), ἡ,** *first day of the month*, Jo.Nic.*nativ.* (M.96.1445A); ἀρχιμηνία †Andr.Cr.*cycl.*(M.19.1332B).

ἀρχοντικός, 1. *able to rule, with authority over*, of Christ πνευμάτων ἀ. Eus.*d.e.*4.4(p.155.5; M.22.257D); **2.** freq. of angels; **a.** *ruling, chief* ἀ. ἄγγελος ἐν ἡλίῳ Clem.*ecl.*56(p.153.12; M.9.725A); δαίμονές τινες πικροὶ καὶ ἀ. Nil.*epp.*2.52(M.79.224A); **b.** *pertaining to the rulers* i.e. angelic hierarchy, *angelic* τὰ ἐπουράνια καὶ τὰς τοποθεσίας τὰς ἀγγελικὰς καὶ τὰς συστάσεις τὰς ἀ. Ign.*Trall.*5.2; ᾧ [sc. τῷ θεῷ] πᾶσα δύναμις ἀ. ὑποτέτακται *A.Jo.*79(p.190.16); **c.** usu. of evil angels, *demonic* τὸν διάβολον καὶ τὰς μετ' αὐτὸν ἀ. καὶ πονηρὰς δυνάμεις Eus.*d.e.*9.7(p.422.24; M.22.681A); *ib.*6.13(pp.263.26,265.19; 433B,436D); Pall.*h.Laus.*22(p.73.10,13, v.l. ἀρχικός M.34.1083B); esp. of those who inspire spiritual, opp. moral, error, acc. author of *Apophth.Mac.Aeg.*3(M.34.212B); **3.** subst.; **a.** of Gnost. seven evil angels who created and rule world ἀγγέλων ἑπτὰ...τῶν μὲν τοῦ φωτός, ἑτέρων δὲ τῶν ὀνομαζομένων ἀ. ... τὸν ἄρχοντα τῶν ὀνομαζομένων ἀ. λέγεσθαι θεὸν κατηραμένον Cels.ap.Or.*Cels.*6.27(p.97.10f.; M.11.1333A); in form of various animals, *ib.*6.33(p.102.28; 1348A); cf.*ib.*6.30(p.99.31ff.; 1337Df.); **b.** name of Gnost. sect akin to Ophites (name derived from 3.a), Epiph.*haer.*40.1(p.80.25ff.; M.41.677B); ἀρχοντικοί. οὗτοι...εἰς πολλοὺς ἄρχοντας τὸ πᾶν ἀναφέρουσι. καὶ τὰ γενόμενα ἐκ τούτων γεγενῆσθαι λέγουσιν id.*anac.*40(p.2.15; M.41.580B); φάσκουσι [sc. οἱ Σευηριανοί] καὶ τὴν γυναῖκα εἶναι ἔργον τοῦ σατανᾶ, καθάπερ καὶ οἱ ἀ. τοῦτο ἔφασαν id.*haer.*45.2(p.200.17; M.41.833B); οἱ δὲ αὖ πάλιν Μαρκίωνες καὶ ἀ. καλούμενοι *ib.*78.3(p.453.19; M.42.701C); Thdt.*haer.*1.11 tit.(4.303); Jo.D.*haer.*40(M.94.701B).

***ἀρχοποιός,** *which creates all rule*, of God τὴν ἀ. ἀρχὴν Dion.Ar. *c.h.*9.1(M.3.257B); αὐτῆς τῆς ἀ. ἀρχῆς ἀναφαίνει τὴν ὑπερούσιον ταξιαρχίαν αὐτῇ ἡ τῶν ἀρχῶν τάξις Max.*schol.c.h.*9.1(M.4.84A).

ἄρχ-ω, usu. c. genit., **A.** *begin*; **1.** *make a beginning* οἱ ἀρχόμενοι *beginners*, of catechumens τῶν ἄρτι ἀ. καὶ εἰσαγομένων καὶ οὐδέπω τὸ σύμβολον τοῦ ἀποκεκαθάρθαι ἀνειληφότων Or.*Cels.*3.51(p.247.9; M.11.988A); of the simple and uninstructed, Thdt.*Cant.*3:10(2.87) cit. s. νυμφοστολέω; novices πρὸς οἰκοδομὴν...τῶν ἀ. ἀσκεῖν ‡Pall. *h.mon.*proem.12(p.4.8; M.65.445B); **2.** *begin, have a beginning*, opp. the eternal οὔ ποτε τοῦ εἶναι υἱὸς ἠργμένος Gr.Naz.*or.*25.16(M.35.1221D); τὰς θείας πράττομεν ἐντολὰς καὶ τοῦ ἀγαθοῦ...τὸ κακὸν διακρίνομεν, ὡς ἀπὸ μὴ ἠργμένου ἠργμένον ‡Proc.G.*Pr.*2:3(M.87.1236A); *ib.*9:1(1301A); Jo.D.*f.o.*1.6(M.94.804A).

B. *rule, govern, command*; **1.** as governor of province; hence of chief city of province, Nicomedia τὴν...Βιθυνῶν ~ουσαν Eus.*v.C.*3.50 (p.98.24; M.20.1109B); cf.id.*l.C.*9(p.221.2; M.20.1369B); **2.** as bishop, *Const.App.*2.26.4; hence οἱ ἀρχόμενοι *those under* episcopal *authority* opp. ἱερεύς (= bishop), Chrys.*sac.*4.8(p.124.5; 1.413D); *ib.*5.4 (p.131.16; 417A); Thdt.*h.e.*4.6.6(3.953); Thdr.Stud.*epp.*1.7(M.99.932A); **3.** as superior of religious community, ‡Just.*ep.Zen.et Ser.*1 (M.6.1184A).

ἄρχων, ὁ, 1. in gen., *ruler*; of Father, Or.*princ.*1.2.10(p.42.14; M.11.140A); cf.*ib.*3.1.19(p.231.8; 289A); of Christ ὁ λόγος, ὃν ἄ. εἰλήφαμεν γνώσεώς τε καὶ βίου Clem.*str.*7.16(p.70.18; M.9.537B); καὶ ἄ. χρήσασθαι αὐτῷ καθ' ὃ ποιμήν ἐστιν Or.*Jo.*19.6(p.305.27; M.14.536D); ref. Ezech.37:23ff. προφητεύεται ἄ. καὶ ποιμὴν γενήσεσθαι ὁ Δαυὶδ...τοῦ Δαυὶδ τὸν Χριστὸν αἰνιττομένου Eus.*e.th.*3.17(p.176.21; M.24.1037A); of apostles τοὺς ἄ. τοῦ πνευματικοῦ 'Ισραὴλ Or.*hom.18.1 in Jos.*(p.406.24)ap.Proc.G.*Jos.*18:4(M.87.1028A); of Titus ἄ. πνευματικόν Thdt.*2Cor.*7:15(3.326); of bishops τῇ ἐν Τράλλεσι... ἄλλην, ἧς ἄ. τότε ὄντα Πολύβιον ἱστορεῖ Eus.*h.e.*3.36.5(M.20.288C); *Const.App.*2.28.6; *ib.*8.4.3 al.; **2.** as an official title; *governor* of province; *magistrate*; ἄ. τῶν μοναστηρίων *superintendent* of monasteries, CNic.(787)*act.*4(H.4.268D); **3.** *angelic power* τὰ ἐπουράνια καὶ ἡ δόξα τῶν ἀγγέλων καὶ οἱ ἄ. ὁρατοί τε καὶ ἀόρατοι Ign.*Smyrn.*6.1 (cf.id.*Trall.*5.2 s.v. ἀρχοντικός); οὐχ...ὑπηρέτην τινὰ πέμψας ἢ ἄγγελον ἢ ἄ. *Diogn.*7.2; ref. Ps.23:7,9 οἱ ἐν τοῖς οὐρανοῖς ταχθέντες ὑπὸ τοῦ θεοῦ ἄ. ἀνοῖξαι τὰς πύλας τῶν οὐρανῶν Just.*dial.*36.5(M.6.553D); ref. Ps.81:7 πλειόνων...ἀ. γενομένων, εἰς πέπτωκεν Or.*Jo.*32.18(11; p.457.6; M.14.792B); of evil angels, demonic powers φοβηθήτωσαν δαίμονες, θραυσθήτωσαν ἄ. *A.Jo.*114(p.214.7); Χριστὲ...ἡ δύναμις... ἡ τὸν ἐχθρὸν καταστρέψασα, καὶ ἡ φωνὴ ἡ ἀκουσθεῖσα τοῖς ἄ. *A.Thom.* A 10(p.115.3); *ib.*156(p.265.4); esp. of Satan (Mt.9:34; Jo.12:31; Eph.2:2) ὁ πονηρὸς ἄ. *Barn.*4.13; τὸν ἄδικον ἄ. *M.Polyc.*19.2; ὁ τῆς ὕλης καὶ τῶν ἐν αὐτῇ εἰδῶν ἄ. Athenag.*leg.*24.4(M.6.948B); ὁ ἄ. τοῦ αἰῶνος τούτου (Jo.12:31 etc.) Or.*hom.6 in Lc.*(p.37.18); Meth.*res.*2.4 (p.337.18; M.41.1169C); ἄ. τῆς ἀκρασίας id.*symp.*10.1(p.122.13; M.18.193A); ὁ ἄ. τοῦ σκότους id.*res.*1.38(p.281.9; cf.M.41.1105B); Cyr.H. *catech.*19.4; τὸν ἄ. τῆς κακίας ‡Ath.*Apoll.*2.8(M.26.1144C); ref. Eph.2:2 ἄ. τῆς ἐξουσίας τοῦ κινεῖν τὸν ἀέρα Cosm.Ind.*top.*2(M.88.117D); abs. ὁ κύριος...ἐκ παρθένου ἐτέχθη...ἵνα δείξῃ τῷ ἄ. καὶ δίχα συνουσίας ἀνθρωπίνης δυνατὴν εἶναι τῷ θεῷ τὴν ἀνθρώπου πλάσιν †Just.*fr.res.*(p.39; M.6.1577A); **4.** Gnost.: Peratic, of fashioner of matter, identified with Devil, ref. Jo.8:44 τὸν ἄ. καὶ δημιουργὸν τῆς ὕλης λέγει Hipp.*haer.*5.17(p.115.10; M.16.2178A); title of the Gnost. hebdomad, seven creative angels (Carpocrates) τῶν κοσμοποιῶν ἀ. Iren.*haer.*1.25.2(cf.M.7.681A); (Basilides) ἐγεννήθη ἀπὸ τοῦ κοσμικοῦ σπέρματος...ὁ μέγας ἄ. Hipp.*haer.*7.23(p.200.25; 3310B); (Ophites) Cels.ap.Or.*Cels.*6.30(p.99.31; M.11.1337D); *Const.App.*6.10.3; of whom God of Jews was one (Saturninus) τὸν τῶν 'Ιουδαίων θεὸν ἕνα τῶν ἀγγέλων εἶναί φησι, καὶ διὰ τὸ βούλεσθαι τὸν πατέρα καταλῦσαι πάντας τοὺς ἄ., παραγενέσθαι τὸν Χριστὸν ἐπὶ καταλύσει τοῦ τῶν 'Ιουδαίων θεοῦ Iren.*haer.*1.24.2(cf.M.7.675A); (Basilides) Clem.*str.*2.8(pp.132.1,133.11; M.8.972A,973B); ὁ ἑβδομάδος ἄ. ὁ λαλήσας τῷ Μωϋσῇ Hipp.*haer.*7.25(p.203.12; 3314A); cf.Iren.*haer.*1.24,4f.(M.7.676B,677B,678A); (Docet.) Hipp.*haer.*8.9(p.228.26; M.16.3351D); **5.** (Manich.) of angelic powers who created material world, Hegem.*Arch.*8(p.12.3f.; M.10.1440A); ὁ ἄ. ὁ μέγας...ὁ θερισμὸς ἄ. *ib.*9(p.14.7,11; 1441A) al.; συνίστανται οἱ ὄμβροι ὡς ἱδρῶτές εἰσι τῶν ἀ. τῆς ὕλης Tit.Bost.*Man.*1.14(M.18.1085D); Epiph.*haer.*66.21 (p.50.1; M.42.65D); in whose image man is made ἄ. ἐστίν, ὁ εἰπὼν τοῖς ἑτέροις ἄ. ... δότε μοι ἐκ τοῦ φωτὸς οὗ ἐλάβομεν, καὶ ποιήσωμεν ἄνθρωπον κατὰ τὴν ἡμῶν, τῶν ἀ., μορφήν, καθ' ἣν εἴδομεν, ὅ ἐστι πρῶτος ἄνθρωπος...καὶ τὴν Εὔαν ὁμοίως ἔκτισαν...καὶ διὰ τούτων γέγονεν ἡ πλάσις τοῦ κόσμου ἐκ τῆς τοῦ ἄ. δημιουργίας Hegem.*Arch.* 12(p.20.1ff.; 1448A); φησὶ...ὁ Μάνης εἶναι ἡμᾶς μορφὰς ἀρχόντων καὶ ὑπὸ τῶν ἀ. γεγονότας Epiph.*haer.*66.76(p.117.23f.; 149B); identified with God as worshipped by Jews and Christians, Hegem.*Arch.*12 (p.20.14; 1448B); φάσκει...τὸν θεὸν τὸν λαλήσαντα ἐν τῷ νόμῳ ἕτερον ὄντα παρὰ τὸν θεὸν τοῦ εὐαγγελίου. κἀκείνῳ μὲν ὄνομα ἄρχοντος τίθησιν Epiph.*haer*.66.42(p.78.32; 92B).

***ἀρωγ-έω**, = ἀρήγω, *aid, succour*, of H. Ghost ἁγιασμὸν καὶ δημιουργικὴν δύναμιν…καὶ ἐν πᾶσιν ~οῦσαν Didym.*Trin*.2.11(M.39.661B).

ἄρωμα, τό, *spice*; met., of Law with which Bride was made ready for divine fragrance of Christ ἐπὶ μὲν τῆς εὐαγγελικῆς πολιτείας ὀσμὴν ἔφη· ἐπὶ τῆς νομικῆς λατρείας αὐτὰ τέθεικα τὰ ἀ. δηλῶν ἐκείνης τὸ ὑπερέχον καὶ πνευματικόν, ταύτης δὲ τὸ πάχυ Proc.G.*Cant*.1:2(M.87.1549A); cf.Or.*Cant*.1:1(pp.97.26–98.24; M.13.90C–91B); of chastity, Clem.*paed*.2.8(p.197.3; M.8.472B) cit. s. μύρον; Meth.*symp*.7.1(p.72.13; M.18.125C); of spiritual life εἰς πᾶν ἄνθος εὐωδίας ἢ ἄ. ἐκ τῶν ποικίλων τῆς ἀρετῆς λειμώνων ἀνθολογήσας Gr.Nyss.*hom.3 in Cant*.(M.44.824B); τὰ ἀ. σου τῶν πόνων ‡Nil.*tract*.14(M.79.1112A).

***ἀρωματοπράτης, ὁ,** *dealer in spices*, Thdr.Stud.*epp*.1.7(M.99.932D).

***ἀρώματος,** *fragrant* κιννάμωμον ἀ. *Apoc.En*.30.2; neut. as subst., *ib*.29.2; *ib*.31.2.

***ἀρῶνα,** v. *ἀαρών.

***ἄς,** (corruption of ἄφες) c. subj., *in order that, Mir.Artem*.32 (p.46).

***ἀσαγήνευτος,** *un-netted* ἀ. ἄγραν ‡Nil.*perist*.12.7(M.79.952D); met. τῶν ἐθνῶν ἡ πληθὺς ἀ. … ἦν ἔτι Cyr.*Jo*.12.1(4.1115A).

***ἀσαγής,** *not saddled, without saddle*, Just.*dial*.53.1(M.6.592B); met. ἀποφορτίζει τὸν νοητόν σου ὄνον ἀχθοφοροῦντα τοῖς δαίμοσι, καὶ ἀ. ποιήσας, ἐπιβαλεῖ σοι τὰ τῶν ἀποστόλων ἱμάτια…καὶ ἐπικαθεσθεὶς τῷ νοΐ σου ὥσπερ τῇ ὄνῳ ποτέ Nil.*epp*.2.81(M.79.237A).

***ἀσάρκης,** *free from sensuality*; of celibate life, Gr.Naz.*carm*.2.2 (epitaph.)115.5(M.38.70A).

ἀσαρκία, ἡ, 1. *absence of sensuality* προεισενέγκατε…αἱ παρθένοι τὴν ἀ., αἱ γυναῖκες τὴν εὐκοσμίαν ἀρετῆς Gr.Naz.*or*.24.18(M.35.1192B); ἀγγέλων…ἀ. id.*carm*.1.2.6.5(M.37.644A); μελέτησον ἀ. ἐν σώματι Thdt.*Cant*.2:14(2.72); **2.** *condition of not being incarnate, not taking flesh* ἐπῆγεν ἐν τῇ ὑποστάσει αὐτῆς τὸ τῆς ἀ. ἴδιον κατηγόρημα Leont.H.*Nest*.1.30(M.86.1496D); *ib*.(1496C).

ἄσαρκος, A. *without flesh, stripped of flesh*; of mangled remains, Thdr.Mops.*Am*.3:11f.(M.66.264C); of a seed, Meth.*res*.1.53(p.310.5; M.41.1129A); hence *disembodied*, ref. descent into Hades ἄ. καὶ γυμνὸς οὗ ἀνειλήφει σώματος ἐπὶ τὸ τῶν ἐχθρῶν κατῄει χωρίον Eus. *d.e*.8.1(p.363.14; M.22.589C).

B. *without flesh*; **1.** *immaterial*, i.e. *spiritual*; **a.** of Father ἄ. … ὁ τέλειος θεός Tat.*orat*.15(p.16.20; M.6.837B); *cat.Ac*.2:24(p.44.29); **b.** of Logos before Inc. θεὸς ἀληθινὸς ὁ ἄ. ἐν σαρκὶ φανερωθείς Apoll.*fid.sec.pt*.31(p.179.1; M.10.1117A); ἐσαρκώθη ὁ ἄ. *Const.App*. 8.28.31; Gr.Naz.*or*.38.2(M.36.313B); ὡς τὸν Ἐφραὶμ ἐκδιδάσκει…κατῆλθεν ὢν ἄ., ὡς θεοῦ λόγος, ἀνῆλθεν ὢν ἔνσαρκος, ὡς ἡμῶν γένος Geo.Pis.*Sev*.609(M.92.1668A); εἰς οὐρανοὺς ἀνιὼν μετὰ τῆς σαρκὸς αὐτοῦ ὅθεν κατεληλύθει ἄ. Jo.D.*jej*.2(M.95.65D); **c.** also after Inc. in respect of essence ἄ. μὲν τὴν οὐσίαν, σεσαρκωμένη δέ ἐστι τὴν ὑπόστασιν Leont.H.*Nest*.2.44(M.86.1597B); ἄ. μένει τὴν φύσιν *ib*.4.36 (1704D); **d.** of angelic powers ἄ. … δύναμιν…ἀγγέλου *Hom.Clem*. 17.16; Gr.Naz.*carm*.1.2.4.8(M.37.641A); *ib*.1.2.10.892(744A); Didym. *Ps*.9:18(M.39.1197A); opp. σάρκινος, id.*Trin*.2.6(M.39.540B); of demons, *Const.App*.6.26.3; **e.** ? iron., of certain antinomian heretics περὶ ἀ. τινῶν ψευδομάντεων ταῦτα εἰρῆσθαι Or.*Apoc*.13(p.26); **2.** *without a body*, not synonymous with ἀσώματος in τὴν ἄ. ἰδέαν οὐ λέγω δύνασθαι πατρὸς ἢ υἱοῦ ἰδεῖν *Hom.Clem*.17.16; τῷ μέρει συνονομάζεται τὸ λειπόμενον…ὁ Ἰακὼβ ἐν ἑβδομήκοντα πέντε ψυχαῖς …ἐπιξενούμενος οὐκ ἄνους, οὔτε ἄ. … ἱστορεῖται; Gr.Nyss.*Apoll*.10 (M.45.1144C); οὐ πνεύμασι…γυμνοῖς…οὐδὲ ἀ. καὶ ἀναμφιέστοις ψυχαῖς Cyr.*Jo*.1.9(4.84D); Cyr.*expl.xii cap*.2(p.18.5; 6¹.148C); not to be predicated of incarnate Word οὐκ ἄ. … ὁ λόγος, ἀλλ' ἐν σώματι ἡ εὐδοκία Epiph.*haer*.42.11(p.144.9; M.41.755B); σφραγίζεται…παρὰ τοῦ πατρός, οὐ γυμνὸς ἢ ἄ. ὁ ἐκ τῆς οὐσίας αὐτοῦ λόγος Cyr.*Jo*.3.5(4. 302C); Gnost. [sc. Χριστόν] οὐκ…ἄ. εἶναι ⟨τὸν⟩ φανέντα λέγει, ἀλλ' ἐκ τῆς τοῦ παντὸς οὐσίας μεταλαβόντα μερῶν σῶμα πεποιηκέναι Hipp.*haer*.7.38(p.224.11; M.16.3346B); **3.** of incarnate Logos, *devoid of true humanity, having no human nature* ἄρα οὖν ἄ. ὁ Χριστὸς… καὶ λέλυται ἡ ἕνωσις καὶ πάντῃ ἡμῖν ἀκοινώνητον τὸ θεῖον ἐν Χριστῷ Leont.H.*monoph*.34(M.86.1789D); *ib*.(1777A); εἰ δὲ οὐκ εἰκονίζεται· οὐκ ἄνθρωπος, ἀλλὰ ἄ.· καὶ οὔπω ἧκε Χριστός Thdr.Stud.*epp*.2.21 (M.99.1184D).

C. *not of flesh*; **1.** *not consisting of flesh* ὡς ἄ., καὶ μόνος δοκῶν ἔχειν ἢ σῶμα χαλκοῦν ἢ σιδηρᾶν καρδίαν Geo.Pis.*Heracl*.1.172(M.92. 1312A); **2.** *spiritual* opp. physical τὴν ἔνθεον καὶ ἄ. παιδοποιίαν Eus. *d.e*.1.9(p.42.9; M.22.81A).

D. *free from carnal appetites* ζῆσαι…ἐν τῇ σαρκὶ βίον…ὡς ἄ. Clem.*str*.7.12(p.56.21; M.9.509A); μηδενὶ τῶν παθῶν…περιπίπτοντι, ἀλλ' οἷον ἀ. ἤδη *ib*.(p.62.9; 521A); Pall.*h.Laus*.18(p.53.3; M.34. 1058B); Βαρσανούφιος…ἐν σαρκὶ τὸν ἄ. διήθλησε βίον Evagr.*h.e*.4.33 (p.182.17; M.86.2764B).

***ἀσάρκως,** *without flesh* ἐν σαρκὶ ὁ κύριος οὐκ ἀ. ἐπεδήμησε τῷ κόσμῳ Apoll.*ep.Dion*.8(p.259.20; ἄσαρκος M.*PL*.8.934B).

ἀσάφεια (-ία), ἡ, 1. *want of clearness, uncertainty* πᾶς δογματικὸς ἔν τισιν ἐπέχειν εἴωθεν, ἤτοι παρὰ γνώμης ἀσθένειαν ἢ παρὰ πραγμάτων ἀ. Clem.*str*.8.5(p.90.5; M.9.581A); ἡ…ὑπερβολὴ τῆς διαβολῆς… εἰς πολλὴν ἀ. ἄγει Ath.*apol.Const*.6(M.25.604A); **2.** *want of clarity, obscurity* in expression, Bas.*hom*.3.1(2.16E; M.31.200A); ἀ. … καὶ περιττολογίᾳ Philost.*h.e*.6.2(M.65.533B); opp. σαφήνεια, Isid.Pel. *epp*.5.145(M.78.1412A); esp. of obscurities in scripture, Or.*sel.in Ps*.1(M.12.1080B); σιωπῆς…εἶδος καὶ ἡ ἀ. ᾗ κέχρηται ἡ γραφὴ δυσθεώρητον κατασκευάζουσα τῶν δογμάτων τὸν νοῦν Bas.*Spir*.66 (3.56A; M.32.189B); τὴν ἐν ταῖς γραφαῖς ἀ. … διεγείρων αὐτοῦ [sc. τοῦ νοῦ] τὴν ἐνέργειαν ἐπετήδευσε †Bas.*Is*.proem.6(1.382B; M.30.128C); Cyr.*Am*.75(3.335E); καὶ τὰ ἀσαφίᾳ τινὶ κεκρυμμένα τῆς ἀσαφίας ἐλευθεροῖ Thdt.*Dan*.5:12(2.1164); Isid.Pel.*epp*.4.113(M.78.1184B); of Law, ref. 2Cor.3:15 ἵνα μή τις νομίσῃ τῆς ἀ. τοῦ νόμου εἶναι τὸ εἰρημένον Chrys.*hom.7.3 in 2Cor*.(10.484D); of parables, Or.*hom.12.13 in Jer*. (p.100.25; M.13.397B); of theological terms τὴν τοῦ ὁμοουσίου λέξιν ὡς ἐκ τῆς ἀ. ὕποπτον, ἐπροφασίζοντο Ath.*syn*.12(p.240.4; M.26.701C); **3.** myst., *obscurity* of divine darkness, Gr.Nyss.*hom.1 in Cant*. (M.44.773B) cit. s. γνόφος.

***ἀσβέστιον, τό,** *unquenched* or ? *unquenchable fire* βάλλετε αὐτοὺς [sc. τοὺς θεοὺς ὑμῶν] εἰς κάμινον. δύνανται γὰρ εἰς ὀλίγα ἀ. ὑμῖν χρησιμεῦσαι *V.Aberc*.4(p.5.16).

ἄσβεστος, *unquenchable*; met., *immortal* τὰ ὀνόματα…ἄ. Esaias *or*.4.9(p.26; cf.M.40.1118B).

***ἀσβολόεις,** *foul as soot*, Gr.Naz.*carm*.1.2.29.224(M.37.900A).

ἀσβολόω, 1. *cover with soot*, Chrys.*hom.13.3 in 1Cor*.(10.113C); *ib*.20.6(10.177E); Jo.Mosch.*prat*.106(M.87.2965C); as a disgrace, *Apophth.Mac.Aeg*.1.1(M.34.236C); *V.Alex.Acoem*.40(p.689.9); as cosmetic ἠσβολωμένας ὀφρῦς Chrys.*hom.30.5 in Mt*.(7.355B); ἠσβολωμένοι *buffoons* with blackened faces, *ib*.35.3(402A); **2.** met., *befoul, vilify* αἱ εὐχαί σου…τοὺς φίλους σου ἠσβόλωσαν Thphn.*chron*. p.120(M.108.337A).

***ἀσεβάρχης, ὁ,** *leader of impiety*, Thdr.Stud.*epp*.2.30(M.99. 1201A); *ib*.2.63(1284C).

ἀσέβεια, ἡ, *disregard for God, impiety*; **1.** properly of sin against God, opp. man, *2Clem*.10.1; Just.*1apol*.58.3(M.6.416B); *ib*.4.7(333B); opp. ἁμαρτία: πολλὴν διαφορὰν ἁμαρτία πρὸς ἀ. ἔχει Thdt.*Ps*.30:18 (1.797); cf. ἀδικήματα…οὐκ ἀσεβήματα id.*qu.13 in 1Reg*.(1.367); **2.** of idolatry, paganism, Apoll.*fid.sec.pt*.6(p.169.21; M.10.1108B); Chrys.*hom.20.4 in 1Cor*.(10.174B); *ib*.19.3(163B); Philost.*h.e*.3.27 (M.65.513C); **3.** of heresy, Didym.(‡Bas.)*Eun*.5(1.308B; M.29.740A); ἵνα μὴ…μεῖζον τὸ πνεῦμα νομίσωσι, καὶ εἰς ἀσεβείας ὑπόθεσιν… ἐμπέσωσι Chrys.*hom.78.2 in Jo*.(8.460D); τὰς ἐπ' ἀ. συνόδους Philost. *h.e*.6.5(M.65.536C); Arianism, Gel.Cyz.*h.e*.2.23.12(M.85.1297C); Nestorianism, Thdt.*haer*.4.12(4.370); **4.** as manifested in evil conduct ἔπραττον πᾶσαν ἀνομίαν καὶ ἀσέλγειαν καὶ ἀ. Arist.*apol*.11(p.107.13); ἀ. καὶ ἡδοναῖς Meth.*creat*.1(p.493.5,8,10; M.18.332A); *Hom.Clem*.14. 5; εὑρέτις τῶν κακῶν ἡ ἀ. Gr.Naz.*or*.21.14(M.35.1097A); τὴν πηγὴν …τοῦ κακοῦ, τὴν ἀ. τὴν ἀπὸ τῶν δογμάτων Chrys.*hom.4.2 in Rom*. (9.456C); *ib*.3.3(452A); ὑποβάθρα…τῆς παρανομίας γεγένηται ἡ ἀ. Thdt.*Rom*.1:25(3.26); cf. ὑποβάθρα τῆς ἀ. ἡ παρανομία γεγένηται id. *Ezech*.23:25(2.870).

ἀσεβ-έω, 1. *show no regard for God, be impious, ungodly* εἰ… ταὐτὸν ὕλη καὶ θεὸς…τοὺς λίθους…οὐ νομίζοντες θεοὺς ~οῦμεν Athenag.*leg*.15.1(M.6.920A); *ib*.14.2(917B); *Ep.Lugd*.ap.Eus.*h.e*.5.1. 31(M.20.420C); Bas.*hom*.21.11(2.172C; M.31.561B); **2.** *utter impieties, blaspheme*, Eus.*h.e*.5.13.9(M.20.461C); Meth.*res*.2.24(p.379.16; M.18. 289B); ὁ λέγων αὐτὸν γεννητὸν ~εῖ ‡Ath.*dial.Trin*.2.5(M.28.1164B); **3.** *behave impiously, live an ungodly life* ~ήσαντας καὶ παραλογισαμένους τὰς ἐντολάς *2Clem*.17.6; Meth.*symp*.4.4(p.50.10; M.18.92C); ἐν τῇ πίστει εὐσεβοῦντας, διὰ τοῦ βίου ~εῖν Chrys.*hom.7.1 in 1Tim*. (11.584E); **4.** by holding heret. opinions, Or.*hom.17.4 in Jer*.(p.147. 6; M.13.457C); Gr.Naz.*or*.21.33(M.35.1121C); **5.** *deny the Faith; profess paganism* μὴ πείσας αὐτὰς ~ῆσαι *M.Thdot.1* 13(p.69.8); Chrys.*hom.5.1 in Rom*.(9.461E).

ἀσεβής, 1. *not worshipping God, atheistic* ἄθεος…ἀ. Clem.*str*. 6.14(p.489.17; M.9.337C); εἶπε…ἀ. ἐπειδὴ οὐδένα σέβεται ‡Ath.*dial. Trin*.2.4(M.28.1161C); ἀσεβεῖς…φίλον τῇ…γραφῇ καλεῖν τοὺς ἀθεΐαν, ἢ πολυθεΐαν θρησκεύοντας Thdt.*Ps*.1:1(1.611); hence *ungodly, impious, sacrilegious*, of persons εἰς τέλος ἀ. *Barn*.10.5; *M.Thdot.1* 13 (p.69.7); ὑβρίζων ὁ ἀ. τὴν εὐσέβειαν *ib.*(p.69.9); ἀ. ... καὶ παράνομοι Chrys.*hom.33.5 in 1Cor.*(10.306A); of Ahab, id.*hom.88.3 in Jo.* (8.529D); of words, *ib.69.2*(410B); of dispositions and acts ζῆλον ἄδικον καὶ ἀ. *1Clem.*3.4; Just.*2apol.*2.4(M.6.444B); **2.** *not worshipping the true God*; **a.** in pre-Christian times, Chrys.*hom.11.2 in Col.* (11.407B); of the Magi, id.*hom.24.5 in 1Cor.*(10.218B); **b.** *idolatrous, pagan*, opp. θεοσεβής: οὐ...θεοσεβεῖς ἦσαν βασιλεῖς, ἀλλὰ ἀσεβεῖς ἀσεβεῖς διαδεχόμενοι Chrys.*hom.6.1 in 1Tim.*(11.579B); id.*hom.15.8 in Mt.*(7.198C); ὅτι τῶν Ἑλληνιστῶν τὰ ἀτοπώτατα κατὰ τῶν Χριστιανῶν...παλαμωμένων, καὶ τόδε τοῖς ἀ. κατὰ Παλαιστίνην δεδραματούργηται Philost.*h.e.*7.4(M.65.541A); Thdt.*Ps.*1:1(1.611); **c.** of heretics, Philost.*h.e.*9.3(M.65.569A); of heretical opinions, Clem. *str.*7.17(p.74.29; M.9.545C); Or.*Jo.*6.39(23; p.148.18; M.14.268B).

***ἀσεβοκαύστης**, ? *burning with impiety*, Thdr.Stud.*epp.*2.75(M. 99.1312B).

ἄσειστος, **1.** *unshakable*, freq. of foundations etc., lit. and met. ὡς ὑποβάθραν...ἄ., τὴν γεωμετρίαν Gr.Thaum.*pan.Or.*8(M.10.1077C); τοὺς ἀ. θεμελίους τῆς Σιών †Bas.*Is.*289(1.598E; M.30.625B); τῇ ἀ. βάσει τῇ τῶν δογμάτων σου [sc. τῆς ἐκκλησίας] Jo.Mon.*hymn.Bas.*10 (M.96.1377B) etc.; of the Church, *Lit.*ap.*Const.App.*8.10.4; *ib.*8.12. 40; Chrys.*hom.2.2 in Ac.princ.*(3.62C); *Hymn.*(*KlT* p.26); neut. as subst., of Christ πέτρα μὲν διὰ τὸ ἐν τῇ ῥώμῃ αὐτοῦ ἄ. Mac.Aeg.*ep.* (M.34.417B); **2.** *unshaken, steady*; of reason as a test of sobriety, Clem.*paed.*2.2(p.169.25; M.8.413C); of apostles' faith οἰκίαν ἄ. Chrys. *hom.24.4 in Mt.*(7.304E); *undisturbed* αἱ τῶν κακῶν ἄ. εὐημερίαι Pall.*v.Chrys.*20(p.134.4; M.47.75); neut. as adv., of S. Peter τὸ ἄ. ἔχων ἐν τῇ πίστει Or.*schol.in Lc.*9:27(M.17.341A).

[*]**ἀσεκρέτις**, v. ἀσηκρῆτις.

[*]**ἀσεκρῆτις**, v. ἀσηκρῆτις.

***ἀσέλαστος**, *not lighted; without light*, Paul.Sil.*Soph.*862(M.86. 2152A).

***ἀσεμνότης**, ἡ, *dishonour* ἕστηκεν...ἡ τοιαύτη ἐν τῇ πολυκοίνῳ ἀ. i.e. prostitution, Epiph.*haer.*66.2(p.17.21; M.42.32C).

[*]**ἀσηκρήτης**, v. ἀσηκρῆτις.

ἀσηκρῆτις, (variant spellings) (Lat. *a secretis*) *private secretary*, ἀσεκρῆτις Jo.Mal.*chron.*18 p.494(M.97.713C); ἀδσηκρῆτις Heracl.*ep.* (M.92.1021A,1025A); *Chron.Pasch.*pp.338,340(M.92.884A,888B); Anast. Ap.*a.Max.*1.10(M.90.124B); ἀσεκρέτις CCP(681)*act.*2(H.3.1064C); ἀσεκρῆτις Jo.VI CP *ep.*(M.96.1428C); Thphn.*chron.*(M.108.612A; v.l. p.243); v.l. ap.*A.Jo.*27(p.165.17).

ἀσήμαντος, **1.** *unrestrained* οἶστρος ἀ. φορεύμενος ἀφραδίῃσιν Gr.Naz.*carm.*1.2.1.116(M.37.531A); **2.** *unsealed; unmarked*; hence **a.** *not understood* or *comprehended*; of Christ's words, Nonn.*par.Jo.* 3:3(M.43.765B); *ib.*10:6(833A); **b.** *incomprehensible* ἀόριστόν ἐστι τὸ κατ' οὐσίαν ἀ. θεός Anast.S.*hod.*2(M.89.53A); **3.** *giving* or *leaving no sign*; **a.** *trackless* ἀ. δι' ἐρήμης Gr.Naz.*carm.*1.2.2.166(M.37.591A); **b.** *unseen* τὸν καθαρὸν...καὶ ἀ. νυμφίον...τὴν ψυχὴν συνοικίζοντα Gr. Nyss.*hom.12 in Cant.*(M.44.1016C).

ἀσημείωτος, *not marked* or *branded*, fig., of baptismal sealing πρόβατον ἀ. ἀκινδύνως ἐπιβουλεύεται Bas.*hom.*13.4(3.117C; M.31. 432C).

***ἀσθενάριος**, ὁ, *indisposed* μὴ τὴν ἡμέραν εἰς τὴν γαστριμαργίαν ὑγιεῖς, καὶ ἐν τῇ νυκτερινῇ εὐχῇ ἀσθενάριοι Ephr.1.117C.

ἀσθένεια, ἡ, *want of strength, weakness*; **1.** in gen. ἀ. λέγεται ἡ τοῦ σώματος ἀρρωστία...λέγεται πάλιν ἀ. τὸ μὴ πεπηγέναι ἐν τῇ πίστει ἁπλῶς...καὶ τρίτον ἕτερον, ὃ καλεῖται ἀ. ... οἱ διωγμοί, αἱ ἐπιβουλαὶ κτλ. Chrys.*hom.29.2 in 2Cor.*(10.641D,E); in moral purpose and fibre opp. ἀνδρεία, Ath.*gent.*16(M.25.33D); of sin, Chrys.*hom.28.1 in Mt.*(7.327D); ref. Heb.7:28 ἀ. ... ἢ τὴν ἁμαρτίαν φησίν, ἢ τὸν θάνατον id.*hom.13.3 in Heb.*(12.135B) v. 3; in reasoning κατηγορεῖ ἀσθενείας τοῦ λογισμοῦ Or.*hom.20.2 in Jer.*(p.178.1; omitted by misprint from M.13.501B); **2.** (= בָּשָׂר) *frailty* of the flesh, not necessarily denoting sin; **a.** as gen. characteristic of man, Herm.*mand.*4.3.4; Or. *princ.*3.1.12(p.216.4; M.11.272A); ὁ θεὸς...συγκαταβὰς τῇ ἀ. τῶν δούλων σου *Lit.Jac.*(*NBP* 10².101) etc.; **b.** of incarnate Word ἰσχυροποιηθῶμεν ἀπὸ τῆς ἀ. τοῦ Ἰησοῦ Or.*hom.8.9 in Jer.*(p.63.8; M.13. 348A); ref. 2Cor.13:4 ἀ. ... τί ἕτερόν ἐστιν, ἢ τῆς καθ' ἕξιν δυνάμεως ἀλλοίωσις καὶ μεταβολή; Leont.B.*Nest.et Eut.*2(M.86.1344C); cf. Thdt.*2Cor.*13:4a(3.354); **3.** of tribulations τί ἐστιν 'ἐν ἀ.'; ἐν διωγμοῖς, ἐν κινδύνοις, ἐν πειρασμοῖς, ἐν ἐπιβουλαῖς, ἐν θανάτοις Chrys. *hom.29.2 in 2Cor.*(10.642A); *ib.*26.3(622A); cf.Thdt.*2Cor.*13:4b(3. 354).

***ἀσθενογενής**, *innately weak*, ‡Jo.D.*hom.*5(M.96.657C).

***ἀσιάντως**, error for ἀσινάντως.

***ἀσιγήτως**, *ceaselessly*, of praising God, Bas.Sel.*or.*1.3(M.85. 34A); Max.*myst.*(M.91.701B); †Jo.D.*B.J.*16(M.96.1004D).

***ἀσίναντος**, *unharmed*, Thdr.Stud.*epp.*2.89(M.99.1337A).

***ἀσινάντως**, *without being harmed*, Anast.S.*qu.et resp.*96(M.89. 748B ἀσιάντως).

ἀσιτέω, *fast*, Cyr.*Jon.*22(3.384A); πάντες σήμερον [sc. Good Friday] διὰ σταυρὸν ἀ. Jo.D.*hom.*3.2(M.96.592C).

ἀσιτία, ἡ, *lack of food; fasting; fast*, abrogated during Easter, Eus.*h.e.*5.23.1(M.20.492A); id.*pasch.*5(M.24.700B); observations on the practice, Cyr.*Joel.*11(3.209E); id.*Ps.*37:4(M.69.956C); Thdt.*h.rel.* proem.(3.1103); Jo.Jej.*poenit.cont.virg.*(M.88.1960B).

ἀσιώπητος, *never silent* ἀσιγήτοις χείλεσι καὶ ἀ. καρδίᾳ *Lit.Marc.* (p.125.25).

[*]**ἀσκαλαβώς**, ὁ, *house lizard, gecko*, Cyr.*glaph.Num.*(1.406B).

§**ἀσκαλώνιον**, τό, a measure of wine, Leont.N.*v.Jo.Eleem.*20 (p.37.19).

[*]**ἀσκαμμωνία**, ἡ, a kind of *convolvulus* from which *scammony*, a strong purgative, is derived, Geo.Pis.*hex.*955(M.92.1507A).

ἀσκανδάλιστος, **1.** of persons; **a.** *not stumbling* or *falling, void of offence*, and therefore *unharmed* ἀ. τὰς θλίψεις ὑπομένοντες Clem. *str.*4.9(p.282.5; M.8.1285A); Ephr.1.89D; *A.Andr.fr.*8(p.41.26) cit. s. ἀσυμπαθής; perh. *proof against stumbling, impeccable*, Pall.*h.Laus.* 32(p.94.3; M.34.1100D); **b.** *not causing* others *to stumble, giving no offence*, *A.Jo.*82(p.192.1); **2.** of things, *free from occasion of scandal, giving no offence*, i.e. *harmless* τὴν ἀ. ὑπόβασιν τῆς ἀληθείας Meth. *symp.*8.10(p.92.12; M.18.153A); Bas.*renunt.*5(2.207C; M.31.637C); of fasting in secret ἀπρόσκοπος καὶ ἀ. Eus.Al.*serm.*1(M.86.321C).

***ἀσκανδαλίστως**, **1.** *without stumbling*, Pall.*h.Laus.*37(M.34. 1188A); Jo.Mosch.*prat.*204(M.87.3096A); **2.** *without giving offence, without being an occasion of scandal* ἵνα ἡ ἐκκλησία ἀ. συναγομένη διαφυλαχθήσηται †Ath.*fr.Mt.*5:29(M.27.1369D).

[*]**ἀσκαρδαμυκτεί**, for ἀσκαρδαμυκτί, *without blinking*, Geo.Pis. *hex.*880(M.92.1501A).

[*]**ἀσκαρδαμυτί**, for ἀσκαρδαμυκτί, *without blinking*, Jo.VI H. *v.Jo.D.*11(M.94.445C).

***ἀσκελίστως**, *without stumbling* or *tripping*, Ephr.3.549F.

***ἀσκεπτί**, adv. of ἄσκεπτος, *without consideration, unadvisedly*, CSard.*ep.Alex.*(p.115.33; M.25.312C).

ἄσκευος, *unfurnished*; with arms, i.e. *lightly-armed, LS*; with comforts, of ascetic life τὸν ἄ. καὶ ἄυλον διαθλευόντων βίον Evagr. *h.e.*2.9(p.61.10; M.86.2529B); ᾤκησας ἐρήμους...ἄ., ἄτροφος Jo.Mon. *hymn.Chrys.*2(M.96.1377D).

ἀσκευώρητος, *devoid of cunning*; neut. as subst., *integrity*, Max.*schol.Dion.Ar.*proem.(M.4.21A).

ἀσκ-έω, **1.** *train* the soul, esp. by affliction ~ούμενος καὶ ταλαιπωρῶν Chrys.*virg.*45(1.304D); ἐν τούτοις...τοῖς γυμνασίοις [sc. θλίψεσιν] τὰς ψυχὰς ~ηθῶμεν *Apophth.Patr.*(M.65.424C); **2.** *practise, cultivate*, virtues ἀ. πᾶσαν ὑπομονήν Polyc.*ep.*9.1; δικαιοσύνην ἀ. Herm.*mand.* 8.10; *A.Jo.*68(p.183.23); ἀγάπην οὖν ~εῖν τὸν τέλειον χρή Clem.*str.* 4.13(p.289.15; M.8.1300C); *ib.*3.7(p.222.30; 1161B); ἀλήθειαν ἄ. id. *q.d.s.*40(p.187.2; M.9.645B); εὐσέβειαν ἀ. Or.*Cels.*7.10(p.161.32; M.11. 1436A); Eus.*h.e.*1.4.14(M.20.80C); monastic virtues, e.g. σιγὴν ἀ. Nil.*epp.*1.291(M.79.189A); τάγμα...~ουμένων τὴν σεμνότητα id.ap. Proc.G.*Cant.*4:3(M.87.1645C); ἡσυχίαν...ἀ. Ammonas *ep.*1(p.433.4); chastity, Or.*Cels.*7.48(p.199.30; M.11.1492B); id.*hom.20.4 in Jer.* (p.182.21f.; M.13.508C); Meth.*symp.*4.6(p.52.12; M.18.96B); *ib.*5.3 (p.56.13; 101B); Chrys.*hom.28.7 in Heb.*(12.269A); monastic life τοῖς τὸν μονήρη βίον ~οῦσι Ath.*ep.mon.*(M.26.1185C); **3.** abs., *practise asceticism, lead an ascetic life*; **a.** in gen., Ath.*v.Anton.*12 (M.26.861B); *ib.*14(864B); of a woman penitent πάντα τὸν χρόνον οὕτως ἠσκεῖτο Chrys.*hom.67.3 in Mt.*(7.606B); *Apophth.Patr.*(M. 65.264A); *ib.*(312A); Marc.Er.*opusc.*9(M.65.1109D); **b.** faults and shortcomings in practice καθ' αὑτὸν μὲν ~ῶν καὶ διαπονούμενος ἀπάθειαν ὁ ἄνθρωπος μηδὲν ἀνύει Clem.*q.d.s.*21(p.173.16; M.9.625B); connected with a certain selfishness ὁ...ἑαυτῷ ~ῶν εἰς ἑαυτὸν μόνον περιίστησι τὴν ὠφέλειαν Chrys.*sac.*2.4(p.36.5; 1.375D); ἐάν ~ῇ τις, ἢ διὰ κενοδοξίαν, ἢ ἔχων ὅτι ἀρετὴν ποιεῖ, οὐκ ~εῖ ὁ τοιοῦτος ἐν γνώσει Dor.*doct.*14.3(M.88.1777D); **4.** *abstain* from ἠσκεῖτο καὶ ἀπὸ οἴνου Epiph.*haer.*67.3(p.136.16; M.42.177A); τὸ ἀψύχοις ~εῖσθαι *ib.* 67.7(181D; ἀρκεῖσθαι p.139.29); **5.** *study*, also *teach, profess* παρ' ἄλλων τῶν ~ησάντων...τὸ εὐαγγέλιον Serap.Ant.ap.Eus.*h.e.*6.12.6 (M.20.545B); ἐν τοῖς μαθήμασιν, ἅτινα ἤσκουν ἐν Βαβυλῶνι οἱ...σοφοί Or.*Cels.*3.45(p.242.8; M.11.980B); **6.** ptcpl. as subst. ὁ ~ούμενος *one who leads religious life, hermit* or *monk*, Bas.*reg.fus.*19.1(2.362C; M.31.968A); id.*ascet.*1.4(2.321D; M.31.877A); ὁ ~ῶν ‡Bas.*const.*tit. (2.533A; M.31.1322); Thdt.*qu.24 in 2Reg.*(1.423).

***ἀσκήδιον**, τό, *wine-skin*, Leont.N.*v.Sym.*10.56(M.93.1740B).

***ἀσκήνως**, *unfeignedly, sincerely*, Synes.*ep.*137(M.66.1528C).

ἄσκηπτος, *unfeigned*, i.e. sincere, Pall.*v.Chrys.*16(p.98.21; M.47.55).

ἄσκησις, ἡ, *exercise, practice, training*; **1.** *study*, esp. of scripture, Or.*Cels.*7.60(p.211.4; M.11.1508B); *τὴν ἄ. καὶ μελέτην τῶν γραφῶν* Meth.*symp.*9.4(p.118.21; M.18.185B); Eus.*h.e.*6.2.15(M.20.525C); id. *d.e.*8.3(p.393.13; M.22.636B); *τὴν ἐν ταῖς ἐλευθερίοις τέχναις ἄ.* Cyr. *Juln.*7(6^2.222D); **2.** *practice*, esp. of piety *ἡ ἄ. τῆς εὐσεβείας* Bas. *reg.fus.*38(2.385B; M.31.1017B); id.*ep.*2.2(3.72B; M.32.225C); †Bas. *Is.*31(1.405C; M.30.181C); Chrys.*hom.12.2 in 1Tim.*(11.612B); and virtue *πάσης ἀρετῆς ἄ.* Athenag.*res.*15(p.67.2; M.6.1005A); Meth. *symp.*9.4(p.118.12; M.18.185A); Max.*Pyrr.*(M.91.309B); of evil *ἄ. πονηρίας* Nil.*Magn.*47(M.79.1029A); **3.** in gen., *devout life ἡ κατὰ λόγον ἄ. ἐκ πίστεώς τε καὶ φόβου παιδαγωγουμένη* Clem.*str.*7.16(p.72.5; M.9.541A); *περὶ τῆς φαινομένης ἀ. ... ἀλλήλων ἐκδέδενται πᾶσαι αἱ ἀρεταί* Mac.Aeg.*hom.*40.1(M.34.761D); *τὸ κατὰ τὰ βρώματα παρακολούθημα εἶναι τῆς ἀ.* †Bas.*Is.*31(1.404E; M.30.181A); Socr.*h.e.* 4.23.10(M.67.512A); *religious practice, worship*, of Essenes *ἔστι γὰρ ἡ κατὰ τούτους ἄ. περὶ τὸ θεῖον ἀρχαιοτέρα πάντων ἐθνῶν* Hipp.*haer.* 9.27(p.261.6; M.16.3406A); in connexion with Easter *ταῖς δὲ τῆς σωτηρίου ἑορτῆς* [sc. Easter] *ἡμέραις ἐπιτείνων τὴν ἄ. πάσῃ ῥώμῃ ψυχῆς* Eus.*v.C.*4.22(p.125.24; M.20.1169A); *ὡς γὰρ τὰς πρώτας τῆς τοῦ πάσχα ἑορτῆς συνεπλήρου ἀσκήσεις ib.*4.60(p.142.16; 1212B); **4.** *spiritual exercise, training, discipline ἡ κυριακὴ ἄ. ἀπάγει τὴν ψυχὴν τοῦ σώματος εὐχαρίστως* Clem.*str.*4.6(p.260.7; M.8.1240A); of virtues, chastity etc. as *γνωστικῆς ἀ. προγυμνάσματα ib.*4.21 (p.306.33; 1344A); ref. apostles *ἐν ἕξει ἀσκήσεως ἀεὶ μένοντες ἀναλλοίωτοι μετά γε τὴν τοῦ κυρίου ἀνάστασιν ib.*6.9(p.467.19; M.9.292D); *οἱ μὲν ἐκ πρώτης ἡλικίας εἰς ἔσχατον γῆρας τὴν ἑαυτῶν ἐκτείναντες ἄ. ἐν τοῖς ἀρχομένοις εἰσίν* Chrys.*sac.*1.4(p.14.5; 1.366D); *ἕξις ἡμῖν ἡ ἄ. γέγονεν* Nil.*Magn.*55(M.79.1041A); **5.** *austere life, asceticism*; in gen., involving restraint in food; adduced to discredit charges of cannibalism brought against Christians *Βλανδίνα ἐπαρρησιάσατο, πῶς ἄν, εἰποῦσα, τούτων ἀνάσχοιντο οἱ μηδὲ τῶν ἐφειμένων κρεῶν δι' ἄ. ἀπολαύοντες;* Iren.*fr.*13(M.7.1236C); *ταχ' ἄν τις τῶν γνωστικῶν καὶ ἀσκήσεως χάριν σαρκοφαγίας ἀπόσχοιτο* Clem.*str.*7.6(p.26.4; M.9.448A); coupled with prayer *διά τε ἀ. καὶ εὐχῶν κτησώμεθα τὰ ἀγαθά* Or.*sel.in Ps.*4:6(M.12.1161C); *ἐν ἐγκρατείᾳ καὶ ἀ.* Bas.*ep.*81.1 (3.174C; M.32.457A); Gel.Cyz.*h.e.*3.10.2; Jo.Mosch.*prat.*65(M.87.2916C); involving toil, Cyr.*hom.pasch.*14(5^2.187E); *οἱ ἐν ἀ. δὲ ζῶντες, μισοῦσι τὰς ἑαυτῶν ψυχάς* id.*Jo.*8(4.703A); ref. Jo. Bapt., who lived *ταῖς εἰς ἄ. ὑπερβολαῖς ib.*1.7(4.63B); of Chrys. *προνοίας, πρὸς τὸ χρήσιμον τῆς ἐκκλησίας διὰ τῆς ἀσθενείας τῶν τῆς ἀ. πόνων αὐτὸν ἀπελασάσης* Pall.*v.Chrys.*5(p.29.6; M.47.18); Jo.Mon.*hymn.Chrys.*1 (M.96.1377D); **6.** as technical term for eremitical and monastic life and its practices; **a.** *monastic life ἀγαθὴν ἅμιλλαν ἐνεστήσασθε πρὸς τοὺς ἐν Αἰγύπτῳ μοναχοὺς...ὑπερβάλλεσθαι τούτους προελόμενοι τῇ κατ' ἀρετὴν ὑμῶν ἀ.* Ath.*v.Anton.*proem.(M.26.837A); *ἀπῃτήσατε καὶ παρ' ἐμοῦ περὶ τῆς πολιτείας τοῦ μακαρίου Ἀντωνίου, μαθεῖν θέλοντες ὅπως τε ἤρξατο τῆς ἀ. ib.*; id.*h.Ar.*25(M.25.721C); *χρὴ τὸν ἀσκητὴν βεβαίᾳ κρίσει προσιέναι τῇ ἀ.* ‡Bas.*const.*19(2.563B; M.31.1388A); Cyr.*ep.*1(p.107; 5^2.1B); Thal.*cent.*3.8(M.91.1448D); as special state *μοναστήρια ἐν τῇ αὐτῇ Γοτθίᾳ ἐγένετο καὶ πολιτεία καὶ παρθενία τε καὶ ἄ.* Epiph.*haer.*70.14(p.247.30; M.42.372B); *οἱ ἐν κλήρῳ, οἱ ἐν παρθενίᾳ, οἱ ἐν ἀ., οἱ ἐν χηρείᾳ* Jo.Mosch.*prat.*79(M.87.2937B); †Jo.D. *B.J.*12(M.96.968A); **b.** of the various penitential and other practices involved in it *εἰ χρὴ ἐν ἀδελφότητι τῷ ἐξαμαρτήσαντί ποτε φροντίδα τινὰ ἐγχειρίζειν μετὰ πολλὴν ἄ.* Bas.*reg.br.*18(2.421A; M.31.1093C); *μοναχοὶ...μυρίαν ἄ. ἐπιδειξάμενοι* Chrys.*hom.25.6 in Rom.* (9.709D); *Apophth.Patr.*(M.65.372A); Proc.G.*Is.*45:9ff.(M.87.2428C); Jo.Mosch.*prat.*91(M.87.2948D); *πόνοι...ἀσκήσεως, οἷον νηστεία, ἀγρυπνία, ὑπομονή, μακροθυμία* Thal.*cent.*3.14(M.91.1449B); **c.** solitude as one of its essentials *ἔστω τοίνυν τὸ χωρίον τοιοῦτον...ἐπιμιξίας ἀνθρώπων ἀπηλλαγμένον, ὡς ὑπὸ μηδενὸς τῶν ἔξωθεν τὸ συνεχὲς τῆς ἀ. διακόπτεσθαι* Bas.*ep.*2.2(3.72B; M.32.225C); *ἐξανύων τοὺς τῆς ἀ. ἄθλους ἱκανὸν χρόνον ἐπὶ τῆς ἐρημίας* Nil.*epp.*4.62(M.79.580C); **d.** sometimes used also in more restricted sense, esp. of abstinence from pleasures of sense, as dist. from poverty, silence etc. *τὰ τρία ταῦτα κεφάλαια εἶχεν ὑπὲρ πολλούς· τὴν ἀκτημοσύνην, τὴν ἄ., καὶ τὸ φεύγειν τοὺς ἀνθρώπους Apophth.Patr.*(M.65.188D); *ποιοῦντες ἀγρυπνίας, ἡσυχίας καὶ ἀ. ib.*(313D); **7.** fruits of asceticism: victory over sin *κακία χρονίσασα, ἀ. δεῖται χρονίας* Thal.*cent.*3.7(M.91.1148D); and passions *ἐξ ἀ. εἰς ἀπάθειαν* Clem.*str.*7.3(p.10.24; M.9.417A); *ὁ σύντονος...περὶ τὴν ἄ., βέβαιος...εἰς τὸ καὶ αὐτῶν τῶν τῆς σαρκὸς καταγωνίζεσθαι παθῶν* Cyr.*thes.*11(5^1.104A); hence freedom *οἰκεῖον ἀσκήσει ἐλευθερία* ‡Pion.*v.Polyc.*9; wisdom *μετὰ ἀ. καὶ διδασκαλίας τὴν γνῶσιν τῆς ἀληθείας ἐπανῃρημένον* Clem.*str.*2.16(p.152.24; M.8.1013B); *ἐν τῇ ψυχῇ ἡ ἐπὶ τὸ τέλειον τῆς σοφίας πρόοδος δι' ἀ. τοῖς μετιοῦσι προστίθεται* Gr.Nyss.*Apoll.*28(M.45.1185B); purity of heart, †Bas.*Is.*42(1.413A; M.30.200B); strength of soul, Thal.*cent.* 3.53(M.91.1453A); miracles, Jo.Clim.*scal.*2(M.88.657B); hence *λαμπροὶ οἱ καρποὶ τῆς ἀ. M.Thdot.*1 2(p.62.12); **8.** degrees of asceticism; moderation counselled for beginners *μὴ οὖν εὐθέως εἰς ἀκρότητα ἀσκήσεως ἐκτείνῃς σεαυτόν· μάλιστα μηδὲ θαρρήσῃς σεαυτῷ, ἵνα μὴ ἐξ ἀπειρίας ἀφ' ὕψους τῆς ἀ. πέσῃς* Bas.*ep.*42.2(3.126D; M.32.349C); summit attainable only by perfect abnegation, Ath.*v.Anton.*3(M.26.844C); **9.** of asceticism taught by pagan philosophers *λέγοντες θανάτου καταφρονεῖν καὶ τὴν αὐτάρκειαν ἀσκεῖν (οἱ γὰρ παρ' ὑμῖν φιλόσοφοι τοσοῦτον ἀποδέουσι τῆς ἀ.)* Tat.*orat.*19(p.20.28; M.6.848B); or practised by heretics from contempt of the body *εἴ τις ἀνδρῶν διὰ νομιζομένην ἄ. περιβολαίῳ χρῆται...*CGangr.*can.*12; *εἴ τις ἐπίσκοπος ἢ πρεσβύτερος...γάμου καὶ κρεῶν καὶ οἴνου οὐ δι' ἄ., ἀλλὰ διὰ βδελυρίαν ἀπέχεται Can.App.*51; or by others from indolence *οὐδὲν οὕτως ἄχρηστον εἰς ἐκκλησίας προστασίαν ὡς αὐτὴ ἡ ἀργία καὶ ἡ ἀμελετησία, ἣν ἕτεροι μὲν ἄ. τινα θαυμαστὴν εἶναι νομίζουσιν* Chrys. *sac.*6.7(p.153.20; 1.427A); true asceticism being distinguished by its moderation *πῶς οὖν διακρίνωμεν τὴν θείαν...ἄ. τῆς...δαιμονιώδους; δῆλον ὡς ἀπὸ τῆς συμμετρίας Apophth.Patr.*(M.65.425C).

ἀσκητήριον, τό, *monastery τῶν ἐν Αἰγύπτῳ μοναστηρίων μνήμην ἐποιησάμην...τὰ ἐν Αἰγύπτῳ ἀ. ...* Socr.*h.e.*4.23.2(M.67.509C); *αἱ εἴσοδοι τῶν ἀ. ταῖς μὲν γυναιξὶν κλεισθήτωσαν* Bas.*ascet.*1.4(2.322B; M.31.877C omits); *τὰ ἀ. τῶν μοναχῶν* Nil.*epp.*2.290(M.79.344D); Pall.*h.Laus.*14(p.38.4; M.34.1036A); Thdt.*ep.*80(4.1138); Jo.VI H. *v.Jo.D.*13(M.94.449A); of women, Justn.*nov.*59.4(p.320); of monasteries of heretics, Jo.D.*haer.*102(M.94.776A); also *hermitage*, of S. Anthony *ὑπέστρεφεν εἰς τὸν ἴδιον τοῦ ἀ. τόπον* Ath.*v.Anton.*4(M.26.845B); dist. from monastery *ἀ. καὶ μοναστήρια* Gr.Naz.*or.*43.62(M.36.577B); hence met., of moral faculty, ref. Eve *μήπω λαχούσης γεγυμνασμένα τὰ τῆς ψυχῆς ἀ. πρὸς καλῶν καὶ μὴ τοιούτων διάκρισιν* Sophr.H.*mir.Cyr.et Jo.*34(M.87.3536D).

ἀσκητής, ὁ, *one who trains*, or *practises an art*, esp. of athletes; hence principal term for those esp. devoted to spiritual life; **1.** in gen., *ascetic*; met., ref. Christian life *τίς...ἀ. ὤν, καταμαθὼν τῆς φιλοδοξίας τὴν ὁδὸν...οὐκ ἐπὶ τὸν στέφανον ἵεται καὶ αὐτός;* Clem. *paed.*3.8(p.261.32; M.8.616A); formally applied to class of Christians, living in the world, who practised continence and certain austerities *ἵνα δὲ μᾶλλον νοήσῃς τὸ 'ταλαιπωρίαν ἐπικαλέσομαι', διαγράψω τι γινόμενον τοῖς ἀ. πολλάκις γὰρ παρακειμένου τοῦ γῆμαι καὶ μὴ ἔχειν πρᾶγμα ἐπανισταμένης τῆς σαρκὸς τῷ πνεύματι, αἱρεῖταί τις οὐ καταχρήσασθαι τῇ τοῦ γαμεῖν ἐξουσίᾳ, ἀλλὰ ταλαιπωρεῖν καὶ κάμνειν, 'ὑπωπιάζειν τὸ σῶμα' νηστείαις 'καὶ δουλαγωγεῖν αὐτό'* Or.*hom.20.7 in Jer.*(p.188.25; M.13.517B); also of Jo. Bapt., *A.Pil.*B(p.324); characterized by humility *ἔλεγε δέ τις τῶν ἁγίων, φύλλα εἶναι τῶν ἀ. τὴν ταπεινοφροσύνην, σκέπουσαν αὐτῶν τοὺς καρπούς, καὶ μηδέποτε πίπτουσαν* Or.*Ps.*1:3(p.446); *οὐδὲ θέλει ἐπαινεῖσθαι, ὡς ἀ.* Dor.*doct.* 14.3(M.88.1777D); furnishing numerous martyrs *ζηλωτὴν ἑαυτὸν καταστήσας τῶν τῆς θεοσεβείας ἀ.* Eus.*m.P.*11(p.943.4; M.20.1508C); **2.** as t.t., *solitary* or *monk*; **a.** in gen. *μονάζοντες καὶ ἀ.* Ath.*apol. Const.*28(M.25.632A); of Athanasius, because he had lived with Anthony in the desert *Χριστιανὸν ἕνα τῶν ἀ., ἀληθῶς ἐπίσκοπον* CAlex.*ep.*(p.92.26; M.25.260A); *ὄνομα ἔχει πρεσβυτέρου, ἢ ἐπισκόπου, ἢ διακόνου, ἢ ἀ.* †Ath.*fr.*(M.26.1253B); *περὶ μὲν οὖν τοῦ καθέκαστον ἀ., καὶ τοῦ τὸν μονήρη βίον ἀσπασαμένου...ἐπεὶ δὲ οἱ πλεῖστοι τῶν ἀ. κατὰ συστήματα πολιτεύονται* ‡Bas.*const.*18.1(2.560D; M.31.1381B); of Egyptian monks, Epiph.*haer.*67.1(p.133.19; M.42.173A); *παρθέναι καὶ ἀ.* Pall.*v.Chrys.*11(p.68.20; M.47.39); *ὁ μὲν πρότερος Ἰσαὰκ ἕκατον πεντήκοντα εἶχεν ὑφ' ἑαυτὸν ἀ. ib.*17(p.106.25; M.47.60); **b.** duties and practices: should imitate Elijah, Ath.*v.Anton.*7(M.26.853B); *τῶν ἀ. τὴν νηστείαν, τὴν ἀγρυπνίαν, τὰς εὐχάς, τὸ πρᾶον, τὸ ἥσυχον, τὸ ἀφιλάργυρον, τὸ ἀκενόδοξον, τὴν ταπεινοφροσύνην, τὸ φιλόπτωχον, τὰς ἐλεημοσύνας, τὸ ἀόργητον, καὶ προηγουμένως τὴν εἰς τὸν Χριστὸν εὐσέβειαν ib.*30(889A); zealously undertake humblest works, ‡Bas.*const.*23(2.547A; M.31.1409D); practise restrictions of food and sleep *ὥρα μία τροφῆς ἀποτεταγμένη...μίαν εἶναι μόλις ταύτην τὴν προσαναλισκομένην τῷ σώματι· τὰς δὲ λοιπὰς ἐν τῇ κατὰ νοῦν ἐνεργείᾳ ἀπασχολεῖσθαι τὸν ἀ. ... ἀλλ' ὅπερ τοῖς ἄλλοις ὁ ὄρθρος ἐστί, τοῦτο τοῖς ἀ. τῆς εὐσεβείας τὸ μεσονύκτιον, μάλιστα σχολὴν τῇ ψυχῇ τῆς νυκτερινῆς ἡσυχίας χαριζομένης* Bas.*ep.*2.6(3.75A,B; M.32.233A); but with moderation *τύφου παντὸς ἀπηλλάχθαι προσήκει τὸν ἀ., καὶ τὴν μέσην ὄντως καὶ βασιλικὴν ὁδὸν πορευόμενον...μήτε τὴν ἄνεσιν ἀσπαζόμενον, μήτε τῇ ὑπερβολῇ τῆς ἐγκρατείας ἀχρειοῦντα τὸ σῶμα* ‡Bas.*const.*4.2(546A; M.1350B); Epiph.*exp.fid.*22(p.523.12; M.42.828B); *πρεσβύτερος καὶ ἀ. μέγας, νηστεύων δύο δύο, πολλάκις δὲ* καὶ τὴν ἑβδομάδα ἕλκων, ἄρτον μόνον ἐσθίων καὶ ἅλας *Apophth.Patr.*(M.65.169C); *ib.*(249A); Marc.Er.*opusc.*7.1(M.65.1072A); οἱ ἀ. ...ἀντήλλαξαν τὸν πλοῦτον αὐτῶν μετὰ τῶν πενήτων, καὶ ἠγόρασαν τὸν παράδεισον Eus.Al.*serm.*21.21(M.86.449A); ἀ. ταπεινόφρων καὶ ἄπλαστος, καὶ λεῖος κατὰ ψυχὴν τῆς ὑλικῆς δασύτητος Max.*cap.theol.*1.17(M.90.1089A); **c.** powers and influence γεωργὸς γὰρ πνευματικός ἐστιν ὁ δόκιμος ἀ., τὴν πρὸς αἴσθησιν τῶν ὁρατῶν θεωρίαν...πρὸς τὴν τῶν νοητῶν χώραν μεταφυτεύων *ib.*(1089B); ὁ ἀ. καταλαβόμενος δαίμονας id.*qu.Thal.*56(M.90.581D); **d.** in communities οὐδὲ θόρυβον ἕξει ὁ οἶκος τῶν ἀ. Bas.*reg.fus.*15.2(2.256B; M.31.953A); οἱ τῶν ἀ. ... χοροί, τὸν ἐσταυρωμένον ὑμνοῦντες, καὶ τὸν ἐκείνου πατέρα, καὶ τὸ ἅγιον πνεῦμα Thdt.*affect.*9(p.228.18; 4.934); heret. ἀποσχίσται... τοὺς εὐχίτας, ἤγουν Μασσαλιανούς, ζηλώσαντες, τοῖς ἀ. λέγουσι μὴ παραμένειν ἐκκλησιαστικαῖς συνάξεσιν, ἀσκεῖσθαι δὲ ταῖς ἐν ἀσκητηρίοις αὐτῶν εὐχαῖς Jo.D.*haer.*102(M.94.776A); **e.** eccl. legislation οὐ δεῖ ἱερατικοὺς...τοῦ τάγματος τῶν ἀ., εἰς καπηλεῖον εἰσιέναι CLaod.*can.*24; ranged after ψάλται in hierarchical order, *Lit.*ap.*Const.App.*8.13.14; **3.** epithet of Jacob, the *wrestler* ὁ συγγυμναζόμενος καὶ ἀλείφων κατὰ τοῦ πονηροῦ τὸν ἀ. Ἰακώβ Clem.*paed.*1.7(p.123.29; M.8.317C); *ib.*(p.124.8; 320A); †Jo.Jej.*serm.*(M.88.1968B); spiritually interpreted πλείοσι [sc. γυναιξί, representing virtues] δὲ συνέρχεσθαι ὁ Ἰακὼβ λέγεται ὡς ἂν ἀ. ἑρμηνευόμενος (διὰ πλειόνων δὲ καὶ διαφερόντων αἱ ἀσκήσεις δογμάτων) Clem.*str.*1.5(p.20.13; M.8.724B; cf. Philo *de congressu eruditionis gratia* 34–37); of active opp. contemplative life ἀντὶ δὲ τοῦ Ἰακὼβ ὁ θεὸς αὐτῷ τὸ τοῦ Ἰσραὴλ ὄνομα δωρεῖται, τὸν ἀ. καὶ πρακτικὸν ἐπὶ τὸν θεωρητικὸν μεταστησάμενος Eus.*p.e.*11.6(519A; M.21.860D); **4.** as adj., *ascetic* ἠγάπα δὲ ὁ ἀββᾶς Ἀγάθων τὸν ἀββᾶν Ἀλέξανδρον, ὅτι ἀ. ἦν καὶ ἐπιεικής *Apophth.Patr.*(M.65.116D).

ἀσκητικός, 1. *suitable for exercise* ἀσκητικώτατόν γέ τοι γυμνοῖς χρῆσθαι τοῖς ποσὶν καὶ ὑγιείαν καὶ εὐκολίαν εὔθετον Clem.*paed.*2.11 (p.227.6; M.8.537B); of Jacob, *fit for struggle* Ἰσραὴλ οὗτος μετονομάζεται ὁ τῷ ὄντι διορατικὸς ὡς ἂν πολύπειρός τε καὶ ἀ. id.*str.*1.5 (p.20.15; M.8.725A); **2.** *ascetic, austere* ὁ δὲ δεύτερος τρόπος τῆς ἁγνείας ἐστὶν ὁ τῆς χηρείας...ὁ δὲ τρίτος τῆς πανάθλου ἁγνείας ἀ. τρόπος, τίνας οὐκ ἔχει ὑπερβολάς; ‡Pion.*v.Polyc.*16; ἡ δὲ προαίρεσις... ἀ. προτροπὰς αὐθεκουσίως ἀγαπήσασα Eus.*p.e.*6.6(247D; M.21.421A); ἔργα ἀ. Nil.*epp.*3.243(M.79.501B); of Jo. Bapt. ὁ μὲν γὰρ Ἰωάννης δι' ἀ. βίου τὰ τῆς σαρκὸς ἐνέκρου, οὐ μὴν δι' ἀ. πόνων βοηθούμενος Cyr.ap.*cat.Mt.*11:20(p.87.6f.); ὁ τῆς στείρας ἀ. κλάδος Procl.CP *or.*6 (M.65.744A); ref. S. Barnabas τὸ σχῆμα ἀ. Alex.Sal.*Barn.*2.25(444E); comp. μὴ εἴπῃς ἐν τῇ καρδίᾳ σου κατὰ τοῦ ἀδελφοῦ σου, λέγων, ὅτι νηφαλιώτερός εἰμι καὶ ἀσκητικώτερος *Apophth.Patr.*(M.65.440C); τὰ ἰσχυρὰ ἔργα τοῖς ἰσχυροτέροις...τὰ δὲ ἄτονα τοῖς ἀσκητικωτέροις Pall.*h.Laus.*32(p.89.4; M.34.1099D); superl. ἑωράκαμεν ἀββᾶν Παῦλον, ἄνδρα...ἀσκητικώτατον Jo.Mosch.*prat.*41(M.87.2896B); **3.** *monastic*; **a.** of religious life ἀ. βίος Bas.*ascet.*2.1(2.323D; M.31.881B); id.*ep.*119(3.211B; M.32.537B); Epiph.*haer.*64.5(p.414.11; M.41.1080A ἀσκητῶν); Thdr.Lect.*h.e.*2.14(M.86.189B); Diad.*perf.*40(p.46.13); CTrull.*can.*46; also ἀ. ζωή Bas.*ascet.*2.1(2.323E; M.31.881B) = Nil.*epp.*3.22(M.79.540A); ἀ. πολιτεία Thdt.*h.rel.*proem.(3.1106); **b.** of religious community ἀ. σύστημα ‡Bas.*const.*22.5(2.573A; M.31.1409C); ἀ. παλαίστρα †Jo.D.*B.J.*28(M.96.1132A); **c.** of things connected with religious life: monastic cell ἀ. καλύβη Thdt.*h.e.*4.28.2(3.1007); habit, Jo.Mosch.*prat.*32(M.87.2881A); a book on monastic discipline which some ascribe to Eust. (perh. ‡Bas.*const.*) τὴν ἐπιγεγραμμένην Βασιλείου τοῦ Καππαδόκου ἀ. βίβλον Soz.*h.e.*3.14.31 (M.67.1080A); **4.** *dedicated, sacred*, of virginity ἡ παρθενία...ἀ. ἐγκαλλώπισμα Amph.*or.*2(M.39.44D); of Cassandra ἀ. παρθένος Jo.Mal.*chron.*5 p.106(M.97.196C); **5.** as subst.; **a.** masc., *monk, religious* τὸν ἀ. μὴ θηρᾶσαι τὸν ἀνθρώπειον ἔπαινον Thdt.*Ps.*118:27 (1.1445); **b.** neut., *exercise, practice* τὸ τούτων [sc. ὁδῶν...φερουσῶν ἐπὶ τὴν...θέαν τῶν προκειμένων] ἀ. Or.*fr.14 in Lam.*1:4(p.241.6; M.13.613A).

ἀσκητικῶς, *ascetically, austerely* τούτων δὲ ἀ. βιοτευόντων Thdt.*Dan.*1:10(2.1072); τῷ Χριστῷ ἠκολούθησαν, οἱ μὲν μαρτυρικῶς...οἱ δὲ ἀ. ἀγωνισάμενοι †Jo.D.*B.J.*15(M.96.992D).

ἀσκήτρια, ἡ, 1. *dedicated virgin* αὐτοπαρθένους ἀ. Eus.*m.P.*5 (p.919.12; M.20.1480A); **2.** *nun* κατοικτειρήσας τὸ τάγμα τῶν ἀ. ... ᾠκοδόμησε μέγα μοναστήριον, καὶ συνήγαγε πάσας Pall.*h.Laus.*29 (p.84.7; M.34.1097C); *ib.*70(p.166.19); Nil.*epp.*2.46(M.79.217B); Max.*ep.*11 tit.(M.91.453A); legislation for burial δεῖ δὲ τὸ μὲν ἐπιβάλλον τοῦ χρυσίου μέρος ταῖς...ἀ. δίδοσθαι παρὰ τῶν...οἰκονόμων Justn.*nov.*59.3(p.319); dist. from κανονικαί, *ib.*(p.320); and from διακόνισσαι id.*cod.*1.3.46.9; **3.** *ascetic* Ἄννα προφῆτις, ἐγκρατὴς εὐλαβεστάτη, καὶ ἀ. Cyr.H.*catech.*10.19.

***ἀσκοδρουγῖται, οἱ,** nickname of Montanist sect, Jo.D.*haer.*48 (M.94.708A) = τασκοδρουγῖται.

***ἀσκοδρουπῖται, οἱ,** = foreg., Thdt.*haer.*1.10 tit.(4.302).

***ἀσκοδρούται, οἱ,** = foreg., Thdt.*haer.*1.10 tit.(4.302).

§ἀσκόομαι, *swell like a wine-skin*, Thdt.*qu.2 in Jos.*(1.305).

***ἀσκότιστος,** *undimmed* ἐν πάσχα φωτεινὸν καὶ ἀ. ὅλον τὸν χρόνον αὐτοῖς τῆς ζωῆς ἐργάζεσθαι Gr.Nyss.*res.*1(M.46.621B).

***ἀσκυβάλιστος,** *free from defilement*; of Church, *Const.App.*2.43.4.

ἄσκυλτος, *undisturbed*; **1.** *unharmed*, Tim.Ant.*Sym.*(M.86.240A); **2.** of the head, *untrimmed*, i.e. with long hair, *Const.App.*1.3.8; **3.** *unflinching*, *M.Polyc.*13.3.

ἀσκύλτως, 1. *without flinching*, *M.Polyc.*ap.Eus.*h.e.*4.15.31(M.20.356A; ἄσκυλτον *M.Polyc.*13.3); **2.** *without budging*, Nil.*epp.*4.60(M.79.577A); **3.** *without trouble*, ‡Nil.*perist.*9.3(M.79.865D).

ἄσκωμα, τό, *inflated skin* (ref. Jos.3:16) τὸ...πῆγμα, ἄ. ὁ Σύμμαχος ἡρμήνευσεν Thdt.*qu.2 in Jos.*(1.305).

ᾆσμα, τό, *song, canticle*; **1.** of two kinds, either elevating or debasing the soul; latter must be banished and replaced by psalms, Or.*Jo.*2.15(9; p.72.6; M.14.141A); Dion.Ar.*ep.*9.1(M.3.1105B); unseemly songs as work and delight of demons, Ephr.3.215D; Chrys.*hom.1.5 in Col.*(11.330B); id.*exp.in Ps.*41(5.132A); positive value of song οὐδὲν οὕτως ἀνίστησι ψυχὴν καὶ πτεροῖ καὶ τῆς γῆς ἀπαλλάττει καὶ τῶν τοῦ σώματος ἀπολύει δεσμῶν καὶ φιλοσοφεῖν ποιεῖ καὶ πάντων καταγελᾶν τῶν βιωτικῶν ὡς μέλος συμφωνίας καὶ ῥυθμῷ συγκείμενον θεῖον ᾆ. οὕτω γοῦν ἡμῶν ἡ φύσις πρὸς τὰ ᾆ. καὶ τὰ μέλη ἡδέως ἔχει καὶ οἰκείως *ib.*(131C); τῷ ᾆ. τὸν ἐκ τῶν ἔργων πόνον παραμυθήσασθαι σπεύδοντες *ib.*(131E); cf.*Const.App.*1.6.5; **2.** of psalms as spiritual songs used in Christian worship πᾶσα μὲν γὰρ ἱερὰ καὶ ἁγιόγραφος δέλτος...θείων ἐρώτων ᾄσματα καὶ ἐνθέους εἰκόνας...ταῖς ἱεραῖς τῶν τελετῶν καὶ θεοειδέσιν ἀναγωγαῖς συνερρίζωσεν Dion.Ar.*e.h.*3.3.4(M.3.429Cf.); τὴν δὲ πνευματικὴν τῶν θείων ᾆ. τερπνότητα τὴν ἐμφαντικὴν δηλοῦν ἔφασκε τῶν θείων ἡδονὴν ἀγαθῶν Max.*myst.*11 (M.91.689C); perfected by use of Christian hymns πρῶτον τῆς παλαιᾶς ψάλλονται οἱ ψαλμοί, εἶτα τῆς νέας χάριτος ᾄσματα ‡Sophr.H.*liturg.*12(M.87.3992C); **3.** myst., of new song of gospel sung by Christ the perfect bard, Clem.*prot.*1.2,5,6(p.4.19; p.5.10; p.6.27; M.8.56A,57B,60B); this being σωτήριον ᾆ. *ib.*1.6(p.7.3; 61A); Nil.*epp.*1.242(M.79.172B); **4.** combining lit. practice and myst. theory Or. develops idea of ascending progress from psalms, through biblical ᾆ. already occupying special place in Church worship, to ᾆ. τῶν ᾀσμάτων the consummation of the mystic union, cf.Or.*hom.1.1 in Cant.*(p.28.2ff.; M.13.37Bff.) and (with one variant) id.*Cant.*proem.(p.81.4ff.; M.13.77Cff.); **5.** praise of Song of Songs, cf. *cum universa transieris, ad altiora conscende ut possis anima decora cum sponso et hoc canere canticum canticorum*, Or.*hom.in Cant.*1.1(p.28.18; M.13.38A); *anima beata...istud epithalamii carmen per spiritum canit quo ecclesia sponso caelesti Christo conjungitur*, id.*Cant.*proem.(p.74.12; M.13.72C); ἀκούσατε τοῦ μυστηρίου τοῦ ᾆ. τῶν ᾆ. Gr.Nyss.*hom.1 in Cant.*(M.44.765A); ἐν τῇ προκειμένῃ τοῦ ᾆ. τῶν ᾆ. φιλοσοφίᾳ διὰ τοῦ ᾆ. τῶν ᾆ. ἐντὸς τῶν θείων ἀδύτων μυσταγωγεῖ τὴν διάνοιαν ἐν οἷς τὸ μὲν ὑπογραφόμενον ἐπιθαλάμιός τίς ἐστι διασκευή, τὸ δ' ἐννοούμενον τῆς ἀνθρωπίνης ψυχῆς ἡ πρὸς τὸ θεῖόν ἐστιν ἀνάκρασις *ib.*(769D).

***ᾀσματίζ-ω,** *sing a song of rejoicing* τὴν ὁδὸν τῶν ἐντολῶν σου δραμόντες πρακτικῶς ~ουσιν *cat.Apoc.*18:14(p.443.15).

***ᾀσματικός,** *lyrical, of song* τὸ στεφάνωμα οὐράνιον, τοῖς ἀ. ἄνθεσιν ...συμπλεκόμενον Thdr.Stud.*epp.*2.77(M.99.1316C); as subst., *lyric, song*, *Const.App.*1.6.5.

***ᾀσματικῶς,** *in the style of Canticles* παρθένος, ᾀ. εἰπεῖν, κῆπος κεκλεισμένος Thdr.Stud.*epp.*2.125(M.99.1408A).

ᾀσμάτιον, τό, dimin. of ᾆσμα, *verse, jingle* ὁ...ἐν ᾀσματίοις Ἄρειος ...μυθολογεῖ Ath.*decr.*16(p.13.29; M.25.'449'(441)D).

ᾀσματογράφος, *writer of songs* or *hymns*; of David, Thdr.Stud.*antirr.*3 proem.(M.99.389A).

***ᾀσμενοειδῶς,** *gladly*, ‡Gr.Nyss.*or.2 in Gen.1:26*(M.44.297A).

ἀσολοικίστως, *without solecism, without making a mistake*, Leont.Abb.*v.Gr.Agr.*4(M.98.556B).

ἄσοφος, *without wisdom*; at all times inapplicable to God, Hipp.*Noët.*10(p.251.17; M.10.817A) cit. s. ἀβούλευτος; πῶς δέ, εἰ λόγος καὶ σοφία ἐστὶ τοῦ θεοῦ ὁ υἱός, ἦν ποτε ὅτε οὐκ ἦν; ἴσον γάρ ἐστι αὐτοὺς [i.e. Arians] λέγειν ἄλογον καὶ ἄ. ποτε τὸν θεόν Alex.Al.*ep.encycl.*4 (p.9.6; M.18.576B); Ath.*Ar.*2.32(M.26.216B); *ib.*3.63(456C); Cyr.*thes.*21(5^1.210D); *ib.*32(285A).

ἀσπάζ-ομαι 1. *welcome readily, greet*; as opening formula in letters, Ign.*Magn.*; id.*Trall.* and in conclusion, id.*Smyrn.*12.1; 13.1 etc.; **2.** met.; **a.** *receive with joy, embrace*; Christian teaching, Just.

1apol.45.5(M.6.397A); Or.Jo.32.10(7; p.442.5; M.14.768A); Thdt. affect.6(p.180.14; 4.882) etc.; study of scripture, Eus.d.e.3.3(p.109. 3; M.22.188B); grace, id.p.e.1.1(3B; M.21.25A); **b.** *enter eagerly upon* a race Mac.Mgn.apocr.3.40(p.138.23); *follow eagerly, embrace* virtues σωφροσύνην Just.1apol.14.2(M.6.348B); ἁγνείαν Meth.symp.11 (p.129.18; M.18.205A); **c.** *adhere firmly to*, of a soldier's allegiance τοὺς...στρατιώτας καὶ πρὸ τῆς ἑαυτῶν ζωῆς...τὴν ὑμετέραν ~εσθαι ὁμολογίαν Just.1apol.39.5(M.6.388C); *be attached to, cling to* with the affections, of Helena ἀ. ... τὸ χωρίον...ὅτι...Λουκιανὸς ὁ μάρτυς ἐκεῖσε τύχοι...ἐκκομισθείς Philost.h.e.2.12(M.65.476C); **3.** *embrace, kiss*; liturg.; **a.** *give kiss of peace* ἀλλήλους φιλήματι ~όμεθα παυσάμενοι τῶν εὐχῶν Just.1apol.65.2(M.6.428A); διὰ τοῦτο καὶ ἐν τοῖς μυστηρίοις ~όμεθα ἀλλήλους, ἵνα οἱ πολλοὶ γενώμεθα ἕν Chrys.hom. 77.4 in Jo.(8.464D); id.hom.18.3 in 2Cor.(10.568C); Anast.S.synax. (M.89.840A); at some point between dismissal of the catechumens and the anaphora; after lavatorium εἶτα βοᾷ ὁ διάκονος...ἀλλήλους ~ώμεθα...σημεῖον τοίνυν ἐστὶ τὸ φίλημα τοῦ ἀνακραθῆναι τὰς ψυχὰς καὶ πᾶσαν ἐξορίζειν μνησικακίαν Cyr.H.catech.23.3; before prayer for faithful, Const.App.2.57.17; ~όμενοι...ἀλλήλους μέλλοντος τοῦ δώρου προσφέρεσθαι Chrys.compunct.1.3.(1.127B); ἀσπασαμένων ἀλλήλους ἁπάντων, ἡ μυστικὴ τῶν ἱερῶν πτυχῶν ἀνάρρησις ἐπιτελεῖται Dion.Ar. e.h.3.1.2(M.3.425C); Lit.Jac.(p.184.12); at beginning of anaphora in Lit.Marc.(p.123.15); in memory of Resurrection, Thdr.Stud.antirr. 1.10(M.99.340C); originally given indiscriminately, but abuses led to its restriction to members of the same sex καὶ ~έσθωσαν οἱ τοῦ κλήρου τὸν ἐπίσκοπον, οἱ λαϊκοὶ ἄνδρες τοὺς λαϊκούς, αἱ γυναῖκες τὰς γυναῖκας Lit.ap.Const.App.8.11.9; Const.App.2.57.17, cf.CLaod.can. 19; **b.** *salute* καὶ μετὰ τὴν ἀνάγνωσιν τοῦ νόμου καὶ τῶν προφητῶν, τῶν τε ἐπιστολῶν ἡμῶν καὶ τῶν πράξεων καὶ τῶν εὐαγγελίων ἀσπασάσθω ὁ χειροτονηθεὶς τὴν ἐκκλησίαν Lit.ap.Const.App.8.5.11; the newly ordained πάντες...ὅσοι πάρεισι τῶν ἱερατικῶν ὄντες τάξεων, ἀλλὰ καὶ αὐτὸς ὁ τελέσας ἱεράρχης, ~ονται τὸν τετελεσμένον Dion. Ar.e.h.5.3.6(M.3.513B); ib.5.2(509B); **c.** after religious profession, ib.6.2(533B); ib.6.3.4(536B); **d.** *salute, kiss* dead before burial ὁ ἱεράρχης...~εται τὸν κεκοιμημένον, καὶ ἑξῆς οἱ παρόντες ἅπαντες Dion.Ar.e.h.7.3.8(565A); ib.7.2(556D); ib.7.3.4(560A); **e.** *kiss* any sacred object: altar, ib.2.2.4(393C); images, Jo.D.haer.103(M.94. 777A); ‡Jo.D.Const.7(M.95.324B); at eucharist ὁ μὲν ἱερεὺς προσκυνήσας τρὶς ~εται τὰ ἅγια...καὶ ὁ διάκονος...~εται...τὸ ὠράριον αὐτοῦ Lit.Chrys.(p.382.26,31); ib.(p.355.12).

ἀσπάρακτος, *inviolate, entire*, of faith of Nicaea ἀ. μένειν εὔχομαι Amph.ep.syn.(M.39.96A).

ἄσπαρτος, **1.** *unsown, uncultivated*; met., i.e. not evangelized ἀ. ... γένος Thdt.Gal.proem.(3.358); **2.** of plants, *not propagated by seed*, Mac.Mgn.apocr.2.17(p.29.7); of birth of Christ, *without seed* τὰς ἀ. ... ὠδῖνας Thdt.qu.42 in Dt.(1.290); ἄ., καὶ ἀνήροτον σκηνὴν διαπλάττει id.inc.23(M.75.1460D).

ἀσπασμός, ὁ, **1.** *salutation, greeting*; ref. Lc.1:29 οὐδ' ἀνδρί που εἴρηται τοῦτο, ταύτῃ δὲ ἐτηρεῖτο ὁ ἀ. οὗτος Or.hom.6 in Lc.(p.40.1); θεοῦ μνήμη σύνεστι τῷ ἀ. cat.Lc.1:28(p.11.19); διεπλάσθη [sc. human nature of Christ]...μετὰ τὸν ἀγγελικὸν ἀ. Thdt.eran.2(4.99); as subst., *reception, levée*, A.Xanthipp.5(p.61.16); plur., ib.(p.61.19); **2.** liturg.; **a.** *kiss of peace* at eucharist ἐν τῇ θείᾳ ἀναφορᾷ ὁ διάκονος προσφωνεῖ πρὸ τοῦ ἀ. Tim.I Al.resp.(M.33.1301C); Chrys.prod.Jud. 1.6(2.385D) cit. s. φίλημα; ὁ θειότατος ἀ. Dion.Ar.e.h.3.3.8(M.3.437A); Max.myst.13(M.91.692C); its symbolism, ib.17(693D); ‡Bas.h.myst. 55(p.392.4); **b.** *salutation* of newly ordained ὁ δὲ πρὸς τῷ τέλει τῆς ἱερατικῆς τελειώσεως ἀ. ἱερὰν ἔμφασιν ἔχει Dion.Ar.e.h.5.3.6(M.3. 513B); ib.5.2(509B); **c.** *kiss* given to dead μετὰ...τὸν ἀ. ἐπιχέει τῷ κεκοιμημένῳ τὸ ἔλαιον ὁ ἱεράρχης ib.7.3.8(565A); Euchol.(p.446); ib. (p.471); v. ἀσπάζομαι.

***ἀσπαστήριος**, *welcoming*; *for reception* ἀ. οἶκος *guest room, reception room*, Thdt.ep.145(4.1245).

***ἀσπερμάντως**, *without seed*, of BMV τὸν στάχυν τῆς ἀφθαρσίας Χριστόν, ἀ., ἀγεωργήτως ἐτελεσφόρησας Andr.Cr.or.5(M.97.897A).

***ἀσπιδόγονος**, ὁ, *offspring of vipers*; of Jewish race, Mir.Artem. 38(p.63.16).

***ἀσπιδογοργών**, ὁ, *serpent that devoured its own tail*, Epiph. haer.22.2(p.247.7; M.41.297A); ib.30.26(p.369.17; 449D).

ἀσπιδοποιΐα, ἡ, *making of the shield*, name for Homer Il.18, LS; also Vergil Aen.8, Jo.Mal.chron.9 p.220(M.97.341B).

***ἀσπιδοχελώνη**, ἡ, *shield-tortoise, shield-turtle*; name of fabulous sea-monster, ‡Eust.hex.(M.18.724D); τί τὴν τῆς ἀ. ὕπουλον ἀγάπην προτιμᾷς τῆς τοῦ ἀδελφοῦ γνησίας ἀγάπης; †Bas.contub.9(M.30. 824C).

ἄσπιλος, *spotless, undefiled*, met. ἄ. καὶ ἄμωμον μέχρι θανάτου πᾶσαν τὴν ἐντολὴν τοῦ κυρίου φυλάξαντες †Bas.bapt.2.13.2(2.673E; M.31.1628C); ἱερωσύνην...ἄ. Gr.Naz.or.17.12(M.35.980A); ἄ. ... διακονίαν Lit.Jac.(p.208.20); esp. of virginity, Gr.Naz.carm.1.2.1.658 (M.37.572A); M.Thdot.1 13(p.69.13); A.Andr.fr.8(p.41.24); of BMV καθαρὰ καὶ ἄ. ψυχή Procl.CP or.6.1(M.65.721C); ib.6.4(728A); Μαρίαν, ὡς ἄ. περιστεράν Jo.Eub.concept.BMV 15(M.96.1484A); of Christ as sinless, Just.dial.110.6(M.6.732A); of the elect as free from sin, Herm.vis.4.3.5; δός μοι σῶμα ἄ. Const.App.7.45.3; Mac.Aeg.hom.2.3 (M.34.465A).

***ἀσπίλως**, *spotlessly, with a pure intention* ἱερωσύνη...μέγας βαθμός, ἐὰν τελεῖται ἀ. Ephr.1.73A; *without error* τὴν...ἁγίαν πίστιν φυλαξάντων ἀ. Gel.Cyz.h.e.2.12.7(M.85.1252A).

***ἀσπλαγχνία**, ἡ, *heartlessness, inhumanity*, Chrys.poenit.3.2(2. 296B); ib.4.3(306B); ὅταν...θέλωσιν ἀσπλαγχνίαν ἐνδείξασθαι...ἀναμνησθῶσι τῆς ἑαυτῶν ἁμαρτίας ‡Chrys.Petr.et El.4(2.740A); ib.2(2.734B); Olymp.Job 42:11(M.93.457C); towards the dead ἀ. ἐπιδείκνυσθαι ἐπὶ νεκρῷ ὡς καὶ βαρβάρων ὠμότητα ὑπερβαίνειν V.Pach.Λ(p.128.23); causes ἀ. ἣν φιλοχρηματία γεννᾷ Nil.exerc.73(M.79.805D); ἐκ...τῆς κακῆς προαιρέσεως ἔρχεται καὶ εἰς ἀ. ὁ ἄνθρωπος Eus.Al.serm.21.23 (M.86.452B); a mark of infidelity, Jo.D.hom.2.6(M.96.585C).

***ἀσπλαγχνίζω**, *be heartless, show no mercy*, Olymp.Job 41:2(M.93. 437A).

ἄσπονδος, *without drink offering*; hence **1.** of sacrifice, *inefficacious, not making reconciliation* θυσίαι ἄ. καὶ ἀνίεροι Eus.d.e.8.2 (p.389.29; M.22.629B); **2.** *deprived of civil rights, outlawed*, Pall.v. Chrys.9(p.57.5; M.47.33).

ἀσπορία, ἡ, **1.** *barrenness*; *state of not having been sown*, Orac.Sib. 3.542; **2.** *procreation, generation, without seed* ὡς...οὐκ οὐσία θεοῦ τὸ ἀγέννητον καὶ γεννητόν...οὕτως οὐδὲ σπορὰ καὶ ἀ. φύσις...ἀνθρωπότητος Max.opusc.(M.91.61A); of BMV χαῖρε κρίνον...ῥοδωνία τοῦ πνεύματος ἐξ ἧς Χριστὸς ἀνόθευτον ἐξ ἀ. στολὴν περιεβάλετο Thdr. Stud.nativ.BMV 7(M.96.692C).

ἄσπορος, **1.** of land, *untilled*; met., of BMV ὦ γῆς ἀ. καρπὸν βλαστησάσης οὐράνιον Procl.CP or.4(M.65.709A); **2.** of plants, *unsown, uncultivated*; of manna ἄ. καὶ ἀνήροτον Bas.hom.8.6(2.68D; M.31.320B); Thdt.qu.54 in Ex.(1.158); **3.** *not propagating by seed*; met., of BMV τὴν ἄ. κόχλον Jo.Eub.concept.BMV 4(M.96.1465A); **4.** of Inc., *without seed*; **a.** *bearing without impregnation, virgin* ἀσπίλους τὰς σὰς γονὰς ἐν ἀ. φέρουσα νηδύι Meth.symp.11.2(p.135. 24; M.18.212C); ἐν τῇ γεννήσει ἄσπορος ὠράθη τόκος Leont.H.Nest. 1.19(M.86.1480C); ἄ. αὐτοῦ κύησις ib.2.20(1580D); ἀλεύρῳ ἀζύμῳ, λοχείας ἀ. ἀντιτύπῳ ‡Meth.Sym.et Ann.9(M.18.372A); freq. with σύλληψις, Isid.Pel.epp.1.377(M.78.396B); Leont.H.Nest.1.10(1441D); Sophr.H.ep.syn.(M.87.3176A); id.or.2.14(M.87.3232D); Max.ep.19 (M.91.592D) cit. s. ἄφθορος; **b.** *begotten without seed* τὸ ἄ. βρέφος Pers.(p.13.18; M.10.101C); Jo.Mon.hymn.Nic.7(M.96.1388B); Paul. Sil.Soph.694(M.86.2146A).

***ἀσποροσύλληψις**, ἡ, *conception without seed, virgin conception*, Jo.D.disp.1(M.94.1597B).

***ἀσπόρως**, **1.** *without seed*; met., ref. BMV καρπὸν ἀ. ἐβλάστησας Sophr.H.or.2.22(M.87.3241C); **2.** *without* human *seed, virginally*; of Inc., Arist.apol.15.1 cit. s. ἀφθόρως; ἀ. καὶ ἀφθάρτως γεγένηται Chron. Pasch.p.12(M.92.92C); σῶμα ἔμψυχον...τῆς...θεοτόκου Μαρίας ἀ. ἐστολίσω Lit.Jac.(NBP 10² p.106); freq. with γίγνομαι and γέννησις: ἄνω γεννηθεὶς ἀχρόνως καὶ κάτω ἀ. ‡Cyr.H.occurs.10(M.33.1197B); cf.Eulog.palm.10(M.86.2929C); Leont.H.Nest.4.3(M.86.1657D); ib. 4.9(1669C); with γεννάω, of BMV ὡς αὐτὴ γεγέννηκας ἀ. Jo.Mon. hymn.Bas.1(M.96.1372B); with συλλαμβάνομαι and σύλληψις, Isid. Pel.epp.1.23(M.78.197A); ἐπὶ τὴν ἀ. οἰκονομηθεῖσαν σύλληψιν Leont. B.Nest.et Eut.2(M.86.1328A); Jo.D.f.o.1.2(M.94.792D); with συλλαμβάνω, of BMV, Anast.S.fr.(M.89.1286C) cit. s. ἀφθόρως; with τίκτομαι: μονογενῆ...ἐκ μόνης μητρὸς ἀ. τεχθέντα Bas.Sel.or.10.2(M. 85.141B); Oecum.Apoc.1:13(p.41.4); Sergia, Olymp.13(p.50.21); **3.** *not by generation*, ref. Adam in comparison with Christ προήνεγκε τὸ θῆλυ ἀ. Cosm.Ind.top.5(M.88.224B).

ἄσπουδος, *not in earnest*, Gr.Nyss.Eun.11(2 p.265.11; M.45.873B).

ἄσπρος, *white* κολόβιον ἄ. συγκεκλεισμένον πορφύρᾳ A.Barth.2 (p.131.22); τῆς ἱερωσύνης στολὴν ἄ. Ep.ap.CSyr.(518–19)act.(ACO 3 p.95.18; H.2.1369C); Jo.Mal.chron.12 p.286(M.97.433A); ib.p.310 (465D); of a leucoma, Leont.N.v.Sym.52(M.93.1733B); of skin, complexion ἀσπροτάτην ὡσεὶ χιών...παρθένον Chron.Pasch.p.312 (793D); neut. plur., *white clothes*, V.Dan.(p.61.26).

***ἀσπρόσαρκος**, *white of flesh, fair*, A.Barth.2(p.131.19).

***ἀσπρότης**, ἡ, *whiteness*, Anast.S.hod.2(M.89.64C); met. ? *candour* ἀντὶ μὲν τῆς ἀ. τὴν ὀρθὴν καὶ ἀμίαντον καὶ ἁπλῆν πίστιν· ἀντὶ δὲ τῆς ὀξύτητος τὴν ὑπομνητικὴν ἐλπίδα ‡Tit.Bost.palm.7(M.18.1276D).

***ἀσπροφορέω**, *wear white*, Jo.Mosch.*prat*.66(M.87.2917B); *Chron. Pasch*.p.383(M.92.981C).

***ἀσσάλιος**, (? = *axilla*) *winged*, sc. χιτών a kind of *garment*, or perh. ὁ ἀ. *wallet*, ref. Satan disguised as a beggar ἐπέθετο τοῖς ὤμοις ἀ. *T.Job* 7(p.107.16).

***ἀσσοβαθός**, ? *near the deep water*; islands, Cosm.Ind.*top*.11(M. 88.445C).

***ἀσσόκουρος**, *closely shorn*, Jo.Mal.*chron*.12 p.302(M.97.456B).

***ἄστα**, ἡ, (Lat. *hasta*) *pike, spear*, Thphn.*chron*.p.305(M.108. 744A).

***ἀστάθεια**, ἡ, *instability*, Chrys.*hom.15.4 in 2Cor*.(10.549A).

***ἀσταθ-έω**, *be unstable* ὕδατος ∼έοντος Eudoc.*Cypr*.2(M.85.849B); ∼ούσης τῆς φυσικῆς δυνάμεως *cat.Apoc*.10:3(p.329.23).

ἄστακτος, *immovable, everlasting*, Leont.N.*v.Sym*.64(M.93.1748A).

***ἀσταλαξία**, ἡ, ? *stillness, silence* τοῦ δὲ ἐνεχθέντος καὶ ἀ. οὔσης διήκουον αὐτοῦ *M.Pers*.1.9(p.429.8).

***ἀσταρεῦσις**, f.l. ap.Or.*fr.in Mt*.28:18(M.17.309D; κατὰ ῥεῦσιν p.235).

ἄστατος, **1.** *never standing still, unresting*, of time τὸ...ἄ. ... τοῦ χρόνου †Dion.Al.*fr.3 in Job*(p.205.16); Ammon.ap.*cat.Jo*.11:9 (p.315.16); Nonn.*par.Jo*.14:29(M.43.872B); **2.** *restless* πονηροῦ καὶ ἀ. πνεύματος Proc.G.*Is*.16:2(M.87.2104B); **3.** of things, *subject to change, unstable*; characteristic of matter, Gr.Naz.*carm*.1.1.32.10(M. 37.512A); Chrys.*hom.2.5 in Ac*.(9.21B); Max.*ambig*.(M.91.1104A); and of the false τὸ ψεῦδος ἄ. φύσει ‡Hipp.*fr.42 in Pr*.9:12(p.173.9); opp. divine nature οὐδὲ γὰρ ἄ. ἐστι θεοῦ φύσις ἢ ῥέουσα Gr.Naz. *carm*.1.1.3.68(M.37.413A); **4.** of persons, *unsteady, unstable* ἄ. καὶ πρὸς τὰς κρίσεις εὐκίνητοι Bas.*reg.fus*.10.1(2.352D; M.31.945A); characteristic of youth, Clem.*paed*.2.7(p.190.8; M.8.457A); Or.*princ*. 3.1.5(p.201.2; M.11.256A); νεώτερος, οὐ διὰ τὸν χρόνον νεώτερος ἀλλὰ διὰ...τὴν γνώμην ἄ. *cat.Lc*.15:11f.(p.117.29); of various human faculties, freq. γνώμη: τὸ πολύτροπον καὶ ἄ. τῆς ἀνθρωπίνης γνώμης Clem. *str*.8.7(p.93.20, M.9.588B); Bas.*reg.fus*.41.1(2.387B; M.31.1021C); of heret. opinion, *inconstant* τὴν τούτων ἄ. γνώμην Iren.*haer*.1.11.1 (M.7.560A).

ἀστάτως, *unsteadily, unstably*, Isid.Pel.*epp*.1.80(M.78.237C); Geo. Pis.*Pers*.3.161(M.92.1244A).

ἀστάφυλος, *without grapes*, ref. miracle at Cana οἶνον ἀ. Thdt. *inc*.25(M.75.1464B).

ἀστειότης, ἡ, **1.** *beauty* νοητὴν ἀ. Cyr.*ador*.12(1.411B); ἀ. τὴν πνευματικήν id.*Is*.4.4(2.676B); **2.** *good manners*, in Christian society of holy life τῆς εὐαγγελικῆς πολιτείας ἐξηγεῖται τὴν ἀ. *ib*.1.1(19E); *ib*.(21D); in spiritual things, *goodness, nobility*, Gr.Nyss.*Eun*.3(2 p.40.6; M.45.608A); Cyr.*Ps*.37:7(M.69.960C); *ib*.46:10(1057D); Anast. Ant.ap.Jo.D.*jej*.(M.95.76A).

ἄστειπτος, = ἀστιβής 1, met., *not oppressed* λύπαις δ' ἄστειπτος ψυχὰ πραεῖαν ζωὰν ἕλκοι Synes.*hymn*.5.40(p.37, v.l. ἄστιπτος M.66. 1609).

ἀστείως, **1.** *delicately, with refinement* κατονειδίζων ἀ. ὡς λήθην εἰσδεδεγμένους Cyr.*Mic*.54(3.446D); freq. ref. figurative language (exeg. Is.6:6) συνήσεις ἀ. ὅτι πίστιν...καθάπερ τινὶ λαβίδι δεχώμεθα διὰ νομικῶν τε ἅμα καὶ προφητικῶν παιδευμάτων id.*Is*.1.4(2.108C); ἑκάστη...τῶν...ὁράσεων ἔμφασίν τινα...ἀ. ἡμῖν ὑπαινίττεται *ib*.2.4 (282E); ἐστι...παραβολῆς τρόπος ἐσχηματισμένος ἀ. id.*Lc*.16:19 (M.72.824A); **2.** *cleverly, aptly*, ‡Meth.*Sym.et Ann*.4(M.18.356D); **3.** *joyfully* ἀ. τὴν αὐτοῦ ἐδέξαντο σφαγήν Thphn.*chron*.p.348(M.108. 837A).

***ἀστεκτέω**, f.l. for ἀτακτέω *be undisciplined, disorderly*, Pall. *v.Chrys*.8(M.47.28; ἀτακτῶν p.48.11).

***ἀστενοχώρητος**, *not straitened, unconstricted*, *cat.Apoc*.18:14 (p.444.10); of incarnate Logos in womb of BMV θεὸν ἀχώρητον, ἐν σοὶ δὲ χωρητὸν καὶ ἀ. ‡Epiph.*hom*.5(M.43.492A).

***ἀστενοχωρήτως**, **1.** ref. Inc.; act., *without constricting*, ‡Jo.D. *hom*.5(M.96.656A); Jo.Mon.*hymn.Blas*.4(M.96.1401D); **2.** pass., *without being straitened* or *constricted* γαστέρα παρθένου πλατυτέραν τῆς κτίσεως. ὁ γὰρ ἐκεῖ μὴ χωρούμενος, ἐνταῦθα ἀ. ἐχώρησε Procl.CP *or*. 4(M.65.709B); ἐν τῷ παρθενικῷ σηκῷ ἀ. οἰκήσας Leont.B.*parasc*. (M.86.1997C); Hesych.H.*serm*.4(M.93.1453B).

ἀστερίσκος, ὁ, **1.** *little star*; liturg., metal framework composed of two bars crossed and bent to keep the veil from disarranging the bread on the δίσκος: ἀ. καθὼς τὰ τέσσαρα ζῷα ἐπικαλύπτει τὸν οὐράνιον ἄνθρακα ‡Sophr.H.*liturg*.(M.87.3985B); cf. ὁ ἱερεὺς θυμιάσας τὸν ἀ. τίθησιν ἐπάνω τοῦ ἁγίου ἄρτου *Lit.Chrys*.(p.360.1); *ib*. (p.385.14); also called ἀστήρ, *ib*.(p.395.31); **2.** a kind of *heron*, Or. *exp.in Pr*.7:22(M.17.184A).

***ἀστερόμαντις**, *divining by stars*, Thdt.*Zach*.10:2(2.1639).

***ἀστερόμουσος**, *star-spangled*; of heaven, Cosm.Mel.*schol*.(M.38. 531) in Gr.Naz.*carm*.2.1.44.36.

***ἀστεροπρόσωπος**, *starry-faced, with face shining as a star*, ‡Hesych.H.*m.Long*.15(M.93.1557C).

ἀστεροσκοπέω, *watch the stars*, Hipp.*haer*.4.4(p.36.16; M.16. 3063C); Meth.*symp*.8.13(p.99.5; M.18.161B).

ἀστεροσκοπία, ἡ, *observation of the stars*, *Apoc.En*.8.3.

***ἀστεροσκοπικός**, *observing the stars* ὁδῶν προγνωστικῶν τὴν ἀ. ...τὴν γενεθλιαλογικήν Or.*comm.in Gen*.(M.12.77A)ap.Eus.*p.e*.6.11 (293D).

***ἀστεροφανία**, ἡ, *appearance of the star*; to Magi, *Pers*.(p.16.2; -εια M.10.105A).

***ἀστηλίτευτος**, *without memorial*, Pall.*h.Laus*.51(p.155.4; M.34. 1227D).

ἀστήρ, ὁ, *star*; **1.** in gen.; pagan attribution of divinity condemned, Clem.*prot*.2(p.19.14; M.8.96A); *ib*.5(p.50.21; 169A); control over human action denied πάντων...κακῶν μέγιστον...τὸ τὰς αἰτίας τῶν ἁμαρτημάτων εἰς τὰς τῶν ἀ. κινήσεις ἀναφέρειν Meth.*symp*.8.13 (p.99.3; M.18.161A); εἰ...τὴν τῶν ἀ. ... κίνησιν...διέπει...οἱ δὲ ἀ. τὰς ποιότητας τῆς κακίας καὶ τῆς ἀρετῆς ἐκτελοῦσι τῷ βίῳ...αἴτιον τῶν κακῶν τὸν θεὸν ἀποφαίνονται καὶ δότην *ib*.8.16(p.105.10 ff.; 168D); a form of heavenly writing ὥσπερ ἔστιν ἐν βιβλίῳ γράμματα, τοῦτο ἐν οὐρανῷ ἄστρα. δι' ἑκατέρων οὖν γνῶσιν τῶν ὄντων λαμβάνουσιν οἱ ἄνθρωποι διὰ μὲν τῶν γραμμάτων τὴν ὑπόμνησιν τῶν λόγων, διὰ δὲ τῶν ἀ. τὴν τῶν καιρῶν καὶ σημείων κατὰ τὴν γραφικὴν διάγνωσιν Max.*fr*.(*Catalogus Codicum Astrologorum* 7, F. Boll, Brussels 1908, p.100); speculations on their nature οἱ ἀ., σώματα πνευματικά, κεκοινωνηκότα ἀγγέλοις ἐφεστῶσι διοικούμενα, οὐκ αἴτια γενέσεως, σημαντικὰ δὲ τῶν γινομένων τε καὶ ἐσομένων καὶ γενομένων Clem.*ecl*. 55(p.152.14; M.9.724B); οὓς...οὐ διὰ τὸ...αἰσθητὸν φῶς ἐχρῆν προσκυνεῖσθαι ἀλλὰ διὰ τὸ νοητὸν καὶ ἀληθινόν, εἴπερ καὶ οἱ ἐν οὐρανῷ ἀ. ζῷά εἰσι λογικά...καὶ γὰρ τὸ μὲν αἰσθητὸν φῶς ἔργον ἐστὶ τοῦ... δημιουργοῦ· τὸ δὲ νοητὸν τάχα καὶ αὐτῶν καὶ ἐκ τοῦ ἐν αὐτοῖς αὐτεξουσίου ἐληλυθὸς Or.*Cels*.5.10(p.11.13; M.11.1196B); cf.id.*princ*.1.7.3 (p.88.9ff.; M.11.172C); clothed in ethereal bodies, *ib*.1.7.5(p.92.10; 174C); as knowing God ἄτοπον γὰρ λέγειν...ὅτι...ὁ χορὸς τῶν ἀ. ... οὐκ ἔγνωσαν τὸ ἀληθινὸν φῶς id.*comm.in Mt*.13.20(p.235.26; M.13. 1149B); as praying πειθόμενοι δὲ καὶ...ἀ. εὔχεσθαι τῷ...θεῷ διὰ τοῦ μονογενοῦς αὐτοῦ, κρίνομεν μὴ δεῖν εὔχεσθαι τοῖς εὐχομένοις id.*Cels*. 5.11(p.12.12; 1197B); true nature yet to be revealed, id.*princ*.2.11.7 (p.191.6; 246C); inanimate, Bas.*hom.in Ps*.48:12(1.185A; M.29.449C); εἴ τις λέγει...τοὺς ἀ. καὶ αὐτὰ τῆς αὐτῆς τῶν λογικῶν ἑνάδος ὄντα ἐκ παρατροπῆς τῆς ἐπὶ τὸ χεῖρον γεγονέναι τοῦτο, ὅπερ ἐστίν· ἀνάθεμα ἔστω CCP(543)*anath*.3(p.228; H.3.284D); v. ἄστρον; **2.** partic. of star seen by Magi, Gr.Naz.*or*.5.5(M.35.669C); explanations οὐ τῶν πολλῶν εἷς ὁ ἀ. οὗτος ἦν, μᾶλλον δὲ οὐδὲ ἀ. ... ἀλλὰ δύναμίς τις ἀόρατος Chrys.*hom.6.2 in Mt*.(7.87B); id.*hom.div*.8.5(12.378D); but gen. thought to be an unusual star, Ign.*Eph*.19.2; τὸν...ἀ. ... καινὸν εἶναι νομίζομεν καὶ μηδενὶ τῶν συνήθων παραπλήσιον...ἀλλὰ...κομῆται ἢ δοκίδες Or.*Cels*.1.58(p.109.28; M.11.768B); ξένος δὲ ἦν καὶ οὐ συνήθης οὐδὲ τῶν πολλῶν τῶν γνωρίμων εἷς, ἀλλά τις καινὸς καὶ νέος ἀ. ἐπιφανεὶς τῷ βίῳ σημεῖον ξένου φωστῆρος ἐδήλου...Χριστός Eus.*d.e*.9.1 (p.405.32; M.22.653D); or unusual course of a star, Isid.Pel.*epp*.1. 378(M.78.396C); **3.** met., of an *illustrious person* Νεστόριος πρεσβύτερος ἐνθ[άδε] κῖτε ἀ. ὃς ἐν[έλ]αμπεν ἐν ἐκλησίησιν Θεοῖο *MAMA* 1.238; **4.** liturg. = ἀστερίσκος q.v.

ἄστης, ὁ, *singer*, Pall.*v.Chrys*.20(p.134.22; M.47.75).

ἀστιβής, **1.** *untrodden*; met., *untouched, unaffected*, Cyr.*hom. pasch*.15(5².205C); **2.** *not treading* ψυχὴ...ταῖς τῶν ἡδονῶν ἐκτόποις... οὐκ ἀ. id.*Is*.5.4(2.825A).

ἄστιπτος, v. ἄστειπτος.

ἀστοιχείωτος, *ignorant of the first elements*; of animals, *unbroken, untrained*, Cyr.*Os*.12(3.33C).

ἀστομάχητος, *without anger, good-tempered*, Herm.*vis*.1.2.3.

***ἀστοχάστως**, *aimlessly, without purpose*, *A.Andr.fr*.14(p.43.30).

ἀστοχ-έω, **1.** abs.; **a.** *miss the mark*, ref. 1Tim.1:6 καλῶς εἶπεν '∼ήσαντες', τεχνῆς γὰρ δεῖ, ὥστε εὐθέα βάλλειν καὶ μὴ ἔξω τοῦ σκοποῦ Chrys.*hom.2.1 in 1Tim*.(11.555F); θέλει γὰρ οὗτος ∼εῖν ὁ τοξότης Geo.Pis.*hex*.467(M.92.1472A); **b.** in gen., *fail* in attainment of an ideal οἱ τῶν 'Ελλήνων σοφοί, ἰδίᾳ δυνάμει τὴν θεοσέβειαν ζητήσαντες, ἠστόχησαν Meth.*fr.Job*(p.513.2 n.; M.18.405A); Cyr.*Ps*.100:3(M.69. 1261C); βλέπετε...πῶς τὴν ὁμολογίαν χειρογράφητε· μὴ ∼ήσητε ἵνα μὴ μεθοδευθῆτε *Rit.Bapt*.(p.439); hence *err* i.e. act unjustly παντὶ ∼οῦντι κατὰ τοῦ ἑτέρου μηδεὶς λαλείτω *Did*.15.3; ? *fail* to make harbour, *be lost*, of a ship, *T.Sal*.18.28(p.57.4; M.122.1345A) cf. 2.a; *fail* in business, Jo.Mosch.*prat*.193(M.87.3072C); of land ἦν γὰρ

~ήσασα ἡ χώρα διὰ τὴν λειψυδρίαν τοῦ Νείλου Leont.N.*v.Jo.Eleem*.30 (p.62.14); **2.** c. genit.; **a.** *fail to reach* or *achieve* τοῦ τῆς ἀληθείας ~ήσας λιμένος Clem.*paed*.2.2(p.173.20; M.8.424A); ἡ ζήτησις...τῆς καταλήψεως ἠστόχει Nil.ap.Proc.G.*Cant*.3:1(M.87.1617C); ‡Caes. Naz.*dial*.147(M.38.1097); τῆς...ἐλπίδος τοῦ θεοῦ ἀ. Areth.*Apoc*.6 (M.106.541C); hence *be lacking in* ὥστε θεῷ μὲν ἀνατιθέναι ὅσον ὀφείλεται, ἐπὶ δὲ τῶν ἄλλων ἑκάστου, τοῦ προσήκοντος μέτρου μὴ ~ῆσαι Gr.Nyss.*hom.4 in Cant*.(M.44.848B); τοῦ μείζονος κατορθώματος τῆς ταπεινώσεως ~εῖ Isid.Pel.*epp*.1.286(M.78.352A); Cyr. *Juln*.3(6^2.75B); **b.** *go astray, err* from ἀ. τῆς ἀληθείας Socr.*h.e*.1.9.28 (M.67.88B); *be in error* concerning μήτε τῆς περὶ θεὸν δόξης... ~ήσωμεν, μήτε τὴν ἡμετέραν φύσιν ἀγνοήσωμεν Iren.*haer*.5.2.3(M.7. 1127D); **c.** *fail to obtain, miss, lose* τῆς...εὐποιΐας αὐτῆς οὐκ ἠστόχησεν οὐδείς Pall.*h.Laus*.54(p.146.6); γυναικὸς ἀ. *A.Paul.et Thecl*.10(p.243. 2); Isid.Pel.*epp*.1.195(M.78.308C); **d.** *fail to keep, lose*; ships, Leont. N.*v.Jo.Eleem*.28(p.61.6); life πάντα δρῶσιν ὡς ἂν ταύτης μὴ ~ῆσαι Jo.D.*hom*.1.16(M.96.569B).

ἀστόχημα, τό, *error* of thought, of Quartodecimans περιέπεσον... ἀστοχήμασι καὶ αὐτοί Epiph.*haer*.50.1(p.245.3; M.41.884A); of act, i.e. *sin* τὸ ἐκείνων ἀ. ὅτι ἑκόντες ἐπιθύουσιν *M.Pion*.4.3.

ἀστοχία, ἡ, *loss* συνήδεσθαι μὲν...ταῖς εὐπορίαις αὐτῶν, συναθυμεῖν τε ταῖς ἀ. ‡Bas.*const*.20.2(2.565D; M.31.1392B); Leont.N.*v.Jo.Eleem*. 28(p.61.4).

***ἀστραγαλόω,** v.l. for στραγγαλόω.

ἀστραγαλωτός, *reaching to the ankle* or *wrist* τὸν χιτῶνα τὸν ἀ., ὁ μὲν Ἀκύλας καρπωτὸν ἡρμήνευσεν...οἱ νῦν δὲ αὐτὸν καλοῦσι πλουμαρικόν· ὁ δὲ Ἰώσηππος, τὸν μέχρις ἀστραγάλων διήκοντα Thdt.*qu.28 in 2 Reg*.(1.429).

***ἀστραπητόκος,** *producing lightnings*, Hesych.S.*temp*.2.69(M.93. 1533C).

ἀστραπηφόρος, *clothed with lightning, flashing*; of an angel, *A.Pil*.B 13.1(p.316).

***ἀστραπικός,** *wielding lightning* ἄγγελοι...ἀ. τινα ἔχοντες κατὰ τοῦ κόσμου...ἐξουσίαν Hipp.*haer*.5.26(MS reading; cj. σατραπικήν p.128.21; M.16.3198A).

***ἀστραποβροντοχαλαζορειθροδάμαστος,** *overcome by lightning, thunder, hail, and flood*, †Bas.*ep*.365(3.467A; M.32.1109A).

***ἀστραπόκαυστος,** *struck by lightning*, *Vaticin*.2(p.52).

ἀστράτευτος, *not having seen service*; fig., of those not yet baptized, Sever.*1Cor*.14:16(p.268.23).

ἀστρατήγητος, *without a general*, Socr.*h.e*.7.30.6(M.67.805C); Cyr.*Os*.proem.(3.4D); neut. as subst., Serap.*Man*.32(p.48).

***ἀστρογοητεία, ἡ,** *juggling with astrology* τὴν φιλοψευδῆ καὶ ἀργυροκάπηλον ἀ. Cyr.*hom.pasch*.14(5^2.195A); id.*ador*.6(1.193E); ἀστρογοητείαι...καὶ ψευδομαντείαι...πρέποιεν ἂν...τοῖς...προτεθυμένοις τὴν...εἰδωλολατρείαν εἰσοικίζεσθαι κατὰ νοῦν *ib*.(183B).

***ἀστρόδουλος, ὁ,** *slave of the stars*; of Chosroes, Geo.Pis.*Heracl*. 1.2(M.92.1297A).

ἀστροθεάμων, *concerned with observation of the stars* τέχνην Philost.*h.e*.8.9(M.65.564B); σοφίαν †Jo.D.*B.J*.3(M.96.877D).

ἀστροθεσία, ἡ, *arrangement of planets*, Tat.*orat*.8(p.8.5; M.6. 821A); *ib*.9(p.9.29; 825B); Clem.*exc.Thdot*.74(p.130.19; M.9.693A).

ἀστροθετέω, *number among the stars*, Tat.*orat*.9(p.10.18; M.6. 825C).

***ἀστροκίνητος,** *star-moved*; of Magi, Sophr.H.*ep.syn*.(M.87. 3176A).

***ἀστροκτονία, ἡ,** *star-slaughter, destruction of stars*, ‡Caes.Naz. *dial*.109(M.38.980).

ἀστροκύων, ὁ, *? vulture* τοῦτον [sc. νεανίσκον τεθνηκότα] ἀπέφερον ἐπὶ τοὺς ἀ. ... ἔθος δέ ἐστιν περὶ τοὺς Πέρσας τοὺς τελευτήσαντας βρωθῆναι Jo.Disc.*v.Epiph*.18(M.41.44C).

***ἀστρολάβιον, τό,** *astrolabe*; astronomical instrument for determining position of celestial bodies, v.l. ap.Synes.*astrolab*.tit.(p.132. 3; M.66.1577A).

ἀστρολογία, ἡ, *astrology* μήτε ἀ. μήτε ὀρνεοσκοπίαις...πρόσεχε Cyr.H.*catech*.4.37; *ib*.9.8; Bas.*hom*.12.6(2.102C; M.31.397B); ἀ. καὶ μαγείας Epiph.*haer*.3(p.177.7; M.41.185B); opp. ἀστρονομία, Clem. *prot*.6(p.51.22; M.8.172C); equated with ἀστρονομία, Chrys.*hom.6.1 in Mt*.(7.84B–85A).

ἀστρολόγος, ὁ, *astrologer* τὴν τῶν ἀ. τέχνην Hipp.*haer*.4.2(p.33. 18; M.16.3059C); Gr.Naz.*carm*.1.1.5.57,63(M.37.428A,429A); of Abraham, ‡Caes.Naz.*dial*.108(M.38.976); as subject of eccl. legislation ἀ., μάντις,...χρόνῳ [sc. δοκιμαζέσθωσαν] *Const.App*.8.32.11; οὐ δεῖ... κληρικοὺς...εἶναι ἢ μαθηματικοὺς ἢ ἀ. CLaod.*can*.36; power of prediction nullified by effects of baptism, Clem.*exc.Thdot*.78(p.131. 16; M.9.693D).

ἀστρομαντεία, ἡ, *divination by stars, astrology*, Cyr.*ador*.6(1. 186A).

ἄστρον, τό, 1. (usu. plur.) *the stars*; **a.** their arrangement symbolic of Christian economy, Thphl.Ant.*Autol*.2.15(M.6.1077B); a form of heavenly writing Max.*fr*.(*Catalogus Codicum Astrologorum* 7, F. Boll, Brussels 1908, p.100) cit. s. ἀστήρ; do not influence men's actions, Clem.*ecl*.55(p.152.18; M.9.724B); Gr.Nyss.*fat*.(M.45. 152B,C et passim); nor control affairs on earth, ref. Ps.72:8f. 'ἀδικίαν γε εἰς τὸ ὕψος' λαλοῦσι πάντες ὅσοι παρὰ τὴν τῶν ἄ. σχέσιν φασὶν εἶναι τὴν αἰτίαν πάντων τῶν ἐπὶ γῆς Or.*comm.in Mt*.13.6 (p.194.14; M.13.1108B); **b.** speculations as to their nature; beings of an order higher than man εἰ...τὰ...ἄ. ... εἰς διορισμὸν...χρόνου γεγονότα...θεῖά ἐστιν καὶ κρειττόνα τῶν ἀνθρώπων Meth.*symp*.8.15 (p.104.2ff.; M.18.168A); *ib*.8.16(p.104.15ff.; 168C); share in redemption by Christ ἄτοπον...αὐτὸν φάσκειν γεγεῦσθαι θανάτου οὐκ... ὑπὲρ ἄλλου τινὸς παρὰ τὸν ἄνθρωπον ἐν ἁμαρτήμασι γεγενημένον, οἷον ὑπὲρ ἄστρων Or.*Jo*.1.35(40; p.45.27; M.14.93B); Christian refusal to worship them defended, id.*Cels*.5.10(p.9.23ff.; M.11.1193Bf.); v. ἀστήρ; **2.** of the *sun*, Chrys.*hom.56.4 in Mt*.(7.571E); id.*hom. 4.3 in 1Tim*.(11.571A).

ἀστρονομία, ἡ, 1. *astronomy*; as scientific study of the stars, Just.*dial*.2.4(M.6.477B); *ib*.3.6(481C); τῶν ἱερῶν μαθημάτων γεωμετρίαν μὲν...καὶ ἀ. Gr.Thaum.*pan.Or*.8(p.22.18; M.10.1077C); opp. ἀστρολογία, Clem.*prot*.6(p.51.23; M.8.172C); Thdt.*affect*.1(p.9.26; 4.699) but cf. Clem.*prot*.6(p.53.14; M.8.176B); Thdt.*Jer*.10:2(2.463); corrupted by astrology διεβάλλετο...ἀσκεῖσθαι τῆς ἀ., ὃ μέρος ἀποτελεσματικὸν καλοῦσι Soz.*h.e*.3.6.5(M.67.1045C); **2.** identified with *astrology* Χαλδαίων ἀ. καὶ γενεθλιαλογία Gr.Naz.*or*.39.5(M.36. 340B); εἱμαρμένη καὶ ἀ. παρ' αὐτοῖς [sc. τοῖς Φαρισαίοις] σφόδρα ἐχρημάτιζεν Epiph.*haer*.15.2(p.211.13; M.41.249B); οὐ κατὰ ἀ. ἀλλὰ θεοσέβειαν ‡Caes.Naz.*dial*.108(M.38.976); ἡ πολυθρύλλητος ἀ., ἡ πολυάσχολος ματαιότης Bas.*hex*.1.3(1.4C; M.29.9C); as such condemned, Epiph.*exp.fid*.24(p.525.9; M.42.829D); ματαίᾳ ἀ. id.*mens*.15 (M.43.261C); ‡Caes.Naz.*dial*.108(M.38.977); its origin Ἐνὼχ φησιν τοὺς παραβάντας ἀγγέλους διδάξαι τοὺς ἀνθρώπους ἀ. Clem.*ecl*.53 (p.152.9; M.9.724A).

ἀστρονόμος, ὁ, 1. *astronomer*; of Abraham, ‡Caes.Naz.*dial*.108 (M.38.976); **2.** *astrologer*, Bardesanes ap.Eus.*p.e*.6.10(278C; M.21. 473B); *Dial.Tim.et Aquil*.118 v°.

***ἀστροπολεύω,** *concern oneself with the stars*, Gr.Naz.*carm*.1.1.5. 59(M.37.428A).

***ἀστροπόλος, ὁ,** *astrologer*, Ant.Mon.*hom*.84(M.89.1688C).

***ἀστροτέκτων, ὁ,** *maker of the stars*; of God, ‡Caes.Naz.*dial*.108 (M.38.977).

***ἀστροτύπως,** *in starry wise* τὸ τοῦ σταυροῦ σημεῖον μεσούσης ἡμέρας...γράμμασιν ἀ. ῥωμαϊκοῖς διασημήνας αὐτοῦ τὴν...νίκην ‡Jo.D. *Artem*.45(M.96.1293B).

***ἀστροφόρητος,** *star-bearing*, Synes.*hymn*.2.15(p.43; M.66.1592).

ἀστυκός, = ἀστικός, *of the city*; as subst., *citizen* opp. ξένος, Const.Diac.*laud*.5(M.88.485A).

***ἀστυμέριμνος,** *caring for the city*, Synes.*hymn*.3.59(p.8; M.66. 1594).

***ἀστυπόλος, ὁ,** *citizen*, Synes.*regn*.24(p.53.14; M.66.1100D).

ἀσυγγενής, *not comformable to one's nature, unnatural*; of vice, †Nil.*vit*.2(M.79.1141C).

ἀσύγγνωστος (ἀσύγνωστος), 1. *not pardoning*; **a.** of persons, *relentless, merciless* ἀ. δικασταί Chrys.*sac*.3.18(p.93.4; 1.400A); id. *Petr.et El*.1(2.732B); ἀ. ... καὶ πικροὶ τοῖς ἀδικοῦσιν Isid.Pel.*epp*.2. 133(M.78.576A); neut. as subst., *mercilessness*, ‡Just.*qu.et resp*.104 (M.6.1349C); **b.** of things, *unrelenting, inexorable*; *inevitable* ἀ. καὶ ὧδε καὶ μετὰ ταῦτα τὴν τιμωρίαν...ὑπομείνωσιν Ath.*ep.Serap*.1.33 (M.26.608B); κίνδυνος ἀ. ἐν ἡμέρᾳ κρίσεως Ath.*gent*.47(M.25.96C); φεύγων ὡς ἀ. τῆς ἀπειθείας τὸν κίνδυνον Max.*ambig*.(M.91.1033B); freq. of eternal punishment τὴν...ἀ. ὑποίσονται καταδίκην Ath.*Ar*. 3.55(M.26.440B); Chrys.*virg*.21(1.283E); spelt ἀσύγνωστος Procl.CP *or*.6.6(M.65.732A); **2.** *unpardonable*; **a.** of persons, Chrys.*hom.4.1 in Rom*.(9.454E); *ib*.17.3(625B); ὅσῳ...ἀσθενέστερος ὁ ἀνταγωνιστής, τοσούτῳ ἀ. μᾶλλον αἱ νικηθεῖσαι id.*hom.78.1 in Mt*.(7.751D); Proc.G. *Is*.43:28(M.87.2400A); comp., Chrys.*hom.44.3 in Mt*.(7.472B); **b.** of things, *inexcusable*, Tit.Bost.*Man*.1.18(M.18.1092D); πονηρὰ...ἡ πρᾶξις...ἀ. ἡ ἐπιχείρησις Chrys.*hom.64.5 in Gen*.(4.615E); ἀ. ... Ἰουδαίων κατάγνωσις ἡ τῶν ἐθνῶν ἐπίγνωσις Bas.Sel.*or*.20.1(M.85. 245D); of sin against H. Ghost, Isid.Pel.*epp*.1.59(M.78.221A); comp. ἐν...τοῖς τοιούτοις τάχα τὸ μετριάζειν τοῦ χαλεπαίνειν ἐστὶν ἀσυγγνωστότερον Gr.Nyss.*ep*.29.6(M.45.240A); neut. as subst. διελέγχων αὐτῶν τὸ ἀ. Chrys.*hom.67.3 in Mt*.(7.665C); τοὺς τὰ ἀ. ἁμαρτάνοντας id.*hom.14.9 in Rom.*(9.589C); εἰ ἀ. καὶ πρὸς θάνατον ἡμαρτήκαμεν Jo.Jej.*poenit.cont.virg.*(M.88.1953D); Jo.D.*spir.neq.*(M.95.92A).

ἀσυγγνώστως, *inexorably; relentlessly*, Thdr.Heracl.*Is.*30:18(M.18.1321D); Chrys.*hom.72.1 in Mt.*(7.702C).

***ἀσυγκαλύπτως**, *openly, unreservedly*, Nil.*epp.*1.70(M.79.113A).

ἀσυγκέραστος, met., *not forming close friendships, aloof* or *unsociable* ἐν Λέοντι τύπος...φύσεως· ἰδίας ἀποφάσεως, ἀ., ἀρέσκοντες ἑαυτοῖς Hipp.*haer.*4.19(p.51.15; M.16.3086B).

***ἀσυγκοινώνητος**, *incommunicable*; of divine essence, Epiph.*haer.*77.34(p.446.23; M.42.692C).

***ἀσυγκρασία, ἡ**, *unwillingness to share; exclusiveness*, Herm.*vis.*3.9.4.

ἀσύγκριτος, *incomparable*;

A. in gen.; **1.** *not comparable* τῷ μεγάλῳ δούλῳ πρὸς τοὺς συνδούλους ἡ σύγκρισις· τῷ υἱῷ δὲ πρὸς οἰκέτας, ἀ. ἡ ὑπεροχή Cyr.H.*catech.*3.6; Chrys.*hom.37.2 in Mt.*(7.417A); Leont.H.*Nest.*1.19(M.86.1477A); **2.** *beyond compare, unparalleled*, i.e. surpassing; def. ὁ...ἀ., πρὸς πάντα κατὰ πάντα ὑπερέχων [sc. λέγεται] Didym.(‡Bas.)*Eun.*4(1.294C; M.29.705C); ἡ πρᾶξίς σου ἀ. ἔσται Herm.*mand.*7.1; ἀ. ... ὁ δεσποτικὸς τόκος Gr.Nyss.*fr.*4(M.46.1112B); (ref. Mal.1:11) νοητῆς θυσίας τὴν ἀ. εὐωδίαν Cyr.*ador.*2(1.57D) etc.; of persons ἀσπάζομαι...Δάφνον τὸν ἀ. Ign.*Smyrn.*13.2; *Hom.Clem.*2.43; Ant.Mon.*hom.*37(M.89.1549C); freq. with ὑπεροχή and διαφορά, *immeasurable*, Isid.Pel.*epp.*2.89(M.78.532D); of emperor ἀ. διαφοραῖς τῶν ἄλλων ἁπάντων ἀνεστηκώς Cyr.*Thds.*(p.42.13; 5².1A); id.*Jo.*1.7(4.60A); **3.** *unparalleled*, i.e. unheard-of, ref. Ps.109:1 ὅτι...ἑαυτὸν κύριον προσηγόρευσεν, ἀβέβαιον καὶ ἀνίσχυρον, καὶ ἀ. οὐ γὰρ τοιαύτην συνήθειαν εὕρομεν πώποτε †Gregent.*disp.*(M.86.652D); **4.** in bad sense, *incomparable, unequalled* τῇ...ἀ. ἁμαρτίᾳ *Hom.Clem.*11.12; ἀ. τινα νοσοῦντες ἀβουλίαν Cyr.*glaph Ex.*2(1.273E); id.*Jo.*3.6(4.322A).

B. theol.; both senses A.1 and A.2 are found, sometimes combined; cf. ἀπαράβλητος; *incomparable*; **1.** abs. of God τὸ μὲν ἀ. οὐδέν ἐστιν ἕτερον ἢ αὐτὸ τὸ ὄν Tat.*orat.*15(p.16.18; M.6.837B); *Hom.Clem.*2.45; θεὸς...ἀ. ἐστι πρᾶγμα Ath.*Ar.*1.57(M.26.132A); *Lit.*ap.*Const.App.*8.5.1; τὸν πατέρα υἱὸν ἔχοντα ἀληθινῶς...οὐ τὸ ἀ. ἀφανίζοντα Epiph.*haer.*76.35(p.385.21; M.42.588D); in Eunomius of Father opp. Son εἷς ὁ...θεὸς ἀγέννητος καὶ ἀ. Eun.*apol.*11(M.30.848A); *ib.*26(864A); ἀ. ... τὸν θεὸν λέγει, ἵνα δείξῃ υἱὸν ἴσον ὄντα τῇ κτίσει Bas.*Eun.*1.27(1.237C; M.29.569C); Aët.*synt.*ap.Epiph.*haer.*76.12(p.358.6; M.42.541D) cit. s. αὐτοουσία; τὸ ἐν οὐσίᾳ ἀ. ‡Ath.*dial.Trin.*2.13(M.28.1177B); δογματίσαι...ἀ. εἶναι τὸν πατέρα Isid.Pel.*epp.*3.334(M.78.992A); in orth. doctrine, of Father and Son alike τοῖς ἀμεγέθεσι καὶ ἀ. Gr.Nyss.*Eun.*1(1 p.107.14; M.45.341A); Ἡσαΐας...ἀ. αὐτόν, ὡς τὸν θεὸν πατέρα...βοᾷ Didym.*Trin.*1.27(M.39.397A); ref. Bar.3:36 πῶς...ἂν ἄλλος εἴη ἀ. πρὸς τὸν υἱόν; *ib.*(400A); εἰ ἀ. ὁ πατὴρ κατὰ πάντα πρὸς τὸν υἱόν...οὐκ ἄλλως πρὸς τὸν υἱόν, ἑτέρως δὲ πρὸς τὴν κτίσιν, ἀλλ' ὁμοίως id.(‡Bas.)*Eun.*4(1.280D; M.29.676A); [sc. θεόν] ἀ. ... διὸ ἀ. μονογενῆ υἱὸν ἀσυγκρίτως γεννήσας Epiph.*haer.*76.37(p.388.31; M.42.593C); Chrys.*hom.4.2 in Jo.*(8.29C); *ib.*5.2(38A); of H. Ghost τὴν ἀ. δόξαν τοῦ θεοῦ πατρός Didym.*Trin.*2.8(M.39.608A); *ib.*2.1(452C); τῆς ἀ. οὐσίας πατρός, καὶ υἱοῦ, καὶ ἁγίου πνεύματος Epiph.*haer.*76.39(p.394.5; M.42.604A); **2.** of God opp. creation ὁ...τὸν ἥλιον κατασκευάσας, αὐτὸς πρότερον ὀφείλει πολλῷ μᾶλλον ἀ. εἶναι Cyr.H.*catech.*4.5; Cyr.*Ps.*9:22(M.69.777C); id.*inc.unigen.*(5¹.683C); Zach.Mit.*opif.*(M.85.1108B) cf. ἀ. πάντα...πρὸς τὴν...τοῦ θεοῦ οὐσίαν Gel.Cyz.*h.e.*2.22.11(M.85.1292D); **3.** opp. angels ἀ. ... πρᾶγμα θεότητος καὶ ἀπαράβλητον Cyr.*thes.*20(5¹.205C); **4.** opp. man συγκρίνεις τὰ ἀ., θεὸν καὶ ἄνθρωπον Gr.Naz.*or.*20.8(M.35.1073C); οὐ...χρὴ τὸν ἀ. θεὸν τῇ ἡμετέρᾳ συγκρίνειν φύσει Epiph.*haer.*76.37(p.388.28; M.42.593C); Thdt.*Trin.*7(M.75.1156C); **5.** of Logos πολλῷ πλέον μείζονι φαντασίᾳ καὶ ἀ. ὑπεροχῇ τοῦ λόγου τὴν δύναμιν Ath.*gent.*45(M.25.89A); of body of Christ τὸ σῶμα τοῦ...υἱοῦ...ὑπερέχει κριῶν καὶ ταύρων· οὐκ ἐκ συγκρίσεως, ἀ. γὰρ ἡ ὑπεροχή †Bas.*bapt.*2.2(2.653E; M.31.1584A); of Christ opp. Jo. Bapt., Chrys.*hom.6 in Jo.*(8.43E); Cyr.*thes.*11(5¹.96C); **6.** of various divine attributes: ἰσχύς Thphl.Ant.*Autol.*1.3(M.6.1028C); δύναμις Ath.*inc.*45.3(M.25.177A); ἡμερότης Cyr.*Jon.*29(3.388E); of grace χάριν...ἀ. τὴν τοῦ ἁγίου πνεύματος μετουσίαν Nil.*epp.*2.314(M.79.353C).

ἀσυγκρίτως, **1.** with comparative expressed or implied, *incomparably* ἀ. ἀμείνους Or.*Cant.*1:7(p.145.27; M.17.257B); Chrys.*hom.4.2 in Jo.*(8.29C); ἐνδοξοτέραν ἀ. τῶν σεραφίμ *Lit.Chrys.*(p.449.26) cit.ap.Mod.*dorm.*4(M.86.3289A); **2.** elliptically, *much more, greatly, more excellently* ἅγιον αὐτοῖς τὸν ἐπιστάτην ἄγγελον ὑπισχνεῖται θεός, ἀλλ' ἀ. Cyr.*Juln.*4(6².149D); ‡Proc.G.*Pr.*25:3(M.87.1472D); hence **3.** *absolutely, without any reference to* ὁ κύριος...πρωτότοκος ἀ. ἐστι πρὸς τοὺς ἰδίους τῶν ἀνθρώπων Gr.Nyss.*fr.*4(M.46.1112D); Epiph.*haer.*76.46(p.400.2; M.42.613B); *ib.*76.37(p.388.32; 593C) cit. s. ἀσύγκριτος; Leont.H.*Nest.*1.19(M.86.1476D).

[*]**ἀσύγνωστος**, v. ἀσύγγνωστος.

***ἀσυγχυτικός**, *not to be confused*, v.l. for συγχυτικός Jo.Jej.*canonar.*1(*SS* 4 p.437).

ἀσύγχυτος, *without fusion; unconfused; distinct*;

A. in gen.; **1.** of physical objects: different luminaries ἓν φῶς τὰ πάντα κατὰ τὸν γενικὸν ὀνομάζεσθαι λόγον, ἀ. δὲ καὶ διῃρημένην τὴν ἐν τούτοις διαφορὰν θεωρεῖν Gr.Nyss.*hex.*65(M.44.116A); iron in the fire ἐν σώμασίν ἐστιν εὑρεῖν ἀ. κρᾶσιν Thdt.*eran.*2(4.116); wine and water blended οὐδὲ πάντως τὸ ἐκ δύο τινῶν συνενηνεγμένον ἀσύγχυτα ἐφύλαξεν τὰ ἐξ ὧν Eust.Mon.*ep.*(M.86.913A); a peacock's colours τὰς πολυμόρφους συνθέσεις τῶν χρωμάτων, ὅλας ἀ. τε καὶ μεμιγμένας Geo.Pis.*hex.*1249(M.92.1529A); **2.** of intellectual operations πρὸς τὸ ἀ. ἡμῖν γίνεσθαι τῶν σεσημειωμένων τὴν γνῶσιν Gr.Nyss.*tres dii*(M.45.121B); ἔσται...ἀ. καὶ σαφὴς...ἡ θεωρία Cyr.*Mich.*44(3.433C); id.*Zeph.*40(3.617E); of expression, id.*Os.*proem.(3.2D); of human personality ἐν τῷ...ἰδιάζοντι βίῳ τῆς ζωῆς κατορθοῦται, ὡς ἀνεπίμικτον καὶ ἀ. εἶναι τὴν φύσιν Gr.Nyss.*ep.*2(M.46.1012A); of relation between thing known and the knower καθάπερ τὰ συνεφθαρμένα, καὶ ἑνούμενα μένειν ἀ. καὶ ἀδιάφθορα, ὡς τὰ παρακείμενα Nemes.*nat.hom.*3(M.40.593B); cf.*ib.*(597A); of relation between created things αἱ πάντων...κοινωνίαι...καὶ ἀ. φιλίαι, καὶ ἁρμονίαι τοῦ παντός Dion.Ar.*d.n.*4.7(M.3.704C); *ib.*8.5(892C,D); *ib.*11.2(949C); of relation between soul and body in man ἡ ψυχή, ἑνουμένη τῷ σώματι, μένει παντελῶς ἀ. Nemes.*nat.hom.*3(597B); *ib.*(596B); ψυχῇ μὲν καὶ σώματι δίδως ἀ. ἕνωσιν Thdt.*eran.*2(4.109); πῶς ἑνοῦται σώματι [sc. ἡ ψυχή]...σώζουσα τὴν ἰδίαν οὐσίαν ἀ. καὶ ἀδιάφθορον; Melet.*nat.hom.*31(M.64.1296C); of eccl. hierarchy ἐν τάξει δὴ οὖν τῇ ἀ. τὰ ἱερά Cyr.*ador.*13(1.462D); of angelic hierarchy αὐταῖς αἱ ὑπερκόσμιαι τάξεις, αἱ πρὸς ἑαυτὰς ἑνώσεις...αἱ ἀ. διακρίσεις Dion.Ar.*d.n.*4.2(M.3.696A); τῆς ἀ. τῶν ἀγγελικῶν διακόσμων ταξιαρχίας id.*c.h.*11.2(M.3.285A).

B. Trin.; **1.** in human thought ἀμήχανον...μὴ ἐν τοῖς ἑκάστου ἰδιώμασι τὴν διάνοιαν γενομένην ἀ., δυνηθῆναι πατρὶ καὶ υἱῷ καὶ ἁγίῳ πνεύματι τὴν δοξολογίαν ἀποπληρῶσαι Bas.*ep.*210.4(3.316A; M.32.773C); τὴν τρανὴν καὶ ἀ. πατρὸς καὶ υἱοῦ...ἔννοιαν id.*Eun.*2.28(1.265B; M.29.637B); **2.** in essence, ref. 1Cor.8:6 τοῦ ἐξ οὗ καὶ δι' οὗ, καὶ ἐν ᾧ μὴ φύσεις τεμνόντων...ἀλλὰ χαρακτηριζόντων μιᾶς καὶ ἀ. φύσεως ἰδιότητας Gr.Naz.*or.*39.12(M.36.348A); *ib.*31.9(p.156.4; 144A); Amph.*Seleuc.*213(M.37.1591A); πατήρ, καὶ υἱός, καὶ ἅγιον πνεῦμα...ἐν ἀ. καὶ διακεκριμένῃ τῇ ἁγίᾳ τριάδι μίαν εἶναι τὴν φύσιν Gr.Nyss.*ep.*3(M.46.1017C); ὦ πάτερ καὶ λόγε καὶ πνεῦμα, ἡ τριυπόστατος οὐσία...ἡμᾶς τοὺς ὁμολογοῦντάς σου τὰς ἀ. καὶ ἀδιαιρέτους ὑποστάσεις ‡Chrys.*hom.*11(13.247C); τριάδα...ταῖς ἀ. τρισὶν ὑποστάσεσι Sophr.H.*ep.syn.*(M.87.3153D); Max.*myst.*23(M.91.700D) cit. s. ἀσυγχύτως; ἀ. ἔχουσαι τὴν ἐν ἀλλήλαις περιχώρησιν Jo.D.*f.o.*1.14(M.94.860B); ἡ ἁγία τριὰς...ἀ. ἀδιαίρετος Jo.V H.*icon.*4(M.96.1352C).

C. Christol.; **1.** pre-CChalc.; **a.** in human thought διαμένει...ἀ. τῶν τε τῆς σαρκὸς καὶ τῶν τῆς θεότητος ἰδιωμάτων ἡ θεωρία Gr.Nyss.*Eun.*5(2 p.123.23; M.45.705B); **b.** of Logos in womb of BMV ἀ. καὶ ἀθόλωτος ἐν τῇ τοσαύτῃ τῶν σαρκῶν κοινωνίᾳ διαμείνας Eus.*d.e.*10.8(p.481.34; M.22.776A); **c.** of union of natures τῇ ἀ. φυσικῇ ἑνώσει τοῦ λόγου ‡Ath.*Apoll.*1.10(M.26.1109B); Χριστὸς δύο ὑπάρχων φύσεις ...μοναδικὸν πρόσωπον, ἀ. ὅμως Gr.Nyss.ap.Leont.H.*monoph.*(M.86.1828B); ref. Jo.2:19 ἀποσώζων...τῶν δύο φύσεων τῶν ἑτεροουσίων ἀ. τὴν ἰδιότητα Amph.*fr.*9(M.39.105B); τοὺς δὲ...μὴ ὁμολογοῦντας...Χριστὸν δύο εἶναι οὐσίας ἀ., ἕν τε πρόσωπον...ἀναθεματίζει ἡ...ἐκκλησία Ambr.ap.Jo.D.*Jacob.*(M.94.1496A); ἀ. ... καὶ τροπῆς ἐλευθέρα πάντως ἡ ἕνωσις Cyr.*apol.Thdt.*11(p.144.12; 6¹.238D); id.*ep.*50(p.91.24; 5².159E); Procl.CP *or.laud.BMV* 8(p.107.4; M.65.689B); **2.** post-CChalc.; **a.** of Inc. ἀ. καθ' ἡμᾶς ἐνανθρωπήσει Dion.Ar.*e.h.*3.3.13(M.3.444C); **b.** of natures after union εἴσω τῆς καθ' ἡμᾶς ἐγεγόνει φύσεως...ἀμετάβολον καὶ ἀ. τῶν οἰκείων ἱδρύσεως id.*d.n.*1.4(M.3.592B); id.*e.h.*3.3.11(M.3.441B); εἰ λέγετε ἀ. τὰ ἑνωθέντα...ἐξ ἀνάγκης δύο φύσεις εἰσάγετε †Leont.B.*sect.*7.5(M.86.1245A) al.; οἶδεν [sc. Κύριλλος]...καὶ τὴν τῶν φύσεων διαφορὰν καὶ τὸ ἀ. αὐτὰς ἀλλήλαις ἐν μιᾷ ὑποστάσει φυλάττεσθαι Justn.*conf.*(p.80.13; M.86.1003A); *ib.*(p.78.24; 1001B); μὴ διέλητε τὴν ἀνθρωπότητα αὐτοῦ ἀπὸ τῆς θεότητος αὐτοῦ· ἀδιαίρετος γὰρ αὕτη καὶ ἀ. μετὰ τὴν ἕνωσιν Gr.Ant.*bapt.*2.6(M.88.1877A); ἀ. ... μεμενηκέναι...καὶ μετὰ τὸ ἑνωθῆναι· τοῦ ἀ. αὐτὰς [sc. δύο φύσεις ἀνομοίους] μεμενηκέναι λέγειν, οὐ διαίρεσιν τὴν οἱανοῦν παρεισάγοντος...ἀλλὰ τὴν διαφορὰν ἄτρεπτον μένειν σημαίνοντος Max.*ep.*12(M.91.469A); *ib.*15(553C); ἡ ἐκκλησία...τὴν κατ' οὐσίαν διαφορὰν διὰ τὸ ἀ. πρεσβεύει id.*opusc.*(M.91.145B); τῶν δὲ φύσεων ἐχουσῶν τὸ ἀ., καὶ τὰ προσόντα ταύταις ἀ. τὰς θελήσεις καὶ τὰς ἐνεργείας φημί ‡Cyr.*Trin.*18(6^3.24D; M.77.1157B); τὰ ἐξ ὧν ἡ ἕνωσις γέγονε...καὶ ἀ. μετὰ τὴν αὐτῶν φυσικὴν καὶ καθ' ὑπόστασιν ἕνωσιν μένοντα Cyrus Al. *cap.*7(H.3.1341D); Χριστὸν...ἐν δυσὶν ἀδιαιρέτοις καὶ ἀ. ταῖς φύσεσι γνωριζόμενον Jo.D.*hom.*1.1(M.96.545B); ἡ...θεότης ἀδιαίρετος καὶ ἀ. καὶ τῇ ψυχῇ ἡνωμένη ἦν τῷ σώματι Jo.V H.*icon.*9(M.96.1356D); **c.** of the union, usu. ἕνωσις: ἀδιαίρετον...λόγου καὶ σαρκὸς δοξάζομεν ἕνωσιν, ἀδιαίρετον ὑπὲρ ἕνωσιν ψυχῆς καὶ σώματος, πυρὸς καὶ σιδήρου, πορφύρας βαφῆς καὶ βύσσου· ἀλλὰ καὶ ἀ. Eulog.*fr.Trin.*4.8(p.371); Thal.*cent.*2.97(M.91.1448A); Andr.Cr.*Apoc.*6(M.106.540B); Jo.V H. *icon.*7(M.96.1356A); also σύνοδος: τῶν φύσεων...τὴν σύνοδον ἴστε, καὶ σὺν ἡμῖν τὸ ἀ. ὁμολογεῖτε τῶν συνελθόντων Leont.H.*monoph.*25(M. 86.1785B); ref. Is.7:11 σημεῖον ἐκ βάθους καὶ ἐξ ὕψους κατὰ σύνοδον ἀ. καὶ ἀδιαίρετον ‡Meth.*Sym.et Ann.*11(M.18.376C); of περιχώρησις (expressing substantial union of Word with humanity): ὁ θεὸς λόγος...ἀμεταβλήτως τὴν σάρκα ἐθέωσε διὰ...τῆς αὐτοῦ σαρκὸς ἀ. παραχωρήσεως [l. περιχωρήσεως] Jo.D.*imag.*1.21(M.94.1253B); **3.** of two natures in union κατ' εὐδοκίαν, Thdr.Mops.*ep.Domn.*(p.339.3; M.66.1013A) cit. s. ἕνωσις; in Nestorius' teaching ἀ. τὴν τῶν φύσεων τηρῶμεν συνάφειαν Nest.*fr.*C 8 ap.Cyr.*Nest.*2.14(p.52.27; 6.60C); *ib.* C 9(p.224.5)ap.CLater.*act.*5(H.3.896C) cit. s. συνάπτω; εἰ...αἱ φύσεις μένουσιν ἀ., μένει δὲ καὶ ἡ ἕνωσις, φαμὲν δὲ τὰ τῆς προσκυνήσεως καὶ δυνάμεως καὶ ἀξίας καὶ αὐθεντίας, ὡς ἑνὶ υἱῷ προσφέρεσθαι ἄξιον, μενουσῶν τῶν φύσεων ἐν τῇ ἑνώσει ἀ. Episc.orient.ap.Cyr.*apol.orient.* 11(6.191B); **4.** ref. monophysite doctrine τὸ λέγειν...τὴν...θεότητα ...μὴ δυνηθῆναι...τὴν οἰκείαν φύσιν ἀ. διασῶσαι Thdt.*eran.*2(4.109); of monophysite *compositio* ἡ σύνθεσις ἡ ἀ. Leont.H.*monoph.*7(M.86. 1773B); συνταράσσων [sc. Severus] τὰς ἀ. φύσεις Geo.Pis.*Sev.*274(M. 92.1643A); Σεύηρος...οὔτε τὴν ἕνωσιν οἶδεν ἀ. κἂν προσποιεῖται λέγειν Max.*ep.*15(M.91.568C).

ἀσυγχύτως, *without confusion*; *while remaining distinct*; **1.** lit. ἑνοῦται τῷ ἀέρι τὸ φῶς, ἀ. ἅμα καὶ κεχυμένως Nemes.*nat.hom.*3(M.40. 597B); **2.** of mental operations, *without confusion, distinctly* ἔργον... τῆς φωνῆς σαφηνίζειν τὸ σημαινόμενον, ὅπως ἀ. ἐπιβάλλειν δυνηθῶσιν τῷ δηλουμένῳ λόγῳ Or.*fr.17 in Jo.*(p.497.5); Gr.Nyss.*infant.*(M.46. 164B); **3.** *without confusion*; i.e. *without losing one's identity*; of relation between soul and body, Nemes.*nat.hom.*3(M.40.596A); †Leont.B.*sect.*7.5(M.86.1245A); of relation between created things ἡ μία...πάντων συμπλοκὴ...ἐναρμόζεται...ἀ. Dion.Ar.*d.n.*11.2(M.3. 949D); **4.** *without confusion*, i.e. *in due order*, of individual virtues ὧν οὐκ οὐσῶν ἐν ἡμῖν ἀ. ... πᾶσά πως ἀνάγκη ταράττεσθαι τὴν ψυχήν Cyr.*Ps.*6:3(M.69.744C); of angels τὰς θεαρχικὰς ἐνεργείας...ἀ. ἑστηκυίας Dion.Ar.*e.h.*5.1.7(M.3.509A); **5.** theol., *without confusion* or *mixture*; Trin., Amph.*Seleuc.*210(M.37.1591A); ἀδιαστάτως τε μεριζόμενον καὶ ἀ. ἑνούμενον Gr.Nyss.*Eun.*2(2 p.298.30; M.45.469B); ‡Cyr. *Trin.*7(6^3.8D; M.77.1132C) // Jo.D.*f.o.*1.8(M.94.809A); Dion.Ar.*d.n.* 2.5(M.3.641D); μονάδα καὶ τριάδα ἀσύγχυτόν τε καὶ ἀ. τὴν ἕνωσιν ἔχουσαν Max.*myst.*23(M.91.700D); **6.** Christol.; **a.** pre-CChalc. ἕνα υἱόν, δύο φύσεών φημι, ἀ., ἀτρέπτως, ἀδιαιρέτως Amph.*fr.*15(Holl p.55; M.39.113B), so Holl pp.248ff. but acc. Cavallera, *Revue d'histoire eccl.*8(Louvain 1907)p.490, post-CChalc.; of Word οὐκ ἀποθέμενος ὃ ἦν ἐγένετο ἀ. καὶ ὃ οὐκ ἦν Didym.*Trin.*3.13(M.39.861A); διὰ φιλανθρωπίαν γέγονεν ἀ. ὅπερ ἐσμέν...μείνας εἷς καὶ ὁ αὐτός *ib.*3.20(896A); Χριστὸς Ἰησοῦς...νοεῖται λόγος...ὅτε...ἀ. ἐνεπλάκη σαρκί Cyr.*Thds.* 36(p.66.4; 5^2.32E); γέγονεν ἄνθρωπος ἀτρέπτως καὶ ἀ. id.*hom.div.*5 (p.93.19; 5^2.360B); πρὸς ἕνωσιν ἀ. ἀναβαινούσης αὐτῆς [sc. τῆς σαρκός] πρὸς τὸν θεὸν λόγον id.*Jo.*11.12(4.1001D); ἴδιον ἐποιήσατο τὸ ἑνωθὲν αὐτῷ σῶμα ἀφράστως, ἀπερινοήτως, ἀτρέπτως τε καὶ ἀ. id.*apol.orient.* 11(p.60.29; 6^1.194D); *ib.*(p.58.33; 192C); δύο φύσεις συνῆλθον ἀλλήλαις ...ἀ. καὶ ἀδιαιρέτως id.*Lc.*2:4(M.72.484C); **b.** CChalc., *Symb.Chalc.* (p.129.31; H.2.456C) cit. s. φύσις; cited: Evagr.*h.e.*2.4(p.49.31; M. 86.2508D); CLater.*act.*4(H.3.848D); cf. ἔστιν εἷς καὶ ὁ αὐτὸς ἐν ἑκατέραις ταῖς φύσεσιν ἀ. καὶ ἀδιαιρέτως γνωριζόμενος Justn.*Or.* (p.195.3; M.86.957B); **c.** post-CChalc., most commonly with ἑνοῦμαι, ἕνωσις, εἷς etc. εἷς ἐξ ἀμφοῖν ὁ Χριστός, ἀτρέπτως καὶ ἀ. Ammon. *Jo.*3:8(M.85.1409B); μιᾶς ὑποστάσεως κηρύττομεν τὸν Χριστόν, ἐκ δύο φύσεων ἡνωμένων ἀλλήλαις ἀ. ‡Cyr.*Trin.*18(6^3.24D; M.77.1157B); φύσεις...ἑνοῦσθαι ἀ. ἀλλήλαις δύνανται ἐν ὑποστάσει τινὶ μὴ ἀναιρούμεναι ὑπ' ἀλλήλων τοὺς οἰκείους λόγους Leont.H.*Nest.*2.7(M.86.1552A); id.*monoph.*8(M.86.1773B); λόγος τοῦ θεοῦ...ἡνώθη τῷ ἀνθρωπίνῳ σώματι ἀ., ἀληθινῶς, ἀδιαιρέτως †Leont.B.*sect.*1.3(M.86.1197B); ἑκατέρας οὐσίας καὶ φύσεως ἐξ ὧν ἡμῖν ἀ. ἐπὶ Χριστοῦ γέγονεν ἡ ἕνωσις Sophr.H.*ep.syn.*(M.87.3172B); with various words ἀναλλοιώτως ἡμῖν καὶ ἀ. κεκοινώνηκε Dion.Ar.*d.n.*2.10(M.3.649A); τῶν ἀ. συνελθουσῶν φύσεων εἰς μίαν ὑπόστασιν Justn.*conf.*(p.84.10; M.86. 1007B); τῆς...διαφορᾶς τῶν ἐξ ὧν ἐστι φύσεων ὁ Χριστὸς ἀ. σωζομένης καὶ μετὰ τὴν ἕνωσιν Max.*ep.*18(M.91.585D); [sc. τῶν φύσεων] εἰς μίαν ὑπόστασιν σύνθετον συνδραμουσῶν ἀ. καὶ ἀδιαιρέτως Jo.D. *Jacob.*79(M.94.1476D); **d.** of union of wills ἐν αὐτῷ...δύο φυσικὰς ἐνεργείας ἀδιαιρέτως, ἀτρέπτως, ἀμερίστως, ἀ. ... κηρύττομεν *Symb. CP*(681)(H.3.1400C); **e.** monophysite and monothelite φήσαντος... οὐ συνομολογεῖν ἰδιότητα τῶν φύσεων ἐξ ὧν ἀ. ἐστὶν ὁ Χριστός, καὶ πάλιν εἰς μίαν οὐσίαν...τὸ πᾶν...συγχέοντος Sev.Ant.ap.Eust.Mon.*ep.* (M.86.908D); ὡς εἶναι οὖν τὸν Ἐμμανουὴλ ἐκ θεότητός τε καὶ ἀνθρωπότητος τελείως ἐχουσῶν ἑκάστῃ τῶν φύσεων κατὰ τὸν οἰκεῖον λόγον, ἀ., ἀτρέπτως, ἀναλλοιώτως, ἀφαντασιάστως. μετὰ δὲ τὴν ἄφραστον ἕνωσιν πεπείσμεθα ἓν πρόσωπον καὶ μίαν ὑπόστασιν καὶ μίαν ἐνέργειαν Oecum.*Apoc.*22:16(p.255); εἰ...προσθῇς ὡς ἀ. λέγεις, φράγμον τε βάλλειν ἀξιοῖς τῇ συνθέσει Geo.Pis.*Sev.*298(M.92.1643B).

ἀσυγχώρητος, **1.** *not authorized* or *allowed, forbidden* ἀ. μοί ἐστιν ἐξηγήσασθαι τὰ γεγονότα *A.Thom.*A 71(p.187.12); neut. as subst., of a breach of canon law διορθώσασθαι τὸ ἀ. *Cod.Afr.*48; **2.** *without forgiveness, without pardon*; **a.** act., *inexorable*; of wrath, Gr.Naz. *or.*41.14(M.36.448D); of judgement, Gr.Nyss.*Maced.*20(M.45.1325D); †Cyr.*hom.div.*14(5^2.411D); **b.** pass., *unforgivable* μὴ διὰ τῆς ἀνθρωπίνης ἀνταποδόσεως ἀ. ποιεῖν τὰ ἑαυτῶν κακά Marc.Er.*opusc.*7.2(M. 65.1073A); φεύγωμεν τὸ πονηρὸν τοῦτο καὶ ἀ. ἁμάρτημα [sc. μνησικακίαν] Anast.S.*synax.*(M.89.844C); freq. of sin against H. Ghost, Bas.*Spir.*70(3.59E; M.32.200A); Didym.*Trin.*3.2(M.39.805A); Isid. Pel.*epp.*1.59(M.78.221B).

[*]**ἀσυζυγής**, v. ἀσύζυγος.

ἀσύζυγος (-ής), **1.** *without consort*; of Gnost. aeon, Iren.*haer.*1.2.4 (M.7.457A) cit. s. ἀθήλυντος; **2.** *not combined with other things*, (gram.) of a word, *absolute* (ref. Heb.1:6) ἀπόλυτόν τε καὶ ἀσυζυγῆ τὴν φωνὴν [sc. πρωτότοκος] παρατίθεται Gr.Nyss.*Eun.*2(2 p.327.7; M.45.501B); philos., *not composite, simple* ὅσ' ἅττα μοναδικὰ καὶ ἀ. τῆς μιᾶς...φύσεως ἐν τρισίν ἐστι προσωπικαῖς ὑποστάσεσιν Sophr.H. *ep.syn.*(M.87.3157A,3168B); id.*or.*2.20(M.87.3240D).

***ἀσύζωος**, *not dwelling together*; met., *not united, incongruous*, Dion.Ar.*e.h.*3.3.12(M.3.444B).

***ἀσυλαγώγητος**, *that cannot be plundered*, †Ath.*fr.Mt.*6:20(M.27. 1373B).

ἀσύλληπτος, *not arrested*, ‡Just.*qu.et resp.*122(M.6.1372C).

ἀσυμβίβαστος, **1.** *incomparable, without equal*, of God σοφίᾳ ἀ. Thphl.Ant.*Autol.*1.3(M.6.1028C); **2.** *unreconciled* φιλονεικησάντων καὶ ἀ. μενόντων Leont.N.*v.Jo.Eleem.*15(p.31.7).

***ἀσυμβούλευτος**, *without counsel* ἀ. ἄνθρωπος πλοῖόν ἐστιν ἀκυβέρνητον †Bas.*Is.*106(1.452B; M.30.289A).

***ἀσύμβουλος**, *inadvisable*, Eus.*p.e.*8.1(349A; M.21.585D).

***ἀσυμμιγής**, *without commixture of* ἀ. τοῦ χείρονος πολιτείαν Cyr. *Am.*21(3.271D); id.*hom.pasch.*25(5^2.297E); ἀ. φαυλότητος...ψυχήν id. *ador.*10(1.357B).

ἀσυμμιξία, ἡ, *freedom from admixture, state of remaining unmixed* or *pure* αἱ κοινωνίαι τῶν ἐναντίων, αἱ ἀ. τῶν ἡνωμένων Dion. Ar.*d.n.*4.7(M.3.704B).

ἀσυμπαθής, **1.** *without fellow-feeling* or *sympathy, irresponsive*; of the children in the market-place, Cyr.*Lc.*7:32(M.72.620C); of the parts of the cosmos τὸ...ἓν οὕτως ἂν σῴζοι, καὶ οὐκ ἀ. πρὸς ἄλληλα τὰ μέρη θησόμεθα Synes.*provid.*2.7(p.128.7; M.66.1277A); **2.** *without inclining* to, *adamant* ἀσκανδάλιστον, ἀ. πρὸς τὰ τοῦ Κάιν ἔργα *A.Andr.fr.*8(p.41.27); **3.** *heartless, harsh*, †Bas.*Is.*53(1.419E; M.30. 216B); ἀρρωστήμασι δὲ τοῖς περὶ τὴν σάρκα...ἀνεθελήτως συμβαίνουσι, τὸ ἐπιτιμᾶν, οἶμαί που σκληρὸν καὶ ἀ. Cyr.*ador.*12(1.412E); †Jo.Jej. *poenit.*(M.88.1916D); of sufferings, Eus.*h.e.*8.12.7(M.20.772B); neut. as subst. εἰς ἐσχάτην ὠμότητα καὶ τὸ ἀ. Chrys.*hom.23.3 in Mt.*(7. 287C).

ἀσύμπλοκος, **1.** *not entangled* with, *not involved* in, *free* from τὴν καθαρὰν νομοθεσίαν τὴν ἀ. τῷ κακῷ Ptol.*ep.*(p.453.29; M.41.561B); Meth.*res.*3.5(p.396.7; M.18.320B); τὸ δὲ θεῖον παθῶν ἀ. id.*symp.*8.16 (p.106.9; M.18.169B); of pre-incarnate Word ἀ. τῆς τοῦ δούλου μορφῆς Cyr.*Jo.*2.5(4.186A); of risen Christ οἰηθῇς...μὴ μετὰ...σώματος ἐγηγέρθαι τὸν κύριον...ἀ. ... τοῦ ληφθέντος ναοῦ *ib.*12.1(1091A); **2.** abs., *uncompounded, simple, absolute* εἴπῃς περὶ θεοῦ, ὦ Ἀέτιε, αὐτὸ ὅλον ἐστὶν ἀ., ἀσύγκριτον Epiph.*haer.*76.37(p.388.30; M.42.593C); of divine essence μένει...ἐφ' ἑαυτῆς καθαρὰ...ἀ. φυσικῶς Cyr.*thes.*6(5^1.44B).

ἀσυμπλόκως, *without being implicated*; *without intermixture* δύναμιν θείαν...ἀ. τὰ πάντα ἐπιπορευομένην Eus.*p.e.*3.5(97A; M.21.177C).

ἀσύμπτωτος, **1.** *not falling in, collapsing*; hence met., *without change, immutable*; of the two natures in Christ, Max.*ep.*15(M.91. 561B); **2.** *not falling together*; hence met., *without coinciding, not agreeing*, of things of different essence ἕτερον καὶ ἕτερον ἀποδίδωσι θάτερον τῆς οἰκείας οὐσίας πρὸς τὸν θατέρου λόγον ἀ. *ib.*(553A).

ἀσυμφανής, 1. *dark, obscure*; met.; **a.** of pre-Christian revelation ἦν ἰσχνὴ καὶ ἀ. ἐν τοῖς ἁγίοις ἡ ἀποκάλυψις Cyr.*Os*.2(3.10C); οὐκ εὐσύνοπτά πως τοῖς ἀρχαιοτέροις ἦν...μᾶλλον δὲ ἀ. ὁ λόγος (i.e. of Trin.) id.*Jo*.11.7(4.962A); but cf. τὸ Χριστοῦ μυστήριον...οὐκ ἀ. τοῖς τῶν ἱερῶν γραμμάτων ἐπιστήμοσιν id.*Ps*.39:2(M.69.981B); **b.** of Christian mysteries: of Inc., id.*glaph.Gen*.2.4(1.50C); id.*Jo*.4.4 (4.388B); of worship in spirit, id.*ador*.1(1.8C); **c.** of language, of prophetic utterance ἀ. μὲν ἀεὶ τῶν ἁγίων προφητῶν ὁ λόγος id.*Is*. proem.(2.*); id.*Nah*.31(3.508C); of parables, id.*Lc*.8:4(M.72.624C); and other sayings of Christ, id.*Jo*.4.3(4.366B); of dogma or other statements ἔστι τοίνυν οὐδενὶ τῶν ὀρθὰ φρονεῖν εἰωθότων ἀ. id.*apol. orient*.3(p.40.5; 6^1.166D); id.*ador*.2(1.68C); id.*inc.unigen*.(5^1.691C) etc.; of a threat, id.*Zach*.9(3.664A); **d.** neut. as subst., *obscurity*, Gr.Agr. *Eccl*.7.11(M.98.1048D); **e.** freq. οὐκ ἀ. *clear, evident*, Cyr.*Os*.118(3.148E); id.*Is*.1.4(2.107B); id.*ador*.1(1.37A); **2.** *obscure, hidden*, of first coming of Christ διπλαῖ αἱ κάθοδοι, μία ἡ ἀ. ... καὶ δευτέρα ἡ ἐπιφανής Cyr.H.*catech*.15.1.

ἀσυμφανῶς, 1. *obscurely*, Cyr.*Os*.proem.(3.2C); of speaking in parables, id.*Lc*.16:1(M.72.809C); *symbolically* εἰς οἶνον...τὸ ὕδωρ μετέβαλε...ἀ. διδάξαι βουληθείς Didym.*Trin*.2.13(M.39.689C); hence οὐκ ἀ., *manifestly, clearly*, Cyr.*ep*.46(p.161.15; 5^2.144D); **2.** *hiddenly, in secret*, of Devil οὕτως ἀ. πάλιν μυριοπαθεῖς ἡμᾶς ποιήσας Bas.*renunt*. 3(2.205A; M.31.632D).

***ἀσυμφθάστως**, *prematurely*, ‡Jo.D.*fid.dorm*.8(M.95.253B).

***ἀσυμφιλία, ἡ**, *one-sided friendship*, Thdr.Stud.*epp*.1.5(M.99.925A).

[*]**ἀσυμφορής**, ? for ἀσύμφορος *prejudicial* οἱ δρομεῖς εἰς πονηρίαν καὶ ἀσυμφορεῖς τοῖς πολλοῖς Or.*adnot.in Dt*.14:5(conj. ἀσυμφανεῖς M.17.25C).

ἀσύμφορος, 1. *without advantage, unprofitable*, *2Clem*.6.1; *Hom. Clem*.4.14; Gennad.*fr.Gal*.4:3(p.420.5; M.85.1732B); **2.** *unsuitable, inexpedient* ταῦτα...πάντα μωρά ἐστι καὶ κενὰ καὶ ἄφρονα καὶ ἀ. τοῖς δούλοις τοῦ θεοῦ Herm.*mand*.5.2.2; *ib*.5.1.4; Nil.*epp*.2.211(M.79.312A); **3.** logically *absurd, irrational* πρὸς τὸ ἀδύνατον καὶ ἀ. φασιν ὑπάρχειν τὴν ταύτης [sc. τῆς σαρκός] σωτηρίαν †Just.*fr.res*.(p.38; M.6.1573C).

ἀσυμφυής, 1. *unnatural*; of vice, Clem.*paed*.2.10(p.210.23; M.8.501C); **2.** *incompatible*, Cyr.*Jo*.2.1(4.117E); ἀνάρμοστον...καὶ ἀ. id. *ador*.6(1.191B); id.*Is*.4.4(2.686C).

***ἀσύμφυρτος, 1.** *without being merged, unmixed, distinct* πάντα ἀπὸ πάντων ἀμιγῆ καὶ ἀ. διασώζουσα [sc. ἡ θεία δικαιοσύνη] Dion.Ar.*d.n*.8.7(M.3.896A); *ib*.8.5(892C); *without confusion, unconfused* μετὰ τὴν ἕνωσιν αἱ...φύσεις ἀ., καὶ αἱ τούτων...ἰδιότητες ἀλώβητοι Jo.D.*f.o*.3.17(M.94.1069B); **2.** *without confusion, orderly*, of the angels τὴν εὔκοσμον καὶ ἀ. ... εὐταξίαν Dion.Ar.*c.h*.8.1(M.3.240A); of Christian ministry, id.*e.h*.1.5(M.3.377A) cit. s. εὐσταθής; μελῶν τὴν ἁρμονίαν ἄθραυστον καὶ ἀ. Max.*ambig*.(M.91.1364B).

ἀσυμφωνία, ἡ, *want of harmony, discord*; met.; **a.** *dissension*, Tat.ap.Clem.*str*.3.12(p.232.29; M.8.1181A); Hipp.*Dan*.4.6.4; *ib*.4.7.5; id.*haer*.5.8(p.93.10; M.16.3146B); **b.** literary *discrepancy, disagreement* between authors, Tat.*orat*.31(p.32.17; M.6.872A); εἰ...ἐξετάζοι τὰ εὐαγγέλια περὶ τῆς κατὰ τὴν ἱστορίαν ἀ. Or.*Jo*.10.3(2; p.173.27; M.14.312A).

ἀσύμφωνος, *not harmonious*; *at variance*; *not in agreement, inconsistent*, freq. of heresy ταῦτα τὰ δόγματα ἀ. ἐστιν τῇ ἐκκλησίᾳ Iren.*ep.Flor*.ap.Eus.*h.e*.5.20.6(M.20.484C); ‡Ath.*Apoll*.2.15(M.26.1157A); of Montanus ἀ. ... τῶν θείων γραφῶν εὑρέθη Epiph.*haer*.48.11(p.234.5; M.41.872B); abs., *discrepant, inconsistent*; ref. gospel narrative οὕτω ἐτάραξέν τινας ὡς ἀ. τὸ εἰρημένον Or.*Jo*.32.32(19; p.479.34; M.14.828C); neut. as subst. τὰ τῶν γραφῶν ἀ. ... μεταρρυθμίζειν *Clem.ep.Petr*.1(M.2.25B).

ἀσυναίσθητος, *without perception, not perceiving*, Or.*Jo*.4.2(p.98.9; M.14.185A); ὦ βραδεῖς καὶ ἀ. τῶν συμφερόντων Nil.ap.Proc.G. *Cant*.2:7(M.87.1592B).

ἀσύνακτος, *not admitted to the assembly, outcast*, i.e. from God, Gr.Naz.*carm*.2.1.43.24(M.37.1348A); hence *excommunicate*, Thphl. Al.*Agath*.(M.65.44D); †Polyb.*v.Epiph*.60(M.41.101A).

***ἀσυναλάλητος**, ? f.l. for ἀσυνάλλακτος, *without intercourse*, Jo. Mosch.*prat*.171(M.87.3040A).

***ἀσυναλγής**, *unsympathetic*; of Dives, Cyr.*Lc*.16:19(M.72.828B).

ἀσυναλείπτως, *without confusion*, of unity in Trin. τρία ἐν ἀλλήλοις φῶτα, ἀ. καὶ ἀχωρίστως ἡνωμένα ‡Caes.Naz.*dial*.2(M.38.857); *ib*.3(860).

***ἀσυνάπτως**, *without being combined*, Anast.*fid*.p.272.

***ἀσυναρίθμητος**, *not to be numbered with* ἀ. ... ἑτέρῳ θεῷ θεὸς ὢν μόνος Cyr.*Juln*.10(6^2.344D).

***ἀσυνάρπακτος**, *not to be carried away* or *distracted* ἀ. ἡ ἀρετὴ τῇ κακίᾳ Didym.*Man*.13(M.39.1101C conj. ἀσυνύπαρκτος); ἀ. ... τὸ ὄμμα τῆς ψυχῆς γίγνεται, ὅταν τὸ ἑαυτῆς παραπέτασμα, τὸ σῶμα λέγω, εἰς λεπτότητα...διὰ τῆς ἐγκρατείας ἐξυφήνῃ Diad.*perf*.71(p.88.10).

***ἀσυνάρπαστος**, *not carried away*, met. ἀ. τὴν ἀκοὴν ἔχουσα Cyr. ap.CEph.(431)*act*.4(*ACO* 1.1.3 p.18.26; H.1.1489D).

***ἀσυναρπάστως**, *without being rushed* (mentally), *gently* οὐ... παραιτεῖται τὸν ἐν πνεύματι φωτισμόν, ἐξ αὐτοῦ δὴ μάλιστα πρὸς τὸ δύνασθαι νοεῖν ἀ. χειραγωγούμενος Cyr.*Jo*.2.1(4.155E).

***ἀσυναρτησία, ἡ**, *inconsistency, incoherence*, Epiph.*haer*.66.48 (p.86.5; M.42.101D).

***ἀσυναρτήτως**, *incoherently, inconsequently* (ref. 1Cor.8:6) περὶ τοῦ...λόγου εἴρηται...οὐ γὰρ ἂν περὶ σαρκὸς ἀ. οὕτως εἶπεν ἂν Eus.*e.th*. 1.20(p.90.20; M.24.881C); *ib*.3.21(p.182.4; 1045C); Eun.ap.Gr.Nyss. *Eun*.1(1 p.156.16; M.45.397B); Gr.Nyss.*Eun*.9(2 p.215.15; 813C); id. *hom.2 in Cant*.(M.44.796B).

ἀσυναφής, 1. *unconnected, without contact, unrelated* ὁ τοῦδέ τινος πράγματος ὑπουργός, οὐκ ἀ. ... νοοῖτ' ἂν...τῷ λαβόντι πρὸς ὑπουργίαν Cyr.*Chr.un*.(5^1.733C); of things of different genus, id.*ador*.8(1.262D); of opposites, id.*Mich*.36(3.423C); ψυχαῖς βεβήλοις...ἀ. ὁ Χριστός id.*ador*.12(1.434C); *ib*.14(487E); Christol., ref. doctrine of a 'heavenly humanity' ἕτερον ἄνθρωπον ἄρριζον καὶ ἀ. πρὸς τὴν ἡμετέραν φύσιν ἀναπλάσσει τῷ λόγῳ Gr.Nyss.*Apoll*.33(M.45.1196D); **2.** *not joined, not united* by betrothal to Christ; of unbaptized catechumen, Cyr.*ador*.8(1.258E); †Cyr.*coll.VT*(6^4.40A; M.77.1233D); of separation of two natures of Christ διϊστὰς μὲν τὰς φύσεις... ἀσυναφῆ τε εἶναι θατέραν λέγων Cyr.*Heb*.1:9(p.378.4).

***ἀσυνδιάθετος**, *not sympathetically disposed, not inclined* φυλάξαι σεαυτὴν...ἀ. ταῖς ὁμιλίαις τοῦ ἀλλοτρίου ἡμῶν *A.Andr.fr*.8(p.41.24).

[*]**ἀσυνδίαστος**, *unconnected* with, *not involved* in ἀ. ἡμᾶς πρὸς τὰς τοιαύτας κινήσεις εἶναι βουλόμενοι Marc.Er.*opusc*.7.21(M.65.1101D); v. ἀσυνδύαστος.

***ἀσύνδιος**, *without mate*; of Adam, Anast.S.*hex*.12(conj. ἀσυνδύαστος M.89.1053C; perh. f.l. for ἀσύμβιος).

***ἀσυνδρομία, ἡ**, *inability to be united*, Thdr.Stud.*epp*.2.107(M.99.1368B).

ἀσυνδύαστος, 1. *of non-duality, uncoupled* ἐπὶ...τῶν ἄλλων ἁπάντων τὸ ἓν ἀ. ἔχει τὴν σημασίαν Gr.Nyss.*Eun*.11(2 p.257.13; M.45.864D); **2.** *unconnected with, not implicated in*, Mac.Aeg.*hom*. 4.1(M.34.472D) cit. s. ἀσύνθετος; καὶ ἀ. εἰς τὸ κακίας μέρος *ib*.4.27 (493C); **3.** *unpaired, without mate*; of birds, Bas.*hex*.8.6(1.76B; M.29.177C); Gr.Nyss.*hom.3 in Cant*.(M.44.816A); **4.** of *virginal* conception, Gr.Nyss.*hom.13 in Cant*.(M.44.1053A); id.*or.catech*.23(p.86.14; M.45.61B).

***ἀσυνδυάστως**, *without pairing*, of birds τοὺς...γῦπας φασὶν ἀ. τίκτειν Bas.*hex*.8.6(1.76D; M.29.180A); *virginally, without union*, of BMV ἀ. ἐκυοφόρησας Anast.Ant.*serm*.3.2(M.89.1388B); of the virgin birth διὰ μὲν τοῦ ἐκ γυναικὸς γεννηθῆναι δεικνὺς ὅτι ἄνθρωπος, διὰ δὲ τοῦ ἀ. ... μαρτυρούμενος ὅτι ἐστὶ θεός Procl.CP *Arm*.11(p.192.23; M.65.868A); σαρκούμενος ἐκ...τῆς...παρθένου ἀ. τίκτεται Jo.D.*hom*. 9.15(M.96.744B); of generation of Son ἐκ πατρὸς...ἀ. γεγεννημένος id.*f.o*.4.24(M.94.1209C).

***ἀσυνέζωστος**, *ungirt*; of a wrestler, Or.*exc.in Ps*.36:24(M.17.133D).

ἀσυνείδητος, 1. *without conscience* ἀσυνέτους δὲ τοὺς ἀ. Gennad. *fr.Rom*.1:29(p.360.14; M.85.1669B); of Judas Iscariot ἀναιδέστατε καὶ λαίμαργε, ἀ., φιλάργυρε Rom.Mel.(*SBBAW* 1901 p.746); partic. *conscienceless* with regard to claims of others, Chrys.*hom.1.1 in 2Tim*.(11.660B); ἔστω τις λῃστὴς καὶ πρὸς πάντας ἀ. id.*hom.2.5 in Ac*.(9.22A); hence **2.** *ungrateful, graceless* ἀ. ... πρὸς τὸν εὐεργέτην Bas.*reg.br*.294(2.519A; M.31.1289B); ἀ. ... καὶ ἀγνώμων περὶ τὸν εὐεργέτην Chrys.*hom.23.2 in Rom*.(9.688E); neut. as subst. καὶ τὸ ἀ. ... αὐτῶν δείκνυται καὶ τὸ σφόδρα ἀνόητον id.*hom.12.2 in 1Cor*. (10.99B); id.*fr.in Jer*.17:11(M.64.917B).

ἀσυνειδήτως, 1. *without proper consideration, heedlessly*, Ath. *Dion*.21(p.62.4; M.25.512A); **2.** *without conscience, ungratefully* (ref. 1Cor.11:29) ὥσπερ...ἀ. καὶ ἀνωφελῶς τοσοῦτον καὶ τοιοῦτον ἀγαθὸν καταργῶν †Bas.*bapt*.1.3.3(2.651C; M.31.1577B).

***ἀσυνειδότως**, *unconsciously*, Chrys.*hom.5.4 in Jo*.(8.40C).

***ἀσυνείθιστος**, *not experienced, unaccustomed*, Leont.N.*v.Sym*.12 (M.93.1685A).

ἀσυνείκαστος, 1. *not to be compared, defying comparison* παρισαζόντων τὰ ἀ. Bas.*Spir*.36(3.30C; M.32.133A); **2.** *inestimable* ἀ. ἡ κατὰ τὸ ἀνθρώπινον τοῦ κυρίου ὑπεροχή †Bas.*Is*.67(1.428A; M.30.233C); Epiph.*ep.Arab*.ap.*haer*.78.24(p.474.33; M.42.737D); ‡Chrys.*Zach*.(2.791B); hence *immense* νηὸς...φόρτον...ἀ. ἐμβαλλομένης Epiph.*haer*.

56.1(p.340.6; M.41.992A); ib.66.45(p.82.20; M.42.97A); **3.** theol.; *unimaginable, incomprehensible, immense,* of Trin. ἀσύνθετος, ἀ. †Epiph.*num.myst.*2(M.43.509A); of God incarnate λεγόμενον ἀδιανόητον, καὶ διανοούμενον ἀ. Thdr.Stud.*nativ.BMV* 7(M.96.696B); neut. as subst., *incommensurability, immensity* τὸ ἀ. καὶ μέγα τῆς θεότητος Didym.*Trin.*1.15(M.39.308B).

***ἀσυνεικάστως**, *without likeness* to, Didym.*Trin.*2.7(M.39.565B).

***ἀσυνετελής**, f.l. in Bas.*mor.*8.9(3.521B; M.32.1233B) for ἀσυντελής, Bas.*hom.*8.3(2.65B; M.31.312B).

***ἀσυνηγόρητος**, *without advocate, undefended* γύμνη ἡ ἀλήθεια, ἀ. Bas.*hom.*23.3(2.186D; M.31.593A); of man at the judgement ἀ., ἀναπολόγητος *ib.*7.6(58B; M.296B); οὐ γὰρ ἀ. ἔδει παρεθῆναι τὴν τοῦ μεγάλου [sc. Βασιλείου] ὑπόληψιν Gr.Nyss.*ep.*29(M.45.240A); *without support* or *authority* ἀ. ἐκτίθεται κατ' αὐτοῦ τὴν ἀσέβειαν id.*Eun.* 2(2 p.377.6; M.45.557C).

ἀσύνθετος, A. (from συντίθημι), *uncompounded*; **1.** in gen.; **a.** gram., of a word *standing alone,* Dion.Al.ap.Ath.*Dion.*18(p.60.6; M.25.508A); **b.** [sc. σχῆμα] a rhetorical figure opp. polysyntheton, cf. *dialyton vel asyntheton est figura, quae...sine conjunctionibus solute ac simpliciter effertur, ut: venimus, vidimus, placuit,* Isid.H.*etym.*1.36.20; **c.** philos., *not composite, simple* οἱ τῶν ἀτόμων τομεῖς...καὶ τῶν ἀ. συναγωγεῖς Dion.Al.ap.Eus.*p.e.*14.25(778A; M.21.1280B); esp. of human soul τὸ...ἀ. λύσιν οὐκ ἐπιδέχεται· ἀλλὰ παραμένει μὲν τῷ μερισμῷ τοῦ συνθέτου ἡ ἀ. φύσις Gr.Nyss.*Apoll.*17(M.45.1156B); Leont.H.*Nest.*1.1(M.86.1404C); Max.*opusc.*(M.91.20B); **2.** theol., *not composite, uncompounded,* i.e. simple; freq. coupled with ἁπλοῦς; **a.** of God ἀσώματος [sc. ὁ τοῦ θεοῦ νοῦς] καὶ ἀ. καὶ ἀμερής Eus.*p.e.*3.10(106B; M.21.192C); ‡Ath.*Sabell.*13(M.28.117B) cit. s. ἀναλλοιώτος; Apoll.*quod un.Chr.*9(p.300.12; M.28.129A) cit. s. μονοειδής; πῶς οὐκ ἀ. ὁ κατὰ τὴν οὐσίαν ἁπλοῦς; Bas.*Eun.*2.29(1.266B; M.29.640B); Gr.Nyss.*Apoll.*2(M.45.1128B); ὁ...θεὸς ἁπλοῦς, καὶ ἀ. καὶ ἀσχημάτιστος Chrys.*incomprehens.*4.3(1.474E); id.*hom.15.1 in Jo.*(8.85B); θεὸς...ἁπλοῦς, ἀ., ἀσώματος Jo.D.*f.o.*1.2(M.94.792C); *ib.*1.4(797B); *ib.*1.7(805A); used in *reductio ad absurdum* arguments showing that to create and to beget are not the same in God, Cyr.*thes.*18(5^1.184A–D); πῶς ὁ θεὸς ἀ. λέγεται τὴν ἐκ δύο προσώπων...καὶ ἑνὸς προσώπου τὴν σύνθεσιν ἔχων; ‡Just.*qu.et resp.*129(M.6.1380B); heret., of Father opp. Son (as begotten), Eun.*apol.*19(M.30.853D); **b.** of the Son ὁ υἱὸς ἁπλοῦς...καὶ ἀ., καὶ ὅμοιος [sc. τῷ πατρί]...κατ' αὐτὴν τὴν οὐσίαν Bas.*Eun.*1.23(1.234D; M.29.564A); εἰ δὲ μήτε δι' ἑαυτόν, μήτε δι' ἕτερον συντεθήσεται ὁ θεὸς λόγος, ἀ. ἄρα Leont.H.*Nest.*1.12(M.86.1448C); prior to Inc. ὁ νῦν ἄνθρωπος, καὶ ἀ. ἦν Gr.Naz.*or.*29.19(p.102.8; M.36.100A); in Inc. ὁ φανερωθεὶς ἡμῖν ἐν σαρκὶ θεὸς...ἀφανὴς καὶ ἀ. Gr.Nyss.*Apoll.*18(M.45.1160A); *ib.*5(1132C); but acc. Apoll. person of Christ μένει...ἀ. καθὸ οὐ συμπεριορίζεται τῷ σώματι Apoll.*fr.*133(p.239.22)ap.Thdt.*eran.*2(4.172); denied of Christ as God and man by orthodox τοὺς...συγχέοντας τὰ περὶ τοῦ πρωτοτόκου πάσης κτίσεως τοῖς περὶ τῆς ψυχῆς καὶ τοῦ σώματος Ἰησοῦ, τάχα δὲ καὶ τοῦ πνεύματος αὐτοῦ, καὶ ἓν πάντῃ ἀ. οἰομένους, εἶναι τὸ ὀφθὲν καὶ ἐπιδημῆσαν τῷ βίῳ Or.*comm.in Mt.*16.8(p.500.8; M.13.1400A); πλὴν οὐκ ἀ. τὴν ὑπόστασιν εἰ καὶ τὴν φύσιν ἁπλοῦς Max.*opusc.*(M.91.73B); id.*ep.*15(556A); comp. ἀσυνθετότερον ἰδίωμα τῆς τοῦ λόγου γέγονεν ὑποστάσεως, πλειόνων ἐπισωρευθέντων ἐν αὐτῇ τῶν ἁπλῶν ἰδιωμάτων μετὰ τὴν σάρκωσιν Leont.H.*Nest.*1.20(M.86.1485D); **3.** Christol., *not united*; Nestorian, ref. relation of human nature of Christ to divinity τὸν κατ' αὐτοὺς θάτερον τῶν υἱῶν Χριστόν, τὸν ἀ. τῷ λόγῳ, τίνι φασὶν ὁμοούσιον; Leont.H.*Nest.*3.6(M.86.1621B); *ib.*1.19(1481A); v. σύνθεσις; **4.** of angels, Max.*schol.c.h.*2.2(M.4.37B).

B. (from συντίθεμαι); **1.** *bound by no covenant* ἡμᾶς δὲ ἀ. εἶναι καὶ ἀσυνδέτους Gr.Naz.*or.*22.3(M.35.1133C); **2.** *breaking covenant, faithless* ἀ. δὲ τοὺς ταῖς συνθήκαις μὴ ἐμμένοντας Gennad.CP *Rom.*1:29ff.(p.360.15; M.85.1669B); **3.** *making no covenant* or *pact* ἀσυνδύαστοι καὶ ἀ. πρὸς τὰς τῆς κακίας ὑποθέσεις Mac.Aeg.*hom.*4.1(M.34.472D); of selfish living ἀ. τοὺς ἀκοινώνητον καὶ πονηρὸν βίον ἀσπαζομένους Thdt.*Rom.*1:31(3.28).

ἀσυνθέτως, 1. *without composition* or *mixture, simply*; hence *absolutely* τὸ ἀθάνατον, καὶ τὸ ἄκακον...οὐκ...ἀ. ταῦτα, εἴπερ οὐσίαι Gr.Naz.*or.*29.10(p.88.12; M.36.88B); ὁ ἀσύνθετος ἀ. ἀσύνθετα ποιεῖ ‡Just.*qu.Chr.*3(M.6.1440D); of God τὸ ἓν καὶ τὸ τρεῖς πρόσεστι τῷ 'πι' καὶ τῷ θεῷ· ἀλλὰ τῷ μὲν 'πι' γενητῶς καὶ συνθέτως, τῷ δὲ θεῷ ἀγενήτως τε καὶ ἀ.‡Just.*qu.et resp.*129(M.6.1380C); ἀ. αὐτός ἐστι σοφός CAnc.(358)*ep.syn.*ap.Epiph.*haer.*73.6(p.276.18; M.42.413C); αὐτὸς ἀ. ἐστὶ ζωὴ ὁ πατήρ CAnc.*ib.*73.8(p.279.3; 417C); of Son ὁμοίως πάντα κατ' οὐσίαν, καὶ ἀ. ὡς ὁ πατήρ CAnc.*ib.*(p.279.7; 417C); CAnc.*ib.*(p.279.5; 417C); **2.** *disconnectedly, separately*; ref. relation between natures of Christ ὅτε ἀ. ἔχει...ἢ ὅτε...συνετέθη Leont.H.*Nest.*1.19(M.86.1481A).

***ἀσυνόδευτος, 1.** *not having a companion, companionless,* Ephr. 3.262E; Anast.S.*defunct.*(M.89.1196A); **2.** *not being a companion, not accompanying, cat.Job* 2(p.59).

***ἀσυνοήτως**, *foolishly, Didasc.Jac.*5.20(p.90.25).

ἀσύνοπτος, 1. *not easily perceived*; **2.** *not perceptive, obtuse,* Isid. Pel.*epp.*1.297(M.78.356B).

***ἀσυνουσία, ἡ,** *solitary life,* Dan.Raith.*v.Clim.*(M.88.600A).

***ἀσυνουσίαστος**, *holding no intercourse, solitary,* Chrys.*sac.*6.12(p.164.5; 1.431E).

***ἀσυνόψισις, ἡ,** error for ***ἀσύνοψις**, *state of not having seen one another, absence of direct encounter,* Thdr.Stud.*epp.*2.145(M.99.1453C).

ἀσύντακτος, 1. *not of the same order* or *category, not to be classed with,* esp. of God in relation to creatures ἐξῃρημένον μὲν καὶ ἀ. παντελῶς τῶν ὅλων, συντεταγμένον δὲ...τῆς πρωτίστης...φύσεως Didym.*Trin.*2.11(M.39.661A); εἰ πάντων προέχει τῶν παρὰ τοῦ υἱοῦ γεγονότων ἀ. ἐστι τῇ λοιπῇ κτίσει τὸ πνεῦμα τὸ ἅγιον Gr.Nyss.*Eun.*2(2 p.380.20; M.45.561C); γεγεννῆσθαι...καὶ οὐ πεποιῆσθαί φασιν, ἀ. μὲν οὐσιωδῶς τῇ κτίσει διὰ τὸ μὴ πεποιῆσθαι νοοῦντες αὐτόν Cyr.*ep.*55(p.52.22; 5^2.178D); in logic, of a *non sequitur* οὗτοι οἱ λόγοι ἀ. ‡Nil.*Epict.*63(M.79.1308D); **2.** *not comprehended in, apart* ἔξων...ἐπὶ τῶν βιβλίων,...ἀ. πάσῃ πόλει καὶ πολιτείᾳ Synes.*ep.*91(M.66.1457A).

ἀσυντάκτως, *without notice*; of a departure, *without farewell,* Thdt.*ep.*80(4.1137).

***ἀσυντελέω**, *be unprofitable,* Max.*opusc.*(M.91.136C).

ἀσυντελής, *not liable for, exempt from* οὐδὲ τὰ ἄλογα ἀ. τῆς τιμωρίας Bas.*hom.*8.3(2.65B; M.31.312B).

ἀσύντριπτος, 1. *unbroken,* Bas.*hom.in Ps.*33(1.156C; M.29.381C); **2.** *immortal,* of human nature as originally created, Gr.Nyss. *v.Mos.*(M.44.397B); and as restored by Inc., *ib.*(397C); **3.** *that cannot be shattered, indestructible,* of Christ στερροτάτην καὶ ἀ. σχόντος τὴν ὑποβάθραν διὰ τὸ θείως καὶ μὴ σαρκικῶς συστῆναι τὸ σῶμα ‡Chrys. *pasch.*2(8^2.257C).

ἀσυντρόχαστος, *individually distinct, separate* τὸ...τούτων τῶν ποιοτήτων ἴδιον καὶ ἀ. πρὸς ἕτερον Or.*or.*24.2(p.354.2; M.11.492B); id.*Apoc.*18(p.29.1).

***ἀσυσκίαστος**, *not to be hidden,* †Chrys.*pan.Bab.*2.15(2.560D).

ἀσυστασία, ἡ, *inconsistency* ἡ τῆς αἱρέσεως ὑπόθεσις ἀσυστασίᾳ μᾶλλον περιπίπτουσα καὶ οὐκ ἀληθείᾳ Epiph.*haer.*23.4(p.252.13; M.41.301D).

***ἀσυστάτως**, *inconsistently*; *incoherently* ἀ. πιστεύειν ‡Just.*qu.Gr.*11.20(M.6.1484C); ref. heretical teaching, Epiph.*haer.*24.8(p.265.18; M.41.317C); *ib.*47.1(p.217.2; 852C).

[*]**ἄσυστος**, = ἀσύστατος, *chaotic, Ev.Barth.*(Vassiliev, p.12).

***ἀσυστρεφής**, *careless,* Philost.*h.e.*8.12a(M.65.566A).

***ἀσυστρέφω**, *? lapse* εἰ...συμβῇ αὐτὸν ἀσυστραφῆναι, πόθεν οἶδας πόσα ἠγωνίσατο; Dor.*doct.*6.5(M.88.1689D), cf. ἀσυστροφέω.

***ἀσυστροφ-έω, 1.** *become lax* or *careless* εἰ βλέπει ἄλλον...λαλοῦντα πολλά, εἴτε δήποτε ~οῦντα Dor.*doct.*16.2(M.88.1796C); **2.** *let oneself go, take things easily* ἐγώ, ἐὰν συμβῇ μοι πρᾶγμα, ἡδέως ἔχω γίνεσθαι γνώμῃ τοῦ πλησίου καὶ ~ῆσαι μετὰ γνώμης αὐτοῦ, ἐὰν ἀπαντήσῃ ἢ καὶ στοιχῆσαι τῇ ἰδίᾳ γνώμῃ καὶ εὐσυστροφῆσαι *ib.*19(1809B); **3.** *make mistakes*; *be unsuccessful* ἄνθρωπος θέλων μαθεῖν τέχνην...πρῶτον παραμένει ποιῶν καὶ ~ῶν, ποιῶν καὶ ἀφανίζων, καὶ οὕτως κατὰ μικρὸν κοπιῶν καὶ ὑπομένων, μανθάνει τὴν τέχνην *ib.*8.5(1713D); ποιεῖ τις κόπον τῆς ἀρετῆς, καὶ ἐκ τοῦ μὴ ποιεῖν ἐν γνώσει, ἀναλύει αὐτόν, ἢ μένει ~ῶν *ib.*14.3(1776D).

***ἀσυστρόφημα, τό,** *laxity*; *relaxation* of discipline οὐ δεῖ ὅρον τιθέναι κατὰ τῶν νεοκατηχητῶν...ἐάνπερ κριθῇ δίκαιον τὸ ἀ. Ephr. 1.318B.

***ἀσυστροφία, ἡ,** *negligence, carelessness,* Ephr.2.110E; Dor.*doct.*18(M.88.1804D).

ἀσύστροφος, *slovenly, untidy* εἰ ἔβλεπε τὸ κέλλιον αὐτοῦ ἀ., ἀφιλοκάλητον...οὐδέποτε ἔλεγε περί τινος ὅτι οὗτος ἀ. ἢ οὗτος πέρπερος Dor.*doct.*16.4(M.88.1800A); *ib.*4.7(1668A).

ἀσύφηλος, *foolish*; *worthless*; *vile*; of the mind, Cyr.*glaph.Gen.*2.3(1.48D); of an opinion, id.*apol.orient.*(p.39.36, v.l. ἀσύμφυλον 6^1.166C); ἀ. πεφλυαρηκότας id.*Juln.*3(6^2.76C); of a man, Eudoc.*Cypr.*1.149(M.85.837C).

ἄσφακτος, *unslain* τὴν ἄθυτον θυσίαν· τὴν σφαγὴν ἐκείνην τὴν ἄ. Germ.CP *or.*2(M.98.280A).

ἀσφαλίζ-ω, *secure*; **1.** act. and pass.; **a.** *secure*; *shut up*; hence *fortify*; met., *confirm* ἠσφαλισμένην ἔχοντες τὴν διάνοιαν Ath.*ep.Aeg.Lib.*1(M.25.537A); id.*apol.Const.*12(M.25.609B); ἀ. σου τὴν ψυχήν

Chrys.*exp.in Ps.*3(5.1B); τοῖς εὐαγγελικοῖς με ἀσφαλίσατε λόγοις Cyr. ap.Proc.G.*Cant.*2:5(M.87.1585D); **b.** *protect* [sc. θηρία] ποικίλοις πλεονεκτήμασιν ἠσφαλισμένα Tit.Bost.*Man.*2.24(M.18.1181C); **2.** med., *secure* or *safeguard oneself*; *be on one's guard* ἀ. μήπως...ἐμπέσῃ εἰς τὸ...κρίμα Bas.*reg.br.*147(2.465A; M.31.1180B); *ib.*169(472A; 1193B); παρ' αὐτοῦ τοῦ κυρίου παιδευόμεθα ~εσθαι †Bas.*bapt.*2.8.6(2.664A; M.31.1605C); τούτοις ~όμενος τοῖς λόγοις νῆφε Cyr.H.*catech.*19.10; **3.** med., trans.; **a.** *make secure, assure* ἠσφαλίσατο νόμῳ...τὴν δοθεῖσαν αὐτοῖς χάριν Ath.*inc.*3.4(M.25.101D); id.*Ar.*2.60(M.26.276A); Diod.*Gen.*27:41(M.33.1576C); Didym.*Trin.*2.4(M.39.481A); hence *assert*, Thdr.Mops.*Ps.*17:10(p.114.23; M.66.664B); **b.** *watch over, protect*, Ign.*Philad.*5.1; πανταχοῦ...~εται τοὺς ἁγίους Cyr.*Am.*30(3.279E) al.; Nil.*Magn.*10(M.79.984A); **c.** *fortify, strengthen* κατὰ τῶν εἰδώλων ~όμενος αὐτούς Eus.*proph.*(M.22.1269B); ἠσφαλίζοντο...τοὺς πιστοὺς ταῖς παραινέσεσιν Ath.*fug.*21(M.25.672A); τῷ βαπτίσματι τοῦτον ἀσφαλισάμενος καὶ περιτειχίσας Anast.S.*Ps.*6(M.89.1108B); **d.** *put on one's guard, warn* ἔξεστιν εἰπεῖν τι περί τινος φαῦλον...ὅταν χρεία γένηται ἀσφαλίσασθαί τινας Bas.*reg.br.*25(2.423D; M.31.1100C); Chrys.*hom.*75.2 *in Mt.*(7.724E); Cyr.*ador.*7(1.250C).

ἀσφάλισμα, τό, *guarantee*, †Bas.*Is.*210(1.537A; M.30.481C); Chrys.*hom.*14.2 *in Heb.*(12.142B).

ἀσφαλτόω, *smear with pitch*, †Jo.D.*B.J.*6(M.96.904A).

***ἀσφάλτως,** *unerringly, infallibly*, Didym.*Trin.*2.7(M.39.584C).

ἀσφράγιστος, 1. *unsealed, unmarked*; esp. ref. marking of houses in Egypt to avert destruction of first-born, partic. as type of baptism [sc. Αἴγυπτον] τὴν ἀ. τοῦ αἵματος Mel.*pass.*16 p.3.12; ἐν...ταῖς ἀ. [sc. οἰκίαις] κατεφόνευε τὰ πρωτότοκα· ἀ. θησαυρὸς εὐεπιχείρητος κλέπταις Bas.*hom.*13.4(2.117B; M.31.432C); ἀ. ... πρόβατον, εὐάλωτον τοῖς λύκοις Didym.*Trin.*2.15(M.39.717B); cf.Eus.Al.*serm.*5(M.86.349B); with sign of cross, Sophr.H.*mir.Cyr.et Jo.*70(M.87.3673A); **2.** met., of unrighteous as unmarked with sign of God's ownership (exeg. 2Tim.2:15) μὴ...τὸ σήμαντρον τὸ βασιλικὸν...ἀποθώμεθα ἵνα μὴ ἀ. ὦμεν Chrys.*hom.*5.3 *in 2Tim.*(11.688F); esp. of those unsealed by baptism, Or.*fr.in Pr.*1:6(M.17.156B) = Chrys.*Pr.*1:6(M.64.661D); exeg. Gen.3:24 ὅταν...ἴδῃ...τινὰ τῶν ἀ., κατὰ στόμα [sc. τῆς ῥομφαίας] προσαπαντᾷ Bas.*hom.*13.2(2.115D; M.31.428C); of soul after death πῶς [ὑποδέχονται οἱ ἄγγελοι] τὴν ἀ.; Gr.Nyss.*bapt.diff.*(M.46.424B); of infants κρεῖσσον ἀναισθήτως ἁγιασθῆναι, ἢ ἀπελθεῖν ἀ. καὶ ἀτέλεστα Gr.Naz.*or.*40.28(M.36.400A); ὀφείλει [sc. baptism] ταχινωτέρα...δίδοσθαι...ἵνα...μὴ ἐξέλθῃ ἀ. Ast.Am.*hom.*20(M.40.445C); cf. Bas., Didym., Chrys. *supra*.

ἀσχάλλ-ω, *be reluctant* or *unwilling* μονονουχὶ δὲ καὶ ~οντος καταδράττεται καὶ πρὸς ἀβουλήτους ἀποφέρει ῥοπάς Cyr.*hom.pasch.*19.2(5².250E).

ἄσχετος, 1. *not to be controlled* or *held* τοῦτο...ἐστι πρὸς τὸ κρεῖττον ἐστράφθαι, καὶ ἄ. εἶναι τοῦ χείρονος Synes.*insomn.*10(p.165.3; M.66.1300B); **2.** *unrestrained, unchecked* τῶν μὲν ἄγαν ἀ. φιλοσοφώτερον...τῶν δὲ φιλοσοφούντων ἀμέτρως ἀνθρωπινώτερον Gr.Naz.*ep.*165(M.37.273B); id.*or.*28.28(p.65.18; M.36.65C); neut. as subst., *ib.*27.2(p.3.12; 13B); ὅπως...τὸ ἄ. τῆς...θείας ὀργῆς ἡ φιλανθρωπία συνέχηται Areth.*Apoc.*2(M.106.517C); neut. plur. as adv., *without restraint* οὐδὲν...ἄλλο ἐστὶν ἢ συκοφαντία καὶ...θυμὸς ἄσχετα φρονῶν CAlex.*ep.*ap.Ath.*apol.sec.*5(p.91.28; M.25.257A); **3.** *unlimited, boundless, infinite* πένθει...ἀ. Chrys.*sac.*1.2(p.6.11; 1.363E); τόλμης ἀ. Jo.D.*hom.*4.29(M.96.629C); of praise, *unqualified*, Max.*ambig.*(M.91.1105C); esp. in Dion. Ar. of what pertains to God, *illimitable*; *incomprehensible* αἱ ἄ. μεταδόσεις...τῆς πάντων αἰτίας ἀγαθότητος Dion.Ar.*d.n.*2.5(M.3.644A); ἔρωτος ἄ. αἰτία *ib.*4.16(713C); πάσης οὐσίας...ἀρχὴ...καὶ πάντων...ἀ. συνοχὴ περιδεδραγμένη id.*c.h.*7.3(M.3.212D); **4.** *not relative, unconditioned, absolute*; **a.** gram., Bas.*Eun.*2.14(1.249D; M.29.600A); ἀπόλυτον εἶναι τὴν τοῦ υἱοῦ προσηγορίαν καὶ ἄ. Gr.Naz.*or.*30.15(p.133.1; M.36.124B); τῶν ὀνομάτων τὰ μὲν ἀπόλυτά τε καὶ ἄ., τὰ δὲ πρός τινα σχέσιν ὠνομασμένα ἐστίν Gr.Nyss.*Eun.*1(1 p.182.7; M.45.425D); *ib.*10(2 p.240.24; 844A); **b.** philos. ἄ. μὲν τὸ αὐτὸ εἶναι, σχετικὸν δὲ τὸ ἄλλου εἶναι ‡Just.*qu.et resp.*113(M.6.1361C); οὐκ ἔστιν...ὅλως σῶμα δυνατὸν ἢ ψυχὴν εὑρεῖν ἢ λέγειν ἄ. Max.*ambig.*(M.91.1101C); of the will, id.*opusc.*(M.91.25D); of the Godhead ἡ θεότης...τῆς πρὸς ἄλλο πᾶν πάσης συναφείας...ἐλευθέρα...ἄ. γάρ id.*ambig.*(M.91.1185D).

ἀσχέτως, *uncontrollably, without restraint*; hence *unconditionally, absolutely* καὶ τοῦτ' ἔστι...κατιόντα μὴ κατιέναι, ὅταν ἀ. ὁ κρείττων ἐπιμεληταὶ τοῦ χείρονος Synes.*insomn.*11(p.167.3; M.66.1301B).

ἀσχημάτιστος, *without form*; **1.** *formless*, i.e. without specific determination, *chaotic*; in gen. τὸ μὲν αὐτῆς [sc. τῆς ὕλης] ἄπειρον καὶ ἀ. ... τὸ δὲ κεκοσμημένον Tat.*orat.*12(p.12.25; M.6.829C); Eus.*l.C.*12(p.232.1; M.20.1389C) cit. s. ἄψυχος; in pagan philosophy, v. ἄποιος; of primary matter in Gnost. systems ἀσχημοσύνη δέ ἐστιν ἡ πρώτη καὶ μακαρία κατ' αὐτοὺς ἀ. οὐσία, ἡ πάντων σχημάτων τοῖς σχηματιζομένοις αἰτία Hipp.*haer.*5.7(p.83.1; M.16.3131C); *ib.*5.17(p.114.22; 3175C) cit. s. ἄποιος; Meth.*arbitr.*3(p.154.3; M.18.248B); **2.** *without shape* or *form*; *indescribable*; *that cannot be represented by a figure* τὸ ἀ. ... οὐ σχῆμα ἔχει, οὐκ εἶδος, οὐ τύπον Chrys.*hom.*5.3 *in Col.*(11.362C); ὁ στῦλος...δηλοῖ τὸ...ἄτρεπτον αὐτοῦ [sc. τοῦ θεοῦ] φῶς, καὶ ἀ. Clem.*str.*1.24(p.102.19; M.8.909C); ἡ κυριακὴ φωνὴ λόγος ἀ. *ib.*6.3(p.448.15; M.9.252C); προβέβληνται...καὶ τὰ σχήματα τῶν ἀ. Dion.Ar.*c.h.*2.2(M.3.140A); *ib.*2.1(137B); in association with ἄμορφος, ἀειδής, ἀνείδεος etc., Clem.*exc.Thdot.*47(p.122.8; M.9.681B); not applicable to man οὐδὲ γὰρ ἀνείδεος οὐδ' ἀ. ... δημιουργεῖται Clem.*str.*4.23(p.315.2; M.8.1360B); save of his mind, Eus.*p.e.*3.10(106C; M.21.192D); and soul, Eustrat.*stat.anim.*7(p.367); with ἀσώματος, ἀφανής, ἀόρατος etc. τίς δὲ τὰς ἀφανεῖς καὶ ἀ. ἰδέας, καὶ τὴν ἀσώματον καὶ ἀσχημάτιστον οὐσίαν τοῖς ἐπὶ γῆς ἐξηγόρευσεν; Eus.*l.C.*4(p.202.29; M.20.1333A); Gr.Nyss.*ep.*24(M.46.1092C); id.*hex.*16(M.44.80A); Dion.Ar.*d.n.*1.1(M.3.588B); πῶς...σῶμα τὸ ἄπειρον...καὶ ἀ.; Jo.D.*f.o.*1.4(M.94.797B); with ἀνωνόμαστος: τὸ ἓν...ἀ. καὶ ἀνωνόμαστον Clem.*str.*5.12(p.380.24; M.9.121B); **3.** *not employing figures of speech* hence *unpretentious, unaffected, simple* ἀ. φωνή Chrys.*sac.*6.3(p.143.21; 1.422D); of monastic life ἡ...τῶν τριχῶν ἀπόκαρσις ἐμφαίνει τὴν καθαρὰν καὶ ἀ. ζωήν Dion.Ar.*e.h.*6.3.3(M.3.536A); *unfeigned* ταπεινοφροσύνην...ἀληθινὴν καὶ ἀ. Marc.Er.*opusc.*7.16(M.65.1096A); neut. as subst., *simplicity*, Chrys.*ep.*2.9(3.546A); **4.** theol., *without form*, of God as above all differentiation therefore form, also as without visible form ὁ περὶ πάντων περιεκτικός, ἀ. τε καὶ ἀόρατος δηλοῦται θεός Clem.*str.*5.6(p.350.19; M.9.61B); Gr.Nyss.*Eun.*1(1 p.89.11; M.45.321A) cit. s. ἀειδής; ἐν σχήμασι τὸν ἀ. ἐπιζητοῦντες Chrys.*hom.*3.2 *in Rom.*(9.450D); ἡ θεία φύσις ἀνείδεός τε καὶ ἀ. Thdt.*qu.*60 *in Ex.*(1.163); τῷ ἀναφεῖ καὶ ἀ. θεῷ Dion.Ar.*d.n.*9.5(M.3.913A); ‡Caes.Naz.*dial.*166(M.38.1129); *cat.Jo.*15:16(p.357.21); προφάσει δοξολογίας ἀ. αὐτὸν λέγουσιν ἵνα ἄμορφος καὶ ἀνείδεος ὢν μηδενὶ ὁρατὸς ᾖ, ὅπως μὴ περιπόθητος γένηται *Hom.Clem.*17.11; freq. associated with ἁπλοῦς: ὁ γὰρ θεὸς ἁπλοῦς...καὶ ἀ. Chrys.*incomprehens.*4.3(1.474E); id.*hom.*15.1 *in Jo.*(8.85B); Thdt.*qu.*20 *in Gen.*(1.25); Dion.Ar.*d.n.*1.4(M.3.592B); ‡Cyr.*Trin.*12(6³.18A; M.77.1148A); also with ἄποσος: πῶς διαλάβω...τὸ ἄποσον, τὸ ἄποιον, τὸ ἀ.; Gr.Nyss.*beat.*3(M.44.1225B); ‡Bas.*struct.hom.*1.4(1.326A; M.30.16A); Cyr.*ep.Calos.*(p.604.7; 6².364A); of divine essence as common to Father and Son τὴν...ἀνείδεον καὶ ἀ. φύσιν ἐν αὐτῇ τῇ οὐσίᾳ λείπεται ἔχειν τὴν ὁμοιότητα Bas.*Eun.*1.23(1.234D; M.29.564A); of Son in his divine nature ἄλλο τι εἰπεῖν τὸν υἱὸν ἢ ἀσώματον καὶ ἀνείδεον καὶ ἀ. *ib.*(1.234B; M.561C); ἁπλοῦς ὢν τὴν φύσιν...καὶ ἀ. ... εἰκὼν τοῦ ἀοράτου Sever.*sigill.*1(M.63.533); Jo.D.*fid.Nest.*46(p.579); of Logos οὐδ' αὐτὸς ἄμορφος καὶ ἀ. ... ἐστιν· ἀλλὰ καὶ μορφὴν ἔχει ἰδίαν Clem.*exc.Thdot.*10.1(p.109.18; M.9.660B); of H. Ghost πνεῦμα μὲν ἐστιν...ἀ. ἐκπορευτὴ ὕπαρξις Anast.S.*hod.*2(M.89.56B).

ἀσχημον-έω 1. *behave unseemly*; by interrupting, Just.*dial.*9.2(M.6.496A); in drinking, Clem.*paed.*2.1(p.163.6; M.8.397C); by uncontrolled exhibition of grief, Bas.*hom.*4.6(2.30B; M.30.229C); **2.** *behave reprehensibly, disgrace oneself*, by bearing false witness, Alex.Thess.*ep.Ath.*(p.145.11; M.25.368B); Isid.Pel.*epp.*2.153(M.78.608B); in gen., Ephr.1.237E; hence *be humiliated* or *discomfited*, *be put to shame* ὁρῶντες ἑαυτοὺς λοιπὸν ~οῦντας, καὶ μηδὲν εὔλογον ἔχοντας Ath.*h.Ar.*66(p.219.20; M.25.772B); *Hom.Clem.*19.24; Dor.*doct.*5.3(M.88.1680C); med. ὁ μὲν [sc. διάβολος] μεῖζον ~ῆται ὑπὸ τῶν ἡττόνων νικώμενος Cyr.H.*catech.*8.4; **3.** *behave indecently*, Clem.*paed.*3.3(p.248.10; M.8.584A); Chrys.*hom.*36.5 *in 1Cor.*(10.341A); id.*hom.*6.8 *in Mt.*(7.101B); partic. of adultery and profligacy ληραίνει...τῶν παρ' ὑμῖν ἐθῶν τὰ ἐπιτηδεύματα καὶ διὰ τῆς γυναικωνίτιδος ~εῖ Tat.*orat.*33(p.34.8; M.6.873B); Or.*hom.*4.2 *in Jer.*(p.24.26; M.13.288B); of any moral impropriety οὐδεὶς τὴν ἀγάπην ἔχων ἀσχημόν τι πράττει· ἐὰν οὖν ποτε ἀδελφοὶ ἡμῶν...πέσωσι προφάσει ἀγάπης, λέγωμεν αὐτοῖς ὅτι οὐκ ἔχουσι τὴν ἀγάπην· ἡ γὰρ ἀγάπη οὐκ ~εῖ Or.*comm.in 1Cor.*13:5(*JTS* 10 p.34); Meth.*symp.*1.2(p.9.25; M.18.40C); **4.** *be ill-clad, go half-naked* ὁ τοὺς ἵππους κοσμῶν, τὸν ἀδελφὸν ~οῦντα περιορᾷς; Bas.*hom.*7.4(2.55B; M.30.288C); τοὺς γυμνοὺς καὶ ~οῦντας περιβάλλων τῇ τῆς φιλοσοφίας στολῇ Chrys.*laud.Paul.*1(2.480A); hence *be shamed*, of a beggar ὁ μὲν κατ' εἰκόνα τοῦ θεοῦ γεγενημένος ἔστηκεν ~ῶν διὰ τὴν σὴν ἀπανθρωπίαν id.*hom.*11.6 *in Rom.*(9.539C); id.*hom.*21.6 *in 1Cor.*(10.188A); †Nil.*mal.cog.*6(M.79.1208B); of a woman, *be dishonoured*, Pall.*v.Chrys.*9(p.57.29; M.47.33).

***ἀσχημονθέα, ἡ,** *unseemly spectacle*, Jo.Clim.*scal.*14(M.88.869B).

***ἀσχημοποιός**, *indulging in obscenity*, *Schol.Clem.prot.*2.37(p.308.25; M.9.783D).

ἄσχιστος, *indivisible*; *undivided*, of the Godhead ὥστε δύο μὲν εἶναι πατέρα καὶ υἱόν, μονάδα δὲ θεότητος ἀδιαίρετον καὶ ἄ. ‡Ath.*Ar.*4.1(p.44.4; M.26.468B); ἡ δὲ φύσις μία ἐστὶν...κἂν ἐν πλήθει φαίνηται ἄ. Gr.Nyss.*tres dii*(M.45.120B).

ἀσωματία, ἡ, *incorporeity*; of Christ's body, asserted by one school of Apollinarians and denied by another οὐ γὰρ δὴ καὶ ὁμοούσιον γενέσθαι τὸ σῶμα τῷ ἀσωμάτῳ θεῷ δυνατὸν διὰ τὴν ἕνωσιν· ὅπερ ἀφρόνως...λέγουσιν...ἐπιτιθέναι τῷ σώματι βουλόμενοι τὴν ἀδύνατον ἀ. Val.Apoll.*apol.*(p.288.16)ap.Leont.B.*Apoll.*(M.86.1953C).

***ἀσωματοειδής**, *without bodily form*, *of incorporeal nature* οἱ Πυθαγόρειοι μὴ ἰσχύοντες λόγῳ παραδοῦναι τὰ ἀ. ... παρεγένοντο ἐπὶ τὴν διὰ τῶν ἀριθμῶν δήλωσιν Cyr.*Juln.*1(6².20A).

ἀσώματος, *incorporeal*; neut. freq. as subst., *incorporeality*; def. ἀ. δέ ἐστιν ὃ μὴ συμπληροῦται σώματι, ἢ οὗ τὸ εἶναι οὐκ ἔστι κατὰ τὸ πλάτος Clem.*fr.*39(p.220.7; M.9.769B); ἀ. ... τὸ χωρὶς σώματος τὴν ὑπόστασιν ἔχον Gr.Nyss.*Eun.*12(1 p.378.7; M.45.1105A); term not found in scripture ὄνομα ἀσωμάτου οὐκ ἴσασιν οὐ μόνον οἱ πολλοί, ἀλλ' οὐδὲ ἡ γραφή Or.*princ.*proem.8(p.14.14; cf.M.11.119B); which prefers ἀόρατος, equated with πνευματικός (cf. A.3) or νοητός (v. A.1) διχῶς...τὸ φῶς ὀνομάζεται σωματικόν τε καὶ πνευματικόν, ὅπερ ἐστὶν...ὡς μὲν αἱ γραφαὶ ἂν λέγοιεν ἀόρατον, ὡς δ' ἂν Ἕλληνες ὀνομάσειεν ἀ. id.*Jo.*13.22(p.246.5, v.l. ὁρατόν...ἀόρατον M.14.436B); νοητὸν...καὶ ἀόρατον καὶ ἀ. *ib.*13.23(p.246.25; 437A).

A. in gen.; **1.** of what pertains to intelligible opp. sensible world, Just.*2apol.*7.8(M.6.456C); Athenag.*leg.*36.2(M.6.972A); Or.*Jo.*19.20(5; p.321.26; M.14.564C); τὸ φυσικὸν διαιρούμενον...εἴς τε τὴν τῶν νοητῶν καὶ ἀ. ἐποπτείαν, καὶ εἰς τὴν τῶν αἰσθητῶν φυσιολογίαν Eus.*p.e.*11.7(521A; M.21.864C); Gr.Nyss.*or.catech.*6(p.29.9; M.45.25C) cit. s. ἀνείδεος; being apprehended by mind ἡ τῶν ἀ. νόησις Just.*dial.*2.6(M.6.477C); ἵνα τῷ λόγῳ τὴν τῶν νοητῶν καὶ ἀ. καὶ θείων ἐποπτεύωμεν οὐσίαν Hipp.*haer.*6.24(p.151.4; M.16.3230B); διττοῦ τοῦ θεωρεῖν ὄντος, αἰσθητικοῦ τε καὶ νοητικοῦ, τὸ μὲν τῶν σωμάτων τὸ δὲ τῶν ἀ. ἐστὶν ἀντιληπτικόν Or.*fr.13 in Jo.*1:18(p.494.26); κάμνει ἐκβῆναι τὰ σωματικὰ ὁ ἡμέτερος νοῦς, καὶ γυμνοῖς ὁμιλῆσαι τοῖς ἀ. Gr.Naz.*or.*28.13(p.43.5; M.36.44A); by way of senses ἵνα...διὰ σωμάτων αἰσθήσεως τῆς τῶν νοητῶν καὶ ἀ. ἐννοίας ἐπιλαβώμεθα αὐτὸς ὁ θεὸς λόγος ⟨ἄνθρωπον⟩ ἀνελάμβανε Eus.*d.e.*7.1(p.302.3; M.22.493D); differing essentially from σώματα, cf.Iren.*haer.*1.5.2(M.7.494A); ὅμοιον ...τῷ λέγειν μεταβάλλειν τι ἀπὸ σώματος εἰς ἀ.· ὡς ὑποκειμένου τινὸς κοινοῦ τῆς τῶν σωμάτων καὶ ἀ. φύσεως Or.*Jo.*13.61(59; p.293.18f.; M.14.516C); so that words with exclusively material connotation are not applicable to ἀσώματα, Ath.*syn.*45(p.270.6; M.26.772D) cit. s. ὁμοούσιος; but both are part of one universe governed by Son, Eus.*d.e.*4.2(p.152.14; M.22.253C); both participating in Son, *ib.*5.1(p.214.9; 356B); characteristics: ἀπαθὲς τὸ ἀ. Just.*dial.*1.5(M.6.476A); not susceptible of increase or decrease, Or.*or.*27(p.367.13f.; M.11.512A); Eus.*e.th.*2.6(p.103.20; M.24.908A); without form etc., ‡Ign.*Smyrn.*3; not confined to space, Or.*fr.37 in Jo.*3:8(p.513.7); Gr.Nyss.*Eun.*1(1 p.72.5; M.45.301B); indivisible, Proc.G.*Gen.*2:23(M.87.176C); cf. *ultimae insipientiae...ut incorporeae naturae substantialis divisio possit intellegi*, Or.*princ.*1.2.6(p.35.15; M.11.135A); **2.** of mental categories, *abstract*, Clem.*str.*8.9(p.97.3; M.9.593B); συμβεβηκότα γένη ἀ. ἐννέα...ποιὸν καὶ ποσόν κτλ. Hipp.*haer.*6.24(p.150.29; M.16.3230B); **3.** with religious connotation; *spiritual* opp. material or physical, Clem.*ecl.*25(p.144.3f.; M.9.709C); of hell fire τοῦ πυρὸς τὸ μὲν σωματικὸν σωμάτων ἅπτεται πάντων, τὸ δὲ...ἀ. ἀσωμάτων φασὶν ἅπτεσθαι, οἷον δαιμόνων id.*exc.Thdot.*81.1(p.131.31; M.9.696B); ἀντὶ τῶν αἰωνίων σκηνῶν τῷ αἰωνίῳ καὶ ἀ. πυρὶ παραδοθήσονται *cat.Lc.*16:1ff.(p.122.24); of anointing of Christ ἀ. καὶ ἐνθέου χρίσεως Eus.*h.e.*1.3.19(M.20.76A); ref. Eph.6:16 τὴν πίστιν, ἀ. θυρεὸν κατ' ἐχθροῦ μὴ φαινομένου Cyr.H.*catech.*5.4; cf. Nil.*epp.*3.33(M.79.392A); οὐ...δείσομεν μή ποτε νοῆται σωματικῶς τὰ ἀ. Gr.Naz.*or.*42.17(M.36.477C); Amph.*Seleuc.*29(M.37.1579A); ἀ. ... λατρείαν Thdr.Mops.*Phil.*3:4(p.233.16; M.66.924C); τὸν σωματικὸν πέπλον ἀπεδύσαντο, καὶ τὴν ἀ. τῆς ὁμολογίας δόξαν ἀνεδύσαντο Mac. Mgn.*apocr.*2.7(p.6.17); met., of Church, Chrys.*a.exil.*2.2(3.422D); myst., Gr.Nyss.*hom.1 in Cant.*(M.44.780D) cit. s. ἁφή.

B. pre-eminently of God; **1.** Platonic τὸν μὲν θεόν φησιν ἀ. τε καὶ ἀνείδεον καὶ μόνοις σοφοῖς ἀνδράσι καταληπτὸν εἶναι Hipp.*haer.*1.19(p.19.12; M.16.3041B); and in other Greek philosophers, Cyr.*resp.*2(p.578.2; 6².386A); not understood by some τούτους...θαυμάζειν χρή, τοὺς οὐδὲ ἔννοιαν ἀσωμάτου λαβόντας θεοῦ; Chrys.*hom.66.3 in Jo.*(8.399B); **2.** Christian σῶμά τις εἶναι λέγει τὸν τέλειον θεόν, ἐγὼ δὲ ἀ. Tat.*orat.*25(p.27.6; M.6.861A); οὐσία θεία ἐστὶν ἀΐδιόν τι καὶ ἄναρχον ἀ. Clem.*fr.*37(p.219.18; M.9.749D); Or.*Jo.*13.21(p.244.20ff.; M.14.432C); *ib.*20.18(16; p.351.10; 613D); id.*Cels.*7.38(p.188.12; M.11.1473B); σύνθετόν τι ὑποτίθεται...ὅπερ οὐ θέμις ἐπὶ τῆς ἀγενήτου καὶ ἀ. φύσεως παραδέχεσθαι Eus.*e.th.*3.3(p.157.8; M.24.1001B); ὁ θεὸς ἄυλος καὶ ἀ. Ath.*decr.*10(p.9.26; M.25.'441'(433)B); τὸ ἀ. [sc. σημαίνει] τὸ μὴ ὑπάρχειν αὐτοῦ τριχῇ διαστατὴν τὴν οὐσίαν Bas.*Eun.*1.9(1.221E; M.29.533A); τὸ...ἀ. σαρκὸς ὄμμασιν ὑποπίπτειν οὐ δύναται id.*mor.*15.3(3.555B; M.32.1309B); ἔστιν ἀ. ἡμῖν τὸ θεῖον Gr.Naz.*or.*28.10(p.37.1; M.36.37C); Chrys.*incomprehens.*2.3(1.456B) cit. s. ἀναλλοίωτος; ἀμεγέθης...ἄποσός τε καὶ ἀ. ἡ θεία νοεῖται καὶ ἔστι φύσις Cyr.*Jo.*1.3(4.25D); αἱ νοεραὶ δυνάμεις ὤφθησαν καὶ αὐτὸς ὁ φύσει ἀόρατος θεὸς καὶ ἀ. CNic.(787)*act.*4(H.4.161B); Jo.D.*f.o.*1.4(M.94.800A); id.*Man.*2(M.96.1321A); of God uniquely ὁ θεὸς μόνος...ἀ. ὤν, διὸ καὶ ἀόρατος Meth.*res.*3.18(p.415.12; M.18.328A); as transcending the incorporeal, Or.*Jo.*13.21(p.244.21; M.14.432C); ὀνομάζομεν αὐτὸν ἀ. καίτοι εἰδότες αὐτὸν ἐπέκεινα ὑπάρχοντα τοῦ ἀ. ὡς τούτου δημιουργόν ‡Just.*qu.Gr.*2(M.6.1469D); neut. as subst. τὸ ἀ. ... τοῦ πατρός Eus.*Marcell.*1.4(p.22.26; M.24.760C); Jo.D.*f.o.*1.8(M.94.813C) = ‡Cyr.*Trin.*7(6³.10C,D; M.77.1133D); = πνεῦμα (exeg. Jo.4:24): φησὶ...ὁ λόγος, ὅτι πνεῦμα ὁ θεός, τουτέστιν ἀ., καὶ τοὺς προσκυνοῦντας αὐτόν, μὴ σωματικῶς δύνασθαι προσεγγίζειν τῷ ἀ. Gr.Nyss.*Apoll.*47(M.45.1240A); ὅταν...εἴπῃ πνεῦμα ὁ θεός, οὐδὲν ἄλλο δηλοῖ ἢ τὸ ἀ. Chrys.*hom.33.2 in Jo.*(8.191D); πνεῦμα κέκληκε [sc. ἡ γραφή] καὶ τὸν πατέρα καὶ τὸν υἱόν, τὸ ἀ. καὶ ἀπερίγραφον τῆς θείας φύσεως...σημαίνουσα Thdt.*eran.*1(4.9); (Arian) εἰ δὲ [sc. ὁ υἱός] ὡς μέρος αὐτοῦ ὁμοουσίου...σύνθετος ἔσται ὁ πατὴρ...ὁ ἀ. θεός Ar.*ep.Alex.*(p.244.20; M.26.712A); **3.** of Logos οὐ δεῖ ταράττεσθαι τὸν νοῦν, γένεσιν καὶ σῶμα...περὶ τὸν ἄυλον καὶ ἀ. τοῦ θεοῦ λόγον ἀκούοντα Eus.*d.e.*4.13(p.170.29; M.22.285A); ὁ τοῦ θεοῦ λόγος...ὁ ἀπερίληπτος, ὁ ἀ. Gr.Naz.*or.*45.9(M.36.633C); ὁ ἀ. σάρκα προσλαβόμενος *cat.Lc.*2:8(p.20.9); Cyr.*ador.*11(1.379C); οἱ οὐδέποτε ἰδόντες αὐτὸν διὰ τὸ ἀ. νοεραὶ δυνάμεις Eulog.*palm.*12(M.86.2936A); θεϊκῶς...ἐγεννήθη ὁ θεὸς λόγος...καὶ ὥσπερ ἀ. καὶ ἀσχημάτιστος καὶ ἀπερίγραπτός ἐστιν Hier.H.*Trin.*(M.40.857D); denied of Logos οὐδὲ τὰ πνευματικὰ καὶ νοερὰ...οὐδὲ μὴν οὐδ' αὐτὸς ἄμορφος...καὶ ἀ. ἐστιν Clem.*exc.Thdot.*10(p.109.18; M.9.660B); **4.** of H. Ghost τὸ ἀ. πνεῦμα τὸ ἅγιον *cat.Ac.*2:24(p.44.29).

C. Christol.; **1.** of Christ as Word incarnate ἄνθρωπος [sc. Jo. Bapt.] θεὸν δείκνυσι καὶ σωτῆρα τὸν ἀ. Or.*Jo.*2.22(26; p.90.9; M.14.172B); Eus.*d.e.*4.13(p.172.9; M.22.285A) cit. s. ἄυλος; *ib.*7.1(p.302.12; 496A); *ib.*10.8(p.483.17; 777A); ἀ. ὢν τῇ φύσει, καὶ λόγος ὑπάρχων ...ἐν ἀνθρωπίνῳ σώματι...πεφανέρωται Ath.*inc.*1.3(M.25.97C); μεταβαίνει τόπον ἐκ τόπου ὁ μηδενὶ τόπῳ χωρούμενος...ὁ ἀ. Gr.Naz.*or.*37.2(M.36.284C); οὐ γὰρ ἐξ ὧν ὡς ἄνθρωπος οἰκονομικῶς διαλέγεται, ἐν τούτῳ ἡ ἀ. οὐσία χαρακτηρίζεται Cyr.*thes.*10(5¹.72C); **2.** of Christ's human soul opp. body τοῦ μὲν τάφου σωματικὴν ἐπιδεχομένου τὴν ἐπίβασιν...τοῦ δὲ ᾅδου ἀ. ‡Ath.*Apoll.*1.13(M.26.1117B); **3.** denied of Christ after Resurrection οὐκ εἰμὶ δαιμόνιον ἀ. Ign.*Smyrn.*3.2 [ascribed by Or.*princ.*proem.8(p.15.2; M.11.119C) to *Keryg.Petr.*; also cit. ap. Eus.*h.e.*3.36.11(M.20.292A)]; **4.** and in eucharist ὁ ἄρτος ὁ ἐκ τοῦ οὐρανοῦ καταβάς, οὐκ ἀ. τι χρῆμά ἐστι. πῶς γὰρ ἂν σώματι τροφὴ γένοιτο τὸ ἀ.; Gr.Nyss.*v.Mos.*(M.44.368C); **5.** Docet. and Gnost., of Christ's human nature τὸν δὲ πατέρα [l. σωτῆρα] ἀγέννητον ὑπέθετο, καὶ ἀ. ... δοκήσει δὲ ἐπιπεφηνέναι ἄνθρωπον Iren.*haer.*1.24.2(cf.M.7.674B); ψηλαφῶντός μου αὐτὸν ἄυλον ἦν καὶ ἀ. τὸ ὑποκείμενον καὶ ὡς μηδὲ ὅλως ὄν *A.Jo.*93(p.196.22); οἱ μὲν ἀνειλῆφέναι σῶμα, οἱ δὲ ἀ. αὐτοῦ τὴν ἐπιδημίαν γεγενῆσθαι διοριζόμενοι Bas.*ep.*260.8(3.400C; M.32.965B); **6.** in Apollinarian Christology τὸν σαρκωθέντα, καὶ ὄντα οὐχ ἕτερον παρὰ τὸν ἀ., ἀλλὰ τὸν αὐτὸν καθ' ὁμοίωσιν ἡμετέρας ἐν σαρκὶ ζωῆς Apoll.*fr.*67(p.220.15)ap.Gr.Nyss.*Apoll.*35(M.45.1200B); οὐ μεταβληθείσης τῆς σαρκὸς εἰς τὸ ἀ. ἀλλ' ἐχούσης καὶ τὸ ἴδιον τὸ ἐξ ἡμῶν κατὰ τὴν ἐκ παρθένου γέννησιν καὶ τὸ ὑπὲρ ἡμᾶς κατὰ τὴν τοῦ θεοῦ λόγου [σύγκρασιν ἤτοι] ἕνωσιν id.*fid.inc.*7(p.199.25; M.*PL.*8.877D); ἡνωμένη ἡ σὰρξ τῷ λόγῳ...μηδέποτε...χωριζομένη... αὐτοῦ τοῦ θεοῦ λόγου...τοῦ ὁμοουσίου τῷ θεῷ καὶ οὐχ ὁμοούσιος τῇ ἀ. οὐσίᾳ τοῦ ἀρρήτου πατρός Job.Ep.*symb.*(p.287.2; M.86.3320C); οὐ γὰρ δὴ καὶ ὁμοούσιον γενέσθαι τὸ σῶμα τῷ ἀ. θεῷ δυνατὸν διὰ τὴν ἕνωσιν... ἀλλὰ δοξασθῆναι τῇ δόξῃ τοῦ ἀ. θεοῦ δυνατὸν καὶ πρέπον τῇ φορούσῃ αὐτὸ θεότητι Val.Apoll.*apol.*(p.288.13ff.)ap.Leont.B.*Apoll.*(M.86.1953C); of Apollinarian Christ ὁ οὖν μήτε ἄνθρωπος, τῷ μηδὲν ἔχειν τοῦ ἀνθρωπίνου γένους, μήτε θεός, τῷ μὴ εἶναι ἀ. Gr.Nyss.*Apoll.*25(M.45.1177B).

D. of angelic creation; **1.** in gen. μεμέρισται πᾶσα ἡ λογικὴ κτίσις εἴς τε τὴν ἀ. καὶ τὴν ἐνσώματον φύσιν· ἔστι δὲ ἀγγελικὴ μὲν ἡ ἀ., τὸ δὲ ἕτερον εἶδος ἡμεῖς οἱ ἄνθρωποι Gr.Nyss.*or.dom.*4(p.74.12f.; M.44.1165B); ἄγγελοι...καὶ πάντα τὰ ἀ. ἀρχὴν τοῦ εἶναι ἔχοντα

Didym.(‡Bas.)*Eun.*4(1.282C; M.29.680B); διὰ τοῦτο [sc. τὴν προαίρεσιν] ἐν τοῖς ἀ. ἀνθρώπων χείρους καὶ ἀλόγων εὑρέθησαν Chrys.*hom.* 75.5 *in Jo.*(8.445B) etc.; ἀζώματος *CIG* 9060.5ff.; **2.** of good angels οὐρανίων...ὡς τῶν ἀ. φύσεων ‡Ign.*Trall.*9; ἄπειροι δῆμοι ἀ. δυνάμεων Chrys.*incomprehens.*2.4(1.457E); id.*hom.6.4 in Heb.*(12.68D); ‡Bas. *h.myst.*49(p.390.22); abs., of Logos described as angel διὰ τῆς τοῦ πυρὸς μορφῆς καὶ εἰκόνος ἀ. τῷ Μωϋσεῖ...ἐφάνη Just.*1apol.*63.16 (M.6.425B); *ib.*63.10(424C); τῶν ἀ. τὸ ᾆσμα βοῶντες ‡Bas.*h.myst.*34 (p.266.2); **3.** of evil spirits δαίμονας καὶ τὰς ἀ. δυνάμεις Chrys. *hom.1.6 in Mt.*(7.12C); διὰ τὴν ἀρετὴν τῶν ἀ. περιγίνεσθαι δυνάμεων id.*hom.10.1 in Eph.*(11.76B); *ib.4.1*(26B); cf. οὐ γὰρ σωματικοὺς εἰς ἀ. ἐγὼ προσκαλοῦμαι πόλεμον Mac.Mgn.*apocr.*2.7(p.4.10); διὰ τί μηδὲν τοὺς δαίμονας τὸ ἀ. ὤνησε; Chrys.*hom.17.4 in 1Cor.* (10.150D).

E. of man; **1.** *disembodied, without a body,* of Docetists at resurrection καθὼς φρονοῦσιν, καὶ συμβήσεται αὐτοῖς, οὖσιν ἀ. καὶ δαιμονικοῖς Ign.*Smyrn.*2; ref. Rom.8:9, Chrys.*hom.53.1 in Jo.* (8.310E); hence of Hades as place of disembodied souls τίς ἐστιν οὗτος ὁ παραγενόμενος ἐν τοῖς ἀ. χωρίοις ἐνσώματος; Eulog.*palm.*12 (M.86.2936A); **2.** of soul; **a.** Platonic ὑποστησάμενοι ἀθάνατον καὶ ἀ. τὴν ψυχήν, οὔτε...ἡγοῦνται δώσειν δίκην (ἀπαθὲς γὰρ τὸ ἀ.) Just.*dial.* 1.5(M.6.476A); Meth.*res.*3.18(p.414.20; M.18.325B); **b.** Christian, asserted by some of νοῦς: ἐμφαίνει...τὴν ἀ. φύσιν καὶ νοητὴν τοῦ ἡγεμονικοῦ ἡμῶν Or.*comm.in Eph.*1:17(p.399); ὁ...σωτὴρ...φωτίζει οὐ σώματα ἀλλὰ ἀ. δυνάμει τὸν ἀ. νοῦν id.*Jo.*1.25(24; p.31.18; M.14.68C); τὸ μὲν γὰρ [sc. λογικόν] πάντη καθαρὸν καὶ ἀ. ... τὸ δ' ἐν σαρκὶ πεπιλημένον Eus.*p.e.*11.6(516D; M.21.857A); †Bas.Anc.*virg.*30(M.30.729C); ἀ. ... ὢν καθ' ἑαυτὸν ὁ νοῦς Gr.Nyss.*Eun.*8(2 p.186.4; M.45.780C); of ψυχή, *Const.App.*6.11.8; δεῖ τοίνυν τοῦ ἀ. καὶ τὴν λατρείαν...διὰ τοῦ ἐν ἡμῖν ἀ. προσφέρεσθαι· τουτέστιν διὰ τῆς ψυχῆς καὶ τῆς τοῦ νοῦ καθαρότητος Chrys.*hom.33.2 in Jo.*(8.191D); id.*hom.28.2 in Mt.*(7.336D); id.*hom.24.3 in Rom.*(9.697D); ἡ μὲν ψυχὴ ὡς ἀ. τῶν οὐρανίων καλῶν [sc. ὀρέγεται], τὸ δὲ σῶμα ὡς χοῦς τῆς ἐπιγείου τροφῆς Diad.*perf.*24(p.26.8); Proc.G.*Gen.*2:23(M.87.176C); Max.*ep.*6(M.91.428C); *ib.*tit.(424C); ἔλθωμεν εἰς ἀ. κτίσμα *ib.*(425B) cf. *omnes animae atque omnes rationabiles naturae...quae omnes secundum propriam naturam incorporeae sunt...nihilominus factae sunt,* Or.*princ.*1.7.1 (p.86.7; M.11.171A); of pre-existent souls, id.*Jo.*1.17(p.21.12; M.14.52B); Cyr.*Jo.*1.9(4.78A); denied by others ἀκολουθεῖ γὰρ τῷ ἀ. αὐτὴν [sc. τὴν ψυχήν] ὑπάρχειν καὶ τὸ ἀπαθῆ εἶναι καὶ ἀπερίσπαστον... ἀσώματον...σώματι ἢ σῶμα ἀσωμάτῳ οὐκ ἄν ποτε συμπάθοι...εἰ δὲ συμπάσχοι τῷ σώματι...ἀ. εἶναι οὐ δύναται Meth.*res.*3.18(p.415.5ff.; M.18.325B–328A); cf. *corporalium et incorporalium passiones inter se non communicare,* Tert.*de anima* 5(M.*PL.*2.694A); id.*de resurrectione carnis* 17(M.*PL.*2.863A); *requirendum...videtur si possibile est penitus incorporeas remanere rationabiles naturas...quod mihi quidem difficillimum et paene impossibile videtur...solius...trinitatis incorporea vita existere recte putabitur,* Or.*princ.*2.2.1f.(p.112.7,21; M.11.187A,B); but cf. his views, *ib.*2.3.2; **3.** met., of ascetics, as having freed themselves from body πλὴν ὀλίγων τινῶν καὶ ἀ. γεγόνασι Chrys.*hom.70.5 in Mt.*(7.693B); μετὰ σώματος ὡς ἀ. Isid. Pel.*epp.*1.477(M.78.444A); ὁ τῶν ἀ. ... τὸν βίον ἐν σώματι μιμησάμενος Thdt.*h.e.*3.24.1(3.941); and of ascetic life, Bas.*ascet.*1.2(2.320A; M.31.873B).

ἀσωματότης, ἡ, *incorporeity,* of God οὐδὲ...θεὸν ὁρῶσιν...οὐ διὰ... ἀσθένειαν ἀλλὰ διὰ τὴν τοῦ θεοῦ ἀ. Or.*fr.13 in Jo.*1:18(p.495.9); θεοῦ λεπτότητα, ἢ ἀ. ... πῶς ἂν ἐθεάσατο [sc. Μωϋσῆς]; Gr.Naz.*or.*37.3 (M.36.285B); of Son ὅμοιος τῷ πατρὶ κατὰ τὴν θεότητα καὶ ἀ. CAnc.(358)*ep.syn.*(p.279.30; M.42.420B); exeg. 2Cor.5:4 οὐκ εἶπεν ἵνα καταποθῇ τὸ σῶμα ὑπὸ τῆς ἀσωματότητος, ἀλλὰ...τὸ θνητὸν ὑπὸ τῆς ζωῆς Chrys.*res.mort.*6(2.432D).

ἀσωμάτως, *incorporeally, without a body;* **1.** of Father in relation to Son and H. Ghost ὁ μὲν γεννήτωρ καὶ προβολεύς, λέγω δὲ ἀπαθῶς ...καὶ ἀ. Gr.Naz.*or.*29.2(p.75.10; M.36.76B); ὁ...θεός, τῷ μονογενεῖ θεῷ...ἀΰλως τε καὶ ἀ. τῶν ἰδίων κοινωνῶν βουλευμάτων Gr.Nyss. *Eun.*12(1 p.274.11; ἀσωμάτῳ M.45.980D); **2.** of Logos in generation υἱός ἐστιν ἐμός, ἐκ τῆς ἐμῆς οὐσίας ἀ. ... ἐκλάμψας Gr.Ant.*bapt.*2.2 (M.88.1873A); τοῦ...θεοῦ λόγου...δύο γεννήσεις, τήν τε πρὸ αἰώνων ἀ., καὶ τὴν ἐπ' ἐσχάτων τῶν ἡμερῶν κατὰ σάρκα Justn.*conf.anath.*2 (p.90.22; M.86.1013D); as pervading all things λόγος...θεοῦ παντοδύναμος διὰ πάντων ἑαυτὸν ἁπλώσας, καὶ ἄνω τε πρὸς ὕψος καὶ κάτω πρὸς βάθος ἑαυτὸν ἀ. ἐκτείνας Eus.*l.C.*11(p.228.19; M.20.1384B); acc. Eus., in relation to his human body ἡ ἀσώματος τοῦ θεοῦ δύναμις...σώματος ἀ. ἐπαφωμένη id.*d.e.*4.13(p.171.3; M.22.285A); **3.** of Christ's descent to Hades ἐκεῖ παρὼν ὁ κύριος ἀ. ‡Ath.*Apoll.* 1.14(M.26.1117B); of his birth, heret. ἀ. ἐκ μήτρας προῆλθεν ὁ κύριος Thdr.Pharan.ap.CLater.*act.*3(H.3.772D); walking on the sea, *ib.* (772E); **4.** of man; of pre-existent soul δόντες...ἀ. τὰς ψυχὰς... βεβαιωκέναι Meth.*res.*1.57(p.318.11; M.41.1152D); *ib.*1.29(p.259.26; 1137B); *ib.*1.58(p.320.18; 1153D); not applicable to human perception, even when perceiving the incorporeal οὐκ ἔχομεν οὐδὲ ταύτην [sc. τὴν νοητὴν φύσιν καὶ ἐπουράνιον] ἀ. ἰδεῖν, εἰ καὶ ἀσώματος Gr. Naz.*or.*28.31(p.70.3; M.36.72A).

ἄσωμος, *without a body,* i.e. existing independently of a body οὐδὲ...ἄχροον εὗρον ἐγὼ δέμας, ἤ τιν' ἄ. χροιὴν Gr.Naz.*carm.*1.1.4.9 (M.37.416A).

ἄσωστος, *past recovery* ἀσώτους αὐτοὺς οἱ καλέσαντες πρῶτοι εὖ μοι δοκοῦσιν αἰνίττεσθαι τὸ τέλος αὐτῶν, ἀ. αὐτοὺς...νενοηκότες Clem. *paed.*2.1(p.158.20; M.8.389A); βίος ἄσωτος καὶ ἄ. Eus.*l.C.*5(conj. M.20.1336A; cf.p.204.1); neut. as subst., *irredeemability,* exeg. Eph. 5:18 τὸ ἄ. τῆς μέθης διὰ τῆς ἀσωτίας αἰνιξάμενος Clem.*paed.*2.2 (p.173.23; 424B).

[*]**ἀσωτέω,** = ἀσωτεύω, *lead a profligate life,* Chrysipp.*enc.in Jo. Bapt.*13(p.45.14).

ἀσωτία, ἡ, 1. *profligacy* ἐν τῷ γάμῳ ἡ ἀ. [sc. κέκρυπται] *T.Aser* 5.1; of the prodigal son δίκην ἐξέτισε τῆς ἀ. Gr.Thaum.*pan.Or.*16 (p.36.22; ἀσώτου M.10.1097B); μήτε τῇ ἀσιτίᾳ εἰς ἀτονίαν, μήτε πολυσιτίᾳ εἰς ἀ. Isid.Pel.*epp.*1.424(M.78.417C); **2.** *concupiscence* ἡ ...τῶν δαιμόνων ἀ. τοῖς ἐν τῷ κόσμῳ πρὸς τὸ κακοποιεῖν ἐχρήσατο Tat.*orat.*17(p.19.16; M.6.844B); διὰ τὴν ἀ. ἑαυτοὺς εἰς τὸ φονευθῆναι πιπράσκουσιν *ib.*23(p.25.22; 857B); ἀσωτίᾳ ὑποτάσσεσθαι Pall.*h.Laus.* 3(p.19.8; M.34.1012C).

***ἀσωτοποσία, ἡ,** *drinking to excess,* †Cyr.*hom.div.*14(5^{2}.405E).

***ἀσωφρόνιστος,** *uncontrolled,* Bas.Sel.*v.Thecl.*2.12(M.85.588C).

***ἀσώφρονος,** *intemperate,* Chrysipp.*enc.in Jo.Bapt.*13(p.44.9).

[*]**ἀτάζω,** *strike with terror* (= ἀτύζω), Gr.Naz.*carm.*2.1.13.46 (M.37.1231A); †Apoll.*met.Ps.*2:5(M.33.1316A; ἀτύξει p.10).

***ἄταικτος,** vox nihili τινὲς δέ φασιν αὐτοὺς [sc. onyx stones] ἐξ ὕδατος ἀ. πεπῆχθαι Epiph.*gemm.*12(M.43.301B).

ἀταλαιπώρητος, *without trouble* or *affliction,* Chrys.*hom.15.5 in Phil.*(11.318D).

ἀταλαίπωρος, 1. *free from labour,* of Adam βίον ἀ. ἔζη Chrys.*hom. 59.2 in Mt.*(7.595B); **2.** *not demanding labour, effortless* ἀ. χαριεῖται τὴν περὶ αὐτοῦ γνῶσιν Cyr.*Jo.*6.1(4.651E); οὐρανὸς...ἐγεωργεῖ τὸ μάννα...σχεδιάζων τοῖς πεινῶσιν ἀ. τράπεζαν ‡Nil.*perist.*12.7(M.79.952C); neut. as subst. δεικνὺς [sc. Jo. Bapt.]...τὸ ἀ. τῆς πρὸς ζωὴν χρείας τοῦ σώματος Nil.*exerc.*60(M.79.793A); **3.** *not difficult* ἰδεῖν ἀ. Cyr.*ador.*2(1.66D); id.*Mich.*27(3.414B; Aubert οὐ ταλαίπωρον); id. *Is.*1.5(2.135D).

***ἀταλάντευτος,** *not weighed, not pondered* τὸ τῆς γλώσσης ἀ. μὴ ἐξιέτω πρόβλημα Ephr.3.405F.

***ἀταλαφρόνως,** *through mental immaturity,* Leont.H.*monoph.* (M.86.1845A).

ἀταπείνωτος, 1. *not humiliated* ἀ. γὰρ ὁ κατὰ ἀγάπην τῷ πλησίον ὑποτασσόμενος Bas.*ep.*65(3.158A; M.32.421B); ἀ. βλέπει τὴν θείαν μεγαλοπρέπειαν ὁ προφήτης Gr.Nyss.*hom.2 in Eccl.*(M.44.637B); ref. Inc. τὸ ἀ. αὐτοῦ ὕψος ἀταπεινώτως ταπεινώσας Jo.D.*f.o.*3.1(M.94.984B); **2.** *not downcast* or *dispirited* τὸ καταπεπτωκὸς ὑπὸ πενίας ἐγείρει, καὶ ἀ. εἶναι παρασκευάζει Synes.*Dion* 2(p.239.11; M.66.1120A); Jo.Mosch.*prat.*171(M.87.3040B); ἀ. ... τὸ τῆς ψυχῆς φρόνημα διασῴζων [sc. Job] Bas.*ep.*2.3(3.73B; M.32.228C); ἡ δὲ ψυχὴ μένει ἀ. Olymp.*Job* 10:1(M.93.129D); neut. as subst., *avoidance of dejection, invincibility,* of spirit τὸ τῆς ψυχῆς ἀκιβδήλευτόν τε καὶ ἀ. Gr. Nyss.*v.Macr.*(p.386.16; M.46.973D); **3.** *not humbled, not submissive* ἐνάγειν εἰς μετάνοιαν τὴν ὑψηλὴν καὶ...ἀ. καρδίαν τοῦ λαοῦ †Bas.*hom. in Ps.*28:5(1.360B; M.30.77C).

***ἀταπεινώτως, 1.** *without humiliation* or *abasement;* ref. Inc. Jo.D.*f.o.*3.1(M.94.984B) cit. s. ἀταπείνωτος; προσκυνῶ τὸν κτίστην κτισθέντα τὸ κατ' ἐμέ, καὶ εἰς κτίσιν ἀ. ... κατεληλυθότα id.*imag.*3.6 (M.94.1325A); **2.** *without being downcast, with unbroken spirit* φέρειν πενίαν εὐγενῶς καὶ ἀ. †Bas.*Is.*256(1.575C; M.30.572A).

ἀταραξία, ἡ, 1. *impassivity, calm, detachment;* a pre-Christian ideal καθάπερ οἱ παλαιοὶ δίκαιοι ἀπάθειαν ψυχῆς καὶ ἀ. καρπούμενοι Clem.*str.*4.7(p.274.1; M.8.1268B); cultivated also by Christians τέλος ἡμῖν ἡ ἀ. καὶ τοῦτο ἄρα ἐστὶν τὸ 'εἰρήνη σοι' id.*paed.*2.7(p.192.15; M.8.461B); ῥύθμιζε τὸν μὲν τρόπον ἐπιεικείᾳ, τὸ δὲ ἦθος ἀταραξίᾳ Gr.Naz.*ep.*244(M.37.388A); ‡Proc.G.*Pr.*4:27(M.87.1261A); a state of soul ἡ ἀνθρωπίνη φύσις...τὸ μακρόθυμον, τὸ καθαρὸν...δεξαμένη, ἑκάστου τούτων ἐπισημαίνει τὸν χαρακτῆρα τῇ καταστάσει τῆς ψυχῆς ἐν ἀ. γαληνιάζουσα Gr.Nyss.*hom.4 in Cant.*(M.44.833A); a state of mind τῶν λογισμῶν ἀ. Ath.*v.Anton.*36(M.26.896C); *ib.*43(908A); Cyr.*Ps.*36:8(M.69.928C); as attribute of God, *Pap.Chr.*(p.446); to be esp. cultivated by monks, ‡Bas.*const*.proem.2(2.534C; M.31.1324C); **2.** *freedom from distraction* τὴν...ἐν ταῖς εὐχαῖς ἀ. Chrys.*hom.5.1 in Mt.*(7.513D); ἡ μόνωσις...ἀταραξίας ἐστὶ μήτηρ *cat.Mt.*14:23(p.117.14).

***ἀταρτηρῶς**, *malevolently*, Eudoc.*Cypr*.1.1(M.85.832A).

***ἀτασθαλέω**, *be presumptuous* or *insolent*, Gr.Naz.*carm*.2.1.45.189(M.37.1366A); Nonn.*par.Jo*.9:3(M.43.824B).

ἄτεγκτος, *not to be softened*, met.; **1.** *immune, impervious* τὸν γνωστικὸν...ἀπαθῆ, ταῖς ἡδοναῖς τε καὶ λύπαις ἄ. Clem.*str*.7.11(p.49.4; M.9.493C); *ib*.7.12(p.53.23; 504A); abs. ζωητόκος χάρις ἄτεγκτος...παρθένος Meth.*symp*.11.2(p.135.23; M.18.212C); **2.** *stiff-necked, obdurate* σκληροὶ καὶ ἄ. Cyr.*Os*.79(3.112D); id.*glaph.Gen*.5(1.166E).

ἀτεκν-έω, *be barren*; ref. 4Reg.2:19ff., *Const.App*.7.37.3; ἅλατι Ἐλισσαῖος τὰ...ῥεύματα ∼οῦντα ἰάσατο Isid.Pel.*epp*.1.16(M.78.189B).

ἀτεκν-όω, *make childless, bereave of children*; of a bear robbed of its cubs, Cyr.*Os*.151(3.184D); properly of persons οὗτός ἐστιν ὁ...τὴν ἀδ[ι]κίαν ∼ώσας ὡς Μωυσῆς Αἴγυπτον Mel.*pass*.68 p.11.13; ∼ώσει αὐτοὺς μάχαιρα Thdt.*Bar*.2:27ff.(2.635); of mothers of Holy Innocents, Sophr.H.*trop*.(M.87.4008C); met., ref. Gen.27:45 ἐπιτίμησον...τῇ ταραχῇ τῆς καρδίας ἡμῶν, καὶ μὴ ∼ωθῇς...τῇ ἁμαρτίᾳ Dor.*doct*.17.2(M.88.1801B); of Judaism ἠτεκνώθη διὰ Χριστόν Proc.G.*Is*.54:1(M.87.2533B).

ἀτέλεια, ἡ, *imperfection, incompleteness*; hence *need, poverty* νικῆσαι τὴν φιλαργυρίαν, ἀγάπα τὴν ἀκτημοσύνην καὶ τὴν ἀ. Jo.D.*spir.neq*.5(M.95.81A).

***ἀτέλεσμα, τό**, *something worthless, trash*; of persons, Dor.*doct*.7.1(M.88.1697C).

ἀτέλεστος, *uninitiated*, of the unbaptized ἄθλιος ἀπελθεῖν καὶ ἀ., ποθῶν τὸ πνευματικὸν ὕδωρ Gr.Naz.*or*.18.31(M.35.1024C); *ib*.40.28(M.36.400A); id.*carm*.2.1.1.324(M.37.994A); ἐδεδίει...ἀ. τοῦ παιδὸς ὄντος ἔτι τὰ τοῦ θείου βαπτίσματος Niceph.Ur.*v.Sym*.240(M.86.3205D).

ἀτελεσφόρητος, **1.** *immature*; of fruit not fully ripened, Eus.*Is*.28:4(M.24.285C); of human embryo, Gr.Nyss.*Maced*.15(M.45.1320A); met. οἱ τῶν αἱρέσεων παρεστηκότες...καταβιάζονται ψυχὰς ἀθλίας καὶ ...ὠμὴν ὥσπερ τινὰ καὶ ἀ. αὐτοὺς τὴν πίστιν ἀπαμβλίσκειν παρασκευάζουσι Cyr.*Am*.12(3.263A); Oecum.*Apoc*.14:15f.(p.166); **2.** *that will not come to maturity, arrested* in development; *aborted* ἄτροφόν τε καὶ ἀ. ... ἔμεινε σπέρμα Gr.Nyss.*anim.et res*.(M.46.157C); Cyr.*Joel*.13(3.212B); met. ἀ. γεννῶσι σοφίαν Meth.*symp*.2.3(p.18.18; M.18.52B); Gr.Nyss.*v.Mos*.(M.44.329B); ref. Eunomian heresy ἀ. γέννημα id.*Eun*.1(1 p.22.9; M.45.249C); ἀ. ἐν ἑαυτοῖς τὴν τοῦ Χριστοῦ μόρφωσιν ἀπετελοῦν Cyr.*ador*.8(1.260E).

***ἀτελεσφόρος**, *not bringing* fruit *to perfection*, Eus.*Is*.18:5f.(M.24.217A).

***ἀτελευτ-άω**, *be endless* πάντας...πρὸς τὴν ∼ῶσαν αὐτοῦ ζωὴν ἐπαγόμενος [sc. Christ] Sophr.H.*ep.syn*.(M.87.3180B).

ἀτελεύτητος, *without an end, everlasting*; **1.** ref. the divine or the world to come; **a.** of God θεὸν ἄναρχον, ἀ. Heraclides ap.Or.*dial*.2(p.122.12); ὁ ἄναρχος θεὸς καὶ ἀ. *Const.App*.8.37.2; *ib*.8.35.5; *ib*.8.41.4; Thdt.*Trin*.28(M.75.1188C); Jo.D.*f.o*.1.2(M.94.792C); *ib*.1.5(801A); neut. as subst. τὸ ἄναρχον τοῦ θεοῦ...τὸ ἀ. δηλῶν Oecum.*Apoc*.1:17(p.38); **b.** of Christ εἰ...ἀρχὴν ἄνωθεν ἔχει, κἂν ἀ. ᾖ, ἄπειρος ὅμως οὐκ ἔστι Chrys.*hom.4.2 in Jo*.(8.30A); id.*hom.12.2 in Heb*.(12.122A); of assumption of flesh εἰς ἑαυτὸν λαβόμενος, πάλιν ἀνακαινίζει...πρὸς διαμονὴν ἀ. ‡Ath.*Ar*.4.33(p.82.12; M.26.520A); **c.** of his kingdom, opp. Marcellus μηδ'...εἰς ἄπειρον καὶ ἀ. ζωήν τε καὶ βασιλείαν τῷ Χριστῷ διδούς Eus.*Marcell*.1.1(p.6.6; M.24.721C); οὔτε τέλος ἔχειν τὴν βασιλείαν αὐτοῦ, ἀλλὰ καὶ τὴν βασιλείαν ἄναρχον καὶ ἀ. CSard.*ep.cath*.ap.Ath.*apol.sec*.45.1(p.122.3; M.25.332C); of kingdom of God, *Const.App*.7.35.9; **d.** of eternity; exeg. Ps.91:8, Gr.Nyss.*hom.8 in Cant*.(M.44.941B); ἀ. ὥσπερ ὁ μέλλων αἰὼν καὶ ἡ ζωὴ τῶν ἀγγέλων Leont.H.*Nest*.1.48(M.86.1508D); in concluding doxology νῦν καὶ εἰς τοὺς ἀ. αἰῶνας τῶν αἰώνων Ath.*decr*.32.5(p.28.26; M.25.476C); *Lit*.ap.*Const.App*.8.12.50; Chrys.*hom.45.4 in Jo*.(8.268D); Thdt.*Ezech*.48(2.1052); **e.** of punishment πυρὸς αἰωνίου καὶ σκώληκος ἀ. *Const.App*.5.7.7; Chrys.*hom.80.3 in Jo*.(8.475E); id.*hom.10.3 in 2Cor*.(10.510D); Isid.Pel.*epp*.1.147(M.78.281B); Justn.*Or*.(p.207.23; M.86.979B); **f.** of life won for man by Christ πρὸς τέλος ἄγει τὸ ἀ. καὶ τέλειον Clem.*str*.7.10(p.41.16; M.9.480B); *ib*.2.22(p.187.4; M.8.1081D); ὑπὲρ ὀδύνης προσκαίρου ἀ. δωρεῖται ἄνεσιν *M.Thdot.3*(p.141.11); τῆς ἐξ αὐτοῦ καὶ δι' αὐτὸν ἐλπιζομένης ἀ. καὶ αἰωνίου παλινζωΐας Areth.*Apoc*.1(M.106.508A); of which a foretaste is given in baptism τοῦ ἁγίου βαπτίσματος χάριτι...εἰς ἀρχὰς ἀναφέρουσα...ἀ. ...ζωῆς Cyr.*Ps*.50:10(M.69.1097A); **2.** of space, *limitless* ὃ γάρ ἐστιν ἀνέφικτον παντὶ καὶ ἀ., τοῦτ' ἐλάχιστόν ἐστι παρὰ τῷ θεῷ †Dion.Al.*fr.2 in Job*(p.204.9).

***ἀτελευτήτως**, *everlastingly, for ever*, also *from everlasting, eternally*, of God φύσει τε καὶ δόξῃ θεὸν ἕνα ἀνάρχως...ἀ. Eun.*exp.fid*.1(p.254); ἡ...ἀγένητος φύσις ἀ. πάσης ἐξουσίας κρείττων ἐστί Geo.Laod.*ep.dogm*.ap.Epiph.*haer*.73.21(p.294.9; M.42.441A); ἀ. ἀεὶ τῆς τριάδος ἀκτίστου μενούσης καὶ ἀ. ὑπαρχούσης Epiph.*haer*.76.49(p.404.4; M.42.620D); ‡Cyr.*Trin*.7(6^3.10D; M.77.1136A); ref. Son τὴν...ζωὴν ...ἀνάρχως εἶναι καὶ ἀ. Chrys.*hom.4.3 in Jo*.(8.30A); τὸ θεῖον τοῦ λόγου...ἀ. ἔχον Leont.H.*Nest*.1.48(M.86.1509C); ref. eternal punishment, Jo.D.*Man*.2.36(M.94.1541C).

***ἀτελευτότης, ἡ**, *everlasting life* κρατοῦντος ἡμᾶς ἐν ἀφθαρσίᾳ τε καὶ ἀ. Thdr.Mops.*Rom*.8:2(M.66.817C; ἀτρεπτότητι p.133.29).

ἀτελής, **1.** *not brought to an end* or *issue, unaccomplished*; of an argument *ad infinitum*, neut. as subst., Leont.H.*Nest*.1.48(M.86.1508D); **2.** *imperfect*; morally, of persons, Eus.*e.th*.3.15(p.172.26; M.24.1029B); ἵνα ὦσιν ἅγιοι...καὶ μηδεὶς...ᾖ κολοβὸς ἢ ἀ. *Lit*.ap.*Const.App*.8.11.4; of Law τέλειος μέν, εἰ νοοῖτο πνευματικῶς...ἀ. δὲ αὖ εἰ μέχρις ἴοι τοῦ γράμματος...ὁ νοῦς Cyr.*Os*.33(3.60C); of persons; in fear of God, *Hom.Clem*.17.12; οὐδεὶς...ἀ. ἐν ἐκείνῳ τῷ τόπῳ [sc. Scete] δύναται παραμεῖναι ‡Pall.*h.mon*.30.1(p.92.8); in spiritual understanding, Chrys.*hom.22.4 in Mt*.(7.279D); id.*hom.30.2 in Jo*.(8.173A); id.*hom.19.1 in Ac*.(9.154A); τοῖς ἀ. ... τὰ στοιχειώδη Thdt.*qu.1 in Gen*.(1.3); neut. as subst., id.*qu.20 in Jud*.(1.338); in nature as a whole, of Adam ἀ. γὰρ ἦν ἔτι καὶ ὁ ὑπ' αὐτοῦ [sc. the Devil] πρῶτος ἀπατηθεὶς ὁ Ἀδάμ †Dion.Al.*fr.1 in Job* 2:10(p.202.10); ἀ. γὰρ ἡ φύσις ἐν τῷ πρώτῳ ἀνθρώπῳ γενομένη, καὶ ἀ. ζῇ, καὶ ἀ. καταλήγει, προσδεομένη τοῦ τελειωτοῦ Proc.G.*Num*.20:4(M.87.853C); of Marcionite demiurge ἀ. καὶ οὐκ ἀγαθοῦ τυγχάνοντος Or.*princ*.4.2.1(p.307.12; M.11.357C); of Son, affirmed of Christ's human body ὁ τέλειος τοῦ θεοῦ λόγος τὸ ἀ. περιτίθεται σῶμα Ath.*Ar*.2.66(M.26.288B); denied of divinity ἠσέβησεν ὥστε...φρονεῖν ὅτι ἡ θεότης ...ἀ. ἐκ τελείου γέγονεν id.*ep.Epict*.2(p.4.16; M.26.1053A); εἰ...ἀ. ἦν [sc. ὁ λόγος] ἐν θεῷ ὤν, γεννηθεὶς δὲ τέλειος γέγονεν ‡Ath.*Ar*.4.11(p.55.6; M.26.481B); Gr.Nyss.*Eun*.1(1 p.99.14; M.45.332D); **3.** act., *not accomplishing one's purpose*; *ineffectual* ἀ. ἡ χάρις ἑνός τινος οἵου δήποτε τῶν ἐκ τῆς ἁγίας τριάδος ὀνομάτων παραλειφθέντος ἐν τῷ σωτηρίῳ βαπτίσματι Gr.Nyss.*ep*.5(M.46.1032A); **4.** *uninitiated*, because of baptism in name of two Persons of Trin. only οὐδὲν λαμβάνει, ἀλλὰ κενὸς καὶ ἀ. αὐτὸς καὶ ὁ δοκῶν διδόναι διαμένει Ath.*ep.Serap*.1.30(M.26.597C); met. ἀμύητοι καὶ ἀτελεῖς τοῦ τῆς ἀληθείας ἀπομείνωσι δράματος Meth.*symp*.8.2(p.82.9; M.18.140B).

ἀτελῶς, **1.** *inadequately* ὡς ἀ. τῶν ἀποστόλων διδασκόντων Chrys.*hom.23.2 in 2Cor*.(10.597C); **2.** *imperfectly*, of understanding spiritual truth τὰ μυστήρια...τὰς θύρας κλείσαντες ἐπιτελοῦμεν, καὶ τοὺς ἀμυήτους εἴργομεν...ἐπειδὴ ἀτελέστερον οἱ πολλοὶ πρὸς αὐτὰ ἔτι διάκεινται id.*hom.23.3 in Mt*.(7.288C); *ib*.*49.1*(505A); πρὸς Κορινθίους τοὺς ἀτελέστερον διακειμένους id.*virg*.49(1.310D).

ἀτενής, *unyielding*; hence *not to be gainsaid, valid* argument, *good* case ἣν ἄν τις αὐτοῖς...πρὸς τοὺς ἄλλους ἀ. λόγος Or.*Cels*.8.12(p.229.12; M.11.1533A).

***ἄτεξ**, *without issue, childless*, of Sarah στεῖρά τε καὶ ἄ. Cyr.*Is*.4.5(2.700C); of gentile world before Inc. χήρα...ἄγονός τε...καὶ ἄ. *ib*.5.2(756E); of BMV ἄ. κατὰ γαμικὴν σύνοδον καὶ τοκὰς κατὰ θείαν σύλληψιν Thdr.Stud.*nativ.BMV* 7(M.96.696C).

[*]**ἀτεράμνων**, ? variant of ἀτεράμων; *hard; stubborn* ἀ. τισι καὶ ἀπαιδευτάτοις Nil.*epp*.3.152(M.79.453D).

ἀτεράμων, *hard, stubborn*; of persons, Meth.*symp*.9.3(p.117.9; M.18.184A); *ib*.10.3(p.125.22; 197B); of Pharaoh, Cyr.*glaph.Ex*.2.1(265C); of the Jews δεινοί τε καὶ ἀ. καὶ τὴν διάνοιαν ἀκαμπεῖς Cyr.*Os*.12(3.33D); Thdt.*Jer*.15:8f.(2.490); of the mind or opinions τὴν ἀ. καταμαλάξῃ καρδίαν id.*qu.57 in 1Reg*.(1.392); id.*Jer*.5:3(2.438).

***ἀτέρμαντος**, *boundless*, †Apoll.*met.Ps*.20:7(M.33.1337C).

ἀτερμάτιστος, **1.** *boundless* ἀ. ἀντλήσεις βάθος Geo.Pis.*hex*.1579(M.92.1557A); met. ἡ...τοῦ κυρίου εἰρήνη...ἀ. †Bas.*Is*.226(1.550D; M.30.513B); **2.** *unsteady*, of a ship *without ballast* καθάπερ σκάφος ἀ. φέρεσθαι εἴασεν Thdt.*Rom*.1:24(3.25).

ἄτευκτος, *not gaining* or *attaining*; of Pharisees, Cyr.*Jo*.5.2(4.483D); ref. Inc. πῶς τινα ἄνθρωπον ἔλαβε γυμνόν, ἄ. ἔτι τῆς προλήψεως αὐτοῦ; Leont.H.*Nest*.5.21(M.86.1744A); prob. f.l. for ὑετός (cf. Ps.71:6) στακτὴ δὲ γέγονεν, ὡς ἄ. ἐπὶ πόκον Gr.Nyss.ap.Proc.G.*Cant*.1:12(M.87.1565B).

ἀτέχναστος, *not artificial*, of Christ in comparison with Jo. Bapt. οὐσιῶδες καὶ ἀ. καὶ αἰώνιον φῶς Max.*ambig*.(M.91.1244C); of a system of ethics, *ib*.(1368A).

***ἀτεχνολόγητος**, *without artifice, artless* τὴν ἁπλῆν καὶ ἀ. τοῦ πνεύματος διδασκαλίαν Bas._Spir_.5(3.5D; M.32.76C); ἡ τοῦ θεοῦ δύναμις...ἀ. Gr.Nyss._bapt.Chr_.(M.46.584D); neut. as subst. τὸ ἁπλοῦν καὶ ἀ. τῆς πίστεως...συνταράττων σοφίσμασι Thdt._haer_.4.12 (4.369).

ἄτεχνος, **1.** _not trained to any craft_ or _profession, without a trade_, _Clem.ep_.8(M.2.44B); **2.** _artless, unsophisticated_, Jo.D._hom_.2.3(M.96.580D).

ἀτέχνως, _simply, artlessly_ οὕτως ἀ. τὰ γεγραμμένα λεγέτω καὶ ψαλλέτω Ath._ep.Marcell_.31(M.27.41D).

ἀτημελέω, _neglect_, _1Clem_.38.2; Chrys._fr.Job_ 38:36(M.64.649B, for ἀτημέλισται).

*__ἀτιθασσεύτως__, _untameably_, Bas._Spir_.75(3.64C; M.32.209B).

[*]__ἀτίθασσος__, _untamed, savage_ θηρίων Eus._Is_.19:1(M.24.221A); ἔθνεσιν Dion.Ar._c.h_.8.2(M.3.240D); τὸν τῆς γεένης ἀ. σκώληκα Jo.D._hom_.4.38(M.96.641C); met., of Pharisees ἀ. καὶ μισάνθρωποι Chrys._hom.40.1 in Mt_.(7.437B); ἀ. ἡδοναῖς Cyr._Is_.1.2(2.54C); ἀ. ... φρόνημα _ib_.3.1(377E); neut. as subst. ἀπὸ τοῦ τιθασσοῦ ἐπὶ τὸ ἀ. ... μεταβαλεῖν Pall._v.Chrys_.20(p.141.11; M.47.78).

ἀτιμαγέλης ([*]__ἀτιμάγελος__), _despising the herd_; met., of persons, _despising one's associates_ or _ignoring one's social obligations_ οἱ δὲ [sc. ἐξ Ἰσραὴλ]...ἄπιστοι γεγόνασι...καὶ ἀ. δεινοὶ καὶ ἀγέρωχοι Cyr._Is_.4.4(2.659C); id._hom.pasch_.12(5^{2}.165B); in form ἀτιμάγελος, id. _Juln_.2(6^{2}.65A).

*__ἀτιμαστήριον, τό__, _source of dishonour_ οὐ μεταβαλὼν εἰς πάθος τὸ ἀπαθὲς τῆς θεότητος...ἵνα μὴ τὸ ἡμῖν σωτήριον, γένηται αὐτῷ ἀ. Eulog._palm_.7(M.86.2924C).

ἀτιμία, ἡ, _worthlessness_, cf. Rom.9:21 etc. ὀστράκινα ὑπὸ τῆς ἀ. φυλάσσεται ὅτι οὐδεὶς...ὀστράκινον ὀρέγεται κλέψαι θεόν _Hom.Clem_. 10.8.

*__ἀτιμοποιός__, _dishonouring, bringing disgrace_ ἀ. ... ἡ ἁμαρτία †Bas._Is_.167(1.498E; M.30.396A); Cyr._ador_.16(1.579C); id._Am_.75(3.336B); ‡Proc.G._Pr_.3:25(M.87.1253A); _ib_.12:16(1341C).

*__ἀτιμωρησία, ἡ__, _impunity_, Chrys._hom.16.2 in 1Cor_.(10.136A).

ἀτιμωρητί, _with impunity_; **1.** act., i.e. without exacting punishment, Eus._l.C_.7(p.214.26; M.20.1356B); **2.** pass., i.e. without suffering punishment, Chrys._hom.28.1 in Jo_.(8.160A); id._hom.1.5 in Heb_.(12.23A); Isid.Pel._epp_.5.269(M.78.1493B); Olymp._Job_ 21:16(M.93.228D).

*__ἀτληπαθής__, _impatient of hardship_ ἀ. τὸ φρόνημα καὶ πολὺ πρόχειρος εἰς ἀκηδίαν ὁ νοῦς Cyr._glaph.Ex_.3(1.311C); neut. as subst., id._ador_.5(1.153E); _ib_.(162D).

ἄτμητος, **1.** _uncut_; met., _entire_ φιλαδελφίαν ἄ. ‡Chrys._hom_.13(13.253B); **2.** _indivisible_, of the divine nature ἄ. τε καὶ ἀδιαίρετον Gr.Nyss._tres dii_(M.45.124D); ref. relation of Logos to Father ἄ. ... καὶ ἀχώριστον τοῦ πατρὸς ταύτην τὴν δύναμιν ὑπάρχειν Just._dial_.128.3 (M.6.776A); of man's union with God ὁ...θεῷ ἑνωθεὶς...ἀδιαίρετον...ἔχειν καὶ ἄ. τὴν πρὸς αὐτὸν...συνάφειαν Isid.Pel._epp_.1.199(M.78.309C); of indwelling Christ ἀμερῶς ἑαυτὸν ἐπιμερίζοντα καὶ τοῖς μετέχουσιν...διὰ τὴν κατὰ φύσιν ἄ. ὀντότητα τῆς ἑνότητος Max._ambig_.(M.91.1172C).

ἀτμήτως, _indivisibly_, Trin. ἀ. ἡ μονὰς χωρίζεται Amph._Seleuc_.212 (M.37.1591A); in analogy of human logos ὁ λόγος ὁ σὸς...προφορικὸς μέν ἐστι, γεννᾶται δὲ ἀ. ἐκ τοῦ σοῦ νοῦ Gel.Cyz._h.e_.2.21.31(M.85.1289B).

ἀτμίς, ἡ, _steam, vapour_, ref. rel. of Logos to Father (cf. Sap. 7:25) πνεύματος...ὄντος...ἀναλόγως...ὁ Χριστὸς ἀ. λέλεκται Dion.Al. ap.Ath._Dion_.15(p.57.18; M.25.504A); Thgn._hypot.fr_.2(p.76; M.10.240A) cit. s. ἀπόρροια; ὅταν...ἀπὸ τῶν γραφῶν λέγῃ λόγον...ἀ. καὶ ἀπαύγασμα τοῦ πατρός Ath._Dion_.9(p.52.4; 492B).

*__ἀτολμήτως__, _beyond what may be dared, outrageously_, Epiph. _haer_.77.32(p.444.14; M.42.688C).

ἄτομος, **1.** _that cannot be cut, indivisible_; hence neut. as subst., the ultimate indivisible; of time, _instant_ οὔτ' ἐπινοίᾳ οὔτ' ἀ. τινὶ προάγει ὁ θεὸς τοῦ υἱοῦ Ar._ep.Eus_.(p.2.2; M.42.212A); **2.** _individual, particular_; also neut. as subst., _individual_ opp. genus or species κατὰ...τὴν πατέρων διδασκαλίαν ἣν ἔχει διαφορὰν τὸ κοινὸν ὑπὲρ τὸ ἴδιον, ἢ τὸ γένος ὑπὲρ τὸ εἶδος ἢ τὸ ἄ. Thdt._eran_.1(4.7); ὑπόστασιν...ἤτοι πρόσωπον καλοῦσιν [sc. οἱ πατέρες] ὅπερ οἱ φιλόσοφοι ἄ. οὐσίαν λέγουσι †Leont.B._sect_.1.1(M.86.1193A); τὰ...περιεχόμενα λέγονται καὶ ἄ. καὶ ὑποστάσεις καὶ πρόσωπα. καὶ ἄ. μὲν διὰ τὸ μηδὲν αὐτῶν τομὴν ἢ διαίρεσιν ὑποδέχεσθαι ‡Cyr._Trin_.13(6^{3}.19C; M.77.1149A); Γαβριὴλ ...Μιχαὴλ καὶ τῶν λοιπῶν ἀγγέλων ἕκαστον, ἄτομα προσαγορεύουσι Jo.D._haer_.83(M.94.745C); **3.** theol., _Person_ of Trin. ἐν μέν τι τούτων εἶναι τὸ ἀποτέλεσμα, ὃ εἴτε πρόσωπον, εἴτε ὑπόστασιν, εἴτε ἄ. ... οὐ διαφέρομαι Leont.B._Nest.et Eut_.1(M.86.1305C); ἐπὶ τῆς θεότητος μίαν οὐσίαν...ἀ. δὲ τρία, τρεῖς ὑποστάσεις, τρία πρόσωπα ‡Cyr._Trin_. 13(6^{3}.19E; M.77.1149B); **4.** Christol., _a particular person, human individual_, ref. Inc. πῶς ἂν περιελήφθη τῷ ἀ. τὸ ἄπειρον; Gr.Nyss. _or.catech_.10(p.54.10; M.45.41B); φύσιν ὁ λόγος ἀναλαβὼν ἀνθρωπίνην, τὴν ἐν τῷ εἴδει θεωρουμένην, ἢ τὴν ἐν ἀ. ἀνέλαβεν; Leont.B._arg.Sev_. (M.86.1917A); οὔτε...οὐσίας...δηλωτικὸν ὡς εἴδους τὸ Χριστὸς ὄνομα ὑπάρχει, τῶν κατὰ πολλῶν καὶ διαφερόντων ταῖς ὑποστάσεσι κατηγορουμένων ἀ. Max._ep_.12(M.91.488B).

ἀτον-έω, **1.** _be relaxed_, hence _be exhausted, worn-out_; **a.** physically; by illness, Jo.Jej._poenit.cont.virg_.(M.88.1953A); hence _be in weak health_ ~οῦντας...ἐγκρατεύεσθαι...προτρέπονται [sc. οἱ δαίμονες] Evagr.Pont._cap.pract_.28(M.40.1229A); met. πλείους...τῆς κεφαλῆς ἀποτομὴν ὑπομείναντας...ὡς ἀμβλύνεσθαι φονεύοντα τὸν σίδηρον ~οῦντά τε διαθλᾶσθαι Eus._h.e_.8.9.4(M.20.760C); **b.** logically; _be in a weak position_, Cyr._Jo_.proem.(4.4A); **c.** morally; _be exhausted_, of patience, Cyr._ador_.8(1.267A); _be weakened_; of virtue in man, id. _Ps_.6:3(M.69.744C); of demons ἡμεῖς δὲ οἱ δαίμονες ~οῦμεν μὴ ἔχοντες βάσιν...ἀναπαύσεως _T.Sal_.20.16(p.62.13; M.122.1349C); of Devil vanquished by Christ, ‡Ath._Apoll_.2.10(M.26.1149A); **2.** abs., _be too relaxed, be powerless, ineffectual_, Serap._Man_.3.9(p.62; M.18.1229C); ἵνα καὶ ἐν τοῖς ἁπάντων ~ήσῃ σώμασιν ἡ φθορά Cyr._ep_.1(p.22.16; 5^{2}.18A); intellectually, _be inadequate, deficient_ ~ούντων...πρὸς τὴν ἀπολογίαν Bas._ep_.226.4(3.349C; M.32.849D); αὐτοῦ τοῦ προφήτου περὶ τὴν διήγησιν ~ήσαντος Thdt._Ezech_.1:5(2.683); of an argument, _fail, not hold good_ ἐπὶ μὲν τῶν ἄλλων ἁπάντων ἀληθὴς ἔσται λόγος... ~ήσει δὲ ἐπὶ μόνου Χριστοῦ Cyr._Jo_.4.3(4.376E); **3.** _be too relaxed_ to, hence _prove unequal_ to, _be incapable_ of ἠτόνησεν εἰπεῖν ὑφ' οὗ γέγονεν Thphl.Ant._Autol_.2.5(M.6.1053B); σοῦ...μὴ δυναμοῦντος ~ῶ πρὸς ἐπιστροφήν Or._fr.57 in Jer_.38:18–20(p.226.19); Bas._hom_.16.4 (2.138C; M.31.481C); τὸ μὲν οὖν ἀραῖς κατὰ τῶν ὑπεναντίων χρῆσθαι, τίς οὐκ οἶδεν ὅτι τῶν ~ούντων ἐστὶ περὶ ἃ σπουδάζουσιν ἴδιον; Gr. Nyss._Apoll_.26(M.45.1180A); πᾶσα τῶν ἀνθρώπων ἡ φύσις ~εῖ πρὸς τὴν τούτου [sc. God] κατάληψιν Gr.Ant._bapt_.2.3(M.88.1872C); Nil. _exerc_.57(M.79.789C); exeg. Jo.8:43 'οὐ δύνασθε' φησίν, ~οῦντας ἐλέγχων περὶ τὸ τελείως ἀγαθόν Cyr._Jo_.5.5(4.556C); τὴν εἰσδοχὴν τοῦ φωτὸς ἀ. Thdt._rect.conf_.17(M.6.1237C,1240A); freq. of Law ὁ...νόμος ...τῇ κατορθώσει τῆς ἀρετῆς ~ῶν Thdr.Mops._Rom_.8:3(p.134.2; M.66.820A); ὁ νόμος τοῦτο ἐσπούδαζε δίκαιον ποιῆσαι τὸν ἄνθρωπον, ἠτόνει δέ Chrys._hom.16.2 in Mt_.(7.206B); id._hom.7.4 in Rom_.(9.488E); Gennad._fr.Rom_.8:3–4(p.375.14; M.85.1689A); of law of sin ἠτόνησε μὲν τῆς ἁμαρτίας ὁ νόμος, κεκράτηκε δὲ ὁ τοῦ πνεύματος Cyr._Arcad_.(p.103.2; 5^{2}.103C); of death ἵνα λοιπὸν ~ήσῃ τοῦ θανάτου τὸ κράτος id._Pulch_.(p.56.12; 5^{2}.172D); Bas.Sel._or_.13.3(M.85.181A); **4.** _grow weary in well-doing, be slack; be faint-hearted_, _cat.Lc_.10:30ff.(p.88.5); Jo.Carp._cap_.77(M.85.1852); met., of seedlings, ref. Mt. 13:5 ἐξανατείλασιν, ἐν δὲ καιρῷ καρπῶν ~ήσασι Isid.Pel._epp_.1.372 (M.78.393B); in spiritual life of Christians ἐν οἷς πεπιστεύμεθα μὴ ~οῦντες Hipp._haer_.1.proem.6(p.3.9; M.16.3020C); ~ήσας...ἀπὸ τῆς θλίψεως id._Dan_.4.12.2; μὴ...~ήσωμεν πρὸς τὴν ἐπαγγελίαν ‡Bas. _const_.1.5(2.539C; M.31.1336B); αὐτοὺς σαθρωθέντας ἢ ~ήσαντας διὰ τοῦ...αὐτοῦ λόγου ἀνεκούφιζεν Ammon._Ac_.18:22f.(M.85.1572B); of Elisabeth ἐξέλιπεν ἡ γονή, ἀλλ' οὐκ ἠτόνησεν ἡ εὐχή Antip.Bost. _Jo.Bapt_.4(M.85.1768A); **5.** not of God τῆς θελήσεως αὐτοῦ οὐκ ἀπορουμένης οὐδὲ ~ούσης, δύναται ὑποστῆσαι ὃ βούλεται [sc. ὁ θεός] Or._comm.in Gen_.(M.12.48A)ap.Eus._p.e_.7.20(335A). ὁ θεὸς... μηδὲν ἐλαττούμενος, μηδὲ ~ῶν ἐκ τῆς δημιουργίας τῆς πολλῆς Chrys._hom.5.3 in Jo_.(8.38E); id._hom.7.2 in Rom_.(9.485B); Cyr. _Is_.2.5(2.329E,330B); not of Christ οὐκ ~ήσει μου ὁ κύριος _A.Jo_.52 (p.177.8); οὐχ ὡς αὐτοῦ ~οῦντος ζωογονῆσαι τὴν σάρκα Chrys._hom. 29.3 in 2Cor_.(10.643E); id._hom.17.2 in 1Cor_.(10.147A); _ib_.39.5(10.370C).

ἀτονία, ἡ, **1.** _slackness_; of solids, _lack of resistance, fragility_, Gr.Nyss._hom.4 in Cant_.(M.44.837C); of water, _sluggishness_, id._virg_. 7(p.280.15; M.46.352B); **2.** _mental torpor_ or _weakness, dullness_, of certain who fall into heresy ὑπὸ ἀ. τε καὶ μικροψυχίας Gr.Nyss. _Eun_.8(2 p.189.15; M.45.784C); τὴν ἀσθένειαν καὶ ἀ. τοῦ λογισμοῦ Nil. _epp_.1.213(M.79.161B); hence _weakness_ in power of self-expression, _paucity_ of style, Gr.Nyss._Apoll_.12(M.45.1148A).

*__ἀτονιάω__, _become exhausted_, ‡Chrys._fug.spec_.(1.816A).

ἄτονος, **1.** _relaxed, feeble_; mentally _too weak_ to, _incapable_ of ἀτονώτερον...πρὸς τὸ γινώσκειν τινὰ πνευματικά Iren._haer_.1.5.4(M.7.497A); **2.** morally _slack, torpid_ ὁ νοῦς ἡμῶν ἄ. ὑπάρχων _M.Thdot_.1 1 (p.61.18); Dor._doct_.4.10(M.88.1672B); opp. πρόθυμος, Tit.Bost._fr.Lc_. 6:27(p.162); **3.** in gen., _impotent, weak_ πανταχοῦ ἄ. ἡ ψυχή Chrys. _hom.7.5 in 1Cor_.(10.57A); _too weak_ to, _unequal_ to εἰ...ἀσθενὲς...τὸ σῶμα, ὥστε νηστεύειν διηνεκῶς, ἀλλ' οὐ...πρὸς ὑπεροψίαν γαστρὸς ἄ. id._hom.57.4 in Mt_.(7.581D); ἐλέγχων ἡμῶν τὸ πρὸς δικαίωσιν ἄ., μᾶλλον δὲ πάντῃ ἀδύνατον Thdr.Mops.*Gal.*3:21(p.50.28; M.66.904D); id.*Os.*13:10f.(M.66.204A); *cat.Jo.*11:25(p.317.11).

ἀτοπέω, *act outrageously* τοῖς μεγάλα ἠτοπηκόσι Serap.*Man.*50 (p.71; M.18.1245B).

ἄτοπος, *out of place*; *out of the way*; hence **1.** *obtrusive* ἐπαχθὴς ἡ δίψα...ἄ. τὸ σῶμα Ast.Am.*hom.*14(M.40.384B); **2.** *outrageous*; *wicked*, Eus.*h.e.*3.17(M.20.252A); λογισμῶν ἀ. Mac.Aeg.*libert.ment.*4 (M.34.937D); Chrys.*sac.*6.3(p.145.5; 1.423B); id.*hom.45.4 in Jo.*(8.267A); partic. of sexual vice, Polyc.*ep.*5.3; Bas.*ep.*53.1(3.147A; M.32.396D); *ib.*55(149D; M.404A); Chrys.*hom.43.2 in Mt.*(7.460D); id.*sac.*6.12(p.162.1,9; 1.431A).

ἀτόπως, *improperly* οἱ δὲ...πρὸς μόνῃ τῇ θεραπείᾳ τοῦ θεοῦ γινόμενοι γνησίως κατὰ τὴν διαφορὰν τῶν εἰς τοῦτο κινημάτων λευῖται καὶ ἱερεῖς οὐκ ἀ. λεχθήσονται Or.*Jo.*1.2(3; p.5.22; M.14.25A); *ib.*1.17 (p.22.9; M.14.53A); Chrys.*hom.11.1 in 2Cor.*(10.513B).

ἀτράγῳδος, *unhistrionic*; *unobtrusive, without fuss*, Nil.ap.Proc. G.*Cant.*3:9f.(M.87.1632D).

***ἀτρανής,** *not clear* οὐκ ἄχρηστον...καὶ ἀ. φωνὴν ἱέντας θεῷ Cyr. *Am.*54(3.308B); ψυχοῖς τε καὶ ἀ. ... λογισμοῖς *ib.*57(313E).

***ἄτρανος,** = foreg.; superl., Meth.*res.*2.16(p.365.10; M.18.312B).

ἀτρανῶς, *not plainly*, Leont.H.*Nest.*5.5(M.86.1729B).

ἀτράνωτος, *not clear, ill-defined* χωρὶς μὲν ἀγάπης, γλῶσσα κἂν ἀγγέλων ἐν ἀνθρώποις...ἀ. ἐστιν Or.*comm.in 1Cor.*13:2(*JTS* 10 p.33); ἐπὶ σκιαῖς καὶ ὀνείρασι καὶ ἀ. φαντασίαις Isid.Pel.*epp.*5.3(M.78.1328A); Leont.B.*Nest.et Eut.*1(M.86.1296B).

***ἀτρανώτως,** *not plainly, without elucidation*, Or.*Cels.*5.54(p.58.15; M.11.1268A); id.*comm.in Mt.*17.27(p.660.15; M.13.1557A).

ἀτράπεζος, *without board* or *food*, of S. Paul ἄστεγος...καὶ ἀ. Gr. Nyss.*hom.5 in Eccl.*(M.44.685A); id.*ep.*17(M.46.1061C).

***ἀτραπία,** ἡ, ? error for ἀτροπία, *unchangeability, fixedness*, Cyr. *glaph.Lev.*(1.361B).

ἄτραχυς, *without asperity, smooth* εὐθεῖαν...φησὶ γενέσθαι τῶν εὐσεβῶν τὴν ὁδόν, πῶς γὰρ οὐκ εὐθεία καὶ ἄ.; Cyr.*Is.*3.1(2.360C); of the way to God οὐκ ἄ. τὸ χρῆμά ἐστιν id.*Os.*172(3.196C); of a life of ease τὸ ἡδύ τε καὶ ἄ. id.*ador.*5(1.154A); of a task, *simple, easy*, id. *Ps.*1:3(M.69.720A); freq. in last sense οὐκ ἄ. *difficult* to understand, id.*ador.*16(577C); id.*Zach.*52(3.729B); id.*inc.unigen.*(5^1.687D).

[*]**ἀτρεκία,** ἡ, *truth*, ‡Caes.Naz.*dial.*38(M.38.904).

ἀτρεπτί, *without erring*, Gel.Cyz.*h.e.*proem.23(M.85.1197B).

ἄτρεπτος, **I.** *immutable, unchangeable*;

A. theol.; **1.** of divine essence τὸν ἄ. καὶ ἀεὶ ὄντα θεόν Just.*1apol.*13.4(M.6.348A); ἀπεμφαίνει, ἀ. ὄντος τοῦ θεοῦ...εὔχεσθαι, οἰόμενον μετατρέψειν...αὐτοῦ τὴν πρόθεσιν Or.*or.*5(p.311.1; M.11.433B); *ib.*24 (p.354.8; 492C); τὸν ἄ. καὶ ἀναλλοίωτον θεόν Meth.*creat.*2(p.494.25; M.18.333C); Eus.*h.e.*1.2.8(M.20.57A); τὴν ἄ. καὶ ἀναλλοίωτον οὐσίαν Bas.*Eun.*2.23(1.258E; M.29.621C); ὁ θεός, ἡ ἀνώλεθρος καὶ ἄ. φύσις Chrys.*hom.3.4 in Rom.*(9.453A); Cyr.*Heb.*2:14(p.464.4; M.74.965A); αὐτοῦ τὸ ἄ. ἔδειξεν μακάριον ὀνομάσας. ὁ γὰρ φύσει μακάριος οὐδεμίαν τροπὴν ἐπιδέχεται Thdt.*1Tim.*6:15(3.672); id.*Heb.*1:12(3.553); ‡Cyr. *Trin.*1(6^3.1A; M.77.1120A); Jo.D.*f.o.*1.13(M.94.853Cf.); fundamental to Christian doctrine of God, Cyr.H.*catech.*4.4; upheld by Jews and Christians opp. Stoics, Or.*Cels.*1.21(p.72.16; M.11.697A); and Epicureans, *ib.*4.14(p.284.20; 1045A); as divine title τὸν παναλκῆ καὶ ἄ. καλοῦντες εἰς ἐπικουρίαν Cyr.*Ps.*36:15(M.69.933B); **2.** of Trin., Ath.*Ar.*1.18(M.26.49B); ἄ. καὶ ἀναλλοωτος ἡ αὐτὴ τριὰς ἀεί Gr.Thaum.*symb.*(p.3.12; M.10.988A); ‡Ath.*Apoll.*1.3(M.26.1097A); Didym.(‡Bas.)*Eun.*5(1.314C; M.29.753B); τριάδα ἄκτιστον, ἄ., ἀναλλοίωτον ‡Chrys.*Trin.*4(1.840A); Thdt.*eran.*1(4.9); as of one substance, ‡Ath.*dial.Trin.*1.15(M.28.1140C); Thdt.*Trin.*28(M.75.1188C) cit. s. αὐτοζωή; **3.** of Father, Or.*Jo.*6.38(22; p.147.7; M.14.265B); πιστεύομεν...εἰς μόνον ἀγέννητον πατέρα, οὐδένα τοῦ εἶναι αὐτῷ τὸν αἴτιον ἔχοντα, ἄ. τε καὶ ἀναλλοίωτον Alex.Al.*ep.Alex.*12(p.27.1; M.18.565A); ἔσται πατὴρ ἀεί, τὸ ἄ. ἔχων καὶ ἀναλλοίωτον ὡς θεὸς Cyr.*Jo.*1.4(4.36E); id.*thes.*13(5^1.124E); Thdt.*Trin.*9(M.75.1157C); **4.** of Son ἄ. τοῦτον καὶ ἀναλλοίωτον ὡς τὸν πατέρα Alex.Al.*ep.Alex.*12(p.27.13; M.18.565B); ὁ υἱός...ἐγεννήθη...ἄ. ἐξ ἀτρέπτου †Ath.*exp.fid.*3(M.25.205A); τῆς δὲ οὐσίας τοῦ πατρὸς οὔσης ἀ., ἄ. ἂν εἴη καὶ τὸ ἐξ αὐτῆς ἴδιον γέννημα Ath.*Ar.*1.35(M.26.85A); *ib.*1.36(88A); ὁ...λόγος...τοῦ θεοῦ ἄ. ἐστι...πῶς πάντα τὰ τοῦ πατρὸς τοῦ υἱοῦ ἐστιν, εἰ μὴ καὶ τὸ ἄ. καὶ ἀναλλοίωτον τοῦ πατρὸς ἔχει; *ib.*1.52(120B); id.*decr.*23.2(p.19.15; M.25.456D); Cyr.*inc.unigen.*(5^1.684A), v. I.B.1 infra; **5.** of H. Ghost, Ath.*ep.Serap.*1.26(M.26.592B) cit. s. ἀεί; ἀθάνατόν ἐστι πάντως, ὅτι ἄ. τε καὶ ἀναλλοίωτον...ἐκ πατρὸς ἐκπορευόμενον Gr. Nyss.*Maced.*10(M.45.1313B); τὸ μὲν πνεῦμα φύσει ἐστὶν ἄ., οἱ δὲ μετέχοντες αὐτοῦ κατὰ μετοχὴν ἄ. ‡Ath.*dial.Trin.*1.25(M.28.1153C); Epiph.*haer.*69.56(p.203.20; M.42.289C); *ib.*(p.204.16; 292B); **6.** of divine action and attributes, Clem.*str.*1.24(p.102.19; M.8.909C) cit. s. ἀσχημάτιστος; τὸ...ἀγέννητον κάλλος...ἄ. καὶ ἀγήρων Meth.*symp.*6.1(p.64.15; M.18.113B); *Const.App.*7.35.9 cit. s. διαμονή; ἐκ τοῦ τοῦ θεοῦ [ἀτ]ρέ[πτου καὶ ἀμεταβ]όλο[υ λογισμοῦ] *POxy.*1493.14 = *Pap. Chr.*(p.396); τὸ οὖν 'μεταμεμέλημαι' τὸ ἄ. αὐτοῦ [sc. θεοῦ] ἐμφαίνει τὸ κατὰ τὸ μὴ συγγινώσκειν. τὸ δὲ 'μετενόησεν ὁ κύριος' τὸ ἄ. αὐτοῦ δηλοῖ τὸ κατὰ τὸ συγγινώσκειν. ἄ. γάρ ἐστιν ὁ θεός, καὶ ἀεὶ ἐν τοῖς αὐτῷ πρέπουσι ποιεῖν διαμένει ‡Just.*qu.et resp.*36(M.6.1284A); ὅπως ἄ. ἐέλδωρ πατρὸς ἐμοῦ τελέοιμι Nonn.*par.Jo.*4:34(M.43.780B); **7.** of God opp. creation; **a.** opp. matter, Iren.*fr.*32(M.7.1248B) cit. s. 9.a; Dion.Al.ap.Eus.*p.e.*7.19(334A; M.21.564B) cit. s. 9.a; Proc.G.*Gen.*proem.(M.87.29B); **b.** opp. man ἐν τούτῳ...τῆς ἑτερότητος τοῦ κατ' εἰκόνα γενομένου πρὸς τὸ ἀρχέτυπον οὔσης ἐν τῷ τὸ μὲν ἄ. εἶναι τῇ φύσει, τὸ δὲ μὴ οὕτως ἔχειν...ἀλλοιούμενον δὲ μὴ πάντως ἐν τῷ εἶναι μένειν Gr.Nyss.*or.catech.*21(p.82.6; M.45.60A); **c.** opp. creation in gen. οὐδενὸς τῶν παρὰ τὸν θεὸν ζώντων ἔχοντος τὴν ἄ. καὶ ἀναλλοίωτον ζωήν Or.*Jo.*2.17(11; p.75.1; M.14.145B); Gr.Nyss.*or.catech.*39(p.155.1; M.45.100A); id.*Eun.*1(1 p.103.8; M.45.336D) cit. s. I.B.1.a; θεοδίδακτος ὤν, τῇ μὲν φύσει τῶν γενητῶν προσέρριψε τὴν τροπὴν...τετήρηκε δὲ τὸ ἄ. τῷ ἐπὶ πάντας θεῷ Cyr.*synous.*2(p.478.28); τρεπτή...ἐστιν [sc. ἡ κτίσις] καὶ τοῖς δημιουργήσαντος ἀκολουθεῖ νεύμασιν· αὐτὸς δὲ ἄ. ἔχει τὴν φύσιν καὶ ἀναλλοίωτον Thdt. *eran.*1(4.10); **8.** heret.; **a.** name of ultimate principle of existence in Valent. Gnosticism, Val.Gn.ap.Epiph.*haer.*31.5(p.390.9; M.41.481B); **b.** as attribute of God made basis of argument for eternity of matter ἀλλοιοῦσθαι...τὸν ἄ. καὶ ἀναλλοίωτον συμβήσεται θεόν. εἰ γὰρ ὕστερον πεποίηκε τὸ πᾶν δῆλον ὅτι ἀπὸ τοῦ μὴ ποιεῖν εἰς τὸ ποιεῖν μετέβαλε Meth.*creat.*2(p.494.25; M.18.333C); **c.** of Manich. principles of good and evil δύο ῥίζας ἀ. ὑπέθου Adam.*dial.*3.4(p.118.23; M.11.1796A); cf. *inconvertibiles quidem sunt utraeque, quantum spectat ad contraria, convertibiles vero, quod spectat ad propria*, Hegem.*Arch.*17(p.28.13; M.10.1456A); Epiph.*haer.*66.59(p.96.13; M.42.117D); antinomy involved in arguing for an immutability outside and independent of God exposed, Meth.*creat.*3ff.(pp.494ff.); Hegem.*Arch.*17(p.28.7ff.; 1455C); Adam.*dial.*3.3f.(p.118.17ff.; 1796); Epiph.*haer.*66.59(p.96.11ff.; 117D–120C); **9.** nature of τὸ ἄτρεπτον; **a.** ἄτρεπτος associated with ἀγέννητος (or ἀγένητος): εἰ ἀγέννητος ἡ ὕλη, πάντως κατά τινα ποιότητα πεποίηται, καὶ ταύτην ἄ., οὐκ ἂν εἴη πλειόνων ποιοτήτων δεκτική· οὐδ' ἂν κοσμοποιοῖτο Iren.*fr.*32(M.7.1248B); εἰπάτωσαν...τὴν αἰτίαν, δι' ἥν, ἀμφοτέρων ὄντων ἀγενήτων, ὁ μὲν θεὸς ἀπαθής, ἄ., ἀκίνητος, ἐργαστικός· ἡ δὲ ἐναντία [sc. ὕλη] παθητή, τρεπτή, ἄστατος, μεταποιουμένη Dion.Al.ap.Eus.*p.e.*7.19 (334A; M.21.564B); τὸ...ἀγένητον, αὐτοτελὲς καὶ ἄ. φανθέν Meth.*creat.*7(p.498.19; M.18.340C); Eus.*d.e.*5.19(p.243.25; M.22.401B); **b.** and with ἀπαθής, Epiph.*haer.*69.26(p.176.19; M.42.244D); οἶδα καὶ ἀπαθῆ τὴν τοῦ θεοῦ φύσιν καὶ ἄ. καὶ ἀναλλοίωτον Cyr.*ep.*53(M.77.288A); cf. Thdr.Heracl.*Is.*28:21(M.18.1320A); **c.** moral as well as metaphysical, cf. *ut aliqui...qui creati sunt, pro eo quod non naturaliter, id est substantialiter, inesset eis bonum sed accidens, non valentes inconvertibiles et incommutabiles permanere...conversi atque mutati de statu suo deciderent*, Or.*princ.*1.2.4(p.31.19; M.11.133A); *ib.*1.7.2 (p.87.8; 172A); φύσει τυγχάνον ἀγαθὸν ἄ. καὶ ἀΐδιον Mac.Mgn.*apocr.*2.9(p.13.20); **d.** contrasted with man's free will ὁ θεὸς ἄ., ὁ δὲ ἄνθρωπος τρεπτὸς...εἴπερ μὴ τὸ αὐτεξούσιον, ἄ. ἦν ὁ ἄνθρωπος. ὁ δὲ ἄ. ἀθάνατος, ὁ δὲ ἀθάνατος θεός Adam.*dial.*3.10(p.128.20ff.; M.11.1801A,B); Arian argument εἰ μὲν οὖν [sc. ὁ υἱός] αὐτεξούσιός ἐστι προαιρέσει φαίνοιτ' ἂν εἰκότως καλός. τὸ δὲ προαιρέσει καὶ οὐ φύσει περί τι κρατούμενον, δύναιτ' ἂν ἐφ' ἕτερα μεταβάλλεσθαι...εἰ δὲ ἄ. ἐστιν, ... ὡς λίθος ἄρα...ἕστηκεν...καὶ τὸ αὐτεξούσιον οὐκ ἔχων Cyr. *thes.*13(5^1.125A,B); cf.Ar.*Thal.fr.*9 ap.Ath.*Ar.*1.35(M.26.84B); otherwise explained ἄ. ὢν τὴν φύσιν, ἄ. ἔχει τὸ μὴ βούλεσθαί τι κακὸν δρᾶσαι· ὥστε δύναται μέν, οὐ δρᾷ δὲ ἀ. τῇ τοῦ μὴ βούλεσθαι φύσει Tit.Bost.*Man.*2.5(M.18.1141B); **e.** excludes alike diminution or deterioration and addition or improvement, Ath.*Ar.*1.18(M.26.49B); ὅτι...ἄ. ... καὶ ἀναλλοίωτος...οὔτε πρὸς τὸ χεῖρον, οὔτε πρὸς τὸ βέλτιον τραπῆναι δυνάμενος Gr.Nyss.*ep.*3(M.46.1020B); **f.** its essence, truth ἐστὶ τῶν λογικῶν δυνάμεων ἡ τροπὴ τὸ ψεύσασθαι. θεὸς δὲ ἄ. ὢν καὶ ἀψευδής ἐστι ‡Ath.*dial.Trin.*1.22(M.28.1149C).

B. esp. ref. Inc.; **1.** of Logos; as **a.** one in essence with Father and remaining so when incarnate, in this opp. man ἡ υἱότης αὐτοῦ κατὰ φύσιν τυγχάνουσα τῆς πατρικῆς θεότητος...ὑπεροχῇ διαφέρει τῶν δι' αὐτοῦ θέσει υἱοθετηθέντων. ὁ μὲν γὰρ ἀ. φύσεως τυγχάνει...οἱ δὲ εἰς ἑκάτερα τροπῇ ὑποκείμενοι Alex.Al.*ep.Alex.*7(p.24.11f.; M.18.557C); cf.Or.*princ.*1.2.10(p.44.18; M.11.142B); τὸ...ἄ. ἡ κτίσις ἐν τῇ φύσει οὐκ ἔχει...δι' ὧν δὲ τῆς κτίσεως ἀφίσταται, διὰ τῶν αὐτῶν τούτων πρὸς τὸν πατέρα τε καὶ υἱὸν ἔχει τὴν οἰκειότητα. εἷς γὰρ καὶ ὁ αὐτὸς ἐπὶ τῶν κατὰ φύσιν ἀνεπιδέκτων τοῦ χείρονος ὁ τοῦ ἀ. καὶ ἀναλλοιώτου λόγος Gr.Nyss.*Eun.*1(1 p.103.8ff.; M.45.336D–337A); εἰ μή ἐστιν οὐσίας ἀξιώματι ἄ. ὁ τοῦ θεοῦ υἱός, τίνι διαφέρει τῶν ἄλλων λογικῶν δυνάμεων, καὶ αὐτῶν ἐχουσῶν τὸ ἄ. ἐν τῇ γνώμῃ τοῦ κτίσαντος; ‡Ath.*dial.Trin.*2.18(M.28.1185C); εἰ δὲ ἄβατά...ἐστιν ἑτέρᾳ φύσει τὰ τῆς θεότητος ἴδια...ὅμοιος ἄρα ἐστὶ κατὰ πάντα τοῦ πατρός· οὐκ ἔκ τινος προκοπῆς...ἀλλὰ τέλειος ἐκ τελείου, καὶ ἄ. ἐξ ἀ. Cyr.*thes.*13(5^{1}.126B); id.*resp.*7(p.589.11; 6^{2}.383B); id.*Jo.*1.4(4.33B); id.*ep.*39(p.18.23; 5^{2}.107D); πόσον διαφέρει τὸ ὁμολογεῖν, ὅτι ἔχει υἱὸν ὁ θεὸς...ἄ., ἀπαθῆ, ὑπὲρ τὸ ὀνομάζειν ἀνθρώπους...τρεπτοὺς καὶ θνητούς, υἱοὺς θεοῦ; Hier.H.*Trin.*(M.40.849C); **b.** suffering no change in Inc. μένων...τῇ οὐσίᾳ ἄ. συγκαταβαίνει...τοῖς ἀνθρωπίνοις πράγμασιν Or.*Cels.*4.14(p.284.18; M.11.1045A); πῶς ὁ τῷ πατρὶ ὁμοούσιος υἱὸς...παθητὸς ἂν λέγοιτο, ἄ. ὤν...εἰ μὴ ἐγένετο ἄνθρωπος ἵνα καὶ ἄνθρωπος ᾖ ἐν τῷ πάθει, καὶ ἄ. ᾗ θεὸς ὤν; ‡Ath.*Apoll.*2.2(M.26.1136A); Gr.Nyss.*ep.*3(M.46.1020B) cit. s. ἀπεμφαίνω; ὁ...θεὸς λόγος...ἄνθρωπος ἄ. ἀσυγχύτως...ὡς οἶδε καὶ ἐβουλήθη, ἐκ τῆς παρθένου...ἐγένετο, μείνας ὃ ἦν, καὶ ἔστι, καὶ ἔσται, εἷς καὶ ὁ αὐτός Didym.*Trin.*2.7(M.39.589A); ἐπὶ γῆς καὶ ⟨ἐν⟩ οὐρανῷ ὁ αὐτὸς θεὸς λόγος ὑπῆρχεν, ἄ. ὢν καὶ ἀναλλοίωτος Epiph.*haer.*57.8(p.354.14; M.41.1008B); υἱοῦ δὲ ἐνσωμάτου γενομένου, ἀλλὰ ἀτρέπτου *ib.*69.65(p.214.3; M.42.308B); id.*anc.*5(p.11.13; M.43.24C); οὔτε...τὴν σάρκα φαμὲν εἰς θεότητος τραπῆναι φύσιν οὔτε μὴν εἰς φύσιν σαρκὸς τὴν...τοῦ θεοῦ λόγου παρενεχθῆναι φύσιν· ἄ. γάρ ἐστιν καὶ ἀναλλοίωτος παντελῶς Cyr.*ep.*17(p.35.22; 5^{2}.70B); τὸ...θεῖον, ὡς ἦν πρὸ σαρκώσεως, ἔστι καὶ μετὰ σάρκωσιν, κατὰ φύσιν...ἄ. ‡Hipp.*Ber.Hel.*1(p.322.13; M.10.832C); οὔτε...ὁ λόγος σαρκούμενος, τρέψας ἑαυτοῦ πρὸς σάρκα τὴν φύσιν σεσάρκωται...ἀλλ' ἔμεινεν ἄ. Sophr.H.*or.*2.47(M.87.3281A); synthesis of Johannine and Pauline teaching διὰ μὲν γὰρ τοῦ 'ἐγένετο' [Jo. 1:14] τὸ ἀδιαίρετον τῆς ἄκρας ἑνώσεως ὁ εὐαγγελιστὴς ὑπαινίττεται ...τὸ δὲ 'ἔλαβε' [Phil.2:7] βοᾷ τὸ ἄ. τῆς φύσεως...οὔτε γὰρ ἐξ οὐκ ὄντων παρήχθη ὁ ἀεὶ ἄναρχος, οὔτε ἐξ ὄντων ἐτράπη ὁ ἀναλλοίωτος λόγος· διὰ τοῦτο δι' ἑκατέρων καὶ τὸ ἄ. τῆς θεότητος, καὶ τὸ ἀδιαίρετον τοῦ μυστηρίου...ἵνα διὰ μὲν τοῦ προτέρου τὸ ἑνικὸν τοῦ προσώπου παραστήσῃ, διὰ δὲ τοῦ ἑτέρου τὸ ἀναλλοίωτον τῆς φύσεως ἐκβοήσῃ Procl.CP*Arm.*6(p.190.9ff.; M.65.861B); v. ἀπαθής, πάσχω; **c.** morally immutable, ref. Ps.44:8 οὐχ...τρεπτὴν δεικνύον τοῦ λόγου τὴν φύσιν, ἀλλὰ...τὸ ἄ. αὐτοῦ σημαῖνον Ath.*Ar.*1.51(M.26.117B); οὐδὲ ἡ πρὸς κακίαν τροπὴ τῶν ἀνθρώπων ἀμφίβολον ἐπὶ τῆς θείας φύσεως εἶναι παρασκευάζει τὸ ἄ. Gr.Nyss.*Eun.*4(2 p.51.12; M.45.621A); *ib.*12(2 p.285.11; 897A); Isid.Pel.*epp.*1.416(M.78.413B); θεοπρεπῶς οὖν...παθεῖν οὐκ ἀνέχεται τὴν ἁμαρτίαν, ὅτι μὴ φύσεως ἦν γενητῆς οὐκ ἐχούσης οὐσιωδῶς τὸ ἄ. Cyr.*Pulch.*(p.51.2; 5^{2}.164E); **2.** of divine nature opp. body of Christ ἡ γὰρ θεότης αὐτοῦ ἀκοίμητος ἄπτωτος ἀκράτητος ἄ. Epiph.*haer.*64.67(p.511.16; M.41.1188B); and opp. human soul, ref. Jo.11:33 ταῦτα...οὔτε σαρκὸς ἀνοήτου ἂν εἴη, οὔτε θεότητος ἀ., ἀλλὰ ψυχῆς νόησιν ἐχούσης ‡Ath.*Apoll.*1.15(M.26.1121B); **3.** of Christ; **a.** in both natures εἰ...καὶ ἠκολούθουν [sc. οἱ μαθηταί] ἐκ προαιρέσεως, ἀλλ' εἶχον τὸ τρεπτὸν τοῦ ἀνθρώπου. μόνος δὲ ἄ. ἦν καὶ θεότητι καὶ ἀνθρωπότητι ὁ τοῦ θεοῦ υἱός Or.*fr.*141 *in Mt.*(p.72; M.17.292C); οὐκ ἐπειδὴ γέγονεν ἄνθρωπος...ἐτράπη· ἀλλὰ...μένων ἄ., καὶ ὁ αὐτός ἐστι διδοὺς καὶ λαμβάνων, διδοὺς μὲν ὡς θεοῦ λόγος, λαμβάνων δὲ ὡς ἄνθρωπος Ath.*Ar.*1.48(M.26.112C); πῶς οὐ δύο φύσεις ἄ. ἐν τῷ Χριστῷ; Leont.H.*monoph.*16(M.86.1780A); ὁ...τῆς ἑνώσεως λόγος...καὶ τηρεῖ συνδράμοντα πρὸς ἕνωσιν ἄτρεπτα, καὶ τῶν ἡνωμένων μερισμὸν οὐκ εἰσδέχεται Sophr.H.*ep.syn.*(M.87.3165B); **b.** in human nature μεμένηκε...ἡ σὰρξ ἀναλλοίωτος, καὶ πάσης ἔξω τροπῆς καὶ συγχύσεως...ἔχουσα...τὸ πρὸς ἡμᾶς ὁμοούσιον ἄ. id.*or.*2.47(M.87.3281B); **4.** heret.; **a.** denied of Son by Arius οὐκ ἐστὶν ἄ. ὡς ὁ πατήρ, ἀλλὰ τρεπτός ἐστι φύσει ὡς τὰ κτίσματα Ar.*Thal.fr.*3 ap.Ath.*Ar.*1.9(M.26.29B); φασὶν αὐτὸν τρεπτῆς εἶναι φύσεως, ἀρετῆς τε καὶ κακίας ἐπιδεκτικόν...τῆς θείας...συναναιροῦντες γραφὰς αἳ τὸ ἄ. τοῦ λόγου...σημαίνουσιν...ὅπερ οὐ φυσικόν ἐστι τῷ σωτῆρι ὄντι φύσεως ἀ. Alex.Al.*ep.Alex.*2(p.21.13ff.; M.18.552B); Leont.H.*monoph.*(M.86.1853C); v. II.A.2; **b.** Apollinarian, v. νοῦς; **c.** of flesh of resurrection body μετὰ δὲ θανάτου κατάλυσιν περὶ τὴν σάρκα τὴν ἁγίαν ἀπάθεια διηνεκὴς καὶ ἄ. ἀθανασία Apoll.*fid.sec.pt.*2(p.168.13; M.10.1105C).

II. *unchanged*, i.e. *unchanging*, which does not in fact change; **A.** theol. (heret.), moral aspect of word being uppermost; freq. equivalent of *without sin*; **1.** Adoptionist Χριστὸς πάσχων κατὰ φύσιν, θαυματουργῶν κατὰ χάριν. τῷ γὰρ ἀ. τῆς γνώμης ὁμοιωθεὶς τῷ θεῷ καὶ μείνας καθαρὸς ἁμαρτίας ‡Paul.Sam.*fr.*1(p.339.2); **2.** Arian in sense I (v. I.B.4) of Father only; allowed of Son in above sense οἴδαμεν ἕνα θεὸν...ἄ. καὶ ἀναλλοίωτον...γεννήσαντα υἱὸν μονογενῆ...ὑποστήσαντα ἰδίῳ θελήματι ἄ. καὶ ἀναλλοίωτον κτίσμα τοῦ θεοῦ τέλειον Ar.*ep.Alex.*(p.12; M.26.709A); πιστεύομεν...εἰς ἕνα κύριον...ἄ. τε καὶ ἀναλλοίωτον *Symb.Ant.*(341)2(p.249.16; M.26.721C); cf. ἀλλὰ καὶ αὐτὸν τρεπτῆς τυγχάνοντα φύσεως διὰ τρόπων ἐπιμέλειαν καὶ ἄσκησιν μὴ τρεπόμενον ἐπὶ τὸ χεῖρον, ἐξελέξατο Alex.Al.*ep.Alex.*2f.(p.21.21f.; M.18.552B,C); τὸ ἄ. ... ὅτι γέγραπται 'οὐδὲν ἡμᾶς χωρίσει ἀπὸ τῆς ἀγάπης τοῦ Χριστοῦ' Ath.*decr.*20.2(p.16.37; M.25.452A); allowed in this sense by Anomoeans εἰ τὸ γέννημα ἄ. τὴν φύσιν ἐστὶ διὰ τὸν γεννήσαντα, τὸ ἀγέννητον οὐσίᾳ ἐστὶν ἄ. οὐ διὰ τὴν γνώμην, ἀλλὰ διὰ τὸ ἐν οὐσίᾳ ἀξίωμα Aët.*synt.*15(p.355.4; M.42.537D); ὡς ὁ Χριστὸς τρεπτὸς μὲν τῇ γε φύσει τῇ οἰκείᾳ, ἐπιμελείᾳ δὲ τῶν ἀρετῶν ἀνυπερβλήτῳ εἰς τὸ ἄ. ἀνυψωθῆναι Philost.*h.e.*8.3(M.65.557B); **3.** Thdr.Mops. ἔσχεν μὲν πολλὴν πρὸς τὸ κακὸν τὴν ἀπέχθειαν, ἀσχέτῳ δὲ στοργῇ πρὸς τὸ καλὸν ἑαυτὸν συνάψας, ἀνάλογόν τε τῇ οἰκείᾳ προθέσει καὶ τὴν τοῦ θεοῦ λόγου συνέργειαν δεχόμενος, ἄ. λοιπὸν τῆς ἐπὶ τὸ χεῖρον μεταβολῆς διετηρεῖτο Thdr.Mops.*fr.inc.*7(p.296.36; M.66.977B); cf.Or.*princ.*2.6.5(p.144.28; M.11.213C); prob. with some approximation to sense I when referring to post-resurrection state ἄνθρωπον ἐξ ἡμῶν ἕνα λαβὼν ἀθάνατόν τε καὶ ἄ. ποιήσας εἰς οὐρανὸν ἀνήγαγεν ἑαυτῷ συνάψας Thdr.Mops.ap.Jo.Philop.*opif.*6.10(p.247.24); cf. *resuscitavit de mortuis et ad vitam constituit meliorem; immutabilem quidem animae cogitationibus, incorruptum autem et indissolutum et carne faciens*, id.*fr.or.catech.*(Swete 2 p.326.15; M.66.1015A); εἴ τις ἀντιποιεῖται Θεοδώρου τοῦ Μοψουεστίας τοῦ εἰπόντος...τὸν Χριστὸν ὑπὸ παθῶν ψυχῆς...ὀχλούμενον καὶ ἐκ προκοπῆς ἔργων βελτιωθέντα καὶ...μετὰ τὴν ἀνάστασιν ἄ. ταῖς ἐννοίαις καὶ ἀναμάρτητον παντελῶς γενόμενον...ἀ. ἔ. Justn.*conf.anath.*11(p.92.31; M.86.1017B); **4.** Nestorius τῷ κατ' οὐσίαν λόγῳ φύσει φύσις οὐχ ἑνοῦται χωρὶς ἀφανισμοῦ...ἡ δὲ κατὰ τὴν θέλησιν ἕνωσις καὶ τὴν ἐνέργειαν ἀ. αὐτὰς τηρεῖ καὶ ἀδιαιρέτους, μίαν αὐτῶν δεικνῦσα πεποιημένην τὴν θέλησιν καὶ τὴν ἐνέργειαν Nest.*fr.*B 6(p.219.21)ap.*Doct.Patr.*41(p.305.1).

B. as imparted to creation; **1.** one of two fundamental categories; characterizing heaven opp. earth, hence characteristic of life to come, cf. *in duos status divisit Deus creaturam, praesentem et futurum; in illo quidem ad immortalitatem et immutabilitatem omnia ducturus, in praesenti vero creatura in mortem et mutabilitatem interim nos dimittens*, Thdr.Mops.*Gen.*(M.66.633A); *ib.*(633C–634A); of destined glory of Church, Ign.*Eph.*proem.; as state of individuals in next life εἰς τὴν πατρῴαν αὐλὴν...ἐσόμενος...φῶς ἑστὸς καὶ μένον ἀϊδίως, πάντῃ πάντως ἄ. Clem.*str.*7.10(p.42.15; M.9.481B); Nil.*epp.*2.247(M.79.328C); ὁ μέλλων...βίος· ἐν ἐκείνῳ...τῶν μὲν σωμάτων ἀφθάρτων, τῶν δὲ ψυχῶν γενομένων ἀ. Thdt.*Jer.*31:34(2.550); id.*haer.*5.21(4.451); the two principles blended by God ἐναλλάξασα τὰς ἰδιότητας ἡ τοῦ θεοῦ σοφία, τῷ μὲν ἀεικινήτῳ τὸ ἄ., τῷ δὲ ἀκινήτῳ τὴν τροπὴν ἐνεποίησε...ἡ μὲν γῆ στάσιμός ἐστι, καὶ οὐκ ἄ.· ὁ δὲ οὐρανὸς τοῦ ἐναντίου τὸ τρεπτὸν οὐκ ἔχων, οὐδὲ στάσιμον ἔχει, ἵνα τῇ μὲν φύσει ἑστώσῃ τὴν τροπήν, τῇ δὲ μὴ τρεπομένῃ τὴν κίνησιν ἡ θεία συμπλέξασα δύναμις Gr.Nyss.*hom.opif.*1.4(M.44.129D); **2.** in this life; **a.** among rational creatures taking form of moral stability ὅπως...ἡμᾶς διατηρήσας...ἀ., ἀμέμπτους, ἀνεγκλήτους *Lit.* ap.*Const.App.*8.12.49; ἄ. πρὸς ἁμαρτίαν *Const.App.*5.8.2; *ib.*8.48.3; αἱ ψυχαὶ καὶ οἱ ἄγγελοι...ἐὰν καὶ φθορᾷ γνώμης μὴ ὑποπέσωσιν, τοῦτ' ἔστιν, εἰ ἄ. διαμείνωσιν Didym.*Trin.*3.16(M.39.873A); τὸ ἄτρεπτον ἐν θεῷ φυσικῶς, οὕτω δὲ καὶ ἐν ἡμῖν οὐδαμῶς, ἀσφάλεια δέ τις ἡμᾶς ὡς πρὸς αὐτῷ σχηματίζει Cyr.*Jo.*3.5(4.305C); *Disp.Phot.*(M.88.577C); of angelic creation ἀτρέπτους...νοεῖν δεῖ [sc. the seraphim] κατ' ἐκεῖνο καθ' ὅ εἰσιν...ἐν τούτοις γὰρ καὶ ἀμεταβόλους οὐσιωδῶς, καὶ εἰς τὸ μὴ τρέπεσθαι εἰς ἐκφύλους ἐπιθυμίας, ἅτε καὶ αὐτεξουσίους, ὁ θεὸς συνέχει αὐτοὺς καὶ διατηρεῖ Max.*schol.c.h.*13.4(M.4.101B); **b.** approximating to ἀπαθής: κἂν νόσος ἐπίῃ...τῷ γνωστικῷ, καὶ δὴ μάλιστα ὁ φοβερώτατος θάνατος, ἄ. μένει κατὰ τὴν ψυχήν Clem.*str.*7.11(p.44.28; M.9.485C); ὥστε πάντων ἀλλοιουμένων τε καὶ μεθισταμένων πόρρω τῇ διανοίᾳ γενόμενος, ἐν ἀ. τε καὶ ἀκλινεῖ τῇ τῆς ψυχῆς καταστάσει, τὸν ἄ. καὶ ἀναλλοίωτον διὰ τῆς γνώμης πρότερον οἰκειώσασθαι Gr.Nyss.*or.dom.*2(p.32.19; M.44.1140C); **c.** mark of Christ's redemptive work, ref. Ps.44:8 ἐκ τούτου τὸ ἄ. αὐτοῦ σημαίνον. ἐπειδὴ γὰρ τῶν γενητῶν ἡ φύσις ἐστὶ τρεπτή...διὰ τοῦτο πάλιν ἀ. χρεία ἦν...ἐπειδὴ γὰρ ὁ πρῶτος ἄνθρωπος Ἀδὰμ ἐτράπη...διὰ τοῦτο τὸν δεύτερον Ἀδὰμ ἔπρεπεν ἄ. εἶναι Ath.*Ar.*1.51(M.26.117B,C); εἰκότως ὁ κύριος ὁ ἀεὶ καὶ φύσει ἄ., ἀγαπῶν δικαιοσύνην χρίεται,...ἵνα ὁ αὐτὸς...διαμένων, τὴν τρεπτὴν σάρκα λαβὼν...ἐλευθέραν...αὐτὴν κατασκευάσῃ εἰς τὸ δύνασθαι λοιπὸν τὸ δικαίωμα τοῦ νόμου πληροῦν ἐν αὐτῇ *ib.*(120A); ὁ ἄ. ἐν τῷ τρεπτῷ γίνεται, ἵνα...μεταβαλὼν ἐκ τοῦ χείρονος τὴν ἐμμιχθεῖσαν τῇ τρεπτῇ διαθέσει κακίαν, ἐξαφανίσῃ ἀπὸ τῆς φύσεως Gr.Nyss.*Eun.*5(2 p.119.25; M.45.700D); ἀεὶ ἄ. ὂν τὸ θεῖον τῇ οὐσίᾳ...ἐν τῇ τρεπτῇ...γίνεται φύσει, ἵνα τῷ ἰδίῳ ἀ. τὴν ἡμετέραν πρὸς τὸ κακὸν τροπὴν ἐξιάσηται id.*Apoll.*2(M.45.1128A); Χριστὸς θεοῦ δύναμις καὶ θεοῦ σοφία, ἀεὶ ἄ., ἀεὶ ἄφραστος, κἂν ἐν τῷ τρεπτῷ καὶ φθαρτῷ γένηται, οὐκ αὐτὸς μολυνόμενος, ἀλλὰ τὸ μολυνθὲν καθαρίζων id.*ep.*3(M.46.1024A); ἵνα...ψυχὴν δὲ ἰδίαν τὴν ἀνθρωπίνην ποιούμενος ἁμαρτίας αὐτὴν ἀποφήνῃ κρείττονα, τῆς ἰδίας φύσεως τὸ πεπηγός τε καὶ ἄ. ... ἐγκαταχρώσας αὐτῇ Cyr.*Thds.*20(p.54.30; 5^2.17E); ψυχὴν ἔλαβε...ἵνα πᾶσα ψυχὴ...μετάσχῃ τῆς ἀτρεπτότητος· εἰ γὰρ ἀθάνατοί εἰσιν αἱ ψυχαί, ἀλλ' οὐκ ἄ. ... μετὰ δὲ τὴν ἀνάστασιν, ἀπολαύει μὲν ἀθανασίας καὶ ἀφθαρσίας τὰ σώματα, ἀπολαύουσι δὲ ἀπαθείας καὶ ἀτρεπτότητος αἱ ψυχαί Thdt.*ep.*145(4.1249); Cosm.Ind.*top.*5(M.88.277B); **d.** applied in baptism ἵνα βιάσηται ἕκαστος ἡμῶν κατὰ τὸ βάπτισμα μὴ τρέπεσθαι ἐπὶ τὸ κακόν, ἀλλ' ἐμμένειν εἰς τὸ ἀγαθόν...ἠδύνατο ἐλευθερῶσαι ἡμᾶς ὁ θεός, καὶ ἀ. βίᾳ ποιῆσαι Marc. Er.*opusc.*4(M.65.989B); τὸ...ὕδωρ ἐποιεῖτο τῆς συνειδήσεως κάθαρσιν· καὶ τὸ...πνεῦμα τὴν ἄ. ἐν ἡμῖν τοῦ καλοῦ...ἐνήργει τελείωσιν Max. *qu.Thal.*6(M.90.281B); **e.** of man in a state of innocence ἀναστάντος...τοῦ ἀνθρώπου...ἀφθάρτου καὶ ἀθανάτου καὶ ἀ. Cosm.Ind.*top.*2 (M.88.128A); acc. others its lack provided occasion for redemption εἰ ἄ. οἱ ἄνθρωποι, ὁ θεὸς ἀγαθὸς πῶς ἐδείκνυτο μὴ ὄντων τῶν χρείαν ἐχόντων τῆς τοῦ θεοῦ ἀγαθότητος;...εἰ γεγόνασιν οἱ ἄνθρωποι ἄ., περισσαὶ ἦσαν αὗται [sc. τοῦ θεοῦ] αἱ ἐνέργειαι Adam.*dial.*3.10(p.130.2–10; M.11.1801B); cf. *si quidem statim ab initio immortales nos fecerit et immutabiles, nullam differentiam ad irrationabilia haberemus...ignorantes enim mutabilitatem, immutabilitatis ignorabamus bonum...nescientes malorum experimentum, bonorum illorum non poteramus scientiam mereri*, Thdr.Mops.*Gen.*(M.66.633B); **f.** of BMV in respect of her corruptible human nature τὴν...θεοτόκον παρθένον ...ἄ. διαμεῖναι [i.e. after coming upon her of H. Ghost] Leont.B. *Nest.et Eut.*2(M.86.1329A); cf.*ib.*(1328A,B).

III. theol., *not causing change*, i.e. to the divinity τὰ περὶ τῆς ἀρρητοτάτης καὶ ἀτρεπτοτάτης...ἐνανθρωπήσεως αὐτοῦ Didym.*Trin.* 3.1(M.39.780B).

***ἀτρεπτότης**, ἡ, *immutability*; **1.** as attribute of Deity, Nil.*epp.* 2.33(M.79.213A); hence of divinity of Christ, ‡Ath.*Apoll.*2.17(M.26.1161B); *ib.*2.18(1164B); **2.** moral aspect predominant μακάριον αὐτὸν...καλεῖ, ὡς ἂν αὐτοῦ μὲν τὸ μακάριον ἔχοντος ἐν τῇ φύσει διὰ τῆς ἀ. ἡμῖν δὲ χάριτι τοῦτο περιποιοῦντος Thdr.Mops.*1Tim.*1:11(p.77.19; M.66.937B); cf. *discere peccatum...et nostram infirmitatem in his demonstrandam, ad ostendendum magnitudinem immutabilitatis* id.*Gen.*(M.66.634C); of the human soul of glorified Christ, cf. *ita et animam utpote humanam et immortalem constitutam et sensus participem prius accipiens et per resurrectionem in immutabilitatem constituens*, id.*fr.Apoll.*10(p.317.26; M.66.996D); σὺν τῇ ἀφθαρσίᾳ καὶ ἀθανασίᾳ καὶ τὴν ἀ. τῆς ψυχῆς κομισάμενος Cosm.Ind.*top.*2(M.88.121D); **3.** in moral sense, *sinlessness, freedom from sin*, by grace of God made attainable by man ultimately in life to come μακάριον αὐτὸν ἐκάλεσεν ἐπὶ συστάσει τῆς μελλούσης προσέσεσθαι ἡμῖν ἀ. Thdr. Mops.*1Tim.*6:16(p.184.18; M.66.944C); *ib.*1:11(p.77.19; 937B) cit. s. 2; ψυχὴν ἔλαβε τὴν κυβερνῶσαν τὸ σῶμα, ἵνα πᾶσα ψυχὴ διὰ ταύτης μετάσχῃ τῆς ἀ. ... μετὰ...τὴν ἀνάστασιν...ἀπολαύουσι...ἀπαθείας καὶ ἀ. αἱ ψυχαί Thdt.*ep.*145(4.1249); τὸ περὶ ἀθανασίας μελλούσης ἢ ἀ. Proc.G.*Gen.*2:9(M.87.165D); ἐν τῇ μελλούσῃ καταστάσει...πᾶσι χαρίζεται ἀθανασίαν, καὶ ἀφθαρσίαν καὶ ζωὴν καὶ ἀ. Cosm.Ind.*top.*5(M.88.285B).

ἀτρέπτως, **A.** *immutably, without change*; **1.** of God; **a.** in his nature πρέπον τῇ μακαρίᾳ φύσει...τὸ ἀιδίως δοξάζειν αὐτὴν εἶναι καὶ μόνην ἐν ἀτρεψίᾳ οὐδενὸς δεομένην τῶν γεγενημένων...ἵν' ᾖ μόνου θεοῦ τὸ...ἀ. εἶναι Zach.Mit.*opif.*(M.85.1112B); **b.** in dealings with creation πρὸς τὸ συγγινώσκειν, καὶ πρὸς τὸ μὴ συγγινώσκειν ἀ. ἔχει. συγγινώσκει γὰρ ἀ. τοῖς διορθοῦσι τὰ ἑαυτῶν πταίσματα· τοῖς δὲ ἀδιορθώτως ἔχουσι πρὸς τὰ κακά, ἀ. οὐ συγγινώσκει ‡Just.*qu.et resp.* 36(M.6.1281D,1284A); **c.** of Logos, *without undergoing change* τὸ γὰρ ἀ. πατέρα ἰδεῖν υἱοῦ μόνου ἐστίν *Hom.Clem.*17.16; in his nature τὸ ἀ. εἶναι...τῇ τοῦ λόγου φύσει τηρεῖν Cyr.*synous.*10(p.486.1); γέγονε [sc. ὁ λόγος]...σὰρξ οὐ κατὰ μετάστασιν...εἰς τὴν τῆς σαρκὸς φύσιν μεταβαλὼν...(ἀμήχανον γάρ, ἐπείπερ ἐστὶ κατὰ φύσιν ἀ. τε καὶ ἀναλλοιώτως ἔχων) id.*ep.*55(p.54.28; 5^2.181D); **2.** most freq. ref. Inc.; **a.** as not impairing divine Logos, *not incurring change* ἐπιτιμᾷ τῷ πάθει, ἵνα μάθωμεν ὅτι ἄνθρωπος γέγονεν ἀ. ὡς ἡμεῖς Or.*fr.84 in Jo.*11:38 (p.549.21); τὸ ἐκ τῆς παρθένου σῶμα...τῇ θεότητι ἀ. ἥνωται καὶ τεθεοποίηται Hymen.*ep.*(p.329.3); ὁ ὑψηλὸς ὡς θεὸς καὶ ὑπὸ πόδας ἔχων πᾶσαν τὴν κτίσιν γέγονεν ἀ. ἄνθρωπος Ath.*exp.Ps.*98:5(M.27.421C); Gr.Nyss.*Apoll.*21(M.45.1165A); Didym.*Trin.*3.6(M.39.844B); *ib.*3.18 (884D); υἱὸν...ἐνανθρωπήσαντα τελείως...ἀ. καὶ ἀναλλοιώτως ‡Chrys. *Trin.*4(1.840A); Cyr.*Ps.*113:16(M.69.1269A); id.*hom.div.*15.4(p.14.23; M.77.1093A); σαρκοῦται μὲν ἀ. ὁ ἀνείδεος, τίκτεται δὲ κατὰ σάρκα ὁ ἄναρχος Procl.CP ap.Cyr.*ep.*55(p.60.15; 5^2.189E); Justn. *conf.*(p.76.10; -ος M.86.997D); ‡Caes.Naz.*dial.*24(M.38.884); **b.** as preserving both natures free from change, *without involving change* ἑνοῦντες...ἡμεῖς τῇ ἁγίᾳ σαρκί, ψυχὴν ἐχούσῃ τὴν νοεράν,...τὸν ἐκ θεοῦ πατρὸς λόγον, ἀσυγχύτως, ἀ., ἀμεταβλήτως, ἕνα υἱὸν καὶ Χριστὸν... ὁμολογοῦμεν Cyr.*ep.*45(p.153.8; 5^2.137B); ὁρῶμεν ὅτι δύο φύσεις συνῆλθον ἀλλήλαις καθ' ἕνωσιν ἀδιάσπαστον ἀσυγχύτως καὶ ἀ. *ib.* (p.153.18; 137C); οὐκ εἰς φύσιν θεότητος τὴν ἀ. τε καὶ ἀσυγχύτως σάρκα μεταστοιχειώσας ὁρᾶται, δόξῃ δὲ μᾶλλον ἰδίᾳ καταφαιδρύνας αὐτὴν νοοῖτ' ἂν id.*synous.*8(p.484.19); Ammon.*Jo.*3:8(M.85.1409B) cit. s. ἀσυγχύτως; *Symb.Chalc.*(p.129.31; H.2.456C) cit. s. φύσις; ἐν τῇ ὑποστάσει τοῦ λόγου τὴν ἀρχὴν τῆς ὑπάρξεως ἔλαβεν. ὅθεν αὐτὸν τὸν θεὸν λόγον ἀ. ἄνθρωπον γεγενῆσθαι ὁμολογοῦμεν, καὶ οὐκ εἰς ἄνθρωπόν τινα αὐτὸν ἐληλυθέναι Justn.*conf.*(p.88.12; M.86.1011B); τὸ μὲν ὑπῆρχεν ἀεί, ὡς φύσιν ἔχων ἀίδιον, τὸ δὲ δι' ἡμᾶς ἐν χρόνοις ἐσχάτοις ἀ. ἐγένετο, ὡς φύσιν προσλαβὼν τὴν ἀνθρωπείαν Sophr.H. *ep.syn.*(M.87.3165D); οὐ τραπεὶς εἰς τὴν κάτω φύσιν...οὐ φαντάσας σαρκὸς εἴδει...τὴν οἰκονομίαν...ἀλλ' αὐτὴν...τὴν ἀνθρωπίνην προσλαβὼν φύσιν ἥνωσεν ἑαυτῷ καθ' ὑπόστασιν ἀ. καὶ ἀναλλοιώτως καὶ ἀμειώτως καὶ ἀδιαιρέτως Max.*ambig.*(M.91.1320C); its implications εἰ...ὄντως ἡνώθη τινὰ ἀ. καὶ ἀμειώτως, πάντα τὰ τούτων ἑκατέρῳ καταφασκόμενα, καὶ τοῦ συνθέτου ἑνὸς ἀποτελέσματος αὐτῶν καταφάσκεται Leont.H.*Nest.*3.1(M.86.1604C); **c.** heret. ἔφη [sc. Eutyches] τὸν θεὸν λόγον ἀνθρώπειον ἐκ τῆς παρθένου λαβεῖν, ἀλλ' αὐτὸν ἀ. τραπέντα...· τοῖς γὰρ καταγελάστοις αὐτοῦ κέχρημαι λόγοις Thdt.*haer.*4.13(4.372); φύσις...Χριστοῦ μία μόνη θεότης, εἰ καὶ σεσάρκωται ἀ. Tim.II Al.*fr.* ap.Eust.Mon.*ep.*(M.86.904B); **d.** as characterizing union of two wills αὐτὸς ὁ τῶν ὅλων θεός, ἀ. γενόμενος ἄνθρωπος οὐ μόνον ὡς θεὸς ὁ αὐτὸς καταλλήλως τῇ αὐτοῦ θεότητι ἤθελεν, ἀλλὰ καὶ ὡς ἄνθρωπος ὁ αὐτὸς καταλλήλως τῇ αὐτοῦ ἀνθρωπότητι Max.*Pyrr.*(M.91.297B); ἐν αὐτῷ...δύο φυσικὰς ἐνεργείας ἀδιαιρέτως, ἀ., ἀμερίστως, ἀσυγχύτως... κηρύττομεν *Symb.CP*(681)(H.3.1400C); **e.** ref. Passion εἴ τις λέγει· ἄλλος ὁ παθὼν καὶ ἄλλος ὁ μὴ παθών, καὶ μὴ ὁμολογεῖ αὐτὸν τὸν ἀπαθῆ θεὸν λόγον σαρκὶ ἰδίᾳ παθόντα ἀ. ... ἀναθεματιζέσθω Gr. Thaum.*fid.cap.*7(p.147.4; M.10.1132A).

B. *irreversibly, fixedly, steadfastly* ἀ. ... πᾶσαν προσβολὴν ὑπομεῖναι Bas.*ep.*79(3.173A; M.32.453D); of adhesion of soul of Christ to righteousness, cf. *haec anima, quae Christi est, ita elegit diligere justitiam, ut pro immensitate dilectionis inconvertibiliter ei atque inseparabiliter inhaereret...ut quod in arbitrio erat positum longi usus affectu jam versum sit in naturam*, Or.*princ.*2.6.5(p.144.28; M.11.213C); of Inc. τὴν...τοῦ θεοῦ λόγου σάρκωσιν, τὴν εἰς ἀεὶ ἀ. τε καὶ ἀμερίστως ἐν αὐτῷ διαμένουσαν ‡Meth.*Sym.et Ann.*9(M.18.369D); and perh. νυμφικῶς ἑνώσαντα ἑαυτῷ Ἀδὰμ ἀ. *ib.*3(356A); for usual force of word in this connexion v. A.2.

C. *unchanging*; in moral sense, *without sin*, of men ἀ., ἀμέμπτως, ἀνεγκλήτως προσφέροντά σοι...θυσίαν *Lit.*ap.*Const.App.*8.5.7; *Const. App.*8.18.3.

***ἀτρεψία**, ἡ, *immutability*; **1.** of essence, but moral aspect not excluded; **a.** an attribute of Deity, Zach.Mit.*opif.*(M.85.1084A); *ib.* (1112B); shared alike by Father and Son πῶς ὁ τοιοῦτος εἰκὼν τοῦ πατρὸς εἶναι δύναται, οὐκ ἔχων τὸ ὅμοιον τῆς ἀ.; Ath.*Ar.*1.35(M.26.85A); τὴν τοῦ υἱοῦ ὁμοίωσιν καὶ ἀ. id.*decr.*20.3(p.17.10; M.25.452B); denied by Arius Ἄρειος μίαν φύσιν τοῦ θεοῦ καὶ λόγου σεσαρκωμένην φησί, βουλόμενος δεῖξαι ὡς οὐ πάντη τῆς τοῦ πατρὸς φυσικῆς ἀ. ἐστὶ καὶ ὁ υἱός Leont.H.*monoph.*(M.86.1809C); **b.** preserved in Inc. because of very nature εἰ δὲ φύσει ἄτρεπτός ἐστι...καὶ ἀπαθής, κἂν ἐν σώματι γένηται, σώζοι ἂν τὸν ἴδιον τῆς ἀπαθείας καὶ ἀ. λόγον Leont.B.*Nest.et Eut.*1(M.86.1284C); εἴπερ ἡμῖν γέγονεν ἄνθρωπος... ἡμῖν δηλονότι καὶ τὴν ἀ. κατώρθωσε τῆς προαιρέσεως, ὡς ἀτρεψίας δημιουργὸς Max.*opusc.*(M.91.29D); ἔδει τὸν ἄτρεπτον τοῦ θεοῦ λόγον ἑαυτὸν ὑπὲρ ἡμῶν ἀντιθεῖναι τῷ πονηρῷ, ἵν' ὥσπερ διὰ τῆς ἐκείνου τροπῆς ἐνικήθημεν, οὕτω διὰ τῆς ἀ. τοῦ λόγου κρατήσωμεν Cyr.*thes.*20 (5^1.198D); of Christ's humanity as preserving its distinct identity and operations in the union οὔτε μὴν εἰς τὸ αὐτὸν αὐτῷ φέρεσθαι φύσεώς ποτε καὶ φυσικῆς ἐνεργείας, ἕως ἂν ἑκάτερον τῆς ἰδίας ἐντὸς μένει φυσικῆς ἀ. ‡Hipp.*Ber.Hel.*3(p.323.28; M.10.836B); ἵνα τὴν ἀληθότητα τῆς κατὰ Χριστὸν θεότητός τε καὶ ἀνθρωπότητος, καὶ τὴν τούτων ἀ. καὶ ἐπιμονὴν καὶ ἀσυγχυσίαν σημάνῃ Thdr.Raith.*praep.* (p.189.9; M.91.1489A); **c.** in this sense not possessed by creatures, Cyr.*inc.unigen.*(5^1.683E); **d.** though it may be used of relationship of soul and body in man δύο φύσεις ὁ ἄνθρωπος λέγεται...διὰ τὴν τῶν μερῶν ἀ. Leont.B.*Nest.et Eut.*1(M.86.1292B); **2.** in moral sense; **a.** *impeccability* of God made man ἦν...ἡ πηγὴ τῶν ἀρετῶν...καὶ ἡ ἀ. καὶ ἡ ἀναμαρτησία Zach.Mit.*opif.*(M.85.1125D); **b.** what is possessed by nature by divine Persons is imparted in form of *moral* *stability* to angels ὁ θεὸς...αὐτὸς καὶ τὰς πρώτας οὐσίας συνέχει καὶ διατηρεῖ πρὸς ἀ. καὶ ἀμεταπτωσίαν...εἰς τὸ μὴ τρέπεσθαι εἰς ἐκφύλους ἐπιθυμίας Max.*schol.c.h.*13.4(M.4.101B); and men τὸ παρέχον ἄλλοις τὴν ἀ., ἀνάγκη ἄτρεπτον εἶναι τῇ φύσει...τὸ μὲν πνεῦμα φύσει ἐστὶν ἄτρεπτον, οἱ δὲ μετέχοντες αὐτοῦ κατὰ μετοχὴν ἄτρεπτοι ‡Ath.*dial. Trin.*1.25(M.28.1153C); as the end of redemption πιστεύων ὅτι διὰ... τὸ δῆσαι πρὸς ἀτρεψίαν τὸ πᾶν, ὁ τῶν ὅλων δημιουργὸς...δίχα τροπῆς ...γέγονεν ἄνθρωπος ‡Hipp.*Ber.Hel.*8(p.325.32; M.10.840A); θείας δυνάμεως...ψυχῆς ἀ. καὶ σώματος ἀφθαρσίαν ἐργαζομένης Max.*ambig.* (M.91.1044A); on man's side being gained by contemplation, †Marc.Er.*temp.*7(M.65.1056C); and purifying of the active life, ‡Proc.G.*Pr.*18:16(M.87.1408D).

[*]**ἀτρομία, ἡ,** = ἀτρεμία, *keeping still, intrepidity, Ep.Lugd.*ap. Eus.*h.e.*5.2.4(M.20.436A).

ἄτροπος, *unchangeable, eternal,* Gr.Naz.*carm.*1.2.1.145(M.37. 533A).

ἀτροφία, ἡ, *want of food* or *nourishment,* met. ἀ. μὲν ἡ ἄγνοια τῆς ψυχῆς, τροφὴ δὲ ἡ γνῶσις Clem.*str.*7.12(p.52.9; M.9.500C); ἐκτήκων... τὸν νοῦν ἐν ἀ. Bas.*hom.*1.9(2.8A; M.31.180A).

ἄτροφος, *ill-fed, under-nourished,* met., *growing no larger, constant in size,* of stars ἄ. ἐστι πυρὸς φύσις Gr.Naz.*carm.*1.1.5.68(M.37. 429A); Gr.Nyss.*hex.*5(M.44.68A).

ἄτρυγος, *without lees, clarified, pure,* Meth.*symp.*4.5(p.51.9; M. 18.93C); χορηγητέον...τὸ ἄ. ἔλαιον...τῶν καλῶν ἔργων...καὶ τῆς συνέσεως *ib.*6.4(p.68.17; 120A).

ἄτρυφος, *free from luxury,* Socr.*h.e.*7.37.5(M.67.824A; ἄτυφος p.819).

***ἀτρύχως,** *indefatigably,* Meth.*symp.*8.4(p.85.9; M.18.144B).

***ἄτρωκτος,** *uneatable*; met., *unconsumable,* Germ.CP *or.*2(M.98. 285B).

ἄτρωτος, 1. *unwounded,* met. ὁ...θεός...σε...ἄ. φυλάξειε τοῖς πάθεσι Gr.Naz.*ep.*223(M.37.368A); ref. those wounded in soul by sin, Bas.*hom.in Ps.*7:3(1.99C; M.29.232C); Gr.Nyss.*Eun.*1(1 p.44.26; M.45.272D); *inviolate, whole* ἄ. φυλάττων τὴν γνῶσιν τῆς πίστεως Didym.*Trin.*2.8(M.39.604A); ὁμολογίαν καὶ πίστιν...ἄ. καὶ ἀπαρεγχείρητον ἐν Χριστῷ διαφυλάξομεν Cyr.S.*v.Sab.*57(p.153.12); cf. τῶν Χριστοῦ τὴν πίστιν...τηρεῖν προαιρουμένων ἄ., καὶ ἀπαρεγχείρητον Jo.D.*hom.*12.6(M.96.789D); neut. as subst., *wholeness, innocence* ὁ Ἐμμανουήλ,...τὸ ἀκέραιον καὶ ἄ. ... τοῦ Ἀδὰμ ἐμιμήσατο Proc.G.*Is.* 7:10ff.(M.87.1965B); **2.** *invulnerable,* usu. met. ἄ. ὑπὸ τῶν χρημάτων Clem.*q.d.s.*26(p.177.22; M.9.632C); μεῖνον ἀπαθής, μεῖνον ἄ. Chrys. *hom.*50.3 *in Ac.*(9.375C); ἐὰν...μνησθῶμεν τῶν κακῶν τῶν δαιμόνων, ἐσόμεθα ἄ. *Apophth.Patr.*(M.65.277D); *invincible* καθωπλισμένους τοῖς τῆς πίστεως λόγοις ἀ. οὖσιν †Just.*fr.res.*1(p.37; M.6.1573C); ref. Eph.6:13ff. ταῦτα ἡμῶν τὰ ὅπλα τὰ ἄ. Clem.*prot.*11(p.82.13; M.8.236C).

Ἀττικός, *Attic*; as fem. subst., a coin, *Athenian drachma,* Clem. *paed.*2.10(p.226.10; M.8.536B); Eus.*h.e.*9.8.4(M.20.816C).

ἄτυπος, *without a type,* ref. 1Cor.10:11 τύπου...προάγοντος... νουθετεῖσθαι τοὺς ὁρῶντας, ἄ. δὲ νουθεσία οὐκ ἄν ποτε δειχθείη Adam. *dial.*2.18(p.96.3).

***ἀτύπως,** *without a type* ταῦτ' ἀ. συνέβαινεν ἐκείνοις 1Cor.10:11 cit.ap.Adam.*dial.*2.18(p.94.9; M.11.1788B ταῦτα τύπος).

ἀτύπωτος, 1. *unformed, shapeless* τίκτει δὲ τὸ ζῷον [sc. she bear] σάρκα ἀ. Clem.*str.*6.6(p.457.12; M.9.272C); τί...τὸν ἀ. χαλκὸν ἢ λίθον οὐ προσκυνεῖς; †Bas.*Is.*82(1.436C; M.30.253B); Chrys.*hom.*17.2 *in 1Cor.*(10.148C); **2.** *incapable of being stamped* or *struck,* of a seal, Dion.Ar.*d.n.*2.6(M.3.644C); **3.** *unstruck by* τὸ πολύαθλόν σου σῶμα... βασάνων σφύραις μένον ἀ. Jo.Mon.*hymn.Geo.*9(M.96.1400C); **4.** *unmoulded by material images* (v. τυπόω) ἡ γνῶσις ἡ πνευματικὴ ἀφίστησι τὸν νοῦν τῶν νοημάτων τῶν τυπούντων αὐτόν, ἀ. δὲ αὐτὸν παρίστησι τῷ θεῷ †Nil.*mal.cog.*24(M.79.1229A); **5.** = ἄτυπος, *typeless, non-symbolical,* Dion.Ar.*c.h.*1.3(M.3.121C); *ib.*2.2(140A); ὥσπερ γὰρ ἄληπτα καὶ ἀθεώρητα τοῖς αἰσθητοῖς ἐστι τὰ νοητά, καὶ τοῖς ἐν πλάσει καὶ τύπῳ τὰ ἁπλᾶ καὶ ἀ. id.*d.n.*1.1(M.3.588B); Max.*schol. c.h.*1.3(M.4.36B); εἰκόνες εἰσὶ τὰ ὁρατὰ τῶν ἀοράτων καὶ ἀ., σωματικῶς τυπουμένων πρὸς ἀμυδρὰν κατανόησιν Jo.D.*imag.*1.11(M.94. 1241A).

ἀτυράννευτος, *free from tyranny,* met. διαρρήξας μὲν τοὺς ἐκείνων δεσμοὺς...τὸ δὲ...ἀ. τῆς δικαιοσύνης ἀναδησάμενος καύχημα Cyr.*Jo.*4.7(4.433B); *not mastered* ἀ. ... τὴν διάνοιαν ἔχοντες ταῖς τῆς σαρκὸς ἡδοναῖς id.*Juln.*3(6².92D).

***ἀτυραννεύτως,** *without subjection to tyranny,* met. οὐ γάρ εἰσιν [sc. οἱ ἄγγελοι] ἐν ἀγνοίᾳ τοῦ κακοῦ, πλὴν ἀ. καὶ ἐλευθέρως Cyr.*Juln.*3 (6².93A).

[*]**ἀτυράννητος,** *not ruled by a tyrant,* Clem.*str.*4.26(p.325.1; M. 8.1381A); neut. as subst., *freedom from tyranny,* Apoll.*quod un. Chr.*11(p.301.23; M.28.129C).

ἀτυφία, ἡ, 1. *freedom from arrogance, humility* ὅταν μὲν τὰ ἐλάττονα λέγῃ, ἑαυτῷ αὐτὰ προσάγει, οὐ γάρ ἐστιν ἐπιδεικτικὸς δι' ἀ. Didym.*Job* 12:4(M.39.1148B perh. emend διὰ τυφίαν); **2.** *frugality* τῆς κατὰ τὰ βρώματα ἀ. καὶ ἁπλότητος ‡Bas.*const.*25 tit.(2.575C; M.31.1413B) and perh. in following passages also as the τέλος acc. Antisthenes, Clem.*str.*2.21(p.184.18; M.8.1077A); Thdt.*affect.*11 (p.274.8; 4.985).

αὐγάζ-ω, 1. *see distinctly,* med. Μωσῆς...τούτου τὴν οἰκονομίαν ~εται ἣν τυπικῶς...μεμυσταγώγητο Jo.D.*hom.*1.2(M.96.548A); **2.** *set in a clear light,* of activity of H. Ghost under old dispensation Χριστοῖο μέγα κλέος ηὐγάζεσκε παύροισιν πινυτοῖσι Gr.Naz.*carm.*1.1. 3.25(M.37.410A); αἱ...Χριστοῦ πανηγύρεις ὅσαι τὸ φῶς τῆς περὶ ἡμᾶς οἰκονομίας ~ουσι Const.Diac.*laud.*1(M.88.480A); **3.** *illumine,* spiritually τῆς θείας αὐτὸν...μικρὸν αὐγασάσης ἐλλάμψεως Eus.*h.e.*1.13.8 (p.88.3 not.; M.20.121C); **4.** *shine* ἐξ ἡλίου τις αὐγάσας ἀστὴρ μέγας Thdr.Stud.*iamb.*80(M.99.1800D).

αὐγασμός, ὁ, *splendour, brilliance,* spiritual ὁ αὐ. τῆς δόξης τοῖς πεφωτισμένοις, ἡ τύφλωσις τοῖς ἀπίστοις Cyr.H.*catech.*6.29.

***αὐγαστικός,** *radiant, glorious,* Thdr.Stud.*or.*8.3(M.99.761B).

αὐγέω, *shine,* Thdr.Stud.*epp.*2.89(M.99.1337D).

αὐγή, ἡ, *light,* plur. *rays*; met., of divine light Χριστοῦ...τοῦ τὴν θείαν αὐ. καταλάμποντος ἐξ οὐρανοῦ Clem.*fr.*44(p.222.22); ὅπερ [sc. soul of Pharaoh] ὡς πηλὸς ὑπὸ ἡλίου σκληρύνεται, οὕτως ὑπὸ τῶν αὐ. τοῦ θεοῦ...ἐσκληρύνθη Or.*Cant.*2(p.129.24; M.13.113B); ἤρκει...ὁ εἷς λόγος, ὡς δικαιοσύνης ἥλιος ἀνατείλας, ἀπὸ τῆς Ἰουδαίας ἐκπέμψαι τὰς ἐπὶ τὴν ψυχὴν τῶν βουλομένων αὐτὸν παραδέξασθαι φθανούσας αὐ. id. *Cels.*6.79(p.150.18; M.11.1417B); of truth ἡ τῶν πολλῶν ἀπιστία τε καὶ ἄγνοια τῇ αὐ. τῆς ἀληθείας ἐπίπροσθε φέρεται Clem.*str.*5.12(p.378.4; M.9.116B); ταῖς τοῦ λόγου αὐ. ἀκολουθήσαντα Or.*Cels.*6.66(p.136.23; 1400A); ταῖς λαμπροτάταις τῆς αὐτοῦ διδασκαλίας αὐ. Eus.*l.C.*17(p.258. 7; M.20.1437A); of virtue τὴν αὐ. τῆς ἀρετῆς Meth.*symp.*10.2(p.124. 15; M.18.196C); *ib.*6.4(p.69.14; 119B); Eus.*l.C.*5(p.204.19; 1336C).

αὖγος, τό, *dawn* αὐ. δὲ γενομένου καὶ διαφαύσαντος κλάσας ἄρτον κοινωνοὺς αὐτοὺς κατέστησεν τῆς εὐχαριστίας τοῦ Χριστοῦ *A.Thom.*A 27(p.143.10); τῇ τρίτῃ ἡμέρᾳ πρὸ τοῦ αὐ. ἠγέρθη *A.Thadd.*6(p.277.8); ἀπὸ ἑσπέρας ἕως αὐ. Jo.Mal.*chron.*18 p.477(M.97.692D).

Αὐγούστα, Αὐγοῦστα, (Lat. *Augusta*) *Augusta, wife of emperor* or *lady honoured with the imperial title,* e.g. emperor's mother οὕτω ...ἀξιώματι βασιλικῷ τετιμηκότα, ὡς...αὐ. βασιλίδα ἀναγορεύεσθαι Eus.*v.C.*3.47(p.97.21; M.20.1108A); Ἑλένη αὐ. *ib.*3.43(p.96.8; 1104B); ἡ Αὐ. Εὐδοξία...ἡ βασίλισσα Εὐδοξία Socr.*h.e.*6.11.19(M.67.700A); ζῶν ὁ κοινὸς αὐτῶν πατὴρ διαδήματί τε αὐτὴν ἐταινίωσεν καὶ Αὐ. ἐπωνόμασεν Philost.*h.e.*3.22(M.65.512A).

[*]**Αὐγουσταῖον, τό,** atrium built in Constantinople by Constantine in honour of Helena, *Chron.Pasch.*p.284(M.92.709B); another built in A.D. 459, *ib.*p.321(M.92.817C); Thphn.*chron.*p.154 (*Αὐγουστέον* M.108.417B).

***Αὐγουσταλιανή, ἡ,** v. *Αὐγουσταμνική.

Αὐγουστάλιος, ὁ, (Lat. *Augustalis*) **1.** *priest of municipal cult of Augustus* κακοδαίμονός τινος Αὐ. Synes.*ep.*105(M.66.1488C); *MAMA* 1.169a; Θεοδώρου τοῦ...δεκουρίωνος καὶ δουκὸς καὶ Αὐ. τῆς Θηβαίων χώρας *CIG* 8646(Egypt 577); **2.** *prefect of Egypt,* Pall.*v.Chrys.*7 (p.39.4; M.47.24); id.*h.Laus.*46(p.134.16; M.34.1225B); Κορνήλιον Γάλλον, ᾧτινι ἔδωκεν ἀξίαν αὐ. τοῦ ἰδίου ὀνόματος σήμαντρον Jo.Mal. *chron.*9 p.224(M.97.348C).

***Αὐγουσταμνική, ἡ,** *cohort under the prefect of Egypt,* Ath.*apol. sec.*83(p.162.21; *Αὐγουσταλιανή* M.25.397B).

***Αὐγουστέον, τό,** v. [*]*Αὐγουσταῖον*.

***Αὐγουστεύς, ὁ,** *bronze column* in forum of Augustus at CP, Thphn.*chron.*p.189(M.108.489C); *ib.*p.157(M.108.424C).

***Αὐγουστεών, ὁ,** forum of Augustus which contained statue of Justinian, Jo.Mal.*chron.*18 p.482(M.97.700A).

***αὐγούστιον, τό,** a measure ξέσται χάλκεοι β' ἔχοντες τρία αὐ. *IGC As.Min.*290.

Αὔγουστος, ὁ, (Lat. *Augustus*) **1.** title of C. Caesar Octavianus, Afric.*chron.*17.1(M.10.84C); Eus.*h.e.*1.5.2(M.20.81A); ‡Chrys.*hom.in Lc.*2:1(2.803C); **2.** title of his successors, Ath.*apol.sec.*76(p.156.13; M.25.385C); Evagr.*h.e.*2.1(p.37.13; M.86.2488B); Thphn.*chron.*p.59 (M.108.201B); **3.** borne at times not only by reigning emperor but by heir to throne Κωνσταντῖνος ὁ Αὐ. καὶ οἱ υἱοὶ αὐτοῦ Κωνστάντιος καὶ Κώνστας οἱ Αὐ. Ath.*v.Anton.*81(M.26.956A); **4.** highest title of emperor, superior to that of Caesar which was often borne, esp. from Diocletian onwards, by junior colleagues in empire οἳ καισάρων μὲν ἔτι πρότερον μετεῖχον τιμῆς νυνὶ δ'...αὐτοκράτορες αὐ.

σεβαστοὶ βασιλεῖς...ἀνεδείχθησαν Eus.*v.C.*1.1(p.7.18; M.20.912B); αὐ. ὃ δὴ πρώτιστον καὶ μέγιστον τῆς ἀνωτάτω βασιλείας γίγνοιτ' ἂν σύμβολον *ib.*4.68(p.146.6; 1224B); Κωνστάντιος ὁ Αὔ. μόνος βασιλεύων Γάλλον...κοινωνὸν τῆς ἑαυτοῦ βασιλείας Καίσαρα ἀναγορεύσας Thphn. *chron.*p.33(M.108.140C); = σεβαστός Eus.*v.C.*1.18(p.17.6; 933B); **5.** *month of August*, Epiph.*haer.*11(p.204.20; M.41.233B); Evagr.*h.e.* 4.9(p.159.32; M.86.2720A).

***αὐδαῖος**, *expressed in speech* φωνὴν μὲν ὑποληπτέον τὴν νοερὰν τῆς διανοίας πρὸς τὸν...θεὸν ἱκεσίαν· οὐ γὰρ τὴν κραυγὴν λέγει, ἀλλὰ τὴν αὐ. τῆς διανοίας εὐχήν Ath.*exp.Ps.*3:5(M.27.69B).

αὐδή, ἡ, *human voice, speech*; theol. ἀεὶ ὢν πατὴρ παιδὸς μονογενοῦς, αὐ. ἐνυποστάτου ‡Caes.Naz.*dial.*3(M.38.861).

***Αὐδιανός, ὁ,** member of sect which arose in Syria in 4th century, Thdt.*haer.*4.10(4.364) also known as Ὠδιανοί, Epiph.*haer.*70.1 (p.232.17; M.42.340A); not a heresy, but a schism, *ib.*proem.1(p.161. 5; M.41.164B); id.*anc.*13(p.22.2; M.43.40D); id.*anac.*6(p.230.4; M.42. 336B); Jo.D.*haer.*70(M.94.720B); with anthropomorphic ideas about God, Epiph.*haer.*70.3ff.(p.235ff.; M.42.341Df.); Thdt.*h.e.*4.10.1(3. 963); id.*haer.*4.10(4.364); ascetic ἐν μοναστηρίοις τὴν κατοίκησιν κέκτηνται ἀναχωροῦντες Epiph.*haer.*70.1(p.232.17; 340A); *ib.*70.15 (p.248.28; 373A); other ideas and practices, *ib.*(pp.233–249; 340–373); Thdt.*haer.*4.10(364f.); Jo.D.*haer.*70(M.94.720Bf.).

Αὐδυναῖος (-εος), ὁ, name of month in Macedonia, Crete, etc.; corresponding to January, Eus.*m.P.*10(p.930.30; M.20.1497A); ref. date of Nativity ἐστὶ κατὰ Ῥωμαίους πέμπτη Ἰανουαρίου ἑσπέρα εἰς ἕκτην ἐπιφώσκουσα...κατὰ Σύρους εἴτ' οὖν Ἕλληνας Αὐδυναίου ἕκτη Epiph.*haer.*51.24(p.293.3; Αὐδυνέου M.41.932B); Chrys.*nativ.*5(2. 362B); ἐβαπτίσθη τῇ ἕκτῃ...τοῦ Αὐ. μηνός *Chron.Pasch.*p.209(M.92. 512C).

αὐθάδεια, ἡ, *self-will*; *arrogance*, ref. inaudible and loud speech τὸ μὲν ἀγεννείας, τὸ δὲ αὐ. τεκμήριον Clem.*paed.*2.7(p.192.14; M.8. 461B); ἡ...μεγαλοφροσύνη πάσης αὐ. καθαρεύουσα Isid.Pel.*epp.*2.241 (M.78.681D).

αὐθάδης, 1. *self-willed, stubborn*; neut. as subst., *self-will* τῷ αὐ. καὶ θρασυτέρῳ Or.*Jo.*10.25(16; p.197.28; M.14.352B); **2.** *arrogant* μὴ βαρὺς ἐν ἐπιτιμήσεσι γίνου...αὐ. γὰρ τὸ τοιοῦτον Bas.*hom.*20.7(2. 162B; M.31.537C).

αὐθαδιάζ-ω, 1. *be self-willed* or *self-assertive*; med.; **a.** in good sense, *act with determination*, Gr.Naz.*or.*4.57(M.35.580C); **b.** *assert contumaciously* μίαν γεγενῆσθαι φύσιν ~εσθε Jo.D.*Jacob.*45(M.94. 1457A); **2.** act., *be obstinate* σκληρυνόμενος σκληρυνθῇς καὶ αὐθαδιάσεις Thdr.Stud.*epp.*1.9(M.99.940B).

***αὐθαδιασμός, ὁ,** *self-assertion, arrogance* ἵνα μὴ νομισθῇ κόμπος εἶναι καὶ αὐ. οὗτος τῆς διδασκαλίας ὁ τρόπος Chrys.*hom.25.1 in Mt.* (7.307C); *ib.16.5*(210C); μή τοι δέξῃ τὴν ὑπόμνησιν ἡμῶν ὡς αὐ., ἀλλ' ὡς ἀγαπητικὸν τρόπον Thdr.Stud.*epp.*2.207(M.99.1628C).

***αὐθαδικῶς,** *violently*; comp., Thphyl.*exc.Rom.*1(p.221.22; M.113. 928B).

***αὐθάδιος,** s.v.l., *obstinate* ὀργὴν...κατ' ἀλλήλων αὐθάδιον *PLond.* 1912.80, perh. emend [καὶ] αὐθαδίαν.

***αὐθαδισμός, ὁ,** *cat.Mt.*5:21(p.469.25; cf. αὐθαδιασμός Chrys. *hom.16.5 in Mt.*(7.210C).

αὐθαδῶς, *arrogantly, insolently* τὰ...ἀπὸ τῶν θεοπνεύστων γραμμάτων ῥήματα, οἷς...ποικίλλουσιν...τὴν δόξαν, δικαιοσύνην αὐ. καὶ ἀλήθειαν ὀνομάζοντες Meth.*res.*1.28(p.257.17; M.41.1136B); Didym. *Trin.*2.6(M.39.548A).

***αὐθαιρετικῶς,** *voluntarily*, Didym.*Trin.*3.12(M.39.860C).

αὐθαιρέτως, *of one's own accord, independently, freely* δι' οὗ [sc. Χριστοῦ] ἐὰν μὴ αὐ. ἔχωμεν τὸ ἀποθανεῖν... Ign.*Magn.*5.2; θέλησίς ἐστι...νοῦς περί τι αὐ. κινούμενος Clem.*fr.*40(p.220.16; M.9.752A); τῷδε ⟨τῷ⟩ ἔργῳ ὡς αὐ. ὑπ' αὐτοῦ γενομένῳ Hipp.*haer.*6.48(p.180.6; M.16.3274B); Const.ap.Eus.*h.e.*10.5.18(M.20.888A).

***αὐθάς,** *voluntary, self-chosen*, Jo.D.*Jacob.*1(M.94.1436B).

αὐθέδραστος, *self-subsistent, having independent existence*; of substances opp. accidents, Jo.D.*dialect.*50(M.94.632A); of God ἡ μακαρία...αὐ. φύσις *cat.Apoc.*12:9(p.360.15).

***αὐθεκούσιος,** *freely-willed, voluntary*, Eus.*d.e.*4.1(p.150.24; M.22. 252B) cit. s. ἄφετος; *ib.*4.10(p.164.27; 276A); id.*p.e.*6.6(253A; M.21. 429C); τῆς τοῦ φωτὸς αὐ. ἀναχωρήσεως *ib.*7.16(328C; M.556A); τὴν... αὐ. ὑπακοήν id.*e.th.*3.15(p.172.22; M.24.1029A); neut. as subst., *free will*, id.*p.e.*6.6(245B; M.417A); τὸ αὐ. τῆς ψυχῆς *ib.*(247C; M.420D).

***αὐθεκουσίως,** *voluntarily*, Eus.*p.e.*6.6(247D; M.21.421A).

[*]**αὐθεντεία,** v. αὐθεντία.

αὐθεντ-έω, 1. *hold sovereign authority, act with authority*, abs.; **a.** of God βαπτίζοντας αὐτοὺς εἰς τὸ ὄνομα...τοῦ μὲν πατρὸς ~οῦντος καὶ δωρουμένου τὴν χάριν, τοῦ δὲ υἱοῦ...διακονουμένου...τοῦ δὲ ἁγίου πνεύματος...χορηγουμένου Eus.*e.th.*3.5(p.163.23; M.24.1013A); οὔτε ἔβρεξεν ἀφ' ἑαυτοῦ [sc. τοῦ υἱοῦ], ἀλλὰ παρὰ κυρίου, ~οῦντος δηλαδὴ τοῦ πατρός *Symb.Sirm.*1 *anath.*18; of Son ὡς τοῦ υἱοῦ τὰ πάντα ποιοῦντος καὶ ~οῦντος καὶ ἐξουσιάζοντος καὶ τῷ πατρὶ παραδιδόντος... τοὺς ὑποτασσομένους Epiph.*haer.*69.75(p.224.5; M.42.325A); ref. raising of Lazarus οὔτε πάντα ὡς ~ῶν ἐργάζεται...οὔτε πάντα εὐχόμενος ποιεῖ Chrys.*hom.16.1 in Mt.*(7.204A); **b.** of men Μάρκος...βραχὺ συνέταξεν εὐαγγέλιον, ᾧπερ ἐντυχὼν Πέτρος ἐδοκίμασε καὶ τῇ ἐκκλησίᾳ ἀναγνωσθησόμενον ~ήσας ἐξέδωκε Hier.*vir.ill.*(tr.Sophr.Pal.)8(p.8. 21; αὐθεντίσας M.*PL.*23.622B); ὁ δὲ Φίλιππος παραχωρεῖ τῷ Ἀνδρέᾳ ...οὐδὲ οὗτος ἁπλῶς ~εῖ Chrys.*hom.66.2 in Jo.*(8.396D); ‡Chrys. *hom.*13(13.256B); of Pope ἐπιστεῖλαι τῷ ἐπισκόπῳ Ῥώμης...ἵν' ἐπειδὴ ἀπὸ κοινοῦ καὶ συνοδικοῦ δόγματος ἀποσταλῆναί τινας δύσκολον τῶν ἐκεῖθεν, αὐτὸν ~ῆσαι περὶ τὸ πρᾶγμα Bas.*ep.*69.1(3.162C; M.32.432A); πάσης...πλάνης ἀποκινηθείσης, διὰ τῆς συγκροτηθείσης ταύτης συνόδου, σοῦ ~οῦντος Marcian.Imp.*ep.Leo.*1(p.10.14; M.*PL.*54.900B); **c.** of things οὐδὲ γὰρ ἐκείνην [sc. τὴν ψυχήν] βούλεται ~εῖν· ἀλλὰ καὶ ἐκείνης τὴν ἐξουσίαν ὑπὸ τῇ τοῦ πνεύματος ἔθηκε δυνάμει Chrys.*hom. 14.2 in Rom.*(9.577B); ὁ μὲν [sc. νόμος] ὑπηρετεῖ, ἡ δὲ [sc. χάρις] ~εῖ Procl.CP *or.*17.5(M.65.816A); **2.** *possess authority* over ἐβούλετο ...ἐνδείξασθαι τῷ δήμῳ ὅτι κρατεῖ καὶ ~εῖ τοῦ παιδός Chrys.*hom. 44.1 in Mt.*(7.467C); id.*serm.4.1 in Gen.*(4.660A); **3.** *assume authority*; *act on one's own authority*, abs. οὐ δεῖ τινα ἑαυτῷ ~εῖν καὶ καινοτομίας εἰσάγειν ἐν τῇ πίστει Ammon.*Ac.*10:18(M.85.1537B); *ib.* 15:7(1549A); *ib.*15:25(1552B); ὁ διάκονος...ὀφείλει...εἰς τὸν λαὸν μηδὲν ~εῖν, ἀλλὰ πάντα κελεύσει τοῦ πρεσβυτέρου διοικεῖν Eus.Al.*serm.*5 (M.86.348D); Socr.*h.e.*2.34.2(M.67.296B); οὗτος [sc. Διόσκορος]... Εὐτυχῆ...καθαιρεθέντα κανονικῶς...~ήσας ἀκανονίστως εἰς κοινωνίαν ἀνεδέξατο episcopi Romani ap.Evagr.*h.e.*2.18(p.77.25; M.86.2564C); εἰ...προφήτης ~εῖ κατὰ τοῦ νόμου Vict.*Mc.*2:25f.(p.292.29); *play the despot, act arbitrarily* μή...ἐπειδὴ ὑποτέτακται ἡ γυνή, ~εῖ Chrys. *hom.10.1 in Col.*(11.396C); *ib.11.2*(406E); *presume on one's own authority* θεοτόκον τὴν μητέρα τοῦ Ἰησοῦ λέγειν ἡμεῖς οὐκ ~ήσομεν Leont.H.*Nest.*4.49(M.86.1720D); **4.** *be primarily responsible for, instigate*; *authorize* τῆς...κρίσεως ~εῖ ὁ ὕψιστος θεός Const.ap.Eus.*v. C.*2.48(p.62.3; M.20.1025C); τοῖς δὲ μὴ ~οῦσι μὲν τῆς ἀσεβείας, παρασυρεῖσι δὲ δι' ἀνάγκην καὶ βίαν,...δίδοσθαι μὲν συγγνώμην Ath.*ep. Rufin.*(M.26.1180C); ἑτέροις ἀκολουθῶν, ἢ αὐτὸς κατάρχων καὶ ~ῶν τοῦ τολμήματος; Bas.*ep.*51.1(3.143D; M.32.389A); Chrys.*hom.3.3 in Ac.*(9.26D); Leo Mag.*ep.*30.1(p.46.1; M.*PL.*54.788A); pass., *be authorized*; of a law or code, *be given force of law, come into force* τούτῳ τῷ ἔτει ὁ Ἰουστινιανὸς κῶδιξ ἐπληρώθη καὶ ἐκελεύσθη ~εῖσθαι *Chron. Pasch.*p.335(M.92.872A); *ib.*p.344(896B).

αὐθεντία (-εία), ἡ, A. *absolute sway, sovereign power, supreme authority*; **1.** divine τὰς γραφὰς...κυρίας οὔσας ἐξ αὐ. παντοκρατορικῆς ἐπιδείξαντας Clem.*str.*4.1(p.248.22; M.8.1216B); ἐν μὲν τῷ εἰπεῖν τὸ προστακτικὸν ἀπὸ αὐ. φάσκειν σημαίνεσθαι, ἐν δὲ τῷ 'ἐλάλησε' τὸ διδασκαλικόν Or.*fr.95 in Jo.*12:49f.(p.558.18); ἐπὶ τῆς κατ' ἐξουσίαν αὐ. παραπλήσια...περὶ πατρὸς καὶ υἱοῦ καὶ ἁγίου πνεύματος παραδέδοται Thdt.*rect.conf.*7(M.6.1220B); ἰσοσθενὴς...ἡ θεία τριὰς...ἐν μιᾷ... αὐ. ‡Caes.Naz.*dial.*3(M.38.861); *ib.*167(1129); **a.** of Father τοῦ μὴ νόμῳ φύσεως αὐτὸν δουλεύειν ἀλλὰ αὐθεντίᾳ βουλήσεως τὸ δοκοῦν ἐργάζεσθαι ‡Just.*confut.*proem.(M.6.1493B); λαβόντες ἐντολὴν...κηρῦξαι...καὶ βαπτίσαι...ἐπὶ αὐθεντίᾳ τοῦ θεοῦ τῶν ὅλων...καὶ μαρτυρίᾳ πνεύματος *Const.App.*5.7.30; τὸ μὴ τυραννικῇ τινι χρήσασθαι...αὐ. Gr.Nyss.*or.catech.*22(p.85.1; M.45.60D); Chrys.*hom.3.1 in Eph.*(11. 17A); opp. second and third Persons of Trin. Χριστοῦ...καὶ ἁγίου πνεύματος παρ' ἑκάτερα τῆς τοῦ πατρὸς αὐ. τὰς δευτέρας αὐγὰς τοῦ φωτός Eus.*h.e.*10.4.65(M.20.876B); id.*e.th.*1.20(p.81.21; M.24.865C); τὸν πατέρα ἐν τῇ πατρικῇ αὐ. ὑφεστῶτα νοοῦντες Geo.Laod.*ep.dogm.* ap.Epiph.*haer.*73.16(p.289.4; M.42.433B); plur. μυσταγωγῶν τὸν θεόφιλῆ τὰς περὶ τοῦ πατρὸς αὐ. Eus.*d.e.*1.4(p.22.18; M.22.48B); **b.** of Son ὁ υἱὸς τὴν εἰκόνα τοῦ πατρὸς ἔχων ἐν ἑαυτῷ ἐξ αὐ. τε αὐτοῦ... διαταττόμενος Eus.*e.th.*2.21(p.131.19; M.24.957A); id.*Is.*40:10(M.24. 369A); εἰπὼν ὅτι δι' αὐτοῦ ἐποίησε τὰ πάντα, ἐνταῦθα δίδωσιν αὐτῷ τὴν αὐ. Chrys.*hom.2.1 in Heb.*(12.14B); ref. Gen.1:26f. αὐ. προσώπων [sc. of Father and Son] σημαίνει Gel.Cyz.*h.e.*2.16.10(M.85.1261C); of Son incarnate ἐξ αὐ. κυριακῆς Clem.*paed.*2.3(p.178.21; M.8. 433B); συγχωρεῖ τὰς ἁμαρτίας ἐξ αὐ. τῶν ἀνθρώπων Gr.Nyss.*tres dii* (M.45.124B); δεῖξαι ὅτι τὴν αὐτὴν αὐ. ἔχει τῷ πατρί Chrys.*paralyt.*7 (3.45C); ref. Mc.13:32 οὐχ ὥσπερ ἐκ τῆς οἰκείας αὐ. τοῦτο ὁρίσας εἰδέναι ἐπαγγέλλεται, ἀλλ' ὅτι ἐν τῇ τοῦ πατρὸς βουλήσει, ἤτοι εἰδήσει, οἶδε τοῦτο καὶ αὐτός †Diad.*Ar.*6(M.65.1160C); and glorified οὐκέτι αἰτούμενος δίδωσιν, ἀλλ' αὐθεντίᾳ τὰ ἴδια [Jo.20:22] Epiph.*haer.* 69.30(p.179.16; M.42.249C); Chrys.*hom.90.2 in Mt.*(7.841C); as principle of operation of divine nature in hypostatic union ἐνεργεῖ...

ὁ Χριστὸς καθ' ἑκάτεραν αὐτοῦ τῶν φύσεων...τοῦ μὲν λόγου κατεργαζομένου ἅπερ ἐστὶ τοῦ λόγου, διὰ τὴν αὐ. ... τῆς θεότητος...τοῦ δὲ σώματος, πρὸς τὸ βούλημα τοῦ ἑνωθέντος αὐτῷ λόγου, οὗ καὶ γέγονεν ἴδιον Jo.D.*f.o.*3.15(M.94.1060A); ‡Jo.D.*ep.Thphl.*3(M.95.348C) cit. s. B.3; **c.** of H. Ghost, ref. Jo.3:8 τὴν...αὐτὴν αὐ. καὶ ἐξουσίαν μαρτυρῶν τῷ πνεύματι ὁ σωτήρ Didym.(‡Bas.)*Eun.*5(1.299A; M.29.717B); τὸ πνεῦμα αὐ. φύσεως χρώμενον *ib.*(300C; M.721A); τὸ ἴσον τῆς πρὸς τὸν πατέρα φύσεως, καὶ αὐ. τοῦ ἁγίου πνεύματος id.*Trin.*2.8 (M.39.628A); οὐ δοῦλον τυγχάνει τὸ πνεῦμα, ἀλλὰ τῆς αὐτῆς θεότητος, τὴν αὐτοῦ αὐ. ὑποδεικνύντες [sc. οἱ ἀπόστολοι] Epiph.*haer.*74.13 (p.331.11; M.42.500B); id.*anc.*16(p.25.12; M.43.45C); Sever.ap.*cat. Ac.*15:28(pp.253.34,254.6); **2.** in Thdr. Mops. and Nest., one of elements forming the ground of union between Logos and humanity ἡ κατ' εὐδοκίαν τῶν φύσεων ἕνωσις μίαν ἀμφοτέρων τῷ τῆς ὁμωνυμίας λόγῳ ἐργάζεται τὴν προσηγορίαν...τὴν ἐνέργειαν, τὴν αὐ. ... μηδενὶ τρόπῳ διαιρουμένην Thdr.Mops.*ep.Domn.*(p.338.24; M.66.1012C); ὁ ...τῆς κατ' εὐδοκίαν ἑνώσεως τρόπος...ἐν ἀμφοτέρων τὸ πρόσωπον δείκνυσιν καὶ...μίαν τὴν ἐνέργειαν μετὰ τῆς ἑπομένης τούτοις μιᾶς αὐ. *ib.*(p.339.5; 1013A); id.*fr.inc.*15(p.312.2; cf.M.66.994A, Lat.); τῶν δύο φύσεων μία ἐστὶν αὐ. ... καὶ ἓν πρόσωπον κατὰ μίαν ἀξίαν Nest.*fr.* A 11(p.196.15)ap.Justn.*conf.*(p.98.7; M.86.1021B); προσκυνῶ...σὺν τῇ θεότητι τοῦτον ὡς τῆς θείας συνήγορον αὐ. Nest.*fr.*C 9(p.260.7)ap.Cyr. *Nest.*2.9(p.47.12; 6.52C); τῶν δύο ἡ αὐ. κοινή Nest.*fr.*D 4(p.354.9)*ib.* 2.6(p.41.24; 6.44A); Nest.*fr.*D 4(p.354.15)*ib.*3.6(p.72.36; 6.90E); condemned by Cyr. εἴ τις ἐπὶ τοῦ ἑνὸς Χριστοῦ διαιρεῖ τὰς ὑποστάσεις ...μόνῃ συνάπτων αὐτὰς συναφείᾳ τῇ κατὰ τὴν ἀξίαν ἢ γοῦν αὐ. ... ἀ. ἔ. Cyr.*expl.xii cap.*3(p.18.22; 6[1].149B); id.*ep.*17(p.36.14; 5[2].71A); ἄνθρωπον...συναφθέντα θεῷ σχετικῶς κατὰ μόνην τὴν ἰσοτιμίαν ἢ γοῦν αὐ. *ib.*40(p.27.8; 116E); τοὺς...φάσκοντας...κατὰ μόνην τὴν ἀξίαν ἤτοι αὐ. ἀνθρώπου γενέσθαι συνάφειαν πρὸς θεόν, τῆς ὀρθῆς...πίστεως ἀλλοτρίους εἶναί φαμεν id.*expl.xii cap.*2(p.18.11; 6[1].148E); and by later Fathers, Leont.H.*Nest.*1.36(M.86.1497D,1500A); μία...αὐ. ... καὶ μία ἀξία...οὐκ ἐπὶ διαφόρων φύσεων, ἀλλ' ἐπὶ διαφόρων προσώπων καὶ τῆς αὐτῆς οὐσίας λέγεται...ὅθεν καὶ οἱ ἅγιοι πατέρες ἀνεθεμάτισαν τοὺς κατ' αὐ. ... ἢ ἀξίαν...λέγοντας τὸν θεὸν λόγον τῷ Χριστῷ ἡνῶσθαι Justn.*conf.*(p.98.9,12; M.86.1021C); εἴ τις λέγει, κατὰ...ἰσοτιμίαν ἢ κατ' αὐ. ... τὴν ἕνωσιν τοῦ θεοῦ λόγου πρὸς ἄνθρωπον γεγενῆσθαι...ἢ κατ' εὐδοκίαν...ἀ. ἔ. id.*conf.anath.*4(p.90.29; M.86.1015A); αὐ. ... καὶ ἀξία...ὧν ἔφασκε Νεστόριος εἶναι τὴν ἕνωσιν, γνώμης ὑπάρχει κινήματα...ἀλλ' οὐ φύσεως Max.*opusc.*(M.91.41D); cf.Jo.D.*f.o.*3.15(M. 94.1060A) cit. s. A.1.b; **3.** Gnost., *the supreme Divine Power* τὸν ἄνθρωπον...ἀγγέλων εἶναι ποίημα, ἄνωθεν ἀπὸ τῆς αὐ. φωτεινῆς εἰκόνος ἐπιφανείσης Iren.*haer.*1.24.1(M.16.3322A); τῆς ὑπὲρ τὰ ὅλα αὐ. Hipp.*haer.*10.21(p.281.7,12; M.16.3438C); ἐκ τῆς ἰσχυροτέρας δυνάμεως...καὶ τῆς ἄνωθεν αὐ. Epiph.*haer.*38.1(p.63.1; M.41.653D).

B. *supreme authority*; **1.** eccl.; **a.** as committed to the Church ὑποταγῆναι τοῦ λοιποῦ τῇ αὐ. τῆς ἐκκλησίας Bas.*ep.*92.3(3.186B; M.32.484A); plur. εἴπερ τινὰ εἰσί τινι σχήματι θρησκείας δεδεγμένα, ἰσχὺν ἔχειν οὐ δύνανται τοσαύταις αὐ. καταπαλαιούμενα Horm.*ep.cler.* (p.56.7; M.*PL.*63.421B); **b.** for teaching: of Law, ref. Mt.24:20 'μηδὲ σαββάτου'...διὰ τὴν αὐ. τὴν ἀπὸ τοῦ νόμου Chrys.*hom.76.1 in Mt.*(7.732D); id.*comm.in Gal.*3:22(10.703B); of gospel τὴν αὐ. τοῦ κατὰ τὸ εὐαγγέλιον νόμου Eus.*d.e.*1.7(p.35.10; M.22.69A); Leo Mag. *ep.*93(p.31.27; M.*PL.*54.940A); of apostolic writings, plur. οὐκ ἐπὶ τὰς τῶν ἀποστόλων γραφάς, οὐκ ἐπὶ τὰς εὐαγγελικὰς αὐ. *ib.*28.1(p.11.10; 758A); μετὰ βραχὺ τοῦ χρόνου προϊόντος αὐ. τινὸς ἐπελάβετο [sc. epistle of S. James] Hier.*vir.ill.*(tr.Sophr.Pal.)2(p.3.24; M.*PL.*23.640B); of apostolic and patristic tradition κατὰ τὴν ἀποστολικὴν παράδοσιν...ἧς τινος τῇ αὐ. ἐν πᾶσιν ἑπόμεθα Agath.Papa *ep.syn.* (M.*PL.*87.1226B); Πολυκράτης...διδάσκων ὀφείλειν Ἰωάννου τοῦ ἀποστόλου καὶ τῇ παλαιᾷ ἐξακολουθεῖν αὐ. Hier.*vir.ill.*(tr.Sophr.Pal.) 45(p.32.17; 693A); καὶ μὴ θαρρήσωμεν καινίσαι φωνήν, ἐφ' ᾗ καταφυγὴν οὐκ ἔχομεν τὴν πατρικὴν αὐ. Max.*opusc.*(M.91.32C); **c.** for ruling, of councils and canons ἡ ἐν Χαλκηδόνι σύνοδος...τῶν προλαβουσῶν [sc. συνόδων] ὁμοίως τὰ δόγματα ἢ τηλαυγέστερον ἐφανέρωσεν ἢ ἐπαναληφθεῖσα τῇ αὐ. ἐβεβαίωσεν Horm.*ep.Epiph.*(p.58.16; M.*PL.*63.520B); *ib.*(p.57.22; 518C); **d.** in person of S. Peter 'σὺ κληθήσῃ Κηφᾶς', ἐκεῖνο γὰρ αὐ. ἦν καὶ ἐξουσίας μείζονος Chrys.*hom. 19.1 in Jo.*(8.112E); and his successors ἔχοντάς τε τὴν αὐ. τούτου παρ' οὗ ἀπεστάλησαν CSard.*can.*5; εἰλήφαμεν...παρὰ τοῦ ἁγιωτάτου Πέτρου καὶ κορυφαίου τῶν ἀποστόλων, ὡς ἔχειν τὴν αὐ. ἐκδικεῖν τὴν ἀλήθειαν ὑπὲρ τῆς ὑμῶν εἰρήνης Leo Mag.*ep.*43(p.3.12; M.*PL.*54. 822A); of bishops ἵνα μὴ κατευτελίζηται τὸ τοῦ ἐπισκόπου ὄνομα καὶ ἡ αὐ. CSard.*can.*6; μηδὲ ἐπαναφέρειν ἡμῖν καταδεχόμενοι, εἰς ἑαυτοὺς τὴν ὅλην περιεστήσατε αὐ. Bas.*ep.*54(3.148C; M.32.400C); ref. 1Tim. 3:1 ἐγὼ...οὐ τοῦ ἔργου, τῆς δὲ αὐ. ... ἐπιθυμεῖν εἶπον εἶναι δεινόν Chrys.*sac.*3.10(p.66.18; 1.388B); ὥστε μὴ τῆς ἀρχῆς καὶ τῆς αὐ. ἐφίεσθαι μόνον, ἀλλὰ τῆς προστασίας id.*hom.10.1 in 1Tim.*(11.598B); of see of Alexandria τὴν αὐ. τῆς εὐαγγελικῆς διαδοχῆς Synes.*ep.*66 (M.66.1409D); τὴν αὐ. εἰς τὴν ἱερατικὴν καθέδραν ἀνέπεμψα *ib.*67 (1425A); ὁλοτελῆ τῆς ἐκκλησιαστικῆς διοικήσεως τὴν αὐ. εἶχον τότε, καὶ πάντα ἀπήρτητο τῆς αὐτῶν γνώμης Thdr.Mops.*1Tim.*3:8(p.120. 16); Leo Mag.*ep.*28.6(p.19.15; 780A); **2.** inherent in moral law ἀναζώσασθαι τὴν αὐ. τῆς δικαιοσύνης Horm.*ep.Epiph.*(p.57.39; M. *PL.*63.520A); **3.** civil; kingly and imperial: of emperor, Eus.*v.C.*3. 51(p.99.12; M.20.1112B); as held under divine sovereignty of Christ ἐνδεικνύντος [sc. Constantine] τὴν τοῦ ἐπουρανίου βασιλέως αὐ. πρὸς τὸν ἐπίγειον γεγοννῖαν ‡Jo.D.*ep.Thphl.*3(M.95.348C); of David, Ast. Am.*hom.*13(M.40.360A); of Helena, Thphn.*chron.*p.20(M.108.109C).

C. *authority* in gen. (not necessarily absolute); **1.** *authority, firmness* μετὰ πολλῆς τῆς αὐ. ἐπάγει τὴν τομήν Chrys.*hom.10.1 in Phil.*(11.276A); μετὰ αὐ. καὶ μετὰ ἐξουσίας πολλῆς...ἐπιτάττειν id. *hom.5.3 in Tit.*(11.760A); *ib.2.2*(739C); id.*hom.13.1 in 1Tim.*(11. 617C); opp. ἐπιείκεια, *ib.*(617E); opp. συγκατάβασις, *ib.12.1*(611D); opp. προσήνεια, *ib.17.1*(647C); **2.** *power, licence*, for some particular end, e.g. monastic rule, Bas.*reg.fus.*41 tit.(2.386E; M.31.1021A); teaching διδασκαλικῆς αὐ. Chrys.*hom.10.3 in Heb.*(12.106C); ὁ διδασκαλίας αὐ. ἔχων id.*hom.72.1 in Mt.*(7.702B); priestly jurisdiction τίς ἐστιν, ὃς ἑαυτῷ ἐν ἀλλοτρίοις θεσπίσμασι τοῦ κελεύειν τὴν αὐ. δύναται προσλαβεῖν; Horm.*ep.cler.*(p.55.34; M.*PL.*63.421A); ἐν ἱερέως αὐ. κρίνων τοῖς πᾶσι Thdr.Mops.*Zach.*3:6f.(M.66.525B); ἵνα μηδεμία ἐξουσία ἢ αὐθεντία αὐτῷ [sc. Meletius] δοθείη CNic.(325)*ep.*(p.50.8; M.67.81B); presidency at a synod, Evagr.*h.e.*2.18(p.69.32; M.86. 2552A); and for evil-doing ὡς ἂν μάθῃ...οὐδεμίαν...ὕβρεώς τε καὶ ἀτιμίας τὴν αὐ. ἔχων Gr.Nyss.*ep.*1(M.46.1008C); **3.** *authority, sanction* οὓς προσκαλέσασθαι ἐξ αὐ. τοῦ γράμματος τούτου δυνήσεσθε Const.ap. Eus.*v.C.*3.53(p.100.16); *ib.*4.36(p.132.2; M.20.1185B); Jo.D.*haer.*80 (M.94.733C); **4.** *freedom, independence* λαβεῖν γυναῖκα...εὐπορωτέραν ...εἰς αὐ. καὶ ἐλευθερίαν τὸν ἄνδρα [sc. ἔβλαψε] Chrys.*Thdr.*2.4(1. 40C); τὴν χηρείαν αἱροῦνται...ἵνα μετὰ πλείονος αὐ. ἅπαντα πράττωσι id.*hom.13.3 in 1Tim.*(11.620C); of Esau opp. Jacob ἐν ἀδείᾳ καὶ αὐ. πολλῇ id.*hom.26.1 in Heb.*(12.235C); id.*hom.62.5 in Gen.*(4.599B); hence ἐξ ἰδίας αὐ. *independently, on one's own initiative*, Eus.*h.e.* 9.9.13(M.20.824C); Bas.*reg.br.*184(2.477D; M.31.1205B).

D. in bad sense; **1.** *irresponsibility, licence* (cf. C.4) λέγονται μετὰ πάσης ἀναιδείας καὶ αὐ. Euther.*confut.*proem.(M.28.1337B); hence αὐθεντίᾳ, ἐξ αὐ. *arbitrarily, on one's own responsibility, unauthorized* ἐχειροτόνησε τὸν Φαῦστον ἰδίᾳ αὐ. καὶ ἰδίᾳ χειρί Bas.*ep.*122(3.213B; M.32.541B); τῆς μὲν τοῦ κυρίου...διδασκαλίας ἀφισταμένου...ὅρους ἰδίους ἐκδικοῦντος ἐξ αὐ. id.*jud.*2(2.214D; M.31.656A); σαφῶς ἐλέγχεται συνομολογῶν οὐ δικαίως, ἀλλ' αὐ. τὸν θεὸν τὰ ἀνθρώπινα πράττειν Gennad.*fr.Rom.*9:19ff.(p.392.7; M.85.1708D); *Chron.Pasch.*p.278(M. 92.692B); **2.** *private notion, personal view* τὴν ἰδίαν αὐ. τῆς τοῦ πνεύματος νομοθεσίας ἔμπροσθεν ἄγουσι Euther.*confut.*10(M.28.1368C); **3.** *high-handedness*; *tyranny* τὸν ἀρχιδιάκονον καλέσας τὸν ἐμὸν ἐξ αὐ. πολλῆς, ὥσπερ ἤδη χηρευούσης τῆς ἐκκλησίας Chrys.*ep.Innoc.*1.1 (p.9.25; 3.516D); *ib.*1.2(p.11.1; 517D); of evil powers, Thdr.Mops.*Col.* 2:15(p.291.17; M.66.929C); βίᾳ με ἔξωσον, ἵνα ἔχω ἀπολογίαν τῆς λειποταξίας τὴν σὴν αὐθεντείαν Pall.*v.Chrys.*9(p.55.17; M.47.32).

αὐθεντίζω, variant of αὐθεντέω.

αὐθεντικός, **1.** *principal, chief* μηδενὶ ἐξεῖναι ἐπισκόπῳ καταλειφθείσης τῆς αὐ. αὐτοῦ καθέδρας πρός τινα ἐκκλησίαν ἐν διοικήσει καθεστῶσαν ἑαυτὸν ἀποφέρειν *Cod.Afr.*71; **2.** *authentic, authoritative*, of way of salvation τὴν βασιλικήν τε καὶ αὐ. εἴσοδον Clem.*str.*1.7 (p.25.22; M.8.733B); τὴν ἐκτεθεῖσαν αὐ. πίστιν ἐν τοῖς Ἐγκαινίοις τοῖς κατὰ Ἀντιόχειαν *Symb.Sel.*(p.257.33; M.26.744B); οὐδὲν ἐπιτακτικὸν γράφοντα, οὐδὲν αὐ., ἀλλὰ συνεσταλμένον καὶ καθυφειμένον Chrys. *hom.8.1 in Eph.*(11.52E); **3.** *independent, spontaneous*; of ἐξουσία etc., ref. Mt.8:9, Gr.Nyss.*hom.10 in Cant.*(M.44.981B); of God, Cyr.H.*catech.*11.22; αὐ. ... καὶ θεϊκῆς ἐξουσίας Gr.Nyss.*or.catech.*15 (p.64.7; M.45.48C); of Son, id.*Eun.*2(2 p.351.15; M.45.529A) cit. s. αὐτοκρατορικός; of H. Ghost, ref. 1Cor.12:11 οὐδὲν ἕτερον ἢ αὐ. καὶ δεσποτικὴν ἐξουσίαν αὐτῷ μαρτυρεῖ Bas.*Eun.*3.4(1.275E; M.29.664B); Didym.*Trin.*2.3(M.39.465A); **4.** *authentic, genuine, actual* τῆς τοῦ κυρίου φωνῆς, εἴτε τῆς αὐ. εἴτε καὶ τῆς διὰ τῶν ἀποστόλων ἐνεργούσης Clem.*str.*6.6(p.455.27; M.9.269B); of Christ ταῖς αὐ. καὶ δεσποτικαῖς χρῆσθαι φωναῖς Bas.*Spir.*21(3.18C; M.32.105B); of Christian baptism opp. baptism of John, Didym.*Trin.*2.14(M.39.708B); **5.** of documents; **a.** *in author's hand, autograph*, Eus.*v.C.*2.23(p.50.27; M.20. 1001A); αὐτοῦ...τοῦ κατηγόρου...προεκόμισε χεῖρα ὁλόγραφον αὐ. Jul. Papa *ep.Dian.*(p.107.34; M.25.296A); neut. as subst. οὐδεὶς...τὸ ἀντίτυπον φθείρας τὸ αὐ. μεταλήψεται 2*Clem.*14.3; **b.** *original* opp.

transcribed ἔνθα λέγονται τὰ αὐτὰ ψηφίσματα δύνασθαι τὰ αὐ. ... εὑρεθῆναι *Cod.Afr.*134; ὁ δὲ ἀσεβὴς βασιλεὺς τὸν αὐ. χάρτην τῶν πεπραγμένων ἐν Χαλκηδόνι...πρὸς διάρρηξιν ἔσπευδεν Thphn.*chron.* p.133(M.108.365A); neut. as subst., opp. τὰ ἴσα, *Cod.Afr.*proem.; **c.** *authentic* [*copy*] τὰ αὐ. τῆς ἐν Νικαίᾳ συνόδου ἀπὸ Γραικοῦ μεταβληθέντα *Cod.Afr.*135 tit.; τὰ...ὑπομνήματα ἔν τισι μὲν βιβλίοις... ἐντέτακται, ἐν δὲ τοῖς αὐ. ... οὐδαμῶς ηὕρηται Justn.*conf.*(p.100.5; M.86.1023C); id.*ep.Thdr.Mops.*(p.66.15; M.86.1087A); τὰ...ἴσα, ἤτοι ῥέγιστρα, ἢ καὶ αὐ. CCP(681)*act.*13(H.3.1348D).

αὐθεντικῶς, **1.** ref. God, *authoritatively, sovereignly*; **a.** of Father αὐ. ... ποιῶν, ὅσα...καὶ οἷα...καὶ ὅτε βούλεται ποιεῖ ‡Just.*qu.Chr.*3.2 (M.6.1436A); **b.** ref. Son ὁ Χριστὸς...οὐ δεῖται τοῦ πατρός, ἀλλ' αὐ. ποιεῖ Chrys.*hom.27.4 in Heb.*(12.251A); σοί, Πέτρε, δίδωμι αὐ. τὰς κλεῖδας Nil.*epp.*1.116(M.79.133B); comp., *with supreme authority*, Ammon.*Jo.*15:9(M.85.1496A); denied of Son οὔτε ἴσα ἐστὶ τῷ θεῷ, ἀλλὰ θεῷ, οὔτε αὐ. ὡς ὁ πατήρ CAnc.(358)*ep.syn.*ap.Epiph.*haer.*73.9 (p.280.2; M.42.420B); ὁ δὲ υἱὸς...οὐκ αὐ. ποιεῖ ὡς ὁ πατήρ, ἀλλ' ὁμοίως Geo.Laod.*ep.dogm.*ap.Epiph.*haer.*73.18(p.290.31; 436C); opp. ὑπουργικῶς, *ib.*(p.291.6; 436D); **c.** of operation of H. Ghost, exeg. 1Cor. 12:11 τουτέστιν αὐ., οὐ δουλικῶς Or.*fr.116 in Lam.*4:20(p.277.7; M. 13.660B); οὐ λειτουργικῶς...ἀλλ' αὐ. διαιρεῖ τὰ χαρίσματα Bas.*hom.*14. 3(2.133E; M.31.472A); τὸ...ἅγιον πνεῦμα...αὐ. ... προστάττει ὡς θεὸς καὶ δεσπότης Didym.*Trin.*2.6(M.39.537B); *ib.*2.7(572C); ὅλα ταῦτα τὴν ἐπιφάνειαν τοῦ πνεύματος αὐ. δηλοῖ γεγενῆσθαι *ib.*2.17(M.725C); ‡Caes.Naz.*dial.*42(M.38.908) cit. s. αὐτοκρατορικῶς; **2.** ref. man, *with authority*; **a.** in virtue of one's office, *authoritatively*, ref. S. Peter μετὰ κοινῆς πάντα ποιοῦντα γνώμης· οὐδὲν αὐ. οὐδὲ ἀρχικῶς Chrys.*hom.3.1 in Ac.*(9.23D); of S. Paul οὐκέτι...ὡς παρεξετάζων ἐκείνοις ἑαυτὸν λέγει, ἀλλ' αὐ. id.*hom.14.2 in 1Cor.*(10.119D); οὐ γὰρ αὐ., οὐδὲ δεσποτικῶς, οὐδὲ μετ' ἐξουσίας, ἀλλ' πατρικῶς id. *hom.5.1 in 1Tim.*(11.574F); of S. James οὐχ ὡς ἐπίσκοπος αὐ. διαλέγεται id.*hom.46.1 in Ac.*(9.345C); comp. ἐπιτάττειν χρὴ τὸν ἱερέα καὶ αὐθεντικώτερον διαλέγεσθαι id.*hom.13.1 in 1Tim.*(617D); id.*hom.4.3 in 2Tim.*(683B); **b.** *with authorization, sanction* τοὺς στρατιωτικοὺς ἄρχοντας δουλικῶς χρᾶσθαι τοῖς ἐπισκόποις καὶ κληρικοῖς ἐκέλευσε καταγομένους αὐ. ἐν τοῖς ἐπισκοπείοις καὶ μοναστηρίοις, καὶ καταχρᾶσθαι τὰ αὐτῶν Thphn.*chron.*p.414(M.108.981B); **3.** of one's own will, *spontaneously* δυναμεῖς λειτουργικαὶ πεμπόμεναι...οὐκ αὐ., οὐδὲ αὐτεξουσίως παραγινόμεναι Proc.G.*Is.*6:6(M.87. 1941B) cf. 1; **4.** *expressly*; **a.** of copying *exactly* οὐ γὰρ αὐ. εὑρέθη μορφή Val.Gn.ap.Clem.*str.*4.13(p.287.25; M.8.1297B); **b.** of naming *directly, expressly* τῶν προφητῶν, ἃ μὲν διὰ παραβολῶν, ἃ δὲ δι' αἰνιγμάτων, ἃ δὲ αὐ. καὶ αὐτολεξεὶ τὸν Χριστὸν Ἰησοῦν ὀνομαζόντων *Keryg.Petr.*ap.Clem.*str.*6.15(p.496.27; M.9.352B).

***αὐθεντίμιος**, *original*; of a document, *Apoc.Paul.*2(p.35).

αὐθέντρια, ἡ, fem. of αὐθέντης, one in authority; **a.** *author* ἐνώπιον τῆς...τριάδος, ἥτις φύλαξ οὖσα ὑμετέρα καὶ αὐ. τῆς βασιλείας Leo Mag.*ep.*44.2(p.26.24; M.*PL.*54.830C); **b.** *mistress* ἡ αὐ. τῆς κόρης Leont.N.*v.Sym.*39(M.93.1717B).

***αὐθερμήνευτος**, *self-interpreting* τὸ μὲν οὖν ἐνύπνιον δοκεῖ αὐ. εἶναι Hipp.*Dan.*3.6.1; ‡Chrys.*hom.in Ps.*100:2–6(5.639A); Max. *Pyrrh.*(M.91.320B).

αὖθις, *again*, etc.; *afterwards, at another time*, Tat.*orat.*1(p.2. 15; M.6.805B); δεξάμενοι τὸ πνεῦμα ἐπ' ἐλπίδι τῆς ἀναστάσεως...αὖ. ὡς θνητοί τινες ὑπὸ τὴν τοῦ νόμου φυλακὴν ἑαυτοὺς ποιεῖτε; Thdr. Mops.*Gal.*3:4(p.38.23); ‡Caes.Naz.*dial.*30(M.38.892).

***αὐθονία**, error for ἀφθονία, *abundance*, Ephr.3.122B.

αὐθύπαρκτος, *self-subsistent*; **1.** characteristic of all οὐσία: πρᾶγμα αὐ. [sc. ἡ οὐσία], μὴ δεόμενον ἑτέρου πρὸς τὴν ἑαυτοῦ σύστασιν Anast. Ant.*fid.*(M.89.1401A); Jo.D.*Man.*1.17(M.94.1524B); ὅν ἐστι πρᾶγμα ἢ αὐ. ... ἢ τὸ μὴ καθ' ἑαυτὸ δυνάμενον εἶναι...οὐσία δέ ἐστιν πρᾶγμα αὐ. id.*dialect.*10(M.94.564A); Melet.*nat.hom.*31(M.64.1305A); of human soul, Leont.H.*Nest.*1.1(M.86.1405B); ‡Ath.*def.*5(M.28.544D) cit. infra; of world to come μήπω φανείσης τῆς αὐ. κατὰ τὸ εἶδος τῶν μελλόντων ἀγαθῶν ὑποστάσεως Max.ap.*cat.1Jo.*3:2(p.122.4); **2.** theol., of hypostatic union αὐ. συνδρομῇ καὶ συνόδῳ Anast.S.*hex.*12(M.89. 1053B); καθ' ὑπόστασιν ἕνωσίς ἐστιν ἡ αὐ. ἐν τῇ μήτρᾳ...τῶν δύο φύσεων συνδρομή...σὰρξ ἔμψυχος...ἐν αὐτῷ ὑπέστη καθάπερ...καὶ ἐπὶ τῆς ἡμετέρας συλλήψεως, αὐ. ἡ ψυχὴ συντρέχει τῷ σώματι ‡Ath.*def.*5 (M.28.544D) cf. Anast.S.*hod.*2(ἀμφύπαρκτος M.89.69C).

αὐθυπόστατος, **1.** = αὐθύπαρκτος, *self-subsistent, having hypostatic existence, existing independently* ἐνυπόστατον...σημαίνει...οὐ μόνον τὴν οὐσίαν ἣν αὐ. ... ὑπογράφουσιν, ἀλλὰ καὶ τὰ συμβεβηκότα... κἂν ἐν ἑτέρῳ ἔχουσι τὸ εἶναι Leont.B.*fr.*(M.86.2009D); cf.†Leont.B. *sect.*7.2(M.86.1240C); ἡ τῶν αὐ. καὶ καθ' ἑαυτὰ εἶναι δυναμένων πρὸς ἄλληλα ποιὰ σχέσις Leont.B.*Nest.et Eut.*1(M.86.1304B); Leont.H. *Nest.*4.40(M.86.1716A); οὐσία ἐστὶ...αὐ. πρᾶγμα μὴ δεόμενον ἑτέρου πρὸς σύστασιν Max.*opusc.*(M.91.276A); οὐσία ἐστὶ πᾶν ὅτιπερ αὐ. ἐστι, καὶ μὴ ἐν ἑτέρῳ ἔχει τὸ εἶναι Jo.D.*dialect.*39(M.94.605B); of human soul αὐ. δι' ἑαυτὴν φύσει Max.*ep.*7(M.91.436D); εἰ δὲ αὐ. οὐκ ἔστιν, οὐδὲ οὐσία ἐστὶ δηλονότι, οὐσία δὲ αὐ. μὴ οὖσα συμβεβηκὸς ἔσται *ib.*(437B); the following, as referring to God, might bear meaning 2: ὁ μὲν γὰρ Νεστόριος, εἰ καὶ ψιλὸν ἄνθρωπον ἔλεγε τὸν Χριστόν, ἀλλ' οὖν τὸν αὐ. λόγον τοῦ θεοῦ, καὶ υἱὸν ἔλεγε γενέσθαι ἐν τῷ ἀνθρώπῳ ἐκείνῳ...ὁ δὲ Παῦλος ὁ Σαμοσατεὺς οὐκ ἔλεγε τὸν αὐ. λόγον γεγενῆσθαι ἐν τῷ Χριστῷ, ἀλλὰ λόγον ἔλεγε τὴν κέλευσιν καὶ τὸ πρόσταγμα †Leont.B.*sect.*3.3(M.86.1216A); ὁ θεὸς πόθου τοῖς ἀξίοις γινόμενος πλήρωσις, ὡς ἀπόλαυσις ἀγαθῶν αὐ. Max.*opusc.*(9A); τῆς αὐ. σοφίας *ib.*(16D); ἡ...βουλὴ...ὅταν οὐκ ἔστι τὰ ἀμφίβολα, τῆς αὐ. πᾶσιν ἐμφανοῦς ἀληθείας δεχθείσης *ib.*(24C); θεὸς ὁ Χριστὸς δύναμις ἦν αὐ. id.*Pyrr.*(M.91.321C); **2.** *self-substantial, possessing aseity, self-existent* ὁ ἅγιος καὶ αὐ., ζῶν θεὸς καὶ λόγος σαρκοφορῶν ‡Caes. Naz.*dial.*155(M.38.1108).

αὐθυποστάτως, *hypostatically, as an individual, independently*, of πρόσωπον as denoting 'the particular' opp. 'face' ἐκεῖνο, κατά τε ἀψύχων καὶ ἐμψύχων, καὶ σωμάτων καὶ ἀσωμάτων...λέγεται, ἤγουν τὸ ἀντὶ τῆς ὑποστάσεως· παντὸς γὰρ ὄντος αὐ., ἐστὶ καὶ ὑπόστασις· τοῦτο δὲ ἐπὶ μόνων τῶν ἐμψυχωθέντων σωμάτων κυρίως Leont.H. *Nest.*2.16(M.86.1572D).

αὐθωρός, neut. as subst., *suddenness*, ref. Ac.2:3 τὸ αὐ. τῆς παρουσίας ‡Chrys.*pent.*4(12.813B).

***αὐλακηδόν**, *furrow-wise* αὐ. τὰ τῆς ψυχῆς βάθη προοδοποιῶν ‡Chrys.*pasch.*6.10(p.137.16; 8.267B).

αὐλακίζω, *furrow, plough*, Mac.Mgn.*apocr.*4.11(p.171.1); Nil. *Magn.*15(M.79.989A).

***αὐλαναῖον**, τό, ? *tax for expenses of court* ὃν...ἔταξεν ἐπὶ ταῖς ἀπαιτήσεσιν τοῦ στρατιωτικοῦ χρυσίου, τοῦ καλουμένου Τιρωνικοῦ, καὶ συνῆψε τὰ αὐ. Synes.*ep.*79(M.66.1445A).

αὖλαξ, ὁ, ἡ, **1.** lit., properly *furrow* made in ploughing; hence *rut*, Const.*or.s.c.*24(p.190.17; M.20.1309A); *channel* worn by water τοῦτο [sc. τὸ ὕδωρ] διαιρεθὲν πολλὰς ἐποίησεν αὔ. Thdt.*Ps.*73:15 (1.1130); **2.** met.; **a.** of the womb, Clem.*paed.*2.10(p.212.23; M.8. 508A); Meth.*symp.*2.1(p.16.6; M.18.48D); **b.** of lines of writing, Bas.*ep.*334(3.452C; M.32.1077B); **3.** fig., of the ear-passages τῇ μακέλλῃ τοῦ λόγου τὰς κεχερσωμένας τῶν ἀκοῶν ἀνευρύνωμεν αὔ. Thdt.*affect.*1(p.7.7; 4.695); of the voice, Nonn.*par.Jo.*4:38(M.43. 781A); of spiritual cultivation τὰς χεῖράς μου ἐπέθηκα τῷ ἀρότρῳ... ἵνα οἱ αὔ. μὴ σκαμβασθῶσιν *A.Thom.*A 147(p.255.19); cf.*A.Phil.*135 (p.66.4); οὐδεὶς τὴν Χριστοῦ αὔ. τέμνει, τὴν ἀκανθοφόρον ἀσπαζόμενος φιλοπάθειαν Isid.Pel.*epp.*1.220(M.78.321A); ἕλκει καὶ διατέμνει τῆς δικαιοσύνης τὰς αὔ. Thdt.*Cant.*4:9(2.99).

αὐλάρχης, ὁ, *master of the royal household*, ref. Mt.16:19 κλειδάρχην αὐτὸν ποιήσας καὶ αὐ. τῆς ἄνω βασιλείας Mac.Mgn.*apocr.*3.27 (p.117.5).

αὐλή, ἡ, **1.** *courtyard*; *atrium* of a church αὐ. πρώτη στοιαί τ' ἐπὶ ταύτῃ καὶ ἐπὶ πᾶσιν αἱ αὔλειοι πύλαι Eus.*v.C.*3.39(p.94.24; M.20. 1100A); κρήνας εἶναι ἐν ταῖς αὐ. τῶν εὐκτηρίων οἴκων νενόμισται Chrys.*hom.3.11 in 2Cor.4:13*(3.289D); **2.** *steading, fold*; hence met., of Church οὐδέ...τις τοῦτο τῶν θεοπνεύστων ἢ εἶπεν ἢ παρεδέξατο, οὐδὲ τῆς ἡμετέρας αὐ. ὁ λόγος Gr.Naz.*or.*28.9(p.35.3; M.36. 36C); τῆς ἡμετέρας αὐ., ἤγουν τῆς καθολικῆς τοῦ θεοῦ καὶ ἀποστολικῆς ἐκκλησίας Max.*opusc.*(M.91.88C); **3.** *imperial court*; *court* of heaven, *MAMA* 1.412.

αὐλήτρια, ἡ, *flute-girl*, *A.Thom.*A 5(p.108.1,5).

ἀϋλία, ἡ, *immateriality*, of God τοῦ θεαρχικοῦ πνεύματος ὑπὲρ πᾶσαν νοητὴν ἀ. καὶ θέωσιν ὑπεριδρυμένου Dion.Ar.*d.n.*2.8(M.3. 645C); ἔρωτα θεῖον...ἐννοῆσαι χρὴ τῆς ὑπὲρ λόγον...ἀ. id.*c.h.*2.4(M.3. 144A); of angels, *ib.*7.1(205D); and angelic intuition ἔστιν αὐταῖς ἡ νοερὰ δύναμις...συνοπτικὴ τῶν θείων νοήσεων ἀμερίᾳ καὶ ἀ. id.*d.n.*7.2 (868B); of human intellect πῶς ἐν ὕλῃ τὴν ἀ. ἔχει εἰ μηδὲν αὐτὸν ὑλικὸν περιγράφει; Geo.Pis.*hex.*742(M.92.1491A); fig., of spiritual, opp. lit., meaning of scripture, †Cyr.*coll.VT*(6^{4}.26B).

αὔλισμα, τό, *court*; of king etc., *cat.1Petr.*2:16(p.55.26).

***αὐλοειδής**, *pipe-like, tubular* ἀφ' ἧς [sc. τῆς καρδίας] αὐ. πόροι... διαφυόμενοι, παντὶ τῷ σώματι τὸ πυρῶδες...διαχέουσι πνεῦμα Gr. Nyss.*hom.opif.*31.11(M.44.245A) = ‡Caes.Naz.*dial.*140(M.38.1075).

***αὐλοειδῶς**, *through a pipe, by tubes* τὸν περιεκτικὸν τοῦ ἐγκεφάλου ὑμένα, ὃς ἄνωθεν ἐπὶ τὸ βάθος αὐ. διήκων, διὰ τῶν καθεξῆς σπονδύλων... τῇ βάσει συναπολήγει τῆς ῥάχεως Gr.Nyss.*hom.opif.*31.24(M.44.249D) = ‡Caes.Naz.*dial.*140(M.38.1076).

αὐλός, ὁ, **1.** *pipe, flute*; of prophets συγχρησαμένου τοῦ πνεύματος, ὡσεὶ καὶ αὐλητὴς αὐ. ἐμπνεῦσαι Athenag.*leg.*9.1(M.6.908A); **2.** *tube*, *duct*, or other *passage* in the body ὁ οἶνος...τοὺς τῆς αἰσθήσεως ἅπαντας καὶ πόρους καὶ αὐ. καὶ μήνιγγας πληροῖ Isid.Pel.*epp*.1.479 (M.78.444B).

ἄϋλος, *immaterial*;

A. in gen.; **1.** *immaterial, noumenal*; **a.** of all that pertains to sphere of intellect opp. senses τὰ δὲ ἄ. νῷ μόνῳ ληπτά ἐστι Clem. *str*.8.8(p.95.2; M.9.589B); πάντων τῶν λογικῶν τὴν παραγωγὴν νόας ἀσωμάτους καὶ ἀ. γεγονέναι δίχα παντὸς ἀριθμοῦ Or.*princ*.2.8.3 (p.159.5); τὸ...τῇ φύσει νοερόν τε καὶ ἄ. πόρρω τῆς κατὰ τόπον ἐννοίας ὁμολογεῖται Gr.Nyss.*Eun*.1(1 p.72.7; M.45.301B); αἱ νοηταὶ καὶ νοεραὶ...οὐσίαι...ὡς ἀσώματοι καὶ ἄ. νοοῦνται Dion.Ar.*d.n*.4.1 (M.3.693C); εἴ τις λέγει...ὅτι τέλος ἐστὶ τοῦ μυθευομένου ἡ ἄ. φύσις, καὶ οὐδὲν ἐν τῷ μέλλοντι τῶν τῆς ὕλης ὑπάρξει, ἀλλὰ γυμνὸς ὁ νοῦς ἀ. ἔ. CCP(543)*anath*.11(p.229; H.3.285D); **b.** of partic. things εἶδεν ἐν ἀ. ἅρματι ἀναλαμβανόμενον προφήτην Procl.CP *or*.19.2(M.65.825A); τὸ εἶδος [sc. τοῦ σταυροῦ] διπλοῦν, τὸ μὲν ἐξ ὕλης...ὃ καὶ ἀφαιρεῖται... ὑπὸ κλεπτῶν· τὸ δὲ ἄ.· οὐ γὰρ ἐξ ὕλης αὐτοῦ ἡ ὑπόστασις, ἀλλ' ἀπὸ πίστεως ἡ οὐσία, ἀπὸ διαθέσεως τοῦ ποιοῦντος ἡ ὕλη ‡Chrys.*ador*.1.4 (3.824B); **c.** opp. ἔνυλος: δύναμίς ἐστιν ἔνυλος ἐνέργεια· ἐνέργεια, ἄ. δύναμις Max.*opusc*.(M.91.153A); **d.** a property of spirit, Bas.*Spir*.22 (3.19A; M.32.108A); πνεῦμα μέν ἐστι λεπτὴ καὶ ἄ. καὶ ἀσχημάτιστος ἐκπορευτὴ ὕπαρξις Anast.S.*hod*.2(M.89.56B); **e.** of soul ὁ ἄνθρωπος... τὴν ψυχὴν ἔχων ἄ. καὶ τὸν νοῦν θεοῦ εἰκόνα Clem.*fr*.38(p.220.2)ap. Max.*opusc*.(M.91.268A); Nemes.*nat.hom*.2(M.40.540B); Aen.*dial*.(M. 85.953B); Jo.D.*Man*.1.16(M.94.1521B); **f.** heret., of man, *A.Andr. fr*.6(p.40.32); **2.** *without matter*; **a.** τίς δ' ὕλην ποτ' ὄπωπεν ἀνείδεον, ἢ τίς ἄ. μορφήν; Gr.Naz.*carm*.1.1.4.7(M.37.416A); ὥσπερ ἡ ὕλη ἐστὶν ἄμορφος, οὕτω καὶ τὸ εἶδός ἐστιν ἄ. ‡Just.*confut*.5(M.6.1505B); **b.** in sphere of mental operations, *abstract* τὰς...νοήσεις οὐκ ἀφαντάστους ποιούμεθα, πλὴν εἰ δή τις ἐν ἀκαρεῖ ποτε ἐπαφὴν ἔσχεν εἴδους ἀ. Synes.*insomn*.7(p.56.4; M.66.1292D).

B. theol.; **1.** of the Godhead μηδὲ...δύνασθαι τὴν ἄ. καὶ νοερὰν καὶ ἀσώματον φύσιν σωματικόν τι πάθος ὑφίστασθαι Eus.*ep.Caes*.4 (p.44.6; M.20.1540A); Ath.*decr*.10.5(p.9.26; M.25.'441'(433)B); τὸ δὲ ταὐτὸν ὑπερουσίως...ἐφ' ἑαυτοῦ μένον...ἀναλλοίωτον, ἀμιγές, ἄ. Dion. Ar.*d.n*.9.4(M.3.912B); τοῦ ἀ. καὶ ἀμεροῦς ἀγαθοῦ id.*myst*.3(M.3. 1033A); ὁ...θεὸς ἄ. ὢν καὶ ἀπερίγραπτος ἐν τόπῳ οὐκ ἔστιν Jo.D. *f.o*.1.13(M.94.852A); *ib*.1.14(860A); **2.** of Aristotelian quintessence, Gr.Naz.*or*.28.8(p.33.7; M.36.36A); cf.Jo.D.*f.o*.1.4(M.94.797C); **3.** ref. allusions to bodily parts of God μόνος...ἄνθρωπος...τοῖς ἀ. κατεκοσμήθη δακτύλοις Nil.*epp*.2.191(M.79.300D); and divine operations τοῦ...λόγου πρόοδον...ἀσύνθετον, ἄ. τε καὶ νοητήν Cyr.*Ps*.44:2(M.69. 1028A); τὸ παχὺ τοῦτο σαρκίον περικειμένους, τὰς θείας...καὶ ἀ. τῆς θεότητος ἐνεργείας νοεῖν ἢ λέγειν ἀδύνατον ‡Cyr.*Trin*.12(6^3.18A; M.77. 1148A); **4.** of Son μένων [sc. in Inc.]...αὐτὸς ἄ. καὶ ἀσώματος Eus.*d.e*. 4.13(p.172.9; M.22.285D); ὁ ἀσώματος καὶ ἄφθαρτος καὶ ἄ. τοῦ θεοῦ λόγος Ath.*inc*.8.1(M.25.109A); ὁ φανερωθεὶς ἐν σαρκὶ θεὸς...ἄ. καὶ ἀφανής Gr.Nyss.*Apoll*.18(M.45.1160A); *ib*.20(1164B); ‡Epiph.*hom*.2 (M.43.452A); Jo.D.*hom*.2.1(M.96.576C); ‡Meth.*Sym.et Ann*.13(M.18. 380B); as φῶς ἄϋλον, ‡Caes.Naz.*dial*.2(M.38.857); [ref. Transfiguration] φωτὶ...ἀ. ταυτίζεται [sc. τὸ πρόσωπον αὐτοῦ] καθ' ὑπόστασιν Jo.D.*hom*.1.4(M.96.552C); ‡Meth.*Sym.et Ann*.13(M.18.380A); heret., of Christ's body ψηλαφῶντός μου αὐτὸν ἄ. ἦν καὶ ἀσώματον τὸ ὑποκείμενον καὶ ὡς μηδὲ ὅλως ὄν *A.Jo*.93(p.196.22); **5.** of H. Ghost τὸ ἄ. καὶ θεῖον πῦρ φωτίζει μὲν ψυχὰς καὶ δοκιμάζειν εἴωθεν Mac.Aeg. *hom*.25.9(M.34.673B).

C. of what pertains to 'the other world'; **1.** in gen. ἄ. πάντῃ καὶ ἀσώματον ζωὴν ζώντων ἐν μακαριότητι τῶν ἁγίων Or.*Jo*.1.17(p.21. 12; M.14.52B); *ib*.19.20(5; p.321.25; 564C); Bas.*hex*.6.2(1.51D; M.29. 121B); Gr.Nyss.*v.Mos*.49(M.44.317C); νῦν τὸν οὐρανὸν κατοικῶν...καὶ ταῖς ἀ. σκηναῖς ἐμφιλοχωρῶν *M.Thdot*.2 4(p.87.28); ταῖς μὲν ὑπερουρανίοις ζωαῖς τὴν ἄ. ... ἀθανασίαν Dion.Ar.*d.n*.6.2(M.3.856C); **2.** partic. of angels as pure spirits, Gr.Naz.*or*.38.9(M.36.320D) = *ib*.45.5 (629B); τῶν ἀ. καὶ νοερῶν οὐσιῶν Dion.Ar.*c.h*.2.4(M.3.144B); *ib*.1. 3(121C); Geo.Pis.*Pers*.1.1(M.92.1197A); Jo.D.*carm.theog*.28(p.206; M.96.821B); τῶν...ἀγγελικῶν...ἀ. τάξεων ‡Bas.*h.myst*.49(p.390.22); ‡Sophr.H.*liturg*.3(M.87.3984B).

D. *spiritual*, opp. physical or material, ref. Gen.11:3 ἵνα διὰ τῶν ὑλικῶν ἐπιβουλεύσωσι τοῖς ἀ. Or.*Cels*.5.30(p.32.1; M.11.1225D); τὴν πνευματικήν τε καὶ ἄ. τῆς ψυχῆς κατάστασιν Gr.Nyss.*hom.in Cant*. proem.(M.44.756B); νυμφοστολεῖται τρόπον τινὰ ἡ ψυχὴ πρὸς τὴν ἀσώματόν τε καὶ πνευματικὴν καὶ ἀ. τοῦ θεοῦ συζυγίαν id.*hom.1 in Cant*.(765A); *ib*.(768C); ἕξιν...ἀυλοτέραν καὶ καθαρωτέραν Cyr.*Jo*. 3.6(4.314A); of beauty τὸ ἄ. καὶ πνευματικὸν...κάλλος Meth.*symp*. 7.1(p.72.17; M.18.125C); Gr.Nyss.*ep.can*.6(M.45.232D); of spiritual light, id.*laud.Bas*.(M.46.809C); of knowledge ἀ. καὶ ἀνείδεον γνῶσιν Evagr.Pont.*or*.68(M.79.1181B); of spiritual perception τὴν...τοῦ... πατρὸς φωτοδοσίαν...ἀΰλοις...νοὸς ὀφθαλμοῖς εἰσδεξάμενοι Dion.Ar. *c.h*.1.2(M.3.121B); id.*e.h*.4.3.6(M.3.480D); of worship ἐν τῇ ἀ. καὶ καθαρᾷ θεραπείᾳ θεοῦ †Bas.*Is*.29(1.402B; M.30.176A); Cyr.*Is*.4.2(2. 617A); προσκομίζομεν...εἰς ὀσμὴν εὐωδίας τῷ θεῷ...πίστιν, ἐλπίδα, ἀγάπην...καὶ τὰς ἑτέρας τῶν ἀρετῶν, ἀυλοτάτη γὰρ αὕτη θυσία τῷ κατὰ φύσιν ἁπλῷ καὶ ἀ. πρέπουσα θεῷ id.*Juln*.10(6^2.345D); of contemplative prayer μὴ δεῖν...παραμένειν τῷ πράγματι...ἀλλὰ μεταβαίνειν πρὸς τὴν ἄ. καὶ νοητὴν θεωρίαν Gr.Nyss.*hom.in Cant*.proem. (757C); αἱ ψυχαὶ...προβαίνουσιν...διὰ τῆς ἀ. καὶ ἀμεροῦς νοήσεως ἐπὶ τὴν ὑπὲρ νόησιν ἕνωσιν Dion.Ar.*d.n*.11.2(M.3.949D); τὰς ἀ. τῶν οὐρανίων οὐσιῶν νοήσεις id.*c.h*.15.8(337B); ἆρα ἀπηλλάγημεν τῶν ἐμπαθῶν νοημάτων, καὶ τῆς καθαρᾶς καὶ ἀ. ἀπολαύομεν προσευχῆς; Thal.*cent*.3.26(M.91.1449D); of mind at prayer μὴ σχηματίζῃς τὸ θεῖον ἐν ἑαυτῷ προσευχόμενος...ἀλλ' ἄ. τῷ ἀ. πρόσιθι καὶ συνήσεις Evagr.Pont.*or*.66(M.79.1181A); μακάριός ἐστιν ὁ νοῦς, ὁ κατὰ τὸν καιρὸν τῆς προσευχῆς ἄ. καὶ ἀκτήμων γίνεται *ib*.119(1193B); ὅταν ...ἄ. καὶ ἀνείδεον...ἔχῃς τὸν νοῦν Max.*carit*.4.42(M.90.1057A); of spiritual opp. lit. meaning of scripture, Dion.Ar.*e.h*.1.4(M.3.376C); of patristic tradition τῶν ἀ. ... πατρικῶν λόγων τε καὶ δογμάτων Max.*opusc*.(M.91.72A).

E. of persons; **1.** *detached from material things, ascetic* ἢ μόνος οἰκεῖ, ἢ μετὰ ἀνθρώπων ἀ. καὶ ὁμοφρόνων ‡Ath.*inst.mon*.(M.28. 848B); Gr.Naz.*or*.21.10(M.35.1093A); ἄ. [sc. μοναχός] ὥσπερ εὔστολος ὁδοιπόρος Ephr.1.92E; τὸν...ἄ. διαθλευόντων βίον Evagr.*h.e*.2.9(p.61. 10; M.86.2529B); *ib*.4.7(p.157.25; 2716A); **2.** of one who has reached heights of contemplation, *spiritualized* κατὰ τὴν ἕξιν τῆς ἀρετῆς καὶ τῆς γνώσεως ἀ. καὶ ἀνείδεος πάντῃ γενόμενος, διὰ τὸν δι' ἡμᾶς ἐν ὕλῃ καὶ εἴδει καθ' ἡμᾶς...γενόμενον θεὸν λόγον, τὸν κατὰ φύσιν...ἄ. καὶ ἀνείδεον Max.*ambig*.(M.91.1273C).

ἀϋλότης, ἡ, *immateriality* σεσάρκωται...ὁ λόγος καὶ τῆς οἰκείας ἀ. οὐκ ἐξέστηκε Jo.D.*f.o*.3.7(M.94.1012B).

αὐλύδριον, τό, *small courtyard*, *Apophth.Patr*.(M.65.152C,D).

ἀΰλως, 1. *immaterially*; *spiritually* opp. corporeally; of H. Ghost, Didym.*Trin*.2.4(M.39.484B) cit. s. ἀνειδέως; in language, *figuratively, spiritually* opp. literally ἐπὶ τὰς καθαρὰς...τῶν θείων νοήσεων πηγὰς ἀ. ποιμανθήσονται Andr.Caes.*Apoc*.20(M.106.285B); **2.** of knowing *intuitively* opp. discursively by way of the senses; **a.** ref. God ὁ...θεὸς τῷ μονογενεῖ θεῷ παραπλησίως, μᾶλλον δὲ ὡσαύτως ἀ. τε καὶ ἀσωμάτως τῶν ἰδίων κοινωνῶν βουλευμάτων Gr.Nyss.*Eun*.12 (1 p.274.11; ἀΰλῳ M.45.980D); ἑαυτὴν...ἡ θεία σοφία γινώσκουσα, γνώσεται πάντα, ἀ. τὰ ὑλικὰ...καὶ τὰ πολλὰ ἑνιαίως Dion.Ar.*d.n*.7.2 (M.3.869B); **b.** of angels τὰς ἀρχικὰς ἐλλάμψεις ἀ. καὶ ἀμιγῶς εἰσδεχόμεναι...καὶ νοερὰν ἔχουσαι τὴν πᾶσαν ζωήν id.*c.h*.4.2(M.3.180A); id. *d.n*.7.2(868B); **3.** of prayer, *contemplatively, in contemplation* μετὰ πλήθους ὑμνῶν οὐ δυνήσῃ ἀ. προσεύξασθαι Jo.Clim.*scal*.19(M.88.937D); ἀ. στῶμεν...καὶ ἐποπτεύσωμεν νοΐ θεότητα ἄϋλον...ἐν υἱῷ...ἀπαστράπτουσαν Jo.D.*carm.transfig*.(M.96.849D).

[*]αὐξ-έω, later form of αὐξάνω, *increase* ~είτω ἡ πίστις Θεοδώρου Cyr.*ep*.69(p.16.11; 5^2.197E).

αὖξις, ἡ, *growth, increase* αὖξιν ἐπιδιδόναι κατὰ τόνδε τὸν βίον Thdr.Mops.*Rom*.9:22–24(M.66.841B; αὔξειν καὶ ἐπιδιδόναι p.147. 40); *waxing* of the moon, Cyr.*ador*.6(1.204D).

***αὐράριος, ὁ,** (Lat. aurarius) *goldsmith, MAMA* 1.214,215.

αὐσταλέος, *rough, squalid* αὐ. βιοτῆς Eudoc.*Cypr*.1.158(M.85. 837C).

αὐστηρία, ἡ, 1. *harshness, bitterness*; of medicine, Clem.*prot*.10 (p.77.29; M.8.225B); **2.** met., of persons; *severity*, opp. both χρηστότης and ἀποτομία, Clem.*paed*.1.12 tit.(p.148.12; M.8.368A); id.*str*.2.20(p.180.10; M.8.1068C); ἐμβλέψας...αὐτὸν...μετὰ πολλῆς αὐ. ‡Ath.*doct.Ant*.21(M.28.585D); τῶν βημάτων αἱ αὐ. Isid.Pel.*epp*.1.148 (M.78.281C); Olymp.*Eccl*.7:4(M.93.561A); **3.** in bad sense, *harshness* τοῦ Ἀρειανοῦ ἐπισκόπου, τοῦ πολλὰ ἰσχύσαντος πλούτῳ τε καὶ αὐ. Epiph.*haer*.30.5(p.340.15; M.41.413A); **4.** *austerity* in morals, *A. Thom*.A 14(p.119.18); Pall.*h.Laus*.3(p.18.22; M.34.1012B); *asceticism* τῇ αὐ. καὶ τῇ στυφότητι *ib*.45(p.133.12; 1218A).

αὐστηρότης, ἡ, 1. *austerity* ἐὰν ἴδῃ [sc. ὁ φιλήδονος] αὐ. πατέρων ἀηδίζεται Ephr.1.17B; κτῆσαι αὐ. πρὸς πᾶσαν ἐπιθυμίαν *ib*.1.166F; Chrys.*sac*.6.2(p.143.12; 1.422D); Nil.*Eulog*.27(M.79.1129C); **2.** *severity* ἔστι...πνεῦμα πραότητος καὶ πνεῦμα αὐ. Chrys.*hom.14.2 in 1Cor*.(10. 119E); id.*hom.div*.1.3(12.327C); Max.*ambig*.(M.91.1173B).

[*]αὐταγαθός, v. αὐτοαγαθός.

[*]αὐταγαθότης, v. αὐτοαγαθότης.

***αὐτάγγελτος,** *self-announced*, Bas.*ep*.116(3.209A; M.32.533A).

αὐτάγρετος, 1. *self-chosen, of one's own choice*; of Christ's death, Nonn.*par.Jo*.7:33(M.43.809C); *ib*.10:18(836A); **2.** *obtained* *by one's own effort*; of Pilate's power to condemn Christ, *ib*.19.11 (900B).

αὐτάδελφος, ὁ, *full brother*, *A.Pil.*B 27(p.332); ἀδελφὸς γάρ, ὁ ἐκ τῆς αὐτῆς δελφύος, ἤγουν μήτρας· καὶ ὁμόδελφος, ὁ αὐ. Melet.*nat.hom.* synops.(M.64.1085A); met., of virtues τὰς αὐ. ἀρετὰς καὶ συντρόφους διττοῖς μερίζει τῶν λόγων νοήμασι Geo.Pis.*Pers*.1.71(M.92.1202A).

***αὐταίτιος,** *self-caused*; term inapplicable to God, who is caused neither by himself nor any other, *Const.App*.6.11.1; and to created things, which would otherwise be ἀγένητα, Max.*ambig*.(M.91.1072B).

***αὐτακολούθησις, ἡ,** *consequential relationship*, Synes.*Dion* 8(M.66.1137C; ἀντ- p.257.6).

***αὐτακούω,** *hear with one's own ears*, Gr.Nyss.*bapt.Chr.*(M.46.584C).

***αὐταπόδεικτος,** *self-evident*, Didym.*Trin*.2.8(M.39.585D).

αὐταρέσκεια, ἡ, *self-pleasing*; **1.** in gen., equivalent to αὐθάδεια, Gr.Naz.*carm*.1.2.34.85(M.37.951A); Marc.Er.*opusc*.7.10(M.65.1085D); ὁ τῆς φιλοχρηματίας καὶ αὐ. ἔρως ἤτοι δαίμων Ammon.*Ac*.17:10 (M.85.1564A); contrary to obedience to God's laws, Jo.D.*hom*.2.7 (M.96.588B); **2.** esp. as besetting sin of monks κίνδυνος δὲ παρέπεται τῇ μοναστικῇ ζωῇ...πρῶτος μὲν καὶ μέγιστος ὁ τῆς αὐ. Bas.*reg. fus*.7.3(2.347B; M.31.932C); contrary to monastic principle, *ib*.7.2 (2.346B; M.929C); causing some to embark on unregulated eremitic life, Nil.*epp*.3.72(M.79.421C); to aim at extravagant asceticism, Ephr.2.188F; to leave monastic life to seek popularity as secular clergy, *ib*.2.187F; preoccupation with literary elegance must be avoided when reading ἵνα μὴ ὁ τῆς αὐ. δαίμων πλήξῃ σὴν καρδίαν *ib*.2.62B.

αὐταρεσκέω, *please oneself*, †Jo.D.*B.J*.16(M.96.1001A).

αὐτάρεσκος, *self-pleasing, selfish*; of a monk who refuses to obey orders ὁ τοιοῦτος καὶ αὐθάδης καὶ αὐ. ἐστι Bas.*reg.br*.117(2.455E; M.31.1161B); to become such is special temptation of religious solitary, Nil.*Eulog*.4(M.79.1100B); τὸ αὐ. equivalent to φιλαυτία and αὐθάδεια, Max.*schol.c.h*.9(M.4.84D); opp. θεάρεστος, ‡Proc.G.*Pr*.17:18(M.87.1400A); in prayer μὴ βούλου πρὸς τὸν ἴδιον σκοπὸν πανταχῇ τὰ πράγματα γίνεσθαι, καὶ μάλισθ' ὅτε...αὐ. εἴ, καὶ οὐ πάντως ἀρέσκει τῷ κυρίῳ ἡ σὴ πληροφορία Nil.*epp*.2.331(M.79.361D).

αὐτάρκεια, ἡ, *contentment, self-sufficiency, frugality*; **1.** in gen., *sufficiency*, Just.*dial*.73.6(M.6.648C); μηδενὸς εἶναι λέγων ἄξιον τὸ πάθος πρὸς αὐταρκείαν τῆς αἰωνίου ἀνταποδόσεως *A.(Pass.)Andr*.11 (p.27.8); **2.** *frugality, moderation in diet*, Bas.*hom*.1.4(2.4A; M.31.169A); **3.** *moderation, contentment, satisfaction with little*; **a.** among philosophers Διογένης, πιθάκνης καυχήματι τὴν αὐ. σεμνυνόμενος Tat.*orat*.2(p.2.19; M.6.805C); *ib*.19(p.20.27; 848A); **b.** as Christian virtue, Clem.*paed*.1.12(p.149.9; M.8.368B); μήτηρ δὲ αὐτῶν [sc. λιτότητος, ἱκανότητος] ἡ δικαιοσύνη, τιθηνὴ δὲ ἡ αὐ. *ib*.2.12(p.233.23; 552C); opp. πλεονεξία, id.*str*.3.12(p.237.9; M.8.1189B); *Hom.Clem*.9.12; *ib*.13.18; Chrys.*sac*.3.17(p.91.15; 1.399C); id.*hom.27.3 in Ac.*(9.218D); αὐ. ἐν τῇ χρείᾳ τούτων ὁρίζεται, ὧν ἄνευ ζῆν οὐκ ἔνι id.*hom.19.3 in 2Cor.*(10.575C); id.*comm.in Gal*.6:6(10.725D); πορισμὸς μέγας ἡ εὐσέβεια μετὰ αὐταρκείας οὐχ ὅταν χρήματα ἔχῃ, ἀλλ' ὅταν μὴ ἔχῃ id.*hom.17.1 in 1Tim.*(11.648E); φεύγειν προσήκει τὴν πλεονεξίαν, καὶ τὴν αὐ. στέργειν Thdt.*1Tim*.6:6(3.669).

αὐταρκ-έω, 1. *be sufficient* οὐ γὰρ ~εῖ μόνον ἡ φιλοσοφία Clem. *prot*.7(p.55.16; M.8.180B); Chrys.*hom.28.1 in Gen.*(4.269C); of Christ τέλειον γὰρ αὐτὸν ἐγέννησεν ὁ πατήρ, καὶ ~οῦντα ἑαυτῷ, καὶ οὐδὲν ἀτελὲς ἔχοντα id.*hom.24.2 in Jo.*(8.139D); **2.** *be sufficient* for, *capable* ~ῶ ἐγὼ εἰς παραμυθίαν σου *A.Xanthipp*.3(p.60.9); ηὐτάρκησε στῆναι μετὰ τοῦ ἀρχιεπισκόπου ἐν λέξεσιν †Gregent.*disp*.(M.86.652A).

***αὐτεκδίκητος,** *self-avenging*, Thdr.Stud.*epp*.1.28(M.99.1000C).

***αὐτέλεγκτος,** *self-convicted*, ‡Ath.*Apoll*.1.4(M.26.1097C); ‡Pamph. Abyd.*ep.Petr*.(p.9.33; H.2.849E).

***αὐτεναντίος,** *contradicting oneself*, Jo.Clim.*scal*.18(M.88.932B).

αὐτενέργητος (αὐτοεν-), *spontaneous, self-motivated*, Dion.Ar.*d.n.* 4.14(M.3.712C) cit. s. αὐτοκίνητος; οὐδὲν γὰρ τῶν ὄντων παντελῶς ἐστιν αὐ. Max.*ambig*.(M.91.1217B); αὐτοενέργητος Dion.Ar.*ep*.9.1(M.3.1104C) cit. s. αὐτοκίνητος.

***αὐτεξουσιάζ-ω,** *act as free agent*, ref. Is.1:19 ταῦτα γὰρ ὡς ~οντι, καὶ οὐχ ὡς ὑπὸ δεσμὰ καὶ ἀνάγκην ἀγομένῳ ἐρρήθη Meth.*res*.1.32 (p.269.6; αὐτῷ ἐξουσιάζοντι M.41.1144C).

***αὐτεξουσίαστος,** *of one's own free will, voluntary*, *Pers*.(p.44.6).

αὐτεξούσιος, αὐτεξουσίως, adj., *possessing free will*; adv., *by an act of free will*; **A. 1.** in gen. πᾶν λογικόν, αὐ.· πᾶν δ' αὐ., προαιρετικόν ‡Cyr.*Trin*.15(6³.21C; M.77.1152D); τοῦ λογικοῦ τὸ αὐ. ἴδιον Thdt. *qu.36 in Gen.*(1.47); Jo.D.ap.*cat.Rom*.8:39(p.300.35); in def. of θέλησις, Iren.*fr*.5(M.7.1232B); Clem.*fr*.40(p.220.15; M.9.752A), Max. *Pyrr*.(M.91.304C) citt. s. θέλησις; αὕτη ἡ ὄρεξις αὐ. ἐστιν· αὐτεξουσίως γὰρ ὀρεγόμενος, νοεῖ...καὶ κρίνει Jo.D.*volunt*.15(M.95.144C); **2.** of Trin., Jo.D.*f.o*.1.14(M.94.860A); ὥσπερ ὁ πατὴρ καὶ ὁ υἱὸς πάντα πράττουσιν αὐτεξουσίως, οὕτως καὶ τὸ πνεῦμα τὸ ἅγιον *cat.Ac*.13:2 (p.212.11); **3.** of God ἡ θεία φύσις ἀναμάρτητος καὶ αὐ. θέλησις Jo.D. *volunt*.28(M.95.161B); **4.** of Logos, at Creation, Procl.CP *or*.15.1(M.65.800C); **5.** Christol.; **a.** of Christ's divine and human nature, Jo.D.*f.o*.1.2(M.94.793A) = †Jo.D.*B.J*.19(M.96.1029A); εἶχε καὶ τὴν θείαν ἐνέργειαν, καθ' ἣν αὐτεξουσίως θέλων ἐνήργει τὰ θεῖα σὺν τῷ πατρὶ καὶ τῷ πνεύματι· εἶχε δὲ καὶ ἀνθρωπίνην ἐνέργειαν, καθ' ἣν αὐτεξουσίως ἐνήργει τὰ ἀνθρώπινα id.*volunt*.42(M.95.181C); **b.** of the divine nature ἐγὼ [sc. Jo. Bapt.] ὑπεξούσιος, αὐτὸς δὲ αὐ. †Hipp. *theoph*.3(p.259.2; M.10.853D); Ambr.ap.CLater.*act*.5(H.3.857C); Jo. D.*volunt*.11(M.95.141B); controlling powers of nature, as shown in healing of man blind from birth, Gel.Cyz.*h.e*.2.16.20(M.85.1264D); τὸν ἐκ γενετῆς τυφλὸν ἄνευ τέχνης ἰατρικῆς θεραπεύσας, τῆς θεϊκῆς δυνάμεως αὐτοῦ ἐνεφάνισε τὸ αὐ. Leont.B.*mesopent*.(M.86.1984C); **c.** of the human nature, ‡Cyr.*Trin*.15(6³.21C; M.77.1152D) cit. s. προαιρετικός; Jo.D.*volunt*.28(M.95.165D); εἰ οὖν τὸν κατ' εἰκόνα αὐτοῦ γενόμενον ἀνέλαβεν ἄνθρωπον, πάντως νοερὰν καὶ λογικὴν φύσιν ἀνέλαβεν· ἀνέλαβε δὲ καὶ θέλησιν αὐ. *ib*.38(M.95.177C); voluntarily conforming to divine will, *ib*.27(160B); ὑπετάσσετο γὰρ αὐτεξουσίως ἡ ἀνθρωπίνη αὐτοῦ θέλησις τῷ θείῳ αὐτοῦ καὶ πατρικῷ θελήματι, καὶ ταῦτα ἤθελεν, ἃ ἤθελεν ἡ θεία αὐτοῦ θέλησις θέλειν αὐτήν *ib*.39(180A); ref. Christ's death, Or.*Jo*.19.18(4; p.318.16; M.14.560A); **6.** of H. Ghost ἐνεργοῦν αὐτεξουσίως οὐ διακονικῶς ἐφ' οὓς βούλεται τὸν ἁγιασμὸν *Lit.Marc.*(p.134.3); **7.** of angels; in gen., Bas.*Spir*.38(3.32D; M.32.137B); ἄγγελος οὐσία ἐστὶ νοερὰ...αὐ. Jo.D.ap.*cat.Rom.* 8:39(p.300.26); of angels and men, granted by God in creation in divine image, Jo.D.*volunt*.30(M.95.168B); opp. God's παντεξούσιον, Adam.*dial*.3.9(p.128.8; M.11.1801A); limited in time χρόνους ὥρισε μέχρις οὗ ἐγίνωσκε καλὸν εἶναι τὸ αὐ. ἔχειν αὐτούς Just.*dial*.102.4(M.6.713B); source of good ἐποίησεν [sc. ὁ θεός] αὐ. πρὸς δικαιοπραξίαν *ib.*; Tat.*orat*.7(p.7.13; M.6.820B); of good and evil, Just.*dial*.88.5 (685C); id.*2apol*.7.5(M.6.456B); **8.** as occasion by which some angels became demons, Tat.*orat*.7(p.8.3; M.6.821A); ref. Devil αὐ. προαιρέσει ἐτράπη ἐκ τοῦ καλοῦ εἰς τὸ κακόν †Jo.D.*B.J*.6(M.96.908A); yet being capable of repentance, Clem.*str*.1.17(p.54.4; M.8.797C); **9.** of human free will; **a.** in relation to God; **i.** granted by God, Iren.*haer*.4.37.3(M.7.1101C); Const.*or.s.c*.13(p.172.21); Gr.Nyss.*or. catech*.5(p.26.8; M.45.24C); in creation in divine image μίμημα τῆς θείας φύσεως κατεσκευάσθη ὁ ἄνθρωπος, τοῖς τε λοιποῖς τῶν ἀγαθῶν καὶ τῷ αὐ. τῆς προαιρέσεως τὴν πρὸς τὸ θεῖον διασῴζων ὁμοίωσιν *ib*.21(p.81.6; 57C); Const.Diac.*laud*.14(M.88.496C); Max.*Pyrr*.(M.91.304C); proved by proclamation of Law οὗ [sc. τοῦ ἀνθρώπου] αὐ. ὄντος νόμος ὑπὸ θεοῦ ὡρίζετο οὐ μάτην· εἰ γὰρ μὴ εἶχεν ὁ ἄνθρωπος τὸ θέλειν καὶ τὸ μὴ θέλειν, τί καὶ νόμος ὡρίζετο; Hipp.*haer*.10.33 (p.290.17; M.16.3450C); οὐκ ἀγνοοῦντος τοῦ θεοῦ τὸ ἐσόμενον, ἀλλὰ νομοθετοῦντος τὸ αὐ. Gr.Naz.*or*.45.28(M.36.661B); Bas.Sel.*or*.3.2(M.85.52A); **ii.** recognized by God οὐ προφθάνει τὰς ἡμετέρας βουλήσεις, ἵνα μὴ λυμήνηται τὸ αὐ. ἡμῶν Chrys.*hom.12.3 in Heb.*(12.124D); Nil.*epp*.2.328(M.79.361A); although some are unfaithful οὔτε τὸ αὐ. τῶν ἀρχομένων διὰ τοὺς ἀφισταμένους ἐξεῖλε Aen.*dial.*(M.85.972B); even after sin, Cyr.*Ps*.50 proem.(M.69.1085C); ἐμμένοντας δὲ τῇ ἀσεβείᾳ εἴασεν, οὐ γὰρ ἐξ ἀνάγκης ἐφέλκεται ἑαυτῷ λατρεύειν, ἵνα μὴ ὑβρίσῃ τὸ αὐ. *cat.Ac*.7:42(p.121.5); **iii.** granted by God to bring man to repentance ἐμφαίνει τὸ θεῖον τὸ φιλάνθρωπον τὸ αὐτοῦ τῷ αὐ. τῆς ψυχῆς ἀφορμὰς μετανοίας χαριζόμενος Clem.*paed*.1.9(p.134.26; M.8.341A); Or.*hom.18.6 in Jer.*(p.160.8; M.13.477B); Chrys.*hom. 19.1 in Gen.*(4.161E); *cat.Ac*.7:42(p.121.7); to make mercy possible, Eleutherius Tyanensis ap.Leont.et Jo.*sacr*.2.3(M.86.2061C); **iv.** not opp. grace οὐ μὴν ἐπειδὴ δωρεὰ [sc. ἡ χάρις], διὰ τοῦτο τὸ αὐ. ἀνῄρηται Chrys.*hom.45.1 in Mt.*(7.476B); id.*hom.8.2 in Phil.*(11.258B); Ammon.*Jo*.6:44(M.85.1437A); τὸ αὐ. ἡμῶν εἰς τὸ πᾶν μὴ δεδεμένον τῷ δεσμῷ τῆς χάριτος Diad.*perf*.85(p.116.18); nor God's providence ἡ τοῦ λόγου δύναμις ἔχουσα παρ' ἑαυτῇ τὸ προγνωστικὸν κατὰ πᾶν τὸ μέλλον ἀποβαίνειν οὐ καθ' εἱμαρμένην τῇ δὲ τῶν αἱρουμένων αὐ. γνώμῃ τῶν μελλόντων προὔλεγε τὰς ἀποβάσεις Tat.*orat*.7 (p.7.21; M.6.820C); Chrys.*hom.3.1 in 1Thess.*(11.562C); ὁ θεὸς εἰδὼς τὸ ἐσόμενον, πλὴν διδοὺς τῷ ἀνθρώπῳ πράττειν ὃ θέλει διὰ τὸ αὐ. *cat. Jac*.1:13(p.5.13); nor God's power πάντα μὲν ἐπὶ τῷ θεῷ· ἀλλ' οὐχ οὕτως, ὥστε τὸ αὐ. ἡμῶν βλάπτεσθαι Chrys.*hom.12.3 in Heb.*(12.124C); but attainment of salvation depends on its exercise προαίρεσιν ἡμῖν αὐ. ἐμβαλεῖ [sc. ὁ θεός] τὴν δυναμένην ποιῆσαι ἡμᾶς ὁμοιωθῆναι θεῷ ‡Bas.*struct.hom*.1.20(1.333B; M.30.29D); *V.Aberc*.34; τὸ αὐ. δέδοται ἡμῖν παρὰ θεοῦ, καὶ ἐν ἡμῖν σωθῆναι καὶ ἀπολέσθαι Leont.

et Jo.*sacr*.2.3(M.86.2053C); **b.** in relation to Christ; **i.** taught by Christ θείως τὸ 'εἰ θέλεις' τὸ αὐ. τῆς προσδιαλεγομένης αὐτῷ ψυχῆς ἐδήλωσεν Clem.*q.d.s*.10(p.165.26; M.9.613B); recognized by Christ, Ammon.*Jo*.5:40(M.85.1432C); **ii.** proved by Christ's life, Hipp.*haer*.10.33(p.291.24; M.16.3451C); **iii.** re-established by Christ τὸ αὐ. τῶν ἀνθρώπων πάλιν ἀφῆκεν ἐλεύθερον *Const.App*.6.22.1; **iv.** proving Christ's free will, Didym.(‡Bas.)*Eun*.4(1.290E,291A; M.29.697C); **c.** must conform to law, Tat.*orat*.7(p.7.17; M.6.820B); Meth.*arbitr*.17(p.189.12; M.18.264A); id.*res*.1.38(p.281.6; M.18.268A); Gr.Naz.*or*.14.25(M.35.892A); ἡ δὲ λογικὴ [sc. ὄρεξις] καὶ αὐ., ὅπως αὐτεξουσίως χαλιναγωγήσῃ πᾶσαν φυσικὴν κίνησιν, καὶ ὑποταγῇ καὶ ὑποτάξῃ τῷ νόμῳ τοῦ κτίσαντος Jo.D.*volunt*.18 bis(M.95.148B) al.; **d.** as essential part of human nature, Jo.D.*volunt*.28(M.95.165D); property of reason, Clem.*q.d.s*.14(p.169.5; M.9.617D); τὸ αὐ., πρῶτον ἀγαθόν, τῇ λογικῇ φύσει πρέπον· καὶ τὸ κεχρῆσθαι τῷ αὐ., καὶ κατεξουσιάζειν καὶ κρατεῖν τῶν ἀλόγων παθῶν, ἀρετή· τὸ δὲ προδιδόναι τὸ αὐ. καὶ ἡττᾶσθαι τοῖς ἀλόγοις πάθεσι, τοῦτο ἁμαρτία Jo.D.*volunt*.19(149C); τὰ οὖν ἄλογα αἰσθητικῶς ὀρέγεται, ἀλλ' οὐ λογικῶς, οὐδὲ αὐτεξουσίως· ὁ δὲ ἄνθρωπος ζῷον ὑπάρχων λογικόν, ὡς μὲν ζῷον, ζωτικῶς καὶ αἰσθητικῶς ὀρέγεται· ὡς δὲ λογικός, λογικῶς καὶ αὐτεξουσίως *ib*.25(156C); of soul, *Const.App*.6.11.7; Dor.*doct*.12.6(M.88.1757C); **e.** granted to Adam by God, ‡Ath.ap.Jo.D.*volunt*.28(M.95.161A) = ‡Ath.*Apoll*.1.15(M.26.1120B); **f.** source of good or evil, Hipp.*Dan*.4.59.6(p.336.17); Or.*schol.in Cant*.2:15(M.17.265B); Bas.*Eun*.3.2(1.274C; M.29.660C); Gr.Nyss.*hom.12 in Cant*.(M.44.1017C); ἐμμένειν ἢ μὴ ἐμμένειν ταῖς ἐντολαῖς τῷ αὐ. ἡμῶν θελήματι παρεχώρησεν [sc. ὁ θεός] Marc.Er.*opusc*.4(M.65.989C); *cat.Lc*.15:11(p.117.31) ∾ Tit.Bost.*fr.Lc*.15:12(p.215); **g.** source of good, Meth.*symp*.8.13(p.98.18; M.18.161A); *M.Tar*.8(p.467); man being good by act of will, God by nature τῷ κατὰ φύσιν ἀγαθῷ οὐκ ἐπισυμβαίνει τὸ κακόν, ἀλλὰ τῷ κατὰ θέσιν ἀγαθῷ διὰ τὸ αὐ. Adam.*dial*.3.9(p.126.24; M.11.1800B); essence of virtue τὸ αὐ. ἔχοντες, τὸ ἀρετῆς συστατικὸν (οὐ γὰρ ἀρετὴ τὸ βίᾳ γινόμενον) Jo.D.*volunt*.19(M.95.149A); in those who accept gospel, Or.*Cels*.6.2(p.72.11; M.11.1292A); [sc. ὁ υἱὸς θεοῦ] τῷ αὐ. τῶν δεχομένων τὸν λόγον βουλήματι ἐπιτρέπων τὴν ἐργασίαν καὶ μὴ τὸ πᾶν αὐτὸς κατεργαζόμενος· ἵνα μὴ ἀκούσιον ἡμῶν ᾖ τὸ ἀγαθόν Vict.*Mc*.4:25(p.309.13); opp. those who lived under Law νηπίους μὲν τοὺς ἐν νόμῳ λέγει, ἄνδρας δὲ τοὺς λόγῳ πειθηνίους καὶ αὐ. κέκληκεν Clem.*paed*.1.6(p.110.3; M.8.289B); source of repentance, Didym.*Ac*.8:22(M.39.1669A); of conversion νικᾷ δὲ [sc. τὸ εὐόλισθον] ὅμως γνώμῃ καὶ πόνοις, ἀλλ' οὐκ ἀνάγκῃ κρατεῖται διὰ τὸ αὐ. Cyr.*Ps*.50:7(M.69.1089C); faith is act of free will, a truth denied by Basilides οὐχὶ ψυχῆς αὐ. λογικὴν συγκατάθεσιν λέγει τὴν πίστιν Clem.*str*.5.1(p.327.24; M.9.12B); **h.** source of evil, Iren.*haer*.4.39.3(M.7.1111B); ἀπώλεσεν ἡμᾶς τὸ αὐ.· δοῦλοι γεγόναμεν οἱ ἐλεύθεροι Tat.*orat*.11(p.12.14; M.6.829B); Hipp.*haer*.10.33(p.290.14; M.16.3450B); ἀρχὴ καὶ ῥίζα τῆς ἁμαρτίας τὸ ἐφ' ἡμῖν καὶ τὸ αὐ. Bas.*hom*.9.3(2.74A; M.31.332D); ἡ ψυχὴ αὐ. τρόπῳ προσαποχρωμένη, καὶ τὴν τῆς ἐλευθερίας τιμὴν ἀφορμὴν ἁμαρτίας ἐργαζομένη Bas.Sel.*or*.35.1(M.85.376A); Jo.D.*imag*.1.16(M.94.1245C); **i.** continually being tested, Diad.*perf*.82(p.110.22); **j.** limited to lifetime, Epiph.*haer*.43.2(p.188.30; M.41.820D); τῇ ἰδίᾳ ἕκαστος ἐφεῖται αὐ. προαιρέσει, ἕως ἐν τῷ παρόντι βίῳ ἐστί †Jo.D.*B.J*.15(M.96.996B); **k.** vindicated by pagan philosophers, ‡Just.*monarch*.6(M.6.325A); in Plato θεόσδοτος ἡ σοφία προτρέπει ἡμῶν τὸ αὐ. Clem.*str*.5.13(p.381.30; M.9.125A); **l.** discussion of biblical passages which seem to indicate contrary, Or.*princ*.3.1 passim(p.195ff.; M.11.249ff.); **10.** in Valent. system; of πνευματικοί opp. ψυχικοί, Iren.*haer*.1.6.1(M.7.504B); τὸ μὲν οὖν πνευματικὸν φύσει σῳζόμενον· τὸ δὲ ψυχικόν, αὐ. ὄν, ἐπιτηδειότητα ἔχει πρός τε πίστιν καὶ πρὸς ἀπιστίαν Clem.*exc.Thdot*.(p.125.19; M.9.685C); **11.** Arian; of Son, Ath.*Ar*.1.22(M.26.57C); proving inferiority to Father, Cyr.*thes*.13(5^1.125A); involving capacity for sin, Ath.*Ar*.1.35(M.26.84A); τῷ ἰδίῳ αὐ., ἕως βούλεται, μένει καλός· ὅτε μέντοι θέλει, δύναται τρέπεσθαι καὶ αὐτὸς ὥσπερ καὶ ἡμεῖς Ar.*Thal.fr*.9 ap.Ath.*ep.Aeg.Lib*.12(M.25.564B); **12.** in Apollinarianism, of angels and men, proving impossibility of Christ's perfect human nature εἰ ἄνθρωπον οἴεταί τις ἑνοῦσθαι θεῷ παρὰ πάντας ἀνθρώπους καὶ ἀγγέλους,...ποιήσει μὴ αὐ. τοὺς ἀγγέλους καὶ τοὺς ἀνθρώπους, ὡς οὐδὲ ἡ σὰρξ αὐ. φθορὰ δὲ τοῦ αὐ. ζῴου τὸ μὴ εἶναι αὐ.· οὐ φθείρεται δὲ ἡ φύσις ὑπὸ τοῦ ποιήσαντος αὐτήν· οὐκ ἄρα ἑνοῦται ὁ ἄνθρωπος θεῷ Apoll.*fr*.87(p.226.2ff.)ap.Gr.Nyss.*Apoll*.45(M.45.1232A); **13.** of heavenly bodies τὸ μὲν αἰσθητὸν φῶς ἔργον ἐστὶ τοῦ δημιουργοῦ· τὸ δὲ νοητὸν τάχα καὶ αὐτῶν καὶ ἐκ τοῦ ἐν αὐτοῖς αὐ. ἐληλυθός Or.*Cels*.5.10(p.11.17; M.11.1196C).

B. *left to one's own choice* τῶν ἐντολῶν αἱ μέν εἰσιν ἐπιτεταγμέναι, αἱ δὲ οὐκ ἐπιτεταγμέναι ἀλλ' αὐ. καὶ τῇ προαιρέσει ἐπιτετραμμέναι ὑπὸ τοῦ θεοῦ Or.*comm.in 1Cor*.7:25(*JTS* 9 p.508); of virtue, Proc.G.*Is*.54(M.87.2549C); καρποῦ παντὸς τῶν ἐν παραδείσῳ φυτῶν ἀπόλαυσιν ἐπέτρεψεν αὐ. Nil.*Magn*.14(M.79.988B).

C. *consisting in free will* τὸν ἄνθρωπον τῇ αὐ. χάριτι κατεκόσμησεν Gr.Nyss.*or.dom*.5(p.110.33; M.44.1189C); ἔδωκε τῇ λογικῇ φύσει τὴν αὐ. χάριν id.*hom.2 in Cant*.(M.44.796C).

D. *wanton* αὐ. ἀπαιδευσία Clem.*paed*.3.5(p.254.20; M.8.600B).

αὐτεξουσιότης, ἡ, *free will*; **1.** in gen. αὐ. ἐστὶ νοῦς κατὰ φύσιν κινούμενος ἢ νοερὰ τῆς ψυχῆς κίνησις αὐτοκρατής Clem.*fr*.40(p.220.16; M.9.752B)ap.Max.*opusc*.(M.91.276C) = †Jo.D.*B.J*.15(M.96.996B); τοῦτο τῆς αὐ. ἐστι τὸ ἰδίωμα, τὸ κατ' ἐξουσίαν ἀναιρεῖσθαι τὸ καταθύμιον Gr.Nyss.*or.catech*.5(p.28.7; M.45.25A); αὐ. ἐστί, ψυχῆς λογικῆς θέλησις ἀκωλύτως γινομένη πρὸς ὅπερ ἂν βούληται Diad.ap.Max.*opusc*.(M.91.277C) = †Jo.D.*B.J*.15(M.96.996B); αὐ. δὲ οὐδὲν ἕτερόν ἐστιν, εἰ μὴ ἡ θέλησις Jo.D.*f.o*.3.14(M.94.1037B); **2.** of Son λέγων [sc. Ἄρειος] αὐτεξουσιότητι κακίας καὶ ἀρετῆς δεκτικὸν τὸν υἱὸν τοῦ θεοῦ CNic.(325)*ep*.(p.48.3)ap.Socr.*h.e*.1.9.3(M.67.77C) = Gel.Cyz.*h.e*.2.26.1(M.85.1308A); **3.** of H. Ghost, Didym.*Trin*.2.8(M.39.600B); Gel.Cyz.*h.e*.2.21.25(M.85.1288D); **4.** of Devil τὸ μὲν πρότερον ἄγγελον ὑπὸ τοῦ θεοῦ γενόμενον καὶ φωτὸς μετέχοντα, ὕστερον δὲ τῇ αὐ. τραπέντα ἐπὶ τὸ χεῖρον Adam.*dial*.3.13(p.134.15; M.11.1804D); Epiph.*haer*.66.16(p.40.1; M.42.52D); **5.** of man, Eus.*d.e*.4.6(p.160.11; M.22.265D); ἐπιγνῶμεν τὴν δοθεῖσαν ἡμῖν τῆς ἐλευθερίας αὐ. παρὰ τοῦ κτίσαντος ἡμᾶς, ἵνα ἐφ' ἡμῖν ᾖ τὸ καὶ τῶν κρειττόνων ὀρέγεσθαι, καὶ τῶν χειρόνων ἀπέχεσθαι Mac.Aeg.*ep*.(M.34.412A); οὐ διὰ τὴν τῶν προνοουμένων αὐ. τὰ θεῖα φῶτα τῆς προνοητικῆς ἐλλάμψεως ἀπαμβλύνεται Dion.Ar.*c.h*.9.3(M.3.260C); Leont.B.*Nest.et Eut*.2(M.86.1332D); ὥσπερ ἡ φυσικὴ ὄρεξις πάσῃ αἰσθητικῇ φύσει ἔγκειται, οὕτως ἡ αὐ. πάσῃ λογικῇ φύσει ἔγκειται Jo.D.*inst.el*.10(M.95.112A); of souls in purgatory, Eustrat.*stat.anim*.25(p.533).

αὐτεξουσίως, v. αὐτεξούσιος.

***αὐτεπαινετός**, ὁ, *one who praises himself* αὐ. μισεῖ ὁ θεός *1Clem*.30.6.

αὐτεπίβουλος, *plotting against one's own interests*; of S. Peter resisting the *pedilavium*, †Cyr.*hom.div*.10(5^2.376E).

***αὐτεπίσκοπος**, ὁ, *eyewitness*, Cyr.*Jo*.2.2(4.165D).

αὐτεπίσπαστος, *self-incurred*, Cyr.*Jo*.6.1(4.634C).

αὐτίκα, **1.** adv.; **a.** *further*, Clem.*str*.1.9(p.29.13; M.8.740C); *ib*.4.6(p.261.26; 1241C); *ib*.4.23(p.315.23; 1360C); **b.** *therefore*, Thdt.*qu.10 in Lev*.(1.188); id.*Is*.65:13(p.254.22; 2.395); **2.** prep., c. genit., *immediately after*, Philost.*h.e*.9.19(M.65.584A).

αὐτοαγαθός ([*]αὐταγ-), *essentially good, absolutely good*; **1.** of God θέλει δὲ ἀγαθὰ πάντα, ὅτι δὴ καὶ αὐ. τὴν οὐσίαν τυγχάνει Eus.*l.C*.12(p.230.2; M.20.1388A); δέον ἕν τι θεῖον...αὐτοζωήν, αὐτοκαλόν, αὐ. ὄντα id.*e.th*.2.14(p.115.17; M.24.928D); οὐκ ἀπὸ βουλήματος μόνον ὑπῆρξεν αὐτῷ τοῦτο [sc. creation]...μελλητικῶς...ἀλλὰ κατὰ τὸ αὐ. πέφυκε γὰρ αὐ. συμπρεπόντως αὐτῷ τὰ πάντα ἔχων καὶ ποιῶν καὶ ἐργαζόμενος Epiph.*haer*.76.35(p.385.9; M.42.588C); Dion.Ar.*d.n*.1.5(M.3.593B); Max.*schol.d.n*.4.20(M.4.277C) cit. s. αὐτοειδοποιός; αὐταγ- Zach.Mit.*opif*.(M.85.1121A); **2.** of Son; **a.** as not the absolute principle of goodness, but image of goodness of God ἐπὶ τοῦ σωτῆρος καλῶς ἂν λεχθήσεσθαι ὅτι εἰκὼν ἀγαθότητος τοῦ θεοῦ ἐστιν, ἀλλ' οὐκ αὐ. Or.*princ*.1.2(p.47.4; M.11.143C αὐτὸ ἀγαθόν); **b.** as himself αὐ.: αὐ. ἐκ τῆς...πατρικῆς ἀγαθότητος προελθόντα Bas.*Eun*.2.25(1.261E; M.29.629B); †Bas.*Is*.139(1.477A; M.30.345B); **3.** of H. Ghost οὐ μετοχῇ ἀγαθότητος ἀγαθόν ἐστιν, ἀλλ' αὐ., ἤγουν ἀγαθότης, ἐστὶν ‡Ath.*dial.Trin*.1.16(M.28.1141B); αὐ. καὶ πηγὴ ἀγαθότητος Gr.Naz.*or*.41.9(M.36.441C); Didym.*Trin*.2.8(M.39.601A).

αὐτοαγαθότης ([*]αὐταγ-), ἡ, *absolute goodness*; of God, Epiph.*haer*.76.35(p.384.33; M.42.588B); τὴν θεαρχικὴν ὅλην ὕπαρξιν ὅ τί ποτέ ἐστιν ἡ αὐ. ἀφορίζουσα καὶ ἐκφαίνουσα...ὕμνηται Dion.Ar.*d.n*.2.1(M.3.636C); ὁ δημιουργὸς...ἀγαθὸς ὢν μᾶλλον δὲ ἡ αὐταγαθότησι καὶ τἀγαθὸν Zach.Mit.*opif*.(M.85.1133B); αὐταγ- ‡Cyr.*Trin*.7(6^3.8C; M.77.1132B) = Jo.D.*f.o*.1.8(M.94.808D) cit. s. αὐτοζωή; †Jo.D.*B.J*.31(M.96.1164A).

***αὐτοαγάπη**, ἡ, *absolute love*; of God, ‡Proc.G.*Pr*.29:5(M.87.1513C); †Jo.D.*B.J*.31(M.96.1164A).

***αὐτοαγγελικός**, *actually angelic*, Max.*schol.d.n*.6.2(M.4.337B).

***αὐτοαγένητος**, *absolutely unoriginate*; of God, Dion.Al.ap.Eus.*p.e*.7.19(p.333D; αὐτὸ ἀγένητον M.21.564A).

***αὐτοαγέννητος**, *absolutely unbegotten*; τὸ αὐτο⟨α⟩γέννητον *essential ingenerateness*, Epiph.*haer*.76.36(p.387.11; M.42.592B; αὐτογέννητον MSS).

***αὐτοαγιασμός**, ὁ, *absolute holiness*; of Christ, Or.*hom.17.4 in Jer*.(p.147.3; M.13.457C); id.*Jo*.1.9(11; p.15.14; M.14.41B); Ath.*gent*.47(M.25.93C).

***αὐτοάγιος**, *absolutely holy*, ref. Son οὐδὲ γὰρ ὁ κατὰ χάριν ἅγιος αὐ. Didym.(‡Bas.)*Eun*.4.3(1.290E; M.29.697C); of H. Ghost ὡς καὶ διὰ τοῦτο ὀρθῶς εὐφημεῖσθαι αὐ. τε καὶ πνεῦμα ἁγιωσύνης, ἀντὶ τοῦ φύσει καὶ ἀφ' ἑαυτοῦ ἅγιον Didym.*Trin*.2.6(M.39.524C).

***αὐτοαγιότης**, ἡ, *absolute holiness*; attribute of God, Dion.Ar. *d.n*.12.1(M.3.969B); of each Person of Trin., Gr.Naz.*or*.23.11(M.35. 1164A); of H. Ghost ἀληθῶς ἅγιον τὸ πνεῦμα τὸ ἅγιον· οὐ γὰρ καὶ ἄλλο τοιοῦτον, οὐδὲ οὕτως, οὐδὲ ἐκ προσθήκης ὁ ἁγιασμὸς ἀλλ' αὐ. *ib*. 25.16(1221B).

***αὐτοαγιωσύνη**, ἡ, *absolute holiness*; of Christ, Andr.Caes.*Apoc*.8 (M.106.245B).

***αὐτοαδαμάς**, *like adamant itself*, Chrys.*coemet*.2(2.399B); id. *Stag*.2.9(1.194C).

***αὐτοαθανασία**, ἡ, *immortality itself*; of Christ, Chrys.*hom*.*18.1 in 1Tim*.(11.654C).

***αὐτοαΐδιος**, *eternal in oneself*; of God, Epiph.*haer*.76.21(p.368.8; M.42.557C) cit. s. αὐτόθεος.

***αὐτοαίσθησις**, ἡ, *perception itself*, Epiph.*haer*.76.37(p.388.31; M.42.593C) cit. s. αὐτοθέλημα.

***αὐτοαιτής**, s.v.l., ? *being himself blameworthy*, Meth.*res*.1.45 ap. Leont.et Jo.*sacr*.2(M.86.2056C), αἴτιος (GCS p.294.6).

***αὐτοαιών**, ὁ, *absolute eternity*, of the Godhead διότι καὶ αὐ., καὶ τὰ ὄντα, καὶ τὰ μέτρα τῶν ὄντων, καὶ τὰ μετρούμενα, δι' αὐτοῦ καὶ ἀπ' αὐτοῦ Dion.Ar.*d.n*.5.10(M.3.825B).

***αὐτοακατέργαστος**, *essentially indigestible*, Chrys.*ecl*.19(12.554B), cited from ‡Chrys.*prov*.1(2.753B) reading αὐτῷ ἀκατέργαστον.

***αὐτοακολασία**, ἡ, *principle of licentiousness* τί γάρ ἐστιν αὐ. δίχα τοῦ εἴδους τοῦ ἀκολασταίνειν; Max.*schol.d.n*.4.20(M.4.281A).

***αὐτοαλήθεια**, ἡ, *absolute truth, truth itself*; **1.** in gen., of reality opp. type ἄρτον δὲ ἀληθινὸν καλεῖ ἐκεῖνον, οὐκ ἐπειδὴ ψευδὲς ἦν τὸ θαῦμα τὸ ἐπὶ τὸ μάννα, ἀλλ' ὅτι τύπος ἦν, οὐκ αὐ. Chrys.*hom*.*45.1 in Jo*.(8.263B); of absolute truth opp. human virtue of truth, Gr. Nyss.*hom*.*1 in Cant*.(M.44.781B); **2.** of God; **a.** Manich., as attribute of the good principle, contrasted with opposite attribute of the evil principle ἐὰν μέντοι καλέσωμεν τὸν θεὸν αὐ., δηλονότι τὸ ἐναντίον ψεῦδος κεκλήσεται Tit.Bost.*Man*.1.11(M.18.1084A); in orthodox reply αὐ. τυγχάνων ὁ θεὸς οὐκ ἀδυναμίᾳ ψεύδους ἀπέχεται, ἀλλὰ μὴ βουλόμενος ψεύσασθαί ποτε *ib*.2.19(1173A); **b.** in gen. ἔστι δὲ αὐ. ὁ θεὸς ἡμῶν Bas.*ep*.233.2(3.356D; M.32.865C); Thdt.*eran.suppl*.(4.268); **3.** of Christ αὐτοδικαιοσύνη ἐστὶν ὁ σωτήρ, αὐ. Or.*hom*. *17.4 in Jer*.(p.147.3; M.13.457C); id.*comm.in Mt*.14.7(p.289.20; M.13. 1197B) cit. s. αὐτοβασιλεία; id.*Jo*.6.6(3; p.114.22; M.14.209D); id. *Cels*.3.41(p.237.6; M.11.973A) cit. s. αὐτολόγος; Alex.Al.*ep.Alex*.7 (p.24.13; M.18.557D); Ath.*gent*.46(M.25.93C); Chrys.*hom*.*14.1 in Jo*. (8.78B) cit. s. αὐτοπηγή; **4.** of H. Ghost, Bas.*Spir*.48(3.40D; M.32. 156B); in inspiration of prophets, Cyr.*Am*.2(3.284C, v.l. ἀλήθεια Aubert); τὴν...ἐνυπόστατον...ἀλήθειαν ἥγουν αὐ., ἥτις ἐστὶ...τοῦ... πατρὸς...λόγος...οἷς συνανίσχει καὶ τῆς ἐκπορευτικῆς ὑποστάσεως ἡ αὐ. τουτέστι τὸ πνεῦμα τῆς ἀληθείας ‡Gr.Nyss.*hom*.*5.31 in Jo*.(p.183. 21,32).

αὐτοαληθής, *true in oneself, essentially true*; of Christ, Ath.*syn*. 45.4(p.270.8; M.26.772D).

***αὐτοαμαρτία**, ἡ, *very principle of sin*, Gr.Naz.*or*.37.1(M.36. 284A); of Devil, Bas.*reg.br*.268(2.508B; M.31.1268A).

***αὐτοαμετάβλητος**, (sic) emphatic for ἀμετάβλητος Val.Apoll. *apol*.3(p.288.24; better written *divisim* as M.86.1953D).

***αὐτοάμετρος**, *absolutely unlimited*, Max.*schol.d.n*.4.20(M.4.277C).

***αὐτοαναμάρτητος**, *absolutely sinless*; of H. Ghost, Didym.*Trin*. 2.20(M.39.553A).

***αὐτοανδρία**, ἡ, *principle of courage*, Max.*schol.d.n*.4.17(M.4. 269D).

***αὐτοανείδεος**, *absolutely formless*, Max.*schol.d.n*.4.20(M.4.277C).

***αὐτοαόργητος**, *absolutely free from anger*; of God, Epiph.*haer*. 76.36(p.387.10; M.42.592B).

***αὐτοαπείθεια**, ἡ, *principle of disobedience*; of Devil, Bas.*reg.br*. 268(2.508B; M.31.1268A).

***αὐτοαπολελυμένως**, *absolutely* ἀλήθειαν τὴν αὐ. καὶ ἀναιτίως ἀλήθειαν Max.*schol.myst*.5(M.4.432C).

***αὐτοαπολύτρωσις**, ἡ, *absolute redemption*; of Christ, Or.*Jo*.1.9 (11; p.15.14; M.14.41B).

***αὐτοαπροσδεής**, *essentially in need of nothing*, of H. Ghost ὑπάρχον αὐ. ἀγαθόν Didym.*Trin*.2.8(M.39.529C).

***αὐτοαρετή**, ἡ, *principle of virtue*; of God, Epiph.*haer*.76.35 (p.385.15; M.42.588C); of Logos, Ath.*gent*.46(M.25.93C).

***αὐτοβασιλεία**, ἡ, *absolute kingship*, of Christ αὐτὸς γάρ ἐστιν ὁ βασιλεὺς τῶν οὐρανῶν, καὶ ὥσπερ αὐτός ἐστιν ἡ αὐτοσοφία καὶ ἡ αὐτοδικαιοσύνη καὶ ἡ αὐτοαλήθεια, οὕτω μήποτε [? l. δήποτε] καὶ ἡ αὐ. Or.*comm.in Mt*.14.7(p.289.20; M.13.1197B).

***αὐτοβασιλεύς**, ὁ, *very king*, Chrys.*hom*.*5.3 in Rom*.(9.464C).

***αὐτοβοηθός**, *able to help oneself*, Nil.*Eulog*.33(M.79.1137D).

***αὐτοβουλή**, ἡ, *absolute counsel* or *will*, Nemes.*nat.hom*.33(M. 40.736A); of Christ εἰ βουλῆς ἐστιν εἰκών, οὐκέτι αὐ.· εἶναι δύναται Marcell.*fr*.86 ap.Epiph.*haer*.72.6(p.261.4; M.42.389C).

***αὐτοβούλητος**, *self-devised*, Iren.*haer*.1.14.7(M.7.608B).

***αὐτοβουλία**, ἡ, **1.** *self-will* αὐθεντία καὶ...αὐ. ἔρημόν τε καὶ πτωχὸν καθίστησι τὸν ἄνθρωπον τῶν πνευματικῶν...χαρισμάτων Ephr. 3.255F; **2.** *singleness of will*; ref. Christ, Max.*opusc*.(M.91.180A) where prob. read ταὐτοβουλίαν.

***αὐτογέεννα**, ἡ, *hell itself*, ref. Mt.23:15 υἱὸν δὲ γεέννης φησί, τουτέστι, αὐτογέενναν Chrys.*hom*.*73.1 in Mt*.(7.708C).

***αὐτογενέθλιος**, *in whom generation itself consists*, of Christ θεοτόκε, δι' ἧς ἡμῖν γεννᾶται ὁ αὐ. ‡Jo.D.*hom*.5(M.96.653A).

αὐτογένεθλος, *self-originate*, of God Ἑβραῖοι, αὐ. ἄνακτα σεβαζόμενοι θεὸν ἁγνῶς Anon. [? Choerilus, cf. Eus.*p.e*.9.9(412A; M.21.696C)] ap.Eus.*d.e*.3.3(p.110.9; M.22.189B); Gr.Naz.*carm*.1.1.35.4(M.37.517A); Nonn.*par.Jo*.1:18(M.43.752C); *ib*.5:18(788B); *ib*.13:20(864B); in Gnost. theology θεὸν...ἄγνωστον δοξάζειν καὶ μὴ εἶναι πατέρα τοῦ Χριστοῦ μηδὲ τοῦ κόσμου δημιουργόν, ἀλλ' ἄλεκτον, ἄρρητον, ἀκατονόμαστον, αὐ. *Const.App*.6.10.1; ἡμεῖς δὲ...θεὸν καταγγέλλομεν...οὐκ αὐταίτιον καὶ αὐ., ὡς ἐκεῖνοι οἴονται, ἀλλ' ἀΐδιον καὶ ἄναρχον *ib*.6.11.1; as logical consequence of Eunomian teaching, of Christ εἰ οὖν ἠλλοτρίωται τῆς τοῦ υἱοῦ γεννήσεως ὁ πατήρ, ἢ ἄλλον τινὰ πατέρα τοῦ υἱοῦ διὰ τοῦ τῆς γεννήσεως ὀνόματος ἀναπλάσσουσιν, ἢ αὐτογέννητόν τινα καὶ αὐ. τὸν υἱόν...ἀποδεικνύουσιν Gr.Nyss.*Eun*.10(2 p.236.18; M.45.837D); of the phoenix ξεῖνον γόνον αὐ. Gr.Naz.*carm*.1.2.2.528 (M.37.620A).

αὐτογενής, *self-originate*; **1.** of God αὐ. ἀγένητος ἅπαντα κρατῶν διὰ παντός *Orac.Sib.fr*.1.17; αὐ. θεὸν καὶ πατέρα Didym.*Trin*.2.1 (M.39.448C); ‡Just.*qu.Chr*.3.5(M.6.1441B) cit. s. αὐτοπάρακτος; **2.** as Gnost. aeon, cf. *de Ennoia et de Logo Autogenem emissum dicunt*, Iren.*haer*.1.29.2(M.7.692B); ἀποροῦσιν...πότερόν ποτε ἐκ τοῦ προόντος ἐστὶν [sc. ἡ ψυχή] ⟨ἢ⟩ ἐκ τοῦ αὐ. Hipp.*haer*.5.7(p.81.3; M.16.3130B); ἔστι τὸ μὲν πρῶτον ἀγέννητον, ὅπερ ἐστὶν ἀγαθόν· τὸ δὲ δεύτερον ἀγαθὸν αὐ.· τὸ τρίτον γεννητὸν *ib*.5.12(p.104.23; 3162A); *ib*.(p.105.9; 3162B); Thdt.*haer*.1.13(4.305).

αὐτογένητος, *self-originate*; of God, *Orac.Sib*.8.429; ‡Just.*coh. Gr*.11(M.6.264A); Gnost., of Devil, Adam.*dial*.3.3(p.118.12; M.11. 1793C).

αὐτογέννητος, *self-begotten*; **1.** of God τοῦ πατρὸς τὸ μὴ γεγεννῆσθαί ἐστιν, υἱοῦ δὲ τὸ γεγεννῆσθαι· γεννητὸν δὲ ἀγεννήτῳ ἢ καὶ αὐ. οὐ συγκρίνεται *Hom.Clem*.16.16; ὁ ὢν αὐ. θεός Aët.*synt*.36 ap.Epiph. *haer*.76.12(p.359.27; M.42.545A); ‡Just.*qu.Chr*.3.5(M.6.1444A); **2.** of Christ in *reductio ad absurdum* of Eunomian theology, Gr.Nyss. *Eun*.10(2 p.236.18; M.45.837D) cit. s. αὐτογένεθλος; **3.** in threefold division of universe postulated by Peratae κόσμον...καλεῖ τὰς δύο μοίρας τὰς ὑπερκειμένας, τήν τε ἀγέννητον καὶ τὴν αὐ. Hipp.*haer*.5. 12(p.105.19; M.16.3162C); **4.** Gnost. and Manich., of darkness as evil principle σκότος, οὐ παρ' ἑτέρου τὸ εἶναι ἔχον, ἀλλὰ κακὸν αὐ. Bas.*hex*.2.4(1.15D; M.29.36C).

***αὐτογεννήτωρ**, *self-originating*; of Christ, Iren.*haer*.1.14.3(M.7. 601B).

αὐτόγλυφος, *self-excavated*, exeg. Jer.4:29 τὸ δὲ σπήλαιον αὐ. ὄν, σημαίνει καὶ τὸ τῆς ψυχῆς αὐτεξούσιον Olymp.*fr.Jer*.4:29(M.93. 637C).

***αὐτόγραπτος**, *written with one's own hand*, Evagr.*h.e*.3.32(p.130. 6; M.86.2665A).

***αὐτοδεσποτέω**, *have absolute power*, Hesych.H.*Ps.tit*.9(M.27. 680C).

αὐτοδέσποτος, *being one's own master, free, self-determined*; **1.** in gen. τὸ τῶν Ῥωμαίων αὐ. κράτος Heracl.ap.Thphn.*chron*.p.257(M. 108.641B); **2.** of free will αὐτεξούσιος γὰρ ὢν...ὁ ἄνθρωπος, καὶ αὐ. βούλησιν καὶ αὐτοπροαίρετον πρὸς τὴν αἵρεσιν...τοῦ καλοῦ λαβὼν Meth.*res*.1.38(p.280.10; M.41.1105A) = Leont.et.Jo.*sacr*.2.3(M.86. 2056A); αὐ. βουλῇ κακίαν εἵλατο *ib*.1.45(p.294.10; 1116A); *ib*.2.1(p.330. 3; M.18.297A); ἄνθρωπος...αὐ. ἔχων τὴν πρόθεσιν Bas.Sel.*or*.3.2(M.85. 52A); in the material universe μηδὲν ἡμᾶς αὐ. βλέπειν Geo.Pis.*hex*. 348(M.92.1460B); **3.** as subst.; **a.** *absolute power* ὅταν...εἴπῃ ἡ γραφὴ ...ὅτι ἑαυτὸν ἐκένωσεν, σημαίνει τὸ αὐ. καὶ βασιλικόν, ὅτι ἑκὼν ἐσαρκώθη Ammon.*Jo*.1:6(M.85.1396B); **b.** *free will* ἐῶν τὸ τῶν λογισμῶν αὐ., σωφρονίζει τιμωρίαις τὸν πλημμελήσαντα Bas.Sel.*or*.3.2(M.85.52B).

***αὐτοδεσπότως**, *freely, with free will*, Meth.*symp*.8.13(p.98.19; M.18.161A); Jo.D.*carm.pent*.111(p.217; M.96.837B).

***αὐτοδιάλυτος**, *self-dissolving*; of the body, Olymp.*Job* 13:28 (M.93.165B).

αὐτοδικαιοσύνη, ἡ, *absolute righteousness*; **1.** of righteousness of God and Word ὁ λόγος τοῦ θεοῦ...τῇ αὐ. ... τὸ κατ' ἀξίαν ἑκάστου τῶν ὄντων ἀπονέμειν ἀπὸ θεοῦ δύνασθαι λαβὼν καὶ κρίνειν Or.*Jo*.2.6(4; p.60.25; M.14.120B); of God's righteousness as absolute, opp. all other righteousness, Gr.Nyss.*hom.1 in Cant*.(M.44.781B); ‡Proc.G.*Pr*.10:3(M.87.1309D); βασιλεία γὰρ θεοῦ...αὐ. Max.*qu.Thal*.(M.90.616B); **2.** of God as absolute righteousness, Evagr.Pont.*ep*.7(M.32.257A); **3.** of Christ, Or.*comm.in Mt*.14.7(p.289.20; M.13.1197B) cit. s. αὐτοβασιλεία; id.*hom.15.6 in Jer*.(p.130.12; M.13.436C); id.*fr.in Pr*.5:1(M.17.153B); ἡ γὰρ αὐ. ἡ οὐσιώδης Χριστός ἐστιν id.*Jo*.6.6(3; p.115.2; M.14.212B); Ath.*gent*.46(M.25.93C); ὁ δὲ θεὸς λόγος αὐ. ὢν...ἐγένετο ἡμῖν δικαιοσύνη ‡Ath.*dial.Trin*.5.25(M.28.1277B); Evagr.Pont.*ep*.9(M.32.261B); Chrys.*hom.11.3 in 2Cor*.(10.517E); **4.** of H. Ghost as partaking of essence of God, Bas.*Spir*.48(3.40D; M.32.156B).

αὐτοδόξα, ἡ, *absolute glory*, Acac.Caes.*fr.Marcell*.(p.262.13; M.42.392C); of God, Epiph.*haer*.76.35(p.385.14; M.42.588C); Areth.*Apoc*.45(M.106.701D) cit. s. αὐτοδύναμις.

***αὐτοδοξάζομαι**, *be absolute glory*, of God θεότητος...ἐχούσης...τὸ αὐτοδεδοξασμένον Epiph.*haer*.69.74(p.222.14; M.42.321D).

***αὐτοδοξία, ἡ**, *absolute glory*, Epiph.*haer*.72.9(M.42.393C; conj. αὐτοδόξαν p.263.18).

αὐτοδουλεία, ἡ, *voluntary servitude*, Mart.Ant.*pan*.6(M.47.xlviii).

αὐτοδύναμις, ἡ, *absolute power, power itself*; **1.** in gen., Dion.Ar.*d.n*.4.20(M.3.747C); πάντα γὰρ τὰ ἐκ θεοῦ, καὶ μετὰ θεόν, πάσχει τῷ κινεῖσθαι, ὡς μὴ ὄντα αὐτοκίνησις, ἢ αὐ. Max.*Pyrr*.(M.91.352A) = Jo.D.*f.o*.3.15(M.94.1061C); Trin. δύναμις γὰρ οὐκ ἀδυναμίαν γεννᾷ, ἀλλὰ αὐτοδύναμιν Acac.Caes.*fr.Marcell*.(p.262.13; M.42.392C); **2.** attribute of God θεοῦ μὲν οὐσίαν τίς ἐστιν οὐ γινώσκομεν· τὴν δὲ αὐτοσοφίαν καὶ τὴν αὐ. ἐν νῷ λαβόντες, τὸν θεὸν ἀνειληφέναι τῇ διανοίᾳ πιστεύομεν Gr.Nyss.*hex*.(M.44.72C); **3.** of God as absolute power ἐκ τῆς αὐ. ἡ τοῦ θεοῦ δύναμις ἐξεφάνη Bas.*Eun*.2.27(1.264B; M.29.636A); Dion.Ar.*d.n*.11.6(M.3.953C); οὐ γὰρ διαστολὴ θεοῦ καὶ τῆς δυνάμεως αὐτοῦ. αὐ. γὰρ καὶ αὐτοδόξα ὁ θεός Areth.*Apoc*.45(M.106.701D); of God as transcending αὐτοδύναμις, Dion.Ar.*d.n*.8.2(889D); **4.** of Christ αὐ. θεοῦ Or.*Jo*.1.33(38; p.43.9; M.14.89B); αὐ. ἰδία τοῦ πατρός ἐστιν Ath.*gent*.46(M.25.93C); Gr.Nyss.*or.catech*.8(p.50.22; M.45.40A); Epiph.*haer*.77.35(p.447.16; M.42.693B).

***αὐτοδύναμος**, *possessing absolute power*; of Christ, Cyr.*apol.Thdt*.4(6.215A; αὐτοδύναμιν p.121.12); of H. Ghost, Gr.Naz.*or*.41.9(M.36.441B).

***αὐτοειδοποιός**, *having absolutely the power of forming*; as subst., of God ὁ θεὸς...αὐ. καὶ αὐτοαγαθὸν οὐσιῶδες Max.*schol.d.n*.4.20(M.4.277C).

αὐτοεῖδος, τό, *pure form*, Max.*schol.d.n*.6.3(M.4.340B).

***αὐτόειμι**, *be in oneself, be self-existent*, of Christ εἰκὼν ζῶσα, μᾶλλον δὲ αὐτοοῦσα ζωή Bas.*Eun*.1.18(1.230A; M.29.552C); of God, Dion.Ar.*d.n*.6.1(M.3.856B); *ib*.11 tit.(948C); *ib*.11.6(953D).

***αὐτοειρήνη, ἡ**, *principle of peace*; of God, Dion.Ar.*d.n*.4.21(M.3.721D); *ib*.11.2(949C); Zach.Mit.*opif*.(M.85.1069B).

αὐτοενέργεια, ἡ, *self-activity*; ref. Christ's Resurrection, Leont.H.*Nest*.1.19(M.86.1476C).

αὐτοενέργητος, v. αὐτενέργητος.

***αὐτοένωσις, ἡ**, *principle of unity*, Dion.Ar.*d.n*.5.5(M.3.820B).

αὐτοέπαινος, *intrinsically praiseworthy* αὐ. ἐστιν ὁ κύριος καὶ ἐπαινούμενος ὑπὸ τοῦ Ἰσραήλ, ἢ αὐτὸς ἔπαινος ὤν Or.*Ps*.21:4(p.477); id.*sel.in Ps*.21:4(M.12.1253B).

αὐτοεπιστήμη, ἡ, *knowledge itself, absolute knowledge*; of the Creator, Max.*ambig*.(M.91.1177A); of Christ, Proc.G.*Is*.52:13–15(M.87.2517A).

***αὐτοετεροούσιος**, (sic) emphatic for ἑτεροούσιος, Val.Apoll.*apol*.3(p.288.23; better written *divisim* as M.86.1953D).

***αὐτόζηλος, ὁ**, *absolute jealousy*; of Devil and his angels, Or.*sel.in Ezech*.8:3(M.13.796D).

***αὐτοζωή, ἡ**, *principle of life, absolute life, life in itself*; **1.** in gen. πᾶν γὰρ τὸ δι' ἕτερον ζῶν αὐ. εἶναι οὐ δύναται Evagr.Pont.*ep*.4(M.32.253A); οὐ γὰρ αὐ. ὁ ἄνθρωπος, ἀλλὰ ζωῆς δεκτικός Chrys.*hom.5.1 in Jo*.(8.36B); **2.** of God ἐξαίρετον γάρ τι ἐχρῆν παραστῆσαι ἐν τῷ λεγομένῳ περὶ τοῦ θεοῦ καὶ πατρὸς τῶν ὅλων, ὡς ζῶντος παρά τε τὴν αὐ. καὶ τὰ μετέχοντα αὐτῆς Or.*comm.in Mt*.12.9(p.83.24; M.13.996B); Eus.*e.th*.2.14(p.115.17; M.24.928D) cit. s. αὐτοαγαθός; ἡ μὲν θεότης αὐ. ἐστι Gr.Nyss.*Eun*.8(2 p.201.8; M.45.797A); αὐ. κατὰ φύσιν ἐστὶν ὁ πατήρ Cyr.*thes*.32(M.75.549B; αὐτὸ ζωὴ 5^1.323B); μίαν δὲ τῆς τριάδος τὴν φύσιν ἀσώματον, ἄτρεπτον...αὐ. Thdt.*Trin*.28(M.75.1188C); αὐτόφως, αὐτοαγαθότητα, αὐ. ‡Cyr.*Trin*.7(6^3.8C; M.77.1132B) = Jo.D.*f.o*.1.8(M.94.808D); of God as transcending life itself καὶ ἔστιν αὐτὸ καθ' αὐτὸ τὸ εἶναι πρεσβύτερον τοῦ αὐ. εἶναι Dion.Ar.*d.n*.5.5(M.3.820A); ζῆν εἴ τις φαίη τὴν αὐ. ... οὐκ ὀρθῶς ἐρεῖ *ib*.2.8(645D); τῆς αὐ. ἐστιν ἡ ὑπὲρ ζωὴν ἡ θεία ζωή *ib*.6.1(856B); **3.** of Christ δένδρον ζωῆς ὁ Χριστός ἐστιν...καὶ ὡς αὐ. τοὺς τῆς γνώσεως καὶ ἀρετῆς καρποὺς ὡς δένδρον ἐβλάστησεν Hipp.*fr.17 in Pr*.(p.162.25); ὁ...τοῦ θεοῦ λόγος, αὐ. τυγχάνων Eus.*d.e*.4.13(p.173.3; M.22.288C); ὁ...πατὴρ τὸν υἱὸν ὑφίστη, αὐ. ὄντα ζωοποιὸν τῶν ὅλων id.*e.th*.1.8(p.66.33; M.24.837D); ὁ μὲν κύριός ἐστιν ἡ αὐ. καὶ ἀρχηγὸς τῆς ζωῆς Ath.*ep.Serap*.1.23(M.26.584B); *ib*.4.20(669B); ‡Ath.*Ar*.4.32(p.81.8; M.26.517A); αὐ. εἶναι τὸν λόγον οἴεσθαι, οὐ ζωῆς μετουσίαν Gr.Nyss.*or.catech*.1(p.9.15; M.45.13D); Chrys.*hom.14.1 in Jo*.(8.78B) cit. s. αὐτοπηγή; εἰ μὲν γὰρ ζῇ καὶ δίχα τοῦ πατρός, ὡς ὑπάρχων οὐσιωδῶς καὶ αὐ., οὐκέτι ζῇ διὰ τὸν πατέρα, τουτέστι, διὰ τὴν ἐκ πατρὸς μετάληψιν Cyr.*Jo*.4.3(4.370C); ref. eucharist μεταλαμβάνωμεν ἡμεῖς τῆς αὐ. σῶμα †Cyr.*hom.div*.10(5^2.378D).

***αὐτοζωία, ἡ**, *absolute life, self-originate life* ζωὴ ὁ θεός ἐστι· τῆς δὲ τρισσοφαοῦς αὐ. ἡ πηγή Or.*exp.in Pr*.16(M.17.196B).

***αὐτοζώωσις, ἡ**, *absolute principle of bringing to life*, Dion.Ar.*d.n*.11.6(M.3.956A) cit. s. αὐτοθέωσις; Max.*schol.d.n*.6(M.4.401C).

***αὐτοθαῦμα, τό**, *principle of wonder*; of God, Epiph.*haer*.76.35(p.385.15; M.42.588C).

***αὐτοθέλημα, τό**, *absolute will*, of God αὐτοαίσθησις γάρ ἐστι καὶ αὐ. Epiph.*haer*.76.37(p.388.31; M.42.593C).

***αὐτοθέλητος**, *following one's own will, supreme*; of God, Agath.*v.Gr.Ill*.94.

***αὐτοθεμέθλος**, *founded on itself*, Nonn.*par.Jo*.14:23(M.43.872A).

αὐτόθεος, *very God, God in his very essence*; **1.** of Father in contradistinction to Son τότε μὲν αὐ. ὁ θεός ἐστι, διόπερ καὶ ὁ σωτήρ φησιν...ἵνα γινώσκωσι σὲ τὸν μόνον ἀληθινὸν θεόν· πᾶν δὲ τὸ παρὰ τὸ αὐ. μετοχῇ τῆς ἐκείνου θεότητος θεοποιούμενον οὐχ 'ὁ θεὸς' ἀλλὰ 'θεὸς' κυριώτερον ἂν λέγοιτο, οὗ πάντως ὁ πρωτότοκος πάσης κτίσεως...ἐστὶ τιμιώτερος Or.*Jo*.2.2(p.54.30; M.14.109A); ὡς γὰρ αὐ. καὶ ἀληθινὸς θεὸς ὁ πατὴρ πρὸς εἰκόνα καὶ εἰκόνας τῆς εἰκόνος...οὕτως ὁ αὐτολόγος πρὸς τὸν ἐν ἑκάστῳ λόγον. ἀμφότερα γὰρ πηγῆς ἔχει χώραν, ὁ μὲν πατὴρ θεότητος, ὁ δὲ υἱὸς λόγου *ib*.2.3(p.55.18; 109C); δέον...τὸ ἐπέκεινα τῶν ὅλων ὁμολογεῖν αὐ. ... τὸν δὲ τούτου μονογενῆ υἱὸν...καὶ αὐτὸν θεὸν καὶ νοῦν...αὐτοῦ τε τοῦ καλοῦ καὶ ἀγαθοῦ εἰκόνα Eus.*e.th*.2.14(p.115.16; M.24.928D); **2.** neut. as subst., of essential nature of Father φύσις...ἀτελευτήτως ἔχουσα τὸ ἀξίωμα, οὐ διά τι ἕτερον, ἀλλὰ διὰ τὸ αὐ. καὶ αὐτοΐδιον Epiph.*haer*.76.21(p.368.8; M.42.557C); **3.** of Son, Eus.*h.e*.10.4.16(M.20.856B; *GCS* αὐτὸν θεόν); ὁ θεὸς λόγος...αὐ. ὤν Epiph.*haer*.77.35(p.447.16; M.42.693B); id.*fid*.17(p.518.24; M.42.817A).

αὐτοθεότης, ἡ, *Godhead itself, absolute principle of deity*, Epiph.*haer*.74.11(M.42.496D; p.329.16 ἡ αὐτὴ θεότης cf.id.*anc*.6(p.13.12)); αὐτοεῖναι καὶ αὐτοζωὴν καὶ αὐ. φαμεν Dion.Ar.*d.n*.11.6(M.3.953D); Max.*schol.d.n*.1.1(M.4.188A).

***αὐτοθερμότης, ἡ**, *principle of heat*, Evagr.Pont.*ep*.4(M.32.253A).

***αὐτοθέωσις, ἡ**, *deification itself* τὰς ἐκδιδομένας ἐκ θεοῦ...δυνάμεις, τὴν αὐτοουσίωσιν, αὐτοζώωσιν, αὐ., ὧν τὰ ὄντα οἰκείως ἑαυτοῖς μετέχοντα, καὶ ὄντα καὶ ζῶντα καὶ ἔνθεα Dion.Ar.*d.n*.11.6(M.3.956A); Max.*schol.d.n*.11.6(M.4.401C).

***αὐτοθήριον, τό**, *very beast*, Chrys.*hom.2.6 in Rom*.(9.445B); id.*ep*.3.11(3.564E).

***αὐτόθροος**, *speaking for oneself*, Nonn.*par.Jo*.5:31(M.43.789C).

***αὐτοϊσχύς, ἡ**, *very strength*; of God, Or.*sel.in Ps*.17:2(M.12.1224C).

***αὐτοκάθαρσις, ἡ**, *principle of purification*; of Christ, Gr.Naz.*or*.40.29(M.36.400C).

αὐτόκακον, τό, *evil in itself, absolute principle of evil* τὸ μὲν αὐ. οὔτε ὂν οὔτε ὄντων ποιητικόν Dion.Ar.*d.n*.4.20(M.3.717C); *ib*.(721A); Max.*schol.d.n*.4.19(M.4.273C).

***αὐτοκαλλοιός**, error for αὐτοκαλλοποιός.

***αὐτοκαλλοποιός**, *absolutely beautifying*, Dion.Ar.*d.n*.11.6(M.3.956B reading αὐτοκαλλοιόν).

αὐτόκαλος, *absolutely beautiful, beautiful in itself*; of God, Eus.*e.th*.2.14(p.115.17; M.24.928D) cit. s. αὐτοαγαθός; of God's wisdom, id.*d.e*.4.2(p.152.1; M.22.253A).

αὐτοκατάκριτος, *self-condemned*; **1.** in gen. ἀνάλγητός ἐστιν ἄφρων φιλόσοφος αὐ. ἐξηγητής Jo.Clim.*scal*.18(M.88.932B); **2.** of Jews, through their disbelief in Christ's Resurrection, Chrys.*hom.43.2 in Mt*.(7.459D); through their rejection of Christ, ref. Mt. 21:31, *ib*.67.2(664C); οὐδὲ γὰρ οὕτως ἀφ' ἑαυτοῦ λέγοντι ἐπείθοντο, ὡς αὐ. τὴν ψῆφον εἶχον id.*hom.29.3 in Jo*.(8.168E); Cyr.*Jo*.3.4(4.286C); **3.** of heretics ὅσοι δὲ ἀφίστανται τῆς ἐκκλησίας καὶ τούτοις τοῖς γραώδεσι μύθοις πείθονται, ἀληθῶς αὐ. Iren.*haer*.1.16.3(M.7.663B); αὐ. ἐστιν αὐτῶν ἡ καρδία Ath.*Ar*.3.47(M.26.424A); **4.** of wicked in gen., who are judged by themselves ἤγουν ἐν κρίσει οὐκ ἀναστήσονται· ἀλλ' ἀναστήσονται μέν, οὐ κριθήσονται δέ, τυγχάνοντες αὐ.· ὁ γὰρ μὴ πιστεύων εἰς ἐμέ, φησίν, ἤδη κέκριται Didym.*Ps*.1:5(M.39.1160B).

***αὐτοκατακρίτως**, *as condemning oneself* τίς δὲ κοσμήσει τὸν αὐ. ἑαυτὸν διαστρέφοντα; Epiph.*haer*.42.11(p.153.26; M.41.772A) citing Eccl.1:15.

***αὐτοκατάρα, ἡ**, *principle of cursing*, Gr.Naz.*or*.37.1(M.36.284A).

***αὐτοκαταφύσιν**, *by very nature*, Cyr.*hom.pasch*.13(5².184D); of Christ ἡ αὐ. ζωή Sev.Ant.ap.*cat.Ac*.8:33(p.145.30).

***αὐτοκατήγορος**, *self-condemning*, CCP(518)*ep*.(*ACO* 3 p.64.21; H.2.1324E).

αὐτοκέλευστος, **1.** *self-bidden*, hence *self-appointed* κοίρανον αὐ., ὃν οὐκ ἐστέψατο Ῥώμη Nonn.*par.Jo*.19:15(M.43.901A); **2.** *unbidden, free, acting as free agent, spontaneous*; of Christ, *ib*.5:15(783A); *ib*. 18:4(889B); of H. Ghost θεῖον μένος, αὐ. Gr.Naz.*carm*.1.1.3.8(M.37.408A); ἔχεις αὐ. ἱερεῖον, τί τὸν δεσμώτην ταῦρον ἀνανεύοντα συμποδίζεις; Chrys.*pan.Rom*.2.3(2.621D); αὐ. ἐγείρει γνῶσις Cyr.*glaph.Gen*.1(1.15E); αὐ. ... βουλαῖς id.*Am*.2(3.251B); Nil.*Magn*.62(M.79.1053B); **3.** *voluntary* ζητοῦσιν μὲν γὰρ αὐτὸν πιάσαι...ὡς ἐθελούσιον καὶ αὐ. τὴν ἐπὶ τοῖς ἐλέγχοις πονησάμενοι σιωπήν Cyr.*Jo*.5.1(4.451C); *ib*. (455A); **4.** *voluntarily accepted* πάντα γὰρ δουλεύει προθύμως τῇ ἐπιθυμίᾳ ἑκουσίως τυραννούμενα...ἐθελουσίῳ καὶ αὐ. ἀνάγκῃ Nil.*narr*. 2(M.79.601B).

αὐτοκέραστος, *undiluted*; met., *with absolute power*, *Orac.Sib*. 8.135.

***αὐτοκέφαλος**, *autonomous*, of churches independent of patriarchal jurisdiction περιγεγόνασι Κύπριοι τὸ αὐ. εἶναι τὴν κατὰ αὐτοὺς μητρόπολιν, καὶ μὴ τελεῖν ὑπὸ Ἀντιόχειαν Thdr.Lect.*h.e*.2.2(M.86.184C); list of αὐ. ἀρχιεπισκόπων, ‡Epiph.*patr*.(p.535; M.86.789B).

αὐτοκίνησις, ἡ, *essential movement, principle of motion* ὁ ἐν ἀνθρώποις λόγος, ἰδίως μὲν ἀνούσιος ὢν...ὅλον δὲ αὐ. ... τυγχάνων Eus.*d.e*.5.5(M.22.377B; p.228.28 αὐτὸ κίνησις); πάντα γὰρ τὰ ἐκ θεοῦ, καὶ μετὰ θεόν, πάσχει τῷ κινεῖσθαι, ὡς μὴ ὄντα αὐ. Max.*Pyrr*.(M.91.352A) = Jo.D.*f.o*.3.15(M.94.1061C); Max.*ambig*.(M.91.1073B).

***αὐτοκινητικός**, *self-moving*, Dion.Ar.*d.n*.4.17(M.3.713D).

αὐτοκίνητος, *self-moved, self-determined*; **1.** of God ἐρωτικὴν κίνησιν, ἁπλῆν, αὐ., αὐτενέργητον, προοῦσαν ἐν τἀγαθῷ, καὶ ἐκ τἀγαθοῦ τοῖς οὖσιν ἐκβλυζομένην Dion.Ar.*d.n*.4.14(M.3.712C); μίαν τινὰ δύναμιν, ἁπλῆν, αὐ., αὐτοενέργητον...γνῶσιν πασῶν γνώσεων ὑπάρχουσαν id.*ep*.9.1(M.3.1104C); of Gnost. demiurge ἅτε γὰρ Δημιουργὸς ἀδήλως κινούμενος ὑπὸ τῆς Σοφίας οἴεται αὐ. εἶναι Clem.*exc.Thdot*.53(p.124.24; M.9.685A); of H. Ghost φανεροῦν αὐτοῦ τὴν ἐνέργειαν, οὐ πνοὴν ἄσθματος ἐννοοῦμεν·...ἀλλὰ δύναμιν οὐσιώδη αὐτὴν ἐφ' ἑαυτῆς...θεωρουμένην...καθ' ὑπόστασιν οὖσαν, προαιρετικήν, αὐ., ἐνεργόν Gr.Nyss.*or.catech*.2(p.15.7; M.45.17C) = ‡Cyr.*Trin*.6(6³.7B; M.77.1129B); **2.** of soul τί γὰρ λείπει τῇ ψυχῇ...πρὸς τὸ εἶναι οὐσίαν ἀσώματον αὐ.; τοῦτο γὰρ αὐτῆς δηλοῖ καὶ τὸ ἀθάνατον Leont.B.*Nest.et Eut*.1(M.86.1281B); ὥσπερ ἡ ψυχὴ αὐ. ἐστιν, οὐδέποτε τοῦ εἶναι διαλείπει· ἀκολουθεῖ γὰρ τῷ αὐ., τὸ ἀεικίνητον εἶναι Max.*anim*.(M.91.357D); Christol., of Christ's human soul, Apoll.*fr*.74(p.222.9)ap.Gr.Nyss.*Apoll*.38(M.45.1209C) cit. s. νοῦς; ἡ σὰρξ ἑτεροκίνητος οὖσα...εἰς τὸ γενέσθαι ζῶον ἐντελὲς συντεθειμένη, πρὸς ἑνότητα τῷ ἡγεμονικῷ συνῆλθεν καὶ συνετέθη πρὸς τὸ οὐράνιον ἡγεμονικόν...οὕτω γὰρ ἓν ζῶον ἐκ κινουμένου καὶ κινητικοῦ συνίστατο καὶ οὐ δύο ἢ ἐκ δύο τελείων καὶ αὐ. *ib*.107(p.232.17)ap.Justn.*monoph*.(p.17.5; M.86.1124A); οὐδὲ τοῦτο συνιδεῖν ἠδυνήθησαν...ὅτι ὁ μὲν θεῖος νοῦς αὐ. ἐστι καὶ ταυτοκίνητος, ἄτρεπτος γάρ, ὁ δὲ ἀνθρώπινος αὐ. μέν, οὐ ταυτοκίνητος δέ, τρεπτὸς γάρ, καὶ ὅτιπερ ἀτρέπτῳ νῷ τρεπτὸς οὐ μίγνυται νοῦς εἰς ἑνὸς ὑποκειμένου σύστασιν *ib*.151(p.247.30)ap.*Doct.Patr*.41(p.307.12); **3.** of material things ἐν ἑαυτοῖς δὲ ἔχει τὴν αἰτίαν τοῦ κινεῖσθαι ζῶα καὶ φυτὰ καὶ...ὅσα ὑπὸ φύσεως ἢ ψυχῆς συνέχεται· ἐξ ὧν φασιν εἶναι καὶ τὰ μέταλλα, πρὸς δὲ τούτοις καὶ τὸ πῦρ αὐ. ἐστι Or.*princ*.3.2(p.196.10; M.11.249B).

αὐτοκινήτως, *of one's own initiative*, Dion.Ar.*c.h*.6.1(M.3.200C); οὐ γὰρ αὐ. οἱ ἅγιοί τι διαπράττονται, ἀλλ' ἐκ πνεύματος ἁγίου κινούμενοι Leont.N.*serm*.1(M.93.1576A).

***αὐτόκληρος**, *choosing one's own lot*, Cyr.*Jo*.3.4(4.286C).

αὐτόκλητος, **1.** *self-invited, unbidden* ηὐχόμην οὕτως ἔχειν τοῦ σώματος, ὥστε παρεῖναι ὑμῖν καὶ αὐ. Gr.Naz.*ep*.221(M.37.361A); Antip.Bost.*Jo.Bapt*.10(M.85.1772D); **2.** *of one's own accord, unprompted*, Chrys.*sac*.4.2(p.105.5; 1.405D); id.*hom.35.2 in Jo*.(8.203E); Cyr.*Os*.3(3.15A); id.*hom.pasch*.11.8(5².160B); Bas.Sel.*or*.10.2(M.85.141C); οὐ γὰρ αὐ. προσέδραμε τῇ μαρτυρίᾳ Ammon.*Jo*.5:33(M.85.1432A); **3.** *self-induced, voluntary* αὐ. ὥσπερ τῆς ἰδίας κεφαλῆς κατέχουσα δίκην Cyr.*glaph.Dt*.(1.416A); id.*Os*.132(3.166B); id.*Jo*.1.7(4.61A).

αὐτοκρατής, *independent*, of God τὸ διὰ πάντων πρὸς τὸ θεῖον ὡμοιωμένον ἔδει πάντως ἔχειν...τὸ αὐ. καὶ ἀδέσποτον Gr.Nyss.*or.catech*.5(p.27.1; M.45.24D); Jo.D.*f.o*.1.14(M.94.860A); of human free will, Clem.*fr*.40(p.220.17; M.9.752B)ap.Max.*opusc*.(M.91.276C) cit. s. αὐτεξουσιότης; τὸ ἀδέσποτον καὶ αὐ. τοῦ ἐναρέτου φρονήματος Gr.Nyss.*hom.15 in Cant*.(M.44.1113A); τὸ αὐ. τε καὶ αὐτεξούσιον τῆς ἀνθρωπίνης προαιρέσεως id.*hom.opif*.16(M.44.185A); πεποίηταί γε μὴν [sc. ἄνθρωπος] αὐ. καὶ ἐλεύθερος Cyr.*Juln*.8(6².277C); αὐ. ὢν τῆς ἑαυτοῦ προαιρέσεως καὶ ὥσπερ ἀδέσποτος Proc.G.*Gen*.1:26(M.87.117A).

***αὐτοκρατητικός**, *having authority over*, Dion.Ar.*c.h*.15.2(M.3.329B).

[*]αὐτοκρατορέω, *become emperor*, Thphn.*chron*.p.346(M.108.833A).

αὐτοκρατορικός, **1.** *imperial*, Eus.*Is*.6:11(M.24.129D); **2.** *ruling with absolute power* αὐ. τις αὐθεντεία Gr.Nyss.*hom.10 in Cant*.(M.44.980D); Isid.Pel.*epp*.5.255(M.78.1485B); of God the Son τὴν αὐθεντικὴν καὶ αὐ. ἐξουσίαν Gr.Nyss.*Eun*.2(2 p.351.16; M.45.529A); **3.** *in one's own power, as a matter of free will*, of Christ αὐ. ἐξουσίᾳ καὶ σὺ φύσεως ἀνάγκῃ διαζεύγνυσι τὴν ψυχὴν ἐκ τοῦ σώματος id.*res*.1(M.46.612B); in gen. αἵρεσιν...δεδόσθαι τοῖς ἀνθρώποις αὐ. παρὰ τοῦ κυρίου Clem.*str*.2.4(p.119.5; M.8.944A); μεταβάλλει πᾶν τὸ ἐνάρετον εἰς ἀμείνους οἰκήσεις, τῆς μεταβολῆς αἰτίαν τὴν αἵρεσιν τῆς γνώσεως ἔχον, ἣν αὐ. ἐκέκτητο ἡ ψυχή *ib*.7.2(p.10.2; M.9.416B); τῷ αὐ. καὶ αὐθαιρέτῳ κρίνοντι προθέσει Meth.*symp*.3.14(p.44.13; M.18.85A); ζῶα προαιρετικά, λελυμέναις καὶ αὐ. ταῖς ὁρμαῖς κεχρημένα Bas.*hex*.6.7(1.56C; M.29.132D); ‡Nil.*narr*.2(M.79.601B); ἡ τροπὴ οὐ περὶ αὐτὴν τῆς ψυχῆς ὑπάρχει τὴν οὐσίαν, ἀλλὰ κατὰ τὴν κίνησιν τὴν ἐφ' ἡμῖν, τῷ αὐ. θελήματι συμφερομένη Max.*ep*.6(M.91.432B).

αὐτοκρατορικῶς, **1.** *with absolute authority* αὐθεντικῶς καὶ αὐ. τοῦ πνεύματος προστάττοντος ‡Caes.Naz.*dial*.42(M.38.909); **2.** *as a matter of free will* τούτου δὲ τοῦ αὐτεξουσίου κινήματος αὐ. πρὸς τὸ δοκοῦν ἡμᾶς ἀγαγόντος Gr.Nyss.*hom.2 in Cant*.(M.44.796D).

αὐτοκράτωρ, **1.** *ruling with absolute power*; of emperor, Arist.*apol*.proem.; Just.*1apol*.1.1(M.6.328A); id.*2apol*.2.8(M.6.445A); Athenag.*leg*.proem.(M.6.889A); *M.Perp*.6(p.71.16); Eus.*h.e*.2.8.1(M.20.156C); of God, *A.(Pass.)Andr*.13(p.31.10); αὐ. γὰρ ἡμεῖς τὸν θεὸν καὶ κύριον αὐτὸν ἑαυτοῦ εἰδότες Ath.*syn*.26.8(p.253.26; M.26.733A); **2.** *controlling one's own actions*; **a.** of man, *possessed of free will* αὐτεξούσιος γὰρ καὶ αὐ. ὁ ἄνθρωπος, καὶ αὐτοδέσποτον βούλησιν καὶ αὐτοπροαίρετον πρὸς τὴν αἵρεσιν τοῦ καλοῦ λαβών Meth.*res*.1.38(p.280.10; M.41.1105A); Eus.ap.Leont.et Jo.*sacr*.2.3(M.86.2061B); **b.** of faculties of man, Clem.*fr*.40(p.220.15; M.9.752A)ap.Max.*opusc*.(M.91.276C) cit. s. θέλησις; πολλοὶ δὲ ἐνταῦθα πνεῦμα ἡγεμονικὸν ἐκάλεσαν τὸν αὐ. λογισμόν Or.*Ps*.50:14(p.52); ἡμέτερον προκρίνειν γὰρ τὰ κρείττω καὶ προτάσσειν πρὸ τῶν γηγενῶν, αὐ. καὶ αὐτεξούσιον τὸν λογισμὸν εἰληφότας καὶ πάσης ἀνάγκης ἐκτὸς εἰς τὸ αὐτοδεσπότως αἱρεῖσθαι τὰ ἀρέσκοντα οὐ δουλεύοντας εἱμαρμένῃ καὶ τύχαις Meth.*symp*.8.13(p.98.17; M.18.161A); τοῦτο γέρας ἐξαίρετον παρὰ θεοῦ λαβοῦσα [sc. ἡ ψυχή], ἐλευθέρα καὶ αὐ. τυγχάνει, τῆς οἰκείας ὁρμῆς τὸ κριτήριον εἰς ἑαυτὴν ἀναδεδεγμένη Eus.*p.e*.6.6(250A; M.21.425A); πνεῦμα ἡγεμονικὸν τὸν αὐ. λογισμὸν ἐκάλεσε Thdt.*Ps*.50:14(1.941); τὸν αὐ. νοῦν τῶν παθῶν ἡνίοχον id.*provid*.1(4.485); **c.** of the φιλόσοφος βασιλεύς as exercising self-control, Eus.*l.C*.5(p.204.15; M.20.1336C).

***αὐτοκρεμαστός**, *hung by oneself*, of rope by which Judas hanged himself αὐτοκρεμαστοῖς ἐν βρόχοις ἠρτημένος ‡Gr.Naz.*Chr.pat*.1428(M.38.250A).

***αὐτόκρισις, ἡ**, *principle of judgement*; of Christ, Or.*Jo*.2.6(p.60.25,30; M.14.120B).

αὐτόκτητος, *made one's own possession* οἱ ἅγιοι οὐκ εἶχον γῆς οὐδὲ τὸ τυχὸν μέτρον εἰς αὐθεντίας λόγον αὐ. Nil.*Magn*.18(M.79.993A); θεὸς δὲ τὴν οἰκείαν δόξαν ἔχων αὐ. *ib*.46(1028B).

***αὐτόκτιστος**, *self-originated*, Chrys.*hom.7.1 in 1Cor*.(10.51A).

***αὐτοκτονία, ἡ**, *suicide*, *Hom.Clem*.12.14.

***αὐτοκύριος**, *very Lord*; of H. Ghost, Jo.D.*f.o*.1.13(M.94.856B) citing Gr.Naz.*or*.31.29(p.183.4; M.36.165B) where MSS read αὐτὸ κύριος.

***αὐτοκυρίως**, *in one's own right, independently*, in Eunomian doctrine of Christ ὁ μονογενής,...οὐκ ἔστιν αὐ. ὁ λόγος αὐτοῦ· ἀλλ' ὁ μὲν ἐνδιάθετος λόγος τοῦ θεοῦ...ἐν αὐτῷ κινεῖται Cyr.*Jo*.1.4(4.30B); *ib*. (31B); in orthodox Christology τὸ ζωῆς μετέχον οὐκ αὐ. ἐστὶ ζωή, ἕτερον γάρ τι ὑπάρχον ἐν αὐτῷ φαίνεται· εἰ τοίνυν μεθεκτὸς ὁ υἱὸς τοῖς γενητοῖς ὡς ζωή, ἕτερος ἂν εἴη παρὰ τὰ μετέχοντα αὐτοῦ καὶ ζωῆς δεόμενα ib.1.6(4.52A).

*αὐτολαμπής, who is light itself; of H. Ghost, ‡Jo.D.carm.pent. 112(p.217; M.96.837C).

*αὐτόλεκτος, 1. word for word τὰς αὐ. τῶν γραφῶν προεκθέσεις Geo.Pis.Sev.509(M.92.1660A); 2. spoken by someone in person, Thdr.Stud.epp.1.34(M.99.1025D).

*αὐτολέκτως, in so many words, Thdr.Stud.nativ.BMV 7(M.96.696A).

αὐτολεξεί, = foreg., Just.1apol.32.1(M.6.377B); Eus.d.e.3.7(p.142.4; M.22.240A); ἕκαστος σπεύδει ἃ λέγει δεῖξαι τοὺς πατέρας εἰρηκότας, εἰ καὶ μὴ αὐ., ἀλλὰ δυνάμει †Leont.B.sect.8.5(M.86.1257B); Jo.D.imag.3.11(M.94.1333B).

*αὐτολίθινος, made all of stone, Chrys.hom.54.1 in Ac.(9.405E); id.ep.2.13(3.551E).

*αὐτόλιθος, genuine stone, Chrys.hom.87.1 in Mt.(7.818D, v.l. αὐτὸς λίθος); id.hom.27.3 in 1Cor.(10.245E); Dion.Ar.d.n.1.6(M.3.596C).

*αὐτολογέω, talk about oneself, Or.comm.in Mt.17.1(M.13.1473B; ἀντιλογῆσαι p.576.29).

*αὐτολογία, ἡ, invented story, Jo.Thess.dorm.BMV 1.2(p.378.3).

*αὐτολογιότης, ἡ, principle of reason; of God, Max.schol.c.h.2.3 (M.4.40C).

αὐτολόγος, ὁ, very Word, very Reason, of Christ [sc. Χριστιανοῖς ἐγκαλεῖ ὡς] σοφιζομένοις ἐν τῷ λέγειν τὸν υἱὸν τοῦ θεοῦ εἶναι αὐ.,... ἐπεὶ λόγον ἐπαγγελλόμενοι υἱὸν εἶναι τοῦ θεοῦ ἀποδείκνυμεν οὐ λόγον καθαρὸν καὶ ἅγιον ἀλλὰ ἄνθρωπον ἀτιμότατα ἀπαχθέντα Cels.ap.Or.Cels.2.31(p.158.22; M.11.852A); ὃν μὲν νομίζομεν...ἀρχῆθεν εἶναι θεὸν καὶ υἱὸν θεοῦ, οὗτος ὁ αὐ. [i.e. very reason] ἐστὶ καὶ ἡ αὐτοσοφία καὶ ἡ αὐτοαλήθεια Or.Cels.3.41(p.237.6; 973A); ib.6.47(p.119.13; 1372D); cf.id.princ.2.6.2(p.140.28; M.11.210C); of Christ as αὐ. contrasted with Father as αὐτόθεος, id.Jo.2.3(p.55.20; M.14.109C) cit. s. αὐτόθεος; τίς δὲ τὰς αἰνέσεις τοῦ θεοῦ ποιεῖ ἀκουστάς, ἢ ὁ αὐ.; id.Ps.115:2(p.91); ib.143:5(p.132); αὐ. καὶ αὐτοσοφίαν σοφῶς τὰ πάντα καὶ λογικῶς ὑφιστάμενόν τε καὶ διοικοῦντα Eus.e.th.1.8(p.67.1; M.24.837D); ib.2.14(p.115.17; 928D); τὸν...ζῶντα καὶ ἐνεργῆ θεὸν αὐ. Ath.gent.40(M.25.81A); ib.46(93B); id.inc.54.3(M.25.192C); ‡Ath.Ar.4.2 (p.45.13; M.26.469B); Leont.H.Nest.1.50(M.86.1513A).

αὐτολόχευτος, self-originate; of God, Orac.Sib.1.20; Synes.hymn.6.1(p.39; M.66.1609); Gnost., of heavenly Christ ἐν τῷ ὀγδόῳ οὐρανῷ Χριστὸν ἄλλον αὐ. καὶ Χριστὸν τοῦτον τὸν κατελθόντα Epiph.haer.26.10(p.287.11; M.41.345C); of pagan deities, Cyr.Is.4.2(2.589C).

*αὐτομακαριότης, ἡ, principle of blessedness, Chrys.hom.18.1 in 1Tim.(11.654B).

*αὐτομανία, ἡ, very madness, Chrys.hom.10.6 in Gen.(4.78A).

αὐτόμαρτυς, ὁ, witness in oneself, of Christ αὐ. αὐτὸς εἰσβήσεται λέγων Cyr.Chr.un.(5¹.767D); ἡ ἔκβασις αὐ. εἰσβήσεται id.Abac.1 (3.534A, v.l. μάρτυς Aubert); id.Is.1.2(2.36E).

αὐτοματί, of itself, Meth.symp.2.7(p.24.10; M.18.57B).

αὐτοματισμός, ὁ, self-movement, self-actuation; 1. in gen., Pers. (p.13.9; M.10.101B); 2. of automatic working of natural forces, as explanation of universe ἕτεροι δέ φασιν [sc. Epicureans] αὐ. τῶν πάντων εἶναι Thphl.Ant.Autol.2.4(M.6.1052A); τὸν δὲ θεὸν ὁμολογῶν [sc. Ἐπίκουρος] εἶναι ἀΐδιον...φησι μηδενὸς προνοεῖν, καὶ...πρόνοιαν μὴ εἶναι μηδὲ εἱμαρμένην, ἀλλὰ πάντα κατὰ αὐ. γίνεσθαι Hipp.haer.1.22(p.26.19; M.16.3049B); A.Xanthipp.6(p.61.29); Meth.creat.7 (p.498.1; M.18.340A); Eus.Is.40:12(M.24.369D); Hom.Clem.11.34; ib.15.3; τὸ ποιεῖν καὶ τὸ πάσχειν αὐτοματισμῷ ἀναθετέον Anomoean ap.‡Ath.dial.Trin.2.29(M.28.1201A); οἱ μὲν αὐ., οἱ δ' εἱμαρμένην, οἱ δ' εἰκῇ φέρεσθαι τὰ πάντα ἀπεφήναντο Isid.Pel.epp.4.57(M.78.1108C); Cyr.Juln.2(6².47C); ‡Caes.Naz.dial.113(M.38.993); οἱ Σαδδουκαῖοί εἰσι, κατὰ τὸν τῆς ἀναγωγῆς λόγον, οἱ τὸν αὐ. εἰσάγοντες δαίμονες, ἢ λογισμοί Max.qu.Thal.38(M.90.389B).

*αὐτοματιστής, ὁ, believer in αὐτοματισμός; of Epicureans, Jo.Mal.chron.10 p.251(M.97.381B).

*αὐτοματόκριτος, condemning by itself μετάνοιά ἐστι αὐ. λογισμός Jo.Clim.scal.5(M.88.764B).

αὐτόματος, 1. growing of itself, wild, Bas.hom.1.7(2.6C; M.31.176A); Gr.Nyss.ep.20(M.46.1081B); 2. spontaneous, ref. atomic theory αὐ. τινὶ καὶ ἀπροαιρέτῳ συναχθέντα φιλίᾳ Meth.res.2.10 (p.350.3); Eus.p.e.1.7(21D; M.21.56B); οὐδὲν αὐ. ἐν τῇ γενέσει τῶν ὄντων· ἐπειδὴ ἑαυτὸν ποιῆσαί τις οὐ δύναται. τὸ γὰρ αὐ. ἑαυτῷ μάχεται Ephr.1.124A,B; 3. neut. as subst., as a philosophical principle of the universe, Clem.str.1.19(p.60.14; M.8.809B); τῷ αὐ. ἐπιτρέψαι ὀφείλομεν τὰ κατὰ τὰς προειρημένας [i.e. ποσότητα καὶ ποιότητα] Anomoean ap.‡Ath.dial.Trin.2.23(M.28.1192C); φέρει πολλὰ τὸ αὐ. ἐν τοῖς ἡμετέροις Gr.Naz.or.7.8(M.35.764C); 4. c. prep., adverbially ἀπὸ ταὐτομάτου ‡Just.confut.12(M.6.1516B); ἐξ αὐτομάτου Hom.Clem.9.16.

*αὐτόμελον, τό, troparion having its own rhythm and melody and used as a pattern for imitation, Lit.Chrys.(p.369.7); cf. ἰδιόμελον, προσόμοιον.

*αὐτομεμφής, self-reproaching, Hesych.S.temp.2.39(M.93.1524A).

*αὐτομεμψία, ἡ, self-reproach, Jo.Clim.scal.23(M.88.969D); Hesych.S.temp.1.34(M.93.1492C).

*αὐτομεταβάλλω, emphatic for μεταβάλλω, Val.Apoll.apol.3 (p.288.24; better written divisim as M.86.1953D).

*αὐτομετοχή, ἡ, essential participation, Dion.Ar.d.n.5.5(M.3.820C); ib.12.4(972B).

αὐτόμετρος, measuring in itself; neut. as subst., measure in itself, principle of measure, of God ὁ θεὸς πάντων αὐτοπέρας καὶ αὐ. Max.schol.d.n.4.20(M.4.277C).

αὐτομήτωρ, ἡ, very mother, Val.Gn.ap.Epiph.haer.31.6(M.41.485A; αὐτοπάτορος p.394.1).

*αὐτόμοιος, essentially like, Thdr.Stud.antirr.3.3.8(M.99.424C) cit. s. ἑτεροπροσκύνητος.

αὐτομολέω, 1. desert; 2. go of one's own accord, Chrys.scand.24 (3.513A); Isid.Pel.epp.1.289(M.78.352C); 3. resort to, Clem.prot.10 (p.68.17; M.8.205B); Chrys.hom.69.4 in Mt.(7.686A); id.hom.7.8 in 1Cor.(10.62E); 4. attach oneself to; virtue, Gr.Nyss.v.Macr.(M.46.965C); Chrys.hom.2.6 in 2Cor.4:13(3.275B); vice, Gr.Nyss.or.dom.5(p.102.19; M.44.1184C); Chrys.hom.60.5 in Jo.(8.357E); 5. involve oneself in; guilt, Ath.Ar.1.30(M.26.73B); misfortune, Gr.Nyss.or.catech.22(p.85.9; M.45.60D).

*αὐτομόλης, ὁ, one who performs or contrives miracles independently opp. τῶν...παρὰ θεοῦ θεσπισμάτων κομιστής Cyr.glaph.Ex.2 (1.298C).

αὐτόμολος, 1. going on one's own initiative, Eus.Marcell.2.4 (p.58.19; M.24.824A); Cyr.ador.11(1.376B); Thdt.affect.3(p.99.5; 4.791; v.l. αὐτομόλως); 2. emigrant, Philost.h.e.2.5(M.65.469A); 3. voluntary μάρτυς ὑπὲρ Χριστοῦ αὐ. Thphn.chron.p.349(v.l. αὐτομόλως M.108.840C).

*αὐτονοερός, absolutely spiritual, Eus.h.e.10.4.56(M.20.872A).

*αὐτονόητος, purely conceptual or spiritual, Dion.Ar.d.n.4.16 (M.3.713C).

αὐτόνους, ὁ, absolute intelligence; of God, Eus.e.th.2.14(p.115.16; M.24.928D); id.p.e.7.15(327A; M.21.552C); of Christ, id.d.e.4.2(p.151.32; M.22.253A); Epiph.haer.77.35(p.447.16; M.42.693B).

*αὐτοξηρότης, ἡ, absolute dryness, Tit.Bost.Man.2.30(M.18.1192B).

αὐτοομοιότης, ἡ, principle of resemblance, Dion.Ar.d.n.5.5(M.3.820A); ὁ θεός ἐστιν αὐτῆς τῆς αὐ. ὑποστάτης ib.9.6(913D).

*αὐτοόμοούσιος, (sic) emphatic for ὁμοούσιος, Val.Apoll.apol.3 (p.288.23; better written divisim as M.86.1953D).

αὐτοουσία, ἡ, self-existence, of God αὐ. ἐστὶν ὁ θεὸς πατὴρ καὶ ὁ υἱὸς καὶ ἅγιον πνεῦμα Epiph.haer.76.46(p.400.5; M.42.613B); ‡Cyr.Trin.7(6².8C; M.77.1132B); ἡ θεότης οὐκ αὐ. ἐστὶ τοῦ θεοῦ, ἀλλὰ τῆς οὐσίας δόξα Max.schol.e.h.4.11(M.4.157D); of Son, argument that εἰ οὐσίας ἐστὶν εἰκών, οὐκέτι αὐ. δύναται εἶναι Marcell.fr.86 ap.Epiph.haer.72.6(p.261.3; M.42.389C); οὐχ οἷά τις πάλιν ἡ παρ' ἡμῖν εἰκών, ἕτερον μὲν ἔχουσα τὸ κατ' οὐσίαν ὑποκείμενον, ἕτερον δὲ τὸ εἶδος, ἀλλ' ὅλον αὐτὸ εἶδος ὤν, καὶ αὐτοουσίᾳ τῷ πατρὶ ἀφομοιούμενος Eus.d.e.5.1(p.213.35; M.22.356A); εἰ τῇ τοῦ γεννήματος οὐσίᾳ συνεμφαίνεται ὡς αἰτία ἡ ἀγέννητος ὑπόστασις, κατὰ πάσης αἰτίας τὸ ἀπαράλλακτον ἔχουσα, αὐ. ἐστὶν ἀσύγκριτος Aët.synt.ap.Epiph.haer.76.12(p.358.5; M.42.541D); cf.Anomoean ap.‡Ath.dial.Trin.2.25(M.28.1196B).

*αὐτοούσιος, self-existent, Acac.Caes.fr.Marcell.(p.262.15; M.42.392C).

*αὐτοουσιώδης, self-existent, of Christ αὐ. ἀλήθεια Andr.Caes.Apoc.8(M.106.245B).

*αὐτοουσίωσις, ἡ, actual effecting of existence; of God, Dion.Ar.d.n.11.6(M.3.956A) cit. s. αὐτοθέωσις.

αὐτοπαγής, self-formed αὐ. βροτὸς ἦλθε [sc. Χριστός] Gr.Naz.carm.1.1.9.69(M.37.462A).

*αὐτοπαθέω, suffer in one's own person, Hom.Clem.19.19.

*αὐτοπαράκλητος, offering assistance of one's own accord, Chrys.ep.151(3.688A).

*αὐτοπάρακτος, self-originate εἰ ἄναρχος καὶ ἀΐδιός ἐστι θεός, οὔτε αὐ. ἐστιν οὔτε ἑτεροπάρακτος· ὁ γὰρ ἁπλῶς αὐ. οὐδενὶ λόγῳ ἐστὶν ἀΐδιος καὶ ἄναρχος ‡Just.qu.Chr.3.1(M.6.1432B); ib.3.5(1440B,C); οὐδὲν διαφέρει αὐ. τοῦ αὐτογενοῦς ib.(1441B).

***αὐτοπαράκτως**, *as being self-originate*, ‡Just.*qu.Chr.*3.5(M.6.1440C).

***αὐτοπαραξία, ἡ**, *self-production*, ‡Just.*qu.Chr.*3.5(M.6.1441C).

***αὐτοπάρθενος**, *absolutely virgin*, Eus.*m.P.*5(p.919.11; M.20.1480A).

***αὐτοπαρουσίως**, *in one's own person*; of Christ, *A.Xanthipp.*9 (p.63.26).

***αὐτοπατήρ, ὁ**, *very father*, Gr.Nyss.*castig.*(M.46.316A).

***αὐτοπείραστος**, *self-tempted*, Jo.Carp.*cap.*suppl.(M.85.1859).

***αὐτοπέρας, τό**, *absolute limit*, Max.*schol.d.n.*4.20(M.4.277C) cit. s. αὐτόμετρος.

***αὐτοπηγή, ἡ**, *very source*, of Christ οὐ μεθεκτὴν...ἔχει τὴν δωρεάν, ἀλλ' αὐ. καὶ αὐτορίζα ἐστὶ πάντων τῶν καλῶν, αὐτοζωὴ καὶ αὐτόφως καὶ αὐτοαλήθεια Chrys.*hom.14.1 in Jo.*(8.78B).

***αὐτοπικρία, ἡ**, *bitterness itself*, Chrys.*hom.15.2 in Eph.*(11.112D).

***αὐτοπλάστης, ὁ**, *very creator*; of Christ, ‡Gr.Naz.*Chr.pat.*2394 (M.38.324A) cit. s. αὐτόρριζος.

αὐτοποίητος, *self-made*, Athenag.*leg.*34.1(M.6.968B); ‡Just.*qu.Chr.*3.5(M.6.1444A).

***αὐτοποιότης, ἡ**, *quality in the abstract*, Max.*schol.d.n.*5.5(M.4.320A).

αὐτόπρακτος, *voluntarily done*, Melet.*nat.hom.*31(M.64.1308D).

αὐτόπρεμνος, 1. *together with the root, root and branch*, Meth.*res.*1.40(p.285.9; M.18.268D); *ib.*1.42(p.288.7; M.41.1112A); Isid.Pel.*epp.*2.282(M.78.713A); *ib.*3.34(756B); **2.** *self-rooted* αὐτὸς ἐγώ, μεδέων τε πατὴρ ἐμός, ἓν γένος ἐσμέν, ἔμφυτον, αὐ. Nonn.*par.Jo.*10:30(M.43.837A).

***αὐτοπροαίρεσις, ἡ**, *self-determination*, Epiph.*haer.*66.64(p.103.28; M.42.129A).

αὐτοπροαίρετος, 1. *possessed of free choice*; of God, Gr.Nyss.*Eun.*9(2 p.207.28; M.45.805A); of Son, Cyr.*thes.*13(5[1].126A); of man ὁ ἄνθρωπος,...αὐτοδέσποτον βούλησιν καὶ αὐ. πρὸς τὴν αἵρεσιν...τοῦ καλοῦ λαβών Meth.*res.*1.38(p.280.11; M.41.1105A) = Leont.et Jo.*sacr.*2.3(M.86.2056A); **2.** *self-chosen*, Eus.*d.e.*9.4(p.412.9; M.22.664D); Leont.H.*Nest.*1.51(M.86.1513D); †Jo.Jej.*poenit.*(M.88.1909D); **3.** neut. as subst., *power of choice*, Cyr.*Jo.*4.1(4.346C); Max.*schol.c.h.*10.1(M.4.89C); *cat.Ac.*13:48(p.230.15).

αὐτοπροαιρέτως, *of one's own choice*, Cyr.H.*catech.*2.1.

***αὐτοπρονοία, ἡ**, *providence itself*, Nemes.*nat.hom.*44(M.40.800A).

***αὐτοπροσαῖτις, ἡ**, *very beggar woman*, Chrys.*hom.div.*8.2(12.374D).

***αὐτοπροσκόπτης, ὁ**, name of a class of schismatics, those who separate themselves from Church for trivial causes, and after separation commit same offences to which they have objected within Church, Jo.D.*haer.*100(M.94.761B).

***αὐτοπροσωπέω**, *speak in one's own person*, Clem.*paed.*1.10 (p.143.23; M.8.357C).

αὐτοπροσώπως, *personally*, ref. action ὁ σατανᾶς ὀργάνῳ κέχρηται ἐκείνῳ, αὐ. δι' αὐτοῦ ἐνεργῶν Cyr.H.*catech.*15.14; Synes.*ep.*139(M.66.1529A); ref. speech, Clem.*str.*3.11(p.228.14; M.8.1172C); Eus.*e.th.*3.1(p.138.5; M.24.969C); Gr.Nyss.*Eun.*1(1 p.108.10; M.45.341C); ἐκ στόματος τῶν ταύτην ἐπιχειρούντων φύσει αὐτὰ αὐ. ἐνηχήθην Epiph.*haer.*26.17(p.297.17; M.41.360B); *in so many words* οὐκέτι ἐξ ὁμοιώσεως, ἀλλ' αὐ. περὶ τοῦ διαβόλου νοεῖται τὰ εἰρημένα Olymp.*Job* 41:25 (M.93.449C); of vision, Ath.*syn.*26.6(p.253.9; M.26.732B); presence, Cyr.*Jo.*3.6(4.317C); *face to face* οἱ ἐπὶ τοῦ ἀντιχρίστου αὐτῷ σατανᾷ αὐ. πολεμήσουσι Cyr.H.*catech.*15.17; Gr.Nyss.*Melet.*(M.46.861B).

***αὐτοπτοθεία, ἡ**, *personal vision of God*, *Lit.Jac.*(*NBP* 10[2] p.109).

***αὐτορίζα, ἡ**, *very root*; of Christ, Chrys.*hom.14.1 in Jo.*(8.78B) cit. s. αὐτοπηγή.

αὐτόρριζος, 1. *entire, root and branch*, Eus.*v.C.*3.56(p.104.9; M.20.1124A); Bas.*hom.in Ps.*61:3(1.194E; M.29.473A); **2.** *having one's own resources*, of Christ αὐ. ...εὐεργέτης ‡Gr.Naz.*Chr.pat.*1736(M.38.275A); **3.** *self-rooted*, of Christ τὸν αὐ., αὐτοπλάστην δεσπότην *ib.*2394(M.38.324A); of living rock, Nonn.*par.Jo.*1:19(M.43.753A); *ib.*19:42 (908A).

***αὐτόσαρξ**, *utterly carnal*, Chrys.*scand.*7(3.477A); *ib.*22(510A).

***αὐτοσέβαστος**, *absolutely august*; of H. Ghost, †Diad.*Ar.*9(M.65.1165D).

***αὐτοσθενής**, *absolutely mighty*; of God, ‡Hipp.*Ber.Hel.*1(p.322.13; M.10.832C).

αὐτοσοφία, ἡ, *absolute wisdom*; of God, Gr.Nyss.*virg.*16(M.46.385D); Dion.Ar.*d.n.*5.5(M.3.820A); Max.*qu.Thal.*54(M.90.512C); of Logos, Ath.*Ar.*2.80(M.26.316C); Eus.*p.e.*4.10(316C; M.21.536A); ‡Proc.G.*Pr.*17:24(M.87.1401B); Son, Or.*comm.in Mt.*14.7(p.289.18; M.13.1197B) cit. s. αὐτοβασιλεία; Ath.*gent.*46(M.25.93B); Cyr.*apol.Thdt.*4(p.121.12; 6[1].215A); Christ, †Bas.*Is.*176(1.507D; M.30.416A); Max.*ambig.*(M.91.1081D); Jo.D.*hom.*11.2(M.96.764C).

***αὐτοστερέωμα, τό**, *principle of firmness*; of God, Or.*sel.in Ps.*17:2(M.12.1224C).

αὐτόστοιχος, *self-reliant, independent*, Ant.Mon.*hom.*34(M.89.1541D).

***αὐτοσύνεσις, ἡ**, *prudence itself*; of Christ, Epiph.*haer.*77.30 (p.442.34; M.42.685B).

αὐτοσύστατος, 1. *made by itself, self-framed*, Meth.*arbitr.*22 (p.206.4); **2.** *existing by itself, self-supporting* τῆς ἀληθείας ἀεὶ ἑδραίας οὔσης καὶ μὴ χρείαν ἐχούσης βοηθείας, ἀλλὰ αὐ. οὔσης Epiph.*haer.*44.1(p.190.8; M.41.821C); αὐ. (v.l. αὐτοσυστάτης M.42.44D) οὔσης τῆς ἀληθείας *ib.*66.10(p.31.14); **3.** *self-commendatory* οὐκ ἔδει τὸ πνεῦμα αὐ. γίνεσθαι ἑαυτοῦ [i.e. as inspirer of the scriptures] *ib.*55.9 (p.335.24; M.41.988B), cf. σύστασις, *ib.*57.5(p.350.30; 1004B).

αὐτόσωμα, τό, *abstract, ideal body*, Max.*schol.d.n.*5.5(M.4.320A).

***αὐτοσωτηρία, ἡ**, *principle of salvation*, Or.*sel.in Ps.*61:2(M.12.1484C).

***αὐτοτάγαθος**, *possessing the principle of goodness*; neut. as subst., of God, Dion.Ar.*d.n.*1.5(M.3.593B).

***αὐτόταξις, ἡ**, *principle of order*, Dion.Ar.*d.n.*5.5(M.3.820B).

αὐτοτέλειος, *absolutely perfect*; of Christ, Epiph.*haer.*69.74(p.222.15; M.42.321D); *ib.*77.35(p.447.16; 693B); of H. Ghost, †Diad.*Ar.*9 (M.65.1165C).

***αὐτοτελεταρχία, ἡ**, *absolute self-origination*; of God, Dion.Ar.*c.h.*3.2(M.3.165C).

αὐτοτελής, 1. *perfect in itself*; of Trin. τρία πρόσωπα αὐ. Photinus et al.*ep.*ap.Epiph.*haer.*72.11(p.266.5; M.42.397B); **2.** *perfectly fulfilled* αὐ. τοῦ ὄφεως τὴν ἐπαγγελίαν ἐπὶ τῆς ἐκβάσεως τῶν ἔργων ἐδέξατο [sc. ὁ Ἀδάμ] Gennad.*fr.Gen.*3:22(M.85.1640A); τῷ δὲ τὴν ἐπαγγελίαν ὡς εὐεργεσίαν αὐ. δεξαμένῳ Niceph.Ur.*v.Sym.*230(M.86.3197B); **3.** *independent* τὰ δὲ πράγματα ἰδιάζουσαν καὶ αὐ. τὴν ὕπαρξιν ἔχειν, οὐδεὶς ἀμφιβάλλει Bas.*ep.*210.4(3.316A; M.32.773B).

αὐτοτελῶς, 1. *completely*, Clem.*str.*6.2(p.442.3; M.9.241A); Eus.*p.e.*6.6(244C; M.21.416C); **2.** *absolutely* αὐ. δὲ λέγω τὸν κύριον πάντων, οὐδενὸς ὑπολειπομένου κατὰ ἐξαίρεσιν Clem.*str.*6.17(p.509.28; M.9.381C); ἐπὰν μὴ μέρος φιλοσοφίας, ἀλλὰ τὴν αὐ. φιλοσοφίαν πολυπραγμονῶσι *ib.*(p.511.5; 385A).

***αὐτοτοιοῦτος**, *such as it is*, Or.*comm.in Gen.*(M.12.49B)ap.Eus.*p.e.*7.20(M.21.565C; αὐτὸν τοιοῦτον p.335D).

αὐτότροφος, *supplying one's own daily bread*, Euthal.Diac.*epp.Paul.*(M.85.760B).

***αὐτουιός, ὁ**, *very son*; of Christ, Or.*Jo.*32.28(18; p.473.20; M.14.817C).

***αὐτοϋμνηγορία, ἡ**, *principle of praise*; of God, Epiph.*haer.*76.35 (p.385.15; M.42.588C).

***αὐτοϋπαρξις, ἡ**, *absolute existence*; of God, Max.*carit.*3.27(M.90.1025A).

***αὐτοϋπεραγαθότης, ἡ**, *principle of super-goodness*, Dion.Ar.*d.n.*5.6(M.3.820C).

***αὐτοϋπερούσιος**, *absolutely super-essential*; of God, Dion.Ar.*d.n.*5.2(M.3.816C).

***αὐτοϋπομονή, ἡ**, *endurance itself*; of Christ, Or.*hom.17.4 in Jer.*(p.147.3; M.13.457C).

***αὐτοϋπόστασις, ἡ**, *actual existence*, Max.*schol.d.n.*4.32(M.4.305B).

αὐτουργία, ἡ, 1. *personal labour, working* with one's own hands, Eus.*h.e.*3.20.3(M.20.253A); Thdt.*h.e.*5.19.4(3.1052); commended as virtuous, Clem.*paed.*2.9(p.205.15; M.8.492B); Nil.*epp.*3.101(M.79.432D); Cyr.*ador.*12(1.437C); **2.** *activity* (Arian) τὸ ἀδύνατον εἶναι τὴν γενητὴν φύσιν μετασχεῖν τῆς τοῦ θεοῦ αὐ. Ath.*Ar.*2.26(M.26.201B); Cyr.*Juln.*2(6[2].61C); *ib.*(68D); **3.** plur., *one's own concerns*, Zach.Mit.*opif.*(M.85.1017A); **4.** *property*, CNic.(787)*can.*6.

***αὐτουργικῶς**, *as one's own work, without assistance*, of Creator τὰ τῆς ἀνακτίσεως...αὐ. αὐτὸς ὑπεδύσατο Leont.H.*Nest.*1.18(M.86.1469B).

αὐτουργός, 1. *acting by oneself, operating with one's own resources, without assistance*, Chrys.*hom.31.3 in Jo.*(8.178D); of Christ αὐ. εἰς ἡμᾶς ἀναδεδειγμένος, καὶ καινῆς...χρηματίσας διαθήκης ἄγγελος *cat.Ac.*7:37(p.118.29); of Christian revelation διὰ πίστεως παρειλήφαμεν λόγον, αὐ. σοφίᾳ πεπαιδευμένοι Clem.*str.*1.20(p.63.15; M.8.816C); **2.** *acting independently, in one's own right* ὁ Μωυσῆς...αὐ. μὲν αὐτὸς ἐπ' οὐδενὶ τῶν θαυμάτων...ὑπηρέτης δὲ μᾶλλον, καὶ ὑπουργός Cyr.*Jo.*3.6(4.311A); (Arian) ὑπουργός ἐστι καὶ οὐχὶ αὐ. ὁ υἱός ‡Ath.*disp.*7(M.28.444C); **3.** c. genit., *effecting by oneself* αὐ. τῶν ...ἐπιταγμάτων Chrys.*hom.21.6 in 1Cor.*(10.188E); Bas.Sel.*or.*7.2(M.

85.108A); *personally concerned with* τῶν ἰδίων προβάτων αὐ. ὁ ποιμήν Cyr.*Mich*.48(3.437C).

***αὐτουσιόω**, pass., *be inherent in the essence*, Max.*schol.c.h*.7.1 (M.4.65C).

***αὐτοφερώνυμος**, *bearing the very name of*, Euthal.Diac.*epp. Paul*.(M.85.708B).

***αὐτοφθορά, ἡ**, *principle of destruction*, Dion.Ar.*d.n*.4.20(M.3. 717C).

***αὐτοφιλανθρωπία, ἡ**, *principle of loving-kindness*, Gr.Naz.*or*. 23.1(M.35.1152B); Max.*ambig*.(M.91.1352A).

***αὐτοφονευτής, ὁ**, *suicide, self-murderer* ὁ ἀκρωτηριάσας ἑαυτόν... αὐ. ἐστιν *Can.App*.22; Eus.*h.e*.2.7(M.20.156B φονευτήν); *Const.App*. 8.2.5; Nil.*epp*.2.140(M.79.261C).

***αὐτοφρούρητος**, *self-guarded*, ‡Just.*qu.Chr*.5.1(M.6.1456C).

αὐτοφυής, 1. *self-grown, natural*, Clem.*paed*.2.10(p.222.9; M.8. 525C); *ib*.3.3(p.247.4; 580C); Eus.*d.e*.3.6(p.136.34; M.22.232A); Procl. CP *or*.17.2(M.65.809D); Synes.*ep*.4(M.66.1333C); *ib*.51(1380B); of words, *spontaneous*, Gr.Nyss.*Eun*.12(1 p.218.30; M.45.912D); **2.** *self-originate*; of God, *Orac.Sib*.3.12; Pall.*ep.Laus*.(p.7.1; M.34.1001); of Manich. principles of good and evil, Hegem.*Arch*.7(p.9.12; M.10.1437A) cit. s. ἀντίκειμαι; as Valent. aeon, Iren.*haer*.1.1.3(M. 7.449A); Hipp.*haer*.6.30(p.157.15; M.16.3238C); Epiph.*haer*.31.2 (p.386.5; M.41.477A).

αὐτόφυσις, ἡ, dat. αὐτοφύσει as adv., *by its own nature, naturally*, Meth.*symp*.3.7(p.33.21; M.18.69C); Leont.H.*Nest*.5.20(M.86. 1741D).

***αὐτοφώνως**, *with his own mouth*, Bas.*hom*.8.8(2.70D; M.31.324C).

αὐτόφως, τό, *absolute light*; of God, Dion.Ar.*d.n*.2.8(M.3.645D); ‡Cyr.*Trin*.7(6³.8C; M.77.1132B) = Jo.D.*f.o*.1.8(M.94.808D) cit. s. αὐτοζωή; of Son, Eus.*d.e*.4.13(p.173.3; M.22.288C); id.*l.C*.14(p.243. 32; M.20.1412C); id.*e.th*.1.8(p.66.33; M.24.837D); Ath.*gent*.46(M.25. 93C); Epiph.*haer*.77.35(p.447.17; M.42.693B); Chrys.*hom.14.1 in Jo*.(8.78B) cit. s. αὐτοπηγή; ‡Gr.Nyss.*hom.1.23 in Jo*.(p.101.21); *ib.1.44*(p.108.28).

***αὐτόφωτος**, *absolute light*; of Logos, Anast.S.*hod*.13(M.89.240C).

***αὐτοχάλκευτος**, *self-forged*, Procl.CP *or*.17.2(M.65.809D); Geo. Pis.*hex*.920(M.92.1504A).

αὐτοχειροτόνητος, *self-appointed* ἱερεὺς ἦν ἴσως αὐ. [sc. Μελχισεδέκ] Chrys.*hom.35.5 in Gen*.(4.356E); γενοῦ αὐ. οἰκονόμος πενήτων. ἡ φιλανθρωπία ταύτην σοι δίδωσι τὴν ἱερωσύνην id.*hom.43.1 in 1Cor*. (10.401B); αὐ. [sc. οἱ δίκαιοι], μᾶλλον δὲ παρὰ θεοῦ χειροτονηθέντες βασιλεῖς Hesych.H.*fr.Ps*.101:16(M.93.1276B); αὐ. πρεσβύτερος Max. *schol.epp.Dion.Ar*.8.1(M.4.544C).

***αὐτοχολή, ἡ**, *very gall*, Chrys.*hom.15.2 in Eph*.(11.112D).

***αὐτοχολωτέω**, *be one's own enemy, contradict oneself*, Didym. *Trin*.2.27(M.39.760B).

αὐτόχρημα, 1. *actually, really and truly*, Const.ap.Gel.Cyz.*h.e*. 3.19.1(M.85.1344D); Niceph.Ur.*v.Sym*.201(M.86.3172A); ὡς αὐ. βασιλέα ἀτιμάσας [sc. εἰκόνα] Anast.Ant.*sabb*.(M.89.1405A); **2.** *in very deed, of its own* ὁ σοφοῦν ἑτέρους δυνάμενος οὐκ αὐ. ἐστιν ἡ σοφία, ἀλλὰ τῆς ἐνούσης ἐν αὐτῷ σοφίας διάκονος Cyr.*Jo*.1.9(4.73E); id.ap. *cat.Rom*.8:11(p.234.9); **3.** *absolutely* θανάτου κρείττων ἐστὶν ὁ τοῦ θεοῦ λόγος, μᾶλλον δὲ αὐ. ζωή Cyr.*apol.Thdt*.12(p.145.24; 6¹.240A); id.*glaph.Ex*.2(1.299B); Cosm.Ind.*top*.5(M.88.253C); **4.** *veritable* ὁ αὐ. Μακκαβαῖος Synes.*ep*.4(M.66.1333A); *ib*.44(1372C).

αὐτοψεί, 1. *with one's own eyes*, Chrys.*ep*.20(3.606D); Eust. *engast*.5(p.22.22; M.18.621C); Amph.*hom*.3.3(M.39.61C); **2.** *manifestly*, Hipp.*antichr*.45(p.29.3; M.10.764B); ‡Jo.D.*Artem*.41(M.96. 1289B).

***αὐτώροφος**, *with a natural roof*, Gr.Naz.*carm*.2.1.88.102(M.37. 1439A).

αὔχημα, τό, 1. *glorious achievement*, Cyr.*glaph.Gen*.5(1.140C); **2.** *honourable distinction*, in gen., Meth.*symp*.1 proem.(p.6.18; M.18.36A); Cyr.*ador*.9(1.287A); Sophr.H.*or*.7.7(M.87.3332C); of God ὅσον μὲν ἦν δεκτικὸν θείων αὐ. τὸ ἀνθρώπινον τοῦ Χριστοῦ, μετέσχεν ὑπ' αὐτοῦ τοῦ λόγου διὰ τὴν ἕνωσιν ‡Cyr.*Trin*.17(6³.24B; M.77.1156D); τῶν μὲν οὖν οἰκείων αὐ. ἡ θεότης τῷ σώματι μεταδίδωσιν Jo.D.*f.o*.3.15 (M.94.1057C); of Son κοινὰ γὰρ πάντα τοῦ ἑνὸς σεσαρκωμένου θεοῦ λόγου γεγένηται...ἕτερον δὲ τὸ ἐξ οὗ κοινὰ τὰ τῆς δόξης αὐ., καὶ ἕτερον ἐξ οὗ κοινὰ τὰ πάθη γνωρίζεται id.*hom*.1.13(M.96.565C); **3.** *moral splendour, ornament of the character*, Cyr.*glaph.Gen*.2(1.26A); id. *Is*.1.1(2.20C); id.*hom.pasch*.26(5².304D).

αὐχηματικός, *arrogant*, Didym.*Trin*.3.29(M.39.948B).

***αὐχηματικῶς**, *as something to be proud of*, Thdr.Stud.*nativ.BMV* 7(M.96.696A).

αὐχμηρός, 1. *living on dry land, land* animal, Mac.Mgn.*apocr*. 4.2(p.159.21); **2.** *austere*, Just.*2apol*.11.5(M.6.461C); Eus.*h.e*.5.3.2 (M.20.436D); Jo.D.*virt*.(M.95.88A) = Ephr.3.425F; **3.** hence of sun in eclipse ὁ ἥλιος πάλιν αὐχμηρότερος γέγονεν, ἐν ὥρᾳ τῆς κυριακῆς ἡμέρας Thphn.*chron*.p.32(M.108.137A).

αὐχμώδης, *austere*, Pall.*h.Laus*.2(p.16.26; M.34.1011A).

***ἀφαγιάζω**, *consecrate*, Epiph.*haer*.29.5(p.327.16; ἀφηγησαμένων M.41.400B).

ἀφαγνίζω, 1. *sanctify*, Cyr.ap.*cat.Heb*.13:11(p.273.11); **2.** med., *profane, desecrate*, Gr.Naz.*or*.4.52(M.35.576B).

ἀφαγνισμός, ὁ, *purification*; of Levites, Cyr.*ador*.11(1.406D citing Num.8:7, LXX ἁγνισμός).

***ἀφαγνιστέον**, *one must purify, cleanse*, Clem.*str*.2.23(p.192.12; M.8.1093B).

ἀφαίρεσις, ἡ, 1. *taking away, removal*; theol., in negative or 'apophatic' theology τὰ μὲν οὖν ἡνωμένα τῆς ὅλης θεότητός ἐστιν τὸ ὑπεράγαθον, κτλ., καὶ ὅσα τῆς ὑπεροχικῆς ἐστιν ἀ. Dion.Ar.*d.n*.2.3 (M.3.640B); τὸν ὑπερούσιον ὑπερουσίως ὑμνῆσαι διὰ τῆς πάντων τῶν ὄντων ἀ. id.*myst*.2(M.3.1025A); explained ἐνταῦθα δέ, ἀπὸ τῶν ἐσχάτων ἐπὶ τὰ ἀρχικώτατα τὰς ἐπαναβάσεις ποιούμενοι, τὰ πάντα ἀφαιροῦμεν *ib*.(1025B); Jo.D.*f.o*.1.4(M.94.800B); Christol., ref. kenosis τῆς κατὰ ἀ. λαμβανομένης φύσεως ἐκ τοῦ κοινοῦ τῶν ἀνθρώπων Leont.H.*monoph*.58(M.86.1801B); ref. eternal Logos, ‡Proc.G.*Pr*. 23:5(M.87.1452A) cit. s. ἀποφατικῶς (A); **2.** logical *negation* in gen., *species definitionis, quam Graeci* κατὰ ἀ. τοῦ ἐναντίου *Latini per privantiam contrarii ejus, quod definitur, dicunt*, Isid.H.*etym*.2.29.9; Thal.*cent*.4.83(M.91.1468A); **3.** *removal, remission*; of sins, *Hom. Clem*.15.9; **4.** of obscuration of moon, Meth.*arbitr*.2(p.149.16; M. 18.244C); **5.** *loss*, Chrys.*hom.49.3 in Mt*.(7.508E); Gel.Cyz.*h.e*.2.32. 11(M.85.1330).

ἀφαιρετής, ὁ, *one who remits*, of Christ ἁμαρτιῶν ἀ. †Hipp. *theoph*.3(p.259.2; M.10.853D).

ἀφαιρετικός, *negative* εἴτε ἀ., εἴτε ἀπαγορευτικὸν ἢ ἀρνητικόν Bas. *Eun*.1.10(1.223A; M.29.536B); ὀνόματα στερητικὰ ἢ ἀ. Gr.Nyss.*Eun*. 12(1 p.378.13; M.45.1105A).

[*]**ἀφαίρησις, ἡ**, = ἀφαίρεσις, *loss*, *T.Job* 11(p.111.1).

***ἀφανδής**, *displeasing*, Gr.Naz.*carm*.2.2(poem.)7.205(M.37.1567A).

***ἀφάνερος**, *invisible*, Marc.Er.*opusc*.1.62(M.65.913A).

ἀφανίζω, 1. *deprive* of ἀφανισθεὶς τῆς ἑαυτοῦ φύσεως Eus.*d.e*.4.13 (p.172.10; M.22.288A); **2.** *lead astray* πολλοὺς πλανῶντες ἀ. Hipp. *haer*.6.39(p.171.9; M.16.3258B).

ἀφανιστής, ὁ, 1. *destroyer*, *A.Andr*.A 9(p.51.16); Epiph.*haer*.42. 11(p.140.28; M.41.749D); **2.** *corrupter*, *A.Thom*.A 106(p.218.12).

ἀφαντασίαστος, 1. *not disturbed by dreams*, Chrys.*hom.43.4 in 1Cor*.(10.406A); ὕπνοι ἄλυποι καὶ ἀ. Ast.Am.*hom*.14(M.40.372D); **2.** *free from vain fancies* διδασκαλίαν ἀ. καὶ ἀκόμπαστον Epiph. *haer*.35.3(p.43.27; M.41.632D); **3.** *without mental power* εἰ ἄψυχον τὴν ψυχὴν εἴπωμεν σῶμα, ἀναίσθητον καὶ ἀ. ἔσται Max.*ep*.6.5(M.91.428B); **4.** *not a fantasy, real*; of human body of Christ, Thdot.Anc.*hom. BMV et Sym*.4(M.77.1393D); of union of natures οὐ διαιρουμένων μετὰ τὴν ἄφραστον καὶ ἀ. ἕνωσιν Oecum.*Apoc*.1:1,2(p.32).

ἀφαντασιάστως, *not as a fantasy, in reality*, of Son συγκατέβη ἀτρέπτως, ἀ. Didym.*Trin*.1.26(M.39.389A); of his perpetual existence, Martin.*ep*.4(M.*PL*.87.152B); Christol., Oecum.*Apoc*.22:16 (p.255) cit. s. ἀσυγχύτως.

***ἀφαντασίως**, = foreg., ‡Rom.Mel.(*AS* 1 p.213).

ἀφάνταστος, 1. *free from fancy*, νοήσεις, φρόνησις, Synes.*insomn*.7 (p.156.2,6; M.66.1292D); διάνοια, Diad.*perf*.11(p.12.20); ὕπνος, Hyper. *mon*.129(M.79.1485C); **2.** *not imaginary*, of reality of Christ's human nature agst. doctrine of 'heavenly Christ' τὸ ἀληθὲς καὶ ἀ. τῆς ψυχῆς αὐτοῦ Mel.*fr*.(p.310; M.5.1221A); ref. Gen.19:11 θύρα τοῦ δικαίου ἀληθὴς καὶ ἀ. Nil.*epp*.3.120(M.79.437D); ἀναμφίβολος καὶ ἀ. κίνησις Diad.*perf*.33(p.36.18); **3.** c. genit., *without a vision of* ἀ. [sc. Devil] τοῦ θεοῦ Didym.*Job* 1:12(M.39.1124D).

ἀφαντάστως, *really, not imaginarily* ἀ. τὴν ὑπὲρ ἡμῶν οἰκονομίαν πεπλήρωκεν Max.*ambig*.(M.91.1049D).

***ἀφάντωσις, ἡ**, *abolition*, Epiph.*haer*.45.4(p.202.15; M.41.836C).

***ἀφαπλόω**, *spread out*, Anast.S.*Ps.6*(M.89.1084C).

ἀφαρεί, *needlessly*, Dor.*doct*.3.3(M.88.1656D); *ib*.4.11(1673B); *ib*. 16.2(1796A).

ἀφαρμόζω, *be unsuitable*, ‡Bas.*struct.hom*.1.4(1.326A; M.30.16A).

ἄφατος, *beyond words, unspeakable*; of action or attributes of God, Or.*princ*.4.1.7(p.303.6; M.11.353B); *M.Das*.7.2; Eus.*e.th*.1.3 (p.64.7; M.24.832D); Cyr.H.*catech*.7.7; Cyr.*Am*.46(3.300C); id.*Jo*. 3.4(4.277B); of action or attributes of Christ, Chrys.*hom.68.1 in Jo*. (8.405B); *ib.70.1*(414C); of operation of H. Ghost, *ib.51.1*(300B); of human qualities, Gel.Cyz.*h.e*.3.2.1; Chrys.*comm.in Gal*.4:14(10.

706E); of number, size, intensity, Meth.*symp*.1.5(p.14.21; M.18.48A); Const.ap.Gel.Cyz.*h.e*.3.18.5; Thdt.*Jer*.9:22(2.461).

ἀφάτως, *in a way that cannot be described, abundantly*, ref. Eph. 1:8 'ἐπερίσσευε', τουτέστιν, ἀ. ἐξεχύθη Chrys.*hom.1.3 in Eph*.(11.7B).

ἀφεγγής, **1.** *without light*; lit., Ath.*Ar*.1.24(M.26.61B); Gr.Naz.*or*.33.5(M.36.221A); Cyr.*Joel*.42(3.240E); met., *unenlightened*, Ath.*ep.Serap*.2.2(M.26.609B); Cyr.*Lc*.14:21(M.72.792A); **2.** *gloomy*, id.*Mich*.42(3.430C); **3.** *obscure*, Clem.*str*.5.5(p.345.1; M.9.52B); **4.** *blind*, Gr.Naz.*carm*.1.2.9.50(M.37.671A); Nonn.*par.Jo*.17:6(M.43.884C).

***ἀφεδράζω,** *set apart*, of Marcosian aeon Σωτήρ: ὁ ἀφεδρασθεὶς ἐν τῷ πατρί Iren.*haer*.1.14.5 ap.Hipp.*haer*.6.46(p.178.13; M.16.3270B).

ἀφεδρών, ὁ, **1.** *privy*, Clem.*prot*.4(p.39.18; M.8.144A); Epiph.*haer*.69.10(p.160.21; M.42.217C); Socr.*h.e*.1.38.7,9(M.67.177A); **2.** *stomach*, *T.Job* 38(p.127.19); **3.** *vent*, †Jo.Jej.*poenit*.(M.88.1909B).

ἀφειδία, ἡ, *extravagance* ἀπόσχου τῆς ἀ. καὶ χρῆσαι τῇ συμμετρίᾳ Isid.Pel.*epp*.1.277(M.78.345B); Cyr.*Joel*.16(3.215B).

***ἀφεκτέος,** *to be abstained from*, Ptol.*ep*.ap.Epiph.*haer*.33.5 (cj. p.454.9 for ἀφθέγκτων M.41.564A); Clem.*ecl*.19(p.142.7; M.9.708A).

ἀφέλεια, ἡ, **1.** *simplicity* of mind, Clem.*paed*.1.4(p.96.17; M.8.261A); Chrys.*hom.58.2 in Mt*.(7.587D); **2.** *want of intelligence*, id.*hom.3.4 in 1Cor*.(10.20C).

ἀφελής, *whole, healthy*, Ephr.2.115A.

***ἀφελκυσμός, ὁ,** *distraction*, Bas.*hom.in Ps*.28:2(1.117A; M.29.288B).

ἀφελότης, ἡ, *simplicity*; of the divine light, Hipp.*haer*.10.16 (p.278.3; M.16.3434B); of the mind, Epiph.*haer*.73.23(p.297.6; M.42.448B); *Apophth.Patr*.(M.65.160A,B).

ἀφελπίζω, = ἀπελπίζω, *despair of*; reflex., *despair*, Herm.*vis*.3.12.2; Hipp.*Dan*.3.4.6; med., *despair*, Or.*Jo*.13.28(p.252.17; M.14.448B).

[*]**ἀφελπισμός, ὁ,** = ἀπελπισμός, Nil.*epp*.2.222(M.79.316B).

[*]**ἀφελπιστία, ἡ,** v. ἀπελπιστία.

ἀφερέπονος, *indolent, ease-loving* εἰς ὑπόδειγμα τοῖς ἀ. ὡς ὁ Λάζαρος Bas.*reg.fus*.55.4(2.400A; M.31.1049C); Dor.*doct*.13.3(M.88.1764B); neut. as subst. εἰώθασι φιλοῦντες ἐν διωγμοῖς τὸ ἀ. ἀγαπᾶν Or.*adnot.in Dt*.20:5(M.17.29A).

ἀφερεπόνως, *with unwillingness to bear pain*, Epiph.*haer*.66.22 (p.50.14; M.42.68B).

ἀφέσιμος, ἀ. [sc. γράμματα] *letters of pardon*, Geo.Pis.*hex*.435 (M.92.1468A).

ἄφεσις, ἡ, **A.** *remission* of sins; **1.** in gen., through Christ, v. ἁμαρτία; **2.** in baptism, *Barn*.11.1; Just.*dial*.14.1(M.6.504C); δύο γὰρ συνέστη τὰ ἄ. ἁμαρτημάτων παρεχόμενα, πάθος διὰ Χριστόν, καὶ βάπτισμα †Mel.*fr*.(p.313); Iren.*haer*.1.21.2(M.7.657B); οὐκ ἔστιν ἄ. ἁμαρτημάτων χωρὶς βαπτίσματος λαβεῖν Or.*mart*.30(p.26.21; M.11.600C); *Hom.Clem*.9.23; *Symb*.ap.*Const.App*.7.41.8; Chrys.*hom.28.1 in Jo*.(8.158E); v. βάπτισμα; **3.** through repentance, Just.*dial*.141.2(M.6.797D); *Const.App*.2.18.2 etc.; v. μετάνοια; **4.** ref. problem of remission of post-baptismal sin in Marcosian system, Hipp.*haer*.6.41(p.172.24; M.16.3259B); in Novatianism, not granted in case of deadly sin, Socr.*h.e*.1.10.3(M.67.101A); granted by orthodox to lapsed when in danger of death, Dion.Al.*fr*.(p.60.2); v. ἁμαρτάνω, μετάνοια, βάπτισμα; **5.** obtained through faith, Clem.*ecl*.15(p.141.6; M.9.705A); †Bas.*bapt*.1.2.7(2.634A; M.31.1536C); **6.** in Holy Communion, *Lit*.ap.*Const.App*.8.12.39 al.; *Lit.Jac*.(p.232.21); **7.** through work of BMV, Jo.D.*carm.dorm.BMV* 160(p.232; M.96.1368A).

B. ἄ. τῶν λόγων *rendering* of accounts, *V.Pach.Φ* 122(p.79.7).

ἀφετηρία, ἡ, **1.** *start* for a debate, *opening gambit*, Mac.Mgn.*apocr*.3.23(p.103.8); **2.** *outlet* of a reservoir, Hipp.*haer*.5.21(p.124.12; M.16.3190C).

ἀφετικός, *ready to remit*; of God, Clem.*str*.2.15(p.148.18; M.8.1004B).

ἄφετος, **1.** *free*; **a.** of divine nature of Christ, freed from body at his death φωνήσας γοῦν μέγα ἀ. ἀνεχώρει τοῦ σώματος Eus.*d.e*.4.12 (p.169.20; M.22.281D); ἄ. αὐτὸς ἀφ' ἑαυτοῦ τὴν ἐκ τοῦ σώματος ἀναχώρησιν ἐποιεῖτο id.*theoph.fr*.3(p.5.1; M.24.612A); **b.** of human free will ψυχὰς ἀνθρώπων ἄφετον ἐπὶ τῆς αὐθεκουσίου περὶ τὸ καλὸν ἢ τοὐναντίον αἱρέσεως τὴν φύσιν ἐπαγομένας id.*d.e*.4.1(p.150.23; M.22.252B); **c.** of human body free from death and sin, participating in kingdom of God, Meth.*res*.2.18(p.371.9; M.18.313C); **2.** *loose*, neut. as subst. ἐξηγεῖται...τὸ...ἄ. εἰς τρυφάς Cyr.*Am*.59 (3.315E); **3.** *abandoned, corrupt* ἀφέτους εἶναι τοὺς νέους Chrys.*hom.59.7 in Mt*.(7.604B); id.*hom.5.2 in 1Thess*.(11.462B); **4.** ?*free*, *open* to the public λουτῆρες ἄφετοι †Gregent.*disp*.(M.86.725C); **5.** name of a Valent. aeon, Val.Gn.ap.Epiph.*haer*.31.6(p.395.7; M.41.485B).

ἀφή, ἡ, *touch, sense of touch*;

A. lit.; **1.** def. τῆς ζωῆς [sc. εἰκών] ἡ ἀ. Max.*ambig*.(M.91.1248C); **2.** cause of sin ἡ κατὰ τὴν ἀ. αἴσθησις, πάντων ἔσχατον τῶν ἁμαρτανομένων ἐστί...καὶ οὐδὲ πρεπὸν ἅμα τοῖς σεμνοτέροις τῶν λόγων παραμιγνύειν, ὅσα τῆς ἀ. ἐστι κατηγορήματα Gr.Nyss.*or.dom*.5(p.106.14, 20; M.44.1185D); cf.id.*hom.11 in Cant*.(M.44.993B); **3.** ref. Inc. ὁ ἅγιος λόγος...ὑπὸ ἀφὴν ἐγένετο καὶ σάρκα ἔλαβε Epiph.*anc*.31(p.40.7; M.43.72D).

B. met.; **1.** of spiritual touch, as one of senses of soul ὁ ἔξω ἄνθρωπος ἔχει ἀ. τὴν αἰσθητήν, καὶ ὁ ἔσω ἄνθρωπος ἔχει ἀ., ἐκείνην τὴν ἀ. ᾗ ἥψατο ἡ αἱμορροοῦσα τοῦ κρασπέδου τοῦ Ἰησοῦ...ἐκείνη δὲ μόνη ἔχουσα θείαν τινὰ ἀ. ἥψατο τοῦ Ἰησοῦ καὶ διὰ τοῦτο ἐθεραπεύθη· καὶ ἐπεὶ θείᾳ αὐτοῦ ἀ. ἥψατο, διὰ τοῦτο δύναμις τοῦ Ἰησοῦ ἐξῆλθεν ἐπὶ τὴν θείαν αὐτῆς ἀ. ... περὶ ταύτης τῆς θειοτέρας ἀ. Ἰωάννης λέγει· καὶ αἱ χεῖρες ἡμῶν ἐψηλάφησαν περὶ τοῦ λόγου τῆς ζωῆς Or.*dial*.19,20 (p.160.1–11); 'ὅτι αἴσθησιν θείαν εὑρήσεις' [Pr.2:5], καὶ ὄντων εἰδῶν ταύτης τῆς αἰσθήσεως, ὁράσεως...καὶ ἀ., καθ' ἣν Ἰωάννης φησὶ ταῖς χερσὶν ἐψηλαφηκέναι 'περὶ τοῦ λόγου τῆς ζωῆς' id.*Cels*.1.48(p.98.18; M.11.749B); ἔστι δέ τις καὶ ἀ. τῆς ψυχῆς, ἡ ἁπτομένη τοῦ λόγου, διά τινος ἀσωμάτου καὶ νοητῆς ἐπαφῆς ἐνεργουμένη Gr.Nyss.*hom.1 in Cant*.(M.44.780D); **2.** of touch of Christ Ἰησοῦς ἥψατο τοῦ λεπροῦ, ἵν' αὐτὸν καθαρίσῃ, ὡς ἐγὼ οἶμαι, διχῶς...λέπρας αἰσθητῆς δι' αἰσθητῆς ἀ. ἀλλὰ καὶ τῆς ἄλλης διὰ τῆς ὡς ἀληθῶς θείας αὐτοῦ ἀ. Or.*Cels*.1.48 (p.99.3,4; M.11.749C); **3.** of H. Ghost διὰ τῆς πρὸς τὴν ψυχὴν αὐτῶν [sc. the prophets], ἵν' οὕτως ὀνομάσω, ἀ. τοῦ καλουμένου ἁγίου πνεύματος διορατικώτεροί τε τὸν νοῦν ἐγίνοντο καὶ τὴν ψυχὴν λαμπρότεροι Or.*Cels*.7.4(p.156.3; M.11.1425B).

ἀφηγ-έομαι, ptcpl. ὁ ~ούμενος, *abbot*, Call.*v.Hipp*.(p.4).

ἀφήγησις, ἡ, *ruling*; of office of abbess, Thdr.Stud.*epp*.2.182 (M.99.1564A).

ἀφηγητής, ὁ, *guide* τῶν θείων ἀ. καὶ μυσταγωγῶν Nil.*epp*.3.196 (M.79.473D).

***ἀφηλικία, ἡ,** *childhood*, ‡Bas.*Lac*.6(2.592A; M.31.1449A).

ἀφῆλιξ, *not of full age, young*, Tit.Bost.*fr.Lc*.15:12(p.215); Didym.*Trin*.2.14(M.39.708B); Jo.Mosch.*prat*.79(M.87.2937B).

ἀφηλ-όω, **1.** *unnail*, Just.*dial*.108.2(M.6.728A); **2.** *draw out* a nail, Sophr.H.*mir.Cyr.et Jo*.35(M.87.3545C); **3.** met., *detach* ἡ ἐκκλησία, ὑπὲρ αὐτῆς βλέπουσα αὐτὸν τῷ σταυρῷ προσηλωμένον, ἵνα ἐκείνη τῆς ἁμαρτίας ~ωθῇ Ph.Carp.*Cant*.221(M.40.140A).

ἄφημος, *silent* ἔχε στόμ' ἄ. *Orac.Sib*.5.439 (v.l. for στόμα φιμῷ).

ἀφηνιάζ-ω, *set in opposition* ἤμελλον αἱρέσεις ~ειν τὸν Χριστὸν ἀπὸ τοῦ πατρῴου θελήματος Epiph.*haer*.69.59(p.207.10; M.42.296C) al.

***ἀφηνιαστικός,** *refractory, rebellious*; neut. as subst., Or.*Jo*.10.29 (18; p.202.25; M.14.360B); Cyr.*Ps*.31:9(M.69.868C).

***ἀφηνιάω,** cf. ἀφηνιάζω; **1.** *throw off the reins*, ‡Pion.*v.Polyc*.9; **2.** met., *rebel*; **a.** abs., Eus.*v.C*.4.5(p.119.22; M.20.1153B); Chrys.*Jud*.8.3(1.677D); Cyr.*Os*.119(3.150C); **b.** c. genit., *rebel* against, ‡Ign.*Phil*.11; Thdt.*provid*.5(4.559); CChalc.*can*.8.

ἀφθαρσία, ἡ, *incorruption* (physical, moral, and spiritual); *immortality* (the two meanings cannot always be clearly distinguished);

I. as divine attribute;

A. of God, Tat.*orat*.7(p.7.9; M.6.820B); ἐπιβάλωμεν τῇ τοῦ θεοῦ ἀ. Clem.*str*.4.6(p.260.10; M.8.1240A); ὁ δὲ θεὸς...ἀ. Meth.*res*.1.34 (p.272.3); Ath.*inc.et c.Ar*.15(M.26.1012A); Gr.Nyss.*Apoll*.55(M.45.1257A); as attribute of both Father and Son, defended against Eunomius περὶ τῆς ἀ. τοῦ πατρὸς διαλέγεται [sc. Eunomius] ὡς οὐκ ἐξ ἐνεργείας προσούσης αὐτῷ. ἐγὼ δὲ εἰ μὲν ἐνέργειά τίς ἐστιν ἡ ὄντως ζωὴ ἑαυτὴν ἐνεργοῦσα καὶ εἰ ταὐτόν ἐστι τῷ σημαινομένῳ τὸ δὲ ἀεὶ ζῆν καὶ τὸ μηδέποτε εἰς φθορὰν διαλύεσθαι οὔπω τῷ λόγῳ προστίθημι...ὅτι μέντοι μία ⟨ἡ⟩ τῆς ἀ. ἐστὶ διάνοια ὡσαύτως ἐπί τε τοῦ πατρὸς καὶ τοῦ υἱοῦ νοουμένη καὶ κατ' οὐδὲν τὸ τοῦ πατρὸς ἄφθαρτον τῆς ἀ. τοῦ υἱοῦ παραλλάσσει, οὔτε ὑφέσει τινὶ καὶ ἐπιτάσει οὔτε τινὶ ἄλλῳ διαφορᾶς τρόπῳ τῆς κατὰ τὴν ἀ. παραλλαγῆς εὑρισκομένης, τοῦτο καὶ νῦν φημι...ὡς ἂν μηδεμίαν ἔχοι διὰ τούτου χώραν ὁ λόγος αὐτῷ τῇ κατὰ τὴν ἀ. ἐννοίᾳ τῷ πατρὶ προσμαρτυρῶν τὸ πρὸς τὸν υἱὸν ἀκοινώνητον. ὡς γὰρ περὶ τὸν πατέρα ἡ ἀ. καταλαμβάνεται, οὕτως καὶ ἐπὶ τοῦ μονογενοῦς εἶναι οὐκ ἀμφιβάλλεται, τὸ γὰρ τῆς φθορᾶς ἀπαράδεκτον, ὅπερ ἀ. καὶ ἔστι καὶ λέγεται, ἴσον μᾶλλον δὲ τὸν αὐτὸν ἔχει λόγον ἐφ' οὗπερ ἂν λέγηται. τί οὖν παθὼν μόνῳ προσμαρτυρεῖ τῷ ἀγεννήτῳ θεῷ τὸ μὴ ἐξ ἐνεργείας εἶναι τὴν ἀ. αὐτῷ, ὡς διὰ τούτου τὴν κατὰ τοῦ μονογενοῦς παραλλαγὴν τοῦ πατρὸς δεικνύων; εἰ μὲν γὰρ φθαρτὸν ὑποτίθεται τὸν κτιστὸν ἑαυτοῦ θεόν, καλῶς τῇ τοῦ φθαρτοῦ πρὸς τὸ ἄφθαρτον διαφορᾷ τὴν κατὰ φύσιν παραλλαγὴν ἀποδεικνυσιν· εἰ δὲ ἀνεπίδεκτος φθορᾶς ὡσαύτως ἑκάτερος καὶ οὔτε τὸ μᾶλλον οὔτε τὸ ἧττον ἐν τῇ κατὰ φύσιν ἀ. καταλαμβάνεται, πῶς δείκνυσι τοῦ πατρὸς πρὸς τὸν μονογενῆ υἱὸν τὸ ἀσύγκριτον; Gr.Nyss.*Eun.*12(1 p.319.17–320.9; M.45.1033C–1036A).

B. of Christ, Clem.*paed.*1.6(p.109.16; M.8.289A); ὁ κύριος, ἡ ἀ. νικήσασα τὸν θάνατον Meth.*symp.*3.7(p.34.25; M.18.72B); Ath.*fr. Cant.*4(M.27.1356C); νοοῦμεν τὸν κύριον, ὅς ἐστι...ἀ. Gr.Nyss.*hom.11 in Cant.*(M.44.1008C); ‡Meth.*Sym.et Ann.*14(M.18.381C); ref. Nativity ἔπρεπε γὰρ τὸν ἐπὶ ἀ. τοῦ παντὸς ἐν τῷ ἀνθρωπίνῳ βίῳ γενόμενον, ἀπὸ τῆς ὑπηρετούσης αὐτοῦ τῇ γεννήσει τῆς ἀ. ἄρξασθαι Gr.Nyss.*nativ.*(M.46.1136B).

II. in men;

A. Christ as its source; **1.** in gen. ἡ νύμφη πρὸς τοὺς ἑταίρους τοῦ νυμφίου φησὶν ὡς οὐδεμίαν ἔχουσα πρὸς τοὺς ἀλώπεκας μετουσίαν· ἐκοινώνησαν γὰρ ἡμῖν, φησίν, αἵματος καὶ σαρκός, καὶ ἡμεῖς αὐτῷ τῆς ἀ. Or.*schol.in Cant.*2:16(M.17.265C); σὺ γὰρ εἶ μόνος κύριε... ἡ πηγὴ τῆς ἀ. *A.Jo.*109(p.208.6); Ammon.*Jo.*14:6(M.85.1488B); ‡Chrys.*hom.*2(13.208A); ἥξει πάντως ἐφ' ἡμᾶς καὶ τὰ ἐν Χριστῷ, τοῦτ' ἔστιν, ἡ ἀ. Cyr.*ep.*45(p.155.18; 5².139B); id.*Jo.*1.9(4.95B) al.; Anast.S.*qu.et resp.*143(M.89.796C); **2.** having restored it by his saving work, Iren.*haer.*3.18.7(M.7.937B) cit. s. συνενόω; οὐκ ἄλλου ἦν τὸ φθαρτὸν εἰς ἀ. μεταβαλεῖν, εἰ μὴ αὐτοῦ τοῦ σωτῆρος τοῦ καὶ τὴν ἀρχὴν ἐξ οὐκ ὄντων πεποιηκότος τὰ ὅλα Ath.*inc.*20.1(M.25.129C); *ib.*7.5(109A); *ib.*8.4(109D); τὸ ὑπὲρ ἡμῶν σφάγιον, ἔνδυμα ἀφθαρσίας, καὶ ὄν, καὶ καλούμενον Gr.Naz.*or.*45.13(M.36.640C); ὄντος [sc. Christ] τοῦ διὰ τῆς οἰκείας πείρας εἰς ἀ. ἐξαιρουμένου τὸν ἄνθρωπον Gr.Nyss.*Eun.*12(2 p.291.9; M.45.904C); Χριστὸς...ῥίζα...τεθειμένος τῶν εἰς καινότητα ζωῆς ἀναμορφουμένων ἐν πνεύματι, καὶ τὴν τοῦ σώματος ἀ. Cyr.*inc.unigen.*(5¹.692A); *ib.*(692B) cit. s. ἀνακομιδή; ἐν ἡμῖν γὰρ ἐστιν ὁ Χριστὸς διὰ τοῦ πνεύματος, μετατρέπων εἰς ἀ. τὸ φθείρεσθαι πεφυκός id.*Jo.*9.1(4.824B); id.*Is.*1.5(2.132D); ὑπέμεινε...σταυρόν, ἵνα σαρκὶ παθὼν τὸν θάνατον καὶ οὐ φύσει θεότητος, γένηται πρωτότοκος ἐκ τῶν νεκρῶν, καὶ ὁδοποιήσῃ τῇ ἀνθρώπου φύσει τὴν εἰς ἀ. ὁδόν id.*ep.*45(p.155.26; 5².139C); μετὰ τὸ πάθος τῆς ἀθανασίας καὶ τῆς ἀ. μετέδωκε Thdt.*Ps.*108:31(1.1390); ἐνανθρωπήσας γὰρ ὁ θεὸς λόγος κατέλυσε τοῦ θανάτου τὸ κράτος· καταλύσας δὲ ἐπηγγείλατο ἡμῖν τὴν ἀνάστασιν· τῇ δὲ ἀναστάσει ἀ. ... συνέζευκται· τῆς δὲ ἀφθαρσίας μεθέξει καὶ τὰ ὁρώμενα id.*Heb.*2:9(3.558); Proc.G.*Is.*11:1–10(M.87.2041A); hence of BMV ζωοδόχον σῶμα αὐτῆς, τὸ πηγάσαν ...ἀ. ἐν τῇ...φθαρτῇ ἡμῶν φύσει Mod.*dorm.*12(M.86.3308C); ‡Gr.Naz. *Chr.pat.*2572(M.38.336A) cit. s. ἀμφίον.

B. human *immortality* (not always to be distinguished from t.t. with certainty), cf. ἀνάστασις; **1.** discussion of its possibility; **a.** ref. soul, in controversy with Heracleon οὐκ οἶδα δὲ πῶς καὶ περὶ ἀθανασίας ψυχῆς ἀπιστεῖ [sc. Heracleon]...εἰ μὲν γὰρ ὅτι δεκτικὴ ἁμαρτίας, ψυχὴ δὲ ἡ ἁμαρτάνουσα αὐτὴ ἀποθανεῖται, καὶ ἡμεῖς ἐροῦμεν αὐτὴν θνητήν· εἰ δὲ τὴν παντελῆ διάλυσιν καὶ ἐξαφανισμὸν αὐτῆς θάνατον νομίζει, ἡμεῖς οὐ προσησόμεθα οὐδὲ μέχρι ἐπινοίας ἰδεῖν δυνάμενοι οὐσίαν θνητὴν μεταβάλλουσαν εἰς ἀθάνατον, καὶ φύσιν φθαρτὴν ἐπὶ τὸ ἄφθαρτον· ὅμοιον γὰρ τοῦτο τῷ λέγειν μεταβάλλειν τι ἀπὸ σώματος εἰς ἀσώματον· ὡς ὑποκειμένου τινὸς κοινοῦ τῆς τῶν σωμάτων καὶ ἀσωμάτων φύσεως, ὅπερ μένει, ὥσπερ μένειν φασὶ τὸ ὑλικὸν οἱ περὶ ταῦτα δεινοὶ τῶν ποιοτήτων μεταβαλλουσῶν εἰς ἀ. οὐ ταὐτὸν δέ ἐστιν ⟨τὸ⟩ τὴν φθαρτὴν φύσιν ἐνδύεσθαι ἀ., καὶ τὸ τὴν φθαρτὴν φύσιν μεταβάλλειν εἰς ἀ. τὰ δ' αὐτὰ καὶ περὶ τῆς θνητῆς λεκτέον, οὐ μεταβαλλούσης μὲν εἰς ἀθανασίαν, ἐνδυομένης δὲ αὐτήν Or.*Jo.*13.61(59; p.293.21 ff.; M.14.516C); **b.** ref. body τοῦ θεοῦ οὖν δυνατοῦ ὄντος ζωοποιεῖν τὸ πλάσμα τοῦ ἑαυτοῦ, καὶ τῆς σαρκὸς δυναμένης ζωοποιεῖσθαι, τί λοιπὸν τὸ κωλύον αὐτὴν μετέχειν τῆς ἀ.; Iren.*haer.*5.3.3(M.7.1132C); possibility of its immortality proved by Elijah and Enoch δείκνυται...διὰ τούτου [sc. Elijah] ἀφθαρσίας ἡμῶν ὑπάρχον τὸ σῶμα δεκτικόν, καθάπερ ἐδείχθη καὶ ἐπὶ τοῦ Ἐνὼχ μετατιθεμένου, εἰ μὴ γὰρ ἀ. ἠδύνατο δέξασθαι, οὐκ ἂν οὐδὲ διέμεινεν ἐν ἀπαθείᾳ τοσούτῳ χρόνῳ Meth.*res.*3.5(p.396.10ff.; M.18.320C); and by Resurrection of Christ τοῦτο γὰρ ἦν κατὰ τοῦ θανάτου τρόπαιον ταύτην ἐπιδείξασθαι πᾶσιν, καὶ πάντας πιστώσασθαι τὴν παρ' αὐτοῦ γενομένην τῆς φθορᾶς ἀπάλειψιν, καὶ λοιπὸν τὴν τῶν σωμάτων ἀ., τὸ πᾶσιν ὥσπερ ἐνέχυρον καὶ γνώρισμα τῆς ἐπὶ πάντας ἐσομένης ἀναστάσεως τετήρηκεν ἄφθαρτον τὸ ἑαυτοῦ σῶμα Ath.*inc.*22.4(M.25.136B); πῶς...τὸ τοῦ θανάτου τέλος ἐδείκνυτο, καὶ ἡ κατὰ τούτου νίκη, εἰ μὴ ἐπ' ὄψει πάντων προσκαλεσάμενος αὐτὸν ἤλεγξε νεκρὸν κενωθέντα λοιπὸν τῇ τοῦ σώματος ἀ.; *ib.*23.4(137A); though during earthly life his body had not yet attained to ἀ., Chrys.*hom.80.2 in Jo.*(8.475C); ἀ. implying ἀπάθεια, Thdt.*Ps.*50:7(1.937); **2.** ref. man's state in paradise, immortality his destined state, lost through sin εἰ γὰρ καθ' ὑπόθεσιν ἡ γυνὴ μὴ ἠπάτητο καὶ ὁ Ἀδὰμ μὴ παραπεπτώκει, κτισθεὶς δὲ ὁ ἄνθρωπος ἐπὶ ἀφθαρσίᾳ κεκρατήκει τῆς ἀ., οὔτ' ἂν εἰς χοῦν θανάτου καταβεβήκει Or.*Jo.*1.20(22; p.25.4; M.14.57C); πεποίητο ...ἐπὶ ἀ. Cyr.*Rom.*5:18(p.186.24; M.74.789A); *ib.*5:11f.(p.182.11; 784A); id.*Ps.*6:3(M.69.745A); Proc.G.*Is.*45:9ff.(M.87.2425A); cf.id. *Gen.*3:18(M.87.216C,D); promised only for future life εἰ...μένοιεν καλοί, ἔχωσι τὴν ἐν παραδείσῳ ἄλυπον...ζωήν, πρὸς τῷ καὶ τῆς ἐν οὐρανοῖς ἀ. αὐτοὺς τὴν ἐπαγγελίαν ἔχειν Ath.*inc.*3.4(M.25.101C); peculiar view of Adam's state ἔτι γὰρ πηλουργούμενον τὸν Ἀδάμ, ὡς ἔστιν εἰπεῖν, καὶ τηκτὸν ὄντα καὶ ὑδαρῆ, καὶ μηδέπω φθάσαντα δίκην ὀστράκου τῇ ἀ. κραταιωθῆναι Meth.*symp.*3.5(p.31.16; M.18.68B); **3.** as hope and reward of Christians; **a.** promised by Christ, Just. *1apol.*42.4(M.6.392C); Ath.*inc.*9.2(M.25.112B); *ib.*32.6(152C); **b.** goal and reward of truly Christian life νῆφε, ὡς θεοῦ ἀθλητής· τὸ θέμα ἀ. καὶ ζωὴ αἰώνιος Ign.*Polyc.*2.3; Χριστιανοὶ παροικοῦσιν ἐν φθαρτοῖς, τὴν ἐν οὐρανοῖς ἀ. προσδεχόμενοι *Diogn.*6.8; διὰ τὸ ἐλέσθαι τοὺς αἱρουμένους τὰ αὐτῷ [sc. θεῷ] ἀρεστὰ καὶ ἀ. καὶ συνουσίας καταξιωθῆναι Just.*1apol.*10.3(M.6.341A); τοῖς [μὲν] [sc. the innocent] ἀπ' ἀρχῆς, τοῖς δὲ ἐκ μετανοίας, ζωὴν χαρισάμενος ἀ. δωρήσηται, καὶ δόξαν αἰωνίαν περιποιήσῃ Iren.*haer.*1.10.1(M.7.552A); τῷ ἀγαπᾶν τὸν πατέρα εἰς οἰκείαν ἰσχὺν καὶ δύναμιν ἀ. κομιζομένους Clem.*q.d.s.*27(p.178.15; M.9.633B); reward of almsgiving, *ib.*32(p.181.6; 637B); πιστὸς...μήτε...ἀναγώνιστος μείνας...τῶν στεφάνων τῆς ἀ. ἐλπιζέτω μεταλαβεῖν *ib.*3(p.161.31; 608B); ὅταν ἐπὶ τὸ πέρας ἔλθωσι [sc. οἱ ἱερώτατοι ἄνδρες] τοῦ τῇδε βίου τὴν εἰς ἀ. αὐτῶν ὁδόν, ὡς ἐγγυτέραν ἤδη γεγενημένην, ἐμφανέστερον ὁρῶσι Dion.Ar.*e.h.*7.1.2(M.3.553D); Leont.et Jo.*sacr.*(M.86.2061C); **c.** prize of martyrdom ἐστεφανωμένον...τὸν τῆς ἀ. στέφανον *M.Polyc.*17.1; *ib.*19.2; *A.Phil.*146(p.88.3); *A.Jo.*4(p.153.8); *Ep.Lugd.*ap.Eus.*h.e.*5.1.36(M.20.421C); *ib.*5.1.42(424C).

C. *incorruption*; **1.** of man's situation between corruption and incorruption, Meth.*symp.*3.7(p.34.2ff.; M.18.69C–72A) cit. s. φθορά; id.*res.*2.18(p.368.13ff.; M.18.312Cff.); ὥσπερ ἡ λογικὴ ψυχὴ οὐκ οὖσα ἀρετὴ ἢ κακία δεκτικὴ ἀμφοτέρων ἐστὶ τούτων, οὕτω καὶ τὸ ἡμέτερον σῶμα οὐ φθορὰ ἢ ἀ. τυγχάνον δέχεται κατὰ διαφόρους χρόνους τὰς ἐγκειμένας οὐσιώδεις ποιότητας. ἀμέλει γοῦν οὐ φθορὰ σπείρεται καὶ ἐγείρεται οὐκ ἀ., ἀλλ' 'ἐν ἀ.' Didym.*1Cor.*15:42f.(p.10.2ff.); all creation (τὰ πάντα) originally made ἐπὶ ἀφθαρσίᾳ, Cyr.*Lc.*22:19(M.72.908C); **2.** as state of Church and its members, Ign.*Magn.*6.2; id.*Eph.*17.1 cit. s. μύρον; τοῦ πάλιν ἐν ἀ. γενέσθαι διὰ πίστιν τὴν ἐν αὐτῷ [sc. Christ] αἰτήσεις πέμποντες Just.*1apol.*13.2(M.6.345B); **3.** given through sacraments; **a.** baptism, Meth.*symp.*3.8(p.36.10; M.18.73C) cit. s. ἀναγεννάω; τὸ λουτρὸν λάβω τῆς ἀ. *A.Thom.*A 120(p.229.24 v.l.); ὁ γὰρ τὸ ἔνδυμα τῆς ἀ. μὴ δεξάμενος, πόρρω... καθίσταται τῆς πρὸς θεὸν ὁμοιώσεως ‡Bas.*struct.hom.*1.21(1.334E; M.30.133B); Gr.Naz.*or.*40.4(M.36.361C); *ib.*40.31(404B); ὁ νυμφίος ἐκπορευθεὶς ἡρμόσατο ἑαυτῷ παρθένον ἡμᾶς διὰ τῆς μυστικῆς ἀναγεννήσεως τὴν τοῖς εἰδώλοις ἐκπορνευθεῖσαν, εἰς ἀ. παρθενικὴν ἀναστοιχειώσας τὴν φύσιν Gr.Nyss.*hom.11 in Cant.*(M.44.997A); Diad.*perf.*78(p.98.23); in prayer for catechumens καταξιώσας αὐτοὺς τοῦ λουτροῦ τῆς παλιγγενεσίας, τοῦ ἐνδύματος τῆς ἀ. *Lit.*ap.*Const.App.*8.6.6; ἐπειδὴ ἄφεσιν εἶπεν ἁμαρτιῶν, διὰ τῶν ἑξῆς αὐτὴν πιστοῦται λέγων, τοῦ ἐνδύματος τῆς ἀ. ὁ γὰρ υἱότητα ἐνδυόμενος, δῆλον ὅτι ἄφθαρτος γίνεται Chrys.*hom.*2.7 *in 2Cor.*(10.439B); baptismal water as ἀφθαρσίας πηγή *Rit.Bapt.*(p.400); ἔνδυμα ἀφθαρσίας *ib.*(p.401); **b.** eucharist, Clem.*paed.*2.2(p.168.2ff.; M.8.409B–412A) cit. s. αἷμα; *ib.*1.6(p.118.9; 305B); Mac.Mgn.*apocr.*3.23(p.107.4); τρέφει δὲ καὶ σαρκὶ τῇ ἰδίᾳ πρὸς ἀ. ἡμᾶς διαμορφῶν Cyr.*Is.*5.6(2.906D); **4.** through gospel τὸ δὲ εὐαγγέλιον ἀπάρτισμά ἐστιν ἀφθαρσίας Ign.*Philad.*9.2; Meth.*symp.*9.3(p.118.6; M.18.185A); **5.** through conversion and a Christian life, with which it is sts. almost equated ὁ τὸν τῆς ἀ. ἀγῶνα φθείρας *2Clem.*7.5; ὑποταγὴ δὲ θεοῦ, ἀ. Iren.*haer.*4.38.3(M.7.1108A); οὐ γὰρ πεσούμεθα εἰς φθορὰν οἱ διαβαίνοντες εἰς ἀ. Clem.*paed.*1.9(p.139.28; M.8.352A); ἁμαρτία φθορὰ οὖσα οὐ δύναται κοινωνίαν ἔχειν μετὰ τῆς ἀ., ἥτις ἐστὶ δικαιοσύνη id.*str.*3.17(p.244.18; M.8.1208B); *ib.*6.15(p.492.31; M.9.344D); Ἡρακλέων...εἰς δὲ τὸν 'ὅπου ἐγὼ ὑπάγω ὑμεῖς οὐ δύνασθε ἐλθεῖν' φησι· 'πῶς ἐν ἀγνοίᾳ καὶ ἀπιστίᾳ καὶ ἁμαρτήμασιν ὄντες ἐν ἀ. δύνανται γενέσθαι;' μηδὲ ἐν τούτῳ κατακούων ἑαυτοῦ· εἰ γὰρ οἱ ἐν ἀγνοίᾳ καὶ ἀπιστίᾳ καὶ ἁμαρτήμασιν ὄντες ἐν ἀ. οὐ δύνανται γενέσθαι, πῶς οἱ ἀπόστολοι ἐν ἀγνοίᾳ ποτὲ καὶ ἐν ἀπιστίᾳ καὶ ἐν ἁμαρτήμασιν γενόμενοι ἐν ἀ. γεγόνασιν δύνανται οὖν οἱ ἐν ἀγνοίᾳ...γενόμενοι γενέσθαι ἐν ἀ. εἰ μεταβάλλοιεν Or.*Jo.*19.14(3; p.314.17ff.; M.14.552B,C); **6.** ἀφθαρσία and virginity, exeg. Eph. 6:24 διηγήσαντό τινες εἶναι τὸ 'ἀγαπᾶν αὐτὸν ἐν ἀ.' καθαρεύοντα ἀπὸ τῶν ἔργων τῆς φθορᾶς· ἔργα δὲ τῆς φθορᾶς ἐστι τὰ κατὰ τὴν συνουσίαν, ὅθεν καὶ ἡ συνήθεια 'ἀφθόρους' ὀνομάζει τοὺς καθαροὺς ἀπὸ συνουσίας, καὶ 'ἐφθαρμένους' τοὺς μίξεως γευσαμένους. ὅρα δὲ εἰ δύναται πᾶσα μὲν ἁμαρτία φθορὰ εἶναι ψυχῆς, ἡ δὲ παντελὴς αὐτῆς ἀποχὴ ἀ. Or.*comm.in Eph.*6:24(p.576.13ff.); virginity leading to ἀ.: εἰς τὸ μὴ μοιχοὺς γεγονέναι, καὶ αὖ πάλιν εἰς σωφροσύνην, καὶ ἀπὸ σωφροσύνης εἰς παρθενίαν, ἔνθα μελετήσαντες τῆς σαρκὸς ὑπερφρονεῖν εἰς τὸν τῆς ἀ. εὔδιον ἀφόβως ὁρμίζονται χῶρον Meth.*symp.*1.2 (p.10.24; M.18.41B); μοὶ δοκῶ, ὅτι τῆς εἰς τὸν παράδεισον ἀποκαταστάσεως καὶ τῆς εἰς τὴν ἀ. μεταβολῆς...οὐδὲν αἴτιον οὕτως ἄλλο γέγονε ...ὡς ἁγνεία *ib.*4.2(p.46.10; 88B); ἐπίκουρον εἰς ἀφθαρσίας κτῆσιν τὴν παρθενίαν ὁ θεὸς ἐδωρήσατο *ib.*4.4(p.49.19; 92B); of virginal incorruption of BMV ὅτι τὸ ἐν αὐτῇ γεννηθὲν ἐκ πνεύματος ἁγίου ἦν... οὐδὲν ἧττον ἡ ἀ. συνδιεφυλάχθη τῷ τόκῳ Gr.Nyss.*Eun.*4(2 p.56.17; M.45.628A); τῷ κυρίῳ Ἰησοῦ ἐστιν ἐγκεκλεισμένη τε καὶ τηρουμένη ἐν ἀ. †Gregent.*disp.*(M.86.657A); ὁ θεὸς...αὐτὴν ἐνέδυσεν ἀ. σύσσωμον Mod.*dorm.*5(M.86.3289C); of BMV as τὸ ἄνθος τῆς ἀ. Andr.Cr. *or.*14(M.97.1100A); **7.** as aspect of spiritual life; **a.** in gen. ὅρασις δὲ θεοῦ περιποιητικὴ ἀφθαρσίας Iren.*haer.*4.38.3(M.7.1108C); cf.Clem. *str.*6.25(p.492.32; M.9.344D); ἐπίγνωσις τοῦ θεοῦ, ἥτις ἐστὶ κοινωνία ἀφθαρσίας *ib.*4.6(p.260.11; M.8.1240B); equated with Christ as author of spiritual life, id.*prot.*11(p.82.33; M.8.237A); Sever.*Eph.* 6:24(p.313.2); **b.** ref. 'garment of incorruption' (1Cor.15:53), gen. interpreted of state of grace in this life νύμφη...λαμβάνουσα...τῆς ἐπαγγελίας καὶ τῆς ἀ. τὸ ἔνδυμα Or.*schol.in Cant.*7:1(M.17.280D); φόρεσον ἔνδυμα ἀφθαρσίας, ἐν ἔργοις ἀγαθοῖς διαπρέπων Cyr.H.*catech.* 15.26; τίς γὰρ ἂν βλέπων περὶ ἑαυτὸν τὸν ἡλιοειδῆ τοῦ κυρίου χιτῶνα, τὸν διὰ καθαρότητος καὶ ἀ. αὐτῷ περιτεθέντα...εἶτα καταδέχεται τὸ πτωχόν τε καὶ ῥακῶδες ἱμάτιον; Gr.Nyss.*hom.11 in Cant.* (M.44.1005C); Geo.Pis.*hex.*1368(M.92.1539A); Anast.S.*hex.*12(M.89. 1064B).

D. Gnost., ref. the aeon Sophia ὅπως...διὰ τὴν ἀπαλλαγὴν τοῦ πληρώματος, ὀρεχθῇ τῶν διαφερόντων, ἔχουσά τινα ὀδμὴν ἀφθαρσίας, ἐγκαταλειφθεῖσαν αὐτὴν τοῦ Χριστοῦ Iren.*haer.*1.4.1(M.7.480A); name of aeon, Thdt.*haer.*1.13(4.304); Manich. εἰ καλοῖεν [sc. Manicheans] τἀγαθὸν ἀ., φθορὰν ὀνομάσουσι τὸ κακόν Tit.Bost.*Man.*1.11(M.18. 1084B).

***ἀφθαρτίζω**, *immortalize*, of body of Christ τὸ βαρὺ καὶ γεῶδες εἰς οὐρανοὺς ἀνελήφθη μετὰ τὴν ἀνάστασιν ἀφθαρτισθέν Iren.*fr.*26 (M.7.1244C); ἔχων καὶ μετὰ τὴν ἀνάστασιν τὴν ἡμῶν μορφὴν ἀφθαρτισθεῖσαν Thdr.Stud.*epp.*2.8(M.99.1133A); of men, through death and Resurrection of Christ ἀφ' οὗ ἀνέστη τὸ ἐξ ἡμῶν αὐτῷ προσληφθὲν ἀφθαρτίσας σαρκίον ὄντως ἠφθαρτίσμεθα Jo.D.*imag.*1.21(M.94.1253B); †Jo.D.*B.J.*7(M.96.916B); ‡Gr.Naz.*Chr.pat.*proem.22(M.38.135A); of BMV, Thdr.Stud.*or.*5.2(M.99.721B).

***ἀφθαρτοδοκῆται, οἱ**, *teachers of the natural incorruptibility of the pre-resurrection body of Christ*, criticized by Leont.B.*Nest.et Eut.*2 tit.(M.86.1316C); Eustrat.*v.Eutych.*37(M.86.2317A); Jo.D.*haer.* 84(M.94.753D); cf.Evagr.*h.e.*4.39(p.190.17; M.86.2781B); Jo.D.*f.o.*3. 28(M.94.1100B).

***ἀφθαρτοποιέω**, *render incorruptible*, Jo.Clim.*scal.*30(M.88.1157B).

***ἀφθαρτοποιός**, *rendering incorruptible*, Leont.H.*Nest.*5.20(M.86 1741D).

ἄφθαρτος, *incorruptible; immortal; uncorrupted;*

A. in gen., description of an incorruptible essence (ref. Christ's humanity) ἀ. γὰρ οὐσία οὐ γεννᾷ, οὐ γεννᾶται, οὐκ αὔξει, οὐχ ὑπνοῖ, οὐ πεινᾷ, οὐ διψᾷ, οὐ κοπιᾷ, οὐ πάσχει, οὐ θνήσκει, οὐ τιτρᾶται ὑπὸ ἥλων καὶ λόγχης, οὐχ ἱδροῖ, οὐχ αἱμορροεῖ. τοιαῦται οὐσίαι εἰσὶν ἥ τε τῶν ἀγγέλων, ἥ τε τῶν ψυχῶν τῶν ἐκ σωμάτων ἀπηλλαγμένων Hipp. *fr.res.*(p.254.6; M.10.861C).

B. of God and Christ; **1.** in gen.; **a.** pagan τῶν Πλατωνικῶν...τὸν δὲ θεὸν οἱ μὲν ἕνα φασὶν αὐτὸν εἰπεῖν ἀγένητον καὶ ἀ. Hipp.*haer.*1.19 (p.20.12; M.16.3041C); Ἐπίκουρος...τὸν δὲ θεὸν ὁμολογῶν εἶναι ἀΐδιον καὶ ἀ. *ib.*1.22(p.26.18; 3049B); in teaching of Val. Gn., Heracleon, and other followers of Platonist and Pythagorean teaching, *ib.*6. 29(p.155.23; 3235B); iron., of pagan gods τῶν δ' ἀ. ἐκείνων τάφους τε καὶ θήκας ἐπιδεικνύουσιν αὐτοί...ἀγνοοῦντες τὸ ἀληθῶς μακάριον καὶ ἀ. ἀνενδεὲς ὑπάρχον Const.*or.s.c.*4(p.158.2,5; M.20.1241C); **b.** Christian (cf. 1Tim.1:17), Arist.*apol.*4.1 cit. s. ἀναλλοίωτος; μόνος ἀ. ... ὁ θεός Just.*dial.*5.4(M.6.488B); †Just.*fr.res.*(p.45; M.6. 1585B); ὁ θεὸς...μένει μακάριος καὶ ἀ. Clem.*str.*6.12(p.484.24; M.9. 325B); ὁ πατὴρ αὐτὸς ἕλκει πρὸς αὐτὸν πάντα τὸν καθαρῶς βεβιωκότα καὶ εἰς ἔννοιαν τῆς μακαρίας καὶ ἀ. φύσεως κεχωρηκότα *ib.*5.13(p.381. 17; 124B); *ib.*5.10(p.369.1; 97A); Or.*Cels.*4.14(p.284.27; M.11.1045B); Ath.*gent.*22(M.25.44D); τὸ θεῖον ἀ. ... αὐτὸ γὰρ ὅ τί ποτέ ἐστιν, ἀ. ἐστιν· ἡ δὲ τοῦ ἀ. ἔννοια αὕτη, τὸ μὴ εἰς φθορὰν τὸ ὂν διαλύεσθαι. οὐκοῦν ἀ. εἰπόντες, ὃ μὴ πάσχει ἡ φύσις εἴπομεν Gr.Nyss.*tres dii*(M. 45.121B,C); Chrys.*hom.in Mt.26:39*(3.21A); Cyr.*dial.Trin.*7(5[1].635B); Thdt.*affect.*2(p.63.7; 4.755); **2.** of H. Ghost, in controversy with Macedonians, Gr.Nyss.*Maced.*22(M.45.1328D) cit. s. ἀναλλοίωτος; **3.** in Eunomian controversy; **a.** Eunomius made fact that God is ἀ. a reason why Father cannot communicate his substance to Son τὸν...υἱὸν πρὸ πάντων...τῇ ἑαυτοῦ δυνάμει καὶ ἐνεργείᾳ ἐγέννησέ τε καὶ ἔκτισε καὶ ἐποίησεν, οὐδὲν τῆς ἑαυτοῦ ὑποστάσεως μεταδοὺς τῷ γεννηθέντι. ἀ. γὰρ...ὁ θεός· ὁ δ' ἀ. τῆς ἑαυτοῦ οὐσίας οὐ μεταδίδωσιν Eun.*apol.*28(M.30.868A); holding ἀ. and ἀγέννητος to be mutually exclusive εἰ κατὰ τὸ ἀτελεύτητον, φησί [sc. Eunomius], τῆς ζωῆς μόνον ἐστὶν ἀ. καὶ κατὰ τὸ ἄναρχον μόνον ἀγέννητος, καθ' ὃ μή ἐστιν ἀ., φθαρτὸς ἔσται, καὶ καθ' ὃ μή ἐστιν ἀγέννητος, γεννητὸς ἔσται. καὶ ἐπαναλαβὼν πάλιν τὸ αὐτό φησιν ἔσται ἄρα κατὰ μὲν τὸ ἄναρχον ἀγέννητος ὁμοῦ καὶ φθαρτός, κατὰ δὲ τὸ ἀτελεύτητον ἀ. ὁμοῦ καὶ γεννητός Gr.Nyss.*Eun.*12(1 p.357.2ff.; M.45.1080A); **b.** orthodox view ἀ. γὰρ καὶ ἀγέννητον εἶναι τὸν θεὸν τῶν ὅλων λέγομεν, κατὰ διαφόρους ἐπιβολὰς τοῖς ὀνόμασι τούτοις προσαγορεύοντες. ὅταν μὲν γὰρ εἰς τοὺς κάτοπιν αἰῶνας ἀποβλέψωμεν,...ἀγέννητον αὐτὸν λέγομεν· ὅταν δὲ τοῖς ἐπερχομένοις αἰῶσι τὸν νοῦν ἐπεκτείνωμεν... προσαγορεύομεν ἀ. ὡς οὗ τὸ ἀτελεύτητον τῆς ζωῆς, ἀ.· οὕτω τὸ ἄναρχον αὐτῆς, ἀγέννητον ὠνομάσθη Bas.*Eun.*1.7(1.218E–219A; M.29.525B,C); τὸ ἀ. τὸ μὴ προσεῖναι τῷ θεῷ φθορὰν σημαίνει...τίνος μὲν ἕξεως προλαβούσης στέρησιν ἐμφαίνει τὸ ἀ.; *ib.*1.9(221D,E; M.532C–533A); **c.** Gr. Nyss., after citing Bas.*Eun.*1.7 (v. supra) refutes Eunomius τό τε γὰρ μὴ ἐξ αἰτίας εἶναί τινος διὰ τῆς τοῦ ἀνάρχου τε καὶ ἀγεννήτου φωνῆς ἐξαγγέλλομεν, καὶ τὸ μηδενὶ περιγράφεσθαι τέλει μηδὲ εἰς φθορὰν διαλύεσθαι, τοῦτο ἡ τοῦ ἀ. τε καὶ ἀτελευτήτου διασημαίνει λέξις· καὶ τούτῳ διορίζεται τὸ δεῖν ἐπὶ τῆς θείας ζωῆς τὸ μὲν τὴν ἀρχὴν μὴ ἔχειν ἀγεννήτως εἶναι λέγειν, τὸ δὲ ἀτελευτήτως εἶναι ἀ. κατονομάζειν...τὸν οὖν μηδέποτε τοῦ εἶναι παυόμενον ἀλλότριόν τε τῆς κατὰ φθορὰν διαλύσεως ὄντα ἀ. ὀνομάζεσθαι λέγει Gr.Nyss.*Eun.*12(1 p.358.6ff.; M.45.1080C,D); ἀ. and ἀγέννητος being not mutually exclusive, but complementary, *ib.*(1 p.359.29; M.45.1081D); *ib.*1 (1 p.182.18; 428A); *ib.*12(1 p.252.20f.; 953B,C); **4.** of Christ as ἀ. in his divinity, *Diogn.*9.2 cit. s. λύτρον; ὁ λόγος ὁ τοῦ θεοῦ ἄσαρκος ὢν ἐνεδύσατο τὴν ἁγίαν σάρκα...μίξας τὸ φθαρτὸν τῷ ἀ. Hipp.*antichr.*4 (p.7.1; M.10.732B); Ath.*inc.*9.1(M.25.112A) cit. s. ἀνάστασις; ἐπὶ μὲν τῆς οἰκείας δυνάμεως ἀ., ἐπὶ δὲ τῆς ἀσθενείας τῆς ἡμῶν παθητός Leo Mag.*ep.*35(p.41.17; M.*PL.*54.807D); ref. Passover, Jewish and Christian ἐστίν...φθαρτὸν καὶ ἀ. ... φθαρτὸν κατὰ τὴν τοῦ προβάτου σφαγήν, ἀ. διὰ τὴν τοῦ κυρίου ζωήν Mel.*pass.*2,3 p.1.7,12; **5.** of Christ's body; **a.** orthodox, of risen body δείξῃ δὲ ἑαυτὸν καὶ θανάτου κρείττονα, ἀπαρχὴν τῆς τῶν ὅλων ἀναστάσεως τὸ ἴδιον σῶμα ἀ. ἐπιδεικνύμενος Ath.*inc.*20.2(M.25.132A); μετά γε τὴν ἀνάστασιν ἦν... τὸ σῶμα...οὐ γὰρ ἔτι πείνης, ἢ κόπου...δεκτικόν...ἀλλὰ λοιπὸν ἀ. Cyr.*ep.*45(p.156.4; 5[2].139D); οὐκοῦν καὶ θνητόν ἐστι καὶ παθητὸν μετὰ τὴν ἀνάστασιν; οὐδαμῶς, ἀλλ' ἀ. Thdt.*eran.*2(4.121); discussion of how incorruptible risen body could be capable of eating etc. ἄξιον δὲ διαπορῆσαι πῶς σῶμα ἀ. τύπους ἐδείκνυτο τῶν ἥλων, καὶ ἁπτὸν ἦν θνητῇ χειρί. ἀλλὰ μὴ θορυβηθῇς· συγκαταβάσεως γὰρ ἦν τὸ γινόμενον...ὥστε πιστευθῆναι τὴν ἀνάστασιν, τοῦτο δείκνυται Chrys. *hom.87.1 in Jo.*(8.520C); *ib.87.2*(521C); **b.** its incorruptibility used as argument against Marcellus' alleged theory that it was separated from Word after Resurrection ⟨αὐ⟩τοῦ δὲ τοῦ πρόοντος ἐν θεῷ λόγου ἀφοριζομένου μὲν τοῦ σώματος (κἂν ἀθάνατον τοῦτο καὶ ἀ. ᾖ) τῷ δὲ θεῷ συναφθησομένου Eus.*Marcell.*1.1(p.6.17, v.l. ἄφθιτον M.24.724B); οὐκοῦν ἄνευ λόγου μόνον τὸ σῶμα στήσεται ἐν...ἀ. ἀλογίᾳ...; *ib.*2.4(p.57.4; 820C) et passim; ἑνῶν μὲν τὸν λόγον τῷ θεῷ τὴν δὲ σάρκα χωρίζων τῆς τοῦ λόγου ἐνεργείας καὶ καταλιπὼν αὐτὴν οὐκ οἶδ' ὅπως ἀθάνατον μὲν καὶ ἀ. ἄψυχον δὲ καὶ ἀνενέργητον ὑπὸ τοῦ λόγου id.*e.th.*3.10(p.167.13; M.24.1020C); **c.** heret., of Christ's body before Resurrection ἄλλη γὰρ ἀπώλεια τῶν Μανιχαίων...καὶ ἄλλο πάλιν τῶν λεγόντων ἀ. σῶμα ἀναλαβεῖν ἐκ τῆς ἁγίας θεοτόκου τὸν...Χριστόν ‡Ath.*qu.Ant.*116(M.28.672B); as heresy of Gaianites Γαϊανῖται ὁμολογοῦσι τὸν θεὸν λόγον ἐνανθρωπῆσαι ἐκ τῆς παρθένου τελείως καὶ ἀληθινῶς· ἀπὸ δὲ τῆς ἑνώσεως ἀ. ὁμολογοῦσιν εἶναι τὸ σῶμα †Leont.B.*sect.*10.1(M.86.1260B); ὅταν οὖν εἴπῃ τις τῶν πατέρων, ὅτι οὐχ ὑπέμεινε φθορὰν τὸ σῶμα τοῦ Χριστοῦ, τοῦτο λέγει, ὅτι οὐ διαμπὰξ ἐλύθη...ἐν πολλοῖς γὰρ πρὸ τῆς ἀναστάσεως φθαρτὸν αὐτὸ λέγουσι, μετὰ δὲ τὴν ἀνάστασιν, ἀ. *ib.*10.2(1261D); several schools of thought within this sect Γαϊανῖται,...οἵτινες λέγουσιν, ἐξ αὐτῆς τῆς ἑνώσεως τὸ τοῦ κυρίου σῶμα κατὰ πάντα τρόπον ἀ. εἶναι Tim. CP *haer.*(M.86.44B); οἵτινες οὐ κατὰ πάντα τρόπον ἀ. λέγουσι τὸ σῶμα τοῦ κυρίου...ἀλλὰ δυνάμει μὲν φθαρτόν, μηδόλως δὲ φθαρῆναι τῇ ἐπικρατείᾳ τοῦ λόγου *ib.*; ἄλλοι, οἵτινες καλοῦνται καὶ ἀκτιστῆται· λέγουσι γὰρ ὅτι οὐ μόνον ἀ. ... ἀλλὰ καὶ ἄκτιστον γεγονέναι τὸ τοῦ κυρίου σῶμα ib.(M.86.44C); Justinian's opinion ὡρμήθη λέγειν...ἄ. τὸ σῶμα τοῦ...Χριστοῦ ἐξ αὐτῆς ἑνώσεως γεγενῆσθαι...ἁμαρτίας φθορά, τὸ λέγειν ἄ. πρὸ τῆς ἀναστάσεως τὸ σῶμα τοῦ κυρίου...εἰ γὰρ τοῦτο δοθήσεται, φαντασία, οὐκ ἀλήθεια, ἡ σάρκωσις καὶ ἐνανθρώπησις τοῦ θεοῦ λόγου γέγονεν Eustrat.*v.Eutych.*33(M.86.2313B,C); Evagr.*h.e.* 4.39(p.190.17; M.86.2781B).

C. of future life; **1.** in gen. ἀναστήσει ἡμᾶς ὁ θεὸς διὰ τοῦ Χριστοῦ αὐτοῦ καὶ ἀ. ... ποιήσει Just.*dial.*46.7(M.6.576C); *ib.*117.3(748A); τῆς ἀτελευτήτου καὶ ἀ. ζωῆς Eus.*e.th.*3.16(p.174.23; M.24.1033A); *Const. App.*5.7.1; Dion.Ar.*d.n.*1.4(M.3.592B); id.*e.h.*7.1.1(M.3.553B); ‡Bas. *h.myst.*62(p.397.15); **2.** of kingdom of God οὐκ ἔχει ἐπιθυμίαν ἡ ἄ. βασιλεία, ἀλλὰ παρουσίαν πάντων τῶν ἀγαθῶν Clem.*fr.*46(p.223.31); ἄ. καὶ ἀγήρω...τὴν βασιλείαν ἔσεσθαι Eus.*e.th.*3.17(p.176.34; M.24. 1037B); *ib.*(p.178.7; 1040B); **3.** of resurrection body ἡμῶν...τὰ σκηνώματα ἐκ τοῦ χοὸς ἄ. ἀνίστανται Meth.*res.*2.21(p.375.7; M.18. 285C); *ib.*3.14(p.411.7)ap.Oecum.*Phil.*3:20f.(M.118.1312D); Eus.*e.th.* 3.16(p.175.13; M.24.1033C); id.*Marcell.*2.1(p.33.26; M.24.780C); **4.** incorruption a reward of Christian virtue and martyrdom οἳ [sc. ἄνθρωποι] ἐὰν ἀξίους τῷ ἐκείνου [sc. θεοῦ] βουλεύματι ἑαυτοὺς δι' ἔργων δείξωσι, τῆς μετ' αὐτοῦ ἀναστροφῆς καταξιωθῆναι προσειλήφαμεν συμβασιλεύοντας, ἀ. καὶ ἀπαθεῖς γενομένους Just.*1apol.*10.2(M.6. 341A); οἱ τῷ Χριστῷ πιστεύοντες...ἴσασι...ὅτι ἀποθνήσκοντες...ἄ. διὰ τῆς ἀναστάσεως γίνονται Ath.*inc.*27.2(M.25.144A); of martyr's crown καταξιωθῆναι τοῦ ἀ. στεφανοῦ *Const.App.*5.1.2; **5.** of the change of soul (Origenist) after death ἀνεστοιχειοῦτο...αὐτῇ ψυχῇ [i.e. of Helena] ἐπὶ τὴν ἄ. καὶ ἀγγελικὴν οὐσίαν, πρὸς τὸν αὐτῆς ἀναλαμβανομένη σωτῆρα Eus.*v.C.*3.46(p.97.10; M.20.1105D); **6.** spiritual joy an indication of immortality, Diad.*perf.*25(p.28.5) cit. s. χαρά; **7.** exeg. 1Cor.15:48f. τοῦτο εἶπεν διὰ τὸ ἐξ οὐρανοῦ εἶναι τὸν θεὸν λόγον τὸν ἀτρέπτως γεγονότα ἄνθρωπον...εἰκόνα δὲ νῦν λέγει πεφορηκέναι ἡμᾶς τοῦ χοϊκοῦ κατὰ τὸ τεθνήξεσθαι, εἰκόνα δὲ τοῦ ἐπουρανίου κατὰ τὸ ἀναστήσεσθαι καὶ διαμενεῖν ἀφθάρτους Thdr.Mops.*1Cor.* 15:48f.(p.195.26).

D. ref. man's condition; **1.** Adam would have remained ἄ. if he had not sinned, Ath.*inc.*4.6(M.25.104C); but οὐκ ἔχων ἐξ οἰκείας φύσεως τό τε ἄ. καὶ ἀνώλεθρον Cyr.*Jo.*1.9(4.94E); discussion of question ζητητέον, εἰ ἄ. ἦν Ἀδάμ, πῶς ὑπεδέξατο τοῦτον φθορά; εἰ δὲ φθαρτός, τί πλέον ἀπὸ τῆς ἀποφάσεως λεγούσης, 'ᾗ δ' ἂν ἡμέρᾳ φάγητε ἀπ' αὐτοῦ, θανάτῳ ἀποθανεῖσθε'· ἄ. οὖν μὲν ὁ γηγενὴς οὐκ ἐπλάσθη· οὐ γὰρ ἄ. τὸ ἀφ' οὗ πέπλασται· μετὰ δὲ τὴν πλάσιν 'ἐνεφύσησεν ὁ θεὸς εἰς τὸ πρόσωπον αὐτοῦ πνοὴν ζωῆς'...ἔχει τοίνυν ἄ. μὲν τὴν ψυχήν, φθειρόμενον δὲ τὸ σῶμα Proc.G.*Gen.*3:18(M.87.216C,D); **2.** human soul immortal; **a.** in pagan thought τὴν ψυχὴν οἱ μέν [sc. τῶν Πλατωνικῶν] φασιν αὐτὸν [sc. Plato] ἀγένητον λέγειν καὶ ἄ. Hipp. *haer.*1.19(p.21.5; M.16.3044A); **b.** Christian ἡ μὲν ψυχὴ ἐστιν ἄ., μέρος οὖσα τοῦ θεοῦ καὶ ἐμφύσημα †Just.*fr.res.*(p.46; M.6.1588A); μεταδεδωκέναι τὸν θεὸν τοῦ ἀ. πνεύματος τῷ ἀνθρώπῳ Or.*Cels.*4.37 (p.308.18; M.11.1085C); ἄ. γὰρ φύσιν πεποίηκε [sc. God] τὴν νοερὰν καὶ αὐτῷ συγγενῆ id.*princ.*3.1.13(p.218.11; M.11.273A).

E. *incorrupt*, of Christian life on earth; **1.** in gen. θέωμεν τὴν ὁδὸν τὴν εὐθεῖαν, ἀγῶνα τὸν ἄ. *2Clem.*7.3; ἡ ζωὴ ἣν ἐγὼ διδάσκω ἄ. ἐστιν *A.Thom.*A 127(p.236.5); **2.** its causes αὐτὸς [sc. Christ] ἐν ἡμῖν κατοικῶν...μετάνοιαν διδοὺς ἡμῖν εἰσάγει εἰς τὸν ἄ. ναόν *Barn.* 16.9; οἱ δὲ νενοηκότες τὰ προσόντα τῷ ὄντι καλὰ καὶ ἄ. τῇ ἀρετῇ Just. *2apol.*11.8(M.6.464A); τούς τε ἀγγέλους καὶ τοὺς ἀνθρώπους ὁ θεὸς... ἐποίησεν, εἰ μὲν τὰ εὐάρεστα αὐτῷ αἱροῖντο, καὶ ἀ. ... αὐτοὺς τηρῆσαι id.*dial.*88.5(M.6.685C); ἀγάπη τῆς γνώσεως ἄ. ποιεῖ Clem.*str.*6.15 (p.492.33; M.9.345A); ἄρτον ζωῆς ὃν οἱ ἐσθίοντες ἄ. διαμείνωσιν *A.Thom.*A 133(p.240.7); λῦσαι φθορὰν προῆλθες [sc. κύριε], ἵνα ἄ. πάντα τεύχοις ‡Meth.*Sym.et Ann.*14(M.18.381C); **3.** of fruits of Christian life οὗτοι γὰρ οὐκ εἰσὶν φυτεία πατρός· εἰ γὰρ ἦσαν, ἐφαίνοντο ἂν κλάδοι τοῦ σταυροῦ, καὶ ἦν ἂν ὁ καρπὸς αὐτῶν ἄ. Ign.*Trall.*11.2; δέχονται τροφὴν ἄ. Max.*cap.*2.25(M.90.1229C); **4.** = *virginal*, of BMV ὁ μόνος ἐξ ἁγίου πνεύματος ἀπὸ ἀ. παρθένου Leo Mag.*ep.*35 (p.42.1; M.*PL.*54.808B); **5.** *incorruptible*; Gnost., of the 'spiritual' τὴν δὲ μίαν λέγει [sc. Heracleon] τὴν ἄ. τῆς ἐκλογῆς φύσιν (opp. πολλοί who are ψυχικοί) Or.*Jo.*13.51(50; p.280.2; M.14.493B).

F. neut., esp. as subst.; **1.** of imperishable (i.e. spiritual) things εἰ γὰρ ἐν τῷ ἀ. κοινωνοί ἐστε, πόσῳ μᾶλλον ἐν τοῖς φθαρτοῖς; *Barn.*19.8; ἐκεῖνα ἀγαπῆσαι, τὰ ἀγαθὰ τὰ ἄ. *2Clem.*6.6; ἵνα μικρὰ καὶ ἐπίκηρα μεγάλοις καὶ ἀ. παραβάλωμεν Clem.*q.d.s.*3(p.161.21; M.9. 608A); Dion.Ar.*d.n.*10.3(M.3.937C); **2.** *incorruptibility*; **a.** as attribute of God τῷ δὲ ἀγενήτῳ ἀκολουθεῖν πάντως καὶ τὸ ἄ. Hipp.*haer.* 1.19(p.20.4; M.16.3041B); ‡Just.*qu.Chr.*5.2(M.6.1457B); Jo.D.*f.o.*1.4 (M.94.800A); **b.** of the sky τὸ ἄφθαρτον τῆς οὐσίας αὐτοῦ [sc. οὐρανοῦ] ἀφορῶντες ‡Just.*qu.Chr.*5.2(M.6.1457A).

ἀφθάρτως, *without suffering corruption*; **1.** i.e. remaining divine, of Son οὐ γὰρ ὑπόστασιν ἑτέραν ἑαυτῷ λαβὼν ἥνωσεν, ἀλλὰ φύσιν ἥρμοσεν ἀ. τῇ ἑαυτοῦ ὑποστάσει Anast.Ant.*fr.*(M.89.1281D) v.l. for ἀφράστως ap.*Doct.Patr.*21.8(p.135.10); **2.** i.e. remaining a virgin, of BMV ἀ. ἐγγέννησεν ἡ Μαρία τὸν Ἰησοῦν *A.Phil.*77(p.30.14).

***ἄφθαστος**, *that cannot be caught up, outrunning all*, of S. John ὁ τοῦ οὐρανίου βυθοῦ ἐρευνητὴς ἄ. Thdr.Stud.*or.*9.2(M.99.772C); hence of τῶν δογμάτων ὁ βυθός, *inexplicable, not to be plumbed*, *ib.*

***ἀφθέγμων**, *unutterable, ineffable*; of God, Dion.Ar.*c.h.*15.8(M.3. 336D).

***ἀφθεγξία, ἡ, 1.** *silence*, of God τῆς θείας εἰρήνης καὶ ἡσυχίας, ἣν ὁ ἱερὸς Ἰοῦστος ἀ. καλεῖ Dion.Ar.*d.n.*11.1(M.3.949A); **2.** *speechlessness*; of Zacharias, ‡Thdt.*nativ.Jo.Bapt.*(5.90); of infant Jesus, Anast.S. *hod.*13(M.89.233A); of mystics in the presence of God δι' ἀφθεγξίας τῷ ἀδύτῳ τῶν ἀδύτων παρακύψαντες Max.*ep.*12(M.91.505C); **3.** *ineffability*, Geo.Pis.*hex.*1077(M.92.1517A; p.636 ἀφθαρσίας); Andr.Cr. *or.*12(M.97.1061A).

***ἀφθιτοεργός, ὁ**, *one who works unceasingly*; of Christ, Eudoc. *Cypr.*1.84(M.85.836B).

ἀφθιτόμητις, *of eternal counsel*; of the Word, Gr.Naz.*carm.*1.2. 31.31(M.37.913A).

***ἀφθονόπλουστος**, *most copious*, *Hymn.*(*AS* 1 p.564).

ἀφθορία, ἡ, 1. *chastity, purity*; of a celibate man, Bas.*ascet.* 1.1(2.319B; M.31.872B); of a woman, Gr.Naz.*carm.*1.2.3.19(M.37. 634A); of BMV τὸ παιδίον ἐγεννήθη καὶ τὴν τῆς μητρὸς ἀ. οὐκ ἐλυμήνατο Gr.Nyss.*Eun.*2(2 p.318.17; M.45.492B); διὰ τῆς παρθενικῆς ἀ. ἐπὶ τὸν ἀνθρώπινον βίον διαπεράσας Gr.Nyss.*nativ.*(M.46.1128B); Anast.Ant.*serm.*3.2(M.89.1388B); in gen., †Bas.Anc.*virg.*tit.(M.30. 669); Gr.Naz.*carm.*2.1.92.5(1447A); **2.** *purity*, spiritual as well as bodily, Thdr.Stud.*epp.*2.54(M.99.1268A); **3.** = ἀφθαρσία, *incorruptibility, immortality* ὅσα τῷ πατρὶ καὶ τῷ υἱῷ ἐφαρμόζεται, ταῦτα καὶ περὶ τὸ ἅγιον θεωρεῖται πνεῦμα· ἡ ἀ., ἡ μακαριότης Gr.Nyss.*fid.*(M. 45.144A).

ἄφθορος, 1. *chaste, virgin*; of a boy or celibate man, Clem.*str.* 3.4(p.208.2; M.8.1132A); Evagr.*h.e.*4.36(p.185.22; M.86.2769A); of Christ ἄ. ἐφύλαξεν ἐν παρθενίᾳ τὴν σάρκα κοσμήσας Meth.*symp.*1.5 (p.13.13; M.18.45B); of a woman: Eve, Just.*dial.*100.5(M.6.712A); BMV, Gr.Nyss.*or.catech.*23(p.86.15; M.45.61B); Sophr.H.*ep.syn.*(M. 87.3176A); τὴν ἄσπορον σύλληψιν καὶ τὴν ἄ. γέννησιν Max.*ep.*19(M.91. 592D); in gen., Just.*1apol.*15.6(M.6.349B); Meth.*symp.*1.1(p.8.9; M. 18.37B); Socr.*h.e.*3.13.11(M.67.413C); neut. as subst. τὸ ἄ. ἐπὶ τῆς παρθενίας λεγόμενον, σημαντικόν ἐστι τῆς ἐν αὐτῇ καθαρότητος Gr. Nyss.*virg.*1(M.46.320C); **2.** of spiritual purity ἡ ἄ. ψυχὴ παρθένος ἐστί, κἂν ἄνδρα ἔχῃ Chrys.*hom.28.7 in Heb.*(12.269A); **3.** = ἄφθαρτος, *incorruptible, immortal* τὸ ἀγένητον, ἄτρεπτον φανθέν, καὶ ἀπροσδεὲς καὶ ἄ. ἔσται Meth.*creat.*7(p.498.20; M.18.340C).

***ἀφθόρως**, *without loss of virginity* ἐκ παρθένου ἁγίας γεννηθεὶς ἀσπόρως τε καὶ ἀ. σάρκα ἀνέλαβε Arist.*apol.*15.1; ἀσπόρως συνέλαβε καὶ ἀ. ἔτεκεν Anast.S.*fr.*(M.89.1286C); Jo.D.*f.o.*1.2(M.94.792D); ‡Meth.*Sym.et Ann.*9(M.18.369C).

***ἄφιγμα, τό**, *story* τῶν βασιλέων τὸ ἄ. *the Book of Kings*, Sophr. H.*nativ.*(p.513.31).

***ἀφιδιάζω**, v. *ἀπιδιάζω.

***ἀφιδιαστικός**, v. *ἀπιδιαστικός.

ἀφιερ-όω, 1. *hallow, treat as holy*, ref. Jewish worship σχεδὸν ὡς τὰ ἔθνη ~ωσαν αὐτὸν [sc. God] ἐν τῷ ναῷ *Barn.*16.2; **2.** *consecrate, dedicate*; in gen., Clem.*str.*6.4(p.449.13; M.9.253B); προσευκτήρια καὶ ναοὶ τῷ θεῷ ~ωμένα Eus.*p.e.*5.1(179C; M.21.312B); Gr.Nyss.*or. dom.*2(p.30.11; M.44.1137C); τὸ ~ωμένον τῷ θεῷ ἀνάθημα ὀνομάζεται Thdt.*Rom.*9:3(3.98); med., of setting apart of eucharistic bread for consecration, ‡Sophr.H.*liturg.*10(M.87.3989D); of setting apart canonical books as sacred, Eus.*p.e.*12.23(597C; M.992B); of a ruler consecrated by God, *Chron.Pasch.*p.402(M.92.1028A); of consecration of persons to God in Christian service and ascetic life τούτῳ τέθνηκεν ἡ σάρξ, ζῇ δὲ αὐτὸς μόνος ~ώσας τὸν τάφον εἰς ναὸν ἅγιον κυρίῳ Clem.*str.*4.22(p.309.10; M.8.1348B); τὸ ~ωμένον...τῷ θεῷ σῶμα Bas.*ascet.*1.2(2.319D; M.31.872D); Didym.*Trin.*2.4(M.39.745B); αὐτὴν τὴν καρδίαν, αὐτὸν τὸν νοῦν ἀ. Mac.Aeg.*hom.*14.3(M.34.572B); τοὺς λογικοὺς ναοὺς ἀ. τῷ θεῷ Thdt.*1Cor.*3:16(3.184); Dion.Ar.*e.h.*1.1 (M.3.372B); Dor.*doct.*15.1(M.88.1788B); of humanity of Christ as consecrated temple, Eust.*engast.*10(p.31.14; M.18.633B); **3.** met., *assign* τὸν ἐγκέφαλον ἀ. τῷ λογισμῷ Gr.Nyss.*hom.opif.*12.1(M.44. 156D); **4.** *honour* Ὀνώριον τῇ συνήθει καθοσιώσει ἀ. *IGC.As.Min.* 281.

***ἀφιέρωμα, τό**, *consecrated object, votive offering*, *A.Andr.*A 11 (p.53.6 not.); Eus.*v.C.*3.51(p.99.8; M.20.1112A); ζωῆς τε ἀθανάτου καὶ βασιλείας ἐνθέου λαμπρὰ ἀ. id.*l.C.*18(p.259.27; M.20.1440B).

ἀφίημι, (for ἀφίω q.v.); **1.** med., *let loose* tongue, voice, Tat.*orat.* 1(p.2.12; M.6.805B); **2.** *stretch out,* Eus.*d.e.*8.1(p.363.21; M.22.589D); Nonn.*par.Jo.*19:24(M.43.904A); **3.** *forgive*; **a.** abs. or c. dat., Ign. *Philad.*8.1; Polyc.*ep.*6.2; Clem.*str.*7.13(p.58.1; M.9.512C); **b.** c. acc., Dion.Al.*fr.*(p.60.10); τοὺς ἀπαλλαττομένους τοῦ βίου ἀφίεσθαι id. ap.Eus.*h.e.*6.44.4(M.20.632A); **4.** *reserve* δίδωσιν αὐτὸ τοῖς πτωχοῖς, μηδὲν ἀφήσας ἑαυτῷ Jo.Mosch.*prat.*202(M.87.3092C); **5.** *place* ἀφίεται τὸ θεῖον σῶμα ἐν τῇ προθέσει ὥσπερ ἐν Βηθλεέμ ‡Sophr.H.*liturg.*10 (M.87.3989D); **6.** intrans. c. genit., *neglect* μὴ ἀφείσης τοῦ δρέπειν καρποὺς πνευματικούς Nil.*epp.*4.1(M.79.545A); **7.** med., *give up,* Socr. *h.e.*3.17.9(M.67.425A).

ἀφικνέομαι, 1. *reach,* of a rumour, announcement ἀφῖκται εἰς ἐμὲ Εὐφρόνιόν τε καὶ Γεώργιον εἶναι τὴν πίστιν δοκιμωτάτους Const. ap.Eus.*v.C.*3.62(p.110.18; M.20.1137A); **2.** of coming of day of the Lord and Messiah, Thdt.*Cant.*6:9(2.133 citing Joel 2:31; LXX ἐλθεῖν); id.*Is.*1:28,29(p.11.33; 2.182); Cyr.*Lc.*4:16(M.72.536C); hence ὁ ἀφικόμενος *the coming one, the Messiah* (cf. Mt.11:3 ὁ ἐρχόμενος), Eus.*e.th.*1.6(p.64.34; M.24.833C).

***ἀφιλάδελφος,** *without brotherly love,* ‡Bas.*const.*30(2.578C; M.31. 1420C).

***ἀφιλαλληλία, ἡ,** *lack of mutual love,* Cyr.*Mal.*25(3.841E, v.l. φιλίας Aubert).

***ἀφιλάλληλος,** *without mutual love,* Cyr.*ep.*78(5^2.210B); id.*Os.*35 (3.64B); id.*Am.*9(3.261C).

***ἀφιλαλλήλως,** *in an unloving manner,* Cyr.*glaph.Ex.*1(1.255A); id.*Am.*73(3.333D).

***ἀφιλανθρώπευτος,** *contrary to humanity, anti-social,* Ephr.3. 388F.

***ἀφιλαργυρέω,** *have no love of money,* Cyr.*Jo.*3.4(4.277A).

***ἀφιλάρετος,** *not caring for virtue,* Cyr.*Lc.*16:15(M.72.817C); id. *Juln.*5(6^2.167E).

***ἀφίλαρχος,** *indifferent to power, V.Pach.Φ* 107(p.70.18); neut. as subst., *indifference to power,* Ephr.1.204C.

ἀφίλαυτος, *free from self-love, unselfish,* Isid.Pel.*epp.*1.278(M.78. 345C); neut. as subst., Jo.D.*virt.*(M.95.88A) = Ephr.3.425F.

***ἀφιλαύτως,** *unselfishly,* Clem.*str.*8.1(p.81.7; M.9.561A).

***ἀφιλεργέω,** *shrink from labour, love idleness,* Cyr.*hom.pasch.*27 (5^2.313D); *ib.*29(336D); id.*Ag.*18(3.648A); ἀφιλοερ- id.*glaph.Ex.*2(1. 288B).

***ἀφιλεργής,** *idle, lazy,* Cyr.*hom.pasch.*26(5^2.303B).

***ἀφιλεργία, ἡ,** *idleness, laziness,* Cyr.*Is.*3.1(2.374B); id.*Lc.*9:26 (M.72.651B); id.*hom.pasch.*26(5^2.303B).

***ἀφιλέταιρος,** *without society of friends,* Bas.*ep.*2.2(3.71E; M.32. 225B).

ἀφιλήδονος, *not yielding to pleasure,* ‡Chrys.*pasch.*2(8.255E).

***ἀφιλοδοξία, ἡ,** *indifference to glory* ὑπογραμμὸς γὰρ ἡμῖν ἀφιλοδοξίας εὑρίσκεται Χριστός Cyr.*Jo.*3.4(4.286E).

***ἀφιλοεργέω,** v. *ἀφιλεργέω.

***ἀφιλοθεάμων,** *not liking contemplation,* Cyr.*dogm.*3(6^2.369E).

***ἀφιλοθεΐα, ἡ,** *enmity to God,* Cyr.*Is.*5.3(2.802B); τὰ τῆς τῶν Ἰουδαίων ἀ. τολμήματα id.*hom.pasch.*30(5^2.349B); id.ap.CLater.*act.*5 (H.3.876C).

***ἀφιλόθεος,** *impious, at enmity with God,* Pall.*v.Chrys.*5(p.31.24; M.47.20); ἀ. ... ὁ μαντείαις προσέχων Cyr.*Is.*2.4(2.290A); *ib.*3.2 (395A) al.; ὦ τῆς ἀ. τῶν Ἰουδαίων ψυχῆς Leont.N.*serm.*2(M.93. 1592A); παρὰ τὴν παράδοσιν...περιπατεῖ ὁ ἀ. Thdr.Stud.*epp.*2.131 (M.99.1424C); neut. as subst., Cyr.ap.*cat.Mt.*21:14(p.170.15); id. *ador.*14(1.486A).

***ἀφιλοθέως,** *out of enmity* or *in a state of enmity to God, impiously,* Didym.*Trin.*1.11(M.39.293B); Cyr.*hom.pasch.*11(5^2.150E); Leont.N. *serm.*2(M.93.1592D).

***ἀφιλοικτιρμόνως (-ειρμόνως),** *pitilessly,* (-ει-) Cyr.*ador.*6(1.181A); id.*glaph.Ex.*2(1.281B); *ib.*(286B).

ἀφιλοικτίρμων, *unmerciful, pitiless,* Eus.*Is.*13:17(M.24.189A); ἀ. αἱρετικῶν Cyr.*ador.*14(1.484C); Olymp.*Job* 22:10(M.93.244D).

ἀφιλοκάλητος, *unadorned, uncared for,* Dor.*doct.*16.4(M.88.1800A) cit. s. ἀσύστροφος; Jo.D.*trisag.*5(M.95.33A).

***ἀφιλοκομπέω,** *be averse to arrogance,* Cyr.*Jo.*9(4.727C).

***ἀφιλοκομπία, ἡ,** *dislike of boasting, humility,* Cyr.*Is.*3.5(2. 536E).

***ἀφιλόκομπος,** *averse to arrogance, not boastful,* Ammon.*Jo.* 11:34(M.85.1468D); ἀ. τὸ θεῖον ἀεί Cyr.*glaph.Lev.*(1.375E); id.*Am.*15 (3.266A).

ἀφιλόλογος, *averse to reasoning,* Diad.*perf.*45(p.52.1).

***ἀφιλομαθής,** *not desirous of learning,* Cyr.*Jo.*2.1(4.149C); *ib.*2.5 (201A).

***ἀφιλομαθία, ἡ,** *absence of desire to learn, voluntary ignorance,* Cyr.*Zach.*117(3.815A).

***ἀφιλόμαχος,** *not fond of fighting,* Cyr.*Joel.*41(3.238D); id.*Jo.*10 (4.840A).

[*]ἀφιλόνικος, *not desirous of victory,* Clem.*str.*5.5(p.345.25, v.l. ἀφιλόνεικος M.9.53B).

[*]ἀφιλονίκως, *not for the sake of victory* πύθεσθε παρὰ τῶν εἰδότων ἀ. καὶ ἀδηρίτως Clem.*str.*5.1(p.330.27; ἀφιλονείκως M.9.17C); *ib.*8.1 (p.80.24; 561A).

***ἀφιλοξενέω,** *be inhospitable,* Cyr.*Jo.*3.4(4.284D).

***ἀφιλοξενία, ἡ,** *lack of hospitality, 1Clem.*35.5; *Orac.Sib.*8.304.

***ἀφιλόπλουτος,** *despising wealth,* Cyr.*Lc.*6:20(M.72.589C).

***ἀφιλοπόλεμος,** *averse to war, unwarlike,* Cyr.*ador.*1(1.44C); id. *Jo.*10(4.840A); id.*hom.pasch.*26(5^2.303B).

***ἀφιλοπραγμόνως,** *without meddlesomeness, without distraction,* Cyr.*Ps.*100:2(M.69.1261A).

***ἀφιλοστοργέω,** *be wanting in natural affection,* Cyr.*Is.*2.4(2. 314A).

ἀφιλοστοργία, ἡ, *want of natural affection* (of members of a family); ref. Edom, Cyr.*Am.*9(3.261B); plur., *unnatural unkindnesses,* id.*Abd.*6(3.360A).

***ἀφιλοτεκνία,** *want of love towards one's children,* Thdr.Stud.*epp.* 2.115(M.99.1384B).

***ἀφιλόϋλος,** *hostile to matter* or *material things,* Thdr.Stud.*or.*11. 2.13(M.99.816B).

***ἀφιλοχρηματέω,** *be free from love of riches,* Cyr.*thes.*26(5^1.244E).

ἀφιματ-όω, *strip* someone *of clothing* ∼ῶσαι πειρώμενον τὸν πλησίον Meth.*arbitr.*3(p.150.11; M.18.245A) = Adam.*dial.*4.2(p.138. 4, v.l. ἀμφαιματῶσαι M.11.1808A).

ἄφιξις, ἡ, *coming*; **1.** of Inc. τοῦτο τῆς εἰς ἀνθρώπους ἀ. τέλος ἦν, τὸν πάλαι τῆς τοῦ πατρὸς γνώσεως ἀποπεπλανημένον εἰς τὴν οἰκείαν ἐπαναγαγεῖν Eus.*d.e.*4.15(p.173.19; M.22.289B); τῆς πρώτης αὐτοῦ ἀ. id.*fr.Lc.*(M.24.592D); προφῆται οἱ τούτου τὴν ἄ. προκηρύξαντες id.*p.e.*1.2(5D; M.21.29B); **2.** of second coming τὴν ἐσομένην ἐν τῇ κρίσει δευτέραν ἄ. αὐτοῦ Didym.*Trin.*3.38(M.39.977B); Thdr. Heracl.*fr.Mt.*10:23(p.78.27); οἱ μετ' αὐτοῦ μεταξὺ [before] τῆς ἀ. ὑπὸ Ἰησοῦ Χριστοῦ ἐρράγησαν Thdt.*h.e.*4.8.10(3.958).

ἀφιστάνω, *stand apart from, beware,* Or.*Cant.*1:7(M.17.257A; p.144.28 ἐφιστάνειν).

ἀφίστημι, 1. *withdraw from communion* with Church ἀφιστάμενος τῆς τῶν ἀδελφῶν συνοδίας Iren.*haer.*3.4.2(M.7.857A)ap.Eus.*h.e.*4.11.1 (M.20.328C); **2.** *apostatize,* Herm.*sim.*8.8.2; ἔνιαι εἰς τὸ παντελὲς ἀπέστησαν Iren.*haer.*1.13.7(M.7.592A) al.; τὸν Ἄρειον αὐτοῦ τε καὶ τῆς ἐκκλησίας ἀποστῆναι Philost.*h.e.*2.1(M.65.465C); **3.** *give up, cease*; c. ptcpl., Clem.*str.*7.16(p.66.2; M.9.529A); Chrys.*hom.15.2 in Jo.*(8.87D); id.*hom.11.6 in Rom.*(9.539D).

[*]ἀφί-ω, = ἀφίημι; **1.** *forgive* τὸ ἀ. τοῖς ὀφειλέταις τὰ ὀφειλήματα Ephr.3.398D; **2.** *leave, abandon* ∼ουσιν τὴν ὁδὸν αὐτῶν τὴν ἀληθινήν Herm.*vis.*3.7.1; Eus.Al.*serm.*15(M.86.400B); folld. by predicate οὐκ ∼ω ὑμᾶς ὀρφανούς Jo.14:18 cit.ap.Epiph.*haer.*69.63(p.212.29; M. 42.305B); **3.** c. acc. pers. et infin., *suffer, permit,* Ath.*fug.*15(p.79. 8; M.25.664C) = Socr.*h.e.*3.8.42(M.67.404A); *Const.App.*3.8.3.

***ἀφλέκτως,** *without being burnt,* ‡Bas.*inc.*(p.241.34).

***ἀφλεξία, ἡ,** *incombustibility,* Geo.Pis.*hex.*1486(M.92.1549A).

***ἄφλεψ,** *without veins,* Melet.*nat.hom.*1(M.64.1149B).

ἀφλόγιστος, *unburnt,* ‡Pall.*h.mon.*11.28(p.61.17; M.34.1155C).

ἀφοβία, ἡ, 1. *absence of godly fear, impiety, Barn.*20.1; ὁ ψευδοπροφήτης ᾧ ἕπεται ἄδεια καὶ ἀ. Miltiades ap.Eus.*h.e.*5.17.2(M.20. 473A); εἰ σοφίας ἀρχὴ φόβος θεοῦ, ἀ. καὶ ἀθέτησις τοὐναντίον ἂν γένοιτο τῆς σοφίας Thdt.*Ps.*13:1(1.682); **2.** *serenity, freedom from anxiety,* Sophr.H.*ep.syn.*(M.87.3149A).

ἀφόδευσις, ἡ, *vent, Barn.*10.6 = Clem.*paed.*2.10(p.208.22; M.8. 497C); *Schol.Clem.paed.*(p.330.29; M.9.789D).

ἀφολκή, ἡ, *drawing away, distraction,* Clem.*str.*2.23(p.189.16; M. 8.1088B).

***ἀφομοιάζω,** *make like,* Epiph.*haer.*73.24(p.297.16; M.42.448C).

***ἀφομοιότης, ἡ,** *resemblance,* Thdot.Anc.*hom.BMV et Sym.*6(M. 77.1397C).

ἀφομοίωσις, ἡ, 1. *becoming like, assimilation to* τοὺς ἐχομένους τῆς πρὸς τὸ θεῖον ἀ. Clem.*ecl.*33(p.147.12; M.9.716B); ἧς ἐτύχομεν πρὸς τὸ θεῖον ἀ. Eus.*p.e.*7.10(316B; M.21.536A); **2.** *symbolical representation* τῇ κατὰ τὴν τάξιν Μελχισεδὲκ ἀ. ὑπὲρ πάντων τῶν ἐθνῶν λύτρον ἑαυτὸν τῷ πατρὶ προσηγάγετο ‡Gr.Nyss.*occurs.*(M.46. 1165D); ἄ. καὶ ὑπόστασις ταὐτὸν οὐκ ἔστι· τὸ μὲν γὰρ τύπος, τὸ δὲ ἀλήθεια τυγχάνει Marc.Er.*opusc*.10.3(M.65.1120D); ‡Meth.*Sym.et Ann*.9(M.18.369C).

ἀφορίζ-ω, **A.** *cast out, banish* ὁ θεὸς τὸν παρ' αὐτοῦ ἐπισπείραντα τὸ ζιζάνιον ἀφώρισε τῆς ἰδίας μετουσίας Iren.*haer*.4.40.3(M.7.1114A); †Bas.*bapt*.2.9.1(2.666D; M.31.1612C); διὰ τοῦ ἀφορίσαντος ἐκ παραδείσου τρυφῆς τὴν εἰς παράδεισον αὖθις ἐπανάζευξιν ἐχαρίσω ‡Meth. *Sym.et Ann*.8(M.18.368A).

B. *cut off*, spiritually τοῦ μὴ ~οντος καὶ ἀποσταυροῦντος ἑαυτὸν τῶν παθῶν Clem.*str*.2.20(p.172.12; M.8.1053A) al.; pass., *separate oneself from*, *ib*.3.11(p.229.13; 1173C).

C. *excommunicate*; **1.** in gen., Or.*fr.in Mt*.18:21(p.164.13; M.17.300B); Eus.Al.*serm*.5(M.86.348B); Proc.G.*Dt*.12:32(M.87.909A); **2.** of minor excommunication of priests, i.e. suspension from office, and temporary exclusion from Communion, *Const.App*.8.28.3 al.; ὁ τὴν εὐσέβειαν μὴ διδάσκων ἐπίσκοπος, ~εται· καθαιρεῖται δὲ μένων ἀδίδακτος Sophr.H.*conf*.(M.87.3368D); **3.** of laity; **a.** of major excommunication; **i.** by which offender is cut off entirely from Church, †Hipp.*Artem*.ap.Eus.*h.e*.5.28.9(M.20.513B); τοὺς ἀθέους αἱρεσιώτας ἀμετανοήτως ἔχοντας ἀφορίσατε ἀπὸ τῶν πιστῶν καὶ τῆς ἐκκλησίας τοῦ θεοῦ ἐκκηρύκτους ποιήσατε *Const.App*.6.18.1; Thdt. *1Cor*.5:5(3.193); **ii.** a less severe form in which offender, though not cut off from Church, is reduced to second grade of penitents (οἱ ἀκροώμενοι), Bas.*ep*.188 *can*.4(3.271D; M.32.673A); **b.** of minor excommunication, by which offender is temporarily deprived of Communion, being reduced to fourth grade of penitents (*consistentes*) τοὺς λέγοντας μετανοεῖν ~ειν χρόνον ὡρισμένον κατὰ τὴν ἀναλογίαν τοῦ ἁμαρτήματος *Const.App*.2.16.4; Pall.*h.Laus*.33(p.97.20; M.34.1106A).

D. *refer, assign to* εἰ μιᾷ τις ἀφορίσῃ ὑποστάσει τὸ 'ὁ θεός', ἐκβάλλει τὴν ἑτέραν Didym.*Trin*.2.19(M.39.736A); λόγους, οὓς οὐδέποτε σὺ ταῖς περὶ σαυτοῦ γνώσεσιν ἀφώρισας Gel.Cyz.*h.e*.3.19.4(M.85.1345B); γνώσεως, ἥτις μόνη τῇ τριάδι ἀφώρισται Phot.*cod*.222(M.103.768B).

E. *devote* ἀφώρισεν ἑαυτὸν εἰς ἔργα καὶ θλίψεις Philox.*ep*.37(p.185).

F. *set apart by itself* τῶν Αἰγυπτίων ἱερέων οἱ σοφώτατοι τὸ τῆς Ἀθηνᾶς ἕδος ὕπαιθρον ἀφώρισαν Clem.*str*.5.5(p.344.15; M.9.49B); *station*, Jo.Mal.*chron*.14 p.374(M.97.557A).

G. *set apart* for a special purpose, c. dat.; **1.** persons ἀφόρισον αὐτοὺς τῷ λόγῳ καὶ τῷ κηρύγματι Chrys.*hom.82.1 in Jo*.(8.484A); **2.** things ὁ παράδεισος, πρὸς ἄλυπον ἀνάπαυσιν τοῖς ἁγίοις ἀφωρισμένος Meth.*res*.1.55(p.313.8; M.41.1148B); Thdt.*h.e*.2.26.1(3.892); Philost.*h.e*.3.22(M.65.512B); **3.** in judicial matters, *reserve, assign*, *Const.App*.7.2.8; CAnt.(445)*act*.(p.77.6; H.2.588E).

H. *place* in a particular class τὸν μέν, ὡς τελείων διανοιῶν διδάσκαλον, τοῖς ὑπὲρ τοὺς πολλοὺς ~ομεν Dion.Ar.*d.n*.3.2(M.3.681B).

I. *put away* in monastery prison, Thdr.Stud.*poen*.17(M.99.1736B).

ἀφορισμός, ὁ, **1.** *casting out* εἰς ἀ. παντὸς πνεύματος πονηροῦ Serap.*euch*.29; **2.** *separation*, of a sinner, acc. Law ἀπέχεσθαι παλαιᾶς συνηθείας καὶ ἀφορισμῶν *Const.App*.6.19.1; ἰουδαϊκοὺς ἀ. *ib*.6.30.1; **3.** *excommunication*; in gen., Dion.Al.*fr*.(p.62.6); Gr.Nyss.*castig*.(M.46.312D); ‡Jo.D.*ep.Thphl*.20(M.95.372B); of priests, *minor excommunication*, *Can.App*.13,32; of laity; *major excommunication*; most severe form, Gr.Nyss.*ep.can*.5(M.45.232A); less severe form, Bas.*ep*.188 *can*.4(3.271E; M.32.673A); *minor excommunication*, *Const.App*.3.8.1; **4.** *section* of a book, Eus.*qu.Steph*.11(M.22.921B); **5.** *seclusion* in monastery prison τέως μὲν ἀ. καὶ ἀσιτίας [sc. ἄξιός ἐστιν] Bas.*reg.br*.44(2.429B; M.31.1109D).

ἀφοριστικός, **1.** *defining, delimiting* ἀ. ἔννοιαι περὶ τοῦ πνεύματος Bas.*Spir*.9(3.19A; M.32.108A); θεῖα θελήματα, τῶν ὄντων ἀ. καὶ ποιητικά Dion.Ar.*d.n*.5.8(M.3.824C); **2.** *distinctive* τῇ ἀ. ἰδιότητι τῇ ἀπὸ τοῦ πατρός Leont.B.*cap.Sev*.25(M.86.1909C); τῶν ἀ. αὐτοῦ ἀπὸ τοῦ κοινοῦ ἰδιωμάτων [i.e. of Logos] Eulog.*fr.dogm*.(M.86.2948A); **3.** *rejecting* τὰς ἀ. ἔχουσιν οἱ ἱεράρχαι δυνάμεις Dion.Ar.*e.h*.7.3.7(M.3.564B); ἀγαθῶν ποιητικὸς καὶ κακῶν ἀ. Proc.G.*Is*.7:10–17(M.87.1964A); **4.** *keeping apart* ἐν τῷ ἀ. μοναστηρίῳ ὡς κατάκριτον ἐξώριζεν Jo.Clim.*scal*.4(M.88.685A).

***ἀφοριστρία**, ἡ, *monastery prison* ἀ., ἐν αἷς οἱ ἀπειθεῖς καὶ δυσήνιοι κατακλείονται *Const.Stud*.25(M.99.1713A).

***ἀφορκίζω**, *exorcize, treat by means of a charm*, Cyr.*Nah*.17(3.496C, v.l. ἐφορκίζειν Aubert); *Pers*.(p.24.23); med., *IGC As.Min*.210.69.

***ἀφορκισμός**, ὁ, *exorcism*, *Euchol*.pp.275,276; *amulet containing a charm*, *IGC As.Min*.210.28.

***ἀφορμολογία**, ἡ, *plea*, Anast.S.*hod*.21(M.89.280C).

ἀφοσιόω, **1.** act.; *acquit oneself of*, Mac.Aeg.*perf*.11(M.34.849A); **2.** med.; **a.** *satisfy, be acceptable to*, Gr.Naz.*or*.21.34(M.35.1124B); **b.** *propitiate, appease*, *ib*.7.16(776A); **c.** *make a formal recognition of*, Gr.Nyss.*ep*.1(M.46.1004B); **d.** *abominate*, Eus.*v.C*.1.10(p.11.28; M.20.921C); Gr.Naz.*ep*.10(M.37.40C); **e.** *raise objections*, Jo.Ant.*ep.Cyr*.4(p.155.28; M.77.248D); **f.** perf. ptcpl., *perfunctory*, Bas.*ep*.244.2(3.378A; M.32.913D).

***ἀφοσιωμένως**, v. *ἀφωσιωμένως.

ἀφοσίωσις, ἡ, *execration*, Leo Mag.*ep*.15(p.50.37; M.*PL*.54.844A).

***ἀφότε**, = ἀφ' ὅτε, *from the time when*, Jo.Mal.*chron*.7 p.176(M.97.281C).

***ἀφραστότης**, ἡ, *ineffability*, ‡Ath.*Apoll*.2.18(M.26.1164B).

Ἀφροδίτη, ἡ, *Aphrodite*; ἡμέρα Ἀφροδίτης *Friday*, Clem.*str*.7.12(p.54.6; M.9.504B).

***ἀφρόμορφος**, *foam-like*; epithet of jelly-fish, in comparison of latter with a clergyman's face, Geo.Pis.*carm*.1.32.

***ἀφροποιέω**, *foam, froth*, Meth.*lepr*.5(p.456.2); id.*symp*.2.2(p.16.21; M.18.49A).

***ἀφρόφορος**, *foaming*, Sever.*fic*.2(M.59.590); Nil.*epp*.2.94(M.79.241D).

ἄφρων, *foolish*, esp. of unbelievers γενόμενος ἄ. ἐρεῖς ὅτι οὐκ ἔστι θεός ‡Ath.*dial.Trin*.3.6(M.28.1212B); Bas.*reg.br*.260(2.502D; M.31.1256B); ἄ. ἡ γραφὴ τὸν δυσσεβῆ εἴωθεν ὀνομάζειν Thdt.*Zach*.11:16(2.1649).

ἀφυβρίζω, *cease to rage*, Synes.*ep*.4(M.66.1336C).

ἀφυλίζω, *strain off*, Meth.*symp*.6.4(p.68.18; M.18.120A).

***ἀφυλλορρόως**, *without shedding leaves*, ‡Epiph.*hom*.1(M.43.429D).

***ἄφυπνος**, *awake*, Cyr.*Jo*.7(4.679D).

ἄφυρτος, *not confused*, Max.*ambig*.(M.91.1228C).

ἀφύσικος, *beyond nature* πᾶσιν αὐτοῖς ἀ. εἶναι λέγων εἰς κατάληψιν Alex.Al.*ep.Alex*.21(p.23.8; M.18.556B)ap.Thdt.*h.e*.1.4.21(v.l. οὐ φυσικήν 3.735).

ἀφυσιολόγητος, *not explained by science*, Gr.Nyss.*hex*.25(M.44.88C).

ἀφύτευτος, met., *accidental, unexpected* μὴ περιιδεῖν ἀθεράπευτον τὴν ἄρριζόν τε καὶ ἀ. ταύτην δυσμένειαν Gr.Nyss.*ep*.1(M.46.1001A).

***ἀφυῶς**, *foolishly, inappropriately*, Adam.*dial*.4.7(p.152.16; M.11.1817A); Gennad.*fr.Gen*.49:27(M.85.1661C); Max.*ambig*.(M.91.1352D).

***ἀφφώ** (*ἀπφώ), (Hebr. אף הוא *even he*) in explanations of ποῦ ὁ θεὸς Ἠλιοὺ ἀ.; 4Reg.2:14: ἀ. ἑρμηνεύεται ἄμφω, τουτέστι τὸ πνεῦμα τὸ διπλοῦν ‡Ath.*comm.essent*.6(M.28.37A); τὸ ἀπφὼ προσφώνησίς ἐστιν ἀδελφική Didym.*Trin*.2.11(M.39.656A); ἀ. ὁ κρύφιος ἑρμηνεύεται, κατὰ τὴν ἔκδοσιν τῶν ἄλλων ἑρμηνευτῶν Thdt.*qu.9 in 4Reg*.(1.516).

***ἀφωσιωμένως**, *perfunctorily*, Chrys.*cruc*.2.5(2.420B); ἀπω- Bas.*hom.in Ps*.28(1.122E; M.29.301C); ἀφο- Ammon.*Jo*.13:4(M.85.1481B).

ἀφώτιστος, **A.** lit.; **1.** *not illuminated*, of moon in its phases τὸ εἶναι καθόλου τῇ ἰδίᾳ φύσει ἀφεγγὲς καὶ ἀ. Gr.Nyss.*anim.et res*.(M.46.33A); Proc.G.*Gen*.1:15(M.87.88A); of primeval darkness τῶν σωμάτων ἡ φύσις...πάντως ἀ. ἦν *ib*.1:2(44B); of persons τὸ φῶς... πάντα δοκεῖ...τὸν ἀέρα πληροῦν, πλὴν εἰ μή τις ἐν ἀντρίοις οἰκίσκοις καθειργμένος ἀ. διαμένοι Thdt.*eran*.2(4.115); **2.** *without light, giving no light*, of fire δικαίοις μὲν φωτιστικήν, ἀλλ' οὐ καυστικήν, ἁμαρτωλοῖς δὲ καυστικήν, ἀλλ' ἀ. Andr.Caes.*Apoc*.58(M.106.401A); ἀδύνατον ...εἶναι πῦρ ἀ. Jo.D.*Man*.1.4(M.94.1509C); **3.** *blind* ἀ. βλεφάρων Nonn.*par.Jo*.9:21(M.43.828B); *ib*.9:1(824B); Dion.Ar.*e.h*.3.3.6(M.3.433A).

B. met.; **1.** *unenlightened, uninstructed* ἀ. ψυχὴ ἀδύνατός ἐστι πρὸς νόησιν Bas.*Eun*.2.16(1.251C; M.29.604B); εἰ φωτίζει πάντα ἄνθρωπον ἐρχόμενον εἰς τὸν κόσμον, πῶς ἀ. μεμενήκασι τοσοῦτοι; Gr.Naz.*or*.33.11(M.36.228C); Chrys.*hom.8.1 in Jo*.(8.48C); οὔτε ἀ. ὄντα δεῖ ἐπιβάλλειν τοῖς πνευματικοῖς θεωρήμασιν Diad.*perf*.8(p.10.4); Dion.Ar.*ep*.8.2(M.3.1092B); **2.** esp. *unbaptized* τί με ποιεῖς νεοφώτιστον καὶ ἀ.; Gr.Naz.*or*.33.17(M.36.236C); οὐ φέρω ἀ. εἶναι μετὰ τὸ φώτισμα *ib*.34.11(252B); *ib*.40.22(388B); αἰσχυνθῆτε ὅσοι ἀ. τυγχάνετε Chrys.*hom.19.2 in Ac*.(9.155A); Pall.*v.Chrys*.7(p.39.14; M.47.24).

***Ἀχααβιτικός**, *like Ahab, murderous* ἡ Ἀ. χείρ Thdr.Stud.*epp*.2.106(M.99.1365A).

***Ἀχαβαϊκός**, = foreg., Thdr.Stud.*epp*.2.49(M.99.1256B).

***ἀχάλαζος**, *free from hail*, *Orac.Sib*.3.369.

***ἀχαλιναγώγητος**, *unbridled*, Iren.*haer*.5.8.3(M.7.1144A); Hipp.*fr.22 in Gen*.(p.59.19); Ephr.2.180A.

ἄχαλκος, *without money*, Gr.Naz.*carm*.2.1.12.200(M.37.1180A); Max.*ambig*.(M.91.1368A).

ἀχανής, **1.** *dead* τυπτόμεναι ἔμενον ἀ. Petr.II Al.*encycl*.1(M.33.1277A)ap.Thdt.*h.e*.4.22.5(3.988); **2.** *stunned*, met. ὁρῶντες τὴν ἀπορίαν ἀ. ἔμενον Ath.*decr*.3.1(p.3.5; M.25.420C); Chrys.*sac*.6.12 (p.165.10; 1.432C); ‡Nil.*narr*.6(M.79.657A).

***ἀχανιάω**, *become mute*, Thdr.Stud.*epp*.2.37(M.99.1228C).

***ἀχαρακτήριστος**, *without distinctive feature*; **1.** in gen., Gr.Nyss. *Eun*.8(2 p.193.15; M.45.788D) = id.*deit*.(M.46.561A); καθ' ἑαυτὸν ἀ. πᾶς καθέστηκε νοῦς Max.*cap*.5.19(M.90.1356B); **2.** in Valent. system Μεσότητος τέκνα ἀ. ἦσαν Val.Gn.ap.Epiph.*haer*.31.6(p.394.5; M.41. 485A); **3.** of the divine reason (Naassene) ὁ Χριστός, ὁ ἐν πᾶσι τοῖς γενητοῖς υἱὸς ἀνθρώπου κεχαρακτηρισμένος ἀπὸ τοῦ ἀ. λόγου Hipp. *haer*.5.7(p.87.6; M.16.3138A); τὸ εἶδος τὸ κατελθὸν ἄνωθεν ἀπὸ τοῦ ἀ. ὁποῖόν ἐστιν εἶδεν οὐδείς *ib*.5.8(p.91.24; 3143B).

ἀχάρακτος, *undimmed* νυκτιφανὴς ἀ. ἀστήρ Nonn.*par.Jo*.20:1 (M.43.908B).

***ἀχαρίεις**, *unpleasant*; of weals, Sophr.H.*mir.Cyr.et Jo*.11(M.87. 3452D).

***ἀχαρίτωτος**, *not winning grace*, Jo.Clim.*scal*.7(M.88.808A).

***ἄχαυνος**, *inaccessible to* ταῖς ἐναντίαις θέλξεσιν ἄ. Thdr.Stud. *nativ.BMV* 7(M.96.693C).

***ἀχαύνωτος**, *unwavering* τὸν τῆς εὐσεβείας τόνον εἶχεν ἀ. Gel.Cyz. *h.e*.3.17.8; ἀμείλικτον, ἤτοι ἀνένδοτον καὶ ἀ. Max.*schol.c.h*.2.4(M.4. 44B).

***ἀχειμαστί**, *without disturbance*, Meth.*symp*.11.3(p.139.16; M.18. 217C).

ἀχειραγώγητος, *refusing to be led, obstinate* ἡ τῶν Ἰουδαίων ἀ. γνώμη Cyr.*Jo*.5.2(4.477C); *ib*.6.1(624E).

***ἀχειρί**, *of its own accord* ἀ. καὶ αὐτοματί ‡Epiph.*hom*.2(M.43. 457C).

ἀχειρίδωτος, *without sleeves*, Soz.*h.e*.3.14.7(M.67.1069C).

***ἀχειρόθετος**, *not involving imposition of hands* ἀ. ὑπηρεσία Bas. *ep*.217(3.325C; M.32.796A).

***ἀχειρομίαντος**, *not defiled by the work of the hands*, i.e. by being fashioned as an image; of God, Isid.Pel.*epp*.4.207(M.78.1301B).

***ἀχειρόπλαστος**, *not made by hands* ὁ χερσὶν ἀ. ἐκ πηλοῦ διαπλάσας τὸν ἄνθρωπον ‡Cyr.H.*occurs*.10(M.33.1197A); ‡Jo.D.*hom*.5(M.96. 652D).

ἀχειροποίητος, *not made by hands*, ref. impression of his face sent by Christ to Abgar (v. *A.Thadd*.3) εἰκόνα ἐποίησε τὴν λεγομένην ἀ. ‡Jo.D.*Const*.4(M.95.320A); fig., of body of BMV as ἀ. tabernacle of Christ, Mod.*dorm*.13(M.86.3309A).

***ἄχειρος**, *without hands*, Meth.*res*.3.15(p.412.1; M.18.317A); Geo. Pis.*Heracl*.1.46(M.92.1302A).

***ἀχειρότευκτος**, *not made by hands* τῶν ἐν οὐρανοῖς ἀ. σκηνωμάτων †Jo.D.*B.J*.16(M.96.1001A).

***ἀχειρότμητος**, *not cut by hands*, Jo.D.*hom*.4.30(M.96.632C).

ἀχειροτόνητος, *unordained*, Isid.Pel.*epp*.3.75(M.78.784A).

ἀχείρωτος, **1.** lit.; **a.** *invincible* σταυρὸς τὸ ὅπλον τὸ ἀ. Chrys.*hom. in Mt*.26:39(3.19D); of Trin., ‡Caes.Naz.*dial*.3(M.38.860); **b.** *impregnable* ἀ. σηκός Isid.Pel.*epp*.1.174(M.78.297A); **2.** met.; **a.** of persons, *not to be overcome* ἀ. ἔσται ὁ ἐνάρετος Chrys.*hom.24.3 in Mt*.(7.304A); φιλανθρωπία ψυχὴν ἀ. πᾶσιν ἐργάζεται *ib*.64.5(641D); πρὸς τὸ μέλλον ἀ. id.*stat*.7.4(2.89D); **b.** of things, *not to be mastered* τὸ ἀ. χειρώσασθαι Isid.Pel.*epp*.2.40(M.78.484A); *ib*.5.181(1432D); **c.** *unaffected* τῇ τῶν φωστήρων φλογὶ μένειν ἀ. ‡Just.*qu.et resp*.93 (M.6.1333C); Chrys.*hom.3.2 in Ac.princ*.(3.73A); φύσις πρὸς ἅπαν πάθος ἀ. Bas.Sel.*or*.3.2(M.85.49D).

[*]**Ἀχέρουσος**, *of Acheron* (river in nether world) Ἀχέρουσα λίμνη *Apoc.Paul*.22.

ἀχθοφορικός, *suitable for bearing burdens*, †Bas.*Is*.14(1.388A; M. 30.141B).

***ἀχλεύαστος**, *not mocked at*, Ath.*inc*.41.1(M.25.168C).

***ἀχλοηφόρος**, *without grass*, ‡Chrys.*salt.Herodiad*.1(8^2.40B).

***ἀχλυοποιός**, *causing mist*, Diad.*perf*.75(p.92.25).

ἀχόρταστος, *insatiable*, Eus.Al.*serm*.15(M.86.400B); Isid.Pel.*epp*. 2.233(M.78.668C).

***ἀχραντία**, ἡ, *purity*; of BMV, Thdr.Stud.*nativ.BMV* 7(M.96. 693A).

ἄχραντος, *undefiled* by sin, in gen. ἄ. τὴν ψυχὴν ἔχειν χρή Clem. *str*.7.7(p.36.27; M.9.469A); Bas.*ep*.45.1(3.134A; M.32.368A); Cyr. *Am*.77(3.339E); of God ἄ. ἡ θεία φύσις Heracleon ap.Or.*Jo*.13.25 (p.248.29; M.14.440D); cf. οὐ νομιστέον τὸ ἓν ἐπὶ τοῦ θεοῦ τῶν ὅλων τῷ ἀ. χωρὶς Χριστοῦ Or.*dial*.4(p.128.5); *M.Ner.et Ach*.12(p.12.14); Jo.D.*hom*.4.21(M.96.620A); of Christ θεὸς ἐν ἀνθρώπου σχήματι ἄ. Clem.*paed*.1.2(p.91.23; M.8.252C); τῇ προσθήκῃ τοῦ ὕδατος τὴν ἄ. καθαρότητα ἐδήλου καὶ ὅτι τοῦ θεοῦ τὸ σῶμα ‡Ath.*Apoll*.1.18(M.26. 1125B); τὸ χωρῆσαι δυνάμενον ἄ. σῶμα πᾶν τὸ πλήρωμα τῆς θεότητος σωματικῶς ‡Ath.*serm.fid*.13(p.9; M.26.1269C); of H. Ghost, *M. Eupl*.2; of Trin., Thdt.*Ps*.57:6(1.986); of eucharist μεταλάβοι τῶν μυστικῶν καὶ ἀ. σώματός τε καὶ αἵματος Χριστοῦ Nil.*epp*.3.280(M. 79.521D); μεταλαβεῖν τοῦ ἀ. θύματος Philost.*h.e*.2.13(M.65.476C); παραφυλαττέσθωσαν ἄ. κοινωνίαν †Jo.Jej.*serm*.(M.88.1929D); of BMV θεός, ἐξ ἀ. κόρης Eus.*d.e*.4.10(p.169.3; M.22.281B); τῆς ἀ. παστάδος Gr.Nyss.*hom.9 in Cant*.(M.44.953D); νοητὸν θυσιαστήριον ἐξ ἀ. λαγόνων θεῷ δεδομημένον Thdr.Stud.*nativ.BMV* 7(M.96.693C); of gospels, *M.Eupl*.1; of Church, Pall.*h.Laus*.proem.(p.9.9; M.34.1002).

***ἀχραντόσωμος**, *with body undefiled*, Meth.*symp*.11.2(p.133.13; M.18.209B).

ἀχράντως, **1.** *without defilement*; **a.** ref. generation of Son ὁ θεὸς ἀφ' ἑαυτοῦ ἐγέννησε τὸν μονογενῆ ἀ. Epiph.*haer*.69.15(p.165.1; M.42.225A); τῆς ἀγεννησίας ἐξ αὐτῆς ἀ. γεννησάσης τὸν μονογενῆ *ib*. 76.45(p.399.11; 612D); **b.** ref. Christ's birth, id.*exp.fid*.15(p.516.8; M.42.812B); ἄνω ἐκ πατρὸς τελείως γεγέννηται ἀχρόνως καὶ ἀνάρχως καὶ κάτω ἐκ μητρὸς μόνης ἀ. καὶ ἀμολύντως id.*haer*.69.25(p.176.4; M.42.244C); **2.** *without suffering defilement* εἰς τὴν ἀπάθειαν θεούμενος ἄνθρωπος ἀ. μοναδικὸς γίνεται Clem.*str*.4.23(p.315.26; M.8.1361A); δύναμις [sc. θεοῦ] ἀ. ταῖς ὅλαις οὐσίαις ἐπιβατεύουσα ‡Cyr.*Trin*.7(6^3. 8B; M.77.1132A); **3.** *without causing defilement* τῶν ἀτελέστων ἀ. ἀποδιαστέλλουσι τὰ ἅγια Dion.Ar.*c.h*.2.5(M.3.145A).

ἀχρειοσύνη, ἡ, *misdoing*, *Cod.Afr*.138.

***ἀχρειώδης**, *useless*, *A.Thom*.A 79(p.195.2).

***ἀχρείωσις**, ἡ, *disablement* τὴν τοῦ σώματος κατάλυσιν καὶ ἀ. Nil. *epp*.3.268(M.79.517B); ref. Fall 'πάντες...ἠχρειώθησαν' τὴν ἀπὸ τῆς ἁμαρτίας τοῦ Ἀδὰμ ἀ. Areth.*Apoc*.11(M.106.577A).

ἀχρημάτιστος, *deprived of revenues*, Jo.Mal.*chron*.13 p.324(M.97. 484C).

ἄχρι, *until, as far as*; *during* ἄ. τῆς αὐτοῦ ζωῆς Jo.Mal.*chron*.8 p.210(M.97.328B).

***ἀχριστιανός**, *un-Christian*, †Gregent.*disp*.(M.86.693D).

ἄχρονος, *independent of time*; **1.** of God τῆς ἀ. καὶ ἀνάρχου καὶ ἀγενήτου καὶ ἀναλλοιώτου οὐσίας, ἐφ' ἧς τὸ εἶναι μόνον ἐπιπρέπει νοεῖν Eus.*e.th*.2.9(p.108.31; M.24.917A); Gr.Naz.*or*.23.8(M.35.1160C); Bas.Sel.*or*.1.3(M.85.36C); Aen.*dial*.(M.85.960B); **2.** of generation of Son τὸ 'ὅτε ἐγένετο' ἀόριστον ἐκφορὰν καὶ ἄ. μηνύει Clem.*str*.6.16 (p.506.19; M.9.376B); τὸ ἄ. τῆς τοῦ Χριστοῦ ἐκ πατρὸς ὑποστάσεως CAnc.(358)*anath*.ap.Epiph.*haer*.73.11(p.283.26; M.42.424D); Bas. *Eun*.2.16(1.251D; M.29.604C); ἣν γὰρ πρὸ Ἀβραὰμ καὶ πρὸ Νῶε καὶ πρὸ Ἀδὰμ καὶ πρὸ πάντων τῶν κτισμάτων, ἄ. ὤν Epiph.*haer*.54.5 (p.322.24; M.41.969B); τὴν ἄ. τοῦ θεοῦ ἐκ πατρὸς γέννησιν Cyr.*Mich*. 46(3.436C); **3.** of Trin., Aen.*dial*.(M.85.960B); ‡Caes.Naz.*dial*.10(M. 38.868); **4.** in Marcosian system, of ogdoad, Iren.*haer*.1.17.2(M.7. 641A).

ἀχρόνως, **1.** *timelessly*; **a.** ref. generation of Son ὁ υἱὸς ἀ. γεννηθεὶς ὑπὸ τοῦ πατρός Ar.*ep.Alex*.(p.244.9; M.26.709B); *Symb.Ant*.(345)3 (p.252.15; M.26.729B); ἀ. καὶ ἀπαθῶς ἐξ ἑαυτοῦ αὐτὸν γεννήσας *Symb. Sirm*.1 *anath*.25; Leont.H.*Nest*.1.39(M.86.1500C); **b.** of working of H. Ghost πᾶν ἀγαθὸν πρᾶγμα ἐν τῇ δυνάμει τοῦ πνεύματος διὰ τοῦ μονογενοῦς θεοῦ ἀ. εἰς τελείωσιν ἄγεται Gr.Nyss.*tres dii*(M.45.129A); κατὰ τὴν πνευματικὴν ἀναγέννησιν τὴν φύσιν τῆς σαρκὸς εἰς πνεῦμα ἀ. ἀναγεννώμεθα Leont.H.*Nest*.2.20(M.86.1581B); **2.** *incorrectly as to time* οὐ γὰρ...ἀ. ... ψεύσαιτο προφήτης Eust.*engast*.15(p.41.3; M.18. 645B).

ἀχρύσωτος, *made without employment of gold*, Cyr.*ador*.9(1.303B).

***ἀχυροφαγέω**, *eat chaff*, Cyr.*Is*.2.1(2.200C).

***ἀχυροφάγος**, *eating chaff*, Chrys.*fr.in Jer*.45:15(M.64.1021B).

***ἀχώλευτος**, *firm* στηρίγματα ἀ. ‡Chrys.*pasch*.6.3(p.157.17; 8. 269C).

***ἀχώλωτος**, *not mutilated*; of a biblical text, Epiph.*mens*.6 (M.43.245C).

ἀχώνευτος, *not melted down*, Socr.*h.e*.5.16.12(M.67.605B).

ἀχώρητος, **A.** *not to be contained*; **1.** in space, *infinite, unlimited*; **a.** of God ὁ θεός, πάντα χωρῶν, μόνος δὲ ἀ. ὤν Herm.*mand*.1.1; ὁ τόπῳ τε ἀ. καὶ τῷ κόσμῳ ὅλῳ Just.*dial*.127.2(M.6.772B); Thphl.Ant. *Autol*.1.5(M.6.1032A); Gr.Nyss.*or.catech*.14(p.62.11; M.45.45D); of Father τὸν ἀ. πατέρα χωρητὸν διὰ τῆς ἐνανθρωπήσεως ὑποτίθενται *Symb.Ant*.(345)7(p.253.16; M.26.732C); ἡ τῶν γενητῶν φύσις τῆς ἀ. πατρικῆς οὐσίας διεστῶσα Eus.*d.e*.4.6(p.159.25; M.22.265C); Max. *ambig*.(M.91.1184D); **b.** of Son ἀ. ἐστι καὶ ὁ υἱὸς ὡς ὁ πατήρ, καὶ πάντα περιέχει Hipp.*pasch*.3(p.269; M.10.701B); esp. ref. Inc. ὀπτανόμενος οὐ καθόσον αὐτός ἐστιν, ἀ. γάρ Mac.Aeg.*elev*.8(M.34.896B); Cyr. *Juln*.8(6^2.287A); ἀ. ὢν τῇ φύσει γίνεται χωρητός Thdt.*Ezech*.3:12(2. 703); **c.** of H. Ghost ἀ., ἀναλλοίωτον, ἄποιον Gr.Naz.*or*.41.9(M.36. 441B); **d.** in Valent. system, of the ultimate principle, Iren.*haer*.1. 1.1(M.7.445A); **2.** met., *incomprehensible* τὸ ἀ. λογισμοῖς ἀνθρωπίνοις

τῆς θείας δυνάμεως Gr.Nyss.*hom.1 in Cant.*(M.44.781C); ἀ. ἐστι τῷ πλήθει τὸ ἑνιαῖον τοῦ θείου ἔρωτος Dion.Ar.*d.n.*4.12(M.3.709C); τὴν νυνὶ μὲν ἀ. γνῶσιν, χωρηθησομένην δὲ κατὰ τὸ ἐνδεχόμενον ἐν τῷ μέλλοντι αἰῶνι Isid.Pel.*epp.*2.56(M.78.500A); ἀ. αὐτοῖς [sc. τοῖς σοφοῖς τοῦ κόσμου] ἡ τοῦ θεοῦ ἀποκάλυψις Sever.*1Cor.*2:14(p.235.5).
B. act., c. genit.; **1.** *unable to contain*, Gr.Nyss.*Eun.*12(1 p.250.26; M.45.952B); id.*Spir.*(M.46.697A); **2.** *unable to comprehend* τὸ ἀ. εἶναι τὴν ἀνθρωπίνην πτωχείαν τῶν ὑπὲρ λόγον τε καὶ ἔννοιαν διδαγμάτων Gr.Nyss.*Eun.*8(2 p.188.1; M.45.781C); id.*hom.opif.*8(M.44.148A).

ἀχώριστος, **A.** *inseparable*; **1.** of Trin. θεὸν ἕκαστον ἂν θεωρῆται μόνον, τοῦ νοῦ χωρίζοντος τὰ ἀ. Gr.Naz.*or.*23.11(M.35.1164A); οὐκ ἀφορίζων τὸ πνεῦμα τῆς δυάδος...ἀλλὰ...ἑνῶν καὶ δηλῶν ἐν πατρὶ καὶ υἱῷ τὸ πνεῦμα τὸ ἀ. Didym.(‡Bas.)*Eun.*5(1.310E; M.29.745B); ἀ. ὁρῶ τὴν ἐνέργειαν τοῦ πατρός, καὶ τοῦ υἱοῦ, καὶ τοῦ ἁγίου πνεύματος *ib.*(317D; M.761A); διὰ πάντων βεβαιούσης ἡμῖν τῆς θείας γραφῆς τὴν διάνοιαν, ἀ. περὶ πατρὸς καὶ υἱοῦ καὶ ἁγίου πνεύματος κεκτῆσθαι τὴν ἔννοιαν Thdt.*rect.conf.*5(M.6.1217A); cf. ἀδιαίρετος; **2.** of Father and Son πεπιστεύκαμεν αὐτοὺς ἀ. ὑπάρχειν ἑαυτῶν *Symb.Ant.*(345) 9(p.253.37; M.26.733B); ἀ. ἐστιν ὡς τῇ φύσει καὶ τοῖς θελήμασι καὶ τοῖς προορισμοῖς τοῦ πατρός †Diad.*Ar.*6(M.65.1160C); ὥσπερ ἀχώριστον ἀνθρώπου πᾶν τὸ φύσει προσὸν αὐτῷ, οὕτω καὶ θεοῦ πᾶν τὸ ἐν αὐτῷ καὶ ἐξ αὐτοῦ. ἐν πατρὶ δὲ καὶ ἐκ πατρὸς ὁ λόγος· ἀ. ἄρα καὶ συναΐδιος Cyr.*thes.*4(5^1.26E); **3.** Christol., of union of natures, Ath. *Ar.*2.41(M.26.233A); ἀ. πρὸς τὴν θείαν φύσιν ἔχων τὴν συνάφειαν Thdr.Mops.*symb.*(p.98.26; M.66.1017C); ἀ. τοῦ φαινομένου θεός Nest.*fr.*C 9(p.262.4); ἦν ἀ. ὁ λόγος τῆς ἰδίας σαρκός, ἐν ἑκάστῳ καιρῷ Eulog.*palm.*8(M.86.2925B); τριὰς γὰρ ἔμεινεν ἡ τριάς, καὶ μετὰ τὴν ἕνωσιν τοῦ μονογενοῦς, ἀ. μεινάσης τῆς ἁγίας αὐτοῦ σαρκός, καὶ ἔτι μετ' αὐτοῦ μενούσης καὶ εἰς τὸν αἰῶνα *Euchol.*p.254; of Christ's pre-existence ἀνεπινόητον τῆς ἀρχῆς τὸ πρεσβύτερον, ἀ. δὲ ταύτης τοῦ θεοῦ λόγου τὸ εἶναι Bas.*Eun.*2.14(1.249E; M.29.600B); **4.** of H. Ghost ἐν πατρὶ καὶ υἱῷ τὸ πνεῦμα τὸ ἀ. Didym.(‡Bas.)*Eun.*5(1.311A; M.29.745B); ‡Cyr.*Trin.*9(6^3.13D; M.77.1140C); τὴν ἀ. καὶ συγγενῆ τῆς θείας οὐσίας τοῦ πνεύματος τοῦ ἁγίου ὑπόστασιν Isid.Pel.*epp.*1.60(M.78.221C); of union of hypothetically sinless man with God, Gr.Nyss.*Apoll.*54(M.45.1256D) cit. s. ἀναμάρτητος.
B. of mental states, *determined, profound* ἀ. μνήμη *Clem.ep.*10; ἀ. λήθη *cat.Lc.*17:11(p.129.11).

ἀχωρίστως, *inseparably*; **1.** Trin., ‡Caes.Naz.*dial.*2(M.38.857) cit. s. ἀσυναλείπτως; ref. Father and Son ἀ. ἀεὶ ὄντος τοῦ πατρὸς πρὸς τὸν υἱὸν καὶ τοῦ υἱοῦ πρὸς τὸν πατέρα Gel.Cyz.*h.e.*2.15.4(M.85.1257D); ὁ υἱός...ἐκ πατρὸς γεννηθεὶς ἀ. καὶ ἀδιαστάτως ‡Cyr.*Trin.*8(6^3.11B; M.77.1136C); *Narr.Jos.*3.4; Jo.D.*hom.*1.18(M.96.572D) cit. s. ἀνεκφοιτήτως; ref. Son and H. Ghost, Gr.Nyss.*diff.ess.*4(M.32.329C); ref. H. Ghost in Godhead μετὰ θεοῦ ἀ. ὂν ἀεὶ Didym.(‡Bas.)*Eun.*5(1.314E; M.29.753D); Procl.CP *Arm.*13(p.193.26; M.65.869B); **2.** Christol. ἀ. ἐν τῷ ἑνὶ προσώπῳ θεότητα καὶ ἀνθρωπότητα Thdt.*eran.*2(4.173); διὰ τῶν ἀνθρωπίνων ἄγει τὴν ἀνθρωπότητα· οἰκῶν μὲν ἀ., οἰκονομῶν δὲ θεοπρεπῶς Bas.Sel.*or.*25.3(M.85.293B); *Symb.Chalc.* cit. s. φύσις.

ἀψηλάφητος, *not to be handled*; **1.** lit., Nil.*epp.*3.155(M.79.457B) = Jo.Carp.*cap.*76(M.85.1852); **2.** met., *untouchable*; of God, Ign.*Polyc.*3.2; ἵνα ψηλαφηθῇ κατὰ τὴν φύσιν τῆς λεπτότητος τῆς ψυχῆς ὁ ἀ. Mac.Aeg.*hom.*4.11(M.34.480D); Chrys.*hom.32.1 in Heb.*(12.293D); of Son, ‡Cyr.H.*occurs.*8(M.33.1196B); ‡Ath.*disp.*21(M.28.464B); of angels ἀ. σχῆμα, ‡Chrys.*Zach.*1(2.791B); **3.** *that cannot be felt* ἐν τῷ ψηλαφητῷ σκότει ὁ ἀ. θάνατος ἐκρύβετο Mel.*pass.*23(p.4.12).

ἀψήφιστος, *not worth reckoning in one's own eyes, humble*, neut. as subst. τὸ ἀ., τὸ μὴ μετρεῖν ἑαυτόν, τὸ ἔχειν ἑαυτὸν γῆν καὶ σποδὸν Bars.*resp.*(M.86.900D); ὁ κατέχων τὸ ἀ. ἐν γνώσει, ἐπιτελεῖ πᾶσαν τὴν γραφήν *Apophth.Patr.*(M.65.373B).

ἀψικόρως, *being*, or *so as to be, quickly sated*, Cyr.*ador.*8(1.284D); id.*fr.Mt.*(M.72.420A); id.*Lc.*6:12(M.72.580C).

ἄψιλος, prob. f.l. for ἄψυχος, Max.*opusc.*(M.91.32C).

ἀψίς (ἁψίς), ἡ, **1.** *arch*; **a.** lit., plur., *arched bridge*, Jo.Mal.*chron.* 13 p.339(M.97.505A); **b.** met., *top, highest rank* εἰς τὴν τῆς ἁγιωσύνης ἀ. ἀναβεβηκέναι Nil.*Eulog.*33(M.79.1137C); εἰς τὴν ἀ. τῆς ἐπισκοπῆς διαβῆναι CSard.*can.*10; **2.** *space beneath vault of a church*, (ἁ-) *Cod. Afr.*43.

ἄψυχος, *without soul*; **1.** of Christ as maintained by Apollinarius, Apoll.*fr.*2(p.204.16)ap.Anast.S.*monoph.*(M.89.1184A) cit. s. ἄνους; ἵνα τὴν ἄ. ἐκείνην σάρκα συζεύξῃ τῷ...θεῷ Gr.Nyss.*Apoll.*45(M.45.1233B); Leont.H.*monoph.*(M.86.1865C) cit. s. ἄνους; denied by orthodox, †Gr.Thaum.*fid.cap.*2(p.149.17; M.10.1133B); Ath.*tom.*7 (M.26.804B) cit. s. ἀνόητος; CCP(381)*ep.*ap.Thdt.*h.e.*5.9.12(3.1032) cit. s. ἄνους; **2.** of men, Chrys.*hom.13.4 in 1Tim.*(11.622E); **3.** of animals, Or.*hom.16.1 in Jer.*(p.132.13; ἄλογοι M.13.437D); **4.** of first matter τὴν ἄμορφον καὶ ἀνείδεον ἄ. τε καὶ ἀσχημάτιστον οὐσίαν... φωτίσας τε καὶ ψυχώσας Eus.*l.C.*12(p.231.31; M.20.1389C).

***ἀψυχόω,** pass., *be despondent*, conj. for MS ἠντικότει, Pall.*v. Chrys.*5(M.47.19; ἠντισκότει p.30.11).

B

βαβαί, exclamation of surprise and wonder, *Oh!*; in serious contexts, ‡Eust.*Laz.*16(p.40.6) cit. s. ἔντριτος; β. τῆς τοῦ θεοῦ φιλανθρωπίας Chrys.*hom.57.1 in Jo.*(8.333A); *ib.71.2*(419C); β. πόση ἡ ἀναισθησία *ib.72.2*(424A); id.*hom.22.2 in Eph.*(11.167C); κληρονόμοι τοῦ θεοῦ· β. τῆς τιμῆς Isid.Pel.*epp.*5.197(M.78.1449D).

***βαβαλίζω,** *lull to sleep* (cf. βαβαλιστήριον, *cradle*), met. δουλεύσει τὸ ἡγεμονικὸν βαβαλίσαντι...ἔρωτι Nil.*epp.*3.331(M.79.541B).

Βαβυλών, ἡ, *Babylon*; **1.** interpreted by derivation from Hebr. בַּלְבֵּל as type of confusion and disorder, and freq. translated σύγχυσις (q.v.), Or.*hom.20.4 in Jer.*(p.314.3; M.13.532D); Meth.*symp.*4.4(p.49.13; M.18.92A); †Bas.*Is.*272(1.587A; M.30.597C); Oecum.*Apoc.*17:5(p.185); ‡Germ.CP *contempl.*(M.98.401B); as type of present world, Areth.*Apoc.*52(M.106.713C); **2.** as disguised name for Rome, *Orac.Sib.*5.143,159; esp. exeg. 1Petr.5:13 and Apoc.14:8, cf.Iren.*haer.*5.26.1(M.7.1192C); Eus.*h.e.*2.15.2(M.20.173A); Hier.*vir. ill.*(tr.Sophr.Pal.)8(p.9.1; M.*PL*.23.622B); Oecum.*Apoc.*16:19(p.182); Areth.*Apoc.*52(M.106.713C) etc.; but 1Petr.5:13 interpreted lit. of Babylon and missionary work there of Thaddaeus, Cosm.Ind.*top.* 2(M.88.113D); **3.** similarly used for CP, Areth.*Apoc.*52(M.106.713C); on ground that many orthodox were slain there by Arians; cf.*ib.* 53(720A).

***βάγυλος, ὁ,** (Lat. *bajulus*) *counsellor*, Thphn.*chron.*p.83(v.l. βάγιλόν; βαϊοῦλον M.108.252A); *ib.*p.393(937B).

[*]βαδδείμ ([*]βαδδήν, βαδδίν), τό, (Hebr. בַּדִּים) *fine linen*, Hipp.*Dan.*4.36.5(M.10.657B); Thdt.*Dan.*10:5(2.1258D); Andr.Caes.*Apoc.*19(M.106.277B).

***βάδιμος,** s.v.l., = βάσιμος 2, *possible*, Cyr.*glaph.Ex.*1(1.245A).

βάδισις, ἡ, *walking*; met., *progress*; of spread of leprosy, Clem.*fr.*34(p.218.9); *way of life* τῆς ἐμῆς β. τὸν τρόπον, τουτέστι, τῆς ἀναστροφῆς τοῦ βίου Chrys.*hom.12.2 in Phil.*(11.293E).

***βαθμίδιον, τό,** *step*, Jo.Mosch.*prat.*61(M.87.2913C).

βαθμίς, ἡ, **1.** *step*, Gr.Nyss.*v.Mos.*(M.44.401B); in spiritual ascent, Gr.Naz.*carm.*1.2.2.30(M.37.580A); μίαν β. τῆς τῶν ἀρετῶν κλίμακος ἀναβῆναι Nil.*epp.*4.42(M.79.569C); Diad.*perf.*92(p.134.3); **2.** a measure of height, Proc.G.*Dt.*11:29(M.87.908A).

βαθμός, ὁ, *step, grade, degree*; **1.** of degrees of kinship β. τῆς συγγενείας ‡Bas.*const.*20.1(2.564E; M.31.1389C); **2.** of degrees or stages of progress in intellectual and spiritual life τελειῶσαι σωτηρίῳ ἡμᾶς β. εἰς παίδευσιν Clem.*paed.*1.1(p.91.16; M.8.252B); Ματθίας ἐν ταῖς παραδόσεσι παραινῶν 'θαύμασον τὰ παρόντα', β. τοῦτον πρῶτον τῆς ἐπέκεινα γνώσεως ὑποτιθέμενος id.*str.*2.9(p.137.3; M.8.981A); πρῶτον εὐσεβείας β. Eus.*d.e.*1.6(p.27.34; M.22.56C); Mac.Aeg.*hom.*8.3(M.34.529C); *ib.*8.4(529C); *V.Pach.Φ* 49(p.32.1); ἐπὶ τὴν θείαν ἑνότητα...τοὺς β. Max.ap.*cat.1Jo.*4:18(p.135.13); of Mosaic dispensation as first stage in progress to Christian way of life, Eus.*d.e.*1.6(p.29.15; 57D); **3.** *rank*; **a.** in state and army, Eus.*h.e.*8 5 (M.20.752A); Evagr.*h.e.*2.1(p.37.9; M.86.2483B); **b.** in Christian ministry, *order*; **i.** in gen. τοῖς ἐν βαθμῷ Bas.*ep.*188 *can.*1(3.269B; M.32.668A); κληρικοὶ δὲ ὄντες τοῦ β. καθαιροῦνται *ib.*217 *can.*55(326A; M.797A); id.*renunt.*10(2.211B; M.31.648A); Pulch.*ep.Strat.*(p.29.22; H.2.48C); Philost.*h.e.*8.4(M.65.560A); Gennad.*encycl.*(p.80.5; M.85.1616C); **ii.** partic. of the three major orders, *Can.App.*82; οἱ τρεῖς β. διὰ τῆς καθιερώσεως συμπλεγμένοι *Cod.Afr.*3; opp. subdeacons, readers, exorcists, etc., Bas.*ep.*217 *can.*51(3.325C; M.32.796A); Thdr.Mops.*1Tim.*3:14f.(p.132.10; M.66.941C) cit. s. ἀναγνώστης; of episcopate, CSard.*can.*5; Gr.Nyss.*ep.*1(M.46.1008C); Pall.*v.Chrys.*8 (p.47.18; M.47.28); CEph.(431)*can.*1(p.27.29); of priesthood, Ephr. 1.73A; Gr.Naz.*ep.*8(M.37.33D); Nil.*epp.*4.1(M.79.544C); Sophr.H.*mir.Cyr.et Jo.*36(M.87.3549A); of diaconate, ‡Pion.*v.Polyc.*11; Bas.*ep.*170(3.259D; M.32.645A); Philost.*h.e.*3.4(M.65.484A); Max.*ep.*14(M.91.536A); of office of deaconess, Gr.Nyss.*v.Macr.*(p.402.15; M.46.988D); **iii.** of ministerial ranks as steps in orderly cursus of eccl. promotion, CSard.*can.*10; *Const.App.*8.18.3; cf. exeg. 1Tim.3:13, *ib.*8.22.4; Chrys.*hom.11.1 in 1Tim.*(11.605C); *Lit.Jac.*(p.208.20); **4.** *grade* of penitents in disciplinary system of Church ἐάν... μοιχεύσῃ τις, ἐν ἑπτὰ ἔτεσι δεῖ αὐτὸν τοῦ τελείου τυχεῖν κατὰ τοὺς β. τοὺς προάγοντας CAnc.(314)*can.*20; Gr.Nyss.*ep.can.*(M.45.232A); Jo.D.*haer.*80(M.94.733C); **5.** theol., of grades introduced by subordinationist doctrine of Trin., exeg. Ex.20:26 γραφὴ ἐκώλυσεν ἐν τῷ θυσιαστηρίῳ, ἐν ᾧ ἡ τριὰς δοξάζεται, ἀναβαθμοὺς ποιεῖν· ὥστε μὴ ὡς ἐν βαθμοῖς διορίζεσθαι ἀνθρώπους, καθ' ὕφεσίν τινα εἶναι τὰς θείας ὑποστάσεις Didym.*Trin.*1.18(M.39.348B); βαθμῷ μόνον αὐτὸ [sc. τὸ ἅγιον πνεῦμα] διαφέρειν τῶν ἀγγέλων [Pneumatomachan] Ath.*ep. Serap.*1(M.26.531A); ref. Origen ἐπὶ τῆς...τριάδος βαθμοὺς ἐπινοήσας Justn.*Or.*(p.190.16; M.86.947D); ref. Apollinarius περὶ τῆς θείας φύσεως κιβδήλοις ἐχρήσατο λόγοις, β. τινας ἀξιωμάτων γεννήσας Thdt. *h.e.*5.3.3(3.1016); **6.** *order* of service ἡ ἀκολουθία τοῦ ἐκκλησιαστικοῦ β. Mac.Aeg.*carit.*29(M.34.932C); **7.** *step, stride* ἄνθρωπος χοϊκὸς μετὰ ἑνὸς β. ἀνέβη εἰς τὸν οὐρανόν Barth.Edess.*Agar.*(M.104.1440D).

***βαθμ-όω**, *make into steps*, ref. Ascension τὸν λεπτομερέστατον ἀέρα ~ώσας ‡Epiph.*hom.*4(M.43.480C).

βάθος, τό, *depth*; **1.** of the primeval abyss, Meth.*symp.*8.14 (p.100.11; M.18.164A); γῆν ἐκ τοῦ β. διαλελυμένην ἀνέσπασε Procl. CP *or.*2.2(M.65.693B); **2.** of depths of the mind τὰ β. τῆς καρδίας καὶ τοῦ νοῦ Just.*dial.*121.2(M.6.757B); Clem.*paed.*3.2(p.241.20; M.8. 509A); εἰς τὸ β. τῆς ψυχῆς...τὸ φῶς id.*str.*7.7(p.29.12; M.9.453B); Or.*Jo.*6.58(37; p.166.28; M.14.301A); Meth.*symp.*3.8(p.35.17; M.18. 73A); Mac.Aeg.*carit.*31(M.34.933D); **3.** of recondite or advanced knowledge τὰ β. τῆς θείας γνώσεως *1Clem.*40.1; Max.*ep.*21(M.91. 604C); esp. of spiritual sense of scripture τὰ β. τοῦ εὐαγγελικοῦ νοῦ Or.*Jo.*1.8(10; p.13.17; M.14.37C); τὰ β. τῆς γραφῆς *ib.*20.10(p.339.12; 596A); Meth.*symp.*5.4(p.57.11; M.18.101D); id.*res.*1.45(p.294.15; M. 41.1116B); Bas.*hex.*2.1(1.12A; M.29.28C); Chrys.*stat.*1.2(2.3A); β. ... τῶν ἱερῶν γραφῶν...ἡ κεκρυμμένη...γνῶσις Cyr.*1Cor.*2:10(p.257.11; M.74.865B); ref. Gnostics φάσκοντες μόνοι τὰ β. γινώσκειν Hipp.*haer.* 5.6(p.78.3; M.16.3126A); **4.** of depths of God τοῖς τοῦ πατρὸς λογισμοῖς...ἐνοπτεύων τὰ ἐν αὐτῷ β. Eus.*e.th.*3.3(p.154.33; M.24. 997C); Cyr.H.*catech.*4.16; Dion.Ar.*d.n.*9.5(M.3.913B); **5.** of Valent. first principle σιγὴ...μητὴρ...τῶν προβληθέντων ὑπὸ τοῦ β. Clem. *exc.Thdot.*29(p.116.24; M.9.673B); **6.** *inside* of a book, Gr.Nyss. *v.Ephr.*(M.46.840D).

βάθρον, τό, 1. *base, foundation*; met. ὁμολογίαν...ὁ Πέτρος...ὡς κρηπῖδα καὶ β. ἀπέθετο Isid.Pel.*epp.*1.235(M.78.328C); **2.** *foot*, Geo.Pis.*carm.vit.*32; **3.** *pavement*, Chrys.*hom.4.10 in Mt.*(7.65C); **4.** *bench* in church, Eus.*h.e.*10.4.44(M.20.865C); upon which to lay a corpse, Chrys.*hom.1.5 in 2Cor.*(10.425D; vv.ll. βόθρου, θρόνου, βαράθρου).

βαθύγειος, *deep in the earth*, Ephr.3.386B.

***βαθύγλυπτος**, *deeply carved*, Paul.Sil.*ambo.*185(M.86.2259A).

***βαθύγνοφος**, *deep in gloom*, ‡Gr.Naz.*Chr.pat.*1512(M.38.257A).

βαθύκνημος, *high-shouldered*; of a lofty roof-vault, Paul.Sil. *Soph.*403(M.86.2135A).

βαθυκρήπις, *with deep foundations*; of the earth, Nonn.*par.Jo.* 6:59(M.43.801B).

***βαθυκρύσταλλος**, *deep in ice*, Paul.Sil.*Soph.*637(M.86.2143B).

βαθυκύμων, 1. *with deep waters*, Nonn.*par.Jo.*3:23(M.43.769C); **2.** *with roots going deep for water, fruitful*, Synes.*hymn.*9.55(p.55; M.66.1616).

βαθύν-ω, 1. *make deep, hollow out*, Nonn.*par.Jo.*6:13(M.43.706A); *ib.*19:41(908A); **2.** *make to descend, lower* ὁ...λόγος καὶ κατὰ γῆν ἑαυτὸν ~ας Eus.*l.C.*11(p.228.26; M.20.1384C); Synes.*Dion* 6(p.249. 22; M.66.1129B); **3.** *make dense* καπνὸς ἢ ὁμίχλη ~ει...τὸν ἀέρα Gr. Nyss.*Eun.*12(1 p.311.3; M.45.1024C); **4.** intrans.; **a.** *sink, degenerate*, Cyr.*glaph.Ex.*2(1.300D); id.*Jo.*1.4(4.31B); **b.** *go deeply, have profound meaning* τοῦ δὲ λόγου ~οντος, τὸν νοῦν ἀναπτυκτέον Didym. *Trin.*1.7(M.39.276A).

***βαθυπρήων**, *lofty*, Paul.Sil.*Soph.*636(M.86.2143B).

βαθύς, *deep*; **1.** *profound*; of peace, Or.*Jo.*6.1(p.107.4; M.14. 197C); Chrys.*hom.19.9 in Mt.*(7.258A); Synes.*ep.*29(M.66.1357C); of divine mysteries θεὸς ἐν οὐρανῷ ἀποκαλύπτων βαθέα καὶ ἀπόκρυφα *Pers.*(p.4.2); of spiritual sense of scripture and profound truths of Christianity τῆς περικοπῆς...τὸ νόημα τὸ β. Or.*hom.19.11 in Jer.* (p.166.33; M.13.485C); θεωρημάτων βαθυτέρων *ib.8.9*(p.62.32; 345C); id.*Jo.*2.29(24; p.86.10; M.14.164D); ἀνατρέχειν εἰς τοὺς βαθυτέρους λόγους *ib.*20.39(31; p.382.16; 668B); Epiph.*haer.*75.4(p.336.16; M.42. 509A); Cyr.*ador.*2(1.71B); of persons μὴ βαθεῖς τὴν διάνοιαν Gr.Naz. *or.*21.24(M.35.1109B); **2.** *deep-rooted, steadfast* στερροί τινες καὶ β. Eus.*d.e.*3.5(p.125.4; M.22.213A); οἱ β. Ἑβραῖοι Chrys.*hom.21.1 in Ac.*(9.169E); **3.** *ancient, original*; of language, Epiph.*haer.*26.1 (p.276.2; M.41.332B); *ib.*66.13(p.35.5; M.42.48C); **4.** *deep-set*; of eyes, Jo.Mal.*chron.*11 p.269(M.97.409C); **5.** *advanced*; of old age, Chrys. *hom.49.6 in Mt.*(7.512E); Synes.*ep.*9(M.66.1345C); Thphn.*chron.*p.16 (M.108.97B).

***βαθύχειλος**, *obscure of speech*, Cyr.*Jon.*21(3.383B).

βάϊνος, *of palm-wood*, *Apophth.Patr.*(M.65.280A); Hier.*v.Paul.*2 (p.13.4); †Jo.D.*B.J.*29(M.96.1133A).

βαίν-ω, *go*; **1.** met. ἔξω τοῦ εὐαγγελίου μὴ β. Or.*Jo.*32.1(p.425.15; M.14.740C); περαιτέρω ~οντες ἑαυτοὺς ταῖς ἀσεβείαις ἐνέφυρον Ath. *gent.*9(M.25.20A); β. ὁμοδόξως id.*Ar.*1.5(M.26.21A); **2.** β. γονυκλισίας *genuflect*, Barth.Edess.*Agar.*(M.104.1405C); **3.** perf. ptcpl., *established, firm*, Eus.*h.e.*8.7.4(M.20.757A); Gr.Nyss.*Eun.*4(2 p.79.28; M. 45.653C); Chrys.*hom.20.4 in Rom.*(9.663B).

βάϊον, τό, 1. *palm-branch*, used by monks for basket-making, ‡Pall.*h.mon.*28(p.87.3; M.34.1050A); *Apophth.Patr.*(M.65.92C); *ib.* (276B); as sign of triumph or victory, *T.Neph.*5.4; Gr.Mag.*dial.* (tr.Zach.)3.7(M.*PL.*77.231A); ref. Christ's entry into Jerusalem φοῖνιξ...τὰ β. παράσχων παισὶ...εὐφημοῦσι Cyr.H.*catech.*10.19; ὡς νενικηκότι τὸν θάνατον ὑπήντησαν αὐτῷ μετὰ βαΐων Ammon.*Jo.*12:13 (M.85.1473C); hence ref. Palm Sunday τῆς ἑορτῆς ἐγγιζούσης λάβωμεν τὰ β. τῶν φοινίκων Ath.*ep.fest.*28(p.296.13; M.26.1433C); Eulog. *palm.*1(M.86.2913A); ‡Sophr.H.*v.Mar.Aeg.*8(M.87.3704B); as prize in chariot-race, Cyr.S.*v.Sab.*44(p.135.4); Jo.Mosch.*prat.*152(M.87. 3017A); hence **2.** *heat, course*, in hippodrome τῷ πέμπτῳ β. Jo. Mal.*chron.*13 p.340(M.97.508A); ἄχρις ἀπολύσεως τοῦ πρώτου β. Thphn.*chron.*p.313(M.108.760C).

***βαϊπάντησις, ἡ,** for βαϊαπάντησις, *meeting with palms*, i.e. greeting of Christ on Palm Sunday, Sophr.H.*carm.*7 tit.(M.87.3765A).

***βαίτων**, v. βαιών.

βαιών, ὁ, a kind of snake, Epiph.*haer.*50.3(p.248.15, v.l. βέωνος M.41.888C); *ib.*40.8(p.90.4 conj. for βαίτων M.692A).

***βακάντιβος, ὁ,** (Lat. *vacantivus*) *absentee bishop*, Synes.*ep.*67 (v.l. βασκάντιβος M.66.1428C).

***βακλίζω**, *cudgel, smite*, *Didasc.Jac.*4.7(p.70.8).

βακτηρία, ἡ, *stick, staff*;

A. exeg.; **1.** of Passover staff (Ex.12:11) περὶ δὲ τῆς β. οὕτως ἔχω...τὴν μὲν ὑπερειστικὴν οἶδα, τὴν δὲ ποιμαντικήν τε καὶ διδασκαλικήν, καὶ τὰ λογικὰ πρόβατα ἐπιστρέφουσαν. ἀλλὰ σοὶ νῦν τὴν ὑπερείδουσαν ὁ νόμος διακελεύεται, μήπου τὸν λογισμὸν ὀκλάσῃς...μήπου περιενεχθῇς ἀθέως Gr.Naz.*or.*45.19(M.36.649B); **2.** ref. Ps.22:4 interpreted **a.** of upright part of Cross, signifying strength and guidance, Thdt.*Ps.*22:4(1.749); of divine strength, Hesych.H.*fr.Ps.*104:16(M.93.1293C); **b.** of H. Ghost, Gr. Nyss.*ascens.*(M.46.692B); **3.** ref. Is.36:6, Ezech.29:9 ἡ πολυδόνητος γνώμη, ἡ β. νομιζομένη, καὶ βέλος εὑρισκομένη Isid.Pel.*epp.*1.419 (M.78.416B); **4.** of Christ as scion of Jesse, with play on meaning, *staff* ἔρριψα τὴν β. ὡς ὁδηγὸν ἀνόμματον. τοῦτον γὰρ [sc. Χριστόν] ἔγνων εἶναι τὴν β. Ἰεσσαὶ τὴν βλαστήσασαν ‡Bas.*inc.*51 (p.245.25).

B. as emblem of philosopher's vocation, Nil.*exerc.*1(M.79.720A).

C. met., *support* ὁ ταξίαρχος τῶν ἀποστόλων Πέτρος, ἡ τῶν νοητῶν θρεμμάτων β. Geo.Pis.*carm.*82.4.

βακχεία, ἡ, *frenzy, rage*; of raving of heathen prophets, Clem. *prot.*12(p.84.18 conj. for βαγχικήν M.9.240C); of addiction to heathen worship, Thdt.*h.rel.*17(3.1226); of demonic possession, Chrys.*Stag.*1(1.175D); Thdt.*h.rel.*9(1188); of fury of warfare, Chrys. *hom.4.4 in Ac.*(9.38D); of wanton behaviour, †Gregent.*leg.Hom.* 20(M.86.592A).

βακχεύ-ω, 1. intrans.; *act as though frenzied, rage*, ‡Nil.*narr.*5 (M.79.645C); of Devil, Chrys.*hom.87.1 in Mt.*(7.817D); id.*hom.4.4 in Ac.*(9.39C); εἰς τὴν πόλιν...β. id.*stat.*2.1(2.20D); **2.** pass.; **a.** *be inspired with frenzy* κατὰ τοὺς ~ομένους τῷ Διονύσῳ Chrys.*hom.81.3 in Mt.*(7.777E); ‡Nil.*narr.*1(M.79.593C); Thdt.*h.rel.*13(3.1209); **b.** *be inspired* (in good sense) θείῳ ~όμενος πνεύματι Jo.D.*trisag.*6(M.95. 37C).

***βαλά**, ? ἡ, ? *clash* of cymbals, *dicta autem cymbala, quia cum ballematia simul percutiuntur; cum enim Graeci dicunt σύν, β. ballematia*, Isid.H.*etym.*3.22.11.

βαλανεῖον, τό, *bath-house, bath*; lit., ref. eccl. regulations against mixed bathing, CLaod.*can.*30; *Const.App.*1.6.6; *ib.*1.9.1; CTrull.*can.*77; met. β. γάρ ἐστιν ἡ ἐκκλησία πνευματικόν Chrys. *hom.15.5 in 2Cor.*(10.551A).

βαλανηφαγέω, *live on acorns*, Marcell.*fr.*112 ap.Eus.*Marcell.*1.3 (p.17.16; M.24.749B).

βαλανικός, *of* or *for the bath*; neut. as subst., *price of a bath*, Leont.N.*v.Jo.Eleem.*38(p.76.24).

***βαλαντιαῖος**, *of the eye-ball* or *sac* in which the humours of the eye are contained, Sophr.H.*mir.Cyr.et Jo.*69(M.87.3661A).

βαλάντιον, τό, 1. *box* γενέσθαι ἐκ ξύλων β. τέσσαρα †Jo.D.*B.J.*6 (M.96.904A); **2.** *eye-ball* or *sac* containing the humours of the eye, Sophr.H.*mir.Cyr.et Jo.*69(M.87.3661A).

***βαλαντιόσκοπος, ὁ,** *purse-watcher, covetous person*, Pall.*v.Chrys.* 5(p.32.1; M.47.20).

βαλβίς, ἡ, 1. *rope* forming starting and finishing line of a race, met.; **a.** *beginning* of a career, Chrys.*hom.25.3 in 2Cor.*(10.617B); id.*anom.*8.5(1.520D); of beginning of Creation, Eudoc.*Cypr.*1.82 (M.85.836B); of foundation of Temple, Nonn.*par.Jo.*2:20(M.43. 764B); of an argument, Thdt.*provid.*1(4.487); Jo.D.*imag.*1.2(M.94. 1233A); of baptismal rebirth, Nonn.*par.Jo.*3:7(768A); **b.** *anything to be attained, goal, object* τοῖς λόγοις...ὤτων οὐκ ἐδίδου βαλβῖδα Thphyl.*exc.gent.*13(p.487.23;M.113.949C); **2.** *limit, boundary*, Eudoc. *Cypr.*2.214(M.85.853B); met., of restraint of passions, Nil.*praest.*3 (M.79.1064C).

***βαλίσσηνος,** sens. dub. βαλισσήνοις βάκλοις τύπτειν Jo.Mal. *chron.*7 p.187(M.97.297A).

βαλλίστρα, ἡ, (Lat. *ballistra*) *catapult*, Mac.Aeg.*hom.*52.2(p.25).

[*]**βαλλιστράριος, ὁ** (βαλλιστάριος *LS*), Lat. *ballistarius, worker of a catapult, artilleryman*, *CIG* 8621; Justn.*nov.*85.2,3(p.415.13,22,24).

βάλλ-ω, A. *hit*; hence **1.** *stone*, Ath.*Ar.*2.28(M.26.205C); **2.** *blow*, of the wind ἔπαρμα θέντες τῇ ~ομένῃ (i.e. *to windward*) Pall.*v. Chrys.*15(p.89.1; M.47.50); **3.** *attack, harm*, Const.ap.Gel.Cyz.*h.e.*2.7. 41(M.85.1241B); Thdt.*qu.33 in Lev.*(1.211); **4.** *vex*, Chrys.*hom.11.1 in Eph.*(11.80C, v.l. δάκνεσθαι); Thdt.*Ps.*76:2(2.1143); *ib.*105:33 (1361); **5.** ὅρκοις β. τινα *adjure*, Thphn.*chron.*p.236(M.108.593C).

B. *throw out, stretch out*, Leont.N.*v.Sym.*45(M.93.1725B); hence **1.** φωνὴν β. *cry out*, *PMich.*220.22(Winter, *Michigan Papyri* 3 p.295); **2.** *recite* an office, *Apophth.Mac.Aeg.*33(M.34.256C); Ephr. 2.105C; id.2.115A; **3.** β. μετάνοιαν *make obeisance* of apology or reverence, *Apophth.Patr.*(M.65.276A,277B); Dor.*doct.*9.2(M.88.1720A); Leont.N.*v.Jo.Eleem.*14(p.30.1); Anast.S.*qu.et resp.*60(M.89.641A); of prostration in prayer, Jo.Mosch.*prat.*40(M.87.2893A); *ib.*100(2960A).

C. *place, set* ἵνα βάλω αὐτὴν εἰς μοναστήριον Leont.N.*v.Jo.Eleem.* 24(p.51.27); *ib.*43(p.87.21); hence **1.** *plant* a vine, Jo.Eleem.*v.Tych.* 10(p.120); **2.** β. ῥίζαν *strike* root, *ib.*; **3.** *pour* water, Dam.*troph.* 2.5(p.226.14); **4.** *lay* to mind, Clem.*prot.*10(p.76.3; M.8.221B); Gr. Thaum.*pan.Or.*5(p.12.17; M.10.1065B); **5.** *set about, begin*, *Apophth. Patr.*(M.65.97A); *ib.*(149A); *ib.*(436A); **6.** *proceed* μὴ ἐφ' ἡσυχίας ~εσθαι τὸ πρᾶγμα Eus.*d.e.*3.4(p.119.5; M.22.204A); **7.** pass., *fall* in love ἐβλήθη εἰς ἔρωτα αὐτῆς Jo.Mal.*chron.*2 p.45(M.97.117B); **8.** ἔξω β. *excommunicate*, *Const.App.*2.16.1.

***βαλσαμουργία, ἡ,** *distilling of balsam*, of BMV στακτή, ἡ ἐκ παρθενικῆς β. ἀποστάξασα Χριστῷ Thdr.Stud.*nativ.BMV* 7(M.96. 692D).

***βαλσαμουργός, ὁ,** *balsam-worker*, Pall.*h.Laus.*8(p.27.20; M.34. 1025C).

***βαλσαμών, ὁ,** *balsam-garden*, Pall.*h.Laus.*8(p.27.20; M.34.1025C).

βαλτίδιον, τό (written βαλτίδιν), *belt*, *Mir.Artem.*32(p.46.27); *ib.* (p.47.24).

βάμμα, τό, *dye*; *dyed fringe to a garment*, ref. Num.15:38 τὸ κόκκινον β. περιτιθέναι αὐτοῖς ἐνετείλατο ὑμῖν Just.*dial.*46.5(M.6.576B).

***βαναυσέω,** *work with one's hands*, Synes.*regn.*14(p.45.1; M.66. 1092A).

***βαναυσοποιΐα, ἡ,** *performance of vulgarity*, Epiph.*exp.fid.*11 (p.511.24; M.42.801C).

βάναυσος, *mechanical*; of persons, *artisan*; hence **1.** *vulgar, illiberal*, *1Clem.*49.5; Just.*dial.*3.3(M.6.481A); ref. Petr. Full. ὅστις οὐχ οὕτω φρονεῖ κοινωνός ἐστι τῆς τοῦ κναφέως τοῦ β. σκαιότητος Jo.D.*trisag.*26(M.95.57A); **2.** *low, sordid* ἀτιμάζει...αὐτὴν [sc. ἁγνείαν] ...β. ἐπιθυμίαις Meth.*symp.*11.1(p.129.23; M.18.205A); **3.** *slack, effeminate* οἱ β. καὶ ῥάθυμοι Chrys.*hom.44.3 in Mt.*(7.472A); ἐν τοῖς πολέμοις χαῦνοι καὶ β. id.*hom.3.4 in 1Thess.*(11.446B); id.*hom.17.2 in 1Tim.*(11.650D); of things, *luxurious* ἐπὶ τὸ β. τὰ πλείονα... ἐξήγαγον, τὸ ἀναγκαῖον...διαφθείραντες Chrys.*hom.49.4 in Mt.*(509D); id.*hom.10.5 in Phil.*(11.281D).

βαναυσουργός, ὁ, *artisan, mechanic*, Just.*1apol.*55.3(M.6.412B).

βάνδον, τό, 1. *ensign, banner*, Cosm.Ind.*top.*11(M.88.444A); *Chron.Pasch.*p.383(M.92.981C); **2.** *detachment, band* of soldiers (*vexillum*), Jo.Mal.*chron.*18 p.461(M.97.673C); Anast.Ap.*a.Max.*2. 31(M.90.168C); Thphn.*chron.*p.265(M.108.657C).

***βανιάρι(ο)ν, τό,** (Lat. *balnearium*) *public baths*, Jo.Mal.*chron.* 9 p.222(M.97.345B).

***βαπτέον,** *one must dye*, Clem.*paed.*3.11(p.271.27; M.8.637B).

βαπτίζ-ω, I. *submerge, sink, plunge*;

A. pass. intrans., of ships, *sink* ναῦς ~ομένη Clem.*q.d.s.*34(p.182. 29; M.9.640C); Chrys.*hom.1.3 in Jo.*(8.5E); id.*hom.34.3 in Heb.*(12. 316C); Nil.*exerc.*42(M.79.772B); Cyr.*Jo.*2.8(4.232E).

B. *plunge*; a sword, Chrys.*hom.1.3 in Eph.*(11.12E); *ib.14.2* (105D); Bas.Sel.*or.*7.2(M.85.112A); the hand, *dip*, Chrys.*hom.3.6 in 2Cor.*(10.451E); id.*hom.5.3 in 1Thess.*(11.464B); id.*hom.25.3 in Heb.* (12.232B).

C. *submerge*; **1.** med. intrans., *sink* in water, Afric.*chron.*9(M. 10.69C); pass., of persons οὐ μὴν ὅλος ἐβαπτίσθη [sc. ἐν βορβόρῳ ὁ Ἱερεμίας] οὐδὲ γὰρ ζῆν οὕτως ἠδύνατο Chrys.*fr.in Jer.*38:6(M.64. 1001D); Jo.Mosch.*prat.*44(M.87.2900A); **2.** *drown* β. σε τὰ κύματα Chrys.*Laz.*6.5(1.779B); pass., Gr.Naz.*or.*45.21(M.36.652C); Chrys. *hom.33.1 in Jo.*(8.189E); **3.** met., *sink, overwhelm*; **a.** persons ὑπὸ μέθης ~όμενος εἰς ὕπνον Clem.*paed.*2.2(p.172.17; M.8.421A); ὁ διάβολος...βαπτίσας τὸν ἀκροατὴν ὕπνῳ Chrys.*hom.43.1 in Ac.*(9.325D); Cyr.*Jo.*2.1(4.126E); esp. of effects of sin ἡμᾶς βεβαπτισμένους ταῖς βαρυτάταις ἁμαρτίαις Just.*dial.*86.6(M.6.681C); ignorance ἀγνοίᾳ βεβαπτισμένος Clem.*prot.*1(p.5.11; M.8.57A); and other spiritual hindrances πολλῇ βαπτισθέντες περιουσίᾳ Chrys.*hom.63.2 in Mt.* (7.630A); ὑπὸ τῆς ἡδονῆς...~εται *ib.*40.5(443E); πτωχείᾳ βαπτισθῆναι id.*fr.Job* proem.(M.64.508C); **b.** faculties of mind and soul ὁ νοῦς βεβαπτισμένος τῷ οἴνῳ †Bas.*Is.*291(1.600C; M.30.629A); Mac.Aeg. *hom.*45.3(M.34.788C); Chrys.*hom.47.4 in Ac.*(9.356D); Nil.*exerc.*64 (M.79.797A); βεβάπτισται...εἰς ἀβουλίαν ὁ νοῦς Cyr.*hom.pasch.*1(5^2. 11D); **c.** things λήθῃ ~οντες τὸ πολλάκις ἀνεγνωσμένον Cyr.*Jo.*3.3 (4.268A).

II. *wash, baptize* (v. βάπτισμα);

A. of ceremonial lustrations of Jewish Law τὸ ~εσθαι ἁψάμενόν τινος ὧν ἀπηγορεύεται ὑπὸ Μωυσέως Just.*dial.*46.2(M.6.573C); Clem. *str.*3.12(p.234.4; M.8.1184B); Gr.Naz.*or.*39.17(M.36.353C) cit. s. B; of similar purificatory washing practised by Christians, *Hom.Clem.* 11.30.

B. of John's baptism, Just.*dial.*51.2(M.6.588D); †Hipp.*theoph.*3 (p.259.5; M.10.853D); ἐβάπτισε Μωϋσῆς, ἀλλ' ἐν ὕδατι· καὶ πρὸ τούτου, ἐν νεφέλῃ καὶ ἐν θαλάσσῃ...τυπικῶς δὲ τοῦτο ἦν...ἐβάπτισε καὶ Ἰωάννης, οὐκ ἔτι μὲν Ἰουδαϊκῶς· οὐ γὰρ ἐν ὕδατι μόνον, ἀλλὰ καὶ εἰς μετάνοιαν...~ει καὶ Ἰησοῦς, ἀλλ' ἐν πνεύματι Gr.Naz.*or.*39.17 (M.36.353C); of Christ's baptism by John, associated with sonship κατὰ θέλημα καὶ δύναμιν Ign.*Smyrn.*1.1; cleansing and sanctifying baptismal water, id.*Eph.*18.2; Clem.*ecl.*7(p.138.28; M.9.701B); giving example to Christians to be baptized, †Hipp.*theoph.*5(p.260.8; 856D); Procl.CP *or.*7.3(M.65.760D); washing away sins, Or.*comm. in Mt.*16.6(p.485.21; M.13.1385A); does not imply that Christians are subject to Jewish Law, id.*Cels.*2.4(p.131.21; M.11.801C).

C. of Christian baptism (v. βάπτισμα); **1.** scope of verb; **a.** at times used loosely in sense of *perform service of baptism*, including water-baptism, unction, and imposition of hands, cf. *baptizati simus in aquis istis visibilibus, et in chrismate visibili*, Or.*comm. in Rom.*5.8(M.14.1038C); cf.Cyr.H.*catech.*21.1; and βαπτιζόμενοι is used of candidates for baptism, *Lit.*ap.*Const.App.*8.8.5; **b.** but gen. signifies baptizing in water alone, *V.Ath.*2(M.25.clxxxviD); χρίσεις δὲ πρῶτον ἐλαίῳ· ἔπειτα β. ὕδατι, καὶ τελευταῖον σφραγίσεις μύρῳ *Const.App.*7.22.2; v. ὕδωρ; **c.** or occasionally denotes baptizing in water and baptizing with H. Ghost as separate actions, ref. Ac.8:1ff. ὁ μὲν Φίλιππος...ἐβάπτιζεν ὕδατι, ὁ δὲ Πέτρος τῷ πνεύματι Or.*comm.in 1Cor.*1:17(*JTS* 9 p.234); **2.** ref. formula of baptism; **a.** administration in name of Christ ἐν τῷ ὀνόματι Ἰησοῦ Χριστοῦ...β. *A.Paul.et Thecl.*34(p.260.7); cf.Herm.*vis.*3.7.3; cf.Or. *comm.in Rom.*5.8(M.14.1039C); Bas.*Spir.*28(3.23B; M.32.116C); **b.** in the threefold name β. εἰς τὸ ὄνομα τοῦ πατρὸς καὶ τοῦ υἱοῦ καὶ τοῦ ἁγίου πνεύματος (cf. Mt.28:19) *Did.*7.1; β. εἰς τὸ ὄνομα τῆς ἁγίας καὶ ὁμοουσίου τριάδος *A.Phil.*86(p.34.5); Or.*fr.36 in Jo.*3:5(p.512.20), cf.Firmilianus *ep.Cypr.*9(M.*PL.*3.1211A); τρισμακαρίᾳ τινὶ ἐπονομασίᾳ *Hom.Clem.*13.4; Gr.Nyss.*bapt.Chr.*(M.46.585C); for theological implications of Trinitarian formula v. βάπτισμα; **c.** formula of administration; **i.** act. voice not often used in actual words of administration, but ~ομέν σε εἰς ὄνομα κτλ. *A.Xanthipp.*21(p.73. 13); **ii.** use of med. indicates self-baptism in case of Thecla ὑστέρᾳ ἡμέρᾳ ~ομαι *A.Paul.et Thecl.*34(p.260.7); but this case recognized as exceptional and highly irregular, Bas.Sel.*v.Thecl.*1(M.85.536B); in standard formula ~εται Θεόδωρος εἰς τὸ ὄνομα τοῦ πατρὸς κτλ. Jo.Mosch.*prat.*176(M.87.3045A); Thdr.Stud.*epp.*2.24(M.99.1192A) etc., verb is prob. pass.; outside actual formula of administration ~ομαι (med.) = *get oneself baptized* τοῖς ὑπὸ Ἰησοῦ βαπτισαμένοις Or.*Jo.*32.7(p.437.5; M.14.760B); χθὲς...ὁ δεσπότης...ὕδατι ἐβαπτίσατο, σήμερον δὲ δοῦλος αἵματι ~εται Chrys.*pan.Lucn.*2(2.526A); but med. used interchangeably with pass. τί οὖν...οὐκ ἐβαπτίσθησαν οὗτοι;...ἀλλὰ ἐβαπτίσαντο id.*hom.*30.2 *in* 2*Cor.*(10.651E); and pass. is at least as common as med. οἱ...θέλοντες βαπτισθῆναι Herm.*vis.*3.7.3; *Hom.Clem.*8.23; ‡Just.*qu.et resp.*44(M.6.1289A).

βάπτισις, ἡ, *baptizing, baptism* (= βάπτισμα, q.v.); **1.** of Christ's baptism, ‡Ath.*qu.script.*41(M.28.725A); Sophr.H.*carm.*5 tit.(M.87.3756A); depicted in art, Jo.D.*imag.*1.8(M.94.1240A); ‡Jo.D.*Const.*3 (M.95.313D); **2.** of Christian baptism ἐμυήθη τὴν ἱερὰν β. [sc. ὁ Κωνστάντινος] Soz.*h.e.*2.34.1(M.67.1029D); of Julian αἵματι σφαγίων τὴν καθ' ἡμᾶς β. ἀπονίψασθαι *ib.*5.2.2(1212B); of Eunomian method of administering baptism, *ib.*6.26.2(1361C).

βάπτισμα, τό, *dipping, baptism* (N.B. for convenience some references to the verb βαπτί-ζω q.v. are included in this article, prefaced (like references to Latin texts) by 'cf.'. Where another word denoting baptism or a kindred idea (e.g. ἀναβαπτίζω, ὕδωρ) is used in a text which is not cited, this word is indicated in parentheses);

I. of Jewish baptism; which Christ's advent rendered valueless τί...ὄφελος ἐκείνου τοῦ β., ὃ τὴν σάρκα καὶ μόνον τὸ σῶμα φαιδρύνει; Just.*dial.*14.1(M.6.504C); *ib.*29.1(537C); the many β. prescribed by Law being comprehended in one Christian baptism, Clem.*str.*3.12 (p.234.6; M.8.1184B); cf.Or.*comm.in Rom.*2.13(M.14.912C); which, being carnal and not spiritual, resembled heretical Christian baptism, cf.Firmilianus *ep.Cypr.*13(M.*PL.*3.1166B); but typified Christian baptism, cf.Gr.Naz.*or.*39.17(M.36.353C) cit. s. βαπτίζω; δέδοται...διὰ τῆς Μωύσεως ἐντολῆς...τὸ ὕδωρ τοῦ ἁγιασμοῦ, τύπον ἐπέχον τοῦ...ἁγίου...β.,...τοῦ ἐν Χριστῷ Cyr.*Lc.*11:37(M.72.712B); followed 'baptisms' of Flood and Red Sea as third in series, Gr.Naz.*or.*39.17(M.36.356A).

II. of John's baptism, in gen., Just.*dial.*88.2(M.6.685B); *ib.*88.7 (688A); historicity attested by Josephus, cf.Or.*Cels.*1.47(p.97.1; M.11.745C); as fulfilment of old dispensation, not beginning of new, cf.Or.*comm.in Rom.*5.8(M.14.1039B); contrast παλαιᾶς τὸ τέλος, καὶ τῆς καινῆς διαθήκης ἀρχὴ τὸ β. Ἰωάννης γὰρ ἦν ἀρχηγός Cyr.H.*catech.*3.6; ended by Christ's advent, cf.Just.*dial.*51.2(M.6.588D); effects: no regeneration conferred, cf.Or.*Jo.*6.33(17; p.143.12; M.14.257B); nor adoptive sonship, but only remission of sins, †Hipp.*theoph.*3(p.259.5; M.10.853D); Cyr.H.*catech.*20.6; not mere washing, but given εἰς μετάνοιαν, cf.Gr.Naz.*or.*39.17(M.36.353C) cit. s. βαπτίζω; could not confer H. Ghost, Ammon.*Ac.*18:25(M.85.1572C); hence superior to Jewish baptism, cf.Gr.Naz.*or.*39.17(M.36.353C); Chrys.*hom.*17.2 *in Jo.*(8.98D); but imperfect, *ib.*; τὸ...θεῷ β. τελείως ἔχει ἄφεσιν ἁμαρτιῶν ἐξ αὐτοῦ τοῦ ~ζεσθαι, τὸ δὲ Ἰωάννου εἰς αὐτὸ μὲν εἶχεν ἄφεσιν ἁμαρτιῶν, διὰ μετάνοιαν δέ, ἀτελὴς γὰρ ἦν *cat.Lc.*3:2(p.28.19); not inferior to that administered by Christ's disciples during his ministry ἑκάτερα γὰρ [sc. β.] ὁμοίως τῆς ἐκ τοῦ πνεύματος χάριτος ἄμοιρα ἦν Chrys.*hom.*29.1 *in Jo.*(165C); but inferior to Christian baptism ἐγὼ μετανοίας βαπτίζω β., αὐτὸς δὲ υἱοθεσίας δωρεῖται χάρισμα †Hipp.*theoph.*3(p.259.5; M.10.853D); Or.*Jo.*6.33 (17; p.143.8; M.14.257B); Ἰωάννης μὲν γὰρ τὸ αἰσθητὸν πρῶτον ἐβάπτισεν β., Ἰησοῦς δὲ τὸ νοητόν id.*fr.*76 *in Jo.*(p.543.7); hence τὸ πρῶτον β. πέραν τοῦ Ἰορδάνου δίδωσιν Ἰωάννης, ὃ ἑρμηνεύεται 'κατάβασις', τὸ δὲ δεύτερον ἐν Αἰνών, ἐγγὺς τοῦ Σαλήμ. Αἰνὼν δὲ ἑρμηνεύεται 'ὀφθαλμὸς βασάνου' καὶ Σαλὴμ 'αὐτὸς ὁ ἀναβαίνων'. ... ἔπρεπέ γε τὸ πρῶτον εἶναι β. παρὰ καταβάσει, τὸ δὲ δεύτερον παρὰ ἀναβαίνοντι *ib.*(p.543.20ff.); Cyr.*Jo.*2.1(4.156E); preparation involved instruction in prayer, cf.Or.*or.*2.4(p.302.26; M.11.421C).

III. of Christ's baptism by John;

A. historicity of NT account defended, cf.Or.*Cels.*1.40ff.(p.90.24ff.; M.11.733Dff.).

B. its significance and purpose; **1.** associated with Christ's sonship κατὰ θέλημα καὶ δύναμιν, cf.Ign.*Smyrn.*1.1; by it Christ partook of υἱοθεσία κατὰ τὸ ἀνθρώπινον, cf.Thdr.Mops.*fr.inc.*8(p.298.24; M.66.980D); heret. doctrine that Christ's sonship began at baptism denied, Epiph.*haer.*51.20(p.278.11; M.41.925A); cf. theory of Ebionites, Val. Gn., Marcus, and Cerinthus, that aeon Christ descended on human Jesus at baptism, Iren.*haer.*1.7.2(M.7.513A); *ib.*1.14.6(608A); *ib.*1.26.1(686B); cf.Epiph.*haer.*28.1(p.314.5; M.41.380A); *ib.*30.14(p.351.18; 429C); **2.** cleansing and sanctifying of baptismal water, cf.Ign.*Eph.*18.2; cf.Clem.*ecl.*7(p.138.28; M.9.701B); cf.Procl.CP *or.*7.3(M.65.760D); and sanctifying of whole baptismal rite, Cyr.H.*catech.*3.11; *ib.*12.15; **3.** as example to Christians βάπτισόν με, Ἰωάννη, ἵνα μηδεὶς β. καταφρονήσῃ †Hipp.*theoph.*5 (p.260.8; M.10.856D); Gr.Naz.*or.*39.14(M.36.349D); cf.Apoll.*quod un.Chr.*11(p.302.15; M.28.132A); cf.*Const.App.*7.22.5; cf.Procl.CP *or.*7.3(l.c.); **4.** washing away sins, Or.*comm.in Mt.*16.6(p.485.21; M.13.1385A); **5.** delivering from fire τὸ β. αὐτοῦ πυρὸς ἡμᾶς ἐξείλετο καὶ τὸ πάθος πάθους Clem.*exc.Thdot.*76(p.131.1; M.9.693B); **6.** at baptism Christ as God sent forth H. Ghost, and as man received him, Nil.*epp.*2.293(M.79.345B); **7.** baptism attested truth of John's mission, cf.*Const.App.*7.22.5; and ended it, Clem.*str.*1.21(p.84.18; M.8.872A); **8.** discussion of question why Christ (who had no need of baptism of repentance, Just.*dial.*88.4(M.6.685B); cf.Clem.*ecl.*7 (p.138.28; M.9.701B); cf.Cyr.H.*catech.*3.11; cf.Procl.CP *or.*7.3(M.65.760D) etc.) underwent baptism, cf.Gr.Naz.*or.*39.15(M.36.352B); cf. Epiph.*exp.fid.*15(p.516.13ff.; M.42.842B,C); **9.** Christol. cf. τὸ μὲν οὖν σχῆμα κατὰ τὴν σάρκα ἐν ὕδατι ~ζεται Apoll.*quod un.Chr.*11(p.302.15; M.28.132A); οὐκ ἔστιν ἄλλος ὁ βαπτισθείς, καὶ ἄλλος ὁ μὴ βαπτισθείς. ἀλλ' οὗτός ἐστιν ὁ υἱός μου Gr.Ant.*bapt.*2.6(M.88.1877A).

C. that a Jew baptized Christ does not imply that Christians must observe Jewish Law, v. βαπτίζω.

D. Christ's age at baptism interpreted; **1.** by Marcosians, as representing 30 aeons contained in him, Iren.*haer.*1.14.6(M.7.608A); **2.** as fixing minimum age for priest's ordination, cf. (φωτίζω) CNeocaes.*can.*11; **3.** as perfect age, so that those dying as children will be raised up as men of 30, cf.‡Ath.*qu.Ant.*24(M.28.612C).

E. festival of Christ's baptism, observed **1.** by some on 8 November, cf.Epiph.*haer.*51.16(p.270.14; M.41.920A); **2.** by Basilidians (with all-night readings) on 15 Tybi or 11 Tybi, Clem.*str.*1.21(p.90.21; M.8.888A) (11 Tybi being 6 January, Epiph.*haer.*51.24(p.293.2; M.41.932B)); **3.** gen. at Epiphany (6 Jan.), cf.†Hipp.*theoph.*(p.257; M.10.852); Gr.Naz.*or.*39.1(M.36.336A); and other Epiphany homilies; τὴν τῶν ἐπιφανίων ἑορτὴν ἀργείτωσαν διὰ τὸ ἐν αὐτῇ ἀνάδειξιν γεγενῆσθαι τῆς τοῦ Χριστοῦ θεότητος...ἐν τῷ β. *Const.App.*8.33.7; cf.Procl.CP *or.*7.1(M.65.757C); Cosm.Ind.*top.*5(M.88.197B); cf.*Chron.Pasch.*p.209(M.92.513C); day corresponding to fifth day of Creation, cf.*ib.*p.210(l.c.) at first celebrated in conjunction with Epiphany, but later separated from it, Jo.Nic.*nativ.*(M.96.1440A), partly owing to Jerusalem priests' difficulty in celebrating at Bethlehem and Jordan on same day, *ib.*(1441B,1445C); contrast Cosm.Ind.*top.*5(197B); Armenians retained earlier practice, Jo.Nic.*nativ.*(1449B); festival supposedly originated by John's disciples on day of the baptism, *ib.*(1440D).

F. story that baptism kindled fire in Jordan, cf.Just.*dial.*88.3 (M.6.685B); πῦρ [i.e. Χριστός] ἐν ὕδατι ~ζόμενον Procl.CP *or.*7.2(M.65.760A); cf.*Ev.Ebion.*ap.Epiph.*haer.*30.13(p.351.1; M.41.429A); cf. (ὕδωρ) *Chron.Pasch.*p.225(M.92.548A).

G. application of Ps.73:13–14 to Christ's baptism, v. δράκων.

IV. exeg. Mc.10:38, Lc.12:50, interpreted of Cross, and as signifying mystical death with Christ in baptism (v. infra VI. E.9), Chrys.*hom.*25.2 *in Jo.*(8.146D); of Ascension, Or.*Jo.*6.56f.(37; p.165.15ff.; M.14.297Df.); of martyrdom, which confers remission of sins, v. infra VII; as type of voluntary works of virtue τὸ τοῦ κυρίου β. τῶν ὑπὲρ ἀρετῆς κατὰ πρόθεσιν ἑκουσίων καὶ ἡμετέρων πόνων τύπος ὑπάρχει Max.*qu.Thal.*30(M.90.368D); id.*cap.*2.99(M.90.1220D); of mortification of earthly desire τὸ τοῦ κυρίου β. ἐστιν ἡ παντελὴς πρὸς τὸν αἰσθητὸν κόσμον τῆς προαιρέσεως ἡμῶν νέκρωσις *ib.*2.98(1220C).

V. of baptism administered by disciples during Christ's ministry; question whether Jesus baptized cf. παρὰ τῷ Ἰωάννῃ Ἰησοῦς γινώσκεται παρὰ τοῖς Φαρισαίοις ~ζων, ἐν τοῖς μαθηταῖς αὐτοῦ ~ζων...ὁ δὲ παρὰ τοῖς τρισὶν Ἰησοῦς οὐδαμῶς ~ζει Or.*Jo.*10.8(6; p.178.8; M.14.320A); Χριστὸς οὖν ἐν ὕδατι οὐ ~ζει...ἑαυτῷ δὲ τηρεῖ τὸ ἁγίῳ πνεύματι ~ζειν *ib.*6.23(13; p.133.33; 241C); this baptism not superior in effect to John's, Chrys.*hom.*29.1 *in Jo.*(8.165C); discussion of question by whom Apostles were baptized, cf.Clem.*fr.*6(p.196.21; M.9.745C); ‡Chrys.*ascens.Ac.*13(3.770A); also BMV, cf.‡Thdt.*fr.bapt.*(M.92.1077A).

VI. of baptism in Church;

A. types and foreshadowings; **1.** in OT, v. ὕδωρ; **a.** types: many discussed, Gr.Nyss.*bapt.Chr.*(M.46.588B); ‡Ath.*qu.script.*101(M.28.760A); cf.Didym.*Trin.*2.14(M.39.696A); commonest types: Spirit and water of Gen.1:2, Clem.*ecl.*8(p.138.33; M.9.701B); Proc.G.*Gen.*1:2(M.87.48B); fifth day of Creation, v. λουτρόν; Flood, Procl.CP *or.*7.3(M.65.760C); Jo.D.*f.o.*4.9(M.94.1124A); and Ark, cf.Firmilianus *ep.Cypr.*15(M.*PL.*3.1216A); cloud and Red Sea (1Cor.10:1–4), cf.Or.*Jo.*6.44(p.153.16; M.14.276D); Bas.*Spir.*31(3.26C; M.32.124B); Chrys.*hom.in* 1*Cor.*10:1(3.235A); Bas.Sel.*or.*13.2(M.85.176A) etc.; passage of Jordan, typical of baptism into Jesus (Joshua), Or.

*Jo.*6.44(26; p.153.16; M.14.276D); trans-Jordan tribes typify those justified by Law, those settled on this side of river typify gentile Christians whose knowledge and conduct is perfected by baptism, Nil.*epp.*1.51(M.79.105B); laver in tabernacle, Cyr.H.*catech.*3.5; Cyr.*ador.*9(1.312A); Elijah's Carmel sacrifice, Bas.*hom.*13.3(2.115E; M.31.428D); Gr.Nyss.*bapt.Chr.*(M.46.592C); Naaman's cleansing, cf.Iren.*fr.*33(p.497; M.7.1248B); cf.Or.*Jo.*6.47(28; p.156.5ff.; M.14.281B); Gr.Nyss.*bapt.Chr.*(592D); and gen. cleansing of lepers, Cyr.*glaph.Lev.*1(1.358A); fountain of Is.7:3, id.*Is.*1.4(2.117A); voice of Lord over waters (Ps.28:3), Bas.*hom.in Ps.*28:3(1.118A; M.29.289C) etc.; ὕδατα πολλά of Ps.92:4, Diod.ad loc.(M.33.1626D); Ps.74:13, Cyr.H.*catech.*3.11; cf.‡Epiph.*hom.*2(M.43.460B); *Rit.Bapt.*(p.400); **b.** prophetic foreshadowings; many cited, *Barn.*11; Is.1:16–19, Gr.Nyss.*bapt.Chr.*(593A); Ezech.47:3, †Mel.*fr.*(p.313); Ezech.26:25, Gr.Nyss.*bapt.Chr.*(593A) etc.; **2.** in NT ἡ προβατικὴ κολυμβήθρα (Jo.5:2), Chrys.*hom.36.1 in Jo.*(8.207B); man with pitcher (Lc.22:10), Cyr.*Lc.*22:10(M.72.904C); **3.** in Greek poets, Clem.*str.*4.22(p.311.2; M.8.1352B); **4.** in Nature, cf.Mel.*bapt.*(p.310); water and Spirit in baptism represented symbolically in thunderstorm, ‡Ath.*dial.Trin.*3.27(M.28.1245A) cit. s. βροντή.

B. def. (ἅγιον β. freq.; τὸ τοῦ Ἰησοῦ β. Or.*Jo.*32.7(6; p.436.21; M.14.757C); Gr.Nyss.*bapt.Chr.*(M.46.593B) etc.); **1.** sts. β. means entire initiatory rite, including water-baptism and subsequent unction and imposition of hands, cf. *per impositionem manuum apostolicarum spiritus sanctus dabatur in baptismo*, Or.*princ.*1.3.2(p.50.4; M.11.147B); *ib.*2.10.7(p.181.7; 239B); id.*Jo.*6.33(17; p.143.4; M.14.257A); cf. *omnes baptizati simus in aquis...visibilibus et in chrismate visibili*, id.*comm.in Rom.*5.8(M.14.1038C); cf.Cyr.H.*catech.*21.1; cf.Didym.*Trin.*2.12(M.39.680Af.); **2.** but usu. denotes water-baptism with Trin. formula, or even baptismal water alone τὸ ὕδωρ...τὸ β. γινόμενον Clem.*exc.Thdot.*82(p.132.13; M.9.696C); cf. *per impositionem manuum apostolorum post baptismi gratiam et renovationem sanctus spiritus tradebatur*, Or.*princ.*1.3.7(p.58.20; M.11.153A); id.*Jo.*32.7(6; p.436.21; M.14.757C); id.*fr.36 in Jo.*(p.512.12); CLaod.*can.*48; cf.*Const.App.*7.22.2; Tim.CP *haer.*(M.86.13A).

C. baptismal rite; **1.** largely warranted by unwritten tradition, not scripture, Bas.*Spir.*66(3.55A; M.32.188B); **2.** descriptions: immersion, threefold pouring of water with threefold name, *Did.*7.1; removal of garments, blessing and exorcism of oils, renunciation of Satan and unction with exorcized oil, threefold immersion with credal interrogations, unction, robing, bishop's unction, consignation, and imposition of hands, cf.Hipp.*trad.ap.*21–22; full account, Cyr.H.*catech.*19–21; cf.*Const.App.*7.22.1ff.; cf. (σφραγίζω) Dion.Ar.*e.h.*2.2.5–7(M.3.396Aff.); cf.Jo.D.*f.o.*4.9(M.94.1120A,B); **3.** essential elements; **a.** water, v. ὕδωρ, κατάδυσις; **b.** Trin. formula, cf. *ut salutare baptismum non aliter nisi excellentissimae omnium trinitatis auctoritate, id est patris et filii et spiritus sancti cognominatione compleatur*, id.*princ.*1.3.2(p.50.7; M.11.147C); v. βαπτίζω, λουτρόν; Ath.*ep.Serap.*4.12(M.26.653A); explanation of formula, Gr.Nyss.*bapt.Chr.*(M.46.585C); mention of each Person necessary, id.*ep.*5(M.46.1032A); discussion of question why, when Christ ordered use of Trin. formula, *apostolus solius Christi in baptismo nomen assumpserit*, Or.*comm.in Rom.*5.8(M.14.1039C); Bas.*Spir.*28(3.23B; M.32.116C); cf. description of baptism as εἰς τὸ ὄνομα τοῦ κυρίου Herm.*vis.*3.7.3 etc.; cf.*A.Paul.et Thecl.*34(p.260.7); theol. implications of formula, cf.Ath.*decr.*31.3(p.27.23; M.25.473C); id.*Ar.*2.41(M.26.236A); ‡Ath.*Ar.*4.21(p.67.17; M.26.500A); Bas.*Eun.*3.5(1.277A; M.29.665C); Didym.*Trin.*2.15(M.39.717A); **4.** other parts of rite; **a.** renunciation of Devil, Clem.*exc.Thdot.*77(p.131.8; M.9.693C); cf. (λουτρόν) †Hipp.*theoph.*10(p.263.13; M.10.861A); cf.Or.*mart.*17(p.16.20; M.11.585A); cf. (ἀποτάσσομαι) Cyr.H.*catech.*19.4; full account of procedure, *ib.*19.2–11; ἄλλα δὲ ὅσα περὶ τὸ β., ἀποτάσσεσθαι τῷ σατανᾷ καὶ τοῖς ἀγγέλοις αὐτοῦ Bas.*Spir.*66(3.55B; M.32.188C); cf.Chrys.*hom.6.4 in Col.*(11.369C); cf.Cyr.*Juln.*7(6².248D); full account, cf. (ἀποταγή) Dion.Ar.*e.h.*2.2.6(M.3.396B); Cosm.Ind.*top.*1(M.88.60B); *ib.*5(313B); **b.** use of creed; **i.** in gen. ὁ τὸν κανόνα τῆς ἀληθείας...ἐν ἑαυτῷ κατέχων, ὃν διὰ τοῦ β. εἴληφε Iren.*haer.*1.9.4(M.7.545B); †Hipp.*theoph.*10(p.263.15; M.10.861A); cf.Chrys.*hom.40.1 in 1Cor.*(10.379B); cf.Cosm.Ind.*top.*5(M.88.221B); **ii.** credal interrogation during actual baptism, cf.Hipp.*trad.ap.*21; ἐπὶ τὴν ἁγίαν τοῦ θείου β. ἐχειραγωγεῖσθε κολυμβήθραν...καὶ ὡμολογήσατε τὴν σωτήριον ὁμολογίαν, καὶ κατεδύετε τρίτον εἰς τὸ ὕδωρ Cyr.H.*catech.*20.4; **iii.** declaratory creed recited, after renunciation, before actual baptism τούτου σύμβολον, τὸ στραφῆναί σε ἀπὸ δυσμῶν πρὸς ἀνατολὴν...τότε σοι ἐλέγετο εἰπεῖν· πιστεύω εἰς τὸν πατέρα, καὶ εἰς τὸν υἱόν, καὶ εἰς τὸ ἅγιον πνεῦμα, καὶ εἰς ἓν β. μετανοίας *ib.*19.11; cf.Bas.*Spir.*26(3.21E; M.32.113A); cf. δεῖ τοὺς φωτιζομένους τὴν πίστιν ἐκμανθάνειν καὶ τῇ πέμπτῃ τῆς ἑβδομάδος ἀπαγγέλλειν τῷ ἐπισκόπῳ ἢ τοῖς πρεσβυτέροις CLaod.*can.*46; cf.*Symb.*ap.*Const.App.*7.41.4; cf. *fides...et testamentum, quod disposuimus ad patrem et filium et spiritum sanctum, ad sacrum lavacrum regenerationis venientes, confessi sic: 'credo in deum patrem omnipotentem'*, etc., †Ath.*Trin.et Spir.*7(M.26.1197B); but Elchezaites κέχρηνται...β. ἐπὶ τῇ τῶν στοιχείων ὁμολογίᾳ Thdt.*haer.*2.7(4.333); **c.** removal of garments, interpreted symbolically, cf. (ἀποδύω) Bas.Sel.*pasch.*2.5(M.28.1085D); Gr.Nyss.*bapt.diff.*(M.46.420C); Chrys.*hom.6.4 in Col.*(11.369D); cf.Dion.Ar.*e.h.*7.3.8(M.3.565A); and removal of sandals, the task of the baptizer, Gr.Nyss.*hom.11 in Cant.*(M.44.1008B); interpreted symbolically, *ib.*(l.c.); **d.** assumption of baptismal robe, cf.Cyr.H.*catech.*3.3; Gr.Naz.*or.*40.25(M.36.393C); symbolically interpreted, Gr.Nyss.*bapt.diff.*(M.46.420C); id.*bapt.Chr.*(M.46.593B); Chrys.*hom.39.5 in Gen.*(4.403D); Ast.Soph.*Ps.6*(M.40.441C); Dion.Ar.*e.h.*2.3.8(M.3.404C); in a mock baptism on the stage, *Chron.Pasch.*p.276(M.92.685A); τὴν ἁγίαν...στολήν, ἣν αὐτὸν ἡ τοῦ ἁγίου β. ἠμφιάσατο χάρις †Jo.D.*B.J.*30(M.96.1140D); **e.** giving of 'Christian name' ὁ Βαρνάβας ἀνεγνώρισεν αὐτόν...ᾧ καὶ πνεῦμα ἅγιον ἐδόθη ἐπὶ τοῦ β., μετωνόμασέν τε αὐτὸν Ἡρακλείδην *A.Barn.*17(p.298.12); τῶν μετονομασάντων με Μάρκον ἐν τῷ ὕδατι τοῦ β. *ib.*26(p.302.5); cf. *A.Thadd.*1(p.273.7); cf.Gr.Nyss.*bapt.diff.*(M.46.417B); †Gregent.*disp.*(M.86.781A); **f.** unction with chrism, cf.Hipp.*trad.ap.*22; cf. ‡Hipp.*can.*134; cf. (σφραγίζω) Corn.ap.Eus.*h.e.*6.43.15(M.20.624A); Cyr.H.*catech.*21.1; Bas.*Spir.*66(3.55A; M.32.188B); δεῖ τοὺς φωτιζομένους μετὰ τὸ β.... χρίεσθαι...χρίσματι ἐπουρανίῳ, καὶ μετόχους εἶναι τῆς βασιλείας τοῦ Χριστοῦ CLaod.*can.*48; cf.*Const.App.*7.22.2; cf.*ib.*7.44.1; μόνον β. ὑποδέξηται, καὶ τὸ χρῖσμα ῥώσῃ· εὐθὺς ἵλεως εὑρίσκεται ἡ...τριάς Didym.*Trin.*2.14(M.39.712A); cf. (σφραγίζω) Dion.Ar.*e.h.*2.2.7(M.3.396D); cf.Tim.CP *haer.*(M.86.13A); τὸ ἔλαιον βαπτίσματι παραλαμβάνεται, μηνύον τὴν χρῖσιν ἡμῶν, καὶ χριστοὺς ἡμᾶς ἐργαζόμενον Jo.D.*f.o.*4.9(M.94.1125B); not practised by Novatianists, who are therefore anointed on joining Church, cf.Thdt.*haer.*3.5(4.345); cf. (σφραγίζω) ‡CCP(381)*can.*7; contrast CNic.(325)*can.*8; **g.** signing with cross, cf.Serap.*euch.*25.2; cf.Didym.*Trin.*2.14(M.39.697A); Chrys.*hom.13.1 in Phil.*(11.298A) etc.; **h.** formula of administration, v. βαπτίζω; **i.** sponsors at baptism, cf.Hipp.*trad.ap.*20.2; Dion.Ar.*e.h.*2.2.7(396C); †Gregent.*disp.*(781A); must be orth., Thdr.Stud.*epp.*2.219 *qu.*14(M.99.1665B), v. ἀνάδοχος; registration of candidate and sponsors, (σφραγίζω) Dion.Ar.*e.h.*2.2.5(396A); **j.** carrying of lamps by candidates, cf.*A.Thom.*A 26(p.142.6); *ib.*27(p.143.5); Gr.Naz.*or.*40.46(M.36.425A); *ib.*45.2(624C); hence ἐὰν τὸν χιτῶνα τῆς πίστεως μὴ...ῥυπώσωμεν· ἐὰν τὴν λαμπάδα τῆς χάριτος ...μὴ κατασβέσωμεν Bas.Sel.*pasch.*1.5(M.28.1081A); **k.** candidate's offering ποῦ δέ μοι τὸ καρποφορούμενον ἐπὶ τῷ β.; Gr.Naz.*or.*40.25(393C); **5.** heret. forms of rite; **a.** without immersion (certain Marcosians), cf. (ὕδωρ) Iren.*haer.*1.21.4(M.7.664B); **b.** with irreg. immersion (Eunomian), Thdt.*haer.*4.3(4.356); Socr.*h.e.*5.24.6(M.67.649A), v. κατάδυσις; *Can.App.*50; cf. κατὰ κεφαλῆς ἄνω τοὺς πόδας στρέφοντες τῶν βαπτιζομένων (ref. Eunomians), Epiph.*anac.*66(p.232.9; M.42.337C); **c.** in which formula is irreg. (Marcosian), cf.Iren.*haer.*1.21.3(M.7.661A); (heretics in Egypt), Dion.Al.ap.Eus.*h.e.*7.9.2(M.20.653B); (Montanist) τίνα οὖν λόγον ἔχει τὸ β. ἐγκριθῆναι τῶν ~ζόντων εἰς πατέρα καὶ υἱὸν καὶ Μοντανὸν ἢ Πρίσκιλλαν; Bas.*ep.*188 *can.*1(3.269D; M.32.668B); (Arian) ~ζεται Βάρβας εἰς τὸ ὄνομα τοῦ πατρός, δι' υἱοῦ, ἐν ἁγίῳ πνεύματι Thdr.Lect.*h.e.*2.25(M.86.196B); (Eunomian) εἰς ὄνομα θεοῦ ἀκτίστου...καὶ υἱοῦ κεκτισμένου καὶ... πνεύματος...ὑπὸ τοῦ κεκτισμένου υἱοῦ κτισθέντος Epiph.*haer.*76.54(p.414.3; M.42.637B); **d.** in which other initiatory rites were employed, e.g. Carpocratian branding of right ear, v. καυτηριάζω; cf. Heracleon ap.Clem.*ecl.*25(p.143.22; M.9.709B); **e.** in which rite was frequently repeated (Elchezaite), cf.Hipp.*haer.*9.16(p.254.17; M.16.3391C); (Ebionite), Epiph.*haer.*30.16(p.353.9; M.41.432B); (Marcionite), *ib.*42.3(p.99.7; 700C); (Valentinian), Or.*comm.in Eph.*4:5(p.413.1); **6.** days of administration, usu. Easter, Cyr.H.*catech.*18.32; τί δ' ἂν γένοιτο τῆς ἡμέρας τοῦ πάσχα συγγενέστερον πρὸς τὸ β.; Bas.*hom.*13.1(2.114A; M.31.424D); cf.Pall.*v.Chrys.*9(p.56.22; M.47.33); Easter, Pentecost, Epiphany, cf.Gr.Naz.*or.*40.24(M.36.392A); in Jerusalem on dedication feast of Church of Holy Sepulchre, cf.Soz.*h.e.*2.26.4(M.67.1008C) cit. s. μύησις; v. πάσχα; **7.** private administration in emergency, Thdr.Stud.*epp.*2.219 *qu.*14(M.99.1665A); forbidden as regular practice, cf.CCP(536)*act.*4(*ACO* 3 p.181.22; H.2.1261C); **8.** minister of baptism; **a.** self-baptism, cf.*A.Paul.et Thecl.*34(p.260.7); explained as an irregularity permissible ἐν καιρῷ μὲν κινδύνων, ἐν ἀμηχανίᾳ δὲ τοῦ πράγματος ἐπινοηθέντος Bas.Sel.*v.Thecl.*1(M.85.536B); **b.** clergy; **i.** bishop, whose presence is necessary, cf.Ign.*Smyrn.*8.2; present, but not actually baptizing, cf.Hipp.*trad.ap.*21; normal minister, cf.Dion. Ar.*e.h.*2.2.7(M.3.396D); **ii.** priest, Cyr.H.*catech.*17.35; whose part is esp. to bless water, Gr.Nyss.*bapt.diff.*(M.46.421D); cf.*Const.App.*3.11.1; cf. τοῖς μὲν ἀφελεστέροις τῶν πρεσβυτέρων τοῦτο ἐγχειρίζομεν Chrys.*hom.3.3 in 1Cor.*(10.19A); **iii.** deacon, apparently baptizes, cf.Hipp.*trad.ap.*21; permitted to do so, Cyr.H.*catech.*17.35; in absence of bishop and when priests neglect duty, cf.Chrys.*hom.46.3 in Ac.*(9.349E); in absence of priest, Thdt.*qu.in 2Par.*29:30(1.596); Proc.G.*2Par.*29:34(M.87.1217A); forbidden to do so, cf.*Const.App.*3.11.1; cf.*ib.*8.46.11; cf.Max.*schol.e.h.*3(M.4.49C); **iv.** minor clergy, forbidden, cf.*Const.App.*3.11.1; **c.** laymen, usu. forbidden, cf.Bas.*ep.*188 *can.*1(3.270B; M.32.669A); *Const.App.*3.10.1; cf.Jo.Mosch.*prat.*176(M.87.3044D); laymen in emergency perform baptism with sand, repeated subsequently with water, cf.*ib.*(3045A); monk or layman permitted in emergency, cf.Thdr.Stud.*epp.*2.24(M.99.1192A); cf.*ib.*2.157(M.99.1492A,B); baptisms performed by Athanasius as a child recognized and completed by bishop's unction, *V.Ath.*2(M.25.clxxxvi D); cf.Jo.Mosch.*prat.*197(3084C); Thdr.Stud.*epp.*2.157(M.99.1492B); **d.** women, forbidden, Epiph.*haer.*79.3(p.477.33; M.42.744B); cf.Jo.Mosch.*prat.*3(2853D); cf.*Const.App.*3.9.1,4; women may only assist at baptism of women, v. λουτρόν; permitted by heretics: (Marcionites), Epiph.*haer.*42.4(p.100.5; M.41.700D); (Montanists), cf.Firmilianus *ep.Cypr.*11(M.*PL.*3.1213B); woman who drowned herself and children in persecution is minister of martyr's 'baptism', Chrys.*pan.Bern.*6(2.643D); v. infra VII.

D. gift of H. Ghost in baptism; **1.** in gen., distinctive of Christian baptism, Just.*dial.*29.1(M.6.537A); cf.Or.*princ.*2.10.7(p.181.7; M.11.239B); πνεῦμα ἅγιον ἐδόθη ἐπὶ τοῦ β. *A.Barn.*17(p.298.11); Cyr.H.*catech.*3.3; cf.Gr.Naz.*or.*39.17(M.36.353C); id.*or.*40.8(368A); Gr.Nyss.*bapt.Chr.*(M.46.581B); Didym.(‡Bas.)*Eun.*5(1.310E; M.29.745A); Thdr.Mops.*Rom.*6:17(p.123.18; M.66.804C); τὸ ὕδωρ...τοῦ β. ... παντὸς...ἡμᾶς ἀπαλλάττει ῥύπου, ὥστε καὶ ναὸν ἡμᾶς ἅγιον γενέσθαι θεοῦ, καὶ τῆς θείας αὐτοῦ φύσεως κοινωνοὺς διὰ μετοχῆς τοῦ ἁγίου πνεύματος Cyr.*Lc.*22:8(M.72.904D); cf. (ἀναγέννησις) id.*Jo.*2(4.147C); τὸ πνεῦμα τοῦ θεοῦ οἰκεῖ ἐν αὐτοῖς, ὅπερ ἐκομίσαντο ἐν τῷ β. Hier.H.*bapt.*(M.40.861B); τὸ ἅγιον πνεῦμα δεχόμεθα διὰ τοῦ β. ἐπειδὴ δὲ καὶ πνεῦμα θεοῦ λέγεται, καὶ πνεῦμα Χριστοῦ· τούτου χάριν διὰ τοῦ πνεύματος τὸν πατέρα καὶ τὸν υἱὸν δεχόμεθα Marc.Er.*opusc.*4(M.65.1008D); Jo.Clim.*scal.*25(M.88.1004B); **2.** in rel. to particular elements in rite; **a.** sacramentally conferred through water-baptism, v. ὕδωρ; **b.** connected especially with chrismation, v. χρῖσμα; cf. (σφραγίζω) Corn.ap.Eus.*h.e.*6.43.15(M.20.624A); **c.** and (ref. Ac.8:18) with imposition of hands, cf.Or.*princ.*1.3.2(p.50.4; M.11.1478B); *ib.*1.3.7(p.58.20; 153A); cf. (ἀναβαπτίζω) Anast.S.*qu.et resp.*86(M.89.712C); **3.** (Gnost.) Spirit conferred in νοητὸν β. dist. from αἰσθητὸν δι' ὕδατος Clem.*exc.Thdot.*81(p.132.3; M.9.696B); **4.** reception of Spirit implies indwelling of Christ, cf.Firmilianus *ep.Cypr.*12(M.*PL.*3.1214A); Marc.Er.*opusc.*4(M.65.1028B); Thdr.Stud.*antirrh.*1.7(M.99.336D); and of Trin., Bas.*hom.*24.5(2.194A; M.31.609D); Didym.(‡Bas.)*Eun.*5(1.317E; M.29.761B).

E. effects of baptism; **1.** remission of sins τὸ β. τὸ φέρον ἄφεσιν ἁμαρτιῶν *Barn.*11.1; Just.*dial.*14.1(M.6.504C); †Mel.*fr.*(p.313) cit. s. ἄφεσις; Marcosian distinction between τὸ...β. τοῦ φαινομένου Ἰησοῦ ἀφέσεως ἁμαρτιῶν and τὴν...ἀπολύτρωσιν τοῦ ἐν αὐτῷ κατελθόντος Χριστοῦ εἰς τελείωσιν...τὸ μὲν ψυχικόν, τὴν δὲ πνευματικὴν εἶναι ὑφίστανται Iren.*haer.*1.21.2(M.7.657B); Clem.*paed.*1.6(p.120.16; M.8.309B); *A.Thom.*A 132(p.239.8); hence it is Παιώνιον φάρμακον Clem.*paed.*1.6(p.108.3; 285C); and recipients are διϋλιζόμενοι βαπτίσματι *ib.*(p.109.4; 288B); cf. (ἀναγεννάω) id.*ecl.*7(p.138.31; M.9.701B); Or.*mart.*30(p.26.21; M.11.600C) cit. s. ἄφεσις; *Hom.Clem.*8.22; Cyr.H.*catech.*3.15; Gr.Nyss.*bapt.Chr.*(M.46.580D); Chrys.*hom.27.1 in Gen.*(4.256D); id.*hom.9.3 in Heb.*(12.97B); Ammon.Aeg.*ep.*20(p.109.26); Cyr.*Is.*1.1(2.17C); hence τὸ τοῦ β. καθάρσιον †Hipp.*theoph.*10(p.263.13; M.10.861A); including remission of pre-baptismal apostasy, CAnc.(314)*can.*12; remission of original sin in infant baptism emphasized, cf.Or.*hom.8.3 in Lev.*(p.398.13; M.12.496B); *Cod.Afr.*110; which doctrine is grudgingly conceded, Isid.Pel.*epp.*3.195(M.78.880B); but remission effective only if candidate not in state of sin, Or.*hom.21 in Lc.*(p.139.24); not magical or applicable to bodily diseases, Cyr.*Juln.*7(6².247D); does not include perseverance in sinlessness, Thdr.Mops.*1Tim.*3:2(p.101.27; M.66.940A); cf.*ib.*3:6(p.112.9); Marc.Er.*opusc.*4(M.65.988B); baptism repeated by Elchezaites for remission of post-baptismal sins, Hipp.*haer.*9.13(p.252.1; M.16.3387C); cf.*ib.*9.15(p.253.14; 3391A); in creeds β. ... εἰς ἄφεσιν ἁμαρτιῶν *Symb.Hier.*(M.33.533B); *Symb.*ap.Epiph.*anc.*118(p.147.15; M.43.232D); *Symb.Nic.-CP*(p.80.15; H.2.288B); β. ... ἀφέσεως ἁμαρτιῶν ‡Ath.*interpr.*(p.66.26; M.26.1232B); **2.** qualification for entry into kingdom of heaven; **a.** necessity, v. βασιλεία; participation in kingdom of Christ connected esp. with chrismation, CLaod.*can.*48; **b.** baptismal grace itself being βασιλεία...ἐντὸς ὑμῶν (Lc.17:21), Hier.H.*bapt.*(M.40.861B); cf.Marc.Er.*opusc.*4(M.65.1005B); and 'Jerusalem within the heart', *ib.*(1009B); **c.** pre-Christian righteous souls admitted to kingdom through Christ's vicarious baptism, cf.Thdr.Abuc.*opusc.*17(M.97.1541B); **d.** but baptism insufficient without perseverance in good living, *2Clem.*6.9; admits to Church, but not yet to τὰς ἄνω μονάς, Cyr.*glaph.Lev.*1(1.358A); **3.** salvation, v. σωτηρία; not all baptized are saved, cf.Jo.Clim.*scal.*1(M.88.636C); and some are baptized εἰς κατάκρισιν, cf.Or.*hom.6.5 in Ezech.*(p.383.7 n.; M.13.713D n.); negatively, unbaptized are to be condemned, Epiph.*haer.*28.6(p.318.19; M.41.384D); as are those who reject baptism, Cyr.*Is.*5.6(2.916B); **4.** liberation from death, *A.Phil.*117(p.47.13); cf. βαπτιζόμενοι... ἀπαθανατιζόμεθα Clem.*paed.*1.6(p.105.21; M.8.281A); διὰ τοῦ β. λύεται τοῦ θανάτου τὸ κέντρον Cyr.H.*catech.*3.11; Bas.Sel.*or.*13.2(M.85.176A); baptism being means of gaining immortality δεῦτε...ἐπὶ τὴν τοῦ β. ἀθανασίαν †Hipp.*theoph.*8(p.262.13; M.10.860B); *Hom.Clem.*13.10; φυτεία γὰρ πρὸς ἀθανασίαν τὸ β. Bas.Sel.*pasch.*1.5(M.28.1080C); cf. Gr.Nyss.*bapt.diff.*(M.46.420C); τὸ β. τῆς ζωῆς Didym.(‡Bas.)*Eun.*5(1.310E; M.29.745A); β. δύναμίς ἐστι πρὸς τὴν ἀνάστασιν Bas.*hom.*13.1(2.114A; M.31.424D); hence ζωοποιόν, Cyr.H.*catech.*19.1; **5.** deification, cf. ὁ τῆς ἀθανασίας πατὴρ τὸν...υἱὸν...ἀπέστειλεν...ὃς ἀφικόμενος εἰς τὸν ἄνθρωπον λούσασθαι ὕδατι καὶ πνεύματι...ἐνεφύσησεν ἡμῖν πνεῦμα ζωῆς. ... εἰ οὖν ἀθάνατος γέγονεν ὁ ἄνθρωπος, ἔσται καὶ θεός †Hipp.*theoph.*8(p.262.5; M.10.860A); εἰ μὲν γὰρ οὐ προσκυνητόν [sc. τὸ πνεῦμα], πῶς ἐμὲ θεοῖ διὰ τοῦ β.; Gr.Naz.*or.*31.29(p.181.12; M.36.165A); Nil.*epp.*2.293(M.79.345B) cit. s. κατοικέω; Cyr.*Lc.*22:8(M.72.904C); Dion.Ar.*e.h.*2.3.6(M.3.404A); **6.** regeneration, Clem.*exc.Thdot.*77(p.131.8; M.9.693C); id.*ecl.*5(p.138.15; M.9.700D); cf. (ἀναγέννησις) *ib.*7(p.138.26; 701A); Or.*Jo.*6.33(17; p.143.12; M.14.257B); *A.Thom.*A 132(p.239.11); Bas.Sel.*pasch.*1.5(M.28.1080D); cf. (ἀναγεννάω) Cyr.H.*catech.*3.4; cf. (γεννάω) *ib.*20.4; spiritual rebirth explained, Gr.Nyss.*bapt.Chr.*(M.46.580Dff.); cf.Didym.*Trin.*2.12(M.39.680B); τῆς νοητῆς τῆς διὰ τοῦ β. γεννήσεως Chrys.*hom.25.2 in Jo.*(8.145E); cf.Isid.Pel.*epp.*3.195(M.78.880C); Jo.D.*f.o.*4.9(M.94.1121A); †Jo.D.*B.J.*8(M.96.920B); cf. (ἀναγέννησις) Dion.Ar.*e.h.*2.2.1(M.3.392A) and use of θεογενεσία as synonym for βάπτισμα, v. ἀναγέννησις, παλιγγενεσία, λουτρόν; **7.** renewal and re-creation ἀνακαινίζοντος αὐτὸν Ἀνανίου τῷ β. Meth.*symp.*3.9(p.37.19; M.18.76B); cf.Bas.*Spir.*28(3.23D; M.32.117A); πνεῦμα...τὸ ἀνακτίζον διὰ τοῦ β. Gr.Naz.*or.*31.29(p.184.2; M.36.165C); cf. (ὕδωρ) Chrys.*hom.6.4 in Col.*(11.370A); Marc.Er.*opusc.*4(M.65.1025B); β. ὅπερ ἐστὶ καινῆς σύμβολον κτίσεως Proc.G.*Gen.*1:9–10(M.87.77C); cf. (ὕδωρ) Jo.D.*f.o.*4.9(M.94.1121A); and restoration of divine image ἄλλοι δὲ λέγουσιν οὔτε ἐν ψυχῇ οὔτε ἐν σώματι, ἀλλὰ ἀρετὴν εἶναι τὸ κατ' εἰκόνα· ἕτεροι δὲ φάσκουσι μὴ εἶναι τὴν ἀρετήν, ἀλλὰ τὸ β. καὶ τὸ χάρισμα τὸ ἐν β. Epiph.*haer.*70.3(p.235.13; M.42.344A); v. εἰκών; **8.** divine sonship by adoption, v. υἱοποιέω, υἱοθεσία, υἱοθετέω; cf. *secunda...nativitas quae est in baptismo filios Dei generat*, Firmilianus *ep.Cypr.*14(M.*PL.*3.1215A); enabling baptized to say 'Our Father', Isid.Pel.*epp.*4.24(M.78.1076A); making them coheirs with Christ, Cyr.H.*catech.*3.15; Isid.Pel.*epp.*3.195(880B,C); this sonship κατὰ θέσιν dist. from Christ's sonship κατὰ φύσιν, Cyr.H.*catech.*3.14; mediated through Church as bride of Christ, cf. Firmilianus *ep.Cypr.*14(1215A); baptism producing children to Church, Meth.*symp.*8.5(p.87.12); **9.** myst. death and resurrection with Christ, whose burial and rising β. symbolizes ἔστι γὰρ καὶ ταφῆναι μετὰ Χριστοῦ καλῶς διὰ τοῦ β. Or.*hom.19.14 in Jer.*(p.172.24; M.13.493C); cf.id.*comm.in Rom.*5.8(M.14.1038A); Cyr.H.*catech.*20.7; *ib.*20.4; cf.*ib.*3.12; Bas.*Spir.*35(3.28E; M.32.129A); ὥσπερ ὁ Χριστὸς ἀπέθανε καὶ...ἀνέστη· οὕτω καὶ ἡμεῖς ἐν τῷ β. θνήσκοντες ἀνιστάμεθα ‡Ath.*qu.script.*92(M.28.753B); Bas.Sel.*pasch.*1.5(M.28.1080C); ‡Just.*qu.et resp.*137(M.6.1389C); cf. μέρος γενόμενοι τοῦ σώματος τοῦ Χριστοῦ διὰ τῆς κατὰ τὴν ἀνάστασιν κοινωνίας, ἧς ἐν τῷ β. πληροῦν τοὺς τύπους ἡγούμεθα Thdr.Mops.*Rom.*7:4(p.124.16; M.66.805B); Marc.Er.*opusc.*4(M.65.985D); Dion.Ar.*e.h.*2.2.6(M.3.404A); cf.*ib.*4.3.10(484B); Eutych.*pasch.*5(M.86.2397A); Jo.D.*f.o.*4.9(M.94.1117B); v. ὕδωρ, συσταυρόω; **10.** conquest of evil powers, cf.Clem.*exc.Thdot.*76(p.131.3; M.9.693C); δοῦλος θεοῦ ἅμα τῷ ἀνελθεῖν τοῦ β. καὶ κύριος τῶν ἀκαθάρτων λέγεται πνευμάτων *ib.*77(p.131.12; 693C); cf. (γένεσις) id.*ecl.*7(p.138.30; M.9.701B); Nil.*epp.*2.16(M.79.

208A) cit. s. δαίμων; liberation from fate and the stars, Clem.*exc. Thdot.*78(p.131.15; 693D); and provision of weapons for spiritual warfare, Marc.Er.*opusc.*4(M.65.997A); **11.** illumination, cf. ∼ζόμενοι φωτιζόμεθα Clem.*paed.*1.6(p.105.20; M.8.281A); cf.*ib.*(p.106.22; 284A); ὃ εἴτε β., εἴτε φώτισμα...βούλοιτό τις ὀνομάζειν Gr.Nyss.*or.catech.*32 (p.122.12; M.45.84A); cf. ὁ δὲ μὴ βαπτισθεὶς οὐ πεφώτισται Bas.*hom.* 13.1(2.113E; M.31.424C); Hier.H.*bapt.*(M.40.861A); Cyr.*Juln.*7(6².248C); Thdr.Stud.*epp.*2.219 *qu.*14(M.99.1665A); v. λουτρόν; cf. freq. use of φώτισμα, φωτισμός as synonyms for βάπτισμα; **12.** perfecting of knowledge πρὸ τοῦ...β., ἀτελής πως καὶ νηπιώδης δείκνυται γνῶσις καὶ πολιτεία Nil.*epp.*1.51(M.79.105B); Diad.*perf.*76(p.94.26); v. λουτρόν; **13.** freedom, esp. from Law, Nil.*epp.*1.211(M.79.161A); **14.** sanctification and moral reformation, Just.*dial.*14.2(M.6. 504D); cf. *baptismi sanctificationem*, Firmilianus *ep.Cypr.*9(M.*PL.* 3.1211A); Gr.Nyss.*bapt.Chr.*(M.46.596C); οἱ ἅγιοι, ἐν οἷς οἰκεῖ... ἁγιότης μία πατρὸς καὶ υἱοῦ καὶ ἁγίου πνεύματος διὰ τὸν ἕνα τοῦ β. ἁγιασμόν Didym.(‡Bas.)*Eun.*5(1.317E; M.29.761B); rendering body lighter and better able to contend for spiritual prizes, Isid.Pel.*epp.* 4.204(M.78.1292B); protecting baptized person against approach of sin, Bas.*hom.in Ps.*28(1.123D; M.29.304C); but baptismal grace not irresistible, Marc.Er.*opusc.*4(M.65.1020C); hence baptism must be preserved by good living, *2Clem.*6.9; which enables it to issue in ἀνάπαυσις, *A.Paul.et Thecl.*6(p.239.5); and is freq. inculcated, cf. Bas.*Spir.*26(3.22A; M.32.113B); Bas.Sel.*pasch.*1.5(M.28.1081A); Cyr. *Is.*1.1(2.18C); Marc.Er.*opusc.*4(985C); Jo.D.*f.o.*4.9(M.94.1121C); baptismal grace itself enables men to do good works, Marc.Er. *opusc.*4(992D); without which faith and baptism cannot save from hell, Nil.*inst.*(M.79.1240A); **15.** conferring of seal (v. σφραγίς); **a.** baptism as seal of faith, Bas.*Eun.*3.5(1.276E; M.29.665C); **b.** as unbreakable seal, Bas.*hom.*13.5(2.117D; M.31.433A); by which angels will recognize faithful, cf. (σφραγίς) *ib.*13.4(117B; M.432C); preserving faithful from fiery sword at entrance to paradise, *ib.*13. 2(115C; 428C); as mark of Christ's ownership, cf. (σφραγίς) Gr.Naz. *or.*40.4(M.36.364A); **c.** as covenant seal, hence replaces Jewish circumcision, v. περιτομή; **16.** admission to eucharist, cf. (σφραγίζω) Dion.Ar.*e.h.*2.2.7(M.3.396D); cf.Cyr.H.*catech.*19.1; **17.** care of guardian angel, beginning at baptism, *Apophth.Mac.Aeg.*(M. 34.221B); *Rit.Bapt.*(p.394); for assistance of angels at baptism v. ἄγγελος; **18.** effects summarized, Clem.*paed.*1.6(pp.105–8; M.8. 280–1); Cyr.H.*procatech.*16; Bas.*hom.*13.5(2.117D; M.31.433A); cf. (φώτισμα) Gr.Naz.*or.*40.3(M.36.361B,C); Isid.Pel.*epp.*3.195(M.78. 880Bf.).

F. post-baptismal sin, v. λουτρόν, ἁμαρτάνω; **1.** regarded as unforgivable, interpreted as blasphemy against H. Ghost (Mt.12:24–32) by Or. and Thgn. acc. Ath.*ep.Serap.*4.9(M.26.649B); **2.** one repentance permitted, cf.Herm.*mand.*4.3.6 cit. s. μετάνοια; **3.** such sin to be expiated in future life, Clem.*str.*6.14(p.486.26; M.9.332A); through baptism of fire, Or.*hom.2.3 in Jer.*(p.19.9; M.13.281A); Gr.Naz.*or.*39.19(M.36.357C); **4.** regarded as pardonable through penance, cf. doctrine of Elchezaites and of Callistus, Hipp.*haer.*9.13 (p.252.1; M.16.3387C); *ib.*9.12(p.251.2; 3387A); **5.** and assumed as inevitable, Jo.Clim.*scal.*7(M.88.804A); **6.** H. Ghost remains present to soul of the baptized, if necessary awaiting his conversion from sin, cf. (σφραγίζω) Bas.*Spir.*40(3.34D; M.32.141C); **7.** Rom.7:13 explained as not referring to S. Paul's post-baptismal experience, Marc.Er.*opusc.*4(M.65.992D); **8.** Novatianist doctrine attacked, cf. (λουτρόν) Ath.*ep.Serap.*4.13(M.26.653D); Gr.Naz.*or.*39.19(M.36.357B); Epiph.*haer.*59.2(p.365.15; M.41.1020B); v. μετάνοια.

G. baptism not to be repeated; **1.** repetition alleged against Callistus, Hipp.*haer.*9.12(p.251.2; M.16.3387A); and practised by heretics, v. ἀναβαπτίζω; **2.** no repetition permissible, cf.Or.*mart.* 30(p.26.22; M.11.601A); id.*comm.in Eph.*4:5(p.413.2); Ath.*ep.Serap.* 4.13(M.26.656A); Cyr.H.*procatech.*7; on pain of minister's deposition, *Can.App.*47; *Const.App.*6.15.2; Nil.*epp.*1.24(M.79.92A); **3.** ἓν βάπτισμα in creeds, Cyr.H.*catech.*19.9; ‡Ath.*interpr.*(p.66.26; M. 26.1232B); *Symb.*ap.Epiph.*anc.*118,119(pp.147.15,149.2; M.43.232D, 236B); *Symb.Nic.-CP*(p.80.15; H.2.288B); **4.** conditional baptism in cases of doubt, cf.*Cod.Afr.*72; cf.Sophr.H.*conf.*(M.87.3369A).

H. conditions for effective reception; **1.** faith, cf. (λουτρόν) †Hipp.*theoph.*10(p.263.14; M.10.861A); Cyr.H.*catech.*3.4; cf.*ib.*3.15; πίστις μὲν γὰρ τελειοῦται διὰ β. β. δὲ θεμελιοῦται διὰ τῆς πίστεως Bas.*Spir.*28(3.24A; M.32.117B); πᾶν ὕδωρ ἐπιτήδειον εἰς τὴν τοῦ β. χρείαν, μόνον ἐὰν εὕρῃ πίστιν τοῦ λαμβάνοντος Gr.Nyss.*bapt.diff.* (M.46.421D); Cyr.*Juln.*7(6².248C); cf.Marc.Er.*opusc.*4(M.65.985D); ἡ...ἁμαρτιῶν ἄφεσις πᾶσιν ὁμοίως διὰ τοῦ β. δίδοται· ἡ δὲ χάρις τοῦ πνεύματος κατὰ τὴν ἀναλογίαν τῆς πίστεως Jo.D.*f.o.*4.9(M.94. 1121C); coupled with γνῶσις, *Disp.Phot.*(M.88.572C); **2.** repentance, Clem.*paed.*1.6(p.109.4; M.8.288B); Bas.*hom.*13.1(2.114B; M.31.425A); Cyr.H.*catech.*3.15; ‡Ath.*interpr.*(p.66.26; M.26.1232B); unworthy reception resulting in possession by evil spirits, Clem.*exc.Thdot.* 83(p.132.15; M.9.696D); and leading to baptism of fire, cf.Or.*hom. 26 in Lc.*(p.165.10); hence baptism to be denied to unrepentant, Isid.Pel.*epp.*4.181(M.78.1273B); **3.** worthiness of minister; **a.** implied to be necessary, cf.Firmilianus *ep.Cypr.*9(M.*PL.*3.1211A); **b.** unnecessary for validity, cf.Gr.Naz.*or.*40.26(M.36.396B); cf. Cyr.H.*catech.*17.35; μέγα...τὸ β. ἀλλὰ μέγα αὐτὸ οὐχ ὁ ∼ζων ποιεῖ, ἀλλ' ὁ καλούμενος εἰς τὸ β. Chrys.*hom.3.2 in 1Cor.*(10.18A); *ib.8.1* (66C); cf. (φωτίζω) Isid.Pel.*epp.*2.37(M.78.481A); for heretical baptism, v. infra N.

I. preparation for baptism; **1.** its necessity, Clem.*exc.Thdot.*83 (p.132.15; M.9.696D); cf.Or.*hom.6.5 in Ezech*(p.383.5; M.13.713C); Gr.Naz.*or.*39.14(M.36.349D); cf.Cyr.H.*procatech.*3; id.*catech.*3.15; Jo.D.*f.o.*4.9(M.94.1121C); **2.** includes catechetical teaching, cf.Or. *or.*2.4(p.302.26; M.11.421C); Cyr.H.*catech.* passim; cf.Tim.CP *haer.* (M.86.72B); **3.** fasting πρὸ...τοῦ β. προνηστευσάτω ὁ ∼ζων καὶ ὁ ∼ζόμενος καὶ εἴ τινες ἄλλοι δύνανται. κελεύεις δὲ νηστεῦσαι τὸν ∼ζόμενον πρὸ μιᾶς ἢ δύο *Did.*7.4; cf.Clem.*exc.Thdot.*84(p.132.20; M.9.696D); *Hom.Clem.*13.11 al.; *Const.App.*7.22.6; **4.** confession, cf.*A.Thadd.*7(p.278.1); Cyr.H.*catech.*1.5; Gr.Naz.*or.*40.27(M.36. 397A); **5.** exorcism, cf.Hipp.*trad.ap.*20.3,8; Cyr.H.*procatech.*9; id. *catech.*1.5; Gr.Naz.*or.*40.27(M.36.397A).

J. infant baptism; **1.** its practice; **a.** perhaps implied, *M.Polyc.* 9.3; **b.** regular practice, cf.Or.*hom.8.3 in Lev.*(p.398.13; M.12. 496B); cf. *ecclesia ab apostolis traditionem suscepit, etiam parvulis baptismum dari*, id.*comm.in Rom.*5.9(M.14.1047B); presupposed, cf. Hier.H.*bapt.*(M.40.860C); Jo.Clim.*scal.*7(M.88.804A); cf.Thdr.Stud. *epp.*2.157(M.99.1492A); strongly recommended, cf.Isid.Pel.*epp.*1. 125(M.78.265C); recommended at 3 years, except in emergency, Gr.Naz.*or.*40.28(M.36.400A); baptism at 2 years, Niceph.Ur.*v.Sym.* 9(M.86.2993D); **c.** children frequently unbaptized owing to exposure by parents, cf.Hier.H.*bapt.*(860D); and, in Mauretania, many children ransomed from barbarians whose baptism is uncertain, *Cod.Afr.*72; **2.** its purpose; **a.** true remission of sin, cf. Or.*hom.8.3 in Lev.*(p.398.11; M.12.496B); asserted against Pelagian τύπος τοῦ εἰς ἄφεσιν ἁμαρτιῶν βαπτίσματος οὐκ ἀληθής *Cod.Afr.*110; **b.** primarily, to secure positive benefits of baptismal grace, Isid. Pel.*epp.*3.195(M.78.880Bff.); obtained through faith of those bringing children to baptism, ‡Just.*qu.et resp.*56(M.6.1297C); **3.** unbaptized children lose advantages of baptized in resurrection, cf. *ib.*; cf. οὔτε εἰς βασιλείαν εἰσέρχονται· ἀλλ' οὔτε πάλιν εἰς κόλασιν ‡Ath.*qu.Ant.*115(M.28.672A); cf. (ἀβάπτιστος) Anast.S.*qu.et resp.*82 (M.89.709C).

K. clinical baptism; **a.** death-bed baptism of newly-converted pagan, cf. (λουτρόν) Bas.*ep.*269.2(3.416C; M.32.1001B); **b.** baptism postponed by Christians until dangerously ill, for fear of post-baptismal sin; by Constantine, cf.Eus.*v.C.*4.62(p.143.16; M.20. 1216A); by Constantius, cf.Ath.*syn.*31(p.260.4; M.26.749A); by Theodosius I, Socr.*h.e.*5.6.3(M.67.572C); former regarded as proof of resurrection and as 'baptism for dead' (1Cor.15:29), cf.Epiph. *haer.*28.6(p.318.24; M.41.385A); to be supplemented by catechetical instruction when possible, cf. (φώτισμα) CLaod.*can.*47; latter disqualifies from ordination, cf. (περιχέω) Corn.ap.Eus.*h.e.*6.43.17(M. 20.624B); cf. (φωτίζω) CNeocaes.*can.*12; and is strongly deprecated, Gr.Nyss.*bapt.diff.*(M.46.417D); *ib.*(432A); Chrys.*hom.1.8 in Ac.* (9.14A); Cyr.*glaph.Ex.*2(1.273C); id.*Lc.*3:25(M.72.525A); †Jo.D.*B.J.* 8(M.96.920C); cf.Gr.Naz.*or.*40.11(M.36.373A).

L. 'baptism for dead' (1Cor.15:29), interpreted **1.** by Cerinthians, of vicarious baptism on behalf of unbaptized dead, Epiph. *haer.*28.6(p.318.19; M.41.384D); so by Marcionites, Chrys.*hom.40.1 in 1Cor.*(10.378C); cf.Tertullianus *adversus Marcionem*, 5.10(M.*PL.* 2.494Cff.); **2.** by Theodotus, of baptism undertaken for men by angels in name of 'aeon' Christ, cf.Clem.*exc.Thdot.*22(p.113.28; M. 9.668); **3.** of clinical baptism (v. K supra), cf.Epiph.*haer.*28.6 (p.318.24; M.41.385A); **4.** of baptismal profession of belief in resurrection of body, cf.Chrys.*hom.40.1 in 1Cor.*(10.379C); Jo.D. *1Cor.*15:29(M.95.693D); v. νεκρός; **5.** of symbolical death with Christ in baptism, Thdt.*1Cor.*15:29(3.275).

M. baptism of dead; forbidden, cf.*Cod.Afr.*18.

N. heret. baptism; **1.** not true or genuine τὸ β. τὸ αἱρετικὸν οὐκ οἰκεῖον καὶ γνήσιον ὕδωρ λογιζομένη [sc. ἡ σοφία] Clem.*str.*1.19(p.62. 3; M.8.813A); carnal and akin to Jewish baptism, cf.Firmilianus *ep.Cypr.*13(M.*PL.*3.1215A); conferring no regeneration, *ib.*14(l.c.);

antinomian Gnostics baptize εἰς πορνείαν, cf.Clem.*str*.3.18(p.246.28; M.8.1212C); **2.** Trinitarian formula no guarantee of valid baptism if used by unorthodox, cf.Firmilianus *ep.Cypr*.9(1211A); cf.Ath. *Ar*.2.42(M.26.237A); Bas.*ep*.199 *can*.47(3.297A; M.32.732A); cf.Gr. Nyss.*or.catech*.39(p.156.8; M.45.100B); **3.** all heret. baptism considered invalid, cf.Firmilianus *ep.Cypr*.23(1221B); by Cyprian and Firmilian, because οἱ...τῆς ἐκκλησίας ἀποστάντες οὐκέτι ἔσχον τὴν χάριν τοῦ ἁγίου πνεύματος ἐφ' ἑαυτοῖς...λαϊκοὶ γενόμενοι, οὔτε τοῦ ~ζειν...εἶχον τὴν ἐξουσίαν, οὐκέτι δυνάμενοι χάριν πνεύματος... ἑτέροις παρέχειν, ἧς αὐτοὶ ἐκπεπτώκασι Bas.*ep*.188 *can*.1(3.270A; M.32.668B); by early African and Asian councils, cf.Dion.Al.ap. Eus.*h.e*.7.7.5(M.20.649A); μήτε...τὸ [sc. βάπτισμα] παρὰ τῶν ἀσεβῶν δεκτὸν ὑμῖν ἔστω *Const.App*.6.15.2; invalid orders render baptisms invalid, cf.Jo.Nic.*fr*.ap.‡Tim.CP *haer.suppl*.(M.86.73A); cf.Cyr.H. *procatech*.7(some MSS only); **4.** heret. baptism regarded as valid (therefore not to be repeated when heretics enter Church), cf. Stephen's theory, Dion.Al.ap.Eus.*h.e*.7.5.4(M.20.645A); τοῦτον ἐγὼ τὸν κανόνα...παρὰ τοῦ μακαρίου πάπα...Ἡρακλᾶ παρέλαβον. τοὺς γὰρ προσιόντας ἀπὸ τῶν αἱρεσέων...συνήγαγεν...οὐ δεηθεὶς ἐπ' αὐτῶν ἑτέρου β. Dion.Al.*ib*.7.7.4(M.20.649A); heret. baptism formerly received by an Alexandrian communicant not treated as invalid, id.ap.Eus.*h.e*.7.9.1(653A); heretic to be anointed only διὰ τί οἱ ὀρθόδοξοι τὸν προσφεύγοντα τῇ ὀρθοδοξίᾳ αἱρετικὸν οὐ βαπτίζουσιν, ἀλλ' ὡς ἐν ἀληθεῖ τῷ νόθῳ ἐῶσι β.;...τὸ σφάλμα...τοῦ...β. [sc. διορθοῦται] τῇ ἐπιχρίσει τοῦ ἁγίου μύρου ‡Just.*qu.et resp*.14(M.6. 1261Cf.); cf. (ἀναβαπτίζω) Epiph.*exp.fid*.13(p.513.24; M.42.808A); cf. (ἀναβαπτίζω) Anast.S.*qu.et resp*.86(M.89.712C); **5.** distn. between heret. and schismatical baptism, Bas.*ep*.188 *can*.1(3.269B; M.32. 668A) cit. s. ἀθετέω; and between heresies whose baptism is recognized, and those whose adherents are baptized afresh on entering Church; latter include most Gnost. and extremer Trinitarian heresies, cf.CNic.(325)*can*.19; Bas.*ep*.188 *can*.1(3.269C; M.668); cf. CLaod.*can*.8; cf.‡CCP(381)*can*.7; Didym.*Trin*.2.15(M.39.720A); Tim.CP *haer*.(M.86.13Af.); CTrull.*can*.95; cf.Thdr.Stud.*epp*.1.40 (M.99.1052C); cf.*ib*.2.24(1192A); **6.** children baptized in Donatism without their consent to be eligible for ordination, cf.*Cod.Afr*.57; **7.** heret. rejection of baptism, Or.*or*.5(p.308.20; M.11.429B); by Ascodrugitae, cf. λύτρωσιν καλοῦσι τὴν ὅλων ἐπίγνωσιν Thdt.*haer*. 1.10(4.302); (Tascodrugi) Tim.CP *haer*.(M.86.13B).

VII. martyrdom as baptism of blood, v. αἷμα; cf.†Mel.*fr*. (p.313); β. τὸ μαρτύριον εὐλόγως λέγοιτ' ἂν Or.*comm.in Mt*.16.6 (p.484.16; M.13.1384B); οὐκ ἔστιν ἄφεσιν ἁμαρτημάτων χωρὶς β. λαβεῖν...β. ἡμῖν δίδοται τὸ τοῦ μαρτυρίου id.*mart*.30(p.26.23; M.11. 601A); εἴ τις μὴ λάβῃ τὸ β., σωτηρίαν οὐκ ἔχει· πλὴν μόνων μαρτύρων, οἳ καὶ χωρὶς τοῦ ὕδατος λαμβάνουσι τὴν βασιλείαν Cyr.H.*catech*. 3.10; cf.Bas.*Spir*.36(3.30C; M.32.132D); Gr.Naz.*or*.39.17(M.36.356A); cf.Chrys.*pan.Lucn*.2(2.526A); τῷ διὰ τοῦ θανάτου β. Bas.Sel.*v.Thecl*. 1(M.85.536A); †Jo.D.*B.J*.12(M.96.964A); of Jo. Bapt., cf.Jo.D.*f.o*. 4.9(M.94.1125B).

VIII. penitential 'baptism' of tears, v. δάκρυον.

IX. baptism by 'Spirit and fire' (Lc.3:16);

A. interpreted as identical τὸ...αὐτὸ β. τοῖς μὲν ἀναξίοις καὶ κακοῖς ~ζομένοις εἰς πῦρ καὶ εἰς κρῖμα γίνεται, τοῖς δὲ καλῶς καὶ ἐπὶ σωτηρίᾳ καταβαίνουσιν εἰς πνεῦμα ἅγιον καὶ σωτηρίαν γίνεται Or.*hom. 26 in Lc*.(p.165.11); at Pentecost πνεύματι ἁγίῳ καὶ πυρὶ τοὺς ἀποστόλους ἐβάπτισεν Cyr.H.*catech*.3.9; fire is symbol of H. Ghost, cf.Cyr.*ador*.12(1.436C); together represent Christian baptism in sanctifying and purifying aspects, cf.id.*Is*.1.1(2.17E); thus Spirit and fire represent H. Ghost in different modes of activity, as ἐνεργητικόν and καθαρτικόν, Max.*cap.theol*.2.63(M.90.1152C) cit. s. πῦρ; Christ as ὁ αὐτὸς...β. ὕδατος καὶ πνεύματος καὶ πυρός, τισὶν δὲ καὶ αἵματος Or.*Jo*.6.43(26; p.152.19; M.14.276B); Eunomian interpretation τῷ περὶ τῆς γεέννης τὸ πνεῦμα τὸ θεῖον συγκατατάττεις, διὰ τὸ λέγειν τὸν Ἰωάννην, 'αὐτὸς...~σει ἐν πνεύματι ἁγίῳ καὶ πυρί' Didym.(‡Bas.)*Eun*.5(1.308B; M.29.740A).

B. interpreted as distinct; those who have preserved Spirit-baptism undefiled, rise in first resurrection; post-baptismal sinners receive purificatory fire-baptism hereafter, Or.*hom.2.3 in Jer*.(p.19.15; M.13.281A); Spirit-baptism interpreted of Pentecost, fire-baptism of purificatory baptism (in fiery river at entrance to paradise) given by Christ to those who have preserved their water-and-Spirit-baptism intact, cf.id.*hom.24 in Lc*.(p.158.20; M. 13.1864C); cf.*Orac.Sib*.2.204,252,315; Or.*sel.in Ps*.36:14(M.12.1337C); Spirit-baptism represents Christian rite, fire-baptism the testing of final judgement, Bas.*Spir*.36(3.30B; M.32.132C) cit. s. πῦρ; cf. Didym.(‡Bas.)*Eun*.5(1.308D; M.29.740B).

C. interpreted literally and as warrant for branding of ears in baptism, v. VI.C.5.d supra.

D. contrasted with washing of disciples' feet (Jo.13:10), cf.Or. *Jo*.32.7(6; p.437.5; M.14.760B).

X. 'baptism of desire', discussed ἀντὶ β. ποιεῖται τὴν ὁρμὴν τοῦ β. and rejected as true equivalent of baptism, Gr.Naz.*or*.40.22(M. 36.388B).

XI. interpretation of water and blood (Jo.19:34) ref. baptism; cf. ὁ ἐκχέας ἐκ τῆς πλευρᾶς αὐτοῦ τὰ δύο...καθάρσια, ὕδωρ καὶ αἷμα, λόγον καὶ πνεῦμα Claud.*fr.pasch*.(M.5.1300A); interpreted of baptism and martyrdom, Gr.Naz.*carm*.1.2.34.217(M.37.961A); cf. Tertullianus *de baptismo* 16(M.*PL*.1.1217A); of baptism and eucharist, cf. (ὕδωρ) Chrys.*hom.85.3 in Jo*.(8.507E); Cyr.*Jo*.12(4.1074C); *Chron.Pasch*.p.220(M.92.536D); as providing a baptism for dead, cf.Thdr.Abuc.*opusc*.17(M.97.1541C).

XII. baptism as ground of an oath ὁρκώσας αὐτὸν εἰς τὸ ἅγιον β. μὴ προδοῦναι *Chron.Pasch*.p.325(M.92.833B).

XIII. fanciful etymology β., βάπταισμα, ἐν ᾧ βάλλεται, ἤγουν πίπτει, τὸ πταῖσμα Anast.S.*hod*.2(M.89.81C).

XIV. s.v.l., *baptistery* ᾠκοδόμησεν ἐκκλησίας καὶ βαπτίσματα Agath.*v.Gr.Ill*.143.

βαπτισμός, ὁ, *dipping, baptism*; usu. synon. with βάπτισμα, but used of orthodox Christian baptism chiefly in comment on Heb.6:2, 9:10; **1.** of Jewish ceremonial ablutions, Cyr.*Heb*. 9:10(M.74.984B); **2.** of John's baptism, Or.*Jo*.6.26(14; p.136.9; M. 14.245C); **3.** of Christian baptism; **a.** exeg. Heb.6:2 τί δέ ἐστι, βαπτισμῶν διδαχῆς; οὐχ ὡς πολλῶν ὄντων τῶν β., ἀλλ' ἑνός. τί οὖν αὐτὸ πληθυντικῶς εἶπε; διὰ τὸ εἰπεῖν, μὴ πάλιν θεμέλιον καταβαλλόμενοι μετανοίας. εἰ γὰρ πάλιν αὐτοὺς ἐβάπτισε...διηνεκῶς ἔμελλον ἀδιόρθωτοι μένειν Chrys.*hom.9.2 in Heb*.(12.95B); τὸ βάπτισμα...ὃ πληθυντικῶς ὠνόμασεν διὰ τὸ πλῆθος τῶν καταξιουμένων, εἴρηκε δὲ βαπτισμῶν Sever.*Heb*.6:2(p.349.14); **b.** in gen. τῇ χάριτι τοῦ β. ‡Chrys.*pasch*.3(8.258B); **c.** of schismatic baptism τυπωθήτω τοὺς ἀπὸ τοῦ β. ἐκείνων προσερχομένους χρίεσθαι Bas.*ep*.188 *can*.1(3. 270D; M.32.669C), where synon. with βάπτισμα in same passage; **d.** of heret. ablutions; **i.** of frequent ritual washings of Ebionites εἰ συναντήσειέ τινι ἀνιὼν ἀπὸ τῆς τῶν ὑδάτων καταδύσεως καὶ βαπτισμοῦ, ὡσαύτως πάλιν ἀνατρέχει βαπτίζεσθαι Epiph.*haer*.30.2(p.334. 19; M.41.408B); **ii.** of Marcionite repetition of baptism for remission of post-baptismal sins ἔξεστιν ἕως τριῶν λουτρῶν, τουτέστι τριῶν β., εἰς ἄφεσιν ἁμαρτιῶν δίδοσθαι id.*haer*.42.3(p.98.18; M.41.700B); **iii.** of Sampsaean baptisms θεὸν δὲ ἕνα λέγουσι· καὶ δῆθεν αὐτὸν σέβουσι β. τισι χρώμενοι id.*haer*.53.1(p.315.13; M.41.960B).

***βαπτιστήρ, ὁ,** *baptistery* μάρμαρα τῆς εἰσόδου τοῦ β. λαβὼν ἐν τῷ βαλανείῳ...προσέθηκεν Pall.*v.Chrys*.14(p.83.23; M.47.48); Thphn. *chron*.p.14(M.108.92A).

βαπτιστήριον, τό, *baptistery*; building usu. adjoining or attached to church, cf.Ath.*ep.encycl*.3(p.172.7,16; M.25.228C,229A); in outer room of which renunciation and recitation of creed took place before baptism, Cyr.H.*catech*.19.2; where baptism was performed, Gr.Nyss.*bapt.diff*.(M.46.420A) etc.; dist. from κολυμβήθρα q.v., Socr.*h.e*.7.4.4(M.67.745B); in which sanctuary might be sought, Thdr.Lect.*h.e*.1.35(M.86.181C); Evagr.*h.e*.2.8(p.56.19; M.86.2524A); τῷ καθαρτικῷ β. Dion.Ar.*e.h*.4.3.10(M.3.484B); met., in baptismal context ὕδωρ...τὸ τοῦ ἡλίου β. Mel.*bapt*.(p.311); v. φωτιστήριον.

βαπτιστής, ὁ, *baptizer, baptist*; **1.** freq. of Jo. Bapt., Just.*dial*. 50.2(M.6.585C); Clem.*exc.Thdot*.5(p.107.2; M.9.656B); Or.*Jo*.1.5(7; p.10.9; M.14.33A); without name, *ib*.6.27(14; p.137.5; 248B); Eus. *e.th*.2.7(p.105.2; M.24.909C); **2.** of minister of Christian baptism, Gr.Naz.*or*.34.12(M.36.252C); *ib*.40.25(393C); **3.** plur., a Jewish sect, Just.*dial*.80.4(M.6.665B); corresponding to Hemerobaptists, cf. Epiph.*haer*.17(p.214.5; M.41.256A).

***βαπτιστικός,** *baptismal*, Didym.*Trin*.2.14(M.39.700B); Thphn. *chron*.p.341(M.108.821B).

βάπτω, *dip*; eucharistic wafer in chalice, *Lit.Jac*.(pp.228.24,28; 230.10); of baptism τὸ μὲν σῶμα β. ὕδατι [sc. Simon Magus] Cyr.H.*procatech*.2; Χριστὸς...ἦλθε...ἵνα μὲν τάχιστα βάψῃ ἐν Ἰορδάνου ῥεέθροις Sophr.H.*carm*.5.91(M.87.3760A); with baptismal ref. [βεβά]μμεθα ἐν ὕδασι ζω[ῆς αἰωνίου] *POxy*.840.43.

βάραθρον, τό, *pit*; met., of destruction etc. ἀσεβείας β. Ath.*Ar*. 1.20(M.26.53B); β. τῆς ἀπωλείας Cyr.*Jo*.2.1(4.150A); τοῦτο τὸ β. [sc. φιλαργυρία] Chrys.*hom.50.3 in Mt*.(7.518A); without definition διὰ μικροῦ σοφίσματος...ἑαυτοὺς ὠθοῦσιν ἐπὶ τὸ β. Bas.*hom*.24.6(2.195A; M.31.612C); ἄγεις τὰς νέας οὐ πρὸς θεόν, ἀλλ' εἰς β. id.*ep*.170(3.159D; M.32.645A).

***βαραθρόω,** *cast into a pit*, ‡Chrys.*remiss*.(9.846D).

***βαρβαρεύ-ω**, *be in hands of barbarians* ~θείσης ποτὲ τῆς Παλαιστήνης ὁδοῦ, γέγονεν...σπάνη τοῦ ἐλαίου †Anast.S.*relat.*9(*OC* 2 p.65.23).

***βαρβαρέω**, = foreg., ‡Jo.D.*ep.Thphl.*11(M.95.357C).

***βαρβαρία, ἡ**, *strange country*, Epiph.*gemm.*7(M.43.300B).

βαρβαρικός, *non-Greek, foreign, uncivilized*; of biblical writings, Clem.*str.*1.9(p.29.17; M.8.741A); τὸ β. *the country of the barbarians*, outside Roman empire, Jo.Mal.*chron.*12 p.295(M.97.445B); τὰ β. CChalc.*can.*28.

βαρβαρισμός, ὁ, *use of foreign language, barbarism*; of false religions of heathen, Epiph.*haer.*80.10(p.495.6; M.42.772B); id.*exp.fid.*6(p.502.16; M.42.784C); esp. of state of religion between Adam and Noah, id.*anac.*1(p.162.6; M.41.165C); †Hipp.Th.*fr.*8b(p.35.19; M.117.1048C); Jo.D.*haer.*1(M.94.677D).

***βαρβαρόθυμος**, *of barbarous mind*, *Orac.Sib.*3.332.

***βαρβαρολέξις, ἡ**, *use of foreign words*, cf. *barbarismus in verbo latino fit, dum corrumpitur; quando autem barbara verba Latinis eloquiis inferuntur, barbarolexis dicitur*, Isid.H.*etym.*1.32.2.

βάρβαρος *non-Greek, foreign, uncivilized*; **1.** of Jews and Christians, as described by pagans, *Hom.Clem.*1.11; *ib.*4.13; cf. Porphyry ap.Eus.*h.e.*6.19.7(M.20.565A); as described by Christians, Just.*1apol.*5.4(M.6.336B); *ib.*7.3(337A); Tat.*orat.*1(p.1.1; M.6.804A); Clem.*str.*6.6(p.453.17; M.9.265A); *ib.*6.17(p.509.33; 381C); **2.** of gentiles opp. Jews, Thdt.*Ps.*82:1(1.1189C); id.*Ezech.*3:17(2.704C); **3.** in association with Ἕλλην of pagans and heretics opp. orthodox Christians Ἕλληνες ἔσεσθε καὶ Οὐαλεντῖνοι καὶ β. Eun.ap.Gr.Nyss.*Eun.*12(1 p.346.11; M.45.1065C); **4.** τὸ β. *the barbarians* collectively, Men.*exc.Rom.*9(p.197.32; M.113.892C).

***βαρβαρόφρων**, *of barbarous mind*, *Orac.Sib.*1.342, 5.96.

βαρβαρόω, pass., *be uncivilized* παρᾳδῶμεν τῷ ἄρχοντι τῷ νῷ τὸν λογισμὸν ἐκεῖνον, τὸν βεβαρβαρωμένον μέν, κατεσκευασμένον δὲ ἐσθῆτι πολιτικῇ Chrys.*hom.37.3 in Ac.*(9.285A); hence *degenerate, become savage* βεβαρβάρωταί τις τυχόν, ἀλοὺς παρ' ἐκείνοις ἐν ἡλικίᾳ μικρᾷ Cyr.*hom.pasch.*9(5^2.115A).

βαρβαρώδης, *barbaric, uncivilized*, Jo.Clim.*scal.*3(M.88.668C).

***βαρβαρωνυμία, ἡ**, *barbarous nomenclature*; of a Gnost. aeon, Epiph.*haer.*25.3(p.271.2; M.41.324D).

***βαρβαρώνυμος**, *with barbarous name*; of a Gnost. aeon, ‡Epiph.*epit.haer.*(p.354.22).

***βαρβᾶτος**, (Lat. *barbatus*) *bearded*; as surname, *Chron.Pasch.* p.340(M.92.885C).

***βαρβηλίτης (-ιώτης), ὁ**, member of a Gnost. sect (v. βαρβηλώ); known also (prob. derisively) as βορβορῖται, βορβοριανοί, Iren.*haer.*1.29.1; Epiph.*rescr.*4(p.158.5; M.41.161B); id.*haer.*26.3(p.279.26; M.41.337A); Thdt.*haer.*1.13(4.304C).

***βαρβηλώ (-ώθ, -ρώ), ἡ**, name of primary aeon in a Gnost. system, Iren.*haer.*1.29.1; Epiph.*haer.*21.2(p.240.12; M.41.288C); *ib.*25.2(p.269.2; 321C); *ib.*26.10(p.288.17; 348A); Thdt.*haer.*1.13(4.304C).

βαρ-έω, **1.** *weigh down, oppress*; pass., *be burdened*; of the body κεκλήρωται ἡ ψυχὴ συνεζεῦχθαι τῷ γηΐνῳ καὶ ~οῦντι σώματι Or.*Jo.*6.52(p.161.18; M.14.292B); τὰ ~οῦντα πάθη *Hom.Clem.*11.16; *crush, overcome* δικαιοσύνη β. τὴν ἀδικίαν ‡Caes.Naz.*dial.*172(M.38.1137); **2.** *place a weight*, Nil.*exerc.*42(M.79.772B); met. ἐκ τοῦ ἡμετέρου φορτίου ~ήσον εἰς τὸ ἔλεος σοῦ Anast.S.*Ps.*6(M.89.1093B); **3.** *find oppressive* ὅταν ~ῶνται τὸν λέγοντα Or.*hom.20.6 in Jer.*(p.186.28; M.13.313D); ~ούμενοι τὴν...διατριβὴν Chrys.*hom.4.11 in Mt.*(7.68A); μηδὲ τὸν ἄρτον βεβαρημένον ἐσθίωσιν [i.e. *burdensomely earned*] Epiph.*fid.*23(p.525.1; M.42.829C); **4.** intrans., *incline, have a bias* towards πρὸς κακίαν β. Gr.Nyss.*or.catech.*6(M.45.29A; βρίσας p.35.14).

***βαρζαμανᾶται, οἱ**, Persian officers, perh. *superintendents*, Jo.Mal.*chron.*11 p.271(M.97.412A); conj. for βαρζαμαρ- *ib.*(409C).

βάρησις, ἡ, *heaviness, grossness* εὐχῆς...ἐμπόδια, ἀκηδία, β. σώματος Ephr.3.345E; Gr.Nyss.*instit.*(p.81.18; M.34.433D).

βάρις, ἡ, *castle* β. τὰς οἰκίας φησίν, ἅσπερ βασιλείας ἐξέδωκε Σύμμαχος Or.*fr.47 in Lam.*(p.256.6; M.13.633B); β. ... τὰς τῶν οἰκοδομημάτων περιγραφὰς ἐν τετραγώνῳ τῷ σχήματι Gr.Nyss.*Pss.titt.*B 12(M.44.556B).

***βάρρις, ἡ**, *dove-cote*, ‡Caes.Naz.*dial.*140(M.38.1072).

***Βαρσανουφίτης, ὁ**, *follower of Barsanuphius*, member of a monophysite sect, Tim.CP *haer.*(M.86.45A); Jo.D.*haer.*7(M.94.756B).

***βαρυαλγία, ἡ**, *grievous suffering*, Germ.CP *or.*2(M.98.269B).

***βαρυαχθέω**, *be heavily burdened*, Hyper.*mon.*137(M.79.1488A).

βαρύγλωσσος, **1.** *grave of speech*, Or.*sel.in Ezech.*3(M.13.773C); **2.** *speaking offensively*, Nonn.*par.Jo.*10:34(M.43.837A).

***βαρύγχητος**, *heavy-flowing, mournful* Ῥαχὴλ...β. ἐκπέμπει μέλος ‡Jo.D.*hom.*5(M.96.652B).

***βαρύδαρτος**, *beating heavily*, Thdr.Stud.*epp.*2.47(M.99.1252B).

βαρυκάρδιος, *slow of heart, obstinate*; of unbelievers, *A.Petr.et Andr.*18(p.125.10); Gr.Nyss.*ep.*3(M.46.1017B); Thdt.*Ps.*4:5(1.631); neut. as subst., *obstinacy*; of Jews in rejecting Christ, Didym.*Ps.*4:3(M.39.1165D).

***βαρύκρανος**, *heavy-headed*, Gr.Naz.*carm.*1.2.28.245(M.37.874A).

[*]**βαρυκτυπής**, *heavy-sounding*, *Orac.Sib.*8.432.

βαρύλλιον, τό, *little weight*; of a weight attached to a ὑδροσκόπιον (instrument for measuring specific gravity of liquids) to keep it upright when placed in water, Synes.*ep.*15(M.66.1352B).

***βαρύναχθος**, *heavily laden*, Eudoc.*Cypr.*2.105(M.85.849B).

***βαρύνουσος**, *badly diseased*, Nonn.*par.Jo.*6:2(M.43.793A).

βαρύν-ω, *weigh down, oppress*; pass., *be hardened* against μὴ ~θῇς, κύριε..., κατὰ τῆς δούλης σου *V.Dan.*10(p.381.14).

***βαρυογκώδης**, *weighing heavily*; superl. (neut. as subst.) τὰ β. τοῦ σώματος Melet.*nat.hom.*synops.(M.64.1085D).

***βαρυπαθής**, *very painful*, Eus.*h.e.*10.4.12(M.20.852C).

***βαρυπειθής**, *slow to believe*, Nonn.*par.Jo.*3:12(M.43.768B).

***βαρυσθενής**, *very mighty*, *Orac.Sib.*14.101.

***βαρυσταθμία, ἡ**, *making the balance heavy, weighting*, *Mir.Artem.*38(p.62.6).

***βαρυστονέω**, *groan loudly*, Epiph.*haer.*70.1(p.233.23; M.42.340C).

βαρύσωμος, *heavy in body*, ‡Just.*qu.et resp.*43(M.6.1289B).

βαρυφωνία, ἡ, *gravity, impressiveness of speech*, Sophr.H.*or.*7.17(M.87.3348C).

βαρύφωνος, *grave of speech*, Sophr.H.*or.*7.17(M.87.3348C).

***βαρυχυμία, ἡ**, *excess of fluid*; causing disfigurement of the complexion, Gr.Nyss.*Eun.*12(1 p.375.30; M.45.1101C).

βαρυωπέω, *be dim-sighted*, ‡Caes.Naz.*dial.*24(M.38.884).

βασανισμός, ὁ, *torture*; mental, Jo.Carp.*cap.*suppl.(M.85.1857).

βασανιστήριον, τό, *torture-chamber* τὸ σῶμα...β. τῆς ψυχῆς Meth.*res.*1.57(p.319.18; M.41.1153C).

[*]**βασανῖτις**, *testing*; β. λίθος *touchstone* ἡ β. λίθος τὸν χρυσὸν δοκιμάζει, ἐξ ἧς λίθου οἶμαι καὶ τὸ βασανίζεσθαι ὠνοματοπεποιῆσθαι Isid.Pel.*epp.*5.270(M.78.1493C).

[*]**βάσανον, τό**, *torture* (= βάσανος, ἡ, *LS*), Thphn.*chron.*p.19(M.108.108B).

βασιλεία, ἡ, *sovereignty, reign, kingdom*;

I. secular;

A. *rule, sovereignty*; classified into four types in order of moral excellence, Clem.*str.*1.24(p.99.22; M.8.905B).

B. *reign*; as chronological period, Tat.*orat.*39(p.39.24; M.6.881B); Eus.*p.e.*10.9(484D; M.21.805D); Philost.*h.e.*9.5(M.65.572A).

C. *king's majesty*, Gr.Nyss.*prof.Chr.*(p.137.5; M.46.245A); Jo.Ant.*relat.imp.*1(p.125.17; M.83.1441C); Evagr.*h.e.*2.18(p.68.4; M.86.2548C).

D. plur., *Books of Kings*, *Const.App.*1.5.2; Chrys.*hom.38.1 in Jo.*(8.217A); Thdt.*qu.28 in Ex.*(1.167).

II. theol.;

A. of kingdom of God (βασιλεία or βασίλειον); **1.** God's sovereignty regarded as twofold, consisting in his absolute sovereignty as Creator and his rule, by grace, over faithful who voluntarily submit to it, Chrys.*hom.39.6 in 1Cor.*(10.371E); **2.** God's sovereign authority as essential attribute, ‡Cyr.*Trin.*7(6^3.8D; M.77.1132B); Jo.D.*f.o.*1.8(M.94.809A); compared with power bestowed by God on earthly rulers, Athenag.*leg.*18.1(M.6.925B); expressed in universal order, Dion.Ar.*d.n.*12.2(M.3.969B); **3.** God's kingdom over faithful; **a.** β. τοῦ θεοῦ gen. identified with β. τῶν οὐρανῶν but this equation questioned, Isid.Pel.*epp.*3.206(M.78.889A); and, for purposes of a particular myst. explanation, denied, Evagr.Pont.*cap.pract.*A 2,3(M.40.1221D); Max.*cap.theol.*2.90(M.90.1168C); different usage explained, Or.*fr.36 in Jo.*3:5(p.512.30ff.); **b.** regarded as central item in apostolic preaching, *1Clem.*42.3; **c.** interpreted eschatologically; **i.** of kingdom to be established at gen. resurrection and final consummation, *1Clem.*50.3; Just.*1apol.*11.12(M.6.341B); Chrys.*hom.16.4 in Mt.*(7.208B); id.*hom.4.3 in Eph.*(11.29B); ‡Just.*qu.et resp.*120(M.6.1369C); Petr.Laod.*fr.in Mt.*26:26(M.86.3325C); **ii.** of first and second advents of Christ, exeg. Mt.3:2, Chrys.*hom.10.2 in Mt.*(7.142A); **iii.** of future state of blessed, *2Clem.*5.5; *M.Polyc.*20.2; Eus.*Marcell.*2.1(p.33.30; M.24.780C); Serap.*euch.*13.8; Thdt.*affect.*11(p.297.16; 4.1010); as form of divine beauty put on by those who shall 'bear image of the heavenly', Max.*cap.theol.*2.93(M.90.1169A); distinguished from paradise, Chrys.*serm.*7.5 *in Gen.*(4.681B); identified with 'heaven' opp. γέεννα or κόλασις, Just.*dial.*117.3(M.6.748A); Adam.*dial.*2.11(p.78.26; M.11.1777B); Chrys.*hom.30.5 in Mt.*(7.354D); id.*hom.15.5 in*

Rom.(9.601A); id.*hom.2.3 in 1Cor.*(10.12B); id.*hom.13.4 in Phil.*(11.302C); Procl.CP *or.*1.5(M.65.837B); identified with 'Abraham's bosom', Chrys.*hom.26.4 in Mt.*(7.319D); cf. Marcionite denial, Adam.*dial.*2.11(p.78.10; M.11.1776B); including grades of blessedness, Chrys.*Thdr.*1.19(1.33D); regarded as place in second heavenly plane, Cosm.Ind.*top.*3(M.88.177C); cf.Proc.G.*Gen.*1:6(M.87.65D); hence Manich. theory of spherical heaven rejected, Cosm.Ind.*top.*6(336B); **iv.** as consisting in immortality, Ign.*Eph.*19.3; Meth.*res.*1.61(p.326.9; M.41.1160A); Cyr.*1Cor.*15:50(M.74.912B) etc.; as *ζωὴ αἰώνιος*, a present reality but not fully realized in this life, *2Clem.*5.5; Hipp.*haer.*5.8(p.91.12; M.16.3142C); Meth.*res.*2.18(p.371.3; M.18.284D); Mac.Aeg.*hom.*4.15(M.34.484B); v. *ζωή*; associated with *ζωὴ αἰώνιος* in credal formularies, Ar.*ep.Const.*(p.64.10; M.67.1012B); *Symb.*ap.Epiph.*anc.*119(p.149.3; M.43.236B); *Symb.*ap.*Const.App.*7.41.8; **d.** consisting in present apprehension of divine truth, Or.*sel.in Ps.*144:13(M.12.1673B); id.*or.*25(p.357.9; M.11.496C); Gr.Naz.*or.*45.23(M.36.656A); Max.*cap.*3.55(M.90.1284C); hence identified with **i.** *φῶς* and union with God through faith, Iren.*haer.*5.28.1(M.7.1198A); **ii.** vision of God, Clem.*q.d.s.*19(p.172.7; M.9.624B); Gr.Naz.*or.*20.12(M.35.1080C); *ib.*40.45(M.36.424C); id.*carm.*1.2.34.258(M.37.964A); Gr.Nyss.*perf.*(p.205.14; M.46.277D); **e.** consisting in regeneration and gift of H. Ghost; **i.** exeg. Lc.11:2 [reading *ἐλθέτω τὸ ἅγιον πνεῦμά σου ἐφ' ἡμᾶς καὶ καθαρισάτω ἡμᾶς* for *ἐλθέτω ἡ β. σου* (cf. codd.700,162)], Gr.Nyss.*or.dom.*3(p.60.23; M.44.1157D); Max.*or.dom.*(M.90.885B); **ii.** exeg. Mt.11:11, Chrys.*hom.37.2 in Mt.*(7.417B); Isid.Pel.*epp.*1.68(M.78.228C); for different interpretation, cf.Clem.*q.d.s.*31(p.180.15; M.9.636D); **iii.** in gen., Or.*sel.in Ps.*67:15(M.12.1508C); Cyr.*dial.Trin.*7(5^1.654B); id.*thes.*11(5^1.105E); id.*fr.Mt.*12:28(M.72.408D); hence associated with baptism, id.*Jo.*2(4.147C); **f.** as *βασιλεία ἐντὸς ὑμῶν* (Lc.17:21), identified with indwelling of Logos in believer, Or.*comm.in Mt.*10.14(p.17.28; M.13.870A); being *ἐντὸς* it requires only *ἡ ἀρετὴ τοῦ θέλειν ἡμῶν* for its apprehension, Ath.*v.Anton.*20(M.26.873A); Gr.Nyss.*virg.*12(p.300.18; M.46.372D); is joy of H. Ghost as present *ἀρραβών* of eternal joy, id.*instit.*(p.79.1; M.46.304A); is union with God through *ἀφθαρσία*, id.*perf.*(p.205.14; M.46.277D); Cyr.*Lc.*17:21(M.72.841A); Max.*cap.theol.*92(M.90.1169A); identified with baptismal grace, v. *βάπτισμα*; with knowledge of God, cf.Or.*hom.36 in Lc.*(p.216.12; M.13.1895A); with faith and knowledge of God, Ath.*gent.*30(M.25.60C); v. *ἐντός*; **g.** as indwelling of Logos, Or.*Jo.*19.12(p.312.11; M.14.548C); **h.** as present condition of those who live virtuously, Clem.*fr.*21(p.223.21)ap.Jo.D.*parall.*(M.95.1264C); Or.*comm.in Mt.*12.14(p.97.13; M.13.1012C); hence **i.** as consisting in, or closely associated with, virtues, Meth.*symp.*10.2(p.122.19; M.18.193B); Evagr.Pont.*or.*38(M.79.1176A); Chrys.*hom.23.5 in Gen.*(4.213D); esp. with *ἀπάθεια* and *γνῶσις*, Evagr.Pont.*cap.pract.*A 2(M.40.1221D); hence Rom.14:17 rewritten as *οὐκ ἔστιν ἡ β. ... βρῶσις καὶ πόσις, ἀλλὰ δικαιοσύνη καὶ ἀπάθεια καὶ μακαριότης* Gr.Nyss.*hom.5 in Eccl.*(M.44.696B); identified with *αὐτοδικαιοσύνη*, Max.*qu.Thal.*(M.90.616B); **j.** associated with divine wisdom, Clem.*str.*2.19(p.167.16; M.8.1044A); **k.** equated with divine revelation in scripture, Or.*comm.in Mt.*10.12(p.13.28; M.13.861C); †Bas.*Is.*309(1.612D; M.30.657A,B); with Christ's teaching, Or.*comm.in Mt.*10.14(p.17.28; 869A); with preaching of gospel, Isid.Pel.*epp.*2.198(M.78.644B); Cyr.*Lc.*13:19(M.72.772C); **l.** manifested in power and truth, Epiph.*haer.*76.37(p.389.26; M.42.596B); **m.** as kingdom of light, opp. reign of darkness, Meth.*res.*1.32(p.269.14; M.18.268C); Mac.Aeg.*hom.*2.5(M.34.468A); *ib.*(468B); opp. reign of sin, Or.*or.*25(p.358.28; M.11.497D); Cyr.H.*catech.*23.13; opp. kingdom of 'rulers of this world', *Hom.Clem.*20.2; opp. tyranny of Devil, Mel.*pass.*68 p.11.17; Isid.Pel.*epp.*4.24(M.78.1073B); **n.** dist. from visible Church: explicitly, *Did.*9.4; *ib.*10.5; Cyr.H.*catech.*18.28; implicitly, but connected with 'church of the first-born' (Heb.12:23), Clem.*prot.*9(p.62.21; M.8.193B); and with heavenly Church, id.*paed.*2.1(p.157.24; M.8.388A); closely related to Church, Herm.*sim.*9.12.5; *Lit.*ap.*Const.App.*8.8.2; **4.** entry into kingdom; **a.** kingdom regarded as conferred or established by grace alone; **i.** as gift of God, *1Clem.*61.1; *Diogn.*10.2; as inheritance bestowed by God, Clem.*ecl.*44(p.149.16; M.9.720A); not earned as reward, Jo.Clim.*scal.*23(M.88.973C); **ii.** to be awaited by faithful, *2Clem.*12.1; to come *ὅταν τὰ δύο ἕν, καὶ τὸ ἔξω ὡς τὸ ἔσω, κτλ.* *ib.*12.2; Clem.*str.*3.13(p.238.24; M.8.1193A); **iii.** entered through power of God, *Diogn.*9.1; through name of Christ, Herm.*sim.*9.12.5; through H. Ghost, Bas.*Spir.*36(3.29E; M.32.132B); **iv.** through grace of baptism, indispensable for all save martyrs, Herm.*sim.*9.16.2; *Hom.Clem.*13.21; Cyr.H.*catech.*3.4; *ib.*3.10; †Bas.*bapt.*1.2.4(2.631D; M.31.1532A); Gr.Naz.*or.*40.3(M.36.361B) cit. s. *κλείς*; Bas.*hom.*13.2(2.115A; M.31.428A); Jo.3:5 rewritten as *ἐὰν μὴ ἀναγεννηθῆτε ὕδατι ζῶντι, εἰς ὄνομα πατρός, υἱοῦ, ἁγίου πνεύματος, οὐ μὴ εἰσέλθητε εἰς τὴν β. τῶν οὐρανῶν* *Hom.Clem.*11:26; but baptismal grace must be preserved by good living, *2Clem.*6.9; and regeneration is linked with observance of commandments *ἐὰν...μὴ γεννηθῇς ἄνωθεν, καὶ τὴν τῶν δογμάτων παραλάβῃς ἀκρίβειαν...πόρρω τῆς β. εἶ τῶν οὐρανῶν* Chrys.*hom.24.2 in Jo.*(8.140A); **v.** not to be inherited by 'flesh and blood' (1Cor.15:50), but flesh can be 'inherited' by the Spirit and be transformed in order to enter kingdom, Iren.*haer.*5.9.4(M.7.1146B); Meth.*res.*2.18(p.371.3; M.18.284D); flesh and blood will share in resurrection, but must put on incorruptibility in order to enter kingdom, Sever.*1Cor.*15:50(p.277.3); Thdr.Mops.*1Cor.*15:50(p.195.30); Cyr.*1Cor.*15:50(M.74.912B); *σάρξ*, which cannot inherit kingdom, identified with *πονηρὰ πρᾶξις*, Chrys.*hom.42.1 in 1Cor.*(10.461B); cf. *πᾶς ὁ τὴν ἑαυτοῦ σάρκα τρέφων εἰς κόρον, οὐ δύναται βασιλείας θεοῦ κληρονομῆσαι* Thdt.*1Cor.*15:50(3.279); **b.** regarded as attainable by human endeavour, or as reward of virtue; **i.** as reward, Clem.*prot.*1(p.6.33; M.8.60B); Eun.*apol.*27(M.30.865D); to be purchased, Clem.*q.d.s.*32(p.181.10; M.9.637C); esp. by almsgiving, freq. emphasized as nec. qualification for entry, *ib.*(p.181.14; 637C); Bas.*hom.*7.1(2.51D; M.31.281A); id.*reg.fus.*8.2(2.350A; M.31.937D); Chrys.*hom.47.4 in Mt.*(7.492A); **ii.** as goal attained by perseverance in Christ's service, Ath.*v.Anton.*94(M.26.976A); **iii.** as attainable by good living, Ign.*Eph.*16.1; *2Clem.*6.9; *Barn.*21.1; Just.*dial.*117.3(M.6.748A); Clem.*prot.*11(p.83.6; M.8.237B); id.*paed.*3.11(p.281.3; M.8.660B); Chrys.*hom.31.3 in Ac.*(9.244B); Thdt.*Ezech.*39:29(2.1017); **iv.** attained through faith, Iren.*haer.*5.28.1(M.7.1197C); Thdt.*qu.38 in Gen.*(1.52); id.*affect.*11(p.297.16; 4.1010); **v.** faith and works as keys of kingdom, Gr.Nyss.*hom.11 in Cant.*(M.44.1024C); **vi.** *γνῶσις* as key of kingdom, v. *γνῶσις*; **vii.** attained through *ἀπάθεια*, Evagr.Pont.*cap.pract.*A 2(M.40.1221D); cf.Gr.Nyss.*hom.5 in Eccl.*(M.44.696B); **viii.** *ἡσυχία* as *ὁδὸς βασιλείας*, ‡Chrys.*pat.et consumm.*(12.819C); **ix.** attained through subjugation of flesh, Meth.*res.*1.61(p.326.9; M.41.1160A); through virginity, id.*symp.*1.1(p.7.13; M.18.37A); *ib.*2.7(p.25.19; 60B); necessity of virginity alleged by Hieracas, Epiph.*haer.*67.1(p.134.2; M.42.173B); denied, Chrys.*hom.47.4 in Mt.*(7.492A); **x.** entered with difficulty by rich, Clem.*q.d.s.*16(p.170.13; M.9.620D); *ib.*18(p.171.5; 621C); Chrys.*hom.3.5 in Phil.*(11.211B); **xi.** obtained through violence (Mt.11:12), i.e. through striving with God in prayer, learning, and asceticism, Clem.*str.*5.3(p.336.16; M.9.33A), *ib.*4.2(p.250.10; M.8.1217B) citt. s. *βιαστής*; *ib.*6.17(p.509.7; M.9.381A); id.*q.d.s.*21(p.173.22; M.9.625C) cit. s. *βιάζω*; Ant.Mon.*hom.*130(M.89.1841B) cit. s. *βιαστός*; **xii.** forfeited by schismatics, Ign.*Philad.*3.3; regained when those baptized in schism are admitted to Church by consignation with chrism, CLaod.*can.*48; **xiii.** SS. Michael and Peter as *κλειδοῦχοι τῆς β. τῶν οὐρανῶν* v. *κλειδοῦχος*.

B. of Christ's kingdom; **1.** distinction of Son's participation with Father in eternal and absolute sovereignty from incarnate Christ's derivative and 'economic' kingdom, which is sometimes said to have had temporal beginning and to be destined to be consummated at parousia, Or.*Jo.*1.28(30; p.35.21; M.14.76B); *οὐκοῦν ὅρον τινὰ ἔχειν δοκεῖ ἡ κατὰ ἄνθρωπον αὐτοῦ οἰκονομία τε καὶ β. οὐδὲν γὰρ ἕτερον βούλεται ἢ τοῦτο τὸ ὑπὸ τοῦ ἀποστόλου ῥηθέν, ἕως ἂν θῇ τοὺς ἐχθροὺς αὐτοῦ ὑποπόδιον...ἐπειδὰν τοὺς ἐχθροὺς σχῇ ὑποπόδιον τῶν ποδῶν οὐκέτι χρῄζει τῆς ἐν μέρει ταύτης β. ... συμβασιλεύει γὰρ τῷ θεῷ καὶ πατρὶ οὗ ὁ λόγος ἦν τε καὶ ἐστίν* Marcell.*fr.*104 ap.Eus.*Marcell.*3.4(p.54.3; M.24.816A); Eus.*Is.*9:7(M.24.153B); *διπλῆ γὰρ ἡ τοῦ σωτῆρος β. ἡ μὲν προαιώνιος καὶ ἀρχὴν οὐκ ἔχουσα, ἡ δὲ μετὰ τοὺς αἰῶνας, ἀρχὴν ἀπὸ τῆς οἰκονομίας λαμβάνουσα* ‡Chrys.*hom.in Ps.96*:1(5.611E); cf. *οἶδεν οὖν ὁ Δαβὶδ τὸν Χριστὸν καὶ προαιώνιον ἔχοντα τὸν τῆς θεότητος θρόνον...οἶδεν αὐτὸν καὶ β. δεχόμενον ἀνθρωπίνως ἐν χρόνῳ, διὰ τὸ τῆς οἰκονομίας νεώτερον* Cyr.*Ps.*2:7(M.69.721A,B); *ὡς γὰρ θεός, ἔμφυτον ἔχει τὴν β., ὡς δὲ ἄνθρωπος, χειροτονητὴν δέχεται ταύτην* Thdt.*Ps.*2:6(1.620); cf. *ὡς γὰρ θεός, ὁ υἱὸς αἰώνιον ἔχει τὸν θρόνον, ἀλλ' ἔλαβεν ὡς ἄνθρωπος, ὅπερ εἶχεν ὡς θεός* *ib.*109:1(1392); **2.** of Son's sovereignty as essential attribute of divinity *ἑνὸς ὄντος θεοῦ τοῦ δὲ υἱοῦ...μία ἔσται ἀρχὴ καὶ β. μία* Eus.*e.th.*2.7(p.104.6; M.24.908C); *μονογενὴς τοῦ θεοῦ υἱὸς...πρόεισι μὲν τῆς πατρικῆς θεότητός τε καὶ β.* *ib.*2.17(p.121.13; 940A); *ὁ δὲ σωτὴρ...θεὸς ὢν καὶ τὴν β. τοῦ πατρὸς ἀεὶ βασιλεύων* Ath.*Ar.*1.46(M.26.108A); *τὴν μὲν θεότητα καὶ τὴν πατρικὴν β. αὐτοῦ* *ib.*1.49(113C); *συναΐδιον καὶ προαιώνιον τὴν β. ἔχων, ὡς ὁ γεννήσας αὐτόν. κοινὴ γὰρ ἡ β.* ‡Chrys.*palm.*1.2(8.234B); **3.** as 'economic' kingdom over mankind, awaiting consummation hereafter; **a.** associated with final judgement ὄψονται τὴν δόξαν αὐτοῦ καὶ τὸ κράτος οἱ ἄπιστοι, καὶ ξενισθήσονται ἰδόντες τὸ βασίλειον τοῦ κόσμου ἐν τῷ Ἰησοῦ *2Clem.*17.5; *Orac.Sib.*2.347; Heges.ap.Eus.*h.e.*3.20.4(M.20.253B); Cyr.H.*catech.*4.15; Chrys.*hom.9.1 in 2Tim.*(11.715B); **b.** equivalent to β. τοῦ θεοῦ or τῶν οὐρανῶν as heavenly state of blessed τάξεις προφητῶν, μαρτύρων τε καὶ ἀποστόλων εἰς β. Χριστοῦ ἀναπαυόμενοι Hipp.*antichr.*59(p.40.9; M.10.780A); χαρήσονται ἐν τῇ β. τοῦ θεοῦ τῇ ἐν Χριστῷ Ἰησοῦ *Const.App.*7.32.5; attainable by body if obedient to divine law, Meth.*res.*1.61(p.326.13; M.41.1160A); in prayer for departed κύριε...μνήσθητι ἡμῶν ἐν τῇ βασιλίᾳ σου. ἀμήν *MAMA* 1.382; **c.** identified with H. Ghost with whom Christ was anointed as king, Gr.Nyss.*Maced.*16(M.45.1321A); **d.** question of its eternity; **i.** eternity freq. asserted Χριστὸς πάλιν παραγινόμενος...καὶ αἰώνιον τὴν β. ἔχων κεκήρυκται Just.*dial.*34.2(M.6.548B); ‡Tit.Bost.*palm.*3(M.18.1268D); Epiph.*haer.*29.4(p.325.13; M.41.396B); ‡Chrys.*palm.*1.2(8.234A); ἡ τούτου β. ἀκατάλυτος ἔσται καὶ αἰώνιος Cosm.Ind.*top.*2(M.88.112B); **ii.** problem whether it has beginning or ending discussed, ref. 1Cor.15:24 and Ps.96:1: kingdom interpreted as consisting in community over which Christ reigns τὸ γὰρ παραδοῦναι αὐτὸν τῷ πατρὶ τὴν β., ταὐτόν ἐστι κατὰ τὴν διάνοιαν τῷ παραγαγεῖν τοὺς πάντας τῷ θεῷ Gr.Nyss.*hom.in 1Cor.15:28*(M.44.1325C); β. οὖν καλεῖ τὸ ἔθνος, τὸν λαόν, τὴν οἰκουμένην τὴν ὑπὸ τὸν βασιλέα...παραδίδωσιν οὖν ὁ σωτὴρ τὴν β., ἤγουν τὴν ἀνθρωπότητα τήν ποτε βασιλευθεῖσαν τῇ ἁμαρτίᾳ,...ἵνα...παραστήσῃ αὐτὴν τῷ θεῷ καὶ πατρί ‡Chrys.*hom.in Ps.96:1*(5.613A); interpreted as *sovereignty* and passages explained in non-subordinationist and wholly Trinitarian terms οὐ γὰρ διακόπτεται αὐτοῦ ἡ β.· κρατεῖ γὰρ καὶ ἰσχύει καὶ μένει, ἕως ἂν πάντα κατορθώσῃ Chrys.*hom.39.5 in 1Cor.*(10.369E); παραδίδωσι τὴν β. τῷ θεῷ...οὐκ αὐτὸς τῆς β. γυμνούμενος, ἀλλὰ τὸν τύραννον διάβολον...ὑποτάττων, καὶ πάντας ὑποκύψαι παρασκευάζων, καὶ...ἐπιγνῶναι θεόν Thdt.*1Cor.*15:24(3.270); cf. τὸ δὲ ἕως, οὐ χρόνου σημαντικόν, ἀλλ' ἰδίωμα τῆς θείας γραφῆς...πῶς δὲ καὶ οἱ ἅγιοι συμβασιλεύουσιν ἢ τίνι συμβασιλεύουσι, τοῦ τὴν β. ὑποσχομένου ἀποτιθεμένου τὴν β.; id.*Ps.*109:1(1.1393); and distn. emphasized between eternal and economic kingdoms (v. supra B.1) τῆς... νοουμένης β. οὐκ ἔσται πέρας· τῆς δευτέρας δέ, τί; τὸ λαβεῖν ἡμᾶς ὑπὸ χεῖρα σωζομένους Gr.Naz.*or.*30.4(p.113.12; M.36.108B); beginning of kingdom explained as being ἀπὸ τοῦ μὴ ἄρχειν τῶν ἁμαρτανόντων μετανοησάντων ἥκειν ἐπὶ τὴν β. Didym.*Ps.*96:1(M.39.1508A); **iii.** ref. teaching of Marcellus, Marcell.*fr.*99 ap.Eus.*Marcell.*2.3(p.51.29; M.24.809C) cit. s. βασιλεύς; ὁ λόγος ἀρχὴν βασιλείας εἴληφεν, ἀλλ' ὁ ἀπατηθεὶς ὑπὸ τοῦ διαβόλου ἄνθρωπος διὰ τῆς τοῦ λόγου δυνάμεως βασιλεὺς γέγονεν, ἵνα βασιλεὺς γενόμενος τὸν πρότερον ἀπατήσαντα νικήσῃ διάβολον id.*fr.*104 *ib.*2.4(p.54.10; 816A); ἀρχὴν βασιλείας ἀπό τινος λαβόντος χρόνου τοῦ δεσπότου ἡμῶν Χριστοῦ id.*fr.*100 *ib.*2.3(p.51.36; 812A); [Ps.2:6 etc.] ἀρχὴν βασιλείας εἴληφεν ὁ ἄνθρωπος διὰ τοῦ λόγου. εἰ οὖν εἴληφεν ἀρχὴν βασιλείας πρὸ ἐτῶν ὅλων οὐ πλειόνων ⟨ἢ⟩ τετρακοσίων, οὐδὲν παράδοξον, εἰ τὸν πρὸ οὕτως ὀλίγου χρόνου τῆς β. ταύτης τυχόντα ὁ ἀπόστολός φησιν παραδώσειν τὴν β., δηλονότι τῷ θεῷ τῷ καταστήσαντι αὐτόν, ὡς ἡ γραφή φησιν, βασιλέα id.*fr.*102 *ib.*2.4(p.52.30; 812C); οὐ δι' ἑαυτόν, ἀλλὰ δι' ἡμᾶς, τὴν ἀνθρωπίνην ἀνείληφε σάρκα· εἰ δὲ δι' ἡμᾶς ἀνειληφὼς φαίνεται...ἐν τῷ καιρῷ τῆς κρίσεως τέλους τεύξεται, οὐκέτι οὐδὲ ταύτης τῆς ἐν μέρει βασιλείας ἔσται χρεία id.*fr.*106 *ib.*2.4(p.55.7; 816Cff.); μέγιστον ἡμῖν μυστήριον...ὁ ἀπόστολος ἀνακαλύπτει, τέλος μὲν ἔσεσθαι φάσκων τῆς Χριστοῦ β. id.*fr.*101 *ib.*2.4(p.52.21; 812C); Marcellus admitted eternity of Christ's kingdom in profession of faith made to Julius, prob. in sense of eternal divine sovereignty of Logos within Godhead, id.*ep.*ap.Epiph.*haer.*72.2(p.257.25; M.42.385B); refutation of Marcellus νεωτερίζεις...ἀρχήν τε πρόσκαιρον καὶ νεωτέραν τῇ β. τοῦ Χριστοῦ διδοὺς καὶ ταύτης τέλος ὑφιστάμενος Eus.*Marcell.*2.4(p.56.19; 820A); id.*e.th.*3.16(p.175.20; M.24.1033B) cit. s. βασιλεύω; Acac.Caes.*fr.Marcell.*(p.262.8; M.42.392C); Didym.*Trin.*3.20(M.39.893A) cit. s. βασιλεύς; ref. Heb.12:28 ἂν ἐροίμην τοὺς παυθῆναί ποτε τὴν β. Χριστοῦ νομίζοντας, τίνος β. διαμεμνῆσθαι νῦν τὸν ἀπόστολον φήσομεν...πότερα τὴν υἱοῦ β. ἐν τούτοις φησίν, ἢ γοῦν τὴν αὐτοῖς τοῖς ἁγίοις δοθησομένην; εἰ μὲν οὖν ἀμείνω τοῦ μεταπίπτειν εἶναί φασι τήν τε β. καὶ ὑπεροχὴν τοῦ υἱοῦ, πεφλυαρηκότας εἰκῇ κατερυθριάσειν οἶμαι τοὺς δι' ἐναντίας· εἰ δὲ δή, μεθέντες τὸν υἱόν, ἀπαραποίητον ἔσεσθαι τοῖς ἁγίοις τὸ βασιλεύειν ἐροῦσι, πρῶτον μὲν ἀμείνους καὶ αὐτοῦ φανήσονται τοῦ Χριστοῦ. ... τὸ οὖν, ὅταν παραδῷ τὴν β., οὐ τοιοῦτόν ἐστιν, ὅτι ταύτην ἀποθήσει, ἀλλ' ὅτι ὑφ' ἑτέρων ἐχομένην ἐκσπάσας προσάξει τῷ πατρί· συγκατάρξει γε μὴν τούτῳ καὶ αὐτός Cyr.*Heb.*12:28(M.74.996C–997B); **iv.** eternity asserted in credal statements, cf.*Symb.Ant.*(341)1(p.249.7; M.26.721A) cit. s. βασιλεύς; *Symb.Ant.*(341)4(p.251.10; M.26.725C); οὗ ἡ β. ἀκατάπαυστος οὖσα διαμενεῖ εἰς τοὺς ἀπείρους αἰῶνας *Symb.Ant.*(345)1(p.251.31; M.26.728B); CSard.*ep.cath.*ap.Thdt.*h.e.*2.8.48(3.839); Cyr.H.*catech.*15.1; *Symb.*ap.*Const.App.*7.41.6; *Symb.Nic.–CP*(p.80.12; H.2.288B); **v.** as coeternal with Roman empire, which is to be superseded only at final consummation, ‡Anast.S.*Jud.disp.*1(M.89.1212C); **e.** prepared for by succession of Davidic monarchy, Thdt.*qu.32 in 1Reg.*(1.376); **f.** Christ's kingdom to be consummated on earth acc. millenarian teaching, esp. of Cerinthus, Caius R.ap.Eus.*h.e.*3.28.2(M.20.273D); Dion.Al.ap.Eus.*h.e.*7.25.3(M.20.697A); Thdt.*haer.*2.3(4.330); of Irenaeus, *haer.*5.32.1(M.7.1210B); *ib.*5.33.3(1213B); of Nepos, Dion.Al.ap.Eus.*h.e.*7.24.4(693A); of Apollinarius, Epiph.*haer.*77.37(p.450.2; M.42.697B); hence woes will be included in times of Christ's kingdom, *Barn.*8.6; **g.** Christ's reign 'from the tree' (Ps.95:10 reading ἀπὸ ξύλου), *Barn.*8.5; cf.Just.*1apol.*41.4(M.6.392B); id.*dial.*73.1(M.6.645B); (cf.Tertullianus, *adversus Marcionem*, 3.19; id.*adversus Judaeos* 10, and many Latin writers); **h.** Christ as himself the β.: Χριστὸς ὁ βασιλεὺς τῶν οὐρανῶν, ἡ β. τῶν οὐρανῶν, ὡμοιωμένη θησαυρῷ κεκρυμμένῳ ἐν τῷ ἀγρῷ Or.*comm.in Mt.*10.5(p.6.1; M.13.845B); ὥσπερ αὐτός ἐστιν ἡ αὐτοσοφία... οὕτω...καὶ ἡ αὐτοβασιλεία...κἂν ζητῇς τὸ 'αὐτῶν ἐστιν ἡ β. τῶν οὐρανῶν', δύνασαι λέγειν, ὅτι αὐτῶν ἐστιν ὁ Χριστός, καθὸ αὐτοβασιλεία ἐστίν *ib.*14.7(p.289.17; 1197B); **i.** Christ's kingdom attainable by soul in present life, Mac.Aeg.*hom.*2.5(M.34.468B); variously interpreted in this aspect, either as vision of Christ attainable through suffering οἱ θέλοντές με ἰδεῖν καὶ ἅψασθαί μου τῆς β., ὀφείλουσιν θλιβέντες καὶ παθόντες λαβεῖν με *Barn.*7.11; or as preaching of Word, and acts of righteousness οἶμαι νοεῖσθαι...Χριστοῦ βασιλείαν τοὺς προϊόντας σωτηρίους τοῖς ἀκούουσι λόγους καὶ τὰ μὲν ἐπιτελούμενα ἔργα δικαιοσύνης καὶ τῶν λοιπῶν ἀρετῶν Or.*or.*25(p.357.10; M.11.496C); **j.** Christ's kingdom consisting of the faithful over whom he rules, Gr.Nyss.*hom.in 1Cor.15:28*(M.44.1325C); **k.** his royalty symbolized by Magi's gift of gold, Iren.*haer.*3.9.2(M.7.871A); Clem.*paed.*2.8(p.195.28; M.8.469B); Gr.Naz.*or.*38.17(M.36.332A); cf.†Bas.*Chr.generat.*6(2.601C; M.31.1472A); **l.** as inheritor of Davidic throne, Christ transfers regal and high-priestly status to ἀρχιερεῖς of Church, Epiph.*haer.*29(p.325.10; M.41.396B).

C. of kingdom of undivided Trinity, Thdt.*Trin.*28(M.75.1188C); *Didasc.patr.*proem.(p.8.9).

D. of kingdom of believers; **1.** of kingly status of all believers (cf. 1Petr.2:9) πάντες...οἱ πιστοί, κεκλημένοι εἰς β. κατά τε τὴν ἐπίγνωσιν, κατά τε τὴν κληρονομίαν Clem.*ecl.*44(p.149.16; M.9.720A); τὸν εἰς β. κεχρισμένον λαόν *ib.*64(p.155.9; 728D); Mac.Aeg.*hom.*2.5(M.34.465D); **2.** of future reign of saints with Christ (cf. Dan.7:27); **a.** as millennial or earthly kingdom, Iren.*haer.*5.35.1(M.7.1219A); Andr.Caes.*Apoc.*62(M.106.413B); **b.** not explicitly millennial χαρήσονται ἐπὶ τῇ β. τοῦ κυρίου αὐτῶν εἰς τοὺς αἰῶνας Clem.*prot.*10(p.69.18; M.8.208B); Hipp.*Dan.*4.55.5(M.10.665D); Chrys.*Dan.*7:27(6.241D); Cyr.*Heb.*12:28(M.74.996D); Thdt.*Dan.*7:27(2.1209); **c.** interpreted as prophecy fulfilled in Constantine's celebration of tricennalia, and association of Dalmatius and Hannibalianus in empire, Eus.*l.C.*3(p.201.1; M.20.1329A); **d.** to be obtained by the worthy, Hipp.*Dan.*4.60.1 citing alleged saying of Christ to Judas.

E. of Adam's royal estate, exchanged for tyranny as result of Fall, Mel.*pass.*49 p.8.19; Marcell.*fr.*99 ap.Eus.*Marcell.*2.3(p.51.29; M.24.809C) cit. s. βασιλεύς; Gr.Nyss.*hom.opif.*21(M.44.204A).

F. of kingdom of spirit, opp. kingdom of letter, corresponding to kingdoms of David and Saul, Max.*qu.Thal.*65(M.90.772C); cf. Jo.D.*Heb.*12:28(M.95.993A).

G. of kingdom of world divided among apostles when missionary spheres were allotted to them, Thdt.*Ps.*67:15(1.1063).

H. of David's kingdom transferred through Christ to bishops of Church, Epiph.*haer.*29.4(p.325.10; M.41.396B); his kingdom being Christ, *A.Mt.*2(p.219.6).

I. of kingship of philosopher (Stoic), Clem.*str.*2.4(p.123.3; M.8.952B).

J. of rule of evil powers; **1.** antichrist, Iren.*haer.*5.25.4(M.7.1191B); Hipp.*Dan.*4.55.3(M.10.665D); id.*antichr.*54(p.36.8; M.10.773A); Meth.*symp.*6.4(p.68.23; M.18.120A); Cyr.H.*catech.*15.11; *ib.*15.13; **2.** Devil, Pall.*v.Chrys.*20(p.145.22; M.47.81); **3.** evil, cf. ἡ παλαιὰ β. Ign.*Eph.*19.3; Meth.*symp.*10.1(p.122.3; M.18.192D); but, since evil is man's own work, it can have no β., Gr.Naz.*or.*40.45(M.36.424A); **4.** death, Clem.*exc.Thdot.*58(p.126.8; M.9.685D); Gr.Nyss.*hom.in 1Cor.15:28*(M.44.1316A); **5.** darkness, Mac.Aeg.*hom.*2.5(M.34.468B); **6.** present age, equated with secular power of Rome τὴν β. τοῦ νῦν αἰῶνος οὐ γινώσκω...ἐπιγινώσκω τὸν κύριον ἡμῶν *M.Scill.*6; **7.** Gnost. demiurge, Heracleon ap.Or.*Jo.*13.60 (p.291.21; M.14.513A) cit. s. βασιλικός.

βασίλειος, *royal*;

A. in gen. (less freq. than βασιλικός), ref. Christ as king τὴν ἀντίτυπον τοῦ β. σώματος Χριστοῦ δεκτὴν εὐχαριστίαν προσφέρετε *Const.App.*6.30.2; ref. Cross ὅπου τὸ συμπέρασμα τῆς...οἰκονομίας, ὅπου τὸ πλήρωμα τῶν ἀγώνων τῶν μυστικῶν, ὅπου τὸ β. ὄντως τὸ διάδοχον Mac.Mgn.*apocr.*3.14(p.92.14).

B. neut. as subst.; **1.** *palace, royal house*, freq. plur.; hence *church*, Eus.*h.e.*10.4.42(M.20.865B); *ib.*10.4.63(876A); met., ref. catechumens ἤδη περὶ τὸ προαύλιον τῶν β. γεγόνατε Cyr.H.*procatech.* 1; **2.** *imperial court, seat of government* ἐν Ῥώμῃ εἶχον πάλαι Ῥωμαίων οἱ βασιλεῖς τὰ β. Thdt.*Rom.*1:18(3.17); Socr.*h.e.*3.13.1 (M.67.412C); **3.** *sovereign authority*, *2Clem.*17.5; *A.Jo.*5(p.153.11); Eus.*p.e.*7.6(304C; M.21.516C); Sophr.H.*ep.syn.*(M.87.3200A); hence, in formal address, the *emperor's majesty* δέομαι τοῦ β. σου *Pet.Ar.*3 (M.26.821C); **4.** *kingdom, empire*, Eus.*d.e.*3.7(p.145.29; M.22.245B); Epiph.*haer.*20.1(p.225.14; M.41.272A); Cosm.Ind.*top.*2(M.88.113C); Jo.Mal.*chron.*2 p.52(M.97.128A); of kingdom of God, v. βασιλεία.

C. fem. as subst., *queen, empress*, Philost.*h.e.*7.6(M.65.633C); met., of Rome as imperial city (cf. βασιλίς), Aberc.*epitaph.*7 cit. s. βασίλισσα.

D. as proper name; of Basil of Caesarea, in acrostic Βασίλειος ἀληθῶς | ἡ βάσις τῶν ἀρετῶν | ἡ βίβλος τῶν ἐπαίνων | ὁ βίος τῶν θαυμάτων Ephr.*enc.Bas.*13(p.145).

βασιλεύς, ὁ, I. *king*;

A. of secular rulers; **1.** def. of true king β. τοίνυν ἐστὶν ὁ ἄρχων κατὰ νόμους, ὁ τὴν τοῦ ἄρχειν ἑκόντων ἐπιστήμην ἔχων. οἷός ἐστιν ὁ κύριος, τοὺς εἰς αὐτὸν καὶ δι' αὐτοῦ πιστεύοντας προϊέμενος Clem.*str.* 1.24(p.100.22; M.8.908B); β. dist. from τύραννος, Synes.*regn.*13(p.39. 11; M.66.1085C); **2.** of emperor, to be prayed for by Christians, Thphl.Ant.*Autol.*1.11(M.6.1041A); emperors as *foederati* of heavenly king, cf.Xyst.Papa *ep.Jo.Ant.*(M.*PL.*50.609B); righteous sovereign's priestly status πᾶς β. δίκαιος ἱερατικὴν ἔχει τάξιν Iren.*haer.* 4.8.3(M.7.995A); **3.** souls of kings, together with priests and prophets, indwelt by Achamoth (Valent.), Iren.*haer.*1.7.2(M.7. 516B); **4.** idea that changes in succession of kings are indicated by appearance of comets rejected in connexion with star of Bethlehem, †Bas.*Chr.generat.*6(2.601D; M.31.1472B).

B. of divine rulers; **1.** of God, freq.; as β. τῶν αἰώνων *1Clem.* 61.2; Cosm.Ind.*top.*5(M.88.204D); *Lit.Jac.*(p.200.8) et freq.; as β. opp. Devil as τύραννος, Thdt.*Cant.*1:2(2.30); as king of heaven, opp. this world, *Hom.Clem.*20.2; **2.** of Christ; **a.** in gen., freq. κυρίῳ ἡμῶν καὶ θεῷ καὶ β. *Lit.*ap.*Const.App.*8.15.9; σωτῆρα, β., καὶ θεὸν ἡμῶν *Const.App.*2.24.7; ἐν τῷ διοπετεῖ ἱερῷ Διὶ Ἡλίῳ θεῷ μεγάλῳ β. Ἰησοῦ τὸ Περσικὸν κράτος ἀνέθηκεν *Pers.*(p.18.4); ἀπόστολον ἔχων τιμὴν Χριστοῦ βασιλῆος *MAMA* 1.238; Pamph.Mon. *Soter.*1(p.114.22); **b.** opp. emperor, as king of kings ἐπιγινώσκω τὸν κύριον ἡμῶν καὶ β. τῶν βασιλέων *M.Scill.*6; **c.** as β. τῶν αἰώνων Chrys. *hom.*4.2 *in 1Tim.*(11.654C); Thdt.*1Tim.*1:17(3.644); ‡Meth.*Sym.et Ann.*6(M.18.361D); indwelling soul of believer (cf. βασιλεία ἐντὸς ὑμῶν) λαλεῖν...τῷ β. τῶν αἰώνων ἐν σοὶ κατοικοῦντι Clem.*q.d.s.*35 (p.183.15; M.9.641A); **d.** as king of all creation, *Const.App.*7.47.3; ἐθελήσας...τῷ σπέρματι αὐτοῦ [i.e. David] φυλάξαι τὴν βασιλείαν, διὰ τὸν ἐξ αὐτοῦ τεχθησόμενον κατὰ σάρκα β. τῆς κτίσεως Thdt.*qu.* 32 *in 1Reg.*(1.376); **e.** as eternal king διαμένοντα β. καὶ θεὸν εἰς τοὺς αἰῶνας *Symb.Ant.*(341)1(p.249.7; M.26.721A); **f.** of Christ's divine nature as β., Or.*Jo.*1.28(30; p.35.27; M.14.76C); **g.** ref. incarnate life; as king Christ was anointed with H. Ghost who is his sovereign power, Gr.Nyss.*Maced.*16(M.45.1321A); ἐτέχθη τὸν βασιλέαν Χριστόν [sic] *Pap.Chr.*(p.438); as man he was 'economically' a king ὁ...τὴν σάρκα...προλαβὼν κατεστάθη β. ἐπὶ τὴν ἐκκλησίαν ἵνα διὰ τοῦ λόγου ὁ τῆς βασιλείας τῶν οὐρανῶν πρότερον ἐκπεπτωκὼς ἄνθρωπος βασιλείας τυχεῖν δυνηθῇ· τοῦτον οὖν τὸν ἄνθρωπον τὸν πρότερον διὰ τὴν παρακοὴν τῆς βασιλείας ἐκπεπτωκότα κύριον καὶ θεὸν γενέσθαι βουλόμενος ὁ θεὸς ταύτην τὴν οἰκονομίαν εἰργάσατο Marcell. *fr.*99 ap.Eus.*Marcell.*2.3(p.51.29; M.24.809C); ὅσα λέγεται λαμβάνειν, ἵνα ἡμεῖς μετασχῶμεν, εἴληφεν. κεχειροτόνημαι, φησίν, εἰς β. παρὰ τοῦ θεοῦ καὶ πατρὸς ὥστε διαγγέλλειν τὸ πρόσταγμα αὐτοῦ Cyr.*Ps.* 2:6(M.69.720C); as king in this sense Christ reigns as second Adam, and will hand over his kingdom to Father, Marcell.*fr.*102 ap.Eus. *Marcell.*2.4(p.52.25ff.; 812C) cit. s. βασιλεία; ἀποτίθεσθαι τὸν μονογενῆ τὴν βασιλείαν, καὶ μὴ εἶναι β. αἰώνιον ὑποτάσσεσθαί τε τῷ θεῷ ὥς τινα ἀντίθεον...καὶ εἶναι μόνον τὰ πάντα ἐν πᾶσι τὸν πατέρα φαντάζονται, ἀφ' ὧν...Παῦλος ἔγραψε Didym.*Trin.*3.20(M.39.893A); such kingship dist. from his eternal status as king, Ath.*Ar.*1.49(M.26. 113B); **h.** as king over Church, Marcell.*fr.*99 ap.Eus.*Marcell.*2.3 (p.51.30; M.24.809C) cit. s. g; *ib.*(p.51.27; 809C); Ath.*exp.Ps.*67:13 (M.27.296C); ‡Chrys.*hom.in Ps.96*:1(5.613A); as β. τοῦ Ἰσραὴλ *Lit. Ant.*(p.180.3); his function as β. coercing transgressors, dist. from his function as shepherd of willing believers, Bas.*Spir.*17(3.14E; M.32.97A); **3.** of H. Ghost; discussion whether he is king as Father and Son are king καὶ τὸ πνεῦμα β. λέγεις;...πῶς οὐχὶ τὸ πνεῦμα τῆς ζωῆς βασιλεύει ἡμῖν; ἡμεῖς λέγομεν ὅτι ὁ πατήρ ἐστι β. καὶ ὁ υἱός· τὸ δὲ πνεῦμα ὑπηρέτης. ... ὁ γὰρ ὑπηρέτης, κἂν μὴ ᾖ β., τῆς αὐτῆς ἐστι τῷ β. οὐσίας ‡Ath.*Maced.dial.*2.17(M.28.1320A).

C. of the faithful, Clem.*str.*617(p.509.8; M.9.381A); id.*ecl.*44(p.149. 15; M.9.720A); *A.Thom.*A 137(p.244.4); οἱ γὰρ ἐκλεκτοὶ αὐτοῦ χρίονται τὸ ἁγιαστικὸν ἔλαιον, καὶ γίγνονται ἀξιωματικοὶ καὶ β. Mac.Aeg.*hom.* 15.35(M.34.600B).

D. of apostles β. μὲν τοὺς ἄρξαντας ἀποστόλους τῆς κληρονομίας αὐτοῦ φησι Ath.*exp.Ps.*67:15(M.27.297A); Didym.*Ps.*67:15(M.39. 1445B); Thdt.*Ps.*67:15(1.1063); cf. τὴν οἰκουμένην ἅπασαν ἐπέδραμον οἱ ἀπόστολοι,...βασιλέων δυνατώτεροι Chrys.*exp.in Ps.*44:13(5. 181C).

E. of a bishop οὗτος ὑμῶν β. καὶ δυνάστης *Const.App.*2.26.4; *ib.* 2.34.1.

F. of Moses, *Orac.Sib.*11.38.

G. of Melchizedek, Cosm.Ind.*top.*5(M.88.236D); ὁ μόνος ἱερεὺς καὶ β. *ib.*(237A).

H. of man as ruler of creation, Cosm.Ind.*top.*3(M.88.153B).

I. of the philosopher, Clem.*str.*2.19(p.167.20; M.8.1044B).

J. of Devil, *Hom.Clem.*8.22.

K. (Manich.) of rulers of realms of light and darkness, Hegem. *Arch.*7(p.10.1; M.10.1437A).

L. met., of an excellent orator β. σὺ τῶν λόγων Gr.Naz.*ep.*24 (M.37.60B).

II. as adj., *royal* τῷ β. ... πολίσματι Sophr.H.*v.Anast.*(M.92. 1684C); of Father in rel. to H. Ghost μὴ λέγοντες βασιλεύτερον ἢ προγενέστερον αὐτοῦ Didym.*Trin.*2.17(M.39.721B).

βασιλεύ-ω, I. *make king, appoint as king* ἐν χαρᾷ...~ουσιν αὐτόν Ephr.3.138B; Bas.Sel.*or.*14.1(M.85.189A); Jo.Nic.*nativ.*(M.96.1445C).

II. *reign, rule as king, govern*;

A. secular ἡ ~ουσα πόλις (or with ellipse of πόλις) *capital city* as seat of imperial rule; of Rome, Eus.*d.e.*3.7(p.144.10; M.22. 241D); of CP, id.*v.C.*3.47(p.97.13; M.20.1108A); Socr.*h.e.*1.17.13(M. 67.121A); CChalc.*can.*9; Thphn.*chron.*p.35(M.108.145A); *ib.*p.80 (244B); ‡Jo.D.*ep.Thphl.*14(M.95.301D); of Jerusalem as seat of God's rule, *Lit.Jac.*(p.208.22).

B. divine; **1.** of God; in gen., v. βασιλεία; χερουβὶμ καλεῖ πᾶν τὸ δυνατόν· οὕτως λέγει, ὁ καθήμενος ἐπὶ τῶν χερουβίμ, ἀντὶ τοῦ, ὁ δυνατῶς ~ων Thdt.*qu.*40 *in Gen.*(1.55); as reigning over souls of faithful, Or.*or.*25(p.357.3; M.11.496C); **2.** of Christ, v. βασιλεία; **a.** exercising absolute divine sovereignty, Ath.*Ar.*1.46(M.26.108A) cit. s. βασιλεία; **b.** in his 'economic' sovereignty; ref. Ps.96:1 ~ει ὁ κύριος, οὐκ ἀπὸ τοῦ μὴ ~ειν καθάπαξ ἐπὶ τὸ ~ειν ἐληλυθώς, ἀλλ' ἀπὸ τοῦ μὴ ἄρχειν τῶν ἁμαρτανόντων μετανοησάντων ἥκειν ἐπὶ τὴν βασιλείαν Didym.*Ps.*96:1(M.39.1508A); βασιλεῦσαι δὲ τὸν κύριον ἔφη, οὐχ ὡς τὸ τηνικαῦτα τὴν βασιλείαν δεξάμενον, ἀλλ' ὡς τότε τοῖς ἀνθρώποις τὴν οἰκείαν δείξαντα βασιλείαν Thdt.*Ps.*96:1(1.1296); **c.** eternity of Christ's rule, asserted against Marcellus οὐδὲ γὰρ παύεσθαι αὐτὸν τῆς βασιλείας ὁ...ἀπόστολος ἔφη, ἢ γὰρ ἂν τἀναντία ἔγραψε τῷ Γαβριὴλ θεσπίσαντι...~σειν αὐτὸν εἰς τοὺς αἰῶνας...ἀλλὰ παραδώσειν τὴν βασιλείαν, δηλαδὴ τοὺς ὑπ' αὐτῷ ~ομένους, τῷ θεῷ Eus.*e.th.*3.16(p.175.20; M.24.1033B); Cyr.H.*catech.*15.29; Cyr.*Heb.* 12:28(M.74.996C–997B); cf. Χριστὸν σὺν διαβόλῳ ~θησόμενον Jo.D. *haer.*64(M.94.716A); **d.** his reign over all things, Ath.*Ar.*1.49(M.26. 113C); over his people, Eus.*e.th.*3.16(p.175.20; M.24.1033B) etc.; **e.** his reign associated with suffering ἐβασίλευσε...διὰ τοῦ πεπονθέναι τὸν σταυρόν Or.*Jo.*1.38(p.49.11; M.14.100A); **f.** exercised 'from the tree', Just.*1apol.*41.4(M.6.392B); id.*dial.*73.1(M.6.645B); **g.** of Christ's heavenly reign, contrasted with earthly reign of emperors ~όντων Μαξιμιανοῦ καὶ Διοκλητιανοῦ...ἐν οὐρανοῖς δὲ ~οντος τοῦ κυρίου ἡμῶν *M.Das.*12.2; and freq. in *Acta Martyrum*; **3.** of H. Ghost, Gr.Nyss.*or.dom.*3(p.60.21; M.44.1157C); id.*Maced.*16(M.45. 1321B); πῶς οὐχὶ τὸ πνεῦμα τῆς ζωῆς ~ει ἡμῖν; ‡Ath.*Maced.dial.*2.17 (M.28.1320A); **4.** of future reign of saints with Christ οἱ ἀξίως μεταλαμβάνοντες τῶν ἐκεῖ ἀγαθῶν ἀναπαύονται καὶ ἀναπαυόμενοι ~ουσιν *A.Thom.*A 136(p.243.10); ὅταν τοίνυν πάντα τὰ ὀγδοήκοντα ἔτη, ἢ καὶ ἑκατὸν διαμείνωμεν ἐν τῇ ἀσκήσει, οὐκ ἴσα τοῖς ἑκατὸν ἔτεσι ~ομεν, ἀλλ'...αἰῶνας αἰώνων ~ομεν Ath.*v.Anton.*16(M.26.868B); Oecum.*Apoc.*20:4(p.219).

C. of reign of evil powers, esp. of sin and death (cf. Rom.6:12), Or.*or.*25(p.357.22; M.11.497A); Meth.*res.*2.8(p.345.6; M.18.308B); Ath.*inc.*4.4(M.25.104B); ‡Ath.*Maced.dial.*2.17(M.28.1320A); of reign of demons of this world, ‡Chrys.*hom.in Ps.96*:1(5.611E).

***βασιλιδίπολις, ἡ,** *capital city* (cf. βασιλὶς πόλις); of Constantinople, Jo.Nic.*nativ.*(M.96.1448A).

βασιλίζ-ω, 1. *behave like royalty,* of Hagar μετὰ τὸ κυῆσαι τὴν παῖδα, καὶ ~ουσαν ἴσως ἀτιμάσαι τὴν δέσποιναν, ὡς τῆς ἡγεμονίας εἰς τὸν ἐξ αὐτῆς τεχθησόμενον περιστησομένης Isid.Pel.*epp.*2.274(M.78.704C); **2.** *have royal status,* of Rome as imperial city ~ουσα πόλις Bas.Sel.*v.Thecl.*1(M.85.541C).

βασιλικός, I. adj.; **A.** *belonging to a king*; **1.** *of the emperor*; of an imperial edict, v. πρόσταγμα, πρόγραμμα; ἡ β. αὐλή *imperial court,* Iren.*ep.Flor.*ap.Eus.*h.e.*5.20.5(M.20.485A); Epiph.*haer.*64.3(p.405.14; M.41.1073A); β. οἰκία Philost.*h.e.*7.10(M.65.548B); of imperial treasury, †Bas.*Is.*47(1.417A; M.30.209A); imperial robe, Philost.*h.e.*3.22(M.65.512A); β. ὁδός *king's highway, A.Paul.et Thecl.* 3(some MSS only; p.237.4); met., *royal road,* of the *via media* in ethics προσήκει τὸν ἀσκητήν, καὶ τὴν μέσην ὄντως καὶ β. ὁδὸν πορευόμενον, ἐπὶ θάτερα μηδαμῶς ἀποκλίνειν ‡Bas.*const.*4.2(2.546A; M.31.1349B); of way of Lord, Eus.*e.th.*1.8(p.66.1; M.24.837A) cit. s. ὀρθοτομέω; Thdt.*Cant.*7:1(2.140C); *Apophth.Patr.*(M.65.329C); β. πόλις *royal* or *capital city,* Eus.*Marcell.*2.4(p.58.8; M.24.821D); abs. ἡ β. *Chron.Pasch.*p.384(M.92.985B); **2.** ref. God as king; of abodes of blessed after death as royal storehouses (cf. Mt.13:30), †Bas.*Is.* 132(1.471D; M.30.333A); of baptism, like circumcision of Old Covenant, as seal of royal ownership, Thdt.*Cant.*1:2(2.30); Cosm. Ind.*top.*1(M.88.76C); of chrism signifying royal character χρῖσμα δέ, ὡς ἱερὸν καὶ β. Gr.Naz.*or.*40.4(M.36.364A); of Prodigal's robe ὁ ἄσωτος υἱὸς ἐν τῇ ἐπιστροφῇ τὸν β. χιτῶνα περιεβάλετο Anast.S.*hex.* 12(M.89.1053A).

B. *worthy of a king, splendid, excellent,* Eus.*v.C.*1.31(p.22.7; M.20.945B); id.*d.e.*3.4(p.119.8; M.22.204A); Chrys.*hom.1.8 in Mt.* (7.17B); description of β. ἄνθρωπος, Clem.*str.*7.7(p.28.7; M.9.452B); descriptive of man's proper state, Gr.Nyss.*hom.opif.*4(M.44.136C); of the νοῦς βασιλικώτατος, Marc.Er.*opusc.*8(M.65.1008B); medic., of main artery ἡ β. φλέψ ‡Ath.*corp.*(M.28.1433C).

II. as subst.; **A.** *imperial* or *royal official,* Eus.*v.C.*1.16(p.15.26; M.20.932A); *ib.*4.43(p.135.14; 1193A); Jo.Eub.*concept.BMV* 17(M.96.1489A); ὁ β. βασίλειος *CIG* 8811(? saec. viii); β. καὶ σπαθαρίῳ *CIG* 8902; Thdr.Stud.*epp.*2.106(M.99.1364D); ref. Jo.4:46 β. interpreted by Heracleon as type of demiurge ἐπεὶ καὶ αὐτὸς ἐβασίλευεν τῶν ὑπ' αὐτοῦ· διὰ δὲ τὸ μικρὰν αὐτοῦ καὶ πρόσκαιρον εἶναι τὴν βασιλείαν...β. ὠνομάσθη Heracleon ap.Or.*Jo.*13.60(p.291.19; M.14.513A).

B. βασιλική, ἡ (for βασιλικὴ οἰκία) *aisled hall for public business, basilica*; **1.** in gen., Jo.Mal.*chron.*p.318(M.97.476C); **2.** of senate-house built by Constantine κτίσας ἐγγὺς καὶ β. ἔχουσαν κόγχην... ἥνπερ ἐκάλεσεν σενᾶτον *Chron.Pasch.*p.284(M.92.709A); **3.** of a judgement hall, ‡Jo.D.*Artem.*58(M.96.1305B); **4.** of place where Cumaean Sibyl delivered oracles, ‡Just.*coh.Gr.*37(M.6.308A); **5.** of a church β. τῶν πανταχοῦ βελτίονα...τὴν δὲ τῆς β. καμάραν, πότερον λακωναρίαν ἢ δι' ἑτέρας τινὸς ἐργασίας γενέσθαι...δοκεῖ; Const.ap. Eus.*v.C.*3.31f.(p.92.13,27; M.20.1092B,C); *Cod.Afr.*92; *Inscr.*(*BZ* 5 p.160)(Caesarea Palestina, saec. vi).

βασιλίς, ἡ, A. subst., *queen*; **1.** in gen., Eus.*h.e.*2.1.13(M.20.137C); Thdt.*Ps.*79:12(1.1175) etc.; of the empress, Eus.*v.C.*3.43(p.95.25; M.20.1104A); Thdt.*h.e.*5.28.1(3.1069); Evagr.*h.e.*1.20(p.28.26; M.86.2473A); *Hymn.*ap.*Mir.Geo.*(p.150.21); of a princess, Clem.*str.*1.23(p.95.5; M.8.897A); of a royal lady, Thdt.*h.rel.*17(3.1228); **2.** of Church, Eus.*h.e.*10.4.41(M.20.865B); Bas.*hom.in Ps.*44:17(1.169D; M.29.413C); Gr.Naz.*or.*36.6(M.36.273A); μυσταγωγοῦσι [sc. apostles] τὴν β. Cyr.*Ps.*44:11(M.69.1041C); **3.** of BMV, ‡Jo.D.*hom.* 5(M.96.648B); ‡Jo.D.*hom.*6.11(M.96.677C); Andr.Cr.*or.*5(M.97.893B); *ib.*13(1080B); Jo.Eub.*concept.BMV* 14(M.96.1481B); ‡Meth.*Sym.et Ann.*5(M.18.360A); ‡Sophr.H.*triod.*(M.87.3905B); **4.** of soul united to Christ, Mac.Aeg.*ep.*2(M.34.417A); **5.** of a particular quality as 'queen' of virtues, Sophr.H.*nativ.*(p.513) cit. s. διάκρισις; humility, Jo.Clim.*scal.*25(M.88.989B) etc.

B. adj., *royal*; **1.** in gen. τοῖς γε μὴν οὖσιν ἐν εὐπαθείαις καὶ πνευματικοῖς ἀναθήμασιν, τὴν ἁπάντων β. φύσιν ἀντιγεραίρουσιν Cyr.*hom.pasch.*9(5².108E); id.*ador.*2(1.69D); id.*Os.*57(3.89A); *ib.*77(111B); **2.** of man's nature, as sovereign of creation, Gr.Nyss.*hom.opif.*4(M.44.136C); **3.** of Trin., Sophr.H.*ep.syn.*(M.87.3160B); Andr.Caes.*Apoc.*1(M.106.224A); **4.** freq. with πόλις, *capital city*; of Rome, Just.*1 apol.* 26.2(M.6.368A); Eus.*v.C.*1.26(p.20.4; M.20.941A); Bas.*hex.*8.7(1.77E; M.29.181C); of CP, Gr.Naz.*ep.*88(M.37.161C); Evagr.*h.e.*1.17(p.27.2; M.86.2469A); Sophr.H.*mir.Cyr.et Jo.*32(M.87.3524D); of Alexandria, Synes.*provid.*15(p.97.12; M.66.1245C).

βασίλισσα, ἡ, *queen, empress*; **1.** in gen., Tat.*orat.*33(p.35.6; M.6.876A); Pall.*v.Chrys.*9(p.56.8; M.47.32); Cyr.*Pulch.*(5².129B; βασιλίσι p.26.31); **2.** of Church, Meth.*symp.*7.9(p.80.5; M.18.137A) cit. s. ἀναμάρτητος; βασιλέα μὲν καλῶν τὸν Χριστόν, β. δὲ τὴν ἀπὸ τῶν πιστῶν συνεστῶσαν ἐκκλησίαν Thdr.Mops.*Ps.*44:2(p.279.31); Cyr.*Ps.*44:10(M.69.1041B); **3.** of BMV ἡ τεκοῦσα αὐτὸν β. καὶ κυρία καὶ θεοτόκος δογματίζεται ‡Ath.*annunt.*13(M.28.937A); ‡Jo.D.*hom.*5(M.96.653D); Andr.Cr.*or.*14(M.97.1104A); **4.** ἑξήκοντά εἰσι β., καὶ ὀγδοήκοντα παλλακαί (Cant.6:7) interpreted respectively of those who spontaneously desire to follow Christ and of those who act virtuously through fear of punishment, Gr.Nyss.*hom.15 in Cant.* (M.44.1112D); Thdt.*Cant.*6:7(2.127); **5.** met., of city of Rome or perh. of Church εἰς Ῥώμην ὃς ἔπεμψεν ἐμὲ βασιλείαν ἀθρῆσαι καὶ β. ἰδεῖν χρυσόστολον χρυσοπέδιλον Aberc.*epitaph.*8.

βάσιμος, 1. *passable, accessible,* Clem.*str.*5.6(p.348.18; M.9.60A); Bas.*Spir.*66(3.55B; M.32.189A); met. καρδίαν οὐ β., οὐχ ἱππήλατον τοῖς ἀκαθάρτοις πνεύμασιν Cyr.*Joel.*43(3.242D); ἵνα...λιταῖς β. ἀποφήνῃ τὴν τοῦ πατρὸς ἀκοήν id.*apol.Thdt.*10(p.139.22; 6¹.234A); **2.** *possible* β. αὐτῇ τὸ χρῆμα τιθέντος θεοῦ id.*Zach.*41(3.717A); v. βάδιμος; **3.** *clear* πάσης ἀποδείξεως βασιμώτερον ὁμολογίαν καὶ πίστιν διδούς Max.*cap.theol.*9(M.90.1085C).

βάσις, ἡ, 1. *going, movement*; in list of diabolical persons and things, ? *dance* φόνοι, μοιχοί...χάλαζαι, ταραχαί, βάσεις *Contrad.*1 p.5; **2.** *lower part, basis* εἰ μὴ περιλυθείη τῶν τῆς ψυχῆς β. ἡ νεκρὰ... τῶν δερμάτων περιβολή Gr.Nyss.*v.Mos.*(M.45.333A); **3.** *foundation,* met. πεφυκὼς δογμάτων, πατέρ, β. ἀνωμαλούσας δεικνύεις τὰς αἱρέσεις Geo.Pis.*carm.*12.1.

βασκανία, ἡ, 1. *evil eye, bewitchment,* Eus.Al.*serm.*7(M.86.356B); **2.** *jealousy, envy, malignity* β. ἐν ὑμῖν μὴ κατοικείτω Ign.*Rom.*7.2; Meth.*res.*1.43(p.289.16; M.18.272A); οὐδὲν φθόνου χεῖρον καὶ βασκανίας Chrys.*hom.48.1 in Jo.*(8.283A); *ib.83.4*(494D); ἡ παμφάγος... τῆς β. ... φλόξ id.*sac.*3.14(p.73.23; 1.391D); φθόνον...ἐπὶ τοῖς τοῦ πλησίον καλοῖς β. Gennad.*fr.Rom.*1:29(p.360.2; M.85.1669A); coupled with φθόνος as cause of schism, CHier.(335)*ep.*ap.Ath.*syn.*21(p.247.31; M.26.717C); esp. of Devil, ‡Just.*monarch.*1(M.6.313A); Gr.Naz.*carm.*2.2(poem.)1.347(M.37.1476A); Cyr.*Joel.*38(3.235B).

βάσκανος, *envious, malignant,* Mel.*fr.*1.3(p.308; M.5.1212A); β. καὶ πλεονεκτικῷ κεχρημένος ὀφθαλμῷ ‡Hipp.*fr.44 in Pr.*(p.174.1); ὁ β. εἰς ἓν ὁρᾷ μόνον, τὴν ἐπιθυμίαν πληρῶσαι τὴν ἑαυτοῦ Chrys.*hom.55.3 in Jo.*(8.325A); of Cain β. πρῶτος Cyr.H.*catech.*2.7; of Devil, *M.Polyc.*17.1; Gr.Naz.*carm.*1.1.7.66(M.37.441A); *ib.*1.1.27.8(499A); of God ὁ θεὸς δεῖ λέγεσθαι β. Juln.Imp.ap.Cyr.*Juln.*3(6².93E); fig. νεφέλαι...β. πρὸς ὀλίγον τὸ φῶς...ἐπισκιάζουσιν Meth.*symp.*8.4(p.85.14; M.18.144C).

βασκοσύνη, ἡ, *sorcery* διαφύλαξον τὸν οἶκον τοῦτον...ἀπὸ β. πάσης ἀερίνων πνευμάτων *Pap.Chr.*(p.422), saec. iv.

***βασμίδιον, τό,** = βασμίς, Gr.Mag.*dial.*(tr.Zach.)3.24(M.*PL*.77.278B).

βασμίς, ἡ, = βαθμός, Anton.Hag.*v.Sym.Styl.*27(p.64.6).

βασταγάριος, ὁ, *porter, carrier,* Jo.Mal.*chron.*18 p.444(M.97.653C); official of S. Sophia at CP ὁ β., ἵνα βαστᾷ τὸν τῆς ἐκκλησίας ἅγιον εἰς λίτας καὶ ἑορτὰς ἐπισήμους *Euchol.*(p.230).

***βασταγή, ἡ, 1.** *conveyance, transport,* ‡Chrys.*hom.suppl.*3.11(M.64.441C); Cosm.Ind.*top.*1(M.88.97A); *ib.*5(216A); met. μερίμνη τῆς τοῦ ἑαυτῶν κρίματος β. Jo.Clim.*scal.*27(M.88.1108A); **2.** *load* ἔχοντες β. τριάκοντα ἀλόγων Cyr.S.*v.Sab.*59(p.160.4).

***βασταγμός, ὁ,** *lifting, carrying,* Jo.Mal.*chron.*11 p.276(M.97.417C); *Mir.Artem.*30(p.43.1).

***βασταγός,** *capable of endurance,* Jo.Clim.*past.*13(M.88.1196B); Ant.Mon.*hom.*110(M.89.1769D).

βαστάζ-ω, 1. *bear, carry,* met. ἀμφότερα τὰ μυστήρια εἰς αὐτῶν βαστάσαι οὐκ ἦν δυνατός Just.*dial.*111.2(M.6.732B); of man bearing image of God, *Hom.Clem.*3.7; *ib.*11.4; of Christ τὰς ἀσθενείας ἡμῶν βαστάσαντος Gr.Naz.*or.*14.15(M.35.876B); Chrys.*hom.32.3 in Rom.* (9.757D); of the Christian bearing the cross, *V.Pach.Φ* 24(p.15.5); *ib.*74(p.50.9); **2.** *bear* a child, Jo.Thess.*dorm.BMV* 2.13(p.428.14); **3.** *undertake* ἀπορρήτους ἐβάστασα τελετάς Synes.*ep.*57(M.66.1389A); **4.** *tolerate, bear with, endure,* Meth.*symp.*5.7(p.62.7; M.18.109B); Ath.*decr.*8(p.7.23; M.25.429A); Mac.Aeg.*hom.*27.7(M.34.697D); ~ε, καὶ ὅτε θέλει ἰᾶσεταί σε *V.Pach.Φ* 90(p.61.5); ~ω σε τὸ ἅπαξ τοῦτο *ib.*142(p.89.4); **5.** *support, uphold,* lit., Herm.*vis.*3.8.2; id.*sim.*9.4.2; Gel.Cyz.*h.e.*2.7.3(M.85.1232D); met., Meth.*symp.*6.3(p.67.12; M.18.117B).

***βαστακτῶς**, *by being carried*, ref. a drunken man β. ἀποφέρεσθαι Mac.Mgn.*apocr*.3.43(p.149.8).

***βάσταξις, ἡ**, *holding, carrying*, Or.*Jo*.6.36(20; p.145.17; M.14. 261C).

***βατᾶν, τό**, ? *ciborium* πίπτει τὸ β. καὶ ὁ τροῦλλος τῆς ἐκκλησίας Ἐδέσης Thphn.*chron*.p.296(M.108.724B).

βάτος, ὁ, *bath* (Hebrew measure), Epiph.*mens*.21(M.43.272B); Thdt.*qu.21 in 3Reg*.(1.466).

βάτος, ὁ, ἡ, *bramble bush*; **1.** of burning bush (Ex.3:2), *1Clem*. 17.5; Just.*1apol*.62.3(M.6.421C) etc.; interpreted symbolically; **a.** of Israel's survival despite Egyptian persecution, Thdt.*qu.6 in Ex*.(1.122); and Egypt's ferocity, avenged by divine wrath, Eus. *d.e*.5.13(p.237.21; M.22.392C); **b.** of Church's continual renewal after persecution, Thdt.*affect*.9(p.228.1; 4.934); **c.** fact that no image of God could be carved from a β. is reason for God's appearance in bush, id.*qu.6 in Ex*.(1.122); **d.** since β. is a thorny plant, manifestation of Logos to Moses at beginning of process of redemption corresponds to Ascension after crowning with thorns at close of that process, Clem.*paed*.1.8(p.203.17; M.8.488A); **e.** typifying union of human and divine natures in Christ, the humanity remaining entire, Cyr.*glaph.Ex*.1(1.262B); id.*Is*.1.4(2.107D); id.*Chr.un*.(5¹. 737C); cf.Nest.*Heracl*.1.3.228(p.138); *ib*.1.3.229(p.138); *ib*.1.3.234 (p.141); ὥσπερ μία ἦν καὶ ἀδιαίρετος ἡ τῆς...β. ὑπόστασις...ἀβλαβῶς περιειλημμένη τῷ πυρὶ...μηδ' αὐτῆς ἐνεργείας τῆς φλογὸς λυμαινομένης τῷ φυτῷ, οὕτω δὴ ἐν τῷ ἑνικῷ προσώπῳ Χριστοῦ ἀμαχεί μοι νόει τὴν θείαν καὶ ἀνθρωπίνην ἰδιότητα Ephr.Ant.*fr*.(M.86.2108A); cf.Gr.Nyss.*v.Mos*.(M.44.332cf.); **f.** typifying BMV, Gr.Nyss.*nativ*. (M.46.1136B); ‡Epiph.*hom*.5(M.43.493D); Thdt.*qu.6 in Ex*.(1.122); Procl.CP *or.laud.BMV* 1(p.103.14; M.65.681A); Thdot.Anc.*hom*.2.2 (p.74.21; M.77.1372A); †Gregent.*disp*.(M.86.657A); Max.*ambig*.(M. 91.1148D); hence as epithet of BMV, Ephr.3.529D; χαῖρε ἡ β. ἡ καιομένη τῷ νοητῷ πυρί Chrysipp.*enc.in BMV* 1(p.337.9); χαῖρε, β., τὸ πυρίπλοκον θαῦμα Thdr.Stud.*nativ.BMV* 7(M.96.689B); **g.** interpreted by Docetae as denoting the air through which the ἰδέαι descend θεὸν ἀπὸ τοῦ β. λαλήσαντα, τουτέστιν ἀπὸ τοῦ σκοτεινοῦ ἀέρος —β. γάρ ἐστι πᾶς ὁ σκότει ὑποκείμενος ἀήρ—...εἴρηκεν Μωϋσῆς, ὅτι ἄνωθεν κάτω πᾶσαι διέβησαν τοῦ φωτὸς αἱ ἰδέαι βατὸν ἔχουσαι τὸν ἀέρα· οὐδὲν δὲ ἧττον καὶ ἡμῖν ὁ λόγος ἀπὸ τοῦ β. γνωρίζεται· φωνὴ γάρ ἐστι σημαντικὴ τοῦ λόγου πλησσόμενος ἀήρ, οὗ δίχα λόγος ἀνθρώπινος οὐ γνωρίζεται Hipp.*haer*.8.9(p.228.28; M.16.3354A); **h.** as symbol of Christ's redemptive work πῦρ τὸ διὰ βάτου σύμβολόν ἐστι φωτὸς ἁγίου τοῦ διαβαίνοντος ἐκ γῆς καὶ ἀνατρέχοντος αὖθις εἰς οὐρανὸν διὰ τοῦ ξύλου Clem.*str*.1.24(p.103.5; δι' ἀβάτου M.8.912A); **i.** as type of Christian altar τύπος τῆς τραπέζης τῆς μυστικῆς ἡ β.· τύπος δὲ τῶν ἁμαρτημάτων τὰ ὑποδήματα *Pers.capt*.(M.86.3244C); **2.** name of monastery on site of burning bush, ‡Nil.*narr*.4(M.79.628A).

***βατραχώδης**, *frog-like* β. ... φωνάς Gr.Nyss.*Eun*.2(2 p.361.4; M. 45.540B); *plagued by frogs* τῆς β. ζωῆς id.*v.Mos*.(M.44.348C); met., *filthy, corrupt*, *ib*.(345D,348D).

βατταρίζ-ω, *stutter*; hence **1.** *babble, talk foolishly*, Cyr.*Juln*.10 (6².332D); id.*resp*.18(6.388B); Porphyry ap.Thdt.*affect*.1(p.13.3; 4. 702B); med., Nil.*epp*.3.229(M.79.489C); **2.** *say foolishly* μυρία δεινὰ ~οντες Sophr.H.*ep.syn*.(M.87.3181B); εἴδωλα τὰς σεβασμίους εἰκόνας ~οντας ‡Jo.D.*ep.Thphl*.21(M.95.373A); Thdr.Stud.*epp*.1.8(M.99. 937A).

[*]**βαττάρισμα, τό**, *stammering*; hence *babbling, nonsensical talk*, Taras.*ep*.5(M.98.1465C); Thdr.Stud.*epp*.2.154(M.99.1480A); *ib*.2.162 (1505C).

βαττολογ-έω, *speak stammeringly*; hence **1.** *babble foolishly*, in gen. μὴ ἐπιστάμενος, ἀλλὰ ~ῶν καὶ λέγων Dam.*troph*.2.4.4(p.224.11); esp. of 'vain repetition' in prayer (Mt.6:7) προσευχόμενοι μὴ ~ήσωμεν ἀλλὰ θεολογήσωμεν Or.*or*.21(p.345.3; M.11.480C); Gr.Nyss. *or.dom*.1(p.16.32; M.44.1129B); Didym.*Trin*.3.10(M.39.857B); Chrys. *hom.43.2 in Jo*.(8.257D); **2.** *say foolishly, prate* τοιαῦτα ~οῦσι Ath. *Ar*.1.8(M.26.25C); Chrys.*hom.2.5 in Mt*.(7.29C); ‡Nil.*perist*.6.1(M. 79.856A).

***βαττολογητέον**, *one must babble, use 'vain repetitions'* in prayer, Or.*or*.8(p.316.26; M.11.441B).

βαττολογία, ἡ, *stammering speech*; hence *unintelligent utterance, foolish babbling* οὐκ ἔστι λόγος, ἀλλὰ β.· ὡς ἂν τις Ἑλληνικώτερον ἑρμηνεύων εἴποι τὸν νοῦν, φλυαρία Gr.Nyss.*or.dom*.1(p.12.36; M.44. 1128A); Chrys.*hom.19.3 in Mt*.(7.249A); Ast.Soph.*hom.1 in Ps*.5(M. 40.397B).

***βαττόλογος**, *speaking stammeringly*; hence *speaking foolishly, babbling* λῆρός τίς ἐστι καὶ β. Gr.Nyss.*or.dom*.1(p.14.28; M.44.1128C); Chrys.*hom.in Mt*.7:14(3.27C).

***βαῦδος, ἡ**, (Hebr. בַּד) *branch* βαστάζων β. ἐξ ἰτέας κατέστρεψε τοὺς λάκκους διὰ τῆς β. *Ev.Thom*.B 2.2.

βαυκάλη, βαύκαλις, ἡ, Alexandrian name for a fat, narrow-necked, earthenware vessel, Philost.*h.e*.1.4(M.65.464A); hence used as nickname of Alexander, an Alexandrian presbyter, *ib*.(462C); also name of a church in Alexandria of which Arius was presbyter, Epiph.*haer*.68.4(p.144.5; M.42.189B); *ib*.69.1(p.152.21; 201D).

βαυκάλιον, τό, dim. of foreg., Pall.*h.Laus*.(p.50.13, v.l. καυκάλιον M.34.1057A); *Apophth.Patr*.(M.65.276C); *ib*.(169D); also καυκάλιον *ib*.(205B); Cyr.S.*v.Sab*.19(p.31.4); Jo.Mosch.*prat*.19(M.87.2865B).

βαφή, ἡ, **1.** *dipping*, of baptism διὰ τῆς ἁγνοτάτης β. ἀναγεννηθῆναι θεῷ *Hom.Clem*.7.8; **2.** *dyeing*; met., *colour, tincture* ἀποσπᾶσαι τῆς ψυχῆς αὐτοῦ τὴν ἀπὸ τοῦ λόγου ἐγγινομένην β. Or.*Jo*.32.22(14; p.465.12; M.14.805A).

βδέλυγμα, τό, *object of loathing, abomination*; **1.** in gen.; of body afflicted by disease, Philost.*h.e*.7.13(M.65.549D); of evil speech ὅσα κακῶς λέγομεν βδελύγματά εἰσιν ἐν τῷ στόματι ἡμῶν Or. *hom.5.11 in Jer*.(p.40.13; M.13.309C); of immoral practices in gen., †Bas.*Is*.82(1.436A; M.30.253A); of human pride β. ἔναντι κυρίου Thdt.*Ezech*.28:1(2.908); **2.** esp. of idols, †Bas.*Is*.82(1.436B; M.30. 253A); Cyr.*ador*.1(1.41A); Thdt.*qu.3 in 4 Reg*.(1.513); and paganism in gen. ἐπιμιγήσεσθε ἐν βδελύγμασιν ἐθνῶν *T.Jud*.23.2; Ath.*gent*.27 (M.25.52C); *Const.App*.2.22.8; **3.** β. ἐρημώσεως *abomination of desolation* (Dan.11:31, Mt.24:15) Νέρων...ἐν τῇ ἁγίᾳ πόλει Ἱερουσαλὴμ ἔστησεν τὸ 'β.' Clem.*str*.1.21(p.79.3; M.8.857A); δύο οὖν β. προείρηκεν Δανιήλ, ἓν μὲν ἀφανισμοῦ, ἓν δὲ ἐρημώσεως. τί τὸ τοῦ ἀφανισμοῦ ἀλλ' ἢ ὃ ἔστησεν ἐκεῖ κατὰ τὸν καιρὸν ὁ Ἀντίοχος; καὶ τί τὸ τῆς ἐρημώσεως, ἀλλ' ἢ τὸ καθ' ὅλου, ὡς πάρεσται ὁ ἀντίχριστος; Hipp.*Dan*.4.54.1(M.10.665B); ἐπὶ τέλει [i.e. at fall of Jerusalem to Titus] τὸ...β. τῆς ἐρημώσεως ἐν αὐτῷ κατέστη τῷ πάλαι τοῦ θεοῦ περιβοήτῳ νεῷ Eus.*h.e*.3.5.4(M.20.224B); β. ἐρημώσεως καθολικῶς ὁ ἀντίχριστος, γέγονε δὲ καὶ β. τῆς ἐρημώσεως Ἱερουσαλὴμ ἡ εἰκὼν Καίσαρος, ἣν ἀνέστησε Πιλᾶτος ἐν τῷ ναῷ Thdr.Heracl.*fr.Mt*.24:15 (p.196.33); τὸν ἀνδριάντα τοῦ τότε τὴν πόλιν ἑλόντος φησίν, ὃ ὁ ἐρημώσας τὴν πόλιν καὶ τὸν ναὸν ἔστησεν ἔνδον Chrys.*hom.75.2 in Mt*.(7.726B); τὰς προρρήσεις...τὰς περὶ τῆς ἁλώσεως τῶν Ἱεροσολύμων, ἅς...ὁ Δανιὴλ τοῦ β. τῆς ἐρημώσεως μνησθείς...προανεφώνησαν id.*hom.4.9 in Ac.princ*.(3.96B); πρῶτον μὲν εἰσενήνεκται τὸ 'β. τῆς ἐρημώσεως' εἰς τὸν...νεών, ὅτε τὸν βωμὸν τῷ Διῒ ἀνέστησεν ὁ δυσσεβὴς βασιλεὺς Ἀντίοχος· καὶ χοῖρον γὰρ ἐν αὐτῷ προσενήνοχεν εἰς θυσίαν... εἶτα...Πιλᾶτος ἡγεμονεύων...νύκτωρ εἰς τὸν...ναὸν τὰς βασιλικὰς εἰσεκόμισεν εἰκόνας, παρὰ τὸν θεῖον νόμον. μετὰ τούτους δὲ ἐπὶ τῆς συντελείας τοῦτο γενήσεται· τὸ γὰρ ἀληθινὸν 'β. τῆς ἐρημώσεως' τοῦ κόσμου, ἤτοι 'ὁ ἄνθρωπος τῆς ἀνομίας...', λέγω δὴ ὁ ἀντίχριστος, καθεσθήσεται εἰς τὸν ἐν Ἱεροσολύμοις ναὸν βλασφημῶν Thdt.ap.*cat. Mt*.24:15(p.197.3); cf.id.*Dan*.11:31(2.1284); *ib*.9:27(1251); ἀνδριάντος ὃν ἐν τῷ ναῷ καθίδρυσε [sc. Titus] ‡Bas.Sel.*or*.38.4(M.85.416A); spiritual interpretation μένει δὲ μόνον ἐν τῷ ναῷ τὸ εἴδωλον τῆς ἁμαρτίας, περὶ οὗ φησὶν ὁ κύριος· 'ὅταν ἴδητε τὸ β. τῆς ἐρημώσεως,' ...ὅτι δὲ τόπος ἅγιος καὶ ναὸς ὁ νοῦς ὑπάρχει τοῦ ἀνθρώπου, μαρτυρεῖ ὁ Παῦλος Thal.ap.*cat.Mt*.24:15(p.197.25); of Arius ἔπεμψ' Ἄρειον τὸ β. ἐρημίας Gr.Naz.*carm*.2.1.11.578(M.37.1069A).

βδελυγμία, ἡ, *filth, nastiness*, Chrys.*hom.73.3 in Mt*.(7.711C); Nil. *epp*.3.4(M.79.365B); Thdt.*qu.3 in 4 Reg*.(1.513).

***βδελύζομαι**, *loathe*, Jo.Clim.*scal*.1(M.88.637D).

βδελυκτός, *abhorred, loathsome* πᾶν σχίσμα β. ἦν ὑμῖν *1Clem*.2.6; β. ἐπιθυμίας *ib*.30.1; ἀκάθαρτα καὶ β. βρώματα Or.*Jo*.5.8(p.105.10; M.14.196A); ἐὰν εἴδητε ἑαυτοὺς...β. id.*mart*.39(p.36.13; M.11.613C); τοῖς δικαίοις...ἡ ἀδικία β. Meth.*symp*.8.16(p.105.19; M.18.169A); of heresies, Ath.*Ar*.1.1(M.26.13B); id.*syn*.20(p.247.10; M.26.717A); esp. of Manicheans, Isid.Pel.*epp*.1.52(M.78.216A); ‡Gr.Nyss.*hom.7 in Jo*. (p.242.26).

***βδέλυξις, ἡ**, *loathing*, Ant.Mon.*hom*.7(M.89.1453B).

***βδελυρωπός**, *foul-visaged*, Eudoc.*Cypr*.1.94(M.85.836C).

βδελύσσ-ομαι, *abhor* τῆς...ταύτης τάξεως...ἐβδέλυκται ἡ ἐνέργεια Serap.Ant.ap.Eus.*h.e*.5.19.2(M.20.481A); ~εται...τὸ ἅγιον μολύνεσθαι Clem.*paed*.2.10(p.217.11; M.8.517A); τῶν ~ομένων τὸν γάμον id.*str*. 3.6(p.219.28; M.8.1153B); ὁ νόμος...οὐ β. ... ἀνθρώπου γένεσιν *ib*. 3.12(p.234.10; 1184B); β. τὴν παιδουργίαν Meth.*symp*.2.2(p.17.6; M. 18.49B); Μανιχαῖον...βδελυξόμεθα Isid.Pel.*epp*.1.245(M.78.332C).

***βεβαιόπιστος**, *firmly believing, steadfast in the faith*, Marc.Er. *opusc*.2.1(M.65.929C); Nil.*epp*.3.319(M.79.537C); Leont.N.*mesopent*. 1(M.93.1580C); β. γνώμῃ Thdr.Stud.*epp*.2.178(M.99.1553A).

βέβαιος, *firm, steadfast, reliable*; of the faithful, *confident, sure*, Just.*1apol*.12.10(M.6.345A); id.*dial*.35.2(M.6.549C); of Church, *firmly established*, *1Clem*.47.6; *secure, valid*, of eucharist ἐκείνη β.

εὐχαριστία ἡγείσθω, ἡ ὑπὸ τὸν ἐπίσκοπον οὖσα...ἵνα...ᾖ...β. πᾶν ὃ πράσσετε Ign.*Smyrn*.8.1,2; of baptism, ‡Just.*qu.et resp*.14(M.6.1261C).

βεβαίωσις, ἡ, 1. *firm establishment* τοῦ θεοῦ λόγου, τὴν ἐπὶ τῆς ἐκκλησίας...στάσιν τε καὶ β., ἣν ὄρος ἐλαιῶν...ὀνομάζει Eus.*d.e*.6.18(p.277.17; M.22.456C); Gennad.*fr.Gen*.49:9(M.85.16–7D); **2.** *assurance* πειθὼ ἡ β. τῆς πίστεως Clem.*str*.1.11(p.34.3; M.8.749B); ἐὰν δὲ γένηται [sc. ἡ ψυχή] ἐν β. τῆς μακαριότητος ὥστε ἀνεπίδεκτος εἶναι τοῦ θανάτου Or.*dial*.26(p.170.20); *certainty*, Philox.*ep*.30(p.179); **3.** *guarantee* ἔστιν οἷον εἰπεῖν ἔγγραφος διδασκαλίας β. Clem.*ecl*.27(p.145.1; M.9.712C); ἀμὴν ἀμὴν...μετὰ διορισμοῦ καὶ β. Chrys.*hom.44.1 in Jo*.(8.258C); Gel.Cyz.*h.e*.2.33.5(M.85.1337B); **4.** *affirmation* τό, ὡς, πῇ μὲν ἐπὶ ὁμοιώσεως εἴληπται παρὰ τῇ...γραφῇ· πῇ δὲ ἐπὶ β. ...τὸ δεύτερον· ὡς ἀγαθὸς ὁ θεός Thdr.Stud.*epp*.2.65(M.99.1288A).

***βεβαιωσύνη, ἡ,** *firm assurance*, Ign.*Philad*.proem.

***βεβαιωτικῶς,** *in an affirmative sense*, Thdr.Stud.*epp*.2.65(M.99.1288B).

βεβασανισμένως, *with severe scrutiny*, Or.*Cels*.2.51(p.174.15; M.11.877B); *ib*.3.38(p.234.22; 969A).

βέβηλος, *profane, unhallowed*, in gen. β. γενόμενος καταλείπει ἁγιασμόν Or.*hom.17.3 in Jer*.(p.147.10; M.13.457C); defined as γαστρίμαργος, ἀκρατής, κοσμικός, τὰ πνευματικὰ ἀπεμπολῶν Chrys.*hom.31.1 in Heb*.(12.286A); β. ... τὸ μὴ ἅγιον, τουτέστι τὸ κοινόν Thdt.*Is*.56:2(p.220.32; 2.365); β. ... τὸ κοινὸν καὶ τῶν θείων κεχωρισμένον id.*Ezech*.22:26(2.852); of persons τὰ λόγια μεταδώσομεν β. καὶ ἀναξίοις ἀνδράσιν Hipp.*antichr*.1.1(p.4.14; M.10.728B); of sacrifices offered to idols βρώματα...τῇ ἰδίᾳ φύσει λιτὰ ὄντα, τῇ ἐπικλήσει τῶν δαιμόνων β. γίνεται Cyr.H.*catech*.19.7; β. τῆς ἀπωλείας...βρώματα *M.Sab*.6.3.

βεβηλ-όω, *profane, make common* ἵνα μὴ ~ωθῇ τὸ ὄνομα αὐτοῦ Just.*dial*.21.1(M.6.520B); Thdr.Heracl.*Is*.57:15(M.18.1364A); Ath.*Ar*.3.1(M.26.324A); hence *defile, pollute* ~οῦνται πάντως αἱ ὁδοί Cyr.*Ps*.9:25(M.69.781A); Jo.Mon.*hymn.Nic.Myr*.6(M.96.1385D).

βεβήλωσις, ἡ, 1. *profanation*; of sabbath desecration, Epiph.*haer*.19.5(p.222.21; M.41.268B); idolatrous worship, Cyr.*Os*.5(3.107E); pagan mythology, id.*Zach*.4(743A); **2.** *pollution*, Meth.*symp*.6.1(p.65.3; M.18.113C).

βεβιασμένως, 1. *by compulsion*, Eus.*p.e*.6.6(250B; M.21.425B); **2.** *by violence*, Iren.*haer*.1.16.3(M.7.633B); of forced exegesis, Meth.*res*.1.54(p.310.14; M.41.1129A); Eus.*p.e*.1.9(32A; M.21.72D).

***βεελζεβούλ, ὁ,** *Beelzebul* (cf. Mt.12:24), Hipp.*haer*.6.33(p.162.3; M.16.3243D); Cyr.*Os*.3(3.65E); β. τῶν δαιμονίων ὁ ἔξαρχος *T.Sal*.3.6(M.122.1320D).

***βελία, βελίαρ, ὁ,** *Beliar*, a name of Devil (cf. 2Cor.6:15 and OT *Belial*) υἱοὶ Βελίαρ Or.*Cels*.6.43(p.113.29; M.11.1365A); Βελίῃ γὰρ ἐμὸς νόος ἐστὶν ἐδητύς Gr.Naz.*carm*.2.1.345(M.37.996A); Βελίαρ, τῇ Ἑβραϊκῇ φωνῇ τὸν ἀποστάτην καλέσας οὕτως Chrys.*hom.13.3 in 2Cor*.(10.533D); φεῦγ' ἀπ' ἐμῶν μελέων, ὄφι, πῦρ, Βελίαρ κακορέκτα *CIG* 9065.

βελοθήκη, ἡ, *quiver*, Or.*enarr.in Job* 2:10(M.17.61C); interpreted mystically of flesh assumed by Logos, Eus.*Is*.49:2(M.24.429C); met. τῇ β. τῆς ἀληθείας χρησάμενος Nil.*epp*.1.147(M.79.144C); of the armoury of the Devil, ‡Chrys.*pent*.1(3.791B) cit. s. ἐκκλησία; ‡Nil.*perist*.10.7(M.79.900C); Cosm.Mel.*schol*.(M.38.409) in Gr.Naz.*carm*.2.1.19.31.

βέλος, τό, *arrow, dart*; of divine vengeance, *Hom.Clem*.16.20; by means of disease βέλει θεοῦ πεπυρωμένῳ πληγεὶς πρηνὴς ἔκειτο Eus.*v.C*.1.58(p.35.16; M.20.973A); exeg. Ps.37:3 οἱ λόγοι τοῦ κυρίου β. εἰσίν...ὁ λέγων οὖν τὸν λόγον τοῦ κυρίου β. ἀφίησι· καὶ ἐπὰν λέγῃ ἐπιστρεπτικά, τῷ β. τούτῳ τιτρώσκει τὸν...ἀκροατήν Or.*Ps*.37:3(p.14) = Didym.*Ps*.37:3(M.39.1341B); δηλοῖ δέ ποτε τὰς κολάσεις τὰ β. καί ποτε δὴ καὶ τὰ πεπυρωμένα β. τοῦ διαβόλου...τὰ πρὸς ἐπιθυμίαν κινήσαντα *ib*.(p.15) ∞ Didym.*Ps*.37:3(1341B); δοκεῖ τὰ ἐνταῦθα λεγόμενα β. λογικὰ εἶναι· μᾶλλον δὲ αὐτοὺς τοὺς τοῦ θεοῦ λόγους, νύττοντας καὶ τιτρώσκοντας...τὴν ψυχήν, καὶ τὴν συνείδησιν ...κολάζοντας †Bas.*hom.in Ps*.37(1.364C; M.30.88B); Cyr.*Ps*.37:3(M.69.956A); exeg. Ps.90:5 β. ἐν ἡμέρᾳ πετόμενον, τὴν ὡς ἐν φωτὶ καὶ ἐναργῶς ἐπιβουλήν *ib*.90:5(1220A); exeg. Job 6:4 ὁ Ἰὼβ τὰ τοῦ διαβόλου β.,...ἐπειδὴ κατὰ συγχώρησιν ἐγίγνετο τοῦ θεοῦ, β. κυρίου ὠνόμασεν †Bas.*hom.in Ps*.37(364D; M.88C); β. γὰρ τὰς τιμωρίας λέγει Olymp.*Job* 6:4(M.93.88D); exeg. Is.49:2 πλεῖστα μὲν γὰρ τὰ τοῦ θεοῦ β. γεγόνασι, καὶ ὑπὲρ πάντα Χριστὸν κρυπτόμενον μέν,..., ὡς ἐν φαρέτρᾳ τῇ προγνώσει τοῦ πατρὸς Cyr.*Is*.4.4(2.658A); τοῦτο τὸ ἐκλεκτὸν β. ἀναιρεῖ...τὸν σατανᾶν...ἀναιρεῖ δὲ...τοὺς τῆς ἀληθείας ἐχθρούς,...τιτρώσκει δὲ...εἰς ὄνησίν τε καὶ σωτηρίαν *ib*.(658B); β. ... αὐτὸν τὸν τιτρώσκοντα τὰς ἐρώσας αὐτοῦ ψυχάς Thdt.*Is*.49:2(p.193.20; 2.348); τέθειται δὲ καὶ β. ... ἐκλεκτόν, ἵνα τιτρώσκῃ τοὺς ἀξίους τῶν...κέντρων...ὃ καὶ αὐτό, ὡς ἐν φαρέτρᾳ λανθάνει τῇ σαρκί, ἣν ἀνείληφεν, τοῖς ἀξίοις μόνοις ὁρώμενον Proc.G.*Is*.49:2(M.87.2464C); exeg. Eph.6:16 β. τοῦ πονηροῦ οἱ πονηροί εἰσι διαλογισμοί Or.*comm.in Eph*.6:16(p.574); ‡Bas.*const*.17.2(2.559E; M.31.1380B); β. δὲ αὐτοῦ καὶ τοὺς πειρασμούς φησι, καὶ τὰς ἐπιθυμίας τὰς ἀτόπους Chrys.*hom.24.1 in Eph*.(11.180B); exeg. 2Cor.10:3 οὐ σαρκικὰ τῶν ἁγίων τὰ β., πνευματικὰ δὲ μᾶλλον καὶ δυνατὰ τῷ θεῷ, χρήσιμά τε πρὸς καθαίρεσιν ὀχυρωμάτων, τῶν ἑλληνικῶν δογμάτων...καὶ αἱρετικῶν Cyr.*2Cor*.10:3(p.358.8; M.74.948C); of the 'dart of love' (exeg. Cant.2:5) Gr.Nyss.*hom.4 in Cant*.(M.44.852B); *ib*.5(860A) cit. s. ἀγάπη; τὸ ἐκλεκτὸν β. ἐν τῇ καρδίᾳ δεξαμένη διὰ τῆς γλυκείας πληγῆς *ib*.6(889A); *ib*.13(1045B) cit. s. τιτρώσκω; Cyr.*fr.Cant*.2:6(M.69.1281D); Thdt.*Cant*.2:5 cit. s. τιτρώσκω.

βελοστασία, ἡ, *battery of warlike engines*, fig. β. τῆς γαστριμαργίας ‡Chrys.*hom.in Lc*.15:11(10.839C).

βελτιότης, ἡ, *superior goodness*, Epiph.*haer*.64.67(p.509.18).

βελτι-όω, *improve*, in gen. κακουργουμένη σιτίοις καὶ ποτοῖς ἡ ψυχὴ ~οῦται *Diogn*.6.9; ἐνδιατριβὴ...τοῦ...πάσχα ὀλίγῳ ~ουμένη παρ' αὐτὸ καὶ κρείττων τυγχάνουσα Or.*Jo*.10.19(14; p.190.19; M.14.340C); τῶν ὑπὸ τῆς δυνάμεως τοῦ σωτῆρος ~ωθέντων *ib*.13.61(59; p.293.32; 516D); Ath.*ep.Afr*.7(M.26.1041B) cit. s. μιμέομαι; τῇ προσθήκῃ τῆς ...ἐπιγνώσεως ~ούμεθα †Bas.*Is*.225(1.549D; M.30.512B); Christol. φαίνεται γὰρ μηδὲν ~ώσας αὐτὸς τὴν σάρκα, ἀλλὰ μᾶλλον αὐτὸς δι' αὐτῆς ~ωθείς, εἴ γε...τότε ὑψώθη καὶ υἱὸς ἐλέχθη, ὅτε γέγονεν ἄνθρωπος Ath.*Ar*.1.38(M.26.89C); τὸν Χριστὸν...ἐκ προκοπῆς ἔργων ~ωθέντα Justn.*conf*.11(p.92.28; M.86.1017A).

βελτίωσις, ἡ, *improvement*, ref. Arian doctrine of Son εἰ μὲν οὖν κατὰ τὴν πρώτην [sc. διάνοιαν i.e. in sense of 'son by grace'] οἷοί εἰσι καὶ οἱ ἐκ β. τρόπων ἐπικτώμενοι τὴν τοῦ ὀνόματος χάριν...ἵνα υἱοὶ θεοῦ γένωνται...οὐδὲν διαφέρειν ἡμῶν δόξειεν Ath.*decr*.6(p.6.12; M.25.425C); ἐξ ἀρετῆς ἄρα καὶ β. ταῦτα ἐσχηκώς, εἰκότως ἐλέχθη διὰ ταῦτα...υἱός,...καὶ οὐκ ἔστιν ἀληθινὸς υἱός id.*Ar*.1.37(M.26.89A); εἰ ἐξ ἀρετῆς ἕπεται τὸ θέλειν καὶ τὸ μὴ θέλειν, καὶ τρόπων β., ὅμοιος καθ' ὑμᾶς ὁ υἱός ἐστι τῷ πατρί· ταῦτα δὲ ποιότητος ἴδια· δηλονότι σύνθετον τὸν θεὸν ἐκ ποιότητος καὶ οὐσίας λέγετε id.*ep.Afr*.8(M.26.1044B).

***βελτιωτής, ὁ,** *improver, reformer*, Cyr.*thes*.13(5^{1}.129B).

***βελτιωτικός,** *making better, improving*; of philosophy and contemplation, Clem.*str*.7.1(p.4.15ff.; M.9.405A).

***βενετίζω,** *be a supporter of the Blues* (circus and political faction), Thphn.*chron*.p.156(M.108.424A).

***βενεφίκιον, τό,** (Lat. *beneficium*) *gift, bribe*, CNic.(325)*can*.12.

***βέργιον, τό,** *rod, wand*, *Mir.Artem*.25(p.35.26).

***βέργος, τό,** *osier, withy* εἴς τι χαλάδριον βέργεσι πεπλεγμένον τοῦτον ἐνθέμενοι *V.Max*.39(M.90.108B).

βέρεδον, τό, (Lat. *veredus*) *post-horse*, Jo.Mal.*chron*.15 p.377(M.97.561A).

[*]βεριδάριος ([*]βηρι-), ὁ, (Lat. *veredarius*) *courier* βηρι- *Ep.Aeg*.ap.Ath.*apol.sec*.77(p.157.11; M.25.388C); Thphn.*chron*.p.162(M.108.437A).

***βέρνακλος, ὁ,** (Lat. *vernaculus*) *public slave*, Jo.Mal.*chron*.7 p.187(M.97.297A).

***βεστήτωρ, ὁ,** (Lat. *vestitor*) *keeper of the wardrobe*, Thphn.*chron*.p.191(M.108.497C; βεστίτορες de Boor); Thdr.Stud.*epp*.2.114 tit.(M.99.1380C).

***βεστιάριον, τό,** (Lat. *vestiarium*); **1.** *wardrobe* πραιποσίτῳ β. *CIG* 8903(Nicaea); **2.** *clothing*, Phot.*nomoc*.2.1(M.104.569A).

***βεστιάριος, ὁ,** (Lat. *vestiarius*) *keeper of the wardrobe*, Thdr.Stud.*iamb*.15(M.99.1785B); *MAMA* 3.287.

βεστίον, τό, (Lat. *vestis*) *clothing*, Jo.Mal.*chron*.13 p.323(M.97.484A).

***βετερᾶνος, ὁ,** (Lat. *veteranus*) *discharged soldier*, ‡Ath.*serm.fid*.1(M.26.1265A).

***βῆλον, τό,** (Lat. *velum*); **1.** *curtain, hanging*; placed before, or instead of, a door, *A.Thom*.A 98(p.211.5); *T.Job* 25(p.118.10); esp. of curtain screening imperial presence-chamber, Ath.*apol.Const*.3(M.25.600C); Cyr.S.*v.Sab*.51(p.142.17); or screening emperor's bed-chamber, Jo.Mal.*chron*.14 p.355(M.97.529A); of curtain enclosing judicial *secretarium*, so arranged as to screen off both court-room and antechamber, *M.Eupl*.1.1; cf.Chrys.*hom.5.4 in 2Tim*.(11.690C); used in churches as door-curtain or sanctuary-screen, Ath.*h.Ar*.56(p.214.36; M.25.760D); **2.** *banner*; used to decorate streets for imperial progresses, Leont.N.*serm*.1(M.93.1568B); hung out at hippodrome as sign that races were being held, Jo.Mal.*chron*.18 p.474(M.97.689B) al.; **3.** *veil*, used as mark of honour for saint's image [sc. τὴν εἰκόνα] ἰδόντες μετὰ φώτων καὶ β. δοξαζομένην Arc.C.*v.Sym*.(M.94.1393D).

βῆμα, τό, A. *step, going*; hence **1.** *gait*, Clem.*fr*.44(p.221.28); Chrys.*hom.72.4 in Mt*.(7.704A); **2.** met., *way of life* περὶ β. καὶ λόγου ἄργου ἀπολογίαν δώσουσι Ephr.2.94B; **3.** *pace*; as measure of length, Chrys.*hom.48.1 in Gen.*(4.481B); Pall.*h.Laus.*47(p.136.14; M.34.1196A); id.*v.Chrys.*10(p.62.18; M.47.36).

B. *platform*; **1.** *rostrum* τραγικῇ φωνῇ ἀνεβόησεν ἐπὶ τὸ β. ἀναβάς Just.*2apol.*12.11(M.6.465A); Jo.Mal.*chron.*13 p.329(M.97.492B); **2.** *tribunal* of magistrate, *Ep.Lugd.*ap.Eus.*h.e.*5.1.29(M.20.420B); Ath.*ep.encycl.*5(p.173.10; M.25.232A); erected by Paul of Samosata in imitation of secular magistrates, Malch.*ep.*ap.Eus.*h.e.*7.30.9(712C); of judgment-seat of God, *Orac.Sib.*8.82; Pall.*v.Chrys.*4(p.27.2; M.47.17); Cyr.*Os.*140(3.173E); *Lit.Jac.*(p.218.13); of Christ, Chrys.*hom.82.4 in Jo.*(8.488D); λέγεται [sc. τὸ θυσιαστήριον] παρὰ πᾶσι καὶ β., διὰ τὸ μέλλον τοῦ Χριστοῦ β. Jo.Jej.*liturg.*(p.441); προσευχή ἐστι...β. κυρίου, πρὸ τοῦ β. μέλλοντος Jo.Clim.*scal.*28(M.88.1129B); παραδίδωμι ἐμαυτὴν τῷ φοβερῷ καὶ φρικτῷ β. τοῦ Χριστοῦ Marc.Diac.*v.Porph.*67; met. δίκαζε τοὺς λογισμοὺς ἐν τῷ β. τῆς καρδίας Nil.*Eulog.*12(M.79.1108D); **3.** hence, met., *legal business* τοῖς ἄλλο τι θεραπεύουσιν ἀντὶ τοῦ β. Synes.*ep.*104(M.66.1476C); *judicial authority* of a bishop, Gr.Naz.*or.*17.8(M.35.976A).

C. eccl.; **1.** *tribune, chancel, sanctuary* of church (i.e. raised platform whereon stood altar and seats of bishop and other clergy, for whom access to it was exclusively reserved) οὐ δεῖ πρεσβυτέρους πρὸ τοῦ ἐπισκόπου καθέζεσθαι ἐν τῷ β. CLaod.*can.*56; μετῆλθες εἰς τὸ β. καὶ κρατεῖς θρόνου Gr.Naz.*carm.*2.1.12.437(M.37.1197A); id.*or.*40.46(M.36.425A); *Lit.*ap.*Const.App.*8.11.10; οὐρανίων δυνάμεων ἅπαν τὸ β. καὶ ὁ περὶ τὸ θυσιαστήριον πληροῦται τόπος Chrys.*sac.*6.4(p.147.18; 1.424C); id.*hom.31.2 in Rom.*(9.746D); τοῦ θείου τῶν ἀρχιερέων β. Thdt.*haer.*4(4.371); ἀντὶ τοῦ σπηλαίου τὸ ἱερατικὸν ἀσπασώμεθα β. Procl.CP *or.*17.2(M.65.809C); εἰσέρχεται εἰς τὸ ἅγιον β., καὶ θυμιάσας τὴν τράπεζαν *Lit.Chrys.*(p.361.27); ἐντὸς τοῦ ἁγίου β. *Euchol.*(p.5); of sanctuaries of martyrs, Gr.Naz.*or.*7.15 (M.35.773C); *ib.*44.12(M.36.620C); β. likened to place of Christ's session with apostles because of arrangement of presbyters' seats on either side of bishop's chair, ‡Bas.*h.myst.*6(p.259.13); and to heavenly sanctuary, ‡Sophr.H.*liturg.*(M.87.3984C); hence **2.** the *clergy* τὴν τάξιν τοῦ β. Gr.Naz.*or.*43.27(M.36.553B); *ib.*43.52(564A); Pall.*h.Laus.*71(M.34.1242A); of pagan 'clergy' instituted by Julian, Soz.*h.e.*5.16.2(M.67.1261A); **3.** *pulpit*, placed in middle of church or nearer altar, from which Gospel and Epistle were read and sermons preached, cf. ἄμβων, Soz.*h.e.*8.5.2(M.67.1528C); *ib.*9.2.11 (1600C); Gr.Ant.*bapt.*2.1(M.88.1872C).

D. (Manich.) focal object of ceremony at which passion of Moses was commemorated, and theme of Judgement emphasized, before judgement-seat containing picture of Moses and Manich. scriptures, cf. *Manichaean Psalm-book* (Manich. MSS in Chester Beatty Collection), v. *JTS* 39 pp.344–5; *Zeitschrift für die neutestamentliche Wissenschaft* 37 pp.2–10; cf. Augustinus *contra epistulam Fundamenti* 8(M.*PL.*42.179).

***βηματέω**, *set foot upon, enter*, †Gregent.*disp.*(M.86.769B).

βηματίζω, *enter upon the* βῆμα, *officiate in the sanctuary*, Areth. ap.*cat.Apoc.*8:4(p.300.23).

***βημόθυρον, τό**, *sanctuary door*, shutting off βῆμα from body of church ὁ ἱερεὺς...θυμιᾷ τὸν λαὸν μικρὸν προελθὼν τῶν β. *Lit.Chrys.* (p.378.19); *Euchol.*(p.5).

***βήναβλον (-αυλον), τό**, (Lat. *venabulum*) *hunting-spear*, Jo. Mal.*chron.*6 p.163(M.97.265B); βήναυλον Ephr.1.83D.

***βήξιλλον, τό**, (Lat. *vexillum*) *standard*, of military standard as example of Cross οἱ τῇδε βασιλεῖς, πάσης πονηρᾶς ἕξεως ἐπὶ σκεδασμῷ, τὸ σταυροειδὲς παραλαμβάνεσθαι αἰσθόμενοι σχῆμα, τὰ καλούμενα τῇ Ῥωμαϊκῇ διαλέκτῳ β. ἐμηχανήσαντο Meth.*Porph.*1(p.504.29; M.18.400C).

[*]**βηριδάριος**, v. [*]βεριδάριος.

[*]**βῆρος, ὁ**, = βίρρος, *cloak*; as lay dress opp. garb of ascetics, CGangr.*can.*12.

βήσαλον, τό, *brick*, Gr.Mag.*dial.*(tr.Zach.)4.36(M.*PL.*77.383D, conj. βισ-); *Exorc.*13 (p.337).

βήχιον, τό, *cough* τὸ β. δεινῶς αὐτὸν διεσπάραττεν *Mir.Artem.*33 (p.50.15).

βία, ἡ, **1.** *force, violence*, ref. God's dealings with man in redemption β. γὰρ οὐ πρόσεστι τῷ θεῷ *Diogn.*7.4; ref. human free will β. θεῷ οὐ πρόσεστι· ἀγαθὴ δὲ γνώμη πάντοτε συμπάρεστιν αὐτῷ Iren.*haer.*4.36.8(M.7.1099B); exeg. Mt.11:12, Clem.*q.d.s.*21(p.173.23; M.9.625C) cit. s. βιάζω; ref. problem whether Son was begotten by Father's will or by constraint, Gr.Naz.*or.*29.6(p.81.4; M.36.81A); v. βιάζω; **2.** *haste* ἠκολούθησεν αὐτῷ μετὰ β. *T.Sal.*3.4; **3.** *necessity* τοῦτο ποιείτο μεγάλης β.· εἰ δὲ χωρὶς β. μηδόλως λειτουργήτω [i.e. after contact with impurity] *Nomoc.*117.

***βιαγωγή, ἡ**, *manner of life*, Gr.Mag.*dial.*(tr.Zach.)1.3(M.*PL.*77.163B).

βιάζ-ω, **1.** *constrain, compel, treat with violence*; med. and pass., *constrain* oneself ~ομένη ἑαυτὴν ἐπέμενεν Just.*2apol.*2.5(M.6.444B); Or.*Jo.*19.8(2; p.308.6; M.14.541A); Mac.Aeg.*hom.*19.3(M.34.644D); theol. υἱὸν...ἔπεμψεν [sc. θεός], ὡς πείθων οὐ ~όμενος *Diogn.*7.4; μήτε τοῦ θεοῦ ~ομένου, εἰ μὴ θέλοι τις κατασχεῖν αὐτοῦ τὴν τέχνην. τὰ οὖν...παραβάντα...παρὰ τὴν αὐτῶν ἀπέστησαν αἰτίαν Iren.*haer.*4.39.3(M.7.1111B); τὸ μὲν γὰρ ἄκοντας σώζειν ἐστὶ ~ομένου, τὸ δὲ αἱρουμένους χαριζομένου. οὐδὲ τῶν καθευδόντων...ἐστὶν ἡ βασιλεία τοῦ θεοῦ, ἀλλ' οἱ [Mt.11:12b] Clem.*q.d.s.*21(p.173.21; M.9.625C); θέλων ...ὑπέστησεν ὁ θεὸς τὰ πάντα ἢ βιασθείς; Gr.Naz.*or.*29.6(p.81.10; M.36.81A); ref. Son's generation οὐ γὰρ βιασθεὶς ὁ πατὴρ ὑπὸ ἀνάγκης φυσικῆς ἀχθείς, ὡς οὐκ ἤθελεν, ἐγέννησε τὸν υἱόν *Symb.Sirm.*(351) *anath.*25; exeg. Mt.11:12 αὕτη βία καλή, θεὸν βιάσασθαι καὶ παρὰ θεοῦ ζωὴν ἁρπάσαι Clem.*q.d.s.*21(p.173.23; 625C); οἱ δὲ ~όμενοί εἰσιν οἱ τῇ εἰδωλολατρείᾳ ἀποταττόμενοι *cat.Mt.*11:12(p.85.23); v. βιαστής; **2.** med., *make an effort* to ἡ ψυχὴ φέρειν ῥᾷον ~εται τὰς γεγενημένας ἐπιβουλάς Or.*Jo.*6.2(1 p.108.9; M.14.201A); Chrys.*sac.*3.9(p.63.1; 1.387A); Thdt.*h.rel.*26(3.1271); **3.** *wrest, distort, do violence to* τὸν νοῦν ἐβιάσατο Meth.*res.*1.58(p.320.9; M.41.1153C); of wresting the meaning of words, Clem.*str.*1.5(p.18.26; M.8.720B); Or.*Jo.*13.11(p.235.25; M.14.416B); Eus.*e.th.*3.3(p.151.19; M.24.992C).

βίαιος, **1.** *violent* οὐ β. ὁ θεός Clem.*fr.*29(p.217.16); exeg. Mt.11:12 γενοῦ β. ἐκεῖ, γενοῦ ἅρπαξ [sc. τῆς βασιλείας] Chrys.*hom.10.4 in 2Tim.*(11.726C); **2.** *enforced, compulsory* αὐθαίρετος γάρ, ἀλλ' οὐ β. ὁ πόνος Thdt.*h.rel.*28(3.1287); **3.** *forced, wrested*; of exegesis and interpretations, Or.*Jo.*13.46(p.272.11; M.14.480C); Eus.*e.th.*3.3(p.151.1; M.24.992A); Proc.G.*Gen.*4:16(M.87.277B); **4.** neut. as subst., *violence*, Thphn.*chron.*p.222(M.108.565B).

βιαστής, ὁ, *man of violence*, exeg. Mt.11:12 οἱ γὰρ ἁρπάζοντες τὴν βασιλείαν 'β.', οὐ τοῖς ἐριστικοῖς λόγοις, ἐνδελεχείᾳ δὲ ὀρθοῦ βίου ἀδιαλείπτοις τε εὐχαῖς ἐκβιάζεσθαι εἴρηνται Clem.*str.*5.3(p.336.17; M.9.33A); βιαστῶν ἐστιν ἡ βασιλεία τοῦ θεοῦ *ib.*4.2(p.250.10; M.8.1217B); Bas.*renunt.*2.9(2.211A; M.31.645C); Chrys.*hom.54.4 in Jo.*(8.320C); Isid.Pel.*epp.*4.136(M.78.1217B); v. βιάζω.

βιαστός, *subject to violence*, ref. Mt.11:12 β. γάρ ἐστιν βασιλεία τῶν οὐρανῶν Ant.Mon.*hom.*130(M.89.1841B).

βιάτωρ, ὁ, (Lat. *viator*) *apparitor, summoner* β. ἀπὸ πρημικιρήων (*viator ex primiceriis*), official concerned with administration of imperial estates, *MAMA* 1.243(Ladik, c. 500).

***βιβάσκω**, *advance, take strides* μακρὰ ~ων †Apoll.*met.Ps.*103:3 (M.33.1465B; p.211.8 βιβάσθων).

βιβλαρίδιον, τό, *little book*, Herm.*vis.*2.1.3; *ib.*2.4.3.

βιβλιδάριον, τό, = foreg.; of a New Testament, or extracts therefrom, Pall.*h.Laus.*8(p.27.11; βιβλίον γεγραμμένον M.34.1025B); self-depreciatory, of author's own work, *ib.*25(p.80.17; 1091A); in gen., Oecum.*Apoc.*10:2(p.121).

βιβλίδιον, τό, *little book, treatise*, Ign.*Eph.*20.1; Herm.*vis.*1.2.4; *ib.*2.1.3; depreciatory, of author's own work, Gel.Cyz.*h.e.*1.10.2 (M.85.1212B); sarcastic, of heret. writings, Sophr.H.*ep.syn.*(M.87.3190B); of Jewish phylacteries, Isid.Pel.*epp.*2.150(M.78.604C); of a memorandum (*libellus*) sent to emperor or governors, Just.*1apol.*29.2(M.6.373A); id.*2apol.*2.8(M.6.445A); *ib.*14.1(468A).

βιβλίον, τό, *strip of* βύβλος (papyrus); hence

A. *document, writing*; of Jewish phylacteries, Chrys.*hom.72.2 in Mt.*(7.703B); of a dictionary, Thdt.*qu.54 in 1Reg.*(1.389); of an indictment (*libellus*), Pall.*v.Chrys.*14(p.85.8; M.47.48); a letter, Thphyl.*exc.gent.*6(p.484.36; M.113.945C); a certificate, Marc.Diac. *v.Porph.*6.

B. *book*; **1.** *division* or *volume* of a work, Tat.*orat.*36(p.38.14; M.6.880B); Or.*Jo.*10.46(30; p.225.13; λόγον M.14.397C); Iren.*haer.*5.33.4(M.7.1214A); hence of the separate books of the Bible, Just. *dial.*75.1(M.6.652A); Ath.*ep.encycl.*4(p.173.19; M.25.232B); Chrys. *hom.42.1 in Jo.*(8.248B); plur.; **a.** the *Old Testament* (as Christian scripture) τὰ β. καὶ οἱ ἀπόστολοι...λέγουσιν *2Clem.*14.2; (as Jewish scripture) Or.*hom.14.12 in Jer.*(p.117.4; M.13.417C); **b.** *the Bible*, Or.*Jo.*6.8(5; p.117.20; M.14.216B); Cyr.H.*catech.*19.5; Chrys. *hom.47.3 in Mt.*(7.491A); **2.** *a complete work*, even if composed of many divisions; **a.** of a gospel-book used in administering oaths, Chrys.*stat.*15.5(2.159A); **b.** of a New Testament β. ἔχον ὅλην τὴν νέαν διαθήκην Jo.Mosch.*prat.*134(M.87.2997A); **c.** of a Bible, Chrys. *hom.32.3 in Jo.*(8.189B); *ib.*54.3(313E); **d.** of the books of divine judgement, *T.Abr.*B 10(p.114); *1Apoc.Jo.*4(p.72); **e.** abs., of a book of magic εἰ βούλει Χριστιανὸς γενέσθαι, φέρε μοι τὸ β. σου καὶ πάντα τὰ περίεργά σου Call.*v.Hyp.*(p.90).

***βιβλιοτάφος**, ὁ, *book-sepulchre*, of a library collector who does not read his books βιβλιοφόρος ἢ β. καὶ σητοτρόφος καλούμενος Isid.Pel.*epp*.1.127(M.78.268B).

***βιβλιοφορέω**, *carry books*, Isid.Pel.*epp*.1.234(M.78.328A).

***βιβλιοφόρος**, *book-carrying*, of the synagogue κτῆνος...β. ‡Caes.Naz.*dial*.183(M.38.1160); as subst., Isid.Pel.*epp*.1.127(M.78.268B) cit. s. βιβλιοτάφος.

[*]**βιβλιοφυλακεῖον**, τό, *library, record-office*, Ammon.*Jo*.21:25 (M.85.1524A).

βιβλιοφύλαξ, ὁ, *librarian, registrar*, *Dial.Tim.et Aquil*.116 r°; ὁ κύριος Ἰσίδωρος ὁ β. τοῦ πατριαρχείου Anast.S.*hod*.10(M.89.185A); Στέφανος μοναχὸς καὶ β. ἀνέγνω CNic.(787)*act*.1(H.4.53C).

βίβλος, ἡ, **A.** *papyrus* ἐκ β. ... σκεῦός τι ποιησάμενοι Clem.*str*.1.23 (p.94.6; M.8.897A).

B. *written roll* of papyrus; hence *book*, whether roll or codex, irrespective of its material; **1.** of individual books of Bible, Just. *dial*.20.1(M.6.517C); ἐν ταῖς τῶν προφητῶν β. id.*1apol*.31.7(M.6.377A); Or.*hom.10.4 in Jer*.(p.74.16; M.13.361C); Meth.*symp*.1.5(p.13.18; M.18.45B); **2.** plur.; **a.** of collected works of one author, e.g. books of Moses, *1Clem*.43.1; or Psalms, books of Solomon, etc., Meth. *symp*.7.4(p.75.19; 129C); **b.** of complete Bible, Or.*Jo*.1.22(p.26.33; M.14.61A); Eus.*v.C*.4.17(p.124.2; M.20.1165A); Ath.*ep.encycl*.3(p.172.16; M.25.229A); Chrys.*hom.32.3 in Jo*.(8.188D); **3.** sing., the *Bible*, Gr.Nyss.*Eun*.12(1 p.291.13; M.45.1000D); Leont.H.*monoph*.(M.86.1816D); Proc.G.*Gen*.15:18(M.87.345A); **4.** sing. or plur., of the book of life, Herm.*vis*.1.3.2; Or.*Jo*.5.7(4; p.104.1; M.14.193A); Gr.Naz. *carm*.2.2(poem.)1.343(M.37.1475A); interpreted as NT, *Didasc.Jac*. 1.13(p.751.1); **5.** met., of images βίβλοι τῶν ἀγραμμάτων Jo.D.*imag*. 2.10(M.94.1293C); of conscience πᾶσάν μου τῆς συνειδήσεως ἀναγνοὺς τὴν β. Max.*ep*.40(M.91.633C).

***βίγκας**, (Lat. *vincas*) *mayest thou conquer*, as shout of acclamation Αὔγουστε Ἰουστινιανέ, τοῦ βίγκας [*tu vincas*] *Chron.Pasch*. pp.338,341(M.92.881A,889B); Anast.Ap.*a.Max*.1.2(M.90.112C).

***βίγλα**, ἡ, (Lat. *vigilia*) *guard*, Thphn.*chron*.p.258(M.108.641C).

βιζάκιον, τό, *pebble, small piece of stone*, Mac.Aeg.*hom*.17.7(M.34.628D); Dor.*doct*.4.10(M.88.1672B); Ant.Mon.*hom*.66(M.89.1628A).

***βικαρία**, ἡ, (Lat. *vicaria*) *office of vicar* of an imperial diocese Μακάριός τις ἀπὸ β. Pall.*h.Laus*.62(p.157.19; M.34.1233B).

***βικάριος**, ὁ, (Lat. *vicarius*) *deputy*; **1.** of deputy of praetorian prefect, *vicar* of an imperial diocese, Ath.*h.Ar*.7(p.187.1; M.25.701C); Firminus *ep.Bas*.(M.32.533C); Bas.*ep*.237(3.365B; M.32.885B); Nil.*epp*.2.162 tit.(M.79.277B); Socr.*h.e*.7.12.2(M.67.760A); **2.** of bishop of Thessalonica as vicar of Pope of Rome over E. Illyricum from time of Damasus, Martin.*ep*.12(M.*PL*.87.191D); **3.** of Pope as vicar (i.e. representative, one who supplies the place) of SS. Peter and Paul, Hadr.Papa *ep.Const*.(M.*PL*.96.1218D); **4.** *lieutenant* (*vicarius cohortis*), Jo.Mal.*chron*.13 p.332(M.97.496A); Thphn.*chron*.p.278(M.108.688C); v. οὐικάριος.

***βικεννάλια**, τά, (Lat. *vicennalia*) *festival in honour of the twentieth year of a reign*, *Chron.Pasch*.p.282(M.92.704C).

βικίον, τό, *jar* or *cask*, Epiph.*mens*.24(M.43.284A).

***βίνδιξ**, ὁ, (Lat. *vindex*) *imperial tax-collector*, Nil.*epp*.2.282 tit. (M.79.341A); *ib*.2.327 tit.(360C); Cyr.S.*v.Sab*.54(p.145.22); τοὺς πολιτευομένους ἅπαντας ἐπῆρε [sc. Anastasius] τῆς βουλῆς, καὶ ἐποίησεν ἀντ' αὐτῶν τοὺς λεγομένους β. εἰς πᾶσαν πόλιν τῆς Ῥωμανίας Jo.Mal. *chron*.16 p.400(M.97.592C); *Chron.Pasch*.p.339(M.92.885B).

βιοδώτωρ, *life-giving*, Nonn.*par.Jo*.10:38(M.43.837B); Paul.Sil. *Soph*.973(M.86.2156A).

βιοθανατ-έω, *die by violence* οὐ γὰρ αἱ ψυχαὶ τῶν ~ούντων δαίμονες γίνονται Chrys.*Laz*.2.1(1.727E).

βιοθάνατος, ὁ, **1.** *one who dies by violence* αἱ ψυχαὶ τῶν β. οὐ γίνονται δαίμονες Chrys.*Laz*.2.1 tit.(1.726D); **2.** in gen., in bad sense, of criminals ὁ μοιχὸς καὶ κυνηγὸς καὶ β. [sc. Ἄδωνις] Arist.*apol*.11.4; *A.(Pass.)Andr*.15(p.36.14; M.2.1247A); *Chron.Pasch*.p.340(M.92.888A); and of suicides, cf. *vitam biothanati morte conclusit* [sc. Judas], Cassianus *institutis coenobiorum* 7.14(M.*PL*.49.304A); id. *collationes* 2.5(M.*PL*.49.530B); hence as term of abuse esp. applied by heathen to Christians, cf. *lupus tibi sum visus et non rex, biothanate?*, *M.Babylae* 1.2(*ASS* Januarii 24 p.571); and to Christ, †Gregent.*disp*.2(M.86.657B).

***βιοθανέω**, *commit suicide*, †Jo.Jej.*serm*.(M.88.1924B).

***βιοθανής**, ὁ, *one who dies by violence*, hence **1.** a *suicide* β. ἐστιν ὁ ἰδίᾳ προαιρέσει ἐξάγων ἑαυτὸν τοῦ βίου *M.Pion*.13.7; †Jo.Jej.*serm*. (M.88.1924B); **2.** a *criminal*, as term of abuse applied to Christ by pagans ὁ Χριστὸς...ἀνεπαύσατο ὡς β. *M.Pion*.13.3.

βιολογέω, *describe the life of*, Eust.*engast*.25(p.56.4; M.18.665B).

***βιοπαίγμων**, ? *playing with life*, Geo.Pis.*carm.vit*.1.

βιοπλανής, **1.** *wandering in search of a living*, Nonn.*par.Jo*.13:29 (M.43.865A); hence *erring, inconstant*, *ib*.15:19(876B); *ib*.20:23 (912B); **2.** *winding* β. λαβυρίνθου Geo.Pis.*carm.vit*.19.

***βιοποριστέω**, *provide for one's living*, Or.*exc.in Ps*.36:16(M.17.129D).

***βιοποριστικός**, **1.** *providing a livelihood*, Eus.*p.e*.1.5(15C; M.21.45A); **2.** *of providing a livelihood* β. χρείαν Olymp.*Eccl*.2:17(M.93.501D).

βίος, ὁ, **A.** *life, mode of life* (opp. ζωή); **1.** *period of life, life-time* τὸν πάντα μου τῆς ζωῆς β. *Hom.Clem*.1.14; Eus.*h.e*.10.4.60(M.20.873A); Thdt.*h.rel*.16(3.1223); **2.** the outward *activities* or *circumstances of life* ἔν τε ἐσθῆτι καὶ διαίτῃ καὶ τῷ λοιπῷ β. *Diogn*.5.4; Clem.*str*.7.16(p.68.4; M.9.533A); τὸ τὸν β. ἡμῶν τῇ νεκρότητι σβέννυσθαι (of the extinction of life's outward activities) opp. τὴν ζωὴν ἡμῶν διαλύεσθαι Gr.Nyss.*or.catech*.8(p.41.6); **3.** *livelihood, means of subsistence, property* εἰς Ἰουδαίαν ὁρμήσω, πρότερον τὸν ἐμὸν διαθεὶς β. *Hom.Clem*.1.8; Eus.*v.C*.3.1(p.76.16; M.20.1053B); *Const.App*.5.1.3; **4.** *manner of life, conduct, behaviour* ὁ β. ὁ Χριστιανῶν...σύστημά τί ἐστι λογικῶν πράξεων Clem.*paed*.1.13(p.151.24; M.8.376A); Or.*hom.14.16 in Jer*.(p.122.11; M.13.1424D); id.*Jo*. 20.36(p.377.11; M.14.660B); Chrys.*hom.24.2 in Rom*.(9.696E); id. *hom.6.3 in 2Tim*.(11.695D); = πολιτεία: τὸ γὰρ 'β.' ἀντὶ τῆς πολιτείας ἔλεξε...τῷ δὲ βρέφει, ὥσπερ οὐκ ἔστι πολιτεία, οὕτως οὐδὲ β. ‡Just.*qu.et resp*.88(M.6.1329C); but occasionally in opp. sense, *essential character of life*, contrasted with πολιτεία (its outward ordering and conditions) τὴν πολιτείαν ἀμείψας, τὸν β. οὐ συμμετέβαλεν Thdt.*h.rel*.17(3.1229); and contrasted with σχῆμα, Eustrat. *v.Eutych*.55(M.86.2337C); of particular modes of life πολλοὶ...τῆς εὐσεβείας οἱ β., μοναδικοὶ καὶ κοινωνικοί, κτλ. Thdt.*Ps*.24:12(1.760); of the 'gnostic' life, Clem.*str*.7.16(p.73.19; M.9.544B) al.; prophetic and apostolic, Or.*hom.14.14 in Jer*.(p.120.23; M.13.424A); 'philosophical', Bas.*ascet*.2.1(2.323E; M.31.881B); monastic, Pall.*h.Laus*. proem.(p.10.1; M.34.1001); secular ἐλήλυθεν ἐκ τοῦ ἔξωθεν βίου Bas.*reg.fus*.20.2(2.364C; M.31.971C); β. ἀδιάφορος, *worldly life*, Soz. *h.e*.3.3.3(M.67.1037C); of the lives of the saints, Bas.*ep*.2.3(3.73C; M.32.229A); **5.** abs., *good life*; contrasted with πίστις, Chrys.*hom. 34.1 in Heb*.(12.311D) al.; with δόγματα, id.*hom.64.4 in Mt*.(7.640C); id.*hom.9.3 in 1Thess*.(11.490B) al.; with μάθησις, Clem.*str*. 7.7(p.33.29; M.9.464C); with λόγος, *ib*.3.5(p.216.15; M.8.1148B); β. ἄνευ λόγου πλεῖον ἐνεργεῖν πέφυκεν ἢ λόγος ἄνευ β. *Apophth.Patr.al*. (p.246); with circumcision, Chrys.*hom.6.4 in Rom*.(9.477B); but associated with ἔργων ἐπίδειξις, id.*hom.46.3 in Mt*.(485B) al.; and with knowledge of God, id.*hom.2.2 in Col*.(11.335E); and equated with ἁγιασμός, id.*hom.9.2 in 1Tim*.(11.596C); its relationship to θεωρία, Gr.Naz.*or*.21.6(M.35.1088B); *Lit.Jac*.(*NBP* 10² p.109) cit. s. σύγκρασις; **6.** of this earthly, temporal life τῷ νῦν β. *2Clem*.20.2; ὁ β. οὗτος Ign.*Rom*.7.3; κοινός Clem.*str*.7.7(p.37.18; M.9.469C); σωματικός Or.*princ*.1.8.4(p.103.18); τρεπτός (opp. ἄτρεπτος ζωή) Gr.Nyss. *or.catech*.39(p.156.9; M.45.100B); Ζήνων ἔτι νέος ὢν β. καὶ γάμῳ ἀπαγορεύσας Soz.*h.e*.7.28.6(M.67.1505A); likened to sleep, Chrys. *hom.24.2 in Rom*.(9.697A); to a dream, id.*Thdr*.1.9(1.13A); id. *hom.15.3 in 1Tim*.(11.639B); a stage, *ib*.; an inn, id.*Eutrop*.2.5 (3.390D); a rood, id.*ep*.60(3.626D); a contest, Clem.*q.d.s*.3(p.162.6; M.9.608B); Bas.Sel.*or*.27.1(M.85.308D); Ant.Mon.*hom*.112(M.89.1781B); hence ἱερεὺς ἀπὸ β. *secular priest* (opp. ἀββαδοπρεσβύτερος) *Nomoc*.44; τοῖς ἐν τῷ β. (opp. monks) Thdr.Stud.*epp*.1.10(M.99.940D); **7.** *the present age, this world-order* (= αἰών) τὴν ἐπὶ συντελείᾳ τοῦ β. δευτέραν...ἐσομένην...παρουσίαν Eus.*d.e*.1.1(p.4.11; M.22.17B); *ib*.7.3(p.342.3; M.557B); *Clem.ep*.10(M.2.45B); τὸ τοῦ β. τέλος Thdt.*Gal*.4.4(3.386); **8.** *world* in general πλήρης ὁ β. δικαστηρίων τε καὶ βουλευτηρίων καὶ ἐκκλησιῶν Clem.*str*.8.7(p.93.30; M.9.588B); Eus.*h.e*.4.28(M.20.400A); id.*p.e*.6.11(296A; M.21.505B); Epiph.*haer*.66.2(p.18.17; M.42.33A); †Jo.D.*B.J*.32(M.96.1168B).

B. = ζωή *life to come, eternal life* εἰς μακάριον β., γέρας εὐζωΐας, ζωὴν αἰώνιον Clem.*paed*.1.10(p.146.29; M.8.364C); ἵνα β. αἰώνιον ἔχωμεν Cels.ap.Or.*Cels*.4.30(p.299.29; M.11.1072C); Or.*Cels*.4.31(p.301.10; M.11.1073D); freq. in Gr. Nyss. ἡ ἀνθρωπίνη ζωή...πρὸς τὸν μακάριον καὶ ἀπαθῆ β. ἐπαναδράμοι Gr.Nyss.*hom.opif*.22.2(M.44.204C); τέλειος β. id.*v.Mos*.2(M.44.300A); *ib*.6(301A); τῶν ἀγγέλων ὁ β. id.*mort*.(M.46.516C); ἡ ὄντως ζωὴ δι' ἐλπίδος ἀπόκειται, ἡ δὲ παροῦσα ζωὴ οἱονεὶ σπέρμα τῆς μελλούσης ἐστί...ὁ νῦν β. ἀναλογεῖ πρὸς τὸν κόκκον· ὁ δὲ προσδοκώμενος β., ἐν τῷ κάλλει τοῦ στάχυος δείκνυται id.*Pulch*.(M.46.876C); Thdt.*Ps*.26:14(1.773); ἐν ἐκείνῳ τῷ β. id.*h.e*.3.16.5(3.932); τοῦ β. τούτου coupled with τοῦ ἀναισθήτου β. *CIG* 9474.

C. *biography*, Or.*Cels*.2.12(p.141.14; M.11.817B); *ib*.6.8(p.78.7; 1300C); Pall.*h.Laus*.proem.(p.11.20; M.34.1003).

βιοσσόος, *saving life, life-supporting*, Nonn.*par.Jo*.3:28(M.43.772B); *ib*.5:26(789A); *ib*.14:27(872A).

***βιοσφαγῶς**, *by violent slaughter*, Cyr.H.*catech*.13.6; *ib*.13.33.

***βιότευσις (*βιώτευσις)**, ἡ, **1.** *life, way of life*, ‡Caes.Naz.*dial*.169 (M.38.1133); **2.** *habitation* πολίχνη βιωτεύσεως Δαυΐδ AQ ap.Eus.*Is*. 29:1(M.24.296D).

βιοτεύ-ω, *live*, of the life of the soul ἔθνη τινὰ τῶν ψυχῶν ἀποτίθεται...πρὸς τὴν ἐν σώματι ζωὴν ~οντα Or.*princ*.1.8.4(p.102.13); ἵνα μὴ...χοιρώδη βίον...τὴν ψυχὴν ~ειν παρασκευάσωσιν [sc. ἡδοναί] Meth.*creat*.1(p.494.15; M.18.333B).

βιοτή, ἡ, **1.** *mode, way of life*, Clem.*paed*.3.12(p.292.39; M.8.684A); Synes.*hymn*.1.30(p.58; M.66.1588); **2.** this earthly, temporal life τὴν ἐνθάδε β. Just.*2apol*.12.2(M.6.464B); **3.** *eternal life, spiritual life* (= ζωή) β. ἕξειν αἰώνιον Cels.ap.Or.*Cels*.2.77(p.199.13; M.11.916C); Cels.*ib*.5.14(p.15.20; 1201B); Or.*ib*.5.24(p.25.9; 1217B); Nonn.*par.Jo*.12:25(M.43.853C); τὴν μέλλουσαν...β. Thdt.*Is*.61:2(p.240.31; 2.383).

βιότης, ἡ, **1.** *lifetime, length of life* διὰ τὸ ἄπειρον τῆς β. (i.e. of demons) Tat.*orat*.14(p.16.3; M.6.837A); **2.** *this life, human life*, Thdt.*h.e*.1.32.1(3.822); **3.** = ζωή *spiritual life* ὁδοὺς βιότητος ἐλέγχει παιδεία (cf. Pr.6:23) Clem.*str*.1.29(p.111.8; M.8.928B).

βιοτήσιος, **1.** *pertaining to this earthly life* κυμάτων β. Synes.*hymn*.1.105(p.62; M.66.1589); Eudoc.*Cypr*.2.330(M.85.857C); **2.** *life-giving*, Nonn.*par.Jo*.4:15(M.43.776C); *ib*.4:31(780B); *ib*.4:52(784B).

βίοτος, ὁ, *life, physical life*, Nonn.*par.Jo*.21:23(M.43.920C).

βιοτρόφος, *life-sustaining*, Geo.Pis.*hex*.695(M.92.1489A).

***βιοφορέομαι**, *be treated violently, be distressed*, Epiph.*haer*.66.24 (p.52.3; M.42.69B); *ib*.68.7(p.147.18; 196A); *ib*.69.10(p.160.11; 217B).

βιόω, **A.** *live*; *pass one's life* (opp. ζάω = exist physically); **1.** in gen. of living a good life, Clem.*str*.7.7(p.36.6; M.9.468C); κατὰ τὸν νόμον...β. Or.*Cels*.7.28(p.179.19; M.11.1461A); κατ' ἀρετὴν β. id.*princ*.3.1.15(p.222.5; M.11.280A); Gr.Nyss.*or.catech*.40(p.163.3; M.45.104D); **2.** more rarely, a bad life, Or.*hom.20.6 in Jer*.(p.186.1; M.13.313A); Gr.Nyss.*anim.et res*.(M.46.149C); Synes.*Dion* 5(p.248.1; M.66.1128B).

B. ? *live a married life* τινες...ἐγκρατεύονται ἀπὸ γάμου μετὰ τὸ βιῶσαι Epiph.*haer*.13.1(conj. μετὰ τὸ οὕτως βιῶσαι p.206.2; M.41.237A); ref. Church's rejection of married men from ordination τὸν ἔτι ⟨συμ⟩βιοῦντα καὶ τεκνογονοῦντα...οὐ δέχεται *ib*.59.4(conj. συμβιοῦντα p.367.16; 1024A).

C. τὰ βεβιωμένα *the events of life, conduct of one's life* τῶν εὖ ἢ κακῶς βεβιωμένων ἡ δικαία κρίσις Athenag.*res*.19(p.72.15; M.6.1013A); Bas.*hex*.1.4(1.5A; M.29.12B); Chrys.*hom.27.6 in Gen*.(4.264A).

[*]βιρίν, τό, *hooded cloak* for outdoor wear, Pall.*h.Laus*.63(p.158.12, v.l. βιρρίον M.34.1235B).

***βιρροφόρος (βυρρ-)**, ὁ, *wearer of a* βιρρίον (= βιρίν), of ordinary citizens at Athens, opp. philosophers τριβωνοφόροι τε καὶ β. Pall.*h.Laus*.37(p.111.4; βυρρ- M.34.1186A).

***βίσεξτος (βίσεκστος, βίσσεξτος)**, (Lat. *bisextus*) *of the doubled sixth, bissextile*, properly of intercalated day with which in every fourth year the 6th day before Kalends of March (i.e. 24th Feb.) was duplicated in Julian calendar, but used also of year in which this intercalation occurs ἡ τετραετία τοῦ λεγομένου β. Anast.Ant.*serm*.2.6(M.89.1381D); ἔτους τετραετηρίδος βισσέξτου *Chron.Pasch*. p.10(M.92.88A) al.; ἡμέρα, ἥτις λέγεται β. Jo.D.*f.o*.2.7(M.94.897A); neut. as subst. Καῖσαρ 'Ιούλιος...τὸ β. ἐφηῦρε Jo.Mal.*chron*.9 p.215 (M.97.336A); μετὰ τὸ βίσεκστον *Chron.Pasch*.p.221(537B); τὰ βίσεξτα *ib*.p.388(996A); Max.*comput*.17(M.19.1233D,1236A).

***βισσίον, τό, (βίσσα, ἡ)**, *wine-jar*, cf. βῖκος; *Pers*.(p.25.12); Leont.N.*v.Sym*.33(M.93.1712A; in form βίσσα, 1712B); *ib*.49(1729D).

***βιώδης**, *of livelihood* β. πορισμόν Epiph.*haer*.76.1(p.341.20; M.42.517A).

βιώσιμος, *alive, vital*, Gr.Naz.*or*.21.34(M.35.1124A); neut. as subst., Areth.*Apoc*.67(M.106.776D).

***βιωσίμως**, *in the enjoyment of life* σὲ δὲ πολλάκις γένοιτο συνεορτάσαι...β. ἔχοντα Gr.Naz.*ep*.120(M.37.216A).

βίωσις, ἡ, *way of life*, Const.*or.s.c*.11(p.168.6; M.20.1264B); ‡Just.*qu.et resp*.124(M.6.1373A).

***βιώτευσις**, v. *βιότευσις.

βιωτικός, **1.** *belonging to this life*; hence, of persons, *worldly, of the world*, Mac.Aeg.*libert.ment*.27(M.34.960D); esp. opp. monks, Chrys.*hom.16.5 in 1Cor*.(10.141D); id.*sac*.3.15(p.79.19; 1.394A); id.*Laz*.3.1 (1.737B); υἱὸς δὲ τοῦ...'Ιωσήφ ἐστιν [sc. 'Ιάκωβος] ἐκ τῆς β. αὐτοῦ γυναικός [i.e. Salome, opp. BMV] Hipp.Th.*fr*.1.6(p.7.6; M.117.1040B); of things, *temporal, earthly*, Herm.*vis*.1.3.1; Hipp.*Dan*.4.52.1; Gr.Nyss.*hom.4 in Cant*.(M.44.852A); φροντίδος...βιωτικωτέρας Chrys.*hom.85.4 in Mt*.(7.810B); Nil.*epp*.3.152(M.79.453C); τὰ β. *worldly possessions* or *advantages*, Clem.*q.d.s*.15(p.169.29; M.9.620B); Or.*Cels*.1.67 (p.121.26; M.11.785C); *Const.App*.2.4.3; **2.** *secular, lay*; of children to be educated in monasteries, Bas.*reg.br*.292 (2.518A; M.31.1288A); of laymen opp. clergy or monks, Chrys.*compunct*.1.5(1.130E); Nil.*epp*.3.153(M.79.453D); Marc.Er.*opusc*.7.11(M.65.1088B); laywomen opp. nuns, Chrys.*hom.4.5 in Heb*.(12.46D); of civil authorities β. δυναστείας Leo Mag.*ep*.93.1(p.31.8; M.*PL*.54.938A); ἀμήχανον...β. κριτηρίῳ παραβάλλεσθαι τὸ θεῖον κριτήριον Thdr.Stud.*epp*.2.129(M.99.1420A); of a secular building, Cyr.S.*v.Sab*.27(p.111.21); **3.** *belonging to public life* ἐν τοῖς β. ... ἐν τοῖς ἰδιωτικοῖς Chrys.*hom.15.5 in Phil*.(v.l. δημοτικοῖς 11.318E); **4.** *belonging to spiritual* or *eternal life* β. παραίνεσις Clem.*paed*.3.12 (p.284.20; M.8.665C); β. ὠφέλεια id.*str*.6.17(p.515.11; M.9.393C).

βιωτικῶς, **1.** *in a worldly* or *unspiritual manner* τοὺς β. περιπατήσαντες Chrys.*hom.16.3 in 1Cor*.(10.138B); οὐ κοσμικῶς ἐχάρην...οὐδὲ β., ἀλλ' ἐν κυρίῳ id.*hom.15.1 in Phil*.(11.310A); βιωτικώτερον ζῶντα id.*Stag*.1.1(1.155D); *ib*.3.12(221E); **2.** *in the world, in ordinary* (opp. monastic) *life* ἐπικουρεῖν ἐμοὶ β. θαλαττεύοντι Sophr.H.*ep.syn*.(M.87.3149C).

βιωφελῶς, *in a way profitable for life*, Eus.*v.C*.2.15(p.47.12; M.20.993A); Const.*or.s.c*.9(p.164.18; βιωφελές M.20.1256D); Euthal.Diac.*Ac*.(M.85.632A); superl., Clem.*paed*.2.7(p.193.2; M.8.464A).

***βλαβοποιός**, *injurious*, Meth.*res*.1.41(p.287.6; M.18.269C); id.*lepr*.5(p.455.16); τὰ...β. τοῦ πονηροῦ βλαστήματα ‡Chrys.*hom.in Lc*.*15:11*(10.839D).

βλακεία, ἡ, **1.** *stupidity*, Or.*Jo*.10.27(17; p.200.18; M.14.356C); Chrys.*Thdr*.1.3(1.4C); id.*hom.8.1 in Col*.(11.380A); **2.** *foolish ostentation, display*, Clem.*paed*.2.3(p.178.13; M.8.433A); ἀλαζονείας, κενοδοξίας, β. πληροῦσι Chrys.*hom.87.3 in Mt*.(7.821D); Nil.*epp*.2.84(M.79.240C); **3.** *luxury, softness* περὶ μύρων καὶ τῆς ἄλλης β. Chrys.*hom.8.3 in 1Tim*.(11.593B); Ast.Am.*hom*.1(M.40.168D); Nil.*Alb*.(M.79.697B); **4.** *fastidiousness* πόσης...β. ... τὸ μὴ δύνασθαι πένησι συγκαθέζεσθαι Chrys.*hom.1.3 in Col*.(11.327B); **5.** *slackness, weakness, indolence*, Chrys.*hom.55.2 in Mt*.(7.557E); id.*hom.5.4 in 1Thess*.(11.465D); Cyr.*Am*.34(3.288E).

βλάκευμα, τό, *act of luxury* or *pleasure*, Gr.Naz.*carm*.1.2.10.612 (M.37.724A); *ib*.2.1.88.35(1436A); τὰ β. τῆς νέας ἡλικίας Nil.*epp*.1.140 (M.79.141A).

βλακεύ-ω, **1.** *be slack, indolent*, ref. Mt.11:12 οὐδὲ τῶν καθευδόντων καὶ ~όντων ἐστὶν ἡ βασιλεία τοῦ θεοῦ Clem.*q.d.s*.21(p.173.22; M.9.625C); Chrys.*sac*.3.14(p.72.19; 1.391A); **2.** *be luxurious, soft*, id.*hom.8.3 in 1Tim*.(11.593A); **3.** med., *boast foolishly*, Didym.*2Cor*.3:4(M.39.1693B).

βλακικός, *luxurious, soft, effeminate*, Clem.*paed*.2.9(p.205.6; M.8.492A); Bas.*ep*.2.6(3.74C; M.32.232B).

βλακώδης, *effeminate, luxurious*; of persons, Gr.Nyss.*or.dom*.5 (p.34.35; M.44.1141C); β. ... σωτάδεια id.*Eun*.1(1 p.25.10; M.45.253A); β. διάχυσις id.*hom.6 in Cant*.(M.44.900C); β. λογισμόν Chrys.*hom.20.1 in 2Cor*.(10.578A); β. ἐπιθυμίας id.*compunct*.1.9(1.138C).

βλακωδῶς, *with foolish arrogance*, ‡Just.*ep.Zen.et Ser*.10(M.6.1193C).

βλάξ, **1.** *slack, indolent*, Nil.*epp*.2.49(M.79.221A); **2.** *luxurious, lascivious*, *Const.App*.8.32.11; Chrys.*Dan*.1(6.201D); id.*hom.6.4 in 2Tim*.(11.697B).

βλαπτικός, *hurtful, mischievous*; superl., Thphyl.*exc.gent*.5 (p.482.24; M.113.941D); neut. as subst., Gr.Nyss.*fat*.(M.45.161B); neut. superl. as subst., Eus.*p.e*.1.4(12A; M.21.40C).

βλαστάνω, **1.** trans., *make to grow, produce*; met., of the fruits of virtues etc., Clem.*q.d.s*.28(p.178.33; M.9.633C); Meth.*symp*.8.11 (p.93.16; M.18.153D); τοῦτο βλαστησάτω ἡμῶν τὰ χείλη Chrys.*hom.33.4 in Heb*.(12.308B); **2.** intrans., *shoot forth, bud, sprout*; of Aaron's rod, *1Clem*.43.5; Thdt.*qu.34 in Num*.(1.242); as type of Cross, cf.Or.*hom.9.7 in Num*.(p.63.18; M.12.632B); and of Christ, *ib*.9.9(p.66.23; 635A); Cyr.*Is*.2.1(2.129B).

βλαστάω, = βλαστάνω, Herm.*sim*.4.2 cit. s. δένδρον.

βλαστ-έω, = foreg. ~οῦντας καρπούς Eus.*l.C*.13(p.237.8; M.20.1400B).

βλάστη, ἡ, *growth, crop, flowering*; met., of 'flowers' of immortal life, Meth.*symp*.8.11(p.94.1; M.18.153D); of fruits of pagan sensuality, Eus.*l.C*.7(p.213.10; M.20.1353A); of growth which chokes the word in parable of Sower, Chrys.*hom.44.4 in Mt*.(7.472C); of general resurrection, Thdt.*Is*.66:14(p.260.8; 2.400); of new creation in Christ, Cyr.*ador*.10(1.331D).

βλάστημα, τό, 1. *plant, flower*; met., of S. Barnabas τὸ πολύανθες τῆς πίστεως β. Alex.Sal.*Barn.*(p.437C); **2.** *growth, crop, product*, of mixture in human nature of body and soul τὸ διφυὲς τουτὶ β. Eus. *p.e.*6.6(246B; M.21.420A); τὰ τῆς τέχνης β. Thdt.*provid.*6(4.580); of Christian doctrine as spiritual pasturage [sc. ποίμνιον] τρέφειν ἐνθέοις τισὶ καὶ ὠφελίμοις β. Sophr.H.*ep.syn.*(M.87.3197B); **3.** *scion, offspring*, of Christ τὸ πρωτόγονον τοῦ θεοῦ καὶ πρῶτον β. Meth. *symp.*3.4(p.30.20; M.18.65B); hence *native* of a country οὗτος τῆς Γαλατῶν γῆς β. γέγονεν Nil.*Alb.*(M.79.700C).

βλάστησις, ἡ, *growth, germination*; of plants etc., ‡Eust.*hex.* (M.18.713C); Bas.*hex.*5.1(1.40B; M.29.96A); ‡Just.*qu.et resp.*111(M.6. 1360C); met. τὴν Εὐτυχοῦς ἐκτρέπων φιλοσύγχυτον β. Sophr.H.*ep. syn.*(M.87.3172D).

βλαστόν, τό, *shoot, plant*, Arist.*apol.*6.1; *ib.*12.1.

βλαστός, ὁ, 1. *growth, shoot*; met. ἀνεφύοντο...ἀγαθῶν δύο β., ἡ Ῥωμαίων ἀρχὴ καὶ ἡ εὐσεβὴς διδασκαλία Eus.*l.C.*16(p.249.17; M.20. 1424A); of BMV compared with burning bush, Gr.Nyss.*v.Mos.* (M.44.332D); of budding of Aaron's rod, *Const.App.*5.7.26; as type of Christ as Branch, Just.*dial.*86.4(M.6.681B); of Christ as Branch, *T.Jud.*24.4; *Const.App.*6.11.10; of Son and H. Ghost as offshoots from Father's deity, Dion.Ar.*d.n.*2.7(M.3.645B) cit. s. θεόφυτος; **2.** *fruit*, *Barn.*7.8; Eus.*v.C.*3.43(p.96.13, v.l. καρπούς M.20.1105A).

***βλαστώδης,** *germinative*, Anast.S.*hod.*2(M.89.65D).

βλασφημ-έω, A. in gen., *slander, discredit*; esp. **1.** of treasonable utterances against state, *Hom.Clem.*11.9; Evagr.*h.e.*1.7(p.16.22; M.86.2444A); *ib.*6.5(p.225.21; 2849C); **2.** of discreditable statements about Church ὥστε τὸ σεμνὸν...ὄνομα ὑμῶν μεγάλως ∼ηθῆναι *1Clem.* 1.1; Ign.*Trall.*8.2; *Diogn.*5.14; Hipp.*haer.*7.32(p.220.2; M.16.3339B).

B. *speak irreverently of divine things, blaspheme*; **1.** against God and God's name, *2Clem.*13.1; Hipp.*haer.*1 proem.(p.2.7; M.16. 3020A); Bas.*reg.fus.*10(2.354A; M.31.948B); Chrys.*hom.72.4 in Jo.* (8.428C); **2.** against Christ, freq.; equated with blasphemy against whole Trinity, ‡Ath.*comm.essent.*49(M.28.76A); consisting in denial of Christ under persecution, *M.Polyc.*9; Just.*1apol.*31.6(M.6.377A); **3.** against H. Ghost (Mt.12:24–32), freq.; interpreted as post-baptismal sin, Or.*Jo.*28.15(13; p.408.23; M.14.713A); this view rejected by Athanasius, who interprets 'Son of Man' and 'H. Ghost' of human and divine natures of Christ, cf.*ep.Serap.*4.17(M.26. 664A); so, ‡Ath.*comm.essent.*49(M.28.76D) = ‡Ath.*qu.Ant.*72(M.28. 644B); Isid.Pel.*epp.*1.59(M.78.221A); applied to Montanist ascription of title 'Paraclete' to Montanus and Priscilla, Bas.*ep.*188 *can.*1 (3.269C; M.32.668A); v. βλασφημία; **4.** of assertion of heret. doctrines, Ign.*Smyrn.*5.2; Apollon.ap.Eus.*h.e.*5.18.5; Clem.*str.*3.17 (p.243.10; M.8.1205A); ‡Ath.*Apoll.*2.18(M.26.1165A) etc.; of rejection of Old Testament by Marcionites and Manicheans, Eus.*h.e.* 5.13.9(M.20.461C); Jo.D.*haer.*66(M.94.217A); **5.** of blasphemy against pagan gods, Cels.ap.Or.*Cels.*8.38(p.253.4; M.11.1573B).

C. *act irreverently towards, blaspheme by deed*, Herm.*sim.*6.2.3; Chrys.*hom.76.3 in Jo.*(8.449C); Thdt.*Rom.*2:24(3.34).

D. *assert blasphemously* τινὲς δὲ αὐτῶν καὶ τὴν ἀντικειμένην εἶναι ∼οῦσιν αὐτοῦ δύναμιν Chrys.*hom.8.2 in Jo.*(8.50C); Gel.Cyz.*h.e.*2.22. 4(M.85.1292A).

***βλασφημητέος,** *to be discredited*, Clem.*str.*1.10(p.30.28; M.8. 744B).

***βλασφημητήριον, τό,** *collection of blasphemies*; of a book by a Macedonian heretic, Didym.*Trin.*2.8(M.39.608C).

βλασφημία, ἡ, I. *evil-speaking*;

A. ref. men; **1.** *ill-omened word* or *speech* βούλομαι μὲν εἰπεῖν τι καὶ τολμηρότερον, φείδομαι δὲ τῆς β. αἰδοῖ τῆς ἡμέρας Gr.Naz.*or.*11.5 (M.35.837D); **2.** *slander, reviling*, Ign.*Eph.*10.2; φθόνου καὶ μίσους καὶ β. ... καὶ διαβολῆς ἐκτὸς ὄντος Clem.*ecl.*30(p.146.14; M.9.713C); καταλαλιὰν δέ, τὴν εἰς ἀπόντας ὑπό τινων β. Gennad.*fr.Rom.*1:29 (p.360.7; M.85.1669B); **3.** *treasonable language* against emperor, Evagr.*h.e.*5.5(p.201.21; M.86.2801B).

B. in relation to God and holy things, *blasphemy*; **1.** against God, Ign.*Smyrn.*5.2; Herm.*sim.*8.6.4; Hipp.*haer.*proem.(p.2.7; M. 16.3020A) et freq.; **2.** against Christ εἰσελθε εἰς τὰς τῶν Ἰουδαίων συναγωγάς, καὶ ἴδε τὸν Ἰησοῦν ὑπ' αὐτῶν τῇ γλώσσῃ τῆς β. μαστιγούμενον Or.*hom.19.12 in Jer.*(p.168.5; M.13.488B); Eus.*Marcell.*1.1 (p.2.14; M.24.713B); Thdt.*haer.*4.7(4.361); **3.** against H. Ghost, Bas. *Spir.*28(3.82E; M.32.200A); Gr.Nyss.*Eun.*1(1 p.79.8; M.45.309C); Chrys.*hom.41.3 in Mt.*(7.448E); Isid.Pel.*epp.*1.59(M.78.220C); exeg. Mt.12:24–32, as rejection of teaching of H. Ghost (of which only the perfect are recipients) contrasted with teaching of Son given to the uninstructed, Thgn.*hypot.fr.*1(p.76.17; M.10.241A); this view rejected by Athanasius, *ep.Serap.*4.17(M.26.664A); interpreted of blasphemy against H. Ghost contrasted with blasphemy against human nature of Christ, Chrys.*hom.41.3 in Mt.*(7.449A); applied to Pneumatomachoi, Bas.*Spir.*28(3.59E; M.32.200A); v. βλασφημέω; **4.** of doctrines of heretics, freq.; e.g. Marcion, Just.*1apol.*26.5(M. 6.369A); Patripassians τὴν εἰς τὸν πατέρα β. Hipp.*haer.*9.12(p.249. 10; M.16.3386A); Arius, Ath.*Ar.*1.7(M.26.25A) al.; Arians and Sabellians, Bas.*hom.*24.2(2.190C; M.31.601C); Nestorius βλασφημίας πατήρ Evagr.*h.e.*1.7(p.12.20; M.86.2436A); of a schismatic, Dion.Al.ap. Eus.*h.e.*7.8(M.20.652B); of heret. baptism ἀσεβείας γὰρ ἐκεῖνο καὶ βλασφημιῶν πεπληρῶσθαι *ib.*7.9.3(656A); **5.** produced by substitution of vain reasonings for faith, Meth.*res.*1.27(p.256.7; M.41. 1133C); Chrys.*hom.5.2 in 1Tim.*(11.576A); by the vices resulting from pride, *Const.App.*7.7.2; and by literal interpretation of scripture, ‡Ath.*qu.Ant.*72(M.28.640C); **6.** consisting in evil-living, Chrys.*hom.68.3 in Jo.*(8.403E).

II. *discredit, dishonour, scandal*, esp. of what is discreditable to reputation of Christians ὥστε καὶ βλασφημίας ἐπιφέρεσθαι τῷ ὀνόματι κυρίου διὰ τὴν ὑμετέραν ἀφροσύνην *1Clem.*47.7; *Const.App.* 3.5.4; Chrys.*hom.19.3 in Jo.*(8.113D); hence *occasion of scandal*, of attendance at heathen games etc. τοῦτο δὲ πᾶσι τοῖς Χριστιανοῖς ἀεὶ κεκήρυκται, ὥστε ὅπου β. εἰσί, μὴ προσιέναι *Cod.Afr.*15.

III. in neutral or good sense; **A.** neutral, *charge, accusation* (which may be true or false) εἰ δέ τινες ἐν βλασφημίαις τοῦ μὴ καλῶς ὁδεύειν...ἐλέγχοιντο *Const.App.*2.47.3.

B. in good sense, *reproof, merited rebuke* ὁ κύριος...οἱονεὶ μάστιγι τῇ β. τὸ νωθρὸν τῆς διανοίας ἐπεγείρων Clem.*paed.*1.8(p.128.33; M.8. 329B); *ib.*(p.129.2; 329B).

***βλασφημόγλωσσος,** *having blaspheming tongues* ἄλλο ἔπεσεν ἐπὶ τὰς ἀκάνθας, τὰς...β. αἱρέσεις ‡Epiph.*hom.*4(M.43.485A).

βλάσφημος, A. *slanderous, evil-speaking*; **1.** against men μετὰ τὸ...ἀποβληθῆναι τοὺς πονηροὺς καὶ ὑποκριτὰς καὶ β. Herm.*sim.*9. 18.3; β., κατηγορίαις χαίροντες Thdr.Mops.*2Tim.*3:2(p.214.20; M.66. 945C); **2.** against God and holy things, *blasphemous*; **a.** against heathen gods etc. παρεγγράφειν μὲν εἰς τὰ ἐκείνης [sc. Σιβύλλης] πολλὰ καὶ β. εἰκῇ δύνασθε Cels.ap.Or.*Cels.*7.53(p.203.27; M.11.1497B); **b.** against God, Christ, and H. Ghost; of apostates, Herm.*sim.* 9.19.1; of those who assert false doctrines of Creation, Meth.*res.* 1.50(p.304.4; M.18.280B); of pagan persecutors, Eus.*v.C.*3.1(p.76.9; M.20.1053A); of Jewish opposition to Christ, Chrys.*hom.55.2 in Jo.*(8.324C); of blasphemous speech against Son of Man (Mt.12:32), Isid.Pel.*epp.*1.59(M.78.221A); of heretics in gen., Iren.*haer.*1.1 (M.7.440A); Hipp.*haer.*9.2(p.239.24; M.16.3370A); Adam.*dial.*1.27 (p.54.15; M.11.1757B); Ath.*Ar.*1.17(M.26.48A); θεοκαταγνῶσται, οἱ καὶ β. Jo.D.*haer.*92(M.94.757B).

B. as subst.; **1.** masc., *slanderer, blasphemer*; **a.** against men, *Const.App.*4.6.5; **b.** against God, Hipp.*haer.*1 proem.(p.2.12; M.16. 3020A); τὸν Σαβέλλιον ἡ ἐκκλησία...ἐν ἀθέοις καὶ β. κατέλεξεν Eus. *e.th.*2.4(p.102.35; M.24.905B); of Jewish charges against Christ β., Μωσέως παραβάτην *Const.App.*5.14.9; Chrys.*hom.64.1 in Jo.*(8. 382A); **2.** neut.; **a.** *ill-omened speech* ὀκνῶ λέγειν τὸ β. Gr.Naz.*or.* 19.11(M.35.1056A); **b.** *blasphemous speech*, Dion.R.ap.Ath.*decr.*26 (p.22.19; M.25.464B); τὰ β. Gr.Nyss.*Eun.*4(2 p.60.16, v.l. βλασφήματα M.45.632B).

***βλασφημοσύνη, ἡ,** *evil-speaking* ἁγνεῦσαι δ' ἀκοὰς β. ἀλεγεινῆς Anon.ap.Synes.*ep.*57(M.66.1393D).

βλασφήμως, *blasphemously*, Clem.*str.*3.18(p.244.22; M.8.1208C); β. ζῆν Gr.Mag.*dial.*(tr.Zach.)4.18(M.*PL.*77.350D).

βλάττα, ἡ, (Lat. *blatta*) *purple* λίθος σάπφειρος πορφυρίζων, ὡς β. πορφύρας τῆς μελαίνης τὸ εἶδος [where πορφύρας is prob. a gloss] Epiph.*gemm.*5(M.43.297A).

βλαύτη, ἡ, *slipper* β. ἢ φαικασίοις χρηστέον· κονίποδας αὐτὰ ἐκάλουν οἱ Ἀττικοί Clem.*paed.*2.11(p.227.9; M.8.537B); ᾗ γε καὶ προσάλλονται β. Ἀττικῆς ἀκριβέστερον Synes.*calv.*13(p.215.10; M.66.1192A).

βλέμμα, τό, 1. *look, glance* τὸ β. εἶχε περίπικρον Herm.*sim.*6.2.5; αἰδὼς δὲ πρὸς γυναῖκας καὶ β. τετραμμένον εἰς γῆν Clem.*fr.*44(p.221. 30); μή σου τὸ β. ἁμαρτανέτω Cyr.H.*procatech.*8; ἵνα μὴ τὸ β. ῥεμβόμενον ποιήσῃ ῥέμβεσθαι καὶ τὴν καρδίαν *ib.*9; ἱκετεύομεν τὴν σὴν ἐπιείκειαν, ἵνα...γαληναίῳ β. τοὺς ἡμετέρους πρέσβεις ἀθρήσειας CArim.*ep.Const.*1(p.238.16; M.26.700A); τὸν καιρόν, ὃν λέγετε φθάνειν ὑμᾶς, βλέμματος γοργότερον παρέρχεται *Pers.*(p.34.18); τὸ δὲ ἔργον τῆς ταπεινώσεώς ἐστιν...τὸ β. ἔχειν χαμαί Esaias *or.*20(M.40.1157A); of God οὗ τὸ β. ξηραίνει ἀβύσσους *Lit.*ap.*Const.App.*8.7.6; of Son in Creation πάντα αὐτὸς ἐδημιούργησεν ὁ υἱός...νεύματι πατρικῷ οὐκ ὀφθαλμῶν βλέμματι Gel.Cyz.*h.e.*2.19.20(M.85.1280B); of Christ looking upon S. Peter, Chrys.*hom.85.1 in Mt.*(7.805B); **2.** the sense of *sight* θυρίδες δὲ ἡμῖν ὑπάρχουσι τὰ τοῦ σώματος αἰσθητήρια, β., ἀκοή, καὶ τὰ ἄλλα Epiph.*haer*.9.4(p.202.17; M.41.229D); **3.** *eye*; **a.** lit., *Hom.Clem*.3.34; Gel.Cyz.*h.e*.3.19.35(M.85.1353B); **b.** met., of the mind's eye etc. ὡς ἀγαθὸς πύκτης, ἀμετεώριστον ἔχε τὸ τῆς ψυχῆς β. Bas.*hom*.3.4(2.20B; M.31.208A); τοῦ φρονήματος τὸ β. Mac.Mgn.*apocr*.2.21(p.44.3); τῷ τῆς διανοίας β. Gel.Cyz.*h.e*.2.19.22 (M.85.1280C); σκότος...τῆς ψυχῆς τῷ β. *Lit.Jac*.(p.178.10); hence αὐτὸς γὰρ ἐπ' αὐτὴν εἶχεν τὸ β. τῇ γνώμῃ στηριζόμενον (*he had his eye on it*) Philost.*h.e*.4.6(M.65.520C).

βλέπ-ω, A. c. prep. or dependent clause; **1.** *perceive, understand* ὅταν ~ητε...οὕτως ἐγκαταλελεῖφθαι αὐτούς *Barn*.4.14; ~εις οὖν ὅτι ἡ μετάνοια σύνεσίς ἐστι μεγάλη Herm.*mand*.4.2.2; ~εις δὲ πολλοὺς...μετανενοηκότας id.*sim*.8.6.6; abs. ἵνα οἱ μὴ ~οντες ~ωσι Or.*Cels*. 7.39(p.190.10; M.11.1476D); Chrys.*hom.45.2 in Mt*.(7.477D); **2.** *consider, mark* ~ετε, ἐπὶ τίνων τέθεικεν *Barn*.13.6; β. μή *consider whether* ~ετε μὴ τὸν χρηματίσαντα τῷ ἑκατοντάρχῃ ἄγγελον, τὸν ἅγιον τῶν ἁγίων σωτῆρα εἶπεν Didym.*Trin*.2.8(M.39.588A); **3.** *look to, have regard* to μὴ πρὸς ἀπέχθειαν ~ων, ἀλλὰ πρὸς ἀλήθειαν Gel. Cyz.*h.e*.2.20.8(M.85.1281D); εἰς...ὁμόνοιαν...β. *ib*.2.7.39(1242B); πρὸς τὴν ἀνάζευξιν ἔβλεπεν Thphyl.*exc.Rom*.(p.226.22; M.113.933D); **4.** *look reverently* towards τὸ πρὸς τὴν κτίσιν ~ειν...πρὸς τὴν ἀληθινὴν θεότητα ~ειν Gr.Nyss.*Eun*.5(2 p.103.24,26; M.45.681D); **5.** with ἵνα or μή *take heed that, beware lest* ~ε μήποτε...βλάψῃς σου τὴν σάρκα Herm.*vis*.3.10.7; id.*sim*.1.5; Chrys.*hom.12.2 in Col*.(11.414A); ‡Jo. D.*Const*.13(M.95.329B); **6.** *have reference* to τὸ μὴ πρὸς τὸν...σταυρωθέντα ~ειν τοῦ ἀποστόλου τὸν λόγον Gr.Nyss.*Eun*.6(2 p.143.27; M. 45.729B); **7.** *result* in ἡ καινὴ αὕτη σοφία πρὸς ἀτιμίαν οἴεται ~ειν *ib*. 4(2 p.99.21; 677A); **8.** *look towards, face*; of a building, Clem.*str*.7.7 (p.33.2; M.9.461A).

B. c. acc.; **1.** *consider, have regard to* μηδεὶς κατὰ σάρκα ~έτω τὸν πλησίον Ign.*Magn*.6.2; *Barn*.10.11; Chrys.*hom.5.1 in 1Cor*.(10.33E); hence *consider as* οὐ ~ει τοὺς ἀνθρώπους ἀνθρώπους *ib*.9.4(78E); **2.** *have reference to* οὐδὲν ἂν εἴη ἐμποδὼν μὴ οὐχὶ τὸν αὐτὸν [sc. τὸν σωτῆρα] ~ειν καὶ τὴν παροῦσαν Eus.*d.e*.7.3(p.347.17; M.22.565B); **3.** *look up to, admire* κοινὸν δ' ὥσπερ ἄγαλμα δι' ἀρετὴν τοῖς ὁμοδόξοις ἐβλέπετο Philost.*h.e*.3.6(M.65.489A); **4.** *look out, seek* ~ε μοι βιβλίον Jo.Mosch.*prat*.134(M.87.2997A); **5.** *examine, feel* χερσὶ γηραιαῖς με νήπιον ~ῃς Geo.Pis.*carm*.52.1; **6.** exeg. Phil.3:2 ~ετε τοὺς κύνας; no clear parallel for rendering *beware of*, but cf. εἴπατε Ἀρχίππῳ, ~ε τὴν διακονίαν...φοβοῦντός ἐστι τοῦτο τὸ ῥῆμα πανταχοῦ, ὡς ὅταν λέγῃ, '~ετε τοὺς κύνας', '~ετε μή τις ὑμᾶς ἔσται ὁ συλαγωγῶν'...καὶ πανταχοῦ οὕτω φησὶν ὅταν φοβῇ. '~ε, φησί, τὴν διακονίαν' Chrys.*hom.12.2 in Col*.(11.414A).

C. ptcpl.; **1.** ὁ ~ων, ἡ ~ουσα *seer, prophet(ess)*, Hipp.*haer*.5.8 (p.89.14; M.16.3139B); Thdt.*qu.17 in 1Reg*.(1.369); **2.** τὰ ~όμενα *the visible universe*, Or.*princ*.4.2.1(p.308.3; M.11.360A); Chrys.*hom. 35.8 in Gen*.(4.360E); **3.** ~ων *true* τὸν ~οντα πλοῦτον Didym.*Ps*. 30:11(M.39.1313C).

βλεφαρίζω, *wink*, Clem.*paed*.3.11(p.274.26; M.8.645A).

βλέφαρον, τό, *eyelid* ὀφθαλμοὺς καὶ β. καὶ ὦτα...εὑρίσκοντες γεγραμμένα τοῦ θεοῦ...μεταλαμβάνομεν εἰς ἀλληγορίαν τὰ γεγραμμένα Or.*Jo*.13.22(p.245.24; M.14.436B); τὰ β. καὶ αἱ ὀφρύες, τὸ τῶν θεοπτικῶν νοήσεων φρουρητικόν Dion.Ar.*c.h*.15.3(M.3.332B).

***βλήσκ-ω,** *cast* τόπος ἔνθα ~ονται οἱ φάρμακοι *Apoc.Paul*.38 (p.60); *ib*.41(p.62).

βλητέον, *one must cast, put* τὸν μηδέποτε παλαιούμενον τῆς ἀληθείας νοῦν εἰς τὸν καινὸν ἄνθρωπον β. Bas.*hom.in Ps*.32(1.137C; M. 29.337B).

βλήχημα, τό, *bleating*, Bas.*hex*.6.6(1.55E; M.29.132A); ‡Caes.Naz. *dial*.111(M.38.988).

***βληχηματώδης,** *bleating*, Nil.*epp*.2.236(M.79.321A).

***βληχηρός,** = foreg., of the noise made by locusts eating, Cyr. *Joel*.17(3.215D conj. βληχράν).

***βληχητικός,** = βληχηματώδης, Bas.*hom.in Ps*.28(1.114E; M.29. 281D).

[*]**βλήχομαι,** *bleat*, ‡Caes.Naz.*dial*.64(M.38.932).

βληχώδης, *bleating*, *Const.App*.8.40.3.

βλοσυρέω** (βλοσσυρέω**), *look grim* βλοσσυροῖ τὸ ὄμμα αὐτοῦ †Anast.S.*relat*.20(p.72.2); †Jo.D.*B.J*.12(M.96.976B).

***βλοσυρία, ἡ,** *brazen-facedness*, ‡Caes.Naz.*dial*.109(M.38.981).

βλύσις, ἡ, *gushing forth, flow* εἰκὼν τῆς...θεοτόκου ἐκ τῆς...παλάμης...τὴν τοῦ μύρου β. προχέουσα Germ.CP *ep.dogm*.4(M.98. 185B).

βλύσμα, τό, *bubbling up*, Geo.Pis.*Pers*.2.12(M.92.1213B).

βλυστάν-ω, 1. intrans., *gush forth* ὡς ὕδωρ...ἄλλους ἐξ ἄλλων νοτίζον καὶ πάλιν πρὸς ἄλλους ~ον Isid.Pel.*epp*.1.274(M.78.344C); met. σοφίαν πρὸς τὰς χρείας ποικίλως ~ουσαν Max.*cap*.2.29(M.90. 1232B); **2.** trans., *pour forth* αἱ τῶν ὑδάτων πηγαὶ...τὸ ὕδωρ ~ουσι ‡Chrys.*jej*.4(9.799A); met. ὦ στεναγμὸς...~ων φιλόχριστα νάματα ‡Chrys.*hom.in Ps.83*(5.608C).

***βοασμός, ὁ,** *cry*, *Exorc*.13(p.336).

βο-άω, 1. *cry aloud* in entreaty; **a.** in gen. σύνετε, ~ῶ, ὅτι... Just.*dial*.24.1(M.6.528B); **b.** of God appealing to men ἐπὶ τὸ λουτρὸν...παρακαλεῖ μονονουχὶ ~ῶν καὶ λέγων Clem.*prot*.10(p.69.4; M.8.208A); Hipp.*haer*.5.8(p.92.4; M.16.3143B); **c.** in prayer, *1Clem*. 34.7; ταύτην...πρὸς τὸν θεὸν ὤφειλες ~ῆσαι τὴν φωνήν...σὺ δὲ ταῦτα ...πρὸς τὸν θεὸν οὐκ ἐβόησας τὴν φωνήν σου Mel.*pass*.76,77 p.12.24, 31; Meth.*symp*.4.3(p.48.18; M.18.89C); Thdt.*qu.9 in Num*.(1.222); **2.** *call for* οὐρανόθεν βασιλῆος ἀρηγόνα χεῖρα ~ήσας †Apoll.*met.Ps*. 17:7(M.33.1332B); **3.** *proclaim*; **a.** ref. sacred proclamation of Eleusinian hierophant, Hipp.*haer*.5.8(p.96.17; M.16.3150C); **b.** of promulgation of philosophical tenets Παρμενίδης...τὸν κόσμον ἀγέννητον λέγων εἶναι ~ᾷ Thdt.*affect*.2(p.65.6; 4.757); **c.** in divine revelation and teaching, hence freq. introducing scriptural citations; of Christ, Serap.*Man*.36(p.54; M.18.1216B); Nonn.*par.Jo*.8:30(M.43. 817B) al.; ἐν εὐαγγελίοις ὁ αὐτὸς υἱὸς ~ᾷ, 'ἐγὼ καὶ ὁ πατὴρ ἕν ἐσμεν' Gel.Cyz.*h.e*.2.15.5(M.85.1257D); Cosm.Ind.*top*.2(M.88.124A); of God, Logos, or H. Ghost speaking through prophets, Just.*dial*.24.3(M. 6.528C); *ib*.25.1(529A); Clem.*paed*.2.10(p.214.24; M.8.512A); Eus. *e.th*.2.22(p.132.7; M.24.957D); Thdt.*Ezech*.2:5(2.697); of preaching of prophets, Just.*dial*.12.1(500B); Meth.*symp*.4.4(p.50.9; M.18.92C); Acac.Mel.*hom*.(p.91.33; M.77.1472B); of any utterances of inspired writers, Eus.*Marcell*.1.1(p.3.30; M.24.717A); id.*e.th*.1.20(p.83.3; 869A); Cyr.*Jo*.1.3(4.24B); Thdt.*Ps*.9:1(1.656); Cosm.Ind.*top*.2(125B); of scriptural teaching ~ῶσιν αἱ θεῖαι γραφαί Cyr.*Jo*.1.3(4.24B); Gel. Cyz.*h.e*.2.16.15(M.85.1264B); of Law's commandments, Thdt.*h.e*.1. 21.7(3.802); of precepts of NT ~ᾷ τὸ θεῖον ἐπίταγμα Nil.*epp*.2.25 (M.79.212A); **4.** *talk of, declare* εἰ στρατιὴν πτερόεσσαν ἢ αἰθέρος ἔργα βοήσω Nonn.*par.Jo*.3:12(M.43.768B); *ib*.5:39(792B); of Christian confessors ~ῶντας ὅτι εἰσὶ Χριστιανοί CAnc.(314)*can*.3; hence **a.** *reveal, make manifest*, of persons or things τῶν πραγμάτων ἁπάντων αὐτὰ ~ώντων Chrys.*hom.17.6 in Mt*.(7.230D); Cyr.*Os*.34(3.62C); **b.** *noise abroad, celebrate*; κακῶς β. *defame* λοιδοροῦνταί τε καὶ κακῶς ἡμᾶς ~ῶσι Jo.Eleem.*v.Tych*.3(p.114); pass., *be extolled, be famous*, Eus.*h.e*.5.1.1(M.20.408C); id.*v.C*.1.8(p.11.7; M.20.921A); Firm.*ep*.44(M.77.1512C); in bad sense, *be notorious*, Chrys.*hom.1.6 in Mt*.(7.14A).

***βοεργάζ, τό,** *coffer*, rendering of בָּאַרְגָּז (1Reg.6:8) found in LXX by Thdt.*qu.10 in 1Reg*.(1.365) where MSS read βερεχθάν, βερσεχθάν, ἀργόζ.

βοή, ἡ, *cry*; **1.** of divine or heavenly utterances οὐ παρεδέξατο τὴν βοή⟨ν τὴν⟩ θείαν τὴν πρὸς αὐτόν Or.*engast*.7(p.291.14 conj. for βοήθειαν M.12.1024C); ταῖς τῶν ἀγγέλων ἐξ οὐρανοῦ φερομέναις β. Meth.*symp*.3.6(p.32.17; M.18.69A); **2.** of inspired utterances, Eus. *Marcell*.2.3(p.48.20; M.24.805A); id.*e.th*.2.23(p.134.18; M.24.961D); **3.** of prayer οὐ φωνὴν δὲ ἐνταῦθα καὶ β. τὴν κραυγὴν νοητέον, ἀλλὰ τὴν τῆς ψυχῆς προθυμίαν. ... ὁ θεὸς πρὸς σιγῶντα...ἔφη Μωσῆν· τί βοᾷς πρός με; β. τὴν σιγὴν ὀνομάζων διὰ τὴν σπουδαίαν τῆς διανοίας εὐχήν Thdt.*Ps*.3:4(1.627); Nonn.*par.Jo*.9:31(M.43.829B); **4.** of acclamation, Meth.*symp*.11(p.133.6; M.18.209A); *ib*.(p.135.2; 212A); **5.** *baa, bleating* of sheep βρυγμοὺς λεόντων, β. προβάτων, κραυγὰς ὀνάγρων Gr.Mag.*dial*.(tr.Zach.)3(M.*PL*.77.226A).

***βοήδιον, τό,** v. βοΐδιον.

βοήθεια, ἡ, 1. *help, aid*, medical ἡ τῶν...νοσημάτων β. ἰατρικὴ καλεῖται Clem.*paed*.1.2(p.93.10; M.8.256A); *Const.App*.2.41.5; divine, hence equivalent to *grace*, Clem.*str*.6.17(p.514.21; M.9.393A); τὴν παρὰ τοῦ θεοῦ β. ἐπ' ἀνθρώποις αἰτοῦ id.*fr*.44(p.223.15); Or.*princ*.3. 1.17(p.226.3; M.11.284A); τὴν ἀπὸ τοῦ θεοῦ β. id.*Jo*.20.5(p.333.19; M.14.584D); β. γὰρ δεόμεθα ἵνα μὴ ἄλλο τι παρὰ τὴν ἀλήθειαν φρονήσωμεν [i.e. in reading scripture] id.*dial*.11(p.146.6); ἔφθασεν ἐπί σε [i.e. convert requesting baptism] ἡ β. τοῦ θεοῦ *A.Thom*.B 27(p.34. 11); Bas.*hom.in Ps*.45(1.173E; M.29.424B); μὴ ἀποστήσῃς ἀφ' ἡμῶν τὴν σὴν β. *Lit.Jac*.(p.168.8); **2.** military *force* ἐκύκλωσεν ἡ β. τὸν οἶκόν σου *A.Xanthipp*.25(p.76.16); *Narr.Jos*.2.4(p.463); Pall.*v. Chrys*.9(p.51.14; M.47.30).

βοήθημα, τό, *means of assistance, aid, resource*, Clem.*paed*.1.8 (p.128.3; M.8.328B); Or.*Cels*.4.78(p.348.8; M.11.1149C); ὁ θεὸς... κατέπεμψεν...τὸ ἄριστον καὶ εὐκλεέστατον β., τὴν ἁγνείαν Meth.*symp*. 4.2(p.47.11; M.18.89A); of Inc. δι' ὀργάνου θνητοῦ, καταλλήλου β., τοῖς θνητοῖς εἰς ὁμιλίαν κατῄει Eus.*l.C*.14(p.241.23; M.20.1408C); medic., *remedy*, Or.*Jo*.1.35(40; p.45.8; M.14.92D); Eus.*l.C*.14(p.242. 30; 1409D); Chrys.*paralyt*.5(3.41A).

βοηθός, ὁ, 1. *helper*, of God and Christ Χριστὸν...τὸν...β. τῆς ἀσθενείας ἡμῶν 1Clem.36.1; Just.dial.30.3(M.6.540A); ἐπὶ πατρὸς καὶ υἱοῦ καὶ ἁγίου πνεύματος, ἐφ' ὧν μαρτύρων καὶ β. αἱ ἐντολαὶ... φυλάσσεσθαι ὀφείλουσιν Clem.ecl.13(p.140.21; M.9.704D); ταπεινῶν ἐστι θεὸς...β. Or.Jo.13.28(p.252.16; M.14.448B); καλεῖν τὴν σοφίαν παραστῆναί οἱ βοηθόν Meth.symp.10.1(p.121.14; M.18.192B); β. καὶ κύριε τῶν ἁπάντων Serap.euch.3.1; **2.** *assistant secretary* ὁ καθωσιωμένος β. τοῦ θείου κονσιστορίου CChalc.act.14(ACO 2.1.3 p.64.39; H.2.572D); Evagr.h.e.2.18(p.74.22; M.86.2560B); **3.** *member of a* βοήθεια of troops or police, Marc.Diac.v.Porph.27.

βόησις, ἡ, *loud utterance, shouting*, ‡Pion.v.Polyc.18.

[*]**βοητός, ὁ,** for βοηθός, ‡Petr.I Al.phys.22.

βοθρεύω, 1. *dig a pit* or *ditch*, Thdr.Stud.poen.1.79(M.99.1744B); **2.** *plant in a trench*, Jo.Eleem.v.Tych.10(p.120); ib.41(p.152).

βοθρίζω, *bury in a pit*; met., *submerge, overwhelm* τοὺς Χριστοῦ στρατιώτας...κενοδοξίᾳ καὶ γαστριμαργίᾳ βοθρίσας †Cyr.hom.div.14 (5^{2}.415E).

βόθρος, ὁ, *pit*, met. κατασπᾷ [sc. Satan] σε εἰς β. κακῶν Cyr.H. catech.2.3; τὸν τῆς παρανομίας β. ‡Ath.Apoll.1.21(M.26.1129B); εἰς β. πορνείας †Cyr.hom.div.14(5^{2}.415E); β. ... διαβολικόν, τὴν πλεονεξίαν Cyr.Lc.12:15(M.72.733A).

βοΐδιον, τό, *calf, heifer*, Ath.h.Ar.56(p.215.4; M.25.761A); Gr. Naz.or.26.18(M.35.1252A); Chrys.fr.in Jer.31:18(M.64.976C); in form βοήδια, τά *oxen*, Mir.Geo.5(p.47.11).

***βοϊλᾶς, ὁ,** *boyar, Slav nobleman*, Thphn.chron.p.367(M.108. 877C).

***βοκάλιος, ὁ,** (Lat. *vocalis*) *singer*; of Hebrew psalm-singers, Cosm.Ind.top.5(M.88.248D); Chron.Pasch.p.86(M.92.244B).

***βολβιτόω,** *make of cow-dung*; perf. ptcpl. pass., *savouring of cow-dung, stinking* ἡ κοπρώδης αὐτοῦ καὶ βεβολβιτωμένη φωνή Gr. Nyss.Eun.12(1 p.340.26; M.45.1060B).

βολβός, ὁ, 1. *eye-ball*, ‡Jo.D.Artem.61(M.96.1308D); **2.** a kind of shell-fish, T.Sal.6.10(p.27.13; M.122.1325B).

βολή, ἡ, 1. *bolt* κεραυνῶν β. Const.ap.Eus.v.C.17(p.178.14; M.20. 1284C); **2.** *ray*, Eus.l.C.13(p.237.7; M.20.1400B); fig. τὰς β. τῶν θαυμάτων Geo.Pis.carm.24.2; **3.** *glance*, met. οὐσία...νοῦ μόνου ληπτὴ βολαῖς Gr.Naz.carm.1.2.10.91(M.37.687); **4.** *casting away, putting off* οὐ κατὰ β., ἀλλὰ κατὰ πρόσληψιν Cyr.Ps.76:11(conj. for καταβολήν M.69.1192C; perh. read κατ' ἀποβολήν).

βολίς, ἡ, *missile, javelin*, fig. τὴν τῆς κατάρας β. Gr.Mag.dial.(tr. Zach.)3(M.PL.77.254A).

βολιστικός, *capable of sinking* or *sounding*, of a sounding-lead πῶς...ἡ τῶν σωμάτων [edd. ὑδάτων] φύσις, β. κατὰ φύσιν ὑπάρχουσα, ὁρᾶται ἄδυτος καὶ ἀβόλιστος ἐν τοῖς ὕδασι τῆς Μαρμαρικῆς Πενταπόλεως; ‡Ath.qu.Ant.136(M.28.684A) [where, if ὑδάτων should be read, βολιστική = *capable of being sounded*].

***βομβαίνω,** *babble, talk nonsense*, Nil.epp.3.174(M.79.465B).

βομβ-έω, A. intrans.; **1.** *buzz*, Hipp.haer.4.28(p.55.26, v.l. ἐπιβομβεῖ M.16.3091B); of bees, Meth.res.2.2(p.333.7; M.41.1165B); of the heart, *beat audibly, thump* ἐβόμβει ἡ καρδία μου T.Zeb.2.5; hence **2.** *talk meaninglessly, chatter idly*; of Paul of Samosata and Nestorius, Sophr.H.ep.syn.(M.87.3161C).

B. trans., *buzz round* μέλιτται κηρίον ~οῦσαι Chrys.stat.2.1(2.21A).

***βόμβημα, τό,** *buzzing*, hence *idle chatter* τὰ ἐξ ἀπιστίας β. Leont.H.Nest.4.19(M.86.1685B).

βόμβησις, ἡ, 1. *buzzing, empty noise*, hence *tiresome repetition* of a sound τὴν δοκοῦσαν εἶναι β. εἰς λειότητα μετέβαλον [sc. LXX], φήσαντες, 'ἔζησε δὲ Ἀδὰμ τριάκοντα καὶ ἐννακόσια ἔτη' [i.e. for Hebr. and AQ 'ἐννακόσια ἔτος καὶ τριάκοντα ἔτος'] Epiph.mens.2(M.43. 240B); **2.** *crowd, multitude*, Gr.Naz.or.42.5(M.36.464C).

βομβύκιον, τό, *small buzzing insect*; hence met., *useless trifling* τοιαῦτά τινα κινεῖ β. [sc. ὁ διάβολος] Ath.ep.Amun.(M.26.1172A).

[*]**βόμβυλος, ὁ,** (= βομβύλιος II, LS), *vessel, jar*, Thdt. provid. 4(4.539).

***βομβωνάρια, τά,** *linen drawers*, Cosm.Ind.top.5(M.88.213C); Jo.Mal.chron.12 p.288(M.97.436A).

***βοόζυξ,** *like an ox-yoke*; of crescent moon, Eudoc.Cypr.1.71 (M.85.836A).

βοοστάσιον, τό, *ox-stall*, Bas.hex.9.3(1.82E; M.29.193B); Chrys. hom.52.4 in Mt.(7.534C); ib.88.4(830D).

βοράτινος, *of juniper* δένδρα...ἀρκεύθινα καὶ β. M.Thdot.1 11 (p.67.30).

***βορβοριανοί, οἱ,** name of adherents of a Gnostic sect, also called βορβορῖται, βαρβηλιωταί, ναασσινοί, κοδδιανοί, notorious for evil living (βόρβορος = *mud*), Ephr.2.242C; Epiph.haer.26.3(p.279. 18; M.41.336D); Philost.h.e.3.15(M.65.505C); Thdt.haer.1.13(4.304).

βορβορῖται, οἱ, = foreg., Epiph.haer.25.2(p.268.21); Tim.CP haer.(M.86.20A).

***βορβοροκοίλιστος,** *wallowing in mud* χοῖρος β. †Anast.S.relat. 49(p.70).

βόρβορος, ὁ, *mud*; smeared on children's foreheads as apotropaic charm against evil eye, Chrys.hom.12.7 in 1Cor.(10.107C); met., *moral filth*, Clem.prot.10(p.68.8; M.8.205A); Dion.Al.ap.Eus. h.e.7.7.2(M.20.648B); Cyr.Am.53(3.307D).

βορβορόω, *smear with mud*, Chrys.hom.12.7 in 1Cor.(10.107D); *make muddy* ἡ βεβορβορωμένη θάλασσα T.Abr.A 19(p.101.14); met., *defile*, Cyr.H.procatech.4; id.catech.6.34; Ephr.3.165E; Chrys.hom. 12.2 in Col.(11.414F); Nil.epp.3.171(M.79.464C); πῶς...διαμένοιεν ἂν ...οὐχὶ βεβορβορωμένη [sc. ἡ ἐκκλησία]; Thdr.Stud.epp.1.48(M.99. 1080A).

βορβορώδης, *filthy*, met. β. βίῳ Clem.q.d.s.1.1(p.159.10 not.; M.9.604A); Gr.Nyss.v.Mos.(M.44.345D); Nil.epp.3.171(M.79.464C); τὸ β. τῶν Νικολαϊτῶν Areth.Apoc.5(M.106.536D).

βορβόρωσις, ἡ, *defilement*, Thdr.Stud.epp.1.6(M.99.928C).

[*]**βορδονάριος, ὁ,** v. βουρδωνάριος.

***βορδόνη, ἡ,** v. *βορδώνη.

***βορδόνιον, τό,** *young mule*, Jo.Mosch.prat.101(M.87.2960B); ib. 125(2988B).

[*]**βορδών,** v. βουρδών.

***βορδώνη, ἡ,** *female mule*, Thphn.chron.p.155(v.l. βορδόνη M.108. 421A).

βορεινός, *northern*, Ath.fr.Cant.(M.27.1356A); Bas.hex.7.4(1.67B; M.29.157B); Cyr.S.v.Sab.37(p.126.14).

***βορειοτικός,** *northern*, Or.sel.in Ezech.8(M.13.796C).

***βορρόφορος, ὁ,** *north wind*, Thdr.Stud.epp.1.3(M.99.917C).

βόσκημα, τό, *fed beast*, plur. *cattle*; met., of heretics and their herds of followers, Epiph.haer.13.2(p.207.2; M.41.237C); ib.42.11 (p.107.10; 709D).

***βοσκητός, ὁ,** *herdsman*, ‡Barth.Edess.Muham.(M.104.1449D).

βοσκός, ὁ, *grass-eating ascetic*; of Mesopotamian monks, Soz.h.e. 6.33.2(M.67.1395A); of monks in Palestine, Evagr.h.e.1.21(p.30.24; M.86.2480B); Jo.Mosch.prat.21(M.87.2868B); Leont.N.v.Sym.14(M. 93.1688C).

βόσκ-ω, *graze*; hence *live as an ascetic eating grass* περὶ τὴν Νεκρὰν θάλασσαν ἔβοσκε Jo.Mosch.prat.159(M.87.3028A); med. ἀναχωρητὴς εἰς τὰ ὄρη ταῦτα ἦν...πολλὰ ἔτη ποιήσας ~όμενος ib.84(2941A).

***βότα, τά,** (Lat. *vota*) *dies votorum* (3rd Jan.), in class. times day of *nuncupatio* of vows for emperor's safety and of payment of vows for previous year (cf. Pliny, *panegyricus* 94.2; Tert.de corona 12); as day of pagan rejoicing τὰς λεγομένας καλάνδας, καὶ τὰ λεγόμενα β. ... ἐκ τῆς τῶν πιστῶν πολιτείας περιαιρεθῆναι βουλόμεθα CTrull.can.62.

βοτάνη, ἡ, *herbage, plant*, met. ἵνα μὴ τοῦ διαβόλου β. τις εὑρεθῇ ἐν ὑμῖν Ign.Eph.10.3; ἀλλοτρίας β. ἀπέχεσθε, ἥτις ἐστὶν αἵρεσις id. Trall.6.1; ἀπέχεσθε τῶν κακῶν β. ἅστινας οὐ γεωργεῖ...Χριστός id. Philad.3.1; Clem.str.6.7(p.461.25; M.9.281A) cit. s. γῆ; Gr.Thaum. pan.Or.7(p.19.24; M.10.1073D).

***βοτανοφάγιον, τό,** *diet of herbs*, Ephr.3.166F.

βότρυς, ὁ, *bunch of grapes*, met., exeg. Gen.49:11 αἵματι... σταφυλῆς...τῆς ἁγίας σαρκὸς αὐτοῦ ὡς β. ἐπὶ ξύλον θλιβείσης Hipp. antichr.11(p.10.18; M.10.737A); in eucharist ἀπὸ τῆς ἀμπέλου τρεῖς β. ἀποθλίψαντες ἐν ποτηρίῳ συγκοινωνήσατέ μοι A.Mt.25(p.253.1); of Christ, Gr.Nyss.hom.3 in Cant.(M.44.829C); ἡ ἄμπελος [sc. BMV] τὸν β. βλαστήσασα τῆς ζωῆς Abr.Eph.occurs.9(p.454.6); of the prophets, Clem.paed.2.2(p.167.24; M.8.409A); of graces, Meth.symp. 5.5(p.59.4; M.18.105B) cit. s. ἄμπελος; also neut., met., of truth, Or.Jo.1.30(33; p.37.20; M.14.80A) cit. s. ἄμπελος.

[*]**βοττίον, τό,** v. [*]βουττίον.

βούβρωστις, ἡ, name of an insect, ? = βούπρηστις, *a poisonous beetle*, Phot.nomoc.9.25(M.104.768C).

***βοῦγλιν, τό,** *dagger*, Jo.Mal.chron.18 p.493(M.97.713B).

βούγλωσσος, ὁ, *bugloss, ox-tongue*, a species of plant; of a golden βούγλωσσος among spoils stolen by Achan (Jos.7:21; γλῶσσαν LXX), Niceph.Ur.v.Sym.60(M.86.3041C).

βουζύγιος, *pertaining to the yoking* of an ox with an ass, ref. Dt.22:10 οὐκ ἂν ἐκφύγοιεν τὴν β. ἀράν Clem.str.2.23(p.189.24; M.8. 1089A).

βουθήλεια, ἡ, *cow*, Hier.(tr.Sophr.Pal.)vir.ill.57(p.38.1).

***βουθυτία, ἡ,** *sacrifice of oxen*, Pers.(p.26.12).

***βουκάκρατον, τό,** *bread steeped in wine*, ‡Ath.Melch.(M.28.529C).

***βουκέλλατος, ὁ,** *biscuit bread*, Pall.h.Laus.18(p.48.8; M.34. 1051B).

βουκίν, τό, v. *βουκίον.*

***βούκινον, τό,** (Lat. *bucina*) *trumpet,* Jo.Mosch.*prat.*152(M.87.3017B).

βουκί(ο)ν ([*]**βουκκίον**), **τό,** *biscuit, morsel of bread, Apophth. Patr.*(M.65.88A); *βουκκία* Dor.*doct.*11.8(M.88.1745A); Anast.S.*hod.*2 (M.89.57A).

βουκόλησις, ἡ, *deception, beguilement,* Or.*Cels.*2.79(p.201.27; M.11.920B).

βούκρανον, τό, *ox-head,* hence the constellation *Taurus,* Meth. *symp.*8.14(p.102.9; M.18.165B).

***βουκτασία, ἡ,** *slaughter of oxen,* Gr.Naz.*carm.*2.2(epigr.)87.4 (M.38.124A).

βουλαῖος, *of the council,* epithet of Themis, Synes.*regn.*20(15; p.46.4; M.66.1093A).

***βουλευματικός,** *able to take counsel, purposive ὁ ἄνθρωπος...β. ἐστι ζῷον* Melet.*nat.hom.*30(M.64.1276D, v.l. *βουλευτικόν*).

βούλευσις, ἡ, *deliberation μετὰ τὴν βούλησιν, ζήτησις, καὶ σκέψις· καὶ μετὰ ταῦτα, εἰ τῶν ἐφ' ἡμῖν ἐστι, γίνεται βουλή, ἤγουν β.* Jo.D. *f.o.*2.22(M.94.945A).

βουλευτήριον, τό, 1. *council;* of the senate, Synes.*regn.*20(15; p.46.2; M.66.1093A); of local councils, Isid.Pel.*epp.*2.146(M.78.596A); **2.** hence the *curia,* ref. Christians enrolled as *curiales* during the last persecution, released from their obligations by Constantine and Licinius, Eus.*v.C.*2.20(p.49.16; M.20.997C); ref. simoniacal ordination sought in order to evade curial *munera,* Pall.*v.Chrys.*15 (p.90.12,16; M.47.51); ref. ineligibility of *curiales* for ordination, CIllyr.*ep.*ap.Thdt.*h.e.*4.9.5(3.962); **3.** of Church *τὸ κοινὸν τῶν ψυχῶν β.* †Bas.*Is.*106(1.452E; M.30.289B); **4.** *counsel, deliberation,* Serap. *ep.mon.*7(M.40.932D); of the deliberative faculty of the mind *τῆς ψυχῆς τὸ β.* Chrys.*hom.59.6 in Mt.*(7.603C); Thdt.*Ps.*118:112(1.1466); of the counsel of God, Gr.Nyss.*or.1 in Gen.1:26*(M.44.260B).

βουλή, ἡ, I. *deliberation, counsel, design;*

A. of men; **1.** *deliberation β. δέ ἐστι ζήτησις περὶ τοῦ πῶς ἂν ἐν τοῖς παροῦσι πράγμασιν διεξάγοιμεν* Clem.*str.*2.15(p.150.10; M.8.1008C); its objects, like those of *προαίρεσις,* are matters falling within the scope of free choice, Melet.*nat.hom.*synops.(M.64.1116D); and man's possession of this faculty argues that his actions are not determined, Nemes.*nat.hom.*39(M.40.764B); associated with *προαίρεσις* which is *ὄρεξις βουλευτική,* Melet.(l.c.); and defined as a function of the appetitive will *ὄρεξις ζητητική,* Max. *opusc.*(M.91.16B); Jo.D.*f.o.*2.22(M.94.945A); where, however, it is equated with *βούλευσις* and dist. from *προαίρεσις* which is defined as *ὀρέξεως καὶ βουλῆς καὶ κρίσεως σύνοδος* Max.*opusc.*(13A); equated with *σκοπός* as object of deliberation, Thdt.*Ps.*13:6(1.684); **2.** *counsel;* **a.** of good counsel as a Christian virtue, *1Clem.*2.3; Clem.*ecl.*65(p.155.13; M.9.728D); and as gift of H. Ghost (cf. Is.11:2), Just. *dial.*39.2(M.6.560C); bestowed esp. on Daniel, *ib.*87.4(684B); **b.** of evil counsel, *Did.*2.6; Herm.*sim.*6.3.5 etc.; esp. *πονηρὰ β. evil impulse* (perh. equivalent to Hebr. יֵצֶר הָרָע), Herm.*vis.*1.2.4; id. *sim.*9.28.4; **c.** *β. λαμβάνω intend,* Gel.Cyz.*h.e.*1.4.2(M.85.1201B); *λαμβάνει β. τινος* Leont.N.*v.Jo.Eleem.*11(p.21.11); also *β. εἶχες ib.*(p.22.13); **3.** *will;* of man's free will, Meth.*symp.*5.1(p.53.11; M.18.97A); id.*fr.mart.*2(p.520.6) cit. s. *συμπέρασμα; ἐν τῇ β. κείσθω τῇ σῇ* [sc. the decision whether or not to follow the counsel of perfection (Mt.19:21)] Chrys.*poenit.*6.3(2.321E).

B. of God; **1.** of Father; **a.** *counsel;* **i.** in gen. *οὐδὲν λέληθεν τὴν β. αὐτοῦ 1Clem.*27.6; Just.*dial.*103.3(M.6.716C) et freq.; **ii.** ref. Creation, Herm.*vis.*1.3.4; as cause of creation of angels and spirits, *Hom.Clem.*3.33; nothing created apart from it, Meth.*res.*1.36(p.277.6; M.41.1101C); of God's counsel in creating man *ἐν...τῇ πρώτῃ β. λέγων ὁ θεός, 'ποιήσωμεν ἄνθρωπον κατ' εἰκόνα', καὶ τὸ 'καθ' ὁμοίωσιν' προσέθηκεν· δεικνὺς ὅτι καὶ προαίρεσιν ἡμῖν αὐτεξουσίαν ἐμβαλεῖ,...ἐν δὲ τῇ κατασκευῇ ὕστερον μόνον εἶπε τὸ 'κατ' εἰκόνα'* ‡Bas.*struct.hom.*1.20(1.333A; M.30.29C); identical with God's *δύναμις,* Gr.Nyss.*hex.*7 (M.44.69A); perfect and incontrovertible, Cyr.*glaph.Gen.*1.3(1.7A); **iii.** ref. continuous providence, Meth.*res.*2.10(p.350.6); **iv.** as defining duration of man's life, ‡Ath.*qu.Ant.*113(M.28.668C); **v.** its immutability signified in scripture by God's 'oath', ‡Cyr.*Trin.*12 (6^3.18E; M.77.1148C); **vi.** as the source of all good, Gr.Nyss.*tres dii* (M.45.129A); **vii.** served by seraphim, Meth.*res.*1.49(p.303.13; M.18.280A); revealed by angels, Dion.Ar.*c.h.*8.2(M.3.241A); esp. by Christ as *ἄγγελος μεγάλης β.* (Is.9:6) Just.*dial.*126.1(M.6.768C); *β. τῆς μεγάλης μέγαν ἄγγελον CIG* 4.9595a; Ath.*Ar.*3.63(M.26.457A); †Bas.*Is.*226(1.550A; M.30.512C); Cyr.*Is.*1.5(2.155C); Thdt.*Is.*9:6(p.49.17; 2.235); Dion.Ar.*c.h.*4.4(M.3.181D); executed by Son, Eus.*e.th.*3.3(p.155.30; M.24.1000B); *Symb.Sirm.*1 *anath.*18(p.255.32; M.26.737D); ‡Ath.*dial.Trin.*2.9(M.28.1169A); **viii.** ref. generation of Son by Father's *βουλή: οὐκ ἔστιν ἀνθρώπινον ἔργον, ἀλλὰ τῆς β. τοῦ προβάλλοντος αὐτὸν πατρός* Just.*dial.*76.1(M.6.652C); *ib.*100.4(709C) cit. s. *δύναμις; γεγεννῆσθαι ἀπὸ τοῦ πατρός, δυνάμει καὶ β. αὐτοῦ, ἀλλ' οὐ κατὰ ἀποτομήν ib.*128.4(776B); this doctrine asserted by Arians *τὸ γὰρ κεφάλαιον εἶναι...ἐπὶ τὴν β. τοῦ πατρὸς ἀνενεγκεῖν τοῦ υἱοῦ τὴν γένεσιν, καὶ μὴ πάθος ἀποφῆναι τοῦ θεοῦ τὴν γονήν* Ast. Soph.*fr.*18 ap.Eus.*Marcell.*1.4(p.19.14; M.24.756A); and refuted by orthodox who maintained that Son is himself Father's *βουλή,* Ath.*Ar.*3.63(M.26.457A); *ib.*3.67(464C); *ib.*2.2(152A) cit. s. *ἐνούσιος; αὐτός...ἐστιν ἡ ζῶσα καὶ ἐνυπόστατος β. τε καὶ θέλησις τοῦ γεννήσαντος αὐτόν* Cyr.*Jo.*5.5(4.527D); id.*hom.pasch.*29(5^2.337E); id.*thes.*7(5^1.54E); id.*dial.Trin.*2(5^1.455A); **ix.** ref. Inc. and death of Christ *λόγος αὐτοῦ ὑπάρχων...τῇ β. αὐτοῦ γενόμενος ἄνθρωπος* Just.*1apol.*23.2(M.6.364A); id.*dial.*75.4(M.6.652C); *ib.*87.2(684A); *τοῦ ὑπομείναντος κατὰ τὴν τοῦ πατρὸς β. ... παθεῖν ib.*95.2(701C); Gel.Cyz.*h.e.*2.24.6(M.85.1300B); Max.*opusc.*(M.91.48C); **b.** plur., *commandments* of God, Dion.Ar.*ep.*8(M.3.1085A); **c.** *will,* equivalent to *βούλησις,* dist. from *οὐσία* of God *ἡ οὐσία τοῦ θεοῦ τὸ μὴ εἶναι οὐσία οὐ δέχεται· ἡ δὲ β. ... δέχεται τὸ μὴ βούλεσθαι* ‡Just.*qu.Chr.*3.1(M.6.1432A); **2.** of Son; *will;* **a.** ref. pre-existent Christ subsisting by his own will *θελήματι καὶ β. ὑπέστη πρὸ χρόνων καὶ πρὸ αἰώνων πλήρης θεός* Ar.*ep.Eus.*(p.3.1; M.42.212B); **b.** ref. harmony of Son's will with Father's, ‡Dion.Al.*fr.in Lc.22:42*(p.235.11; M.10.1598C); of their identity, Thdr.Mops.*fr.in Jo.*5:19(p.326.5; M.66.744C); **c.** ref. unity of Christ's will in Nestorius' view, Nest.*fr.*B 9(p.224.15)ap. CLater.*act.*5(H.3.896C) cit. s. *θέλημα;* **3.** of Trin., *will,* ref. unity of will in Godhead *οὔτε γὰρ χρόνῳ διαιρεῖται ἀλλήλων τὰ πρόσωπα τῆς θεότητος, οὔτε τόπῳ, οὐ β.* Gr.Nyss.*comm.not.*(M.45.180C); Sever.*creat.*5.2(M.56.472); *συντρέχει τῆς ἁγίας τριάδος εἰς μίαν β. τε καὶ γνώμην ἀεὶ τὰ θελήματα* Cyr.*Jo.*4.1(4.334B); Gel.Cyz.*h.e.*2.15.4 (M.85.1257D).

II. *senate β. σύγκλητος;* of Rome, Eus.*h.e.*5.21.4(M.20.488B); of CP, Philost.*h.e.*2.9(M.65.472B); abs., Eus.*h.e.*2.2.3(140B); hence *senate-house ὁ μὲν ἐπὶ τὴν β. βαδίζει, ὁ δὲ ἐπὶ τὴν ἐκκλησίαν* Ath.*gent.*43(M.25.85D); of eccl. elders as *σύμβουλοι τοῦ ἐπισκόπου...συνέδριον καὶ β. τῆς ἐκκλησίας Const.App.*2.28.4.

βούλημα, τό, I. *act of will, will, purpose;*

A. of men; ref. free will involving moral responsibility *οἰκείῳ τοίνυν β., καὶ οἰκείᾳ ἐξουσίᾳ ἢ στεφανοῦται ἢ τιμωρεῖται ὁ ἄνθρωπος* Nil.*epp.*2.328(M.79.361A).

B. of God; **1.** ref. God's power, Gr.Nyss.*Eun.*12(1 p.279.13; M.45.985D); *οὐδὲν ἐναντιοῦται τῷ αὐτοῦ β.* Epiph.*haer.*70.7(p.239.20; M.42.350C); *δύναμιν...μόνῳ...τῷ οἰκείῳ β. μετρουμένην* ‡Cyr.*Trin.*7 (6^3.8A; M.77.1132A); Jo.D.*f.o.*1.8(M.94.808C); **2.** ref. Creation *γῆν...ἥδρασεν ἐπὶ τὸν ἀσφαλῆ τοῦ ἰδίου β. θεμέλιον 1Clem.*33.3; *μόνον αὐτοῦ τὸ β. κοσμοποιία* Clem.*prot.*4(p.48.16; M.8.164A); Gr.Naz.*or.*20.9 (M.35.1076B); Gr.Nyss.*Eun.*12(1 p.281.6; M.45.988D); **3.** ref. Son's generation: (Arian) *οὕτω καὶ αὐτὸς τῷ β. τοῦ θεοῦ, οὐκ ὢν πρότερον, γέγονεν* Ath.*ep.Aeg.Lib.*12(M.25.565B); (orthodox) *ἄμεσός ἐστι τοῦ υἱοῦ ἡ πρὸς τὸν πατέρα συνάφεια, καὶ οὐκ ἐξωθεῖται οὐδὲ ἐξείργεται ὑπὸ τῆς ἀδιαστάτου συναφείας τὸ β. τὸ τῇ ἀγαθῇ φύσει διὰ παντὸς ἐνυπάρχον* Gr.Nyss.*Eun.*8(2 p.182.10; M.45.776B); **4.** ref. procession of H. Ghost *ἐκ τοῦ πατρὸς β. ἀφορμᾶται* Gr.Nyss.*tres dii*(M.45.129A); **5.** ref. Son as agent of Father's will, Just.*dial.*61.1(M.6.613C); *ib.*103.3(717A); Bas.*Eun.*2.20(1.257B; M.29.617C); **6.** of God's will ref. Inc. and Atonement, *1Clem.*8.5; Just.*dial.*103.3(M.6.717A); Clem.*paed.*1.6(p.106.10; M.8.281B); **7.** of God's providence exercised over Church by angels, Or.*or.*31.6(p.398.21; M.11.556B); **8.** of God's will as standard and guide of human morality, Tat.*orat.*7 (p.7.18; M.6.820B); Or.*Jo.*19.3(p.301.14; M.14.529A); Gr.Nyss.*or. dom.*4(p.70.18; M.44.1164A); **9.** as implanted in soul *καὶ ἐν τοῖς ἐσφαλμένοις ἴχνη τινὰ σώζει τοῦ θεοῦ β.* Or.*mart.*47(p.43.4; M.11.629B); **10.** ref. identity of will in Father and Son, ‡Dion.Al.*fr.in Lc.*22:42(p.234.3; M.10.1598B); *θρησκεύομεν οὖν τὸν πατέρα...καὶ τὸν υἱὸν...ὄντα δύο τῇ ὑποστάσει πράγματα, ἓν δὲ τῇ ὁμονοίᾳ καὶ τῇ συμφωνίᾳ καὶ τῇ ταυτότητι τοῦ β.* Or.*Cels.*8.12(p.230.2; M.11.1533C); Bas.*Spir.*18(3.16A; M.32.100C); *οὐ μόνον κοινὰ τὰ ἔργα ἀλλὰ καὶ... τοῦ β. ἡ ταυτότης* Thdr.Mops.*fr.in Jo.*5:19(p.326.5; M.66.744B); **11.** ref. one will in Trin. *ἓν γὰρ...τὸ β. τοῦ θεοῦ ἐν μιᾷ ταὐτότητι* Clem.*str.*6.16(p.504.14; M.9.369C); *κατὰ τὸ ἓν καὶ ταὐτὸ τῆς θεότητος ...κίνημά τε καὶ β. καὶ τὴν τῆς οὐσίας ταὐτότητα* Gr.Naz.*or.*20.7(M.35.1073A); *οὐδεμιᾶς παρατάσεως ἐν τῇ τοῦ θείου β. κινήσει ἀπὸ τοῦ πατρὸς διὰ τοῦ υἱοῦ ἐπὶ τὸ πνεῦμα γινομένης* Gr.Nyss.*tres dii*(M.45.129B).

II. *principle, norm καθαρὰν ἀποδεικνύουσαν τὴν πολιτείαν καὶ* ἀποκαθισταυομένην εἰς τὸ β. τῆς φύσεως τοῦ λόγου Or.*Jo.*32.21(p.462.27; M.14.800D); τὸ β. τῆς φύσεως καταμαθεῖν ἔστιν, ἐξ ὧν οὐ διαφερόμεθα πρὸς ἀλλήλους ‡Nil.*Epict.*33(M.79.1297D).

III. *purport, meaning, intention*; of meaning of divine revelation οἱ προφῆται ἐν τῷ λέγειν οὐ τὰ ἴδια ἀλλὰ τὰ τοῦ θείου β. Or.*or.*28.8(p.380.14; M.11.528C); τὸ β. τοῦ ἐν τοῖς προφήταις πνεύματος id. *Cels.*6.19(p.89.31; M.11.1320A); of the 'mind' of Church in formulation of doctrine τηροῦμεν καὶ τὸ β. τῆς ἐκκλησίας *ib.*5.22(p.23.20; 1216B); of sense of a passage or thesis of a writer, Clem.*str.*2.9(p.135.20; M.8.977C); τὸ β. μυστικόν Or.*hom.4.1 in Jer.*(p.22.7; M.13.284C); β. ... τῶν γραμμάτων *ib.19.11*(p.167.1; 485C); οὐκ ἔχων... ἐκ τῶν θείων γραφῶν τὸ ἑαυτοῦ κατασκευάσαι β. Marcell.*fr.*76 ap. Eus.*Marcell.*1.4(p.20.14; M.24.756C).

βούλησις, ἡ, I. *will, purpose*;

A. in gen. τὴν μὲν θέλησιν νοῦν εἶναι ὀρεκτικὸν...τὴν δὲ β. εὔλογον ὄρεξιν ἢ τὴν περί τινος θέλησιν Clem.*fr.*41(p.220.22)ap.Max.*Pyrr.*(M.91.317C); usu. in good sense, dist. from ἐπιθυμία: ὥστ' ἂν τὸ μὲν ἀστεῖον β. ὀνομάσαι, ἣν ὁρίζονται εὔλογον ὄρεξιν, τὸ δὲ φαῦλον ἐπιθυμίαν, ἥν φασιν εἶναι ἄλογον ὄρεξιν Or.*Jo.*20.22(20; p.355.20; M.14.621C); but λέγονται γάρ [sc. in scripture] τινες εἶναι καὶ θεοῦ ἐπιθυμίαι, ὀνομαζομένων οὕτως αὐτοῦ τῶν β. *ib.*20.23(20; p.356.1; 624A); β. also used of evil desire or purpose παρόντος χρόνου τῆς ἀνοσίου β. Const.ap.Gel.Cyz.*h.e.*3.1.3; β. οἶδα, νοῦ ῥοπὴν καὶ συνδρομὴν τῶν ὅσσ' ἐφ' ἡμῖν Gr.Naz.*carm.*1.1.34.35(M.37.948A); in rel. to evil τὸ κακὸν παρὰ τὴν ὁδὸν καὶ...παρὰ τὴν β. ... στέρησις ἄρα ἐστὶ τὸ κακόν...καὶ μηδαμῶς μηδαμῇ μηδὲν ὄν Dion.Ar.*d.n.*4.32(M.3.732D); dist. from προαίρεσις: τὴν αὐτὴν...ἀναλογίαν ἣν ἔχει τὸ βουλευτὸν πρὸς τὸ βουλευτόν, ἔχειν τὴν β. φασι πρὸς τὴν προαίρεσιν· εἴπερ ταῦτα μόνα προαιρούμεθα, ἃ δι' ἡμῶν οἰόμεθα δύνασθαι γενέσθαι. βουλόμεθα δὲ καὶ τὰ μὴ δι' ἡμῶν οἷά τε γενέσθαι Max.*opusc.*(M.91.13C); β. γὰρ εἶναί φασιν, οὐ τὴν ἁπλῶς φυσικήν, ἀλλὰ τὴν ποιάν· τουτέστι, τὴν περί τινος θέλησιν *ib.*(21A).

B. ref. men; **1.** of free will, Meth.*res.*1.37(p.278.14; M.18.293B); ὁ ἄνθρωπος...αὐτοδέσποτον β. καὶ αὐτοπροαίρετον πρὸς τὴν αἵρεσιν... τοῦ καλοῦ λαβών *ib.*1.38(p.280.10; M.41.1105A); οὐ προφθάνει τὰς ἡμετέρας β., ἵνα μὴ λυμήνηται τὸ αὐτεξούσιον ἡμῶν· ὅταν δὲ ἡμεῖς ἑλώμεθα, τότε πολλὴν εἰσάγει τὴν βοήθειαν ἡμῖν Chrys.*hom.12.3 in Heb.*(12.124D); **2.** of man's will, rendered ineffective by his lack of corresponding δύναμις, Gr.Nyss.*Eun.*9(2 p.210.12; M.45.808C); of weakness of man's will as a cause of evil, Dion.Ar.*d.n.*4.35(M.3.736A); ref. the 'gnostic' ἡ β. καὶ ἡ κρίσις καὶ ἡ ἄσκησις ἡ αὐτή Clem.*str.*2.16(p.153.23; M.8.1016B).

C. ref. God; **1.** in gen., *1Clem.*9.1; plur., Or.*Jo.*20.23(p.356.1; M.14.624A); ποίησις θεοῦ, αὐτή ἐστιν ἡ β. Isid.Pel.*epp.*1.353(M.78.384C); dist. from οὐσία of God, ‡Just.*qu.Chr.*3.1(M.6.1429C); equated with God's wisdom, Cyr.*thes.*7(5^1.51D); power, Gr.Nyss.*hex.*7(M.44.69A); and Spirit in Church, Const.ap.Socr.*h.e.*1.9.44(M.67.93A); as illuminating minds of heavenly hierarchy, Dion.Ar.*c.h.*1.4(M.3.376B); **2.** in Creation, ‡Just.*qu.Chr.*2.7(M.6.1428B); Bas.*Eun.*2.21(1.257B; M.29.617C); Gr.Nyss.*hex.*5(M.44.69A); *Const.App.*5.7.18; of divine purpose in Creation συνάναρχον...τῇ μακαρίᾳ φύσει τὴν περὶ τῶν...δημιουργεῖσθαι μελλόντων ἐκέκτητο β. Zach.Mit.*opif.*(M.85.1097A); **3.** of Providence, ref. distinction between God's positive will for good and his permission of evil οὐθ' οἱ διωκόμενοι βουλήσει τοῦ θεοῦ διώκονται,...ἀλλὰ μὴν οὐδὲν ἄνευ θελήματος τοῦ κυρίου Clem.*str.*4.12(p.286.8; M.8.1293D); τῶν γὰρ γινομένων ἃ μὲν κατὰ β. γίνεται, ἃ δὲ κατ' εὐδοκίαν, ἃ δὲ κατὰ συγχώρησιν Or.*fr.57 in Lc.*(p.261); οὐ μὴν ἐνέργειαν καλοῦμεν τὴν β. κακῶν γὰρ ἀναίτιος ὁ θεός Thdt.*haer.*5.23(4.456); in sustaining the universe, *Const.App.*7.35.2; in miracles, *ib.*8.1.7; **4.** of divine purpose of redemption, Dion.Ar.*d.n.*2.6(M.3.644C); **5.** ref. generation of Son; **a.** by will of Father, especially in Arian doctrine, *Symb.Ant.*(345)2(p.252.8; M.26.728C); Eun.*apol.*23(M.30.860A); καθὸ καὶ εἰκόνα βουλήσεως ὀνομάζουσιν Bas.*Eun.*1.24(1.235D; M.29.565B); *Lit.*ap.*Const.App.*8.12.7; Cyr.*thes.*6(5^1.43B); *ib.*7(51A); ‡Jo.D.*Artem.*65(p.155.7 n.; M.96.1313A) cit. s. θέλησις; **b.** denial of this doctrine by orthodox, Ath.*Ar.*3.62(M.26.453B–456A) cit. s. ἀνάγκη; and assertion that Son *is* βούλησις of Father υἱὸν δέ, τοῦτ' ἔστι τὴν τοῦ πατρὸς β. Const.*ep.*(Opitz 3 p.58.4); εἴ τις βουλήσει τοῦ θεοῦ ὡς ἓν τῶν ποιημάτων γεγονέναι λέγοι τὸν υἱὸν τοῦ θεοῦ, ἀνάθεμα ἔστω *Symb.Sirm.*1 *anath.*24; ἐπεὶ φύσει καὶ μὴ ἐκ β. ἐστιν ὁ υἱός Ath.*Ar.*3.66(M.26.461C); *ib.*3.67(465B); *ib.*2.2(149C); γεννηθέντος δὲ τοῦ υἱοῦ ἐκ πατρὸς ἀληθινῇ γεννήσει, οὐ ποιήσει τῇ ἐκ β. Apoll.*fid.sec.pt.*34(p.180.16; M.10.1117C); ὡς μήτε ἐκβάλλειν τοῦ δόγματος τὴν ἐπὶ τῷ υἱῷ β. τοῦ γεννήσαντος, οἷον στενοχωρουμένην ἐν τῇ συναφείᾳ τῆς... ἑνότητος, μήτε...τὴν ἀδιάστατον διαλύειν συνάφειαν, ὅταν ἐνθεωρῆται τῇ γεννήσει βούλησις Gr.Nyss.*Eun.*8(2 p.181.19; M.45.773D); οὐ β. γεννᾷ τὸν υἱόν, ἀλλὰ φύσει Cyr.*thes.*7(5^1.53D); ἤτοι σοφία, ἤτοι β., ἢ ἕτερόν τι τῶν ὅσα καθ' ἑαυτὰ οὐκ ἐνυπόστατα μέν, ἐνυπάρχει δὲ ὅμως τῶν ὄντων τισίν...ἐνυπόστατος ὢν ὁ υἱὸς τοῦ θεοῦ, τῇ ἀνυποστάτῳ β. κατ' οὐδὲν ἔσται προσεοικώς *ib.*8(61Df.); *ib.*15(153B) cit. s. ἐνούσιος; ‡Ath.*dial.Trin.*2.9(M.28.1169C); **6.** of unity of will subsisting bet. Father and Son, ‡Paul.Sam.*fr.*3(p.339.14) cit. s. προκοπή; Eun.*apol.*24(M.30.860B) cit. s. ἐνέργεια; Bas.*Eun.*4(1.282E; M.29.680C); ὡς μία θεότης, οὕτω καὶ β. Gr.Naz.*or.*30.12(p.126.16; M.36.120A); Chrys.*anom.*7.6(1.511B); Isid.Pel.*epp.*1.353(M.78.384C); **7.** of the one will of Trin., Sophr.H.*ep.syn.*(M.87.3157A).

D. ref. Christ; **1.** of Christ's will to reveal himself, Clem.*exc.Thdot.*5(p.107.7; M.9.656C); to suffer, ‡Dion.Al.*fr.Lc.22:43*(p.243.2); **2.** of one will in Christ μία αὐτοῦ ἡ φύσις ἐστὶ καὶ ἡ β. καὶ ἡ ἐνέργεια Aët.*fr.*ap.*Doct.Patr.*41(p.312.6); *ib.*(p.311.15).

E. ref. H. Ghost τῇ εὐδοκίᾳ τοῦ πατρὸς καὶ β. τοῦ υἱοῦ ἀοράτως παρὸν ὑποδεικνύει τὴν ἐνέργειαν τὴν θείαν ‡Bas.*h.myst.*60(p.395.16); ref. identity of his will and power, Jo.D.*f.o.*1.7(M.94.805C).

II. *sense, meaning*; of an author or speaker, Clem.*str.*1.28(p.110.5; M.8.925A); *ib.*5.8(p.360.24; M.9.80C); Or.*Jo.*10.13(p.183.12; M.14.328B).

***βουλητικός,** *capable of willing*, Epiph.*haer.*72.7(p.262.11; M.42.392C).

***βουλητικῶς,** *by willing*, Max.*schol.d.n.*1.4(M.4.193C).

βουλητός, *willed, object of will* οὔτε δυνατὸν ἦν ⟨οὔτε⟩ β. εἶναί μοι εἴποιμ' ἂν Gr.Thaum.*pan.Or.*1(p.3.5; M.10.1053A); Dion.Ar.*d.n.*4.32(M.3.733A); τέλος οὖν εἶναί φασι τὸ β. ... πρὸς τὸ τέλος δέ, τὸ βουλευτόν Max.*opusc.*(M.91.13C); of object of God's will τὸ τῷ θεῷ β. πάντως εἶναι δυνατόν Athenag.*res.*11(p.59.19; M.6.993B).

βούλκανος** (βουρκ-**), **ὁ,** (Lat. *Vulcanus*) *volcano*, Gr.Mag.*dial.*(tr.Zach.)4.30(M.*PL.*77.370B); met. βούρκανος ἀσεβείας ‡Jo.D.*ep.Thphl.*9(M.95.356B).

βοῦλλα, ἡ, (Lat. *bulla*) *seal*, Leont.N.*v.Jo.Eleem.*46(p.99.11); CCP(681)*act.*15(H.3.1376A).

***βουλλόω,** *seal*, Leont.N.*v.Jo.Eleem.*46(p.96.19); *ib.*(p.97.3); CCP(681)*act.*13(H.3.1349A); ref. sending of robe of BMV to Constantinople under seal, Jo.D.*hom.*9.18(M.96.752A).

βούλ-ομαι, I. *wish*;

A. of men; **1.** of rational willing in rel. to desire and reason προηγεῖται τοίνυν πάντων τὸ ∼εσθαι· αἱ γὰρ λογικαὶ δυνάμεις τοῦ ∼εσθαι διάκονοι πεφύκασι Clem.*str.*2.17(p.153.12; M.8.1016B); οὐδεὶς ζητεῖ, μὴ ∼ηθείς· καὶ οὐδεὶς ∼εται, μὴ λογισάμενος· καὶ οὐδεὶς λογίζεται μὴ ὀρεγόμενος· καὶ οὐδεὶς λογικῶς ὀρέγεται, μὴ ὑπάρχων φύσει λογικός Max.*opusc.*(M.91.24A); **2.** of free will in rel. to grace γίνωσκε ὅτι ψυχὴν ἔχεις αὐτεξούσιον...ζῶον λογικὸν ἄφθαρτον... ἐξουσίαν ἔχον ποιεῖν ἃ ∼εται Cyr.H.*catech.*4.18; ἡμῶν γὰρ τὸ προελέσθαι καὶ ∼ηθῆναι, θεοῦ δὲ τὸ ἀνύσαι καὶ εἰς τέλος ἀγαγεῖν Chrys.*hom.12.3 in Heb.*(12.125A); ὁμολογουμένου μὲν γὰρ τοῦ παρ' ἡμῖν εἶναι τὴν ἐξουσίαν τῆς τε τῶν καλῶν καὶ τῶν χειρόνων αἱρέσεως, συναπηλέγχετο καὶ τὸ τὰ περὶ ἡμᾶς γινόμενα ἀπὸ τῆς ἡμετέρας συμβαίνειν αἰτίας. τῆς δέ γε τοῦ ποιεῖν ἐξουσίας ἅπερ ἂν ∼ώμεθα ἐν ἡμῖν οὐκ οὔσης, οὐδὲ τὰ περὶ ἡμᾶς γινόμενα ἑτέρως γινόμενα ἐφαίνετο ἀλλ' ἢ κατὰ τὸ δοκοῦν τῷ ποιοῦντι θεῷ Thdr.Mops.*Rom.*9:14(p.144.37; M.66.836C); but τὸ ∼εσθαι παρὰ θεοῦ Gr.Naz.*or.*37.13(M.36.300A); **3.** ref. importance of right motive in moral action τοῖς μὲν γὰρ ὁμοῦ τῷ θέλειν καὶ τὸ δύνασθαι πάρεστιν...οἱ δέ, εἰ καὶ μήπω δύνανται, τὸ ∼εσθαι ἤδη ἔχουσιν. ἔργον δὲ τὸ μὲν ∼εσθαι ψυχῆς, τὸ πράττειν δὲ οὐκ ἄνευ σώματος. οὐδὲ μὴν τῷ τέλει παραμετρεῖται μόνῳ τὰ πράγματα, ἀλλὰ καὶ τῇ ἑκάστου κρίνεται προαιρέσει Clem.*str.*2.5(p.127.9; M.8.961B); ὁρᾷς ὅτι...πλείονα καρποῦσθαι τὸν ἔπαινον τόν γε ἑλόμενον καὶ ∼ηθέντα, ἢ ἀναγκασθέντα καλὸν εἶναι Chrys.*laud.Paul.*6(2.509A); **4.** of evil desire, Gr.Naz.*or.*42.8(M.36.468D).

B. of God; **1.** of relation of God's will to his power ὁ θεὸς εἰ ὅσα μὲν ∼εται ποιεῖν, δύναται ποιεῖν, οὐχ ὅσα δὲ δύναται ποιεῖν, ∼εται ποιεῖν· οὐ ταὐτὸν ἄρα παρ' αὐτῷ τὸ εἶναι τῷ ∼εσθαι ‡Just.*qu.Chr.*3.2(M.6.1433B); θεοῦ δὲ τὸ ∼εσθαι πρᾶξίς ἐστιν Gr.Naz.*or.*20.9(M.35.1076C); οὐ γὰρ πάθει συνέχεται τὸ θεῖον, ἵνα ὃ ∼εται μὴ πράττῃ ἢ πράττῃ ὃ μὴ ∼εται· δυνατὸς γάρ ἐστι ποιεῖν ὃ ∼εται Epiph.*haer.*70.7(p.239.20; M.42.349C); **2.** of God's will in Creation ψιλῷ τῷ ∼εσθαι δημιουργεῖ Clem.*prot.*4(p.48.18; M.8.164A); **3.** of God's providence in rel. to evil οὔτε πάθοιμεν ἄν τι, μὴ ∼ομένου θεοῦ, οὔτε μὴν ὧν πάσχομεν βλαβερόν τί ἐστιν, ἢ τοιοῦτον, ὥστε ἐνεῖναι βέλτιόν τι κἂν ἐπινοίᾳ λαβεῖν Bas.*hom.*9.3(2.74A; M.31.332C); τούτου δὴ χάριν ἐνδίδωσιν ὁ πάνσοφος ἐπιφανῆναι τὸν ἀλιτήριον. εὔδηλον γὰρ ὡς οὐκ ἂν ὤφθη μὴ ∼ομένου θεοῦ· οὐ μὴν ἐνέργειαν καλοῦμεν τὴν βούλησιν. κακῶν γὰρ ἀναίτιος ὁ θεός Thdt.*haer.*5.23(4.456); **4.** of God's will in rel. to Son's generation: (Arian) τότε ἐγέννησεν ὅτε ἐβούλετο Eun. ap.Gr.Nyss.*Eun.*9(2 p.209.12; M.45.808A); (orthodox), Gr.Naz.*or.* 20.9 (M.35.1076C); εἰ γὰρ 'τότε ἐγέννησε τὸν υἱόν, ὅτε ἐβούλετο',... ἐβούλετο δὲ τὸ ἀγαθὸν ἀεί, σύνδρομος δὲ τῇ βουλήσει ἡ δύναμις, ἀεὶ ἄρα ὁ υἱὸς μετὰ τοῦ πατρὸς νοηθήσεται, τοῦ ἀεὶ καὶ ~ομένου τὸ καλόν, καὶ δυναμένου ἔχειν ὃ ~εται Gr.Nyss.*Eun.*9(2 p.211.20; M.45.809B); **5.** of identity of will in Father and Son ἔλεγεν, 'εἰ ~ει', οὐχ ἕτερόν τι ~όμενον εἰδὼς εἶτα τοῦτο πυνθανόμενος, ἀλλ' ἀκριβῶς εἰδὼς ὅτι ~εται παρενεγκεῖν ἀπ' αὐτοῦ τὸ ποτήριον, ἠπίστατο δικαίως ὃ ~εται δυνατὸν αὐτῷ ‡Dion.Al.*fr.in Lc.22:42*(p.235.1; M.10.1598C); Chrys. *hom.in Mt.26:39*(3.18E); **6.** of one will in Trin., Sever.*creat.*5.2 (M.56.472).

II. *mean, signify*, Clem.*str.*2.8(p.133.28; M.8.973C); ἐρωτῆσαι...τί ~εται αὐτοῖς ἡ τοσαύτη δαπάνη Chrys.*hom.3.5 in Jo.*(8.23D); Evagr. Pont.*or.*50(M.79.1177B).

III. *maintain* in argument, Clem.*paed.*1.6(p.119.7; M.8.308B); id.*str.*2.8(p.134.8; M.8.976A).

***βουνευρίζω**, *beat with whip formed of tendon of an ox*, Leont.N. *v.Jo.Eleem.*16(p.34.12); Marc.Diac.*v.Porph.*99.

***βούνευρον, τό,** *whip made of tendon of an ox*, *V.Dan.*(p.388.24); Cyr.S.*v.Euthym.*58(p.81.19); †Jo.D.*B.J.*28(M.96.1129B); as a torment in hell, †Cyr.*hom.div.*14(5².411C).

βουνίζω, *heap up, mass together*, Epiph.*mens.*21(M.43.272C).

βουνός, ὁ, 1. *hill, mound*, Herm.*vis.*1.3.4; *Hom.Clem.*3.45; Thdt. *qu.42 in 2 Reg.*(1.445); Gel.Cyz.*h.e.*2.17.20(M.85.1269B); as symbol of Creation πρὸ τῶν β. (Pr.8:25) †Ath.*exp.fid.*3(M.25.203C); interpretations; **a.** Pr.8:25 ὄρη and βουνοί equated with apostles and their successors, Marcell.*fr.22* ap.Eus.*e.th.*3.3(p.150.19; M.24.989C); and with τὰς θείας καὶ ὑπερκοσμίους δυνάμεις, Eus.*e.th.*1.11(p.70.24; 845B); **b.** Jer.3:23 ὄντως εἰς ψεῦδος ἦσαν οἱ β. interpreted of pagan gods and heroes, Or.*hom.5.3 in Jer.*(p.34.2; M.13.300D); **2.** *heap* of corn, *Apophth.Patr.*(M.65.192D); as measure, Epiph.*mens.*21(M.43.272C).

***βουοπρόσωπος,** *ox-faced*, *T.Sal.*18.1(one MS; M.122.1341A).

[*]βουρδουνάριος, ὁ, v. βουρδωνάριος.

βουρδών ([*]βορδών), ὁ, (Lat. *burdo*) *mule*, βορ- Eustrat.*v.Eutych.* 72(M.86.2356C); βορ- Jo.Mosch.*prat.*101(M.87.2960B); *Chron.Pasch.* p.113(M.92.297B).

βουρδωνάριος ([*]βορδον-, [*]βουρδουν-), ὁ, (Lat. *burdonarius*) *muleteer*, Cyr.S.*v.Sab.*8(p.92.13); βορδον- Jo.Mosch.*prat.*125(M.87. 2988B); βουρδουν- Leont.N.*v.Sym.*56(M.93.1737C).

[*]βουριχάλιον (βουρικ-), τό, a kind of carriage, plur. βουρικ- Gr.Naz.*test.*(M.37.392D); *Chron.Pasch.*p.309(M.92.788B).

***βούρκανος, ὁ,** v. *βούλκανος.

βοῦς, ὁ, ἡ, 1. *sea-cow*, ‡Gr.Nyss.*or.1 in Gen.1:26*(M.44.265D); **2.** a district of Constantinople (=*forum boarium*), *Chron.Pasch.* p.382(M.92.981A).

***βουτιστής, ὁ,** *baptizer*, an official in Church of S. Sophia at CP ὁ β. ἵσταται ἐν τῇ ἁγίᾳ κολυμβήθρᾳ, καὶ ὁ ἱερεὺς λέγει τὰς εὐχάς. ὁ δὲ ἀρχιερεὺς σταυρώνει τὸ ὕδωρ, ὁ δὲ β. βαπτίζει τὸν μέλλοντα βαπτισθῆναι *Euchol.*(p.225); *ib.*(p.230).

[*]βουττίον ([*]βοττ-), τό, *cask*, Jo.Mal.*chron.*12 p.314(βοττ- cod., M.97.473A) = *Chron.Pasch.*p.276(M.92.685A).

βοῦττις, ἡ, *cask*, Jo.Mal.*chron.*12 p.314(M.97.473A).

βούτυρον, τό, *butter*, ref. Is.7:15 τὸ β. τρέφεσθαι ἄρτου παρίστησι λιμόν Eus.*Is.*7:21–22(M.24.140A); παιδικῇ τροφῇ χρῆται ὁ 'Εμμανουὴλ διὰ τὴν σάρκα, β. †Bas.*Is.*202(1.529E; M.30.465B); Thdt.*Is.* 7:15(p.39.6; 2.218D).

βραβεῖον, τό, *prize, reward*; **1.** of heavenly reward (freq.); **a.** of Christ's conquest of death τὸν τὰ β. τῆς κατὰ τοῦ θανάτου νίκης ἀναδησάμενον Eus.*l.C.*15(p.247.24; M.20.1420B); **b.** of reward of virtue, *1Clem.*5.5; Eus.*d.e.*3.7(p.146.27; M.22.245D); Chrys.*sac.*1.8 (p.20.14; 4.369B); with nature of reward specified, e.g., immortality, *M.Polyc.*17.1; Eus.*v.C.*1.9(p.11.14; M.20.921B); eternal life, Clem.*q.d.s.*1(p.160.13; M.9.605B); understanding, Const.ap.Gel.Cyz. *h.e.*2.7.6(M.85.1233B); H. Ghost, Bas.*Spir.*40(3.35A; M.33.144A); of a palm Μαρία, ἐγερθεῖσα, λάβε τοῦτο τὸ β., ὃ ἔδωκέ μοι ὁ φυτεύσας τὸν παράδεισον Jo.Thess.*dorm.BMV* 1.3(p.378.23); cf. τὸ δὲ β. ἦν φοῖνιξ *ib.*2.5(p.414.7); **2.** of reward of evil-doing, Tat.*orat.*33(p.35. 12; M.6.876A).

βραβευτής, ὁ, *awarder, judge at contest*; of God, Synes.*ep.*137 (M.66.1525B); of Christ ὁ β. ὁ μονογενὴς υἱός Clem.*str.*7.3(p.14.25; M.9.424D).

***βραδεύ-ω,** *come slowly, delay in coming* ~οντες εἰς τὸ βάπτισμα Eustrat.*stat.anim.*17(p.471).

***βραδυγλωσσία, ἡ,** *slowness of speech*, Cyr.*Os.*3(3.12E); Sophr.H. *ep.syn.*(M.87.3196C); id.*or.*7.17(M.87.3348C).

***βραδυγράφος,** *slow at writing*, Geo.Pis.*Heracl.*1.153(M.92. 1327A).

***βραδυνόητος,** *slow of intellect*, Melet.*nat.hom.*8(M.64.1188A).

***βραδυπαθέω,** *make way slowly*, ‡Nil.*perist.*11.22(M.79.936C).

***βραδυπευθής,** *slowly heard*, Nonn.*par.Jo.*5:7(M.43.785A).

***βραδύπιστος,** *slow of belief*, Ph.Carp.*Cant.*239(M.40.149A).

βραδύς, *slow*, neut., *late* ὀψὲ καὶ β. περὶ τὴν νύκτα ‡Ath. *azym.*(M.26.1329B); comp. adv. βράδιον *later, too late*, *1Clem.*1.1; Or.*princ.*1.14(p.219.9; M.11.276B); Eus.*qu.Marin.*3.4(M.22.952C); *Apophth.Patr.*(M.65.220A); v. πρᾶος.

***βραδυστομέω,** *be slow of utterance*, Cyr.*Jon.*proem.(3.366B).

***βραδυτοκέω,** *delay in giving birth*, ‡Chrys.*concept.Jo.Bapt.*(2. 950).

***βραδυφαγέω,** *eat slowly*, Ant.Mon.*hom.*7(M.89.1453A).

***βραδυφαγία, ἡ,** *eating slowly*, Ephr.3.425F.

βράσις, ἡ, 1. *boiling* (of water), Anast.S.*qu.et resp.*92(M.89.728C); **2.** *throwing up*; of Jonah's ejection from great fish, Gr.Naz.*carm.* 2.1.68.65(M.37.1414A).

βράσμα, τό, 1. *boiling*, Jo.Mosch.*prat.*29(M.87.2877A); Jo.Mon. *hymn.Geo.*7(M.96.1397C); **2.** *boiled* (i.e. cooked) *food*, *Nomoc.*255; **3.** *surging* (of fire), Geo.Pis.*hex.*954(M.92.1508A); of fires of hell, *Apoc.Esd.*(p.28); βράσματα βελιάρ †Cyr.*hom.div.*14(5².410A); hence **a.** *shaking* γέλως παρειᾶς β. Gr.Naz.*carm.*1.2.34.111(M.37.953A); **b.** *tumult, turmoil*; of persecution, Petr.I Al.*ep.can.*11(M.18.496A); of passion, Gr.Naz.*carm.*1.2.1.544(M.37.563A); *ib.*1.2.3.27(635A); *ib.* 2.1.45.306(1375A); of secular life, id.*or.*42.24(M.36.488B); of this world, Max.*cap.*5.76(M.90.1380C); of turmoil produced by rise of heresy, Anast.S.*hod.*8(M.89.136C).

***βρασματώδης,** *spluttering*; of laughter, Gr.Naz.*or.*5.23(M.35. 692B).

***βρασμώδης,** *boiling, effervescent*, Gr.Nyss.*hom.opif.*12(M.44. 160C); met., *tumultuous*, Melet.*nat.hom.*synops.(M.64.1136B,1137B).

[*]βραυκάνομαι, *cry*; of children, Philost.*h.e.*11.6(M.65.600B).

βραχιάλιον ([*]βραχιάριον), τό, 1. *bracelet*, AQ ap.Thdt.*qu.2 in 2Reg.*(1.404); βραχιάριον AQ ap.Proc.G.*2Reg.*1:10(M.87.1120C); **2.** a part of the defences of CP, *Chron.Pasch.*p.398(M.92.1009A).

βραχιόλιον, τό, = foreg. 1, Leont.N.*v.Jo.Eleem.*7(p.14.5).

βραχίων, ὁ, *arm*, as symbol of strength β. τὴν δύναμιν καλεῖ Thdt. *Is.*51:5(p.203.37; 2.354); τὸν β. ἐπὶ τῆς ἐνεργείας...ἔλαβε id.*Ps.*88:14 (1.1234); δικαιοσύνης β. καὶ ὅπλα Thphyl.*exc.gent.*(p.482.23; M.113. 941D); of Son τὸν υἱόν...'Ησαίας β. ἀπεκάλει Eus.*e.th.*1.20(p.95.27; M.24.892B); β. ... μὴ ἄλλον τοῦ λόγου καὶ τῆς σοφίας καὶ αὐτοῦ τοῦ κυρίου, ὅς ἐστιν ὁ Χριστὸς...νόμιζε id.*d.e.*6.24(p.293.29; M.22.481D); ἐκλήθη β., ὅτι ὁμοούσιος...τῷ πατρί Chrys.*Eutrop.*2.8(3.393B); β. δὲ τοῦ πατρὸς ὀνομάζει τὸν υἱόν· ἐνεργεῖ γὰρ δι' αὐτοῦ τὰ πάντα Cyr.*Ps.* 88:11(M.69.1212B); of H. Ghost εἴωθεν ἡ γραφὴ...ἢ χεῖρα ἢ β. καλεῖν τὸ πνεῦμα Gel.Cyz.*h.e.*2.21.12(M.85.1286B); dat. as adv., *violently* εἰσελθεῖν βραχίονι διεβεβαιώσατο Gr.Mag.*dial.*(tr.Zach.)3.29(M.*PL.* 77.286C).

***βραχυδίαιτος,** *of sparing appetite*, Jo.Carp.*cap.*48(M.85.1847B).

***βραχυεπῶς,** *in few words*, Just.*1apol.*49.6(M.6.401B); id.*2apol.* 9.1(M.6.460A).

***βραχυμέριμνος,** *full of short-lived cares*, Chrys.*fr.in Jer.*5:24 (M.64.817A).

βραχύνομαι, *shorten, reduce to small compass*, Meth.*Porph.*2 (p.505.11,14; M.18.481D).

***βραχυπορέω,** *take a short cut, pass quickly through*, Meth.*res.*2.6 (p.339.17; M.41.1172C); Cyr.*ador.*3(1.82A).

βραχύσκιος, *with a short shadow*, Or.*or.*17.1(p.338.12; M.11. 469D).

βραχυτελής, *speedily ending, brief*, Dion.Al.ap.Eus.*p.e.*14.25 (774C; M.21.1276B); Isid.Pel.*epp.*1.31(M.78.201B); *ib.*1.493(449D).

βραχύτης, ἡ, *shortness*; **1.** of stature, Philost.*h.e.*10.11(M.65. 592A); of range (of sun's rays) εἴ τι αὐτῶν οὐ μετέχει, τοῦτο οὐ...τῆς β. ἐστι τῆς φωτιστικῆς αὐτοῦ διαδόσεως Dion.Ar.*d.n.*4.4(M.3.697D); **2.** *smallness* (of children), of incarnate Christ πάσης γενόμενον ἥττονα β. ‡Meth.*Sym.et Ann.*14(M.18.381B); **3.** in polite address, as term of self-depreciation, *your humble servant* παρὰ τῆς β. ἡμῶν, οὐκ ἄκαιρον...ἀκοῦσαί σου τὴν σεμνοπρέπειαν Gr.Naz.*ep.* 202(M.37.332B); Epiph.*haer.*40.1(p.81.22; M.41.680A); Ammon.Aeg. *ep.*23(p.110.36); *Supplicatio* ap.Evagr.*h.e.*3.5(p.105.11; M.86.2605A); **4.** *poverty*, Thphn.*chron.*p.298(M.108.728B).

***βραχύτιμος,** *cheap*, Thdr.Stud.*or.*11.3(M.99.817C).

***βραχυφαγέω,** *eat sparingly*, Ant.Mon.*hom.*7(M.89.1453A).

***βραχυφαγία, ἡ,** *light diet, eating sparingly*, Ephr.3.425F; Thal. *cent.*4.31(M.91.1461B).

βρέβιον, τό, (Lat. *breviarium*) **1.** *brief, document*; **2.** *summary*, *Cod.Afr.*94 tit.; of the Hippo Breviary (393), *ib.*33,34; **3.** *inventory*, Pall.*v.Chrys.*3(p.19.16; M.47.14); **4.** *accounts*, *ib.*5(p.32.8; M.47.20); *ib.*12(pp.70.7,72.12; M.47.39,41).

***βρεγκάριος, ὁ,** (?) *water-carrier*, Ephr.2.176A.

βρεκτός, *soaked*; of soaked pulse as article of monastic diet, Pall.*h.Laus.*18(p.48.6; M.34.1051A); Marc.Diac.*v.Porph.*10; Jo.Mosch.*prat.*107(M.87.2968A); Niceph.Ur.*v.Sym.*14(M.86.3000A).

[*]βρένθιον, τό, *luxurious scent*, Clem.*paed.*2.8(p.196.9; M.8.469B).

βρεφικός, *of an infant* βοήν...β. Petr.Rav.*ep.*(p.45.27; M.*PL*.54.742A).

***βρεφοκτονία, ἡ,** *infanticide*, Jo.Schol.*nomoc.*40(p.25.27).

***βρεφοπρεπής,** *suitable to a child*, Nil.*epp.*4.61(M.79.577D); Diad.*perf.*61(p.70.7).

***βρεφοπρεπῶς,** *as* or *like an infant*, Nil.*epp.*2.49(M.79.221A); Jo.Mon.*hymn.Chrys.*7(M.96.1381D).

***βρεφοτρεφής,** *nourishing an infant*, Thdr.Stud.*nativ.BMV* 7 (M.96.696A).

***βρεφοτροφεῖον, τό,** *foundling-hospital*, CCP(536)*act.*1(*ACO* 3 p.129.42; H.2.1192C).

***βρεφουργέω,** *form into an embryo, engender*, ‡Ath.*occurs.*3(M.28.976C); Melet.*nat.hom.*synops.(M.64.1085B); *ib.*25(1244A); met., of spiritual rebirth, ‡Proc.G.*Pr.*23:25(M.87.1456C).

***βρεφοφανής,** *appearing as an infant*, ‡Ath.*occurs.*12(M.28.988C).

βρεφόω, pass., *become an infant*, ‡Rom.Mel.29.44(*AS* 1 p.231).

βρέχω, 1. *rain*; exeg. Gen.19:24, v. κύριος; **2.** pass., *descend* upon; hence *happen* to ὄντως νομίζομεν πρᾶγμά σοι ἐβράχη Leont.N.*v.Jo.Eleem.*22(p.45.22); **3.** pass., *meet* with ἡ καλῶς βραχεῖσά μοι κόρη *ib.*24(p.51.17).

***βριαρῶς,** *vigorously, strongly* β. αὐτῷ διαλεχθῆναι Gr.Mag.*dial.*(tr.Zach.)1.4(M.*PL*.77.174B).

***βρῖθον, τό,** *vigour, strength*, Call.*v.Hyp.*p.48.

***βριμηδόν,** *with groans*, Nonn.*par.Jo.*11:38(M.43.845A).

βρισαύχην, *haughty, bombastic*, Gr.Naz.*carm.*1.2.14.101(M.37.763A).

***βρόμα, τό,** v. βρῶμα.

***βρομιαῖος,** *crackling*, ‡Jo.D.*ep.Thphl.*13(M.95.361B).

***βροντέος,** *thunderous*, Gr.Nyss.*Eun.*4(M.45.624A; βρονταία 2 p.53.1).

βροντή, ἡ, *thunder*, exeg. ἰδοὺ ἐγὼ στερεῶν β. (Am.4:13): πρεπόντως ἂν νοηθείη ἡ στερεουμένη β. ὁ πιστὸς λόγος, καὶ ἀσάλευτος τοῦ πνεύματος ὁ νόμος. τούτου γὰρ ὑπηρέτας εἶναι θέλων τὸν Ἰακὼβ καὶ τὸν Ἰωάννην, ἐκάλεσεν ὁ κύριος βοανεργές, ὅ ἐστιν, υἱοὶ βροντῆς Ath.*ep.Serap.*1.10(M.26.556A); on meaning of υἱοὶ βροντῆς (Mc.3:17): γεννώμενοι ἀπὸ τῆς μεγαλοφωνίας τοῦ θεοῦ βροντῶντος καὶ μεγάλα οὐρανόθεν βοῶντος τοῖς ἔχουσιν ὦτα καὶ σοφοῖς Or.*comm.in Mt.*12.32 (p.140.41; M.13.1057A); υἱοὺς β. κεκλημένους διὰ τὴν μεγαλοφωνίαν τῶν νοημάτων καὶ δογμάτων αὐτῶν id.*Apoc.*36(p.40.5); β. ... τὸ κήρυγμα τὸ εὐαγγελικὸν αἰνίττεται...διὸ καὶ τοὺς ἀποστόλους...βοανῆργες ὠνόμαζεν Eus.*Ps.*76:18(M.23.897C); υἱοὶ β. ... διὰ τὸ μέγα καὶ διαπρύσιον ἠχῆσαι τῇ οἰκουμένῃ τῆς θεολογίας τὰ δόγματα Vict.*Mc.*3:14ff.(p.297.15); υἱοὺς β. ... τουτέστι βαπτίσματος υἱούς. ἐπειδὴ γὰρ ἡ β. συνίσταται ἐξ ὕδατος καὶ πνεύματος, τοῦτο δέ ἐστιν ἡ τοῦ ἁγίου βαπτίσματος μυσταγωγία, συμβολικῶς τὸ βάπτισμα β. καλεῖ ἐστερεωμένην ὑπὸ τοῦ ἁγίου πνεύματος ‡Ath.*dial.Trin.*3.27(M.28.1245A).

***βροντηδόν,** *like thunder*, *Orac.Sib.*5.345; *Hymn.*(*AS* 1 p.505).

***βρόντησις, ἡ,** *thundering*, Thdt.*Ps.*80:8(1.1182).

***βροντοηχ-έομαι,** *be called by voice of thunder* τὸν...∼ούμενον ἐξ οὐρανοῦ Chrysipp.*enc.in Jo.Bapt.*3(p.33.17).

***βροντοηχής,** *sounding like thunder*, Germ.CP *or.*1(M.98.221C).

***βροντόλογος,** *uttering thunder*, Procl.CP *or.*15.6(M.65.805A).

***βροντόπαις, ὁ,** *son of thunder*; of S. John, ‡Caes.Naz.*dial.*29 (M.38.889).

***βροντόφωνος,** *with voice of thunder*, Chrysipp.*enc.in Jo.Bapt.*3 (p.33.14).

***βροτογενής,** *born of mortal man*, Mod.*dorm.*(M.86.3297C).

βροτοειδής, *like mortal man*, Nonn.*par.Jo.*1:14(M.43.752B); *ib.* 8:15(816A); *ib.*14:9(868B).

***βροτόμορφος,** *in mortal form*, Mod.*dorm.*(M.86.3297B).

***βροτοπλάστης, ὁ,** *former of mortal men*, Mod.*dorm.*(M.86.3297C).

***βροτοπορία, ἡ,** *movement, transport of men*, ‡Caes.Naz.*dial.*156 (M.38.1113).

βροτοσσόος, *saving mortals*, Jo.D.*carm.pent.*106(p.217; M.96.837B).

***βροτοφόρος, ὁ,** *bearer of mortals*, Ephr.3.537A.

***βροτοφυής,** *in mortal nature*, Mod.*dorm.*(M.86.3285C).

***βροτόω,** *make mortal*; of incarnate Christ, Gr.Naz.*carm.*1.1.9.42 (M.37.460A); ‡Gr.Naz.*Chr.pat.*511(M.38.177A).

***βρουμάλιον, τό,** (usu. plur.) *brumalia*, the Roman winter-solstice festival; instituted by Romulus, Jo.Mal.*chron.*7 p.179(M.97.285B); *Chron.Pasch.*p.114(M.92.300) quoting authority of Licinius Macer (cf. Pliny, *naturalis historia* 4.3); observance forbidden (along with that of τὰ βότα) to Christians, CTrull.*can.*62; observed by Leo III τὸ κατ' ἐκεῖνο καιρὸν βρουμάλιον, ἤτοι ἑορτὴν δαιμονιώδη, ἐξετέλει, Διόνυσον καὶ Βροῦμον εὐφημῶν εἰς τὴν αὐτὴν τελετήν, ὡς τῶν σπερμάτων καὶ τοῦ οἴνου γενεσιουργούς Steph.Diac.*v.Steph.*(M.100.1170B).

βροῦχος, ὁ, *wingless locust*, Nil.*epp.*3.153(M.79.457A); as divine plague, *Apoc.Bar.*16(p.94.11); κάμπη, ἀκρίς, β., ἐρυσίβη interpreted respectively of Tiglath-pileser, Shalmaneser, Sennacherib, Nebuchadnezzar, Thdr.Mops.*Joel.*1:4(M.66.213B); exeg. Joel 2:25 (ἡ ἀκρὶς καὶ ὁ β. ... ἡ δύναμίς μου) text employed by Arians to minimize significance of δύναμις when applied to Son, Ath.*decr.*20 (p.16.38; M.25.452A); ὥσπερ ἡ κάμπη καὶ ὁ β. λέγονται δύναμις, οὕτω καὶ αὐτὸς λέγεται δύναμις τοῦ πατρός id.*ep.Aeg.Lib.*12(M.25.565B).

***βροχθισμός, ὁ,** *gulping*, ‡Nil.*narr.*5(M.79.645B).

βροχίζω, *ensnare*, Hipp.*Dan.*4.33.4; ‡Chrys.*hom.*8(13.231E).

***βρόχιος,** *of* or *by a noose* θανεῖν ἐθέλει βρόχιον μόρον Nonn.*par. Jo.*8:22(M.43.816C).

***βρόχισμα, τό,** *noose*, Nil.*epp.*2.226(M.79.317B).

***βροχισμός, ὁ,** *gulp, mouthful*, Epiph.*haer.*66.34(p.74.2; M.42.84A).

βρυγμός, ὁ, *roaring* β. τῶν λεόντων Hier.*vir.ill.*16(p.19.27; M.*PL*.23.636A).

***βρυερῶς,** *vigorously, powerfully* β. τούτῳ ἀντέλεγεν Thphn.*chron.* p.236(M.108.593B, ? for βριαρῶς).

βρύζ-ω, *ferment, abound in* ἀρτιτόκοις ἐπέεσσι τόσος ∼ες Gr.Naz *carm.*2.2(epitaph.)4(M.38.13A); *foam*, Agath.*v.Gr.Ill.*110(p.56).

***βρυκτικός,** *given to roaring*, ‡Caes.Naz.*dial.*140(M.38.1072).

***βρύλλιον, τό,** *reed*, Jo.Clim.*scal.*15(M.88.881C).

βρύσις, ἡ, *spring*; of the fountain of divine grace, ‡Proc.G.*Pr.* 5:18(M.86.1265B); of Christ ἡ β. ἡ γλυκεῖα *A.Thom.*A 39(p.157.5).

βρυτήρ, ὁ, *one who causes to spring forth*, Thdr.Stud.*nativ.BMV* 7(M.96.692C); of Christ β. νοημάτων *Hymn.*(*AS* 1 p.630).

βρυχητικός, *given to roaring*, ‡Gr.Nyss.*or.1 in Gen.1:26*(M.44.268A).

***βρυχικός,** *able to roar* ἀπολέσας...τὸ β. ὁ λεών, οὐκ ἔστι λεών Anast.Ap.*a.Max.*8(M.90.121D).

βρυώδης, *mossy*; met., *useless* β. συγγραφὰς ἀποπτύεις Geo.Pis.*Sev.*101(M.92.1629A).

βρῶμα, τό, A. *food*; **1.** esp. plur., of foods forbidden by Jewish Law, *Did.*6.3; *Barn.*10.9; Eus.*e.th.*2.20(p.127.14; M.24.949C); **2.** βρωμάτων ἀποχή etc., of Christian abstinence; **a.** in gen., Bas.*jej.*1.1 (2.2B; M.31.164B); Eus.Al.*serm.*1(M.86.317D); Jo.D.*jej.*3(M.95.69B); in form βρομάτων Pamph.H.*can.*5; **b.** of heret. vegetarianism and excessively scrupulous abstinence from certain foods, Hipp.*haer.* 1.24(p.28.2; M.16.3052A); Epiph.*haer.*48.8(p.230.22; M.41.868B); *Const.App.*6.26.3; of supply of food to Manichean 'elect' by the 'hearers', Hegem.*Arch.*10(p.16.13; M.10.1444A); 1Tim.4:3 (κωλυόντων γαμεῖν, καὶ ἀπέχεσθαι βρωμάτων) discussed, Isid.Pel.*epp.*4.112 (M.78.1177C); **3.** of food for use in heathen sacrifices; **a.** in gen. τὰ ...β. τῆς πομπῆς τοῦ σατανᾶ, τῇ ἰδίᾳ φύσει λιτὰ ὄντα, τῇ ἐπικλήσει τῶν δαιμόνων βέβηλα γίνεται Cyr.H.*catech.*19.7; Chrys.*hom.17.1 in 1Cor.*(10.115D); **b.** by Christians under persecution; **i.** of food tasted under compulsion, CAnc.(314)*can.*3; **ii.** of food taken by Christians to scene of pagan festivals, but not offered as sacrifice, *ib.*7; **4.** met.; **a.** of faith and knowledge as food of soul, Clem.*paed.* 1.6(p.112.26; M.8.296A); id.*str.*5.11(p.373.1; M.9.105B) al.; **b.** exeg. 1Cor.3:1–3 ὁ ἀπόστολος δυνατὸς ἦν διδόναι τὸ β., οἷς γὰρ ἂν ἐπετίθουν χεῖρας, ἐλάμβανον πνεῦμα ἅγιον, ὅ ἐστι β. ζωῆς Iren.*haer.*4.38.2(M.7.1106C); γάλα μὲν ἡ κατήχησις...β. δὲ ἡ ἐποπτικὴ θεωρία Clem.*str.*5.10(p.370.15; M.9.101A); v. γάλα; **5.** of eucharist β. σωτήριον Sever.*creat.*6 ap.Cosm.Ind.*top.*10(p.306.14; θυσιαστήριον M.56.488).
B. *voracity*; *edacitas...Graece β. appellatur*, Isid.H.*etym.*5.35.6.

βρωματίζ-ω, *feed*, pass., of Christ χολὴν ∼εται Gr.Naz.*or.*29.20 (p.105.16; M.36.101B); met., of S. Paul, c. dupl. acc. ∼ων αὐτοὺς ...τὴν φυσικὴν τῶν ὁρατῶν θεωρίαν Max.*ep.*36(M.91.629C).

βρωμέω, *stink*, †Cyr.*hom.div.*14(5^2.411E).

βρῶσις, ἡ, A. *food*; **1.** of diet forbidden by Jewish Law, *Barn.* 10.9; *Diogn.*6.3; Just.*dial.*57.3(M.6.605C); **2.** of fruit of Eden, *A.Andr.et Mt.*20(p.92.1); Nil.*epp.*2.318(M.79.356B); ‡Anast.Ant.

*serm.*4(M.89.1389C); **3.** of eucharist, Eus.*e.th.*3.12(p.169.1; M.24.1024A); Chrys.*hom.47.1 in Jo.*(8.275D); ἡ αὐτοζωὴ τοῖς θνητοῖς ἑαυτὸν εἰς β. ... χαρίζεται †Cyr.*hom.div.*10(5^{2}.372B); *ib.*(378C); **4.** met., exeg. Jo.6 β. γὰρ καὶ πόσις τοῦ θείου λόγου ἡ γνῶσίς ἐστι τῆς θείας οὐσίας Clem.*str.*5.10(p.370.20; M.9.101A); good works as οὐκ ἀπολλυμένη β. Chrys.*hom.44.1 in Jo.*(8.260A); τὴν τῆς ψυχῆς β. Leont.N.*v.Jo.Eleem.*1(p.7.10,12); Gr.Mag.*dial.*(tr.Zach.)2.22(M.*PL.*66.176D).

B. *rust*, only in citations of Mt.6:19, e.g. Just.*1apol.*15.11(M.6.352A); Chrys.*hom.20.2 in Mt.*(7.262C).

βρωστήρ, ὁ, *devourer*; hence *moth*, Cyr.*Os.*58(3.90E).

***βύβλον, τό,** = βίβλος, *book*, Eudoc.*Cypr.*2.77(M.85.852C).

***βυζάνω,** *suckle*, †Jo.Jej.*poenit.*(M.88.1924A).

***βύζια, τά,** *breasts*, *V.Dan.*(p.52.26); *T.Sal.*18.35(p.58.7).

βύθιος, 1. *deep*; of a well, Nonn.*par.Jo.*4:15(M.43.776C); **2.** *in the deep*; of ark of Moses, Gr.Nyss.*v.Mos.*(M.44.329A); of Israelites at Red Sea, *ib.*33(312A); of a catch of fish, Nonn.*par.Jo.*21:6(916B); **3.** *of the deep* τὴν β. ἄμμον Chrys.*hom.17.3 in 1Tim.*(11.651C); Nonn.*par.Jo.*21:10(M.43.917A); as subst., *fish* ἔστι καὶ ἐν βυθίοισι πόθου νόμος Gr.Naz.*carm.*2.2(poem.)4.27(M.37.1507A); **4.** met., *deep* β. καὶ σκοτεινὲ διάβολε *M.Seb.*5(p.175.27); of a deep sigh, Nil.*epp.*3.274(M.79.520C); **5.** Valent., one of the first pair (βύθιος and μίξις) of aeons of the decad, Iren.*haer.*1.1.2(M.7.449A); Hipp.*haer.*6.30(p.157.15; M.16.3238C); Val.Gn.ap.Epiph.*haer.*31.5(p.392.14; M.41.484A).

***βυθοδρόμος, ὁ,** *ranger of the deep, diver*, Geo.Pis.*hex.*1007(M.92.1512A).

βύθοθεν, *from the abyss*, Jo.Mon.*hymn.Blas.*8(M.96.1405A).

βυθός, ὁ, 1. *depth*; of the sea, *Barn.*10.5; Herm.*vis.*3.2.5; Eus.*v.C.*1.15(p.15.20; M.20.929C); of primeval 'sea' as symbol of death, Herm.*vis.*3.5.2; of water of baptism ὁ β. διὰ σωφροσύνην θνησκούσῃ βάπτισμα ἐγίνετο πρὸς ψυχῆς σωτηρίαν *Hom.Clem.*13.20; connected with Red Sea, Cosm.Mel.*hymn.*2(M.98.465B); **2.** met.; **a.** usu. in bad sense εἰς β. ἀτοπίας...ἐκπεπτωκότα Eus.*Marcell.*2.4(p.55.19; M.24.817B); Chrys.*hom.56.2 in Mt.*(7.568B); Gel.Cyz.*h.e.*2.20.4(M.85.1281C); **b.** in good sense τὸ πάντων αἴτιον...ἐν ἀπορρήτῳ β. γνώσεως τεταμιευμένον Eus.*l.C.*12(p.229.24; M.20.1385B); **3.** Gnost.; **a.** one of primary elements (with σκότος and ὕδωρ) in Nicolaitan doctrine of Creation, Epiph.*haer.*25.5(p.272.19; M.41.328B); **b.** the primary aeon, with σιγή, of Valent. ogdoad, Val.Gn.*ib.*31.2(p.386.1; 476D); **4.** Manich., abode of θέλησις, *Disp.Phot.*(M.88.536D); **5.** of depths of mysteries ὁ ἡσυχίαν καταλαβὼν ἔγνω β. μυστηρίων Jo.Clim.*scal.*27(M.88.1100C); **6.** of depths of soul ἀρχὴ μὲν ἡσυχίας τὸ ἀποσείεσθαι κτύπους, ὡς τὸν β. ταράσσοντας *ib.*(1097B).

***βυθοστροφία, ἡ,** *upheaval from the depths*, Nil.*Magn.*62(M.79.1052D); ‡Nil.*perist.*2.5(M.79.821C).

***βύλαρος, ὁ,** *dung-beetle*, Epiph.*haer.*40.1(p.83.26; M.41.681B).

***βυρροφόρος, ὁ,** v. *βιρροφόρος.

βυρσεῖον, τό, *tannery*, Pall.*h.Laus.*39(p.96.3; M.34.1105B).

βυρσεύω, *make out of leather*; ref. Origen's objection that literal interpretation of Gen.3:21 would make God a leather-worker, Epiph.*anc.*62(p.74.14; M.43.128C); ref. book-production out of parchment Ἰουδαῖε, διὰ τί...προσκυνεῖς τὸ βιβλίον τοῦ νόμου, ἐπειδὴ ἐκ δερμάτων τυγχάνει...βεβυρσευμένον; ‡Anast.S.*Jud.disp.*2(M.89.1233C).

***βυρσοδεύτης, ὁ,** *leather-worker*, Epiph.*anc.*62(M.43.128C; βυρσοδέψης p.74.13).

βυρσοτόμος, ὁ, *cutter of leather*, exeg. Gen.3:21, ‡Caes.Naz.*dial.*152(M.38.1105); cf.Epiph.*anc.*62(p.74.13; M.43.128C).

***βυτίον, τό,** a sound indicative of ridicule διέσυρε τὸ λαλούμενον, βυτία ποιῶν καὶ λαιβία Anast.Ap.*a.Max.*1.3(M.90.113C).

***βωβόομαι,** pass., *become dumb*, *M.Ner.et Ach.*22(p.21.18).

βῶλος, ὁ, ἡ, 1. *lump, clod* of earth; used in medicine to staunch flow of blood, Geo.Pis.*hex.*1516(M.92.1551A); ref. Jews deprived of their country οὐδ' ὁποῖά τις β. οὐδ' ἑστία λείπεται Cels.ap.Or.*Cels.*8.69(p.286.6; M.11.1621A); fig. ἄνθρωπος...δεκτικὸς ὢν ἀγαθοῦ καὶ πονηροῦ, ὡσεὶ β. τῶν ἑκατέρων σπερμάτων Mel.*pass.*48 p.8.7; **2.** *lump, nugget*; of gold, Clem.*str.*2.20(p.175.29; M.8.1060B); of another mineral, Gr.Nyss.*hom.14 in Cant.*(M.44.1072C); **3.** Manich., of mass of matter to be destroyed by fire in final consummation, Hegem.*Arch.*11(p.19.4; M.10.1445B); *ib.*13(p.21.7; 1448C); Tit.Bost.*Man.*1.30(M.18.1113A).

βωμός, ὁ, A. *altar*; **1.** usu. of pagan altars, *1Clem.*25.4; Hipp.*antichr.*49(p.33.5; M.10.769A); *A.Thom.*A 76(p.191.16); **2.** of Jewish altars (as rarely in LXX): of altar of sacrifice of Isaac, ‡Eust.*hex.*(M.18.764D); and of Jephthah's daughter, Meth.*symp.*11(p.134.20; M.18.212A); of an altar erected by Joshua, Thdt.*qu.19 in Jos.*(1.316); **3.** Christian; **a.** freq. met. β. δὲ ἀληθῶς ἅγιον τὴν δικαίαν ψυχήν Clem.*str.*7.6(p.24.17; M.9.445A); in reply to charge of Celsus that Christians have no β.: βωμοὶ μέν εἰσιν ἡμῖν τὸ ἑκάστου τῶν δικαίων ἡγεμονικόν Or.*Cels.*8.17(p.234.18; M.11.1541A); ref. widows θεοῦ εἰσιν ἔμψυχος β. Meth.*symp.*5.8(p.62.21; M.18.112A); Chrys.*hom.65.3 in Jo.*(8.393A); **b.** rarely lit., Synes.*catast.*1(M.66.1573B); in inventory of Church furniture in Egypt, *Pap.Chr.*(p.161.21) (saec. v or vi).

B. *base* of a pillar, Paul.Sil.*ambo.*155(M.86.2257B).

***βωμόσκοπος,** v. μωμόσκοπος.

Γ

***γαβέξ,** sign denoting *six*; used at Alexandria, Ammon.*Jo.*19:14(M.85.1512B).

γάγ(γ)ραινα, ἡ, *gangrene*; met., of heresy, Gr.Nyss.*Maced.*1(M.45.1301C); of addiction to sin, †Nil.*mal.cog.*10(M.79.1212C); Thdt.*2Tim.*2:17(3.684); term of abuse ταῦτα λαλήσει ἡ γ. *Vaticin.*2(p.56).

Γάδειρα, τά, *Cadiz*; met., *extreme limits* πέρατα...τὰ τῆς φύσεως Γ. Jo.D.*hom.*11.2(M.96.764C).

γαζαρηνός, ὁ, *diviner*; ? for γαληνοῦ, Gr.Nyss.*Apoll.*38(M.45.1209C); as name of a class of Babylonian magicians, Epiph.*exp.fid.*12(p.512.19; M.42.804C).

γαζοφυλάκιον, τό, 1. *offertory box* γ. ... ἐστὶν τόπος νομισμάτων εἰς τιμὴν θεοῦ καὶ οἰκονομίαν ἀναπαύσεως πενήτων προσφερομένων Or.*Jo.*19.7(2; p.306.31; M.14.537D); as symbol of charity, Chrys.*hom.43.1 in 1Cor.*(10.401B); id.*eleem.*4(3.254A); **2.** *repository* for Jewish scriptures, i.e. *genizah*, Epiph.*haer.*30.3(p.338.6,10; M.41.409C).

γαζοφύλαξ, ὁ, = γαζοφυλάκιον, Nonn.*par.Jo.*8:20(M.43.816B).

***Γαιανῖται, οἱ,** *followers of Gaius*, sect with monophysite tendencies, Tim.CP *haer.*(M.86.44B); †Leont.B.*sect.*7(M.86.1245Bff.); *ib.*10(1260B,1261D).

γαι-όω, *make earthy, solid*; met., of the soul κακυνομένης δὲ παχύνεται καὶ ~οῦται Synes.*insomn.*6(M.66.1292B; γεοῦται p.155.5).

γάλα, τό, *milk*; **1.** met.; **a.** of rudiments of Christian doctrine (cf. 1Cor.3:2, Heb.5:12) γ. ἔτι ἐδέοντο, τῆς εἰσαγωγικῆς...τοῦ εὐαγγελίου διδασκαλίας Bas.*hom.*12.13(2.108E; M.31.412D); Chrys.*hom.8.3 in Heb.*(12.87B); Cyr.*Joel.*44(3.243C); cf.Dion.Ar.*ep.*9.4(M.3.1112A); ἀνατραφεὶς ἐν τῷ γ. τῶν ἐντολῶν Philox.*ep.*6(p.161); **b.** symbolizing whole doctrine of Christ, cf. 1Petr.2:2 ὁ ἀναγεννήσας ἡμᾶς ἐκτρέφει τῷ ἰδίῳ γ., τῷ λόγῳ· πᾶν γὰρ τὸ γεννῆσαν ἔοικεν εὐθὺς παρέχειν τῷ γεννωμένῳ τροφήν. καθάπερ δὲ ἡ ἀναγέννησις, ἀναλόγως οὕτως καὶ ἡ τροφὴ γέγονεν τῷ ἀνθρώπῳ πνευματική...τὸ αὐτὸ ἄρα καὶ αἷμα καὶ γ. τοῦ κυρίου πάθους καὶ διδασκαλίας σύμβολον Clem.*paed.*1.6(p.119.19ff.; M.8.309A) al.; and his blood, *ib.*(p.118.13; 305B); exeg. Is.55:1 οἶνος δὲ καὶ γ. τὰ μυστικὰ τῆς ἀναγεννήσεως σύμβολα. οἱ γὰρ ἐξ ὕδατος καὶ πνεύματος ἀναγεννώμενοι, ὡς ἀρτιγέννητα βρέφη τῷ λογικῷ τρέφονται γάλακτι, οἶνόν τε πίνουσι, περὶ οὗ φησι· τοῦτό μού ἐστι τὸ αἷμα Proc.G.*Is.*55:1(M.87.2552A); v. αἷμα; gospel of S. Luke compared with milk, ‡Germ.CP *contempl.*(M.98.413B); **c.** of Christ's humanity ὡς νηπίοις, ὁ ἄρτος ὁ τέλειος τοῦ πατρός, γ. ἡμῖν ἑαυτὸν παρέσχεν, ὅπερ ἦν ἡ κατ' ἄνθρωπον αὐτοῦ παρουσία Iren.*haer.*4.38.1(M.7.1106A); **d.** exeg. Gen.49:12 ἤτοι τοὺς ἀποστόλους ἐσήμανεν τοὺς ὑπὸ τοῦ λόγου ἁγιασθέντας καὶ ὡς γ. γεννηθέντας...ἢ...τὰς ἐντολὰς τοῦ κυρίου λέγει...γ. δὲ ἡμῖν γεγενημένας Hipp.*ben.Jac.*19(p.35.5); **2.** liturg.; milk mixed with honey given to newly baptized, as symbol of entry into land of promise and as food suitable for babes, *Barn.*6.17; cf.Hipp.*trad.ap.*16; ‡Hipp.*can.*144,148; cf.Tertullianus *de corona* 3, *adversus Marcionem* 1.14; interpreted as symbolizing reception of Christian doctrine, Clem.*paed.*1.6(p.120.11; M.8.309B).

[*]**γαλάγρα** ([*]**γαλαιάγρα**), **ἡ,** = γαλεάγρα, **1.** *cage* for lions, *T.Job* 27(p.120.1); **2.** *trap*, -αιάγρα, Nil.*epp.*2.96(M.79.244A).

***γαλαδοτέω,** *suckle*, *Orac.Sib.*2.192.

[*]**γαλαιάγρα, ἡ,** v. [*]γαλάγρα.

***γαλακτικός,** *milky*, of colour λίθος γ. Hipp.*haer.*4.33(p.59.23; M.16.3098A).

***γαλακτοδοτέω,** *suckle*, Or.*sel.in Ps.*21:10(M.12.1253C).

γαλακτοειδής, *milk-like*, Clem.*paed.*1.6(p.119.10; M.8.308B).

***γαλακτοροία, ἡ,** *flow of milk*, plur., Jo.Eub.*innoc.*(M.96.1505B).

***γαλακτόροος**, *flowing with milk*, *Hymn.*(*AS* 1 p.468).

***γαλακτορροέω**, *flow with milk*, Anast.S.*hod.*13(M.89.220A).

γαλακτοτροφ-έω, *nourish with milk*, *suckle*, in gen., Chrys.*hom.* *17.6 in Mt.*(7.230E); id.*Laz.*3.1(1.736E); ref. Christ, as sign of his real humanity σαρκωθεὶς...καὶ ~ηθεὶς ἀληθῶς Cyr.H.*catech.*4.9; Chrys.*hom.80.1 in Mt.*(7.766D); Eus.Al.*serm.*11(M.86.376A); met., of rudiments of Christian doctrine ἐκ τῶν αὐτῶν μαζῶν ~ούμεθα, τῆς τε παλαιᾶς καὶ τῆς καινῆς διαθήκης ‡Ath.*v.Syncl.*21(M.28.1500A); of bishops τοὺς τῷ λόγῳ ~ήσαντας *Const.App.*2.33.2.

γαλακτοτροφία, ἡ, *nourishing with milk*, *suckling*, Isid.Pel.*epp.* 3.180(M.78.872A); of Christ, Chrys.*hom.8.3 in Mt.*(7.124A); of OT in contrast with solid food of NT, id.*hom.2.3 in 2Cor.4:13*(3.272B); acc. Nestorius attributed to the Godhead by Arians and Apollinarians γαλακτοτροφίας κοινωνὸν διὰ τὴν οἰκειότητα τὸν θεὸν λόγον ποιεῖν Nest.*ep.Cyr.*2(p.31.32; M.77.56B); sign of reality of Inc. τὴν μέχρι σαρκὸς καὶ αἵματος καὶ γ. ἐνανθρώπησιν τοῦ θεοῦ Areth.*Apoc.* 67(M.106.773D).

***γαλακτουργία, ἡ**, *milk-feeding*, of humanity of Christ διὰ τῆς τοιαύτης γ. ἐθισθέντες τρώγειν καὶ πίνειν τὸν λόγον τοῦ θεοῦ Iren.*haer.* 4.38.1(M.7.1106A).

***γαλακτουχία, ἡ**, *weaning*, Clem.*str.*2.18(p.163.6; M.8.1033A); *ib.* 3.11(p.228.25; 1173A); *ib.*(p.229.1; 1173B).

***γαλακτοφαής**, *milk-coloured*, †Ath.*fr.Mt.*(M.27.1388D).

***γαλακτοφορέω**, *yield milk*, Gr.Nyss.*hom.9 in Cant.*(M.44.956C).

γαλακτώδης, *milky*; met., *suitable for babes*; of teaching given to beginners, Eus.*h.e.*4.23.8(M.20.388A); Cyr.H.*catech.*4.3; Thdt. *qu.6 in Dt.*(1.264).

***γαλαποτίζω**, s.v.l., *feed with milk*, Or.*exp.in Pr.*17(M.17.197B).

***Γαλατιστί**, *in the Galatian language*, Tim.CP *haer.*(M.86.16A).

***γαλατρωπρόσωπος**, *having a milk-white face*; of the moon, *Ev.Barth.*(Vassiliev p.14).

***γαλβιανός, ὁ**, a medicinal herb, Sophr.H.*mir.Cyr.et Jo.*19(M.87. 3477D).

***γαλεύομαι**, *live on milk*, Jo.D.*haer.*101(M.94.772B).

γαληναῖος, **1.** *calm*, *tranquil*, of souls who receive Christ ὁ... λόγος ἁπάσης ψυχῆς τὸ εὐσταθὲς καὶ γ. ... σημαίνει τῆς τὸν γεννηθέντα θεὸν παραδεξαμένης Eus.*d.e.*7.1(p.307.19; M.22.501D); Gr.Nyss.*virg.* 14(p.311.1; M.46.384A); γ. ... δεῖ τὴν τῆς παρθένου ψυχήν †Bas.Anc. *virg.*49(M.30.765C); **2.** *serene*, *benign* of countenance; of emperor, CArim.*ep.Const.*1(p.238.16; M.26.700A) cit. s. βλέμμα; γ. τῇ προσόψει *ib.*2(p.278.18; M.26.792C); of Christ, Nonn.*par.Jo.*1:43(M.43.757A).

γαληναίως, *peacefully*, *tranquilly* γ. ἔχωμεν Meth.*symp.*4.2(p.47. 13; γαλήνην ἔχομεν M.18.89A).

***γαληνεύω**, *calm*, met., Isid.Pel.*epp.*1.183(M.78.301B).

***γαληνέω**, *be calm*, Eus.Al.*serm.*1(M.86.317A).

γαλήνη, ἡ, *calm*, esp. *interior calm*, *tranquillity*; **1.** in gen. ὁ Χριστιανὸς...γ. καὶ εἰρήνης οἰκεῖός ἐστιν Clem.*paed.*2.7(p.193.30; M.8.465A); *ib.*2.10(p.224.18; 532B); Or.*Ps.*44:3f.(p.55); γυνὴ καθάπερ ἐν τινὶ διδασκαλείῳ φιλοσοφίας τῇ οἰκίᾳ καθημένη...διηνεκῶς δύναται ἀπολαύειν γ. Chrys.*hom.61.3 in Jo.*(8.366A); **2.** esp. of quiet from passions εἰσὶν ἀνεπίδεκτοι πάντῃ καὶ κατὰ τὴν σάρκα καὶ κατὰ τὴν καρδίαν οὗτοι τῆς ἐπιθυμίας, γ. ἄγοντες τῶν παθημάτων Meth. *symp.*11(p.138.16; M.18.216C); *ib.*(p.138.21; 216C); necessary for approaching Holy Communion, Chrys.*nativ.*1.7(2.365B); Thdt.*h.e.* 5.36.5(3.1072); quality of Christian life effected by Inc., Procl.CP *or.*13.2(M.65.792B); **3.** myst. ὑπ' αὐτοῦ [sc. Χριστοῦ] ὁδηγούμενοι ἐν πολλῇ γ. ἐσόμεθα Mac.Aeg.*hom.*14.3(M.34.572B); ἡ ἀληθὴς γίνεται γ., ὅταν μὴ μόνον αἱ ἐνέργειαι, ἀλλὰ καὶ αἱ περὶ αὐτῶν μνῆμαι σχολάζουσαι καιρὸν παρέχωσι τῇ ψυχῇ δυνηθῆναι τοὺς ἐνεσφραγισμένους τύπους ἰδεῖν Nil.*exerc.*48(M.79.777C); of calm of prayer when discursive thought is stilled, ‡Chrys.*pat.et consumm.*(12.819D); ὁ διὰ πνεύματος ἁγίου γ. κτησάμενος, οὐκ ἀγνοεῖ τὸ θεώρημα Jo.Clim.*scal.*27(M.88. 1109B); **4.** *serenity*; as style of address to emperor, CCP(681)*act.*2 (H.3.1061C).

***γαληνιαῖος**, *calm*, *tranquil*, Const.ap.Eus.*v.C.*4.10(p.122.9; M. 20.1160B); Gr.Nyss.*virg.*21(p.329.18; M.46.401C); Olymp.*Job* 38:11 (M.93.401B).

γαληνιάω, *be calm*, *find peace* ~ῶντας ἁγίῳ συμφέρεσθαι πνεύματι Clem.*paed.*3.12(p.291.6; M.8.680C); resulting from faith, id.*str.*4.6 (p.262.17; M.8.1244B); from presence of a saint, Ath.*v.Anton.*87 (M.26.965B); from absence of desire, ‡Just.*or.Gr.*5(M.6.240A); Bas. *hom.in Ps.*33(1.153E; M.29.376B); from divine revelation, Cyr.*Jo.*10 (4.839D).

γαλήνιος, *calm*, Eus.*v.C.*1.17(M.20.933A; conj. γαληνὸν p.16.24); Epiph.*exp.fid.*1(p.496.21; M.42.773C).

***γαληνόμορφος**, *calm*, Jo.D.*carm.pent.*12(p.213; M.96.833A).

γαληνότης, ἡ, **1.** *calm*, *tranquillity*, of Trin. ἡ αὐτὴ ὁδηγία καὶ γ., ἡ αὐτὴ καὶ οὐσία Didym.*Trin.*2.8(M.39.629B); esp. of divine clemency in regard to man τῆς ἑνούσης γ. τῷ θεῷ νικώσης ἀεὶ τὰς ἀνθρωπίνας μικροψυχίας Cyr.*Is.*3.1(2.378C); id.*Joel.*30(3.221D); id. *glaph.Num.*(1.386A,B); Isid.Pel.*epp.*2.123(M.78.576B); **2.** *serenity*, as term of polite address to emperor, Cyr.*ep.*31(p.73.21; 5^2.97C); Thdr.Scyth.*libell.*(M.86.232C); *Ep.*ap.CCP(536)*act.*1(*ACO* 3 p.131. 19; H.2.1193D); and bishops, Max.*ep.*18(M.91.589A).

***γαληνοφόρος**, *bringing peace*, v.l. for γαμνοφόροι, †Cyr.*hom.div.* 11(5^2.379C); Alex.Sal.*Barn.*proem.6(p.438D).

***Γαλιλαῖοι, οἱ**, *Galileans*; **1.** Jewish sect, founded by Judas Galilaeus (cf. Ac.5:37), Just.*dial.*80.4(M.6.665B); **2.** term of abuse for Christians used by emperor Julian who wrote κατὰ Γαλιλαίων and used the word in his letters, e.g. *ep.*89(p.146.5); Γαλιλαίους ἀντὶ Χριστιανῶν ὀνομάσας Gr.Naz.*or.*4.76(M.35.601B); *M.Thdot.1* 31 (p.80.15); **3.** term of abuse used for orthodox by Manes, *ep.Add.* (M.86.904A).

§**γαλλάζω**, *vex oneself*, Ephr.3.220E.

***γαλλικόν, τό**, *soap*, Thphn.*chron.*p.292(M.108.716C).

***γαλοπάροχος**, *providing milk*, met. γ. τοῦ Χριστοῦ φιλανθρωπίαν Andr.Cr.*or.*19(M.97.1225A).

γαλουχ-έω, *suckle*; ref. Christ, a sign of true humanity, Nil.*epp.* 1.149(M.79.144D); Amph.*hom.*1.3(M.39.40C); met. (cf. γάλα) *feed with milk*, of elementary Christian doctrine οὐδέπω τέλειος...ἐν Χριστῷ γεννᾶται πρότερον καὶ ~εῖται Meth.*symp.*3.9(p.37.18; M.18.76A); Vict.*Mc.*9:48(p.368.4); of Judaism as preparation for Christianity, Eus.*Is.*28:9(M.24.288D); of penitence, Ephr.3.164F; of an evil influence ~εῖ τὸ βρέφος τῷ τῆς μαγείας μαζῷ Sophr.H.*v.Anast.*(M. 92.1684A).

***γαλούχησις, ἡ**, *suckling*, Sophr.H.*or.*2.32(M.87.3257B); *ib.*7.3 (3325B); Anast.S.*hod.*13(M.89.233A).

γαλουχία, ἡ, **1.** *suckling*, Diad.*perf.*86(p.118.15); **2.** *possession of milk*, Thdr.Stud.*nativ.BMV* 7(M.96.696A).

***γαλουχικός**, *consisting of milk*, Thdr.Stud.*epp.*2.144(M.99. 1453A).

γαμ-έω, *marry* εἰ...τις ἐν κλήρῳ ὢν ~οίη, μένειν τὸν τοιοῦτον ἐν τῷ κλήρῳ ὡς μὴ ἡμαρτηκότα [i.e. under Callistus] Hipp.*haer.*9.12(p.249. 25; M.16.3386B).

***γαμιαῖος**, *matrimonial*, *Pers.*(M.10.105C; προγαμιαίων p.17.9).

γαμικός, *of marriage*, *bridal*, ref. Cant. γ. τις διασκευή, δίδωσι τῇ θεωρίᾳ τὰς ὕλας Gr.Nyss.*hom.6 in Cant.*(M.44.892B); εἰκὼν γ. τίς ἐστι κατασκευή, ἐν ᾗ κάλλους ἐπιθυμία μεσιτεύει τῷ πόθῳ *ib.1*(772B).

γαμικῶς, *as in marriage*, *like married people*, Or.*hom.20.4 in Jer.*(p.182.23; M.13.508C); fig. ψυχὴ πρακτική,...ἣν...πᾶς τις τὴν θείαν μετιὼν φιλοσοφίαν γ. εἰσοικίζεται Max.*ambig.*(M.91.1372A).

***γαμνοφόρος**, v. *γαληνοφόρος.

***γαμοκλοπία, ἡ**, *illicit intercourse*, *Orac.Sib.*2.52; *ib.*5.430.

γάμος, ὁ, *marriage*;

A. lit.; **1.** as divine institution; **a.** in gen., common way of life, willed by God for procreation of children, Clem.*str.*2.23(p.188.26; M.8.1085C); Gr.Naz.*or.*37.9(M.36.293B); βίου κοινωνίαν εἶναι τὸν γ. Chrys.*laud.Max.*3(3.216E); Ast.Am.*hom.*5(M.40.228C); **b.** instituted after the Fall ὁ προσηγούμενος σκοπὸς τοῦ θεοῦ ἦν τοῦ μὴ διὰ γ. γενέσθαι ἡμᾶς καὶ φθορᾶς, ἡ δὲ παράβασις τῆς ἐντολῆς τὸν γ. εἰσήγαγε διὰ τὸ ἀνομῆσαι τὸν Ἀδάμ Ath.*exp.Ps.*50:7(M.27.240C) cit. Max. *qu.dub.*3(M.90.788B); Chrys.*virg.*17(1.282B); to prevent fornication, *ib.*19(282E); id.*hom.in 1Cor.7:2*(3.195A); **c.** a χάρισμα endowed with special blessings, Clem.*str.*3.12(p.231.31; M.8.1180A); Or.*comm.in Mt.*14.16(p.324.9; M.13.1229A); [sc. κοινωνία γάμου]...ὁ τῆς φύσεως δεσμός, ὁ διὰ τῆς εὐλογίας ζυγός Bas.*hex.*7.5(1.68A; M.29.160B); Chrys.*hom.12.4 in Col.*(11.418E); **2.** marriage and eccl. law; **a.** a concern of bishops πρέπει δὲ τοῖς γαμοῦσι καὶ ταῖς γαμουμέναις μετὰ γνώμης τοῦ ἐπισκόπου τὴν ἕνωσιν ποιεῖσθαι, ἵνα ὁ γ. ᾖ κατὰ κύριον Ign.*Polyc.*5.2; celebrated in their presence, Gr.Naz.*ep.*193(M.37. 316C); **b.** with heretics εἰ δὲ τὸν οὐκ ἔχοντα τὴν τῆς πίστεως συμφωνίαν οὐ διέλυσε γ., δῆλον ὅτι τὸν γ. ἔννομον, ἀλλ' οὐ παράνομον οἶδεν Thdt.*haer.*5.25(4.469); **c.** forbidden to persons consecrated to God τῶν κανονικῶν τὰς πορνείας εἰς γ. μὴ καταλογίζεσθαι Bas.*ep.*188 *can.*6(3.272B; M.32.673B); *ib.*199 *can.*18(292A; M.720B); to bishops, priests, and deacons after ordination, *Const.App.*6.17.1; to deaconesses who have received imposition of hands, CChalc.*can.* 15; to consecrated virgins and monks, *ib.*16; **3.** in heret. opinion; attacked by Saturninus and Marcion, Iren.*haer.*1.28.1(M.7.691A); by Hieracas as contrary to gospel, Epiph.*haer.*67.1(p.133.23; M.42. 173A); by Tatian and his school as fornication, *ib.*46.2(p.205.6; M.41.840B); Thdt.*haer.*1.20(4.312); by Gnostics as work of Devil, *ib.*1.3(291); defended by orthodox εἴ τις τὸν γ. μέμφοιτο...ἀ. ἔ. CGangr.*can.*1; *ib.*9; †Bas.Anc.*virg.*38(M.30.745C); Chrys.*hom.4.2f. in Is.6*:1(6.123C); *Const.App.*6.14.3 al.; cf. ἀποτάσσω; **4.** inferior to virginity, v. παρθενία; **5.** second marriage (cf. δίγαμος, διγαμία) opposed ἢ οἷός τις ἐτέχθη, μένειν, ἢ ἐφ' ἑνὶ γ. ὁ γὰρ δεύτερος εὐπρεπής ἐστι μοιχεία Athenag.*leg.*33.2(M.6.965A); regarded as fault to be expiated by prayer and fasting before admission to Communion, CLaod.*can.*1; admitted as concession to human weakness, Clem.*str.*3.1(p.197.14; M.8.1104C); but forbidden to priests, Epiph.*haer.*59.4(p.367.14; M.41.1024A); who may not assist at wedding meal of a second marriage, CNeocaes.*can.*7; man who has contracted second marriage ineligible for holy orders, *Can.App.*17; more than two marriages opposed ὀνομάζουσι δὲ τὸ τοιοῦτον οὐκ ἔτι γ., ἀλλὰ πολυγαμίαν Bas.*ep.*188 *can.*4(3.271D; M.32.673A); *ib.*199 *can.*50 (297D; M.732C); but from later 4th cent. more lenient view taken based on 1Cor.7:39, widow may marry as often as she loses her husband and thus remain ἐν σεμνῷ γ. Epiph.*haer.*59.6(p.371.11; M.41.1028B); καλὸν μὲν καὶ ὁ δεύτερος γ. Chrys.*hom.in 1Tim.5*:9(3.325C); discussed, Thdt.*haer.*26(4.469); marriage with deceased wife's sister forbidden, Bas.*ep.*160.2(3.249C; M.32.624B).

B. met.; **1.** of Christ and Church, v. νύμφη, νυμφίος; exeg. Ex. 2:21 διὰ τοῦ γ. Μωυσέως ὁ τοῦ Ἰησοῦ νοητὸς γ. ἐδείκνυτο, καὶ διὰ τῆς Αἰθιοπικῆς νύμφης, ἡ ἐξ ἐθνῶν ἐκκλησία ἐδηλοῦτο Iren.*haer.*4.20.12 (M.7.1042C); cf.Cyr.*glaph.Ex.*1.8(1.259A); Thdt.*qu.4 in Ex.*(1.121); ref. Eph.5:23–32 ἅγιος ὁ γ. τὸ μυστήριον τοίνυν τοῦτο εἰς τὸν Χριστὸν καὶ τὴν ἐκκλησίαν ἄγει ὁ ἀπόστολος Clem.*str.*3.12(p.234.30; M.8.1185A); id.*paed.*2.8(p.200.16; M.8.480B); Chrys.*hom.20.5 in Eph.* (11.149E); Thdt.*Eph.*5:31(3.435); Andr.Cr.*triod.*(M.97.1409C); exeg. Apoc.19:7ff. πνευματικὸς γ. τοῦ κυρίου ἐπὶ τῇ πρὸς τὴν ἐκκλησίαν μνηστείᾳ ἐστί, καὶ οὕτω τέλειος γ. Areth.*Apoc.*57(M.106.740A); **2.** of spiritual marriage of Christ with individual soul, Mac.Aeg.*hom.*47.17(M.34.808C) cit. s. νύμφη; Gr.Nyss.*virg.*15(p.311.23; M.46.384D); id.*hom.1 in Cant.*(M.44.765A); ἐπὶ τοῦ κόσμου παρθένοι μένουσι πρὸ τοῦ γ., μετὰ δὲ τὸν γ. οὐκέτι. ἐνταῦθα δὲ οὐχ οὕτως· ἀλλὰ κἂν μὴ ὦσι παρθένοι πρὸ τοῦ γ. τούτου, μετὰ τὸν γ. παρθένοι γίνονται Chrys.*hom.23.1 in 2Cor.*(10.595E); ‡Chrys.*pasch.*6.5(p.181.5; 8².272C); Jo.Clim.*scal.*7(M.88.813C); **3.** in pagan and Gnost. symbolism, of numbers γ. παρὰ τοῖς Πυθαγορείοις...ἡ ἑξὰς καλεῖται Clem.*str.*5.14(p.387.24; M.9.137A); *ib.*6.16(p.502.24; 365A); of spiritual marriage enacted in Valent. mysteries, Iren.*haer.*1.21.3(M.7.661A); connected with 'marriage' of those who are admitted as the saved into the pleroma, this marriage being related to the syzygies of aeons, Clem.*exc.Thdot.*64(p.128.19; M.9.689C).

γαμοστολέω, *prepare for wedding,* Jo.Mal.*chron.*p.244(M.97.373B).

***γανοφόρος,** *joy-giving,* v.l. for γαμνοφόρος, †Cyr.*hom.div.*11(5².379A).

γάν(ν)υμαι, *be glad, rejoice,* ref. spiritual joy, Clem.*paed.*1.1(p.90.5; M.8.249A); ὁ υἱὸς...γ. ἐπὶ τῇ τοῦ πατρὸς θέᾳ Eus.*e.th.*3.3(p.156.3; M.24.1000B); γάνν- Chrys.*hom.53.5 in Mt.*(7.544D); *radiate* [sc. αἰτία]...εἰς τὴν εὔτακτον ταυτότητα...γαννυμένη Dion.Ar.*d.n.*12.3(M.3.972A).

***γάνυσμα, τό,** *exultation,* Gr.Naz.*carm.*2.1.88.128(M.37.1440A); †Cyr.*hom.div.*10(5².374A).

***γαράμαντες, οἱ,** parrot-like birds, so called from Garamantidae (African tribe which exported them), Philost.*h.e.*3.11(M.65.500A).

γαργαλίζω, *tickle, titillate;* met., *tempt, seduce,* ref. Sophists κνήθοντες καὶ γ. Clem.*str.*1.3(p.15.5; M.8.712C); of lasciviousness, id.*paed.*2.4(p.122.15; M.8.441A); id.*prot.*10(p.77.29; M.8.225B); Mac.Aeg.*hom.*15.50(M.34.609C); of Devil, Ath.*v.Anton.*5(M.26.848B); Cosm.Ind.*top.*2(M.88.120D).

γαργαρίζω, *gargle,* Melet.*nat.hom.*10(M.64.1196B).

***γάργαρος, ὁ,** *throat,* Sophr.H.*mir.Cyr.et Jo.*41(M.87.3580B).

γαστήρ, ἡ, 1. *belly, stomach;* met., as seat of lower appetites τὰ ὑπὸ γαστέρα Clem.*paed.*2.10(p.211.24; M.8.504C); id.*str.*1.5(p.19.18; M.8.724A); Gr.Naz.*or.*14.17(M.35.880B); †Jo.D.*B.J.*24(M.96.1084A); τὸ κατὰ γαστρός Clem.*str.*8.4(p.87.4; M.9.576A); τοῖς μετὰ γαστέρα Isid.Pel.*epp.*5.28(M.78.1341A); **2.** *womb;* met., of generative power of God (Ps.109:3) esp. ref. begetting of Son γ. ἐπὶ θεοῦ...πνευματικόν τι...αὐτὸ τὸ γεννητικὸν τοῦ θεοῦ Didym.(‡Bas.)*Eun.*5(1.316C; M.29.757C); ‡Ath.*dial.Trin.*1.19(M.28.1148A) cit. s. στόμα; ἡ ὑπόστασις τὸ εἶναι σημαίνει· ἡ γ. τὸ γεννητικόν *ib.*1.20(M.l.c.); Mac.Aeg.*hom.*30.2(M.34.721D); μυσταγωγεῖται γ. θεὸν ἀγέννητον, τουτέστι τὸν...πατέρα, γ. πρὸ ἑωσφόρου καὶ πρὸ αἰώνων τὸν υἱὸν γεννῶσαν, καθὼς λέγει [Ps.109:3b] ‡Bas.*h.myst.*60(p.395.10); **3.** a kind of earthen pot, *Exorc.*31(p.342).

***γαστρέομαι,** *be distended,* Melet.*nat.hom.*21(M.64.1225A).

γαστρίδουλος, ὁ, *slave of the belly,* Chrys.*hom.44.1 in Jo.*(8.258C); Pall.*v.Chrys.*15(p.92.12; M.47.52).

γαστριμαργέω, *be gluttonous,* Chrys.*hom.4.8 in Mt.*(7.61A); Isid.Pel.*epp.*2.135(M.78.577B); Nil.*epp.*3.46(M.79.413D).

γαστριμαργία, ἡ, *gluttony* ἡ γ. ἀκρασία περὶ τὴν τροφήν Clem.*paed.*2.1(p.162.13; M.8.397A); μήτηρ τῶν ἀλόγων παθῶν γ. τοὺς πρώτους ἀνθρώπους τῆς τρυφῆς ἐξεώσατο Isid.Pel.*epp.*1.69(M.78.228D); γ. ... τὸ ὀξέως ἐσθίειν καὶ πολλά, λαιμαργίαν δὲ τὸ ἐνηδόνεσθαι βρώμασιν ‡Nil.*vit.cog.*(M.79.1437D); ἡ μανία περὶ τὸ πληροῦσθαι τὴν γαστέρα...λέγεται γ. ... ὅταν γένηται περὶ τὸν λαιμὸν...ἡ ἡδονή, καλεῖται λαιμαργία Dor.*doct.*15.2(M.88.1789C); ref. institution of salaried church officials by Montanus ἵνα διὰ τῆς γ. ἡ διδασκαλία...κρατύνηται Apollon.ap.Eus.*h.e.*5.18.2(M.20.476B).

***γαστριμαργικός,** *gluttonous,* Meth.*res.*1.60(p.324.22; M.41.1157B); †Cyr.*hom.div.*14(5².406A).

γαστρίμαργος, *gluttonous* ὁ νοῦς...πτερνίζει τὰ πάθη τὰ γ. Isid.Pel.*epp.*1.192(M.78.305B); as subst., Clem.*paed.*2.1(p.155.16; M.8.381A); γ. ἔξω ἔστω τῆς ἐκκλησίας Or.*hom.7.3 in Jer.*(p.54.3; M.13.333A); τῶν γ. ὧν θεὸς ἡ κοιλία Amph.*Seleuc.*115(M.37.1585A).

***γαστρόφιλος, ὁ,** *belly-lover,* Gr.Naz.*carm.*2.2(poem.)5.141(M.37.1532A).

***γαστρόφρων,** *gluttonous,* Steph.Diac.*v.Steph.*(M.100.1120A).

***γαύδιον, τό,** measure of length used in Ceylon (Taprobana), about 3 Roman miles, Cosm.Ind.*top.*11(M.88.445C).

[*]**γαυνάκης, ὁ,** = καυνάκης; *thick rug,* Clem.*paed.*2.9(p.204.21; M.8.489B).

***γεγεννημένως,** *as being generated,* of Son ὑπόστασις χαρακτηρίζεται...ἐπὶ τῆς θείας οὐσίας ἀπὸ τρόπου ὑπάρξεως· καθ' ὃν ἡ μὲν γεννητικῶς, ἡ δὲ γ., ἡ δὲ ἐκ πορευτικῶς Leont.H.*Nest.*2.4(M.86.1537C).

***γεγωνόφωνος,** *loud-voiced,* Isid.Pel.*epp.*3.280(M.78.957A).

γέεννα, ἡ, *gehenna* (Hebr. גֵּי הִנֹּם *valley of Hinnom*), *hell;* **1.** place of future punishment, Just.*1apol.*19.8(M.6.357B); Chrys.*hom.38.4 in Jo.*(8.221D); habitation of fallen angels, *Orac.Sib.*1.103; demons confessing its existence, Chrys.*hom.13.5 in Mt.*(7.175B); though ἡ γέεννα οὐ φαίνεται τοῖς ἀπίστοις id.*Laz.*4.3(1.755B); **2.** characterized by fire, Chrys.*hom.25.3 in Jo.*(8.147C); as a punishment for fire of lust, Max.*ep.*1(M.91.385D); by fiery river running through it, Clem.*exc.Thdot.*38(p.118.30; M.9.677B); emptiness, *ib.*; separation from God, Chrys.*hom.23.8 in Mt.*(7.295C); but comprising degrees of punishment, Mac.Aeg.*hom.*40.3(M.34.764C); *ib.*(765A); **3.** eternity questioned by Or., *hom.19.15 in Jer.* (p.175.5; M.13.497C); defended esp. by Chrys., *hom.36.3 in Mt.*(7.411A); εἰ τέλος ἔχει τὸ τῆς γ. πῦρ. ὅτι μὲν οὐκ ἔχει, ὁ Χριστὸς ἀπεφήνατο id.*hom.9.1 in 1Cor.*(10.73C); †Cyr.*hom.div.*14(5².404A); **4.** revelation of gehenna due to God's mercy ἡ γ. γὰρ τῇ βασιλείᾳ συμπράττει, τοὺς ἀνθρώπους τῷ φόβῳ ὠθοῦσα πρὸς αὐτήν Chrys.*hom.15.3 in 1Tim.*(11.638C); id.*hom.3.2 in Philm.*(11.790C); Jo.Jej.*serm.* (M.88.1961B); though God should be desired μὴ φόβῳ γ., ἀλλ' ἐπιθυμίᾳ βασιλείας Chrys.*hom.15.4 in 1Tim.*(639E); **5.** symbolized by Flood, *ib.15.3*(638D); **6.** Manich., place of imprisonment of matter, Jo.D.*Man.*1.68(M.94.1565B); v. ᾅδης.

***γεεννικός,** *of gehenna,* ‡Caes.Naz.*dial.*71(M.38.940).

[*]**γεημόρος, ὁ,** = γημόρος, *husbandman,* Gr.Naz.*carm.*1.1.5.42 (M.37.427A).

γεη-πονέω, -πόνος, v. γη-.

[*]**γεηπονικός,** *agricultural,* Bas.*ep.*260.4(3.398B; M.32.960C); Cyr.*glaph.Gen.*1(1.14E).

γεῖσος, τό, *projecting part of the roof, cornice,* Chrys.*stat.*11.3 (2.118D).

[*]**γείσσωμα, τό,** *cymatium,* exeg. אֵילָם *waved moulding* round door of Temple, Thdt.*qu.40 in Ezech.*40:26(2.1022).

[*]**γειτονιάρχης, ὁ,** *chief officer of a ward, local administrator* κατέστησεν ἀνὰ ἑκάστῳ ῥεγεῶνι τοὺς λεγομένους γ. †Gregent.*leg.Hom.* (M.86.577D); fig. ἐγέννησεν ἡ Ἐλισάβετ τὸν γ. τῶν οὐρανῶν Chrysipp.*enc.in Jo.Bapt.*(p.33.5).

γ(ε)ιώρας ([*]**γηόρας**), **ὁ,** *stranger,* (representing Hebr. גֵּר, i.e. not a Jew) sts. equated with proselyte, γηόρ-, Just.*dial.*122.1(M.6.760A); τούς τε καλουμένους γ. τοὺς ἐπιμίκτους Afric.*ep.Arist.*5(M.10.61A); γιώρ-, Thdt.*Is.*14:1(p.70.3; 2.266).

γελασῖναι, αἱ, *dimples,* Jo.Mal.*chron.*5 p.106(M.97.196B) perh. for γελασῖνοι.

***γελαστέον,** *one must laugh,* Clem.*paed.*2.5(p.185.24; M.8.448B); *ib.*(p.186.17; 449A).

γελ-άω, **1.** *laugh* ἂν δὲ ~ῶμεν καὶ παίζωμεν,...καὶ πρὸ τῆς συμβολῆς ὑπὸ τῆς οἰκείας καταπεσούμεθα ῥᾳθυμίας. οὐ τοίνυν ἡμέτερον τὸ ~ᾶν διηνεκῶς Chrys.*hom.*6.7 *in Mt.*(7.99A); to laugh may lead into sin τὸ ~ᾶν...οὐ δοκεῖ μὲν ὡμολογημένον ἁμάρτημα εἶναι, ἄγει δὲ εἰς ὡμολογημένον ἁμάρτημα id.*stat.*15.4(2.157A); τὸ ~ᾶν ὅλως Χριστιανοῖς οὐκ ἐπιτρέπεται, μάλιστα δὲ μοναχοῖς Ant.Mon.*hom.*95 (M.89.1721C); of spiritual 'mirth' σοφία γελῶσα Synes.*hymn.*1.38 (p.58; M.66.1589); **2.** *laugh at, deride,* of pagans deriding Christians ~ᾶτε δὲ ὑμεῖς, ὡς καὶ κλαύσοντες Tat.*orat.*32(p.33.14; M.6.872B); of Sophists ἀπιστεῖν ἐθέλοντες, ~ῶσι τῆς ἁπάσης σεμνότητος ἀξίαν ἀλήθειαν Clem.*str.*1.3(p.14.21; M.8.712A); ταῦτα [sc. Christian funeral rites] μὲν εἴπερ ἴδοιεν...οἱ ἀνίεροι πρὸς ἡμῶν τελούμενα... γελάσουσιν Dion.Ar.*e.h.*7.3.1(M.3.556D); of Christians ridiculing pagan errors; ref. followers of Aristotle γελάσαιμι δ' ἂν καὶ τοὺς μέχρι νῦν τοῖς δόγμασιν αὐτοῦ καταχρωμένους Tat.*orat.*2(p.3.4; M.6. 808B); *ib.*3(p.4.6; 812A); v. γέλως.

γελοιάομαι, *make oneself ridiculous,* Epiph.*exp.fid.*11(p.511.23; M.42.801C).

***γελοίασμα, τό,** *jest,* Thdr.Stud.*epp.*1.13(M.99.953C); *ib.*2.114 (1381B).

***γελοιάστρια, ἡ,** *female buffoon,* Ath.*virg.*13(p.48.3; M.28.268A).

***γελοιολογία, ἡ,** *jesting language,* Ath.*Ar.*1.4(M.26.20B).

γελοιότης, ἡ, *absurdity,* Cyr.*Os.*83(3.116A).

***γελοποιός,** *mirth-provoking; hilarious* γ. καὶ ἐμβρόντητον... ἑστίασιν ‡Meth.*Sym.et Ann.*1(M.18.349B); as subst., *jester,* Nil.*epp.* 2.13(M.79.205D).

[*]**Γελώ, ἡ,** [-οῦς, plur. -οῦδες] kind of female *vampire,* believed to fly through the air, enter by closed doors and suffocate children λέγουσιν ὅτι γυναῖκές εἰσι Στρύγγαι αἱ καὶ Γελοῦδες λεγόμεναι Jo.D. *drac.*(M.94.1604A).

γέλως, ὁ, A. *laughter*; **1.** def. and descriptions γ., παρειᾶς βράσμα, παλμὸς καρδίας Gr.Naz.*carm.*1.2.34.111(M.37.953A); εὐκολίαν τινὰ τῇ διεξόδῳ τοῦ πνεύματος μηχανωμένη ἡ φύσις, ἀνευρύνει τὸν περὶ τὸ στόμα πόρον, ἑκατέρωθεν περὶ τὸ ἆσθμα τὰς παρείας διαστέλλουσα. ὄνομα δὲ τῷ γινομένῳ γ. ἐστίν Gr.Nyss.*hom.opif.*12.5(M.44.160C); οὕτως γὰρ καὶ αὐτὸν ὁρίζονται· βρασμώδη κίνησιν τῶν περὶ τὸ πρόσωπον μυῶν, ἤτοι τοῦ μυώδους πλατύσματος ἐκ τῶν ἔνδοθεν σπλάγχνων τοῦ κινουμένου πνεύματος ὠθουμένου. παρὰ τὸ γελῶ γ. ἐκλήθη· τὸ δὲ γελῶ παρὰ τὸ ἕλη, ὃ σημαίνει τὴν θερμασίαν· οἱ γὰρ θερμοὶ πολλὰ γελῶσιν Melet.*nat.hom.*synops.(M.64.1137B); for etymology of Ἰσαάκ v.s.v.; **2.** permissible and objectionable laughter ἡ...καθ' ἁρμονίαν τοῦ προσώπου...κόσμιος ἄνεσις μειδίαμα κέκληται... σωφρονούντων [ὁ] γ.· ἡ δὲ ἐκμελὴς τοῦ προσώπου ἔκλυσις, εἰ μὲν ἐπὶ γυναικῶν γίνοιτο, κιχλισμὸς προσαγορεύεται, γ. δέ ἐστι πορνικός, εἰ δὲ ἐπὶ ἀνδρῶν, καγχασμός, γ. ἐστιν οὗτος μνηστηριώδης κἀξυβρίζων Clem. *paed.*2.5(p.186.2ff.; M.8.448C–449A); τὸ γὰρ γ. ἀκρατεῖ...κατέχεσθαι, ἀκρασίας σημεῖον...ἄχρι μὲν γὰρ μειδιάματος φαιδροῦ τὴν διάχυσιν τῆς ψυχῆς ὑποφαίνειν οὐκ ἀπρεπές Bas.*reg.fus.*17(2.359D; M.31.961A); ταῦτα λέγω, οὐ τὸν γ. ἐκκόπτων, ἀλλὰ τὴν διάχυσιν ἀναιρῶν Chrys. *hom.*6.6 *in Mt.*(7.97A); **3.** moderation counselled, Gr.Naz.*carm.* 1.2.32.13(M.37.917A); Chrys.*pasch.*5(3.756E); right use κατακαλύπτεις...τὴν κεφαλήν, καὶ γελᾷς, ὦ γύναι, ἐν ἐκκλησίᾳ καθημένη; εἰσῆλθες ἐξομολογήσασθαι τὰ ἁμαρτήματα...καὶ μετὰ γ. τοῦτο ποιεῖς;...καὶ τί κακὸν ὁ γ., φησίν. οὐ κακὸν ὁ γ., ἀλλὰ κακὸν τὸ παρὰ μέτρον, τὸ ἄκαιρον. ὁ γ. ἔγκειται ἐν ἡμῖν, ἵνα, ὅταν φίλους ἴδωμεν διὰ μακροῦ χρόνου, τοῦτο ποιῶμεν...ὁ γ. ἔγκειται τῇ ψυχῇ τῇ ἡμετέρᾳ, ἵνα ἀνῆται ποτε ἡ ψυχή, οὐχ ἵνα διαχέηται id.*hom.*15.4 *in Heb.*(12.156B,C); **4.** very often condemned; **a.** in gen. οὐδέποτε καιρὸς γέλωτός ἐστι τῷ πιστῷ Bas.*reg.br.*31(2.425C; M.31.1104B); γ. γέλωτος εὖ φρονοῦσιν ἄξιος, μάλιστα μὲν πᾶς, τὸν πλέον δ' ὁ πορνικὸς γ. ἄτακτος ἐκφέρει καὶ δάκρυον Gr.Naz.*carm.*1.2.33.77ff.(M.37.933A,B); id.*or.*8.9(M.35.800A); ἐχθρὸν ἑαυτοῦ ποιεῖ καὶ τὸν γ., καὶ περιφορὰν ὀνομάζει τὸ πάθος, ὅπερ ἴσόν ἐστι κατὰ διάνοιαν τῇ παραφορᾷ τε καὶ παρανοίᾳ. εἴ τι γὰρ ἄλλο τις ὀνομάσειε κυρίως τὸν γ., ὃ μήτε λόγος ἐστί, μήτε ἔργον ἐπί τινι σκοπῷ κατορθούμενον. διάλυσις δὲ στόματος ἀπρεπής, καὶ πνεύματος κλόνος, καὶ βρασμὸς ὅλου τοῦ σώματος...τί ἂν ἄλλο εἴη τοῦτο, φησί, καὶ οὐ παράνοια; Gr.Nyss.*hom.*2 *in Eccl.*(M.44.645C); **b.** incompatible with Christian vocation and virtues; the example of Christ who never laughed, Bas.*reg.fus.*17(2.360A; M.31.961C); οὐ γὰρ εἰς μετεωρισμὸν ἐκλήθημεν, καὶ γ. Ant.Mon.*hom.*95(M.89.1721D); εἰ οὐδὲν οὕτω τῇ ταπεινοφροσύνῃ ὡς τὸ πένθος συνέρχεται, οὐδὲν πάντως αὐτῇ ὡς ὁ γ. ἀνθέστηκεν Jo.Clim.*scal.*7(M.88.804B); ὁ γ. ὁ ἄκαιρος, ποτὲ μὲν ἐκ πορνείας δαίμονος, ποτὲ δὲ ἐκ κενοδοξίας,... ποτὲ δὲ ἐκ τρυφῆς *ib.*26(1021D); **c.** its evil consequences μάλιστα γὰρ μειρακίοις καὶ γυναιξὶν ὄλισθος εἰς διαβολὰς ὁ γ. ἐστίν Clem.*paed.*2.5 (p.186.21; M.8.449B); εἰς γ. ἐκκαλούμενοι πορνείας πρόδρομον *ib.*3.4 (p.253.17; 597A); ὁ γ. τὸν μακαρισμὸν τοῦ πένθους ἔξω βάλλει...τὸ πνεῦμα τὸ ἅγιον λυπεῖ, ψυχὴν οὐκ ὠφελεῖ, σῶμα διαφθείρει, τὰς ἀρετὰς διώκει· οὐκ ἔχει μνήμην θανάτου...περίελε ἀπ' ἐμοῦ τὸν γ., καὶ δώρησόν μοι πένθος καὶ κλαυθμόν, ὃν ζητεῖς παρ' ἐμοῦ ὁ θεός Ephr.ap. *Schol.*35 in Jo.Clim.*scal.*26(M.88.1045A); πολλάκις γοῦν ἀπὸ γ. αἰσχρὰ ῥήματα τίκτεται, ἀπὸ ῥημάτων αἰσχρῶν πράξεις αἰσχρότεραι· πολλάκις ἀπὸ ῥημάτων καὶ γέλωτος λοιδορία καὶ ὕβρις Chrys.*stat.*15.4(2.157A); Nil.*paraen.*77(M.79.1256B); τῶν γὰρ ἀφρόνων ἐστὶν ὁ γέλως Ant. Mon.*hom.*95(M.89.1724C); **5.** as expression of spiritual joy 'ὅτι πικρῷ λόγῳ μου γελάσομαι'. ἔστι τις ἐπαγγελία γ. ἧς ἐπαγγελίας ἐπώνυμός ἐστιν ὁ πατριάρχης Ἰσαάκ· ἑρμηνεύεται γὰρ Γ. ὅτι ἐπαγγελία γ., δῆλον [ὅτι] ἐκ τοῦ 'μακάριοι οἱ κλαίοντες νῦν'· ἡ δὲ ἐπαγγελία 'ὅτι γελάσονται' Or.*hom.*20.6 *in Jer.*(p.185.21ff.; M.13.512Df.); διὰ τοῦ κλαυθμοῦ ἄγει ἐπὶ τὸν μακαριζόμενον γ. *ib.*(p.186.14; 513B); τὸν ἐν ἐπαγγελίᾳ γ. ποθῶν καὶ τὴν θείαν ἱλαρότητα id.*fr.*10 *in Lam.* (p.239.20; M.13.612A); Bas.*reg.fus.*17(2.360B; M.31.961C); μακάριοι οἱ κλαίοντες...ὅτι...αὐτοὶ γελάσουσι. γ. δὲ λέγει οὐ τὸν διὰ τῶν παρειῶν ἐκπίπτοντα ψόφον ἐν τῷ αἵματος ἀναβρασμῷ, ἀλλὰ τὴν ἄκρατον καὶ ἀμιγῆ παντὸς σκυθρωποῦ ἱλαρότητα id.*hom.*4.4(2.28D; M.31.228A); ὁ γ. σημεῖον τῆς ἔνδον φαιδρότητος Gr.Nyss.*Placill.*(M.46.880C).

B. *derision*; objects for Christians: heathen worship, Clem.*paed.* 3.2(p.238.11; M.8.560B); id.*prot.*2(p.13.11; M.8.76B); exeg. Am.7:9 'γέλως' μὲν οὖν...ἡ παντὸς εἰδώλου ποίησις· πρέποι δ' ἄν, οἶμαι, κυρίως τε καὶ ἰδικῶς 'γέλωτα' νοεῖσθαι τὸν Βεελφεγώρ, διάτοι καὶ αὐτὸ τὸ τοῦ σχήματος ἀκαλλές Cyr.*Am.*68(3.325E); cf.Thdr.Mops. *Am.*7:4–9(M.66.289A); things of this world, ‡Nil.*perist.*9.2(M.79. 865A); for pagans, certain Christian practices, such as infant baptism and Holy Communion, Dion.Ar.*e.h.*7.3.11(M.3.565D); ἀπέθανε θάνατον γέλωτος *a ridiculous death,* Philox.*ep.*39(p.186).

***γελωτοκάρηνος,** *with a comedian's mask,* Geo.Pis.*carm.vit.*70.

***γελωτολόγος,** *making idle jests, Sent.App.*(p.84).

***γελωτοποιητέον,** *one must play the buffoon,* Clem.*paed.*2.5(p.185. 18; M.8.448B).

γέμ-ω, *be full*; **1.** lit., c. genit., Chrys.*hom.*72.4 *in Mt.*(7.706A); c. acc. θησαυρὸν εὗρον ~οντα ταῦτα Thphn.*chron.*p.128(M.108.353B); abs. ἀνάθεμα...ἔστω...πᾶς ἀνύγων τὸ μνῆμα...ἐπειδὴ ~ει *CG–CI* 1 pp.118–19(Eleutheropolis, 588); **2.** met. θεοῦ ~ετε Ign.*Magn.*14.1; ~οντες ἁμαρτιῶν *Barn.*11.11; θειότητος ~ων τοῦτο ποιεῖ *Hom.Clem.* 1.6; τοῦ φρίκης ~οντος βήματος Jo.D.*hom.*4.34(M.96.637B); c. acc. ὁδὸν...~ουσαν θλίψεις Nil.*epp.*4.1(M.79.545B); c. prep. ἀκροατήριον ~ον ἐπὶ τοῖς λεγομένοις Or.*hom.*20.6 *in Jer.*(p.186.11; γελῶν M.13. 313B).

γενάρχης, ὁ, 1. *first ancestor* Ἀδὰμ ὁ ἀνθρώπων γ. Bas.*ep.*362(3. 464C; M.32.1104A) etc.; **2.** *originator,* of God as πάντων γ. Areth.ap. *cat.Apoc.*4:4(p.241.19); **3.** neut., *first principle* τὰ δὲ ἐκ τῶν γ. γεγενημένα ‡Just.*confut.*proem.(M.6.1493B); τὰ μὲν γ. ἐστὶν ἔργα θεοῦ ‡Just.*qu.et resp.*49(M.6.1293B).

***γεναρχικός,** *originating,* Bas.*ep.*362(3.464C; M.32.1104A).

γενεά, ἡ, *generation*; liturg. εἰς γενεὰς γενεῶν Serap.*euch.*13.19; consisting of **1.** period of about thirty years, Clem.*str.*1.21(p.85.2; M.8.872B); **2.** length of time between birth of one group of contemporaries and death of their last surviving member, cf.*1Clem.* 5.1; Eus.*h.e.*3.32.8(M.20.284C); ref. date of Apoc. ἐπὶ τῆς ἡμετέρας γ. πρὸς τῷ τέλει τῆς Δομετιάνου ἀρχῆς Iren.*haer.*5.30.3(M.7.1207B).

γενεαλογ-έω, *trace one's descent*; **1.** of Christ's humanity εὐαγγελισταὶ ~οῦσι τὸν Χριστὸν τὸ κατὰ σάρκα ‡Ath.*Apoll.*1.9(M.26. 1108D); θεολογεῖται μὲν ὁ λόγος, ~εῖται δὲ ὁ ἄνθρωπος †Ath.ap. CLater.*act.*5(H.3.881D); κατὰ σάρκα γὰρ ~εῖται Χριστὸς ὁ θεός *Dial.Christ.et Jud.*12(p.69.25); **2.** of Christians, who trace their descent from Christ, Arist.*apol.*15.1; Ph.Carp.*Cant.*4:4(M.40.92B).

γενεαλογία, ἡ, *line of descent, genealogy*; **1.** exeg. 1Tim.1:4 and Tit.3:9, interpreted as referring to Gnost. aeons, Iren.*haer.*proem. (M.7.437A); Jews tracing their descent from Abraham and David, Chrys.*hom.*6.1 *in 1Tim.*(11.765E); Thdt.*1Tim.*1:3f.(3.640); those Jews who search genealogy of Christ in order to deny descent from Abraham and David, Thdr.Mops.*1Tim.*1:3f.(M.66.937Af.); Greek theogonies, Jo.D.*1Tim.*1:3(M.95.1000A); **2.** of genealogies of Christ and their difficulties, Or.*Cels.*2.32(p.159.9f.; M.11.852C); **3.** name for Book of Genesis, *Chron.Pasch.*p.22(M.92.109B).

γενεθλιακός, 1. *of a birthday* τοῦ γ. ἱππικοῦ *Chron.Pasch.*p.285 (M.92.712A); **2.** astrol., *belonging to nativity casting* κατά τινα τερατείαν τῶν γ. λόγων Gr.Nyss.*Eun.*11(2 p.268.5; M.45.876D).

γενεθλιαλογέω, *cast nativities, practise astrology,* Or.*Cels.*1.36 (p.87.29; M.11.729A); Gr.Nyss.*fat.*(M.45.172D); *ib.*(173B).

γενεθλιαλογία, ἡ, *casting of nativities, astrology*; condemned as deceitful, Or.*Cels.*6.80(p.151.21; M.11.1420B); Bas.*hex.*6.5(1.54A; M.

29.128A); as against scripture, ‡Ath.*synops*.15(M.28.348C); Olymp. *Eccl*.7:1(M.93.557D); as work of demons, Gr.Nyss.*fat*.(M.45.172C); its origin attributed to Chaldaeans, Thdt.*affect*.1(p.10.1; 4.699).

***γενεθλιάς**, *congenital*, Nonn.*par.Jo*.9:1(M.43.824B).

γενέθλιος, freq. with subst., e.g. ἡμέρα, understood; **1**. (*of a*) *birthday*, celebration condemned in early Church ἐπ' οὐδεμιᾶς γραφῆς εὕρομεν ὑπὸ δικαίου γ. ἀγόμενον Or.*comm.in Mt*.10.22(p.30.4; M.13.896A); id.*sel.in Gen*.(M.12.132A); **2**. *anniversary of martyrdom* as birthday to eternal life, *M.Polyc*.18.3; *M.Pion*.2.1; *M.Ariadn*.(p.123); not to be observed during Lent, CLaod.*can*.51; cf.*can*.52 where ordinary birthdays seem to be referred to; **3**. *Nativity* of Christ (v. γένεσις, γέννησις) identified with ἐπιφάνεια q.v. until later 4th cent.; from that time a separate feast, also called τὰ θεοφάνια; γ. ἥτις ἡμῖν ἐπιτελείσθω εἰκοστῇ πέμπτῃ τοῦ ἐνάτου μηνός. μεθ' ἣν ἡ ἐπιφάνιος *Const.App*.5.13.1f.; *ib*.8.33.6; Jo.Nic.*nativ*.(M.96.1449A); from 5th cent. γ. reserved to Nativity, v. θεοφάνεια; celebrated in Roman church on 25th Dec., date adopted by other churches, cf.Chrys.*nativ*.1.1 and 4f.(2.354–62); Χριστοῦ γενέθλιον ὅπερ ἁπλανῶς λίαν ἑορτάζει ἡ...ἐκκλησία τῇ εἰκάδι πέμπτῃ τοῦ κατὰ Ῥωμαίους Δεκεμβρίου μηνὸς *Chron.Pasch*.p.11(M.92.89A); πάντες...διδάσκαλοι τῆς ἐκκλησίας...ὡρίσαντο εἶναι τὴν γ. ἡμέραν τοῦ Χριστοῦ τῇ πρὸ ὀκτὼ καλανδῶν Ἰανουαρίων Alex.Sal.*cruc*.(M.87.4029C); Jo.Nic.*nativ*.(M.96.1445B); description of feast at Alexandria, Sophr.H.*mir.Cyr.et Jo*.12(M.87.3460C); **4**. of particular birthdays: of BMV, ‡Jo.D.*hom*.6.1(M.96.661B); Jo.Eub.*concept.BMV* 10(M.96.1476A); Andr.Cr.*or*.2(M.97.841A); of Jo. Bapt., *Chron.Pasch*.p.11 (M.92.89A).

***γενεογραφία, ἡ**, *genealogy*, Andr.Cr.*or*.2(M.97.852C).

***γενεσία, ἡ**, *generation* περαιτέρω τετάρτης...γ. Ath.Scholast.*coll*.9.11(p.106).

γενεσιάρχης, ὁ, *creator, originator* κτίστης καὶ γ. τῆς ὅλης...κτίσεως Clem.*exc.Thdot*.19(p.113.9; M.9.668A); Epiph.*haer*.69.57 (p.205.24; M.42.293B); Gr.Agr.*Eccl*.3.17(M.98.876A); of Father as *author* of Logos, Eus.*l.C*.12(p.232.28; M.20.1392B).

γενέσιος, *of a birthday anniversary*; neut. as subst., *birthday* (cf. γενέσια plur., *LS*); Anast.Ant.*serm*.3.8(M.89.1384D); Thdr.Stud.*nativ.BMV* tit.(M.96.680C).

γενεσιουργ-έω, **1**. *create* τὸ φῶς οὐ ∼εῖ τὴν ἑαυτοῦ αὐγήν, ἀλλὰ γεννᾷ Didym.*Trin*.2.22(M.39.553C); Cosm.Ind.*top*.1(M.88.80A); Jo.D.*Man*.1.24(M.94.1529B); **2**. *bring into being* from existing principles, Gr.Nyss.*res*.3(M.46.673C); **3**. *generate*, of Gnost. aeons δυνάμεις...ἀπορρυεῖσαι ἐγενεσιούργησαν τὸν...Ἰησοῦν Iren.*haer*.1.15.3(M.7.620B); Hipp.*haer*.6.51(p.183.12; M.16.3279B).

γενεσιουργία, ἡ, *generation*; in gen., of the earth ἀνενέργητος πρὸς...γ. Gr.Agr.*Eccl*.3.1(M.98.844C); theol., Eus.*d.e*.4.15(p.180.24; M.22.301D); id.*Marcell*.1.1(p.5.26; M.24.721B).

γενεσιουργός, (adj. and subst.) *creator*; **1**. of God as revealed in creation, ref. Sap.13:5, Or.*sel.in Ps*.1(M.12.1081D); Ath.*gent*.44 (M.25.88D); †Bas.*Is*.154(1.488D; M.30.372B); **2**. gen., epithet of God, Clem.*str*.3.10(p.227.3; M.8.1169B); Cyr.*Jo*.1.5(4.44B); id.*Juln*.1 (6².14D); **3**. theol., ref. Son's generation γεννητὸν γάρ ἐστι τὸ πατέρα ἔχον, γενητὸν δὲ τὸ γ. ἔχον ‡Ath.*dial.Trin*.2.10(M.28.1173A); ἡ κτίσις τοιῶσδε [sc. γεννᾷ], ὁ γ. ἐναντίως Didym.*Trin*.1.15(M.39.312B); **4**. of Logos in relation to Creation, Max.*ep*.12(M.91.501A); **5**. of nature γ. φύσεως Clem.*paed*.2.10(p.209.26; M.8.500C).

γένεσις, ἡ, **1**. *origin, source, beginning*, Tat.*orat*.12(p.12.29; M.6.832A); Meth.*arbitr*.8(p.164.14); ἀρχὴ γενέσεως *principle of origin*, Athenag.*leg*.19.1(M.6.928B); Meth.*creat*.7(p.498.18; M.18.340B); denied of God ἀρχῆς γ. αὐτοῦ...οὐχ εὑρισκομένης Or.*Jo*.1.29 (32; p.37.11; M.14.77D); denied of Son's divinity ὁ ἄπειρος γένεσιν ἔχειν οὐ δύναται Didym.*Trin*.3.5(M.39.841A); but used to describe Son's generation, Eus.*e.th*.1.2(p.63.21; M.24.832B); id.*d.e*.5.1(p.212.26; M.22.353A) cit. s. δημιουργία; counterpart of φθορά: γ. δὲ καὶ φθορὰν τὴν ἐν κτίσει προηγουμένως γίνεσθαι ἀνάγκη Clem.*str*.3.9 (p.225.12; M.8.1165B); Cels.ap.Or.*Cels*.6.52(p.123.3; M.11.1377C); Hipp.*haer*.5.15(p.110.25; M.16.3170C); Eus.*p.e*.11.9(523D; M.21.868C); **2**. *Creation* of world, Iren.*haer*.1.14.1(M.7.593A); Hipp.*haer*.5.15(p.110.18; M.16.3170B); Gr.Nyss.*or.1 in Gen.1:26*(M.44.257A); defended against Gnostics as divine work ἁγία δὲ γ. δι' ἣν ὁ κόσμος συνέστηκεν Clem.*str*.3.17(p.243.26; M.8.1205C); βλασφημοῦσι...τὴν γ. διαβάλλοντες *ib*.(p.243.11; 1205A); of creation *ex nihilo*, *ib*.5.14 (p.411.16; M.9.185C); of man, Or.*fr.11 in Mt*.(p.19.14; M.17.289B); γ. ... ἡ ἐκ θεοῦ πρώτη πλάσις· γέννησις δέ, ἡ...διὰ τὴν παράβασιν ἐξ ἀλλήλων διαδοχή Jo.D.*f.o*.2.30(M.94.976B); God of OT as ὁ θεὸς τῆς γ. Adam.*dial*.1.10(p.22.1; M.11.1733A); *ib*.1.13(p.28.20; 1737C); **3**. *created universe, creatures*, Hipp.*haer*.5.16(p.111.17,18; M.16.3171C); Cyr.*Jo*.5.4(4.504A); **4**. *Book of Genesis*, Just.*dial*.20.1(M.6.517C); Or.*or*.23.3(p.351.15; M.11.489A); *Const.App*.1.6.5; **5**. *procreation, generation*, Clem.*paed*.3.3(p.247.21; M.8.581B); not to be condemned, id.*exc.Thdot*.67(p.129.5; M.9.689D); foreshadowing spiritual regeneration ὁ νόμος τὴν ἀναγέννησιν ἡμῶν προφητεύων διὰ σαρκικῆς γ. id.*str*.3.12(p.234.9; M.8.1184B); *Const.App*.6.29.2; Gnost., of generation of aeons, Iren.*haer*.1.3.1(M.7.468A); hence Pythagorean name for duality, Anat.Laod.*decad*.(p.31); **6**. *birth*; in gen., Iren.*haer*.1.18.3(M.7.645B); Or.*hom.1.11 in Jer*.(p.10.3; M.13.268B); Gr.Nyss.*or.catech*.33(p.123.3; M.45.84A); of Christ's birth, Just.*dial*.43.3(M.6.568B); speculations on its date, Clem.*str*.1.21(p.90.18; M.8.885A); Or.*Jo*.2.37(30; p.96.8; M.14.181B); Μαρκίων τὴν γ. τοῦ σωτῆρος...παρῃτήσατο...νομίζων...χωρὶς γ. ... κατεληλυθότα αὐτόν Hipp.*haer*.7.31(p.217.5; M.16.3335A); Gr.Nyss.*or.catech*.13(p.61.10; 45C); λόγος, γ. σαρκὸς ἀνθρωπίνης ἀνασχόμενος ‡Ath.*Apoll*.1.12(M.26.1113A); γ. τοῦ δεσπότου...κατὰ σάρκα Cosm.Ind.*top*.2(M.88.121B, v.l. γεννήσει); ref. human (sinful) nature τὴν παλαιὰν γ. παραιτούμενος Tat.*orat*.11(p.12.12; M.6.829B); τῆς φθαρτῆς γ. Ath.*ep.Marcell*.18(M.27.32A); **7**. baptismal *rebirth* γ. ... καινῆς τε καὶ πνευματικῆς Clem.*ecl*.7(p.138.32; M.9.701B); παλιγγενεσίας γ. Or.*Jo*.2.18(11; p.457.28; M.14.792D); Bas.*ep*.199 *can*.20(3.292E; M.32.721A); Chrys.*hom.7.3 in Col*.(11.374C); **8**. astrol., *nativity*; hence *fate, destiny* cf. εἱμαρμένη: οὔτε γὰρ θεὸς ἔστιν, οὔτε πρόνοια, ἀλλὰ γ. τὰ πάντα ὑπόκειται *Hom.Clem*.14.3; ἡ γέννησις τοῦ σωτῆρος γενέσεως ἡμᾶς...ἐξέβαλεν Clem.*exc.Thdot*.76(p.130.30; M.9.693B); Epiph.*haer*.5.1(p.184.5; M.41.201C); detailed refutation of idea, Chrys.*hom.1.3 in 1Tim*.(11.553B); εἰ γ. ἐστι, πίστις οὐκ ἔστιν· εἰ γ. ἐστι, θεὸς οὐκ ἔστιν· εἰ γ. ἐστιν, οὐκ ἔστιν ἀρετή, οὐκ ἔστι κακία· εἰ γ. ἐστι, πάντα μάτην...ποιοῦμεν καὶ πάσχομεν ‡Chrys.*prov*.5(2.772B); Marc.Diac.*v.Porph*.85.

***γενετάρχης, ὁ**, *Creator*, *cat.Apoc*.16:17(p.422.10).

γενετήρ, ὁ, *father*; of God, *Orac.Sib*.3.278; *ib*.3.296; Nonn.*par.Jo*.1:1(M.43.749A); *ib*.1:12(752B).

***γενετήριος**, *of the Father*, Synes.*hymn*.2.41(p.45; M.66.1592).

γενέτης, ὁ, *father*; of God the Father, Gr.Naz.*carm*.1.2.2.688 (M.37.632A); Nonn.*par.Jo*.1:17(M.43.752C); of Christ, Gr.Naz.*carm*.2.2(poem.)3.4(M.37.1480A).

***γένη, ἡ**, *jaw*, Gr.Nyss.*hom.opif*.9(M.44.244C).

***γενῄτης**, *bearded*, Jo.Mal.*chron*.11 p.282(M.97.428A).

***γενηματικός**, ἐπὶ γ. Proc.G.*Gen*.1:27(M.87.128D) error for ἐπιγενηματικός.

***γένησις, ἡ**, error for γέννησις, e.g. Ath.*exp.Ps*.32:9(M.27.165B); and γένεσις, e.g. Bas.Sel.*or*.2(M.85.45B).

γενητός [owing to confusion of MSS and printed sources it is in many cases virtually impossible to decide whether word used by author in particular passage was γενητός or γεννητός. Entries under both these headings follow text of critical editions, where available], *having come into existence, originated*; hence *created*; **1**. of creatures in gen., Or.*Cels*.3.34(p.231.8; M.11.964C); id.*fr.10 in Jo*.(p.493.5); with idea of their being perishable Σωκράτης...γ. καὶ φθαρτός Athenag.*leg*.8.2(M.6.905A); *Orac.Sib.fr*.3.1; εἰ μὲν γ. καὶ ἀγένητον, δύναται τὸ ἀγένητον ἄφθαρτον τὸ δὲ γ. φθαρτόν Adam.*dial*.3.8(p.126.14f.; M.11.1800B); of pagan gods θεοὺς γ., καὶ διὰ μὲν τὸ γεγενῆσθαι...φθαρῆναι Hipp.*haer*.1.19(p.20.19; M.16.3041D); of changeable nature of elements, Clem.*str*.1.11(p.34.11; M.8.749C); of angels ὅλως γὰρ τὸ γ. οὐκ ἀνούσιον id.*exc.Thdot*.10(p.109.21; M.9.660C); **2**. of human nature of Christ τοῦ σωτῆρος ἡμῶν καὶ ἀρχιερέως γ. θεοῦ Or.*sel.in Ps*.1(M.12.1080B); λόγος ὢν δημιουργός, ὕστερον πεποίηται ἀρχιερεύς, ἐνδυσάμενος σῶμα τὸ γ. καὶ ποιητόν Ath.*Ar*.2.8(M.26.164A); *ib*.1.60(137B); Ign.*Eph*.7.2 which in texts has γεννητὸς καὶ ἀγέννητος is quoted by Ath. as γ. καὶ ἀγένητος *syn*.47(p.271.29; M.26.776C); and interpreted by him γενητὸν αὐτὸν λέγων διὰ τὴν σάρκα *ib*.(p.272.3; 777A); **3**. of the Arian conception of Son δύο κυρίοις λατρεύειν, ἑνὶ μὲν ἀγενήτῳ, τῷ δὲ ἑτέρῳ γ. καὶ κτίσματι Ath.*Ar*.3.16(M.26.353C); amounting to ditheism λέγουσι δύο θεούς, καὶ τούτους διαφόρους ἔχοντας τὰς φύσεις, τὸν μὲν γ., τὸν δὲ ἀγένητον *ib*.(356A); which includes him among γενητά, Athanasius Nazarbonensis ap.eund.*syn*.17(p.245.1; M.26.712C); *ib*.19(p.246.23; 716B); Ast.Soph.*fr*.3; γεννητός ἐστιν ἅμα καὶ γ. CSard.*ep.cath*.ap. Thdt.*h.e*.2.8.37(3.844); view repudiated by orthodox μὴ τῶν γ. ἐστιν ὁ λόγος Ath.*Ar*.2.28(M.26.205C); τίς ἡ χρεία...γ. θεοῦ τῷ ἀγενήτῳ θεῷ; †Diad.*Ar*.2(M.65.1153D); in gen. in subordinationist terminology ἑτέροις παρὰ Χριστὸν...γ. Or.*Jo*.2.28(23; p.85.7; M.14.161D); Eus.*d.e*.5.1(p.211.12; M.22.352A); Epiph.*haer*.64.8(p.417.14; M.41.1084A); **4**. (Sabellian) also applied to Godhead ἕνα καὶ τὸν αὐτὸν θεὸν εἶναι πάντων δημιουργὸν καὶ πατέρα, εὐδοκήσαντα δὲ πεφηνέναι... ὄντα ἀόρατον·...οὕτως...ἀγένητος ⟨καὶ γ.⟩ Hipp.*haer*.9.10(p.244.17; M.16.3378A); οἶδα ἕνα θεὸν Χριστὸν Ἰησοῦν, καὶ πλὴν αὐτοῦ ἕτερον οὐδένα γ. καὶ παθητόν *ib*.9.11(p.246.3; 3379A).

*__γενητῶς__, *in the manner of created things*, ‡Just.*qu.et resp*.129 (M.6.1380C) cit. s. συνθέτως; ‡Just.*confut*.2(M.6.1497B).

*__γενίζ-ω__, prob. facetious word, *boast of one's pedigree* μή μοι γένος ∼ε Gr.Naz.*carm*.1.2.10.372(M.37.707A).

γενικός, **1.** *general, universal*; **a.** in gen. οὐκ ἂν...λέγοιμεν ἔχειν ἀπὸ θεοῦ τὸ εἰδικὸν τόδε, τὸ κινεῖσθαι πρὸς τὸ τύπτειν...ἀλλὰ τὸ μὲν γ., τὸ κινεῖσθαι Or.*princ*.3.1.20(p.235.4; M.11.293B); of the Deuteronomic curse, †Bas.*bapt*.2.5.2(2.659A; M.31.1593D); of laws, Diod. *fr.Gen*.20:5(M.33.1583C); v. γενικῶς; **b.** theol.; of divine providence, Athenag.*leg*.24.3(M.6.948A); of man's punishment for Fall and redemption through Christ, Cyr.*dogm*.(p.561.7; 6^2.376B); of redemption, id.*Abac*.33(3.547E); of grace of Christ, id.*Ps*.32:13(M. 69.877D); Christol. εἰ...ὁ Χριστὸς συνθετός ἐστι φύσις...ᾗ γ. πάντως ἐστί, ἢ μοναδική Max.*ep*.13(M.91.517D); *ib*.(521A); **2.** *principal*; of the four elements τὰ γ. σώματα, Or.*fr.29 in Jo*.(p.546.25); the four principal passions (Stoic) τὰ πάθη τὰ γενικώτατα Clem.*paed*.1.13(p.150.22; M.8.372B); Or.*fr.25 in Jer*.(p.211.2); four cardinal virtues, Nil.*epp*.1.223(M.79.164D); Areth.*Apoc*.10(M.106. 572A); of heresies, Chrys.*hom.46.3 in Ac*.(9.348D); **3.** *belonging to a class* γ. ἔχουσι τὸ γέρας οἱ ἱερεῖς Thdt.*qu.1 in 2Par*.(1.592); **4.** *of general application*, of laws δέκα εἶναι τὰς γ. ἐντολάς Bas.*hom.in Ps*.32(1.133B; M.29.328B); γ. νομοθεσίας Diod.*Ex*.22:5(M.33.1583D); Heracl.*nov*.25(p.48); Thphn.*chron*.p.45(M.108.168C); βασιλικὸς δὲ τύπῳ γ. τὴν ἐν Χαλκηδόνι σύνοδον ἐξέβαλεν *ib*.p.104(304A); opp. τοπικός, Ath.Scholast.*coll*.1.12(p.20); **5.** *concerned with the public treasury*, Thdr.Stud.*epp*.2.82 tit.(M.99.1324A).

γενικῶς, *generically*; **a.** *as a class*, opp. ἰδικώτερον, Or.*Jo*.20.10 (p.339.27; M.14.596B); opp. τοῖς καθ' ἕκαστον, Gr.Nyss.*v.Mos*.48 (γενικός M.44.317C); **b.** *as a whole*, opp. τοῖς μέρεσιν, Chrys.*hom. 5.1 in Rom*.(9.460D).

*__γενισταί, οἱ__, Jewish sect; name perh. indicating claim of descent from Abraham, Just.*dial*.80.4(M.6.665A).

γέννα, ἡ, *birth* hence *birthday*; of Nativity of Christ, †Bas.Sel. *or*.41(M.85.469B); Cosm.Ind.*top*.5(M.88.197A); *Const.Stud*.13(M.99. 1709A); as neut. plur. τὰ δὲ Χριστοῦ γ. †Jo.Jej.*poenit*.(M.88.1913A); ‡Anast.Ant.*serm*.4(M.89.1392A).

γεννάδας, ὁ, *man of noble birth, gentleman*; iron., *excellent fellow*; esp. of heretics, Or.*Cels*.4.81(p.350.20; M.11.1153A); Gr.Nyss.*Apoll*. 24(M.45.1173B); *ib*.27(1184A).

*__γενναιοζωία, ἡ__, *nobility*, *Pers*.(p.33.4).

[*]__γεννάρχης, ὁ__, = γενάρχης, *generator, founder*; of Adam, Gr. Agr.*Eccl*.1.3(M.98.761A); *ib*.4.2(924A).

γενν-άω, *beget, engender*; **1.** of generation of Logos, taught in gen. terms by 2nd-cent. Apologists ὁ λόγος τῆς σοφίας,...ἀπὸ τοῦ πατρὸς τῶν ὅλων ∼ηθείς Just.*dial*.61.1(M.6.613C); id.*2apol*.6.3(M.6. 453A) al.; ὁ λόγος ἐν ἀρχῇ ∼ηθεὶς ἀντεγέννησε τὴν καθ' ἡμᾶς ποίησιν Tat.*orat*.5(p.6.8; M.6.817A); **2.** of eternal generation of Son; **a.** affirmed by Origen οὐχὶ ἐγέννησεν ὁ πατὴρ τὸν υἱὸν καὶ ἀπέλυσεν αὐτὸν ὁ πατὴρ ἀπὸ τῆς γενέσεως αὐτοῦ, ἀλλ' ἀεὶ ∼ᾷ αὐτόν Or.*hom. 9.4 in Jer*.(p.70.14ff.; M.13.357A); *ib*.(p.70.24–27; 358A); id.*princ*. 4.4.1(p.348.9; M.11.401B); **b.** opposed by Arians, in controversy with whom this became key word, esp. in phrase οὐκ ἦν πρὶν ∼ηθῇ freq. cited, e.g. Ar.*Thal.fr*.3 ap.Ath.*decr*.6(M.25.433A); id.ap. eund.*ep.Aeg.Lib*.12(M.25.564B); εἰ ἀγέννητός ἐστιν ὁ θεὸς τὴν οὐσίαν, οὐκ οὐσίας διαστάσει τὸ ∼ηθὲν ἐγεννήθη Aët.*synt*.5(p.353.14; M.42. 536C); ἡμᾶς χρονίτας ὠνόμασε...ἐπειδὴ ∼ᾶσθαι λέγομεν ἐκ τοῦ πατρὸς τὸν υἱόν· τὸ δὲ ∼ᾶσθαι τοῖς Ἀρειανοῖς χρονικήν [l. χρονικόν] ‡Ath.*dial. Trin*.2.11(M.28.1173C); **c.** affirmed ∼ηθέντα, οὐ ποιηθέντα *Symb.Nic*. (325)(p.51; M.20.1540B); and defended by orthodox, human analogy supporting consubstantiality with Father οἰκίαν μὲν οὖν τις βουλευόμενος κατασκευάζει, υἱὸν δὲ ∼ᾷ κατὰ φύσιν Ath.*Ar*.3.62(M.26. 453B); τοιοῦτον εἶναι τὸν λόγον οἷός ἐστιν ὁ ∼ήσας αὐτὸν *ib*.1.31(76C); τὸν ἐκ τοῦ θεοῦ θεὸν ∼ηθέντα Cyr.H.*catech*.4.7; and expressing the divine relationship ὁ γὰρ ∼ηθεὶς πρὸς τὸν γεγεννηκότα...τὴν ἀναφορὰν ἔχει Gr.Nyss.*Eun*.4(2 p.88.22; M.45.664D); ὁμοούσιος ὁ ∼ηθεὶς τῷ ∼ήσαντι Chrys.*anom*.7.2(1.502E); ἣν ὡς θεὸς συναΐδιος τῷ ∼ήσαντι πατρί, καὶ ἐξ αὐτοῦ κατὰ φύσιν ἀπορρήτως γεγεννημένος Cyr.*Chr.un*. (5^1.717B); though comparison cannot be pressed, Ath.*Ar*.1.23 (M.26.60B); because generation of Son is timeless τὸν πρὸ πάντων αἰώνων ἐκ τοῦ πατρὸς γεγεννημένον...οὐχ ὁμοίως μὲν τοῖς λοιποῖς γεννητοῖς ὑποστάντα οὐδὲ ζωὴν ἐμφερῆ τοῖς δι' αὐτοῦ γεγεννημένοις ζῶντα Eus.*e.th*.1.8(p.66.18,22; M.24.837Bf.); οὐ χρόνοις ὑπόκειται, ἵνα ὑπέρχρονος ᾖ ὁ γεννήτωρ τοῦ ∼ηθέντος ‡Caes.Naz.*dial*.18(M.38. 873) and without 'passion' ὁ λόγος ὁ υἱὸς ὀνομάζεται ὡς ἀπαθῶς ∼ηθείς Thdt.*Trin*.10(M.75.1157D); but rather τὸν υἱὸν ἐγέννα ὥσπερ τινὸς φωτὸς ἀκτῖνα Eus.*e.th*.1.8(p.66.29; 837C); ‡Chrys.*Jud*.(1. 825B); **3.** of double generation (divine and human) of Son from Father and BMV (v. γέννησις), affirmed against Nestorius ἐκ θεοῦ πατρὸς λόγον, ∼ηθέντα μὲν θεϊκῶς πρὸ παντὸς αἰῶνος...ἐν ἐσχάτοις δὲ ...καιροῖς...κατὰ σάρκα ἐκ γυναικός Cyr.*Chr.un*.(5^1.734B); id.*ep*.44 (p.36.2; 5^2.134A); ἐκ τοῦ πατρὸς ∼ηθέντα κατὰ τὴν θεότητα,...ἐκ Μαρίας...κατὰ τὴν ἀνθρωπότητα Evagr.*h.e*.2.4(p.49.26; M.86.2508C); Jo.D.*fr*.(M.96.816B); cf. ∼ωμένης τῆς σαρκὸς ἐκ τῆς θεοτόκου Μαρίας, αὐτὸς λέγεται γεγεννῆσθαι Ath.*Ar*.3.33(M.26.393B); **4.** of human birth of Christ Ἰησοῦ Χριστοῦ...τοῦ ἐκ Μαρίας, ὃς ἀληθῶς ἐγεννήθη Ign.*Trall*.9.1; id.*Eph*.18.2; Just.*dial*.45.4(M.6.573A); Heraclides ap.Or.*dial*.1(p.118.9); from BMV and H. Ghost, Cyr. H.*catech*.4.9; *Symb.App*.(pp.23,24); *Symb.Nic*.(359)ap.Thdt.*h.e*.2. 21.4(3.880); on 25th Dec. ἡ γὰρ πρώτη παρουσία τοῦ κυρίου ἡμῶν...ἐν ᾗ γεγέννηται ἐν Βηθλεέμ...πρὸ ὀκτὼ καλανδῶν Ἰανουαρίων Hipp.*Dan*. 4.23.3(M.10.645A) (prob. later interpolation); **5.** of generation of Gnost. aeons τὴν δύναμιν τῶν γεγεννηκότων αἰώνων Hipp.*haer*. 6.30(p.157.25; M.16.3239A); Epiph.*haer*.31.3(p.387.11; M.41.477C); **6.** spiritually, esp. in pass., *be engendered* or *born*, cf. Jo.3:3ff.; **a.** in gen. of Christians being born anew οὐ γὰρ ἅπαξ ἐρῶ τὸν δίκαιον γεγεννῆσθαι ὑπὸ τοῦ θεοῦ, ἀλλ' ἀεὶ ∼ᾶσθαι, καθ' ἑκάστην πρᾶξιν ἀγαθήν, ἐν ᾗ ∼ᾷ τὸν δίκαιον ὁ θεός Or.*hom.9.4 in Jer*.(p.70. 11ff.; M.13.357A); πιστεύσατε ἐπὶ τῷ ∼ηθέντι Χριστῷ ἵνα οἱ ∼ηθέντες διὰ τῆς αὐτοῦ ζωῆς ζήσωσιν *A.Thom*.A 79(p.194.5); ἄνωθεν αὐτοὺς [i.e. Christians] ἐκ θεοῦ γεγεννῆσθαι Mac.Aeg.*hom*.5.4(M.34.497B); Proc.G.*Gen*.5:3(M.87.264A); **b.** baptismal διὰ γὰρ τοῦ ἀποθανεῖν τῇ σαρκὶ περιγίνεται ἡμῖν τὸ ∼ηθῆναι τῷ πνεύματι Bas.*hom*.13.1(2.113D; M.31.424B); Chrys.*hom.7.2 in Col*.(11.374B); priests begetting children to Church by baptism πατέρας...∼ᾷ [sc. the episcopal order] τῇ ἐκκλησίᾳ Epiph.*haer*.75.4(p.336.5; M.42.508D); **c.** myst., of Word engendered in hearts of saints οὗτος [sc. ὁ λόγος] ὁ ἀπ' ἀρχῆς...καὶ πάντοτε νέος ἐν ἁγίων καρδίαις ∼ώμενος ‡*Diogn*. 11.4; of Christ bringing forth spiritual children, Mac.Aeg.*hom*. 30.2(M.34.721C); of soul born to spiritual life, *ib*.5.3(497A); of soul bringing forth Christ Χριστὸς ∼ᾶται μυστικῶς...καὶ μητέρα παρθένον ἀπεργαζόμενος τὴν ∼ῶσαν ψυχήν Max.*or.dom*.(M.90. 889C).

γέννημα, τό, *that which is begotten* or *born, offspring*; also *product*;

A. of Christ; **1.** in 2nd and 3rd cent.; **a.** of Son as begotten of Father, opp. ποίημα, v.s.v.; and κτίσμα· τὸ γ. πρὸ πάντων...τῶν κτισμάτων Just.*dial*.129.4(M.6.777B) al.; πρῶτον γ. εἶναι τῷ πατρί, οὐχ ὡς γενόμενον Athenag.*leg*.10.2(M.6.909A); **b.** of Christ as mere man, in view attributed to Simon Magus Χριστὸς...γ. γυναικός, ἐξ αἱμάτων καὶ ἐπιθυμίας σαρκικῆς...γεγεννημένος Hipp.*haer*.6.9(p.136. 6; M.16.3207C); **2.** in early stages of Arian controversy; **a.** orthodox, Eus.*h.e*.1.2.3(M.20.53C) cit. s. δημιουργία; ἀγαθοῦ πατρὸς ἀγαθὸν γ. id.*d.e*.4.2(p.152.4; M.22.253B); freq. defended agst. Arian usage εἰ ἀγένητος ὁ θεός, οὐ γενητή, ἀλλὰ γ. ἐστιν ἡ τούτου εἰκών Ath. *Ar*.1.31(M.26.76C); id.*syn*.48(p.272.26; M.26.777C) cit. s. ποίημα; **b.** used by Arius as almost synon. with κτίσμα: κτίσμα τοῦ θεοῦ τέλειον...γ. ἀλλ' οὐχ ὡς ἓν τῶν γεγεννημένων Ar.*ep.Alex*.(p.12.10; M.26.709A)cit.ap.Epiph.*haer*.69.7(p.158.11, M.42.213B reading γ. for γεγεννημένων); εἴ τις λέγει τὸν υἱὸν κτίσμα ὡς ἓν τῶν κτισμάτων, ἢ γ. ὡς ἓν τῶν γ., ἢ ποίημα ὡς ἓν τῶν ποιημάτων...ἀ. ἔ. *Symb.Ant*.(341)2 ap.Ath.*syn*.23(p.249.37f.; M.26.724B); **3.** in later stages; **a.** by Eunomians in derogatory and subordinationist sense τοῦτο καὶ λεγόμενον ἀληθῶς γ., υἱὸν ὑπήκοον, ὑπουργὸν τελειότατον, πρὸς πᾶσαν δημιουργίαν καὶ γνώμην πατρικὴν ὑπηρετήσαντα Eun.*apol*.27(M.30. 864C); as expressing substance of Son opp. the ἀγέννητον of Father γ. τοίνυν τὸν υἱόν φαμεν...οὐχ ἕτερον μέν τι τὴν οὐσίαν νοοῦντες, ἕτερον δέ τι παρ' αὐτὴν τὸ σημαινόμενον· ἀλλ' αὐτὴν εἶναι τὴν ὑπόστασιν, ἣν σημαίνει τοὔνομα *ib*.12(848B); cf.Bas.*Eun*.2.6(1.242D; M.29.584A); **b.** hence rejected by Basil as unscriptural παιδίον γάρ, φησίν, ἐγεννήθη ἡμῖν...οὐχὶ γ. ... καίτοι εἴπερ τὸ γ. οὐσίας ὑπῆρχε σημαντικόν, οὐκ ἂν ἕτερον ὄνομα παρὰ τοῦ πνεύματος ἐδιδάχθημεν *ib*.2.7(243A; M. 584C); and as designating a thing rather than a person, *ib*.2.8 (244A; M.585C); οὕτω μὲν οὖν ἀλλοτρία τῆς τε κοινῆς συνηθείας καὶ τῆς τῶν γραφῶν χρήσεως ἡ φωνὴ τοῦ γ. ἀπελήλεγκται *ib*.(244C; M.588B); **c.** but used once by Basil γεννητῶς ὑπάρχων ἐκ τοῦ πατρὸς ὁ υἱός,... ὡς δὲ γ., τὸ ὁμοούσιον διασώζει id.*hom*.24.4(2.192C; M.31.608A); following most contemporary Fathers who assert identity of nature between γεννήτωρ and γ., e.g. Gr.Naz.*or*.29.10(p.88.2; M.36.88A);

distinguishing γ. from ποίημα and κτίσμα agst. Eunomian identification, Gr.Nyss.*Eun*.4(2 pp.80.7–81.8; M.45.653D–656B); Chrys.*hom. 10.2 in 1Cor*.(10.82E); Cyr.*Jo*.6.1(4.652B) cit. s. γινώσκω; id.*thes*.15 (5^1.147E) cit. s. ποίημα; consequence of identification discussed εἰ, εἴ τι κτίσμα θεοῦ, τοῦτο καὶ γ., οὐδὲν τῶν γεγονότων λείπεται τῆς υἱοθεσίας *ib*.18(182D); εἰ κτίσμα καὶ γ. ταὐτόν ἐστιν, ὁ κτίζων ἔσται καὶ πατήρ. εἰ δὲ κτίζει ὁ υἱός, ἔσται ὁ αὐτὸς καὶ πατήρ *ib*.(183B); used less freq. by later writers, e.g. Jo.D.*Trin*.5(M.95.16C).

B. of Gnost. aeons δευτέραν τετράδα, γ. πρώτης τετράδος Iren. *haer*.1.18.1(M.7.641B); τῶν αἰώνων τὰ γ. Hipp.*haer*.6.31(p.158.18; M.16.3239C).

C. of H. Ghost, ref. Jo.15:26 ὁ γ. ἐστι τῆς οὐσίας τοῦ θεοῦ †Leont. B.*sect*.4.1(M.86.1220B).

D. met. καθάπερ ἂν ἰδίου γ. ... ὁ...σωτὴρ ἀναδέχεται τὰς ὠφελείας Clem.*str*.7.3(p.15.19; M.9.426B); τὰ ἐκ τῆς ἀδικίας...ἐκφύοντα γ. Const.*or.s.c*.16(p.176.23; M.20.1280C); τὸ ψεῦδος γ. τοῦ διαβόλου Bas.*ep*.223.4(3.339C; M.32.828B); of spoken word as analogy of Logos γ. ... ἐστι τοῦ νοῦ Sever.*sigill*.6(M.63.542).

γέννησις, ἡ, *generation, engendering,* also *birth*; **1.** of divine Son; **a.** eternal generation [v. γεννάω] τὴν ἄναρχον...παρὰ τοῦ πατρὸς γ. Alex.Al.*ep.Alex*.12(p.28.2; M.18.568B); not to be conceived of in terms of human generation, Ath.*Ar*.1.28(M.26.69A); **b.** denied by Arians as incompatible with divine essence ἡμεῖς δὲ...μήτε τῆς οὐσίας τοῦ θεοῦ παριεμένης γέννησιν, ὡς ἀγεννήτου,...μήτε μὴν ἑτέρας τινὸς ὑποκειμένης εἰς υἱοῦ γ., μὴ ὄντα φαμὲν γεγεννῆσθαι τὸν υἱόν Eun.*apol*.15(M.30.849C); πρὸ τῆς ἰδίας γ. μὴ εἶναι τὴν οὐσίαν τοῦ μονογενοῦς id.ap.Gr.Nyss.*Eun*.4(2 p.184.4; M.45.777B); and with divine impassibility εἰ μὲν τὸ ἀπαθὲς εἴη, μὴ εἶναι τὴν γ. Gr.Nyss. *ib*.(2 p.52.27; 621D); πάσης...γ. οὐκ ἐπ' ἄπειρον ἐκτεινομένης Eun. *ib*.(2 p.212.22; 809D); **c.** affirmed by orthodox οὔτε τοῦ πατρὸς ἐκστάντος τῆς ἀγεννησίας, διότι γεγέννηκεν, οὔτε τοῦ υἱοῦ τῆς γ. ὅτι ἐκ τοῦ ἀγεννήτου Gr.Naz.*or*.39.12(M.36.348B); because οὐσία...τοῦ υἱοῦ ἡ γ. Bas.*hom*.24.4(2.192B; M.31.605D); id.*Eun*.1.9(1.221E; M.29. 533A); human analogy not to be too closely pressed οὐ χρὴ τὰ τῆς σαρκικῆς γ. ἰδιώματα ἐφαρμόζειν τῇ θείᾳ φύσει Gr.Nyss.*fid*.(M.45. 140A); id.*Eun*.8(2 p.186.20; M.45.780D); for γ. is ἀπαθής, *ib*.4(p.85.1; 660C); Thdt.*Trin*.9(M.75.1157C); not temporal, Gr.Nyss.*Eun*.9 (2 p.213.29; 812C); Thdt.*Trin*.5(1152B); and an ineffable mystery, Chrys.*nativ*.2(6.394B); Cyr.*inc.unigen*.(5^1.707A); constituting difference between Persons of Father and Son, Anast.*fid*.(p.272); Jo.D.*f.o*.3.7(M.94.1008C); **2.** of incarnate Son; **a.** human γ. of Logos denied by Marcion and other heretics, ‡Ath.*Apoll*.2.5(M.26. 1140A); and by Nestorius, *fr*.C 14(p.287.7)ap.Cyr.*Nest*.1.8(6^1.24E) al.; also called ἡ κάτω γ., ‡Ath.*nativ.Chr*.4(M.28.965B); **b.** 'double generation' from Father and BMV maintained against Nestorius, Eutyches, and monophysites γεγέννηκε ὁ...πατὴρ τὸν υἱὸν ἐξ ἑαυτοῦ γ. μιᾷ· πλὴν εὐδόκησεν ἐν αὐτῷ τὸ ἀνθρώπινον ἀνασῶσαι γένος...διὰ γ. δηλονότι τῆς ἐκ γυναικός Cyr.*Chr.un*.(5^1.721E); *ib*.(747A); id.*Jo*.5 (4.447B,C); μονογενὴς...ὠνόμασται κατὰ τὴν ἄνωθεν γ., πρωτότοκος δὲ...ὡς πρῶτος τῆς ἐπὶ τὴν ζωὴν φερούσης γ. τὰς ὠδῖνας λύσας Thdt. *Trin*.10(M.75.1160C); ὁμολογῶ δύο γ., ἐκ θείας καὶ ἐκ σαρκός·...δύο γ. ἐν ἑνὶ προσώπῳ Valerius ap.CCP(448)*act*.2(*ACO* 2.1.1 p.119.34; H.2.136B); and affirmed esp. in Three Chapters controversy εἴ τις οὐχ ὁμολογεῖ, τοῦ θεοῦ λόγου εἶναι τὰς δύο γεννήσεις, τήν τε πρὸ αἰώνων ἐκ τοῦ πατρός,...τήν τε ἐπ' ἐσχάτων τῶν ἡμερῶν...ἐκ τῆς... Μαρίας...ἀ. ἔ. CCP(553)*anath*.2 ∞ Justn.*conf.anath*.2(p.90.22; M.86. 1013D); Eulog.*palm*.10(M.86.2929C); Evagr.*h.e*.1.11(p.18.29; M.86. 2449B); δύο γ. ... τήν τε...ἀσωμάτως καὶ ἀιδίως, καὶ τὴν...σαρκικῶς CLater.*can*.4; **3.** *the Nativity*; **a.** in gen., Ign.*Magn*.11.1; Iren. *haer*.3.19.1(M.7.939A); Gr.Nyss.*Apoll*.28(M.45.1184B) cit. s. γήϊνος; its purity defended, Or.*Cels*.6.73(p.142.24; M.11.1408C); and its reality affirmed, *ib*.(p.143.3; 1408D); ἡ δὲ γ. αὐτοῦ διπλῆ γέγονε, καθ' ἡμᾶς καὶ ὑπὲρ ἡμᾶς id.*fr.11 in Mt*.1:18(p.20.1; M.17.289C); Bas.*hom*.3.3(2.597D; M.31.1464A); source of grace to world, Gr. Nyss.*laud.Bas*.(M.46.789A); parallel with eternal generation, †Chrys.*nativ*.2(6.394A); foretold by prophets, Chrys.*nativ*.1(2.355D); threefold birth of Christ (Nativity, Baptism, Resurrection) dist. by Jo.Nic.*nativ*.(M.96.1440A); **b.** of feast of Nativity (v. γενέθλιος); as source of all other feasts, Chrys.*Philogon*.6(1.497C); kept 12 days before Epiphany, Cosm.Ind.*top*.5(M.88.197C); on 25th Dec., Jo.Nic.*nativ*.(1440A); *ib*.(1445C); **4.** *spiritual birth, regeneration* (v. ἄνωθεν), through practice of virtue γίνεται...ἡ ἄνωθεν γ. ... ἐξ ἀναλήψεως ἀρετῆς καὶ τηρήσεως τῶν ἐντολῶν αὐτοῦ Or.*fr.35 in Jo*. (p.510.14); Chrys.*hom.25.1 in Jo*.(8.143D); through baptism, Or. *fr.35 in Jo*.(p.510.21,25); νοητῆς τῆς διὰ τοῦ βαπτίσματος γ. Chrys. *hom.25.2 in Jo*.(8.145E); hence of man's threefold birth, physical, baptismal, and in resurrection, Gr.Nyss.*Eun*.4(2 p.64.21; M.45. 636C); Max.*ambig*.(M.91.1325B); **5.** = γένεσις *creation*, Hipp.*haer*. 5.25(p.126.27; M.16.3194B); πρὸ γὰρ τοῦ ὁρωμένου...γεννήσεως, ἐγὼ γεγέννηκά σε Ath.*exp.in Ps*.109:3(M.27.461D); Gr.Nyss.*Eun*.4(2 p.58.3; M.45.628D); *ib*.8(p.185.10,22; 780A,B).

γεννήτειρα, ἡ, *mother*, of BMV γ. ἐστι τοῦ λόγου Leont.H.*Nest*.3 (M.86.1609A); met. [sc. παρρησία] γ. ... πάντων τῶν παθῶν Dor.*doct*. 4.5(M.88.1665A); cf.*Apophth.Patr*.(M.65.109A) cit. s. γεννήτρια.

***γεννητή, ἡ,** = γενετή *birth* in phrase ἐκ γ.: τίς γὰρ...ὁ ἅγιος ἐκ γ.; Apoll. *fr*.56(p.217.19)ap.Gr.Nyss.*Apoll*.28(M.45.1184D); Cyr.*inc. unigen*.(5^1.703C); Call.*v.Hyp*.(p.96); *Mir.Artem*.24(p.34.7).

γεννητικός, *generative, productive*; **1.** of men κάτοχος ἐπιθυμίας γ. Meth.*symp*.2.2(p.17.3; M.18.49B); Isid.Pel.*epp*.1.139(M.78.273C); ref. types of baptismal regeneration in OT ὁ νόμος τὴν ἀναγέννησιν ἡμῶν προφητεύων διὰ σαρκικῆς γενέσεως ἐπὶ τῇ γ. [sc. καταβολῇ] τοῦ σπέρματος προσέφερε τὸ βάπτισμα Clem.*str*.3.12(p.234.9; M.8.1184B); **2.** of eternal generation of Son, Father's nature being ἀεὶ γ., Ath. *Ar*.3.66(M.26.464B); ‡Ath.*dial.Trin*.1.20(M.28.1148A) cit. s. στόμα; Didym.(‡Bas.)*Eun*.5(1.316C; M.29.757C) cit. s. γαστήρ; Leont.H. *Nest*.1.29(M.86.1496A) cit. s. ἀνεκπόρευτος; as dist. from Son, Ath. *Ar*.1.22(57A); of whom term appears to be used passively ὁ υἱὸς λόγος τοῦ θεοῦ, υἱικῶς γ. Didym.*Trin*.2.2(M.39.464C); **3.** Gnost., of Father μόνον [i.e. without female aeon] εἶναι καὶ γ. Hipp.*haer*.10.13 (p.273.27; M.16.3427A); **4.** met. ἀπείθεια ἁμαρτίας ἐστὶ γ. Clem.*paed*. 1.13(p.150.26; M.8.372B); of number ten which is γ. τελειότητος Gr. Naz.*or*.45.14(M.36.641C); of baptismal waters ὁ ἄρρητός σου λόγος... γ. αὐτὰ κατασκευασάτω Serap.*euch*.19.2; of episcopal order as πατέρων γ. τάξις Epiph.*haer*.75.4(p.336.5; M.42.508D); of original of a translation ἀνῄρηται ὁ λόγος ἀπὸ τοῦ γ. τόπου id.*mens*.7(M.43. 248B).

***γεννητικῶς,** *by way of generation,* ‡Ath.*dial.Trin*.1.6(M.28. 1125A) cit. s. δημιουργικῶς; Didym.(‡Bas.)*Eun*.5(1.298B; M.29. 716B); id.*Trin*.1.35(M.39.437C); οὐκέτι γ. ... ἀλλὰ κτιστικῶς Epiph. *haer*.76.40(p.394.28; M.42.604D); Leont.H.*Nest*.2.4(M.86.1537C) cit. s. γεγεννημένως.

***γεννητοαγέννητος (*γεννηταγέννητος),** *begotten-unbegotten* εἰ ταὐτόν, φασί, ὁ υἱὸς τῷ πατρὶ κατ' οὐσίαν, ἀγέννητος δὲ ὁ πατήρ, ἔσται τοῦτο καὶ ὁ υἱός· καλῶς, εἴπερ οὐσία θεοῦ τὸ ἀγέννητον, ἵν' ᾖ τις καινὴ μίξις γεννητοαγέννητον Gr.Naz.*or*.29.12(p.90.9; M.36.89A); Μακεδ.· εἰ μία θεότης ἐστίν, ἀγέννητος δέ ἐστιν ἡ τοῦ πατρός, γεννητὴ δέ ἐστιν τοῦ υἱοῦ, γ. ἐστιν ἡ θεότης ‡Ath.*dial.Trin*.3.8(M.28.1213B).

γεννητός, [v. ἀγέννητος, and γενητός (with which it is freq. confused in MSS];

A. *begotten, generated*; **1.** of creatures; **a.** as having a beginning, not eternal, thus in Gr. philosophy (s.v.l.) τὸ μὲν ἀεὶ ὄν, τὸ νοητόν, ἀγέννητον εἶναι διδάσκει [sc. Plato]· τὸ δὲ οὐκ ὄν, τὸ αἰσθητόν, [γ.] Athenag.*leg*.19.1(M.6.929A); hence objections of Arians agst. eternal generation of Son (v. 3.b); **b.** of Gnost. aeons γ. ... ἀπὸ τοῦ ἀγεννήτου πατρός Iren.*haer*.1.11.1(M.7.561A); Hipp.*haer*.6.30 (p.157.6; M.16.3239A); **c.** ref. Gnost. conception of world οὐκ ἐκτισμένα τὰ κτιστὰ ὁρίζεται, ἀλλὰ γ. καὶ ἀπὸ μετουσίας Epiph.*haer*.32.2 (p.441.5; M.41.545C); **2.** owing to confusion with γενητός freq. = *created*, esp. in early Fathers μόνος γὰρ ἀγέννητος καὶ ἄφθαρτος ὁ θεὸς...τὰ δὲ λοιπὰ πάντα μετὰ τοῦτον γ. καὶ φθαρτά Just.*dial*.5.4(M. 6.488B); τὰ θνητά τε καὶ γ. Clem.*str*.2.11(p.141.3, v.l. γενητά M.8. 988B); Hipp.*haer*.6.12(p.138.9; M.16.3211B); Eus.*d.e*.3.3(p.112.11,16; M.22.192D,193A reading γενητόν); **3.** of divine Son; **a.** this confusion raised difficulties in the application of term to Son; sts. used before Nicaea to express relationship between Father and Son, in a possibly subordinationist sense, opp. ἀγέννητος: ὁ μὲν [sc. Father] ἀγέννητος, ὁ δὲ [sc. Son] γ. Eus.*d.e*.5.1(p.213.28; M.22.353D); *ib*.4.3(p.154.13; 257A); but during Arian controversy begins to be dist. from γενητός: τὰ δὲ γενητὰ ἀδύνατον, δημιουργήματα ὄντα, λέγεσθαι γ., εἰ μὴ ἄρα, μετὰ ταῦτα μετασχόντα τοῦ γ. υἱοῦ, γεγεννῆσθαι καὶ αὐτὰ λέγονται Ath.*Ar*.1.56(M.26.129B), though Athanasius does not always differentiate between the two spellings, which are constantly confused in MSS; **b.** as Arian term to express view that Son is creature, or at least subordinate divine being; ἀγέννητος expressing essence of divinity is applicable only to Father, γ. characterizes Son ἀγέννητον δὲ αὐτόν φαμεν διὰ τὸν τὴν φύσιν γ. Ar.*Thal.fr*.2 ap.Ath.*syn*.15(M.26.705D); εἰ δὲ τὸ γ. αὐτὸν λέγεσθαι ὑπόφασίν τινα παρέχει...οὐ περὶ αὐτοῦ μόνου τὸ γ. εἶναί φησιν ἡ γραφή, ἀλλὰ καὶ ἐπὶ τῶν ἀνομοίων αὐτῷ Eus.Nic.*ep.Paulin*.(p.16. 16,18; M.82.916A); term rejected as unscriptural by CAnc.(358)*ep. syn*.ap.Epiph.*haer*.73.3(p.271.14; M.42.408B); Geo.Laod.*ep.dogm*. (pp.291.29–292.3; M.42.437B,C); all likeness between the ἀγέννητος and the γ. being denied by Anomoeans ἀγέννητος...ἐκφύγοι... κοινωνίαν τὴν πρὸς τὸ γ. Eun.*apol*.9(M.30.843B); *ib*.11(845D); **c.** hence comparatively rarely used by later Fathers γ. δὲ τὸν υἱὸν οὐκ ἀρνούμεθα, ἀλλ' οὐχὶ κτιστόν· οὔτε γάρ, ἐὰν τὸν υἱὸν γ. ὁρισώμεθα, ἐκ θεοῦ πατρὸς τὴν οὐσίαν ἔχειν ἀρνεῖσθαι δυνάμεθα Epiph.*haer*.76.29 (p.378.4; M.42.576A); ‡Gr.Nyss.*Ar.et Sab*.5(M.45.1288C); Jo.D.*f.o*. 1.7(M.94.817C); and clearly dist. from γενητός, Epiph.*haer*.64.8 (p.417.16–19; M.41.1084A); Cyr.*thes*.2(5^{1}.15A); ‡Ath.*dial.Trin*.1.18 (M.28.1144A).

B. *born*; **1.** plur., *mortals* ἀπὸ πάντων τῶν γ. Or.*or*.23.5(p.253.11; M.11.492A); Eus.*d.e*.proem.(p.445.12; M.22.716B); Bas.*Spir*.63(3. 52E; M.32.184A); γεννητοὶ γυναικῶν (cf. Mt.11:11; Lc.7:28) Or.*Jo*. 20.44(33; p.388.19; M.14.677C); Gr.Nyss.*or.dom*.5(p.100.15; M.44. 1181D); *Hom.Clem*.2.17; **2.** in sense of *creature* πῶς γὰρ ἂν συνεγγίσαι ποτὲ τὸ γ. τῷ ἀγεννήτῳ; Clem.*str*.2.2(p.115.23; M.8.936B); Eus. *e.th*.1.8(p.66.23; M.24.837C); Chrys.*hom.59.3 in Mt*.(7.596D); **3.** of human nature of Christ, opp. divine, Ign.*Eph*.7.2 cit. s. ἰατρός; γ. φύσει Or.*Jo*.2.18(12; p.75.21; M.14.145D); post-Nicene οὔτε ἀγέννητος οὐσία τῇ γ. κατὰ φύσιν συντίθεται Bas.Sel.*or*.25(M.85.297B); **4.** of human birth of Christ, Just.*dial*.66.1(M.6.628B); θεὸς...γ. κατὰ σάρκα Cyr.*Chr.un*.(5^{1}.725D); **5.** of Father (Sabellian) λέγων [sc. Noëtus] ἕνα τὸν πατέρα καὶ θεὸν τῶν ὅλων...γ. δέ, ὅταν γεννᾶται ἐκ παρθένου Hipp.*haer*.10.27(p.283.8; M.16.3442A); of Adam οὐ γ., ἀλλ' ἐκ τῆς θείας διαπλασθέντα χειρός Thdt.*rect.conf*.3(M.6.1209C); **6.** of spiritual birth γεννητοὶ πνεύματος ἐσόμεθα Cyr.*Chr.un*.(5^{1}. 725B); id.*thes*.34(5^{1}.364B) al.

γεννήτρια, ἡ, *mother, source* οὐσία θεοῦ γ. ἐστιν Const.*or.s.c*.6 (p.160.26; M.20.1249A); Epiph.*exp.fid*.21(p.522.8; M.42.824B); [sc. παρρησία] γ. ... τῶν παθῶν *Apophth.Patr*.(M.65.109A); cf.Dor.*doct*. 4.5(M.88.1665A) cit. s. γεννήτειρα; ref. *Tome* of Leo ὀρθοδοξίας γ. Sophr.H.*ep.syn*.(M.87.3188D); of BMV θεοῦ...γ. Horm.*ep.cler*.(p.55. 5; M.*PL*.63.419B); Sophr.H.*or*.2(M.87.3245A); ‡Jo.D.*carm.annunt*. 175(p.242; M.96.853A).

γεννήτωρ, ὁ, *begetter, father*; theol. ὁ πατὴρ ἀρχὴ τοῦ υἱοῦ καὶ γ. ἐστί Ath.*Ar*.1.14(M.26.41A); id.*ep.Aeg.Lib*.16(M.25.573C); Bas.*hom*. 24.2(2.190D; M.31.601C); μὴ ὡς δημιουργὸν...λέγειν τὸν πατέρα, ἀλλ' ὡς γ. φυσικῶς Cyr.*thes*.10(5^{1}.76D); Jo.D.*f.o*.1.6(M.94.804A); of godparents, Gr.Naz.*or*.40.26(M.36.396C); of the Devil γ. τῶν κακῶν Cyr.H.*catech*.2.4.

γεννητῶς, *by generation*; theol., Bas.*hom*.24.4(2.192C; M.31.608A) cit. s. γέννημα; Gr.Naz.*or*.20.10(M.35.1077A); Gr.Nyss.*Eun*.4(2 p.79.15; M.45.653B); Cyr.*Jo*.1.5(4.46B); of Abel Ἄβελ γ. ὑποστάντος Gr.Nyss.*Eun*.3(2 p.26.27; M.45.592C).

***γενολόγιον, τό,** *brood*, *Exorc*.6(p.334).

γένος, τό, *family, class, race*; of Christians as a race or people (cf. 1Petr.2:9) καινὸν τοῦτο γ. *Diogn*.1; τοῦ...γ. τῶν Χριστιανῶν *M.Polyc*.3.2; of Church as γ. τῶν δικαίων Herm.*sim*.9.17.5; ἐκ... τῆς Ἑλληνικῆς παιδείας, ἀλλὰ καὶ ἐκ τῆς νομικῆς εἰς τὸ ἓν γένος τοῦ σωζομένου συνάγονται λαοῦ οἱ τὴν πίστιν προσιέμενοι Clem.*str*.6.5 (p.452.25; M.9.261B).

***γεντίλιοι, οἱ,** (Lat. *gentiles*) *gentiles* περὶ τῶν Σαρακηνῶν...οἱ νῦν λεγόμενοι γ. Chrys.*fr.in Jer*.9:26(M.64.860A).

γε-όομαι, pass., *become earth* τῆς ~ωθείσης σαρκός Gr.Nyss.*ep.can*. 7(M.45.233D); id.*res*.3(M.46.660C); †Cyr.*coll.VT*(6^{4}.1B); ref. state of man before Inc., Max.*ambig*.(M.91.1044D) cit. s. θεουργέω.

[*]**γεο-πονέω,** [*]**-πονία,** v. γη-.

γεοῦχος, *landlord*, Cyr.H.*catech*.15.23; *Apophth.Patr*.(M.65. 181B).

γεραίρω, *do honour*; esp. to God, *worship*, *Diogn*.3.5; Clem.*paed*. 2.4(p.183.10; M.8.444A); Eus.*h.e*.1.3.20(M.20.76B); Meth.*symp*.3.6 (p.32.15; M.18.69A); Nil.*epp*.1.232(M.79.168C).

γέρας, τό, 1. *privilege*, of S. John resting on breast of Christ τοῦ γ. τούτου ἀξιωθείς Or.*Jo*.23.20(13; p.461.25; M.14.800A); *prerogative*, of priesthood γενικὸν ἔχουσι τὸ γ. οἱ ἱερεῖς Thdt.*qu.1 in 2Par*. (1.592); id.*qu.1 in Lev*.(1.183); **2.** *reward*, in gen. εὐδαιμονία...τῆς σοφίας γ. Just.*dial*.3.4(M.6.481A); θεοῦ...γ. ἀξιοῦντος, καὶ κολάζοντος ἕκαστον κατὰ τὴν ἀξίαν Or.*or*.24.2(p.354.17; M.11.492D); id.*Cels*.4.30 (p.299.31; M.11.1072D); of happy death of Theodosius τοῦτο γ. ἐξενεγκών Philost.*h.e*.11.2(M.65.596B); of eternal life as reward for sufferings and martyrdom, *1Clem*.6.2; Mel.*fr*.1.2(M.5.1209); Cyr. *Lc*.9:27(M.72.652C); for good life on earth, Clem.*paed*.1.10(p.146.29; M.8.364C); id.*str*.7.2(p.8.31; M.9.413B).

γερδία, ἡ, (female) *weaver*, Cyr.S.*v.Sab*.80(p.186.9,11).

***Γερμανολέτης, ὁ,** *destroyer of Germany*, *Orac.Sib*.14.45.

***γεροδοσία, ἡ,** *prize-giving*, †Jo.D.*B.J*.39(M.96.1232C).

γεροντικός, *of old men*, hence τὸ [βιβλίον] γ. or τὰ γ., name of a book containing tales of desert fathers τοὺς βίους τῶν πατέρων σὺν τὰ γ. Nil.*epp*.4.1(M.79.545A); Dor.*doct*.1.13(M.88.1633C); Jo.Mosch. *prat*.55(M.87.2909B).

γερουσία, ἡ, *senate*; *synod* ἱερατικῆς...γ. Bas.Sel.*v.Thecl*.2.17 (M.85.613A); Gel.Cyz.*h.e*.2.22.21(M.85.1293D).

γέρων, ὁ, *old man*, as title of dignity; **1.** of desert fathers διδασκαλίας τῶν γ. Evagr.Pont.*cap.pract*.proem.(M.40.1221C); *ib*. 99(1252B); *Apophth.Patr*.(M.65.73A); Dor.*doct*.1.17(M.88.1640D); **2.** (*senex*), title of primate of African church, *Cod.Afr*.90; *ib*.92; *ib*.100; **3.** met., of God κἀκεῖνος ἀΐδιος γ. ὁ τῶν ὄντων πρεσβύτερος Clem.*paed*.3.3(p.246.9; M.8.580A); as symbol of decay, id.*str*.5.7 (p.354.16; M.9.69A).

γεῦμα, τό, *foretaste, first-fruits* γ. ... τῆς χάριτος Bas.*hom.in Ps*.33 (1.149A; M.29.365A); γ. τῆς κρίσεως Chrys.*hom.5.4 in Heb*.(12.57B); γ. ... ἁγίου πνεύματος Antip.Bost.*annunt*.16(M.85.1785C).

γεῦσις, ἡ, 1. *tasting*, of forbidden tree, *Const.App*.6.7.3; Isid.Pel. *epp*.1.181(M.78.301A); of food after a fast, Dion.Al.*ep.can*.(p.102.5; M.10.1277A); met., of enjoyment of sinful pleasures, Bas.*hom*.21.1 (2.164B; M.31.541D); γ. ἁμαρτίας Jo.Clim.*scal*.15(M.88.893D); of spiritual tasting τῶν μελλόντων δοὺς ἀπαρχὰς ἡμῖν γεύσεως *Barn*.1.7; ἡ τοῦ πνεύματος γ. Mac.Aeg.*hom*.18.13(M.34.632C); γ. ἐξ οὐρανοῦ id. *carit*.2(M.34.909A); ἡ τοῦ θεοῦ γ. *ib*.(909B); Didym.*Ps*.33:9(M.39. 1329A); of perception of flesh of Christ διὰ γ. ἡμῖν νοητῆς Bas.*hom. in Ps*.33(1.149A; M.29.364D); Cyr.*Ps*.33:9(M.69.888A); **2.** *taste, flavour*, *Hom.Clem*.8.15.

γεύστης, ὁ, *taster of food*, Gr.Naz.*carm*.1.2.8.146(M.37.659A).

γευστός, *that may be tasted* εἰ γ. ἐστιν ὁ κύριος, διὰ τῆς πίστεώς ἐστι γ. Or.*sel.in Ps*.33(M.12.1308C).

γεύ-ω, med., *taste*; met. **1.** *taste, experience*, in gen., e.g. death διὰ σταυροῦ θανάτου ἐγεύσατο Arist.*apol*.15(p.110.19; M.96.1121B); Gr. Nyss.*hom.9 in Cant*.(M.44.976C); life, Meth.*res*.1.40(p.285.2; M.41. 1108D); ‡Caes.Naz.*dial*.109(M.38.981); joy, Clem.*paed*.2.1(p.160.6; M.8.393A); truth, id.*q.d.s*.34(p.182.23; M.9.640C); **2.** spiritually διὰ τούτου [sc. Christ] ἠθέλεν ὁ δεσπότης τῆς ἀθανάτου γνώσεως ἡμᾶς ~σασθαι *1Clem*.36.2; the will of God, Clem.*str*.7.11(p.44.7; M.9. 485A); the divine sweetness, cf. Ps.33:9 τοῦ ἀληθινοῦ ἄρτου... ~σασθε, τοῦ καταβάντος ἐξ οὐρανοῦ Ath.*exp.Ps*.33:9(M.27.168D); Didym.*Ps*.33:9(M.39.1329A); †Apoll.*met.Ps*.33:9(M.33.1356B); Procl. CP *or*.6.5(M.65.728C), Dor.*doct*.4.1(M.88.1657D) citt. s. γλυκύτης; ref. ἀπάθεια, Jo.Clim.*scal*.29(M.88.1148C).

γέφυρα, ἡ, 1. *bridge*; met., of BMV γ. κόσμου παντὸς πρὸς τὸν ὑπερκόσμιον οὐρανόν Ephr.3.528F; ἡ μόνη θεοῦ πρὸς ἀνθρώπους γ. Procl.CP *or.laud.BMV* 1(p.103.18; M.65.681B); Mod.*dorm*.9(M.86. 3300B); ‡Sophr.H.*triod*.(M.87.3968C); Thdr.Stud.*can.imag*.8(M.99. 1777B); of John's baptism γ. τις ὃν ἑκατέρων τούτων τῶν βαπτισμάτων [sc. Jewish and Christian] Chrys.*bapt.Chr*.3(2.370C); of charity, id.*hom.1.2 in Ac.princ*.(3.54A); of Christ's descent into Hades, Procl.CP *or*.11.4(M.65.785C); of prayer, as bridge across, means of passing over, temptations προσευχὴ...πειρασμῶν γέφυρα Jo.Clim.*scal*.28(M.88.1129A); **2.** *platform* in circus, *M.Perp*.19 (p.91.1).

***γεφυροποιΐα, ἡ,** *building of bridges*, Justn.*cod*.1.4.26(*CJC* p.42) cit. s. ὁδοστρωσία.

γεφυρ-όω, *connect by a bridge, link together* ὁ τὴν γῆν καὶ τὸν οὐρανὸν ~ώσας τῷ ἁγίῳ σου ὀνόματι ‡Gr.Ant.*bapt*.1.4(M.10.1181D).

[*]**γεωδεσία, ἡ,** *land-measuring, surveying*, Anat.Laod.*arith*. (M.10.733D).

[*]**γεωδέτης, ὁ,** *surveyor*, Anat.Laod.*arith*.(M.10.733B).

γεώδης, *earthy, earthly*; **1.** in bad sense, of pagans οἷς βίος ἐστὶ σαρκικός, γ. τε Cyr.*Abac*.49(3.563A); and their worship, Eus.*v.C*.4.10 (p.121.28; M.20.1157C); demons, *Hom.Clem*.9.12; heretics γ. πλάττοντες ἀπάτας Eust.*fr*.55(p.90; M.18.689B); and all kinds of error, Eus.*l.C*.15(p.248.2; M.20.1420B); Cyr.*Os*.67(3.102B); **2.** opp. spiritual; of animal part of man ψυχὴν γ. Clem.*exc.Thdot*.50(p.123.10; M.9.684A); which is purified by fear of God ἀπὸ πάσης τῆς γ. παχύτητος Diad.*perf*.16(p.18.24); Gr.Nyss.*or.dom*.2(p.40.26; M.44.1145B); Gennad.*encycl*.(p.79.12; M.85.1616A); of earthly opp. heavenly life, Eus.*v.C*.3.46(p.97.9; M.20.1105D); of earthly counterparts of spiritual realities ἐν...γεωδεστέροις διαμορφοῦντες...τὰ πνευματικά Cyr.*Os*.3(3.15E); of Mosaic worship λατρείαν ὡς γεωδεστέραν id. *Jo*.6(4.563A).

γεωμέτρης, ὁ, *land-measurer*; met., iron., of Aëtius γ. τῆς ἡμετέρας εἰς Χριστὸν σωτηρίας Epiph.*haer*.76.8(p.348.23; M.42. 529A).

***γεωπετής,** *cast to the earth*; of Osiris, ‡Caes.Naz.*dial*.112(M.38. 993).

γεω-πονία, -πόνος, v. γη-.

γεωργ-έω, *be a husbandman*; *cultivate*, met.; **1.** *cultivate*; **a.** of Christ's work διὰ ὕβρεως δόξαν ἐγεώργησεν Procl.CP *or*.2.2(M.65.693C); in souls, Ign.*Philad*.3.1 cit. s. βοτάνη; and in Church θεία χάρις ταύτην ~εῖ τὴν ἐκκλησίαν Chrys.*anom*.12.1(1.547D); hence of work of bishops etc. τοὺς πολλοὺς ~οῦντα τῆς ἐκκλησίας ἡγούμενον Eus.*d.e*.2.3(p.77.33; M.22.140C); ~εῖν τὰς τῶν ἀνθρώπων πεπιστευμένας ψυχάς Thdt.*2Tim*.2:6(3.682); †Thdt.*Nest*.(4.1042); in gen., of spiritual direction μετὰ γὰρ τὸ πάντα ὑποτάξαι τὰ πάθη...καλὸν τὸ ~εῖν ἑτέρους Nil.*exerc*.31(M.79.760B); and improvement [sc. the Christian] αὐτοῦ [sc. of the pagan] ~εῖ τὴν ψυχήν Chrys.*hom*.*43.5 in Mt*.(7.466B); **b.** virtues ~οῦμεν εὐσέβειαν Just.*dial*.110.3(M.6.729B); Or.*Jo*.20.2(p.329.6; M.14.576B); *ib*.20.3(p.330.6; 577B); Jo.Carp.*cap*.9(M.85.1840); and vices τῶν...τὴν ἀσέβειαν ~ησάντων Bas.*ep*.92.2(3.184D; M.32.480A); Gr.Nyss.*or.dom*.4(p.86.17; M.44.1173C); Cyr.*Jo*.5.1(4.462E); **c.** by cultivating virtue eternal life is obtained, hence ~εῖν τὴν ζωήν Meth.*res*.1.51(p.305.12; M.18.281B); id.*symp*.9.4(p.119.16; M.18.185A); ~ήσωμεν τὸν οὐρανόν Chrys.*hom*.*7.9 in Rom*.(9.496E); *ib*.*21.2*(9.673C); **2.** *implant* ἐν ὅλῃ τῇ φύσει καὶ τῇ γραφῇ ~ούμενον θεῖον λόγον ‡Proc.G.*Pr*.31:16(M.87.1537D); **3.** *harvest*, met., of reaping evil, Mel.*pass*.88 p.15.30; Pall.*v.Chrys*.20(p.125.29; M.47.71); **4.** neut. of pres. ptcpl. as subst., *farmers* τὸ αὐτόθι ~οῦν Malchus *exc.Rom*.9(p.169.8; M.113.777D).

***γεωργητικός,** *given to cultivating*, met., Anast.S.*hod*.2(M.89.64C).

γεωργία, ἡ, *cultivation*, met.; **1.** of cultivation of virtues etc., Or.*dial*.22(p.164.1); Esaias *or*.6.4(p.20) etc.; **2.** of evangelization ἐνετείλατο κύριος γ. Clem.*str*.7.12(p.57.11; M.9.512A); ἡ γ. δὲ διττή· ἡ μὲν γὰρ ἄγραφος, ἡ δ' ἔγγραφος *ib*.1.1(p.6.12; M.8.693A); Chrys.*anom*.12.1(1.548A); Isid.Pel.*epp*.1.488(M.78.448C); as work of Father, Cyr.*Jo*.10.2(4.861D); of pastoral care, Eus.*h.e*.3.37.3(M.20.293B); **3.** of God's care and tending, Thdt.*qu.72 in Gen*.(1.84); **4.** *cultus* of pagan worship as γ. τοῦ ἐχθροῦ *A.Phil*.119(p.48.12); **5.** of sexual intercourse, Thdt.*qu.1 in Ruth*(1.346).

γεωργικός, *cultivating*, *concerned with husbandry*, c. genit. [sc. πῦρ] ἀγαθῶν γ. ‡Eust.*Laz*.6(p.31.10).

γεώργιον, τό, 1. *cultivated field*, *tillage*; of Church, Or.*hom*.*17.5 in Jer*.(p.157.2; M.13.473A); τοῦ γ. τῶν ἀποστόλων Cyr.*Ps*.51:7(M.69.1105C); θεοῦ γ. ὁ Ἰσραήλ id.*Os*.31(3.57B); of apostles as γ. τοῦ ἄνω καλλιέργου Rom.Mel.(*AS* 1 p.171); in pun on S. George as τὸ τοῦ δεσπότου πολύχουν γ. *Mir.Geo*.4(p.41.3); **2.** *crop*, met., Clem.*paed*.2.2(p.174.25; M.8.425A); ‡Ath.*dial.Trin*.1.12(M.28.1137A); ἐν ...γ. ... τὴν...ἁμαρτίαν Ast.Am.*prod*.(p.109.33).

γεωργός, ὁ, *husbandman*, *vine-dresser*, *gardener*, met.; **1.** of Jewish leaders, Cyr.*Joel*.9(2.208A); of Christian teachers, Just.*1apol*.44.13(M.6.396C) cit. s. δεσπόζω; Jo. Bapt. ὁ τῆς ἐρήμου γ. Clem.*prot*.1(p.9.33; M.8.65B); τὸν τοῦ Ἰορδάνου γ. Chrysipp.*enc.in Jo.Bapt*.(p.37.18); apostles εὑρίσκεις αὐτοὺς γ. τὴν ἄμπελον τῆς ψυχῆς ἐργαζομένους Mac.Aeg.*hom*.28.6(M.34.713D); Chrys.*pent*.1.2(2.460E); Gr.Nyss.*hex*.proem.(M.44.64B); ascetics, Max.*cap.theol*.1.17(M.90.1089B) cit. s. ἀσκητής; **2.** of God, Clem.*str*.1.7(p.24.17; M.8.732B) cit. s. σπείρω; id.*paed*.2.8(p.200.18; M.8.480B); Or.*engast*.9(p.294.9; M.12.1028B); of Father as husbandman of Christ, the true vine, id.*Jo*.6.57(37; p.165.26; M.14.300A); and of heaven, Gr.Nyss.*beat*.2(M.44.1213B); of men γ. δέ φησι τὸν πατέρα...οὐδὲ γὰρ ἄπρακτος ἢ ἀεργος εἰς ἡμᾶς ὁ πατήρ Cyr.*Jo*.10.2(4.858B); from whom Christ, though called ἄμπελος (Jo.15:1) does not differ in nature (against Arian interpretation of passage), *ib*.(860C); metaphor being only symbol of paternal care, *ib*.(862A) citt. s. ἄμπελος; **3.** of Christ ὁ τοῦ θεοῦ γ. Clem.*prot*.11(p.80.29; M.8.232C); Ἰησοῦς ὡς καλὸς γ. λόγου θεοῦ δεδύνηται τὴν πολλὴν Ἑλλάδα καὶ τὴν πολλὴν βάρβαρον ἐπισπεῖραι καὶ πληρῶσαι λόγων Or.*Cels*.5.62(p.65.22; M.11.1281A); cultivator of chastity, Meth.*symp*.7.1(p.71.19; M.18.125A); Mac.Aeg.*hom*.28.7(M.34.713D); Gr.Nyss.*v.Mos*.(M.44.389B); **4.** in gen., Clem.*str*.7.12(p.53.9; M.9.501C) cit. s. ἀμπελών; καὶ σὺ γ. γενοῦ σεαυτοῦ Or.*hom*.*5.13 in Jer*.(p.42.15; M.13.313A); of a human father γ., ὁ ἔμψυχον σπείρων ἄρουραν Clem.*paed*.2.10(p.208.6; M.8.497A); of Devil, *ib*.6.8(p.465.26; M.9.289A); ὁ γάμος, γ. τῶν κτισμάτων γενόμενος Bas.Sel.*or*.4.2(M.85.65C).

γῆ, ἡ, 1. *earth*; **a.** as stuff of which man is made (cf. Gen.3:19), *Barn*.6.9; Gr.Nyss.*v.Macr*.(p.397.7; M.46.984C); met., of human minds γῇ δὲ ἀγόνῳ...παραδεδωκότες ἀγρίαις συνεπνίξαντο βοτάναις, καθάπερ οἱ Φαρισαῖοι Clem.*str*.6.7(p.461.24; M.9.281A); v. Ἀδάμ, ἄνθρωπος, παρθένος; **b.** met., of realm of material things ἡμεῖς δὲ ἐν ἀλλοτρίᾳ γῇ τὸν ἀλλότριον τῆς γ. προσκυνοῦμεν θεόν, ἀλλότριον τῶν ἐπὶ τῆς γ. πραγμάτων Or.*hom*.*7.3 in Jer*.(p.54.15f.; M.13.333B); τὴν γ. πρὸ τοῦ οὐρανοῦ ζητῶν Chrys.*hom*.*6.5 in Mt*.(7.83B); abode of devils, *Chron.Pasch*.p.239(M.92.576C); **2.** *land*; **a.** esp. of Promised Land τὴν ἁγίαν γ. Or.*Cels*.7.28(p.179.18; M.11.1461A); as type of heaven, Cosm.Ind.*top*.5(M.88.248A); **b.** and in gen. of heaven τῆς...γ. ἀγαθῆς καὶ πολλῆς, ἐν ᾗ ἐστιν ἡ ἐπουράνιος Ἱερουσαλήμ Or.*Cels*.7.29(p.180.10; M.11.1461C); exeg. Ps.26:13 γῆ ζώντων ἐκλήθη ἡ ἐν ἐπαγγελίαις γῆ, κατὰ τὴν αἰώνιον ζωήν Didym.*Ps*.26:13(M.39.1308A); Gr.Nyss.*beat*.2(M.44.1212A); Thdt.*Ps*.26:14(1.773); and beatitude Mt.5:5 εὑρήσομεν ἐκεῖ τὴν ὑπερουράνιον γ. Gr.Nyss.*beat*.2(M.44.1209A); *ib*.(1213B); this exegesis contested ποίαν γ.;...τινὲς νοητήν φασιν. ἀλλ' οὐκ ἔστι τοῦτο· οὐδαμοῦ γὰρ εὑρίσκομεν ἐν τῇ γραφῇ γ. νοητήν...αἰσθητὸν τίθησιν ἔπαθλον Chrys.*hom*.*15.3 in Mt*.(7.188B,C); **c.** of Church ἐν τῇ γῇ τοῦ θεοῦ, τῇ ἐκκλησίᾳ Or.*hom*.*7.3 in Jer*.(p.53.34; M.13.333A); id.*or*.26.4(p.361.20; M.11.501C); Cyr.*Os*.31(3.57B); **3.** met., in gen. ψυχὴ οὖσα μὲν ἐν γῇ ἐρήμῳ Cyr.*Ps*.62:3(M.69.1120D); ἔστι γῆ...σατανική, οὗ διάγουσι...αἱ δυνάμεις τοῦ σκότους...καὶ ἔστι γῆ φωτεινὴ τῆς θεότητος Mac.Aeg.*hom*.14.6(M.34.573B,C).

γηγενής, *earthborn*; **1.** of Adam, Or.*Cels*.4.36(p.307.8; M.11.1084C); Euthal.Diac.*epp.Paul*.(M.85.752A); implying imperfection and sinfulness τὸν γ. εἰς ἅγιον καὶ ἐπουράνιον μεταπλάσας ἄνθρωπον Clem.*paed*.1.12(p.148.21; M.8.368A); κακοήθεις ἀνθρώπους καὶ γ. id.*str*.4.6(p.261.30; M.8.1241C); τῶν γ. πράξεων Meth.*symp*.8.16(p.105.2; M.18.168C); of the mind of the flesh τοὺς γ. φρόνημα ἔχοντες Clem.*ecl*.(p.138.3; M.9.700C); τὸ γ. ... ἐνδεικνύμενοι id.*paed*.2.10(p.220.13; M.8.524A); of the children of Israel opp. prophets and apostles, Eus.*d.e*.2.3(p.79.32; M.22.144A); of man opp. pagan gods, Diodorus Siculus ap.Eus.*p.e*.2.1(49A; M.21.100C); **2.** as subst., *mortal*, *man* τίς ἰσχὺς γηγενοῦς; *1Clem*.39.2; opp. angels, *T.Sal*.5.3; of Christ as man θεὸς ὤν, καὶ γ. γενόμενος ‡Jo.D.*hom*.6.3(M.96.665A).

γήινος, *of earth*, *earthly*; **1.** lit. τὸν ποιητὴν τῶν οὐρανίων καὶ γ. ... θεόν Just.*1apol*.58.1(M.6.416A); τῆς γ. αὐτοῦ [sc. Χριστοῦ] γεννήσεως Gr.Nyss.*Apoll*.28(M.45.1184B); νεκρώσας...τὰ γ. μέλη Isid.Pel.*epp*.1.193(M.78.306D); **2.** of the body; freq. in sense of *material* opp. spiritual, Clem.*str*.5.14(p.392.7; M.9.149A); Or.*Jo*.6.14(7; p.123.34; M.14.225C); *ib*.6.42(25; p.151.17; 273B); Thdt.*h.e*.5.3.4(3.1016); **3.** of worldly things in gen. τὸ οὐράνιον φυτὸν τὸν ἄνθρωπον...γ. προσανέχειν...πλάσμασιν Clem.*prot*.2(p.19.12; M.8.96A); of Mosaic ordinances in lit. sense, Or.*Jo*.10.15(12; p.186.3; M.14.332D); of physical opp. spiritual birth, Chrys.*hom*.*25.1 in Jo*.(8.145D); ἐπὶ τὴν γ. [sc. τροφήν] τρέχετε *ib*.44.1(260B); δόξας γ.,...διαδήματα...πρόσκαιρα Thdr.Stud.*epp*.2.177(M.99.1549B); τὰ γ. *the things* or *concerns of this world*, Just.*1apol*.58.3(M.6.416B); Or.*Jo*.10.24(16; p.196.30; M.14.349C); διαιρεῖ τὰ γ. ἀπὸ τῶν οὐρανίων Chrys.*hom*.*34.2 in Jo*.(197C); scorned by Christians, Isid.Pel.*epp*.1.227(M.78.324C); Nil.*epp*.4.1(M.79.545A); **4.** connoting *imperfect*, *sinful* κακία γ. Clem.*prot*.11(p.78.28; M.8.228C); of unclean spirits, *ib*.4(p.43.26; 152C); τὰ πρὸ τῆς ἀπὸ Ἰησοῦ παιδεύσεως γ. ... κινήματα Or.*Jo*.10.24(16; p.196.24; M.14.349B); φρόνημα γ. id.*Ps*.2:4(p.448); τῶν γ. ἐνθυμημάτων Ph.Carp.*Cant*.proem.(M.40.29A); of the foolish virgins ἀγάπῃ τινὶ γ. κατασχεθεῖσαι Mac.Aeg.*hom*.4.6(M.34.471A).

***γηίνως,** *in an earthly manner* τῶν πολιτευομένων γ. Or.*hom*.*17.4 in Jer*.(p.147.22; M.13.460A); τοὺς...γ. φρονήσαντας Didym.*Trin*.1.27(M.39.396C).

[*]**γηνός,** for καινός, *new* τῆς γ. διαθήκης *PRyl*.3.465.11.

[*]**γηόρας,** v. γειώρας.

γηπον-έω (**γεηπονέω,** [*]**γεοπονέω**), *till the ground*, *cultivate*, γεηπ-, Eus.*p.e*.1.4(10C; M.21.37B); Cyr.*ador*.8(1.253C); id.*Am*.85(3.351C); met. τοῦ ~οῦντος τὴν ἐκκλησίαν τουτέστι τοῦ Χριστοῦ id.*Is*.5.2(2.785C); γεοπονήσας τῷ σταυρῷ τὴν ἄρουραν τῆς διανοίας Jo.Mon.*hymn.Geo*.1(M.96.1393C).

γηπονία ([*]**γεοπονία, γεωπονία**), **ἡ,** *tillage*, *agriculture* γεοπ-, ‡Hipp.*fr.9 in Pss*.(p.138.16); τοὺς τὰς γ. ... ἐσχηκότας ἀνθρώπους †Dion.Al.*fr.Eccl*.(p.211.8); γεωπ-, Chrys.*hom.in Mt*.*7:14*(3.26A); ὁ τῆς γ. νόμος Cyr.*Jo*.6.4(4.392D); Thdt.*qu.110 in Gen*.(1.116).

***γηπονικῶς,** *by working on the land* γ. ζήσαντες Thphn.*chron*.p.412(M.108.977C).

γηπόνος (**γεηπόνος, γεωπόνος**), **ὁ,** *tiller of the ground*, *husbandman*, lit. γεωπ- Eus.*d.e*.2.3(p.77.34; M.22.140C); γεηπ- Gr.Nyss.*ep*.10(M.46.1040C); Chrys.*hom*.*15.4 in 2Cor*.(10.548D); in comparison with Christians διανείμωμεν ἑαυτοῖς τὰς ἀρετάς, καθάπερ τὴν γεωργίαν οἱ γ. id.*hom*.*24.3 in Heb*.(12.225C); Isid.Pel.*epp*.1.488(M.78.448C); met., of Jewish leaders ἀγρῷ παρείκασε τὴν...γῆν, καὶ γηπόνους ὠνόμασε τοὺς προεστηκότας Cyr.*Joel*.9(3.208C); id.*Os*.121(3.152A).

[*]**γηραλαῖος**, *of old age, mature, M.Eleuth.*5; neut. as subst., Sophr.H.*or.*7(M.87.3348D).

***γηραλεότης**, ἡ, *old age*, Tim.Ant.*nativ.Jo.Bapt.*1(M.28.905C).

γῆρας, τό, *cast skin, slough* of serpent; met., of sin ἀποδύεται... τὸ γ. τῆς ἁμαρτίας Thdt.*Ps.*22:2(1.748); *ib.*50:12(940); id.*2Cor.* 5:17(3.317); id.*Eph.*5:27(3.434).

γηράσκω, **1.** *grow old*, met. ⟨ἐ⟩γηράσατε πρὸς δεισιδαιμονίαν, νέοι ἀφίκεσθε πρὸς θεοσέβειαν Clem.*prot.*10(p.77.12; M.8.225A); **2.** perf., of things, *be antiquated* μύθων...γεγηρακότων Eus.*v.C.* 3.54(p.102.24; M.20.1120B); Cyr.*Is.*2.3(2.276C); Thphyl.*exc.gent.*3 (p.479.17; M.113.937B).

γηροκομεῖον, τό, *home for old people, almshouse*, †Gregent.*leg. Hom.*55(M.86.609B); Cyr.S.*v.Euthym.*35(p.53.6); Leont.N.*v.Jo. Eleem.*45(p.93.20); Max.*ep.*44(M.91.648A).

γηροτροφεῖον, τό, *almshouse*, †Gregent.*leg.Hom.*56(M.86.612A).

γιγαντιαῖος, *gigantic*; met., *extraordinary, of surpassing excellence*, Agath.*v.Gr.Ill.*85(p.43).

***γιγαντιαίως**, *in the manner of a giant*, Agath.*v.Gr.Ill.*124 (p.63).

***γιγαντι-άω**, *behave like a giant*, Zach.Mit.*opif.*(M.85.1052A); of Chosroes ∼ᾷ δὲ καὶ τυραννῆσαι θέλει Geo.Pis.*Heracl.*1.30(M.92. 1300A).

γιγαντικός, **1.** *of the giants* (cf. Gen.6:4), Eus.*p.e.*5.4(186A; M.21. 324A); **2.** *gigantic, enormous*, ‡Caes.Naz.*dial.*125(M.38.1020).

γιγάντιος, *gigantic* δαίμονές τινες...τιτανικοὶ ἢ γ. Or.*Cels.*4.92 (p.365.9; M.11.1169C).

***γιγαντογενής**, **1.** *giant-born*, *Chron.Pasch.*p.36(M.92.145A); *ib.* p.38(149B); **2.** *giant-like* γύνη...γ. ὑπάρχουσα τὴν ἡλικίαν Jo.Mal. *chron.*17 p.412(M.97.609B); Thphn.*chron.*p.147(M.108.400A).

***γιγαρτικός**, *grapestone-like*, Or.*enarr.in Job* 28:18(M.17.89C).

γίγας, ὁ, *giant*; **1.** ref. Gen.6:4 γ.... σκολιοὶ μιαρῶς δύσφημα χέοντες *Orac.Sib.*1.124; *T.Reub.*5.7; offspring of angels and women, Athenag.*leg.*24.5(M.6.948B); whose souls are wandering demons, *ib.*25.1(948C) cit. s. δαίμων; *A.Andr.et Mt.*20(p.92.3); which later became pagan gods, Eus.*p.e.*5.4(186D; M.21.324A); *Hom.Clem.*8.18; not to be identified with giants of pagan mythology, *ib.*8.15; variously characterized as long-lived, impious, and abnormally tall, Thdt.*qu.48 in Gen.*(1.62); Gennad.*fr.Gen.*6:4(M.85.1644A); **2.** met., of Marcion ὁ θεομάχος οὗτος γ. Clem.*str.*3.4(p.207.10; M.8. 1129A); of any heretics, Ath.*Ar.*3.42(M.26.412B); of persecutors of Christians τὸ τῶν θεομάχων γ. στῖφος Eus.*l.C.*9(p.219.3; M.20.1364C); of passions οὐχ ἁμαρτάνει δὲ ὁ ἄνθρωπος...εἰ μὴ πρότερον οἱ κραταιοὶ οὗτοι γ. [sc. φιληδονία, φιλοδοξία, φιλαργυρία]...περιγένωνται Jo.D. *spir.neq.*(M.95.89A); **3.** as complimentary epithet of Chosroes βασιλεὺς βασιλέων...γ. γιγάντων Men.*exc.Rom.*3(p.176.15; M.113. 860B).

γί(γ)ν-ομαι, [aor. ptcpl. γενάμενος Didym.*Pss.*proem.(M.39.1157A); *CG–CI* 1.17(Corinth saec.vii); 3 pl. perf. indic. γέγοναν *Pers.*(p.19.25, p.20.21)]; **1.** *be made* or *created* τοὺς ὑπὸ τοῦ ἀγεννήτου γεγονότας Athenag.*leg.*23.2(M.6.941C); ἐν τῇ ἕκτῃ τῶν ἡμερῶν...ἄνθρωπον γεγονέναι Iren.*haer.*1.14.6(M.7.608A); ref. God αἰτία τοῦ γενέσθαι καὶ γενομένους εἶναι Clem.*str.*5.12(p.380.17; M.9.121A); πάντων τῶν ὑπὸ τοῦ πατρὸς διὰ Χριστοῦ γεγενημένων Or.*Jo.*2.10(6; p.65.21; M.14. 129A); τὰ ὑπὸ τοῦ Ἰησοῦ παράδοξα γεγενημένα id.*Cels.*1.46(p.95.31; M.11.744C); Eus.*p.e.*7.11(320A; M.21.541A); ἀγέννητος ὁ Μινώταυρος ...οὐ τῷ ἀγεννήτως εἶναι, ἀλλὰ τῷ μὴ γενέσθαι ὅλως Gr.Nyss.*Eun.*7 (2 p.166.18; M.45.756D); hence τὰ γεγονότα *created things*, Iren.*haer.* 4.38.1(1105A); ὁ πατὴρ πάντων τῶν γεγονότων Hipp.*haer.*9.9(p.242.6; M.16.3374A); Cyr.*Jo.*9(4.773C); Max.*ambig.*(M.91.1085B); theol. οὐκ ἦν ὁ μονογενὴς θεὸς πρὶν γενέσθαι, καθώς φησιν ὁ Εὐνόμιος Gr. Nyss.*Eun.*8(2 p.193.10; M.45.788D); **2.** *become*, Christol., ref. Jo. 1:14 εἰ τὸν λόγον φάσκει σάρκα γεγενῆσθαι καὶ μὴ ἀνειληφέναι σῶμα ἀνθρώπου, φρασάτω τί ἐστι τὸ πεπονθὸς ἐπὶ τοῦ σταυροῦ Adam.*dial.* 4.17(p.175.21; M.11.1832B); Ath.*Ar.*1.62(M.26.141A); υἱὸς ἀνθρώπου γέγονέ τε καὶ κεχρημάτικεν ὁ μονογενὴς Cyr.*Jo.*1.9(4.94C); text explained, Procl.CP *Arm.*6(p.189.34; M.65.861B); μείνας θεὸς ὅπερ ἦν, γέγονεν ἄνθρωπος ὅπερ οὐκ ἦν ‡Cyr.*Trin.*14(6³.21A; M.77.1152B); theol. [Arians] λέγοντας πρότερον βεβουλῆσθαι τὸν πατέρα, εἶθ' οὕτως ἐλθεῖν ἐπὶ τὸ γενέσθαι πατέρα Gr.Nyss.*Eun.*8(2 p.181.8; M.45.773C); **3.** with (ἑνὸς) μόνου *aim at, be concerned with one thing only* ἑνὸς ∼εται μόνου τοῦ μὴ φλοχθῆναι Chrys.*virg.*34(1.292E); id.*hom. 19.2 in Ac.*(9.155D); id.*hom.2.3 in Heb.*(12.76B); **4.** c. genit., *gain control of*, Men.*exc.Rom.*3(p.184.34; M.113.872D); ∼εσθαι ἑαυτοῦ *recover, rest oneself* ἀπέλθατε οὖν γενέσθαι ἑαυτῶν (ἐστὲ γὰρ ἀπὸ κόπου) Marc.Diac.*v.Porph.*40; **5.** impers., *come to pass* γένοιτο δὲ ἵνα καὶ ὁ καρπὸς τέλειος ᾖ Cyr.H.*procatech.*1; id.*catech.*1.4; ‡Ath. *disp.*10(M.28.448D); τῷ σε γεννήσαντι...κράτος ἐλθεῖν γένοιτο Geo. Pis.*carm.*4.165; **6.** *become of* τί ἐγένετο τὸ ἔνδυμα *A.Phil.*28(p.15. 16).

γι(γ)νώσκ-ω, *know*; **1.** of God; **a.** knowing all things as being their cause αὐτὴ [sc. divine knowledge] γὰρ ἑαυτὴν ἡ πάντων αἰτία ∼ουσα...ὁ θεὸς τὰ ὄντα ∼ει, οὐ τῇ ἐπιστήμῃ τῶν ὄντων, ἀλλὰ τῇ ἑαυτοῦ Dion.Ar.*d.n.*7.2(3.869C); not by intellectual or sensible knowledge, but ὡς ἴδια θελήματα ὁ θεὸς τὰ ὄντα ∼ει Max.*ambig.* (M.91.1085B); and fully known only by Son ∼εται δὲ ὑπὸ μόνου τοῦ ἰδίου γεννήματος Cyr.*Jo.*6.1(4.652B); **b.** God's knowledge of man precedes man's knowledge of God τοὺς πρὸ καταβολῆς κόσμου εἰς πίστιν ἐγνωσμένους θεῷ Clem.*paed.*1.7(p.125.13; M.8.321B); οὐ γὰρ ἡμεῖς αὐτὸν ἔγνωμεν, ἀλλ' αὐτὸς ἡμᾶς ἔγνω Chrys.*hom.20.2 in 1Cor.* (10.171A); Cyr.*Jo.*6.1(4.654D); and unites men to him ἔγνω κύριος τοὺς ὄντας αὐτοῦ ἀνακραθεὶς αὐτοὺς καὶ μεταδεδωκὼς αὐτοῖς τῆς ἑαυτοῦ θειότητος Or.*Jo.*19.4(1; p.303.5; M.14.532B); dist. from ἐπίστασθαι: διττοῦ...τοῦ τῆς γνώσεως ὀνόματος...ὅτε μὲν τὸ ἐπίστασθαι, ὅτε δὲ τὸ ἡνῶσθαι καὶ ἀνακεκρᾶσθαι τὸν ∼οντα τῷ ∼ομένῳ. κατὰ τὸ πρότερον σημαινόμενον, πάντας ∼ει ὁ θεός...κατὰ δὲ τὸ δεύτερον σημαινόμενον, μόνους τοὺς δικαίους εἰδέναι λέγεται Didym.*Ps.*17:45 (M.39.1264B); **2.** of man knowing God ἐφωτίσθημεν γάρ· τὸ δὲ ἔστιν ἐπιγνῶναι τὸν θεόν. οὔκουν ἀτελὴς ὁ ἐγνωκὼς τὸ τέλειον. καί μου μὴ λάβησθε ὁμολογοῦντος ἐγνωκέναι τὸν θεόν; Clem.*paed.*1.5(p.105.2f.; M.8.280B); ∼ομεν...τουτέστιν, ἐλθεῖν εἰς οἰκειότητα τῶν προβάτων αὐτοῦ Cyr.*Jo.*6.1(4.653E); through Jesus, *ib.*1.8(p.132.4; 336C); Gr. Naz.*or.*40.45(M.36.421C); of man's knowledge in relation to faith τοῦ ∼ειν τὸν θεὸν παρὰ τὸ πιστεύειν Or.*Jo.*19.3(1; p.301.15; M.14. 529A); εἰ δὲ λέγεις τὸν πιστεύοντα καὶ ∼ειν· ἀφ' ὧν πιστεύει, ἀπὸ τούτων καὶ ∼ει...ἀφ' ὧν ∼ει ἀπὸ τούτων καὶ πιστεύει. ∼ομεν δὲ ἐκ τῆς δυνάμεως τὸν θεόν. ὥστε πιστεύομεν μὲν τῷ γνωσθέντι, προσκυνοῦμεν δὲ τῷ πιστευθέντι Bas.*ep.*234.3(3.358C; M.32.872A); ὁ μὴ ∼ων τὴν ἀλήθειαν, οὔτε ἀληθῶς πιστεύειν δύναται Hesych.S.*temp.*1.60(M.93. 1500A); esp. of knowledge of contemplatives ὁ γνωστικὸς ἐργάτης... περὶ δὲ ὧν ἔγνω, τῶν μελλόντων καὶ ἔτι ἀοράτων πεπεισμένος ἀκριβῶς Clem.*str.*7.12(p.53.30; M.9.504A); *ib.*2.17(p.153.19; M.8.1016A); who know God in a way expressed in paradoxes ἐν πᾶσιν ὁ θεὸς ∼εται, καὶ χωρὶς πάντων· καὶ διὰ γνώσεως ὁ θεὸς ∼εται, καὶ διὰ ἀγνωσίας... οὐδὲ ἔν τινι τῶν ὄντων ∼εται...καὶ ἐκ πάντων πᾶσι ∼εται, καὶ ἐξ οὐδενὸς οὐδενί Dion.Ar.*d.n.*7.3(M.3.872A); because [sc. θεὸς] ὑπὲρ νοῦν ∼εται id.*ep.*1(M.3.1065A); and perfectly only in heaven, Clem. *str.*6.14(p.486.21; M.9.332A); knowledge of God producing holiness, *ib.*7.7(p.35.19; 468A); *ib.*1.7(p.25.17; M.8.733B); and union with Christ ὥσπερ...ἡ γνῶσις γνοῦσα ἐκεῖνο ὃ γνῶναι ἠθέλησεν, ἑνοῦται τῷ γνωσθέντι...οὕτως οἱ πιστοὶ τῇ γνώσει ἑνωθέντες τῷ γνωσθέντι Χριστῷ...ὑπὸ θεοῦ ἐγνώσθησαν Max.*schol.d.n.*7.4(M.4. 353C,D); knowing being identified with doing, Or.*hom.10.1 in Jer.* (p.72.6f.; M.13.360A); and lack of knowledge meaning sin οὐκ ἔγνω τὸν κύριον ὁ λαὸς ὁ πεπλανημένος Clem.*paed.*2.8(p.202.22; M.8. 485B); id.*prot.*9(p.64.9; M.8.197A); **3.** of Christ's human knowledge, v. γνῶσις; **4.** in phrase χάριν γινώσκειν *owe thanks*, Clem.*str.*3.3 (p.201.10; M.8.1116A); ‡Ath.*dial.Trin.*2.17(M.28.1184D).

[*]**γιώρας**, v. γειώρας.

***γλαυκαίνω**, *be bluish-grey*; of colour of leprosy, Meth.*lepr.*5 (p.455.11); *ib.*(p.456.5).

***γλαύκη**, ἡ, = γλαύξ, *owl*, ‡Caes.Naz.*dial.*140(M.38.1072).

γλαφυρός, *polished, elegant* of style; hence title of work of Cyr. Γλαφυρῶν εἰς Γένεσιν (Ἔξοδον κτλ.) Λόγοι (1.1,244 etc.).

γλεῦκος, τό, *new wine, must*; also of a barbarian drink not made from grapes, Men.*exc.Rom.*8(p.194.4; M.113.885D); met., of inspiration of H. Ghost, Gr.Nyss.*Spir.*(M.46.701A).

γλισχρολογέομαι, *dispute about trifles, quibble*, Or.*mart.*2(p.4.15; M.11.565B).

γλισχρώδης, *sticky*; neut. as subst., Epiph.*haer.*64.72(p.522.21; M.41.1197D).

γλίχ-ομαι, *desire*, pass. ὦ θαυμάσιοι θεῷ ∼όμενοι Serap.*ep.mon.*9 (M.40.936A).

[*]**γλιχόνη**, ἡ, = γλήχων, *pennyroyal*, a species of mint, Leont. N.*v.Sym.*56(M.93.1740A).

γλοιόομαι, *become thick, viscous*, Leont.H.*monoph.*(M.86.1816C).

***γλούττων**, ὁ, (Lat. *glutto*) *glutton*, Pall.*h.Laus.*21(M.34.1073D; v.l. p.65.8 n.).

γλυκαίν-ω, **1.** *sweeten*, met. [sc. Χριστὸν] τὸν γλυκάναντα λόγοις θείοις Isid.Pel.*epp.*1.293(M.78.353C); τὸν γὰρ φάρυγγα ἔχει γλυκασμὸν οὐ ∼όμενον, ἀλλὰ ∼οντα Nil.ap.Proc.G.*Cant.*7:10(M.87.1693C); χρηστότης...∼ουσα τὰς ψυχάς *V.Pach.Φ* 131(p.83.12); τίς δὲ συντυχὼν οὐ γεγλύκασται; Thdr.Stud.*epp.*2.29(M.99.1200B); of the gospel τὰ λόγια κυρίου...ἐγλύκαινεν αὐτούς *A.Paul.et Thecl.*1(p.236. 3 v.l. ἐγγλυκαίνειν); ∼εται τῷ λόγῳ τὰ τῆς ψυχῆς αἰσθητήρια Gr. Nyss.*hom.4 in Cant.*(M.44.844D); of use of imagery to make discourse palatable, Chrys.*hom.34.2 in Jo.*(8.197B); of Christian τῷ ξύλῳ [i.e. Cross] γλυκανθείς Gr.Nyss.*v.Mos.*(M.44.368A); **2.** *taste (the sweetness of)* τῶν ∼όντων τὴν τοῦ ὑψίστου χρηστότητα Or.*exc.in Ps.* 77:30f.(M.17.145A); pass., *taste sweet* ἕως γλυκανθῇ ἐν τῷ στόματι ἡμῶν τὸ γάλα αὐτῆς [sc. μετανοίας] Esaias *or.*25.18(p.170; M.40. 1186A).

γλυκασία, ἡ, *sweetness*, Meth.*symp.*2.7(p.25.8; M.18.60A); *V. Mac.*2(p.147); met. ὄψις ἀγαθὴ ὡς εἶδος τῆς γ. *A.Mt.*2(p.219.1); Nil.*epp.*4.24(M.79.561A).

γλύκασμα, τό, 1. *sweetness*, met. ψαλμῳδίας...γ. Nil.*epp.*3.318 (M.79.537B); id.*paup.*62(M.79.1052C); εὐχῆς...γ. Diad.*perf.*68(p.84. 8f.); CNic.(787)*act.*3(H.4.153D); **2.** plur., *sweet things, sweets*; of honey, ‡Ath.*synops.*(M.28.380A); met. τὰ τῆς εὐσεβείας γ. Gr.Nyss. *Spir.*(M.46.701B); id.*ordin.*(M.46.544C).

γλυκασμός, ὁ, *sweetness*, exeg. Cant.5:16 ὁ γ. τοῦ φάρυγγος τοῦ σωτῆρος Or.*sel.in Dt.*(M.12.809B); οὗ [sc. Christ] τὴν φωνὴν ἑαυτῷ [sc. S. Paul] χρήσας, γ. ἦν δι' ἐκείνου φθεγγόμενος Gr.Nyss.*hom.14 in Cant.*(M.44.1084C); Jo.D.*hymn.exod.*(M.96.1368B); †Jo.D.*B.J.* 24(M.96.1077C); ‡Gr.Naz.*Chr.pat.*810(M.38.203A); of BMV, Jo. Mon.*hymn.Nic.Myr.*(M.96.1384D); of Chrys., id.*hymn.Chrys.*6(M. 96.1381B); of eloquence ῥεῖθρα γλυκασμοῦ γλῶσσα βλύζει στωμύλη Gr.Naz.*carm.*1.2.32.25(M.37.918A); of truth and righteousness, Gr.Agr.*Eccl.*9.11(M.98.1101D); γ. ὀρθοδοξίας Geo.Pis.*carm.*91.1.

γλύκιος, *sweet*, met. γ. ἀδελφούς Thdr.Stud.*epp.*1.1(M.99.908B).

***γλυκολογ-έω,** *cloak with honeyed words* ∼οῦντι τὸ πταῖσμα Nil. *Eulog.*21(M.79.1120D).

***γλυκολογία, ἡ,** *honeyed words*, Thphn.*chron.*p.163(M.108.437A).

***γλυκορήμων,** *sweet-speaking*, Ant.Mon.*hom.*16(M.89.1476D).

[*]γλυκόφωνος, *sweet-voiced*, ‡Caes.Naz.*dial.*140(M.38.1072).

γλυκυδερκής, *sweet to behold*, *Orac.Sib.fr.*1.30.

γλυκύδωρος, *bearing sweet gifts*, of BMV γ. γεννῆτορ φωτός ‡Meth.*Sym.et Ann.*14(M.18.381B).

***γλυκυμυθία, ἡ,** *honeyed speech*, Meth.*symp.*11.1(p.129.15; M.18. 204C).

***γλυκύνομαι,** *enjoy sweetness*, Ph.Carp.*Cant.*206(M.40.129C).

γλύκυσμα, τό, *sweetness* παντὸς γ. ... γλυκύτερος...ὁ κατ' ἀρετὴν... βίος Gr.Nyss.*v.Mos.*(M.44.365B).

***γλυκυσταγής,** *sweetly dropping*, met. τὰ γ. τῆς μελιχρᾶς σου γλώττης ῥεῖθρα Thdr.Stud.*cant.*15.2(p.369).

γλυκύτης, ἡ, *sweetness*, met.; **1.** of God, *loving-kindness, mercy* χρηστευσώμεθα ἑαυτοῖς κατὰ τὴν...γ. τοῦ ποιήσαντος ἡμᾶς *1Clem.* 14.3; ἡ γ. τοῦ θεοῦ μου ἀνήγαγεν ὑμᾶς ἐκ τῆς ἀβύσσου *A.Phil.*139 (p.72.11); of Trin. ἡ πηγὴ πάσης γ. Epiph.*haer.*74.12(p.329.30; M.42. 497B); of Christ ὁ ἔχων τὴν γ. *A.Phil.*141(p.77.4); τῆς δεσποτικῆς ἐγεύσατο γ. Procl.CP *or.*6.5(M.65.728C); *V.Pach.Φ* 110(p.72.6); **2.** of soul united to God, Or.*hom.2.1 in Jer.*(p.17.3; M.13.277B); Gr.Nyss. *v.Mos.*(M.44.389C); γευσάμενος αὐτῆς τῆς γ. τοῦ εἶναι μετὰ τοῦ θεοῦ Dor.*doct.*4.1(M.88.1657D); ἡσυχαστὴς...ἐκκοπὴν γλυκύτητος θεοῦ λαβεῖν μὴ βουλόμενος Jo.Clim.*scal.*27(M.88.1100D); **3.** *suavity*, as style of polite address, Thds.Imp.*ep.Licin.*(p.8.12; M.*PL.*54.878C); Thphn.*chron.*p.87(M.108.261C).

***γλυκυφανής,** *seemingly pleasant*, Nil.*epp.*2.186(M.79.297A).

***γλυκυφόρος,** *yielding sweet* water πηγὰς...ἁλμυροφόρους καὶ γ. Chrys.*hom.in Ps.115:1–3*(p.357.13).

***γλυός,** prob. f.l. for γλοιός *glutinous*, Melet.*nat.hom.*28–29(M.64. 1260C).

γλυπτός, 1. *carved*; of pagan images, Clem.*str.*6.14(p.487.15; M.9.333A); Ath.*gent.*18(M.25.37C); neut. as subst., *carved image*, *A.Petr.et Paul.*26(p.190.6); Eus.*d.e.*9.1(p.404.34; M.22.653A); Cyr. *Os.*116(3.148A); **2.** *hewn* τύμβος...γ. Nonn.*par.Jo.*19:41(M.43.908A).

γλῶσσα, ἡ, 1. *tongue*, as instrument of speech; κατὰ τὴν γ. *oral* μαρτύριον Clem.*str.*7.8(p.38.21; M.9.473A); **a.** rational function, Clem.*str.*7.9(p.39.12; M.9.473C); ἡ γ. ... διάκονος...διαλεκτικῆς ἐνεργείας Cyr.H.*catech.*4.22; Thdt.*provid.*3(4.513); **b.** function in service of God: in prayer, †Bas.Anc.*virg.*20(M.30.712C); γ. δὲ ἐδόθη ...ἵνα ὑμνῇς τὸν ποιητήν Chrys.*diab.*2.3(2.264A); χείρ ἐστιν ἡ γ. τῶν εὐχομένων, καὶ δι' αὐτῆς κατέχομεν τὰ γόνατα τοῦ θεοῦ id.*hom.51.5 in Mt.*(7.526D); in imitating Christ ἡ γ. σου ὡς ἡ γ. ... τοῦ Χριστοῦ *ib.78.3*(755D); **c.** requires bridle because of its proneness to sin οὐκ ἀπέχεται τῆς γ., ἐν ᾗ πονηρεύεται Herm.*vis.*2.2.3; γ. ... ὄλισθος ἀνθρώποις μὴ λόγῳ κυβερνωμένη Gr.Naz.*or.*3(M.35.524B); Isid.Pel. *epp.*1.325(M.78.372A); **d.** ref. Pentecost ἐν γλώσσαις δὲ διὰ τὴν πρὸς τὸν λόγον οἰκείωσιν Gr.Naz.*or.*41.12(M.36.445A); Chrys.*pent.*2.2(2. 472B); Jo.D.*carm.pent.*3(p.213; M.96.832C); **2.** *language*; **a.** ref. confusion of tongues (Gen.11:7) traditionally held to number 70 or 72 διεσκέδασε γὰρ αὐτῶν τὰς γ. καὶ ἀπὸ μιᾶς εἰς ἑβδομήκοντα δύο διένειμεν Epiph.*haer.*2(p.176.4; M.41.134B); *ib.*39.8(p.78.4; 673C); seventy, *Hom.Clem.*18.4; †Gregent.*disp.*(M.86.704A); **b.** of languages spoken at Pentecost ἐλάλουν...ξέναις γ. ... τὸ σημεῖον τοῖς ἀπίστοις Gr.Naz.*or.*41.15(M.36.449A); reason for miracle and its cessation in later times discussed, Chrys.*pent.*1.4(2.464B,C); contrasted with Babel, *ib.*2.2(472D); τοῖς...ἀποστόλοις ἡ χάρις τοῦ πνεύματος τὴν τῶν γ. εἴδησιν ἐδεδώκει, ἐπειδὴ τῶν ἐθνῶν ἁπάντων διδασκάλους ἀποφανθέντας ἔδει τὰς ἁπάντων εἰδέναι φωνάς Thdt.*1Cor.*12:1(3.241); Sever.ap.*cat.Ac.*2:7(p.27.22); **c.** γένη γλωσσῶν (1Cor.12:10, al.) interpreted as speech in foreign tongues χάρισμα εὐχῆς ἔχοντες πολλοὶ μετὰ γλώττης,...καὶ ἡ γ. ἐφθέγγετο, ἢ τῇ Περσῶν ἢ τῇ Ῥωμαίων φωνῇ εὐχομένη, ὁ νοῦς δὲ οὐκ ᾔδει τὸ λεγόμενον Chrys.*hom.35.3 in 1Cor.*(10.325C); its nature dist. from gift at Pentecost οἱ μὲν ταῖς γ. ἐλάλουν, καίτοι πρὸ οὐκ εἰδότες αὐτὰς...τὸ γλώσσαις λαλεῖν, οὐχ ὡς ἐν μοίρᾳ χαρίσματος [as at Pentecost], ἀλλ' ὡς ἐν τάξει σημείου τοῖς πιστοῖς Cyr.*1Cor.*12:9(M.74.888C); its effects εἰς τύφον ἐξώγκωσε τὸ χάρισμα τῶν γ. Thdt.*1Cor.*12:1(3.241); **3.** met. ἡ γ. τὸ ψαλτήριον κυρίου Clem.*paed.*2.4(p.182.22; M.8.441A); τὸν Ἰησοῦν ...τῇ γ. τῆς βλασφημίας μαστιγούμενον Or.*hom.19.12 in Jer.*(p.168. 5; M.13.488B); **4.** *thong* ἐν πλατείαις ταῖς κρηπῖσι καὶ γ. τῶν ὑποδημάτων προϊόντες [sc. Φαρισαῖοι] Epiph.*haer.*16.1(p.211.7; M.41.249A); **5.** *ingot*, of gold (LXX Jos.7:21), Gr.Naz.*carm.*1.2.2.435(M.37. 612A).

γλωσσαλγ-έω, 1. *have a diseased tongue*, hence *blaspheme*; of heretics, Gr.Naz.*or.*38.2(M.36.313B); Steph.Afr.*ep.*(H.3.740A); τῶν ἀπίστων...περὶ τῆς θεότητος τοῦ Χριστοῦ ∼ούντων Anast.S.*hod.*14 (M.89.252A); **2.** *have an itching tongue, speak much*, Ephr.1.7D; Nil.*Eulog.*17(M.79.1113D); ‡Nil.*perist.*11.12(M.79.920D).

γλωσσαλγία, ἡ, 1. *talkativeness*, Gr.Naz.*carm.*1.2.4.11(M.37.641A); **2.** *blasphemy*; ref. heretics, Gr.Naz.*ep.*41(M.37.85B); Cyr.*Mich.*1 (3.392A); Max.*ambig.*(M.91.1209D); Jo.D.*carm.theog.*83(p.207; M.96. 821D).

***γλωσσαλλαγή, ἡ,** *confusion of tongues*; at Babel, *Apoc.Bar.*3 (p.86.14).

γλωσσαργία, ἡ, *loquacity*, Clem.*paed.*2.6(p.189.14; M.8.456A).

***γλωσσίζ-ω,** *kiss*; fig., of fire, *lick* πῦρ ∼ον καὶ ἐξερχόμενον διὰ ...θυρίδων †Anast.S.*relat.*1(p.60).

γλωσσόκομον, τό, 1. *casket*, Ath.*apol.sec.*60(p.141.1; M.25.360A); Marc.Diac.*v.Porph.*14; Chrys.*hom.47.5 in Jo.*(8.281D); **2.** *coffin*, *A.Mt.*24(p.251.7); Thdt.*h.e.*3.23.3(3.940); Cyr.S.*v.Euthym.*40(p.60. 25); *Chron.Pasch.*p.309(M.92.788B).

***γλωσσοκοπ-έω,** *cut out the tongue of* ἐγλωσσοκόπησαν Μαρτῖναν Thphn.*chron.*p.283(M.108.697B); pass. ἐπισκόπων τῶν διὰ τὴν ὀρθόδοξον πίστιν ∼ηθέντων Gr.Mag.*dial.*(tr.Zach.)3.32(M.*PL.*77. 294B).

***γλωσσοκόπος,** *sharp-tongued*, *Sent.App.*(p.84).

***γλωσσολογία, ἡ,** *chatter*, ‡Proc.G.*Pr.*10:31(M.87.1321D).

***γλωσσομανία, ἡ,** *insane talk*, Tat.*orat.*3(p.4.10; M.6.812A).

***γλωσσοπύρσευτος,** *like tongues of fire* τὸ πνεῦμα τεύχει γ. θεῷ Jo.D.*carm.pent.*108(p.217; M.96.837B).

***γλωσσοπυρσόμορφος,** *shaped like tongues of fire*; of H. Ghost, Sophr.H.*carm.*20.57(M.87.3821A); Jo.D.*carm.pent.*55(p.215; M.96. 836A).

γλωσσότμητος, *with the tongue cut out*, ‡Just.*or.Gr.*3(M.6.236B).

γλωσσοτομέω, *cut out the tongue of*, *M.Tar.*9; *M.Pers.*1.15(p.433. 13); pass., *have one's tongue cut out* ἐγλωσσοτομήθη πρῶτον Or.*mart.* 23(p.21.5; M.11.592B); CChalc.*act.*1(*ACO* 2.1.1 p.180.36; H.2.216C); *Chron.Pasch.*p.380(M.92.973B).

***γλωσσοτομία, ἡ,** *cutting out of the tongue*, Anast.S.*serm.imag.*3 (M.89.1156C).

γλώττημα, τό, *tongue*, Jo.D.*carm.pent.*14(p.214; M.96.833A).

***γλωττιαῖος,** *of the tongue*, Tim.Ant.*nativ.Jo.Bapt.*2(M.28.909D).

***γλώττισμα, τό,** *daintiness of language*, Soz.*h.e.*3.16.2(M.67. 1088A).

***γλωττοφόρος,** *having a tongue, uttering speech*, Gr.Nyss.*Thdr.* (M.46.737D).

γνάμψις, ἡ, *bending*, Melet.*nat.hom.*7(M.64.1184C).

***γνησιάζω,** *be familiar with*, ‡Ath.*synops.*46(M.28.380B).

***γνησιεύω,** *be genuine*, Thdr.Stud.*epp.*2.31(M.99.1204A); *ib.*2.177 (1549B).

***γνήσιμος,** *sincere*, Tim.Ant.*cruc.*(M.86.257A).

***γνησιοδίδακτος,** *truly taught*, ‡Chrys.*ador.*2(11.824A).

γνήσιος, 1. *belonging to the race*, i.e. *lawfully begotten, legitimate*, e.g. of Isaac opp. Ishmael, Chrys.*hom.16.6 in Rom.*(9.612B); hence of Son, expressing genuine sonship υἱὸς τοῦ νοῦ γ. ὁ θεῖος λόγος Clem.*prot.*10(p.71.25; M.8.212C); τὸν τοῦ θεοῦ παῖδα γ. καὶ μονογενῆ Eus.*h.e.*1.2.3(M.20.56A); Χριστὸς γέννημα γ. Chrys.*hom.10.2 in 1Cor.*(10.82E); Cyr.*Jo.*1.3(4.23A); Thdt.*Col.*1:13(3.476); **2.** met., *genuine*; **a.** of spiritual children ὁ τοῦ πιστοῦ Ἀβραὰμ υἱὸς γ. Clem.*exc. Thdot.*56(p.126.4; M.9.685C); γ. ... τῆς ἐκκλησίας τέκνα Cyr.H.*catech.*19.1; γ. ... τέκνον τῆς χάριτος Gel.Cyz.*h.e.*2.23.3(M.85.1296B); **b.** of other relationships ὁ τοῦ Ἰησοῦ γ. μαθητὴς Παῦλος Or.*Cels.*1.13(p.66.12; M.11.680B); γ. τῆς ἀληθοῦς φιλοσοφίας ἐραστής Eus.*h.e.*4.8.3(M.20.324A); γ. φίλῳ *Hom.Clem.*1.16; γ. τῶν ἄνω μύστας Gr.Naz.*or.*8.6(M.35.796B); **3.** of things; **a.** of biblical books, *authentic*, e.g. of 2 and 3 Jo. οὐ πάντες φασὶ γ. εἶναι ταύτας Or.*Jo.*5.3(p.101.33; M.14.189A); *ib.*13.17(p.241.15; 424C); τὰ μὲν ὀνομαζόμενα Πέτρου, ὧν μόνην μίαν γ. ἔγνων ἐπιστολήν Eus.*h.e.*3.3.4(M.20.217A); of an interpretation of scripture, *Barn.*9.9; **b.** of virtues etc., *genuine, true*, *1Clem.*62.2; Eus.*theoph.fr.*9(p.24.3; M.24.633A τοῖς...γνησίοις); Chrys.*hom.2.2 in Rom.*(9.439A); id.*comm. in Gal.*4:13f.(10.707A); Thdt.*ep.*97(4.1167); **4.** as subst.; **a.** masc., *friend*, Ath.*ep.Serap.*1.1(M.26.529A); Chrys.*comm. in Gal.*6:11f.(10.727A); **b.** neut., *genuineness, reality* τὸ γ. τῆς ἀγάπης *Ep.Lugd.*ap.Eus.*h.e.*5.2.6(M.20.436B); Cyr.*Nah.*3(3.476D); of eternal generation of Son τὸ γ. τοῦ υἱοῦ Ath.*Ar.*1.61(M.26.140A); τὸ γ. τῆς υἱότητος Chrys.*hom.71.2 in Mt.*(7.696B); τὸ γ. τῆς γεννήσεως Thdt.*Heb.*1:3(3.548); αἱ κλήσεις αὗται [sc. υἱός, πατήρ] τὸ γ. καὶ οἰκεῖον γνωρίζουσιν Gr.Naz.*or.*29.16(p.98.9; M.36.96A); τὰ γ. *legitimate things*, i.e. true religion, Geo.Pis.*Pers.*1.22(M.92.1199A).

***γνησιοτέρως**, adv. from comp. of γνήσιος, *courteously*, Dam.*troph.*2.8.3(p.234.6).

γνησιότης, ἡ, **1.** *legitimacy, true sonship*, Chrys.*hom.29.2 in Heb.*(12.272C); theol. ὁ σωτὴρ...γ. ἐμφανίζων Alex.Al.*ep.Alex.*8(p.24.30; M.18.560B); Ath.*Ar.*3.66(M.26.464B); μονῆς τῆς γ. ἐπὶ τοῦ θεοῦ καὶ πατρός Gr.Nyss.*Eun.*3(2 p.28.2; M.45.593B); CAnc.(358)*ep.syn.*ap. Epiph.*haer.*73.2(p.269.21; M.42.405A); Epiph.*anc.*30(p.39.22; M.43.72B); ἡ γ. τοῦ υἱοῦ Chrys.*hom.15.2 in Jo.*(8.87C); *ib.*38.2(219B); of Father–Son relationship τῆς αὐτῆς γ. πατρὸς πρὸς τὸν υἱόν, καὶ υἱοῦ πρὸς τὸν πατέρα Epiph.*haer.*62.8(p.397.26; M.41.1061B); **2.** met., *sincerity, truth*; **a.** of men towards God μετὰ τῆς γ. ... τὴν εὐχαριστίαν τῷ θεῷ τελεῖν Thdr.Mops.*Ps.*32:1(p.143.5; M.66.668C); τῆς εἰς θεὸν...γ. ... ἐπίδειξιν Cyr.*Ps.*11:1(M.69.793D) al.; id.*ador.*7(1.229C); and Christ, Eus.*h.e.*7.29.2(M.20.709A); Oecum.*Apoc.*3:8(p.61); **b.** between men, Cyr.*Zach.*55(3.734A); Thal.*cent.*1.21(M.91.1429B); **c.** generally, *friendly relationship*, Epiph.*ep.Arab.*(p.464.11; M.42.720A); of husband and wife, id.*exp.fid.*6(p.502.6; M.42.784B); hence *friendship*, Eus.*v.C.*3.60(p.108.15; M.20.1132B); Chrys.*comm.in Gal.*6:11(10.727B); Gr.Mag.*dial.*(tr.Zach.)4.11(M.*PL.*77.335B); of searching of hearts by H. Ghost οὐκ ἀγνοίᾳ...ἀλλὰ γ. ‡Caes.Naz.*dial.*1.14(M.38.869D); **3.** as style of address, *your sincerity*, Bas.*ep.*124(3.214C; M.32.545A); *M.Areth.*(p.42, v.l. ὁσιότης).

γνησίως, **1.** *legitimately, truly*, ref. Christ ὑπ' αὐτοῦ γ. γεγεννημένος Epiph.*haer.*69.55(p.202.2; M.42.288B); ref. Christians as truly members of Christ, Chrys.*hom.20.3 in Eph.*(11.147A); of discipleship etc. τοὺς τῷ Ἰησοῦ γ. μεμαθητευμένους Or.*Jo.*1.26(24; p.32.11; M.14.69B); Gr.Naz.*or.*7.20(M.35.780B); ref. a loyal servant γ. δουλεύοντα *CG–CI* 1.2(Corinth, saec. vi); **2.** *sincerely, affectionately* γ. τε αὐτὸν ἑώρακε Ath.*h.Ar.*22(p.194.18; M.25.717D); *Hom.Clem.*18.11; Chrys.*hom.60.3 in Mt.*(7.609C).

γνόφος, ὁ, *darkness*; **1.** lit.; **a.** *darkness*, ref. Ex.20:21, *Hom.Clem.*2.44; Gr.Nyss.*v.Mos.*45(M.44.316B); **b.** plur., *storm clouds* τοὺς ἀνέμους τῶν γ. *Apoc.En.*17.7(p.46.3); ἄγγελοι νεφελῶν καὶ γ. Epiph.*mens.*22(M.43.276C); **2.** met.; **a.** of sins γ. ἁμαρτημάτων Thdr.Heracl.*Is.*1:16(M.18.1309C); Gr.Naz.*or.*35.2(M.36.260A); of unbelief, exeg. Ex.20:21 γ. ... ἡ τῶν πολλῶν ἀπιστία Clem.*str.*5.12(p.378.3; M.9.116B); and mental confusion, Philost.*h.e.*6.2(M.65.533B); **b.** myst., of divine darkness where God dwells, ref. Ex.20:21 ὁ γ. τῆς ἀσαφείας...ἐν ᾧ ἐστιν ὁ θεός Gr.Nyss.*hom.1 in Cant.*(M.44.773B); Dion.Ar.*myst.*1.3(M.3.1000C); as symbol of transcendence θεὸν... γνόφῳ τῇ ἀκαταληψίᾳ πανταχόθεν διειλημμένον Gr.Nyss.*v.Mos.*(M.44.377A); ὁ θεῖος γ. ἐστὶ τὸ ἀπρόσιτον φῶς Dion.Ar.*ep.*5(M.3.1073A); hence associated with contemplation of mysteries, ref. Moses ὁ ἐν τῷ θείῳ γ. ὀξυωπῶν, καὶ βλέπων ἐν αὐτῷ τὸ ἀόρατον Gr.Nyss.*Pss.titt.* A 7(M.44.457A); whose entering into darkness is type of mystical experience, id.*hex.*(M.44.65C); being progress from rational knowledge to mystical 'un-knowing', id.*v.Mos.*(376D); ἡ...ὁδεύουσα πρὸς τὰ ἄνω ψυχὴ...ἐντὸς τῶν ἀδύτων τῆς θεογνωσίας γίνεται, τῷ θείῳ γ. πανταχόθεν διαληφθεῖσα id.*hom.11 in Cant.*(1000D); εἰς τὸν γ. τῆς ἀγνωσίας εἰσδύνει τὸν ὄντως μυστικὸν καθ' ὃν ἀπομύει πάσας τὰς γνωστικὰς ἀντιλήψεις Dion.Ar.*myst.*1.3(1001A); def. as τὸ ὑπὸ θεῖον γ. γενέσθαι, τὸ δι' ἀβλεψίας καὶ ἀγνωσίας ἰδεῖν καὶ γνῶναι τὸ ὑπὲρ θέαν καὶ γνῶσιν Max.*schol.in myst.*2(M.4.421); the place of mystical knowledge ἃ προεπαιδεύθη διὰ τοῦ γ., πάλιν διὰ τοῦ γ. διδάσκεται Gr.Nyss.*v.Mos.*(377B); εἰς τὸν γ. εἰσελθών, τὸν ἀειδῆ καὶ ἄυλον τῆς γνώσεως τόπον Max.*cap.theol.*1.84(M.90.1117C); used as synonym of contemplation πολλάκις ἔγνωμεν αὐτὸν [sc. Basil] καὶ ἐντὸς τοῦ γ. γενόμενον, οὗ ἦν ὁ θεός Gr.Nyss.*laud.Bas.*(M.46.812C); τὸν ὑπὲρ νοῦν εἰσδύνοντες γ. Dion.Ar.*myst.*3(1033B); and for the mystical presence of God κατὰ τοῦτον ἡμεῖς γενέσθαι τὸν ὑπέρφωτον εὐχόμεθα γ. *ib.*2(1025A); κατὰ τὸν θεῖον ἐκεῖνον καὶ ὑπέρφωτον καὶ ἀόρατον γ. Andr.Cr.*or.*7(M.97.949C).

γνωματεύω, *judge, consider* ἐγνωμάτευσε δὲ ὅπως τὰ ἡμαρτημένα εὖ διαθείη Men.*exc.Rom.*6(p.192.12; M.113.884C).

γνώμη, ἡ, many meanings ποτὲ μὲν γὰρ δηλοῖ τὴν παραίνεσιν... ποτὲ δὲ βουλήν...ποτὲ δὲ ψῆφον...ποτὲ δὲ ἐπὶ πίστεως, ἢ δόξης, ἢ φρονήματος, καὶ ἁπλῶς εἰπεῖν, κατὰ εἴκοσι ὀκτὼ σημαινόμενα λαμβάνεται τὸ τῆς γ. ὄνομα Jo.D.*f.o.*3.14(M.94.1045B); cf.Max.*Pyrr.*(M.91.308B,C);

A. *mind*; **1.** in gen. ὡς θεοῦ γνώμην κεκτημένος Ign.*Polyc.*8.1; Just.*dial.*44.2(M.6.569B); τὴν γ. ὑγιῆ κεκτῆσθαι Clem.*str.*5.1(p.329.30; M.9.16C); its instability, *ib.*8.7(p.93.20; 588B); made strong in the true Christian, Bas.*ep.*293(3.432A; M.32.1036A); ἀκόρεστον τοῦ διαβόλου γ. Chrys.*hom.7.7 in Rom.*(9.492A); **2.** in sense of *spirit, character* διὰ τὸ ἀσθενὲς τῆς γ. Just.*dial.*47.2(M.6.577A); opp. body Tat.*orat.*32(p.33.29; M.6.873A); μηδὲ τὴν τῆς γ. νόσον παραπλησίαν τῇ τῶν εἰς τὰ σώματα δυστυχησάντων Bas.*leg.lib.gent.*8(2.184E; M.31.589A).

B. *opinion, view, doctrine*, esp. of heretics εἴ τις ἐν ἀλλοτρίᾳ γ. περιπατεῖ, οὗτος τῷ πάθει οὐ συγκατατίθεται Ign.*Philad.*3.3; contrasted with true γνῶσις, Iren.*haer.*1 proem.(M.7.440A); Just.*dial.*35.4,6(M.6.552Af.); Heges.ap.Eus.*h.e.*4.22.7(M.20.381A); γ. ἑτεροδοξούντων Or.*Jo.*13.1(p.227.9; M.14.401A); *ib.*13.27(p.251.21; 445C).

C. *will*; **1.** of God; **a.** gen. συντρέχητε τῇ γ. τοῦ θεοῦ Ign.*Eph.*3.2; expressed by Christ, *ib.*; id.*Rom.*8.3; γ. θεοῦ ὑπηρετοῦντες Just.*dial.*95.2(M.6.701C); τῆς θείας προνοίας καὶ γ. Clem.*str.*6.17(p.513.23; M.9.392A); μονογαμία...κατὰ γνώμην θεοῦ ὑπάρχουσα *Const.App.*3.2.2; **b.** opp. ἀνάγκη: εἰ μὲν γὰρ ἁπανταχοῦ παρὼν τῇ εὐδοκίᾳ, ἑτέρως πάλιν ἀνάγκῃ δουλεύων εὑρίσκετο, οὐκέτι κατὰ γ. τὴν παρουσίαν ποιούμενος, ἀλλὰ τῷ ἀπείρῳ τῆς φύσεως, καὶ τὴν γ. ἑπομένην ἔχων Thdr.Mops.*fr.inc.*(p.295.24f.; M.66.973D); **c.** of Father, ref. generation of Son, Eus.*d.e.*4.3(p.153.14; M.22.256B) cit. s. προαίρεσις; εἶναι δὲ γεννηθεῖσαν [sc. hypostasis of Son]...γνώμῃ τοῦ θεοῦ καὶ πατρός Eun.*apol.*12(M.30.848B); **2.** of Christ πρεσβυτέροις...ἀποδεδειγμένοις ἐν γ. Ἰησοῦ Χριστοῦ Ign.*Philad.*proem.; Const.ap.Eus.*v.C.*3.60(p.107.15; M.20.1129B); μὴ...παρὰ γ. αὐτὸν [sc. Christ] τὸ σωτήριον ὑπομεῖναι πάθος Thdt.*Zach.*13:7(2.1658); οὐ γὰρ διαμάχεται ἐν τῷ...θεῷ γ. καὶ φύσις Leont.H.*Nest.*1.41(M.86.1501B); this application freq. rejected by later writers because of equivocal uses of γ.: διχῶς δὲ τῆς γ. λεγομένης· λέγεται γὰρ γ. καὶ ἡ ἁπλῶς ῥοπὴ πρὸς τὸ θελητόν...λέγεται γ. καὶ ἡ ἐκ προβουλεύσεως καὶ κρίσεως περί τι διάθεσις· οὐκ ἀσφαλὲς ἢ γ. ἢ θέλημα γνωμικὸν εἰπεῖν ἐπὶ τοῦ Χριστοῦ κατὰ τὸ τῆς γ. δεύτερον σημαινόμενον διὰ τὸ συνεισάγεσθαι τούτοις τὴν ἄγνοιαν ‡Cyr.*Trin.*21(6^3.26D,E; M.77.1160Dff.); hence γ. λέγοντες ἐπὶ Χριστοῦ...ψιλὸν αὐτὸν δογματίζουσιν ἄνθρωπον Max.*Pyrr.*(M.91.308C); Jo.D.*f.o.*3.14(M.94.1044B,C); v. θέλημα; **3.** of man's will; **a.** *free will, choice* τῇ...τῶν αἱρουμένων αὐτεξουσίων γ. Tat.*orat.*7(p.7.21; M.6.820C); Clem.*paed.*1.2(p.92.4; M.8.253A); κυρία τῶν ἐν αἱρέσει πρακτέων ἡ ἑκάστου γ. Cyr.*ador.*6(1.202D); opp. ἀνάγκη: ταῦτά σε βούλεται ποιεῖν τῇ γ., ἃ καὶ ἀνάγκῃ σε δεῖ ποιῆσαι Chrys.*hom.76.4 in Mt.*(7.738A); Cyr.*ador.*1(1.33E); assisted by divine protection, Thdt.*Dan.*1:9(2.1071); // ἀγάπη: ἔστι δὲ καὶ τοῖς νοήμασι συμφωνοῦντα, μηδέπω καὶ τῇ γ. συμφωνεῖν· οἷον, ὅταν τὴν αὐτὴν πίστιν ἔχοντες, μὴ ὦμεν συνημμένοι κατὰ τὴν ἀγάπην Chrys.*hom.3.1 in 1Cor.*(10.15C); = *motive*, Bas.Sel.*or.*29.2(M.85.329B); opp. φύσις: ἐξουσία...καὶ αὐθεντία...γ. προδήλως, ἀλλ' οὐ φύσεως ὑπάρχει κινήματα [hence condemned as basis for union of wills in Christ] Max.*Pyrr.*(M.91.829D); γνώμῃ *of one's own accord, voluntarily*, Rom.Mel.(*BZ* 24 p.4); **b.** of will weakened by sin τὴν ἀπὸ γ. καὶ ἔργων τοῖς ἀνθρώποις προσοῦσαν ἁμαρτίαν Didym.*Trin.*3.10(M.39.857C); Bas.Sel.*or.*4.1(M.85.64A); *ib.*4.3(69A); **4.** of Devil, Ign.*Philad.*6.2; and demons, Tat.*orat.*16(p.17.28; M.6.841A).

D. *decision, judgement*, Tat.*orat.*32(p.33.14; M.6.872B); κύριον εἶναι τὸν κριτὴν τῆς ἑαυτοῦ γ. Clem.*str.*4.11(p.283.13; M.8.1288B); Philost.*h.e.*8.4(M.65.560B); ἄνευ τῆς ἐμῆς γ. *CG–CI* 1.23(Corinth, saec. v); of conciliar ordinances, applied to spurious *Gnomes* of CNic.(325), cf. Pitra, *SS* 1 pp.523ff.

E. *advice* γ. ἀγαθή *Barn.*21.2; ‡Chrys.*Spir.*3(3.801D).

γνωμικός, A. *of the mind* or *will*; **1.** *intentional, purposely effected* ἰατρευόμενος ἀπὸ τῆς ἰδίας γ. αὐτοῦ κακίας ‡Just.*qu.et resp.*123(M.6.1373A); opp. φυσικός: οὐ φυσικὴν ἀλλὰ γ. νοοῦμεν συγγένειαν Thdt.*Cant.*proem.(2.10); ref. Christ [Ps.44:8a] γ. γὰρ ταῦτα αἱρέσεως, οὐ φυσικῆς δυνάμεως id.*Ps.*44:8(1.891); τοῖς γ. κατορθώμασι opp. physical descent, id.*2Cor.*11:22(3.345); **2.** *of free will* [LXX ἑκούσια] τῶν θυσιῶν τὰ μὲν νομικά, τὰ δὲ γ. id.*Ps.*118:108(1.1465); id. *Ezech.*46:12(2.1037).

B. θέλημα γ. *moral will* or *will of choice* which is variable; **1.** of men in gen., v. θέλημα; **2.** Christol., v. θέλημα; by making the union of divinity and humanity one of θελήματα γ. which remain distinct after the union Nestorius συνήγαγε τῇ τῶν γ. θελημάτων διαφορᾷ καὶ τὴν τῆς γνώμης παραλλαγήν· καθ' ἣν οὐχ ἡ κατὰ φύσιν διαφορὰ δείκνυσθαι πέφυκεν, ἀλλ' ἡ καθ' ὑπόστασιν, ποιουμένη τῆς ἀγαθότητος ἐν τῇ διαφορᾷ τῶν γ. θελημάτων, ἄνεσιν καὶ ἐπίτασιν Max. *opusc.*(M.91.44C); cf. ὁ μὲν γὰρ [sc. Nest.] ποιοτήτων γ. εἰσηγούμενος ἕνωσιν...ὁ δὲ [sc. Severus] ποιοτήτων φυσικῶν λέγων μόνον εἶναι διαφορὰν μετὰ τὴν ἕνωσιν *ib.*(44A).

C. neut. as subst., *proverb, sentence*, Pall.*v.Chrys.*16(p.94.26; M. 47.53).

γνωμικῶς, 1. *succinctly* τὴν ἀπόδειξιν...γ. σχηματίσας Thdt.*Heb.* 11:6(3.614); comp., Clem.*str.*5.3(p.337.21; M.9.36B); superl., *ib.*5.14 (p.416.5; 196A); **2.** *deliberately* ἑκουσίως καὶ γ. τὰ πάθη κατεδέξατο ὁ Χριστός Anast.S.*hod.*23(M.89.304A); **3.** *by the will* ὁ θεὸς λόγος γ. δύναται ἑνωθῆναι τῇ κτιστῇ φύσει, φυσικῶς δὲ οὐ δύναται Leont.H. *Nest.*1.41(M.86.1501A); **4.** *spiritually* κατὰ σάρκα ζῇ...γ. ἀποθνήσκων Max.*qu.Thal.*63(M.90.669D).

***γνωμοδοσία, ἡ,** *counsel*, Cyr.*ador.*12(1.427C).

***γνωμοδοτ-έω, 1.** *give advice, counsel*, ‡Chrys.*Spir.*4(3.801D); Cyr. *ador.*3(1.95A); iron. ~ῆσαι τῷ θεῷ id.*Is.*4.2(2.609E); **2.** *give as an opinion*, Nil.*Eulog.*22(M.79.1121D).

***γνωμοδότης, ὁ,** *adviser, counsellor*, Didym.*Trin.*2.7(M.39.565A); Ast.Soph.*Ps.*7(M.40.461B); Oecum.*1Cor.*7:25ff.(p.436.20).

***γνωμοδότις, ἡ,** fem. of foreg. αὕτη [sc. πλεονεξία] γ. εὐμήχανος ‡Nil.*perist.*8(M.79.880C).

***γνωμόνως,** *purposefully*, Evagr.Pont.*or.*73(M.79.1184A).

***γνωμοφθόρος,** *mind-corrupting*; of heretics, Pall.*v.Chrys.*9 (p.56.23; M.47.33).

γνώμων, ὁ, 1. *one that knows*, hence *guide* ἀκριβεῖς γ. τῆς ἀληθείας ...οἱ γνωστικοί Clem.*str.*7.16(p.68.3; M.9.533A); γ. χρήσασθαι τοῦ προβλήματος Πλάτωνι Eus.*p.e.*11 proem.(508B; M.21.844C); σωφροσύνη...εὐχῆς γ. †Nil.*vit.*2(M.79.1141C); **2.** *rule, norm*, of faith τῶν πατέρων...παράδοσιν, ὥσπερ τινὰ γ. καὶ κανόνα προεκθέμενοι Eun. *apol.*4(M.30.840B); τὸν γ. τῆς ἀληθείας Bas.*Eun.*1.4(1.213D; M.29. 513B); of divine law, Chrys.*hom.13.4 in 2Cor.*(10.536A); Synes. *regn.*3(p.14.4; M.66.1061C); of behaviour, Nil.*epp.*3.193(M.79.437A); **3.** a measure ὁ μόδιος...καλεῖται δὲ καὶ γ. Epiph.*mens.*23(M.43. 280B).

***γνωνιώδης,** error for γωνιώδης, *angular*, Proc.G.*Ex.*26:15(M.87. 645C).

γνωρίζ-ω, A. *make known*; supernaturally, **1.** God through Christ ἔδει γὰρ τὸν μεσίτην θεοῦ τε καὶ ἀνθρώπων...ἀνθρώποις... γνωρίσαι τὸν θεόν Iren.*haer.*3.18.7(M.7.937B); ὁ λόγος, ᾧ...ὁ θεὸς... ~εται Clem.*paed.*1.7(p.124.4; M.8.320A); id.*exc.Thdot.*10(p.110.5; M. 9.661A); who is known in Inc., Meth.*symp.*8.9(p.91.14; M.18.152B); Gel.Cyz.*h.e.*2.19.25(M.85.1280D) cit. s. διαφορά; and in created order, Ath.*inc.*2.2(M.25.100A); **2.** mysteries of the faith ἐγνώρισεν...ἡμῖν ὁ δεσπότης διὰ τῶν προφητῶν τὰ παρεληλυθότα καὶ τὰ ἐνεστῶτα *Barn.* 1.7; *ib.*5.3; τῆς ἀμπέλου Δαυὶδ...ἧς ἐγνώρισας ἡμῖν διὰ Ἰησοῦ *Did.* 9.2; *ib.*9.3; *ib.*10.2; **3.** pass.: **a.** of a dream, *appear* ἐνύπνιον...σοὶ μὲν γνωρισθέν Thdt.*Dan.*2:7(2.1080); **b.** *seem* ὁ μάρτυς ὡς ἄλλου πάσχοντος ἐγνωρίζετο ‡Jo.D.*Artem.*37(M.96.1285B).

B. *know*; **1.** in gen., Just.*1apol.*12.11(M.6.345A); ὁ γνωστικός, τά τε ὄντα καὶ τὰ ἐσόμενα ~ων Clem.*str.*7.11(p.47.12; M.9.492A); *ib.* 7.14(p.63.17; 524A); in sense of *pay attention to* Λάζαρον, ὃν ἐπὶ τοῦ ἐδάφους ἐρριμμένον...οὐκ ἐγνώριζες ‡Nil.*perist.*15(M.79.844B); **2.** *recognize* οἱ ἐν οὐρανῷ ἄρχοντες...οὐ ~οντες αὐτόν Just.*dial.*36.6(M.6. 556A); *ib.*92.3(696A); Leont.N.*v.Jo.Eleem.*46(p.99.7); **3.** *acknowledge* ~ομεν ὅτι...τοῦτό ἐστι τὸ ὕδωρ τῆς ζωῆς Just.*dial.*14.1(M.6. 504C); σὲ βασιλέα ~ομεν Const.ap.Eus.*v.C.*4.20(p.125.7; M.20.1168B); hence *profess*, Const.*ib.*4.9(p.121.14; 1157B); ὀφείλει...ἐκκλησία... τούτους [sc. Nicene canons] ~ειν Innoc.*ep.cler.*(M.52.538); **4.** *deem* οἱ δ' ἂν μὴ εὑρίσκωνται βιοῦντες ὡς ἐδίδαξε, ~έσθωσαν μὴ ὄντες Χριστιανοί Just.*1apol.*16.8(M.6.353A); id.*dial.*102.4(713B); **5.** pass., *be well-known, famous*, Eus.*h.e.*5.11.1(M.20.456C); id.*p.e.*10.14(503D; M.21.837D); id.*v.C.*1.8(p.11.7; M.20.921A); Philost.*h.e.*3.4(M.65. 485A); Cyr.*Juln.*6(6².206B).

γνώριμος, *well-known*; **1.** as subst. masc., *pupil, disciple*; of the Twelve οἱ γ. αὐτοῦ πάντες ἀπέστησαν Just.*1apol.*50.12(M.6.404A); Clem.*paed.*1.5(p.97.3; M.8.261C); Eus.*d.e.*3.4(p.115.5; M.22.197A); of S. Paul's converts ὑπὲρ τῶν γ. οὓς αὐτὸς ἐγέννησεν ἐν πίστει Clem. *str.*7.9(p.39.28; M.9.477A); **2.** as subst. neut.; *knowledge*, Ath.*gent.*1 (M.25.4A); *familiarity* τὸ γ. τοῦ σαρκικοῦ γένους Vict.*Mc.*6:1(p.321. 24).

γνώρισμα, τό, *that by which a thing is known, mark*; **1.** in gen., *characteristic*, Ath.*decr.*4(p.4.2; M.25.421C); Didym.*Ps.*8:1(M.39. 1185A); Gr.Nyss.*or.catech.*40(p.159.14; M.45.101D); εὐεργετεῖν... πεφυκότες [sc. βασιλεῖς], καὶ ἰδιαίτατον...ἔχοντες τοῦτο γ. Anast. Ant.*redit.*(p.254); **2.** of God, *property* τῆς ἐκ τοῦ πατρὸς γεννήσεως ...γ. Ath.*decr.*17(p.14.14; M.25.444C); υἱόν...ἐν τοῖς τοῦ πατρὸς γ. χαρακτηριζόμενον Gr.Nyss.*diff.ess.*6(M.32.337A); ἴδιον θεότητος γνώρισμα, τὸ ἀληθῶς εἶναι id.*Eun.*10(2 p.238.15; M.45.840D); ἴδιον δὲ γ. τῆς θείας φύσεώς ἐστι τὸ παντὸς ὑπερκεῖσθαι γνωρισμάτος id. *v.Mos.*(M.44.404B); Max.*Pyrr.*(M.91.300B); **3.** *distinctive feature*, of baptism πῶς δὲ σὺ ἐρεῖς, τοῦ θεοῦ εἰμι, μὴ ἐπιφερόμενος τὰ γ.; Bas.*hom.*13.4(2.117B; M.31.432C); of charity τὸ γ. τῶν τοῦ Χριστοῦ μαθητῶν Chrys.*sac.*2.4(p.40.23; 1.377D); id.*hom.4.7 in Mt.*(7.59C); **4.** *sign, proof*, ref. Christ's Messiahship τὸ καθεσθέντα αὐτὸν ὄνῳ... τοῖς ἀνθρώποις γ. ἔφερεν ὅτι αὐτός ἐστιν ὁ Χριστός Just.*dial.*88.6 (M.6.688A); of contrition μέγα γ. παλιγγενεσίας Clem.*q.d.s.*42(p.190. 18; M.9.649D); id.*str.*5.1(p.330.19; M.9.17B); Eus.*e.th.*3.3(p.157.28; M.24.1001C); Ath.*h.Ar.*3(p.184.13; M.25.697A); Gr.Nyss.*v.Mos.*(M. 44.429A); τὸ γ. τῆς ἀποστολικῆς εἰκόνος Chrys.*hom.2.3 in Ac.princ.* (3.66B); **5.** hence *document*, Phil.Thm.*ep.*ap.Eus.*h.e.*8.10.2(M.20. 764A); Cyr.*Is.*3.2(2.423C); *profession* of faith λέγε...τῆς σεαυτοῦ πίστεως τὸ γ. Const.ap.Gel.Cyz.*h.e.*3.19.13(M.85.1348C); **6.** *sign, symbol*, Eus.*d.e.*1.6(p.24.3; M.22.49C); of Cross γ. τοῦ ἁγιωτάτου πάθους Const.ap.Eus.*v.C.*3.30(p.91.23; M.20.1089C); **7.** *signification, name*, Leont.H.*Nest.*4.37(M.86.1705D); αὐτὸς δὲ Μαγουνδὰτ τῷ γ. Sophr.H.*v.Anast.*(M.92.1684A); Max.*schol.c.h.*15.8(M.4.113D).

γνωρισμός, ὁ, *faculty of knowledge*, Nil.*Magn.*62(M.79.1052C).

***γνωριστήριον, τό,** *distinguishing feature* τὸ θεῖον καὶ τὰ ἁπλᾶ πάντα...τοῦ εἴδους γ. φέρουσι Leont.H.*Nest.*1.1(M.86.1408C); τὸ ἰδιώτατον θεοῦ γ. *ib.*4.37(1705C).

γνωριστικός, 1. *making known, indicative of, revealing* ὄνομα γ. τοῦ τῆς σῆς θεότητος μύρου Gr.Nyss.*hom.1 in Cant.*(M.44.781D); *ib.13*(1045A); ὡς ὑπέρκειται [sc. ἡ θεία φύσις] παντὸς γ. νοήματος id.*v.Mos.*47(v.l. γνωστικοῦ M.44.317B); ὁ παράκλητος...γ. ἐστιν ὄνομα Chrys.*hom.5.1 in Jo.*(8.36A); †Leont.B.*sect.*7.5(M.86.1245B); **2.** *characteristic, distinctive* γ. τινας ἰδιότητας...τὸ γεννητὸν καὶ τὸ ἀγέννητον Bas.*Eun.*2.28(1.265B; M.29.637B); Gr.Nyss.*Eun.*4(2 p.51. 16; M.45.621A); Chrys.*hom.4.3 in Jo.*(8.30D); **3.** neut. as subst., *distinguishing faculty*, Just.*2apol.*14.2(conj. for γνωριστόν M.6. 468B).

***γνωριστός,** *recognized*, Or.*adnot.in Ex.*13(M.17.20A).

***γνωσιμάχοι, οἱ,** *opponents of knowledge*; name of an heretical sect opposed to all doctrine, holding that God demands only good works, Jo.D.*haer.*88(M.94.757A); Thdr.Stud.*epp.*1.48(M.99.1080D).

γνῶσις, ἡ, *knowledge*;

A. def. and scope; **1.** in gen. γ. δὲ ἐπιστήμη τοῦ ὄντος αὐτοῦ Clem. *str.*2.17(p.153.8; M.8.1013C); ἕξις ἡ γ., εἴτε διάθεσις *ib.*4.22(p.309.28; 1349A); γ. ... ἐστὶ θεωρία τῆς φύσεως τῶν ὄντων Olymp.*Eccl.*1:16ff. (M.93.492D); **2.** its twofold nature λέγεται...διττὴ ἡ γ. ἡ μὲν κοινῶς, ἡ ἐν ἀνθρώποις ὁμοίως σύνεσίς τε καὶ ἀντίληψις...ἣν οὐκ ἄν ποτε ἔγωγε γ. τε ὀνομάσαιμι...ἡ δέ, ἐξαιρέτως ὀνομαζομένη γ. ἀπὸ τῆς γνώμης καὶ τοῦ λόγου χαρακτηρίζεται· καθ' ἣν μόναι αἱ λογικαὶ δυνάμεις γνώσεις γενήσονται Clem.*str.*6.1(p.423.17ff.; M.9.209B,C); ἡ μὲν [sc. γ.] ἐπιστημονική, ἡ δὲ...πρακτική Max.*cap.*1.22(M.90.1092B); **3.** freq. identified with Christian doctrine, as Christianity in gen., sometimes called γ. ἀληθή or ἀληθείας, ‡*Diogn.*12.6; Iren.*haer.*4.33. 8(M.7.1077B) cit. s. B.3.d infra; Or.*fr.2 in Jo.*1:4(p.486.22); opp. Gnost. fancies, Hipp.*haer.*10.31(p.288.5; M.16.3446C); Cosm.Ind. *top.*1(M.88.57B); opp. worldly knowledge, Philox.*ep.*4(p.159f.); **4.** of the spiritual meaning of scripture, *Barn.*9.8; *ib.*10.10; *ib.* 13.7; cf.Herm.*vis.*2.2.1.

B. of gen. human knowledge of God; **1.** its object; **a.** God in himself, transcending all knowledge, Gr.Nyss.*ep.*24(M.46.1089D); ἐν τῷ θείῳ πᾶσα γ. ἀργεῖ Max.*schol.d.n.*1.3(M.4.200C); Jo.D.*f.o.*1.4 (M.94.800B); **b.** in his mysteries ,to which γ. holds the key (ref.

Lc.11:52) πύλη ἐστὶ κεκλεισμένη, τὰ μυστήρια...τὰ ἀκατάκλειστα. ἡ γ. κλεῖδα ἔχει Or.*fr.in Ezech.*44:1(M.17.288C); cf.*Hom.Clem.*18.15; of Trin. τὴν χάριν τῆς γ. τῆς ἁγίας τριάδος Eus.*Marcell.*1.1(p.3.10; M.24.716B); of the gospel, *A.Phil.*142(p.80.5); of the kingdom, Chrys. *hom.66.2 in Jo.*(8.396C); **2.** its character; **a.** diversity οὐ συγγενᾶται τοῖς ἀνθρώποις, ἀλλ' ἐπίκτητός ἐστιν ἡ γ. καὶ...δεῖται κατὰ τὰς ἀρχὰς ἡ μάθησις αὐτῆς, ἔπειτα...εἰς ἕξιν ἔρχεται, οὕτως ἐν ἕξει τελειωθεῖσα τῇ μυστικῇ ἀμετάπτωτος δι' ἀγάπην μένει Clem.*str.*6.9(p.470.22; M.9.297C); πολλαχῶς ἡ γ. ... ἥ τε γὰρ τοῦ κτίσαντος ἡμᾶς σύνεσις, καὶ ἡ τῶν θαυμασίων αὐτοῦ κατανόησις Bas.*ep.*235.3(3.360A; M.32.873C); **b.** a higher mystical and lower discursive knowledge, Mac. Aeg.*hom.*29.6(M.34.720B); former distinguished as γ. ἄληστος, Dion. Ar.*d.n.*4.35(M.3.736A); interpreted as ἄληστον δὲ τὴν γ. ... τὴν ἐκ φυσικῆς θεωρίας ἢ ἐλλάμψεως ἀδιδάκτως προσγινομένην Max.*schol. d.n.*4.35(M.4.308C); id.*myst.*5(M.91.676C); **3.** its attainment; **a.** in rudimentary form derived from senses, Clem.*str.*4.26(p.320.24; M.8.1373A); Dion.Ar.*ep.*7.2(M.3.1080B); πᾶσι...ἡ γ. τοῦ εἶναι θεὸν ὑπ' αὐτοῦ φυσικῶς ἐγκατέσπαρται Jo.D.*f.o.*1.1(M.94.789B); **b.** in higher forms a gift, Clem.*str.*5.1(p.334.6; M.9.28A); Or.*schol.in Cant.*7:4(M.17.281C); κατηξιώθη χαρίσματος γνώσεως Pall.*h.Laus.*38 (p.120.14; M.34.1194B); **c.** obtained through Christ, *1Clem.*36.2 cit. s. γεύω; *2Clem.*3.1; Clem.*str.*6.7(p.462.21; 284A); who is himself called γ., Ign.*Eph.*17.2; Clem.*str.*6.1(p.423.16; 209B); Manich. τὸ δὲ ἐν παραδείσῳ φυτὸν ἐξ οὗ γνωρίζουσι τὸ καλόν, αὐτός ἐστι ὁ Ἰησοῦς, ἡ γ. αὐτοῦ, ἡ ἐν τῷ κόσμῳ Hegem.*Arch.*11(p.18.4; M.10.1445A); **d.** contained in teaching of apostles and in Church γ. ἀληθής, ἡ τῶν ἀποστόλων διδαχή Iren.*haer.*4.33.8(M.7.1077B); ἐν... τῇ ἀρχαίᾳ ἐκκλησίᾳ ἡ...γ. Clem.*str.*7.15(p.65.21; 528D); in scripture οἶμαι...τῆς ὅλης γ. στοιχεῖα...ὅλας γραφάς Or.*Jo.*13.5(p.230.14; M.14.405C); Chrys.*hom.51.1 in Mt.*(7.299E); **e.** passed on through instruction, Serap.*Euch.*3.2f.; Eus.*h.e.*2.1.13(M.20.137D); Cyr.H. *procatech.*11; **4.** its aim and effects: to enhance man's responsibility, *1Clem.*41.4; to teach him to despise death, Tat.*orat.*19(p.21.10; M.6.849A); and to discern good and evil, Chrys.*hom.13.1 in Rom.*(9.558D); and to lead him to the First Cause, Dion.Ar.*d.n.*5.9(M.3.825A); **5.** its relation; **a.** to πίστις; γ. and πίστις closely connected ἵνα μετὰ τῆς πίστεως ὑμῶν τελείαν ἔχητε τὴν γ. *Barn.*1.5; πίστις perfected by γ.: ἔστιν...ἡ γ. τελείωσίς τις ἀνθρώπου ὡς ἀνθρώπου...πίστις μὲν...ἐνδιάθετόν τί ἐστιν ἀγαθόν...ὅθεν χρή, ἀπὸ ταύτης ἀναγόμενον τῆς πίστεως...τὴν περὶ αὐτοῦ κομίσασθαι...γ. Clem.*str.*7.10(p.40.21ff.; M.9.477C); *ib.*6.18(p.516.26; 397A); Or.*Jo.*10.37(21; p.211.25; M.14.373D); γ. unattainable without πίστις: οὐδ' ἄνευ πίστεως γ. ἐπακολουθῆσαι Clem.*str.*2.6(p.129.29; M.8.968A); *ib.*5.1(p.326.9; M.9.9A); ὅταν γὰρ πίστις μὴ ᾖ, γ. οὐκ ἔστιν Chrys. *hom.18.2 in 1Tim.*(11.655C); Gnost. divorce of the two rejected, Clem.*str.*2.3(p.118.5; M.8.941B); natural knowledge of God precedes faith, Bas.*ep.*235.1(3.358E; M.32.872A,B); ἡ γὰρ γ. κατὰ φύσιν προηγεῖται τῆς πίστεως Marc.Er.*opusc.*1.112(M.65.920A); Hesych.S. *temp.*1.60(M.93.1500A); **b.** to σοφία: ἣ μὲν γάρ τί ἐστι γ., ταύτῃ πάντως καὶ σοφία τυγχάνει, ἣ δέ τι σοφία, οὐ πάντως γ.· ἐν μόνῃ γὰρ τῇ τοῦ προφορικοῦ λόγου τὸ τῆς σοφίας ὄνομα φαντάζεται Clem.*str.*7.10(p.40.29ff.; M.9.477C); σοφία...γ. θείων καὶ ἀνθρωπίνων πραγμάτων...γ. δὲ ἐστι θεωρία τῆς φύσεως τῶν ὄντων Olymp.*Eccl.*1:16ff.(M.93.492D); **c.** to ἀγάπη: ὁ δὲ εἰς γ. ἐπαναβαίνων τῆς ἀγάπης τὴν τελειότητα αἰτήσεται Clem.*str.*7.7(p.34.25; 465B); *ib.*7.10(p.41.7f.; 480A); **d.** to θεωρία, Just.*2apol.*8.3(M.6.457B); Clem.*str.*4.22(p.308.23; M.8.1345C); Evagr.Pont.*ep.*7(M.32.257B); οἶδε...καὶ ἐπὶ τῆς ἀκριβοῦς γ. θεωρίαν λέγειν Chrys.*hom.75.1 in Jo.*(8.440A); τῆς ἐπ' αὐτῷ θεωρίας συλλέγων τὴν γ. Cyr.*Jo.*5.4(4.505B); **e.** to ζωή, v.s.v.; **f.** to σωτηρία, v.s.v.; **6.** as charisma; of OT prophets, Eus.*p.e.*11.7 (521B; M.21.864C); given to understand mysteries, Or.*Jo.*32.8 (6; p.438.6ff.; M.14.761A); ‡Pall.*h.mon.*28(p.12.1; M.34.1116D); of Daniel's interpretation of dreams, Thdt.*Dan.*2:30(2.1088).

C. contemplative or mystical knowledge; **1.** in gen., Clem.*str.*3.5 (p.216.19ff.; M.8.1148B); γ. ... θέα τίς ἐστι τῆς ψυχῆς τῶν ὄντων... τελειωθεῖσα δὲ τῶν συμπάντων *ib.*6.8(p.466.24; M.9.292A); **2.** its transcendence; expressed in paradoxes, Dion.Ar.*d.n.*7.3(M.3.872A) cit. s. γινώσκω; id.*ep.*1(M.3.1065A) cit. s. ἀγνωσία; ἡ περὶ θεὸν ἀγνωσία...οὐκ ἔστιν ἀμαθία, ἀλλὰ γ. Max.*schol.d.n.*7.1(M.4.341A); **3.** its growth; after victory over passions, Clem.*str.*3.5(p.215.27; M.8.1145C); cf.*ib.*6.12(p.482.11; M.9.321B); given to each acc. his progress, id.*ecl.*57(p.154.1; M.9.725C); fostered by the practice of the virtues, esp. temperance, id.*str.*7.12(p.50.18; 497A); humility, Max.*carit.*4.58(M.90.1061A) = Hesych.S.*temp.*1.67(M.93.1501D) cit. s. ταπείνωσις; and reception of the sacraments, Dion.Ar.*e.h.*6.3.5 (M.3.536C); **4.** its transmission; not intended for all, Clem.*str.*1.1 (p.4.2; M.8.689A); but given to SS. James, John, and Peter after Resurrection, id.*fr.*13(p.199.22; M.20.136B); and handed down to the few in unwritten traditions of apostles, id.*str.*6.7(p.462.28; M.9.284A); and by other Christian teachers, esp. bishops, Dion.Ar. *e.h.*1.3(M.3.373C); id.*ep.*8.6(M.3.1097C); **5.** its perfection; loving union with God διὰ γνώσεως...εἰσελθὼν ὁ νυμφίος ταῖς ἡγιασμέναις ἐνοικήσῃ ψυχαῖς Thdt.*Cant.*5:3(2.111); ἡ γ. ἑνωτικὴ τῶν ἐγνωκότων καὶ ἐγνωσμένων Dion.Ar.*d.n.*7.4(M.3.872C); Max.*schol.d.n.*7.4(M.4.353C) cit. s. γινώσκω; ἡ γ. τῇ πείρᾳ τὸν ἄνθρωπον συνάπτει τῷ θεῷ Diad.*perf.*9(p.10.22); and assimilation to him ὁ δ' ἐν γ. καθεστώς, ἐξομοιούμενος θεῷ Clem.*str.*4.26(p.323.8; M.8.1377A); ‡Just.*fr.*18 (M.6.1600B) cit. s. ὁμοίωσις; but never completely attained in this life, Or.*Jo.*2.28(23; p.85.5; M.14.161D); Thdt.*rect.conf.*8(M.6.1221B); Areth.ap.*cat.Apoc.*14:5(p.388.6); **6.** its effects: repentance and purification βραδεῖα γὰρ γ. μετάνοια· γ. δὲ ἡ πρώτη ἀναμαρτησία Clem.*str.*2.6(p.127.14; M.8.961B); ἡ γ. ... ἀπὸ τῶν παθῶν ἀπάγων καὶ χορίζων τὴν ψυχήν *ib.*7.12(p.51.19; M.9.500A); nourishment of the soul, *ib.*5.10(p.370.21; 101A) cit. s. βρῶσις; illumination, id.*paed.*1.6 (p.107.30; M.8.285B) cit. s. φωτισμός; φῶς ἐστι γ. ἀληθινῆς τὸ διακρίνειν...τὸ καλὸν ἐκ τοῦ κακοῦ Diad.*perf.*6(p.8.11); Esaias *or.*24.2 (p.184); joy, Clem.*paed.*1.6(p.111.31; 293B); good works ἕπεται... τὰ ἔργα τῇ γ. ὡς τῷ σώματι ἡ σκιά id.*str.*7.13(p.59.11; 516B); immortality, *ib.*6.8(p.466.11f.; 289C); preparation for beatific vision, *ib.*6.7(p.462.31; 284A); **7.** its nature; holy, Clem.*str.*6.15(p.498.12; M.9.356B); Diad.*perf.*80(p.102.13); ἐκκλησιαστική Clem.*str.*6.16 (p.507.9; 377A); θεία Dion.Ar.*d.n.*4.9(M.3.705B); Max.*or.dom.*(M.90.889D); καθαρά Dion.Ar.*d.n.*4.6(701B); θεουργική id.*e.h.*5.2(M.3.501B).

D. divine knowledge; **1.** characteristics; fullness of perfection, Dion.Ar.*d.n.*7.2(M.3.869A); itself the source of all knowledge, *ib.* (869C); *ib.*1.6(596B); a knowledge *sui generis*, Max.*schol.myst.*5 (M.4.429D); **2.** mutual knowledge of Father and Son within Trin., ref. Lc.10:22 αὕτη ἡ ἀντιταλαντεύουσα γ. ἐπ' ἴσης δικαιοσύνης... σύμβολον Clem.*paed.*1.9(p.142.3; M.8.356B); from which H. Ghost is not excluded, Bas.*ep.*236.1(3.361A; M.32.877A); Thdt.*Trin.*23 (M.75.1180C); **3.** God's knowledge of creatures; no knowledge of wicked, in sense of love or sympathy, but only of righteous, Or.*sel.in Ps.*1:6(M.12.1100B); id.*hom.1.8 in Jer.*(p.7.20; M.13.264D); ‡Proc.G.*Pr.*10:7(M.87.1313A).

E. Christ's knowledge; **1.** perfect knowledge of his human soul due to hypostatic union ἡ τοῦ κυρίου ψυχὴ...ἔχουσα...πᾶσαν γ. τῶν γεγονότων, τῶν ὄντων, τῶν ἐσομένων, οὐ φύσει, οὐ χάριτι, διὰ δὲ τὴν... καθ' ὑπόστασιν ἕνωσιν ‡Cyr.*Trin.*21(6^3.26E; M.77.1161A); Jo.D.*f.o.*3.21(M.94.1085A); **2.** its apparent defectiveness (Mc.13:32) utilized by Arians, Ath.*Ar.*3.44(M.26.417B); *ib.*3.37f.(404B–405A); *ib.*3.42 (412B); his 'ignorance' variously interpreted as indication that ἐκ ...τοῦ πατρὸς αὐτῷ ὑπῆρχε δεδομένη ἡ γ. Bas.*ep.*236.4(3.362C; M.32.880B); Gr.Naz.*or.*30.15f.(pp.131.12,133.8; M.36.124A,C); as a feigning of ignorance, Didym.(‡Bas.)*Eun.*4(1.289E; M.29.696B,C); cf.id. *Ps.*68:6(M.39.1453A); ‡Caes.Naz.*dial.*20(M.38.877,880); as speaking acc. human, not divine, nature, Gr.Naz.*or.*30.15(p.132.3; 124A); Cyr.*thes.*22(5^1.218–24); as speaking as judge, not knowing judgement as a present but as a future event, ‡Caes.Naz.*dial.*21(880); **3.** his perfect knowledge of Father ἐπὶ τελείαν γ. ἣν γινώσκει ὁ υἱὸς τὸν πατέρα Or.*Jo.*32.28(18; p.473.14; M.14.817B); Ath.*Ar.*3.46 (M.26.421B); Chrys.*hom.50.2 in Jo.*(8.295B); **4.** acc. monophysites μία...ἡ γ. ἐπὶ Χριστοῦ, καθάπερ καὶ ἡ θέλησις Them.*fr.*ap.*Doct.Patr.*41.39(p.314.3).

F. angelic knowledge; **1.** not discursive, but intuitive, Dion.Ar. *d.n.*7.2(M.3.868B); filled with immutable divine love, id.*e.h.*4.5(M.3.480C); and with purifying power, id.*c.h.*7.3(M.3.209D); against gen. opinion (based on Mt.18:10) held to be defective and not face to face, ref. Mc.13:32 οὐδὲ οἱ ἄγγελοι, φησίν, ἴσασι...παχεία γὰρ καὶ τούτων ἡ γ., συγκρίσει τοῦ πρόσωπον πρὸς πρόσωπον Evagr.Pont. *ep.*7(M.32.257A); **2.** its transmission; in hierarchical order, Dion. Ar.*c.h.*7.4(M.3.212A); τῶν θεολογικῶν γ. οἱ πρῶτοι τοῖς δευτέροις μεταδιδόασιν *ib.*10.2(273B); *ib.*12.2(293B); also to men, e.g. of Inc., *ib.*4.4(181B).

G. Gnost.; **1.** denoting a secret science, Clem.*str.*7.7(p.31.8; M.9.457A); so hymn of Naassenes τὰ κεκρυμμένα τῆς ἁγίας ὁδοῦ, γ. καλέσας, παραδώσω ap.Hipp.*haer.*5.10(p.104.3; M.16.3159B); Gnost. claim to have τελεία γ. in contrast to ordinary Christians οἱ ψυχικοὶ ἄνθρωποι, οἱ δι' ἔργων καὶ πίστεως ψιλῆς βεβαιούμενοι, καὶ μὴ τὴν τελείαν γ. ἔχοντες Iren.*haer.*1.6.2(M.7.505A); whom they seek to seduce under pretext of γ., Or.*Jo.*5.8(p.105.4; M.14.196A); alleging gospel to be source of their secret knowledge, Hipp.*haer.*

7.27(p.207.5; M.16.3319A); γ. and baptism ἔστιν δὲ οὐ τὸ λουτρὸν μόνον τὸ ἐλευθεροῦν, ἀλλὰ καὶ ἡ γ., τίνες ἦμεν, τί γεγόναμεν Clem. *exc.Thdot.*78(p.131.17; M.9.696A); Manich. denial of salvation to orthodox ὅτι οὐκ ἔμαθε τὴν γ. τοῦ παρακλήτου Hegem.*Arch.*11 (10; p.19.4; M.10.1445B); they themselves being saved γνώσει καὶ πίστει *Disp.Phot.*(M.88.572C); **2.** their doctrine πνεῦμα γνώσεως... ἐν γ. προέβαλε τὸν μονογενῆ Clem.*exc.Thdot.*7(p.108.3ff.; M.9.657B); fall of an aeon attributed to desire to snatch τὸ ὑπὲρ τὴν γ. *ib.* 31(p.117.10; M.9.676A); beginning of perfection is γ. ἀνθρώπου [i.e. Adamas, the heavenly man], Hipp.*haer.*5.6(p.78.13ff.; M.16. 3126B).

H. *relationship* with a person ἡ θεία γραφὴ γ. οἶδε τὴν οἰκειότητα Cyr.*Jo.*6.1(4.652D); hence *sexual intercourse,* Clem.*str.*3.17(p.244.6; M.8.1208A); Hipp.*haer.*5.25(p.126.21; M.16.3194B).

I. *list, order, certificate* ἐπιδίδωσιν αὐτῷ...γ. ξενίου πέντε κεντηναρίων χρυσίου Leont.N.*v.Jo.Eleem.*11(p.21.15); γ. συνηθείων ἃς παρεῖχον...τῶν στενῶν οἱ ναύκληροι *IGC As.Min.*4.17.

γνώστης, ὁ, *one who knows*; **1.** divine, of Christ ὁ...τῶν κρυπτῶν γ. *A.Xanthipp.*28(p.78.17); τὸν πάντων γ. ‡Just.*monarch.*1(M.6. 313B); as one of divine names, Dion.Ar.*d.n.*1.6(M.3.596B); **2.** human, *A.*(*Pass.*)*Andr.*4(p.48.11); of bishops as οἱ γ. τῶν γραφῶν *Const. App.*2.25.7; equivalent to *seer, diviner,* Cyr.*Am.*31(3.281D); τοὺς μάντεις γ. ἐκάλουν, ὡς καὶ γινώσκειν τὰ κεκρυμμένα οἰομένους καὶ προγινώσκειν τὰ μηδέπω γεγενημένα Thdt.*qu.32 in 4Reg.*(1.531).

γνωστικός, I. adj.; **A.** *of* or *for knowing*; **1.** *cognitive* opp. practical τῆς ἀληθείας τὸ μέν ἐστι γ., τὸ δὲ ποιητικόν ἐρρύηκεν δὲ ἀπὸ τοῦ θεωρητικοῦ Clem.*str.*6.11(p.477.25; M.9.312C); Dion.Ar.*myst.*1.3 (M.3.1001A); Max.*ambig.*(M.91.1205D); **2.** *producing knowledge* εἶδος ...γ. διδασκαλίας Clem.*str.*6.15(p.492.3; M.9.344A); id.*ecl.*16(p.141. 10; M.9.705B); **3.** of the *Gnostic* sects τῆς λεγομένης γ. αἱρέσεως Iren.*haer.*1.11.1(M.7.560A); v. II.B.

B. applied to spiritual life; **1.** *wise, prudent, enlightened* ἡ πίστις ἡ γ. Clem.*str.*6.8(p.466.6; M.9.289B); *ib.*6.9(p.469.32; 297A); ἀνὴρ ὁ γ. πάντα ἐν μέτρῳ ἐργάζεται Ephr.2.101D; of teachers ὁ γ. Μωυσῆς Clem.*str.*5.11(p.376.6; 112B); Pall.*h.Laus.*47(p.138.2; M.34. 1196D); Evagr.Pont.*Gnost.*ap.Socr.*h.e.*4.23.70(M.67.520C); Thdr. Stud.*epp.*2.110(M.99.1372B); **2.** *spiritual*; **a.** in gen., esp. in Clem., of a way of life τὴν γ. ἀγωγήν Clem.*str.*6.15(p.498.1; M.9.356A); *ib.*5.4(p.342.13; 45B); which leads to heaven, *ib.*4.6(p.262.11; M.8. 1244A); of virtue, *ib.*4.22(p.313.5; 1356B); of perfection, *ib.*5.4 (p.342.2; M.9.45A); βρώματος γ. μεταλαμβάνουσιν *ib.*(p.342.10; 45A); of spiritual exercises, *ib.*4.21(p.306.33; 1344A); of truth, *ib.*5.14 (p.384.21; 129B); of love, ref. 1Cor.13 δι' ἀγάπης γ. ἀγαπήσω *ib.*4. 18(p.297.16; 1320B); opp. φόβος, *ib.*4.21(p.306.4; 1341A); bracketed with πνευματικός, *ib.*5.4(p.341.22; 44C); in title of *Stromateis* at end of several books, e.g. ὁ...κατὰ τὴν ἀληθῆ φιλοσοφίαν γ. ὑπομνημάτων πρῶτος...Στρωματεύς *str.*1.29(p.112.5; 929A); *ib.*3.18(p.247.15; 1213B); **b.** as comprising both action and contemplation, Clem. *ecl.*37(p.148.9; M.9.717A) cit. s. πρακτικός; πρᾶξις καὶ θεωρία μίαν κατὰ σύνοδον σοφίαν ἀποτελεῖ γ. *Schol.*32 in Max.*qu.Thal.*63(M.90. 692A); **c.** of spiritual interpretation of scripture τὴν διάπτυξιν... τὴν γ. τῶν γραφῶν Clem.*str.*6.15(p.498.9; M.9.356B); *ib.*6.16(p.499. 13; 357C); of esoteric tradition, handed down by apostles through oral teaching τὴν γ. παράδοσιν, ἣν μεταδοῦναι αὐτοῖς παρὼν [sc. S. Paul] παροῦσι ποθεῖ, οὐ γὰρ δι' ἐπιστολῆς οἷά τε ἦν ταῦτα μηνύεσθαι *ib.*5.10(p.369.16f.; 100A); *ib.*6.7(p.462.19; 284A); **3.** *perfect,* i.e. having attained to fullness of Christian life (not always clearly distinguishable from 2.a) τὸν γ. ἡμᾶς παρακελεύεται βίον ἔργῳ τε καὶ λόγῳ ζητεῖν, τὴν ἀλήθειαν προτρέπει Clem.*str.*4.6(p.263. 27; M.8.1245C); which life leads to God, *ib.*4.23(p.315.29; 1361A); and is a perfect μαρτυρία, *ib.*4.4(p.255.21; 1229A); *ib.*4.21(p.306.3; 1341A); of the soul γυμνὴν τῆς ὑλικῆς δορᾶς γενομένην τὴν γ. ψυχήν *ib.*5.11(p.371.8; M.9.104A); which is an earthly image of God, *ib.*7. 11(p.46.19; 489B); *ib.*7.2(p.10.7; 416C); compared with wise virgins, *ib.*7.12(p.52.10; 500C); ἡσυχαστὴς γ. οὐ δεηθήσεται λόγων Jo.Clim. *scal.*27(M.88.1097B); **4.** *contemplative* or *mystical,* freq. in connexion with θεωρία and kindred words μεταλαμβάνειν...τῶν γ. θεωρημάτων Clem.*str.*6.17(p.509.16; M.9.381B); *ib.*7.3(p.10.27; 417A); Eus.*p.e.*11.6(519B; M.21.860D) cit. s. θεωρητικός; ἐν πνεύματι γ. θεωρίας Max.*ambig.*(M.91.1237D); id.*ep.*1(M.91.380B); opp. πρακτικός, Or.*Jo.*19.8(2; p.307.32; M.14.541A) cit. s.v.; γεύεται δὲ καὶ ὁ θεολόγος...τῆς πείρας τῆς γ. καὶ ὁ γνωστικός...ἔχει μέρος τῆς θεωρητικῆς πρὸς ὀλίγον ἀρετῆς Diad.*perf.*72(p.90.1); and which effects purification, Geo.Pis.*hex.*26(M.92.1428A).

II. masc. as subst., *one who possesses true knowledge*;

A. the *perfect Christian,* with Clement a t.t. expressing his ideal of holiness, described esp. in *str.*7; his twofold perfection τέλος...τοῦ γ. ... διττόν, ἐφ' ὧν μὲν ἡ θεωρία ἡ ἐπιστημονική, ἐφ' ὧν δὲ ἡ πρᾶξις Clem.*str.*7.16(p.72.7; M.9.541A); a friend of God who loves him, *ib.*7.11(p.49.12; 496A); a mirror of divine perfection ἡ τοῦ γ. ὁσιότης...τὴν εὐεργεσίαν ἐπιδείκνυσι τοῦ θεοῦ *ib.*7.7(p.31.28; 457C); constant in prayer, *ib.*(p.30.30; 456C); through which he rises above the world, *ib.*(p.30.25; 456B); not subject to passions, *ib.*6.9(p.468.27; 296A); *ib.*7.3(p.13.19; 424A); Diad.*perf.*72(p.88.23) al.; a lover of truth, Clem.*str.*4.3(p.252.9; M.8.1221B); perfectly orthodox and living acc. the gospel, *ib.*7.16(p.73.15,19; M.9.544A,B); desiring both his own and his neighbour's salvation, *ib.*7.3(p.12.3; 420B); which he identifies with his own advantage, *ib.*7.9(p.39.8; 473C); doing good only for love, *ib.*4.22(p.308.16; M.8.1345B); eager to obey and ready for martyrdom, *ib.*4.4(p.254.6; 1225B); a deified man, *ib.*7.13(p.58.25; M.9.513B); *ib.*4.23; (p.314.23; M.8. 1360A); who combines action with contemplation, ‡Max.*cap.al.*188 (M.90.1445A); but esp. of contemplative opp. active Christian, *ib.*162(1440A); whose main concern is θεωρία, Clem.*str.*7.3(p.12. 22; M.9.421A); who prays that his θεωρία may continue and increase, *ib.*7.7(p.34.26; 465B); and teaches it to others, *ib.*7.1(p.4. 22; 405A); whose end is ἡ θεωρία τῶν ἀρετῶν ‡Max.*cap.al.*143(M. 90.1434C); who is the true Christian though believed insane by his brethren, Max.*schol.d.n.*7.3(M.4.356A); pursued by demons πολεμοῦσιν οἱ δαίμονες...τοὺς δὲ γ., ἵνα ἐγχρονίζωσιν ἐν αὐτοῖς οἱ ἐμπαθεῖς λογισμοί id.*carit.*2.90(M.90.1013B); acc. Socr.*h.e.*4.23.60(M. 67.520A) ὁ Γ., title of a book by Evagrius Ponticus, prob. dealing with the ideal of the contemplative monk; cf. ἐπιστήμη.

B. plur., *Gnostics,* members of one or more sects; modern use of term for a variety of 2nd-cent. dualistic heresies is prob. of 18th-cent. origin. Irenaeus seems to have confined its use to Ophites, Valentinians, and Carpocratians, *haer.*1.11.1(M.7.560A); cf.*ib.*1.30.15(704A); 1.31.3(705A,B); split into various schools, *ib.*2. 13.10(748B); comp., iron. of some Valentinians who invent other aeons antecedent to Βυθός and Σιγή: τελείων τελειότεροι φανῶσιν ὄντες, καὶ γνωστικῶν γνωστικώτεροι *ib.*1.11.5(569A); and of Carpocratians, *ib.*1.25.6(685B); so also Hipp. of Naassenes, otherwise called Ophites, Hipp.*haer.*5.2(p.77.4; M.16.3123A); *ib.*5.6(p.78.2; 3125A); and their offshoots, *ib.*5.23(p.125.23; 3191C); Epiph., also of Ophites, *haer.*26 passim, which states their doctrines in detail; and of Valentinians, *ib.*31.1(p.382.18; M.41.473B); Jo.D.*haer.*26(M. 94.692B); of followers of false γνῶσις of 1Tim.6:20, Chrys.*hom. 18.2 in 1Tim.*(11.655C).

III. neut. as subst.;

A. *sphere of* (*greater*) *knowledge,* in comp. ἐπὶ τὸ ὑψηλότερον καὶ γνωστικώτερον ἐπεκτεινόμενος Iren.*haer.*1.11.3(M.7.565A).

B. *cognitive faculty,* Dion.Ar.*c.h.*7.1(M.3.205C); *ib.*13.3(304A).

γνωστικῶς, 1. *intellectually, concerning knowledge* (opp. faith) τὸ αὐτὸ γοῦν ἔργον...ἤτοι διὰ πίστεως ἢ καὶ γ. ἐνεργούμενον Clem.*str.*4. 18(p.298.17; M.8.1321B); Dion.Ar.*c.h.*14(M.3.321A); *ib.*15.3(332A); **2.** *wisely* κατ' ἐκλογὴν τῶν καλῶν τἀγαθὸν ἑλομένῳ γ. Clem.*str.*4. 23(p.313.27; M.8.1357A); Max.*or.dom.*(M.90.889A); **3.** *spiritually*; **a.** ref. spiritual life τὸν γ. πολιτευόμενον Clem.*str.*4.5(p.257.33; M.8. 1233C); *ib.*3.10(p.227.19; 1172A); ἀπανδροῦσθαι γ. *ib.*4.21(p.307.5; 1344B); of love, *ib.*6.9(p.468.23; M.9.296A); νόμος...τῆς καινῆς [sc. διαθήκης]...τὸν νοῦν γ. ἀναβιβάζει Max.*cap.*1.67(M.90.1205C); in sense of *perfectly* ὁ μίαν ἔχων ἀρετὴν γ. πάσας ἔχει Clem.*str.*2.18(p.155. 3; M.8.1020A); *ib.*4.7(p.272.22; 1265A); Max.*qu.Thal.*25(M.90.333B); **b.** of spiritual (mystical) interpretation of scripture ὁ νόμος πνευματικὸς ὢν καὶ γ. νοούμενος Clem.*str.*3.12(p.234.20; M.8.1184C); γνωστικώτερον...ὁ τόπος οὗτος τῆς γραφῆς κατανοούμενος Max.*qu. Thal.*63(M.90.681C).

***γνωστοποιέω,** *make known, Hymn.*ap.*Mir.Geo.*(p.150.20).

γνωστός, *known, knowable*; *filled with, characterized by, knowledge* γ. δὲ ἡ πίστις Clem.*str.*2.4(p.121.7; M.8.948A); *giving knowledge* τοῦ 'τῆς ζωῆς' ξύλου καὶ τοῦ γ. 'καλοῦ τε καὶ πονηροῦ' Meth. *symp.*3.7(p.34.10; M.18.72A); Pall.*h.Laus.*25(p.80.18; τοῦ γινώσκειν M.34.1091A); Procl.CP *or.*6.3(M.65.725A); Bas.Sel.*or.*3.2(M.85.52C); plur. as subst., *relatives* γνωστοὺς οὖν ἔθος ἀποκαλεῖν τοῖς Ἑλλήνων παισὶν οὐχ ὅπως τοὺς κατὰ γένους οἰκείους μόνον, ἀλλὰ καὶ ὁμαίμους ἀδελφούς Cyr.*Jo.*6.1(4.652D).

γνωστῶς, *intelligibly, clearly,* of Psalms which foretell Christ ἐν ἀπορρήτῳ δὲ καὶ οὐ γ. Or.*Jo.*19.5(1; p.304.3; M.14.533B); ref. Ex. 33:13 τῷ...Μωσῇ γ. ἰδεῖν αἰτήσαντι τὸν θεόν Thdt.*Ezech.*3:9(2.703); explained τὸ γ. ὁρώμενον εὔδηλον ὡς θεωρίᾳ μόνον, καὶ οὐκ αἰσθήσει καταλαμβάνεται Didym.*Ex.*33:13(M.39.1113D).

***γνωτοκτόνος, ὁ,** a *fratricide,* Eudoc.*Cypr.*1.39(M.85.833C).

[*]**γνωφερός,** for γνοφερός, *gloomy*, †Anast.S.*relat*.40(p.85).

γογγύζω, *murmur, grumble*; pass., *be murmured at* or *against*, of bishops τί μέγα ἂν γογγυσθῶμεν, οἱ τοῦ σταυρωθέντος διάκονοι; Gr.Nyss.*castig*.(M.46.516D); of Moses εἰ μὴ ὁ γογγυσθεὶς ἱκέτευσεν, οὐκ ἂν τὴν τιμωρίαν διέφευγεν Ast.Am.*hom*.13(M.40.361B).

γογγυστικός, *inclined to grumble*, neut. as subst. πάτριον γὰρ τὸ γ. τοῖς θεομάχοις οὐκ ἐπιστραφήσεται Germ.CP *or*.2(M.98.244C).

***γογγύστρια,** ? adj. fem., *cooing* ἡ περιστερὰ γ. ‡Caes.Naz.*dial*. 140(M.38.1072).

γοητεία, ἡ, *magic, witchcraft*; **1.** lit., pagan explanation of Christ's miracles, Or.*Cels*.2.49(p.171.16; M.11.873A); pagan designation of Christianity ἄλλος τῶν ἐκ τῆς αὐτῆς γ. Cels.*ib*.2.55(p.178.26; 884C) etc.; **2.** met., *magic of Nature, deceitful attraction of world of sense*, as in Philo and Plotinus ἡ ἡδονὴ...νύκτωρ ἐν αὐτοῖς τοῖς ἐνυπνίοις μετὰ γ. ... ἐπιβουλεύουσα Clem.*str*.2.20(p.178.18; M.8.1065A); hidden in pagan mysteries, id.*prot*.2(p.11.12; M.8.69B) cit. s. ἐγκρύπτω; defined γ. δὲ ἀκούσας, νόησόν μοι τὴν ποικίλην τῆς ζωῆς ταύτης ἀπάτην, δι' ἧς οἱ ἄνθρωποι...εἰς ἀλόγων μορφὰς μεταπλάττονται Gr.Nyss.*v.Mos*.(M.44.428C); of pleasures of present life ἡ διὰ τῶν ἡδονῶν γ. id.*hom.11 in Cant*.(M.44.996B); opp. εὐσέβεια, id.*Pss.titt*.A 7(M.44.457A).

γοητεύ-ω, *bewitch*; **1.** lit., δακτυλίους Ἐξηκέστου...γεγοητευμένους Clem.*str*.1.21(p.83.4; M.8.868C); ὁ μάγος [sc. S. Thomas]...ἐλαίῳ καὶ ὕδατι καὶ ἄρτῳ...σὲ οὐδέπω ἐγοήτευσεν *A.Thom*.A 152(p.261.16); **2.** met., *beguile, entice, seduce*, of Devil τὸ θηρίον ~ον καταδουλοῦται ...τοὺς ἀνθρώπους Clem.*prot*.1(p.8.3; M.8.61C); †Dion.Al.*fr.1 in Job* (p.202.7); of sinful pleasures that beguile soul, Meth.*symp*.6.5 (p.70.5; M.18.121A); of women, Isid.Pel.*epp*.1.213(M.78.317A); of Potiphar's wife, *ib*.2.236(673C); of deceivers in gen., Ammon.*Ac*. 17:32f.(M.85.1568C); **3.** *use artifices* ὁ δὲ ἡμέτερος διδάσκαλος οὐδέν τι τοιοῦτο ἐγοητεύσατο *Hom.Clem*.3.15.

γοήτης, ὁ, *sorcerer*, Leont.Abb.*v.Gr.Agr*.53(M.98.641B).

γοητικός, *magic, of witchcraft* γ. πράγματος *Apoc.Adam* 4(p.142); γ. βίβλους Gr.Naz.*or*.24.12(M.35.1184A); of staffs of Egyptian magicians γ. ξύλα Gr.Nyss.*v.Mos*.24(M.44.308C); Chrys.*hom.8.4 in 2Cor*.(10.497B); γ. μαγγανείαις Thphn.*chron*.p.11(M.108.85A).

***γοητόστομος,** *bewitching with* one's *speech*, of Eve γύναι γ. ‡Chrys.*hom.in Ps.92*:3(5.622E).

***γοήτρια, ἡ,** *sorceress*, *M.Pers*.3.4(p.442.8); Agath.*v.Gr.Ill*.86 (p.44).

***γοητρίς, ἡ,** *sorceress*, Gr.Nyss.*engast*.(p.63.22; M.45.108A).

γομάρι(ο)ν, τό, *load of a beast*, Jo.Mosch.*prat*.24(M.87.2869B,C); Dor.*doct*.7.3(M.88.1700D).

***γομᾶτος,** *laden, filled* δόρκωνα...γ. σίτου Leont.N.*v.Jo.Eleem*.10 (p.19.7).

***γομεύς, ὁ,** *loader, stevedore*, *CG–CI* 1(p.123).

γομ-όω ([*]γωμόω), **1.** *load*, γωμ-, *T.Job* 9(p.109.1); *ib*.25(p.118.13); Adam.*dial*.1(p.26.27; M.11.1737A); intrans., of the waxing moon ὁ τῆς σελήνης φόρτος, ἵνα ἄρξηται πάλιν ἀπὸ νεομηνίας ~οῦν Epiph.*haer*.66.23(p.51.17; M.42.69A); met., c. dupl. acc. ~ώσας τὸν ἀέρα λόγους *Dial.Tim.et Aquil*.(79 v°); **2.** *fill* ~οῦνται...οἱ...λάκκοι Cyr.S.*v.Euthym*.44(p.66.4, v.l. γεμοῦνται); ἐγομώθησαν *ib*.(p.66.9, v.l. ἐγεμίσθησαν).

***γομφότομος,** *pierced* or *fastened with nails*, Nonn.*par.Jo*.19:15 (M.43.901A).

***γομφώδης,** *articulated*, ‡Caes.Naz.*dial*.140(M.38.1077).

γομφωτός, *fastened with nails*, Nonn.*par.Jo*.19:15(M.43.901A).

***γονατίς, ἡ,** *knot* or *joint* of a reed, Epiph.*haer*.64.68(p.513.15; M.41.1189D).

***γόνατον, τό,** *knee*, *Apoc.Paul*.34(p.58).

γονατόομαι, *be furnished with knees*; exeg. Phil.2:10 λέγομεν μὴ πάντως τὰ ἐπουράνια ἔχειν σώματα γεγονατωμένα Or.*comm.in Eph*.3:14(p.410).

***γονάχιον, τό,** *covering*, prob. *cloak*, used alternately with παλλίν, Leont.N.*v.Jo.Eleem*.21(p.38.9f.); *ib*.(p.39.14).

γονεύς, ὁ, *parent*; of Christ and Church, apostles and prophets, as spiritual parents of believers, ‡Petr.I Al.*phys*.21; of Athanasius as spiritual parent, Constantius Imp.ap.Ath.*h.Ar*.24(M.25.721B).

[*]**γονία, ἡ,** for γωνία, *corner*, *A.Pil*.B 15.5(p.321).

***γονικάρχης, ὁ,** *one who has right of ownership by inheritance* κυριεύσει ὁ γ. *Nomoc*.105; *ib*.106.

γονικός, **1.** *ancestral, parental* τῷ πλούτῳ...γ. *Asen*.14(p.55.14); Cyr.S.*v.Euthym*.47(p.68.10); Jo.Mosch.*prat*.188(M.87.3065B); **2.** neut. as subst., *ancestral property*; sing., *Nomoc*.105; plur., *A.Thom*.A 61(p.177.20).

***γονιμοποιός,** *fertilizing*, Dion.Ar.*c.h*.15.8(M.3.337A).

γονιμότης, ἡ, *fertility, fecundity*; **1.** lit., Cyr.*Mal*.39(3.860C); Dion.Ar.*c.h*.15.9(M.3.337C); of BMV ἡ ἄχραντος γ. Horm.*ep.Epiph*. (p.58.33; M.*PL*.63.520D); **2.** met., of divine fecundity ἀδύνατον γὰρ τὸν θεὸν...ἔρημον τῆς φυσικῆς γ. ἡ δὲ γ. ... ἐκ τῆς ἰδίας οὐσίας, ὅμοιον κατὰ φύσιν γεννᾶν ‡Cyr.*Trin*.7(6[3].9C; M.77.1133A) = Jo.D.*f.o*.1.8 (M.94.812B); of Trin., Dion.Ar.*d.n*.1.4(M.3.592A) cit. s. ἔκφανσις; Ant.Mon.*hom*.1(M.89.1433C); of divine fecundity received into the mind, Max.*ambig*.(M.91.1260D).

***γονοποιός,** *fertilizing, generating*; of soul held by some philosophers to be ὕδωρ γ., ‡Just.*coh.Gr*.7(M.6.256B); Hermias *irris*.1 (M.6.1169A).

γόνυ, τό, *knee*, γόνυ (γόνατα) τίθημι, κλίνω, κάμπτω *bend one's knees*, in posture of Christian prayer, v. γονυκλισία; **1.** in private prayer; **a.** in gen. τοὺς...στρατιώτας...γ. θέντας ἐπὶ τὴν γῆν κατὰ τὸ οἰκεῖον ἡμῖν τῶν εὐχῶν ἔθος Eus.*h.e*.5.5.1(M.20.441A); κλίνας τὰ γ. καὶ τὰς χεῖρας ἐκτείνας προσηύχετο Ath.*v.Anton*.54(M.26.921A); Nil. *epp*.1.57(M.79.121A); Jo.Clim.*scal*.15(M.88.900C); of Christ as man, proving his bodily incarnation, ‡Ath.*serm.fid*.24(p.20; M.26.1277C); **b.** esp. of intercession ἔκλιναν τὰ γ. ὑπὲρ αὐτοῦ πρὸς τὸν κύριον *A.Phil*.31(p.16.17); of S. James κείμενος ἐπὶ τοῖς γ., καὶ αἰτούμενος ὑπὲρ τοῦ λαοῦ ἄφεσιν, ὡς ἀπεσκληκέναι τὰ γ. αὐτοῦ δίκην καμήλου Heges.ap.Eus.*h.e*.2.23.6(M.20.197A); and as sign of sorrow for sins θεὶς τὰ γ. ἐξωμολογούμην τῷ κυρίῳ πάλιν τὰς ἁμαρτίας μου Herm. *vis*.3.1.5; met. παιδεύθητε εἰς μετάνοιαν, κάμψαντες τὰ γ. τῆς καρδίας ὑμῶν *1Clem*.57.1; cf.*Const.App*.2.22.14; **c.** as ascetical exercise, of Palestinian monks εἰσὶ δὲ γονάτων αὐτοῖς συχναὶ καὶ ἀδιάκοποι κλίσεις Evagr.*h.e*.1.21(p.32.6; M.86.2481C); ‡Sophr.H.*v.Mar.Aeg*. 1.9(M.87.3704D); **2.** liturg.; **a.** at beginning of anaphora after penitents and catechumens have left, deacon says: ὅσοι πιστοί, κλίνωμεν γ. *Lit*.ap.*Const.App*.8.10.2; **b.** forbidden on Sunday κυριακὴν δὲ χαρμοσύνης ἡμέραν ἄγομεν διὰ τὸν ἀναστάντα ἐν αὐτῇ, ἐν ᾗ οὐδὲ γ. κλίνειν παρειλήφαμεν Petr.I Al.*ep.can*.15(M.18.508B); and in Paschaltide, *A.Paul*.(p.1.13); ἐπειδή τινές εἰσιν ἐν τῇ κυριακῇ γ. κλίνοντες καὶ ἐν ταῖς τῆς πεντηκοστῆς ἡμέραις...ἑστῶτας ἔδοξε τῇ ἁγίᾳ συνόδῳ τὰς εὐχὰς ἀποδιδόναι τῷ θεῷ CNic.(325)*can*.20; οὐδ' ἐν ταῖς εὐχαῖς γ. κλίνομεν...τοὺς γὰρ τῆς κατὰ θεὸν ἀναστάσεως ἠξιωμένους οὐκέτ' αὖθις οἷόν τε ἐπὶ γῆς πίπτειν Eus.*pasch*.5(M.24.700C); custom traced back to Irenaeus τὸ δὲ ἐν τῇ κυριακῇ μὴ κλίνειν γ. σύμβολόν ἐστι τῆς ἀναστάσεως...ἐκ τῶν ἀποστολικῶν δὲ χρόνων ἡ τοιαύτη συνήθεια ἔλαβε τὴν ἀρχήν, καθώς φησιν ὁ μακάριος Εἰρηναῖος ‡Just.*qu.et resp*.115(M.6.1364B) = Iren.*fr*.7(M.7.1233A); later detailed legislation: Sev.Ant.ap.*cat.Ac*.2:1(p.16.11); ταῖς κυριακαῖς μὴ γ. κλίνειν ἐκ τῶν...πατέρων κανονικῶς παρελάβομεν...δῆλον τοῖς πιστοῖς καθιστῶμεν, ὥστε μετὰ τὴν ἐν τῷ σαββάτῳ ἑσπερινὴν τῶν ἱερωμένων πρὸς τὸ θυσιαστήριον εἴσοδον...μηδένα γ. κλίνειν μέχρι τῆς ἐφεξῆς κατὰ τὴν κυριακὴν ἑσπέρας, καθ' ἣν μετὰ τὴν ἐν τῷ λυχνικῷ εἴσοδον αὖθις τὰ γόνατα κάμπτοντες CTrull.*can*.90; spiritual interprn. πεντηκοστὴ γάρ ἐστιν ἀνάστασις ψυχῆς...τοῦτο γὰρ καὶ σύμβολόν ἐστι τὸ μὴ κλίνειν ἡμᾶς γ. ἐν τῇ ἁγίᾳ ἐκκλησίᾳ πᾶσαν τὴν πεντηκοστήν Dor.*doct*.15.1(M.88.1789A); τὸ μὴ κλίνειν γ. τῇ ἀναστασίμῳ ἡμέρᾳ τῆς ἁγίας κυριακῆς, σημαίνει τὴν τῆς καταπτώσεως ἡμῶν ἀνόρθωσιν γενομένην διὰ τῆς...τοῦ Χριστοῦ ἀναστάσεως. τὸ δὲ μέχρι τῆς πεντηκοστῆς μὴ κλίνειν γ., ἔστι τὰς ἑπτὰ ἡμέρας μετὰ τὸ ἅγιον πάσχα ἑπταπλουμένας κρατεῖν τῇ διακαινησίμῳ ‡Germ.CP *contempl*.(M.98.392C); **c.** γ. κλίνοντες *penitents*, either as special category of penitents or more prob. in gen. of those supplicating for reconciliation and undergoing discipline, CNeocaes.*can*.5 cit. s. κατηχέω; **d.** at renunciation of Devil, Chrys.*hom.2.7 in 2Cor*.(10.438D); **3.** ref. Phil.2:10 ἐπὶ τῆς ἀναστάσεως...ὅτε πάντες...ἄγγελοι, οἵ τε ἄνθρωποι καὶ...νεκροὶ ἀνιστάμενοι γ. κλινοῦσιν ἐν τῷ ὀνόματι Ἰησοῦ τῷ θεῷ Cosm.Ind.*top*.2(M.88.132A).

γονυκλινέω, *kneel*, Ph.Carp.*Cant*.88(M.40.85C).

γονυκλινής, *on bended knee, kneeling*, *Hom.Clem*.3.1; Eus.*v.C*. 4.67(p.145.16; M.20.1221B).

***γονυκλισία, ἡ,** *bending the knee, genuflexion*, v. γόνυ; **1.** in private prayer; **a.** of kneeling posture in prayer, Clem.*exc.Thdot*.84 (p.132.20; M.9.697A); Nil.*epp*.1.87(M.79.121A); **b.** esp. in intercession, Marc.Diac.*v.Porph*.20; Leont.N.*v.Jo.Eleem*.26(p.54.10); and as sign of penitence ἡ γ. δὲ ὅτι ἀναγκαία ἐστίν, ὅτε τις μέλλει τῶν ἰδίων ἐπὶ θεοῦ ἁμαρτημάτων κατηγορεῖν Or.*or*.31.3(p.396.21; M.11.552A); ἐπαύσαντο αἱ ἀποστασίαι [i.e. after the persecutions], καὶ ἤκμασαν αἱ γ. Ast.Soph.*hom.5 in Ps.5*(M.40.436A); performed before confession, †Jo.Jej.*poenit*.(M.88.1889D); imposed as a penance, Thdr.Stud.*epp*.2.219(M.99.1661A); τὸ δὲ ἐπιτίμιον, γ. πεντεκαίδεκα *ib*.(1661D); **c.** among monks, as ascetical exercise, Nil.*epp*.3.68(M.79.429D); where genuflexions were multiplied πολλὰς ὥρας γ. ποιῶν ηὔχετο Eustrat.v.Eutych.5.38(M.86.2320B); Jo.Mosch. prat.80(M.87.2937C); Thdr.Stud.or.11.16(M.99.817D); ἑβδομήκοντα ἑπτὰ γ. ποιοῦντες V.Alex.Acoem.30(p.680.17); also addressed to men, accompanying a request, Jo.Clim.scal.4(M.88.689B); **d.** symbolizing spiritual submission τὸ κάμπτειν τὰ γόνατα σύμβολόν ἐστιν ἄλλης γ. τῆς γινομένης ἐν τῷ ὑποτάσσεσθαι τῷ θεῷ Or.comm.in Eph. 3:14(p.410); τὴν δὲ νοητὴν γ., οὕτως ὀνομαζομένην παρὰ τὸ ὑποπεπτωκέναι τῷ θεῷ id.or.31.3(p.396.26; M.11.552B); and of sinfulness ἡ...γ. σύμβολόν ἐστι τῆς ἐν ταῖς ἁμαρτίαις πτώσεως ἡμῶν ‡Just. qu.et resp.115(M.6.1364B); Bas.Spir.66(3.56D; M.32.192C) cit. s. διανάστασις; **e.** as synonym of prayer, id.ascet.1.4(2.321D; M.31.877A); αὐτῶν τῇ γ. προσκαρτερούντων Gr.Nyss.mart.2(M.46.760A); **2.** in liturg. prayer; **a.** in gen., of a certain prayer of the synaxis, recited with people kneeling, styled εὐχὴ γονυκλισίας, Serap.euch.12 tit.; of genuflexions after each psalm in divine office, Ath.virg. 20(p.55.22; M.28.276C); εὐχὰς...προστάσσεται [sc. ἡ ἐκκλησία] μετὰ πάσης...γ. ἐν ταῖς τεταγμέναις ὥραις (v.l. ἡμέραις) Epiph.exp.fid.24 (p.525.17; M.42.832A); **b.** ref. eccl. legislation forbidding genuflexion and kneeling on Sunday and at paschal season τῆς πεντηκοστῆς ὅλης τῶν πεντήκοντα ἡμερῶν, ἐν αἷς οὔτε γ. γίνονται, οὔτε νηστεία προστέτακται ib.22(p.523.6; 828A); Phot.nomoc.7.4(M. 104.1076A); ib.7.5(1076C); sometimes also on Saturday σάββατον καὶ κυριακήν· ταύτας τὰς ἡμέρας οὔτε γ. ... βαλεῖν Nomoc.36; ib.290; ib.298; τὰς δὲ σαββατοκυριακὰς καὶ τὰς ἑορτὰς γ. κάτω μὴ ποιῶμεν, ἀλλὰ προσκυνήσεις μόνον Jo.Jej.canonar.3.3(p.440); at Quinquagesima no meat to be eaten until after first genuflexion at vespers, Nomoc.39; **3.** in exorcism μετὰ δευτέραν γ. ἐξέβαλε τὸ πνεῦμα Pall.h.Laus.36(p.107.21; M.34.1180A).

γονυκλιτέω, *kneel*, †Jo.Jej.poenit.(M.88.1916D); †Jo.D.B.J.30(M. 96.1149C).

γονυπετ-έω, *fall on one's knees, genuflect* αἰτεῖ ~ῶν ἀθανασίαν Clem.q.d.s.8(p.165.2; M.9.612C); ib.42(p.190.13; 649C); Eus.v.C.4.22 (M.20.1169A); ἐν κυριακῇ...μήτε ~εῖν...μήτε ἐν πεντηκοστῇ ‡Ath. syntag.2.17(M.28.840A); c. acc. and εἰς, *kneel for* something *to* someone ταῦτα ~ῶν εἰς τὸν ἅγιον Mir.Geo.8(p.97.3).

***γονυπέτησις, ἡ**, *genuflexion*, Thdr.Stud.or.11(M.99.813C).

***Γοραθηνοί, οἱ**, v. *Γορθηνοί.

γοργεύ-ω, act. and med.; **1.** *hasten, move eagerly* towards, Mac. Aeg.hom.4.6(M.34.476D); Nil.epp.1.26(M.79.92C); **2.** *be eager, keen* ~ου ἐν ταῖς προσευχαῖς ‡Ath.renunt.2(M.28.1409C); Ephr.3.272C.

***γοργονεύ-ω**, *be diligent, watchful* ~σον, ἵνα μὴ ἔξω μείνῃς μετὰ τῶν μωρῶν παρθένων Nil.epp.4.1(M.79.545D).

γοργότης, ἡ, **1.** *swiftness*, Anast.S.hod.2(M.89.64C); **2.** *vigour, zeal* ἐν ποίᾳ νήψει καὶ γ. πίστεως Mac.Aeg.hom.5.6(M.34.512C); τὸ... ἐζῶσθαι τὴν ὀσφύν, γοργότητος...σύμβολον Cyr.glaph.Ex.2(1.274C); **3.** *ferocity*, ref. Devil μηχανημάτων γ. Bas.Sel.pasch.2.6(M.28.1089A).

***Γορθηνοί (*Γοραθηνοί, *Γορθηωνοί, *Γοροθηνοί), οἱ**, adherents of early heresy mentioned by Heges.ap.Eus.h.e.4.22.5(Γοραθηνοί; Γορθηωνοί M.20.380A); of Samaritan origin, observing festivals with Jews, Epiph.haer.12(p.205.5ff. Γοροθηνοί, v.l. Γορθηνοί M.41.236Af.); Jo.D.haer.10(M.94.685A); offshoot of Simonians, Thdt.haer.1.1(4. 288).

***γούλα, ἡ**, (Lat. *gula*) *throat*, Leont.N.v.Jo.Eleem.38(p.76.24).

§γοῦνα, ἡ, *fur, fur garment*, Barth.Edess.Agar.(M.104.1405A).

***γουνάριος, ὁ**, *furrier*, Chron.Pasch.p.337(M.92.880A); cf.CG-CI 1(p.56).

§γοώδης, *magic*; neut. plur. as subst., *magic devices*, Eust.engast. 9(p.27.12; M.18.629C).

***γοωδῶς**, *by trickery*, Eust.engast.12(p.35.5; M.18.637C).

Γραικιστί, *in Greek*, CCP(678)act.16(H.3.1384B).

***γραϊκός**, *old-womanish* μυθολογῶν ὕθλῳ γ. Clem.prot.6(p.51.12; M.8.172B); id.paed.3.4(p.252.29; M.8.596B); Chrys.hom.1.1 in 2Thess. (11.511E).

γραῖς, ἡ, *woman of mature years, old woman*, A.Phil.1(p.1.5); Ath.apol.Const.15(M.25.613A); Pall.h.Laus.61(p.155.4; M.34.1228A); id.v.Chrys.8(p.45.18; M.47.27).

γράμμα, τό, **1.** *written character*, ref. Gal.6:11, variously interpreted; of S. Paul's awkward Gr. handwriting ἐνταῦθα οὐδὲν ἄλλο αἰνίττεται, ἀλλ' ὅτι αὐτὸς ἔγραψε τὴν ἐπιστολὴν ἅπασαν...τὸ δέ, πηλίκοις, ἐμοὶ δοκεῖ οὐ τὸ μέγεθος, ἀλλὰ τὴν ἀμορφίαν τῶν γ. ἐμφαίνων λέγειν Chrys.comm.in Gal.6:11(10.727B,C); Thdt.Gal.6:11(3.394); as emphasizing seriousness of his admonitions μείζοσιν ἐχρήσατο γ. ἐμφαίνων ὅτι οὔτε αὐτὸς ἐρυθριᾷ, οὔτε ἀρνεῖται τὰ λεγόμενα Thdr. Mops.Gal.6:11(p.107.23; M.66.912A); as signifying sublimity of doctrine and intimating that it was his own handwriting, Jo.D. Gal.6:11(M.95.817D,820A); **2.** of scripture (v. γραφή); **a.** with distinctive attribute, e.g. ἱερόν, Cyr.ador.4(1.139E); Cosm.Ind.top.2 (M.88.92D); plur. ἱερὰ...ὡς...τὰ ἱεροποιοῦντα καὶ θεοποιοῦντα γ. Clem.prot.9(p.65.5; M.8.197C); Or.Cels.4.27(p.296.15; M.11.1068A); Cyr.inc.unigen.(5^{1}.681A); θεῖον, Gr.Thaum.pan.Or.6(p.18.23; M. 10.1073B); Epiph.haer.80.1(p.485.17; M.42.757A); plur., Or.Cels.4.9 (p.280.23; 1040A); ἅγιον, plur., Or.Jo.6.40(24; p.150.2; M.14.269C); Ath.gent.41(M.25.84B); τῶν ἐκ τοῦ οὐρανοῦ γ. Chrys.hom.19.9 in Mt.(7.257D); **b.** of OT or NT, Or.comm.in Mt.12.3(p.73.17; M.13. 981A); id.Jo.10.30(18; p.203.24; M.14.361A) cit. s. παλαιός; **c.** of particular books τοῦ προφητικοῦ γ. Didym.(‡Bas.)Eun.5(1.301A; M.29.721C); τὰ γ. ἀποστολικὰ τείχη τῶν ἐκκλησιῶν ἐστιν Chrys.hom. in 2Tim.3:1(6.282B); of Canticles, Thdt.Cant.proem.(2.3); **d.** of partic. passages τὸ ἀποστολικὸν γ. τὸ λέγον CNic.(325)can.2; Thdt. rect.conf.6(M.6.1217B); γ. θεῖον ἀντιτιθεὶς ἀγράφῳ παραδόσει ἀνθρώπων Vict.Mc.7:9(p.334.19); **3.** *letter* opp. Spirit (cf. 2Cor.3:6 al.) ὁ νόμος κατὰ τὸ γ. ... τῷ νόμῳ κατὰ τὸ πνεῦμα Or.Jo.13.8(p.232.23; M.14.409C); ib.10.26(17; p.199.24; 353D); ἔνδυμα τῆς ἀσεβείας...ἡ φιλία τοῦ γ. Gr.Naz.or.31.3(p.147.10; M.36.136B); Gr.Nyss.Eun.12 (1 p.286.17; M.45.996A); of OT contrasted with NT πεπαλαίωται τὰ τοῦ γ., ἀνακεκαίνωται τὰ τοῦ πνεύματος Didym.Job 9:5(M.39.1144A); Max.myst.(M.91.684B,C); v. πίστις; **4.** *rescript, imperial letter*, Chrys. exp.in Ps.3(5.1B); γ. βασιλικῶν Evagr.h.e.1.3(p.8.15; M.86.2425C); Chron.Pasch.p.341(M.92.889B); γ. κανονικά issued by bishop to travelling clergy, CLaod.can.41; Bas.ep.224.2(3.343B; M.32.836C); γράμματα τιμῆς *letter of congratulation*, sent by one patriarch to another on his enthronement, Apoll.ep.Diocaes.(p.255.21; M.86. 1969C); **5.** Gnost. interprn. of letters of alphabet, Hipp.haer.6.46 (p.178.3; M.16.3270B) cit. s. ἀπόρροια.

γραμματεύς, ὁ, *scribe*, Jewish καλεῖ μὲν σοφὸν τὸν τῇ Ἑλληνικῇ στωμυλίᾳ κοσμούμενον· γ. δέ, τὸν τῶν Ἰουδαίων διδάσκαλον Thdt. 1Cor.1:20(3.170); believed to be descendants of Simeon, Hipp. ben.Jac.(p.29.19); regarded as one of seven Jewish sects, Epiph. anac.14(p.167.4; M.41.172A); id.haer.17.1(p.214.6; M.41.256A).

γραμματίζω, perf. pass., *be learned* οἱ ⟨ἐν⟩ Κριῷ γεννώμενοι... γεγραμματισμένοι Hipp.haer.4.15(p.50.1; M.16.3083B).

***γραμματοδιακομιστής, ὁ**, *letter-carrier*, Ep.Tib.(p.79.19).

***γραμματοκομιστής, ὁ**, *letter-carrier*, Ep.Abg.ap.Eus.h.e.1.13.8 n. (M.20.121C).

[*]γραμματόκυφος, *that binds under the letter* (of the Law), *of slavery to the letter* ἀπολυθῶ τοῦ γ. ζυγοῦ ‡Meth.Sym.et Ann.8 (M.18.368C).

γραμματοφύλαξ, ὁ, *keeper of records*, Socr.h.e.1.19.6(M.67.128A).

***γραμμιστής, ὁ**, *image designer*, Thphn.chron.p.247(M.108.620B).

γραμμοειδής, *like a straight line*; of lightning, Jo.D.drac.(M.94. 1601C).

***γραοπρεπής**, *old womanish*, Cyr.ador.6(1.197C); ib.(210E); id. Chr.un.(5^{1}.749E).

***γραοπρεπῶς**, *like an old woman*, Cyr.ep.50(p.91.2; 5^{2}.158E).

***γραοτέρα**, comp. fem. formed from γραῦς, *older* γραοτέρας πρεσβυτίδας Epiph.haer.79.4(p.478.28; M.42.745A).

***γραπτοάγραπτος**, *both able to be depicted and not able to be depicted*, of Christ εἴη ἂν οὔτε γραπτός, οὔτε ἄγραπτος· ἀλλὰ γ. ἐξ ἡμισείας συνηνεγμένος. καὶ κατ' οὐδ' ἕτερον τέλειος Thdr.Stud.probl.1 (M.99.477B).

γραπτός, *able to be depicted*; of Christ, Thdr.Stud.probl.1(M.99. 477B).

γραφεῖον, τό, **1.** *pencil, paint brush*, met. γ. νηστείας Jo.Clim. scal.18(M.88.933D); **2.** *writing, book*, applied to third group of OT books (hagiographa), hence of Psalter λέγει...τὸ γ. 1Clem.28.2; also of historical books (Jos., Jud. with Ruth, 1 and 2 Par., 1–4 Reg.), Epiph.mens.4(M.43.244B); Jo.D.f.o.4.17(M.94.1180A,B); cf.Epiph. haer.29.7(p.329.8; M.41.401B); of scripture as a whole, Didym.Trin. 2.8(M.39.608C); of Gnost. books, Epiph.haer.26.12(p.290.19; 349C).

γραφή, ἡ, *writing, written document*;

A. *scripture*; **1.** use of term; **a.** in gen., for OT λέγει γὰρ ἡ γ. 1Clem.34.6; 2Clem.6.8; 14.1; Barn.4.7,11; of OT and NT indifferently (from end of 2nd cent.), Iren.haer.1.1.3(M.7.452A); Or. princ.4.1.1(p.292.11; M.11.341B) cit. s. διαθήκη; Alex.Lyc.Man.5 (p.8.22); τῆς νέας καὶ ἀρχαιοτέρας γ. Cyr.inc.unigen.(5^{1}.678E); ταῖς γ. αὐτῶν [sc. Ἰουδαίων] περιέτυχον καὶ τὰς ὑμῶν [sc. Χριστιανῶν] ἔγνων Pers.(p.9.20); **b.** of individual books: γ. ... εὐαγγελίου [sc. Mt.] Iren.haer.3.1.1(M.7.844B); γ. τοῖς Κορινθίοις ib.3.3.3(850A); of gospels, Clem.paed.1.13(p.152.7; M.8.376B); 1Cor., ib.1.6(p.111.17; 292D); Rom., id.str.4.16(p.292.5; M.8.1305B); Gr.Nyss.diff.ess.6(M. 32.336C); Chrys.hom.1.6 in Mt.(7.13B); of apocryphal writings, Iren.haer.1.20.1(M.7.653A); **c.** of partic. texts; in OT, 1Clem.23.3;

περὶ τῆς γ. ἣν ἔφη Ἡσαΐας Just.*dial*.65.1(M.6.625B); in NT, of Mt. 9:13 ἑτέρα δὲ γ. λέγει *2Clem*.2.4; indifferently in OT or NT, Or. *princ*.4.2.5(p.314.6; M.11.365B); Gr.Nyss.*Apoll*.12(M.45.1145C); accompanied by a title, feature of Mohammedan scriptures ἡ γ. τῆς γυναικός Jo.D.*haer*.101(M.94.769B); γ. τῆς καμήλου τοῦ θεοῦ *ib*. (769D); **2.** distinctive epithets ἱερά, *1Clem*.53.1; Thphl.Ant.*Autol*. 1.14(M.6.1045A); Eus.*h.e*.6.25.1(M.20.580A); ἁγία, Thphl.Ant.*Autol*. 2.19(1081B); Polycr.ap.Eus.*h.e*.5.24.7(M.20.497A); plur., Hipp.*haer*. proem.(p.3.17; M.16.3021A); Or.*mart*.2(p.3.15; M.11.565A); θεία, Thphl.Ant.*Autol*.2.22(1088A); Or.*Cels*.1.6(p.59.32; M.11.668A); Chrys. *hom.58.3 in Gen*.(4.566B); plur., Iren.*haer*.2.27.1(M.7.802C); Or.*Cels*. 2.20(p.149.3; 836C); κανονική, plur., *Cod.Afr*.24; v. θεῖος, θεϊκός, θεόπνευστος, κυριακός; **3.** characteristics; **a.** unity τολμητέον εἰπεῖν πασῶν τῶν γ. εἶναι ἀπαρχὴν τὸ εὐαγγέλιον Or.*Jo*.1.2(4; p.6.5; M.14. 25C); Chrys.*hom.22 in 2Cor.4:13*(M.3.270D) cit. s. σῶμα; **b.** difficulties, intended to lead men to deeper understanding, Or.*princ*.4.2. 9(p.321.6; M.11.373B); σιωπῆς δὲ εἶδος καὶ ἡ ἀσάφεια, ᾗ κέχρηται ἡ γ., δυσθεώρητον κατασκευάζουσα τῶν δογμάτων τὸν νοῦν, πρὸς τὸ τῶν ἐντυγχανόντων λυσιτελές Bas.*Spir*.66(3.56A; M.32.189Bf.); τὴν ἐν ταῖς γ. ἀσάφειαν ἐπ' ὠφελείᾳ τοῦ νοῦ, διεγείρων [sc. God] αὐτοῦ τὴν ἐνέργειαν ἐπετήδευσε †Bas.*Is*.proem.6(1.382B; M.30.128C); due to anthropomorphism, Chrys.*hom.75.2 in Jo*.(8.441A); ἡ γ. τὴν ἀλήθειαν πεζῷ λόγῳ ἡρμήνευσεν Isid.Pel.*epp*.4.67(M.78.1125A); **c.** but unimpaired veracity τὰς γ. τὰς ἀληθεῖς *1Clem*.45.2; αἱ κυριακαὶ γ., τὴν ἀλήθειαν ἀποτίκτουσαι καὶ μένουσαι παρθένοι μετὰ τῆς ἐπικρύψεως τῶν τῆς ἀληθείας μυστηρίων Clem.*str*.7.16(p.66.23; M.9.529B); Epiph.*haer*.9. 2(p.199.11; M.41.225C); Chrys.*hom.68.2 in Jo*.(8.406C); though in *Hom.Clem*. difficult passages of scripture are called 'lies' τὰ τῶν γ. ψευδῆ εὐλόγως πρὸς δοκιμὴν ἔχοντα τυγχάνει, 3.4, 3.5; **d.** role as a tutor, Clem.*prot*.9(p.65.21; M.8.200B); ἐξετάζοντες...εὑρίσκομεν διὰ τῆς τῶν γ. ὁδηγίας Gr.Nyss.*tres dii*(M.45.125D); **e.** sufficiency, Ath.*gent*.1(M.25.4A) cit. s. θεόπνευστος; οὐδὲν ἔλειπεν, οὐδὲ παρεσιώπησε τῶν συμφερόντων ἡμῖν ἡ θεία γ. ‡Chrys.*pseud*.1(8².73B); Thdt.*qu.4 in Gen*.(1.8); Cyr.*glaph.Gen*.2(1.25B); **f.** canon of scripture, v. κανών; **4.** interpretation of scripture; **a.** necessity τὰ ἀσαφῆ τῆς γ. ... οὐ δεῖ ἀναγιγνώσκειν, εἰ μή τις αὐτῶν σαφηνίζει τὸν νοῦν τῇ διηγήσει Or.*comm.in 1Cor*.14:7(*JTS* 10 p.36); Chrys.*hom. 57.1 in Jo*.(8.331E); *ib.53.3*(313B); **b.** gen. rules ἡ ἀλήθεια δὲ οὐκ ἐν τῷ μετατιθέναι τὰ σημαινόμενα εὑρίσκεται,...ἀλλ' ἐν...τῷ βεβαιοῦν ἕκαστον τῶν ἀποδεικνυμένων κατὰ τὰς γ. ἐξ αὐτῶν πάλιν τῶν ὁμοίων γ. Clem.*str*.7.16(p.68.20f.; M.9.533C); οὗτος τῆς γ. ἐστιν ὁ τρόπος, ὡς αἰτιολογίαν τιθεμένης τὰ ἐκ τῆς ἐκβάσεως συμβαίνοντα. καὶ δεῖ πάντα μετὰ ἀκριβείας ἐξετάζειν, καὶ τὸν τρόπον τοῦ λέγοντος, καὶ τὴν ὑπόθεσιν, καὶ τοὺς νόμους τοὺς τῆς γ., εἴ γε μὴ μέλλοιμεν παραλογίζεσθαι Chrys.*hom.81.2 in Jo*.(8.481A); οὐ γὰρ ἀρκεῖ τὸ λέγειν, ὅτι ἐν ταῖς γ. γέγραπται, οὐδὲ ἁπλῶς παρασπῶντας ῥήματα καὶ σπαράσσοντας τὰ μέλη τοῦ σώματος τῶν θεοπνεύστων γ., ἔρημα καὶ γυμνὰ τῆς οἰκείας αὐτῶν συναφείας λαβόντας...ἀλλὰ χρὴ καὶ τὴν ἀκολουθίαν ἀναγνῶναι πᾶσαν id.*hom.in Jer.10:23*(6.160C,D); v. ἀλληγορέω; **c.** threefold sense, elaborated esp. by Or. who developed principles of Philo to facilitate exegesis of difficult texts ὥσπερ γὰρ ὁ ἄνθρωπος συνέστηκεν ἐκ σώματος καὶ ψυχῆς καὶ πνεύματος, τὸν αὐτὸν τρόπον καὶ ἡ οἰκονομηθεῖσα ὑπὸ θεοῦ εἰς ἀνθρώπων σωτηρίαν γ. Or.*princ*.4. 2.4(p.313.4; M.11.365A); thus ἡ...ὁδὸς ποῦ πῶς δεῖ ἐντυγχάνειν ταῖς γ. ... ἐστι τοιαύτη.... τριχῶς ἀπογράφεσθαι δεῖ εἰς τὴν ἑαυτοῦ ψυχὴν τὰ τῶν ἁγίων γραμμάτων νοήματα· ἵνα ὁ μὲν ἁπλούστερος οἰκοδομῆται ἀπὸ τῆς οἱονεὶ σαρκὸς τῆς γ., οὕτως ὀνομαζόντων ἡμῶν τὴν πρόχειρον ἐκδοχήν, ὁ δὲ ἐπὶ ποσὸν ἀναβεβηκὼς ἀπὸ τῆς ὡσπερεὶ ψυχῆς αὐτῆς, ὁ δὲ τέλειος...ἀπὸ τοῦ πνευματικοῦ νόμου *ib*.(p.312.2ff.; 364B); Chrys. *fr.in Pr*.22:20(M.64.728C); Andr.Caes.*Apoc*.proem.(M.106.217C) cit. s. ἀναγωγή; some texts without literal sense εἰσί τινες γ. τὸ σωματικὸν οὐδαμῶς ἔχουσαι...ἔστιν ὅπου οἱονεὶ τὴν ψυχὴν καὶ τὸ πνεῦμα τῆς γ. μόνα χρὴ ζητεῖν Or.*princ*.4.2.5(p.314.6; M.11.365B); περὶ πάσης τῆς θείας γ., ὅτι πᾶσα μὲν ἔχει τὸ πνευματικόν, οὐ πᾶσα δὲ τὸ σωματικόν *ib*.4.3.5(p.331.13; 385B); another interprn. of threefold sense τὸν ποιήσαντα τῇ γ. σῶμα καὶ ψυχὴν καὶ πνεῦμα, σῶμα μὲν τοῖς πρὸ ἡμῶν, ψυχὴν δὲ ἡμῖν, πνεῦμα δὲ τοῖς ἐν τῷ μέλλοντι αἰῶνι κληρονομήσουσι ζωὴν αἰώνιον id.*hom.2 in Lev*.ap.*philoc*.1.30 (p.36.15; M.12.421C); τὴν...γ., ἄνθρωπον...εἶναι· τὴν μὲν παλαιὰν διαθήκην ἔχουσαν σῶμα, ψυχὴν δὲ καὶ πνεῦμα καὶ νοῦν, τὴν καινήν, καὶ πάλιν, ὅλης τῆς ἁγίας γ., παλαιᾶς τέ φημι καὶ νέας, τὸ καθ' ἱστορίαν γράμμα, σῶμα· τὸν δὲ νοῦν τῶν γεγραμμένων...ψυχήν Max. *myst*.6(M.91.684A,B); superiority of spiritual sense ἡ ἁγία γ., τὸ μὲν φαινόμενον γράμμα, παρερχόμενον ἔχουσα· τὸ δὲ κρυπτόμενον τῷ γράμματι πνεῦμα, μηδέποτε τοῦ εἶναι παυόμενον *ib*.(684B); **5.** authority and inspiration; **a.** in gen. scripture to be preserved intact τοῦ προσθέντος ἢ ἀφελόντος τι τῆς γ., ἐπιτιμίαν οὐ τὴν τυχοῦσαν ἔχοντος Iren.*haer*.5.30.1(M.7.1204C); ὅσα...κηρύσσουσιν αἱ θεῖαι γ. ἴδωμεν, καὶ ὅσα διδάσκουσιν ἐπιγνῶμεν...μὴ κατ' ἰδίαν προαίρεσιν...μηδὲ βιαζόμενοι τὰ ὑπὸ τοῦ θεοῦ δεδομένα, ἀλλ' ὃν τρόπον αὐτὸς ἐβουλήθη διὰ τῶν ἁγίων γ. δεῖξαι, οὕτως ἴδωμεν Hipp.*Noët*.9(p.251.6; M.10.817A); μὴ οὖν ἐπίσπειρε ζιζάνια τῷ ἀγρῷ τῆς θείας γ. ‡Ath. *dial.Trin*.2.9(M.28.1169B); ἐὰν δέ τις ἐγκαλῇ τῇ θείᾳ γ. ... καταμανθανέτω πᾶσαν τὴν τῶν ἀνθρωπίνων διακόσμησιν †Bas.*Is*.proem.6 (1.381E; M.30.128B); not to be neglected, Chrys.*hom.85.4 in Mt*. (7.810B); Isid.Pel.*epp*.3.292(M.78.965D); **b.** scripture as rule of faith, Ath.*exp.in Ps*.118:137f.(M.27.504A); ‡Ath.*dial.Trin*.2.3(M.28. 1161B); Gr.Nyss.*Trin*.3(p.73.10; M.32.688A); κανόνι παντὸς δόγματος καὶ νόμῳ κεχρημένοι τῇ ἁγίᾳ γ. ... τοῦτο δεχόμεθα μόνον, ὅ τί περ ἂν ᾖ συμφωνοῦν τῷ τῶν γεγραμμένων σκοπῷ id.*anim.et res*.(M.46.49C); Chrys.*hom.53.3 in Jo*.(8.313B); **c.** inspiration, the work of H. Ghost τὰς γ. ... τὰς διὰ τοῦ πνεύματος τοῦ ἁγίου *1Clem*.45.2; Iren. *haer*.2.28.3(M.7.806Af.) cit. s. πνευματικός; μυρίας ἂν ἔχοιμί σοι γραφὰς παραφέρειν, ὧν οὐδὲ κεραία παρελεύσεται μία...τὸ γὰρ στόμα κυρίου, ἅγιον πνεῦμα, ἐλάλησεν ταῦτα Clem.*prot*.9(p.62.9; M.8.192D); τὰς γ. αἷς πεπιστεύκαμεν κυρίας οὔσας ἐξ αὐθεντείας παντοκρατορικῆς id.*str*.4.1(p.248.21; M.8.1216B); *ib*.5.13(p.382.13; M.9.125B); Or. *princ*.4.1.6(p.301.10; M.11.352B); τῷ ἐν ταῖς θεοπνεύστοις γ. λαλοῦντι πνεύματι id.*Jo*.6.48(29; p.157.2; M.14.284A); ἃ δὲ αἱ γ. φθέγγονται, ταῦτα ὁ δεσπότης ἐφθέγξατο· ὥστε κἂν νεκρὸς ἀναστῇ, κἂν ἄγγελος ἐξ οὐρανοῦ καταβῇ, πάντων ἔστωσαν αἱ γ. ἀξιοπιστότεραι Chrys.*Laz*. 4.3(1.755B); οὐδὲν ἁπλῶς ἐν ταῖς θείαις γ. κεῖται· πνεύματι γὰρ εἰρημέναι εἰσὶν ἁγίῳ id.*hom.50.1 in Jo*.(8.293E); Thdt.*2Tim*.3:16(3.690); *ib*.(691); **d.** scripture and tradition, v. παράδοσις; **6.** scripture and spiritual life; produces deification ὁ δὲ...κατακούσας τῶν γ. ... οἷον ἐξ ἀνθρώπου θεὸς ἀποτελεῖται Clem.*str*.7.16(p.67.15; M.9.532B); τροφὴ ψυχῆς ἡ γ. Euther.*confut*.2(M.28.1314B); all are urged to read it for spiritual advancement, Bas.*reg.br*.95(2.449A; M.31. 1148D); Chrys.*hom.2.6 in Mt*.(7.30B–32B); **7.** use by heretics; **a.** their methods of interprn. τὴν μὲν τάξιν καὶ τὸν εἱρμὸν τῶν γ. ὑπερβαίνοντες, καί, ὅσον ἐφ' ἑαυτοῖς, λύοντες τὰ μέλη τῆς ἀληθείας Iren.*haer*.1.8.1(M.7.521A); κἂν τολμήσωσι προφητικαῖς χρήσασθαι γ. καὶ οἱ τὰς αἱρέσεις μετιόντες, πρῶτον μὲν οὐ πάσαις, ἔπειτα οὐ τελείαις, οὐδὲ ὡς τὸ σῶμα καὶ τὸ ὕφος τῆς προφητείας ὑπαγορεύει Clem.*str*.7.16(p.68.8; M.9.533A); *ib*.(p.73.2f.; 541D); Ath.*exp.Ps*. 67:27(M.27.301B) cit. s. διαιρέω; or complete abandonment of scripture μὴ γὰρ μαθόντες τὰ τῆς γνώσεως τῆς ἐκκλησιαστικῆς μυστήρια,...παρεπέμψαντο τὰς γ. Clem.*str*.7.16(p.69.12; 536B); **b.** appealed to (esp. by Arians) agst. conciliar definitions παρὰ τὸ βούλημα τῆς θεοπνεύστου γ. τοιαῦτα [sc. eternal generation of Son] τετολμήκασι περὶ αὐτοῦ διορίσασθαι *Symb.Ant*.(345)8(p.253.25; M.26.733A); ἐν ταῖς θείαις γ. οὐ γέγραπται περὶ τούτων [sc. ὁμοούσιος and ὁμοιούσιος] *Symb.Sirm.2* ap.Ath.*syn*.28(p.257.6; M.26.741B); *Symb.Sirm.3* ap. Ath.*syn*.8(p.236.11,14; 693B,C); CSel.*ep*.ap.Epiph.*haer*.73.25(p.298. 24; M.42.452A); cf. μαθέτωσαν ἀπὸ τῶν γ., ὅτι καὶ ὁ τὰς αἱρέσεις ἐπινοήσας διάβολος διὰ τὴν ἰδίαν τῆς κακίας δυσωδίαν κιχρᾶται τὰς λέξεις τῶν γ. Ath.*Ar*.1.8(M.26.25C); of Eutyches μόνας δὲ τὰς γ. ἐρευνᾶν, ὡς βεβαιοτέρας οὔσας τῆς τῶν πατέρων ἐκθέσεως CCP(448) *act*.3(*ACO* 2.1.1 p.124.23; H.2.141A).

B. (royal) *edict*, Eus.*v.C*.2.21(p.49.30; M.20.1000A); *ib*.2.23(p.50. 21; 1000D).

C. *indictment, accusation*; in gen., apart from legal proceedings ἀπειθίας...γ. Cyr.*Ps*.36:7(M.69.928B); id.*Jo*.9(4.724B); Thdt.*qu.37 in Gen*.(1.48); id.*Tit*.1:14(3.702).

D. ? *image, picture* ὅπερ μόνον ἐγκαλεῖν ἡμῖν ἔχετε, ὅτι μὴ...ἐν γραφαῖς στεφάνους καὶ θυσίας φέρομεν Just.*1apol*.24.2(M.6.365A conj. ταφαῖς).

E. met. θεοῦ...γ. ... δημιουργία τοῦ κόσμου Clem.*str*.6.16(p.499. 17; M.9.357C).

γραφία, ἡ, *writing, treatise*, Gr.Nyss.*Eun*.11(M.45.873A; λογογραφίας 2 p.265.7).

γραφικός, 1. *of drawing* or *writing*; γ. ἄσκησις as ascetical exercise, Pall.*h.Laus*.13(p.36.14; M.34.1035C); **2.** *of scripture, scriptural*, Mac.Aeg.*hom*.5.24(M.34.492A); Bas.*fid*.6(2.229D; M.31.692A); γ. ... προβάλλει μαρτυρίας Diod.*fat*.(M.103.872B); θεορρύτους πηγὰς γ. Dam.*troph*.2.2.3(p.220.3); †Jo.D.*B.J*.28(M.96.1128A); **3.** *skilled, versed in the scriptures* γ. ἐστιν καὶ μέγας διδάσκαλος *Didasc.Jac*.3.2 (p.53.7); ἐπισκόπους οὓς ἐδόκουν γ. ὑπάρχειν Anast.S.*hod*.(M.89. 185D); γραφικώτατος ὑπάρχων †Anast.S.*relat*.49(p.69); **4.** neut. as subst., *scriptural passage*, Pall.*v.Chrys*.12(p.69.4; M.47.39); Jo. Mosch.*prat*.40(M.87.2893D); plur., *the scriptures*, Gr.Nyss.*Eun*.10 (2 p.242.12; M.45.845A).

γράφ-ω, **1.** *write*; pass., γέγραπται *it stands written* [sc. in scripture] and hence is authoritative; of OT and NT, *1Clem.*4.1; *Barn.* 4.3; Just.*dial.*100.1(M.6.709A); Or.*princ.*3.1.19(p.232.6; M.11.289B); Bas.*ep.*160.3(3.249D; M.32.624C) etc.; more rarely in act. ~ει γάρ, μὴ ἀποκρίνου Didym.*Trin.*3.42(M.39.989B); τὸ γεγραμμένον *passage* or *word of scripture*, *1Clem.*13.1; Or.*fr.12 in Jo.*1:17(p.494.7); ‡Ath. *pass.*21(M.28.221D); plur., ‡*Diogn.*12.1; Or.*Jo.*1.15(p.19.32; M.14. 49B); Bas.*ep.*160.3(3.250D; 625C); **2.** *depict* (fig.), *typify* τὸ τίμιον δὲ τῶν νοημάτων βάθος τὸ πορφυραυγὲς εἰκότως ἴον ~ει Geo.Pis. *carm.*107.19.

***γράψιμον, τό**, *handwriting*, Zos.*alloquia* 12(M.78.1696C).

***γραωδῶς**, *like an old woman*, Or.*Jo.*10.42(26; p.219.25; M.14. 389A).

γρηγορ-έω, *be vigilant, watch*; **1.** as characteristic of God, Gr. Naz.*or.*31.22(p.172.12; M.36.157B); **2.** of spiritual vigilance ~ει ἀκοίμητον πνεῦμα κεκτημένος Ign.*Polyc.*1.3; ass. psalmody, *Pss. Sal.*3.2; with expectation of the Lord, Meth.*symp.*5.3(p.55.18; M. 18.100D); with fasting ἐν ἡμέρᾳ ἂν ~ῇ τις, μὴ νήφῃ δέ, μυρίοις περιπεσεῖται δεινοῖς Chrys.*hom.9.3 in 1Thess.*(11.489D); *ib.*1.3(429D); as defence against Devil, Gr.Nyss.*instit.*(M.46.301A); ὅτι ἂν ~ῶμεν, οὐ δεησόμεθα τῆς ἑτέρων βοηθείας Chrys.*hom.1.3 in 1Thess.*(11. 429E); Cyr.*Lc.*12:35(M.72.744D); *ib.*(745A); **3.** liturg., of paschal vigil ἀγρυπνοῦντες καὶ ἐπὶ τὸ αὐτὸ ἐν τῇ ἐκκλησίᾳ συναθροιζόμενοι ~εῖτε *Const.App.*5.19.3.

γρηγόρησις, ἡ, *wakefulness, vigilance*; **1.** in gen., Hipp.*Dan.* 3.15.5; Epiph.*haer.*16.1(p.210.22; γρήγορσιν M.41.249A); **2.** of spiritual vigilance, *Pss.Sal.*3.2; ἔνυξέ με...ἐπὶ τὴν γ. αὐτοῦ [sc. θεοῦ] *ib.*16.4; ass. sobriety, Epiph.*haer.*26.13(p.293.21; M.41.353B); and fasting, Chrys.*hom.9.3 in 1Thess.*(11.489D); Cyr.*Lc.*12:35(M.72.744D).

***γρηγορητέον**, *one must watch*, Eus.*fr.Lc.*12:39(M.24.564A); Thdr.Stud.*epp.*2.122(M.99.1400C).

***Γρηγοριολόγοι, οἱ**, *those who speak like Gregory* (of Nazianzus), Cosm.Mel.*schol.*proem.(M.38.343).

***γρήγορος**, *wakeful, vigilant*, *Orac.Sib.*1.98; Mac.Aeg.*hom.*7.8 (M.34.528B); neut. as subst., *vigilance*, Serap.*Man.*54(p.78; M.40. 924A).

γρήγορσις, ἡ, *vigilance*, Cyr.*ador.*14(1.509B); id.*Jo.*6.1(4.647C).

[*]**γρήπισμα, τό**, for γρίπισμα, *rapacious act*, *T.Reub.*3.6.

γριπίζω, *seize, lay hold of*, Leont.N.*v.Sym.*42(M.93.1724A); of netting a profit, Gr.Nyss.*ep.*27(p.81.13; M.32.1092).

γριφοειδής, *enigmatical*; of Eunomian manner of argument, Gr. Naz.*or.*28.11(p.38.14; M.36.40A).

***γριφοειδῶς**, *enigmatically*, Zach.Mit.*opif.*(M.85.1081C).

***γρονθίζω**, *beat with fists*, Thphn.*chron.*p.208(v.l. γροθιζόμενον M.108.533B).

γρόνθος, ὁ, *fist*; hence *blow of the fist*, Polyc.*ep.*2.2; *M.Ner.et Ach.*3(p.3.7).

***γρυγμός, ὁ**, *grunting* of a pig, Gr.Mag.*dial.*(tr.Zach.)3.4 (M.*PL.*77.226A) perh. for γρυσμός.

***γρυλλοειδής**, *hideous*, Jo.Jej.*poenit.cont.virg.*(M.88.1972C).

***γρυπόρυγχος**, *hook-nosed*, Jo.Mal.*chron.*10 p.258(M.97.392B).

γρυτάριον, τό, *frivolity* τελευτῶν...καταλιμπάνει τὰ γ. Pall.*h.Laus.* 13(p.37.8; M.34.1035C).

***γυγγλυσμός, ὁ**, = γίγγλυμος, kind of *joint*, Melet.*nat.hom.* synops.(M.64.1120B, v.l. γυγλυσμός).

γυμνάζ-ω, **1.** *train, exercise*, esp. ref. Christian life; of this life as training for next ~όμεθα τῷ νῦν βίῳ, ἵνα τῷ μέλλοντι στεφανωθῶμεν *2Clem.*20.2; for salvation, ‡Dion.Al.*fr.in Lc.22:46*(p.248.2); of martyrs, *M.Thdot.1* 3(p.63.8); of faith requiring training, *Ep. Lugd.*ap.Eus.*h.e.*5.1.43(M.20.425A); Clem.*ecl.*36(p.148.4; M.717A); sometimes provided by heresies, Or.*Cels.*3.13(p.212.26; M.11. 936B); ~ομένων τῶν ἀγαθῶν ἐν αὐτῷ [sc. τῷ κακῷ] Proc.G.*Gen.*1:26 (M.87.113A); divine love being its ultimate cause ἡ ἀγάπη... γυμνάσασα κατασκευάζει τὸν ἴδιον ἀθλητήν Clem.*str.*7.11(p.48.22; M.9.493B); Cyr.*Jo.*3.4(4.276E); in higher stages of spiritual life τοῖς εἰς γνῶσιν ~ουσιν Clem.*str.*6.10(p.471.19; 300C); *ib.*7.7(p.35.5; 465C); esp. organs of moral and spiritual perception διὰ τὴν ἕξιν τὰ αἰσθητήρια γυμνάσαντι πρὸς διάκρισιν καλοῦ καὶ κακοῦ Or.*Cels.* 4.50(p.323.10; M.11.1109B); †Bas.*Is.*172(1.503B; M.30.405A); Cyr.H. *catech.*4.3; ἡ γεγυμνασμένη τὰ αἰσθητήρια ψυχή Gr.Nyss.*hom.4 in Cant.* (M.44.844C); Chrys.*hom.8.4 in Heb.*(12.88E); **2.** *dispute*, Athenag.*res.* 7(p.56.14; M.6.988B); κακῶς γυμνασθὲν κατὰ τοῦ θεοῦ Thdr.Heracl. *Is.*49:15(M.18.1349B); Socr.*h.e.*3.7.4(M.67.392A); **3.** *discuss* ἐπὶ πολὺ γυμνάσας τὸ πρόβλημα Eus.*h.e.*7.7.5(M.20.649A); Ath.*decr.*27(p.23. 20; M.25.465B); id.*ep.Epict.*3(p.6.16; M.26.1056A); Chrys.*hom.55.1 in Mt.*(7.555D); **4.** *examine* γυμνάσωμεν τὰ κατὰ τὸν τόπον Or.*Jo.*32. 24(16; p.467.22; M.14.808C); τὸν περὶ τῆς πίστεως ~ων λόγον Chrys. *hom.10.3 in 1Cor.*(10.84E); **5.** *explain* γύμνασον καὶ τὸν ἄλλον λόγον Or. *hom.1.7 in Jer.*(p.5.31; M.13.261C); Eus.*d.e.*2.3(p.80.4; M.22.144B); σαφέστερον...ἐπὶ ὑποδείγματος αὐτὸ γυμνάσωμεν Chrys.*hom.65.3 in Mt.*(7.647D); **6.** *meditate on* τοὺς περὶ προνοίας καὶ κρίσεως κατὰ σαυτὸν ἀεὶ ~ε λόγους Evagr.Pont.*Gnost.*ap.Socr.*h.e.*4.23.70(M. 67.520C); ~ε τοὺς λόγους τῶν ἁγίων γερόντων Dor.*doct.*4.11(M.88. 1673D); **7.** *investigate* legally ἐν ταῖς ἐπαρχίαις τὰ τῶν ἐπαρχιῶν ~εσθαι Chrys.*ep.Innoc.*1.1(3.516D); Pall.*v.Chrys.*2(p.15.9; M.47.12); Heracl.*nov.*25(p.46); Thphn.*chron.*p.77(M.108.238C).

γυμνασία, ἡ, *exercise, training*; in gen. of spiritual exercise, Iren.*haer.*4.38.2(M.7.1107A) cit. s. αἰσθητήριον; ἀναγκαία γὰρ ἡ γνῶσις...πρὸς ψυχῆς γυμνασίαν Clem.*ecl.*28(p.145.26; M.9.713A); Jo. Clim.*scal.*4(M.88.712A); of fasting, Chrys.*hom.12.2 in 1Tim.*(11. 612A) cit. s. σωματικός; *ib.*(612B); Euthal.Diac.*Ac.*proem.(M.85. 632A); of study of scripture, Dion.Ar.*d.n.*2.9(M.3.648B).

γυμνάσιον, τό, **1.** *exercise, training, discipline*; **a.** in gen. ἄτυφον ἡ αὐτουργία γ. Clem.*paed.*3.10(p.266.15; M.8.625A); opp. αὐτάρκεια: δικαιοσύνης...κοινωνικῆς τὸ γ. *ib.*(p.266.18; 625B); id.*q.d.s.*3(p.161. 26; M.9.608A); Or.*Cels.*proem.5(p.54.25; M.11.649A); **b.** of external events as means of training soul τῷ θεῷ, ἃ βούλεται πρὸς γυμνάσιον ἡμῶν διατασσομένῳ Or.*or.*10.1(p.319.27; M.11.445B); ἡ νόσος...γ. δὲ καὶ δοκίμιον Dion.Al.ap.Eus.*h.e.*7.22.6(M.20.688B); of sufferings, Eus.*d.e.*3.5(p.125.4; M.22.213A); Chrys.*hom.50.1 in Mt.*(7.514C); of tortures of martyrs as γ. ἀρετῆς Thdt.*h.e.*4.22.19(3.994); and other evils as a training τοῦ βίου τὰ δυσχερῆ φιλοθείας γ. Bas.Sel.*or.*17.2 (M.85.220A); Proc.G.*Gen.*1:26(M.87.113A); **c.** of spiritual training γ. μέν φαμεν εἶναι τῆς ψυχῆς τὴν ἀνθρωπίνην σοφίαν, τέλος δὲ τὴν θείαν Or.*Cels.*6.13(p.83.16; M.11.1309B); γ. γὰρ ταπεινοφροσύνης ἡ ἐν τοῖς εὐτελεστέροις πράγμασι διατριβή Bas.*reg.br.*289(2.517B; M.31.1285B); and pious exercises, Eus.*d.e.*4.7(p.161.6; 268C); Cyr.*Ps.*76:11(M.69. 1192B); **2.** *training ground*; met., of Palestine, for the apostles, Chrys.*hom.32.2 in Mt.*(7.367B); εἰς τὸ τῶν θλίψεων κατιέναι γ. Thdt. *Ps.*33:20f.(1.818); ἐν τῷ τῆς ἀρετῆς γ. Jo.Clim.*scal.*4(M.88.724C).

γύμνασμα, τό, *exercise, training*; of sufferings of martyrs, *Ep. Lugd.*ap.Eus.*h.e.*5.1.42(M.20.424C); and of the just, Or.*sel.in Ps.* 4:6 ap.*philoc.*26.5(p.236.29; M.12.1157A); of ascetical practices, Clem.*paed.*3.8(p.260.13; M.8.612B); διὰ τῶν τῆς ταπεινοφροσύνης γ. Bas.*reg.br.*289(2.517B; M.31.1285B); γ. τι πρὸς εὐπείθειαν Cyr.*Juln.* 8(6[2].277D); θεῖα γ. Jo.Clim.*scal.*4(M.88.685B).

***γυμνασμός, ὁ**, *exercise* τοῦ γ. τῆς χάριτος Mac.Aeg.*hom.*19.11 (M.34.641B).

γυμναστής, ὁ, *trainer of athletes*; of a spiritual guide, Jo.Clim. *scal.*4(M.88.724B); *ib.*(725C).

γυμναστικός, neut. as subst., *what is suitable for* spiritual *training* εὑρήσεις δὲ ἐν τῇ θείᾳ γραφῇ μίγμα τοῦ ὡσὰν ἱστορικοῦ πρὸς τὸ γ. Or.*fr.74 in Jo.*10:31(p.541.15).

γυμναστικῶς, *by way of* spiritual *discipline* αἱ κακώσεις...ἐπιφέρονται...καὶ γ. ἵνα δοκιμασθῶσιν οἱ δίκαιοι Olymp.*Job* 15(M.93.172C).

***γυμνήτευσις, ἡ**, *nakedness, poverty* ἡ γ., τοῦ τῆς ἀθανασίας περιβολαίου [sc. πρόξενον] Thdr.Stud.*epp.*2.58(M.99.1272D).

[*]**γυμνιτεύω**, = γυμνητεύω, *be naked*, Or.*or.*11.2(p.322.24; M.11. 449B).

***γυμνοκέφαλος**, *bare-headed*, *A.Thom.*A 56(p.173.1).

***γυμνόκριθον, τό**, a kind of wheat, *Schol.* in *Can.App.*3(*Mon.*2 p.642).

γυμνοποδέω, *be barefooted*, Gr.Naz.*or.*45.19(M.36.649B).

γυμνός, **A.** *naked*, of Adam and Eve before Fall οὐδὲ γὰρ ᾔδεισαν ὅτι γ. ἦσαν, τῆς δόξης τῆς ἀφάτου περιστελλούσης αὐτούς Chrys.*hom. 16.1 in Gen.*(4.124A); ἡ τῶν ὀφθαλμῶν διάνοιξις [sc. παρέσχεν αὐτοῖς] γνῶναι ὅτι γ. ἐτύγχανον, καὶ αἰσχύνεσθαι Diod.*Gen.*3:8(M.33.1568B); Cyr.*glaph.Gen.*1.2(1.6C); Andr.Cr.*triod.*(M.97.1401B).

B. met.; **1.** *unadorned, plain, (as it is) in (it)self* γ. δικαιοσύνης ἐπιδείξω τὸ σχῆμα Clem.*prot.*12(p.85.10; M.8.241B); θεὸς...γ. ἔσωθεν τὴν ψυχὴν βλέπων id.*str.*6.17(p.512.21; M.9.388C); Eus.*h.e.*1.3.12(M. 20.73A); ‡Ath.*qu.al.*20(M.28.793C,D.) cit. s. διαβολότης; hence *plain, clear* ἴχνη Eus.*h.e.*1.1.3(49B); of a pronouncement, Bas.*jud.*8(2. 222A; M.31.672C); esp. of truth τὴν ἀλήθειαν γ. Meth.*symp.*9(p.115. 3; M.18.180A); Eus.*p.e.*7.8(312D; M.21.528D); Eun.*apol.*3(M.30. 840A); Bas.*hom.*23.3(2.186D; M.31.593A); **2.** of divinity of Christ, *unveiled, unclothed*, i.e. by manhood; **a.** γ. ἔτι παρὰ πατρὶ λόγος Cyr.*Jo.*2.5(4.186A); †Gregent.*disp.*(M.86.636A); not thus would Devil have attacked him φύσιν οὐκ εἶχεν ἡ ἐναντία δύναμις...γυμνὴν ὑποστῆναι αὐτοῦ τὴν ἐμφάνειαν Gr.Nyss.*or.catech.*24(p.92.18; M.45. 64D); *ib.*26(p.96.14; 68A); ἐννόησον...πῶς...ἀντιπαρετάξατο ὁ διάβολος, μᾶλλον δὲ οὐ θεῷ γ., ἀλλὰ θεῷ ἀνθρωπίνῃ κρυπτομένῳ φύσει Chrys.

hom.2.1 in Mt.(7.20A); Const.Diac.*laud.*16(M.88.497D); as such incapable of suffering, Thdot.Anc.*exp.symb.*16(M.77.1337B); θεὸς δὲ πάσχειν οὐ πέφυκεν ‡Caes.Naz.*dial.*133(M.38.1036); normal term for unincarnate Godhead, as ψιλός for mere manhood μήτε θεὸν γ. οὔτε ἄνθρωπον ψιλὸν ὑποπτεύσητε Gr.Ant.*bapt.*2.6(M.88.1877B); Thdr.Raith.*praep.*(p.199.12; M.91.1501B) cit. s. ἐνανθρωπέω; Max. *ep.*19(M.91.593A); **b.** c. genit., *without* (v. infra C) λόγον γ. τῶν ὑποδεεστέρων καθ' αὐτόν Or.*Jo.*6.35(19; p.144.34; M.14.261B); acc. Apollinarius γ. εἶναι τὴν θεότητα τοῦ σώματος [i.e. after Ascension] Gr.Naz.*ep.*101(M.37.181A).

C. with genit., *not having*, often best translated by Eng. prep., *without*; **1.** *free* from, *devoid* of γυμνὸν αἰσθητῶν πνευματικόν Or.*Jo.*13.40(p.265.29; M.14.469A); νοῦς...πάσης κακίας γ. *Hom.Clem.*6.16; esp. armour, in context of spiritual life γ. τοῦ θυρεοῦ τῆς πίστεως καρδίαν Or.*Jo.*32.2(p.429.5; 745B); ψυχὴ ἡ γ. ... ἀπὸ κοινωνίας πνεύματος Mac.Aeg.*hom.*18.2(M.34.636C); *ib.*18.3(636D); **2.** *freed* from, *divested*, *stripped* of, fig. γυμνὴν τῆς ὑλικῆς δορᾶς γενομένην τὴν γνωστικὴν ψυχήν Clem.*str.*5.11(p.371.7; M.9.104A); *ib.*4.25(p.319.7; M.8.1368C); met. γ. πάσης ἀγνοίας...κατὰ τὸ δυνατὸν αὐτὸν ὀψόμενοι Or.*fr.10 in Jo.*(p.493.7); γ. [sc. ψυχὴν] διαμεῖναι σώματος Meth.*res.*1.29(p.259.2; M.41.1136D); γυμνὸν ἡμῖν αὐτὸν [sc. διάβολον] ὁ Χριστὸς τῶν μηχανημάτων κατέστησεν ‡Ath.*pasch.*2.7(M.28.1089C); in spiritual life, *detached* πρὸς τούτων γυμνὸς...Χριστῷ ἀκολούθει Jo.Clim.*scal.*2(M.88.653C); as condition of prayer, *ib.* 20(940C); *ib.*4(700D); abs., [sc. arms] *without defence*, Chrys. *hom.9.3 in 1Thess.*(11.490A); ‡Ath.*pass.*29(M.28.236A); of souls at Judgement γ. ἑστώτων πάντων Andr.Cr.*triod.*(M.97.1408B); *ib.*(1408D).

D. *bare, mere*, often where Eng. would use the adverbial *only*, *nothing but* ἐκ προαιρέσεως γ. Clem.*str.*7.12(p.53.11; M.9.501C); id.*prot.*1(p.3.7; M.8.52A); Or.*princ.*4.3.4(p.329.13; M.11.384B); ἐξ οὐκ ὄντων γ. τῷ βουλήματι...ὃ βούλεται [sc. θεὸς] ποιεῖν Meth.*creat.*9(p.498.25; M.18.341A); Chrys.*hom.14.1 in Rom.*(9.575E); ἐκεῖ δὲ τῆς ψυχῆς γ. ἐστι τὸ κατόρθωμα *ib.*8.5(505D); Vict.*Mc.*7:14f.(p.335.24); of unaccompanied chant γ. φωνῇ, μὴ συνηχοῦντος αὐτῇ τοῦ ὀργάνου Bas.*hom.in Ps.*44(1.160A; M.29.392A).

E. in phrase γ. (τῇ) κεφαλῇ *bareheaded*, i.e. *fearlessly*; **1.** in good sense, *freely, boldly*, Clem.*paed.*2.10(p.211.11; M.8.504B); Chrys. *hom.34.2 in Mt.*(7.390D); id.*hom.10.1 in Phil.*(11.276A); **2.** more freq. in bad sense, *shamelessly*, Clem.*prot.*7(p.58.26; M.8.185C); Or.*princ.*3.1.9(p.209.11; M.11.264A); Eus.*h.e.*3.32.8(M.20.284C); Chrys.*hom.48.3 in Mt.*(7.498A); Jo.D.*Jacob.*(M.94.1473B); Thdr. Stud.*epp.*1.8(M.99.937A); in same sense also γ. τῇ φωνῇ ref. Eunomius denying equality of Father and Son, Gr.Nyss.*Eun.*1 (1 p.152.18; M.45.393A).

γυμνότης, ἡ, *nakedness*, of Adam and Eve πρὸ τῆς παρακοῆς ἀναισθήτως ἔχειν τῆς γ. ... μετὰ δὲ τὴν παρακοὴν εἰς ἔννοιαν ἐλθεῖν τῆς γ. Diod.*Gen.*3:8(M.33.1568C); Proc.G.*Gen.*2:25(M.87.180A); τὴν γ. ... ἐκ τοῦ ἀπολωλεκέναι τὴν ἀρετὴν ἔνδυμα θεῖον ὑπάρχουσαν *ib.*3:7(193C).

γυμνοφανής, *openly visible, manifest, Const.App.*7.33.1.

γυμν-όω, *strip naked*; **1.** met., *strip, deprive*; **a.** in gen., Clem.*prot.*2(p.20.27; M.8.100A); Or.*sel.in Gen.*9:20f.(M.12.109C); Meth.*symp.*3.10(p.38.11; M.18.76C); of God, acc. opinion attributed to Origen ὁ θεὸς...οὐδὲν οὐδαμῶς δημιουργήσας ἐγύμνωτο τοῦ πατὴρ καὶ προκράτωρ εἶναι Meth.*creat.*12(p.500.2; M.18.344B); of Christ's divinity after death and before Resurrection τρέμει ὁ ᾅδης θεὸν σαρκὸς γεγυμνωμένον Procl.CP *or.*13.3(M.65.792D); of Christ on Cross, Cyr. H.*catech.*20.2; ~ωθεὶς οὖν ἀπὸ τοῦ παντός ‡Ath.*pass.*25(M.28.228C); *ib.*32(241C); of Jews, whom God deprived of their privileges, Chrys. *hom.6.2 in Rom.*(9.474D); *ib.*6.6(480B); Andr.Cr.*triod.*(M.97.1401B); of Devil after third temptation γυμνωθεὶς τῶν βελῶν Bas.Sel.*pasch.*2.7(M.28.1089C); and at Passion μόνον γὰρ τοῦτο αὐτῷ [sc. διαβόλῳ] περιελείπετο λοιπὸν τὸ ἆθλον, πάντων ~ωθέντι ‡Ath.*pass.*14(M.28.209C); *ib.*29(236A,B); **b.** spiritually ~ωθεὶς τῆς ἐκ θεοῦ ἐλπίδος Eus. *v.C.*1.58(p.35.10; M.20.975A); τοὺς τῆς θεοσεβείας κατ' ἐπήρειαν τοῦ διαβόλου...γεγυμνωμένους Nil.*epp.*2.190(M.79.300C); *ib.*2.322(357B); of Adam and Eve, ‡*Diogn.*12.3; παραβάντες τὴν ἐντολὴν τοῦ θείου χαρίσματος ἐγυμνώθησαν Gel.Cyz.*h.e.*2.24.5(v.l. ἐστερήθησαν M.85.1300B); of Eve ἐγυμνώθη τῆς θείας σωφροσύνης Nil.*epp.*2.318(356B); **c.** more rarely in good sense, *deliver, free* from τὴν ψυχὴν...~ῶσαι τῶν ὑπόντων παθῶν Clem.*q.d.s.*12(p.167.15; M.9.616C); Jo.Clim. *scal.*7(M.88.801D); **2.** met., *lay bare, discover*; **a.** *reveal, make manifest* ~ώσω γὰρ τὸ ἦθος τὸ ἐμαυτοῦ Clem.*paed.*3.12(p.284.7; M.8.665B); τὰ ἀπόρρητα ~οῦντες Eus.*l.C.*11(p.223.26; M.20.1376A); Nil. *epp.*3.102(M.79.432D); Thdt.*Cant.*1:5(2.41); id.*Ezech.*20:33(2.832); **b.** unfavourably, *expose* τὴν γοητείαν...~ώσαντες Meth.*symp.*8.14(p.99.18; M.18.161C); Cyr.*Os.*11(3.31E); **3.** *unsheathe*, Meth.*arbitr.*3(p.151.1; M.18.245A); Jo.Mosch.*prat.*15(M.87.2861D); Jo.D.*hom.*3.8(M.96.600A); **4.** *leave empty*, of Christ ὁ μὴ ~ώσας τὸν πατρικὸν θρόνον, σαρκωθεὶς ἐκ παρθένου Procl.CP *or.*15.6(M.65.894D); pass., *be emptied* οἶνον...ἀμφιφορῆες...ἐγυμνώθησαν Nonn.*par.Jo.*2:3(M.43.760C); **5.** *set aside, disregard* οἱ Ἕλληνες...τοὺς τῆς φύσεως ~οῦντες νόμους Chrys.*hom.4.6 in 1Cor.*(10.33A).

γυμνῶς, **1.** *openly, plainly*, opp. ἠνιγμένως, μυστικῶς, Clem.*exc. Thdot.*66(p.128.26; M.9.689C); Or.*Jo.*2.30(24; p.88.1; M.14.168B); Meth.*symp.*1.3(p.12.5; M.18.44B); *ib.*5.7(p.61.24; 109B); τότε μὲν κεκαλυμμένως, τότε δὲ γ. Eus.*d.e.*2.3(p.81.15; M.22.145B); Ath.*ep. Epict.*3(p.6.12; M.26.1056A); Proc.G.*Gen.*3:1(M.87.181D); comp., Or.*Jo.*1.1(p.3.7; 21A); Eus.*d.e.*2.3(p.81.7; 145A); Ath.*syn.*17(p.244.29; M.26.712B); **2.** *simply, merely*, of Logos οὐ γ. εἶναι αὐτὸν 'πρὸς τὸν θεόν' ἀλλὰ ὄντα 'ἐν τῇ ἀρχῇ' Or.*Jo.*1.39(42; p.51.10; M.14.101D).

γύμνωσις, ἡ, **1.** *stripping*, fig. σοῦ, Χριστέ, γυμνωθέντος, εὗρεν ἡ φύσις γ. ὄντως ψυχικῆς ἁμαρτάδος Geo.Pis.*carm.*30.2; **2.** *nakedness*, of Adam and Eve, Meth.*res.*1.29(p.260.18; M.41.1137C); Diod.*Gen.*3:22(M.33.1569A); regarded as a gift from God, Nil.*exerc.*65(M.79.800A,B); ἔδει μὴ γινώσκειν τὴν γ., ἵνα μὴ τῆς πρὸς θεὸν ἀτενίσεως ὁ ἄνθρωπος ἀφελκόμενος περισπᾶται περὶ τὴν τοῦ ἐλλείποντος ἀναπλήρωσιν Proc.G.*Gen.*2:25(M.87.177B); ἀθάνατον εἶχον τὸ φρόνημα, μηδὲν γυμνώσεως αἰσθανόμενοι *ib.*(177C); of Noah, Just.*dial.*139.1(M.6.793C); Clem.*paed.*2.6(p.188.11; M.8.453B); of those possessed by demons, Epiph.*haer.*30.10(p.345.25; M.41.421C); Chrys.*hom. 81.3 in Mt.*(7.777E); of Adamites, Epiph.*haer.*52.3(p.313.25; M.41.957B); met., of Christ redeeming nakedness of mankind, Gr.Naz. *carm.*1.2.34.196(M.37.959A); ἐλευθεροῦτο τῆς γ. ἡ γῆ Procl.CP *hom.* 1.2(M.65.836A).

***γυναιάζω,** *be addicted to women*, Thdr.Stud.*epp.*2.107(M.99.1368A).

***γυναικαδέλφη, ἡ,** *wife's sister*, Pall.*h.Laus.*55(p.148.16, v.l. γυναῖκα ἀδελφήν M.34.1244A).

***γυναικοαρρενομανία, ἡ,** *erotomania*, †Jo.Jej.*serm.*(M.88.1921D).

***γυναικόδουλος, ὁ,** *slave of women*, Chrys.*subintr.*6(1.236C); id. *hom.62.5 in Mt.*(7.627B); Isid.Pel.*epp.*2.53(M.78.497A).

γυναικοειδής, *womanish*, Cyr.*ador.*3(1.104C).

γυναικοιέραξ, ὁ, *woman-hunter*, Pall.*h.Laus.*65(p.161.14; M.34.1251C); id.*v.Chrys.*12(p.77.30; M.47.44); *Max.invect.*(M.90.204B).

γυναικομανία, ἡ, *madness for women*, Clem.*str.*3.9(p.225.9; M.8.1165B); Eus.*l.C.*5(p.204.7; M.20.1336B); †Bas.*contub.*10(M.30.825A).

***γυναικομαστοβορέω,** *eat the breasts of women*, ‡Caes.Naz.*dial.*110(M.38.985).

[*]**γυναικονῖτις, ἡ,** v. γυναικωνῖτις.

***γυναικόπαιδα, τά,** *women and children*, Thphn.*chron.*p.325(M.108.785C).

***γυναικοπρεπῶς,** *like a woman*, Cyr.*Mich.*64(3.459C).

[*]**γυναικοτραφής,** *reared by women, effeminate*, Chrys.*hom. 33.2 in 1Cor.*(10.301D).

γυναικωνῖτις (-ονῖτις), ἡ, **1.** *women's apartments*; hence **a.** women's part of church ἡ γ. γέγονεν ἵνα διαιρῶνται αἱ γυναῖκες ἀπὸ τῶν ἀνδρῶν ‡Sophr.H.*liturg.*4(M.87.3985A); cf.Procopius Caesariensis *de Sancta Sophia*(M.87.2836A); of convent of women, -ονῖτις, Thdt. *h.rel.*9(3.1192); **b.** *womankind, women* collectively, Clem.*str.*1.13(p.36.20; M.8.756A); Gr.Naz.*or.*27.2(p.3.10; M.36.13B); Pall.*v.Chrys.*16(p.95.5; M.47.54); Isid.Pel.*epp.*4.71(M.78.1129C); **c.** *wooldresser's shop* (where women carried on the work), Cels.ap.Or.*Cels.*3.55(p.251.7; M.11.993B); **2.** as adj.; **a.** *of women*, Epiph.*haer.*79.4(p.478.32; M.42.745B); **b.** *of the wooldressing trade* γ. ἐργάνη Clem.*paed.*3.4(p.252.11; M.8.593B).

γυνή, ἡ, *woman*;

A. in relation to man; **1.** her spiritual equality with man; **a.** due to both being made in image of God, ‡Gr.Nyss.*or.1 in Gen. 1:26*(M.44.276A); οὐκ ἐχρῆν μόνον τὸν ἄνδρα εἰκόνα λέγεσθαι, ἀλλὰ καὶ τὴν γ. γυναικὸς γὰρ καὶ ἀνδρὸς εἷς ὁ τύπος καὶ ὁ χαρακτήρ, καὶ ἡ ὁμοίωσις μία Chrys.*serm.2.2 in Gen.*(4.654A); but cf. Diod.*Gen.*1:26(M.33.1564C,D) cit. s. εἰκών; **b.** and being redeemed in same way ὑπὲρ ἀνδρὸς σὰρξ ἐγένετο; τοῦτο καὶ ὑπὲρ γ. ὑπὲρ ἀνδρὸς ἀπέθανε; καὶ ἡ γ. τῷ θανάτῳ σώζεται Gr.Naz.*or.*37.7(M.36.289C); **c.** hence human nature and virtue are same in man and woman οὐκ ἄλλην τοίνυν πρὸς τὴν ἀνθρωπότητα φύσιν ἔχειν ἡ γ., ἄλλην δὲ ὁ ἀνὴρ φαίνεται, ἀλλ' ἢ τὴν αὐτήν, ὥστε καὶ τὴν ἀρετήν Clem.*str.*4.8(p.275.10; M.8.1272A); *ib.*(p.275.15; 1272B); τὴν γ. οὐχ ἑτέρωθέν ποθεν διέπλασεν, ἀλλ' ἐκ τοῦ ἀνδρός...διά τοι τοῦτο καὶ τοὺς αὐτοὺς νόμους καὶ ἀνδράσι προσφέρει καὶ γ.· ἐπειδήπερ ἐν τῷ τοῦ σώματος σχήματι, καὶ οὐκ ἐν τῇ ψυχῇ τὸ διάφορον Thdt.*affect*.5(p.139.11; 4.836); οὔτε ἀνὴρ χωρὶς γ., οὔτε γυνὴ χωρὶς ἀνδρὸς ἐν κυρίῳ· εἰ γὰρ καὶ δευτερεύει τῷ σώματι, ἀλλ' οὖν κατὰ ψυχὴν ἀθάνατόν τε οὖσαν καὶ λογικὴν οὐδὲν τοῦ ἄρρενος διενήνοχεν Proc.G.*Gen*.2:18(M.87.172A); but γ. δὲ ἀνδρὸς πολλῷ ἐλάττω λαχοῦσα τὴν φύσιν †Bas.Anc.*virg*.34(M.30.740A); **d.** their equality in martyrdom, Clem.*str*.4.8(p.275.4; M.8.1272A); *ib*.(p.278.32; 1280A); Ath.*inc*.27.3(M.25.144A); Chrys.*pan.Barn*.1(2.634B); id. *pan.Barl*.4(2.686E); **e.** and in spiritual life ὡς γὰρ σώφρονα τὸν ἄνδρα καὶ τῶν ἡδονῶν κρείττονα δεῖν εἶναί φαμεν, οὕτω καὶ τὴν γ. σώφρονά τε ὁμοίως ἀξιώσομεν εἶναι Clem.*str*.4.8(p.275.31; 1272C); *ib*.6.12(p.482.14; M.9.321B); πότε δύναται ἀνθρώπου φύσις ἁμιλληθῆναι γυναικὸς φύσει καρτερικῶς διαγούσῃ τὸν ἑαυτῆς βίον; πότε τὸ ἐν νηστείαις εὔτονον γυναικῶν μιμήσασθαι δύναται ἄνθρωπος, τὸ ἐν προσευχαῖς φιλόπονον, τὸ ἐν δάκρυσι δαψιλές, τὸ περὶ εὐποιΐας ἕτοιμον; ‡Gr.Nyss.*or.1 in Gen.1:26*(M.44.276B); Bas.*hom*.2.2(2.11E; M.31.188A); **2.** physical inferiority and subjection to man; **a.** due to method of creation ὁ ἀνὴρ ἐκ τῆς γῆς καὶ ἡ γ. ἐκ τοῦ ἀνδρός Isid. Pel.*epp*.1.141(M.78.276D); and esp. to Fall ἔστι τοίνυν ἀρχὴ καὶ δουλεία πρώτη, καθ' ἣν καὶ γυναικῶν οἱ ἄνδρες κρατοῦσι· μετὰ γὰρ τὴν ἁμαρτίαν ἡ ταύτης ἐγένετο χρεία. πρὸ γὰρ τῆς παρακοῆς ὁμότιμος ἦν τῷ ἀνδρί Chrys.*serm.4.1 in Gen*.(4.659A); but with qualifications εἰ γὰρ ὑποτέτακται ἡμῖν ἡ γ., ἀλλ' ὡς γ., ἀλλ' ὡς ἐλευθέρα καὶ ὡς ὁμότιμος id.*hom.26.2 in 1Cor*.(10.229E); **b.** relating only to physical matters τὸ γοῦν κυοφορεῖν καὶ τὸ τίκτειν τῇ γ. προσεῖναί φαμεν, καθὸ θήλεια τυγχάνει, οὐ καθὸ ἄνθρωπος...ἢ μὲν τοίνυν ταὐτόν ἐστι, κατὰ ψυχήν Clem.*str*.4.8(p.275.21; M.8.1272B); ‡Bas.*struct.hom*.1.22(1.335A; M.30.33D).

B. position in Christianity; **1.** position in world, inferior to that of man, Chrys.*laud.Max*.4(3.217D); γυναιξὶν ἀναγκαῖον...τὸ τῶν οἰκείων προνοεῖσθαι παίδων, καὶ εἰς φιλοσοφίαν αὐτοὺς ἐνάγειν id. *Anna* 1.4(4.705C); ἐπέτρεψε...τῇ γ. ... τὴν οἰκίαν...ἱστὸς γὰρ καὶ ἠλακάτη τῆς γ. αὐτὸς γὰρ ἔδωκε τῇ γ. ὑφάσματος σοφίαν id.*hom.34.4 in 1Cor*.(10.316B); Gr.Naz.*or*.28.24(p.59.8; M.36.60B); **2.** position in Church; **a.** debarred from teaching and priestly functions οὐκ ἐπιτρέπομεν οὖν γ. διδάσκειν ἐν ἐκκλησίᾳ, ἀλλὰ μόνον προσεύχεσθαι *Const.App*.3.6.1; γ. τὸ σῶμα τυγχάνεις...πέπαυσο τοίνυν τοὺς ἄνδρας διδάσκουσα ἐπὶ τῆς ἐκκλησίας Nil.*epp*.2.116(M.79.249D); from baptizing, *Const.App*.3.9.1; reasons ὁ Χριστὸς...γυναῖκας οὐδαμοῦ ἐξαπέστειλεν εἰς τὸ κήρυγμα...εἰ γὰρ ἦν ἀναγκαῖον γυναιξὶν διδάσκειν, αὐτὸς ἂν ἐκέλευσε πρῶτος *ib*.3.6.2; ἡ ἐξ ἀρχῆς τῆς γ. διδασκαλία οὐ καλῶς τὸ κοινὸν ἔβλαβε γένος Didym.*Trin*.3.41(M.39.989A); cf.Anast.S.*qu. et resp*.59(M.89.625C); εἰ ἱερατεύειν γ. θεῷ προσετάσσοντο ἢ κανονικόν τι ἐργάζεσθαι ἐν ἐκκλησίᾳ, ἔδει μᾶλλον αὐτὴν τὴν Μαρίαν ἱερατείαν ἐπιτελέσαι ἐν καινῇ διαθήκῃ...ἀλλ' οὐδὲ βάπτισμα διδόναι πεπίστευται Epiph.*haer*.79.3(p.477.27; M.42.744A); *ib*.79.7(p.482.4; 749D); *Const. App*.3.9.4; **b.** eccl. legislation οὐ δεῖ γ. ἐν τῷ θυσιαστηρίῳ εἰσέρχεσθαι CLaod.*can*.44; ἄνευ τῆς διακόνου μηδεμία προσίτω γ. τῷ διακόνῳ ἢ τῷ ἐπισκόπῳ *Const.App*.2.26.2; to sit apart in church, *ib*.2.57.4; and receive Holy Communion κατακεκαλυμμέναι τὴν κεφαλήν, ὡς ἁρμόζει γυναικῶν τάξει *ib*.2.57.21; **c.** in Montanist sect γυναῖκες...εἰς ἐπισκοπὴν καὶ πρεσβυτέριον καθίστανται διὰ τὴν Εὔαν Epiph.*haer*.49.3(p.343.18; M.41.881B); **3.** in monasticism; strict separation of women from monks, ‡Bas.*const*.3.1(2.543C; M.31.1344C); *ib*.3.2(2.544C; 1345C); Nil.*epp*.3.150(M.79.453A); ἀνάρμοστον γὰρ τοῖς ἅπαξ φυγοῦσι τὸν κόσμον ὁμιλεῖν γυναιξίν, ἢ γλίχεσθαι συντυχίας γυναικῶν Ant.Mon.*hom*.17(M.89.1480A); same applies to nuns παρεκτὸς μέντοι τοῦ πρεσβυτέρου καὶ τοῦ διακόνου οὐδεὶς περᾷ εἰς τὸ μοναστήριον τῶν γ. Pall.*h.Laus*.33(p.97.2; M.34.1105C); **4.** woman and spiritual life, her restoration to grace by faith in resurrection ἡ γ. ἐξαπατηθεῖσα ἐν παραβάσει...πρώτη τῆς ἀναστάσεως γίνεται μάρτυς, ἵνα τὴν ἐκ τῆς παραβάσεως καταστροφὴν διὰ τῆς κατὰ τὴν ἀνάστασιν πίστεως ἀνορθώσῃ Gr.Nyss.*Eun*.12(2 p.280.2; M.45.892A); αἱ γ. ἐκκαεῖ τοῦ διδασκάλου τῷ φίλτρῳ πυρούμεναι,...τῶν ἀποστόλων τὴν παρρησίαν ἐνίκησαν,...ἔδει γὰρ δι' ὧν διηκονήθη ὁ θάνατος, διὰ τούτων λειτουργηθῆναι καὶ τὴν ἀνάστασιν Jo.D.*hom*.4.33(M.96.636B); contemplative nature of her life ἡ δὲ γ. καθάπερ ἔν τινι διδασκαλείῳ φιλοσοφίας τῇ οἰκίᾳ καθημένη, καὶ τὸν νοῦν συνάγουσα εἰς ἑαυτήν, καὶ εὐχαῖς προσέχειν καὶ ἀναγνώσεσι καὶ τῇ ἄλλῃ δυνήσεται φιλοσοφίᾳ Chrys.*hom.61.3 in Jo*.(8.365D); her mission αἱ...γ. διὰ τῆς αἰδοῦς καὶ πραότητος τὴν θεοσέβειαν ἐνδείκνυσθε εἰς ἐπιστροφὴν καὶ προτροπὴν πίστεως καὶ τοῖς ἐκτὸς πᾶσιν *Const.App*.1.10.3; exercised esp. by wives towards their husbands οὐδὲν ἰσχυρότερον γ. εὐλαβοῦς καὶ συνετῆς, πρὸς τὸ ῥυθμίζειν ἄνδρα, καὶ διαπλάττειν αὐτοῦ τὴν ψυχὴν ἐν οἷς ἂν θέλῃ Chrys.*hom.61.3 in Jo*.(8.366A); Jo.D.*1Cor*.7:16f.(M.95.624C); [1Tim.2:12] περὶ τῆς ἐν τῷ βήματι διδασκαλίας λέγει,...ἰδίᾳ δὲ παραινεῖν καὶ συμβουλεύειν οὐκ ἐκώλυσεν Chrys.*hom.1.3 in Rom. 16:3*(3.177A); **5.** woman's moral qualities; **a.** virtues, her true ornaments, Gr.Naz.*or*.8.10(M.35.800C); Chrys.*hom.1.5 in Ps.48:17*(5.513A); Isid.Pel.*epp*.2.53(M.78.496C); **b.** vices τῶν γ. ὅσαι λίαν ἐπιδεικτικαὶ καὶ ῥάθυμοι, καὶ τὸ κάλυμμα τῆς αἰδοῦς ἀτιμάζουσαι Gr.Naz. *or*.8.9(M.35.800A); οὐδὲν αἰσχρότερον γ. τρυφώσης, οὐδὲν αἰσχρότερον μεθυούσης. ... πῶς ἐστιν ἀήδης οἴνου ἀποπνέουσα γ. ὀδωδότος, σεσηπότος Chrys.*hom.27.2 in Ac*.(9.218A); id.*hom.15.3 in Eph*.(11.112E,114A); γ. δεινὸς καταγοητεῦσαι ῥήτωρ τοὺς μὴ προσέχοντας, καὶ παλαιὸν τοῦ διαβόλου ὅπλον Isid.Pel.*epp*.4.71(M.78.1129C); τί γ.; ἐπὶ γῆς ναυάγιον, πηγὴ κακίας, θησαυρὸς ῥυπαρίας Anast.S.*qu.et resp*.59(M.89.636Cf.).

C. exeg.; **1.** 1Tim.3:15, as ref. good education of her children, Chrys.*Anna* 1.3(4.704D,E); cf.Isid.Pel.*epp*.1.316(M.78.365B); or BMV ἡ δὲ γ. ἐξαπατηθεῖσα ἐν παραβάσει γέγονε· σωθήσεται δὲ διὰ τῆς τεκνογονίας...Μαρίας ‡Chrys.*trid*.(2.826A); **2.** 1Cor.9:5, not of wives, but of pious women ministering to apostles 'γ.' εἰπὼν καὶ προσθεὶς 'ἀδελφήν', τὸ πρέπον καὶ σῶφρον καὶ καθαρὸν τῆς συνεκδημούσης ἐδήλωσεν Sever.*1Cor*.9:5(p.256.4); τὸ δὲ ἀδελφὴν γ. περιάγειν τινὲς οὕτως ἡρμήνευσαν, ὅτι καθάπερ τῷ κυρίῳ εἵποντο γ. πισταί...οὕτω καί τισι τῶν ἀποστόλων ἠκολούθουν τινὲς θερμοτέραν ἐπιδεικνυμέναι πίστιν Thdt.*1Cor*.9:5(3.219); γ. ἠκολούθουν, οὐ παιδοποιίας, οὐδὲ συμβιώσεως ἕνεκεν, ἀλλ' ἐκ τῶν οἰκείων χορηγοῦσαι Isid.Pel.*epp*.3.176(M.78.865D); **3.** 1Cor.11:5, ref. Church ἡ γ. κεῖται εἰς τύπον τῆς ἐκκλησίας· καὶ ὥσπερ...ἐκεῖναι εἶχον ἐξηπλωμένας τὰς τρίχας ἀντὶ σκεπάσματος· οὕτω καὶ ἡ ἐκκλησία τὰ τέκνα αὐτῆς ἐνδύει...ἐνδύμασι θεϊκοῖς Mac.Aeg.*hom*.12.15(M.34.565C); in series of myst. interprn. understood as part of soul, e.g. γ. ... νοὸς εἶναί φαμεν, αὐτὴν τὴν ἕξιν τῆς πράξεως,...κατακεκαλυμμένην πρακτικοῖς τε λογισμοῖς καὶ ἤθεσι Max.*qu.Thal*.25(M.90.329D); γ. ... ἡ σύνοικος αἴσθησις δι' ἧς ἐπιβατεύει [sc. ὁ νοῦς] τῇ φύσει τῶν αἰσθητῶν *ib*.(M.90.332B); πᾶσα γ., διάνοια...νοός, προσευχομένη ἢ προφητεύουσα ἀκατακαλύπτῳ κεφαλῇ, τουτέστιν, ἄφετος τῆς ἐπ' αὐτῇ τοῖς πολλοῖς πεπυκνωμένης μυστικοῖς θεωρήμασι νοερᾶς δυνάμεως, καταισχύνει τὴν κεφαλὴν αὐτῆς, ἀποβαλλομένη τὴν ὡς κεφαλὴν καλύπτουσαν τὸν νοῦν, θείαν...γνῶσιν *ib*.(333D); ὀφείλει οὖν ἔχειν...πᾶσα τοιαύτη γ., τὴν ἐξουσίαν τοῦ λόγου διὰ παντὸς ἐπὶ τῆς κεφαλῆς, λέγω δὲ τὴν λογικὴν ἐπιστασίαν *ib*.(336B).

D. as synonym of Eve, Iren.*fr*.14(p.484; M.7.1237B); τί λέγει ἡ γ. τῷ θεῷ; Or.*hom.20.3 in Jer*.(19; p.182.5; M.13.508B); Gr.Naz.*or*.45.8(M.36.633A); *ib*.37.7(289C); *Lit*.ap.*Const.App*.8.12.20; contrasted with BMV ἐκκλείσασα τὸν θάνατον τὸν ἐκ γ. πάλιν ὁ διὰ γυναικὸς ἡμῖν ζωὴ γεγεννημένος Epiph.*ep.Arab*.(p.469.13f.; M.42.729A); id. *haer*.79.9(p.483.24f.; M.42.753B); Andr.Cr.*or*.1(M.97.809C); Jo.Eub. *concept.BMV* 21(M.96.1496B) cit. s. ἀνάκλησις; with BMV and Elisabeth πρὸ Ἰωάννου Ἐλισάβετ προφητεύει, πρὸ τῆς γενέσεως τοῦ σωτῆρος ἡμῶν ἡ Μαρία προφητεύει. καὶ ὥσπερ ἤρξατο ἡ ἁμαρτία ἀπὸ τῆς γ. καὶ μετὰ τοῦτο ἔφθασεν ἐπὶ τὸν ἄνδρα, οὕτω καὶ τὰ ἀγαθὰ ἀπὸ τῶν γ. ἤρξατο, ἵνα προτραπῶσιν αἱ γ., τὴν ἀσθένειαν...ἀποθέμεναι, ζηλῶσαι τοὺς βίους τῶν μακαρίων τούτων Or.*hom.8 in Lc*.(p.55.2–5); with Canaanitish woman γ. ... τὸ παλαιὸν ὅπλον τοῦ διαβόλου, ἡ τοῦ παραδείσου με ἐκβαλοῦσα, ἡ μήτηρ τῆς ἁμαρτίας,...'Ιουδαῖοι φεύγουσι, καὶ ἡ γ. καταδιώκει Chrys.*dimiss.Chan*.4(3.435C); cf. s. Ἀδάμ passim.

E. met., of soul ὁ μὲν [sc. νόμος] τοῦ νοός (τουτέστιν ὁ πνευματικός) ἀνήρ ἐστι, πρὸς ὃν ἡρμόσθη ἀπὸ θεοῦ γ. (ἡ ψυχὴ) ἀνδρὶ (τῷ νόμῳ) Or. *comm.in Mt*.12.4(p.73.28; M.13.981B); of heresy πᾶσα γὰρ αἵρεσις φαύλη γ. Epiph.*haer*.79.8(p.483.11; M.42.752D); of weakness and imbecility σημεῖον μὲν γὰρ ἡ γ. καὶ φρονήματος ἀνάνδρου, καὶ κεκλασμένου τύπος Cyr.*Os*.5(3.25B); id.*Zach*.30(3.698A).

F. heret. φάσκουσι [sc. Severians] δὲ καὶ τὴν γ. εἶναι ἔργον τοῦ σατανᾶ, καθάπερ καὶ οἱ ἀρχοντικοὶ τοῦτο ἔφασαν Epiph.*haer*.45.2(p.200.16; M.41.833B).

***γύπειος**, *of a vulture*, Bas.*ep*.236.4(3.363D; M.32.881D).

***γυρευτής**, ὁ, *vagabond, restless person* μοναχὸς γ. οὐκ οἴσει καρπὸν ἀρετῆς Ant.Mon.*hom*.26(M.89.1516B); Jo.Clim.*scal*.27(M.88.1112D).

γυρεύ-ω, **A.** trans.; **1.** *move in circles through* γύψ, διὰ τὸ ~ειν ὕψη Anast.S.*hod*.2(M.89.68D); hence *witness, see* Γαβριὴλ...μετὰ στρατιᾶς ἀγγέλων οἵτινες ἐγύρευσαν πάσας τὰς κολάσεις *Apoc.Paul*.43(p.62); *see to, attend to, Euchol*.(p.225) cit. s. ἔξαρχος; **2.** *roam, wander in* πλατείας ~ειν Gr.Mag.*dial*.(tr.Zach.)1.10(M.*PL*.77.202C); πᾶσαν πόλιν καὶ χώραν ~οντες Jo.Mosch.*prat*.110(M.87.2973B); *ib*.185(3060B); **3.** *encompass* τί κακὸν εὑρὼν εἰς τὸν Ἰησοῦν ἐγύρευσας τὴν ἀπώλειαν αὐτοῦ; *A.Pil*.B 23(p.330); **4.** *seek, Mir.Geo*.5(p.45.10); *inquire into*, †Hipp.Th.*fr*.8 c.6(p.39.27; M.117.1045C); **5.** *surround* ~σαντες τὴν οἰκίαν *V.Mac*.A(p.138).

B. intrans.; **1.** ref. movements made in pain, *writhe*, Leont.N. *v.Sym*.31(M.93.1709A); **2.** *wander* about, *A.Phil*.B 15.1(p.319); Jo. Clim.*scal*.27(M.88.1113A); μοναχοῦ ~οντος ἐν τῇ πόλει μετὰ μιᾶς κόρης

Leont.N.*v.Jo.Eleem.*24(p.49.17); *ib.*(p.51.26); **3.** *trace a circle, Mir. Artem.*41(p.69.3).

***γυρηδόν**, *all round*, Mac.Mgn.*apocr.*3.13(p.86.2).

***γυρίζω**, *whirl round, T.Gad* 1.3, v.l.; Cosm.Mel.*schol.*(M.38.532) in Gr.Naz.*carm.*2.2(epigr.)25.

***γυροβολέω**, *turn in a circle, Vaticin.*2(p.56).

γυροειδής, *circular, round*; of tonsure of priests, ‡Germ.CP *contempl.*(M.98.392D).

γῦρος, ὁ, *circle, ring*; of the earth, Gr.Nyss.*Eun.*2(2 p.347.19; M.45.524C); *ib.*(p.361.19; 540D); Chrys.*Thdr.*1.12(1.17C); Jo.Mosch. *prat.*76(M.87.2929C); of dancers, *A.Jo.*94(p.197.15).

[*]**γύρωθεν**, = *γυρόθεν, in a circle, round about, A.Pil.*B 10.2 (p.304); cf.*Lit.Chrys.*(p.371.19); as prep. c. genit., *round*, Barth. Edess.*Agar.*(M.104.1392B).

***γυψοπλασία, ἡ**, *plaster casting*, Nil.*epp.*4.61(M.79.577C).

[*]**γωμόω**, v. *γομόω*.

γωνία, ἡ, *angle, corner*; met., of Christ as corner-stone *ὥσπερ τινὰ γ. συνείρων εἰς ὁμοψυχίαν* Cyr.*Mich.*35(3.422A); with prep., *in a corner, in some obscure place, secretly* (cf. Eng. 'hole and corner'), ref. false prophet *κατὰ γωνίαν...προφητεύει* Herm.*mand.* 11.13; pagan philosophers, Tat.*orat.*26(p.28.13; M.6.364A); heretics, Ath.*apol.sec.*2(p.88.18; M.25.249C); agst. idea that Christ thus disposed of his body at Resurrection, id.*inc.*23.1(M.25.136C); with *μία* esp. implying belittlement *τὸν τοῦ θεοῦ λόγον ἀπὸ μιᾶς γ. ἐπισπεῖραι* Or.*Cels.*5.50(p.55.4; M.11.1262A); *εἰς μίαν γ. ἔπεμψε τοῦτο ὅ φατε πνεῦμα* Cels.*ib.*6.78(p.149.25; 1416D).

γωνιόομαι, *become angular, have corners ἀνάβασις...περὶ τὸν οἶκον τοῦ θεοῦ μὴ γεγωνιωμένη, ἀνακλάσεις εὐθειῶν ἔχουσα. γέγραπται γὰρ 'καὶ ἑλικτὴ ἀνάβασις'* Or.*Jo.*10.40(24; p.218.1; M.14.385B); *ὁδοῦ Ἰησοῦ Χριστοῦ...οὐδὲ ὅλως γεγωνιωμένης* id.*or.*19.3(p.343.12; M.11.477B); met. *πᾶς ἅγιος οὐ γεγωνίωται οὐδὲ ἔχει τι σκολιόν* Cyr. *Ps.*77:19(M.69.1193B).

Δ

Δαβ-, v. *Δαυ-*.

δαγύς, ἡ, *wax doll, Schol.Clem.prot.*(p.314.22; M.9.787A).

δᾳδίς, ἡ, *torch*, Cyr.*Os.*46(3.77E).

δᾳδουχ-έω, **1.** *carry as a torch*, of BMV *ἡ ὡς λυχνία...~ήσασα αὐτὸν ἐν κόσμῳ* Mod.*dorm.*12(M.86.3308C); **2.** *conduct with torches πρὸς τὸν νυμφίον ἠπείγετο ~ούντων αὐτήν* Chrys.*pan.Dros.*4(2.694C); **3.** *celebrate by carrying torches in procession*, ref. mysteries *τὴν πλάνην καὶ τὴν ἁρπαγὴν καὶ τὸ πένθος αὐταῖν Ἐλευσὶς ~εῖ* Clem. *prot.*2(p.11.22; M.8.72A); **4.** (since *δᾳδοῦχος* and hierophant were chief officers in Eleusinian mysteries) *enlighten, initiate ~οῦμαι τοὺς οὐρανοὺς καὶ τὸν θεὸν ἐποπτεῦσαι...ἱεροφαντεῖ δὲ ὁ κύριος* *ib.*12(p.84.23; M.8.241A); *περιλάμπει* [sc. S. Philip] *τὸν Ναθαναὴλ δᾳδουχήσας αὐτῷ τὸ τῆς εὐσεβείας μυστήριον* Gr.Nyss.*hom.15 in Cant.*(M.44.1089A); intrans. *ἀποστόλοις ~οῦσι πρὸς τὴν ἀλήθειαν* Thdt.*Is.*8:20(p.46.20); **5.** *illuminate*, in gen. *νεφέλης...νύκτωρ μὲν ~ούσης ib.*4:6(p.22.27; 2.196); *τοὺς ἐξ ἐθνῶν πάντων τῷ φωτὶ τῆς ἀστραπῆς ἐδᾳδούχησε* [sc. Sion] Hesych.H.*serm.*8(M.93.1480B); ref. H. Ghost *παρ' οὗ νοῦς ἀνθρώπων ~εῖται ὁρᾶν* Hesych.S.*temp.*1.29 (M.93.1489A); ref. teachers *λάμποντες καὶ ~οῦντες* ‡Caes.Naz.*dial.*1 (M.38.856); of Christ, Jo.D.*hom.*1.13(M.96.564D).

δᾳδουχία, ἡ, *torch-bearing*, esp. in mysteries; hence *illumination διὰ τῆς ἄνωθεν δ. Χριστοῦ καθιέντος εἰς νοῦν...οἱάπερ ἀκτῖνα λαμπράν* Cyr.*Os.*172(3.196B); *διὰ τῆς τοῦ πνεύματος δ. προεγνωκὼς ὁ προφήτης* id.*Is.*3.1(2.363D); *προφητικῆς δ.* Thdt.*affect.*1(p.33.19; 4.724); Geo. Pis.*carm.*51.1.

δᾳδοῦχος, ὁ, *torch-bearer*, esp. in mysteries; met., of BMV *θεογεννῆτορ καὶ δ. τῶν πιστῶν* ‡Meth.*Sym.et Ann.*10(M.18.372C); of fathers at Chalcedon *σύνταγμα τῶν...δ. τῆς πίστεως* Sophr.H.*ep. syn.*(M.87.3185A).

***δαιδαλόγλωσσος**, *subtle-tongued*, Synes.*hymn.*3.257(p.14; M.66. 1597).

δαιδαλοεργός, ὁ, *skilful worker*, Paul.Sil.*ambo*.123(M.86.2256B).

δαίδαλον, τό, *cunningly worked thing*, plur., Paul.Sil.*Soph.*605 (M.86.2142B); id.*ambo*.97(M.86.2255B).

δαιμον-άω, *be possessed by a devil*; **1.** lit., *Hom.Clem.*7.10; Gr. Nyss.*v.Macr.*(M.46.1001A; *δαιμόνων* p.414.3); ‡Just.*qu.et resp.*40(M. 6.1285B); such possession better than sin, Chrys.*hom.83.6 in Mt.* (7.789E); id.*hom.48.3 in Jo.*(8.287B); of witch of Endor, Eust. *engast.*4(p.21.14; M.18.620D); **2.** with underlying sense of *rage*; of pagan actors, Tat.*orat.*22(p.24.26; M.6.856A); Clem.*prot.*1(p.4.25; M.8.56A); esp. of heretics, Anon.ap.Eus.*h.e.*5.16.8(M.20.468A); Rhod.*ib.*5.13.2(460B); †Hipp.*Artem.ib.*5.28.18(516A); *~ῶσα αἵρεσις* Eus.*h.e.*7.31.1(720C); Chrys.*stag.*2.2(1.182A); **3.** ref. accusation brought against Christ by Jews, Chrys.*hom.56.1 in Jo.*(8.326B); *οὐδὲ γὰρ ~ῶντος ἦν τοσαύτην ἐπιδείκνυσθαι ἐπιείκειαν· οὐ ~ῶντος τὸ τὰ ἀπόρρητα εἰδέναι* id.*hom.41.1 in Mt.*(7.445A); Leont.N.*serm.*2 (M.93.1592A).

δαιμονιακός, v. *δαιμονικός*.

***δαιμονιάριος, ὁ**, *maniac τὸν ἅγιον Ἐπιφάνιον...ἀπεκάλει* [sc. Chrysostom] *δ.* CQuerc.(M.103.107A); *δ. ἐστιν καθαρός* Leont.N.*v. Sym.*34(M.93.1712C); *ὁ ταξεώτης τοῦ ἐπάρχου...ὁ ἐπιλεγόμενος ἀπὸ Δαιμονιαρίων Chron.Pasch.*p.383(M.92.981B).

***δαιμονιασμός, ὁ**, *demonic possession*, Or.*comm.in Mt.*13.6(p.195. 15; M.13.1109A).

δαιμον-ιάω, = *δαιμονάω*, mostly lit., Just.*2apol.*1.2(M.6.444A); Clem.*ecl.*15(p.141.4; M.9.705A); Chrys.*dimiss.Chan.*11(3.443E); *~ιῶντας γὰρ ἐκάλουν* [sc. the Jews] *τοὺς εἰδωλολάτρας, διὰ τὸν ἐν αὐτοῖς ὄντα διάβολον* Cyr.*glaph.Num.*(1.381C).

δαιμονίζ-ομαι, *be possessed by a devil, T.Sal.*17.3; Or.*fr.79 in Jo.*(p.547.3); *A.Mt.*5(p.222.10); Pall.*h.Laus.*18(p.51.17; M.34.1059C); legislation on reception of sacraments by those possessed *ἐὰν ~όμενος κατηχούμενος ᾖ, καὶ θελήσῃ αὐτός, ἢ οἱ ἴδιοι αὐτοῦ, ἵνα λάβῃ τὸ ἅγιον βάπτισμα...ἐὰν ὁ ~όμενος μὴ καθαρισθῇ ἀπὸ τοῦ ἀκαθάρτου πνεύματος, οὐ δύναται λαβεῖν τὸ ἅγιον βάπτισμα· περὶ δὲ τὴν ἔξοδον βαπτίζεται. ἐὰν πιστός τις ὢν ~εται, ὀφείλει μεταλαβεῖν τῶν ἁγίων μυστηρίων...ἐὰν μὴ ἐξαγορεύῃ τὸ μυστήριον, μήτε ἄλλως πως βλασφημῇ, μεταλαμβανέτω· μὴ μέντοι καθ' ἑκάστην* Tim.I Al.*resp.*(M.33. 1297B,C).

δαιμονικός, -ιακός, **1.** *phantom-like, ghostly*, ref. Docet. *καθὼς φρονοῦσιν καὶ συμβήσεται αὐτοῖς, οὖσιν ἀσωμάτοις καὶ δ.* Ign.*Smyrn.* 2; **2.** *of* or *pertaining to evil spirits αἱ ἀπὸ τοὐναντίου πνεύματος δ. κινήσεις* Athenag.*leg.*25.3(M.6.949B); Or.*Cels.*8.61(p.277.17; M.11. 1608A); Eus.*e.th.*1.12(p.72.31; M.24.849B); *φανερὸν ἂν εἴη...μὴ εἶναι δ. τινα δύναμιν...Χριστόν* Ath.*inc.*48.8(M.25.184A); Chrys.*sac.*3.6 (p.57.3; 1.384C); Nil.*epp.*3.153(M.79.456A); Thdt.*h.rel.*6(3.1169); *μὴ ἀνθρωπίνοις λογισμοῖς θέλειν...περιγενέσθαι λογισμῶν δ.* Dor.*ep.*1 (M.88.1840A); esp. *belonging to* or *caused by demons* (i.e. heathen gods), Eus.*v.C.*2.61(p.65.27; M.20.1036A); *ib.*3.27(p.90.29; 1088C); *ἀπέχεσθε...πάσης τῆς τῶν εἰδώλων πομπῆς...καὶ πάσης θέας δ. Const. App.*2.62.4; Chrys.*hom.20.1 in 1Cor.*(10.168E); Bas.Sel.*or.*8.2(M.85. 120A); Euthal.Diac.*epp.cath.*(M.85.688A); **3.** *possessed by evil spirits, demoniac*, Clem.*str.*6.12(p.481.9; M.9.320B); *-ιακός* Eus. *p.e.*4.15(154D; M.21.269A); *-ιακός Apophth.Mac.Aeg.*5.3(M.34.213B); esp. of heretics *δ. τις ὢν* [sc. Manes] *καὶ μανιώδης* Eus.*h.e.*7.31.1 (M.20.720C); *οἱ ἐκ τῆς δ. ἐκκλησίας* Jo.Nic.*nativ.*(M.96.1448B); **4.** *τὸ δ.* = *δαιμόνιον T.Sal.*1.1(v.l. *δαιμόνιον* M.122.1316A).

***δαιμονιόθυτος**, *sacrificed to demons* (i.e. to heathen gods), Or. *Cels.*8.21(p.238.13; M.11.1549A).

***δαιμονιόληπτος**, *possessed by an evil spirit*, Just.*1apol.*18.4 (M.6.356B); id.*2apol.*6.6(M.6.453B) cit. s. *δαίμων*.

***δαιμονιόμορφος**, *having the shape of demons*, ‡Jo.D.*hom.*5(M.96. 657A).

δαιμόνιον, τό, **1.** *spirit, phantom ψηλαφήσατέ με, καὶ ἴδετε ὅτι οὐκ εἰμὶ δ. ἀσώματον* Ign.*Smyrn.*3.2; *δ. ... ἄσαρκα φανταζόμενοι ἐκ νεκρῶν ἀναστήσεσθαι Const.App.*6.26.3; **2.** *genius*, ref. Socrates, Clem.*str.*1.17(p.54.11; M.8.797D); Or.*Cels.*6.8(p.78.18; M.11.1301A); **3.** *evil spirit*; **a.** in gen., *Barn.*16.7; Herm.*mand.*2.3 cit. s. *καταλαλία*; *μέγα...δ. ἐστιν ἡ αὐθάδεια* id.*sim.*9.22.3; *ib.*9.23.5; *Μένανδρον. ...ἐνεργηθέντα...ὑπὸ τῶν δ.* Just.*1apol.*26.4(M.6.368B); id.*dial.*78.9 (M.6.660C); Iren.*haer.*1.5.4(M.7.497B); *τὰ δ. ἀσώματα εἴρηται, οὐχ ὡς σῶμα μὴ ἔχοντα. ... ἀλλ' ὡς πρὸς σύγκρισιν τῶν σωζομένων πνευματικῶν σκιὰ ὄντα ἀσώματα εἴρηται* Clem.*exc.Thdot.*14(p.111.15; M.9.664B); *οἱ...πολλοὶ παῖδες ἄχρηστοι γίνονται, ὑπὸ δ. ὀχλούμενοι. ... γίνονται γὰρ ἢ σεληνιαζόμενοι. ... ἢ πηροὶ...ἢ μωροί A.Thom.*A 12 (p.117.8); Or.*Cels.*1.31(p.82.29; M.11.720A); *οὐκ ὤκνησαν...καὶ τὰ νομισθέντα ἂν ἐλάχιστα εἶναι τῶν ἁμαρτημάτων δαιμονίοις προσάψαι οἱ φήσαντες τὴν ὀξυχολίαν δ. εἶναι, ὁμοίως δὲ...τὴν καταλαλίαν* id.*Jo.*20. 36(29; p.376.4; M.14.657B); *τὸ δ. ὁ σεληνιασμός* id.*hom.12.12 in Jer.* (p.98.17; M.13.393C); *ἵνα δ. νοῆτε τὰ ἐφεδρεύοντα πνεύματα τοῖς ἀψύχοις μορφώμασι* id.*Apoc.*35(p.39.5); *χάρισαι δύναμιν θεραπευτικὴν ἐπὶ τὰ κτίσματα ταῦτα* [sc. water and oil] *ὅπως...πᾶν δ. καὶ πᾶσα νόσος...ἀπαλλαγῇ* Serap.*euch.*17.2; *δ. μεσημβρινόν* (Ps.90:6), identified with *ἀκηδία*, Cyr.*Ps.*90:6(M.69.122A); *Euchol.*(p.277);

b. exeg. 1Reg.28:3ff., v. δαίμων; **c.** of heathen gods regarded as evil spirits ψευδοπροφῆται. ... τὰ τῆς πλάνης πνεύματα καὶ δ. δοξολογοῦσιν Just.*dial*.7.3(M.6.492C); Tat.*orat*.19(p.21.17; M.6.849A); δεισιδαίμων...ὁ δεδιὼς τὰ δ. Clem.*str*.7.1(p.5.12; M.9.408A); πάντων τῶν παρὰ τοῖς ἔθνεσι νομιζομένων θεῶν καταφρονεῖν ὡς οὐ θεῶν ἀλλὰ δ. Or.*Cels*.3.2(p.204.29; M.11.924A); τῷ τοῦ τόπου δ. *ib*.8.36(p.251.23; 1572C); μή ποτε εἰδωλολατρήσωμεν καὶ τοῖς δ. ἑαυτοὺς ὑποτάξωμεν· τὰ γὰρ εἴδωλα τῶν ἐθνῶν δ. id.*mart*.32(p.28.7; M.11.604B); τὸ λαοπλάνον δ. Eus.*h.e*.7.17(M.20.680A); τὰ λίχνα δ., θερώμενα τὴν ἀπὸ τῶν αἱμάτων...τῶν θυσιῶν ἀπόλαυσιν, περὶ τοὺς βωμοὺς εἱλεῖται †Bas.*Is*.236(1.558E; M.30.532D); τὰ...δ., τὰ προσδιατρίβοντα τῷ περιγείῳ τόπῳ...εἰς τὸν οἰκεῖον τῆς ἀβύσσου ἀπελαθήσεται τόπον *ib*.(559B; M.533B); Gr.Nyss.*Eun*.4(2 p.75.16; M.45.648D); Chrys.*hom.in Is*.45:7(6.154A); Philost.*h.e*.7.8(M.65.545B); ἡ τῶν ἐθνῶν πληθύς, ἡ...καθέδρα δαιμονίων τυγχάνουσα Job.Mon.*inc*.1(M.86.3316A); **4.** *Devil, Satan* τοῦ δ. ἡμᾶς νικήσαντος Or.*Jo*.20.36(29; p.376.32; M.14.660A); Nonn.*par.Jo*.17:12(M.43.885B).

δαιμόνιος, 1. *supernatural, divine* ὄνομα δ. ἔσχε Μωϋσῆς Cels.ap.Or.*Cels*.1.21(p.72.4; M.11.696C); Cels.*ib*.5.24(p.36.23; 1233A); Cels.*ib*.8.48(p.263.6; 1588B); **2.** *demonic, caused by demons* δ. νόσου Gr.Nyss.*Eun*.8(2 p.194.15; M.45.789B).

δαιμονισμός, ὁ, *demonic possession,* Or.*Cels*.8.58(p.275.17; M.11.1605B); *ib*.8.66(p.282.5; 1616A).

δαιμονιώδης, *devilish,* Or.*princ*.2.8.3(p.160.9) cit. s. κατάστασις; δ. αἵρεσις Ath.*decr*.5(p.5.22; M.25.425A); δ. διδασκαλίας Epiph.*haer*.42.14(p.183.28; M.41.813B); δ. ἐπιβουλὰς δι' ὧν ἐπάγεται τοῖς ἀνθρώποις τὰ πονηρὰ πρὸς ἁμαρτίαν συμπτώματα Gr.Nyss.*or.dom*.1(p.20.14; M.44.1132B); Nil.*epp*.3.33(M.79.392C) cit. s. θυμός; ἐγκόσμιον...καὶ δ. καὶ ψυχικὴν σοφίαν Cyr.*Ps*.9:23(M.69.780A); ‡Jo.D.*ep.Thphl*.9(M.95.356C) cit. s. οἰώνισμα.

***δαιμονιωδῶς,** *devilishly, madly, like one possessed,* Pall.*h.mon*.8(p.40.6; M.34.1140B); Thphn.*chron*.p.93(M.108.276B); δαιμωνιωδῶς Sophr.H.*ep.syn*.(M.87.3184A).

δαιμονίως, *by supernatural power, miraculously,* Cels.ap.Or.*Cels*.3.26(p.222.11; M.11.952A).

***δαιμονομανία, ἡ,** *madness of demon-worship*; of pagan cult, Areth.*Apoc*.27(M.106.636A).

δαιμονόπλοκος, *woven by the Devil* σειρά τις εἶναι δ. ἡ καθόλου αἵρεσις Thdr.Stud.*epp*.1.40(M.99.1053C).

***δαιμονοποιός,** *making* men *into demons* ἀποσχέσθαι αὐτὸν τῶν σκοτεινῶν...καὶ δ. φθεγμάτων Thdr.Stud.*epp*.2.116(M.99.1385C).

δαιμονώδης, *devilish,* Chrys.*exp.in Ps*.11(5.120B).

***δαιμοχαίρων,** *demon-loving* Βεελφεγὼρ...ἑρμηνεύεται εἶδος ἀσχημοσύνης, καὶ δαιμοχαίρων Hesych.H.*Ps.tit*.105.58(M.27.1117C).

δαίμων, ὁ, [acc. δαίμοναν *Mir.Geo*.13(p.133.5)]; *demon, devil, evil spirit*; etym. δ. ... οὐχ ἧπερ Ἕλλησι δοκεῖ παρὰ τὸ δαήμονας εἶναι καὶ ἐπιστήμονας, ἀλλ' ἢ παρὰ τὸ δειμαίνειν, ὅπερ ἐστὶ φοβεῖσθαι καὶ ἐκφοβεῖν, δαίμονάς τινας προσφυῶς ὀνομάζεσθαι Eus.*p.e*.4.5(142B; M.21.248C); cf. *daemonas autem grammatici dictos aiunt quasi* δαήμονας *id est penitos ac rerum scios,* Lactantius *divinae institutiones* 2.15(M.*PL*.6.331A).

A. origin; **1.** older view, offspring of marriages between 'angels' and women (cf. Gen.6:4), or these angels themselves, Just.*2apol*.5.3(M.6.452B); αἱ τῶν γιγάντων ψυχαὶ οἱ περὶ τὸν κόσμον εἰσὶ πλανώμενοι δ. Athenag.*leg*.25.1(M.6.948C); **2.** later refutation ἀναγκαῖον...ἡμᾶς...εἰπεῖν...ἐπειδὴ δὲ οἱ υἱοί, φησίν, τοῦ ἐπικληθέντος θεοῦ, τουτέστι, τοῦ Ἐνώς, τὰς ἐκ τοῦ Κάιν θυγατέρας τεθέανται, ἃς καὶ τῶν ἀνθρώπων θυγατέρας εἶπεν ἡ γραφή· εἶτα προσεφθάρησαν αὐταῖς... ἀσύνετον δὲ τὸ οἴεσθαι τοὺς ἀσωμάτους δ. ἐνεργεῖν δύνασθαι τὰ σωμάτων, καὶ τὸ παρὰ φύσιν ἰδίαν ἐπιτελεῖν Cyr.*resp*.15(p.601.18; 6².385B); id.*glaph.Gen*.2(1.28B); ‡Caes.Naz.*dial*.48(M.38.917).

B. nature and destiny; **1.** discussion whether material; **a.** old view that they have a certain kind of body δ. δὲ πάντες σαρκίον μὲν οὐ κέκτηνται, πνευματικὴ δέ ἐστιν αὐτοῖς ἡ σύμπηξις ὡς πυρὸς καὶ ἀέρος. μόνοις γοῦν τοῖς πνεύματι θεοῦ φρουρουμένοις εὐσύνοπτα καὶ τὰ τῶν δ. ἐστὶ σώματα, τοῖς λοιποῖς δὲ οὐδαμῶς, λέγω δὲ τοῖς ψυχικοῖς Tat.*orat*.15(p.16.27; M.6.840A); Clem.*str*.7.6(p.24.5; M.9.444B); cf.id.*exc.Thdot*.81(p.131.32; M.9.696B); cf. *tale corpus quale habent daemones, quod est naturaliter subtile quoddam et velut aura tenue, et propter hoc vel putatur a multis vel dicitur incorporeum,* Or.*princ*.1 proem.8(p.15.12; M.11.120A); for they must be fed, id.*mart*.45(p.41.31; M.11.624B); id.*Cels*.4.32(p.302.14; M.11.1076C,D); *ib*.8.30(p.245.6; 1560B); **b.** later view, that they do not possess bodies; †Bas.*Is*.97(1.447B; M.30.277B); yet given to material lusts *ib*.; τῶν δ. ἕκαστος, οὔτε ὄψα προσφέρεται, οὔτε πολυποσίας, ἢ μέθης δέχεται κατηγόρημα. φύσις γὰρ αὐτοὺς τῆς τῶν βρωμάτων μετουσίας ἐχώρισεν Gr.Nyss.*paup*.1(M.46.456A); ‡Chrys.*indict*.1.1(8².94C); Thdt.*Is*.13:21(p.69.15; 2.265); Dion.Ar.*d.n*.4.27(3.728D); **c.** whether they differ in nature from angels ἅγιοι ἄγγελοι ἄλλης εἰσὶ φύσεως καὶ προαιρέσεως παρὰ τοὺς ἐπὶ γῆς πάντας δ. Or.*Cels*.3.37(p.233.25; M.11.968B); later view τί παρήλλακται ἡ οὐσία τῶν δ. τῶν ἀγγέλων; ἡ οὐσία οὐ παρήλλακται, ἀλλ' ἡ προαίρεσις ‡Ath.*qu.Ant*.(M.28.604A); †Bas.*Is*.97(1.447B; M.30.277B); **d.** not souls of the dead, Tat.*orat*.16(p.17.11; M.6.840B); Chrys.*hom.28.2 in Mt*.(7.336B); **2.** demons and evil; **a.** not created evil δεῖ...περὶ δαιμόνων ἀκριβέστερον διειληφέναι ὅτι τε μή εἰσι, καθὸ δ. εἰσι, δημιουργήματα τοῦ θεοῦ, ἀλλὰ μόνον καθὸ λογικοί τινες, καὶ πόθεν ἐληλύθασιν ἐπὶ τὸ τοιοῦτοι γενέσθαι, ὡς ἐν καταστάσει δαιμόνων αὐτῶν ὑποστῆναι τὸ ἡγεμονικόν Or.*Cels*.4.65(p.336.13; M.11.1133C); κατὰ δὲ ἡμᾶς πάντες δ. ἀποπεσόντες τῆς ἐπὶ τὸ ἀγαθὸν ὁδοῦ, πρότερον οὐκ ὄντες δ.· καὶ ἔστιν εἶδος τῶν ἐκπεσόντων θεοῦ τὸ τῶν δ. *ib*.7.69(p.218.18ff.; 1517C); οἱ δ. οὐ καθ' ὃ δ. καλοῦνται, οὕτω γεγόνασιν· οὐδὲν γὰρ κακὸν ἐποίησεν ὁ θεός· ἀλλὰ καλοὶ μὲν γεγόνασι καὶ αὐτοί Ath.*v.Anton*.22(M.26.876A); Gr.Naz.*or*.39.7(M.36.341B); τούτους [sc. δ.]...οὐ πονηροὺς ἐξ ἀρχῆς παρὰ τοῦ θεοῦ τῶν ὅλων δημιουργηθῆναί φαμεν, οὐδὲ τοιάνδε φύσιν λαχεῖν· ἀλλὰ τῇ παρατροπῇ τῆς γνώμης, ἀπὸ τῶν ἀμεινόνων εἰς τὰ χείρω μεταπεσεῖν Thdt.*affect*.3(p.97.6; 4.788f.); id.*haer*.5.8(4.407); Dion.Ar.*d.n*.4.34(M.3.733C); view that demons are evil by nature elaborately refuted, *ib*.4.23(M.3.724C–725C); πλῆθος πολὺ...τῶν ἀγγέλων, οἵτινες, κακοὶ γεγονότες τὴν προαίρεσιν, καί, ἀντὶ τοῦ ἀγαθοῦ, τῇ ἀποστασίᾳ ἐξακολουθήσαντες τοῦ ἄρχοντος αὐτῶν, δ. ὠνομάσθησαν †Jo.D.*B.J*.7(M.96.908A,B); **b.** but all are now evil, without possibility of repentance ἡ τῶν δ. ὑπόστασις οὐκ ἔχει μετανοίας τόπον Tat.*orat*.15(p.17.1; M.6.840A); Clem.*prot*.3(p.33.3; M.8.128B); τὸ τῶν δ. ὄνομα οὐδὲ μέσον ἐστὶν ὡς τὸ τῶν ἀνθρώπων, ἐν οἷς τινὲς μὲν ἀστεῖοι τινὲς δὲ φαῦλοί εἰσιν...ἀεὶ δ' ἐπὶ τῶν φαύλων ἔξω τοῦ παχυτέρου σώματος δυνάμεων τάσσεται τὸ τῶν δ. ὄνομα Or.*Cels*.5.5(p.5.15ff.; M.11.1188A); *ib*.8.31(p.246.24; 1561C); Eus.*p.e*.4.5(142A; M.21.248B); **c.** and cause all evil in the world, Tat.*orat*.17(p.19.16; 844B); **d.** cause of their apostasy; man ὑπόθεσις δὲ αὐτοῖς τῆς ἀποστασίας οἱ ἄνθρωποι γίνονται *ib*.8(p.8.4; 821A); Eus.*d.e*.4.9(p.162.14; M.22.272A); whose honourable place in Creation they envied, ‡Bas.*Lac*.8(2.592E–593B; M.31.1452B,C); cf.†Bas.*Is*.279(1.591E–592A; M.30.609A,B); pride, Thdt.*haer*.5.8(4.407); ἐξ ἀγγέλων δ. τινὰς αὕτη [sc. οἴησις] πεποίηκε Jo.Clim.*scal*.25(M.88.1001B); transgression and ignorance, Tat.*orat*.7(p.8.1; 821A); **e.** demons and passion, v. πάθος; **3.** their ultimate fate; **a.** eternal punishment, cf. ἀθανασία, ἀθάνατος; Just.*1apol*.28.1(M.6.372B) al.; *M.Carp*.7; Thdt.*haer*.5.8(4.406); view that Christ died also for them is condemned, Nil.*epp*.1.204(M.79.160A); **b.** acc. Or. they participate in final *apocatastasis* πάντων ἀσεβῶν ἀνθρώπων καὶ πρός γε δ. ἡ κόλασις πέρας ἔχει καὶ ἀποκατασταθήσονται ἀσεβεῖς τε καὶ δ. εἰς τὴν προτέραν αὐτῶν τάξιν Or.*princ*.2.10.8(p.183.3f.)ap.Justn.*Or*.(M.86.975A); δ. ... τὴν αὐτὴν τοῖς ἁγίοις τάξιν διὰ τῆς ἀποκαταστάσεως λαμβάνειν Justn.*ib*.(p.205.28; M.86.975C); †Leont.B.*sect*.10(M.86.1265C); **4.** their present habitat; earth itself or air surrounding earth, Or.*Cels*.8.33(p.248.28; M.11.1565B); id.*mart*.45(p.41.17; M.11.621A); Eus.*p.e*.5.2(181D; M.21.316A); Chrys.*exp.in Ps*.41(5.137D).

C. pagan gods as demons; **1.** in gen., Just.*1apol*.5.2(M.6.336B); οἱ δ. αὐτοὶ μετὰ τοῦ ἡγουμένου [αὐτῶν] Διός Tat.*orat*.8(p.8.18; M.6.824A); Clem.*prot*.2(p.30.15ff.; M.8.121B); a demon confessing προσκυνούμεθα ὑπ' αὐτῶν [sc. pagans] ὡς θεοί· ἀλλ' ἐν ἀληθείᾳ ἐσμὲν δ. *A.Barth*.6(p.142.20); ἑορταῖς...αἵτινες ἐπὶ τιμῇ τῶν δ. ἐπιτελοῦνται *Const.App*.2.62.3; *ib*.5.11.1; **2.** individual pagan gods called demons, e.g. Apollo, Clem.*prot*.3(p.33.18; M.8.129A); Or.*Cels*.3.28(p.225.20; M.11.956B); Proteus, Clem.*paed*.3.1(p.236.8; M.8.556B); Ὀλυμπιακός, ἣ δαίμονος ἑορτή Bas.Sel.*or*.27.1(M.85.309B); **3.** pagan gods and heroes, demons in disguise, Eus.*p.e*.5.3(182C; M.21.316C); *ib*.4.15(153D–154B; M.268B,C); **4.** demons in statues δ. ἐνιδρυμένοι τισὶν ἀγάλμασι Or.*Cels*.8.41(p.256.12; M.11.1577C); Ath.*exp.Ps*.5:7(M.27.73D); Chrys.*exp.in Ps*.134(5.395B,C).

D. demons' relationships with men, apart from possession; **1.** demon (i.e. Satan) caused Fall, Bas.*hex*.6.1(1.50C; M.29.117C,D); cf.id.*hom*.9.8(2.80E; M.31.348B); **2.** demons generally hostile to man, producing droughts, famines, storms etc. πάντα ταῦτα δ. αὐτουργοῦσι δήμιοι, κρίσει τινὶ θείᾳ λαβόντες ἐξουσίαν ἐν καιροῖς τισι ταῦτ' ἐνεργεῖν εἴτε εἰς ἐπιστροφὴν ἀνθρώπων Or.*Cels*.8.31(p.247.3ff.; M.11.1564A); Gr.Nyss.*anim.et res*.(M.46.72A); ὁ...δ., καθάπερ ἐχθρὸς καὶ πολέμιος, πολεμεῖ τῇ φύσει τῇ ἀνθρωπίνῃ Chrys.*exp.in Ps*.44(5.161C); οἱ δ. πανταχοῦ τοὺς ἀνθρώπους εἰς ἀθυμίαν ἐμβάλλειν ἐσπουδάκασι, καὶ πανταχοῦ χαίρουσι τῇ ἀπωλείᾳ id.*hom.28.3 in Mt*.(7.338A); Synes.*ep*.57(M.66.1384C); χαρὰ τοῖς δ. ἡ τῶν ἀνθρώπων ἀπώλεια, καὶ τρυφῶσιν ἐκεῖνοι τοῖς ἡμετέροις κακοῖς Bas.Sel.*or.*23 (M.85.277B); **3.** in paganism; **a.** instigators of idolatry οἱ μὲν περὶ τὰ εἴδωλα αὐτοὺς ἕλκοντες οἱ δ. εἰσιν...οἱ προστετηκότες τῷ ἀπὸ τῶν ἱερείων αἵματι καὶ ταῦτα περιλιχμώμενοι Athenag.*leg.*26.1(M.6.949D); *ib.*27.2(953A); Eus.*p.e.*4.14(153B; M.21.265C); of belief in fate τοιοῦτοί τινές εἰσιν οἱ δ. [οὗτοι] οἳ τὴν εἱμαρμένην ὥρισαν Tat.*orat.*9(p.9.23; M.6.825A); and of other evils δ. φαῦλοι, ἐπιφανείας ποιησάμενοι, καὶ γυναῖκας ἐμοίχευσαν καὶ παῖδας διέφθειραν Just.*1apol.*5.2(M.6.336A); Tat.*orat.*14(p.15.12; 836B); through sacrifice offered to them, demons obtain power over men, cf.1Cor.10:20, *Hom.Clem.*9.9; *Const.App.*7.21; **b.** as objects of worship τὸν...παρελθόντα εἰς τὸν βίον δ. τοῖς τὰ ἐπὶ γῆς εἰληχόσιν εὐχαριστητέον καὶ ἀπαρχὰς καὶ εὐχὰς ἀποδοτέον, ἕως ἂν ζῶμεν, ὡς ἂν φιλανθρώπων αὐτῶν τυγχάνοιμεν Cels. ap.Or.*Cels.*8.33(p.248.17; M.11.1565A); equated with angels ἀγγέλους θεοῦ ἢ δ. ἀγαθούς Or.*ib.*3.37(p.234.6; 967C); *ib.*4.24(p.243.27; 1061B); Plato's view δαιμόνων δὲ φύσεις ἀποδέχεται, καὶ τοὺς μὲν ἀγαθοὺς εἶναί φησιν αὐτῶν, τοὺς δὲ φαύλους Hipp.*haer.*1.19(p.21.3; M.16.3044A); **c.** Christian refutation of pagan views οὐχ ὑποκείμεθά γε δαίμοσιν ἀλλὰ τῷ ἐπὶ πᾶσι θεῷ διὰ τοῦ ἡμᾶς προσαγαγόντος Ἰησοῦ τοῦ Χριστοῦ, καὶ κατὰ νόμους μὲν θεοῦ οὐδεὶς εἴληχε δ. τὰ ἐπὶ γῆς· διὰ ⟨δὲ⟩ τὴν σφῶν παρανομίαν τάχα μὲν αὐτοῖς διελόντες τοὺς τόπους Or.*Cels.*8.33(p.248.26ff.; M.11.1565B); Κέλσος μὲν οὐ θέλει ἡμᾶς ἀχαρίστους εἶναι πρὸς τοὺς τῇδε δ., οἰόμενος ἡμᾶς ὀφείλειν αὐτοῖς χαριστήρια· καὶ ἡμεῖς δὲ...φαμὲν πρὸς τοὺς μηδὲν εὐεργετοῦντας ἀλλὰ καὶ ἐκ τοῦ ἐναντίου ἱσταμένους μηδὲν ἀχάριστον ἡμᾶς ποιεῖν, ὅταν αὐτοῖς μὴ δύωμεν *ib.*8.57(p.273.31; 1601D); *ib.*8.25(p.241.21; 1553C); **d.** pagan opinion that demons govern world had to be opposed even by later Christians οὐχ οὕτως ἥλιος φανός, ὡς ἡ τοῦ θεοῦ πρόνοια σαφής· ἀλλ' ὅμως τολμῶσί τινες λέγειν, ὅτι δ. τὰ καθ' ἡμᾶς διοικοῦσι Chrys.*diab.*1.6(2.255D); εἰ δ. διῴκουν, οὐδὲν τῶν δαιμονιώντων ἀνθρώπων ἄμεινον διεκείμεθα, μᾶλλον δὲ κἀκείνων χείρους ἂν ἦμεν *ib.*(256D); μὴ δαίμοσι λογιζώμεθα τοῦ κόσμου τὴν οἰκονομίαν ‡Chrys.*prov.*1(2.753C); **4.** their activities among Christians; **a.** in gen., seek to draw men away from God and Christ, Just.*1apol.*58.3(M.6.416B); *ib.*58.1(416A); Or.*Cels.*8.64(p.280.15ff.; M.11.1613A); δ., οἵτινες ἡμᾶς ἐξαφανίσαι ἀπὸ τῶν σωζομένων καὶ ἐρημῶσαι σπουδάζουσι Nil.*epp.*3.99 (M.79.432A); Cyr.*Ps.*118:11(M.69.1272A); cause Christians to be persecuted, Just.*2apol.*1.2(M.6.444A); and are both tempters and accusers αὐτοὶ γὰρ διεγείρουσιν ἡμᾶς εἰς τὸ ἁμαρτεῖν, καὶ αὐτοὶ κατήγοροι γίνονται...αὐτοί οἱ δ. λέγοντες· οὐχ ἡμεῖς ὑπηρέται ὑμῶν γεγόναμεν εἰς τὸ ὀργισθῆναι, ἢ κενοδοξῆσαι Jo.Jej.*poenit.cont.virg.* (M.88.1965A); **b.** being responsible for many vices τῶν δὲ ἀμφὶ τὰς φλεγμαινούσας κυπταζόντων τραπέζας, τὰ σφέτερα τιθηνουμένων πάθη, δ. καθηγεῖται λιχνότατος, ὃν ἔγωγε οὐκ ἂν αἰσυνθείχην 'κοιλιοδαίμονα' προσειπεῖν [καὶ] δαιμόνων κάκιστον Clem.*paed.*2.1(p.165.9f.; M.8.404A); ὁ δ. τοῦ θυμοῦ, ὁ δ. τῆς κενοδοξίας, ὁ δ. τῆς λύπης καὶ... ἑκάστου πάθους ἡ δύναμις Or.*hom.6.11 in Ezech.*(p.390.18f.; M.13.719D); ἔστι μὲν ὅτε καὶ ἄλλοι ἄλλας διαφόρους σατανικὰς διανοίας ἐκτελοῦσιν οἱ δ. πρὸς πειρασμόν, καὶ βλάβην τῶν ἀνθρώπων· ἔστι δὲ ὅτε καὶ εἷς δ. πολλὰς τεκταίνει φαυλότητας Nil.*epp.*1.294(M.79.189C); †Nil.*mal.cog.*1(M.79.1200D); Jo.Clim.*scal.*3(M.88.664D); *ib.*23(965B); Max.*carit.*2.19(M.90.989B); but not so as to exonerate man from responsibility for sin, Clem.*str.*6.12(p.481.7; M.9.320A); theory that there are two kinds of demons, the one to tempt soul, the other to tempt body, fully propounded, Diad.*perf.*81(p.104.8ff.); **c.** deceiving by magic διὰ τῆς τῶν ἐνεργούντων δ. τέχνης δυνάμεις ποιήσας μαγικάς Just.*1apol.*26.2(M.6.368A); ἵνα...πιστεύσωμέν τινας, ἐκ τῆς ἀσήμου φωνῆς τῶν ὀρνίθων μαθόντας ὅτι ἀπίασί ποι οἱ ὄρνιθες καὶ ποιήσουσι τόδε ἢ τόδε, προδηλοῦν, καὶ τοῦτ' ἐροῦμεν ἀπὸ τῶν δ. συμβολικῶς ἀνθρώποις δεδηλῶσθαι κατὰ σκοπὸν τὸν περὶ τοῦ ἀπατηθῆναι ὑπὸ τῶν δ. τὸν ἄνθρωπον καὶ κατασπασθῆναι αὐτοῦ τὸν νοῦν ἀπ' οὐρανοῦ καὶ θεοῦ ἐπὶ γῆν καὶ τὰ ἔτι κατωτέρω Or.*Cels.*4.97(p.370.27; M.11.1177A); cf. *sive auguratio, sive extispicium, sive quaelibet immolatio, sive etiam sortitio aut quicumque motus avium vel pecudum ...ut aliquid de futuris videatur ostendere, in operatione daemonum fieri non dubito, dirigentium vel avium vel pecudum...motus aut sortium secundum ea signa, quae docuerunt idem daemones observari ab his, quibus artis hujus scientiam tradiderunt,* id.*hom.16.7 in Num.*(p.147.24ff.; M.12.698A); id.*Cels.*4.93(p.366.15ff.; 1172B,C); Eus.*h.e.*8.14.5(M.20.781C); occupation with which is forbidden to Christians, cf.Or.*hom.16.7 in Num.*(pp.148.28–149.2; 699A); εἰ δὲ ἀπὸ δαιμόνων ἐνεργείας ἀπατηλὰ περιπέτονται, μή μοι καθέζου δαιμόνων ἀπάταις προσκεχηνώς, μηδὲ γίνου διαβολικαῖς ἔκδοτος ἐνεργείαις †Bas.*Is.*77(1.434A; M.30.248C); *ib.*78(434D; M.249B); demonic predictions not true prophecy, Jo.Clim.*scal.*3(M.88.669C); ἐν τοῖς πειθομένοις τῷ δ. πολλάκις προφήτης ἐγένετο· ἐν τοῖς δὲ ἐξουθενοῦσιν αὐτόν, ἀεὶ ἐψεύσατο...οὐδὲν τῶν μελλόντων ἐκ προγνώσεως οἴδασιν *ib.*(672A); because they are liars, should never be believed, Chrys.*hom.13.2 in Mt.*(7.170C); Cyr.*Jo.*12(4.1039C); speak truth only if compelled by higher power, Eust.*engast.*4(p.20.30; M.18.620C); **d.** tempting and vexing Christians in other ways πολλῆς τοῖς ἀγωνιζομένοις διὰ τοὺς ἀνταγωνισμένους δ. χρεία τῆς νήψεως...τῶν ἀντιπάλων φυλάξασθαι τὰς ἐπιβουλὰς πολλῶν ὄντων, καὶ ἀοράτων, καὶ πάθεσιν ἡμετέροις καὶ αἰσθήσεσιν ὅπλοις καθ' ἡμῶν κεχρημένων Nil.*Magn.*59(M.79.1048B); ἀλλήλοις...βοηθοῦσιν οἱ δ., εἰς ἀπώλειαν τῶν τούτοις [sc. sins] περιπιπτόντων συμφωνοῦντες, τάχα πῶς ὁ ἄνθρωπος τῆς οἰκείας ἀπογνῷ σωτηρίας id.*epp.*3.42(M.79.408C); καὶ τοῖς ἔξωθεν πράγμασι κέχρηνται πρὸς τὰς φαντασίας οἱ δ. †Nil.*mal.cog.*4(M.79.1205A); ἐν ταῖς καθ' ὕπνον φαντασίαις τυποῦσιν ἡμῶν τὸ ἡγεμονικὸν καὶ σχηματίζουσιν οἱ δ. *ib.*(1204C); πρὸ μὲν τοῦ πτώματος, φιλάνθρωπον· μετὰ δὲ τὸ πτῶμα ἀπότομον τὸν θεὸν λέγουσιν οἱ δ. Jo.Clim.*scal.*5 (M.88.780A); εἰσὶν ἀκάθαρτοι πονηρῶν πονηρότεροι δ., οἳ τὴν ἁμαρτίαν ἡμᾶς κατεργάζεσθαι μόνους οὐ συμβουλεύουσιν· ἀλλὰ κοινωνοὺς ἡμᾶς πρὸς τὸ κακόν, καὶ ἑτέρους ἔχειν συμβουλεύουσιν *ib.*26(1060D); freq. also in disguise ὁ δ. ὁ ἐν τῷ στρατιωτικῷ σχήματι φανεὶς *A.Mt.*14 (p.232.6); Evagr.Pont.*or.*107(M.79.1192A); **e.** receiving souls of wicked after death, *Hom.Clem.*9.9; Mac.Aeg.*hom.*22(M.34.660A); and detaining those not yet perfectly purified, *ib.*43.9(777C); ἐὰν ἐξέλθῃ ἡ ψυχὴ μὴ γνοῦσα τὴν ἀλήθειαν, παραδίδοται τοῖς δ., ὅπως δαμάσωσιν αὐτὴν ἐν ταῖς γεένναις τοῦ πυρός Hegem.*Arch.*11(p.18.10; M.10.1445A); **5.** demons in spiritual life (for special demon of accidie, the noonday devil, v. ἀκηδία); **a.** distractions in prayer caused by demons λίαν βασκαίνει ὁ δ. ἀνθρώπῳ προσευχομένῳ, καὶ πάσῃ χρᾶται μηχανῇ, λυμήνασθαι τὸν τούτου σκοπόν· οὐ παύεται οὖν τὰ νοήματα κινῶν τῶν πραγμάτων διὰ τῆς μνήμης, καὶ ὅλα τὰ πάθη ἀναμοχλεύων διὰ τῆς σαρκός, ἵνα ἐμποδίσαι δυνηθῇ τῷ ἀρίστῳ αὐτοῦ δρόμῳ Evagr.Pont.*or.*46(M.79.1176D); τοὺς μὲν ἄκρως προσευχομένους πολεμοῦσιν οἱ δ., ἵνα τὰ νοήματα τῶν αἰσθητῶν ψιλὰ μὴ ἀναλαμβάνωσι· τοὺς δὲ γνωστικούς, ἵνα ἐγχρονίζωσιν ἐν αὐτοῖς οἱ ἐμπαθεῖς λογισμοί Max.*carit.*2.90(M.90.1013B); distinction between distractions that come from man himself and those caused by demons εἰ...χρημάτων, ἢ δόξης ἀνάμνησις γένοιτο, ἐκ τοῦ πράγματος δῆλον ὅτι ὁ θλίβων ἡμᾶς ἐπιγνωσθήσεται· καὶ ἐπὶ τῶν ἄλλων δὲ λογισμῶν ὡσαύτως, ἀπὸ τοῦ πράγματος εὑρήσεις τὸν παρεστῶτα, καὶ ὑποβάλλοντα τὰς φαντασίας δ. οὐ πάσας δὲ τὰς μνήμας τῶν τοιούτων πραγμάτων ἐκ δαιμόνων λέγω συμβαίνειν· ἐπειδὴ πέφυκε καὶ αὐτὸς ὁ νοῦς κινούμενος ὑπὸ ἀνθρώπου τῶν γεγονότων ἀναφέρειν τὰς φαντασίας, ἀλλ' [viz. ἐκ δαιμόνων] ὅσαι τῶν μνημῶν θυμόν, ἢ ἐπιθυμίαν παρὰ φύσιν συνεπισπῶνται †Nil.*mal.cog.*2(M.79.1201C); **b.** special temptations in prayer ἐπὰν καθαρῶς... προσεύχηται ὁ νοῦς...οἱ δ. ... ὑποτίθενται...αὐτῷ δόξαν θεοῦ, καὶ σχηματισμόν τινα τῶν τῇ αἰσθήσει φίλων, ὡς δοκεῖν τελείως τετεῦχθαι αὐτὸν τοῦ περὶ προσευχῆς σκοποῦ. τοῦτο δέ,...ὑπὸ τοῦ τῆς κενοδοξίας πάθους γίνεσθαι, καὶ ὑπὸ τοῦ δαίμονος τοῦ ἁπτομένου, τοῦ κατὰ τὸ ἐγκέφαλον τόπου, καὶ φλεψὶ πάλλοντος Evagr.Pont.*or.*72(M.79.1181D); ὁ παμμίαρος φιλεῖ πολλάκις παρ' αὐτὰς τὰς ἁγίας συνάξεις...δυσφημεῖν τὸν κύριον. ... ὅθεν...μανθάνομεν σαφῶς μὴ οὖσαν τὴν ἡμετέραν ψυχὴν τὴν τὰ ἄθεσμα...καὶ ἄρρητα λόγια ἔνδοθεν φθεγξαμένην· ἀλλὰ τὸν μισόθεον δ. Jo.Clim.*scal.*23(M.88.976C); through visions, Evagr. Pont.*or.*94(1188B); **c.** in eremitical and monastic life, †Nil.*mal. cog.*8(M.79.1209C) cit. s. ἀναχωρητής; εἴθισται τῷ δ. καὶ μάλιστα ἐν τοῖς ἀγωνιζομένοις, καὶ τὸν μονήρη βίον μετερχομένοις πολλάκις πᾶσαν αὐτοῦ τὴν ὁρμὴν...ἐν τοῖς παρὰ φύσιν μόνον...αὐτοὺς παρασκευάζειν πολεμεῖσθαι Jo.Clim.*scal.*15(M.88.885B); **d.** principal temptations and remedies ἐν πάσαις ἡμῶν ταῖς κατὰ θεὸν ἐργασίαις τρεῖς ἡμῖν βοθύνους οἱ δ. ὀρύσσουσι. καὶ πρῶτον μὲν παλαίουσιν, ἵνα τὸ ἀγαθὸν κωλύσωσι γενέσθαι· δεύτερον δὲ μετὰ τὴν πρώτην αὐτῶν ἧτταν, ἵνα μὴ κατὰ θεὸν τὸ τυχὸν γένηται. ὅταν δὲ καὶ τούτου οἱ κλέπται τοῦ σκοποῦ ἀποτύχωσι, τότε λοιπὸν ἡσυχίως ἐπιστάντες ἐν τῇ ἡμετέρᾳ ψυχῇ μακαρίζουσιν ἡμᾶς, ὡς κατὰ θεὸν ἐν πᾶσιν πολιτευομένους. τοῦ μὲν προτέρου ἐχθρός, σπουδὴ καὶ μέριμνα θανάτου· τοῦ δὲ δευτέρου, ὑποταγὴ καὶ ἐξουδένωσις· τοῦ δὲ τρίτου, τὸ ἑαυτὸν διηνεκῶς καταμέμφεσθαι *ib.*26(1013C); *ib.*23(977D); **6.** limitations of their power; **a.** cannot truly prophesy, heal, or help men in other ways, Tat.*orat.*18(p.20.15; M.6.845B); *ib.*17(p.18.24; 844A); Or.*Cels.*8.57(p.274.9; M.11.1604A); τοῦτο [sc. προφητεία]...ἔργον θεοῦ, ὅπερ οὐδὲ μιμήσασθαι δύναιντ' ἂν οἱ δ., κἂν σφόδρα φιλονεικῶσιν...εἰ δέ που καὶ δ. τοῦτο πεποιήκασιν, ἀλλ' ἀπατῶντες τοὺς ἀνοητοτέρους Chrys.*hom.19.2 in Jo.*(8.112D); δ. οὐ θεραπεύουσιν. εἰ δέ ποτε, καὶ συγχωροῦντος τοῦ θεοῦ, ἐπιτύχοιέν τινος θεραπείας, καθάπερ ἄνθρωποι, εἰς δοκιμὴν τὴν σὴν ἡ συγχώρησις γίνεται, οὐκ ἐπειδὴ θεὸς ἀγνοεῖ, ἀλλ' ἵνα σὺ παιδευθῇς, μηδὲ θεραπευόντων ἀνέχεσθαι τῶν δ. id.*Jud.*1.7(1.598E); τῶν ἐσομένων οὐδὲν οἱ δ. ἴσασι· καταστοχαζόμενοι δὲ τῶν πραγμάτων,

...προλέγειν ἐπιχειροῦσι Thdt.*Ezech.*21:22(2.845); Jo.D.*f.o.*2.4(M.94.877A); do not know secrets of heart, †Nil.*mal.cog.*27(M.79.1232B); **b.** cannot harm Christians οὐ Χριστιανὸς...ὑποτάξας ἑαυτὸν μόνῳ τῷ θεῷ καὶ τῷ λόγῳ αὐτοῦ, πάθοι τι ἂν ὑπὸ τῶν δαιμονίων, ἅτε κρείττων δαιμόνων τυγχάνων Or.*Cels.*8.36(p.251.28; M.11.1572C); *ib.*8.27(p.243.7; 1556C); τὸ μὲν παρὰ δαίμονος ἐνοχλεῖσθαι χαλεπὸν οὐδέν· οὐ γὰρ εἰς γέενναν ἐμβαλεῖν τὸ δαιμόνιον δύναται Chrys.*hom.in 1 Tim.* 5:9(3.321B); οὐδεὶς...τῶν πονηρῶν δ. τοῦ ἐναρέτου ποτὲ κωλύει τὸ πρόθυμον Max.*qu.Thal.*56(M.90.581B,C); Jo.D.*f.o.*2.4(M.94.877B); but only those who subject themselves to them, Or.*Cels.*8.36(p.251.15; 1572B); *ib.*8.34(p.250.6; 1569A); being dependent on permission of God for man's good διὰ πέντε αἰτίας φασὶ παραχωρεῖσθαι ἡμᾶς ὑπὸ θεοῦ πολεμεῖσθαι ὑπὸ δαιμόνων καὶ πρώτην...ἵνα πολεμούμενοι καὶ ἀντιπολεμοῦντες, εἰς διάκρισιν τῆς ἀρετῆς καὶ τῆς κακίας ἔλθωμεν. δευτέραν δέ, ἵνα πολέμῳ...τὴν ἀρετὴν κτώμενοι, βεβαίαν αὐτὴν...ἕξωμεν. τρίτην δέ, ἵνα προκόπτοντες εἰς τὴν ἀρετήν ...μάθωμεν ταπεινοφρονεῖν. τετάρτην δέ, ἵνα πειρασθέντες τῆς κακίας, τέλειον μῖσος αὐτὴν μισήσωμεν. πέμπτην δὲ ἐπὶ πάσαις, ἵνα ἀπαθεῖς γενόμενοι, μὴ ἐπιλαθώμεθα τῆς οἰκείας ἀσθενείας Max.*carit.*2.67(M.90.1005B); their power limited to this world, Chrys.*incomprehens.* 4.2(1.474B) cit. s. κοσμοκράτωρ.

E. possession, freq. described in same bridal imagery as mystic union between Christ and soul; **1.** close relationship between certain men and demons (familiar spirits), cf. *ostenditur ab adversariis spiritibus quosdam a prima aetate possessos, id est nonnullos cum ipso daemone esse natos, alios vero a puero divinasse historiarum fides declarat, alii a prima aetate daemonem, quem Pythonem nominant, id est ventriloquum, passi sunt,* Or.*princ.*3.3.5(pp.261.19–262.1; M.11.318B,C); *A.Thom.*A 42 tit.(p.159.8); *ib.*43(p.161.9); οἱ μὲν κοινωνοῦσι Χριστῷ καὶ τοῖς ἀγγέλοις αὐτοῦ, οἱ δὲ τῷ σατανᾷ καὶ τοῖς δ. Mac.Aeg.*hom.*15.32(M.34.597B); *ib.*26.13(684A); *ib.*27.19(708A); οἱ δ. ... οἰκήτορες ἀνθρώπων ἐγίνοντο Bas.Sel.*or.*23.1(M.85.272B); its cause τὸ δὲ τοὺς δ. γλίχεσθαι εἰς τὰ τῶν ἀνθρώπων εἰσδύειν σώματα, αἰτία αὕτη. πνεύματα ὄντες καὶ τὴν ἐπιθυμίαν ἔχοντες εἰς βρωτὰ καὶ ποτὰ καὶ συνουσίαν, μεταλαμβάνειν δὲ μὴ δυνάμενοι διὰ τὸ πνεύματα εἶναι καὶ δεῖσθαι ὀργάνων τῶν πρὸς τὴν χρῆσιν ἐπιτηδείων, εἰς τὰ ἀνθρώπων εἰσίασιν σώματα, ἵνα, ὥσπερ ὑπουργούντων ὀργάνων τυχόντες, ὧν θέλουσιν ἐπιτυχεῖν δυνατοὶ ὦσιν *Hom.Clem.*9.10; **2.** before Christ all men possessed by demons, cf. *omnes daemones ante adventum domini et salvatoris nostri, quieti et securi humanas animas possidentes, in earum mentibus corporibusque regnabant,* Or.*hom.14.1 in Jos.*(p.376.21; M.12.893B); *per singula peccata, quae committimus, maxime si...studio affectuque peccamus, illi...daemoni, cui peccatum illud, quod admisimus, inoperari curae est, consecramur. et fortasse continget nobis tot daemoniis esse consecratos, quot peccata committimus...per alia peccata,...aliis daemonibus homines consecrantur. ...si senseris malignum spiritum loqui in corde tuo, ut te ducat ad aliquod opus peccati, intellige quia te ducere vult, ut consecret te alicui daemoni; ducere te vult, ut suscipias mysteria diabolica,* id.*hom.20.3 in Num.*(p.193.13ff.; M.12.732C–733A); *si infelix anima divini verbi dereliquerit sancta connubia et in adulterinos se complexus diaboli aliorumque daemonum illecebris decepta tradiderit, generabit sine dubio etiam inde filios, ib.*20.2(p.188.22; 729A); Jews possessed by demons both before and after Christ, Chrys.*Jud.*1.6(1.596B,C); **3.** description of possession ὁ...ἀκάθαρτος δ., ὅταν ἔρχηται ἐπὶ ψυχὴν ἀνθρώπου...ὡς λύκος αἱμοβόρος ἕτοιμος εἰς βορὰν...ἔρχεται· ἀγριωτάτη ἡ παρουσία, βαρυτάτη ἡ αἴσθησις, σκοτώδης ἡ διάνοια γίνεται...σώματι γὰρ ἀλλοτρίῳ, ὡς ἰδίῳ κεχρῆσθαι βιάζεται, καὶ ὀργάνῳ ἀλλοτρίῳ. τὸν ἑστῶτα καταβάλλει. οἰκεῖος γάρ ἐστι τοῦ πεσόντος ἐξ οὐρανοῦ. παρατρέπει τὴν γλῶσσαν. στρεβλοῖ τὰ χείλη. ἀφρὸς ἀντὶ ῥημάτων. σκοτοῦται ὁ ἄνθρωπος. ἤνοικται ὁ ὀφθαλμός, καὶ δι' αὐτοῦ οὐ βλέπει ἡ ψυχή· καὶ σπαίρει τρομικῶς ὁ ἄθλιος ἄνθρωπος πρὸ θανάτου. ἐχθροὶ τῶν ἀνθρώπων ἀληθῶς οἱ δ. Cyr.H.*catech.*16.15; Chrys.*Stag.*1.1(1.156D,E); which demonstrates wickedness of demons and goodness of God ὅταν ἴδῃς ἄνθρωπον ὑπὸ δ. κινούμενον, προσκύνησον τὸν δεσπότην, μάθε τῶν δ. τὴν πονηρίαν· ἀμφότερα γάρ ἐστιν ἰδεῖν ἐπὶ τῶν δαιμονώντων τούτων, καὶ τὴν τοῦ θεοῦ φιλανθρωπίαν, καὶ τὴν τῶν δ. κακίαν· τὴν μὲν τῶν δ. κακίαν, ὅταν ταράττωσι καὶ θορυβῶσι τὴν ψυχὴν τοῦ παραπαίοντος· τὴν δὲ τοῦ θεοῦ φιλανθρωπίαν, ὅταν οὕτως ἄγριον δαίμονα...κατέχῃ id.*diab.*1.6(2.256B); Thdt.*h.e.*3.20.1(3.936); a difference to be made between diabolic possession and natural depression ὡς καὶ πολλάκις σε ἀναπείθειν τὸν δ. εἰς πέλαγος, ἢ κατὰ κρημνῶν ἀφανίσαι σαυτόν...οὐ γὰρ ἐκείνου μόνον ἐστὶν αὕτη ἡ συμβουλή, ἀλλὰ καὶ τῆς ἀθυμίας τῆς σῆς, καὶ ταύτης μᾶλλον ἢ ἐκείνου, τάχα δὲ καὶ μόνης ταύτης Chrys.*Stag.*2.1(179C); οὐχ ὁ δ. ἐστὶν ὁ τὴν ἀθυμίαν κινῶν, ἀλλ' ἐκείνη ἡ ποιοῦσα τὸν δ. ἰσχυρόν *ib.*(180A); **4.** exorcism, practised from earliest times δαιμονιολήπτους...ἰῶνται, καταργοῦντες καὶ ἐκδιώκοντες τοὺς κατέχοντας τοὺς ἀνθρώπους δ. Just.*2apol.*6.6(M.6.456A); εἰ ἠπίστατό γε [sc. Celsus] τὸν περὶ δαιμόνων λόγον...οὐκ ἂν ἐνεκάλεσεν ἡμῖν, φάσκουσιν ὅτι οὐ χρὴ θεραπεύειν δ. ὅστις σέβει τὸν ἐπὶ πᾶσι θεόν. καὶ τοσοῦτόν γε ἀποδέομεν τοῦ θεραπεύειν δ., ὥστε καὶ ἀπελαύνειν αὐτοὺς εὐχαῖς...ἀπὸ τῶν ἀνθρωπίνων ψυχῶν καὶ ἀπὸ τῶν τόπων, ἐν οἷς ἱδρύκασιν Or.*Cels.*7.67(p.216.19ff.; M.11.1516B); *ib.*8.73(p.291.7; 1628B); Dion.Al.ap.Eus.*h.e.*7.10.4(M.20.660A); *A.Phil.*12(p.6.22) and freq. in popular literature; performed not by human power, but through Christ, *Const.App.*8.1.3; **5.** eccl. legislation on possession, v. προσδέχομαι.

F. defeat of demons through Christ and Church; **1.** through Inc. and Passion ὁ δὲ πέμψας τὸν Ἰησοῦν θεὸς ἐκλύσας πᾶσαν τὴν τῶν δ. ἐπιβουλήν Or.*Cels.*3.29(p.227.2; M.11.957B); ὁ νομιζόμενος ἄνθρωπος πρὸς τὸ ἀποθανεῖν ἐπὶ καθαιρέσει μεγάλου δ. καὶ δαιμόνων ἄρχοντος, ὑποτάξαντος ὅλας...ψυχάς *ib.*1.31(p.83.4; 720A); *ib.*1.60(p.111.4; 769C); cf. *una hostia omnis daemonum cultura depulsa,* id.*hom.17.1 in Num.*(p.155.5; M.12.703C); *ib.*17.6(p.165.13; 710D); ἐπεδήμησεν ὁ υἱὸς τοῦ θεοῦ Χριστός...ἵνα δὴ τὰ κράτη τῶν τυραννούντων ἀνατρέψας δ. ἐξέληται τῆς πικρᾶς τὰς ψυχὰς δουλείας Meth.*Porph.*1(p.503.3; M.18.397C); τούτου γὰρ ἕνεκα καὶ σάρκα ἐφόρεσεν ὁ κύριος Ἰησοῦς... ὅπως δι' ἧς σαρκὸς οἱ δ. ἀναδεῖξαι θεοὺς ἠλαζονεύσαντο...διὰ ταύτης ἀνατραπέντες κατοπτευθῶσιν οὐκ ὄντες θεοί *ib.*(p.503.15; 397D); *ib.*(p.504.3ff.; 400A,B); ἀπὸ χρόνων τῆς ἐπιφανείας τοῦ...Χριστοῦ... δαιμόνων θάνατοι μνημονεύονται Eus.*d.e.*5 proem.(p.203.34; M.22.337C); Porphyry himself testifying to it περὶ δὲ τοῦ μηκέτι δύνασθαί τι κατισχύειν τοὺς φαύλους δ. μετὰ τὴν τοῦ σωτῆρος ἡμῶν εἰς ἀνθρώπους πάροδον, καὶ αὐτὸς ὁ καθ' ἡμᾶς τῶν δ. προήγορος ἐν τῇ καθ' ἡμῶν συσκευῇ...μαρτυρεῖ id.*p.e.*5.1(179D; M.21.312C); *ib.*(178D; M.309C); εἰ ὁ ἐχθρὸς τοῦ γένους ἡμῶν διάβολος ἐκπεσὼν ἀπὸ τοῦ οὐρανοῦ, περὶ τὸν ἀέρα τὸν ὧδε κάτω πλανᾶται, κἀκεῖ τῶν σὺν αὐτῷ δ. ὡς ὁμοίων ἐν τῇ ἀπειθείᾳ ἐξουσιάζων, φαντασίας μὲν δι' αὐτῶν ἐνεργεῖ τοῖς ἀπατωμένοις, ἐπιχειρεῖ δὲ τοῖς ἀνερχομένοις ἐμποδίζειν...ἦλθε δὲ ὁ κύριος, ἵνα τὸν μὲν διάβολον καταβάλῃ, τὸν δὲ ἀέρα καθαρίσῃ...ποίῳ δ' ἂν ἄλλῳ θανάτῳ ἐγεγόνει ταῦτα ἢ τῷ ἐν ἀέρι γενομένῳ, φημὶ δὴ τῷ σταυρῷ; μόνος γὰρ ἐν τῷ ἀέρι τις ἀποθνήσκει, ὁ σταυρῷ τελειούμενος...οὕτως γὰρ ὑψωθείς, τὸν μὲν ἀέρα ἐκαθάριζεν ἀπό τε τῆς διαβολικῆς καὶ πάσης τῶν δ. ἐπιβουλῆς Ath.*inc.*25.5,6(M.25.140B,C omitted in 'short recension'); Cyr.H.*catech.*19.3 cit. s. ἀμνός; Gr. Nyss.*or.catech.*18(p.75.1; M.45.53C); Chrys.*exp.in Ps.*41(5.133B); Bas.Sel.*or.*23.1(M.85.272B); **2.** through Holy Name ὁ ἡμέτερος Ἰησοῦς, οὗ τὸ ὄνομα μυρίους ἤδη ἐναργῶς ἑώραται δ. ἐξελάσαν ψυχῶν καὶ σωμάτων Or.*Cels.*1.25(p.76.14; M.11.708A); *ib.*3.36(p.233.10; 968A); Eus.*d.e.*3.6(p.138.31; M.22.233C); Chrys.*exp.in Ps.*110(5.275D); **3.** through sacraments and sacramental signs; **a.** baptism δ. ... ἐν τῷ σωτηρίῳ ὕδατι ἀφανίζεται Cyr.H.*catech.*19.3; *ib.*20.3; τῷ κατὰ Χριστὸν γινομένῳ βαπτίσματι ἀκροτηριάζονται...οἱ πρὸ τῆς πίστεως ἡμᾶς δουλωσάμενοι, καὶ τὰς ψυχὰς ἀποκτείναντες δ. Nil.*epp.*2.16(M.79.208A); **b.** eucharist, Chrys.*hom.46.3 in Jo.*(8.273A) cit. s. αἷμα; **c.** sign of cross τοῦ σταυροῦ γενομένου...δαιμόνων φαντασία τῷ σημείῳ τούτῳ ἀπελαύνεται Ath.*gent.*1(M.25.5A); Thdt.*h.e.*3.3.4(3.913); **4.** through saints, esp. martyrs αἱ ψυχαὶ τῶν διὰ Χριστιανισμὸν ἀποθνησκόντων δι' εὐσέβειαν...καθῄρουν τὴν δύναμιν τῶν δ. Or.*Cels.*8.44(p.258.28; M.11.1581C); *ib.*8.55(p.272.17; 1601A); ἡ τέφρα τῶν ἁγίων μαρτύρων πονηροὺς ἀπελαύνει δ. Chrys.*stat.*8.2(2.93B); id.*pan.Juln.*2(2.674D); id.*pan.Bab.*2.13(2.558A,B) al.; ‡Chrys.*indict.* 1.1(8².94C); Thdt.*affect.*3(p.99.2; 4.791); **5.** through vigorous spiritual life, Mac.Aeg.*hom.*9.11(M.34.537D) cit. s. ἀγωνίζομαι; Chrys.*hom.14.5 in Gen.*(4.114A); *ib.*37.1(373C); and the virtues οὐδεμίαν γὰρ τῶν ἀρετῶν σχεδὸν οὕτω δεδοίκασιν οἱ δ., ὡς πραΰτητα †Nil.*mal.cog.*14(M.79.1216C); ἀσθενοῦσι μὲν οἱ δ., ὅταν διὰ τῶν ἐντολῶν μείωνται τὰ πάθη τὰ ἐν ἡμῖν· ἀπόλλυνται δέ, ὅταν εἰς τέλος διὰ τῆς ἀπαθείας τῆς ψυχῆς ἐξαφανίζωνται Max.*carit.*2.22(M.90.992A).

G. exeg.; **1.** 1Reg.28:3ff.; view that demon feigned Samuel's appearance πῶς γὰρ ἠδύνατο δ. ψυχήν, οὐ λέγω δικαίου μόνον, ἀλλὰ καὶ τοῦ τυχόντος, τὴν ἀπελθοῦσαν, ἣν οὐκ ᾔδει ποῖ διάγει, καλέσαι;... ἀλλὰ Σαοὺλ οὐκ εἶδεν, ἀλλ' ἀκούσας παρὰ τῆς γυναικός, ὅπερ ἔβλεπεν, σχῆμα τῶν ἀνιόντων ἑνὸς καὶ ἐπιγνοὺς ὡς Σαμουήλ, τοιούτῳ ἐχρᾶτο, προσεκύνησεν. οὐδὲν δὲ τῷ δ. μορφῶσαι, ὅπερ ᾔδει, σχῆμα τοῦ Σαμουήλ ‡Hipp.*engast.*(p.123.3ff.; M.10.605C); cf. οὐχ ὅτι οὖν ἀνήγαγε τὸν Σαμουήλ, ἀλλὰ τῇ ἐγγαστριμύθῳ καὶ τῷ ἀποστάτῃ Σαοὺλ δ. ταρταραῖοι ἐξομοιωθέντες τῷ Σαμουὴλ ἐνεφάνισαν ἑαυτούς *M.Pion.*14.11; cf. reasons advanced by Origen agst. demon's having spoken in Samuel's person δαιμόνιον δὲ οὐ δύναται εἰδέναι τὴν βασιλείαν Δαβὶδ τὴν ὑπὸ τοῦ κυρίου χειροτονηθεῖσαν Or.*engast.*5(p.287.19; M.12.1020A); cf. reply of defender of traditional view οὐκ ἔστι Σαμουήλ, ψεύδεται τὸ δαιμόνιον, ἐπεὶ οὐ δύναται ψεύδεσθαι ἡ γραφή. τὰ δὲ ῥήματα τῆς γραφῆς [ἐστιν] οὐκ ἔστιν ἐκ προσώπου τοῦ δαιμονίου [αὐτοῦ], ἀλλ' ἐκ προσώπου αὐτῆς *ib.*6(p.288.8ff.; 1020B,C); cf. ἐγὼ δὲ οὐ δύναμαι διδόναι δαιμονίῳ τηλικαύτην δύναμιν, ὅτι προφητεύει περὶ Σαοὺλ [Σαμουὴλ] καὶ τοῦ λαοῦ τοῦ θεοῦ, καὶ προφητεύει περὶ βασιλείας Δαβὶδ ὅτι μέλλει βασιλεύειν *ib.*8(p.292.10; 1025A); ἡ ψυχὴ τοῦ Σαμουὴλ ἀνελθοῦσα ἐκ τοῦ ᾅδου διά τινα οἰκονομίαν, καὶ λαλήσασα τῷ Σαούλ, καὶ προειποῦσα αὐτῷ τὸν...θάνατον...ὅπερ δ. οὔτε ἐγίνωσκεν, οὔτε προειπεῖν ἠδύνατο, κἂν τινες οὕτω νομίζωσιν Anast.S.*serm.imag.* 3(M.89.1176A); this view refuted δαιμόνιον δὲ λέγων [sc. Origen] οὐ δύναται εἰδέναι τὴν βασιλείαν Δαβὶδ κτλ. ... εἰ μὲν οὖν ἄδηλος ἦν ἡ βασιλεία, ἐξῆν ἂν ἴσως ἄγνοιαν ὑποκρίνεσθαί τινα σκηπτόμενον· εἰ δὲ μεμαρτύρητο μὲν ὑπὸ θεοῦ, κέχριστο δ' ἐπὶ τούτοις ὑπὸ τοῦ Σαμουήλ, ἔν τε τοῖς πολέμοις ἀριστεύων ἀεί...εἰ δὲ ταῦτα...καθεστήκει σαφῆ, τί ξένον...εἰ τὴν οὖσαν καὶ κεχειροτονημένην ὑπὸ τοῦ κυρίου διὰ τοῦ προφήτου βασιλείαν ἐπεγίνωσκεν ὁ δ.; Eust.*engast.*23(p.52.3; M.18.660C); cf. answer to second objection from inspiration of scripture τροπολογῶν [sc. Origen] οὐ φρίττει 'μύθους' ὀνομάζειν ὅσα δεδημιουργηκέναι μὲν ἱστορεῖται θεός...ἀλλ' ἐκ τῶν ἐναντίων, ἅπερ ὁ μῦθος ἐν γαστρὶ πλαττόμενος ἀφανῶς ὑπηχεῖ, ταῦτα δογματικῷ βεβαιοῖ προγράμματι, δεικνύων ἀληθῆ *ib.*21(p.48.13ff.; 656A,B); to third οὐκοῦν ἀπορίᾳ προγνώσεως οὐδὲν ἀληθὲς ἐξεῖπεν ὁ δ. (οὐ γὰρ ἂν ἐναντία τῶν γεγονότων ἀπήγγειλεν), ἀλλὰ τὰ τῷ Σαμουὴλ εἰρημένα πρότερον, ὡς ἔφην, ὑποκλέψας, ὀλίγα ἄττα προσετίθη τούτοις, ἐκ τῶν εἰκότων ὁμοιότροπα συμπλέξας *ib.*13(p.37.16; 641A); traditional view of apparition being a demonic fraud defended, Gr.Nyss.*engast.* (p.66.1; M.45.112A); ‡Just.*qu.et resp.*52(M.6.1296C); third view, based on 1Par.10:13f., that God, in order to punish Saul for impiety in consulting woman of Endor, announced his doom through mouth of Samuel δ. δέ τινα λαοπλάνον ἔφησαν δεῖξαι τὸ σχῆμα τοῦ Σαμουήλ...ἀνοίας...ἐστι...αὐτὴν τοῖς τοῦ ψεύδους διδασκάλοις ἀνέθεσαν δαίμοσιν...δῆλον...ὡς αὐτὸς ὁ τῶν ὅλων θεός, σχηματίσας...τὸ εἶδος τοῦ Σαμουήλ, ἐξήνεγκε τὴν ἀπόφασιν, οὐ τῆς ἐγγαστριμύθου δρᾶσαι τοῦτο δυνηθείσης Thdt.*qu.63 in 1Reg.*(1.398f.); opinion that ἐγγαστρίμυθος prophesied nothing that she could not have known by natural means rejected, *ib.*(400); cf.*cat.Tit.*1:12 (p.91.14); **2.** allegorical: Ex.11:5, cf. *quosdam primogenitos etiam in Aegyptiis, id est in contrariis potestatibus, quasi electos in malitia et primos inter daemones; qui nisi percussi fuerint..., sanctificationem percipere Istrahelitarum primogeniti omnino non possunt. quis ergo est, qui primogenitos Aegyptiorum, id est 'principatus et potestates' daemonum percussit? nonne dominus meus Jesus Christus?* Or.*hom.3.4 in Num.*(p.19.5ff.; M.12.597D–598A); Ps.20:8, cf. *dixit de his qui in daemonibus confidebant: 'hi in curribus et hi in equis'... illi invocant 'currus et equos' id est daemones,* id.*hom.15.3 in Jos.* (p.384.15ff.; M.12.899A,B); Ps.16:7 ἀνθεστηκότας τῇ δεξιᾷ τοῦ θεοῦ· τοὺς δαίμονάς φησι,...φυλαχθείημεν καὶ ἡμεῖς ἀπὸ δαιμόνων τῶν ἐναντιουμένων τῇ δεξιᾷ Cyr.ad loc.(M.69.816B,C).

H. heret.; **1.** in teaching ascribed to Simon Magus, v. ὀνειροπομπός; **2.** in dualist heresies; demons uncreated τὸν δὲ διάβολον καὶ τοὺς ὑπ' ἐκείνῳ τελοῦντας δ., κατὰ τοὺς Μαρκίωνος, καὶ Κέρδωνος, καὶ τοὺς Μάνεντος μύθους, οὐκ ἀγενήτους εἶναί φαμεν Thdt.*haer.* 5.8(4.406); themselves creators of world, Chrys.*hom.18.3 in 1Cor.* (10.155D); assisting especially the wicked, Hipp.*haer.*7.28(p.209.12; M.16.3323A); and givers of Law, Chrys.*hom.8.2 in Jo.*(8.50C); 'familiar demons' possessed by Marcus and Carpocratians, Iren.*haer.*1.13.3(M.7.581B); Epiph.*haer.*27.3(p.303.16; M.41.365D); **3.** Euchite (Messalian) λέγουσιν ὅτι ἑκάστῳ ἀνθρώπῳ τικτομένῳ παραυτίκα δ. οὐσιωδῶς συνάπτεται, ἐκ τῆς καταδίκης τοῦ Ἀδὰμ τούτου κεκληρωμένου· καὶ ὅτι οὗτος ὁ δ. εἰς τὰς ἀτόπους πράξεις κινεῖ τὸν ἄνθρωπον, οὐσιωδῶς αὐτῷ συνημμένον Tim.CP *haer.*(M.86.48B); λέγουσιν ὅτι τὸ ἅγιον βάπτισμα οὐδὲν συμβάλλεται εἰς τὴν τοῦ δ. τούτου δίωξιν...ὅτι μόνη ἡ ἐκτενὴς προσευχὴ διώκειν δύναται τοῦτον τὸν δ. διὰ χρέμψεως καὶ ἀποπτύσεως τοῦ προσερχομένου, φυγαδευομένου τούτου τοῦ δ. ὡς καπνοῦ ὁρωμένου *ib.*; λέγουσιν ὅτι σπέρμα καὶ λόγος ἐνέπεσεν εἰς τὴν Μαρίαν· καὶ ὅτι τὸ σῶμα ὃ ἀνέλαβεν ἐξ αὐτῆς ὁ κύριος, δαιμόνων ἦν πεπληρωμένον, καὶ ἐξέβαλεν τὰ δαιμόνια, καὶ οὕτως αὐτὸ ἐνεδύσατο *ib.*(49A); cf.Thdt.*h.e.*4.11.7(3.966).

I. in folk-lore, v. *T.Sal.* passim; κἀγὼ Σολομῶν...ἔδωκα αὐτοῖς [sc. Israelites] ὥστε εἰδέναι τὰς δυνάμεις τῶν δ. καὶ τὰς μορφὰς αὐτῶν καὶ τὰ ὀνόματα αὐτῶν τῶν ἀγγέλων ἐν οἷς καταργοῦνται οἱ δ. *T.Sal.*15.14 (M.122.1340A); female demons, *ib.*4.1(1320D); used for Solomon's building activities, *ib.*10.10(1332C); though by nature instigators of many evils, *ib.*8.1ff.(1328A); but view that demons were subject to Solomon vigorously opposed, Leont.B.*mesopent.*(M.86.1980B).

J. term of abuse, Socr.*h.e.*3.23.42(M.67.445B); Evagr.*h.e.*3.41 (p.139.27; M.86.2684C).

K. of antichrist, Or.*hom.9.3 in Jer.*(p.410.32; M.13.736A).

***δαιμωνιωδῶς**, v. *δαιμονιωδῶς.

[*]**δαίρω**, = δέρω, *beat*, Herm.*sim.*6.2.6.

δάκν-ω, **1.** *bite, sting*, met. ~ων...καὶ κατεσθίων τὸν πλησίον Or.*Jo.*20.37(29; p.378.28; M.14.661C); ὅταν γὰρ ὁ ὑβρίσας ἴδῃ μὴ καθικνουμένην αὐτοῦ τὴν πληγὴν τῆς τῶν λοιδορηθέντων ψυχῆς, αὐτὸς ~εται μειζόνως Chrys.*stat.*2.8(2.33D); Sever.*serp.*5(M.56.508); **2.** *stab*, Jo.Mosch.*prat.*60(M.87.2913B).

***δακρυηρός**, *tearful*, Germ.CP *or.*2(M.98.272A).

***δακρυολογία, ἡ**, *tearful speech*, Ephr.3.186A.

δάκρυον, τό, *tear*; [dat. plur. δάκρυσι];

A. causes and explanations διὰ τῆς λύπης μύουσιν αἱ λεπταὶ...τῶν πόρων διαπνοαί, καὶ διασφίγξασαι τὴν ἔνδοθεν τῶν σπλάγχνων διάθεσιν, ἐπὶ τὴν κεφαλὴν καὶ τὰς μήνιγγας τὸν νοτερὸν ἀτμὸν ἀναθλίβουσιν, ὃς πολὺς ἐναποληφθεὶς ταῖς τοῦ ἐγκεφάλου κοιλότησι, διὰ τῶν κατὰ τὴν βάσιν πόρων ἐπὶ τοὺς ὀφθαλμοὺς ἐξωθεῖται, τῆς τῶν ὀφρύων συμπτώσεως ἐξελκομένης διὰ σταγόνων τὴν ὑγρασίαν (ἡ δὲ σταγὼν δ. λέγεται) Gr.Nyss.*hom.opif.*12.5(M.44.160C); γίνεται τῶν τῆς ψυχῆς τραυμάτων ὥσπερ αἷμα τὸ δ. id.*Placill.*(M.46.880C); Jo.Clim.*scal.*7(M.88.808B); τὸ...ἐξ ἀγαθῶν ἄρξασθαι τοῦ πένθους δακρύων, καὶ εἰς πονηρὰ καταλῆξαι, οὐ θαῦμα. τὸ δὲ ἐξ ἐναντίων ἢ φυσικῶν εἰς πνευματικὰ μετεγκεντρίσαι ἀξιέπαινον *ib.*(808C); οὐκ ἦν ἐν τῷ Ἀδὰμ πρὸ τῆς παραβάσεως δάκρυον· ὥσπερ οὐδὲ μετὰ τὴν ἀνάστασιν *ib.*(809C).

B. right use τὸ δ. οὐκ ἔστι νομοθεσία πρὸς τὸ θρηνεῖν, ἀλλὰ μέτρον... καὶ κανὼν ἀκριβής, καθ' ὃν προσῆκε σεμνῶς...τοῖς τῆς φύσεως ὅροις ἐμμένοντας διαφέρειν τὰ λυπηρά. οὔτε οὖν γυναιξίν, οὔτε ἀνδράσιν ἐπιτέτραπται τὸ φιλοπενθὲς καὶ πολύδακρυ, ἀλλ' ὅσον ἐπιστυγνάσαι τοῖς λυπηροῖς, καὶ μικρόν τι δ. ἀποστάξαι, καὶ τοῦτο ἡσυχῇ, μὴ ἀναβρυχώμενον μηδὲ ὀλολύζοντα, μηδὲ καταρρηγνύντα χιτῶνα Bas.*hom.*4.6 (2.30B; M.31.229C); ὅταν ἀδελφὸν παρακαλῶμεν ἁμαρτάνοντα, κλαίειν δεῖ...ὅταν παραινῶμέν τινι, ὁ δὲ μὴ προσέχῃ, ἀλλὰ ἀπολλύηται, κλαίειν δεῖ. ταῦτα φιλοσοφίας τὰ δ.· ὅταν μέντοι πένης τις γένηται, ὅταν ἐν νόσῳ ᾖ σωματικῇ, ὅταν ἀποθάνῃ, οὐκέτι· ταῦτα γὰρ οὐ δ. ἄξια... διαβάλλομεν...τὰ δ., ἀκαίρως αὐτὰ μεταχειρίζοντες Chrys.*hom.12.4 in Col.*(11.417C); bad results if suppressed; paralysis or apoplexy, Bas.*hom.*4.5(2.29E; M.31.229B); Isid.Pel.*epp.*2.176(M.78.628C); to be shed in accordance with reason, Jo.Clim.*scal.*7(M.88.805A).

C. tears of repentance; **1.** in gen., ref. S. Mary Magdalene ἐπισπένδουσα τῷ κυρίῳ μετανοίας δ. Clem.*paed.*2.8(p.194.8; M.8.465B); τὸ γὰρ ὄντως ἐκ πολλῆς θλίψεως καὶ συνοχῆς καρδίας προχεόμενον δ., ἐν γνώσει ἀληθείας μετὰ καὶ πυρώσεως σπλάγχνων, βρῶσίς ἐστι ψυχῆς χορηγουμένη ἐκ τοῦ ἐπουρανίου ἄρτου, οὗ προηγουμένως μετέσχε Μαρία καθεσθεῖσα πρὸς τοῖς ποσὶ τοῦ κυρίου Mac.Aeg.*hom.*25.8(M.34.672D); Bas.*hom.*5.7(2.41C; M.31.256C); ἐν οὐδενὶ μῶμον εὑρίσκων οὔτε παρὰ τῷ ἐπισκόπῳ οὔτε μὴν παρὰ τῷ ὑπ' αὐτὸν τεταγμένῳ λαῷ, αἰσχυνθεὶς μετὰ αἰδοῦς καὶ πολλῶν δ. ἐξελεύσεται εἰρηνικῶς κατανενυγμένος...καὶ τὸ ποίμνιον ὅλον, θεασάμενον ἐκείνου τὰ δ. *Const.App.*2.10.4; Evagr.Pont.*or.*78(M.79.1184C); **2.** efficacy μεγάλη γὰρ ἀρετή ἐστι τὸ δ., μέγα κατόρθωμα, μεγάλαι ἁμαρτίαι...διὰ δ. ἀπαλείφονται Ath.*virg.*17(p.51.24; M.28.272B); S. Peter as proof, *ib.* (p.52.5; M.l.c.); πορνεία...καὶ ὅσα τοιαῦτα...πρὸς τὸ μηδὲ εἶναι χωρεῖ, λυθέντα τοῖς δ. Bas.*hom.*21.7(2.168D; M.31.552D); Gr.Naz.*carm.*2.1.46.27(M.37.1379A); exeg. Ps.6:7 ἀκουέτωσαν οἱ τὰς ἀργυρᾶς κλίνας ἔχοντες, οἷα τοῦ βασιλέως ἦν ἡ κλίνη· οὐ λιθοκόλλητος...ἀλλὰ δάκρυσι λελουμένη...ἴσασιν οἱ πεῖραν λαβόντες ὃ λέγω, ὅσην εὐφροσύνην ἔχουσιν αὗται τῶν δ. αἱ πηγαί. ταῦτα τὰ δ. τὸ ἄσβεστον πῦρ σβέσαι δύνανται, τὸν ποταμὸν ἐκεῖνον τὸν πρὸ τοῦ βήματος ἑλκόμενον...οἱ νήφοντες...ὥσπερ ὑετῷ τοῖς δ. κεχρημένοι τούτοις, καὶ τὰ σπέρματα τῆς ἀρετῆς αὔξοντες. πάσῃ κακίᾳ...ἄβατός ἐστιν εὐνὴ τοιαῦτα δ. σταλάζων, οὐδὲν ἡγεῖται τὰ ἐπὶ τῆς γῆς, ἀλλὰ πάσης πολιορκίας ἀπαλλάττει τὴν ψυχὴν Chrys.*exp.in Ps.*6(5.46A–C); δ. καταφερομένων γαλήνη γίνεται, καὶ εὐδία, καὶ τὸ ἐκ τῶν ἁμαρτημάτων ἀφανίζεται σκότος. καὶ ὥσπερ ἐξ ὕδατος καὶ πνεύματος, οὕτως ἀπὸ δ. καὶ ἐξομολογήσεως καθαιρόμεθα πάλιν...ἐκεῖνα ζητῶ τὰ δ. τὰ μὴ πρὸς ἐπίδειξιν, ἀλλὰ πρὸς κατάνυξιν γινόμενα id.*hom.6.5 in Mt.*(7.96A); id.*hom.12.4 in Col.*(11.417D) cit. s. ἀποσμήχω; id.*hom.in 1Cor.7:39*(3.210B); id.*Laz.*1.8(1.718B); μέγας σπόγγος τὰ δ. τῶν ἁμαρτιῶν· μεγάλη ἡ δύναμις τῶν δ. εἴπω σοι, πόσον ἰσχύει τὰ δ.;...οἱ μάρτυρες ἐκχέουσιν αἷμα, οἱ ἁμαρτωλοὶ ἐκχέουσι δ. καὶ ἵνα μάθῃς ὅσην δύναμιν ἔχει τὰ δ., ἡ πόρνη μὴ αἷμα ἐξέχεεν; οὐ πηγὴν δακρύων ἐξέχεε, καὶ ἐξήλειψε τὰ ἁμαρτήματα;...ὁ Πέτρος, οὐκ ἠρνήσατο τὸν Χριστόν...; οὐ πηγὰς δ. ἐξέχεε...καὶ ἀπεσμήξατο αὐτοῦ τὸ ἁμάρτημα; ‡Chrys.*hom.3.5 in Ps.*50(5.589B,C); Ant.Mon.*hom.*107(M.89.1761B–D); ἀναιρετικὸν...τὸ δ. τὸ ἀγνὸν παντὸς φαινομένου, καὶ νοουμένου ῥύπου Jo.Clim.*scal.*7(M.

88.808B); *ib.*(808D); **3.** tears identified with repentance, Clem.*paed.*2.8(p.194.20; M.8.465C); εἰ μὲν οὐ μεταγνόντας, δικαίως [sc. Novatian treated sinners]...εἰ δὲ τοὺς ἐκτακέντας τοῖς δ., οὐ μιμήσομαι Gr.Naz.*or.*39.19(M.36.357B); **4.** danger of pride in tears Evagr. Pont.*or.*7(1169A); μὴ ἐπαρθῶμεν ἐν τῇ προσευχῇ ἡμῶν ἐκχέοντες δ. οὐ γὰρ ἐξ ἡμῶν τὰ δ., ἀλλ' ἐκ τῆς ἐπιχορηγούσης χάριτος Ant.Mon. *hom.*104(M.89.1748C); ὁ ἐπὶ τοῖς ἑαυτοῦ δ. ψυχικῶς φυσιούμενος, καὶ τοὺς μὴ δακρύοντας κατακρίνων, ὅμοιός ἐστι τῷ ὅπλον κατὰ τοῦ ἑαυτοῦ ἐχθροῦ...αἰτησαμένῳ, ἑαυτὸν δὲ ἐν τούτῳ διαχειρησαμένῳ Jo.Clim.*scal.*7(M.88.809B); to be judged by pain they express, *ib.*(805C); **5.** discussion of inability to shed physical tears τί ποιήσω, ὅτι ἐπιθυμῶ τοῦ...πενθῆσαι ἐπὶ ταῖς ἁμαρτίαις μου...καὶ οὐκ ἔρχεται εἰς ὀφθαλμόν μου δ.;...πρὸς ὅπερ φημί, ὅτι ὠφέλιμόν ἐστι τὸ ὅλως ἐπιθυμεῖν δακρύων...ἔστι δὲ καὶ κατασκευὴ ἔν τισιν ἀνθρώποις φυσική, εὐχερῶς δ. μὴ παρέχουσα. τί οὖν χρὴ δακρύων ἐπιθυμοῦντα; λέξω σοι. ἐὰν μὴ δύνῃ διὰ τῶν ὀφθαλμῶν τῶν φαινομένων δακρῦσαι, ποίησον τὴν διάνοιάν σου, ὥσπερ καθ' ὕπνον κλαίουσαν πολλάκις τεθέασαι, οὕτως καὶ γρηγοροῦσαν, ἐνώπιον τοῦ θεοῦ...τῇ ἐνθυμήσει,...ἐκχέον δ. ... συνεχῶς γὰρ...καὶ πυκνὰ τὴν καρδίαν κεντοῦντες τῇ μνήμῃ τῶν τοῦ θεοῦ θαυμάτων, παρεσκεύασαν ἔξωθεν ἀπὸ ἔσω βλύσαι ἀπὸ λιθίνων ὀφθαλμῶν τὸ τῶν δ. νᾶμα Nil.*epp.*3.257(M.79.512A–513A).

D. tears and baptism τοῖς δ. βαπτιζόμενος ἐκ δευτέρου Clem.*q.d.s.*42(p.190.11; M.9.649C); οἶδα καὶ πέμπτον [sc. βάπτισμα] ἔτι, τὸ τῶν δ.· ἀλλ' ἐπιπονώτερον, ὡς ὁ λούων καθ' ἑκάστην νύκτα τὴν κλίνην αὐτοῦ...τοῖς δ. Gr.Naz.*or.*39.17(M.36.356A); δεύτερον β. διὰ τῶν δ. Chrys.*poenit.*3.4(2.301A); μείζων τοῦ βαπτίσματος μετὰ τὸ βάπτισμα τῶν δ. πηγὴ καθέστηκεν, εἰ καὶ τολμηρόν ἐστί πως τὸ λεγόμενον· διότι ἐκεῖνο μὲν τῶν προγεγονότων ἐν ἡμῖν κακῶν ἐστι καθαρτήριον· τοῦτο δὲ τῶν μεταγεγονότων...καθαρτήριον Jo.Clim.*scal.*7(M.88.804A); ὥσπερ γὰρ διὰ τοῦ ἐν τῷ βαπτίσματι ὕδατος ἀναγεννώμεθα, οὕτω διὰ δ. καὶ κατανύξεως ἀναβαπτιζόμενοι καθαιρόμεθα. πλήν, οὔτε τὸ βάπτισμα, οὔτε ἡ τῶν δ. κατάνυξις, ἄνευ τοῦ ἁγίου δίδοται πνεύματος. καὶ μὴ θαυμάσῃς· τὴν χάριν γὰρ ἣν ἐν τῷ βαπτίσματι νήπιοι βαπτιζόμενοι λαμβάνομεν, ταύτην ἀπολλύντες διὰ ῥαθυμίας...διὰ μετανοίας, καὶ τῆς τῶν δ. πηγῆς ἀπολαμβάνομεν Anast.S.*Ps.*6(M.89.1129C).

E. tears and prayer τίς γὰρ οὐκ ἐπίσταται ὑμῶν, ὅτι μάλιστα μὲν ἡ μετὰ οἴκτου καὶ δ. εὐχὴ μειλίσσεται τὸν θεόν; Just.*dial.*90.5(M.6.692A); Ath.*virg.*16(p.51.12; M.28.272A); Bas.*ep.*45.1(3.134A; M.32.368A); κέχρησο τοῖς δ. πρὸς παντὸς αἰτήματος κατόρθωσιν· λίαν γὰρ χαίρει σου ὁ δεσπότης ἐν δ. προσευχὴν δεχόμενος Evagr.Pont.*or.*6(M.79.1169A); τὸ φυτὸν τῆς εὐχῆς αἱ πηγαὶ τῶν δ. ποτίζουσαι Chrys.*Anna* 3.1(4.721E); ἐν κατανύξει μένει διηνεκεῖ, πηγὰς συνεχεῖς ἀφιεὶς δ.,...οὐδὲν γὰρ οὕτως συγκολλᾷ καὶ ἑνοῖ τῷ θεῷ, ὡς τὰ τοιαῦτα δ. id. *hom.*6.5 *in Mt.*(7.95A); Nil.*sent.*58(M.79.1245B) cit. s. λουτήρ; Bas. Sel.*v.Thecl.*2.28(M.85.613C); χρὴ οὖν, πρὸ παντὸς αἰτήματος, κατόρθωσιν κεχρῆσθαι τοῖς δ. πάνυ γὰρ χαίρει ὁ δεσπότης ἡμῶν δεχόμενος προσευχὴν ἐν δ. μετὰ ταπεινῆς καρδίας...ὅθεν ὄντως ἔστιν ἰδεῖν τὰ σπέρματα τῆς εὐχῆς μετὰ δακρύων ἐν τῇ γῇ τῆς καρδίας ἐνσπειρόμενα διὰ τὴν ἐλπίδα τῆς τοῦ θερισμοῦ χαρᾶς Ant.Mon.*hom.*107(M.89.1761B–D); *ib.*106(1757A).

F. gift of tears οὐχ οἱ πολλοὶ ἔχουσι τὸ χάρισμα τῶν δ., ἀλλ' ὅσοι τὸν νοῦν ἔχουσιν ἄνω, ὅσοι τῶν γηΐνων ἐπιλανθάνονται, ὅσοι τῆς σαρκὸς πρόνοιαν οὐ ποιοῦσιν, οἵτινες οὐκ ἐπίστανται ὅλως, εἰ ἔνι κόσμος, οἵτινες ἐνέκρωσαν τὰ μέλη τὰ ἐπὶ τῆς γῆς· τούτοις μόνοις δίδοται πένθος δακρύων Ath.*virg.*17(p.52.12; M.28.272C); Mac.Aeg.*hom.*15.26(M.34.593B); περὶ λήψεως δ. προσεύχου, ἵνα διὰ τοῦ πένθους μαλάξῃς τὴν ὑπάρχουσαν ἐν τῇ ψυχῇ σου ἀγριότητα Evagr.Pont.*or.*5(M.79.1168D).

G. exeg.; **1.** tears of Christ (Jo.11:35) τὸ δ. αὐτοῦ, χαρὰ ἡμετέρα Ath.*inc.et c.Ar.*5(M.26.992A); κύριος...τὸ δ. προσήκατο, τὸ φυσικὸν τῇ σαρκὶ ἐπιγίνεσθαι σύμπτωμα συγχωρῶν. ὅπερ συμβαίνει, ὅταν τὰ κοῖλα τοῦ ἐγκεφάλου τῶν ἐκ τῆς λύπης ἀναθυμιάσεων πληρωθέντα, οἷον δι' ὀχετῶν τινων τῶν κατὰ τοὺς ὀφθαλμοὺς πόρων τοῦ ὑγροῦ τὸ βάρος ἀποσκευάζηται...εἶτα, οἶμαι, ὥσπερ τὸ νέφος εἰς ψεκάδα, οὕτως τὸ πάχος τῶν ἀτμῶν εἰς δ. διαλύεται Bas.*hom.*4.5(2.29Df.; M.31.228Df.); *ib.*(29A; M.228B) cit. s. ἐμπαθής; μέτρα γὰρ ὁρίζει τῇ ἀνθρωπίνῃ φύσει μέχρι πόσου ἐπιστάζειν δεῖ τοῖς κειμένοις τὸ δ., καὶ μὴ πέρα τοῦ προσήκοντος ἐπὶ νεκρῶν πρὸς θρήνους ἐξάγεσθαι Thdr. Mops.*Jo.*11:35(p.365.19; M.66.764D); Cyr.*Jo.*7(4.686A) cit. s. δακρύω; **2.** rel. of Mt.5:5 to Phil.4:4 πῶς σύμφωνα ταῦτα, φασί, τῷ 'πάντοτε χαίρετε'; οὐδὲ γὰρ ἐκ τῶν αὐτῶν ἀρχῶν δ. τε καὶ χαρὰ τὴν γένεσιν ἔχουσι...πρὸς δὴ ταῦτα ἐροῦμεν, ὅτι...τὰ δ. τῶν ἁγίων διὰ τὴν πρὸς θεὸν ἀγάπην ἐγίγνοντο. ἀεὶ οὖν ἐνορῶντες τῷ ἀγαπητῷ, καὶ τὴν ἐκεῖθεν ἑαυτοῖς εὐφροσύνην συναύξοντες, τὰ περὶ τοὺς ὁμοδούλους ἑαυτῶν ᾠκονόμουν· πενθοῦντες τοὺς ἁμαρτάνοντας, ἐπανορθούμενοι αὐτοὺς διὰ τῶν δ. ... ὑπὲρ τῶν εἰς τὸν ἀδελφὸν δ., τῆς χαρᾶς τοῦ κυρίου καταξιούμενοι...κλαίειν οὖν μετὰ κλαιόντων συγχωρεῖ ὁ ἀπόστολος, ἐπειδὴ τὸ δ. τοῦτο οἱονεὶ σπέρμα...γίνεται τῆς αἰωνίου χαρᾶς Bas.*hom.*4.4(2.28B; M.31.225B); τὴν ἐκ τῶν δ. τούτων λέγων ἡδονήν. ὥσπερ γὰρ ἡ διὰ κόσμον χαρὰ λύπην ἔχει συγκεκληρωμένην, οὕτω τὰ κατὰ θεὸν δ. χαρὰν βλαστάνει διηνεκῆ καὶ ἀμάραντον Chrys.*hom.*6.5 *in Mt.*(7.95B); **3.** exeg. Lc.7:37 δ. δέ ἐσμεν οἱ ἁμαρτωλοὶ μετανενοηκότες Clem.*paed.*2.8(p.194.28; M.8.468A).

H. tears of fallen angels, alleged Christian belief οὓς [sc. ἀγγέλους] δὴ γενέσθαι κακοὺς καὶ κολάζεσθαι δεσμοῖς ὑποβληθέντας ἐν γῇ, ὅθεν καὶ τὰς θερμὰς πηγὰς εἶναι τὰ ἐκείνων δ. Cels.ap.Or.*Cels.*5.52(p.56.9; M.11.1261C); refuted 'τὰς θερμὰς πηγὰς εἶναι τὰ ἐκείνων δ.', πρᾶγμα οὔτε λεγόμενον οὔτ' ἀκουόμενον ἐν ταῖς ἐκκλησίαις τοῦ θεοῦ...οὐδὲ γὰρ ἀνόητος οὕτως τις ἦν, ἵνα σωματοποιήσῃ δ. παραπλήσια τοῖς τῶν ἀνθρώπων ἐν τοῖς καταβεβηκόσιν ἐξ οὐρανοῦ ἀγγέλοις...λεκτέον ὅτι οὐκ ἄν τις εἶπε τὰς θερμὰς πηγάς, ὧν αἱ πλεῖσται γλυκεῖαί εἰσι, δ. εἶναι τῶν ἀγγέλων, ἐπεὶ ἡ φύσις τῶν δ. ἐστὶν ἁλμυρά· εἰ μὴ ἄρα οἱ κατὰ τὸν Κέλσον ἄγγελοι γλυκέα δακρύουσιν Or.*ib.*5.55(p.59.10ff.; 1269A).

***δακρυρῶς**, *tearfully*, Thdr.Stud.*epp.*1.3(M.99.917D).

δακρυσταγής, *tearful*, Meth.*symp.*11(p.136.9; M.18.212D).

***δακρυτικός**, *lamentable*, Ath.*apol.Const.*23(M.25.624B).

δακρύ-ω, *weep*; **1.** in gen., of pagan deities ~οντες θεοί Clem. *prot.*4(p.43.16; M.8.152B); ref. Celsus' allegation of Christian belief that hot springs are caused by tears of fallen angels, v. δάκρυον; of weeping as denoting spiritual affliction ἔστι καὶ ἔσω τὸ ~ειν *V.Pach.Φ* 33(p.20.21); δι' ὧν εἰς αἴσθησιν ὁ νοῦς ἔρχεται, καὶ βρίθει μὲν ~ουσα ἡ ψυχή *ib.Λ* 20(p.145.26); **2.** of Christ as man τίς δὲ χρεία ~ειν ὃ ἔμελλεν ἀνιστᾶν μετ' ὀλίγον; ἀλλ' ἐδάκρυσεν ὁ Ἰησοῦς, ἵνα τὸ συμπαθὲς καὶ τὸ φιλάνθρωπον...ἡμῖν ὑποδείξῃ· ἐδάκρυσεν ὁ Ἰησοῦς ἵνα τὸ κλαίειν μετὰ κλαιόντων ἔργῳ μᾶλλον ἢ λόγῳ διδάξῃ. ... ἐδάκρυσεν, οὐκ ἐπένθησεν, τὸ μὲν ἀδάκρυτον...ὡς...ἀπάνθρωπον παραιτούμενος, τὸ δὲ φιλοπενθὲς ὡς ἀγενὲς καὶ ἄνανδρον διωθούμενος· τάξιν δὲ ἐπιτιθεὶς τῇ συμπαθείᾳ ἐδάκρυσεν †Hipp.*Laz.*(p.244.14; M.62.777); οὕτως εἰδότες αὐτὸν ἄνθρωπον γενόμενον οὐκ ἀρνούμεθα τὰ περὶ αὐτοῦ ἀνθρωπίνως λεγόμενα οἷά ἐστι...τὸ δακρῦσαι Ath.*ep.Serap.*2.8(M.26.621B); ‡Ath.*serm.fid.*24(p.20; M.26.1277A); ὅταν οὖν λέγηται...~ειν ...δέχεται παρ' ἡμῶν καὶ τῷ πατρὶ ἀναφέρει, πρεσβεύων ὑπὲρ ἡμῶν ἵνα ἐν αὐτῷ ἐξαφανισθῇ ‡Ath.*Ar.*4.6(p.50.11; M.26.476B); τάχα καὶ ~ει, ἵνα τὸ δάκρυον ἐπαινετὸν ἀπεργάσηται Gr.Naz.*or.*37.2(M.36.284C); ~ει δὲ ὁ κύριος, ἑωρακὼς τὸν κατ' ἰδίαν εἰκόνα γεγονότα ἄνθρωπον κατεφθαρμένον, ἵνα τὸ ἡμῶν περιστείλῃ δάκρυον...~ει δὲ μόνον καὶ εὐθὺς ἐπέχει τὸ δάκρυον, ἵνα μὴ δόξῃ τις ὠμὸς...εἶναι, καὶ ἡμᾶς ἐπὶ τοῖς αὐτοῖς παιδεύων μὴ ἐπὶ πολὺ ἐκλύεσθαι ἐπὶ τοῖς τεθνηκόσι...διὰ τοῦτο οὖν συνεχώρησε τῇ ἰδίᾳ σαρκὶ κλαῦσαι ὀλίγον, καίπερ ὢν τῇ φύσει ἄδακρυς καὶ ἁπάσης ἀνεπίδεκτος λύπης ὅσον εἰς ἰδίαν φύσιν...ἐνόμιζον δὲ οἱ Ἰουδαῖοι ὅτι διὰ τὸν θάνατον ἐδάκρυσε Λαζάρου, αὐτὸς δὲ πᾶσαν τὴν ἀνθρωπίνην φύσιν κατελεῶν ἐδάκρυσεν...ὅτι πᾶσα ἡ ἀνθρωπότης γέγονεν ὑπὸ θάνατον δικαίως Cyr.*Jo.*7(4.686A); v. δάκρυον.

δακρυώδης, **1.** *tearful*; of drunken men, Bas.*hom.*14.3(2.124E; M.31.449B); δ. φωνάς Isid.Pel.*epp.*1.191(M.78.305A); **2.** *sorrowful*, hence *repentant* ἐν τῷ καιρῷ τῆς θεωρίας...δ. αὐτῷ [sc. τῷ νῷ]...ἐννοίας περιποιήσομεν Diad.*perf.*68(p.84.6); *ib.*73(p.90.17); ὅταν ἡ ψυχὴ ...δ. καὶ κάθυγρος...γένηται, ὁ...κύριος...ἐλήλυθε Jo.Clim.*scal.*7(M.88.805D).

δακτύλιος, **ὁ**, *ring*; **1.** signet ring as symbol of gifts of H. Ghost τί γὰρ ἂν εἴη σφραγὶς ἢ δ. ἀλλ' ἢ τοῦ πνεύματος τὰ δῶρα, καὶ χάρις, καὶ εἰς υἱοθεσίαν ἀνάκλησις; Job.Mon.*inc.*5(M.86.3320A); exeg. Lc.15:22 δότε...δ. τὸ σημεῖον τῆς πίστεως τὸ κατὰ τοῦ διαβόλου Tit.Bost.*fr.Lc.*15:22[3](p.223); ὅ τε περὶ τὴν χεῖρα δ., διὰ τῆς ἐν τῇ σφενδόνῃ γλυφῆς τὴν τῆς εἰκόνος ἐπανάληψιν ὑποσημαίνει Gr.Nyss.*or.dom.*2(p.40.1; M.44.1144D); **2.** *ring* or *staple* to secure a bolt, Cosm.Ind.*top.*5(M.88.204B).

***δακτυλοδεικνέω**, = (perh. f.l. for) δακτυλοδεικτέω, Ast.Am. *hom.*1(M.40.165D); Thdr.Stud.*antirrh.*3.1.31(M.99.404C).

δακτυλοδεικτ-έω, **1.** *point the finger at*; lit., Clem.*paed.*3.11(p.276.24; M.8.649B); Epiph.*anc.*106(p.128.10; M.43.209A); Cosm.Ind.*top.*5(M.88.212B); esp. in derision, Chrys.*fem.reg.*6(1.261C); id.*hom.in 1Tim.*5:9(3.319B); Jo.D.*hom.*12.18(M.96.808A); met., *indicate*, *point to*, Cyr.H.*catech.*18.18; Gel.Cyz.*h.e.*2.20.4(M.85.1281C); **2.** hence *symbolize*, *point to* Σὴμ δὲ καὶ Ἰαφὲτ ~οῦσι τοὺς περὶ τὸν Ἰωσὴφ ἐντυλίξαντα τὸ σῶμα τοῦ σωτῆρος Nil.*epp.*1.85(M.79.120C).

***δακτυλοδείκτης**, **ὁ**, *pointer-out*, *indicator*; of Jo. Bapt. as one who pointed to Christ, Chrysipp.*enc.in Jo.Bapt.*3(p.33.5).

***δακτυλοδειξία**, **ἡ**, *pointing with the finger*, *indication*, Cyr.*Jo.*2.5(4.195E).

***δακτυλοκοπέω**, *mutilate by cutting off fingers*, *M.Pers.*1.14(p.433.4).

δάκτυλος, ὁ, *finger*; of God, interpreted **1.** as power, ref. Ex. 31:18 δ. γὰρ θεοῦ δύναμις νοεῖται θεοῦ, δι' ἧς ἡ κτίσις τελειοῦται οὐρανοῦ καὶ γῆς ὧν ἀμφοῖν αἱ πλάκες νοηθήσονται σύμβολα Clem.*str.* 6.16(p.499.15; M.9.357C); **2.** as H. Ghost; **a.** in gen. τὸ ἅγιον πνεῦμα δ. θεοῦ καλεῖ Ath.*inc.et c.Ar.*19(M.26.1020A); δ. δὲ θεοῦ... εἴρηται τὸ πνεῦμα, οὐχ ὅτι μικρά τίς ἐστι τῷ θεῷ συνοῦσα δύναμις... ἀλλ' ἐπειδὴ ἕν τι τῶν κατὰ διαίρεσιν χαρισμάτων αὐτοῦ ἐστι τὸ χάρισμα τῶν σημείων καὶ ἰαμάτων, τὸ ἕν τι, καὶ οὐχὶ τὰ ὅλα χαρίσματα τοῦ πνεύματος δ. καλεῖ [1Cor.12:8–11] Didym.(‡Bas.)*Eun.*5(1.298D; M. 29.716C); πνεῦμα...ὃ καὶ δ. θεοῦ εἶναι διδασκόμεθα, ἐν τῷ εὐαγγελίῳ ...[Lc.11:20] *ib.*(306A; M.733B); δ. θεοῦ τὸ πνεῦμα λέγων τὸ ἅγιον. δ. δὲ...τῆς οὐσίας ἐστὶ τοῦ σώματος. τὴν τοίνυν ἀχώριστον...τῆς θείας οὐσίας τοῦ πνεύματος...ὑπόστασιν τῷ τοῦ δ. ὀνόματι ἐφανέρωσε Isid. Pel.*epp.*1.60(M.78.221C); ἐνεχάραξε...ταῖς ἁπάντων καρδίαις ὁ τοῦ πατρὸς κάλαμος, τουτέστιν ὁ υἱὸς τὴν παντὸς εἴδησιν ἀγαθοῦ, οἱονεί τινι δ. θεοῦ, τῷ τε τοῦ πατρὸς καὶ τῷ ἰδίῳ χρώμενος πνεύματι Cyr.*ador.* 1(1.8A,B); δ. δὲ λέγεσθαι τὸ πνεῦμα μαρτυρεῖ Job.Mon.*inc.*5(M.86. 3320A); **b.** esp. in OT; as instrument in plagues of Egypt, Ath.*ep. Serap.*4.22(M.26.673A); ὁ δ. τοῦ θεοῦ ὁ μεταβαλὼν...τὸν χοῦν εἰς ζῶα...ὁ παράκλητος ἦν, τὸ πνεῦμα τῆς ἀληθείας Didym.(‡Bas.)*Eun.*5 (1.298B; M.29.716B); δ. ἀντὶ τοῦ τῇ θεοῦ ἐνεργείᾳ ταῦτα γίνεται, καὶ οὐκ ἀνθρώπων...ἐπεὶ...ἠρέμα ἐγίνοντο τὰ γινόμενα, δ. ἐκάλεσαν, ἀλλ' οὐ χεῖρας...ἡ μὲν οὖν τρίτη μάστιξ δ. εἴρηται· ἡ δὲ πέμπτη ὡσανεὶ συμπληρωθέντων πέντε δ. ... χεὶρ ὠνόμασται· ἃς τὸ πνεῦμα τὸ θεῖον ἐνήργησε Proc.G.*Ex.*8:22(M.87.553A); through whose power commandments were written down καὶ ἔλαβεν [sc. Μωυσῆς] παρὰ κυρίου τὰς δύο πλάκας τὰς γεγραμμένας τῷ δ. τῆς χειρὸς κυρίου ἐν πνεύματι *Barn.*14.2; **c.** as God's instrument in souls of men τὰς τοῦ θεοῦ ἐντολὰς ἐν τῷ τῆς ψυχῆς πίνακι καὶ τῇ τῆς καρδίας πλακὶ δ. θεοῦ πνεύματι ἁγίῳ ἀναγεγραμμένας ἔχων ‡Pion.*v.Polyc.*4; μεταμελόμενος γὰρ πάλιν λέξει, δ. θεοῦ ἐστιν ἐν αὐτῷ Cosm.Ind.*top.*3(M.88. 164B); **d.** as instrument of Inc. αὐτὸς τῆς ἰδίας σαρκὸς γίνεται λατόμος [cf.Ex.24:12, 31:18, 34:1] τῆς τῷ θείῳ δ. καταγραφείσης... πάλιν τὸ ἀσύντριπτον ἔσχεν ἡ φύσις, ἀθάνατος γενομένη τοῖς τοῦ δ. χαράγμασιν [cf.Lc.1:35] Gr.Nyss.*v.Mos.*2(M.44.398B).

δαλίον, τό, *small torch*, Cyr.*Am.*29(3.294D, v.l. δᾳδίον; δαλίδιον Aubert).

[*]δαλματάκιον, τό, dim. of δαλματική, ‡Epiph.*epit.haer.*15(p.350. 31).

δαλματική, ἡ, *robe*, worn by Scribes and Pharisees, Epiph.*haer.* 15.1(p.209.15; M.41.245A); σχήματα ἐθελοθρησκευτικὰ τῆς ἐνδυσίας... τῶν δ. ἤγουν κολοβίων Jo.D.*haer.*15(M.94.688A).

[*]δαλματίκιον, τό, dim. of foreg., Gr.Mag.*dial.*(tr.Zach.)4.40 (M.*PL.*77.398A).

δαμάζ-ω, 1. *tame, subdue*; Manich., ref. punishment of soul after death, Hegem.*Arch.*11(p.18.11; M.10.1445A); of God ὁ πᾶσαν ἐνέργειαν κακωτικὴν ~ων *A.Jo.*75(p.187.25); **2.** *assail*, Nonn.*par.Jo.* 18:23(M.43.893B).

***δαμασμός, ὁ,** *taming, chastening*, Mac.Aeg.*hom.*23.2(M.34.661B); Nil.*epp.*1.169(M.79.149B); Pall.*h.Laus.*2(p.16.21; M.34.1011A).

***δαμαστήριον, τό,** *place of chastisement*; lit., Petr.II Al.*encycl.*4 (M.33.1281C)ap.Thdt.*h.e.*4.22.15; met. ἐγκράτεια...λογισμῶν δ. †Nil. *vit.*2(M.79.1141B); ἀγρυπνία...πνευμάτων δ. Jo.Clim.*scal.*20(M.88. 940D).

***δαμάτωρ, ὁ,** *subduer*, Thdr.Stud.*epp.*2.17(M.99.1169B).

***Δαμιανισταί, οἱ,** an heretical sect (monophysite), Tim.CP *haer.* (M.86.45B); cf.*ib.*(41B).

***δανατζᾶνος, ὁ,** *janitor*, Leont.Abb.*v.Gr.Agr.*54(M.98.644C).

δανείζ-ω, 1. *lend on usury*; met., to God ὃ ἑτέρῳ μέλλεις ~ειν χρυσίον τοῦτο δάνεισον ἐμοί, καὶ ἐπὶ πλείοσι Chrys.*hom.76.4 in Mt.* (7.738A); **2.** *lend*; met., of prophets τὴν γλῶτταν μὲν οὗτος ἐδάνεισεν Chrys.*hom.21.1 in Gen.*(4.181E); Cyr.*Mich.*4(3.393A); of a priest, Chrys.*hom.87.4 in Jo.*(8.518E); **3.** *bestow* ἐδάνεισας χάριν *Hom.Clem.* 1.16; καθάπερ ἐκείνη [sc. the poor widow] δύο κατέβαλεν ὀβόλους... οὕτω καὶ σὺ δύο δάνεισον ὥρας τῷ θεῷ Chrys.*bapt.*1(2.368B); of BMV σὺ ἐδάνεισας θεῷ θείαν σάρκωσιν ἣν οὐκ εἶχε ‡Meth.*Sym.et Ann.* 10(M.18.373A); **4.** med., *borrow*; met. εἰ μὴ ἄρα παρὰ...Ἰουδαίων καὶ τοῦ Καϊάφα δανείσωνται τὰς δυσφημίας Ath.*Ar.*3.67(M.26.468A); Chrys.*hom.52.4 in Mt.*(7.534C); ἡμέρα καὶ νὺξ...παρ' ἀλλήλων τὸν χρόνον ~όμεναι Thdt.*Ps.*18:3(1.719); τῶν ἀγγέλων τὸν ὕμνον ~ομαι Sophr.H.*nativ.*(p.503.27).

δάνειον, τό, *loan*, met. παρὰ σοῦ [sc. God] τὸ δ. εἰς τὸ μέλλον ἐκδέχεσθαι, καὶ ἐπίμετρον ζωῆν αἰώνιον Didym.*Trin.*2.27(M.39. 765B).

δανειστής, ὁ, *money-lender, creditor*, met. τρισὶ δ. περιέπεσα [sc. covetousness, greed, harlotry], Pall.*h.Laus.*37(p.111.7; M.34.1185D); of God εὖγε ἡ ὑποχρέων ἔχουσα [i.e. BMV] τὸν πάντων δ. ‡Meth. *Sym.et Ann.*10(M.18.373A).

δαπάνη, ἡ, 1. *cost*; met., of compensation for sin αὕτη τῶν ἁμαρτημάτων μου ἡ δ., τὸ...διὰ τοιούτων ὁδεύειν πειρασμῶν Chrys.*ep.* 14.1(3.595C); δ. τυγχάνει τῶν ἡμετέρων ἁμαρτημάτων ἡ πρὸς τοὺς λυπήσαντας καταλλαγή id.*hom.27.7 in Gen.*(4.267B); **2.** *consumption*; of waste of time, id.*hom.32.5 in Jo.*(8.182E); hence *material for consumption, food* for, Bas.*hex.*3.5(1.27C; M.29.65A); πυρὸς δ. Chrys.*hom.14.4 in Jo.*(8.76E); Philost.*h.e.*9.17(M.65.581B); *fodder, provisions*, *V.Pach.A* 9(p.133.17); *Chron.Pasch.*p.392(M.92.1005C); *ib.*p.397(1016B); Thphn.*chron.*p.332(M.108.801A).

δαπάνησις, ἡ, *consumption, expenditure*, Jo.Mosch.*prat.*185(M.87. 3060B).

δαπανητικός, 1. *consuming*; *devouring*, ‡Eust.*Laz.*6(p.31.7); πῦρ ...δ. τοῦ ὕδατος Gr.Nyss.*hex.*5(M.44.68A); comp. τοῦ πυρὸς τούτου δαπανητικωτέραν...φλόγα Chrys.*hom.7.6 in Rom.*(9.490D); id.*hom. 28.5 in Mt.*(7.340B); **2.** *destructive, wasteful*, Bas.*hex.*1.7(1.8B; M. 29.20B); *ib.*2.4(16B; M.37B); δ. ... πλούτου ἡ θεραπεία τῶν δεομένων id.*hom.*7.1(2.52B; M.31.281B); δ. τῶν καθομιλούντων παθῶν ἐγκράτειαν Gr.Nyss.*v.Mos.*(M.44.388A); **3.** neut. as subst., *destruction*, Gr.Naz.*or.*30.18(p.136.8; M.36.128A); Chrys.*hom.16.8 in Rom.*(9. 615C); Nil.*epp.*2.235(M.79.320D).

***δάπτριος (*δαπτρεῖος),** *destructive* πρὶν πτόρθου γλυκεροῖο φυγεῖν δαπτρεῖαν ἐδωδήν Gr.Naz.*carm.*1.1.8.121(M.37.456A); -τρια *ib.*2.2 (poem.)3.33(1482A); -τρια *ib.*2.1.50.15(1386A).

***δαρήσιμος,** *liable to beating*, Thdr.Stud.*epp.*2.14(M.99.1160A).

***δαρμός, ὁ,** *beating*, *Const.App.*4.11.4; Max.*carit.*4.81(M.90. 1068C); Thdr.Stud.*epp.*1.51(M.99.1097B).

***δασμογράφος, ὁ,** *tax-collector's clerk*, Gr.Naz.*carm.*1.2.15.64 (M.37.770A).

δασμολογ-έω, *exact tribute from*, met. ὁ Μαμωνᾶς...~ῶν τοὺς ὑποχειρίους Gr.Nyss.*ep.*18(M.46.1069C); Nil.*Magn.*18(M.79.993A); Cyr. *ador.*4(1.132D).

δασμολόγος, ὁ, *collector of tribute*, Cyr.*glaph.Ex.*1(1.260C).

δασμός, ὁ, *tribute*; met., of gifts of Nature to man, Thdr.*provid.* 2(4.510).

***δασυκέφαλος,** *with thick hair*, *A.Barth.*2(p.131.18).

***δασύκομος,** *with thick foliage*, *V.Mac.A*(p.148).

δασύτης, ἡ, *roughness*; of Syrian pronunciation of Greek, Soz. *h.e.*8.10.1(M.67.1541B); τὴν προσοῦσαν αὐτοῖς [sc. Syrians] δ. ἐδόκει πρὸς τὴν συνήθη ἡμῶν διηλλάχθαι φωνήν, τοῦτ' ἔστι τοῦ η στοιχείου εἰς τὸ ει μεταβολὴν ἢ τὸ ἀνάπαλιν Call.*v.Hyp.*(p.4).

***δασύφωνος,** *hoarse-voiced*, Chrys.*exp.in Ps.*41(5.133C).

***δάτιβος,** (Lat. *dativus*) *appointed* ὁ ἐπίσκοπος, δ. γενόμενος δικάστης Ath.Scholast.*coll.*4 paratit.1(p.90).

***Δαυίδ, *Δαβίδ, *Δαυείδ, ὁ,** *David*;

A. as ancestor of Christ ὁ Χριστὸς...ἐκ σπέρματος μὲν Δ., πνεύματος δὲ ἁγίου Ign.*Eph.*18.2; id.*Trall.*9.1; Just.*dial.*43.1(M.6.568A); ὁ...κύριος υἱὸς μὲν τῇ οὐσίᾳ...τοῦ θεοῦ ἐστι, τὸ δὲ κατὰ σάρκα ἐκ σπέρματός ἐστι Δ. Ath.*ep.Epict.*2(p.5.13; M.26.1053B); Cyr.H.*catech.* 11.5 cit. s. πατήρ; ‡Ath.*Apoll.*1.9(M.26.1108C,D); Chrys.*hom. 2.3 in Mt.*(7.24Aff.); Cyr.*hom.pasch.*15(5.209B); Andr.Cr.*or.*1(M.97. 817B,C); but with qualification, cf.Mt.22:42–45, *Barn.*12.10; not implying that Christ is mere man, Ath.*Dion.*8(p.51.11ff.; M.25. 489C–492A); ref. Gen.49:9, David as λέων and Christ as σκύμνος λέοντος, Andr.Cr.*or.*2(M.97.832A,B); chronology of his life etc., Clem.*str.*1.21(p.71.22ff.; M.8.837B).

B. in relation to Christ ὁ δὲ ἐκ Δ. καὶ πρὸ αὐτοῦ, ὁ τοῦ θεοῦ λόγος, λύραν μὲν καὶ κιθάραν, τὰ ἄψυχα ὄργανα, ὑπεριδών...τὸν ἄνθρωπον, ψυχήν τε καὶ σῶμα αὐτοῦ, ἁγίῳ πνεύματι ἁρμοσάμενος, ψάλλει τῷ θεῷ διὰ τοῦ πολυφώνου ὀργάνου καὶ προσᾴδει τῷ ὀργάνῳ τῷ ἀνθρώπῳ... ναὶ μὴν ὁ Δ. ... προὔτρεπεν ὡς τὴν ἀλήθειαν, ἀπέτρεπε δὲ εἰδώλων, πολλοῦ γε ἔδει ὑμνεῖν αὐτὸν τοὺς δαίμονας ἀληθεῖ πρὸς αὐτοῦ διωκομένους μουσικῇ Clem.*prot.*1(p.6.11ff.; M.8.60A); type of Christ, exeg. Ezech.34:23, Or.*Jo.*1.23(p.28.26; M.14.64C); cf.*ib.*1.36(41; p.46. 12; 93D); exeg. Os.3:5, Cyr.*Os.*34(3.62E); exeg. Am.9:11 σκήνη γὰρ ἡ πεσοῦσα τοῦ ἐκ σπέρματος Δ. τὸ κατὰ σάρκα Χριστοῦ, πρώτη πρὸς ἀφθαρσίαν διὰ τῆς δυνάμεως τοῦ...πατρὸς ἐξεγήγερται id.*Jo.*4.5 (4.403A); Δ. ἐστι νοητὸς...Χριστός Max.*qu.Thal.*53(M.90.501A); elaborated in myst. exegesis of biblical narratives, *ib.*(501Bff.); desired Christ, Chrys.*compunct.*2.3(1.144A); and prophesied him, Nil.*epp.*1.289(M.79.188C); liturg. εὐχαριστοῦμέν σοι...ὑπὲρ τῆς ἁγίας ἀμπέλου Δ. τοῦ παιδός σου, ἧς ἐγνώρισας ἡμῖν διὰ Ἰησοῦ *Did.*9.2; cf. οὗτος [sc. Christ] ὁ τὸν οἶνον, τὸ αἷμα τῆς ἀμπέλου τῆς Δ., ἐκχέας ἡμῶν ἐπὶ τὰς τετρωμένας ψυχάς Clem.*q.d.s.*29(p.179.11; M.9.636A).

C. and Christians; his kingdom continued in Church, Epiph.

haer.29.3(p.323.5ff.; M.41.392A); ref. Am.9:11, David's tabernacle being identified with Church, Chrys.*hom.33.2 in Ac*.(9.255D); resurrection of body, Meth.*res*.1.53(p.308.18ff.; M.41.1128B,C); prophets *λέγουσιν αὐτοῖς παραγίνεσθαι Δ. καὶ ἀνίστασθαι, οὐ περὶ ἐκείνου λέγοντες τοῦ τετελευτηκότος, ἀλλὰ τῶν ζηλούντων τὴν ἀρετὴν τὴν ἐκείνου* Chrys.*hom.2.3 in Mt*.(7.24C); Gregory of Nyssa's fight against Eunomius compared with fight with Goliath, Gr.Nyss.*Eun*.12(1 p.217.27; M.45.912A).

D. ref. Psalms as equivalent for Psalmist, *1Clem*.52.2; *Barn*.10.10; Just.*1apol*.41.1(M.6.392A); Clem.*paed*.1.5(p.97.28; M.8.264C); view that David is not author of all Psalms repudiated, Cosm.Ind.*top*.5(M.88.249B).

E. significance of certain incidents in his life: his dancing before the ark *ἣν ἡγοῦμαι τῆς εὐκινήτου καὶ πολυστρόφου κατὰ θεὸν πορείας εἶναι μυστήριον* Gr.Naz.*or*.5.35(M.36.709C); his sparing Saul (1Reg.24:8) *οὐ γὰρ ὡς στρατηγὸς στρατιωτῶν, ἀλλ' ὡς ἱερεύς, οὕτως αὐτῶν προειστήκει, καὶ ἦν ἐκκλησία τὸ σπήλαιον ἐκεῖνο λοιπόν* Chrys.*David* 2.1(4.761A); which was a greater victory than that over Goliath, *ib*.2.2(761C,D); his sin and repentance discussed, id.*hom.26.6 in Mt*.(7.321Dff.); cf.*ib.2.6*(31C); id.*exp.in Ps*.6(5.45C,D); *Δ. ἥμαρτε, καὶ μέγιστα ἁμαρτήματα ἐπλημμέλησεν· ἀλλ' οὐ κατέλιπεν, ἣν ὥδευσεν ὁδόν, ἀλλὰ...πεσὼν ἀνέστη* Thdt.*Ezech*.3:20(2.706); Andr.Cr.*or*.15(M.97.1120B); his eating the shewbread *ἵνα διὰ τούτου πάλιν ἡ τῶν ἐθνῶν πίστις καὶ ἀπὸ μέρους τῶν ἐξ 'Ισραὴλ σημαίνηται* Cyr.*Jo*.4.4(4.390A).

F. various qualities: pattern of penitence, Cyr.H.*catech*.2.11f.; of meekness, Gr.Naz.*or*.5.30(M.35.704A); *ib*.14.2(861A); esp. in his attitude to Saul, Chrys.*David* 1.3(4.751Dff.) et passim; *ὁ μέγας θεραπευτής, ὁ καὶ πνευμάτων πονηρῶν κατεπᾴδων διὰ τοῦ ἐν αὐτῷ πνεύματος* Gr.Naz.*or*.17.2(968B); id.*carm*.1.2.25.202(M.37.827); of patience, Chrys.*David* 2.1(4.759D); humility, *ib*.2.4(766E); generosity, id.*hom.in Rom.12:20*(3.169D); faith, id.*hom.3.8 in 2Cor.4:13*(3.286B); living by law of gospel, Thdt.*Ps*.34:29(1.827); *Δ. τὴν εὐαγγελικὴν προθεωρῶν πολιτείαν, κατ' ἐκείνην ἤθελε βιοῦν ib*.140:4(1.1544); cf. *ἔκστασις*.

Δαυϊτικός** (Δαβιδικός**, ***Δαβιτικός**), *of David Δαυϊτικὸν...θησαύρισμα* Didym.*Trin*.1.18(M.39.356A); *ψαλτήριον Δαβιτικόν* ‡Ath.*synops*.1(M.28.285D); *τὴν Δαβιδικὴν...λύραν* Sophr.H.*v.Anast*.(M.92.1705D).

Δαυϊτικῶς** (Δαβιτικῶς**), *in the words of David, after the manner of David Δαυϊτικῶς ἐπιφθέγγεσθαι· τοῦ ἐχθροῦ ἐξέλιπον αἱ ῥομφαῖαι* Leont.H.*Nest*.1.13(M.86.1452B); Sophr.H.*nativ*.(p.514.21); *ἡ γῆ...Δαβιτικῶς ἀλαλάζουσα* Germ.CP *or*.2(M.98.252A); Thdr.Stud.*nativ.BMV* 7(M.96.696D).

***δαφνηδαία, ἡ,** *laurel* or *bay tree εἶδε δαφνηδαίαν Protev*.2(vv.ll. *δαφνιδίαν, δαφνηδέαν, δαφνίδα, δάφνην* p.6); *ib*.3(vv.ll. *δαφνηδέᾳ, δάφνῃ* p.7).

***δαφνόω,** *crown with laurels*, pass., Jo.Mal.*chron*.12 p.307(M.97.464A).

***δαψίλαιος,** *rich, fertile ἐν δ. χώρῳ A.Thom*.A 130(p.238.15, conj. *διψαλέῳ*).

δαψίλεια, ἡ, 1. *abundance, plenty*; hence in bad sense *excess* δ. ... *χρήζει ἡ τρυφή* Clem.*paed*.1.12(p.149.16; M.8.369A); Bas.*hom*.1.4(2.3D; M.31.168C); **2.** *liberality μετὰ...τῆς ἄλλης ἀρετῆς καὶ τὴν περὶ τοὺς πένητας δ. ἐπιδεικνυώμεθα* Chrys.*hom.3.6 in Gen*.(4.21B); *ἐλεημοσύνην μετὰ δαψιλείας ἐργαζόμενος ib.5.2*(33C); *εἶδες...οὐκ ἐν τῇ πολυτελείᾳ τῆς τραπέζης τὴν φιλοξενίαν ἐπιδεικνυμένην, ἀλλ' ἐν τῇ δ. τῆς γνώμης; ib.43.3*(439A); **3.** *imperial treasury* (*largitio*), Men.*exc.gent*.23(p.464.6; M.113.828B).

δαψιλής, 1. *large, ample ἡ ἐπαγγελία ὡς δ.* Gr.Naz.*or*.41.13(M.36.448A); Synes.*ep*.4(M.66.1340C); Bas.Sel.*or*.8.1(M.85.116A); **2.** *full, copious*; of speech and writing, Eus.*d.e.2* proem.(p.52.7; M.22.96A); Gr.Naz.*or*.16.1(M.35.936A); **3.** neut. as subst.; **a.** *abundance, largeness τὸ δ. τῆς διακονίας* Bas.*hom.in Ps*.14(1.357C; M.29.264B); **b.** *liberality, munificence*, Cyr.H.*procatech*.3; **4.** neut. as adv., with *γελάω*, laugh *heartily καὶ γελάσαι μοι λοιπὸν δ. ἐνταῦθα ἐπέρχεται* Chrys.*hom.22.5 in 1Cor*.(10.199D); id.*hom.13.10 in Rom*.(9.573D).

δαψιλῶς, 1. *abundantly, plentifully*, Clem.*paed*.1.6(p.120.8; M.8.309A); Or.*fr.48 in Jo*.(p.523.20); Eus.*h.e*.6.2.15(M.20.525C); **2.** *excessively, inordinately*, Tit.Bost.*Man*.2.10(M.18.1152D); Nil.*epp*.1.185(M.79.153A); Isid.Pel.*epp*.1.329(M.78.372C); **3.** with *γελάω*, *heartily, deeply*, Chrys.*sac*.3.18(p.93.26; 1.400C).

***δεδειγμένως,** *conclusively*, ‡Just.*qu.Chr*.4.1(M.6.1445D).

***δέδιξις, ἡ,** *terror*, Sophr.H.*or*.2.24(M.87.3244B).

***δεδοκιμασμένως,** *in approved fashion*, Or.*or*.29.15(p.390.21; M.11.544A).

δέησις, ἡ, *entreaty, supplication, petition*; **1.** def. and characteristics, exeg. 1Tim.2:1, Or.*or*.14.2(p.331.4; M.11.460C) cit. s. *εὐχή*; *δ. μέν ἐστιν, ὑπὲρ ἀπαλλαγῆς τινων λυπηρῶν ἱκετεία προσφερομένη* Thdt.*1Tim*.2:1(3.646); to be addressed not only to God but also to holy men, though not to others, Or.*or*.14.6(p.333.11,14; 464C); *δ. λέγεται, ὅταν τις ἀξιοῖ τὸν θεὸν εἰς πρᾶγμα* ‡Chrys.*inc*.6(8^2.224D); in contradistinction to *προσευχή*: *δ. οἵου, τὴν αἴτησιν ἐνδεῶν· τὴν δὲ προσευχὴν ἴσθι τῶν ἀμεινόνων* Gr.Naz.*carm*.1.2.34.138(M.37.955A); *ἡ μὲν προσευχὴ τὴν ἱκετηρίαν δηλοῖ τὴν πρὸς τὸν θεόν, καὶ τὴν παράκλησιν· ἡ δὲ δ. τὴν αἴτησιν τὴν περὶ ὧν βούλεται αὐτῷ δεομένῳ παρασχεθῆναι* ‡Chrys.*hom.1.1 in Ps.101*(5.644B); *δ. ἐστιν ἡ ἔνδεια καὶ τὸ λεῖμμα οὗ ἕκαστος ἀπορεῖ...οὕτως πτωχός εἰμι καὶ ταπεινὸς πνεύματι, ὅτι αὕτη μου ἡ ἔνδεια...ὡς χάρτης δεήσεως τῶν κατορθωμάτων διὰ γραμμάτων βοᾷ* Ast.Soph.*hom.4.3 in Ps.5*(M.40.439C); **2.** *supplication*, expressed in words, opp. mental prayer *τοῖς μὲν οὖν ἐξ ἁμαρτιῶν μετανενοηκόσι...διὰ τῶν δεήσεων παρέχει ὁ θεὸς τὰ αἰτήματα, τοῖς δ' ἀναμαρτήτως καὶ γνωστικῶς βιοῦσιν ἐννοησαμένοις μόνον δίδωσιν* Clem.*str*.6.12(p.482.23; M.9.321C); reinforced by fasting, Polyc.*ep*.7.2; *A.Jo*.84(p.192.29); and tears, Chrys.*poenit*.4.2(2.304D); its efficacy *ἐπειδὰν δὲ ἀποκαθαρθεῖσα ψυχὴ τῆς περὶ θεοῦ ἀγνοίας, ἀνενέγκῃ δεήσεις, ἐν τῇ λαμπρότητι τῆς λογικῆς καὶ πνευματικῆς ἡμέρας γενομένη, εἰσακούοντα ἔχει τῆς φωνῆς τὸν θεόν* †Bas.*Is*.162(1.494B; M.30.384C); *κατὰ δύο τρόπους ἐνεργουμένην οἶδα τοῦ δικαίου τὴν δ.· καθ' ἕνα μέν, ὁπόταν μετὰ τῶν κατ' ἐντολὴν ἔργων τῷ θεῷ τὴν ταύτης ποιεῖται προσαγωγὴν τῆς δ. ὁ εὐχόμενος...εὐχῆς γὰρ καὶ δ. ὑπόστασις, ἡ διὰ τῶν ἀρετῶν ὑπάρχει προδήλως ἐκπλήρωσις· καθ' ἣν ἰσχυρὰν καὶ πάντα δυναμένην ὁ δίκαιος ἔχει τὴν δ., ἐνεργουμένην ταῖς ἐντολαῖς. καθ' ἕτερον δὲ τρόπον ὁπόταν ὁ τῆς εὐχῆς τοῦ δικαίου δεόμενος, τὰ ἔργα τῆς εὐχῆς διαπράττεται, τόν τε πρότερον διορθούμενος βίον, καὶ τὴν δ. τοῦ δικαίου ἰσχυρὰν ποιούμενος διὰ τῆς οἰκείας καλῆς ἀναστροφῆς δυναμουμένην* Max.*qu.Thal*.57(M.90.589D–592A); **3.** esp. *intercessory prayer*; **a.** in gen., *Barn*.12.7; *ἐνορκίζοντες αὐτὸν μνήμην αὐτῶν ἔχειν ἐν ταῖς δ. αὐτοῦ A.Thom*.A 68(p.185.7); Clem.*str*.4.19(p.300.25; M.8.1329A); **b.** liturg. *ἡ πρώτη δὲ δ. ἐλέους γέμει, ὅταν ὑπὲρ τῶν ἐνεργουμένων παρακαλῶμεν· καὶ ἡ δευτέρα πάλιν, ὑπὲρ ἑτέρων τῶν ἐν μετανοίᾳ,...καὶ ἡ τρίτη...ὑπὲρ ἡμῶν αὐτῶν* Chrys.*hom.71.4 in Mt*.(7.699E); *καθ' ἑκάστην ἡμέραν...καὶ ἐν ἑσπέρᾳ καὶ ἐν πρωΐᾳ...ὑπὲρ παντὸς τοῦ κόσμου, καὶ βασιλέων καὶ πάντων τῶν ἐν ὑπεροχῇ ὄντων ποιούμεθα τὴν δ.* id.*hom.6.1 in 1Tim*.(11.579B); of prayers for dead *μεγίστην ὄνησιν πιστεύοντες ἔσεσθαι ταῖς ψυχαῖς ὑπὲρ ὧν ἡ δ. ἀναφέρεται τῆς ἁγίας καὶ φρικωδεστάτης προκειμένης θυσίας* Cyr.H.*catech*.23.9; **4.** combined with other terms denoting petition *τὴν δ. καὶ ἱκεσίαν ποιοῦμενοι 1Clem*.59.2; *μία προσευχή, μία δ.* Ign.*Magn*.7.1; *τῇ εὐχῇ καὶ τῇ δ. A.Thom*.A 67(p.184.12); *νηστεῖαι, δ., εὐχαί* Clem.*exc.Thdot*.84(p.132.20; M.9.697A); *Const.App*.2.26.2; *πρόσδεξαι ὁ θεὸς τὴν δ. ἡμῶν καὶ ποίησον ἡμᾶς ἀξίους γενέσθαι τοῦ προσφέρειν σοι δ. καὶ ἱκεσίας καὶ θυσίας ἀναιμάκτους Lit.Chrys*.(p.316.19); v. *εὐχή*; **5.** written *petition χωρὶς ψηφισμάτων καὶ χωρὶς δ.* Maximinus Daia ap.Eus.*h.e*.9.7.13(M.20.813C); Firminus *ep.Bas*.(M.32.533C); *δ. δὲ ἔγγραφον οὐδεὶς ἀρχόντων ἐπιδέχηται, ἀλλὰ βασιλεὺς μόνον* Ast.Soph.*hom.1 in Ps.5*(M.40.401B); Socr.*h.e*.1.8.18(M.67.64C).

***δεητήριον, τό,** *place of prayer*, Germ.CP *or*.1(M.98.236C).

δεητικός, *supplicatory*; neut. as subst., *petition*, Leont.Abb *v.Gr.Agr*.86(M.98.704A).

δειγμάτιζω, 1. *make a show of, expose*, *Ascens.Is*.A 3.13(p.92); *ἔλεγεν...ἵνα μὴ μόνον ἀπὸ τῆς τοῦ Σίμωνος ἀπάτης φύγωσιν, ἀλλὰ καὶ δειγματίσουσιν αὐτόν A.Petr.et Paul*.33(p.194.3); *εὖ...τὸ 'μὴ θέλων αὐτὴν δειγματίσαι' εἰρῆσθαι δοκεῖ ὑπὸ τοῦ εὐαγγελιστοῦ· οὐ γὰρ ἔφησε 'μὴ θέλων αὐτὴν παραδειγματίσαι' ἀλλὰ 'μὴ δειγματίσαι θέλων'· πολλῆς οὔσης διαφορᾶς...τὸ μὲν γὰρ παραδειγματίσαι τὴν ἐπὶ κακῶς πράξαντι εἰς πάντας φανέρωσίν τε καὶ διαβολὴν ὑποβάλλει νοεῖν· τὸ δὲ δειγματίσαι τὸ φανερὸν ἁπλῶς ποιῆσαι* Eus.*qu.Steph*.1.3(M.22.884C,D); *ἀποδῦσαι τὸ κάλυμμα τῆς ἀσεβείας καὶ δειγματίσαι τὴν αἵρεσιν* Ath.*ep.Aeg.Lib*.11(M.25.564A); *ὅτε...ἐπεδήμησεν ὁ σωτήρ, τότε ἡ πᾶσα φαντασία αὐτοῦ* [sc. Devil] *ἐδειγματίσθη* id.*fr.Job*(M.27.1348B); *ἵνα...γυμνὸν αὐτὸν τῶν ἀρετῶν στήσαντες τοῖς ἀγγέλοις δειγματίσωσι* Nil.*Eulog*.28(M.79.1132A); **2.** *make a show of, display*, in good sense *τοῦτο...εἰπὼν ἑαυτὸν ἐδειγμάτισεν* ‡Chrys.*hom.in Ps.76:4*(10.740D); **3.** *make an example of μὴ τὸν κακοπαθήσαντα χαροποιῆσαι πένητα μηδὲ τὸν τρυφήσαντα δειγματίσαι πλούσιον* Mac.Mgn.*apocr*.4.30(p.225.14).

δεικτήριον, τό, *pulpit, platform*, Bas.Sel.*v.Thecl*.2.27(M.85.612D).

δειλαίν-ω, A. act.; **1.** *fear*; c. acc., Herm.*sim*.9.1.3; with dependent clause, Sophr.H.*mir.Cyr.et Jo*.32(M.87.3528A); **2.** *terrify, frighten*, *A.Xanthipp*.21(p.73.21); pass., Pall.*h.Laus*.35(p.103.15; M.34.1114B); Thphn.*chron*.p.74(M.108.232C); **3.** *make a coward of* ἐγὼ...σιγῆσαι βούλομαι, διότι ~ει με ὁ ἀνθρώπινος λογισμός *A. Xanthipp.*14(p.68.1).

B. med., *be afraid*, Ign.*Rom.*5.2; Chrys.*exp.in Ps.*3(5.5C); Jo. Clim.*scal.*21(M.88.945B).

δειλανδρέω, *be cowardly*, *A.Paul.et Thecl.*25(p.253.6); Ephr.3. 393D; Eun.ap.Gr.Nyss.*Eun.*2(2 p.388.9; M.45.569C); †Cyr.*hom.div.* 11(5².382C).

***δειλανδρία,** ἡ, *cowardice*, Geo.Pis.*Pers.*3.42(M.92.1238A).

***δειλανδρίζω,** **1.** *play the coward*, *M.Seb.*11(p.180.1); **2.** c. acc., *fear*, *A.(Pass.)Andr.*8(p.21.25, v.l. ἐκφοβεῖν M.2.1233B).

[*]**δειλητήριον, τό,** = δηλητήριον, *poison*, Dam.*troph.*4.1(p.261.10).

δειλιαίνομαι, *be a coward*, Jo.Clim.*scal.*21(M.88.945C).

δειλιάω, *be afraid*; trans., *fear*, †Jo.Jej.*serm.*(M.88.1921B) cit. s. ἐξαγορεύω.

δειλοκοπέω, *terrify*, Nil.*Eulog.*23(M.79.1124D).

δειλός, *cowardly*; in good sense, *reverent, fearing God*, of bishop εἰ καὶ νέος, ἀλλὰ πρᾶος ὑπαρχέτω δ. τε καὶ ἡσύχιος *Const.App.*2.1.3.

***δειλοψυχέομαι,** *be disheartened*, ‡Ath.*pat.*6(M.26.1304B).

***δειμάζω,** *fear*, *Apophth.Patr.*(M.65.196B).

***δειμαλέως,** *timidly, in fear*, *Orac.Sib.*1.228.

δεινολογέω, *complain loudly*, Or.*Cels.*4.52(p.325.16; M.11.116A).

δεινοπαθ-έω, *suffer acutely* πολλὰ δ. *Mir.Geo.*4(p.29.3); τὰ εὖ πεπονθότα πρόσωπα καὶ τὰ ~ήσαντα ὑφ' ἡμῶν Thdr.Stud.*epp.*2.99 (M.99.1352D).

***δεινοπαθῶς,** *movingly*, Philost.*h.e.*9.8(M.65.576A).

***δεινοποίησις,** ἡ, *dreadful composition*, of books of Manichean heresy πλασματικῆς δ. Epiph.*haer.*66.4(p.22.5; M.42.36C).

[*]**δεῖνος,** ὁ, late form of δεῖνα, *such a one*, used to indicate that the name of a person is to be inserted by the reader or speaker, cf. Lat. and Eng. 'N.' ὑπὲρ τοῦ ἀρχιεπισκόπου ἡμῶν, ὁ δ. *Lit.Chrys.*ap. *Euchol.*(p.50).

δεινῶς, *cleverly*, Iren.*haer.*1.3.6(M.7.477B; conj. δεινοτέρως ap. Epiph.*haer.*31.15(p.409.13)).

δείνωσις, ἡ, = δεινότης, *ability, cleverness*, Cyr.*apol.orient.* (p.62.23; 6¹.197A); id.*Is.*4.2(2.597A).

δειπνάριον, τό, (dim. of δεῖπνον), used contemptuously, *wretched dinner*, Clem.*paed.*2.1(p.156.13,17,18; M.8.384B).

δειπνίζ-ω, *entertain*; of a spiritual feast, Or.*Jo.*13.32(31; p.257. 7; M.14.456A); τίνα...τρόπον...ἀλείφεται καὶ ~εται καὶ δοξάζεται [sc. ὁ Ἰησοῦς] *ib.*1.11(12; p.17.15; 45A).

δειπνοκλήτωρ, ὁ, *one who invites to a feast*, Cyr.*ador.*1(1.113D); id.*glaph.Ex.*2(1.294C); id.*Lc.*14:23(M.72.792C).

δειπνολόχος, *hanging around at feasts, parasitic*, *Orac.Sib.*2.258; Gr.Naz.*carm.*1.2.29.121(M.37.893A).

δεῖπνον, τό, **δεῖπνος,** ὁ, *dinner, supper*; **1.** in gen., ref. Lc.7:37 ἀλάβαστρον μύρον παρὰ τὸ δ. τὸ ἅγιον κομίσασα ἡ γυνή Clem.*paed.*2.8 (p.194.1; M.8.465B); ref. Cana, *A.Thom.*A 146(p.254.5,14); ref. Mt.22:4 ἰδοὺ τὸ δ. ἕτοιμον καὶ μακάριος ὁ καλούμενος *A.Phil.*135 (p.67.7); ref. feeding of five thousand ὁ τοὺς ἰχθύας θηρεύων [sc. ὁ Ἰησοῦς] εἰς τὸ ἄριστον καὶ εἰς τὸ δ. *A.Thom.*A 47(p.164.8); symbolical interpretation ἄριστον μέν ἐστιν ἡ πρώτη...τροφή· δ. δὲ ἡ τελευταία καὶ τοῖς ἤδη ἐπὶ πλεῖον προκεκοφόσι παρατιθεμένη...ἄριστον μὲν εἶναι τὸν νοῦν τῶν παλαιῶν γραμμάτων, δ. δὲ τὰ ἐναποκεκρυμμένα τῇ καινῇ διαθήκῃ μυστήρια Or.*Jo.*32.2(p.426.14,16; M.14.741B); **2.** of Last Supper τὸ μὲν δ. ἐδείπνησε πρὸ τοῦ πάσχα, τὸ δὲ πάσχα οὐκ ἔφαγεν Hipp.*pasch.fr.*5(p.270.11; M.92.80C); περὶ τοῦ δ. τοῦ δεσποτικοῦ Jo.Philop.*pasch.*(p.209.5); κυριακὸν δ. *ib.*(p.212.7); ἣν δὲ ἡ μεγάλη τοῦ μυστικοῦ δ. ... ἡμέρα Niceph.Ur.*v.Sym.*224(M.86.3192C); τὸν μυστικὸν τοῦ κυρίου μετὰ τῶν μαθητῶν δ. *Chron.Pasch.*p.225(M.92. 548C); **3.** of eucharist τὸ μὴ κοινωνεῖν τῶν μυστικῶν δ. ἐκείνων λιμὸς καὶ θάνατος Chrys.*hom.24.5 in 1Cor.*(10.218D); id.*scand.*14 (3.500E); id.*hom.6.3 in Is.6:1*(6.142C); τοῦ μυστικοῦ δ. πᾶσαν ἡμέραν μέτεχε Nil.*paraen.*120(M.79.1260D); †Cyr.*hom.div.*10(5². 371B); Dion.Ar.*e.h.*3.3.1(M.3.428B); Max.*schol.e.h.*3.3.1(M.4.137B); Geo.Pis.*carm.*74 tit.; esp. κυριακὸν δ. (1Cor.11:20), Bas.*reg.br.*310 (2.525E; M.31.1304C); Thdt.*1Cor.*11:20(3.236); ἐξῃρημένης μιᾶς ἐτησίας ἡμέρας ἐν ᾗ τὸ κυριακὸν δ. ἐπιτελεῖται *Cod.Afr.*41; Oecum. *1Cor.*11:17(p.441.1; M.118.801C); **4.** Θυέστεια δ. cannibal *feasts*, of which Christians were accused by pagans, Athenag.*leg.*3.1(M.6. 896C); id.*res.*4(p.52.22; M.6.981C); *Ep.Lugd.*ap.Eus.*h.e.*5.1.14(M.20. 413B); **5.** τὸ ἔσχατον δ. given to condemned before martyrdom τὸ ἔσχατον ἐκεῖνο δ. ὅπερ ἐλεύθερον ὀνομάζουσι. ὅσον δὲ ἐφ' ἑαυτοῖς οὐκ ἐλεύθερον δ. ἀλλ' ἀγάπην ἐπεκάλουν τῇ αὐτῶν παρρησίᾳ *M.Perp.* 17(p.87.8).

δειπνοποιΐα, ἡ, *preparation of a feast*, Gr.Naz.*carm.*1.2.32.47(M. 37.919A).

δεῖπνος, ὁ, v. δεῖπνον.

***δειροπέδη,** ἡ, *necklace*, Gr.Naz.*carm.*1.2.29.229(M.37.901A).

δεῖσα, ἡ, *mud, filth*, *Schol.Clem.prot.*4(p.313.31; M.9.786C); *Schol. Clem.paed.*3.11(p.339.7; M.9.794B).

***δεισαλέος,** *filthy*, Clem.*prot.*4(p.43.26; M.8.152C); id.*paed.*3.11 (p.278.8; M.8.653A).

δεισιδαιμον-έω, **1.** *hold false religious beliefs*; **a.** ref. popular paganism, Clem.*prot.*10(p.77.4; M.8.224C); οἱ φιλοσοφοῦντες καὶ διδασκόμενοι μὴ ~εῖν Or.*Cels.*5.35(p.38.15; M.11.1236A); τίς ἀπόδειξις περὶ τοῦ εἶναι τούτους θεοὺς γένοιτ' ἂν τοῖς ἐν τούτοις ~οῦσιν; Ath. *gent.*18(M.25.37A); εἰς Ἡλιούπολιν ἔνθα ~ῶν πᾶς Petr.II Al.*encycl.* 7(M.33.1287A)ap.Thdt.*h.e.*4.22.26; **b.** ref. heresy οὐ ~οῦμεν κατὰ τοὺς αἱρετικούς, μήπως ἡ τοῦ θεοῦ κτίσις κόσμος οὖσα ἐν τῷ πονηρῷ ἵδρυται *cat.1Jo.*5:19(p.144.14); Leont.H.*monoph.*testimonia(M.86. 1877C); συνόδων οὖν διαφόρων δεισιδαιμονησασῶν κατήργηνται συνόδοις μὲν κυριωτέραις τὰ ὑπ' αὐτῶν *ib.*(1889A); **2.** *have scruples, be hesitant* (for religious reasons) εἰ μὴ ~οῦντές γε περὶ τὰ ὀνόματα, ἀλλὰ βλέποντες τὰ πράγματα Or.*Jo.*19.15(4; p.315.29; M.14.553C); ref. Ac. 10:13 τὸ πνεῦμα...ἦλθε πρὸς αὐτὸν [sc. S. Peter] ἔτι ~οῦντα id.*Cels.* 2.2(p.129.16; M.11.800A); ~οῦμεν πῇ μὲν εἰπεῖν δύο θεούς, πῇ δὲ εἰπεῖν ἕνα θεόν id.*dial.*2(p.122.9).

δεισιδαιμονία, ἡ, *false religion, superstition*, in gen. ἀθεότης καὶ δ. Clem.*prot.*2(p.18.22; M.8.93A); ἡ...δ. πάθος, φόβος δαιμόνων οὖσα ἐκπαθῶν τε καὶ ἐμπαθῶν id.*str.*2.8(p.134.9; M.8.976A); Or.*exp.in Pr.* 22:28(M.17.221A); of paganism τῆς Ἑλληνικῆς δ. Clem.*str.*7.4(p.16. 15; M.9.428C); τῇ, ὡς ἡμεῖς ὀνομάζομεν, εἰδωλολατρείᾳ, ὡς δὲ οἱ πολλοὶ λέγοιεν ἂν...τῇ δ. Or.*Cels.*6.17(p.87.28; M.11.1316B); Dion. Al.ap.Eus.*h.e.*6.41.1(M.20.605B); Ἑλληνισμόν...τὴν κατὰ τὰ πάτρια τῶν ἐθνῶν ἁπάντων εἰς πλείονας θεοὺς δ. Eus.*d.e.*1.2(p.7.30; M.22. 24B); *ib.*(p.8.12; 24C); of Judaism, *Diogn.*1; πᾶσαν Ἰουδαϊκὴν δ. Or. *Cels.*7.41(p.192.7; 1480C); Gr.Nyss.*or.catech.*18(p.77.7; M.45.50B); of Christianity as seen by pagans, Maximinus Daia ap.Eus.*h.e.*9. 9ᵃ.5(M.20.825C); within Christianity, Or.*Cels.*3.79(p.269.30; 1021D); οἱ τὰ ὀρθὰ φρονοῦντες μηδεμίᾳ δ. τῶν τόπων [ref. Donatist martyrshrines] καταδεσμῶνται *Cod.Afr.*83; Socr.*h.e.*7.25.9(M.67.793C).

δεισιδαίμων, *superstitious* μὴ προλήψει μηδ' ἀνθρωπαρεσκείᾳ τῇ δ. κατεχομένους Just.*1apol.*2.3(M.6.329B); Ἑλλήνων τοὺς δ. Clem.*prot.*2 (p.12.6; M.8.73A); μεταβάλλειν...ἐκ δ. εἰς εὐσεβῆ τὸν παραδεξάμενον τὴν τοῦ λόγου...ἐπιδημίαν Or.*Cels.*4.5(p.278.12; M.11.1036B); τοὺς δ. τῶν εἰδώλων Epiph.*haer.*62.7(p.396.7; M.41.1060B); applied to Christians by pagans, Or.*Cels.*3.79(p.270.1; 1021D).

δέκα, *ten*; **1.** perfect number symbolizing perfection μέγιστος ...ἀριθμὸς ὁ δ. κατὰ τοὺς Πυθαγορικοὺς ὁ τετρακτύς τε ὢν καὶ πάντας τοὺς ἀριθμητικοὺς καὶ τοὺς ἁρμονικοὺς περιέχων λόγους Athenag.*leg.* 6.1(M.6.901A); Or.*Jo.*10.1(p.171.7; M.14.308A); τὸν δ. τέλειον ὄντα καὶ οἰκεῖον θεοῦ (δεκάται γὰρ ἐν τῇ δεκάτῃ τῶν ἱλασμῶν ἀναφέρονται, καὶ δεκάλογος ἡ πρώτη νομοθεσία) id.*fr.62 in Jer.*(p.228.27); cf. *decem numerus ubique perfectus invenitur; totius enim numeri ex ipso ratio et origo consurgit*, id.*hom.13.4 in Lev.*(p.473.7; M.12. 548B); ἔθος τῇ θείᾳ γραφῇ τὸν ἀριθμὸν τὸν δ., τέλειον ἀεὶ προσδέχεσθαι καὶ εἰδέναι πληρέστατον, ἐπείπερ ἡ τῶν ἐφεξῆς ἀριθμῶν πάροδός τε καὶ θέσις, ἀνακύκλησίν τινα καὶ πολυπλασιασμὸν τῶν αὐτῶν εἰς τὰ αὐτὰ δεχομένη, πρὸς ὅπερ ἄν τις ἐθελήσαι βαδίζει καὶ ἐκτείνεται Cyr.*Jo.*4.2 (4.356E); Areth.*Apoc.*62(M.106.753B); **2.** in Gnost. theory (Valentinian); of number of aeons produced by Λόγος and Ζωή, Iren. *haer.*1.1.2(M.7.449A); *ib.*11.1(561A); *ib.*12.4(576A); symbolized by ι', first letter of Ἰησοῦς *ib.*3.2(469A).

***δεκάγλωσσος,** *ten-tongued*, i.e. *eloquent*, Geo.Pis.*bell.Avar.*86 (M.92.1270A).

δεκαδικός, *tenfold, multiplied by ten*, Gr.Naz.*or.*28.9(p.36.14; M.36.37B); Areth.*Apoc.*62(M.106.753B).

***δεκαδρομ-έω,** *outrun, exceed ten*, of seventeen nonads as representing the number of fathers at Council of Ephesus εἷς ἣν ἀριθμὸς ἑπτασυνθέτους ἔχων ~ούσας εἰς ἑαυτὸν ἐννάδας Geo.Pis. *Sev.*120(M.92.1632A).

δεκαέξ, *sixteen*, Jo.Eleem.*v.Tych.*(p.123); †Anast.S.*relat.*49(p.69).

***δέκαθλος,** ὁ, *tenfold contest*, Geo.Pis.*carm.*20.1.

***δεκακέρατος,** **1.** *with ten horns*, name applied to monophysite heretics τοὺς λεγομένους δεκακεράτων συνομοκεράτους, καὶ ὑπὸ τοῦ ἐν ἁγίοις Σωφρονίου ἐν τῷ λιβέλλῳ αὐτοῦ ἀναθεματιζομένους Thdr. Stud.*test.*(M.99.1816B); **2.** neut. as subst., *heresy of the Ten Horns* Σευῆρος...εἶπεν ἀποτελεῖσθαι μίαν φύσιν τὸν Χριστόν. ὡσαύτως καὶ Εὐτυχής, καὶ Διόσκορος, Τιμόθεός τε, καὶ Γαϊανός, καὶ Ἰουλιανός, Ἰάκωβος, καὶ Πέτρος ὁ Γναφεύς, καὶ Βαρσανούφιος, καὶ Θεοδόσιος τὸ δ. τῆς πλάνης...παρέλαβον τὸ λέγειν, τὴν φύσιν πρόσωπον καὶ οὐκ ἔστι φύσις ἀπρόσωπος Anast.S.*hod.*6(M.89.108B).

***δεκάκτινος**, *ten-rayed* θεοτόκε, δι' ἣν τὸ δ. κάλλος τῶν ἀποστόλων ἐκλέλεκται †Cyr.*hom.div.*11(5^2.381A; ? f.l. for δωδεκάκτινον).

δεκάλογος, ἡ, *decalogue* ἡ δ. ... προσηγορίαν σωτηρίαν ἁμαρτιῶν περιγράφουσα Clem.*paed.*3.12(p.285.1; M.8.668A); ὑπόδειγμα...εἰς σαφήνειαν γνωστικὴν ἡ δ. id.*str.*6.16(p.499.13; M.9.357C); Hipp.*haer.* 8.14(p.234.8; M.16.3362A) cit. s. ἀλληγορέω; Or.*fr.62 in Jer.*(p.228. 28) cit. s. δέκα; τὸν νόμον θεοῦ...παρασχόμενον αὐτοῖς τέλειον ἀριθμοῦ δ. *Const.App.*6.3.2.

***δεκάνευρος**, *ten-stringed*, Or.*sel.in Ps.*32:2(M.12.1304C).

***δεκανομέω**, *have ten* nummi, Thdr.Stud.*epp.*2.180(M.99.1557D).

δεκανός (δικανός), ὁ, **1.** *court usher*, Chrys.*hom.13.5 in Heb.*(12. 137C); CQuerc.(M.103.108A); μεταπέμπεται ἡμᾶς ὁ κουβικουλάριος ...διὰ δύο δεκανῶν ἀπελθεῖν εἰς τὸ παλάτιον Marc.Diac.*v.Porph.*39; *ib.* 40; Thal.CP *libell.*3(p.8.28; δικανῶν M.91.1476A); **2.** church worker who buried the dead, Just.*nov.*43 proem.et 1(pp.270.3,271.8); *ib.* 59.2(p.319.5,15); Hypat.*fr.*(p.126.15, see note p.116) = *IGC* As.Min. 108 [c. 538]; Θεοδόρο δεκανοῦ *MAMA* 3.397; **3.** astrol.; plur., *decans*, thirty-six divinities each of whom presided over ten degrees of the zodiac, Jo.D.*f.o.*2.7(M.94.897C).

***δεκάνουμον**, τό, *ten* nummi, exeg. Mt.10:29 ἀσσάριον δ. εἶναι. δηλοῦται δὲ διὰ τοῦ δέκα, τοῦ ἰῶτα γράμματος· ἀρχὴ δέ ἐστι τοῦτο τοῦ ὀνόματος...'Ιησοῦ Χριστοῦ Max.*qu.dub.*6(M.90.789B).

δεκαπέντε, *fifteen*, Pall.*h.Laus.*32(p.94.7; M.34.1100D); *Didasc. Jac.*5.3(p.73.12).

δεκαπλασιάζω, *multiply by ten*, Hipp.*haer.*4.43(p.65.21; M.16. 3106C) cit. s. ἑκατοντάς; Or.*comm.in Mt.*14.9(p.296.15; M.13.1205A); Meth.*symp.*8.11(p.94.11; M.18.156A).

***δεκαπλασιασμός**, ὁ, *multiplying by ten*, Gr.Nyss. *hom.15 in Cant.*(M.44.1113B); Max.*ambig.*(M.91.1404B).

δεκάπληγος, ἡ, *ten plagues* of Egypt, Hipp.*haer.*8.14(p.234.10; M.16.3362A); ‡Ath.*synops.*6(M.28.297A); *Const.App.*2.26.2 cit. s. δεκάς; †Bas.*hom.in Ps.*37(1.363D; M.30.85C).

***δεκάπλωσις**, ἡ, *multiplication by ten*, Max.*qu.Thal.*55(M.90. 541D).

***δεκάριθμος**, *ten in number*, *Hymn.*(*AS* 1 p.624).

δεκάς, ἡ, **A.** as subst.; **1.** *decad, group* or *series of ten*; **a.** in Gnost. system (Valentinian); of ten aeons produced by Λόγος and Ζωή, Iren.*haer.*1.1.3(M.7.449B); (Marcosian) formed from the tetrad ἐκ μονάδος καὶ δυάδος φάσκοντες τὰ ὅλα συνεστηκέναι· καὶ ἀπὸ μονάδος ἕως τῶν τεσσάρων ἀριθμοῦντες οὕτω γεννῶσι τὴν δ. μία γὰρ καὶ δύο καὶ τρεῖς καὶ τέσσαρες συντεθεῖσαι ἐπὶ τὸ αὐτὸ τὸν τῶν δέκα αἰώνων ἀπεκύησαν ἀριθμόν *ib.*1.16.1(629A); typified astronomically ἑπτὰ μὲν σωματικὰ κυκλοειδῆ, ἃ καὶ οὐρανοὺς καλοῦσιν· ἔπειτα τὸν περιεκτικὸν αὐτῶν κύκλον, ὃν καὶ ὄγδοον οὐρανὸν ὀνομάζουσι· πρὸς δὲ τούτοις ἥλιόν τε καὶ σελήνην. ταῦτα δέκα ὄντα τὸν ἀριθμὸν εἰκόνας λέγουσιν εἶναι τῆς ἀοράτου δ. τῆς ἀπὸ Λόγου καὶ Ζωῆς προελθούσης *ib.*1.17.1(637A); by objects of natural creation μεθ' ἣν τῆς δ. μνημονεύοντα [sc. τὸν Μωυσῆν] φῶς λέγειν, καὶ ἡμέραν καὶ νύκτα στερέωμά τε καὶ ἑσπέραν, καὶ ὃ καλεῖται πρωΐ, ξηράν τε καὶ θάλασσαν, ἔτι τε βοτάνην, καὶ...ξύλον· οὕτω δὲ διὰ τῶν δέκα ὀνομάτων τοὺς δέκα αἰῶνας μεμηνυκέναι *ib.*1.18.1(644A); by various passages in scripture τὴν δ. σημαίνεσθαι διὰ τῶν δέκα ἐθνῶν, ὧν ἐπηγγείλατο ὁ θεὸς τῷ Ἀβραὰμ εἰς κατάσχεσιν δοῦναι, λέγουσι...ἔτι τε Ῥοβοὰμ ὁ τὰ δέκα σκῆπτρα λαμβάνων, καὶ τῆς σκηνῆς αἱ δέκα αὐλαῖαι...καὶ οἱ δέκα υἱοὶ 'Ιακὼβ...καὶ οἱ δέκα ἀπόστολοι οἷς φανεροῦται μετὰ τὴν ἔγερσιν ὁ κύριος *ib.*1.18.3(648A); refutation, cf. *quid quia ex Logo et Zoe decem emissi sunt Aeones et non plures aut minus...universum quoque pleroma, quid utique tripartitum est in octonationem et decadem et duodecadem, et non alterum quendam praeter hos numerum? ib.*2.15.1(758A); **b.** in other contexts ὁ δέκατος ἀριθμὸς τετήρηται ὡς ἅγιος, οὐκ ὀλίγων μυστηρίων ἐν τῇ δ. ἀναγραφομένων Or.*Jo.*2.36(29; p.95.16; M.14.180C); ἄκουε, ἱερὰ καθολικὴ ἐκκλησία, ἡ τὴν δεκάπληγον ἐκπεφευγυῖα...καὶ τὴν δ. ἐγνωκυῖα καὶ ἐπὶ τὸ ἰῶτα, ὅπερ ἐστὶν ἀρχὴ ὀνόματος 'Ιησοῦ, πεπιστευκυῖα *Const.App.*2.26.2; **2.** the number *ten* as a sacred number, Clem.*str.*6.16(p.499.13; M. 9.357C); as a perfect number, *ib.*6.11(p.473.30; 305A); Anat.Laod. *decad.*(p.39); cf. δέκα; in man ἡ τὸν ἄνθρωπον συνέχουσα δ. ... εἴη δ' ἂν σῶμά τε καὶ ψυχὴ αἵ τε πέντε αἰσθήσεις καὶ τὸ φωνητικὸν καὶ σπερματικὸν καὶ τὸ διανοητικὸν ἢ πνευματικόν Clem.*str.*2.11(p.139.25; M. 8.985B); cf.*ib.*6.16(p.500.1; M.9.360A); in various passages in scriptures, cf. *at...Istraheliticus populus honorat decadem perfectionis numerum; decem enim verba legis accepit; sed et in novo testamento similiter venerabilis est decas, sicut et fructus spiritus denis exponitur germinare virtutibus, et servus fidelis de negationis suae lucris decem mnas offert Domino, et decem civitatium accepit potestatem*, Or.*hom. 16.6 in Gen.*(p.143.15,18; M.12.252A); symbolized by ι', first letter of 'Ιησοῦς: τὸ δεκάχορδον ψαλτήριον (Ps.32:2) τὸν λόγον τὸν 'Ιησοῦν μηνύει, τῷ στοιχείῳ τῆς δεκάδος φανερούμενον Clem.*paed.*2.4(p.183. 33; M.8.444C).

B. as adj.; *tenfold*, †Apoll.*met.Ps.*32:2(M.33.1353B); *ib.*143:9 (1529A).

δεκατηλόγος, ὁ, *tithe-exactor*, Bas.*hom.in Ps.*14(1.113C; M.29. 280B).

***δεκατήμερος**, *every ten days*, Thdr.Stud.*or.*11.15(M.99.917C).

***δεκατία**, ἡ, *tithing*, Dor.*doct.*15.1(M.88.1788D).

***δεκατοπεντάς**, ἡ, *the fifteenth day*, Jo.Thess.*dorm.BMV* A suppl.(p.438.5).

δέκατος, *tenth*; **1.** neut. [sc. μέρος]: προστιθεμένου τοῦ σαββάτου μεγάλου καὶ τοῦ ἡμίσεως τῆς...φωτοποιοῦ νυκτὸς τριάκοντα ἕξ... ἡμέραι εἰσίν· ὅπερ ἐστὶ τὸ δ. ... τοῦ ἐνιαυτοῦ Dor.*doct.*15.1(M.88. 1788D); **2.** fem.; **a.** [sc. μερίς] *tenth part* οὐ γὰρ ὥς τινες ὑπενόησαν δ. τῶν τοῦ ἐνιαυτοῦ νηστεύειν νενομοθετήμεθα Jo.D.*jej.*3(M.95.68C); *tithe*; given to God, Clem.*str.*2.11(p.140.9; M.8.988A); to bishops, *Const.App.*2.27.6; to other clergy, *ib.*8.30.2; **b.** [sc. ἡμέρα] *tenth day* ἡ τοῦ πάσχα ἑορτὴ ἀπὸ δ. ἤρχετο Clem.*str.*2.11(p.140.10; 988A); Or.*fr.62 in Jer.*(p.228.28) cit. s. δέκα.

***δεκάτωσις**, ἡ, *tithing*, Didym.*Trin.*1.15(M.39.321B); Epiph. *haer.*16.1(p.211.2; M.41.249A); *ib.*50.2(p.246.13; 885B).

δεκάφυλος, *consisting of ten tribes*, *Orac.Sib.*2.171(conj. for δωδεκάφυλος).

δεκάχορδος, *ten-stringed*, of an instrument used in psalmody, ref. Ps.32:2 εἶχον δὲ ἓξ ψαλμοὺς καὶ δ. κιθάραν *T.Job* 14(p.111.22); δ. δὲ τὸ ψαλτήριον λέγεται...τὸ σῶμα, ὡς πέντε αἰσθήσεις ἔχον, καὶ πέντε ἐνεργείας ψυχῆς Or.*sel.in Ps.*32:2(M.12.1304C); *psalterium autem Hebraei decachordon usi sunt propter numerum Decalogi legis*, Isid.H.*etym.*3.22.7; as symbolizing name of Jesus (ι' = 10), Clem.*paed.*2.4(p.183.33; M.8.444C); neut. as subst. ἐν τῷ παναρμονίῳ δ. πρὸς τὸν θεὸν ἐκελάδει Didym.*Trin.*2.16(M.39.721B).

***δεκαχῶς**, *ten times*, Max.*ambig.*(M.91.1293B).

***δεκάωρος**, *of ten hours*, Mac.Mgn.*apocr.*4.11(p.173.7).

***Δεκέμβριος**, (Lat. *Decembrius*) (*of*) *December*, *A.*(*Pass.*)*Andr.* 15(p.37.8); δ. μηνός *Chron.Pasch.*p.11(M.92.89A) cit. s. γενέθλιος; Thphn.*chron.*p.167(M.108.445C).

***δεκέμπριμος**, ὁ, (cf. Lat. *decemprimi*) *corporal*, Nil.*epp.*2.299 tit. (M.79.348D).

***δεκουρίων**, ὁ, (Lat. *decurio*) *decurion*, Ath.*apol.sec.*56(p.136.10; M.25.349C); *IGC Aeg.*584.6.

***δέκρετον**, τό, (Lat. *decretum*) *decree*, *Cod.Afr.*56.

***δεκτήριον**, τό, *receptacle*, Gel.Cyz.*h.e.*3.19.19(M.85.1349B).

δεκτικός, **1.** *capable of receiving*; in gen., *capable* of γεννητοῦ δὲ παντὸς ἥδε ἡ φύσις, κακίας καὶ ἀρετῆς δ. εἶναι Just.*2apol.*7.6(M.6. 456C); ἀφθαρσίας ἡμῶν ὑπάρχον τὸ σῶμα δ. Meth.*res.*3.5(p.396.11; M.18.320C); denied by heretics μὴ γὰρ εἶναι τὴν ὕλην δ. σωτηρίας Iren.*haer.*1.6.1(M.7.505A); τὴν σάρκα ταύτην μὴ εἶναι ταύτην ἀθανασίας δ. Meth.*res.*1.40(p.284.11; M.41.1108C); δι' ἁμαρτίαν...πάθους γέγονε δ. [sc. ὁ ἄνθρωπος] *Hom.Clem.*19.15; of man in relation to divine gifts ὁ νοῦς δ. πως ὑπάρχει τῆς τοῦ θεοῦ δυνάμεως Clem.*str.*3.5 (p.215.24; M.8.1145C); ὁ λόγος σὰρξ ἐγένετο, ἵνα τὸν ἄνθρωπον δ. θεότητος ποιήσῃ Ath.*Ar.*2.59(M.26.273A); δ. γινόμεθα τῆς δημιουργοῦ σοφίας καὶ δι' αὐτῆς γινώσκειν δυνάμεθα τὸν αὐτῆς πατέρα *ib.*2.78 (312C); τὸ πνεῦμα...παρακαλοῦν τοὺς δ. αὐτοῦ ‡Ath.*Ar.*4.29(p.77.22; M.26.513A); ref. Inc. τὴν σάρκα δ. τοῦ λόγου κατασκευάσας Ath.*Ar.* 1.60(137C); Christol. ἴδιον ἑαυτοῦ σῶμα...δ. θανάτου *ib.*1.44(104A); παύσονται δὲ καὶ οἱ εἰπόντες μὴ εἶναι δ. θανάτου τὴν σάρκα, ἀλλὰ τῆς ἀθανάτου φύσεως εἶναι ταύτην id.*ep.Epict.*8(p.13.10; M.26.1064B); heret. αὐτὴν...τὴν θεότητα...ἐρεῖτε δ. εἶναι θανάτου ‡Ath.*Apoll.*1. 11(M.26.1112B); αὐτὸν ἀπαθῆ θεὸν λόγον καὶ πρὸ τῆς σαρκώσεως... ἐρεῖτε δ. εἶναι πάθους *ib.*2.2(1136A); (Arian) κακίας καὶ ἀρετῆς δ. αὐτὸν εἶναι τὸν υἱὸν τοῦ θεοῦ Gel.Cyz.*h.e.*2.26.1(M.85.1308A); Trin. ἀλλήλων φημὶ γεγονέναι δ. καὶ χωρητικούς...ὁ πατὴρ καὶ ὁ υἱὸς κατὰ τοῦ αὐτοῦ κεχωρηκότες τόπου καὶ ἀλλήλων δ. γεγονότες καὶ ἐν ὄντες ‡Gr.Nyss. *Ar.et Sab.*12(M.45.1297B,D); **2.** = δεκτός, *acceptable* ἵνα τοῦ λόγου τὸ κέρδος δ. αὐτοῖς γένηται Thdt.*Rom.*10:2(3.111).

***δεκτικῶς**, *hospitably, kindly*, *Hom.Clem.*4.1.

δεκτός, **1.** *acceptable*; to God, in gen. εἰς τὸ φανῆναι δ. [sc. the people] τῷ κυρίῳ Dion.Al.ap.Eus.*h.e.*7.11.21(M.20.669B); δ. γὰρ τὰ εὐδοκούμενα Thdt.*qu.33 in Dt.*(1.297); of religious observances, *Barn.*15.8 cit. s. σάββατον; νηστεία...δ. τῷ κυρίῳ Herm.*sim.*5.1.3; Clem.*str.*5.11(p.370.26; M.9.101B); τὰς προσευχὰς ἀναπέμπουσα κυρίῳ δ. εἰς ὀσμὴν εὐωδίας Meth.*symp.*5.8(p.63.10; M.18.112C); τὴν ἀντίτυπον τοῦ βασιλείου σώματος Χριστοῦ δ. εὐχαριστίαν προσφέρετε *Const.App.*6.30.2; μετανοοῦντας γενέσθαι δ. Proc.G.*Gen.*3:7(M.87.

196C); of a martyr ὥσπερ...ὁλοκαύτωμα δ. τῷ θεῷ ἡτοιμασμένον *M.Polyc.*14.1; neut. as subst. τὸ τῆς ἀγάπης δ. ἀναφέρειν τὸν κύριον Clem.*paed.*2.8(p.197.23; M.8.473B); **2.** *capable of being admitted*, to Church, of heretics εἰ δὲ μεταγνοῖεν καὶ ἀναθεματίζοιεν ἕκαστον τούτων τῶν κακῶς λεχθέντων δ. αὐτοὺς γίνεσθαι C.Gangr.*can.*proem. (p.80.27); CCP(360)*ep.*ap.Thdt.*h.e.*2.28.6(3.901); Bas.*ep.*199 *can.*18 (3.291B; M.32.717A); δ. ... τῇ ἐκκλησίᾳ *ib.can.*20(292D; M.720D); τοὺς ἑπομένους αὐτῷ [sc. Marcellus] ἀναγκαῖον, ἀναθεματίσαντας ἐκείνην τὴν αἵρεσιν οὕτω δ. γενέσθαι τῇ κοινωνίᾳ *ib.*265.3(410E; M. 989A); to priesthood οὗτοι [i.e. insubordinate clergy] οὐδαμῶς δ. ὀφείλουσιν εἶναι ἐν ἑτέρᾳ ἐκκλησίᾳ CNic.(325)*can.*16; Bas.*ep.*188 *can.* 14(275D; M.681C); **3.** *admissible* τὸ βάπτισμά ἐστιν δ. *ib.can.*1 (270B; M.669A); μήτε δὲ τὸ παρὰ τῶν ἀσεβῶν δ. ὑμῖν ἔστω *Const. App.*6.15.2; of writings τὰ ἐν τοῖς σοῖς γεγραμμένοις βίβλοις, οὐκ ἔστιν δ. *Dial.Tim. et Aquil.*99 r°; πῶς οὖν μὴ δ. ἔσονται οἱ οβ̄ μᾶλλον ἢ Ἀκύλας; *ib.*119 r°; **4.** *capable of receiving* κεῖνος δεκτὸν ἔθηκε καλοῦ Gr.Naz.*carm.*1.2.9.98(M.37.675A).

δεκτρία, ἡ, *receptacle*, Gr.Naz.*carm.*1.2.17.22(M.37.783A).

δελεάζ-ω, 1. *entice*; met., *allure*, in good sense ἡ γραφὴ...πρὸς ὁμοιότητα προθέσεως ~ουσα Bas.Sel.*or.*14.1(M.85.184B); in bad sense ἀπολαύσεις ~ουσας τὴν γεῦσιν Clem.*str.*7.7(p.28.16; M.9. 452B); ~όμενος τῇ...πρωτοκαθεδρίᾳ †Hipp.*Artem.*ap.Eus.*h.e.*5.28.12 (M.20.513C); Meth.*symp.*4.4(p.50.17; M.18.93A); ἡδονῇ βραχείᾳ δελεασθεὶς Bas.*hom.*14.1(2.122E; M.31.445A); **2.** *catch by bait, deceive*, ref. Inc. ὁ θεότητος ἐλπίδι δελεάσας [sc. Devil] τὸν ἄνθρωπον σαρκὸς προσλήμματι εἰκότως δελεασθήσεται Jo.D.*hom.*1.10(M.96.561C); ἐπειδὴ θεότητος ἐλπίδι ὁ ἐχθρὸς ~ει τὸν ἄνθρωπον σαρκὸς προβλήματι ~εται id.*f.o.*3.1(M.94.981C); **3.** pass., *be offered as bait*, Epiph.*haer.* 64.30(p.448.17; M.41.1105A); *ib.*69.43(p.191.13; M.42.269B).

δέλεαρ, τό, *bait*, fig. τούτῳ [sc. wealth] καθάπερ δ. ἀγκιστρεύουσιν τοὺς ἀθλίους Clem.*paed.*3.5(p.254.25; M.8.601A); ref. Inc. κατὰ τοὺς λίχνους τῶν ἰχθύων...τῷ δ. τῆς σαρκὸς συγκατασπασθῇ τὸ ἄγκιστρον τῆς θεότητος Gr.Nyss.*or.catech.*24(p.93.3; M.45.65A); ὥσπερ γάρ τι δ. αὐτῷ τὴν οἰκείαν σάρκα προβαλλόμενος, διὰ τῶν οἰκείων ἥλων, ὡς δι' ἀγκίστρων, ἰχθὺν ἤγρευσεν Olymp.*Job* 40:20(M.93.432D); in a good sense τὸ τῆς δικαιοσύνης δ. Clem.*paed.*2.1(p.163.21; M.8.400A); in bad sense, *allurement* τῆς ἐπιθυμίας τὰ δ. id.*str.*4.6(p.266.12; M.8. 1252B); τοῖς τῆς ἡδονῆς δ. ... κατέσπα ψυχάς Eus.*d.e.*4.9(p.163.12; M.22.272D); Nil.*serm.*8(M.79.1276B).

δελέασμα, τό, *bait*, fig. οὗτος νόμου πολιτείαν προβάλλεται δελεάσματος δίκην Hipp.*haer.*9.14(p.252.18; M.16.3390B); hence *seduction, temptation* μακάριος ὁ μὴ περιτραπεὶς ἐκ τῶν τῆς ἡδονῆς δ. Bas. *hom.in Ps.*1(1.95E; M.29.224B); ὁ προαπατήσας τὸν ἄνθρωπον τῷ τῆς ἡδονῆς δ. Gr.Nyss.*or.catech.*26(p.98.13; M.45.68D); ἡ τῶν τοῦ πονηροῦ δ. προτίμησις id.*or.dom.*5(p.98.22; M.44.1181B); Nil.*Magn.* 52(M.79.1037B).

δελεασμός, ὁ, *allurement, temptation*, Epiph.*haer.*69.73(p.221.22; M.42.321A); Nil.*Magn.*2(M.79.972A).

***δελεαστικός,** *seductive*, Clem.*str.*2.20(p.173.27; M.8.1056A); Cyr. H.*catech.*12.34.

***δελεαστικῶς,** *in seductive manner*, Clem.*str.*2.20(p.178.18; M.8. 1065A).

δελτίον, τό, *small book*, Cyr.*ador.*1(1.1A).

δελτωτός, *in the shape of the letter Δ*; neut. as subst., the constellation *Triangle* τὸ...διὰ τὴν Σικελίαν ἀστροθετούμενον Δ. Tat.*orat.* 9(p.10.19; M.6.825C).

***δελφιναῖος,** *of a dolphin*, *A.Mt.*19(p.240.18).

δέμα, τό, 1. *bundle, bunch*, Pall.*h.Laus.*18(p.49.18; M.34.1052B); *ib.*2(p.17.8; 1011B); Soz.*h.e.*6.29.5(M.67.1373C); **2.** *something that binds, charm* περὶ δ. καὶ λύματος †Jo.Jej.*serm.*(M.88.1924A).

δεμάτιον, τό, *small bundle*, *Apophth.Patr.*(M.65.349A).

***δενδροκόλαψ, ὁ,** *wood-cutter*, Melet.*nat.hom.*27(M.64.1253A, v.l. δενδροκόλαφος).

***δενδροκοπία, ἡ,** *cutting down of trees*, plur., Thdr.Al.*libell.* (p.16.18; H.2.324C); Isch.*libell.*(p.17.21; H.2.325C).

δένδρον, τό, *tree*, fig. ταῦτα...τὰ δ. τὰ βλαστῶντα οἱ δίκαιοι εἰσιν οἱ μέλλοντες κατοικεῖν εἰς τὸν αἰῶνα τὸν ἐρχόμενον Herm.*sim.*4.1; τοὺς ἀγνίνους...κλάδους...τὸ δ. τῆς ἁγνείας Meth.*symp.*9.4(p.119.6; M.18. 188A); as figure of Church, Clem.*fr.*54(p.226.4; M.9.744B); of trees in paradise ἀποστείλῃ [sc. ὁ θεός] τὸν ἄγγελον αὐτοῦ εἰς τὸν παράδεισον καὶ δώσῃ μοι ἐκ τοῦ δ. ἐν ᾧ ῥέει τὸ ἔλαιον ἐξ αὐτοῦ *Apoc.Mos.*9(p.5); τὸ θυμίαμα τῶν δ. τῶν ζώντων *Apoc.Bar.rel.*9.3; τὸ δ. τῆς ζωῆς... ποιήσει πάντα τὰ δ. τὰ ἄκαρπα ποιῆσαι καρπόν *ib.*9.14; δ. παμμεγέθη ὡραῖον, ἐν ᾧ ἐπανεπαύετο τὸ πνεῦμα τὸ ἅγιον, καὶ ἐκ τῆς ῥίζης αὐτοῦ ἐξήρχετο πᾶν εὐωδέστατον ὕδωρ, μεριζόμενον εἰς τέσσαρα ὀρύγματα *Apoc.Paul.*45(p.64); of Cross as δ. ἀειθαλές, ‡Chrys.*serm.pasch.*37.

δενδροτομέω, *cut down trees*, Clem.*str.*2.18(p.164.16; M.8.1037A).

δενδροτομία, ἡ, *laying waste*, Synes.*calv.*1(p.190.14; M.66.1168A).

δενδροφυής, *growing as trees*, Hipp.*haer.*5.7(p.79.16; M.16.3127B).

δενδρ-όω, pass., *become like a tree* in shape φλὸξ...~ωθεῖσα δὲ εἰς ὕψος εἴρψεν Pall.*v.Chrys.*10(p.62.10; M.47.35).

δέννω, (= δέω), *bind* δέννω σε⟨,⟩ Σκόρπιε Ἀρτεμίσιε *Pap.Chr.*3 R. 2(p.422).

***δεξιολαβέω,** *receive kindly*, pass., ‡Jo.D.*ep.Thphl.*11(M.95. 360A).

δεξιός, A. adj.; **1.** *right*, in gen. διὰ τοῦτο ἐκείνων [sc. martyrs] ἐστὶν τὰ δ. μέρη τοῦ ἁγιάσματος Herm.*vis.*3.2.1; τῆς γὰρ ἀριστερᾶς χειρὸς κατεχούσης τὸ χρῆμα, ἤτοι τὸ βαλάντιον, ἡ δ. χεὶρ σπείρει τὸν καλὸν σπόρον εἰς τὴν χώραν τῆς καρδίας τῶν πενήτων †Ath.*fr.Mt.*6:3 (M.27.1372B); of hand of God θεὸς δὲ αὐτὸς...ἄνωθεν αὐτῷ δ. χεῖρα προτείνων Eus.*l.C.*10(p.223.15; M.20.1373C); οὐ βούλεται δὲ ὁ μονογενὴς εἰδέναι τοὺς σαρκικοὺς λογισμοὺς τί ποιεῖ ἡ δ. χεὶρ τοῦ ἁγίου πνεύματος, ἵνα μή ποτε τῇ ἀγαθῇ προθέσει καὶ τῇ πλουσίᾳ προαιρέσει προσεμποδίζωσι †Ath.*fr.Mt.*6:3(1372B); neut. as subst. ἐὰν μὴ ποιήσητε...τὰ ἀριστερὰ εἰς τὰ δ. οὐ μὴ εἰσέλθητε εἰς τὴν βασιλείαν *Agraph.*73[a](p.279); cf.*A.Petr.c.Sim.*38(p.94.10); **2.** neut. as subst., *right hand* of God τὸ γὰρ δ. οὐ τὴν κάτω χώραν δηλοῖ...ἀλλὰ τὴν πρὸς τὸ ἴσον σχέσιν Bas.*Spir.*15(3.11D; M.32.89C); **3.** *on the right hand*, Gnost. τὸν σωτῆρα γεν⟨ν⟩ητὸν καὶ παθητὸν διὰ τοὺς ἀριστ⟨ερ⟩ούς... καὶ κατὰ τὸ πνευματικὸν ἐξ ἁγίου πνεύματος καὶ παρθένου, ὡς οἱ δ. ἄγγελοι γινώσκουσιν Clem.*exc.Thdot.*23(p.114.26; M.9.672A); οἱ δ. ... οὐκ εἰσιν ἱκανοὶ παρακολουθοῦντες σώζειν καὶ φυλάσσειν ἡμᾶς· οὐ γάρ εἰσι τέλεον προνοητικοί, ὥσπερ ὁ ἀγαθὸς ποιμὴν *ib.*73(p.130.8; 692D); ref. just men δ. τόποι στηκέτωσαν, ἀριστεροὶ μὴ μενέτωσαν *A.Jo.*114 (p.214.7); but usu. in phrase ἐκ δεξιῶν, in gen. οἱ πρεσβύτεροι ἐκ δ. αὐτοῦ [sc. ἐπισκόπου] *Lit.*ap.*Const.App.*8.12.3; ὃν ἐθεάσατο Στέφανος ...ἑστῶτα ἐκ δ. τῆς δυνάμεως *Const.App.*6.30.10; Marc.Er.*opusc.* 3.11(M.65.981B); ref. souls of just οἱ τοιοῦτοι ἐκ δ. ἵστανται τοῦ ἁγιάσματος Clem.*str.*4.6(p.261.12; M.8.1241A); Or.*sel.in Ps.*44:10 (M.12.1432A); ref. place of Son in relation to Father θρόνον ἐκ δ. αὐτοῦ Polyc.*ep.*2.1; λόγος θεός...ὁ ἐκ δ. τοῦ πατρός Clem.*paed.*1.2 (p.91.24; M.8.252C); ἐκ δ. γοῦν καθήμενος, ἀριστερὸν οὐ ποιεῖ τὸν πατέρα· ἀλλ' ὅπερ ἐστὶ δ. καὶ τίμιον ἐν τῷ πατρί, τοῦτο καὶ ὁ υἱὸς ἔχει...διὰ τοῦτο γὰρ καὶ καθήμενος ἐκ δ. ὁ υἱὸς ὁρᾷ τὸν πατέρα καὶ αὐτὸς ἐκ δ. ... ὁ υἱὸς ἐν τῷ πατρὶ καὶ ὁ πατὴρ ἐν τῷ υἱῷ. δ. γὰρ ὄντος τοῦ πατρὸς ἐν τῷ δ. ἐστιν ὁ υἱός· καὶ καθημένου τοῦ υἱοῦ ἐκ δ., ὁ πατήρ ἐστιν ἐν τῷ υἱῷ Ath.*Ar.*1.61(M.26.140B); οὔτε κάθηται ἐκ δ. ἀφ' ἑαυτοῦ ἀλλ' ἀκούει λέγοντος τοῦ πατρός [Ps.109:1] *Const.App.* 7.25.2; in creeds: *Symb.Ant.*(341)3(p.250.14; M.26.724D); *Symb. Ant.*(345)1(p.251.29; M.26.728B); *Symb.Sirm.*1 *anath.*18; *Symb. Sirm.*3(p.236.4; M.26.693B); *Symb.Nic.*(359)ap.Thdt.*h.e.*2.21.6(3. 880); *Symb.*ap.Epiph.*anc.*118(p.147.10; M.43.232D); *Symb.App.* (p.32); **4.** *right hand* man, Eus.*v.C.*4.44(p.136.1; M.20.1193C); **5.** *courteous, kindly*, neut. as subst. διὰ τὸ δ. τῆς προαιρέσεως μὴ δυνάμενον [sc. τὸν θεόν] παρορᾶν τὸν δεδεημένον τῶνδέ τινων Or.*or.* 11.4(p.323.29; M.11.453A); **6.** ψυχὴν πίστεως καὶ θεοῦ δ. ὁπόταν ἴσον τὸ τῆς ἐπαγγελίας καταστήσῃ *A.Jo.*69(p.184.16, conjj. ἀξίαν, δεκτικήν).

B. as fem. subst.; **1.** *right hand*, imposed by bishop in baptismal rite διὰ τοῦ ἐπισκόπου σου ὁ θεὸς υἱοποιεῖταί σε, ἄνθρωπε· γνώριζε, υἱέ, τὴν δ., τὴν μητέρα σου καὶ στέργε, καὶ τὸν μετὰ θεὸν γενόμενόν σου πατέρα σέβου *Const.App.*2.33.1; in rite of consecration ὁ δὲ ἱερεὺς... ἐπὶ κεφαλῆς ἔχει τὴν τοῦ τελοῦντος αὐτὸν ἱεράρχου δ. Dion.Ar.*e.h.* 5.2.2(M.3.509B); of God, symbol of honour, glory, and power δ. δὲ τοῦ θεοῦ ὅταν ἀκούσῃς, τὴν δόξαν καὶ τὴν τιμὴν τοῦ θεοῦ εἶναι νόει ‡Ath.*qu.script.*45(M.28.728C); δ. ... τὴν θείαν οὕτως ὀνομάζων ἐνέργειαν Thdt.*Ps.*19:7(1.727); δ. δὲ τὴν ἐπὶ τοῖς αἰτίοις αὐτοῦ βοήθειαν Jo.D.*f.o.*1.11(M.94.844A); δ. δὲ τοῦ πατρὸς λέγομεν τὴν δόξαν καὶ τὴν τιμὴν τῆς θεότητος *ib.*4.2(1104B); giving life, help, protection διὰ τῆς δ. ζωοποιῆσαι δύναται *Hom.Clem.*7.3; Eus.*h.e.*6.3.4(M.20. 528B); θεός...δ. αὐτοῖς ἐπήκοον παρέχων id.*m.P.*13(p.949.7; M.20. 1517A); ποίμανον αὐτοὺς ὑπὸ τὴν δ. σου *Const.App.*8.41.8; as heavenly place of Christ καθίζοντα αὐτὸν ἐν δ. αὐτοῦ [sc. θεοῦ] Just.*dial.*32.3 (M.6.544B); ἐν δ. ὢν αὐτοῦ [sc. θεοῦ] Or.*Jo.*13.8(p.233.5; M.14. 412A); Eus.*e.th.*3.14(p.171.14; M.24.1028A); ἐκάθισεν ἐν τῇ δ. τοῦ πατρός. δ. γὰρ τοῦ πατρὸς λέγω, οὐ τοπικήν, ἢ περιγραπτήν· ἀλλὰ λέγω δ. τοῦ θεοῦ εἶναι, τὴν ἄναρχον, καὶ προαιώνιον δόξαν, τὴν ἔχων ὁ υἱὸς πρὸ τῆς ἀνθρωπήσεως καὶ μετὰ τὴν ἐνανθρώπησιν ταύτην ἔσχηκε *Euchol.*(p.254); in the creeds, *Symb.Ant.*(341)1(p.249.5; M.26.721A); *ib.*2(p.249.25; 724A); *ib.*4(p.251.8; 752C); *Symb.Sirm.*1 (p.254.27; M.26.736B); cf.*Symb.Sard.Orient.*(pp.190,191); Marcell. *ep.*(p.258.10; M.42.385D); *Symb.App.*(pp.24,30,31,34); *Symb.*ap.

Epiph.*anc*.119(p.148.24; M.43.236A); ‡Ath.*interpr*.(p.66.20; M.26.1232B); *Symb*.ap.*Const.App*.7.41.6; *Symb.Nic.-CP*(p.80.11, v.l. ἐκ δεξίων H.2.288B); name for the Son ἡ δ. τοῦ φωτὸς ἡ καταστρέφουσα τὸν πονηρὸν ἐν τῇ ἰδίᾳ φύσει *A.Thom*.A 48(p.164.12); ὁ λόγος τοῦ θεοῦ καὶ σοφία ὁμοίως χρηματίζει...καὶ δ. ‡Ath.*Ar*.4.33(p.82.4; M.26.517C); ἡ δ. τοῦ θεοῦ ἡ ποιητικὴ πάντων τῶν ὄντων, ἥτις ἐστὶν ὁ κύριος ...αὕτη τὸν ἐνωθέντα πρὸς αὐτὴν ἄνθρωπον εἰς τὸ ἴδιον ὕψος ἀνήγαγε διὰ τῆς ἀνακράσεως Gr.Nyss.*Eun*.5(2 p.117.4; M.45.697B); δ. τοῦ πατρὸς τὴν τοῦ θεοῦ λέγομεν δύναμιν τὴν ποιητικὴν τοῦ παντός, ἥτις ἐστὶν ὁ κύριος *ib*.6(p.135.25; 720C); δ. γὰρ τοῦ θεοῦ καὶ πατρὸς ὁ υἱός Cyr.*glaph.Gen*.3(1.76A); Manich. ἡ δ. τοῦ φωτός Hegem.*Arch*.5(p.6.1; M.10.1433B); *ib*.7(p.10.14; 1437B); fig., of the good man σώζει δὲ [sc. ὁ θεός] καὶ εὐεργετεῖ διὰ τῆς δ., τοῦτ' ἔστι διὰ τοῦ...ἀγαθοῦ *Hom.Clem*.20.3; **2.** *right hand, pledge*, plur. θεῷ δ. ἔδωκα Pall.*h.Laus*.21(p.65.16; M.34.1074B); sing. συνείδησις πίστεως...τῆς μελλούσης τρυφῆς δ. ἀπολαμβάνει *Const.App*.7.33.3.

δεξιότης, ἡ, *uprightness, righteousness*, Gr.Thaum.*pan.Or*.6(p.16.17; M.10.1069D); Gr.Nyss.*Eun*.1(1 p.54.12; M.45.284A).

δεξι-όω, 1. act., *alleviate*, Gr.Ant.*exerc*.ap.Evagr.*h.e*.6.12(p.229.17; M.88.1884B); **2.** med.; **a.** *entertain* δέκα ἄρτοις...ἑκατὸν ἐδεξιώσαντο ‡Nil.*perist*.11.20(M.79.932A); **b.** *welcome, receive as a friend*, Ath.*ep.Aeg.Lib*.22(M.25.589A); ‡Nil.*perist*.12.12(965A); **c.** *receive kindly, treat kindly*, Eus.*d.e*.8 proem.(p.351.1; M.22.572A); Euthal. Diac.*epp.cath*.(M.85.688C); **d.** *honour*, Gr.Nyss.*hom.4 in Cant*.(M.44.845D); **e.** *honour, endow* τοῖς ἐντεῦθεν χρηστοῖς πολλάκις ∼οῦται τὸ θεῖον τοὺς εὐσεβεῖς Gr.Naz.*or*.14.19(M.35.881B); **f.** *greet*; *embrace* φιλήματι τὸν τράχηλον δεξιώσασθαι Gr.Nyss.*or.dom*.2(p.38.30; M.44.1144D); **g.** *embrace, accept* μαθόντες...∼οῦσθαι τὰ βλάπτοντα Nil.*Magn*.39(M.79.1016D); **3.** med., in pass. sense, *be received* σατανᾶς...πολλοὺς σπεύδει λυπῆσαι τοῦ ∼ώσασθαι Ephr.3.80A; **4.** pass., *be received*; of repentant sinners, Eus.*h.e*.4.23.6(M.20.385B).

δεξίωσις, ἡ, 1. *graciousness, kind treatment*; plur., Eus.*h.e*.8.1.2(M.20.740C); sing., Gr.Nyss.*bapt.diff*.(M.46.429A); Chrys.*hom.43.2 in Gen*.(4.437E); **2.** *hospitality*, Eus.*v.C*.4.44(p.136.5; M.20.1193C); Gr.Naz.*or*.8.12(M.35.801C); Bas.Sel.*v.Thecl*.1(M.85.481D); **3.** *protection, kindly assistance*; plur., Eus.*l.C*.18(p.259.13; M.20.1440A); id.*h.e*.4.15.47(M.20.361A); Chrys.*hom.1.5 in Phil*.(11.201B); **4.** *relief, comfort*, ‡Bas.*struct.hom*.2.5(1.340E; M.30.48A); **5.** *gift, offering*, Eus.Al.*serm*.8(M.86.357D); *bribe*, ‡Gr.Naz.*Chr.pat*.2271(M.38.315A).

***δεξιώτης, ὁ,** *guest-master*, Pall.*h.Laus*.52(p.145 n.(one MS); M.34.1217A).

δέος, τό (A), 1. *fear*; godly, Just.*dial*.82.4(M.6.672A); Eus.*e.th*.1.10(p.69.5; M.24.841D); **2.** *ground for* godly *fear* δ. γάρ τι ἔχουσιν [sc. οἱ τοῦ σωτῆρος λόγοι] ἐν ἑαυτοῖς Just.*dial*.8.2(M.6.492D).

§δέος, τό (B), *lack* πενία...καὶ τὸ δ. τῶν ἀναγκαίων Chrys.*hom.2.4 in Eph*.(11.14C).

***δεπορτατίων, ἡ,** (Lat. *deportatio*) *exile*, Ath.Scholast.*coll*.10.2(p.114); Phot.*nomoc*.9.26(M.104.769D).

***δεπόσιτον, τό,** (Lat. *depositum*) *deposit*, Ign.*Polyc*.6.2 cit. s. ἄκκεπτα.

***δερβᾶς,** Persian word, = *praetorium* τὴν τάξιν...τοῖς προπυλαίοις τοῦ δ. ἐφιζάνοντες, ὃ δὴ φίλον ἀρχεῖον παρ' Ἕλλησιν ὀνομάζεσθαι Sophr.H.*v.Anast*.(M.92.1697B).

δέρμα, τό, 1. *skin, hide*, Gr.Nyss.*or.catech*.8(p.46.6; M.45.36C); used as clothing by prophets (Heb.11:37) διὰ τῆς...τῶν κτηνογενῶν δ. ἐνδύσεως, καὶ ἡ ἔνσαρκος οἰκονομία τοῦ Χριστοῦ προδιετυποῦτο Anast.S.*hex*.12(M.89.1053A); **2.** *bark* of a tree, Thdt.*qu.39 in Gen*.(1.53); **3.** *parchment*, Pall.*v.Chrys*.20(p.125.17; M.47.70); **4.** *leather* ἐσκεπασμένοις...τοῖς ποσὶν ὑπὸ παχέων τινῶν δ. Gr.Thaum.*pan.Or*.2(p.5.20; M.10.1056C).

***δερμακατούδιον, τό,** ? *garment of cat's fur*, Barth.Edess.*Agar*.(M.104.1405B).

δερμάτινος, *of skin*, ref. Gen.3:21, v. χιτών.

δερματοφόρος, *wearing skins*, Anast.S.*hex*.12(M.89.1053B).

δερματόω, *clothe with skin*, Geo.Pis.*hex*.1366(M.92.1539A).

***δερμοκουκούλιον (-κουλον), τό,** *leather cowl*, Nil.*epp*.2.178(M.79.292C); δερμοκούκουλον Niceph.Ur.*v.Sym*.117(M.86.3096B).

δερμότυλον, τό, *leather cushion*, Pall.*h.Laus*.55(p.149.1; M.34.1244B).

***δεσέρτωρ, ὁ,** v. *δησέρτωρ.

δέσις, ἡ, *binding together, bond* λῦσαι τὴν δ. τῆς συμβιώσεως Clem.*paed*.2.7(p.190.17; M.8.457B); of body and soul at Creation ἡ δὲ μὲν ἀρχεγόνοιο βροτοῦ δ. Gr.Naz.*carm*.1.1.8.78(M.37.452A); at resurrection ἀνάστασις, ἡ δ. τοῦ συνθέτου *ib*.1.2.34.251(963A).

***δέσμευσις, ἡ,** *imprisonment*, Sophr.H.*v.Anast*.(M.92.1720A).

δεσμεύω, δεσμέω, *bind*, ref. powers of Church in regard to sin οὐ γὰρ ἄνθρωπός ἐστιν ὁ δεσμῶν, ἀλλ' ὁ Χριστὸς ὁ τὴν ἐξουσίαν ταύτην ἡμῖν δεδωκώς Chrys.*hom.4.6 in Heb*.(12.49C); αὐτῷ μεταδίδωμι τὴν ἐξουσίαν τοῦ δεσμεύειν καὶ λύειν *Clem.ep*.2(M.2.36B); ἐν χειρὶ γὰρ τῆς ἱερωσύνης ἐλύετο καὶ ἐδεσμεύετο τὰ ἁμαρτήματα Epiph.*anc*.97(p.118.11; M.43.193A); this power is from God σὺ δὸς ἐξουσίαν...λύειν ἃ δεῖ λύειν, καὶ δεσμεῖν ἃ δεῖ δεσμεῖν *Hom.Clem*.3.72; ref. Mt.7:1 εἰ γὰρ μὴ μέλλουσι κρίνειν ἁπάντων ἔσονται ἄκυροι καὶ μάτην τοῦ δεσμεῖν καὶ τοῦ λύειν ἐξουσίαν εἰλήφασι Chrys.*hom.24.1 in Mt*.(7.284C); ref. imposed penances ὅσα ἂν ἔτη ἔλαβον παρὰ τοῦ δεσμεύσαντος αὐτούς †Jo.Jej.*poenit*.(M.88.1905C); δεσμήσαντος †Jo.Jej.*serm*.(M.88.1929D); ref. observances πότε γὰρ τὸ σάββατον ἐπὶ ἀγαθῇ προφάσει οὐ λέλυται; πότε δὲ οὐκ ἐδεσμεύθη ἀπὸ πονηρίας οὐ μόνον τὸ σάββατον, ἀλλὰ πᾶσα ἡμέρα; Epiph.*haer*.66.82(p.124.3; M.42.157B); of the soul δεσμεῖται φόβῳ *Hom.Clem*.17.2; c. εἰς *bind to*, ‡Petr.I Al.*phys*.3(p.34).

δεσμίδι(ο)ν, τό, dim. of δεσμίς, *small bundle*, *A.Petr.et Andr*.6(p.120.19,23).

***δεσμολύτης (δεσμόλυτος), ὁ,** *one who releases from bonds, liberator*, ‡Gr.Naz.*Chr.pat*.447(M.38.172A); δεσμόλυτος *ib*.2529(332A).

δεσμός, ὁ, 1. *bond*; of physical bonds as ornament of martyrs, Ign.*Eph*.11.2; id.*Smyrn*.11.1; Polyc.*ep*.1.1; met., in good sense, of God's love etc. τὸν δ. τῆς ἀγάπης τοῦ θεοῦ τίς δύναται ἐξηγήσασθαι; *1Clem*.49.2; μεμαθηκὼς τὰ θεῖα δ. Thdt.*qu.50 in 1Reg*.(1.386); of human love ἡ τῆς ἀναλύσεως τῶν ἱερῶν τῶν φιλίων τούτων δ. ἐξουσία Gr.Thaum.*pan.Or*.6(p.18.3; M.10.1072D); of chastity, Meth.*symp*.4.6(p.52.3; M.18.96B); in bad sense; in gen., *2Clem*.20.4; τοῦ δ. καταμεγαλοφρονοῦντες τοῦ σαρκικοῦ Clem.*str*.7.7(p.30.24; M.9.456B); of Mosaic Law ἔλυσεν γὰρ ἡμᾶς ὁ κύριος ἐκ τῶν δ. *Const.App*.6.12.11; ἦλθεν...λύων...τὰ πεπεδημένα δεσμοῖς τῆς κατάρας Epiph.*haer*.29.8(p.331.11; M.41.404B); heret., of relationship between body and soul δ. αὐτῇ τὸ σῶμα δεδόσθαι τιμωρόν Meth.*res*.1.29(p.260.12; M.41.1137C); δ. ... τὸ σῶμα μεμηχανῆσθαι κατὰ τῆς ψυχῆς *ib*.1.30(p.261.19; 1140B); ἔφης δ. εἶναι τῆς ψυχῆς τὸ σῶμα Adam.*dial*.3.1(p.116.35; M.11.1793B); ref. Inc. ἐλύετο...πᾶς δ. ... θεοῦ ἀνθρωπίνως φανερουμένου Ign.*Eph*.19.3; ref. Christ at Ascension λύσας πάλιν τὸν δ. τοῦ σώματος Hipp.*haer*.8.38(p.224.20; M.16.3346C); **2.** *restriction*; met., in gen., Thdt.*ep*.113(4.1192); id.*Jon*.1(2.1464); CCP(381)*ep*.ap. Thdt.*h.e*.5.9.3(3.1028); **3.** *censure, discipline*, of God δέχου τὸν δ. ᾧ ὁ θεὸς...γίνεται σύμψηφος Thdt.*h.e*.5.18.4(3.1047); of Church τὰ τῆς ἱερωσύνης αὐτοῖς δεσμὰ περιτέθεικα id.*h.rel*.21(3.1237); id.*h.e*.5.18.8(3.1048); τῆς ἐκκλησιαστικῆς αὐτὸν κοινωνίας ἐκώλυσε, καὶ τὸν δ. ἐπιθεὶς ὑπεχώρησεν *ib*.5.37.1(3.1078); id.*ep*.154(4.1319); this power of Church comes through Christ, Chrys.*hom.4.6 in Heb*.(12.49C,D); **4.** *chain of argument*, Gr.Mag.*dial*.(tr.Zach.)4.6(M.*PL*.77.331A).

***δεσμόω,** *bind together*, *A.Mt*.14(p.234.1); Melet.*nat.hom*.22(M.64.1229D).

δεσμώτης, ὁ, *prisoner*; eccl., *one under censure*, Chrys.*hom.4.6 in Heb*.(12.49D).

***δεσμωτικός,** *of prison*, Eus.*h.e*.8.10.11(M.20.768A).

δεσπόζ-ω, 1. abs., *be lord* or *master*, of man προσετάγη τῷ...∼ειν Meth.*res*.1.35(p.274.1; M.41.1100B); of God ὡς γεωργοὶ γὰρ ἀγαθοὶ παρὰ τοῦ ∼οντος τὴν ἀμοιβὴν ἕξομεν Just.*1apol*.44.13(M.6.396C); of Christ εἰ ὁμοῦ θεὸς καὶ ἄνθρωπος ὁ Χριστός, δηλονότι ὁμοῦ ∼ει καὶ ∼εται Leont.H.*Nest*.1.43(M.86.1504A); cf. 2 fin.; **2.** c. genit., *be lord* or *master of*, of man τὸν ∼ειν...παντὸς τοῦ ὁρωμένου κόσμου λαχόντα Max.*ep*.10(M.91.449B); of BMV πάντων ∼ουσα Ephr.3.526E; of angels δ. τῆς κτίσεως πάσης Herm.*vis*.3.4.1; of God τοῦ πάντων ∼οντος Just.*1apol*.14.3(M.6.348C); Ath.*gent*.29(M.25.57B); ∼οντα τῶν στοιχείων Cyr.*Am*.46(3.300E); τὸ θεῖον...οὐδὲ μόνον Ἰουδαίων ∼ον Thdt.*Ezech*.1:3(2.681); pass., *be a servant, be ruled*, Leont.H.*Nest*.1.43 cit. supra; εἰ...κύριος καὶ Χριστὸς...ἐποιήθη ὑπὸ τοῦ θεοῦ ὁ Ἰησοῦς, πῶς ἔτι ὑπὸ τοῦ θεοῦ ∼εται; *ib*.5.14(M.86.1736C); **3.** *keep charge of*, c. genit. τῶν...χρυσῶν ἐδέσπωσεν [sic] *Mir.Geo*.8(p.94.9).

δέσποινα, ἡ, *mistress*; *queen*; of BMV, Petr.I Al.*fr*.(M.18.517B) cit. s. θεοτόκος; Ἰωάννης...υἱὸς ὢν θέσει τῆς δ. Leont.H.*Nest*.3.9(M.86.1641D); †Gregent.*disp*.(M.86.669B); Jo.Mosch.*prat*.45(M.87.2900B) cit. s. ἐκτύπωμα; *Chron.Pasch*.p.11(M.92.89A); Thphn.*chron*.p.90(M.108.269C); ἐδυνήθη...ὁ θεῖος λόγος...ἐνανθρωπῆσαι ἐν τῇ δ. Jo.V H.*icon*.7(M.96.1356B); ἡ δ. πάντων καὶ θεοτόκος Niceph.Ur.*v.Sym*.145(M.86.3121B); as form of address παρθένε δ. Ephr.3.526C; Mod.*dorm*.10(M.86.3305); Jo.D.*carm.dorm.BMV* 32(p.229; M.96.1364B); Jo.Mon.*hymn.Nic.Myr*.7(M.96.1388C); ‡Gr.Naz.*Chr.pat*.634(M.38.187A).

***δεσποινιακός,** *with authority of empress*, Sym.Styl.J.*ep.Just*.(M.86.3217C).

δεσπόσυνος, *belonging to the Lord*, of relatives of Christ δ. καλούμενοι διὰ τὴν πρὸς τὸ σωτήριον γένος συνάφειαν Afric.*ep.Arist.*5 (p.61.20; M.10.61A).

δεσποτεία, ἡ, **1.** *ownership*; in legal sense, Eus.*v.C.*2.36(p.57.5; M.20.1013B); Gr.Naz.*test.*(M.37.392A); Chrys.*hom.20.6 in Mt.*(7.267D); Thdt.*Ezech.*46:16(2.1037); met., of the things of this life ῥήματι μόνον ἐστὶν ἡ δ. Chrys.*hom.11.2 in 1Tim.*(11.608B); **2.** *lordship*, as title μὴ προσδεχομένης τῆς ἡμερωτάτης ὑμῶν δ. Sym.Styl.J.*ep.Just.*(M.86.3217C); **3.** *mastery, power*, of Trin. μία θεότης, μία δ., μία κυριότης Epiph.*haer.*57.4(p.349.23; M.41.1001B); of God εἰ τοῦ εἶναι καὶ τοῦ μὴ εἶναι ἡμᾶς δεσπόζει θεός, πῶς οὐκ ἔσται ἀπὸ τῆς αὐτῆς αὐτοῦ δ. τὸ γίνεσθαι ἡμᾶς ἀθανάτους; εἰ δὲ τὸ γενέσθαι ἡμᾶς ἀθανάτους, ἔξωθεν τῆς τοῦ θεοῦ δ. καθέστηκε, πῶς οὐκ ἔσται θεὸς τοῦ μὴ εἶναι ἡμᾶς μὴ δεσπόζων; ‡Just.*qu.Gr.*11.43(M.6.1489A); πάνθ' ὑποτετάχθαι τῇ ἐκείνου δ. μόνου Const.*or.s.c.*3(p.156.20; M.20.1240A); Chrys.*hom.45.2 in Mt.*(7.478D); δοῦλον δὲ τῆς τοῦ θεοῦ δ. id.*hom.42.5 in Jo.*(8.253B); οὐ διὰ τὸν φόβον, οὐδὲ διὰ δ. μόνον, ἀλλὰ καὶ δι' αὐτὴν τὴν τῶν πραγμάτων φύσιν εὐχαριστοῦμεν id.*hom.2.2 in Col.*(11.336A); τὸ ἐπικείμενον ἡμῖν τῆς σῆς δ. ὄνομα Thdt.*Dan.*3:33(2.1116); of Christ, Eus.*d.e.*5.6(p.230.4; M.22.380B) cit. s. δευτέρως; ὁ γὰρ βασιλεὺς πάσης τῆς γῆς καὶ τοῦ μέρους πάντως τὴν δ. ἔχει Gr.Nyss.*hom.7 in Cant.*(M.44.909A); *Const.App.*6.23.5; πῶς οὖν οὐκ ἐσχάτης ἀνοίας τῆς οὕτω προσηνοῦς δ. ... ἀμελοῦντας, ἀχαρίστῳ καὶ ἀγνώμονι δουλεύειν τυράννῳ; Chrys.*hom.8.2 in Jo.*(8.51D); ἡ δὲ Μωσέως καὶ Ἡλίου παρουσία τὴν ζώντων καὶ νεκρῶν ἐμαρτύρησεν αὐτῷ δ. [i.e. at Transfiguration] Isid.Pel.*epp.*1.239(M.78.329B); Gel.Cyz.*h.e.*2.21.17 (M.85.1285D); of Devil μὴ γὰρ ἑαυτοὺς ἠλευθερώσατε ὅτι πάλιν ἐπὶ τὴν προτέραν τρέχετε δ. Chrys.*comm.in Gal.*5:1(10.712D).

δεσπότης, ὁ, *lord, master* (usu. = κύριος q.v.); **1.** in gen., as having authority ἄμπελος...οὐκέτι εὔχρηστός ἐστι τῷ δ. ἑαυτῆς...καὶ τοιοῦτοι ἄνθρωποι...γίγνονται ἄχρηστοι τῷ κυρίῳ ἑαυτῶν Herm.*sim.*9.26.4 al.; ὥστε...τὸν δ. ἥκειν ἐπὶ τὸ νίπτειν τοὺς πόδας τοῦ πιστεύοντος δούλου Or.*Jo.*32.12(7; p.444.33; M.14.772B); of a husband καὶ δ. σὲ οἶδα καὶ κύριον τῆς ἐμῆς ζωῆς Pall.*h.Laus.*61(p.155.13; M.34.1228A); fig. ἀγοράζει...ἡμᾶς κύριος τιμίῳ αἵματι, δ. πάλαι τῶν πικρῶν ἀπαλλάσσων ἁμαρτιῶν Clem.*ecl.*20(p.142.10; M.9.708A); δ. ... γεγόνασιν ὑμῶν ἐκεῖνοι [sc. idols] *Hom.Clem.*10.7; δύνασθε δ. γενέσθαι πάλιν *ib.*10.25; **2.** partic., of Devil ὁ τοῦδε τοῦ κόσμου δ. Hipp.*haer.*5.16(p.112.24; M.16.3174B); normal title of emperors; of princes, Thphn.*chron.*p.312(M.108.757B); as form of address to bishops, Alex.Thess.*ep.Ath.*(p.145.7; M.25.368A); Jo.Ant.*ep.Cyr.*2(p.9.19; M.77.173B); of priest (liturg.) εὐλόγησον, δ. cf.*Lit.Chrys.*(p.362.23); **3.** esp. of God; **a.** in gen. ἐν γενεᾷ καὶ γενεᾷ μετανοίας τόπον ἔδωκεν ὁ δ. *1Clem.*7.5; σύ, δ. ἔδωκας...αὐτοῖς...οἷς δός, κύριε... *ib.*61.1; δ., ἐπουράνιε βασιλεῦ *ib.*61.2; *Barn.*1.7 cit. s. γνωρίζω; Herm.*vis.*2.2.5; βλασφήμους εἰς τὸν ἑαυτῶν εὑρίσκεσθαι δ. Iren.*haer.*2.26.1(M.7.803A); ὁ ὤν, δ. κύριε ὁ θεὸς ὁ παντοκράτωρ *Lit.*ap.*Const.App.*8.5.1; σὺ οἶδας, δ., ὅτι... *V.Pach.A* 18(p.142.3); **b.** of Father, *1Clem.*64; *Did.*10.3; τοῦ πατρὸς πάντων καὶ δ. θεοῦ υἱός Just.*1apol.*12.9(M.6.345A); *ib.*61.10(421B); Clem.*prot.*10(p.78.13; M.8.228A) cit. s. ἐξισόω; ὦ τῶν πάντων ἔχων τὸ κῦρος δ. ὦ τῆς μονήρους δυνάμεως πάτερ Const.ap. Gel.Cyz.*h.e.*3.19.26(M.85.1352A); δ., δ. τῶν ἁπάντων, κύριε οὐρανοῦ καὶ γῆς..., ὁ πατὴρ τοῦ κυρίου ἡμῶν Ἰησοῦ Χριστοῦ *Lit.Bas.*(p.322.17); **c.** of Christ, Clem.*str.*4.7(p.267.9; M.8.1253B); διὰ τὴν πρόσταξιν ὡς δ. τοῦ Χριστοῦ Or.*Jo.*28.7(6; p.398.26; M.14.696D); ὁ πάσης κτίσεως δ. ὁ μονογενὴς υἱός Gr.Nyss.*ep.*1(M.46.1004D); οὐ γὰρ κύριος ὁ ἄνθρωπος τῆς διατάξεως τῆς τοῦ σωτῆρος, ἐπείπερ ὁ μὲν δ., ὁ δὲ ὑπήκοος *Const.App.*7.22.6; ἵνα...τῆς παρὰ τοῦ δ. φιλοτιμίας ἀπολαύσωμεν Chrys.*hom.30.1 in Gen.*(4.294B); μήτηρ τοῦ δ. σου γέγονε id.*hom.53.3 in Jo.*(8.314B); Thdt.*1Cor.*2:8(3.176); τὴν τοῦ δ. σταύρωσιν Anast.S.*hod.*12(M.89.196C); id.*synax.*(M.89.841A).

δεσποτικός, *of* or *for a lord* or *master*; **1.** theol.; **a.** *of, for,* or *towards the Lord*, objectively προΐετο [sc. Judas] φόνον δ. Chrys.*hom.81.3 in Mt.*(7.777B); δ. φίλος ἐστίν Antip.Bost.*Jo.Bapt.*7(M.85.1772A); ὁ λῃστὴς...πόθῳ δεσποτικῷ τῶν ἥλων τὸν πόνον οὐ λογιζόμενος Bas.Sel.*or.*17.1(M.85.217A); θείῳ καὶ δ. φόβῳ ‡Proc.G.*Pr.*15:27(M.87.1380A); †Jo.D.*B.J.*19(M.96.1032B) cit. s. ἐκτύπωμα; **b.** *of the Lord, belonging to the Lord*, freq. τὸν δ. τόκον Antip.Bost.*Jo.Bapt.*13(M.85.1776B); πάθει Areth.*Apoc.*60(M.106.748D); θάνατον Chrys.*hom.27.1 in Heb.*(12.245D); κοινωνίαν τοῦ σώματος καὶ αἵματος τοῦ δ. Didym.*Trin.*2.14(M.39.716B); κοινωνήσας τῶν δ. συμβόλων Pall.*v.Chrys.*11(p.68.9; M.47.38); θέλημα Cyr.*Ps.*7:11(M.69.753A); δόγμασι id.*Abac.*10(3.525E); νόμῳ Gennad.*encycl.*(p.79.31; M.85.1617C); οἰκός ἐστι δ. ἡ ἐκκλησία ‡Chrys.*prov.*3(2.763B); **c.** esp. of festivals etc., *dominical* νηστεία Pall.*v.Chrys.*9(p.55.2; M.47.32); ἑορτῆς [i.e. Hypapante] Cyr.*hom.div.*12(5^2.385E); ἡ δ. ἡμέρα τῇ ἀναστάσει τετιμημένη Thdt.*1Cor.*16:2(3.281); ἑορτῶν Andr.Cr.*or.*17 (M.97.1172A); *Const.Stud.*4(M.99.1704D); **2.** secular; **a.** *royal* τῶν δ. παιδίων Pall.*v.Chrys.*17(p.111.11; M.47.61); τὸ δ. βρέφος [i.e. Christ] *Pers.*(p.17.5; M.10.105C); hence **b.** *imperial* τῷ δ. καθίσματι τοῦ Ἱππικοῦ *Chron.Pasch.*p.339(M.92.884C); *Euchol.*(p.5).

δεσποτικῶς, *with the authority of a master*; of Father, ref. Inc. τὸν ἀποστείλαντα οὐ δ. ἀλλὰ πατρικῶς Jo.D.*hom.*1.18(M.96.573B); of Son δ. εἰπεῖν μὴ ῥίπτεσθαι μαργαρίτας Thdt.*Ezech.*proem.(2.671); τῶν ἀνθρώπων τὴν σωτηρίαν, ἣν δ. πραγματεύεται id.*Heb.*8:2(3.594); of H. Ghost δ. τὴν ἐλευθερίαν οἷς ἐθέλει χαρίζεται id.*Trin.*21(M.75.1177B).

***δέτης, ὁ**, *one who binds*, Gr.Naz.*carm.*1.1.8.51(M.37.450A).

δετός, *that may be bound*, Gr.Naz.*carm.*1.1.2.15(M.37.403A).

δευσοποι-έω, *dye*, met. δόγματα ~ήσαντα...καὶ ποιώσαντα...τὴν ψυχήν Or.*Cels.*1.52(p.103.6; M.11.757A); ὡσπερεὶ ~ηθέντες ἀπὸ τῆς κακίας *ib.*3.65(p.259.5; 1005B).

δευσοποιός, 1. *deeply dyed* οἱονεὶ δ. τις βαφὴ γίνεται...περὶ τὴν ψυχήν Or.*comm.in Rom.*4:15(*JTS* 13 p.360); Gr.Thaum.*pan.Or.*13 (p.29.26; M.10.1088C); τοῖς...καθάπερ τινὰ δ. βαφὴν τὴν αἱρετικὴν παραδεδεγμένοις Gr.Nyss.*or.catech.*7(p.38.11; M.45.32A ψευδοποιόν); καθάπερ τις δ. βαφὴ καὶ δυσέκνιπτος ἡ ἀπάτη id.*Eun.*9(2 p.212.11; M.45.809D); met. ὅταν ἁμάρτῃ δευσοποιά τε καὶ ἀναπόνιπτα Synes.*ep.*44(M.66.1369A); **2.** as subst., *dyer*, Bas.*leg.lib.gent.*2(p.43; M.31.568A); Chrys.*hom.20.5 in 1Cor.*(10.177B); Thdt.*Is.*1:18(p.9.8; 2.179).

δευσοποιῶς, *in deeply dyed fashion*; hence met., *ineffaceably*, *cat.Apoc.*12:9(p.361.27).

***δευτεραρία, ἡ**, *prioress, deputy head of nunnery*, *V.Dan.*5 (p.69.20).

***δευτεράριος, ὁ**, *second in command*, ‡Ath.*doct.Ant.*18(M.28.581A); Cyr.S.*v.Euthym.*48(p.70.13); Φλαβιανὸς πρεσβύτερος καὶ δ. τῆς Μοδέστου CCP(536)*act.*2(*ACO* 3 p.157.18; H.2.1232A); *prior* of monastery, Gr.Mag.*dial.*(tr.Zach.)1.2(M.*PL.*77.158A).

***δευτεράω**, v. δευτερόω.

δευτερεῖος, plur. δευτερεῖα, τά *second rank*, of Son ὡσανεὶ τοῦ πατρὸς ὑπάρχοντα δύναμιν καὶ σοφίαν ἰσοκλεῆ καὶ τὰ δ. τῆς κατὰ πάντων βασιλείας τε καὶ ἀρχῆς ἐμπεπιστευμένον Eus.*h.e.*1.2.11(M.20.60A); πρωτείοις μὲν τῆς τῶν ὅλων ἀρχῆς δ. δὲ τῆς πατρικῆς βασιλείας ἐνδοξαζόμενος id.*l.C.*1(p.198.26; M.20.1324B); of sin πολὺ γὰρ δεινὸν ἡ μοιχεία τοσοῦτον ὅσον τὰ δ. ἔχειν αὐτὴν τῆς κολάσεως *Clem.ep.*7(M.2.41B).

δευτερεύ-ω, 1. *hold second place*; in rank, of Son in relation to Father ἄξιον εἶναι τῆς ~ούσης μετὰ τὸν θεὸν...τιμῆς Or.*Cels.*7.57 (p.206.26; M.11.1501D); τὸν δὲ τούτῳ [sc. τῷ πανηγεμόνι] ~οντα θεῖον λόγον Eus.*h.e.*1.2.5(M.20.56B); πατὴρ...ἀγαθοῦ γεννητικός, ~οντος δὲ καὶ ὡς ἂν ἀπὸ πρώτης καὶ ἡγουμένης οὐσίας ἐπιχορηγουμένου τοῦ υἱοῦ id.*d.e.*5.1(p.214.16; M.22.356B); ~ούσης δὲ μετὰ τὸν πατέρα τῆς δημιουργικῆς ὁμοῦ καὶ φωτιστικῆς δυνάμεως τοῦ θείου λόγου id.*p.e.*7.15(325A; M.21.549B); ὁ γὰρ ἐν ἔργοις ἴσος ὢν τῷ πατρὶ πῶς ἂν ~ων κατὰ φύσιν αὐτοῦ; Cyr.*fr.*ap.CLater.*act.*5(H.3.861E); of H. Ghost ἀξιώματι μὲν γὰρ ~ειν τοῦ υἱοῦ Bas.*Eun.*3.1(1.272B; M.29.653B); **2.** *come second* in time, of Inc. μὴ πρὸ τῆς καθόδου νοεῖσθαι τὴν σάρκα, ἀλλὰ ~ειν μετὰ τὴν κάθοδον Gr.Nyss.*Apoll.*9(M.45.1141A); of Christ in relation to Jo. Bapt. ἐχὼν μὲν τὸ πρωτεύειν καθὸ λόγος ἐστί. ~ων δὲ κατὰ τὴν σάρκα Cyr.*Pulch.*(p.109.24; 5^2.113C); **3.** *repeat* ~σαντος δὲ τοῦ προφήτου, δῆλον ὡς ταῖς αὐταῖς λέξεσιν ἕτερα πάλιν τὸ πνεῦμα ἐμήνυσεν Or.*Ps.*58:15(p.66).

***δευτερογαμέω**, *marry a second time*, Epiph.*haer.*61.1(p.381.19; M.41.1041A); Phot.*nomoc.*13.2(M.104.1168B); readers marrying a second time to be ineligible for preferment, Ath.Scholast.*coll.*1.1 (p.3); Jo.Scholast.*coll.cap.*47 tit.(p.388).

***δευτερογαμία, ἡ**, *second marriage*, Afric.*ep.Arist.*(p.58.19; M.10.56A); *Const.App.*3.2.1; Ath.Scholast.*coll.*9.10(p.105); ὁ πολιτικὸς νόμος οὐ κολάζει τὴν δ. Phot.*nomoc.*13.2(M.104.901A).

***δευτερόγαμος**, *twice married*, hence ineligible for priesthood, Epiph.*exp.fid.*21(p.522.11; M.42.824B); Ath.Scholast.*coll.*1.1(p.2).

***δευτερογραφέω**, *copy*, Mac.Mgn.*apocr.*3.10(p.74.11).

***δευτεροδεκάδη, ἡ**, *tenth part of a tithe*, Hier.*comm.in Ezech.*14.45 (M.*PL.*25.450D) prob. f.l. for δευτεροδεκάτη.

***δευτεροκῆρυξ, ὁ**, *later preacher*; ref. 2Cor.11:14, Marc.Er.*opusc.*10.10(M.65.1136B).

δευτερολογέω, *repeat*, Epiph.*haer.*76.46(p.399.30; M.42.613B).

δευτερολογία, ἡ, *repetition*, Epiph.*mens.*2(M.43.240B).

***δευτερόνοια, ἡ**, *second thought*, Marc.Er.*opusc.*4(M.65.996D).

δευτερονόμιον, τό, *Deuteronomy*, fifth OT book, *Barn.*10.2; written by Moses, Or.*Cels.*2.54(p.178.5; M.11.884A); Chrys.*hom.*

9.4 *in Mt.*(7.135B); ε´ δὲ βίβλος ἐστὶ τὸ δ. οὐ διὰ στόματος θεοῦ ὑπαγορευθέντα· διὸ οὔτε ἐτέθη ἐν τῷ ἀρῶνα τοῦτ᾽ ἔστιν ἐν τῇ κιβωτῷ τῆς διαθήκης *Dial.Tim.et Aquil.*77 r°.

δευτερόπρωτος, (cf. Lc.6:1) *second after the first*; of Low Sunday τῆς δ. κυριακῆς Eustrat.*v.Eutych.*96(M.86.2381B); δ. δὲ σάββατον καλεῖ τοῦτο τὸ σάββατον, οὐ μόνον ὡς ἑβδόμης ἡμέρας οὔσης, ἐν ᾗ ἡ πρώτη τῶν ἀζύμων εὑρέθη, ἀλλὰ καὶ διὰ τὸ ἀπ᾽ αὐτῆς ἀριθμεῖν τὰς ν´ ἡμέρας, καὶ ἑορτάζειν τὴν ἑορτήν, ἣν ἑορτὴν τῶν ἑβδομάδων ὁ θεῖος προσαγορεύει νόμος...εἴτε οὖν τὴν ιε´ τῆς σελήνης, ὡς ἐν σαββάτῳ φθάσασαν, μετὰ τὸ θῦσαι τὸν ἀμνόν, δεύτερον ὠνόμασε σάββατον ὁ εὐαγγελιστής, εἴτε ὡς πρώτην οὖσαν τῆς πεντηκοστῆς, ἤγουν τῶν ἑπτὰ τῆς ἐν τούτῳ τῷ ἔτει πεντηκοστῆς, πανταχόθεν φαίνεται ὅτι τὴν ἐν τούτῳ τῷ ἔτει τοῦ πάσχα ἑορτὴν δηλῶσαι βουλόμενος ὁ εὐαγγελιστὴς δ. ὠνόμασε σάββατον *Chron.Pasch.*p.211(M.92.516C, 517B,C); neut. as subst. τί δέ ἐστι ἐν δ.; ὅταν διπλῆ ἡ ἀργία ᾖ καὶ τοῦ σαββάτου τοῦ κυρίου, καὶ ἑτέρας ἑορτῆς διαδεχομένης Chrys.*hom.39.1 in Mt.*(7.431D); δ. εἴρηται ἐπειδὴ δεύτερον μὲν ἦν τοῦ πάσχα πρῶτον δὲ τῶν ἀζύμων Isid.Pel.*epp.*3.110(M.78.816B).

δεύτερος, *second*; **1.** in rank; **a.** of Son's relationship to Father υἱὸν...θεοῦ μαθόντες, καὶ ἐν δ. χώρᾳ ἔχοντες Just.*1apol.*13.3(M.6.348A); οὕτω καὶ σοφία καὶ ἀλήθειά ἐστιν ὁ κύριος, καὶ οὐκ ἔστιν ἄλλης σοφίας δ. Ath.*Dion.*25.3(p.65.9; M.25.517B); ἡ ἐκ τοῦ πατρὸς μεγαλιότητος δ. μεγαλιότης *Pap.Chr.*4.16.1.14(p.446); in subordinationist sense ὁ υἱός...δ. γάρ ἐστι τοῦ πατρός Or.*princ.*1.3.5(p.56.3; M.11.150B); ὁ δέ, ὡς ἐξ αἰτίου γεγονὼς υἱὸς δ. οὗ ἐστιν υἱὸς καθέστηκεν ...βουληθεὶς γὰρ ὁ θεὸς γέγονεν υἱοῦ πατὴρ καὶ φῶς δ. κατὰ πάντα ἑαυτῷ ἀφωμοιωμένον ὑπεστήσατο Eus.*d.e.*4.3(p.153.11,15; M.22.256B); τὸν πρῶτον κύριον ὡς ἂν καθόλου τῶν ἁπάντων δεσπότην, Ἑβραῖοι ἀνεκφωνήτῳ προσρήσει τῇ διὰ τῶν τεσσάρων στοιχείων ἀνηγόρευον· τὸν δὲ δ. οὐκέθ᾽ ὁμοίως, ἰδίως δ᾽ αὐτὸν κύριον ὠνόμαζον *ib.*5.3(p.219.13; 361C); δ. εἰκότως καὶ αὐτὸς ἂν εὐσεβῶς χρηματίζοι κύριος *ib.*5.6(p.230.6; 380B); Eunomian δ. ἔσται τοῦ πατρὸς ὁ υἱός, αἴτιον αὐτὸν ἔχων Cyr.*thes.*9(5[1].68C); **b.** of man in relation to God, Max.*ep.*10(M.91.452D); **2.** in time λέγει ἡ θεία γραφὴ περὶ τοῦ δ. οὐρανοῦ...[Gen.1:8] Cosm.Ind.*top.*2(M.88.81C); of economy of Creation and Inc. in relation to generation of Son, ref. Pr.8:22, Ath. *Ar.*2.50(M.26.252C); εἰ γὰρ εἰς ἔργα φησὶν ἐκτίσθαι, φαίνεται μὴ τὴν οὐσίαν ἑαυτοῦ σημᾶναι θέλων, ἀλλὰ τὴν εἰς τὰ ἔργα αὐτοῦ οἰκονομίαν γενομένην, ὅπερ δ. ἐστι τοῦ εἶναι *ib.*2.51(256A); μηδὲ κατὰ τὴν πρώτην αὐτοῦ, μηδὲ κατὰ δ. γέννησιν τινὶ τῶν πάντων κοινωνοῦντα Leont. H.*Nest.*4.9(M.86.1669B); τὴν ἐπίκτησιν τῶν ἐκ τῆς δ. γεννήσεως προσληφθέντων *ib.*4.12(1673D); of Second Advent, v. παρουσία; met. δ. φύσις ἡ συνήθεια *Hom.Clem.*5.25; ref. Mt.20:16 δ. πλάσιν ἐπ᾽ ἐσχάτων ἐποίησεν *Barn.*6.13; fem. as subst., *second day of week, Monday*, *V.Dan.*10(p.371.7); Jo.Jej.*canonar.*3.3(p.439); neut. as adv. πρότερον μὲν θεὸς λόγος ὤν, γενόμενος δὲ δ. υἱὸς ἀνθρώπου Eus.*d.e.* 8.1(p.364.8; M.22.592B).

δευτεροστάτης, ὁ, *soldier of the second line*, Or.*sel.in Ex.*14:7 (M.12.288C).

***δευτερότης, ἡ,** *duplication* καὶ υἱὸς μὲν κυρίως ἐστὶ δ. ὑποστάσεως ἐν ταυτότητι φύσεως Anast.S.*hod.*2(M.89.56A).

***δευτερότοκος,** *second-born*, Didym.*Trin.*3.4(M.39.836C).

***δευτεροφανῶς,** *by a secondary manifestation*, Dion.Ar.*c.h.*8.1 (M.3.240B); *ib.*15.6(336A).

δευτερ-όω (*-άω), 1. *put in second place*, Procl.CP *hom.*1.4(M.65.837A); **2.** *discuss in the second place*, Mac.Mgn.*apocr.*2.20(p.37.1); *ib.*3.41(p.141.2); **3.** *teach tradition* (δευτέρωσις), cf. *discipulis suis solent dicere* οἱ σοφοὶ ∼οῦσιν, *id est, sapientes docent traditiones*, Hier.*ep.*121.10(*CSEL* p.49.18,v.l.(one MS); ∼ῶσιν M.*PL.*22.1034); **4.** med., *repeat oneself*, *Dial.Tim.et Aquil.*79 v°.

δευτέρως, *secondarily*, Or.*Jo.*13:16(p.240.2; M.14.421C); of relationship between Father and Son ὀνομάζει κύριον δὲ τὸν...λόγον, τὸν δὴ καὶ δ. ἡμῖν μετὰ τὸν τῶν ὅλων θεὸν κυριολογούμενον Eus.*d.e.*4.7 (p.160.32; M.22.268B); δ. τὴν κυρείαν καὶ δεσποτείαν παρὰ τοῦ πατρὸς ὁ τοῦ θεοῦ λόγος ἀναδεξάμενος *ib.*5.6(p.230.4; 380B).

δευτέρωσις, ἡ, 1. *second rank*, Dion.Ar.*c.h.*8.2(M.3.240C); **2.** *second quarter* of Jerusalem, interprn. of מִשְׁנֶה SM ap.Proc.G. *2Par.*34:22(M.87.1217D); **3.** *repetition*, Gr.Nyss.*hom.8 in Cant.* (M.44.949C); hence **4.** Jewish *tradition*, Eus.*p.e.*12.4(576A; M.21.956C); *Const.App.*1.6.3; *ib.*2.5.6 cit. s. διαστολεύς.

***δευτερωτής, ὁ,** *interpreter*, Cosm.Mel.*schol.*(M.38.466) in Gr. Naz.*carm.*1.1.10; esp. Jewish *scribe* ναὶ μὴν καὶ τῶν πρώτων μαθημάτων δ. τινες ἦσαν αὐτοῖς· (οὕτω δὲ φίλον τοὺς ἐξηγητὰς τῶν παρ᾽ αὐτοῖς γραφῶν ὀνομάζειν) Eus.*p.e.*11.5(513C; M.21.852B); Proc. G.*Is.*22:1(M.87.2176D); Jo.D.*haer.*14(M.94.685B).

***δεφενσίων, ἡ,** (Lat. *defensio*) *defence*, Ath.Scholast.*coll.*6.3 (p.81).

***δεφένσωρ, ὁ,** (Lat. *defensor*) *protector*, Gr.Mag.*dial.*(tr.Zach.) 1.4(M.*PL.*77.171C).

δέχ-ομαι, *receive*; Sophr.H.*conf.*(M.87.3365B); of receiving or admitting into Church, Jul.Papa *ep.Dian.*ap.Ath.*apol.sec.*31(p.111.4; M.25.301B); *Chron.Pasch.*p.336(M.92.872A); of receiving back penitents, CAnc.(314)*can.*5; Bas.*ep.*199 *can.*22(3.293C; M.32.724A); †CCP(381)*can.*2; Thdr.Scyth.*libell.*proem.(M.86.232C); and reconciled heretics, Bas.*ep.*188 *can.*5(3.272A; M.673B); ‡CCP(381)*can.*7; of hearing confession ἐξαγόρευσιν ∼όμενοι †Jo.Jej.*serm.*(M.88.1929D); of God accepting sinners, Ammon.*ep.*17(p.106.24); in Inc.; of Christ taking human nature to himself, Isid.Pel.*epp.*1.193(M.78.305C).

[*]**δηάκων, ὁ,** v. διάκων.

***δηκτήρ,** *biting*, ‡Nil.*perist.*2.4(M.79.820D).

***δηλατόρευσις, ἡ,** *work of an informer*, Leont.B.*mesopent.*(M.86.1985C).

***δηλατορεύω,** *inform against*, Heges.ap.Eus.*h.e.*3.20.1(M.20.253A); Pall.*v.Chrys.*17(p.108.6; M.47.60); *V.Olymp.*3(p.411).

***δηλάτωρ, ὁ,** (Lat. *delator*), **1.** *informer*, Thdt.*ep.*43(4.1103); **2.** *public prosecutor*, †Gregent.*leg.hom.*22(M.86.592C).

δηλαυγῶς, *clearly*, *Dial.Tim.et Aquil.*110 v°.

***δηληγάτωρ, ὁ,** (Lat. *delegatus*) *delegation*, Jo.Mal.*chron.*13 p.319(M.97.477B).

δηλητήριος, met., *noxious*; hence, neut. as subst., *poison* τερπνὰ δ. Gr.Naz.*carm.*2.1.12.338(M.37.1190A); of diabolical inducements to sin, Eus.*h.e.*10.4.14(M.20.853C); Chrys.*hom.62.3 in Mt.*(7.624A).

δηλητηριώδης, *noxious*; neut. plur. as subst., Nemes.*nat.hom.*1 (M.40.532A).

***δηλοποιέω, 1.** *make clear, reveal*, †Bas.*parad.*1(1.347F; M.30.64A); ‡Proc.G.*Pr.*3:11(M.87.1244D); *Contrad.*1(p.6); **2.** *make celebrated* τοῦ...ἀνδρὸς τὸ φαιδρὸν ὄνομα ἐδηλοποιήθη Gr.Mag.*dial.* (tr.Zach.)3.1(M.*PL.*77.215D).

δῆλος, *clear, manifest*; as subst. δῆλοι, οἱ *Urim* εἶπεν ὁ ἱερεὺς διὰ τῶν δ. ‡Epiph.*v.proph.Elisaei* A 6(p.32; M.43.396D); τά...δῆλα Hesych.S.*temp.*2.93(M.93.1541C); hence *oracles, revelations* δότε ἡμῖν δήλους· τί ἄρα ἀποβήσεται ἡμῖν; *Pers.*(p.8.18).

***δηλοσιεύω,** error for δημοσιεύω, †Anast.S.*relat.*49(p.69).

***δηλοτικός,** v. δηλωτικός.

δηλ-όω, 1. *make clear, manifest; signify* ἀνέστη [sc. Χριστός]... ὡς καὶ...αἱ...γραφαὶ ἐδήλουν Just.*dial.*85.1(M.6.676B); exeg. Am.4:12 κτίζειν πνεῦμα λέγεται...τοῦ τοῖς ἀποστόλοις ἐμπνεύσαντος Χριστοῦ ∼ουμένου Eus.*d.e.*4.16(p.189.29; M.22.316D); Gel.Cyz.*h.e.*2.7.23(M.85.1237A); **2.** *mean* ∼οῖ δὲ [sc. προτίκτωρ]...τὸν προσκεπαστὴν Men. *exc.Rom.*19(p.216.26; M.113.920C); ∼οῖ δὲ ἡ λέξις [i.e. χαβάρ] τὴν μεγάλην ‡Barth.Edess.*Muham.*(M.104.1448B); pass. ptcpl. as subst., *meaning*, Or.*Apoc.*14(p.27.6); **3.** *order* ∼οῦσιν αὐτῷ· ἐλθέ Call. *v.Hyp.*(p.76); Gr.Mag.*dial.*(tr.Zach.)3.10(M.*PL.*77.235C); **4.** *declare* war, *Chron.Pasch.*p.286(M.92.716A); **5.** pass. ptcpl., *aforesaid*, Eus.*h.e.*1.5.1(M.20.81A); *ib.*6.14.8(552B); id.*v.C.*1.58(p.34.25; M.20.972C).

δήλωμα, τό, 1. *indication, proof*, Dion.Al.ap.Ath.*Dion.*18(p.60.9; M.25.508A); ‡Dion.Al.*fr.in Lc.*22:42(p.234.13; M.10.1598B); **2.** *news*, Gr.Nyss.*v.Macr.*(p.411.23; M.46.997A); id.*Eun.*2(2 p.328.25; M.45.504B); **3.** *communication, report*, CEph.(431)*act.*4(*ACO* 1.1.3 p.17.23; H.1.1488E); Heracl.*ep.*(M.92.992B); *Chron.Pasch.*p.392(M.92.1005B); Thdr.Stud.*epp.*1.24(M.99.981D); *ib.*2.159(1497B).

δήλως, *clearly*, Chrys.*hom.80.3 in Mt.*(7.769C).

δήλωσις, ἡ, 1. *manifestation, indication* οὐδέπω γὰρ ἀποκεκάλυπτο ἡ τῶν προφητικῶν δ. μυστηρίων πρὸ τῆς τοῦ κυρίου παρουσίας Clem. *str.*5.14(p.385.22; M.9.132B); τῶν τῆς κιβωτοῦ μέτρων ὁ λόγος τῆς τριάδος δ. Cyr.*glaph.Gen.*2(1.37A); ‡Sophr.H.*liturg.*2(M.87.3981D); **2.** *Urim*, Gr.Nyss.*laud.Bas.*(M.46.812C); Epiph.*gemm.*(M.43.301C); Proc.G.*Dt.*33:8(M.87.984A).

δηλωτικός, *significant, indicative*, in gen. ὄνομα [sc. τοῦ Χριστοῦ] μύρου κεκενωμένου δ. Eus.*d.e.*4.16(p.195.20; M.22.325A); Σαβὲκ... τοῦ μυστηρίου τοῦ σταυροῦ δ. Diod.*Gen.*22:13(M.33.1575C); καὶ τί θαυμαστὸν εἰ ἐπὶ θεοῦ, ὅπου γε οὐδὲ ἐπὶ ἀγγέλου εὕροι τις ἂν ὄνομα τῆς οὐσίας δ. Chrys.*hom.2.2 in Heb.*(12.17C); of prophecy τὸ δὲ [sc. Gen.49:10] σύμβολον δ. ἦν τῶν γενησομένων τῷ Χριστῷ Just.*1apol.* 32.5(M.6.380A); τὸ δὲ 'ὅτι ἔρχεται κρῖναι τὴν γῆν' γένοιτ᾽ ἂν δ. καὶ τῆς δευτέρας αὐτοῦ παρουσίας Eus.*d.e.*6.6(p.256.33; 421C); δηλοτικός Max.*ep.*12(M.91.469B).

δημαγωγ-έω, *be a leader of the people*, Chrys.*hom.80.3 in Mt.*

(7.770D); hence *govern* τοῦ πνεύματος πάντα ~οῦντος id.*hom.36.4 in 1Cor.*(10.339C).

δημαγωγικός, *fit to lead the people*; neut. as subst., Chrys.*hom.* 56.2 *in Mt.*(7.567D).

***δημαίτητος**, *demanded by the people*, Synes.*ep.*13(M.66.1349C).

δήμαρχος, ὁ, 1. *leader of the people* τὸν Ἰακὼβ πατέρα εἶναι τῶν δώδεκα πατριαρχῶν, κἀκείνους τῶν δ. Or.*princ.*4.3.7(p.333.12,14; M.11.388A); **2.** *leader of one of the circus factions*, Thphn.*chron.* p.241(M.108.608B).

***δημεκδικ-έω**, *be a* defensor civitatis ὁ ~ῶν Marc.Diac.*v.Porph.*25.

δημεύ-ω, 1. *make public*; **a.** *divulge* τὰ τῶν Καβίρων ~οντι μυστήρια Athenag.*leg.*4.1(M.6.897A); pass., Clem.*prot.*2(p.25.20; M.8.112A); **b.** *admonish publicly*, †Gregent.*leg.Hom.*22(M.86.593B); *ib.*30(597B); *ib.*48(605D); **2.** *punish by fining*, Ath.*ep.encycl.*4(p.173.11; M.25.232A); Chrys.*hom.7.7 in 1Cor.*(10.61A); *Chron.Pasch.*p.327 (M.92.844A); c. acc. of respect τοῖς ~θεῖσι τὰς οὐσίας αὐτῶν Gel. Cyz.*h.e.*1.8.2(M.85.1208D).

***δημηγέρτης, ὁ,** *seditious person*, Leont.et Jo.*sacr.*2 tit.(M.86.2021D).

[*]δημηγορεύω, *proclaim publicly*, ‡Caes.Naz.*dial.*177(M.38.1145).

δημηγορέω, *make a public speech*, Eus.*h.e.*2.10.1(M.20.157C); Chrys.*hom.83.3 in Jo.*(8.492C); Isid.Pel.*epp.*3.300(M.78.973A).

δημηγορία, ἡ, 1. *idle talk*, Or.*Cels.*6.33(p.103.6; M.11.1348B); **2.** *public speech, oration*, *ib.*6.10(p.80.11; 1305A); Chrys.*hom.54.2 in Jo.*(8.317D); Bas.Sel.*v.Thecl.*1(M.85.480B); hence *sermon*, Or.*Cels.*4.5 (p.277.25; M.11.1033D); Chrys.*hom.48.1 in Jo.*(284A); Philost.*fr.* (M.65.636C).

δημιουργ-έω, 1. *fashion*, Tat.*orat.*33(p.35.17; M.6.876B); *Hom. Clem.*10.20; Eus.*d.e.*4.5(p.157.2; M.22.261C); **2.** *effect, produce* εἰρήνην ~ῆσαι Or.*hom.12.5 in Jer.*(p.91.29; M.13.385A); κακοδοξίαν ~εῖ Gr.Naz.*ep.*183(M.37.301A); Chrys.*hom.58.3 in Mt.*(7.589B); **3.** *create*; **a.** of God in gen., Arist.*apol.*13.8; Just.*1apol.*59.1(M.6.416C); ψιλῷ τῷ βούλεσθαι ~εῖ Clem.*prot.*4(p.48.18; M.8.164A); οὐκ ἄλλῳ τινὶ κελεύει ~εῖν, ἀλλὰ τὰ μὴ ὄντα καλεῖ Thdt.*qu.9 in Gen.* (1.13); applied also to God's activity in fashioning existing entities θεὸς καὶ ἐξ ὄντων καὶ ἐκ μὴ ὄντων ~εῖ *ib.20*(1.26); καὶ ἐκ μὴ ὄντων ποιεῖ, καὶ ἐξ ὄντων ~εῖ· τὸν μὲν γὰρ πρότερον οὐρανὸν ἐκ μὴ ὄντων ἐδημιούργησε, τὸν δὲ δεύτερον ἐξ ὑδάτων ἐποίησεν *ib.14*(1.17); **b.** through the second Person ὁ λόγος ἐν ἀρχῇ γεννηθείς, ἀντεγέννησε τὴν καθ' ἡμᾶς ποίησιν, αὐτὸς ἑαυτῷ τὴν ὕλην ~ήσας Tat.*orat.*5 (p.6.9; M.6.817A); Athenag.*leg.*6.3(M.6.901C); τοῦ κατὰ τὴν ἀρχὴν ...~ήσαντος λόγου Ath.*inc.*1.4(M.25.97C); τὸ δὲ ἐξ οὐκ ὄντων ~εῖσθαι τὸν κόσμον νεωτέραν ἔχει τὴν ὑπόστασιν καὶ πρόσφατον τὴν γένεσιν, ὑπὸ τοῦ πατρὸς διὰ τοῦ υἱοῦ πάντων εἰληφότων τὴν τοιαύτην οὐσίωσιν Alex.Al.*ep.Alex.*4(p.22.17; M.18.553B); ἀρχὴ γὰρ τῶν ὄντων μία, δι' υἱοῦ ~οῦσα καὶ τελειοῦσα ἐν πνεύματι Bas.*Spir.*38(3.31E; M.32.136B); this being special function of Son in relation to other Persons τοῦ μὲν πατρὸς εὐδοκοῦντος καὶ κελεύοντος, τοῦ δὲ υἱοῦ πράσσοντος καὶ ~οῦντος, τοῦ δὲ πνεύματος τρέφοντος καὶ αὔξοντος Iren.*haer.*4.38.3 (M.7.1108B); but creation through Son is due to Father's will, not to necessity οὕτω γὰρ ἂν οὔτε πατὴρ προσδεηθείη υἱοῦ, μόνῳ τῷ θέλειν ~ῶν, ἀλλ' ὅμως θέλει διὰ υἱοῦ Bas.*Spir.*38(32A; M.136B); question addressed to those who said Father created Son to serve him in creating world εἰ γὰρ καλὸν τὸ ~εῖν (ὥσπερ οὖν καλόν, καὶ μόνον ἴδιον, καὶ μόνον ἐξαίρετον τῆς θεϊκῆς ἀφθόνου φύσεως, ἵν' ἔχοι καὶ ὑπὸ τοῦ δοξάζηται), ἀνθότου μὴ πάντα δι' ἑαυτοῦ ἔκτισεν, ἀλλ' οἷον εἴπως κατώκνησεν; Didym.*Trin.*1.8(M.39.276C); heret. ἐκ μὴ ὄντων ἑκάτερον αὐτῶν πέφυκε ~εῖν Philost.*h.e.*10.3(M.65.585A); **c.** as activity of Trin. τριὰς...ἁγία...ὅλη τοῦ κτίζειν καὶ ~εῖν οὖσα Ath.*ep. Serap.*1.28(M.26.596A); CCP(543)*anath.*6(p.228; H.3.285A) cit. s. δημιουργικός; **d.** Son not himself created, Thdt.*Trin.*8(M.75.1157A); οὗτός ἐστιν ὁ πρὸ πάντων τῶν αἰώνων ἐξ ἐμοῦ γεννηθεὶς οὐ δημιουργηθείς Gr.Ant.*bapt.*2.1(M.64.33; οὐ δ. om. M.88.1872C); as asserted by Arians υἱὸς...ὡς τὰ κτίσματα διὰ τὸ δεδημιουργῆσθαι Ath. *decr.*22(p.19.5; M.25.456B); τότε γὰρ γέγονεν ὅτε βεβούληται αὐτὸν ὁ θεὸς ~ῆσαι id.*ep.Aeg.Lib.*12(M.25.564B); **e.** ref. Inc. ὁ θεὸς λόγος ...ἐν τῇ γαστρὶ τῆς...ἀεὶ παρθένου Μαρίας ἐδημιούργησεν ἑαυτῷ ἐξ αὐτῆς ἐν τῇ ἰδίᾳ ὑποστάσει σάρκα ὁμοούσιον ἡμῖν Just.Imp.*edict.* ap.Evagr.*h.e.*5.4(p.200.12; M.86.2800A); ὁ τεχνίτης ἐν σοὶ πρὸς ἑαυτοῦ ἀσπόρως βρέφος ~ηθήσεται Jo.D.*fr.*(M.96.816A); **f.** ref. 'nature miracles', Chrys.*hom.42.3 in Jo.*(8.251D); *cat.Jo.*2:6(p.198.35); **g.** ref. man's creation ὁ πλάσας ἡμᾶς καὶ ~ήσας 1Clem.38.3; Clem.*exc.Thdot.*51(p.123.19; M.9.684A); Εὔα οὐκ ἐγεννήθη, ἀλλ' ἐδημιουργήθη ‡Ath.*disp.*23(M.28.465D); **h.** ref. new creation by spiritual regeneration, of H. Ghost ~εῖ δὲ τὴν πνευματικὴν ἀναγέννησιν Gr.Naz.*or.*41.14(M.36.448B); ~εῖ τὸ μέγα κτίσμα τὸν ἄνθρωπον, καὶ ἐκ νεκρῶν ἐγείρει, καὶ ζωοποιεῖ καὶ εἰς οὐρανὸν ἐπιστρέφει...τὸ πνεῦμα τὸ ἅγιον Didym.*Trin.*2.7(M.39.564A); ἑτέραν ἐδημιούργησε κτίσιν...ἐν Χριστῷ Chrys.*hom.26.1 in Jo.*(8.148D); *ib.25.2*(145C); in baptism, Eustrat.*v.Eutych.*8(M.86.2284A); **i.** angels cannot create, being themselves creatures, Ath.*Ar.*2.21(M.26.192A); but man's creative capacity imitates that of God though it is restricted to fashioning of existing material, Thdt.*qu.20 in Gen.*(1.26); **j.** angels prob. created along with heaven and earth, *ib.4*(1.8); **4.** ptcpl. as subst.; **a.** *creator*, Athenag.*res.*5(p.52.31; M.6.981D); Ath.*decr.*18(p.15.23; M.25.448B); Gr.Naz.*or.*4.15(M.35.545A); **b.** neut., *creature, created thing*, Ath.*syn.*35(p.262.31; M.26.756B); †Bas.*Is.*161 (1.493C; M.30.384A).

δημιούργημα, τό, 1. *work, product*; in gen., fig. ἐπιορκίαι...τῆς γλώσσης...δ. Bas.*hom.in Ps.*33(1.153A; M.29.373C); λοιδορίαν...τῆς κακίας δ. Gr.Nyss.*instit.*(p.76.10; M.46.301A); **2.** *created thing, creature*; **a.** in gen., Clem.*prot.*11(p.81.13; M.8.233B); ἀρχὴ δημιουργημάτων ὁ δημιουργός Or.*Jo.*1.17(p.22.10; M.14.53A); πάντα μὲν καλὰ καὶ καλὰ λίαν τὰ τοῦ θεοῦ καὶ σωτῆρος ἡμῶν δ. †Hipp.*theoph.*1 (p.257.3; M.10.852A); αἰσθητὸς κόσμος...θεοῦ δ. Eus.*l.C.*12(p.233.4; M.20.1392C); οὐκ ἠδύνατο μὴ δι' αὐτοῦ [sc. Logos] γενέσθαι τὰ δ. Ath.*Ar.*2.31(M.26.212B); ἑνὸς δημιουργοῦ ἀγαθοῦ ἐστι πάντα τὰ ἄλογα ζῷα δ. ‡Just.*qu.et resp.*127(M.6.1377D); θαυμαστὰ...δ. ὁ οὐρανὸς καὶ ἡ γῆ Cyr.*Ps.*8:5(M.69.760A); **b.** of man, Clem.*paed.*2.1 (p.157.1; M.8.385B); σὸν γὰρ ἦν [sc. ὁ ἄνθρωπος] δ. *Lit.*ap.*Const. App.*8.12.20; κοινὸν γὰρ τῆς θεότητος δ. τὸ πλαττόμενον Bas.Sel.*or.*1.3 (M.85.36A); Gnost. denial that man's physical nature is creature of God τὴν μὲν σάρκα...τοῦ πονηροῦ λέγοντες εἶναι δ. *cat.Judae* 8(p.158.20); **c.** of angelic powers ἀρχαὶ καὶ κυριότητες καὶ ταῦτα δοῦλα καὶ ταῦτα δ. ‡Chrys.*hom.*8(13.221E); **d.** of Devil τὸ πονηρὸν καὶ κακὸν οὐκ ὄν. καὶ τάχα τοῦτο ἔσηνε τοὺς εἰπόντας τὸν διάβολον μὴ εἶναι θεοῦ δ.· καθὸ γὰρ διάβολός ἐστιν οὐκ ἔστι θεοῦ δ., ᾧ δὲ συμβέβηκε διαβόλῳ εἶναι, γενητὸς ὤν, οὐδενὸς κτιστοῦ ὄντος παρὲξ τοῦ θεοῦ ἡμῶν, θεοῦ ἐστι κτίσμα· ὡς εἰ ἐφάσκομεν καὶ τὸν φονέα μὴ εἶναι θεοῦ δ., οὐκ ἀναιροῦντες τὸ ᾗ ἄνθρωπός ἐστι πεποιῆσθαι αὐτὸν ὑπὸ θεοῦ Or.*Jo.*2.13 (7; p.69.18; M.14.136B); **e.** of Son τὸ τέλειον τελείου δ. Eus.*d.e.*4.2 (p.152.3; M.22.253B); denied against Arians οὗτοι [sc. Arians]...τὸν κτίστην τῶν ἁπάντων κτίσμα ἢ δ. βλασφημῆσαι ἐτόλμησαν Ath.*inc.et c.Ar.*1(M.26.985B); μὴ λεγέσθω θελήματος δ. ὁ υἱός id.*Ar.*2.67(M.26.464C); ἀσεβὲς...τὸ τὸν κτίστην τοῖς δι' αὐτοῦ κεκτισμένοις δ. παραβάλλειν id.*syn.*26.8(p.253.31; M.26.733A); εἰ μὲν δ. ὁ μονογενής, οὐ παρίστησιν ἡμῖν τοῦ πατρὸς τὴν οὐσίαν· εἰ δὲ γνωρίζει ἡμῖν δι' ἑαυτοῦ τὸν πατέρα, οὐχὶ δ. ἀλλὰ υἱὸς ἀληθὴς καὶ εἰκὼν τοῦ θεοῦ Bas.*Eun.* 2.32(1.269E; M.29.648D); ‡Gr.Nyss.*Ar.et Sab.*9(M.45.1293C); **f.** of H. Ghost (Arian), Bas.*Eun.*2.33(1.270A; M.29.649A).

***δημιουργητικός**, *creative*; neut. as subst., *creative power*, of God, Hesych.H.*Ps.tit.*78.21(M.27.1028C); Anast.S.*serm.imag.*3(M.89.1165A).

***δημιουργητικῶς**, *by way of creation*, ref. Son τὸ μὲν εἶναι γεννητῶς καὶ οὐ δ. Jo.D.*f.o.*4.18(M.94.1181C).

***δημιουργητός**, *created*, ‡Just.*coh.Gr.*22(M.6.281A).

δημιουργία, ἡ, A. *creation*; **1.** in pagan thought ποτὲ μὲν φύσιν λέγουσι ποιηταί, ποτὲ δὲ νοῦν ἀρχηγὸν γενέσθαι τῆς ὅλης δ. *Hom.Clem.* 6.19; δημιουργὸν αὐτὸν [sc. God]...ἀλλὰ ὕλης πρὸς δημιουργίαν δεόμενον Gr.Nyss.*v.Mos.*(M.44.337B); ὕλην...τὴν πρόφασιν αὐτῷ τῆς δ. παρέχουσαν ‡Just.*coh.Gr.*6(M.6.253B); **2.** Gnost. and Manich. ascription of Creation to inferior or evil creator, Hegem.*Arch.*12 (p.20.7; M.10.1448A); τὸν πονηρὸν μηδὲν ἔχειν κοινὸν πρὸς τὸν ἀγαθὸν θεὸν εἰς τὴν τοῦ κόσμου δ. Cyr.H.*catech.*6.13; εἰ γὰρ ἀγαθῆς φύσεως ἡ κατὰ τὸ ἀγαθὸν ἐνέργεια πάντως ἐστίν, ὁ λυπηρὸς οὗτος καὶ ἐπίκηρος βίος οὐκέτ' ἄν, φησίν, εἰς τὴν τοῦ ἀγαθοῦ δ. ἀνάγοιτο Gr.Nyss.*or. catech.*7(p.38.8; M.45.32A); Gennad.*fr.Gen.*1:1(M.85.1625D); **3.** orthodox; **a.** in gen., *1Clem.*20.6; τὴν ἐπὶ πάσης τῆς δ. θεωρουμένην ἀγαθότητα καὶ σοφίαν Athenag.*res.*12(p.62.10; M.6.997B); ἐπαναπαύεται δὲ τερπόμενος τῇ δ. Clem.*str.*2.2(p.116.8; M.8.937A); τὸ σάββατον δημιουργίας ἐστὶν ὑπόμνημα *Const.App.*7.23.3; ἤρκει τῆς δ. ὁ τρόπος δεῖξαι τοῦ νόμου τὸν δεσπότην Chrys.*hom.40.1 in Mt.*(7.438A); creation of evils justified εἰ τοίνυν μέμφεταί τις τῇ τῶν πονηρῶν δ., ἀποστερεῖ ἄρα τῶν τῆς νίκης βραβείων τοὺς τῆς ἀρετῆς ἀθλητάς Thdt.*qu.36 in Gen.*(1.47); in heret. determinist view γέγονασί τινες ἐξ αὐτῆς τῆς δ. οἱ μὲν ἀγαθοὶ τὸν τρόπον, οἱ δὲ κακοί Cyr. *Ps.*57:4(M.69.1169B); **b.** of man's place in it ἐπὶ τέλει τῆς δ. αὐτὸν προήγαγεν Clem.*exc.Thdot.*41(p.119.30; M.9.680A); τῆς τοῦ θεοῦ δ. ἐχθρὸς [i.e. self-mutilator] *Can.App.*22; πάντες...γὰρ ἄνθρωποι τοῦ θεοῦ...κατὰ τὸν τῆς δ. λόγον Chrys.*hom.17.2 in 1Tim.*(11.649C); ἡμεῖς αὐτοὶ τὸ κεφάλαιον τῆς δ. Gennad.*fr.Rom.*8:23(p.381.17; M.

85.1697C); ref. sonship τὸ δέ, τέκνον, ἢ καὶ αὐτῷ πιστεύσαντι, ἢ κατὰ τῆς δ. λόγον Vict.*Mc.*2:5(p.285.10); method of man's creation as Christol. illustration ὡς γὰρ ὁ πρῶτος ἄνθρωπος ἐκ θεοῦ καὶ τῆς γῆς οὐ κατὰ μῖξιν, ἀλλὰ κατὰ δ., οὕτως...Χριστὸν ἐκ πνεύματος ἁγίου καὶ Μαρίας τῆς παρθένου *Dial.Ath.et Zach.*45(p.31); **c.** ref. Person and work of Son, cf.Eus.*h.e.*1.2.3(M.20.53C) cit. s. F; ἄλλη γὰρ υἱοῦ γένεσις καὶ ἄλλη ἡ διὰ τοῦ υἱοῦ δ. id.*d.e.*5.1(p.212.26; M.22.353A); συνόντα... πρὸ αἰώνων τῷ...πατρὶ καὶ πρὸς πᾶσαν διακονησάμενον αὐτῷ τὴν δ. εἴτε τῶν ὁρατῶν εἴτε τῶν ἀοράτων *Symb.Ant.*(345)6(p.253.7; M.26. 732B); εἴ τις λέγων θεὸν τὸν Χριστὸν πρὸ αἰώνων υἱὸν τοῦ θεοῦ ὑπουργηκότα τῷ πατρὶ εἰς τὴν τῶν ὅλων δ. μὴ ὁμολογῇ, ἀ. ἔ. *Symb. Sirm.anath.*3; Arian objection πολλοὺς λαλεῖ λόγους ὁ θεός. ποῖον αὐτῶν ἄρα λέγομεν...λόγον μονογενῆ τοῦ πατρός;...μικροῦ δεῖν ἄνθρωπον τὸν θεὸν ὑπολαμβάνουσιν...ὥσπερ οὐκ ἀρκοῦντος ἑνὸς ἐκ τοῦ θεοῦ λόγου πᾶσαν τὴν ἐκ τοῦ βουλήματος τοῦ πατρὸς δ. ... πληρῶσαι Ath.*decr.*16(p.13.34; M.25.'444'(452)A); Eunomian, Eun.*apol.*27(M. 30.864C) cit. s. γέννημα; *ib.*15(852A); **d.** of H. Ghost οὔτε υἱὸς ἐλλιπῆ τὴν δ. μὴ τελειουμένην παρὰ τοῦ πνεύματος Bas.*Spir.*38(3.31E; M.32. 136B); Gr.Nyss.*Maced.*9(M.45.1313D); hence of Trin. οὐδὲ τῆς τοῦ παντὸς δ. υἱοῦ καὶ πνεύματος τὴν ἐνέργειαν κεχωρισμένην τοῦ πατρός Thdt.*rect.conf.*5(M.6.1217A); Gel.Cyz.*h.e.*2.21.6(M.85.1284D); (Eunomian) H. Ghost included in Creation, Eun.*apol.*25(M.30.861C); **e.** angels having no part in Creation, Didym.*Trin.*2.6(M.39.549A).

B. spiritual *creation* or *recreation* in Christ, *Diogn.*9.5; αὕτη μείζων ἡ δ. Chrys.*hom.8.3 in 2Cor.*(10.495C); εἴ τις ἐπίστευσεν αὐτῷ...εἰς ἑτέραν ἦλθε δ. *ib.11.2*(10.515A); esp. in baptism, id.*hom. 25.1 in Jo.*(8.144C); as work of whole Trin., Thdt.*haer.*5.3(4.392).

C. *working*, of God's providence κατὰ δ. τοῦ ἀγαθοῦ...θεοῦ περιέπεσαν αὐτοὶ οἱ Πέρσαι *Chron.Pasch.*p.395(M.92.1012C); in gen., *T.Sal.*D 2.1.

D. *construction*, Gr.Nyss.*v.Mos.*(M.44.320A); *ib.*(321B); Chrys. *sac.*5.7(p.136.7; 1.419B).

E. *procreation*, Thdt.*provid.*6(4.576).

F. concrete, *creation*, *creatures* δ. τὴν ὑπ' αὐτοῦ γεγενημένην... προσκυνεῖν οὐ θέλω Tat.*orat.*4(p.5.6; M.6.813B); πρὸ πάσης...δ. ὁρωμένης τε καὶ ἀοράτου τὸ πρῶτον καὶ μόνον τοῦ θεοῦ γέννημα Eus.*h.e.* 1.2.3(M.20.53C).

δημιουργικός, A. *of a craftsman*; as subst., *craftsmanship* δραστήριος ἡ δ. Clem.*prot.*4(p.45.6; M.8.156B).

B. *creative*; **1.** of man in procreation, Clem.*paed.*2.10(p.212.16; M.8.505B); **2.** of God; **a.** in gen. ἐπὶ δὲ θεοῦ χεὶρ μὲν τὸ δ. Or.*fr.4 in Reg.*(p.295.26; M.17.44B); τὸν...τῶν καθόλου τε καὶ κατὰ μέρος δ. νοῦν Eus.*p.e.*3.6(97A; M.21.177C); εἶχε γὰρ ἐν ἑαυτῷ τὸ ἀεὶ δ. καὶ τέλειον Epiph.*haer.*76.38(p.391.21; M.42.600A); οὐ κτιστή τις οὖσα ἐν τῇ τοῦ θεοῦ οὐσίᾳ φύσις, ἀλλὰ δ. τῶν πάντων *ib.*76.50(p.405.14; 624A); θεότητος...γνώρισμα τὸ δ. Chrys.*hom.68.2 in Ac.*(9.289A); Proc.G. *Gen.*1:6(M.87.72A); θεοῦ δὲ χεῖρες αἱ...δ. τε καὶ ἐνεργητικαὶ δυνάμεις Eustrat.*stat.anim.*7(p.365); μίαν ἀρχὴν...μίαν κίνησιν...τῶν μετ' αὐτὴν ὄντων ἁπάντων δημιουργικήν Sophr.H.*ep.syn.*(M.87.3157A); **b.** Manich. ἡ ἀγαθὴ ἀρχὴ τῶν Χριστιανῶν ἄρχει, ἡ δὲ δ. τῶν Ἰουδαίων Adam.*dial.*1.3(p.4.26; M.11.1720A); **c.** of Person and work of Son τὸ δ. αἴτιον Ath.*syn.*49(p.273.16; M.26.780B); Bas.*Spir.*38(3. 31D; M.32.136B) cit. s. προκαταρκτικός; Chrys.*hom.4.3 in Jo.*(8.30E); χεὶρ...ἡ δ. τῶν ὄντων ἁπάντων δύναμις,...υἱὸς τοῦ θεοῦ Proc.G.*Is.*8:11 (M.87.1984A); **d.** of H. Ghost, Bas.*hom.in Ps.*32(1.135D; M.29. 333A); δ. κατὰ φύσιν τὸ πνεῦμα Cyr.*thes.*31(5[1].331B); denied by Eunomius θεότητος μὲν καὶ δ. δυνάμεως ἀπολειπόμενον [sc. τὸ πνεῦμα], ἁγιαστικῆς καὶ διδασκαλικῆς πεπληρωμένον Eun.*apol.*25(M. 30.861D); **e.** ref. doctrine of operation of Trin. in Creation εἴ τις λέγει...ὅτι οὐχ ἡ παναγία καὶ ὁμοούσιος τριὰς ἐδημιούργησε τὸν κόσμον...ἀλλ' ὁ νοῦς, ὅν φασι δ., προϋπάρχων τοῦ κόσμου καὶ τὸ εἶναι αὐτῷ τῷ κόσμῳ παρέχων, γενητὸν ἀνέδειξεν, ἀ. ἔ. CCP(543)*anath.*6 (p.228; H.3.285A).

C. *pertaining to Creation*, hence *natural* τρεῖς εἰσιν οὗτοι θεῖοι σύμπαντος νόμοι· εἷς μὲν ὁ φυσικὸς ὁμοῦ καὶ δ. καθ' ὅν...τὸ δέον γινώσκομεν Cyr.*Ps.*19:8(M.69.832A); κόσμος διττῶς λέγεται, καὶ ἡ σύστασις ἡ δ. καὶ τῶν ἀνθρώπων τὸ σύστημα τὸ πονηρόν Sever.*Eph.* 2:2f.(p.307.27).

D. *relating to, concerned with, Creation* κατὰ μὲν οὖν τὸν δ. λόγον, ἐξ ὑδάτων καὶ ἐν ὕδασι ἔχει τὸ εἶναι ἡ γῆ...κατὰ δὲ τὸν θεωρητικὸν καὶ τροπικὸν ὁ φθαρτὸς οὗτός ἐστι κόσμος, διύγροις πράξεσι...διεξαγόμενος *cat.Apoc.*17:11(p.433.18).

δημιουργικῶς, *by way of creation*, in gen. πάντα διὰ τοῦ υἱοῦ ἐγένετο...δ. *cat.Heb.*1:2(p.292.31); φωτίζει...δ. μὲν υἱός...κατὰ μετοχὴν δὲ ἡ κτίσις ‡Just.*qu.et resp.*49(M.6.1293C); Cyr.*Is.*5.3(2. 809E) cit. s. ἐκπόρευσις; Trin. τὰ μὲν ἔστιν ἐκ τῆς ἐντολῆς αὐτοῦ δ.· ὁ δὲ υἱὸς ἐκ τῆς ὑποστάσεως γεννητικῶς τὸ δὲ πνεῦμα ἐκπορευτικῶς ‡Ath.*dial.Trin.*1.6(M.28.1125A); Didym.(‡Bas.)*Eun.*5(1.298A; M.29. 716A); id.*Trin.*1.9(M.39.281C); ‡Cyr.*Trin.*23(6[3].28E; M.77.1164C); ref. Inc. τῆς τοῦ πνεύματος παρουσίας...δ. αὐτὸ [sc. Christ's body] διαπλαττούσης Leont.B.*Nest.et Eut.*2(M.86.1352C).

δημιουργός, ὁ, A. as subst.; **1.** *craftsman*; met., *maker, author* ὁ δ. τῆς...ἐπιστολῆς Synes.*ep.*101(M.66.1469B); of Devil πάσης κακίας δ. Cyr.H.*catech.*19.4; and δ. τῆς ὑπερηφανίας †Bas.*Is.*88(1. 440B; M.30.261C); αὐτὸς δ. τῆς ἁμαρτίας Chrys.*hom.13.2 in Eph.* (11.98B); hence, fig., *cause* ἔννομος ζωὴ παρρησίας δ. Ath.*exp.Ps.* 118:46(M.27.488C); Gr.Naz.*carm.*2.1.11.458(M.37.1061A); βία γὰρ ἢ φόβος ἀρετῆς οὐκ ἄν ποτε γένοιτο δ. Bas.Sel.*v.Thecl.*1(M.85.500B); *practiser* οἱ τῆς ἀρετῆς δ. Isid.Pel.*epp.*5.188(M.78.1445A); **2.** *creator*; **a.** of God, in gen. κτίστην καὶ δ. τῶν ἁπάντων Arist.*apol.*15.3; *Hom. Clem.*17.4; τὰ γὰρ κτίσματα μηνύει τὸν ἑαυτῶν δ. Ath.*Ar.*1.12(M.26. 36C); ἀποσεσιώπηται μὲν ὁ τρόπος τῆς κτίσεως τῶν οὐρανίων δυνάμεων, ἀπὸ γὰρ τῶν αἰσθητῶν μόνον τὸν δ. ἡμῖν ὁ τὴν κοσμογονίαν συγγραψάμενος ἀπεκάλυψε Bas.*Spir.*38(3.31D; M.32.136A); **b.** esp. of Father, *1Clem.*20.11; Just.*1apol.*8.2(M.6.337B); ἔστι δὲ οὗτος ὁ δ., ὁ κατὰ μὲν τὴν ἀγάπην πατήρ, κατὰ δὲ τὴν δύναμιν κύριος, κατὰ δὲ τὴν σοφίαν ποιητής Iren.*haer.*5.17.1(M.7.1169A); Clem.*str.*1.11(p.34. 10; M.8.749C); Or.*Jo.*20.30(24; p.367.23; M.14.644A); *Hom.Clem.*2. 45; Ath.*gent.*2(M.25.5C); πιστεύομεν εἰς ἕνα τὸν μόνον...πατέρα...δ. τῶν πάντων *Symb.Sirm.*3(p.235.25; M.26.692B); ref. 1Cor.8:6 τὸ μὲν γὰρ 'ἐξ οὗ' τὸν δ. σημαίνειν Bas.*Spir.*4(3.4D; M.73C); Chrys.*hom. 22.2 in Mt.*(7.277D); Jo.D.*f.o.*1.3(M.94.796C); **c.** of Son, *Diogn.*7.2; Tat.*orat.*7(p.7.12; M.6.820B); Clem.*prot.*1(p.7.31; M.8.61C); Or.*Jo.* 1.19(p.22.18; 56B); Ath.*Ar.*3.28(384B); δ. ἀθανάτων καὶ θνητῶν, δ. τῶν πνευμάτων καὶ πάσης σαρκός Eun.*exp.fid.*2(p.256); Cyr.*Is.*3.5 (2.527A); **d.** of H. Ghost ὡς δ. καὶ ἀγαθὸς θεὸς μένων εἰς ἀεὶ τὸ πνεῦμα Didym.*Trin.*2.7(M.39.564C); *ib.*3.41(801C); ‡Cyr.*Trin.*9(6[3]. 13C; M.77.1140B); cf.Sev.Ant.*fr.*(*SR* 10 p.204), Jo.D.*hom.*4.6(M.96. 608C) citt. s. B; **e.** denied of Father in relation to Son, Cyr.*thes.* 10(5[1].76D) cit. s. γεννήτωρ; τοῦ δὲ ἰδίου γεννήματος οὐκ ἔστι δ. ἀλλὰ κατὰ φύσιν πατήρ id.*hom.pasch.*11(5[2].159A); **f.** in pagan thought δ. ... πάντων φησὶν ὁ Πυθαγόρειος λόγος τὸν μέγαν γεωμέτρην καὶ ἀριθμητὴν ἥλιον Hipp.*haer.*6.28(p.154.14; M.16.3234D); περὶ τοῦ δ. φησι [sc. Πλάτων] 'τόν...πατέρα...τοῦ παντὸς εὑρεῖν τε ἔργον· καὶ εὑρόντα εἰς πάντας ἐξειπεῖν, ἀδύνατον' Zach.Mit.*opif.*(M.85.1089A); **g.** Gnost. ὁ δὲ Καρποκράτης ἀγγέλους τοῦ κόσμου δ. εἶναί φησι Ath. *Ar.*1.56(M.26.129C); Valentinian τὸν δ. δὲ καὶ αὐτὸν ἄγγελον θεῷ ἐοικότα Iren.*haer.*1.5.2(M.7.496A); τὸν μὲν γὰρ δ. ὡς θεὸν καὶ πατέρα κληθέντα εἰκόνα τοῦ ἀληθινοῦ θεοῦ καὶ προφήτην προσεῖπεν Clem.*str.* 4.13(p.287.28; M.8.1297B); ἐάν...ἀπολογούμενοι περὶ θεοῦ, ἕτερον μὲν εἶναι λέγωσι τὸν ἀγαθόν, οὐδενὸς τούτων ἔχοντα τὴν ἀρχήν, τῷ δὲ δ. πάντων τὰ τοιαῦτα προσάπτωσι... Or.*comm.in Gen.*ap.Eus.*p.e.*6.11 (282C; M.12.53B); cf. ὁ πρῶτος δ. ἐδημιούργησεν *A.Thom.*A 6(p.109. 11); **h.** Marcionite δ. ... τοῦ κόσμου πονηρόν...ἀγαθὸν...θεὸν καταλύοντα τὰ τοῦ δ. ποιήματα Hipp.*haer.*7.30(p.216.1; M.16.3334B); *ib.*6. 33(p.162.5; 3246A); ἄλλον δὲ εἶναι ὁρατὸν θεὸν καὶ κτίστην καὶ δ. Epiph. *haer.*42.3(p.97.5; M.41.697D); οἱ μὲν τὰ Μαρκίωνος νοσοῦντες λέγουσι περὶ τοῦ δ. τοῦ δικαίου μόνον, καὶ οὐκ ἀγαθοῦ, ταῦτα εἰρῆσθαι Chrys. *hom.8.2 in 2Cor.*(10.493D); **i.** Manich., Thdr.Heracl.ap.*cat.Mt.*15:32 (p.127.16); Chrys.*hom.83.4 in Jo.*(8.496A); δ. τῆς κτίσεως ἕτερον ἐπεισαγαγεῖν παρὰ τὸν ὄντα βουλόμενοι id.*hom.8.2 in 2Cor.*(10.493D); φύσεως...δ. ὁ διάβολος ‡Ath.*Apoll.*1.15(M.26.1120C); **j.** ref. Arian argument φασί,...ἀεὶ ποιητής ἐστιν ὁ θεός, καὶ οὐκ ἐπιγέγονεν αὐτῷ τοῦ δημιουργεῖν ἡ δύναμις· ἆρ' οὖν, ἐπειδὴ δ. ἐστιν, ἀΐδιά ἐστι καὶ τὰ ποιήματα, καὶ οὐ θέμις εἰπεῖν οὐδὲ ἐπὶ τούτων, οὐκ ἦν πρὶν γεννηθῇ; ἄφρονες...· τί γὰρ ὅμοιον υἱὸς καὶ ποίημα; Ath.*Ar.*1.29(M.26.72A); εἰ ἐκ διδασκαλίας τὸ δημιουργεῖν τινι προσγίνεται, φθόνον...περὶ τὸν θεὸν εἰσάγουσιν...ὅτι μὴ πολλοὺς δημιουργεῖν ἐδίδαξεν, ἵν' ὥσπερ πολλοί...ἄγγελοι, οὕτω καὶ πολλοὶ δ. περὶ αὐτὸν ὦσιν *ib.*2.29(208B); δ. αὐτοὶ ἀντεισάγουσι τοῦ κόσμου, ἵνα καὶ τοῦ δημιουργεῖν τὸν υἱὸν ἀφέλωνται *ib.*2.38(228C); **k.** in argument agst. Jews: [sc. if they ascribe Christ's healing miracles to Beelzebul] φρονήσουσί ποτε καὶ δ. εἶναι τὸν Βεελζεβοὺλ τῆς ἀνθρωπίνης φύσεως Ath.*ep.Serap.*4.21(M.26.672B).

B. as adj., *creative*, esp. of Son ὁ δ. λόγος Bas.*hom.in Ps.*32 (1.135E; M.29.333B); Epiph.*haer.*69.52(p.199.16; M.42.284B); of H. Ghost δ. τὸ πνεῦμα ὡς ὁ υἱός Sev.Ant.*fr.*(*SR* 10 p.204); τὸ πνεῦμα ...τὸ ζωοποιὸν καὶ δ. Jo.D.*hom.*4.6(M.96.608C); of wisdom, Ath.*Ar.* 2.40(M.26.232A); *ib.*2.77(312A); Didym.*Trin.*3.3(M.39.812B); of fire acc. Messalians, Jo.D.*haer.*80(M.94.732A).

δημοβόρος, *devouring the people*; met., *grasping* δ. βασιλεῖς *Orac.Sib.*11.225; τῶν δ. ἔξαρχος Isid.Pel.*epp.*3.153(M.78.844D).

***δημοδιδάσκαλος, ὁ,** *demagogue*, Synes.*ep.*154(M.66.1553B).

δημοθοινία, ἡ, *public feast*, ref. 1Cor.11:22ff. πανδαισίας καὶ δ. πληροῦντες ἐν ἐκκλησίαις Cyr.*Nest*.4.5(p.86.8; 6^{1}.111D).

***δημοθόρυβος**, *disturbing people*; of ravens' cries, ‡Caes.Naz. *dial*.140(M.38.1072).

δημοκατάρατος, *cursed by the people*, Or.*exp.in Pr*.11:26(M.17. 192B).

δημοκῆρυξ, ὁ, *public crier*, CEph.Orient.*act*.(*ACO* 1.1.5 p.120.21; H.1.1452B).

δημοκοπέω, *force into public life*; pass., Bas.*ep*.33(3.112E; M.32. 320A).

δημοκοπία, ἡ, *popular appeal* πομπείας καὶ δ. τῶν λόγων Bas.Sel. *v.Thecl*.1(M.85.500D).

***δημοκοπικῶς**, *so as to gain popular support* οὔτε δ. τὴν ταπεινοφροσύνην ἐπιτηδεύειν Bas.*reg.fus*.21(2.366C, vv.ll. δημοκοπητικῶς, δημοτικῶς; M.31.976C).

δημοκρατέω, *be in power*; of a circus faction, Jo.Mal.*chron*.10 p.244(M.97.373C); Thphn.*chron*.p.142(M.108.385B).

δημοκρατία, ἡ, **1.** *democracy*; met., of heavenly bodies θαυμαστή γε τῶν ἀτόμων ἡ δ. ... εἰς μίαν...συνοικίαν ἐπειγομένων Dion.Al.ap. Eus.*p.e*.14.25(776D; M.21.1277B); **2.** *popular pressure*, Attic.*ep.Cyr*. (p.23.33; M.77.349D); *ib*.(p.24.11; 352A); **3.** *change of power* among circus factions, Thphn.*chron*.p.154(M.108.416D).

δῆμος, ὁ, **1.** *people*, plur. τοῦ ἐκείνου [sc. God] δ. Const.ap.Eus.*v. C*.2.71(p.70.12; M.20.1045A); τοῖς Χριστοῦ δ. Bas.Sel.*or*.27.1(M.85. 312A); **2.** *company, band*, plur. δ. μαρτύρων ἄπειροι Chrys.*hom. 12.4 in Rom*.(9.547D); τῶν μαρτύρων οἱ δ. Thdt.*Ps*.46:6(1.1571); τῶν ἀοράτων οἱ δ. id.*Eph*.1:10(3.405); **3.** *township, commune* τῷ δ. τῆς Ἀλεξανδρείας Ath.*h.Ar*.48(p.211.7; M.25.752C); **4.** *circus faction* τὸν πλοῦτον ἑαυτοῦ θηριομάχοις προσαναλίσκων, καὶ ταῖς ματαίαις τῶν δ. φωναῖς ἐπαγαλλόμενος Bas.*hom.in Ps*.61(1.196B; M.29.477A); τῶν δ. ἀλλήλοις συναφθέντων Evagr.*h.e*.4.13(p.163.12; M.86.2728A); οἱ δ. τῶν πρασίνων *Chron.Pasch*.p.336(M.92.873A); **5.** *family* Σάτυρος ἱστορῶν τοὺς δ. Ἀλεξανδρέων Thphl.Ant.*Autol*.2.7(M.6.1057A).

Δημοσθενίζω, *imitate Demosthenes*, Gr.Naz.*ep*.190(M.37.312A).

***δημοσίευσις**, ἡ, *publicity, making manifest*; of Second Advent λαθὼν ἦλθον· τότε δὲ μετὰ πολλῆς τῆς δ. Chrys.*hom.53.2 in Mt*. (7.541A); id.*incomprehens*.5.7(1.490D); ἐπαισχύνῃ τῶν αἰσχρῶν τὴν δ. Nil.*Eulog*.14(M.79.1112C); πρὸς...δημοσίευσιν τῶν κεκρυμμένων ἐπενοήθη ἡ εἰκών Jo.D.*imag*.3.17(M.94.1337C).

δημοσιεύ-ω, **A.** *reveal*; **1.** *make known publicly*; in gen., Isid. Pel.*epp*.2.109(M.78.549D); Ammon.*Jo*.12:50(M.85.1480C); οὐράνιος ἀστὴρ ἐδημοσίευσεν αὐτὸν καὶ τὴν γέννησιν αὐτοῦ *Pers*.(p.28.8); ref. Jo. Bapt. μέσος τῶν δύο διαθηκῶν τῆς μὲν καταλύων τὸ γράμμα, τῆς δὲ ~ων τὸ πνεῦμα Gr.Naz.*or*.43.75(M.36.597B); ὁ πρόδρομος...τὸ φῶς τὸ ἀπρόσιτον...~ειν ἀποστελλόμενον Jo.D.*hom*.1.3(M.96.549B); of Christ τὴν πατρικὴν αὐτοῦ περὶ ἡμᾶς ἀγάπην ἐδημοσίευσεν *ib*.2.2 (580A); **2.** *admit to, confess*, sins, Nil.*epp*.1.37(M.79.100D); Bas.Sel. *or*.17.3(M.85.225B); Niceph.Ur.*v.Sym*.15(M.86.3000D); **3.** *bring to light*, Gr.Nyss.*hom.6 in Cant*.(M.44.892A); Pall.*v.Chrys*.20(p.146.22; M.47.82); Thdt.*Ps*.72:1(1.1114); **4.** *show up* a person, to his credit, Bas.Sel.*or*.7.2(M.85.105A); to his discredit, Chrys.*hom.35.4 in Mt*. (7.403C); Anast.S.*Ps*.6(M.89.1084A); **5.** *display publicly*, Gr.Naz. *or*.27.2(p.3.2; M.36.13A); id.*ep*.45(M.37.93B); good works, Sev.Ant. ap.*cat.Mt*.6:3(p.43.18); **6.** *utter publicly*, Bas.*ep*.2.5(3.74A; M.32. 229C); Gr.Naz.*ep*.114(M.37.209C); Synes.*insomn*.14(p.174.10; M.66. 1307B); **7.** *publish* in writing τὸ...ἀπόρρητον...ἐν βίβλοις γράφων ~ει Bas.*Eun*.1.13(1.226A; M.29.544A); **8.** *mark publicly*, Cain σημεῖον εἶχε ~ον αὐτόν †Epiph.*num.myst*.5(M.43.513C); **9.** *appear in public*, Or.*Jo*.28.23(18; p.419.10; M.14.732A); Bars.*resp*.(M.88. 1813C).

B. *be in public service, in public use*, Eus.*h.e*.9.9.10(M.20.824A); Didym.*Ac*.8:39(M.39.1669C); of things, Chrys.*hom.82.4 in Jo*.(8. 487E); ptcpl. as subst., *police*, Marc.Diac.*v.Porph*.99.

δημόσιος, *public*; **1.** fem. as subst., *harlot*, *T.Jud*.23.2; **2.** neut. as subst.; **a.** *public building*; of an amphitheatre, *Ep.Lugd*.ap. Eus.*h.e*.5.1.37(M.20.421C); of public baths, *Chron.Pasch*.p.314 (M.92.797C); **b.** *tax*, Phot.*nomoc*.1.34(M.104.557C); plur., *public affairs*, Chrys.*sac*.6.4(p.149.7; 1.425B); **3.** δημοσίᾳ *publicly*, Just. *2apol*.3.2(M.6.449A); Tat.*orat*.25(p.26.26; M.6.860B); Or.*Cels*.2.63 (p.185.4; M.11.896A).

δημοσίως, *publicly*, Gr.Mag.*dial*.(tr.Zach.)3.37(M.*PL*.77.311B).

***δημοσκοπέω**, *court the populace*, Nil.*epp*.2.215(M.79.312D).

δημότεροι, οἱ, *the people* δημοτέρων ἔριδός με...σάωσον †Apoll. *met.Ps*.18:44(M.33.1333D).

δημοτεύω, *compel to serve as soldiers*, Thphn.*chron*.p.197(M.108. 512A).

δημότης, ὁ, *partisan, member of circus faction*; plur., *Chron. Pasch*.p.337(M.92.880A); *ib*.p.340(887A).

δημοτικός, **1.** *of the common people*; *of the laity* χρῆναι τούτοις, ἐν ταῖς δ. καθέδραις Synes.*ep*.67(M.66.1432A); **2.** neut. as subst., *the people*, Cyr.*ador*.13(1.452D); ἐξείργεται τὸ δ. παντὸς ἱεροῦ πράγματος *ib*.(454D).

δημοφθόρος, *destroying the people*, Geo.Pis.*hex*.343(M.92.1460A).

δημοχαρής, *courting the populace*, Ephr.3.450D; Nil.*Eulog*.22 (M.79.1121C).

δημώδης, **1.** *public* δ. λεηλασίᾳ †Mel.*fr*.(p.307; M.5.1209); **2.** *popular*; **a.** *usual* τῷ δ. ὀνόματι Athenag.*leg*.23.5(M.6.944C); **b.** *proverbial* τὸ δ. ῥῆμα Dion.Al.ap.Eus.*h.e*.7.22.7(M.20.689A); **c.** *common* δ. πλῆθος Eus.*p.e*.11.7(522D; M.21.865C); κόσμον ἐνταῦθα τὸ δ. πλῆθός φησι *cat.Jo*.1:10(p.184.20); **d.** *vulgar, low, coarse* ταῖς δ. ἑστιάσεσιν Clem.*paed*.2.1(p.161.26; M.8.396B); χρῆσιν...τὴν δ. μέν, λαθραίως δὲ καὶ μοιχικῶς ἐπιτελουμένην Ath.*ep.Amun*.(M.26.1173B); neut. as subst. τὸ λαϊκὸν καὶ δ. καὶ ⟨τὸ⟩ ἄναγνον Clem.*paed*.2.10(p.213.16; M.8.508B).

δημωδῶς, *in public*, Or.*Cels*.2.63(p.185.10; M.11.896A).

δηνάριον, τό, *denarius*; met., of BMV χαίροις, καλλιέμπορε τοῦ παρθενικοῦ δ. Thdot.Anc.*hom.BMV et Sym*.3(M.77.1393C).

***δηναρισμός**, ὁ, *valuation in terms of* δηνάρια, Epiph.*mens*.24 (M.43.292A).

***δηπουτᾶτος**, ὁ, (Lat. *deputatus*) *deputy*, Thdr.Al.*libell*.(p.16.2; δηποτᾶτον H.2.324A).

***δησέρτωρ** (*δεσ-), ὁ, (Lat. *desertor*) *deserter* δεσέρτωρ Ign.*Polyc*. 6.2; Bas.*ep*.268(3.414E; M.32.997C).

διά, **I.** c. genit., *through*; v. B;

A. in gen.; **1.** *because of* δ. τῆς ἐνδείας Didym.*Trin*.2.8(M.39.612A); **2.** *at intervals of*, idiom in form δ. δύο (δυῶν, δυοῖν) [sc. ἡμερῶν] *every second* [etc.] *day*; δ. δύο ἐσθίοντες Epiph.*haer*.29.5(p.326.10; M.41.397B); cf.Cyr.S.*v.Cyriac*.(p.225.7); Jo.Disc.*v.Epiph*.9(M.41. 33C); δ. πέντε Pall.*h.Laus*.43(p.130.8; M.34.1210C).

B. theol.; *through, by means of* an agent; **1.** exeg. Jo.1:3, Or. *Jo*.2.10(6; p.64.12; M.14.125A); εἰ πάντα δ. τοῦ λόγου ἐγένετο οὐχ ὑπὸ τοῦ λόγου ἐγένετο *ib*.(p.64.29; 125C); τὸ δὲ δ. τοῦ θεοῦ ἁπλούστερον εἴρηται ἀντὶ τοῦ παρὰ τοῦ θεοῦ...τὸ μὲν ἐκ, ὡς ἐξ ὕλης· τὸ δὲ ὑπό, ὡς αἰτίου, τὸ δὲ δ., ὡς ὀργάνου Proc.G.*Gen*.4:1(M.87.233B); but cf. οἶδε γὰρ τὸ δ. οὗ, τὸ ὑφ' οὗ λέγειν ἡ γραφή...οὐ τὸ δεύτερον αἴτιον ἀλλὰ τὸ πρῶτον τιθεῖσα Chrys.*hom.59.3 in Mt*.(7.598C); **2.** ref. Father; **a.** who works through Son, Thphl.Ant.*Autol*.1.7(M.6. 1036A); Or.*Jo*.2.10(6; p.65.21; 129A); Ath.*ep.Serap*.1.28(M.26.596A); **b.** who is made known through Son, Cyr.ap.*cat.Heb*.suppl.1:8 (p.355.28); cf. εἰς μίαν ἄναρχον τῶν ὅλων ἀρχὴν δ. υἱοῦ...τὰ πάντα ἀνάγομεν *Symb.Sirm*.1 *anath*.26; and creates through Son, Bas. *Spir*.4(3.4D; M.32.73B) etc.; **c.** glorified through Son; **i.** as high priest σὲ δοξάζω διὰ τοῦ...ἀρχιερέως Ἰησοῦ Χριστοῦ...δι' οὗ σοι σὺν αὐτῷ καὶ πνεύματι ἁγίῳ δόξα *M.Polyc*.14.3; αἰνοῦμέν σε, ὑμνοῦμέν σε, δοξολογοῦμέν σε...διὰ τοῦ μεγάλου ἀρχιερέως *Const.App*.7.47.2; **ii.** in doxologies applied esp. to second Person Ἰησοῦ Χριστοῦ, δ. οὗ ἐστιν αὐτῷ ἡ δόξα *1Clem*.58.2; *ib*.64; δ. τοῦ παιδὸς αὐτοῦ τοῦ... Ἰησοῦ Χριστοῦ, δόξα, τιμή, κράτος, μεγαλωσύνη *M.Polyc*.20.2; δ. οὗ τῷ πατρὶ ἡ δόξα καὶ τὸ κράτος Ath.*ep.Afr*.11(M.26.1047C); id.*ep. Serap*.2.6(M.26.617C) cit. s. ἐν; *Const.App*.7.47.3; *ib*.7.49; Gr.Nyss. *Melet*.(M.46.864A); for further reff. v. μετά; with ἐν for third Person v. ἐν; with σύν for third Person v. σύν; in Arian sense, Bas. *Spir*.13(3.10C; M.32.88B) cit. s. μετά; ἐνταῦθα...τὴν δ. οὗ, ἣν οἱ τὰ Ἀρείου καὶ Εὐνομίου φρονοῦντες προσνέμουσι τῷ υἱῷ, ἐπὶ τοῦ πατρὸς τέθεικεν Thdt.*1Cor*.1:1(3.165); defended by Arians as more scriptural, Bas.*Spir*.16(3.13B; M.93B); Basil's refutation ἐν μὲν...τῷ λέγειν 'δ. οὗ ἐλάβομεν χάριν'...τὴν...χορηγίαν ἐμφαίνει· ἐν δὲ τῷ λέγειν 'δ. οὗ τὴν προσαγωγὴν ἐσχήκαμεν', τὴν ἡμετέραν πρόσληψιν...δ. Χριστοῦ πρὸς τὸν θεὸν...παρίστησιν. ἆρ' οὖν ἡ ὁμολογία τῆς ἐνεργουμένης παρ' αὐτοῦ πρὸς ἡμᾶς χάριτος, ὑφαίρεσίς ἐστι τῆς δόξης; *ib*. 17(3.14B; M.96C); *ib*.(3.15A; M.97B) cit. s. μετά; defence of Eusebius of Caesarea's use of δ., Socr.*h.e*.2.21.4f.(M.67.240B); to second and third Persons, Just.*1apol*.65.3 cit. s. προΐστημι; ὁ πατὴρ...ᾧ δ. τοῦ παιδὸς Ἰησοῦ Χριστοῦ...καὶ δ. τοῦ ἁγίου πνεύματος εἴη δόξα, τιμή, κράτος Clem.*q.d.s*.42(p.191.10; M.9.652B); **3.** ref. H. Ghost; **a.** who proceeds from Father through Son, Geo.Laod.*ep.dogm*.(p.289.7; M.42.433B); Epiph.*haer*.76.44(p.398.13; M.42.609D); **b.** is known through Son, Gr.Thaum.*symb*.(p.3.7; M.10.985A); Eus.*e.th*.3.6 (p.163.31; M.24.1013B); cf.*Symb.Sirm*.2(p.257.26; M.26.744A); ‡Cyr. *Trin*.10(6^{3}.17A; M.77.1145A); **c.** through whom comes revelation, Cyr.*thes*.33(5^{1}.333D); perfection, Bas.*Spir*.38(3.32A; M.32.136C); Cyr.*thes*.34(344E); id.*dial.Trin*.7(5^{1}.652D); indwelling of God in men,

Ath.*Ar*.3.25(M.26.376B); Bas.*Eun*.3.5(1.276D; M.29.665B); **d.** who comes into existence through Son (Eunomian), Eun.*apol*.26(M.30.864A); *ib*.(864B); **4.** ref. Inc. ἄνθρωπον αὐτὸν δ. παρθένου γεννηθῆναι Just.*dial*.75.4(M.6.652C); ὁ θεὸς λόγος...ἐτέχθη δ. παρθένου Thdt. Anc.*hom*.2.7(p.77.23; M.77.1377B); (Valent.) of Christ as διά and not ἐκ BMV, v. ἐκ, σωλήν; as mediator between God and man δ. σοῦ γὰρ τὸ μεσότοιχον τοῦ φραγμοῦ τὴν ἔχθραν κατέλυσεν...δ. σοῦ ...εἰρήνη τῷ κόσμῳ ἐδωρήθη ‡Epiph.*hom*.5(M.43.501B); πέπαυται γὰρ δ. σοῦ τὰ τῆς Εὔας στυγηρά· ὤλοντο διὰ σοῦ τὰ φαῦλα Thdt. Anc.*hom.BMV* 12(p.331.9f.); Mod.*dorm*.1(M.86.3281A); indwelling of God in men achieved through Christ, Cyr.*Jo*.9.1(4.824B).

II. c. acc.; **1.** of time, *throughout*, Jo.Mosch.*prat*.137(M.87.3000C); **2.** *by using* δ. ταύτην τὴν πρόφασιν Hegem.*Arch*.8(p.12.9; M.10.1440A); δ. τέχνην...ποιοῦνται Chrys.*hom.3.4 in Phil*.(11.217B); Pall.*h.Laus*.32(p.94.12; M.34.1105A); **3.** *with a view to*, esp. with infin. δ. τὸ εἶναι Epiph.*haer*.52.2(p.312.29; M.41.956C); Jo.Mal. *chron*.15 p.388(M.97.576B); **4.** *with reference to, about, concerning*, Jo.Mal.*chron*.5 p.102(M.97.189B); εἶπεν αὐτῇ δ. Μαρκιανόν *Chron. Pasch*.p.319(M.92.812B).

διαβάθρα, ἡ, 1. *ladder*, met. θεοῦ κάθοδος ἐπ' ἄνθρωπον...δ. [sc. ἐστί] τῶν ἐπειρομένων ἀπολαῦσαι τοῦ ἐκεῖ φωτός Meth.*Porph*.1 (p.504.24; M.18.400C); **2.** *staircase*, Jo.Mosch.*prat*.73(M.87.2925C); **3.** *bridge*; met., of boats, Thdt.*h.e*.3.25.2(3.942).

διαβαίν-ω, 1. *pass through*, Or.*fr.20 in Jo*.(p.500.32); met., temptations, Ath.*v.Anton*.5(M.26.848C); trials, Thdt.*Ezech*.24:6 (2.877); pass. πάντων αὐτῷ διαβαθέντων τῶν κατ' εὐσέβειαν τρόπων Max.*ep*.2(M.91.401D); id.*ambig*.(M.91.1216C); **2.** *pass over, go beyond*, met. νῷ καὶ αὐτὴν τὴν ἀγγελικὴν φύσιν διέβην Thdt.*Cant*.3:4 (2.79); hence *transcend* τὴν ἕξιν δ. Eus.*d.e*.1.8(p.39.6; M.22.76B); **3.** *go over, be transferred*, to ταύτην τέθεικε τὴν αἰτίαν...ἢ πάλιν εἰς τὴν τοῦ θεοῦ δόξαν διέβαινεν Chrys.*hom.17.5 in Mt*.(7.228E); id. *hom.12.1 in 2Cor*.(10.521A); **4.** *progress*; met., ref. etymology of πάσχα: ~ων ἀεὶ τῷ λογισμῷ...ἀπὸ τῶν τοῦ βίου πραγμάτων ἐπὶ τὸν θεόν Or.*Cels*.8.22(p.239.22; M.11.1552A); in gen. δ. ἐπὶ τὸ...φθάσαι τῆς ἀληθείας θεάματα id.*Jo*.13.48(46; p.275.26; M.14.485C); ὁ δὲ ~ων ἀναβαίνει καὶ ἐπὶ τὸ πιστεῦσαι εἰς τὸν υἱὸν τοῦ θεοῦ id.*fr.71 in Jo*. (p.539.20); ἐκ τοῦ παιδὸς ἐπὶ τὸν νεανίαν δ. Eus.*v.C*.1.19(p.17.20; M.20.936A); εἰς τὸν...πατέρα ἡ πίστις ~ει δι' ἐμοῦ [sc. Christ] Apoll. ap.*cat.Jo*.12:44(p.333.14); **5.** *proceed, pass on*; met., Eus.*v.C*.3.35 (p.93.25; M.20.1096A); ἐπὶ τὸν ὕστατον αὐτοῦ τῆς ζωῆς διαβησόμεθα χρόνον *ib*.4.39(p.132.31; 1188C); **6.** perf. ptcpl., *advanced* λόγον... δεόμενον σοφοῦ...καὶ ἐπὶ πλεῖον διαβεβηκότος Or.*Cels*.7.32(p.182.22; M.11.1465A); hence *consummate* διαβεβηκόσι καὶ τελεωτέροις ἀθληταῖς id.*or*.29.2(p.382.18; M.11.532B).

διαβάλλω, *reprove, reproach* (without malice) μετὰ πολλῆς δ. [sc. Jo. Bapt.] τῆς παρρησίας Chrys.*hom.11.1 in Mt*.(7.149E); τοὺς ἄρχοντας...δ. [sc. Christ] *ib.68.2*(7.672B).

διαβαπτίζομαι, *overwhelm, submerge*, Tit.Bost.*Man*.2.7(M.18.1145B).

διάβασις, ἡ, 1. *crossing over, passage*; hence *Passover* in etym. of πάσχα: ἡ τοῦ πάσχα ἑορτὴ...παντὸς πάθους καὶ παντὸς αἰσθητοῦ δ. οὖσα Clem.*str*.2.11(p.140.10; M.8.988A); τὸ πάσχα τοῦτο...φάσκα τοῖς Ἑβραίοις προσαγορεύεται...δηλοῖ δὲ...τὴν δ. Gr.Naz.*or*.45.10(M.36.636B); Cyr.*ador*.17(1.598D) cit. s. διαβατήριος; φασὲκ ὁ τῆς ἑορτῆς... καιρός, δηλοῖ δὲ δ. id.*Lc*.22:8(M.72.904B); πάσχα κυρίου, δ. ἀπὸ κακίας Dor.*doct*.22(M.88.1821C); *Chron.Pasch*.p.226(M.92.549B); met., freq. with etym. of πάσχα in mind ἀθυμίας νέφος...οὐκ ἀφίησιν εὔκολον γίνεσθαι τὴν τοῦ λόγου δ. Chrys.*stat*.2.3(2.23B); ἡμῖν δ. βαπτίσματος Cosm.Ind.*top*.5(M.88.196A); προκάλυμμα τῆς...τοῦ νοῦ πρὸς τὰ νοητὰ δ. Max.*ambig*.(M.91.1124B); **2.** *means of crossing, conduit*, ‡Epiph.*v.proph.Is*.1(p.20; M.43.397B,420B).

***διαβασκαίνω,** *continually begrudge, show ill will* to, c. dat., Or. *Ps*.5:9(p.455).

διαβαστάζ-ω, 1. *carry over*, met. χεῖρα τὸν μακάριον αἰτῶ προτεῖναί μοι μάρτυρα ~οντα τὸν λόγον ἐν τῷ πελάγει τοῦ θαύματος Sophr.H.*v.Anast*.(M.92.1708A); **2.** *carry, bear*, *A.Andr.et Mt*.16 (p.84.9); †Jo.D.*B.J*.40(M.96.1232D); abs., Niceph.Ur.*v.Sym*.179 (M.86.3152B); met., *sustain* τὸ σῶμα ἀναπαύλαις ~όμενον Clem. *paed*.2.9(p.207.21; M.8.496C); Eus.*Is*.49:23(M.24.440A); of God ἐν αὐτῷ [sc. temptation]...~ων ἡμᾶς Chrys.*paralyt*.2(3.36A); **3.** *endure, tolerate*, Epiph.*haer*.59.4(p.368.13; M.41.1024C); Chrys.*hom.70.1 in Jo*.(8.414A); id.*hom.11.2 in Col*.(11.407D); abs., id.*hom.27.2 in Rom*. (9.720C).

***διαβαστάω,** *contain*, Melet.*nat.hom*.22(M.64.1229B).

διαβατήριος, 1. *of the Passover*, Gr.Naz.*ep*.120(M.37.213C); **2.** neut. as subst., *crossing over, passage*; **a.** *Passover* in etym. of πάσχα: πάσχα ὅπερ ἑρμηνεύεται διαβατήρια, διαβαίνων ἀεὶ τῷ λογισμῷ ...ἀπὸ τῶν τοῦ βίου πραγμάτων ἐπὶ τὸν θεόν Or.*Cels*.8.22(p.239.22; M.11.1552A); Eus.*pasch*.1(M.24.696A); πάσχα...ἐστὶ κυρίου, τουτέστι, διάβασις ἤτοι διαβατήρια Cyr.*ador*.17(1.598D); *Chron.Pasch*.p.227 (M.92.552C); **b** met. θάνατος δ. γίνεται τῆς ἀιδίου ζωῆς †Jo.D.*B.J*.4 (M.96.888B).

διαβατικός, *penetrating* γεγόναμεν...διαβατικοὶ τὴν διάνοιαν Gr. Naz.*or*.4.124(M.35.664C); comp., ‡Thdt.*nativ.Jo.Bapt*.(5.91).

διαβεβαιωτικός, *affirmative*; gram., *indicative* τὸ ὁριστικὸν ὑπό τινων καλούμενον δ. Or.*sel.in Ps*.4:5(M.12.1141D).

***διαβεβλημένως,** *slanderously*, *cat.Apoc*.16:13ff.(p.418.19).

διάβημα, τό, *step*; fig., Or.*exc.in Ps*.16:14(M.17.109E); Gr.Naz.*or*. 8.12(M.35.801C); ‡Pion.*v.Polyc*.16; met., exeg. Ps.17:37 διαβήματα λέγει καθ' ἃ ἐκ κακίας εἰς ἀρετήν, καὶ ἐξ αἰσθητῶν ἐπὶ νοητά, καὶ ἀπὸ τοῦ παρόντος αἰῶνος εἰς τὸν μέλλοντα διαβαίνει Cyr.*Ps*.17:37(M.69.825B); exeg. Ps.16:5 διαβήματα...τῆς πράξεως τὴν ὁρμὴν προσηγόρευσεν Thdt.*Ps*.16:5(1.696); διὰ δακρύων ἀποκαθαρθῆναι τοὺς πόδας ἤτοι τὰ σαρκικὰ δ. Eulog.*fr.Novat*.(M.104.388A).

διαβήτης, ὁ, *pair of compasses*, Dor.*doct*.6.9(M.88.1696B).

***διαβίωσις, ἡ,** *course of life*, Epiph.*haer*.24.1(p.256.21; M.41.308D); Gr.Nyss.*v.Ephr*.(M.46.832D); Thdr.Stud.*epp*.1.31(M.99.1013C); *ib*. 2.69(1297C).

διαβιώσκω, *survive*, *cat.Apoc*.6:6(p.269.21).

***διάβλεψις, ἡ,** *clear vision*, Or.*comm.in Mt*.11.14(p.58.6; M.13.949B).

***διαβλητέος,** *necessarily to be found fault with*, Tat.*orat*.4(p.5.14; M.6.813B); neut., *one must find fault with*, Clem.*str*.2.6(p.129.2; M.8.965A).

διαβλήτωρ, ὁ, *slanderer*, Thdr.Stud.*conf*.6(M.99.1724C).

διαβλύζ-ω, *pour forth*, fig. αἱ τῆς δεσποτικῆς φιλανθρωπίας πηγαὶ τοῖς πιστεύουσι ~ουσι τἀγαθά Thdt.*ep*.26(4.1089).

διαβο-άω, *make to resound* with πᾶσαν...Ἑλλάδα...ψευδέσι φήμαις ~ῶσιν Const.*or.s.c*.10(p.164.29; M.20.1257B).

διαβόησις, ἡ, *crying out* or *aloud*; plur., Const.*or.s.c*.11(p.167.16; M.20.1261B).

***διαβοήτως,** *loudly*, Thdr.Stud.*epp*.1.48(M.99.1073D).

διαβολή, ἡ, 1. *censure* κατηγορίας ἄξιος καὶ δ. Chrys.*hom.6.3 in 2Tim*.(11.696F); id.*hom.23.4 in Heb*.(12.217B); ταῖς ἐκ νόμου δ. ὑπενηνεγμένους Cyr.*ador*.14(1.503A); **2.** *ground for censure* ἡδονὴ... ἢ μὴ πρόσεστι τὸ χρειῶδες, ἤθους ἐστὶν ἑταιρικοῦ διαβολή Clem.*paed*. 2.8(p.198.21; M.8.476B); οὐδὲ...εἰ θαυμαστὸν οἶκον...λάβοι...λῃστής, δ. τῆς οἰκίας τὸ γινόμενον Chrys.*hom.13.3 in Rom*.(9.561C); id.*hom. 48.1 in Jo*.(8.284B); *blameworthiness* διαβολῆς τῆς ἐσχάτης...ἀνάπλεων τὴν...νόσον Cyr.*ador*.6(1.178B); *ib*.(1.179D); **3.** *dislike, hatred* αὐτόματον ἔχομεν τὴν πρὸς τὰ λυποῦντα δ. Bas.*hex*.9.4(1.83D; M.29.196C).

διαβολικός, 1. *belonging to the Devil*, acc. Valentinus of human body ἐκ τῆς δ. οὐσίας πεπλασμένος Hipp.*haer*.6.34(p.163.13; M.16.3246C); ἡ κακία ἐπλήμμυρε τῇ δ. ... φύσει Gr.Nyss.*res*.1(M.46.609C); of power, Or.*fr.54 in Jer*.(p.225.17); id.*Ps*.35:13(p.9); Cyr.H. *catech*.22.7; Nil.*epp*.2.314(M.79.353C); of demons and men, *M.Pion*. 14.9; Ath.*apol.Const*.7(M.25.604D); Cyr.*Abac*.1(3.531E); **2.** *inspired by the Devil, emanating from the Devil*; of persons, Ath.*Ar*.3.8(M.26.337A); of acts and practices, *A.Pil*.B 1.1(p.288); Ath.*fug*.23 (p.83.28; M.25.673B); Chrys.*hom.26.3 in Heb*.(12.240C); τὸ ἐν ταῖς θλίψεσι σαλεύεσθαι δ. ἐστι id.*hom.4.1 in 1Thess*.(11.452D); of paganism, id.*hom.4.1 in Rom*.(9.454D) cit. s. δόγμα; esp. of idolatry, Cyr.*Jo*.11.7(4.963B); Olymp.*fr.in Jer*.48:13(M.93.708B); ‡Jo.D. *Artem*.69(p.100.33; M.96.1317A); of mental states and processes, Ath.*Ar*.2.38(M.26.228B); ‡Bas.*const*.7.1(2.553A; M.31.1365B); Cyr. *Os*.4(3.97B); of temptation, Const.ap.Eus.*v.C*.2.71(p.70.9; M.20.1045A); *Lit.Jac*.(p.54.7); of wine (Encratite view), Epiph.*haer*.47.1 (p.216.12; M.41.852B); **3.** *like that of the Devil, diabolical*; of deceit, Or.*enarr.in Job* 2:9(M.17.61A); Bas.Anc.al.*libell*.(H.4.41E); of cruelty, Const.ap.Eus.*v.C*.3.20(p.87.18; M.20.1080B); freq. of immorality, Clem.*str*.3.12(p.233.2; M.8.1181B); Chrys.*hom.51.5 in Mt*. (7.527A); *ib.73.4*(713E).

***διαβολικῶς,** *diabolically*, Chrys.*hom.28.5 in 1Cor*.(10.256E).

διάβολος, ὁ, A. *calumniator, slanderer*, Polyc.*ep*.5.2; *Const.App*. 3.12.3; Chrys.*hom.8.1 in 2Tim*.(11.706E); ὁ δ. ἐξ ἑαυτοῦ προῆλθεν δ. Proc.G.*Gen*.1:2(M.87.45B).

B. *Devil, Satan*, prince of demons, leader of evil angels; **1.** in gen., Just.*1apol*.28.1(M.6.372B); *V.Aberc*.41(p.31.6); Clem.*str*.5.14 (p.387.5; M.9.136B); Ath.*ep.Aeg.Lib*.1(M.25.540B); **2.** derivation of name; **a.** from διαβάλλω (*calumniate*), Cyr.H.*catech*.2.4; Chrys. *diab*.2.2(2.262B); ‡Caes.Naz.*dial*.123(M.38.1016); cf. *Graece vero* *diabolus criminator vocatur, quod vel crimina...ad deum referat, vel quia electorum innocentiam criminibus fictis accusat*, Isid.H.*etym.* 8.11.18; **b.** from διαβάλλω (*cross over*), Evagr.Pont.*ep.*10(M.32.264A); **3.** origin and nature; **a.** Gnost. etc.; **i.** Valentinian τὴν ὑλικὴν οὐσίαν ἐκ τριῶν παθῶν συστῆναι...φόβου τε, καὶ λύπης, καὶ ἀπορίας. ... ἐκ...τῆς λύπης τὰ πνευματικὰ τῆς πονηρίας...γεγονέναι· ὅθεν τὸν δ. τὴν γένεσιν ἐσχηκέναι Iren.*haer.*1.5.4(M.7.497A); ὁ δ. ... ἄρχων τοῦ κόσμου Hipp.*haer.*6.34(p.162.13; M.16.3246A); ἡ σοφία... ἐξέπεσε τῶν οὐρανῶν. ... εἶτα στενοῦσα, ἐκ τῶν στεναγμῶν ἐγέννα τὸν δ. ... καὶ...ὁ δ. ἐγέννησεν ἄλλους, οἵτινες κατεσκεύασαν τὸν κόσμον Cyr.H.*catech.*6.18; **ii.** Marcionite τὸν δ. αὐτοφυῆ...καὶ αὐτογένητον Adam.*dial.*3.3(p.118.12; M.11.1793C); **iii.** Manich., God and Devil as eternal principles, Epiph.*haer.*66.8(p.29.4; M.42.41B); **iv.** equated by other heretics with σκότος, Proc.G.*Gen.*1:2(M.87.45B); **b.** orthodox; **i.** a creature, Or.*Jo.*2.13(7; p.69.20; M.14.136C); Meth.*res.*1.36(p.276.10; M.41.1101B,C); Ath.*Ar.*2.70(M.26.296A); ref. Job 40:14 τὸν δ. πρῶτον κτίσμα εἶναι λέγει Didym.*Trin.*1.17(M.39.341B); Areth.*Apoc.*54(M.106.720C); being an archangel ἀγαθὸς κατασκευασθείς, δ. γέγονεν ἐξ οἰκείας προαιρέσεως...ἀρχάγγελος γὰρ ὤν, δ. ὕστερον ἐκλήθη Cyr.H.*catech.*2.4; Hesych.H.*fr.Ps.*81:7(M.93.1260B); one of cherubim, Ath.*ep.Serap.*1.26(M.26.592B); **ii.** mutable, Evagr.Pont.*ep.*10(M.32.264A); **iii.** of same essence as good angels, Or.*Jo.*20.23(20; p.357.20; M.14.625B); Ath.*ep.Serap.*1.26(592B); having authority of angel, ‡Bas.*Lac.*8(2.592E; M.31.1452B); immortal, Gr.Nyss.*Eun.*2(1 p.367.17; M.45.1092B); Antip.Bost.*fr.*(M.86.2077B); incorporeal, Gr.Nyss.*paup.*(M.46.456A); Chrys.*hom.* 22.2 *in Gen.*(4.196B); Thdt.*haer.*5.8(4.407); not evil by nature, as proved from Rom.7:13, Didym.*Rom.*7(p.3.37); and from 2Cor. 11:14, id.*2Cor.*11:13ff.(p.40.12); possessing free will, Adam.*dial.*3.9(p.128.10; M.11.1801A); Bas.*hom.*9.8(2.80B; M.31.345D); Epiph.*haer.* 66.16(p.40.1; M.42.52D); ‡Ath.*dial.Trin.*1.15(M.28.1141A); **iv.** place of origin δεικνυσιν ὁ ἀπόστολος ὅτι οὐκ ἀπ' οὐρανοῦ ἄγγελος ἦν ὁ δ., ἀλλ' ἀέριόν τι πονηρὸν πνεῦμα Sever.*Eph.*2:2f.(p.308.5); **4.** fall; **a.** pre-cosmic, Chrys.*hom.*22.2 *in Gen.*(4.195D); ‡Caes.Naz.*dial.*123(M.38.1016); **b.** due to his own wickedness, Or.*princ.*1.8.3(p.100.4); result of exercise of free will, Cyr.H.*catech.*2.4; Bas.*hom.*9.8(2.80C; M.31.348A); Chrys.*diab.*2.2(2.262B); Petr.Laod.*or.dom.*(p.111.8; M.86.3333C); Thdt.*affect.*3(p.97.4; 4.789); voluntary, id.*haer.*5.8(4.409); Jo.D.*drac.*(M.94.1600A); †Jo.D.*B.J.*6(M.96.908A); due to pride, Or.*princ.*3.1.12(p.216.8; M.11.272A); cf.Ath.*virg.*5(p.39.17; M.28.257A); Chrys.*hom.*16.4 *in Jo.*(8.94D); Thdt.*haer.*5.8(4.407) cit. s. ἔκπτωσις; Jo.Clim.*scal.*25(M.88.1001C); Anast.S.*hod.*4(M.89.93C); **c.** post-cosmic, due to envy of man, Meth.*res.*1.37(p.278.11; M.18.293B); *Const.App.*6.27.6; ‡Bas.*Lac.*8(2.593E; M.31.1452B); **d.** irretrievable, Cyr.H.*catech.*4.1; ‡Bas.*Lac.*8(2.594B; M.31.1453C); Chrys.*poenit.*1.2(2.281D); hence οὐκ ἔστι τῷ δ. μέρος ἐν παραδείσῳ Synes.*ep.*58(M.66.1401C); cf.Clem.*fr.*24(p.214.1; M.9.738A); **5.** destiny, to be cast into fire with his hosts, Just.*1apol.*28.1(M.6.372B); ‡Hipp.*consumm.* 40(p.305.24; M.10.941C); Chrys.*Thdr.*1.9(1.11A); Jo.D.*f.o.*2.4(M.94.877B); cf.Iren.*haer.*3.23.2; before Christ's advent, being ignorant of his future destiny, Devil did not dare to blaspheme against God, Epiph.*haer.*39.9(p.78.20; M.41.673D); ἐπειδὴ δὲ ἧκεν...ὁ σωτήριος λόγος, τῷ...δ. ... προμηνύων τὴν ἀναμένουσαν αὐτὸν δίκην... σφοδρότερον ἔπνευσε καθ' ἡμῶν, καὶ τὰς αἱρέσεις ἔτεκε Isid.Pel.*epp.* 2.90(M.78.533C); **6.** has power given to him over the air, Ath.*inc.* 25.5f.(M.25.140B) cit. s. δαίμων; Gr.Nyss.*paup.*1(M.46.456B); Thdt.*haer.*5.8(4.407); Bas.Sel.*or.*23.1(M.85.269C); **7.** relations with man; **a.** as enemy of God, always hostile to man as God's image, Or.*Jo.*20.23(20; p.356.27; M.14.624C); ‡Bas.*Lac.*9(2.594E; M.31.1456C); Chrys.*stat.*20.5(2.206C); id.*hom.*4.3 *in Tit.*(11.752C); Thdt.*affect.*3(p.97.4; 4.789); **b.** is envy personified ἐν δὲ τῷ δ. ... οὐκ ἔστιν εἰκὼν ζήλου, ἀλλ' αὐτόζηλος Or.*sel.in Ezech.*8:4(M.13.796D); Bas.*hom.*9.8(2.80C; M.31.348A); Chrys.*hom.*48.1 *in Jo.*(8.283A); Eus.Al.*serm.*7(M.86.356B); ἤγειρεν ἡ θέα [sc. of Adam's happiness] πρὸς βασκανίαν δ. Bas.Sel.*or.*3.3(M.85.53C); **c.** contrived man's fall by deceit, Ath.*ep.Aeg.Lib.*2(M.25.540C); Chrys.*hom.*16.2 *in Gen.*(4.124D–125C); †Jo.D.*B.J.*7(M.96.908B); so brought death to man, Meth.*symp.*5.5(p.59.8; M.18.105B); Cyr.*Jo.*1.9(4.86B); **d.** deceit to be expressed in last days ὁ δ. ἐκ μιαρᾶς γυναικὸς ἐξελεύσεται... τίκτεται ἐν πλάνῃ ἐκ παρθένου. ὁ γὰρ θεὸς ἡμῶν σαρκικῶς ἡμῖν ἐπεδήμησε...ὁ δὲ δ. εἰ καὶ σάρκα ἀναλάβοι, ἀλλὰ ταῦτα ἐν δοκήσει ‡Hipp.*consumm.*22(p.298.5; M.10.925A); **e.** surrounding man with snares, Ign.*Trall.*8.1; *2Clem.*18.2; Herm.*mand.*4.3.4; *Const.App.*7.32.4; accompanies men in person of his emulators, Clem.*str.*4.14(p.290.1; M.18.1301C); in whom he dwells, *T.Neph.*8.6; Didym.*Rom.*7(p.5.18); ‡Ath.*Maced.dial.*1.11(M.28.1305D); as being his children, Or.*hom.*9.4 *in Jer.*(p.70.5; M.13.356C); Cyr.H.*catech.*2.4; Chrys.*hom.*54.3 *in Jo.*(8.318D); called by his name, *ib.*75.4(444A); esp. Judas, Epiph.*haer.*38.4(p.67.15; M.41.660C); Cyr.*Jo.*4.4(4.395A); Ammon.*Jo.*6:71(M.85.1441B); the wicked being of his essence ὁμοουσίους τινὰς τῷ διαβόλῳ λέγων [sc. Heracleon] ἀνθρώπους Or.*Jo.*20.20(18; p.352.33; M.14.617A); **f.** responsible for all sin, Meth.*res.*2.2(p.331.18; M.18.297C); Cyr.H.*catech.*19.5; Ath.*ep.Aeg.Lib.*1(M.25.540B); equated with ἁμαρτία, Didym.*Rom.*7(pp.1.11,3.20,37); Diod.*Rom.*7:8(p.87.21); fomenter of evil desires, Herm.*mand.*12.2.2; Meth.*res.*2.2(p.331.3; M.18.297B); †Bas.*bapt.*1.2.19(2.643D; M.31.1560B); inspirer of ridicule, Chrys.*hom.*84.3 *in Jo.*(8.502A); sower of sinful thoughts, ‡Ath.*Apoll.*2.6(M.26.1141A); esp. of heresy, Ath.*ep.Aeg.Lib.*3(M.25.544C); Isid.Pel.*epp.*2.90(M.78.533C); acc. one view ἡ...Ἑλληνικὴ φιλοσοφία...ἐκ τοῦ δ. τὴν κίνησιν ἔχει Clem.*str.*1.16(p.52.17; M.8.796A); **8.** defeated by Christ, *Lit.* ap.*Const.App.*8.12.33; ‡Ath.*pass.*29(M.28.236A); Chrys.*hom.*2.1 *in Mt.*(7.20B); subjected to God's will and power, Cyr.H.*catech.*8.4; Antip.Bost.*fr.*(M.86.2077C); so that faithful need not fear, Herm.*mand.*7.2; *T.Neph.*8.4; Chrys.*hom.*32.3 *in Jo.*(8.188C); has involuntarily benefited mankind, id.*Stag.*1.4(1.163D); id.*diab.*2.4(2.264D); *ib.*3.2(269A); being created, despite God's foreknowledge of his fall, for man to be able to prove himself in contest and win crown of victory, Cyr.H.*catech.*8.4; ‡Ath.*qu.Ant.*11(M.28.604C); Thdt.*qu.*36 *in Gen.*(1.47); **9.** as antichrist, v. σατανᾶς, ἀντίχριστος; **10.** equated with God's wrath, Or.*Apoc.*30(p.6.25); Proc.G.*2Reg.* 22:1(M.87.1144B).

C. as jocular mode of address to slave ἐλθέ, δ., ἐξυπόλυσόν με Gr.Mag.*dial.*(tr.Zach.)3.20(M.*PL.*77.270C).

D. as adj., *slanderous, tale-bearing*, *Hom.Clem.*3.46; *Const.App.* 3.12.3; Thdr.Mops.*2Tim.*3:2(p.214.23; M.66.945C).

***διαβολότης, ἡ,** *form proper to the Devil* οὐ προσῆλθε τῇ Εὔᾳ γυμνῇ τῇ ἑαυτοῦ δ. ‡Ath.*qu.al.*20(M.28.793C,D).

***διαβομβέομαι,** *sound meaninglessly*, Dion.Ar.*d.n.*4.11(M.3.708C).

διαβούλιον, τό, 1. *counsel, plan*, †Bas.*Is.*120(1.462C; M.30.312C); Cyr.*Ps.*9:23(M.69.780A); **2.** *inclination* τὰ δύο δ. ἐν στέρνοις ἡμῶν *T.Aser* 1.3.

διαβρέχω, *water*; met., Chrys.*hom.*29.4 *in Heb.*(12.278A).

διαβριθής, 1. *weighed down*, Cyr.*ador.*5(1.151C); **2.** *heavy, burdensome*, Cyr.*Os.*132(3.165D); id.*Am.*69(3.327B); id.*Juln.*9(6^2.325B).

διαβρωτικός, *consuming*, neut. as subst. τὸ δ. αὐτοῦ [sc. fire] Chrys.*hom.*20.1 *in Heb.*(12.187B).

***διαγαργαλίζ-ω,** *titillate*; met., *tempt, seduce*, of things of sense ὑπερεθίζει γὰρ ταῦτα καὶ ∼ει καὶ παρακαλεῖ τὴν ψυχὴν προσπάσχειν αὐτοῖς Mac.Aeg.*carit.*20(M.34.925B).

διαγγελία, ἡ, *announcement*, Or.*comm.in Gen.*ap.*philoc.*23.20(p.209.12; M.12.84B).

διαγγέλλ-ω, *announce, proclaim, preach* χάρις...∼ουσα καιρούς ‡*Diogn.*11.5; ἄγγελος...καλεῖται...ἐκ τοῦ ∼ειν τοῖς ἀνθρώποις τὰ παρὰ τοῦ πατρός Just.*dial.*60.3(M.6.613A); διήγγελτο τὸ εὐαγγέλιον αὐτοῖς Hipp.*haer.*7.26(p.204.26; M.16.3315B); ἐκεῖνοι [sc. OT prophets]... τὰ τοῦ δεσπότου διήγγελον, οὗτος δὲ τὰ τοῦ πατρός Chrys.*hom.*16.5 *in Mt.*(7.211A); hence *make evident*, Philost.*h.e.*11.3(M.65.597A).

διάγγελμα, τό, *announcement*, Nil.*epp.*1.188(M.79.153C); Leo Mag.*ep.*44(M.*PL.*54.828B; ἀγγέλῳ p.25.23); †Jo.D.*B.J.*1(M.96.864A); of Annunciation, Sophr.H.*or.*2.18(M.87.3237B).

διάγγελος, ὁ, 1. *preacher*, Gr.Naz.*carm.*1.2.10.560(M.37.720A); **2.** as adj., *proclaiming* ναῦς ναυπηγοῖο διάγγελος *ib.*2.2(poem.)7.68(1556A).

***διάγγελσις, ἡ,** = διάγγελμα, Cyr.*hom.pasch.*11(5^2.144A).

***διαγγελτήρ, ὁ,** *messenger*, *Orac.Sib.*7.33.

διάγλυφος, *carved*, Gr.Nyss.*hom.*4 *in Cant.*(M.44.840A); id.*ep.*25(M.46.1100A).

διαγλύφω, *pick* the teeth, Clem.*paed.*2.7(p.193.23; γλύφοντες M.8.465A).

***διαγνεύω,** *purify thoroughly* δ. ... τὴν καρδίαν Meth.*symp.*5.4(p.58.5; M.18.104B).

***διαγνίζ-ω,** *clean thoroughly* ∼εται...τὰ ταῖς θυσίαις ὑπηρετοῦντα σκεύη Cyr.*ador.*12(1.442C).

διαγνώμων, ὁ, *arbitrator*, Cyr.*ador.*13(1.476C).

διάγνωσις, ἡ, 1. *discerning* ἡ δὲ ἀληθὴς φρόνησις δ. ἐστι τῶν ποιητέων καὶ οὐ ποιητέων Bas.*hom.*12.6(2.103A; M.31.400A); **2.** *discernment* τὴν ψυχὴν...πάσης πληροῦν ἀληθοῦς δ. Max.*ambig.*(M.91.1125A); hence *judgement* τὴν τοῦ μέλλοντος ἡμέραν τῆς οἰκουμενικῆς δ. Nil.*epp.*3.133(M.79.445A); τῇ φοβερᾷ ἡμέρᾳ τῆς δ. Thdt.*Cant.*3:4(2.78).

διαγογγύζω, 1. *mutter* or *murmur among themselves* δ. κατὰ τοὺς

Ἰουδαίους Ath.*decr.*1(p.1.10; M.25.416A); abs., *T.Job* 14(p.112.5); **2.** *grumble at*; c. acc., Clem.*str.*3.4(p.213.22; M.8.1141C); c. dat., Ast.Am.*prod.*(p.107.7).

διαγόρευσις, ἡ, 1. *declaration*, Thdr.Mops.*symb.*(p.98.15; M.66. 1017B); **2.** *precept* of Law, id.*Rom.*7:5(p.125.33; M.66.808B); Thdt.*1Tim.*1:10(3.641).

***διαγορευτικός,** *declaratory*, Chrys.*hom.2.2 in 1Tim.*(11.557C).

διαγραφή, ἡ, 1. *description* τῆς τοῦ Νείλου δ. Clem.*str.*6.3(p.449. 12; M.9.253B); **2.** *delineation* ἀποβλέψαντας ἐκ τῆς δ. τὸν δημιουργήσαντα νοῆσαι θεόν *Hom.Clem.*1.18; **3.** *outline*, i.e. *foundations* of a building, Jo.Mosch.*prat.*92(M.87.2952A); **4.** *levy, tax*, *Chron.Pasch.* p.389(M.92.997A).

διαγράφ-ω, 1. *paint* ἡ μὴ χρώμασι ∼ουσα τὸ πρόσωπον Chrys. *hom.4.3 in 1Tim.*(11.571C); fig., id.*hom.13.3 in 1Cor.*(10.112C); **2.** *imagine, conceive* διάγραψόν μοι δύο ἡμαρτηκότας τὴν αὐτὴν... ἁμαρτίαν Or.*hom.20.9 in Jer.*(p.191.18; M.13.521A); *ib.*(p.191.26; 521B); πρότερος...ὁ λογισμὸς ∼ει τὴν ἁμαρτίαν Thdt.*ep.*145(4.1250); **3.** ? *write down to pay, make to pay*, c. dupl. acc. Εὐθάλιος, ὃν...εἰς μείζω τάξιν μεταχωρήσαντα, ∼ειν ἐπιχειροῦσι χρυσὸν οἱ τῆς ἡγεμονικῆς τάξεως Gr.Naz.*ep.*9(M.37.36B); med., *reckon* at τοὺς ἀναιρεθέντας ∼ονται εἰς τριακοσίας μυριάδας ‡Hipp.Th.*fr.*20 (p.54.24).

διαγρηγορέω, 1. *be fully awake*, Nil.*epp.*4.62(M.79.580D); **2.** *start into full wakefulness*, Cyr.*apol.Thdt.*3(p.118.14; 6¹.212A).

διαγυμνάζ-ω, 1. *keep in hard exercise*; met., of God ∼οντος...τοὺς ἁγίους Cyr.*Mich.*63(3.464A); δ. τὴν ἐκκλησίαν id.*Soph.*18(3.599B); δ. ... τῶν ἁγίων τὴν πίστιν id.*Zach.*8(3.663A); pass., Petr.I Al.*ep.can.* 1(M.18.468B); Ephr.3.214C; εἰ...πρὸς ἄσκησιν ἀρετῆς τὸν λόγον ∼οιμεν τὸν ἐν ἡμῖν, ὥσπερ σῶμα τῇ εὐμέτρῳ κινήσει Tit.Bost.*Man.*2(M.18. 1136A); med. ∼εσθαι τὴν τῶν μαθητῶν ψυχὴν εἰς τὸ πιστεύειν τῇ θείᾳ αὐτοῦ δυνάμει Thdr.Mops.*Mt.*15:34(M.66.709D); **2.** *wrestle with*, met. πρέπει τὴν ψυχὴν...τὰ περὶ τοῦ θείου νόμου ∼ειν Constantius Imp.ap.Ath.*syn.*55(p.278.3; M.26.792A); Cyr.*Nest.*1.7(p.27.25; 6¹. 23B); pass., id.*ador.*16(1.582A); Max.*schol.c.h.*2.4(M.4.44A); **3.** *make suitable* καιροῦ πρὸς τοῦτο τοὺς λόγους ∼οντος ἀκονιτὶ διαδείξομεν Cyr.*Juln.*5(6².160B).

***διαγυμνασία, ἡ,** *hard exercise*; met., of spiritual conflict τὴν αὐτάρκη δ. Eus.*h.e.*10.4.15(M.20.853C); id.*d.e.*1.5(p.22.21; M.22. 48B).

διαγωγή, ἡ, 1. *way, manner* βιβλίον...ἐν ᾧ ὅλην τὴν τοῦ μύθου αὐτῶν δ. ... γνώσεται Hipp.*haer.*5.27(p.133.19; M.16.3203C); τὴν καθαράν...τοῦ βίου δ. Gr.Nyss.*v.Macr.*(p.372.7; M.46.961A); **2.** *way of life*, Chrys.*hom.9.2 in Jo.*(8.56A); Nil.*exerc.*7(M.79.725D); of monks τὸν χῶρον...ἐν ᾧ τὴν δ. εἶχον Gr.Nyss.*v.Macr.*(p.410.23; M.46. 996C); Chrys.*sac.*6.6(p.151.6; 1.426A); of Christians, Just.*1apol.*8.2 (M.6.337B); of Christ on earth, Ath.*inc.*19.4(M.25.129C).

διαγωνίζομαι, *decide the conflict*; hence *be decisive*; of an argument, Zach.Mit.*opif.*(M.85.1120B).

διαδάκν-ω, *bite*; hence *feed on* οὓς γὰρ ἂν φιλῶμεν, καὶ ∼ομεν πολλάκις. ... καὶ ὁ Χριστὸς τῶν σαρκῶν αὐτοῦ ἔδωκεν ἡμῖν πλησθῆναι, εἰς φιλίαν πλείονα ἡμᾶς ἐπισπώμενος Chrys.*hom.24.4 in 1Cor.* (10.218A).

διαδατέομαι, *divide*, fut. διαδάσσομαι for LXX διαμεριῶ †Apoll. *met.Ps.*107:8(M.33.1480C).

διαδέχ-ομαι, 1. *succeed to, receive in succession*, in Church; ref. leadership of Alexandrian catechetical school τῆς...κατηχήσεως τὴν διατριβὴν ∼εται Διονύσιος Eus.*h.e.*6.29.4(M.20.589A); ref. succession of ἐπίσκοποι and διάκονοι appointed by apostles ἀπόστολοι... ἐπινομὴν δεδώκασιν ὅπως, ἐὰν κοιμηθῶσιν, διαδέξωνται ἕτεροι δεδοκιμασμένοι ἄνδρες τὴν λειτουργίαν αὐτῶν *1Clem.*44.2; ∼εται τὴν ἐκκλησίαν μετὰ τῶν ἀποστόλων ὁ ἀδελφὸς τοῦ κυρίου Ἰάκωβος Heges.ap.Eus.*h.e.*2.23.4(M.20.197A); ἄλλοι τὴν ἐπισκοπὴν διεδέξαντο ἀπὸ τῶν ἀποστόλων Epiph.*haer.*27.6(p.308.8; M.41.372B); ref. regular episcopal succession παρὰ Ἀνικήτου ∼εται Σωτήρ Heges.ap. Eus.*h.e.*4.22.3(377D); Iren.*haer.*3.3.3(M.7.849B); Eus.*h.e.*3.14(249A); *ib.*3.15(249A) etc.; ref. prophetic succession, lacking among Montanists εἰ γὰρ μετὰ Κοδρᾶτον καὶ...Ἀμμίαν, ὥς φασιν, αἱ περὶ Μοντανὸν διεδέξαντο γυναῖκες τὸ προφητικὸν χάρισμα, τοὺς ἀπὸ Μοντανοῦ καὶ τῶν γυναικῶν τίνες παρ' αὐτοῖς διεδέξαντο, δειξάτωσαν Anon.*ib.*5.17.4(473B); ref. heret. teachers, Iren.*haer.*2.9.2(734B); διαδεξάμενος δὲ αὐτὸν [sc. Cerdo] Μαρκίων *ib.*1.27.2(688A); **2.** *come upon, overtake*; of disaster, Gr.Thaum.*pan.Or.*16(p.36.28; M.10. 1097C); Eus.*h.e.*1.8.3(M.20.101A); Philost.*h.e.*9.6(M.65.573A); **3.** *receive back* into office, *Chron.Pasch.*p.300(M.92.753B); Thphn.*chron.* p.221(M.108.564A).

***διαδήλως,** *very clearly*, Eus.*theoph.fr.*3(p.7*.13; M.24.613A).

διάδημα, τό, 1. *diadem, crown*; met. τοῖς ἁγιοπρεπέσιν δεσμοῖς, ἅτινά ἐστιν δ. τῶν ἀληθῶς ὑπὸ θεοῦ καὶ τοῦ κυρίου ἡμῶν ἐκλελεγμένων Polyc.*ep.*1.1; τὸ δ. τῆς δικαιοσύνης Clem.*paed.*2.8(p.202.29; M.8. 485C); ἀλήθειαν...τὸ δ. τῆς ἀϊδίου βασιλείας *Hom.Clem.*13.20; hence *imperial power* ἐν...τῷ δ. ... δύο καὶ ἥμισυ διανύσαντα ἔτη [sc. Ἰουλιανόν] Philost.*h.e.*7.15(M.65.553C); **2.** *head covering* ἀποσκεπάζει αὐτόν [sc. before absolution], ἐάν ἐστι καὶ ὁ τὸ δ. φορῶν Jo.Jej. *serm.*(M.88.1924C).

διαδιδράσκ-ω, *escape*, fig. τούς...τῶν λέξεων ἐχομένους καὶ περὶ ταύτας ἀσχολουμένους ∼ει τὰ πράγματα Clem.*str.*2.1(p.114.14; M.8. 933A); ἵνα μηδὲν ἡμᾶς τῶν ἀναγκαίων διαδρᾶναι δυνηθῇ Meth.*symp.* 7.5(p.76.4, v.l. ἀποδρᾶναι M.18.132A); Eus.*h.e.*2.2.1(M.20.140A).

διαδίδωμι, 1. *distribute* τὸ διαδοῦναι τὴν κλάσιν τοῖς κληρικοῖς Serap.*euch.*15 tit.; **2.** *spread abroad, publish* τὸ πλάσμα τῶν κατὰ τοῦ σωτῆρος ἡμῶν ὑπομνήματα...διαδεδωκότων Eus.*h.e.*1.9.3(M.20. 108B); **3.** pass., *spread*, of disease εἰς τὸ σῶμα διαδοθέν Meth.*lepr.*6 (p.458.2); *ib.*7(p.460.11).

διαδικάζ-ω, *bring into judgement* πᾶσα ἀρετὴ πρὸς πᾶσαν κακίαν ∼εται Bas.*hom.*12.10(2.106D; M.31.408B).

διάδικος, ὁ, *prosecutor*, Isid.Pel.*epp.*2.92(M.78.537A); *MAMA* 4.325[Phrygia, saec. iv–v].

***διαδονέω,** *shake violently*, Chrys.*paralyt.*2(3.35D); Dion.Ar.*ep.* 8.6(M.3.1100A).

***διαδονίζομαι,** *be agitated*, Dion.Al.*fr.*(p.164.1).

***διαδόσιμος,** *transmitted*, Synes.*ep.*58(M.66.1401C); id.*Dion* 5 (p.277.13; M.66.1127A); of death and sin through Adam, Olymp. *Eccl.*9:18(M.93.593C).

διάδοσις, ἡ, 1. *distribution*, of eucharist, Just.*1apol.*67.5(M.6. 429C); Eustrat.*v.Eutych.*37(M.86.2317C); *Chron.Pasch.*p.390(M.92. 1001C); **2.** *diffusion*, of light, Dion.Ar.*c.h.*13.3(M.3.301A); Max. *schol.c.h.*9.2(M.4.85A); **3.** *transmission*: of disease etc., Dion.Al. ap.Eus.*h.e.*7.22.10(M.20.689B); Bas.*hom.in Ps.*1(1.96C; M.29.225A); of grace τοῖς μετ' ἐκείνους [sc. first disciples] ἐκ δ. τὴν αὐτὴν ἐποίησαν χάριν Gr.Nyss.*hom.1 in Cant.*(M.44.785B); νοῶμεν θελήματος δ. ... ἐκ πατρὸς εἰς υἱὸν...διϊκνουμένην Bas.*Spir.*20(3.17E; M.32.104C).

διαδότης, ὁ, *distribution, dispenser*, Leont.N.*v.Jo.Eleem.*2 (p.8.18); *ib.*7(p.14.10).

***διαδοτικός,** *derivative, transmitted*, Dion.Ar.*c.h.*13.3(M.3.301B).

***διαδοχεύ-ω,** *pour forth* ∼σει ⟨ἐπ'⟩ αὐτὸν ὁ θεὸς σοφίαν Gel.Cyz. *h.e.*2.17.18(M.85.1269A); σοφία ἡ ∼σασα ἐπὶ Σολομῶντα *ib.*2.17.30 (1272C).

διαδοχή, ἡ, A. temporal *succession*; **1.** of time, *course* τοῦτο τῇ δ. τοῦ χρόνου συνέστησεν Synes.*ep.*74(M.66.1440D); **2.** with emphasis on idea of continuity or transmission, Meth.*symp.*6.4(p.68.16; M.18.117D); τὰ νῦν ἐκ τῆς γῆς φυόμενα ἐκ τῆς σπερματικῆς δ. ἀπὸ τῆς πρώτης κτίσεως εἰς ἀεὶ διαμένει Gr.Nyss.*Eun.*12(1 p.369.28; M.45. 1093D); πῶς δύναται ἡ ἐν συνηθείᾳ τῆς ἁμαρτίας γενομένη φύσις, καὶ δ. τῆς ἁμαρτίας διαδεξαμένη, χωρὶς ἁμαρτίας εἶναι; ‡Ath.*Apoll.*2.8 (M.26.1144B); **3.** of succession in office; **a.** of OT priesthood as continuing in Christ μὴ μετετέθη ἡ ἱερωσύνη...ἀλλὰ μόνον δ. Leont. H.*Nest.*3.5(M.86.1616C); **b.** of episcopate, i.e. succession of occupants of a particular see, Iren.*haer.*1.27.1(M.7.687B) cit. s. ἐπισκοπικός; μετὰ τὴν Ἰακώβου μαρτυρίαν...λόγος κατέχει...βουλὴν...τοὺς πάντας [sc. surviving apostles, disciples, and earthly relatives of Christ] περὶ τοῦ τίνα χρὴ τῆς Ἰακώβου δ. ἐπικρῖναι ἄξιον ποιήσασθαι Eus.*h.e.*3.11(M.20.245B); Ἰγνάτιος, τῆς κατ' Ἀντιόχειαν Πέτρου δ. δεύτερος τὴν ἐπισκοπὴν κεκληρωμένος *ib.*3.36.2(288B); *ib.*4.1(303B) cit. s. κατάγω; Ἀθανάσιον, ὃν ἐξ ἀρχῆς ὁ θεὸς ἡμῖν δέδωκε κατὰ διαδοχὴν τῶν πατέρων ἡμῶν clergy of Alexandria ap.Ath.*h.Ar.*81(p.230.14; M.25.796B); Ἀνικήτου ἐπισκόπου Ῥώμης τοῦ κατὰ τὴν δ. Πίου Epiph.*haer.*27.6(p.308.8; M.41.372B); εἰς ἐμὲ ...ἡ τῆς ἐπισκοπῆς κατήντησε δ. Cyr.*hom.pasch.*1(5².4B); of Marcionite bishops ἐξ ὅτου Μαρκίων ἐτελεύτησεν τοσούτων ἐπισκόπων, μᾶλλον δὲ ψευδεπισκόπων, παρ' ὑμῖν διαδοχαὶ γεγόνασι Adam.*dial.* 1.8(p.18.1; M.11.1729B); **4.** of succession of pupils and teachers, hence of transmission of tradition of teaching; **a.** in gen. ὥς τινες λέγουσιν...ἐκ δ. ἀκούσαντες *Chron.Pasch.*p.284(M.92.709A); ἐκ πλάνης τῆς πρὶν κρατούσης δ. δεδεγμένοι Geo.Pis.*Pers.*1.159(M.92.1209A); **b.** of recognized succession of teachers and teaching in philosophical schools στασιώδεις δὲ ἔχοντες τῶν δογμάτων τὰς δ. Tat.*orat.*25 (p.27.4; M.6.860C); φιλοσοφίας...τρεῖς γεγόνασι δ. ἐπώνυμοι τῶν τόπων περὶ οὓς διέτριψαν Clem.*str.*1.14(p.39.15; M.8.761A); ἐκ τῆς Κυρηναϊκῆς δ. *ib.*2.21(p.184.19; 1077A); τῆς ἐπ' Ἀλεξανδρείας Ἀριστοτέλους δ. Eus.*h.e.*7.32.6(M.20.724B); Gr.Nyss.*ep.*3(M.46.1024C, conj. διδαχαῖς); Σωπάτρῳ...κατ' ἐκεῖνο καιροῦ προεστῶτι τῆς Πλωτίνου δ. Soz.*h.e.*1.5.1(M.67.869A); **c.** of teachers and teaching in Church; in gen. *ἀλλόκοτα ἀναπλάσματα, καὶ μὴ ἀρέσκοντα τοῖς τῆς ἀπὸ τοῦ Ἰησοῦ δ.* Or.*Cels.*5.61(p.65.3; M.11.1277B); *τὴν αὐθεντίαν τῆς εὐαγγελικῆς δ.* Synes.*ep.*66(M.66.1409D); *τούτῳ δὲ τῷ...ἀρχηγῷ γενομένῳ τῶν τῇδε μοναστηρίων* [sc. Amoun], *πολλοὶ...ἐγένοντο μαθηταί, ὡς αἱ δ. ἐπιδείξουσι. πολλὰ δὲ καὶ θεσπέσια ἐπ' αὐτῷ συμβέβηκεν ἃ μάλιστα τοῖς κατ' Αἴγυπτον μοναχοῖς ἠκρίβωται, περὶ πολλοῦ ποιουμένοις, διαδοχῇ παραδόσεως ἀγράφου ἐπιμελῶς ἀπομνημονεύειν τὰς τῶν παλαιοτέρων ἀσκητῶν ἀρετάς* Soz.*h.e.*1.14.4(M.67.901B); of heret. teachers, Hipp.*haer.*9.7(p.240.26; M.16.3371A); ref. Theodotion *ἀπὸ τῆς δ. Μαρκίωνος τοῦ αἱρεσιάρχου Chron.Pasch.*p.263 (M.92.644A); esp. of doctrinal succession derived from apostles, (Gnost.) *μαθήσῃ γὰρ...ἀξιουμένη τῆς ἀποστολικῆς παραδόσεως, ἣν ἐκ δ. καὶ ἡμεῖς παρειλήφαμεν μετὰ καὶ τοῦ κανονίσαι πάντας τοὺς λόγους τῇ τοῦ σωτῆρος ἡμῶν διδασκαλίᾳ* Ptol.*ep.*ap.Epiph.*haer.* 33.7(p.457.15; M.41.568B); of tradition of *γνῶσις* handed down from apostles by 'successions', Clem.*str.*6.7(p.462.28; M.9.284A); *ἐχομένοις τοῦ κανόνος τῆς Ἰησοῦ Χριστοῦ κατὰ διαδοχὴν τῶν ἀποστόλων οὐρανίου ἐκκλησίας* Or.*princ.*4.2.1(p.308.15; M.11.360B); cf. *servetur...ecclesiastica praedicatio per successionis ordinem ab apostolis tradita, ib.*proem.2(p.8.26; 116B); ref. Gnostic exegesis *non debemus aliter credere, nisi quemadmodum per successionem ecclesiae dei tradiderunt nobis,* id.*comm.ser.46 in Mt.*(p.94.29; M.13.1667D); *τὰς τῶν...ἀποστόλων δ. ... ὅσα τε...πραγματευθῆναι...λέγεται, καὶ ὅσοι...ἐν ταῖς...παροικίαις...προέστησαν, ὅσοι τε κατὰ γενεὰν ἑκάστην ...τὸν θεῖον ἐπρέσβευσαν λόγον* [i.e. successions from apostles of bishops and leading teachers] Eus.*h.e.*1.1.1(M.20.48B); *ib.*1.1.4 (52A); cf.*ib.*7.32.2(721B); of Clement's teachers *τοὺς ἐμφανεστέρους ἧς κατείληφεν ἀποστολικῆς δ. ἐπισημηνάμενος ib.*5.11.2(457A); cf.*ib.* 6.13.8(549A); **d.** of bishops as transmitters and upholders of apostolic doctrine *ἐν ἑκάστῃ δὲ δ. καὶ ἐν ἑκάστῃ πόλει οὕτως ἔχει ὡς ὁ νόμος κηρύσσει καὶ οἱ προφῆται καὶ ὁ κύριος* Heges.*ib.*4.22.2(377D); cf. *traditionem itaque apostolorum...in omni ecclesia adest perspicere omnibus qui vera velint videre, et habemus annumerare eos qui ab apostolis instituti sunt episcopi in ecclesiis, et successiones eorum usque ad nos, qui nihil tale docuerunt...quale ab his* [sc. Gnostics] *deliratur,* Iren.*haer.*3.3.2(M.7.848B); ref. episcopal successions *τῇ αὐτῇ τάξει καὶ τῇ αὐτῇ διδαχῇ* [v.l. *διαδοχῇ*] *ἥ τε ἀπὸ τῶν ἀποστόλων ἐν τῇ ἐκκλησίᾳ παράδοσις...κατήντηκεν εἰς ἡμᾶς ib.*3.3.3(851B); cf. *cum episcopatus successione charisma veritatis certum...acceperunt, ib.*4.26.2(1053C); Eus.*Is.*2:27(M.24.100C); Gr.Naz.*or.*21.8(M.35. 1089B); **5.** of bishops as successors to apostles in exercise of high-priesthood and guardianship of Church as well as in doctrine, cf. Hipp.*haer.*1 proem.(p.3.3; M.16.3020C) cit. s. *διάδοχος*; in gen. (in consecration prayer) *ποίησον ὁ θεὸς τῆς ἀληθείας καὶ τόνδε ἐπίσκοπον ζῶντα, ἐπίσκοπον ἅγιον τῆς δ. τῶν ἁγίων ἀποστόλων* Serap.*euch.*28.1; **6.** of succession of prophets in Church, Anon.ap.Eus.*h.e.*5.16.7 (M.20.465C) cit. s. *παράδοσις*; **7.** of succession of generations; **a.** in gen. *κατὰ γὰρ τὰς δ. τῶν γενῶν ἕτεροι καὶ ἕτεροι ἐγένοντο προφῆται* Just.*1apol.*31.8(M.6.377B); of Christ *τοῦ...Ἰακὼβ...κατὰ γένους διαδοχὴν υἱός ib.*32.14(380C); of pagan priests *οἱ κατὰ διαδοχὴν γένους παῖς παρὰ πατρός, ὡς τὴν ἱερωσύνην καὶ τὴν ἱστορίαν διαδεχόμενοι* Athenag.*leg.*28.3(M.6.956A); Meth.*arbitr.*15(p.183.10); id. *symp.*7.5(p.76.9; M.18.132A); *ἐκ προγόνων δ.* Eus.*h.e.*2.3.2(M.20. 144A); Ath.*Ar.*1.21(M.26.56C); ‡Ath.*diab.*8(p.9.25); Thdt.*Ezech.* 17:22(2.805); **b.** of generations by which Christians were removed from apostles *ὁ Ἡγήσιππος ἐπὶ τῆς πρώτης τῶν ἀποστόλων γενόμενος δ.* Eus.*h.e.*2.23.3(M.20.196D); *τῶν κατὰ τὰς δ. ἐκκλησιαστικῶν ib.*3. 25.6(269B); of Ignatius, Quadratus, etc. *τὴν πρώτην τάξιν τῆς τῶν ἀποστόλων ἐπέχοντες δ. ib.*3.37.1(292D); **8.** of succession by inheritance, Eus.*v.C.*2.35(p.56.21; M.20.1013A).

B. *succession list, order* or *catalogue of succession*; **1.** of kings, Tat.*orat.*39(p.40.8; M.6.881C); **2.** of leaders of philosophical schools, Clem.*str.*1.14(p.41.5; M.8.765A); **3.** of bishops in their sees *γενόμενος δὲ ἐν Ῥώμῃ, διαδοχὴν ἐποιησάμην μέχρις Ἀνικήτου* Heges.ap. Eus.*h.e.*4.22.3(M.20.377D); *τῶν ἐπὶ Ῥώμης τὴν δ. ἐπισκόπων... παραθέμενος* [sc. Irenaeus] *εἰς Ἐλεύθερον...τὸν κατάλογον ἵστησιν* Eus.*ib.*5.5.9(441B); *ἡ τῶν ἐν Ῥώμῃ ἐπισκόπων δ. ταύτην ἔχει τὴν ἀκολουθίαν* Epiph.*haer.*27.6(p.310.6; M.41.373B); Soz.*h.e.*1.14.4(M.67. 901B) cit. s. A.4.c.

C. *being succeeded, appointment of a successor πᾶς ἄρχων μετὰ δ. τὰς νενομισμένας...ἡμέρας ἐν τῇ...ἐπαρχίᾳ προσμενέτω* Ath.Scholast. *coll.*4.18(p.60).

D. *passing over* into death *πρὶν ἐπέλθῃ ἡ δ. ὑμῶν* Eus.Al.*serm.*21.6 (M.86.432C).

E. *successor*, met. *ἐσχάτην εὐλογίαν, ἥτις δ. οὐκ ἔχει Protev.*6.2 (p.13); *τρεῖς γὰρ δ. εἰσι* [sc. in NT] *τῶν δέκα λόγων* Jo.Eub.*concept. BMV* 2(M.96.1497C).

F. *ἐκ δ. ᾄδειν* sing *antiphonally*, Thdt.*h.e.*2.24.9(3.889).

***διαδοχικῶς**, *successively*, *Disp.Phot.*3(M.88.561A).

διάδοχος, **1.** adj., *succeeding τὸ βασίλειον...τὸ δ.* Mac.Mgn. *apocr.*3.14(p.92.14); *τοῦ θαύματος θαῦμα δ.* Bas.Sel.*or.*1.2(M.85. 29B); **2.** subst., *successor ὁ χρόνος...Ἰησοῦν...ἔχει τὸν παντὸς ὄντα καὶ χρόνου καὶ αἰῶνος δ.* Max.*ambig.*(M.91.1164B); succession of generations, Meth.*arbitr.*16.2(p.186.10); succession in office: of kings, Just.*dial.*103.3(M.6.716C); Or.*comm.in Gen.*ap.Eus.*p.e.*6.11 (285C; M.12.60B); with idea of inheritance of authority, privileges etc. *εἰς μέγα...τὸ Ῥωμαίων ηὐξήθη κράτος· οὗ σὺ δ. εὐκταῖος γέγονας* Mel.*fr.*1.3(p.308; M.5.1212A); of bishops, Ath.*ep.encycl.*2 (p.170.28; M.25.225B); Gr.Naz.*or.*21.8(M.35.1089B); Ammon.Aeg.*ep.* 32(p.119.4); of abbots in monasteries, *V.Pach.Φ* 106(p.69.29); *ib.* 117(p.76.3); *ib.*145(p.92.4); succession in performance of function: of Joshua as successor of Moses, *V.Pach.Λ* 41(p.164.27); apostles as successors of Christ *ὁ θεὸς λόγος...ἀνερχόμενος εἰς τὸν οὐρανὸν προκατεστήσατο δ. αὐτοῦ τοὺς ἀποστόλους V.Pach.Φ* 135(p.85.29); bishops and teachers of Church as successors of apostles, Or.*hom. 34 in Lc.*(p.202.19); cf.id.*hom.6.4 in Is.*(p.274.26); bishops as successors of apostles in various aspects of their work *τὸ ἐν ἐκκλησίᾳ παραδοθὲν ἅγιον πνεῦμα, οὗ τυχόντες πρότεροι οἱ ἀπόστολοι μετέδοσαν τοῖς ὀρθῶς πεπιστευκόσιν· ὧν ἡμεῖς δ. τυγχάνοντες τῆς τε αὐτῆς χάριτος μετέχοντες ἀρχιερατείας τε καὶ διδασκαλίας καὶ φρουροὶ τῆς ἐκκλησίας λελογισμένοι* Hipp.*haer.*proem.(p.3.3; M.16.3020C); of Pope *πρὸς Πέτρον ἤτοι τὸν αὐτοῦ δ.* Thdr.Stud.*epp.*1.33(M.99. 1017B); of heret. teachers as successors in pupil–teacher relationship, Hipp.*haer.*9.10(p.244.9; 3378A); Serap.Ant.ap.Eus.*h.e.*6.12.6 (M.20.545B); of those who continue in a tradition (ref. idolatry) *τέκνα τοὺς δ. τῆς τοιαύτης ὀνομάζων βδελυρίας* Areth.*Apoc.*6(M.106. 544A).

διαδύνω, *immerse oneself* in, *study εἰς τὴν τῶν ἀοράτων θεωρίαν διαδυεῖσα...ἡ διάνοια* Gr.Nyss.*hom.1 in Eccl.*(M.44.632A); med., id. *fat.*(M.45.156C); id.*tres dii*(M.45.121D).

διαέριος, **1.** *through the air νεφῶν τε δ. πορεῖαι* Eus.*l.C.*1.4(p.197. 28; M.20.1321B); Gr.Nyss.*Eun.*10(2 p.227.24; M.45.828C); ‡Nil. *perist.*10.5(M.79.893D); **2.** *in the air θυρεοὶ οὐκ ἐπὶ γῆς κείμενοι, ἀλλὰ δ. περὶ αὐτὸν θεωρούμενοι* Gr.Nyss.*hom.7 in Cant.*(M.44.933D); Jo.Mon.*hymn.Petr.*3(M.96.1392C).

διαζεύγνυμι, *part, separate*; of soul and body in death, Ephr. 1.265D; Thdt.*rect.conf.*11(M.6.1228B); theol. *οὐ γάρ ἐστιν ἐπινοῆσαι τομὴν ἢ διαίρεσιν κατ' οὐδένα τρόπον...τὸ πνεῦμα τοῦ υἱοῦ διαζευχθῆναι* Gr.Nyss.*diff.ess.*4(M.32.332D); *τὰς τῆς ἁγίας τριάδος ὑποστάσεις οὐ διεζευγμένας* Gel.Cyz.*h.e.*2.22.5(M.85.1292A).

διάζευξις, **ἡ**, *separating, parting*; in gen., Gr.Naz.*or.*6.2(M.35. 721C); Chrys.*sac.*5.2(p.129.10; 1.416A); ‡Nil.*narr.*2(M.79.604A); *ib.* 6(660B); of death, Meth.*res.*1.38(p.280.9; M.41.1105A); Gr.Naz.*or.* 7.22(784C); Eustrat.*v.Eutych.*98(M.86.2384D).

διαζήτησις, **ἡ**, *quest, inquiry*, Or.*fr.64 in Jo.*9:8(p.535.18).

διαζωγραφέω, *paint in divers colours*; met., of words, writings etc., Gr.Nyss.*hom.14 in Cant.*(M.44.1065C); Leont.N.*v.Jo.Eleem.* proem.(p.3.16); Areth.*Apoc.*44(M.106.696C).

διαζωγράφησις, **ἡ**, *depicting*, *cat.2Tim.*1:13(p.61.4).

***διαθαλάττιος**, prob. f.l. for *δυσθαλάττιος*.

διαθάλπω, med., *warm oneself*, Bas.*hex.*7.3(1.65C; M.29.153B).

διαθερμαίνω, *warm through*; met., pass., *be warmed, moved*, with emotion, Chrys.*David* 2.5(4.768A); id.*hom.22.4 in Rom.*(9.684E); id. *hom.32.4 in 1Cor.*(10.292E).

διάθεσις, **ἡ**, **1.** *disposition, arrangement*; of facial expression, Chrys.*sac.*3.18(p.93.25; 1.400C); **2.** *arrangement, ordering*; in art or rhetoric, Ath.*Ar.*2.4(M.26.153C); *τούτῳ δὲ κεχρήμεθα τῆς δ. τῷ τρόπῳ* Chrys.*hom.5.1 in Phil.*(11.227E); **3.** *disposition, attitude*; of will, purpose, Or.*or.*2.3(p.301.2; M.11.420B); id.*schol.in Cant.*6:7 (M.17.277C); *ἡ μὲν γὰρ πίστις ἀπὸ δ. ψυχῆς γίνεται* Ath.*v.Anton.*77 (M.26.952A); *ἵνα...τὴν ἡμετέραν περιπτυξώμεθα δ.* id.*tom.*2(M.26. 797A); *λέγουσι γὰρ κἂν μὴ γνησίᾳ δ. τὴν ἀλήθειαν* Serap.*Man.*29 (p.44; M.18.1116B); *ἡ...ἐμπαθεστέρα δ.* Gr.Nyss.*v.Mos.*(M.44.328A); *ἔχουσιν Ἑλληνικὰς δ. ἐν ἑαυτοῖς* Cyr.*Ps.*67:7(M.69.1145B); id.*Is.*5.5 (2.871C); Gnost. *τῶν δύο δ. τούτων, ἢ καὶ δυνάμεων, τῆς ἐννοίας καὶ τῆς θελήσεως...τύπους...τῶν δύο δ. τοῦ πατρὸς προελθεῖν* Iren.*haer.* 1.12.1(M.7.572A); in complimentary address *τὰ γράμματα τῆς σῆς ἱερᾶς δ.* Ath.*ep.Serap.*1.1(M.26.529A); id.*decr.*2(p.2.19; M.25.420A); Ursac.*ep.Ath.*(p.138.14; M.25.353C).

διαθέ-ω, **1.** *run to and fro*, met. *τὸ γὰρ θεὸς ὄνομα φύσεώς ἐστι θεωρουμένης εἴτουν ~ούσης τὰ πάντα δηλωτικόν* ‡Ath.*Maced.dial.*1.1

(M.28.1292B); **2.** *run a race*, met. ὠκυπόδως ἐνάρετον ~ουσι στάδιον ‡Caes.Naz.*dial*.1(M.38.856).

***διαθήγω**, *stimulate*, Cyr.*hom.pasch*.14.1(5².187E).

διαθήκη, ἡ, 1. *testament, will*; for theol. application v. infra 2.c.iii; **2.** *compact, covenant*; **a.** in gen., Ath.*ep.Aeg.Lib*.6(M.25.549C); dist. from συνθήκη: τὴν συνθήκην, τουτέστι τὴν ἐπαγγελίαν, δ. ἡ...καλεῖ γραφὴ διὰ τὸ βέβαιον. ... συνθῆκαι μὲν γὰρ πολλάκις ἀνατρέπονται, δ. δὲ νόμιμοι οὐδαμῶς Isid.Pel.*epp*.2.196(M.78.641D); ἔθος γὰρ τῇ...γραφῇ δ. ἀποκαλεῖν τὰς ἐπαγγελίας Cyr.*Os*.112(3.144C); **b.** of natural man with Devil ὅταν...τῷ σατανᾷ ἀποτάττῃ, πᾶσαν τὴν πρὸς αὐτὸν δ. λύσας Cyr.H.*catech*.19.9; **c.** of God with man; **i.** various forms δ. πλείους γεγόνασι τῇ ἀνθρωπότητι...καὶ...ἑκάστης τῶν δ. ὁ χαρακτήρ Iren.*haer*.1.10.3(M.7.556A); τέσσαρες ἐδόθησαν καθολικαὶ δ. τῇ ἀνθρωπότητι [i.e. with Noah and Abraham, through Moses and Christ] *ib*.3.11.8(889B); with Abraham, Or.*Jo*.9.39(23; p.217.4; M.14.384A); with Jacob, Esaias *or*.4(p.15); the Greeks, Clem.*str*.6.8(p.465.20; M.9.288C); but δυνάμει [sc. αἱ δ.] μία οὖσαι, ἡ μὲν παλαιά, ἡ δὲ καινή, διὰ υἱοῦ παρ' ἑνὸς θεοῦ χορηγοῦνται *ib*. 2.6(p.128.23; M.8.964C); μία τῷ ὄντι δ. ἡ σωτήριος ἀπὸ καταβολῆς κόσμου εἰς ἡμᾶς διήκουσα *ib*.6.13(p.485.17; M.9.328B); δύο δὲ τῶν καλλινίκων οἱ χοροὶ μαρτύρων, εἷς μὲν τῆς δ. τῆς καινῆς, θάτερος δὲ τῆς παλαιᾶς Meth.*res*.1.56(p.316.9; M.41.1149D); Chrys.*hom.4.4 in Eph*.(11.30F); δύο μὲν αἱ δ., εἷς δὲ ὁ νομοθέτης id.*hom.16.7 in Mt*.(7.213C); **ii.** Old Covenant Μωυσῆς δὲ φαίνεται τὸν κύριον δ. καλῶν...ἐπεὶ καὶ πρότερον εἶπεν δ. μὴ ζητεῖν αὐτὴν ἐν γραφῇ· ἔστι γὰρ δ. ἣν ὁ αἴτιος...θεός τίθεται, θεὸς δὲ παρὰ τὴν θέσιν εἴρηται Clem.*str*.1.29(p.111.23; M.8.929A); passed from Israel, *Barn*.4.8; Cyr.*Os*.112(3.144C); culminating in work of Jo. Bapt. ἑτοιμάζων κυρίῳ λαὸν κατεσκευασμένον ἐπὶ τέλει τῆς παλαιᾶς γενομένης δ., ἥ ἐστι σαββατισμοῦ κορωνίς Or.*Jo*.2.33(27; p.91.2; M.14.172C); μέχρι τοῦ βαπτίσματος ὁ Χριστὸς ἐν τῷ τῆς παλαιᾶς δ. καιρῷ ὑπάρχων, τὰ τῆς παλαιᾶς ἔπραττεν *Disp.Phot*.(M.88.549D); in rel. to New Covenant ἡ δὲ παλαιὰ δ. ... μετὰ φόβου καὶ τρόμου διετάγη τοῖς πατράσιν Just.*dial*.67.9(M.6.632B); ὁ παράκλητος...ἐνεργῶν νῦν τῇ ἐκκλησίᾳ τῆς αὐτῆς οὐσίας ἐστὶ...τῷ...ἐνεργήσαντι κατὰ τὴν παλαιὰν δ. Clem.*exc.Thdot*.24(p.115.9; M.9.672B); εἰς ἑνότητα πίστεως μιᾶς, τῆς κατὰ τὰς οἰκείας δ., μᾶλλον δὲ κατὰ δ. τὴν μίαν διαφόροις τοῖς χρόνοις id.*str*.7.17(p.76.13; M.9.552B); cf. *apostoli enim...duo quidem testamenta in duobus populis fuisse docuerunt; unum autem et eundem esse deum, qui disposuerit utraque ad utilitatem hominum*, Iren.*haer*.4.32.2(M.7.1071B); being transitory and providing types of New Covenant, Ath.*exp.Ps*.49 proem.(M.27.229B); Cyr.H.*catech*.22.5; cf. τύπος, νόμος; Jo. Bapt. being ὁ μέσος τῆς παλαιᾶς καὶ καινῆς δ. Cosm.Ind.*top*.5(M.88.277A); **iii.** New Covenant; effected through Christ, *Barn*.14.5; Just.*dial*.12.2(M.6.500B); ζηλωτὴν ὄντα τῆς δ. Χριστοῦ *Ep.Lugd*.ap.Eus.*h.e*.5.4.2(M.20.440A); καινῷ...καὶ νέῳ λαῷ καινὴ καὶ νέα δ. δεδώρηται Clem.*paed*.1.7(p.125.1; M.8.321A); Or.*Cels*.2.75(p.196.14; M.11.912C); Eus.*d.e*.1.6(p.28.24; M.22.57B) cit. s. ἀνανεόω; through his death, hence interpreted as *testament, will*, Chrys.*hom.16.1 in Heb*.(12.158A); δ. διδομένης καινῆς, ἔδει γενέσθαι τὸν θάνατον. μετὰ γὰρ τὴν τῶν διατιθεμένων τελευτὴν αἱ δ. λαμβάνουσι τὴν ἰσχύν Thdt.*Heb*.9:16(3.601); Jo.D.*Heb*.9:16(M.95.972B); as being Christ himself, Just.*dial*.118.3(M.6.749C); *ib*.122.6(760C); eucharistic τροφὴ δὲ αὐτῷ καὶ ποτὸν γενέσθω τεταγμένον ἡ καινὴ δ. τοῦ κυρίου Clem.*q.d.s*.3(p.162.2; M.9.608B); exeg. Apoc.2:17 ὄνομα καινὸν γράφεται κατὰ τὴν καινὴν δ. ... ἀεὶ καινόν ἐστι κατὰ τὴν ἀδιάδοχον καινὴν δ. Or.*Apoc*.14(p.27); *Lit*.ap.*Const.App*.8.5.7; ‡Pion.*v.Polyc*.2; *Lit.Jac*.(p.194.3); esp. in words of institution τοῦτό μού ἐστι τὸ αἷμα τὸ τῆς καινῆς δ. *ib*.(p.202.18); *Lit.Chrys*.(p.328.17); cf.*Lit.Marc*.(p.133.12); *Lit.Bas*.(p.405.10); of S. Stephen as ὁ τῆς νέας δ. πρωτομάρτυς καὶ πρωτοδιάκονος Cosm.Ind.*top*.5(M.88.297A); **iv.** no such covenant with heathen 'λαὸς ὃν οὐκ ἔγνων ἐδούλευσέν μοι'· κατὰ διαθήκην οὐκ ἔγνων Clem.*ecl*.43(p.149.12; M.9.720A); **3.** *written covenant, scriptures of Old* or *New Testament*; **a.** in gen. πάντων μὲν γὰρ αἴτιος τῶν καλῶν ὁ θεός...ὡς τῆς τε δ. τῆς παλαιᾶς καὶ τῆς νέας, τῶν δὲ...ὡς τῆς φιλοσοφίας Clem.*str*.1.5(p.17.37; M.8.717D); Ἰησοῦς...ὀχούμενος τῇ...ὄνῳ, λέγω δὲ τοῖς ἀφελέσι τῆς παλαιᾶς δ. γράμμασι. ... ὀχεῖται δὲ καὶ τῷ...πώλῳ, τῇ καινῇ δ. Or.*Jo*.10.28(18; p.201.25; M.14.357C); πεπιστευμένων...θείων γραφῶν, τῆς τε λεγομένης παλαιᾶς δ. καὶ τῆς καλουμένης καινῆς id.*princ*.4.1.1(p.292.12; M.11.341C); id.*fr.comm.in Ezech*.(p.60.22; M.13.664B) cit. s. ἐγκρίνω; τά τε τῆς παλαιᾶς καὶ τὰ τῆς νέας δ. βιβλία †Ath.*synops*.4(M.28.296A); *ib*.74 tit.(432A); τὰ κανονικὰ τῆς καινῆς καὶ παλαιᾶς δ. CLaod.*can*.59; *Can.App*.85; Cyr.H.*catech*.4.33 cit. s. ἐκκλησία; γαλακτοτροφίᾳ προσέοικεν ἡ τῆς παλαιᾶς δ. παιδαγωγία, στερεᾷ δὲ τροφῇ τῆς καινῆς δ. ἡ φιλοσοφία Chrys.*hom.2.3 in 2Cor.4:13*(3.272B); Isid.Pel.*epp*.4.209 (M.78.1304A); Cosm.Ind.*top*.1(M.88.57B); Max.*qu.Thal*.63(M.90.676D) cit. s. ἐκκλησία; **b.** partic. of Old Testament τὰ τῆς παλαιᾶς δ. βιβλία Mel.*fr*.3(p.309; M.5.1216A); ἐν τῇ παλαιᾷ δ. νομοθετεῖ Clem.*str*.3.6(p.221.15; 1160A); ἡ γραφὴ...ἐκ τῆς παλαιᾶς ἤρτηται δ. *ib*.4.21(p.307.32; 1345A); Or.*princ*.3.1.16(p.224.11; M.11.281B); id.*or*.22(p.346.13; M.11.481C); Meth.*symp*.10.2(p.122.18; M.18.193B); danger to foolish, †Bas.*ep*.42.3(3.127E; M.32.353A); **c.** of NT ἡ καινὴ δ. Or.*Jo*.2.33(27; p.90.20; M.14.172C); ἄριστον μὲν γὰρ οἱ εἰσαγωγικοὶ λόγοι...ἢ τὰ παλαιὰ λόγια, δεῖπνον δὲ οἱ ἐν προκοπῇ λόγοι μυστικοὶ ἢ οἱ τῆς νέας δ. id.*fr.68 in Lc*.14:12(p.267); τῆς νέας καὶ καινῆς δ. Eus.*e.th*.2.9(p.110.16; M.24.920B); ἐν ταύταις ὁ βλέπων ἱερῶς ὄψεται τὴν ἑνοειδῆ ...σύμπνοιαν, ὡς ὑφ' ἑνὸς...πνεύματος κεκινημένην· ὅθεν...μετὰ τὴν ἀρχαιοτέραν παράδοσιν ἡ καινὴ δ. κηρύσσεται Dion.Ar.*e.h*.3.3.5(M.3.432B); **4.** *record*, *T.Sal*.26.8(M.122.1357B); *V.Zos*.21(p.108.12); *Dial.Tim.et Aquil*.83 r°.

[*]**διαθηλύομαι**, *be wanton*, Areth.*Apoc*.53(M.106.717A).

διαθλεύω, *struggle desperately*, Evagr.*h.e*.1.13(p.23.25; M.86.2457C).

***δίαθλος**, s.v.l., *full of conflict* δ. καὶ διαυγῆ καὶ διαστεφῆ ἀγῶνα Thdr.Stud.*epp*.2.140(M.99.1445A).

διαθολ-όω, *darken*; met., *tarnish* ~ῶσαι...τὸν νοῦν Niceph.Ur.*v.Sym*.137(M.86.3113B).

***διαθρέπτω**, *nourish, feed*, of BMV ἡ...ἄρτον ζωοποιὸν ἐκ τοῦ καρποῦ αὐτῆς τὴν οἰκουμένην διαθρέψασα Abr.Eph.*occurs*.9(p.454.9).

διαθρυλ(λ)έω, 1. *spread abroad*, doctrines, reports, rumours etc., Ath.*h.Ar*.44(p.208.32; M.25.748B); Chrys.*hom.2.1 in 1Thess*.(11.432E); -λλει Jo.D.*haer*.101(M.94.765A); **2.** pass., *ring with the noise of, be deafened*, met. ἐκκλήσιαν ὑπὸ τῆς νέας ταύτης...προφητείας... διατεθρυλημένην Anon.ap.Eus.*h.e*.5.16.4(M.20.465A); βασιλέα ὑπὸ πολλῶν τὰ ὦτα διαθρυλλούμενον Chrys.*hom.58.4 in Mt*.(7.590E); διατεθρυλλημένος Aen.*dial*.(M.85.892A).

***διαθρύλλητος**, *famous*, ‡Caes,Naz.*dial*.154(M.38.1103).

***διάθρυψις, ἡ**, *voluptuousness* κινημάτων δ. Chrys.*sac*.6.2(p.143.5; 1.422C).

διαίρεσις, ἡ, I. *division*;

A. theol.; **1.** denied within Trin., v. τομή; although μονάδα γὰρ ἐν τριάδι καὶ τριάδα ἐν μονάδι προσκυνοῦμεν, παράδοξον ἔχουσαν καὶ τὴν δ. καὶ τὴν ἕνωσιν...διαιρεῖται γὰρ ἀδιαιρέτως ἵν' οὕτως εἴπωμεν καὶ συνάπτεται διῃρημένως Just.Imp.*edict*.(p.198.19; M.86.2796B); against Monarchian view of those who *numerum et dispositionem trinitatis, divisionem praesumunt unitatis*, Tert.*adversus Praxeam* 3(M.*PL*.2.180C); δεῖ δὲ καὶ τὴν ἀσεβῆ σύγχυσιν ἐκείνου [sc. Sabellius] καὶ τὴν μανιώδη τούτου [sc. Arius] δ. ἀποστρέφεσθαι καὶ φεύγειν τὴν μὲν θεότητα πατρὸς καὶ υἱοῦ καὶ ἁγίου πνεύματος μίαν ὁμολογοῦντας προστιθέντας δὲ καὶ τὰς τρεῖς ὑποστάσεις Chrys.*sac*.4.4(p.115.16; 1.410A); οὐ τρία ἀλλόφυλά τε καὶ ἑτεροούσια...κατὰ τὴν Ἀρείου δ. τε καὶ ἀλλοτρίωσιν Thdt.*Trin*.28(M.75.1188C); of which error Sabellius accused the orthodox, ‡Ath.*Apoll*.1.21(M.26.1129C); **2.** Christol., denied of Person of Christ ἐπειδὴ καὶ φύσις ὅλη τοῦ λόγου ἐν ἐπιδείξει μορφῆς τῆς ἀνθρωπίνης καὶ σαρκὸς τῆς ὁρωμένης τοῦ δευτέρου Ἀδάμ, οὐκ ἐν δ. προσώπων ἀλλ' ἐν ὑπάρξει θεότητος καὶ ἀνθρωπότητος ‡Ath.*Apoll*.2.10(M.26.1148C); πᾶσαν συναίρεσίν τε καὶ δ. τοῦ κατὰ Χριστὸν μυστηρίου...ἀποπέμπεται Max.*opusc*.(M.91.88B); ἐπὶ δὲ τοῦ πάντων ἡμῶν σωτῆρος Χριστοῦ συνεισενεγκὼν εἰς ἕνωσιν τὴν ἀληθῆ τε καὶ καθ' ὑπόστασιν παραιτοῦ τὴν δ.· ἕνα γὰρ οὕτως ὁμολογήσεις Χριστὸν καὶ υἱόν Cyr.*Nest*.2.8(p.45.37; 6.50B); on other hand, statement of monophysite doctrine μία φύσις ἐστίν, ἐπειδὴ πρόσωπον ἓν οὐκ ἔχον εἰς δύο διαίρεσιν, ἐπεὶ μηδὲ ἰδίᾳ φύσις τὸ σῶμα καὶ ἰδίᾳ φύσις ἡ θεότης κατὰ τὴν σάρκωσιν Apoll.*ep.Dion*.2(p.257.16) ap.Leont.H.*monoph*.(M.86.1869C); is refuted, Leont.B.*cap.Sev*.29(M.86.1912Df.); ὁ ἀριθμὸς...καθ' ἑαυτὸν οὔτε διαιρεῖ οὔτε συνάπτει· ἀλλ' ἀμφότερα δέχεται τῇ ποιᾷ σχέσει· οἷον ἡ δυάς, ἡ τετράς...ὥστε ...τὴν φύσιν τοῦ ἀριθμοῦ μηδὲν ἀφωρισμένον ἔχειν, μήτε τὸ διῃρημένον, μήτε τὸ ἡνωμένον...ἀπαίδευτον οὖν τὸ τῇ φύσει τοῦ ἀριθμοῦ, ἀναγκαίως τὴν δ. τῶν πραγμάτων ἕπεσθαι νομοθετεῖν...εἰ μὲν ὁ ἀριθμὸς φύσεσιν ἐπιφημισθῇ, οὐ τὸ ποσὸν αὐτῶν προηγουμένως ἀλλὰ τὸ ἑτερογενὲς συνίστησιν...οὕτω δὴ καὶ ἐπὶ τῆς οἰκονομίας, δύο λέγοντες τὰς φύσεις, τὸ ἑτεροειδὲς αὐτῶν οὐ τὸ κεχωρισμένον δηλοῦμεν, ἐκβάλλοντες αὐτῶν εἰ καὶ μὴ εἶεν ἀνυπόστατοι τὸν τῶν ὑποστάσεων ἀριθμόν· ὥσπερ ἐκεῖ τὸν τῶν οὐσιῶν, κἂν μηδ' ὁπότερα ὑπόστασις τὸ ἀνούσιον, ὥσπερ οὐδὲ ἐνταῦθα τὸ ἀνυπόστατον, ἔχειν ὡμολόγηται id.*arg.Sev*.(M.86.1920Bff.); hence εἰ ὁ ἀριθμὸς πάντως χωρίζει τὰ ἀριθμούμενα, οὐχ ὁ τῶν φύσεων μόνος ἀριθμὸς χωρίσει τὰς φύσεις, ἀλλὰ καὶ ὁ τῶν ἰδιοτήτων χωρίσει πάντως ἀριθμός. πῶς τοίνυν ἰδιότητας λέγοντες, οὐχὶ καὶ αὐτοὶ τῇ αἰτίᾳ τῆς δ. ὑποκείσονται;

id.*cap.Sev.*10(1903C); complex unity analysed, id.*arg.Sev.*(1932C); *οὔτε δὲ τὸ τῇ ἐπινοίᾳ διαιρετόν, εἰς ταὐτὸν τῷ τῇ ἐνεργείᾳ φέρειν εὐσεβές...καὶ διὰ τοῦτο τῆς κατ' ἐνεργείαν δ. τὰς ὑποστάσεις ἐχούσης τε καὶ τιθεμένης, ἡ κατ' ἐπίνοιαν δ. τὸν τῶν ὑποστάσεων ἀριθμὸν οὐ παραδέχεται* *ib.*(1933B); *εἰ μὲν οὖν ἦν ποτε ὅτε οὐκ ἦν ταῦτα ἡνωμένα, σκοπείτω τις αὐτὰ οὕτως, ὡς πάντῃ κεχωρισμένα· εἰ δὲ σύνδρομον τῇ ὑπάρξει τῆς ἀνθρωπότητος, τοῦ θεοῦ λόγου ἴσμεν τὴν ἕνωσιν, πῶς τὰ μηδέποτε ἀλλήλων κεχωρισμένα, τὸν τῶν πάντῃ διαιρετῶν ὑποδέξεται λόγον; ἐπινοίᾳ μὲν οὖν ταῦτα λόγῳ ἄν τις διέλοι, οὐ μὴν αἰσθήσει καὶ ἐνεργείᾳ καὶ τοῦτο μετὰ τὴν ἕνωσιν, καὶ οὔ τί γε πρὶν συναφθῆναι· καθόλου γὰρ λαμβάνειν δ. πρὸ τῆς ἑνώσεως ἄτοπον...οὔτω τοίνυν ἐπὶ τῆς δ.· οὐ γὰρ προεπινοεῖται τῶν πραγμάτων ἐν οἷς αὐτὴ θεωρεῖται, ἀλλ' οὐδὲ αὐτῆς τῆς ἑνώσεως...ἐπινοίᾳ ἀλλ' οὐκ ἐνεργείᾳ ἡ ἀνθρωπότης ἀπὸ τῆς θεότητος ἑνωθεῖσα χωρίζεται...ἀλλ' οὐδὲ ὅλως ἔσται ἡ κατ' ἐπίνοιαν δ., μὴ ἐνεργείᾳ ὄντων τῶν καθ' ὧν ἡ ἐπίνοια, εἰ καὶ ὁμοῦ ταῦτα καὶ ἐν ταὐτῷ εἶεν* *ib.*(1937Aff.); illogical position of extreme views pointed out *εἰ δὲ μήτε τὴν δ. αἱ ὑποστάσεις κατ' ἐκείνους* [sc. Nestorians], *μήτε τὴν σύγχυσιν ἡ μιὰ φύσις κατὰ τούτους* [sc. monophysites] *εἰσάγει, λεγέτω τις ὁποῖόν τι ἕτερον εἶναι βούλεται τὸ τῆς δ. ἢ συγχύσεως ἀποτέλεσμα...πῶς δὲ τὰς δύο φύσεις παραιτούμενοι, ὡς πάντως τῆς δυάδος κατ' αὐτοὺς τὴν δ. εἰσαγούσης, δύο ἰδιότητας λέγειν οὐ παραιτοῦνται;* *ib.*(1936A); *εἰ δὲ πάλιν ἐξ ὑποστάσεων ἤγουν προσώπων λέγων γεγενῆσθαι τὴν ἕνωσιν, τὴν Ἐβιῶνος, Παύλου τε τοῦ Σαμωσατέως καὶ Νεστορίου δ. ἀποδειχθῇ φρονῶν, ἕτοιμον αὖθις σχοίη τὸ ψεῦδος συνήγορον, ἀντὶ φύσεων εἰρηκέναι τὰς ὑποστάσεις ἀποφαινόμενος...Νεστόριος...γὰρ κατὰ μόνην ψιλὴν τὴν προσηγορίαν, ὀνομάζων τὴν ἕνωσιν, κατ' ἐνεργείαν τὴν τῶν πραγμάτων εἰσῆγε δ.· καὶ οὗτος ψιλὴν τὴν διαφορὰν πρεσβεύων μετὰ τὴν ἕνωσιν, κατὰ μὲν τὴν ἐπίνοιαν εἶναι φρονεῖ τῶν διαφερόντων τὴν ὕπαρξιν· κατὰ δὲ τὴν ἐνέργειαν, τὴν αὐτῶν ἐπιδιατίθεται σύγχυσιν. ... εἰ μὴ ψιλὴν ἐκήρυττε τὴν διαφοράν, οὐ παρῃτεῖτο λέγειν ἐν Χριστῷ μετὰ τὴν ἕνωσιν τὴν ἄτμητον καὶ ἀδιαίρετον τῶν διαφερόντων ποιότητα* Max.*opusc.*(M.91.40C–41B); *πᾶσαν συναίρεσίν τε καὶ δ. τοῦ κατὰ Χριστὸν μυστηρίου... ἀποπέμπεται* *ib.*(88B).

B. of other forms of division; **1.** *incision*, medic., Epiph.*mens.*8 (M.43.248C); **2.** *separation*; of husband and wife, Sophr.Al.*libell.* (p.23.21; H.2.336D); from righteousness, hence *transgression* *διὰ δὲ τῆς εἰδωλοθύτων ἐδωδῆς ἔοικε καὶ τὰς ἄλλας δ. συντάττειν* Areth. *Apoc.*6(M.106.541B); **3.** *distribution*; of gifts of H. Ghost, Didym. (‡Bas.)*Eun.*5(1.298D; M.29.716D); of property, Gr.Nyss.*Placill.*(M. 46.892B); **4.** *selection* of offering, Cyr.*Juln.*10(6^2.347B).

II. *distinction*;

A. theol.; **1.** used correctly of Trin. *θεὸν πατέρα καὶ υἱὸν θεὸν καὶ πνεῦμα ἅγιον, δεικνύντας αὐτῶν καὶ τὴν ἐν τῇ ἑνώσει δύναμιν καὶ τὴν ἐν τῇ τάξει δ.* Athenag.*leg.*10.3(M.6.909B); *ib.*12.2(913C); *ὁμολογουμένως δ. δηλουμένης τοῦ ἁγίου πνεύματος παρὰ τὸν υἱὸν ἐν τῷ* [Mt.12:32] Or.*Jo.*2.10(6; p.65.12; M.14.128A); *μονὰς...παράδοξον ἔχουσα τὴν δ. τῶν προσώπων καὶ τὴν ἕνωσιν* ‡Bas.*h.myst.*60(p.395. 27); cf. I.A.1 supra; but term must be applied with caution *οὔτε τὴν ἕνωσιν σύγχυσιν ἐργαζόμενοι, οὔτε τὴν δ. ἀλλοτρίωσιν* Gr.Naz. *or.*39.11(M.36.348A); *ἐπὶ μὲν οὖν πάντων τῶν κτισμάτων ἡ μὲν τῶν ὑποστάσεων δ. πράγματι θεωρεῖται (πράγμασι γὰρ ὁ Πέτρος τὸν Παῦλον κεχωρισμένως θεωρεῖται)· ἡ δὲ κοινότης καὶ ἡ συνάφεια καὶ τὸ ἓν λόγῳ καὶ ἐπινοίᾳ...ἐπὶ δὲ τῆς ἁγίας...τριάδος τὸ ἀνάπαλιν. ἐκεῖ γὰρ τὸ μὲν κοινὸν καὶ ἓν πράγματι θεωρεῖται διὰ...τὸ ταὐτὸν τῆς οὐσίας καὶ τῆς ἐνεργείας...ἐπινοίᾳ δὲ τὸ διῃρημένον...οὔτε γὰρ τοπικὴν διάστασιν...δυνάμεθα ἐπὶ τῆς ἀπεριγράπτου λέγειν θεότητος... οὔτε θελήματος διαφορὰν...ἅτινα τὴν πραγματικὴν καὶ διόλου ἐν ἡμῖν γεννῶσι δ.*‡Cyr.*Trin.*10(6^3.14E–16A; M.77.1141C–1144B); *οὔτε τῷ ἑνὶ Σαβελλίζοντες κατὰ τῶν τριῶν, καὶ συναιρέσει κακῇ τὴν δ. λύοντες. οὔτε τοῖς τρισὶν Ἀρειανίζοντες κατὰ τοῦ ἑνός, καὶ πονηρᾷ δ. τὸ ἓν ἀνατρέποντες* Gr.Naz.*or.*42.16(M.36.476C); **2.** of cardinal importance in Christology of Theodore of Mopsuestia and Nestorius *εἷς δὲ υἱὸς ὁμολογεῖται δικαίως. ἐπείπερ ἡ τῶν φύσεων δ. ἀναγκαίως ὀφείλει διαμένειν, καὶ ἡ τοῦ προσώπου ἕνωσις ἀδιασπάστως φυλάττεσθαι* Thdr. Mops.*fr.inc.*(p.304.3; M.66.985B); *τὴν μὲν τῶν φύσεων ἐπήνουν δ. κατὰ τὸν τῆς ἀνθρωπότητος καὶ θεότητος λόγον καὶ τὴν τούτων εἰς ἑνὸς προσώπου συνάφειαν* Nest.*ep.Cyr.*2(p.30.18; M.77.52C); but not without regard to hypostatic union *Σευῆρος κακούργως ταὐτὸν εἶναι λέγει τῇ φύσει τὴν ὑπόστασιν, ἵνα τὴν σύγχυσιν διὰ τῆς μιᾶς κυρώσῃ φύσεως...καὶ πάλιν τὴν διαίρεσιν εἰσηγήσηται τὴν ἐξ ὑποστάσεως πρεσβεύων ἕνωσιν καὶ ὅτι καθάπερ Νεστόριος ψιλὴν λέγων τὴν ἕνωσιν, πραγματικὴν εἰσῆγε δ.· οὕτω καὶ Σευῆρος ψιλὴν λέγων φύσεων διαφοράν, πραγματικὴν ποιεῖται τὴν σύγχυσιν* Max.*opusc.*(M.91.40A).

B. in logic, *division* of an argument *μετὰ δ. καὶ τεχνολογίας Ἑλληνικῆς* Or.*Cels.*3.39(p.236.8; M.11.972B).

C. *exegesis, explanation*, [Is.44:3f.] *διὰ κρυφίων ἔχει νοητὴν δ.* Didym.*Trin.*2.6(M.39.556A).

D. *difference*; of divine titles, Thdr.Mops.*Eph.*1:3(p.120.16; M.66.912C); of aspects of revelation of the Word (cf. Jo.14:6), Or.*Jo.*6.46(28; p.155.30; M.14.281A); in gen., Ephr.1.121D.

διαιρ-έω, A. *divide, separate*; **1.** in gen.; of Pharisees separating themselves from rest of Jews, Or.*fr.34 in Jo.*(p.510.6); **2.** ref. distribution of eucharistic bread *ἄρτον εἰς πολλὰ διελών* Dion.Ar. *e.h.*3.3.12(M.3.444A); *τὸ θεῖον σῶμα...τῷ θιάσῳ πάντῃ ἀτμήτως ~ούμενον* ‡Caes.Naz.*dial.*169(M.38.1133); **3.** theol.; **a.** of Marcionite separation of God of justice from God of love *~οῦντες τὴν θεότητα* Or.*fr.49 in Jo.*(p.523.24); *τῶν ~ούντων τὴν κατὰ τὸ εὐαγγέλιον θεότητα ἐκ τῆς νομικῆς θεότητος* id.*Cels.*7.25(p.176.17; M.11.1456D); hence *τοὺς ~οῦντας τὴν παλαιὰν καὶ νέαν γραφήν* Ath.*exp.Ps.*67:27 (M.27.301B); **b.** Trin., ref. Sabellius, Ar.*ep.Alex.*(p.12.12; M.26. 709A) cit. s. *υἱοπάτωρ*; ref. materialistic conception of God *ἐκ τῆς οὐσίας φάσκειν τοῦ πατρὸς γεγεννῆσθαι τὸν υἱόν, οἱονεὶ μειουμένου καὶ λείποντος τῇ οὐσίᾳ...τοῦ θεοῦ, ἐπὰν γεννήσῃ τὸν υἱόν...καὶ σῶμα λέγειν τὸν πατέρα καὶ τὸν υἱόν, καὶ διῃρῆσθαι τὸν πατέρα* Or.*Jo.*20.18 (16; p.351.9; M.14.613D); allegation agst. Dion. Al. *ὅτι πατέρα λέγων...οὐκ ὀνομάζει τὸν υἱὸν καὶ πάλιν υἱὸν λέγων οὐκ ὀνομάζει τὸν πατέρα, ἀλλὰ ~εῖ καὶ μακρύνει καὶ μερίζει τὸν υἱὸν ἀπὸ τοῦ πατρός* Ath.*Dion.*16(p.58.12; M.25.504C); in Arian and Eusebian teaching attacked by Marcellus *διελεῖν γὰρ τὸν λόγον τοῦ θεοῦ τολμήσας καὶ ἕτερον θεὸν τὸν λόγον ὀνομάσαι οὐσίᾳ τε καὶ δυνάμει διεστῶτα τοῦ πατρός* Marcell.*fr.*72 ap.Eus.*Marcell.*1.4(p.26.14; M.24.765C); id. *fr.*65 *ib.*2.2(p.38.30; 789A); id.*fr.*58 ap.Eus.*e.th.*2.19(p.123.18; M.24. 944B); id.*fr.*60 *ib.*3.4(p.158.9; 1004B) cit. s. *πλατύνω*; ref. Arian doctrine *ἀναθεματίζειν δὲ καὶ τοὺς λέγοντας κτίσμα εἶναι τὸ πνεῦμα τὸ ἅγιον καὶ διῃρημένον ἐκ τῆς οὐσίας τοῦ Χριστοῦ· τοῦτο γάρ ἐστιν ἀληθῶς τὸ ἀποπηδᾶν ἀπὸ τῆς...αἱρέσεως τῶν Ἀρειάνων, τὸ μὴ ~εῖν τὴν ἁγίαν τριάδα καὶ λέγειν τι ταύτης εἶναι κτίσμα* Ath.*tom.*3(M.26. 800A); *ἄν τε διέλῃ πάλιν, ἕτερον μὲν τὸν πατέρα, ἕτερον δὲ τὸν υἱὸν καὶ τὸ πνεῦμα δὲ...ἕτερον εἶναι λέγων, ἐφέστηκεν Ἄρειος* Chrys.*sac.* 4.4(p.115.12; 1.410A); by an interval of time, Bas.*Spir.*59(3.50D; M.32.177B) cit. s. *διάστημα*; in orthodox thought, Gr.Naz.*or.*6.22 (M.35.749C) cit. s. *συνάπτω*; *δύο ταῦτα ἔστι πρόσωπα διῃρημένα* Didym.ap.*cat.Heb.*1:7(p.132.6); *ὑποστάσεσι...ἀσυγχύτως ἡνωμέναις καὶ ἀδιαστάτως ~ουμέναις...εἰς πατέρα καὶ υἱὸν καὶ ἅγιον πνεῦμα* ‡Cyr.*Trin.*7(6^3.8E; M.77.1132C); *Lit.Jac.*(p.162.1) cit. s. *μοναδικῶς*; **4.** Christol.; **a.** of Apollinarian division of Christ's humanity (by denying the human *νοῦς*), Gr.Naz.*or.*22.13(M.35.1145B); **b.** of Person of Christ; **i.** divided by early heretics *ἡ...κακόνοια Οὐαλεντίνου καὶ Μαρκίωνος καὶ Μανιχαίου...ὧν οἱ μὲν...δόκησιν εἰσηγήσαντο, οἱ δὲ ~οῦντες τὰ ἀδιαίρετα ἠρνήσαντο τὸ 'ὁ λόγος σὰρξ ἐγένετο'* Ath. *ep.Adelph.*2(M.26.1073B); **ii.** by Nestorius and his followers *τὸ θεοτόκος εἰσάγειν, ὡς κράσεως γινομένης καὶ τῶν δύο φύσεων μὴ ~ουμένων* Nest.*fr.*C 10(p.273.9)ap.Cyr.*apol.orient.*4(p.42.27; 6^1. 170B); *~οῦντες γάρ, φασίν, τὰς ὑποστάσεις ἑνοῦμεν τὸ πρόσωπον* Cyr.*ep.*50(p.100.5; 5^2.170C); cf. *ὁ ~ῶν τὰς φύσεις δύο υἱοὺς λέγει* id.*dial.Nest.*(M.76.252C); *ἕνα μὲν Χριστὸν καὶ υἱὸν ὁμολογεῖν ὑποπλάττονται καὶ ἓν αὐτοῦ πρόσωπον εἶναί φασι· ~οῦντες δὲ πάλιν εἰς ὑποστάσεις δύο κεχωρισμένας ἀλλήλων* id.*ep.*50(p.97.26; 167C); *οὐ γὰρ ἀνθρωπότης διεστήκει θεότητος, ὡς οἱ νῦν ~οῦντες τὸν Χριστὸν φασι* Thdot.Anc.*exp.symb.*2(M.77.1316D); *ib.*7(1324A); id.*hom.*3.4 (p.72.33; M.77.1388D) cit. s. *δοῦλος*; *Νεστόριος...τὰς φύσεις ~ούμενός τε καὶ σπαραττόμενος* Evagr.*h.e.*1.2(p.7.4; M.86.2424A); **iii.** orthodox denial of such teaching *προσκυνοῦμεν οὐ ~οῦντες τὸν υἱὸν καὶ τὸν λόγον, ἀλλ' αὐτὸν τὸν λόγον εἰδότες εἶναι τὸν υἱόν* Ath.*ep.Epict.*12 (p.17.23; M.26.1069A); *δύο φύσεων...μήτε συγχεομένων...ἢ διαιρεθεισῶν* id.ap.Leont.H.*monoph.*(M.86.1832D); *ἡ κατ' εὐδοκίαν ἕνωσις μίαν ἀμφοτέρων...ἐργάζεται τὴν προσηγορίαν, τὴν θέλησιν, τὴν ἐνέργειαν...μηδενὶ τρόπῳ ~ουμένην* Thdr.Mops.*ep.Domn.*(p.338.26; M.66.1012C); *μετὰ τὴν ἕνωσιν οὐ ~οῦμεν τὰς φύσεις ἀπ' ἀλλήλων... ἀλλ' ἕνα φαμὲν υἱόν* Cyr.*ep.*45(p.153.21; 5^2.137D); *προσκύνησον ὡς ἕνα, μὴ διελὼν εἰς δύο μετὰ τὴν ἕνωσιν* id.*ep.*1(p.23.13; 19B); id.*ep.* 17 *anath.*3(p.40.28; 76B) cit. s. *συνάφεια*; id.*ep.*50(p.92.11; 160D); *μηδ' ἂν ἐκεῖνο...τολμήσῃς εἰπεῖν ὅτι τὸ προκόπτειν ἐν ἡλικίᾳ κτλ. τῷ ἀνθρώπῳ προσάψομεν. τοῦτο γάρ, οἶμαι, ἐστὶν ἕτερον οὐδὲν ἢ διελεῖν εἰς δύο τὸν ἕνα Χριστόν* id.*hom.pasch.*17(5^2.230B); this view accepted by Antiochenes *ἥκιστα μὲν εἰς δύο ~οῦσι τὸν ἕνα υἱὸν καὶ Χριστὸν καὶ κύριον* id.*ep.*40(p.25.9; 114E); *ἓν αὐτοῦ τὸ πρόσωπον εἶναι πιστεύουσι κατ' οὐδένα ~οῦντες τρόπον εἰς δύο υἱούς* id.*ep.*50 (p.100.31; 171C); *ἀνάθεμα τῷ ~οῦντι* CChalc.*act.*1(*ACO* 2.1.1 p.93. 6; H.2.100E); *ἕνα...Χριστὸν...οὐκ εἰς δύο πρόσωπα μεριζόμενον ἢ ~ούμενον* *Symb.Chalc.*(p.130.1; H.2.456D); *γνωρίζομεν τὰς δύο* φύσεις· οὐ ~οῦμεν οὔτε διῃρημένας οὔτε συγκεχυμένας λέγομεν Bas. Sel.ap.CChalc.*act.*1(*ACO* 2.1.1 p.143.25; H.2.165D); οὐκ ἄλλος καὶ ἄλλος, ἀλλ' ὁ αὐτός ἐστιν οὐκέτι ~ούμενος Thdot.Anc.*exp.symb.*7 (M.77.1324C); ὃ ἥνωσεν ἡ χάρις, μὴ ~είτω ἔννοια *ib.*; ἀλλ' εἰ καὶ γέγονε διττός, ἀλλ' εἷς ἐστι μὴ ~ούμενος Proc.G.*Gen.*17:23(M. 87.360C); Sophr.H.*or.*2.46(M.87.3277D); this teaching recognizes separation of natures in unity of person, Leont.H.*Nest.*2.27(M.86. 1588B); ὧν ἐν τῇ ἑνώσει οὐ μένουσιν αἱ ὑποστάσεις φυσικῶς διῃρημέναι, τούτων ἡ ἕνωσις φύσεώς ἐστιν ἀλλοίωσις *ib.*2.28(1588C); **5.** of separation of Christ's spirit, soul, and body at death, Or.*dial.*7 (p.138.2); **6.** met., of man in rel. to God οὐ ~οῦμαι ἀπὸ σοῦ *A.Thom.*A 81(p.196.14); **7.** med., *be divided against* δ. καθ' ἑαυτῶν *ib.*94(p.207.13).

B. *distinguish*; Christol.; of distn. of NT passages applicable to the humanity from those relating to the divinity, Cyr.*ep.*40(p.26. 13; 5^{2}.115E); οὔτε μὴν φυσικὴν παραδέχονται [sc. Antiochenes] τὴν διαίρεσιν, καθὸ φρονεῖν ἔδοξε τῷ τῶν ἀθλίων εὑρημάτων εἰσηγητῇ· ~εῖσθαι δὲ μόνας διατείνονται τὰς ἐπὶ τῷ κυρίῳ φωνάς *ib.*(p.27.17; 117A); τὰς δὲ φωνὰς ~οῦσι μόνας, ~οῦσι δὲ...ὡς τὰς μὲν θεοπρεπεῖς εἶναι λέγειν, τὰς δὲ ἀνθρωπίνας id.*ep.*44(p.36.23; 134C); Jo.Ant.*ep. Cyr.*2(p.9.7; M.77.173A); δύο οὐσίαι ἡνωμέναι καθ' ὑπόστασιν· καὶ διῃρημέναι ὅσον ἐπινοίᾳ μόνῃ, ταῖς τε ποιότησι καὶ ἐνεργείαις, ὅροις τε καὶ θελήσεσιν, μιᾶς οὔσης τῆς συνθέτου ὑποστάσεως καὶ ἑνὸς προσώπου *Lit.Jac.*(*NBP* 10^{2} p.37).

C. *analyse* thoughts etc., †Nil.*mal.cog.*19(M.79.1221B).

D. med., *be set in opposition*, Jo.Mosch.*prat.*66(M.87.2917B).

διαίρω, 1. *remove, transfer*, Epiph.*haer.*66.9(p.30.19; M.42.44B); **2.** *open one's mouth, speak*, Eus.*d.e.*3.7(p.141.12; M.22.237C); Bas. *ep.*226.1(3.346C; M.32.844B); Chrys.*stat.*2.1(2.20D).

διαιτάριος, ὁ, (Lat. *diaitarius*), *steward* of imperial palace, Thdr. Lect.*fr.*(M.86.224D).

διαιτητής, ὁ, *arbitrator*; of Christ, Or.*Cels.*3.37(p.234.18; M.11. 969A).

διαιωνίζ-ω, 1. *endure for ever, be eternal*; in gen., Meth.*lepr.*10 (p.464.14); Diod.*Ps.*88(M.33.1619A); Chrys.*hom.22.7 in Gen.*(4. 204B); of eternal life, id.*hom.in Rom.5:3*(3.141D); Diad.*perf.*41 (p.48.6); Sophr.H.*ep.syn.*(M.87.3184B); theol. τὸν γεννηθέντα σὺν τῷ πατρὶ ~ειν Ath.*gent.*47(M.25.93D); **2.** trans., *perpetuate*, Eus. *v.C.*3.41(p.95.10; M.20.1101A); *ib.*4.60(p.141.25; 1209C); *wish perpetuity to* τὴν ἀρχὴν ~ειν λιπαρῶς ἐναρξάμενοι Mac.Mgn.*apocr.*4.25 (p.208.4); **3.** *be distributed regularly* καλαμίων συντόμια πολλὰ ἄρτων ~όντων Jo.Mal.*chron.*12 p.289(M.97.437A); *ib.*13 p.322(484A); *Chron.Pasch.*p.263(M.92.641B).

διακαθαίρ-ω, 1. *make clear*, Ath.*decr.*22(p.19.1; M.25.456B); *explain, define*, Chrys.*hom.34.5 in 1Cor.*(10.317A); **2.** *order, arrange*; pass., Clem.*str.*6.1(p.423.4; M.9.209A); **3.** *clear away, remove*, *ib.*5.1 (p.333.9; 25A); *ib.*7.15(p.63.22; 524B); **4.** *reap, gather* τὰ δὲ νέα σπέρματα ἐπανθήσαντα ~εται εἰς τοὺς ἀλῶνας συγκομιζόμενα Petr. I Al.*fr.*(M.18.513B).

***διακαθαίρωσις, ἡ,** *thorough cleansing* or *purging*, Chrys.*scand.*7 (3.480A).

***διακαινήσιμος, ἡ,** [sc. ἑβδομάς] *new week* i.e. *Easter week* εἴ τις τὴν ἑβδομάδα τῆς λαμπροφόρου ἀναστάσεως ἤγουν τῆς δ. σμικρύνει μίαν τῶν ἡμερῶν *Poen.App.*1.1; ‡Germ.CP *contempl.*(M.98.392C); *Catech.Stud.*9(M.99.1700C).

διακαλέομαι, 1. *be called* by a name or title, Cyr.*ador.*17(1. 599E); *ib.*5(171B); id.*inc.unigen.*8(5^{1}.704D); **2.** *be called* or *summoned*, *ib.*(679B).

***διακαλλύνω,** *adorn*, Thdt.*affect.*2(p.56.15; 4.748).

***διακάλυμμα, τό,** *dividing veil*, ‡Meth.*Sym.et Ann.*1(M.18.348A).

διακαλύπτομαι, *be covered completely*, Gr.Nyss.*v.Mos.*38(M.44. 312D).

διακάμπτω, *turn away* or *aside*, Epiph.*haer.*59.12(p.377.11; M.41. 1036B).

***διακαπνίζω,** *contend zealously* or *warmly*, ‡Chrys.*hom.in Ps. 38*:7(5.567D).

***διακαταπονέομαι,** *be disturbed* or *distressed*, ‡Chrys.*poenit.*1.8 (9.777A).

***διακατάσχεσις, ἡ,** *occupation*, Just.*dial.*139.4(M.6.796C).

διακατελέγχομαι, *be confuted thoroughly*, ‡Felix III Papa *ep. Petr.*2(p.14.9; H.2.825B).

διακατοχή, ἡ, *possession*, Epiph.*haer.*66.83(p.126.9; M.42.161A).

διάκαυσις, ἡ, *burning heat*, Ath.*gent.*27(M.25.56A).

διάκει-μαι, 1. *be well disposed, feel affection*, Constantius Ant.*ep.* 5(M.52.746); Chrys.*ep.*56(3.625A); id.*hom.62.5 in Mt.*(7.626B); id. *hom.15.2 in Rom.*(9.595D); εἰ ἁπλῶς τῶν περὶ ἡμᾶς ~μένων ἦσθα *if you were one of my ordinary acquaintances*, id.*ep.*47(3.619A); **2.** *be convinced* or *assured*; hence *hold an opinion*, Or.*princ.*4.3.5(p.331. 13; M.11.385B); Cyr.*Jo.*9(4.747C); id.*hom.pasch.*16(5^{2}.217D); περὶ τὸ δόγμα ~μένων *upholding the orthodox doctrine*, Soz.*h.e.*2.13.6 (M.67.965D); **3.** *be ordered* or *arranged* τετραχῇ τῶν στίχων ~μένων Gr.Nyss.*v.Mos.*(M.44.320C); Chrys.*hom.14.1 in Eph.*(11.103D); **4.** *be situated* ἀγρῷ τῆς πόλεως ἔξωθεν ~μένῳ Philost.*h.e.*9.5(M. 65.572B); Cyr.*Soph.*39(3.616C); Jo.Mosch.*prat.*92(M.87.2949B).

***διακεκλασμένως,** *half-heartedly*, Nil.*epp.*3.263(M.79.516B).

***διακεκομμένως,** *asunder, separately*, of Father and Son ἐν μιᾷ ἄμφω τῇ φύσει, διῃρημένως δὲ ἀναμέρος ἑκάτερος, ὡς ὑπάρχων ἰδιοσυστάτως, πλὴν οὐ πάντῃ δ. Cyr.*Jo.*3.5(4.307B).

διακεκριμένως, *with differentiation*, Gr.Nyss.*diff.ess.*4(M.32. 332A); κατὰ γένος δ. Euthal.Diac.*epp.Paul.*(M.85.749D); opp. ἡνωμένως, Const.Diac.*laud.*19(M.88.501B).

***διακέλευσις, ἡ,** *giving of orders*, Philost.*fr.*(M.65.636B).

διακηρύσσ-ω, *proclaim*, *A.Phil.*15(p.8.23); Gr.Nyss.*Eun.*11(2 p.255.4; M.45.861C); Sophr.H.*v.Anast.*(M.92.1685B); c. acc. ὁ νόμος ...~ει...τὸν ἀρχιερέα Cyr.*ador.*7(1.225C).

διακιν-έω, 1. met., *incite, provoke*, Clem.*str.*4.10(p.282.33; M.8. 1288A); **2.** *proceed, walk*; abs., *A.Phil.*128(p.57.3); Ammon.*Ac.*1:13 (M.85.1525A); c. acc. δ. τὴν ἔρημον *Apophth.Patr.*(M.65.85D).

[*]διακιχράω, *lend*, Cyr.*ador.*8(1.273C); id.*Am.*74(3.333C).

διάκλασις, ἡ, *softness*; of a voice, Chrys.*sac.*6.2(p.143.6; 1. 422C); of limbs, id.*hom.37.6 in Mt.*(7.422E).

διακλ-άω, 1. *break in pieces*, Chrys.*hom.72.3 in Mt.*(7.705B); *ib. 89.4*(837E); id.*hom.10.2 in Eph.*(11.77D); ref. eucharist ἀνέχεται ~ώμενος [sc. ὁ Χριστός] ἵνα πάντας ἐμπλήσῃ id.*hom.24.2 in 1Cor.* (10.213D); **2.** met., *weaken* οὐχ ἵνα διακλάσῃ...τὴν ψυχὴν καταφέρεται ἡ πληγή id.*hom.6.6 in Phil.*(11.243D); id.*hom.29.3 in Heb.*(12.275B).

διακλονέω, *shake violently*, Gr.Nyss.*virg.*3(p.262.23; M.46.332D).

***διάκλυσις, ἡ,** *washing*, Thdr.Stud.*epp.*2.219(M.99.1661B).

***διακλώθω,** *weave*, Gr.Naz.*or.*19.8(M.35.1052B).

διακνίζω, pass., *be enraged*, *Chron.Pasch.*p.395(M.92.1012B).

διακοιλαίνω, *hollow*, Cyr.*Ag.*4(3.630B).

***διακολοβόω,** *curtail*, Gr.Nyss.*Eun.*1(1 p.115.2; M.45.349B).

διακομιδή, ἡ, 1. *transportation*, ‡Jo.D.*Artem.*18(p.157.6; M.96. 1268B); **2.** *journey, passage* τὴν τοῦ σωτῆρος...δ. ... εἰς Αἴγυπτον Eus.*d.e.*9.3(p.409.12; M.22.660C).

διακομίζ-ω, *carry, convey*; met. ἄσκησις...τὸν κόσμον...μετὰ ῥᾳστώνης ἀβασάνιστον ἐκεῖ ~ουσα Meth.*symp.*10.6(p.129.3; M.18. 204B); Cyr.*ador.*2(1.50D).

***διακομιστής, ὁ,** *bearer* of a letter, Synes.*ep.*8(M.66.1345B); *ib.*13 (M.1349B); *ib.*69(M.1433A); of an oral statement or message, Ant. Mon.*hom.*29(M.89.1529C); Μωσῆς...τῶν παρὰ θεοῦ νόμων δ. Cyr.*glaph. Ex.*3(1.316B); id.*Zach.*37(3.713C); id.*Ps.*47:4(M.69.1061B).

***διακονάω,** *sharpen* ἡ γνῶσις περιγίνεται...οὐδ' ἐκ παιδείας τῆς ἐγκυκλίου· ἀγαπητὸν γὰρ εἰ παρασκευάσαι μόνον τὴν ψυχὴν καὶ διακονῆσαι δύναιτο Clem.*str.*7.3(p.14.17; M.9.424C) [but perh. from διακονέω, *serve* or *equip* by means of propaedeutic studies].

διακον-έω, I. in gen., *serve, minister to, administer*;

A. *serve*; **1.** of waiting at table, *A.Phil.*94 (p.36.31) etc.; **2.** of personal attendance upon a master, Chrys.*hom.72.3 in Mt.*(7. 705B); id.*hom.4.3 in Tit.*(11.752E); of attendance by διακονητής upon senior monk in a community, *Apophth.Patr.*(M.65.257D); **3.** of work of an animal, Jo.Mosch.*prat.*158(M.87.3025D).

B. hence *promote, further the cause of* οἱ εἰσέτι ~οῦντες τῇ δικαιοσύνῃ τοῦ κηρύγματος Arist.*apol.*15.2(M.96.1121C); Or.*Cels.*6.79 (p.150.19; M.11.1417C).

C. *attend to, have as one's business* τοῖς πράγμασιν ἃ ~οῦνται Or. *Cels.*1.25(p.76.11; M.11.708A); καταξιωθῆς ~ήσασθαί τινι πνευματικῷ πράγματι Chrys.*hom.8.2 in Mt.*(7.122A); τῇ ἐπιστολῇ τοῦ γράμματος ~ησάμενος Thdr.Mops.*Heb.*proem.(M.66.952B); Evagr.*h.e.*2.2 (p.38.28; M.86.2480C); ταῖς ἀποκρίσεσι ~ῶν Ath.Scholast.*coll.* 1.2(p.11); hence *have a particular business* or *mission* ὁ...Γαβριήλ, ~ησάμενος πρὸς τὴν Μαρίαν Didym.*Trin.*2.4(M.39.481D); of worldly business opp. meditation, Cyr.H.*procatech.*13.

D. *supply wants of, afford assistance to, minister*; **1.** of material things ὁ λύχνος ~ήσει τὸ φῶς Clem.*paed.*2.3(p.179.22; M.8.436B); *ib.*1.6(p.117.12; 304B); Chrys.*hom.39.1 in Mt.*(7.432E); esp. of ministrations to poor, and those in receipt of subventions from Church funds χήραν, τὴν καταλεγεῖσαν εἰς τὸν ἀριθμὸν τῶν χηρῶν, τουτέστι, τὴν ~ουμένην ὑπὸ τῆς ἐκκλησίας Bas.*ep.*199 *can.*24(3. 293D; M.32.724B); Chrys.*hom.19.2 in Mt.*(7.246A); ἀπέστειλεν νομίσματα...παρακαλέσασα αὐτὸν ἐκεῖνα ~ῆσαι τοῖς...ἀδελφοῖς Pall.*h. Laus.*58(p.151.22; M.34.1203C); Nil.*epp.*2.105(M.79.248A); **2.** of abstracts Μωυσῆς...πολιτείαν...διηκόνησεν ἀγαθήν· ἡ δέ ἐστι τροφὴ ἀνθρώπων Clem.*str*.1.26(p.104.25; M.8.916B); Μωσέως...ταύτην [sc. χάριν] ∼ησαμένου Eus.*Marcell*.1.1(p.3.12; M.24.716B); Cyr.*Jo*.3.6 (4.311A); pass., *be furnished* τὸ φθαρτὸν...ταῖς...τοῦ πνεύματος βουλαῖς τε καὶ πράξεσιν διηκονεῖτο Eus.*d.e*.7.1(p.302.23; M.22.496B); Ἱερεμίας τοῖς...παρὰ θεοῦ ∼ούμενος λόγοις Cyr.*Is*.1.3(2.82B); Max. *ambig*.(M.91.1253B); **3.** hence *administer*, Evagr.*h.e*.1.22(p.33.1; M.86.2184B).

II. *serve* God;

A. in gen., Or.*Cels*.4.4(p.277.10; M.11.1033B); Nil.*epp*.2.167(M. 79.281C); *cat.Jud*.7(p.158.8).

B. of angels: serving Christ (Mt.4:11), Clem.*exc.Thdot*.85(p.132. 27; M.9.697A); fulfilling behests of God, Ath.*Ar*.3.12(M.26.348A); Gel.Cyz.*h.e*.2.24.16(M.85.1301B); esp. in ministering to men, Just. *dial*.79.2(M.6.661B); Or.*Cels*.1.25(p.76.11; M.11.708A); *ib*.5.4(p.4.18; 1185B); τοῦτο γὰρ ἔργον...τῶν ἀγγελικῶν ταγμάτων τε καὶ δυνάμεών ἐστι τὸ ∼εῖν πρὸς εὐεργεσίαν καὶ τιμὴν τῆς εἰκόνος τοῦ θεοῦ, τουτέστι τοῦ ἀνθρώπου Cosm.Ind.*top*.2(M.88.117D); v. ἄγγελος.

C. within Church; **1.** in gen., of ministry of word, Or.*Jo*.32.17 (10; p.454.2; M.14.788A); Bas.*Spir*.79(3.67D; M.32.217B); v. διακονία; and H. Ghost τὸ πνεῦμα...οὐ διηκονεῖτο Φίλιππος τῷ βαπτιζομένῳ Or.*comm.in 1Cor*.1:14(*JTS* 9 p.234); of ministering to God with liturg. worship οὐδεὶς ἄξιος...προσέρχεσθαι ἢ λειτουργεῖν σοι... τὸ γὰρ ∼ῆσαί σοι μέγα καὶ φοβερόν *Lit.Jac*.(p.178.27); of ministering grace and office of apostleship, Or.*comm.in 1Cor*.12:28(*JTS* 10 p.32.4); **2.** in partic. eccl. offices; **a.** of apostles, Or.*Jo*.32.17(10; p.453.27; M.14.785D); apostles and prophets, *ib*.1.25(24; p.31.22; 68D); **b.** of bishops διαδέχεται...τοῦτον Φαβιανός, ἐπὶ μῆνα τῇ λειτουργίᾳ ∼ησάμενον Eus.*h.e*.6.29.1(M.20.588B); *ib*.7.2.1(640B); **c.** of deacons; **i.** in gen. οἱ ἀπόστολοι καὶ ἐπίσκοποι καὶ διδάσκαλοι καὶ διάκονοι οἱ πορευθέντες κατὰ τὴν σεμνότητα τοῦ θεοῦ καὶ ἐπισκοπήσαντες καὶ διδάξαντες καὶ ∼ήσαντες ἁγνῶς...τοῖς ἐκλεκτοῖς τοῦ θεοῦ, οἱ μὲν κεκοιμημένοι, οἱ δὲ ἔτι ὄντες Herm.*vis*.3.5.1; γενόμενος διάκονος...οὐκ ἤθελε καταδέξασθαι ∼εῖν *Apophth.Patr*.(M.65.193A); Pall.*v.Chrys*.15(p.92.10; M.47.52); **ii.** with emphasis on function of ministering poor-relief διάκονοι...κακῶς ∼ήσαντες καὶ διαρπάσαντες χηρῶν καὶ ὀρφανῶν τὴν ζωήν Herm.*sim*.9.26.2; **iii.** of deacon's office contrasted with priest's οὔτε διάκονοι ἐν τῇ ἐκκλησιαστικῇ τάξει ἐπιστεύθησάν τι μυστήριον ἐπιτελεῖν, ἀλλὰ μόνον ∼εῖν τὰ ἐπιτελούμενα Epiph.*haer*.79.4(p.478.31; M.42.745A); but regarded as a step towards promotion to priesthood οἱ γὰρ καλῶς ∼ήσαντες... τόπον ἑαυτοῖς περιποιοῦνται τὸν ποιμενικόν *Ordo Eccl.App*.23; **iv.** of liturg. functions of deacon οὐ προσφέρει, τοῦ δὲ ἐπισκόπου προσενεγκόντος ἢ τοῦ πρεσβυτέρου, αὐτὸς ἐπιδίδωσι τῷ λαῷ, οὐχ ὡς ἱερεὺς ἀλλ' ὡς ∼ούμενος ἱερεῦσι *Const.App*.8.28.4; Epiph.*haer*.79.4 (p.478.31; 745A); ὁ ∼ούμενος τοῖς μυστηρίοις Chrys.*hom.82.6 in Mt*. (7.790A); of reading of prayers appointed to be said by deacons, *Lit*.ap.*Const.App*.8.6.1; **v.** of deacon's personal attendance upon his superior, *A.Jo*.30(p.167.8); cf.‡Hipp.*can*.5.34; **d.** of deaconesses, in administration of poor-relief to widows, *Const.App*.3.14.2.

III. ref. work of Christ; **1.** as Father's agent in Creation ἑτέρου μὲν πεποιηκότος, αὐτοῦ δὲ ∼ησαμένου Eus.*e.th*.2.14(p.116.11; M.24. 929C); *Symb.Ant*.(345)6(p.253.6; M.26.732B); **2.** as mediator between God and man οὐ μὴν ὁ ἐπὶ πάντων, ἀλλ' ὁ ἐκείνου δεύτερος, τὰ τοῦ πατρὸς εἰς ἀνθρώπους ∼ούμενος Eus.*d.e*.5.10(p.233.13; M.22. 385A); ἵνα, μεσίτης γενόμενος θεοῦ καὶ ἀνθρώπων, τὰ μὲν θεοῦ ἡμῖν, τὰ δὲ ἡμῶν τῷ θεῷ ∼ῇ ‡Ath.*Ar*.4.6(p.50.10; M.26.476B); as mediator of baptismal grace, Eus.*e.th*.3.5(p.163.24; M.24.1013A).

διακόνημα, τό, *office* or *ministry* exercised within Church, Jo. Mosch.*prat*.118(M.87.2981B).

***διακονητής (*-ιτής), ὁ,** *attendant, minister*; of attendant upon a senior monk in monastery, *Apophth.Patr*.(M.65.104A); *ib*.(260A); ὁ δ. ... τοῦ ἀββᾶ Jo.Mosch.*prat*.138(M.87.3001A); of any monastery servant (gardener, cook etc.), *ib*.158(3025D); Dor.*doct*.4.10(M.88. 1672C); of high-ranking servant in monastery -ιτής Ephr.2.176D.

***διακονήτρια, ἡ,** *female attendant, ministrant* (not technical term for *deaconess*), Steph.Diac.*v.Steph*.(M.100.1168B).

διακονία, ἡ, A. in gen.; **1.** *service, function* ἕως ἐκτελέσω τὴν δ. μου εἰς ἣν ἀπεστάλην *A.Andr.et Mt*.7(p.74.2); χειρῶν δ. Dion. Al.ap.Eus.*p.e*.14.26(779D; M.21.1281D); Ath.*Ar*.2.27(M.26.205A); Chrys.*stat*.8.1(2.92D); σατανικὰς δ. ἐκτελοῦσιν οἱ δαίμονες Nil.*epp*. 1.294(M.79.189C); **2.** esp. *ministration* to need, *provision* of money, food etc., Or.*fr.59 in Jo*.(p.531.18); hence = θεραπεία, Clem.*q.d.s*. 35(p.183.10; M.9.641A); **3.** *administration, ministry* δ. θανάτου Clem.*exc.Thdot*.58(p.126.9; M.9.688A); δ. τοῦ πνεύματος...τοῦ νόμου Thdt.*2Cor*.3:8(3.303); δ. τῆς καταλλαγῆς *cat.2Cor*.5:18(p.386.4).

B. ref. service to God; **1.** in gen. ἔχει γάρ...ὁ γάμος ἰδίας λειτουργίας καὶ δ. τῷ κυρίῳ διαφερούσας Clem.*str*.3.12(p.231.29; M.8.1180A); Or.*Jo*.2.30(24; p.87.26; M.14.168A); Marc.Er.*opusc*.2.197(M.65. 961A); of almsgiving as service to God, Herm.*sim*.1.9; Chrys.*hom. 79.5 in Jo*.(8.471C); **2.** of Jo. Bapt., Or.*Jo*.2.30(24; p.87.9; M.14. 165C); **3.** of Levites, *1Clem*.40.5; and priests, Clem.*str*.5.6(p.348. 14; M.9.57B); of prophets, id.*exc.Thdot*.24(p.115.4; M.9.672A); **4.** of angels οὐ μίαν...πιστεύονται δ. εὐαγγελικὴν ἄγγελοι οὐδὲ μόνην τὴν πρὸς τοὺς ποιμένας γεγενημένην Or.*Jo*.1.14(p.18.28; M.14.48B); Bas. *Eun*.2.21(1.257C; M.29.620A) cit. s. ὑπουργός; Cosm.Ind.*top*.2(M.88. 124D); *ib*.5(260C); **5.** exercised within Church; **a.** in gen., of preaching, consolation etc., Herm.*mand*.12.3.3; Clem.*q.d.s*.35(p.183.10; M.9.641A); †Marc.Er.*temp*.26(M.65.1065D); **b.** of charitable service, poor-relief, and ministration to those maintained by Church, Herm.*mand*.2.6; τὴν οὐσίαν καθιερώσασα τῇ...ἐκκλησίᾳ...εἰς τὴν τῶν πτωχῶν δ. Gr.Naz.*test*.(M.37.389A); *Const.App*.3.13.2,4.1.1; hence, plur., *alms*, Cyr.*Mal*.27(3.844C); **c.** of liturg. service, Isid.Pel.*epp*. 1.123(M.78.264D) cit. s. δῶρον; by whole congregation ὁ θέμενος ἡμᾶς εἰς τὴν δ. ταύτην *Lit.Jac*.(p.194.2); **d.** of partic. ministry; **i.** of apostles, Clem.*str*.3.6(p.220.20; M.8.1157A); Or.*Jo*.32.17(10; p.453.14; M.14.785B); **ii.** of bishops ὃν ἐπίσκοπον ἔγνων...κεκτῆσθαι τὴν δ. Ign.*Philad*.1.1; Ποθεινός, ὁ τὴν δ. τῆς ἐπισκοπῆς ἐν Λουγδούνῳ πεπιστευμένος *Ep.Lugd*.ap.Eus.*h.e*.5.1.29(M.20.420A); **iii.** of evangelists, Or.*Jo*.1.12(13; p.17.21; M.14.45B); **iv.** of Seven of Ac. 6 (regarded as διάκονοι), Hipp.*haer*.7.36(p.223.7; M.16.3343B); **v.** of partic. office, *diaconate*, of διάκονοι who are entrusted with δ. Χριστοῦ Ign.*Magn*.6.1; id.*Philad*.10.2; id.*Smyrn*.12.1; office being largely concerned with poor-relief, Herm.*sim*.9.26.2; and compared with OT ministry of Levites, *1Clem*.40.5; as technical term, Ath.*syn*.38(p.265.5; M.26.761A); *Const.App*.8.18.4; Chrys.*sac*.2.7 (p.46.8; 1.380A) (but reference here may poss. be to gen. ministry); dist. from teaching office, Philost.*h.e*.3.17(M.65.509A); regarded as regular stage in eccl. preferment ἠξιώθη μὲν ἐκκλησιαστικῆς δ.· ἠξιώθη δὲ τοῦ πρεσβύτερος εἶναι Synes.*ep*.66(M.66.1408C); ἐνδιατρίψας οὖν χρόνον μικρὸν ἐν τῷ βαθμῷ τῆς δ. κατὰ τοὺς θείους κανόνας, ἵνα εὐεργετήσῃ πλείονας, ἀνάγεται καὶ εἰς τὴν τῶν πρεσβυτέρων καθέδραν Eustrat.*v.Eutych*.15(M.86.2292A); v. βαθμός, διάκονος; hence **vi.** = *body of deacons* collectively, *Lit*.ap.*Const.App*.8.10.2; *Lit.Jac*.(p.208.9); **vii.** of office of deaconess εὔχρηστόν ἐστιν...ταῖς γυναιξὶν δ. καταστῆσαι *Ordo Eccl.App*.24; ἦν τις προτεταγμένη τοῦ χοροῦ τῆς παρθενίας ἐν τῷ τῆς δ. βαθμῷ Gr.Nyss.*v.Macr*.(p.402.15; M.46.988D); Thdr.Mops.*1Tim*.5:9(p.159 n; M.66.944A); γυνὴ...τοῦ τῆς δ. ἠξιωμένη χαρίσματος Thdt.*h.e*.3.14.1(3.927).

C. *of ministry* or *service* of Son ὅσον ὁ υἱὸς διαφέρει δούλου, τοσοῦτον καὶ τῆς δ. τῶν δούλων ἡ τοῦ υἱοῦ δ. κρείττων γέγονε Ath.*Ar*.1.55 (M.26.128A); οὐ δουλικὴν ὑπέμεινε δ. ... οὐδὲ ἐξεδόθη παρά τινος, ἀλλ' ἑαυτὸν ἔδωκεν Chrys.*hom.1.4 in Gal*.(10.663A); of the work of the Logos in Creation 'τὸ δι' αὐτοῦ', οὐ δ. ἕνεκεν αὐτῷ κεῖται, ἀλλὰ συνεργείας Thdr.Mops.*fr.3 in Jo*.(p.312.14; M.66.729C).

D. of the office of H. Ghost τοῦ ἁγίου πνεύματος...ἑτοίμου τε παρεστῶτος εἰς ἣν τέτακται δ. Eus.*e.th*.3.5(p.162.1; M.24.1009C); πνεῦμα...ὡδήγησεν αὐτούς. καὶ μὴ...τὴν ὁδηγίαν πάλιν εἰς ταπεινὴν δ. ἐκλάβῃς. τοῦτο γὰρ καὶ θεοῦ ἔργον Bas.*Spir*.49(3.42A; M.32. 160A); ἡ αὐτὴ δὲ ἡ δ. τοῦ πνεύματος καὶ τοῦ λόγου Epiph.*anc*.69 (p.87.2; M.43.145B).

διακονικός, *of* or *pertaining to ministry, deacon,* or *diaconate*;

A. as adj. ἑτέρα τις ἐπιστολὴ τοῖς ἐν Ῥώμῃ τοῦ Διονυσίου φέρεται διακονικὴ διὰ Ἱππολύτου Eus.*h.e*.6.46.5(M.20.636B); various interprn. **1.** *serviceable* [i.e. containing practical advice]; **2.** = ἐπιστολὴ εἰρηνική (v. εἰρηνικός); **3.** *concerned with deacons*; **4.** *concerned with ecclesiastical administration*, cf. *de ministeriis*, Rufinus ad loc. (*GCS* Eus.*h.e*.p.629.12); **5.** perh., *sent by a deacon* as messenger.

B. neut. as subst., *place in*, or *part of, church, used for ministry of altar*; **1.** of sacristy or vestry, where sacred vessels were kept; used by deacons and forbidden to subdeacons, CLaod.*can*.21; also used by priests, Cyr.S.*v.Euthym*.39(p.57.25); *ib*.48(p.69.13,15,18); esp. by celebrant, Jo.Mosch.*prat*.25(M.87.2872A); cf.*Lit.Marc*. (p.143.10); **2.** as separate building οἶκον εὗρεν μέγαν διακονικοῦ τάξιν ἐπέχοντα Cyr.S.*v.Sab*.18(p.102.4); **3.** either *sanctuary*, i.e. that part of church used by ministers, or *chapel*, containing altar, situated near sanctuary and used as sacristy, *Apophth.Patr*.(M.65. 149A); cf. τὸν δὲ ἀνδριάντα μεταστησάμενοι ἐν τῷ τῆς ἐκκλησίας δ. τὰ πρέποντα ἐθεράπευον...στάσει...σεμνοτέρᾳ Philost.*h.e*.7.3(M.65. 540A); †Anast.S.*relat*.52(p.76.21).

διακονικῶς, *in the manner of a servant*, ref. Martha ταρασσομένην δ. Clem.*q.d.s*.10(p.166.15; M.9.613C); ref. Christ δ. ἐπλάττετο Cyr.

*Is.*4.4(2.662B); of H. Ghost, ref. ἐνεργοῦν...αὐτεξουσίως οὐ δ. *Lit. Marc.*(p.134.4).

διακόνισσα, ἡ, *deaconess* (cf. διάκονος, ἡ); **1.** in gen. τὴν γυναῖκα τοῦ υἱοῦ αὐτοῦ κατέστησεν δ. *A.Mt.*28(p.259.5), where δ. appears to possess status inferior to that of πρεσβῦτις q.v.; CNic.(325)*can.*19; σεμνοτάτῃ γυναικὶ καὶ τῷ θεῷ προσομιλούσῃ, τῇ δ. Σαβινιανῇ Pall. *h.Laus.*41(p.129.5); *IGC As.Min.*258; **2.** function; not exercise of priesthood but ministry to women, esp. assistance at women's baptisms, Epiph.*haer.*79.3(p.478.16; M.42.744D); id.*exp.fid.*21 (p.522.18; M.42.824C) cit s. ἀειπάρθενος; δ. οὐκ εὐλογεῖ· ἀλλ' οὐδέ τι ὧν ποιοῦσιν οἱ πρεσβύτεροι ἢ οἱ διάκονοι ἐπιτελεῖ, ἀλλ' ἢ τοῦ φυλάττειν τὰς θύρας, καὶ ἐξυπηρετεῖσθαι τοῖς πρεσβυτέροις ἐν τῷ βαπτίζεσθαι τὰς γυναῖκας *Const.App.*8.28.4; fulfils many tasks, partic. assistance at baptism, cf.*ib.*3.16.2; **3.** ordination of deaconess; **a.** apptly. receives no imposition of hands, CNic. (325)*can.*19; **b.** but imposition of hands explicitly mentioned, *Const.App.*8.19.2; CChalc.*can.*15; and implied οὐκ ἐπιτρέπομεν δὲ πρεσβυτέροις χειροτονεῖν διακόνους ἢ δ. ... ἀλλὰ μόνοις τοῖς ἐπισκόποις *Const.App.*3.11.3; **c.** ordination by bishop takes place παρεστῶτος τοῦ πρεσβυτερίου καὶ τῶν διακόνων καὶ τῶν δ. *ib.*8.19.2; **d.** ordination prayer for deaconess, *ib.*8.20; **4.** a consecrated person, Justn.*cod.*1.3.53(p.37;) Phot.*nomoc.*9.29(*Mon.*2 p.565); **5.** qualifications for office; **a.** in gen. δ. ... χειροτονεῖσθαι...μετὰ ἀκριβοῦς δοκιμασίας CChalc.*can.*15; **b.** must be μονόγαμοι ἐγκρατευσάμεναι ἢ χηρεύσασαι ἀπὸ μονογαμίας ἢ ἀειπάρθενοι Epiph. *exp.fid.*21(p.522.20; M.42.825A); must not marry after ordination, CChalc.*can.*15; Phot.*nomoc.*9.29(*Mon.*2 p.565); **c.** minimum age for ordination; **i.** deaconess ordained at 17, *A.Mt.*28(p.259.5); **ii.** age fixed at 60 (cf. 1Tim.5:9), cf.*Cod.Thds.*16.2.27; **iii.** at 40, CChalc.*can.*15; CTrull.*can.*14; *ib.*40; **6.** number of deaconesses in a church ἐν τῇ μεγάλῃ ἐκκλησίᾳ Κωνσταντινουπόλεως εἶναι...κ' δ. Phot.*nomoc.*1.30(*Mon.*2 p.477); number raised by Heraclius to 40, *ib.*

***διακονιστής, ὁ,** *minister, attendant,* Ast.Am.*hom.*1(M.40.173B).

***διακονιτής, ὁ,** v. *διακονητής.

διάκονος, ὁ, I. in gen.;

A. *servant*; of waiter at table, Clem.*paed.*2.1(p.161.29; M.8. 396B); of a letter-carrier, Bas.*ep.*200(3.298A; M.32.733B); *ib.*231 (354C; M.861B); of a royal official as king's servant, Cels.ap.Or. *Cels.*8.35(p.250.20; M.11.1569B); of Christ as δ. πάντων Polyc.*ep.*5.2.

B. *agent, ministrant, executant*; of a father μὴ αἴτιον ἡγήσησθε ...μᾶλλον δὲ δ. γενέσεως Clem.*str.*3.12(p.236.25; M.8.1189A); κἂν γεωργός τις ᾖ...δ. ἐστι σπερμάτων καταβολῆς *ib.*6.16(p.507.28; M.9. 377C); ἐν ἀγγέλῳ δ. τῆς τιμωρίας Eus.*d.e.*5.13(p.237.19; M.22.392C); Μωσέα δ. καὶ ὑπηρέτην...τῆς εἰς ἀνθρώπους ἐκδόσεως id.*e.th.*2.14 (p.116.6; M.24.929B); τῆς ἀληθείας δ. Ath.*gent.*41(M.25.84B); ὁ τῆς ...ὀργῆς...δ. Bas.*jud.*7(2.221B; M.31.672A); Cyr.*glaph.Dt.*(1.430A); of Logos as 'minister' of prophecy, Or.*Cels.*5.12(p.14.3; M.11.1200B); met. μαντική...τῶν ἐν κόσμῳ πλεονεξιῶν ἐστί σοι δ. Tat.*orat.*19(p.21. 15; M.6.849A); αἱ...λογικαὶ δυνάμεις τοῦ βούλεσθαι δ. πεφύκασι Clem. *str.*2.17(p.153.22; M.8.1016B); ὕβριν...μέθης εἶναι δ. id.*paed.*2.7(p.189. 20; M.8.456B).

C. esp., *minister, agent, servant* of God, Clem.*str.*1.1(p.6.25; M.8.693B); οἱ μὲν προφῆται...οὐ κλέπται, ἀλλὰ δ. *ib.*1.17(p.53.3; 796B); ἡμεῖς...οἱ δ. Χριστοῦ Cyr.H.*procatech.*4; †Bas.*bapt.*2.9.3 (2.668A; M.31.1616B); of Jo. Bapt. as δ. of Christ's first advent, Or.*hom.* *11 in Lc.*(p.81.10); of minister of Devil, Clem.*str.*1.17(p.55. 12; 800C); Dor.*doct.*9.4(M.88.1724A).

II. in Christian ministry, *servant, agent, deacon*;

A. untechnically, any *minister*, irrespective of particular office, e.g. δ. τῆς ἀληθείας, τῆς καινῆς διαθήκης etc.; of apostles, prophets, and others, Or.*princ.*4.2.7(p.318.10; M.11.372A); id.*Cels.*1.38(p.90. 2; M.11.733B); Eus.*d.e.*1.7(p.35.4; M.22.69A); †Bas.*Is.*57(1.422A; M.30.221A); Gr.Nyss.*Eun.*8(2 p.195.17; M.45.792A).

B. technically, *deacon*; **1.** expressing function, rather than possession of definite title; **a.** associated with ἐπίσκοπος in NT, neither term being restricted to one office τότε γὰρ τέως ἐκοινώνουν τοῖς ὀνόμασι, καὶ δ. ὁ ἐπίσκοπος ἐλέγετο Chrys.*hom.1.1 in Phil.* (11.195A); **b.** in sub-apostolic age associated with ἐπίσκοπος (both terms being connected with Is.60:17), and regarded as of apostolic appointment, *1Clem.*42.4 cit. s. ἐπίσκοπος; hence **2.** διάκονοι as second order in two-fold ministry πρεσβυτέροις καὶ δ. Polyc.*ep.* 5.3; *Did.*15.1 cit s. ἐπίσκοπος; and as third order in threefold ministry, Ign.*Philad.* proem. cit s. πρεσβύτερος; τῷ ἐπισκόπῳ προσέχετε καὶ τῷ πρεσβυτερίῳ καὶ δ. *ib.*7.1; id.*Magn.*13.1; id.*Polyc.* 6.1; necessary with bishops and presbyters for all branches of Church life, id.*Trall.*7.2; freq. after Ignatius, sometimes in conjunction with χῆραι q.v., Clem.*paed.*3.12(p.289.20; M.8.676C); Or. *or.*28(p.377.18; M.11.524C); ἐπίσκοπος, πρεσβύτερος, καὶ δ. ὁμοούσιοί εἰσιν ‡Ath.*dial.Trin.*1.27(M.28.1157B); three orders are μιμήματα ἀγγελικῆς δόξης Clem.*str.*6.13(p.485.11; M.9.328C), third (deacons) being appointed for fulfilment of law of 'three witnesses' (Dt. 19:15), *Ordo Eccl.App.*20; function being ἀντίληψις, cf.Chrys.*proph. obscurit.*2.5(6.188A); **3.** corresponding to Levite in OT ministry, hence deacon freq. called λευίτης q.v.; **4.** deacons in relation to Seven of Ac.6:3; **a.** Seven regarded as first deacons, cf. *Stephanus ...qui electus est ab apostolis primus diaconus*, Iren.*haer.*3.12.10 (M.7.904B); *ib.*4.15.1(1013A); cf.‡Pion.*v.Polyc.*12; τοῖς ἑπτὰ δ. Cyr. H.*catech.*17.24; ὁ ἐκλεξάμενος διὰ τοῦ μονογενοῦς σου τοὺς ἑπτὰ δ. Serap.*euch.*26.1; cf.Bas.*moral.*71.2(2.306A; M.31.845C); *Const.App.* 2.55.2; **b.** deacons unconnected with Seven ὁποῖον...ἀξίωμα εἶχον οὗτοι...ἆρα...τῶν δ.; καὶ μὴν τοῦτο ἐν ταῖς ἐκκλησίαις οὐκ ἔστιν, ἀλλὰ τῶν πρεσβυτέρων ἐστὶν ἡ οἰκονομία· καίτοι οὐδέπω οὐδεὶς ἐπίσκοπος ἦν, ἀλλ' οἱ ἀπόστολοι μόνον. ὅθεν οὔτε δ., οὔτε πρεσβυτέρων οἶμαι τὸ ὄνομα εἶναι δῆλον Chrys.*hom.14.3 in Ac.*(9.115A); CTrull. *can.*16; **5.** deacons believed to have been appointed by apostles, *A.Petr.et Paul.*13(p.185.2); *A.Thom.*A 169(p.284.5); ordained by Thaddaeus, together with bishops and priests, and entrusted with liturgical 'canon', *A.Thadd.*5(p.275.17); **6.** status of deacon; **a.** appointed by Church, Ign.*Philad.*10.1; *Did.*15.1 cit. s. ἐπίσκοπος; **b.** ordained by bishops (v. infra 10); **c.** included in κλῆρος q.v., Hipp.*haer.*9.12(p.249.24; M.16.3386B); by implication, Or.*hom.11.3 in Jer.*(p.81.6; M.13.369D); CAnc.(314)*can.*14; contrast, *non est enim [diaconus] particeps consilii in clero*, Hipp.*trad.ap.*9.3; **d.** normally ranked next in order after πρεσβύτεροι but mentioned after ἀναγνῶσται in *Ordo Eccl.App.*20; **e.** subject to bishop and presbyters, Ign.*Magn.*2; Clem.*str.*7.1(p.4.20; M.9.405A) cit. s. πρεσβύτερος; forbidden to sit among presbyters, CNic.(325)*can.*18; cf. οἱ δ. παριστάσθωσαν *Const.App.*2.57.4; and to be seated before presbyter, CLaod.*can.*20; CTrull.*can.*7; and to communicate before bishop or priest, CNic.(325)*can.*18; **f.** referred to as ὑπηρέται, as λειτουργοί v.s.vv. and as ὑποδρηστῆρες, Gr.Naz.*carm.* 2.1.16.11(M.37.1255A) cit. s. 11; **g.** but are fellow-servants with bishop, Ign.*Smyrn.*12.2; id.*Philad.*4; **h.** and typify Christ ἐντρεπέσθωσαν τοὺς δ. ὡς Ἰησοῦν Χριστόν, ὡς καὶ τὸν ἐπίσκοπον ὄντα τύπον τοῦ πατρός, τοὺς δὲ πρεσβυτέρους ὡς συνέδριον θεοῦ καὶ ὡς σύνδεσμον ἀποστόλων Ign.*Trall.*3.1; cf.id.*Magn.*6.1 cit. s. πρεσβύτερος; Polyc. *ep.*5.3 cit. s. πρεσβύτερος; or θεοῦ ἐντολήν Ign.*Smyrn.*8.1; **i.** and are properly servants of God, *ib.*10.1; Ant.Mon.*hom.*123(M.89.1817D); **j.** receiving honour due to prophets, *Const.App.*2.30.1; **7.** functions; **a.** bishops and deacons perform service of prophets and teachers, *Did.*15.1 cit. s. ἐπίσκοπος; **b.** deacon serves Church, Ign. *Trall.*2.3; ‡Hipp.*can.*5.34; **c.** esp. serves and attends upon bishop; **i.** being closely associated with bishop in lists of ministerial offices, Clem.*paed.*3.12(p.289.20; M.8.676C); and believed to have been closely associated with apostles as personal attendants, *A. Thom.*A 65(p.182.11); *Hom.Clem.*16.1; **ii.** and specially ordained to this function (v. infra 10), cf.Hipp.*trad.ap.*9.2; **iii.** acting as bishop's agent and minister; in gen., *ib.*30; *Const.App.*2.26.5, 2.30.2; as 'bishop's eye', *Clem.ep.*12(M.2.48A); *Const.App.*2.44.4; Isid.Pel.*epp.*4.188(M.78.1277B); reporting to bishop on condition of his people, *Hom.Clem.*3.67; cf.‡Hipp.*can.*5.35; **iv.** attends bishop on rural visitations, ‡Pion.*v.Polyc.*27; **v.** carries episcopal letters, Eus.*h.e.*6.19.19(M.20.572A); and sent by bishop on errands, Ath. *apol.sec.*67(p.145.20; M.25.368C); **vi.** attends councils with bishop or as his representative, Eus.*h.e.*6.43.2(616B); *ib.*7.28.1(708A); Soz. *h.e.*4.16.16(M.67.1157C); **d.** also serves presbyters, ‡Hipp.*can.*5.34; ἐχειροτονήθη...δ., ὡς καὶ τῷ πρεσβυτέρῳ διακονήσων Bas.*ep.*169(3. 258B; M.32.641C); *Const.App.*3.20.2; **e.** with presbyters, deacons represent a church in absence of its bishop, Ign.*Philad.*10.2; **f.** administers almsgiving and poor-relief, cf.Hipp.*trad.ap.*9; ‡Hipp. *can.*5.36; *Ordo Eccl.App.*22; *Const.App.*2.32.1; *ib.*3.19.7; **g.** tends sick, cf.‡Hipp.*can.*34; *Const.App.*3.19.1; **h.** teaches, cf.Hipp.*trad. ap.*33; cf.‡Hipp.*can.*61; ‡Pion.*v.Polyc.*12; and preaches Ξενοφῶντα...τὸν δ. καταλιμπάνω...καὶ γὰρ αὐτὸς ὥσπερ κἀγὼ καταγγέλλει τὸν Ἰησοῦν *A.Thom.*A 66(p.183.7); CAnc.(314)*can.*2; but permission given by Leontius to Aëtius to preach as a deacon regarded as unusual, cf.Philost.*h.e.*3.17(M.65.508C); and censured, Thdt.*h.e.* 2.24.6; bishops refuse to dispute with Aëtius as deacon, Philost. *h.e.*4.12(525A); **i.** in persecution attends upon confessors in prison, *M.Perp.*2(p.65.17); *ib.*6(p.71.25); *ib.*10(p.77.1); **j.** assists at ecclesiastical tribunals, *Const.App.*2.47.1; **k.** has pastoral care of sinners expelled from Church, *ib.*2.16.1; **l.** arranges congregation in church and keeps order, *ib.*2.57.13; Thdt.*h.e.*5.18.21; **m.** guards doors, cf.*Didascalia* 2.57.6(Funk I p.162.3); *διακόνοις...ἡ φυλακὴ τῶν τῆς ἐκκλησίας πυλῶν ἀφώρισται* Max.*schol.epp.Dion.Ar.*8.1(M.4.548C); but cf. id.*schol.e.h.*5.6(M.4.165A) cit. s. *ὑποδιάκονος*; **n.** exorcizes candidates for baptism *ἐν τῷ φωτιστηρίῳ...ἐπιορκιζόντων αὐτοὺς τῶν δ.* CSyr.(p.99.31; H.2.1377A); deacon's function at baptism being that of *καθαρτικὴ...διακόσμησις* involving preparation of candidates, Dion.Ar.*e.h.*5.1.6(M.3.508A); Max.*schol.e.h.*5.6(M.4.164D); deacon descends into water with candidate, cf.Hipp.*trad. ap.*21; **o.** deacon and baptism; **i.** permitted to baptize, Cyr.H.*catech.*17.35; **ii.** in absence of bishop, when priests negligent, deacon baptizes; this a scandal to many, but approved by Chrys.*hom.46.3 in Ac.*(9.349E); permitted in absence of priest, Thdt.*qu.2Par.*29:30 (1.596); Proc.G.*2Par.*29:34(M.87.1217A); **iii.** forbidden, *Const.App.* 3.11.1; *ib.*8.46.11; Max.*schol.c.h.*3.2(M.4.49C); **p.** at eucharist: deacons perform many duties and are *οἱ τοῦ σεπτοῦ θυσιαστηρίου δ.* Isid.Pel.*epp.*4.188(M.78.1277B); cf. *δ. ... μυστηρίων Ἰησοῦ Χριστοῦ* Ign.*Trall.*2.3; partic. functions include **i.** preparation of altar, *A.Thom.*A 49(p.165.18); **ii.** reading *προέτρεπον τὸν μὲν δ. ἀναγινώσκειν ψαλμόν* Ath.*fug.*24(p.84.16; M.25.676A); of Gospel *δ. ἢ πρεσβύτερος ἀναγινωσκέτω τὰ εὐαγγέλια* *Const.App.*2.57.7; *ἀναγινώσκει ἐνθάδε* [sc. Alexandria] *μόνος ὁ ἀρχιδιάκονος· παρὰ δὲ ἄλλοις, διάκονοι* Soz.*h.e.*7.19.6(M.67.1477A); sometimes combining offices and titles of deacon and reader, *CIG* 8882; cf. *εὐαγγέλιον*; **iii.** during service, proclamation of instructions to congregation, warning those at variance with each other to depart before Communion, *Const. App.*2.54.1; and catechumens and uninitiated to leave, *Lit.ib.* 8.6.2; ‡Chrys.*prodig.*1.3(8.37A); *Lit.Jac.*(p.176.15) etc.; announcing subjects of prayer, *Lit.*ap.*Const.App.*8.13.2; *ὅταν...ὁ δ. λέγῃ, ὑπὲρ τῶν κατηχουμένων ἐκτενῶς δεηθῶμεν* Chrys.*hom.2.5 in 2Cor.*(10.435B); *ὁ δ. βοᾷ, ὑπὲρ τῶν ἐν Χριστῷ κεκοιμημένων* id.*hom.21.4 in Ac.* (9.176A); id.*proph.obscurit.*2.5(6.188A); *Lit.Jac.*(p.170.18); and in liturgies passim; calling for silence and attention before readings, Chrys.*hom.3.4 in 2Thess.*(11.527E); id.*hom.19.5 in Ac.*(9.159E); announcing kiss of peace, Cyr.H.*catech.*23.3; and dismissing congregation, *Lit.*ap.*Const.App.*8.15.10; Chrys.*Jud.*3.6(1.614C); cf.*Lit.Marc.* (p.142.27); **iv.** bringing elements to celebrant at offertory, cf. Hipp.*trad.ap.*23.1; ‡Hipp.*can.*3.20; *οἱ δ. προσαγέτωσαν τὰ δῶρα τῷ ἐπισκόπῳ πρὸς τὸ θυσιαστήριον* *Lit.*ap.*Const.App.*8.12.3; and standing by with fans to keep insects from chalices, *ib.*; **v.** bringing water to bishop and priests at altar for ablution of hands, Cyr. H.*catech.*23.2; **vi.** communicating the people, Just.*1apol.*65.5(M.6.428B) cit. s. *εὐχαριστέω*; *ib.*67.5(429C); administering chalice, Hipp.*trad.ap.*23.7–8; ‡Hipp.*can.*31.216; cf.Chrys.*hom.82.6 in Mt.* (7.790A) cit. s. *διακονέω*; and taking Communion to the absent, Just.*1apol.*65.5(M.6.428B); *ib.*67.5(429C); **vii.** distributing milk and honey after Communion to newly baptized, if presbyters are not present, cf.‡Hipp.*can.*19.145; **viii.** introducing energumens at eucharist for prayer to be made on their behalf, Chrys.*incomprehens.*4.4(1.477B); **ix.** forbidden to celebrate, CNic.(325)*can.*18; *Const.App.*8.46.11; but cf. *δ. ὁμοίως θύσαντας...πεπαῦσθαι...πάσης τῆς ἱερᾶς λειτουργίας, τῆς τε τοῦ ἄρτον ἢ ποτήριον ἀναφέρειν* CAnc. (314)*can.*2; **x.** and to communicate priests, CNic.(325)*can.*18; **q.** at *agape*, presbyter or deacon distributes *εὐλογία*, cf.Hipp. *trad.ap.*26; **r.** at episcopal elections and consecrations, deacon ascertains popular will, ‡Pion.*v.Polyc.*22; brings candidate to consecrating bishops, *ib.*23; deacons hold Gospels over head of candidate during consecration, *Const.App.*8.4.6; **s.** deacon's office often combined with partic. official position in Church, e.g., head of monastery *ὁ εὐλαβέστατος...δ. καὶ ἀρχιμανδρίτης Μάξιμος* Cyr.*ep.*69(p.15.27; 5².197A); Thdt.*ep.*27(4.1089); *CIG* 8647; *δ. ... οἰκονόμος* *CIG* 8822; *δ. τε καὶ ἐπορκιστής* Eus.*m.P.*2.1(p.909.7; M.20.1465A); *δ. καὶ ἰατρός* *PLond.*1044.38; *Supplic.*ap.CBeryt.*act.*(*ACO* 2.1.3 p.36.14; H.2.533E); **t.** in gen.: in simile of ship, deacons compared with *τοίχαρχοι*, *Clem.ep.*14(M.2.49A) cit. s. *πρεσβύτερος*; *Const.App.*2.57.2; summary of deacon's duties and privileges, *ib.* 8.28.2; **u.** spiritual interpretations of deacon's office *οὗτος πρεσβύτερός ἐστι τῷ ὄντι...καὶ δ. ἀληθὴς...ἐὰν ποιῇ καὶ διδάσκῃ τὰ τοῦ κυρίου* Clem.*str.*6.13(p.485.11; M.9.328A); *διακόνου λόγον ἐπέχει ὁ πρὸς τοὺς ἱεροὺς ἀγῶνας ἀλείφων τὸν νοῦν, καὶ τοὺς ἐμπαθεῖς ἀπελαύνων λογισμοὺς ἀπ' αὐτοῦ* *Schol.*82 in Jo.Clim.*scal.*4(M.88.757A); cf. *διακονῶν ἐστι, σώματι μὲν ἀνθρώποις παρεστώς, νοΐ δὲ ἐν οὐρανοῖς διὰ προσευχῆς κρούων* Jo.Clim.*scal.*4(M.88.717A); **8.** qualifications for deacon's office; **a.** gen. moral character *δ. ἄμεμπτοι...μὴ διάβολοι, μὴ δίλογοι, ἀφιλάργυροι, ἐγκρατεῖς περὶ πάντα, εὔσπλαγχνοι,* *ἐπιμελεῖς, πορευόμενοι κατὰ τὴν ἀλήθειαν τοῦ κυρίου* Polyc.*ep.*5.2; *δεδοκιμασμένοι...μεμαρτυρημένοι παρὰ τοῦ πλήθους,...εὐμετάδοτοι, κοινωνικοί, κτλ.* *Ordo Eccl.App.*20; *Const.App.*7.31.1; Chrys.*hom. 11.1 in 1Tim.*(11.604D); **b.** age: deacon ordained at 17, *A.Mt.*28 (p.259.3); minimum age fixed at 25, *Cod.Afr.*16; CTrull.*can.*14; **c.** marriage no bar, cf.Iren.*haer.*1.13.5(M.7.588A); Clem.*str.*3.12 (p.237.21; M.8.1192A); *Ordo Eccl.App.*20; provided deacon informs bishop at ordination of his intention to marry, CAnc. (314)*can.*10; *Can.App.*5; CTrull.*can.*13; not to marry after ordination, *Const.App.*6.17.1; *δίγαμοι* not to be admitted, cf.Or.*hom.17 in Lc.*(p.121.4; M.13.1847A); *Ordo Eccl.App.*17; but admitted by Callistus acc. Hipp.*haer.*9.12(p.249.24; M.16.3386B); **9.** number of deacons in a church: at Rome, seven, Corn.ap.Eus.*h.e.*6.43.11 (M.20.621A); Soz.*h.e.*7.19.3(M.67.1476A); this the canonical number based on Ac.6:3 *δ. ἑπτὰ ὀφείλουσιν εἶναι κατὰ τὸν κανόνα, κἂν πάνυ μεγάλη εἴη ἡ πόλις* CNeocaes.*can.*14; but number varies, e.g. Ac.6:3 declared to be irrelevant to question, CTrull.*can.*16; 38 deacons sign letter of Edessan clergy to Photius and Eustathius, *Supplic.*ap.CBeryt.*act.*(*ACO* 2.1.3 p.36.7ff.; H.2.533D); 100 deacons in great church of Constantinople, increased to 150 by Heraclius, Phot.*nomoc.*1.30(M.104.1013C); **10.** ordination: bishop alone imposes hands on deacon, signifying that deacon is ordained to attend upon bishop, cf.Hipp.*trad.ap.*9; ‡Hipp.*can.*5.38; *Const.App.*8. 17.2; ceremony described briefly, Dion.Ar.*e.h.*5.2(M.3.509B); ordination prayer for deacon, cf.Hipp.*trad.ap.*9; Serap.*euch.*26; *Const. App.*8.18.1–3; **11.** dress; **a.** white robe *Πομπόνιος ὁ δ. ... ἦν ἐνδεδυμένος ἐσθῆτα λαμπράν* *M.Perp.*10(p.77.1); cf.‡Hipp.*can.*37. 201; cf. *οἱ δ' ἄρ' ὑποδρηστῆρες ἐν εἵμασι παμφανόωσιν* Gr.Naz.*carm.* 2.1.16.11(M.37.1255A); Chrys.*hom.82.6 in Mt.*(7.789D); **b.** deacon girded for service, *Const.App.*2.57.4; wearing stole on left shoulder, ‡Chrys.*prodig.*1.3(8.37A); his *ὀθόνη* signifying Christ's humility in washing and wiping disciples' feet, Isid.Pel.*epp.*1.136(M.78. 272C); ‡Sophr.H.*liturg.*7(M.87.3988A); **c.** symbolism of deacon's dress fully explained, *ib.*(3988A,B); **12.** maintenance of deacons: offerings are divided among deacons and other clergy by bishop and priests, *Can.App.*4; *ὅσον...ἑκάστῃ τῶν πρεσβυτίδων δίδοται, διπλοῦν διδόσθω τοῖς δ. εἰς γέρας Χριστοῦ* *Const.App.*2.28.3; *αἱ... ἀπαρχαὶ τῶν ἱερέων εἰσί, καὶ τῶν αὐτοῖς ἐξυπηρετουμένων δ.* *ib.*8.30.2; surplus of 'eulogia' divided among bishop, priests, deacons, subdeacons, in proportion of 4, 3, 2, 1, *ib.*8.31.2; **13.** deacon normally promoted to higher office, cf.*Ordo Eccl.App.*22; implied, ‡Pion. *v.Polyc.*11; cf. 1Tim.3:13 as interpreted by *Const.App.*8.22.4; Chrys.*hom.11.1 in 1Tim.*(11.605C); Thdr.Mops.*1Tim.*3:13(M.66. 941C); *Lit.Jac.*(p.208.19); freq. succeeds his bishop, ‡Pion.*v.Polyc.* 27; hence ordination to priesthood a bar to preferment, Eulog.ap. Phot.*cod.*182(M.103.533A); **14.** deposition of deacon for immorality, not necessarily involving excommunication, Bas.*ep.*188 *can.*3 (3.271B; M.32.672B); deacon *ἐν χείλεσι μιανθείς* removed from office, but continues to receive Communion with deacons, id.*ep.*217 *can.* 70(327E; M.801A); removed from office if found guilty of crime, and not restored, even if penitent, Thdr.Stud.*epp.*2.191(M.99. 1581D).

C. *διάκονος, ἡ*, *deaconess*, as teacher and evangelist among women, Clem.*str.*3.6(p.220.24; M.8.1157A); cf.*Ordo Eccl.App.*24–28; as intermediary between lay women and deacon or bishop, compared with H. Ghost in relation to Christ and believers, *Const.App.* 2.26.6; has authority over widows, *ib.*3.7.7; is regular minister of Church, Pall.*v.Chrys.*10(p.61.3; M.47.35); *ib.*16(p.107.3; 60); ‡Jo.D.*Artem.*67(p.174.10; M.96.1316A); δ. of women's community, Pall.*h.Laus.*70(p.166.8; M.34.1242A); freq. as title of individuals *Ἀγαλίασις δ.* *IG* 12.3.1238; *Φαυστῖνα δ.* *MAMA* 1.194; *ib.*1.226; *ib.* 1.326; *ib.*3.744 (saec. v–vi); a consecrated person, Bas.*ep.*199 *can.*44 (3.296B; M.32.729B); ordained with imposition of hands, CChalc. *can.*15; minimum age for ordination, 40; careful testing required, *ib.*

III. theol.;

A. of Son as agent of Father's will, Clem.*paed.*1.2(p.91.24; M.8. 252C); *θεοῦ μὲν υἱός, σωτὴρ δὲ ἀνθρώπων, καὶ τοῦ μὲν διάκονος ἡμῶν δὲ παιδαγωγός* *ib.*3.1(p.237.2; 557A); (Arian), Philost.*h.e.*9.14(M.65. 636C) cit. s. *ὑπηρέτης*; denied *καθὸ λόγος ἐστὶν...ὃς εἰς τὰ ἴδια ἥκει καὶ διαλέγεται μετ' ἐξουσίας, οὐχ ὡς ἄν τις δ. τῶν παρὰ θεοῦ δεδομένων λόγων* Apoll.ap.*cat.Jo.*12:50(p.335.7); cf.Cyr.*Jo.*1.9(4.73E).

B. of H. Ghost *τὸν δ. τοῦ πεπονθότος θεοῦ* Tat.*orat.*13(p.15.5; M.6. 836A); (Basilidean), Clem.*str.*2.8(p.133.8,10; M.8.973B); *ἡ περιστερὰ δὲ σῶμα ὤφθη, ἣν οἱ μὲν τὸ ἅγιον πνεῦμά φασιν, οἱ δὲ ἀπὸ Βασιλείδου τὸν δ.* id.*exc.Thdot.*16(p.112.5; M.9.665A).

C. (Marcosian), of seven letters which represent agent of *Νοῦς* in Creation, Iren.*haer.*1.14.7(M.7.608B).

διακοπή, ἡ, *break, gap, interruption*; met., Or.*Jo.*6.2(1; p.108.15; M.14.201A); ἡ δοκοῦσα δὲ δ. τῶν εἰς Ἱεροσόλυμα ἀνόδων τοῦ Ἰησοῦ... οὕτω μόνως σώζεσθαι δύναται [ref. discrepancy between accounts in fourth gospel and synoptics] *ib.*10.31(18; p.205.10; 364B); δ. τῆς τοῦ κακοῦ συνεχείας [sc. at baptism] Gr.Nyss.*or.catech.*35(p.134.12; M.45.89B); Cyr.*Is.*2.3(2.280D).

***διακοπτικός,** *able to cut through*, Clem.*paed.*1.11(p.147.12; M.8.365A); id.*fr.*(M.9.744A).

***διακοσιονταέτης,** *two hundred years old*, Anast.S.*qu.et resp.*96 (M.89.741C).

διακόσιος, *two hundred*, in myst. exeg. ὁ δὲ δ. πάλιν ἀριθμὸς τὴν τῆς φύσεως ἡμῶν εἰς ἑαυτὴν διὰ τῆς τῶν ἐντολῶν ἐργασίας δηλοῖ ἀποκατάστασιν Thdt.*Cant.*8:12(2.163).

διακοσιοστός, *two-hundredth*, Clem.*str.*1.21(p.74.6; M.8.844A); *ib.*(p.75.16; 848B).

διακοσμ-έω, 1. *order, arrange*; of God ordering universe acc. Plato θεὸν...τὸν ~ήσαντα τὸ πᾶν Hipp.*haer.*1.19(p.19.7; M.16.3041A); of Father, *1Clem.*33.2; τὸν λόγον...δι' οὗ τὰ πάντα ὁ πατὴρ ~εῖ Ath.*gent.*47(M.25.96B); id.*inc.*1.1(M.25.97A); of Son, id.*gent.*40(80D); *ib.*(81A); *ib.*43(88A); **2.** *adorn*, Philost.*h.e.*3.5(M.65.485A); Thdt.*h.e.*1.31.3(3.821); id.*qu.20 in Gen.*(1.29); met. τούτους...ἐπαίνοις οὐκ ἔχει κόρον ~εῖν Philost.*h.e.*8.2(557A).

διακόσμησις, ἡ, 1. *ordering, arrangement*; of universe, by Son, Ath.*gent.*38(M.25.76C); *ib.*41(84A); *ib.*46(92B); Gr.Nyss.*tres dii*(M.45.128A) cit. s. θέλημα; by angels, Papias *fr.*4; **2.** *order, rank, class*; of angels, Gr.Nyss.*hom.6 in Cant.*(M.44.893A); Dion.Ar.*c.h.*2.1(M.3.137A); *ib.*2.2(140B); *ministerial order*, id.*e.h.*2.2.4(M.3.393C); id.*ep.*8.1 (M.3.1088D); **3.** *ordered statement, exposition* ἀληθείας δ. Tat.*orat.*27 (p.29.10; M.6.865B).

διάκοσμος, ὁ, *ornament* ὁ πρόδρομος...μαρτύρων δ. Thdr.Stud.*epp.*2.37(M.99.1228B).

διακουφίζω, *make light, alleviate*, †Jo.D.*B.J.*35(M.96.1193C).

διακράζω, *cry aloud, proclaim*, Cyr.*ador.*5(1.150A); id.*inc.unigen.*(5^1.703D); Dam.*troph.*4.1(p.259.12).

διακρατ-έω, 1. *control, govern, direct* συνῆκα τὸν...~οῦντα εἶναι θεόν Arist.*apol.*1.2(M.96.1108A); Meth.*symp.*8.14(p.101.16; M.18.164C); id.*res.*1.23(p.247.3; M.41.1092D); ὁ λόγος...οὐρανὸν εἰς αἰῶνα ~εῖ Eus.*l.C.*12(p.235.2; M.20.1396B); **2.** *establish, confirm* τὴν ἀπειλὴν τῆς παραβάσεως ~οῦσαν τὴν καθ' ἡμῶν φθοράν Ath.*inc.*8.2 (M.25.109B); **3.** *support, maintain, preserve* τὰ σώματα ἡμῶν ἐν ἁγιασμῷ ~ούμενα Meth.*res.*1.61(p.326.10; 1160A); Bas.*Eun.*1.7 (1.218D; M.29.525B); Chrys.*hom.18.3 in Mt.*(7.237B); *ib.*52.4(535B); **4.** pass., *be checked* or *restrained*, Chrys.*hom.22.3 in Heb.*(12.209A).

διακράτησις, ἡ, 1. *preservation*, Chrys.*hom.div.*9.4(12.387B); **2.** *observance* of laws, Thdr.Stud.*epp.*1.8(M.99.936B).

διακρατητικός, *able to maintain* or *support*, neut. as subst. ζωὴ ἦν, τὸ δ. τῆς κτίσεως δηλῶν Chrys.*hom.2.3 in Heb.*(12.18C).

[*]**διακρητικός,** = διακριτικός, *Const.App.*2.6.4 (v.l. for δικαιοκριτικός).

διακρίν-ω, [aor. pass. ptcpl. διακρινηθέντων Gr.Nyss.*ep.can.*(M.45.225B)]; **A. 1.** *separate*; hence *select, choose*, Nonn.*par.Jo.*15:16 (M.43.876A); **2.** *separate into elemental parts*; hence *expound, explain*, Hipp.*haer.*4.15(p.48.28; M.16.3082D).

B. *distinguish*; **1.** Son from creation εἰ ἐν ψιλῷ καὶ μόνῳ τῷ ὀνόματι διακέκριται θεὸς ὁ υἱός, πλεονεκτήσει τὴν κτίσιν...οὐδέν Didym.*Trin.*3.10(M.39.856B); **2.** *discern* as true or false, *appraise* πάντα προφήτην λαλοῦντα ἐν πνεύματι οὐ...~εῖτε *Did.*11.7; **3.** Christol., ref. the two natures, Amph.*fr.*(M.39.109A) cit. s. ἔκπτωσις; ~ειν γὰρ ἐδίδασκον [sc. opponents of Arius] τῇ τοῦ χρόνου διαστολῇ, τίς τε φύσις ἀσάρκου θεοῦ, τίς τε φύσις κατ' οἰκονομίαν ἀτρέπτως ἀνθρώπου γενομένου id.ap.Eust.Mon.*ep.*(M.86.913D); διακεκριμέναι γὰρ αἱ φύσεις, ἓν δὲ τὸ πρόσωπον τῇ ἑνώσει ἀποτελούμενον Thdr.Mops.*fr.inc.*8(p.299.19; M.66.981B); οὐ γὰρ ἔστιν ἑτέρως [sc. λέγειν]...τὰ πάντη διακεκριμένα, ἢ τὸ λέγειν δύο φύσεις καὶ ὑποστάσεις εἶναι Leont.H.*monoph.*8(M.86.1773C); λέγετε κατά τι ~εσθαι τοῦ ἰδίου πατρὸς τὸν υἱὸν καὶ λόγον, ἢ οὐχί; ἴσμεν οὖν ὅτι λέγετε, καὶ ὅτι τοῦτο εἶναι τὴν ὑπόστασιν ὁμολογεῖτε. ... τῆς ἰδίας σαρκὸς λέγετε κατά τι ~εσθαι τὸν λόγον ἢ οὐχί; εἰ μὲν οὖν κατὰ μηδέν, ἐγγυτέραν ταύτην τῷ λόγῳ καὶ ἡνωμένην μᾶλλον τοῦ πατρὸς παρεστήσατε, εἴπερ τοῦ πατρὸς καθ' ὑπόστασιν· τῆς δὲ σαρκὸς τῆς ἐν αὐτῷ οὐδὲ κατὰ φύσιν οὐδὲ καθ' ὑπόστασιν διακέκριται ὁ λόγος· εἰ δὲ κατά τι, καὶ ταύτην τοῦ λόγου ~ετε διαφορᾶς λόγῳ, καὶ οὐ διαιρέσεως, τί τοῦτο, ἀποκρίνασθε. εἰ μὲν οὖν τῷ αὐτῷ καθ' ὃ καὶ τοῦ πατρὸς διωρίζετο, ὑπόστασις δὲ αὐτή, πρῶτον μὲν δύο τὰς ὑποστάσεις Χριστοῦ δεδώκατε· εἶτα δὲ καὶ ἴσην τῷ πατρὶ κατὰ πάντα τὴν σάρκα παριστάνετε, εἴ γε τοῖς αὐτοῖς καὶ μόνοις ἔκ τε τοῦ πατρὸς καὶ τῆς οἰκείας σαρκὸς ~εται ὁ λόγος *ib.*18 (1780B,C); **4.** of Persons in Trin., Dion.Ar.*d.n.*2.3(M.3.640C); *ib.*2.11 (M.649B); v. διάκρισις.

C. *judge* a person, Eus.*v.C.*2.18(p.48.7; M.20.996A).

D. *examine, consider*, Eus.*l.C.*9(p.217.34; M.20.1361C); Bas.*hom. in Ps.*61(1.197D; M.29.479B); Dion.Ar.*d.n.*3.2(M.3.681B).

E. *ponder* ταῦτά μου...καὶ ~οντος ἐν τῇ καρδίᾳ μου Herm.*vis.*1.2.2; id.*sim.*2.1; Eus.*v.C.*1.27(p.20.23; M.20.941C).

F. med. and pass., *hesitate, be in doubt*, in gen. ἐπαινεῖ τὴν Σαμαρεῖτιν ὡσὰν...μὴ διακριθεῖσαν ἐφ' οἷς ἔλεγεν αὐτῇ Heracleon ap.Or.*Jo.*13.10(p.235.2; M.14.413C); *Hom.Clem.*2.40; κοινωνῆσαι Μακαρίῳ ~ομαι Jo.Mosch.*prat.*96(M.87.2953C); c. acc., *be in doubt about*, Const.ap.Gel.Cyz.*h.e.*3.15.5; also act., Pall.*h.Laus.*81 (M.34.1258B); Jo.Mosch.*prat.*96(M.87.2953C); ptcpl. as subst. οἱ δ., heretics who dissented from decisions of Council of Chalcedon; so-called either because they constituted a third party, *the Hesitaters*, between orthodox and Eutychians, or as gen. name for dissidents from Chalcedon, *the Separatists*, †Leont.B.*sect.*4.7(M.86.1225C); *ib.*5.3(1229C); οἱ τούτου [sc. Διοσκόρου] ἀντιλαμβανόμενοι ἀπέστησαν τῆς...καθολικῆς...ἐκκλησίας, καὶ ὠνόμασαν ἑαυτοὺς δ., διὰ τὸ ~εσθαι αὐτοὺς κοινωνεῖν τῇ καθολικῇ ἐκκλησίᾳ Tim.CP *haer.*(M.86.53A); esp. of one of these, John, who wrote a Church history Ἰωάννης ὁ ~όμενος μετὰ [? l. περὶ] Σεβήρου ἱστορεῖ Thdr.Lect.*h.e.*2.31(M.86.200B); Ἰωάννου τοῦ δ. ἐκ τῆς ἐκκλησιαστικῆς ἱστορίας CNic.(787) *act.*5(H.4.305D).

διάκρισις, ἡ, A. *separation, distinction*; **1.** in gen. δ. ... τῶν πιστῶν ἀπὸ τῶν ἀπίστων Clem.*ecl.*40(p.148.27; M.9.717C); ὁ θάνατος ...δ. ... ψυχῆς ἀπὸ σώματος Meth.*res.*1.38(p.280.3; M.41.1104C); *ib.*2.27(p.384.7); ὁ ἀὴρ τοῖς Αἰγυπτίοις μὲν οὐδεμίαν νυκτὸς καὶ ἡμέρας παρεῖχε δ. Gr.Nyss.*v.Mos.*28(M.44.309A); *ib.*29(l.c.); **2.** of distinction of Persons within Godhead ἄρρητος...ἐν τούτοις καταλαμβάνεται καὶ ἡ κοινωνία καὶ ἡ δ. Gr.Nyss.*diff.ess.*4(M.32.332D); Dion.Ar.*d.n.*2.4(M.3.640D); ἔστι δὲ καὶ δ. ἐν ταῖς ὑπερουσίοις θεολογίαις, οὐχ ἣν ἔφην μόνον, ὅτι κατ' αὐτὴν τὴν ἕνωσιν ἀμιγῶς ἵδρυται, καὶ ἀσυγχύτως ἑκάστη τῶν ἐναρχικῶν ὑποστάσεων· ἀλλ' ὅτι καὶ τὰ τῆς ὑπερουσίου θεογονίας οὐκ ἀντιστρέφει πρὸς ἄλληλα *ib.*(641D); *ib.*(644A); δ. θείαν φαμὲν...τὰς ἀγαθοπρεπεῖς τῆς θεαρχίας προόδους *ib.*2.11(649B); ἐπὶ τῶν θείων αἱ ἑνώσεις τῶν δ. ἐπικρατοῦσι,...καὶ μετὰ τῆς τοῦ ἑνὸς ἀνεκφοίτητον καὶ ἑνιαίαν δ. *ib.*(652A); ἡ κατὰ τὰς ὑποστάσεις δ. μόνη Jo.D.*f.o.*1.7(M.94.808A); **3.** of the two natures in Christ ἐπαλλαττομένων τῶν κατὰ τὴν δ. τε καὶ ἕνωσιν σχέσεων Leont.B.*Nest.et Eut.*1(M.86.1289A).

B. *division* πολλὴ τῆς ἐξουσίας δ. Eus.*v.C.*2.58(p.65.2; M.20.1033A); τὴν τοῦ ὅλου εἰς τὰ μέρη δ. Leont.B.*Nest.et Eut.*1(M.86.1296C).

C. *discernment*; **1.** *power of discrimination* ἤτω σοφὸς ἐν δ. λόγων *1Clem.*48.5; δ. καλοῦ τε καὶ κακοῦ Or.*Jo.*6.51(32; p.160.27; M.14.289C); *Lit.*ap.*Const.App.*8.12.17; Proc.G.*Is.*3:3(M.87.1900B); **2.** *discretion, superior judgement*, Mac.Aeg.*elev.*13(M.34.901C); πηγὴ καὶ ῥίζα καὶ κεφαλὴ καὶ σύνδεσμος πάσης ἀρετῆς ἐστιν ἡ δ. ‡Nil.*vit.cog.*(M.79.1468B); Jo.Mosch.*prat.*56(M.87.2909D); τὴν πασῶν ἀρετῶν βασιλίδα δ. Sophr.H.*nativ.*(p.513); **3.** *examination, scrutiny*, Or.*Jo.*28.8(7; p.399.4; M.14.697B); τὴν δ. ἐποιεῖτο τῶν λεγομένων Eus.*v.C.*4.33(p.130.13; M.20.1181B); Thdt.*h.e.*2.26.10(3.894).

D. *hesitation, doubt*, Clem.*q.d.s.*31(p.180.32; M.9.637B); Bas.*ep.*51.2(3.144C; M.32.392A); ὁ διάβολος...ἐπεισήγαγεν...γογγυσμόν, ἤ, εἰ μηδὲν τούτων, δ. (= διαλογισμός Phil.2:14) Chrys.*hom.8.2 in Phil.*(11.258B).

***διακριτήριον, τό,** *judgement, arbitrament*, Procl.CP *or.*6.13(M.65.745B).

***διακριτής,** *discerning, perceptive* νοῦν...δ. ἀγαθῶν τε καὶ φαύλων Epiph.*anc.*76(p.96.7; M.43.160C).

διακριτικός, A. adj.; **1.** *able to distinguish, distinguishing, discerning*, c. genit. τῆς δ. τῶν σημαινουσῶν τι φωνῶν νοήσεως Clem.*str.*7.7(p.28.27; M.9.453A); δ. γενέσθαι ἀγαθῶν τε καὶ κακῶν Or.*Jo.*13.24 (p.248.5; M.14.440A); οἱ γὰρ ἔχοντες πνεῦμα θεῖον, δ. πνευμάτων Eus.*p.e.*12.5(576D; M.21.936D); Cyr.H.*catech.*10.3; ὁ ἄνθρωπος...δ. παθῶν Mac.Aeg.*hom.*26.1(M.34.676B); **2.** *discerning, possessing superior judgement* ἀνὴρ πνευματοφόρος καὶ δ. Pall.*h.Laus.*11(p.34.11; M.34.1034C); *ib.*24(p.77.14; 1089C); *Apophth.Patr.*(M.65.301C); τὸ...τῶν ἡδέων...ἡδέως ἀπέχεσθαι καὶ διακριτικώτατον καὶ γνωστικώτατον Diad.*perf.*44(p.50.18); Philox.*ep.*31(p.179).

B. neut as subst.; **1.** *faculty of discernment* τὸ δ. ἔχοντες *Hom.Clem.*2.39; ἑπτὰ ὀφθαλμοὺς ἔχουσα [sc. πίστις] διὰ τὸ δ. [ref. seven gifts of Spirit] *Schol.*24 in Max.*qu.Thal.*54(M.90.533A); **2.** *gift* or *power of interpreting* τὸ δ. τῆς θείας γραφῆς Marc.Diac.*v.Porph.*8; **3.** *hesitation, doubt,* Chrys.*hom.8.2 in Phil.*(11.258C).

***διακρουστέον,** *one must repel* or *resist,* Isid.Pel.*epp.*5.28(M.78. 1341C).

διακρουστικός, *capable of resolving* λογικὴ διέξοδος...δ. ... τῶν ἀποριῶν Clem.*str.*6.17(p.512.11; M.9.388B).

***διακτενισμός, ὁ,** *elaborate combing of the hair,* Clem.*paed.*3.3 (p.246.2; M.8.577C).

διακτορίη, ἡ, *office, service* Μάρθα διακτορίην...εἶχε τραπέζης Nonn.*par.Jo.*12:2(M.43.849C); eccl., *office of lector,* Eudoc.*Cypr.* 1.298(M.85.844B); of exorcist, *ib.*301.

διάκτορος, ὁ, *servant, attendant;* as adj., *ministering,* Nonn.*par. Jo.*6:13(M.43.796A); *ib.*1:52(760B); δ. ἔργον *ib.*12:26(853C); *ib.*13:4 (860B); *ib.*13:12(861B).

***διακτυπέω,** *make a noise,* Cyr.*ador.*14(1.509C).

***διακυβέρνησις, ἡ,** *piloting;* met., *guidance, direction,* Meth.*res.* 2.10(p.351.12); Gel.Cyz.*h.e.*3.11.11; Thdr.Stud.*epp.*2.115(M.99. 1384A).

***διακυβερνητικός,** *piloting, guiding;* met., Epiph.*haer.*77.25 (p.438.10; M.42.677A).

διακυβιστάω, *plunge through,* Gr.Nyss.*ep.*20(M.46.1085A).

διακυκ-άω, *make confusion;* abs., Cyr.*Ps.*36:32(M.69.948A); c. acc., *throw into confusion,* Gr.Nyss.*Eun.*1(1 p.65.3; M.45.293C); Cyr.*Joel.*24(3.217A); of an argument ὅπερ ὁ ὑμέτερος...~ᾷ λόγος Zach.Mit.*opif.*(M.85.1096A).

***διακυμβαλίζω,** *attune* to, Gr.Nyss.*Eun.*1(1 p.25.8; M.45.253A).

διακύπτ-ω, 1. *advance* towards; met., of progress towards faith, Chrys.*hom.35.3 in Jo.*(8.205E); **2.** *peer out;* **a.** in gen. διακύψας τῆς θυρίδος (παρακύψας LXX Gen.26:8) Clem.*paed.*1.5(p.103.19; M.8. 277A); Chrys.*hom.24.5 in 1Cor.*(10.218E); Bas.Sel.*v.Thecl.*2.18(M. 85.597A); = ἀναφαίνω (ref. Ps.91:8), Dor.*doct.*13.7(M.88.1769A); hence *appear, dawn* τῆς...πορρηθείσης ἡμέρας ὅσον διακυψάσης μόνον Bas.Sel.*v.Thecl.*2.20(604B); **b.** met., *look to, concern oneself with,* Thdt.*ep.*34(4.1094); of God οὐκ ἀπαξιοῖ ~ειν ἐκ τοῦ οὐρανοῦ πρὸς τὴν ἐπιμελείαν τῶν ἀνθρώπων †Bas.*Is.*183(1.513D; M.30.428C); Thdt. *provid.*1(4.488); **3.** *scrutinize closely* θησαυρὸς δικαιοσύνης ὁ νόμος τοῖς οὐ προσέχουσι τῇ σκιᾷ, ~ουσι δὲ μᾶλλον αὐτήν Cyr.*Is.*3.3(2. 455A).

διακυρίττ-ομαι, 1. *butt against,* Synes.*calv.*13(p.215.6; M.66. 1192A); **2.** met., *contend* with ὁ πάντα τολμῶν οὗτος...ἀρθεὶς ἀφ' ἡμῶν αὐτῷ ~εται τῷ θεῷ id.*ep.*57(M.66.1393C).

διακυρόω, *confirm,* Cyr.*Ps.*36:25(M.69.941A).

διακωδωνίζω, 1. *prove by ringing* [sc. coins]; met., *test, try* ὁ σατανᾶς...διακωδωνίσας...αὐτὸν [sc. Judas] ἐν ἀρχῇ Chrys.*hom.81.3 in Mt.*(7.776E); id.*hom.12.1 in Heb.*(12.120C); Nil.*epp.*3.153(M.79. 456B); abs. διακωδωνήσας (prob. error for -ίσας) Isid.Pel.*epp.*3. 385(M.78.1028B); **2.** *spread abroad,* Chrys.*fem.reg.*6(1.261B).

***διακωθωνίζομαι,** *drink hard,* Gr.Nyss.*Eun.*1(1 p.51.11; M.45. 280B); *ib.*(p.193.19; 440B).

διάκων, ὁ, = διάκονος, Jo.Mosch.*prat.*219(M.87.3109D, v.l. δηάκων).

διαλαλ-έω, 1. *babble* τῶν ἐν ταῖς αἱρέσεσιν...~ούντων ⟨ὡς⟩ σωτήρια τὰ ὀλέθρια Or.*Jo.*32.5(p.434.1; M.14.753B); *speak incoherently,* as one possessed, Leont.N.*v.Sym.*45(M.93.1725B); τοὺς ἐκ δαιμόνων ~οῦντας καὶ προφητεύοντας *ib.*(1725C); *ib.*53(1736B); *speak under inspiration* of H. Ghost, *ib.*(1736B); **2.** *speak of, describe,* Mac.Mgn.*apocr.*2.20(p.39.19); **3.** *decide, pass a resolution* τοῦτο ἀξιῶ τὴν ἁγίαν σύνοδον ~ῆσαι CCP(394)*act.*(M.119.824B); Pall.*v.Chrys.*14(p.87.11; M.47.49); **4.** *make a proposal* in debate διελάλησα ἀναγνωσθῆναι αὐτήν [sc. τὴν ἐπιστολήν] CChalc.*act.*1 (*ACO* 2.1.1 p.84.22; H.2.89A); Evagr.*h.e.*2.18(p.68.9; M.86.2549A); *ib.*(p.89.8; 2581A); **5.** *make a speech,* in the course of a trial, *Chron. Pasch.*p.322(M.92.825A); **6.** *say, speak* = λαλέω, Eus.*e.th.*3.5(p.160. 28; M.24.1008C); ‡Ath.*dial.Trin.*2.29(M.28.1201B); *ib.*3.3(1208A).

***διαλάλητος,** *famed,* Thdr.Stud.*epp.*2.68(M.99.1296C); *ib.*2.82 (1324B); neut. as subst., Gr.Nyss.*v.Ephr.*(M.46.849A).

διαλαλία, ἡ, 1. *discourse,* Epiph.*haer.*64.73(p.523.18 n.); **2.** during the course of a debate; **a.** *resolution, proposal,* CChalc.*act.*1(*ACO* 2.1.1 p.84.6; H.2.89A); Evagr.*h.e.*2.18(p.83.10; M.86.2572C); *ib.* (p.87.28; 2580A); **b.** *speech, declaration* ἡ δ. μου ἀνεγνώσθη CChalc. *act.*1(*ACO* 2.1.1 p.92.26,30; H.2.100C); Justn.*ep.Thdr.Mops.*(p.65. 25; M.86.1085Aff.); **c.** *order* given by emperor, Evagr.*h.e.*2.18(p.91. 28; M.86.2585B).

διαλαμβάν-ω, A. *lay hold of;* **1.** met., *take possession of* κτύπου καὶ ταραχῆς ἀθρόας διαλαβούσης τὸ στρατιωτικόν Eus.*v.C.*2.9(p.44.20; M.20.988C); id.*l.C.*8(p.217.27; M.20.1361B); διαλαβούσης δὲ αὐτοὺς νυκτὸς id.*d.e.*10.7(p.470.16; M.22.757A); *ib.*10.8(p.480.36; 773B); ἡ διορθωτικὴ τῆς φύσεως δύναμις καὶ τῆς ἀρχῆς ἀψαμένη καὶ μεχρὶ τοῦ τέλους [sc. τῆς ζωῆς] ἑαυτὴν ἐπεκτείνασα καὶ τὰ διὰ μέσου τούτων πάντα διαλαβοῦσα Gr.Nyss.*or.catech.*27(p.102.10; M.45.69D); **2.** *attack, overwhelm,* Eus.*v.C.*3.59(p.105.27; M.20.1125C); **3.** *include, comprehend,* Gr.Nyss.*or.catech.*32(p.121.7, v.l. καταλαμβάνει 81C); **4.** *take in hand, commence* ἄρξομαι...τοῦ λέγειν, ὅθεν διέλαβον κακῶς φυτεύειν Epiph.*haer.*69.20(p.169.20; M.42.232D); *ib.*69.28(p.178.9; 248B); **5.** *take in, enclose* a place, Eus.*v.C.*3.39(p.94.23; M.20. 1100A); Cyr.*Ps.*20:4(M.69.836C); pass., *be enclosed* or *covered* πόδες ...διειλημμένοι τοῖς ὑποδήμασι Gr.Nyss.*v.Mos.*(M.44.356C); id. *v.Macr.*(p.399.18; M.46.985C); **6.** *receive;* **a.** an honour, position etc., Eus.*h.e.*4.19(M.20.377A); perf. *hold* τῶν...τὴν ἔπαρχον διειληφότων ἐξουσίαν id.*v.C.*2.44(p.60.3; M.20.1021A); id.*l.C.*10(p.223.7; M.20.1373C); **b.** a conception or understanding τὰ περὶ τοῦ θεοῦ δ. Clem.*str.*7.7(p.34.3; M.9.464C); abs., *have a conception* or *understanding* περὶ...τῶν ὅλων ἀληθῶς...διείληφεν *ib.*7.11(p.43.29; 485A).

B. *catch fire* διέλαβεν πᾶς ὁ ναὸς καὶ ἐκαύθη Marc.Diac.*v.Porph.* 69; met. περισσοτέρως ἀνήφθη καὶ διέλαβεν...ἡ θρησκεία αὐτῶν Agath. *v.Gr.Ill.*68(p.35).

C. *divide;* **1.** *mark off at intervals,* met., pass., *be divided* or *bounded* δοκεῖ...ὁδὸς...ἡ παροῦσα ζωὴ καὶ πορεία διειλημμένη ταῖς ἡλικίαις καθάπερ σταθμοῖς Bas.*hom.*21.2(2.164E; M.31.544B); Gr. Nyss.*or.catech.*27(p.102.6; M.45.69D); **2.** *cut off, bound* by a wall or fortification, *V.Const.*37(p.567.3); **3.** *interrupt* μεταξὺ διαλαβόντες φασί, 'σὺ τίς εἶ;' Cyr.*Jo.*5.4(4.510D); **4.** *discuss;* c. acc., Athenag.*res.* 14(p.65.5; M.6.1001C); Meth.*res.*1.25(p.251.13; M.41.1129B); Ath. *inc.*1.1(M.25.96D); elliptically τοῦ πρώτου βιβλίου τοῦ κατὰ τῶν εἴκοσιν αἱρέσεων ~οντος *which deals with the attack on the 20 heresies* Epiph.*anac.*tit.(*GCS* 1 p.162.1 n.; M.42.840C); c. περί, Clem.*str.*8.2 (p.81.17; M.9.561B); Or.*Cels.*5.45(p.48.16; M.11.1249C); Eus.*h.e.*1.4.1 (M.20.76C); followed by clause, Or.*Jo.*2.1(p.52.3; M.14.104C); *ib.* 28.19(14; p.413.25; 721B); Eus.*d.e.*3.3(p.112.8; M.22.192D); **5.** *define, settle* ἀμφιβολίας...διαλαβόντες Gr.Nyss.*Eun.*1(1 p.70.9; M.45.300A); **6.** *grasp, comprehend,* Or.*exc.in Ps.*41:10(M.17.136C); Eus.*d.e.* 4.15(p.174.33; M.22.292B); **7.** *decide, judge,* Eus.*h.e.*7.30.19(M.20. 720A); διαλαβὼν ὁ προφήτης ἀποκρίνεται Cyr.*Is.*2.4(2.295B).

D. *traverse* κυβερνήτην μυρία διαλαβόντα πελάγη Chrys.*hom.26.9 in Mt.*(7.323D); id.*hom.24.3 in Heb.*(12.224B); *ib.*(226A, v.l. διαβαίνειν).

E. *dawn* διαλαβούσης...τῆς ἕω Eus.*v.C.*4.22(p.125.30; M.20.1169A).

διαλαμπής, *shining* εἵματα...διαλαμπέα Gr.Naz.*carm.*2.2(poem.) 6.7(M.37.1543A).

διαλάμπ-ω, 1. *shine,* Or.*Cant.*3(p.179.27; M.17.261A); **2.** *be illustrious* or *eminent;* of persons, Eus.*v.C.*3.9(p.81.9; M.20.1064A); δ. ἐν ἔργοις ἀγαθοῖς †Bas.*parad.*11(1.351C; M.30.71A); Chrys.*hom.7.6 in Rom.*(9.491A); **3.** *be obvious* or *patent* ἀπὸ τῶν ~όντων τὴν ψῆφον ἐνεργεῖν Isid.Pel.*epp.*5.342(M.78.1536A).

διαλεαίνω, *triturate,* Or.*enarr.in Job* 20:18(M.17.73C); met., *make smooth,* †Jo.D.*B.J.*30(M.96.1145B).

διαλέγ-ω, A. act.; *separate one from another, Orac.Sib.*3.87; *ib.* 8.412.

B. dep.; **1.** *hold converse with* ὅταν ἡμῖν ~ηται μετανοοῦσιν ὁ θεὸς λέγει 'μετανοῶ' Or.*hom.18.6 in Jer.*(p.159.26; M.13.477A); *ib. 18.8*(p.161.17; 480A); in prayer τρία τὰ νοούμενα, ὡς ἑνὶ δὲ ~όμεθα Melitius ap.Thdt.*h.e.*2.31.8(3.909); **2.** *say, utter,* Diad.*perf.*70(p.86. 12); *Didasc.Jac.*1.55(p.780.5); **3.** *discourse, preach,* Malch.*ep.*ap. Eus.*h.e.*7.30.10(M.20.713B); Eus.*ib.*6.19.16(569B); Bas.*hom.*14.1(2. 122E; M.31.445A).

διαλείπ-ω, 1. *cease from,* c. genit. δ. τοῦ ἐν ἀνθώποις εἶναι Heracleon ap.Or.*Jo.*6.39(23; p.147.23; M.14.265C); **2.** *cease to exist,* Eus. *d.e.*7.1(p.318.19; M.22.520D); διαλελοιπότων ἤδη τῶν παρ' Ἑβραίοις προφητῶν id.*p.e.*10.14(505A; M.21.840C); **3.** *abandon, desert* τοὺς μὲν ἐν θαλάσσῃ...οὐ ~εις ‡Rom.Mel.(*AS* 1 p.209).

διαλεκτικός, 1. *skilled in dialectic,* superl. διαλεκτικώτατον ὄντα κατὰ πασῶν τῶν αἱρέσεων Pall.*h.Laus.*86(p.117.5; M.34.1188C); masc. as subst., Clem.*str.*1.28(p.109.14; M.8.924B); Or.*Cels.*2.20(p.149.4; M.11.836C); esp. in bad sense, Clem.*str.*1.28(p.109.12; 924A); Gr. Naz.*or.*27.9(p.16.8; M.36.24A); Cael. *ep.CP* 1(p.85.12; M.*PL.*50. 490A); **2.** fem. as subst., *dialectic, disputation;* def. and scope, Clem.*str.*1.9(p.30.12; M.8.741C); μικτὴ δὲ φιλοσοφίᾳ οὖσα τῇ ἀληθεῖ ἡ ἀληθὴς δ. ... ὑπεξαναβαίνει ἐπὶ τὴν πάντων κρατίστην οὐσίαν τολμᾷ τε ἐπέκεινα ἐπὶ τῶν ὅλων θεόν,...ἐπιστήμην τῶν θείων καὶ οὐρανίων ἐπαγγελλομένη *ib.*1.28(p.109.6; 924A); ἡ δ. φρόνησίς ἐστι περὶ τὰ νοητὰ διαιρετική,...μόνη αὕτη ἐπὶ τὴν ἀληθῆ σοφίαν χειραγωγεῖ *ib.*(p.109.15; 924B); συνεργεῖ...ἡ δ. πρὸς τὸ μὴ ὑποπίπτειν ταῖς...

αἱρέσεσιν *ib.*1.20(p.63.28; 817A); in bad sense τῆς φιλοσοφίας καὶ τῆς δ. εὑρετής [i.e. ὁ διάβολος] *ib.*1.9(p.29.30; 741B).

διάλεξις, ἡ, 1. *speech, conversation*, Clem.*fr.*11(p.199.2); ἡ γὰρ εὐχὴ δ. ἐστι πρὸς τὸν θεόν Chrys.*hom.30.5 in Gen.*(4.301E); εἰς δ. ἐλθεῖν id.*hom.87.2 in Jo.*(8.521E); κατὰ διάλεξιν *word for word*, *Didasc. Jac.*1.55(p.780.6); **2.** *language, dialect*, Chrys.*hom.30.4 in Gen.*(4.300A); id.*hom.31.4 in Jo.*(8.180C); Thdt.*qu.19 in Jud.*(1.337); **3.** *homily, discourse*; hence *treatise*, Eus.*h.e.*5.26(M.20.509A); *ib.*6.13.3(548A).

***διαλεπτουργέω,** *concern oneself with petty details of, niggle over*, Gr.Nyss.*Eun.*12(1 p.284.4; M.45.992C).

διαλεπτύν-ω, *diminish, reduce greatly*, Gr.Nyss.*Eun.*2(2 p.321.10; M.45.493D); pass., c. genit., *be deprived, bereft of* ~όμενος τῶν κέδρων ὁ Λίβανος id.*hom.in Cant.*proem.(M.44.761D).

διαλευκαίνω, *illustrate, make clear*, Or.*exc.in Ps.*36:14(M.17.129B); Cyr.*Ps.*4:2(M.69.733D); id.*Mal.*22(3.838E); followed by clause, id. *ador.*2(1.50B); id.*Ps.*37:20(969A); id.*Is.*3.3(2.475D).

***διαλήγω,** *cease*, *Dial.Tim.et Aquil.*96 v°.

διαληπτέον, *one must discuss, treat*, Clem.*paed.*2.10(p.208.1; M.8.497A); id.*str.*2.23(p.188.26; M.8.1085C); *ib.*3.5(p.214.14; 1144B).

***διαλικμάω,** *winnow away thoroughly*, †Apoll.*met.Ps.*17:43(M.33.1333D).

διαλιμπάν-ω, *intermit*; **1.** *cease*; c. ptcpl., Eus.*Is.*18:7(M.24.217D); Serap.*ep.mon.*6(M.40.932B); Chrys.*hom.8.3 in 2Tim.*(11.710C); abs., id.*comm.in Gal.*4:19(10.708C); id.*ecl.*30(12.659A); c. infin., Thdr.Stud.*epp.*1.44(M.99.1069A); **2.** *leave alone, allow to rest* μάχαι...οὔποτ' αὐτοὺς διελίμπανον Eus.*l.C.*16(p.248.32; M.20.1421B); **3.** *let pass* [sc. time], Chrys.*hom.in Mt.26:39*(3.15B); **4.** *thrust away, repulse* τὸν θεὸν ἀπὸ σοῦ μὴ ~ειν Eus.Al.*serm.*21.11(M.86.437A).

διαλλακτήριος, *reconciling, mediating*, Bas.*hom.in Ps.*1(1.90E; M.29.212C); Gr.Naz.*or.*21.36(M.35.1128A); Andr.Cr.*or.*1(M.97.813A); neut. as subst., of BMV τὸ τοῦ κόσμου δ. Ephr.3.530C.

διάλληλος, 1. *reciprocal*, *cat.Apoc.*3:20(p.235.26); Areth.*Apoc.*6(M.106.540C); **2.** *alternating, corresponding*, Andr.Cr.*or.*19(M.97.1217A); **3.** neut. as subst., *correspondence* ἵνα...τῷ ἰῷ τοῦ χαλκοῦ, τὸν ἰὸν τῆς κακίας ἀντιπαραθείς, ὡς ἐν συγκρίσει, τὸ τοῦ χαλκοῦ παραδείξῃ διάλληλον *ib.*11(1040C).

διαλογή, ἡ, 1. *discourse, description*, Epiph.*haer.*20.3(p.227.1; M.41.273A); **2.** *reasoning, argument, discussion*, *ib.*48.3(p.224.11; 860C); *ib.*77.18(p.431.11; M.42.665B); cf. εἰς διαλογισμοὺς καὶ εἰς δ. λέξεων *quibbles* about words, *ib.*76.9(p.350.22; 532D).

διαλογίζομαι, 1. *reason*, Herm.*vis.*1.1.2; *ib.*4.1.4; Heracleon ap. Or.*Jo.*19.19(4; p.320.14; M.14.561C); Ath.*v.Anton.*42(M.26.995B); **2.** *dispute, argue*, Herm.*vis.*3.1.9; *ib.*4.3; id.*sim.*9.2.6.

διαλογικῶς, 1. *in the manner of a dialogue*, Polychr.*fr.Job* 2:1(p.25); Thdt.*eran.*proem.(4.3); id.*ep.*130(4.1219); **2.** *contentiously, in a contest* Νηφαλίῳ μὲν ὁ Σεβῆρος δ. συμπλέκεται Evagr.*h.e.*3.33(p.132.5; M.86.2669A).

διαλογισμός, ὁ, 1. *thought* οὐδὲν λέληθεν αὐτὸν...τῶν δ. ὧν ποιούμεθα *1Clem.*21.3; 'οὐδεὶς γὰρ καθαρὸς ἀπὸ ῥύπου' καὶ δ. ἀλλοτρίων Or.*hom.21.2 in Jos.*(p.431.23)ap.Proc.G.*Jos.*15:63(M.87.1033C); ὁ δὲ Χριστὸς καὶ τοὺς δ. τῶν ἀνθρώπων ᾔδει Adam.*dial.*1.17(p.36.14; M.11.1744C); of last and perfected stage of thought before utterance ἡ δὲ φρόνησις πλατυνθεῖσα, ποιεῖ τὸν δ. Max.*opusc.*(M.91.21A); **2.** *disputation, argument*, exeg. 1Tim.2:8 δ. τὴν ἀμφιβολίαν λέγει Chrys.*hom.8.1 in 1Tim.*(11.590C); Thdt.*1Tim.*2:8(3.650).

διάλογος, ὁ, 1. *dispute, argument*, Cels.ap.Or.*Cels.*3.1(p.203.12; M.11.921A); **2.** name given to Gr. Mag. as author of *Dialogues* (tr. Pope Zacharias into Greek), ‡Jo.D.*fid.dorm.*16(M.95.261D).

***διάλοιπος,** *remaining*, Pall.*h.Laus.*5(p.21.20, v.l. ὑπολοίπους M.34.1017D).

***διαλοχέω,** *bring forth*; met., Anast.Ap.*a.Max.*2(M.90.204C).

διάλυσις, ἡ, 1. *expiation* of sins, Chrys.*hom.9.2 in Mt.*(7.131E); **2.** *settlement, division* of inheritance, CSyr.*act.*(*ACO* 3 p.99.16; H.2.1376C); **3.** *agreement* συνθήκας καὶ δ. ἐγγράφους Phot.*nomoc.*2.1(M.104.572D).

διαλύτης, ὁ, *one who dissolves, discharges* a debt, Gr.Naz.*ep.*69(M.37.133C).

διαλύ-ω, A. *break up*; **1.** a ship, Dion.Al.ap.Eus.*p.e.*14.24(774B; M.21.1273B); **2.** *dissolve* ὕδωρ ὥσπερ...καταστάζουσα διέλυσεν αὐτὸν [sc. τὸν Ἀδάμ] ἡ ἁμαρτία Meth.*symp.*3.5(p.31.17; M.18.68C); τὸν γὰρ ἄνθρωπον...διέλυσεν εἰς ὕλην πάλιν [sc. ὁ θεός] id.*res.*1.43(p.291.5; M.18.272C); τῷ θανάτῳ τὴν ζωὴν ἡμῶν ~εσθαι Gr.Nyss.*or.catech.*8(p.41.5; M.45.33A); *ib.*37(p.142.9; 93B); marriage, Thdt.*haer.*5.25(4.469) cit. s. γάμος; pass., *perish, decay* ἅτινα [sc. σπέρματα] πεσόντα εἰς τὴν γῆν ξηρὰ καὶ γυμνὰ ~εται *1Clem.*24.5; Just.*1apol.*19.4(M.6.357A); Or.*Jo.*13.33(p.258.3; M.14.456C); **3.** *extinguish* a lamp, Chrys.*hom.50.3 in Jo.*(8.298C); **4.** *dispel*, fig. τῆς συκοφαντίας διαλῦσαι τὰ κύματα Thdt.*ep.*106(4.1176); **5.** *release*, id.*Ps.*73:14(1.1129) cit. s. κραταιόω; **6.** *loose* a bond of excommunication, id.*h.e.*5.37.1,2(3.1079); **7.** *break a fast, keep* a period *free from fasting*, Jo. Jej.*canonar.*3.2(p.439); τὴν...γέννησιν τῆς...θεοτόκου...~ομεν εἰς ἔλαιον καὶ ἰχθύας *Catech.Stud.*5(M.99.1696C); *ib.*9(1700C); τὴν δὲ ἅπασαν ἑβδομάδα τοῦ ἁγίου πνεύματος ~ομεν...ἐν παντὶ βρώματι Anast.*temp.*(p.279); **8.** *discharge* or *pay* one's debts; pass., *be released* from a debt, Chrys.*hom.1.3 in Philm.*(11.777F); met., med., *expiate* ἁμαρτήματα ~όμεθα id.*hom.9.2 in Mt.*(7.132A); *ib.*(132C); *ib.14.4*(183C); pass., of sins, *be expiated*, id.*Laz.*6.3(1.776E); of sinner, *be absolved, have one's sins cancelled* πολλοὶ...καὶ ἐνταῦθα ~ονται καὶ ἐκεῖ κρίνονται *ib.*(l.c.).

B. *relax, weaken*; pass., *be enervated*; of the body, Chrys.*hom.6.3 in 2Cor.*(10.477A); id.*hom.23.2 in Eph.*(11.176A); also act. ~ει... τοὺς ἀμῶντας...τὸ τῆς ὥρας θερμόν Thdt.*Gal.*6:9(3.394); perf. ptcpl. pass., *enervated, slack, dissolute*; of persons, Chrys.*hom.2.8 in 2Cor.*(10.440E); *ib.13.4*(536A); id.*hom.7.3 in 1Tim.*(11.587E); τὸν...διαλελυμένον...βίον id.*hom.1.4 in 2Cor.*(10.423B); so of one laughing unrestrainedly, *helpless, overcome*, id.*hom.4.7 in Mt.*(7.60B).

διαμανθάνω, *learn*, Cyr.*Juln.*1(6².19A).

διαμαντεύω, *consult an oracle*, Thphn.*chron.*p.336(M.108.812A).

διαμάρτημα, τό, *mistake*, Nemes.*nat.hom.*8(M.40.653A).

***διαμάρτησις, ἡ,** *mistake*, Thdr.Stud.*epp.*2.21(M.99.1181D).

***διαμαρτυρητέον,** *one must testify*, Thdr.Stud.*epp.*2.22(M.99.1188A).

διαμαρτυρία, ἡ, 1. legal *appeal* or *plea* for a case to be referred to a higher court ἀνάγκην ἔχομεν ἐπὶ τήνδε τὴν δ. ἐλθεῖν...ἀξιοῦντες ...τηρῆσαι τὴν ἀκρόασιν...αὐτῷ τῷ...βασιλεῖ *Ep.Dion.*2(p.160.3; M.25.392D; **2.** *solemn statement* or *declaration*, *A.(Pass.)Andr.*15(p.35.24; M.2.1248A); *Clem.contest.*tit.(M.2.28C); Thdt.*Ps.*80:9(1.1182).

***διαμαρτύρ-ω, A.** act., *call to witness* ~ε αὐτοῖς τὸν οὐρανόν Thdt. *Ps.*118:152(1.1476); hence, c. dat., *warn*, Chrys.*hom.13.1 in Jo.*(8.72B).

B. usu. med.; **1.** *call to witness*, *Clem.contest.*4(M.2.32A); *Hom. Clem.*18.5; Thdt.*Zach.*3:7(2.1609); **2.** *warn*, id.*Ps.*118:138(1.1472); **3.** abs., *affirm solemnly* διὰ τοῦ Ἰεζεκιὴλ διεμαρτύρατο ὁ θεός Just. *dial.*82.3(M.6.669C); Thdt.*h.rel.*8(3.1180); Andr.Caes.*Apoc.*72(M.106.449D).

***διαμαρυκ-άομαι,** *ruminate*, met. ὥστε...~ᾶσθαι τὰ ῥήματα Chrys.*hom.4.7 in Gen.*(4.29C).

διαμάσησις, ἡ, *mastication*, Nemes.*nat.hom.*23(M.40.693C); Melet. *nat.hom.*10(M.64.1189A).

διαμαστίγωσις, ἡ, *scourging*, Thdt.*affect.*10(p.245.20; 4.953).

διαμαστίζω, *scourge*; met., Eus.*v.C.*4.29(p.129.6; M.20.1177C).

***διαμέλω,** *examine thoroughly*, Cyr.*inc.unigen.*(5¹.678C).

***διαμεριμνάω,** *be anxious, concern oneself about*; c. acc., Anast.S. *synax.*(M.89.828C); c. περί, *ib.*; abs., Taras.*apol.*(M.98.1424C)ap. Thphn.*chron.*p.386(M.108.924B).

διαμέρισις, ἡ, *separation, division*, Epiph.*mens.*22(M.43.276C).

διάμεσος, 1. *intermediate*, Alex.Lyc.*Man.*5(M.18.417C; conj. ἄμεσοι p.9.3); **2.** neut. as subst., *difference* πολὺ τὸ δ. Geo.Al.*v. Chrys.*4(p.163.21).

διαμηνύω, 1. *point out clearly*, Cyr.*ador.*11(1.388E); *ib.*13(471B); **2.** med., *issue a summons* to one's presence διεμηνύσατο δέ, καὶ ἦλθεν πρὸς αὐτὸν ὅλον τὸ συνέδριον *A.Pil.*B 11.2(p.310).

διαμηχαν-άομαι, *contrive, devise* προφάσεως ~ῶμαι *Hom.Clem.* 19.20, conj. προφάσεις.

***διαμίμησις, ἡ,** *imitation*, *V.Chrys.*4(p.299.6).

***διαμόλιβδος,** *leaden*, †Ath.*fr.Mt.*11:29(M.27.1381D).

διαμολύνω, *pollute*, Gr.Nyss.*Eun.*12(1 p.281.21; M.45.989A).

διαμονή, ἡ, *continuance, permanence*; **1.** in concrete sense, *resting-place, dwelling-place*, Cyr.*Ps.*67:7(M.69.1145B); id.*Zach.*69(3.749C); Proc.G.*Cant.*7:2(M.87.1761A); **2.** *permanence, duration* τῶν ἀτόμων ...τῆς περὶ τὴν δ. διαφορᾶς Dion.Al.ap.Eus.*p.e.*14.25(775C; M.21.1276C); 'δι' αὐτοῦ' [sc. τοῦ θεοῦ] τοῖς πᾶσιν ἡ δ. Bas.*Spir.*7(3.7D; M.32.81A); Const.ap.Gel.Cyz.*h.e.*3.19.34(M.85.1353A); Melet.*nat. hom.*30(M.64.1277B); of abstracts τῆς ἀληθείας δ. Clem.*str.*7.3(p.14.20; M.9.424C); τὴν ἁρμόζουσαν δικαίῳ πράξει δ. Or.*enarr.in Job*(M.17.88B); *Clem.ep.Petr.*2(M.2.28A); of human life τῶν ἀνθρώπων ἡ φύσις...ἀνώμαλον ἔχει τὴν ζωὴν καὶ τὴν δ. Athenag.*res.*17(p.68.21; M.6.1008B); Clem.*paed.*2.1(p.154.14; M.8.377C); ‡Bas.*struct.hom.22*(1.335C; M.30.36A); τῶν μαρτύρων...ἡ ἐν Χριστῷ τελεία δ. Leo Mag. *ep.*43(p.4.15; M.*PL.*54.824B); of God τῆς ἀιδίου αὐτοῦ δ. *Clem.ep.*

*Petr.*2(M.2.28A); οὗ...ἄτρεπτος καὶ ἀνελλιπὴς ἡ δ. *Const.App.*7.35.9; ref. Inc. ἡ τοῦ θεοῦ φύσις...ἀκατάσειστον ἔχει τὴν ἐφ' οἷς ἐστι δ. Cyr. *inc.unigen.*(5^1.683B); ἡ τοῦ λόγου φύσις...ἐν ἀκλονήτῳ σώζεται δ. *ib.* (701D); of Christ Γαβριὴλ ὁ ἀρχάγγελος τὰ περὶ τῆς αἰωνίου δ. τοῦ σωτῆρος ἐδίδαξε Cyr.H.*catech.*15.17; of H. Ghost ἡ...ἄπαυστος δ. μεθ' υἱοῦ καὶ πατρὸς θεωρουμένη Bas.*Spir.*63(3.53A; M.32.184B).

διάμονος, *permanent, enduring*, Anon.ap.Eus.*h.e.*5.16.19(M.20. 472B).

διαμορφ-όω, **1.** *give form to, shape*, ref. Creation τὴν...γῆν, ἣν ταῖς σαῖς χερσὶ διεμόρφωσας Gr.Nyss.*v.Macr.*(p.397.8; M.46.984C); Bas.Sel.*or.*29.1(M.85.328A); Sophr.H.*v.Anast.*(M.92.1717C) cit. s. διαπλάσσω; med., Leont.B.*arg.Sev.*(M.86.1932B); fig. Παῦλος... τοὺς ἐκπεσόντας...~οῖ ἀναπλάσσων αὐτοὺς εἰς εὐσέβειαν [Gal.4:19] †Bas.*Is.*13(1.387A; M.30.140A); met. Χριστοῦ ἐν ἡμῖν ~ουμένου Mac.Aeg.*perf.*11(M.34.848D); **2.** *represent allegorically* παραδείξαιμι ...τὰ τοῖς ἀρχαίοις συμβεβηκότα ~ῶν εὐτέχνως εἰς τύπον τῶν νοητῶν Cyr.*ador.*1(1.11D); *ib.*5(153C); διὰ παντὸς...τοῦ γεγονότος ἐν τῇ ἁγίᾳ σκηνῇ, τὸ τοῦ σωτῆρος ἡμῖν ~οῦται μυστήριον *ib.*9(325A); Thdt. *eran.*3(4.179); ἀνθρωπίνως ~οῖ τὸν θεὸν ἡ γραφὴ τὸν ἀσχημάτιστον Olymp.*fr.Jer.*14:19(M.93.660C).

διαμύσσω, *pierce through*, Hipp.*haer.*5.9(p.98.1; M.16.3151C).

***διαμφής**, *rotund*; neut. as subst., Epiph.*haer.*45.1(p.200.9; M.41. 833B).

διαμφιβάλλω, *dispute*, Gr.Nyss.*Eun.*12(1 p.296.22, v.l. διασφαλλόμενος M.45.1005D); Anast.S.*hod.*10(M.89.184B); Thphyl.*exc.gent.* 14(p.488.1; M.113.949D).

***διαμφότεροι**, *both*, Amph.*hom.*1.1(M.39.37B).

***διαμωκίζω**, *mock*, ‡Jo.D.*ep.Thphl.*6(M.95.353A).

διαμωμάομαι, *find fault with*, Cyr.*apol.orient.*(p.60.1; 6^1.193D); id.*inc.unigen.*(5^1.695A); id.*Is.*3.4(2.511A).

διαναβάλλομαι, *put off continually*, Chrys.*hom.22.5 in Mt.*(7. 281D); Cyr.*Zach.*44(3.720B).

***διαναδίδωμι**, pass., *be distributed*, Jo.D.*f.o.*2.7(M.94.896C).

***διανακαλύπτω**, *reveal completely*, Gr.Nyss.*Eun.*12(1 p.383.26; M. 45.1112C).

διαναπαύ-ω, **1.** act.; **a.** *give rest to, refresh* ὁ θεὸς...~ει τοὺς πεπιεσμένους Dion.Al.ap.Eus.*h.e.*7.11.25(M.20.672B); τοῦτον...καμάτου ~σας Eus.*l.C.*6(p.209.1; M.20.1345B); ὁ...φόβος ὁ τοῦ θεοῦ...~ων αὐτούς Chrys.*hom.14.4 in 1Tim.*(11.630A); **b.** *provide a resting-place*, Pall.*h.Laus.*21(p.64.20; M.34.1073C); **c.** *assuage, relieve*, Or. *fr.52 in Jo.*(p.526.18); **d.** *satisfy, indulge* passion, Chrys.*hom.50.2 in Jo.*(8.296C); **e.** *set down* burdens, Eus.*v.C.*4.70(p.146.32; M.20. 1225A); αὐτῷ τὸ σκῆνος τελευτήσαντι τὸν βίον...μέλλοι ~εσθαι *ib.*4. 60(p.142.11; M.1212A); **2.** med., *find refreshment*, Chrys.*hom.51.1 in Jo.*(8.299B).

***διανάπτω**, *enkindle* φῶς διανάψας Chrys.*hom.30.3 in 2Cor.*(v.l. διανοίας 10.654A).

διανάστασις, ἡ, *rising up*, from the knees in prayer καθ' ἑκάστην δὲ γονυκλισίαν καὶ δ., ἔργῳ δείκνυμεν, ὅτι διὰ τῆς ἁμαρτίας εἰς γῆν κατερρύημεν, καὶ διὰ τῆς φιλανθρωπίας τοῦ κτίσαντος ἡμᾶς εἰς οὐρανὸν ἀνεκλήθημεν Bas.*Spir.*66(3.56D; M.32.192C); = erect posture, Chrys.*hom.6.3 in 2Cor.*(10.477B); of growth in height, ‡Gr.Nyss. *or.1 in Gen.1:26*(M.44.269D); met. τί βούλονται αἱ σάλπιγγες καὶ ἡ ἠχή; πρὸς δ., πρὸς εὐφροσύνην Chrys.*hom.76.4 in Mt.*(7.737B); τὴν δὲ τοῦ ζήλου τῆς εὐσεβείας δ. Thdr.Stud.*epp.*1.35(M.99.1029A).

***διανατίθεμαι**, *place on one's shoulders*, Niceph.Ur.*v.Sym.*201 (M.86.3172A); *ib.*205(3173C).

διαναυμαχέω, *enter into conflict at sea*; met., Synes.*ep.*4(M.66. 1329C).

***διάνευμα, τό**, *incitement*, Cyr.*ador.*1(1.38E); Anast.Ap.*a.Max.*2 (M.90.204C).

***διανευρόω**, *brace up*, met., Cyr.*Os.*167(3.194A); id.*Is.*4.4(2.671C); id.*Ps.*33:16(M.69.892B).

***διάνευσις, ἡ**, *inclination*, Cyr.*Os.*172(3.196C).

διανήθω, *spin out*, Cyr.*Abac.*35(3.550C).

διάνηξις, ἡ, *swimming*, Epiph.*haer.*59.3(p.366.13; M.41.1021B).

***διανήφω**, **1.** *be sober* διανήφωμεν ἔννοιαν ἀγαθὴν κτησάμενοι Mac. Aeg.*hom.*4.17(M.34.485A); **2.** *recover consciousness* or *sobriety*, Eus. *Is.*24:6–10(M.24.260D); Ath.*h.Ar.*57(p.215.25; M.25.761C); med., Anast.S.*qu.et resp.*91(M.89.724B); **3.** ? *be conscious of, awaken to*; met., *realize* τῆς ἀληθείας διανήψας τὰ πρότερόν σοι γραφέντα λαμπρᾷ καὶ φιλαλήθει δίελθε φωνῇ Eus.*Hierocl.*43(539D; M.22.857A).

διανήχω, *swim through* or *across*; **1.** act., met. δ. σωτηρίως ἐκ τοῦ παρθενικοῦ πελάγους ‡Meth.*Sym.et Ann.*11(M.18.373D); **2.** usu. med.; met., *traverse*, Tit.Bost.*Man.*2.7(M.18.1145B); Cyr.*ador.*6 (1.201A); id.*hom.pasch.*12(5^2.164D); *cross* a river, Thphyl.*exc.Rom.* 6(p.226.29; M.113.936A); σχεδίας ποιήσαντες τὸν ποταμὸν δ. Thphn. *chron.*p.237(M.108.596C).

διανθέω, med., *have a bouquet*, of wine οἴνου...διηνθημένου Thdt. *Am.*6:6(2.1435, v.l. διηνθισμένου).

διανίημι, *disperse, dissolve* τὰ πάντα συνίστασθαι πηγνυμένου [sc. τοῦ ὕδατος] καὶ πάλιν διανιεμένου (acc. Thales) Hipp.*haer.*1.1(p.4.15; M.16.3021C).

διανίστ-ημι, **A.** act.; **1.** *raise up, make to stand* ~ᾶσιν εἰς προσευχάς [sc. οἱ πρεσβύτεροι τοὺς λαούς] Cyr.*ador.*13(1.454C); met., Clem. *prot.*9(p.63.17; M.8.196A); ἡμᾶς ἐκ θανάτου δ. Cyr.*Jo.*4.1(4.339E); **2.** *arouse, stimulate, excite*, Clem.*paed.*1.8(p.129.2; M.8.329B); τὸ πνεῦμα...πρὸς τὴν τῶν νοητῶν θεωρίαν τὸν...νοῦν δ. †Bas.*Is.*5(1. 381C; M.30.125C); Chrys.*hom.4.2 in Mt.*(7.48C); τὰ ὑποδείγματα καὶ τὸ εἰς εὐλάβειαν βλέπειν δ. τοὺς φοιτητάς Isid.Pel.*epp.*5.263(M.78. 1489C).

B. pass. with perf. and aor. 2 act., *stand up, rise*; **1.** *arise* from the dead, Clem.*str.*5.11(p.375.16; M.9.112A); **2.** *be aroused* πρὸς ἀντίρρησιν ~ασαι Gr.Naz.*ep.*166(M.37.276B); ~αται μὲν πρὸς τὸ ὕψος τῶν λεγομένων τέως, σκοτοῦται δὲ καὶ οὐχ ἵσταται Chrys.*hom. 24.3 in Jo.*(8.141A); of passions, *ib.*4.5(33A); id.*hom.22.6 in Mt.*(7. 282D).

***διανίσχ-ω**, ? *part asunder* αἱ προφητικαὶ ~ουσι νεφέλαι ‡Rom. Mel.(*AS* 1 p.238).

***διανοηματικός**, *meditative, reflective*, Leont.B.*Nest.et Eut.*1 (M.86.1296C); Thdr.Stud.*epp.*1.50(M.99.1096C).

***διανομία, ἡ**, *distribution*, Thdt.*Ps.*148:4(1.1577), perh. f.l. for διανόμην.

***διαντιβάλλω**, *discuss thoroughly*; pass., Eutych.*ep.Vigil.*(M.86. 2405A).

***διανυκτέρευσις, ἡ**, **1.** *vigil by night* τὴν μεγάλην...τοῦ πάσχα δ. Eus.*h.e.*6.9.2(M.20.537C); Jo.Not.*v.Eus.*3(M.86.305C); *Chron. Pasch.*p.267(M.92.656B); **2.** *revelry by night*, Anast.S.*Ps.6*(M.89. 1108B).

διανυκτερεύω, *pass the night* δ. τὴν νύκτα *V.Zos.*9(p.103.5); abs. *LS*; hence *keep vigil*, *A.Mt.*8(p.225.15); Socr.*h.e.*1.20.17(M.67. 134A).

***διανυκτέριος**, *lasting throughout the night*, Andr.Cr.*or.*19(M.97. 1245C).

διανύττω, *prick, sting*; met., *stimulate, arouse* τὰ πάθη Thdr. Heracl.ap.*cat.Mt.*5:27(p.37.19); Cyr.*Os.*149(3.182D).

διαξαίν-ω, **1.** *tear to pieces*, Chrys.*hom.11.5 in Eph.*(11.88B); id. *hom.27.5 in 2Cor.*(10.626B); **2.** met., *analyse* κατὰ μικρὸν ~ομεν ὑμῖν τὰ ἐν ταῖς γραφαῖς κείμενα Chrys.*hom.25.1 in Jo.*(8.143B); Leont.H.*monoph.*testimonia(M.86.1816B).

διαξέω, *scratch*, Zach.Mit.*opif.*(M.85.1136C).

διαπαιγμός, ὁ, *jesting, mocking*, Max.*schol.d.n.*3.1(M.4.237A).

***διαπαίγνιον, τό**, *subject of jest*, Ast.Soph.*hom.2 in Ps.5*(M.40. 412C).

διαπαίζω, **1.** *avoid, elude*, Const.ap.Ath.*apol.sec.*87(p.166.17; M.25.405C); Dial.ap.Thdt.*h.e.*2.16.3(3.864); **2.** *delude*, *A.(Pass.) Andr.*2(p.5.19; M.2.1220B); med., *delude oneself*, Cyr.*Os.*95(3.126D; om. Aubert).

***διαπανάω**, prob. error for δαπανάω, Jo.Jej.*doct.*20(p.232).

διαπαννυχίζω, *keep vigil all night*, Dion.Al.ap.Eus.*h.e.*6.40.6(M.20. 604B).

***διαπαράγ-ω**, *bring* into a certain state or condition τὸν πάντα τὰ ὄντα ~οντα [i.e. God] εἰς γένεσιν Gr.Nyss.*Eun.*5(M.45.729C; διὰ κτίσεως παραγαγόντα 2 p.144.20).

διαπαρατριβή, ἡ, *rubbing up against, friction*, Clem.*str.*1.8(p.26. 18; M.8.736C); Chrys.*hom.17.1 in 1Tim.*(11.648C); Ant.Mon.*hom.* 130(M.89.1841C).

διαπαρθένευσις, ἡ, *deflowering of a virgin*, Cyr.*ador.*8(1.259B); id. *glaph.Dt.*(1.421A).

***διαπεζεύω**, *traverse on foot*, Epiph.*exp.fid.*2(p.497.15; M.42. 776B).

διαπείθομαι, *be persuaded*, Cyr.*ador.*8(1.276D).

***διαπερασμός, ὁ**, *delimitation*, Epiph.*haer.*66.14(p.37.5; M.42. 49C).

***διαπερόνησις, ἡ**, *transfixing*, Max.*schol.d.n.*3.1(M.4.237A).

***διαπεταγμός, ὁ**, *stretching out* of the hands, Nil.*epp.*3.243(M.79. 500D).

***διαπετάζω**, *blow away, make to fly away*, ‡Caes.Naz.*dial.*187 (M.38.1164).

***διαπέτασμα, τό**, *veil*, ‡Ath.*occurs.*18(M.28.997B).

***διαπευθύνω**, *correct*, Olymp.*fr.Sev.Ant.*(M.89.1189B).

***διαπεφωνημένως**, *divergently*, Socr.*h.e.*5.22.16(M.67.628C).

διαπήγνυμι, *set up* ἐκεῖ δ. θυσιαστήριον Cyr.*ador*.3(1.98c); *ib*.10 (355D); met., *establish* τὸ ναὶ καὶ τὸ οὔ...διαπεπήχθω ὀρθῶς *ib*.6 (214B); med. τὸν τῆς ἀναστάσεως δ. ὅρον [sc. ὁ θεός] ‡Ath.*Apoll*.1.14 (M.26.1117B).

διαπιπράσκω, *sell off*, *Dial.Tim.et Aquil*.118 rº; *Chron.Pasch*. p.247(M.92.593A); pass., Chrys.*hom.3.6 in 1Thess*.(11.450D).

διαπιστέω, *disbelieve*, Chrys.*hom.23.3 in Jo*.(8.136A); *ib.40.3* (241B); ἡ ἀνάστασις ἂν διηπιστήθη id.*hom.43.2 in Mt*.(7.459E); id. *hom.62.4 in Jo*.(8.373C); abs., of persons, Mac.Aeg.*pat*.26(M.34. 888B).

διαπλανάω, ? *make to wander about*, s.v.l., *Protev*.6(p.12).

***διαπλασιασμός**, ὁ, *duplication*, Thdt.*Ps*.1:5(1.614).

διάπλασις, ἡ, **1.** *fashioning, formation*; *creation*, of man τῆς τοῦ ἀνθρώπου ἐκ χοὸς δ. Clem.*str*.5.14(p.392.7; M.9.149A); τὴν ἐξ Ἀδὰμ δ. Leont.et Jo.*sacr*.2(M.86.2036A); †Jo.D.*B.J*.6(M.96.905B) etc.; of foetus in womb, Bas.*Eun*.2.5(1.241E; M.29.581A); Gr.Nyss.*Eun*.1 (1 p.150.23; M.45.392A); Nemes.*nat.hom*.2(M.40.572B); of body of Christ at Inc. εἰ γὰρ τῆς φύσεως ἐργαζομένης ἀδύνατον ἑρμηνεῦσαι τῆς δ. τὸν τρόπον, πῶς τοῦ πνεύματος θαυματουργοῦντος δυνησόμεθα ταῦτα εἰπεῖν; Chrys.*hom.4.3 in Mt*.(7.50B); Cyr.*apol.Thdt*.9(p.135. 15; 6^1.229D); τὴν ὑπὸ τοῦ πνεύματος τοῦ σώματος γεγενημένην δ. Thdt.*eran*.1(4.28); of the soul τῆς ψυχῆς τὴν δ., πολλῷ θαυμαστοτέραν τῆς ἐν τοῖς σώμασιν οὖσαν Chrys.*hom.12.2 in Jo*.(8.68E); **2.** *form, shape*, ‡Just.*coh.Gr*.4(M.6.249A); Chrys.*subintr*.5(1.235A); εἰς ἀκεφάλου ἀνδρὸς δ. τυπωθῆναι Thphn.*chron*.p.423(M.108.1001A); met., of that which is formed by the imagination οὐχ ὑπέγραψας πολλάκις μορφὴν εὐειδῆ, καὶ ἔπαθές τι πρὸς τὴν δ.; Chrys.*hom.7.7 in 2Cor*.(10.491D).

διάπλασμα, τό, *form, shape, model*, ‡Bas.*struct.hom*.2.13(1.345E; M.30.57C); Bas.Sel.*or*.6.2(M.85.88A).

διαπλάσσ-ω, *form, mould, fashion*; **1.** of Creation τὸν οὐρανὸν καὶ τὴν γῆν διεμόρφωσε καὶ διέπλασεν [sc. ὁ θεός] Sophr.H.*v. Anast*.(M.92.1717C); of creation of man, Clem.*paed*.1.3(p.94.13; M.8.257B); Chrys.*hom.10.2 in 2Cor*.(10.507D); Bas.Sel.*or*.2.2(M.85. 44A); in gen. τὰ ὄργανα παρὰ τοῦ δημιουργοῦ διαπέπλασται Ath.*ep. Amun*.(M.26.1173A); Thdt.*Jon*.3:1–2(2.1470); **2.** of child in womb τὸ ῥῆμα τοῦ θεοῦ τὸν Ἰσαὰκ διέπλασε Chrys.*hom.16.4 in Rom*.(9. 608E); τὰ δὲ ῥήματα τοῦ θεοῦ διὰ τοῦ ἱερέως λεγόμενα...καθάπερ ἐν νηδύϊ τινὶ ~ει...τὸν βαπτιζόμενον id.*comm.in Gal*.4:28(10.711C); ref. Inc. ἐν τῇ...νηδύϊ ὁ λόγος ἑαυτῷ τὸν οἶκον διεπλάσατο ‡Ath.*Ar*.4.34 (p.83.1; M.26.520B); Chrys.*hom.1.5 in Ac*.(9.9C); ἡ μορφὴ...καθ' ἣν ἐν μήτρᾳ συλληφθεὶς διεπέπλαστο Sophr.H.*ep.syn*.(M.87.3173A); **3.** met.; **a.** of character ὁ παιδοτρίβης...~ων τὸν μανθάνοντα Clem. *str*.6.17(p.514.26; M.9.393A); Gr.Naz.*or*.41.14(M.36.448B); τῷ τῆς ἀρετῆς ἢ κακίας λόγῳ ~όμενοι Gr.Nyss.*v.Mos*.(M.44.328B); med. τοιούτους...φαίνεσθαι καὶ ~εσθαι τοὺς Χριστῷ τελουμένους, οἵους σφᾶς ἐν ἐκκλησίαις ἐπὶ τὸ σεμνότερον σχηματίζουσι Clem.*paed*.3.11 (p.280.16; M.8.657B); **b.** of a description or explanation, Chrys. *hom.30.5 in Mt*.(7.354B); Cyr.*Ps*.40:1(M.69.992C); ὡς ἐξ ὁμοιότητος τῶν καθ' ἡμᾶς πραγμάτων δ. τὰ νοητά *ib*.9:5(764C); id.*ador*.13(1. 471E); of future events foreshadowed in past τὰ γὰρ μέλλοντα διεπλάττετο...ὡς ἐν σκιᾷ, τοῖς προτέροις Chrys.*hom.7.4 in 1Cor*. (10.55D).

***διάπλαστος**, *pliable*, Athenag.*res*.17(M.6.1008B; ἀδιαπλάστῳ p.68.25).

διαπλοκή, ἡ, **1.** *combination* τὸ δὲ ποικίλον τοῦτο τῆς σοφίας εἶδος, τὸ ἐκ τῆς πρὸς τὰ ἐναντία δ. συνιστάμενον Gr.Nyss.*hom.8 in Cant*.(M.44.948D); astrol., id.*fat*.(M.45.166B); **2.** *engagement, contest* τὰς ἐν δικαστηρίῳ δ. Bas.*hom*.12.11(2.107B; M.31.408D).

διάπλοκος, *interwoven, plaited*, Gr.Naz.*ep*.10(M.37.40B); Gr. Nyss.*v.Mos*.(M.44.320C); Sophr.H.*v.Anast*.(M.92.1724C).

διαπλ-όω, *extend, spread out*; **1.** act. τὰς...χεῖρας πρὸς οὐρανὸν δ. Ast.Am.*hom*.11(M.40.337C); of God οὐρανὸν ~ώσας Bas.*hom.in Ps*.32(1.134C; M.29.329C); fig. τὸ τῆς ἀφθαρσίας ἔνδυμα, ὅπερ ὁ Χριστός σοι ~ώσας προτείνεται Gr.Nyss.*bapt.diff*.(M.46.420C); met. τὸν ἄπειρον βυθὸν τῆς Οὐαλεντίνου πολυπλανοῦς ὕλης εὐτονώτατα ~ώσας Eus.*h.e*.4.11.3(M.20.329A); **2.** med. and pass., Gr.Nyss.*hom. 4 in Cant*.(M.44.828B); †Cyr.*coll.VT*(6^4.7D; M.77.1185B); met. ὑποκάτωθεν αὐτοῦ φῶς ~ούμενον *A.Xanthipp*.15(p.68.22).

διάπνευσις, ἡ, *evacuation* of the bowels, Jo.Clim.*scal*.14(M.88. 865B).

***διαποβλέπω**, *turn one's gaze penetratingly upon*; met., Chrys. *hom.48.5 in Jo*.(8.282A).

διαποιμαίνω, *feed*, Cyr.*ador*.2(1.61D); id.*glaph.Gen*.1(1.19A); id. *Soph*.42(3.620B).

διαπόμπησις, ἡ, v. διοπόμπησις.

διαπόνησις, ἡ, *exercising*, Clem.*paed*.3.10(p.264.25; M.8.621A); *ib*.(p.266.4; 625A).

***διαπονητέον**, *one must toil*, Clem.*paed*.3.10(p.266.1; M.8.624B).

διαπορέω, **1.** trans., *trouble, vex*, Chrys.*hom.50.4 in Mt*.(7. 519C); *ib.64.3*(639C); *ib.80.2*(768A); **2.** pass., *be at a loss*, Vict.*Mc*. 6:34(p.327.26).

διαπορητικῶς, *in soliloquy*, Bas.*hom.in Ps*.61(1.193E; M.29. 472A).

***διαπόρθμευσις**, ἡ, **1.** *transportation, conveying*, Epiph.*haer*.66.9 (p.30.24; M.42.44B); **2.** *that which is conveyed* [sc. through senses] αἱ ἐπιδηλότεραι τῶν αἰσθήσεων δ., οἱ σαφέστεροι λόγοι, τὰ τρανέστερα τῶν ὁρατῶν Dion.Ar.*d.n*.4.11(M.3.709A).

***διαπορθμευτής**, ὁ, *conveyer* ὁ υἱὸς γεννητὸς...διαπορθμευτὴς τοῦ ἁγίου πνεύματος Leont.H.*Nest*.1.20(M.86.1485B).

***διαπορθμευτικός**, *permeating*, Dion.Ar.*c.h*.13.3(M.3.301B); *ib*. 15.6(333D).

***διαπορθμευτικῶς**, *as one who transmits*, Dion.Ar.*e.h*.7.3.7(M.3. 564C).

διαπορθμεύ-ω, **1.** *convey, transmit*, of Christ οὐκ ἄνθρωπος αὐτὴν [sc. τὴν σωτηρίαν] διεπόρθμευσεν εἰς τὴν γῆν...ἀλλ' αὐτὸς ὁ μονογενής Chrys.*hom.3.4 in Heb*.(12.32A); Bas.Sel.*v.Thecl*.1(M.85.481D); Max.*ambig*.(M.91.1137A); of the faculties γλῶττα δ. τοῖς ἔξω τὸν νοῦν Ath.*fr.Pss.comm*.(M.27.565B); Dion.Ar.*d.n*.4.1(M.3.696A); a report or statement, Bas.*ep*.221(3.334C; M.32.816C); Thdt.*h.e*. 5.20.9(3.1054); Gel.Cyz.*h.e*.2.28.14(M.85.1312C); a divine message ~ων δὲ εἰς ἡμᾶς τὰς ἄνωθεν καὶ παρὰ πατρὸς φωνὰς...ὁ υἱός Cyr.*ador*. 10(1.369C); προφῆται...τοὺς παρὰ τοῦ πνεύματος ~οντες λόγους id. *Jo*.2.5(4.199E); Thdt.*Ezech*.1:28(2.692); pass., *be translated*, Areth. *Apoc*.51(M.106.712B); **2.** *accomplish* a journey or voyage, Isch. *libell*.(p.18.21; H.2.328C); **3.** *traverse, cross* a river, Chrys.*hom.25.1 in 2Cor*.(10.613C).

***διαπορπάω**, *pin together*, met. ὁ ἐκ ῥυπαρῶν τε καὶ παρακεκομμένων λεξειδίων διαπεπορπημένος τῶν ἐναντίων λόγος Gr.Nyss.*Eun*.9 (2 p.205.18; M.45.801C).

διαπρίζω, *saw through*, Chrys.*exp.in Ps*.44(5.174D).

διαπρί-ω, *saw asunder*; pass., met., *be cut to the quick, be goaded* with envy or rage τῷ φθόνῳ...~εσθαι Or.*hom.12 in Lc*.(p.84.1); Cyr.*Jo*.3.2(4.261C); id.*hom.pasch*.6(5^2.79B).

***διάπρυμνος**, ? *with stern like the prow*, Thphn.*chron*.p.198(M. 108.512C).

διαπρύσιος, *brilliant, distinguished*; of persons, Thdr.Stud.*epp*. 1.7(M.99.933A); *ib*.1.17(961D).

διαπρυσίως, *clearly, penetratingly*; met., ‡Meth.*palm*.5(M.18. 392D); ὁ τῆς ἀληθείας δ. πᾶσιν ἐμβοᾷ λόγος Max.*ep*.13(M.91.529D); ‡Jo.D.*fid.dorm*.22(M.95.268D).

***διάπταισμα**, τό, *fault*, Thdr.Stud.*epp*.2.220(M.99.1668C).

διαπταίω, *err*; **1.** in doctrine, *be mistaken*, Ptol.*ep*.ap.Epiph. *haer*.33.3(p.451.6; M.41.557B); **2.** in morals, *fall*, Bas.*reg.fus*.15(2. 356A; M.31.952C); *ib*.83(445C; M.1141B); Cyr.*Ps*.14:3(M.69.805C); ἐπανόρθωσιν τῶν διαπταισμένων id.*glaph.Gen*.1(1.16B); id.*Juln*.8 (6^2.278C).

***διαπτερνιστής**, ὁ, *supplanter* (cf. πτερνιστής), Clem.*exc.Thdot*. 53.1(p.124.18; M.9.684C).

διάπτυξις, ἡ, *explication* δ. ... γνωστικὴν τῶν γραφῶν Clem.*str*.6.15 (p.498.9; M.9.356B).

διάπτωσις, ἡ, **1.** *fall*; met., *error* ἔχει πολλὴν δ. [sc. in argument] Meth.*res*.1.49(p.302.4; M.18.277A); **2.** *bursting* of a tumour, Gr. Nyss.*anim.et res*.(M.46.21B); *dissolution* of elements, Bas.*hex*.1.11 (1.11C; M.29.25D).

διαπυτίζω, *spit out*, Clem.*paed*.2.2(p.171.25; M.8.420B).

***διαπώλησις**, ἡ, *selling*, Jo.VI H.*v.Jo.D*.26(M.94.468A).

***διάραιος**, *frail*; of a body, opp. ἰσχυρός, ‡Chrys.*prov*.1(2.753A).

***διαρετίζομαι**, *contend in virtue*, Synes.*regn*.25(p.56.5; M.66. 1101C).

***διαρίζω**, *provide with an allowance*, Jo.Scholast.*coll.cap*.19.

διάριον, τό, (Lat. *diarium*) *day's allowance*, Cyr.S.*v.Sab*.6(p.90. 4); Ath.Scholast.*coll*.1.2(p.9).

δίαρμα, τό, *elevation, loftiness*; **1.** lit., of a mountain, †Bas.*Is*.256 (1.574D; M.30.569A); **2.** met., of prayer μετὰ δ. ἐνθέου τῆς εὐχῆς Clem.*str*.7.7(p.34.6; M.9.465A); esp. of soul, *exaltation*, Or.*Jo*.10.23 (16; p.195.3; M.14.348A); †Bas.*Is*.228(552A; M.517A); Proc.G.*Is*. 33:5(M.87.2296D).

***διαρμένιος**, *having two sails*; of a merchant-ship, Synes.*ep*.4 (M.66.1329C); *ib*.130(1513A).

***διάρπαγμα**, τό, *snatching away, robbery*, ‡Bas.*Lac*.7(2.592C; M.31. 1449C).

διαρράπτω, *stitch, interweave,* Chrys.*hom*.49.5 *in Mt*.(7.510B).

***διαρραψῳδέω,** *declaim,* Gr.Nyss.*Eun*.1(1 p.50.18; M.45.280A); id.*Apoll*.40(M.45.1216C).

***διαρρηγμός, ὁ,** *rending* δ. τῶν ἱματίων Anast.S.*qu.et resp*.38 (M.89.580D).

διαρρήκτης, ὁ, *one who breaks,* fig. δ. τῆς εὐαρμοστίας τοῦ βίου Meth.*symp*.2.5(p.22.13; M.18.56B).

[*]διαρριν-έω, (late form of διαρρινάω), ? *snort* τοῖς μυξωτῆρσιν ἐν ἀλλήλοις ~οῦντες Just.*dial*.101.3(conj. for διερινοῦντες M.6.712C).

διαρριπίζω, *cool by driving a current of air upon, fan,* Ath.*h.Ar*.12 (p.189.12; M.25.708A); ὁ πνεύμων...τὸ ἔνδον ἡμῶν θερμὸν δ. καὶ ἀναψύχει Bas.*hex*.7.1(1.63E; M.29.149B); Bas.Sel.*v.Thecl*.1(M.85.513B).

***διαρτία, ἡ,** *form, formation* σύμμορφος πηλίνης εὐτελοῦς δ., Χριστέ, γεγονώς Cosm.Mel.*hymn*.2.40(p.166; M.98.461A).

***διασαλπίζω,** *noise abroad,* Ephr.3.406B cit. s. ἅρπαγμα.

διασάφησις, ἡ, *explanation, interpretation, A.Petr.et Andr*.15 (p.124.5); Cyr.*Nah*.31(3.509C); Max.*opusc*.(M.91.249D).

διάσεισμα, τό, *extortion,* ‡Ath.*syntag*.6.6(p.126.10; M.28.841D).

***διασκαλιδεύω,** *investigate, search closely* δ. καὶ καλλιεργεῖν τὸν νοητὸν τῶν θείων γραφῶν παράδεισον Olymp.*Job* proem.(M.93.17B); id.*Eccl*.5:8(M.93.544C).

διασκεδάννυμι, 1. *bring to nought,* ref. Ps.33:10 τὴν βουλὴν αὐτῶν διεσκέδασεν ὁ θεός Thphn.*chron*.p.332(M.108.800A); **2.** *put a stop to, silence,* Dam.*troph*.3.6(p.247.3); **3.** pass., *be diverted* from διασκεδασθῆναι ἐξ αὐτῆς [sc. τῆς θείας ἀδολεσχίας] †Anast.S.*relat*.23(p.74).

διασκεδασμός, ὁ, 1. *scattering* τὸν δ. ὃν διεσκεδάσθησαν [sc. Jews] φεύγοντες τὰς...συμφοράς Eus.*Is*.6:12(M.24.132A); **2.** met., *perturbation, unrest,* Jo.Clim.*scal*.26(M.88.1057D).

διασκελίζω, *stretch* with a stride ἐσκάλωσα τὸν ἕνα μου πόδα εἰς τὰ Ἱεροσόλυμα, καὶ τὸν ἕτερόν μου διεσκέλισα εἰς τοὺς οὐρανούς Barth.Edess.*Agar*.(M.104.1440C).

***διασκέλισις, ἡ,** *stride* εἰς τοὺς ⟨οὐρανοὺς⟩ ἀνέβης μίαν δ. Barth. Edess.*Agar*.(M.104.1433A).

διασκεπάζω, *cover, protect,* Melet.*nat.hom*.1(M.64.1156D).

διασκευάζω, 1. *deal with,* Philost.*h.e*.6.1(M.65.532B); **2.** pass., *be composed* or *expressed in words* ἀνθρωπίνως δ. ταῦτα Areth.*Apoc*.55(M.106.728A).

διασκευαστής, ὁ, *one who contrives* or *arranges,* Cyr.*Jo*.11.12(4.1020E).

διασκευή, ἡ, 1. *arrangement* of an argument, *account,* Gr.Nyss. *hom.1 in Cant*.(M.44.769D) cit. s. ᾆσμα; Cyr.*ador*.7(1.217B); id.*Jo*. 1.4(4.33E); *ib*.11.3(947A); **2.** *ordering,* of reformation πάντα...δι' αὐτοῦ [sc. τοῦ θεοῦ] τὴν εἰς τὰ ἀμείνω δέχεται δ. id.*Ps*.15:11(M.69.813C).

***διασκολιεύομαι,** *traverse crooked passages,* c. genit., ‡Caes.Naz. *dial*.78(M.38.945).

***διασκοπητέον,** *one must examine* or *consider well,* Eus.*e.th*.1.19 (p.80.20; M.24.864C).

διασκορπίζ-ω, 1. *scatter abroad* τὸν λαὸν αὐτοῦ διεσκόρπισα *T. Jud*.3.2; Or.*hom.12.3 in Jer*.(p.90.5; M.13.384A); fig. ὁ θεός...~ει αὐτούς [sc. τοὺς δαιμονιώδεις λογισμούς] Nil.*epp*.2.139(M.79.257C); **2.** *overthrow,* Pall.*h.Laus*.41(p.128.15; M.34.1233D); met. δ. τὴν βουλὴν αὐτῶν *A.Phil*.48(p.21.13); Eus.*Ps*.140:6(M.24.44D).

διασκορπισμός, ὁ, *scattering;* of money, Diad.*perf*.66(p.80.11); Jewish *dispersion, T.Lev*.16.5.

***διασκύλλω, 1.** *distort,* Mac.Mgn.*apocr*.3.43(p.151.7); **2.** *trouble, annoy,* Pall.*v.Chrys*.5(p.29.23; M.47.19).

διασμήχ-ω, *rub well, cleanse,* Bas.*hom.in Ps*.7(1.105B; M.29.245C); met. θεοῦ...τὴν καρδίαν...~οντος Cyr.*Ps*.37:1(M.69.952B); *ib*.37:20(968D); id.*Os*.34(3.62C).

διασμύχ-ω, 1. trans., *burn up, consume,* met. τοῦ πένθους οἱονεὶ πυρός τινος...τὰς ψυχὰς ~οντος Gr.Nyss.*v.Macr*.(p.400.8; M.46.985D); **2.** intrans., *smoulder,* met. ἐπὶ τῷ σώματι τοῦ πυρετοῦ ~οντος id.*nativ*.(M.46.1132A); Max.*ep*.1(M.91.381D).

διασπαθάω, *squander,* Chrys.*hom.7.3 in Eph*.(11.50B, vv.ll. διαπτῶσι, διασπῶσι); id.*hom.3.3 in Phil*.(11.215B, vv.ll. διασπαθίζοντας, διασκορπίζοντας).

διασπαθίζω, = foreg., Chrys.*hom.3.3 in Phil*.(11.215B).

***διασπαραγμός, ὁ,** *tearing, rending,* ‡Chrys.*serm.jej*.4(11.837C); Leont.N.*v.Sym*.24(M.93.1700D).

***διασπαργανόω,** *enwrap,* Melet.*nat.hom*.1(M.64.1153B).

διασπασμός, ὁ, *tearing in pieces, T.Jud*.23.3.

διασπ-άω, *tear asunder;* **1.** act., mentally, *Symb.Chalc*.(p.129.17; H.2.456B) cit. s. δυάς; *cancel* a bond, Gr.Naz.*or*.40.31(M.36.404B); *dissolve* a marriage, ‡Jo.Jej.*can*.(p.438); **2.** pass.; **a.** *be strained* or *torn,* met. τῶν νεύρων ~ωμένων Chrys.*hom.68.4 in Mt*.(7.675B); id. *hom.36.6 in 1Cor*.(10.341E); *ib*.37.4(349B); of BMV πῶς οὐ ~ᾶται τὸν κύριον φέρουσα; †Ephr.*nativ*.41(p.86); **b.** of property; *be divided,* opp. community of goods of early Christians at Jerusalem, Chrys.*hom.11.3 in Ac*.(9.93E); **c.** of persons, *be separated* οὗτος... διεσπασμένος λίαν πόρρω Thdr.Stud.*epp*.2.57(M.99.1272A).

διασπεύδω, *hasten,* Cyr.*ador*.2(1.76E); *ib*.3(81B).

διασπορά, ἡ, *scattering, dispersion, dispersal;* **1.** met. ἡ...ἐκ πολλῶν ἕνωσις ἐκ πολυφωνίας καὶ δ. ἁρμονίαν λαβοῦσα θεϊκὴν μία γίνεται συμφωνία Clem.*prot*.9(p.65.31; M.8.200C); **2.** *scattering, bestowing* of money, Diad.*perf*.66(p.80.7); **3.** meton.; **a.** of persons, *scattered band* τοὺς γονεῖς...τὴν δ. ἐπαναγαγεῖν βουλομένους Bas.*ep*. 169(3.259A; M.32.644B); (exeg. Jo.7:35) οὕτω τὰ ἔθνη ἐκάλουν οἱ Ἰουδαῖοι, διὰ τὸ πανταχοῦ διεσπάρθαι καὶ ἀδεῶς ἀλλήλοις ἐπιμίγνυσθαι Chrys.*hom.51.3 in Jo*.(8.297D); ταῖς τῶν Ἑλλήνων δ. Cyr.*Jo*.5.1 (4.467C); **b.** of region of exile [sc. οἱ ἐπίσκοποι] οἳ νῦν εἰσιν ἐν τῇ δ. Bas.*ep*.195(3.287A; M.32.708C); of Jews, *Const.App*.6.24.5; ἐν τῇ δ. τῆς γῆς Andr.Caes.*Apoc*.19(M.106.281C).

***διασποράδην,** *scatteredly, here and there,* Clem.*str*.1.12(p.36.4; M.8.753B).

[*]διασπορέη, ἡ, = διασπορά, *dispersion* of Jews, †Apoll.*met. Ps*.138 tit.(M.33.1521A).

διάσταλμα, τό, *ordinance, command* μελετώντων ὃ ἔλαβον δ. ῥήματος ἐν τῇ καρδίᾳ *Barn*.10.11.

διαστασιάζω, trans., *cause to disagree, set at variance* τὰ περὶ τὴν πρεσβείαν καὶ πάνυ λαμπρῶς διεστασίασεν ἡμᾶς Synes.*ep*.95(M.66.1464A).

διάστασις, ἡ, *separation,* theol. υἱόν...γεννώμενον...οὐ κατὰ δ. ἢ τομὴν ἢ διαίρεσιν ἐκ τῆς τοῦ πατρὸς οὐσίας προβεβλημένον Eus.*d.e*. 4.3(p.154.17; M.22.257B); *ib*.5.1(p.211.25; 352B); Aët.*synt*.5(p.353.13; M.42.536C) cit. s. γεννάω; οὐκ οὐσίας δ. τὸ γεννηθὲν ἐγεννήθη ‡Ath.*dial.Trin*.2.13(M.28.1177C).

διαστατός, *having extension* or *dimension,* denied of God τὸ ἀσώματον τὸ μὴ ὑπάρχειν αὐτοῦ τριχῇ δ. τὴν οὐσίαν [sc. σημαίνει] Bas.*Eun*.1.9(1.221E; M.29.533A).

διαστατῶς, *separately, apart,* ref. Eunomians οἱ...ἐκβεβηκέναι τοῦ πατρὸς τὴν οὐσίαν οἰόμενοι τὸν υἱὸν δ. τε καὶ κεχωρισμένως Cyr. *thes*.6(5^1.49D).

διαστείβω, *express exactly,* Cyr.ap.*cat.Heb*.1:8(suppl.)(p.355.29).

διαστείχ-ω, A. lit.; **1.** *go one's way, proceed,* Nonn.*par.Jo*.4:28 (M.43.780A); *ib*.10:23(836B); *ib*.12:35(856C); **2.** *go through* or *across, ib*.2:23(764C); *ib*.7:1(804C); *ib*.18:1(888C); c. genit., *go* or *walk upon* Χριστόν...~οντα θαλάσσης *ib*.6:19(796C); **3.** c. genit., *go from, leave, ib*.11:42(845C).

B. met.; **1.** *extend to* εἰς πάντας ἐν ἴσῳ...~ει βλάβη Cyr.*ador*.6 (1.206B); **2.** *continue, pursue an inquiry* οὐκ ἀτραχὺ...τὸ χρῆμα... ἀλλὰ...θεῷ πίσυνοι ~ωμεν *ib*.9(289A); Thdr.Stud.*epp*.2.75(M.99.1312B).

διαστέλλ-ω, A. *divide* δ. τὸ μέλος τῷ διαψάλματι Cyr.*Ps*.3:4(M.69.725C); hence *distinguish, differentiate between;* **1.** trans., Clem.*str*. 2.8(p.133.29; M.8.973C); δ. τά τε κοινὰ καὶ τὰ ἴδια *ib*.6.10(p.472.25; M.9.304A); τὴν δεισιδαιμονίαν...δ. ἀπὸ τῆς εὐσεβείας Synes.*ep*.67 (M.66.1421A); exeg. Jo.6:63 τὸ πνεῦμα πρὸς τὸ κατὰ σάρκα διέστειλεν [sc. ὁ Χριστός] ἵνα μὴ μόνον τὸ φαινόμενον ἀλλὰ καὶ τὸ ἀόρατον αὐτοῦ πιστεύσαντες μάθωσιν Ath.*ep.Serap*.4.19(M.26.665C); εἰ δὲ ἔργον ἦν ὁ λόγος, πάντως ἂν καὶ αὐτὸς ἐν σοφίᾳ ἐγεγόνει, καὶ οὔτ' ἂν διέστελλεν αὐτὸν ἀπὸ τῶν ἔργων ἡ γραφή id.*Ar*.2.72(M.26.300B); μόνον ὀνόμασι τὴν ἁγίαν τριάδα δ. Cyr.*Jo*.1.2(4.15B); id.*thes*.12(5^1.109E), *ib*. 23(225C) citt. s. δυάς; med., Or.*Jo*.4.21(12; p.130.32; M.14.237B); Eus.*p.e*.11.7(522D; M.21.865C); pass., *be distinguished* διασταλέντων τοῦ 'ἡμῖν' καὶ τοῦ 'ἁπλῶς' Or.*Jo*.1.34(40; p.44.20; M.14.92B); **2.** intrans., *make a distinction, distinguish precisely,* med., Clem.*paed*.1.8 (p.198.4; M.8.473C); id.*str*.1.20(p.63.7; M.8.816B); Or.*Jo*.20.24(20; p.359.6,18; M.14.628C,629A).

B. med., *expand, increase,* met. πῶς ~ονται καὶ οὐ συστέλλονται τὴν προπέτειαν; Serap.*Man*.39(p.57; M.18.1221A).

C. med., *command* ~εται μὴ τὸν πάντα λαὸν συναναβαίνειν ἑαυτῷ Clem.*str*.5.12(p.377.29; M.9.116B); ὁ νόμος σωματικῶς μὲν ~όμενος Epiph.*haer*.8.5(p.190.22; M.41.212C); *ib*.50.2(p.247.2; 885C); ptcpl. pass. as subst. τὰ ἐν τῷ...Σινᾷ...τὴν τοῦ ~ομένου γνῶσιν ὠδίνοντα Cyr.*glaph.Num*.(1.383E).

***διαστεφής,** *concerned with, leading to a crown* δ. ἀγῶνα Thdr. Stud.*epp*.2.140(M.99.1445A).

***διαστήκω,** *remain in,* fig. πολὺ δ. τῆς βασιλικῆς λεωφόρου, τοῦτ' ἔστι τῆς ἀποστολικῆς πίστεως Gel.Cyz.*h.e*.2.20.4(M.85.1281C).

διάστημα, τό, A. *interval;* **1.** temporal, between two events;

a. in gen., *Barn.*9.8; Clem.*str.*1.21(p.87.2; M.8.876B); Meth.*symp.* 6.4(p.68.21; M.18.120A); *πέντε ἡμέρας ἐπὶ τῆς οἰκίας κατέχεται τὸ πρόβατον* [sc. before Passover]...*ἔπειτα...θύεται. ... πέντε διαστήματα χρόνου δηλοῦται ταῖς πέντε ταύταις ἡμέραις ἀπὸ Ἀδὰμ μέχρι συντελείας* ‡Chrys.*pasch.*5.2(8².263A); cf.*ib.*5.1(252A); *season* of the year *μετοπωρινῷ* δ. Eus.*l.C.*6(p.209.2; M.20.1345B); plur., *watches* of the night, Cyr.*Ps.*6:7(M.69.745D); *span* of time *τῆς ἐπιούσης ἡμέρας... οὐκ οἶδας εἰ τὸ δ. ὄψει* Chrys.*hom.19.5 in Mt.*(7.252A); *ἀνήλωσεν ἐν ματαιότητι τὸ δ. τῆς ἡμέρας* Esaias *or.*10(p.67; M.40.1135B); **b.** before generation of Son, alleged by Arians *προηγεῖται κατ' αὐτοὺς τῆς τὰ ὅλα δημιουργούσης τοῦ θεοῦ σοφίας ἐκεῖνο τὸ δ. ἐν ᾧ φασι μὴ γεγενῆσθαι τὸν υἱὸν ὑπὸ τοῦ πατρός· ψευδομένης κατ' αὐτοὺς καὶ τῆς 'πρωτότοκον' αὐτὸν εἶναι 'πάσης κτίσεως' ἀναγορευούσης γραφῆς* Alex.Al.*ep.Alex.*6(p.23.21; M.18.557A); orthodox statement *ἀεὶ δὲ παρόντος αὐτῷ* [sc. *τῷ πατρί*]...*οὐ χρονικῶς, οὐδὲ ἐκ* δ. *οὐδὲ ἐξ οὐκ ὄντων γεννήσας τὸν μονογενῆ υἱόν ib.*7(p.23.31; 557B); *οὐδὲ τὸ ἦν ποτε ὅτε οὐκ ἦν ἐξ ἀγράφων ἐπισφαλῶς λέγοντας χρονικόν τι* δ. *προενθυμητέον αὐτοῦ Symb.Ant.*(345)3(p:252.14; M.26.729A); *τὸ λεγόμενον ἐν τῷ...ψαλμῷ πρὸς τὸν υἱὸν 'ἡ βασιλεία σου βασιλεία πάντων τῶν αἰώνων' οὐκ ἐπιτρέπει τινὰ κἂν τὸ τυχὸν* δ. *λογίσασθαι ἐν ᾧ μὴ ὑπῆρχεν ὁ λόγος* Ath.*Ar.*1.12(M.26.37A); *ὅτε οὐκ ἦν, ὥς φατε* [sc. Eunomians] *τί ἦν ἐκεῖνο τὸ* δ.; *τίνα αὐτῷ προσηγορίαν ἐπινοήσετε; ἡ μὲν γὰρ κοινὴ συνήθεια ἢ χρόνοις ἢ αἰῶσιν ἅπαν* δ. *ὑποβάλλει* Bas.*Eun.*2.13(1.248A; M.29.596B); *οἱ χρονικοῖς* δ. *τοῦ μὲν πατρὸς τὸν υἱόν, τοῦ δὲ υἱοῦ τὸ πνεῦμα τὸ ἅγιον διαιροῦσι* [sc. Sabellians and Arians] id.*Spir.*59 (3.50D; M.32.177B); *ὁ πρεσβυτέραν τῆς τοῦ υἱοῦ ζωῆς τὴν τοῦ πατρὸς δογματίζων* δ. *τινι τὸν μονογενῆ τοῦ ἐπὶ πάντων θεοῦ πάντως διΐστησι· τοῦτο δὲ ἢ ἄπειρον...ἢ τισι πέρασι καὶ σημείοις φανεροῖς ὁριζόμενον. ἀλλ' ἄπειρον μὲν εἰπεῖν οὐκ ἐάσει ὁ τῆς μεσότητος λόγος ἢ παντελῶς τὴν τοῦ πατρός τε καὶ υἱοῦ ἔννοιαν διαγράφει τῷ λόγῳ. ... οὐκοῦν... οὐδεμίαν ἕξει χώραν ἄπειρον ἐννοεῖν τὸ* δ., *ἀλλὰ πεπερασμένῳ τινὶ κατὰ πᾶσαν ἀνάγκην τὸν μονογενῆ τοῦ πατρὸς διαστήσουσι. ... ὁ λόγος οὗτος οὐκ ἐξ ἀϊδίου εἶναι τὸν ἐπὶ πάντων θεόν· ἀλλ' ἀπό τινος ὡρισμένου σημείου τὴν ἀρχὴν ἐσχηκέναι κατασκευάσει. ὃ δὲ λέγω, τοιοῦτόν ἐστι ...τὸ μετά τι γενόμενον διὰ τοῦ πρὸ ἑαυτοῦ* δ. *ὁρίζει καὶ τὴν τοῦ προϋπονοουμένου ὑπόστασιν* Gr.Nyss.*Eun.*1(1 p.122.30ff.; M.45.357D–360B); **c.** ref. Heb.2:9 *οὐκ εἶπεν ἀποθάνῃ· ὥσπερ γὰρ ὄντως γευσάμενος, οὕτω μικρὸν ἐν αὐτῷ ποιήσας* δ., *εὐθέως ἀνέστη* [sc. *ὁ Χριστός*] Chrys.*hom.4.2 in Heb.*(12.41D); **2.** spatial; **a.** of distance between two points; **i.** in gen., *M.Perp.*7(p.73.19); *λεπροὶ ἐκ* δ. *μόνον ἐνορῶντες Clem.epit.* A 6(M.2.476A); *ἐν ἀγῶνι...σταδίοις ὥρισται τὰ* δ. Eus.*l.C.*6(p.207.22; M.20.1344A); ? as a measure of days' journeys *πολλοῖς* δ. *εἴσω χωρῆσαι τῆς χώρας πεποίηκεν* Thphn.*chron.*p.125(M.108.348C); of the capacity or span of the hand, Chrys.*hom.22.4 in Ac.*(9.183A); met. *οἱ ἀπὸ Βασιλείδου πίστιν ἅμα καὶ ἐκλογὴν οἰκείαν εἶναι καθ' ἕκαστον* δ. Clem.*str.*2.3(p.118.18; M.8.941B); of intervals between numbers, *ib.*6.16(p.503.29; M.9.369A); of repetition or multiplication *ὁ δέκατος ἀριθμὸς...τῷ δεκαδίκῳ* δ. *τὸν ἑκατὸν ἀπετέλεσε* Areth. *Apoc.*62(M.106.753B); **ii.** astron. *ἄστρα τάξει καὶ* δ. *φερόμενα* Arist. *apol.*4.2(M.96.1109A); *τῶν κόσμων ἄνισα τὰ* δ. Hipp.*haer.*1.13(p.17.3; M.16.3037B); Jo.VI H.*v.Jo.D.*11(M.94.448A); **iii.** ref. unity of Father and Son *χωρίζομεν αὐτὸν* [sc. *τὸν υἱόν*] *τοῦ πατρός, τόπους καὶ* δ. *τινα μεταξὺ τῆς συναφείας αὐτῶν σωματικῶς ἐπινοοῦντες Symb. Ant.*(345)9(p.253.35; M.26.733B); denial of Anomoean doctrine *οὐδενὸς* δ. *μεσιτεύοντος τῇ φυσικῇ πρὸς τὸν πατέρα τοῦ υἱοῦ συναφείᾳ* Bas.*Spir.*14(3.10D; M.32.88C); **b.** *division περατουμένης τῆς ὕλης καθ' ἑκάτερον* δ. *ὕδατος βουλήσει τοῦ θεοῦ* (ref. crossings of Red Sea and Jordan) Clem.*ecl.*6(p.138.22; M.9.701A); **c.** *distance, extent,* Clem.*str.*6.10(p.471.26; M.9.301A); *βραχεῖ* δ. Or.*Jo.*10.27(17; p.200.6; M.14.356B); †Jo.D.*B.J.*22(M.96.1061B); **d.** in concrete sense, *extension* to a building *προσθεὶς ἄλλο* δ. *πολὺ τῷ τείχει* Jo.Mal. *chron.*13 p.320(M.97.480A).

B. f.l. for διάδημα, Areth.*Apoc.*53(M.106.716D).

διαστηματικός, 1. temporal; **a.** *occurring within time τὰ... κτίσματα...*δ. *ἀρχὴν τοῦ εἶναι ἔχει...ὁ δὲ τοῦ θεοῦ λόγος οὐκ ἔχων ἀρχὴν τοῦ εἶναι...ἦν ἀεί* Ath.*Ar.*2.57(M.26.268C); *τὴν* δ. *τῶν αἰώνων παράτασιν* Gr.Nyss.*Eun.*12(1 p.343.29; M.45.1064A); Cyr.*thes.*5(5¹. 35E); **b.** *involving the concept of time ἡ γὰρ 'ἀρχή'* (Gen.1:1) *παντὸς* δ. *νοήματος ἀλλοτρίως ἔχει* Gr.Nyss.*hex.*8(M.44.72A); *αἰτίαν* [sc. God]... *παντὸς* δ. *νοήματος ὑπερκειμένην* id.*infant.*(M.46.172C); ref. generation of Son *μηδὲν εἶναι...ὃ μεταξὺ τῆς τοῦ υἱοῦ πρὸς τὸν πατέρα συναφείας εὑρίσκεται, μὴ* δ. *τι νόημα* id.*Eun.*4(1 p.85.28; M.45.661B); **2.** spatial, *contained within dimensions τῆς σωματικῆς καὶ* δ. ... *φύσεως* opp. *ἡ νοερά τε καὶ ἀδιάστατος φύσις* Gr.Nyss.*anim.et res.* (M.46.48B); id.*hom.opif.*23.3(M.44.212A); *τὸ θεῖον μηδὲ τόπῳ περιληπτὸν ἢ* δ. *τὰς μεταβάσεις ποιεῖσθαι πεφυκός* Cyr.*Jo.*2.1(4.128A).

διαστηματικῶς, *temporally, in time,* characteristic of created opp. divine being *αὕτη* [sc. created being] *διαστηματικῇ τινι παρατάσει συμπαρεκτείνεται, καὶ χρόνῳ καὶ τόπῳ περιειργομένη, ἐκείνη* [sc. divinity] *ὑπερεκπίπτει πᾶσαν διαστήματος ἔννοιαν...οὔτε ἀρχὴν οὔτε τέλος προσίεται...οὐ* δ. *ἔκ τινος εἴς τι τῇ ζωῇ διοδεύουσα* Gr.Nyss.*Eun.*12(1 p.236.6; M.45.933B); *ib.*(p.344.22; 1064C).

διαστίζω, 1. *spot, mottle,* Bas.*ascet.*1.2(2.320B; M.31.873B); **2.** *distinguish, make a distinction between κἂν πιστεύσῃς ὡς ἀληθὲς εἴη τὸ σῶμα τοῦ Χριστοῦ, καὶ προσκομίσῃς τῷ θυσιαστηρίῳ πρὸς μεταποίησιν, μὴ διαστίξῃς δὲ τὴν τοῦ σώματος καὶ τῆς θεότητος φύσιν, ἐροῦμεν καί σοι* [Gen.4:7] Ambr.*fr.*ap.Thdt.*eran.*2(4.145).

διάστιξις, ἡ, 1. legal *distinction, differentiation τὴν...*δ. *περὶ τῶν διχονοούντων δικαστῶν* Ath.Scholast.*coll.*4.17(p.60); *ib.*8.4(p.94); Phot.*nomoc.*11.1(M.104.841A); **2.** *prescript, regulation, ib.*13.3(904C).

διαστολεύς, ὁ, *one who separates* or *distinguishes;* of Aëtius, Epiph.*haer.*76.28(p.376.29; M.42.573A) cit. s. *ὁροθέτης; one who discriminates* δ. *ἀγαθὸς γινέσθω, νόμον καὶ δευτέρωσιν διαιρῶν Const. App.*2.5.6.

διαστολή, ἡ, 1. *separation;* **a.** lit., of parting of lips in prayer, Gr.Nyss.*v.Macr.*(p.398.21; M.46.985A); **b.** of a pause or interval between words *κατὰ τὴν* δ. *τῆς ἀναγνώσεως τοιαύτην ἀποδεξώμεθα διάνοιαν* Clem.*paed.*1.6(p.111.4; M.8.292B); **c.** *distinction, difference;* between Son and creatures *τὸ πνεῦμα ἐν ψαλμοῖς μετὰ καλλίστης* δ. *εἴρηκεν ὅτι 'εὐθὺς ὁ λόγος τοῦ κυρίου καὶ πάντα τὰ ἔργα αὐτοῦ ἐν πίστει'* Ath.*Ar.*2.71(M.26.300A); *ib.*2.72(300B); between Father and Son *οὐ γάρ ἐστι σωματική τις* δ., *ἀλλὰ λόγος ἐνυπόστατος, υἱὸς ἐκ πατρὸς ὤν, πνεῦμα ἐκ πνεύματος καὶ θεὸς ἐκ θεοῦ* Epiph.*haer.*76.35 (p.385.21; M.42.588D); between Persons of Trin. *ἀνατρέψει τὴν τῶν προσώπων* δ. *ἡ τῆς φύσεως ταυτότης* Cyr.*Jo.*1.4(4.36B); **d.** plur., in concrete sense, *separate passage θρηνεῖ περικοπάς τινας καὶ* δ. *περιγράφων ἀρχομένας ἑξῆς ἀπὸ τῶν παρ' Ἑβραίοις στοιχείων* Or. *fr.1 in Lam.*(p.235.8; M.13.605C); δ. *κεφαλαίων τῶν ἐν ταῖς γραφαῖς ζητουμένων* Eus.*h.e.*2.18.1(M.20.184C); **e.** of a contrasted statement *τὸ ῥητὸν μόνον...ἐπειπών, τὴν πᾶσαν* δ. *παρελθών* Epiph.*haer.*64.2 (p.405.8; M.41.1072B); Chrys.*hom.14.3 in Heb.*(12.144D); **f.** plur., *changes* or *differences* of time, Meth.*res.*1.34(p.273.1; M.41.1097D); **2.** *distinctness* of letters in writing, Andr.Cr.*Agath.*7(M.97.1437C); **3.** *precept, command* of God, Anon.ap.Eus.*h.e.*5.16.8(M.20.468A); *ὅσα κατὰ* δ. *τοῦ νόμου φυλάττειν προσετάχθησαν* Epiph.*haer.*8.5 (p.190.17; M.41.212B).

διαστράπτω, *glance like lightning, flash, Schol.*1 in Max.*qu.Thal.*55 (M.90.560A); trans., *lighten ἄμμι διαστράψοις δνοφερὸν κνέφας ἐκ σέθεν αἴγλης* †Apoll.*met.Ps.*17:29(M.33.1333B).

διάστρεμμα, τό, *contention, argumentation,* Anast.S.*hod.*12 (M.89.201A).

***διαστρεπτέον,** *one must turn aside, divert,* in argument, Clem.*str.* 3.6(p.217.5; M.8.1149A).

διαστρέφω, *turn different ways, twist about;* **1.** *displace* a burden, Thphn.*chron.*p.218(M.108.556C); pass., of letters of the alphabet, *be put out of order* or *disarranged,* Chrys.*hom.11.8 in Mt.*(7.159A); **2.** pass., of the hair, *be parted,* ‡Hipp.Th.*fr.*21(p.55.16); **3.** met., *disturb greatly,* Chrys.*hom.21.1 in Heb.*(12.194B); *ἵνα μὴ διαστραφῶσιν, ὡς τἀναντία κελευόμενοι* id.*hom.4.3 in 2Cor.*(10.458C); **4.** *pervert τὸ σχίσμα ὑμῶν πολλοὺς διέστρεψεν 1Clem.*46.9; *ib.*47.5; *οὐκ ἐγένετο χρήσιμος ὁ πλασθεὶς ἀλλὰ διεστράφη* Chrys.*hom.7.5 in Gen.*(4.681C); *οἱ ἀκόλαστοι καὶ διεστραμμένοι* id.*stat.*1.12(2.19A); of words *πικροῖς τε καὶ διεστραμμένοις...λόγοις τῶν πλανωμένων τὸν νοῦν* Cyr.*Jo.* proem.(4.2D); **5.** of a text; *be corrupt,* Or.*Jo.*6.41(24; p.150.24; M.14.272B).

διαστροφεύς, ὁ, *one who distorts* or *perverts,* Eus.*d.e.*3.4(p.119.16; M.22.204B); *σοφισταὶ καὶ τῶν λόγων* δ. Epiph.*haer.*69.56(p.203.25; M.42.289D).

διαστροφή, ἡ, *turning aside from what is right;* **1.** *perversity, error,* Clem.*str.*7.3(p.11.3; M.9.417B); *ib.*7.16(p.72.33; 541C); Const. ap.Ath.*apol.sec.*87(p.166.16; M.25.405C); Bas.*hom.in Ps.*7(1.102C; M.29.240B); **2.** *debasement* of coinage, Jo.Mal.*chron.*18 p.486(M.97.704C); **3.** *leading astray πολλαί εἰσιν αἱ* δ. *τοῦ ἐχθροῦ A.Phil.*B 142 (p.82.4); **4.** *refutation,* ‡Ath.*synops.*77(M.28.436A).

διάστροφος, *twisted, distorted;* met., *perverted τὴν* δ. *ἑτεροδοξίαν* Eus.*h.e.*7.30.1(M.20.709A); id.*e.th.*1.18(p.80.12; M.24.864B); *ἐν* δ. *νουθεσίᾳ ἀπολέσαι τοιαύτην κόρην* Agath.*v.Gr.Ill.*86(p.44); of persons *τοὺς* δ. *διὰ τοῦ φθόνου* Gr.Mag.*dial.*(tr.Zach.)3.15(M.*PL.*77.251C).

διαστρόφως, *in a distorted manner ἀπ' αὐτῆς* [sc. Epistle to Philippians in Marcion's canon], *διὰ τὸ* δ. *παρ' αὐτῷ κεῖσθαι, οὐδὲν ἐξελεξάμεθα* Epiph.*haer.*42.12(p.182.5; M.41.812A).

διαστρώννυμι, *lay down* met.; **1.** *place together,* Clem.*str.*4.2

(p.249.21; M.8.1217A); **2.** pass., *be allayed, subside*, Bas.Sel.*v.Thecl.*1 (M.85.500D).

διαστύφ-ω, *conserve, preserve* ἅλας εἰδότες...τὴν θείαν διδασκαλίαν τὴν ~ουσαν τὰ σεσηπότα Thdt.*Cant.*proem.(2.11).

διασυνίστημι, *construct*, Ath.*decr.*9(p.8.18; M.25.432A).

***διασυντηρέω**, *keep, retain*, †Bas.Anc.*virg.*13(M.30.697A).

***διασυριτικός**, *bringing disparagement* or *ridicule*, Clem.*paed.*1.9 (p.137.13; M.8.345C) cit. s. διάσυρσις.

***διασυριτικῶς**, *mockingly*, Thdr.Mops.*Nah.*2:10f.(M.66.416A).

διασυρμός, ὁ, *disparagement, ridicule*; a rhetorical figure, cf. *diasyrmos ea, quae magna sunt, verbis minuit, aut minima extollit*, Isid.H.*etym.*2.21.42.

διάσυρσις, ἡ, *ridicule* δ. ... ἐστι ψόγος διασυριτικός Clem.*paed.*1.9 (p.137.13; M.8.345C).

διασύρτης, ὁ, *disparager*, Ephr.1.114A.

διασύρω, **1.** *drag roughly, A.Andr.et Mt.*25(p.102.8); *ib.*26(p.103. 4); Ath.*ep.encycl.*3(p.172.20; M.25.229B); **2.** *draw out* or *extend the time* βουλόμενος διασῦραι εἰς ὑπέρθεσιν Marc.Diac.*v.Porph.*22; *Pers.* (p.11.12); trans., Hegem.*Arch.*5(p.7.13; M.10.1436B); pass., *be prolonged* ἔμεινεν ὁ ἦχος διασυρείς †Anast.S.*relat.*3(p.61); abs., *tarry, linger*; of persons, *V.Dan.*10(p.371.19); Jo.Mal.*chron.*13 p.338(M.97. 505A); *ib.*p.348(520B).

διασύστασις, ἡ, *commending, making oneself commendable* (cf. 2Cor.6:4ff.), Clem.*str.*4.21(p.306.15; M.8.1341B).

***διασυστατικός**, *able* or *calculated to commend itself* ἡ πολυμαθία δ. τυγχάνει Clem.*str.*1.2(p.13.23; M.8.709A).

διασφαγή, ἡ, *breach, gap* in a wall, Epiph.*haer.*59.12(p.377.9; M.41.1036B); Cyr.*Abd.*4(3.357C).

διασφάλλω, *overturn utterly*; pass., met., *be wrong, be disproved*; of a statement, Bas.*renunt.*3(2.205B; M.31.633A); Didym.*Trin.*3.20 (M.39.897A); Nemes.*nat.hom.*18(M.40.684C).

διασφίγγω, *bind tightly*, fig. ταῖς ἀλύτοις ἀνάγκαις δ. τὸν λόγον Gr.Nyss.*Eun.*9(2 p.209.25; M.45.808B); id.*Apoll.*45(M.45.1232A); Max.*cap.*3.12(M.90.1264D).

***διασφύζω**, *throb with life, stir*, Hipp.*haer.*5.9(p.97.26; M.16. 3151C); of Sonship, acc. heresy of Basilides ταύτης τῆς υἱότητος... τὸ...λεπτομερὲς...διέσφυξε καὶ ἀνῆλθε...κάτωθεν ἄνω *ib.*7.22(p.198.30; M.3305D); διέσφυξε καὶ ἐγεννήθη ἀπὸ τοῦ κοσμικοῦ σπέρματος καὶ τῆς πανσπερμίας τοῦ σωροῦ ὁ μέγας ἄρχων *ib.*7.23(p.200.24; M.3319B).

διασχηματίζ-ω, **1.** *form, fashion* εἰς ἑκατέρας χρείας διεσχημάτιστο [sc. τὸ πάλαι φρούριον] Synes.*ep.*67(M.66.1211C); **2.** *picture, describe* ὀφθαλμοῖς αὐτὰ ἡ θεία πανταχόθεν ~ει γραφή [sc. cherubim and seraphim] †Diad.*Ar.*1(M.65.1152A).

διασχίζω, **1.** *tear apart*; **a.** fig. μὴ ἐπιτρέψετε διασχισθῆναι τὰ μέλη τοῦ Χριστοῦ Ath.*apol.sec.*34(p.112.24; M.25.305B); **b.** met., *divide, cause disagreement among*, Chrys.*hom.35.1 in Mt.*(7.397C); med. and pass., *be divided* αἱ...διεσχισμέναι...ἐκκλησίαι Dion.Al.ap.Eus. *h.e.*7.5.1(M.20.641B); οἱ ἐξ Ἀρείου τὴν πρὸς τὸν πατέρα τοῦ μονογενοῦς ὁμοιότητα εἰς πολλὰς αἱρέσεις διεσχίσαντο Philost.*h.e.*3.10(M.65. 585A); **2.** pass., *be broken*, of a treaty, Thphyl.*exc.Rom.*3(p.223.9; M.113.929C).

διάσχισις, ἡ, *cleaving, rending* ἡ τῶν πετρῶν δ. Anast.S.*hod.*1 (M.89.45A).

διασχοινίζω, *separate*; pass., *be separated* τὴν ἐπ' αἰτίαις εὐλόγοις ἀνδρὸς διεσχοινισμένην [sc. γυναῖκα] Cyr.*ador.*8(1.283E); met. γένος... ὡς ἐν φαυλότητι δογμάτων διεσχοινισμένον *ib.*11(398C); id.*Is.*4.3 (2.632E); of the two natures in Christ τὰ πολὺ τῆς ἀλλήλων ὁμοουσιότητος διεστηκότα τε καὶ ἀμετρήτῳ διαφορᾷ διεσχοινισμένα id.*inc. unigen.*(5^1.695D); id.*Nest.*2(p.33.13; 6^1.31D).

διασώζ-ω, **1.** *save*; **a.** in gen. τὰ ὑπάρχοντα...δ. Hipp.*Dan.*4.51.4; met., *preserve, maintain* οὕτω γὰρ ἂν ἡ θεία τριάς, καὶ τὸ ἅγιον κήρυγμα τῆς μοναρχίας ~οιτο Dion.R.ap.Ath.*decr.*26(M.25.465A); Max.*ep.*15(M.91.557A); **b.** of salvation wrought by Christ, Cyr. *Lc.*4:16(M.72.536C); διὰ γυναικὸς ὁ ἄνθρωπος ἐθανατώθη· διὰ γυναικὸς πάλιν διεσώθη Eulog.*fr.Trin.*3.6(p.367); **2.** *escort* or *conduct safely, A.Xanthipp.*32(p.81.14); Heracl.*ep.*ap.*Chron.Pasch.*p.399(M.92. 1021B).

***διάσωσις, ἡ**, *saving, preserving* τὴν ἐν ξυλίνῃ λάρνακι μικρὰν τοῦ γένους δ. [sc. of Noah] Gr.Nyss.*v.Ephr.*(M.46.844A); τὴν ὁδὸν ἐδιδάχθη τὴν πρὸς δ. μᾶλλον ἐπιτηδείαν *ib.*(849B); καστελλάτους καράβους παρασχεθῆναι εἰς δ. αὐτῶν Const.Pogon.*sacr.*1(M.*PL.*87.1154B).

διασωστής, ὁ, *guard*, Heracl.*ep.*(M.92.1021B).

***διασωφρονίζομαι**, *compete in virtue*, Synes.*regn.*18(p.56.4; M.66.1101C).

διαταγή, ἡ, **1.** *command, commandment, order*, Bas.*reg.fus.*12 (2.354B; M.31.948C); Chrys.*hom.40.3 in Jo.*(8.240E); Areth.*Apoc.*54 (M.106.724B); title of work αἱ δ. ὑμῖν δι' ἐμοῦ Κλήμεντος...προσπεφωνημέναι *Can.App.*85; διαταγαὶ τῶν ἁγίων ἀποστόλων *Const.App.* tit.; **2.** *regulation* τῆς ἐκκλησίας δ. Ath.*h.Ar.*34(p.202.10; M.25. 732D).

διατακτικῶς, *by way of differentiation*, Or.*or.*27.8(p.368.11; M.11. 512B).

διατάκτωρ, ὁ, *one in command*, Ephr.1.114B.

διάταξις, ἡ, *regulation*, Didym.*Pr.*1:8(M.39.1624C); Epiph.*haer.* 45.4(p.202.5; M.41.836B); *ib.*70.10(p.243.2; M.42.356C); *ib.*75.7(p.338. 20; 513A).

διατατικῶς, *in a wider sense* ἀφανίζων τὴν ὕβριν τῶν ὑπερηφάνων, οὐχ ἓν μόνον τῶν κακῶν ἐξαναλίσκει, ἀλλ' ἀπὸ ἑνὸς ἁμαρτήματος δ. ἐφ' ὅλα τὰ εἴδη τῆς κακίας ἐξακούειν προσήκει τῆς ὕβρεως †Bas.*Is.*267 (1.583A; M.30.589A).

διατείν-ω, **1.** act., *be conducive* to εἰς σωτηρίαν καὶ ἀίδιον ὑγιείαν δ. Clem.*paed.*1.8(p.128.14; M.8.329A); φιλοσοφία...~ουσα ἐπὶ τὴν... εἴδησιν id.*str.*1.20(p.62.33; M.8.816B); **2.** med., *stretch oneself*; **a.** lit., Chrys.*hom.57.4 in Mt.*(7.581C); id.*hom.24.1 in Rom.*(9.695A); id. *hom.14.3 in 1Tim.*(11.629E); **b.** met., *exert oneself, endeavour*, Cyr. *Mich.*32(3.419D); **3.** pass., *reach, extend* τὸ ᾆσμα...ἀπὸ τῶν ἄκρων ἐπὶ τὰ μέσα διαταθέν Clem.*prot.*1(p.6.8; M.8.57D).

διατειχίζω, **1.** *obstruct*, ‡Caes.Naz.*dial.*140(M.38.1077); **2.** *hinder, prevent*, Chrys.*ep.*19(3.606B).

διατείχισμα, τό, *wall* of partition or separation; met., of cloud of Exodus, Or.*exc.in Ps.*77:31(M.17.141B); Gr.Nyss.*v.Mos.*32(M.44. 309C); *ib.*44(314D).

διατεκταίνω, *fashion*; **1.** act.; met., Cyr.*Nah.*5(3.480B); **2.** med., *fashion for oneself*; in gen., id.*Ps.*32:9(M.69.876B); of God creating world, id.*glaph.Gen.*1(1.4A); id.*Mich.*37(3.425A).

***διατελεστέον**, *one must persevere*, Clem.*str.*3.5(p.215.23; M.8. 1145C).

διατέμν-ω, **1.** *cut through, dissever*; **a.** met., *disunite*, Chrys.*hom. 19.1 in Heb.*(12.183A); Cyr.*Os.*10(3.31A); Christol. κατὰ μηδένα τρόπον ~εσθαι δεῖν [sc. τὸν λόγον ἑνωθέντα τῇ σαρκί] id.*apol.Thdt.*3 (p.118.23; 6^1.212B); **b.** *cut out, omit* a passage, cf.Or.*comm.in Rom.* 10.43(M.14.1290B); **2.** *lay waste*, Thphn.*chron.*p.228(M.108.577C).

διατετραίνω, *bore through*, fig. ὦτα εἰς αἴσθησιν διατετρημένα Clem.*paed.*2.12(p.234.9; M.8.553A).

διατήρησις, ἡ, **1.** *keeping, preservation*; of paschal lamb, chosen on first day of week, Eutych.*pasch.*2(M.86.2393A); in sense of eternal life μενοῦμεν εἰς δ. Cyr.*hom.pasch.*24(5^2.294E); **2.** *observance* δογμάτων ἀκριβῶν δ. Chrys.*hom.47.3 in Mt.*(7.491C); id.*hom.7.4 in Phil.*(11.239B).

διατηρητέον, *one must observe*, Clem.*paed.*2.10(p.211.12; M.8. 504B).

διατηρητικός, *disposed for keeping* or *binding together* τὸ πάντων δ. τῶν συντιθεμένων Leont.H.*Nest.*1.13(M.86.1452B); of creative Logos πάντων...δ. τε καὶ διοριστικός ἐστιν, ἐπεὶ καὶ προακτικός *ib.*

διατίθημι, [pres. infin. διατιθεῖν *Const.App.*1.3.10; 3 plur. opt. aor. med. διάθοιντο Men.*exc.gent.*21(p.462.8; M.113.824D)]; **A.** act.; **1.** *arrange, put in order*; met., *set right* ἐπαγιώθη τὸν ἄρχοντα τοῦ Δάρας διατιθέναι τὸ πλημμεληθέν Men.*exc.Rom.*1(p.181.23; M.113.868B); **2.** *inflict upon* ὅσα διέθεσαν αὐτὸν οἱ ἀπὸ τοῦ γένους ὑμῶν Just.*dial.*67.6(M.6.629D); Or.*Cels.*3.5(p.206.24; M.11.925C); Chrys.*Stag.*3.7(1.218B); also med., Epiph.*haer.*66.4(p.23.7; M.42. 36D); *ib.*76.1(p.341.11; 516D); Chrys.*hom.11.4 in Eph.*(11.86E); **3.** *dispose, arrange*; hence *assimilate* εἰ γὰρ κυριώτερον τοῦ σώματος ἡ ψυχή, οὐκ ἰσχύει τὰ ἀκρότερα αὐτὴν διαθεῖναι πρὸς ἑαυτά Chrys. *hom.80.4 in Mt.*(7.771D).

B. pass.; **1.** *be confident* διατεθέντες ὅτι θεοῦ κρίσει ταῦτα ἐπιτελεῖται Didym.*Ps.*17:23(M.39.1252C); Cyr.*Is.*4.5(2.701A,702B); **2.** *delight in* πάνυ...διατεθέντες ἐν τῷ ἀποστόλῳ *A.Thom.*A 26(p.140.10).

διατίλλω, *tear in pieces*, Gr.Nyss.*Melet.*(M.46.861D).

διατίμησις, ἡ, *valuation* ὑπὲρ διατίμησιν *beyond value*, Pall.*h. Laus.*6(p.23.14; M.34.1018D).

διατιμητικός, *fixing a penalty, penal*, Hipp.*haer.*5.20(p.121.18; M.16.3186B).

διατμέω, *evaporate*, Bas.*hex.*3.7(1.29C; M.29.69B).

***διατομῖται, οἱ**, *those who separate* or *divide*; name given to Arian heretics, Jo.D.*haer.*69(M.94.720A).

διατορνεύω, **1.** *round off*; abs., *become round*; of moon at the full, Cyr.*ador.*6(1.206E); **2.** *shape, fashion*, id.*hom.pasch.*11(5^2.155D).

διατρανόω, *make clear, show* or *state clearly*, Gr.Nyss.*Eun.*12 (1 p.301.6; M.45.1012C); Cyr.*Ps.*34:13(M.69.904A); Zach.Mit.*opif.* (M.85.1120B); pass., Philost.*h.e.*4.8(M.65.521B).

***διατρεπτικῶς,** *dissuasively*; superl., Clem.*str*.2.10(p.138.10; M.8.984B).

διατρέχ-ω, **1.** *pass over* to ~ούσης εἰς αὐτὸν [sc. the Son] τῆς τοῦ γεννήσαντος ἀρχῆς τε καὶ κυριότητος Cyr.*thes*.(5^1.226A); **2.** *pass away*, of time ἕκτη...διέτρεχε...ὥρη Nonn.*par.Jo*.4:6(M.43.773C).

διάτρητος, *perforated, interstitial*, Thdt.*qu.2 in 4Reg*.(1.513).

διατρυπάω, *pierce through*; pass., fig. ψυχὴν...διατετρυπημένην... ὑπὸ φροντίδων Chrys.*hom.47.4 in Mt*.(7.492C).

διάττ-ω, **A.** intrans; **1.** *rush* or *dart rapidly*, fig. ὁ νοῦς...~ει πρὸς τὸ εὐθύ Cyr.*ador*.9(1.289E); εἰς πᾶν εἶδος ἀκαθαρσίας...~οντες id. *Os*.11(3.32D); **2.** *arrive, attain*, id.*ador*.1(1.29B); id.*glaph.Gen*.4 (1.128B); εἰς τὰ τῶν ἀρετῶν ὑψώματα...~ειν *ib*.7(240D); **3.** *penetrate* ἠχὴ...εἰς τὸ ἄνω ~ουσα id.*glaph.Ex*.2(1.296E); id.*ador*.16(1.562B); ~ει...ἡ δικαιοῦσα χάρις εἰς πάντας ἐν ἴσῳ id.*Rom*.3:21(p.179.3; M.74. 780A); **4.** *surpass* παντὸς ἐπέκεινα κακοῦ ~ουσαν δίκην id.*ador*.6 (1.186B); *ib*.15(543D).

B. trans.; **1.** *attain* ψυχὴ...τρίβον οὐκέτι τὴν προτεθεῖσαν ~ουσα Cyr.*Os*.32(3.45A); **2.** *travel, traverse* a road, fig. οἶμον ὀρθήν τε καὶ ἀπλανῆ ~οι τις ἄν id.*ador*.16(1.576D); **3.** *pass on, transmit* ἀμαθὲς γὰρ οἴεσθαι...τὸν Ἀδὰμ...τῆς ἐπ' αὐτῷ γενομένης ἀρᾶς τὴν δύναμιν... ~οντα φυσικῶς id.*glaph.Gen*.1(1.12A).

διατυπ-όω, **1.** *form perfectly, mould* ἐκεῖ χαλκὸς τὸ κρεμάμενον ἦν εἰς σχῆμα ὄφεως διατυπωθείς Chrys.*hom.27.2 in Jo*.(8.155C); of the embryo, id.*hom.4.3 in Mt*.(7.51A); id.*hom.7.2 in 1Thess*.(11.475C); **2.** *represent* ἐπὶ τοῦ ἱεροῦ καλουμένου πυλῶνος διατετύπωται παιδίον μὲν γενέσεως σύμβολον Clem.*str*.5.7(p.354.16; M.9.69A); ταῦτα διετύπου ἃ δὴ φωναὶ προφητῶν...ἐβόων Eus.*v.C*.3.3(p.78.21; M.20. 1057B); Gr.Nyss.*or.catech*.35(p.132.21; ἀποτυποῦται M.45.88C); Areth.*Apoc*.58(M.106.745B); **3.** *imagine, conceive, form in the mind*, Eus.*e.th*.3.3(p.154.27; M.24.997B); οὐδὲ διάνοια διατυπῶσαι τὸ τοιοῦτον δύναιτ' ἂν ὁποῖός ἐστιν ὁ θεός Chrys.*serm.2.2 in Gen*.(4.654B); Eus. Al.*serm*.21.11(M.86.437B); **4.** *signify* καθὼς ἂν αὐτοὶ διατυπώσητε Eus.*v.C*.3.53(p.100.12); *ib*.4.56(p.140.31; M.20.1208B); in Chrys. esp. in phrase ἄνωθεν ~οῦν of God's communication to man τοῦτο ἄνωθεν αὐτῷ διατετυπωμένον ἦν Chrys.*comm.in Gal*.4:30(10.712A); *ib*.4:31(10.712C); id.*hom.2.1 in Eph*.(11.10C); ἄνωθεν ταῦτα ὁ θεὸς ἐβούλετο, καὶ οὕτω διατετύπωτο id.*hom.5.1 in Col*.(11.358A, v.l. διετ-); αἰτεῖ δὲ τὸν πατέρα, καὶ τὸ τῆς εὐχῆς σχῆμα ~οῖ Cyr.*Jo*.8 (4.705A); id.*Juln*.9(6^2.308C); ταῖς ἀσθενεστέραις συγκατιὼν ἀκοαῖς ταῦτα ~οῖ Thdt.*Ezech*.44:1(2.1032); Ammon.*Ac*.16:8(M.85.1556B); Areth.*Apoc*.2(M.106.516C); τὴν ἄνω διετυπώσατο Ἱερουσαλὴμ *cat. Ac*.3:13(p.62.20); **5.** *dispose* οὐδὲ γὰρ ἦν ἑτέρως ἀναστῆναι αὐτὴν [sc. τὴν σκηνὴν Δαυΐδ] μὴ τοῦ τὴν ἀρχὴν διαπλάσαντος αὐτῇ χεῖρα ὀρέξαντος καὶ διατυπώσαντος ἄνωθεν τῇ δι' ὕδατος ἀναγεννήσει καὶ πνεύματος Chrys.*hom.11.2 in Jo*.(8.65A); Cyr.*Nah*.11(3.488C); esp. as a testamentary legal term προσήκει ~οῦν αὐτὸν τὸν οἶκον αὐτοῦ id.*Is*.3.4(2.495A); *Chron.Pasch*.p.311(M.92.793A); **6.** *appoint* ὁ βασιλεὺς...τὸν...Αἰδέσιον οἰνοχοεῖν αὐτῷ διετύπωσεν Gel.Cyz.*h.e*. 3.9.6; **7.** *indite* τοῖς αὐτοῖς δὲ ἄλλην [sc. ἐπιστολὴν] περὶ εἰρήνης ~οῦται Eus.*h.e*.6.46.5(M.20.636B); id.*v.C*.3.24(p.89.6; M.20.1084D); Isid.Pel.*epp*.2.96(M.78.540D); **8.** *prescribe, enact* ἡμέραν δ' εὐχῶν ἡγεῖσθαι...διετύπου Eus.*v.C*.4.18(p.124.6; M.20.1165A); Ath.*decr*.5 (p.4.17; M.25.424A); Bas.*ep*.22.2(3.100B; M.32.292A); Chrys.*hom. 16.2 in 1Cor*.(10.136A); Ἰουδαίους μέν, οἷς ἅπαντα τὰ σωματικὰ διετετύπωτο id.*virg*.30(1.290A); Cyr.*ador*.3(1.83D); τούτων...μετὰ πάσης...ἐμμελείας παρ' ἡμῶν διατυπωθέντων *Symb.Chalc*.(p.130.4; H.2.456D); Justn.*ep.Thdr.Mops*.(p.64.36; M.86.1083B); Max.*ep*.10 (M.91.449C); pass., *be dealt with by edict*, cf. τύπος [πά]ντων διατυπωθ[έντων] ἤτοι κ[αὶ] ἐξωρισθέντων ἀνοσίων...Ἑλλήνων *IGC As.Min*.324; **9.** *figure, symbolize* οἱ δέκα ἀπόστολοι...τὴν ἀόρατον διετύπουν...δεκάδα Iren.*haer*.1.18.3(M.7.648A); τοῦτο καὶ ὁ πάλαι νόμος αὐτοῖς ὡς ἐν σκιαῖς διετύπου, καὶ προανεκήρυττε τὴν χάριν διὰ τοῦ ἁγίου βαπτίσματος Cyr.*Is*.1.1(2.17C).

διατύπωσις, ἡ, **1.** *impression, mark, sign* ἐπεὶ τοίνυν ἐσημειώθη τὸ φῶς τοῦ προσώπου κυρίου ἐφ' ἡμᾶς σταυρικαῖς διαγραφαῖς καὶ δ. Germ.CP *or*.1(M.98.224B); **2.** used to describe the atomic effluence of sound, hence perh. *formation, configuration*; perh. *percussion* αἱ μὲν [sc. φωναὶ] φέρονται διὰ τῶν φωνητικῶν ὀργάνων· αἱ δὲ [sc. ἀκοαὶ] ὑποδέχονται διὰ τῆς ἐν μέσῳ τοῦ ἀέρος πληγῆς καὶ δ. Melet. *nat.hom*.30(M.64.1284B); **3.** *signification* ἕτοιμον ὑποδέξασθαι τῇ καρδίᾳ τὰς ἐκ τῆς θείας διδασκαλίας ἐγγινομένας δ. Bas.*ep*.2.2(3.71E; M.32.225B); Areth.*Apoc*.2(M.106.516C); hence *purpose, plan* ὥστε τὴν τῷ θεῷ δοκοῦσαν καὶ νῦν ἐξενεχθῆναι περὶ ἡμῶν δ. Nest.*fr*.A 13 (p.199.18)ap.Evagr.*h.e*.1.7(M.86.2440C); **4.** *disposition, arrangement* τὴν κρίσιν τῆς δ. ἐπέτρεψεν τοῦ καθ' αὐτὸν βίου Const.*or.s.c*.13(p.172. 22); οὐ γὰρ δὴ μόνον ἀπὸ τῆς δημιουργίας φαίνεσθαι βούλεται, ἀλλὰ καὶ ἀπὸ τῆς δ. Chrys.*fr.in Jer*.5:22(M.64.816B); **5.** *form, pattern, system* ψυχαὶ...ταύτην λαβοῦσαι τὴν δ. τῆς μορφῆς Meth.*res*.3.18 (p.415.15; M.18.328A); πρὸς μίαν δ. ἄγεσθαι τοῦτο ἡ θεία πρόνοια βούλεται Const.ap.Eus.*v.C*.3.18(p.86.16; M.20.1077A); ἐπὶ τὸ κορυφαιότατον τῆς ἐκκλησιαστικῆς δ. ὁ λόγος ἡμᾶς ἐπείγει *Const.App*. 8.3.2; **6.** *testamentary disposition*, *Cod.Afr*.81; τὴν δ. πάντων τούτων τῶν ἀγαθῶν ἔγραψε, καὶ μάρτυρας ἀνατέθεικε Anast.S.*qu.et resp*.96 (M.89.736C); **7.** *regulation, ordinance* τὰς κανονικὰς δ. τῶν κοινοβίων ‡Ath.*ep.Cast*.1.1(M.28.849C); εἰς ἁρμονίαν αὐτοὺς καταστῆσαι ταῖς ἐκκλησιαστικαῖς δ. Thdr.Mops.*Tit*.1:5(p.236.20; M.66.948B); CChalc. *can*.8; πρὸς ἀποτέλεσμα τῆς θείας διατυπώσεως Leo Mag.*ep*.33.1 (p.43.22; M.*PL*.54.798B); *ib*.106.2(p.56.36; 1004B); Socr.*h.e*.7.13.6 (M.67.761B); Evagr.*h.e*.2.18(p.89.22; M.86.2581B); Leont.N.*v.Jo. Eleem*.3(p.10.7); **8.** *rule* of monastic orders μοναστήριον γυναικῶν... τὴν αὐτὴν ἔχον δ., τὴν αὐτὴν πολιτείαν Pall.*h.Laus*.33(p.96.7; M.34. 1105B).

***διατυχέω,** *fail to accomplish* διητύχησε δὲ τοῦ βουλεύματος Thphn.*chron*.p.221(M.108.564D).

διατωθάζω, *mock, laugh to scorn*, Olymp.*Job* 22:19(M.93.248B).

***διαυαίνω,** *dry completely*, Thdt.*qu.11 in Gen*.(1.15); id.*h.e*. 2.30.7(3.906).

διαυγάζω, **1.** *be transparent*, *Anaph.Pil*.B 4(p.445); **2.** *illuminate* ὁ θεὸς...διαυγάσῃ τὰ ζεζοφωμένα τῶν διανοημάτων Epiph.*anc*.101 (p.122.1; M.43.200A); **3.** of day, *dawn*, *A.(Pass.)Andr*.B 8(p.18.30); Cyr.*Ps*.7:7(M.69.749D); id.*Os*.120(3.151C).

διαυγασμός, ὁ, *dawn*, Cyr.*Os*.124(3.156B).

διαύγεια, ἡ, *splendour, glory*; of God, Dion.Ar.*c.h*.2.4(M.3.144A); Areth.*Apoc*.10(M.106.572A).

διαυγής, **1.** *clear, pellucid*, met. τὸν δ. καὶ καθαρὸν Ἰησοῦν Clem. *paed*.2.12(p.228.6; M.8.540C); δ. ... λόγους id.*str*.1.12(p.35.25; M.8. 753A); νῷ δ. καὶ καθαρῷ νοούμενον τὸν...θεοῦ λόγον Eus.*l.C*.11(p.226. 22; M.22.1380D); νηστείᾳ διαυγεστέραν ἐποίησε τὴν ψυχήν Bas.*hom*. 1.9(2.8D; M.31.180C); **2.** neut. as adv., *clearly*; ref. sound, Chrys. *hom.28.2 in 2Cor*.(10.636D).

διαυθεντέω, *domineer*, for αὐθεντέω in 1Tim.2:12, ‡Chrys.*poenit*. 1.9(9.778E).

***διαυθεντίζω,** *assert authoritatively*, ‡Jo.D.*Artem*.33(M.96.1281C).

δίαυλος, ὁ, *double course*, in a race; **1.** fig. πόδας...τὸν τῆς ἀρετῆς δ. ἐξανύσαντας Thdt.*provid*.10(4.670); **2.** met., *stretch, tract*; of words in a speech κἂν μυρίους περιβάληται λόγων δ. Chrys.*ep*.94(3.643D); id.*hom.6.1 in 1Cor*.(10.44A); Pall.*v.Chrys*.4(p.26.6; M.47.17).

διαφάνεια, ἡ, *transparency*, Bas.*hex*.3.4(1.26A; M.29.61B).

διαφανής, **1.** *bright* τόπῳ δ. καὶ ἀμιάντῳ Clem.*ecl*.37(p.148.15; M.9.717B); **2.** *illustrious*; of deeds, Tat.*orat*.39(p.40.9; M.6.881C); δ. ἐκκλησίας Eus.*h.e*.5.1.2(M.20.408C); of persons, *ib*.5.21.1(488A); Cyr.*Mich*.24(3.412B).

διάφαυμα, τό, *dawn*, *Protev*.23(p.46); Ath.*virg*.20(p.56.2; M.28. 276D); †Jo.D.*B.J*.22(M.96.1056D).

διάφαυσις, ἡ, *dawn*, Jo.Mosch.*prat*.186(M.87.3064C).

[*]διάφαυσμα, τό, = διάφαυμα, Jo.Thess.*mul.ung*.2(M.59.638); *Const.Stud*.14(M.99.1709B) cit. s. ἐκκλησιάρχης.

[*]διαφαύω, = διαφαύσκω, *dawn*, *A.(Pass.)Petr.et Paul*.5(p.122. 6); Thphn.*chron*.p.194(M.108.501C); †Jo.D.*B.J*.39(M.96.1232A); abs. πρὸ τοῦ διαφαῦσαι (unless from διαφαύσκω) ‡Eust.*hex*.(M.18. 776B).

[*]διαφάω, = διαφαύσκω, *dawn*, *A.Barth*.4(p.134.25); *Chron. Pasch*.p.378(M.92.969A) al.; Jo.Mal.*chron*.14 p.369(M.97.549B).

διαφέρ-ω, **1.** *differ*, Trin. ᾤοντο [sc. Monarchians]...παρίστασθαι μὴ ~ειν τῷ ἀριθμῷ τὸν υἱὸν τοῦ πατρός, ἀλλ' ἓν οὐ μόνον οὐσίᾳ ἀλλὰ καὶ ὑποκειμένῳ τυγχάνοντας ἀμφοτέρους, κατά τινος ἐπινοίας διαφόρους, οὐ κατὰ ὑπόστασιν λέγεσθαι πατέρα καὶ υἱόν Or.*Jo*.10.37(21; p.212.13; M.14.376B); not in essence μοναρχία...κἂν ἀριθμῷ ~ῃ, τῇ γε οὐσίᾳ μὴ τέμνεσθαι Gr.Naz.*or*.29.2(p.75.6; M.36.76B); εἷς ἐστιν ὁ θεὸς τῇ συνυπάρξει τῶν τριῶν...ὑποστάσεων, τῶν ~ουσῶν ἀλλήλων οὐ τῇ οὐσίᾳ, ἀλλὰ τοῖς τῆς ὑπάρξεως τρόποις ‡Just.*qu.et resp*.139(M.6. 1392C); v. διαφορά; **2.** *make a difference, be of importance* τῷ δεσπότῃ δ. ταῦτα Chrys.*hom.26.2 in Rom*.(9.702E); id.*hom.8.1 in Eph*.(11. 52F); med., *concern oneself* οὐδὲν ~ομαι id.*hom.39.1 in 1Cor*.(10. 362C); **3.** c. dat., *belong to*; **a.** of property, *A.Thom*.A 24(p.138.10); Const.ap.Eus.*h.e*.10.5.11(M.20.884B); Pall.*v.Chrys*.9(p.55.15; M.47. 32); also c. genit. κυμητήρ[ιον] δ[ια]φέρον Ἀνδρέου *CG–CI* 54(? saec. vi); *ib*.17(saec.vii); *ib*.45(? saec.vii); **b.** met., ref. Ac.5:4 ἃ ἐπαγγελλόμεθα θεῷ, οὐκ ἔτι λοιπόν ἐστιν ἡμῶν, ἀλλὰ θεῷ ~ει ‡Ath.*pass*.3 (M.28.188D); *be proper* to, *appertain* to οὐ...~ει ἀνθρωπίνῃ φύσει τὸ ἀγαθόν, ἀλλὰ θεῷ Ath.*inc.et c.Ar*.7(M.26.993B); ῥημάτων ἰδιότης... ~ουσα τοῖς εὐσεβέσιν Bas.*reg.fus*.13(2.354E; M.31.949B); μηδὲν τῇ ἡμετέρᾳ θρησκείᾳ ~ουσῶν ἱστοριῶν ‡Just.*coh.Gr.*9(M.6.257B); Thdt. *eran.*2(4.81); *refer* to ὅσα...εὐτελῆ ῥήματα ὑπὸ τοῦ κυρίου εἴρηται, τῇ πτωχείᾳ αὐτοῦ ~ει Ath.*inc.et c.Ar.*8(996A); **c.** ptcpl., of persons; **i.** *kinsfolk*, *A.Thom.*A 73(p.189.1); Epiph.*haer.*66.3(p.21.9; M.42.36B); *Apophth.Patr.*(M.65.252A); **ii.** *partisans, adherents* οἱ ~οντες Ἀθανασίου *PLond.*1914.8; **4.** med., *decline, refuse* μηδὲν δ. Soz.*h.e.*2.9.4(M.67.956D); *ib.*5.13.4(M.1252D); **5.** trans., *endure* πόνους ~ομένων Proc.G.*Gen.*3:7(M.87.197A).

διαφθέγγομαι, *speak, utter*, Meth.*res.*1.61(M.41.1157D; ἀνα- p.325.22).

διαφθον-έω, *envy*; med., c. dat., Or.*sel.in Ps.*29:2(M.12.1292C); Cyr.*ador.*14(1.486C); Jo.Mal.*chron.*2 p.35(M.97.105B); hence *withhold* information *out of envy*, s,v.l., οὗτος...πολλὰ...διὰ βασκανίαν ~εῖται Chrys.*hom.9.1 in Col.*(11.391C).

διαφίημι, **1.** *abandon*, Gr.Nyss.*ep.*4(M.46.1028A); **2.** *allow to depart*, Synes.*ep.*121(M.66.1500B).

[*]**διαφιλονεικέω**, *contend against* in rivalry, Clem.*str.*4.13(p.288.25; M.8.1300A).

διαφλέγω, *burn thoroughly*, *M.Tar.*8(p.468); Gr.Nyss.*res.*3(M.46.660C); *Chron.Pasch.*p.263(M.92.644C).

διαφοιτάω, *spread, penetrate*, Dion.Al.ap.Eus.*h.e.*7.23.3(M.20.692B); Isid.Pel.*epp.*1.51(M.78.213C); of God's power τὰ καθολικώτατα τῶν ἐνεργημάτων αὐτοῦ [sc. τοῦ θεοῦ] διαπεφοίτηκεν ἐπ' ἴσης πάντα Clem.*str.*5.14(p.417.8; M.9.197A); id.*fr.*23(p.202.22); of Logos penetrating universe, Or.*Jo.*6.39(23; p.147.16; M.14.265C).

***διαφοίτησις**, ἡ, *spreading*; of gospel, Gr.Nyss.*Steph.*1(M.46.708C).

διαφορά, ἡ, **1.** *difference, distinction*; **a.** in gen. δ. δίδωμι *make a distinction*, Or.*Jo.*28.9(8; p.400.2; M.14.700A); λύω τὴν δ. *resolve a distinction*, *ib.*(p.400.7; 700A); **b.** theol., denied in Trin. ἕνα...θεὸν ἐκ θεοῦ, ἀλλ' οὐ πλείους. ἐν γὰρ πλείοσιν ἑτερότης ἔσται καὶ δ. Eus.*d.e.*4.3(p.152.22; M.22.253D); i.e. not in substance τῆς...κατὰ τὴν φύσιν ἰδιότητος μηδεμίαν ἑτέρου πρὸς τὸ ἕτερον ἐπινοεῖσθαι διαφοράν, ἀλλ' ἐν τῇ κοινότητι τῆς οὐσίας τὰς γνωριστικὰς ἰδιότητας ἐπιλάμπειν ἑκάστῳ Gr.Nyss.*diff.ess.*5(M.32.336B); ἐν...ὄνομα...ἡμῖν τὴν ἑνότητα τῆς οὐσίας τῶν ἐν τῇ πίστει προσώπων διερμηνεύει...διὰ γὰρ τῶν κλήσεων τούτων οὐ φύσεως διαφορὰν διδασκόμεθα ἀλλὰ μόνας τὰς τῶν ὑποστάσεων γνωριστικὰς ἰδιότητας id.*Eun.*2(2 p.301.21; M.45.472D); μήτε παρὰ τὸ πλέον καὶ ἔλαττον τὴν δ. ἐξευρίσκοι, διότι τὴν ἐλάττωσιν ὁ τῆς τελειότητος οὐ παραδέχεται λόγος id.*or.catech.*proem.(p.5.11; M.45.12C); τὸ θεῖον...κατὰ πάντα τέλειον. εἰ οὖν πολλοὺς ἐροῦμεν θεοὺς ἀνάγκη διαφορὰν ἐν τοῖς πολλοῖς θεωρεῖσθαι. εἰ γὰρ οὐδεμία δ. ἐν αὐτοῖς, εἷς μᾶλλόν ἐστι καὶ οὐ πολλοί. εἰ δὲ δ. ἐν αὐτοῖς, ποῦ ἡ τελειότης; ‡Cyr.*Trin.*4(6^{3}.5C; M.77.1128A); but in Person ὥστε ἀριθμῷ μὲν τὴν δ. ... ὑπάρχειν καὶ ταῖς ἰδιότησι, ἐν δὲ τῷ λόγῳ τῆς θεότητος, τὴν ἑνότητα θεωρεῖσθαι Bas.*Eun.*1.19(1.231C; M.29.556B); οὔτε τῆς τῶν ὑποστάσεων δ. τὸ τῆς φύσεως συνεχὲς διασπώσης οὔτε τῆς κατ' οὐσίαν κοινότητος τὸ ἰδιάζον τῶν γνωρισμάτων ἀναχεούσης Gr.Nyss.*diff.ess.*4(M.32.333A); *ib.*7(337D); cf. ἡμᾶς...τήν τε τῆς φύσεως ἑνότητα [sc. of Peter and Paul] καὶ τὴν τῶν ὑποστάσεων δ. παραστήσαντες id.*Eun.*7(2 p.168.3; M.45.757C); ‡Cyr.*Trin.*10(6^{3}.15E; M.77.1144A); διὰ τοῦ μὲν λέγειν τρεῖς ὑποστάσεις ἡ δ.· διὰ τοῦ ὁμολογεῖν δὲ μίαν οὐσίαν ἡ ἕνωσις ὁμολογεῖται Max.*opusc.*(M.91.148A); of Father and Son οὐκοῦν ἡ τῶν ὀνομάτων δ. λαμβάνεται μὲν ἐπὶ τῶν ὁμοουσίων...δέδεικται γὰρ ὡς οὐκ ἀνατρέφει τῶν ὁμοφυῶν τὴν πρὸς ἄλληλα φυσικὴν ὁμοιότητα τῶν ὀνομάτων ἡ δ. Cyr.*thes.*19(5^{1}.187Af.); **2.** *difference* between divine and human natures of Christ τὴν δ. τῆς τε τοῦ λαβόντος φύσεως καὶ τῆς τοῦ ληφθέντος ἡμῖν ὑποδείκνυσιν ἡ θεία γραφή Thdr.Mops.*fr.Apoll.*(p.321.14); id.*fr.inc.*8(p.299.17; M.66.981B); cf.*Symb.Chalc.*(p.129.32; H.2.456C) cit. s. φύσις; θεωρεῖ μέν τινα δ. φύσεων ὁ νοῦς· ταὐτὸν γὰρ οὔτι που θεότης τε καὶ ἀνθρωπότης Cyr.*inc.unigen.*(5^{2}.21E); εἷς γὰρ ἐξ ἀμφοῖν Χριστός...γνωριζομένης τῆς δ. τῶν οὐσιῶν Gel.Cyz.*h.e.*2.19.25(M.85.1280D); οὐδὲ ὅλως γάρ φαμεν οὔτε δ. ὑποστάσεων ἐν τῇ μιᾷ ὑποστάσει τοῦ κυρίου—μὴ γένοιτο—εἰ καὶ ὑποστατικῶν μερικῶν ἰδιωμάτων ἴσμεν δ. Leont.H.*Nest.*2.13(M.86.1561C); εἴ τις οὐχ ὁμολογεῖ...τὴν κατ' οὐσίαν τῶν φύσεων δ. μετὰ τὴν...ἕνωσιν ἐξ ὧν ὁ εἷς...ὑπάρχει Χριστός...εἴη κατάκριτος CLater.*can.*7; οὐκοῦν εἴπερ δ. ἐπὶ Χριστοῦ μετὰ τὴν ἕνωσιν λέγομεν...οὐ διαιροῦμεν τῷ ἀριθμῷ τὰ σημαινόμενα παντελῶς, ἀλλὰ δηλοῦμεν σωζομένην τῶν ἡνωμένων τὴν ὕπαρξιν Max.*ep.*15(M.91.561C); μίαν ἀμφοτέρων ἐκ τῆς ἑνώσεως τοῖς εὐσεβέσιν οὐκ ἐδίδου γνωρίζεσθαι φύσιν...μὴ σώζουσα τὴν κατ' οὐσίαν δ. μετὰ τὴν ἕνωσιν· ἀλλ' ὑπόστασιν μίαν παρεῖχεν ὁρᾶν ἐκ τῆς ἑνώσεως σύνθετον *ib.*(556C); cf.*ib.*11(M.469B); οὐχ ὡς τῶν δύο φύσεων ἀποτελεσασῶν μίαν σύνθετον φύσιν, ἀλλ' ἑνωθεισῶν ἀλλήλαις κατ' ἀλήθειαν εἰς μίαν ὑπόστασιν σύνθετον τοῦ υἱοῦ τοῦ θεοῦ, καὶ σώζεσθαι αὐτῶν τὴν οὐσιώδη δ. ὁριζόμεθα Jo.D.*f.o.*3.3(M.94.993C); in monophysite doctrine Νιοβῖται...τὴν δ. τῆς σαρκὸς καὶ τῆς θεότητος μετὰ τὴν ἕνωσιν ἀναιροῦσιν Tim.CP *haer.*(M.86.44A); ποιοτήτων λέγων [sc. Severus of Antioch] φυσικῶν, ἀλλ' οὐ φύσεων, ἤγουν οὐσιῶν ἐπὶ Χριστοῦ διαφορὰν μετὰ τὴν ἕνωσιν Max.*opusc.*(M.91.41A); εἷς οὖν Νεστορίῳ τε τῶν Σευήρῳ περὶ τοῦ δυσσεβεῖν ὑπάρχει σκοπός. ... ὁ μὲν γὰρ διὰ τὴν σύγχυσιν...τὴν οὐσιώδη δ. προσωπικὴν ποιεῖται διαίρεσιν· ὁ δὲ διὰ τὴν διαίρεσιν τὴν οὐσιώδη μὴ λέγων δ., τὴν καθ' ὑπόστασιν ἕνωσιν φυσικὴν ἐργάζεται σύγχυσιν· δέον μήτε σύγχυσιν ἐπὶ Χριστοῦ, μήτε διαίρεσιν· ἀλλ' ἕνωσιν τῶν κατ' οὐσίαν διαφερόντων, καὶ διαφορὰν τῶν καθ' ὑπόστασιν ἡνωμένων ὁμολογεῖν *ib.*(56C); in monothelite confession ὁμολογοῦμεν...τὸν...Χριστὸν...μίαν ὑπόστασιν σύνθετον ἐν δύο καὶ μετὰ τὴν ἕνωσιν κηρύττοντες φύσεσι, τὴν δ. ἑκατέρας γνωρίζοντες φύσεως κατὰ τὴν αὐτῶν ἰδιότητα Paul.CP *ep. Thdr.*(M.*PL.*87.95A); for problem of Christ's human and divine will v. θέλημα; **3.** *advantage* εἰς δ. καὶ προτροπὴν τῶν ἐκπαιδευομένων ταῦτα γέγραπται Just.*1apol.*21.4(M.6.360B); **4.** *divulsion, destruction* τὴν ἐκ τοῦ κατακλυσμοῦ δ. ἐνίκησεν ἂν ἡ τοῦ λόγου φορά Bas.Sel.*or.*6.3(M.85.96C).

διαφορία, ἡ, = διαφορά, s.v.l., τὴν ἐκ τῆς ὁμωνυμίας δ. Ath.*syn.*36(p.263.1; M.26.756C).

***διαφορῖται**, οἱ, an alternative name for a sect of monophysites, also called Νιοβῖται, Tim.CP *haer.*(M.86.44A).

διάφορος, comp., *superior, excelling others*, Clem.*exc.Thdot.*17(p.112.12; M.9.665B); *ib.*41(p.119.16; 677C); Thphn.*chron.*p.261(M.108.649B).

διάφραγμα, τό, *barrier*, fig. ἐνταῦθα μὲν γὰρ...πολλοῖς διεστήκασι, χρώματι, σχήματι κτλ. ... ἐκεῖ δὲ τούτων οὐδέν ἐστι τῶν δ. Chrys.*hom.1.1 in 1Tim.*(11.550B); ἐπειδὴ αἱ ἁμαρτίαι διϊστῶσιν ἡμᾶς ἀπὸ τοῦ θεοῦ τοῦ ἐγγίζοντος, περιέλωμεν...τὸ...δ. Cyr.*Ps.*72:27(M.69.1185C).

διαφράσσω, *form a barrier*; pass., met., *be separated from* τοὺς...ποικίλῃ πλάνῃ θεοῦ διαπεφραγμένοις Eulog.*fr.Novat.*(M.104.349B).

διαφρουρέω, *guard, garrison*, Thphn.*chron.*p.235(M.108.592C).

***διαφύλαξις**, ἡ, *safe keeping*, ‡Ath.*synops.*77(M.28.436C).

διαφυλάσσω, **1.** *keep safe*, Const.ap.Eus.*v.C.*3.60(p.109.2; M.20.1133A); Const.*ib.*4.42(p.135.11; 1192C); **2.** *observe* a custom, Eus.*h.e.*5.24.1(M.20.493B).

***διαφυρόω**, *mix, confound, confuse*, med., Gr.Nyss.*hom.opif.*13.3(M.44.165D).

***διαφύρ-ω**, s.v.l., *mix, confound* τριὰς τελεία...οὐ συναλοιφή τις οὖσα οὐδὲ πρὸς ἑαυτὴν ~ομένη Epiph.*haer.*76.31(M.42.593D; conj. διαφερομένη p.389.8).

διαφωνέω, **1.** *utter*, *Apoc.Mos.*37(p.20); **2.** ? *grow weary*, *T.Job* 13(p.111.13); *ib.*27(p.120.4,10).

διαφώτισις, ἡ, *elucidation* (sc. of scripture), ‡Ath.*synops.*4(M.28.293D).

***διάφωτος**, *illuminated, light*, Jo.Mal.*chron.*14 p.360(M.97.536B).

[*]**διαχαίνω**, = διαχάσκω, *gape, crack*, Chrys.*hom.8.4 in 1Cor.*(10.70D); Evagr.*h.e.*1.17(p.27.4; M.86.2469A).

διαχαλάω, *relax*; pass., *be enervated*; of persons, Chrys.*hom. 23.1 in Eph.*(11.175A).

διαχαράσσω, **1.** *sever*, Jo.Mosch.*prat.*47(M.87.2901D); **2.** med., *scratch, lacerate*, Men.*exc.Rom.*14(p.207.17; M.113.905B); **3.** *describe* or *make* sign of cross, *A.Thom.*A 50(p.166.18); *mark out* διαχάραξόν μοι πῶς γίνεται τὸ ἔργον...καὶ...κάλαμον λαβὼν διεχάρασσεν μετρῶν τὸν τόπον *ib.*18(p.127.5,7); Eus.*onomast.*(p.2.11); met. τοὺς τύπους τῆς ἀληθείας, οὓς οἱ προφῆται...διέτυπον, διεχάραττον, κατήγγελλον Epiph.*ep.Arab.*ap.*haer.*78.4(p.454.27; M.42.704C); **4.** *indite upon tablets, write*, Eus.*h.e.*5.3.4(M.20.437B); Bas.*ep.*45.1(3.133A; M.32.365A); Gr.Nyss.*ep.*20(M.46.1080B).

***διαχαυν-όω**, *slacken, soften*; met. ἐπειδὰν...ἡμᾶς ~ώσῃ [sc. ὁ διάβολος], καθάπερ τις χειμάρρους ἐπιχέεται Chrys.*hom.14.2 in Eph.*(11.105A); med., *relax* δ. τὴν διάνοιαν Tit.Bost.*Man.*2.14(M.18.1160C).

διαχειμάζομαι, *be tempestuous, rage*; met., of persons, Tit.Bost. *Man.*2.2(M.18.1133C).

***διαχειραγωγ-έω**, *lead*, met. θεοφιλὲς...ἀπὸ τῆς γλώττης ἐπὶ τὰ ἔργα τὸ κόσμιον ~εῖν Clem.*str.*2.23(p.193.4; M.8.1096B); pass., of persons ἐπὶ τὴν θεωρίαν ~ούμενοι id.*fr.*60(p.227.24).

***διαχερσόω**, *dry up*, ‡Caes.Naz.*dial.*152(M.38.1105).

διαχέω, **1.** perf. ptcpl. pass., *dissolute* pleasures, Cyr.*Ps.*65:10(M.69.1136D); **2.** *break* a treaty, Thphyl.*exc.Rom.*3(p.222.24; M.113.929B).

διαχρίω, *besmear*, Gr.Nyss.*v.Mos.*17(M.44.304D); Chrys.*hom. 88.3 in Mt.*(7.829B); Const.Diac.*laud.*25(M.88.508C).

[*]**διαχύν-ω**, late form of διαχέω; **1.** *pour out*; met., Hipp.*haer*. 5.14(p.109.1; M.16.3167B); **2.** *spread abroad, disperse*; pass., Ath. *h.Ar*.77(p.226.14; M.25.788A); τὰ ἀπὸ τῆς Ἰνδικῆς εἴδη ἐκεῖσε τῇ Θηβαΐδι ~εται Epiph.*haer*.66.1(p.17.5; M.42.32A).

***διάχυτος**, *diffused*, Andr.Cr.*or*.21(M.97.1277B).

διαχωρίζ-ω, **1.** *separate* ἐτόλμησαν...ἀσεβῶς τὸν ἕνα θεὸν διαχωρίσαι τῷ λόγῳ Cyr.H.*catech*.4.4; c. genit. ὅτι οὐδὲ μιᾶς ἐνεργείας τῆς παρὰ πατρὸς ἐνεργουμένης τὸ ἅγιον πνεῦμα διακεχώρισται Gr.Nyss. *Trin*.7(p.80.4); **2.** *distinguish*, Clem.*paed*.2.4(p.182.19; M.8.441A); ἑτεροδόξους ~οντας δίκαιον θεὸν ἀπὸ ἀγαθοῦ Or.*comm.in Eph*.6:1 (p.568.8); pass. impers., *a distinction is made* διακεχώρισται...ἀνὰ μέσον ὕδατος καὶ ὕδατος Hipp.*haer*.5.27(p.133.7; M.16.3203B); **3.** *tear in pieces*, Jo.Mosch.*prat*.69(M.87.2920B).

***διαχωριστικός**, *separative* τὸ πνεῦμα δ. ἔχει δύναμιν ἐνεργειῶν ὑλικῶν Clem.*ecl*.25(p.143.29; M.9.709B); Epiph.*exp.fid*.9(p.506.29; M.42.792D).

διάψαλμα, τό, *selah* (Hebr. סֶלָה) a musical or liturgical direction marking a division of the psalm; **1.** various interpretations ἐστοχασάμεθα μήποτε ὑπεσήμαναν οἱ θέντες αὐτὸ [sc. τὸ δ.] ῥυθμοῦ τινος ἢ μέλους ἢ μέρους μεταβολὴν γεγονέναι κατὰ τοὺς τόπους ἢ κρουμάτων ἀνακωχήν, ἢ καὶ ἐποχὴν τοῦ ἁγίου πνεύματος μάλιστα, ἢ...ἀπὸ νοήματος εἰς νόημα μεταβολήν, ἢ καὶ τρόπου διδασκαλίας εἰς ἕτερον τρόπον ἢ διανοίας καὶ δυνάμεως λόγου ἐνάλλαγμα. οὔτε δὲ παρὰ τῷ Ἀκύλᾳ κεῖται οὔτε ἐν τῷ Ἑβραϊκῷ, ἀλλ' ἀντὶ δ. γέγραπται 'ἀεί' ‡Hipp. *fr.13 in Pss*.(p.143.3; M.10.720A); cf.Or.*sel.in Pss*.proem.(M.12. 1057C,1060C); Thdt.*Pss*.proem.(1.606,607); marking a change either of metre τὸ δ. διὰ τὰς ἐναλλαγάς προσκεῖσθαι τῶν ῥυθμῶν, οὐχὶ δὲ διὰ τὴν ὑποχώρησιν τοῦ ἁγίου πνεύματος, ὥς τινες ἐφαντάσθησαν †Ath.*fr*.(M.26.1321D); or of singers, Cosm.Ind.*top*.5(M.88.248D); or of theme, Ath.*exp.Ps*.3:5(M.27.69C); Cyr.*Ps*.43:10(M.69.1021C); Hesych.H.*fr.Ps*. 82:9(M.93.1260D); this interprn. rejected by Gr. Nyss.*Pss.titt*.B 10(M.44.533D); = a pause ἔστιν οὖν τὸ δ. ... μεταξὺ τῆς ψαλμῳδίας γενομένη κατὰ τὸ ἀθρόον ἐπηρέμησις, πρὸς ὑποδοχὴν τοῦ θεόθεν ἐπικρινομένου νοήματος...ὡς δ' ἂν μὴ νομισθείη τοῖς πολλοῖς σημεῖον γίνεσθαι τὴν σιωπὴν τοῦ ἐπιλελοιπέναι τὸν προφητεύοντα τὴν τοῦ ἁγίου πνεύματος δύναμιν, τούτου χάριν τινὲς τῶν ἑρμηνέων ἀντὶ τοῦ δ. τὸ 'ἀεί' τοῖς διαλείμμασι τούτοις ἐγγράφουσιν *ib*.(536B); Isid. H.*etym*.6.19.15; **2.** of the portion of the psalm after *selah*, Just. *dial*.47.1(M.6.556B).

διαψεύδω, *deceive*; med., abs., Hipp.*haer*.4.7(p.40.7; M.16.3070B); *ib*.6.21(p.149.10; 3227A); Or.*fr.67 in Jo*.(p.537.11).

διαψηφιστής, ὁ, **1.** *supporter* δ. τῆς ἀσεβείας Bas.*Spir*.42(3.36B; M.32.145B); Nil.*Eulog*.20(M.79.1120A); **2.** *accountant*, (Lat. *rationalis*) Bas.*ep*.215(3.323B; M.32.789D).

***διάψοφος**, s.v.l., *noisy* δ. καὶ σαθρὰς φωνάς CNic.(787)*refut*.(H. 4.424E).

***διάψυχος**, *living*, Areth.*Apoc*.55(M.106.736A).

***διαψυχραίνω**, *grow cool*; of faith, Niceph.Ur.*v.Sym*.139(M.86. 3116A).

δίβουλος, *of two wills*, Max.*opusc*.(M.91.56B) cit. s. θέλημα.

***διγαμέω**, *marry a second time*, Or.*hom.20.4 in Jer*.(p.182.24; M.13.508C); CNeocaes.*can*.7; Anast.S.*hod*.2(M.89.68D).

***διγαμία, ἡ**, *second marriage* οἱ νόμῳ ἀνθρωπίνῳ διγαμίας ποιούμενοι ἁμαρτωλοὶ παρὰ τῷ ἡμετέρῳ διδασκάλῳ εἰσί Just.*1apol*.15.5 (M.6.349B); ref. 1Cor.7:8,9 οὐκ αὐτὸ τοῦτο δ. ἀποφηνάμενος [sc. ὁ Παῦλος] εἶναι καλὸν ἀλλ' ἄμεινον κρίνας τῆς ἐκπυρώσεως Meth.*symp*. 3.12(p.41.7; M.18.80B); condemned by Novatianists τῆς δ. ὡς πορνείας κατηγοροῦσιν Thdt.*1Cor*.8:39(3.212); cf. γάμος.

δίγαμος, *twice married* ἤρξαντο ἐπίσκοποι...καὶ διάκονοι δίγαμοι... καθίστασθαι εἰς κλήρους Hipp.*haer*.9.12(p.249.24; M.16.3386B); μετέχει μὲν σωτηρίας τινὸς καὶ ἡ δ., οὐ μὴν τοσαύτης μακαριότητος, ὅσης παρὸν διγαμεῖν καθαρεύσασα Or.*hom.20.4 in Jer*.(p.182.30; M.13.508C); τοὺς δ. παντελῶς ὁ κανὼν τῆς ὑπηρεσίας ἀπέκλεισε Bas. *ep*.188 *can*.12(3.275C; M.32.681B); cf.Or.*hom.17 in Lc*.(p.121.13; M. 13.1847A); second marriage condemned by Novatianists τοὺς Καθαροὺς...ὁμολογῆσαι...προσήκει...δ. κοινωνεῖν CNic.(325)*can*.8; οἱ Ναυατιανοὶ οἱ περὶ Φρυγίαν διγάμους οὐ δέχονται Socr.*h.e*.5.22.60 (M.67.641A); cf. γάμος.

διγενής, *of twofold generation*, Anast.S.*hod*.7(M.89.117C).

***δίγλυφος**, *carved with two faces* or *facing each way*, Gr.Naz.*carm*. 2.2(poem.)7.136(M.37.1561A); Cosm.Mel.*schol*.ad loc.(M.38.489).

***διγλωσσία, ἡ**, *deceitfulness*, *Did*.2.4 = *Barn*.19.7.

δίγλωσσος, *double-tongued* οὐκ ἔσῃ διγνώμων οὐδὲ δ. *Did*.2.4 = *Barn*.19.7; *Orac.Sib*.3.37; masc. as subst., Socr.*h.e*.1.23.6(M.67. 141B).

δίγνωμος, *of two practical wills*; of Christ, Max.*opusc*.(M.91.56B).

διγνώμων, *of two opinions* οὐκ ἔσῃ δ. *Did*.2.4 = *Barn*.19.7; Hipp. *haer*.10.15(p.276.15; M.16.3431A).

***διγύναιος**, *who has married a second wife*, Ath.*h.Ar*.73(p.223.22; M.25.781B).

δίδαγμα, τό, *instruction, teaching*; plur., of teaching of apostles, Meth.*creat*.1(p.494.2; M.18.333A); †Hipp.*Laz*.12(p.215.24; M.62. 777); ‡Ath.*Apoll*.1.1(M.26.1093B); Oecum.*Apoc*.22:14(p.253); of ten commandments τὰ θεῖα δ. Gr.Nyss.*v.Mos*.45(M.44.316C); of teaching of Christ, Just.*2apol*.2.2(M.6.444A); Cyr.*Jo*.4.3(4.378D); τῶν δεσποτικῶν δ. Thdt.*Trin*.11(M.75.1161C).

διδακτικός, **1.** of persons, *apt at teaching*, Chrys.*hom.6.3 in Eph*. (11.42E); 'δ.' οὐ τὸν εὐγλωττίᾳ λέγει κεκοσμημένον, ἀλλὰ τὸν τὰ θεῖα πεπαιδευμένον, καὶ παραινεῖν δυνάμενον τὰ προσήκοντα Thdt.*1Tim*. 3:2(3.654); τὸν τοῦ νόμου δ. ‡Meth.*Sym.et Ann*.5(M.18.360B); **2.** met., *instructive* δ. ... τὴν σοφίαν Clem.*str*.1.5(p.20.8; M.8. 724B); Cyr.H.*catech*.21.7; Gr.Nyss.*tres dii*(M.45.128D).

***διδακτικῶς**, *as a teacher, instructively*, Or.*fr.46 in Jo*.(p.521.30); κηρυττέτω δὲ τὴν εὐαγγελικὴν ὁ λόγος πίστιν ἁπλοϊκῶς οὕτω καὶ δ. Thdt.*Trin*.2(M.75.1149B); ‡Cyr.*Trin*.23(6^3.28E; M.77.1164C).

διδακτός, *taught, learnt*; of persons (ref. Jo.6:45) *taught, instructed* δ. θεοῦ γεγονότες Cyr.*Ps*.22:1(M.69.840C).

***διδάκτρια, ἡ**, *mistress*; of Eve, ‡Chrys.*hom.3.3 in Gen*.(6.547A); ὦ πόσων κακῶν Εὔα δ. ‡Chrys.*hom.in Ps.92*:3(5.623D).

***διδακτῶς**, *by means of teaching* or *instruction*, Cyr.*Ps*.44:1(M.69. 1028C); κεῖται γὰρ ἐν ἀμφοῖν [sc. Father and Son] ἡ ἑκατέρου γνῶσις ἀκριβής, οὐ δ. ἀλλὰ φυσικῶς id.*Jo*.2.6(4.223A); id.*thes*.15(5^1.152A).

διδασκαλεῖον, τό, **1.** *teaching-place*, of a church τὸ καθ' ἡμᾶς δ. Ath.*ep.encycl*.6(p.176.10; M.25.236C); **2.** *school of thought* ὁ Πλάτων ...συνέστησε τὸ δ. Hipp.*haer*.1.18(p.19.2; M.16.3041A); Or.*Cels*.3.51 (p.247.20; M.11.988B); Eus.*h.e*.4.7.3(M.20.316C); **3.** *teaching, doctrine*, Just.*2apol*.2.13(M.6.445B); Iren.*haer*.1.27.2(M.7.688A); Chrys. *hom.4.6 in Ac.princ*.(3.89E); **4.** *position* or *office of teacher* οὐκ ἐμὸν ...τὸ δ. σήμερον ‡Meth.*palm*.2(M.18.385B).

διδασκαλία, ἡ, **1.** *teaching, instruction*; **a.** of Christ τὴν διδασκαλίαν τοῦ σωτῆρος, ἥτις ἐστὶ βρῶμα ἡμῶν πνευματικόν Clem.*str*. 7.16(p.73.27; M.9.544B); ἀδύνατόν ἐστιν ἄνευ τῆς τούτου δ. ἀληθείᾳ σωζούσῃ ἐπιστῆναι *Hom.Clem*.3.54; Ath.*gent*.1(M.25.4A); of apostles, Clem.*str*.7.17(p.76.23; M.9.552C) cit. s. παράδοσις; πίστις ...ἐκ δ. ἀποστολικῆς ὁρμωμένη καὶ παραδόσεως τῶν πατέρων, βεβαιουμένη ἔκ τε νέας καὶ παλαιᾶς διαθήκης Ath.*ep.Adelph*.6(M.26. 1080A); and of their successors σῴζοντες διδασκαλίας παράδοσιν εὐθὺς ἀπὸ τῶν...ἀποστόλων Clem.*str*.1.1(p.9.4; M.8.700A); τὴν ἐξ ἀρχῆς παράδοσιν καὶ δ. καὶ πίστιν τῆς καθολικῆς ἐκκλησίας, ἣν ὁ μὲν κύριος ἔδωκεν, οἱ δὲ ἀπόστολοι ἐκήρυξαν, καὶ οἱ πατέρες ἐφύλαξαν Ath.*ep.Serap*.1.28(M.26.593D); *Symb.Nic*.(787)(H.4.456B); of scripture opp. tradition, v. παράδοσις; gen. of Christian teaching, esp. of orthodox faith, Clem.*str*.7.2(p.9.19; M.9.416A); τῇ ἐκκλησιαστικῇ δ. Eus.*Marcell*.1.3(p.17.29; M.24.749D); Ath.*gent*.1(M.25. 4B); but also of heret. teaching, Ign.*Eph*.17.1; Clem.*ecl*.29(p.146. 8; M.9.713B); Ath.*apol.sec*.77(p.156.30; M.25.388A); as function of bishops, Hipp.*haer*.1 proem.(p.3.4; M.16.3020C) cit. s. διάδοχος; *Clem.ep*.2(M.2.36A); v. ἐπίσκοπος; **b.** in title of work καθολικὴ δ. περὶ λαϊκῶν *Const.App*.1.1 tit.; **c.** in teaching of Arius ref. creative Logos ἡ σοφία τοῦ θεοῦ ἐκ δ. ἐκτήσατο τὸ δημιουργεῖν Ath. *Ar*.2.28(M.26.208A); denied by Athanasius οὐκ ἐκ δ. γέγονε δημιουργὸς ὁ λόγος *ib*.2.29(208A); **2.** *statement*, of a formal petition, CChalc.*act*.14(*ACO* 2.1.3 p.65.27; H.2.573B).

διδασκαλικός, **1.** *of* or *for teaching, instructive*; ref. H. Ghost, Eun.*apol*.25(M.30.861D) cit. s. δημιουργικός; **2.** *characteristic of* or *belonging to a teacher* τὴν δ. τῆς παραδόσεως φροντίδα Clem.*ecl*.27 (p.144.27; M.9.712B); Chrys.*comm.in Gal*.6:6(10.725A); id.*hom.3.5 in Heb*.(12.34B); of office or position of teacher τὸν δ. θρόνον Meth. *lepr*.12(p.466.10); Chrys.*hom.67.2 in Mt*.(7.663C); *ib.72.3*(704B); **3.** neut. as subst., *formal statement* or *document*, CChalc.*act*.14 (*ACO* 2.1.3 p.64.34,35; H.2.572D); CSyr.*act*.(*ACO* 3 p.93.7,9,12; H.2. 1365C,D); CCP(536)*act*.1(*ACO* 3 p.134.6; H.2.1197E).

διδασκάλιον, τό, **1.** *instruction, teaching*, Rhod.ap.Eus.*h.e*. 5.13.4(M.20.460C); Bas.*hom*.24.2(2.190D; M.31.604A); Pall.*v.Chrys*.8 (p.47.5; M.47.28); **2.** *school* πάσης τῆς οἰκουμένης ἦσαν [sc. prophets] δ. ἱερὸν τῆς περὶ θεοῦ γνώσεως Ath.*inc*.12.5(M.25.117B).

διδάσκαλος, ὁ, *teacher*; **1.** in gen., of apostles τῶν κοινῶν τῆς οἰκουμένης δ. Chrys.*hom.in Philm*.proem.(11.773B); of S. Paul, *A.Xanthipp*.7(p.62.11); of S. Peter, †Jo.D.*B.J*.11(M.96.960B); of Chrysostom, Thdt.*h.e*.5.32.8(3.1072); of bishops, *M.Polyc*.16.2; v. ἐπίσκοπος; of Christ, Just.*1apol*.12.9(M.6.345A); *A.Petr.et Andr*.8

(p.121.21); Chrys.*hom.79.2 in Jo.*(8.468B); **2.** as an order in Church προφητῶν καὶ δ. *Did.*15.1,2; Herm.*vis.*3.5.1; Clem.*ecl.*23(p.143.6; M.9.708D).

διδάσκ-ω, **1.** *teach*; of Christ, Polyc.*ep.*2.3; τὸν υἱόν...τὸν τὴν ἀλήθειαν περὶ τοῦ θεοῦ διδάξαντα Clem.*str.*7.10(p.43.2; M.9.481C); ὁ σωτὴρ τοὺς ἀποστόλους ἐδίδασκεν, τὰ μὲν πρῶτα τυπικῶς καὶ μυστικῶς, τὰ δὲ ὕστερα παραβολικῶς καὶ ἠνιγμένως, τὰ δὲ τρίτα σαφῶς καὶ γυμνῶς κατὰ μόνας id.*exc.Thdot.*66(p.128.24; M.9.689C); Ath.*inc.*14.6(M.25.121B); in gen., of those teaching Christian faith, Herm.*vis.*3.5.1; Ath.*gent.*46(M.25.93B); esp. of bishops, v. ἐπίσκοπος; of scripture, id.*Ar.*1.36(M.26.85D); *Symb.Sirm.*3 ap.Ath. *syn.*8(p.236.15; M.26.693C); *Symb.Ant.*(345)*ib.*26(729A); of God in Arian theology ὡς δὲ παρὰ διδασκάλου καὶ τεχνίτου μεμάθηκε τὸ δημιουργεῖν [sc. ὁ λόγος] καὶ οὕτως ὑπηρέτησε τῷ διδάξαντι θεῷ Ath. *Ar.*2.28(M.26.205C); **2.** *demonstrate, give proof of*, id.*apol.sec.*45 (p.120.26; M.25.328B); Thdt.*Ps.*19:1(1.725); id.*Jon.*3:10(2.1473); **3.** *give directions* or *orders* βασιλέων ἴδιον τὸ δ., τὸ δὲ ~εσθαι τῶν ἀρχομένων id.*Ps.*118:100(1.1463).

διδαχή, ἡ, *teaching*; **1.** of Christian teaching or doctrine, *Barn.* 16.9; Just.*dial.*35.8(M.6.553A); Gr.Nyss.*or.catech.*proem.(p.1.4; M. 45.10A); **2.** title of work δ. κυρίου διὰ τῶν δώδεκα ἀποστόλων τοῖς ἔθνεσιν *Did.*tit.; Ath.*ep.Amun.*(M.26.1177D); plur., Eus.*h.e.*3.25.4 (M.20.269A).

***διδί,** (Hebr. יְדִידִי) *my beloved, Dial.Tim.et Aquil.*83 r°.

διδυμεύ-ω, *bear twins*, exeg. Cant.4:2 ~ουσαι δὲ ἄλλως, διὰ τὸ διττὸν τῆς νοήσεως τῆς τερπνῆς (sic) καὶ πνευματικῆς Or.*schol.in Cant.*4:2(M.17.269D); ~ειν τῇ μὲν ψυχῇ τὴν ἀπάθειαν, τῷ δὲ σωματικῷ βίῳ τὴν εὐσχημοσύνην γεννῶντας Gr.Nyss.ap.Proc.G.*Cant.*4:2 (M.87.1641C), cf.Gr.Nyss.*hom.7 in Cant.*(M.44.928B); Nil.ap.Proc. G.*Cant.*4:2(1644A).

διδυμοτοκία, ἡ, *production of twins*, met. μηκέτι εἴπῃς...εἰ... προήγαγεν ὁ πατὴρ...τὰ ἀμφότερα [sc. Son and H. Ghost] ἅμα, ἆρα ἂν ἀδελφοθεῖα καὶ δ. ἐστιν ἐν τῇ τριάδι; ‡Gr.Nyss.*imag.*(M.44. 1340D); Nil.ap.Proc.G.*Cant.*4:2(M.87.1644A).

διδυμοτόκος, *producing twins*, Bas.*hex.*9.5(1.85A; M.29.200A); Gr.Nyss.*hom.7 in Cant.*(M.44.925B,928B); εἰ δὲ ἐν τῷ ἅμα προῆλθον [sc. Son and H. Ghost] εὔδηλον ὅτι δ. ἐστὶν ὁ πατὴρ Anast.S.*hod.*22 (M.89.288B).

***διδυμοφυῶς,** *in twofold nature*; ref. Inc., Anast.S.*hex.*12(M.89. 1053B).

***διδύσκω,** *sink back* πάλιν τὸ ὕδωρ ἐδίδυσκεν εἰς τὸν τόπον αὐτοῦ *V.Zos.*6(p.100.4); *ib.*11(p.104.5).

δίδωμι, [pres. indic. δίδει *Poen.App.*1.17; διδόαμεν Or.*comm. in Gen.*ap.Eus.*p.e.*6.11(288A; M.12.65A); Chrys.*hom.40.2 in 1Cor.* (10.380D); Jo.Jej.*poenit.cont.virg.*(M.88.1956D); infin. δίδειν †Jo.Jej. *poenit.*(M.88.1912D); ptcpl. διδοῦντες Jo.Mal.*chron.*18 p.443(M.97. 653A); imper. δίδος Jo.Mosch.*prat.*195(M.87.3077D); aor. ptcpl. δώσας *ib.*186(3064C); δόσας Jo.Mal.*chron.*2 p.26(M.97.92B); subj. δώσῃς Eus.Al.*serm.*8(M.86.361B)]; *give*; **1.** *administer* Communion οὐ δεῖ ὑπηρέτην ἄρτον διδόναι CLaod.*can.*25; **2.** ptcpl., *supporter, benefactor*, abs., of those who maintain Church widows, *Const. App.*3.5.2; **3.** of God; **a.** abs. ἑτοιμότερον γὰρ ἑαυτὸν λέγει ὁ κύριος εἰς τὸ διδόναι τοῦ αἰτοῦντος *2Clem.*15.4; pass., of spiritual gifts εἰρήνη...ἐδέδοτο πᾶσιν *1Clem.*2.2; τὴν δοθεῖσαν ὑμῖν πίστιν Polyc. *ep.*3.2; Gel.Cyz.*h.e.*2.7.4(M.85.1233A); of H. Ghost, given by Father through Son, or by Son ἐγὼ λόγος ὢν τοῦ πατρὸς αὐτὸς ἐμαυτῷ ἀνθρώπῳ γενομένῳ δίδωμι τὸ πνεῦμα Ath.*Ar.*1.46(M.26.108B); Μωυσεῖ μὲν ἐδίδου καὶ τοῖς ἄλλοις τοῖς Ἑβδομήκοντα [sc. ὁ λόγος τὸ πνεῦμα] *ib.*1.48(112B); ὁ αὐτός [sc. Christ] ἐστι διδοὺς καὶ λαμβάνων, διδοὺς μὲν ὡς θεοῦ λόγος, λαμβάνων δὲ ὡς ἄνθρωπος *ib.* (112C); ὁ τὸ πνεῦμα διδοὺς κύριος *ib.*1.50(116A); διὰ τίνος δὲ καὶ παρὰ τίνος ἔδει τὸ πνεῦμα δίδοσθαι ἢ διὰ τοῦ υἱοῦ, οὗ καὶ τὸ πνεῦμά ἐστι; *ib.*(117A); τὸ πνεῦμα...παρὰ τοῦ πατρὸς δι' υἱοῦ δίδοσθαι πεπιστεύκαμεν id.*ep.Serap.*4.6(M.26.645D); **b.** *grant, allow* ὡς ἡ τοῦ θεοῦ χάρις ἔδωκεν Cyr.H.*catech.*19.9; θεοῦ διδόντος Gr.Nyss.*engast.* (p.63.21; M.45.108B); *ib.*(p.68.19; 113C); **4.** catachrestically for παραδίδωμι: τοὺς ἐν μετάλλοις ἐπὶ τιμωρίᾳ δεδομένους Eus.*h.e.*9.1.7 (M.20.801A); id.*m.P.*5(p.919.5; M.20.1480A); **5.** met.; **a.** *offer* prayers αἱ γὰρ [παρ'] ὑμῶν διδόμεναι εὐχαί *PLond.*1929.7 [saec. iv]; **b.** *render, show*, Hegem.*Arch.*10(p.16.11; M.10.1444A); **c.** *offer, dedicate* δῶμεν ἑαυτούς [sc. τῷ θεῷ] Cyr.H.*procatech.*9; **6.** c. νοεῖν *give* or *cause* one to understand ὁ λόγος...νοεῖν δίδωσι Gr.Nyss.*hex.* 1.16(M.44.79A); *ib.*1.18(81A); Chrys.*hom.2.1 in 2Thess.*(11.515C); **7.** *put forward, recommend* a candidate for office, id.*sac.*3.15(p.81. 16; 1.394E); **8.** c. dat., *strike, give a blow to*, *T.Jud.*3.3; Jo.Mosch. *prat.*15(M.87.2861D); Leont.N.*v.Sym.*33(M.93.1712B); *Chron.Pasch.* p.383(M.92.981B); also c. acc., Jo.Mosch.*prat.*70(M.87.2924B); **9.** *sound forth* ἡ φωνὴ ἔδωκεν διὰ...τῆς πόλεως *T.Job* 40(p.129.22).

διεγγυάω, med., met., *asseverate*, Synes.*ep.*132(M.66.1517C).

διεγείρ-ω, **1.** *arouse, stimulate*; met., Or.*Cels.*4.44(p.317.9; M.11. 1100C); Eus.*v.C.*1.10(p.12.11; M.20.924A); Chrys.*hom.2.6 in Col.* (11.342E); of God ὁ κύριος...~ων, νουθετῶν Clem.*prot.*9(p.63.16; M.8.196A); ὁ σωτὴρ...ἐπὶ τὸν ἔλεον τὸν ἡμέτερον ~ει τὸν πατέρα Cyr. *Ps.*68:19(M.69.248C); **2.** *raise up*, Chrys.*hom.18.1 in 2Cor.*(10. 564C,D); *cat.2Cor.*8:16(p.404.15); **3.** med. and pass.; **a.** *stand upright*, Ath.*v.Anton.*8(M.26.856B); **b.** met., *arouse oneself, be aroused*, *A.Petr.et Paul.*32(p.193.8); Chrys.*hom.34.1 in Jo.*(8.195A); *ib.45.4* (274D); hence *arise* εὔχεται τὸν μονογενῆ...διεγερθῆναι Cyr.*Ps.*9:20 (M.69.776C); **c.** ptcpl. neut. as subst., τὸ διεγηγερμένον *liveliness, vehemence*, Or.*hom.15.1 in Jer.*(p.125.19; M.13.429A); fig., ref. Jo. 4:14 οὕτω δὲ τὸ πνεῦμα καλεῖ...τὸ δ. καὶ θερμὸν τῆς χάριτος Chrys. *hom.31.1 in Jo.*(8.184A).

διέγερσις, ἡ, *arousing*; **1.** met. τὴν τῆς προσοχῆς δ. Vict.*Mc.*4:34 (p.312.3); τὴν...εἰς τὸ ἀγαθὸν δ. Proc.G.*Cant.*8:5(M.87.1772C); **2.** meton., of a *rousing cry*, Thphn.*chron.*p.254(M.108.636A).

διεγερτικός, *stimulating* ἐπιστολὴ...δ. πίστεως Eus.*h.e.*4.23.2 (M.20.384B); ἡ τοῦ κυρίου ἐπιφάνεια δ. ... [sc. ἐστί] τῶν τῆς ψυχῆς ἰδιωμάτων Bas.*ep.*260.7(3.400A; M.32.964D); neut. as subst. τῆς ἐπιστολῆς τὸ...δ. πρὸς ζήτησιν τῆς ἀληθείας Nicol.*ep.*(M.65.1052C).

***διεγκαρτερέω,** Dion.Al.*ep.can.*1(M.10.1277A) error for ἐγκαρτερέω (p.101.5).

***διεγκολπίζομαι,** *carry in the heart*, Nil.*epp.*3.252(M.79.505A).

***διεγχειρέω,** *attempt, undertake*, Thphyl.*exc.gent.*5(p.482.32; M. 113.944A).

δίεδρος, *pure, undefiled*; superl., Pyrr.ap.CLater.*act.*3(H.3. 801B).

διεζευγμένως, *distinctively* ἐὰν δ. λέγωμεν τὸν υἱὸν ποτὲ μὲν υἱὸν τοῦ πατρὸς ποτὲ δὲ υἱὸν τοῦ θεοῦ ἀλλὰ δ. αὐτὸν οὐδέποτε νοοῦμεν ‡Just.*qu.et resp.*18(M.6.1264D).

διειδής, *transparent, clear*; **1.** met. τὸ δ. νᾶμα τοῦ βίου Bas.*hom.* 21.11(2.172D; M.31.561B); Gr.Nyss.*v.Mos.*(M.44.345A); τῆς...διδασκαλίας τὸ δ. Thdt.*qu.110 in Gen.*(1.116); **2.** of an eye, *clear, unobscured*, Chrys.*hom.90.4 in Mt.*(7.844A); superl., Jo.D.*dialect.*1 (M.94.529C); **3.** *intelligible*, Clem.*str.*6.15(p.490.18; M.9.340C).

διεκβολή, ἡ, **1.** *source* or *spring* of a river, Or.*Jo.*10.32(18; p.206. 11; M.14.365A); Epiph.*haer.*4.1(p.181.10; M.41.197A); met., *origin* τοῖς οὐκ ἄναρχον ἔχουσιν εἰς τὸ εἶναι δ. Cyr.*ador.*6(1.205C); **2.** *side-channel, secondary river*, Meth.*res.*1.55(p.313.11; M.41.1148B); fig. δ. ἐργάζονται, παροχετεύοντες τὴν θείαν διδασκαλίαν Olymp.*fr.Jer.* 12:14(M.93.656B); hence *offshoot* of a vine, Cyr.*Mich.*61(3.454B); *speech* or *address inserted* [i.e. in a narrative] ἔχεται πάλιν τῆς τοῦ θεοῦ δ.· καί φησιν, ὡς πρός γε τὴν τῶν Ἰουδαίων συναγωγήν id.*Is.*3.3 (2.464D).

διεκδικ-έω, **1.** *vindicate, claim justice for, defend*, Chrys.*hom.17.7 in Mt.*(7.233B); Cyr.*Jo.*6(4.571E); ἐπιστολαὶ...ἐν αἷς εὕρηνται ποικίλαι βλασφημίαι τοὺς περὶ Ἄρειον ~οῦσαι CNic.(787)*refut.*(H.4.409A); **2.** *avenge* ~ῶν ὁ θεὸς τὸν ἑαυτοῦ θεράποντα...θάνατον ἐπήγαγεν Anast.S.*qu.et resp.*62(M.89.648D); **3.** *claim for oneself* οἷα τυραννίδας τὰς φιλαρχίας ~οῦντες Eus.*h.e.*8.1.8(M.20.741C); CSard.*can.*19; *Cod.Afr.*56.

***διεκδικία, ἡ,** *penalty*, Jo.Scholast.*coll.cap.*66 tit.

***διέκδοσις, ἡ,** *cat.Apoc.*20:1(p.469.31) error for διέκδυσις, Areth. *Apoc.*60(M.106.749B).

διεκδρομή, ἡ, *an issuing forth*; **1.** *stream* of water τὰς τῶν ῥείθρων δ. Philost.*h.e.*3.9(M.65.492C); **2.** *course* or *passage*; of time, Clem.*paed.*2.9(p.204.19; M.8.489B); Cyr.*ador.*6(1.206A); of events τὰ μεγάλα...τῶν πραγμάτων...οὐκ ἀθαύμαστον ἔχει τὴν εἰς πέρας δ. id.*Zach.*41(3.717A); **3.** of generation of Son Παῦλος...δεικνὺς τὴν ἐκ πατρὸς οἱονεί πως εἰς τὸ ἔξω δ. id.ap.*cat.Heb.*1:3 suppl.(p.301.21).

[*]**διεκδύν-ω,** (cf. διεκδύομαι *LS*) *escape from* ~αι τὴν νόσον Cyr. *ador.*15(1.526B); id.*Os.*97(3.129B); Olymp.*Eccl.*7:19(M.93.569B); c. genit., Cyr.*Zach.*92(3.780B).

***διεκθλίβω,** *press, constrain*, pass., ‡Caes.Naz.*dial.*191(M.38.1169).

διεκθρώσκω, *leap out from*; met., c. genit., Clem.*prot.*2(p.19.2; M.8. 93B); abs., Meth.*symp.*6.3(p.67.14; M.18.117B).

***διεκκαλέω,** *summon*; pass., *Cod.Afr.*28.

διεκλάμπω, *flash forth*, Andr.Cr.*or.*17(M.97.1176A).

***διεκνεύω,** *avoid, shun*; c. genit., Cyr.*ador.*1(1.26A); c. acc., id. *Nah.*33(3.511D); c. infin., id.*Mich.*64(3.459A).

***διεκνήφω,** *become sober*, Cyr.*Os.*88(3.120A).

διεκπίπτω, c. genit., *miss* or *fail to attain*; a goal, Anast.S.*haer.*

(p.258); an object of prayer πάσης διεξέπεσες τῆς εὐχῆς Ephr. 3.456E.

***διεκπλήσσομαι**, *be panic-stricken*, Tit.Bost.*Man*.2.38(M.18.1208A).

***διεκσείω**, *drive out*, Eus.*d.e*.4.9(p.162.30; M.22.272B).

***διέκτασις**, ἡ, *stretching* [sc. oneself], Clem.*paed*.2.9(p.207.19; M.8.469B).

διεκτελέω, **1.** *accomplish*, Evagr.*h.e*.1.21(p.32.4; M.86.2481C); **2.** *spend* one's life, Chrysipp.*enc.in BMV* 2(p.337.33).

διεκτρέχω, *run out of the way*, Cyr.*ador*.15(1.523C).

***διεκφάντωρ**, ὁ, *one who makes clear* or *sheds light upon*, Ephr. 2.268D.

***διέκχυσις**, ἡ, v. πρόσχυσις.

***διέλαιος**, *with two wicks* ἄναψον λύχνους ἑπτὰ δ. *T.Abr*.A 4(p.80.24).

διελαύνω, **1.** *pass through*, met. οἱ...εἰς τὸ τῆς ἀληθείας διελάσαντες φῶς Cyr.*Ps*.47:12(M.69.1064C); τοὺς εἰς κατάληξιν ἤδη καιρῶν διεληλακότας id.*ador*.17(1.618C); **2.** *arrive at*, met. τοσοῦτον...διήλαυνεν ἀτοπίας ἡ...θέα Eus.*v.C*.2.61(p.66.14; M.20.1036B).

***διελεγκτικός**, *capable of refuting*; c. genit., Clem.*str*.6.11(p.477.16; M.9.312B).

***διελεγκτικῶς**, *in complete refutation*, Epiph.*haer*.76.37(p.388.1; M.42.592D).

διέλευσις, ἡ, *transit, passing* δ. τῶν ἡμερῶν Evagr.*h.e*.1.4(p.9.11; M.86.2429A).

***διέμπαιγμα**, τό, *illusion, deceit*, ‡Chrys.*hom.in Ps*.92:3(5.623C).

***διεμπράσσω**, *perform* τὰ παράδοξα ἔργα διεμπεπραγμένα Eus.*Is*.49:4(M.24.432C).

διενεκτέον, *one must dispute*, Synes.*regn*.21(p.51.1; M.66.1097B).

διένεξις, ἡ, *difference, disagreement*, Leont.H.*monoph*.testimonia (M.86.1805A); ‡Proc.G.*Pr*.25:8–10(M.87.1473B,1504A); Jo.VI CP *ep*.(M.96.1432B).

***διενηνεγμένως**, *separately* εἰς μίαν δ' οὖν ὅμως θεότητα φυσικῶς ἀναφέροντες αὐτά, καὶ τὸ πάντη δ. εἶναι νοεῖν παραιτούμενοι Cyr.*Jo*.1.5(4.46E).

διενθυμέομαι, **1.** *hold an opinion, think, consider*, trans., Const. ap.Eus.*v.C*.3.60(p.107.13; M.20.1129B); Cyr.*Nest*.2.3(p.38.30; 6^1.39E); id.*Jo*.5.4(4.508A); c. dependent clause, *ib*.(516B); id.*inc.unigen*.(5^1.686C); **2.** *take into consideration, ponder*, id.*Ps*.44:3(M.69.1032C); *ib*.86:6(1208D); †Jo.D.*B.J*.5(M.96.893D).

***διενιζάνω**, *settle, deposit oneself on* or *in*, ‡Caes.Naz.*dial*.140(M.38.1053).

διενοχλέω, *be annoying*, c. dat., *LS*; **1.** abs., Eus.*v.C*.3.5(p.79.9; M.20.1057D); Chrys.*hom.3.6 in Jo*.(8.25B); Isid.Pel.*epp*.2.62(M.78.505A); **2.** trans., *annoy*, Gr.Nyss.*usur*.(M.46.452A); Chrys.*hom.65.5 in Mt*.(7.651B); id.*hom.4.2 in Tit*.(11.752A).

***διεντέλλω**, *enjoin*, Max.*schol.d.n*.1.5(M.4.209C).

***διεξαγορεύω**, *proclaim publicly*, Eus.*Hierocl*.48(544D, v.l. ἐξαγ- M.22.865D).

διεξάγ-ω, **A.** act.; **1.** *extend* application of a term, Epiph.*haer*.30.22(p.364.4; M.41.444B); **2.** *order, arrange*, Jo.Mon.*hymn.Bas*.1(M.96.1372A); ~ων δὲ τοῦ βίου τὸν ἄξονα [sc. ὁ θεός] Geo.Pis.*hex*.341(M.92.1460A); pass., *be arranged* or *administered*, Gr.Nyss.*or*.28.16(p.47.3; M.36.48A); cf.‡Cyr.*Trin*.2(6^3.3C; M.77.1124B); **3.** *lead, pass* one's life, Clem.*str*.4.20(p.304.21; M.8.1337B); Gr.Nyss.*anim.et res*.(M.46.108C); med., Max.*ambig*.(M.91.1057C); abs., *live*, Clem.*str*.2.15(p.150.11; M.8.1008C); **4.** pass., *be perpetuated* πρὸς τὸ διηνεκὲς τὸ γένος ἡμῶν ~εται Gr.Nyss.*or.catech*.28(p.107.9; M.45.73C); **5.** of a trial, *be conducted*, *Const.App*.2.17.2.

B. med.; **1.** *pass from*, Gr.Nyss.*tres dii*(M.45.128A) cit. s. θέλημα; **2.** *go out against* in battle, c. acc., Areth.*Apoc*.54(M.106.724B).

διεξαγωγή, ἡ, **1.** *performance, execution*, Cyr.*Jo*.4.7(4.431C); **2.** *administration, direction* of universe by God, Max.*ambig*.(M.91.1121A); *ib*.(1176C); βούλησις θεοῦ, δι' ἣν πάντα...τὴν πρόσφορον δ. λαμβάνει *ib*.(1189B); **3.** *arrangement* of a literary work, Dion.Al. ap.Eus.*h.e*.7.25.8(M.20.697D); **4.** *way of living, life; mode of existence*, of God τὸ ἀκίνητον...τῆς τοῦ θεοῦ δ. Bas.*Spir*.15(3.12E; M.32.93A).

διεξανύω, *accomplish; complete*, a course in a race, Eus.*l.C*.6(p.207.21; M.20.1344A); one's life, id.*v.C*.1.17(p.16.21; M.20.933A).

διεξέρχομαι, *go completely through*; met., *accomplish*, Olymp. *Eccl*.7:19(M.93.569A); ‡Proc.G.*Pr*.24:27(M.87.1468D); †Gregent. *leg.Hom*.(M.86.584A,B).

***διεξέτασις**, ἡ, *legal inquiry* or *examination*, ‡Chrys.*hom.in Ps*.95:1(5.636E).

***διεξηχέω**, *utter*, †Gregent.*disp*.(M.86.746C).

[*]διεξιτητέον, *one must go through, investigate*, Eus.*Hierocl*.42(537D; M.22.853C).

διεξοδεύω, **1.** *investigate* a subject *thoroughly*, Or.*Cels*.3.67(p.260.13; M.11.1009A); Gr.Nyss.*or.catech*.21(p.82.12; M.45.60A); Max. *ambig*.(M.91.1232A); **2.** *speak at length concerning, give a full account of*, Eus.*e.th*.3.3(p.153.29; M.24.996C); id.*d.e*.10.8(p.490.11; M.22.788A); *ib*.5.2(p.217.26; 360A); **3.** *meditate*, Or.*Jo*.2.32(26; p.89.25; M.14.169D); **4.** *carry through to the end, accomplish*, *cat. Apoc*.10:1(p.327.23).

διεξοδικός, **1.** *describing* or *narrating in detail*, Clem.*str*.1.8(p.26.10; M.8.736B); †Bas.*Is*.164(1.496B; M.30.389A); Olymp.*Eccl*.7:12(M.93.565B); hence *detailed*, *LS*; comp., Max.*myst*.(M.91.708B); *diffuse*, Gr.Nyss.*Eun*.4(2 p.81.17; M.45.656C); **2.** *flowing continually* μόνη ἡ νύμφη δ. ἐν ἑαυτῇ ἔχει τὸ ὕδωρ Gr.Nyss.*hom.9 in Cant*.(M.44.977C); **3.** *departing, leaving this world* τοῦ καθ' ἑαυτὸν δ. τέλους Euthal.Diac.*epp.Paul*.(M.85.705B).

διέξοδος, ἡ, **1.** *going forth*; of martyrs entering arena and running the gauntlet of whips at the entrance ὑπέφερον...τὰς δ. τῶν μαστίγων *Ep.Lugd*.ap.Eus.*h.e*.5.1.38(M.20.424A); met. τὴν...πρὸς τὸ τέλος δ. τῆς ζωῆς ‡Proc.G.*Pr*.30:12(M.87.1525D); **2.** *emission, expression* φωνὴ ἡ φθάνουσα πρὸς θεὸν...ἐστι...ἡ τοῦ ἡγεμονικοῦ καθαρὰ...δ. τῶν πρὸς θεὸν ἀναπεμπομένων λόγων Or.*sel.in Ps*.4:4(M.12.1141B); **3.** *discussion* ἡ...περὶ τῶν νοηθέντων λογικὴ δ. ... διαλεκτικὴ λέγεται Clem.*str*.6.17(p.512.9; M.9.388B); **4.** *process of discernment* 'ἡ διάνοια', ἥτις ἐστὶν δ. λογική Or.*comm.in Eph*.4:18(p.416).

***διεξοίχομαι**, *escape from*, Cyr.*ador*.8(1.271B); *ib*.14(1.504A).

***διεξομολογέομαι**, *make a confession*, Ph.Carp.*Cant*.131(M.40.101A).

***διεξωθέω**, *drive back, repel*, Chrys.*hom.3.4 in 1Thess*.(11.445E).

***διεπαγγέλλω**, *promise faithfully* τὸ πάλαι διεπηγγελμένον διὰ φωνῆς Ἡσαΐου Cyr.*ador*.9(1.319E).

διέπ-ω, *conduct, manage, administer*; **1.** of God ordering the universe, Meth.*symp*.8.16(p.105.11; M.18.168D); Ath.*gent*.36(M.25.72C); *ib*.43(172C); **2.** *hold, occupy* a position or office, Diod.*Ps*.88:29(M.33.1622A); Eudoc.*Cypr*.1.308(M.85.844C); Proc.G.*Is*.16:1–5(M.87.2108C); of a bishop ~ων τὸν τόπον τῆς ἐπισκοπῆς Alex.H.*fr*.ap. Eus.*h.e*.6.11.3(M.20.544A); Gel.Cyz.*h.e*.2.10.1(M.85.1245C); Evagr. *h.e*.1.4(p.9.3; M.86.2428B).

***διεργής**, s.v.l., *vigilant*, *A.Jo*.69(p.184.10).

διερείδ-ω, *support*, met. ὀστᾶ...λέγει τοὺς σώφρονας λογισμούς, τοὺς τὴν ψυχὴν ~οντας Cyr.*Ps*.6:3(M.69.744C).

διερευνητικός, *fit for examining* or *investigating*, Gr.Nyss.*hom. opif*.5.2(M.44.137C).

***διερινέω**, v. [*]διαρρινέω.

διερμηνεύ-ω, *interpret*; med., *reveal oneself*, of God τὸν...~όμενον τοῖς ἁγίοις Serap.*euch*.13.4.

διέρπ-ω, **1.** *pass* or *progress* to ἐξ ὁμοιώσεων...ὁ λόγος τῶν σωματικῶν ~ει...ἐπὶ τὰ νοητά Cyr.*ador*.16(1.574D); **2.** of persons, *reach, attain* ἀρετῆς εἰς τοῦτο ~ειν *ib*.9(312D); *ib*.15(523B); **3.** *extend* or *apply* to ὁ νόμος...εἰς πάντα ~ει χρόνον *ib*.12(413C).

***διερρέω**, *waste away*, Ast.Am.*hom*.1(M.40.172A).

διερριμμένως, *disconnectedly*, Clem.*str*.1.12(p.36.4; M.8.753B); *ib*. 7.18(p.78.20; M.9.556C).

***διερυθραίνομαι**, *become very red*, Gr.Nyss.*v.Mos*.(M.44.417D).

διέρχομαι, **1.** *pass through*; in Bardesanes' Christology ὥσπερ...ὕδωρ διὰ σωλῆνος διέρχεται, μηδὲν προσλαμβάνον, οὕτω καὶ ὁ λόγος διὰ Μαρίας καὶ οὐκ ἐκ Μαρίας Adam.*dial*.5.9(p.191.25; M.11.1845A); Cyr.H.*catech*.4.9; **2.** *go through* district or world, *go about*, of God ὁ θεὸς...ὃς διῆλθεν διὰ τοῦ δούλου αὐτοῦ εὐεργετῶν πάντας *A.Andr*.A 10(p.52.11).

διερωτητέον, *one must ask*, Anast.S.*hod*.13(M.89.207B).

διεσθί-ω, *eat, consume*; of persons, Bas.Sel.*or*.6.3(M.85.93A); of animals, Or.*hom.10.8 in Jer*.(p.78.14; M.13.368A); met. τὰς καρδίας ~ομένας ὑπὸ τῶν δυνάμεων τῶν ἀντικειμένων *ib*.(p.78.15; 368B); καθάπερ...τὸν σῖτον ὁ σὴς...οὕτω τὰς...ψυχὰς ἡ ὠμότης...διέφαγε Chrys.*hom.15.8 in 1Cor*.(10.375D); id.*hom.10.3 in Eph*.(11.78E); of fire, *consume*, Gr.Nyss.*hex*.12(M.44.76A).

διεσμιλευμένως, *in polished style*, Cyr.*glaph.Gen*.2(1.48B); id.*inc. unigen*.(5^1.678C).

διεσπαρμένως, *in a disjointed manner, disconnectedly*, Or.*princ*. 4.6(p.332.5; M.11.386C); Chrys.*hom.12.6 in 1Cor*.(10.267D); Gennad. *fr.Rom*.9:32–33(M.85.1712B); *intermittently*, Chrys.*hom.15.4 in 1Cor*.(10.356B).

διεσπασμένως, **1.** *separately*, Bas.*Spir*.58(3.49C; M.32.176A); **2.** *at a different time*, Chrys.*hom.1.5 in Ac*.(9.9D).

***διεσταλμένως**, *separately, apart from others*, ‡Gr.Nyss.*occurs.*(M.46.1161A); Cyr.*Am.*2(3.248C).

διεστραμμένως, *perversely, preposterously, distortedly* τὸ καλὸν... δόγμα δ. ἀκηκοότες Clem.*str.*3.4(p.209.21; M.8.1133C); πάντα δ. ἔπραττον Ath.*ep.Serap.*4.22(M.26.674A); Chrys.*hom.in Jer.10:23* (6.160D,161B).

***διετοιμασία, ἡ**, *preparation*, Nil.*epp.*3.7(M.79.369A).

***διευδιάζ-ω**, *enjoy calm*, fig. πρὸς τὴν προκειμένην τοῦ βίου ναυτιλίαν ~οντες Gr.Nyss.*paup.*2(M.46.489B).

διευθετέω, *arrange*, Philost.*h.e.*8.8(M.65.564A).

***διευθυμέομαι**, *rejoice*, Bas.*hom.*4.1(2.25A; M.31.217D); Cyr.*ador.* 17(1.590D); c. ἐπί, id.*Jo.*10.2(4.886A).

διευθύν-ω, **1.** *set right, order aright*; of God, *1Clem.*20.8; Meth. *symp.*8.15(p.103.18; M.18.168A); ὦ τὰς ἀΰλους [sc. οὐσίας] τῶν ἄνω στρατευμάτων τριὰς ~ουσα Geo.Pis.*Pers.*1.2(M.92.1197A); **2.** med., *set people to rights, settle a question*, Gr.Naz.*or.*29.9(p.87.5; M.36.85C); **3.** med., *be prosperous, flourish*; of persons, Nil.*epp.*2.113(M.79. 249A); **4.** *establish firmly* οὕτω τὰ τῆς ἀρχῆς...~εται Thphn.*chron.* p.360(M.108.864C).

διευκρινέω, *distinguish clearly*, theol. οὐ χωρισθεὶς [sc. ὁ υἱός] τῆς τοῦ πατρὸς ὑποστάσεως, ἀλλ'...ἰδιοποιεῖται τὴν ἐνανθρώπησιν ἵνα διευκρινηθῶσιν αἱ ὑποστάσεις ‡Ath.*dial.Trin.*3.15(M.28.1225B); οὕτως εἴρηται...διὰ τὸ μὴ σύγχυσιν νοῆσαι τῶν θείων ὑποστάσεων, ἑκάστην δὲ διευκρινηθῆναι Didym.*Trin.*3.23(M.39.924C).

διευκρινής, *clear*, Gel.Cyz.*h.e.*2.22.7(M.85.1292B).

διευλύτωσις, ἡ, *release, relief* from disease, Jo.Eleem.*v.Tych.*32 (p.142).

***διευμαρίζ-ω**, *make easy* ῥᾴδια...τὰ τῶν ἐντολῶν ἔσται, τῆς τοῦ θεοῦ ἀγάπης αὐτὰ ~ούσης Mac.Aeg.*perf.*14(M.34.852A).

διευρύνω, *open*, Geo.Pis.*hex.*1840(M.92.1575A); met., *expand*, Thdt.*affect.*8(p.211.5; 4.915).

***διεφθαρμένως**, *corruptly, perversely*, Pall.*h.Laus.*47(p.138.16; διεφθαρμένῳ σκοπῷ M.34.1201B).

***διεχειρόμενοι**, f.l. for διεγειρόμενοι, Thdt.*Rom.*8:27(3.90).

διεχθρεύ-ω, *be at enmity*; abs., Clem.*str.*7.14(p.61.20; M.9.520B); med., met. ἡ ἀλήθεια...οὐ ~εταί τινι *ib.*(p.60.34; 517C).

***διζήμων**, *seeking*, Nonn.*par.Jo.*8:21(M.43.816B).

***διζήτωρ, ὁ**, *seeker*, Gr.Naz.*carm.*2.2(epigr.)92(M.38.127A).

διηγέομαι, *explain* a phrase, Heracleon ap.Or.*Jo.*10.11(9; p.180. 19; M.14.324A); Or.*hom.6.2 in Jer.*(p.48.19; M.13.324C); *ib.11.3* (p.80.21; 396C); c. dupl. acc., *explain* or *interpret as*, Heracleon ap. eund.*Jo.*13.60(59; p.291.24; 513A); c. ἀντί, *ib.*13.31(30; p.255.30; 453A).

διήγημα, τό, *setting forth, statement* τὸ δὲ εὐαγγέλιον δ. νόμου καὶ πλήρωμα Mel.*pass.*40 p.6.33; Meth.*arbitr.*1.2(p.147.8; M.18.241B); Ath.*Ar.*1.55(M.26.125C).

διήγησις, ἡ, **1.** *declaration*, Gr.Nyss.*hex.*11(M.44.73C); **2.** *interpretation, explication*, Or.*princ.*3.12(11; p.214.7; M.11.269B); id. *hom.6.2 in Jer.*(p.49.7; M.13.325A); id.*Jo.*13.46(p.272.12; M.14. 480C).

***διηδής**, *very sweet*, Chrys.*prod.Jud.*3(2.721A).

***διηδύνω**, pass., *be allured* or *coaxed* Εὔα...ἐπεὶ ἐγεύσατο ἡδονῆς, διηδύνθη πρὸς σωματικὴν ἐπιθυμίαν Diad.*perf.*56(p.62.13).

διήλυσις, ἡ, *opening*; of sleeve of a garment, Paul.Sil.*ambo.*287 (M.86.2262B); at top of ascent to pulpit, *ib.*295 (l.c.).

***διημέρευσις, ἡ**, *way of spending time, occupation*, Sophr.H. *v.Anast.*(M.92.1720A).

***διημερινός**, *daily*, Sophr.H.*v.Anast.*(M.92.1708B).

***διήμερος**, *on the second day*, Evagr.*h.e.*4.29(p.178.23; M.86. 2756A).

διῃρημένως, *separately*, theol. δ. ὁρᾶται καὶ ἐν μονάδι καταλαμβάνεται Gr.Nyss.*or.catech.*3(p.16.1; M.45.17D); Cyr.*Jo.*3.5(4. 307B) cit. s. διακεκομμένως; Just.Imp.*edict.*ap.Evagr.*h.e.*5.4(p.198. 23; M.86.2796B); Christol., in denial of suggestion that at Inc. Son entered an already existing body ὁ κύριος τὸ ἡμέτερον ἀνέλαβε σῶμα ...ἀλλ' οὐ δ. αὐτὸ ἀνέλαβεν...ἀλλ' ἀδιαίρετον ἐκ μήτρας ἐποιήσατο τὴν ἕνωσιν Marc.Er.*opusc.*10.5(M.65.1124A).

***διθεΐα, ἡ**, *belief in two gods*, Gr.Naz.*or.*26.18(M.35.1224B); *ib.*31. 13(p.162.6; M.36.148C).

***διθεΐτης, ὁ**, *one who believes in two gods* οἱ τὸν υἱὸν σέβοντες... ὑμεῖς...οὐ δ.; Gr.Naz.*or.*31.13(p.162.1; M.36.148C).

***διθελής**, *having two wills* οὔκουν δ. ὁ τῆς Μαρίας υἱὸς ἵνα μὴ κατὰ τοὺς Μανιχαίων νόμους σαρκικῷ θελήματι ἀντιστρατεύηται τὸ θέλημα τοῦ θεοῦ Anast.S.*monoph.*(M.89.1181A).

***δίθεος**, *believing in two gods*, Hipp.*haer.*9.11(p.246.7; M.16. 3379B).

δίθυμος, *at variance*, Or.*exp.in Pr.*26:20(M.17.240C).

***διθυραμβιστής, ὁ**, *one who uses bombastic language*, Gr.Nyss. *Eun.*12(1 p.259.27; M.45.964A).

***διθυραμβωδῶς**, *dithyrambically, bombastically*, Synes.*regn.*15 (p.34.3; M.66.1080C).

***διϊδρύω**, *establish firmly*, Cyr.*Is.*4.5(2.714A); med., *continue firm* or *settled*; in one's faith, id.*hom.pasch.*24.3(5^{2}.289B).

διΐημι, **1.** act.; *spread out* wings, Cyr.*Ps.*26:5(M.69.853B); **2.** pass.; *be soaked in* or *permeated with*, Hipp.*haer.*4.34(p.60.25; M.16.3099A).

διϊθύν-ω, *steer, guide*; met., Cyr.*hom.pasch.*25.2(5^{2}.298E); of God δεσπότην τῶν ὅλων...τὸ πᾶν ~οντα id.*Abac.*32(3.547D); id.*Is.*4.2 (2.595D); of one explaining a difficult passage, Max.*ambig.*(M.91. (1272B).

***διΐκτωρ, ὁ**, *one who tells* of; c. genit., ‡Ath.*palm.*8(M.26.1308B).

διϊππεύ-ω, **A.** trans.; **1.** *ride over* or *across*; ptcpl. pass., of a road *that can be ridden over*, Thdt.*h.rel.*4(3.1151); **2.** *traverse*, Cyr. *Jo.*4.3(4.381A); Eus.*v.C.*3.26(p.90.7; M.20.1088A); ‡Caes.Naz.*dial.*1 (M.38.853); abs., ‡Jo.D.*Artem.*42(p.162.24; M.96.1289B); **3.** *pass by*; met., in proverbial saying, *bring no profit to* ὁ δεύτερος ὑμᾶς οὐ διϊππεύσει πλοῦς Isid.Pel.*epp.*2.171(M.78.621C).

B. intrans.; **1.** of time, *pass, elapse*, *A.Jo.*7(p.155.3); Cyr.*Jo.*2.5 (4.199A); Sophr.H.*mir.Cyr.et Jo.*51(M.87.3613C); **2.** *progress*; of the course of speech or argument, Cyr.*Jo.*6(4.585E); pass., id.*hom. pasch.*5.3(5^{2}.49D); **3.** *pass unnoticed* μὴ ~ειν ἐὰν τὰ ἐν τῇ θεοπνεύστῳ γραφῇ θεωρήματα id.*Jo.*11.12(4.1006B); **4.** *attain* ἁγνὴ καὶ ὁμόφρων ἡ συζυγία ~ει πρὸς τὰς οὐρανίας πύλας Sever.ap.*cat.1Petr.*3:7 (p.60.21).

***διΐππι(ο)ν, τό**, *circus*, Thphn.*chron.*p.342(M.108.824B); *ib.*p.341 (824A).

διΐστ-ημι, **A.** trans., *divide, separate* τὴν θάλασσαν...διέστησαν προφῆται δύο Clem.*ecl.*6(p.138.21; M.9.701A); Bas.*ep.*203.3(3.301B; M.32.741A); Christol. θεόν τε ὁμοῦ καὶ ἄνθρωπον, οὐ ~αντες εἰς ἄνθρωπον ἰδικῶς...καὶ εἰς θεὸν λόγον ἰδικῶς Cyr.*expl.xii cap.*2 (p.18.7; 6^{1}.148D); God the Son from Father, by an interval of time, Gr.Nyss.*Eun.*1(1 pp.122.31,123.13; M.45.357Dff.) cit. s. διάστημα.

B. intrans.; **1.** *pause, stop*, Clem.*paed.*1.6(p.111.3; M.8.292C); **2.** *move away*, Philost.*h.e.*10.9(M.65.589C).

δικάζ-ω, **1.** *act as judge, sit in judgement*; of Christ, Chrys.*hom. 25.3 in Jo.*(8.147D); met. ὀφθαλμοὶ...~ουσιν ὑγιαίνοντες μέν, ὀρθῶς Thdt.*Ezech.*proem.(2.669); **2.** *judge*, c. dat., *LS*; c. acc., Athenag. *leg.*12.1(M.6.913B); Epiph.*haer.*42.11(p.140.22; M.41.749D); Chrys. *hom.3.3 in 2Tim.*(11.676A); pass., Herm.*mand.*2.5; ὁ Χριστιανός, ἐν ᾧ ἐστι Χριστὸς ~όμενος...καταδεδυνάστευται ὑπὸ τοῦ ἀδίκου Or. *hom.14.17 in Jer.*(p.124.3; M.13.428A); Chrys.*hom.61.1 in Mt.*(7. 611B); Thdt.*ep.*113(4.1190).

***δικαιοεύρετος**, *rightly found* δ. σταυρόν ‡Chrys.*ador.*2(11.824B).

δικαιοκρισία, ἡ, *righteous judgement*; **1.** in gen., Or.*exp.in Pr.* 26:17(M.17.240B); Bas.*hex.*6.7(1.57B; M.29.133C); Thdt.*ep.*116(4. 1197); **2.** of God, title of work of Clem. περὶ προνοίας καὶ δ. θεοῦ Anast.S.*qu.et resp.*96(M.89.741D); ἡ τοῦ θεοῦ δ. ταῖς ἡμετέραις διαθέσεσιν ἐξομοιοῦται Meth.*fr.*(p.520.11; M.18.408B); Eus.*v.C.*1.58 (p.35.8; M.20.972D); Ath.*exp.Ps.*100:1(M.27.424D); †Bas.*hom.in Ps.*37(1.363E; M.30.85C); *Const.App.*1.6.11; Chrys.*hom.31.4 in Rom.*(9.751A); Cyr.*Is.*4.4(2.684E); Jo.D.*f.o.*3.1(M.94.981A).

δικαιοκρίτης, ὁ, *righteous judge*; **1.** in gen., *M.Pers.*1.4(p.423.17); **2.** of God, Hipp.*antichr.*49(p.33.9; M.10.769B); Gr.Nyss.*ep.*16(M.46. 1057A); Thdt.*Col.*3:25(3.497); id.*1Tim.2*:1(3.646); Hesych.H.*Ps. tit.*118.137(M.27.1200D); **3.** of Christ φιλάνθρωπος γάρ εἰμι, ἀλλὰ καὶ δ. ‡Hipp.*consumm.*47(p.308.25; M.10.950A); *Pers.capt.*(M.86. 3240A).

***δικαιοκριτικός**, *righteous in judgement*; of bishop's character, *Const.App.*2.6.4(vv.ll. δίκαιος κριτικός, διακρητικός).

***δικαιόκριτος**, = foreg., Or.*sel.in Ps.*145:7(M.12.1676A).

***δικαιοκτονέω**, *slay righteous men*, Eust.*engast.*25(p.55.27; M.18. 665A).

δικαιολογ-έομαι, *justify oneself*; in gen. ~εῖται περὶ τῶν κακολογούντων αὐτόν Or.*hom.14.11 in Jer.*(p.115.17; M.13.416C); Chrys. *hom.51.5 in Ac.*(9.386C); id.*hom.41.5 in 1Cor.*(10.394A); οὐκ ἔστιν οὐδεὶς τῶν ἁγίων τοιαῦτα ~ούμενος, ὡς φθόνου...ὑπάρχοντες καθαροί *cat.Lc.*15:24(p.120.15); of God οὐδὲ...ἁπλῶς ἐκφέρει τὴν καταδίκην, ἀλλὰ πρότερον ~εῖται Chrys.*hom.in Mt.18:23*(3.13A); id.*fr.in Jer.*27:4(M.64.961A).

δικαιολογία, ἡ, *plea in justification*, Gr.Nyss.*or.catech.*22(p.85.3; M.45.60D); Chrys.*David* 2.1(4.760E); Thphl.Al.*common.*3(M.65.37A);

ἐναντιοῦται ἀλλήλοις δ. καὶ ταπείνωσις Marc.Er.*opusc.*1.126(M.65.921A); Bas.Sel.*or.*4.1(M.85.65B); c. genit. δ. τῇ τῶν κανόνων Pall. *v.Chrys.*9(p.53.11; M.47.31).

***δικαιομετρία**, ἡ, *just measure*, Ant.Mon.*hom.*76(M.89.1656D).

δικαιοπραγής, *acting justly*, Thphyl.*exc.gent.*5(p.482.10; M.113.941C).

***δικαιοπραγματεία**, ἡ, *righteous dealing*, Thdr.Heracl.*Is.*59:17 (M.18.1365A).

***δικαιοπρακτικός**, *acting righteously*, Or.*sel.in Gen.*1:26(M.12.96A).

***δικαιοπραξία**, ἡ, *righteous dealing*, Just.*dial.*44.2(M.6.569B); *ib.* 46.7(576C).

δίκαιος, *just, righteous*;

A. with primary connotation of *just*; of God; **1.** in gen. δ. ἐν τοῖς κρίμασιν *1Clem.*27.1; θεὸν τῶν πάντων ἐπόπτην δ. οἴδαμεν Just. *2apol.*12.6(M.6.465A); problem discussed of how God who is ἀγαθὸς καὶ δίκαιος can be said to 'harden Pharaoh's heart', Or. *princ.*3.1.9(p.209.1ff.; M.11.264ff.); problem of reconciling God's character as *benignus* with his character as *justus* in respect of judgement and punishment, cf.id.*hom.8.1 in Num.*(p.51.13ff.; M. 12.622Dff.); Eus.*e.th.*2.20(p.129.26; M.24.953C); οἴδαμεν ἕνα θεὸν... δ. καὶ ἀγαθόν Ar.*ep.Alex.*(p.12.6; M.26.709A); δ. δὲ ὁ αὐτός ἐστιν, ὅταν κρίνων τὰ κατ' ἀξίαν ἑκάστῳ ἀπονέμῃ *V.Aberc.*32(p.68.4); ὁμολογεῖται...μὴ μόνον δυνατὸν εἶναι...τὸ θεῖον, ἀλλὰ καὶ δ., καὶ ἀγαθόν, καὶ σοφόν. ... οὔτε τὸ ἀγαθὸν ἀληθῶς ἐστιν ἀγαθόν, μὴ μετὰ τοῦ δ. τε καὶ σοφοῦ καὶ τοῦ δυνατοῦ τεταγμένον Gr.Nyss.*or.catech.*20(pp.78.12, 79.4; M.45.56D); εἰ γάρ ἐστι θεός, δ. ἐστιν· εἰ δὲ δ. ἐστι, τὸ κατ' ἀξίαν ἀπονέμει ἑκάστῳ· εἰ δὲ οὐδέν ἐστι μετὰ ταῦτα, ποῦ τὸ κατ' ἀξίαν ἀπολήψεται ἕκαστος; ‡Chrys.*prov.*4(2.767A); ἦν γὰρ...ὅτι μάλιστα πρέπον τῷ δ. πατρὶ τὸ καταρραχθὲν ἐκ πλεονεξίας ὑψῶσαι πάλιν Cyr.*Jo.*11.12(4.1007B); ὅσα δὲ λέγομεν ἐπὶ θεοῦ καταφατικῶς, οὐ τὴν φύσιν, ἀλλὰ τὰ περὶ τὴν φύσιν δηλοῖ. κἂν ἀγαθόν, κἂν δ. ... κἂν ὅ τι ἂν ἄλλο εἴπῃς, οὐ φύσιν λέγεις θεοῦ, ἀλλὰ τὰ περὶ τὴν φύσιν Jo.D. *f.o.*1.4(M.94.800B); **2.** heret. distn. between 'just God' of OT and 'good God' of NT; **a.** Cerdon and Marcion, Iren.*haer.*1.27.1(M.7. 688A) cit. s. ἀγαθός; Hipp.*haer.*7.37(p.223.15; M.16.3343C); cf. *dixerint aliud esse justum, aliud bonum, et hac divisione etiam in divinitate usi sunt, adfirmantes bonum quidem deum esse patrem... Christi, et non justum, justum vero legis et prophetarum deum, nec tamen bonum*, Or.*princ.*2.4.5(p.132.16; M.11.203C); *ib.*2.5.2(p.135.4; 205D); id.*hom.8.6 in Ex.*(p.230.18; M.12.358D); *deus legis non est bonus, sed justus, et Moysi lex non bonitatem continet, sed justitiam*, id.*hom.9.4 in Num.*(p.59.1; M.12.628C); id.*hom.18 in Lc.*(p.125.6; M. 13.1849A); δ. μὲν εἶναι τὸν δημιουργόν, ἀγαθὸν δὲ τὸν τοῦ Χριστοῦ πατέρα id.*Jo.*1.35(40; p.44.32; M.14.92C); Thdt.*haer.*1.24(4.314); **b.** acc. Apelles εἶναί τινα θεὸν ἀγαθόν,...τὸν δὲ πάντα κτίσαντα εἶναι δ.,...καὶ τρίτον τὸν Μωσεῖ λαλήσαντα...καὶ τέταρτον ἕτερον, κακῶν αἴτιον Hipp.*haer.*7.38(p.224.3; M.16.3346A); **c.** acc. Prepon τρίτην... δ. εἶναι ἀρχὴν καὶ μέσην ἀγαθοῦ καὶ κακοῦ τεταγμένην *ib.*7.31(p.216.19; 3334C); **d.** acc. Valentinians τρίτος θεὸς πάρεστιν...οὔτε τὴν κακίαν ἔχων καὶ ἀδικίαν...οὔτε τὴν ἀγαθότητα καὶ φωτεινὴν οὐσίαν, μεσαίτατος δὲ ὢν δ. Epiph.*haer.*33.10(p.461.11; M.41.573B); **3.** ref. Rom.3:26, cf. *justum namque apud deum visum est, ut quia futurum saeculum ad judicium statuerat, praesens sustentationi et patientiae deputaret. nam si puniret in hoc tempore peccatorem, justum non videretur iterum ad judicium quem punierat evocare. si ...sustentet...in praesenti saeculo, recte erit justus judex in futuro*, Or.*comm.in Rom.*3.8(M.14.951D); Chrys.*hom.7.2 in Rom.*(9.485D) cit. s. δικαιοσύνη; ἔδει...τὰς πρὸς τὸν Ἀβραὰμ πληρωθῆναι ὑποσχέσεις ...τῷ μὴ μόνον εἶναι δ. τὸν θεόν, ἀλλὰ καὶ τῷ δικαιοῦν τὸν διὰ τῆς πίστεως τοῦ Ἰησοῦ οἰκεῖον θεοῦ καὶ λαὸν γινόμενον Oecum.*Rom.* 3:25–26(p.423.10); Jo.D.*Rom.*3:26(M.95.465A); **4.** ref. treatment of Devil in Atonement, Gr.Nyss.*or.catech.*26(p.97.8; M.45.68B).

B. with primary connotation of *righteous*; **1.** of man in natural state φύσει δ' αὖ κοινωνικοὺς καὶ δ. ὁ θεὸς ἡμᾶς ἐδημιούργησεν Clem. *str.*1.6(p.23.3; M.8.729A); **2.** of OT saints, *1Clem.*9.3; πατράσιν ἡμῶν τοῖς δ. *ib.*30.7; *ib.*33.7; *ib.*45.3,4; *2Clem.*6.9; Herm.*sim.*9.15.4; of those before the Law, Just.*dial.*19.5(M.6.517A); *ib.*20.1(517B); οἱ τοσοῦτοι δ. μηδὲν τούτων τῶν νομίμων πράξαντες μεμαρτύρηνται ὑπὸ τοῦ θεοῦ *ib.*29.3(537B); μέχρι Μωυσέως οὐδεὶς ἁπλῶς δ. οὐδὲν ὅλως τούτων...ἐφύλαξεν οὐδὲ ἐντολὴν ἔλαβε φυλάσσειν, πλὴν τὴν ἀρχὴν λαβούσης ἀπὸ Ἀβραὰμ τῆς περιτομῆς *ib.*46.4(576A); *ib.*67.7(632A); *ib.*85.3(676C); of prophets, *ib.*7.1(492A); *ib.*105.4(721B); of Noah, *ib.* 138.1(793A); cf. *omnis multitudo eorum, qui ante Abraham fuerunt justi, et...patriarcharum, qui ante Moysem fuerunt, et sine his quae praedicta sunt, et sine lege Moysi justificabantur*, Iren.*haer.*4.16.2 (M.7.1017A); Clem.*str.*2.20(p.180.21; M.8.1069A); ref. Encratite theory οὔθ' οἱ πρὸ τῆς παρουσίας δ. οὔθ' οἱ μετὰ τὴν παρουσίαν γεγαμηκότες...σωθήσονται *ib.*3.12(p.238.4; 1192A); ὁ Χριστὸς γέγονε πρὸς Μωσέα,...πρὸς ἕκαστον τῶν δ. Or.*hom.9.1 in Jer.*(p.64.12; M.13.349A); cf. *fuerit licet justus Abraham, justus Moyses, justus unusquisque illustrium virorum, sed ad comparationem Christi non sunt justi*, id.*hom.9.3 in Ezech.*(p.411.15; M.13.736B); of Noah, Chrys.*hom.23.5 in Gen.*(4.212E); of Job, *ib.23.4*(212A); Thdt.*qu.58 in Gen.*(1.71); ref. Rom.5:14 πολλοὶ δ.· καὶ οὐδεὶς αὐτῶν τῆς τοῦ θανάτου ἐξουσίας ἑαυτὸν ἠδυνήθη λυτρώσασθαι Gel.Cyz.*h.e.*2.24.26 (M.85.1304C); ὁ χορὸς τῶν δ. καὶ προφητῶν Cosm.Ind.*top.*2(M.88. 76B); *ib.*(93C); Νῶε ὁ τέλειος δ. ὢν *ib.*5(232C); of Abel, Clem.*paed.*1.6 (p.118.18; M.8.305C); Cosm.Ind.*top.*5(228A); *Lit.Jac.*(p.220.10 n.); μνήσθητι...τῶν ἁγίων προφητῶν καὶ πατριαρχῶν καὶ δ. *ib.*(p.214.20); object of Christ's preaching in Hades, Clem.*exc.Thdot.*18(p.112.20; M.9.665C); his descent giving them redemption, Cyr.H.*catech.*4.11; **3.** of Christ μετέλαβον τοῦ ῥήματος τοῦ δ. Herm.*vis.*3.7.6; ἵνα ἀνομία μὲν πολλῶν ἐν δ. ἑνὶ κρυβῇ, δικαιοσύνη δὲ ἑνὸς πολλοὺς ἀνόμους δικαιώσῃ *Diogn.*9.5; ἀπεκτείνατε γὰρ τὸν δ. Just.*dial.*16.4(M.6.512A); τῆς κατὰ τοῦ δ. ... κακῆς προλήψεως αἴτιοι *ib.*17.1(512B); τοῦ μόνου ἀμώμου καὶ δ. φωτός *ib.*17.3(513B); *ib.*86.4(681B); μετὰ τὸ ἀναιρεθῆναι τὸν δ. *ib.*119.3(752B); μισεῖν, ὃν ἐφονεύσατε, δ. *ib.*136.2(789C); as antitype of Abel τύπος γὰρ ὁ δ. ὁ παλαιὸς τοῦ νέου δ. Clem.*paed.*1.6(p.118.21; M.8.305C); and of Noah, cf.Or.*hom.2.3 in Gen.*(p.30.17; M.12. 167C); *ib.*(p.31.15; 168C); v. Νῶε; id.*Jo.*10.6(4; p.176.15; M.14. 316B); ὡς θεὸς ὢν καὶ λόγος...κριτής ἐστι δ. ... δ. οὖν φύσει καὶ ὅσιος ὤν, διὰ τοῦτο ἀγαπᾶν λέγεται δικαιοσύνην Ath.*Ar.*1.52(M.26.120B); **4.** of H. Ghost, Herm.*mand.*5.2.7 cit. s. κενός; **5.** of righteous angels, id.*sim.*6.3.2; **6.** of Christians; **a.** in gen. κολληθῶμεν οὖν τοῖς...δ.· εἰσὶν δὲ οὗτοι ἐκλεκτοὶ τοῦ θεοῦ *1Clem.*46.4; ἐν καθαρᾷ καρδίᾳ δουλεύσωμεν τῷ θεῷ, καὶ ἐσόμεθα δ. *2Clem.*11.1; ἐμμείνωμεν οὖν ἐφ' οἷς ἐπιστεύσαμεν δ. καὶ ὅσιοι *ib.*15.3; οἱ δὲ δ. εὐπραγήσαντες... ἔσονται 'δόξαν διδόντες τῷ θεῷ' *ib.*17.7; μετὰ δ. καὶ ταπεινῶν ἀναστραφήσῃ *Did.*3.9 = *Barn.*19.6; *Barn.*10.11 cit. s. αἰών; Herm.*vis.*1.1.8; ἡ γὰρ μετάνοια τοῖς δ. ἔχει τέλος *ib.*2.2.5; ἀνομία οὐκ ὀφείλει ἀναβαίνειν ἐπὶ καρδίαν ἀνδρὸς δ. id.*mand.*4.1.3; ἐν τῷ αἰῶνι τούτῳ οὐ φαίνονται οὔτε οἱ δ. οὔτε οἱ ἁμαρτωλοί, ἀλλὰ πάντες ὅμοιοί εἰσιν id.*sim.*3.3; σεμνοὶ καὶ δ. καὶ λίαν πορευθέντες ἐν καθαρᾷ καρδίᾳ καὶ τὰς ἐντολὰς κυρίου πεφυλακότες *ib.*8.3.8; συναγωγὴ ἀνδρῶν δ. as scene of manifestations of spirit of prophecy, id.*mand.*11.9; *ib.*11.13–14; ὁ θεός... παντὸς...τοῦ γένους τῶν δ. *M.Polyc.*14.1; Devil as ὁ ἀντικείμενος τῷ γένει τῶν δ. *ib.*17.1; ὅστις...ἀγαπᾷ κύριον τὸν θεόν...δ. ἀληθῶς ἂν εἴη Just.*dial.*93.3(M.6.697C); of penitent sinner ἡ γὰρ χρηστότης...τοῦ θεοῦ...τὸν μετανοοῦντα...ὡς δ. ... ἔχει *ib.*47.5(580A); state of being δ. received from Christ, *ib.*136.2(789C); Tat.*orat.*7(p.7.16; M.6. 820B); Clem.*paed.*3.6(p.257.12; M.8.605B); *ib.*3.11(p.278.18; 653A); ᾗ μὲν οὖν τίς ἐστι δ., πάντως οὗτος καὶ πιστός, ᾗ δὲ πιστός, οὐδέπω καὶ δ. τὴν κατὰ προκοπὴν καὶ τελείωσιν δικαιοσύνην λέγω, καθ' ἣν ὁ γνωστικὸς δ. λέγεται id.*str.*6.12(p.483.18; M.9.324B); μίαν εἶναι τὴν ἀληθῆ ἐκκλησίαν...εἰς ἣν οἱ κατὰ πρόθεσιν δ. ἐγκαταλέγονται *ib.*7.17 (p.76.6; 552A); ὅταν οὖν μὴ κατὰ ἀνάγκην ἢ φόβον ἢ ἐλπίδα δ. τις ᾖ, ἀλλ' ἐκ προαιρέσεως, αὕτη ἡ ὁδὸς λέγεται βασιλικὴ *ib.*7.12(p.53.1; 501B); ὁ ἄνθρωπος ὁ δ. καὶ ὁ Χριστὸς πνεῦμα ἕν Or.*dial.*3(p.126.8); cf. Logos as *vinum, quo etiam inebriari justis...optabile ducitur*, id.*Cant.*3(p.185.21; M.13.155B); οὐ γὰρ ἅπαξ ἐρῶ τὸν δ. γεγεννῆσθαι ὑπὸ τοῦ θεοῦ, ἀλλ' ἀεὶ γεννᾶσθαι καθ' ἑκάστην πρᾶξιν ἀγαθήν, ἐν ᾗ γεννᾷ τὸν δ. ὁ θεὸς id.*hom.9.4 in Jer.*(p.70.12; M.13.357A); οὐκ ἔστιν οὔτε δ. εἶναι χωρὶς Χριστοῦ οὔτε ἅγιον χωρὶς αὐτοῦ *ib.17.3*(p.147.4; 457C); cf. *qui justus est, justitiam reginam habet*, id.*hom.36 in Lc.* (p.216.21); id.*Cels.*8.20(p.237.17; M.11.1548B); τοὺς δ. παρωνύμους εἶναι Χριστοῦ τῆς δικαιοσύνης id.*comm.in Mt.*12.11(p.88.27; M.13. 1004A); Dion.Al.ap.Eus.*p.e.*14.25(777B; M.21.1277D); δ. γενέσθαι ἐκ τῆς αὐτοῦ δικαιοσύνης καὶ ἁγίους ἐκ τῆς αὐτοῦ ἁγιωσύνης Eus.*e.th.*3.15 (p.173.7; M.24.1029C); τοῦ μὲν δ. ἡ ψυχὴ χωριζομένη τῆς πρὸς τὸ σῶμα συμπαθείας, τὴν ζωὴν ἔχει κεκρυμμένην σὺν τῷ Χριστῷ ἐν τῷ θεῷ Bas.*hom.in Ps.*7(1.100B; M.29.233D); πᾶς δ. ἐν ὑψηλοῖς ἔχει τὴν διατριβὴν *ib.*28(121D; M.300B); *ib.*32(132B; M.324D); δ.· διὰ ταύτης τῆς προσηγορίας τὴν καθόλου ἀρετὴν ταύτην ἐμφαίνει. τὸ γὰρ δ. ὄνομα ἔθος ἡμῖν ἐπὶ τῶν πᾶσαν ἀρετὴν μετιόντων λέγειν Chrys.*hom.23.5 in Gen.*(4.212E); δ. ... τὸν ἐνάρετον ἐν ἅπασι λέγει· ἔστι μὲν γὰρ δικαιοσύνη...ἡ καθόλου ἀρετή. ... δ. οὖν ὤν, τουτέστι χρηστὸς καὶ ἐπιεικὴς id.*hom.4.3 in Mt.*(7.52A,B); μόνῳ δὲ τῷ δ. πάντα δεδούλωται, ὥσπερ δεσπότῃ, τὰ πάθη *M.Thdot.1* 2(p.62); μνησθῆναι καταξίωσον...παντὸς πνεύματος δ. ἐν πίστει τοῦ Χριστοῦ σου τετελειωμένου *Lit.Jac.*(p.212.18); **b.** ref. 1Tim.1:8–9, v. νομιμῶς; **c.** as condition of the faithful διὰ τῆς πίστεως τῆς τοῦ Χριστοῦ θεοσεβεῖς καὶ δ. γενόμενοι Just.*dial.*52.4(M.6.592B); ἡμεῖς οὖν, ἐν ἀκροβυστίᾳ... πιστεύοντες τῷ θεῷ διὰ τοῦ Χριστοῦ...δ. καὶ εὐάρεστοι τῷ θεῷ ἐλπίζομεν φανῆναι *ib.*92.4(696B); Clem.*ecl.*60(p.154.27; M.9.728B); contrasted with that of righteous under Law, id.*str.*6.6(p.454.1; M.9.265A); in rel. to baptism ἡ πίστις μὲν ἡμῖν ἐδωρήσατο τῶν ἁμαρτημάτων τὴν ἄφεσιν, καὶ...δικαίους διὰ τῆς τοῦ λουτροῦ παλιγγενεσίας ἀπέφηνε Thdt.*Rom.*5:1–2(3.53); v. δικαιοσύνη, δικαιόω; of those who live well after baptism τῶν γὰρ μετὰ τὸ βάπτισμα ἀπολλυμένων τὸ ὕδωρ τοῦ Ἰορδάνου εἰς τὴν θάλασσαν ἄπεισι τῶν ἁλῶν· τὸ δὲ ἄλλο τὸ ὕδωρ ἐστὶ τῶν δ. Or.*hom.4.2 in Jos.*(p.310.31; M.87.1005D); **d.** difficulty of man's appearing righteous before God, cf. *difficilis res est in conspectu dei justum esse, ut non ob aliam causam quid boni facias, nisi propter ipsum bonum, et deum tantum quaeras boni operis retributorem,* id.*hom.2 in Lc.*(p.16.14; M.13.1807A); **e.** God's assistance to righteous, cf. *justis ergo et electis ipse adest deus, inferioribus vero adsunt angeli,* id.*hom. 24.3 in Num.*(p.232.8; M.12.762D); γίνεται πάντα τῷ δ. βατὰ Ἐρυθρὰν διοδεύοντι θάλατταν καὶ τὴν ἔρημον id.*hom.4.1 in Jos.*(p.308.22; M. 87.1005C); ὁ θεὸς...τέως μὲν βοηθεῖ τοῖς δ. μερικῶς, ὕστερον δὲ ἀποδίδωσι τοὺς μισθοὺς αὐτοῖς τελείως Cyr.H.*catech.*18.4; ἔστι δὲ τῷ δ. ἀληθινὴ βοήθεια ὁ θεός Bas.*hom.in Ps.*45(1.171D; M.29.417D); Chrys.*exp.in Ps.*5:13(5.38B); **f.** reward of righteous εἰ γὰρ τὸν μισθὸν τῷ δ. ὁ θεὸς συντόμως ἀπεδίδου, εὐθέως ἐμπορίαν ἠσκοῦμεν καὶ οὐ θεοσέβειαν. ἐδοκοῦμεν γὰρ εἶναι δ., οὐ τὸ εὐσεβές, ἀλλὰ τὸ κερδαλέον διώκοντες *2Clem.*20.4; Herm.*vis.*1.4.2; id.*sim.*4.2 cit. s. αἰών; τάς τε τῶν δ. ψυχὰς ἀναπαύσεσθαι καὶ αὐτὰς ἐν τῷ τῆς μεσότητος τόπῳ Iren.*haer.*1.7.1(M.7.513A); πρὸ τῆς ἀναστάσεως σὺν Χριστῷ ἐστιν ὁ δ., καὶ ἐν αὐτῇ τῇ ψυχῇ ζῇ μετὰ Χριστοῦ Or.*dial.*23(p.164.20); id. *Cels.*7.21(p.172.24; M.11.1452A); περὶ τοῦ...μέλλοντος αἰῶνος καὶ τῶν ἐν αὐτῷ γερῶν...ἐπὶ τοὺς δ. *ib.*8.48(p.263.15; 1588C); *ib.*8.51(p.266. 12; 1592C); Cyr.H.*catech.*18.4; *ib.*18.18; **g.** liability of δ. to sin μεταπτωτή ἐστι καὶ ἡ τοῦ δ. ψυχή, ὡς μαρτυρεῖ καὶ ὁ Ἰεζηκιὴλ λέγων τὸν δ. ἀφίστασθαι δύνασθαι τῶν ἐντολῶν τοῦ θεοῦ, ὡς μὴ λογίσασθαι αὐτῷ τὴν προτέραν δικαιοσύνην Or.*comm.in Mt.*13.29 (p.260.30; M.13.1172C); **h.** troubles of righteous ὁ δὲ λέγων μὴ πρέπειν τῷ δ. τὴν θλῖψιν, οὐδὲν ἕτερον λέγει ἢ μὴ ἁρμόζειν τῷ ἀθλητῇ τὸν ἀνταγωνιστήν Bas.*hom.in Ps.*33(1.156A,B; M.29.381B); ὁ μὲν γὰρ δ. ἐν συμφοραῖς ἦν· ὁ δὲ μιαρὸς...ἐν εὐπραγίᾳ...ἀλλ' οὔτε ἐκεῖνος... ἐκέρδαινέ τι, οὔτε ὁ ἅγιος οὗτος ἐβλάπτετο Chrys.*exp.in Ps.*7:2 (5.51B); παντὶ δ. αἱ κακώσεις αἴτιαι μισθῶν γίνονται id.*hom.16.3 in Ac.*(9.131D); **i.** ref. Gen.15:5, cf. *justus intus est et in interioribus semper consistit, quia intus in abscondito orat patrem...sed tamen deus educit eum foras, cum res postulat et rerum visibilium ratio deposcit,* Or.*hom.21.2 in Num.*(p.202.19; M.12.739D); **7.** pagan accusation that in Christian view righteous are unacceptable to God, Cels.ap.Or.*Cels.*3.62(p.256.21; M.11.1001C); **8.** title of S. James, Heges.ap.Eus.*h.e.*2.23.7(M.20.197B); Clem.*fr.*13(p.199.21)*ib.*2.1.5 (136B); **9.** etym., of Sadducees ἑρμηνευόμενοι δικαιότατοι Jo.D. *haer.*16(M.94.688A); **10.** of things δ. ἔργα Herm.*mand.*6.2.3; id. *sim.*2.9; etc.

C. *fit, meet,* of persons ἀγαπᾶσθαι δίκαιός ἐστι Bas.*hom.*11.5(2. 96A; M.31.384A); Chrys.*sac.*3.7(1.385D); πειραθῆναι δίκαιοι Thdt. *Zach.*14:5(2.1662); of things, *right, fitting,* liturg. ἄξιον καὶ δ. cf. Hipp.*trad.ap.*4.3; Serap.*euch.*13.1; *Lit.*ap.*Const.App.*8.12.5; *Lit. Jac.*(p.198.18).

D. neut. as subst.; **1.** *justice*; **a.** in gen. τὸ δὲ δ. πᾶν καλόν Meth. *res.*1.31(p.265.1; M.41.1141A); δ. ... τὸ πρὸς ἀξίαν ἑκάστῳ νεμητικόν Gr.Nyss.ap.*Doct.Patr.*33(p.254.28); **b.** of God τί οὖν...τὸ δ.; τὸ μὴ τυραννικῇ τινι χρήσασθαι κατὰ τοῦ κατέχοντος ἡμᾶς αὐθεντίᾳ id.*or. catech.*22(p.84.16; M.45.60D); Thdt.*Ps.*17:23(1.708); ἐπὶ τῆς τιμωρίας ...θεὸς τοῦ δ. τὸν ὅρον ἐφύλαξε id.*Rom.*5:15(3.58); Proc.G.*Lev.*20:2 (M.87.764C); **2.** *righteousness,* Isid.Pel.*epp.*2.85(M.78.529A); plur., *righteous acts,* Or.*fr.13 in Jer.*(p.204.17; M.13.569B); **3.** (= Lat. *jus*) *right*; **a.** civil, Eus.*v.C.*3.62(p.110.7; M.20.1137A); hence τὸ τοῦ νόμου δ. *jurisprudence,* Zach.Mit.*opif.*(M.85.1020A); **b.** of ownership οὐδενὸς τῶν εἰς τὴν δεσποτείαν ἐλαττουμένου δ. Eus.*v.C.*2.39(p.58.13; 1017A); Const.ap.Eus.*h.e.*10.5.11(M.20.884B); ἔθος...τῇ ἐκκλησίᾳ τῆς Ῥώμης, ἀκίνητα μὴ κρατεῖν δ. [i.e. property-rights over immovable possessions] Thdr.Lect.*h.e.*2.55(M.86.212A); **c.** civic δοὺς δίκαιον μητροπόλεως...τῇ...Μύρᾳ Jo.Mal.*chron.*14 p.365(M.97.544A); *Chron.Pasch.*p.335(M.92.869A); **d.** eccl. τῷ δ. τῆς χειροτονίας Basilisc. *antencycl.*(p.52.15; M.86.2612A); τὸ πατριαρχικὸν δ. Evagr.*h.e.*3.6 (p.106.13; M.86.2609A); **e.** in gen. τοῖς δ. κοινωνίας οὐκ ἔχουσι Proc. G.*Lev.*19:9(M.87.757A); **4.** *jurisdiction, Cod.Afr.*59(H.1.897B); τόπων τῷ σῷ δ. ὑπαχθέντων Leo Mag.*ep.*106(p.56.39; M.*PL.*54. 1004B).

δικαιοσύνη, ἡ, A. *justice*; **1.** in gen. ἡ δ. ἀγαθὸν εἶναι λέγεται οὐ τῷ ἀρετὴν ἔχειν (ἀρετὴ γάρ ἐστιν αὐτή), ἀλλὰ τῷ αὐτὴν καθ' αὑτὴν καὶ δι' αὑτὴν ἀγαθὴν εἶναι...κατὰ πάντα ἄρα τὰ μέρη, καθ' ἃ τὸ ἀγαθὸν ἐξετάζεται, καὶ ἡ δ. χαρακτηρίζεται Clem.*paed.*1.8(p.127.23; M.8. 328A); δ. δὲ συμφωνία τῶν τῆς ψυχῆς μερῶν id.*str.*4.26(p.321.3; M.8. 1373A); κἂν ἡ ἕξις ἡ μεταδοτικὴ παρ' ἡμῖν δ. λέγηται *ib.*7.12(p.50.10; M.9.497A); as chief of the cardinal virtues περὶ ἀνδρείας καὶ φρονήσεως καὶ σωφροσύνης τῆς τε ἐπὶ πᾶσι παντελοῦς ἀρετῆς δ. *ib.*7.3 (p.13.8; 421C); τὸ τῆς δ. ὄνομα ταὐτὸν μέν ἐστι παρὰ πᾶσιν Ἕλλησιν· ἤδη δὲ ἀποδείκνυται ἄλλη μὲν ἡ κατ' Ἐπίκουρον δ., ἄλλη δὲ ἡ κατὰ τοὺς ἀπὸ τῆς Στοᾶς, ἀρνουμένους τὸ τριμερὲς τῆς ψυχῆς. ἄλλη δὲ κατὰ τοὺς ἀπὸ Πλάτωνος, ἰδιοπραγίαν τῶν μερῶν τῆς ψυχῆς φάσκοντας εἶναι τὴν δ. Or.*Cels.*5.47(p.51.18; M.11.1253D); ἔστι δ. ἕξις ἀπονεμητικὴ τοῦ κατ' ἀξίαν· δυσθήρατον δὲ τοῦτο, τῶν μὲν...οὐκ ἐξευρισκόντων ἑκάστῳ διανεῖμαι τὸ ἴσον, τῶν δέ, διὰ τὸ προκατέχεσθαι ὑπὸ παθῶν ἀνθρωπίνων, ἀφανιζόντων τὸ δίκαιον, ὅταν πενήτων μὲν καταφρονῶσι, δυνάστας δὲ ἀδικοῦντας μὴ διελέγχωσι Bas.*hom.*12.8(2.104A; M.31.401B); opp. divine justice ἔστι δὲ δ., ἡ μέν τις ἐν ἡμῖν στρεφομένη, ἡ τοῦ ἴσου διανομή...ἡ δέ τις οὐρανόθεν ἐπαγομένη...ἥ τε ἐπανορθωτική, καὶ ἡ ἀνταποδοτική, ἧς πολὺ τὸ δυσθεώρητον, διὰ τὸ ὕψος τῶν ἐναποκειμένων αὐτῇ δογμάτων *ib.*(104D; M.401D); δ. δέ, μὴ πλέον ζητεῖν ἔχειν Gr.Naz.*carm.*1.2.34.59(M.37.950A); δ. ... τὴν ὀρθὴν τῆς ψυχῆς ἡγεμονίαν, καὶ τῶν ὑπηκόων παθῶν τὴν συμμετρίαν Thdt.*provid.*6(4.567); **2.** of God τὸ δὲ μόνον δίκαιον μέτρον, ὁ μόνος ὄντως θεός,...μετρεῖ τε πάντα καὶ σταθμᾶται, οἱονεὶ τρυτάνῃ τῇ δ. τὴν τῶν ὅλων...περιλαμβάνων καὶ ἀνέχων φύσιν Clem.*prot.*6(p.53.5; M.8.176A); ἡ νομοθεσία τὴν τοῦ θεοῦ δ. ἅμα καὶ ἀγαθότητα καταγγέλλει id.*str.*2.18(p.158.11; M.8.1025A); ἀγαθὴ γὰρ ἡ τοῦ θεοῦ δ. καὶ δικαία ἐστὶν ἡ ἀγαθότης αὐτοῦ *ib.*6.14(p.486.29; M.9.332A); cf. *justitia debet creatoris in omnibus apparere,* Or.*princ.*2.9.7(p.171.24; M.11.232B); *alia anima erga amorem justitiae ejus fervens et... providentiae ejus justitiam contuens dicit...vulnerata justitiae ego sum. et alia bonitatis...immensitatem perspiciens similia loquitur,* id.*comm.in Cant.*3(p.194.25; M.13.162B); ἡ [sc. τοῦ θεοῦ] ὑπόστασις καὶ ἀθανασία ἐστί· καὶ...δ. ... καὶ οὐκ ἔστι κατὰ σύνθεσιν ταῦτα ὁ θεός, ἀλλὰ κατὰ διαφόρους ἐπινοίας λεγόμενος· ἀθανασία μὲν διὰ τὸ ἀτελεύτητον...δ. διὰ τὸ ἴσον ‡Ath.*dial.Trin.*1.18(M.26.1144D); αὐτοῦ τοῦ θεοῦ ἡ δ. ἡ ὑπερέχουσα πάντα νοῦν Bas.*hom.in Ps.*7(1.103A; M.29.241A); id.*hom.*12.8(2.104D; M.31.401D); its likeness being found in men, Gr.Nyss.*or.catech.*21(p.81.3; M.45.57Cff.); **3.** ref. Marcion's distinction between 'just' and 'good' deities, cf.Or. *princ.*2.5.1(p.132.25ff.; M.11.204A); cf. *deus legis non est bonus sed justus, et Moysi lex non bonitatem continet sed justitiam,* id.*hom. 9.4 in Num.*(p.59.2; M.12.628C); v. δίκαιος; ἀγαθότης.

B. *righteousness*; **1.** in gen., Clem.*str.*4.25(p.319.21; M.8.1369B) cit. s. εἰρήνη; ἡ δ. τετράγωνός ἐστι, πανταχόθεν ἴση καὶ ὁμοία ἐν λόγῳ, ἐν ἔργῳ, ἐν ἀποχῇ κακῶν, ἐν εὐποιίᾳ, ἐν τελειότητι γνωστικῇ *ib.*6.12 (p.483.15; M.9.324B); δ. δὲ...οὐ τὴν μερικὴν ἀρετήν φησιν, ἀλλὰ τὴν καθόλου Chrys.*exp.in Ps.*4:6(5.20B); δ. τὴν καθόλου ἀρετὴν λέγει, τὴν ἐν τῷ βίῳ εὐσέβειαν, πίστιν, ἀγάπην, πραότητα id.*hom.6.1 in 2Tim.*(11.693C); δ. γάρ ἐστι, μὴ μόνον τὸ κρύπτειν τὰ καλά, ἀλλὰ καὶ τὸ μὴ ἐννοεῖν τι τῶν ἀπηγορευμένων Marc.Er.*opusc.*2.127(M.65.949A); **2.** of God, Just.*1apol.*6.1(M.6.336C); πηγῆς τῆς δ. Const.ap.Gel. Cyz.*h.e.*2.7.25(M.85.1237B); ref. Apollinarian view of Inc. ἐληλυθέναι τὴν θεότητα...ἵνα αὐτὴ ἀναιχμαλώτιστος μείνῃ, καὶ οὕτως ὀφθῇ καθαρὰ δ., πότε γοῦν οὐκ ἦν τῆς θεότητος καθαρὰ ἡ δ.; ‡Ath.*Apoll.*2.11 (M.26.1149B); ref. Rom.3:25ff. δικαιοσύνης ἔνδειξις, τὸ μὴ μόνον αὐτὸν εἶναι δίκαιον, ἀλλὰ καὶ τὸ ἑτέρους ἐν ἁμαρτίᾳ κατασαπέντας ἐξαίφνης δικαίους ποιεῖν Chrys.*hom.7.2 in Rom.*(9.485D); ἠνέσχετο γὰρ ὁ θεός, ἵνα δείξῃ τὴν ἑαυτοῦ δ. ... συγχωρήσας τοίνυν ἁμαρτάνειν ἀθρόαν τὴν ἄφεσιν ἐχαρίσατο Sever.*Rom.*3:25(p.217.3); ἔνδειξιν δ. τὸ μὴ μόνον δειχθῆναι τὸν θεὸν δίκαιον, ἀλλὰ καὶ δικαιοῦντα τοὺς πιστεύοντας εἰς Χριστὸν Jo.D.*Rom.*3:25(M.95.465A); **3.** Christ as righteousness, cf. *justitia est, justitia autem numquam profecto injustitiam capiet,* Or.*princ.*1.8.3(p.100.13; M.11.178B); *quia ergo Christus, sicut verbum et sapientia est, ita etiam justitia est, consequens...erit, ut ea quae in verbo et sapientia facta sunt, etiam in ea justitia, quae est Christus, facta esse dicantur, ib.*2.9.4(p.167.27; 228B); cf.*ib.*4.4.1(p.351.3; 403B); *regnat in nobis justitia ipse dominus noster,* id.*hom.25.3 in Num.*(p.237.19; M.12.767A); δ. θεοῦ αὐτός id.*hom.8.2 in Jer.*(p.57.7; M.13.337C); *ib.14.12*(p.117.22; 420A); id.*comm.in Mt.*12.11(p.88.28; M.13.1004A); ζητεῖν τὸν Ἰησοῦν ζητεῖν ἐστι τὸν λόγον καὶ τὴν σοφίαν καὶ τὴν δ. καὶ τὴν ἀλήθειαν καὶ τὴν δύναμιν τοῦ θεοῦ id.*Jo.*32.31(19; p.478.28; M.14.825C); ref. Is. 41:2 δ. δὲ αὐτὸν ἐκάλουν Eus.*e.th.*1.20(p.94.27; M.24.889B); ref. Ps.97:2, *ib.*(p.95.29; 892C); οὐ μόνον λόγος κεκλημένος...ἀλλὰ καὶ υἱὸς καὶ...δ. καὶ ἥλιος δ. καὶ σοφία *ib*.(p.96.30; 893B); Bas.*hom*.12.9 (2.105B; M.31.404C); Christ as δ. in sense of *justice* οἱ διὰ τοῦ υἱοῦ σωθέντες τῇ δυνάμει τοῦ πατρὸς ἐσώθησαν, καὶ οἱ παρὰ τούτου κρινόμενοι τῇ δ. τοῦ θεοῦ τὴν κρίσιν ὑπέχουσιν. Χριστὸς γάρ ἐστιν ἡ τοῦ θεοῦ δ. ἡ διὰ τοῦ εὐαγγελίου ἀποκαλυπτομένη Gr.Nyss.*Eun*.6(2 p.139.15; M.45.724D); **4.** of Christ's righteousness justifying sinners τί γὰρ ἄλλο τὰς ἁμαρτίας ἡμῶν ἠδυνήθη καλύψαι ἢ ἐκείνου δ.;...ὢ τῆς γλυκείας ἀνταλλαγῆς...ἵνα...δ. ... ἑνὸς πολλοὺς ἀνόμους δικαιώσῃ *Diogn*.9.3,5; in gen. τάχα δὲ διὰ τοῦ ἰῶτα καὶ τῆς κεραίας ἡ δ. κέκραγεν αὐτοῦ Clem.*fr*.58(p.227.1; M.9.765C); ref. Atonement οὐ τοσαύτη ἦν τῶν ἁμαρτωλῶν ἡ ἀνομία, ὅση τοῦ ὑπεραποθνήσκοντος ἡ δ. Cyr.H.*catech*.13.33; **5.** in Christ's human life τεκτονικὰ ἔργα εἰργάζετο...ἄροτρα καὶ ζυγά· διὰ τούτων καὶ τὰ τῆς δ. σύμβολα διδάσκων Just.*dial*.88.8(M.6.688B); αὐτὸς...πρότερος ὥδευσεν τὴν τῆς δ. ὁδόν Thdt.*Ps*.84:14(1.1209); **6.** for the angel of righteousness v. ἄγγελος II.H.10.d; **7.** in men; **a.** natural τὸν τῆς φύσεως δημιουργὸν ἕνα γινώσκομεν, καθὸ καὶ τὴν δ. φυσικὴν εἰρήκαμεν Clem.*str*.1.19(p.60.17; M.8.809B); εἰς πάντας ἐξ ἀρχῆς ἀνάρχου ἴση ἀτεχνῶς ἡ φυσικὴ δ., κατ' ἀξίαν ἑκάστου γένους γενομένη *ib*.5.14(p.421.9; M.9.205B); cf. *justitiae ejus, quam inesse creaturis omnibus credimus*, Or.*princ*.2.9.4(p.168.5; M.11.228C); **b.** obtained through philosophy ἦν μὲν οὖν πρὸ τῆς τοῦ κυρίου παρουσίας εἰς δ. Ἕλλησιν ἀναγκαία φιλοσοφία Clem.*str*.1.5 (p.17.31; M.8.717C); τοὺς ἐν δ. τῇ κατὰ νόμον καὶ κατὰ φιλοσοφίαν βεβιωκότας *ib*.6.6(p.454.21; M.9.268B); **c.** through Law ἐπὶ τοὺς ἀνθρώπους καταβέβηκεν ἡ δ. καὶ γράμματι καὶ σώματι, τῷ λόγῳ καὶ τῷ νόμῳ id.*paed*.1.9(p.142.4; M.8.356B); id.*str*.6.6(p.454.21; M.9.268B); *ib*.(p.457.19; 273A); ἡ ἐπίτασις γὰρ τῆς κατὰ τὸν νόμον δ. τὸν γνωστικὸν δείκνυσιν *ib*.6.18(p.516.21; 397A); εἰς τὸ ἐπὶ πλέον τῆς κατὰ νόμον δ. κατ' ἐπίτασιν προεληλυθέναι *ib*.7.10(p.41.15; 480B); ref. Mt.3:15 δ. γὰρ ἐνταῦθα τὴν ἐκπλήρωσιν καλεῖ τῶν ἐντολῶν ἁπασῶν Chrys.*hom.10.1 in Mt*.(7.140B); Μωυσῆς δείκνυσιν ἡμῖν τὴν ἐκ τοῦ νόμου δ. ... καὶ ἄλλως οὐκ ἔνι δίκαιον γενέσθαι ἐν νόμῳ, ἀλλ' ἢ πάντα πληρώσαντα· τοῦτο δὲ οὐδενὶ γέγονε δυνατόν. οὐκοῦν διαπέπτωκεν ἡ δ. αὕτη id.*hom.17.1 in Rom*.(9.622D,E); but Christian righteousness not at variance with it, cf. *docebat* [sc. Christus]...*adimplens legem, et infigens justificationes legis in nobis*, Iren.*haer*.4.13.1(M.7.1007B); **d.** sources of Christians' righteousness; **i.** God, who gives it in return for sacrifice to him of our own righteousness, cf.Or.*hom.24.2 in Num*.(p.229.10; M.12.760B); love of God, Clem.*paed*.1.9 (p.141.29; M.8.356A); **ii.** Christ, Or.*comm.in Mt*.12.11(p.88.28; M.13.1004A); ἡ γὰρ αὐτοδικαιοσύνη...Χριστός ἐστιν...ἀπ' ἐκείνης δὲ δ. ἡ ἐν ἑκάστῳ δ. τυποῦται ὡς γίνεσθαι ἐν τοῖς σωζομένοις πολλὰς δ. id.*Jo*.6.6(3; p.115.4; M.14.212B); οὕτως καὶ οἱ δίκαιοί ἐσμεν ὡς ἄνθρωποι, οὐχ ὡς ἡ ἁμαρτία δ. ὅθεν ὁ υἱὸς...δ. ἀκούει· ἡμεῖς δὲ μεταλήψει δ. δίκαιοι †Bas.*poenit*.2(2.605B; M.31.1480A); Mac.Aeg.*hom*.31.4(M.34.732A) cit. s. δικαιόω; **iii.** obtained by grace through faith, as in case of Abraham πιστὸς ὤν, ἐσφραγίσθη εἰς δ. Cyr.H.*catech*.5.5; Chrys.*hom.17.2 in Rom*.(9.622E); id.*hom.11.3 in 2Cor*.(10.518B) cit. s. δικαιόω; ἐπειδὴ γὰρ εἰκὸς ἦν αὐτοὺς λέγειν, ὅτι μείζων αὕτη ἡ δ. ἡ διὰ πόνων, δείκνυσιν ὅτι σκύβαλον τοῦτό ἐστι πρὸς ἐκείνην...ποία δέ ἐστιν αὕτη; ἡ ἀπὸ πίστεως τοῦ θεοῦ· τουτέστι, καὶ αὕτη παρὰ θεοῦ δέδοται. θεοῦ ἐστιν αὕτη ἡ δ. id.*hom.11.2 in Phil*.(11.285D); Thdt.*Rom*.4:4(3.47); ἡ χάρις τὴν διὰ πίστεως δ. τοῖς πεπιστευκόσι δωρησαμένη *ib*.5:21(3.60); ἰδίαν δ. τὴν ἄκαιρον τοῦ νόμου προσηγόρευσε φυλακήν...θεοῦ δὲ δ., τὴν κατὰ χάριν διὰ τῆς πίστεως γινομένην ὠνόμασε *ib*.10:3(111); Jo.D.*Rom*.9:30–32(M.95.521A); **iv.** through baptism, cf.Or.*hom.13.4 in Gen*.(p.120.25ff.; M.12.235C); as δικαιοσύνης δωρεά †Bas.*bapt*.1.2.17(2.642B; M.31.1556B); **v.** through fear of God, Clem.*str*.7.12(p.56.11; M.9.509A); *cat.2Cor*.7:1(p.393.33); **vi.** from works, Clem.*str*.4.18(p.299.27; M.8.1325B); contrast Chrys.*hom.11.3 in 2Cor*.(10.518C); depreciation of righteousness of works not implying laxity ῥαθυμίας ὑπόθεσιν εἶναι τὰ λεγόμενα id.*hom.9.1 in Rom*.(9.512A); **vii.** beginning at conversion, Thdt.*Ps*.84:9 (1.1205); **e.** in Christian life, *Barn*.1.4; ἐὰν γάρ τις τούτων [sc. πίστις, ἐλπίς, ἀγάπη] ἐντὸς ᾖ, πεπλήρωκεν ἐντολὴν δικαιοσύνης Polyc.*ep*.3.3; διχῇ οὖν τῆς πάσης δ. τετμημένης, πρός τε θεὸν καὶ ἀνθρώπους, ὅστις...ἀγαπᾷ κύριον...καὶ τὸν πλησίον...δίκαιος ἀληθῶς ἂν εἴη Just.*dial*.93.3(M.6.697C); *ib*.110.3(729B); Iren.*haer*.4.36.7(M.7.1097C); Clem.*prot*.10(p.68.17; M.8.205B); αἱ μὲν εἰς δ. ὁδοὶ...πολλαί τε καὶ ποικίλαι καὶ φέρουσαι εἰς τὴν κυρίαν ὁδόν τε καὶ πύλην id.*str*.1.7(p.25.19; M.8.733B); ᾗ μὲν οὖν τίς ἐστι δίκαιος, πάντως οὗτος καὶ πιστός, ᾗ δὲ πιστός, οὐδέπω καὶ δίκαιος, τὴν κατὰ προκοπὴν καὶ τελείωσιν δ. λέγω, καθ' ἣν ὁ γνωστικὸς δίκαιος λέγεται *ib*.6.12(p.483.20; M.9.324B); ἐξ ἰδιοπραγίας καὶ τῆς πρὸς θεὸν ἀγάπης ἡ δ. *ib*.6.15(p.495.17; 349B); ἡ δ. διπλῆ, ἡ μὲν δι' ἀγάπην, ἡ δὲ διὰ φόβον *ib*.7.12(p.56.11; 509A); id.*ecl*.37(p.148.14; M.9.717B); cf. *eos...qui... reges sunt..., reges ex eo dicti quod...justitiae regnum paraverint in membris suis*, Or.*hom.12.2 in Num*.(p.100.26; M.12.661C); of Antony's hermitage χώραν τινὰ καθ' ἑαυτὴν οὖσαν θεοσεβείας καὶ δ. Ath.*v.Anton*.44(M.26.908B); οἱ τὸν ἀγγελικὸν ἀσπασάμενοι βίον τὴν εὐαγγελικὴν ἐν αὐτοῖς δ. καρποῦνται Thdt.*Ps*.71:3(1.1103); **f.** its relation to eternal or future life καθηράμενος δ. καὶ τῇ ἄλλῃ ἀρετῇ πάσῃ [sc. ὄψεται τὸν θεόν] Just.*dial*.4.3(M.6.484C); Clem.*paed*.3.11(p.278.19; M.8.653B); ὁ δι' ἀγάπην...προσβλέπων τὸ κάλλος...δι' οὗ κάλλους ἐπὶ τὸν τεχνίτην καὶ τὸ ὄντως καλὸν αὐτὸς ἑαυτὸν παραπέμπει, σύμβολον ἅγιον τὸν χαρακτῆρα τῆς δ. τὸν φωτεινὸν ἐπιδεικνύμενος τοῖς ἐφεστῶσι τῇ ἀνόδῳ ἀγγέλοις id.*str*.4.18(p.299.18; M.8.1325A); id.*ecl*.60(p.154.24; M.9.728B); cf.Or.*princ*.2.3.2(p.117.4; M.11.190C); ὁπόταν δ. αἰτία ὁ ἄνθρωπος ἀθάνατος γένηται *Hom.Clem*.19.20; **g.** other effects δ. μετανοεῖν συμβουλευούσης Clem.*paed*.1.10(p.145.9; M.8.360C); ἔργον...τῆς δ. ... ἐπὶ τὸ ἄμεινον αἰεὶ κατὰ τὸ ἐνδεχόμενον ἕκαστον προάγειν id.*str*.7.2(p.9.28; M.9.416A); *ib*.7.11(p.48.22; 493B); cf.Or.*hom.9.9 in Num*.(p.66.28; M.12.635A); *justitiae vero natura contraria est; in initiis videtur amarior, in novissimis vero melle dulcior invenitur, cum virtutis functus attulerit*, id.*hom.14.2 in Jos*.(p.378.10; M.12.894C); ἡ δὲ δ. ... πάντας φίλους, πάντας συνήθεις, πάντας εὐνοϊκῶς διατίθησι πρὸς ἡμᾶς Chrys.*hom.14.2 in Phil*.(11.307E); preserves man's peace with God, Thdt.*Rom*.5:2(3.53); **h.** of BMV πάσης δ. ἀνωτέραν Jo.Eub.*concept.BMV* 18(M.96.1489A); **8.** Gnost. τὴν δ. τοῦ θεοῦ κοινωνίαν τινὰ εἶναι μετ' ἰσότητος...δ. τῆς κοινῆς ἅπασιν ἐπ' ἴσης δοθείσης...δ. γὰρ ἐν αὐτοῖς ἀναφαίνεται ἡ κοινότης Epiph.Gn.ap.Clem.*str*.3.2(p.198.1; M.8.1105A); ἡ δὲ Καρποκράτους δ. καὶ τῶν ἐπ' ἴσης αὐτῷ τὴν ἀκόλαστον μετιόντων κοινωνίαν Clem.*str*.3.6(p.221.6; M.8.1157B); Βασιλείδης δὲ ὑποστατὰς Δ. τε καὶ τὴν θυγατέρα αὐτῆς τὴν Εἰρήνην ὑπολαμβάνει ἐν ὀγδοάδι μένειν ἐνδιατεταγμένας *ib*.4.25(p.320.3; 1372A).

C. plur.; **1.** *judgements* (= δικαιώματα), cf.Or.*hom.10.1 in Ex*.(p.245.7; M.12.369B); **2.** *works of righteousness, righteous deeds*, *Pss.Sal*.9.6; Mac.Aeg.*hom*.10.4(M.34.541D); *Lit.Jac*.(p.192.17); Jo.Thess.*dorm.BMV* 2.4(p.411.3); Jo.D.*Man*.1.75(M.94.1573B).

δικαιοφανής, *self-justifying, plausible*, Isid.Pel.*epp*.5.149(M.78.1413B).

δικαι-όω, A. *set right, correct*, Clem.*str*.4.22(p.312.7; M.8.1353B); 'μετὰ τοσοῦτον αἰῶνα ὁ θεὸς ἀνεμνήσθη ~ῶσαι τὸν ἀνθρώπων βίον',... φήσομεν ὅτι οὐκ ἔστιν ὅτ' οὐκ ἐβουλήθη '~ῶσαι τὸν ἀνθρώπων βίον ὁ θεός', ἀλλὰ καὶ ἀεὶ ἐπεμελήθη διδοὺς ἀρετῆς ἀφορμὰς τοῦ ἐπανορθοῦσθαι τὸ λογικὸν ζῷον Or.*Cels*.4.7(p.279.11; M.11.1037A); †Bas.*Is*.42(1.413A; M.30.200B); hence

B. *deem right*; c. infin., Athenag.*res*.5(p.53.1; M.6.981D); CNic.(325)*can*.17; Const.ap.Ath.*apol.sec*.86(p.165.4; M.25.401D); Cyr.*ador*.10(1.354B); Proc.G.*Gen*.1:5(M.87.61C); *cat.Apoc*.6:4(p.264.28).

C. *hold, think* εἰ...τὸ σχῆμα τοῦ κόσμου ~οῖς μὴ παρέρχεσθαι Mac.Mgn.*apocr*.4.11(p.172.27); ~οῖς...τὸ ἀγέννητον εἶναι τὴν οὐσίαν ‡Ath.*dial.Trin*.2.21(M.28.1189B).

D. *deem to be, pronounce* τοῦτο...ἀνδράσι...ἀνάρμοστον ἐδικαίωσεν *Const.App*.1.3.11.

E. *prove, attest* ~οῦσιν ὡς οὐ διὰ τὴν κρίσιν ἡ ἀνάστασις γίνεται κατὰ πρῶτον λόγον Athenag.*res*.14(p.65.14; M.6.1001D); ἡ κοινὴ συνήθεια ἔχει λέγειν· ὁ δεῖνα ἐδικαιώθη ἀληθινὸς εἶναι υἱὸς τοῦδε Didym.*Trin*.1.27(M.39.404B).

F. *show to be right, vindicate*, Eus.*h.e*.8.2.2(M.20.744C); ἐδικαίωσε γὰρ ἐκ τῶν ἐχθρῶν ἡμῶν τὴν δίκην ἡμῶν Ath.*exp.Ps*.100:1(M.27.424D); Areth.*Apoc*.48(M.106.705D).

G. *put in the right, justify*; **1.** in gen. ~οῖ τὰ πραχθέντα ἡ ψυχή *T.Dan* 3.3; οἱ ~οῦντες ἑαυτοὺς καὶ λέγοντες εἶναι τέκνα Ἀβραάμ Just.*dial*.25.1(M.6.529A); ἴδωμεν τίς ἐδικαιώθη, τίς κατεδικάσθη Or.*hom.4.5 in Jer*.(p.29.6; M.13.293A); Meth.*res*.1.60(p.324.15; M.41.1157B); Ath.*v.Anton*.55(M.26.924A); *Const.App*.2.24.3; Chrys.*fr.Job* 13:5(M.64.613A); Mac.Aeg.*ep*.(M.34.413B); Dor.*doct*.1.9(M.88.1628B); **2.** of man's justification before God; **a.** of gentiles who are without the Law, ref. queen of Sheba τῆς ἀποστολικῆς ἀνεμνήσθην διδασκαλίας, ἣ τοὺς δίχα νόμου ~ωθέντας ἐθαύμασεν...αὕτη γὰρ...ἠρκέσθη τῷ τῆς φύσεως νόμῳ Thdt.*qu.33 in 3Reg*.(1.479); cf. id.*affect*.12(p.310.9ff.; 4.1024); **b.** of Greeks through philosophy, Clem.*str*.1.4(p.17.29; M.8.717C); καθ' ἑαυτὴν ἐδικαίου ποτὲ καὶ ἡ φιλοσοφία τοὺς Ἕλληνας, οὐκ εἰς τὴν καθόλου δὲ δικαιοσύνην, εἰς ἣν εὑρίσκεται συνεργός *ib*.1.20(p.63.19; 816C); **c.** of God's justification of men in OT; **i.** in gen. of righteous before Inc., Eus.*d.e*.2.3(p.91.22; M.22.161B); **ii.** of Adam by his obedience at the first, Clem.*str*.4.23(p.315.9; M.8.1360B); **iii.** of Noah and Enoch, justified like Abraham, Eus.*d.e*.1.5(p.21.7; M.22.45A); **iv.** of Abraham's justification by faith, Just.*dial*.23.4(M.6.528A); cf. *fides enim, quae est ad* *deum altissimum, justificat hominem,* Iren.*haer*.4.5.5(M.7.986B); *dicitur de Abraham, quod ex operibus fidei justificatus sit: quia certum est eum qui vere credit, opus fidei, et justitiae, et totius bonitatis operari,* Or.*comm.in Rom*.4.1(M.14.961C); by works and faith, Cyr. H.*catech*.5.5; Chrys.*hom.8.1 in Rom*.(9.497C,D); *ib.9.1*(511B); κἂν εἰ λέγοιτο τυχὸν ἐξ ἔργων δεδικαιῶσθαι διὰ...τὸ προσενεγκεῖν τὸν Ἰσαὰκ πειραζόμενον, ἀλλ' ἦν καὶ τοῦτο αὐτῷ πίστεως τῆς ἑδραιοτάτης ἀπόδειξις ἐναργής Cyr.*Rom*.4:2(p.181.16; M.74.781B); cf. οὐ γὰρ κατὰ νόμον πολιτευσάμενος ὁ...Ἀβραὰμ τῆς θείας μαρτυρίας τετύχηκεν, ἀλλὰ τῷ κεκληκότι πιστεύσας τῆς δικαιοσύνης τὸν πλοῦτον ἐτρύγησε Thdt.*Rom*.4:3(3.46); **v.** discussion of justification of those between Abraham and Moses, Just.*dial*.92.2(M.6.696A); cf.Iren.*haer*.4.13.1 (M.7.1007A); **vi.** by Law, Or.*Jo*.13.49(47; p.276.14; M.14.488A); †Bas.*bapt*.1.2.11(2.637B; M.31.1544C); **d.** of Pharisees, justified κατὰ ἀποχὴν κακῶν Clem.*str*.6.18(p.516.19; M.9.397A); **e.** of Christ; **i.** his justification through performance of works of Law denied, Just.*dial*.67.6(M.6.629C); but asserted by Ebionites, Hipp.*haer*.7.34 (p.221.11; M.16.3342B); **ii.** ref. 1Tim.3:16 'ἐδικαιώθη ἐν πνεύματι', τοῦτ' ἔστιν ἀπεφάνθη, ἤτ' οὖν ἐβεβαιώθη...ἀληθινὸς εἶναι θεός Didym. *Trin*.1.27(M.39.404B); ἤτοι τοῦτο λέγει· 'καὶ ἐδικαιώθη ἡ σοφία ἀπὸ τῶν τέκνων αὐτῆς'· ἢ ὅτι δόλον οὐκ ἐποίησεν Chrys.*hom.11.1 in 1Tim*. (11.606A); ἀντὶ τοῦ ὤφθη μὲν ἐν σαρκί, ἐδικαιώθη δὲ ἐν πνεύματι πολιτευσάμενος. εἰ γὰρ καὶ ἐν σαρκὶ ἦν, ἀλλ' οὐ κατὰ σάρκα ἐπολιτεύετο, ἀλλ' ὑπέταξε τῷ πνεύματι τὴν σάρκα, δικαιοσύνης ἡμῖν ὑπανοίγων ὁδόν. ἢ καὶ τοῦτό φησιν ὅτι τοῦ πνεύματος σημεῖα ποιοῦντος, ἐδικαιοῦτο κατὰ τὴν ἡμετέραν ὁμολογίαν καὶ πίστιν ὁ...Χριστός Sever.*1Tim*.3:16 (p.339.6); cf. τὴν γὰρ ἀνθρωπείαν φύσιν ἀνειληφώς, ἐλευθέραν ταύτην ἁμαρτημάτων ἐφύλαξεν. ἔχει δὲ καὶ ἑτέραν διάνοιαν τουτὶ τὸ ῥητόν... διὰ τοῦ θείου πνεύματος ἐνεργεῖ τὰ θαύματα...ἀπεδείχθη τοίνυν διὰ τῶν θαυμάτων...ὅτι...θεοῦ υἱός Thdt.*1Tim*.3:16(3.658); ἡ ἐκκλησία ἡ ἐπὶ τῆς γῆς διὰ τῆς ὁμολογίας ἐδικαιώθη ἐν πνεύματι *cat.1Tim*.3:16 (p.31.26); Oecum.*1Tim*.3:16(p.458.15); **f.** of Christians; **i.** in gen. οὐκ ἀποχῇ κακῶν μόνον ~ωθείς, πρὸς δὲ καὶ τῇ κυριακῇ τελειωθεὶς εὐποιΐᾳ Clem.*str*.4.6(p.261.6; M.8.1241A); ἀνατρέχει...ἐπὶ τὸν κύριον ἡ τῶν καλῶν διδασκαλία ἡ ~οῦσα *ib*.6.7(p.461.21; M.9.281A); οὐχ ἡ τῶν πράξεων ἀποχὴ ~οῖ τὸν πιστόν, ἀλλ' ἡ τῶν ἐννοιῶν ἁγνεία καὶ εἰλικρίνεια id.*fr*.65(p.228.20; M.9.753A); Ath.*exp.Ps*.118:135(M.27. 501D); **ii.** by Christ, *Diogn*.9.5 cit. s. δίκαιος; ἐν Χριστῷ...τελειούμενοι ~ωθείημεν Or.*hom.19.15 in Jer*.(p.176.4; M.13.500B); id.*Jo*. 2.7(4; p.61.10; M.14.120C); cf. τοὺς ὑβρίζοντας εἰς ἑαυτόν τε καὶ τὸν πατέρα ~οῖ Cels.ap.Or.*Cels*.2.35(p.161.18; M.11.857A); Diod.*Ps*. 70:22(M.33.1610D); τοὺς ἐν Χριστῷ δεδικαιωμένους *ib*.91:13(1626C) = Cyr.*Ps*.91:13(M.69.1228D); αἱ πισταὶ ψυχαὶ μόνῳ τῷ κυρίῳ ἐλπίζουσιν ἀεί, πᾶσαν δικαιοσύνην αὐτῷ ἀπονέμουσαι· ὥσπερ γὰρ χωρὶς τῆς ἀμπέλου τὸ κλῆμα ψύχεται, οὕτως καὶ ὁ ἄνευ Χριστοῦ ~οῦσθαι θέλων. ὡς ὁ λῃστής...ἐστίν, ὁ μὴ διὰ τῆς εἰσόδου εἰσερχόμενος... οὕτως ὁ ἄνευ τοῦ ~οῦντος ἑαυτῷ ~ούμενος Mac.Aeg.*hom*.31.4(M.34. 732A); Cyr.*Is*.3.3(2.449E); *ib*.5.5(869C); id.*Mich*.41(3.429D); id. *glaph.Gen*.2(1.61D); ἵνα ~ώσῃ τὰ δικαιοσύνην οὐκ ἔχοντα id.*thes*.16 (5^1.177E); id.*Pulch*.(p.56.14; 5^2.172D); **iii.** esp. through Resurrection, cf. *justificat ergo eos Christus tantummodo qui novam vitam exemplo resurrectionis ipsius susceperunt,* Or.*comm.in Rom*.4.7 (M.14.986D); Gr.Ant.*mul.ung*.11(M.88.1861D); **iv.** by grace, Didym. *Trin*.2.14(M.39.716C); τὸν γὰρ δίκαιον...ἐποίησεν ἁμαρτωλόν... μᾶλλον δὲ...ἁμαρτίαν...ἵνα καὶ ἡμεῖς γενώμεθα, οὐκ εἶπε, δίκαιοι, ἀλλὰ δικαιοσύνη, καὶ θεοῦ δικαιοσύνη. θεοῦ γάρ ἐστιν αὕτη, ὅταν μὴ ἐξ ἔργων...ἀλλ' ἀπὸ χάριτος ~ωθῶμεν Chrys.*hom.11.3 in 2Cor*.(10. 518C); δικαιοσύνην δὲ τὴν εὐαγγελικὴν ὑπέδειξε δωρεάν, ἵν' ὅπερ ὁ νόμος κατεπόνει τῷ κρίματι, τοῦθ' ἡ δωρεὰ τοῦ εὐαγγελίου ~ώσῃ τῇ χάριτι Mac.Mgn.*apocr*.4.12(p.175.14); Χριστοῦ δὲ...ἀναλάμψαντος, εἰσβέβηκεν ἡ δικαιοσύνη, ~οῦσα χάριτι, καὶ ἀποσοβοῦσα τῶν ἡμετέρων σωμάτων τὴν φθοράν Cyr.*dogm*.6(p.562.2; 6^2.376E); by grace alone οὐκ ἀπὸ κατορθωμάτων, οὐδὲ πόνων, οὐδὲ ἀμοιβῆς, ἀλλ' ἀπὸ χάριτος μόνης τὸ γένος ἐδικαίωσε τὸ ἡμέτερον Chrys.*Jud*.7.3(1.665E); **v.** through faith οὐ δι' ἑαυτῶν ~ούμεθα οὐδὲ διὰ τῆς ἡμετέρας σοφίας ...ἢ ἔργων ὧν κατειργασάμεθα ἐν ὁσιότητι καρδίας, ἀλλὰ διὰ τῆς πίστεως, δι' ἧς πάντας τοὺς ἀπ' αἰῶνος ὁ...θεὸς ἐδικαίωσεν *1Clem*. 32.4; cf.Iren.*haer*.4.5.5(M.7.986B); by which those before Law were justified, cf.*ib*.4.13.1(1007A); Clem.*str*.2.4(p.119.16; M.8.944B); cf.Or.*hom.15.4 in Num*.(p.137.1ff.; M.12.690A); cf. *qui ex fide justificatur, apud solum deum habet gloriam qui occultorum notitiam habet, et fidei solus inspector est...non autem putes quod si quis habeat talem fidem ex qua justificatus habeat gloriam apud deum, possit simul cum ea habere et injustitiam...indicium igitur verae fidei est ubi non delinquitur...certum est eum qui vere credit, opus fidei, et justitiae, et totius bonitatis operari,* id.*comm.in Rom*.4.1 (M.14.961Bf.); cf. *initium...justificari a deo fides est quae credit in justificantem. et haec fides cum justificata fuerit...haeret in animae solo, ut...surgant in ea rami qui fructus operum ferant, non ergo ex operibus radix justitiae, sed ex radice justitiae fructus operum crescit,* *ib*.(965B); πάντα ἄνθρωπον ἡ πίστις ~οῖ Chrys.*hom.8.4 in Rom*.(9.488A); Thdt.*Rom*.3:28(3.45); Cyr.*ador*.8(1.273D); Jo.D.*Rom*. 5:1(M.95.473B); by faith alone ἡ τελεία...καύχησις ἐν θεῷ, ὅτε μήτε ἐπὶ δικαιοσύνῃ τις ἐπαίρεται τῇ ἑαυτοῦ, ἀλλ' ἔγνω μὲν ἐνδεῆ ὄντα ἑαυτὸν δικαιοσύνης ἀληθοῦς, πίστει δὲ μόνῃ τῇ εἰς Χριστὸν δεδικαιωμένον Bas.*hom*.20.3(2.158E; M.31.529C); cf. οὐ γὰρ δὴ δι' ἔργων ἀξιεπαίνων, ἀλλὰ διὰ μόνης πίστεως τῶν μυστικῶν τετυχήκαμεν ἀγαθῶν (in context referring to baptismal grace) Thdt.*affect*.7 (p.189.20ff.; 4.892); **vi.** through orthodox belief, Cyr.*Jo*.5.4(4. 508E); id:*Heb*.3:2(p.401.20); **vii.** works done prior to faith do not justify τὰ πρὸ τῆς πίστεως ἔργα κἂν δοκῇ εἶναι δεξιὰ οὐ ~οῖ τὸν ποιήσαντα αὐτά Or.*comm.in Rom*.3:28(*JTS* 13 p.222); **viii.** in baptism, †Bas.*bapt*.1.2.11(2.637A; M.31.1544B); 'ἐδικαίωσε'. διὰ τῆς τοῦ λουτροῦ παλιγγενεσίας Chrys.*hom.16.2 in Rom*.(9.595D); cf.id. *hom.7.2 in 2Cor*.(10.481C); τὸ κήρυγμα ἐν τῷ βαπτίσματι...~οῖ καὶ ἁγιάζει *cat.2Cor*.3:9(p.367.32); ~οῖ γὰρ ἡμᾶς ἥκιστα μὲν ὁ νόμος, ἀπαλλάξει δὲ...πλημμελημάτων ἡ διὰ τοῦ...βαπτίσματος χάρις Cyr.*Is*.2.5(2.343B); id.*Joel*.32(3.224E); id.*apol.Thdt*.12(p.145.23; 6^1. 240A); ‡Just.*qu.orth*.44(M.6.1289A); τῆς κατὰ χάριν Χριστοῦ τοῦ θεοῦ δεδικαιωμένης ἐκκλησίας ἐν τῷ βαπτίσματι ‡Meth.*Sym.et Ann*.12 (M.18.377D); **ix.** by the gospel ἐν τῷ ~οῦν δυναμένῳ εὐαγγελίῳ *cat.2Cor*.11:15(p.425.3); **x.** through spiritual sacrifices, cf.Iren. *haer*.4.17.1(M.7.1020B); **xi.** justification by works, *1Clem*.30.3; usu. denied, Bas.*hom.in Ps*.32(1.141C; M.29.348A); v. supra iv–vi; but cf. Herm.*sim*.5.7.1; discussion of Jac.2:17ff., cf.†Didym.*Jac*. 2:26(M.39.1752B); cf.Chrys.*fr.in Jac*.2:17–19(M.64.1045C); Ἀβραὰμ ...ἑκατέρας πίστεως ἐστὶν εἰκών· καὶ τῆς πρὸ τοῦ βαπτίσματος, τῆς μὴ ἐπιζητούσης ἔργα, μόνον δὲ...τὸ ῥῆμα τῆς σωτηρίας, ᾧ ~ούμεθα πιστεύοντες εἰς Χριστόν, καὶ τῆς μετὰ τὸ βάπτισμα, τῆς συνεζευγμένης τοῖς ἔργοις hence SS. Paul and James agree, *cat.Jac*.2:20–21 (p.16.29); Cyr.*Rom*.4:2(p.180.11 n.; M.74.1008B); **xii.** justification reserved for future, *Barn*.4.10; **xiii.** absolute justification (before God) contrasted with relative justification obtained from men, cf.Or.*hom.9.2 in Ezech*.(p.410.3; M.13.735B); exeg. Ps.142:2, id.*Jo*. 2.17(11; p.74.11; M.14.144C); **xiv.** Ebionite doctrine of justification by Mosaic Law, Hipp.*haer*.7.34(p.221.11; M.16.3342B); *ib*.10.22 (p.281.19; 3439A).

δικαίωμα, τό, 1. *righteous act,* Ath.*exp.Ps*.118:117(M.27.500B); †Bas.*bapt*.2.6.2(2.660B; M.31.1597A); *Const.App*.3.12.2; ὅταν... στοιχῶμεν τοῖς δ. ἡμῶν, τότε...ἑαυτοὺς ἐπιβουλεύομεν Dor.*doct*.5.1 (M.88.1676D); **2.** *righteousness,* Meth.*res*.2.8(p.344.13,21; M.41. 1176B,C); **3.** *reason, justification* for an action ποῖον δ. τοῦ συνοικῆσαι εὗρεν; Chrys.*hom.39.1 in Ac*.(9.295C); *ib.40.3*(306A); θάνατος... ἐστὶ τὸ εὑρεθῆναι δ. μετὰ τοῦ θελήματος Dor.*doct*.5.2(M.88.1677B); *ib*.9.1(1717A); **4.** *proof, argument* ἐπὶ...τοῦ πιστοῦ πολλὰ μὲν ἡμῖν τὰ δ. Chrys.*oppugn*.2.2(1.58E); **5.** *document,* esp. of written argument or plea παρεῖναι...Εὐτυχῇ καὶ τοῖς αὐτοῦ δ. χρήσασθαι CEph. (449)*act*.(*ACO* 2.1.1 p.90.3; H.2.96D); **6.** *bond* μετὰ τοῦ ὁμοφύλου καὶ μυρία ἔχων δ., τὸ συγγενές, τὸ λογικόν Chrys.*hom.25.3 in Heb*. (12.232A); **7.** *act of justice, judgement* διὰ τοῦ τῆς μετανοίας δ. παιδευομένην †Bas.*Is*.42(1.413A; M.30.200B); Bas.*reg.fus*.25.1(2. 370A; M.31.984C); Max.*ambig*.(M.91.1132A); **8.** *ordinance,* in gen; Eus.*h.e*.1.2.19(M.20.61C); *Const.App*.6.24.2; of God προστάγματα καὶ δ. τοῦ κυρίου *1Clem*.2.8; *ib*.58.2; *Barn*.1.2; *ib*.2.1; φυλάσσειν ἀγωνιζώμεθα τὰς ἐντολὰς αὐτοῦ, ἵνα ἐν τοῖς δ. αὐτοῦ εὐφρανθῶμεν *ib*.4.11; *ib*.16.9; *ib*.21.5; ἐνεδυναμώθην ἐν πᾶσι τοῖς δ. τοῦ κυρίου Herm.*mand*.12.6.4; Just.*dial*.46.2(M.6.573B); Thphl.Ant.*Autol*. 3.15(M.6.1141B); Or.*sel.in Ps*.18:8–10(M.12.1244B); Eus.*d.e*.1.6(p.24. 15; M.22.49D); †Bas.*Is*.77(1.433E; M.30.248B); *Const.App*.7.38.5; *Lit.ap.Const.App*.8.6.5; δ. δὲ τὰς ἐντολὰς λέγει...τοῦτο γάρ ἐστι τὸ δ. καὶ ἡ ἐντολὴ τοῦ θεοῦ Gennad.*fr.Rom*.1:29(M.85.1672A).

δικαίωσις, ἡ, 1. *vindication, doing justice* to ἡ δ. τῆς χήρας †Bas. *Is*.44(1.414B; M.30.201C); **2.** *justification*; **a.** in gen. τὰ ἁμαρτήματα τοῦ Ἰσραὴλ συγκρινόμενα τοῖς πταίσμασιν Ἰούδα γέγονε δ. τῆς ψυχῆς τῆς Ἰσραὴλ συναγωγῆς Or.*hom.4.1 in Jer*.(p.24.2; M.13.285D); **b.** of God's justification of men; **i.** in gen. θεοῦ...παρέχοντος ἡμῖν...τὴν ἀληθινὴν...δ. ἐν ᾗ καταστησόμεθα, ἁμαρτεῖν οὐκ ἐπιδεχόμενοι τότε. ... σημαίνων δὲ διὰ τῆς δ. τὸ εἶναι αὐτῶν ἐν ἀπολαύσει τότε, δ. τὸ ἁμαρτίαν μὴ ἐπιδέχεσθαι καλῶν—αὕτη γὰρ ἀληθὴς δ. Gennad.*fr.Rom*.8:33 (p.384.8,13,14,15; M.85.1701Cff.); **ii.** through Law, in Jewish system, Thdr.Mops.*Heb*.11:1(p.210.4; M.66.965B); **iii.** through Christ πᾶσά τε προσαγωγὴ καὶ τελείωσις ἐν Χριστῷ...καὶ...πᾶσα δ. ἐν αὐτῷ τε καὶ δι' αὐτοῦ Cyr.*ador*.11(1.388E); ῥεραντίσμεθα δι' αὐτοῦ πρὸς δ. id.*Heb*.3:1f.(p.398.14); id.*resp*.(p.599.3; 6².393E) cit. s. ἀνυπαίτιος; **iv.** by grace, ‡Meth.*Sym.et Ann*.7(M.18.365A); **v.** by faith τῆς κατὰ πίστιν δ. Thdr.Mops.*Rom*.3:28(p.117.24; M.66.793D); and baptism ἐγράφετο δὲ δι' ἀμφοῖν [sc. pillar of cloud and Red Sea] ὁ Χριστός, ἤτοι τὸ ἐπ' αὐτῷ μυστήριον, ἤγουν ὡς ἐν πίστει τε καὶ ἁγίῳ βαπτίσματι, δ. καὶ ἁγιασμός Cyr.*Is*.2.4(2.283A); **vi.** but justification by works implied in view that gift by Ananias and Sapphira of half their property to poor counted for justification, Or.*comm.in Ex*.(M.12:276B).

δικαιωτήριον, τό, 1. *place of punishment*, Const.*or.s.c*.10(p.164.31; M.20.1257B); Bas.*leg.lib.gent*.6(p.54; M.31.580D); Evagr.*h.e*.1.7 (p.16.26; M.86.2444A); **2.** *judgement* θείας κρίσεως δ. προσδοκῶντες Eus.*l.C*.7(p.213.3; M.20.1353A); id.*d.e*.3.6(p.139.15; M.22.236A); *Const.App*.7.39.2; Dion.Ar.*d.n*.4.35(M.3.736B).

δικαιωτής, ὁ, *justifier*; of Messiah in Jewish and Christian thought, Cels.ap.Or.*Cels*.4.2(p.274.13; M.11.1029B).

δικανός, ὁ, v. δεκανός.

***δικαρράφος, ὁ,** *one who fabricates lawsuits, litigious person*, Cyr.*Is*.5.4(2.831E).

δικαστήριον, τό, 1. *law-court, place of judgement*; of Christ's judgement-seat, Meth.*symp*.2.6(p.24.3; M.18.57A); φρικτὸν...τοῦ Χριστοῦ δ. Bas.*hom.in Ps*.33(1.151D; M.29.372A); **2.** *judgement* ἐπὶ τοῦ φοβεροῦ...τῆς κτίσεως πάσης δ. Bas.*Spir*.15(3.12E; M.32.93A); Chrys.*hom.in Mt.18:23*(3.6D); id.*hom.45.4 in Jo*.(8.267A); **3.** *office of judge* προκαθέζεταί σου ὁ νοῦς πεπιστευμένος τὸ δ. Bas.*hom*.12.9 (2.106B; M.31.405C).

δικαστής, ὁ, *judge*; **1.** of secular judges δαίμονες...δ. ἔχοντες ὑποχειρίους...φονεύειν ἡμᾶς παρασκευάζουσιν Just.*2apol*.1.2(M.6. 444A); Athenag.*leg*.2.4(M.6.896A); παντὸς γὰρ εἶναι δ. τοὺς ἱερεῖς τοῦ θεοῦ δοκιμωτέρους Eus.*v.C*.4.27(p.128.1; M.20.1176B); παραιτήσῃ ...δ. παράνομον *Const.App*.4.6.5; **2.** of God and Christ, Tat.*orat*.12 (p.13.25; M.6.832C); τοῦ μεγάλου δ. Athenag.*leg*.12.1(M.6.913A); Or.*hom.12.5 in Jer*.(p.92.14; M.13.385C); *Const.App*.8.4.5; Chrys. *hom.40.4 in Jo*.(8.242A); **3.** in gen., of a critic δ. τῶν λόγων Meth.*res*. 1.33(p.270.15; M.41.1097A); μὴ τῶν ἔργων ἔσο δ. Nil.*Eulog*.15(M.79. 1113A).

δικέρατον, τό, sum consisting of *two siliquae*, Thphn.*chron*.p.345 (M.108.832B).

δίκη, ἡ, 1. *penalty*, of divine judgement πιστεύοντες...κατ' ἀξίαν τῶν πράξεων ἕκαστον τίσειν διὰ πυρὸς αἰωνίου δίκας Just.*1apol*.17.4 (M.6.353D); αἰωνίαν δ. ὑπ' ἐμπύροις θεοῦ τιμωρίαις παθεῖν Meth. *symp*.11(p.135.13; M.18.212B); αἰώνιος δ. Chrys.*stat*.5.2(2.62E); Cyr. *glaph.Gen*.2(1.42A); **2.** partic. *fine* δώσῃ δ. τῷ φίσκῳ τάλαντον *CG-CI* 1.28(Corinth, saec. v).

***δικηλής,** (for [*]διχηλής) *dividing the hoof* δ. τὸν εὐσεβῶς ἐν τῷ αἰῶνι τούτῳ πολιτευόμενον Or.*sel.in Lev*.11:3(M.12.401A); (v. διχηλέω).

δικίδιον, τό, dim. of δίκη, *lawsuit*, Synes.*ep*.105(M.66.1488B).

***δικλήματος,** *with two branches*, ‡Ath.*disp*.36(M.28.488A).

δικόρυμβος, *two-peaked*, Paul.Sil.*Soph*.849(M.86.2151B).

[*]δίκραιρος, (for δικέραιος, metri gratia) *two-horned*, Paul.Sil. *Soph*.856(M.86.2151B).

δικρανοφόρος, masc. as subst., (cf. Lat. *furcifer*) *gaol-bird*; as term of abuse for Arius, Const.ap.Gel.Cyz.*h.e*.3.19.21(M.85.1349C).

δίκρουνος, *with double source* δ. ὑετὸν αἵματος καὶ ὕδατος Germ. CP *or*.2(M.98.285A).

***δικτυάλωτος,** *caught in a net*; of animals, Synes.*insomn*.14 (p.175.16; M.66.1308D).

δίκτυον, τό, 1. *net*; met., of Christian preaching and missionary work χάριν λόγου πεπλεγμένην ὡς δ. καὶ συγκειμένην ἀπὸ τῶν... γραφῶν ὡς ἀμφίβληστρον Or.*hom.16.1 in Jer*.(p.132.6; M.13.437D); γέγονας εἴσω δ. ἐκκλησιαστικῶν Cyr.H.*procatech*.5; εὐαγγελικῆς μυσταγωγίας τὸ δ. ἁπλώσαντες id.ap.*cat.Lc*.5:1(p.40.26; λίνον M.72. 553C); εἴσω τῶν ἀποστολικῶν δ. ἐγένετο Thdt.*Philm*.proem.(3.711); of snares of false reasoning, Eus.*e.th*.1.14(p.74.28; M.24.853B); **2.** *lattice*, ref. Cant.2:9 interpreted of light of revelation mediated by Law, Gr.Nyss.*hom.5 in Cant*.(M.44.864C); ref. 4Reg.1:2 interpreted of consequences of sin, Nil.*exerc*.50(M.79.781B); hence **3.** *balustrade* dividing sanctuary from body of church, fencing in the altar, Eus.*h.e*.10.4.44(M.20.865D).

***δικτύφιον, τό,** *small net*, Clem.*q.d.s*.20(p.172.32; conj. δικτύδια M.9.625A).

δίκυμος, *twin, double* δ. ὄρος *Orac.Sib*.12.84; conj. for δίκμος, *ib*.5.32.

δίλογος, *double-tongued* διάκονοι...μὴ δ. Polyc.*ep*.5.2.

διμέδιμνον, τό, measure of *two bushels* χωρίον...ὁ νοῦς γέγονε τῆς... θεότητος, ὥσπερ...καὶ ἡ σάρξ, οὐ σύνοικος, ὡς ἡ τῶν αἱρετικῶν... πλανᾶται οἴησις, οὐ γὰρ ἂν μεδιμναῖον, λέγουσα, χωρήσει δ., σωματικῶς τὰ ἄυλα κρίνουσα Jo.D.*f.o*.3.6(M.94.1005C); id.*Man*.1.25(M.94. 1529C).

διμερής, *in two parts*; as subst., *faction, division*, Jo.Mal.*chron*. 18 p.492(M.97.712B).

διμηνιαῖος ([*]διμηναῖος), *two months old* ἔφη [sc. Nestorius] ἐγὼ δ. ἢ τριμηνιαῖον θεὸν οὐ λέγω Cyr.*ep*.23(p.66.28; διμηναῖον 5².84E); ἔφη [sc. Nestorius] δ. ἢ τριμηνιαῖον μὴ δεῖν λέγεσθαι θεόν Thdot.Anc. ap.CEph.(431)*act*.1(*ACO* 1.1.2 p.38.10, v.l. διμηναῖον H.1.1397D); ἐγὼ τὸν γενόμενον διμηναῖον...οὐκ ἂν θεὸν ὀνομάσαιμι Thphn.*chron*. p.77(M.108.240A); ὁ διμηναῖος [sc. χρόνος] *space of two months*, Jo. Scholast.*coll.cap*.12.

***διμόδιον, τό,** measure *containing two modii*, Jo.Mal.*chron*.11 p.278(M.97.420C).

διμοιρίτης, ὁ, 1. *leader of a* διμοιρία, *company commander*, Synes. *insomn*.8(p.171.18; M.66.1305B); **2.** name given to Apollinarius and his followers as confessing Christ in only two of the three parts of his human nature and denying the rational soul, Epiph.*anac*.77 (p.415.5; M.42.873C); id.*haer*.78.1(p.452.2; M.42.700B); Eust.Mon. *ep*.(M.86.905D); Jo.D.*haer*.77(M.94.728A).

***διμοιρότριτον, τό,** *half and third*, denoting mathematical fractions, Max.*opusc*.(M.91.269B).

***διοδευτός,** *passable*, Or.*Jo*.6.46(28; p.155.30; M.14.281A).

διοδεύω, 1. *pass through*; **a.** lit.; in Valent. Christology, Iren. *haer*.1.7.2(M.7.513A) cit. s. σωλήν; of soul travelling through αἰσθητὸς κόσμος, Max.*ambig*.(M.91.1252B); **b.** met.; of aeon Sophia passing through πάθος, Iren.*haer*.1.4.5(M.7.485B); of an historian traversing a period, Gel.Cyz.*h.e*.3.1.1; **2.** *pass over, cross* a river, Thphn.*chron*.p.198(M.108.513A); **3.** *extend* πῦρ...διοδεῦσαν κατέφλεξεν Hipp.*Dan*.3.30.3(p.178.11); **4.** *pass away*, Nil.*Eulog*.13 (M.79.1109C).

***διόδμητος,** *wonderfully built*, Paul.Sil.*Soph*.570(M.86.2141A).

διοικ-έω, 1. *control*; **a.** in gen., *LS*; **b.** of moral and spiritual influence ~εῖν τὴν ἀγνωμοσύνην τῶν ἀνθρώπων *Hom.Clem*.3.61; ἔτι ὑπὸ σαρκὸς ~εῖται Bas.*ascet*.2(2.325E; M.31.885C); ~ούμεθα, δέει τε τιμωρίας, καὶ σωτηρίας ἐλπίδι...καὶ ἀσκήσει τῶν ἀρετῶν Gr.Naz. *or*.30.19(p.138.2; M.36.128B); ψυχικὸν κληθὲν σῶμα τὸ ψυχῇ καὶ οὐ πνεύματι ἁγίῳ ~ούμενον Oecum.*1Cor*.15:44(p.443.9); **c.** of divine government of world: pagan θεοὺς τοὺς τὰ πάντα ~οῦντας *M.Carp*.4; Christian τὴν τοῦ δημιουργήσαντος καὶ ~οῦντος τόδε τὸ πᾶν...δύναμιν Athenag.*res*.5(p.52.31; M.6.981D); τοῦ τέχνῃ ἀφάτῳ καὶ δυνάμει ~οῦντος τὰ ὅλα θεοῦ Or.*princ*.4.1.7(p.303.6; M.11.353B); Meth.*symp*. 2.4(p.19.8; M.18.52C); ἀγαθῇ θεοῦ προνοίᾳ...~εῖσθαι τὸν κόσμον *Hom.Clem*.2.36; αὐτοματισμὸς μὲν οὐκ ἔστιν, ἀλλὰ κατὰ πρόνοιαν ~εῖται ὁ κόσμος *ib*.11.34; **d.** of other powers, zodiac (Valentinian) ὡς γὰρ ὑπ' ἐκείνων ἡ γένεσις ~εῖται, οὕτως ὑπὸ τῶν ἀποστόλων ἡ ἀναγέννησις ἐφορᾶται Clem.*exc.Thdot*.25(p.115.13; M.9.672B); angels (Valentinian), Iren.*haer*.1.23.3(M.7.672A); κατ' ἔθνος καὶ κατὰ βασιλείαν ἀρχάγγελοι ~οῦσιν Cosm.Ind.*top*.2(M.88.132C); **2.** *administer*; **a.** of priests' administration on earth of heavenly things, Chrys.*sac*.3.5(p.54.7; 1.383B); **b.** of administration of Church, by an apostle, *Clem.ep*.5(M.2.40B); by bishops, *MAMA* 1.170(Ladik, c. 340); τὸν τοῦ ἐπισκόπου κλῆρον...~ήσαντος Epiph. *haer*.63.3(p.400.9; M.41.1064D); CCP(381)*can*.2; ὁ τὴν ἐκκλησίαν... ~ῶν ἐπίσκοπος CChalc.*can*.12; Thdt.*ep*.86(4.1157); **c.** monastic, by οἰκονόμος of monastery, *V.Pach.Φ* 83(p.56.14); cf.*PLond*.1913.13; **3.** *act as manager* for a circus faction τῷ οἰκείῳ σου δήμῳ παρενοχλοῦσιν, ἵνα ὁ Κρούκης ~ήσῃ Thphn.*chron*.p.241(M.108.608A).

διοίκησις, ἡ, A. *administration, control, ordering*; **1.** in gen. οὐ χρὴ ἐπίσκοπον ἢ πρεσβύτερον καθιέναι ἑαυτὸν εἰς δημοσίας δ. *Can. App*.81; **2.** of ordering of world; **a.** by pagan deities δι' οὓς...ἡ τῶν δημοσίων δ. συνίσταται Maximinus Daia.ap.Eus.*h.e*.9.9a.6 (M.20.825C); **b.** by God οὐρανοὶ τῇ δ. αὐτοῦ σαλευόμενοι ἐν εἰρήνῃ ὑποτάσσονται αὐτῷ *1Clem*.20.1; Just.*dial*.29.3(M.6.537B); of λογικὴ καὶ θεία δ. reflected in human government, Clem.*str*.1.24(p.100.3; M.8.905B); τῇ μιᾷ καὶ θείᾳ τῇ προνοητικῇ δ. *ib*.2.2(p.115.2; 933C); Or. *or*.6.3(p.313.14; M.11.437A); ref. problems of providence, id.*princ*. 3.1.17(p.229.1; M.11.285C); Eus.*p.e*.6.6(249C; M.21.424B); **c.** by Christ, Eus.*e.th*.1.13(p.73.13; M.24.852A); τῆς τῶν ὅλων δ. τὴν πρόνοιαν ἀναδέχεσθαι αὐτόν *ib*.3.2(p.142.13; 977A); ὑπήκοος πρὸς τὴν τῶν ὄντων δημιουργίαν...ὑπήκοος πρὸς πᾶσαν δ. Eun.*exp.fid*.2(p.256); **d.** by angelic powers τινα τῶν πεπιστευμένων τὰς ἐν οὐρανοῖς δ. *Diogn*.7.2; Athenag.*leg*.24.3(M.6.948A); Meth.*res*.1.37(p.278.3; M.41. 1104A); of Devil τὴν τοῦ ἀέρος παρὰ τοῦ δημιουργοῦ κεκληρωμένος δ. Bas.Sel.or.23.1(M.85.269C); **3.** of eccl. administration τὴν δ. τῆς ἐκκλησίας Clem.ep.3(M.2.37A); Hom.Clem.3.64; ἔθος...τὸν ἐν τῇ Ἀλεξανδρείᾳ ἀρχιεπίσκοπον πάσης τε Αἰγύπτου καὶ Θηβαΐδος, Μαρεώτου τε καὶ Λιβύης, Ἀμμωνιακῆς, Μαρμαρίδος τε καὶ Πενταπόλεως ἔχειν τὴν ἐκκλησιαστικὴν δ. Epiph.haer.68.1(p.141.17; M.42.185A); Proc.G.Is.42:1–9(M.87.2364B); monastic, V.Pach.Φ 130 (p.82.27); Sergia Olymp.1(p.44); **4.** of Church *order* οὐδὲν παρακεχαραγμένον τῆς πίστεως...οὔτε τῆς ὁμολογίας, οὔτε τῆς ἐκκλησιαστικῆς δ. καὶ κανόνος καὶ πίστεως Epiph.haer.70.10(p.242.27; M.42.356C).

B. *sphere of administration* or *government*; **1.** in gen., Eus.h.e.2.23.2(M.20.196C); **2.** *a group of civil provinces* governed by a vicar, Const.ap.Eus.v.C.4.36(p.131.30; M.20.1185B); Const.ib.3.19(p.86.26; 1077C); Synes.ep.73(M.66.1437C); **3.** recognized by Church and employed as unit of administration, *group of provinces* administered by exarch or patriarch τοὺς ὑπὲρ διοίκησιν ἐπισκόπους ταῖς ὑπερορίοις ἐκκλησίαις μὴ ἐπιέναι...ἀλλὰ...τὸν μὲν Ἀλεξανδρείας ἐπίσκοπον τὰ ἐν Αἰγύπτῳ μόνον οἰκονομεῖν, τοὺς δὲ τῆς ἀνατολῆς ἐπισκόπους τὴν ἀνατολὴν...διοικεῖν...καὶ τοὺς τῆς Ἀσιανῆς δ. τὰ κατὰ τὴν Ἀσίαν μόνην οἰκονομεῖν CCP(381)can.2; ὁ ἀρχιερεὺς τῆς Αἰγυπτιακῆς δ. Pall.v.Chrys.7(p.39.5; M.47.24); ib.(p.41.12; 25); νενοσηκότων πραγμάτων ὅλης τῆς Ἀσιανῆς δ. δι' ἀπειρίαν...ποιμένων ib.14(p.88.26; 50); κληροῦται...τῆς...Ποντικῆς δ. Ἑλλάδιος..., Γρηγόριος ὁ Νύσσης..., καὶ Ὀτρήιος Socr.h.e.5.8.15(M.67.580A); συνελθοῦσα σύνοδος ...ἐκ τῆς Αἰγυπτιακῆς δ. Cyr.ep.17(p.33.5; 5^{2}.67C); εἰ δὲ πρὸς τὸν τῆς αὐτῆς ἐπαρχίας μητροπολίτην ἐπίσκοπος...ἀμφισβητοίη, καταλαμβανέτω ἢ τὸν ἔξαρχον τῆς δ., ἢ τὸν τῆς...Κωνσταντινουπόλεως θρόνον, καὶ ἐπ' αὐτῷ δικαζέσθω CChalc.can.9; οἱ...πατριάρχαι δ. ἑκάστης id.act.2(ACO 2.1.2 p.78.26; H.2.285B); τοποτηρητῶν τῶν ἀποστολικῶν θρόνων τῆς ἀνατολικῆς δ. CNic.(787)act.3(H.4.124E); **4.** *diocese* governed by bishop, Cod.Afr.53 tit. [= παροικία infra]; ib.56 [interchangeable with παροικία]; ib.117.

C. *digestion*, A.Jo.9(p.156.21).

διοικητής, ὁ, *administrator, controller*, of bishop οἰκονόμον καὶ δ. τῶν ἐκκλησιαστικῶν πραγμάτων Const.App.2.35.3; of God πάντων δ. Ar.ep.Alex.ap.Ath.syn.16(p.243.30; M.26.709A); of Christ τὸν πρῶτον δ. τῶν ὅλων Clem.str.7.2(p.8.14; M.9.413A).

διοικονομέω, **1.** *deal with, attend to*, Or.hom.12.3 in Jer.(p.90.25; M.13.384C); **2.** *arrange, order*, Meth.res.1.43(p.291.2; M.41.1113A); Const.or.s.c.3(p.156.26; M.20.1240B); Germ.CP or.1(M.98.232D).

δίοιξις, ἡ, *opening*, met. τῶν γραφῶν...δ. ταῖς τῶν μανθάνειν ὀρεγομένων ψυχαῖς Clem.str.2.11(p.139.7; M.8.985A).

διολισθαίν-ω, **1.** *slip away* from, *fall away* from, Meth.res.1.61 (p.326.8; M.41.1160B); Eus.e.th.1.13(p.73.6; M.24.849D); Didym. Trin.3.27(M.39.944A); ~ων τῶν...νοημάτων Gel.Cyz.h.e.2.13.4(M.85.1253A); c. ἐκ: ἐκ τῆς μνήμης ~οντος Synes.insomn.12(p.183.16; M.66.1316B); **2.** *slip away* towards, Cyr.glaph.Dt.(1.419D); οὐρανὸς καὶ γῆ...πρὸς πτῶσιν ~οντες Bas.Sel.or.1.2(M.85.29C).

***διομιλέω**, *converse together*, †Jo.D.B.J.38(M.96.1220A).

***διομοσία**, ἡ, *pledge, oral warranty*, Ath.Scholast.coll.5.2(p.71).

***Διονυσιακῶς**, *like Dionysius* (the Areopagite) ἐπείπερ...ταῦτα μιμήματα κἂν οὐκ ἀνθρωπόμορφα· μάτην καὶ ὅσα ἄλλα αἰσθηταῖς εἰκόσι, Δ. εἰπεῖν, παραδέδοται ἡμῖν· δι' ὧν ἐπὶ τὰς νοητὰς...φησίν, ἀναγόμεθα θεωρίας Thdr.Stud.epp.2.36(M.99.1220B).

διοπετής, *fallen from God*, masc. as subst., apptly. a veiled name for Christ, Pers.(p.28.10).

***διοπλίζομαι**, *arm oneself thoroughly*, Epiph.haer.66.70(p.112.4; M.42.141A).

***διοπόμπησις**, ἡ, *dismissal, getting rid of*, Clem.str.7.6(p.25.21, v.l. διαπομπήσει M.9.448A).

***διόρασις**, ἡ, *insight*, Niceph.Ur.v.Sym.216(M.86.3185A); ib.236 (3201D).

διορατικός, **1.** *clear-sighted*, Gr.Nyss.Eun.9(2 p.208.16; M.45.805C); Chrys.hom.4.3 in 1Tim.(11.572D); neut. as subst., Or.schol. in Cant.2:17(M.17.268B); Chrys.hom.5.5 in 2Thess.(11.544E); id. hom.13.3 in 1Tim.(11.622A); **2.** *discerning, perceptive*; **a.** in gen., of spiritual and intellectual insight τὸ δ. τῆς ψυχῆς...ὄμμα Clem. paed.2.9(p.206.31; M.8.496A); ὁ δὴ συνίων καὶ δ. οὗτός ἐστιν ὁ γνωστικός id.str.4.22(p.308.5; M.8.1345B); ψυχὴν...τοῦ τε ἀληθοῦς δ. καὶ τοῦ ψευδοῦς διελεγκτικήν ib.6.11(p.477.15; M.9.312B); ib.7.7 (p.33.23; 464B); ψυχαὶ νοεραὶ καὶ δ. Or.comm.in Mt.11.17(p.63.7; M.13.961A); δ. τῆς ἀληθείας ὄψεις id.Jo.20.32(26; p.369.10; M.14.645C); τὸ λογικὸν...καὶ δ. τῆς φρονήσεως κάλλος Meth.symp.6.1 (p.65.5; M.18.113C); δ. τοῦ βελτίονος Gr.Nyss.v.Mos.19(M.44.305B); ὁ κεκαθαρμένος καὶ δ. τῆς ψυχῆς ὀφθαλμός id.hom.5 in Cant.(M.44.864B); δ. ἐκεῖνος, ὁ δι' ἑνὸς τοῦ τῆς ψυχῆς ὀφθαλμοῦ πρὸς μόνον τὸ ἀγαθὸν βλέπων ib.8(952A); id.Eun.3(2 p.14.2; M.45.577C); ὁ δὲ δ. τὴν ψυχὴν καὶ πεπαιδευμένος, μὴ μόνοις ὀφθαλμοῖς ἐπιτρέπων τὴν τῶν ὄντων ἐπίσκεψιν, οὐ μέχρι τῶν φαινομένων στήσεται...ἀλλὰ καὶ ψυχῆς φύσιν περινοεῖ id.virg.11(p.291.23; M.46.364B); Isid.Pel.epp.2.188 (M.78.637C); ref. Jo.3:23 Αἰνὼν δὲ ἑρμηνεύεται ὀφθαλμὸς βασάνου, τουτέστιν ἐξητασμένη...καὶ ἔγκοπος θεωρία. δ. τοίνυν ἐγένοντο οἱ βαπτισθέντες Nil.epp.1.273(M.79.184A); V.Pach.Φ 42(p.26.20); V. Pach.Σ 8(p.174.7); of demons δ. ... τῶν ὑλικῶν ἰδιωμάτων †Bas.Is. 218(1.543A; M.30.496D); **b.** of prophetic insight or 'second sight', of demons ἔχοντές τι περὶ τῶν μελλόντων δ., ἅτε γυμνοὶ τῶν γηΐνων σωμάτων τυγχάνοντες Or.Cels.4.92(p.365.12; M.11.1169C); ib.7.4 (p.156.4; 1425B) cit. s. ἀφή; καθαρεύουσα ψυχὴ...δύναται, δ. γενομένη, πλείονα καὶ μακρότερα βλέπειν τῶν δαιμόνων Ath.v.Anton.34(M.26.893B); Isid.Pel.epp.1.42(M.78.208D); Apophth.Patr.(M.65.385D); Cyr.Is.2.5(2.341E); ὅταν γὰρ ὁ ἐν αὐτοῖς κύριος...ἀποκαλύπτῃ αὐτοῖς, δ. εἰσιν· καὶ μὴ ἀποκαλύπτοντος, ὡς πάντες ἄνθρωποί εἰσιν, μέντοι γε ἀδιάλειπτον ἕτερον δ. ἔχουσι τὸν κύριον ὁρᾶν V.Pach.Φ 48(p.31.12); Cyr.S.v.Sab.7(p.91.19); Gr.Mag.dial.(tr.Zach.)2.8(M.PL.66.147B); ib.2.14(161A); Marc.Diac.v.Porph.35; Dor.doct.11.6(M.88.1741A); **c.** *consisting in prophetic insight* τὸ δ. χάρισμα as monastic attainment, Ammonas ep.3(p.439.13); Bars.resp.proem.(M.88.1812D); Steph.Diac.v.Steph.(M.100.1168B); **d.** neut. as subst., *insight, discernment* τὸ δ. τῆς ψυχῆς ἀποτείνειν πρὸς τὴν εὕρεσιν Clem.str.5.1 (p.333.8; M.9.25A); Or.fr.6 in 1 Reg.(p.297.19; M.12.993A); Chrys. hom.13.1 in Eph.(11.96A); Procl.CP annunt.2(M.85.429A); of God whose 'eyes' represent τὸ δ., Didym.(‡Bas.)Eun.5(1.316C; M.29.757C); **e.** in interpretation of name Israel ὁ τῷ ὄντι δ. Clem.str.1.5 (p.20.15; M.8.725A); Or.fr.26 in Jo.(p.503.25); Eus.d.e.4.10(p.166.17; M.22.277B); Diod.Ps.71:17(M.33.1613A); Nil.exerc.26(M.79.753B).

***διορατικῶς**, **1.** *with discernment*, Or.Jo.20.33(27; p.370.22; M.14.648C); Bas.hom.in Ps.48(1.182E; M.29.445A); Proc.G.Gen.18:1–3 (M.87.365C); **2.** *with clear perception*, †Bas.Is.182(1.512E; M.30.425D).

διοργανόω, *fashion*, ‡Gr.Nyss.or.2 in Gen.1:26(M.44.293B); Leont.H.Nest.4.9(M.86.1669C).

διορθόω, *correct, set right, amend*; of moral and spiritual amendment, Or.princ.3.1.23(p.241.4; M.11.300B); V.Pach.Φ 70(p.51.17); διορθῶσαί σε τοῦ σφάλματος V.Pach.Λ 2(p.125.5); Sophr.H.mir. Cyr.et Jo.37(M.87.3564C); of work of Christ, Ath.inc.43.7(M.25.173A); τὴν τῶν μαθητῶν πενίαν τῷ πλούτῳ τῆς χάριτος διορθωσάμενος Bas.Sel.or.6.1(M.85.84D).

διόρθωσις, ἡ, *correction, setting right, amendment*, of moral and spiritual amendment ἡ ἐκ μεταμελείας δ. Gr.Nyss.or.catech.35 (p.138.15, v.l. ὄρθωσις M.45.92B); through physical suffering, Nil. epp.3.170(M.79.464B); ἄγγελοι...αὐτῷ φανέντες εἰς δ. V.Pach.Φ 108 (p.71.21); V.Pach.Λ 27(p.155.11); μετάνοιαν καὶ δ. Cyr.Ps.38:5 (M.69.972D); ἡ εἰς τὴν ἐκκλησίαν εἴσοδος παραδηλοῖ...τὴν διὰ μετανοίας δ. Max.myst.9(M.91.689A); of work of Christ, Gr.Nyss.or. catech.27(p.103.3; M.45.72A); μετὰ τὴν δ. τῶν ἀνθρωπίνων πλημμελημάτων ἀναλελυκότα ‡Gr.Nyss.Ar.et Sab.6(M.45.1289B); of Christ's δ. of the Law, Cyr.Ps.16:1(M.69.813D).

διορθωτής, ὁ, *corrector, one who sets right*, Iren.haer.1.13.1(M.7.577B); of emperor ἕνα δὲ καὶ τὸν ἐπὶ γῆς δ. Eus.l.C.10(p.223.11; M.20.1373C); Chrys.hom.60.1 in Mt.(7.606E); of Christ ὁ...λόγος...δ. ... τῶν ἁμαρτιῶν Clem.paed.1.8(p.129.28; M.8.332B); δ. τοῦ παντός Eus.l.C.12(p.231.18; 1389B); ἀδιόρθωτον ἡμῖν τὸ κακόν, σοῦ δεῖται δ. Cyr.H.catech.12.7; Gr.Nyss.v.Mos.(M.44.397C); Mac.Aeg.elev.11 (M.34.900A); of H. Ghost ὁ κοινὸς τοῦ βίου δ. Bas.hom.in Ps.1(1.92A; M.29.216A).

[*]**διορία**, v. διωρία.

διορίζ-ω, **1.** *distinguish*, Meth.res.2.2(p.332.13; M.41.1165A); ἰδέαι...ποιότησι,...διωρισμέναι Hom.Clem.3.34; ἡ τούτων [sc. ἀθανασία ἀγγέλων]...διωρισμένη ἐκείνης [sc. ἀθανασίας θεοῦ] ὅσον δημιούργημα δημιουργοῦ Didym.Trin.3.16(M.39.872A); **2.** *separate, divide*, of function of Logos ᾧ πάντα διατέτακται καὶ ~εται Diogn. 7.2; of Horus in Valentinian system καθὸ μὲν ἑδράζει καὶ στηρίζει σταυρὸν εἶναι, καθὸ δὲ μερίζει καὶ ~ει, ὅρον Iren.haer.1.3.5(M.7.476A); Christol. ~οντες...ἡμῖν γυμνὸν τοῦ ἑνωθέντος λόγου δεικνύντες ἕτερον Χριστὸν καὶ υἱόν Cyr.Heb.2:9(p.390.6).

διορισμός, ὁ, *division, separation*; of σταυρός (Gnost.), A.Jo.98 (p.200.11) cit. s. σταυρός; v. διορίζω, ὅρος.

διοριστικός, **1.** *dividing, separative*; of Horus in Valent. system whose δ. ἐνέργεια is alluded to in Mt.10:34, Iren.haer.1.3.5(M.7.476A); **2.** *determining*, Leont.H.Nest.1.13(M.86.1452B) cit. s. διατηρητικός; **3.** *distinctive* μόναις δὲ ἰδιότησιν χαρακτηριστικαῖς εἴτ' οὖν δ. ἀλλήλων νοεῖσθαι Cyr.apol.orient.(p.51.33; 6^{1}.182C).

διορυγή, ἡ, 1. *place hollowed out, cave, hollow*, Leont.N.*v.Jo. Eleem*.41(p.80.12); Gr.Mag.*dial*.(tr.Zach.)2.1(M.*PL*.66.129C); **2.** *digging through* μνημάτων δ. Isid.Pel.*epp*.1.490(M.78.449A).

***διορυκτής, ὁ,** *one who digs through, burglar*, *T.Sal*.8.9(M.122.1328D).

διορυχή, ἡ, *digging through* for burglary, Esaias *or*.8.17(p.40).

***Διοσκοριανοί, οἱ,** name of monophysite sect who separated from Tim. I Al. after latter received some clergy of Proterius into communion, *followers of Dioscorus*, Tim.CP *haer*.(M.86.44C).

***Διοσκορῖται, οἱ,** = foreg., Dam.*troph*.suppl.(p.283.11); Anast.S.*haer*.(p.261).

διοτρεφής, prob. f.l. for διοπτῆρας, *seers* ἐπὶ γόητας καὶ δ. αὐτομολεῖν ‡Caes.Naz.*dial*.112(M.38.992).

***διούσιος,** *of two substances* δ. ὄντος Χριστοῦ Leont.H.*Nest*.1.24(M.86.1492B).

διόχλησις, ἡ, *annoyance*, Eus.*Ps*.142:11(M.24.52B).

***δίπετρος,** ? *between two rocks* ἐν τῷ φρέατι διπέτρῳ Epiph.*gemm*.10(M.43.300D; conj. τῇ φρεάτιδι πέτρᾳ).

διπλῆ, ἡ, 1. a critical sign, > *diple. hanc scriptores nostri adponunt in libris ecclesiasticorum virorum ad separanda vel [ad] demonstranda testimonia...Scripturarum.* ⪢ *diple* περὶ στίχον. *hanc primus Leogoras Syracusanus posuit Homericis versibus ad separationem Olympi a caelo.* ⋗ *diple* περιεστιγμένη...*hanc antiqui in his opponebant quae Zenodotus...non recte adjecerat, aut detraxerat, aut permutaverat*...⇝ *diple* ὀβολισμένη *interponitur ad separandos in comoediis vel tragoediis periodos*...⩾ *diple superne obolata ponitur ad conditiones locorum ac temporum personarumque mutatas.* >̄< *diple recta et adversa superne obolata ponitur finita loco suo monade, significatque similem sequentem quoque esse*, Isid.H.*etym*.1.21.13ff.; **2.** *a kind of rod*, hence a *blow* of such a rod, †Gregent.*leg.Hom*.5(M.86.584B); *ib*.19(592A).

διπλόη, ἡ, 1. *double-mindedness, inclination to go two ways* εἰς τὴν μίαν ἐκείνην ἕξιν ἐκ τῆς εἰς τὴν δ. ἐπιτηδειότητος ἐκθλίψαντας ἑαυτούς Clem.*str*.7.7(p.35.3; M.9.465C); *ib*.7.18(p.78.3; 556B); id.*ecl*.8(p.139.3; M.9.701B); **2.** *ambiguity*, Or.*Cels*.1.18(p.70.4; M.11.692C); Gr.Naz.*ep*.58(M.37.116B); Cyr.ap.*cat.2Cor*.3:14(p.370.13); **3.** *duplicity*, Gr.Naz.*carm*.1.2.34.64(M.37.950A); plur., *ib*.2.1.14.25(1247A); Chrys.*hom.8.1 in 2Cor*.(10.492E); Cyr.*Ps*.11:1(M.69.793D); **4.** *twofold character*, theol. ἁπλῆς...τῆς τοῦ λόγου φύσεως...οὐδεμίαν δ. καὶ σύνθεσιν ἐν ἑαυτῇ δεικνυούσης Gr.Nyss.*or.catech*.1(p.9.10; M.45.13C); of divine nature πᾶσαν δ. ἀπαναινομένη Dion.Ar.*d.n*.4.9(M.3.825A); Christol. τῶν φύσεων ἀσύγχυτος ἡ δ. γνωρίζεται Sophr.H.*ep.syn*.(M.87.3177B).

διπλοΐς, ἡ, *cloak*, Eus.*h.e*.7.18.2(M.20.680C); of priestly robe, Or.*engast*.3(p.285.11; M.12.1016B); of bishop's cloak, in comparison of Basil with Samuel, Gr.Naz.*or*.43.73(M.36.596A); Jo.Mon.*hymn.Bas*.4(M.96.1372D).

***διπλοκαρδία, ἡ,** *duplicity*, *Did*.5.1; *Barn*.20.1.

***διπλοκίνδυνος,** *doubly dangerous*, Geo.Pis.*Heracl*.1.138(M.92.1310A).

διπλόος, 1. *dual, of two kinds*; **a.** in gen. τὸ βάπτισμα οὖν δ. ..., τὸ μὲν αἰσθητὸν δι' ὕδατος...τὸ δὲ νοητὸν διὰ πνεύματος Clem.*exc.Thdot*.81(p.132.3; M.9.696B); δ. τε ἡ δύναμις τοῦ πυρός, ἡ μὲν πρὸς δημιουργίαν...ἡ δὲ πρὸς ἀνάλωσιν id.*ecl*.26(p.144.16; M.9.712A); of Pentecostal tongues δ. τὴν χρῆσιν...τὸν μὲν διάβολον καταφλέγειν, φωτίζειν δὲ τοὺς καθημένους ἐν σκότει ‡Chrys.*pent*.2(3.792E); **b.** Christol., of Christ as possessing two natures ἀπεστάλη μέν, ἀλλ' ὡς ἄνθρωπος· δ. γὰρ ἦν Gr.Naz.*or*.38.15(M.36.328C); λαβὼν τό, Χριστός, ὡς τῶν δύο φύσεων προσηγορίαν σημαντικήν, ἀκινδύνως αὐτὸν καὶ δούλου μορφήν...καὶ θεὸν ὀνομάζει, τῶν λεγομένων εἰς τὸ τῶν φύσεων ἀλήπτως μεριζομένων δ. Nest.*fr*.C 9(p.254.12)ap.Cyr.*apol.orient*.(p.39.6; 6¹.165C); cf. *numquid ego duplicem Christum solus appello? nonne semetipsum et templum solubile et deum nuncupat suscitantem?* Nest.*fr*.C 9(p.259.8); *duplicem confiteamur et adoremus ut unum*, *ib*.(p.263.14); ὁ υἱὸς τοῦ θεοῦ δ. ἐστὶ τὰς φύσεις *ib*.C 10(p.274.15); ὁ εἷς ἐστι δ., οὐ τῇ ἀξίᾳ, ἀλλὰ τῇ φύσει *ib*. C 12(p.281.8)ap.Cyr.*Nest*.2.6(p.42.6; 6¹.44E); Nest.*fr*.D 4(p.354.13) *ib*.(p.72.34; 6¹.90E); ἀποσώζει δὲ...ἐν τῇ καθ' ἑαυτὸν θεωρίᾳ τὸ ἐν νοήσει δ. διὰ τὴν μετὰ σαρκὸς οἰκονομίαν Cyr.*Jo*.11.9(4.974D); εἰμὶ γὰρ νῦν κατ' οὐσίαν δ., καὶ ἄνθρωπος δηλαδὴ καὶ θεός ‡Gr.Nyss.*hom.6.36 in Jo*.(p.214.11); ὁρᾷς αὐτὸν ἐπὶ πῶλον σήμερον· ἀλλ' ὡς ἄνθρωπον· δ. γὰρ ἦν Eulog.*palm*.8(M.86.2925B); κατὰ Γρηγόριον καὶ τοὺς λοιποὺς πατέρας σὺν Κυρίλλῳ φαμέν, ὅτιπερ δ. κατὰ τὴν οὐσίαν· καὶ πάλιν κατὰ τὸν αὐτὸν Κυρίλλου σκοπόν, ὡς οὐ δ. τῇ χαρακτηριστικῇ ὑποστάσει· εἷς γὰρ ἔμεινε καὶ ἐνανθρωπήσας ὁ θεὸς λόγος Ephr.Ant.*fr*.(M.86.2108D); †Gregent.*disp*.(M.86.644B); τὴν φύσιν ἁπλοῦς· ἅτε διαμείνας θεός...καὶ αὖθις δ. ὡς γενόμενος σάρξ Max.*opusc*.(M.91.73B); **2.** *doubled*, i.e. *two* μετὰ δ. ἦμαρ Nonn.*par.Jo*.4:43(M.43.781B); *ib*.19:18(901B); ποιεῖ δ. μερίδας ἑκάστῳ τῶν κληρικῶν καὶ βάπτει εἰς τὸν κρατῆρα *Lit.Jac*.(p.230.10).

***διπλοσύνθετος,** *combined in pairs*; of the bones round the brain, Melet.*nat.hom*.51(M.64.1152C).

***διπλότειχος,** *having two walls*, †Hipp.Th.*fr*.7.1(p.33.2; M.117.1033C).

***διπλοτομία, ἡ,** *double incision*, *Mir.Artem*.27(p.40.19).

***δίπλουτος,** *doubly rich*, *Schol*.28 in Jo.Clim.*scal*.1(M.88.652D).

δίπλωσις, ἡ, *doubling*, Leont.H.*Nest*.7.4(M.86.1768A); plur., *folds*, Hier.H.*Trin*.(M.40.856C).

***διπροσωπίτης, ὁ,** *one who holds doctrine of two persons in Christ*, Eust.Mon.*ep*.(M.86.924A).

διπρόσωπος, 1. *twofold* δ. κακὸν ὁ θυμὸς μετὰ ψεύδους *T.Dan* 4.7; **2.** *two-faced, deceitful*, *T.Aser* 2.5; *ib*.3.2; δ. τὴν καρδίαν Cyr.*Ps*.61:5(M.69.1117A); **3.** *of two persons*, Christol. ἐφ' ἑνὸς δὲ προσώπου πολλάκις δ. ἡμῖν εἰσφέρεται λόγου σχῆμα καὶ κατ' οὐδένα τρόπον ἀδικεῖ τὴν ἀλήθειαν Cyr.*Pulch*.(p.37.21; 5².144E); μηδὲ διστὰς εἰς ἄνθρωπον ἰδικῶς καὶ εἰς θεὸν λόγον, δ. ἡμῖν ἀνατύπου τὸν Ἐμμανουὴλ id.*inc.unigen*.(5¹.694E); Leont.H.*Nest*.2.16(M.86.1572C); οὐ γὰρ ἂν ἔλεγόν ποτε γνωμικῶν ἐπὶ Χριστοῦ θελημάτων διαφοράν, ἵνα μὴ...δ. αὐτὸν κηρύττωσιν Max.*opusc*.(M.91.56B); Anast.S.*hod*.7(M.89.117C).

δίπτυχος, 1. *doubled, double*; neut. as subst., *writing-tablet*, Jo.Mal.*chron*.5 p.138(M.97.236B); **2.** neut. plur. as subst., *diptychs* from which names of those commemorated at eucharist, living and departed, were read, cf.Epiph.*haer*.75.3(p.335.4; M.42.508A); **a.** in gen., *Lit.Jac*.(p.212.22); cf.*Lit.Chrys*.(p.388.8); significance, cf.Dion.Ar.*e.h*.3.3.8(M.3.437A); **b.** insertion of names as recognition of piety and orthodoxy, cf.Thdt.*h.e*.5.34.12(3.1076); Attic.*ep.Cyr*.(p.24.22; M.77.352B); CChalc.*act*.13(*ACO* 2.1.3 p.49.36; H.2.553C); CCP(536)*act*.5(p.64.4; H.2.1324C); ἐν τοῖς ἱεροῖς δ. Evagr.*h.e*.3.21(p.119.4; M.86.2640B); **c.** names of councils similarly inserted, CCP(536)*act*.4(p.178.35; H.2.1257C); *ib*.5(p.76.20; 1340E); Anast.Ap.*a.Max*.1.13(M.90.128B); **d.** names removed as sign of condemnation, Cyr.*ep*.77(p.67.2; 5².209A); Justn.*conf*.(p.104.3; M.86.1027C); Thdr.Lect.*fr*.(M.86.220B); Jo.Mal.*chron*.18 p.484(M.97.701A).

***διπυλίς, ἡ,** *double gateway*, *M.Pion*.3.6(p.46.22).

***διπυρόω,** pass., *be twice tested by fire*; of gold, Thdr.Stud.*epp*.1.40(M.99.1052A).

***διριγεύω,** (Lat. *dirigo*) *escort*, Jo.Mal.*chron*.13 p.322(M.97.481B).

***δίρριζος,** *with double root* ὁ δὲ μυστικὸς καὶ ἡμέτερος κόκκος, ὡς διφυὴς καὶ δ. ἐστιν· ἄνω μὲν τὸν πατέρα προαιώνιον ῥίζαν αὐχῶν κάτω δὲ τὴν μητέρα, καὶ δι' αὐτῆς...τὸν Ἰεσσαί Germ.CP *or*.2(M.98.265A).

δίς, *twice* ἡ δ. πρὸ ἓξ *the leap-year day*, i.e. Feb.24th (πρὸ ἓξ καλ. Μαρτ.) then occurring twice, Hipp.*can.pasch*.(M.10.879).

***δισάγιος,** *twice holy*, Jo.D.*trisag*.2(M.95.25D).

δισάκκιον ([*]**δισσάκιον**), **τό,** *double sack, pannier*, Cosm.Ind.*top*.11(M.88.441C); δίσσακιον *ib*.5(205A).

***δίσεκτος,** neut. as subst., *leap-year day*, Max.*comput*.5(M.19.1221D); v. δίς.

[*]**δισεξαδέλφη, ἡ,** *second cousin*, †Jo.Jej.*poenit*.(M.88.1893D).

δισεξάδελφος, ὁ, *second cousin*; of Christ as δ. of John Baptist, Hipp.Th.*fr*.6.6(p.32.5).

***δισιγνατεύω,** (Lat. *designo*) *designate*, Jo.Mal.*chron*.7 p.182(M.97.289C).

***δίσκαλμος,** *two-oared*, Synes.*ep*.4(M.66.1337C).

δισκάριον, τό, *paten*, *Chron.Pasch*.p.390(M.92.1001C).

δισκεύ-ω, *hurl, throw down, precipitate*; of Theodotus, Montanist prophet ἀναλαμβανόμενον εἰς οὐρανοὺς παρεκστῆναί τε καὶ καταπιστεῦσαι ἑαυτὸν τῷ τῆς ἀπάτης πνεύματι καὶ ~έντα κακῶς τελευτῆσαι Anon.ap.Eus.*h.e*.5.16.14(M.20.469B); ref. Mt.4:6–7 ἐν τῷ ~σαι τοῦ ὕψους ἄνωθεν αὐτὸν κάτω Mac.Mgn.*apocr*.3.18(p.98.7); ἐμαυτὴν ~σω Pall.*h.Laus*.69(p.165.6; M.34.1241B).

***δίσκηνος,** *of two tabernacles*, Anast.S.*hex*.12(M.89.1065B).

***δισκοκάλυμμα, τό,** *veil covering paten*, ‡Sophr.H.*liturg*.5(M.87.3985C); symbolism δίσκος τὸ ἅγιον πνεῦμα, ὁ πατὴρ δ. Tim.Ant.*descr.BMV* 7(M.28.953D).

δίσκος, ὁ, 1. *orb* of sun or moon, †Hipp.*theoph*.1(p.257.5; M.10.852A); Hegem.*Arch*.8(p.13.3; M.10.1440B); ‡Ath.*annunt*.(M.28.924C); **2.** *plate*, Socr.*h.e*.7.21.3(M.67.781C); **3.** esp. *paten*, sts. made of gold, Evagr.*h.e*.6.21(p.236.18; M.86.2873D); Chosroes *ib*.(p.237.28; 2876D); eucharistic bread deposited thereon by deacons, Jo.Mosch.*prat*.25(M.87.2862D); or priest δεχόμενος ὁ ἱερεὺς...παρὰ διακόνου...

τὴν προσφορὰν...θεὶς...ἐν τῷ ἁγίῳ δ. ‡Bas.*h.myst.*31(p.264.23); symbolizing H. Ghost, Tim.Ant.*descr.BMV*7(M.28.953D); symbolizing cloud (itself symbolizing H. Ghost or BMV), ‡Sophr.H.*liturg.*5(M.87.3985B); or hands of those who buried Christ, ‡Bas.*h.myst.*52(p.391.15); or orb of the νοητὸς ἥλιος [i.e. Christ], *ib.*(p.391.16); ὥσπερ...ὁ ἡλιακὸς δ. χωρεῖ τὸ φῶς, οὕτω καὶ οὗτος χωρεῖ τὸν Χριστὸν θυσιαζόμενον Jo.Jej.*liturg.*(p.442); sts. bearing representation of Last Supper, ‡Jo.D.*ep.Thphl.*28(M.95.381A); blessed by sign of cross in eucharistic action, *Lit.Marc.*(p.124.8); use in administration of Communion τὸν δ. ἐπάρῃ *Lit.Jac.*(p.232.24); **4.** *gong*, Marcell.*fr.*112 ap.Eus.*Marcell.*1.3(p.15.11; M.24.745B).

***δισκούσσωρ, ὁ,** (Lat. *discussor*) *public auditor*, Sophr.H.*mir.Cyr.et Jo.*68(M.87.3657B).

[*]δισσάκιον, v. δισάκκιον.

***δισσεύω,** *repeat*, Pall.*v.Chrys.*4(p.27.10; M.47.17); Steph.Diac. *v.Steph.*(M.100.1076C).

***δισσογραφέω,** *write in two ways*, pass., Areth.*Apoc.*1(M.106.508C).

δισσολογέω, *repeat*, Epiph.*haer.*8.8(p.194.28; δεδισσολογισμένον M.41.220A); id.*mens.*2(M.43.240A); Euthal.Diac.*epp.Paul.*(M.85.724B).

δισσολογία, ἡ, *repetition*, Epiph.*haer.*8.8(p.194.28; M.41.220B); id. *mens.*2(M.43.240A).

***δισσολογίζομαι,** v. δισσολογέω.

δισσόλογος, *double-tongued, deceitful* ὑπαρχέτω...χήρα...μὴ δ. *Const.App.*3.5.1.

***δισσόω,** *double*, Max.*ambig.*(M.91.1393B).

δισταγμός, ὁ, 1. *uncertainty, doubt*; hence *disbelief, want of faith* σχίσμα...διέστρεψεν...πολλοὺς εἰς δ. *1Clem.*46.9; σατανᾶς...ἐνέβαλέ τισι περὶ τοῦ πνεύματος δ. Amph.*ep.syn.*(M.39.96B); μηδὲ παραρρύητε ἀπ' αὐτῆς [sc. τῆς πίστεως] ἔν τινι δ. Ephr.2.243C; Θωμᾶς... δίδυμος ὅ ἐστι δ. Max.*ambig.*(M.91.1381C); **2.** *hesitation*, Herm.*sim.*9.28.4; Const.ap.Eus.*h.e.*10.6.3(M.20.892B).

διστάζ-ω, 1. *be uncertain, be doubtful*, Herm.*mand.*2.4; Hipp.*ep. reg.*(p.253.12; M.10.869B); ~ειν εἰ ἔστι πρόνοια Or.*hom.12.11 in Jer.*(p.97.27; M.13.393B); τίς ~ει εἰ αὐτοδικαιοσύνη ἀγαθόν ἐστι; id.*Jo.*1.9(11; p.15.13; M.14.41B); ~όντων μήποτε Ἰωάννης εἴη Χριστός *ib.*6.8(5; p.116.29; 213D); τὴν αὐτὴν μὲν ἡμῖν διάνοιαν ἔχοντας, περὶ δὲ τὸ ὄνομα μόνον ~οντας Ath.*syn.*41(p.266.32; M.26.765A); id.*Ar.*2.2(M.26.152A); Eus.Al.*serm.*4(M.86.337A); **2.** *disbelieve, be in want of faith*, *1Clem.*11.2 cit. s. δίψυχος; ~οντες εἰς τὸν θεόν Herm.*mand.*9.5; μὴ διστάσαι περὶ θεοῦ Clem.*str.*7.10(p.40.33; M.9.477D); Or.*Jo.*1.31(34; p.39.1; M.14.81A); ~ειν περὶ τῆς...ἀναστάσεως Ath.*inc.*31.3(M.25.149C); Philox.*ep.*17(p.168); *Didasc.Jac.*1.14(p.751.13); **3.** *hesitate*, *Did.*4.7 = *Barn.*19.11; ~ουσιν αἰτεῖσθαι Herm.*sim.*5.4.3; ~ετε πιστεῦσαι Just.*dial.*28.2(M.6.536A); Clem.*str.*4.22(p.308.31; M.8.1348A); Or.*Jo.*6.4(2; p.110.16; M.14.204C); ἵνα...μὴ ~ῃ γινώσκων τὸ θεῖον Ath.*gent.*23(M.25.45B); CSard.*can.*11.

διστακτικός, 1. *doubting, disbelieving* Θωμᾶς...ἐστι πᾶς δ. ἄνθρωπος Max.*ambig.*(M.91.1381C); **2.** *expressing uncertainty* δ. ... φωνήν Or.*Jo.*6.59(38; p.168.13; M.14.304A); Bas.*hom.in Ps.*48(1.180E; M.29.440C); Epiph.*haer.*73.1(p.268.20; M.42.401B).

διστακτικῶς, *uncertainly, hesitatingly*, of Semi-Arians περὶ δὲ τοῦ ἁγίου πνεύματος...οὐ δ. ὁρμῶνται, ἀλλ'...ἀφειδῶς κτίσμα αὐτὸ... ὁρίζονται Epiph.*haer.*73.1(p.268.24; M.42.401C).

***διστασιάζω,** *be at variance*, Nil.*epp.*2.50(M.79.221C).

***δίστασις, ἡ,** *doubt, uncertainty*, Or.*Jo.*1.31(34; p.38.28, v.l. διαστάσεως M.14.81A).

δίστομος, ? *articulate* ὡς γὰρ τὰ δ., οὕτως καὶ ὁ ἀλέκτωρ μηνύει τοῖς ἐν τῷ κόσμῳ κατὰ τὴν ἰδίαν λαλιάν *Apoc.Bar.*6(p.89.18).

***δισύπαρχος, ὁ,** *one who has held prefecture twice*, Gr.Naz.*or.*21.28(M.35.1113C).

***δισυπόστατος,** *of two hypostases*, Leont.H.*Nest.*2.5(M.86.1544B); οὐδὲν γὰρ ὄντων ἐν ἀριθμῷ ὄν, δ. ἐστι *ib.*2.16(1572C).

***δίσχιστος,** *divided*, hence *contradictory*, Gr.Naz.*carm.*2.1.11.1015(M.37.1099A).

δισώματος, *two-bodied*, Athenag.*leg.*18.3(MSS διὰ σώματος M.6.928B); of the female principle in system of Just. Gn., Hipp.*haer.*10.15(p.276.16; M.16.3431A).

δίσωμος, = foreg.; in Peratic system τῶν...ζῳδίων τὰ μὲν ἀρρενικὰ...τὰ δὲ θηλυκά· καὶ τὰ μὲν δ., τὰ δὲ οὔ Hipp.*haer.*5.13(p.106.15; M.16.3163B); of female principle, Just.Gn.*ib.*5.26(p.127.1; 3194C).

***διυλάττω,** *howl*, Ephr.2.236C.

διυλίζ-ω, 1. *strain, filter*; met., ref. Mt.23:23–24, cf. *omnia liquat, qui in omnibus quaecumque agit...segregat quod est sordidum ...ab his quae natura...sincera sunt*, Or.*comm.ser.20 in Mt.*(p.36.22; M.13.1626D); ἄκρατον τῆς γραφῆς...λόγον πάσης τρυγίας διυλισμένον Gr.Nyss.*hom.9 in Cant.*(M.44.976D); **2.** *purify, refine*; of gold, Clem.*str.*2.20(p.176.1; M.8.1060B); met. ~όμενοι βαπτίσματι id.*paed.*1.6(p.109.4; M.8.288B); πνεύματα ἀκάθαρτα συμπεπλεγμένα τῇ ψυχῇ ~εσθαι ἀπὸ τῆς γενέσεως τῆς καινῆς [i.e. baptism] id.*ecl.*7(p.138.31; M.9.701B).

***διυλισμός, ὁ,** *purification*, Iren.*haer.*1.14.8(M.7.612A); Clem. *paed.*1.6(p.108.31; M.8.288B).

διυλιστήρ, ὁ, *filter, strainer*, Epiph.*mens.*24(M.43.284B); Thdt. *affect.*1(p.6.17; 4.695).

διυλιστήριον, τό, *strainer, filter*, interprn. of מְזַמְּרוֹת (*snuffers*), Epiph.*haer.*75.5(p.337.13; M.42.509D).

διυπηρετέω, *serve*, Clem.*ecl.*6(p.138.22; M.9.701A).

[*]διφρελάτης, ὁ, = διφρηλάτης, *charioteer*, ‡Sophr.H.*triod.*(M.87.3977A).

***διφροστάτης, ὁ,** *charioteer*, Geo.Pis.*Heracl.*1.207(M.92.1315A); met., of reason, id.*van.*260(M.92.1600A).

διφυής, A. *having two natures*; **1.** met. διψυχίαν καὶ τὸ οἱονεὶ τῆς γνώμης δ. Cyr.*ador.*7(1.245C); **2.** theol. εἰ δὲ φεύγει τις τὸ λέγειν γέννημα, μόνον δὲ λέγει ὑπάρχειν τὸν λόγον σὺν τῷ θεῷ· φοβηθήτω...μὴ ...ἐμπέσῃ εἰς ἀτοπίαν, δ. τινα εἰσάγων τὸν θεόν ‡Ath.*Ar.*4.3(p.47.8; M.26.472B); ὁ Εὐνομίου θεός, δ. τις ἢ πολυσύνθετος Gr.Nyss.*Eun.*9(2 p.207.17; M.45.804D); **3.** Christol. ἡ γὰρ ὑπόστασις...καθ' ἣν καὶ λόγος θεὸς ὢν τὴν φύσιν νοεῖται, δευτέραν ἔχει ἀρχήν, οὐκ ἔτι ἁπλῆ καὶ μονοφυὴς ἐν τοῖς θείοις προσώποις νοουμένη, ἀλλὰ σύνθετος καὶ δ. Leont.H.*Nest.*4.43(M.86.1716D); Χριστέ,...ὁ δ. ἄνθραξ *Lit.Jac.*(p.162.7); Jo.D.*Jacob.*78(M.94.1473C); μῆτερ τοῦ δ. ‡Gr.Naz.*Chr.pat.*1792(M.38.279A).

B. *relating to two natures* δ. τὴν γνῶσιν ἔχει [sc. ὁ Χριστός] νοεῖται γὰρ ἐν αὐτῷ θεός τε καὶ ἄνθρωπος Cyr.*ador.*9(1.318A).

***διφύλλιον, τό,** *two-leaved book, pamphlet*, CCP(681)*act.*14(H.3.1364A).

***δίφυλλος,** *two-leaved*, Cosm.Ind.*top.*11(M.88.444D).

***διφυσίτης, ὁ,** *diphysite*; monophysite name for Chalcedonian orthodox, *Apophth.Patr.*(M.65.432B); Tim.II Al.*fr.*3(M.86.273D).

***δίφυσος,** *of two natures* ἰχθυοφάγοι ὄρνιθες δ. ... ὄντες ἀκάθαρτοι κρίνονται Ephr.3.184C.

***διχαλακέω,** *break asunder*, ‡Gr.Naz.*Chr.pat.*1691(M.38.271A).

διχηλ-έω, *part the hoof* τί δὲ τὸ ~οῦν; ὅτι ὁ δίκαιος καὶ ἐν τούτῳ τῷ κόσμῳ περιπατεῖ καὶ τὸν ἅγιον αἰῶνα ἐνδέχεται *Barn.*10.11; τὸ ~οῦν δικαιοσύνην ἐμφαίνει τὴν ἰσοστάσιον μηρυκάζουσαν τὴν οἰκείαν δικαιοσύνης τροφήν, τὸν λόγον ἔκτοσθεν εἰσιόντα...διὰ κατηχήσεως, ἔνδοθεν δὲ ἀναπεμπόμενον...εἰς ἀνάμνησιν λογικήν Clem.*paed.*3.11(p.278.14; M.8.653A); τὰ...~οῦντα καὶ μηρυκισμὸν ἀνάγοντα τῶν ἱερείων καθαρὰ καὶ δεκτὰ τῷ θεῷ παραδίδωσιν ἡ γραφή id.*str.*7.18(p.77.4; M.9.556A); ἡ τῶν ~ούντων ἑδραιότης τῶν τὰ λόγια τοῦ θεοῦ... μελετώντων *ib.*(p.77.8; 556A); interpreted of division of this world and its concerns from spiritual things, cf.Or.*hom.7.6 in Lev.*(p.389.3ff.; M.12.489Cff.).

διχηλία, ἡ, *division of the hoof* δ. δέ γε τύπος ἂν εἴη...τοῦ ἐπ' ἄμφω βαίνειν ἡμᾶς ὀρθῶς...δύνασθαι, εἰς τὸ καθ' ἡμᾶς αὐτοὺς καὶ... εἰς ἑτέρους Cyr.*ador.*14(1.500A).

***διχόμητις,** *of divided counsel*, Nonn.*par.Jo.*7:43(M.43.812C); *ib.*11:40(845B); *ib.*20:29(913B).

διχονο-έω, *be at variance, be divided in opinion* πρὸς τὴν τῶν πρὸς ἀλλήλους ~ούντων ὁμόνοιαν βοηθοὺς ἀποστείλαιμι Const.ap.Eus.*v.C.*2.66(p.67.24; M.20.1040A); θεοῦ λαὸν...~εῖν οὔτε πρέπον Const.*ib.*2.71(p.69.24; 1044B); Chrys.*hom.38.5 in Gen.*(4.390C); οἱ ἐν πνεῦμα λαβόντες...οὐκ ὀφείλετε ~εῖν id.*hom.11.1 in Eph.*(11.80D); Ἰσραὴλ... γεγονότος ὑπὸ Χριστοῦ, πῶς ἂν ἀκόλουθον ~εῖν ἔτι; Cyr.*Os.*10(3.31B); ἐρεῖ γὰρ ἴσως τις τοῖς σοῖς...ἑπόμενος λογισμοῖς, ὅτι καὶ ἀπίθανον...τὸ παραιτεῖσθαι τὸ πάθος τὴν τοῦ δούλου μορφὴν καὶ ~οῦσαν ὁρᾶσθαι πρὸς τὸν πατέρα καὶ πρὸς τὸν...ἐνοικήσαντα λόγον id.*apol.Thdt.*4(p.125.9; 6[1].219A); ἀπὸ τῆς ἡμετέρας ~εῖ πίστεως Cael.*ep.Cyr.*1(p.76.24; M.77.93A); Jo.Mal.*chron.*18 p.476(M.97.692B); ~ουσῶν διανοιῶν Jo.VI CP *ep.*(M.96.1432A).

διχόνοια, ἡ, *division of opinion, discord* ἀπόθεσθε...στάσιν...δ. Or.*dial.*15(p.152.14); ὡς μηδὲν ἔτι πρὸς δ. ἢ πίστεως ἀμφισβήτησιν ὑπολείπεσθαι Const.ap.Eus.*v.C.*3.17(p.85.1; M.20.1073C); ἠλέγχθη [i.e. at Nicaea] ἅπαντα...ὅσα...διχονοίας πρόφασιν ἐδόκει γεννᾶν Const.*ep.*(Opitz 3 p.53.3)ap.Socr.*h.e.*1.9.20(M.67.85A); Jul.Papa *ep. Dian.*ap.Ath.*apol.sec.*25(p.105.31; M.25.289B); οὐδὲ γὰρ εὔλογόν ἐστι δ. τινα ἢ στάσιν ἐν ὑμῖν κινηθῆναι Constantius Imp.*ib.*55(p.135.27; 348D); τί τὸ αἴσχιστον καὶ τὸ βλαβερώτατον; ἡ δ. Gr.Naz.*or.*32.2(M.36.176B); τὸ νοσοῦν ἐκ τῆς πίστεως ἐν δ. *Const.App.*2.20.3; μὴ ἀφεῖναι ἐρεσχελίαν τινὰ καὶ δ. εἶναι Chrys.hom.20.6 in Eph.(11.152A); ὥρμησεν ἡ πλάνη καὶ ἡ δ. ὑποσπείρειν ἀπὸ τῆς μιᾶς θεοσεβείας εἰς πολλὰς παραπεποιημένας γνώμας Epiph.haer.8.9(p.197.9; M.41.224A); δεῖ σεμνότερον διανοεῖσθαι, ἵνα μὴ ὑψαυχενίαν κτησώμεθα ἢ δ. id.ep.Arab.(p.471.30; M.42.733A); μέλος ἐστὶν ἡ παρ' ὑμῖν ἐκκλησία τῆς ἁπανταχοῦ. ὥστε δίκαιοι ἂν εἴητε...πᾶσαν δ. ἐκ ποδῶν ποιησάμενοι Isid.Pel.epp.4.103(M.78.1169D); ἐκκλησιῶν, οὐ διεσπαρμένων εἰς δ. ... ἀλλ' ἡνωμένων ἐν πνεύματι Cyr.ador.9(1.315E); id.Os.10(3.31A); Thdt.eran.1(4.34).

***διχονόως**, *contentiously, discordantly*, Ephr.2.243C.

***διχοστάτης**, ὁ, *factious person*, Herm.sim.8.7.6.

***διχότμητος**, *divided*, of Nestorianism ἡ διχότομος δόξα, μᾶλλον δὲ ἡ δ. γλῶσσα Leont.H.Nest.proem.(M.86.1400A).

διχοτομέω, **1.** *cut in two, cut asunder*; ref. Mt.24:51, Lc.12:46, cf. *genus indicat poenae quorum...separandus ab anima spiritus indicatur...id est animae substantia...divisa...ab eo spiritu* [sc. *sancto*]...*si vero hoc non de dei spiritu, sed de natura...animae intelligendum est, pars ejus melior illa dicetur quae ad imaginem...et similitudinem facta est*, Or.princ.2.10.7(p.181.4; M.11.239B); *qui enim peccavit dividitur et pars quidem ejus cum infidelibus ponitur, quod autem non est ejus revertitur ad deum*, id.comm.ser.57 in Mt.(p.132.20; M.13.1691B); id.comm.in Rom.2.9(M.14.893C); Bas.Spir.40(3.34D; M.32.141C) cit. s. διχοτομία; **2.** *separate, divide*, Jo.D.hom.12.9(M.96.793C).

διχοτομία, ἡ, *cutting off*, ref. Mt.24:51 οἱ λυπήσαντες τὸ πνεῦμα τὸ ἅγιον τῇ πονηρίᾳ...διχοτομηθήσονται παντελῶς· τῆς δ. νοουμένης κατὰ τὴν εἰς τὸ παντελὲς ἀπὸ τοῦ πνεύματος ἀλλοτρίωσιν. ... δ. ... ἡ ἀπὸ τοῦ πνεύματος εἰς τὸ διηνεκὲς τῆς ψυχῆς ἀλλοτρίωσις Bas.Spir.40(3.34D; M.32.141C).

***διχοψυχία**, ἡ, *division of soul, double-mindedness*, Or.sel.in Ps.67:6(M.12.1505D).

***δίχρυσον**, τό, *half an ἄργυρον*, Epiph.mens.24(M.43.289A,B).

δίχρως, *two-coloured*; of a turncoat, Anast.S.hod.14(M.89.244D).

***διψαλέως**, *thirstily*, Thdr.Stud.epp.2.148(M.99.1461D).

διψ-άω, *thirst*, spiritually εὗρον πάντας μεθύοντας καὶ οὐδένα...~ῶντα Agraph.(p.69); Or.princ.2.11.2(p.185.16; M.11.242A); exeg. Jo.4:13, Or.Jo.13.3ff.(p.228.8ff.; M.14.404C); id.fr.54 in Jo.(p.528.16ff.); ὁ πίνων ἐκ τοῦ ὕδατος τοῦ νομικοῦ διψώσει πάλιν, ὄρεξιν ἔχων τοῦ εὐαγγελικοῦ πόματος...τὸ δὲ εὐαγγέλιον ἐπεὶ ἀδιάδοχόν ἐστιν, ὁ πίνων ἐξ αὐτοῦ οὐ διψώσει εἰς τὸν αἰῶνα ib.56(p.529.12); Meth.symp.4.5(p.51.2; M.18.93B); ~ῶντι καὶ εὐχομένῳ τῆς ἐν θεῷ τυχεῖν σωτηρίας Const.ap.Eus.v.C.4.62(p.143.6; M.20.1213A); Jul.Papa ep.Alex.ap.Ath.apol.sec.53(p.134.13; M.25.345B); satisfied in baptism, Gr.Naz.or.40.27(M.36.397C); Cyr.Is.4.1(2.567B); id.Jon.16(3.379D); διψῆν μὲν τῆς σωτηρίας Thdt.h.e.5.31.1(3.1070); hence in gen., *desire eagerly*, Anast.S.qu.et resp.89 tit.(M.89.716B).

***διψυχ-έω**, *be double-minded, doubt, hesitate*, Did.4.4; μὴ ~ῶμεν, ἀλλὰ ἐλπίσαντες ὑπομείνωμεν 2Clem.11.4; πάντες οἱ μὴ ~οῦντες καθαρισθήσονται ἀπὸ...ἁμαρτημάτων Herm.vis.3.2.2; id.mand.9.1; ἐὰν δὲ...~ῇς αἰτούμενος, σεαυτὸν αἰτιῶ καὶ μὴ τὸν διδόντα σοι ib.9.8; τί ~εῖς περὶ τῶν ἐντολῶν id.sim.6.1.2; λήψονται ἴασιν παρὰ τοῦ κυρίου τῶν προτέρων ἁμαρτιῶν, ἐὰν μὴ ~ήσωσιν ἐπὶ ταῖς ἐντολαῖς ταύταις ib.8.11.3; Or.dial.6(p.134.12); A.Phil.16(p.9.9); Pall.h.Laus.38(p.119.13; ἐδυσψύχησε M.34.1193D); θεὸς ~εῖν οὐκ ἐᾷ· θαρσεῖν δὲ κελεύει Cyr.Zach.41(3.718C); καλὴ...ἡ πίστις, ἰσχύειν ἐν ἡμῖν τὴν...χάριν παρασκευάζουσα, καὶ τὸ ~εῖν ἐπιζήμιον id.Jo.6.1(4.603C); μηδ' ὅλως ~ήσωμεν αἰτήσασθαί τι παρὰ κυρίου Ant.Mon.hom.85(M.89.1692D).

διψυχία, ἡ, *indecision, doubt, hesitancy* ἐνίοτε πονηρὰ πράσσοντες οὐ γινώσκομεν διὰ τὴν δ. καὶ ἀπιστίαν...ἐν τοῖς στήθεσιν ἡμῶν 2Clem.19.2; τὸ πνεῦμα ὑμῶν...μὴ ἔχον δύναμιν ἀπὸ τῶν μαλακιῶν...καὶ δ. Herm.vis.3.11.2; βλέπετε τὴν δ. ... πονηρὰ γάρ ἐστι...καὶ πολλοὺς ἐκριζοῖ ἀπὸ τῆς πίστεως...καὶ γὰρ αὕτη ἡ δ. θυγάτηρ ἐστὶ τοῦ διαβόλου ...καταφρόνησον οὖν τῆς δ. καὶ κατακυρίευσον αὐτῆς...ἐνδυσάμενος τὴν πίστιν τὴν ἰσχυράν id.mand.9.9; ib.10.1.1; ib.10.2.2; διαβόλῳ...μολύνειν ἡμᾶς διαλογισμοῖς...θέλοντι ἀρνήσεως ἢ δ. Or.mart.11(p.11.7; M.11.577A); id.princ.4.1.7(p.302.13; M.11.353B); Pall.h.Laus.proem.(p.10.11; M.34.1002); ἀπάτη καὶ δόλος...χρῆμα...ἀδελφὴν ἔχον...τὴν δ. Cyr.ador.7(1.245C); id.Zach.41(3.718B); id.Jo.9(4.754A); νοῦν οὐ ταῖς δ. χωλεύοντα id.apol.orient.10(p.54.33; 6^{1}.186E); id.hom.pasch.9(5^{2}.118B); Ammon.Aeg.ep.6(p.143.9); οἱ δὲ ἐρχόμενοι πρὸς αὐτὸν οὐκ ἐν ὅλῃ καρδίᾳ ἀλλ' ἐν δ., καὶ ποιοῦντες τὰ ἔργα αὐτῶν ὥστε δοξασθῆναι ἀπὸ τῶν ἀνθρώπων, οὗτοι οὐκ εἰσακουσθήσονται παρὰ τοῦ θεοῦ ἐν οἷς αἰτοῦσιν αὐτόν ib.(p.148.10); δ. εἰ ἀληθῆ ταῦτά εἰσιν Bars.resp.(M.86.892B); ass. ὀλιγοψυχία, Ant.Mon.hom.85(M.89.1692D); one of the ψυχικὰ πάθη, Jo.D.spir.neq.(M.95.88B).

δίψυχος, **1.** *undecided, uncertain, wavering* οἱ δ. καὶ οἱ διστάζοντες περὶ τῆς τοῦ θεοῦ δυνάμεως εἰς κρίμα...γίνονται 1Clem.11.2; Herm.vis.3.4.3; οἱ δ. ... οὐδὲν ὅλως ἐπιτυγχάνουσι τῶν αἰτημάτων αὐτῶν id.mand.9.5; πᾶς γὰρ δ. ἀνήρ, ἐὰν μὴ μετανοήσῃ, δυσκόλως σωθήσεται ib.9.6; ib.11.4; id.sim.8.7.2; δ., οἱ δὲ τὸν κύριον ἔχοντες ἐπὶ τὰ χείλη, ἐπὶ τὴν καρδίαν δὲ μὴ ἔχοντες ib.9.21.1; δύο πάσχει ὁ Ἰησοῦς ἐν ἀνθρώποις· ὑπὸ μὲν τῶν ἀπίστων καταδικάζεται, ὑπὸ δὲ τῶν δ. διακρίνεται Or.hom.14.8 in Jer.(p.113.21; M.13.413B); μὴ γίνου δ. ἐν προσευχῇ σου, εἰ ἔσται ἢ οὔ Const.App.7.11; Cyr.Ps.11:1(M.69.796A); Ant.Mon.hom.85(M.89.1693A); **2.** *believing in two souls* or (if acc. sing.) *of two souls*, Christol. μὴ τοίνυν ἀποδιοριζέτωσαν [sc. τὸν Χριστόν] ὡς δίψυχοι Cyr.resp.5(p.586.13, v.l. δίψυχον 6^{2}.390C).

[*]**διωγμίτης**, ὁ, *policeman, gendarme*, M.Polyc.7.1; M.Pion.15.1(p.53.32); ib.15.7(p.54.8); τῷ δ. ἄρχοντι apptly. equivalent to εἰρηνάρχῳ, M.Agap.2.1(p.95.24).

διωγμός, ὁ, **1.** *persecution* of Christians by unbelievers Πολύκαρπον ὅστις...κατέπαυσε τὸν δ. M.Polyc.1.1; Δομετιανὸν...καταπαῦσαι ...τὸν κατὰ τῆς ἐκκλησίας δ. Heges.ap.Eus.h.e.3.20.5(M.20.253B); Iren.fr.40(M.7.1260A); Clem.paed.3.8(p.260.13; M.8.612B); ref. problem of divine will for good, id.str.4.12(p.286.9; M.8.1293D); ὁ ἐν τοῖς δ. φεύγων οὐχὶ μὴ εἰς δῶμα μὴ ἀναβαινέτω Or.hom.19.13 in Jer.(p.169.9; M.13.489A); Ἰγνάτιον...τὸν ἐν τῷ δ. ἐν Ῥώμῃ θηρίοις μαχησάμενον id.hom.6 in Lc.(p.37.6; M.13.1815A); as assaults on body of Christ, id.Jo.10.35(20; p.209.26; M.14.372A); Πέτρος...πρὸ τοῦ δ. γέγονεν ἐπίσκοπος, ἐν δὲ τῷ δ. ἐμαρτύρησεν Ath.apol.sec.59(p.139.4; M.25.356B); ref. baptism of water in time of peace, of blood in persecutions, Cyr.H.catech.3.10; τῷ καιρῷ τῶν δ. ἐναθλήσασα Gr.Nyss.v.Macr.(p.371.27; M.46.961A); τοὺς...φεύγοντας...προσλαμβάνεσθε...χαίροντες ὅτι κοινωνοὶ αὐτῶν τοῦ δ. γεγένησθε Const.App.5.3.1; τοῖς δ. τὴν χάριν τοῦ θεοῦ ἀεὶ ἐπανθοῦσαν Chrys.stat.1.7(2.10D); of mortification as equivalent to suffering in persecution, id.hom.74.3 in Jo.(8.437C); Thdt.h.e.1.3.1(3.727); of inward persecution of soul by evil desires, Clem.q.d.s.25(p.176.7; M.9.629B); **2.** *running* of a race, Chrys.hom.25.3 in 2Cor.(10.617B).

διωκάθω, *pursue*, Clem.paed.2.1(p.160.11; M.8.393A).

***διωκτήριον**, τό, *that which drives away*, Andr.Cr.or.10(M.97.1021B).

διώκτης, ὁ, **1.** *persecutor*, Did.5.2; Clem.str.5.5(p.343.4; M.9.48A); Λικινίου τοῦ δ. Const.ap.Socr.h.e.1.9.34(M.67.93B), om. ap.Eus.v.C.2.46(p.60.27; M.20.1024A); Eus.v.C.4.11 tit.(p.114.17; 1145B); of Constantius ὠμότερος τῶν πρὸ αὐτοῦ τυράννων καὶ δ. Ath.h.Ar.40(p.205.17; M.25.740B); of emperor Julian παραλογιστὴς καὶ δ. Gr.Naz.or.21.32(M.35.1121A); id.carm.1.2.10.704(M.37.731A); Δεκίου τοῦ δ. Hier.v.Paul.B(p.5.6); Cyr.Ps.17:33(M.69.824D); of S. Paul, Or.hom.1.16 in Jer.(p.14.30; M.13.273D); δ. ... ὄντος τῇ τοῦ Χριστοῦ πίστει M.Petr.et Paul.39(p.152.5); **2.** *one who drives away* [sc. Χριστέ] δ. τοῦ σκότους A.Thom.A 80(p.196.11); of a heretic δ. ἐστὶ τῆς...πίστεως Gr.Nyss.Eun.2(1 p.316.28; M.45.489C); **3.** adj., *of persecution* δ. καιρός Gr.Naz.carm.1.2.2.515(M.37.619A); ib.1.2.34.218(961A).

διωκτικός, *able to drive away*, Const.App.8.29.3.

***διωκτικῶς**, *to the extent of persecution, so as to persecute* τῆς αἱρέσεως δ. ἀναπαφλασάσης Thdr.Stud.epp.2.121(M.99.1396D).

***διώκτριος**, *putting to flight*; met., of prayer δ. πάσης ἀντικειμένης δυνάμεως Nil.epp.3.155(M.79.457C).

διώκ-ω, **1.** *pursue*; hence *pursue one's way, travel* ἐδίωξε μέχρι Συριῶν Thphn.chron.p.126(M.108.349A, v.l. ἐδηίωσε); **2.** *drive out, expel*, ib.p.39(M.108.153B); in monastic discipline ἄμεινον διῶξαί τινα τῆς μονῆς, ἢ θέλημα ἴδιον ἐᾶσαι τοὺς ὑπηκόους οἰκεῖον ποιεῖν. ὁ μὲν γὰρ διώξας πολλάκις τὸν διωχθέντα ταπεινότερον ἀπειργάσατο Jo.Clim.past.14(M.88.1200B); **3.** *persecute*, Christ ἐδιώχθη ἐπὶ Ποντίου Πιλάτου Ign.Trall.9.1; Christians διὰ ζῆλον καὶ φθόνον οἱ...στῦλοι ἐδιώχθησαν 1Clem.5.2; ἀγαπῶσι πάντας, καὶ ὑπὸ πάντων ~ονται Diogn.5.11; Clem.str.7.1(p.3.6; M.9.401B); Const.App.5.3.1.

διώνυμος, **1.** *having two names*, Or.Ps.72:28(p.97); ref. Jo.10:30 τὰ δύο ἓν εἶναί φατε, ἢ τὸ ἓν δ. ... εἰ τὸ ἓν δ. Σαβελλίου τὸ ἐπιτήδευμα, τὸν αὐτὸν υἱὸν καὶ πατέρα λέγοντος ‡Ath.Ar.4.9(p.53.5; M.26.480A); ref. Abiathar (Mc.2:26), Chrys.hom.39.1 in Mt.(7.432D); of S. Thomas δ. ... Θωμᾶς ὃν Δίδυμον καλέουσι Nonn.par.Jo.11:16(M.43.841A); **2.** *far-famed*, Gr.Nyss.or.catech.18(p.76.12; M.45.56A); id.Eun.1(1 p.31.16; M.45.260A).

διωρία ([*]διορία), ἡ, **1.** *interval* δ. ... τετράμηνον Heracleon ap.Or.Jo.13.41(p.267.8; διορίαν M.14.472B); Pers.(p.25.17); ‡Nil.narr.7(M.79.681A); **2.** *respite*, διορ- A.Thom.A 167(p.281.17n.); Nil.epp.1.234

(M.79.169A); †Gregent.*leg.Hom.*(M.86.577B); **3.** *fixed time,* Nil. *epp.*3.213(M.79.480C); **4.** *opportunity,* Ephr.3.200E; Thphn.*chron.* p.398(M.108.948C).

διωστήρ, ὁ, *bolt* of a door, ‡Nil.*perist.*11.11(M.79.917D).

δόγμα, τό, A. *opinion* (cf. δόξα), Chrys.*hom.25.1 in Mt.*(7.308A); *ib.26.1*(314C); *ταράσσει τοὺς ἀνθρώπους οὐ τὰ πράγματα, ἀλλὰ τὰ περὶ τῶν πραγμάτων δ.· οἷον ὁ θάνατος οὐ δεινόν,...ἀλλὰ τὸ δ. τὸ περὶ τοῦ θανάτου διότι δεινόν* ‡Nil.*Epict.*10(M.79.1289A); Olymp.*Job* 8:4 (M.93.108C).

B. *fixed belief, tenet*; **1.** in gen.; def. *τὸ μὲν δ. ἐστὶ κατάληψίς τις λογική* Clem.*str.*8.5(p.90.2; M.9.581A); *Χριστιανοὶ...οὐδὲ δ. ἀνθρωπίνου προεστᾶσιν ὥσπερ ἔνιοι* *Diogn.*5.3; Tat.*orat.*27(p.29.16; M.6.865B); Athenag.*res.*1(p.48.3; M.6.973A); *ib.*2(p.50.5; 977B); *ἀσεβέσι δ. ἑαυτοὺς ἀνατεθείκασιν* Or.*or.*29.10(p.385.32; M.11.536C); id.*Cels.* 1.64(p.117.19; M.11.781A); id.*Jo.*6.10(7; p.120.4; M.14.220B); Meth. *symp.*5.4(p.57.17; M.18.104A); Const.*or.s.c.*10(p.164.27; M.20.1257B); *δ. περὶ θεοῦ γεγραφέναι ἀπὸ τῆς οἰκείας ἑαυτῶν προαιρέσεως. τὸ γὰρ δ. ὄνομα τῆς ἀνθρωπίνης ἔχεται βουλῆς τε καὶ γνώμης, ὅτι δὲ τοῦθ' οὕτως ἔχει μαρτυρεῖ...τὰ τῶν φιλοσόφων καλούμενα δ.· ὅτι δὲ καὶ τὰ συγκλήτῳ δόξαντα ἔτι καὶ νῦν δ. συγκλήτου λέγεται, οὐδένα ἀγνοεῖν οἶμαι* Marcell.*fr.*76 ap.Eus.*Marcell.*1.4(p.20.17; M.24.756C); *ἡ μὲν ὑποψία τῆς ἀνάγκης...τὸ δὲ δ. τῆς προαιρέσεως* Tit.Bost.*fr.Lc.*6:43 (p.163.11); **2.** of tenets of philosophers *τῶν δ. ἐναντίων ὄντων* Just. *1apol.*7.3(M.6.337A); *τοῖς Πλάτωνος ἔπη δ.* Tat.*orat.*25(p.26.28; M.6. 860B); *δεινὸν καὶ ἀθέμιτον δ.* [i.e. that of transmigration of souls] Thphl.Ant.*Autol.*3.7(M.6.1132A); of philosophical teaching as preparation for knowledge of God, Clem.*str.*1.5(p.20.14; M.8.725A); *ἀσεβῶν δ.* [i.e. of Epicurus] Or.*Cels.*6.26(p.96.26; M.11.1332C); Eus.*p.e.*10.14(505B; M.21.840D); *Ἀριστοτέλους...τὸ ἀνθρωπικὸν τῶν δ.* Gr.Naz.*or.*27.10(p.19.3; M.36.24C); **3.** of beliefs of pagan religion *πῶς τιμητέον τούτους παρ' οἷς δογμάτων ἐναντιότης ἐστὶ πολλή;* Tat.*orat.*8(p.8.21; M.6.824A); Cels.ap.Or.*Cels.*8.68(p.284.15; M.11.1620A); *Χριστοῦ τὰ περὶ τῶν ἐθνικῶν εἰδώλων καταργήσαντος δ.* Or.*fr.35 in Jer.*(p.216.22); Gr.Naz.*or.*27.5(p.8.11; M.36.17B); *διάβολος τῶν οὐκ ὄντων θεῶν τὰ δ. ἀκολασίας ἐνέπλησε* Thdt.*1Thess.*4:7 (3.516); **4.** in Judaism; of tenets of Moses, Tat.*orat.*40(p.41.4; M.6. 884B); Cels.ap.Or.*Cels.*5.41(p.44.25; M.11.1245B); *εἴ τίς γε ἐντύχοι τοῖς ψαλμοῖς εὕροι ἂν πολλῶν καὶ σοφῶν δ. πλήρη τὴν βίβλον* Or.*ib.* 3.45(p.240.24; 977B); id.*Jo.*19.15(4; p.315.21; M.14.553B); *δ. ... Σαδδουκαίων* Meth.*res.*1.51(p.304.19; M.41.1124C); Eus.*p.e.*11.9(524B; M.21.869A); Chrys.*hom.26.1 in Jo.*(8.150A); **5.** of Christian doctrines; **a.** in gen. *φατὲ μὴ δεῖν δεδιέναι τὸν θάνατον, κοινωνοῦντες ἡμῶν τοῖς δ.* Tat.*orat.*19(p.21.9; M.6.849A); Athenag.*leg.*11.1(M.6.912A); Clem.*str.*7.16(p.73.17; M.9.544A) cit. s. *ὀρθοτομία*; *τὰ Χριστιανῶν δ.* Cels.ap.Or.*Cels.*3.76(p.268.14; M.11.1020C); *εὐχαὶ...πεπληρωμέναι ἀπορρήτων καὶ θαυμασίων δ.* Or.*or.*2.5(p.303.5; M.11.424A); *ἵνα μὴ ...ἀποστῶμεν τῶν δ.* id.*princ.*4.2.9(p.321.10; M.11.373B); *τῆς ἀληθείας τὰ δ.* id.*fr.12 in Jer.*22:13(p.203.19; M.13.568C); id.*Jo.*10.18(13; p.189.2; M.14.337B); *τὸ περὶ ἀναστάσεως κατὰ τὰς γραφὰς δ.* id.*Cels.* 5.22(p.23.11; 1216A); id.*Cant.*1(p.92.31; M.17.253A); *ἐν τῷ βάθει κρύπτει* [sc. *ὁ νύμφιος*] *τὰ θεωρήματα...δηλῶν τὰ σιωπώμενα δ.* id. *schol.in Cant.*4:3(M.17.272A); Eus.*h.e.*1.3.12(M.20.73A); *τὰ περὶ ψυχῆς ἀθανασίας καὶ νεκρῶν ἀναστάσεως ἐκκλησιαστικὰ δ.* *ib.*3.26.4 (272C); *τὸ...τῆς ἐκκλησίας δ.* id.*e.th.*1.10(p.68.26; M.24.841C); *περὶ δ. ... κοινοῦ ἐκκλησιαστικοῦ* Ath.*apol.sec.*69(p.147.20; M.25.372C); *τὰ εὐαγγελικὰ δ.* id.*exp.in Ps.*24:4(M.27.144C); Bas.*hex.*6.2(1.51B; M.29.120D); *τὸ εὐσεβὲς δ. τῆς μοναρχίας* id.*Spir.*47(3.39E; M.32. 153C); Gr.Naz.*or.*28.2(p.23.3; M.36.28B); *πόθος τις...τῶν θείων δ. καὶ τῆς περὶ ἐκεῖνα φιλοσοφίας* Evagr.Pont.*ep.*1(M.32.248A); *τὸ ἅγιον πνεῦμα ἐν ὑμῖν ὁ κύριος ἔδωκεν ἐν τῇ χειροθεσίᾳ, δι' οὗ ἅγια δ. μεμαθήκατε* *Const.App.*2.32.3; *τὰ τῆς εὐσεβείας δ.* *ib.*3.5.3; Chrys. *hom.6.2 in Phil.*(11.235C); *τῆς ἀκραιφνοῦς ὀρθότητος τῶν ἐκκλησιαστικῶν δ.* Cyr.*Is.*5.2(2.771D); id.*Jo.*2.3(4.168A); *τελείων τῆς θεολογίας δ.* ‡Gr.Nyss.*hom.5.13 in Jo.*(p.178.14); ref. disciples *ἐπιτηδειότεροι ...πρὸς τὴν μυσταγωγίαν καὶ τὴν ἀνάληψιν...τῶν ἀπορρητοτέρων... τῆς θεολογίας δ.* *ib.7.19*(p.241.22); ref. doctrine of angels *τῶν ἀθέων Ἑλλήνων τὰ δ. περὶ τῶν παρὰ σφίσιν ἐθνάρχων μηδὲν κοινὸν ἔχοντα τοῖς...τῆς ἐκκλησίας δ.* Oecum.*Apoc.*22:8(p.251); ref. Apoc. 22:14 *διὰ τῶν πυλώνων, τουτέστι τῶν ἀποστολικῶν δ. καὶ διδαγμάτων* *ib.*(p.253); Cosm.Ind.*top.*2(M.88.73B); of patristic tradition *ἁγίων καὶ ἐκκρίτων πατέρων...οὓς...κοινοὺς διδασκάλους ὁμολογοῦμεν, ὧν τὰ δ. νόμον αἱ ἅγιαι...ἐκκλησίαι γινώσκουσι* Serg.*ep.*3(H.3.1316B); **b.** in relation to ethical conduct, Athenag.*leg.*3.2(M.6.897A); *ἐκκλησίαν...τυγχάνουσαν ἁγνὴν παρθένον διὰ τὴν τῶν δ. καὶ ἠθῶν ὀρθότητα* Or.*fr.45 in Jo.*(p.520.16); *ὁ γὰρ θεοσεβείας τρόπος ἐκ δύο τούτων συνέστηκε, δ. εὐσεβῶν καὶ πράξεων ἀγαθῶν· καὶ οὔτε τὰ δ.* *χωρὶς ἔργων ἀγαθῶν εὐπρόσδεκτα τῷ θεῷ, οὔτε τὰ μὴ μετ' εὐσεβῶν δ. ἔργα τελούμενα προσδέχεται ὁ θεός* Cyr.H.*catech.*4.2; ref. Mt.28:19 *διαιρῶν εἰς δύο τὴν τῶν Χριστιανῶν πολιτείαν, εἴς τε τὸ ἠθικὸν μέρος καὶ εἰς τὴν τῶν δ. ἀκρίβειαν, τὸ μὲν σωτήριον δ. ἐν τῇ τοῦ βαπτίσματος παραδόσει κατησφαλίσατο, τὸν δὲ βίον ἡμῶν διὰ τῆς τηρήσεως τῶν ἐντολῶν αὐτοῦ κατορθοῦσθαι κελεύει* Gr.Nyss.*ep.*24(M.46.1089A); Chrys.*hom.2.2 in Rom.*(9.437A); ref. 1Thess.5:8 *βίον μετὰ δ. ὀρθῶν αἰνίττεται* id.*hom.9.3 in 1Thess.*(11.490B); *τῶν μὲν δ. ἕνεκεν πολλάκις ἂν αὐτοὺς διαβάλλοιεν Ἕλληνες, βίου δὲ ὀρθοῦ οὐκ ἂν ἐπιλάβοιντο* id.*hom.10.2 in 1Tim.*(11.602B); **c.** of heretical doctrines *ταῦτα τὰ δ. ... οὐκ ἔστιν ὑγιοῦς γνώμης· ταῦτα τὰ δ. ἀσύμφωνά ἐστι τῇ ἐκκλησίᾳ* Iren.*ep.Flor.*ap.Eus.*h.e.*5.20.4(M.20.484C); Clem.*str.* 7.16(p.68.24; M.9.533C); Hipp.*haer.*9.11(p.245.23; M.16.3379A); Or. *hom.16.9 in Jer.*(p.141.6; M.13.449C); Dion.Al.ap.Eus.*h.e.*7.6(M.20. 648A); ref. Marcellus' doctrine *τὴν τοῦ Ἰουδαϊκοῦ τούτου δ. ἀτοπίαν* Eus.*Marcell.*2.2(p.43.20; M.24.797A); Ath.*Ar.*2.43(M.26.240A); Gr. Naz.*or.*28.11(p.39.2; M.36.40A); *ἐκτόπων δ.* *Const.App.*6.8.1; Cyr. *thes.*15(5[1].150A); *τὸν ὑπὲρ Ἀετίου καὶ τοῦ δ. τόμον* Philost.*h.e.*8.2 (M.65.556A); Evagr.*h.e.*4.37(p.186.17; M.86.2772A); Thdr.Raith. *praep.*(p.185.13; M.91.1484A); **d.** of esoteric traditions opp. public *κήρυγμα* of Church; **i.** of myst. sense of scripture, ref. the 318 of Gen.17:23,27 *Ἀβραὰμ...προβλέψας εἰς τὸν Ἰησοῦν περιέτεμεν, λαβὼν τριῶν γραμμάτων δ.* *Barn.*9.7; *τρία ἔλαβεν ἐν τῇ συνέσει δ.* *ib.*10.1; **ii.** of liturg. tradition and its significance, ref. baptismal formula *ὁ μὲν κύριος ὡς...σωτήριον δ. τὴν μετὰ πατρὸς σύνταξιν τοῦ ἁγίου πνεύματος παραδέδωκε* Bas.*Spir.*25(3.21D; M.32.112C); *τῶν ἐν τῇ ἐκκλησίᾳ πεφυλαγμένων δ. καὶ κηρυγμάτων, τὰ μὲν ἐκ τῆς ἐγγράφου διδασκαλίας ἔχομεν, τὰ δὲ ἐκ τῆς τῶν ἀποστόλων παραδόσεως διαδοθέντα ἡμῖν ἐν μυστηρίῳ παρεδεξάμεθα...οὗτος ὁ λόγος τῆς τῶν ἀγράφων παραδόσεως, ὡς μὴ καταμελετηθεῖσαν τῶν δ. τὴν γνῶσιν εὐκαταφρόνητον τοῖς πολλοῖς γενέσθαι διὰ συνήθειαν. ἄλλο γὰρ δ., καὶ ἄλλο κήρυγμα. τὸ μὲν γὰρ σιωπᾶται, τὰ δὲ κηρύγματα δημοσιεύεται. σιωπῆς δὲ εἶδος καὶ ἡ ἀσάφεια, ᾗ κέχρηται ἡ γραφή, δυσθεώρητον κατασκευάζουσα τῶν δ. τὸν νοῦν πρὸς τὸ τῶν ἐντυγχανόντων λυσιτελές* *ib.*66(54D,55E; M.188A,189Bf.); *δυσωπητικὰ γάρ πως τὰ παλαιὰ τῶν δ.* *ib.*71(60B; M.200C); *τῶν ἐν τῇ ἐκκλησίᾳ παραδιδομένων...διδαγμάτων τὰ μέν ἐστι δ., τὰ δὲ κηρύγματα. καὶ ἡ διαφορά, τὰ μὲν δ. μετ' ἐπικρύψεως καὶ σοφίας ἀπαγγέλλεται, καὶ τὴν ἀσάφειαν πολλάκις ἐξεπίτηδες περιβάλλεται, ὡς ἂν 'μὴ βεβήλοις εἶεν τὰ ἅγια ἔκθετα...', τὰ δὲ κηρύγματα χωρίς τινος ἐπικρύψεως ἀπαγγέλλεται...εἶναι δὲ καὶ τῶν δ. ἔτι τινὰ μυστικώτερα, ἃ παντελῶς ὡς τὸ ἔπος φάναι σεσίγηται, ἐκείνοις δὲ μόνοις μυστικῶς παραδέδοται, οἳ...ἔχουσι πνευματικὴν σοφίαν πιστοῖς ταῦτα παρατίθεσθαι* [i.e. acc. Eulogius] Phot.*cod.*230(M.103.1028B); **6.** *principle,* Or.*fr.in Ezech.*30:25(M.17.288A).

C. *system of belief, religion, creed*; **1.** in gen. *μιασμὸν...τό τινος ἅψασθαι ἤτοι θιγεῖν ἄλλου τινὸς ἀνθρώπου ἀπὸ ἄλλου δ.* Epiph.*haer.*9.3 (p.200.17; M.41.228B); Justn.*conf.*(p.94.9; M.86.1017C); **2.** of pagan religion *οὐ τὸ δ. ... σατανικὸν μόνον ἦν, ἀλλὰ καὶ ὁ βίος διαβολικός* Chrys.*hom.4.1 in Rom.*(9.454D); id.*hom.11.2 in Col.*(11.407D); Just. Imp.ap.*Chron.Pasch.*p.333(M.92.864A); **3.** of Judaism, Gr.Nyss.*or. catech.*3(p.16.9; M.45.17D); **4.** of Christianity *τὸ δ. ... τῆς ἀληθείας* Arist.*apol.*15(p.110.26); *βάρβαρον ἄνωθεν εἶναι τὸ δ.* Cels.ap.Or.*Cels.* 1.2(p.57.1; M.11.656A); Cels.*ib.*2.4(p.130.27; 801A); *τοῦ καθ' ἡμᾶς δ.* Eus.*h.e.*2.13.2(M.20.168A); *ἐπίσκοποι τοῦ δ.* *ib.*7.30.19(720A); *ib.*9.5.2 (808A); Gr.Naz.*or.*4.74(M.35.600A); *τοῖς ἔξω τοῦ καθ' ἡμᾶς δ.* Gr. Nyss.*or.catech.*1(p.7.5; M.45.13A); *τὸ κατὰ τὴν ἀκολουθίαν τοῦ δ. εὐσεβές* id.*Eun.*7(2 p.155.19; M.45.744B); *τὸ δ. τὸ ἡμέτερον* Chrys. *hom.33.6 in 1Cor.*(10.307D); *τοῦ Χριστιανικοῦ δ.* Thdr.Mops.*1Tim.* 1:4(p.71.23; M.66.937A); Justn.*conf.*(p.102.36; M.86.1027B); Jo.VI CP *ep.*(M.96.1420C); **5.** of heret. systems, Hipp.*haer.*proem.(p.3.26; M.16.3021A); Epiph.*haer.*26.4(p.280.13; M.41.337B).

D. *precept, ordinance*; **1.** in gen., Athenag.*res.*19(p.72.10; M.6. 1012D); *τὰ τῆς γενέσεως δ., οἷον τὸ ἀδικῆσαι* Meth.*symp.*8.16(p.107. 17; M.18.169D); **2.** of precepts of Christian conduct *κατὰ τὸ δ. τοῦ εὐαγγελίου* (cf. Mt.10:40), *οὕτω ποιήσατε* *Did.*11.3; Ign.*Magn.*3.1; *τρία οὖν δ. ἐστιν κυρίου· ζωῆς ἐλπὶς ἀρχὴ καὶ τέλος πίστεως ἡμῶν, καὶ δικαιοσύνη κρίσεως ἀρχὴ καὶ τέλος, ἀγάπη εὐφροσύνης...μαρτυρία* *Barn.*1.6; Clem.*str.*7.16(p.70.27; M.9.537C); *λόγος...βεβαιωθεὶς τοῖς δ. πρὸς τὸ καλόν* Or.*princ.*3.1.4(p.199.9; M.11.253A); of Christ's teaching as *σωτηρίας δ.* *ib.*4.1.2(p.296.5; 345B); id.*Jo.*20.39(31; p.382.23; M.14.668C); Meth.*res.*1.61(p.326.8; M.41.1160A); **3.** of precepts of Mosaic Law, *Orac.Sib.*8.301; *παρὰ τὸ δ. τοῦ νόμου* Thdt. *Ps.*33:1(1.813); ref. Eph.2:15, Or.*comm.in Eph.*2:15(p.406.14ff.); v. *νόμος*; *πολλὴν γὰρ ἐνταῦθα διαφορὰν φησὶν ἐντολῆς καὶ δογμάτων· ἢ τὴν πίστιν φησί, δ. αὐτὴν καλῶν...ἢ τὴν παραγγελίαν* Chrys.*hom.* *5.2 in Eph.*(11.35B); *τὸν νόμον...ἐν δ., τοῖς ἰδίοις, καταργήσας* Sever.

*Eph.*2:15(p.309.8); τὸν νόμον ἔπαυσεν, ὃς τοῖχόν τινα μιμούμενος, ἀπ' ἀλλήλων ὑμᾶς διείργει...τοῦτο γὰρ εἶπε τὸν νόμον τῶν ἐντολῶν... δ. δὲ τὴν εὐαγγελικὴν διδασκαλίαν ἐκάλεσεν Thdt.*Eph.*2:15(3.414); **4.** of divine decrees in gen., *Orac.Sib.*3.656; Epiph.Gn.ap.Clem. *str.*3.2(p.199.13; M.8.1109A); οὐ δύναται νικηθῆναι τὸ δ. τοῦ θεοῦ ὑπὸ δ. ἀνθρωπίνου *M.Apollon.*24(p.32.27); Meth.*symp.*2.2(p.17.17; M.18.49C); id.*res.*1.45(p.294.11 M.41.1116B); Const.*or.s.c.*11(p.168.5; M.20.1264B); ἀνάγκη τὴν ὁμοίωσιν...ἐπ' αὐτὴν τὴν οὐσίαν τοῦ υἱοῦ φέρειν. εἰ γὰρ μὴ οὕτω τις λάβοι οὔτε πλέον τι τῶν γενητῶν ἔχων φανήσεται...οὔτε τοῦ πατρὸς ὅμοιος ἔσται, ἀλλὰ τῶν τοῦ πατρὸς ὅμοιος ἔσται δ.· καὶ τοῦ πατρὸς διαφέρει ὅτι ὁ μὲν πατὴρ πατήρ ἐστι, τὰ δὲ δ. ... τοῦ πατρός ἐστιν. εἰ τοίνυν κατὰ τὰ δ. ... ὅμοιός ἐστιν ὁ υἱὸς τῷ πατρί, ὁ μὲν πατὴρ κατ' αὐτοὺς ὀνόματι μόνον πατὴρ ἔσται Ath. *Ar.*3.11(M.26.344B); Alex.Lyc.*Man.*4(p.7.20; M.18.416D); Bas.Sel. *or.*11.3(M.85.156B); **5.** hence of scriptures as θεῖα δ. Const.ap.Eus. *v.C.*3.60(p.108.3; M.20.1132A); Eus.*ib.*4.45(p.136.14; 1196A); **6.** of authoritative decrees of Church councils and authorities; **a.** of 'Apostolic Council', Chrys.*hom.*5.3 *in Mt.*(7.78A); Sever.*Gal.*2:18 (p.300.11); δ. καὶ κρίσει τῶν ἀποστόλων Euthal.Diac.*Ac.*(M.85.657B); **b.** in later history, ref. Quartodeciman controversy σύνοδοι...δι' ἐπιστολῶν ἐκκλησιαστικὸν δ. τοῖς πανταχόσε διετυποῦντο Eus.*h.e.* 5.23.2(M.20.492B); ref. baptismal controversy δ. περὶ τούτου γέγονεν ἐν ταῖς μεγίσταις τῶν ἐπισκόπων συνόδοις Dion.Al.*ib.*7.5.5 (645A); ref. excommunication of Novatian δ. παρίσταται τοῖς πᾶσιν, τὸν μὲν Νοουάτον...ἐν ἀλλοτρίοις τῆς ἐκκλησίας ἡγεῖσθαι Eus.*h.e.* 6.43.2(M.20.616B); of Nicene definition τὰ τῆς συνόδου δ. κυρῶν ἐπεσφραγίζετο id.*v.C.*3.23(p.88.34; M.20.1084C); τουδὲ τοῦ δ. συγγραφεῖς CArim.*ep.Const.*1(p.237.28; M.26.697B); of additions thereto τὰ προσυφαινόμενα τῇ πίστει ἐκείνῃ δ. Bas.*ep.*258.2(3.393D; M.32. 949C); Gr.Nyss.*Apoll.*19(M.45.1161A); τίς νόμος...ποῖον συνόδου δ. τοιοῦτον ἡμῖν παρακατέθετο; *ib.*34(1200A); Horm. *ep.Epiph.*3(p.58. 15; M.*PL.*63.520B); ἐκ τῆς τῶν παραβατῶν λύμης χωρισθέντες εἰς τὰ τῆς ἀποστολικῆς καθέδρας δ. καὶ ἐντολὰς ἐπανέρχεσθε id.*ep.cler.* (p.54.11; M.*PL.*63.417B); **7.** of secular decrees; **a.** δ. συγκλήτου *senatus consultum*, *Orac.Sib.*8.45; τὸ δ. τῆς συγκλήτου ἐστὶν Χριστιανοὺς μὴ εἶναι *M.Apollon.*23(p.32.25); **b.** of imperial edicts, Eus. *h.e.*4.6.3(M.20.313A); *V.Aberc.*1(p.59.20); *M.Glyc.*(p.12*); of decree of Augustus (Lc.2:1) as divinely inspired, Chrys.*nativ.*1.2(2.356D); **c.** perh. also of decrees of local authorities διώκεται τὸ τῶν θεοσεβῶν γένος καινοῖς ἐλαυνόμενον δ. κατὰ τὴν Ἀσίαν Mel.*fr.*ap.Eus.*h.e.* 4.26.5(M.20.393A); **8.** met., *prompting* τῷ δ. τῆς ὀργῆς ‡Just.*ep. Zen.et Ser.*2(M.6.1184C).

δογματίζ-ω, **A.** *lay down an opinion* or *doctrine, teach as a doctrine*; **1.** tenets of philosophical schools, Just.*1apol.*2.1(M.6.329A); *ib.*4.8(333B) cit. s. δοξάζω; Στωϊκοὶ...τὸν θεὸν εἰς πῦρ ἀναλύεσθαι ~ουσι *ib.*20.2(357C); ὡς οἱ Στωϊκοὶ ~ουσι Tat.*orat.*6(p.6.17; M.6. 817B); Εὐριπίδης...ὡς ἔστιν θεὸς ~ων Athenag.*leg.*5.1(ὡς ἐκεῖνος ~ων M.6.900A); τὸ δι' ὅλου κεχωρηκὸς πνεῦμα θεὸν ~ουσι Thphl.Ant. *Autol.*2.4(M.6.1052A); ~ειν μὴ εἶναι πρόνοιαν *ib.*3.2(1124A); Clem. *prot.*5(p.51.4; M.8.172A); id.*str.*5.14(p.386.22; M.9.136A); τὸν ὅ τί ποτ' οὖν ~οντα...λέγῃς σοφόν Or.*Cels.*3.72(p.264.4; M.11.1013D); πολλὰ καὶ διάφορα ἐδογμάτισαν, τὴν οἰκείαν τῶν ὑποθέσεων ἀκολουθίαν ἀλήθειαν εἶναι νομίσαντες *Hom.Clem.*2.8; τὴν μονάδα καὶ πρόνοιαν, καὶ τὸ κωλύειν θύεσθαι τοῖς...θεοῖς, Πυθαγόρας ἐδογμάτισεν Jo.D. *haer.*5(M.94.681C); **2.** pagan religious beliefs τῇ κτίσει χρῆναι προσκυνεῖν...~ουσιν Cyr.*Mich.*37(3.424E); **3.** Jewish beliefs, Just. *dial.*62.3(M.6.617B); **4.** Christian doctrine, CCarth.*act.*(H.1.161A); Dion.Al.ap.Eus.*h.e.*7.24.5(M.20.693B); ὁ παρὰ σοὶ ~όμενος ὅρος Eust.*engast.*4(p.20.29; M.18.620C); Eus.*e.th.*1.7(p.65.18; M.24.836B) cit. s. ἐνοικέω; Gr.Naz.*or.*28.5(p.28.13; M.36.32C); οὐδὲ γὰρ τὸν ἄνθρωπον χωρίζομεν τῆς θεότητος, ἀλλ' ἕνα καὶ τὸν αὐτὸν ~ομεν id.*ep.*101(M.37.177B); Chrys.*hom.*20.3 *in 1Cor.*(10.171E); Isid.Pel. *epp.*3.112(M.78.817C); ἐν δύο φύσεσι τὸν κύριον...~εσθαι CEph.(449) *act.*(*ACO* 2.1.1 p.181.10; H.2.216D); ἀσώματον δὲ αὐτὸν δογματίσαι Socr.*h.e.*6.7.5(M.67.684B); Bas.Sel.*or.*9.3(M.85.137B); Dam.*troph.* 1.1(p.192.12); **5.** heret. teaching αὐτοὺς δὲ μὴ διὰ πράξεως, ἀλλὰ διὰ τὸ φύσει πνευματικοὺς εἶναι...σωθήσεσθαι ~ουσιν Iren.*haer.*1.6.2 (M.7.505B); ἀσαφέστατον ἐδογματίζετο αὐτῷ πρᾶγμα Rhod.ap.Eus. *h.e.*5.13.5(M.20.461A); παρὰ τίνι γὰρ ἡ ἀλήθεια ἄλλων ἄλλα ~όντων; Clem.*str.*7.15(p.63.27; M.9.524B); Ναασσηνοὶ...ἐκεῖνα ~ουσιν ἃ πρότερον οἱ...φιλόσοφοι ἐδογμάτισαν Hipp.*haer.*5.2(p.77.5; M. 16.3123A); *ib.*6.3(p.134.9; 3206B); Μαρκίων...ἐδογμάτισε δύο εἶναι τὰ τοῦ παντὸς αἴτια *ib.*7.29(p.210.12; 3323B); Eus.*e.th.*2.9(p.109. 5; M.24.917A); Ath.*Ar.*2.19(M.26.188A); ‡Ath.*Apoll.*2.16(M.26. 1160C).

B. *teach, declare*; of teaching of Christ, prophets, apostles, †Bas. *ep.*42.2(3.126B; M.32.349A); †Bas.*bapt.*1.2.22(2.645B; M.31.1564A); *Const.App.*3.5.5; Chrys.*hom.*71.2 *in Mt.*(7.697B).

C. *decree, lay down a law*; **1.** of secular legislation, esp. imperial edicts, c. acc., Meth.*symp.*8.16(p.108.4; M.18.172A); μὴ δογματίσοι κατὰ Κομεντιόλου τὸν θάνατον Thphyl.*exc.Rom.*1(p.222.12; M.113. 929A); **2.** of eccl. ordinances; **a.** episcopal ἐδογμάτισεν [sc. Callistus] ὅπως εἰ ἐπίσκοπος ἁμάρτοι τι, εἰ καὶ πρὸς θάνατον, μὴ δεῖν κατατίθεσθαι Hipp.*haer.*9.12(p.249.22; M.16.3386B); **b.** conciliar, CSard.*ep.Alex.*ap.Ath.*apol.sec.*40(p.118.20; M.25.317B); τοῖς ἐν συνοδικῷ γράμματι κανονικῶς...δεδογματισμένοις Bas.*ep.*92.3(3.186C; M. 32.484A); *ib.*263.2(405E; M.977B); **3.** of divine decrees οὐδὲν μὴ παρέλθῃ τῶν δεδογματισμένων ὑπ' αὐτοῦ *1Clem.*27.5; *Clem.ep.*2(M. 2.36B); **4.** error in Gennad.*fr.Rom.*7:5(M.85.1680B; ἐδαμάζετο p.369.17).

δογματικός, **1.** *laying down an opinion* or *doctrine* οὐ μόνον οἱ ἐφεκτικοί, ἀλλὰ καὶ πᾶς δ. Clem.*str.*8.5(p.90.4; M.9.581A); **2.** *theoretical, concerned with general principles* ἡ δ. τῶν ἰατρῶν τέχνη Marcell. *fr.*76 ap.Eus.*Marcell.*1.4(p.20.20; M.24.757A); **3.** *doctrinal, concerned with doctrine*, Clem.*str.*5.1(p.332.23; M.9.24B); Or.*Ps.*36:21 (p.11); δ. θεωρήμασι Eus.*p.e.*11 proem.(508B; M.21.844C); οὗτος [sc. ὁ ψαλμός] δογματικώτερος ὤν id.*Ps.*140 proem.(M.24.44A); δ. θεολογίαις id.*v.C.*4.33(p.131.14; M.20.1181B); id.*d.e.*3.3(p.113.8; M. 22.193C); δ. μαθήμασιν τοῦ σωτῆρος *ib.*(p.113.22; 193D); Cyr.*Jo.* proem.(4.5C); opp. practical, concerned with practice or ethics, Eus.*p.e.*7.8(313A; M.529A); Cyr.H.*catech.*5.10; εἰς τὸν ἠθικὸν ἐμπεσὼν λόγον, πάλιν ἀναμίγνυσι τὸν δ. Chrys.*comm.in Gal.*5:13(10.718A); Cyr.*ador.*5(1.166B); δ. εὐτεχνίας καὶ πρακτικῆς ἀστειότητος id.*Ps.* 46:10(M.69.1057C); δύο νεβροί, ἡ ἠθικὴ καὶ ἡ δ. διδασκαλία id.*fr.Cant.* 4:5(M.69.1288B); Thdt.*Ps.*1:1(1.609); neut. as subst., Clem.*paed.* 1.1(p.90.23; M.8.249C); καταλύσας...τὸν τῶν ἠθικῶν λόγον, ἐπὶ τὰ δ. ἐκβαίνει Chrys.*hom.*13.2 *in Rom.*(9.544B); *ib.*21.3(660D); ‡Chrys. *fid.*3(1.831A).

δογματικῶς, *doctrinally, as concerned with doctrine* οὐ δ. εἴρηται, ἀλλ' ἀγωνιστικῶς Bas.*ep.*210.5(3.316D; M.32.776A); πολλὰ δι' ὀλίγων δ. ἐκπαιδεύει ὁ λόγος Gr.Nyss.*hom.*2 *in Cant.*(M.44.796C); τῶν...ἐν ἱστορίας χαρακτῆρι δ. εἰρημένων id.*Eun.*12(1 p.279.5; M.45.985C); Didym.*Trin.*3.8(M.39.849B).

***δογματισμός, ὁ**, *dogmatic principle*, Meth.*res.*1.26(p.253.4; M.41. 1132A).

***δογματιστής, ὁ**, *one who lays down a doctrine*; **1.** of philosophers οἱ τῶν Ἑλλήνων δ. Hipp.*haer.*10.6(p.265.24; M.16.3414C); **2.** of Christ δ. ἀξιόπιστον Isid.Pel.*epp.*1.20(M.78.196A); *ib.*1.109(256C); **3.** of theologians, Gr.Naz.*or.*34.4(M.36.244C); ironically, of would-be theologians, Corn.ap.Eus.*h.e.*6.43.8(M.20.620A); Eust.*engast.*7 (p.24.20; M.18.624D); δ. καὶ μυθολόγων Gr.Naz.*or.*31.18(p.166.13; M.36.152C); Gr.Nyss.*Eun.*1(1 p.135.6; M.45.373A); *ib.*8(2 p.190.8; 785A); τοῖς νέοις δ. Cyr.*ep.*21(p.117.15; 5².82D); Max.*ep.*13(M.91. 520C).

***δογματοθεσία, ἡ**, *issuing of an edict*, Tim.Ant.*descr.BMV* 6 (M.28.953B).

δογματοποιΐα, ἡ, *fabrication of doctrine*; ref. heresies, Gr.Nyss. *v.Mos.*(M.44.332A); id.*Eun.*3(2 p.5.18); id.*Apoll.*37(M.45.1208C); Eustrat.*v.Eutych.*30(M.86.2309A); *ib.*36(2316C); *V.Max.*29(M.90. 97D).

δοκ-έω, **1.** *think* τί ~εῖτε; *1Clem.*43.6; Herm.*vis.*2.4.1; Hipp.*haer.* 8.10(p.231.9; M.16.3355C); **2.** *hold an opinion about* τὰ μὲν περὶ... Μοντανὸν ὁμοίως ~οῦσι *ib.*10.26(p.282.23; 3439C); **3.** *seem*; Christol.; **a.** orthodox τὸν σαρκωθέντα λόγον...ἐν τοῖς ἀνθρωπότητος καθικέσθαι μέτροις, διὰ τοῦ ~εῖν ὑπομεῖναι τὰ αὐτῆς Cyr.*Lc.*22:39(M.72.920D); id.*Thds.*28(p.60.21; 5².25C); τὸ ὑψοῦσθαι ~εῖν id.*Pulch.*(p.55.5; 5². 170E); τὸ μὴ εἰδέναι ~εῖν id.*apol.Thdt.*4(p.124.20; 6¹.218B); θεὸς γὰρ ὤν, ἐδόκει ἄνθρωπος εἶναι δι' ἣν ἀνείληφε φύσιν Thdt.*eran.*1(4. 42); **b.** in docetic heresies, Ign.*Smyrn.*4.2; ἄπιστοι, λέγουσιν, τὸ ~εῖν πεπονθέναι αὐτόν *ib.*2 = id.*Trall.*10; (Marcion) δοκήσει πεφηνότα, οὔτε γένεσιν ὑπομείναντα οὔτε πάθος, ἀλλὰ τῷ ~εῖν Hipp.*haer.*10.19 (p.280.13; M.16.3438A); ἡμεῖς τὸ ~εῖν ἐπὶ τοῦ παθεῖν οὐ τάσσομεν Or.*Cels.*2.16(p.145.12; M.11.828A); Meth.*res.*2.18(p.370.8; M.18. 284D); ἐδόκει σῶμα ἔχειν, μὴ ἔχων Ath.*Ar.*2.43(M.26.237C); **c.** adv. τῷ ~εῖν or τὸ ~εῖν *seemingly, in appearance*, Ign.*Trall.*10; cf. *et partus virginis et ipsius exinde infantis ordo* τὸ ~εῖν *haberentur*, Tert.*de carne Christi* 1(M.*PL.*2.754C); Hipp.*haer.*10.19(cit. supra); cf. *non* τὸ ~εῖν *juxta veteres haereticos*, Hier.*adversus Pelagianos* 2.14 (M.*PL.*23.550B); τῷ ~εῖν ἀνεχώρησαν Sophr.H.*mir.Cyr.et Jo.*(M.87. 3573D); Thphn.*chron.*p.187(M.108.484C); *hypocritically* εἶπεν αὐτῷ τῷ ~εῖν· ἀπέλθωμεν Jo.Thess.*dorm.BMV* 2.10(p.421.32); **4.** *seem good*; **a.** in gen., *LS*; c. ἵνα et infin., Const.ap.Eus.*h.e.*10.5.19(M.

20.888A); **b.** of eccl. enactments, freq. dist. from apostolic tradition of doctrine περὶ μὲν τοῦ πάσχα 'ἔδοξε τὰ ὑποτεταγμένα'. τότε γὰρ ἔδοξε πάντας πείθεσθαι· περὶ δὲ τῆς πίστεως ἔγραψαν οὐκ 'ἔδοξεν', ἀλλ' 'οὕτως πιστεύει ἡ καθολικὴ ἐκκλησία' Ath.*syn.*5(p.234.9; M.26.688C); **5.** *be seen, be apparent,* Const.ap.Ath.*apol.sec.*70 (p.148.19; M.25.373B); CSard.*ep.cath.*ap.Ath.*apol.sec.*44(p.121.36; M.25.332B); **6.** *be on watch for* ἄλγεα τεκταίνοντας ἄναξ δοκέεσκεν ὀπωπαῖς †Apoll.*met.Ps.*33:17(M.33.1356D).

§**δοκή, ἡ,** = δοχή, *reception,* Thal.*cent.*2.19(M.91.1440B).

δόκησις, ἡ, 1. *appearance* opp. reality; **a.** Christol., of docetic heresies; cf. (Saturninus) *salvatorem...putative...visum hominem,* Iren.*haer.*1.24.2(M.7.674B); (Valentinian) οὐ γὰρ δοκήσει...ἀλλ' ἐν ὑποστάσει ἀληθείας ἐγίνετο *ib.*5.1.2(1122A); δοκήσει τινὲς αὐτὸν πεφανερῶσθαι ὑπέλαβον Clem.*str.*6.9(p.467.12; M.9.292C); (Saturninus) σωτῆρα ἀγέννητον...καὶ ἀσώματον...δοκήσει δὲ ἐπιπεφηνέναι ἄνθρωπον Hipp.*haer.*7.28(p.209.5; M.16.3322B); (Marcion and Cerdon), *ib.*10.19(p.280.12; 3438A); (Marcion, Valentinus, and Gnostics), id.*fr.in Mt.*25:24(p.209.8; M.10.868A) cit. s. φασματώδης; εἰρηκέναι τινὰ τῶν ἐν ταῖς αἱρέσεσι δοκήσει τὸν Ἰησοῦν...πεπονθέναι οὐ πεπονθότα Or.*Cels.*2.16(p.145.8; M.11.828A); οὐ δ. ἀλλ' ἀλήθειαν εἶναι...κατὰ τὴν...εἰς ἀνθρώπους ἐπιδημίαν *ib.*4.19(p.288.20; 1052B); id.*Jo.*10.6(4; p.176.16; M.14.316B); id.*fr.*53 *in Jo.*(p.527.18); περὶ ἕνα τῶν ἀριθμῶν τῆς τριάδος διεσφαλμένοι...ὅτε δὲ τὸν τοῦ υἱοῦ, ὡς Ἀρτεμᾶς καὶ οἱ δοκήσει αὐτὸν ἀποφηνάμενοι πεφηνέναι Meth.*symp.*8.10(p.93.4; M.18.153B); ἀληθείᾳ γὰρ καὶ οὐ δ. ἦν ὃ ἐφάνη id.*res.*2.8 (p.344.20; M.41.1176C); Alex.Al.*ep.Alex.*12(p.28.15; M.18.568C); (Manicheans) Ath.*ep.Epict.*7(p.11.9; M.26.1061A); (Valentinus, Marcion, Manicheans) id.*ep.Adelph.*2(M.26.1073B); (Apollinarians) ἢ ἀλλοίωσιν τοῦ λόγου φαντάζονται, ἢ δ. τὴν οἰκονομίαν τοῦ πάθους ὑπολαμβάνουσι ‡Ath.*Apoll.*1.2(M.26.1096A); (Simonians) ἑαυτὸν μὲν εἶναι τὸν...ὡς πατέρα φανέντα· παρὰ δὲ Ἰουδαίοις ὕστερον οὐκ ἐν σαρκί, ἀλλὰ δοκήσει ὡς Χριστὸν...φανέντα Cyr.H.*catech.*6.14; οὐ γὰρ νεώτερον τοῦτο τῆς δ. τὸ ἀσέβημα, ἀλλὰ πάλαι ἀπὸ τοῦ ματαιόφρονος ἀρξάμενον Οὐαλεντίνου Bas.*ep.*261.2(3.402C; M.32.969C); Gr. Naz.*carm.*2.1.11.1183(M.37.1110A); Gr.Nyss.*ep.*3(M.46.1020D) cit. s. κατασχηματίζω; (Apollinarians) τίς οὖν ὁ ἄνθρωπος ὁ...ἐπὶ βρώσει τε καὶ τῇ πόσει ὀνειδιζόμενος;...εἰ μὲν μὴ μετεῖχε, δ. ἦν· εἰ δὲ μετεῖχε, γήινον τὸ μετεχόμενον· τὸ δὲ οὐράνιον διὰ τῶν γηίνων οὐ τρέφεται id. *Apoll.*34(M.45.1197B); (Simonians) Epiph.*haer.*21.1(p.238.12; M.41.285B); (Gnostic) σάρκα δὲ αὐτὸν μὴ εἰληφέναι, ἀλλ' ἢ μόνον δ. εἶναι *ib.*26.10(p.287.15; 345D); (Archontics) *ib.*40.8(p.89.7; 689B); (Cerdon) μὴ εἶναι δὲ τὸν Χριστὸν γεγεννημένον...ἀλλὰ δοκήσει ὄντα καὶ δοκήσει πεφηνότα, δοκήσει δὲ τὰ ὅλα πεποιηκότα *ib.*41.1(p.91.11; 692C); (Marcion) *ib.*42.11(p.126.6; 729A); *ib.*(p.128.10; 732C); τὸ δεῖραι καὶ τὸ τύψαι...οὐ δ. ἦν, ἀλλὰ ἀφῆς ἐστι σωματικῆς καὶ ἐνσάρκου ὑποστάσεως δηλωτικόν *ib.*(p.151.15; 768B); (Bardesanes) *ib.*56.2 (p.341.12; 992C); εἶπεν...'ἐν τῇ καρδίᾳ τῆς γῆς', ἵνα καὶ τὸν τάφον δηλώσῃ, καὶ μηδεὶς δ. ὑποπτεύσῃ Chrys.*hom.*43.2 *in Mt.*(7.459D); id. *hom.*4.4 *in Heb.*(12.44A); Cyr.*glaph.Gen.*7(1.240A); id.*inc.unigen.* (5^1.681B); cf. μηδὲν νοεῖν κατὰ δ., ἀλλὰ πάντα καθ' ὑπόστασιν καὶ ἀλήθειαν Euther.*confut.*13(M.28.1377D); (monophysite) ἀναθεματίζεσθαι...κατὰ...δ. τερατευομένων [sc. monophysites] Basilisc.*encycl.* (p.51.2; M.86.2601B); v. φαντασία; **b.** theol., of generation of Son γεννήσαντα οὐ δ., ἀλλ' ἀληθείᾳ Ar.*ep.Alex.*(p.12.8; M.26.709A); hence **2.** *docetic heresy* ὁ τῆς δ. ἐξάρχων Ἰούλιος Κασσιανός Clem. *str.*3.13(p.238.9; M.8.1192C); *ib.*3.17(p.243.11; 1205A); **3.** *pretence* ταύτης δ. ἐστιν ἡ εἰρωνεία Gr.Naz.*carm.*1.2.34.87(M.37.952A); **4.** *decision, resolve* ὁ...λόγος...ἰδίᾳ δ. ... ἐνηνθρώπησε Epiph.*haer.*69.52 (p.199.18; M.42.284B).

***δοκησισκοπία, ἡ,** *consideration of, deference to, opinion,* Nil. *serm.*7(M.79.1276A).

***δοκησισοφέω,** *have a conceit of wisdom, pretend to* or *make a display of wisdom,* Cyr.*Jo.*1.10(4.110A); *ib.*5.5(537C); of pagan teachers, id.*Zach.*67(3.746E).

δοκησισοφία, ἡ, *conceit of wisdom; sham wisdom,* Cyr.*Jo.*3.5(4.308A); *ib.*9(755C); id.*Joel.*40(3.237E).

***δοκηταί, οἱ,** *docetists,* those who maintain illusory character of Inc.; **1.** as distinct sect, with peculiar system of belief Φρυγῶν... ἐγκρατητῶν...δ. Clem.*str.*7.17(p.76.26; M.9.553A); Hipp.*haer.*8.2 (p.225.9; M.16.3347A); οἵ γ' ἑαυτοὺς δ. ἀπεκάλεσαν *ib.*8.8(p.226.6; 3347C); τῆς τῶν δ. πολυπλόκου...αἱρέσεως *ib.*8.11(p.231.18; 3358A); *ib.*10.16(p.277.15; 3434A); **2.** of followers of Marcion and others who deny reality of Christ's human body, Serap.Ant.ap.Eus.*h.e.*6.12.6 (M.20.545B); Cyr.*inc.unigen.*(5^1.680D); *ib.*(690E); including Marcion, Valentinus, and Manes, Thdt.*ep.*82(4.1142); of monophysites, Eust.Mon.*ep.*(M.86.916D).

***δοκιανή, ἡ,** (cf. Lat. *ducianus*) *office of* dux, Max.*ambig.*(M.91.1284B).

[*]**δοκίδη, ἡ,** variant of δοκίς, a kind of meteor, Thdt.*qu.*15 *in Gen.*(1.18).

δοκιμάζ-ω, 1. *test*; ref. prophets δοκιμάσαντες αὐτὸν γνώσεσθε *Did.*12.1; οὕτω δοκιμάσεις τὸν προφήτην καὶ τὸν ψευδοπροφήτην Herm.*mand.*11.7; **2.** *approve after testing,* id.*vis.*1.2.4; δοκιμασθέντες...οἱ μάρτυρες ἐν ταῖς κατὰ τοὺς πειρασμοὺς...προσβολαῖς Meth.*res.*1.56(p.315.7; M.41.1149B); of candidates for Valentinian initiation, Hipp.*haer.*6.41(p.172.26; M.16.3259B); for baptism, cf. id.*trad.ap.*20.1; *Const.App.*8.32.11; for eccl. office, of prophets προφήτης δεδοκιμασμένος...οὐ κριθήσεται *Did.*11.11; of ἐπίσκοποι and διάκονοι: χειροτονήσατε...ἑαυτοῖς...ἄνδρας...ἀληθεῖς καὶ δεδοκιμασμένους *ib.*15.1; of those converts who were appointed as bishops and deacons by apostles καθίστανον τὰς ἀπαρχὰς αὐτῶν, δοκιμάσαντες τῷ πνεύματι *1Clem.*42.4; and successors of such ministers ὅπως...διαδέξωνται ἕτεροι δεδοκιμασμένοι ἄνδρες τὴν λειτουργίαν αὐτῶν *ib.*44.2; of bishops, *Const.App.*2.1.3; οὕτως γὰρ ~έσθω...εἰ ἔστι σεμνός, πιστὸς καὶ κόσμιος, κτλ. *ib.*2.2.3; ~έσθω εἰ ἄμωμός ἐστι περὶ τὰς βιωτικὰς χρείας *ib.*2.3.1; of deacons, *ib.*3.16.1; of bishops, priests, and deacons, *ib.*7.31.1; **3.** *decide, resolve,* Eus. *v.C.*4.52(p.139.12; M.20.1204A); Ath.*decr.*32(p.28.20; M.25.476B); Gr. Nyss.*v.Macr.*(p.375.22; M.46.964D).

δοκιμασία, ἡ, *test, testing*; **1.** eschatological ἥξει ἡ κτίσις τῶν ἀνθρώπων εἰς τὴν πύρωσιν τῆς δ. ... καὶ ἀπολοῦνται *Did.*16.5; τὸ τοῦ πυρὸς βάπτισμα τὴν ἐν τῇ κρίσει δ. λέγων Bas.*Spir.*36(3.30B; M.32.132C); **2.** of temptations, Mac.Aeg.*pat.*27(M.34.888C); Cyr.*Ps.*32:19(M.69.881B); Diad.*perf.*76(p.96.5); **3.** of self-examination of one to be appointed to priestly office, Chrys.*sac.*4.2(p.106.16; 1.406B).

δοκιμαστής, ὁ, *tester, prover*; of God as judge, Tat.*orat.*6(p.6.23; M.6.817C).

δοκιμαστικός, *testing* ποταμοῦ πυρὸς δ. τῶν ἀνθρώπων Cyr.H. *catech.*15.21.

δοκιμή, ἡ, 1. *testing, trial* Ἰὼβ οὐ μισηθεὶς ὑπὸ κυρίου, ἀλλὰ δ. χάριν εἰς τὸ τοῦ παρανόμου πέπτωκε στόμα Or.*exp.in Pr.*22:14(M.17.220B); τὸν πονηρὸν πρὸς δοκιμὴν ἀνθρώπων ἐγρηγορότα *Hom.Clem.*3.3; τὰ τῶν γραφῶν ψευδῆ εὐλόγως πρὸς δοκιμὴν ἔχοντα τυγχάνει *ib.*3.4; οἱ...τῶν πραγμάτων αὐτόπται διὰ πυρὸς καὶ σιδήρου δ. τὴν ὑπὲρ ὧν ἐμαρτύρησαν ἀλήθειαν ἐπιστώσαντο Eus.*d.e.*3.6(p.137.23; M.22.232C); **2.** *affliction, trial* χήρα ἐν δ. πολλῇ ‡Pion.*v.Polyc.*27.

δοκίμιος, *approved, reliable* δ. δόγματα Sophr.H.*ep.syn.*(M.87.3152B); τὸ δ. *reliability,* Eus.*d.e.*2.3(p.74.28).

***δοκιμότης, ἡ,** *excellence, worth* δ. φράσεως ‡Just.*coh.Gr.*35 (M.6.304C); δ. τῆς ἀρετῆς Chrys.*hom.*24.3 *in Ac.*(9.197C).

δοκίμως, *worthily,* Eus.*ep.Caes.*(p.43.4; M.20.1537A).

δοκίς, ἡ, *beam,* name given to a kind of meteor because of its shape κομῆται ἢ δοκίδες ἢ πωγωνίαι ἢ πίθοι Or.*Cels.*1.58(p.109.31; M.11.768B); Eus.*d.e.*9.1(p.406.7; M.22.656A); *Chron.Pasch.*p.323(M.92.828A); v. [*]δοκίδη, δοκίτης.

δοκίτης, ὁ, variant of foreg., Thphn.*chron.*p.279(M.108.689C).

δολιεύ-ομαι, 1. *practise cunning* or *behave treacherously towards,* Ephr.3.214A; Epiph.*haer.*59.7(p.372.10; M.41.1029A); ref. Ps.33:13b ἐστὶ τὸ μὴ ~σασθαι τὸν πλησίον Dor.*doct.*4.3(M.88.1661D) etc.; **2.** *use wiles*; of women, *T.Reub.*5.1,5.

***δολιολάλος,** *speaking guile,* Leont.B.*Nest.et Eut.*1(M.86.1301C).

***δολιοπλόκος,** *weaving wiles, Orac.Sib.*12.48.

δολιότης, ἡ, *deceit, cunning,* Herm.*sim.*8.6.2; Mac.Aeg.*hom.*3.4 (M.34.469D); οὐ ῥᾳδιουργία ἡ δ. ἐστίν, ἀλλὰ πλήρης τούτων τυγχάνει Didym.ap.*cat.Ac.*13:10(p.215.32); as practised by Devil, Ath.*ep. Aeg.Lib.*4(M.25.545C); †Nil.*mal.cog.*27(M.79.1232D); by antichrist ὑπὸ πολλῆς δ. ὁ παγκάκιστος ὥσπερ πρᾶος ἐλεύσεται Rom.Mel. (*SBBAW* 1898^2 p.171); of women's *wiles, T.Jos.*4.3.

***δολιοτρόπως,** *deceitfully,* El.H.*cant.*1.6(p.290).

***δολομέτρης, ὁ,** *one who uses false measures, Const.App.*4.6.5.

δολοποιέω, *act treacherously towards,* Marc.Er.*opusc.*1.124(M.65.921A).

δόλος, ὁ, *guile, deceit*; defined ἔστι δὲ ὁ δ. κακοποιΐα λαθραία ἐν προσποιήσει τῶν βελτιόνων τῷ πλησίον προσφερομένη Bas.*hom.in Ps.*33(1.153B; M.29.373D); δ. τὸ πρὸς ἐπιβουλὴν περίεργον, ὅταν τις, ἀγαθόν τι σχηματισάμενος, καὶ τοῦτο, ὥσπερ δέλεαρ, τινὶ προθείς, δι' αὐτοῦ τὰ τῆς ἐπιβουλῆς κατεργάσηται id.*reg.br.*77(2.442D; M.31.1136D).

***δολότροπος,** *guileful, wily*; of Devil, ‡Epiph.*hom.*4(M.43.481B).

δολουργός, = δολοεργός, *treacherous,* Bas.*renunt.*5(2.207C; M.31.637C).

***δολουργῶς**, *guilefully*, Nil.*epp*.3.142(M.79.449B); Hesych.S. *temp*.1.74(M.93.1504B).

δολοφονία, ἡ, *murderous intent*, Gr.Mag.*dial*.(tr.Zach.)2.8(M.*PL*. 66.147D).

***δολοφωνέω**, *address guilefully*, *T.Gad* 6.5.

δόμα, τό, *gift*, Hipp.*Dan*.3.6.2; Or.*Jo*.10.13(11; p.184.22; M.14. 329C); ‡Pion.*v.Polyc*.10; τοῖς τοῦ θεοῦ δ. *Const.App*.2.24.7; of offerings to clergy, *ib*.2.28.5; for widows, *ib*.3.4.2; *ib*.4.8.1; κυρίως γὰρ δ. μὲν τὰ τοῖς ἐνδεέσι διδόμενα, δῶρα δέ, τὰ τοῖς ἀπροσδεέσιν εἰσκομιζόμενα...δῶρα μέν, οἱ ἐνυπάρχοντες ἑκάστῳ εἴδει τῶν συμπληρούντων τὴν κτίσιν πνευματικοὶ λόγοι, δι' ὧν ὁ τῆς κτίσεως γνωρίζεται ποιητής..., δ. δέ, οἱ ἐνόντες ἑκάστῳ τούτων αὖθις φυσικοὶ νόμοι· τοῦτ' ἔστι τὰ φυσικὰ πλεονεκτήματα, δι' ὧν παιδεύεταί τις πρὸς ἀρετήν †Cyr.*coll.VT*(6[a].64B; M.77.1272A); Thdt.*qu*.9 *in Dt*.(1.269).

δομαῖος, *belonging to, part of, the building*, Paul.Sil.*ambo*.187 (M.86.2259A).

[*]**δομάτιον, τό**, v. δωμάτιον.

δομάω ([*]**δομ-έω**), *build*, Gr.Naz.*carm*.1.2.32.82(M.37.922A); med., *Orac.Sib*.3.384; Thdt.*qu*.45 *in 2Reg*.(1.454); -εῖται *Chron. Pasch*.p.323(M.92.828B); pass., Thdt.*qu*.45 *in Dt*.(1.295); id.*qu*.55 *in 4 Reg*.(1.551).

***δομέστικος, ὁ**, (Lat. *domesticus*) title of palace or other imperial *official*; **1.** of palace official δ. τῆς βασιλικῆς τραπέζης CCP (681)*act*.1(H.3.1056C); **2.** of subaltern of minister, governor or general δ. τοῦ ἐπάρχου Isid.Pel.*epp*.1.300 tit.(M.78.357A); τὸν πραιπόσιτον...καὶ...τὸν τοῦ αὐτοῦ...δ. Jo.Mal.*chron*.17 p.410(M.97. 608A); δ. τοῦ στρατηγοῦ Anast.Ap.*a.Max*.2.31(M.90.169A); **3.** of head of a division of the *scholae* under the *comes*, Pall.*h.Laus*.44 (p.131.7; M.34.1209C); Thds.Imp.*syn*.(p.120.12; H.1.1345C); Jo. Mal.*chron*.13 p.333(M.97.497A); **4.** of a taxation officer, Malchus *exc.gent*.6(p.573.28; M.113.788D); **5.** of officer of ceremonial bodyguard, Thphn.*chron*.p.235(M.108.785B); **6.** of eccl. leader of choir, *Euchol*.(p.225).

[*]**δομέω**, v. δομάω.

δόμημα, τό, *building*, Eus.*h.e*.10.4.43(M.20.865B).

δομήτωρ, ὁ, *builder*, fig., †Max.*hymn*.2(M.91.1421A); of God ὁ δ. οὐρανοῦ Jo.Mon.*hymn.Blas*.6(M.96.1404D).

δόμος, ὁ, *house*; of a church, *CIG* 8654(Gerasa, 496); *IGC As. Min*.215(Naxos, saec. vii–ix); of Persian fire-temples, Geo.Pis. *carm*.4.168.

***δονακοτρεφής**, *nurtured in a reed*; of a spice (here aloes, but cf. Ex.30:23, Cant.4:14), Nonn.*par.Jo*.19:39(M.43.905D).

δον-έω, *agitate*; ? *beat*, in token of grief ∼ούμενος...τὸ πρόσωπον Serap.*ep.mon*.6(M.40.932C).

δόξα, ἡ, **A.** *intention*, Eus.*v.C*.4.26(p.127.24; M.20.1176A).

B. *doctrine, system of belief* τῆς ἀποστολικῆς καὶ ἐκκλησιαστικῆς δ. Eus.*h.e*.4.7.5(M.20.317A); ὡς μὴ ὀρθὴν ἐχόντων...δ. id.ap.Marcell. *fr*.73 ap.eund.*Marcell*.1.4(p.27.21; M.24.768C); cf.CSard.*ep.cath*.ap. Ath.*apol.sec*.46(p.122.28; M.25.333B); τὴν ὑγιαίνουσαν πίστιν καὶ εὐσεβῆ δ. Bas.*jud*.8(2.223C; M.31.676C); περὶ λατρείας καὶ περὶ τῆς τοῦ θεοῦ δ. Chrys.*hom*.7.6 *in 1Cor*.(10.59D); Philost.*h.e*.3.12(M.65. 501A); ὁ Ἰωσὴφ...δ. ἑτέρας ἦν, οὐ τῆς Αἰγυπτιακῆς Chrys.*hom*.4.4 *in Tit*.(11.754C); Cyr.*Jo*.9.1(4.811E); Christianity described by opponents as τὴν ἄθεον...δ. Licinius ap.Eus.*v.C*.2.5(p.43.1; M.20.984B).

C. *honour, distinction, glory*; coming **1.** from good reputation, def. ὁρίζονται εἶναι δ., τὸν ἀπὸ τῶν πολλῶν ἔπαινον Or.*Jo*.32.26(17; p.471.14; M.14.813C); in gen. ἐν ταῖς ἐντολαῖς...περὶ πρωτείων ἢ περὶ δ. τινὸς οὐκ ἔστιν Herm.*sim*.8.7.6; Meth.*symp*.8.2(p.82.17; M.18. 140C); Gr.Naz.*or*.15.5(M.35.920B); ἀπετάξατο [sc. Christ]...τρυφῇ, δ., πλούτῳ *Const.App*.5.5.3; καταφρονήσωμεν τῆς τῶν πολλῶν δ. Chrys.*hom*.3.6 *in Jo*.(8.25C); Cyr.*Jo*.1.9(4.98E); as having no permanent effect on men, Bas.*hom*.23.2(2.186B; M.31.592C); endangering faith ὅταν γὰρ διὰ δ. πίστιν ἀμείβωσιν ὀρθήν Chrys.*hom*. 3.5 *in Jo*.(8.24A); **2.** from something which exalts one in men's eyes or in one's own, e.g. children δ. πατέρων ὁσιότης παίδων *Const.App*. 7.24.8; learning, †Bas.*Is*.238(1.560D; M.30.537A); **3.** from God, *1Clem*.32.2; *ib*.3.1 cit. s. πλατυσμός; σύ...δίδως τοῖς υἱοῖς τῶν ἀνθρώπων δ. καὶ τιμὴν καὶ ἐξουσίαν *ib*.61.2; δ. παρὰ θεῷ καὶ τιμὴν παρὰ ἀνθρώποις οἴσει Chrys.*hom*.77.5 *in Jo*.(8.457D); and Christ εἰ καὶ πᾶσα ἡ δ. σου ἐν τῷ κυρίῳ...Χριστῷ ὑπάρχει ἐστηριγμένη καὶ οὐκ ἐξ ἀνθρωπίνου, ἀλλ' ἐκ θείου ἀξιώματος ἐγκαυχᾶσαι *M.Ner.et Ach*.9 (p.8.13); **4.** but not to be sought τὸ μὲν δ. ἐρᾶν ἀδοξία, δ. δὲ ὄντως τὸ ταύτης ὑπερορᾶν Chrys.*hom*.3.6 *in Jo*.(8.25D); and contrasted with heavenly glory τῶν δὲ χοϊκῶν καὶ κατὰ σάρκα ζώντων, ἡ δ. αὐτῶν κατασκηνοῦν εἰς τὸν χοῦν λέγεται Bas.*hom.in Ps*.7(1.100D; M.29.236A); and glory of God, †Gregent.*leg.Hom*.48(M.86.608A).

D. *glory, majesty*, *A.Thom*.B 20(p.32.28); as title of address, *ib*.10 (p.30.7); of a king, †Jo.D.*B.J*.16(M.96.1004A); of reverence accorded to bishop, *Const.App*.3.13.1.

E. *vainglory, boastfulness* φυσιώμενοι...διὰ δόξης Tat.*orat*.26(p.28. 10; M.6.864A); πόρρω...ἦν δόξης, καὶ τύφου...ἐλεύθερος Chrys.*hom*. 17.5 *in Rom*.(9.629C); id.*hom*.35.5 *in 1Cor*.(10.328A); φιλοτιμίᾳ δὲ καὶ κενῇ δ. δεδουλωμένους Thdt.*h.e*.1.2.7(3.725).

F. *glory*, i.e. dazzling splendour which is in OT and NT peculiar attribute of Godhead and manifestation of divine presence (cf. Ex.16:10, 3Reg.8:11, Is.6:1); **1.** of God; **a.** in gen. οἱ ἄγγελοι τῆς δ. τοῦ προσώπου κυρίου *T.Lev*.18.5; Herm.*mand*.12.4.2; οἱ ἀληθινοὶ προσκυνηταὶ...ἀφομοιοῦνται τῇ δ. τοῦ θεοῦ καὶ εἰσὶν μετ' αὐτοῦ ἀθάνατοι *M.Carp*.7; οὗτος ὁ τόπος...ἀπόβλητός ἐστι τῆς δ. τοῦ θεοῦ *Apoc.Paul*.41(p.62); *ib*.44(p.63); τὰ χερουβὶμ τῆς δ. κατασκιάζοντα τὸ ἱλαστήριον Ath.*ep.Adelph*.7(M.26.1080D); ἄστεκτος ἡ μεγαλοπρέπεια τῆς δ. σου *Const.App*.2.22.12; δ. δὲ πολλάκις ἡ γραφὴ λέγει αὐτὴν τοῦ θεοῦ οὐσίαν· ἐπειδὴ γὰρ ἀψηλάφητος καὶ ἀνέφικτος, δ. αὐτὴν ὠνόμασεν. ... πρῶτος τὴν οὐσίαν τοῦ θεοῦ δ. λέγει Ἰεζεκιὴλ...θεασάμενος τὸν θεὸν καθεζόμενον, καὶ ἐπάγων· τοῦτο ὁμοίωμα τῆς δ. κυρίου. ...ἣν οὖν εἶπε δ. ὁ Ἰεζεκιήλ, ταύτην ὁ θεός φησι τὸ ἐγώ Sever.*Eph*.1:17 (p.306.24ff.); **b.** meton. for God ὁ θρόνος τῆς δ. σου *Apoc.En*.9.4; *T.Lev*.3.4; ἐνώπιον τῆς ἁγίας δ. σου *T.Abr*.B 4(p.108.22); τοὺς... λειτουργήσαντας τῇ...δ. αὐτοῦ *1Clem*.9.2; ὁ θεός,...ἡ...ἀκίνητος δ. Chrys.*hom*.3.4 *in Rom*.(9.453A); εὐλογημένον εἴη τὸ ὄνομα τῆς δ. αὐτοῦ †Jo.D.*B.J*.17(M.96.1013C); **c.** dist. as outward manifestation from invisible divine essence οὐ τὴν οὐσίαν τοῦ θεοῦ ἔβλεπον [sc. οἱ προφῆται] ἀλλὰ τὴν δ. ‡Ath.*qu.Ant*.28(M.28.616A); ἐπωχεῖτο...ἡ τοῦ θεοῦ δ., οὐκ αὐτὸς ὁ θεός,...ἀλλ' ἡ τούτου δ. ἡ πρὸς τὰς οἰκονομίας ἐπιφαινομένη Thdt.*Ezech*.10:18(2.743); ὁρῶσι [sc. angels]...δ. τινὰ τῇ αὐτῶν φύσει συμμετρουμένην. ... μετὰ μέντοι τὴν ἐνανθρώπησιν ὤφθη...οὐχ ὁμοιώματι δ. ἀλλ' ἀληθεῖ...χρησάμενος id.*eran*.1(4.22); **d.** ass. divine power, v. δύναμις; **e.** effects of manifested glory ὀφθεῖσα ἡ δ. τοῦ θεοῦ τοὺς μὲν εἰς γῆν κατήνεγκεν, τοὺς δὲ πυρὶ κατέφλεξεν *Const.App*.6.3.2; when communicated to Moses θείας ἐνεπλήσθη δ. τοῦ νομοθέτου τὸ πρόσωπον καὶ τὸ σέλας ἐκεῖθεν ὑπὲρ ἀστραπὴν ἐκπεμπόμενον ἀντιβλέπειν οὐκ εἴα τοὺς ἐντυγχάνοντας Thdt. *qu*.69 *in Ex*.(1.173); **2.** partic. of Father Χριστοῦ, δι' οὗ ἐκάλεσεν ἡμᾶς...ἀπὸ ἀγνωσίας εἰς ἐπίγνωσιν δόξης ὀνόματος αὐτοῦ *1Clem*.59.2; *T.Job* 50(p.136.5); Or.*hom*.1.8 *in Jer*.(p.8.6; M.13.265A); πατρικῆς δ. Eus.*e.th*.1.13(p.74.3; M.24.852C); †Jo.D.*B.J*.31(M.96.1161B); **3.** Son being image, reflection, or lustre of Father's glory εἰκὼν γάρ ἐστι τῆς ἀγαθότητος αὐτοῦ καὶ ἀπαύγασμα οὐ τοῦ θεοῦ ἀλλὰ τῆς δ. αὐτοῦ καὶ τοῦ ἀϊδίου φωτὸς αὐτοῦ...καὶ ἀπόρροια εἰλικρινὴς τῆς παντοκρατορικῆς δ. αὐτοῦ Or.*Jo*.13.25(p.249.30; M.14.444A); ὅλης μὲν οὖν οἶμαι τῆς δ. τοῦ θεοῦ αὐτοῦ ἀπαύγασμα εἶναι τὸν υἱόν...φθάνειν μέντοι γε ἀπὸ τοῦ ἀπαυγάσματος τούτου τῆς ὅλης δ. μερικὰ ἀπαυγάσματα ἐπὶ τὴν λοιπὴν λογικὴν κτίσιν· οὐκ οἶμαι γάρ τινα τὸ πᾶν δύνασθαι χωρῆσαι τῆς ὅλης δ. τοῦ θεοῦ ἀπαύγασμα ἢ τὸν υἱὸν αὐτοῦ *ib*.32.28 (p.474.7; 820A,B); πότε γὰρ ὁ θεὸς...ἀπαύγασμα οὐκ εἶχε τῆς ἰδίας δ.; id.*princ*.4.4.1(p.349.19; M.11.401C); φῶς ἱλαρὸν ἁγίας δ. ἀθανάτου πατρὸς...Ἰησοῦ Χριστέ *Hymn*.(*AGC* p.40); ἀπόρροια τῆς τοῦ παντοκράτορος δ. εἰλικρινής Eus.*d.e*.4.3(p.154.1; M.22.256D); Ast. Soph.*fr*.21 ap.Marcell.*fr*.85 ap.Eus.*Marcell*.1.4(p.25.7; M.24.764C); τῆς...οὐσίας...δυνάμεως καὶ δ. τοῦ πατρὸς ἀπαράλλακτον εἰκόνα *Symb.Ant*.(341)2(p.249.17; M.26.721C); ὁ μὲν υἱὸς ἐν τῷ πατρί, ὡς τὸ ἐπὶ τῆς εἰκόνος κάλλος ἐν τῇ ἀρχετύπῳ μορφῇ...ἐκεῖ δὲ οὐκ ἔστι χωρίσαι τοῦ ἑτέρου τὸ ἕτερον...οὔτε τῆς θείας δ. τὸ ἀπαύγασμα. ... ἐκ γὰρ τῆς δ. ἐστὶ τὸ ἀπαύγασμα Gr.Nyss.*Eun*.1(1 p.200.12; M.45. 448A,B); τὸ τῆς δ. ἀπαύγασμα καὶ πάντα ὅσα τοιαῦτα τὸ μὴ ἀναρμόστως ἔχειν τοῦ υἱοῦ τὴν οὐσίαν πρὸς τὸν πατέρα μαρτύρεται *ib*.4(2 p.94.26; 672A); ὅταν τοῦτο εἴπῃς, οὐδὲ τὴν δ. πάντως εἶναι δώσεις...οὐ γὰρ ἔστι...τυφλὴν...νομισθῆναι τὴν δ. εἶναι...ὥστε εἰ τὸ ἀπαύγασμα οὐκ ἦν, οὐδὲ ἡ δ. ἦν *ib*.8(2 p.191.12; 785D); δ. δὲ ὁ πατήρ, ὅθεν τὸ μονογενὲς φῶς ἀπηυγάσθη *ib*.(2 p.193.23; 789A); ὤφθη...ἡ δ. κυρίου... ἤτοι γέγονεν ἐμφανὴς ὁ υἱός, ἡ δ. τοῦ θεοῦ καὶ πατρὸς Cyr.*ador*.11 (1.402A); revealing Father's glory to the saints, Serap.*euch*.13.4; **4.** of Son, *A.Jo*.88(p.194.7); ἔοικεν ἡ θειότης αὐτοῦ ἰδίως κατὰ τὴν γραφὴν δ. αὐτοῦ ὀνομάζεσθαι...ἀπὸ τοῦ πλούτου...τούτου τῆς θειότητος καὶ τῆς δ. αὐτοῦ μεταδιδοὺς Or.*comm.in Eph*.3:16(p.410); τῆς παρὰ τῷ θανάτῳ δ. αὐτοῦ id.*Jo*.19.18(4; p.318.27; M.14.560B); Χριστοῦ ἐπιδημίαν...τὴν νοητὴν γεγονέναι...τοῖς τεθεαμένοις Χριστοῦ τὴν δ. προφήταις *ib*.1.7(9; p.11.30; 36C); ἐκ τῶν ὀστῶν καὶ ἐκ τῆς σαρκός, τουτέστιν ἐκ τῆς ἁγιωσύνης καὶ ἐκ τῆς δ. Meth.*symp*.3.8(p.36.7; M.18. 73B); συναπεγεννήθη ἐκ τοῦ πατρὸς ἀϊδίως ἡ ὁμοία δ. καὶ δύναμις †Ath.*exp.fid*.2(M.25.204C); ἐπαγγελίαν τῆς δ. τοῦ μονογενοῦς υἱοῦ τοῦ θεοῦ *A.Phil*.97(p.38.9); θεός ἐστιν καὶ ἐκ θεοῦ κατὰ φύσιν καὶ τῆς δ.

κύριος Cyr.*apol.Thdt.*55(p.131.12; 6^1.225C); as denoting Son's full divinity δ. αὐτὸν καλεῖ, ἅτε φυσικῶς ἀπαύγασμα ὄντα τῆς πατρικῆς δ. Didym.*Trin.*1.32(M.39.429A); exeg. Eph.1:17 ἐνταῦθα τὴν οἰκονομίαν διώρισε· καὶ δ. μὲν τὸν μονογενῆ καλεῖ· Ἰησοῦν δὲ Χριστὸν τὸ κήρυγμα τῆς οἰκονομίας· τῆς μὲν γὰρ οἰκονομίας θεός, τῆς δὲ δ. πατήρ ‡Ath. *comm.essent.*31(M.28.60B); τὸν αὐτὸν τοῦ αὐτοῦ καὶ θεὸν ἐκάλεσε καὶ πατέρα· θεὸν μὲν ὡς ἀνθρώπου, πατέρα δὲ ὡς θεοῦ, δ. γὰρ τὴν θείαν φύσιν ὠνόμασεν Thdt.*Eph.*1:17(3.407); cf. διὰ τοῦ ἀνθρώπου, οὗ ἀνέλαβεν ἡ δ. ἐκείνη ἀκατάληπτος, ἥτις δι' ἀνθρώπου τοῖς ἀνθρώποις συνελθεῖν κατηξίωσεν *A.Petr.et Paul.*22(p.128.8); **5.** characteristics and qualities of Son's glory; **a.** derived from Father; **i.** orthodox, in gen. v. 3 supra; ref. Jo.6:27 ἐν τῇ μορφῇ τοῦ θεοῦ ἐστι, καὶ ἐν τῷ πατρὶ ὢν ἐσφράγισται τῇ πατρῴᾳ δ. Gr.Nyss.*Eun.*4(2 p.94.23; M.45.672A); **ii.** subordinationist and Arian οὐ γὰρ ἀγένητον οὐδὲ ἄναρχον ...εἶχε τὴν δ. ἀλλὰ παρὰ τοῦ πατρὸς λαβών Eus.*e.th.*1.20(p.82.29; M.24.868D); τὴν δοθεῖσαν αὐτῷ ἐξουσίαν Ἀστέριος δ. ὀνομάζει Marcell. *fr.*93 ap.eund.*Marcell.*2.2(p.40.5; M.24.792A); τὸ ζῆν καὶ τὸ εἶναι παρὰ τοῦ πατρὸς εἰληφότα καὶ τὰς δ. Ath.*syn.*16(p.244.5; M.26.709B); **b.** before Creation οὐκοῦν εἰ καὶ πρὸ τοῦ τὸν κόσμον γενέσθαι τὴν δ. εἶχεν ὁ υἱός Ath.*Ar.*1.38(M.26.92B); ὁ...θεὸς λόγος ὁ πρὸ κόσμου ἔχων τὴν τοῦ πατρὸς δ. Gr.Nyss.*hom.in 1Cor.15:28*(M.44.1320D); πῶς ὡς δόξης ἐπιδεὴς τὴν προκόσμιον αὐτοῦ δ. αἰτεῖ; Cyr.*apol.Thdt.*55 (p.131.13; 6^1.225C); **c.** Son as ἥλιος τῆς δ. Jo.Mon.*hymn.Bas.*3(M.96.1372C); id.*hymn.Chrys.*8(M.96.1384B); id.*hymn.Nic.Myr.*7(M.96.1388B); **d.** glory hidden in Inc., Eus.*d.e.*6.1(p.252.8; M.22.413C); blasphemed, *A.Thom.*B 62(p.43.18); but not lost οὐ χωρισθεὶς τῆς δ. τοῦτο λέγει, ἀλλ' ἐν ἀδόξῳ σώματι γεγονώς, ἵνα δείξῃ οὐ χωριζομένην τῆς θεϊκῆς δ. τὴν τοῦ δούλου μορφήν, ἀλλὰ ταύτην ἐπιδεικνυμένην, διὸ λέγει· 'καὶ ἐδόξασα καὶ πάλιν δοξάσω', μίαν τὴν πρὸ σώματος καὶ ἐν σώματι δ. δεικνύς ‡Ath.*Apoll.*2.15(M.26.1157B); Cyr.*hom.pasch.*17 (5^2.226C); **e.** glory of Christ's body οὐ γὰρ ὁ κύριος τῆς δ. δοξάζεται, ἀλλ' ἡ σὰρξ τοῦ κυρίου τῆς δ. αὕτη λαμβάνει δ. συναναβαίνουσα αὐτῷ εἰς οὐρανόν Ath.*inc.et c.Ar.*3(M.26.989B); εἰ δὲ καὶ ἤγειρεν ἐκ νεκρῶν τὸ ἑαυτοῦ σῶμα...οὐχ ἑτέρῳ τινὶ παρ' ἑαυτὸν τὴν ἐπὶ τούτῳ κεχάρισται δ. Cyr.*apol.Thdt.*7(p.131.10; 6^1.225B); in Transfiguration ὅτε ἐν δ. ὤφθη τοῖς ἀποστόλοις ἐπὶ τοῦ ὄρους, οὐ δι' ἑαυτὸν ἐποίησεν δεικνὺς ἑαυτόν, ἀλλὰ διὰ τὴν ἐκκλησίαν Clem.*exc.Thdot.*4(p.106.24; M.9.656B); τίς...ἡ δ. τοῦ σώματος...παρεδείχθη τοῖς μαθηταῖς...ἐπὶ τοῦ ὄρους; Or.*fr.85 in Lc.*(p.274); id.*Cels.*2.64(p.186.3; M.11.896D); τὴν δ. μὴ δυνάμενοι φέρειν...τὰ πρόσωπα καὶ τὰ γόνατα κλίνωσιν ἐπὶ τὴν γῆν ἐκ τῆς δ. τῆς θεότητος ‡Ath.*serm.fid.*24(p.21; M.26.1277C); **f.** the Cross as δ., Chrys.*hom.77.4 in Jo.*(8.455C); Ammon.*Jo.*12:28(M.85.1476B); **6.** of H. Ghost τὸ δὲ πνεῦμα λέγεται πνεῦμα δυνάμεως καὶ πνεῦμα τῆς δ. Ath.*ep.Serap.*1.25(M.26.589A); Bas.*Spir.*55(3.47C; M.32.172A); πῶς οὖν τὸ πνεῦμα συμμαρτυρήσει...εἴπερ αὐτὸ τῆς τοῦ υἱοῦ δ. ἀλλότριον; Didym.(‡Bas.)*Eun.*5(1.302B; M.29.725A); as identical with divine glory τὸ δὲ συνδετικὸν τῆς ἑνότητος ταύτης, ἡ δ. ἐστί· δ. δὲ λέγεσθαι τὸ πνεῦμα τὸ ἅγιον, οὐκ ἄν τις...ἀντείποι. ... 'τὴν δ.' γάρ φησι 'ἣν ἔδωκάς μοι δέδωκα αὐτοῖς.' ἔδωκε γὰρ...τοῖς μαθηταῖς τοιαύτην δ., ὁ εἰπὼν πρὸς αὐτούς· 'λάβετε πνεῦμα ἅγιον.' ἔλαβε δὲ ταύτην τὴν δ., ἣν πάντοτε εἶχε πρὸ τοῦ τὸν κόσμον εἶναι, ὁ τὴν ἀνθρωπίνην φύσιν περιβαλλόμενος, ἧς δοξασθείσης διὰ τοῦ πνεύματος ἐπὶ πᾶν τὸ συγγενὲς ἡ τῆς δ. τοῦ πνεύματος διάδοσις γίνεται Gr.Nyss.*hom.15 in Cant.*(M.44.1117A,B); δ. λέγειν αὐτὸν οἶμαι τὸ πνεῦμα τὸ ἅγιον id.*hom.in 1Cor.15:28*(M.44.1320C); cf. δ. σου [sc. πνεύματος] τῇ δ. *A.Jo.*94(p.197.20); **7.** of Trin. μία δ. τῆς ἁγίας τριάδος Ath.*Ar.*1.18 (M.26.48C); cf.*A.Phil.*24(p.13.19); **8.** of angels, Ign.*Smyrn.*6.1; οἱ... ἄγγελοι ἐκτὸς ὄντες σαρκὸς ἐν μακαριότητος ἀκρότητι διὰ τοῦτο καὶ δόξης εἰσίν Meth.*res.*1.49(p.302.8; M.18.277A); Ath.*Ar.*2.23(M.26.196B); forfeited by rebel angels, *ib.*3.10(341B); τῶν ἀγγέλων καὶ... πάσης τῆς περὶ τὰ ὑπερκόσμια δ. †Bas.*Is.*237(1.559E; M.30.536B); ref. man's original state ἵνα ἔμεινεν ἴσος τῆς δ. ... τῶν...ἀγγέλων *V.Zos.*19 (p.107.19); ἀγγελικὴ δ. as heavenly state of the blessed, *A.Phil.*144 (p.87.2); of angels of divine presence ἄγγελοι πρὸ προσώπου καὶ ἄγγελοι τῆς δ. Epiph.*mens.*22(M.43.276C); δόξαι as angelic order, *A.Jo.*11(p.158.9); ἀρχάγγελοι, δ. καὶ δυνάμεις ἐπουράνιοι ‡Pion. *v.Polyc.*32; **9.** of divine mysteries and holy things τοιαύτης δ. [i.e. eucharist] ἐν ταῖς χερσὶν ἐφαπτόμενοι *Pers.capt.*(M.86.3241D); ἄκουε τὰς δ. τοῦ θεοῦ Herm.*vis.*1.3.3; *A.Jo.*93(p.196.19); τολμηροὶ...καὶ αὐθάδεις, δ. οὐ τρέμοντες Ath.*hom.in Mt.11:27*(M.25.217C); οὐ μὴ παύσηται ἡ δ. τοῦ θεοῦ ἐκ τοῦ νόμου αὐτοῦ ‡Epiph.*v.proph.Jer.*14(p.22; M.43.400D,421D); of Law and new covenant αἰσθητὴ ἦν ἡ δ. [sc. Μωυσέως]...ἡ δὲ τῆς καινῆς νοητή Chrys.*hom.7.1 in 2Cor.*(10.479E); *cat.2Cor.*3:10(p.456.13); of new Jerusalem ἥτις ἐστὶ δ. θεοῦ αἰώνιος *T.Dan* 5.12; δ. τῆς ἁγνείας Meth.*symp.*8.4(p.85.3; M.18.144B); Serap. *euch.*10.1; **10.** of divine glory as communicated to creatures, Or. *or.*23.5(p.353.12; M.11.492A); esp. to men; **a.** as divine gift virtually equivalent to grace ὥσπερ ὁ Ἀδὰμ...τῆς δ. τοῦ θεοῦ ἐγυμνώθη, οὕτως καὶ οἱ νῦν ἄνθρωποι τῆς τοῦ θεοῦ δ. μακρὰν γίνονται *Apoc. Bar.*4(p.87.36); δός τὴν δ. ἵνα ἴδω τὰ μυστήριά σου *Apoc.Esd.*(p.24); Or.*Cels.*5.60(p.64.2; M.11.1276D); τοῦτο...ἡμῶν τὸ σῶμα σῶμα δ. ἦν πρὸ τῆς παραβάσεως Meth.*res.*3.14(p.410.32); δ. θεοῦ ἐστιν ἀληθῶς ἐπ' αὐτούς *A.Phil.*89(p.35.4); δεκτικὸς δὲ τῆς τοῦ πνεύματος δ. γενόμενος δι' ἀπαθείας καὶ καθαρότητος Gr.Nyss.*hom.15 in Cant.*(M.44.1117B); Thdt.*Is.*9:4(p.48.24; 2.234); δ. λέγει τὴν τῶν σημείων καὶ... ὁμοψυχίας...λέγει δὲ τὴν τοῦ πνεύματος χάριν Ammon.*Jo.*17:22(M.85.1504D); of apostles ὧν...ἡ δ. ἡ αὐτή Alex.Sal.*Barn.*4(437C); identified with revelation of divine truth τὰ περὶ θεοῦ ἀκριβῶς γινωσκόμενα ...δ. ἂν λέγοιτο εἶναι θεοῦ ὀφθεῖσα Or.*Jo.*32.27(17; p.472.28; M.14.816D); **b.** as reward of the blessed in resurrection life, esp. of martyrs μαρτυρήσας ἐπορεύθη εἰς τὸν...τόπον τῆς δ. *1Clem.*5.4; οἱ... ὑπομένοντες...δ. ... ἐκληρονόμησαν *ib.*45.8; ἐκ δεξιῶν κάθηνται καὶ ἔχουσιν δ. Herm.*vis.*3.2.1; id.*mand.*4.4.2; id.*sim.*5.3.3; *Ep.Lugd.*ap. Eus.*h.e.*5.2.2(M.20.433A); ἵν' εἰς δ. τὴν ἐν Χριστῷ ἀναστῶμεν Or.*hom.16.10 in Jer.*(p.142.26; M.13.452A); ὅταν...ἀναστῶσιν οἱ δίκαιοι ἐν δ. ἐν τῇ δευτέρᾳ Χριστοῦ παρουσίᾳ id.*fr.22 in Lc.*(p.243); Meth.*res.*1.44(p.293.8; M.41.1113D); ἵνα τὴν δ. παρ' αὐτῷ κτήσωνται μείζονα [sc. martyrs], διὰ πολλῶν αὐτοὺς ἤλεγξε πόνων *ib.*1.56(p.315.11; 1149B); ἵνα...συναριθμηθῶ ἐν τῇ δ. ὑμῶν ἐν τοῖς οὐρανοῖς *A.Phil.*30 (p.16.13); ἐν τῇ μετὰ τὴν ἀνάστασιν τῆς σαρκὸς δευτέρᾳ δ. Marcell. *fr.*96 ap.Eus.*Marcell.*2.3(p.51.1; M.24.809B); ἐν τῇ τῆς δ. ἀποπληρώσει Bas.*Spir.*26(3.22B; M.32.113C); δ. ... ἐστεφάνωται ὁ κοινὸς ἄνθρωπος, καὶ δ. ... παντὶ τῷ ποιοῦντι τὸ ἀγαθὸν...ἀπόκειται...καὶ μεγάλη...ἡ δ. τοῦ δικαίου *ib.*55(47B; M.169B); τῶν μὲν ἁγίων...ἡ δ. ἐστὶν ἐν τοῖς οὐρανοῖς id.*hom.in Ps.*7(1.100C; M.29.236A); δ. αἰώνιος id.*hom.*6.3 (2.46B; M.31.268A); αἰωνίου ζωῆς καὶ δ. *Const.App.*2.47.3; τὴν μέλλουσαν δ. καὶ παρρησίαν Chrys.*hom.77.5 in Jo.*(8.457E); ἵνα...τὴν ἡμῶν οὐσίαν τῇ οὐρανίῳ τιμήσῃ δ. †Jo.D.*B.J.*31(M.96.1161C); ἔρριψε [sc. ὁ θεός]...αὐτὸν [sc. Devil] ὡς ἀνάξιον τῆς ἄνωθεν δ. *ib.*7(908A); **11.** of glory as visible light or halo, *Apoc.Mos.*18(p.10); Or.*Jo.*32.26(17; p.471.23; M.14.816A); *A.Jo.Bapt.*4(p.529.9); Chrys.*hom.7.1 in 2Cor.*(10.479E) cit. s. 9 supra; Thdt.*qu.69 in Ex.*(1.173) cit. s. 1.e supra.

G. *glory, praise, worship,* as offered; **1.** in gen. to God συνέρχεσθαι εἰς εὐχαριστίαν θεοῦ καὶ εἰς δ. Ign.*Eph.*13.1; id.*Magn.*15; *2Clem.*17.7; by deeds, *A.Jo.*18(p.161.5); ἐν πράξεσιν ὁ διδοὺς δ. ... τῷ θεῷ Or.*hom.12.11 in Jer.*(p.97.16; M.13.393A); id.*Jo.*1.37(42; p.47.23; M.14.97A); Didym.*Trin.*1.25(M.39.380A); **2.** partic. to Father, Eus.*e.th.*3.15(p.172.21; M.24.1029A); v. 3 infra; to Son, *A.Jo.*43(p.172.7); Eus.*e.th.*3.15(p.172.18; 1029A); *cat.2Cor.*2:10 (p.361.7); to H. Ghost δ. σοι τὸ πνεῦμα· δ. σοι ἅγιε *A.Jo.*94(p.197.19); **3.** to God, liturg.; **a.** in *Gloria in excelsis*, Ath.*virg.*20(p.56.3; M.28.276D); cf.*Const.App.*7.47.2 cit. s. διά; *A.Mt.*25(p.245.3); **b.** in *Sanctus* πλήρης ἐστὶν ὁ οὐρανός, πλήρης ἐστὶν καὶ ἡ γῆ τῆς μεγαλοπρεποῦς σου δ. κύριε τῶν δυνάμεων Serap.*euch.*13.10; *Lit.Marc.*(p.132.2); **c.** in eucharistic prayer σοὶ ἡ δ. εἰς τοὺς αἰῶνας *Did.*9.2; σοῦ ἐστιν ἡ δ. καὶ ἡ δύναμις διὰ Ἰησοῦ Χριστοῦ *ib.*9.4; Just.*1apol.*65.3(M.6.428A) cit. s. προΐστημι; **d.** in other parts of liturgy δι' οὗ σοὶ ἡ δ. καὶ τὸ ⟨κράτος⟩ ἐν ἁγίῳ πνεύματι Serap.*euch.*5.11; *ib.*1.4; *Lit.*ap.*Const.App.*8.5.7; **e.** doxology, to Father ᾧ ἡ δ. εἰς τοὺς αἰῶνας τῶν αἰώνων *1Clem.*38.4; *Did.*9.2; ‡*Diogn.*12.9; *Const.App.*3.18.2; αὐτῷ ἡ δ. καὶ τὸ κράτος Gr.Nyss.*hom.opif.*2.34(M.44.297A); Chrys.*hom.59.7 in Mt.*(7.605C); to Son ᾧ ἡ δ. καὶ ἡ μεγαλωσύνη *1Clem.*20.12; *M.Polyc.*21; ᾧ ἐστιν ἡ δ. καὶ τὸ κράτος κτλ. Or.*hom.1.16 in Jer.*(p.16.11; M.13.276C); Ath.*v.Anton.*94(M.26.976B); Chrys. *hom.41.4 in Mt.*(7.451B); Thdt.*provid.*10(4.686); to H. Ghost, Gr. Nyss.*hom.14 in Cant.*(M.44.1088A); to the three Persons δ. ἀναπέμποντες τῷ πατρὶ καὶ τῷ υἱῷ καὶ τῷ ἁγίῳ πνεύματι id.*res.*3(M.46.681A); Chrys.*hom.in Mt.7:14*(3.32A); Jo.D.*virt.*(M.95.97B); *Lit. Jac.*(p.224.25); also without καί: δ. σοι πάτερ· δ. σοι λόγε· δ. σοι πνεῦμα ἅγιον *A.Jo.*96(p.199.2); *ib.*94(p.197.19); in grace after food, Ath.*virg.*14(p.49.7,19; M.28.268Df.); Chrys.*hom.55.5 in Mt.*(7.561A); *ib.*55.6(563C); cf. σοὶ δ. ἡ τῶν σπλάγχνων ἀγάπη· σοὶ δ. τὸ τοῦ Χριστοῦ ὄνομα· σοὶ δ. ἡ ἐν Χριστῷ δύναμις ἱδρυμένη *A.Thom.*A 132 (p.239.26); to God in three Persons, Gr.Naz.*or.*19.17(M.35.1064B); *ib.*31.33(p.190.11; M.36.172B); *ib.*45.30(664B); to Trinity, *ib.*26.19 (M.35.1252D); Nil.*Eulog.*34(M.79.1140A); theol. relation of doxology to baptismal formula, Gr.Nyss.*ep.*24(M.46.1092B); for other forms and their Trin. implications v. διά; ἐν; μετά; σύν.

H. as synonym for *doxology*, ‡Bas.*h.myst.*35(p.266.10); τῶν τροπαρίων ψαλλομένων μετὰ τὴν δ. Thdr.Stud.*praesanct.*(M.99.1688C); cf.*Lit.Chrys.*(p.353.19).

δοξάζ-ω, **A.** *think, form an opinion*; intrans., *LS*; trans., *hold* a belief or opinion τὰ ἐναντία δ. καὶ δογματίσαντες Just.*1apol.*4.8(M.6.333B); τὰ περὶ τὴν ἀνάστασιν ~όμενα Hipp.*haer.*9.30(p.264.17; M.16.3411B); οἱ μετεμψύχωσιν ~οντες Or.*hom.4 in Lc.*(p.29.6); οὐκ ἔδει [sc. name of Jesus]...ἀπ' ἀνθρώπων πρῶτον κληθῆναι οὐδὲ...δοξασθῆναι *ib.14*(p.95.27); τοῦ τεθνεῶτος ἀναβίωσιν τὴν τοῦ παιδὸς κράτησιν ἐδόξαζον Eus.*v.C.*1.22(p.18.30; M.20.937C); τῶν τὸ ὁμοούσιον ~όντων Philost.*h.e.*8.17(M.65.568A); in form δεδόξακαν, Hipp.*haer.*6.30(p.157.4; 3238B).

B. *glorify, give honour to*; **1.** of glorification of divine Persons by man; **a.** in gen. οὕτως ἐποίησεν [sc. Moses] εἰς τὸ δοξασθῆναι τὸ ὄνομα τοῦ ἀληθινοῦ *1Clem.*43.6; ~ω Ἰησοῦν Χριστὸν τὸν θεόν Ign.*Smyrn.*1.1; δοξάσαι τὸ ὄνομα id.*Philad.*10.1; id.*Trall.*1.2; ἐὰν πάσχωμεν διὰ τὸ ὄνομα...~ωμεν αὐτόν Polyc.*ep.*8.2; οἱ πάσχοντες ἕνεκεν τοῦ ὀνόματος ~ειν ὀφείλετε τὸν θεόν Herm.*sim.*9.28.5; *M.Polyc.*14.3 cit. s. διά; Clem.*paed.*2.8(p.200.9; M.8.485C); πίστις ὁμολογοῦσα εἶναι τοῦτον [sc. God] καὶ ~ουσα ὡς ὄντα id.*str.*7.10(p.40.27; M.9.477C); ἔδει...τέλειον ὄντα τὸν πατέρα, ἀριθμῷ ~εσθαι τελείῳ Hipp.*haer.*6.29(p.156.27; M.16.3238B); εὔλογον...καταπαύειν τὴν εὐχήν...~οντα τὸν τῶν ὅλων πατέρα διὰ Ἰησοῦ Χριστοῦ ἐν ἁγίῳ πνεύματι Or.*or.*33.6(p.402.33; M.11.561A); διὰ Χριστοῦ...~ειν τὸν θεόν id.*Jo.*1.12(13; p.18.6; M.14.45C); διὰ τούτων [sc. τῶν αἰσθητῶν] ~οντας τὸν πεποιηκότα *ib.*1.28(30; p.36.23; 77A); *ib.*32.4(p.431.25; 749C); ~ομεν ...σὲ καὶ τὸν ἀόρατόν σου πατέρα καὶ τὸ ἅγιόν σου πνεῦμα καὶ τὴν μητέρα πασῶν κτίσεων *A.Thom.*A 39(p.157.16); πνεύματι ~οντες Ἰησοῦν Meth.*arbitr.*1(p.147.5; M.18.241B); πολλῶν...~όντων ἐπὶ τῇ μαρτυρίᾳ τοῦ Ἰακώβου Eus.*h.e.*2.23.14(M.20.200C); *POxy.*924.13 (saec. iv); Bas.*Spir.*54(3.46E; M.32.169A); δεῖ...ἡμᾶς βαπτίζεσθαι μέν, ὡς παρελάβομεν· πιστεύειν δέ, ὡς βαπτιζόμεθα· ~ειν δέ, ὡς πεπιστεύκαμεν, πατέρα καὶ υἱὸν καὶ ἅγιον πνεῦμα id.*ep.*125.3(3.216D; M.32.549B); Amph.*ep.syn.*(M.39.96D); Gr.Nyss.*ep.*24(M.46.1092B); CHier.(350)*ep.*(p.137.15; M.25.352C), *Can.App.*34 citt. s. ἐν; δ. τὸν θεόν, οὐκ ἐκείνῳ δόξαν χαριζόμενοι, ἀλλ' ἑαυτοὺς τὴν ἀθάνατον δόξαν ἐνδύοντες Sever.*serp.*1(M.56.499); προφητῶν, ἀποστόλων, μαρτύρων, δι' οὓς ὁ δεσπότης ἡμῶν ~εται Χριστός *V.Pach.Σ* 90(p.269.18); H. Ghost, cf. πνεῦμα, συνδοξάζω; **b.** in eucharistic prayer, *A.Jo.*109(p.207.9); cf.Hipp.*trad.ap.*4.13; in liturg. prayer to Christ ~ομέν σε καὶ αἰνοῦμεν καὶ εὐλογοῦμεν καὶ εὐχαριστοῦμεν τὴν πολλήν σου χρηστότητα καὶ μακροθυμίαν ἅγιε Ἰησοῦ *A.Jo.*77(p.189.23); in doxology, Thdt.*haer.*4.1(4.350) cit. s. ἐν; **c.** through good living ἀλήθειαν ἀγάπα...ἵνα τὸ πνεῦμα, ὃ ὁ θεὸς κατῴκισεν ἐν τῇ σαρκὶ ταύτῃ, ἀληθὲς εὑρεθῇ παρὰ πᾶσιν ἀνθρώποις, καὶ οὕτως δοξασθήσεται ὁ κύριος ὁ ἐν σοὶ κατοικῶν Herm.*mand.*3.1; κυριακὴν ἐκείνην τὴν ἡμέραν ποιεῖ, ὅταν ἀποβάλλῃ φαῦλον νόημα...τὴν ἐν αὐτῷ τοῦ κυρίου ἀνάστασιν ~ων Clem.*str.*7.12(p.54.20; M.9.505A); id.*ecl.*42(p.149.9; M.9.720A); ~εται ὁ θεὸς διὰ τῆς εὐωδίας τοῦ βίου τῶν δικαίων Or.*fr.10 in Lc.*(p.236); Meth.*symp.*6.3(p.67.22; M.18.117B); ~ωμεν τὸν υἱὸν μὴ τῇ δόξῃ ταύτῃ μόνον, ἀλλὰ καὶ τῇ διὰ τῶν ἔργων Chrys.*hom.52.4 in Jo.*(8.309A); *ib.57.3*(336C); Cyr.*Jo.*9(4.746C); Thdt.*1Cor.*6:20(3.199); τινὰ τοσοῦτον τὸν θεὸν ἀγαπῶντα...ὥστε τὸν μὲν θεὸν ἐν αὐτῷ ~εσθαι, ἑαυτὸν δὲ ὡς μήτε ὄντα εἶναι Diad.*perf.*13(p.16.1); **d.** through martyrdom δοξάσωμεν...καὶ ἡμεῖς ὑψώσαντες τῷ ἑαυτῶν θανάτῳ τὸν θεόν, ἐπείπερ ὁ μαρτυρῶν τῷ ἑαυτοῦ θανάτῳ δοξάσει τὸν θεόν Or.*mart.*50(p.47.3; M.11.636A); **2.** of God's glorification by angels, Clem.*prot.*12(p.84.14; M.8.240C); *Const.App.*2.56.1; **3.** the Son by the universe κόσμος σε ~ει *Hymn.*(*AGC* p.40); **4.** of Son's glorification of Father, Or.*Jo.*2.13(7; p.69.14; M.14.136B); Eus.*e.th.*1.11(p.70.16; M.24.845B) cit. s. ἀντιδοξάζω; οὐ γὰρ ὁ υἱὸς μόνον, ἀλλὰ καὶ ὁ πατὴρ ἐδοξάσθη· πρὸ μὲν γὰρ τοῦ σταυροῦ οὐδὲ Ἰουδαῖοι αὐτὸν ᾔδεσαν...μετὰ δὲ τὸν σταυρὸν ἡ οἰκουμένη...προσέδραμεν Chrys.*hom.80.1 in Jo.*(8.473B); Cyr.*Jo.*9(4.746A,B); **5.** Son as glorified by Father, Ath.*inc.et c.Ar.*4(M.26.989B) cit. s. ἀνθρωπότης; **a.** through Passion, *Barn.*11.9; Chrys.*pent.*1.3(2.461E); id.*hom.51.2 in Jo.*(8.301A); cf.*ib.72.2*(425B,C); μέλλων σταυροῦσθαι ἔλεγε·...'δόξασόν σου τὸν υἱόν', δόξαν τὸν σταυρὸν καλῶν id.*hom.in Mt.26:39*(3.19A); Cyr.*Jo.*8(4.705D); Ammon.*Jo.*13:32(M.85.1485A); **b.** through Resurrection, *Const.App.*7.25.2; ποῦ ἐδόξασεν; ἐν τοῖς πρὸ τούτων γενομένοις· καὶ πάλιν δοξάσω μετὰ τὸν σταυρόν Chrys.*hom.67.2 in Jo.*(8.402B); μετὰ τὸ δοξασθῆναι Χριστόν, τουτέστι μετὰ τὴν ἀνάστασιν Cyr.*Jo.*5.2(4.473D); Ammon.*Jo.*12:23(M.85.1473D); **c.** through Ascension, Chrys.*hom.80.2 in Jo.*(8.475C); Cyr.*Jo.*9(4.745E); **d.** through his manifestation to world and his dominion and authority, ref. Jo.17:10 τουτέστιν, ἢ ὅτι ἐξουσίαν αὐτῶν ἔχων, ἢ ὅτι δοξάσουσιν ἐμέ Chrys.*hom.81.1 in Jo.*(8.479C); 'δόξασόν με', ἀντὶ τοῦ, φανέρωσόν με Cyr.*thes.*30(5^{1}.259B); **6.** Son as glorified by H. Ghost ὁ παράκλητος...~ων τὸν Χριστὸν περιμένει τὸ ἐκείνου θέλημα *Const.App.*2.26.6; ἐδόξασε...τὸν Ἰησοῦν τὸ πνεῦμα...ὡς πνεῦμα αὐτοῦ, καὶ οὐκ ἀλλοτρία δύναμις Cyr.*apol.Thdt.*9(p.135.6; 6^{1}.229C); opp. Nestorian conception of δύο Χριστούς...τὸν μὲν ~όμενον...τὸν δὲ ~οντα *ib.*(p.135.11; 229C); *A.Barth.*7(p.144.27) cit. s. ἐν; **7.** men as glorified by God, *1Clem.*32.3; ~ειν...Χριστὸν τὸν δοξάσαντα ὑμᾶς Ign.*Eph.*2.2; ὁ...ταῦτα ποιῶν ἐν τῇ βασιλείᾳ τοῦ θεοῦ δοξασθήσεται *Barn.*21.1; ἀτιμοῦνται [sc. Χριστιανοί] καὶ ἐν ταῖς ἀτιμίαις ~ονται *Diogn.*5.14; τῇ δοθείσῃ αὐτῷ παρὰ τοῦ πατρὸς δόξῃ τοὺς θεοσεβεῖς ἐδόξασεν ἀνθρώπους Marcell.*fr.* 95 ap.Eus.*Marcell.*2.3(p.50.30; M.24.809A); *Const.App.*3.13.1; *ib.*7.39.3; εἰ ~ομεν ἐν ἑαυτοῖς τὸν θεόν, προσδοκήσωμεν ὅτι δοξασθησόμεθα παρ' αὐτοῦ Cyr.*Jo.*9(4.746C); Thdt.*Is.*12:2(2.258); **8.** in gen., *honour* τούτους Κελτοὶ ὡς προφήτας...~ουσι Hipp.*haer.*1.25(p.29.21; M.16.3053A); τῶν παρ' αὐτοῖς ~ομένων βίβλων *ib.*5.14(p.108.13; 3166C); τὸν λαλοῦντά σοι τὸν λόγον τοῦ θεοῦ δοξάσεις *Const.App.*7.9.1; Gel.Cyz.*h.e.*2.24.24(M.85.1304B).

C. *say the doxology* ψάλλει...ψαλμὸν ἕκτον...καὶ ~ει †Jo.Jej.*poenit.*(M.88.1889A); *Euchol.*(p.491); or simply *sing* ὁ λαὸς τὸ τροπάριον ~ει *Const.Stud.*2(M.99.1705A).

***δοξάριοι, οἱ,** members of sect, otherwise called ἀποσχίσται who separated themselves from organized Church life τὴν ἰδίαν δόξαν ζητοῦντες Jo.D.*haer.*102(M.94.776A).

δοξάριον, τό, 1. *paltry, contemptible opinion* or *doctrine* τὰ τῶν ἀνοσίων αἱρετικῶν δ. Cyr.*glaph.Gen.*5(1.175A); Zach.Mit.*opif.*(M.85.1057A); **2.** *paltry, contemptible glory,* Or.*Cels.*3.9(p.210.7; M.11.932B); οὐ...διὰ δοξάριον ἀσκοῦσι τὴν...παρθενίαν *ib.*7.48(p.199.30; 1492B); Bas.*hex.*5.6(1.46A; M.29.109A); id.*ep.*238(3.366D; M.32.889A); Gr.Naz.*carm.*1.2.25.447(M.37.844A); τὸ δ. τοῦ κόσμου τούτου Isid.Pel.*epp.*5.563(M.78.1640A); Cyr.*Ps.*36:35(M.69.949B); id.*Jo.*9(4.727C).

***δοξαστήρ, ὁ,** *one who glorifies* τοῦ ἁγίου πνεύματος...οὐ...σε εἶναι δ. ἀληθινὸν ἀκούοντες Bas.*ep.*50(3.143A; M.32.388B).

δοξαστικός, *glorifying,* of H. Ghost οὐδὲ τὴν δ. δύναμιν ἐπιδείξεται, ὃ ἂν μὴ αὐτὸ ᾖ δόξα Gr.Nyss.*Maced.*22(M.45.1329A).

δοξαστός, *to be glorified, cat.2Cor.*4:4(p.374.31).

***δοξοκαθαιρέτης, ὁ,** *subverter of true doctrine,* Eust.Mon.*ep.*(M.86.909C).

δοξοκαλία, ἡ, *false estimate of beauty,* Clem.*paed.*2.3(p.179.28; M.8.436B); *ib.*2.10(p.222.30; 528B).

***δοξολογ-έω, A.** *glorify, give glory to, praise*; **1.** God, by martyrs before execution, *M.Scill.*16; λελάληκεν γὰρ ἐν τῇ διαλέκτῳ τῶν χερουβίμ, ~οῦσα τὸν δεσπότην τῶν ἀρετῶν ἐνδειξαμένη τὴν δόξαν αὐτῶν *T.Job* 50(p.136.2); ~οῦντες αὐτὸν...ἤγουν εὐλογοῦντες Or.*exc. in Ps.*36:22(M.17.132C); †Dion.Al.*fr.2 in Job* (p.204.1); Epiph.*haer.*70.8(p.241.9; M.42.353A); τὴν...τριάδα ~οῦμεν *ib.*76.47(p.401.5; 616B); τῶν ἐν ταῖς ἐκκλησίαις...τὸν τῶν ὅλων ~ούντων θεόν Cyr.*Is.*2.5(2.343E); ~εῖσθαι τὸ ὄνομα αὐτοῦ *ib.*4.1(543E); id.*Am.*19(3.268E); id.*Jo.*11.6(4.955D); Procl.CP *hom.*1.3(M.65.836C); ~εῖν τὴν σοφίαν τοῦ ποιήσαντος id.*or.*2.4(M.65.697A); πρόσωπα τρία ~εῖν Sophr.H.*ep.syn.*(M.87.3156A); ὁ θεὸς ἡμῶν, ὁ ἐν τριάδι καὶ μονάδι ~ούμενος Jo.D.*f.o.*2.5(M.94.880A); by angels ἀγγέλοις ἔργον ~εῖν τὸν θεόν Bas.*hom.in Ps.*28(1.122E; M.29.301C); by seraphim with whom worshippers at eucharist are associated, Chrys.*hom.14.4 in Eph.*(11.108B); **2.** partic. Father, Afric.*ep.Arist.*1(p.56.31; M.10.53C); πατὴρ ~εῖται· υἱὸς συμπροσκυνεῖται· τὸ πνεῦμα τὸ ἅγιον καταγγέλλεται ‡Eust.*alloc.*(M.18.673D); Gr.Naz.*carm.*1.1.31.12(M.37.511A); Thdt.*haer.*4.1(4.350) cit. s. ἐν; in eucharistic prayer ἄξιον...ἐστίν σε τὸν ἀγένητον πατέρα...αἰνεῖν ὑμνεῖν ~εῖν Serap.*euch.*13.1; *Lit.Jac.*(p.198.21); *Const.App.*7.47.2 cit. s. διά; **3.** Son, Or.*Jo.*1.22(23; p.27.18; M.14.61C); Bas.*Spir.*16(3.13C; M.32.93C) cit. s. μετά; τοὺς τέμνοντας τὰ βάϊα...καὶ ~οῦντας αὐτόν †Bas.*Is.*217(1.542B; M.30.493D); Epiph.*haer.*69.62(p.211.18; M.42.304B); τῷ παρὰ πάσης ~ουμένῳ τῆς κτίσεως Cyr.*Jo.*1.5(4.47D); *ib.*5.5(523C); id.*inc.unigen.*(5^{1}.700C); ἔσται...κατὰ τίνα τρόπον...ἐν τοῖς ~οῦσιν ὁ ~ούμενος; id.*thes.*15(5^{1}.148B); **4.** the Resurrection τὴν ἁγίαν σου ἀνάστασιν δοξωλογοῦμεν *Pap.Chr.*(p.434) saec. vii–viii; **5.** sacred things ἐδοξολόγησεν τοῦ ὑψηλοῦ τόπου τὸ ποίημα *T.Job* 49(p.135.20); **6.** evil spirits (ironically) τὰ τῆς πλάνης πνεύματα...~οῦσιν Just.*dial.*7.3(M.6.492C).

B. abs., *praise God,* Afric.*ep.Arist.*1(p.53.7)ap.Eus.*qu.Steph.*4.1(M.22.900A); Cyr.*Ps.*29:10(M.69.857A); σωτήριον χρῆμα τὸ ~εῖν id.*Is.*2.1(2.211A); ~εῖν κατὰ τὸν...Δαβίδ Proc.G.*Is.*48:12–22(M.87.2460B).

***δοξολογητικῶς,** *so as to glorify,* Germ.CP *or.*8(M.98.364D).

δοξολογία, ἡ, A. *ascription of glory* or *praise*; **1.** to God; **a.** in gen. προπύλῳ ἑνὶ...τῆς τοῦ...ἑνὸς καὶ μόνου θεοῦ δ. τὸν πάντα νέων κατακοσμῶν Eus.*h.e.*10.4.65(M.20.876A); εἰς δ. τοῦ ἑνὸς καὶ ἐπὶ πάντων θεοῦ id.*e.th.*2.23(p.133.22; M.24.961A); τῷ ψαλμῷ τῆς δ. †Bas.*Is.*93(1.444D; M.30.272B); συμφυές ἐστιν ἀξίωμα τῷ θεῷ, αὐτὴ ἡ θεότης, ἡ σοφία...τὸ ἀγαθὸν εἶναι...καὶ εἴ τι ἄλλο τῶν εἰς δ. παρὰ τῆς ...γραφῆς εἰρημένων ἐστίν Gr.Nyss.*Eun.*1(1 p.154.12; M.45.396A); ἡ δὲ τῶν τριῶν ὑμνῳδία παίδων, πνεύματα καὶ ψυχὰς δικαίων πρὸς κοινωνίαν τῆς δ. παραλαμβάνουσα id.*Apoll.*47(M.45.1237B); Σαβαὼθ οὐκ ὄνομά τινος εἶπεν, ἀλλ' ὄνομα δοξολογίας τῆς θεότητος Epiph. *haer.*26.10(p.288.21; M.41.348B); Nil.*epp.*3.252(M.79.505A); **b.** as offered by creation, Bas.*hex.*8.7(1.77C; M.29.181A); εἰς τὴν δ. παραλαμβάνεται ξύλα καρποφόρα †Bas.*Is.*90(1.444C; M.30.268A); εἰ τὴν δημιουργίαν τῆς οὔσης κτίσεως ἐπηχύνθη δι' ἑαυτοῦ ποιῆσαι ὁ θεός, καὶ τὴν δ. αὐτῆς οὐ προσίεται Didym.(‡Bas.)*Eun.*4(1.286E; M. 29.689A); αἶνον τὴν δ. καλεῖ, ἥτις αὐτῷ παρὰ τῆς κτίσεως ὅλης φυσικοῖς κινήμασιν αὐτὸν δοξολογούσης προσφέρεται. ἡ ἐκκλησία τοίνυν οὐ μόνον τὴν μετὰ τῆς κτίσεως δ. προσφέρειν ἐπαγγέλλεται, ἀλλὰ μετ' ᾠδῆς δοξάζειν, τουτέστι πνευματικὴν καὶ νοερὰν ὑμνῳδίαν προσφέρειν Hesych.H.*fr.Ps.*68:31(M.93.1232C); **c.** by angels, Ath. *hom.in Mt.11*:37(M.25.217C); πῶς εἴπῃ τὰ σεραφίμ, ἅγιος, ἅγιος, ἅγιος, μὴ διδαχθέντα παρὰ τοῦ πνεύματος, ποσάκις ἐστὶν εὐσεβὲς τὴν δ. ταύτην ἀναφωνεῖν; Bas.*Spir.*38(3.33B; M.32.140A); †Bas.*Is.*188 (1.519A; M.30.441A); ἐξουσίαι τεταγμέναι...διὰ τὴν ἄνω ἀκήρατον δ. Epiph.*haer.*40.4(p.85.9; M.41.684C); Chrys.*hom.55.6 in Mt.*(7.563B) cit. infra **e**; *V.Zos.*15(p.105.36); Cosm.Ind.*top.*3(M.88.165B); **d.** of Jewish musical worship, Cyr.*Am.*54(3.307E); **e.** Christian; **i.** in rel. to prayer, Or.*or.*14.2(p.331.6; M.11.461A) cit. s. εὐχή; εὔλογον δὲ ἀρξάμενον ἀπὸ δ. εἰς δ. καταλήγοντα καταπαύειν τὴν εὐχήν *ib.*33.6 (p.402.32; 561A); προσευχῆς...δύο εἰσὶ τρόποι· ὁ μέν, ὁ τῆς δ. μετὰ ταπεινοφροσύνης· δεύτερος δέ, ὁ τῆς αἰτήσεως ὑποβεβηκώς ‡Bas.*const.* 1.2(2.536C; M.31.1328D); μὴ...ἐγκάλωμεν τοῖς ἀγγέλοις...ὅτι καταλύσαντες τὸν λόγον εἰς δ. πάλιν ἄρχονται τῶν ὕμνων...ἀποστολικοῖς γὰρ ἕπονται νόμοις, ἀπὸ δ. ἀρχόμενοι, καὶ εἰς τοῦτο τελευτῶντες, καὶ μετὰ τὴν τελευτὴν ταύτην προοιμιαζόμενοι πάλιν Chrys.*hom.55.6 in Mt.*(7.563B); id.*hom.7.2 in Eph.*(11.48F); ‡Germ.CP *contempl.*(M. 98.401A); **ii.** based on commemoration of God's benefits to man, Bas.*Spir.*17(3.14B; M.96C); **iii.** offered in form of good living δύο δ. τρόποι· εἷς μέν, ὁ διὰ ῥημάτων, ἕτερος δέ, ὁ δι' ὄψεως, καὶ τρίτος δὲ μετὰ τούτων, ὁ διὰ βίου καὶ ἔργων. καὶ γὰρ ἀνθρώπων οὐ φθεγγομένων μόνον, ἀλλὰ καὶ σιγώντων, δόξα ἀναφέρεται τῷ θεῷ Chrys.*exp.in Ps.* 148:3–6(5.490C); **iv.** as office performed by widows ἐν εὐχαριστίᾳ καὶ δ. διάγουσι id.*hom.30.4 in 1Cor.*(10.274E); **v.** as spiritual sacrifice, †Bas.*hom.in Ps.*115(1.375D; M.30.113B); **vi.** expressed in form of doxology at end of sermon, Chrys.*hom.16.10 in Rom.*(9. 620E); ἔθος ἀεὶ τῷ Παύλῳ εἰς εὐχὰς καὶ δ. κατακλείειν τὴν παραίνεσιν *ib.27.1*(718C); **2.** partic. to Father, Or.*or.*33.2(p.402.11; M.11.560B); offered on men's behalf by Christ as high priest, Eus.*d.e.*4.16(p.186. 4; M.22.309C); Epiph.*inc.*3(p.231.15; M.41.277C); **3.** to Son, Afric. *ep.Arist.*1(p.56.8; M.10.53B); Or.*Jo.*1.3(5; p.7.6; M.14.28C); *ib.*6.30 (15; p.140.9; 252D); *ib.*13.25(p.249.22; 441C); Eus.*d.e.*7.1(p.299.30; M.22.492A); id.*e.th.*1.20(p.81.4; M.24.865B); ἡ ἐν Ἱεροσολύμοις δ. [i.e. of Christ's entry] Ath.*exp.Ps.*117:25–27(M.27.480B); Bas.*Eun.*1.18 (1.229E; M.29.552B); Epiph.*haer.*42.11(p.151.6; M.41.768A); Chrys. *paralyt.*1(3.34B); id.*hom.10.2 in 2Tim.*(11.722F); μυρίαις δ. στεφανοῦσθαι Χριστόν Oecum.*Apoc.*5:10(p.82); **4.** to H. Ghost δ. πνεύματός ἐστιν ἡ τῶν προσόντων αὐτῷ ἀπαρίθμησις Bas.*Spir.*54 tit. (3.46C; M.32.168C); id.*ep.*52.4(3.146C; M.32.396B); *ib.*258.2(393D; M.949B); **5.** not ascribed to angels along with God, Didym.*Trin.* 2.19(M.39.549A); **6.** theol. implications, esp. ref. doxology (v. infra); **a.** Trin. μετὰ πατρὸς ἀποπληροῦμεν τῷ μονογενεῖ τὴν δ., καὶ τὸ ἅγιον πνεῦμα μὴ διϊστῶμεν ἀπὸ τοῦ υἱοῦ Bas.*Spir.*13(3.10B; M.32. 88A); *ib.*16(3.13D; M.96A) cit. s. μετά; ὡς γὰρ ἡ κρατοῦσα ἡμῶν ἀρχὴ καὶ ἡ ἐξουσία μία, οὕτω καὶ ἡ παρ' ἡμῶν δ. μία, καὶ οὐ πολλαί· διότι ἡ τῆς εἰκόνος τιμὴ ἐπὶ τὸ πρωτότυπον διαβαίνει *ib.*45(3.38B; 149C); id.*ep.*52.4(3.146C; M.32.396B); μία...δ. τοῖς τρισὶν ὡς ἑνὶ θεῷ ‡Bas. *struct.hom.*1.3(1.325F; M.30.13C); Amph.*ep.syn.*(M.39.97B); ref. baptismal formula, Epiph.*inc.*3(p.231.15; M.41.277C); τρεῖς ὑποστάσεις μία κυριότης μία θεότης μία δ. id.*haer.*25.6(p.273.25; M.41.328D); *ib.* 69.32(p.181.26; M.42.253B); πῶς οὐκ ἴσος τῷ πατρί, τὴν αὐτὴν δ. ἣν καὶ ἐκεῖνος λαμβάνων; Chrys.*hom.10.2 in 2Tim.*(11.722F n.); Thdt. *rect.conf.*4(M.6.1213A); τὴν τριαδικὴν δ. ‡Meth.*Sym.et Ann.*12(M.18. 377B); **b.** Christol. ἀναθεματίζομεν τοὺς οὕτως ἀσεβοῦντας, τοὺς ἄνθρωπον ἐν τῇ θείᾳ δ. τιθέντας Apoll.*fid.sec.pt.*31(p.179.6; M.10. 1117A); μίαν μὲν...τὴν δ. προσφέρομεν τῷ...Χριστῷ καὶ τὸν αὐτὸν θεὸν ὁμοῦ καὶ ἄνθρωπον ὁμολογοῦμεν...τῶν δὲ φύσεων τὰς ἰδιότητας οὐ παραιτησόμεθα λέγειν Thdt.ap.Cyr.*apol.Thdt.*8(p.132.2; 6[1].226A); δ. καὶ τὸν τῆς ἑνώσεως λόγον προφέροντες, ἕνα Χριστὸν...τὸν τοῦ θεοῦ λόγον σεσαρκωμένον...ὁμολογοῦμεν Justn.*conf.*(p.88.30; M.86. 1013A); **7.** partic. of doxology, v. ἐν, σύν; Bas.*Spir.*74(3.63B; M.32. 208A); ὥστε σύμφωνον τῷ...βαπτίσματι τὴν δ. ἀποπληροῦσθαι τῇ... τριάδι id.*ep.*91(3.183C; M.32.476D); cf.Amph.*ep.syn.*(M.39.97B); ‡Germ.CP *contempl.*(M.98.401A); of threefold sanctus, ‡Bas.*h.myst.* 59(p.394.4); and Trisagion, Phot.*cod.*228(M.103.957B); **8.** of observance of ninth hour ἐν ὕμνοις καὶ δ. ... ὅτι ἐν αὐτῇ τῇ ὥρᾳ ὁ κύριος...ἀπέδωκε τὸ πνεῦμα Ath.*virg.*12(p.46.9ff.; M.28.265B); **9.** of *Gloria in excelsis*, Dion.Ar.*c.h.*4.4(M.3.181C); as μεγάλη δ. (when sung on Sundays and festivals), *Euchol.*(p.1).

B. virtually equivalent to *glory* οὐρανὸς καὶ τὰ ἐν οὐρανῷ πάντα πλήρη τυγχάνει τῆς δ. αὐτοῦ, ἀλλὰ καὶ πᾶσα ἡ γῆ τῆς αὐτῆς μετέσχεν δυνάμεως Eus.*d.e.*7.1(p.299.26; M.22.489D); τὴν τοῦ...λόγου ἔνσαρκον δ. καὶ τελείαν θεότητα Epiph.*haer.*69.36(p.184.12; M.42.257B); Bas. Sel.*or.*30.1(M.85.336B).

***δοξολογικός,** *concerned with praise* δ. τε καὶ εὐχαρίστου φωνῆς Gr.Nyss.*Pss.titt.*A 9(M.44.481C); δ. ἀγρυπνίαν Steph.Diac.*v.Steph.* (M.100.1076D).

***δοξολόγος,** *giving glory, praising* τῶν δ. πνευμάτων, ἃ αἰνίσσεται χερουβίμ Clem.*str.*5.6(p.350.20; M.9.61C); ζῷα τὰ δ. τὰ Ἠσαΐου ἀλληγορούμενα *ib.*7.12(p.57.18; 512A).

δοξομανέω, *be crazy for fame*, Or.*Jo.*32.2(p.429.2; M.14.745B); Bas.*renunt.*3(2.205A; M.31.632D); Chrys.*hom.62.5 in Mt.*(7.627B).

δοξομανία, ἡ, *mad desire for fame*, Tat.*orat.*11(p.11.29; M.6.829A); Clem.*paed.*2.12(p.232.11; M.8.549A); Bas.*Spir.*76(3.65C; M.32.212C).

***δοξοποιέω,** *fabricate a doctrine*, Epiph.*haer.*66.53(p.90.13; M.42. 109B).

***δοξοποιΐα, ἡ,** *invention of theory* or *doctrine*, Clem.*prot.*2.(p.20. 29; M.8.100A).

***δοξοχαρής,** *delighting in glory*, Evagr.Pont.*or.*148(M.79.1200A).

§δορκαλίς, ἡ, *hook, claw*, instrument of torture (*ungula*), Gr. Naz.*or.*5.40(M.35.717A).

δορκάς (*δορκή), ἡ, δόρκων, ὁ, *gazelle*; **1.** ref. Pr.6:5 δορκαὶ [v.l. δορκάς] Or.*fr.62 in Lc.*(p.263); ἡ δ. ζῷόν ἐστιν ὀξυδερκές, ἐπώνυμον τῇ ἑαυτοῦ ὀξυδορκίᾳ. ... δ. ἔσω πρὸς τὸ τὰ κάτω ἐρευνᾶν †Bas.*hom.in Pr.6*:4(2.618C; M.31.1500C); **2.** ref. Cant.2:9 ἡ δ. σημαίνει τὴν ὀξυωπίαν τοῦ τὸ πᾶν ἐπιβλέποντος...δ. μὲν ὁμοιοῦται ὁ ἐκ τῶν οὐρανῶν ἐπὶ τὴν γῆν ἐπιβλέψας Gr.Nyss.*hom.5 in Cant.*(M.44. 861A); similar explanation with addition that Christ resembles the δ. as a destroyer of serpents, Thdt.*Cant.*2:9(2.62); δόρκωνι Ph.Carp. *Cant.*49(M.40.65B); **3.** ref. Ac.9:39 φερώνυμος ἦν, οὕτως ἐγρηγορυῖα καὶ νήφουσα, ὥσπερ δ. Chrys.*hom.21.2 in Ac.*(9.171D).

δόρκων, ὁ, 1. = δορκάς q.v.; **2.** a kind of *boat*, Leont.N.*v. Jo.Eleem.*10(p.19.6); *ib.*13(p.28.1).

***δορυκοίρανος, ὁ,** *lord of the spear*, *Orac.Sib.*14.261.

δορυφορ-έω, 1. *attend as bodyguard, escort*, esp. emperors; pass. ptcpl., *with a bodyguard*, of Paul of Samosata βαδίζων δημοσίᾳ καὶ ∼ούμενος Malch.*ep.*ap.Eus.*h.e.*7.30.8(M.20.712B); **2.** *attend upon*, of Moses and Elijah at Transfiguration, Eus.*fr.Lc.*9:28(M.24.549A); ∼ούμενον ὑπὸ νόμου καὶ προφητῶν δεσπότην Cyr.*Lc.*9:27(M.72.653B); of angels, Meth.*symp.*7.9(p.80.3; M.18.136C); Eus.*p.e.*7.16(328B; M. 21.553C); Χριστὸν...προσδόκα...ὑπ' ἀγγέλων ∼ούμενον Cyr.H.*catech.* 4.15; σεραφὶμ...∼οῦντα τὸν υἱόν Cyr.*ador.*10(1.334E); attending upon eucharistic elements, *Lit.Praesanct.*(p.349.12); pass., of BMV ὑπὸ στρατιᾶς οὐρανίου...ἀγγέλων ∼ουμένην [sc. κιβωτόν] Mod.*dorm.*4 (M.86.3289A); *ib.*10(3304B); **3.** *accompany* τοὺς τῶν ἁγίων ∼οῦμεν θανάτους Bas.*hom.*17.1(2.139A; M.31.484A); δύο διαθῆκαι...τὸν ἕνα δεσπότην ∼οῦσι ‡Chrys.*hom.in Lc.*2:1(2.801A); ψυχὴν ἀρεταῖς ∼εῖσθαι Synes.*ep.*101(M.66.1472A); **4.** *serve, wait upon*, Athenag. *res.*11(p.60.1; M.6.993B); Mod.*dorm.*1(M.86.3280B).

δορυφορία, ἡ, 1. *escort, guard*; of imperial bodyguard, Eus.*v.C.* 1.22(p.18.27); *ib.*3.47(p.97.13; M.20.1108A); of escorts of high officials, Chrys.*hom.9.1 in Eph.*(11.69B); Pilate's guards, Thdt.*Ps.* 58:8(1.994); of military escorts in gen., Ath.*apol.sec.*72(p.151.27; M.25.377C); met. περὶ τὸν ἐγκέφαλον ὥσπερ ἄρχοντα...τῶν αἰσθήσεων ἡ δ. Dion.Al.ap.Eus.*p.e.*14.26(779C; M.21.1281C); **2.** of God's angelic retinue ὡς κύριος ἐκτὸς τῆς βασιλικῆς δ. πρὸς τὸν Ἰωάννην παραγέγονεν [sc. Χριστός] †Hipp.*theoph.*4(p.259.14; M.10.856A); δ. τε θείας ἀμφὶ τὸν πάντων βασιλέα Eus.*l.C.*proem.(p.196.9; M.20. 1317C); οὐκ ἂν δὲ ἔπαθεν ὑπὲρ ἡμῶν...εἰ οἷά τις ἔνδοξος βασιλεὺς μετὰ δ. ἐνθέου...ἐπήει id.*qu.Steph.*14(M.22.928C); of seraphim, ‡Meth. *Sym.et Ann.*2(M.18.352C); **3.** *attendance* δ. φίλων προσποιητῶν Bas. *hex.*5.2(1.41E; M.29.97D); Chrys.*hom.53.5 in Mt.*(7.545A); ‡Chrys. *Abr.*2(2.744B); hence **4.** *honour*, Jo.D.*haer.*80(M.94.733B); **5.** *pomp* τὸν κόσμον φησὶ...τὴν δ., τὴν δόξαν Chrys.*comm.in Gal.*6:14(10. 728D); id.*hom.9.5 in 1Thess.*(11.493B); Cyr.*Is.*5.1(2.742E); Gr.Agr. *Eccl.*2.9(M.98.832B).

δορυφορικός, *of* or *for a guard*; neut. as subst., *that which acts as a guard* ἔστι δὲ ὁ θυμὸς τὸ δ. τοῦ λογισμοῦ Jo.D.*f.o.*2.16(M.94.933A).

***Δοσιθεανοί, οἱ**, (with variant spellings), *followers of Dositheus*, an ascetic sect of the Samaritans, -θιανοί, Heges.ap.Eus.*h.e.*4.22.5(M.20.380A); first sect described by Hippolytus in σύνταγμα, Phot.*cod.*121(M.103.404A); Dositheus declared himself son of God οἱ δὲ Δ. οὐδὲ πρότερον ἤκμασαν· νῦν δὲ παντελῶς ἐπιλελοίπασαν, ὥστε τὸν ὅλον αὐτῶν ἱστορεῖσθαι ἀριθμὸν οὐκ εἶναι ἐν τοῖς τριάκοντα Or.*Cels.*6.11(p.81.26; M.11.1308A); Δοσίθεός τις ἀναστὰς ἔφασκεν ἑαυτὸν εἶναι τὸν προφητευμένον χριστόν, ἀφ' οὗ δεῦρο μέχρι εἰσὶν οἱ Δοσιθεηνοί, φέροντες καὶ βίβλους τοῦ Δοσιθέου καὶ μύθους τινὰς περὶ αὐτοῦ διηγούμενοι ὡς μὴ γευσαμένου θανάτου, ἀλλ' ἐν τῷ βίῳ που τυγχάνοντος id.*Jo.*13.27(p.251.16; Δοσιθεινοί M.14.445B); cf.id.*comm.ser.33 in Mt.*(p.59.23; M.13.1643A); ascetic practices, -θεοί, Epiph.*haer.*13.1(p.205.14ff.; M.41.237A); offshoot of Simonians, Thdt.*haer.*1.1(4.288); unlike Samaritans, believe in resurrection, Δοσθηνοί, Jo.D.*haer.*13(M.94.685B); Δοσθηνοί, cf.Mac.Mgn.*apocr.*3.43(p.151.27) cit. s. ἐγκρατῖται.

δοσοληψία (δοσιληψία), ἡ, 1. *receiving of gifts* or *bribes*, *T.Reub.*3.6; περὶ τοῦ ἀπέχεσθαι τοὺς ἐπισκόπους πάσης δ. CNic.(787)*can.*4 tit. (H.4.488E); **2.** *commerce, giving and taking*, δοσιλ-, Jo.D.*imag.*2.12(M.94.1297B); **3.** δ. τῆς πνοῆς *respiration*, Agath.*v.Gr.Ill.*48(p.27).

δοτός, 1. *given, as a gift* ἦν καὶ οὕτω θεὸς ὡς μὴ δοτὸν ἔχων τὸ φύσει προσὸν αὐτῷ Cyr.*Chr.un.*(5[1].742B); δ. γὰρ ἦν ἐν αὐτῷ [sc. Jo. Bapt.] καὶ οὐκ οὐσιῶδες τὸ ἅγιον πνεῦμα id.*Jo.*2.1(4.125B); δ. ... ἐν ἡμῖν πᾶν...ἀγαθόν, θεῷ δὲ οὐκέτι *ib.*10.2(861E); **2.** *fated, destined*, Eus.Al.*serm.*22.4(M.86.456D).

***δουκανιός**, (Lat. *ducianus*) *of* or *belonging to a* dux τῆς δουκανιῆς τάξεως *CIG* 8646(Egypt, 577).

***δουκάτον, τό**, (Lat. *ducatus*) *office of* dux: τὸ δ. τῆς Ἀλεξανδρέων πόλεως *M.Artem.*(p.167.26); τὸ δ. ἔχοντα Παλαιστίνης Cyr.S.*v.Sab.*56(p.150.1).

δουκηνάριος, ὁ, (Lat. *ducenarius*) *official receiving salary of 200,000 sesterces*, including imperial procurator; ref. secular status assumed by Paul of Samosata, Malch.*ep.*ap.Eus.*h.e.*7.30.8(M.20.712B); of officials who acted as inspectors of police and reported on criminal matters in provinces to emperor's *magister officiorum*, Ath.*apol.sec.*75(p.155.34; M.25.385A); Eulog.*fr.Novat.*(M.104.353B).

δουλαγωγ-έω, *enslave, make a slave of*; **1.** lit., Men.*exc.Rom.*3(p.177.15; M.113.861A); δοῦλος...ἐλευθεροῦται. εἰ δὲ ἀγνοεῖ ὁ δεσπότης, δύναται ἐντὸς ἐνιαυτοῦ τοῦτον ~εῖν Ath.Scholast.*coll.*1.2(p.9); **2.** met., ref. God's dealings with men λόγος...τὸν ἄνθρωπον...οὐ βίᾳ ἀνάγκης ~ῶν, ἀλλ' ἐπ' ἐλευθερίαν ἑκουσίῳ προαιρέσει καλῶν Hipp.*haer.*10.33(p.291.14; M.16.3451B); ~εῖται μὲν ἐπιτάγμασι τοῖς τοῦ πνεύματος ὁ Ἰσραὴλ...υἱοθετεῖται δὲ...ἐκκλησία Didym.(‡Bas.)*Eun.*5(1.309B; M.29.741A); of Arians ~οῦντας τὸν ἐλευθερωτήν Gr.Ant.*bapt.*2.8(M.88.1880B); of sin etc. enslaving men κακία...~εῖ τοὺς χαμαιπετεῖς τῶν ἀνθρώπων Just.*2apol.*11.7(M.6.461D); τί κέρδος ἐκ τῆς ἔξωθεν ἐλευθερίας, ὅταν κυριώτερον ἐν ἡμῖν ~ῆται αἰσχρῶς; Chrys.*hom.in Rom.12:20*(3.162D); of Christ ὦ ἐλευθερία ἄφραστος ~ηθεῖσα παρ' ἡμῶν *A.Jo.*77(p.189.19); of the subjugation of the passions, Athenag.*res.*19(p.72.6; M.6.1012C); ἄνθρωπος...ἑαυτὸν ~ῶν Meth.*arbitr.*16(p.187.10); Ath.*v.Anton.*7(M.26.852B); †Bas.*Is.*31(1.404D; M.30.180C); Chrys.*pan.Macc.*2.2(2.631D); ‡Nil.*perist.*2.2(M.79.820A).

δουλαγωγία, ἡ, *enslavement, subjection*; of passions or flesh, Bas.*reg.fus.*16.1(2.358B; M.31.957B); id.*hom.in Ps.*1(1.95D; M.29.224B).

δουλάριον, τό, *slave*, dim. of δούλη but used of males, Call.*v.Hyp.*(p.76); acting as gladiators, *M.Tar.*10(p.473); v. λουδάριος.

δουλεία, ἡ, 1. *slavery*, of spiritual servitude τὸ ὑποπεσεῖν...τοῖς πάθεσιν ἐσχάτη δ. Clem.*str.*2.23(p.192.21; M.8.1096A); μετάθεσις τοῦ ψυχικοῦ ἐκ δ. εἰς ἐλευθερίαν id.*exc.Thdot.*57(p.126.7; M.9.685D); Or.*hom.8.1 in Ex.*(p.218.30); ἐπεδήμησεν ὁ...Χριστὸς...ἵνα...ἐξέληται τῆς πικρᾶς τὰς ψυχὰς δ. Meth.*Porph.*1(p.504.4; M.18.397C); of man's fallen state, Marcell.*fr.*96 ap.Eus.*Marcell.*2.3(p.51.3; M.24.809B); τὴν...ἁμαρτιῶν κακίστην δ. ἀποθέμενος, τὴν δὲ τοῦ κυρίου μακαριωτάτην δ. κτησάμενος Cyr.H.*catech.*1.2; Bas.*Spir.*29(1.24D; M.32.120A); ἐρρύσατο ὑμᾶς κύριος τῆς δ. τῶν ἐπεισάκτων δεσμῶν *Const.App.*2.35.1; Chrys.*hom.54.1 in Jo.*(8.316A); Thdt.*Jer.*10:25(2.468); of obedient service to God, Herm.*sim.*5.6.7; Or.*Cels.*8.8(p.226.30; M.11.1529B); Eus.*v.C.*4.48(p.137.21; M.20.1200A); πολλοὶ δ. τρόποι· εἷς μὲν ὁ κατὰ τὴν δημιουργίαν...ἕτερος δὲ ὁ ἀπὸ τῆς πίστεως...ἕτερος δὲ ἀπὸ τῆς πολιτείας...κατὰ πάντας τοὺς τρόπους τῆς δ. δοῦλος ἦν ὁ Παῦλος Chrys.*hom.1.1 in Rom.*(9.429E); id.*hom.18.2 in Eph.*(11.128E); Thdt.*Ps.*27:9(1.777); id.*Is.*60:12(p.237.32; 2.380); of Christ ἐδούλευσε καὶ τὴν μέχρι σταυροῦ δ. ὁ Χριστός Just.*dial.*134.5(M.6.788B); *Const.App.*3.19.4; **2.** *service* to men; of deacons, *ib.*3.19.1; of officials, †Gregent.*leg.Hom.*45(M.86.605B); of angels to God δ. τῶν ἀγγέλων ἡ...δοξολογία Eustrat.*stat.anim.*15(p.446); to false gods in pagan worship, Thdt.*qu.19 in Jos.*(1.319); id.*Jer.*3:22(2.428); id.*haer.*5.3(4.392); of service to men contrasted with λατρεία of God, cf. δ. *debetur deo tanquam domino*, λατρεία *vero nonnisi deo tanquam deo*, Aug.*qu.94 in Ex.*(M.*PL.*34.631); **3.** legal *liability*, Phot.*nomoc.*2.1(M.104.565D).

***δουλειανοί, οἱ**, name of Arian sect, so called as τὸν...τοῦ θεοῦ υἱὸν δοῦλον τοῦ πατρὸς τολμήσαντες καλέσαι Thdt.*haer.*4.4(4.359).

***δουλευτής, ὁ**, *servant*, *A.Pil.*B 16.1(p.322.1).

δουλεύ-ω, *be a slave* of, *serve*; **1.** in gen. μηδὲ αὐτοὶ [sc. δοῦλοι] φυσιούσθωσαν, ἀλλ' εἰς δόξαν θεοῦ πλέον ~έτωσαν, ἵνα κρείττονος ἐλευθερίας ἀπὸ θεοῦ τύχωσιν Ign.*Polyc.*4.3; προστάττει...~ειν ὁ δεσπότης..., τὴν δουλείαν γινώσκω Tat.*orat.*4(p.4.24; M.6.813A); **2.** of service to God and Christ; **a.** in gen. τοὺς ἐν...ἀμώμῳ προθέσει ~οντας τῷ θεῷ *1Clem.*45.7; ~σωμεν αὐτῷ μετὰ φόβου καὶ πάσης εὐλαβείας Polyc.*ep.*6.3; ἡ σάρξ, ἐν ᾗ κατῴκησε τὸ πνεῦμα τὸ ἅγιον, ἐδούλευσε τῷ πνεύματι καλῶς ἐν σεμνότητι Herm.*sim.*5.6.5; *ib.*6.3.6; ὀγδοήκοντα καὶ ἓξ ἔτη ~ω αὐτῷ...καὶ πῶς δύναμαι βλασφημῆσαι τὸν βασιλέα μου; *M.Polyc.*9.3; Or.*Jo.*6.55(37; p.164.17; M.14.297A); *Const.App.*8.16.5; τιμὴ γὰρ τῶν εὐσεβῶν, ~ειν θεῷ Thdt.*Ps.*61:5(1.1014); id.*Rom.*12:12(3.133); **b.** of Nature's obedience to creator, Arist.*apol.*5.4; Adam.*dial.*5.18(p.212.4; M.11.1857B); *Const.App.*8.46.2; contrasted with man's voluntary service, Meth.*arbitr.*16(p.186.14); **c.** of angels' ministry to Christ ὁ γὰρ ἀγγέλων ἐν σαρκὶ κρατήσας εὐλόγως ὑπ' ἀγγέλων ἤδη ~εται Clem.*exc.Thdot.*85(p.132.28; M.9.697A); **d.** of Christ's obedience unto death, Just.*dial.*134.5(M.6.788A) cit. s. δουλεία; **3.** of service to pagan gods, *Diogn.*2.5; Or.*Cels.*3.15(p.214.17; M.11.940A); Thdt.*Is.*61:1(p.240.21; 2.383); **4.** of Christian service to others χρὴ οὖν καὶ ὑμᾶς [sc. deacons] ~ειν τοῖς ἀδελφοῖς ὡς Χριστοῦ μιμητάς *Const.App.*3.19.4; **5.** of service to emperor by officials, *CG–CI* 1.2(Corinth, 527–65); **6.** *devote oneself* to virtues, Herm.*vis.*3.8.8; id.*mand.*8.8; *ib.*9.12; to the Law, Or.*Cels.*5.6(p.6.19; M.11.1188D); **7.** met., *be slave* of fate and chance, Meth.*symp.*8.13(p.98.19; M.18.161A); passions etc., Athenag.*leg.*31.2(M.6.961C); Clem.*str.*7.12(p.51.32; M.9.500B); οὐδαμῶς ~ειν θέλοντες τοῖς τῆς ἁμαρτίας νόμοις Or.*Cels.*8.56(p.272.21; M.11.1601A); ἡ κτίσις πᾶσα ~ει· τὸ δὲ πνεῦμα ἐλευθεροῖ Bas.*Spir.*55(3.47E; M.32.172B); ὁ ~ων ἡδοναῖς, δαίμοσιν ὁμιλεῖ †Chrys.*hom.prec.*2(2.785B); letter of scripture, Or.*Jo.*10.40(24; p.217.28; M.14.385B); the time οὐ πρέπει τῷ καιρῷ ~ειν, ἀλλὰ τῷ κυρίῳ Ath.*ep.Drac.*3(M.25.525C); Gr.Naz.*carm.*2.1.11.708(M.37.1078A); **8.** *be subject* to, Thdt.*provid.*3(4.522); ref. Inc. ἐδούλευσε σαρκὶ καὶ γενέσει Gr.Naz.*or.*30.3(p.111.9; M.36.105C); **9.** *be under penitential discipline*, *Nomoc.*481; **10.** of an editor, translator, student etc., *follow* a text *slavishly* Ἀκύλας ~ων τῇ Ἑβραϊκῇ λέξει Or.*ep.*1.2(M.11.52B); Eus.*d.e.*5.1(p.214.18; M.22.356C); *ib.*9.4(p.412.2; 664C); Thdt.*Cant.*3:6(2.82).

δούλη, ἡ, *maidservant, handmaid*; of Christian women as servants of God, *A.Thom.*A 159(p.270.2); *POxy.*924.10(saec. iv); *MAMA* 1.161(saec. iv); δεόμεθά σου περὶ τῆς κοιμήσεως...τοῦ δούλου σου τοῦδε ἢ τῆς δ. σου τῆσδε Serap.*euch.*30.2; ἔπιδε ἐπὶ τὴν δ. σου τήνδε τὴν προχειριζομένην εἰς διακονίαν *Const.App.*8.20.2; of BMV τίς τὴν ἰδίαν δ. μητέρα προσκαλεσάμενος ἐνυβρίζεται; Cyr.*hom.div.*4(p.103.6; 5[2].356C); ἡ δ. καὶ μήτηρ Procl.CP *or.laud.BMV* 1(p.103.17; M.65.681B); id.*or.*5.3(M.65.720B); ‡Epiph.*hom.*5(M.43.497D); of creation as δ. τοῦ λόγου Ath.*Ar.*2.10(M.26.168C).

δουλικός, *servile*; of creaturely condition in rel. to God, Bas.*Spir.*29(3.24C; M.32.117D); *ib.*46(39B; M.152C); of the seventh day ἑβδόμη, ἡ παροῦσα ζωή, δ. δέ, ὡς τῇ φθορᾷ δουλευούσης τῆς κτίσεως *Schol.*20 in Jo.Clim.*scal.*5(M.88.789A); of Christ, Gr.Nyss.*hom.13 in Cant.*(M.44.1048A) cit. s. προσωπεῖον; of Sethian saviour ἐν εἰκόνι δ. Hipp.*haer.*5.21(p.124.12; M.16.3190B); neut. plur. as subst., Leont. N.*v.Jo.Eleem.*1(p.7.5).

***δουλικοσμικός**, *enslaved to the world*, ‡Chrys.*pasch.*5.1(8.262A).

***δουλίριον, τό**, *rein* or *harness*, Jo.Mosch.*prat.*107(M.87.2968C); perh. f.l. for λωρίδιον, dim. of λῶρος.

δουλίς, ἡ, = δούλη, *T.Abr.*A 15(p.95.18); *T.Job* 21(p.116.9); Gr. Nyss.*v.Macr.*(p.378.4; M.46.965D); ‡Chrys.*hom.*10(13.239A); Pall.*h.Laus.*61(p.157.3; M.34.1233A); as adj. δ. ... γυναικῶν Chrys.*hom.3.2 in Mt.*(7.36B).

***δουλογάστριος**, *gluttonous*, Ephr.3.405C.

***δουλογενής**, *slave-born*; hence *like a slave*, Thdr.Stud.*or.*11.12(M.99.813C).

***δουλοδοῦλος, ὁ,** *slave of a slave*, Thdr.Stud.*epp*.2.107(M.99.1368A).

***δουλόμοιος,** *like a slave*, Thdr.Stud.*epp*.2.156(M.99.1489B).

***δουλόμορφος,** *in form of a slave*, Gr.Naz.*carm*.1.2.25.129(M.37.822A).

***δουλοπάθεια, ἡ,** *slavery to passion*, Ephr.1.209F.

***δουλοπαθής,** *enslaved to passion*, Ephr.1.237E.

***δουλοποιητέον,** *one must make into a servant* οὐ γὰρ ἐπειδὴ ἐν πνεύματι λαλῶν κύριον ἐκάλεσε τὸν Χριστόν, διὰ τοῦτο δ. τὸ πνεῦμα Vict.*Mc*.12:35(p.405.28).

***δουλοποιΐα, ἡ,** *enslavement*, Dion.Ar.*c.h*.8.1(v.l. δουλοπρεπεία M.3.237C).

δουλοπρεπής, *befitting a slave, servile* φόβος δ. Chrys.*sac*.3.9 (p.62.9; 1.386D); πῶς υἱοὺς θεοῦ κατασκευάζεις ὁ δ.; Isid.Pel.*epp*.2.65 (M.78.508D); Christol., Cyr.*thes*.9(5[1].72A) cit. s. ἐνανθρώπησις; θεὸς ὢν φύσει...δ. ὑπέδυ μέτρον, τουτέστι τὸ ἀνθρώπινον id.*apol.Thdt*.10 (p.139.4; 6[1].233C).

δοῦλος, ὁ, A. *slave*; **1.** in gen. δ. καὶ δούλας μὴ ὑπερηφάνει Ign. *Polyc*.4.3; δ. ἐὰν ὦ, τὴν δουλείαν ὑπομένω Tat.*orat*.11(p.11.31; M.6.829A); τῇ φύσει δ. οὐδείς...ὥστε κἂν ὁ μὲν δεσπότης, ὁ δὲ οἰκέτης λέγηται, ἀλλ' οὖν πάντες...ὡς κτήματα τοῦ πεποιηκότος ἡμᾶς, ὁμόδουλοι Bas.*Spir*.51(3.42E; M.32.160D); **2.** of imperial officials as δ. of emperor, *CG–CI* 1.1(Corinth, 527–65); **3.** of Christ in his humanity (for μορφὴ δ. ref. Phil.2:8, v. μορφή); δ. ἐν ταῖς γραφαῖς ἐλέχθη, καὶ παιδίσκης υἱός...ἀλλ' ἔχει τὴν πρόφασιν καὶ τὸ αἴτιον εὔλογον...τὰ τοιαῦτα...διότι ἄνθρωπος...γέγονε, λαβὼν τὴν τοῦ δ. μορφήν, ἥτις ἦν ἡ ἀνθρωπίνη φύσις Ath.*ep.Aeg.Lib*.17(M.25.576C); ταπεινῶσαι ἑαυτὸν καὶ δ. ἀνθ' ἡμῶν καὶ ὑπὲρ ἡμῶν γενέσθαι id.*Ar*.1.43(M.26.101B); *ib*. 2.11(169A); τῶν τοῦ Χριστοῦ προσηγοριῶν...τῶν τε ὑψηλοτέρων...καὶ τῶν δι' ἡμᾶς ταπεινοτέρων, τοῦ θεοῦ, τοῦ υἱοῦ...τοῦ ἀνθρώπου, τοῦ δ. Gr.Naz.*or*.2.98(M.35.500C); τὸ δ. ἀκούειν εὖ δουλεύοντα πολλοῖς...τῷ ὄντι γὰρ ἐδούλευσε σαρκί, καὶ γενέσει...διὰ τὴν ἡμετέραν ἐλευθερίαν *ib*. 30.3(p.111.6; M.36.105C); ὁ ἐν τῇ κοιλίᾳ τῆς παρθένου πλασθεὶς κατὰ τὸν λόγον τοῦ προφήτου, ὁ δ. ἐστιν, οὐχ ὁ κύριος· τουτέστιν ὁ κατὰ σάρκα ἄνθρωπος ἐν ᾧ ὁ θεὸς ἐφανερώθη...οὐχ ὁ θεός ἐστιν, ἀλλ' ὁ ἄνθρωπος Gr.Nyss.*fid*.(M.45.137C); πῶς...ὁ μονογενὴς δ. γεγένηται, μείνας ὃ ἦν, καὶ γενόμενος ὃ οὐκ ἦν; Thdot.Anc.*hom*.1.6(p.84.11; M.77.1356D); ποῦ ὁ διαιρῶν τὸν Χριστόν; ποῦ ὁ...Χριστὸν μὲν ἕνα λέγων, δύο δὲ ὑποτιθέμενος, τὸν μὲν δ., τὸν δὲ δεσπότην *ib*.3.4(p.72.35; 1388D); κἂν εἴ τις λέγοι δ. αὐτὸν ὠνομάσθαι...κατ' οὐδένα τρόπον σκανδαλίζεσθαι πρέπει...ἦν μὲν...ἐλεύθερος ὡς υἱός,...ἡμῖν τοῖς ὑπὸ ζυγὰ δουλείας συμμορφούμενος Cyr.*apol.Thdt*.6(p.129.11; 6[1].223C); ὁ δ. τοίνυν τῆς ληφθείσης φύσεως ὄνομα· οὐκ ἐπειδὴ δουλεύει ἐκείνη... ἀλλ' ἵνα δειχθῇ τῆς φύσεως αὐτῆς τὸ ἴδιον Thdt.*Ps*.108:28(1.1390); use of such language rejected, ‡Dion.Al.*ep.Paul.Sam*.7(p.26); ἡ ἀπαρχὴ τῆς ἡμετέρας φύσεως, δι' ἧς καὶ ἡμεῖς τοῦ τῆς υἱοθεσίας χαρίσματος ἠξιώθημεν, τῆς τοῦ δ. προσηγορίας ἀπήλλακται Thdt.ap. Cyr.*apol.Thdt*.6(p.128.12; 6[1].222C); οὐδὲ δ. αὐτὸν λέγειν δυνάμεθα· τὸ γὰρ τῆς δουλείας καὶ τῆς δεσποτείας ὄνομα οὐ φύσεώς εἰσι γνωρίσματα, ἀλλὰ τῶν πρός τι. ... δούλη ἐστὶν ἡ σάρξ, εἰ μὴ ἥνωτο τῷ θεῷ λόγῳ· ἅπαξ δὲ ἑνωθεῖσα, πῶς ἔσται δούλη; εἷς γὰρ ὢν ὁ Χριστός, οὐ δύναται δ. ἑαυτοῦ εἶναι καὶ κύριος Jo.D.*f.o*.3.21(M.94.1085A); **4.** of Christ as son, opp. creation as God's slave, Herm.*sim*.5.5.5; *ib*. 5.6.1; Ath.*Ar*.1.55(M.26.128A) cit. s. διακονία; ὅσῳ διέστηκεν υἱὸς δούλων, δείκνυσιν ἄλλον αὐτὸν εἶναι τῆς τῶν ἀγγέλων φύσεως *ib*.1.57 (132B); his creaturely status asserted by Eunomius, v. s. ὑπηρέτης; **5.** creaturely status as δ. denied of H. Ghost, Bas.*Spir*.49(3.42A; M.32.157C); δ. λέγεις τὸ πνεῦμα; ἀλλ' ὁ δ. ... οὐκ οἶδε τί ποιεῖ ὁ κύριος αὐτοῦ, τὸ δὲ πνεῦμα οὕτως οἶδε τὰ τοῦ θεοῦ, ὡς καὶ τὸ πνεῦμα τοῦ ἀνθρώπου τὰ ἐν αὐτῷ *ib*.50(42D; M.160C); *ib*.51(42E; M.160C,D); ‡Ath.*Maced.dial*.1.20(M.28.1328A); asserted by Eunomians, Thdt. *Ps*.57:6(1.986); **6.** of status of men before redemption ὥσπερ ἡμεῖς οἱ δ. τοῦ θεοῦ υἱοὶ θεοῦ γεγόναμεν, οὕτως ὁ δεσπότης τῶν δ. υἱὸς τοῦ ἰδίου δ. γέγονε θνητός, τουτέστι τοῦ Ἀδάμ, ἵνα οἱ υἱοὶ τοῦ Ἀδὰμ ...υἱοὶ τοῦ θεοῦ γένωνται Ath.*inc.et c.Ar*.8(M.26.996B); id.*Ar*.2.51 (M.26.253C); of slave (opp. μαθητής) of God, Heracleon ap.Or.*Jo*. 6.20(12; p.129.25; M.14.236B); of those who serve God in fear, opp. those who love, Bas.*hom.in Ps*.33(1.148C; M.29.364A); δ. γάρ εἰσι, πιστοί, οἱ φόβῳ τῶν ἠπειλημένων ἐκπληροῦντες τοῦ δεσπότου τὰς ἐντολάς Max.*myst*.(M.91.709D); of those who are unwitting instruments of God, Thdt.*1Tim*.6:11(3.670).

B. *servant*; **1.** of star of nativity as servant of Christ δ. τῆς γνώσεως Ἰησοῦ Or.*Jo*.1.26(24; p.32.30; M.14.72A); **2.** of Christians as servants; **a.** of God, *1Clem*.60.2; *2Clem*.20.1; Herm.*mand*.12.1.2; id.*sim*.9.15.3; Serap.*euch*.5.3; Bas.*hom.in Ps*.33(1.145A; M.29.356A); *Lit*.ap.*Const.App*.8.6.12; ἄκρα δὲ τιμὴ τὸ δ. ὀνομασθῆναι θεοῦ Thdt.*qu.21 in 2Reg*.(1.416); contrasted with δ. ἀσεβείας id.*Ps*. 61:7(1.1015); **b.** of Christ, Herm.*sim*.9.28.4; *A.Thom*.A 163(p.275.12); Ath.*v.Anton*.52(M.26.950A); [κ]ύριε βόητι...[τῷ] δ. σου Τιμ[οθ]έ[ῳ] *MAMA* 1.161(Phrygia, saec. iv); *ib*.3.463 (Corycus); Ἰάκωβος, ἀδελφὸς μὲν κατὰ σάρκα τοῦ Χριστοῦ, δ. δὲ ὡς θεοῦ μονογενοῦς *Const.App*.8.35.1; κεφάλαιον τῶν ἀγαθῶν, δ. εἶναι Χριστοῦ ...ὁ τοῦ Χριστοῦ δ., οὗτος ὄντως ἐλεύθερός ἐστι τῇ ἁμαρτίᾳ, καὶ γνήσιος δ., οὐδενὸς ἄλλου δ. γενέσθαι Chrys.*hom.1.1 in Phil*.(11.194C,D); *Lit.Jac*.(p.226.6); **3.** especially of bishops, priests, and deacons, cf.Hipp.*trad.ap*.3.4; *ib*.8.2; *ib*.9.11; *Lit*.ap.*Const.App*.8.5.6; *Const.App*.8.16.4; *ib*.8.18.2; **4.** of a bishop as self-styled δ. τῶν δ. τοῦ θεοῦ Maur.*ep*.(M.*PL*.87.103B); similarly of popes, Agath.Papa *ep.imp*.(M.*PL*.87.1162); Hadr.Papa *ep.Taras*.(M.*PL*. 96.1234D).

C. met., of slaves of sin etc. δ. ... ἐπιθυμίας Athenag.*leg*.21.4(M. 6.936A); χρημάτων δ. Chrys.*hom.6.5 in Phil*.(11.242D); of literalist exegetes δ. τῆς λέξεως Or.*Jo*.10.18(13; p.188.16; M.14.336D).

D. as adj., *serving, subject to* ἔθνη...δοῦλα δικαιοσύνης Or.*hom.30 in Lc*.(p.185.24; M.13.1878B); Meth.*res*.2.18(p.371.10; M.18.285A); describing hypothetical status of Christ's humanity apart from union with Logos, ‡Cyr.*Trin*.25(6[3].31A; M.77.1169A).

***δουλόσαρκος,** *enslaved to the flesh*, Thdr.Stud.*epp*.2.28(M.99.1197C).

***δουλότροπος,** *servile*, Ast.Am.*hom*.14(M.40.380D).

δουλ-όω, 1. *enslave*, ref. enslavement to sin etc. θανάτῳ ~ουμένους *Barn*.16.9; Meth.*symp*.10.1(p.122.4; M.18.192D); id.*arbitr*.11(p.175.3; M.18.260C); Bas.*hom*.6.6(2.48E; M.31.273A); to false gods, *Diogn*. 2.10; **2.** *gain control over, hold in bondage*, Hipp.*haer*.1 proem.(p.2.11; M.16.3020A); Or.*Jo*.10.25(16; p.198.7; M.14.352C); Meth.*Porph*. 1(p.504.17; M.18.400B).

***δούλωτος,** *enslaved*, *cat.Apoc*.18:14(p.444.32).

δούξ, ὁ, (Lat. *dux*) *military governor* of one or more provinces after separation by Diocletian of civil and military powers ὁ τῆς Αἰγύπτου δ. ‡Eus.*ant.mart.coll*.2(M.20.1533C); *M.Seb*.3(p.173.25); ὁ...δ. τῆς Σκυθίας *M.Sab*.8.1; δ. Ἀρμενίας Ath.*apol.Const*.22(M.25.624A); δ. καὶ Αὐγουσταλίου τῆς Θηβαΐων χώρας *CIG* 8646.6(Egypt, 577); Thphn.*chron*.p.43(M.108.164A); having honorary title of ὕπατος, Marc.Diac.*v.Porph*.50.

***δούπημα, τό,** *crash, clap* of thunder, *Orac.Sib*.8.432.

δουριαλής, ὁ, *captive of the spear*, Gr.Naz.*carm*.2.1.1.355(M.37.996A); *ib*.2.1.16.68(1259A).

***δουροφόρος, ὁ,** *spearman*, *Orac.Sib*.11.193.

***δοχεία, ἡ,** = δοχή, *feast*, Diod.*Ps*.62:6(M.33.1597B).

δοχεῖον, τό, A. *receptacle*; **1.** in gen. θάλασσα...ποταμῶν οὖσα δ. Bas.*hex*.4.7(1.39B; M.29.93A); Gr.Naz.*carm*.1.2.33.8(M.37.928A); *ib*. 1.2.34.226(961A) cit. s. θεηδόχος; Thdt.*Ps*.143:13(1.1557); of vessels for reception of Communion, forbidden since hand only is to be used, CTrull.*can*.101; **2.** Christol. εἰ ἐκ πάντων τῶν ἴσων ἡμῖν ἐστι τοῖς χοϊκοῖς ὁ ἐπουράνιος ἄνθρωπος...οὐκ ἐπουράνιος ἀλλ' ἐπουρανίου θεοῦ δ. Apoll.*fr*.90(p.228.2)ap.Gr.Nyss.*Apoll*.48(M.45.1240D); **3.** of Christ τὸ δ. τῆς σοφίας καὶ τῆς θεότητος Epiph.*anc*.66(p.79.10; M.43.133D); **4.** denial that H. Ghost is δ. ... τοῦ προγεγονότος ἁγιασμοῦ Cyr.*thes*.34(5[1].350D); **5.** of BMV φέγγος ἀενάοιο δοχήϊον Paul.Sil.*Soph*.710(M.86.2146B); δ. τοῦ στήσαντος τὰ ὄρη Jo.Eub. *concept.BMV* 4(M.96.1465A); **6.** of mind or soul as receptacle of instruction, Clem.*str*.7.18(p.77.10; M.9.556A); of Logos, Meth. *symp*.3.8(p.37.14; M.18.76A); of H. Ghost, Chrys.*carit*.2(6.289B); of God δεῖ κενὴν εἶναι παθῶν τὴν ψυχὴν τὴν μέλλουσαν ἔσεσθαι δ. θεοῦ Synes.*ep*.57(M.66.1396C); ψυχῆς δὲ κοιλία, τὸ δ. τῶν πνευματικῶν τροφῶν Cyr.*Ps*.39:9(M.69.989D); **7.** of man as receptacle; **a.** of H. Ghost, Gr.Naz.*or*.32.11(M.36.188A); μάρτυς ἅγιος...δ. τοῦ ἁγίου πνεύματος *Const.App*.5.1.2; Δανιὴλ...θείου πνεύματος δ. γενόμενος Thdt.*Dan*.5:12(2.1164); **b.** of evil spirits, Or.*fr.51 in Lc*.(p.257); or passions, Chrysipp.*enc.in Jo.Bapt*.11(p.41.22); **8.** of Church as receptacle of μακαρία ζωή, Gr.Nyss.*hom.2 in Cant*.(M.44.805D); of monastic life as τῶν κυρίου ἐντολῶν...δ. Isid.Pel.*epp*.1.278(M.78.345C); **9.** of Satan δ. πάσης κακίας Bas.*hom*.9.8(2.80C; M.31.348A); **10.** of skin of Manes τὸ...τῆς κακίστης γνώμης δ. Cyr.H.*catech*.6.30.

B. *cistern*, Thphn.*chron*.p.370(M.108.888B).

C. *guest-house*, Thdr.Stud.*iamb*.107(M.99.1805C).

δοχή, ἡ, 1. *entertainment, feast*; of *agape*, *Const.App*.2.28.1; ‡Ign.*Smyrn*.8; **2.** *reception*; hence *assembly for purpose of reception*, Thphn.*chron*.p.321(M.108.776B); **3.** *funeral-rites*, Thphn.*chron*. p.317(M.108.768B); **4.** *receptacle*, hence *measure* ὕδατος δ. δέκα *T.Sal*.16.7(M.122.1349C); **5.** *received impression* μνήμη...φυλάττει τὰς δ. τῶν πραγμάτων Geo.Pis.*hex*.680(M.92.1488A).

***δόχια, τά,** *funeral-rites* δ. ... προσαγορεύουσι [sc. Huns] τὰ ἐπὶ τοῖς τεθνεῶσι νόμιμα Men.*exc.Rom.*14(p.207.20; M.113.905C).

***δοχμέω,** v. δοχμόω.

δόχμιος, *aslant*; hence met., *oblique, ambiguous* δ. ὀμφήν Nonn. *par.Jo.*16:25(M.43.881C).

δοχμ-όω, 1. *place obliquely*, †Apoll.*met.Ps.*139:6(v.l. δοχμήσαντες M.33.1524B); **2.** *bend down* αὐχένα ~ώσαντες Nonn.*par.Jo.* 8:33(M.43.817B); γούνατα ~ώσαντες *ib.*19:3(897B); med. αὐχένα ~ώσαντο *ib.*4:20(777A); αὐχένα ~ωθέντα *ib.*4:23(777B).

δόχος, *conceiving* ἤκουσεν ἡ παρθένος τὸ 'χαῖρε', καὶ εὐθέως δ. ἀνεδείχθη Abr.Eph.*annunt.*4(p.445.24).

δράγμα, τό, *sheaf*; **1.** ref. Lev.23:10, Cyr.*Os.*96(3.128D); as type of Resurrection on third day τρίτῃ ἀνέστη ἡμέρᾳ, ἥτις ἦν πρώτη τῶν ἑβδομάδων τοῦ θερισμοῦ, ἐν ᾗ καὶ τὸ δ. ἐνομοθετεῖτο προσενεγκεῖν τὸν ἱερέα Clem.*fr.*28(p.217.10; M.9.757B); πρωτότοκος ἐκ νεκρῶν...καὶ ἀπαρχὴ τῆς ἁπάντων ἀναστάσεως...ἐλήφθη μὲν γὰρ ἐξ ἡμῶν...ἵνα καὶ καθάπερ ἐξ ἅλωνος δ. τὸ πρῶτον ἀναφέρηται τῷ θεῷ καὶ πατρί Cyr.*Jo.* 4.2(4.355E); **2.** met., ref. Ps.125:6 δέσμευε τὰ τῆς ἀληθείας δ. Ath.*ep. Serap.*4.23(M.26.676B); ἀμήσατε τῶν σπερμάτων ὑμῶν τὰ δ. Thdt. *qu.7 in Jud.*(1.325); of a first-born son, id.*h.rel.*26.19(p.14.21; 3.1279).

***δρακήν,** adv., *in one's grasp*, *Apoc.Esd.*(p.32).

δρακονάρι(ο)ς, ὁ, v. δρακωνάρι(ο)ς.

***δρακοντιαῖος,** *belonging to a serpent*, hence *of the Devil*, Amph. *mesopent.*(M.39.124C); τῶν δ. συριγμάτων, καὶ οὐ προφητικῶν κατηχημάτων πυθόμενοι ‡Chrys.*hom.in Ps.92:3*(5.622E); Steph. Diac.*v.Steph.*(M.100.1137B); neut. as adv. ὁ τύραννος...δρακοντιαῖόν τε συριεὶς μέγα *ib.*(1157A).

***δρακοντικός,** = foreg., ‡Pamph.Abyd.*ep.Petr.*(p.9.20; H.2. 849C).

δρακόντιον, τό, *serpent*, ‡Ign.*Ant.*6.

***δρακοντογόνος,** *serpent-engendered, devilish*, Geo.Pis.*carm. vit.*52.

δρακοντοειδής, *serpent-like*; **1.** of heavenly powers in Ophite system πρὸς...ἀπόδειξιν φέρουσι τὴν τοῦ ἐγκεφάλου ἀνατομήν, αὐτὸν μὲν τὸν ἐγκέφαλον ἀπεικονίζοντες τῷ πατρὶ διὰ τὸ ἀκίνητον, τὴν δὲ παρεγκεφαλίδα τῷ υἱῷ διά τε τὸ κινεῖσθαι καὶ δ. ὑπάρχειν Hipp.*haer.* 5.17(p.116.4; M.16.3178C); τὸ δὲ διάγραμμα τρίτον 'Ραφαὴλ ἔλεγεν εἶναι δ. Or.*Cels.*6.30(p.100.13; M.11.1341A); δ. ἄρχοντας *ib.*6.37(p.106. 19; 1353A); Gnost. εἶναι δ. τὸν ἄρχοντα τὸν κατέχοντα τὸν κόσμον τοῦτον Epiph.*haer.*26.10(p.288.7; M.41.345D); **2.** of Devil δ. σατανᾶ id.*anac.*45(p.3.23; M.42.861C); Jo.D.*haer.*45(M.94.704C); of a demon, *T.Sal.*14.7(M.122.1337A).

δρακοντοειδῶς, *in the manner of a serpent* εἶναι δὲ ἐξ ὑπαρχῆς ᾠοῦ δίκην τὸ σύμπαν, τὸ δὲ πνεῦμα δ. περὶ τὸ ᾠὸν ὡς στέφανον...περισφίγγειν τότε τὴν φύσιν [sc. acc. Epicureans] Epiph.*haer.*8.1(p.186.18; M.41.205C).

δρακοντοκέφαλος, *with a serpent's head*, Cosm.Mel.*schol.*(M.38. 487) in Gr.Naz.*carm.*2.2(poem.)7.104.

δρακοντόμορφος, *in form of a serpent*; of demons, *T.Sal.*18.1; †Jo.D.*B.J.*37(M.96.1216B).

***δρακοντοπαῖς, ὁ,** *offspring of a dragon*, *T.Sal.*5.4(M.122.1321C), v. δρακοντόπους.

***δρακοντοπνίκτης, ὁ,** *dragon-strangler*; of Heracles, Agath. *v.Gr.Ill.*140(p.71).

δρακοντόπους, 1. *serpent-footed*; of giants in pagan mythology, Gr.Naz.*or.*4.115(M.35.653A); Cosm.Mel.*schol.*(M.38.488) in Gr.Naz. *carm.*2.2(poem.)7.105; of Asmodaeus, *T.Sal.*5.4(v.l. δρακοντοπαῖδα M.122.1321C); **2.** as subst., *serpent-footed monster* in pagan mythology, Chrys.*hom.7.4 in Phil.*(11.376F).

***δρακοντόω,** *turn into a serpent*, Leont.H.*Nest.*2.47(M.86.1600C).

***δρακοντώνυμος,** *dragon-named*, Steph.Diac.*v.Steph.*(M.100. 1165A).

δράκων, ὁ, *serpent, dragon*; **1.** as object of pagan worship, Arist.*apol.*12(p.108.9); μαρτυρήσει...'Ελευσὶς καὶ δ. ὁ μυστικὸς καὶ 'Ορφεύς Tat.*orat.*8(p.9.12; M.6.824C); Σαβαζίων γοῦν μυστηρίων σύμβολον τοῖς μυουμένοις ὁ διὰ κόλπου θεός· δ. δέ ἐστιν οὗτος, διελκόμενος τοῦ κόλπου τῶν τελουμένων Clem.*prot.*2(p.13.19; M.8.77A); Gr.Nyss.*Eun.*2(2 p.339.21; M.45.516B); **2.** of primeval chaos-monster symbolizing power of death and evil (Rahab, Behemoth etc.); **a.** as identified with Devil δαίμων δὲ καὶ δ. καλεῖται, διὰ τὸ ἀποδεδρακέναι αὐτὸν ἀπὸ τοῦ θεοῦ Thphl.Ant.*Autol.*2.28(M.6.1097A); τύραννος καὶ δ. Clem.*prot.*1(p.8.7; M.8.64A); id.*str.*1.21(p.77.17; M.8.852B); *M.Perp.*4(p.67.15,20); Or.*fr.30 in Jer.*(p.214.14; M.13. 597B); ref. Ezech.29:3–5 μήποτε χωρίον ἐστὶν τοῦ ἐχθροῦ ἡμῶν δ. ὁ τῆς Αἰγύπτου ποταμὸς ὁ μηδὲ παιδίον ἀποκτεῖναι Μωσέα δυνηθείς. ὥσπερ δὲ ὁ δ. ἐν τῷ Αἰγυπτίῳ ἐστὶν ποταμῷ, οὕτως ὁ θεὸς ἐν τῷ εὐφραίνοντι τὴν πόλιν τοῦ θεοῦ ποταμῷ Or.*Jo.*6.48(29; p.157.14; M. 14.284B); ref. Apoc.12:1–6 τίνα ἐξέφυγεν ἢ πάντως τὸν δ., ἵνα γεννήσῃ τὸν λαὸν ἡ νοητὴ Σιὼν τὸν ἄρσενα, τὸν τῶν γυναικείων παθῶν καὶ τῆς ἐκλύσεως εἰς τὴν ἑνότητα τοῦ κυρίου καταντήσαντα καὶ ἀπαρσενωθέντα τῇ σπουδῇ; Meth.*symp.*8.7(p.90.1; M.18.149B); *ib.*8.10 (p.92.4; 152C); *ib.*11(p.136.17; 213A); id.*arbitr.*17(p.190.9; M.18. 265C); δ. καὶ ὄφιν, μελανά τε καὶ ἑρπυστικόν, ἰοῦ θανατηφόρου γεννητικόν Eus.*p.e.*7.16(328D; M.21.556A); ref. portrait of Const. τὸ μὲν σωτήριον σημεῖον ὑπερκείμενον τῆς αὐτοῦ κεφαλῆς τῇ γραφῇ παραδούς, τὸν δ' ἐχθρόν...θῆρα τὸν τὴν ἐκκλησίαν τοῦ θεοῦ...πολιορκήσαντα... κατὰ βυθοῦ φερόμενον ποιήσας ἐν δράκοντος μορφῇ id.*v.C.*3.3(p.78. 12; M.20.1057A); Ath.*v.Anton.*6(M.26.849A); *A.Phil.*111(p.43.13); τὸν δωδεκακέφαλον δ. *IGC As.Min.*210³.8(Amorgus); identified with δ. or Behemoth of Job 40:14, Or.*Jo.*1.17(p.21.11; M.14.52B); Chrys. *hom.6.4 in Phil.*(11.240C); **b.** as overthrown by Christ, esp. in his baptism (cf. Ps.73:13) and so in Christian baptism αὐτὸς ἐλθὼν... καὶ συντρίβων τὴν κάραν τοῦ δ. ἐπὶ τοῦ ὕδατος *T.Aser* 7.3; ἔσται δὲ καὶ πλῆθος μετὰ εἰρήνης ἀπὸ τῶν ἐθνῶν ἐν τῇ εἰς 'Ιερουσαλὴμ τοῦ σωτῆρος ἐπιδημίᾳ, ἄρχοντος τῶν ὑδάτων, ἵνα συντρίψῃ τὰς κεφαλὰς τῶν δ. ἐπὶ τοῦ ὕδατος Or.*Jo.*10.32(18; p.206.9; M.14.365A); ὁ δ. ἦν ἐν τοῖς ὕδασι κατὰ τὸν 'Ιώβ, ὁ δεχόμενος τὸν 'Ιορδάνην ἐν τῷ στόματι αὐτοῦ. ἐπεὶ οὖν ἔδει συντρῖψαι τὰς κεφαλὰς τοῦ δ., καταβὰς ἐν τοῖς ὕδασιν ἔδησε τὸν ἰσχυρόν Cyr.H.*catech.*3.11; ὁ ἐν ὕδασι 'Ιορδάνου συντρίψας τὰς κεφαλὰς τῶν δ. ὑμῶν ‡Epiph.*hom.*2(M.43.460B); ἡ τῆς 'Ερυθρᾶς τοῦ βαπτίσματος θάλασσα...ἐν ᾧ καὶ πνεῦμα θεοῦ ἀληθῶς ἐπιφέρεται ὁμοῦ...ἐν ᾧ συντρίβεται ἡ κεφαλὴ τοῦ δ., καὶ ἄρχοντος τῶν δ. τῶν δαιμονικῶν τοῦ διαβόλου λαῶν *ib.*3(469A); τοῦ δεσπότου δὲ βαπτιζομένου ἐν τῇ οἰκονομίᾳ ἐπὶ τῷ τόν τε δ., τὸν ἐπὶ τοῖς ὕδασι δεξάμενον τὸν 'Ιορδάνην, ἐν τῷ στόματι, ὡς ἱστορεῖ...ὁ 'Ιώβ, θανατῶσαι Didym.*Trin.*2.12(M.39.684A); ἐκεῖ δρακόντων κεφαλαὶ τοῖς ὕδασι συντριβόμεναι, καὶ ἐνταῦθα δυναστεῖαι δαιμόνων καταλυόμεναι τῇ τοῦ βαπτίσματος χάριτι Thdt.*Ps.*73:14(1.1131); Cosm.Mel.*hymn.*2(p.37; M.98.465C); **c.** as conquered in martyrdom, *M.Thdot.1* 31(p.80. 25); **d.** of Devil, *A.Thom.*A 167(p.281.12); **e.** of evil spirits, Or.*fr.95 in Lam.*(p.270.1; M.13.652A); *1Apoc.Jo.*(p.94, one MS only); **f.** of dragon surrounding earth, whose belly is Hades, *Apoc.Bar.*5 (p.88.12); cf.Hipp.*haer.*4.47(p.69.10ff.; M.16.3111B); *A.Thom.*A 32 (p.149.1); **g.** at the parousia ὅταν ἐπιτελῶνται σημεῖα καὶ τέρατα ὑπ' αὐτοῦ τοῦ δ. ἐν πολλῇ ἐξουσίᾳ...δεικνύῃ ἑαυτόν, ὥσπερ θεόν...ἐν τῷ ἀέρι ἱπτάμενον, καὶ πάντας τοὺς δαίμονας ἐν τῷ ἀέρι ἐπηρμένους ὥσπερ ἀγγέλους ἔμπροσθεν τοῦ τυράννου Ephr.2.222E; οὗτος ὁ δ. εὑρίσκεται μιαρός, ἀπότομος τῷ γένει τῶν ἀνθρώπων id.2.223C; ὁ δ. τὴν ἑαυτοῦ σφραγῖδα ἀντὶ τοῦ σταυροῦ τοῦ σωτῆρος id.2.225D; id. 3.138ff.; cf. τὴν σφραγῖδα τὴν τοῦ σωτῆρος ἐκ τούτων ἀφαιρεῖται Rom.Mel.(*SBBAW* 1898² p.172); of serpent of Apoc.12:4 interpreted of power of antichrist, cf.Iren.*haer.*2.31.3(M.7.825C); 'δ.' δὲ 'πυρρόν'...ἢ διὰ τὸ φονικὸν αὐτοῦ καὶ αἱμοχαρές, ἢ διὰ τὸ πυρῶδες τῆς ἀγγελικῆς οὐσίας, εἰ καὶ τῶν ἀγγέλων ἐκπέπτωκεν Andr.Caes. *Apoc.*33(M.106.321B); cf. συγγενής εἰμι ἐκείνου τοῦ μέλλοντος ἀπὸ τῆς ἀνατολῆς ἔρχεσθαι...ταῦτα εἰπόντος τοῦ δ. *A.Thom.*A 32f.(p.149. 23); **3.** ref. other interprn. of Ps.73:13 δ. τὸν Φαραώ, κεφαλὰς δὲ αὐτοῦ τοὺς ὑπ' αὐτὸν ἄρχοντας...ἢ δ. τοὺς Αἰγυπτίους, κεφαλὰς δὲ αὐτῶν τοὺς...ἡγουμένους αὐτῶν Eus.*Ps.*73:12–18(M.23.861D); Αἰγυπτίων...κεφαλήν, οὓς καὶ δ. διὰ τὸ πονηρὸν τῆς γλώσσης ὀνομάζει· εἶτα μετ' αὐτῶν καὶ αὐτοῦ τοῦ ἐξάρχοντος αὐτῶν βασιλέως, ὃν καὶ αὐτὸν ὁμοίως δ. προσαγορεύει Ath.*exp.Ps.*73:13(M.27.336C); οἱ δὲ δυσαπόνιπτον ἔχοντες τὴν ἀκαθαρσίαν...καταθοινήσονται τὰς τοῦ δ. κεφαλάς Cyr.*Ps.*73:14(M.69.1188A); **4.** as emblem carried by Devil, *M.Seb.*7(p.176.31); **5.** imagery of δ. as power of evil transferred to human tyrants, e.g. Pompey, *Pss.Sal.*2.29; Licinius, Const.ap. Eus.*v.C.*2.46(p.60.27; M.20.1024A); of heathens in gen., Eus.*l.C.*9 (p.219.3; M.20.1364C); Chosroes, Geo.Pis.*carm.*2.22.

δρακωνάρι(ο)ς (δρακονάρι(ο)ς), ὁ, (Lat. *draconarius*) *bearer of dragon standard, standard-bearer*, Thdt.*ep.*59(4.1112); *ib.*133(1222); δρακωνάρις *Inscr.*(*JHS* 4 p.402); δρακονάρις Jo.Mosch.*prat.*20(M.87. 2868A).

δρᾶμα, τό, 1. *action, drama* on stage; met. τὸ δ. τοῦ βίου Clem.*str.* 7.11(p.47.8; M.9.489C); πανήγυριν τὸν βίον...ἡμᾶς δὲ τὸ δ. τῆς ἀληθείας τὴν δικαιοσύνην ἥκειν ὡς εἰς θέατρον ἐπιδειξομένους Meth. *symp.*8.1(p.81.11; M.18.140A); τῷ μεγάλῳ τοῦ κόσμου δ. Synes. *provid.*13(p.94.4; M.66.1241D); **2.** *made-up story, plot*, Ath.*apol.sec.* 65(p.144.17; M.25.365C); Gr.Naz.*or.*21.15(M.35.1097B); Chrys. *hom. 33.3 in 1Cor.*(10.302D); **3.** *tragic event*, Cels.ap.Or.*Cels.*2.55(p.178. 20; M.11.884B); *A.Thom.*A 100(p.212.20); of a martyrdom, Eus. *m.P.*5(p.918.31); Gr.Naz.*or.*21.14(M.35.1096C); **4.** *spectacular crime* ᾧ ἀναξίου δ. Const.ap.Gel.Cyz.*h.e.*2.7.31(M.85.1240A); Thdt.*h.e.* 2.8.57(3.849); **5.** *crime story* τὸ ἀνιαρὸν...δ. τῆς τὸν υἱὸν...καταφαγούσης συνέγραψε id.*Is.*5:13(p.26.15; 2.201); hence *crime*, Tim.CP *haer.*(M.86.21A); **6.** *fantasy, fable*, of heret. doctrines ἀτοπίαις καὶ δ. χρήσιμα Const.ap.Eus.*v.C.*3.64(p.111.26; M.20.1140C); **7.** any *tale, story*, Chrys.*hom.22.5 in 1Cor.*(10.198C); of Nathan's parable, Thdt.*qu.24 in 2Reg.*(1.425); id.*Is.*3:9(p.19.5; 2.192).

δραματουργ-έω, 1. *represent* on stage, *act*, met. οὐ κατὰ φαντασίαν κατὰ τοὺς τῶν αἱρετικῶν παῖδας ἐδραματούργησεν Ἰησοῦς τὴν ἔνσαρκον αὐτοῦ παρουσίαν Or.*hom.1 in Lc.*(p.7.8); **2.** *invent, devise, fabricate*, Const.ap.Gel.Cyz.*h.e.*3.18.7; CSard.*ep.Alex.*ap.Ath.*apol. sec.*37(p.115.29; M.25.312C); τούτου χάριν εἰρηκέναι τοὺς ἀγγέλους ~εῖ ὁ...γόης Epiph.*haer.*23.1(p.248.18; M.41.300A); ~εῖ...ἄλλην δραματουργίαν ὁ...μιμολόγος *ib.*24.3(p.260.4; 312B); *ib.*32.7(p.447.8; 553B); *ib.*33.8(p.458.30; 569C); Men.*exc.Rom.*19(p.219.20; M.113. 924D); **3.** *devise* a criminal act Ἰουδαῖοι ταῦτα ἐδραματούργουν κατὰ τοῦ δεσπότου Paul.Em.*hom.*2(p.14.9; M.77.1444A); Socr.*h.e.*5.16.4 (M.67.604C); Philost.*h.e.*4.10(p.63.4; M.65.524A); **4.** *stage, enact* αὕτη ζωή, ἡ ἀπ' ἀνθρωπίνων χειρῶν ~ουμένη Meth.*res.*2.15(p.362. 21; M.18.312A); of Christ's human experiences ἃ ~εῖται...ὑπὲρ ἡμῶν Gr.Naz.*or.*30.6(p.115.16; M.36.109B); Gr.Nyss.*ep.*7(M.46. 1036C); Max.*ambig.*(M.91.1124B).

δραματούργημα, τό, 1. *plot* of play; met., *plot, scheming* τῶν περὶ Εὐσέβιον...τὸ δ. Ath.*ep.encycl.*6(p.175.18; M.25.236B); Diod. *fat.*(M.103.873B); Mac.Mgn.*apocr.*2.21(p.43.14); Cyr.*Jo.*5.4(4.520A); Jo.D.*hom.*11.14(M.96.777B); **2.** *invention, fabrication*, Epiph.*haer.* 27.8(p.313.1; M.41.377C); *ib.*31.36(p.437.28; 541B).

δραματουργία, ἡ, 1. *story, drama*, Eus.*h.e.*1.8.4(M.20.101B); id. *m.P.*11(p.939.5; M.20.1505A); id.*qu.Steph.*7.2(M.22.905D); Gr.Naz. *or.*45.25(M.36.657C); **2.** *fable, fictitious tale*, Epiph.*haer.*24.3(p.260.4; M.41.312B); *ib.*26.3(p.278.18; 336B); Thphn.*chron.*p.136(M.108. 373A); **3.** *play-acting*, Epiph.*haer.*44.5(p.197.17; M.41.829C); **4.** *device, machination* δαίμονες...ποικίλαις...δ. τὰς γνώμας...παρατρέπουσι Tat.*orat.*16(p.17.20; M.6.840C); *A.Jo.*74(p.187.8); Epiph. *haer.*73.24(p.297.10; M.42.448B); Nil.*epp.*2.167(M.79.280C).

δραματουργός, 1. *dramatic*, ‡Just.*or.Gr.*3(M.6.236B); **2.** as subst., *schemer, deviser* διάβολος...τῶν ἐχθίστων ὁ δ. αὐτός ἐστιν ἁπάντων Eust.*engast.*14(p.39.8; M.18.644B).

δραπετεία, ἡ, 1. *running away, escape*, ‡Caes.Naz.*dial.*112(M.38. 992); **2.** *expulsion*; of demons, *ib.*43(912).

δραπετεύω, 1. *run away, be an absconder*; met. πλοῦτον τὸν ἀεὶ μένοντα καὶ μηδέποτε δ. Chrys.*hom.33.3 in Jo.*(8.194E); of a disease disappearing, Isid.Pel.*epp.*3.129(M.78.829B); of the ebbing sea, Bas.Sel.*or.*1.2(M.85.32B); **2.** *flee* to, *escape as a fugitive slave* to, met. οὐκ ἐδραπέτευσας πρὸς τὴν ἁμαρτίαν; Gr.Nyss.*or.dom.*5(p.112. 13; M.44.1189D); Cyr.*Jo.*1.4(4.37C).

δραπέτης, ὁ, *runaway slave*; of Devil, Bas.*renunt.*10(2.211C; M. 31.648B); of fallen man δ. τοῦ κατὰ φύσιν δεσπότου Gr.Nyss.*or. dom.*5(p.98.13; M.44.1181B); of Jewish nation ὥσπερ...δ. ... πανταχοῦ διεσπάρησαν Isid.Pel.*epp.*3.128(M.78.829A); met. δ. ἐστὶν ὁ πλοῦτος Chrys.*hom.2.3 in Ps.48*:17(5.522B).

***δραπετοδούλως,** *like runaway slaves*, ‡Epiph.*hom.*2(M.43.457B).

***δραπετοποιός,** *causing desertion*, Chrys.*hom.2.3 in Ps.48*:17 (5.522B).

***δραπετρία, ἡ,** *runaway slave*, Chrys.*hom.15.3 in Eph.*(11.113B); met., of unveiled woman δ. τινὰ τὴν κεφαλὴν ἀποδείκνυσι καὶ φυγάδα τῆς δοθείσης αὐτῇ...ἐξουσίας id.ap.*cat.1Cor.*11:6(p.209.33).

δράσσ-ω, A. act.; *lay hold on, seize*, Eus.Al.*serm.*5(M.86.348B); met. ἀναγκαῖον ἁγιάζεσθαι τῷ αἵματι ~οντας καὶ ἐγγίζειν θεῷ γλιχομένους Cyr.*glaph.Ex.*3(1.331C).

B. med.; **1.** *lay hold on, seize* εἴ τις...~εται γυναῖκα *Poen.App.* 2.2; Thphn.*chron.*p.318(M.108.771A); **2.** *attain to* δραξάμενοι τῶν ὅρων τῆς ζωῆς Clem.*paed.*1.6(p.106.2, v.l. ἀρξάμενοι M.2.281B); **3.** *grasp, take to oneself*; met. μετὰ τοῦ δράξασθαι τῆς ἀληθείας ἐπὶ τοὺς τύπους κατεπέσετε Chrys.*comm.in Gal.*3:3(10.697A); βουλῆς ἀνωμάλου δραξάμενος ‡Jo.D.*Artem.*13(M.96.1264B); **4.** *seize on*; **a.** met., words or ideas (δράζωνται, prob. f.l. for δράξ-), Didym. *Trin.*1.9(M.39.281C); **b.** *take advantage of* δραξάμενοι...οἱ γραμματεῖς τῆς τοῦ σωτῆρος ἀπουσίας Vict.*Mc.*9:16(p.359.11); Men.*exc. Rom.*19(p.215.14; M.113.917B); Marc.Diac.*v.Porph.*64; hence **c.** *profit by*, *ib.*21.

δραστήριος, 1. *active* opp. passive δισσοῦ αἰτίου κατ' αὐτοὺς [sc. Stoics] ὄντος, τοῦ μὲν δ. καὶ καταρχομένου, καθὸ ἡ πρόνοια, τοῦ δὲ πάσχοντος..., καθὸ ἡ ὕλη Athenag.*leg.*19.2(M.6.929A); 'μορφὴν δούλου λαβεῖν' εἴρηται, οὐ μόνον τὴν σάρκα...ἀλλὰ καὶ τὴν οὐσίαν ἐκ τοῦ ὑποκειμένου, δούλη δὲ ἡ οὐσία, ὡς ἂν παθητὴ καὶ ὑποκειμένη τῇ δ....αἰτίᾳ Clem.*exc.Thdot.*19(p.113.13; M.9.668B); opp. contemplative τοῦ διορατικοῦ τῆς ἀληθείας συγκεκραμένου πρὸς τὸ δ. Gr.Nyss.*hom.13 in Cant.*(M.44.1057B); cf.Or.*comm.in Mt.*17.16(p.633.2; M.13.1529A); **2.** *effective* δ. μὲν ἡ δημιουργική Clem.*prot.*4(p.45.5; M.8.156B); δ. ὄντος τοῦ λόγου Or.*Jo.*13.59(p.291.17; M.14.513A); τὴν δ. καὶ προνοητικὴν αὐτοῦ χεῖρα id.*fr.50 in Jo.*(p.525.17); Isid.Pel.*epp.*3.34(M. 78.753C); Dion.Ar.*c.h.*15.2(M.3.329B); theol. οὐ προφορικὸς λόγος ἐν τῷ θεῷ, ἀλλὰ ζῶν καὶ ὑφεστηκώς, καὶ τῶν ὅλων δ. Didym.(‡Bas.) *Eun.*5(1.297C; M.29.713B).

δράστης, ὁ, 1. *fugitive, runaway*, *Orac.Sib.*4.119(conj. for δράτης, ἀστήρ); **2.** as adj., *violent*, *Apophth.Patr.*(M.65.148A).

δραστικός, *powerful, active, efficacious*, Tat.*orat.*16(p.17.13,15; M.6.840B); ἡ τούτου δραστικωτέρα αἰώνιος ζωή Iren.*haer.*5.3.3 (M.7.1132A); μυστηρίοις δ. Clem.*str.*2.20(p.179.17; M.8.1068A); *ib.* 6.16(p.508.20; M.9.380B); δ. ... ἀπόδειξιν Isid.Pel.*epp.*5.375(M.78. 1552A); Jo.D.*f.o.*3.15(M.94.1048A); Thphn.*chron.*p.331(M.108.800A); opp. contemplative δ. τῆς ψυχῆς δύναμιν, ἔτι δὲ...καὶ τὴν θεωρητικὴν Or.*Jo.*28.10(9; p.400.20; M.14.700C); id.ap.*cat.Mt.*22:13(p.180.14) for δραστήριος, id.*comm. in Mt.*17.16(p.633.2; M.13.1529A); of Logos ὁ ...τοῦ σύμπαντος κόσμου δημιουργικός, δ. δυνάμει τοῖς πᾶσιν ἐπιπαρών Eus.*d.e.*4.5(p.157.19; M.22.261D); in Marcellus' theology πρὸ γὰρ τοῦ τὸν κόσμον εἶναι ἦν ὁ λόγος ἐν τῷ πατρί. ὅτε δὲ ὁ παντοκράτωρ... πάντα...ποιῆσαι προέθετο, ἐνεργείας ἡ τοῦ κόσμου γένεσις ἐδεῖτο δραστικῆς· καὶ...τότε ὁ λόγος προελθὼν ἐγίνετο...ποιητής Marcell.*fr.* 54 ap.Eus.*e.th.*3.3(p.153.14; M.24.996A); προῆλθεν ὁ λόγος δ. ἐνεργείᾳ id.*fr.*108 ap.eund.*Marcell.*2.2(p.42.23; M.24.796A); Eus.*ib.*2.4(p.57. 13; 821A) cit. s. σάρξ; μετὰ τὴν σιγὴν...προελθεῖν τὸν λόγον...ἐν ἀρχῇ τῆς κοσμοποιΐας δ. ἐνεργείᾳ id.*e.th.*2.9(p.109.7; 917B); *ib.*2.14(p.118. 3; 933A); *ib.*3.3(p.157.5; 1001B).

δραχμή, ἡ, *drachma*; exeg. Lc.15:8, cf. *si adhibeas tibi illuminationem Spiritus sancti...invenies intra te drachmam. intra te namque collocata est imago regis coelestis*, Or.*hom.13.4 in Gen.*(p.119.14; M.12.234C); *sapientia est quae drachmam perditam quaesivit... Judaei autem...quaerunt de Christo...et non inveniunt*, id.*comm.in Rom.*8.6(M.13.1174C); δ. νόμισμα...ἐστί, χαρακτῆρας ἔχον βασιλικούς. ὅτι δὲ πεσόντες...εὑρήμεθα παρὰ Χριστοῦ καὶ πρὸς αὐτὸν μεμορφώμεθα ...πῶς ἂν ἐνδοιάσειέ τις; Cyr.*Lc.*15:8(M.72.800C); τὴν βασιλικὴν ἀνασώσασθαι εἰκόνα, ὑπὸ τὴν...τῶν παθῶν κόπρον γεγενημένην παραγεγονέναι, διὰ τῆς δ. παραβολικῶς παρῃνίξατο Max.*ep.*11(M.91. 453C); id.*ambig.*(M.91.1277A).

δράω, *do* or *perform rites*, pass. ptcpl., of pagan mysteries παρεδρεύουσιν...τοῖς...Μητρὸς μεγάλης μυστηρίοις, μάλιστα καθορᾶν νομίζοντες διὰ τῶν δρωμένων ἐκεῖ τὸ ὅλον μυστήριον Hipp.*haer.*5.9 (p.100.13; M.16.3155B); of Jewish ceremonies at festivals, Jo. Philop.*pasch.*(p.211.8); met., of spiritual sacrifice ὁ γνωστικὸς παρὰ ὅλον εὔχεται τὸν βίον...ἤδη τὴν τελείωσιν ἀπειληφὼς τοῦ κατὰ ἀγάπην δρωμένου Clem.*str.*7.7(p.30.33; M.9.456C); in fanciful derivation of ἄνθρωπος: παρὰ τὸ δρῶ τὸ βλέπω ἢ πράττω, ἄδρωπος καὶ ἄνθρωπος Melet.*nat.hom.*synops.(M.64.1084B).

δρεπανηφόρος, *bearing a sickle*; of prophet Zechariah (cf. Zach.5:1–2), Didym.*Trin.*2.10(M.39.649A).

***δρεπανιστής, ὁ,** *reaper*, ‡Chrys.*decoll.*2(8.4A); ‡Chrys.*hom.in Lc.* 8:5(10.829A).

δριμυγμός, ὁ, *bitterness of spirit*, Nil.*epp.*1.234(M.79.169A).

δριμύσσ-ω, 1. *cause to smart*; **a.** lit., Gr.Nyss.*or.catech.*8(p.48.7; M.45.37A); pass. intrans., *smart*, id.*ep.*2(M.46.1012B); Ast.Soph. *hom.5 in Ps.5*(M.40.441A); **b.** met. ~ει τὰ τοῦ πατρὸς σπλάγχνα ἡ φωνὴ τοῦ παιδός Gr.Nyss.*deit.*(M.46.569D); ‡Chrys.*hom.*7(13.217D); λίθος ὁ πράσινος...διὰ τῆς καυστικῆς τοῦ...πράσου φύσεως, τὸν καταπιόντα αὐτὸν ἐδρίμυξε θάνατον Procl.CP *or.*6.1(M.65.721D); Max.*qu. Thal.*54(M.90.509B); pass. intrans. τοῦ στόματος τῆς κοιλίας ~ομένου Gr.Nyss.*hom.opif.*12.4(M.44.157D); Pall.*v.Chrys.*7(p.40.15; M.47.24); **2.** *exasperate, annoy*, Amph.*hom.*2.5(M.39.52C); ἐδρίμυττε τοὺς ἀρχιερεῖς...ἀκούειν ἐκ τῶν ὄχλων· 'βασιλεὺς τοῦ Ἰσραήλ' Procl.CP *or.*9.3(M.65.773D); pass. μὴ ὧδε ~ου ‡Chrys.*hom.*13(13.251E); Tim. Ant.*caec.*10(M.28.1016D); Domit.*Jo.Bapt.*18(p.325); Anast.S.*hod.*8 (M.89.136A).

δρομαίως, *at a run, quickly*, *T.Sal.*1.9(v.l. δρομαῖος M.122.1317C); *A.Jo.*49(p.175.18); Epiph.*haer.*66.8(p.28.24; M.42.41A); Chrys.*pan. Rom.*2.3(2.620C); Leont.N.*v.Jo.Eleem.*27(p.56.13).

***δρομοκάμηλος, ἡ,** *dromedary*, †Polyb.*v.Epiph.*67(M.41.112C).

δρόμος, ὁ, 1. *course, race*; met. ἐπὶ τὸν τῆς πίστεως βέβαιον δ. κατήντησαν *1Clem.*6.2; προσθεῖναι τῷ δ. σου Ign.*Polyc.*1.2; τὸν τῆς εὐσεβείας...δράμετε δ. Cyr.H.*catech.*1.1; εἰς τὸν ὑπὲρ παρθενίας δ. ... ἀσκουμένους †Bas.Anc.*virg.*9(M.30.688C); τοῖς τὸν ἐνόπλιον...κατὰ τῶν ἐχθρῶν τῆς ἀληθείας τρέχουσι δ. Gr.Nyss.*Eun.*7(2 p.172.23;

M.45.764B); *M.Thdot.1* 21(p.74.10); *ib.1* 31(p.80.31); Diad.*perf.*79 (p.100.24); of monastic life, Jo.Clim.*past.*12(M.88.1189A); **2.** *order* of worship, Const.ap.Eus.*v.C.*3.18(p.85.16; M.20.1076A); **3.** *concourse*, Ath.*apol.sec.*7(p.93.29; M.25.261B); **4.** δημόσιος δ. *cursus publicus*, made available by emperor to bishops, Eus.*v.C.*3.6(p.79.30; M.20.1060B); *ib.*4.43(p.135.16; 1193A); Ath.*h.Ar.*20(p.193.2; M.25.716B); Νικόβουλον...τῇ τοῦ δ. φροντίδι καὶ τῇ τῆς μονῆς προεδρείᾳ στενοχωρούμενον Gr.Naz.*ep.*126(M.37.221A); Marc.Diac.*v.Porph.*54; περιεῖλε [sc. Juln. Imp.]...τὸν δημόσιον τῶν χρειῶν δ., οἷον ἡμιόνων, βοῶν, καὶ ὄνων· μόνον δὲ τῶν ἵππων ταῖς δημοσίαις χρείαις συνεχώρησεν ὑπουργεῖν Socr.*h.e.*3.1.52(M.67.377B).

***δρομωνάριος,** δ. κάμηλος, *dromedary*, Jo.Mal.*chron.*12 p.300(M.97.453B).

δροσίζ-ω, *bedew, moisten, refresh* τὴν ἐν Συρίᾳ ἐκκλησίαν διὰ τῆς ἐκκλησίας ὑμῶν δροσισθῆναι Ign.*Magn.*14; ὑπὸ τῆς οὐρανίου πηγῆς τοῦ ὕδατος τῆς ζωῆς ~όμενος *Ep.Lugd.*ap.Eus.*h.e.*5.1.22(M.20.417A); τῇ χάριτι ~όμενοι τοῦ θεοῦ Clem.*paed.*2.10(p.219.27; M.8.521B); id.*str.*2.20(p.170.9; M.8.1048C); Hipp.*Dan.*2.31.3(M.10.680A); ἀσθένεια πυρετοὺς ψυχῶν ἀποσοβοῦσα, καὶ ἱδρῶτας βαπτίσματος ~ουσα †Hipp.*Laz.*(p.216.36; M.62.776); Δανιὴλ...τὸν μὲν υἱὸν εἶδε ~οντα τὴν κάμινον Ath.*ep.Serap.*2.6(M.26.617B); Gr.Naz.*or.*5.40 (M.35.716B); ‡Epiph.*hom.*3(M.43.473C); Isid.Pel.*epp.*2.151(M.78.605D); κάμινος πυρὸς ~ει τοὺς τρεῖς παῖδας †Jo.D.*creat.*6(p.146).

δροσισμός, ὁ, *bedewing* ὅρος...ἡ...θεοτόκος. ἐπεὶ ὥσπερ οἱ... φλεγόμενοι...δροσίζονται ὑπὸ τὴν σκιὰν τῶν δένδρων τοῦ ὄρους... τοιούτῳ τρόπῳ...ἡ...παρθένος, τῷ δ. τῆς κυοφορίας...τὰς ψυχὰς τῶν ἀνθρώπων καταφλεγομένας...ἀνεζώωσε ‡Ath.*qu.script.*85(M.28.748C).

δροσοβόλος, *shedding dew* εὖξαι τῇ θείᾳ σκεπασθῆναι δ. νεφέλῃ Jo. Carp.*cap.*60(M.85.1849).

δροσοειδής, *like dew, dewy* νεφέλη δ. ‡Pall.*h.mon.*21.8(p.81.8; M.34.1171D).

δροσοειδῶς, *like dew*, Bas.*hex.*8.4(1.74C; M.29.173B).

***δροσόμματος,** *dewy* νεφέλης...ἐξ ἧς ὥσπερ τινὲς δ. σταγόνες οἱ... μαθηταὶ τῷ τῆς παρθένου καθορμισθέντες...ἐπέστησαν οἴκῳ [sc. at Dormition] Germ.CP *or.*8(M.98.365B).

***δροσ-όομαι,** *be filled with dew*, Or.*exp.in Pr.*3:19(M.17.168D); *be bedewed* τριττοὶ θεουδεῖς ἐμπύρως ~ούμενοι Jo.D.*carm.theoph.*106 (p.212; M.96.832A).

***δροσοποιός,** *making dew*, hence met., *refreshing*, ‡Ath.*haer.*4 (M.28.509B).

δρόσος, ἡ, *dew*; **1.** lit.; exeg. Jud.6:38ff., v. πόκος; **2.** met.; **a.** of cooling moisture ἐγένετο τὸ μέσον τῆς καμίνου δ. λεπτή Hipp.*Dan.* 2.32.9; Or.*or.*16.3(p.337.24; M.11.469C); Chrys.*hom.4.11 in Mt.* (7.68B); **b.** of comfort and refreshment θησαυρὸν...δυνάμει θεοῦ πατρὸς καὶ αἵματι θεοῦ παιδὸς καὶ δ. πνεύματος ἁγίου περιτετειχισμένον Clem.*q.d.s.*34(p.182.22; M.9.640C); Or.*mart.*27(p.23.22; M.11.596B); *ib.*33(p.28.19; 604C); τῆς ἀρετῆς τὸ κάλλιστον...χωρίον, ἔνθα... πάντα τῶν ἀμβροσίων πεπλήρωται δ. Meth.*symp.*8.11(p.93.19; M.18.153D); ref. double effect of river of fire τοῦτο μὲν γὰρ φλὸξ καὶ ὀδύνη, ἐκεῖνο δὲ δ. καὶ ἄνεσις Chrys.*hom.4.11 in Mt.*(7.69B).

***δροσοσυρίζω,** *distil dew*, ‡Meth.*Sym.et Ann.*7(M.18.364C).

***δρουγγάριος, ὁ,** *commander of a* δροῦγγος, Heracl.*ep.*ap.*Chron. Pasch.*p.400(M.92.1021B).

***δροῦγγος, ὁ,** (Lat. *drungus*) *troop* (= μοῖρα third part of a *turma*), *M.Areth.*(p.53); of a band of monks, Chrys.*ep.*14.2(3.596C).

δρυάς, ἡ, *tree*, Meth.*res.*2.9(p.347.27; M.18.309A).

***δρυμόθεν,** *from the coppice*, Gr.Naz.*carm.*2.1.1.191(M.37.984A).

[*]**δρυμός, τό,** *thicket*, met. τῷ δρυμεῖ τῶν κολάσεων τὴν προθυμίαν ἐκκλύσαντες Andr.Cr.*Geo.*7(p.xxiD).

***δρυμοτομική, ἡ,** *woodman's craft*, Chrys.*hom.52.4 in Mt.*(7.534C, v.l. δρυοτομικήν).

δρυμών, ὁ, *thicket*; met., ref. Christ ὁ ἐν τῷ δ. τῆς φύσεως ἡμῶν... ἀναβλαστήσας Gr.Nyss.*hom.4 in Cant.*(M.44.849B).

δρυοτομικός, *suitable for the woodcutter*, Pall.*v.Chrys.*1(p.4.1; M.47.5).

δρύφακτος, ὁ, 1. plur., *cancelli*, barrier separating sanctuary (reserved for clergy) from rest of church, Soz.*h.e.*7.25.9(M.67.1496B); **2.** *balcony*, Chrys.*hom.7.4 in Ac.*(9.62A); id.*hom.12.6 in 1Cor.* (10.106B); Thdt.*h.e.*3.14.8(3.928); **3.** *structure of lattice-work*, id. *qu.60 in Ex.*(1.165).

***δυαρχία, ἡ,** *existence of two principles*, opp. μοναρχία: ἐξ αὐτῆς δὲ τῆς ἀρχῆς ἐστι φύσει υἱὸς ὁ λόγος, οὐχ ὡς ἀρχὴ ἑτέρα καθ' ἑαυτὸν ὑφεστώς...ἵνα μὴ τῇ ἑτερότητι δ. καὶ πολυαρχία γένηται ‡Ath.*Ar.*4.1 (p.44.7; M.26.468B).

δυάς, ἡ, A. *duality*; **1.** Pythagorean ἀρχὴν τῶν ὅλων ἀγέννητον... τὴν μονάδα, γεννητὴν δὲ τὴν δ. καὶ πάντας τοὺς ἄλλους ἀριθμούς. καὶ τῆς μὲν δ. πατέρα...εἶναι τὴν μονάδα, πάντων δὲ τῶν γεγεννημένων μητέρα δ., γεννητὴν γεννητῶν...καὶ ἔστιν ἡ μὲν μονὰς ἄρρεν καὶ πρώτη, ἡ δὲ δ. θῆλυ Hipp.*haer.*6.23(p.149.27; M.16.3227B); Anat. Laod.*decad.*(p.30f.); **2.** Marcosian ἐκ μονάδος καὶ δ. ... τὰ ὅλα συνεστηκέναι· καὶ ἀπὸ μονάδος ἕως τῶν τεσσάρων ἀριθμοῦντες οὕτω γεννῶσι τὴν δεκάδα...πάλιν δ' αὖ ἡ δ. ἀπ' αὐτῆς προελθοῦσα ἕως τοῦ ἐπισήμου, οἷον δύο καὶ τέσσαρες καὶ ἕξ, τὴν δωδεκάδα ἐπέδειξε Iren. *haer.*1.16.1(M.7.628B)ap.Epiph.*haer.*34.12(p.23.22,25); **3.** Valentinian προέβαλεν...ὁ πατὴρ...νοῦν καὶ ἀλήθειαν, τουτέστι δ., ἥτις κυρία καὶ ἀρχὴ γέγονε καὶ μήτηρ πάντων τῶν ἐντὸς πληρώματος... αἰώνων Hipp.*haer.*6.29(p.156.17; M.16.3238A); as aeon in Valent. system, Val.Gn.ap.Epiph.*haer.*31.6(p.393.7; M.41.484C) cit. s. τετράς; **4.** of principles in Manicheism, Epiph.*haer.*66.62(p.99.24; M.42.124B); **5.** Trin.; **a.** of Father and Son; **i.** orthodox, Or.*dial.* 4(p.126.16) cit. s. ἑνάς; Gr.Naz.*or.*29.2(p.75.7; M.36.76B) cit. s. μονάς; ref. Jo.10:27–30 δείξας τὴν τῶν προσώπων δ., ἐκήρυξε τὴν τῆς φύσεως ταυτότητα Thdt.*Trin.*(M.75.1165D); τὴν δ. τῶν προσώπων, ἀλλὰ καὶ τὸ ὁμότιμον τῶν προσώπων id.*Zach.*2:9(2.1606); ref. Gen. 19:24 δυάδα κυρίων ἡμῖν ἐπέδειξε id.*affect.*2(p.55.3; 4.746); esp. in directly anti-Sabellian polemic, ref. Jo.10:30 ἵνα μή τις τὸν αὐτὸν εἶναι πατέρα καὶ υἱὸν ὑπολάβῃ, μόνοις ὀνόμασι διαστελλομένους εἰς δ. ...ἐπιφέρει τὸ 'ἐγὼ ἐν τῷ πατρὶ καὶ ὁ πατὴρ ἐν ἐμοί' Cyr.*thes.*12(5[1].109E); ἐν ἰδιαζούσαις ὑποστάσεσι δ. ... οὐ μόνοις ὀνόμασι διαστελλομένην *ib.*23(225C); τῇ δ. τῶν προσώπων ἐξήλασε τοῦ Σαβελλίου τὴν σύγχυσιν Thdt.*Heb.*1:8(3.553); **ii.** Arian, Ar.*Thal.fr.*2.20ap.Ath.*syn.* 15(p.243.1; M.26.708A) cit. s. μονάς; δ. οὐσίας εἰσάγει, μηδετέραν τῆς ἑτέρας πατέρα τυγχάνουσαν ‡Ath.*Ar.*4.3(p.47.10; M.26.472B); Μαρκίων...φῶ κοινὸν μὲν πρὸς τὸ ὑμέτερον φρόνημα τὴν θεῶν ἡ δ., καὶ τὸ παρηλλάχθαι κατὰ τὴν φύσιν ἑκάτερον πρὸς τὸ ἕτερον οἴεσθαι Gr.Nyss. *Eun.*11(2 p.253.9; M.45.860B); **b.** ref. denial of divinity of H. Ghost τριάς ἐστιν, ἢ δ.; εἰ μὲν οὖν δ. ἐστι, συναριθμείσθω παρ' ὑμῶν τοῖς κτίσμασι τὸ πνεῦμα Ath.*ep.Serap.*1.29(M.26.596C); *ib.*1.30(597B); εἰ δὲ κτίσμα ἐστί, τὰ δὲ κτίσματα ἐξ οὐκ ὄντων ἐστί, δῆλον, ὅτι ἦν ὅτε οὐκ ἦν τριάς, ἀλλὰ δ. *ib.*3.7(636B); **6.** Christol., of duality of natures πῶς οὖν ἀπρόσφορον ἔσται ἐπὶ τῶν συντεθεισῶν φύσεων καὶ τὸ ἓν τέλειον πληρουσῶν δ. λέγειν, μονάδα δὲ ὑποστάσεως; Leont.H.*monoph.* 31(M.86.1788D); ταὐτόν ἐστι...τὸ λέγειν μίαν φύσιν τοῦ θεοῦ σεσαρκωμένην, καὶ δ. φύσεων Χριστοῦ καθ' ὑπόστασιν μίαν ἡνωμένην *ib.* (1805B); acc. monophysites ἀναθεματίζοντες τοὺς διαιροῦντας τὸν ἕνα Χριστὸν μετὰ τὴν ἕνωσιν τῇ δ. τῶν φύσεων Sev.Ant.*ib.*(M.86.1848C); acc. Antiochenes and Nestorians ref. Mt.19:6, Thdr. Mops.*fr.inc.*8(p.299.14; M.66.981A); δ. Χριστῶν Cyr.*inc.unigen.*(5[1].690B); τοῖς...εἰς υἱῶν δ. τὸ τῆς οἰκονομίας διασπᾶν ἐπιχειροῦσι μυστήριον *Symb.Chalc.*(p.129.17; H.2.456B); in monophysite argument δύο δὲ λέγειν παραιτοῦμαι φύσεις, ἵνα μὴ τῇ τῶν υἱῶν περιπέσω δ. Thdt.*eran.*2(4.109); **7.** of matter and form, Eus.*l.C.*6(p.207.10; M.20.1341B); τριάδα τελείαν ἐκ τελείων τριῶν, μονάδος μὲν κινηθείσης διὰ τὸ πλούσιον, δ. δὲ ὑπερβαθείσης (ὑπὲρ γὰρ τὴν ὕλην καὶ τὸ εἶδος), ἐξ ὧν τὰ σώματα, τριάδος δὲ ὁρισθείσης διὰ τὸ τέλειον Gr.Naz.*or.*23.8 (M.35.1160C); δ. ἐστι...πᾶσα τῶν μετὰ θεὸν ὄντων ἡ σύμπηξις, οἷον τὰ μὲν αἰσθητὰ πάντα ὡς ἐξ ὕλης συνεστηκότα καὶ εἴδους ἐστὶ δ., τὰ δὲ νοητά, ὡσαύτως ἐξουσίας καὶ τοῦ εἰδοποιοῦντος αὐτὰ οὐσιωδῶς συμβεβηκότος Max.*ambig.*(M.91.1400C); **8.** of body and mind τὴν ὑλικὴν δ. Gr.Naz.*or.*21.2(M.35.1084C); ‡Nil.*fr.pasch.*1(M.79.1493D).

B. *pair*; **1.** in gen. ἡ δ. τῶν ὀφθαλμῶν Gr.Nyss.*hom.7 in Cant.* (M.44.920D); of Arius and Macedonius as ὀλέθριος δ. Didym.*Trin.* 2.8(M.39.620C); Cyr.*ador.*14(1.486D); **2.** of syzygies in Valentinian system, Iren.*haer.*1.11.1(M.7.561A); Epiph.*haer.*31.2(p.384.26; M.41.476B).

δύν-αμαι, *be able, have power*;

A. in gen., *LS*; freq. in perf. ὡς μὴ δεδυνημένοι λέγειν πρὸς αὐτόν Or.*Cels.*5.53(p.56.25; M.11.1264A); id.*comm.in Mt.*11.5(p.41.21; M.13.916B); Chrys.*fem.reg.*1(1.249A) etc.; **c.** ἵνα: εἰ δύνασαι ἵνα ὡς ἐξέρχῃ οὕτως καὶ εἰσέρχῃ, ὕπαγε *Apophth.Patr.*(M.65.212C).

B. various meanings defined οὐ τῶν καθ' ἕνα τρόπον λεγομένων, τὸ ~ασθαι, ἢ μὴ ~ασθαι· πολύσημον δέ. τὸ μὲν γάρ τι λέγεται κατὰ δυνάμεως ἔλλειψιν, καὶ ποτέ, καὶ πρός τι, ὡς τὸ μὴ ~ασθαι τὸ παιδίον ἀθλεῖν...ἀθλήσει γὰρ ἴσως ποτέ...τὸ δέ, ὡς ἐπὶ πλεῖστον, ὡς τό· 'οὐ ~αται πόλις κρυβῆναι ἐπ' ἄνω ὄρους κειμένη'..., τὸ δέ, ὡς οὐκ εὔλογον· 'οὐ ~ανται οἱ υἱοὶ τοῦ νυμφῶνος νηστεύειν',...τὸ δέ, ὡς ἀβούλητον, ὡς τό, 'μὴ ~ασθαι ἐκεῖ σημεῖα ποιῆσαι'. ... ἔστι δέ τι καὶ τοιοῦτον ἐν τοῖς λεγομένοις, ὃ τῇ φύσει μὲν ἀδύνατον, θεῷ δὲ δυνατὸν βουληθέντι...τούτων δὲ πάντων ἐκτός, τὸ παντελῶς ἀδύνατον καὶ ἀνεπίδεκτον...ὡς...πονηρὸν εἶναι θεὸν ἢ μὴ εἶναι...ἢ τὸ μὴ ὂν εἶναι Gr. Naz.*or.*30.10(p.121.9ff.; M.36.113C).

C. of what is possible because consistent with, or result of, character, nature, law, propriety, etc. πῶς ~αμαι βλασφημῆσαι τὸν βασιλέα μου; *M.Polyc.*9.3; τίς εὑρεθήσεται Παῦλος ὁ ~άμενος λέγειν· 'κάλλιον γὰρ ἀναλῦσαι καὶ σὺν Χριστῷ εἶναι'; ἐγὼ δὲ οὐ ~αμαι τοῦτο λέγειν Or.*hom.20.3 in Jer.*(p.181.8; M.13.505C); οὐ ~αται γὰρ ...κόσμος...ὑμέας ἐχθαίρειν Nonn.*par.Jo.*7:7(M.43.805B); of Christ ὁ υἱὸς τοῦ θεοῦ οὐκ ἠδύνατο παθεῖν εἰ μὴ δι' ἡμᾶς *Barn.*7.2; discussion of Mc.6:5 οὐ γὰρ εἶπεν, οὐκ ἤθελεν, ἀλλ', 'οὐκ ἠδύνατο', ὡς ἐρχομένης μὲν ἐπὶ τὴν ἐνεργοῦσαν δύναμιν συμπράξεως ὑπὸ πίστεως ἐκείνου εἰς ὃν ἐνήργει ἡ δύναμις...ἀκριβῶς δὲ δοκοῦσί μοι ὁ Ματθαῖος καὶ ὁ Μάρκος τὸ ὑπερέχον τῆς θείας δυνάμεως παραστῆσαι βουλόμενοι ὅτι καὶ ἐν ἀπιστίᾳ ~αται, ἀλλ' οὐκ ἐπὶ πλεῖον ~αται, ὅσον ~αται ἐν πίστει..., εἰρηκέναι οὐχ ὅτι οὐκ ἐποίησε δυνάμεις...ἀλλ' οὐκ ἐποίησεν... δυνάμεις πολλάς Or.*comm.in Mt.*10.19(p.25.17; M.13.884B); cf. τὸ δέ, ὡς ἀβούλητον, ὡς τὸ μὴ ~ασθαι...ποιῆσαι...οὐκ οἶδα δέ, εἰ μὴ καὶ τοῦτο τῷ εὐλόγῳ προσθετέον Gr.Naz.*or.*30.10(p.122.5; M.36.116A); τό 'οὐ ~αται ὁ υἱὸς ποιεῖν ἀφ' ἑαυτοῦ οὐδὲν...'οὐκ ἀσθενείας σημεῖον, ἀλλὰ τοῦ μὴ ἐνδέχεσθαι, ἄλλην πατρὸς καὶ ἑτέραν υἱοῦ εἶναι τὴν βούλησιν Isid.Pel.*epp.*1.353(M.78.384B); τὸ μὴ ~ασθαι πῶς εἴρηται σκοπητέον...(ref. Dt.16:5–6) τό, οὐ ~ήσῃ, ἀντὶ τοῦ, μὴ ἐξόντος, μηδὲ ἐγχωροῦντος, μηδὲ συγκεχωρημένου, μηδὲ ἐνδεχομένου τεθεικώς...τί οὖν ἐστιν, οὐ ~ήσῃ; οὐκ ἔξεστί σοι, οὐ προσάξεις, οὐ ποιήσεις...τὸ γὰρ 'οὐ ~αται ὁ υἱὸς ποιεῖν ἀφ' ἑαυτοῦ οὐδέν' οὐκ ἀσθένειαν αὐτοῦ κατηγορεῖ, ἀλλὰ...ῥώμην, ὅτι ἀνεπίδεκτός ἐστι τοῦ ἐναντίον τι τῷ πατρὶ ποιεῖν *ib.*3.335(993A,D).

D. of something possible or natural, *may, might* ἐδύνατο λέγειν Or.*Cels.*1.3(p.57.24; M.11.660A); hence εἰ ~ασαι, εἴ τις ~αται *if you (he) would, please,* id.*hom.8.1 in Jer.*(p.55.18; M.13.336B); ἐν τούτοις, εἴ τις ~αται, τηρείτω *ib.12.10*(p.96.22; 392C); hence ὁ ~άμενος *anyone who chooses* ὁ ~άμενος ἀναγινώσκειν τὸν Ἰεζεκιὴλ *ib.11.5*(p.83.10; 373C).

E. *will,* neg. *refuse* περῆσαι οὐ ~αται βροτὸς οὗτος ἐς...ἑορτήν Nonn.*par.Jo.*11:56(M.43.849B); ref. Jo.12:39 τό, 'οὐκ ἠδύναντο', κεῖται ἀντὶ τοῦ, οὐκ ἤθελον. καὶ γὰρ ἐν ἄλλοις δύναμιν τὴν προαίρεσιν νοοῦμεν Ammon.*Jo.*12:40(M.85.1477C).

F. *have efficacy, prevail* over οὐ ~αται ἡ ἑορτὴ τοῦ υἱοῦ σου πρὸς τὴν ἑορτὴν τοῦ Χριστοῦ μου *M.Ariadn.*2(p.124.2).

δύναμις, ἡ, *power;*

I. def. δ. λέγεται ἡ μὲν κατ' ἐπιτηδειότητα, ἡ δὲ καθ' ἕξιν. κατ' ἐπιτηδειότητα μέν, ὡς ὅταν εἴπωμεν τὸ παιδίον δυνάμει γραμματικὸν εἶναι, καθὸ ἔχει ἐπιτηδειότητα πρὸς τὸ γενέσθαι γραμματικόν, καθ' ἕξιν δέ, ὡς ὅταν εἴπωμεν τὸν ἠρεμοῦντα γραμματικὸν δυνάμει γραμματικὸν εἶναι...δ. πάλιν λέγεται καθ' ἕξιν, ὡς ὅταν εἴπωμεν τὸ παιδίον σπερματικόν, καθ' ὃ πέφυκεν εἶναι σπερματικὸν καὶ ἔστι δυνάμει, εἰ καὶ μήπω τῇ ἐνεργείᾳ. ... δ. λέγεται καὶ ἡ ἰσχύς. δ. λέγεται καὶ ἡ στρατιά El.*fr.*ap.*Doct.Patr.*33(p.256.18).

II. *faculty, physical power;* of blood as δ. ζωτικὴ τῆς ψυχῆς Or.*dial.*22(p.164.15).

III. *property, quality* of things; hence *virtue,* Herm.*vis.*3.8.6,7.

IV. *efficacy* ἐγνώρισα...τῆς ἡσυχίας τὴν δ. Ammonas *ep.*1(p.434.1).

V. *potentiality,* opp. ἐνέργεια *actuality,* Or.*Jo.*2.24(19; p.81.18; M.14.157A); θνητὸς μὲν κατεσκευάσθη, δυνάμενος δέ, ἐκ προκοπῆς τελειούμενος, ἀθάνατος γενέσθαι, τουτέστι δυνάμει ἀθάνατος Nemes.*nat.hom.*1(M.40.516A); ref. generation of Son τὸ ἀναθεματίζεσθαι τὸ πρὸ τοῦ γεννηθῆναι οὐκ ἦν οὐκ ἄτοπον ἐνομίσθη...ἤδη δὲ ὁ...βασιλεὺς τῷ λόγῳ κατεσκεύαζε καὶ κατὰ τὴν ἔνθεον αὐτοῦ γέννησιν τὸ πρὸ πάντων αἰώνων εἶναι αὐτόν, ἐπεὶ καὶ πρὶν ἐνεργείᾳ γεννηθῆναι δυνάμει ἦν ἐν τῷ πατρὶ ἀγεννήτως, ὄντος τοῦ πατρὸς ἀεὶ πατρὸς...δυνάμει πάντα ὄντος, ἀεί τε κατὰ τὰ αὐτὰ καὶ ὡσαύτως ἔχοντος Eus.*ep.Caes.*10(p.46.19; M.20.1544B); ἵν' ἐν μὲν τῷ φῆσαι ἐν ἀρχῇ ἦν ὁ λόγος δείξῃ δυνάμει ἐν τῷ πατρὶ εἶναι τὸν λόγον..., ἐν δὲ τῷ καὶ ὁ λόγος ἦν πρὸς τὸν θεὸν ἐνεργείᾳ πρὸς τὸν θεὸν εἶναι τὸν λόγον Marcell.*fr.*47 ap.Eus.*Marcell.*2.2(p.37.1; M.24.785C); Θεόγνιν· ὃς τὸν θεὸν καὶ πρὸ τοῦ γεννῆσαι τὸν υἱὸν πατέρα οἴεται, ἅτε δὴ τὴν δ. ἔχοντα τοῦ γεννῆσαι Philost.*h.e.*2.15(M.65.477B); δυνάμει ἐστὶν ὃ δύναται γενέσθαι...οὕτω καὶ κατ' εἰκόνα θεοῦ ἐστιν ἕκαστος δυνάμει· ἐὰν δὲ...ἐνδύσηται τὸν καινὸν ἄνθρωπον...τότε γίνεται ἐνεργείᾳ κατ' εἰκόνα τοῦ κτίσαντος Thdt.*eran.*3(4.1014).

VI. *might, power;*

A. of spiritual strength or fortitude ἡ δὲ πραότης αὐτοῦ δ. Ign.*Trall.*3.2; as a virtue τῶν παρθένων τὰ ὀνόματα...ἡ μὲν πρώτη πίστις, ἡ δὲ δευτέρα ἐγκράτεια, ἡ δὲ τρίτη δ. Herm.*sim.*9.15.2; Or.*hom.1 in Lc.*(p.12.3); Procl.CP *or.*17.3(M.65.812C); *Lit.Jac.*(p.240.21).

B. of divine power; **1.** in gen. as divine attribute σοῦ ἐστιν ἡ δ. καὶ ἡ δόξα εἰς τοὺς αἰῶνας *Did.*8.2; *ib.*9.4; *ib.*10.5; πάντα γὰρ ὁ θεός ἐστιν αὐτὸς αὑτῷ,...πνεῦμα, δ., λόγος Athenag.*leg.*16.2(M.6.920D); = δόξα: Μωσεῖ καταφανῆ ἐβούλετο γενέσθαι τὴν αὐτοῦ δ. Clem.*paed.*2.8(p.203.15; M.8.488A); εἰ δή τις νοεῖ θεόν..., νοείτω... φῶς ἀπρόσιτον, πᾶσαν δ. ἀγαθήν...συγκεκληρωμένον id.*ecl.*21(p.142.22; M.9.708B); οὐδ' ὁ θεὸς δύναται ἀδικεῖν· ἐναντίον γάρ ἐστιν αὐτοῦ τῇ θειότητι καὶ τῇ κατ' αὐτὴν πάσῃ δ. ἡ τοῦ ἀδικεῖν δ. Or.*Cels.*3.70(p.262.32; M.11.1012D); ζητεῖσθαι χρὴ...τὴν τοῦ θεοῦ δ., εἰ μεγάλη καὶ ἀξιάγαστος, ὅτε τὸ δρώμενόν ἐστιν οὐκ ἀπεοικὸς τῇ θείᾳ δόξῃ. οὐ γὰρ ὅτι πάντα δύναται, διὰ τοῦτο καὶ τῶν ἀτόπων ἐργάτην αὐτὸν ὁρᾶσθαι προσήκει Cyr.*dogm.*(p.565.11; 6².380E); αὕτη ἡ ὑπόστασις... ἐστι...δ. ... δ. διὰ τὸ μηδὲν αὐτῷ ἀντικεῖσθαι ‡Ath.*dial.Trin.*18(M.28.1144D); δ. ἐστιν ὁ θεός, ὡς πᾶσαν δ. ἐν ἑαυτῷ προέχων καὶ ὑπερέχων, καὶ ὡς πάσης δ. αἴτιος, καὶ πάντα κατὰ δ. ἄκλιτον...παράγων, καὶ ὡς αὐτοῦ τοῦ εἶναι δ. Dion.Ar.*d.n.*8.2(M.3.889C); **2.** esp. in creation θάλασσαν...ἐνέκλεισεν τῇ ἑαυτοῦ δ. *1Clem.*33.3; ὁ ἀοράτῳ δ. ... κτίσας τὸν κόσμον Herm.*vis.*1.3.4; Clem.*prot.*11(p.79.10; M.8.229A); id.*str.*6.16(p.499.16; M.9.357C); Meth.*res.*1.36(p.277.11; M.41.1101D); ὁ πατὴρ μετὰ σοφίας καὶ δ. διὰ τοῦ λόγου πάντα ποιῶν Marcell.*fr.*54 ap.Eus.*e.th.*3.3(p.153.21; M.24.996B); God is himself power, Meth.*res.*1.50(p.304.8; M.18.280B); **3.** in providence πρόνοια...τις...δ. θεϊκῆς Clem.*prot.*10(p.74.5; M.8.217B); id. *fr.*42(p.220.32; M.9.768B); διήκει...ἡ πρόνοια τοῦ θεοῦ διὰ πάντων, ἀλλ' οὐχ ὡς τὸ τῶν Στοϊκῶν πνεῦμα...οὐχ ὡς σῶμα δὲ περιέχον περιέχει...ἀλλ' ὡς δ. θεία καὶ περιειληφυῖα τὰ περιεχόμενα Or.*Cels.*6.71(p.141.14; M.11.1405C); id.*princ.*1.4.3(p.65.12); Eus.*e.th.*3.3(p.146.20; M.24.984C); **4.** in redemption καιρός, ὃν...προέθετο...φανερῶσαι τὴν ἑαυτοῦ χρηστότητα καὶ δ. *Diogn.*9.2; κρυφία δ. τοῦ θεοῦ γέγονε τῷ σταυρωθέντι Χριστῷ, ὃν καὶ τὰ δαιμόνια φρίσσει Just.*dial.*49.8(M.6.585B); Clem.*prot.*11(p.79.10; M.8.229A); **5.** in Inc. προεκήρυξεν, ἵνα ὅταν γένηται, δ. καὶ βουλῇ τοῦ...ποιητοῦ γενόμενον γνωσθῇ Just.*dial.*84.2(M.6.673B); *ib.*139.4(796B); exeg. Lc.1:35, v. 15 infra; **6.** manifested in Christ ὁ πατὴρ αὐτοῦ τοσαύτην ἔδωκεν αὐτῷ δ., ὥστε καὶ τὰ δαιμόνια ὑποτάσσεσθαι τῷ ὀνόματι αὐτοῦ...εἰ δὲ τῇ τοῦ πάθους...οἰκονομίᾳ τοσαύτη δ. δείκνυται παρακολουθήσασα, πόση ἡ ἐν τῇ ἐνδόξῳ...παρουσίᾳ; Just.*dial.*30.3–31.1(M.6.540B); Cels.ap.Or.*Cels.*2.63(p.184.30; M.11.896A); ἔχων ἐκ θεοῦ δ. Or.*hom.29 in Lc.*(p.183.12); Eus.*e.th.*3.17(p.179.4; M.24.1042A); of Christ's word as δ. θεοῦ, Just.*1apol.*14.5(M 6.349A); οὐδὲ ἔχει δ. τινα [ref. Messiah in Jewish tradition who is to be unrecognized until Elijah comes and anoints him] id.*dial.*8.4(493B); Christ's power is Father's will, Heracleon ap.Or.*Jo.*13.38(p.263.19; M.14.465B); **7.** in gen. of divine operation or manifested power, esp. of grace in Christian life ἔρρωσθέ μοι ἐν δ. πατρός Ign.*Smyrn.*13.1; μοι δύναμιν αἰτεῖσθε ἔσωθέν τε καὶ ἔξωθεν, ἵνα μὴ μόνον λέγω, ἀλλὰ καὶ θέλω id.*Rom.*3.2; Herm.*mand.*5.2.1; ἐὰν ἐπιστραφῆτε πρὸς τὸν κύριον...ἕξετε δ. τοῦ κατακυριεῦσαι τῶν ἔργων τοῦ διαβόλου *ib.*12.6.2; maintaining Church, id.*vis.*3.3.5; revealed in life of Church, *Diogn.*7.9; ἵνα...εἰσελθεῖν εἰς τὴν βασιλείαν τοῦ θεοῦ τῇ δ. τοῦ θεοῦ δυνατοὶ γενηθῶμεν *ib.*9.1; in apostolic preaching, Just.*1apol.*39.3(M.6.388B); of miraculous power accompanying gospel, id.*dial.*11.4(M.6.500A); ἡ πίστις δ. τις τοῦ θεοῦ Clem.*str.*2.11(p.138.28; M.8.984C); *ib.*2.2(p.115.23; 936B); τὸ γνῶναι [sc. τὸν πατέρα] ζωὴ αἰώνιος κατὰ μετουσίαν τῆς τοῦ ἀφθάρτου δ. *ib.*5.10(p.36 1; M.9.97A); δύναμιν λαβοῦσα κυριακὴν ἡ ψυχὴ μελετᾷ εἶναι θεός *ib.*6.14(p.488.27; 337A); φιλόσοφος...ἐὰν προσλάβῃ τὴν θείαν διὰ πίστεως δ. *ib.*6.15(p.491.12; 341B); δι' ἀγγέλων γὰρ ἡ θεία δ. παρέχει τὰ ἀγαθά *ib.*6.16(p.514.35; 393B); ἐπίγειος εἰκὼν θείας δ. ἡ γνωστικὴ ψυχή *ib.*7.11(p.46.19; 489A); Or.*Cels.*4.6(p.278.26; M.11.1036C); esp. in miracles, Just.*dial.*79.4(M.6.664A); **8.** of power of Father, Son, and H. Ghost respectively ὁ...πατὴρ συνέχων τὰ πάντα φθάνει εἰς ἕκαστον τῶν ὄντων...ἐλαττόνως δὲ...ὁ υἱὸς φθάνων ἐπὶ μόνα τὰ λογικά ...ἡττόνως τὸ πνεῦμα...ἐπὶ μόνους τοὺς ἁγίους διϊκνούμενον· ὥστε κατὰ τοῦτο μείζων ἡ δ. τοῦ πατρὸς παρὰ τὸν υἱὸν καὶ τὸ πνεῦμα...πλείων δὲ ἡ τοῦ υἱοῦ παρὰ τὸ πνεῦμα...καὶ πάλιν διαφέρουσα μᾶλλον τοῦ...πνεύματος ἡ δ. παρὰ τὰ ἄλλα ἅγια Or.*princ.*1.3.5(p.56.5; M.11.150B); **9.** partic., of power of Christ, Ign.*Eph.*11.2; bestowed on apostles, Just.*1apol.*50.12(M.6.404A); on Moses at burning bush, *ib.*62.4(424A); on apostles by Christ as high priest, id.*dial.*42.1(M.6.565A); *ib.*54.1(593C) cit. s. στολή; Clem.*str.*6.6(p.456.2; M.9.269C); Or.*or.*31.5(p.399.4; M.11.553D); ἵνα μὴ μόνον, ὅτε παρῆν τῷ σώματι, ἀλλὰ καὶ νῦν, ὅτε πάρεστι δυνάμει καὶ τῷ πνεύματι, προφητεύῃ id.*hom.1.12 in Jer.*(p.10.25; M.13.269A); Ath.*inc.*1.1(M.25.97A); δ. νοερᾷ καὶ λογικῇ τὰς κατ' εἰκόνα τὴν αὐτοῦ...πεποιημένας ψυχὰς νοερὰς καὶ λογικὰς ἀπειργάζετο Eus.*e.th.*1.20(p.81.31; M.24.868A); πάλιν ἐρχόμενον μετὰ δόξης καὶ δ. κρῖναι *Symb.Ant.*(341)3 ap.Ath.*syn.*24(p.250.15; M.26.725A); of power of Christ's word, Just.*dial.*83.4(M.6.673A); *ib.*102.5(713C); ref. theophanies in OT δυνάμει φαινόμενος πρότερον ὡς ἀνὴρ καὶ ἄγγελος *ib.*128.1(773B); cf.*ib.*128.4(776B); of Christ's power imparted to apostles by lifting up of hand in blessing, Or.*fr.87 in Lc.*(p.275.18); **10.** partic., of power of H. Ghost, esp. ref. prophecy πνεύματι τῷ ἐρχομένῳ ἀπὸ τοῦ θεοῦ καὶ ἔχοντι δ. opp. πνεύματι τῷ ἐπιγείῳ...ἐν αὐτῷ δ. οὐκ ἔστιν Herm. *mand.*11.17; πᾶν...πνεῦμα ἀπὸ θεοῦ δοθὲν οὐκ ἐπερωτᾶται, ἀλλὰ ἔχον τὴν δ. τῆς θεότητος ἀφ' ἑαυτοῦ λαλεῖ πάντα, ὅτι ἄνωθέν ἐστιν ἀπὸ τῆς δ. τοῦ θείου πνεύματος *ib.*11.5; cf. ὄντος δὲ τοῦ υἱοῦ ἐν πατρὶ καὶ πατρὸς ἐν υἱῷ, ἑνότητι καὶ δ. πνεύματος Athenag.*leg.*10.2(M.6.909A); Clem.*ecl.*25(p.143.29; M.9.709B); *ib.*(p.144.1; 709C); ref. an ecstatic prophet ἐγὼ ὁ θεός εἰμι ἢ θεοῦ παῖς ἢ πνεῦμα θεῖον...καὶ ὄψεσθέ με αὖθις μετ' οὐρανίου δ. ἐπανιόντα Cels.ap.Or.*Cels.*7.9(p.161.10; M.11. 1433B); τὸ φραγέλλιον εἰκόνα τυγχάνειν τῆς δ. καὶ ἐνεργείας τοῦ ἁγίου πνεύματος Heracleon ap.eund.*Jo.*10.33(19; p.207.10; M.14.368A); ἦν γὰρ ἐπὶ τὸν Ἡλίαν πνεῦμα καὶ δ., εἴτ' οὖν πνευματικὸν χάρισμα, ὥσπερ καὶ ἐπὶ ἕκαστον τῶν προφητῶν Or.*hom.4 in Lc.*(p.29.12); χάρις...τὴν τοῦ ἁγίου πνεύματος διὰ τοῦ υἱοῦ τοῖς ἀξίοις ἐπιχορηγοῦσα δ. Eus.*Marcell.*1.1(p.3.24; M.24.716C); Ath.*ep.Serap.*1.25(M.26. 589A) cit. s. δόξα; *ib.*4.4(641C); ἐν ἑαυτοῖς οἰκοῦσαν τὴν δ. τὴν θεϊκήν Ammonas *ep.*1(p.433.4); *ib.*2(p.436.11); πνεῦμα, δι' οὗ τὰς ἡμετέρας ἀσφαλίζεται ψυχάς,...ἀνατειχίζων ὥσπερ ἀρρήτῳ δ. πρὸς ἄμαχον εὐτολμίαν Cyr.*Jo.*11.12(4.1006C); Cosm.Ind.*top.*7(M.88.361B); **11.** Trin., divine δ. sts. being virtually equivalent to *divinity* υἱὸν θεοῦ κατὰ θέλημα καὶ δ. Ign.*Smyrn.*1.1; υἱὸν...πρὸ πάντων ποιημάτων ἀπὸ τοῦ πατρὸς δυνάμει αὐτοῦ καὶ βουλῇ προελθόντα Just. *dial.*100.4(M.6.709C); Athenag.*leg.*10.3(M.6.909B) cit. s. διαίρεσις; *ib.*24.1(945B) cit. s. ἑνόω; εἰ δὲ βούλεται μαθεῖν πῶς εἷς θεὸς ἀποδείκνυται, γιγνωσκέτω ὅτι μία δ. τούτου, καὶ ὅσον μὲν κατὰ τὴν δ. εἷς ἐστιν θεός, ὅσον δὲ κατὰ τὴν οἰκονομίαν τριχῆς ἡ ἐπίδειξις Hipp.*Noët.*8 (p.249.21; M.10.816B); οὐ δύο θεοὺς λέγω...δ. γὰρ μία, ἡ ἐκ τοῦ παντός· τὸ δὲ πᾶν πατήρ, ἐξ οὗ δύναμις λόγος *ib.*11(p.253.11; 817C); ref. Jo. 10:30 τὸ γὰρ 'ἐσμὲν' οὐκ ἀφ' ἑνὸς λέγεται, ἀλλ' ἐπὶ δύο· ⟨δύο⟩ πρόσωπα ἔδειξεν, δ. δὲ μίαν *ib.*7(p.247.13; 813A); ὁμολογοῦμεν δύο θεούς; ναί· ἡ δ. μία ἐστιν Or.*dial.*2(p.124.6); τοὺς...ἀναιροῦντας τὸ...κήρυγμα τῆς ἐκκλησίας,...τὴν μοναρχίαν, εἰς τρεῖς δ. τινὰς καὶ μεμερισμένας ὑποστάσεις καὶ θεότητας τρεῖς Dion.R.ap.Ath.*decr.*26(p.22.3; M.25. 461D); δύο μὲν οὐσίαι καὶ δύο πράγματα καὶ δύο δ. Eus.ap.Marcell. *fr.*72 ap.Eus.*Marcell.*1.4(p.26.20; M.24.765C); εἰ μὴ τῷ πνεύματι προσέχοντες δυνάμει ἀδιαίρετον τὴν μονάδα εἶναι νομίζοιμεν, ἆρα οὐχ ἁμαρτησόμεθα; Marcell.*fr.*68 ap.Eus.*e.th.*2.19(p.124.1; M.24.944C); ἀδιαίρετος καὶ ἀχώριστός ἐστιν, ᾗ δύναμις τοῦ πατρός, ὁ υἱός Marcell. *ep.*ap.Epiph.*haer.*72.3(p.258.21; ἡ δ. M.42.388A); of Marcellus' doctrine λόγον ἔνδον ὑπάρχειν ἐν αὐτῷ τῷ θεῷ, καὶ τοῦτον ποτὲ μὲν ἡσυχάζειν ποτὲ δὲ ἐνεργεῖν δραστικῇ δ. Eus.*Marcell.*2.2(p.43.15; 797A); Chrys.*anom.*7.2(1.502D,504A); εἴ τις λέγει, ὡς οὐδὲ μίαν παντελῶς ἕξει ὁ Χριστὸς πρὸς οὐδὲ ἓν τῶν λογικῶν διαφορὰν οὐδὲ τῇ οὐσίᾳ οὐδὲ τῇ γνώσει οὐδὲ τῇ ἐφ' ἅπαντα δ. ἢ ἐνεργείᾳ CCP(543)*anath.*13; θεὸν δὲ λέγω...τὴν μίαν οὐσίαν καὶ φύσιν καὶ δ. Dam.*troph.*suppl.(p.281.9); **12.** of Christ as δ. of God λόγος...ὑπάρχων καὶ πρωτότοκος καὶ δ. Just.*1apol.*23.2(M.6.364A); *ib.*33.6(381B); ἀρχὴν πρὸ πάντων τῶν κτισμάτων ὁ θεὸς γεγέννηκε δ. τινα ἐξ ἑαυτοῦ λογικήν, ἥτις καὶ δόξα κυρίου ὑπὸ τοῦ πνεύματος τοῦ ἁγίου καλεῖται, ποτὲ δὲ υἱὸς ποτὲ δὲ σοφία id.*dial.*61.1(M.6.613C); λόγος καὶ σοφία καὶ δ. καὶ δόξα τοῦ γεννήσαντος *ib.*61.3(616A); μονογενὴς γὰρ ὅτι ἦν τῷ πατρὶ τῶν ὅλων οὗτος, ἰδίως ἐξ αὐτοῦ λόγος καὶ δ. γεγεννημένος *ib.*105.1(721A); *ib.*128.4(776B); θεὸς ἦν ἐν ἀρχῇ, τὴν δὲ ἀρχὴν λόγου δ. παρειλήφαμεν Tat.*orat.*5(p.5. 16; M.6.813C); λόγος...ὢν πνεῦμα θεοῦ, καὶ ἀρχὴ καὶ σοφία καὶ δ. ὑψίστου κατήρχετο εἰς τοὺς προφήτας Thphl.Ant.*Autol.*2.10(M.6. 1064C); δ. τοῦ θεοῦ ἐστιν ὁ κύριος Clem.*str.*6.6(p.455.29; M.9.269B); δ. οὖν πατρικὴ ὑπάρχων ῥᾳδίως περιγίνεται ὧν ἂν ἐθέλῃ *ib.*7.2(p.8.10; 412C); ἡ δ. ἡ πατρῴα, ὅ ἐστιν λόγος Hipp.*Noët.*16(p.259.24; M.10. 825A); †Hipp.*fr.*23(p.202.20); Χριστὸς...ἡ ἀκαταμάχητος δ. τοῦ πατρὸς καὶ δεξιά Or.*hom.10 in Lc.*(p.70.5); *A.Thom.*A 10(p.115.1); ἀεὶ δὲ ἦν...εἰ λόγος καὶ σοφία καὶ δ. ὁ Χριστός. ταῦτα γὰρ εἶναι τὸν Χριστὸν αἱ θεῖαι λέγουσι γραφαί...ταῦτα δὲ δ. οὖσαι τοῦ θεοῦ τυγχάνουσιν Dion. R.ap.Ath.*decr.*26(p.22.22; M.25.464B); ἀεὶ τὸν Χριστὸν εἶναι, λόγον ὄντα καὶ σοφίαν καὶ δ. ... ἀναλόγως πάλιν ὁ Χριστὸς ἀτμὶς λέλεκται· ἀτμὶς γὰρ...ἐστι τῆς τοῦ θεοῦ δ. Dion.Al.ap.Ath.*Dion.*15(p.57.2,19; M.25.501C,504A); Eus.*p.e.*7.12(320C; M.21.541B) cit. s. οὐσία; θεοῦ δ. καὶ σοφία Ath.*gent.*40(M.25.81B); δ. τοῦ πατρὸς ὁ λόγος Marcell. *fr.*64 ap.Eus.*Marcell.*2.2(p.37.27; M.24.788A); εἰ δυνάμεως εἰκών, οὐκέτι δ. id.*fr.*86 ap.Epiph.*haer.*72.6(p.261.4; M.42.389C); ἀδιαίρετος δ. τοῦ θεοῦ id.*ep.*ap.Epiph.*haer.*72.2(p.257.28; 385C); cf. οὐσίας τε καὶ βουλῆς καὶ δ. καὶ δόξης ἀπαράλλακτον εἰκόνα Ast.Soph.*fr.*21 ∞ *Symb.Ant.*(341)2(p.249.17; M.26.721C); ὁ τοῦ θεοῦ λόγος καὶ ἡ σοφία καὶ ἡ εἰκὼν καὶ ἡ χεὶρ καὶ ἡ δ. Ath.*decr.*17(p.14.13; M.25.444C); id. *Dion.*9(p.52.4; M.25.492B); id.*Ar.*3.1(M.26.324C); οὐ κτίσμα, ἀλλὰ δ. id.*ep.Afr.*5(M.26.1037C); contrast ἡ ἀΐδιος αὐτοῦ δ. ... οὐχ ὁ μονογενὴς υἱός, ἀλλ' ὁ γεννήσας πατήρ. ἄλλην δὲ δ. καὶ σοφίαν διδάσκει θεοῦ εἶναι διὰ Χριστοῦ δεικνυμένην...ἡ δ. ... ἣν ἄναρχόν τε καὶ ἀγέννητον...ἀποφαίνονται λογισμοί, μία ἂν εἴη...καὶ ἡ αὐτή· πολλαὶ δὲ... ὑπ' αὐτοῦ κτισθεῖσαι, ὧν πρωτότοκος καὶ μονογενὴς ὁ Χριστός Ast. Soph.*fr.*2a; τὴν δὲ δ. τοῦ πατρὸς λέγει λαμβάνειν δ. ὁ παράνομος [i.e. Ast. Soph.] Ath.*Ar.*3.2(325B); CSard.*ep.cath.*ap.Thdt.*h.e.*2.8.43 (3.845); λόγον...καὶ σοφίαν καὶ δ. *Symb.Ant.*(345)1(p.251.26; M.26. 728B); *Symb.Sel.*ap.Ath.*syn.*29(p.258.9; M.26.745A); δ. δέ, ὡς συντηρητικὸς τῶν γενομένων Gr.Naz.*or.*30.20(p.139.15; M.36.129B); ἡ τοῦ θεοῦ δ. τε καὶ σοφία, δι' οὗ τὰ πάντα ἐγένετο Gr.Nyss.*Eun.*2 (2 p.323.24; M.45.497B); Cyr.*Nest.*4.2(p.80.15; 6^1.102D); λέγομεν τὸν πατέρα πάντα...διὰ τοῦ...υἱοῦ...ποιεῖν· οὐχ ὡς δι' ὀργάνου λειτουργικοῦ, ἀλλὰ φυσικῆς καὶ ἐνυποστάτου δ. ‡Cyr.*Trin.*8(6^3.12E; M.77.1137D); **13.** of δ. of Son in relation to H. Ghost, Marcell.*fr.*60 ap.Eus.*e.th.*3. 4(p.158.25; M.24.1004C); **14.** of H. Ghost as δ. of Christ, Cyr.*Nest.*4. 1(p.78.26; 6^1.100A); δ. of Father, Jo.D.*f.o.*1.12(M.94.849A); **15.** exeg. Lc.1:35 τὸ πνεῦμα οὖν καὶ τὴν δ. τὴν παρὰ τοῦ θεοῦ οὐδὲν ἄλλο νοῆσαι θέμις ἢ τὸν λόγον Just.*1apol.*33.6(M.6.381B); διὰ δυνάμεως τοῦ λόγου κατὰ τὴν τοῦ πατρὸς...βουλήν, διὰ παρθένου ἄνθρωπος ἀπεκυήθη *ib.* 46.5(397C); cf.Iren.*haer.*5.1.3(M.7.1122D); τὸ οὖν πνεῦμα ἅγιον...τὴν τοῦ σώματος τοῦ κυρίου γένεσιν λέγει, δ. δὲ ὑψίστου...τὴν μόρφωσιν δηλοῖ τοῦ θεοῦ, ἣν ἐνετύπωσεν τῷ σώματι ἐν τῇ παρθένῳ Clem.*exc. Thdot.*60(p.127.2; M.9.688B); ἐνεργέστερον γὰρ τοῦ ἀνδρὸς ἐνεποίησεν ἡ τοῦ θεοῦ δ. ἐπισκιάσασα τῇ παρθένῳ σὺν τῷ ἐπεληλυθότι ἁγίῳ πνεύματι Petr.I Al.*fr.*(*ACO* 1.1.2 p.39.25; M.18.512A); Eus.*d.e.*10.8 (p.481.19; M.22.773C); δ. τοῦ ὑψίστου identified with H. Ghost, agst. theory that it denotes Son, Ant.Ptol.*Adam*(p.650.39); δύο λέγει· πνεῦμα ἅγιον, καὶ δ. τίς ἡ δ. ἐστιν; Χριστὸς θεοῦ δ. ἔρχεται τοίνυν τὰ δύο· καὶ τὸ πνεῦμα τὸ ἅγιον, καὶ ὁ Χριστὸς ὁ μονογενής Antip.Bost.*annunt.*9(M.85.1781A); (Valentinian) πνεῦμά ἐστιν ἡ σοφία...ὕψιστός ἐστιν ὁ δημιουργός...ὁ καινὸς ἄνθρωπος, ὁ ἀπὸ πνεύματος ἁγίου...καὶ τοῦ δημιουργοῦ...οἱ δ' αὖ ἀπὸ τῆς ἀνατολῆς λέγουσιν ...ὅτι πνευματικὸν ἦν τὸ σῶμα τοῦ σωτῆρος· πνεῦμα γὰρ ἅγιον ἦλθεν... τουτέστιν ἡ σοφία, καὶ ἡ δ. τοῦ ὑψίστου, ἡ δημιουργικὴ τέχνη Hipp. *haer.*6.35(p.164.19; M.16.3247C); (Basilidean) ἡ δ. τῆς κρίσεως [prob. for χρίσεως] ἀπὸ τῆς ἀκρωρείας ἄνωθεν διὰ τοῦ δημιουργοῦ μέχρι τῆς κτίσεως, ὅ ἐστι τοῦ υἱοῦ *ib.*7.26(p.205.18; 3318A); **16.** Christol., ref. Gen.49:10–11 αἷμα τῆς σταφυλῆς σημαντικὸν τοῦ ἔχειν μὲν αἷμα τὸν φανησόμενον, ἀλλ' οὐκ ἐξ ἀνθρωπείου σπέρματος ἀλλ' ἐκ θείας δ. Just.*1apol.*32.9(M.6.380B); Nemes.*nat.hom.*3(M.40.605A) cit. s. οὐσία; of natures τῶν δύο φύσεων μία ἐστὶν αὐθεντία καὶ μία δ. Nest.*fr.*A 11(p.196.15; M.86.1021B); union κατὰ δ. condemned, CCP (553)*anath.*4 cit. s. ἕνωσις; of Christ's divinity ὁ κύριος ἀνεβόησε λέγων, ἡ δ. μου, ἡ δ., κατέλειψάς με *Ev.Petr.*5; ἡ κατασκηνώσασα δ. ἐν τῷ σώματι Hipp.*fr.2 in Jo.19:34*(p.211.10; M.10.868B); μὴ καθικνούμενον τῆς δ. τὸ πάθος *ib.3*(p.211.16; 868C); τὴν θείαν δ. ἐνεσταυρῶσθαι τῇ ὕλῃ...λέγουσιν Alex.Lyc.*Man.*24(p.35.22; M.18.444D); ἀσεβὴς οὖν ὁ τὸ πάθος ἀνάγων εἰς τὴν δ. Apoll.*fid.sec.pt.*12(p.171.11; M.10.1109B); οὔτε γὰρ ἄλλαξις...οὔτε περικλεισμὸς ἐν πνεύματι γέγονεν περὶ τὴν...τοῦ θεοῦ δ. *ib.*(p.171.5; 1109A); cf. εἰ γὰρ τὴν φύσιν ἐξ ἀνθρώπων ἔσχεν, ἀλλὰ...τὴν δ. ἐξ οὐρανοῦ id.*fr.*6(p.205.26)ap.Thdt. *eran.*2(4.174); ὡς ἄνθρωπος εὑρεθείς, ὡς υἱὸς ἐν δ. Cyr.*Jo.*9(4.764D); **17.** of prophetic inspiration as divine power (v. 10 supra), Just. *dial.*87.4(M.6.684B); Clem.*str.*1.21(p.84.6; M.8.869B); Hipp.*Noët.*11 (p.253.22; M.10.820A); **18.** of divine power in baptism, Clem.*exc. Thdot.*77(p.131.10; M.9.693C); ἡ δ. τῆς σωτηρίας ἡ ἀπὸ τῆς δ. ἐκείνης ἐρχομένη...ἐλθὲ καὶ σκήνωσον ἐν τοῖς ὕδασι *A.Thom.*A 52 (p.168.17); σοὶ δόξα ἡ ἐν τῷ βαπτίσματι ἀόρατος δ. *ib.*132(p.239.20); ref. pre-baptismal unction Ἰησοῦ ἐλθέτω ἡ νικητικὴ αὐτοῦ δ., καὶ ἐνιδρυσθήτω τῷ ἐλαίῳ τούτῳ ὥσπερ ἱδρύνθη ἐν τῷ συγγενεῖ αὐτοῦ ξύλῳ ἡ τότε αὐτοῦ δ., ἧς τὸν λόγον οὐκ ἤνεγκαν οἱ σταυρώσαντές σε *ib.*157 (p.267.6); partic. of baptismal invocation of Trin., Or.*Jo.*6.33(17; p.142.30; M.14.257A); **19.** in eucharistic consecration ὁ ἄρτος καὶ τὸ ἔλαιον ἁγιάζεται τῇ δ. τοῦ ὀνόματος θεοῦ, τὰ αὐτὰ ὄντα κατὰ τὸ φαινόμενον οἷα ἐλήφθη· ἀλλὰ δυνάμει εἰς δ. πνευματικὴν μεταβέβληται Clem.*exc.Thdot.*82(p.132.10; M.9.696C); of Christ's flesh in Communion τῆς ἁγίας σαρκὸς ἡ δ. συσσώμους ἀποτελεῖ τοὺς ἐν οἷς ἂν γένοιτο Cyr.*Jo.*11.11(4.1000A); **20.** in gospel λόγοις...μεστοῖς πνεύματος θείου καὶ δ. βρύουσι Just.*dial.*9.1(M.6.493C); **21.** of faith as divine power, Ign.*Eph.*14.2; ἡ πίστις ἄνωθέν ἐστι...καὶ ἔχει δ. μεγάλην Herm.*mand.*9.11; cf. ἀπόστολοι...κοιμηθέντες ἐν δ. καὶ πίστει τοῦ υἱοῦ τοῦ θεοῦ id.*sim.*9.16.5; ἡ πίστις δ. τις τοῦ θεοῦ, ἰσχὺς οὖσα τῆς ἀληθείας Clem.*str.*2.11(p.138.28; M.8.984C); cf.Or.*or.*31.7 (p.400.17; M.11.556C); **22.** God's power contrasted with Devil's lack of δ., Herm.*mand.*7.2; and with weakness of ghosts, Tat.*orat.*16 (p.17.15; M.6.840B).

VII. concretely, *power*; **A.** of spiritual beings; **1.** of God καθῆται...ἐκ δεξιῶν τῆς μεγάλης δ. Heges.ap.Eus.*h.e.*2.23.13(M.20.200B); cf. *benignus omnium pater, simul et* εὐεργετικὴ δ. *et* δημιουργική Or.*princ.*1.4.3(p.65.11); **2.** of Son ἡ δὲ πρώτη δ. μετὰ τὸν πατέρα πάντων...καὶ υἱὸς ὁ λόγος ἐστίν Just.*1apol.*32.10(M.6.380B); cf.id.*dial.*61.1(M.6.613C); cf.Or.*princ.*1.2.9(p.40.9; M.11.138A); Eus.*d.e.*4.15(p.179.33; M.22.300B); **3.** of H. Ghost τῆς τρίτης δ. Eus.*p.e.*11.20(541B; M.21.901B); Proc.G.*Gen.* 1:26(M.87.125B); **4.** of cosmic spiritual powers, good and evil ἡ εἱμαρμένη ἐστὶ σύνοδος πολλῶν καὶ ἐναντίων δ., αὗται δέ εἰσιν ἀόρατοι καὶ ἀφανεῖς, ἐπιτροπεύουσαι τὴν τῶν ἄστρων φορὰν καὶ δι' ἐκείνων πολιτευόμεναι Clem.*exc.Thdot.*69(p.129.15; M.9.692A); *ib.*71(p.129.29; 692B); δ. κρειττόνων καὶ χειρόνων Or.*or.*27.12(p.371.10; M.11.516B); identified with στοιχεῖα, Clem.*str.*6.16(p.508.1; M.9.380A); **5.** partic. of angels θεὸς ἀγγέλων καὶ δ. *M.Polyc.*14.1; ἄγγελοι καὶ δ. εἰσίν Just.*dial.*85.4(M.6.677A); Athenag.*leg.*24.2(M.6.945B); Clem.*str.*1.17(p.53.6; M.8.796B); *ib.*5.6(p.351.6; M.9.64A); id.*exc.Thdot.*72(p.130.2; M.9.692C); θεὸν...πάσης δ. καὶ ἀγγέλων πάντων...καὶ αἰώνων...ἰσχυρότερον *A.Jo.*104(p.202.26); ἀγγέλους, ἀρχαγγέλους, δ. ἐξουσίας. ἀπὸ δὲ ἑπτά τινων ἀγγέλων τὸν κόσμον γεγενῆσθαι [i.e. in system of Saturninus] Hipp.*haer.*7.28(p.208.11; M.16.3322A); Or.*princ.*1.5.3(p.71.25; M.11.139B); τάξιν ἀγγελικὴν ἢ δ. ἀρχικὴν ἢ ἐξουσίαν τὴν ἐπί τινων *ib.*1.6.2(p.81.4; 167A); id.*or.*31.5(p.398.16; M.11.553B); αἱ δ. αἱ συνεργοῦσαι τῇ ψυχῇ καὶ τῷ νῷ id.*hom.20.1 in Jos.*(p.418.23; M.12.920B); εὐχομένοις...μυρίαι...συνεύχονται δ. ἱεραί id.*Cels.*8.64(p.280.13; M.11.1613A); Meth.*symp.*3.6(p.33.1; M.18.69A); Eus.*e.th.*1.11(p.70.25; M.24.845B); Ath.*gent.*19(M.25.40C); τῇ ἑαυτοῦ δ. τόν τε ὁρατὸν κόσμον καὶ τὰς ἀοράτους δ. κινεῖ καὶ συνέχει *ib.*44(88C); id.*Ar.*3.51(M.26.432A); Serap.*euch.*1.3; καθαραὶ καὶ νοεραὶ καὶ ὑπερκόσμιοι δ. Bas.*Spir.*38(3.31C; M.32.136A); Chrys.*incomprehens.*2.4(1.457E); ? of guardian angel ἡ ἀγάπη αὐτοῦ ἐξαποστείλῃ ἡμῖν δ. φυλάττουσαν ἡμᾶς ἕως οὗ καταπολεμήσωμεν μεθ' ὧν ἐπράξαμεν τοὺς ἄρχοντας τῆς πονηρίας Ammonas *opusc.*4(p.474.11); Pall.*h.Laus.*18(p.53.21; M.34.1058D); Nil.*epp.*2.188(M.79.297C); Cyr.*Is.*1.4(2.103B); Thdt.*Ps.*23:10(1.754); Dion.Ar.*c.h.*2.2(M.3.137C); **6.** of evil powers αἱ δ. τοῦ σατανᾶ Ign.*Eph.*13.1; ἡ δ. ... ὄφις κεκλημένη καὶ σατανᾶς Just.*dial.*125.4(M.6.768A); Clem.*str.*2.20(p.173.9; M.8.1053C); id.*exc.Thdot.*80(p.131.28; M.9.696B); Or.*mart.*18(p.17.9; M.11.588A); δαίμονες ἢ ἄλλαι τινὲς ἡμῖν ἀόρατοι δ. *ib.*46(p.42.13; 628A); id.*Cels.*3.36(p.233.7; M.11.968A); *ib.*5.5(p.5.20; 1188A); δ. ἀντικειμένων id.*hom.1.13 in Jer.*(p.11.19; M.13.269C); id.*Jo.*20.19(17; p.351.21; M.14.616A); *A.Jo.*23(p.163.26); *ib.*98(p.200.14); *ib.*114(p.214.7); Meth.*symp.*10.5(p.126.30; M.18.200C); id.*Porph.*1(p.503.11; M.18.397D); τὰς δουλωσαμένας ἡμᾶς δ. κατηγωνίσατο διὰ τοῦ σταυροειδοῦς *ib.*(p.504.18; 400B); τὰς ἔξωθεν ἀμφὶ τὸν ἀέρα τοῦτον ἀσάρκους καὶ ἀνθρώποις ἀοράτους δ. Eus.*d.e.*10.8(p.485.2; M.22.780B); καταχθονίους...δ. *ib.*(p.488.19; 784D); Cyr.*Is.*3.5(2.524A); Thdt.*qu.20 in Gen.*(1.31); Jo.Mal.*chron.*6 p.160(M.97.160B); Jo.D.*f.o.*2.4(M.94.873C); **7.** of angelic powers in phrase κύριος τῶν δ. (v. σαβαώθ), where meanings *heavenly powers* and *angelic hosts* or *forces* (*LS*) are combined, Herm.*vis.*1.3.4; applied to Christ, Just.*dial.*29.1(M.6.537A); *ib.*36.2(553B); κύριος τῶν δ. διὰ τὸ θέλημα τοῦ δόντος αὐτῷ πατρός *ib.*85.1(676B); ὁ ἐκ νεκρῶν ἀναστὰς κύριος τῶν δ. *ib.*85.4(677A); name σαβαώθ when translated κύριος τῶν δ. or κύριος στρατιῶν or παντοκράτωρ loses magical efficacy, Or.*Cels.*5.45(p.50.2; M.11.1253A); Christ being greater than these δ. as himself θεοῦ δ., id.*Jo.*1.39(42; p.51.20; M.14.104A); as title proper to Father in relation to creatures, not to the Son, Ath.*Ar.*1.33(M.26.80A); exeg. Ps.23:8 ff. applied to Christ at Ascension, Thdt.*Cant.*2:6(2.81); **8.** of aeons in Gnost. systems προστιθέασιν...Προυνικοῦ τινος ῥέουσαν δ. παρθένου καὶ ψυχὴν ζῶσαν Cels.ap.Or.*Cels.*6.34(p.103.15; M.11.1348C); δ. ἄπειρόν τι πλῆθος...γεγενημένων Hipp.*haer.*5.12(p.104.20; M.16.3162A); of supreme creative power in Peratic system, Gnost.*ib.*5.14(p.108.15ff.; 3167Aff.); of δ. δεξιαί and ἀριστεραί, Gnost. *ib.*(p.109.21ff.; 3167Dff.); Hipp.*ib.*5.16(p.112.15; 3174A) cit. s. ὄφις; δ. σιγή ἀόρατος...μεγάλη δ., νοῦς τῶν ὅλων 'Simon' *ib.*6.18(p.144.13; 3222A); ἑαυτὸν λέγων [sc. 'Simon'] τὴν ὑπὲρ πάντα δ. εἶναι *ib.*6.19(p.146.7; 3223A); *Hom.Clem.*2.22(M.2.89C); Arian οὐκ ἠδύνατο προβάλλειν, εἰ μὴ ὅτε καὶ ἡ τοῦ θελήματος δ. ἐπεγένετο likened to Valent. doctrine of aeons, Ath.*Ar.*3.60(M.26.449A); of Melchizedek as a δ., Hipp.*haer.*10.24(p.282.12; 3439B); Epiph.*haer.*55.1(p.324.4; M.41.972A); acc. Manicheans προβάλλειν ἐξ αὐτοῦ δ., λεγομένην μητέρα τῆς ζωῆς Hegem.*Arch.*7(p.10.5; M.10.1437A); ἑτέρας τρεῖς δ. *ib.*8(p.11.5; 1437C); *ib.*(p.12.4; 1440A); Epiph.*haer.*66.24(p.51.22; M.42.69B).

B. *force, army*; of angelic host, Chrys.*hom.15.4 in 1Tim.*(11.641C) etc.

VIII. *act of power, mighty work*; **A.** of miracles δ. ... μαγικάς Just.*1apol.*26.2(M.6.368A); collectively ἐκ τῶν ἔργων καὶ ἐκ τῆς παρακολουθούσης δ. συνιέναι... δυνατόν, ὅτι οὗτός ἐστιν ὁ καινὸς νόμος id.*dial.*11.4(M.6.500A); *ib.*35.8(553A); *ib.*115.4(741C); *ib.*132.1(781C); Iren.*ep.Flor.*ap.Eus.*h.e.*5.20.6(M.20.485B); Hipp.*haer.*7.33(p.220.13; M.16.3342A); of miracles performed by Christ's disciples and continuing in Church, Or.*Cels.*1.46(p.96.1; M.11.744D); id.*Jo.*6.29(14; p.139.25; M.14.252C); *V.Pach.Φ* 17(p.11.12).

B. of gifts of H. Ghost (Is.11:1–3), Just.*dial.*87.2(M.6.684A); *ib.*88.1(685A).

IX. *intensity, volume*; **A.** *square* of a number, ref. measurements of ark, Or.*Cels.*4.41(p.314.22; M.11.1097A).

B. of *volume* of sound; in deacon's cry urging congregation to sing more loudly, cf.*Lit.Chrys.*(p.370.9).

C. dat. sing., *strongly*, Gr.Mag.*dial.*(tr.Zach.)3.18(M.*PL.*77.267A).

X. *significance, purport*; **A.** *meaning* in gen. μαθεῖν...τίς ἡ δ. τοῦ 'Ισραὴλ ὀνόματος Just.*dial.*125.1(M.6.765C); Or.*Jo.*32.21(13; p.462.22; M.14.800D); τὸ μὲν τοῦ πατρὸς ἕν ἐστιν ὄνομα, ποικίλη δὲ τῆς ἐνεργείας ἡ δ. Cyr.H.*catech.*7.7; of significance of scripture μεταπλάττων...τῆς ἱστορίας τὴν δ. εἰς ἐννοίας πνευματικάς Cyr.*Os.*3(3.12C); id.*Jo.*1.5(4.48B); Proc.G.*Gen.*2:2(M.87.140B).

B. *implication, scope*, Tat.*orat.*18(p.20.14; M.6.845B).

C. dat. sing., *implicitly, virtually, in effect* ὀγδόης ἡμέρας... δυνάμει δ' ἀεὶ πρώτης ὑπαρχούσης Just.*dial.*138.1(M.6.793B); Or.*hom.14.14 in Jer.*(p.119.14; M.13.421B); Cyr.H.*catech.*23.4; Bas.*Eun.*1.10(1.222D; M.29.533C); Gr.Nyss.*or.catech.*37(p.146.12; M.45.96D).

***δυναμοδότως**, *as a source of power*, Dion.Ar.*c.h.*8.1(M.3.240A).

***δυναμοειδής**, *power-reflecting*, contrasted with δυναμοποιός, Dion.Ar.*c.h.*8.1(M.3.240A).

δυναμ-όω, *strengthen*, **1.** in gen. ἐν ἔργοις ~οῖ [sc. θυμός] τὸν ὀργιζόμενον *T.Dan* 4.2; Or.*Jo.*13.32(31; p.257.3; M.14.456A); οὐκ αὐτὸς [sc. ὁ νόμος] τὴν ἁμαρτίαν ἐδυνάμωσεν Chrys.*hom.42.2 in 1Cor.*(10.397E); Synes.*provid.*10(p.84.10; M.66.1232A); **2.** of God ἐδυναμώθητε ἐν τῇ πίστει Herm.*vis.*3.12.3; ἄγγελοι...ἀπὸ τῆς... θεωρίας ~ούμενοι πρὸς τὸ τὰ ἴδια ἔργα ἐπιτελεῖν Or.*or.*27.10(p.369.30; M.11.513B); πάντα τὰ ὅπου ποτὲ ~ούμενα μετέχειν αὐτοῦ, καθ' ὃ δύναμίς ἐστι, πεπιστεύκαμεν id.*Jo.*1.33(38; p.43.14; M.14.89B); τὴν... ~οῦσαν τοῦ θεοῦ δεξιάν Eus.*d.e.*6.2(p.254.17; M.22.417C); τῷ ἐλέει αὐτοῦ ~ούμενος Ath.*narr.fug.*(M.26.981A); of Christ διὰ τὰ ~ούμενα δύναμις λέγεται id.*Ar.*2.38(M.26.228A); †Bas.*Is.*184(1.514E; M.30.432A); ἀδιαστάτως ~ωθεῖσα [sc. ἡ ψυχή] τῷ προστάγματι Gr.Nyss.*hom.8 in Cant.*(M.44.948A); ~οῖ...ὁ τῶν δυνάμεων κύριος οὓς ἂν ἕλοιτο Cyr.*Am.*68(3.325D); ἡ [sc. δύναμις θεοῦ] διὰ τὴν περιουσίαν τοῦ δυνατοῦ καὶ τὴν ἀσθένειαν ~οῖ Dion.Ar.*d.n.*8.2(M.3.892A); **3.** of strengthening by power indirectly given by God ἀλκῆς καὶ ῥώμης ~ούσης τοὺς ἀγωνιζομένους Eus.*v.C.*2.7(p.44.10; M.20.982A); τῷ τε τῆς θεϊκῆς ἐπηγορίας ἐπωνύμῳ ~ούμενος id.*l.C.*2(p.199.7; M.20.1325A); **4.** by other men's prayers ταῖς εὐχαῖς ὑμῶν ~ούμενοι Gr.Nyss.*fr.*1(M.46.1109A).

***δυναμωνομία, ἡ**, *name of power*, Dion.Ar.*d.n.*8.1(M.3.889C).

***δυναμώτερος**, *more powerful*, of BMV τῶν δυνάμεων δ. προελήλυθας δύναμις Sophr.H.*or.*2.18(M.87.3237C).

***δυναμώτης, ὁ**, *strengthener*, Ephr.3.463A.

δυναστεία, ἡ, **A.** *rule, power, authority*; **1.** in gen., of the sun ἡμέρας ἔχει τὴν δ. Gr.Naz.*or.*28.30(p.69.8; M.36.69B); οὐ...συγχωροῦμαι τῷ ἀέρι δοῦναι τὴν ἅπασαν δ. τῶν τοῦ ἀέρος εἶναι νομιζομένων *ib.*28.28(p.65.9; 65C); of human, opp. divine, power, Thdt.*Jer.*17:5(2.496); **2.** of secular powers: imperial, Thdt.*h.e.*5.18.2(3.1046n.); id.*ep.*112(4.1184); of magistracies, Jo.Mosch.*prat.*79(M.87.2937B); hence *province*, Gr.Nyss.*Eun.*1(1 p.64.19; M.45.293A); **3.** of spiritual authority Παῦλος...κατὰ τὴν ἀπὸ τοῦ λόγου δ. ὑποτάσσων τῇ Χριστοῦ...διδασκαλίᾳ τοὺς ἀπὸ τῶν ἐθνῶν Or.*Cels.*7.21(p.173.17; M.11.1452C); Jo.D.*carm.assumpt.Chr.*(M.96.844D); **4.** of divine authority, Const.ap.Gel.Cyz.*h.e.*2.7.26(M.85.1237B); Cyr.*expl.xii cap.*7(p.22.17; 6.153D).

B. *tyranny, oppressive rule*; **1.** in gen., Ath.*syn.*3(p.232.31; M.26.685A); οὐ γὰρ προσεῖχε τῇ δ. τῶν γραμματέων καὶ Φαρισαίων Thdt.*Is.*11:3(p.59.27; 2.250); τὴν πλοῦτον, τὴν δ. id.*Jer.*12:13(2.478); τῆς τῶν Ἀρειανῶν δ. CCP(381)*ep.*ap.eund.*h.e.*5.9.2(3.1028); **2.** of secular tyranny βίᾳ καὶ δ. χρώμενον Ath.*apol.sec.*14(p.98.20; M.25.272C); Chrys.*Laz.*6.1(1.773B); of Julian's reign as δυσσεβὴς δ. opp. εὐσεβὴς βασιλεία, Thdt.*h.e.*3.28.3(3.945); **3.** of demonic tyranny οἱ νικῶντες, καὶ δι' εὐσέβειαν ἀποθνήσκοντες, καθαιροῦσιν αὐτῶν τὴν δ. Or.*Cels.* 8.44(p.259.7; M.11.1581D); *Hom.Clem.*4.5; Thdt.*Abac.*2:5(2.1545).

C. *love of power*; in catalogue of vices, Chrys.*hom.26.3 in 2Cor.* (10.622E).

δυναστεύ-ω, 1. *rule over* Ἄβγαρος τῶν...ἐθνῶν...~ων Eus.*h.e.* 1.13.2(M.20.120B); **2.** *dominate, hold sway over* τὸν τῇ φθορᾷ δεδυναστευμένον ἄνθρωπον Meth.*Porph.*1(p.504.19; M.18.400B); τοῦ θυμοῦ ~οντος Gr.Naz.*or.*21.30(M.35.1117B); Gr.Nyss.*Apoll.*5(M.45.1133A); **3.** *be in the ascendant*; of a star, Clem.*exc.Thdot.*71(p.129.31; M.9.692C).

δυνατός, A. *mighty, powerful*; **1.** of God ὁ μόνος δ. ποιῆσαι ταῦτα ...ἀγαθά *1Clem.*61.3; πρὸ πάντων εὐχαριστοῦμέν σοι, ὅτι δ. εἶ *Did.* 10.4; δι' ἑαυτὸν πλούσιος καὶ δ. τυγχάνει Meth.*creat.*3(p.495.36; M.18.336B); **2.** of H. Ghost in prophetic inspiration τὸ πνεῦμα τὸ θεῖον ἄνωθεν ἐρχόμενον δ. ἐστι Herm.*mand.*11.21; χωρισθέντος ἀπ' αὐτοῦ τοῦ πνεύματος τοῦ δυνατωτέρου θνητὸς γίνεται Tat.*orat.*7(p.7.30; M.6.821A); **3.** of creative principle (Gnost.); **a.** of law of Logos-Creator, cf.Gnosticus Anon.11(*GCS, Koptische-Gnostische Schriften*, p.351.12); **b.** of aeons, *ib.*16(p.357.22); **c.** of creator (Basilidean) δυνατῶν δυνατώτερος Hipp.*haer.*7.23(p.200.27; M.16.3310B); **4.** of inspiration of Sibyl, ‡Just.*coh.Gr.*38(M.6.309C); **5.** of Christians, *1Clem.*48.5; φυλάσσων...τὰς ἐντολὰς τοῦ θεοῦ ἔσῃ δ. ἐν πάσῃ πράξει Herm.*mand.*7.1; δυνατωτάτους...ἀποστόλους Or.*Jo.*20.36(29; p.377.3; M.14.660A); **6.** of soul, Clem.*exc.Thdot.*51(p.124.2; M.9.684B); in Aristotelian view δυνατώτερον...τοῦ σώματος Hipp.*haer.*7.24(p.201.22; M.16.3311A); Meth.*symp.*11.2(p.140.25; M.18.220C); **7.** of faith, Herm.*mand.*9.10.

B. *possible* οὐ γὰρ ἦν δ. ἀφανισθῆναι [sc. τὰ πάθη] διὰ τὸ ἐκτικὰ ἤδη καὶ δ. εἶναι Iren.*haer.*1.4.5(M.7.488A); in phrase ἐν δ.: ἐφ' ὅσον ἦν ἐν δ. ... δηλῶσαι ὑμῖν *Barn.*17.

C. neut. as subst., *power*, Const.*or.s.c.*20(p.184.8; M.20.1296A); Ath.*v.Anton.*28(M.26.883C); τοῦ δ. τῆς ἐνεργείας τοῦ πνεύματος Thdr.Mops.*Eph.*6:17(p.193.15; M.66.920D); Thdt.*1Tim.*6:15–16(3.672); Dion.Ar.*d.n.*8.2(M.3.892A).

***δυογαμία, ἡ,** *bigamy*, Thdr.Stud.*epp.*1.24(M.99.985A).

***δυοπεντεκαιδεκάς, ἡ,** *group* or *band of seventeen*, Thdr.Stud.*epp.* 1.51(M.99.1096D).

***δυοϋπόστατος,** *of two persons*, Thdr.Stud.*icon.*1(M.99.489A).

δυσάγγελος, *announcing evil*, Thdt.*ep.*21(4.1082).

δυσαγέω, *perform an impious deed*, Mel.*pass.*74 p.12.14.

***δυσαγκάλιστος,** *hard to embrace*; met., of heretics, Didym.*Trin.* 3.4(M.39.828C).

***δυσάγρευτος,** *hard to catch*, Dam.*troph.*proem.2(p.190.11).

δυσάγωγος, *hard to lead, refractory*, in gen. δ. πρὸς ἀρετὴν τὸ γένος τῶν ἀνθρώπων Bas.*hom.in Ps.*1(1.90C; M.29.212B); νοῦν...δ. Cyr.*Joel.*8(3.207C); id.*Am.*46(3.301B); τὸ δ. σῶμα Jo.Mon.*hymn. Geo.*8(M.96.1400B); esp. of Israel, †Bas.*Is.*187(1.517C; M.30.437A); Gr.Nyss.*usur.*(M.46.433B); Cyr.*ador.*2(1.74A); id.*glaph.Gen.*5(1.163D).

***δυσάθεος,** *evilly denying God*, superl., Cyr.*ador.*6(1.175E).

***δυσάκουστος,** *hard of hearing*, neut. as subst. τὸ ἄνουν αὐτῆς [sc. τῆς Ἰουδαίων συναγωγῆς] καὶ δ. πρὸς τὰ χρήσιμα Dam.*troph.*4.1(p.259.10).

δυσάλυκτος, *hard to escape*, †Apoll.*met.Ps.*14:5(v.l. δυσάλευτον M.33.1328C).

δυσαμάρτητος, *little liable to sin*, opp. πολυαμάρτητος, Bas.*renunt.*1(2.202D; M.31.628B).

***δυσαναβίβαστος,** *hard to bring back* δ. ἡ ψυχὴ ἐπὶ ταῦτα ἀφ' ὧν ὠλίσθησε καλῶν †Just.*fr.*(p.50; M.6.1593C).

δυσανάγωγος, *hard to lead up* τινές εἰσι πήλινοι, καὶ δ. Chrys.*scand.*7(3.477A); id.*cruc.*1.5(2.409C); id.*hom.3.5 in Jo.*(8.23B); Synes.*calv.*6(p.201.9; M.66.1177B).

***δυσαναθετέω,** *lose heart*, Ephr.3.292D.

***δυσανάφορος,** *hard to bear*, Bas.*hom.*14.3(2.124D; M.31.449A).

***δυσαναφόρως,** *so as to be difficult to lift up*; ref. drowsy eyelids, Philost.*h.e.*11.3(M.65.597A).

***δυσανέγερτος,** *hard to arouse*, Thdr.Stud.*epp.*2.51(M.99.1261D).

***δυσανόδευτος,** *hard to climb*, Sev.Ant.ap.*cat.Jo.*12:19(p.325.31).

δυσάνοικτος, *hard to open*, Jo.Clim.*scal.*19(M.88.937C).

δυσάντης, *hard to climb*; comp., Alex.Lyc.*Man.*21(p.28.24).

δυσάντλητος, *hard to draw* (of water); met., Eustrat.*v.Eutych.* 101(M.86.2388C).

***δυσαπόφορος,** *hard to bear*, Germ.CP *or.*2(M.98.264B).

***δυσαυχεν-έω,** *be refractory* ~οῦντας ἐκ τοῦ θεοῦ Marc.Diac. *v.Porph.*73.

***δυσβασάνιστος,** *hard to test*, *Orac.Sib.*7.128.

***δυσβάτευτος,** neut. as subst., *difficulty of approach*, Thdr.Stud. *cant.*2.6(p.339).

***δύσβουλος,** *ill-advised*, *Orac.Sib.*7.115.

δυσδιακόμιστος, 1. *hard to bear* βαπτιζόμεθα γὰρ εἰς ἀπόθεσιν ἁμαρτίας καὶ οἱονεί τι δ. ἀληθῶς φορτίον ἀποτρεπόμενοι τὴν ἀσέβειαν Cyr.*Is.*2.4(2.283B); met., id.*ador.*14(1.509E); **2.** *hard to carry out* or *perform*; of a task, Cyr.*inc.unigen.*(5[1].680C).

δυσδιάλλακτος, *hard to reconcile, implacable*, Leont.H.*monoph.* testimonia(M.86.1849B).

***δυσδιαπόρευτος,** *hard to pass through*, Evagr.*h.e.*2.13(p.65.15; M.86.2541A).

***δυσδιάτμητος,** *hard to cut through*, Chrys.*hom.10.5 in Rom.* (9.527A).

***δυσδιατύπωτος,** *hard to mould*; met., Chrys.*hom.4.3 in 2Tim.* (11.753A).

δυσδιάφευκτος (-φυκτος), *hard to escape*, Cyr.*Ps.*96:3(M.69.1248D); id.*ador.*7(1.238E); δυσδιάφυκτον id.*Os.*3(3.14C).

δυσδιεξίτητος, *hard to get out of*, Synes.*ep.*104(M.66.1481B).

δυσδιεξόδευτος, = foreg. δ. πραγμάτων πλοκή Gr.Nyss.*v.Gr. Thaum.*(M.46.924D); ἀνάγκη...δ. Chrys.*hom.12.2 in 2Cor.*(10.522E); ‡Jo.D.*ep.Thphl.*3(M.95.348B).

δυσδιήγητος, 1. *hard to describe, indescribable*, Or.*Jo.*20.2(p.328.18; M.14.573D); τὴν δ. σοφίαν [i.e. of God] †Bas.*Is.*119(1.461D; M.30.309C); Pall.*h.Laus.*36(p.106.15, v.l. ἀδιήγητα M.34.1179C); Cyr.*Jo.*1(4.8D); Thdt.*h.rel.*18(3.1231); **2.** *difficult of exegesis*, Or.*Jo.*10.39(23; p.215.21; M.14.381A).

δυσδιόδευτος, *difficult to explain*; of a passage of scripture, Olymp.*Job* 22:15(M.93.245D).

δυσδιόρθωτος, *hard to set right*, †Bas.*Is.*113(1.458A; M.30.301B); Chrys.*hom.60.1 in Mt.*(7.606A); Isid.Pel.*epp.*5.224(M.78.1468B).

δυσείδεια, ἡ, *ugliness*, Chrys.*hom.14.4 in Heb.*(12.146A); Cyr. *hom.pasch.*10.4(5[2].137A); Melet.*nat.hom.*4(M.64.1181A).

δυσείμων, *ill-dressed*, Clem.*q.d.s.*33.5(p.182.11); Jo.VI H.*v.Jo.D.* 26(M.94.468A); met., †Jo.D.*B.J.*2(M.96.868D).

δυσέκβατος, 1. *hard to follow to the end*, Cyr.*hom.pasch.*15(5[2].203A); **2.** *hard to escape*, *Orac.Sib.*7.100.

***δυσεκβάτως,** *so as to be reluctant to go out* δ. εἶχεν ὁ δαίμων ὁ κατοικῶν ἐν αὐτῷ Call.*v.Hyp.*(p.79).

***δυσέκβλητος,** *hard to cast out*; of devil, Gr.Nyss.*or.dom.*4(p.82.22; conj. for δυσέκκλητος M.44.1172B).

***δυσέκφραστος,** *difficult to expound*, Cyr.*Os.*129(3.161C); id.*Juln.* 1(6[2].20A).

δυσεκφώνητος, *hard to put into words* δ. ... τὰ τῆς θείας φύσεως ἴδια Cyr.*Jo.*1 proem.(4.8D); id.*ep.*40(p.28.24; 5[2].118C).

***δυσέκφωνος,** *harshly spoken* or *expressed*, Mac.Mgn.*apocr.*2.21 (p.42.9).

***δυσεμετέω,** *retch*, Areth.*Apoc.*9(M.106.564A).

***δυσέμετος,** *retching*, Synes.*ep.*120(M.66.1500A).

***δυσένδοτος,** *hardly yielding, stubborn* Ἰουδαίων...τὸ σκληρὸν τοῦ τρόπου καὶ πρὸς εὐσέβειαν δ. Eus.*d.e.*7.1(p.304.19; M.22.497D); *ib.*9.5(p.416.11; 672A); Chrys.*stat.*4.4(2.54E); id.*hom.60.1 in Mt.* (7.606D).

***δυσεξάγγελτος,** *of evil report*, Isid.Pel.*epp.*1.247(M.78.332D).

***δυσεξαγόρευτος,** *wrong to utter*, *Schol.*19 in Jo.Clim.*scal.*23(M.88.976D).

***δυσεξάντλητος,** *hard to draw*; of water, ‡Proc.G.*Pr.*20:5(M.87.1424A).

***δυσεξάνυστος,** *difficult to accomplish* δ. τὸ πρᾶγμα Thdr.Stud. *epp.*2.51(M.99.1261D).

δυσεξίτητος, 1. *hard to get out of*, Cyr.*Nah.*20(3.499B); **2.** *hard to get rid of*, id.*ador.*2(1.67B); id.*glaph.Ex.*(1.300C).

δυσέξοιστος, *hard to explain*, Cyr.*Juln.*1(6[2].19D); *ib.*(20A).

***δυσεπίδεκτος,** *slow to receive* δ. τῆς ἀληθείας τετύχηκας ‡Gr. Nyss.*Ar.et Sab.*7(M.45.1289D).

***δυσεπιτήδευτος,** *hard to put into practice*, Cyr.*hom.pasch.*11 (5[2].143A).

***δυσέποπτος,** *obscure*, Cyr.*ador.*6(1.202B).

δυσέργαστος, *unwilling to work*, Cyr.*Ag.*15(3.644A).

δυσέργεια, ἡ, *sluggishness, sloth*, Clem.*str.*4.21(p.305.32; M.8.1341A).

***δυσεύναστος,** *hard to soothe*, Cyr.*glaph.Gen.*6(1.184B).

***δυσεφίκτως,** *so as to be hard to grasp*, Didym.*Trin.*1.18(M.39.348C).

δυσήνεμος, 1. *stormy* τὸ δ. τῶν ἀρκτῴων Bas.*hex.*7.4(1.67C; M.29.157C); **2.** *noisome* δ. ὀδμή Nonn.*par.Jo.*11:39(M.43.845B).

***δυσηνιάστως,** *reluctantly*, Synes.*ep.*57(M.66.1389A).

δυσήνυτος, *hard to accomplish*, Cyr.*Is*.2.3(2.267E).

δύσηχος, *unpleasant in sound*, Gr.Naz.*carm*.1.2.28.245(M.37.874A); Soz.*h.e*.7.23.4(M.67.1489B); Jo.Mon.*hymn.Geo*.2(M.96.1396A).

***δυσθαλάττιος**, *stormy*, Epiph.*haer*.28.8(p.320.25; conj. for διαθαλάττια M.41.388B).

δυσθάνατος, *meeting a hard death* σώματα τῶν ἐν ναυαγίοις... δυσθανάτων Athenag.*res*.4(p.52.3; M.6.981A).

***δύσθνητος**, *dying a hard death* ὁ δύστυχος Θεόδωρος...θανάτῳ ἀώρῳ δ. γεγονώς ‡Jo.D.*ep.Thphl*.28(M.95.381B).

***δύσθρησκος**, *superstitious*, Eudoc.*Cypr*.2.8(M.85.845A).

δυσικός, v. δυτικός.

δύσις, ἡ, *setting*; *west* Παῦλος...κῆρυξ γενόμενος ἔν τε τῇ ἀνατολῇ καὶ ἐν τῇ δ. ... ἐπὶ τὸ τέρμα τῆς δ. ἐλθών *1Clem*.5.7; Ign.*Rom*.2.2; Πέτρος...ὁ τῆς δ. τὸ σκοτεινότερον τοῦ κόσμου μέρος...φωτίσαι κελευσθείς *Clem.ep*.1(M.2.33A); of western portion of empire οἱ κατὰ τὴν δ. ἐπίσκοποι Ath.*apol.Const*.27(M.25.629B); Cyr.*ador*.10(1.335E); Thdt.*ep*.70(4.1120); v. δυσμή.

***δυσκαταληψία, ἡ**, *difficulty of comprehension* ὄψεται...οὕτως οὐδὲ τὸν θεόν, εἰ μή τις εἰσέλθοι τοῦ τῆς δ. ἔνδον παραπετάσματος Or.*exc.in Ps*.17:12(M.17.112C); ὡς ἐν γε τοιαύτῃ δ. θεωρημάτων Cyr.*ador*.13(1.458B).

δυσκατανόητος, *hard to understand*, Hipp.*haer*.5.7(p.80.19; M.16.3130B); Gr.Nyss.*hom.3 in Cant*.(M.44.817C); id.*Eun*.11(2 p.268.33; M.45.877C).

***δυσκατάνυκτος**, *hard to prick* with compunction, Isid.Pel.*epp*.1.460(M.78.436B).

δυσκάτοπτος, *hard to understand* δ. ... τῶν ζητουμένων ἡ γνῶσις Cyr.*ador*.2(1.61C); id.*Ps*.32:4(M.69.872D); id.*Is*.3.2(2.403C); Olymp.*Job* 4:13–16(M.93.73C).

δυσκατόρθωτος, 1. *hard to deal with*; of a difficult reading, Thdr.Mops.*Gal*.1:4(M.66.900D); **2.** *hard to remedy* or *set right*, Marc.Er.*opusc*.5.10(M.65.1045B).

***δυσκίνησις, ἡ**, *tossing* of a boat, Sophr.H.*mir.Cyr.et Jo*.(M.87.3440B).

***δυσκληρία, ἡ**, *misfortune*, Bas.*hom*.8.5(2.66E; M.31.316B); Gr.Nyss.*Eun*.12(1 p.388.32; M.45.1117D); Chrys.*Anna* 2.1(4.712C); Thdt.*Trin*.15(M.75.1168C).

***δυσκουσσίων, ἡ**, (Lat. *discussio*) *examination of accounts*; ref. Lc.12:48, Nil.*epp*.2.22(M.79.209B).

***δυσμαχής**, *rebellious*, Cyr.*Ps*.30:17(M.69.861C).

δυσμάχητος, *hard to fight against*, Thphn.*chron*.p.297(M.108.728A).

δυσμενής, *hostile*; as subst., *the enemy*; of Devil, *A.Thom*.A 44 (p.162.1); Bas.*hom*.21.11(2.171E; M.31.560C); Thdt.*Ezech*.31:11(2.938); ὁ κοινὸς δ. id.*haer*.2 proem.(4.327); Gr.Ant.*bapt*.2.10(M.88.1881A).

***δυσμετακόμιστος**, *difficult to transport, intractable* πρὸς τὴν ἄνω πορείαν δ. [sc. τὸ σῶμα] Nil.*Magn*.4(M.79.973D); Cyr.*ador*.2(1.67B); id.*glaph.Ex*.3(1.339E); id.*Is*.3.1(2.391E); γνώμης...τὸ δ. id.*Os*.135(3.167B).

***δυσμετανόητος**, *hardly to be repented, almost beyond repentance*, Marc.Er.*opusc*.1.55(M.65.912D).

δυσμή, ἡ, 1. *setting, sunset*; met., *close* of life; of end of present age ἐπὶ δυσμαῖς τοῦ παρόντος αἰῶνος Cyr.*Rom*.5:14(p.184.10; M.74.785B); **2.** *west*; ref. baptismal renunciation made by candidate facing west (as realm of darkness and Satan), Cyr.H.*catech*.19.2; *ib*.19.4; σύμβολον τὸ στραφῆναί σε ἀπὸ δυσμῶν πρὸς ἀνατολήν, τοῦ φωτὸς τὸ χωρίον *ib*.19.9; ref. Abac.1:8 δ. δηλοῖ κατὰ τὴν Ἑλλάδα φωνήν...τῆς Ἀραβίας τὸ ὄνομα. νοῶ δὲ...διὰ τῆς Ἀραβίας τὴν σάρκα ταύτην...τὴν ὄντως δύσιν καὶ γενομένην διὰ τὴν ἁμαρτίαν ἀληθῶς λεγομένην Max.*ep*.8(M.91.444A).

δυσνόητος, *hard to be understood*, Herm.*sim*.9.14.4; Epiph.*haer*.42.11(p.124.24; M.41.728A); ref. 2Petr.3:16 δοκεῖ δέ τισιν ὁ...Παῦλος ...τινα λέγειν...δ. ... ὅτι δὲ σοφίας τῆς ἄνωθεν μεμέστωται ταῦτα οὐκ ἔστιν ἀμφιβάλλειν· λαλεῖ γὰρ ἐν αὐτῷ ὁ Χριστός Cyr.*resp*.12(p.596.5; 6^2.379A).

***δυσνοήτως**, *so as to be hard to understand*, Adam.*dial*.1.23(p.44.3; M.11.1749C).

δύσνους, *stupid*, Isid.Pel.*epp*.1.99(M.78.249D).

***δυσοκνέω**, *be lazy* or *slow*, Ephr.2.96C; Leont.N.*v.Jo.Eleem*.30 (p.63.10).

***δυσόρεκτος**, *lacking desire*, Andr.Cr.*or*.7(M.97.936A); θεὸν πρῶτον καλὸν καὶ ἔσχατον ὀρεκτὸν ἀποκαλεῖ καὶ δ. Cosm.Mel.*schol*.117(M.38.552) in Gr.Naz.*carm*.1.1.5–6.

***δυσπαραδεκτέω**, *accept with difficulty*, Or.*Jo*.2.29(24; p.86.22; M.14.165A).

***δυσπαραστάτως**, *obscurely*, ref. Jo.4:42 ὡς ἰδιώτης δὲ τῷ λόγῳ ὁ Ἰωάννης δ. ἔφρασεν ὃ νενόηκεν Or.*Jo*.13.54(53; p.284.11; M.14.500D).

***δυσπαύστως**, *so as to be hard to appease*, *Ep.Lugd*.ap.Eus.*h.e*.5.1.57(M.20.429C).

δυσπετέω, *be impatient, be intolerant*, c. πρός, Const.*or.s.c*.22(p.188.17; M.20.1304C); abs., Mac.Mgn.*apocr*.4.30(p.221.12); ‡Max.*cap.al*.48(M.90.1412B).

***δυσπλοέω**, *have a rough voyage*, Bas.*hom*.14.4(2.125D; M.31.452B).

δύσπλοος, *hard to navigate*, Epiph.*haer*.37.9(p.62.4; M.41.653B).

***δυσπράγημα, τό**, *misfortune*, Gr.Nyss.*hom.in 1Cor*.6:*18*(M.46.492C); Chrysipp.*enc.in Thdr*.(p.60.3).

***δυσπρόσβλητος**, *hard to grapple with*, met., Cyr.*Juln*.3(6^2.98C).

δυσσέβεια, ἡ, *impiety*, in gen.; ref. genealogy in Mt. διὰ τὴν ἄγαν δ. αὐτῶν παρέδραμε [sc. τρεῖς βασιλέας] ὁ εὐαγγελίστης Afric.ap.*cat.Mt*.1:17(p.9.8); δ. τῆς κατὰ θεὸν πολιτείας τοῦ Ἰσραήλ Ath.*exp.Ps*.58 proem.(M.27.264C); δ., καὶ δεισιδαιμονίᾳ, καὶ πάσῃ παρανομίᾳ συζῶντας Thdt.*Ps*.25:1(1.764); κατάλληλος ἡ παρανομία τῇ δ. id.*Rom*.1:27(3.26); of Jewish attitude to Christ, Eus.*d.e*.2.3(p.76.10; M.22.137B); Ath.*exp.Ps*.59 proem.(269A); *Const.App*.5.14.20; of heresy, Eus.*Marcell*.1.1(p.6.19; M.24.724A); ἡ κατὰ τοῦ πνεύματος δ. Didym.(‡Bas.)*Eun*.5(1.312A; M.29.748B); Isid.Pel.*epp*.1.243(M.78.332A); of paganism, *Const.App*.2.23.1; *ib*.5.15.1; Thdt.*Tit*.2:12 (3.705); of Christianity from pagan standpoint, *M.Ariadn*.6 (p.128.25).

δυσσεβ-έω, 1. *be impious* ~ούντων δοξασμάτων Or.*fr.54 in Jo*.(p.528.30); ἐάν τις τῇ ἐπιθυμίᾳ χρῆται πρὸς νόμιμον γάμον, οὐκ ἀσεβεῖ, πρὸς μοιχείαν δὲ ὁρμῶν ~εῖ *Hom.Clem*.19.21; Ath.*exp.Ps*.58:10(M.27.265C); **2.** *speak irreverently, preach impious doctrine*, Philost.*h.e*.8.3(M.65.557B); pass., Evagr.*h.e*.1.4(p.9.30; M.86.2429B); **3.** *treat irreverently, profane*, Geo.Pis.*Pers*.2.373(M.92.1236A); id.*Heracl*.1.5 (M.92.1297A).

δυσσέβημα, τό, *act of impiety*, Const.ap.Eus.*v.C*.3.52(p.99.28; M.20.1113A); μὴ ὀμνύειν...μήτε μὴν τὸν οὐρανόν...Ἑλληνικὸν γὰρ τὸ δ. *Const.App*.5.12.6; Thdt.*h.rel*.7(3.1174); of heresy Ἀρειανῶν τὸ δ. Sophr.H.*ep.syn*.(M.87.3153B).

δυσσεβής, *impious*; of pagans, Didym.(‡Bas.)*Eun*.5(1.308C; M.29.740B); Thdt.*Col*.3:18(3.496); of heresy, Eus.*h.e*.4.7.4(M.20.316C); id.*e.th*.1.5(p.64.20; M.24.833B); Ath.*ep.Serap*.1.1(M.26.532B); Bas.*hex*.2.4(1.15C; M.29.36B); Thdt.*h.e*.1.13.5(3.784); Philost.*h.e*.3.15 (M.65.505C); of heretics, Cyr.H.*catech*.16.9; *Const.App*.6.18.3; Philost.*h.e*.7.2(M.65.537B); Justn.*conf*.(p.90.8; M.86.1013C).

δύστοκος, *bearing children with pain*; of Eve, Geo.Pis.*carm.vit*.53.

***δυστράχηλος**, ? *heavy on the neck*, Geo.Pis.*senar*.76(M.92.1741B).

***δύστρεπτος**, *hard to turn aside, inevitable*, Const.*or.s.c*.22(p.188.20).

***δυστροπεύω**, *be perverse*, Bas.*ep*.299(3.435D; M.32.1044A).

δυστροπία, ἡ, *moral perversity, evil disposition*, Ephr.1.261D; Chrys.*hom.87.1 in Mt*.(7.817E); id.*hom.9.2 in 1Cor*.(10.76B); Pall.*h.Laus*.19(p.58.16; M.34.1065D); of Devil, Diod.*Ps*.90:13(M.33.1625D); Cyr.*ador*.3(1.100C); id.*Ps*.10:3(M.69.792C); id.*Is*.3.1(2.386B); *ib*.(389D); of death, id.*Os*.156(3.189C); id.*Nah*.32(3.510D); id.*Jo*.7(4.692B); Eudoc.*Cypr*.2.136(M.85.849D); plur., *evil ways*, Cyr.*Ps*.7:11(752D); id.*Lc*.17:20(M.72.840D); id.*apol.Thdt*.4(p.123.27; 6^1.217D).

[*]**δύστυχος**, = δυστυχής, *unfortunate*, *A.Mt*.21(p.247.13, one MS only).

***δυσυπότακτος**, *hard to subdue*; of false doctrine, *Apophth.Mac.Aeg*.(M.34.212B).

δυσφημ-έω, 1. *assert slanderously* μήτε ποίημα τὸν υἱὸν ἢ τὸ πνεῦμα ~ήσῃς Didym.(‡Bas.)*Eun*.5(307A; M.29.736C); Philost.*h.e*.4.10(M.65.524B); **2.** *revile* νόμον δὲ καὶ προφήτας ~εῖ [sc. Apelles], ἀνθρώπινα ...φάσκων εἶναι τὰ γεγραμμένα Hipp.*haer*.7.38(p.224.6; M.16.3346A); Meth.*res*.2.24(p.379.14; M.18.289A); ‡Nil.*perist*.11.4(M.79.909A); **3.** *blaspheme* οἱ ~οῦντες αὐτόν [sc. Χριστόν] Just.*1apol*.49.6(M.6.401B); Μαρκίων...εἰς τὸν...δημιουργὸν ~ήσας Hipp.*haer*.7.37(p.223.18; M.16.3346A); *ib*.10.13(p.274.9; 3427B); Or.*Jo*.2.11(6; p.66.9; M.14.129C); παύσασθε ~οῦντες, οἱ εὐφημεῖν καὶ πᾶσαν τιμὴν αὐτῷ ἀπονέμειν ὀφείλοντες *Hom.Clem*.11.8; ~οῦντες ἐν αὐταῖς ταῖς ἐκκλησίαις τὸν κύριον Ath.*ep.encycl*.3(p.172.14; M.25.229A); id.*Ar*.1.8(M.26.28A); τὸ πνεῦμα...τὸ ~ούμενον id.*ep.Serap*.1.15(M.26.568A); Didym.(‡Bas.)*Eun*.5(1.229B; M.29.717C); οὐ γὰρ ἐν τοῖς ~οῦσι τὸν υἱὸν κατοικεῖ [sc. τὸ πνεῦμα] Cyr.*thes*.12(5^1.123C).

δυσφημία, ἡ, 1. *slander* δ. ... καὶ ψιθυρισμῶν Meth.*symp*.5.4(p.57.21; M.18.104A); Cyr.*glaph.Gen*.4(1.114C); **2.** *ill repute*, *Can.App*.40; **3.** *insult*, Or.*hom.14.15 in Jer*.(p.121.3; M.13.424A); id.*Jo*.20.35(28; p.374.15; M.14.653D); Eus.*p.e*.10.9(485A; M.21.808A); id.*e.th*.1.1(p.62.31; M.24.829C); **4.** *blasphemy* ἡ κατὰ Χριστοῦ δ. Hipp.*haer*.5.12(p.104.14; M.16.3159C); ἀθέου δ. *ib*.9.8(p.241.10; 3371B); *ib*.10.18(p.279.19; 3435C); κατὰ τοῦ θείου λόγου δ. Eus.*h.e*.4.7.10(M.20.320A); Ath.*Ar*.1.9(M.26.29C); τὴν τῶν ἀλόγων κατὰ τοῦ πνεύματος δ. (of deniers of divinity of H. Ghost) id.*ep.Serap*.1.15(M.26.565C); κατὰ θεοῦ δ. Cyr.*Nah*.17(3.496A); **5.** *evil foreboding* Ῥεβέκκα...πρὸ ὠδῖνος ...δυσφόρητον...τὴν δ. ἐδέχετο, καὶ ἐν αὐτοῖς ἦν ἤδη τοῖς τοῦ θανάτου δείμασιν id.*glaph.Gen*.4(1.111C).

δύσφημος, 1. *ill-spoken*, *irreverent*, Or.*hom.1.7 in Jer*.(p.6.3; M.13.261D); id.*Jo*.13.6(p.231.18; M.14.408C); Meth.*res*.1.45(p.294.16; M.41.1116B); **2.** *insulting*, *slanderous*, Just.*1apol*.23.3(M.6.364B); *ib*.49.6(401A); of Ebionite statements about S. Paul, Or. *hom.19.11 in Jer*.(p.167.20; M.13.488A); **3.** *blasphemous* τοσαῦτα... δ. περὶ τοῦ θεοῦ id.*Jo*.13.21(p.245.21; M.14.436A); Meth.*res*.1.36(p.276.9; M.41.1101B); δ. ἑτεροδόξων Eus.*v.C*.3.66(p.113.17; M.20.1144B); οὔτε τὸν...υἱὸν αὐτὸν εἶναι τὸν πατέρα τις εἰπὼν διαδράσεται τὴν κατὰ τῶν δ. δίκην id.*e.th*.1.7(p.65.37; M.24.836D); *ib*.1.20(p.88.9; 877C); of Arians δ. καὶ δυσσεβεῖς Ath.*Ar*.1.11(M.26.33B); of Julian and Valens, Andr.Caes.*Apoc*.36(M.106.333A); **4.** *of ill repute* δ. ... ἔργα Just.*1apol*.26.7(M.6.369A).

δυσφορέω, *be angry*, *vexed*; c. κατά et genit., Thphn.*chron*.p.102(M.108.297B).

δυσφόρητος, *hard to bear*, Cyr.*Lc*.11:46(M.72.716C); id.*glaph. Gen*.4(1.111C).

δυσφώρατος, 1. *hard to detect*, Bas.*Spir*.73(3.62A; M.32.204C); Chrys.*hom.19.1 in Mt*.(7.244D); id.*hom.2.5 in Phil*.(11.202A); **2.** *obscure*, *hard to understand* πολὺ ἐν τοῖς εἰρημένοις...ἀσαφὲς καὶ δ. διὰ τὴν ἑρμηνευτικὴν ἀτονίαν Gr.Nyss.*Apoll*.48(M.45.1241A).

***δυσχάλινος,** *hard to keep in check*, Chrys.*stat*.1.4(2.6B).

[*]**δύσχριστος,** for δύσχρηστος, *intractable*, *inconvenient*, ref. Is. 3:10, *Dial.Christ.et Jud*.12(p.69.7); *Max.invect*.(M.90.204B).

***δυσψυχέω,** *be in low spirits*, Pall.*h.Laus*.38(p.119.13; M.34.1193D).

δυσωδία, ἡ, 1. *stench*; **a.** lit.; ref. Jo.11:39 οὐ γὰρ ἂν ἐφάνη ἡ χάρις...εἰ μὴ καὶ ἡ δ. προεχώρησε Chrys.*hom.62.3 in Jo*.(8.372C); ass. with demonic possession, Ath.*v.Anton*.63(M.26.933A); and heresy, *V.Pach.A* 7(p.130.27f.); **b.** met., *being in bad odour*, Gr. Nyss.*ep*.19(M.46.1077C); **2.** *foulness*, *filth* μὴ τὸν μονογενῆ...ἐξ αἵματος καὶ σαρκὸς καὶ τῆς ἄλλης δ. τῶν γυναικῶν γεγεννῆσθαι Hegem. *Arch*.5(p.7.11; M.42.40B); met. δ. τῆς διδασκαλίας τοῦ ἄρχοντος τοῦ αἰῶνος τούτου Ign.*Eph*.17.1; κακίας δ. Ath.*Ar*.1.8(M.26.25C); id.*syn*.20(p.247.6; M.26.716D); of sin, Gr.Naz.*carm*.1.2.8.107(M.37.656A); Gr.Nyss.*hom.1 in Cant*.(M.44.772D); Cyr.*Ps*.37:6(M.69.960A).

δυσωπ-έω, 1. *importune*, *win over* εὔχεται δέ, ὥσπερ ~ῶν τὸ θεῖον Eus.*d.e*.7.1(p.327.2; M.22.533C); μεγάλη...ἡ τῶν δυναμένων ~εῖν τὸν θεὸν βοήθεια Bas.*ep*.174(3.262B; M.32.652A); ~ῆσαι...ὑπὲρ ἐμαυτοῦ *A.Barn*.6(p.294.13); περὶ τῶν μειζόνων ~οῦσι Chrys.*hom. 55.6 in Mt*.(7.563D); id.*hom.24.3 in Eph*.(11.183C); *ib*.(183E); ~ήσωσι [sc. the saints] τὸν φιλάνθρωπον Ἰησοῦν δέξασθαι...εὐχὰς ἡμῶν Eus.Al.*serm*.8(M.86.357B); Jo.Mal.*chron*.5 p.124(M.97.217D); ~ούντων μαθεῖν Leont.N.*v.Jo.Eleem*.2(p.8.10); ~ῶν ἵνα σκεπάζηται αὐτῷ *ib*.21(p.40.3); ταύτην τὴν παράκλησιν ~ῶ τὸ ὄνομά σου *Dorm. BMV* 42(p.109); Anast.S.*qu.et resp*.63(M.89.653B); in polite address, *pray*, *beg* ~ῶ ὑμᾶς, ἀδελφοί, ἵνα...μίαν εὐχὴν ποιήσω *A.(Pass.) Andr*.14(p.32.14); Leont.N.*v.Jo.Eleem*.42(p.86.15); **2.** *convince*, *persuade* ~ῶν ὑμᾶς ἀεὶ μνήμην ἔχειν τοῦ θεοῦ Just.*dial*.46.5(M.6.576B); *ib*.68.7(636A); *ib*.77.1(656A); ~ούντων σε εἰς σωτηρίαν Clem. *prot*.7(p.57.14; M.8.184B); id.*paed*.2.10(p.214.23; M.8.512A); id.*str*.2.10(p.138.10; M.8.984B); ~ῆσαι τὸν βασιλέα...ὡς...τὰ...ὁριζόμενα κύρια εἶναι οὐ νομισθήσεται Hipp.*Dan*.3.25.5; Or.*ep*.1.6(M.11.61A); ~ῶν...ὅτι...οὗτος...ἄξιός ἐστι τοῦ πιστεύεσθαι id.*Cels*.1.44(p.94.16; M.11.741B); Eus.*e.th*.1.20(p.84.22; M.24.872B); παρουσίᾳ...αὐτοὺς ~ῶν· μόνον ἵνα μὴ ἑτέροις δουλεύσωσι Ath.*inc*.13.5(M.25.120A); Chrys.*hom.43.2 in 1Cor*.(10.403A); Jo.Mosch.*prat*.1(M.87.2905B); **3.** *reverence*, *respect* οὐδὲ...φοβοῦνται ἢ ~οῦνται οὐ τοὺς δαίμονας Clem.*prot*.4(p.41.5; M.8.145C); Bas.*hom*.1.3(2.3A; M.31.165C); ~ούμενοι τὴν φωνὴν τοῦ κυρίου *ib*.24.2(190C; M.601B); ref. Jo.2:4 τῷ γὰρ δυσχερᾶναι ἔδειξεν ὅτι σφόδρα αὐτὴν ~εῖται Chrys.*hom.21.3 in Jo*.(8.123E); *ib*.46.1(270E); id.*hom.4.3 in 2Thess*.(11.534A); Cyr. *glaph.Gen*.2(1.43C); id.*Jo*.10.2(4.903D); αὐτὸν...ἐδυσώπει μικροῦ δεῖν ὡς πατέρα Call.*v.Hyp*.(p.71).

δυσώπημα, τό, *ground of persuasion*, hence **1.** *propitiatory offering* τοῦτο ἀντὶ δ. προσάγων, ὅτι ἐν ἀσφαλείᾳ ψυχῆς καὶ ἀληθινῇ καρδίᾳ πεπόρευμαι ἐνώπιόν σου Thdr.Heracl.*Is*.38:3(M.18.1329C); *ib*. 55:13(1361C) = Proc.G.*Is*.55:1–13(M.87.2561C); **2.** *argument* ἀξιόπιστα δ. προβάλλεται εἰς πίστωσιν Thdr.Heracl.*Is*.51:6(1352C); Nil. *serm*.2(M.79.1268A).

***δυσώπησις, ἡ, 1.** *shame*, *sense of shame*, Epiph.*haer*.73.1(p.268.20; M.42.401B); **2.** *refutation*, *putting to shame*, Eus.*Marcell*.1.1(p.2.36; M.24.716A); Serap.*Man*.48(p.67; M.18.1237D); Thdot.Anc. *exp.symb*.10(M.77.1329A); **3.** *appeal*, *persuasion* πλοῦτος ἀσθενὴς πρὸς δ. Eun.*apol*.27(M.30.865C); εἰς δ. τοῦ θεοῦ Diod.*Ps*.85:13(M.33.1617D); ποῖα ῥήματα πρὸς δ. τῷ θεῷ προσήνεγκας; Ast.Soph.*hom. 4 in Ps*.5(M.40.428A); Max.*opusc*.(M.91.197C).

δυσωπητέον, *one must convince*, ‡Ath.*Ar*.4.4(p.48.15; M.26.473A).

δυσωπητικός, 1. *appealing*, *importunate*, Gr.Naz.*or*.19.13(M.35.1060A); Chrys.*hom.2.2 in Philm*.(11.780E); δ. γὰρ πατρὶ...αἷμα υἱοῦ Jo.D.*imag*.1.21(M.94.1253B); superl., Thdr.Mops.*Rom*.12:1(p.159.29; M.66.860B); **2.** *convincing*, *persuasive*, Or.*Cels*.2.11(p.140.1; M.11.816B); id.*Jo*.10.40(24; p.217.18; M.14.385A); **3.** *venerable*, Bas. *Spir*.71(3.60B; M.32.200C).

δυσωπητικῶς, 1. *so as to put to shame*, Tat.ap.Clem.*str*.3.12(p.232.25; M.8.1181A); Or.*Jo*.32.5(p.433.18; M.14.753A); **2.** *persuasively*, Or.*comm.in Ex*.(M.12.281A); id.*Jo*.32.10(7; p.442.8; M.14.768A); Gr.Agr.*Eccl*.3.2(M.98.845B); Max.*ambig*.(M.91.1224D).

δυσωπία, ἡ, 1. *shame*, *shamefacedness* τοῦ μετανοοῦντος δὲ τρόποι δύο, ὁ μὲν κοινότερος φόβος ἐπὶ τοῖς πραχθεῖσιν, ὁ δὲ ἰδιαίτερος ἡ δ. ἡ πρὸς ἑαυτὴν τῆς ψυχῆς ἐκ συνειδήσεως Clem.*str*.4.6(p.265.8; M.8.1249A); Gr.Nyss.*usur*.(M.46.448B); **2.** *discomfiture* Μωυσῆς... ἐσφράγισεν τὰς τῶν οἰκιῶν θύρας...εἰς δ. τοῦ ἀγγέλου Mel.*pass*.15 p.3.6; Clem.*str*.4.16(p.294.12; M.8.1309C); *Hom.Clem*.15.2; **3.** *putting to shame*, *appeal to sense of shame*, Or.*Cels*.4.81(p.352.5; M.11.1153D); **4.** *persuasion*, *Hom.Clem*.3.64; **5.** *respect*, *reverence*, Clem. *q.d.s*.22(p.174.26; M.9.628B); Jo.VI H.*v.Jo.D*.8(M.94.441A).

δυτικός, *western* αἱ τῶν δ. ... μερῶν...ἐκκλησίαι Const.ap.Eus.*v.C*. 3.19(p.86.20; M.20.1077B); διατείνει [sc. ἡ ἐκκλησία] καὶ ἐπὶ τὴν δ. θάλασσαν Eus.*d.e*.6.18(p.279.20; M.22.460B); τοὺς ἐν τοῖς δ. μέρεσιν ἐπισκόπους Ath.*syn*.1(p.231.9; M.26.681A); δ. ἀρχιερέων Gr.Naz.*or*. 43.28(M.36.536A); δ. συνόδου id.*ep*.101(M.37.177A); Epiph.*haer*.71.1(p.249.18; M.42.373C); ἡ τῶν...δ. γλῶττα Anast.S.*hod*.11(M.89.193A); δυσικός *Apoc.Dan*.C(p.115); comp. οἱ ἐκείνων δυτικώτεροι Thdt.*Ezech*.27:9(2.900).

δώδεκα, *twelve*; **1.** of aeons in Valent. system, emanating from Anthropos and Ecclesia, Iren.*haer*.2.14.8(M.7.756A); v. δωδεκάς, ζῴδιον; **2.** of apostles, OT types of apostles and Gnost. application to dodecad of aeons, v. ἀπόστολος; **3.** of the twelve prophets, v. προφήτης.

***δωδεκαγώνιος,** *of twelve sides*, Hipp.*haer*.5.14(p.109.7; M.16.3167B).

δωδεκαετής, 1. *lasting twelve years*, Dion.Al.*ep.can*.(p.103.6; M.10.1281A); *Const.App*.2.1.4; **2.** *twelve years old*, Iren.*haer*.1.3.2(M.7.469A); Hipp.*haer*.5.26(p.131.21; M.16.3202B); *Ev.Thom*.A 19(p.156).

δωδεκαήμερος, *lasting twelve days*; of festival of Christmas, neut. as subst., †Jo.Jej.*poenit*.(M.88.1913C).

δωδεκάθεον, τό, *temple of the twelve gods*, ‡Ath.*Melch*.(M.28.525A).

***δωδεκάκλωνος,** *with twelve branches*, ‡Chrys.*ascens.Ac*.3(3.783A).

***δωδεκάκτινος,** *of twelve rays*, Mac.Mgn.*apocr*.3.41(p.143.30); Leont.B.*mesopent*.(M.86.1992A).

***δωδεκακώδων, ὁ,** *robe with twelve bells*, *Protev*.8.3(p.17).

***δωδεκάλιθον, τό,** the *twelve precious stones* in high priest's breastplate; met., of apostles, ‡Bas.*h.myst*.13(p.261.5); ‡Sophr.H. *liturg*.6(M.87.3988A).

***δωδεκαμελής,** *of twelve members*, Iren.*haer*.1.14.9(M.7.612B).

***δωδεκαμερής,** *in twelve parts*, ‡Just.*ep.Zen.et Ser*.7(M.6.1189D).

***δωδεκάπληγος,** neut. as subst., the *twelve last plagues* of fifth hell, *Apoc.Esd*.(p.28); fem. as subst., *1Apoc.Jo*.(p.94, some MSS only).

***δωδεκαπρόφητον, τό,** *book of the twelve prophets*, Epiph.*mens*.4(M.43.244C); *Dial.Tim.et Aquil*.77 v°; Jo.D.*f.o*.4.17(M.94.1180B).

***δωδεκάπυλος,** *having twelve gates*; **1.** δ. πόλις, fig. of BMV, Rom. Mel.(Maas *KlT* p.9); **2.** neut. as subst., of building in Jerusalem having twelve gates, *Chron.Pasch*.p.254(M.92.613B).

***δωδεκάριθμος, 1.** *twelve in number*, Nonn.*par.Jo*.2:12(M.43.

761D); †Jo.D.*B.J.*1(M.96.864A); **2.** *twelfth, one of the Twelve*, Nonn. *par.Jo.*13:31(865A).

δωδεκάς, ἡ, *group of twelve*; of apostles, †Gregent.*disp.*(M.86.748A); Jo.D.*trisag.*14(M.95.48B); Thdr.Stud.*or.*5.3(M.99.724C); of Marcosian aeons, *dodecad*, Iren.*haer.*1.16.1(M.7.629A) cit. s. δυάς; Val.Gn.ap.Epiph.*haer.*31.5(p.392.8; M.41.484A) al.

***δωδεκάσκηπτρον, τό,** the *company of the twelve tribes*, *1Clem.* 31.4.

δωδεκάφυλ(λ)ος, *of twelve tribes*, *Orac.Sib.*3.249; *ib.*11.36; †Gregent. *disp.*(M.86.704A); neut. as subst., the *twelve tribes of Israel*, *1Clem.* 55.6; Jo.Eub.*concept.BMV* 6(M.96.1468C); as borne on high priest's breastplate τὸ δωδεκάφυλλον *Hymn.*(v.l. -φύλον *AGC* p.543); fem. as subst., *Protev.*1.3(p.3).

***δωδεκάφωτος,** *with twelve lights*, *Lit.Marc.*(p.115.36).

δωδεκάχορδος, *with twelve strings*, Jo.D.*trisag.*14(M.95.48B).

δωμάτιον ([*]δομ-), **τό, 1.** dim. of δῶμα, *cottage* δοματίῳ Eus.Al. *serm.*4(M.86.333A); **2.** = δῶμα, *house*, Chrys.*hom.30.4 in Rom.*(9.743D); id.*hom.1.6 in 2Cor.*(10.426E); Dion.Ar.*d.n.*2.4(M.3.641B); **3.** *structure, building*, Eus.*v.C.*4.58(p.141.14; M.20.1209B); **4.** *chamber*, Chrys.*sac.*1.5(p.22.19; 1.370B); monk's *cell*, Nil.*epp.*2.96(M.79.244B); **5.** *house-top*, Marc.Diac.*v.Porph.*97.

***δωματουργία, ἡ,** *erection of a building*, Eus.*v.C.*3 tit.36(p.74.1; M.20.1050A).

δωμήτωρ, ὁ, 1. *builder*, Gr.Naz.*carm.*2.2(poem.)7.67(v.l. δομήτηρα M.37.1556A); **2.** as adj., *of a builder* δ. τέχνῃ Paul.Sil.*Soph.*456(M.86.2137A).

***Δωνατιανοί (Δωνατικοί, Δωνατισταί), οἱ,** *followers of Donatus, Donatists*; relation of their views to those of Novatianists discussed, Epiph.*haer.*59.13(p.378.28; M.41.1037B); Arianism alleged; martyr-cult, and suicides, Thdt.*haer.*4.6(4.360); *Δωνατικοί· οἱ ἀπὸ Δονάτου τινὸς...ἐναρξάμενοι, τοῦ παραδεδωκότος αὐτοῖς ὀστοῦν τι ἐπὶ χειρὸς αὐτῶν κρατοῦντες, τοῦτο πρότερον ἀσπάζεσθαι, καὶ τηνικαῦτα τῆς προσφορᾶς...μετέχειν* Jo.D.*haer.*95(M.94.757D).

δωρεά, ἡ, *gift, present*; of God's gifts, in gen. ταῖς...ὑπερβαλλούσαις αὐτοῦ δ. τῆς εἰρήνης εὐεργεσίαις τε κολληθῶμεν *1Clem.*19.2; μεταλάβωμεν τῶν ἐπηγγελμένων δ. *ib.*35.4; τῷ δυναμένῳ...ἡμᾶς εἰσαγαγεῖν ἐν τῇ αὐτοῦ χάριτι καὶ δ. εἰς τὴν αἰώνιον αὐτοῦ βασιλείαν *M.Polyc.*20.2; Meth.*arbitr.*22(p.206.8); Chrys.*hom.15.4 in Phil.*(11.316B); esp. of gift of H. Ghost, cf.*Barn.*1.2; in baptism βάπτισμα... πνεύματος ἁγίου δωρεᾶς πρόξενον Cyr.H.*catech.*20.6; CLaod.*can.*47; Bas.*hom.*13.1(2.114D; M.31.425C); id.*hom.in Ps.*32(1.136B; M.29.333D); Chrys.*hom.4.7 in Mt.*(7.60A); *ib.12.3*(164E); ἄφατος ἡ τοῦ πνεύματος χάρις, καὶ πολυειδὴς ἡ δ. id.*hom.86.3 in Jo.*(8.517B); cf. βάπτισμα; esp. ass. post-baptismal chrismation, Serap.*euch.*25.2; σφραγὶς δωρεᾶς πνεύματος ἁγίου ‡CCP(381)*can.*7; hence of baptism as a gift, *Hom.Clem.*13.10; in eucharist ἡ κοινωνία καὶ ἡ δ. τοῦ παναγίου πνεύματος εἴη μετὰ πάντων ὑμῶν *Lit.Jac.*(p.198.13); καὶ νῦν τὰς δ. τοῦ...πνεύματος ἐπιχορήγησον αὐτῇ [sc. ἐκκλησίᾳ] *ib.*(p.208.1); of spiritual benefit of eucharist, cf.Ign.*Smyrn.*7.1; μὴ ἐννοῶν...τὸ μέγεθος τῶν προκειμένων, μὴ λογιζόμενος τὸν ὄγκον τῆς δ. Chrys. *hom.28.1 in 1Cor.*(10.251A); of Christ's teaching as divine gift implanted in soul, *Barn.*9.9.

δωρ-έομαι, *give, bestow*; ref. God as giver δι' ὧν αὐτὸς ἐδωρήσατο λογικῶν δυνάμεων Just.*1apol.*10.4(M.6.341A); διὰ μετανοίας κλῆσις αὐτοῖς δεδώρηται Tat.*orat.*15(p.17.7; M.6.840B); ὁσίως τῷ θεῷ ἀπαρχόμενοι τῶν παρ' αὐτοῦ δεδωρημένων εἰς χρῆσιν...ἀνθρώπων Hipp.*haer.*9.30(p.263.22; M.16.3410C); οὐχ ἡμεῖς τὰ διαφέροντα πεποιήκαμεν, ἀλλ' ἡμεῖς μὲν ἐδόξαμεν, ὁ δὲ θεὸς ταῦτα ἐδωρήσατο Or. *princ.*3.1.20(p.234.11; M.11.293A); Gr.Thaum.*pan.Or.*6(p.16.25; M.10.1072A); χρησιμωτάτην...εἰς ἀφθαρσίας κτῆσιν τὴν παρθενίαν ὁ θεὸς ἐδωρήσατο Meth.*symp.*4.4(p.49.20; M.18.92B); *Hom.Clem.*8.10; ζωὴν αἰώνιον σὺν ἔργοις καλοῖς ~εῖσθαι τὸν θεὸν ἐπὶ τῷ βαπτίσματι *ib.*13.10; Jo.D.*hom.*1.3(M.96.549D); of Son as giver τοῖς πᾶσι τὸ εἶναι ~εῖται, ὡς φύσει ὢν θεός Didym.(‡Bas.)*Eun.*5(1.313D; M.29.752C); *cat.Lc.* 10:30(p.89.3); ref. H. Ghost τὸ πνεῦμα τὸ προφητεῦσαν τὴν σύνεσιν τῶν αὐτοῦ λόγων ἐδωρήσατο Gr.Thaum.*pan.Or.*15(p.34.16; 1093D); τοῦ εἶναι τὴν διαμονὴν ~εῖται μεταλαμβανόμενον Didym.(‡Bas.)*Eun.* 5(1.311D; M.29.748B); of Church ἐπιζητοῦσι ~ουμένη ‡*Diogn.*11.5.

δώρημα, τό, *gift* πᾶσιν γὰρ ὁ θεὸς δίδοσθαι θέλει ἐκ τῶν ἰδίων δ. Herm.*mand.*2.4; πάντα τὰ τοῦ θεοῦ δ. ... μείζονά ἐστι τῆς θνητῆς ὑποστάσεως Or.*fr.incert.in Jer.*(p.195.7); πᾶν δ. τέλειον ἐφ' ἡμᾶς ἔρχεται παρὰ πατρὸς δι' υἱοῦ ἐν ἁγίῳ πνεύματι Cyr.*Lc.*22:19(M.72.908B); Jo.D.*hom.*1.3(M.96.552A).

***δωρημαῖος,** *freely given*, neut. as subst., Cyr.H.*catech.*13.36.

δωρητικός, *apt to give, giving*, of God δ. τῶν εὐαγγελίων Epiph. *haer.*42.12(p.165.14; M.41.788B); of H. Ghost πνεῦμα...πάσης συνέσεώς τε καὶ ζωῆς δ. †Diad.*Ar.*9(M.65.1165C); of Abel as δ. and Cain as διανομεύς with God, Proc.G.*Gen.*4:2(M.87.237C).

δωροδοκ-έω, *bribe, win over by bribes*; ref. almsgiving διὰ πενήτων ὁ ἡμέτερος δικαστὴς ~εῖται Chrys.ap.Jo.D.*parall.*(M.95.1468D); οἶδε ~εῖσθαι Χριστὸς ταῖς τῶν πενήτων χερσίν Bas.Sel.*or.*26.2 (M.85.308C).

***δωροδοκητέον,** *one must win over by gifts*, Tat.*orat.*4(p.5.13; M.6.813B).

***δωροδοσία, ἡ,** *gift* προσευχὴ...τοῦ ἐπὶ πάντων θεοῦ δ. Leont.B. *parasc.*2(M.86.1997C).

δωροδότης, ὁ, *giver*, of God γνώσεως δ. *Lit.Marc.*(p.135.12).

δωρολήπτης, ὁ, *one who accepts bribes*, Tat.*orat.*10(p.11.4; M.6.828B); Hipp.*haer.*9.11(p.245.16; M.16.3378C).

δωροληψία, ἡ, *acceptance of bribes*, of Montanus ὁ ἐπ' ὀνόματι προσφορῶν τὴν δ. ἐπιτεχνώμενος Apollon.ap.Eus.*h.e.*5.18.2(M.20.476B); ἀπληστίας τῶν δ. Ephr.1.132A; bishop warned against δ. in his treatment of sinners, *Const.App.*2.9.2; *ib.*2.17.1; Cyr.*Is.*5.4 (2.831E).

δῶρον, τό, *gift*; **1.** of God's gifts μακάρια...τὰ δ. τοῦ θεοῦ...ζωὴ... λαμπρότης ἐν δικαιοσύνῃ, ἀλήθεια ἐν παρρησίᾳ, πίστις ἐν πεποιθήσει, ἐγκράτεια ἐν ἁγιασμῷ *1Clem.*35.1; δ. καὶ...ἐπαγγελίαι Herm.*vis.* 3.2.1; δ. τὸ μέγιστον...ἑρμηνεὺς εἶναι τῶν τοῦ θεοῦ λόγων Gr.Thaum. *pan.Or.*15(p.34.20; M.10.1096A); of remission of sins in baptism, Bas.*hom.*13.3(2.116E; M.31.432A); of grace of baptism λάβε παρὰ τοῦ δ. τὴν ἀσφάλειαν, καὶ δὸς τῷ δ. τὴν ἁγνείαν Gr.Naz.*or.*40.18(M.36.381C); of remission of sins as distinctive gift of participation in Christ's death in baptism, being absent from John's baptism, Chrys.*hom.10.1 in Mt.*(7.140D); of Communion, Thdt.*1Cor.*11:28 (3.239); Jo.Clim.*scal.*23(M.88.976C); **2.** of man's offerings to God; **a.** in gen. δ. ... καὶ...προσφοραῖς χαίρει Just.*dial.*28.4(M.6.536C); οὐδὲ...φέροιμι ἄν τι παρ' ἐμαυτοῦ δ. ἄξιον εἰς τιμὴν...τῷ πάντων ἡγεμόνι Gr.Thaum.*pan.Or.*3(p.7.27; M.10.1060B); *Hom.Clem.*18.19; of OT sacrifices, *Const.App.*2.25.6; *ib.*2.25.16; **b.** of spiritual sacrifices δ. δέ ἐστιν θεῷ ἡ ἑκάστου προσευχὴ καὶ εὐχαριστία *ib.*2.53.4; ἀνατέθεικα γὰρ ἐμαυτὸν καὶ ὡς δ. ἐπήγγελμαι τῷ θεῷ Cyr.*ador.*7 (1.239A); δ. ... τῷ...θεῷ, τὴν ἰδίαν ἕκαστος ἀνατίθησι ζωήν *ib.*16 (560A); **c.** of eucharistic oblation, *1Clem.*44.4; προσαγαγεῖν τὰ δ. Pall.*v.Chrys.*14(p.85.9; M.47.48); ἄρα αὐτὸ τὸ δ. φυσικὴν ἔχει σωτηρίαν Sever.*creat.*6.4(M.56.488)ap.Cosm.Ind.*top.*10(M.88.425A); ἡ καθαρὰ σινδὼν ἡ ὑφαπλουμένη τῇ τῶν θείων δ. διακονίᾳ Isid.Pel.*epp.*1.123(M.78.264D); v. προσφέρω.

δωροφορ-έω, *bring as a gift* διδάσκει...μὴ πρότερον αἰτεῖσθαί τι παρὰ τοῦ θεοῦ πρὶν αὐτῷ τι τῶν κεχαρισμένων ~ῆσαι Gr.Nyss.*or. dom.*2(p.30.27; M.44.1140A); μεῖζόν ἐστι [sc. πνεῦμα] τῶν ἀπὸ μικρᾶς ...δυνάμεως τὰ κατὰ δύναμιν αὐτῷ ~ούντων id.*Maced.*14(M.45.1317D); τῶν ἐν ἡμῖν τὰ τίμια, τῇ ἀτιμήτῳ φύσει ~οῦντες *ib.*25(1333A); of offering of eucharistic elements, Isid.Pel.*epp.*1.349(M.78.381B); of worship κύριος...ἀξιώσειεν ἡμᾶς σεραφικῶς ~ῆσαι καὶ προσᾷσαι τὴν πολυύμνητον ἐπῳδήν *Lit.Jac.*(p.164.15); Thdr.Stud.*nativ.BMV* 1 (M.96.680D).

***δωροφορητέον,** *one must offer as a gift* δ. τῇ τοῦ λόγου μητρὶ τοὺς λόγους αὐτούς Andr.Cr.*or.*1(M.97.808C).

δωροφορία, ἡ, A. *bringing of gifts, offering*; of gifts to God; **1.** in gen. ἡ...Μάγων δ. Isid.Pel.*epp.*1.18(M.78.193B); Cyr.*Ps.*8:1(M.69.757A); ἱερεὺς...δεχόμενος τὰς παρὰ τῶν λαῶν δ. id.*Os.*40(3.71C); Sophr.H.*ep.syn.*(M.87.3176A); **2.** of spiritual sacrifices τὰς πάλαι μὲν ἀνατρέπων...θυσίας, εἰσφέρων δὲ τὰς τῆς νέας διαθήκης, τὰς δι' αἰνέσεως δ. Ath.*exp.Ps.*49 proem.(M.27.229B); Gr.Nyss.*or.dom.*2 (p.30.23; M.44.1137D); *ib.*(p.30.34; 1140A); θυσίας πνευματικὰς καὶ δ. Cyr.*ador.*16 tit.(1.557A); id.*Jo.*4.5(4.401E); **3.** of eucharist τὴν μυστικὴν δ. Gr.Nyss.*Eun.*11(2 p.269.14; M.45.877D); τῆς μυστικῆς καὶ ζωοποιοῦ δ. ἡ χάρις Cyr.*Lc.*22:19(M.72.908B); **4.** of church offerings in gen. μὴ καὶ τὴν πρόθεσιν τῆς δ. ὑβρίσῃς, τὸν τρόπον τῆς δαπάνης αὐτῆς ἐρευνῶν Isid.Pel.*epp.*1.187(M.78.304A).

B. *giving of presents* ἄνεσίν τε καὶ δ. ἐπαγγελλόμενος Thdr.Mops. *fr.in Jo.*5:43(p.327.2, v.l. δορυφορίαν M.66.745A).

E

***ἑβδομαδάριος**, *on duty for a week*; masc. as subst., *hebdomadarian*, a deacon responsible for church services for a week at a time, CSyr.*act.*(*ACO* 3 p.98.27; H.2.1376A).

ἑβδομαδικός, v. ἑβδοματικός.

***ἑβδομάριος**, *on duty for a week*; as subst., of church officials, Leont.N.*v.Jo.Eleem.*14(p.29.20); of patriarch's servants, *ib.*18 (p.36.13); *ib.*27(p.58.1).

ἑβδομάς, ἡ, **A.** the number *seven*; **1.** as mysterious number, ref. Mt.18:21ff. *οἶδε τὸ μυστήριον τῆς ἑ. Πέτρος...οὔτε ὁ Πέτρος ἄλλον ἠρώτησεν, οὔτε ὁ κύριος ἐξέβη τοῦ κανόνος τοῦ ἑβδοματικοῦ* ‡Gr. Nyss.*or.2 in Gen.1:26*(M.44.288A); signifying 'sabbath' and so 'God' *τοῦτό ἐστιν ἑβδομάδος μυστήριον. αὐτὸς γάρ ἐστιν ἡ τῶν ὅλων ἀνάπαυσις, ὃς τοῖς ἐν μικρῷ μιμουμένοις αὐτοῦ τὸ μέγα αὐτὸν χαρίζεται εἰς ἀνάπαυσιν* *Hom.Clem.*17.10; cf. C infra; **2.** signifying earthly time, Clem.*str.*6.16(p.504.17; M.9.369C); *τὸν αἰσθητὸν διαδεξαμένη χρόνον, τὸν ἐν ἑβδομάσιν ἀνακυκλούμενον* Gr.Nyss.*Pss.titt.*B 5(M.44. 504D); *ib.*(505A); *ib.*6(609C); **3.** signifying rest, Clem.*str.*6.14(p.486. 7; M.9.329A) cit. s. ἀνάπαυσις; *ib.*7.10(p.42.14; 481B); **4.** Valentinian; **a.** as region below ogdoad, ruled by demiurge *ἡ Σοφία ἄνωθεν ἀπὸ τῆς ὀγδοάδος ἐνεργοῦσα ἕως τῆς ἑβδομάδος* Hipp.*haer.*6. 33(p.162.4; M.16.3243D); *ib.*7.24(p.202.9; 3311B); into which region Christ descended from mount of Transfiguration, Iren.*haer.*1.14.6 (M.7.608A) (though by some interpreted as seventh day); *ἀναβάντα εἰς τὸ ὄρος...τὸν καταβάντα καὶ κρατηθέντα ἐν τῇ ἑ.* *ib.*(608A); *ἐπεὶ γάρ ἐστιν ὁ κόσμος διῃρημένος εἰς ὀγδοάδα, ἥτις ἐστὶν ἡ κεφαλὴ τοῦ παντὸς κόσμου...καὶ εἰς ἑ., ἥτις ἐστὶν ἡ κεφαλὴ τῆς ἑ. ... ἀναγκαῖον ἦν τὰ συγκεχυμένα φυλοκρινηθῆναι διὰ τῆς τοῦ Ἰησοῦ διαιρέσεως. ἔπαθεν οὖν τοῦτο ὅπερ ἦν αὐτοῦ σωματικὸν μέρος, ὃ ἦν τῆς ἀμορφίας... ἀνέστη δὲ τοῦτο ὅπερ ἦν ψυχικὸν αὐτοῦ μέρος, ὅπερ ἦν τῆς ἑ., καὶ ἀπεκατέστη εἰς τὴν ἑ.* Hipp.*haer.*7.27(p.207.15ff.; 3319B,C); and which he evangelizes, *ib.*7.26(p.204.19ff.; 3315A,B); **b.** as name of demiurge *ἑπτὰ γὰρ οὐρανοὺς...ὧν ἐπάνω τὸν δημιουργὸν εἶναι λέγουσι· καὶ διὰ τοῦτο ἑ. καλοῦσιν αὐτόν* Iren.*haer.*1.5.2(M.7.493B); *ib.*1.14.7 (609A); *τούτου τοῦ διαστήματος...κύριος ἡ ἑ., καὶ ἔστιν ἡ μὲν ὀγδοὰς ἄρρητος, ῥητὸν δὲ ἡ ἑ.· οὗτός ἐστι...ὁ τῆς ἑ. ἄρχων ὁ λαλήσας τῷ Μωυσῇ* Hipp.*haer.*7.25(p.203.10ff.; M.16.3314A); *ib.*6.36(p.165.21; 3250B); so also acc. Basilides, *ib.*10.14(p.275.26; 3430C); **c.** of soul *τὸ μέρος θνητή τίς ἐστιν ἡ ψυχή, μεσότης τις οὖσα· ἔστι γὰρ ἑ. καὶ κατάπαυσις· ὑποκάτω γάρ ἐστι τῆς ὀγδοάδος* *ib.*6.32(p.161.13; 3243C).

B. *week*; **1.** of Creation *ὁ τὴν τοῦ χρόνου φύσιν κατασκευάσας θεὸς... ἑβδομάδι αὐτὸν ἐκμετρῶν, ἀεὶ τὴν ἑ. εἰς ἑαυτὴν ἀνακυκλοῦσθαι κελεύει, ἐξαριθμοῦσαν τοῦ χρόνου τὴν κίνησιν* Bas.*hex.*2.8(1.21A; M.29.49C); *τὰ κβ' ἔργα, ἃ ἐποίησεν ὁ θεὸς ἐν ταῖς ἓξ ἡμέραις τῆς ἑ.* Epiph.*mens.* (M.43.276B); Jo.D.*disp.*(M.96.1337B); *ib.*(1345C); **2.** of seventy weeks prophesied in Dan. *αἱ ἑβδομήκοντα ἑ. ἐπληρώθησαν ἕως Χριστοῦ ἡγουμένου κατὰ τὸν Δανιήλ* Or.*princ.*4.1.5(p.300.10; M.11.349C); discussed, Eus.*d.e.*8.2(p.374.9ff.; M.22.608Bff.); **3.** liturg.; **a.** esp. of Holy Week, usu. called *ἡ μεγάλη ἑ.* *Const.App.*8.33.3; *μεγάλην δὲ καλοῦμεν τὴν ἑ., οὐκ ἐπειδὴ πλέον ἔχει τὸ μῆκος τῶν ὡρῶν...διὰ τοῦτο τοίνυν μεγάλην τὴν ἑ. καλοῦμεν, ἐπειδὴ τοσοῦτον πλῆθος δωρεῶν ἡμῖν ἐν αὐτῇ κεχάρισται ὁ δεσπότης* Chrys.*hom.30.1 in Gen.*(4.294B,C); id. *hom.in Ps.145:2*(5.525C); Eutych.*pasch.*6(M.86.2400A); *τῇ μεγάλῃ ἑ. φωτίσαι τὰ παιδία* Jo.Mosch.*prat.*165(M.87.3032B); also called *ἡ ἁγία ἑ.* *Const.App.*5.13.4; Proc.G.*Jos.*1:11(M.87.996C); *ἑ. τοῦ πάσχα* Eutych.*pasch.*5(M.86.2397B); *ἑ. τοῦ πάθους* Cyr.*hom.pasch.*1 (5².16C); *ib.*2(31A); **b.** weeks of Lent *τῆς νηστείας ἑ.* Bas.*hom.*14.1 (2.122D; M.31.444D); **c.** of Pentecost *ἑορτῆς, τῆς...πεντηκοστῆς ἑβδομάσι μὲν ἑπτὰ τετιμημένης* Eus.*v.C.*4.64(p.144.11; M.20.1220B); Cyr.*hom.pasch.*1(5².16D); *ib.*2(31B); week of Pentecost to be kept as feast, *Const.App.*5.20.14; week after as fast, *ib.*5.20.18; Ath.*fug.*6 (p.72.8; M.25.652B); **d.** weeks of canonical penance, *Const.App.* 2.16.2; †Jo.Jej.*poenit.*(M.88.1916B); **4.** Gnost. *elegisse* [sc. *Ialdabaoth*] *septem dies, quos et sanctam hebdomadam vocant. et unusquisque eorum suum praeconem assumit ad gloriandum*, Iren. *haer.*1.30.10(M.7.701A).

C. *seventh day, sabbath* *παρ' Ἑβραίοις ὃ καλεῖται σάββατον Ἑλληνιστὶ ἑρμηνεύεται ἑ.* Thphl.Ant.*Autol.*2.12(M.6.1069C); deified in pagan literature, Clem.*str.*5.14(p.398.17; M.9.164B); in Christian dispensation a day of work, *ib.*6.16(p.502.15; 364C); interpreted as 7,000th year, the year of judgement, Meth.*creat.*12(p.499.30; M.18. 344B).

***ἑβδοματιαῖος**, *lasting a week*, Jo.Clim.*scal.*4(M.88.701B).

***ἑβδοματίζομαι**, *spend the week*, Amph.*hom.*2.7(M.39.53C).

ἑβδοματικός (ἑβδομαδικός), **1.** *belonging to seven, of seven*; **a.** in gen., ref. Mt.18:21f. *οὔτε ὁ κύριος ἐξέβη τοῦ κανόνος τοῦ ἑ.* ‡Bas. *struct.hom.*7(1.341F; M.30.49B); **b.** signifying eternal world *διὰ τὸν... ἑ. ἀριθμὸν τὸν εἰς τὸν σαββατισμὸν καταντῶντα τοῦ μέλλοντος αἰῶνος* Andr.Caes.*Apoc.*2(M.106.228B); but more often this world, *ib.*36 (332D); *διὰ τὸ τοῦ ἑ. ἀριθμοῦ τῷ παρόντι φθαρτῷ αἰῶνι σύστοιχον, καταντῶντος δηλαδὴ εἰς τὸν σαββατισμὸν καὶ τοῦ μέλλοντος αἰῶνος* Areth.*Apoc.*2(M.106.513D); cf. ἑβδομάς; ἕβδομος and Church on earth, Andr.Caes.*Apoc.*1(221C,D); **c.** in myst. doctrine of numbers (Pythagorean), Hipp.*haer.*4.14(p.46.34; M.16.3079A) et passim; **2.** *weekly*; **a.** lit. *ἑ. κύκλοις νήστις διατελῶν* Bas.*ep.*45.1(3.133D; M.32.365B); ref. weekly fast of monks *ἑβδομαδικόν* ‡Nil.*narr.*3(M. 79.617A); *τὴν ἑβδομαδικὴν...ἡμέραν week* day, Max.*comput.*20(M.19. 1237B); *ib.*23(1241B); **b.** met. = earthly opp. heavenly (which belongs to eighth day) *τοῦ ἑ. τούτου χρόνου* Bas.*hex.*2.8(1.21D; M. 29.52A); Gr.Nyss.*Ps.6*(M.44.609D); *ἑβδομαδικὸς γὰρ οὗτος ὁ αἰών, τῇ εἰς ἑαυτὸν τοῦ χρόνου περιελίξει πληρούμενος* Max.*ambig.*(M.91.1377D); *ib.*(1396D); *ib.*(1397D); *ἐν τῷ ἑ. τούτῳ βίῳ* Jo.D.*fr.Mt.*12:1(M.96. 1408C); **3.** *of the seventh day, sabbatical*; **a.** lit., Gr.Naz.*or.*15.3(M. 35.916A); Max.*cap.theol.*1.60(M.90.1105A); **b.** met. *ὑπερβὰς δὲ τὸν κόσμον καὶ ἐν τῇ ἑ. ἀναπαύσει γεγενημένος, οὐκ αἰσθήσεται κακώσεως* Didym.*Job* 5:18(M.39.1133C).

ἑβδομήκοντα, *seventy*; **1.** of LXX translators, Just.*dial.*68.7 (M.6.636A); *οἱ ἑ.* *ib.*124.3(765A); *ib.*137.3(792B); full story, Iren.*haer.* 3.21.2(M.7.947B); Clem.*str.*1.22(p.92.16; M.8.892A); ‡Just.*coh.Gr.*13 (M.6.265C); opp. writers of Hebr. original, Or.*hom.12.5 in Lev.* (p.464.15; M.12.542B); **2.** of seventy elders to whom Moses was supposed to have entrusted Law, *Hom.Clem.*2.38; *Clem.ep.Petr.*1 (M.2.25A); *ib.*2(25B); **3.** of seventy disciples, to whom *γνῶσις* was transmitted by apostles, Clem.*fr.*13(p.199.23; M.9.749A); exeg. Ex. 15:27, cf. *'arbores' repperientur 'septuaginta palmarum'. non enim soli duodecim apostoli fidem Christi praedicarunt, sed et alii septuaginta missi...referuntur*, Or.*hom.7.3 in Ex.*(p.209.8,10; M.12.343C); cf. id.*hom.27.11 in Num.*(p.271.2ff.; M.12.792B,C); **4.** as symbolic number (ref. Jer.36:10) *πληρώσας τὸν συμβολικὸν ἀριθμὸν 'τῶν ἐτῶν τῶν ἑ.' σαββάτου καὶ ἀναπαύσεως ὄντα* id.*fr.48 in Jer.*(p.222.20; M.13.577B).

***ἑβδομηκονταετηρίς**, ἡ, *period of seventy years*, Eus.*d.e.*8.2 (p.382.31; M.22.620B).

ἑβδομηκονταετής, *of seventy years*, Clem.*str.*1.21(p.87.12; M.8. 877A); Eus.*d.e.*8.2(p.382.6; M.22.617D).

***ἑβδομηκονταετία**, ἡ, *period of seventy years*, Afric.*chron.*16.1 (M.10.81A); Bas.*ep.*264(3.408A; M.32.984A).

ἑβδομηκοστός, *of seventy years*, Thdt.*Ps.*119:5(1.1483).

ἕβδομος, **A.** *seventh*; **1.** as myst. number *ὁ ἕ. παρὰ Ἰουδαίοις ἀριθμός, τίμιος, ἐν ᾧ αἱ σκηνοπηγίαι...ἕ. ἐνιαυτὸς παρ' ἐκείνοις τίμιος ὁ τῆς ἀφέσεως λεγόμενος κτλ.* ‡Gr.Nyss.*or.2 in Gen.1:26*(M.44. 285D); **2.** *ἡ ἑ.* [sc. *ἡμέρα*], v. ἀνάπαυσις; **a.** a sacred day, Thphl.Ant. *Autol.*2.12(M.6.1069C); even among pagans, Clem.*str.*5.14(p.397.18; M.9.161B); **b.** seventh day of Creation (Gen.2:2) related to last judgement *ὅταν ἐλθὼν ὁ υἱὸς αὐτοῦ καταργήσει τὸν καιρὸν τοῦ ἀνόμου καὶ κρινεῖ τοὺς ἀσεβεῖς...τότε καλῶς καταπαύσεται ἐν τῇ ἡμέρᾳ τῇ ἑ.* *Barn.*15.5; *ἐκείνη ἡ ἑ.* [i.e. judgement]...*ὑπὸ ταύτης τῆς ἑ.* [i.e. sabbath] *διασχηματίζεται...οὐκέτι τὰ τοῦ βίου τούτου ἐν ἐκείνῃ τῇ ἡμέρᾳ ...αὕτη ἡ ἑ. ἐκείνης τῆς ἑ. τύπος* ‡Gr.Nyss.*or.2 in Gen.1:26*(M.44. 289B,C); **c.** circumscribes earthly time *ἡ δὲ ἑ. πέρας γενομένη τῆς κτίσεως, ἐν ἑαυτῇ περιέγραψε τὸν συμπαρεκτεινόμενον τῇ κατασκευῇ τοῦ κόσμου χρόνον* Gr.Nyss.*Ps.6*(M.44.609B); ‡Gr.Nyss.*occurs.*(M.46. 1153C); *ἡ δὲ ἑ., τῆς χρονικῆς ἰδιότητος περιγράφει τὴν κίνησιν* Max. *cap.theol.*1.51(M.90.1101C); *Schol.*18 in Jo.Clim.*scal.*4(M.88.733B); **d.** opp. *ὀγδόη* (v. ὄγδοος) signifying eternity, Just.*dial.*24.1(M.6. 528B); *ὁ ἐν ἑ. σαββατισμός, καὶ ἣν ἔτι τῆς σκιᾶς ὁ καιρός* Cyr.*Mich.*49 (3.438E; ἑβδομάσι Aubert); *μετὰ τὴν ἑ. δουλικήν, τῇ ὀγδόῃ λύεται ἐλεύθερος ἡμέρᾳ* Jo.Clim.*scal.*5(M.88.776D); *Schol.*20 in Jo.Clim.*scal.* 5(789A,B) cit. s. δουλικός; **e.** representing cessation of earthly thoughts, Max.*cap.theol.*1.55(M.90.1104B); cf.*ib.*1.56(1104C); **3.** as subst., name of Valent. aeon, Val.Gn.ap.Epiph.*haer.*31.6(p.393.6; M.41.484C).

B. neut. plur. as subst., *week*, Ath.*fug.*6(p.72.4; M.25.652A).

C. neut. sing. as adv., *seven times*, Jo.Mosch.*prat*.73(M.87.2925C).

D. *sevenfold*, s.v.l., πίστιν τῆς ἑ. χάριτος Didym.*Job* 1:2(M.39.1120C).

***ἐβέλινος**, *of ebony*, Jo.Mal.*chron*.12 p.286(M.97.433A).

***ἐβένιος**, = foreg., in erroneous interpretation of Ezech.27:15 τὰ κέρατα ὁ Σύμμαχος ἐβένους ἡρμήνευσεν, ἀφ' ὧν τὰ ἐβένια καλούμενα γίνεται Thdt.*Ezech*.27:15(2.901); v. s. κέρας.

ἐβέννινος, = foreg., Cosm.Ind.*top*.2(M.88.100A); Anast.S.*hod*.2 (M.89.72A).

***Ἐβιωναῖος, ὁ,** *Ebionite*, member of Judaizing sect rejecting virgin birth of Christ, Pauline epistles, and all gospels except Mt. (v. Ἑβραῖος), cf.Iren.*haer*.1.26.2(M.7.686B); cf.*ib*.3.11.7(884B); Hipp.*haer*.7.8(p.190.10; M.16.3294B); *ib*.7.34(p.221.8; 3342B); etym. ὡς οἱ πτωχοὶ τῇ διανοίᾳ Ἐ., τῆς πτωχῆς διανοίας ἐπώνυμοι (ἐβίων γὰρ ὁ πτωχὸς παρ' Ἑβραίοις ὀνομάζεται) Or.*princ*.4.3.8(22; p.334.1; M.11.389A); id.*comm.in Mt*.16.12(p.513.1; M.13.1413A); id.*Cels*.2.1 (p.126.19; M.11.793A); but acc. Or. οἱ διττοὶ Ἐ., ἤτοι ἐκ παρθένου ὁμολογοῦντες ὁμοίως ἡμῖν τὸν Ἰησοῦν ἢ οὐχ οὕτω γεγεννῆσθαι ἀλλὰ ὡς τοὺς λοιποὺς ἀνθρώπους *ib*.5.61(p.65.7; 1277C); Eus.*h.e*.3.27.1(M.20.273A); OT translator Symmachus an Ebionite, *ib*.6.17(M.20.560A); Epiph.*haer*.30.1(p.333.5; M.41.405B).

***Ἐβιωνεῖς, οἱ,** *Ebionites*, v. foreg., Thdt.*haer*.2.1(4.328).

Ἑβραϊκός, *Hebrew*; **1.** of people, Afric.*chron*.18.3(M.10.92B); Ἑ. προφῆται Clem.*str*.1.17(p.56.3; M.8.801B); **2.** of language, etym. explanation Ἑ. κέκληται, ἀπὸ τοῦ Ἔβερ †Chrys.*synops*.(6.316A); neut. as subst., Or.*Cels*.5.48(p.52.25; M.11.1257A); OT books not written in Hebrew rejected by Jews, id.*or*.14.4(p.332.3; M.11.461C).

Ἑβραῖος, ὁ, *Hebrew* (for etym. v. περάτης, περατικός); **A.** usu. as synonym of Jew, Clem.*str*.1.23(p.92.6ff.; M.8.896Bff.); οὗτοι γὰρ [sc. Ἑλληνισταί] Ἑλληνιστὶ διελέγοντο, Ἑ. ὄντες Chrys.*hom*.*14.1 in Ac*.(9.111D); but exeg. 2Cor.11:22 οὐ γὰρ ἦν πάντας τοὺς Ἑ. Ἰσραηλίτας εἶναι· ἐπεὶ καὶ Ἀμμανῖται καὶ Μωαβῖται τοῦτο ἦσαν Chrys.*hom*.*25.1 in 2Cor*.(10.612C).

B. ref. Epistle to the *Hebrews*; **1.** authorship discussed; **a.** view of Clem. τὴν πρὸς Ἑ. δὲ ἐπιστολὴν Παύλου μὲν εἶναί φησιν γεγράφθαι δὲ Ἑβραίοις Ἑβραϊκῇ φωνῇ, Λουκᾶν δὲ...αὐτὴν μεθερμηνεύσαντα ἐκδοῦναι τοῖς Ἕλλησιν Clem.*fr*.22(p.201.18; M.9.748B); cf.*ib*.(p.202.1; 749B); **b.** view of Or.: used as scriptural proof together with Is., Or.*ep*.1.9(M.11.65B); can be shown to be Pauline despite contrary opinion of some, *ib*.(65Cff.); ὁ χαρακτὴρ τῆς λέξεως τῆς Πρὸς Ἑ. ἐπιγεγραμμένης ἐπιστολῆς οὐκ ἔχει τὸ ἐν λόγῳ ἰδιωτικὸν τοῦ ἀποστόλου ...ἀλλ' ἐστὶν ἡ ἐπιστολὴ συνθέσει τῆς λέξεως Ἑλληνικωτέρα...ἐγὼ δὲ... εἴποιμ' ἂν ὅτι τὰ μὲν νοήματα τοῦ ἀποστόλου ἐστίν, ἡ δὲ φράσις καὶ ἡ σύνθεσις ἀπομνημονεύσαντός τινος τὰ ἀποστολικὰ καὶ ὥσπερ σχολιογραφήσαντός τινος τὰ εἰρημένα ὑπὸ τοῦ διδασκάλου id.*fr.in Heb*.(M.14.1308D)ap.Eus.*h.e*.6.25.11; **c.** view of Eus.: counted by some among ἀντιλεγόμενα, Eus.*h.e*.6.13.6(548C); rejected by Romans, *ib*.3.3.5 (217B); *ib*.6.20.3(573A); cited in *1Clem*., Eus.*h.e*.3.38.1(293C); and by Iren., *ib*.5.26(509A); attributed to S. Paul without question, *ib*. 2.17.12(180A); Ἑβραίοις γὰρ διὰ τῆς πατρίου γλώττης ἐγγράφως ὡμιληκότος τοῦ Παύλου, οἱ μὲν τὸν εὐαγγελιστὴν Λουκᾶν, οἱ δὲ τὸν Κλήμεντα τοῦτον [sc. of Rome] αὐτὸν ἑρμηνεῦσαι λέγουσι τὴν γραφήν· ὃ καὶ μᾶλλον εἴη ἀληθὲς τῷ τὸν ὅμοιον τῆς φράσεως χαρακτῆρα τήν τε τοῦ Κλήμεντος ἐπιστολὴν καὶ τὴν πρὸς Ἑ. ἀποσῴζειν *ib*.3.38.2,3 (293C,D); this testimony cited against Arians by Thdt.*Heb*.proem. (3.542); **d.** cited as Pauline, Alex.Al.*ep.Alex*.6(p.23.23; M.18.557A); Ath.*ep.fest*.39.9(M.26.1437B); Didym.*Trin*.1.15(M.39.308A); **2.** later discussions of authorship, recipients, and date; discussion why S. Paul, being apostle of gentiles, wrote to Hebrews, Chrys.*hom. in Heb*.proem.(12.1Bff.); epistle dated after journey to Spain, before second Roman captivity, and thought to have been written in Palestine, *ib*.(2D,E); οἱ αἱρετικοί φασι μὴ εἶναι Παύλου τὴν ἐπιστολήν, καὶ τούτου πρώτην ἀπόδειξιν προφέρουσι τὸ μὴ προτετάχθαι αὐτοῦ τὸ ὄνομα ὡς ἐν ταῖς ἄλλαις ἐπιστολαῖς· δεύτερον τὸ τὴν φράσιν ἄλλην εἶναι, τοῦτ' ἔστι ξένην παρὰ τὴν Παύλου καὶ τὴν κατασκευήν. δεῖ τοίνυν εἰδέναι ὅτι Παῦλος ἐμισεῖτο ὑπὸ Ἰουδαίων ὡς ἀποστασίαν νόμου διδάσκων...ὠφέλιμα τοίνυν γράφων Ἑβραίοις οὐ προτίθησι τὸ ὄνομα ἑαυτοῦ, ἵνα μὴ τῷ μίσει τῷ πρὸς αὐτὸν ζημιωθῶσι τὴν ὠφέλειαν τὴν ἀπὸ ἐπιστολῆς Sever.*Heb*.proem.(p.345.18); reproduction of Eusebius' view that it was written in Hebrew and translated by S. Luke or, more prob., by Clement of Rome, *ib*.(p.345.21).

C. ref. Gospel acc. *Hebrews* (divergent form of Mt., in Hebr. or Aramaic, used by Jewish-Christian sects of Nazarenes and Ebionites, and believed in antiquity to be original of Mt.); passages cited by Clem.*str*.2.9(p.137.4; M.8.981A); Or.*Jo*.2.12(6; p.67.19; M.14.132C); said to have contained Jo.7:53–8:11, Eus.*h.e*.3.39.17 (M.20.300D); reckoned among disputed books, *ib*.3.25.5(269A); used by Ebionites, *ib*.3.27.4(273B); v. Ἐβιωναῖος, εὐαγγέλιον.

***ἑβραϊσμός, ὁ,** *Hebrew language*, Or.*hom.18.6 in Jer*.(p.159.21; M.13.476D).

ἐγγαμίζω, pass., *be given in marriage*, *1Apoc.Jo*.11(p.79).

***ἔγγαμος,** *married* τὸ πνεῦμα τὸ ἅγιον ἐνήργησεν ἐν τῇ Ἐλισάβετ. οὐ γὰρ μόνον παρθένους οἶδεν, ἀλλὰ γνωρίζει καὶ ἐγγάμους Cyr.H. *catech*.17.7; Epiph.*haer*.67.2(p.134.25; M.42.173D).

[*]**ἐγγαστερίμυθος, ὁ,** = ἐγγαστρίμυθος, *Orac.Sib*.3.226(cj., metr. gr.).

***ἔγγαστρα, τά,** *depths* of a prison ἐγ[γ]άσ[τρ]οις τοῦ δεσμωτηρίου *A.Tit*.(p.551).

ἐγγαστρίμυθος, ὁ, ἡ, *ventriloquist*; def. τί ἐστιν ἐ.; τινὲς ὑπὸ δαιμόνων ἐνεργούμενοι...οὓς ἐντερομάντεις οἱ Ἕλληνες προσηγόρευον, ὡς ἔνδοθεν δοκοῦντες τοῦ δαίμονος φθέγγεσθαι Thdt.*qu.29 in Lev*. (1.207); freq. of women believed to prophesy in this manner; **1.** in gen., Clem.*prot*.2(p.11.5; M.8.69A); id.*paed*.2.1(p.165.11; M.8.404A); abolished by Christianity, Gr.Naz.*or*.5.25(M.35.693C); but still active among non-Christians, ‡Just.*qu.et resp*.81(M.6.1324A); **2.** (fem.), esp. of witch of Endor (1Reg.28:7ff.) cf. δαίμων; **a.** assertion that Samuel was actually called up ὅτι μένουσιν αἱ ψυχαὶ ἀπέδειξα ὑμῖν ἐκ τοῦ καὶ τὴν Σαμουὴλ ψυχὴν κληθῆναι ὑπὸ τῆς ἐ. ... φαίνεται δὲ καὶ ὅτι πᾶσαι αἱ ψυχαὶ τῶν οὕτως δικαίων...ὑπὸ ἐξουσίαν ἔπιπτον τῶν τοιούτων δυνάμεων, ὁποία...ἐν τῇ ἐ. ... ὁμολογεῖται Just. *dial*.105.4(M.6.721B); discussion of arguments of opponents who assert impossibility of Samuel's being in Hades (v. ᾅδης) λέγει ἡ ἐ. ἑωρακέναι τὸν Σαμουήλ, ψεύδεται Or.*engast*.3(p.285.1; M.12.1016B); **b.** denial of this theory, ‡Hipp.*engast*.(p.123.1ff.; M.10.605Cff.); counter-arguments: ἐ. condemned in scripture (e.g. Lev.20:27; 1Reg.18:3ff. etc.), Eust.*engast*.2(p.17.14; M.18.616B); *ib*.25(p.55.24; 665A); ἐ. used illicitly by Saul, *ib*.2(p.18.5ff.; 616C); *ib*.11(p.33.31; 636D); bringing up souls from other world is not in power of ἐ., *ib*.3(p.19.8ff.; 617B); *ib*.16(p.43.2ff.; 648C); ref. 1Reg.28:14 φαίνεται ...ὡς οὐδαμοῦ...ἡ τοῦ θείου γράμματος ἔφησεν ἐκδοχὴ τὸν Σαμουὴλ ἀνῆχθαι διὰ τῆς ἐ. *ib*.3(p.20.7; 620A); a phantom was called up, *ib*.6 (p.23.32; 624B); as appears from very name of ἐ.: πρῶτον ἐδήλωσεν τὸ πρόσωπον ὁποῖόν ἐστιν, ἐμμανὲς *ib*.7(p.25.14; 625B); why prophecy not genuine οὐδὲν ἀπήγγελλεν ξένον ὁ διὰ τῆς ἐ. λεγόμενος ἀνῆχθαι, τὰ δὲ ὑπὸ τοῦ Σαμουὴλ εἰρημένα πρότερον ὡς ἴδια μὲν ἐσχημάτιζε *ib*.12 (p.36.2; 640B); not, as Or. represents it, a question of Samuel being in Hades, but of ἐ. having power to bring him up, *ib*.17(p.44.3ff.; 649B); absurdity of Or.'s here clinging to lit. sense, *ib*.21(p.48.18; 656B); τοιαύτῃ...μεθόδῳ συνήθως ἀλληγορῶν ἅπαντα πανταχῶς, οὐχ οἷός τε ἐγένετο τὰ τῆς ἐ. τροπολογῆσαι ῥήματα μόνον *ib*.22(p.51.8; 660A); Saul deceived by phantoms, Gr.Nyss.*engast*.(p.65.21ff.; M.45.109Dff.); Eustrat.*stat.anim*.(p.507f.); **c.** modifications of this theory, ‡Just.*qu.et resp*.52(M.6.1296Bff.); **3.** (masc.) met., derogatory term for Eunomius, Gr.Nyss.*Eun*.2(2 p.361.10; M.45.540C); cf.id.*Apoll*.45(M.45.1232B).

ἐγγάστριος, *in the womb*; of Christ in womb of BMV, †Ephr. *nativ*.60(p.87); ‡Thdt.*nativ.Jo.Bapt*.(5.88); Sophr.H.*ep.syn*.(M.87.3161A); ref. Jo. Bapt.'s ἐ. σκίρτησις *ib*.(3176A); met. οἱ ἔχουσι μαθήματα ἐναντία τοῖς δόγμασι...ἐγγάστρια αὐτῶν Or.*sel.in Job* 20:15 (M.12.1033D).

***ἐγγαστρόω,** *impregnate*, Jo.Mal.*chron*.7 p.179(M.97.285B); Leont.N.*v.Sym*.39(M.93.1717B).

***ἐγγεωργ-έω,** *produce as by husbandry*, ref. miraculously produced loaves ἕτοιμος ἄρτος ταῖς χερσὶ τῶν διακονούντων ~ούμενος Gr.Nyss.*or.catech*.23(p.88.11; M.45.61D); ταῖς παλάμαις τῶν μαθητῶν ὡς ἀρούραις ~οῦντα κόρον αὐτοσχέδιον ἀγεώργητον Gr.Ant.*bapt*.2.7 (M.88.1877C).

***ἐγγλυκαίνω, 1.** *sweeten*; met., Eus.*Is*.60:6,7(M.24.492C); Areth. *Apoc*.8(M.106.556C); cf.*A.Paul et Thecl*.1 cit. s. γλυκαίνω; **2.** intrans; met., *remove bitterness*, *Ep.Lugd*.ap.Eus.*h.e*.5.1.46(M.20.425B); **3.** *soften, enervate*, †Dion.Al.*fr.Eccl*.2:14(p.220.2; M.10.1584B).

***ἐγγλυφίς, ἡ,** *carved work*, Jo.D.*haer*.101(M.94.769B).

ἐγγλύφω, *carve*; met., *impress on*, Nil.*epp*.3.143(M.79.449D).

ἐγγοητεύω, *induce by charms* ὁ ὄφις...τινὰ κατὰ τὴν αἴσθησιν ἡδονὴν ἐγγοητεύσας τῇ γεύσει Gr.Nyss.*hom.opif*.20(M.44.200C).

***ἐγγόνιον, τό,** *grandchild*, Cyr.S.*v.Euthym*.30(p.47.16).

***ἐγγραπτέον,** *one must inscribe* ἐν σώφρονι ψυχῇ δικαιοσύνην ἐ. Clem.*prot*.10(p.76.26; M.8.224B); Isid.Pel.*epp*.3.289(M.78.964C).

ἔγγραφος, A. *written*; **1.** opp. ἄγραφος: ἡ γεωργία [i.e. apostolic function] δὲ διττή· ἡ μὲν ἄγραφος, ἡ δὲ ἔ. Clem.*str*.1.1(p.6.12; M.8.

693A); ib.4.18(p.297.6; 1320A); of written, opp. *viva voce*, argument, Eus.p.e.1.3(6D; M.21.32A); id.h.e.4.24(M.20.389B); **2.** of official documents; **a.** laws and statutes ἐγγράφους...παρέθετο διδασκαλίας Eus.v.C.3.58(p.105.6; M.20.1125A); id.h.e.9.7.2(M.20.809B); **b.** of confessions of faith ἔ. ἡ τῆς πίστεως...ὀρθοδοξία ib.5.22(489B); ὑποτάξας τοῖς ἑαυτοῦ γράμμασιν ἔ. τὴν τῶν ἀνδρῶν ὀρθοδοξίαν CHier.(335)ep.(p.248.5; M.26.720A); Bas.fid.1(2.223D; M.31.676C).

B. esp. *written in Bible, scriptural*; **1.** in gen.; of Commandments, Clem.str.5.6(p.352.16; M.9.65A); προφητείαν Meth.symp.10.2(p.122.18; M.18.193B); χρησμός Eus.p.e.1.4(9D; M.21.36C); ἀπόδειξις Bas.Spir.67(3.57A; M.32.193A); Hom.Clem.3.10; φωνή ib.16.8; ὁμολογία †Bas.bapt.1.3.1(2.649D; M.31.1573B); **2.** opp. non-scriptural (ἄγραφος); **a.** esp. of OT; ref. Pauline citations ὃ μέν ἐστιν ἐκείνου [sc. non-believer] πλεονέκτημα, ἄγραφον τίθησιν [sc. S. Paul]...ὃ δέ ἐστι τοῦ πιστοῦ προτέρημα, τοῦτο δι' ἐγγράφους μαρτυρίας κατασκευάζει Chrys.hom.8.2 in Rom.(9.499D); id.hom.29.1 in 2Cor.(10.639E); id.hom.18.1 in Heb.(12.175A); of OT laws opp. unwritten law in the heart (Jer.38:33) νομίζεις τοὺς ἐ. τῶν ἀγράφων νόμων κυριωτέρους εἶναι Isid.Pel.epp.3.106(M.78.812B); cf.Ammon.Ac.28:19(M.85.1604D); **b.** ref. non-biblical traditions of Church, Clem.str.6.15(p.498.16; M.9.356B), Bas.Spir.66(3.54D; M.32.188A) citt. s. παράδοσις; acc. Pneumatomachoi τὰς ἐκ τῶν ἐ. ἀποδείξεις ἐπιβοῶνται, τὴν ἄγραφον τῶν πατέρων μαρτυρίαν...ἀποπεμπόμενοι ib.25(21C; M.112C); **c.** ref. orthodoxy opp. unwritten tradition and interpretation of heretics (Arian) τὸ δὲ 'πατὴρ' ἁπλοῦν καὶ ἔ. Ath.Ar.1.34(M.26.81B); τὴν...ἔγγραφον πατρὸς χρῆσιν...ὑπαμείψας ἀγέννητον ἀντὶ τοῦ πατρὸς κατωνόμασεν Gr.Nyss.Eun.2(2 p.335.2; M.45.509D); cf. use of such teaching by Macedonians, Didym.Trin.2.19(M.39.736B); **d.** Arians blaming orthodox for not using scriptural expressions ὅτι καὶ μὴ ἔ. εἰσι πάλιν γογγύζουσιν Ath.decr.21(p.18.2; M.25.453A).

C. *recorded*, hence *approved* οἱ δὲ ὑπομένοντες ἐν πεποιθήσει...ἔ. ἐγένοντο ἀπὸ τοῦ θεοῦ 1Clem.45.8; ἔ. ἔσται ἡ νηστεία αὕτη Herm.sim.5.3.8; opp. eternal ἔ. ἔχουσι τὰ ἐπιτίμια Clem.str.7.16(p.74.28; M.9.545B); of people who are οὐκ ἔ., ib.3.18(p.246.31; M.8.1212C).

D. *educated* πόθεν οὗτος [sc. Christ] ἐρεύγεται ἔ. αὐδήν; γράμματα πῶς δεδάηκεν...; Nonn.par.Jo.7:15(M.43.808A).

E. neut. plur. as subst.; **1.** *documents, writings* κελεύων δι' ἐγγράφων Thphl.Ant.Autol.3.25(M.6.1160B); writings of heretics, Hipp.haer.9.13(p.252.15; M.16.3390B); πεπλασμένοις λόγοις καὶ ἐ. Alex.Al.ep.Alex.2(p.20.27; M.18.552A); documents of a synod, Eus.h.e.6.33.3(M.20.593B); **2.** *scripture* τὰ θεῖα ἔ. Eus.Marcell.1.1(p.8.23; M.24.728C); Cyr.H.catech.18.11; Didym.(‡Bas.)Eun.4(1.295C; M.29.709A).

ἐγγράφ-ω, **1.** *put on record, write down*; **a.** lit. τὰ δὲ ὀνόματα αὐτῶν [sc. Docetists]...οὐκ ἔδοξέν μοι ~ειν Ign.Smyrn.5.3; in scripture, Clem.paed.3.12(p.289.19; M.8.677A); Chrys.hom.16.1 in Mt.(7.203C); **b.** met., of commandments ἐν αὐταῖς ~όμενοι ταῖς καρδίαις Clem.prot.10(p.77.20; M.8.225A); id.str.6.15(p.498.18; M.9.356B); **2.** *enrol*: names of catechumens, Cyr.H.procatech.4; fig., Christians in book of life, Herm.vis.1.3.2; among those who keep commandments, id.sim.5.3.2; among friends of God through love, Clem.str.6.9(p.468.27; M.9.296A); εἰς τὴν ἐκλογὴν τῶν ἀποστόλων ἐ. ib.6.13(p.485.10; 328A); in heaven, id.q.d.s.21(p.174.7; M.9.625D); **3.** *admit*, Bas.Spir.59(3.50B; M.32.177A); to canon of scripture τὰς οὕτω μικρὰς ἐπιστολὰς...ἔδει ἐγγεγράφθαι Chrys.hom. in Philm. proem.(11.772C); **4.** *assign to*, Thphyl.exc.gent.9(p.486.21; M.113.948D); **5.** *inscribe* τοῖς...ἐγγεγραμμένοις ἐν ταύτῃ 'τῇ βίβλῳ τῆς ζωῆς' Hipp.Dan.4.60.2; Meth.symp.3.14(p.45.3; M.18.85B); met. τοῦ σπέρματος ἐγγεγραμμένην ἔχοντος τὴν τῶν ἀνθρώπων φυὴν Athenag.res.17(p.69.12; M.6.1008D).

ἐγγράφως, **A.** *in writing*; **1.** in gen. τὰ ὑπὸ Πέτρου κηρυσσόμενα ἐ. ἡμῖν παραδέδωκεν [sc. S. Mark] Iren.haer.3.1.1(M.7.845A); Clem.str.4.1(p.249.2; M.8.1216B); Ischyras ep.(p.143.18; M.25.364C); i.e. in letters, ref. Ign., Eus.h.e.3.36.4(M.20.288C); τὰ δεινότατα αὐτοὺς ἐ. εἰπών Ath.apol.sec.9(p.95.23; M.25.265B); i.e. in historical documents, Socr.h.e.1.1.3(M.67.33A); ἐμφέρεται ἐν τῇ ἐκκλησίᾳ 'Ρώμης ἐ. Jo.Mosch.prat.147(M.87.3012B); **2.** ref. confessions of faith, private εἰπεῖν ἐ. τὴν ἑαυτοῦ πίστιν Ath.ep.Aeg.Lib.18(M.25.581A); of Symb. Nic.(325) τὴν δὲ τῆς καθολικῆς ἐκκλησίας πίστιν ὡμολόγησαν ἐ. id. ep.Jov.1(M.26.816B)ap.Thdt.h.e.4.3.5; Gr.Naz.or.21.33(M.35.1121C); ἐ. ἐκτίθενται τὸ τῆς καθολικῆς πίστεως σύμβολον Gel.Cyz.h.e.2.26.4(M.85.1308B).

B. *in the scriptures* ἐπὶ τὴν ἀλήθειαν τὴν ἐ. τὰ ἄγραφα δηλοῦσαν Clem.str.1.1(p.8.3; 696C); τὸ κρῖμα τοῦ θεοῦ...ἐ. καταβέβληται Eus.Ps.149:9(M.24.73C); Ath.Ar.2.25(M.26.200B); τὸ πνεῦμα ἐ. φησίν id. gent.7(M.25.16B); Const.App.3.9.4; Hom.Clem.17.15; Ammon.Ac.15:1(M.85.1548C).

ἐγγυητής, ὁ, *one who gives security, guarantor*, whose function is forbidden to bishop, Clem.ep.5(M.2.40A); met., of God πιστευέτω ...ἐ. θεῷ Clem.q.d.s.42(p.190.24; M.9.652A); ‡Nil.perist.13(M.79.965B); of S. Paul ἐ. τῆς ἀναστάσεως Ath.inc.21.2(M.25.132D); Gr.Nyss.hom.2 in Cant.(M.44.804D).

ἐγγυμνάζ-ω, **1.** *train for, exercise*, also *try*; intellectually, Gr.Nyss.hex.6(M.44.68C); of Christ training minds of apostles, Chrys.hom.65.1 in Mt.(7.643E); ib.(644B); id.hom.75.4 in Jo.(8.444D); morally, id.hom.21.3 in 1Cor.(10.183C); id.hom.14.3 in Jo.(8.81D); id.ep.1.1(3.528D); **2.** med. and pass., *exercise oneself in, practise*; intellectual pursuits, Or.Cels.3.13(p.212.28; M.11.936B); moral behaviour, Clem.str.2.18(p.161.10; M.8.1029B); ref. OT Law, Gr.Nyss.hom.5 in Cant.(M.44.877B); ascet., Clem.str.7.7(p.33.27; M.9.464B); ib.7.11(p.44.13; 485B); id.ecl.35(p.147.21; M.9.716C); hence med., *accustom oneself to* ~εσθαι παρασκευάζει πρὸ μὲν τοῦ χειμῶνος τῷ μετοπώρῳ Chrys.hom.11.1 in Gen.(4.83B); pass., Cyr.Ps.7:1(M.69.748C).

***ἐγγύμνασμα, τό,** *preliminary exercise* ταῦτ' ἦν ἀγώνων ὥσπερ ἐ., ἢ καὶ προτέλεια μειζόνων μυστηρίων Gr.Naz.carm.2.1.11.275(M.37.1048).

***ἐγγυμναστήριον, τό,** *training place, school*, Gr.Naz.ep.116(M.37.213A).

***ἔγγυμος,** v. *ἔγκυμος.

ἐγγύς, *near*; **1.** adv.; **a.** of God being near to man, 1Clem.21.3; and πάντα ἐ. αὐτῷ ib.27.3; ἐ. ἐστι τοῖς πιστεύουσι καὶ πόρρω τοῖς ἀθέοις Clem.q.d.s.41(p.187.26; M.9.648A); in sense of *known* τὰ κρυπτὰ ἡμῶν ἐ. αὐτῷ ἐστιν Ign.Eph.15.3; **b.** of creatures being near to God: angels, comp., Ath.hom.in Mt.11:27(M.25.217C); men, ref. martyrs ὁ ἐ. μαχαίρας, ἐ. θεοῦ Ign.Smyrn.4.2; holy people ἐ. θεῷ βιοῦντας Just.1apol.21.6(M.6.361A); Meth.symp.8.16(p.107.4; M.18.169C); being similar to angels, Dion.Ar.c.h.9.4(M.3.261B); **c.** in phrase ἐ. ἔχων τὸ δάκρυον Marc.Diac.v.Porph.8; **2.** comp. as adj. ὁ σατανᾶς...ἐγγύτερός ἐστι τῆς ψυχῆς Mac.Aeg.hom.51.2(p.21); ἐγγύτεροι...γινόμεθα...τῶν ὑπὲρ ἡμᾶς οὐσιῶν Dion.Ar.e.h.1.1(M.3.372B).

ἐγγύτης, ἡ, *nearness*; **1.** in time ἐ. τῆς ἐξόδου Marc.Er.opusc.3.13(M.65.984C); Proc.G.Is.13:1–11(M.87.2080B); **2.** exeg. Jo.14:9 of relationship between Father and Son ποίαν μείζω ταύτης ζητεῖς ἐ.; Chrys.hom.74.1 in Jo.(8.434C); **3.** to God; of cherubim and seraphim, Dion.Ar.c.h.6.2(M.3.201A); achieved by men through prayer, †Jo.D.B.J.20(M.96.1040C); ib.(1041A).

ἔγγων, ὁ, ἡ, *grandchild*, Thphn.chron.p.93(M.108.276B); ib.p.276 (ἐγγόνου 681C).

ἐγείρω, **I.** trans.;

A. *awaken, rouse, stir up*, met. ἤγειρεν θεοσεβείας σπέρμα Clem.prot.1(p.5.16; M.8.57A); the mind to spiritual life, id.str.5.3(p.337.8; M.9.36A).

B. *raise*; **1.** from the dead ὃς [sc. Christ] καὶ ἀληθῶς ἠγέρθη ἀπὸ νεκρῶν, ἐγείραντος αὐτὸν τοῦ πατρὸς αὐτοῦ, ὃς καὶ κατὰ τὸ ὁμοίωμα ἡμᾶς...ἐγερεῖ ὁ πατὴρ αὐτοῦ Ign.Trall.9.2; Polyc.ep.5.2; discussion on how Christ was raised οὐ λέγω, ὅτι τὸ πνεῦμα, ὡς δυνατώτερον τοῦ Χριστοῦ, ἤγειρεν αὐτὸν τὸν Χριστόν, ἀλλ' ὅτι αὐτὸν τὸν ναὸν τοῦ σώματος ἤγειρεν ὁ πατήρ, καὶ ὁ υἱός, καὶ τὸ πνεῦμα κτλ. ‡Ath.dial.Trin.3.28(M.28.1248A); cf.Cyr.inc.unigen.(5^1.712D); ὁ ἑαυτὸν ἐγείρας ἐκ νεκρῶν Leont.B.mesopent.(M.86.1977C); prophets ὃν [sc. Christ] δικαίως ἀνέμενον, παρὼν ἤγειρεν αὐτοὺς ἐκ νεκρῶν Ign.Magn.9.2; Ammon.Ac.17:30(M.85.1568A); met., from death of sin, ‡Proc.G.Pr.29:4(M.87.1513B); **2.** sinners, 1Clem.59.4; **3.** eyes of soul, Cels. ap.Or.Cels.7.39(p.189.21; M.11.1476B).

C. *raise, set up*; **1.** persons: kings, Mel.pass.38 p.14.13; Moses as a leader, Eus.v.C.1.12(p.13.17; M.20.925B); Adam from earth, Hom.Clem.16.19; **2.** things: Church, Clem.fr.36(p.218.29; M.9.769A); Cross above life of this world, Cyr.Soph.45(3.623B); met., ref. Israel passing through Red Sea τῷ θεῷ...ἐγείραντι τρόπαιον Gr.Nyss.v.Mos.34(M.44.312B).

II. intrans.;

A. *be awake, vigilant*; **1.** spiritually ἔνδοθεν ἐγρηγόρασιν Clem.paed.1.6(p.106.18; M.8.284A); ὁ δὲ τὸ φῶς ἔχων ἐγρήγορεν...ἄρα πρὸς τὸν θεὸν ὁ πεφωτισμένος ib.2.9(p.206.4f.; 493A); Bas.hom.21.1(2.163D; M.31.541B); Thdt.Cant.7:4(2.145); τὸ ἐγρηγορός *vigilance*, Or.hom.15.1 in Jer.(p.125.18; M.13.429A); **2.** *be sober*, i.e. free from exaggeration, Cyr.Jo.10.2(4.925B).

B. *rise* from the dead, Hom.Clem.1.6 v. I.B.1.

C. *rise, stand up*; **1.** in gen., Meth.symp.6.4(p.69.2; M.18.120B);

Thph.*chron*.p.389(M.108.929A); **2.** as posture of prayer, *Hom.Clem.* 3.29.

D. c. ἀπό, *arise and leave*, Or.*hom.14.15 in Jer.*(p.121.20,26; M. 13.424C).

***ἔγερμα, τό,** *awakening, arousing*, Procl.CP *or*.18.1(M.65.820B).

***ἐγερσιβόητος,** *raising the cry* ἐ. ἀλέκτωρ Nonn.*par.Jo*.13:38(M. 43.865C).

ἐγέρσιμος, *from which one wakes*, of death of Christ as ἐ. ὕπνος Nonn.*par.Jo*.20:9(M.43.909B); *ib*.21:14(917B).

***ἐγερσίνεκρος,** *awakening the dead*, Meth.*symp*.11(p.131.21; M. 18.208C).

ἔγερσις, ἡ, 1. *awaking* from sleep, of Christ's Resurrection, ref. Ps.3:6, Clem.*str*.5.14(p.397.5; M.9.161A); **2.** *raising*; **a.** met., of opening of eyes of soul, Or.*Cels*.7.39(p.190.14; M.11.1477A); of mind τὴν εἰς ὕψος τῆς διανοίας ἀπὸ τῶν φθειρομένων ἔ. Max.*ep*.25 (M.91.613D); **b.** of dead; of Lazarus, ‡Tit.Bost.*palm*.2(M.18.1264D); in gen., Serap.*Man*.11(p.34; M.40.909B); Chrys.*hom.32.8 in Mt.* (7.376C); Philost.*h.e*.2.8(M.65.629A); **c.** *erection* of buildings etc.: statues, Eus.*v.C*.2.45(p.69.8; M.20.1021B); walls, *ib*.3.31(p.92.16; 1092B); τῶν χωμάτων ἔ. Cyr.*Os*.142(3.176C); fig., of Christ's body τελειοῦται δὲ αὐτοῦ [sc. τοῦ ναοῦ] ἡ ἔ. ἐν...τρισὶν ἡμέραις Or.*Jo*. 10.37(21; p.211.33; M.14.374A); of bodies of Christians 'οἰκοδομὴν ἐκ θεοῦ ἔχομεν' οἷον...τὴν ἔ. *cat.2Cor*.5:1(p.379.20); **3.** *rising*, fig., ref. divine nature ἵδρυσίς τε γὰρ αὐτῆς, θρόνοι τε καὶ ἔ. Cyr.*Mich*.5 (3.394A); met., from fall into sin, Jo.Carp.*cap*.84(M.85.1854); †Jo.D.*B.J*.11(M.96.961A); **4.** *resurrection*; of Christ, *Keryg.Petr.* ap.Clem.*str*.6.15(p.496.30; M.9.352C); Iren.*haer*.1.10.1(M.7.549A); Serap.*Man*.40(p.59; M.18.1225A); τὴν ἔ. τῆς σαρκὸς αὐτοῦ δι' αὐτοῦ ἐποίησε Ath.*inc.et c.Ar*.2(M.26.988B); Jo.D.*hom*.4.30(M.96.632C); of dead, Meth.*res*.3.5(p.396.5; M.18.320B); for discussion of theol. problems v. ἀνάστασις.

***ἐγκαγχάζω,** *laugh loudly*, Bas.*reg.fus*.17.1(2.359E; M.31.961B).

ἐγκαθείργνυμι, *shut up, enclose, infix*; teaching in souls, Cyr. *Jo*. 2.1(4.128E); souls in Hades, id.*Is*.3.3(2.442A).

ἐγκαθείργω, = foreg.; pass., of soul in body, Gr.Thaum.*pan.Or*. 2(p.4.17; M.10.1056A); of teaching in souls, Cyr.*hom.pasch*.9(5^2. 122C); of souls in Hades, *ib*.11(151D); of Christ in womb, Leont.H. *monoph*.23(M.86.1784D).

***ἐγκαθειρκτέον,** *one must enclose*, Clem.*paed*.2.10(p.215.14; M.8. 512C).

ἐγκάθετος, 1. *put in secretly, suborned*; hence *put in deceitfully* νομίζουσιν...ὡς ἐ. ἐκείνην τὴν προβολὴν τῆς πίστεως ἐποιησάμεθα Bas.*ep*.244.5(3.379D; M.32.917C); **2.** *settled, resident*, Jo.Mal.*chron*. 13 p.319(M.97.477B); as subst., *settler*, Epiph.*haer*.8.8(p.195.9,19; M. 41.220C,221A); *ib*.8.9(p.197.7; 224A); **3.** *posted, on garrison duty* οὓς γάρ τινες καλοῦσιν ἐ., ἐστηλωμένους ὠνόμασεν Thdt. *qu.23 in 2Reg*. 8:14(1.421); Jo.Mal.*chron*.7 p.185(M.97.296A); *ib*.13 p.329(492B); Olymp.*Job* 19:12(M.93.205D).

ἐγκαθιδρύω, 1. *install*, Meth.ap.*cat.Rom*.7:23(p.206.3); ἐ. θρόνῳ *enthrone* a bishop, Philost.*h.e*.5.1(M.65.529A); Thdt.*h.e*.4.6.7(3.954); ἐ. ταῖς ἀκοαῖς c. genit., *bring to the attention of*, Isid.Pel.*epp*.5.194 (M.78.1448C); **2.** pass., *reside*, Cyr.*Jo*.4.3(4.380D); of a quality, Philost.*h.e*.12.10(M.65.620B).

***ἐγκαθιερόω,** *consecrate inwardly* ἣν [sc. τριάδα] ταῖς ἡμετέραις διανοίαις ἐγκαθιερωθεῖσαν κατέχομεν *Cod.Afr*.2.

***ἐγκαθικνέομαι,** *come down into* αὐτὴν [sc. τὴν θείαν φύσιν]...τοῖς τῆς κτίσεως ἐγκαθικέσθαι μέτροις Cyr.*Nest*.1(p.15.14; 6^1.4E).

***ἐγκάθισις, ἡ,** *indwelling*, Oecum.*Rom*.7:18(p.427.3).

ἐγκαθισμός, ὁ, *dwelling-in*; in fanciful etym. of Nebuchadnezzar, Or.*fr.9 in Lam*.(p.238.17; M.13.609C).

***ἐγκαθορμάω,** *harbour*; *install* φιλόκοσμος οἴκαδε ἐγκαθώρμηται γυνή ‡Pion.*v.Polyc*.9; ἐπίσκοποι τὸ μὲν πήλινον γένος...στρατείαις καὶ ἀξιώμασιν ἐγκαθώρμησαν Pall.*v.Chrys*.20(p.144.22; M.47.80).

ἐγκαθορμίζ-ω, *anchor*, met. καθάπερ τι πλοῖον...τῷ λιμένι τῆς ἀληθείας ~ει τὸν λόγον Gr.Nyss.*Eun*.9(2 p.204.10; M.45.801A); med. intrans., *run into harbour* ἐπ' ἔλαττον τινασσομένοις κόλποις ~ονται Bas.*hex*.7.4(1.67C; M.29.157C).

ἐγκαίνια, τά, 1. *dedication, consecration*; **a.** of Temple, Clem.*str*. 1.21(p.77.28; M.8.853A); Ath.*apol.Const*.18(M.25.617D); Thdt.*qu.26 in 3Reg*.(1.473); **b.** of churches τὰ ἐ. τοῦ ἐν Ἱεροσολύμοις μαρτυρίου Eus.*v.C*.4.40(p.116.8; M.20.1146A); cf.Gel.Cyz.*h.e*.3.17.8; *Chron. Pasch*.p.285(M.92.713A); not to take place without consent of emperor, Ath.*apol.Const*.14(M.25.612B); dist. from ordinary σύναξις, *ib*.15(613B); which could be held first, as proved by scripture, *ib*.18 (617B–D); Jo.Mal.*chron*.18 p.492(M.97.712A); **2.** annual *feast of dedication* or *consecration* of a church, Eus.*h.e*.10.3.1(M.20.848A); ἐ. τιμᾶσθαι παλαιὸς νόμος, καὶ καλῶς ἔχων· μᾶλλον δέ, τὰ νέα τιμᾶσθαι δι' ἐγκαινίων· καὶ τοῦτο, οὐχ ἅπαξ, ἀλλὰ καὶ πολλάκις, ἑκάστης τοῦ ἐνιαυτοῦ περιτροπῆς τὴν αὐτὴν ἡμέραν ἐπαγούσης, ἵνα μὴ ἐξίτηλα τῷ χρόνῳ γένηται τὰ καλά Gr.Naz.*or*.44.1(M.36.608A); ref. synod at Antioch (341) held προφάσει τῶν λεγομένων ἐ. Ath.*syn*.22(p.248.26; M.26.720C); cf.Socr.*h.e*.2.8.2(M.67.196A); met. γενοῦ καινὸς ἀντὶ παλαιοῦ, καὶ ψυχῆς ἑόρταζε τὰ ἐ. Gr.Naz.*or*.44.6(M.36.613C).

ἐγκαινίζ-ω, 1. *inaugurate*; **a.** in gen., *Chron.Pasch*.p.285(M.92. 712B); *ib*.p.305(776B); **b.** *consecrate*, the Cross ὁ ἐν τῷ σώματι τοῦ Χριστοῦ ἐγκαινισθεὶς *A.(Pass.)Andr*.10(p.24.17); brazen walls (Jer. 1:18) as type of consecration of Christians, Gr.Naz.*or*.44.1,2(M.36. 608A,B); **c.** met., *dedicate* to God; the soul, Or.*or*.24.4(p.355.19; M.11.493C); Ath.*ep.Marcell*.17(M.27.29D); **d.** *celebrate* (*encaenia*), Cyr.*Am*.31(3.281B); met. ἐ. τὴν ἐμαυτοῦ σωτηρίαν Gr.Naz.*or*.44.4 (M.36.612B); ἐ. τὴν ἀνάστασιν *ib*.45.24(657A); **e.** exeg. Heb.9:18 τί ἐστιν, 'ἐγκεκαίνισται'; βεβαία γέγονεν, ἐκυρώθη Chrys.*hom.16.1 in Heb*.(12.159A); Heb.10:20, Ath.*Ar*.2.65(M.26.285A); cf. Χριστὸς... τὴν δὲ εἰς οὐρανὸν ἡμῖν ἄνοδον ~ει id.*ep.fest*.22(p.295.20; M.26.1433A); 'ἣν ἐνεκαίνισε' τουτέστιν, ἣν κατεσκεύασε, καὶ ἧς ἤρξατο Chrys.*hom. 19.1 in Heb*.(12.180D); Cyr.*Jo*.12(4.1076E); id.*Ps*.7:8(M.69.752A); **2.** *renew*, spiritually ~εσθε, καὶ τὸν παλαιὸν ἄνθρωπον ἀπορρίψαντες, ἐν καινότητι ζωῆς πολιτεύεσθε Gr.Naz.*or*.44.6(M.36.613A); *ib*.44.7 (616A); **3.** *innovate, invent*, Areth.*Apoc*.35(M.106.669B).

ἐγκαινισμός, ὁ, 1. *dedication, consecration* of a building; Temple, Ath.*apol.Const*.18(M.25.617D); *Const.App*.7.45.2; exeg. Ps.29:1 κατὰ τὴν ἐπιγραφήν, τοῦ ἐ. τοῦ οἴκου περιέχει τινὰς λόγους. καὶ ἔοικε κατὰ μὲν τὸ σωματικόν, ἐπὶ τῶν χρόνων τοῦ Σαλομῶντος ἀνεγερθέντος τοῦ...ναοῦ ὁ λόγος διεξοδεύεσθαι· κατὰ δὲ τὸ νοητόν, τὴν ἐνσωμάτωσιν τοῦ θεοῦ λόγου σημαίνειν, καὶ τὸν ἐ. τοῦ καινῶς...αὐτοῦ κατασκευασθέντος οἴκου τὴν ἐπιγραφὴν δηλοῦν...ἢ τάχα οἶκον νοῆσαι προσήκει τὴν οἰκοδομουμένην ὑπὸ Χριστοῦ ἐκκλησίαν...ἐ. δὲ τῆς ἐκκλησίας ὑποληπτέον τὴν ἀνακαίνωσιν τοῦ νοός Bas.*hom.in Ps*.29 (1.124D,E; M.29.305C–308A); οἴκου τινὰ ἐγκαινισμὸν ὀνομάζων· ὅστις ἐσμὲν ἡμεῖς, οἱ θεοῦ ναὸς εἶναι...ἠξιωμένοι Gr.Naz.*or*.44.5(M.36. 613A); ἐ. ... οἴκου καλεῖ, τὴν τῆς ἀνθρωπίνης φύσεως νεουργίαν· ἣν ὁ ...Χριστὸς ὑπετέλεσε τὸν ὑπὲρ ἡμῶν καταδεξάμενος θάνατον Thdt. *Ps*.29:1(1.786); *dedication festival* of church, Jo.Eub.*concept.BMV* 23(M.96.1500A); **2.** *renewal* (v. 1 supra), after falling from grace διδοὺς τόπον ἐγκαινισμοῦ †Bas.*poenit*.6(2.608C; M.31.1488A); baptismal (controv. Cathari) ἓν...τὸ βάπτισμα καὶ εἷς ὁ ἐ. but not excluding possibility of repentance, Epiph.*haer*.59.2(p.365.15,20; M.41.1020B,C); **3.** *inauguration*, exeg. Heb.10:20. ἐ. γὰρ λέγεται ἀρχὴ χρήσεως Chrys.*hom.19.1 in Heb*.(12.180D); ἐ. δὲ ὁδοῦ, τὸ πρῶτον διὰ τούτων ὁδεῦσαι Thdt.*Heb*.10:20(3.608); of nativity of Christ ἐ. τῆς βασιλείας Jo.Nic.*nativ*.(M.96.1448D).

ἐγκακ-έω, *lose heart, grow tired* τὰς προσευχὰς ἡμῶν ἁπλῶς ἀναφέρειν πρὸς τὸν θεόν, μὴ ὡς αἱ ὠδίνουσαι ~ῶμεν *2Clem*.2.2.

ἐγκαλλωπίζω, 1. *adorn, make glorious*, Gr.Nyss.*hom.5 in Cant*. (M.44.872A); Thdr.Mops.*Joel*.1:6–9(M.66.213D); **2.** med.; **a.** *take pride* or *glory in*; in gen., Or.*Cels*.3.53(p.249.9; M.11.992A); Isid.Pel. *epp*.2.146(M.78.600A); Nil.*Magn*.8(M.79.980B); Ph.Carp.ap.Proc.G. *Cant*.1:15f.(M.87.1572C); of a philosopher glorying in adversities, Gr.Naz.*or*.26.10(M.35.1241A); of taking pride in one's baptism, Gr.Nyss.*bapt.Chr*.(M.46.596A); in matters which ought to be a source of shame, Chrys.*hom.73.4 in Mt*.(7.713D); of Marcellus glorying in Judaistic doctrine, Eus.*e.th*.1.17(p.78.20; M.24.860D); **b.** *take pleasure in*, ‡Jo.D.*Artem*.47(p.164.19; M.96.1296A); **c.** *boast, give oneself airs* about, Bas.*Eun*.1.5(1.214D; M.29.516C).

ἐγκαλλώπισμα, τό, *ornament, adornment*, met. ὁ καθαρὸς βίος... ζωῆς ἐ. Gr.Nyss.*v.Macr*.(p.402.20; M.46.989A); ‡Pall.*proem*.(p.4. 28; M.34.996); Isid.Pel.*epp*.3.10(M.78.733C); *ib*.4.10(1057C).

***ἐγκαπηλεύω,** *handle deceitfully*, c. dat., Serap.*Man*.36(p.53; M.18.1213B).

***ἐγκαρποφορία, ἡ,** *fruit-bearing*, Ephr.3.121D.

ἐγκαταβάλλω, 1. *cast into*; seed, Meth.*symp*.2.5(p.21.11; M.18. 56A); **2.** met., *implant*, Bas.*reg.fus*.2(2.336C; M.31.908C); *Const. App*.7.40.2; ‡Just.*qu.et resp*.8(M.6.1257B); Cyr.*1Cor*.15:42ff.(p.313. 13; M.74.909A); **3.** *set down* in books, Eus.*p.e*.11.7(522D; M.21. 865D).

***ἐγκατάβρωμα, τό,** *food*, fig., *Hymn.*(*AS* 1 p.460).

***ἐγκαταγέλαστος,** *ridiculous*, *M.Pion*.18.14.

***ἐγκαταγί(γ)νομαι,** *be occupied with*, Adam.*dial*.5.14(p.202.24; M.11.1853A); hence *be possessed by*, Gnost., of Sophia ἐγκαταγενομένην δὲ τοῖς πάθεσι Iren.*haer*.1.2.3(M.7.457A).

ἐγκαταγράφω, 1. *inscribe upon*, met. ἐγκαταγράψαντες τῇ διανοίᾳ *A.Thom*.A 108(p.220.5); **2.** *enrol among*, Cyr.*ador*.4(1.132A).

*__ἐγκαταδείκνυμι__, *indicate*, *Orac.Sib.*8.359.

*__ἐγκαταδεσμεύ-ω__, *bind fast in*, met. τοῖς τῆς ἁμαρτίας ~εσθαι ζυγοῖς Cyr.*ador.*5(1.161E).

*__ἐγκαταδέχομαι__, *receive, accept*, Epiph.*anc.*107(p.130.17; M.43.212A).

__ἐγκαταδέ-ω__, *bind fast in*; met., *link closely with* τῇ ὑποθέσει τῶν ἑορτῶν ἐγκατέδησε τῶν δωρεῶν τὰ ὑπομνήματα ὁ θεός Chrys.*prod. Jud.*1.4(2.382D); id.*hom.82.1 in Mt.*(7.783B); Isid.Pel.*epp.*2.116(M.78.557B); τὸν τοῖς τῆς δουλείας ~οντα ζυγοῖς Cyr.*ador.*1(1.37B); id.*Is.*3.3(2.434B).

*__ἐγκαταθάπτω__, *bury in*, Athenag.*leg.*36.1(M.6.969B).

*__ἐγκαταθετέον__, *one must assign*, Or.*or.*31.1(p.395.19; M.11.549B).

*__ἐγκαταθρέω__, *gaze into*, Cyr.*ador.*1(1.6D).

*__ἐγκατακαί-ω__, *burn into*; met., *inflame* τοῦ ἁγίου πνεύματος...τοῖς ἐσωτάτοις τῆς διανοίας μυχοῖς οἱονεί πως ~οντος Cyr.*Is.*3.4(2.504A).

__ἐγκατάκλειστος__, *imprisoned* παῖς ὀφείλει ἐ. εἶναι *T.Jos.*14.6; *A.Thom.*A 122(p.232.6); Jo.Mosch.*prat.*150(M.87.3016A); of soul ψυχὴ γὰρ ἐλεύθερον καὶ οὐκ ἐγκατάκλειστον οὐδενὶ τρόπῳ Gr.Thaum. *pan.Or.*6(p.17.18; M.10.1072C); Epiph.*haer.*66.44(p.81.18; M.42.96B).

__ἐγκατακλεί-ω__, *shut in*; met., *enclose* ἐν ἡσυχίᾳ διεκαρτέρουν ἐκεῖναι, καὶ τῇ ψυχῇ τὴν ὀδύνην ~ουσαι Gr.Nyss.*v.Macr.*(p.400.1; M.46.985D).

__ἐγκατακλώθω__, *intertwine, insert*; ref. Mosaic laws as used by pagan philosophers τοῖς ἰδίοις λόγοις ἐγκατακλώσαντας Cyr.*Juln.*1 (6^{2}.7E).

__ἐγκατακρούω__, *hammer in*, Clem.*paed.*2.11(p.226.21; M.8.537A).

*__ἐγκατακύπτω__, *look down on*, Bas.*hom.in Ps.*32(1.140A; M.29.344A).

__ἐγκαταλέγ-ω__, **1.** *admit, include*; demons, in second rank inferior to gods, Clem.*prot.*2(p.30.16; M.8.121B); Christians as sons of God, id.*str.*1.27(p.107.27; M.8.921A); *ib.*6.9(p.469.26; M.9.297A); in true Church, *ib.*7.17(p.76.6; 552A) cit. s. ἐκκλησία; among living, Or.*enarr.in Job* 3(M.17.68B); man in second rank to angels, Meth.*res.*1.35(p.273.13; M.41.1100A); among virgins of Church, Bas.*ep.*199 can.18(3.292B; M.32.720B); S. Paul among witnesses of Resurrection, Chrys.*hom.38.4 in 1Cor.*(10.356C); S. Matthias among apostles, id.*hom.5.1 in 1Tim.*(11.574C); things, Clem.*paed.*2.1(p.156.18; M.8.385A); in canon of scripture, Eus.*h.e.*3.38.2(M.20.293C); in a volume, *ib.*4.23.7(385B); in one's writings, Socr.*h.e.*3.23.27(M.67.441C); of sin as included in works of Devil, Cyr.H.*catech.*19.5; *ib.*19.7; **2.** *reckon, comprise in* εἰς...τὰ ἑκατὸν ἔτη τρεῖς ~ονται γενεαί Clem.*str.*1.21(p.85.2; M.8.872B); **3.** *impart*, Clem.*paed.*2.9(p.207.27; M.8.496C).

__ἐγκατάλειμμα, τό__, **1.** *remnant, remains, rest*, ref. idolatrous cult τὰ ἐ. τῶν εἰδώλων (Lat. *reliquias idolorum*) *Cod.Afr.*58; ἐνθύμιον, καὶ ἐ. ἐνθυμίου Niceph.Ur.*v.Sym.*69(M.86.3052A); ‡Gr.Naz.*Chr.pat.*795(M.38.200A); **2.** *moral defect, fault* τῶν ἐννοιῶν τῶν παρὰ τὸν ὀρθὸν λόγον, τῶν ἐ. Clem.*ecl.*62(p.155.2; M.9.728C).

__ἐγκαταλείπ-ω__, *abandon, forsake, desert*; **1.** ref. Mt.27:46, ‡Dion.Al.*fr.in Lc.22:42*(p.239.11); Cyr.*Pulch.*(p.35.2; 5^{2}.141A); **2.** of God abandoning men τοὺς ἐλπίζοντας ἐπ' αὐτὸν οὐκ ~ει *1Clem.*11.1; Herm.*sim.*2.9; id.*mand.*9.2; Or.*Cels.*5.31(p.33.4; M.11.1228B); to divine judgement, id.*princ.*3.1.13(p.217.4; M.11.273A); Jews to captivity, id.*hom.1.3 in Jer.*(p.2.20; M.13.257A); pass., of soul deserted by God, Bas.*hom.*7.7(2.60A; M.31.300B); v. ἐγκατάλειψις; **3.** of man forsaking God, *Hom.Clem.*10.4; Chrys.*poenit.*8.3(2.345B); commandments, *Did.*4.13; virtue, *1Clem.*33.1; **4.** in Basilides' system ἐγκαταλελειμμένης υἱότητος Hipp.*haer.*10.14(p.275.25; M.16.3430C).

__ἐγκατάλειψις, ἡ__, **A.** act., *forsaking, abandonment*; **1.** in gen.; of a wife, for Christ's sake, ‡Just.*qu.et resp.*110(M.6.1357D); of the good, †Bas.*Is.*17(1.389A; M.30.144C); **2.** of man by God προαναφωνεῖ...οὐ...ἐ. οὐδαμοῦ, ἀλλὰ βοήθειαν Chrys.*hom.2.3 in 2Cor.*(10.432A); exeg. Ps.41:10 λήθην δὲ ἐπὶ θεοῦ μὴ πάθος εἶναι νόμιζε, ἀλλὰ τὴν ἐ. Cyr.*Ps.*41:10(M.69.1009D); ἡ ὀργὴ τῆς ἐ. †Cyr.*coll.VT*(6^{4}.65E; M.77.1273B); *ib.*(66B; M.1273C); ref. Christ on Cross οὐκ ἄνθρωπος θεοῦ ἐχωρίζετο οὔτε θεὸς πρὸς ἄνθρωπον ἐ. διηγεῖτο ‡Ath.*Apoll.*2.15(M.26.1157A).

B. pass., *being forsaken, abandonment, dereliction*; **1.** of human nature in gen.; forsaken by God because of Fall, Cyr.*Pulch.*(p.35.1; 5^{2}.141A); ransomed by Christ, id.*Chr.un.*(5^{1}.756E); **2.** as spiritual state of individuals; **a.** in gen., Chrys.*hom.15.4 in Rom.*(9.598E); Oecum.*Heb.*4:12(p.463.18); **b.** as state of sinners, †Bas.*Is.*77(1.433B; M.30.245C); τοῦ δὲ ἁμαρτωλοῦ διὰ τὴν ἐ. περιαιρεῖται πᾶσα ἀσφάλεια *ib.*146(482A; M.356D); cf.Chrys.*hom.12.2 in Col.*(11.414E); **c.** as salutary punishment τὴν αἰτίαν τῆς ἐ. ἀποθέμενος, τουτέστι τὸν τῦφον...πᾶσα οὖν πτῶσις...πρὸς τὴν ἀναλογίαν τῆς ὑπερηφανίας κατ' ἐγκατάλειψιν γίνεται, θεοῦ φειδομένου τῶν ἐγκαταλιμπανομένων Pall.*h.Laus.*47(p.140.6ff.; M.34.1202A,B); ‡Proc.G.*Pr.*11:28(M.87.1333A); **d.** as spiritual trial, exeg. Ps.41:10f., Or.*exc.in Ps.*41:10f.(M.17.136D); Chrys.*hom.9.1 in 2Cor.*(10.498E); πρὸς τὸ...ὠφέλιμον ἡ ἐ. τοῦ θεοῦ Nil.*epp.*3.88(M.79.428B); †Nil.*mal.cog.*10(M.79.1212C); γίνονται γὰρ ἐ., πρὸς τὸ μὴ τοὺς ἁγίους ἐπαίρεσθαι Proc.G.*1Reg.*25:18(M.87.1113A); οἶδε γεννᾶν φόβος...καὶ αἱ ὑπὸ θεοῦ ἐ.... συνέχειαν ἐπιστατικὴν προσοχῆς ἐν τῷ ἡγεμονικῷ τοῦ ἀνθρώπου πειρωμένου τὴν πηγὴν φράξαι τῶν κακῶν λογισμῶν...δι' ἣν καὶ ἐ. ... πρὸς τὴν ἡμῶν τοῦ βίου διόρθωσιν, καὶ μάλιστα τοῖς γευσαμένοις τὴν ἀνάπαυσιν Hesych.S.*temp.*1.7(M.93.1484A); opp. illumination, Diad.*perf.*69(p.86.4); of Job, as proving his virtue, Chrys.*fr.Job* 40:4(M.64.652D); **e.** various forms τέσσαρές εἰσι γενικοὶ ἐ. τρόποι. ἡ μὲν οἰκονομική, ὡς ἐπὶ τοῦ κυρίου, ἵνα διὰ τῆς δοκούσης ἐ. οἱ ἐγκαταλελειμμένοι σωθῶσιν· ἡ δὲ πρὸς δοκιμήν, ὡς ἐπὶ τοῦ Ἰώβ...ἡ δὲ πρὸς παίδευσιν πατρικήν, ὡς ἐπὶ τοῦ ἀποστόλου...ἡ δὲ κατὰ ἀποστροφήν, ὡς ἐπὶ τῶν Ἰουδαίων ‡Ammon.*Mt.*27:46(M.85.1389C); τῶν ἐ., ἡ μὲν ἔστι διὰ κεκρυμμένην ἀρετήν, ἵνα φανερωθῇ, ὡς ἡ τοῦ Ἰώβ· ἡ δὲ δι' ἀποτροπὴν ὑπερηφανίας, ὡς ἐπὶ τοῦ Παύλου· ἡ δὲ πρὸς διόρθωσιν ἄλλου, ὡς ἐπὶ τοῦ Λαζάρου καὶ τοῦ πλουσίου...ἡ δὲ εἰς ἄλλου δόξαν, ὡς ὁ ἐκ γενετῆς τυφλός, εἰς δόξαν Χριστοῦ. ἡ δὲ εἰς ἄλλου ζῆλον, ὡς ἐπὶ τὴν μαρτυρίαν. καὶ ἁπλῶς τῆς ἐ. εἰσὶν εἴδη δύο· ἔστι γὰρ ἐ. οἰκονομικὴ καὶ παιδευτική, καὶ ἔστιν ἐ. τελεία ἀπογνωστική Jo.D.*fr.Mt.*27:5(M.96.1412A); id.*f.o.*2.29(M.94.968A,B) cit. s. ἀνιάτρευτος; **f.** S. Peter's denial due to ἐ., Chrys.*hom.12.3 in Heb.*(12.288A); Πέτρος...πρὸς μικρὸν ἐγκαταλειφθεὶς οἰκονομικῇ τινι ἐ. †Jo.D.*B.J.*11(M.96.960A).

__ἐγκαταλιμπάνω__, = ἐγκαταλείπω, Chrys.*hom.5.4 in Mt.*(7.79B) al.; Pall.*h.Laus.*47(p.138.12; M.34.1201A).

[*]__ἐγκαταλίμπ-ω__, prob. error for foreg. ~ονται οἱ δίκαιοι πρὸς καιρόν Or.*Ps.*36:25(p.12).

__ἐγκαταμίγνυμι__, [pres. ἐγκαταμίσγειν Ath.*h.Ar.*34, v. 2 infra]; **1.** *mix, associate with*, Clem.*ecl.*36(p.148.4; M.9.717A); angels in prayer, Chrys.*hom.19.3 in Mt.*(7.248C); Cyr.*Jo.*1.6(4.49E); **2.** *mix up* incompatibles: false with true prophets, Clem.*str.*1.17(p.54.27; M.8.800B); Church and State, Ath.*h.Ar.*34(p.202.9; M.25.732D); pagan opinions in thought of Arians, Gr.Nyss.*Eun.*12(2 p.289.20; M.45.901C); **3.** met., *blend with, infuse* Χριστιανῶν [sc. πολιτεία] δέ, ᾗ ⟨ὁ⟩ χρυσὸς ὁ βασιλικὸς ἐγκαταμέμικται, τὸ ἅγιον πνεῦμα Clem.*str.*5.14(p.391.5; M.9.148A); of divine love infusing its own goodness into mind of sinners, Isid.Pel.*epp.*5.307(M.78.1516A); **4.** *introduce*, Ath.*h.Ar.*41(p.206.10; M.25.741B); **5.** *insert* in a book, Socr.*h.e.*4.23.14(M.67.512B).

*__ἐγκαταμικτέον__, *one must mingle with*, Clem.*paed.*2.2(p.170.16; M.8.416B).

__ἐγκαταμίσγω__, v. ἐγκαταμίγνυμι.

__ἐγκαταπαίζ-ω__, *mock, deride*; exeg. Job 40:14 ὥστε τὸν διάβολον πρῶτον κτίσμα εἶναι λέγει, ἑαυτὸν ποιήσαντα ~εσθαι ὑπὸ τῶν ἁγίων ἀγγέλων Didym.*Trin.*1.17(M.39.341B); of heretics σεσωρευμέναις γυναιξὶν ~όντων Eus.*h.e.*2.13.8(M.20.169B).

*__ἐγκαταπείρω__, *pierce through*, Cyr.*Jo.*5.2(4.481B); id.*hom.pasch.*7(5^{2}.87C).

__ἐγκαταπήγνυμι__, met., *implant* ἵνα...τὴν ἀσέβειαν ἐγκαταπήξωσι Ath.*apol.sec.*17(p.99.39; M.25.276B); ἐγκαταπέπηκται...τῷ ἐν ἡμῖν λογικῷ...ἡ ἐφ' ἑκάστῳ τῶν πρακτέων ὀρθὴ...κρίσις Cyr.*ador.*11(1.383D).

*__ἐγκαταπηδάω__, *leap down into*; met., Cyr.*Is.*5.2(2.761D).

__ἐγκαταπνίγ-ω__, *suffocate*; met., of mortification ψυχὰς ἑαυτοῖς ~οντες ‡Caes.Naz.*dial.*140(M.38.1048).

*__ἐγκαταπραγματεύομαι__, *be occupied with*, Euthal.Diac.*Ac.* proem.(M.85.632A).

*__ἐγκαταρριζόω__, *implant, infix*, met. τὸ κέντρον τοῦ θανάτου ἐγκατερρίζωται ἡμῖν Mac.Aeg.*hom.*25.4(M.34.669B); ἣν [sc. παράδοσιν] οἱ ἐξ ἀρχῆς διαταξάμενοι παραδιδόντες τοῖς ἐφεξῆς...ταῖς ἐκκλησίαις ἐγκατερρίζωσαν Bas.*Spir.*71(3.60B; M.32.200C).

*__ἐγκαταρρωστέω__, *be sick with*, met. πολλὴν ἐγκατηρρωστηκότας τὴν ἐν ἁμαρτίαις φθοράν Cyr.*ador.*15(1.523A).

__ἐγκατασκευάζω__, pass., *be constituted*, Gr.Nyss.*Apoll.*15(M.45.1152A).

*__ἐγκατασκεύαστος__, *fittingly constituted*, Iren.*haer.*4.38.3(M.7.1107C).

__ἐγκατασκήπτω__, *fall upon*; of lightning or epidemics, *LS*; met. κατῆλθεν [sc. Logos] ἐνταῦθα καὶ προσεκολλήθη καὶ ἐγκατέσκηψεν ἐνανθρωπήσας εἰς αὐτήν [sc. τὴν σάρκα] Meth.*symp.*7.8(p.78.19, v.l. ἐγκατεσκήνωσεν; M.18.136A).

*__ἐγκατασπάω__, *draw down into*, Gr.Nyss.*ordin.*(M.46.552D).

ἐγκατασπείρ-ω, *sow, implant*; **1.** in begetting, Epiph.*haer*.26.5 (p.282.2; M.41.340B); **2.** fig., Gr.Nyss.*or.catech*.23(p.88.15; κατασπ- M.45.61D); in Gnost. eucharistic invocation *χάρις...~ουσα τὸν κόκκον τοῦ σινάπεως εἰς τὴν ἀγαθὴν γῆν* Iren.*haer*.1.13.2(M.7.581A); *τὰ δὲ πνευματικά, ἃ ~ει ἡ Ἀχαμώθ* *ib*.1.7.5 ap.Epiph.*haer*.31.23 (p.421.17) for *ἃ ἂν κατασπείρῃ* Iren.*haer*.1.7.5(M.7.520A, M.41.520B); **3.** met.; **a.** of natural implanting: Gnost. of *πρόνοια* in *οὐσίαι*, Clem.*str*.4.12(p.287.2; M.8.1296C); *σπερματικοὶ λόγοι* in soul, Or.*Jo*. 20.2(p.328.17; M.14.573C); soul in animals and men, Epiph.*haer*. 26.9(p.286.6; M.41.345A); powers in soul, ‡Bas.*const*.2.1(2.541B; M. 31.1340A); immortality in body through soul, Aen.*dial*.(M.85.932C); Zach.Mit.*opif*.(M.85.1124B); knowledge of existence of God *φυσικῶς ἡμῖν ἐ.* ‡Cyr.*Trin*.1(6^{3}.1C; M.77.1121A) = Jo.D.*f.o*.1.3(M.94.793C); **b.** of intellectual implanting; teaching in mind, *A.Jo*.34(p.168.20); Clem.*str*.7.18(p.78.21; M.9.556C); Hipp.*antichr*.1(p.3.13; M.10.728A); Chrys.*hom.8.4 in 1Thess*.(11.484D); Isid.Pel.*epp*.1.415(M.78.413A); **c.** of moral implanting; virtue in soul, Clem.*paed*.2.10(p.213.30; M.8.509A); Chrys.*hom.23.3 in Eph*.(11.178B); **4.** *introduce* heresy in Church, Socr.*h.e*.2.37.89(M.67.320C); pass., of Trin. doctrine in OT, Isid.Pel.*epp*.2.143(M.78.585B); **5.** *overwhelm ~εσθαι συμφοραῖς τὸν ὑπερόπτην* Cyr.*hom.pasch*.11(5^{2}.157D).

***ἐγκατασπορά, ἡ,** *implanting τὴν τῶν δογμάτων ἐ.* Clem.*str*.7.18 (p.79.5; M.9.557A).

ἐγκαταστηρίζω, *fix firmly in*, c. dat., *Diogn*.7.2.

***ἐγκατασφραγίζω,** *seal up in ἡ διαθήκη...Ἰησοῦ ἐγκατασφραγισθῇ εἰς τὴν καρδίαν ἡμῶν* *Barn*.4.8.

ἐγκατασχάζω, f.l. for *ἐγκαγχάζω*, Bas.*reg.fus*.17.1 ap.*Schol*.5 in Jo.Clim.*scal*.7(M.88.820B).

ἐγκατατάσσω, 1. *include*; **a.** persons *τὸν ἐγκαταταγέντα τῇ ἐκλεκτῇ υἱοθεσίᾳ* Clem.*str*.1.27(p.107.29; M.8.921A); *ἐγκαταταγῆναι τῷ πρεσβυτερίῳ* *ib*.6.13(p.486.1; M.9.329A); Chrys.*hom.4.1 in Col*.(11.351D); Max.*ambig*.(M.91.1277D); c. *εἰς*, Or.*mart*.26(p.23.5; M.11.596A); **b.** things *ἐγκατατέτακται τοῖς εὐαγγελίοις* Or.*Jo*.1.11(12; p.17.5; M.14.44D); ‡Proc.G.*Pr*.25:1(M.87.1472C); **2.** *admit, sanction*; pass., Clem.*paed*.2.10(p.214.21; M.8.512A); **3.** *relegate*; pass., Pall.*v.Chrys*. 12(p.70.17; M.47.39); **4.** *put in charge of ἐπίσκοπον ἐγκατατάξας κωμυδρίῳ* *ib*.7(p.38.20; M.47.23).

***ἐγκατατείνω,** *increase, intensify*, Cyr.*ador*.1(1.37A).

ἐγκατατίθημι, *place within, instil*, med.; met., esp. ref. soul *τὸ μέγιστον...τῶν πρὸς τὴν ζωὴν μαθημάτων...ἐ. τῇ ψυχῇ δεῖ* Clem. *q.d.s*.7(p.164.15; M.9.612B); Gr.Thaum.*pan.Or*.8(p.22.14; M.10. 1077C); Chrys.*hom.4.3 in Tit*.(11.753D); Cyr.*Lc*.14:28(M.72.796B).

***ἐγκατατρίβομαι,** *be well versed ἐν πράγμασιν* Synes.*ep*.121(M.66. 1500D).

***ἐγκατατρύχω,** *wear out, exhaust*, Cyr.*ador*.1(1.34A); id.*Jo*.9 (4.743E).

***ἐγκαταυγάζω,** *enlighten*, Epiph.*anc*.103(p.124.11; M.43.204A).

***ἐγκαταυλίζ-ομαι,** *shelter, find refuge in*, met. *ταῖς διὰ Μωσέως ἐντολαῖς...~εσθαι* Cyr.*ador*.3(1.86C).

***ἐγκαταφέρομαι,** *be brought down to*, Gr.Nyss.*or.catech*.24(p.94. 16; M.45.65C).

ἐγκαταφύομαι, *grow up within*, c. dat., Cyr.*Jo*.2.5(4.202C).

***ἐγκαταφύρομαι,** *be mixed up with*, Cyr.*Jo*.4.7(4.437B).

ἐγκαταφυτεύω, *implant*; met., Clem.*prot*.2(p.12.17; M.8.73B); ⟨ἐγ⟩*καταφυτευθεὶς γνώσει* id.*str*.6.15(conj. p.491.13 for *καταφυτευθεὶς* M.9.341B); Or.*Jo*.20.38(30; p.379.11; M.14.664A); *ἐγκαταφυτεύσῃ ἐν αὐτοῖς τὸν ἁγνὸν...φόβον* *Lit*.ap.*Const.App*.8.6.5.

***ἐγκαταχρώννυμι,** *give colour* to; fig., Christol., Cyr.*inc.unigen*. (5^{1}.691D) cit. s. *ἴδιος*.

ἐγκαταχώννυμι, *smother, bury καθάπερ σπινθῆρα πυρὸς ἐγκαταχώσας αὐτοῖς τὴν ζωοποιὸν τοῦ πνεύματος δύναμιν* Cyr.*Jo*.4.1(4.340D, conj. *ἐγκαταχύσας* Aubert).

ἐγκαταχωρίζω, *include*; pass., Or.*comm.in Rom*.1:1(*JTS* 13 p.211; M.14.842C).

ἐγκατοικέω, *indwell*, *Barn*.1.4; Didym.(‡Bas.)*Eun*.5(1.310A; M. 29.744A).

ἐγκατορύσσω, *bury in*, met. *τὸν νοῦν ἐγκατορύξας τῇ κοιλίᾳ* Clem.*paed*.2.1(p.167.8; M.8.408B); id.*str*.7.15(p.65.34; M.9.528C); *λέγει δὲ Πυθαγόρας...τὰς ψυχὰς...εἶναι...θνητὰς μέν, ὅταν ὦσιν ἐν τῷ σώματι, οἱονεὶ ἐγκατορωρυγμένας ὡς ἐν τάφῳ* Hipp.*haer*.6.25(p.152. 18; M.16.3231C); *ib*.5.8(p.93.13; 3146B); Or.*exc.in Ps*.77:31(M.17. 141A); Chrys.*hom.div*.1.1(12.324C).

ἐγκαυστικός, *burnt in, encaustic*, Jo.Mal.*chron*.12 p.294(M.97. 445A); ‡Jo.D.*ep.Thphl*.28(M.95.381A).

ἐγκαυχ-άομαι, *glory, exult*; **1.** in God and divine things, Clem. *paed*.1.6(p.119.24; M.8.309A); abs. *μὴ ἐπαισχυνθῇς τὸν σταυρὸν ὁμολογεῖν· ἄγγελοι γὰρ ~ῶνται* Cyr.H.*catech*.13.22; *M.Ner.et Ach*.9 (p.8.15); **2.** in bad things, exeg. Ps.51:3 *οὐ γὰρ εἶπε, 'τί καυχᾷ;' ἀλλά, 'τί ~ᾷ;' οὐδέποτε δὲ ἐν ἀγαθῷ λέγεται τὸ '~ᾶσθαι'· ἀλλ' εἴ τις ἁμαρτάνει, ~ᾶται* Or.*sel.in Ps*.51:3(M.12.1457A); *φαῦλον μὲν τὸ '~ᾶσθαι', μέσον δὲ τὸ 'καυχᾶσθαι'* *ib*.l.c.; but cf. *κἂν γένῃ...ἀγαθός, ~ήσεταί* [sc. *θεός*] *σοι* id.*exc.in Ps*.36:6(M.17.124A); Ath.*ep.encycl*. 5(p.174.13; M.25.233A); Bas.*reg.fus*.2.4(2.339D; M.31.916B); id.*reg. br*.247(2.498D; M.31.1248C); abs., *boast, exalt oneself*, Jo.Eub.*concept. BMV* 19(M.96.1492C); Thphn.*chron*.p.416(M.108.985C).

ἔγκειμαι, 1. *be in, be innate τοῖς ἀνθρώποις ὄρεξις ἔγκειται* Clem. *prot*.10(p.67.4; M.8.204A); Or.*Jo*.13.41(p.267.25; M.14.472D); Meth. *res*.2.8(p.344.17; M.18.308A); *τὸν ἐγκείμενον τῇ φύσει τῆς κτίσεως λόγον* Gr.Nyss.*hex*.26(M.44.88D); **2.** theol., *inhere*, in Trin. context *νοῦς ἐστιν οἷον λόγος ἐγκείμενος* Dion.Al.ap.Ath.*Dion*.23(p.63.18; M.25.513C); Christol. *τὸ σῶμα κύριος λέγεται διὰ τὴν ἐγκειμένην θεότητα* Gr.Nyss.*ep*.3(M.46.1021D); **3.** *be prone, addicted* to, gen. bad things, c. dat., Or.*Jo*.2.3(p.57.19; ἐκκ- M.14.113C); Gr.Nyss. *fat*.(M.45.148C); c. *ἐπί*, Cyr.*Ps*.50:13(M.69.1100C); **4.** *τὰ ἐγκείμενα*; **a.** *matters, concerns*, Or.*Cels*.3.54(p.249.27; M.11.992B); Meth.*res*.1. 54(p.312.10; M.41.1145D); **b.** *passages* of scripture, Hipp.*fr.Cant*. (p.343.11; M.10.629A); *μὴ μόνον τὰ ἐγκείμενα εἰδέναι, ἀλλὰ καὶ τὴν αἰτίαν τῶν γεγραμμένων* Chrys.*hom.8.4 in Heb*.(12.91B).

***ἐγκειμένως,** *insistently, eagerly*, Const.ap.Eus.*v.C*.3.60(p.107.11, v.l. *ἐγκειμένους* M.20.1129B).

***ἐγκεκαλυμμένως,** *secretly*, Ammon.*Ac*.17:30(M.85.1568A).

ἐγκέλευσις, ἡ, *command*, Thphl.Ant.*Autol*.3.25(M.6.1160B); Clem.*paed*.3.12(p.290.24; M.8.680B).

ἐγκεντρίζ-ω, 1. *goad, spur on*; met., ‡Meth.*Sym.et Ann*.2(M.18. 353A); **2.** *engraft, implant*, fig., Clem.*str*.1.1(p.8.13; M.8.697A); Ath.*Dion*.4(p.49.9; M.25.485B); Mac.Aeg.*pat*.28(M.34.888D); ref. Rom.11:17, Clem.*str*.6.15(p.490.31; M.9.341A); so also met. *ἡ κλῆσις ἡ ἐξ ἐθνῶν...ἐπὶ τὸ ξύλον τοῦ κυρίου ἐγκεντρισθεῖσα* Hipp.*fr.41 in Gen*.(p.67.3; M.10.597C); Gr.Naz.*or*.7.3(M.35.757C); Gr.Nyss.*hom.4 in Cant*.(M.44.844B); Isid.Pel.*epp*.1.64(M.78.225A); of creation engrafted into Christ, Cyr.*thes*.25(5^{1}.238D); similarly, †Gregent.*disp*. (M.86.704B); ref. Cross *στελέχη δὲ πικρὰ ἐγκεντρίσαντες* [sc. Devil and Hades] *αὐτῷ* Rom.Mel.(*AS* 1 p.58); theol. *ἕκαστον τῶν περὶ τὸ θεῖον ὀνομάτων τῇ οὐσίᾳ τοῦ θεοῦ ~οντος* [sc. Eunomius] Gr.Nyss. *Eun*.12(1 p.385.30; M.45.1113D); in gen., Synes.*insomn*.7(p.157.18; M.66.1293C).

ἐγκεντρισμός, ὁ, *grafting*; fig., ref. Rom.11:17, four methods described and applied to 'grafting' of faith on different categories of converts, Clem.*str*.6.15(p.491.18ff.; M.9.341Cff.); contrasted with *θεμέλιον* of Eph.2:20, Chrys.*hom.6.1 in Eph*.(11.39C); cf.Vict.*Mc*. 11:13(p.393.5); ref. heret. sect *ὥσπερ δι' ἐγκεντρισμοῦ...ἕτερα σώματα παραφθείρεσθαι* Epiph.*haer*.25.7(p.274.14; M.41.329C); of soul *φυτὸν οὐράνιον, ἐ. ἀλλότριον οὐ δεξάμενον* Synes.*provid*.1.10(p.85.4; M.66. 1232C).

***ἐγκεντρῶς,** *pointedly, clearly*; comp., Pall.*v.Chrys*.3(p.19.5; M. 47.13).

ἐγκεράννυμι, *mix in, immingle*, Clem.*prot*.1(p.4.21; M.8.56A); Hipp.*haer*.5.21(p.123.9; M.16.3187C); theol., of God *ἐγκέκραται ἡμῖν ὡς συνέχων ἐν τῷ εἶναι τὴν φύσιν* Gr.Nyss.*or.catech*.25(p.96.3; M.45.65D); of relationship of *δύναμις τοῦ ὑψίστου* to human nature in Inc., id.*ep*.3(M.46.1021D).

ἐγκινδυνεύω, *run a risk in*; c. dat., Gr.Nyss.*Eun*.4(2 p.71.2; M. 45.644C).

ἐγκισσάω, 1. *conceive*, cf.Gen.30:38f.; cited Just.*dial*.86.2(M.6. 680C); cf.Hipp.*haer*.5.17(p.114.26; M.16.3175C); Gnost. conception of aeons, Iren.*haer*.1.4.5(M.7.489A); Epiph.*haer*.25.5(p.273.2; M.41. 328B); fig. *ἐ. ἡ γαστήρ μου φρόνησιν* Ephr.2.293A; met. *ὁ διάβολος ...φθόνον ἐ. καθ' ἡμῶν* Meth.*res*.1.37(p.278.11; M.18.293B); *ib*.2.1 (p.330.14; 297B); Epiph.*haer*.31.4(p.389.23; 480D); *ib*.76.7(p.348.6; M.42.528C); *Max.invect*.(M.90.204C); **2.** met., *engender*, Hipp.*Dan*. 1.18.4(M.10.693B); Epiph.*haer*.39.9(p.78.20; M.41.673D); Anast.S. *haer*.(p.260).

***ἐγκίσσημα, τό,** *sexual desire, lust*, Gnost. *κατὰ τὸ ἐ. τῆς δυνάμεως τῆς ἀπὸ τῶν ῥάβδων ἐπὶ τὰ ἐγκεκισσημένα* Hipp.*haer*.5.17 (p.114.27; M.16.3175C); *τὸ ἐ. τοῦ ξύλου* Epiph.*haer*.79.7(p.482.20; M. 42.752B).

ἐγκλεισμός, ὁ, *enclosure*; eremitical and monastic, Pall.*h.Laus*. 45(p.133.3; M.34.1217C); Nil.*epp*.2.96(M.79.244A).

***ἐγκλειστήριον, τό, 1.** *prison*, Chrys.*fr.in Jer*.20:2(M.64.925D); **2.** *cell* of hermit, Cyr.S.*v.Sab*.87(p.195.23); Jo.Mosch.*prat*.69(M.87. 2921B).

***ἐγκλειστικός,** *of a recluse ἐ. ζωή* Thdr.Stud.*or*.11.32(M.99.836A).

***ἔγκλειστος**, *enclosed*; **1.** masc. as subst., *hermit, anchorite*, Jo.Mosch.*prat*.45(M.87.2900B); *ib*.69(2921B); Thphn.*chron*.p.195(M.108.505D); *ib*.p.367(880B); **2.** fem. as subst., *enclosed nun*, Max.*ep*.31(M.91.625B).

***ἐγκλείστρα**, **ἡ**, *hermit's cell* τοὺς...ἐν ἐ. βουλομένους ἀναχωρεῖν...πρότερον ἐν μοναστηρίῳ εἰσιέναι δεῖ CTrull.*can*.41; Andr.Cr.*or*.19(M.97.1245B); Thphn.*chron*.p.367(M.108.880B); eccl. *prison*, Ath.Scholast.*coll*.1.15(p.22).

***ἔγκλειστρον**, **τό**, *hermitage*, Steph.Diac.*v.Steph*.(M.100.1148C).

ἐγκλείω, *shut up, confine* ἐν αἰωνίῳ πυρὶ ἐ. Just.*2apol*.8.3(M.6.457B); reflex., of withdrawal for prayer, Eus.*v.C*.4.22(p.125.22; M.20.1169A); hence of recluses μονάζοντα ἐγκεκλεισμένον Chrys.*ep*.221(3.722B); Pall.*h.Laus*.35(p.100.14; M.34.1107D); *Apophth.Patr*.(p.404.7; M.65.120B); Jo.Mosch.*prat*.70(M.87.2924A).

ἔγκλημα, **τό**, **1.** *accusation, charge*; legal, of pagans against Christians, Athenag.*leg*.1.4(M.6.893B); τρία ἐπιφημίζουσιν ἡμῖν ἐ., ἀθεότητα Θυέστεια δεῖπνα Οἰδιποδείους μίξεις *ib*.3.1(896C); *Ep.Lugd*.ap.Eus.*h.e*.5.1.35(M.20.421B); of Jews against Christ, Chrys.*hom.83.4 in Jo*.(8.495C); *ib.84.2*(500B); gen. of prophets against sinners, Or.*hom.14.4 in Jer*.(p.109.14; M.13.408D); Meth.*symp*.4.4(p.50.9; M.18.92D); hence **2.** *ground of complaint, fault, crime* τοὺς διακόνους...δέον...φυλάσσεσθαι τὰ ἐ. ὡς πῦρ Ign.*Trall*.2.3; Meth.*res*.1.31(p.266.1; M.41.1141C); συγχωρῆσαι ἐ. Chrys.*hom.in Mt.18:23*(3.9C); id.*hom.in Mt.26:39*(3.23E).

ἐγκληματικῶς, **1.** *by way of accusation* τοῦτο ἐ. διηγεῖται Epiph.*haer*.66.63(p.102.16; M.42.128A); **2.** *criminally, on a criminal charge*, Ath.Scholast.*coll*.5.5(p.76); Phot.*nomoc*.9.27(M.104.777A).

ἔγκλησις, **ἡ**, *charge, accusation* ἐ. δέ ἐστι ψόγος ἀδικούντων Clem.*paed*.1.9(p.137.1; M.8.345B); Eus.*v.C*.3.60(M.20.1132B; ἐγκλήματος p.109.8); ‡Jo.D.*Artem*.54(p.90.17; M.96.1301B).

ἔγκλητος, *liable to a charge, blameworthy*; neut. as subst. τὸ ἐ. τῶν λόγων Or.*enarr.in Job 22*:2(M.17.80C); plur., id.*Cels*.2.24(p.153.12; M.11.844A).

***ἐγκλήτως**, *faultily, in blameworthy manner*, Or.*Cels*.5.35(p.38.12; M.11.1233D).

ἐγκλώθω, *intertwine, combine* παραίνεσιν εὐφυεστάτοις ἐλέγχοις ἐγκεκλωσμένην ποιεῖται θεός Cyr.*Is*.4.2(2.583C).

ἐγκοίμησις, **ἡ**, *sleeping in* or *on*, Clem.*paed*.2.9(p.204.25; M.8.489B).

***ἐγκοίμισμα**, **τό**, ? *sarcophagus* ἔχεις τάφον ἔχοντά τι ἔξωθεν ἐ. πάνυ θαυμαστὸν..., ἔσωθεν δὲ δυσωδίας...γέμει Barth.Edess.*Agar*.(M.104.1413D).

***ἐγκοιτάω**, *lie inside*, *Pers*.(p.45.15).

ἐγκολάπτω, *carve upon a stone*; met., *inscribe, engrave* divine teaching in the heart, Chrys.*hom.6.6 in Gen*.(4.47A); the Cross in the mind, id.*hom.54.5 in Mt*.(7.552B); scripture, id.*hom.32.3 in Jo*.(8.188B); Synes.*ep*.44(M.66.1369C).

ἐγκολλ-άω, *glue to*; pass., met., *be united, adhere to* τὰ τῆς ψυχῆς...μέρη τῇ τοῦ θείου πόθου...~ᾶσθαι χρηστότητι Diad.*perf*.34(p.38.27).

ἐγκολπίζω, med., **1.** *embrace, carry in one's arms*; met., of God ἐ. τὰ πάντα Clem.*str*.5.12(p.380.13; M.9.121A); *ib*.2.2(p.115.24; M.8.936B); τοὺς μὲν πονηροὺς ὁ διάβολος ἐ., τοὺς δὲ δικαίους ὁ κύριος Or.*exp.in Pr*.16:33(M.17.197A); Areth.*Apoc*.12(M.106.584B); *enclose*, Chrys.*hom.7.3 in 1Thess*.(11.474F); *contain*; of stone containing a colour, Areth.*Apoc*.67(M.106.773B); *surround*; of sky surrounding earth, Cyr.H.*catech*.6.3; **2.** *receive, possess* in one's heart, Nil.*epp*.1.27(M.79.96B); *ib*.2.183(296B); *ib*.3.51(416C); Ph.Carp.ap.Jo.D.*parall*.(M.95.1381B).

ἐγκόλπιος, **1.** *in the breast* ἐγκόλπιός με τρώσῃς Gr.Naz.*carm*.2.1.88.140(M.37.1440A); met. τὸ δὲ ἐ. ἡμῶν κακὸν ὁ Εὐνόμιος id.*ep*.202(M.37.332A); ἐ. τὸ πῦρ τῆς ἐπιθυμίας Gr.Nyss.*v.Mos*.(M.44.424C); μητρικῆς κοιλίας ἐγγάστριος ὁ τοῦ ἀϊδίου πατρὸς ἐ. Sophr.H.*ep.syn*.(M.87.3161A); πέτρα σχισθεῖσα, ἐ. τὴν ἀμνάδα εἰσδέχεται Jo.D.*hom*.12.10(M.96.793D); **2.** *in the womb*, ref. BMV τὴν θεὸν ἐ. ὑποδέχεσθαι μέλλουσαν Jo.D.*f.o*.4.14(M.94.1160A); τὴν ἐ. ὡς βρέφος τὸν κτιστὴν βαστάσασαν id.*hom*.9.14(M.96.741B).

***ἔγκολπον**, **τό**, *what is in the breast*; of Son in bosom of Father, Anast.S.*hod*.17(M.89.264B).

ἐγκόλπω, med., *put in the fold of one's robe*; hence **1.** *enclose, embrace*, Mac.Mgn.*apocr*.4.11(p.172.19); Philost.*h.e*.3.8(M.65.489C); met., of God and creatures, Cyr.*glaph.Ex*.2(1.300E); Leont.H.*Nest*.2.30(M.86.1589A); Eustrat.*v.Eutych*.2(M.86.2276D); **2.** *pocket, appropriate*, *M.Ariadn*.7(p.128.21); *Chron.Pasch*.p.46(M.92.164D).

ἐγκομβ-όομαι, *be clothed with, gird oneself with*; met., cf.1Petr.5:5; πάσας ἐκκεκομβωμένος...τὰς ἀρετάς Nil.*epp*.2.126(M.79.253C (sic)); πάσας τὰς ἀρετὰς ὁ τοῦ ἀγῶνος ἄνθρωπος ~ώσοιτο Diad.*perf*.85(p.116.9); Ant.Mon.*hom*.127(M.89.1829A).

***ἐγκομίζω**, *carry in* or *on*, *M.Ner.et Ach*.12(p.11.23).

ἔγκομμα, **τό**, *obstacle*, Eus.*v.C*.3.54(p.102.4; M.20.1117C) = id.*l.C*.8(p.216.4; M.20.1360A).

***ἐγκομπάζω**, *boast about*, Hipp.*haer*.4.13(p.45.17; M.16.3078A).

***ἐγκονίζομαι**, *take part in a contest*, Gr.Nyss.*usur*.(M.46.436A).

ἐγκόπτω, **1.** *wound, mutilate*, Athenag.*leg*.26.1(M.6.952A); **2.** *check* ἱδρῶτας Chrys.*hom.58.5 in Jo*.(8.343D); **3.** *interrupt* an argument or speech, Just.*dial*.45.1(M.6.572B); *Hom.Clem*.2.2; *ib*.19.1; an action, Chrys.*hom.16.9 in Mt*.(7.216D); **4.** *hinder, check, thwart*, *Ep.Lugd*.ap.Eus.*h.e*.5.1.11(M.20.413A); Gr.Naz.*or*.14.31(M.35.900B); Chrys.*hom.62.5 in Jo*.(8.374D); Thdr.Mops.*Gen*.3:7(M.66.640B); pass., *be deprived of* ὁ μαθητὴς οὐκ ὠφελεῖται, ἀλλὰ τὸν καρπὸν ἐγκόπτεται Chrys.*hom.9.6 in Phil*.(11.273F).

ἐγκορδυλέω, *wrap up in*, Synes.*regn*.15(p.33.1; M.66.1080B).

***ἐγκορυφόομαι**, *lift* waves *into a crest*, Gr.Nyss.*hom.11 in Cant*.(M.44.996B).

ἐγκόσμιος, *mundane, of this world*; **1.** in gen. νοῦς ἐ. Dion.Ar.*d.n*.4.6(M.3.701A); Melet.*nat.hom*.synops.(M.64.1101C); *Rit.Sacr*.(p.413); pejorative τὸ ἐ. πνεῦμα τῆς πλάνης Mac.Aeg.*libert.ment*.11(M.34.944A); τὴν ἐ. καὶ δαιμονιώδη...σοφίαν Cyr.*Ps*.9:23(M.69.780A); neut. plur., Tat.*orat*.18(M.6.848A; v.l. ἐγκωμίων p.20.22); **2.** *physical* opp. spiritual and eternal, ἐ. opp. ἀγγελικὴ κτίσις, Gr.Nyss.*Eun*.4(2 p.59.18; M.45.629D); id.*Maced*.14(M.45.1317B); φῶς ἐ. opp. φῶς θεῖον καὶ νοητόν, Cyr.*ador*.8(1.264A); cf.id.*Jo*.2.1(4.148C); Dion.Ar.*d.n*.4.16(M.3.713B); Leont.B.*Nest.et Eut*.1(M.86.1284C); neut. plur. παριστῶν ἐκ τῶν ἐ. ... τὰ ὑπερκόσμια ‡Hipp.*fr.32 in Pr*.(p.170.3); ‡Meth.*Sym.et Ann*.13(M.18.380A); ‡Max.*cap.al*.81(M.90.1417C); **3.** ref. God; pagan, distinguishing creator from ἐ. gods, Cyr.*Jo*.8(4.700A); Christian, *immanent* θεὸς ἐ. Synes.*insomn*.14(p.176.13; M.66.1309A); Dion.Ar.*d.n*.1.6(M.3.596B); **4.** *living in this world* ὁ χθὲς ἐ. ἐγκλίνεται τῇ σήμερον *Hymn*.(*AS* 1 p.500).

ἐγκοσμογενής, *of earthly existence* υἱὸν...ἀγαθῶν παροχὰν ἐ. Synes.*hymn*.4.224(p.32; M.66.1607).

ἐγκοτέω, pass.; *be regarded with anger*, Epiph.*haer*.30.11(p.346.18; M.41.424B); *ib*.51.27(p.298.17; 936C).

ἐγκράτεια, **ἡ**, *temperance, continence, abstinence*; **1.** definitions and scope ἐ. διάθεσίς ἐστιν ἀνυπέρβατος τῶν κατὰ τὸν ὀρθὸν λόγον φανέντων Clem.*str*.2.18(p.155.4; M.8.1020A); ἐ. ... σώματος ὑπεροψία κατὰ τὴν πρὸς θεὸν ὁμολογίαν. οὐ μόνον γὰρ περὶ τὰ ἀφροδίσια, ἀλλὰ καὶ περὶ τὰ ἄλλα, ἃ ἐπιθυμεῖ ἡ ψυχὴ κακῶς οὐκ ἀρκουμένη τοῖς ἀναγκαίοις, ἡ ἐ. ἀναστρέφεται. ἔστι δὲ καὶ περὶ τὴν γλῶσσαν καὶ περὶ τὴν κτῆσιν καὶ περὶ τὴν χρῆσιν καὶ περὶ τὴν ἐπιθυμίαν ἐ. οὐ διδάσκει δ' αὕτη σωφρονεῖν μόνον, ἧγε παρέχει σωφροσύνην ἡμῖν, δύναμις οὖσα καὶ θεία χάρις *ib*.3.1(p.197.3ff.; 1104B); *ib*.3.6(p.218.19; 1152B); *ib*.3.7(p.223.5ff.; 1161B,C); ἐ. δὲ λέγομεν οὐ πάντως τὴν παντελῆ ἀποχὴν τῶν βρωμάτων..., ἀλλὰ τὴν ἐπὶ καθαιρέσει τοῦ φρονήματος τῆς σαρκὸς πρὸς τὸν τῆς εὐσεβείας σκοπὸν ἐπιτετηδευμένην ἀποχὴν τῶν ἡδέων Bas.*reg.fus*.16.2(2.359A; M.31.960A); *ib*.16.3(359B; M.960B); ἔστιν οὖν ἡ ἐ., ἁμαρτίας ἀναίρεσις, παθῶν ἀπαλλοτρίωσις, σώματος νέκρωσις μέχρι καὶ αὐτῶν τῶν φυσικῶν παθημάτων...ζωῆς πνευματικῆς ἀρχή, τῶν αἰωνίων ἀγαθῶν πρόξενος, ἐν ἑαυτῇ τὸ κέντρον τῆς ἡδονῆς ἀφανίζουσα *ib*.17.2(360C; M.964A); *ib*.19.1(362B; M.968A); ἐ. δὲ ἡγούμεθα ὁρίζεσθαι, οὐ μόνον τὴν τῶν βρωμάτων ἀποχὴν (τοῦτο γὰρ πολλοὶ καὶ τῶν παρ' Ἕλλησι φιλοσόφων κατώρθωσαν), ἀλλὰ πρό γε πάντων τὸν τῶν ὀφθαλμῶν ῥεμβασμόν ‡Bas.*const*.19(2.564B; M.31.1389B); Ast.Am.*hom*.14(M.40.372C); τοῦτο γάρ ἐστιν ἐ., τὸ μηδενὶ ὑποσύρεσθαι πάθει Chrys.*hom.2.2 in Tit*.(11.739D); *Doct.Patr*.33(p.258.3); two kinds ἐ. αἰσθητή ἐστιν ἔκκλισις ἀπὸ πάντων τῶν διὰ σαρκὸς ἐνεργουμένων παραλόγων πράξεων. ἐ. δὲ νοητή ἐστιν ἔκκλισις νοῦ ἀπὸ ἡδονῆς νοημάτων ἐμπαθῶν *Schol*.7 in Jo.Clim.*scal*.15(M.88.905B); ‡Max.*cap.al*.51(M.90.1412C); cf.*ib*.54(1413A); summary ἡ ἐ. πᾶσι μὲν ἁρμόδιος...ἐ. δέ φαμεν οὐ τῶν βρωμάτων μόνον, ἀλλὰ τὴν περιεκτικήν· τουτέστι, τὴν ἀποχὴν πάντων τῶν ἀπηγορευμένων...ἐ. γὰρ ἔργον ἐστὶ τὸ ἀπέχεσθαι πάσης ἀλόγων ἡδονῆς, καὶ μηδὲν παρὰ τὸ βούλημα ἐντολῶν τοῦ θεοῦ πράττειν. ἐ. ἐστι χαλινὸς ἄρχων τὴν ἐπὶ βρώματα, ἢ χρήματα, ἢ δόξαν, τοῦ ἐπιθυμητικοῦ ὁρμήν. οὐ γὰρ ἔστι τι τῶν ἀγαθῶν τίκτεσθαι ἄνευ... ἐ. Ant.Mon.*hom*.6(M.89.1449A,B); **2.** necessity ἡ δὲ ἡμετέρα φύσις ἐμπαθὴς οὖσα ἐ. δεῖται, δι' ἧς πρὸς τὸ ὀλιγοδεὲς συνασκουμένη συνεγγίζειν πειρᾶται κατὰ διάθεσιν τῇ θείᾳ φύσει Clem.*str*.2.18(p.155.15; M.8.1020B); Bas.*reg.fus*.16.1(2.358A,C; M.31.957A,B) al.; **3.** in conjunction with other virtues and spiritual activities: θεωρία, Clem.*str*.4.3(p.252.2; M.8.1221A); prayer, Ant.Mon.*hom*.6(M.89.1449B); humility, Jo.Clim.*scal*.15(M.88.888C); *Schol.22 ib*.(912B); obedience, Thdr.Stud.*or*.1(M.99.689C); as quality of Christian love, Polyc.*ep*.

4.2; Clem.*str*.3.7(p.222.30; M.8.1161B); personified as daughter of Faith, Herm.*vis*.3.8.4; **4.** Christian ἐ. dist. from pagan ἡ...ἀνθρωπίνη ἐ., ἡ κατὰ τοὺς φιλοσόφους λέγω τῶν Ἑλλήνων, τὸ διαμάχεσθαι τῇ ἐπιθυμίᾳ καὶ μὴ ἐξυπηρετεῖν αὐτῇ εἰς τὰ ἔργα ἐπαγγέλλεται, ἡ καθ' ἡμᾶς δὲ τὸ μὴ ἐπιθυμεῖν, οὐχ ἵνα τις ἐπιθυμῶν καρτερῇ, ἀλλ' ὅπως καὶ τοῦ ἐπιθυμεῖν ἐγκρατεύηται. λαβεῖν δὲ ἄλλως οὐκ ἔστι τὴν ἐ. ταύτην ἢ χάριτι τοῦ θεοῦ...ὡς δὲ ὑγιαίνειν ἄμεινον τοῦ νοσοῦντα περὶ ὑγιείας διαλέγεσθαι, οὕτω...ἡ κατὰ ἀλήθειαν ἐ. τῆς ὑπὸ τῶν φιλοσόφων διδασκομένης Clem.*str*.3.7(p.222.14ff.; M.8.1161A); ἔστι...ἃ καὶ κατὰ ἰδιωτισμὸν πρός τινων κατορθοῦται, οἷον ἡδονῶν ἐ. ὡς γὰρ ἐν τοῖς ἔθνεσιν ἔκ τε τοῦ μὴ δύνασθαι τυχεῖν ὧν ἐρᾷ τις καὶ ἐκ τοῦ πρὸς ἀνθρώπων φόβου, εἰσὶ δ' οἳ διὰ τὰς μείζονας ἡδονὰς ἀπέχονται τῶν ἐν τοῖς ποσὶν ἡδέων, οὕτως κἂν τῇ πίστει ἢ δι' ἐπαγγελίαν ἢ διὰ φόβον θεοῦ ἐγκρατεύονταί τινες. ἀλλ' ἔστι μὲν θεμέλιος γνώσεως ἡ τοιαύτη ἐ. καὶ προσαγωγή τις ἐπὶ τὸ βέλτιον *ib*.7.12(p.50.14ff.; M.9.497A); and from heret. ἐ.: οἴνου δὲ καὶ κρεωφαγίας ἀποχήν, καὶ τὴν ἄλλην ἐ., οὐ τοῖς αἱρετικοῖς παραπλησίως ἀσπάζεται. οἱ μὲν γὰρ ὡς βδελυκτῶν τούτων νομοθετοῦσιν ἀπέχεσθαι. ἡ δὲ ἐκκλησία, οὐδὲν περὶ τούτων νενομοθέτηκεν Thdt.*haer*.5.29(4.479); **5.** practice of ἐ., esp. in abstinence from food; moderation counselled, ‡Bas.*const*.4.1(2.544E–545B; M.31.1348A,B); *ib*.4.2(546A; M.1350B) cit. s. ἀσκητής; should become habitual, Ast.Am.*hom*.14(M.40.381D–384A); different applications ἄλλη ἡ τοῖς ἀνευθύνοις, καὶ ἑτέρα τοῖς ὑπευθύνοις, ἁρμόζουσα ἐ.· οἱ μὲν γὰρ τὴν τοῦ σώματος κίνησιν εἰς σημεῖον κέκτηνται· οἱ δὲ μέχρι θανάτου...πρὸς τοῦτο...ἀδιαλήκτως διάκεινται Jo.Clim.*scal*.14(M.88.865C); **6.** to be treated as gift of God ὁ ἁγνὸς ἐν τῇ σαρκὶ μὴ ἀλαζονευέσθω, γινώσκων, ὅτι ἕτερός ἐστιν ὁ ἐπιχορηγῶν αὐτῷ τὴν ἐ. *1Clem*.38.2; *ib*.35.2; *ib*.64; to be obtained through prayer, Ant.Mon.*hom*.6(M.89.1449B); **7.** foundation of virtues, cf. Philo ap.Eus.*h.e*.2.17.16(M.20.180B) followed by Clem.*str*.2.20(p.170.18; M.8.1049A); Eus.*d.e*.3.6(p.135.15; M.22.228D); Ast.Am.*hom*.14(M.40.372A); ἀρχὴ καρποφορίας, ἄνθος, καὶ ἀρχὴ πρακτικῆς, ἐ. Nil.*spir.mal*.1(M.79.1145A); ‡Nil.*perist*.2.1(M.79.817B); ref. monks, Hyper.*mon*.45(M.79.1477C); **8.** weapon against attacks of sensuality, *Hom.Clem*.19.19; Bas.*renunt*.5(2.207A; M.31.637A); **9.** *chastity*, as state of life; **a.** dist. from παρθενία and γάμος, *Hom.Clem*.3.26; παρθενίαν ἀσκεῖν...καὶ ἁγνείαν καὶ ἐ., τὴν δὲ μονογαμίαν τιμᾷ Epiph.*haer*.48.9(p.231.12; M.41.868C); **b.** of practice of continence by widow(er)s καλὸν μὲν γὰρ ἡ ἐ. ... συγγνωστὸν δὲ καὶ τῷ δευτέρῳ γάμῳ προσελθεῖν Cyr.H.*catech*.4.26; *ib*.6.35; κἂν ἀπολέσῃς γυναῖκα, δόξαζε. ἴσως σε εἰς ἐ. ἀγαγεῖν βούλεται ὁ θεός Chrys.*hom.41.5 in 1Cor*.(10.394C); μηδεὶς δὲ αὐτὸν [sc. S. Paul] οἰέσθω τὴν μὲν ἀγαμίαν τοῖς ἀνδράσι, τὴν δέ γε μετὰ τὸν γάμον ἐ. ταῖς γυναιξὶ μόναις νομοθετεῖν Thdt.*1Cor*.7:8(3.203); **c.** of living continently in marriage; Noah as practising this for a time, *Apoc.Paul*.50(p.68); μετὰ ταύτην [sc. μονότητα] ἐ. ἔπειτα δὲ χηροσύνη Epiph.*fid*.21(p.523.1; M.42.824A); *Lit*.ap.*Const.App*.8.10.11; **d.** in gen. of chaste life; ref. S. Paul, Chrys.*hom.19.2 in 1Cor*.(10.160E); id.*comm.in Gal*.2:4(10.681A); praise of chastity, Ath.*virg*.24(p.59.14; M.28.280C); **10.** effects; **a.** salvation συμβουλίαν ἐποιησάμην περὶ ἐ., ἣν ποιήσας τις οὐ μετανοήσει, ἀλλὰ καὶ ἑαυτὸν σώσει κἀμὲ τὸν συμβουλεύσαντα *2Clem*.15.1; Herm.*vis*.2.3.2; ἐ. σωτηρία ἐστὶν ψυχῆς ὁδηγοῦσα εἰς φῶς εἰσάγουσα εἰς τὴν βασιλείαν τῶν οὐρανῶν Anton.Hag.*v.Sym.Styl*.2(p.20.22); Thdr.Stud.*or*.1(M.99.689B); **b.** spiritual effects; friendship of angels, Ast.Am.*hom*.14(M.40.373B); σωφροσύνην τίκτει ἐ. Nil.*spir.mal*.4(M.79.1148C); διὰ τοῦτο καλὸν ἡ ἐ., ὅτι τὸ φλεγμαῖνον τῶν παθῶν...καταστέλλει, καὶ ταπεινοῖ πρὸς τὸ ἐπιεικέστερον ‡Nil.*perist*.3.5(M.79.821A); οἱ γὰρ τῆς ἐ. ἐρασταί, ἀριδήλως τῷ μὲν σώματι ἄρτιοι ὑπάρχουσι, τὴν δὲ φρένα ὑγιεῖς, τὴν ψυχὴν τῇ εἰς θεὸν θυμηδίᾳ εὐφραινόμενοι, τὸν νοῦν τῶν γηΐνων μὲν ἀφιστάμενον, καὶ τῶν ἄνω ὀρεγόμενον Ant.Mon.*hom*.6(M.89.1449C); Max.*ascet*.23(M.90.920B); **c.** physical effects, Bas.*reg.fus*.16.1(2.358B; M.31.957B); αἱ...λοιπαὶ ἀρεταὶ ἐν τῷ κρυπτῷ κατορθούμεναι, ὀλιγάκις διαφαίνονται τοῖς ἀνθρώποις· ἡ δὲ ἐ. ... γνώριμον ποιεῖ τὸν ἔχοντα...χαρακτηρίζει...τὸν Χριστιανὸν τὸ κατεσκληκὸς τοῦ σώματος, καὶ ἡ ἐκ τῆς ἐ. ἐπανθοῦσα ὠχρία δεικνῦσιν *ib*.17.2(361A; M.964C); as ornament of body, Clem.*paed*.3.2(p.237.28; M.8.560A); **11.** in dualist heresies; **a.** Gnost. (Saturninus), Iren.*haer*.1.24.2(M.7.675A); **b.** Hieracites ἓν δὲ μόνον τοῦτο κατορθῶσαι ἦλθε [sc. Christ], τὸ τὴν ἐ. κηρῦξαι ἐν τῷ κόσμῳ καὶ ἑαυτῷ ἀναλέξασθαι...ἐ.· ἄνευ δὲ τούτου μὴ δύνασθαί ⟨τινα⟩ ζῆν Epiph.*haer*.67.1(p.134.7f.; M.42.173B); **c.** Encratites τοῖς δὲ εὐφήμως δι' ἐ. ἀσεβοῦσιν εἴς τε τὴν κτίσιν καὶ τὸν...θεὸν καὶ διδάσκουσι μὴ δεῖν παραδέχεσθαι γάμον refuted by 1Jo.2:18f., Mt.5:17 etc., Clem.*str*.3.6(p.216.30; M.8.1148D); *ib*.3.18(p.244.23; 1208C); ἔμψυχα δὲ βδελύσσονται, ἀπαγορεύοντες οὐχ ἕνεκεν ἐ. ... ἀλλὰ κατὰ φόβον καὶ ἰνδαλμὸν τοῦ μὴ καταδικασθῆναι ἀπὸ τῆς τῶν ἐμψύχων μεταλήψεως Epiph.*haer*.47.1(p.216.8; M.41.852B); διὰ μὲν κοινωνίας ὁ κόσμος τὴν ἀρχὴν ἔσχε· διὰ δὲ τῆς ἐ. τὸ τέλος θέλει λαβεῖν Mac.Mgn.*apocr*.3.43(p.151.30); **d.** others, Chrys.*hom.4.3 in Tit*.(11.752D); ἡ ἐ. ... εἰς κραιπάλην... λογίζεται τῷ κατὰ τοὺς Ἕλληνας νηστεύοντι, καὶ τῷ κατὰ τοὺς Μανιχαίους ἀσιτοῦντι, καὶ τὰ καλὰ κτίσματα τοῦ θεοῦ βδελυττομένῳ Nil.*epp*.2.10(M.79.205B); *ib*.2.11(205B); **12.** Lent as time of ἐ., Ast.Am.*hom*.14(M.40.377C); Lenten fare as τὰ ὄψα τῆς ἐ. *ib*.(380D); **13.** περὶ ἐ. title of work by Clem. mentioned, Clem.*paed*.2.10(p.213.33; M.8.509A) (possibly, however, alluding to discussion in *str*.2–4); also of Gnost. work by Cassian, id.*str*.3.13(p.238.10; M.8.1192C).

ἐγκρατεύ-ομαι, **1.** *practise self-restraint, abstain*; def. ~εται δὲ ὁ κατέχων τὰς παρὰ τὸν ὀρθὸν λόγον ὁρμὰς ἢ ὁ κατέχων αὑτὸν ὥστε μὴ ὁρμᾶν παρὰ τὸν ὀρθὸν λόγον Clem.*str*.2.18(p.155.5; M.8.1020A); **a.** in gen. τὸ πονηρὸν ~ου...τὸ δὲ ἀγαθὸν μή Herm.*mand*.8.2 et passim, cf.‡Ath.*doct.Ant*.8(M.28.565A et passim); Arist.*apol*.15.6; ~εσθαι...ἀγαθοεργίας κακίας ἔργον Clem.*str*.4.3(p.251.16; M.8.1220B); ~ονται δὲ ὁπότε τὸ σῶμα ὑποτάσσουσι (ἄλλως γὰρ ~εσθαι ἁμαρτίας ἀδύνατον) Meth.*res*.1.59(p.323.14f.; M.41.1156C); **b.** from sensuality πρό γε πάντων χρὴ μοναχὸν ~εσθαι ἀπὸ συντυχίας γυναικῶν, καὶ οἰνοποσίας Bas.*ascet.disc*.2(2.212E; M.31.652A); Ammonas *opusc*.2.19(p.471.1); Ant.Mon.*hom*.6(M.89.1449C); **2.** *live in chastity*; **a.** in gen., Just.*1apol*.29.1(M.6.373A); ἢ δι' ἐπαγγελίαν ἢ διὰ φόβον θεοῦ ~ονταί τινες Clem.*str*.7.12(p.50.18; M.9.497A); Or.*princ*.3.1.4(p.199.1; M.11.253A); κρείσσων ἄρα ἡ ἐπιθυμοῦσα καὶ ~ομένη τῆς μὴ ἐπιθυμούσης ἐστὶν...καὶ ~ομένης Meth.*symp*.11(p.140.30f.; M.18.220C); Ath.*ep.Drac*.7(M.25.532B); **b.** of widowed persons (consecrated widows), Ath.*virg*.2(p.37.5; M.28.253C); Thdt.*haer*.26(4.469); priests τὰ χαρίσματα τῆς ἱερωσύνης διὰ τῶν ἀπὸ μονογαμίας ~ομένων καὶ τῶν ἐν παρθενίᾳ διατελούντων τῷ κόσμῳ προδιετύπου Epiph.*haer*.48.9(p.231.14; M.41.868D); **c.** of married persons living in continence πείσασα [sc. Melania] αὐτὸν καὶ ~εσθαι μετὰ τῆς ἰδίας γυναικός Pall.*h.Laus*.54(p.147.2; M.34.1227A); legislation for priests and other orders εἰ δὲ μὴ εἶεν ἱκανοὶ εἰς ὑπηρεσίαν ἀπὸ μοναζόντων, ἐξ ~ομένων τῶν ἰδίων γυναικῶν ἢ χηρευσάντων ἀπὸ μονογαμίας. δευτερόγαμον δὲ οὐκ ἔξεστι δέχεσθαι ἐν αὐτῇ εἰς ἱερωσύνην, κἄν τε ~όμενος εἴη ⟨ἢ⟩ χῆρος Epiph.*exp.fid*.21(p.522.10ff.; M.42.824B); τὸν ἔτι ⟨συμ⟩βιοῦντα...μιᾶς γυναικὸς ὄντα ἄνδρα, οὐ δέχεται, ἀλλὰ ἀπὸ μιᾶς ἐγκρατευσάμενον ἢ χηρεύσαντα διάκονόν τε καὶ πρεσβύτερον καὶ ἐπίσκοπον καὶ ὑποδιάκονον id.*haer*.59.4(p.367.18; M.41.1024A); id.*exp.fid*.21(p.522.21; M.42.825B); **d.** οἱ ~όμενοι as order besides clergy κληρικοὶ ἢ ἐ. πρὸς χήρας ἢ παρθένους...μὴ εἰσίτωσαν *Cod.Afr*.38; cf.Phot.*nomoc*.8.15(M.104.1092D); dist. from monks, *Didasc.patr*.7(p.17.7); ranking after virgins and widows, *Lit.Jac*.(p.218.16); **3.** *fast*, cf. μέλλων ὁ ἱερεὺς τὴν θείαν ἐπιτελεῖν μυσταγωγίαν ὀφείλει...~εσθαί τε μικρὸν ἀφ' ἑσπέρας *Lit.Chrys*.(p.353.4); **4.** *practise abstinence*, of Essenes μετὰ γὰρ τὸ δεῖξαι εἰ ~εσθαι δύναται [sc. aspirant to sect] Hipp.*haer*.9.23(p.258.16; M.16.3399B); Adamites, Epiph.*anac*.52(p.212.10; M.41.848B); Hieracites, *ib*.67(p.2.1; M.42.12A); Jo.D.*haer*.67(M.94.717B); condemned εἴ τις...~εται, ὡς ἂν βδελύττιον τῶν γάμων ἀναχωρήσας...ἀ. ἕ. CGangr.*can*.9.

ἐγκρατευτής, *temperate*, Jo.Mosch.*prat*.69(M.87.2921B); *Lit.Chrys*.(p.331.18).

ἐγκρατής, **1.** *temperate*; **a.** of Christians; in gen., Herm.*vis*.1.2.4; *2Clem*.4.3; deacons, Polyc.*ep*.5.2 cit. s. διάκονος; martyrs, *Const.App*.2.49.4; **b.** in rel. to ἀπάθεια: ἀνενδεὲς...τὸ θεῖον καὶ ἀπαθές, ὅθεν οὐδὲ ἐ. κυρίως Clem.*str*.2.18(p.155.14; M.8.1020B); οὐκ ἐ. οὗτος [sc. τέλειος ἄνθρωπος] ἔτι, ἀλλ' ἐν ἕξει γέγονεν ἀπαθείας, σχῆμα θεῖον ἐπενδύσασθαι ἀναμένων *ib*.4.22(p.309.11; M.1348B); οὐδὲ ὁ ἐ. ἐστιν ἀπαθής, κρατῶν οὐκ ἀπόνως τῶν παθῶν· ὅταν δὲ ἕξις γένηται, οὐκέτι ἐ. id.*ecl*.45(p.149.20f.; M.9.720A); **c.** ref. non-material things ταπεινόφρων...ἐστιν ὁ περὶ δόξαν ἐ. Bas.*reg.fus*.16.3(2.359C; M.31.960C); δεῖ γὰρ τὸν ἐ., πάσης αἰσχίστης ἡδονῆς, καὶ ἐπιθυμίας ἀνώτερον εἶναι Ant.Mon.*hom*.6(M.89.1449C); **2.** *continent*; **a.** orthodox; of ascetics, Bas.*renunt*.6(2.208B; M.31.640B); as subst. masc., dist. from monks, *Didasc.patr*.1(p.11.2); subst. fem., prob. widows, dist. from παρθένοι, Ath.*ep.encycl*.3(p.172.20; M.25.229B); of either sex τῶν μοναζόντων, τῶν ἁγίων παρθένων, τῶν ἐ., τῶν ἐν γάμῳ σεμνῷ Cyr.*hom.div*.17(M.77.1097D); **b.** heret. ἀπὸ Σατουρνίνου καὶ Μαρκίωνος οἱ καλούμενοι ἐ., ἀγαμίαν ἐκήρυξαν Iren.*haer*.1.28.1(M.7.690A); of Marcionites οὐ τῇ προαιρέσει γίνονται ἐ., τῇ δὲ πρὸς τὸν πεποιηκότα ἔχθρᾳ, μὴ βουλόμενοι χρῆσθαι τοῖς ὑπ' αὐτοῦ κτισθεῖσιν Clem.*str*.3.3(p.201.4; M.8.1113B); Adamites, Epiph.*haer*.52.2(p.313.6; M.41.956D); Hieracites οὐδεὶς δὲ μετ' αὐτῶν συνάγεται, ἀλλὰ εἰ εἴη παρθένος ἢ μονάζων ἢ ἐ. ἢ χήρα *ib*.67.2(p.135.8; M.42.176A).

[*]**ἐγκρατηταί, οἱ**, = ἐγκρατῖται q.v.

***ἐγκρατητικός**, *of continence*, Epiph.*haer*.46.2(p.205.7; M.41.840C).

***ἐγκρατικός**, *continent*, Pall.*h.Laus*.36(M.34.1180C).

***ἐγκρατιστής**, ὁ, *one who practises self-control, ascetic*, Hipp.*haer*.9.26(p.260.23; M.16.3403C).

ἐγκρατῖται ([*]ἐγκρατηταί), οἱ, *Encratites*, sect who abstained from marriage and use of flesh-meat and wine, basing their asceticism on dualist doctrine of evil of matter, cf.Iren.*haer*.1.28.1 (M.7.690A); Clem.*str*.7.17(p.76.25; M.9.553A); their re-baptism defended, Bas.*ep*.199 *can*.47(3.296D; M.32.729C) cit. s. ἀναβαπτίζω; arguments to be used in controversy with them, *ib*.236.4(363C; M.881C); ἐγκρατηταὶ...οὐ Χριστιανοί τινες...πίστεως μὲν εὐαγγελικῆς ἀποστάται...Δοσίθεος ὁ κορυφαῖος παρ' αὐτοῖς...δι' ὀκτὼ βιβλίων ὅλων κρατύνει τὸ δόγμα Mac.Mgn.*apocr*.3.43(p.151.23); full description of tenets, origin being ascribed to Tatian, Epiph.*haer*.47.1–3 (pp.215.1ff.; M.41.849Dff.); followed by Thdt.*haer*.1.20(4.311ff.); Tim.CP *haer*.(M.86.16C) cit. s. σακκοφόροι; *Chron.Pasch*.p.260(M.92.633C); Isid.H.*etym*.8.5.25; a different view ἕτεροι δὲ ἑαυτοὺς ἀποκαλοῦντες ἐ. τὰ μὲν περὶ τοῦ θεοῦ καὶ τοῦ Χριστοῦ ὁμοίως καὶ τῇ ἐκκλησίᾳ ὁμολογοῦσι, περὶ δὲ πολιτείαν πεφυσιωμένοι ἀναστρέφονται Hipp.*haer*.8.20(p.238.26; M.16.3367A).

[*]**ἐγκρέμαμαι**, *be hung up in* ψυχαὶ δὲ ἐνεκρέμαντο ἐν τοῖς τροχοῖς *A.Thom*.A 55(p.171.20).

***ἐγκρεμής**, *hanging upon*, Vict.*Mc*.9:14ff.(p.359.17).

***ἐγκρημνίζ-ω**, *hurl down into*, met. ἀπωλείας ~ονται φάραγξιν Jo.Eleem.*v.Tych*.(p.114).

ἐγκρίν-ω, **1**. *select, admit, accept* persons, of God παῖδας ἀκάκους ἐ. Clem.*prot*.10(p.77.3; M.8.225A); πάντα πράττωμεν πρὸς τὸ ἐγκριθῆναι τῇ αὐτοῦ [sc. Χριστοῦ] ἀγάπῃ Or.*Jo*.32.21(13; p.463.12; M.14.801B); into kingdom of heaven, Meth.*res*.2.4(p.337.6; M.41.1169B); into number of apostles, Chrys.*hom.30.1 in Mt*.(7.348A); to eccl. dignities, id.*sac*.3.15(p.77.4; 1.393A); **2**. *accept, approve*; of God approving mercy, Clem.*str*.1.11(p.33.26; M.8.749B); Chrys.*hom.30.3 in Mt*.(7.350E); scripture as canonical τὰ μὲν τῶν γεγραμμένων ~ουσι [sc. heretics], τινὰ δὲ ἀποδοκιμάζουσιν...εἰσὶν οἵ τε τὴν μὲν καινὴν ~οντες, τὴν δὲ παλαιὰν ἀποδοκιμάζοντες διαθήκην Or.*fr.comm.in Ezech*.(p.60.22; M.13.664B); *ib*.(p.61.28; 665A); **3**. *reckon, sum up in*, ‡Nil.*perist*.12(M.79.964B); **4**. τὰ ~όμενα *things admitted* into the body, ‡Caes.Naz.*dial*.140(M.38.1077).

ἔγκριτος, **1**. *admitted, chosen* τῶν...φίλων τοὺς ἐ. Eus.*v.C*.2.5 (p.42.22; M.20.984B); *ib*.2.8(p.44.12; 988B); οἱ ἔ. of those admitted to knowledge of mysteries by faith, Clem.*str*.6.15(p.495.23; M.9.349B); *ib*.7.10(p.41.12; 480B); to secret science of Egyptians, ‡Just.*qu.et resp*.25(M.6.1272D); εἷς τῶν δώδεκα, τουτέστι, τῶν ἐ. Chrys.*prod.Jud*.2.2(2.389C); id.ap.*cat.Jo*.1:44(p.196.5) for ἐκκρίτους id.*hom.20.1 in Jo*.(8.115D); **2**. *approved, authoritative* ἔστω [sc. he who baptizes] τις τῶν ἐ. Gr.Naz.*or*.40.26(M.36.396B); of orthodox Fathers πατέρες ἔ. Oecum.*Apoc*.proem.(p.30); Anast.S.*hod*.33(M.89.296D); Gr. language, Areth.*Apoc*.7(M.106.549D); hence *established, settled*, ref. alternative of apostasy or martyrdom ἐν πράγματι οὕτως ἐγκρίτῳ οὐδεμία καθίσταται βουλὴ ἢ διάσκεψις *M.Scill*.11(p.25.15); **3**. *chosen, excellent*, of S. Peter ὁ ἔ. τῶν ἀποστόλων †Bas.*bapt*.1.2.13(2.638C; M.31.1548A); of H. Ghost ἡ...ἔ. ... δόξα Didym.*Trin*.2.1(M.39.452C); πόλεις...αἱ ἔ. Thdt.*Am*.6:2(2.1435); Isid.Pel.*epp*.5.109(M.78.1389A); **4**. *real, genuine* τῶν πνευματικῶν... ἔ. ἐραστής Cyr.*Ps*.33:2(M.69.885A).

ἔγκρυμμα, τό, **1**. *ambuscade*, Geo.Pis.*Pers*.2.297(M.92.1230A); **2**. *secret attack*; met., Eus.*v.C*.1.38(p.25.19; M.20.953A); Mac.Aeg.*cust.cor*.11(M.34.832B); ἡ κακία ἔ. ποιοῦσα *ib*.9(829A) = †Marc.Er.*temp*.28(M.65.1069B); σκόπει κατευχόμενος λογισμῶν...μὴ ἔ. πάθης Evagr.Pont.*or*.133(M.79.1169B); **3**. *secret gathering* τὰ τῶν ἑτεροδόξων ἐ. βασιλικῷ προστάγματι διελύοντο Eus.*v.C*.3.66(p.113.4; M.20.1141D).

***ἐγκρυπτάζ-ομαι**, *lurk* τὸ φιλήδονον πνεῦμα τὸ ~όμενον ἐν τοῖς τοῦ σώματος μέλεσι Nil.*epp*.4.2(M.79.552B).

ἐγκρύπτ-ω, intrans., *hide in*, met. ἁμαρτία τοῖς μὲν ζῶσιν...~ει Serap.*ep.Eudox*.(M.40.925A); pass., *be hidden, concealed*, ref. pagan mysteries γοητείαν τὴν ἐγκεκρυμμένην αὐτοῖς Clem.*prot*.2(p.11.12; M.8.69B); of power of faith hidden in soul, id.*str*.5.12(p.379.26; M.9.120B); of soul in body, id.*exc.Thdot*.51(p.124.1; M.9.684B); ἐγκρυβεῖσα ἡ κακία Mac.Aeg.*hom*.27.6(M.34.628B); of hidden meaning of scripture, Chrys.*hom.13.2 in Gen*.(4.100A).

ἐγκρύφιος, *hidden* σπινθὴρ τῆς θεοσεβείας ἐ. ἐγεγόνει πυρσός Sophr.H.*v.Anast*.(M.92.1689B).

ἐγκτίζ-ω, *create within* οὐ γὰρ ἡ ἐν κόσμῳ σοφία κτίζουσά ἐστιν, ἀλλ' ἡ ~ομένη τοῖς ἔργοις Ath.*Ar*.2.79(M.26.313C); *ib*.2.80(316C); *ib*.2.81(317B).

ἐγκυβιστ-άω, *plunge into*, Bas.Sel.*v.Thecl*.2.3(M.85.569C); Sophr.H.*mir.Cyr.et Jo*.53(M.87.3620D); met., Synes.*ep*.73(M.66.1437B); βυθῷ θαυμάτων ~ῶν Antip.Bost.*Jo.Bapt*.3(M.85.1765C).

ἐγκυέω, *engender*, met. πένθος...ὁ διάβολος ἐνεκύησεν ἐν τῇ τῶν ἀνθρώπων διανοίᾳ Epiph.*haer*.52.1(p.312.23, v.l. ἐνοίκησεν M.41.956C).

ἐγκυκλ-έω, *introduce* μεθίσταται μὲν ὁ νοῦς εἰς τὸν λόγον, ὁ δὲ λόγος τὸν νοῦν εἰς τοὺς ἀκροατὰς ~εῖ Dion.Al.ap.Ath.*Dion*.23(p.63.20; M.25.513C); v. ἐκκυκλέω.

***ἐγκύκλησις**, ἡ, v.l. for ἐκκύκλησις q.v.

***ἐγκυκλητής**, ὁ, *one who moves round*, hence *contemplates* τοῖς τῆς ἀληθείας ἐ. Epiph.*anc*.103(p.124.11; M.43.204A).

ἐγκύκλιος, *circular*; ἐπιστολὴ ἐ. *circular letter, encyclical*; of Clement of Rome, Epiph.*haer*.30.15(p.352.7; M.41.432A); of Alexander, *ib*.69.4(p.155.26; M.42.209A); *ib*.69.9(p.159.26; 217A); ref. 1Petr., *cat.1Petr*.1:1(p.41.27); *synodal letter*, Thphn.*chron*.p.17(M.108.101A) etc.

***ἐγκυλινδ-έομαι**, *be involved, wallow* in, Epiph.*haer*.66.88(p.131.24; M.42.172A); ~ούμενος βορβόρῳ Chrys.*hom.in 1Cor*.7:39(3.210D); †Cyr.*hom.div*.14(5².412A); τῷ βορβόρῳ τῶν τῆς ἀτιμίας παθῶν ~ούμενος *cat.Lc*.15:13(p.118.17); †Jo.D.*B.J*.19(M.96.1037B).

***ἐγκυμαίν-ω**, *wave hither and thither* λήια...~οντα Bas.*hex*.2.3(1.15B; M.29.36B); id.*ep*.210.3(3.314E; M.32.772B); met. ~ονται... αἱ ὀρέξεις περὶ τὰ τῆς μέθης ναυάγια Clem.*paed*.2.2(p.169.20; M.8.413C).

***ἐγκυματόομαι**, *be tossed about in*, c. dat., Gr.Nyss.*or.catech*.39 (p.156.13; M.45.100C).

ἐγκυμον-έω, **1**. *become pregnant, conceive* μήτε μὴν ~ούσαις ὁμιλείτωσαν *Const.App*.6.26.8; Epiph.*haer*.26.5(p.282.3; M.41.340B); Anast.S.*hod*.7(M.89.116A); of BMV, Just.*dial*.78.3(M.6.657C); ‡Meth.*Sym.et Ann*.9(M.18.369C); pass., of Christ, Epiph.*inc*.1 (p.228.1; M.41.273C); met. λογισμοὺς ἀθεμίτους...τοῖς τῆς καρδίας ταμείοις ἐ. Gr.Agr.*Eccl*.9.8(M.98.1093C); **2**. *carry in the womb*; pass., of Christ, Epiph.*haer*.30.27(p.370.6; M.41.452C); *ib*.51.29(p.300.20; 940A); reality stressed against Apollinarians, *ib*.77.26(p.438.26; M.42.677C); met. ταῖς ~ούσαις...τὸν θεῖον ἔρωτα ψυχαῖς Isid.Pel.*epp*.1.211(M.78.316C).

***ἐγκυμόνησις**, ἡ, *impregnation, pregnancy*, Epiph.*haer*.63.1 (p.399.23; M.41.1064C); *ib*.77.28(p.441.5; M.42.681C).

***ἐγκυμονικός**, *belonging to pregnancy*, Epiph.*ep.Arab*.ap.*haer*.78.12(p.463.7; M.42.717B).

***ἔγκυμος**, *conceived*, *Orac*.ap.‡Ath.*templ*.(p.109.7, v.l. ἔγγ- M.28.1429A).

***ἐγκυοφορέω**, *carry in the womb*, ‡Petr.I Al.*phys*.22(p.53).

ἐγκύπτω, **1**. *peep into*; a place, *A.Xanthipp*.6(p.61.25); a book, Gel.Cyz.*h.e*.2.8.2(M.85.1244B); hence **2**. *search, penetrate into, study*, *1Clem*.40.1; ref. books, Cosm.Ind.*top*.proem.(M.88.53A); Anast.S.*haer*.(p.257); esp. scripture, *1Clem*.45.2; *ib*.53.1; Polyc.*ep*.3.2; Arist.*apol*.16(p.111.25); Meth.*res*.1.45(p.294.17; M.41.1116C); ‡Bas.*struct.hom*.1.1(1.324B; M.30.12A); Chrys.*hom.72.4 in Mt*.(7.706E); **3**. prob. f.l. for ἐκκύπτω, Jo.D.*hom*.8.11(M.96.716D).

***ἐγκύτιον**, τό, prob. for ἐγκοίτιον, plur., *bedclothes*, †Gregent.*leg.Hom*.53(M.86.609A).

***ἐγκωμίδιον**, τό, *inadequate encomium, paltry praise*, Thdr.Stud.*cant*.6.4(p.347).

ἐγκώμιον, τό, **1**. *praise*, *T.Job* 18(p.114.20); ἐ. τοῦ ἑαυτοῦ βίου Or.*Cels*.proem.2(p.52.11; M.11.644C); μυρμήκων ἐ. *ib*.4.83(p.353.3; 1156B); ὁ ὑπὸ τῶν πολλῶν ψόγος αὐτῷ ἐ. παρὰ θεῷ id.*hom.20.9 in Jer*.(p.192.21; M.13.524A); Eus.*Marcell*.2.4(p.58.6,21; M.24.821D,824B); ref. false praise of pagan gods, Ath.*gent*.16(M.25.36A); *ib*.17(36B,C); ἐ. τῆς παρθενίας id.*virg*.24(p.59.11; M.28.280C); self-praise, Const.ap.Ath.*apol.sec*.62(p.142.1; M.25.361A); *Const.App*.2.45.1; *ground, matter for praise* πολλοὶ ταπεινοὶ...βιαζόμενοι...οὐδὲ τοῦτο ἐ. Chrys.*hom.15.1 in Mt*.(7.185E); **2**. *eulogy, panegyric, song of praise* Χριστὸς ταῖς ἐπὶ πέρατα παρθενίας ἐλθούσαις τὰ ἐ. ψάλλει Meth.*symp*.7.1(p.72.10; M.18.125B); t.t. for praise of saints and other famous dead, *T.Job* 43(p.132.19); ref. BMV, Procl.CP *or*.6.17(M.65.753B); iron., ‡Jo.D.*ep.Thphl*.22(M.95.373C); also in titles of hymns etc.

***ἐγκωφόω**, *be dumb, say nothing* about, c. πρός, Thdot.Anc.*hom.BMV et Sym*.1(M.77.1389D).

ἐγρεσίκωμος, *stirring up to revelry*, Gr.Naz.*carm*.1.1.7.77(M.37.444A).

[*]**ἐγρηγόρησις**, ἡ, *waking, wakefulness* σημαίνει...ὁ ὕπνος...τὴν ἀπροσεξίαν τῆς ψυχῆς· τῆς προσοχῆς ἐ. καλουμένης Or.*sel.in Ps*.3:6 (M.12.1128A); Serap.*ep.mon*.3(M.40.929A); Gr.Nyss.*hom.10 in Cant*.(M.44.992C).

ἐγρήγορος, *wakeful, watchful, vigilant*; **1.** in gen. ἐ. ὀφθαλμῷ *M.Perp.*18(p.87.24); ref. Cyril ἐ. τῷ ὄμματι περιεπατήσας Alyp.*ep.*(p.74.30; M.77.145D); Melet.*nat.hom.*9(M.64.1188B); **2.** spiritually; of indwelling Logos, Clem.*paed.*2.9(p.207.11; M.8.496B); of angels, *A.Thom.*A 36(p.154.1); νοῦς ἐ. *Const.App.*7.45.3; Epiph.*haer.*66.65(p.105.32; M.42.132C); *ib.*69.68(p.216.5; 312A); Chrys.*hom.47.2 in Mt.*(7.489D); **3.** as subst., name for angels ἐ. ἡ γραφὴ τοὺς ἀγγέλους καλεῖ, ὡς παρὰ τῷ Δανιήλ Or.*fr.109 in Lam.*(p.274.8; M.13.656C); ref. Gen.6:4, *T.Reub.*5.6f.; *T.Neph.*3.5; *Apoc.En.*1.5,10.7; Clem.*paed.*2.9(p.206.2; M.8.493A).

ἐγρήγορσις, ἡ, *waking, watchfulness*; **1.** as Christian practice; means of using life more fully, Clem.*paed.*2.9(p.207.15; M.8.496B); assimilating believers to angels, *ib.*(p.207.28; 496C); necessary, esp. for monks, Isid.Pel.*epp.*1.130(M.78.269A); as weapon against passions, Hyper.*mon.*91(M.79.1481C); of watchfulness of mind (in def. of φρόνησις), Thdt.*provid.*6(4.566) cit. s. φρόνησις; *rousing* of mind against evil thoughts, Hesych.H.*temp.*76(M.93.1537A); symbolized by καρυΐνη [sc. ῥάβδος], Cyr.*glaph.Gen.*5(1.148D); †Cyr.*coll.VT*(6⁴.34E; M.77.1228A); λύχνοι, Cyr.ap.*cat.Lc.*12:35(p.103.1; for γρηγόρησιν M.72.744D); myst. ἡ ψυχὴ...καθαρᾷ τῇ διανοίᾳ διὰ τῆς θείας ἐ. δέχεται τοῦ θεοῦ τὴν ἐμφάνειαν Gr.Nyss.*hom.10 in Cant.*(M.44.993D); λεπτὴν ἐνετίθει ἐ. τῷ προφήτῃ θεός Cyr.*Zach.*23(3.682B); **2.** of God in 'symbolic' theology τοῦ θεοῦ...ἐ. δέ, τὴν εἰς τὸ προνοεῖν αὐτοῦ τῶν παιδείας ἢ σωτηρίας δεομένων προσοχήν Dion.Ar.*ep.*9.6(M.3.1113B); id.*myst.*3(M.3.1033B); **3.** of eternal *vigil* of future life, Clem.*paed.*2.9(p.206.18; M.8.493B); cf.*ib.*(p.207.29; 498A).

ἐγχαλκεύ-ω, *impress as on brass*, met. φρόνημα τὸ νεανικὸν καὶ φιλόθεον ∼οντος Cyr.*Jo.*10.2(4.887B).

***ἐγχαραδρ-όω**, *furrow*, met. σὰρξ...ῥεύματι τῶν παθῶν ∼ωθεῖσα Max.*qu.Thal.*47(M.90.425A).

ἐγχαράσσ-ω, **1.** *engrave*; **a.** lit., of Law of Moses engraved on tables, Hipp.*Dan.*3.14.7; Gr.Nyss.*v.Mos.*(M.44.397A); names of patriarchs on stones of priest's ephod (Ex.28:9f.), *ib.*(320B); hence **b.** met., name of God engraved on heart of priest, cf. Ex.28:36, Clem.*exc.Thdot.*27(p.115.24,27; M.9.672C); cf.Andr.Caes.*Apoc.*68(M.106.444D); ὅταν γένῃ τῶν σῶν καρδιῶν λατόμος, ὥστε ἐν ταύταις τὰ θεῖα λόγια ἐγκεχαράχθαι παρὰ τοῦ θεοῦ Gr.Nyss.*v.Mos.*(M.44.428C); id.*hom.14 in Cant.*(M.44.1076B); ὁ τῆς φιλοστοργίας τοὺς νόμους ∼ων τῇ φύσει Cyr.*Mich.*65(3.460B); **c.** and in gen. of spiritual teaching, virtues etc., Or.*Apoc.*21(p.30); Chrys.*hom.5.4 in 2Thess.*(11.543C); Cyr.*Ps.*44:3(M.69.1029C); of divine image impressed on soul, Chrys.*hom.2.4 in 2Thess.*(11.520E); cf. Cyr.*glaph.Gen.*1(1.5D); of teachings of demons, Gr.Nyss.*virg.*8(p.282.17; M.46.353B); evil imaginings, Nil.*epp.*3.288(M.79.525D); theol. οὐ...ἐπιτάττει τῷ λόγῳ ὁ...πατήρ...ὡς δὲ νοῦς ἀδιαστάτως...τῷ ἐγκεχαραγμένῳ...λόγῳ φανερούμενος Cyr.*Jo.*1.5(4.48B); **2.** *inscribe*, fig. τὸν...ἐγκεχαραγμένον τῷ πόλῳ κύκλον Gr.Nyss.*fat.*(M.45.152C); id.*virg.*11(p.295.4; M.46.365D); Firm.*ep.*38(M.77.1508B); Nil.*epp.*3.43(M.79.408D); **3.** εἰς γραφὴν ἐ. *commit to writing*, Clem.*str.*6.1(p.422.9; M.9.208A); so *record*, Alex.Al.*ep.Alex.*55(13; p.28.20; M.18.569A); Eus.*h.e.*10.2.2(M.20.845C); Ath.*ep.Serap.*1.33(M.26.605C); id.*apol.sec.*19(p.101.29; M.25.280C); Ephr.1.201E; **4.** *paint*, Chrys.*hom.14.1 in Jo.*(8.79C); **5.** *outline*, Eus.*v.C.*4.30(p.129.19; M.20.1180B); οὐδὲ γὰρ ἁπλῶς τῷ δακτύλῳ ∼ειν αὐτὸν [sc. sign of cross] δεῖ, ἀλλὰ πρότερον τῇ προαιρέσει μετὰ πολλῆς τῆς πίστεως Chrys.*hom.54.4 in Mt.*(7.551D).

ἐγχάσκω, *gape*; *hold in the open mouth*, ref. Mt.17:27 τὴν ἅλωσιν τοῦ ζῴου τὸν στατῆρα ἐγκεχαμμένου ‡Caes.Naz.*dial.*182(M.38.1156).

***ἐγχαυνόομαι**, *be filled with conceit*, Gr.Nyss.*hom.8 in Cant.*(M.44.944B).

ἐγχειμάζω, pass., *be storm-tossed*, met. τὴν ψυχὴν...ταῖς τοῦ βίου ζάλαις ἐγχειμασθεῖσαν Gr.Nyss.*v.Mos.*13(M.44.304A).

ἐγχείρησις, ἡ, **1.** *undertaking*; hence *duty* διατηρεῖν τὰς τῆς ἱερωσύνης ἐ. CNic.(787)*can.*14; **2.** *argument, proposition*, Clem.*str.*3.8(p.224.15; M.8.1104C); *ib.*6.2(p.423.30; M.9.212A); **3.** deceitful *enterprise, machination*, Eus.*h.e.*3.27.6(M.20.273C); *Hom.Clem.*2.28; **4.** *instigation* ἐ. τῆς ἀσεβείας Bas.*Eun.*1.5(1.216A; M.29.520A).

ἐγχειρίδιον, τό, *maniple* τὰ ἐ. ἅπερ βαστάζουσιν οἱ διάκονοι, εἰσὶ τὰ σουδάρια τοῦ χρωτὸς τῶν ἀποστόλων ‡Sophr.H.*liturg.*8(M.87.3988D).

ἐγχειρίζω, **A.** *put into one's hands, entrust*; **1.** of God entrusting government etc. to men; **a.** orthodox, Clem.*str.*7.7(p.32.13; M.9.460A); knowledge of divine things to those who are worthy, *ib.*7.10(p.41.6; 480A); prophetic ministry, Ath.*ep.Drac.*5(M.25.529B); church government, *ib.*6(l.c.); kingship, id.*h.Ar.*44(p.208.20; M.25.745D); judgement to Son, and thence to apostles (ref. Mt.18:18), Chrys.*sac.*3.5(p.54.21; 1.383D); of Christ οὐδὲ ἐνεχείριζε πάντα τὰ δόγματα *cat.Jo.*2:20(p.202.19); **b.** Arian ὁ θεὸς...τὸν μὲν υἱὸν μόνον εἰργάσατο, τὰ δὲ ἄλλα τῷ υἱῷ ἐνεχείρισεν ὡς βοηθῷ Ath.*Ar.*2.25(M.26.200B); **2.** of men; **a.** eccl. government οἱ...ἀπόστολοι...Λίνῳ τὴν τῆς ἐπισκοπῆς λειτουργίαν ἐνεχείρισαν Iren.*haer.*3.3.3(M.7.849A); **b.** met. ὁσίαις τῶν ἀκουόντων γνώμαις ἐγχειρίζων τὸν λόγον Const.ap.Eus.*v.C.*2.68(p.68.13; M.20.1041A); **3.** pass., *be entrusted* to τὰ λοιπὰ τῶν ἐθνῶν...ἀγγέλοις τισὶν ἐγκεχειρισμένα Eus.*d.e.*4.8 tit.(p.148.18, conj. for ἐγκεχωρισμένα M.22.269B); ἕκαστος...τῶν ἐγχειρισθέντων αὐτῷ λόγον ἀποδώσει Ath.*ep.Drac.*6(M.25.529C); **4.** pass., *be entrusted with*; **a.** angels with worship, Or.*Jo.*10.39(23; p.216.18; M.14.381D); with care of men, Eus.*theoph.fr.*8(p.21.23; M.24.629C); Proc.G.*Num.*22:22(M.87.864A); of demons τὰς ὠδῖνας ἐγκεχειρισμένοι παρὰ τοῦ διαβόλου δαίμονες Nil.*epp.*3.42(M.79.408C); **b.** of bishops with eccl. government, Or.*hom.11.3 in Jer.*(p.81.6; M.13.369D); *ib.14.14*(p.120.9; 421D); Ἰάκωβον, ὃν...τὸν τῆς ἐπισκοπῆς ἐγχειρισθῆναι θρόνον Eus.*h.e.*2.1.2(M.20.136A); with care of flock Εὐδοξίου τὴν Ἀντιόχειαν ἐγχειρισθέντος Philost.*h.e.*4.6(M.65.520C); *ib.*8.2(557A); with other eccl. functions, e.g. ministry of word, Chrys.*hom.in Mt.18:23*(3.7C); id.*comm.in Gal.*1:1(10.659E); **5.** of men, *entrust, commit* cares to God, Thdt.*ep.*14(4.1074).

B. *recommend* a person, Gr.Naz.*ep.*150(M.37.256B).

***ἐγχείριον, τό**, **1.** *handkerchief*, Procl.CP *annunt.*6(M.85.448C); Niceph.Ur.*v.Sym.*6(M.86.2992C); **2.** *maniple*, ‡Sophr.H.*liturg.*7(M.87.3988B); *V.Amph.*5(M.39.24B).

***ἐγχειρουργ-έω**, *model, execute in* εἶδος ∼ήσας τῇ ὕλῃ Gr.Nyss.*hom.opif.*30.30(M.44.253C).

ἐγχορεύ-ω, *dance upon*, met.; **1.** *play about, amuse oneself with*; ref. Manicheans οἱ δὲ εἰληφέναι δοκοῦντες [sc. τὰ εὐαγγέλια]...∼ουσι τοῖς γράμμασι Serap.*Man.*36(p.53; M.18.1213B); **2.** *triumph in*, Procl.CP *or.*17.4(M.65.813A).

***ἐγχριμψις, ἡ**, *attack*, Areth.*Apoc.*26(M.106.621D).

ἔγχρονος, *conditioned by time, temporal*; ref. God, in controversy with pagans whether world is uncreated; pagan argument οὐδὲν ἔ. ἐστι παρὰ τῷ θεῷ. εἰ δὲ μηδὲν ἔ. ... δῆλον ὡς οὔτε τὸ παρεληλυθὸς τοῦ χρόνου ἁρμόζει ἐπιφέρειν τῷ θεῷ. εἰ δὲ τοῦτο μὴ ἁρμόζει, καὶ τὸ πεποιηκέναι τὸν θεὸν τὸ ὁτιοῦν οὐχ ἁρμόττει λέγειν ‡Just.*qu.Chr.*2(M.6.1416B); refuted by Christian, *ib.*(1417A et passim); ὁ αὐτὸς...μένων οὐδὲν ἔχει ἔ. ποιεῖ τοίνυν τὸν κόσμον τάττων αὐτὸν ἀεὶ *ib.*(1425D); ref. creatures ἔργα τῶν γεννητῶν ἔ. *ib.*3(1437A); ἔ. αἰών Dion.Ar.*d.n.*10.3(M.3.937D).

***ἐγχρόνως**, *in time*, ‡Just.*qu.Chr.*3(M.6.1437B); Leont.H.*Nest.*1.39(M.86.1500C).

***ἐγχρωμάτιστος**, *coloured*, Leont.H.*Nest.*2.13(M.86.1560B).

ἐγχώννυμι, **1.** *bury in the earth*, Cyr.*Lc.*8:9(M.72.625A); Dion.Ar.*d.n.*4.2(M.3.696D); **2.** hence *bury in* τὰ μικρὰ τῶν βοτρυδίων...τοῖς φύλλοις ἐγκεχωσμένα Cyr.*Soph.*36(3.613B); met. τοῖς...εἰρημένοις ἱστορικῶς ἢ μυστικὴ...ἐγκέχωσται θεωρία id.*Ag.*1(3.627E); ἐγκεχωσμένον τῷ γράμματι νοῦν id.*Is.*3.1(2.356B); ὁ ταῖς τῶν δαιμονίων ἀπάταις ἐγκεχωσμένος *ib.*2.1(2.211B); Ἰσραὴλ...τῇ τοῦ γράμματος ἐνεχώσθη σκιᾷ id.*Jo.*6.1(4.621D); [sc. λογισμός] ῥίζα πονηρίας ἐγκεχωσμένος ἐν ἡμῖν Eulog.*fr.Novat.*(M.104.348D).

ἐγχωρ-έω, τὸ ∼οῦν *that which is allowable, fitting* δεῖν τὸ ἐ. ὁδῷ καὶ τάξει περὶ τῆς σωτηρίας τοῦ Ἰησοῦ ᾠκονομῆσθαι Or.*Cels.*1.66(p.120.11; M.11.784C); *possibility* τὸ ἐ. διὰ τῆς παραγγελίας ἀναιροῦντες Serap.*Man.*10(p.34; M.40.909A); κατὰ τὸ ἐ. *as far as possible*, Epiph.*haer.*proem.1(p.169.8; M.41.173A); Chrys.*hom.32.5 in Mt.*(7.372D); plur., *things that are possible*, *ib.23.7*(7.294A); *ib.72.1*(701C).

***ἐγχωριάζω**, *reside among*, c. dat., Eus.*Hierocl.*21(525A; M.22.828A); c. παρά, Men.*exc.Rom.*8(p.194.3; M.113.885D).

***ἐγχωρίζω**, v. ἐγχειρίζω.

***ἐγχωρίτης, ὁ**, *rough countryman*, Nil.*epp.*3.230(M.79.489C).

ἐδαφίζ-ω, met., *dash to the ground, destroy* τὴν ἀποστολικὴν παράδοσιν ἐδαφισθεῖσαν Bas.*Spir.*25(3.21C; M.32.112C); οἷον ∼ομένης τῆς ψυχῆς †Bas.*Is.*19(1.392A; M.30.152A); Nil.*exerc.*58(M.79.792B); *Pers.*(p.14.8; M.10.104A).

ἐδάφιον, τό, *foundation, base*; met., *sacred text* πρόσταξον αὐτῷ τὸ ἐ. τοῦ ἀποστόλου ἀναγνωσθῆναι Adam.*dial.*5.23(p.224.8; M.11.1865A); ἐκ τοῦ ἐ. διδασκόμεθα ‡Ath.*dial.Trin.*3.12(M.28.220C); Didym.*Trin.*1.27(M.39.404A).

ἔδαφος, τό, *foundation, pavement*; hence **1.** *earth*, Eust.*fr.*(M.18.688C); **2.** *sacred text* ὁ φιλόπονος ἀναγνοὺς τῆς θείας γραφῆς τὰ ἐ. Gr.Nyss.*Eun.*3(2 p.22.25; M.45.588B); Epiph.*mens.*7(M.43.248B); Cyr.ap.*cat.Mt.*proem.(p.4.22,24).

ἔδεσμα, τό, *meat, food*; prob. eucharistic πνευματικὰ ἐ. Meth. *arbitr.*1(p.147.19; M.18.241C).

***ἔδικτον, τό,** (Lat. *edictum*) *edict*, Ath.Scholast.*coll.*3.4(p.47); *ib.*5.2(p.72).

***ἑδνοφόρος, ὁ,** *bearer of wedding gift*, Gr.Nyss.*hom.1 in Cant.*(M.44.772C).

ἑδράζ-ω, *cause to sit*; hence **1.** *fix, establish*, of creation by God (cf. Pr.8:25) ὁ δημιουργὸς...γῆν...ἥδρασεν ἐπὶ τὸν ἀσφαλῆ τοῦ ἰδίου βουλήματος θεμέλιον *1Clem.*33.3; *ib.*60.1; *Orac.Sib.*1.9; Athenag. *leg.*13.1(M.6.916B); Ath.*gent.*36(M.25.72C); Cyr.*Ps.*8:5(M.69.760A); Cosm.Ind.*top.*2(M.88.80B); **2.** *establish, confirm* ἡδρασμένους ἐν ἀγάπῃ Ign.*Smyrn.*1.1; *ib.*13.2; id.*Polyc.*1.1; ὁ νεὼς τοῦ θεοῦ [i.e. holy man], τρισὶν ἡδρασμένος θεμελίοις, πίστει, ἐλπίδι, ἀγάπῃ Clem. *str.*5.1(p.334.28; M.9.29A); Or.*Pr.*3:19(M.17.168D); of a priest τοὺς δὲ ἑστῶτας ~ει Chrys.*ep.*126(3.672A); **3.** *establish, found*, Church ἐκκλησίᾳ...ἡδρασμένῃ ἐν ὁμονοίᾳ θεοῦ Ign.*Philad.*proem.; τὰ...τῶν Ἰουδαίων λέλυται...τὰ δὲ τῆς ἐκκλησίας ἥδρασται ‡Ath.*Ar.*4.34(p.83.17; M.26.520C); Gnost. περὶ τοῦ Ὅρου αὐτῶν...δύο ἐνεργείας ἔχειν... τὴν ἑδραστικὴν καὶ τὴν μεριστικήν· καὶ καθὸ μὲν ~ει...Σταυρὸν εἶναι Iren.*haer.*1.3.5(M.7.476A); **4.** *anchor, berth*, *A.Jo.*89(p.194.20).

ἑδραῖος, *steadfast, firm*; met., esp. in rel. to faith ὁ δὲ ἅπαξ πιστὸς...τὸ πιστὸν τῆς ὁμολογίας ἐν...ἑ. δείκνυσι βίῳ Clem.*str.*7.8(p.37.25; M.9.472A); ἑ. οὖν γενοῦ...μήποτε τῇ πίστει βαμβαίνων Hipp.*Dan.*2.37.5; Ath.*ep.Aeg.Lib.*4(M.25.548A); ἑδραῖα μένειν... τῆς μακαρίας ἐκείνης ψυχῆς τὰ ἔργα Bas.*ep.*29(3.109D; M.32.312C); neut. as subst., Ath.*syn.*55(p.277.28; M.26.789D); τὸ ἑ. ... τῆς εἰς Χριστὸν δηλοῦται πίστεως Oecum.*Apoc.*1:15(p.42); *established* ἑ. τὸν νοῦν τῆς...γραφῆς Cyr.*Jo.*5(4.448A).

ἑδραιότης, ἡ, *stability, steadfastness* ἐκ τῆς κατ᾽ ἀλήθειαν ἑ. Clem. *str.*1.19(p.62.6; M.8.813A); *ib.*7.7(p.35.7; M.9.565C); *ib.*7.18(p.77.8; 556A); of Satan's fall ἦν ποτε ἐν...ἑ. Tit.Bost.*Man.*1.35(M.18.1128D); of the divine, Cyr.*inc.unigen.*(5^1.683E); of faith, *ib.*(686E); spiritual stability, id.*hom.pasch.*7(5^2.91B); id.*ador.*11(1.400A); id.*Os.*167(3.194A); ἑ. τὴν ἐν πίστει καὶ ἀληθείᾳ Proc.G.*Is.*12:1–6(M.87.2064C).

ἑδραιόω, *establish, confirm*; pass., of faith, Epiph.*haer.*76.15(p.361.16; M.42.548A); in solitary life, *Apophth.Patr.*(M.65.188B).

ἑδραίωμα, τό, 1. lit., *foundation, base* ἑ. τοῦ χερουβικοῦ θρόνου ‡Sophr.H.*liturg.*8(M.87.3988C); **2.** met., *firm base, support*; **a.** of persons Ἄτταλον Περγαμηνὸν τῷ γένει...ἑ. τῶν ἐνταῦθα ἀεὶ γεγονότα *Ep.Lugd.*ap.Eus.*h.e.*5.1.17(M.20.416A); of a bishop, Bas.*ep.*29(3.109B; M.32.312A); defenders of true faith, *ib.*214.4(323A; M.789C); of Christ ἑ. λαμπρὸν ἑαυτὸν...ἀναθείς, φωτίζοντα τοὺς ἐν σκότῳ Cyr. *Zach.*91(3.779C); of S. Peter, Jo.Thess.*dorm.BMV* B 6(p.415.26); **b.** of truths of faith, ref. 1Tim.3:15 πῆξις ἑ. ἀληθείας Epiph. *haer.*44.4(p.196.7; M.41.828C); *ib.*55.9(p.337.12; 988D); *ib.*56.3(p.342.22; 993C); Chrys.*hom.11.1 in 1Tim.*(11.605E); ‡Proc.G.*Pr.*14:26(M.87.1365D).

ἕδρασμα, τό, *seat*; met., *support*, Clem.*str.*2.6(p.129.9; M.8.965B) cit. s. ἀντεπάγω; ξύλον τοῦ σταυροῦ...ψυχῶν ἡμῶν...ἕ. ἀσφαλές Mac. Aeg.*hom.*47.16(M.34.808A); of S. Basil, Thdr.Stud.*cant.*6.3(p.347) cit. s. στῦλος.

ἑδρασμός, ὁ, *a sitting down*, Or.*comm.in Mt.*16.4(p.477.27; M.13.1377B).

***ἑδραστήριος,** *of the seat* or *buttocks*, Isid.Pel.*epp.*4.114(M.78.1188B).

***ἑδρεύω,** *be seated, established* πνεῦμα ἕδρευσεν ἐπὶ τοῦ θρόνου Procl.CP *or.*16.1(M.65.808A).

***ἐδῶ,** = ἔσω, *inside*, *Exorc.*23(p.340); *Mir.Geo.*14(p.135.16).

ἐδωδή, ἡ, *food*, *LS*; *taste* ἐ. δ᾽ ὥσπερ φορολογοῦσα Dion.Al.ap. Eus.*p.e.*14.26(779C; M.21.1281C).

***ἐές,** (Lat. *heus*) *hey!* ἐ., ἄνελθε εἰς τὸν ἄμβωνα CCP(536)*act.*5 (H.2.1333C).

ἐθελακρίβεια, ἡ, *would-be accuracy, hankering after exact definition*, *Schol.Clem.paed.*(p.336.22; M.9.792C); ref. Nestorian exegesis, Cyr.*ep.*55(p.61.4; 5^2.190E).

***ἐθελοακρότης, ἡ,** *desire for excess*, ref. pagans δι᾽ ἐθελοακρότητα δεισιδαιμονίας Didym.*Trin.*3.24(M.39.937A); ref. schismatics οὐ διὰ πίστιν ἀφηνιαζόντων...ἀλλὰ κατὰ ἐθελοακρότητα δικαιοσύνης...σχιζόντων ἑαυτούς Epiph.*anc.*14(p.22.23; M.43.41B).

***ἐθελοβλέπω,** *seek one's own will*, ‡Ath.*polit.*(M.28.1408D).

***ἐθελοδιδάσκαλος, ὁ,** *self-appointed teacher*, Herm.*sim.*9.22.2; ‡Ath.*synops.*(M.28.377C).

***ἐθελοδικαιοσύνη, ἡ,** *affected righteousness*; of Montanists, Epiph.*haer.*48.14(p.239.15; M.41.877B); of Meletius, *ib.*69.3(p.155.1; M.42.208A).

***ἐθελοδόκησις, ἡ,** *arbitrary opinion* or *interpretation*, ref. Marcion ἐν ἐ. τῶν τοῦ...Παύλου ἐπιστολῶν Epiph.*haer.*42.11(p.117.14; M.41.720C).

***ἐθελοδοξία, ἡ,** *self-opinionatedness*, Mac.Aeg.*pat.*1(M.34.868A).

***ἐθελοευλάβεια, ἡ,** *self-chosen piety*, ‡Bas.*const.*25(2.575E; M.31.1413C).

ἐθελοθρησκεία, ἡ, *self-chosen worship, superstition*; **1.** of Jewish worship ἐκπεπτωκότα...ἀπὸ τῆς εἰς Χριστὸν πίστεως ἐπὶ τὴν Ἰουδαϊκὴν ἐ. Eus.*h.e.*6.12.1(M.20.545A); id.*d.e.*1.2(p.9.2; M.22.25B); *ib.*1.6(p.25.14; 52C); id.*qu.Steph.*6(M.22.904C); id.*Is.*1:16f.(M.24.96C); of Scribes, Epiph.*anac.*14(p.167.5; M.41.172A); τῆς ἐ. τῆς κατὰ τὸν σωματικὸν νόμον Proc.G.*Is.*1:20(M.87.1849A); *ib.*49:14ff.(2477D); **2.** of heresy ἐν ἐ. εἰκῇ φυσιούμενος κατὰ τοῦ διδάξαντος τὴν καλὴν ὁμολογίαν ‡Ath.*dial.Trin.*2.16(M.28.1184A); Gr.Nyss.*Eun.*1(1 p.204.6; M.45.452B); *ib.*12(1 p.296.23; 1008A); Epiph.*haer.*42.11(p.133.11; M.41.740C); **3.** of pagan worship, Cyr.*Juln.*2(6^2.43E).

***ἐθελοθρησκευτικός,** *of self-chosen worship, superstitious*, Epiph. *anac.*15(p.167.15; M.41.172B); Jo.D.*haer.*15(M.94.688A).

***ἐθελοθρησκεύω,** *worship according to one's fancy*; ref. heretics, Epiph.*haer.*61.1(p.380.17; M.41.1040C).

***ἐθελόθυτος,** *self-immolated*; ref. religious life, Dan.Raith.*v.Jo. Clim.*(M.88.597A); of a martyr, *Hymn.*(*AS* 1 p.594).

ἐθελοκακ-έω, 1. *do evil deliberately, be ill-disposed*, Athenag.*leg.*31.4(M.6.964A); of Jews against Christ, Ammon.ap.*cat.Jo.*8:14(p.273.35); esp. ptcpl., Meth.*res.*1.45(p.295.6; M.41.1116C); ~οῦντας τοὺς τῆς ἀνατολῆς ἐπισκόπους Pall.*v.Chrys.*3(p.21.26; M.47.15); Cyr. *Am.*30(3.279E); id.*Jo.*3.4(4.271C); Evagr.*h.e.*3.25(p.122.15; M.86.2648C); **2.** *play the coward, lose heart* μὴ τὴν ἑαυτῶν ~οῦντες ἀπογινώσκωμεν σωτηρίαν Mac.Aeg.*elev.*11(M.34.897D); Evagr.*h.e.*3.43(p.145.11; M.86.2696A).

ἐθελοκακία, ἡ, *wilful wickedness*, Constantius Imp.ap.Ath.*apol. sec.*55(p.136.1; M.25.349B); Mac.Aeg.*pat.*2(M.34.868A); ‡Bas.*struct. hom.*1.20(1.333B; M.30.29D).

ἐθελόκακος, *malevolent, wilfully bad*; **1.** of character προαιρέσεως ἐ. Bas.*reg.br.*19(2.421C; M.31.1096B); φρονιμότης, *M.Tar.*5(p.459); γνώμη, Cyr.*Ps.*31:2(M.69.868A); μανία, Cosm.Ind.*top.*10(M.88.436A); **2.** of persons τοὺς ἐ. ἐν Ἰουδαίοις Or.*fr.29 in Jo.*(p.505.22); †Bas.*hom.in Ps.*37(1.369A; M.30.97D); Petr.Full.*ep.Acac.*(p.116.10; M.86.2632A); Anast.S.*Ps.*6(M.89.1108B).

***ἐθελοκακουργία, ἡ,** *wilful wickedness*; of heretics, Leont.H. *Nest.*2.3(M.86.1537B).

***ἐθελοκακοῦργος,** *wilfully doing evil*; masc. as subst., *A.Jo.*16*(p.160.23); neut. as subst., Eust.Mon.*ep.*(M.86.920C).

ἐθελοκάκως, *wickedly*, Isid.Pel.*epp.*4.213(M.78.1308B); Areth. *Apoc.*71(M.106.784D).

ἐθελοκίνδυνος, *ready to face danger*; neut. as subst., Men.*exc. Rom.*19(p.219.28; M.113.924D).

ἐθελοκωφ-έω, *affect deafness, shut one's ears deliberately*; ref. scriptural evidence, Eus.*e.th.*3.3(p.156.23; M.24.1001A); of heretics, Chrys.*comm.in Gal.*1:1–3(10.661C); id.*hom.div.*9(12.384B); ὥσπερ οὖν ἀκούοντες, μᾶλλον δὲ ~οῦντες Cyr.*deip.BMV*(p.26.9; M.76.273C); of idolaters, Proc.G.*Is.*42:16(M.87.2373B); trans., *shut one's ears to* truth, Clem.*str.*6.8(p.465.22; M.9.289A).

ἐθελοκωφία, ἡ, *wilful deafness*, Thdr.Heracl.*Is.*50:2(M.18.1349C).

ἐθελοντής, ὁ, *voluntary agent*; as adv., *willingly*; **1.** of Christ; of his voluntary κένωσις (in reply to Nestorian assertion that ἕνωσις φυσική implies that κένωσις was οὐχ ἑκούσιος): κεκένωκεν ἑαυτὸν οὐκ ἀβουλήτως, ἀλλ᾽ ἐ. ὁ μονογενὴς γέγονεν ἄνθρωπος Cyr.*apol.Thdt.*3(p.119.22; 6^1.213C); of his will to suffer ἐ. τὸν ὑπὲρ τῆς ἁπάντων σωτηρίας ὑπομεμένηκε τὸν σταυρόν id.*Os.*34(3.61D); οὐ γὰρ ἐκ πλεονεξίας Ἰουδαϊκῆς, ἀλλ᾽ ἐ. ἐπὶ τὸν ὑπὲρ ἡμῶν...ἀνέβη σταυρόν id.*Jo.*5.1(4.452A); *ib.*5.3(498E); **2.** ref. generation of Son acc. Arians ἑκουσίως αὐτὸν [i.e. the Father] καὶ ἐ. τὸν υἱὸν γεγεννηκέναι...ὑπειλήφαμεν Symb.Ant.(345)8(p.253.27; M.26.733A).

ἐθελοντί, *voluntarily* ἐ. κατώλισθον εἰς ἀπόστασιν Cyr.*Mich.*21(3.409E); id.*Juln.11–19 fr.*(M.76.1060C).

***ἐθελοπερισσοθρησκεία, ἡ,** *excessive religious observance*; of Pharisees, Epiph.*haer.*16.1(p.211.9; M.41.249A).

***ἐθελοσοφία, ἡ,** *would-be wisdom*, of heretics ἐν σπηλαίῳ ἀναχωρῶν δι᾽ ὑπερβολὴν ἐ. Epiph.*haer.*13(p.206.11; M.41.237B); *ib.*69.28(p.178.7; M.42.248B); *ib.*76.35(p.384.23; 588A).

***ἐθελόσοφος,** *would-be wise*, of pagans ἐθελόσοφε καὶ γνῶσιν ἀνθρώποις ἐπαγγελλόμενε Epiph.*haer.*5.2(p.184.22; M.41.204A); Sabellius, *ib.*62.6(p.394.24; 1057B); Origen, *ib.*64.72(p.522.6; 1197B); of Corinthians, Chrys.ap.*cat.1Cor.*11:13–16(p.213.18).

***ἐθελοταπεινοφροσύνη, ἡ,** *would-be humility*, †Bas.*contub.*11(M.30.828A).

***ἐθελότρεπτος**, *changeable*, Nil.*epp*.2.124(M.79.253B); of angelic nature, Jo.D.*f.o*.2.3(M.94.868A).

ἐθελουργέω, *act freely*, Dion.Al.ap.Eus.*p.e*.14.25(776B; M.21.1277A); Cyr.*Ag*.10(3.637D).

***ἐθελουργία**, ἡ, *freedom of action*, Cyr.*Juln*.3(6^{2}.79A).

ἐθελουργός, *acting of one's own free will, voluntary* ῥοπῇ διανοίας ἐθελουργῷ τῆς ἑαυτῶν καταθλῆσαι ζωῆς Cyr.*hom.pasch*.11(5^{2}.143D); *ib*.16(213C).

***ἐθελοφίλεχθρος**, *deliberately quarrelsome*, Ph.Carp.ap.Cosm. Ind.*top*.10(M.88.436A).

ἐθελοφιλόσοφος, ὁ, *would-be philosopher*, Pall.*h.Laus*.proem. (p.12.26; M.34.1003).

***ἐθελοφρονημότης**, ἡ, *stubbornness, wilfulness*, *M.Tar*.1(p.453).

***ἐθικῶς**, *customarily* τὸ ἐσφραγίσθαι ἢ τὸ κεχρίσθαι ἐ. τέθεικε Cyr.ap.*cat.Jo*.6:27(p.247.18) om. id.*Jo*.3.5(4.300C).

ἔθμη, ἡ, *hot air* for heating a building (ἐθμή *LS*), Epiph.*haer*. 52.2(M.41.956C; v.l. for αἴθμη p.312.30).

***ἐθναγός**, ὁ, *leader of a people*, Dion.Ar.*c.h*.9.4(M.3.261C).

ἐθνάρχης, ὁ, *ruler*; of God of Israel, Dion.Ar.*c.h*.9.4(M.3.261C); pagan national gods, Cyr.*Juln*.4(6^{2}.132D); Oecum.*Apoc*.19:10 (p.204); *ib*.(p.205); as adj., *ruling over nations* ἀξίωμα τοῦ ἐ. ἀγγέλου Bas.*Eun*.3.1(1.272C; M.29.656B).

ἐθναρχία, ἡ, **1.** *governmental district, petty state* τῶν ἀνθρώπων γένος εἰς ἐπαρχίας καὶ ἐ. ... κατετέτμητο Eus.*l.C*.16(p.248.29; M.20.1421B); id.*p.e*.5.1(179A; M.21.312A); id.*d.e*.3.7(p.146.6; M.22.245B); **2.** *office of governor* ὑπὲρ ἀρχιερωσύνης καὶ ἐ. ἐφιλονείκουν Dion.Ar.*ep*.8.1(M.3.1085A); *ib*.(1089B).

ἐθνικός, *national*; **1.** *gentile* opp. Jewish, Heracleon ap.Or.*Jo*. 13.16(p.239.36; M.14.421C); *Hom.Clem*.2.19; Ath.*ep.encycl*.3(p.172.2; M.25.228C); **2.** *pagan* opp. Christian φιλία ἐ. Herm.*mand*.10.1.4; ἐ. ὄντας αὐτοὺς Χριστὸς οὐδὲν ὠφελήσει Hipp.*haer*.7.19(p.195.18; M.16.3302B); Clem.*paed*.3.8(p.261.20; M.8.613B); id.*str*.2.13(p.143.17; M.8.993B); Or.*hom.1.7 in Jer*.(p.6.3; M.13.261C); δόγμα ἐ. id.*Jo*. 13.52(51; p.280.14; M.14.493C); Ath.*ep.encycl*.4(p.173.15; 232A); τῶν ἐ. βιβλίων πάντων ἀπέχου *Const.App*.1.6.1; cf.*ib*.5.10.2; opp. πιστός, *ib*.1.10.1; ἐ. ἐπιθυμίαι *ib*.2.6.3; μὴ ἐρχέσθω ἐπὶ κριτήριον ἐ. *ib*.2.45.1; †Bas.*Is*.191(1.522A; M.30.448B); as subst., Clem.*str*.6.6(p.457.11; M. 9.272C); τῷ ἐ. ἐθνικῶς...ἕκαστα ἀποδίδοται *ib*.7.7(p.34.23; 465B); Or.*Jo*.28.7(6; p.398.4; 696B); Ath.*apol.sec*.14(p.98.12; M.25.272B); coupled with Arians, id.*ep.Adelph*.3(M.26.1073D); **3.** *ordinary, common* ἐ. [sc. ἄνθρωπον] καὶ ἀπαίδευτον Clem.*paed*.2.6(p.187.11; M.8.452B); neut. as adv. τὸ ἐ. ζῆν opp. τὸ εὖ ζῆν *ib*.1.13(p.152.4; 376B).

ἐθνικῶς, **1.** *in gentile fashion* τὸν ἐ. ζῶντα Bas.*hom.in Ps*.48 (1.183C; M.29.445C); **2.** *in pagan fashion, like the heathen*, *A. Jo*.27(p.166.1); Clem.*str*.6.5(p.452.20; M.9.261A); *ib*.7.14(p.62.25; 521B).

***ἐθνίον**, τό, *small nation, tribe*, Hier.H.*bapt*.(M.40.864C).

***ἐθνιστί**, *like a heathen*, *Didasc.Jac*.1.53(p.777.6).

***ἐθνόμυθος**, *of pagan fables, mythological* ἐ. πλάνη Epiph.*haer*.3 (p.179.3; M.41.189B); *ib*.62.7(p.396.15; 1060C); ἡ ἀπὸ τῶν Ἑλλήνων ἐ. διδασκαλία *ib*.64.65(p.505.10; 1184A); neut. as subst., *Const.App*. 1.6.2.

***ἐθνοπάτωρ**, ὁ, *father of nations*; of Abraham, ‡Jo.D.*hom*.5(M. 96.649B).

ἔθνος, τό, **1.** *nation, people*; opp. λαός, ref. Jo.11:50 ἀπέθανεν ὁ ἄνθρωπος οὗτος ὑπὲρ τοῦ λαοῦ, καὶ διὰ τοῦτον οὐχὶ ὅλον τὸ ἔ. ἀπώλετο, καὶ ἐπίστησον εἰ δύνασαι τὸ μὲν ὄνομα τοῦ λαοῦ λαβεῖν εἰς τοὺς ἐκ περιτομῆς, τὸ δὲ τοῦ ἔ. εἰς τοὺς λοιπούς. ἀπέθανεν γὰρ οὗτος ὁ ἄνθρωπος οὐ μόνον ὑπὲρ τοῦ λαοῦ, ἀλλ' ἵνα καὶ μὴ ὅλον τὸ ἔ. ἀπόληται, ὡς εἰ ἔλεγεν τὸ χρηματίζον ἔ. καὶ πάντες οἱ ἐθνικοὶ ἀπόλωνται Or.*Jo*. 28.19(14; p.414.14ff.; M.14.721D–724A); ref. Church (cf. 1Petr.2:9) καινὸν καὶ ξένον ἐ. *A.Jo*.3(p.152.10); Eus.*d.e*.3.6(p.137.28; M.22. 232D); **2.** plur., *gentiles* opp. Jews εἴτε ἐν Ἰουδαίοις εἴτε ἐν ἐ. Ign. *Smyrn*.1.2; *Barn*.16.2; Just.*1apol*.49.1(M.6.400C); *Hom.Clem*.2.19; of gentile Christians, Just.*dial*.29.1(M.6.537A); myst. exeg. Lam. 1:10 ἔ. δὲ κατὰ τὸν τόπον ἀλληγορητέον τὸν ὄχλον τῶν κακιῶν Or.*fr*. *27 in Lam*.(p.248.7; M.13.624A); **3.** plur., *pagans* opp. Christians τὰ ἔ. γὰρ ἀκούοντα ἐκ τοῦ στόματος ἡμῶν τὰ λόγια τοῦ θεοῦ *2Clem*. 13.3; *M.Polyc*.9.2; Herm.*sim*.1.10; Iren.*haer*.2.32.4(M.7.830A); Or.*hom.5.3 in Jer*.(p.33.19; M.13.300C); id.*Jo*.6.54(36; p.163.1; M. 14.293C); *Hom.Clem*.13.4.

***ἐθνόφρονες**, οἱ, *Ethnophrones*, Christian heretics ἐ.· οἱ ταῖς συνηθείαις τῶν ἐθνῶν ἐπακολουθοῦντες, Χριστιανοὶ τἄλλα ὑπάρχοντες Jo.D.*haer*.94(M.94.757C).

ἔθος, τό, *custom, habit*; eccl. *custom, tradition* τὰ ἀρχαῖα ἔ. κρατείτω CNic.(325)*can*.6; ref. paschal controversy οὐκ ἔ. ὄντος τοῦτον ἐπιτελεῖν τὸν τρόπον ταῖς...ἐκκλησίαις ἐξ ἀποστολικῆς παραδόσεως τὸ... ἔ. φυλαττούσαις Eus.*h.e*.5.23.1(M.20.492A); ref. prohibition of marrying deceased wife's sister τὸ παρ' ἡμῖν ἔ. ... νόμου δύναμιν ἔχον Bas.*ep*.160.2(3.249C; M.32.624B); *ib*.188 *can*.2(268C; M.664C); of liturg. practice εἰ γὰρ ἄχρηστος μὲν ἡ τῶν σεμνῶν...τῆς ἁγίας τριάδος ὀνομάτων ὁμολογία, ἀνόνητα δὲ τὰ ἔ. τῆς ἐκκλησίας, ἐν δὲ τοῖς ἔ. τούτοις ἐστὶν ἡ σφραγίς, ἡ προσευχή, τὸ βάπτισμα κτλ. Gr.Nyss.*Eun*. 11(2 p.270.30; M.45.880C).

εἰδαίνω, *know*, ‡Ath.*proph*.2(M.28.1065A).

***εἰδεάρχις**, ἡ, *source of form, formal principle*, Dion.Ar.*d.n*.2.10 (M.3.648C).

εἰδέχθεια, ἡ, *ugliness*, lit. and met. ἡ ψυχὴ ἐνοῦσα μὲν αὐτῷ [sc. σώματι], καλὸν αὐτὸ δείκνυσιν, ὅταν δὲ αὐτὸ ἐρημώσῃ τῆς οἰκείας ἐνεργείας...εἰ. γίνεται πολλή·...οὕτω καὶ τὸ πνεῦμα ὅταν ἔρημον καταλίπῃ καὶ τὸ σῶμα καὶ τὴν ψυχήν, χείρων γίνεται...ἡ εἰ. Chrys.*hom.5.4 in Eph*.(11.37A,B); met. ἐλεπρώθη τῇ εἰ. ... τῆς ἁμαρτίας †Cyr.*coll.VT* (6^{4}.9A; M.77.1188B); Max.*ep*.4(M.91.417C); *cat.Apoc*.6:16(p.420.9).

εἰδεχθής, *ugly*; met., *vile, repulsive* ὁ δὲ ἐπὶ γαστέρα...βίος... εἰ. Clem.*prot*.3(p.258.9; M.8.608B); of actions of heretics, Eus.*v.C*. 3.64(p.111.34; M.20.1140D); Bas.*hom.in Ps*.29(1.129C; M.29.317C); Gr.Nyss.*hom.2 in Cant*.(M.44.789C); neut. as subst., Chrys.*hom*. *34.4 in Mt*.(7.395B); of grave τοῦ τόπου τὸ εἰ. id.*Thdr*.1.9(1.12D); Cyr.*Ps*.41:6(M.69.1005A); id.*Is*.5.4(2.822E); Thdt.*ep*.49(4.1108).

***εἰδεχθῶς**, *repulsively*, Gr.Nyss.*prof.Chr*.(p.132.23; M.46.241A).

εἴδησις, ἡ, *knowledge*; **1.** of religious knowledge, exeg. Mt.19:29 γνῶσιν γὰρ σημαίνει ἡ τοῦ ὀνόματος εἴ. καὶ ἡ τοῦ εὐαγγελίου νόησις Clem.*str*.4.4(p.255.23; M.8.1229A); τὴν τῶν θείων εἴ. *ib*.5.7(p.354.6; M.9.68B); *ib*.6.8(p.464.11; 285C); ἐν τούτῳ γὰρ ἡ ἀληθής ἐστιν εἴ. τοῦ ζητουμένου, τὸ ἐν τούτῳ τὸ ἰδεῖν, ἐν τῷ μὴ ἰδεῖν· ὅτι ὑπέρκειται πάσης εἴ. τὸ ζητούμενον Gr.Nyss.*v.Mos*.(M.44.377A); Epiph.*haer*. 69.43(p.191.17; M.42.269C); exeg. Jo.10:14f. τὴν γνῶσιν ἐν τούτοις οὐχ ἁπλῶς τὴν εἴ. λέγει Cyr.*Jo*.6.1(4.652C); id.*ador*.10(1.360B); of divine knowledge, Dion.Ar.*d.n*.7.2(M.3.869A) cit. s. νοῦς; **2.** of different kinds of knowledge; ref. Gen.4:1 τὴν μὲν πρώτην εἴ. ... περὶ εἴ. καὶ ὁράσεως συνισταμένης λέγει καὶ διὰ ἐννοίας, περὶ δὲ τῆς δευτέρας γνώσεως περὶ εἴ. διὰ χρήσεως ἀπαγγέλλει Epiph.*haer*.69.46 (p.193.17ff.; M.42.273B); **3.** ἐν εἴ. *knowingly* ὁ ἐν εἴ. ἐκδοὺς αἱρετικῷ ἰδίαν κτῆσιν Ath.Scholast.*coll*.2.3(p.37); c. genit., *with the knowledge of*, Phot.*nomoc*.3.14(M.104.609A).

***εἰδογραφία**, ἡ, *painting of figures*, Gr.Naz.*carm*.1.2.29.287(M.37. 905).

εἰδοποι-έω, **1.** *endue with form* τὸ εἶδος, καθ' ὃ ~εῖται ὁ Πέτρος καὶ ὁ Παῦλος Meth.*res*.1.22(p.245.10; M.41.1092A); *ib*.1.23(p.247.4, v.l. ἰδιοποιοῦντος 1092C); as a divine activity τὴν ὕλην προϋποστήσας, εἰ. ὕστερον Gr.Naz.*or*.44.4(M.36.609D); τὸ ἀνείδεον εἰ. Dion.Ar.*d.n*. 4.3(M.3.697A); τὰς ἀμόρφους ~ῶν οὐσίας Geo.Pis.*hex*.1643(M.92. 1563A); cf.Max.*ambig*.(M.91.1228A); ref. clothing of newly-baptized τὸ ἀνείδεον ~εῖται Dion.Ar.*e.h*.2.3.8(M.3.404C); Christol. ὁ γὰρ ἀσώματος, ἑαυτὸν τῇ προσλήψει τῆς σαρκὸς ~ήσας Diad.*ascens*.5(M. 65.1145C); Χριστὸν...τῇ...ἐνανθρωπήσει...ἐξ ἡμῶν ~ούμενον Dion. Ar.*e.h*.3.3.13(M.3.444C); ~εῖται γὰρ νοητῶς τὸ θεῖον οὕτως [sc. in Christ] Cyr.Is.4.4(2.658E); Nestorian εἰδοποιηθέντα θεόν, οὐκ ὄντα δὲ τοῦτο..., ἄνθρωπον id.*Chr.un*.(5^{1}.731E); **2.** *fashion in the pattern of*, Cyr.*Juln*.5(6^{2}.172E); of contemplatives πρὸς τὴν...νοητὴν εὐπρέπειαν...τὸ νοερὸν ἑαυτῶν ἀμεταστρέπτως ~οῦντες Dion.Ar.*e.h*.4.3.1 (M.3.473C); **3.** *constitute a species* οὐκ ἀνάγκη δὲ πάσας λέγειν ἑκάστου τὰς διαφοράς, ἀλλὰ τὰς ~ούσας Clem.*str*.8.6(p.91.9; M.9. 584B); pass., *be divided into species* μίαν μὲν εἶναι τῇ φύσει τὴν ἀρετήν, ~εῖσθαι δὲ αὐτὴν ἐν ταῖς δυνάμεσι τῆς ψυχῆς Evagr.Pont. *cap.pract*.B 98(M.40.1252A).

εἰδοποίησις, ἡ, *making of a form, fashioning to a pattern*, ‡Just. *confut*.51(M.6.1544C); Cyr.*ador*.15(1.555C).

εἰδοποιΐα, ἡ, **1.** *production of forms, engraving images*, as divine activity; in met. interpretation of tables of decalogue θεοῦ... γραφὴ καὶ εἰ. ἐναποκειμένη τῇ πλακὶ δημιουργία τοῦ κόσμου τυγχάνει Clem.*str*.6.16(p.499.18; M.9.357C); Dion.Ar.*d.n*.4.3(M.3.697A); **2.** *characteristic formation, structure*, Max.*schol.c.h*.2.5(M.4.48C); ref. Son ἁπάσης τῆς εἰ. δημιουργός id.*schol.d.n*.2.10(M.4.229A).

εἰδοποιός, *creating* or *giving form*, of Son ἀόρατον λόγον τὸν δὴ τοῦ παντὸς εἰ. Eus.*l.C*.11(p.227.5; M.20.1381A); τοῦ Ἰησοῦ θεότης... εἶδος εἰ. ἐν τοῖς ἀνειδέοις Dion.Ar.*d.n*.2.10(M.3.648C); *ib*.4.18(716A); *ib*.4.35(736B); Zach.Mit.*opif*.(M.85.1101C); Leont.H.*Nest*.1.52(M.86. 1524B); of Devil ὁ εἰ. τῶν παθῶν †Cyr.*coll.VT*(6^{4}.65E; M.77.1269D).

εἶδος, τό, *form*; **1.** def. οὐσία δέ ἐστιν, ἤτοι φύσις, παρ' αὐτοῖς [sc. fathers], ὅπερ οἱ φιλόσοφοι λέγουσιν εἶ. εἶ. δέ, τὸ κατὰ πολλῶν καὶ διαφερόντων τῷ ἀριθμῷ λεγόμενον †Leont.B.*sect*.1.1(M.86.1193A); *Doct.Patr*.33(p.258.15); **2.** *material shape, form*; denied of God, *Hom.Clem*.17.10; **3.** *shape, form, expression*, Christol. εἶ. τοῦ θεοῦ (ref. Gen.32:20) identified with Christ, Cyr.*thes*.12(5¹.117E); τὸ εἶ. αὐτοῦ τοῦ γεγεννηκότος id.*dial.Trin*.5(5¹.558D); Manich., opp. reality ὁ υἱὸς μετεσχημάτισεν ἑαυτὸν εἰς ἄνθρωπον εἶ. ... μὴ ὢν ἄνθρωπος Hegem.*Arch*.8(p.12.11; M.10.1440B); **4.** *kind, species* τὸ τῆς συμβολικῆς ἑρμηνείας εἶ. Clem.*str*.5.8(p.357.4; M.9.73B); εἶ. εὐχῆς *ib*.7.7 (p.30.12; 456A); οὐ μόνον περί τι ἓν εἶ. τὴν ἐγκράτειαν συνορᾶν προσήκει *ib*.3.7(p.223.5; M.8.1161B); *Hom.Clem*.11.27; Serap.*Man*.45(p.63; M.18.1232D); **5.** κατ' εἶδος *according to species*, Cyr.H.*catech*.19.5; hence *individually, in detail*, *Hom.Clem*.4.24; Chrys.*hom.26.8 in Mt*.(7.325B); **6.** ref. 2Cor.5:7, *sight* ἀπὸ τῆς ἐν πίστει χάριτος, εἰς τὴν κατ' εἶδος χάριν Max.*myst*.24(M.91.705A); **7.** *party* ἐκτιθέσθωσαν τὰ ὁμολογηθέντα ἀμφοτέροις εἶ. *Pers*.(p.44.15).

εἴδω, v. ὁράω, οἶδα.

εἰδωλεῖον, τό, *idol temple*, *A.Jo*.38(p.170.1); *ib*.39(p.170.15); *A. Thadd*.5(p.275.15); Afric.*ep.Arist*.4(p.60.19; M.10.60A); λατρεία δέ ἐστι διαβόλου, ἡ ἐν εἰδωλείοις εὐχή Cyr.H.*catech*.19.8; met. εἴ που εἶ. ᾠκοδόμηται εἰς τὴν καρδίαν Or.*hom.1.16 in Jer*.(p.16.7; M.13.276C).

***εἰδωλιανός**, '*idolian*', derogatory name with pun on emperor Julian, Gr.Naz.*or*.4.77(M.35.604A).

εἰδωλικός, 1. *pertaining to idols, of idols*, of worship εἰ. πανηγύρεις Cyr.H.*catech*.19.7; εἰ. θυσίαι ‡Just.*qu.et resp*.83(M.6.1324C); †Jo.D. *B.J*.1(M.96.864A); of sanctuaries, Chrys.*hom.8.5 in 2Tim*.(11. 713B); Thdt.*h.e*.3.3.2(3.913); †Jo.D.*B.J*.2(877B); *Exorc*.(p.344); of names, Eus.*m.P*.11(p.937.1; M.20.1504A); **2.** *worshipping idols, idolatrous* ποιητὴς εἰ. Clem.*prot*.2(p.13.22; M.8.77A); εἰ. πλάνη Eus. *v.C*.4.37(p.132.13; M.20.1185C); Cyr.*ador*.14(1.484C); Thdt.*h.e*.5.22.1 (3.1059); Bas.Sel.*or*.27.2(M.85.313A); Jo.Eleem.*v.Tych*.(p.113); Jo. V H.*icon*.2(M.96.1349D); iconoclastic view [εἰκονικῆς ἀναστηλώσεως] ...μεταληφθείσης...εἰς εἰ. προσκύνησιν τῇ καθολικῇ ἐκκλησίᾳ Thdr. Stud.*antirr*.1.2(M.99.329B); masc. as subst., Petr.II Al.*encycl*.6 (M.33.1285B)ap.Thdt.*h.e*.4.22.22; neut. as subst. τι τῶν εἰ. πρᾶξαι Chrys.*hom.3.5 in 1Thess*.(11.447E); **3.** *idol-like*, alluding to Arian theories, ref. Is.43:10 οὐκ ἐκβάλλων τὸν υἱόν, τοῦτό φησιν, ἀλλ' ὅτι θεὸς εἰ. μετ' ἐμὲ οὐκ ἔστιν Chrys.*hom.4.2 in Jo*.(8.29D); *ib*.(29E).

εἰδωλικῶς, 1. *in a certain form* or *image*, opp. λογικῶς, ‡Just. *qu.Gr*.5(M.6.1473B); **2.** *idolatrously*, Thdr.Stud.*antirr*.3.3.14(M.99. 425D).

***εἰδωλογραφέω**, *represent*, Nil.*praest*.11(M.79.1073A).

***εἰδωλογραφία, ἡ**, *painted idol*, ref. iconoclastic controversy μὴ λέγε ταύτας...στηλογραφίας, ἀλλ' εἰ. Steph.Diac.*v.Steph*.(M.100. 1157B).

***εἰδωλοθύτης, ὁ**, *one who sacrifices to idols, idol-worshipper* οὐκ αἰσχύνονται οἱ 'Ιουδαῖοι εἰ. ἡμᾶς...ὀνομάζοντες *Dial.Christ.et Jud*.13 (p.74.10) ∞ ‡Anast.S.*Jud.disp*.2(M.89.1233B).

εἰδωλόθυτον, τό, *meat sacrificed to idols*, use forbidden to Christians, cf.Ac.15:29; ἀπὸ δὲ τοῦ εἰ. λίαν πρόσεχε *Did*.6.3; Just.*dial*.34. 8(M.6.549B); *ib*.35.1(l.c.); Clem.*paed*.2.1(p.159.12; M.8.392A); *ib*. (p.166.14; 405B); Or.*comm.11.12 in Mt*.(p.54.1; M.13.941C); Ast. Am.*hom*.14(M.40.384C); but allowed by Valentinians εἰ. ἀδιαφόρως ἐσθίουσι Iren.*haer*.1.6.3(M.7.508A); and Basilides, Eus.*h.e*.4.7.7(M. 20.317A).

εἰδωλολατρ(ε)ία, ἡ, *idolatry*; **1.** definitions and scope εἰ. ἐκ τοῦ ἑνὸς εἰς τοὺς πολλοὺς ἐπινέμησίς ἐστι θεούς Clem.*str*.3.12(p.237.10; M.8.1189B); a species of fornication, *ib*.6.16(p.507.14; M.9.377B); *ib*.7.12(p.54.10; 504B); opp. γνῶσις τοῦ θεοῦ, Meth.*symp*.7.6(p.77.7; M.18.132C); greatest sin, *Const.App*.2.23.1; incl. use of charms, Chrys.*hom.8.5 in Col*.(11.387A,C); **2.** in gen., *Barn*.16.7; *ib*.20.1; Just.*dial*.22.1(M.6.521B); Iren.*haer*.5.29.2(M.7.1202A); Clem.*paed*. 2.10(p.210.28; M.8.504A); Or.*Cels*.1.5(p.58.21; M.11.664A); Cyr.H. *catech*.4.6; **3.** causes: drunkenness and other vices, *Did*.3.4; covetousness, *T.Jud*.19.1; sin in gen., ‡Hipp.*fr.21 in Pr*.(p.163.19; M.10.621A); Ath.*gent*.8(M.25.17A); τὰ ἐθνικὰ ἐπιτηδεύματα ἀπὸ κληδονισμῶν τὴν ἀρχὴν λαβόντα, διὰ φιλαργυρίας καὶ ἱππομανίας προκόψαντα, εἰς εἰ. ἐξώκειλε †Bas.*Is*.82(1.436A; M.30.252D); hero-worship, Chrys.*hom.26.4 in 2Cor*.(10.623E); plots of Devil, Bas.Sel. *or*.23.1(M.85.272A); **4.** prohibitions, Clem.*prot*.8(p.61.19; M.8.192A); id.*str*.6.16(p.501.13; M.9.364A); Bas.Sel.*or*.6.2(M.85.89B); εἵλετο [sc. a mother] μᾶλλον νεκρὸν τὸ παιδίον ἰδεῖν, ἢ εἰδωλολατρείας ἀνασχέσθαι Chrys.*hom.8.5 in Col*.(11.386E); **5.** denounced even by pagans, Clem.*str*.5.14(p.401.1; M.9.168B); for whose salvation its rejection is necessary, *ib*.6.6(p.454.4; 265B); **6.** effects οἱ ἐν τῇ εἰ. κατορωρυγμένον ἔχοντες τὸ ἡγεμονικόν Clem.*str*.6.6(p.453.27; M.9.265A); men's perdition, Ath.*gent*.29(M.25.60B); **7.** its destruction by Christ, *ib*.1 (5A); id.*inc*.30.6(M.25.148D); esp. through Resurrection, *ib*.50.6 (185D); through baptism, Chrys.*hom.in 1Cor.10:1*(3.235A); through death of a martyr, *M.Thdot*.3(p.131.18); **8.** metaphors ἐξ εἰ. ... ἣν καλεῖ Βαβυλῶνα Or.*fr.32 in Jer*.(p.215.21); likened to cloud, †Bas. *Is*.224(1.547C; M.30.508D); **9.** exeg. Col.3:5 αὐτὸ [sc. φιλαργυρίαν] εἰ. ἐκάλεσεν ὁ Παῦλος...διατί δὲ εἰ. φησίν; ἔχουσι πολλοὶ χρήματα, καὶ χρήσασθαι αὐτοῖς οὐ τολμῶσιν, ἀλλὰ ἀφιεροῦσιν...καθάπερ τινῶν ἀναθημάτων οὐ τολμῶντες ἅψασθαι Chrys.*hom.65.3 in Jo*.(8.392D); **10.** eccl. legislation, on whether post-baptismal idolatry can be absolved οὐκ οἶδ' ὅπως ἑαυτοῖς τινες ἐπιτρέψαντες τὰ ὑπὲρ τὴν ἱερατικὴν ἀξίαν...αὐχοῦσιν ὡς δυνάμενοι καὶ εἰ. συγχωρεῖν Or.*or*.28.10(p.381.14; M.11.529B); but cf. id.*Cels*.3.51(p.247.22ff.; M.11.988B,C); οἱ δὲ ἐλεύθεροι ἐν τρισὶν ἔτεσιν ἐξετασθήσονται ἐν μετανοίᾳ...τοὺς δὲ συνδούλους ἑαυτῶν ἑλκύσαντες ἐπὶ εἰ. Petr.I Al.*ep.can*.7(M.18.480B); anathematized, CLaod.*can*.35; **11.** heret., Simon Magus' teaching ἐνδιαφορεῖν...πρὸς τὴν εἰ. Or.*Cels*.6.11(p.81.23; M.11.1308A); Arianism πᾶσαν τὴν διὰ τῶν σοφισμάτων κατασκευὴν τὴν περὶ τοῦ μὴ εἶναί ποτε τὸν ὄντως ὄντα...τροπὴν εἰς εἰ. εἶναι διοριζόμεθα Gr.Nyss.*Eun*. 8(2 p.179.1; M.45.772B); called νέα εἰ., *ib*.11(2 p.271.28; 881A); **12.** iconoclasts' fear that veneration of icons might lead to εἰ., Thdr.Stud.*antirr*.2 proem.(M.99.352D).

***εἰδωλολατρεύω**, *worship idols*, †Hipp.*theoph*.10(p.263.2; M.10. 860D); Eus.*e.th*.2.22(p.132.19; M.24.960A).

***εἰδωλολατρ-έω**, *worship idols*; **1.** in gen., *T.Lev*.17.11; Just. *dial*.19.6(M.6.517A); Clem.*paed*.1.10(p.143.4; M.8.357A); Or.*mart*.17 (p.16.1; M.11.584C); opp. θεολατρέω, Meth.*res*.2.4(p.335.18; M.41. 1168D); Eus.*v.C*.2.20(p.49.14; M.20.997B); **2.** οἱ ∼οῦντες condemned by scripture, †Bas.*Is*.219(1.544B; M.30.500A); Chrys.*hom.35.1 in Mt*.(7.399B); **3.** of Christians; through cowardice, Herm.*mand*.11.4; id.*sim*.9.21.3; πεῖσαι μὲν ὁ ἐχθρὸς οὐ δύναται πρὸς τὸ ∼εῖν βιάσασθαι δὲ βούλεται...προσέχωμεν οὖν, μήποτε ∼ήσωμεν Or.*mart*.32(p.28. 3ff.; M.11.604A,B); Chrys.*hom.8.5 in Col*.(11.388A); **4.** of heretics: Samaritans ἡ αἵρεσις...ἐν ἑαυτῇ δὲ ∼οῦσα κατ' ἄγνοιαν Epiph.*haer*. 9.2(p.199.3,9; M.41.224B,C); Arians μήτε διὰ τῆς τοῦ κτίσματος προσκυνήσεως τῷ πτώματι τῶν ∼ούντων συγκαταπίπτοντες Gr.Nyss. *Eun*.4(2 p.71.8; M.45.644C); τί οὖν ποιοῦσιν οἱ λέγοντες, ὅτι κτιστός [sc. Son] ἐστι;...εἰ...προσκυνοῦσιν, ∼οῦσι id.*fid*.(M.45.137A); **5.** fig., of addiction to material beauty, Clem.*paed*.2.10(p.220.17; M.8. 524A); cf.*ib*.2.12(p.233.8; 552A).

εἰδωλολάτρης, ὁ, *idol-worshipper, idolater* καὶ αὐτοὺς [sc. gentiles] εἰ. ὄντας κατηξίωσε [sc. God] γνῶναι τὴν βουλὴν αὐτοῦ Just. *dial*.130.4(M.6.780B); Jews charged with being εἰ., *ib*.93.4(697C); Clem.*prot*.8(p.61.1,5; M.8.189C); Eus.*d.e*.1.6(p.32.28; M.22.64C); †Bas.*Is*.260(1.577A; M.30.573D); tolerated by God's patience, Cyr. H.*catech*.8.4; of persons consulting soothsayers, Herm.*mand*.11.4; avaricious people, Gr.Naz.*carm*.1.2.28.372(M.37.883A); εἰ. δ' Ἄρειος μιμούμενος Amph.*Seleuc*.205(M.37.1590A); εἰ δέ τις υἱοῦ ὄνομα τῇ κτίσει τίθεται, ἐν τοῖς εἰ. τετάξεται Gr.Nyss.*Eun*.4(2 p.90.24; M.45. 668A); Cyr.*Pulch*.(p.60.23; 5².179A); orthodox called εἰ. by iconoclasts, †Gr.II Papa *ep.Leon*.1(H.4.4A).

***εἰδωλολατρικῶς**, *idolatrously*, *M.Pion*.16.1.

***εἰδωλολάτρις, ἡ**, *idolatress*, Chrys.*hom.19.3 in 1Cor*(10.162D, v.l. -ης); id.*hom.8.5 in Col*.(11.386F, vv.ll. -εία, -ία); ‡Jo.D.*fid.dorm*.9 (M.95.253D); as adj. πόλις...πικρὰ καὶ εἰ. Cyr.*Mich*.14(3.403C).

***εἰδωλολατρισμός, ὁ**, *idolatry*, *Apoc.Bar*.13(p.93.18).

***εἰδωλομανέω**, *be idol-mad*, Gr.Nyss.*v.Mos*.(M.44.393A); id.*or. dom*.1(p.22.3; M.44.1132D); of Athenians, id.*deit*.(M.46.557A); id. *Eun*.5(2 p.100.1; M.45.677A); Evagr.*h.e*.1.11(p.18.16; M.86.2449A); ‡Caes.Naz.*dial*.111(M.38.989).

***εἰδωλομανής**, *idol-mad, idolatrous* τῆς ψυχῆς κινήσεις εἰ. Athenag. *leg*.27.1(M.6.953A); Marc.Diac.*v.Porph*.40; εἰ. πλάνη ‡Chrys.*pasch*. 6.2(p.141.5; 8².267D); Cyr.*Os*.1(3.8E); ἀπάτη εἰ. id.*Zach*.59(3.739A); as subst., *Asen*.12(p.56.2); Ph.Carp.*Cant*.11(M.40.45C); Marc.Diac. *v.Porph*.75.

***εἰδωλομανία, ἡ**, *idol-madness, madness of idolatry*, freq.= εἰδωλολατρία, *A.Barn*.16(p.298.1); *A.Thom*.B 2(p.28.16); εἴθε μέχρις ἀρρένων εἱστήκει...ἡ εἰ., καὶ μὴ εἰς θηλείας κατέφερον τὴν θείαν προσηγορίαν Ath.*gent*.10(M.25.21C); εἰ. καὶ ἀθεότης id.*inc*.14.3(M. 25.120D); Αἰγυπτιακὴ εἰ. †Bas.*Is*.6(1.382E; M.30.129A); demons working through it, Gr.Nyss.*or.catech*.18(p.75.3; M.45.53C); id.*v. Gr.Thaum*.(M.46.913D); Epiph.*haer*.32.3(p.442.19; M.41.548C); Nil. *epp*.1.75(M.79.116A); ‡Jo.D.*Artem*.69(p.100.33; M.96.1317A).

εἰδωλόμορφος, *idol-shaped* εἰ. ὗλαι Eust.*engast*.25(p.55.28; M.18. 665A); †Bas.*contub*.7(M.30.821C).

εἴδωλον, τό, A. *false god, idol*, def. εἶδος *graece formam sonat, ab eo per diminutionem εἰ. deductum, aeque apud nos formulam fecit*.

igitur omnis forma vel formula idolum se dici exposcit, Tert.*de idololatria* 3(M.*PL*.1.665A); **1.** of pagan gods, *Barn*.4.8; *ib*.9.6; Just.*1apol*.64.1(M.6.425C); id.*2apol*.12.5(M.6.464C); Athenag.*leg*. 15.1(M.6.920A); Iren.*haer*.1.6.3(M.7.508A); *Hom.Clem*.10.2; Ath. *gent*.15(M.25.32B); **2.** rejected; **a.** by pagan thinkers, Clem.*str*.5.14 (p.402.15; M.9.169B); **b.** by Christians, *2Clem*.17.1; *πῶς...θεοὶ τὰ εἰ. ... ἀκάθαρτα πνεύματα;* Clem.*prot*.4(p.43.25; M.8.152C); *τὰ εἰ. τῶν ἐθνῶν δαιμόνια* Or.*mart*.32(p.28.8; M.11.604B); *Hom.Clem*.8.23; *οὐκ ἔστι σώφρων ἐν τοῖς εἰ.* Ath.*gent*.25(M.25.49D); **c.** pagan objections to Christian attitude *καταγέλαστοι, τοὺς μὲν ἄλλους...θεοὺς ὡς εἰ. βλασφημοῦντες, τὸν δὲ καὶ αὐτῶν ὡς...εἰ. ἀθλιώτερον καὶ μηδὲ εἰ. ἔτι ἀλλ' ⟨ὄντ⟩ως νεκρὸν σέβοντες* Cels.ap.Or.*Cels*.7.36(p.186.24ff.; M.11. 1472A,B); refusal to worship idols discussed, Cels.*ib*.8.24(p.240.28ff.; 1553A,B); **3.** special characteristics; idols dead, hence crowned with flowers, crown being symbol of freedom from care, Clem. *paed*.2.8(p.202.1; M.8.484B); *εἰ. ... τῇ φύσει ἐστὶ ψευδῆ* Or.*hom.16.8 in Jer*.(p.140.23; M.13.449B); being nothing, *Hom.Clem*.11.13; restricted to certain localities and nations, Ath.*inc*.46.5(M.25.180A); no resurrection for them, *ib*.50.6(185C); **4.** liberation from them by Christ, Just.*dial*.113.6(M.6.737A); Ath.*inc*.31.2(M.25.149B); **5.** their pretended powers discussed, Athenag.*leg*.23.1(M.6.941A,B); **6.** their worship instigated by demons, *ib*.26.1(949D) cit. s. *δαίμων*; cf. *ἄνισα εἰ. ... ἐν τῇ...ῥυπώσῃ ψυχῇ κατακέκρυπται* Clem.*prot*.6(p.53. 2; M.8.176A); **7.** opp.; **a.** *εἰκών*: *οὐδὲ τὴν εἰκόνα τοῦ θεοῦ τὴν ζῶσαν δίκην εἰ. τῶν νεκρῶν καταστεπτέον* Clem.*paed*.2.8(p.202.6; M.8. 485A); *Hom.Clem*.11.4; **b.** *ἀλήθεια*, Clem.*prot*.1(p.6.19; M.8.60A); *ib*.7 (p.56.16; 181B); Ath.*inc*.11.4(M.25.116B); **c.** God *πιστεύετε μὲν τοῖς εἰ. ... ἀπιστεῖτε δὲ τῷ θεῷ* Clem.*prot*.4(p.47.17; M.8.160C); Meth.*res*. 1.32(p.268.14; M.41.1144C); *Hom.Clem*.16.14; Ath.*inc*.55.5(M.25. 193D); **8.** heret.; **a.** Gnost. *τὴν μὲν Ἀλήθειαν ὁρῶν εἰ. ὑπὸ Μάρκου γεγονυῖαν* Iren.*haer*.1.15.4(M.7.624A); **b.** Sabellian conception of God called *εἰ.*, Eus.*e.th*.20.1(p.99.12; M.24.900B); **c.** iconoclast *τὴν εἰκόνα τοῦ κυρίου...εἰ. πλάνης βλασφήμως ἀποκαλοίη* Thdr.Stud. *antirr*.2 proem.(M.99.352C); **9.** sts. = *εἰδωλεῖον*: *τῶν ἐν Αἰγύπτῳ οἰκοδομηθέντων εἰ.* Epiph.*haer*.22.2(p.247.2; M.41.297A); Chrys.*hom. 20.1 in 1Cor*.(10.168D).

B. *phantom of the mind*, so prob. ref. pagan god *εἴτε χρόνος ἐστὶν ὁ Κρόνος, μεταβάλλει, εἴτε καιρός, τρέπεται...οὔτε ἄρα ὁ Κρόνος οὔτε τὸ ἐπ' αὐτῷ εἰ. θεός* Athenag.*leg*.22.5(M.6.937C); of mental illusions in pagan worship, *ib*.27.1(952D); with play on double meaning of word, ref. golden calf *τὸ γοῦν ἐκπορνεῦσαν τῆς ἐπιθυμίας εἰς χρυσίον εἰ. γίνεται βασανιζόμενον πυρί, ᾧ μόνῳ τηρεῖται τρυφὴ καθάπερ εἰ., οὐκ ἀλήθεια* Clem.*paed*.2.12(p.232.32; M.8.549C); this Platonic term said to be abandoned by Christians because of meaning A, Or.*Cels*.6.9(p.79.20f.; M.11.1304B); *εἰ.* opp. *ἀλήθεια*, Meth.*symp*.6.2(p.66.4; M.18.116B); id.*res*.1.52(p.308.12; M.41. 1128B); *ἐσκιαγραφημένα...εἰ.* opp. *ἐμφανεῖς εἰκόνες*, Synes.*insomn*.15 (p.178.7; M.66.1312A); ref. contemplation *ἐφορείας ἀξιοῦσθαι νοῦ καὶ θεοῦ, ἀλλὰ μὴ δεξαμενὴν εἶναι τῶν ἀορίστων εἰ.* *ib*.16(p.178.13; 1312A); Serap.*Man*.44(p.62; M.18.1229D); ref. Manichean theory *...ὅτε κατὰ τὴν ὀφθεῖσαν ἐν ἡλίῳ εἰκόνα τῆς ὕλης τὸν ἄνθρωπον δημιούργημα εἶναι λέγωσιν; καὶ γὰρ εἰκόνες εἰ. εἰσὶ τῶν ἀρχετύπων ...εἴδωλον εἰδώλου τὸν ἄνθρωπον ὑπάρχειν οὕτω γε κατ' αὐτοὺς καὶ μηδεμίαν ἔχειν ὑπόστασιν* Alex.Lyc.*Man*.23(pp.32.13,33.2; M.18. 441B,C).

C. *phantom, ghost*, cf. *παῖδες...ὥσπερ εἰ. κατὰ τὰς ἀγορὰς ἀνειλοῦντο* Josephus ap.Eus.*h.e*.3.6.12(M.20.228B); Eus.*v.C*.1.58(p.35.19; M.20. 973A); Chrys.*hom.73.3 in Mt*.(7.711B).

D. *image, likeness*, opp. *ἀπεικονίσματα...ἀειδῆ* Meth.*symp*.8.3 (p.84.1; M.18.141B); *ἀπατηλὸν εἰ.* [sc. *ἁγνείας*] *ib*.10.2(p.123.26; 196B); id.*res*.1.28(p.257.5; M.41.1136A); Chrys.*hom.17.2 in Mt*.(7. 224A).

E. *illustration, example* *κἂν τοῖς φυτοῖς τῶν νῦν λεγομένων εἴδωλα φαίνεται* Aen.*dial*.(M.85.953B).

εἰδωλοπλαστέω, *make idols*, ‡Epiph.*epit.haer*.(pp.342.17,21; 344.27).

εἰδωλοποι-έω, **1.** *make into an idol*, Gr.Nyss.*hom.14 in Cant*.(M. 44.1021B); fig., ref. persons holding false opinions on God *νοητὴν εἰδωλολατρείαν ~οῦντες ἐν ἑαυτοῖς* †Bas.*Is*.96(1.446D; M.30.276C); of Arians *~οῦντες ἑαυτῶν τὴν ὑπόνοιαν* Gr.Nyss.*Eun*.12(1 p.245.1; M. 45.944C); *διὰ τῶν Ἀρείου δογμάτων ~οῦντας τὴν κτίσιν* id.*ep*.3(M.46. 1017B); of Apollinarius *ἐν τῷ σαρκίνῳ θεῷ, ὃν...~ήσας ἀνέπλασε* id. *Apoll*.19(M.45.1160C); **2.** *express by images* *τὰ ἐκ τῆς ἐνθυμήσεως καὶ ~εῖσθαι* ‡Ath.*Ar*.4.11(p.55.2; M.26.481A).

εἰδωλοποίησις, ἡ, *making of idols*, Eus.*Is*.19:14(M.24.229A); Cyr.*Am*.68(3.326A).

εἰδωλοποιΐα, ἡ, *manufacture of idols*, ‡Just.*monarch*.1(M.6.313A); Ath.*gent*.24(M.25.48C); Gr.Nyss.*Eun*.12(2 p.289.21; M.45.901C).

εἰδωλοποιός, *idol-making, idolatrous*; of heresies, ref. Basilides *εἰ. ... διδασκαλία* Epiph.*haer*.24.7(p.264.8; M.41.316B); ref. Collyridians *εἰ. ... αἵρεσις* *ib*.79.1(p.476.22; M.42.741A); *ib*.79.4(p.479.8; 745B); as subst., of Marcus, who made *ἀλήθεια* into an idol (v. *εἴδωλον*), Iren.*haer*.1.15.6(M.7.628A); *Const.App*.4.6.5; *ib*.8.32.8.

***εἰδωλοπρεπής**, *befitting idol-worship* *ἔθη...εἰ.* Cyr.*ador*.7(1.229C); *ib*.10(360E).

[*]**εἰδωλοχαρής**, *delighting in idols*, Synes.*hymn*.3.92(p.9; M.66. 1595).

εἰθισμένως, *in the accustomed way*, Geo.Pis.*Pers*.1.175(M.92. 1209B).

***εἴθοις**, = *εἴθε*, *would that!* *εἰ. Σαββάτης μὴ ἐγεννήθη* Thphn. *chron*.p.155(M.108.421B); *ib*.p.287(705A).

εἰκαιοβουλία, ἡ, *rashness, recklessness*; of worshipping idols, Cyr.*Os*.85(3.117C); *ib*.146(180B); id.*Zach*.90(3.778C); of heret. views, id.*ep*.1(p.16.32; 5².10D); of Judas *ἐπιμένοντα...τῇ εἰ. τῆς προδοσίας* Procl.CP *or*.10.3(M.65.781A).

***εἰκαιόβουλος**, *rash, reckless*, also *stupid*; of opinions etc., Cyr. *Os*.proem.(3.1A); id.*Zach*.95(3.785D); id.*Juln*.2(6².39E); of heretics *εἰ. καὶ ματαιόφρονας* ‡Caes.Naz.*dial*.9(M.38.868); of superstitious people, *ib*.117(1001).

***εἰκαιοδάπανος**, *extravagant*, *Const.App*.2.24.5.

***εἰκαιολατρεία, ἡ**, *vain worship* of idols, Cyr.*ador*.6(1.181D).

***εἰκαιολέσχης, ὁ**, *vain babbler*, ‡Caes.Naz.*dial*.153(M.38.1108).

***εἰκαιολεσχία, ἡ**, *foolish babble*, ‡Caes.Naz.*dial*.170(M.38.1133).

εἰκαιολογέω, *speak aimlessly, talk nonsense*, Cyr.*apol.Thdt*.1 (p.112.9; 6¹.206A); Dion.Ar.*d.n*.3.2(M.3.681A); v. *εἰκοτολογέω*.

εἰκαιολογία, ἡ, *rash talk*; of heret. opinions, Cyr.*Jo*.1.2(4.14D).

εἰκαιομυθέω, *talk nonsense*, Cyr.*glaph.Gen*.2(1.29A); id.*Os*.64(3. 97D); id.*Juln*.6(6².212E); id.*apol.Thdt*.5(p.126.24; 6¹.220D).

εἰκαιομυθία, ἡ, *foolish talk, babble*; of views of opponents, heretics etc., Cyr.*apol.orient*.(p.34.2; 6¹.158D); id.*Ps*.33:14(M.69. 889D); pagan myths, id.*Juln*.2(6².44C); Germ.CP *syn.haer*.3(M.98. 41B); *ib*.9(48A); ‡Meth.*Sym.et Ann*.1(M.18.349B).

***εἰκαιόμυθος**, *talking to no purpose*, Cyr.*Nest*.2.12(p.51.17; 6¹. 58D); id.*hom.pasch*.16(5².217C); neut. as subst., id.*Os*.118(3.149D); id.*Soph*.41(3.620A).

***εἰκαιοπονέω**, *give needless trouble*, Cyr.*Jo*.6.1(4.612D; *ματαιοπ-* Aubert).

***εἰκαιοπονία, ἡ**, *vain toil, vanity* *Ἑλλήνων εἰ.* Cyr.*Jo*.4.5(4.405E).

***εἴκασις, ἡ**, *vain idea, opinion*; of Adam's hope of becoming like God, ‡Ath.*qu.script*.59(M.28.737A).

εἰκασμός, ὁ, *idea, imagining*, Anton.Hag.*v.Sym.Styl*.8(p.28.18).

εἰκονίζ-ω, **1.** *fashion*, Meth.*arbitr*.11(p.174.10; cf.M.18.260B); **2.** *represent, portray*; **a.** lit., in gen. *παντὸς ~ομένου, οὐχ ἡ φύσις, ἀλλ' ἡ ὑπόστασις ~εται* Thdr.Stud.*antirr*.3.34(M.99.405A); of sacred images; **i.** portrayal of God impossible, Jo.D.*imag*.1.7(M.94.1237C); *πάλαι μὲν ὁ θεός, ἀσώματός τε καὶ ἀσχημάτιστος, οὐδαμῶς ~ετο* *ib*.1.16 (1245A); **ii.** God incarnate may be portrayed *οὐ τὴν ἀόρατον ~ω θεότητα, ἀλλ' ~ω θεοῦ τὴν ὁραθεῖσαν σάρκα* *ib*.1.4(1236C); *~ω θεοῦ τὸ ὁρώμενον* *ib*.1.16(1245A); **iii.** portrayal of Christ forbidden *ἕτερον πρόσωπον διδόντες τῇ σαρκί, ὅπερ ~ειν λέγουσιν* CCP(754)*decr*.(H.4. 365A); in gen. *εἴ τις τὸν Χριστὸν εἰκονίσει σταυρούμενον* Jo.D.*imag*.1. 27(1281C); v. *εἰκών*; **b.** met., pass., *be reflected*, of divine image in Christ *ἐν τῷ μόνῳ σου ἀνθρώπῳ ~όμενον* *A.Jo*.109(p.208.10); **3.** *typify* *Ἰακὼβ πρῶτος προσκυνήσας τὸ ἄκρον τῆς ῥάβδου Ἰωσήφ, τὸν σταυρὸν εἰκόνισε* Jo.D.*f.o*.4.13(M.94.1132C); *τοῦτον τὸν ἄρτον οἱ ἄρτοι ~ον* [l. *~ουσι*] *τῆς προθέσεως* *ib*.(1149C); **4.** *symbolize, signify* *τὰς ἐν τῷ νόμῳ σκιάς, αἵτινες ~ουσι τὴν ἀλήθειαν* Cyr.*Ps*.24:4(M.69.848B); Max.*qu.Theop*.(M.90.1397B); *ὁ διπλοῦς στέφανος ἐκ τῆς τῶν τριχῶν σημειώσεως, ~ει τὴν τοῦ κορυφαίου ἀποστόλου τιμίαν κάραν* ‡Sophr.H. *liturg*.6(M.87.3985D); **5.** *imitate, express nature of* *τὸν ἀπαθῶς υἱὸν ~ων ἐν πάθεσιν* Bas.Sel.*or*.1.3(M.85.36C); Geo.Pis.*Pers*.1.135(M.92. 1207A); *Lit.Marc*.(p.122.19); **6.** med., *imagine, form mental picture of* *τῆς θείας χάριτος μορφὴν ~όμενος...χαίρω* Max.*ep*.2(M.91.393A).

εἰκονικός, **1.** *of* or *pertaining to an image, pictorial* *οὓς οὐ βλέπεις σαρκικῶς...τούτους ὁρᾷς πνευματικῶς διὰ εἰ. τυπώσεως* ‡Jo.D.*Const*. 10(M.95.328B); *εἴ τις καὶ τὰς εἰ. ἀναζωγραφήσεις οὐκ ἀποδέχεται, ἀ. ἔ.* CNic.(787)*act*.7(H.4.432D); *ib*.(444B); ‡Jo.D.*ep.Thphl*.21(M.95. 373A); **2.** *pertaining to* or *consisting in the image of God* *διὰ τὴν πρὸς αὐτὸν εὐπρεπεστάτην ὁμοίωσιν καὶ εἰ. περιφάνειαν* Sophr.H.*or*.2.12 (M.87.3229D); ref. Son, Acac.Caes.*fr.Marcell*.ap.Epiph.*haer*.72.9 (p.264.17; M.42.396B); **3.** *symbolical* *τὰ παρ' ὑμῖν εἰκοσιτέσσαρα γράμματα ἀπορροίας ὑπάρχειν...τῶν τριῶν δυνάμεων εἰκονικά* Iren.*haer*.

1.14.5(M.7.604A); **4.** *typical*, Eus.*h.e.*1.3.7(M.20.72A) cit. s. ἀπεργάζομαι; σκιώδη καὶ εἰ., ἀλλ' οὐκ ἀληθῆ Χριστὸν καὶ ἀρχιερέα id.*d.e.*4.15 (p.180.22; M.22.300D); *ib.*5.3(p.221.9; 364D); τὴν υἱῶν προσηγορίαν ἔσχον εἰ. Proc.G.*Is.*1:3(M.87.1829A); **5.** *representative* ἐκ τῆς περὶ αὐτοὺς εἰ. τοῦ Χριστοῦ προσρήσεως Χριστιανοὺς ἐπεφήμισεν Eus.*h.e.* 1.3.10(M.20.72C); **6.** *representative* of an ideal reality, *derivative* δύναται δὲ ἀληθὴς δικαιοσύνη πρὸς ἀντιδιαστολὴν λέγεσθαι τῆς εἰ. Or.*fr.Pr.*1:1(M.17.153A); id.*fr.6 in Jo.*1:8(p.488.14); **7.** *imitative, counterfeit* εἰ. χειροθεσίᾳ Corn.ap.Eus.*h.e.*6.43.9(M.20.620B); Eus.*d.e.* 4.15(p.180.22; M.22.300D) cit. s. ἀντίμιμος.

εἰκονικῶς, *symbolically, figuratively*; **1.** of scriptural types πάσχα...Ἑβραίων παισὶν εἰ. παραδεδομένου Eus.*pasch.*1(M.24.693A); προλαβὼν τὸ μέλλον ὁ θεὸς διὰ συμβόλων εἰ. *ib.*6(700D); ἡ δὲ πέτρα ἦν εἰ. ὁ Χριστός ‡Anast.S.*Jud.disp.*3(M.89.1244C); **2.** in gen., *figuratively* ἐπ' ὀνόματι Βαβυλῶνος εἰ. Ῥώμην σημαίνων Hier.*vir.ill.*(tr. Sophr.Pal.)8(p.9.1; M.*PL.*23.622B).

εἰκόνισμα, τό, 1. *image*, Thdr.Mops.*Am.*6:24–7(M.66.280B); **2.** *likeness*; **a.** of children resembling parents ποίησον αὐτοὺς πατρὸς εἰ. Geo.Pis.*hex.*1845(M.92.1576A); **b.** of ideas in Platonic doctrine of creation τὸ δὲ παράδειγμα τὴν διάνοιαν τοῦ θεοῦ εἶναι, ὃ καὶ ἰδέαν καλεῖ οἷον εἰ. τι ᾧ προσέχων ἐν τῇ ψυχῇ ὁ θεὸς τὰ πάντα ἐδημιούργει Hipp.*haer.*1.19(p.19.10; M.16.3041B); **c.** of earthly reflections of supramundane realities, Max.*schol.c.h.*1.3(M.4.33A); **3.** *type* τὰ κρυπτὰ τοῦ μέλλοντος εἰ. Geo.Pis.*hex.*855(M.92.1500A); τῆς ἀδιαφθορίας προϋπεχάραττεν εἰκονίσματα Germ.CP *or.*2(M.98.264C); Jo.D.*f.o.*4.13(M.94.1149C).

εἰκονισμός, ὁ, 1. *likeness* οὐ πάντως ἀπαράλλακτον ἡμῖν εἰσφέρει τὴν ἰσότητα, ὁμοιότητα δὲ μᾶλλον καὶ εἰ. Cyr.*Jo.*2.8(4.227D); *ib.*3.3 (265D); **2.** *symbol* τύπον...καὶ εἰ. οὐρανοῦ τὸ γράμμα...ποιεῖται...τὴν λίθον Cyr.*ador.*11(1.381B); **3.** divine *image*, Clem.*str.*6.9(p.468.5; M.9.293B); τὸ πνεῦμα...μεταπλάττον...τὰς...ψυχὰς...καὶ τῆς ἀνωτάτω πασῶν οὐσίας ἀποσημαίνεται τὸν εἰ. Cyr.*Jo.*11.11(4.995D); ἐσμεν εἰ. θεοῦ id.*dogm.*3(6^2.372A; codd. εἰκόνες p.555.7); Geo.Pis. *carm.*26 tit.

***εἰκονιστικός**, *significant, representative* of, as a shadow or reflection ὁ χρόνος...καθ' ὃν ἐκράτει...ὁ νόμος, οὐκ ἦν δικαιοσύνης καρπῶν, ἀλλ' εἰ. τῶν ἐν δικαιοσύνῃ καρπῶν Max.*qu.Thal.*20(M.90.309C).

εἰκονογραφ-έω, 1. *make images* πῶς μὴ ~εῖν ὁ νόμος διακελεύεται; Jo.D.*imag.*1.15(M.94.1245A); **2.** *paint a picture of, delineate*, of fashioning of soul after divine image ἔστι δὲ ταῦτα τὰ χρώματα ἅπερ σοι λέγει ζωγραφεῖν πίστις..., γνῶσις, εὐλάβεια,...καὶ ὅλος ὁ τῶν χρωμάτων χορὸς ὁ ~ῶν σου τὴν ψυχήν *A.Jo.*29(p.166.25); of 'portrayal' of Christ by ἁγιωσύνη, ἀμεριμνία, πρᾳότης, *A.Thom.*A 86 (p.202.7); **3.** *present a picture of, portray* ἡ δὲ [sc. πανήγυρις] ὑδάτων ἁγιασμὸν καὶ βαπτίσματος ~εῖ μήτραν Procl.CP *or.*3.2(M.65. 705B).

εἰκονογραφία, ἡ, 1. *making of images* τῆς εἰδωλολατρείας ἕνεκα ἀπαγορεύει τὴν εἰ. Jo.D.*imag.*1.7(M.94.1237C); Thdr.Stud.*antirr.*3.1 (M.99.389C); **2.** *description, representation* τὰς τῶν ἁγίων νόων ἐν τοῖς λογίοις εἰ. Dion.Ar.*c.h.*2.2(M.3.137C); *ib.*(140B); τῶν ἱερῶν λογίων ἀγγελοειδεῖς εἰ. *ib.*2.5(145B); *ib.*15.9(337D); τῆς θεαρχικῆς εἰ. id.*e.h.*3.3.3(M.3.429A); *ib.*4.3.10(481C); *ib.*4.3.11(484C); Max.*ambig.* (M.91.1213C); **3.** *picture* προσκυνοῦμεν εἰκονογραφίας ‡Jo.D.*hom.*5(M. 96.657A).

***εἰκονοθραύστης, ὁ,** *iconoclast*, Jo.VI H.*v.Jo.D.*19(M.94.457D).

***εἰκονοκαύστης, ὁ,** *burner of images*; of Constantine Copronymus, Steph.Diac.*v.Steph.*tit.(M.100.1069A).

εἰκονοκλάστης, ὁ, *iconoclast*, Germ.CP *ep.*4(M.98.189B); εἰ. δέ, ὅτι τὰς...ἁγίας καὶ σεπτὰς εἰκόνας...πυρὶ παραδεδώκασιν Jo.D.*haer.* 102(M.94.773A); τοῖς Χριστιανοκατηγόροις, ἤγουν εἰ., ἀνάθεμα Bas. Anc.al.*libell.*(H.4.41D).

***εἰκονοκτίστης, ὁ,** *image-maker*, Agath.*v.Gr.Ill.*34(p.20).

***εἰκονολάτρης, ὁ,** *image-worshipper*, Agath.*v.Gr.Ill.*34(p.20).

***εἰκονομαχέω**, *war against images*, Thdr.Stud.*or.*10.24(M.99. 828A).

***εἰκονομαχικός**, *warring against images*, Thdr.Stud.*antirr.*2.7(M. 99.356D); id.*or.*11.17(M.99.820B); *Schol.*in CNic.(787)*can.*1(*Mon.*2 p.647).

***εἰκονομάχος**, *hostile to images*; as subst., of iconoclasts, ‡Gr. Nyss.*hom.7.155 in Jo.*(p.279.25); CNic.(787)*act.*1(H.4.60E); Germ. CP *or.*1(M.98.232A); ‡Jo.D.*Const.*10(M.95.328B); Thdr.Stud.*antirr.* 2.1(M.99.353B).

***εἰκονοπερίγραπτος**, *depictable in an icon*; of Christ, *Nomoc.*336.

***εἰκονοποιέω**, *fashion, give form to*, Just.*1apol.*19.1(M.6.356C).

εἰκονοποιός, *making an image* or *likeness* θεῖος δὲ χαρακτὴρ... ὄντως ὢν εἰκὼν εἰ. Didym.(‡Bas.)*Eun.*5(1.302A; M.29.724C).

***εἰκονουργία, ἡ,** *representation*, Thdr.Stud.*antirr.*3.2(M.99. 417C).

***εἰκονοφίλης, ὁ,** *lover of images*, Agath.*v.Gr.Ill.*34(p.20).

***εἰκοσάδρομος**, *having run twenty times* πεντὰς γὰρ αὐτὸν εἰκοσαδρόμου χρόνου μετῆρεν Geo.Pis.*Sev.*353(M.92.1648A).

***εἰκοσαετηρικός**, *for the twentieth anniversary*, i.e. of Constantine's accession εἰ. ὕμνοι Eus.*v.C.*1.1(p.7.4; M.20.912A); *ib.*4.40 (p.133.6; 1188C).

εἰκοσαετηρίς, ἡ, *twentieth year*; *vicennalia*, festival celebrated on twentieth anniversary of a reign, Eus.*v.C.*4.47(p.137.10; M.20. 1197B); id.*h.e.*8.13.9(M.20.777A); id.*m.P.*2(p.909.27; M.20.1468A); Socr.*h.e.*1.16.1(M.67.116B); *Chron.Pasch.*p.282(M.92.704B).

***εἰκοσαόμβη, ἡ,** *sacrifice of twenty*, sc. 12 apostles, 7 deacons, and S. Paul, word formed on analogy of hecatomb Παῦλος ὁ τῆς θείας εἰ. ἐξαίρετος ‡Caes.Naz.*dial.*193(M.38.1176).

***εἰκοσιοκταετηρίς, ἡ,** *period of twenty-eight years*, Max.*comput.* (M.19.1260A).

εἰκοσιπέντε, *twenty-five*, Philost.*h.e.*10.11(M.65.592B *divisim*).

εἰκοσιτρεῖς, *twenty-three*, Socr.*h.e.*2.6.2(M.67.192C).

***εἰκοστοδεύτερος**, *twenty-second*, CTrull.*act.*11(H.3.1253A).

εἰκοτολογέω, *reason from probabilities*, Pall.*v.Chrys.*19(conj. p.121.12 for εἰκαιολογοῦντες M.47.67).

[*]εἴκριον, τό, v. ἴκριον.

εἰκών, ἡ, *likeness, image, picture*;

I. lit.; **A.** def. εἰ. ... ἐστιν ὁμοίωμα καὶ παράδειγμα, καὶ ἐκτύπωμά τινος, ἐν ἑαυτῷ δεικνύον τὸ εἰκονιζόμενον,...πᾶσα εἰ. ἐκφαντορικὴ τοῦ κρυφίου ἐστὶ καὶ δεικτική...διαφοραὶ δὲ εἰκόνων εἰσί· πρώτη...εἰ. ἐστιν ἡ φυσική. ... δεύτερος τρόπος εἰκόνος, ἡ ἐν τῷ θεῷ τῶν ὑπ' αὐτοῦ ἐσομένων ἔννοια, τουτέστιν ἡ προαιώνιος αὐτοῦ βούλησις...τρίτος τρόπος ...ὁ κατὰ μίμησιν ὑπὸ θεοῦ γενόμενος, τουτέστιν ὁ ἄνθρωπος...τέταρτος τρόπος εἰ. τῆς γραφῆς, σχήματα...καὶ τύπους ἀναπλαττούσης τῶν ἀοράτων...πέμπτος...ὁ προεικονίζων καὶ προδιαγράφων τὰ μέλλοντα, ὡς ἡ βάτος...τὴν παρθένον...ἕκτος...ἡ πρὸς μνήμην τῶν γεγονότων... πρὸς τὴν εἰς ὕστερον τῶν θεωμένων ὠφέλειαν...διπλῆ δὲ αὕτη· διά τε λόγου ταῖς βίβλοις ἐγγραφομένου...καὶ διὰ θεωρίας αἰσθητῆς Jo.D. *imag.*3.16–23(M.94.1337A–1341D).

B. of imperial pictures or statues; **1.** permission to erect image a mark of imperial favour, Juln.Imp.*ep.*58(p.64.19); images of unpopular or deposed rulers overthrown, *Chron.Pasch.*p.391(M.92. 1004C); **2.** represent emperor and receive reverence καὶ γὰρ βασιλέως ἀπόντος, εἰ. βασιλέως πληροῖ χώραν βασιλέως· καὶ προσκυνοῦσιν ἄρχοντες...καὶ δῆμοι προσκυνοῦσιν, οὐ πρὸς τὴν σανίδα βλέποντες, ἀλλὰ πρὸς τὸν χαρακτῆρα τοῦ βασιλέως †Sever.*cruc.*(p.898. 42); **3.** as object of adoration imposed on Christians θῦσον...τῇ εἰ. τοῦ αὐτοκράτορος *M.Apollon.*7; **4.** in similes illustrating theol. truths ὥσπερ γὰρ καὶ βασιλέως καταπεμφθεῖσαν εἰ. τιμῶντες τὸ πρωτότυπον τῆς εἰ. αὐτὸν ἂν τιμήσαιμεν τὸν βασιλέα, τὸν αὐτὸν τρόπον ὁ πατὴρ ἂν εἴη διὰ τοῦ υἱοῦ τιμώμενος Eus.*e.th.*2.7(p.106.13; M.24. 912D); ἐν γὰρ τῇ εἰ. τὸ εἶδος καὶ ἡ μορφὴ τοῦ βασιλέως ἐστί...ἐκ δὲ τοῦ μὴ διαλλάττειν τὴν ὁμοιότητα...εἴποι ἂν ἡ εἰ.· ἐγὼ καὶ ὁ βασιλεὺς ἕν ἐσμεν Ath.*Ar.*3.5(M.26.332A); ὃν τρόπον εἴ τις βασιλέως εἰκόνος, καλῶς κατασκευασαμένης...μετενέγκοι τὰς ψηφῖδας...καὶ μεθαρμόσαι, καὶ ποιήσειεν ἐξ αὐτῶν μορφὴν κυνός...καὶ λέγοι ταύτην εἶναι τὴν τοῦ βασιλέως,...τὸν αὐτὸν τρόπον καὶ οἱ αἱρεσιάρχαι...ἐφαρμόζειν βιάζονται τοῖς ἑαυτῶν μύθοις τὰ λόγια τοῦ θεοῦ Nil.*epp.*1.247(M.79.173B); Justn. *conf.anath.*11(p.92.30; M.86.1017B).

C. of images of pagan deities; forbidden by Numa as a Pythagorean, Clem.*str.*1.15(p.45.14; M.8.777A); Pythagoras forbidding all such representations, *ib.*5.5(p.344.7; M.9.49A); cf.Zeno, *ib.*5.11 (p.377.2; 113B); worship of Nebuchadnezzar's image likened to submission to Arian persecution, Bas.*ep.*243.2(3.373D; M.32.905A); worship of pagan images contrasted with Christian prohibition of their use, Clem.*prot.*4(p.47.9; M.8.160B); cause of pagan idolatry ἐπειδὴ ἀπώλεσε τὸ κατ' εἰκόνα...τοῦ θεοῦ ὁ ἄνθρωπος, διὰ τοῦτο κατ' εἰ. καὶ ὁμοίωσιν ἀνθρώπου γέγονεν ὁ θεός Eulog.*fr.Trin.*3.8(p.368).

D. Christian attitude to use of images; **1.** forbidden by Moses ἵνα μηδεμία πρόφασις ᾖ τῆς τῶν ἀγαλμάτων κατασκευῆς, τοὺς ἀνοήτους τῶν ἀνθρώπων...καθελκούσης ἀπὸ τοῦ θεοῦ εἰς γῆν τοὺς ὀφθαλμοὺς τῆς ψυχῆς...νόμος...μὴ ποιήσητε...πᾶσαν εἰ. Or.*Cels.*4.31(p.301. 18; M.11.1076A); Thdt.*affect.*2(p.51.19; 4.742); **2.** use disapproved, esp. images of God or Christ [cf.Iren.*haer.*1.25.5(M.7.685B) infra 3.c; Clem.*prot.*4(p.47.28; M.8.161B); id.*str.*7.5(p.20.18; M.9.436B)]; ὁρᾷ εἰ. περιεστεμμένην πρεσβύτου καὶ παρακειμένους λύχνους...καὶ εἶπε· ...τί βούλεταί σοι τὸ τῆς εἰ. ταύτης;...ὁρῶ γάρ σε ἔτι ἐθνικῶς ζῶντα. καὶ...ἀπεκρίνατο...σὺ εἶ, πάτερ, ὁ ἐν τῇ εἰ. γεγραμμένος μοι, ὃν στέφω καὶ φιλῶ καὶ σέβομαι *A.Jo.*27(p.165.27) [cited by iconoclasts, cf.

CNic.(787)act.5(H.4.296D); cf. εἰσφέρει τὸν Λυκομήδην στεφανοῦντα τὴν εἰ. τοῦ ἀποστόλου, ὥσπερ καὶ οἱ Ἕλληνες τὰ εἴδωλα. Βασίλειος... εἶπε· μὴ γένοιτο, ὅτι...Ἰωάννης...ἐναντίον τῷ εὐαγγελίῳ αὐτοῦ ἐφθέγξατο ib.(300C)]; Christians worship Christ as image of invisible God, instead of ἀγάλματα, Or.Cels.8.17(p.235.5; M.11.1544B); τίνα λέγεις καὶ ποίαν ταύτην, ἣν φῄς τοῦ Χριστοῦ εἰ.; οὐκ οἶδα πόθεν αὐτὴ ὁρμηθεῖσα τοῦ σωτῆρος ἡμῶν διαγράψαι εἰ. προστάττεις. ποίαν τοῦ Χριστοῦ εἰ. ἐπιζητεῖς;...ἔστιν ὅτε ἐν ἐκκλησίᾳ τὸ τοιοῦτον ἢ αὐτή, ἢ παρ' ἄλλου τοῦτο ἤκουσας; Eus.ep.Constant.(M.20.1545A,1548C); ἡμεῖς διὰ τῶν...γραφῶν τῆς τῶν ἁγίων ἀπολαύομεν συνουσίας, οὐχὶ τῶν σωμάτων αὐτῶν, ἀλλὰ τῶν ψυχῶν τὰς εἰ. ἔχοντες Chrys.hom. in Ps.145:2(5.527C) cited at CCP(754)decr.(H.4.396B), but v. ib. infra; cf. *inveni velum pendens in foribus ejusdem ecclesiae...et habens imaginem quasi Christi, vel sancti cujusdam;...cum ergo vidissem, et detestatus essem in ecclesia Christi contra auctoritatem scripturarum hominis pendere imaginem, scidi illud*, Epiph. ep.(M.43.390C,391A); μνήμην ἔχετε...τοῦ μὴ ἀναφέρειν εἰκόνας ἐπ' ἐκκλησίας, μήτε ἐν τοῖς κοιμητηρίοις τῶν ἁγίων...οὐκ ἔξεστι γὰρ Χριστιανῷ δι' ὀφθαλμῶν μετεωρίζεσθαι CNic.(787)refut.(H.4.389D); [cf. εἰ δὲ φῄς...Ἐπιφάνιον...ταύτας ἀπαγορεῦσαι,...παραγεγραμμένος καὶ ἐπίπλαστος ὁ λόγος, ἄλλου μὲν ὢν πόνος...δεύτερον...τάχα τοιοῦτό τι καὶ ὁ...Ἐπιφάνιος ἐπιδιορθώσασθαι θέλων, τὸ μὴ χρῆναι ποιεῖν εἰ. ἐνομοθέτησεν, εἴ γε καὶ αὐτοῦ δῶμεν εἶναι τὸν λόγον Jo.D. imag.1.25(M.94.1257A,B); ib.2.18(1305A)]; ὅσοι δὲ...τῶν πλουτώντων ...τὴν εὐαγγελικὴν ἱστορίαν τοῖς ὑφανταῖς παρέδωκαν...ἐκεῖνα πωλήσαντες, τὰς ζώσας εἰ. τοῦ θεοῦ τιμησάτωσαν. μὴ γράφε τὸν Χριστὸν ...ἐπὶ δὲ τῆς ψυχῆς...τὸν ἀσώματον λόγον περίφερε Ast.Am.hom.1 (M.40.168A,B), but v. ib. infra; τὰς τῶν ἁγίων ἰδέας οὐκ ἐν εἰ. ... ἀναμορφοῦν παρειλήφαμεν, ἀλλὰ τὰς τούτων ἀρετὰς...οἷόν τινας ἐμψύχους εἰ. ἀναμάττεσθαι δεδιδάγμεθα Thdot.Anc.ap.CNic.(787)act. 6(404E); prohibited by Philoxenus, Jo.Diacr.fr.h.e.(H.4.305D); Thphn.chron.p.115(M.108.325C); portrayal of God always disallowed, cf.†Gr.II Papa ep.Leon.1(H.4.5D); cf.Jo.D.imag.1.4(M.94. 1236C), ib.1.16(1245A) citt. s. εἰκονίζω; θεοῦ μὲν γὰρ τοῦ ἀσωμάτου καὶ ἀοράτου...ἀδύνατον ποιεῖν εἰ. ib.2.7(1289C); **3.** use of εἰκόνες; **a.** of cross or sign of cross, cf.Eus.v.C.3.49(p.98.19; M.20.1109B); Juln. Imp.ap.Cyr.Juln.6(6^2.194C) cit. s. σταυρός; cf. ἀθανάτου βασιλέως εἰ. ὁ σταυρός †Sever.cruc.(p.899.2); cf.Nil.epp.4.61(M.79.577D); **b.** Christian symbols on signet-rings, cf.Clem.paed.3.11(p.270.7; M. 8.633A); v. σφραγίς; **c.** in Gnost. cults (Carpocratian) cf. *imagines quasdam depictas...habent, dicentes formam Christi factam a Pilato ...et has coronant, et proponunt eas cum imaginibus mundi philosophorum...et observantiam circa eas, similiter ut gentes, faciunt*, Iren.haer.1.25.5(M.7.685B); Epiph.haer.27.6(p.310.14; M.41.373C); Simonian, cf.Eus.ep.Constant.(M.20.1548D); Manich. τὸν τῆς μανίας ἐπώνυμον ὑπὸ τῶν Μανιχαίων εἰκόνι δορυφορούμενον ib.; **d.** orthodox legend of portrait of Christ obtained by Abgar and preserved at Edessa, Ep.Abg.5(p.282.23); A.Thadd.3(p.274.17); [cf.Evagr.h.e. 4.27(p.175.7; M.86.2748C); Jo.D.imag.1.27(M.94.1261B); ‡Jo.D.ep. Thphl.5(M.95.352C)]; cf. τὰς μὲν ἀπὸ χρυσοῦ κατεσκευασμένας εἰ. τοὺς αὐτοῦ ἀγγέλους [cited by Jo. D. as τῶν ἀγγέλων]...εἰς τιμὴν καὶ δόξαν αὐτοῦ ποιηθέντας νοοῦμεν [where no reference to actual images] Meth. res.2.24(p.379.17; M.18.289B)ap.Jo.D.imag.3.42(1420B); supposed image of Christ at Paneas, Eus.h.e.7.18.3(M.20.680C); [cf.Philost. h.e.7.3(M.65.537Cff.); Gr.II Papa ep.Germ.(M.98.149C); Germ.CP ep.dogm.4(M.98.185D)]; early images of apostles, Eus.h.e.7.18.4 (680C) v. infra 4; martyr's picture ἀνάστητε...ζωγράφοι· τὴν τοῦ στρατηγοῦ κολοβωθεῖσαν εἰ. ... μεγαλύνατε τέχναις...ἐγγραφέσθω τῷ πίνακι καὶ ὁ...ἀγωνοθέτης Χριστός Bas.hom.17.3(2.141B; M.31.489A); †Bas.ep.360(3.463A; M.32.1100B); cf. ὁ ἅγιος Βασίλειος, τί εἶχεν ἀνάγκην...καταβαλέσθαι εἰς Καισάρειαν, ἵνα ἱστορήσῃ τὴν εἰ. τοῦ Χριστοῦ; ‡Jo.D.Const.6(M.95.321D); picture of Abraham's sacrifice, Gr.Nyss.deit.(M.46.572C); cf.Germ.CP ep.dogm.4(176C); of martyr ἐπέχρωσε...ζωγράφος...ἐν εἰ. διαγραψάμενος, τὰς ἀριστείας τοῦ μάρτυρος Gr.Nyss.Thdr.(M.46.737D); ἐν δακτυλίων σφενδόναις καὶ ἐν ἐκτυπώμασι, καὶ ἐν φιάλαις, καὶ ἐν θαλάμων τοίχοις, καὶ πανταχοῦ τὴν εἰ. τὴν ἁγίαν ἐκείνην διεχάραξαν πολλοί Chrys.pan.Melet.1(2. 519D); cf.Ast.Am.hom.11(M.40.337A); legend of S. Luke's portrait of BMV, Thdr.Lect.h.e.1.1(M.86.165A); cf.‡Jo.D.Const.6(M.95. 321C); ‡Jo.D.ep.Thphl.4(M.95.349C); portrait of Christ fashioned by pagan duplicity in style of Zeus, Thdr.Lect.h.e.1.15(M.86. 173A); picture of a miracle, Evagr.h.e.4.26(p.173.26; M.86.2745B); of a saint, Niceph.Ur.v.Sym.171(M.86.3144B); of Christ, CTrull.can. 82 cit. s. ἀμνός; religious images before imperial palace, Germ.CP ep.dogm.4(M.98.185A); 'holy images', 1Apoc.Jo.13(p.80); images of bishops etc. in churches, Thdr.Lect.h.e.2.29(200A); id.fr.(M. 86.220Aff.); cf. Manich. use (v. c supra); **4.** veneration of images; Gnost., Iren.haer.1.25.5(M.7.685B); A.Jo.27(p.166.5); cf.Eus.h.e.7. 18.4(M.20.680C); τοὺς χαρακτῆρας τῶν εἰ. αὐτῶν τιμῶ καὶ προσκυνῶ †Bas.ep.360(3.463A; M.32.1100C); prayer before image, Helladius v.Basilii ap.Jo.D.imag.1.27(M.94.1277B); of Theodosius I προσκυνητὴς τῆς ἁγίας τριάδος, καὶ τῆς Χριστοῦ εἰ. ‡Jo.D.ep.Thphl.28(M. 95.381A); ὁρῶ...εἰ. τῆς...θεοτόκου ἑστῶσαν, καί φημι πρὸς αὐτήν· παρθένε, κτλ. ‡Sophr.H.v.Mar.Aeg.23(M.87.3713B); προσκυνήσας [sc. Abgar] τὴν εἰ. ... ἰάθη A.Thadd.4(p.275.1); ῥίψας ἑαυτὸν ἔμπροσθεν τῆς εἰ. τῆς θεοτόκου...ἔλεγε v.Danieli ap.Jo.D.imag.3.42(1416D); cf. πόσης...ἄξιοί εἰσι καταδίκης...οἱ εἰς τὴν εἰ. τοῦ υἱοῦ...καὶ τῆς...θεοτόκου...τετολμηκότες; Sym.Styl.J.ep.Just.(M.86.3217A); cf.id.imag. (M.86.3220A); λέγει...ὁ δαίμων, μὴ προσκυνήσῃς ταύτῃ τῇ εἰ., καὶ οὐκ ἔτι σε πολεμῶ. εἶχεν δὲ ἡ εἰ. τὸ ἐκτύπωμα τῆς δεσποίνης Jo. Mosch.prat.45(M.87.2900B); Sophr.H.mir.Cyr.et Jo.36(M.87.3557D); ἀχράντῳ καὶ τιμίᾳ εἰ. σου...Χριστέ ‡Ath.imag.Beryt.6(M.28.801D); τὰς θείας μορφώσεις τῶν ἁγίων εἰ. ... ἀσπάζεσθαι Anast.S.synax.(M. 89.832C); Leont.N.serm.3(M.93.1604C); †Gr.II Papa ep.Leon.1(H.4. 5C); prayers offered to Christ, BMV, and saints before their pictures, ib.(8A,B); with lights and incense ἔμπροσθεν τῶν εἰ. τῶν ἁγίων φωταγωγίαν γίνεσθαι καὶ εὐώδη θυμίασιν Germ.CP ep.dogm.4(M.98. 184B); cf.Niceph.Ur.v.Sym.170(M.86.3144A); Steph.Diac.v.Steph. (M.100.1076B–D); ib.(1080A); **5.** miraculous images, Thdr.Lect.fr. (M.86.225C); ἔχρισεν ἀμφοτέρους τῷ ἁγίῳ ἐλαίῳ, τοῦ τε τιμίου σταυροῦ, τοῦ τε τῆς ἁγίας...Μαρίας, τοῦ βρύοντος ἐκ τῆς ἁγίας εἰ. αὐτῆς τῆς οὔσης ἐν Σωζοπόλει Eustrat.v.Eutych.45(M.86.2328A); miracles of Abgar's picture of Christ, Evagr.h.e.4.27(p.175.8; M.86.2749A); of Symeon Junior's portrait, Niceph.Ur.v.Sym.171(M.86.3144B); ἔρριψεν εἰς ἓξ αὐτῶν [sc. Σαρακηνῶν] σαγίταν κατὰ τῆς εἰ. τοῦ ἁγίου Θεοδώρου,...καὶ ἐξῆλθεν αἷμα, καὶ κατῆλθεν ἕως κάτω τῆς εἰ. Anast. S.ap.Jo.D.imag.3.42(M.94.1393A); πόσαι ἀναβλύσεις, πολλάκις δὲ καὶ αἱμάτων ῥύσεις ἐξ εἰ. ... γεγόνασι; Leont.N.serm.3(M.93.1601D); μύρα πολλάκις ἔβλυσαν αἱ ἅγιαι εἰ. ‡Ath.qu.Ant.39(M.28.621C); αὐτὴν [sc. λόγχην] ἄραντες...ἐκέντησαν κατὰ τῆς πλευρᾶς τῆς εἰ. τοῦ σωτῆρος. παρευθὺ δὲ ἐξέβλυσεν αἷμα καὶ ὕδωρ ‡Ath.imag.Beryt.4(M. 28.801A); Germ.CP ep.dogm.4(M.98.185B); of S. Luke's portrait of BMV πολλὰ σημεῖα καὶ...τέρατα ἐν τῇ τῆς...θεομήτορος εἰ. ... διαδείκνυνται ‡Jo.D.ep.Thphl.4(M.95.352B); **6.** iconoclasm and protests against cult of images; by Philoxenus, v. supra 2; images of Christ and BMV removed by Jezid II (720–4) at instigation of Jews, Thphn.chron.p.336(M.108.812A); cf.‡Jo.D.ep.Thphl.9(M.95. 356D); cf. ψιλῇ τῇ τοῦ γράμματος θεωρίᾳ ἐν τῇ τῶν...γραφῶν ἀναγνώσει προσκεχηνώς [sc. Constantine, bishop of Nacoleia],...σύνδρομοι καὶ ἕτεροι τοῦ ἱερατικοῦ καταλόγου γεγόνασιν...κακουργότατα πειρῶνται τοὺς τῶν ἁγίων χαρακτῆρας μεταφέρειν ἐπὶ τὰ εἴδωλα Germ.CP syn.haer.40(M.98.77A–C); proceedings of Leo III σὺ εἶ ὁ διώκτης τῶν εἰ. καὶ ὑβριστὴς καὶ καταλυτής †Gr.II Papa ep.Leon.1(H.4.9D); Thphn.chron.p.339(M.108.817A); θὴρ καὶ λεοντώνυμος...εἶπεν· εἰδωλικῆς τεχνουργίας ὑπαρχούσης τῆς τῶν εἰ. ἀνατυπώσεως, οὐ δεῖ ταύτας προσκυνεῖν Steph.Diac.v.Steph.(M.100.1084C); cf.‡Jo.D.ep. Thphl.12(360B); πυρπολεῖ [sc. Constantine Copronymus] ἁπάσας ἁγίων εἰ. θέαν ib.(360C); iconoclasts' anathema ὁ δὲ τολμῶν... κατασκευάσαι εἰ., ἢ προσκυνῆσαι, ἢ στῆσαι ἐν ἐκκλησίᾳ, ἢ ἐν ἰδιωτικῷ οἴκῳ...ἀναθεματιζέσθω...ὡς ἐναντίος τῶν τοῦ θεοῦ προσταγμάτων, καὶ ἐχθρὸς τῶν πατρικῶν δογμάτων CCP(754)decr.(H.4.417B); ib. (425A); εἴ τις τῆς τοῦ θεοῦ λόγου φύσεως καὶ τῆς σαρκὸς τὴν ἀδιαίρετον καθ' ὑπόστασιν ἕνωσιν...ἐν εἰ. πειρᾶται γράφειν, ὀνομάζων αὐτὴν Χριστὸν...ἀνάθεμα ib.(425D); **7.** iconoclastic arguments; **a.** man alone the earthly image of God, CNic.(787)act.6(H.4.333A); **b.** portrayal of Christ implies Nestorian separation of humanity from divinity, ib.(353D); cf.‡Jo.D.Const.4(M.95.317D); **c.** portrayal of Christ implies monophysite confusion of humanity and deity, latter being uncircumscribed, CNic.(787)refut.(H.4.361C); ib.(424E); **d.** eucharistic elements the only proper image of Christ, CCP(754) decr.(H.4.369A); **e.** purport of second commandment, cf.Jo.D.imag. 1.7(M.94.1288D); **8.** use and veneration defended; **a.** veneration offered not to images but to those whom they depict, Sym.Styl.J. imag.(M.86.3220A); οὐδὲ παρ' ἡμῖν ὡς θεοὶ προσκυνοῦνται οἱ τῶν ἁγίων...εἰ. ... ὡς δὲ φίλους αὐτοῦ [sc. προσκυνοῦμεν] τοὺς ἀποστόλους ...καὶ λοιποὺς ἁγίους Leont.N.serm.3(M.93.1597C,1600A); ἐγὼ μὲν προσκυνῶν εἰ. λέγω δόξα σοι ὁ θεὸς τῶν ἁγίων, καὶ οὐ λέγω δόξα σοι ξύλον ἢ ζωγραφία Dial.Christ.et Jud.(p.74.16); Germ.CP ep.dogm.4 (M.98.181D); Jo.Thess.fr.(H.4.292D); ‡Ath.qu.Ant.39(M.28.621B); ἡ γὰρ τιμὴ τῆς εἰ. εἰς Χριστὸν ἀνατρέχει ‡Jo.D.Const.3(M.95.317C); εἴ τις τὴν κατὰ τὴν εἰ. σχετικὴν προσκύνησιν τοῦ Χριστοῦ, εἰδώλων προσκύνησιν...ἀποφαίνοι, καὶ οὐκ αὐτοῦ Χριστοῦ...αἱρετικός ἐστιν Thdr.Stud.

antirr.1.20(M.99.349C); *ib*.3.3.14(425D); id.*ep.imag*.(M.99.504C); Bas. *Spir*.45(3.38C; M.32.149C) [ἡ τῆς εἰ. τιμὴ ἐπὶ τὸ πρωτότυπον διαβαίνει (which really refers to honours paid to emperor's image as illustrating Trin. worship)] cited to support above doctrine, Jo.D. *imag*.1.21(M.94.1252D); *ib*.1.27(1261D); *ib*.3.42(1361B); Gr.II Papa *ep.Germ*.(M.98.149B); CNic.(787)*refut*.(H.4.360C); ‡Jo.D.*Const*.3 (317B); ‡Jo.D.*ep.Thphl*.30(M.95.384C); Steph.Diac.*v.Steph*.(M.100. 1113B); Thdr.Stud.*antirr*.1.8(337D); **b.** veneration offered is relative, and not λάτρεια, †Gr.II Papa *ep.Leon*.1(H.4.5C); cf.Jo.D.*imag*. 1.8(M.94.1240B); *ib*.1.14(1244A); *ib*.3.41(1357Aff.); Taras.*ep*.1(M.98. 1433B,C); Thdr.Stud.*ep.imag*.(M.99.504B); id.*epp*.2.85(M.99.1329A); **c.** purpose of images; **i.** to arouse devotion οὐ προσκυνεῖς εἰ., μηδὲ τῷ υἱῷ τοῦ θεοῦ προσκύνει, ὅς ἐστιν εἰ. τοῦ ἀοράτου θεοῦ ζῶσα... προσκυνῶ Χριστοῦ εἰ., ὡς σεσαρκωμένου θεοῦ· τῆς δεσποίνης...οἷα μητρὸς τοῦ υἱοῦ...τῶν ἁγίων ὡς φίλων θεοῦ...τούτων τὰς ἀριστείας... ἀναγράπτους καθίστημι, ὡς δι' αὐτῶν ἁγιαζόμενος, καὶ πρὸς ζῆλον μιμήσεως ἀλειφόμενος Jo.D.*imag*.1.21(M.94.1252C,D); ‡Jo.D.*Const*.10 (M.95.328A,B); θύρα δὲ ἡ εἰ. λέγεται, ἥτις διανοίγει τὸν κατὰ θεὸν κτισθέντα νοῦν ἡμῶν πρὸς τὴν ἔνδον τοῦ πρωτοτύπου καθομοίωσιν Steph.Diac.*v.Steph*.(M.100.1113A); ὅταν δὲ ἴδω εἰ. ἀποστόλου ἢ μάρτυρος...ἱστορίαν τῶν παθημάτων αὐτῶν...λέγω· δόξα σοι, ὁ θεὸς τοῦδε ἀποστόλου Jo.V H.*icon*.15(M.96.1360D); τὸ αἰσθητὸν ὄμμα πρὸς τὴν εἰ. ἀτενῶς βλέπων, τὸ νοητὸν τῆς καρδίας ὄμμα σὺν τῷ νῷ εἰς τὸ μυστήριον τῆς ἐνσάρκου οἰκονομίας ἀκοντίζω *ib*.13(1360B); **ii.** to instruct ζωγράφος...ἐν εἰ. διαγραψάμενος τὰς ἀριστείας τοῦ μάρτυρος ...πάντα...ὡς ἐν βιβλίῳ τινὶ γλωττοφόρῳ...τεχνουργησάμενος Gr. Nyss.*Thdr*.(M.46.737D); cf.Jo.D.*imag*.1.27(M.94.1281C); εἰκόνας... βίβλους τῶν ἀγραμμάτων *ib*.2.10(1293C); τοῦτο δ' ἂν καὶ διὰ τοῦ προσέχειν τῇ εἰ. κατὰ τὸν τοῦ εἰ. λόγον γενήσεται. ἃ γὰρ ὁ λόγος τῆς ἱστορίας διὰ τῆς ἀκοῆς παρίστησι, ταῦτα γραφὴ σιωπῶσα διὰ μιμήσεως δείκνυσι Germ.CP *ep.dogm*.4(M.98.172C); **d.** use of images necessitated by practice of invocation of saints, cf.‡Jo.D.*Const*.22(340D); **e.** iconoclasm involves Manichean depreciation of matter, Jo.D. *imag*.1.16(1245Bff.); **f.** veneration of images justified by reference to cult of relics, *ib*.2.19(1305B); and likened to Jewish veneration of roll of Law, Leont.N.*serm*.3(M.93.1600B); **g.** second commandment a temporary, 'paedagogic' law directed agst. Jewish tendency to idolatry; not to be lit. observed by Christians, Jo.D.*imag*.1.8(M. 94.1237C,D); did not exclude making of brazen serpent etc., cf. Sever.ap.Jo.D.*imag*.1.27(1276C); Thdr.Stud.*antirr*.1.6(336A); iconoclasts pervert scripture, ‡Jo.D.*ep.Thphl*.21(M.95.373A); **h.** grace of H. Ghost persists in saints' images, Jo.D.*imag*.1.19(M.94.1249D); ἐν εἰ. εἶναι τὴν θεότητα εἰπών τις οὐκ ἂν ἁμάρτῃ τοῦ δέοντος...ἀλλ' οὐ φυσικῇ ἑνώσει Thdr.Stud.*antirr*.1.12(344B); but εἴ τις προσκυνῶν τὴν εἰ. Χριστοῦ, ἐν αὐτῇ φυσικῶς τὴν θεότητα προσκυνεῖσθαι λέγοι, ἀλλὰ μὴ καθ' ὅσον ἐστὶ σκιὰ τῆς ἑνωθείσης αὐτῇ σαρκός, ἐπεὶ καὶ πανταχοῦ τὸ θεῖον, αἱρετικός ἐστιν *ib*.1.20(349D); **i.** tradition adduced in support, cf.Germ.CP *haer.syn*.41(M.98.77D); from Constantine's time ἐν σανίσιν ἀεὶ...τοῦ ποθουμένου μάρτυρος τὴν εἰ. ἐστηλογράφουν, ἢ καὶ...Χριστοῦ. ἀλλὰ καὶ ἐν ἱεραῖς ἐσθῆσι καὶ ἐν κειμηλίοις αἱ εἰ. παρά τε τῶν ἁγίων πατέρων ἡμῶν...ἀνεζωγραφήνται CNic.(787)*refut*.(H.4.336C,D); cult of images, like many other practices, rests upon tradition, not express words of Christ, ‡Jo.D.*Const*.5(M.95.320B); tradition alleged to go back to apostolic age, Jo.V H.*icon*.16(M.96.1361A); and practice of universal Church, Thdr.Stud.*epp*.2.8(M.99.1132C); **j.** refutation of objections on ground of Nestorianism οὐδεὶς ποτε...ἰδὼν ἀνθρώπου εἰ. ἐλογίσαιτο ὅτι χωρίζεται διὰ τοῦ ζωγράφου ὁ ἄνθρωπος ἐκ τῆς ψυχῆς CNic.(787) *refut*.(H.4.353D); and of monophysitism εἰ συμπεριεγράφη ἀνακειμένου...ἐν φάτνῃ τῇ φύσει τῆς ἀνθρωπότητος ἡ φύσις τῆς θεότητος αὐτοῦ, συμπεριγράφεται καὶ ἐν τῇ...εἰ. τῆς ἀνθρωπότητος...ἡ ἀπερίγραπτος θεότης αὐτοῦ *ib*.(361C); and on ground that eucharistic elements alone are Christ's image οὔτε ὁ κύριος, οὔτε οἱ ἀπόστολοι...εἰ. εἶπον τὴν...θυσίαν, ἀλλὰ αὐτὸ σῶμα καὶ αὐτὸ αἷμα *ib*.(369D); **k.** accusation of idolatry implies failure to distinguish Christian from pagan images, *ib*.(328E); **l.** iconoclasts deny Christ's true humanity, Jo.V H.*icon*.2(M.96.1349C); **m.** Christ's attitude to Caesar's image adduced in support, Jo.D.*imag*.3.11(M.94.1333C); ‡Jo.D.*ep.Thphl*. 24(M.95.376C); Thdr.Stud.*icon*.2(M.99.492C); **n.** possibility of idolatry among ignorant discounted, ‡Jo.D.*Const*.13(M.95.329B,C); **9.** veneration of images officially approved; cf.CNic.(787)*refut*. (H.4.352A); καλῶς εἶναι τὴν τῶν σεπτῶν εἰ. ἀνάθεσιν ἐν τῇ ἐκκλησίᾳ, καὶ πνευματικῶς δι' αὐτῶν ἀνάγεσθαι ἐπὶ τὴν τῶν πρωτοτύπων αὐτῶν ἀνάμνησιν...καὶ τὴν ὀφειλομένην προσκύνησιν ἀπονέμειν...εἰ μή που τὴν κατὰ λατρείαν προσκύνησίν τις ἐννόησεν *ib*.(441C); *Symb.Nic*.(787) (H.4.456A).

II. met.;

A. image as representing a reality; **1.** material likenesses reflecting spiritual realities ἡ σήμερον γὰρ ἀιδίου αἰωνός ἐστιν εἰ. Clem.*prot*. 9(p.64.6; M.8.196C); ἡ δεκάλογος δὲ κατὰ μὲν οὐράνιον εἰ. περιέχει ἥλιον καὶ σελήνην...ἡ δὲ τῆς γῆς εἰ. περιέχει ἀνθρώπους, κτήνη, κτλ. id.*str*.6.16(p.499.19,21; M.9.357C); ἀπὸ...τῶν σωματικῶν, ὡς ἐξ εἰ. ἐναργεστάτης ἀναφοιτᾶν ἀναγκαῖον ἐπὶ τὰ πνευματικά Cyr.*Os*.30(3. 55B); εἰ. ... οὐρανοῦ τὴν λίθον ποιεῖται τὸ γράμμα τὸ ἱερόν id.*ador*.10 (1.380E); τῆς ἀΰλου φωτοδοσίας εἰ., τὰ ὑλικὰ φῶτα Dion.Ar.*c.h*.1.3 (M.3.121D); ταῖς αἰσθηταῖς εἰ. τοὺς ὑπερουρανίους ἀνεγράψατο νοάς *ib*. (124A); id.*d.n*.4.4(M.3.697C); which man needs to lead him to contemplation, id.*e.h*.1.2(M.3.373B); *ib*.1.5(376D); whereas highest angelic orders do not need them, id.*c.h*.7.2(208C) al.; heret. εἰ. δὲ ἐν ἡλίῳ ἑωρᾶσθαι τοιαύτην, οἷόν ἐστι τὸ τοῦ ἀνθρώπου εἶδος Alex.Lyc. *Man*.4(p.7.6; M.18.416D); **2.** of non-material realities of a lower order reflecting those of a higher, Clem.*str*.1.2(p.13.30; M.8.709B) cit. s. φιλοσοφία; *ib*.4.8(p.278.10; 1277B) cit. s. ἐκκλησία; *Hom.Clem*. 2.25; εἰ. ὄντως τῶν ψυχῶν εἰσιν οἱ λόγοι Bas.*ep*.9.1(3.90B; M.32.268C); **3.** of OT as type of NT realities; Jewish and pagan ablutions as image of baptism, Clem.*str*.4.22(p.311.2; M.8.1352B); τὸ θυόμενον πρόβατον Χριστοῦ περιέχει εἰ. Or.*Jo*.10.16(13; p.186.29; M.14.333B); *ib*.13.13(p.237.19; 417C) cit. s. Ἰουδαῖος; τὸν ναὸν εἰ. τυγχάνοντα τοῦ σωτῆρος Heracleon ap.Or.*Jo*.10.38(22; p.214.32; 380B); id.*ib*.10.33 (19; p.206.27; 365C); ὁ τοῦ Ναυῆ Ἰησοῦς τοῦ σωτῆρος ἡμῶν τὴν εἰ. ἔφερεν Eus.*h.e*.1.3.4(M.20.69B); *ib*.1.3.15(73B); ἐκείνη [sc. OT] μὲν ἐν εἰ. τὴν ἀλήθειαν ἔγραψεν Dion.Ar.*e.h*.3.3.5(M.3.432B); sometimes = τύπος and σύμβολον, Eus.*h.e*.1.3.2(69A) cit. s. τύπος; Χριστός... οὐκέτι τύπους οὐδὲ εἰ., ἀλλ' αὐτὰς γυμνὰς ἀρετὰς...παραδούς *ib*.1.3.13 (73A); *ib*.1.2.22(64B); τῶν προφητῶν οἱ μὲν λόγῳ τὸν Χριστὸν προεκήρυξαν...ἄλλοι τῆς οἰκονομίας τύποι ἐγένοντο, ὡς ἐν σκιαγραφίᾳ τὴν εἰ. προδεικνύντες τοῦ μέλλοντος Bas.Sel.*or*.10.1(M.85.137B); **4.** of NT as reflecting divine realities in contrast to mere shades and outlines of OT, Meth.*symp*.5.7(p.62.10; M.18.109C); *ib*.9.2(p.115. 26f.; 180C) cit. s. ἀλήθεια; Cosm.Ind.*top*.5(M.88.193C) cit. s. σκιά; Max.*schol.e.h*.3.3.2(M.4.137D) cit. s. ἀλήθεια; of the Law οὐδὲ εἰ. ἦν ὁ νόμος, ἀλλ' εἰ. προσκίασμα Jo.D.*imag*.1.15(M.94.1244D); **5.** of images in NT; of scourge made by Christ, Heracleon ap.Or.*Jo*. 10.33(19; p.207.10ff.; M.14.368A) cit. s. φραγέλλιον; εἰ. εἰσὶν ὥσπερ αἱ παραβολαὶ [sc. of Christ] πραγμάτων οὐχ ὁρατῶν Cyr.*Lc*.8:4(M. 72.624C); **6.** in gen. of scriptural types, Or.*Jo*.13.59(58; p.290.26; M.14.512B); †Sever.*cruc*.(p.899.21); Jo.D.*imag*.3.22(M.94.1341C) etc.; **7.** liturg.; **a.** of Church and hierarchy (angelic and eccl.) as images of the divine ὁ λεγόμενος ἱεραρχίαν...δηλοῖ εἰ. τῆς θεαρχικῆς ὡραιότητος Dion.Ar.*c.h*.3.2(M.3.165B); αὗται [sc. eccl. hierarchies] δέ εἰσιν αἱ τελεσιουργοὶ τῆς θεαρχικῆς δυνάμεως εἰ. id.*e.h*.5.1.5(M.3. 505B); *ib*.5.1.17(508C); priest as Christ's image, Thdr.Stud.*icon*.4 (M.99.493C,D); bishop, Max.*ep*.30(M.91.624B); ἔστι...ἡ ἁγία ἐκκλησία τύπος, ὡς εἴρηται, καὶ εἰ. τοῦ μὲν θεοῦ id.*myst*.24(M.91.705A); **b.** of sacraments ἡ παροῦσα νῦν ἱερὰ τελετουργία, μόναις ἐν εἰ. ὁρωμένη Dion.Ar.*e.h*.4.3.4(M.3.477B); ἐπὶ τὰς τῶν τελουμένων ἀρχὰς ἀναβλέψαντες...ἐπιγνωσόμεθα τίνων εἰσὶ χαρακτήρων τὰ ἐκτυπώματα, καὶ τίνων ἀφανῶν αἱ εἰ. *ib*.2.3.2(397C); of baptism ἡ δι' ὕδατος ὁλικὴ κάλυψις εἰς τὴν τοῦ θανάτου...εἰ. παρείληπται *ib*.2.3.7(404B); cf. ἀπεδύεσθε τὸν χιτῶνα· καὶ τοῦτο ἦν εἰ. τοῦ τὸν παλαιὸν ἄνθρωπον ἀποδύεσθαι σὺν ταῖς πράξεσιν Cyr.H.*catech*.20.2; of eucharist τὴν εἰ. τοῦ ἰδίου σώματος ποιεῖσθαι παρακελευόμενος Eus.*d.e*.7.1(p.366.21; M.22.596A); μετὰ τὰς εἰ. ... ἐπὶ τὴν θεοειδῆ τῶν ἀρχετύπων ἀλήθειαν Dion.Ar.*e.h*.3.3.1(M.3.428A); εἰ. ἐκάλεσε τῶν ἀληθῶν τὰ νῦν τελούμενα ἐν τῇ συνάξει Max.*schol*.in loc.(M.4.137A); which is an image of spiritual life, Dion.Ar.*e.h*.4.3.4(477B); **8.** of God reflected in creation ἔχει μὲν τὰ αἰτιατὰ τὰς τῶν αἰτίων ἐνδεχομένας εἰ., αὐτὰ δὲ τὰ αἴτια τῶν αἰτιατῶν ἐξῄρηται Dion.Ar.*d.n*.2.8(M.3.645C); *ib*.7.3(869D).

B. of image as inferior to reality; **1.** exeg. Ps.38:7 ἐπειδὴ ἐν εἰ. καὶ οὐκ ἐν ἀληθείᾳ νῦν διαπορεύεται ὁ ἄνθρωπος· ἡ γὰρ ἀληθὴς ζωὴ κατὰ τὸν μέλλοντα αἰῶνά ἐστιν· εἰκότως ὁ ψάλλων τὴν εἰ. ματαιότητα προσεῖπεν Ath.*fr.Pss.comm*.38:7(M.27.557D) = Cyr.*Ps*.38:7(M.69. 976B); as characteristic of transitoriness, Thdt.in loc.(1.852); Ps.72:20 ἡ εἰ. πρόσκαιρον ἔχει τὸ ἄνθος· εἰ. τοίνυν ἀπεικάζει τῶν Βαβυλωνίων τὴν δυναστείαν, εἰς ὀλίγον ἀρκέσασαν χρόνον id.in loc. (1119); **2.** in depreciatory sense, '*figment of the imagination*' τὴν εἰ. ἔλαθεν περιφέρουσα τοῦ πάθους ἡ ψυχή Clem.*str*.2.20(p.174.3; M.8. 1056B); id.*paed*.2.2(p.168.22; M.8.412B); μήτε...ἐμπαθῶς ἐμπαγῆναι τῶν εἰ. ταπεινότητας Dion.Ar.*c.h*.2.2(M.3.140A); Max.*cap*.3.52(M.90. 1284A); **3.** *mere image*; of Christ's humanity in Eutychian teaching, Leo Mag.*ep*.30(p.46.10; M.*PL*.54.788B) cit. s. IV.E infra.

C. *pattern, example*; **1.** of Christ οὗτος ἡμῖν εἰ. ἡ ἀκηλίδωτος, τούτῳ

...πειρατέον ἐξομοιοῦν τὴν ψυχήν Clem.*paed*.1.2(p.91.25; M.8.252C); πεποίηκεν ἃ ἐδίδαξεν, ἵνα ἕκαστος...ἐν εἰ. δὲ βλέπων λαμβάνῃ παρ' αὐτοῦ τὸ παράδειγμα τοῦ ποιεῖν Ath.*ep.Marcell*.13(M.27.25A); **2.** in gen. γέγονεν...ἡ Σοδομιτῶν δικαία τιμωρία τῆς εὐλογίστου τοῖς ἀνθρώποις σωτηρίας εἰ. Clem.*paed*.3.8(p.262.12; M.8.616B); *ib*.(p.262.25; 616C); of Noah ἀρχέτυπος εἰ., ζῶσα καὶ ἔμψυχος,...ὑπόδειγμα τρόπου θεοφιλοῦς παρεσχημένος Eus.*p.e*.7.8(309A; M.21.524A); ἡ ἐν παραδείσῳ διαγωγή, νηστείας ἐστὶν εἰ. Bas.*hom*.1.3(2.3B; M.31.168A); Nil.*epp*.1.232(M.79.168C); πρὸς δὲ τὴν ἀρχέτυπον εἰ. τῆς ἀποστολικῆς ζωῆς ἀποσκοπῶν Thdr.Stud.*or*.11.22(M.99.824D); **3.** *pattern* of thought δείξω σοι τὸν λόγον καὶ τοῦ λόγου τὰ μυστήρια, κατὰ τὴν σὴν διηγούμενος εἰ. Clem.*prot*.12(p.84.7; M.8.240B).

D. *description* ἔγγραπτον τὴν εἰ. τοῦ παραπτώματος ἔχοντες Clem.*paed*.2.2(p.177.16; M.8.432A).

III. of image of God in man; in def. of man ἄνθρωπός ἐστιν ποίημα θεοῦ λογικόν, κατ' εἰκόνα γενόμενον τοῦ κτίσαντος αὐτόν ‡Bas.*struct.hom*.1.16(1.330D; M.30.24D);

A. Persons of Godhead mirrored in soul; **1.** Trin., cf.Nil.*epp*.1.174(M.79.152A); Bas.Sel.*or*.1.3(M.85.36A); ἔχει γὰρ αὐτὴ [sc. ψυχή] καὶ τὸ λογικόν, καὶ τὸ ζωτικὸν ἐν ἑαυτῇ· καὶ γεννᾷ μὲν ὁ νοῦς τὸν λόγον, συμπρόεισι δὲ τῷ λόγῳ πνεῦμα, οὐ γεννώμενον καθάπερ ὁ λόγος, συμπαρομαρτοῦν δὲ ἀεὶ τῷ λόγῳ, καὶ συμπροϊὸν γεννωμένῳ. ἀλλὰ ταῦτα ὡς ἐν εἰ. πρόσεστι τῷ ἀνθρώπῳ· οὗ δὴ χάριν καὶ ἀνυπόστατος ὁ λόγος ἐστί, καὶ τὸ πνεῦμα Thdt.*qu.20 in Gen*.(1.28); τὸ κυριώτατον τοῦ κατ' εἰ. καὶ ὁμοίωσιν...τὸ μοναδικὸν τῆς ἐν τριάδι θεότητος...εὔδηλον ὅτι ἡ ἡμετέρα πάλιν ψυχή, καὶ ὁ ταύτης νοερὸς λόγος, καὶ ὁ νοῦς...ἀγέννητος...ἐστὶν ἡ ψυχὴ καὶ ἀναίτιος εἰς τύπον τοῦ ἀγεννήτου καὶ ἀναιτίου θεοῦ καὶ πατρός· οὐκ ἀγέννητος δὲ ὁ νοερὸς αὐτῆς λόγος, ἀλλ' ἐξ αὐτῆς γεννώμενος...ἀπαθῶς, εἰς τύπον τοῦ γεννητοῦ υἱοῦ· ὁ δὲ νοῦς οὐδὲ ἀναίτιός ἐστιν, οὐδὲ γεννητός, ἀλλ' ἐκπορευτός...καὶ ἀοράτως ψηλαφῶν, κατ' εἰ. καὶ ὁμοίωσιν τοῦ παναγίου καὶ ἐκπορευτοῦ πνεύματος ‡Anast.S.*serm.imag*.1(M.89.1148B,C); cf. αἱ τρεῖς...πάσης τῆς ἀνθρωπότητος ὁμοούσιοι ὑποστάσεις, κατ' εἰ. τινά, ὡς καὶ Μεθοδίῳ δοκεῖ, τυπικῶς γεγόνασι τῆς ἁγίας καὶ ὁμοουσίου τριάδος· τοῦ μὲν ἀναιτίου καὶ ἀγεννήτου Ἀδάμ, τύπον καὶ εἰ. ἔχοντος, τοῦ ἀναιτίου...πατρός· τοῦ δὲ γεννητοῦ αὐτοῦ υἱοῦ, εἰ. ... τοῦ γεννητοῦ υἱοῦ...τοῦ θεοῦ· τῆς δὲ ἐκπορευτῆς Εὔας, σημαινούσης τὴν τοῦ ἁγίου πνεύματος ἐκπορευτὴν ὑπόστασιν...οὐκοῦν ἔχεις τὸ κατ' εἰ. ... τυπικὴν τριάδα ἐν μονάδι, ἐν τρισὶν ὑποστάσεσιν *ib*.(M.89.1145B,C); **2.** second Person ὁρᾶται...ὡς ἐν εἰ. τινὶ καὶ τύπῳ, λέγω ἐν τῷ ἀνθρώπῳ, καὶ διττή τις ἐνεργείας ἔμφασις εἰς εἰ. ... Χριστοῦ· καθάπερ γὰρ ἡ αὐτοῦ θεότης ἐνήργει, καὶ θεανδρικῶς ἐνήργει καὶ θεϊκῶς ἐν οὐρανῷ πρὸ τῆς τοῦ σώματος ἀναπλάσεως...οὕτω καὶ ἡ ψυχὴ ἡ κατ' εἰ. καὶ ὁμοίωσιν τοῦ ἀοράτου θεοῦ λόγου ὑπάρχουσα, ἐνεργεῖ μὲν καὶ ψυχανδρικῶς, τουτέστι σωματοψύχως, εἰς τύπον τοῦ θεανδρικῶς Χριστοῦ *ib*.1(1148D–1149A); cf.Anast.S.*serm.imag*.(M.89.1161C); **3.** third Person τὸ...τὴν θείαν ἡμῖν ἐγχαράττον εἰ., καὶ σημάντρου δίκην ἐμποιοῦν τὸ ὑπερκόσμιον κάλλος, οὐχὶ τὸ πνεῦμά ἐστιν; ἀλλ' οὐχ ὡς θεός, φησίν, ἀλλ' ὡς θείας χάριτος ὑπουργόν. οὐκ αὐτὸ τοιγαροῦν ἡμῖν, ἀλλ' ἡ δι' αὐτοῦ χάρις ἐνσημαίνεται...ἦν οὖν ἀναγκαῖον, εἰ. τῆς χάριτος, καὶ οὐχὶ μᾶλλον εἰ. θεοῦ διακεκλῆσθαι τὸν ἄνθρωπον Cyr.*dial.Trin*.7(5^1.638B,C).

B. of what is made in divine image and in what it consists; **1.** soul or rational part of man (prevalent conception of Alexandrian school), cf.*M.Apollon*.8; εἰ. ... τοῦ θεοῦ ὁ λόγος αὐτοῦ...εἰ. δὲ τοῦ λόγου ὁ ἄνθρωπος ὁ ἀληθινός, ὁ νοῦς ὁ ἐν ἀνθρώπῳ, ὁ κατ' εἰκόνα τοῦ θεοῦ καὶ καθ' ὁμοίωσιν διὰ τοῦτο γεγενῆσθαι λεγόμενος Clem.*prot*.10(p.71.24ff.; M.8.212C–213A); εἰ. ... θεοῦ λόγος θεῖος...εἰ. δ' εἰκόνος ἀνθρώπινος νοῦς id.*str*.5.14(p.388.14ff.; M.9.140A); *ib*.7.14(p.61.25; 520B); Eus.*Marcell*.2.3(p.49.7; M.24.805C); interpretation defended against pagan philosophers by stressing difference between εἰκών (Christ) and man created κατ' εἰ.: ὁ Κέλσος, μὴ ἐνιδὼν τῇ διαφορᾷ τοῦ κατ' εἰ. θεοῦ καὶ τῆς εἰ. αὐτοῦ, ὅτι εἰ. μὲν τοῦ θεοῦ ὁ πρωτότοκος πάσης κτίσεώς ἐστιν ὁ αὐτολόγος...κατ' εἰ. δὲ τοῦ θεοῦ ὁ ἄνθρωπος πεποίηται,...ἀλλ' οὐδ' ἐπιστήσας [sc. Celsus], ἐν τίνι τῶν τοῦ ἀνθρώπου τὸ κατ' εἰ. τοῦ θεοῦ χαρακτηρίζεται,...φησὶ τὸ οὐδ' ἄνθρωπον ἐποίησεν εἰ. αὐτοῦ· οὐ γὰρ τοιόσδε ὁ θεὸς οὔτ' ἄλλῳ εἴδει οὐδενὶ ὅμοιος. οἷον δ' ἐστὶ τοῦ συνθέτου ἀνθρώπου τῷ χείρονι μέρει, λέγω δὲ τῷ σώματι, νομίζειν ἐνυπάρχειν τὸ κατ' εἰ. τοῦ θεοῦ, ὡς δ' ὁ Κέλσος ἐξείληφεν, αὐτὸ εἶναι τὸ κατ' εἰ. αὐτοῦ; εἰ γὰρ τὸ κατ' εἰ. τοῦ θεοῦ ἐν τῷ σώματί ἐστι μόνῳ, ἐστέρηται τὸ κρεῖττον, ἡ ψυχή, τοῦ κατ' εἰ. καὶ ἔστιν ἐν τῷ φθαρτῷ σώματι, ὅπερ οὐδεὶς ἡμῶν λέγει. εἰ δ' ἐστὶν ἐν τῷ συναμφοτέρῳ τὸ κατ' εἰ. τοῦ θεοῦ, ἀνάγκη σύνθετον εἶναι τὸν θεόν...λείπεται δὴ τὸ κατ' εἰ. τοῦ θεοῦ ἐν τῷ καθ' ἡμᾶς λεγομένῳ ἔσω ἀνθρώπῳ καὶ ἀνακαινουμένῳ καὶ πεφυκότι γίνεσθαι κατ' εἰ. τοῦ κτίσαντος νοεῖσθαι Or.*Cels*.6.63(p.133.7–134.5; M.11.1393B–1396A); cf.id.*hom.1.13 in Gen*.(p.15.9; M.12.155D); *ib*.*13.3*(p.118.17; 234A); τῷ γηΐνῳ γὰρ τὴν ψυχὴν ἥνωσε [sc. ὁ θεός] τὴν κατ' εἰ. θεοῦ γεγενημένην Meth.*res*.2.24(p.380.5; M.18.329C); πῶς δὲ τό, κατ' εἰ. θεοῦ, νοητέον; οὐδέν τι σωματικὸν καὶ γήϊνον ἐννοήσασθαι χρή ‡Bas.*struct.hom*.1.4(1.325F; M.30.13D); νοερὰν ψυχὴν καὶ εἰ. θεοῦ οἶδεν ὁ λόγος Gr.Naz.*or*.45.7(M.36.632A); vindicated esp. against Anthropomorphitae ἔστι...ὁμολογουμένως κατ' εἰ. θεοῦ ὁ ἄνθρωπος, ἡ δὲ ὁμοιότης οὐ σωματική· ὁ γὰρ θεὸς ἐστιν ἀσώματος...τὸ δὲ κατ' εἰ. θεοῦ πεποιῆσθαι τὸν ἄνθρωπον, ἑτέρας ἐμφάσεις...ἔχει. μόνος γὰρ αὐτὸς παρὰ πάντα τὰ ἐπὶ γῆς ζῷα λογικός ἐστι...ἐπιτηδειότητα πρὸς πᾶσαν ἀρετὴν ἔχων, λαχὼν δὲ καὶ τὸ ἄρχειν ἁπάντων τῶν ἐπὶ τῆς γῆς καθ' ὁμοιότητα καὶ εἰ. θεοῦ. οὐκοῦν κατὰ τὸ εἶναι ζῷον λογικὸν...ἐν εἰ. θεοῦ πεποιῆσθαι λέγεται. εἰ δὲ νομίζουσι κατὰ τὸ τοῦ σώματος σχῆμα λέγεσθαι τὴν εἰ. οὐδὲν λυπεῖ καὶ τοῖς ἀλόγοις τῶν ζῴων σύμμορφον εἶναι τὸν θεόν Cyr.*ep.Calos*.(6^2.364A–365A); Max.*ep*.6(M.91.429B); **2.** image impressed on whole human compound πρὸς ἰδιότητα τῆς τελείας φύσεως δι' ἀμφοῖν ἀφιγμένῳ, ψυχῆς δὴ λέγω καὶ σώματος, καθάπερ καὶ σφραγῖδα τῆς ἑαυτοῦ φύσεως ἐνέπηξεν ὁ δημιουργὸς τὸ πνεῦμα ἅγιον, τουτέστι, τὴν πνοὴν τῆς ζωῆς, δι' ἧς πρὸς τὸ ἀρχέτυπον διεπλάττετο κάλλος, ἀπετελεῖτο δὲ κατ' εἰ. τοῦ κτίσαντος, πρὸς πᾶσαν ἰδέαν ἀρετῆς δυνάμει τοῦ ἐνοικισθέντος αὐτῷ διακρατούμενος πνεύματος Cyr.*Jo*.9.1(4.822D,E); **3.** freedom from necessity as special characteristic; (view of Gr. Nyss., who places creation of man 'in image' before distinction of sexes), Gr.Nyss.*hom.opif*.16.3–7(M.44.180B–181A); ἐπεὶ δὲ πολὺς τῶν καθ' ἕκαστον ἀγαθῶν ὁ κατάλογος...περιληπτικῇ φωνῇ ἅπαντα συλλαβὼν ὁ λόγος ἐσήμανεν, ἐν τῷ εἰπεῖν, κατ' εἰ. θεοῦ γεγενῆσθαι τὸν ἄνθρωπον...ἓν δὲ τῶν πάντων καὶ τὸ ἐλεύθερον ἀνάγκης εἶναι, καὶ μὴ ὑπεζεῦχθαί τινι φυσικῇ δυναστείᾳ· ἀλλ' αὐτεξούσιον πρὸς τὸ δοκοῦν ἔχειν τὴν γνώμην *ib*.16.10(184B); εἰ. ἦν καὶ ὁμοίωμα...τῆς πάντων τῶν ὄντων βασιλευούσης δυνάμεως. καὶ διὰ τοῦτο καὶ ἐν τῷ αὐτεξουσίῳ τῆς προαιρέσεως πρὸς τὸν ἐξουσιάζοντα πάντων εἶχε τὴν ὁμοιότητα, οὐδεμιᾷ τινι τῶν ἔξωθεν ἀνάγκῃ δεδουλωμένος id.*virg*.12(p.298.10; M.46.369C); αὐτοπροαίρετος ὤν, καὶ τὰς τῶν ἰδίων θελημάτων πεπιστευμένος ἡνίας· μοῖρα γὰρ τῆς εἰ. καὶ αὐτή, κατεξουσιάζει γὰρ τῶν οἰκείων θελημάτων θεός Cyr.*Jo*.9.1(4.822E); **4.** dominion over creation (emphasized esp. by Antiochene school) ὅπου...ἡ τοῦ ἄρχειν δύναμις, ἐκεῖ ἡ τοῦ θεοῦ εἰ. ‡Bas.*struct.hom*.1.8(1.328D; M.30.20C); τινὲς κατ' εἰ. θεοῦ τὸν ἄνθρωπον ἐνόμισαν κατὰ τὸ τῆς ψυχῆς ἀόρατον. καὶ οὐ συνῆκαν, ὅτι καὶ ἄγγελος ἀόρατος, καὶ δαίμων ἀόρατος...πῶς οὖν θεοῦ εἰ. ὁ ἄνθρωπος; κατὰ τὸ ἀρχικόν Diod.*Gen*.1:26(M.33.1564C,D); ἐμάθετε τί ἐστι τό, κατ' εἰ., ὅτι οὐκ οὐσίας ἐστὶν ἀξία, ἀλλ' ἀρχῆς ὁμοιότης, καὶ ὅτι οὐ κατὰ τὴν τῆς μορφῆς εἰ. εἶπεν, ἀλλὰ κατὰ τὸν τῆς ἀρχῆς λόγον, διὸ καὶ ἐπήγαγε· καὶ ἀρχέτωσαν τῶν ἰχθύων κτλ. Chrys.*hom.9.2 in Gen*.(4.67A,B); ποιήσωμεν ἄνθρωπον κατ' εἰ. ἡμετέραν καὶ ὁμοίωσιν, τουτ' ἔστιν, ἵνα ἄρχων ᾖ καὶ τῶν ὁρωμένων ἁπάντων καὶ τῶν ἐν αὐτῷ τικτομένων παθῶν· ἵνα ἀρχῇ, καὶ μὴ ἄρχηται *ib*.23.5(212D); refutation of other views in favour of this, Thdt.*qu.20 in Gen*.(1.24–27); on this view is based idea that woman was not made in image τί δή ποτε οὖν ὁ Παῦλος τὸν μὲν ἄνδρα εἰ. τοῦ θεοῦ λέγει, οὐκ ἔτι δὲ καὶ τὴν γυναῖκα, εἴπερ κατὰ τὸν τῆς ψυχῆς λόγον εἰ. θεοῦ ὁ ἄνθρωπος; λέγει γάρ, ἀνὴρ...εἰ. καὶ δόξα θεοῦ ὑπάρχων, οὐκ ὀφείλει κατακαλύπτεσθαι τὴν κεφαλήν· γυνὴ δὲ δόξα ἀνδρός ἐστιν. εἰ τοίνυν εἰ. θεοῦ ὁ μὴ ὀφείλων καλύπτεσθαι τὴν κεφαλήν, δῆλον ὅτι καλυπτομένη οὐκ εἰ. θεοῦ, τῆς αὐτῆς ψυχῆς ὑπάρχουσα. πῶς οὖν θεοῦ εἰ. ὁ ἄνθρωπος; κατὰ τὸ ἀρχικόν Diod.*Gen*.1:26(1564C,D); **5.** (connected with 4) man, as microcosm, sums up all creation in himself ὥσπερ...βασιλεὺς πόλιν τινὰ μεγίστην κατασκευάσας...μετὰ τὴν ἁπάντων ἐκπλήρωσιν, κελεύσειεν εἰ. αὐτοῦ γενομένην μεγίστην τινά, ἐν μέσῳ πάσης ἑστάναι τῆς πόλεως, εἰς ἔλεγχον τοῦ τῆς πόλεως αἰτίου...οὕτω καὶ ὁ τῆς κτίσεως δημιουργὸς πεποίηκε μὲν πάντα τὸν κόσμον,...τελευταῖον δὲ τὸν ἄνθρωπον ἐν τάξει παρήγαγεν εἰ. οἰκείας, ὡς ἂν ἅπασα ἡ κτίσις τῇ τοῦ ἀνθρώπου χρείᾳ φαίνηται συνδουμένη Thdr.Mops.ap.Thdt.*qu.20 in Gen*.(1.29,30); καὶ τὸ μέν, κατ' εἰ., ταύτην ἔχει τὴν ἔννοιαν, ὅτι ὁ ἄνθρωπος καὶ μόνος, ὡς πάντα ἔχων ἐν ἑαυτῷ ὁρατά τε καὶ ἀόρατα, νοητά τε καὶ αἰσθητά...δεικνύει ἕνα τινὰ δημιουργὸν πάντων τῶν ὄντων εἶναι τὸν θεόν· καὶ κατὰ τοῦτο εἰ. ἐστι τοῦ θεοῦ, διὰ τὸ γνωρίζειν αὐτὸν ἕνα τοῦ παντὸς εἶναι δημιουργόν...διαρρήδην τὸν ἄνθρωπον εἰς δόξαν θεοῦ γεγενῆσθαι φήσας, καὶ κατὰ τοῦτο εἰ. καλέσας, ὡς μόνος ὁ ἄνθρωπος δυνάμενος γνωρίσαι ἕνα εἶναι τοῦ παντὸς τὸν θεὸν δημιουργόν Cosm.Ind.*top*.5(M.88.309B,C); **6.** other views; **a.** immortality and indwelling of H. Ghost λόγος γὰρ ὁ ἐπουράνιος πνεῦμα γεγονὼς ἀπὸ τοῦ πνεύματος καὶ λόγος ἐκ λογικῆς δυνάμεως, κατὰ τὴν τοῦ γεννήσαντος αὐτὸν πατρὸς μίμησιν εἰκόνα τῆς ἀθανασίας τὸν ἄνθρωπον ἐποίησεν, ἵν', ὥσπερ ἡ ἀφθαρσία παρὰ τῷ θεῷ, τὸν αὐτὸν τρόπον θεοῦ μοίρας ἄνθρωπος μεταλαβὼν ἔχῃ καὶ τὸ ἀθάνατον Tat.*orat*.7(p.7.8; M.6.820B); μόνος δὲ ὁ ἄνθρωπος εἰ. καὶ ὁμοίωσις τοῦ θεοῦ...ἄσαρκος μὲν οὖν ὁ τέλειος θεός, ἄνθρωπος δὲ σάρξ· δεσμὸς δὲ τῆς σαρκὸς ψυχή, σχετικὴ δὲ τῆς ψυχῆς ἡ σάρξ. τὸ δὲ τοιοῦτον τῆς συστάσεως εἶδος εἰ μὲν ὡς ναὸς εἴη, κατοικεῖν ἐν αὐτῷ θεὸς βούλεται διὰ τοῦ πρεσβεύοντος πνεύματος *ib.*15(p.16.13; 837A,B); ἡ ἔνδοθεν ἡμῶν ψυχὴ τὴν αὐτοῦ εἰ. πρὸς ἀθανασίαν ἠμφίεσται *Hom. Clem.*16.10; cf. ἀθάνατος; **b.** Word and Wisdom ἵνα δὲ μὴ μόνον ὑπάρχῃ τὰ γενόμενα, ἀλλὰ καὶ καλῶς ὑπάρχῃ, ηὐδόκησεν ὁ θεὸς συγκαταβῆναι τὴν ἑαυτοῦ σοφίαν τοῖς κτίσμασιν· ὥστε τύπον τινὰ καὶ φαντασίαν εἰ. αὐτῆς ἐν πᾶσι...ἐνθεῖναι, ἵνα καὶ σοφὰ τὰ γενόμενα, καὶ ἄξια τοῦ θεοῦ ἔργα δείκνυται. ὡς γὰρ λόγου ὄντος τοῦ υἱοῦ τοῦ θεοῦ εἰ. ἐστιν ὁ ἡμέτερος λόγος, οὕτως...αὐτοῦ σοφίας εἰ. πάλιν ἐστὶν ἡ ἐν ἡμῖν γενομένη σοφία Ath.*Ar.*2.78(M.26.312B,C); **c.** connected with procreation of children κατὰ τοῦτο εἰ. ὁ ἄνθρωπος γίνεται τοῦ θεοῦ, καθὸ εἰς γένεσιν ἀνθρώπου ἄνθρωπος συνεργεῖ Clem.*paed.*2.10(p.208.10; M.8.497B); Meth.*symp.*2.1(p.16.2; M.18.48D); **d.** multiplicity of images οὐ μίαν τινὰ εἰ. καὶ ὁμοίωσιν κέκτηται, ἀλλὰ καὶ δευτέραν, καὶ τρίτην, καὶ τετάρτην, καὶ πέμπτην. ἐξεικονίζων ὥσπερ ἐν ἐσόπτρῳ τινὶ καὶ σκιαγραφίᾳ φυσικῇ, οὐ τυπικῇ, τῆς τρισυποστάτου θεότητος τὸ μυστήριον· οὐ μόνον, ἀλλὰ καὶ τὴν ἐνανθρώπησιν τοῦ ἑνὸς τῆς αὐτῆς τριάδος θεοῦ λόγου σαφῶς προδιαγράφων· καὶ τάχα κατ' εἰ. μὲν ἔστι γυμνὴ ἡ ψυχή, τῆς γυμνῆς θεότητος· καθ' ὁμοίωσιν δὲ τῆς τοῦ λόγου σαρκώσεως τὸ σύνθετον ἡμῶν τῆς ψυχῆς καὶ τοῦ σώματος ‡Anast.S.*serm.imag.*1(M.89.1144D–1145A); ἔχει σου καὶ ἕτερον κατ' εἰ. θεοῦ ἡ ψυχή. λέγω δὴ τὸ ἑτεροούσιον αὐτὴν εἶναι πάσης κτιστῆς φύσεως *ib.*(1148A)∾(M.44.1332C); **7.** summary ὥστε...φιλονεικότερον ἐν τούτῳ διακείμενοι ἐκτὸς...βαίνουσι τῆς κατὰ τὴν ἐκκλησιαστικὴν ὑπόθεσιν παραδόσεως, τῆς πιστευούσης κατ' εἰ. μὲν εἶναι πάντα ἄνθρωπον, μὴ ὁρίζειν δὲ...ἐν ποίῳ τέτακται τὸ κατ' εἰ. ... οἱ μὲν γὰρ λέγουσιν ἐν τῇ ψυχῇ πληροῦσθαι τὸ κατ' εἰ.,...ἄλλοι δὲ λέγουσιν οὔτε ἐν ψυχῇ οὔτε ἐν σώματι, ἀλλὰ ἀρετὴν εἶναι τὸ κατ' εἰ. ἕτεροι δὲ φάσκουσι μὴ εἶναι τὴν ἀρετήν, ἀλλὰ τὸ βάπτισμα καὶ τὸ χάρισμα τὸ ἐν τῷ βαπτίσματι...ἄλλοι δὲ πάλιν τοῦτο οὐ βούλονται, ἀλλὰ θέλουσι λέγειν τότε μὲν εἶναι τὸ κατ' εἰ. ἐν τῷ Ἀδάμ, ἕως ὅτε ἐν παρακοῇ γέγονε καὶ... ἀπώλεσε τὸ κατ' εἰ. καὶ πολλή τίς ἐστι τῶν ἀνθρώπων μυθοποιΐα, οἷς οὐ χρή...τοῖς οὕτω ἢ οὕτω λέγουσιν, ἀλλ' εἶναι μὲν πιστεύειν ἐν τῷ ἀνθρώπῳ τὸ κατ' εἰ. ... ποῦ δέ ἐστιν ἢ ποῦ πεπλήρωται τὸ κατ' εἰ., αὐτῷ μόνῳ ἔγνωσται τῷ θεῷ τῷ κατὰ χάριν τῷ ἀνθρώπῳ δωρησαμένῳ τὸ κατ' εἰ. Epiph.*haer.*70.3(p.235.3–22; M.42.341D–344A); κατὰ πόσους τρόπους λέγεται τό, κατ' εἰ.; κατὰ τὸ λογικόν, καὶ νοερόν, καὶ αὐτεξούσιον, κατὰ τὸ γεννᾷν τὸν νοῦν λόγον, καὶ προβάλλειν πνεῦμα· κατὰ τὸ ἀρχικόν Jo.D.*volunt.*30(M.95.168B).

C. image and original sin, v. Ἀδάμ; **1.** image lost through Fall and restored by Christ; **a.** its loss ὁ μὲν κατ' εἰ. τοῦ θεοῦ γεγονὼς χωρισθέντος ἀπ' αὐτοῦ τοῦ πνεύματος...θνητὸς γίνεται Tat. *orat.*7(p.7.29; M.6.821A); Mac.Aeg.*hom.*12.1(M.34.557A); ὁ ἄνθρωπος κατ' εἰ. θεοῦ ἐγένετο καὶ ὁμοίωσιν· ἡ δὲ ἁμαρτία τὸ κάλλος τῆς εἰ. ἠχρείωσεν, εἰς τὰς ἐμπαθεῖς ἐπιθυμίας τὴν ψυχὴν καθέλκουσα Bas. *ascet.*1.1(2.318D; M.31.869D); Gr.Nyss.*virg.*12(p.299.29; M.46.372B); **b.** its restoration, necessary οὐκ ἔδει δὲ τὰ ἅπαξ κοινωνήσαντα τῆς τοῦ θεοῦ εἰ. ἀπολέσθαι Ath.*inc.*13.6(M.25.120B); through Christ ὡς γὰρ τῆς γραφείσης ἐν ξύλῳ μορφῆς παραφανισθείσης ἐκ τῶν ἔξωθεν ῥύπων, πάλιν χρεία τοῦτον παραγενέσθαι, οὗ καὶ ἔστιν ἡ μορφή, ἵνα ἀνακαινισθῆναι ἡ εἰ. δυνηθῇ ἐν τῇ αὐτῇ ὕλῃ—διὰ γὰρ τὴν ἐκείνου γραφὴν καὶ αὐτὴ ἡ ὕλη ἐν ᾗ καὶ γέγραπται, οὐκ ἐκβάλλεται, ἀλλ' ἐν αὐτῇ ἀνατυποῦται—κατὰ τοῦτο καὶ ὁ...υἱός, εἰ. ὢν τοῦ πατρός, παρεγένετο ἐπὶ τοὺς ἡμετέρους τόπους, ἵνα τὸν κατ' αὐτὸν πεποιημένον ἄνθρωπον ἀνακαινίσῃ *ib.*14.1,2(120C); ‡Ath.*Apoll.*1.5(M.26.1101A); Gr.Naz.*or.*7.23(M.35.785C) cit. s. ἀνασῴζω; Gr.Nyss.*or.dom.*1(p.10.33; M.44.1125B); id.*virg.*12(p.301.18; M.46.373C); Cyr.*dial.Trin.*7(5^1.638E); *Lit.Jac.*(p.200.22); through H. Ghost ἀναπλάττεσθαι...εἰς εἰ. τὴν πρώτην τὴν ἀνθρώπου φύσιν...διὰ μετουσίας τοῦ πνεύματος Cyr.*Jo.*11.10(4.988B); action of Trin. in restoring image τοῦ σωτῆρος... ἡμᾶς ἀνακομίζοντος εἰς τὸ τῆς εἰ. ἀρχέτυπον, τουτέστι, τὸν χαρακτῆρα τοῦ πατρός. χαρακτὴρ...ὁ ἀληθινός...αὐτός ἐστιν ὁ υἱός· ὁμοίωσις... φυσικὴ τοῦ υἱοῦ, τὸ πνεῦμά ἐστι, πρὸς ὃ καὶ ἡμεῖς μορφούμενοι δι' ἁγιασμοῦ, πρὸς αὐτὴν εἰδοποιούμεθα τὴν θεοῦ μορφήν id.*dial.Trin.*7(5^1.639B); through baptism ἀνιόντες [sc. from font]...τὴν γεγραμμένην εἰ. καὶ ὁμοίωσιν τοῦ θεοῦ ἀπολαμβάνομεν, ἣν ἐδεξάμεθα διὰ τοῦ θεϊκοῦ ἐμφυσήματος, καὶ ἀπωλέσαμεν διὰ τοῦ ἁμαρτήματος Didym.*Trin.*2.12(M.39.680A); Didym.(‡Bas.)*Eun.*5(1.303A; M.29.725D); διπλῆν ἡμῖν ἔδωκε καὶ τὴν κάθαρσιν, δι' ὕδατός τε καὶ πνεύματος· τοῦ μὲν πνεύματος, τὸ κατ' εἰ. καὶ ὁμοίωσιν ἐν ἡμῖν ἀνακαινίζοντος, τοῦ δὲ ὕδατος, διὰ τῆς τοῦ πνεύματος χάριτος καθαίροντος τὸ σῶμα τῆς ἁμαρτίας Jo.D.*f.o.*4.9(M.94.1121A); ἐνοικεῖ τοῦ... πνεύματος ἡ χάρις τῇ τοῦ βαπτισθέντος ψυχῇ...τὸ κατ' εἰ. καὶ καθ' ὁμοίωσιν αὐτῇ ἀνακαινίζουσα †Jo.D.*B.J.*8(M.96.920B); by repentance ἐν τῇ δεξιᾷ τοῦ θεοῦ γίνεται πᾶς ὁ τὸ κατ' εἰ. διὰ μετανοίας ἀναλαμβάνων Or.*fr.14 in Jer.*(p.205.1; M.13.569C); **2.** image never lost οὔτε γὰρ ἀπώλεσεν ὁ ἄνθρωπος τὸ κατ' εἰ., ἀλλ' εἰ ἄρα ἐχυδαίωσε τὸ κατ' εἰ., μολύνας ἑαυτὸν ἐν ἀδιαφόροις πράγμασι καὶ ἀνηκέστοις ἁμαρτίαις. ἰδοὺ γὰρ μετὰ τὸν Ἀδὰμ τῷ Νῶε λέγει...πᾶς ὁ ἐκχέων αἷμα ἀνθρώπου...ἐκχυθήσεται τὸ αἷμα αὐτοῦ, ὅτι ἐν εἰ. θεοῦ ἐποίησα τὸν ἄνθρωπον....καὶ ὁρᾷς ὅτι ἐν τῷ ἀνθρώπῳ λέγεται τὸ κατ' εἰ. μετὰ δεκάτην γενεὰν τοῦ τὸν Ἀδὰμ πλασθῆναι; ἅμα δὲ καὶ Δαυὶδ μετὰ πολὺν χρόνον λέγει...ἐν εἰ. διαπορεύεται ἄνθρωπος...καὶ ὅρα ὅτι ἐξέπεσεν ὁ λόγος τῶν λεγόντων τὸν Ἀδὰμ τὸ κατ' εἰ. ἀπολωλεκέναι Epiph.*haer.*70.3(pp.235.24–236.9; M.42.344B–D); Anast.S.*serm.imag.*3(M.89.1169C); but only hidden διὰ δὲ τῆς ζητουμένης δραχμῆς τὴν εἰ. ... τοῦ βασιλέως αἰνίσσεται, τὴν οὐχὶ παντελῶς ἀπολλυμένην, ἀλλὰ ὑποκεκρυμμένην τῇ κόπρῳ. κόπρον δὲ χρὴ νοεῖν...τὴν τῆς σαρκὸς ῥυπαρίαν. ἧς...ἀνακαθαρθείσης διὰ τῆς ἐπιμελείας τοῦ βίου, ἔκδηλον τὸ ζητούμενον γίνεσθαι Gr.Nyss.*virg.*12(p.301.8; M.46.373A); cf. δραχμή; **3.** solution of difficulty by distn. between εἰ. and ὁμοίωσις, latter being lost, former retained; **a.** distn. between εἰ. as constituent of humanity, and ὁμοίωσις as implying spiritual perfection, cf. *cum autem Spiritus hic commistus animae unitur plasmati; propter effusionem Spiritus, spiritualis et perfectus homo factus est: et hic est qui secundum imaginem et similitudinem factus est dei. si autem defuerit animae spiritus, animalis est vere, qui est talis, et carnalis derelictus imperfectus erit; imaginem quidem habens in plasmate, similitudinem vero non assumens per Spiritum,* Iren.*haer.*5.6.1(M.7.1137C–1138A); but cf.Clem.*exc.Thdot.*54.2(p.125.1; M.9.685A); τινὲς τῶν ἡμετέρων τὸ μὲν κατ' εἰ. εὐθέως κατὰ τὴν γένεσιν εἰληφέναι τὸν ἄνθρωπον, τὸ καθ' ὁμοίωσιν δὲ ὕστερον κατὰ τὴν τελείωσιν μέλλειν ἀπολαμβάνειν ἐκδέχονται id.*str.*2.22(p.185.26; M.8.1080C); *ib.*4.6(p.261.15ff.; 1241B); ‡Ath.*qu.script.*55(M.28.733B,C); ὥσπερ εἰ. εἶπε τὴν τῆς ἀρχῆς δηλῶν εἰ., οὕτω καὶ ὁμοίωσιν, ὥστε κατὰ δύναμιν ἀνθρωπίνην ὁμοίους ἡμᾶς γίνεσθαι θεῷ, κατὰ τὸ ἡμέτερον λέγω καὶ πρᾶον ἐξομοιοῦσθαι αὐτῷ Chrys.*hom.*9.3 *in Gen.*(4.67C); τὸ μὲν γὰρ κατ' εἰ., τὸ νοερὸν δηλοῖ καὶ αὐτεξούσιον· τὸ δὲ καθ' ὁμοίωσιν, τὴν τῆς ἀρετῆς κατὰ τὸ δυνατὸν ὁμοίωσιν Jo.D.*f.o.*2.12(M.94.920B); **b.** hence εἰ. in contrast to ὁμοίωσις is linked up with man's creation ἡ βουλὴ [sc. θεοῦ] δύο εἶχε, κατ' εἰ., καὶ καθ' ὁμοίωσιν· ἡ δημιουργία τὸ ἓν ἔχει μόνον, τὸ κατ' εἰ. ‡Bas.*struct.hom.*1.19(1.332D; M.30.29A); ‡Gr.Nyss. *hom.1 in Gen.1*:26(M.44.273A); **c.** and consequently cannot be lost τὸ...κατ' εἰ. φύσει δέδοται ἡμῖν· καὶ ἀμετάβλητον ἐξ ἀρχῆς καὶ εἰς τὸ τέλος συμπάρεστι· τὸ δὲ καθ' ὁμοίωσιν, ἐκ προαιρέσεως, καὶ οἴκοθεν κατορθοῦμεν ὕστερον ‡Bas.*struct.hom.*1.20(1.333A,B; M.30.29C,D); cf. ἄνθρωπον, εἰ. περιφέροντα θεοῦ, εἰ καὶ τὴν ὁμοιότητα ἀπώλεσεν *Hom. Clem.*10.7 (but acc. this work εἰ. resides in body πρόσιτε τῷ θεῷ... οἵ τινες ἔχετε αὐτοῦ ἐν μὲν τῷ σώματι τὴν εἰ., ὁμοίως τε ἔχετε ἐν τῷ νῷ τῆς γνώμης τὴν ὁμοιότητα *ib.*10.6); cf.*Clem.recogn.*5.15(M.1.1336D); **4.** double image in man, cf.1Cor.15:49; **a.** which image is realized depends on conduct εἰ...ἐπιλαθόμενοι τῆς ἐν ἡμῖν κρείττονος οὐσίας ὑποτάξομεν ἑαυτοὺς τῷ ἀπὸ τοῦ χοῦ πλάσματι, καὶ τὸ κρεῖττον τὴν εἰ. τοῦ χοϊκοῦ λήψεται· εἰ δὲ συνέντες τὸ ποιηθὲν κατ' εἰ. καὶ τὸ ληφθὲν ἀπὸ τοῦ χοῦ τῆς γῆς, ὅλοι προσνεύοιμεν ἐπὶ τοῦτον, οὗ κατ' εἰ. γεγόναμεν Or.*Jo.*20.22(20; p.355.13; M.14.621B); *ib.*2.5(4; p.59.30f.; 117C); τὴν εἰ. τοῦ χοϊκοῦ φέροντος ἀνθρώπου, λέγω δὴ τοῦ φιλοσωμάτου καὶ τοῦ κατὰ σάρκα ζῶντος Eus.*Is.*40:6(M.24.368B); Didym.*Ps.*38:7f.(M.39.1349C); εἰκόνα χοϊκοῦ λέγει τὴν ἀναστροφὴν τὴν χοϊκήν, εἰ. ἐπουρανίου τὴν ἐπουράνιον πολιτείαν, ἀντὶ τοῦ ἐμιμησάμεθα τὴν παρακοὴν τοῦ Ἀδάμ, μιμησώμεθα καὶ τοῦ υἱοῦ τοῦ θεοῦ τὴν ὑπακοὴν ὑπακούσαντες Sever.*1Cor.*15:47ff.(p.276.28ff.); Chrys.*hom. 42.1 in 1Cor.*(10.395B); Cyr.*inc.unigen.*(5^1.692A); **b.** interpreted of state of man before and after resurrection of body, Thdr.Mops. *1Cor.*15:48f.(p.195.23); **c.** man by sinning becomes 'image of devil', Or.*Jo.*20.22(20; p.355.3; M.14.621A); **d.** universality of double image ἡ ψυχὴ οὐ τοῦ πρώτου μόνου γέγονε κατ' εἰ., ἀλλὰ παντὸς ἀνθρώπου...καὶ ἔστι πρεσβύτερον ὥσπερ ἐν τῷ Ἀδὰμ ἐκεῖνο ὃ οἱ πολλοὶ νοοῦσι τὸ κατ' εἰ. τοῦ προσειλημμένου αὐτῷ, ὅτε ἐφόρεσε διὰ τὴν ἁμαρτίαν τὴν εἰ. τοῦ χοϊκοῦ, οὕτως ἐν πᾶσι πρεσβύτερον τὸ κατ' εἰ. θεοῦ τῆς εἰ. τῆς χείρονος. ἐφορέσαμεν ἁμαρτωλοὶ ὄντες τὴν εἰ. τοῦ χοϊκοῦ, φορέσωμεν μετανοοῦντες τὴν εἰ. τοῦ ἐπουρανίου. πλὴν ἡ κτίσις γέγονεν ἐν εἰ. τοῦ ἐπουρανίου id.*hom.2.1 in Jer.*(p.17.8–16; M.13.277B,C); Cyr.*Jo.*11.11(4.995B,C).

D. image in spiritual life (in more strictly spiritual contexts εἰ. in soul is considered the meeting place between God and man, and hence freq. equated with those qualities that made man apt to be united to God); **1.** presence in soul presupposes practice of virtue τῷ γὰρ ὄντι εἰ. τοῦ θεοῦ ἄνθρωπος εὐεργετῶν, ἐν ᾧ καὶ αὐτὸς εὐεργετεῖται Clem.*str.*2.19(p.169.2; M.8.1045B); σωτήριος γάρ τις ὁ τῷ σωτῆρι ἐξομοιούμενος, εἰς ὅσον ἀνθρωπίνῃ φύσει χωρῆσαι τὴν εἰ. θέμις, ἀπαραβάτως τὰ κατὰ τὰς ἐντολὰς κατορθῶν *ib.*6.9(p.470.10; M.9.297B); cf. *ipsi animae tuae deus imaginem suam et similitudinem commendavit. istud ergo depositum tam integrum tibi restituendum est quam a te constat esse susceptum. si enim sis misericors... imago dei in te est et integrum depositum servas. ... similiter et cetera omnia, si pius, si justus es, si sanctus,...et omnia quae in deo praesto sunt per naturam si tibi per imitationem subsistant, depositum apud te divinae imaginis salvum est. si vero e contrario agas et pro misericorde crudelis, pro pio impius...abjecta imagine dei diaboli in te imaginem suscepisti et bonum depositum commendatum tibi divinitus abnegasti,* Or.*hom.4.3 in Lev.*(p.318.4ff.; M.12.436B–C); ‡Nil.*perist.*4(M.79.893A); ἔχουσι τοίνυν, φησίν [sc. Christ], οἱ τὸν σὸν...δεξάμενοι λόγον τὴν ἐμὴν ἐν ἑαυτοῖς διαλάμπουσαν εἰ., συμμορφοί τε τῷ σῷ γνησίῳ γεγόνασιν υἱῷ Cyr.*Jo.*11.9(4.983C); id.*dial.Trin.*1(5^{1}.393E); **2.** for only purified soul becomes image of God εἰ τοιούτων ἡ ψυχὴ κινημάτων [i.e. passions] ἐλευθέρα γένοιτο,...ἑαυτὴν ἀκριβῶς εἰδοῦσα, οἵα τῇ φύσει ἐστί, καὶ οἷον ἐν κατόπτρῳ καὶ εἰ. διὰ τοῦ οἰκείου κάλλους πρὸς τὸ ἀρχέτυπον βλέπουσα Gr.Nyss.*anim.et res.*(M.46.89C); γενώμεθα καθαροὶ τῇ καρδίᾳ, ἵνα γινώμεθα μακάριοι, τῆς θείας εἰ. ἐν ἡμῖν μορφωθείσης id.*beat.*6(M.44.1277A); Max.*ambig.*(M.91.1113B); **3.** hence image equated with various aspects of spiritual life; **a.** perfection, Clem.*str.*7.16(p.71.20; M.9.540B); πλησιάζουσι δὲ αὐτῷ [sc. the Spouse] οἱ τετελειωμένοι, καὶ τὴν πρὸς αὐτὸν αὐχοῦσι συγγένειαν οἱ τὴν εἰ. φυλάττοντες ἀδιάφθορον Thdt.*Cant.*5:1(2.108); cf. οὔπω γεγόναμεν ἄδολος πορφύρα βασιλική, οὔτε ἀνόθευτος εἰ. θεϊκή Mac.Aeg.*hom.*25.5(M.34.669D); **b.** ἀγάπη, Esaias *or.*25.12(M.40.1181A Lat.); **c.** ἀπάθεια and kindred virtues πάλιν κατὰ τὴν τοῦ θεοῦ εἰ. ἑαυτοὺς καλλωπίσωμεν, διὰ τῆς ἀπαθείας ὁμοιωθέντες τῷ κτίσαντι. ὁ γὰρ τὸ ἀπαθὲς τῆς θείας φύσεως, καθὼς ἐστι δυνατόν, ἐφ' ἑαυτοῦ μιμησάμενος, οὗτος ἐπανέλαβεν ἐπὶ τῆς ἰδίας ψυχῆς τοῦ θεοῦ τὴν εἰ. Bas.*ascet.*1.1(2.318E; M.31.872A); *ib.*(319A; M.l.c.); Gr.Nyss.*hom.opif.*5.1(M.44.137B); ἀνάρχου βασιλείας ἐστὶν εἰ., ἡ τοῦ νοῦ περὶ τὴν ἀληθῆ γνῶσιν ἀτρεψία, καὶ ἡ τῆς αἰσθήσεως περὶ τὴν ἀρετὴν ἀφθαρσία Max.*cap.*3.55(M.90.1284C); **d.** contemplation, indwelling of God, and spiritual self-knowledge, Clem.*str.*7.3(p.12.22ff.; M.9.421A) cit. s. θεωρία; Or.*hom.1.13 in Gen.*(p.17.26ff.; M.12.157B,C); τῶν...ἁγίων ἡ θεοειδὴς τοῦ πνεύματος εἰ. ἀπὸ τοῦ νῦν ἔνδον ὥσπερ ἐντυπωθεῖσα, καὶ τὸ σῶμα θεοειδὲς ἔξω καὶ οὐράνιον ἀπεργάσεται Mac.Aeg.*libert.ment.*25(M.34.957C); Gr.Nyss.*beat.*6(M.44.1272B); εἰ βούλει γνῶναι θεόν, προλαβὼν γνῶθι σαυτὸν ἐκ τῆς σαυτοῦ...κατασκευῆς...διάκρινον τὴν ταύτης κατασκευήν, καὶ ὄψῃ σαυτὸν κατ' εἰ. καὶ ὁμοίωσιν θεοῦ τυγχάνοντα. ἀνώνυμός σου γὰρ καὶ ἄγνωστος, καὶ νοερά, καὶ ἀθάνατος τῆς ψυχῆς ἡ οὐσία κατ' εἰ. καὶ ὁμοίωσιν τυπικὴν τοῦ ἀνωνύμου καὶ ἀγνωρίστου καὶ ἀθανάτου θεοῦ καθέστηκεν ‡Anast.S.*serm.imag.*1(M.89.1145D); for the reason why man was created in the image was that he should know God, for which the image was sufficient, Ath.*inc.*12.1(M.25.116D); cf.*ib.*11.3(116A,B); **e.** kingdom of heaven τὴν βασιλείαν τῶν οὐρανῶν εἶναί τινες λέγουσι...τὸ εἶδος αὐτὸ τῆς θεϊκῆς ὡραιότητος τῶν φορεσάντων τὴν εἰ. τοῦ ἐπουρανίου Max.*cap.theol.*2.93(M.90.1169A).

E. dignity and beauty conferred by image on soul, cf. *Solomon...ad animam...loquens dicit 'nisi cognoveris temet ipsam, et pulchra inter mulieres', et agnoveris pulchritudinis tuae causas inde descendere, quod 'ad imaginem dei facta es', per quod inest tibi plurimum naturalis decoris, et agnoveris, quam pulchra eras ex initio,... jubeo te 'exire' et in ultimis 'gregum vestigiis' collocari,* Or.*comm.in Cant.*2(p.141.26ff.; M.13.123C); κατ' εἰ. γὰρ δημιουργηθεῖσα τοῦ μονογενοῦς [sc. ἡ ψυχή],...ἀνυπέρβλητον ἔχει τὸ κάλλος Meth.*symp.*6.1(p.64.18ff.; M.18.113B); οὐκ οὐρανὸς γέγονεν εἰ. τοῦ θεοῦ...οὐκ ἄλλο τι τῶν κατὰ τὴν κτίσιν φαινομένων οὐδέν. μόνη σὺ [sc. ψυχή] γέγονας τῆς ὑπερεχούσης πάντα νοῦν φύσεως ἀπεικόνισμα...οὐδὲν οὕτω τῶν ὄντων μέγα, ὡς τῷ σῷ μεγέθει παραμετρεῖσθαι Gr.Nyss.*hom.2 in Cant.*(M.44.805D); οὐκοῦν καὶ τὸ τῆς ἀνθρωπίνης φύσεως κάτοπτρον, οὐ πρότερον ἐγένετο καλόν, ἀλλ' ὅτε τῷ καλῷ ἐπλησίασε, καὶ τῇ εἰ. τοῦ θείου κάλλους ἐνεμορφώθη *ib.*5(868D); ἐπειδὴ κατ' εἰ. θεοῦ ἐκτίσθη, ἠρκέσθη τὸ θεῖον γράμμα τῷ τοσούτῳ ἀξιώματι,...εἰ γὰρ αὐτῆς τῆς ἀγαθότητος εἶχε κεκτημένος τὴν εἰ. ... πῶς ἔτι χρείαν εἶχε μαρτυρίας ⟨τοῦ⟩ ἀκοῦσαι ὅτι ἰδοὺ καλόν, ὁπότε τὴν εἰ. αὐτοῦ τοῦ καλοῦ εἶχε κεκτημένος; Epiph.*haer.*66.18(p.42.14ff.; M.42.56C,D); Max.*cap.*1.11(M.90.1088A); on account of which dignity every man must be honoured, Meth.*res.*2.24(p.380.6ff.).

F. discussion whether other creatures, besides man, were created in image; **1.** angels εἰ. ἐστι τοῦ θεοῦ ὁ ἄγγελος...ἔσοπτρον ἀκραιφνές Dion.Ar.*d.n.*4.22(M.3.724B); cf.id.*c.h.*8.1(M.3.240A); οἱ ἄγγελοι καὶ οἱ ἄνθρωποι κατ' εἰ. Jo.D.*volunt.*30(M.95.168B); **2.** man alone made in image οὐδὲ αὐτοί [sc. ἄγγελοι] εἰσιν εἰ. Ath.*inc.*13.7(M.25.120B); τινὲς μὲν τῶν δυσωνύμων αἱρετικῶν πρὸς τοὺς ἀγγέλους αὐτὸν εἰρηκέναι, καὶ τοὺς πονηροὺς δαίμονας ἔφασαν· οὐ συνιέντες οἱ ἐμβρόντητοι τὸ κατ' εἰ. ἡμετέραν Thdt.*qu.19 in Gen.*(1.22) ∾ ‡Ath.*qu.script.*56(M.28.733D); ἐπὶ...τῆς τῶν ἀγγέλων καὶ τῶν χερουβὶμ καὶ σεραφὶμ δημιουργίας εἴρηται ὅτι...θεὸς εἶπε, καὶ ἐγενήθησαν...· ἐπὶ δὲ τοῦ ἀνθρώπου τοῦ κατ' εἰ. καὶ ὁμοίωσιν θεοῦ ὄντος, οὐχ οὕτως Anast.S.*serm.imag.*3(M.89.1165B); 'image' refers to whole human race as it was first conceived in divine mind, without later sex distinction, Gr.Nyss.*hom.opif.*16.18(M.44.185D); **3.** εἰ. θεοῦ sometimes used as synonym of man, *Apoc.Mos.*10(p.5); *ib.*12(p.6); Cosm.Ind.*top.*2(M.88.120A); **4.** Devil's enmity against man due to man's creation in image, Bas.*hom.*9.9(2.81E; M.31.349C); ‡Bas.*Lac.*9(2.595B; M.31.1456D); ἔργον δὲ τῶν ἀντικειμένων δαιμόνων τὰ πρὸς βλάβην τῆς εἰ. Cosm.Ind.*top.*2(M.88.120A).

G. image in Christian hierarchy, priests τοὺς οὕτω [sc. as true followers of Christ] ζῶντας, ὡς ὁμοιοειδεῖς ἐνσημαίνοντος τῷ σταυροειδεῖ τῆς οἰκείας ἀναμαρτησίας εἰ. Dion.Ar.*e.h.*5.3.4(M.3.512B); bishop, Max.*ep.*30(M.91.624B).

IV. theol.;

A. Gnost.; of double letters of alphabet as images of elements which are images of aeons, Iren.*haer.*1.14.5(M.7.605A); of order of Christ's actions, and evangelists' use of time notes, as image of order of aeons, *ib.*1.14.6(605B); of demiurge as εἰ. τοῦ Μονογενοῦς Clem.*exc.Thdot.*7(p.108.16; M.9.657C); and as εἰ. τοῦ ἀληθινοῦ θεοῦ καὶ προφήτην id.*str.*4.13(p.287.28; M.8.1297B); ζωγράφον δὲ τὴν σοφίαν, ἧς τὸ πλάσμα ἡ εἰ. ... ἐπεὶ ὅσα ἐκ συζυγίας προσέρχεται, πληρώματά ἐστιν, ὅσα δὲ ἀπὸ ἑνός, εἰκόνες *ib.*(p.287.30; 1297B).

B. of Wisdom as God's image ἡ σοφία ἐστὶν ὁ λόγος ᾧ εἶπε, 'ποιήσωμεν ἄνθρωπον' κτλ.· ὡς οὔσης εἰ. τοῦ ἀρχετύπου *Dial.Ath.et Zacch.*8(p.5).

C. of Logos or Son as image of Father (Col.1:13), v. ἀπαράλλακτος; εἰ. μὲν γὰρ τοῦ θεοῦ ὁ λόγος αὐτοῦ...εἰ. δὲ τοῦ λόγου...ὁ νοῦς ὁ ἐν ἀνθρώπῳ Clem.*prot.*10(p.71.24; M.8.212C); ἔστιν οὖν τις, ὁ υἱὸς τοῦ θεοῦ, εἰ. τοῦ θεοῦ, καὶ τούτου εἰ. ἡ λεγομένη εἰ. τοῦ υἱοῦ τοῦ θεοῦ· ἣν νομίζομεν εἶναι ἣν ἔλαβε ψυχὴν ὁ υἱὸς τοῦ θεοῦ ἀνθρωπίνην, γενομένην διὰ τὴν ἀρετὴν τῆς εἰ. τοῦ θεοῦ εἰκόνα· ἣν οἰόμεθα εἰ. εἰ. εἶναι τοῦ θεοῦ Or.*comm.in Rom.*1:49(*JTS* 13 p.211); εἰ ἔστιν εἰ. τοῦ θεοῦ τοῦ ἀοράτου, ἀόρατος εἰ. id.*princ.*4.4.1(p.349.15); id.*Jo.*13.36(p.261.25; M.14.461C); τῆς ἀνεκφράστου καὶ ἀπερινοήτου θεότητος μόνον ἐν αὐτῷ φέροντα τὴν εἰ. Eus.*d.e.*4.2(p.152.9; M.22.253B); *ib.*4.3(p.153.14; 256B) cit. s. προαίρεσις; εἴη δ' ἂν ταύτῃ καὶ εἰ. θεοῦ...ζῶντος θεοῦ ζῶσά τις καὶ καθ' αὑτὴν ὑφεστῶσα...ἀλλ' οὐχ οἵα τις πάλιν ἡ παρ' ἡμῖν εἰ., ἕτερον μὲν ἔχουσα τὸ κατ' οὐσίαν ὑποκείμενον, ἕτερον δὲ τὸ εἶδος *ib.*5.1(p.213.30; 353D); acc. Marcellus τότε [sc. at Inc.] υἱὸν θεοῦ γεγονέναι...εἰ. τε θεοῦ id.*Marcell.*1.1(p.6.4; M.24.721C); οὐδεὶς ἐδύνατο τὸν θεὸν εἰδέναι, οὐδὲ τὸν λόγον γνωρίζειν αὐτοῦ, εἰ μὴ τὴν εἰ. εἰλήφει...δηλαδὴ τὴν σάρκα...διὰ μόνης γὰρ τῆς εἰ. γνωρίζεσθαι τὸν θεὸν καὶ τὸν τούτου λόγον διετείνατο, τὴν σάρκα λέγων εἶναι τὴν εἰ. id.*e.th.*2.25(p.136.21; M.24.965C); but agst. Marcell. εἷς δὲ καὶ μονογενὴς τοῦ θεοῦ υἱός, εἰ. τῆς πατρικῆς θεότητος καὶ διὰ τοῦτο θεός *ib.*1.2(p.63.29; 832C); Ath.*Ar.*2.78(M.26.312B); ἡ δὲ εἰ., ἑτέρου καὶ οὐχ ἑαυτῆς εἰ. οὖσα, καθὰ καὶ σὺ [sc. Marcellus] θέλεις, τοῦ πρωτοτύπου ἐν ἑαυτῇ τοὺς χαρακτῆρας φέρουσα, τὴν ἑτερότητα παρίστησιν, ἑτερότητα δὲ ὡς ὁμοιότητα· οὐχ ἑαυτῆς γάρ, ἑτέρου δέ τινος εἰ. ἐστιν οὗτος...εἰ. οὖν τοῦ πατρὸς ὁ υἱός, ζῶσα ζῶντος Acac.Caes.*fr.Marcell.* ap.Epiph.*haer.*72.10(p.264.24; M.42.396C); εἴ τις εἰ. ἀκούων τὸν υἱὸν τοῦ θεοῦ...ταὐτὸν λέγοι τὴν εἰ. τῷ θεῷ..., ὡς μὴ ὁμολογῶν ἀληθῶς υἱόν, ἀνάθεμα...καὶ...ἀνόμοιον λέγοι [καὶ] κατ' οὐσίαν τὸν υἱὸν εἰ. ὄντα τοῦ θεοῦ...οὐ εἰ. καὶ κατ' οὐσίαν νοεῖται, ὡς ἀληθῶς μὴ λέγων υἱόν, ἀνάθεμα CAnc.(358)*anath.*6,7(p.281.22; M.42.421C); τὸ θεῖον βούλημα...διὰ τῆς οἰκείας εἰ. τοῦ...λόγου πρόεισιν εἰς ἐνέργειαν Bas.*Eun.*2.21(1.257C; M.29.620A); id.*ep.*236.1(3.361B; M.32.877A); Gr.Nyss.*Eun.*11(2 p.264.20; M.45.872D); οὐχὶ τῷ διαφέρειν τοῦ ἀρχετύπου τὴν εἰ. ... ἀλλ' ἵνα δειχθῇ ὅτι ταὐτὸν τῷ πρωτοτύπῳ ἐστίν, κἂν ἕτερον ᾖ id.*diff.ess.*8(M.32.340B); *Pap.Chr.*4.16.1.6(p.445); εἰ. ὢν τοῦ πατρὸς ὁ υἱός, οὐκ ἂν εἴη κτίσις αὐτοῦ Didym.(‡Bas.)*Eun.*4(1.287E; M.29.692B); εἰ. εἰκονοποιός *ib.*5(302A; M.724C); Cyr.*thes.*1(5^{1}.12C); ἔστι δὲ καὶ οὕτως εἰ. τοῦ πατρός, καθ' ὃ καὶ ἔστι θεὸς καὶ ἐξ αὐτοῦ γεγέννηται κατὰ φύσιν id.*2Cor.*4:4(p.342.10; M.74.933B); Procl.CP *or.*2.3(M.65.696C); *Dial.Ath.et Zacch.*19(p.15).

D. of Son as image of attributes of God ὁ δὲ σωτὴρ εἰ. τῆς ἀγαθότητος αὐτοῦ Or.*Jo.*6.57(37; p.166.6; M.14.300B); εἰ. ... τῶν ἐπινοουμένων τῇ οὐσίᾳ τοῦ θεοῦ μεγαλείων, εἰ. δυνάμεως, εἰ. σοφίας, καθὸ εἴρηται Χριστὸς θεοῦ δύναμις καὶ θεοῦ σοφία Bas.*ep.*236.1(3.361B; M.32.877A); τὸν λόγον...[sc. τοῦ πατρός] οὐσίας τε καὶ βουλῆς καὶ δόξης καὶ δυνάμεως ἀπαράλλακτον εἰ. Ast.Soph.*fr.*21 ap.Eus.

*Marcell.*1.4(p.25.8; M.24.764C) ∞ *Symb.Ant.*(341)2(p.249.18; M.26.721C); of Father's will τὸ ἐν αὐτῷ θέλημα εἰ. τοῦ πρώτου θελήματος, καὶ ἡ ἐν αὐτῷ θεότης εἰ. τῆς ἀληθίνης θεότητος Or.*Jo.*13.36(p.261.25; 461C); (Eunomian) εἰ. βουλήσεως ὀνομάζουσιν Bas.*Eun.*1.24(1.235D; M.29.565B); v. βούλησις; of his ἐνέργεια, *ib.*2.31(268C; M.645A); υἱὸς γάρ ἐστι, φησίν, εἰ. καὶ σφραγὶς τῆς τοῦ παντοκράτορος ἐνεργείας Gr.Nyss.*Eun.*2(2 p.360.14; M.45.540A).

E. of Christ's humanity τὴν εἰ. λαμβάνων τῆς ἀνθρωπότητος Procl.CP *or.*6.11(M.65.741A); (Eutychian) τυγχάνειν τῆς ἡμετέρου σώματος εἰ., καὶ μὴ ἀληθείαν Leo Mag.*ep.*30(p.46.10; M.*PL.*54.788B).

F. of H. Ghost; **a.** as image of God, Eus.*e.th.*3.5(p.163.10; M.24.1012C); **b.** as image of Son, Gr.Thaum.*symb.*(p.3.8; M.10.985A); Ath.*ep.Serap.*1.24(M.26.588B); Didym.(‡Bas.)*Eun.*5(1.302A; M.29.724C); Jo.D.*f.o.*1.13(M.94.856B).

εἴλημα, τό, 1. *covering, wrapping*, ref. Christ's burial τὸ εἴ. τῆς σινδόνος Epiph.*haer.*42.11(p.153.18; M.41.769D); **2.** *arch, vault*; of heaven, Geo.Pis.*hex.*86(M.92.1436A); in architecture, Jo.Mal.*chron.* 18 p.490(M.97.709A); *ib.*p.495(716B); **3.** *volume* κεφαλίδα δὲ βιβλίου καλεῖ τὰ εἴ. Thdt.*Jer.*36:1–3(2.562).

***εἰληματικός,** *arched*, Jo.Eleem.*v.Tych.*(p.139).

εἰλητός, A. *wound, wrapped*; neut. as subst.; **1.** liturg.; linen or silk *corporal* placed on altar, symbolizing grave-clothes of Christ, ‡Sophr.H.*liturg.*5(M.87.3985B); ‡Bas.*h.myst.*47(p.389.23); unfolded by deacons (compared with Joseph of Arimathea and Nicodemus) at beginning of mass of faithful, ‡Sophr.H.*liturg.*20 (4000D); or by priest, cf.*Lit.Chrys.*(p.375.6); εὐχὴ πιστῶν μετὰ τὸ ἁπλωθῆναι τὸ εἰ. *Lit.Bas.*(p.316.10); later practically identified with ἀντιμίσιον q.v.; placed by bishop on altar at consecration of church, *Euchol.*(p.660D); **2.** *roll, volume* μεμβράνας ῥωμαϊκώτερον τὰ εἰ. ἐκάλεσεν...ἐν εἰλητοῖς γάρ εἶχον τὸ παλαιὸν τὰ τῆς θείας γραφῆς Thdr.Mops.*2Tim.*4:13(p.228.11); Thdt.ad loc.(3.695).

B. *vaulted*, s.v.l., εἰ. ναῷ Andr.Cr.*imag.*(M.97.1304A).

εἰλικρίνεια, ἡ, *purity* of intention, *sincerity* τῶν λόγων εἰ. Clem.*str.*4.22(p.311.11; M.8.1352C); *ib.*6.7(p.462.8; M.9.281B); id.*fr.*65 (p.228.21; M.9.753A) cit. s. δικαιόω; coupled with πίστις, Const.ap. Eus.*v.C.*4.42(p.134.22; M.20.1192B); *ib.*4.45(p.136.4; 1193C); μετὰ εἰλικρινείας ἀφῶμεν Chrys.*hom.in Rom.12:20*(3.171B); ref. 2Cor. 1:12, id.*hom.3.1 in 2Cor.*(10.442B).

εἰλικρινής, *pure, unmixed*; **1.** def., ref. Phil.1:10 εἰ. λογίζομαι εἶναι τὸ ἀμιγές, καὶ ἄκρως κεκαθαρμένον ἀπὸ παντὸς ἐναντίου, συνηγμένον δὲ καὶ τεταγμένον πρὸς μόνην θεοσέβειαν· οὐ μόνον δέ, ἀλλὰ καὶ πρὸς τὰ ἐν ἑκάστῳ καιρῷ καὶ πράγματι πρὸς τὸν ταύτης σκοπὸν ἀκριβῶς ἐπιζητούμενα· ὥστε μηδὲ πρὸς τὰ συγγενῆ τῶν κατορθωμάτων ἀπομετεωρίζεσθαι τὸν εἴς τι ταχθέντα Bas.*reg.br.*264 (2.505D; M.31.1261B); **2.** of contemplation, Clem.*str.*6.14(p.486.9; M.9.329B); *ib.*7.3(p.10.13; 416C); τὸ τῆς θεωρίας εἰ. Nil.*exerc.*75(M. 79.809B); of Christ to whom is applied Sap.7:25, Or.*Jo.*13.25(p.249. 32; M.14.444A), Eus.*d.e.*4.3(p.154.1; M.22.256D) citt. s. δόξα; his divinity, ‡Ath.*Ar.*4.35(p.84.15; M.26.521B); God called ὁ εἰ., *A.Jo.* 107(p.205.2); of doctrine, Eus.*h.e.*4.24(M.20.389B); τῶν δικαίων ἀξιωμάτων τὸ εἰ. ... κάλλος Cyr.*Mich.*36(3.422D); ref. morsel given to Judas at Last Supper εἰ δύνασαι τὸν εἰ. ἄρτον ἀβαφῆ φάσκειν εἶναι Or.*Jo.*32.22(14; p.465.8; 804D); **3.** morally *pure, uncontaminated*, ref. Christian life τῆς εἰ. ... ζωῆς ἡ ἀρχή [sc. ὁ σωτήρ] Or. *Jo.*1.28(27; p.34.22; M.14.73C); Eus.*h.e.*4.7.13(M.20.320B); id.*d.e.*3.7 (p.147.2; M.22.248A); of prayer δέησις εἰ. *Const.App.*3.7.6; προσευχὴ ...τοῦ νοῦ...εἰ. κρίσις Evagr.Pont.*or.*84(M.79.1185B); εἰλικρινεῖ πρόσελθε τῷ θεῷ διαθέσει Olymp.*Job* 11:13f.(M.93.144D); εἰ. διανοίᾳ Bas. Sel.*or.*4.3(M.85.69A); of God's righteousness, Cyr.*Mich.*67(3.462B); *single-minded, Ep.Dor.*(M.88.1616A); *pure in doctrine*, exeg. Phil. 1:10 ἵνα ἦτε ὑμεῖς εἰ.· τουτέστιν, ἵνα μηδὲν νόθον δόγμα τῷ τῆς ἀγάπης προσχήματι παραδέχησθε Chrys.*hom.2.1 in Phil.*(11.203D); **4.** *sincere*; characterizing believers, *1Clem.*2.5; τὸ μετανοῆσαι ἐξ εἰ. καρδίας *2Clem.*9.8; εἰ. κάθαρσις Clem.*str.*4.23(p.316.1; M.8. 1361A); id.*q.d.s.*40(p.187.7; M.9.645C); Ath.*ep.mon.*(M.26.1188A); of faith, Clem.*q.d.s.*35(p.183.10; M.9.641A); Chrys.*hom.35.1 in Jo.*(8. 202C); εἰ. διανοίᾳ θεραπεύει...[sc. Abel] τὸν τῆς ποίμνης δοτῆρα Bas. Sel.*or.*4.3(M.85.69A).

εἰλικρινότης, ἡ, *sincerity*, as polite form of address ἡ ὑμετέρα εἰ. *Cod.Afr.*56.

εἰλικρινῶς, 1. *purely, in purity* ψυχὴν...ἀμίαντον εἰ. τὸν προσομιλοῦντα τῷ θεῷ Clem.*str.*7.7(p.36.27; M.9.469A); εἰ. θεάσονται τὴν ἀφθαρσίαν Meth.*symp.*1.1(p.8.2; M.18.37A); ἑορτάζομεν κυρίῳ εἰ. *ib.* 9.2(p.116.9; M.181A); Hyper.*mon.*140(M.79.1488A); **2.** *sincerely, 1Clem.*32.1; εἰ. τὸ ἀληθὲς λέγειν Meth.*res.*1.42(p.287.14; M.41.1109D); of believing, *Symb.Ant.*(341)4(p.251.14; M.26.725D); *Symb.Sirm.*1 (p.254.31; M.26.736C); Chrys.*hom.35.1 in Jo.*(8.202).

***εἰλιμμένον, τό,** *chalice veil, Euchol.*(p.86).

***εἰλιτάριον, τό,** *scroll* εἰ. γὰρ οἱ Ἑβραῖοι ἀντὶ τῶν παρ' ἡμῖν βιβλίων ἐκέχρηντο Andr.Caes.*Apoc.*18(M.106.273D); CTrull.*act.*14 (H.3.1360B).

εἱμαρμένη, ἡ, *fate*;

A. def., Clem.*exc.Thdot.*69(p.129.15; M.9.692A) cit. s. δύναμις; εἰ. ... εἱρμός, οἶμαι, τῶν θεῷ τυπουμένων Gr.Naz.*carm.*1.2.34.263(M. 37.964); dist. from πρόνοια and ἀνάγκη: τοῦ μὲν θεοῦ ἔργον, οὐσία καὶ πρόνοια· τῆς δὲ ἀνάγκης, τῶν ἀεὶ ὡσαύτως ἐχόντων ἡ κίνησις· τῆς δὲ εἰ., τὸ ἐξ ἀνάγκης τὰ δι' αὐτῆς ἐπιτελεῖσθαι Jo.D.*f.o.*2.25(M.94. 957A).

B. its reality, affirmed ὅτι δέ ἐστι, φασίν, εἰ. τοῖς ἄλλοις, τὰ ἀποτελέσματα προλεγόμενα δείκνυσιν, ἐναργὴς δὲ ἀπόδειξις καὶ ἡ τῶν μαθημάτων θεωρία Clem.*exc.Thdot.*75(p.130.23; M.9.693B); denied ὁ κατὰ τὴν προσοῦσαν αὐτῷ φύσιν ζῶν οὐδὲν ἁμαρτάνει· οὐ γὰρ ἑαυτὸν ἐποίησε τοιοῦτον, ἀλλ' ἡ εἰ. ... οὐδεὶς οὖν κακός. ἀλλ' εἰσὶ κακοί, καὶ ἡ μὲν κακία...ἐχθρὰ τῷ θεῷ...ἡ δὲ ἀρετὴ προσφιλὴς...θεοῦ διατάξαντος νόμον τιμωρὸν τῶν κακῶν. οὐκ ἄρα εἰ. Meth.*symp.*8.16 (p.110.11ff.; M.18.173A); ποία δ' αὐτῶν εἰ. θεὸν δημιουργὸν ἁπάντων πᾶσιν ἀνθρώποις κατήγγειλεν, εἰ. δὲ μὴ εἶναι φάναι ἐξηνάγκασε; καὶ πῶς ἡ εἰ. μὴ εἶναι ἑαυτὴν λέγειν τε καὶ φρονεῖν ἐβιάσατο; Eus.*p.e.*6.6 (253D; M.21.432A); ἡ παρὰ τοῖς ἄφροσιν Ἕλλησι...εἰ. προσαγορευομένη, οὔτ' ἦν ποτε, οὔτ' ἔστιν, οὔτ' ἔσται πώποτε Nil.*epp.*1.278(M.79. 184D).

C. pagan belief in it, Tat.*orat.*8(p.8.6; M.6.821A,B); *ib.*9(p.9.24; 825A); οἱ δαίμονες αὐτοὶ μετὰ τοῦ ἡγουμένου...Διὸς ὑπὸ τὴν εἰ. πεπτώκασι τοῖς αὐτοῖς πάθεσιν...κρατηθέντες *ib.*8(p.8.19; 824A); οὐδὲ γὰρ τὸν δάκτυλον ἐξεῖναί φασι χωρὶς εἰ. κινῆσαί τινι Meth.*symp.*8.16 (p.108.8; M.18.172A); πάντα...ὑπεζεῦχθαι τῇ τῆς εἰ. ἀνάγκῃ Gr.Nyss. *fat.*(M.45.148C); ἔστι...καὶ νεώς, καὶ πόλεως, καὶ ἔθνους παντὸς εἰ., κατὰ τὴν πρώτην θέσιν τὸ ἐφεξῆς ἐπικλώθουσα *ib.*(165C); philosophers' views: Plato εἰ. φησὶν εἶναι οὐ μὴν πάντα καθ' εἰ. γίνεσθαι Hipp.*haer.* 1.19(p.23.2f.; M.16.3045A); Stoic conception, *ib.*1.21(p.25.16ff.; 3048C,D); Epicurus πρόνοιαν μὴ εἶναι μηδὲ εἰ., ἀλλὰ πάντα κατὰ αὐτοματισμὸν γίνεσθαι *ib.*1.22(p.26.19; 3049B).

D. implications and consequences of this belief; **1.** immorality οἱ διοριζόμενοι μὴ εἶναι τὸν ἄνθρωπον αὐτεξούσιον, ἀλλ' ἀνάγκαις ἀφύκτοις εἰ. λέγοντες οἰακίζεσθαι...εἰς αὐτὸν ἀσεβοῦσι τὸν θεόν, παρεκτικὸν τῶν ἀνθρωπίνων αὐτὸν κακῶν...εἰσηγούμενοι Meth.*res.* 8.16(p.105.7; M.18.168D); πάντα δ' εἰ. διὰ τῶν χρησμῶν ἀναρτήσας ὁ δαίμων...θέα εἰς οἷον κακῶν δογμάτων ὄλεθρον τοὺς αὐτῷ πειθομένους καταβέβληκεν. εἰ γὰρ...εἱμαρμένῃ οὐ μόνα τὰ ἐκτός, ἀλλὰ καὶ τὰς κατὰ λογισμὸν προθυμίας ἀναθετέον...οἰχήσεταί σοι φιλοσοφία...οὐδέ τις ἦν τοῖς σπουδαίοις ἔπαινος ἀρετῆς...εἰ. τὴν αἰτίαν πάντων ἀναδεδεγμένης...εἰ γὰρ ἐξ εἰ. τόδε τι γενήσεσθαι νομίζοι, εἴτε πονοίημεν ἡμεῖς περὶ αὐτό...εἴτε καὶ μή, πῶς οὐκ ἂν τις ἐθελήσειε τὸ ῥᾷον αἱρεῖσθαι... ὡς ἐξ εἰ. ... γενησομένου τοῦ πραχθησομένου; Eus.*p.e.*6.6(242D–243C; M.21.413A–C); καὶ τὴν πρὸς τὸ θεῖον εὐσέβειαν ἀνατρέποι ἂν ἥδε ἡ δόξα, εἴγε μηδὲν ἡμῖν ὁ θεός, μηδὲ μὴν αὐτοὶ οἱ τῶνδε χρησμῳδοί, μήτ' εὐχομένοις, μήτ' εὐσεβοῦσι συμβάλλονται εἱμαρμένης ἀνάγκαις πεπεδημένοις *ib.*(244D; M.416D); ποῦ τὸ δίκαιον;...ποῦ τὸ ὅσιον; ἢ τούτων οὐδενὸς μέλειν φῂς τῇ εἰ., οὐδὲ πρὸς ἀρετὴν βλέπειν...; Gr.Nyss. *fat.*(M.45.160A); Chrys.*hom.26.6 in Mt.*(7.321C); ὥσπερ γὰρ δῆλον ὅτι πονηρὸν τὸ φονεύειν καὶ τὸ μοιχεύειν φαῦλον, οὕτω δῆλον ὅτι τὸ προσέχειν εἱμαρμένῃ πονηρόν...ἐπεὶ ὅτι γε τῶν κεκωλυμένων ἐστίν, ὥσπερ ὁ φόνος, παρὰ τοῖς νόμοις αὐτοῖς τοῖς τῶν Ἑλλήνων, τὸ τῇ γενέσει πείθεσθαι...κατηγορούμενος ἐν δικαστηρίῳ λεγέτω, ὅτι οὐκ ἐγώ, ἀλλ' ἡ γένεσις...ἆρα οὐ διὰ τοῦτο χαλεπωτέραν δώσει δίκην, ὡς καταγέλαστα ἀπολογούμενος; ‡Chrys.*prov.*3(2.761B); ὅρα...πόσα κακὰ συνέστησεν ὁ διάβολος ἀπὸ τῆς εἰ.· ὑπεροψίαν ἀρετῆς· ἐκλύει γὰρ ψυχὴν κἂν σφόδρα πρόθυμος ᾖ πρὸς τοὺς ὑπὲρ αὐτῆς ἱδρῶτας, ὅταν πείσῃ, ὅτι τῶν γενομένων οὐδέν ἐστιν ἐφ' ἡμῖν εὐέμπτωτον πρὸς πονηρίαν ἔργον *ib.*(762D); *ib.*5(769B); **2.** ass. astrology διὰ τῆς...περιφορᾶς τῶν ἄστρων...τῆς αὐτῆς τυχεῖν...εἰ. Eus.*p.e.*6.6(253D; M.21.432A); ἠρόμην αὐτὸν [sc. a pagan philosopher] εἰ θεόν τινα οἴεται τὸν κατὰ πάντων ἔχοντα κράτος, τὸν τῷ ὀνόματι τῆς εἰ. ἀποκαλούμενον...ὁ δὲ πολλήν μου καταγνοὺς...οὔ μοι δοκεῖς κατανενοηκέναι, φησί, τῶν οὐρανίων οὐδέν. ἢ γὰρ ἂν ἔγνως τῆς εἰ. τὴν δύναμιν, καὶ ὅπως κατελήφθη τῶν καθ' εἱρμὸν ἀπαραβάτως γινομένων ἡ δύναμις. ἐμοῦ...πρὸς τοῦτον ξενοφωνουμένου τὸν λόγον, καί τι σαφέστερον ἀξιοῦντος μαθεῖν, πότερον δύναμίν τινα προαιρετικὴν αὐτοκρατῆ...τὴν εἰ. εἶναι φαντάζεται...ὁ τῶν οὐρανίων, φησίν, ἐπισκεμμένος τὴν κίνησιν, τόν τε ζῳδιοφόρον κύκλον...ὁ...τοιαῦτα κατανοήσας, εἴσεται τῆς εἰ. τὸ σημαινόμενον, ὅτι τὸ εἱρμῷ τινι ἀπαραβάτῳ κατὰ τὴν ποιὰν συμπλοκὴν τῶν *ἀστέρων ἀναγκαίως ἀποτελούμενον τῷ ὀνόματι τῆς εἱ. διηρμήνυται* Gr. Nyss.*fat.*(M.45.149B–D); this view discussed, *ib.*(152Aff.); hence **3.** implies absurdity *ζῴων οὐκ ἔστιν, ἐν περιγραφῇ οὐχ ὁρᾶται, θεὸς οὐ νομίζεται...ὃ δὲ μηδέν ἐστι τούτων, τί ἐστιν; ἀλλ' ἔοικε παρ' ὑμῶν τὸ ἀεὶ ἐνεστὼς τοῦ χρόνου, εἱ. λέγεσθαι· πάσῃ γὰρ κινήσει...ὁ χρόνος συμπαρεκτείνεται. διαφέρει δὲ οὐδέν, ἢ ὕδατι προσκαθήμενον τῇ κινήσει τοῦ ῥεύματος ἀποσημειοῦσθαι τὰ ἀκαρῆ διὰ τοῦ ἀεὶ ἐνεστῶτος χρόνου τμήματα,...ἢ κινουμένων ἄστρων. εἷς γὰρ ἐπὶ πάντων τῶν μεταβατικῶς κινουμένων ὅρος κινήσεως...εἰ δὲ οὔτε ἡ τῶν ῥείθρων φορά, οὔτε ἡ τῶν πλοίων κίνησις...τοῦ χρόνου τὰ διαστήματα εἱ. ποιεῖ, πῶς τὰ χρονικὰ σημεῖα τῆς τῶν ἀστέρων κινήσεως εἰς εἱ. γένεσιν πλάσσετε, καὶ φάτε τήνδε τὴν ὥραν, ἢ τῆς ὥρας τὸ πολλοστημόριον ὅπερ τῷδε τῷ σημείῳ τῆς τῶν ἄστρων κινήσεως ἐσημειώθη, εἱ. γίνεσθαι; ib.*(160B,C); *εἰ ταῦτα τὰ φαινόμενα ἡμῖν κατ' ἀνάγκην τινὸς εἱ. ἐστὶ τοιαῦτα, πάντως καὶ τῆς ὑπερκειμένης ἐκείνης ἀνάγκης ἑτέραν αἰτίαν ἀναγκαστικὴν τῆς τοιαύτης καταστάσεως προσεπινοήσει ὁ λόγος, κἀκείνης ἄλλην, καὶ πάλιν ἄλλην τῆς ἄλλης, καὶ οὕτως εἰς ἄπειρον προϊὼν ὁ λόγος, οὐδαμοῦ στήσεται εἱμαρμένην εἱμαρμένης ib.* (161C); *εἰ. δὲ παρεισάγεις, ὡς ἐξ αὐτῆς γίνεσθαι τὰ τῷ ἀνθρώπῳ συμβαίνοντα καὶ ἄλλοις...εἰ γὰρ εἱμαρμένης τὸ σοφίζεσθαι τὸ συνετίζεσθαι τὸ λογικὸν γεννᾶσθαι καὶ ἄλογον...παυσάσθωσαν νόμοι· ἐπικρατεῖ γὰρ ἡ εἱ. μοιχῶν τε καὶ ἄλλων...ἀργείτωσαν αἱ διατριβαί, παυσάσθωσαν σοφισταί τε καὶ ῥήτορες...εἴπερ ἐξ εἱ. τυγχάνει τῶν ἐπιστημῶν καὶ μὴ ἐκ γραμμάτων μαθήσεως ὁ πορισμὸς τῇ ἀνθρωπείᾳ φύσει. εἰ γὰρ εἱ. τὸν πεπαιδευμένον...παρεσκεύασε, μὴ μανθανέτω τις παρὰ τοῦ διδάσκοντος* Epiph.*haer.*5.3(pp.184.27–185.9; M.41.204B,C); ‡Chrys.*prov.*5(2.770A,B); *ἀμέλησον τῶν σαυτοῦ πάντων· πάντως γὰρ ἥξει σοι τὰ τῆς εἱ. ... οὐδὲν ἀπὸ τῆς ῥᾳθυμίας τῆς σῆς ἢ τῆς εἱ. ῥᾳθυμία παραβλαβήσεται ib.*(772A).

E. *εἱ.* and free will; **1.** belief in *εἱ.* destroys scriptural teaching on free will, Chrys.*hom.62.3 in Mt.*(7.623E); ref. Is.1:19f. *τὸ γὰρ στόμα κυρίου ἐλάλησε ταῦτα. εἶδες πῶς ὁ θεὸς φθέγγεται καὶ ποίους τίθησι νόμους; ἄκουσον καὶ τῆς εἱ. ... πῶς ἐναντίους εἰσάγει θεσμούς... εἶπεν ὁ θεός, ἐὰν θέλητε, καὶ ἐὰν μὴ θέλητε, κυρίους ἡμᾶς ποιῶν ἀρετῆς καὶ κακίας...ἐκεῖνος δὲ τί φησιν; ὅτι τὸ εἱμαρμένον οὐ δυνατὸν ἐκφυγεῖν, κἂν θέλωμεν, κἂν μὴ θέλωμεν* ‡Chrys.*prov.*2(2.758B); **2.** even believers in *εἱ.* act on assumption of free will, Eus.*p.e.*6.6 (244B; M.21.416B) al.; ‡Chrys.*prov.*3(2.762B); *εἰ φαύλους καὶ ἀγαθοὺς εἱ. ποιεῖ, τίνος ἕνεκεν παραινεῖς τῷ παιδί, τίνος ἕνεκεν νουθετεῖς;...εἰ πλουσίους καὶ πένητας ποιεῖ, μὴ πέμψῃς εἰς διδασκαλεῖα,...ἀλλ' ἐπίτρεψον τῇ εἱ. τὰ κατ' αὐτόν...ὁρᾷς πῶς ἐν τοῖς ἐλάττοσι διαπιστῶν αὐτῆς τὴν δύναμιν, ἐν τοῖς μείζοσιν αὐτῇ πιστεύεις; εἰ γὰρ ὄντως εἱ. ἐστίν, ἄφες τὸν παῖδα καὶ πονηροῖς ἀνδράσι συγγίνεσθαι ib.*5(770C,D); **3.** free will affirmed against *εἱ.*: *ἡμέτερον ἔργον τὸ βιῶσαι καλῶς ἐστι...οὐδὲ...ὡς οἴονταί τινες, ἀπὸ εἱ.* Or.*princ.*3.1.6(p.201.9; M.11. 256B); *ἡμέτερον προκρίνειν γὰρ τὰ κρείττω...οὐ δουλεύοντας εἱ.* Meth. *symp.*8.13(p.98.20; M.18.161A); *οἴχεται μὲν τὰ τῆς εἱ., καὶ οὐδεμίᾳ ἀνάγκῃ τὰ ἡμέτερα ἄγεται, πάντα δὲ ἐλευθερίᾳ προαιρέσεως τετίμηται* Chrys.*hom.div.*8(12.381D); ref. S. Paul's conversion *ποῦ τοίνυν εἰσὶν οἱ τὴν τῆς εἱ. ἀνάγκην ἐπιτειχίζοντες τῇ τῆς προαιρέσεως ἐλευθερίᾳ;* id.*hom.22.4 in 1Cor.*(10.197C).

F. man not subject to *εἱ.*; **1.** gen. statement *εἰ δὴ οὖν τις τὰ κατὰ φύσιν ἤτοι τοῦ σώματος ἢ καὶ τῆς ψυχῆς, εἱ. ὀνόματι χρώμενος, ὑπ' αἰτίαν ἀνάγκης καταβάλλοι, διαμάρτοι ἂν τῆς οἰκείας προσηγορίας... εἰ γὰρ ἀπαράλλακτόν φασιν εἶναι τὴν εἱ., καὶ μὴ δύνασθαί τι παρ' αὐτὴν γίνεσθαι (ἀνάγκην γὰρ εἶναι ἀπαραίτητον), πολλὰ δέ, ὡς ἔφην, παρὰ τὰ κατὰ φύσιν καὶ ψυχῇ καὶ σώματι συμβαίνει, οὐκ ἂν ὀρθῶς τις ὀνομάζοι, ταὐτὸν εἶναι λέγων εἱ. καὶ φύσιν* Eus.*p.e.*6.6(246C,D; M.21. 420A,B); **2.** proofs, from martyrs' lives, *ib.*(253B; M.429D); from pagan philosophers, *ib.*6.7(261C; M.445A); and from scripture, *ib.*6.9 (272D; M.461D); from difference of individual fortunes *εἰ οὖν καὶ πάντα καὶ ἀεὶ δύναται ἡ εἱ. αὕτη, πάντα ἐπὶ πάντων δυνήσεται. ἀλλὰ μὴν πολλαὶ καὶ ποικίλαι τοῖς ἀνθρώποις τοῦ βίου διαφοραί, κατά τε τὰς ἀξίας καὶ τὰς περιουσίας...ἄρα τὸ μὴ πάντα δύνασθαι τὴν ἀναπλασθεῖσαν ἐκείνην τῷ λόγῳ...εἱ., ἡ τῶν ἀποτελεσμάτων ἀνισότης...ἐπιδείκνυσιν. εἰ γὰρ τὸ μακρόβιον δυνάμεως ἔργον νομίζομεν, ἀσθενείας ...ἐστὶ τὸ ὠκύμορον. οὐκοῦν, τὴν μὲν ἀσθενεῖν τῶν εἱ. τὴν δὲ δύνασθαι δογματίζειν προσήκει* Gr.Nyss.*fat.*(M.45.157A,B).

G. belief in *εἱ.* and Christianity; **1.** incompatible *ὁ...εἱ. εἰσάγων ἄντικρυς θεὸν καὶ θεοῦ πρόνοιαν ἐξωθεῖ· ὥσπερ ὁ τὸν θεὸν ἐφιστὰς τοῖς πᾶσιν ἀνέλοι ἂν τὸν περὶ εἱμαρμένης λόγον. ἢ γὰρ ταὐτὸν ἂν εἴη ὁ θεὸς καὶ εἱ., ἢ θάτερον διεστὼς ἑτέρου. ταὐτὸν μὲν οὖν οὐκ ἂν γένοιτο* Eus.*p.e.*6.6(252A; M.21.428C); detailed refutation of opinion that God and *εἱ.* are identical, *ib.*(252A,B; M.428C–429A); *εἴρηται δὲ ἡμῖν ἐν ἄλλοις λόγοις πολλὰ πρὸς ἀνατροπὴν τῶν γένεσιν καὶ εἱ. νομιζόντων...ἐσχάτη δὲ αὐτοῖς ἀπορία...τοῖς καὶ ἀνάστασιν ὁμολογοῦσιν καὶ κρίσιν δικαίαν ὁριζομένοις. πῶς γὰρ δύναται κρίσις εἶναι καὶ εἱ.;* Epiph.*haer.*16.3(p.212.13ff.; M.41.252B–253A); Chrys.*hom.45.4 in Jo.*(8.267D); discussion of opposition between *εἱ.* and *πρόνοια*, id. *oppugn.*3.10(1.92E); ‡Chrys.*prov.*2(2.756C); **2.** power of *εἱ.* destroyed by Christ *ὁ κύριος...ὁ κατελθὼν εἰς γῆν, ἵνα μεταθῇ τοὺς εἰς τὸν Χριστὸν πιστεύσαντας ἀπὸ τῆς εἱ. εἰς τὴν ἐκείνου πρόνοιαν* Clem.*exc. Thdot.*74(p.130.22; M.9.693A); *ἡ γέννησις σωτῆρος γενέσεως ἡμᾶς καὶ εἱμαρμένης ἐξέβαλεν ib.*76(p.130.30; 693B); *μέχρι τοῦ βαπτίσματος οὖν ἡ εἱ., φασίν, ἀληθής, μετὰ δὲ τοῦτο οὐκέτι ἀληθεύουσιν οἱ ἀστρολόγοι ib.*78(p.131.15; 693D); *εἱ. ἀνεῖλε* [sc. *Χριστός*] Chrys.*hom. 6.1 in Mt.*(7.84B); **3.** superiority of Christianity *ἡμεῖς δὲ καὶ εἱ. ἐσμὲν ἀνώτεροι καὶ ἀντὶ πλανητῶν δαιμόνων ἕνα τὸν ἀπλανῆ δεσπότην μεμαθήκαμεν καὶ οὐ καθ' εἱμαρμένην ἀγόμενοι τοὺς ταύτης νομοθέτας παρῃτήμεθα* Tat.*orat.*9(p.10.7; M.6.825B,C); *πῶς οὖν γένεσιν τὴν καθ' εἱμαρμένην ἀποδέξομαι τοιούτους* [sc. pagan gods] *αὐτῆς τοὺς οἰκονόμους θεωρῶν;...τί μοι καθ' εἱ. ἀγρυπνεῖς διὰ φιλαργυρίαν; τί δέ μοι καθ' εἱ. πολλάκις ὀρεγόμενος πολλάκις ἀποθνήσκεις; ἀπόθνησκε τῷ κόσμῳ παραιτούμενος τὴν ἐν αὐτῷ μανίαν ib.*11(p.11.25; 829A); Eus. *p.e.*6.6(253D; M.21.432A); **4.** *εἱ.* not presupposed by belief in prophecy *ὅπως δὲ μή τινες ἐκ τῶν προλελεγμένων ὑφ' ἡμῶν δοξάσωσι καθ' εἱμαρμένης ἀνάγκην φάσκειν ἡμᾶς τὰ γινόμενα γίνεσθαι. τὰς τιμωρίας ...καὶ τὰς ἀγαθὰς ἀμοιβὰς κατ' ἀξίαν τῶν πράξεων ἑκάστου ἀποδίδοσθαι ...ἀληθὲς ἀποφαινόμεθα· ἐπεὶ εἰ μὴ τοῦτό ἐστιν, ἀλλὰ καθ' εἱμαρμένην πάντα γίνεται, οὔτε τὸ ἐφ' ἡμῖν ἐστιν ὅλως...εἰ δὲ εἵμαρτο ἢ φαῦλον ἢ σπουδαῖον εἶναι, οὐκ ἄν ποτε τῶν ἐναντίων δεκτικὸς ἦν...ἀλλ' οὐδ' οἱ μὲν ἦσαν σπουδαῖοι, οἱ δὲ φαῦλοι, ἐπεὶ τὴν εἱ. αἰτίαν φαύλων καὶ ἐναντία ἑαυτῇ πράττουσαν ἀποφαινοίμεθα...ἀλλ' εἱ. φαμὲν ἀπαράβατον ταύτην εἶναι, τοῖς τὰ καλὰ ἐκλεγομένοις τὰ ἄξια ἐπιτίμια, καὶ τοῖς ὁμοίως τὰ ἐναντία τὰ ἄξια ἐπίχειρα* Just.*1apol.*43.1–7(M.6.392C–393B); *ib.*44.11 (396B).

H. as belief of Pharisees, Hipp.*haer.*9.28(p.262.6ff.; M.16.3407A, B); *Const.App.*6.6.3; and Sadducees, Hipp.*haer.*9.29(p.262.13; 3407B).

I. *εἱ.* not a divinity, Clem.*prot.*10(p.73.25; M.8.217A).

εἰμί, *to be* (*τὸ εἶναι being*; *ὁ ὤν, τὸ ὂν he who is, that which is*; *τὰ ὄντα things that are*, i.e. *creatures*, occur freq. in same passages, hence are not treated separately);

A. God as being and source of all being *πίστευσον ὅτι εἷς ἐστιν ὁ θεός, ὁ...ποιήσας ἐκ τοῦ μὴ ὄντος εἰς τὸ εἶναι τὰ πάντα* Herm.*mand.*1.1; *τοῦ εἶναι πᾶσι τοῖς ἄλλοις αἴτιον, τοῦτο δή ἐστιν ὁ θεός* Just.*dial.*3.5 (M.6.481B); *ὁ λόγος ἡμῶν ἕνα θεὸν ἄγει...αὐτὸν μὲν οὐ γενόμενον (ὅτι τὸ ὂν οὐ γίνεται ἀλλὰ τὸ μὴ ὄν)* Athenag.*leg.*4.2(M.6.900A); *ὁ μὲν θεὸς...συνέχων τὰ πάντα φθάνει εἰς ἕκαστον τῶν ὄντων, μεταδιδοὺς ἑκάστῳ ἀπὸ τοῦ ἰδίου τὸ εἶναι, ὅπερ ἐστίν* Or.*princ.*1.3.5(p.56.1f.; M. 11.150B); *θέλων* [sc. *θεός*] *ὁμοῦ καὶ δυνάμενος...ὕλην ὥσπερ τινὰ καὶ οὐσίαν τῆς τῶν ὅλων γενέσεως...προβεβλημένος, ὡς μηκέτι εὐλόγως φάναι δεῖν ἐξ οὐκ ὄντων εἶναί τι τῶν ὄντων· οὐδὲ γὰρ ἂν εἴη τι τὸ ἐκ μὴ ὄντος. πῶς γὰρ τὸ μὴ ὂν ἑτέρῳ τοῦ εἶναι γένοιτ' ἂν αἴτιον; πᾶν δὲ ὅ τί ποτε καὶ ἔστιν ἐξ ἑνὸς τοῦ μόνου ὄντος καὶ προόντος, τοῦ δὴ καὶ φήσαντος, 'ἐγώ εἰμι ὁ ὤν', τὸ εἶναι λαβὸν ἔχει, ὅτι δὴ μόνος ὢν καὶ ἀεὶ ὢν αὐτὸς πᾶσι, τοῖς ἐξ αὐτοῦ τὸ εἶναι κτησαμένοις, αἴτιος τοῦ εἶναι κατέστη* Eus.*d.e.*4.1(p.151.22ff.; M.22.252D); *θεὸς ἦν μὲν ἀεί, καὶ ἔστι, καὶ ἔσται· μᾶλλον δέ, ἔστιν ἀεί. τὸ γὰρ ἦν, καὶ ἔσται, τοῦ καθ' ἡμᾶς χρόνου τμήματα...ὁ δὲ ὢν ἀεί, καὶ τοῦτο αὐτὸς ἑαυτὸν ὀνομάζει... ὅλον γὰρ ἐν ἑαυτῷ συλλαβὼν ἔχει τὸ εἶναι* Gr.Naz.*or.*45.3(M.36.625C); *τοῦ γὰρ ὄντος ἐξῆπται τὰ ὄντα, καὶ οὐκ ἔνεστιν εἶναί τι μὴ ἐν τῷ ὄντι τὸ εἶναι ἔχον* Gr.Nyss.*or.catech.*25(p.95.6; M.45.65D); id.*anim.et res.* (M.46.136A); *κυριώτερον πάντων τῶν ἐπὶ τοῦ θεοῦ ὀνομάτων εἶναι, τὸ ὂν* [sc. *ὁ ὤν*]. *ὅλον γὰρ ἐν ἑαυτῷ συλλαβὸν ἔχει τὸ εἶναι, οἷόν τι πέλαγος οὐσίας ἄπειρον* ‡Cyr.*Trin.*11(6^3.17C; M.77.1145B); *ἐπειδὴ ὤν ἐστιν ὁ θεὸς ὑπερουσίως, δωρεῖται δὲ τὸ εἶναι τοῖς οὖσι...πολλαπλασιάζεσθαι λέγεται τὸ ἓν ὂν ἐκεῖνο τῇ ἐξ αὐτοῦ παραγωγῇ τῶν πολλῶν ὄντων...τῷ πάντων εἶναι τῶν ὄντων ὑπερουσίως ἐξῃρημένον* Dion.Ar.*d.n.*2.11 (M.3.649B); *ἐκ τοῦ ὄντος, αἰών, καὶ οὐσία, καὶ ὄν...τὰ ἐν τοῖς οὖσιν ὄντα...καὶ ὑφεστῶτα. καὶ γάρ, ὁ θεὸς οὔ πώς ἐστιν ὤν, ἀλλ' ἁπλῶς καὶ προειληφώς· διὸ καὶ βασιλεὺς λέγεται τῶν αἰώνων, ὡς ἐν αὐτῷ καὶ περὶ αὐτὸν παντὸς τοῦ εἶναι καὶ ὄντος καὶ ὑφεστηκότος, καὶ οὔτε ἦν, οὔτε ἔσται...μᾶλλον δὲ οὔτε ἐστίν· ἀλλ' αὐτός ἐστι τὸ εἶναι τοῖς οὖσι· καὶ οὐ τὰ ὄντα μόνον, ἀλλὰ καὶ αὐτὸ τὸ εἶναι τῶν ὄντων, ἐκ τοῦ προαιωνίως ὄντος ib.*5.4(817C,D); *ib.*5.5(820–C) et passim; commented upon *τὸ ὄν, ἐπὶ τοῦ θεοῦ λεγόμενον, ὅλου συλλήβδην τοῦ εἶναι ὑπέρεστι· τοῦτο γάρ φησιν ὑπερούσιον, ἀντὶ τοῦ ὑπὲρ τὸ ἐν γενέσει ὄν· τὸ γὰρ ὂν οὐσία· ἀπὸ γὰρ τοῦ εἶναι τὸ ὄνομα παρῆκται τῆς οὐσίας. ὁ οὖν θεός, ὡς καὶ τοῦ εἶναι ὑπερκείμενος (τὸ γὰρ εἶναι ἐξ αἰτίας τινὸς δηλοῖ εἰς τὸ εἶναι ἀχθῆναι) ὢν ὑπερουσίως νοεῖται· διὸ καὶ αἰὼν λέγεται εἶναι τῶν παρηγμένων ὑπ' αὐτοῦ αἰώνων· ὅπερ γὰρ μήτε ἦν, μήτε ἔσται, ἀλλ'* ἔστι μόνον, τοῦτο ἑστὼς ἔχον τὸ εἶναι, τὸ μὴ μεταβάλλειν εἰς τὸ ἔσται, μήτ' αὖ μεταβεβηκέναι ἀπὸ τοῦ [ἦν εἰς τὸ] ἔστι, τοῦτό ἐστιν αἰών· οὐ γὰρ μόνον τὰ ὄντα πάντα δεῖ παρεῖναι τῷ παντὶ καὶ ὅλῳ, ἀλλὰ τὸ μηδὲν τοῦ ποτε μὴ ὄντος Max.*schol.d.n.*5.4(M.4.313B,C); cf.Dion.Ar.*e.h.*1.3 (M.3.373C); id.*d.n.*1.5(M.3.593D); ὁ ὢν εἰς πάντα τὰ ὄντα ἐκτείνεται, καὶ ὑπὲρ τὰ ὄντα ἐστίν *ib.*5.1(816B).

B. his existence proved τοῦ μὲν γὰρ εἶναι θεόν,...καὶ ὄψις διδάσκαλος, καὶ ὁ φυσικὸς νόμος Gr.Naz.*or.*28.6(M.36.32C); ὅτι μὲν οὖν ἔστι θεός...οὐκ ἀμφιβάλλεται...ἡ γνῶσις τοῦ εἶναι θεὸν φυσικῶς ἡμῖν ἐγκατέσπαρται Jo.D.*f.o.*1.3(M.94.793B,C); ἡ τῆς κτίσεως συνοχή, καὶ συντήρησις, καὶ κυβέρνησις, διδάσκει ἡμᾶς ὅτι ἐστὶ θεός *ib.*(796C); ὅτι μὲν οὖν ἔστι θεός, δῆλον. τί δέ ἐστι κατ' οὐσίαν... ἄγνωστον *ib.*1.4(797B).

C. God as beyond being (negative theology) ὑπερούσιος οὐσία... κατὰ μηδὲν τῶν ὄντων οὖσα· καὶ αἴτιον μὲν τοῦ εἶναι πᾶσιν, αὐτὸ δὲ μὴ ὂν Dion.Ar.*d.n.*1.1(M.3.588B); εἰ δὲ καὶ ὑπὲρ πάντα τὰ ὄντα ἐστίν... τἀγαθόν, καὶ τὸ ἀνείδεον εἰδοποιεῖ...οὐσίας ὑπερβολὴ...καὶ εἰ θεμιτὸν φάναι, τἀγαθοῦ τοῦ ὑπὲρ πάντα τὰ ὄντα, καὶ αὐτὸ τὸ μὴ ὂν ἐφίεται, καὶ φιλονεικεῖ πῶς ἐν τἀγαθῷ καὶ αὐτὸ εἶναι *ib.*2.11(697A); αὐτὸς αἴτιος τοῦ εἶναι τὰ πάντα, καὶ πρὸ τοῦ εἶναι, ὡς ἐντεῦθεν δηλοῦται· τὸ γὰρ αὐτὸ εἶναι οὐκ αὐτό ἐστιν ὁ θεός, διὰ τὸ εἶναι τὸν θεόν, ἀλλὰ διὰ τὸν θεόν. καὶ τὸ εἶναί ἐστι, καὶ λέγεται· διὸ ἐν τῷ θεῷ ἐστι τὸ εἶναι, ὡς ἰδέα· οὐ μὴν ὁ θεός, ἐν τῷ εἶναί ἐστι. πρὸ γὰρ τοῦ εἶναι ἦν· ὅμως διὰ τὸ πάντων αἴτιος εἶναι...καὶ ἔξω πάντων ἐστίν, ὡς αἴτιος τούτων Max.*schol.d.n.* 5.8(M.4.325B).

D. uncreated and created being contrasted; **1.** God as ὁ ὢν or τὸ ὄν; **a.** opp. τὸ μὴ ὄν (= creatures): πανταχόθεν καθαρεύοι τὸ ὄντως ὂν τῆς πρὸς τὸ μὴ ὂν κοινωνίας Gr.Nyss.*Eun.*9(2 p.221.19; M.45.820D); οὐδὲ γάρ ἐστιν ὁ θεὸς ὂν ἤτοι κατὰ τὰ αὐτὰ καὶ ὡσαύτως τοῖς οὖσιν, ἵνα δηλωθῇ τελείως διά τινος τῶν ὄντων, ἀλλ' ὁ ὤν, τουτέστιν ὁ κυρίως ...ἔχων τὴν ὕπαρξιν, παρ' οὗ καὶ πάντα τὰ ὄντα διὰ ἀγαθότητα μόνην ἐξ οὐκ ὄντων προήχθησαν...καὶ καθ' ὁμωνυμίαν ὄντα προσηγορεύθησαν ‡Gr.Nyss.*hom.6.43 in Jo.*(p.216.22ff.); cf. ὃ δὲ ἤρξατο, ἦν ὅτε οὐκ ἦν. οὗ δὲ πρεσβύτερον τὸ οὐκ ἦν, τοῦτο οὐ κυρίως ὄν. τὸ δὲ μὴ κυρίως ὄν, πῶς θεός; Gr.Naz.*or.*42.17(M.36.477C); **b.** opp. τὰ ὄντα: ἔστι γὰρ τοῦτο τῆς πάντων αἰτίας...τὸ πρὸς κοινωνίαν ἑαυτῆς τὰ ὄντα καλεῖν, ὡς ἑκάστη τῶν ὄντων ὥρισται πρὸς τῆς οἰκείας ἀναλογίας. πάντα μὲν οὖν τὰ ὄντα μετέχει προνοίας...οὐ γὰρ ἂν ἦν, εἰ μὴ τῆς τῶν ὄντων οὐσίας καὶ ἀρχῆς μετειλήφει. τὰ μὲν οὖν ἄζωα πάντα, τῷ εἶναι αὐτῆς μετέχει· τὸ γὰρ εἶναι πάντων ἐστὶν ἡ ὑπὲρ τὸ εἶναι θεότης Dion.Ar.*c.h.* 4.1(M.3.177C,D); νοῦς ὤν, ὄντως νοεῖ τὰ ὄντα ὡς ὤν. εἰ οὖν νοῶν ἑαυτὸν τὰ ὄντα νοεῖ, αὐτός ἐστι τὰ ὄντα· ἢ γὰρ ἑτέρωθι ὄντα αὐτὰ νοήσει, ἢ ἐν ἑαυτῷ, ὡς αὐτοῦ ὄντα· ἀλλαχοῦ μὲν ὄντα οὖν οὐ δυνατὸν νοῆσαι· ποῦ γὰρ ὄντα ἐν αἰσθητοῖς; τὰ γὰρ αἰσθητὰ οὐκ εἰσὶν ὄντα, ἅτε τρεπτὰ ὄντα, καὶ γινόμενα, καὶ ἀπολλύμενα. ἑαυτὸν οὖν ἄρα καὶ ἐν ἑαυτῷ νοεῖ. ἐπειδὴ δὲ καὶ ποιητὴς τῶν ὄντων ἐστὶν ὁ θεός, ἐν τῷ μήπω ὄντι νοήσει αὐτά· καὶ ἃ νοεῖ, οὐ τύπους λαμβάνων ἀφ' ἑτέρων, αὐτὸς ὢν τῶν ὄντων παράδειγμα· ὥστε οὔτε αὐτὸς ἐν τόπῳ, οὔτε τὰ ἐν αὐτῷ ὡς ἐν τόπῳ· ἀλλ' ἔχει αὐτὰ ὡς ἑαυτὸν ἔχων, καὶ ἑνῶν αὐτοῖς, πάντων μὲν ὁμοῦ ὄντων, καὶ ἐν ἀμερεῖ ὄντων ἐν αὐτῷ· διακεκριμένων δέ, ἐν τῷ ἀμερεῖ ἀμερῶς. αἱ τοίνυν νοήσεις αὐτοῦ εἰσι τὰ ὄντα· τὰ δὲ ὄντα εἰσὶ τὰ εἴδη Max.*schol.d.n.*5.6(M.4.320B,C); πάντα τὰ ὄντα, ἢ κτιστά ἐστιν, ἢ ἄκτιστα. εἰ γὰρ κτιστά, πάντως καὶ τρεπτά· ὧν γὰρ τὸ εἶναι ἀπὸ τροπῆς ἤρξατο, ταῦτα τῇ τροπῇ ὑποκείσεται πάντως...εἰ δὲ ἄκτιστα...πάντως καὶ ἄτρεπτα. ὧν γὰρ τὸ εἶναι ἐναντίον, τούτων καὶ ὁ τοῦ πῶς εἶναι λόγος ἐναντίος Jo.D.*f.o.*1.3(M.94.796A,B); οὐδὲν γὰρ τῶν ὄντων ἐστὶν [sc. ὁ θεὸς]· οὐχ ὡς μὴ ὤν, ἀλλ' ὡς ὑπὲρ πάντα τὰ ὄντα, καὶ ὑπὲρ αὐτὸ τὸ εἶναι ὢν *ib.*1.4(800B); **2.** Gen.1:1 contrasted with Jo. 1:1 τί γὰρ...κοινὸν ἔχει πρὸς τό, 'ἐποίησε', τό, 'ἦν'; τί δὲ ὁ θεὸς πρὸς τὸν ἄνθρωπον;...ἐνταῦθα γὰρ τό, 'ἦν', οὐ δείκνυσι τὸ ἀΐδιον μόνον, ἀλλὰ καὶ τό, 'ἐν ἀρχῇ ἦν', καὶ τό, 'ὁ λόγος ἦν'. ὥσπερ οὖν τό, ὤν, ὅταν μὲν περὶ ἀνθρώπου λέγηται, τὸν ἐνεστῶτα χρόνον δηλοῖ μόνον· ὅταν δὲ περὶ θεοῦ, τὸ ἀΐδιον δείκνυσιν· οὕτω καὶ τὸ 'ἦν', περὶ μὲν τῆς ἡμετέρας λεγόμενον φύσεως, τὸν παρελθόντα σημαίνει χρόνον ἡμῖν, καὶ αὐτὸν τοῦτον πεπερατωμένον· ὅταν δὲ περὶ θεοῦ, τὸ ἀΐδιον ἐμφαίνει Chrys. *hom.3.2 in Jo.*(8.18E–19A); *ib.*3.3(19D–20A); ὅπου...δημιουργία, ἔταξε Μωυσῆς τὸ ἐποίησεν, ὅπου δὲ δημιουργὸς ἔταξεν ὁ εὐαγγελιστὴς τὸ ἦν. πολὺ δὲ τὸ μέσον τοῦ ἐποίησε καὶ τοῦ ἦν· τὸ μὲν γὰρ ἐγένετο μὴ ὄν, ὁ δὲ ἦν ἀεὶ ὤν. ἐν ἀρχῇ ἐποίησε καὶ ἐν ἀρχῇ ἦν· θεοῦ γὰρ τὸ εἶναι, κτίσματος δὲ τὸ γίνεσθαι, ὥσπερ καὶ ὁ εὐαγγελιστὴς μερίζει...ὃ ἦν ἐν ἀρχῇ ζωὴ ἦν. ἑξάκις λέγει τὸ ἦν, ἵνα ἑρμηνεύσῃ τὸ ὤν. περὶ δὲ τοῦ οἰκέτου, ὅτε ἐκήρυξε τὸν ὄντα, λέγει· ἐγένετο ἄνθρωπος. θεὸς ἦν, ἄνθρωπος δ' ἐγένετο †Jo.D.*creat.*1(p.59); **3.** exeg. 1Cor.1:28 and Rom.4:17 τίνα δὲ τὰ μὴ ὄντα ἢ οἱ ἐστερημένοι τοῦ ὄντος καὶ μὴ μετέχοντες αὐτοῦ, οὕτω καλούμενοι πρὸς ἀντιδιαστολὴν τῶν μετεχόντων τοῦ εἰπόντος, 'ἐγώ εἰμι ὁ ὤν'; καλεῖ δὲ τὰ μὴ ὄντα ἵνα ὑπακούσασιν αὐτοῖς χαρίσηται τὸ εἶναι. ἀλλ' ἴσως τις πρὸς ταῦτα ἐρεῖ, πῶς ὁ ἀπόστολος ἑτέρωθί φησι μεθ' ἕτερα, 'ἐξελέξατο ὁ θεὸς τὰ μὴ ὄντα ἵνα τὰ ὄντα καταργήσῃ'; ἀλλ' εὔδηλον ὡς ἕτερόν ἐστι τοῦτο σημαινόμενον τοῦ ὄντος καὶ μὴ ὄντος ὅσον ἀπὸ πάσης τῆς ἐκεῖσε συμφράσεως· ὄντες μὲν γὰρ ἐνθάδε οἱ κατὰ σάρκα σοφοί...μὴ ὄντες δὲ οἱ ἄλλως παρὰ τούτοις διακείμενοι ὡς πρὸς τὴν ἐκείνων ὑπόληψιν Or.*Rom.*4:17(*JTS* 13 p.361); Eph.1:1 ἐπὶ μόνων Ἐφεσίων εὕρομεν κείμενον τό, 'τοῖς ἁγίοις τοῖς οὖσι' καὶ ζητοῦμεν...τί δύναται σημαίνειν. ὅρα οὖν εἰ μὴ ὥσπερ ἐν τῇ Ἐξόδῳ ὄνομά φησιν ἑαυτοῦ ὁ χρηματίζων Μωσεῖ τὸ ⟨ὁ⟩ ὤν, οὕτως οἱ μετέχοντες τοῦ ὄντος γίνονται ὄντες, καλούμενοι οἱονεὶ ἐκ τοῦ μὴ εἶναι εἰς τὸ εἶναι, 'ἐξελέξατο' γὰρ 'ὁ θεὸς τὰ μὴ ὄντα...ἵνα τὰ ὄντα καταργήσῃ.' καὶ ζητήσει τις, πῶς τὰ ὄντα καταργεῖ...ἐὰν γάρ τις μετεσχηκὼς τοῦ εἶναι ἐπιλαθόμενος τῆς μετοχῆς, ἑαυτῷ καταχαρίσηται τὴν τοῦ εἶναι αἰτίαν, καὶ μὴ τὴν πᾶσαν εὐχαριστίαν ἀναφέρῃ ἐπὶ τὸν ἐκ τοῦ μὴ εἶναι τὸ εἶναι αὐτῷ ὅμοιον κατ' εἰκόνα χαρισάμενον, τότε καταργεῖται τὸ ὂν id.*Eph.*1:1(p.235).

E. the being of the Son; **1.** (Marcellus), ref. Ex.3:14 'ἐγώ εἰμι ὁ ὤν', λέγει μὲν τῷ Μωσεῖ ὁ πατήρ, λέγει δὲ δηλονότι διὰ τοῦ λόγου Marcell.*fr.*56 ap.Eus.*Marcell.*2.2(p.40.35; M.24.792D); πῶς γὰρ ἐγχωρεῖ τὸν λέγοντα 'ἐγώ εἰμι ὁ ὤν' μὴ συνομολογεῖν ὅτι κατὰ ἀντιδιαστολὴν τοῦ μὴ ὄντος ὁ ὢν ἑαυτὸν εἶναί φησιν; εἰ δὲ τὸν υἱὸν ὑποστάσει διῃρημένον τοῦτο φάσκοι λέγειν τό, 'ἐγώ εἰμι ὁ ὤν', ταὐτὸν αὖθις περὶ τοῦ πατρὸς λέγειν νομισθήσεται· ἑκάτερον δὲ τούτων ἀσεβὲς id. *fr.*58 ap.Eus.*e.th.*2.19(p.123.16ff.; M.24.944B); εἴτ' οὖν ὁ πατὴρ λέγοι εἴθ' ὁ υἱὸς τό, 'ἐγώ εἰμι ὁ ὤν', ἀληθεύοι ἂν ἑκατέρως ὁ λόγος. ὅ τε γὰρ πατὴρ 'ὁ ὢν' εἴη ἄν, μόνος αὐτὸς ὢν 'ἐπὶ πάντων, καὶ διὰ πάντων, καὶ ἐν πᾶσιν θεός'...ὅ τε υἱὸς καὶ αὐτὸς χρηματίζων 'ὁ ὢν' ἀληθεύοι ἄν, μόνος ὢν υἱὸς μονογενὴς τοῦ ὄντος· ἀλλὰ καὶ εἰκὼν τοῦ ἀοράτου θεοῦ ὑπάρχων κατὰ τοῦτο εἴη ἂν αὐτοῦ εἰκών, καθ' ὃ μόνος ἦν αὐτὸς ὁ ὤν· διὸ καὶ αὐτὸς χρηματίζοι ἂν 'ὁ ὤν' Eus.*e.th.*2.20(p.129.28ff.; 953C); **2.** in early stages of Arian controversy; **a.** Arian position οὐκ ἦν πρὸ τοῦ γεννηθῆναι...οὐδὲ ἅμα τῷ πατρὶ τὸ εἶναι ἔχει...διὸ καὶ πρὸ τοῦ υἱοῦ ἔστιν [sc. Father]...καθὸ οὖν παρὰ τοῦ θεοῦ τὸ εἶναι ἔχει...κατὰ τοῦτο ἀρχὴ αὐτοῦ ὡς θεὸς αὐτοῦ καὶ πρὸ αὐτοῦ ὢν Ar.*ep. Alex.*(p.13.9; M.26.709B,C); λεγόντων ὅτι ἦν πότε ὅτε οὐκ ἦν ὁ υἱὸς τοῦ θεοῦ, καὶ γέγονεν ὕστερον ὁ πρότερον μὴ ὑπάρχων...'πάντα γάρ', φασίν, 'ὁ θεὸς ἐξ οὐκ ὄντων ἐποίησε', συναναλαμβάνοντες τῇ τῶν ἁπάντων...κτίσει καὶ τὸν υἱὸν τοῦ θεοῦ. οἷς ἀκολούθως καί φασιν αὐτὸν τρεπτῆς εἶναι φύσεως...καὶ τῇ ἐξ οὐκ ὄντων ὑποθέσει καὶ τὰς θείας τοῦ εἶναι αὐτὸν ἀεὶ συναιροῦντες γραφάς Alex.Al.*ep.Alex.*2(p.21. 8ff.; M.18.552A,B); **b.** refuted ὅτι ὁ υἱὸς τοῦ θεοῦ οὔτε ἐξ οὐκ ὄντων γεγένηται, οὔτε ἦν πότε ὅτε οὐκ ἦν, αὐτάρκης ἐπαίδευσεν Ἰωάννης ὁ εὐαγγελιστὴς...[Jo.1:8]...ἀλλὰ γὰρ καὶ ὅτι τοῖς ἐξ οὐκ ὄντων γενομένοις ὁ λόγος τοῦ θεοῦ οὐ συναριθμεῖται, πάντα δι' αὐτοῦ γεγονέναι φησὶν ὁ αὐτὸς Ἰωάννης...εἰ γὰρ πάντα δι' αὐτοῦ ἐγένετο, πῶς ὁ τοῖς γενομένοις τὸ εἶναι χαρισάμενος αὐτός ποτε οὐκ ἦν...αὐτὸς μὲν ἦν ἐν ἀρχῇ, πάντα δὲ δι' αὐτοῦ ἐγένετο [καὶ ἐξ οὐκ ὄντων ἐποίησεν]. ἐναντίον γὰρ δοκεῖ τοῖς ἐξ οὐκ ὄντων γενομένοις τὸ ὂν καὶ ἀφεστηκὸς σφόδρα *ib.*4 (p.22.4ff.; 553A,B); ἀσεβεστάτης οὖν φανείσης τῆς ἐξ οὐκ ὄντων ὑποθέσεως, ἀνάγκη τὸν πατέρα ἀεὶ εἶναι πατέρα· ἔστι δὲ πατὴρ ἀεὶ παρόντος τοῦ υἱοῦ, δι' ὃν χρηματίζει πατήρ...εἰ δὲ καὶ ἡ εἰκὼν τοῦ θεοῦ οὐκ ἦν ἀεί, δῆλον ὅτι οὐδὲ οὗ ἐστιν εἰκὼν ἔστιν ἀεί. ἀλλὰ καὶ τῷ μὴ εἶναι τὸν τῆς ὑποστάσεως τοῦ θεοῦ χαρακτῆρα συναναιρεῖται κἀκεῖνος ὁ πάντως ὑπ' αὐτοῦ χαρακτηριζόμενος *ib.*7(pp.23.28–24.5; 557B,C); **c.** orthodox confession of faith πιστεύομεν...εἰς μόνον ἀγέννητον πατέρα, οὐδένα τοῦ εἶναι αὐτῷ τὸν αἴτιον ἔχοντα...καὶ εἰς ἕνα κύριον Ἰησοῦν Χριστόν...γεννηθέντα οὐκ ἐκ τοῦ μὴ ὄντος, ἀλλ' ἐκ τοῦ ὄντος πατρός *ib.*12(p.27.1ff.; 565A,B); **3.** Athanasian argument ὁ δὲ θεὸς ὤν ἐστι, καὶ οὐ σύνθετος· διὸ καὶ ὁ τούτου λόγος ὤν ἐστι, καὶ οὐ σύνθετος...τῶν μὲν γὰρ γενητῶν ἡ φύσις, ἅτε δὴ ἐξ οὐκ ὄντων ὑποστᾶσα, ῥευστή τις καὶ ἀσθενὴς...τυγχάνει· ὁ δὲ τῶν ὅλων θεὸς ἀγαθὸς...ἐστί... ἀγαθῷ γὰρ περὶ οὐδενὸς ἂν γένοιτο φθόνος· ὅθεν οὐδὲ τὸ εἶναί τινι φθονεῖ, ἀλλὰ πάντας εἶναι βούλεται...ὁρῶν οὖν τὴν γενητὴν πᾶσαν φύσιν...ῥευστὴν οὖσαν καὶ διαλυομένην· ἵνα μὴ...πάλιν εἰς τὸ μὴ εἶναι ἀναλυθῇ τὸ ὅλον...τῷ ἑαυτοῦ λόγῳ...τὴν σύμπασαν διακυβερνᾷ καὶ καθίστησιν, ἵνα, τῇ τοῦ λόγου ἡγεμονίᾳ...φωτιζομένη ἡ κτίσις, βεβαίως διαμένειν δυνηθῇ, ἅτε δὴ τοῦ ὄντως ὄντος ἐκ πατρὸς λόγου μεταλαμβάνουσα καὶ βοηθουμένη δι' αὐτοῦ εἰς τὸ εἶναι· μὴ ἄρα πάθῃ ὅπερ ἂν ἔπαθεν, εἰ μὴ ὁ λόγος αὐτὴν ἐτήρει, λέγω δὴ τὸ μὴ εἶναι Ath. *gent.*41(M.25.81C–84B); τὰ μὲν κτίσματα ὑπὸ τὴν ἀρχὴν πεποίηται, καὶ διαστηματικὴν ἀρχὴν τοῦ εἶναι ἔχει...ἀπὸ γὰρ ἀρχῆς τινος τοῦ μὴ εἶναί ποτε γέγονε καὶ ἐκτίσθη τὰ γενητά...οὐκοῦν τὰ μὲν κτίσματα ἤρξατο γίνεσθαι· ὁ δὲ τοῦ θεοῦ λόγος...οὐκ ἔχων ἀρχὴν τοῦ εἶναι, εἰκότως οὐκ ἤρξατο τοῦ εἶναι, οὐδὲ ἤρξατο γίνεσθαι, ἀλλ' ἦν ἀεί...καὶ τῶν μὲν γενητῶν τὸ εἶναι ἐν τῷ γίνεσθαι μετρεῖται, καὶ ἀπό τινος ἀρχῆς ἄρχεται ταῦτα διὰ τοῦ λόγου ποιεῖν ὁ θεός, ἵνα καὶ τὸ μὴ εἶναι, πρὶν γενέσθαι, ταῦτα γινώσκηται· ὁ δὲ λόγος τὸ εἶναι οὐκ ἐν ἄλλῃ ἀρχῇ ἔχει, ἀλλ' ἐν τῷ πατρί id.*Ar.*2.57(M.26.268C–269B); ref. 2Cor.5:18 ὅτι, τοῦ θεοῦ ὄντος, τὰ πάντα παρ' αὐτοῦ διὰ τοῦ λόγου οὐκ ὄντα πρότερον εἰς τὸ εἶναι γέγονε, διὰ τοῦτο εἴρηται τὸ ἐκ τοῦ θεοῦ· ὁ δὲ λόγος, ἐπεὶ μὴ κτίσμα ἐστίν...ἔστι μόνος ἐκ τοῦ πατρός· τῆς δὲ τοιαύτης διανοίας γνώρισμα τὸ εἶναι τὸν υἱὸν ἐκ τῆς οὐσίας τοῦ πατρός id.*decr.*19 (p.16.14; M.25.449B); **4.** Eunomian controversy; **a.** orthodox position ὁ υἱὸς πρὸ αἰῶνος ὤν, καὶ ἀεὶ ὤν, οὐκ ἤρξατο τοῦ εἶναί ποτε Bas. *Eun.*2.12(1.247B; M.29.593B); **b.** Eunomian contradiction λεγόντων, ἐκ τοῦ μὴ ὄντος αὐτὸν εἰς τὸ εἶναι παρῆχθαι *ib.*(247D; M.593C); ἤτοι γὰρ ὄντα, φησίν [sc. Eunomius], ἐγέννησεν ὁ θεὸς τὸν υἱόν, ἢ οὐκ ὄντα. ἀλλ' εἰ μὲν οὐκ ὄντα, μηδείς μοι, φησί, τόλμαν ἐπεγκαλείτω. εἰ δὲ ὄντα, οὐκ ἀτοπίας μόνον...ἀλλὰ καὶ πάσης εὐηθείας ὑπερβολὴν ὁ λόγος ἔχει· τῷ γὰρ ὄντι οὐ δεῖ γεννήσεως *ib.*2.14(248D,E; M.597B); μὴ ὄντα φαμὲν τὸν υἱὸν γεγεννῆσθαι *ib.*2.18(1.253C; M.609A); **c.** Basil's refutation, exeg. Jo.1:1 οὔτε τό, ἦν, διαβάντας τῷ λογισμῷ, εἰς τὸ ὅτε οὐκ ἦν δυνατὸν ὑπερκύψαι. ἀθέτησις γάρ ἐστι τοῦ ἦν, ἡ τοῦ ὅτι οὐκ ἦν ἐπίνοια *ib.*2.14(249C; M.600A); [Apoc.1:8] οἷον γὰρ τὸ ὤν, τοιοῦτον καὶ τὸ ἦν, ἀΐδιον ὁμοίως καὶ ἄχρονον...ἀνεπινόητον μὲν γὰρ τῆς ἀρχῆς τὸ πρεσβύτερον, ἀχώριστον δὲ ταύτης τοῦ θεοῦ λόγου τὸ εἶναι *ib.*(249D,E; M.600B); οὐ παύσῃ μὴ ὄντα προσαγορεύων...τὸν ὄντως ὄντα...τὸν πᾶσι τοῖς οὖσι τοῦ εἶναι παρεκτικόν;...ἐγὼ γάρ εἰμι, φησίν, ὁ ὤν. καὶ τούτοις οὐδεὶς ἀντερεῖ μὴ οὐχὶ ἐκ προσώπου τοῦ κυρίου εἰρῆσθαι... τίς οὖν ὁ αὐτὸς καὶ ἄγγελος καὶ θεός; ἆρα οὐχὶ περὶ οὗ μεμαθήκαμεν, ὅτι καλεῖται τὸ ὄνομα αὐτοῦ μεγάλης βουλῆς ἄγγελος; *ib.*2.18(253D; M.609A); εἰς τὸν κατόπιν χρόνον ἐπανελθόντες τῷ λόγῳ...μὴ εἶναί ποτε τὸν υἱὸν βλασφημοῦντες, ὡς τῇ μὲν ἑαυτοῦ φύσει μὴ ὄντα, χάριτι δὲ εἰς τὸ εἶναι ὑπὸ τοῦ θεοῦ παραχθέντα; εἶτα ἣν ὁ Παῦλος περὶ τῶν εἰδώλων ἀφῆκε φωνήν, εἰπών· ἐδουλεύσατε τοῖς φύσει μὴ οὖσι θεοῖς *ib.*2.19 (254C,D; M.612B); **d.** refutation by Gr. Nyss. πᾶσαν τὴν διὰ τῶν σοφισμάτων κατασκευὴν τὴν περὶ τοῦ μὴ εἶναί ποτε τὸν ὄντως ὄντα οὐδὲν ἄλλο ἢ παράβασιν τοῦ Χριστιανισμοῦ...εἶναι διοριζόμεθα. καὶ γὰρ εὐαγγελιστοῦ διὰ τῆς θεολογίας πανταχόθεν ἐξορίσαντος τὸ μὴ ὂν ἐκ τοῦ ὄντος καὶ διὰ τῆς συνεχοῦς τοῦ 'ἦν' ἐπαναλήψεως τὴν τοῦ μὴ εἶναι ὑπόνοιαν ἐπιμελῶς ἐξαλείψαντος, μονογενῆ δὲ...λόγον θεοῦ... κατονομάσαντος, παγίαν ἔχομεν ταύτην ἐν ἑαυτοῖς τὴν κρίσιν..., ὅτι εἰ θεός ἐστιν ὁ...υἱός, ἀεὶ χρὴ πιστεύειν αὐτὸν εἶναι, τὸν θεὸν πεπιστευμένον. ἀλλὰ μὴν εἰ ἀληθῶς ἔστι θεός, καὶ ἀεὶ πάντως ἔστι καὶ οὐδέποτε ἐν τῷ μὴ εἶναι καταλαμβάνεται. θεὸς γάρ...εἰ νῦν ἔστι, καὶ ἀεὶ πάντως ἦν. εἰ δέ ποτε μὴ ἦν, οὐδὲ νῦν ἔστιν ὅλως. ἀλλ' ἐπειδὴ τὸ υἱὸν εἶναι τὸν μονογενῆ θεὸν καὶ εἰσαεὶ διαμένειν...ὁμολογεῖται, τοῦτό φαμεν ὅτι ἐν τῷ πατρὶ ὢν οὐ καθ' ἓν μόνον ἐστὶν ἐν αὐτῷ, ἀλλὰ κατὰ πάντα ὅσα νοεῖται ὁ πατήρ, διὰ πάντων ἐστὶν ἐν αὐτῷ Gr.Nyss.*Eun.*8 (2 p.178.28ff.; M.45.772B,C); Eunomian conception of relation of being of Father to being of Son discussed, *ib.*10(2 p.247.29ff.; 852Bff.); *ib.*9(2 p.220.28ff.; 820Cff.); πεπιστευκέναι τὴν ἐκκλησίαν... υἱὸν...κατὰ φύσιν γεννητῶς ἐκ τοῦ ὄντος ὄντα *ib.*4(2 p.79.15; 653B); ὁ τῇ τοῦ ὄντος ἐπωνυμίᾳ ἑαυτὸν γνωρίσας, ὁ μονογενής ἐστι θεὸς *ib.*11(2 p.263.1; 869D); **5.** in later fathers; **a.** Cyril ἀγνοοῦσιν...ὅτι τὸ ὄντως ὂν καὶ κατ' οὐσίαν τίκτειν δυνάμενον, τὸ θεῖόν ἐστιν. αὐτὸ γὰρ δὴ περὶ ἑαυτοῦ φησιν· 'ἐγώ εἰμι ὁ ὤν', ὡς τῶν ἄλλων ἁπάντων, οὐκ ὄντων μὲν πρὶν γενέσθαι, βουλήσει δὲ θείᾳ πρὸς τὸ εἶναι παρενεχθέντων. οὐκοῦν τὸ ὄντως ὄν, ᾧ καὶ τὸ εἶναι κυριώτατον ὄνομα, αὐτὸ δὴ καὶ μόνον κατ' οὐσίαν γεννήσει Cyr.*thes.*13(5^1.133A,B); ref. Jo.1:1 πῶς δὲ ἡμῖν οὐκ ἀρκέσει τὸ 'ἦν', πρὸς ἀνατροπὴν τῶν πεποιῆσθαι λεγόντων αὐτόν; εἰ γὰρ ἦν, οὐκ ἐγένετο· εἰ ἐγένετο, οὐκ ἦν. ἐπειδὴ δὲ ἦν, οὐκ ἐγένετο· τὸ γὰρ ὂν καὶ ὑπάρχον ἤδη, καὶ τοῦτο ἐν ἀρχῇ, οὐκ ἂν λέγοιτο πεποιῆσθαί ποτε *ib.*32(5^1.312C); id.*Jo.*1.1(4.11A); ἐπιπλέκει δὲ τῷ τῆς ἀρχῆς ὀνόματι χρησίμως τὸ 'ἦν', ἵνα μὴ μόνον εὐκλεής, ἀλλὰ νοῆται καὶ προαιώνιος· τέθειται γὰρ ἐν τούτοις τὸ 'ἦν', εἰς βαθεῖάν τινα...καὶ τὴν ἔξω χρόνων ἄρρητον γέννησιν ἀνατεῖνον τοῦ θεωροῦντος τὴν ἔννοιαν *ib.*(14B); *ib.*1.2 (15C); οὐ μόνον ἦν ὁ λόγος πρὸς θεόν, ἀλλ' ἦν καὶ θεός, ἵνα διὰ μὲν τοῦ εἶναι πρὸς θεόν, ἕτερος ὢν παρὰ τὸν πατέρα γνωρίζηται, καὶ υἱὸς ὑπάρχειν...πιστεύηται· διὰ δὲ τοῦ εἶναι θεός, ὁμοούσιός τε καὶ ἐξ αὐτοῦ νοῆται κατὰ φύσιν...ἦν οὖν καὶ θεός· οὐ γέγονεν ὕστερον, ἀλλὰ πάλιν ἦν, εἰ καὶ ὅτι μάλιστα τῷ εἶναι θεὸν ἀκολουθήσει πάντως καὶ τὸ ἀϊδίως εἶναι, ἐπεὶ τὸ ἐν χρόνῳ γεγονός, ἢ καὶ ὅλως ἐκ μὴ ὄντος εἰς τὸ εἶναι παρενεχθέν, οὐκ ἂν εἴη φύσει θεός. ἔχοντος...τοῦ θεοῦ λόγου διὰ μὲν τοῦ ἦν τὸ ἀΐδιον, διὰ δὲ τοῦ εἶναι θεὸν τὸ πρὸς τὸν πατέρα ὁμοούσιον *ib.*1.3(20A,C); **b.** Jo. D. οὐ γὰρ ἐκ τοῦ μὴ ὄντος εἰς τὸ εἶναι παρήχθη ὁ υἱὸς τοῦ θεοῦ...ἀλλ' ἀεὶ ἦν σὺν τῷ πατρί...οὐ γὰρ ἦν ποτε ὁ πατήρ, ὅτε οὐκ ἦν ὁ υἱός...εἰ δὲ ἦν ἡ μὴ ἔχων υἱόν, οὐκ ἦν πατήρ· καὶ εἰ μετὰ ταῦτα ἔσχεν υἱόν, μετὰ ταῦτα ἐγένετο πατήρ, μὴ ὢν πρὸ τούτου πατήρ, καὶ ἐτράπη ἐκ τοῦ μὴ εἶναι πατὴρ εἰς τὸ γενέσθαι πατήρ· ὅπερ πάσης βλασφημίας ἐστὶ χαλεπώτερον Jo.D.*f.o.*1.8(M.94.812A); ἐὰν εἴπῃ ὁ αἱρετικὸς ὁ λόγος γενόμενος ἦν καὶ πρὶν γενέσθαι οὐκ ἦν, τί πλέον ἔσχε τῆς γῆς; καὶ γὰρ περὶ τῆς γῆς εἶπε Μωυσῆς· ἡ δὲ γῆ ἦν. εἰ οὖν τό, ἐν ἀρχῇ, εἰς ποίησιν λαμβάνουσι καὶ οὐ κατὰ τὴν ἀΐδιον φύσιν, οὐδὲν πλέον ἔχει τῆς γῆς· καὶ γὰρ ὁ θεὸς λόγος ἦν καὶ ἡ γῆ ἦν. ἀλλ' ἐκεῖ μὲν ἐν ἀρχῇ ἦν μὴ γενόμενος ὁ ἀεὶ ὤν, ἡ δὲ γῆ γενομένη ἦν †Jo.D.*creat.*1(p.59); cf. Chrys.*hom.2.4 in Jo.*(8.13B,C); **6.** credal οὐ πάντοτε...εἶναι ἠδύνατο, εἰ ἀρχὴν ἔλαβεν, ὅτι ὁ πάντοτε ὢν ἀρχὴν οὐκ ἔχει λόγος CSard.*ep.cath.* ap.Thdt.*h.e.*2.8.42(3.845); ὁμολογοῦμεν...μονογενῆ τὸν λόγον, ὃς πάντοτε ἦν καὶ ἔστιν ἐν τῷ πατρί...ὃ πάντοτέ ἐστιν, οὐδέποτε τοῦ εἶναι ἤρξατο οὐδὲ ἐκλείπειν δύναται *ib.*2.8.44(846); τοὺς δὲ λέγοντας ἐξ οὐκ ὄντων τὸν υἱὸν...καὶ ὅτι ἦν χρόνος ποτὲ ἢ αἰών, ὅτε μὴ ἦν, ἀλλοτρίους οἶδεν ἡ...ἐκκλησία *Symb.Ant.*(345)2(p.252.4; M.26.728C) = *Symb. Sirm.*1 *anath.*1; οὔτε γὰρ ἐξ οὐκ ὄντων τὸν υἱὸν λέγειν ἀσφαλές...ἀλλ' οὐδὲ τὸ ἦν ποτε ὅτε οὐκ ἦν ἐξ ἀγράφων ἐπισφαλῶς λέγοντας χρονικόν τι διάστημα προενθυμητέον αὐτοῦ, ἀλλὰ μόνον τὸν ἀχρόνως αὐτὸν γεγεννηκότα θεόν *Symb.Ant.*(345)3(p.252.10; M.26.729A).

F. of created being; **1.** creation *ex nihilo* ἐκάλεσεν γὰρ ἡμᾶς οὐκ ὄντας καὶ ἠθέλησεν ἐκ μὴ ὄντος εἶναι ἡμᾶς *2Clem.*1.8; ἐκ τοῦ μὴ ὄντος εἰς τὸ εἶναι προαγαγεῖν Eus.*e.th.*1.12(p.71.5; M.24.845D); as activity of Son, *ib.*2.6(p.103.33; 908B); Ath.*inc.*42.2(M.25.169B); id. *Ar.*3.19(M.26.361C); τῷ γὰρ γενικῷ τῆς προσηγορίας ἐν κατὰ πάντων ἐστὶ τῶν ἐκ τοῦ μὴ ὄντος ὑποστάντων τὸ τῆς κτίσεως ὄνομα Gr.Nyss. *Eun.*5(2 p.120.8; M.45.701A); *ib.*9(2 p.223.23; 824A); Epiph.*haer.*69. 59(p.208.3; M.42.296B); affirmed by Christians opp. philosophers, acc. whom δημιουργός...μὴ δυνάμενος ἐκ μὴ ὄντων ὑποστῆναι τὰ ὄντα Proc.G.*Gen.*proem.(M.87.29B); **2.** characterized by having a beginning, Ath.*ep.Afr.*8(M.26.1044A); ‡Ath.*Ar.*4.27(p.75.23; M.26. 509C).

G. not to be predicated of evil ἔξω δὲ αὐτῆς [sc. divine nature] οὐδέν, ὅτι μὴ ἡ κακία μόνη, ἥτις, εἰ κἂν παράδοξον εἰπεῖν, ἐν τῷ μὴ εἶναι τὸ εἶναι ἔχει· οὐ γὰρ ἄλλη τίς ἐστι καὶ κακίας γένεσις, εἰ μὴ τοῦ ὄντος στέρησις. τὸ δὲ κυρίως ὂν ἡ τοῦ ἀγαθοῦ φύσις ἐστίν. ὃ οὖν ἐν τῷ ὄντι οὐκ ἔστιν, ἐν τῷ μὴ εἶναι πάντως ἐστίν Gr.Nyss.*anim.et res.*(M. 46.93B); οὐκ ἔστι τὸ κακόν, ᾗ κακόν, οὔτε ὄν, οὔτε ἐν τοῖς οὖσι Dion. Ar.*d.n.*4.33(M.3.733A).

H. ref. H. Ghost: his being is not derived from creatures; hence he is divine, Ath.*ep.Serap.*3.2(M.26.628B).

I. of flesh of Christ, ref. Pr.8:22 ἔκτισεν γὰρ ἀληθῶς τὸ μὴ ὂν πεποιηκὼς ὁ δεσπότης ἡμῶν θεός· οὐκ οὖσαν ⟨γὰρ⟩ τὴν σάρκα, ἣν ἀνείληφεν ὁ λόγος ⟨ἀλλὰ μὴ οὖσαν ἔκτισεν⟩ Marcell.*fr.*10 ap.Eus. *Marcell.*2.3(p.46.26ff.; M.24.801D).

J. in rel. to time ἡ τῷ χρόνῳ προήκουσα τῆς μεταγενεστέρας οὐσίας τί μᾶλλον ἔχει τὸ εἶναι, κατ' αὐτὸν λέγω τὸν τοῦ εἶναι λόγον, ὥστε τὴν μὲν ἀνωτάτω καὶ κυρίαν λέγειν, τὴν δὲ μὴ οὕτως ἔχειν; Gr.Nyss.*Eun.* 1(1 p.73.20; M.45.304B).

K. εἶναι θείως *exist divinely, be deified,* Dion.Ar.*e.h.*2.1(M.3. 392B).

L. Basilidean: of primal aeon οἱ μὲν...λέγουσι...μήτε ὅλως ὄντα τι Iren.*haer.*1.11.5(M.7.569A); Βασιλείδης...λέγει εἶναι θεὸν οὐκ ὄντα, πεποιημένον κόσμον ἐξ οὐκ ὄντων οὐκ ὄντα...ἔχειν γὰρ ἐν ἑαυτῷ τὰ πάντα οἷον οὐκ ὄντα ὑπὸ τοῦ οὐκ ὄντος θεοῦ γενέσθαι προβεβουλευμένα. ἦν οὖν, φασί, ἐν αὐτῷ τῷ σπέρματι υἱότης τριμερής, κατὰ πάντα τῷ οὐκ ὄντι θεῷ ὁμοούσιος ἐξ οὐκ ὄντων Hipp.*haer.*10.14(p.274.17ff.; M.16. 3427C–3430A).

***εἴποθεν**, *if from anywhere,* Nonn.*par.Jo.*7:31(M.43.809B *divisim*).

***εἰρηναγωγέω**, *lead in peace, peacefully,* Clem.*paed.*1.8(p.128.23; M.8.329A).

εἰρηναῖος, **1.** *peaceable, peaceful* εἰ. ψυχῇ δέξασθαι τοὺς περὶ Ἄρειον Ath.*apol.sec.*84(p.163.5; M.25.400A); εἰ. γράμματα Soz.*h.e.* 8.3.5(M.67.1520D); spiritually εἰ. ὕμνοις Dion.Ar.*d.n.*11.1(M.3. 948D); ἄρτου καὶ ποτηρίου κοινὴ καὶ εἰ. μετάδοσις [i.e. in eucharist] id.*e.h.*3.3.1(M.3.428B); ref. union with God, *ib.*3.3.8(437A); τῆς τριάδος...ἧς οὐδὲν οὕτως...πρὸς ἑαυτὴν εἰρηναῖον Gr.Naz.*or.*22.14 (M.35.1148B); neut. plur. as subst., Ath.*inc.*50.5(εἰρήνην M.25.185C); **2.** *prescribed by peace treaty,* of reparations τὰ εἰ. χρήματα Men.*exc. Rom.*16(p.210.15; M.113.909C); *ib.*20(p.220.31; 925D).

εἰρηνάρχης, ὁ, *prince* or *author of peace*; of Christ, ‡Meth.*palm.*6 (M.18.393D); ὁ πνευματικὸς Σολομών, ὁ εἰ. Jo.D.*hom.*9.12(M.96.740A); ‡Jo.D.*hom.*6.10(M.96.677A).

***εἰρηναρχία**, ἡ, *principle of peace*; as divine name, Dion.Ar.*d.n.* 11.1(M.3.949A).

εἰρηναρχικός, *belonging to the police* εἰ. τάξις *M.Con.*2.2.

εἰρήναρχος, ὁ, *prince of peace*; of Christ, ‡Epiph.*hom.*6(M.43. 504B).

εἰρηνεύ-ω, **1.** *make, establish peace, reconcile*; **a.** in gen. ∼σεις δὲ μαχομένους *Did.*4.3=*Barn.*19.12; Eus.*v.C.*3.15(p.84.2; M.20.1072A);

Gr.Naz.*ep.*185(M.37.301B); eccl. legislation τὰ δικαστήρια ὑμῶν γινέσθω δευτέρᾳ σαββάτων, ὅπως...ἕως σαββάτου ἔχοντες ἄδειαν δυνηθείητε...~σαι εἰς τὴν κυριακὴν τοὺς διαφερομένους πρὸς ἀλλήλους *Const.App.*2.47.1; **b.** of reconciliation of heretics, Ath.*tom.*8(M.26.805A); id.*ep.Epict.*12(p.18.5; M.26.1069A); **c.** spiritual, *pacify* Χριστέ ...~σόν μου τὸν λογισμόν *A.Xanthipp.*18(p.78.20); Mac.Aeg.*hom.* 8.6(M.34.532B); ‡Proc.G.*Pr.*1:1(M.87.1221B); Dor.*doct.*17.2(M.88.1801C); δόξα...τῇ...τριάδι, τῇ...~ούσῃ τὴν ζωὴν ἡμῶν *Lit.Jac.*(p.160.7); **2.** *live, be at peace, have peace*; **a.** of Church τὸ ποίμνιον τοῦ Χριστοῦ ~έτω μετὰ τῶν καθεσταμένων πρεσβυτέρων *1Clem.*54.2; ἐκκλησίᾳ...~ούσῃ ἐν σαρκὶ καὶ πνεύματι τῷ πάθει Ἰησοῦ Χριστοῦ Ign.*Trall.*proem.; through absence of persecution, id.*Polyc.*7.1; Const. ap.Eus.*v.C.*2.49(p.62.13; M.20.1028A); Ath.*apol.sec.*30(p.109.9; M.25.297C); **b.** of Christians having peace with each other, Herm.*vis.* 3.12.3; ἐπίσκοποι, ~ετε μετ' ἀλλήλων *Const.App.*2.44.2; *ib.*2.54.4; *ib.*2.56.4; and with God οὐδὲν βλάβος ἡμῶν, κἂν παρὰ πάντων πολεμώμεθα, τῷ δὲ θεῷ ~ωμεν Chrys.*hom.1.1 in 1Cor.*(10.5C); ἂν τῷ διαβόλῳ πολεμῶμεν, ~ομεν τῷ θεῷ id.*hom.24.1 in Eph.*(11.180A); **c.** having peace with all creation as sign of sanctity, Ath.*v.Anton.* 51(M.26.917B); **d.** as state of angels, Or.*Cels.*6.44(p.115.13; M.11.1368A); **e.** of the heavenly Jerusalem πόλις ~ομένη Mac.Aeg.*hom.* 11.15(M.34.556C); *ib.*25.7(672C).

εἰρήνη, ἡ, *peace*;

A. def. and properties; **1.** material, an essential good without which other good things cannot be enjoyed, Gr.Nyss.*beat.*7(M.44.1281B); **2.** spiritual τελειοτάτη τῶν εὐλογιῶν...ἡ εἰ., εὐστάθειά τις οὖσα τοῦ ἡγεμονικοῦ Bas.*hom.in Ps.*28(1.124A; M.29.305A); ἄνω γάρ ἐστιν ἡ εἰ. ἡ ἀληθής...ζήτησον οὖν εἰ., λύσιν τῶν τοῦ κόσμου τούτου θορύβων...ἵνα κτήσῃ τὴν εἰ. τοῦ θεοῦ id.*hom.in Ps.*33(153E; M.376B, C); εἰ. δὲ τὸ καθ' ἕκαστον αἱρετόν, καὶ ἡ κατὰ τῶν παθῶν δεσποτεία Gr.Naz.*or.*32.15(M.36.1149A); ἔστιν ἡ εἰ. ... ἀγαπητική τις πρὸς τὸ ὁμόφυλον συνδιάθεσις Gr.Nyss.*beat.*7(M.44.1284B); exeg. Rom.1:7 εἰ. δὲ ἡ τῶν ἀοράτων πολεμίων ἀπαλλαγὴ ὧν ἡμᾶς ἀπαλλάσσει Χριστός, καὶ τὸ μὴ στασιάζειν τὸ σῶμα πρὸς τοὺς τῆς ψυχῆς λογισμοὺς καὶ ἡ πρὸς ἀλλήλους εὐσεβὴς συμφωνία Thdr.Mops.*Rom.*1:7(p.113.11); *ib.* 8:5f.(p.135.6ff.; M.66.821A).

B. sources; **1.** divine; **a.** God, *1Clem.*19.2; *ib.*60.4; Clem.*q.d.s.*22 (p.174.17; M.9.628A); cf.*Hom.Clem.*9.19; εἰ. φίλη...ἣν θεοῦ τε εἶναι ἀκούομεν, καὶ ἧς θεόν, τὸν θεὸν καὶ αὐτόθεον Gr.Naz.*or.*22.1(M.35.1132A); Didym.*Trin.*1.26(M.39.384A); ἡ ὄντως εἰ. παρὰ τοῦ θεοῦ Chrys.*hom.1.1 in 1Cor.*(10.5C); Sever.*pac.*2(p.19.23); Dion.Ar.*d.n.* 11.1(M.3.949A); *ib.*11.2(952A); **b.** Christ τὰ παθήματα αὐτοῦ [sc. Χριστοῦ] ἦν πρὸ ὀφθαλμῶν ὑμῶν. οὕτως εἰ. βαθεῖα...ἐδέδοτο πᾶσιν *1Clem.* 2.2; Χριστέ...ὁ ποιῶν εἰ. πάντοτε μετὰ τῶν ἀγαπώντων τὴν εἰ. *A.Xanthipp.*28(p.78.20f.); τίς ὁ τοὺς μισοῦντας ἀλλήλους εἰς εἰ. συνάψας, εἰ μὴ ὁ...τοῦ πατρὸς υἱός; Ath.*inc.*52.1(M.25.188C); ὁ ζητῶν εἰ., Χριστὸν ἐκζητεῖ, ὅτι αὐτός ἐστιν ἡ εἰ. ... ποιῶν εἰ. Bas.*hom.in Ps.*33 (1.153E; M.29.376C); Chrys.*exp.in Ps.*45:10(5.186B); Sever.*pac.*1 (p.16.19ff.); εἰ. ἐστὶν οἷον ὥσπερ χώρας...μεγάλης, διαφόροις δεσποτείαις ὑποβεβλημένης. οἱ ὅροι διατειχίζοντες δεικνύουσιν μέχρι τίνος φθάνει ἡ τούτου δεσποτεία, καὶ πόθεν ἄρχεται ἡ τοῦ ἑτέρου κληρουχία. οὕτως, ἐπειδὴ μεταξὺ δαιμόνων καὶ Χριστοῦ, βραβεύοντος εἰ., κεῖται τὰ τῶν ἀνθρωπίνων ψυχῶν πταίσματα ἢ κατορθώματα, τῶν μὲν Χριστὸν ἀγαπώντων καὶ τὴν αὐτοῦ εἰ. τῶν δὲ δαίμοσι προστρεχόντων ὅριον τίθησιν ὁ τῆς ἀληθείας λόγος εἰ., ἵνα μάθῃς ὅτι, ἕως ὅτε βλέπῃς εἰ., Χριστοῦ ἐστιν δεσποτεία. τὰ ἔξω εἰ. Χριστοῦ ἀλλότρια *ib.*5(pp.21.23–22.2); *ib.*9(p.24.21); exeg. Jo.14:27 ἐξιτήριον δῶρον τοῖς ἑαυτοῦ μαθηταῖς...τὴν ἑαυτοῦ εἰ. ὁ κύριος κατέλιπεν...οὐ δύναμαι πεῖσαι ἐμαυτόν, ὅτι ἄνευ...τοῦ...εἰρηνεύειν πρὸς πάντας δύναμαι ἄξιος κληθῆναι δοῦλος Ἰησοῦ Χριστοῦ Bas.*ep.*203.1(3.300A; M.32.737B); Gr.Naz.*or.*22.16(M.35.1149B); ἡ τοῦ κόσμου εἰ. ἔστιν ὅπου καὶ ἐπὶ κακῷ γίνεται. ἡ δὲ τοῦ Χριστοῦ εἰ. οὐ μόνον πρὸς τοὺς ἔξω εἰρηνεύειν πείθει, ἀλλὰ καὶ πρὸς ἑαυτούς, ἵνα μὴ ἡ σὰρξ στασιάζῃ κατὰ τῆς ψυχῆς Ammon.*Jo.*14:27(M.85.1492D); διατί, δίδωμι; διατί, ἀφίημι; ἐπειδὴ καὶ κατὰ σάρκα καὶ κατὰ θεότητα θεωρεῖται πᾶς ὁ τοῦ Χριστοῦ δοῦλος· ἀπεδήμει δὲ κατὰ σάρκα, μένων κατὰ θεότητα...ἀφίημι, ὡς ἀναλαμβανόμενος· δίδωμι, ὡς συμπολιτευόμενος. εἰ. δὲ ὑπογέγραπται σύνθεμα τοῦ δρόμου τῶν ἀποστόλων, εἰ μὴ σύνθεμα ἔλαβεν εἰ., οὐκ ἂν ἴσχυσεν διελθεῖν τὸν κόσμον πολέμου γέμοντα Sever.*pac.*4(pp.20.30–21.2); **c.** linked with gift of H. Ghost, Pall.*v.Chrys.*1(p.6.19ff.; M.47.7); **2.** angels αἰτησώμεθα τὰ ἐλέη τοῦ κυρίου...τὸν ἄγγελον τὸν ἐπὶ τῆς εἰ. *Const.App.*8.36.3; τὰ ἐπουράνια τάγματα ἀλλήλοις ἐπιπέμπουσιν τὰ τῆς εἰ. δῶρα Sever.*pac.*2(p.19.9); **3.** virtue ἐὰν γὰρ σπουδάσωμεν ἀγαθοποιεῖν, διώξεται ἡμᾶς εἰ. *2Clem.*10.2; τὸ εἰ. ἀπολαύειν τοὺς ἀνακειμένους θεῷ. ... οὐδὲν γὰρ οὕτως εἰ. ποιεῖν εἴωθεν, ὡς ἡ τοῦ θεοῦ γνῶσις, καὶ ἡ τῆς ἀρετῆς κτῆσις Chrys.*exp.in Ps.*4:8(5.25B); οὐκ ἔνι εἰ. εἶναι, μὴ πρότερον ἀρετῆς κατορθωθείσης id.*hom.9.3 in Eph.*(11.73A).

C. as possession of Christians, *Did.*15.3; *Barn.*21.9; Clem.*paed.* 3.12(p.292.61ff.; M.8.684B); ἐν μισοῦντι ἡμᾶς τῷ κόσμῳ παραδόξως εἰ. ἄγομεν Or.*Cels.*8.70(p.287.10; M.11.1621D); *Hom.Clem.*3.31; εἰρήνης ἡμᾶς υἱοὺς χρηματίζειν Bas.*hom.in Ps.*28(1.124B; M.29.305B); ref. Lc.10:5f., *Const.App.*2.54.2; *ib.*6.11.1; ref. deacon's words πορεύεσθε ἐν εἰ. ... αὕτη γάρ ἐστιν ἡ τροφὸς ἡμῶν καὶ μήτηρ...εἰ. δὲ λέγω, οὐ τὴν ἀπὸ προσρήσεως ψιλῆς, οὐδὲ τὴν ἀπὸ τῆς κοινωνίας τῶν τραπεζῶν, ἀλλὰ τὴν κατὰ θεὸν εἰ., τὴν ἐκ τῆς συμφωνίας τῆς πνευματικῆς Chrys.*Jud.*3.6(1.614C,D).

D. in relation to various virtues δικαιοσύνη οὖν ἐστιν εἰ. βίου... ἐφ' ἣν ὁ κύριος ἀπέλυε λέγων· ἄπελθε εἰς εἰ.· Σαλὴμ γὰρ ἑρμηνεύεται εἰ., ἧς ὁ σωτὴρ ἡμῶν ἀναγράφεται βασιλεύς...καὶ δὴ ἑρμηνεύεται ὁ Μελχισεδὲκ βασιλεὺς δίκαιος, συνωνυμία δέ ἐστι δικαιοσύνης καὶ εἰ. Clem.*str.*4.25(pp.319.21–320.2; M.8.1369B–1372A); Gnost., *ib.*(p.320.3; 1372A) cit. s. δικαιοσύνη; ἐὰν γὰρ εἰ. ᾖ, καὶ ἀγάπη ἔσται· ἂν ἀγάπη, καὶ εἰ. ἔσται Chrys.*hom.24.4 in Eph.*(11.185E); εἰ. γεώργιόν ἐστιν ἀληθείας, καὶ ἀμπελὼν δικαιοσύνης, καὶ ποταμὸς εὐσεβείας Sever.*pac.*6(p.22.29); ὅταν φανῇ εἰ., μόνη φαίνεται,...ἀλλὰ συμπαραλαμβάνει μεθ' ἑαυτῆς τὴν ἀδελφὴν αὐτῆς, τὴν δικαιοσύνην *ib.*17 (p.23.21).

E. in the spiritual life τῇ ὑπερεχούσῃ πάντα νοῦν εἰ. χρωμένη ἡ ψυχή, πάσης ταραχῆς ἀλλοτριουμένη Or.*Jo.*6.1(p.106.10; M.14.197A); ref. Solomon and building of Temple, *ib.*(p.107.4ff.; M.197C–200A); ἐὰν οὖν ἡ εἰ. ἡ ὑπερέχουσα πάντα νοῦν φρουρήσῃ τὰς καρδίας ἡμῶν, δυνάμεθα τὴν ταραχὴν...τῶν παθῶν διαφυγεῖν Bas.*hom.in Ps.*29(1.129E; M.29.320A); freeing from fear of Devil and from passions, Chrys.*exp.in Ps.*4:10(5.25E); εἰ. συγκροτεῖ ἱερέως ψυχήν· δίδωσιν ὦτα ἀνεῳγμένα τοῖς ἀκροωμένοις· πρὸ γὰρ τῶν λόγων εἰ. λάμπουσα φωτίζει τῶν ἀκουόντων τὴν διάνοιαν Sever.*pac.*4(p.21.9f.).

F. in relation to Church; **1.** in gen. ἡ ἐκκλησία, ἡ ὅρασις τῆς εἰ., ἐν αὐτῇ [ἐστιν] ἡ εἰ. ἣν ἤγαγεν ἡμῖν, εἴγε ἐσμὲν τέκνα εἰ. ... ὁρᾶται Or.*hom.9.2 in Jer.*(p.65.22f.; M.13.349D); exeg. Lc.7:50 εἰ. δὲ γαληνός ἐστιν ἡ τοῦ Χριστοῦ ἐκκλησία *Const.App.*2.20.10; **2.** opp. heresy and schism; **a.** in gen., Ath.*h.Ar.*36(p.203.16; M.25.736A); id.*fug.*4(p.70.20; M.25.649A); Arsen.Hyps.*ep.*(p.147.13; M.25.372B); Sever.*pac.*1(p.16.2); Pall.*v.Chrys.*3(p.21.18; M.47.14); **b.** necessity of preserving peace μὴ ἐπιτρέψητε διασχισθῆναι τὰ μέλη τοῦ Χριστοῦ, ...ἀλλὰ τὴν τοῦ κυρίου εἰ. προτιμήσατε Ath.*apol.sec.*34(p.112.25; M.25.305B); πάντα γὰρ δεῖ σπουδάσαι δεύτερα ἡγήσασθαι τῆς εἰ. Bas.*ep.* 69.2(3.163C; M.32.433A); Gr.Naz.*or.*22.2(M.35.1133A); **c.** equivalent to *maintenance of communion* with others, Ursac.*ep.Ath.*(p.138.27; M.25.356A).

G. of various kinds; **1.** divine and human πείθουσα ὅτι ὁ θεὸς εἰ. ἐστίν, ὅτι εἰρήνευσεν ἡμῖν...μὴ θυμός, φησί, βραβευέτω,...μὴ ἀνθρωπίνη εἰ.· ἡ γὰρ ἀνθρωπίνη εἰ. ἐκ τοῦ ἀμύνασθαι γίνεται, ἐκ τοῦ μηδὲν πάσχειν δεινόν. ἀλλ' οὐ ταύτην βούλομαι, φησίν, ἀλλ' ἐκείνην, ἣν καὶ ἀφῆκεν αὐτός [sc. Χριστός] Chrys.*hom.8.3 in Col.*(11.383D); **2.** material and spiritual εἰ. ... οὐ ταύτην μόνην τὴν αἰσθητήν, ἀλλὰ καὶ τὴν ταύτης ὑψηλοτέραν, καὶ ὅθεν καὶ αὕτη τίκτεται id.*exp.in Ps.* 124:5(5.351D); material peace useless without spiritual peace, id.*exp.in Ps.*4:10(5.25C); id.*hom.7.1 in 1Tim.*(11.584B,C); **3.** right and wrong kinds, esp. ref. heretics and schismatics ἵνα...αἱ δὲ ἐκκλησίαι εἰ. ἔχωσι πρὸς τὸ τὴν τοῦ κυρίου εἰ. τὴν δοθεῖσαν ἡμῖν παραμεῖναι...ὁμολογῶ γὰρ ὑμῖν τὰ γενόμενα οὐκ εἰ., ἀλλὰ σχίσματος προφάσεις εἰσίν Ath.*apol.sec.*32(p.111.6ff.; M.25.301C); λέγω· ὅτι τὸ τῆς εἰ. καλόν, εἰ μὲν ἐν τῷ ὀνόματι τῆς εἰ. περιγράφεται μόνῳ, καταγέλαστόν ἐστι τὸν δεῖνα καὶ τὸν δεῖνα ἐκλεγομένους, τούτοις μόνον μεταδιδόναι τοῦ εἰρηνεύειν, ἑτέρους δὲ μυρίους ἀποκλείειν τῆς πρὸς τὸ καλὸν κοινωνίας. εἰ δὲ ἡ πρὸς τοὺς βλαβεροὺς συμφωνία ἐν εἰ. προσχήματι τὰ τῶν πολεμίων τοὺς προσδεχομένους ἐργάζεται, σκόπει τίνος εἰσίν, οἷς ἀνέμιξαν ἑαυτούς Bas.*ep.*250(3.385B,C; M.32.932B); id.*reg.br.*215(2.487C; M.31.1225A); μηδεὶς οἰέσθω με λέγειν, ὅτι πᾶσαν εἰ. ἀγαπητέον· οἶδα γὰρ ὥσπερ στάσιν τινὰ βελτίστην, οὕτω καὶ βλαβερωτάτην ὁμόνοιαν...ἀλλ' οὐ μὲν ἂν ᾖ πρόδηλα τὰ τῆς ἀσεβείας, καὶ πυρὶ...καὶ πᾶσι πρότερον ὁμόσε χωρητέον, ἢ τῆς ζύμης μεθεκτέον τῆς πονηρᾶς Gr.Naz.*or.*6.20(M.35.748B); no peace with sinners, *Const.App.*6.18.8; exeg. Mt.10:34 πῶς οὖν αὐτοῖς ἐπέταξεν εἰς ἑκάστην οἰκίαν εἰσιοῦσιν εἰ. ἐπιλέγειν; πῶς δὲ καὶ οἱ ἄγγελοι, ἔλεγον,... καὶ ἐπὶ γῆς εἰ.; ὅτι τοῦτο μάλιστα εἰ., ὅταν τὸ νενοσηκὸς ἀποτέμνηται... οὕτω καὶ ἐπὶ τοῦ πύργου γέγονεν ἐκείνου· τὴν γὰρ κακὴν εἰ. ἡ καλὴ διαφωνία ἔλυσε, καὶ ἐποίησεν εἰ. Chrys.*hom.35.1 in Mt.*(7.397B,C).

H. peace and sacrifice, exeg. Mt.5:23f. διὰ γὰρ τὴν εἰ. τὴν πρὸς τὸν ἀδελφόν σου...ἡ θυσία ἐγένετο. εἰ τοίνυν διὰ τὴν εἰ. τὴν εἰς τὸν πλησίον ἡ θυσία ἐστί, σὺ δὲ οὐ κατορθοῖς τὴν εἰ., εἰ καὶ μετέχεις τῆς θυσίας, ἀνωφελής σοι ἡ μετάληψις γέγονεν ἄνευ τοῦ κατορθώματος τῆς εἰ. ποίησον τοίνυν ἐκεῖνο πρῶτον, λέγω δὲ τὴν εἰ., δι' ὅπερ καὶ ἡ θυσία προσενήνεκται, καὶ τότε αὐτῆς ἀπολαύσεις καλῶς Chrys.*prod. Jud.*2.6(2.395B,C); ref. Jud.6:24 εἰ. τὸ πρῶτον...τοῦ θυσιαστηρίου ὄνομα· ἐν ἀρχῇ γὰρ θυσιαστήριον εἰρήνης ἐκλήθη, ἐπειδὴ πᾶσα μικροψυχία ἐν τῷ θυσιαστηρίῳ λύεται. ἀπ' ἀρχῆς ἔπηξεν ὁ θεὸς ὄνομα τῷ θυσιαστηρίῳ εἰ. Sever.*pac.*4(p.21.17ff.).

I. characteristic of creation οἱ οὐρανοὶ τῇ διοικήσει αὐτοῦ σαλευόμενοι ἐν εἰ. ὑποτάσσονται αὐτῷ...καιροὶ ἐαρινοὶ καὶ θερινοὶ...ἐν εἰ. μεταπαραδιδόασιν ἀλλήλοις...τά τε ἐλάχιστα τῶν ζῴων τὰς συνελεύσεις αὐτῶν ἐν ὁμονοίᾳ καὶ εἰ. ποιοῦνται. ταῦτα πάντα ὁ μέγας δημιουργὸς...ἐν εἰ. καὶ ὁμονοίᾳ προσέταξεν εἶναι *1Clem.*20.1,9–11; πῶς δὲ...ἐφίεται πάντα εἰ.; πολλὰ γὰρ ἑτερότητι καὶ διακρίσει χαίρει...καὶ εἰ μὲν ἑτερότητα καὶ διάκρισιν ὁ ταῦτα λέγων φησὶ τὴν ἑκάστου τῶν ὄντων ἰδιότητα, καὶ ὅτι ταύτην οὐδὲ ἓν τῶν ὄντων ὄν, ὅπερ ἐστίν, ἐθέλει ποτὲ ἀπολλύειν,...καὶ ταύτην εἰρήνης ἔφεσιν ἀποφανούμεθα...καὶ ἔστι καὶ τῆς καθ' ἕκαστον ἀμιγοῦς ἰδιότητος ἡ παντελὴς εἰ. φυλακτική Dion.Ar.*d.n.*11.3(M.3.952B,C).

J. praise of peace οὐδέν ἐστιν ἄμεινον εἰ., ἐν ᾗ πᾶς πόλεμος καταργεῖται ἐπουρανίων καὶ ἐπιγείων Ign.*Eph.*13.2; Bas.*ep.*114(3.206D; M.32.528B); τί γὰρ ἥδιον ἄκουσμα τοῦ τῆς εἰ. ὀνόματος; *ib.*156.1(3.245B; M.613C); Gr.Naz.*or.*22.1(M.35.1132A); εἰ. ... ἡ τῶν ἐν οὐρανοῖς ἀγγέλων ὁμοδίαιτος...εἰ., ὁ τῶν ἀγγέλων ὕμνος. εἰ., τὸ τῶν ἁγίων ἔργον. ... καὶ τὰ ἐπουράνια ὑμνεῖ τὴν εἰ., καὶ τὰ ἐπίγεια Sever. *pac.*2(p.18.20ff.); *ib.*4(p.20.15ff.); *ib.*7(p.23.16ff.).

K. liturg; **1.** in greeting ἡ εἰ. τοῦ θεοῦ εἴη μετὰ πάντων ὑμῶν *Lit.* ap.*Const.App.*8.13.1; in dismissal ἀπολύεσθε ἐν εἰ. *ib.*8.15.10; ὅταν εἰσέλθῃ ὁ τῆς ἐκκλησίας προεστώς, εὐθέως λέγει, εἰ. πᾶσιν· ὅταν ὁμιλῇ, εἰ. πᾶσιν· ὅταν εὐλογῇ, εἰ. πᾶσιν· ὅταν ἀσπάζεσθαι κελεύῃ, εἰ. πᾶσιν· ὅταν ἡ θυσία τελεσθῇ, εἰ. πᾶσι· καὶ μεταξὺ πάλιν, χάρις ὑμῖν καὶ εἰ. Chrys.*hom.3.3 in Col.*(11.348C); id.*Jud.*3.6(1.614C); ἐν τῇ ἐκκλησίᾳ, ὁ προεστὼς δίδωσιν εἰ. id.*hom.32.6 in Mt.*(7.373A); Pall.*v. Chrys.*14(p.84.26; M.47.48); *Lit.Jac.*(p.166.7); **2.** kiss of peace, after offertory, cf.Just.*1apol.*65.2(M.6.428A), Cyr.H.*catech.*23.3 citt. s. φίλημα; cf.Hipp.*trad.ap.*(p.6); τὰς εὐχὰς γίνεσθαι τρεῖς...εἶθ' οὕτως τὴν εἰ. δίδοσθαι· καὶ μετὰ τὸ πρεσβυτέρους δοῦναι τῷ ἐπισκόπῳ τὴν εἰ., τότε τοὺς λαϊκοὺς τὴν εἰ. διδόναι, καὶ οὕτω τὴν ἁγίαν προσφορὰν ἐπιτελεῖσθαι CLaod.*can.*19; *Const.App.*2.57.19; *Lit.*ap.*Const.App.*8.11.8; πῶς δίδως εἰ., πολέμου γέμοντι στόματι; Chrys.*hom.21.5 in Rom.*(9.679A); Dion.Ar.*e.h.*3.2(M.3.425C); *ib.*3.3.8(437A); in baptismal context ἐπειδὴ γὰρ πρὸ τοῦ φωτίσματος ἐχθρὸς ἦν, μετὰ δὲ τὸ φώτισμα γέγονε φίλος τοῦ...δεσπότου...διὰ τοῦτο καὶ τὸ φίλημα εἰ. καλεῖται Chrys.*hom.3.6 in Ac.princ.*(3.81B); given before ordination ἐπίσκοπος...δοὺς εἰ. χειροτονεῖ αὐτὸν διάκονον· καὶ πάλιν δοὺς εἰ. ποιεῖ αὐτὸν πρεσβύτερον *Dial.Tim.et Aquil.*138 v°; **3.** prayer for peace, *Lit.*ap.*Const.App.*8.10.3; *ib.*8.15.4; Chrys.*hom.37.3 in Ac.*(9.284B); *Lit.Jac.*(p.166.15ff.); **4.** angel of peace, *ib.*(p.174.10).

L. τὰ τῆς εἰ. γράμματα episcopal *letters of recommendation*, Ath. *h.Ar.*25(p.197.4; M.25.724A).

M. ὁ ἐπὶ τῆς εἰ. officer in charge of eccl. discipline in Alexandria, Leont.N.*v.Jo.Eleem.*2(p.8.4); cf.Pall.*h.Laus.*116(M.34.1220B).

N. name of a church, founded by Const., Socr.*h.e.*1.16.2(M.67.117A); *Chron.Pasch.*p.337(M.92.877B).

εἰρηνικός, **1.** *peaceful*; **a.** divine attribute, of God τῆς εἰ. ἑνώσεως θεωρήσωμεν φύσιν Dion.Ar.*d.n.*11.2(M.3.949C); *ib.*(952A); of heavenly Jerusalem μεγάλου βασιλέως...εἰ. πόλις *Clem.ep.*13(M.2.49A); of kingdom of Christ, *Hom.Clem.*19.20; hence **b.** of Christians, Bas.*hom.in Ps.*28(1.124A; M.29.305A); **c.** of death ἔξοδον αὐτοῦ εἰ. ... ποίησον Serap.*euch.*30.3; **d.** of state of men after resurrection, Gr.Nyss.*hom.1 in Cant.*(M.44.777A); **e.** interpretation of name Solomon, ‡Hipp.*fr.33 in Pr.*(p.170.2; M.10.616B); **2.** *peaceable*, of Christians, Just.*dial.*131.5(M.6.781B); ἡμεῖς δὲ τὸ εἰ. γένος Clem. *paed.*2.2(p.175.26; M.8.428B); εἰ. ... ὄργανον ὁ ἄνθρωπός ἐστιν...ἑνὶ δὲ ἄρα ὀργάνῳ, τῷ λόγῳ μόνῳ τῷ εἰ., ἡμεῖς κεχρήμεθα *ib.*2.4(p.183.3; 441B–444A); Χριστὸς δὲ εἰρηνικὸν...ἐπιπνεύσας μέλος οὐ συνάξει ἄρα τοὺς εἰ. στρατιώτας τοὺς ἑαυτοῦ; id.*prot.*11(p.82.4f.; M.8.236B); of Christian faith, Const.ap.Ath.*apol.sec.*62(p.142.21; M.25.361C); εἰ. ζωή being the greatest good, Gr.Nyss.*beat.*7(M.44.1281A); neut. as subst., *peaceable disposition, love of peace*, Athenag.*leg.*1.2(M.6.892B); Clem.*str.*4.6(p.266.16; M.8.1252B); Thphyl.*exc.gent.*5(p.482.37; M.113.944B); **3.** *of peace, peace-giving* σωτὴρ...πηγὴ...εἰ. Clem. *prot.*10(p.78.22; M.8.228B); χαρίσαι αὐτοῖς ἄγγελον εἰ. συνοδοιπόρον γενέσθαι Serap.*euch.*5.8; ἄγγελοι εἰ. †Bas.*Is.*260(1.577C; M.30.576B); neut. plur. as subst. εἰ. φρονεῖν *Lit.Marc.*(p.114.27); **4.** τὰ [γράμματα] εἰ., ἡ εἰ. [sc. ἐπιστολή] *letter(s) of commendation* εἰ. δέ ἐστιν ἡ ἄνευ σκανδάλου τινὸς τοῦ ἐπικομιζομένου ἐγχειριζομένη ὑπὸ τοῦ προέχοντος πρός τινας ἀποφέρεσθαι *Schol.*in *Can.App.*12(*Mon.*2 p.642); exchanged between bishops as sign of intercommunion, Ath.*h.Ar.*26(p.197.21; M.25.724C); Arsen.Hyps.*ep.*(p.147.18; M.25.372C); as letters of introduction, CAnt.(341)*can.*7; CChalc.*can.*11; cf. ἡ ἀνατολὴ πρὸς τὴν δύσιν διαφερομένη εἰ. παρ' ἀλλήλων οὐκ ἐδέχοντο Epiph.*haer.*70.9(p.242.16; M.42.356B); **5.** liturg. τὰ εἰ. *litany for peace*, *Euchol.*(p.57); cf.Chrys.*Jud.*3.6(1.614C); **6.** *gentle*, opp. λαῦρος: ἔτι...ὑετὸς εἰ. Or.*exp.in Pr.*28:3(M.17.241D).

εἰρηνικῶς, *peacefully*; ref. contemplation, Clem.*str.*1.5(p.18.20; M.8.720B); τὸν λαὸν εἰ. ποιμαίνων *Const.App.*2.20.3.

***εἰρηνόδωρος**, *giving peace*; of providence, Dion.Ar.*d.n.*11.3(M.3.952C); masc. as subst., as divine name, *ib.*4.21(724A); ref. liturg. praise εἰ. σημειώσεις Max.*myst.*23(M.91.700A).

εἰρηνοποι-έω, **1.** *make, establish peace, reconcile*, ref. Mt.5:9 ∼οῦσι...τοὺς ἐνταῦθα πολεμουμένους τοῖς τῆς ἁμαρτίας στρατηγήμασι, μεταδιδάσκοντες ἐπὶ τὴν πίστιν καὶ τὴν εἰρήνην μετιέναι Clem.*str.*4.6(p.266.19; M.8.125B); **a.** in gen., *Const.App.*3.15.4; Epiph.*haer.*42.7(p.103.3; M.41.705A); Jo.D.*trisag.*26(M.95.57B); **b.** as divine activity, of Father ὡς ἀδελφὰς οἰκοδεσπότης πατὴρ ∼ῶν τὰς ἐναντίας φύσεις Geo.Pis.*hex.*259(M.92.1454A); of Christ, ref. Col. 1:20, †Bas.*Is.*226(1.550B; M.30.513A); *ib.*250(570B; M.560A); Chrys. *hom.3.3 in Col.*(11.346Bff.); id.*prod.Jud.*1.6(2.384E); **c.** as Christian activity οὐδὲν γὰρ οὕτως ἴδιόν ἐστι Χριστιανοῦ, ὡς τὸ ∼εῖν Bas.*ep.*114(3.207A; M.32.528B); Gr.Nyss.*beat.*7(M.44.1281A); pacifying the soul, ‡Proc.G.*Pr.*29:8(M.87.1516A); **2.** *do, make, in peace* ∼οῦ τὴν εἰς οἶκον ἐπάνοδον Sophr.H.*mir.Cyr.et Jo.*16(M.87.3473A); **3.** *give the kiss of peace*, *M.Perp.*12(p.81.24).

***εἰρηνοποίησις**, ἡ, *peace-making*, Clem.*str.*4.6(p.266.15; M.8.1252B); ref. Inc. ἦν εἰ. τῆς γῆς Apoll.*quod.un.Chr.*11(p.302.4; M.28.129D).

***εἰρηνοποιΐα**, ἡ, *peace-making*, Bas.*ep.*156.1(3.245B; M.32.613C); *ib.*219.2(332E; M.813A); Gr.Nyss.*beat.*7(M.44.1289D).

εἰρηνοποιός, *peacemaking*, of Christ ὁ...εἰ. κύριος †Dion.Al.*fr. Cant.*(p.229.7); as subst. masc. Εἰρηναῖος φερώνυμός τις ὢν τῇ προσηγορίᾳ αὐτῷ τε τρόπῳ εἰ. Eus.*h.e.*5.24.18(M.20.508A); *Const. App.*2.1.7; τίς ἐστιν ὁ ὑπὸ τοῦ κυρίου μακαριζόμενος εἰ.; ὁ τῷ κυρίῳ συνεργῶν Bas.*reg.br.*215(2.487B; M.31.1225A); εἰ. δέ ἐστιν ὁ εἰρήνην διδοὺς ἄλλῳ Gr.Nyss.*beat.*7(M.44.1284A); fig. πρὸς τοὺς 'εἰ.' τῶν δογμάτων πορευτέον Clem.*str.*7.16(p.70.28; M.9.537C).

***εἰρηνοφόρος**, *bringing peace*; ref. preaching of gospel, Agath. *v.Gr.Ill.*144(p.73); *ib.*152(p.77).

***εἰρηνοχύτος**, *shedding peace*, Dion.Ar.*d.n.*11.5(M.3.953A).

εἱρμός, ὁ, **A.** *series, chain, sequence*; **1.** in gen. εἰ. τῶν γραφῶν Iren.*haer.*1.8.1(M.7.521A); Clem.*str.*4.1(p.248.23; M.8.1216B); εἰ. ... τῶν...εἰρημένων ἐν τοῖς προφήταις Or.*Cels.*7.11(p.163.2; M.11.1436D); εἰ. ... τῶν μακαρισμῶν id.*or.*18.3(p.340.31; M.11.473D); id.*Jo.*2.23(17; p.79.9; M.14.153A); of generations, Epiph.*haer.*39.8(p.77.30; M.41.673B); of agreement, Gr.Nyss.*or.catech.*6(p.30.5; M.45.25C); **2.** esp. Stoic, of chain of cause and effect τὰ τούτοις ἐφεξῆς καθ' εἰ. ἑπόμενα Athenag.*res.*1(p.48.14; M.6.976A); Or.*or.*6.3(p.313.8; M.11.436D); ἐν τῇ φύσει κατὰ τὸν ἴδιον εἰ. πορευομένη Gr.Nyss.*or.catech.*16(p.67.9; M.45.49B); ref. events of Inc. τὰ δὲ πεπραγμένα εἰ. τινι *ib.*20(p.80.12; 57C); of logical sequence εἰ. τοῦ νοήματος id.*hom.2 in Cant.*(M.44.796A); cf. εἱμαρμένη.

B. liturg., original strophe on pattern of which other strophes of same ode were fashioned, cf.*Lit.Chrys.*(p.388.7); *Max.offic.*2(M.90.216B).

εἴρ-ω, **1.** *fasten, string together*; **2.** *run over* a topic *quickly* τὸ νῦν προκείμενόν ἐστιν οὐ λαβόντα πρόβλημα παρέρχεσθαι καὶ ∼ειν Or. *dial.*3(p.124.12).

εἰρωνεία, ἡ, **1.** *dissimulation, pretence*; ref. Jewish fasts and new moons, *Diogn.*4.1; of heretics: Marcellus σὺν εἰ. δὲ καταψευδόμενος Eus.*e.th.*2.12(p.114.6; M.24.925C); Arians, Epiph.*anc.*6(p.12.15; M.43.25B); *ib.*52(p.61.4; 108A); of pagans, Chrys.*hom.36.2 in Ac.*(9.278B); foreign to true Christians, Nil.*Magn.*47(M.79.1029B); **2.** *irony, sarcasm*, Eus.*h.e.*2.18.8(M.20.188A); Cyr.*Mich.*9(3.399A); *mockery*; of soldiers mocking Christ, Chrys.*hom.83.5 in Jo.*(8.496D); *ib.*84.3(501D).

εἰρωνεύ-ομαι, **1.** *feign ignorance*; through modesty, Just.*dial.*58.2(M.6.608A); Chrys.*sac.*3.14(p.71.13; 1.390C); by way of excuse, id. *hom.48.2 in Ac.*(9.360A); **2.** *pretend*, Bas.Sel.*or.*18(M.85.233C); **3.** *make a jest of, insult*, Just.*dial.*101.3(M.6.712C); Bas.*hom.*6.4(2.47A; M.31.269B); Chrys.*hom.50.4 in Mt.*(7.519A); id.*hom.23.5 in 2Cor.*(10.603A); ? *approach as a game* ὁ πένης [μὴ] ∼έσθω πρὸς τὴν νηστείαν Bas.*hom.*2.2(2.11D; M.31.188A); **4.** *speak ironically* οὐκ ἦλθον καλέσαι δικαίους...∼όμενος...λέγει Chrys.*hom.30.3 in Mt.*(7.

351A); Cyr.*Os*.153(3.186E); Olymp.*Job* 1:20f.(M.93.33C); **5.** c. acc., *deceive*, Socr.*h.e*.3.1.47(M.67.377A); of Herod ~όμενος τοὺς μάγους Chrysipp.*enc.in Jo.Bapt*.14(p.46.7).

εἰρωνευτικός, *pretended* στοργή Max.*ambig*.(M.91.1205B).

***εἰρωνευτικῶς,** *deceivingly*, Max.*ep*.12(M.91.485A).

εἷς, *one*;

A. of unity of God; **1.** in gen., Herm.*mand*.1.1 cit. s. εἰμί; *Diogn*.3.2; Athenag.*leg*.8.1(M.6.904C); discussion, *ib*.4.2ff.(897B); Clem.*paed*.1.8(p.131.18; M.8.336A); Ath.*gent*.3(M.25.9A); in credal statements, *Symb.Caes*.(M.20.1537B); *Symb.Nic*.(325)(p.51; M.20.1540B); *Symb.Hier*.ap.Cyr.H.*catech*.6(M.33.538); **2.** proof of unity of God from unity of universe μιᾶς οὔσης τῆς κτίσεως, καὶ ἑνὸς ὄντος κόσμου, καὶ μιᾶς τῆς τούτου τάξεως, ἕνα δεῖ νοεῖν καὶ τὸν ταύτης ...δημιουργὸν κύριον. διὰ τοῦτο γὰρ καὶ αὐτὸς ὁ δημιουργὸς ἕνα τὸν σύμπαντα κόσμον πεποίηκεν, ἵνα...ἑνὸς ὄντος τοῦ ποιήματος, εἷς καὶ ὁ τούτου ποιητὴς πιστεύηται Ath.*gent*.39(80A,B); but reverse does not follow οὐχ ὅτι εἷς ἐστιν ὁ δημιουργός, διὰ τοῦτο καὶ εἷς ἐστιν ὁ κόσμος· ἠδύνατο γὰρ καὶ ἄλλους κόσμους ποιῆσαι ὁ θεός *ib*.(80B) et passim; **3.** God as τὸ ἕν; **a.** in gen. ἀδιαίρετον γὰρ τὸ ἕν Clem.*str*.5.12 (p.380.22; M.9.121B); Dion.Ar.*e.h*.2.3.5(M.3.401A) al.; **b.** indicating transcendence ἀδιανόητόν ἐστι τὸ ὑπὲρ διάνοιαν ἕν id.*d.n*.1.1(M.3.588B); ἓν ὤν, καὶ παντὶ μέρει καὶ ὅλῳ, καὶ ἑνὶ καὶ πλήθει, τοῦ ἑνὸς μεταδούς, ἕν ἐστιν ὡσαύτως ὑπερουσίως, οὔτε μέρος ὂν τοῦ πλήθους, οὔτε ἐκ μερῶν ὅλον· καὶ οὕτως οὔτε ἕν ἐστιν, οὔτε ἑνὸς μετέχει, οὐδὲ τὸ ἓν ἔχει· πόρρω δὲ τούτων ἕν ἐστιν, ὑπὲρ τὸ ἕν, τοῖς οὖσιν ἕν...πᾶν ἓν καὶ πλῆθος παράγον *ib*.2.11(649C); **c.** reason for this divine name ἓν δέ, ὅτι πάντα ἑνιαίως ἐστὶ κατὰ μιᾶς ἑνότητος ὑπεροχήν, καὶ πάντων ἐστὶ τοῦ ἑνὸς...αἴτιον· οὐδὲν γάρ ἐστι τῶν ὄντων ἀμέτοχον τοῦ ἑνός, ἀλλ' ὥσπερ ἅπας ἀριθμὸς μονάδος μετέχει, καὶ μία δυάς, καὶ δεκὰς λέγεται, καὶ ἥμισυ ἕν...οὕτω πάντα καὶ πάντων μόριον τοῦ ἑνὸς μετέχει, καὶ τῷ εἶναι τὸ ἕν, πάντα ἐστὶ τὰ ὄντα· καὶ οὐκ ἔστι τὸ πάντων αἴτιον ἓν τῶν πολλῶν ἕν, ἀλλὰ πρὸς παντὸς ἑνὸς καὶ πλήθους, καὶ παντὸς ἑνὸς καὶ πλήθους ὁριστικόν *ib*.13.2(977C); κατὰ τὸ ἑνὸς ἑκάστου προεπινοούμενον εἶδος ἡνῶσθαι λέγεται τὰ ἡνωμένα, καὶ πάντων ἐστὶ τὸ ἓν στοιχειωτικόν· καὶ εἰ ἀνέλῃς τὸ ἕν, οὔτε ὁλότης, οὔτε μόριον, οὔτε ἄλλο οὐδὲν τῶν ὄντων ἔσται· πάντα γὰρ ἐν ἑαυτῷ τὸ ἕν...περιείληφε. ταύτῃ γοῦν ἡ θεολογία τὴν ὅλην θεαρχίαν, ὡς πάντων αἰτίαν ὑμνεῖ τῇ τοῦ ἑνὸς ἐπωνυμίᾳ, καὶ εἷς θεὸς ὁ πατήρ, καὶ εἷς Ἰησοῦς Χριστός, καὶ ἓν καὶ τὸ αὐτὸ πνεῦμα *ib*.13.3(980B); **d.** in relation to creatures ἐν ἑνὶ... τὰ ὄντα πάντα *ib*.5.10(825B); οὐδὲ γάρ ἐστι πλῆθος ἀμέτοχόν πῃ τοῦ ἑνός, ἀλλὰ τὸ μὲν πολλὰ τοῖς μέρεσιν ἓν τῷ ὅλῳ· καὶ τὸ πολλὰ τοῖς συμβεβηκόσιν ἓν τῷ ὑποκειμένῳ· καὶ τὸ πολλὰ τῷ ἀριθμῷ...ἓν τῷ εἴδει· καὶ τὸ πολλὰ τοῖς εἴδεσιν ἓν τῷ γένει· καὶ τὸ πολλὰ ταῖς προόδοις ἓν τῇ ἀρχῇ· καὶ οὐδέν ἐστι τῶν ὄντων, ὃ μὴ μετέχει πῃ τοῦ ἑνὸς τοῦ ἐν τῷ κατὰ πάντα ἑνικῷ...καὶ ἄνευ μὲν τοῦ ἑνὸς οὐκ ἔσται πλῆθος, ἄνευ δὲ τοῦ πλήθους ἔσται τὸ ἓν *ib*.13.2(980A); οὐκ ἂν εὕροις τι τῶν ὄντων, ὃ μὴ τῷ ἑνὶ καθ' ὃ πᾶσα ἡ θεότης...ὀνομάζεται, καὶ ἔστι τοῦθ' ὅπερ ἐστί, καὶ τελειοῦται, καὶ διασώζεται...αὐτὸ τὸ ἓν ὂν ὀρίζον, ἐπείπερ τὸ ὂν ἕν, τὸ ἐν τοῖς οὖσιν, ἐνάριθμόν ἐστιν *ib*.13.3(980C); **4.** oneness characteristic of the divine and spiritual οὐδὲν γὰρ ἓν τῆς ὕλης καὶ τῶν σωμάτων, ἀλλ' ἕκαστον τῶν νομιζομένων ἓν ἔσχισται...εἰς πλείονα τὴν ἕνωσιν ἀπολωλεκός· ἓν γὰρ τὸ ἀγαθόν, πολλὰ δὲ τὰ αἰσχρά, καὶ ἓν ἡ ἀλήθεια, πολλὰ δὲ τὰ ψευδῆ, καὶ ἓν ἡ ἀληθὴς δικαιοσύνη, πολλαὶ δὲ ἕξεις ταύτην ὑποκρίνονται, καὶ ἓν ἡ τοῦ θεοῦ σοφία, πολλαὶ δὲ αἱ καταργούμεναι τοῦ αἰῶνος τούτου...καὶ εἷς μὲν ὁ τοῦ θεοῦ λόγος, πολλοὶ δὲ οἱ ἀλλότριοι τοῦ θεοῦ Or.*or*.21.2(p.345.17ff.; M.11.481A); τὸ ἀγαθὸν ἐκ τῆς μιᾶς καὶ τῆς ὅλης αἰτίας· τὸ δὲ κακὸν ἐκ πολλῶν καὶ μερικῶν ἐλλείψεων Dion.Ar.*d.n*.4.30(M.3.729C); *ib*.4.31(732B); cf. εἷς ὢν ὁ θεὸς ἑνὶ ἀνθρώπῳ μίαν ἔκτισε γυναῖκα *Hom.Clem*.13.15; **5.** unity of Father and Son; **a.** affirmed ἑνὸς ὄντος τοῦ πατρὸς καὶ τοῦ υἱοῦ Athenag.*leg*.10.2(M.6.909A); ἡ τοῦ υἱοῦ θεότης τοῦ πατρός ἐστιν...καὶ οὕτως εἷς θεός...ἓν αὐτῶν ὄντων, καὶ μιᾶς αὐτῆς οὔσης τῆς θεότητος Ath.*Ar*.3.4(M.26.329A); id.*decr*.17(p.14.10f.; M.25.444C); **b.** denied by Arian doctrine ἓν τὸ ἀγένητον...οὐκοῦν ὁ υἱὸς τῶν γενητῶν ἐστι id.*Ar*.1.30(M.26.73B); **c.** Arian position refuted εἰ δὲ οἱ μὲν Ἕλληνες ἑνὶ ἀγενήτῳ καὶ πολλοῖς γενητοῖς λατρεύουσιν, οὗτοι [sc. Arians] δὲ ἑνὶ ἀγενήτῳ καὶ ἑνὶ γενητῷ· οὐδ' οὕτω διαφέρουσιν Ἑλλήνων. ὅ τε γὰρ παρ' αὐτῶν λεγόμενος γενητὸς εἷς ἐκ πολλῶν ἐστι· καὶ οἱ πολλοὶ δὲ πάλιν τῶν Ἑλλήνων τὴν αὐτὴν τῷ ἑνὶ τούτῳ φύσιν ἔχουσι *ib*.3.16(356A,B); τὰ μὲν κτίσματα πολλά, ὁ δὲ λόγος εἷς ἐστι· τίς οὐ συνορᾷ καὶ ἐκ τούτων, ὅτι ὁ υἱὸς διέστηκε τῶν πάντων, καὶ οὐ πρὸς τὰ κτίσματα τὴν ἐξίσωσιν ἔχει, ἀλλὰ πρὸς τὸν πατέρα τὴν ἰδιότητα; ὅθεν οὐδὲ πολλοὶ λόγοι, ἀλλὰ μόνος εἷς τοῦ ἑνὸς πατρὸς λόγος, καὶ μία τοῦ ἑνὸς θεοῦ εἰκών ἐστιν *ib*.2.27(204C); id.*ep.Aeg.Lib*.14(M.25.569B); **d.** exeg. Jo.10:30 ἓν γάρ εἰσιν, οὐχ ὡς ἑνὸς πάλιν εἰς δύο μέρη διαιρεθέντος, καὶ μηδὲν ὄντων πλὴν ἑνός· οὐδὲ ὡς τοῦ ἑνὸς δὶς ὀνομαζομένου ...ἕν εἰσιν...τῇ ταὐτότητι τῆς μιᾶς θεότητος id.*Ar*.3.4(328C–329A); Arian exegesis λέγοντες μὴ οὕτως εἶναι τὸν υἱὸν καὶ τὸν πατέρα ἕν...ὡς ἡ ἐκκλησία κηρύσσει, ἀλλ' ὡς αὐτοὶ θέλουσι who admit only moral unity, *ib*.3.10(341A); τὰ δύο ἓν εἶναί φατε, ἢ τὸ ἓν διώνυμον, ἢ πάλιν τὸ ἓν εἰς δύο διῃρῆσθαι. εἰ...τὸ ἓν εἰς δύο διῄρηται, ἀνάγκη σῶμα εἶναι τὸ διαιρεθέν...εἰ δὲ τὸ ἓν διώνυμον, Σαβελλίου τὸ ἐπιτήδευμα, τὸν αὐτὸν υἱὸν καὶ πατέρα λέγοντος...εἰ δὲ τὰ δύο ἕν, ἀνάγκη δύο μὲν εἶναι, ἓν δὲ κατὰ τὴν θεότητα,...ὥστε δύο μὲν εἶναι, ὅτι πατήρ ἐστι καὶ υἱός...ἓν δέ, ὅτι εἷς θεός ‡Ath.*Ar*.4.9(p.53.4ff.; M.26.480A,B); *ib*.4.10 (p.54.8; 480C); for unity in Trin. v. τριάς.

B. unity of Christ, Ign.*Eph*.7.2 cit. s. ἰατρός; *Diogn*.9.5 cit. s. δικαιοσύνη; ἓν γὰρ μάλιστα μετὰ τὴν οἰκονομίαν γεγένηται πρὸς τὸν λόγον τοῦ θεοῦ ἡ ψυχὴ καὶ τὸ σῶμα Ἰησοῦ Or.*Cels*.2.9(p.136.31; M.11.809D); ἀμφότερα [sc. divine and human acts] ἐξ ἑνὸς πραττόμενα βλέποντες Ath.*Ar*.3.35(M.26.397B); εἷς ἦ τὰ ἑκάτερα...θεὸς καὶ ἄνθρωπος ὁ αὐτός ‡Ath.*Apoll*.1.16(M.26.1124A); for μία φύσις v. φύσις.

C. unity of Church and worship μηδὲ πειράσητε εὔλογόν τι φαίνεσθαι ἰδίᾳ ὑμῖν, ἀλλ' ἐπὶ τὸ αὐτὸ μία προσευχή, μία δέησις, εἷς νοῦς, μία ἐλπὶς ἐν ἀγάπῃ...πάντες ὡς εἰς ἕνα ναὸν συντρέχετε θεοῦ, ὡς ἐπὶ ἓν θυσιαστήριον, ἐπὶ ἕνα Ἰησοῦν Χριστόν, τὸν ἀφ' ἑνὸς πατρὸς προελθόντα καὶ εἰς ἕνα ὄντα καὶ χωρήσαντα Ign.*Magn*.7.1,2; id. *Philad*.4.1 cit. s. εὐχαριστία; ἕνα ἄρτον κλῶντες id.*Eph*.20.2; ἔσται ἡ ἐκκλησία τοῦ θεοῦ ἓν σῶμα, μία φρόνησις, εἷς νοῦς, μία πίστις, μία ἀγάπη Herm.*sim*.9.18.4; *ib*.9.13.5; τοῖς εἰς αὐτὸν [sc. Christ] πιστεύουσιν, ὡς οὖσι μιᾷ ψυχῇ καὶ μιᾷ συναγωγῇ καὶ μιᾷ ἐκκλησίᾳ Just.*dial*. 63.5(M.6.621B); μία γάρ ἐστιν ἡ θεότης· καὶ διὰ τοῦτο μία τιμὴ καὶ μία ἐστὶ προσκύνησις ἐν υἱῷ...καὶ ὁ οὕτω προσκυνῶν ἕνα θεὸν προσκυνεῖ Ath.*Ar*.3.6(M.26.333B); εἷς θεὸς υἱὸς καὶ πατήρ, οὐ τῇ ὑποστάσει, ἀλλὰ τῷ αὐτῷ λόγῳ τῆς οὐσίας· ὡς πάντες ἄνθρωποι ἐν Χριστῷ εἷς, οὐ τῇ ὑποστάσει, ἀλλὰ τῷ λόγῳ τῆς οὐσίας καὶ συμφωνίας ‡Ath.*dial.Trin*. 1.12(M.28.1136D); v. ἐκκλησία.

D. Valentinian aeon, Iren.*haer*.1.11.3(M.7.563A).

E. phrases; **1.** ἐν μιᾷ [sc. ἡμέρᾳ] *one day*, Jo.Mosch.*prat*.25(M.87.2869D); *ib*.27(2873B); Leont.N.*v.Jo.Eleem*.8(p.15.10); *ib*.36(p.73.10); **2.** πρὸ μιᾶς *the day before* πρὸ μιᾶς ἀρνούμενος...ὕστερον ὑπογράψας Ath.*decr*.3(p.3.12; M.25.420D).

εἰσάγ-ω, 1. *introduce*; πίστις εἰσάξει Clem.*prot*.9(p.65.20; M.8.200B); Or.*hom.8.9 in Jer*.(p.63.9; M.13.348A); into eternal life ~ει [sc. God] εἰς τὸν ἄφθαρτον ναόν *Barn*.16.9; *M.Polyc*.20.2; Ath.*Ar*.1.42(M.26.100B); Gnost. εἰς τὸ πλήρωμα Clem.*exc.Thdot*.42(p.120.4; M.9.680A); virtues φόβῳ δὲ ἀφοβίαν ~ων id.*str*.2.8(p.134.3; M.8.976A); Or.*hom.19.15 in Jer*.(p.173.32; M.13.496C); Meth.*symp*. proem.(p.5.15; M.18.32B); divisions into Godhead, of Arians, Ath. *Ar*.2.37(M.26.225A); hence heresy into Church, id.*apol.sec*.82(p.161.29; M.25.396C); **2.** *intrude*; heretics into Church, *ib*.17(p.99.39; 276B); id.*ep.Aeg.Lib*.19(M.25.581B); unlawful bishop into a see, id. *h.Ar*.81(p.230.12; M.25.796B); **3.** ὁ εἰσαγόμενος *catechumen*, Or.*Cels*. 3.15(p.214.15; M.11.940A); s.v.l., Eus.*v.C*.3.66(p.113.17; M.20.1144B).

εἰσαγωγεύς, ὁ, *one who introduces*, of Christ ὁ τῆς καινῆς... νομοθεσίας εἰ. Eus.*d.e*.1.6(p.34.29; M.22.68B); *ib*.3.2(p.97.15; 169B); ὁ τῆς ἀληθοῦς θεογνωσίας εἰ. *ib*.8 proem.(p.351.11; 572B); Χριστὸς... θύρα δέ, ὡς εἰ. Gr.Naz.*or*.30.21(p.142.17; M.36.132C); Melchizedekian αὐτὸν [sc. Melchizedek] εἶναι εἰ. πρὸς τὸν θεόν Epiph.*haer*. 55.8(p.334.11; M.41.985C).

εἰσαγωγή, ἡ, 1. *beginning* τοῦ εὐαγγελίου Epiph.*haer*.51.6(p.255.2; M.41.897A); **2.** *introduction, initiation* πρὸς θεογνωσίαν...εἰ. Or. *fr.3 in Lam*.(p.236.9; M.13.608A); id.*fr.in Pr*.1:7(M.17.156D); Eus. *h.e*.1.2.22(M.20.65A); to piety, id.*d.e*.1.6(p.27.35; M.22.56C); εἰ. ἐπὶ τὴν τελειότητα ‡Nil.*perist*.12.6(M.79.952A); **3.** *bringing in* to the world περὶ εἰσαγωγὴν τοῦ πρὸς σωτηρίαν ἡμῶν ἀνθρώπου Ἰησοῦ Χριστοῦ ἀντὶ τοῦ πεσόντος...Ἀδάμ Euthal.Diac.*epp.Paul*.(M.85.749D).

εἰσαγωγικός, 1. *introductory, preliminary* εἰ. ... διδασκαλίαν τῆς ἐκκλησίας Ath.*exp.Ps*.86:2(M.27.377B); †Bas.*Is*.204(1.532B; M.30.472B); ὁ νόμος, τὸ εἰ. τῆς εὐσεβείας γράμμα Gr.Nyss.*usur*.(M.46.441C); Cyr.*ador*.3(1.93D); of baptism εἰ. ... φωτισμός id.*Jo*.3.1(4.250D); ἡ ὑπακοὴ...ἐν εἰ. ἀρεταῖς Ant.Mon.*hom*.39(M.89.1556B); of what is incomplete opp. perfect, John's baptism as εἰ. opp. Christ's as τελειωτικόν, Bas.*hom*.13.1(2.114B; M.31.425A); cf. Jo.D.*f.o*.4.9(M.94.1124A); of fear, Olymp.*Eccl*.12:13(M.93.625D); δύο εἰσὶ φόβοι, εἷς εἰ., καὶ εἷς τέλειος Dor.*doct*.4.1(M.88.1657C); διάφορός ἐστιν ἡ πίστις. ἡ μὲν εἰ., ἡ δὲ τελεία Vict.*Mc*.9:28(p.361.32); **2.** as subst., *beginner, novice* Χριστὸς...τοῖς δὲ εἰ. σκύμνος Or.*sel.in Gen*.49:9(M.12.145B); opp. οἱ τέλειοι, Thdt.*Ps*.110:9(1.1402); Jo.Clim.*scal*.2(M.88.653D).

εἰσαγωγός, *introducing* αἱ παραινέσεις...εἰ. εἰς εὐσέβειαν Bas.*hom. in Ps*.33(1.153C; M.29.376A); εἰ. ἀρεταί Diad.*perf*.41(p.46.21); ἄλλη ἐστὶν ἡ εἰ. χαρὰ καὶ ἄλλη ἡ τελειοποιός *ib*.60(p.66.24); *ib*.(p.68.4).

εἶσαι, = εἶ *thou art* μὴ γὰρ οὐκ εἶσαι πονηρὸς δαίμων; *Mir.Geo.* 13(p.30.12).

***εἰσαιτέω,** *ask for,* Andr.Cr.*Agath.*1(M.97.1437C).

***εἰσάκουσις, ἡ,** *listening to, attention* ἄξιος εἶ...εἰσακούσεως †Gregent.*disp.*(M.86.665B).

***εἰσακουστός,** *hearkened to,* Bas.*hom.in Ps.*33(1.148B; M.29. 364A).

***εἰσακτικός,** *introductory* εἰ. διδασκαλία Eus.*Is.*54:12(M.24.465C); *ib.*60:11(493D); Proc.G.*Is.*60:11(M.87.2632A).

***εἰσαναβάλλομαι,** *put off, delay,* Cosm.Mel.*schol.*(M.38.530) in Gr.Naz.*carm.*2.1.50.75.

εἰσαῦθις, 1. (*till*) *afterwards,* (*for*) *another time* ὥσπερ δὲ ἡμεῖς, οἷς τὸ θνήσκειν ῥᾴδιον ἀποβαίνει νῦν, εἰ. ἢ μετὰ ἀπολαύσεως τὸ ἀθάνατον ἢ τὸ λυπηρὸν μετὰ ἀθανασίας προσλαμβάνομεν, οὕτω καὶ οἱ δαίμονες τῇ νῦν ζωῇ πρὸς τὸ πλημμελεῖν καταχρώμενοι διὰ παντὸς...εἰ. ἕξουσιν τὴν αὐτὴν ἀθανασίαν Tat.*orat.*14(p.15.21ff.; M.6.836C); τοῦτο εἰ. ἀναβαλλομένη μὴ ὀκνήσῃς νῦν...διελθεῖν Meth.*symp.*proem.(p.3.9; M.18.29A); of the wise virgins τροφὴν ἄφθονον καὶ εἰ. ἐπορίσαντο ταῖς...λαμπάσιν *ib.*6.3(p.66.13; 116C); **2.** *recurrently* συνεχῆ...ὄντα τὸν χρόνον...ταῖς τῶν καιρῶν, ὡρῶν τε καὶ ἡμερῶν οἱονεί πως διὰ μέσον παρεγκοπαῖς καὶ ἀνακυκλήσεσι ταῖς εἰ. αὖ μέτροις τε καὶ ἀριθμοῖς ὑπέταξε θεός Cyr.*ador.*6(1.205C).

εἰσβολή, ἡ, 1. *entrance, vestibule,* Cyr.*ador.*10(1.336D); **2.** *entry* τοῦ μὴ ποιεῖσθαι...εἰς τὰ ἅγια τῶν ἁγίων εἰ. id.*glaph.Lev.*(1.370C); διὰ ξύλου σταυροῦ...ἡ εἰ. τοῦ παραδείσου Cosm.Ind.*top.*2(M.88.124D).

***εἰσδεκτήριος,** *acceptable,* ‡Hipp.*fr.17 in Pss.*(p.145.2; M.10. 720D).

εἰσδεκτός, *acceptable, to be admitted*; to Church, Epiph.*haer.*59.5 (p.369.19; M.41.1025C).

***εἴσδεξις, ἡ,** *admission*; to a sect, Epiph.*haer.*61.1(p.380.19; M.41. 1040C).

εἰσδέχομαι, *receive, admit*; **1.** into Church; of repentant heretics, Alex.Al.*ep.Alex.*2(p.21.4; M.18.552A); Const.ap.Gel.Cyz.*h.e.*3.19.9 (M.85.1348A); **2.** met. λόγον Meth.*res.*1.28(p.256.21; M.41.1133D); Thdt.*Zach.*11:5(2.1644); id.*Rom.*6:21(3.67).

εἰσδρομή, ἡ, *entrance* τὴν εἰς ἅγια τῶν ἁγίων εἰ. οὐκ ἔχοντες Cyr. *ador.*10(1.347E); id.*glaph.Lev.*(1.348A).

***εἰσελασία, ἡ,** *charge*; of chariots, Jo.Mal.*chron.*16 p.396(M.97. 585B).

***εἰσέλθει,** prob. f.l. for εἰσέθει (εἰσθέω *run in, LS*), Cyr.*glaph. Lev.*(1.358A); id.*hom.pasch.*16(5^2.216E, v.l.).

εἰσεμβαίν-ω, *enter,* met. ~ει μετὰ τὴν πρᾶξιν αὐτῆς [sc. ἁμαρτίας] μετανοῆσαι Diod.*Ps.*69:1(M.33.1607B).

***εἰσερεύγ-ομαι,** *discharge into* εἰς τὸν...Ὠκεανὸν τὸ ῥεῖθρον ~όμενος Philost.*h.e.*3.10(M.65.493B).

εἰσέρχομαι, *enter*; of a corpse, *be brought* for burial (cf. Lat. *infero*), *Chron.Pasch.*p.304(M.92.772A); *ib.*p.306(777A).

***εἰσευρισκω,** *discover, Hom.Clem.*3.9.

***εἰσεχεῖτο,** vox nihili, Gr.Nyss.*v.Mos.*45(conj. εἰσηχεῖτο M.44. 316C).

εἰσήγησις, ἡ, 1. *instruction, admonition,* ‡Gr.Nyss.*hom.7.48 in Jo.*(p.249.30); Cyr.*Mich.*23(3.411C); *ib.*35(421B); Thdt.*qu.2 in Ruth*(1.349); **2.** *explanation,* id.*Ps.*121:1(1.1495).

εἰσηγητής, ὁ, *one who brings in, author, teacher,* of Christ εἰ. τῶν κατὰ Χριστιανισμὸν...δογμάτων Or.*princ.*4.1.1(p.293.7; M.11.344A); Cyr.*Os.*23(3.46B); of apostles τῶν πρακτέων εἰ. id.*Ps.*44:17(M.69. 1045A); of heresiarchs, Dion.Al.ap.Eus.*h.e.*7.24.9(M.20.696B); Eus. *h.e.*5.28.2(512B).

***εἰσηγητικός,** *introductory,* Clem.*prot.*2(p.19.29; M.8.96B).

***εἰσηγορία, ἡ,** *reproach,* Or.*enarr.in Job* 22:22(M.17.85C).

***εἰσικάριος, ὁ,** (Lat. *isiciarius*) *forcemeat maker, MAMA* 3.343.

εἰσιτήρια, τά, *entry,* Gr.Nyss.*ep.*19(M.46.1076B).

***εἰσκατατάσσω,** s.v.l., *arrange into,* Or.*fr.in Ps.*105:2(p.91.4).

***εἰσκατηχέομαι,** *instruct in the faith,* Phot.*nomoc.*4.6(p.510).

***εἰσκαυχάομαι,** s.v.l., *boast,* c. infin., *Dial.Tim.et Aquil.*94 v°.

***εἰσκεκριμένως,** *accidentally, adventitiously,* Christol. ἐν ἁγιασμῷ, φυσικῶς μὲν...ἐνυπάρχοντι καθ' ὅ...ἐστι θεός, εἰ. δὲ αὖ διὰ τὸ ἀνθρώπινον Cyr.*ador.*10(1.362E); id.*Chr.un.*(5^1.731B); ref. Jo.5:26f. ἔχει...τὴν ζωὴν οὐκ ἐπίκτητον ἢ εἰ., φυσικῶς δὲ μᾶλλον ἐνυπάρχουσάν τε αὐτῷ καὶ οὐσιώδη καρπόν id.*Pulch.*(p.60.6; 5^2.178A); Nestorian view that Christ's powers are ἔξωθεν καὶ εἰ. κερδαίνοντα id.*Nest.*4.1 (p.76.27; 6^1.96E).

***εἰσκλέπτω,** pass.; **1.** *be robbed of* ὃν ποτε εἰσεκλάπην χρόνον *Hom.Clem.*1.8; **2.** *steal in,* i.e. *be inserted* εἰσκλαπέντος...τοῦ ἐπισήμου εἰς τὴν γραφήν Clem.*str.*6.16(p.503.22; M.9.369A).

***εἰσκολπίζομαι,** *form a gulf,* Philost.*h.e.*3.6(M.65.488A).

εἰσκομίζω, 1. *bring in, let in,* Gr.Nyss.*or.dom.*4(p.70.26; M.44. 1164B); Cyr.*Pulch.*(p.60.5; 5^2.178A); **2.** met., *introduce* a subject, id.*Ps.*9:14(M.69.772B); *ib.*36:27(941C); id.*Is.*3.1(2.361A,362A); Thdt. *eran.*3(4.193).

εἰσκρίνω, 1. *bring in* πῦρ ἔξωθεν...εἰσκεκρίσθαι Cyr.*Juln.*10(6^2. 347D); **2.** *cause to enter, introduce* souls into bodies, Clem.*ecl.*50 (p.151.1; M.9.721A); Or.*Cels.*1.32(p.84.21f.; M.11.724A); Eus.*e.th.* 1.12(p.71.21; M.24.848B); Thdt.*affect.*5(p.138.4; 4.834); a subject or opinion in writing, Cyr.*glaph.Gen.*2(1.63D); id.*Zach.*12(3.667E); knowledge in mind, id.*Os.*proem.(3.2A); Christol. οὔτε...μετὰ τὴν ἕνωσιν διαίρεσις...εἰσεκρίνετο Sophr.H.*ep.syn.*(M 87.3164B); **3.** perf. ptcpl. pass., *accidental* οὐδὲν εἰσκεκριμένον...ἐν αὐτῷ [sc. Χριστῷ] Cyr.*ador.*9(1.299A).

εἴσκρισις, ἡ, *entering in, introducing,* of soul τῆς εἰς τὸ γήινον σῶμα εἰ. αὐτῆς Or.*Jo.*6.14(7; p.123.34; M.14.224C); Synes.*insomn.*6 (p.154.16; M.66.1292B).

***εἴσκυρσις, ἡ,** *incursion,* Isid.Pel.*epp.*1.452(M.78.432A; perh. f.l. for εἰς κύρσεις).

εἰσκωμάζω, *burst in upon, invade*; met., Clem.*paed.*2.12(p.228.1; M.8.540C); Chrys.*sac.*3.15(p.79.17; 1.394A); id.*hom.*9.6 *in Mt.*(7. 138B); id.*hom.*64.4 *in Jo.*(8.387D); Isid.Pel.*epp.*1.328(M.78.372B); Thdt.*ep.*146(4.1258).

***εἰσοδέξοδος, ἡ,** *going in and going out, entry and exit* πύλη... θείας εἰ. Thdr.Stud.*iamb.*26(M.99.1789C).

***εἰσόδευσις, ἡ,** liturg., *entrance,* of Great Entrance μετὰ γὰρ τὴν τῶν θείων δώρων εἰ. Thdr.Stud.*praesanct.*(M.99.1689A) = *Lit. Praesanct.*(p.348.23).

εἰσοδεύω, *enter, Apoc.Dan.*C(p.121.14); Andr.Cr.*or.*9(M.97.1004A).

***εἰσοδικόν, τό,** *hymn concluding Little Entrance, introit,* cf.*Lit. Chrys.*(p.368.29).

εἰσόδιος, *for entering, celebrating entrance* ἄνθος εἰ. Gr.Naz.*or.*21. 28(M.30.1113C); τιμᾶται τῶν εἰ. τιμῶν τὴν ἐξόδιον πολυτελεστέραν *ib.* 21.37(1128B); masc. as subst., *entrance,* Gr.Nyss.*hom.3 in Eccl.*(M. 44.656B).

εἴσοδος, ἡ, *entrance*; **1.** of Christ into world μία δὲ εἰ. ἐπὶ τὴν οἰκουμένην, ἡ διὰ τοῦ τόκου ἐστί, καὶ οὐκ ἔστιν ἑτέρως ἐντὸς τοῦ βίου τῶν ἀνθρώπων γενέσθαι, μὴ ταύτῃ τῇ εἰ. χρησάμενον. οὐκοῦν τὴν διὰ σαρκὸς αὐτοῦ γένεσιν εἰ. εἰς τὴν οἰκουμένην ὀνομάζει ὁ λόγος Gr.Nyss. *Apoll.*42(M.45.1224B); ὁ δὲ Παῦλος εἰ. αὐτὴν [sc. Inc.] ὀνομάζει, ἀπὸ μεταφορᾶς τῶν κληρονομούντων Chrys.*hom.3.1 in Heb.*(12.24C); αὐτὸς οὐδὲ ἐν κλίνῃ κατεκλίνετο, ἀλλ' ἐν φάτνῃ ἁπλῶς...τοιαῦτα τῆς εἰ. αὐτοῦ τὰ προοίμια...εἰ. δὲ ὅταν ἀκούσῃς, μὴ τόπου νόμιζε μετάβασιν, ἀλλ' οἰκονομίας συγκατάβασιν id.*hom.div.*8.2(12.374D); **2.** of men, to God and eternal life ὁ υἱὸς τοῦ θεοῦ...μία εἰ. ἐστι Herm.*sim.*9.12.6; cf. exeg. Jo.14:12, Apoll.ap.*cat.Jo.*14:12(p.348. 6); into eternal life, Clem.*str.*7.16(p.66.9; M.9.529A); of soul ἡ εἰς ἑαυτὴν εἰ. ἀπὸ τῶν ἔξω Dion.Ar.*d.n.*4.9(M.3.705A); **3.** of bishops into a see, Ath.*apol.sec.*5(p.91.1; M.25.256B); id.*ep.encycl.*3(p.171.22; M.25.228B); **4.** *admission* of heretics to Church ἅπασι τοῖς βουλομένοις εἰς τὴν ἐκκλησίαν εἰσελθεῖν ἀκώλυτον παράσχου τὴν εἰ. Const. ap.Ath.*apol.sec.*59(p.140.8; M.25.357C); **5.** *privilege of entry, right of access* τὴν πρὸς τὰ ἱερὰ...εἰ. Dion.Ar.*e.h.*5.1.6(M.3.508B); **6.** liturg.; **a.** of Little Entrance, *Lit.Chrys.*(p.312.12); εὐχὴ τῆς εἰ. *ib.*(p.312. 14); in Liturgy of Presanctified ἡ εἰ. χωρὶς τοῦ εὐαγγελίου μετὰ θυμιατοῦ Thdr.Stud.*praesanct.*(M.99.1688C); ἡ εἰ. τοῦ εὐαγγελίου ἐμφαίνει τὴν παρουσίαν καὶ τὴν εἰ. τοῦ ⟨υἱοῦ τοῦ⟩ θεοῦ τὴν εἰς τὸν κόσμον ‡Bas.*h.myst.*33(p.265.12); ἡ εἰ. τοῦ εὐαγγελίου τὴν ἔλευσιν τῆς οἰκονομίας μηνύει Jo.Jej.*liturg.*(p.441); τὰ κηρία ὀψικεύοντα ἐν τῇ εἰ., δεικνύουσι τὸ θεῖον φῶς. ἡ...εἰ. τοῦ ἀρχιερέως τὴν ἐπὶ τοῦ Ἰορδάνου ἀνάδειξιν τοῦ Χριστοῦ ‡Sophr.H.*liturg.*13(M.87.3993C); Max.*myst.*8 (M.91.688C); **b.** of Great Entrance ἡ τῶν ἁγίων...μυστηρίων εἰ. *Lit. Chrys.*(p.318.40); cf.*Lit.Jac.*(p.178); ἡ δὲ μεγάλη εἰ. τύπος ἂν εἴη τῆς φοβερᾶς ἐκείνης ἐλεύσεως, ἣν μέλλομεν πάντες γυμνοὶ καὶ ὡς κατάκριτοι παραστῆναι. εὐθὺς δὲ καὶ μετὰ τὴν αὐτὴν εἰ., ἑτοίμως αἱ θύραι κλείονται Jo.Jej.*liturg.*(p.442); ἡ δὲ τῶν ἁγίων...μυστηρίων εἰ., ἀρχὴ...ἐστιν... τῆς γενομένης ἐν οὐρανοῖς καινῆς διδασκαλίας περὶ τῆς οἰκονομίας τοῦ θεοῦ τῆς εἰς ἡμᾶς Max.*myst.*16(M.91.693C); **c.** ἡ ἐσχάτη εἰ. return of clergy to altar after communion of people, *Lit.Jac.*(p.236.5n.).

εἰσοικέω, *settle*; intrans., Meth.*res.*2.6(p.339.13; M.18.304B); trans., Dam.*troph.*2.2(p.218.1).

εἰσοικίζ-ω, 1. *bring in as a dweller, establish,* reflex., of Inc., Gr. Nyss.*Apoll.*21(M.45.1164D); **2.** *inhabit,* Serap.*ep.mon.*11(M.40. 937B); **3.** med. and pass., *establish oneself, dwell*; met., of God in soul τούτων [sc. sins] γὰρ ἀναιρεθέντων αὖθις εἰς σὲ θεὸς εἰσοικισθήσεται Clem.*q.d.s.*39(p.185.19; M.9.644C); Or.*schol.in Cant.*4:16(M. 17.273A); ὁ μονογενὴς...~εται...ἡμῖν διὰ τῆς πίστεως Cyr.*Jo.*2.4(4.

173B); of evil in man, Meth.*res.*2.2(p.333.5; M.18.300B); *ib.*2.6 (p.340.3; 304B); Christol. τὸν πρεσβύτατον τῶν αἰώνων...εἰς τὸν πρεσβύτατον...τῆς ἀνθρωπότητος ἄνθρωπον εἰσοικισθῆναι τὸν Ἀδάμ id. *symp.*3.4(p.31.5; M.18.68A); *ib.*3.7(p.33.19; 69C); Gr.Nyss.*or.catech.* 24(p.93.4; M.45.65A); **4.** *admit, give entrance to*, met. ψυχὴ καταξιωθεῖσα τὴν ἐξ ὕψους εἰσοικίσασθαι δύναμιν Mac.Aeg.*elev.*9(M.34.896C); word of salvation, faith etc., Cyr.*Jo.*4.2(4.352E); id.*Ps.*33:13(M.69. 889B); exeg. Jo.3:29 ἐν ὠσὶν ~ομαι τὴν φωνήν [sc. Χριστοῦ] id.*Jo.* 2.1(4.159D); diabolic perversity, id.*Is.*3.1(2.386B); virtue, Thdt. *haer.*5(4.418); God into νοῦς, id.*Cant.*3:3f.(2.79); Vict.*Mc.*9:35ff. (p.365.4); Evagr.*h.e.*4.7(p.156.32; M.86.2712A); **5.** *introduce into one's house, marry*, Evagr.*h.e.*1.20(p.28.23; M.86.2473A); met., Max. *ambig.*(M.91.1372A) cit. s. γαμικῶς.

εἰσοικισμός, ὁ, *entrance*; met., Ephr.1.284C.

εἰσπνέω, *breathe into*; met., Dam.*troph.*suppl.(p.278.15).

***εἴσπνοια, ἡ,** *inbreathing*, Max.*schol.c.h.*2.3(M.4.41A).

εἰσποι-έω, med.; **1.** *adopt*; of God adopting men as sons, Clem. *prot.*12(p.86.19; M.8.245A); id.*paed.*3.11(p.270.1; M.8.633A); Bas. *hom.*13.3(2.116B; M.31.429B); Gr.Nyss.*hom.4 in Cant.*(M.44.841C); Gennad.*fr.Rom.*11:25(p.401.6; M.85.1717C); Christol. οὐχὶ δὲ ὁμοίως τοῖς ἔξωθεν ~ούμενος Eus.*d.e.*5.4(p.225.28; M.22.372D); Gr.Nyss. *Eun.*4(1 p.79.14; M.45.653B); met. τοὺς λόγους ἐσεποιήσατο Thphyl. *exc.Rom.*2(p.222.21; M.113.929A); **2.** *incorporate* ὁ κύριος κατῆλθεν... ἡμᾶς...ἑαυτῷ δὲ εἰσποιησόμενος Clem.*exc.Thdot.*67(p.129.10; M.9. 692A); **3.** *call for the inclusion of* μάρτυρας...τούσδε ὁ παρὼν καιρὸς δοκεῖ...~εῖσθαι Eus.*p.e.*8.1(348D; M.21.585C); **4.** *receive into one's house* ~εῖσθαι...τὴν γεγενημένην ἀπόπεμπτον οὐκ ἐᾷ Cyr.*ador.*8(1. 284A).

εἰσποίησις, ἡ, *adoption*; of men by God, Eus.*d.e.*7.3(p.338.28; M. 22.552D); id.*qu.Steph.*9.2(M.22.917B).

εἰσποιητός, 1. *adopted*; Nestorian theory of Christ's adopted Sonship denounced, Cyr.*hom.pasch.*12(5².174A); id.*Chr.un.*(5¹.748E); Thdt.*ep.*146(4.1258); **2.** *received by adoption* ὁ τὴν ἐν πίστει δικαίωσιν εἰ. ἔχων διὰ Χριστοῦ Cyr.*ador.*15(1.535C); **3.** *introduced from outside* εἰ. θεοῖς Didym.*Trin.*3.23(M.39.924B); εἰ. ἁμαρτία Cyr.*Os.*154(3. 187C; εἰς ποιητήν Aubert).

***εἰσποιητῶς,** *from without, adventitiously* εἰ. παρὰ θεοῦ καταπλουτοῦσι [sc. τὰ κτίσματα] τὴν χάριν Cyr.*ador.*10(1.352D).

εἰσπράκτωρ, ὁ, *exactor*, Soz.*h.e.*2.9.2(M.67.956C).

εἴσπραξις, ἡ, 1. *exaction*, Eus.*h.e.*10.8.12(M.20.900A); id.*v.C.*1.13 (p.14.14; M.20.928B); Chrys.*stat.*18.1(2.181B); **2.** *penalty, punishment* ἡ τῶν ἁμαρτημάτων εἰ. Or.*comm.in Mt.*13.1(p.175.17; M.13. 1089A); Alex.Thess.*ep.Ath.*(p.145.12; M.25.368B); Chrys.*hom.1.4 in Is.6:1*(6.102B); Thdt.*Is.*58:3(p.227.15; 2.371).

εἰσπράσσ-ω, 1. *exact, demand*, esp. penalty for sin, *Const.App.* 2.14.9; Cyr.*ador.*5(1.154A); Thdt.*qu.54 in Gen.*(1.67); **2.** med., *have exacted, required from* Χριστὸς εἰσεπράξατο...δίκας αὐτὸν [sc. Satan] τῆς καθ' ἡμῶν ἀσεβείας Cyr.*Is.*5.5(2.860E); Thdt.*haer.*5.20(4.447); **3.** *exact an answer, question* ἐμὲ ~εις...λέγειν Hier.H.*Trin.*(M.40. 849A); τίνα δὲ ταῦτά ἐστιν ~όμενοι Leont.H.*monoph.*17(M.86.1780A); Anast.S.*hod.*1(M.89.41B); **4.** *confer, bestow*, †Gregent.*leg.Hom.*56 (M.86.612A).

***εἰσπροεδρία, ἡ,** *succession to seats of honour*, ref. Mt.20:21ff., Didym.*Trin.*3.29(M.39.948A).

***εἰσρήγνυμι,** *rend, tear* εἰσερράγη τὸ πέπλον τοῦ ναοῦ *Ev.Barth.* 2.16(p.324, v.l. διερρ-).

***εἰσύστερον,** *in time to come, later*, Meth.*symp.*8.1(p.81.1; M.18. 137C).

εἰσφθείρομαι, *intrude perniciously*; of heretics, Bas.*Eun.*1.1(1. 208A; M.29.500C); Gr.Nyss.*Eun.*1(1 p.164.12; M.45.405C); †Thdt. *Nest.*(4.1042); of sin, Gr.Nyss.*virg.*12(p.299.16; M.46.372A); of passions, Max.*qu.Thal.*proem.(M.90.256B).

εἰσφορά, ἡ, *contribution*, esp. for Church, *Const.App.*2.35.1; Chrys.*hom.74.3 in Jo.*(8.438B); of members to body, Thdt.*provid.*6 (4.573).

εἰσφρέω, 1. trans., *admit*; met., into the mind, ‡Gr.Naz.*Chr. pat.*546(M.38.180A); *introduce, intrude*, Nil.*epp.*2.321(M.79.356D); reflex. Μοντανὸς...εἰσέφρησεν ἑαυτόν Epiph.*haer.*48.11(p.234.25; M.41.872D); Thdt.*h.rel.*2(3.1135); **2.** intrans., *enter*; fig. and met., Cyr.*glaph.Gen.*2(1.34E); *ib.*7(229B); Geo.Pis.*carm.*4.14; Jo.D.*hom.* 4.27(M.96.628B); *rush in upon, attack*, Synes.*provid.*2.3(p.118.7; M. 66.1268A); met., Ephr.Ant.*fr.*(M.86.2108D).

***εἰσφρητέον,** *one must admit*, Zach.Mit.*opif.*(M.85.1032B).

εἴσω, ἔσω, (comp. v. ἐσώτερος) **1.** *within*; **a.** fig. οἱ ἔ. of those who understand Christ, Clem.*q.d.s.*5(p.163.24; M.9.609C); οἱ μὲν οὖν 'ἔξω' λεγόμενοι, δηλονότι συγκρίσει τῶν 'ἔ.', οὐ πάντη πόρρω τῶν ἔ. τυγχάνοντες, τῶν ἔ. σαφῶς ἀκουόντων Or.*princ.*3.1.17(p.227.3f.; M.11. 285A); **b.** met., of inner man χρὴ γὰρ εἶναι κοσμίας ἔνδοθεν καὶ τὴν ἔ. γυναῖκα δεικνύναι καλήν Clem.*paed.*2.12(p.230.4; M.8.544B); exeg. Rom.7:22 ἔ. ἄνθρωπον τὸν νοῦν λέγει Thdt.ad loc.(3.79); cf.Cyr.ad loc.(p.208.20; M.74.813C); τὸν ἔ. ἄνθρωπον ὀνομάζει τὸ ἐν ἡμῖν νοερόν Gennad.ad loc.(p.374.3); Gnost. (Heracleon) ἡ τοῦ πνευματικοῦ μῖξις τῷ ψυχικῷ τε καὶ ὑλικῷ, ὃ δὴ λέγεται παρά σοι ἔ. ἄνθρωπος τῷ δευτέρῳ καὶ τρίτῳ ἔξω ἀνθρώπῳ συνημμένος Epiph.*haer.*36.5(p.49.4; M.41. 640A); **2.** *within reach of, subject to* ἡ ἀνθρώπου φύσις, φθορᾶς δὲ εἴ. πεσοῦσα Cyr.*ador.*1(1.11A); Thdt.*Dan.*5:12(2.1164); **3.** εἴ. τὰς χεῖρας ἔχοντας *with folded hands*, i.e. not working, Thdt.*h.rel.*10(3.1197).

***εἴτις,** neut. with article, *anything at all*, Dor.*doct.*7.3(M.88.1700D).

***εἴτουν,** = εἴτ' οὖν *or; that is* [as Lat. *sive*], Pall.*h.Laus.*46(p.134. 2; M.34.1225A); Cyr.*Ps.*9:10(M.69.768A).

ἐκ, *from out of, from*;

A. of place, *beyond, outside*; of state, *besides* παλλακὰς...χιλίας ...ἐκ τῶν τεσσάρων γυναικῶν Jo.D.*haer.*101(M.94.769C).

B. of time; **1.** *beyond*, cf. ἀπό II *LS*; τὸν ἐκ στρατηγῶν καὶ ὑπάτων...τὸν ἐξ ὑπάρχων the *ex*-general etc., Ast.Am.*hom.*4(M.40. 224C); **2.** elliptic ἐξ ἐκείνου *from* that time, Eus.*v.C.*1.8(p.10.23; M. 20.920B); *ib.*1.12(p.13.29; 925C); Chrys.*hom.8.4 in 1 Thess.*(11.483F, 484B); ἐκ μακροῦ *for* a long time, Eus.*v.C.*1.14(p.14.33; M.20.929A).

C. of origin; **1.** theol.; **a.** Trin.; **i.** for Son as ἐκ τοῦ πατρός, ἐκ θελήματος τοῦ πατρός, ἐκ τοῦ θεοῦ, ἐκ τοῦ ὄντος v. υἱός; **ii.** for Son as ἐκ τῆς οὐσίας v. οὐσία, υἱός; **iii.** for Holy Ghost as proceeding v. πνεῦμα, ἐκπορεύω; ἐκ τῆς οὐσίας v. πνεῦμα; Cyr.*Is.*5.3(2.809E) cit. s. φύσις; **b.** Christol.; **i.** Christ born *from* BMV γεγεννημένον ἀληθῶς ἐκ παρθένου Ign.*Smyrn.*1.1; Valent. theory ἡμεῖς ὁμολογοῦμεν ὅτι διὰ Μαρίας ἀλλ' οὐκ ἐκ Μαρίας Adam.*dial.*5.9(p.190.25; M.11.1844D); Valent. theory refuted οὐ γὰρ ἔφη [sc. Gabriel] τὸ γεννώμενον διὰ σοῦ, ἀλλ' 'ἐκ σοῦ' *ib.*(p.192.6; 185A); Σίμων...καὶ Μένανδρος, Κέρδων καὶ Μαρκίων...τὴν ἐκ παρθένου γέννησιν μυθολογίαν ἀποκαλοῦσιν Thdt.*ep.*145(4.1248); Christ born *from* the H. Ghost and BMV ὁ ἐκ πνεύματος καὶ παρθένου τέλειος υἱὸς θεοῦ ἀποδεδειγμένος Hipp.*Noët.*4(p.243.4; M.10.309B); γεννηθεὶς ἐξ ἁγίας παρθένου καὶ ἁγίου πνεύματος Cyr.H.*catech.*4.9; σαρκωθέντα ἐκ πνεύματος ἁγίου καὶ Μαρίας τῆς παρθένου καὶ ἐνανθρωπήσαντα *Symb.Nic.-CP* (p.80.8; H.2.288B); cf. περὶ δὲ τοῦ σωτῆρος οὐκ εἴρηται διὰ γυναικός, ἀλλ' 'ἐκ γυναικός'· ὅτι ἐπὶ παντὸς μὲν ἀνθρώπου χώραν ἔχει τοῦτο, ἐπεὶ πρὸ τοῦ διὰ γυναικὸς γέγονεν ἐξ ἀνδρός, ἐπὶ δὲ τοῦ σωτῆρος μὴ γενομένου ἐξ ἀνδρὸς οὐκ ἔχει τὸ γεγονέναι αὐτὸν διὰ γυναικός· διόπερ ἐκεῖ, ἐπεὶ 'τὸ γεγενημένον ἐκ τῆς σαρκὸς σάρξ ἐστιν' ἡ σὰρξ αὐτοῦ, μὴ γενομένη ἐξ ἀνδρός, 'γέγονεν ἐκ γυναικὸς' καὶ οὐ διὰ γυναικός Or.*comm.in Rom.*3:29(*JTS* 13 p.223); **ii.** for ἐκ δύο φύσεων as alternative form of Chalcedonian definition, v. φύσις; **2.** in phrase ἐκ προσώπου *in* the person (of) ἡ θεία σημαίνει γραφὴ ἐκ προσώπου τοῦ θεοῦ λέγουσα 'ποιήσωμεν ἄνθρωπον κτλ.' Ath.*gent.*34 (M.25.68D); Eun.*apol.*26(M.30.364B); Cyr.*ador.*1(1.14C); cf. ὡς ἐκ τοῦ ἀποστολικοῦ ταῦτα λέγει χοροῦ Thdt.*Is.*25:5(p.101.33; 2.294).

ἑκατόν, *a hundred*; **1.** sacred number, exeg. Mc.6:39f. ἔδει γὰρ τοὺς ἀναπαυσομένους ἐπὶ ταῖς Ἰησοῦ τροφαῖς...ἐν τάγματι εἶναι τῶν ἑ. ... ἱεροῦ ἀριθμοῦ καὶ τῷ θεῷ διὰ τὴν μονάδα ἀνακειμένου Or.*comm. in Mt.*11.3(p.38.21; M.13.909B); cf.id.*hom.2.5 in Gen.*(p.34.15; M.12. 171B); **2.** in Arian heresy, ref. Lc.15:4 Ἀθανάσιος δὲ ὁ ἀπὸ Ναζαρβῶν...ἀπεκάλυπτε τὴν αἵρεσιν ἕνα τῶν ἑ. προβάτων λέγων εἶναι τὸν υἱὸν τοῦ θεοῦ...'ἐν ἑ. γὰρ προβάτοις παραβαλλομένων πάντων τῶν πεποιημένων εἷς ἐστι καὶ ὁ υἱὸς ἐξ αὐτῶν. εἰ μὲν οὖν τὰ ἑ. οὐκ ἔστι κτίσματα...ἢ ἔνι πλέον τι τῶν ἑ., δηλονότι μηδὲ ὁ υἱὸς ἔστω κτίσμα καὶ εἷς τῶν πάντων. εἰ δὲ τὰ ἑ. πάντα γενητὰ καὶ οὐδέν ἐστιν ἐκτὸς τῶν ἑ. πλὴν μόνου τοῦ θεοῦ, τί ἄτοπον λέγουσιν οἱ περὶ Ἄρειον, εἰ ἓν ἐν τοῖς ἑ. περιλαβόντες...τὸν Χριστὸν...εἰρήκασι;' Ath.*syn.*17(p.244. 30ff.; M.26.712B,C).

***ἑκατονταετίζω,** *spend a hundred years*, Thdr.Stud.*epp.*2.48(M. 99.1253D).

***ἑκατονταπλασιασμός, ὁ,** *hundred-fold increase*, Or.*mart.*16(p.15. 22; M.11.584B).

ἑκατοντάς, ἡ, the number *a hundred*, in neo-Pythagorean symbolism of numbers αὕτη [sc. μονάς] δεκαπλασιασθεῖσα γίνεται ἑ. καὶ πάλιν γίνεται μονάς· καὶ ἡ ἑ. δεκαπλασιασθεῖσα ποιήσει χιλιάδα, καὶ αὕτη ἔσται μονάς Hipp.*haer.*4.43(p.65.22; M.16.3106C); exeg. Gen. 14:14f., Clem.*str.*6.11(p.473.30; M.9.305A); symbolizing perfection of rational creation, ref. Lc.15:4 οἱ ἄνθρωποί ἐσμεν ἐκεῖνο τὸ πρόβατον, οἱ τῆς λογικῆς ἑ. ἀποβουκοληθέντες διὰ τῆς ἁμαρτίας Gr. Nyss.*Apoll.*16(M.45.1153A); Max.*ep.*11(M.91.456A).

ἑκατοντάχειρος, *hundred-handed*, Ath.*gent.*11(M.25.25B); Epiph. *haer.*36.1(p.44.18; M.41.633B).

***ἑκατοντόφθαλμος**, *having a hundred eyes*; of Argus, Jo.Mal. *chron.*4 p.70(M.97.148B).

ἑκατοστεύω, *bear a hundredfold*, Proc.G.*Gen.*26:13(M.87.416B); ref. Mt.13:23, †Jo.D.*B.J.*6(M.96.900B,C); *ib.*38(1220C).

ἑκατοστιαῖος, *of one per cent.* per month, Chrys.*hom.56.5 in Mt.*(7.573C); ‡Nil.*perist.*12.13(M.79.965B).

***ἑκατοστολόγος, ὁ**, *exactor of a hundred per cent.*, Bas.*hom.in Ps.*14(1.113C; M.29.280B).

***ἐκβαθρεύω**, v. *ἐκβοθ-.

ἐκβαίνω, **1.** *transcend, pass beyond*, of Moses' fast ἐκβὰς τὴν φύσιν Gr.Nyss.*v.Mos.*(M.44.321B); ἐ. ... τῶν κοσμικῶν πραγμάτων Chrys. *hom.10.3 in 2Tim.*(11.724C); Ἰησοῦς...ὁ πάσης τῆς κατὰ φύσιν τάξεως...ἐκβεβηκώς Dion.Ar.*d.n.*1.4(M.3.592A); **2.** *come forth, emerge from* μέλλωσιν ἐ. τοὺς ἀγῶνας οἱ δίκαιοι Chrys.*hom.50.1 in Mt.*(7.514C); abs., Cyr.*Jo.*1.1(4.11D); **3.** *cease* ἐκβήσεται τοῦ εἶναι... ἀρχή, προεπινοουμένου τινὸς ἑτέρου *ib.*(10E); **4.** *leave, be separated from* οὐκ ἐκβέβηκε [sc. Son] τὸν πατέρα id.*thes.*28(5^1.250D); **5.** *come to pass, be fulfilled*; of prophecies, Or.*princ.*4.1.2(p.296.3; M.11.345B); Chrys.*hom.74.3 in Mt.*(7.719C); id.*hom.24.2 in Jo.*(8.139D); **6.** *subtract* ἔκβα τριακοντάδας, λοιπόν β' *Chron.Pasch.*p.194(M.92.480C).

ἐκβακχεύ-ω, *excite to Bacchic frenzy*; hence **1.** *madden, excite violently* πρὸς τὰς ἡδονὰς ~θείς Ast.Am.*hom.*13(M.40.364C); ὑπὸ τῆς τῶν χρημάτων ἐπιθυμίας ~θέντες Chrys.*compunct.*1.8(1.132E); id. *prod.Jud.*1.3(2.380A); ‡Nil.*perist.*3.3(M.79.820B); esp. ref. demons, Nil.*epp.*3.46(M.79.413D); Philost.*h.e.*8.10(M.65.564C); Thdt.*haer.*4. 11(4366); med. ~όμεναι γὰρ αἱ διάνοιαι ἀεὶ τοὺς κατέχοντας τὴν ἄγκυραν τῆς ἀληθείας Epiph.*haer.*49.3(p.243.16; M.41.881B); **2.** *rage against* ~εις τὴν ἐκκλησίαν Chrys.*Eutrop.*1.1(3.382A).

ἐκβάλλ-ω, **1.** *expel, drive out*; **a.** first man from paradise ὁ ~όμενος διὰ τὴν παράβασιν Meth.*symp.*3.3(p.29.24; M.18.64C); id. *res.*1.39(p.283.14; M.41.1108B); *Hom.Clem.*3.39; Chrys.*hom.13.1 in Mt.*(7.169A); **b.** devils, *A.Phil.*12(p.6.22); Ath.*Ar.*1.50(M.26.116C); id.*v.Anton.*6(M.26.849A); *Const.App.*8.1.3; **c.** met., sin from soul, Meth.*symp.*9.4(p.118.10; M.18.185A); **2.** *cast out* from Church, *excommunicate*; **a.** in gen., sinners ἐξεβλήθησαν ἐκ τοῦ γένους τῶν δικαίων Herm.*sim.*9.17.5; *ib.*9.18.3; Or.*hom.7.3 in Jer.*(p.54.2; M.13.333A); ἥμαρτέ τις, ἐδεήθη μετὰ τὴν ἁμαρτίαν περὶ κοινωνίας. ἐὰν τάχιον ἐλεήθη...αὔξεται ἡ ἁμαρτία ἑτέρων. ἐὰν δὲ...δικαστής... σκοπήσῃ τὴν ἐσομένην ζημίαν τῷ κοινῷ ἐκ τῆς κοινωνίας τοῦ ἑνὸς...δῆλον ὅτι ποιήσει ἐκβαλεῖν τὸν ἕνα, ἵνα σώσῃ τοὺς πολλούς *ib.12.5*(p.92.17; 385C); id.*comm.in 1Cor.*5:3–5(*JTS* 9 p.364.4ff.); Chrys.*hom.14.2 in Rom.*(9.578C); Thdt.*qu.19 in Lev.*(1.196); **b.** heretics Ἀρείου... τῆς ἐκκλησίας ἐκβληθέντος Ath.*apol.sec.*6(p.91.33; M.25.257B); οἱ Ἀρειανοὶ...ἐπὶ ἀσεβείᾳ ἐκβληθέντες *ib.*23(p.104.24; 285C); CEph.(431)*can.*1(p.27.26); **c.** eccl. legislation: on excommunication of clergy, CSard.*can.*14; cf.Bas.*ep.*188 *can.*3(3.271B; M.32.672B); on apostates οἱ δὲ ἄνευ ἀνάγκης μεγάλης παραδόντες τὴν εἰς θεὸν πίστιν... ~εσθαι μὲν ἐν γ' ἔτεσι, καὶ ἐν β' ἀκροᾶσθαι *ib.*217 *can.*81(3.329E; M. 805C); **d.** in Montanist practice ~ουσι γὰρ τὸν δευτέρῳ γάμῳ συναφθέντα Epiph.*haer.*48.9(p.231.20; M.41.869A); **3.** *remove*; from προσευχαί stage of penance, Bas.*ep.*189 *can.*22(3.293C; M.32.724A); *ib.*217 *can.*75(328D; M.804B); **4.** *depose* a bishop, Pall.*v.Chrys.*9(p.51.15; M. 47.30); **5.** *exclude* (from), *put beyond reach* of πάσης ἑαυτοὺς ἀπολογίας ἐξέβαλον Chrys.*hom.29.3 in Jo.*(8.169A); *ib.71.1*(417D); ~ουσι τοῦ εἶναι ἀληθινὸν θεὸν τὸν υἱόν *ib.80.2*(474D); Thdt.*Ps.*109:1(1.1391); **6.** *lead out* (from), Gr.Nyss.*v.Mos.*(M.44.357D); Epiph.*haer.*8.4 (p.190.8; M.41.212A); of Christ τὰ ἴδια πρόβατα ἐ. Didym.*Ps.*32:3 (M.39.1289D); of leading a procession, Thphn.*chron.*p.201(M.108. 517A); ref. Mt.9:38, Lc.10:2 ἐπὶ πάντας...~ειν τοὺς ἐργάτας Cyr.*Lc.* 10:2(p.100.28); **7.** *release* (from), Chrys.*hom.23.9 in Mt.*(7.297D); id.*hom.16.4 in Rom.*(9.609D); met. ἡ γέννησις τοῦ σωτῆρος γενέσεως ἡμᾶς...ἐξέβαλεν Clem.*exc.Thdot.*76(p.131.1; M.9.693B); Chrys.*hom. 4.5 in Heb.*(12.46C); **8.** *bring out* from a store, *produce* οὐδὲ ἐξέβαλεν ἐκ τῶν ταμιείων τὰ ἐπιβλήματα Chrys.*hom.83.4 in Mt.*(7.796B); Jo.Mosch.*prat.*179(M.87.3049C); *Chron.Pasch.*p.338(M.92.884A); waters, Thphn.*chron.*p.338(M.108.816A); **9.** *reject* doctrines etc., Ursac.ap.Ath.*h.Ar.*30(p.199.3; M.25.725D); *Symb.Sel.*(p.258.2; M. 26.745A); Chrys.*hom.16.4 in Mt.*(7.209B); Jo.Ant.*ep.Ruf.*(p.41.2; M.83.1477D); **10.** *open on to, look towards* κατ' αὐτὴν δὲ τὴν πεδιάδα ...~ει θυρώριον Cyr.S.*v.Euthym.*43(p.65.3).

***ἐκβαρύνω**, *depress*; met., *Hymn.*(*AS* 1 p.642).

ἐκβασανίζω, *examine closely*, Cyr.*ador.*10(1.363C); in biblical exegesis, id.*Nah.*4(3.479E); id.*Nest.*1.3(p.22.13; 6^1.15D).

***ἐκβασανιστέον**, *one must examine closely*, Cyr.*ador.*3(1.82A).

ἔκβασις, ἡ, **1.** *departure, leaving behind*, met. θεοποιῶν τι τῶν γενητῶν...ἐ. γνώσεως Clem.*str.*6.16(p.507.12; M.9.377B); τὸ βάπτισμα ...τῆς ὕλης ἐστιν ἐ. id.*ecl.*5(p.138.16; M.9.701A); τῶν προσηκόντων...ἐ. Dion.Ar.*d.n.*4.23(M.3.725B); *overflowing* οὐσίας παράγει [sc. the first cause] κατὰ τὴν ἀπὸ οὐσίας ἐ. *ib.*5.8(M.824C); *escape* from ἡ παρθενεία δ' ἐ. τοῦ σώματος Gr.Naz.*carm.*1.2.34.176(M.37. 958); **2.** *issue, result, accomplishment*, Clem.*str.*1.17(p.53.13; M.8. 797A); Or.*Jo.*28.23(18; p.418.1; M.14.720A); τὴν ἐπὶ σωτηρίᾳ πάντων ᾠκονομήσατο ἐ. Meth.*Porph.*1(p.504.6; M.18.400A); Eus.*Marcell.*2.4 (p.58.24; M.24.824B); Gr.Nyss.*fat.*(M.45.161D); οὐδὲ γὰρ ἀπὸ τῆς ἐ., ἀλλὰ ἀπὸ τῆς προαιρέσεως ἡμᾶς ὁ μακάριος κρίνει Chrys.*sac.*4.6(p.119. 9; 1.411D); hence **3.** *fulfilment* of prophecy, Iren.*haer.*4.26.1(M.7. 1052B); *ib.*5.30.3(1205C); Clem.*paed.*3.3(p.249.23; M.8.585B); id.*str.* 2.12(p.142.16; M.8.992B); Or.*Cels.*2.19(p.148.4; M.11.833D); Chrys. *hom.26.5 in Mt.*(7.319E); **4.** *end* of life, Bas.*hom.in Ps.*1(1.93A; M.29.217A).

***ἐκβατικός**, *resulting from the event, consequential*, Jo.D.*f.o.*4.19 (M.94.1193C).

***ἐκβατικῶς**, *in regard to the result*, Olymp.*Job* 5:3(M.93.81A); *as of a result*, opp. αἰτιολογικῶς, Jo.D.*f.o.*4.19(M.94.1193B).

ἐκβιάζ-ω, **1.** *force out, expel, dislodge*; **a.** antagonist in games; ref. martyrs, *Ep.Lugd.*ap.Eus.*h.e.*5.1.38(M.20.424C); **b.** met. ψεῦδος ...τῇ δὲ χρήσει τῆς ἀληθείας ~όμενον Clem.*prot.*8(p.59.29; M.8.188B); **2.** *force, compel*, med.; **a.** met. διὰ τὴν ἀλήθειαν ~όμενοι *ib.*7(p.57. 15; M.8.184D); ~ονται μετανοεῖν id.*str.*7.2(p.10.5; M.9.416B); Eus. *h.e.*4.15.11(M.20.345C); id.*Marcell.*2.4(p.58.11; M.24.824A); demons to speak, Philost.*h.e.*7.8(M.65.545B); ‡Meth.*Sym.et Ann.*3(M.18. 353A); **b.** *importune, insist*; by prayer, Clem.*str.*5.3(p.336.18; M.9.33A); cf.*ib.*7.11(p.44.19; 485B); τῇ πολλῇ προσεδρίᾳ ἡμᾶς ~ονται [sc. κύνες] Chrys.*hom.13.5 in 1Cor.*(10.116A); *Mir.Geo.*4(p.22.11); **c.** *endeavour* ~όμενοι κατ' ἴχνη βαίνειν τοῦ στύλου τῆς ἀληθείας Or.*Jo.*32.1(p.425.10; M.14.740B); *Pers.*(p.25.18); **d.** *insist*, in argument, Clem.*str.*4.12(p.285.1; M.8.1292C); Leont.B.*Nest.et Eut.*1(M. 86.1304C); **e.** *force* an interpretation, *pervert* ῥητὸν...Ὠριγένους ἀλληγοροῦντος, καὶ εἰς τὴν...Ἰσραηλιτῶν ἐπάνοδον ~ομένου Meth.*res.* 3.9(p.405.5n.; M.18.324A); Eus.*e.th.*3.2(p.144.31; M.24.981A); id.*p.e.* 1.2(6A; M.21.29B).

ἐκβιαστής, ὁ, *exactor*, Leont.B.*mesopent.*(M.86.1993A); met., *one who urges* ὁ τῆς ἀγάπης νόμος καὶ πρὸς τὰ ὑπὲρ δύναμιν ἐ. Jo.Clim. *scal.*3(M.88.669B).

ἐκβιβάζω, *carry out, execute* ὅρκον Synes.*ep.*67(M.66.1421B); ἀπόφασιν Pall.*v.Chrys.*8(p.43.21; M.47.26); αἰτήματα Cyr.*Ps.*33:16 (M.69.892C); τὸ δόξαν Iren.Tyr.*ep.*(p.135.35; H.1.1549C).

ἐκβιβαστής, ὁ, **1.** *one who makes to come out, producer*; iron., of Or. ἐ. τῶν ἐπουρανίων Epiph.*haer.*64.8(p.417.6; M.41.1081D); **2.** *one who drives out, deliverer* Κῦρον καὶ Ἰωάννην...ἐ. τῆς ἐμῆς ἐπηρείας ποιήσομαι Sophr.H.*mir.Cyr.et Jo.*45(M.87.3593C); **3.** *executor*; church functionary, *Cod.Afr.*96; as rendering by AQ of Hebr. שֹׁטְרִים (LXX γραμματεῖς), Proc.G.*Jos.*1:10(M.87.996B).

ἐκβιβαστικός, **1.** *of a tax collector*, Ath.Scholast.*coll.*4.22(p.63); **2.** neut. as subst., *executor's fee*, *ib.*1.3(p.15); *ib.*5 paratit.3(p.78).

ἐκβι-όω, **1.** *pass one's life*, ‡Nil.*Epict.*71(M.79.1312B); **2.** *finish one's life, die* βίου τὸ κέρδος, ~οῦν καθ' ἡμέραν Gr.Naz.*carm.*1.2.30.2 (M.37.909); ‡Hipp.Th.*fr.*16(p.48.7).

***ἐκβίωσις, ἡ**, *passing away, death*, Jo.D.*hom.*9.9(M.96.736A).

***ἐκβλήσκομαι**, *be cast out of*, Thphn.*chron.*p.156(M.108.424B).

ἔκβλητος, **1.** *expelled*; from heaven, of demons, Tat.*orat.*9(p.9. 26; M.6.825B); *ib.*(p.10.24; 828A); from Church, Hipp.*haer.*9.12 (p.249.20; M.16.3386B); ἐ. ... κλήρου ἁγίου id.*Noët.*1(p.235.10; M.10. 804A); **2.** *to be thrown out*; hence **a.** *to be rejected*, Clem.*paed.*3.11 (p.271.18; M.8.637A); Hipp.*Noët.*3(p.239.11; M.10.808A); **b.** *contemptible* σκυβάλων ἐκβλητότερον Eus.*l.C.*16(p.253.26; M.20.1428B); Ath.*h.Ar.*58(p.215.31; M.25.764A).

***ἐκβλητρία, ἡ**, *woman who expels*, of Eve τοῦ Ἀδὰμ ἡ ἐ. Chrys.ap. Jo.D.*parall.*(M.95.1329B).

ἐκβλύζ-ω, **1.** *gush out, leap forth*, of fire ἔσωθεν ἔξω ἐξέβλυσεν Hipp.*Dan.*2.32.9(M.10.677D); of blood and water from side of Christ, Cyr.*ador.*9(1.311C); ‡Jo.D.*azym.*1(M.95.392B); fig., of sources of wisdom ~ουσαι γῆς Clem.*str.*1.5(p.18.13; M.8.720A); ‡Meth.*Sym.et Ann.*10(M.18.372D); †Jo.D.*B.J.*15(M.96.997A); med., met. ~ονται αἱ ἡδοναί Clem.*paed.*3.1(p.236.17; M.8.556C); προνοίας... ἐκ τῆς...θεότητος ~ομένης Dion.Ar.*c.h.*4.1(M.3.177C); id.*d.n.*4.2(M.3. 696C); **2.** trans., *cause to gush out, pour forth*, *A.Jo.*17(p.160.33); Geo.Pis.*hex.*1079 (ἐμβ. M.92.1517A); fig., ref. Jo.4:14 τοὺς μεταλαμβάνοντας τοῦ ἄνωθεν ἐπιχορηγουμένου...αὐτοὺς ἐκβλύσαι εἰς τὴν ἑτέρων αἰώνιον ζωὴν τὰ ἐπικεχορηγημένα αὐτοῖς Heracleon ap.Or.*Jo.*13.10 (p.234.32; M.14.413C).

***ἐκβλυστάνω**, *cause to gush forth, emit*, Ph.Carp.*Cant.*208(M.40.132A); met., of Cerinthus κακοποιὰ φάρμακα ἐ. Epiph.*haer.*28.1(p.313.10; M.41.377D).

ἐκβόησις, ἡ, 1. *acclamation, applause*, Eus.*l.C.*5(p.205.7; M.20.1337B); by congregation in church for teaching of Thdr. Mops., Cyr.*ep.*69(p.116.11; 5².197E); Eustrat.*v.Eutych.*72(M.86.2356B); **2.** *proclamation* ὀνομαστὶ μὴ ἀναθεματισθῶσι τὰ πρόσωπα εἰς τὰς ἐ. CCP(681)*act.*16(3.1385B bis); **3.** liturg., *exclamation* τρισσὴ τοῦ ἁγιασμοῦ τῆς θείας ὑμνολογίας ἐ. παρὰ παντὸς τοῦ πιστοῦ λαοῦ Max.*myst.*19(M.91.696B).

***ἐκβόητος**, neut. as subst., *wide proclamation* τὸ ἐ. τῆς πίστεως Didym.*Trin.*2.23(M.39.557B).

***ἐκβοθρεύω (-όω), *ἐκβαθρεύω**, *dig out*; met., *overthrow, destroy* ἁμαρτίας ἐκβεβοθρωμένης Cyr.*Is.*3.1(2.370E); βωμῶν ἐκβεβοθρευμένων id.*Juln.*7(6².220E); ἐκβαθ- *Hom.Clem.*7.9; *ib.*17.3; *ib.*17.11.

***ἐκβολβέω**, *peel like an onion* Μαξικιανὸς δὲ κακῷ μόρῳ ὀφθαλμίᾳ ...περιπεσών, ἐξεβολβήθη τοὺς ὀφθαλμοὺς αὐτομάτῳ νόσῳ Epiph.*mens.*20(M.43.269C).

ἐκβολή, ἡ, 1. *excommunication* ἀπὸ τῆς ἐκκλησίας ἐ. Chrys.*hom.60.2 in Mt.*(7.608B); **2.** liturg., *dismissal* of catechumens ἐ. διὰ τῶν λειτουργῶν γίγνεται Max.*myst.*14(M.91.693A); *Lit.Bas.*(p.316.6); **3.** *putting forth*, of fish ταῖς τῶν πτερυγίων ἐ. ... διερέττοντα Cyr.*ador.*14(1.503E); **4.** ἐν ἐ. γίνεσθαι *be deprived* of, id.*hom.pasch.*25(5².300D).

§**ἐκβολίζ-ω**, *drag down, degrade*, of a nun addicted to drink ἐὰν αὐτὴν ἐάσωμεν ~ει τὰς ἀδελφάς *V.Dan.*7(p.69.13).

ἐκβομβ-έω, *thunder forth* ~εῖσα [sc. φωνή] οὐρανὸν ἐζόφωσε ‡Jo.D.*ep.Thphl.*14(M.95.364A).

***ἐκβουλεύω**, *devise plots*, Areth.*Apoc.*5(M.106.536B).

ἐκβράζ-ω, 1. *throw up*; pass., of Jonah κηρύξαντος...μετὰ τὸ ἐκβρασθῆναι Just.*dial.*107.2(M.6.724C); ‡Epiph.*v.proph.Jon.*2(p.27; M.43.416B); Isid.Pel.*epp.*1.114(M.78.257D); met., Evagr.*h.e.*1.1(p.6.10; M.86.2421A); **2.** *cast up, produce*, of the earth γῆ...λυμαντικὰ ζῶα ἐξέβρασεν *Hom.Clem.*8.17; fig. οὐχ ἡ γῆ αὐτομάτως...ἡμᾶς ~ει ‡Bas.*struct.hom.*2.1(1.337E; M.30.40C); Chrys.*hom.10.2 in Heb.*(12.104B); χρόνος ἐξέβρασεν Isid.Pel.*epp.*1.388(M.78.401A); **3.** intrans., *gush forth*; of waters, Thdt.*Ezech.*47:3–5(2.1040); med., Proc.G.*Is.*41(M.87.2360D); **4.** *boil over*; met., *be excited* τὴν Ἐνθύμησιν τῆς ἄνω σοφίας...ἀφορισθεῖσαν τοῦ ⟨ἄνω⟩ πληρώματος...ἐκβεβράσθαι κατὰ ἀνάγκην Iren.*haer.*1.4.1(M.7.480A); πρὸς τὸν παράνομον... ἐξεβράσθησαν ἔρωτα Chrys.*hom.4.1 in Rom.*(9.455C); **5.** *pullulate, sprout forth* ~εται τῶν κλημάτων ὁ βότρυς Cyr.*Mich.*61(3.454B); **6.** medic., *break out in*; of the body, Pall.*h.Laus.*38(p.121.9; M.34.1194B); abs., of the person, Sophr.H.*mir.Cyr.et Jo.*8(M.87.3440B); met., of human nature after Fall ἐξέβραττε...σκώληκας Germ.CP *or.*2(M.98.264A).

ἐκβράσματα, τά, 1. *things thrown up, offscourings, refuse* θαλάττης τὰ ἐ. Clem.*paed.*2.12(M.8.540A); met. τὰ...κακίας ἐ. Or.*comm.in Ex.*(M.12.272C); τῶν αἱρετικῶν τὰ ἐ. Cyr.*fr.Ac.*20:29(p.445; M.74.772D); **2.** *castings up* ἰχθύων ἐ. ... γίνεται Epiph.*haer.*30.34(p.382.2; M.41.472D).

***ἐκβραχυπλοῦτος**, *getting rich quickly*, Cyr.*Am.*73(3.332D, conj. for ἐκ βραχὺ πλουτῶν; Aubert ἐν βραχεῖ πλουτούντων).

ἐκγαλακτόω, pass., *be turned into milk*, Clem.*paed.*1.6(p.116.28; M.8.304A).

***ἐκγαμίζω**, *give in marriage*, Epiph.*haer.*30.18(p.357.16; M.41.436A).

ἐκγεννάω, *beget* Son ἀπὸ γαστρὸς ἐκ τῆς ἡμετέρας οὐσίας σε ἐξεγέννησα Cosm.Ind.*top.*5(M.88.256B).

ἔκγονος, *born of, sprung from*; as subst.; **1.** *grandchild*, theol. (view of Pneumatomachoi) εἰ ἐκ τοῦ υἱοῦ λήψεται τὸ πνεῦμα...πάππος ὁ πατήρ, καὶ ἔ. ἐστιν αὐτοῦ τὸ πνεῦμα Ath.*ep.Serap.*4.1(M.26.637C); cf. τὸ πνεῦμα...οὐκ ἀδελφὸν υἱοῦ, οὐκ ἔ. πατρός Epiph.*haer.*62.4(p.392.20, v.l. ἔγγ- M.41.1053D); **2.** fig., spiritual *son*; of priest in relation to bishop who ordained him, Bas.*ep.*81(3.174B; M.32.457A); **3.** met., *offspring* νοητὰ τῆς ψυχῆς ἔ. Meth.*symp.*4.2(p.48.3; M.18.89B); *ib.*7.4(p.75.20; 129D); Ath.*decr.*4(p.4.1; M.25.421C); τἀγαθὸν...ἑνὸς ἔκγονον αἰτίου Dion.Ar.*d.n.*4.19(M.3.717A); *ib.*4.21(724A).

ἐκγυμνάζω, *exercise, train*, spiritually, Meth.*fr.14 in Job*(p.514.20; M.18.405B).

***ἐκγυναικόω**, *make effeminate*, Germ.CP *or.*1(M.98.240B).

***ἐκδαμάζω**, *dominate, master*, Thdt.*Dan.*7:7(2.1195).

***ἔκδαρσις, ἡ**, *flaying*, Nect.*Thdr.*6(M.39.1828B).

ἐκδεδιῃτημένως, *dissolutely, luxuriously*, Thdt.*qu.21 in Jud.*tit.(1 339 v.l. ἐκδιαιτώμενος).

***ἐκδεδίττομαι**, *terrify*, Cyr.*Nah.*1(3.474A).

***ἐκδέησις, ἡ**, *petition*, Evagr.*h.e.*1.9(p.17.12; M.86.2445A).

***ἐκδειμάτωσις, ἡ**, *terror*, Pall.*v.Chrys.*20(p.146.27; M.47.82).

ἐκδεκτέον, *one must take as meaning, interpret*, Clem.*paed.*1.5(p.99.28; M.8.268C); οὐ κακίας, ἀλλὰ δυνάμεως ὄνομα...ἐ. id.*ecl.*26(p.144.11; M.9.709D); id.*q.d.s.*14(p.169.10; M.9.620A); Or.*Jo.*1.37(42; p.48.24; M.14.97D).

***ἐκδενδρόω**, *clear of trees*, Jo.Mal.*chron.*12 p.292(M.97.441B).

[*]**ἐκδεσμέω**, *make binding, secure*, ‡Eust.*hex.*(M.18.724D).

ἐκδέχ-ομαι, 1. *wait for, expect*; esp. life after death, *Barn.*10.11; ~ώμεθα...τὴν βασιλείαν τοῦ θεοῦ ἐν ἀγάπῃ *2Clem.*12.1; Just.*2apol.*11.6(M.6.461C); id.*dial.*5.3(M.6.488B); Cyr.*Ps.*29:10(M.69.857A); opp. receive quickly, *2Clem.*20.3; **2.** *come next*; ptcpl., *adjacent*, Gr.Nyss.*Pulch.*(M.46.868A).

ἐκδημαγωγέω, *proclaim publicly*, Paul.Sil.*Soph.*131(M.86.2124B).

ἐκδημ-έω, 1. *depart (from)*; **a.** in gen. ἐ. τῆς...πατρίδος Marc.Diac.*v.Porph.*6; Thphyl.*exc.gent.*(p.479.5; M.113.937A); **b.** this life τὴν τελευταίαν ἐκδημίαν ἀφ' ἡμῶν ~ήσας Gr.Naz.*ep.*63(M.37.124B); ἐ. ἀπὸ τοῦ σώματος Gr.Nyss.*ep.*2(M.46.1013C); Thdt.*h.rel.*11(3.1201); πρὸς κύριον ἐ. Jo.Mosch.*prat.*182(M.87.3053C); ‡Hipp.Th.*fr.*16(p.49.5); of BMV ~οῦσα γὰρ τῶν τοῦ σώματος, ἐνδημεῖς πρὸς τὰ κρείττονα Jo.D.*hom.*8.10(M.96.716C); *ib.*9.9(736B); **2.** *travel abroad, be in exile*, i.e. on earth τῷ κατὰ θεὸν ~ήσαντι ἀντὶ τοῦ γενέσθαι ἐκεῖ Gr.Nyss.*ep.*2(M.46.1013A); **3.** *travel, go out*, met. διὰ τῶν ὁρωμένων πρὸς τὸν ἀόρατον ~ήσωμεν Thdt.*affect.*4(p.119.12; 4.813).

***ἐκδήμησις, ἡ**, *departure*, sc. from life, Jo.Mosch.*prol.prat.*(p.92).

ἐκδημία, ἡ, *departure*; **a.** from body, or life τελευταία ἐ. Gr.Naz.*ep.*63(M.37.124B); ref. 2Cor.5:6 ἀπὸ τοῦ σώματος ἐ. ἐνδημίαν πρὸς τὸν κύριον id.*or.*7.21(M.35.784A); ἡ ἐντεῦθεν ἐ. Epiph.*haer.*59.10(p.376.5; M.41.1033B); Cyr.*Ps.*16:1(M.69.817B); †Jo.D.*B.J.*39(M.96.1228A); **b.** met., in prayer, *flight* of mind to God δι' εὐχῆς πρὸς θεὸν ἐ. Gr.Naz.*ep.*6(M.37.29C); Evagr.Pont.*or.*46(M.79.1176D); Nil.*Eulog.*2(M.79.1096B); τῆς πρὸς θεὸν ἐ. τε καὶ ἑνώσεως ἡ προσευχὴ τῷ νῷ γίνεται πρόξενος Jo.D.*hom.*1.10(M.96.561B).

***ἐκδιαίνομαι**, *become fluid*, Leont.H.*monoph.*(M.86.1816C).

ἐκδιαιτ-άομαι, 1. *live in an undisciplined way, luxuriously* Ἑβραίων...πλήθεσιν ἔτι ταῖς παλαιαῖς ἀγωγαῖς ἐκδεδιῃτημένοις Eus.*h.e.*1.2.22(M.20.64B); σῶμα ἐκδεδιῃτημένον ἄρτι...σωφρονεῖ Serap.*Man.*18(p.37; M.40.913C); ἐπιθυμίαις ~ώμενος Ast.Am.*hom.*1(M.40.165B); Thdt.*Am.*6:3ff.(2.1435); **2.** *corrupt* ὑπὸ τῶν ἐπαίνων...τὰ ὦτα ἐκδεδιῄτηται Synes.*regn.*2(p.7.10; M.66.1056B).

***ἐκδιαίτημα, τό**, *habitation*, Eus.*Is.*40:19ff.(M.24.373A).

***ἐκδιασώζω**, *preserve*, Thdr.Stud.*cant.*3.9(p.342).

***ἐκδιατρίβω**, *stay, sojourn*, Ath.*v.Anton.*85(M.26.961C) perh. f.l. for ἐνδιατρίβω.

ἐκδίδωμι, 1. reflex., *give* oneself *up, devote* oneself ἡδοναῖς σφᾶς αὐτοὺς ἐ. Clem.*str.*7.16(p.67.2; M.9.532A); Eus.*v.C.*4.29(p.129.5; M.20.1177C); ὁ τῇ διακονίᾳ ἑαυτὸν ἐκδιδούς Mac.Aeg.*or.*9(M.34.860B); δουλεύειν μᾶλλον διὰ τὸν θεὸν ἐκδόντες τῇ ἀδελφότητι ἑαυτούς id.*perf.*9(M.34.848B); pass. ἐκδεδόσθαι νηστείαις Const.ap.Eus.*v.C.*3.18(p.86.14; M.20.1077A); med. σφᾶς αὐτοὺς...ἐκδίδοσθαι ἡδοναῖς Clem.*paed.*2.10(p.214.23; M.8.512A); c. prep. τοῖς...σφᾶς αὐτοὺς ἐκδεδωκόσιν εἰς ὄλεθρον Thdt.*qu.47 in Gen.*(1.61); id.*Is.*64:5(2.391); *V.Dan.*10(p.376.2); pass. βασιλέως...πρὸς τὸ φιλάνθρωπον ἐκδεδομένου Eus.*v.C.*4.31(p.129.27; M.20.1180C); intrans. πρὸς οὐδεμίαν παραμυθίαν ἐκδέδωκεν Jo.Mosch.*prat.*171(M.87.3040A); **2.** *interpret*; **a.** in gen., Clem.*str.*6.16(p.507.4; M.9.377A); τινὲς δὲ τῶν ἑρμηνέων...ἐξέδωκαν ὅτι... *Chron.Pasch.*p.22(M.92.108A); **b.** esp. *render, translate* ὁ Σύμμαχος ἀντὶ τοῦ 'ἠφανισμένοι' ἐξέδωκεν 'ἔρημοι' Or.*fr.35 in Lam.*(p.252.6; M.13.628C); Eus.*e.th.*3.2(p.143.11; M.24.977D); Thdt.*Dan.*9:24(2.1239); **3.** *let out, emit* ἡ γλῶσσα τῇ τροφῇ πιεζομένη...τὴν προφορὰν ἐ. τεθλιμμένην Clem.*paed.*2.1(p.163.11; M.8.400A); **4.** *announce, make public*, id.*str.*1.12(p.36.2; M.8.753B); διὰ προφητῶν μελλούσης αὐτοῦ θεοφανείας ἅπασιν ἐκλάμψειν ἀνθρώποις ἐξεδίδου θεσπίσματα Eus.*e.th.*1.13(p.73.28; M.24.852B); cf.*ib.*2.17(p.120.18; 937B); **5.** *edit, publish* Ἰωάννης...ἐξέδωκε τὸ εὐαγγέλιον Iren.*haer.*3.1.1(M.7.845B); Or.*comm.in Mt.*1(p.3.8; M.13.829A); **6.** *derive*, Max.*ep.*2(M.91.393C); *Schol.*in Max.*ep.*2(M.91.408B); **7.** tr. Lat. *confero*, *betake oneself* ἐν τῷ ὄρει ἑαυτὸν ἐκδέδωκεν Gr.Mag.*dial.*(tr.Zach.)3.16(M.*PL.*77.262A).

ἐκδικ-έω, 1. *vindicate, justify*; bishop's office, Ign.*Polyc.*1.2; oneself, Bas.*ep.*207.1(3.309D; M.32.760B); εἰς τὸν σταυρὸν ἀνελθὼν [sc. Christ]...πᾶσαν ~ήσας τὴν κτίσιν Gr.Ant.*mul.ung.*2(M.88.1849A); **2.** *champion* by taking up a cause: truth, Or.*hom.14.14 in Jer.*(p.120.11; M.13.421D); Ath.*ep.Aeg.Lib.*13(M.25.568A); doctrines, *ib.*10(560B); αἵρεσιν ~ῶν ἐξῆλθε τῆς ἐκκλησίας id.*Dion.*3(p.48.9; M.25.484B); πίστιν id.*decr.*27(p.24.12; M.25.468A): Law, Chrys.

*hom.*48.3 *in Mt.*(7.496C); **3.** *defend* βασιλεὺς κατασκευάσας οἰκίαν... ὡς ἴδιον ἔργον ἐ. καὶ περισώζει Ath.*inc.*10.1(M.25.112C); *M.Ner.et Ach.*10(p.9.28); *Chron.Pasch.*p.392(M.92.1005C); **4.** *claim* τὰ ἄλογα ζῷα διὰ σφραγῖδος δείκνυσι τίνος ἐστὶν ἕκαστον, καὶ ἐκ τῆς σφραγῖδος ~εῖται Clem.*exc.Thdot.*86(p.133.6; M.9.697B); ref. Novatian ἐπισκοπὴν...μὴ ἐπιβάλλουσαν αὐτῷ ~εῖ Corn.ap.Eus.*h.e.*6.43.9(M.20.620B); τὰ ἀλλότρια...~ῆσαι Chrys.*hom.*22.5 *in Mt.*(7.282A).

ἐκδίκησις, ἡ, 1. *revenge, vengeance*, *A.Phil.*131(p.61.17); *Ep. Lugd.*ap.Eus.*h.e.*5.1.60(M.20.432A); Chrys.*hom.*32.6 *in Gen.*(4.325E); esp. of God, *T.Lev.*5.3; *ib.*18.1; θεὸς ἐκδικήσεων *A.Paul.et Thecl.*17 (p.246.11); Cyr.*Ps.*17:9(M.69.821B); ‡Jo.D.*Artem.*59(M.96.1305C); **2.** *vindication, defence* ἐ. ... τῆς ἀληθείας Leo Mag.*ep.*44(p.25.12; M.*PL.*54.828A); ἐ. τῆς καθολικῆς πίστεως *ib.*106.1(p.56.18; 1002C); **3.** *legal representation, advocacy* οἱ τὴν ἐ. τῶν ἐκκλησιῶν ἀναδεξάμενοι *Cod.Afr.*97.

ἐκδικητής, ὁ, *vindicator, champion*, of S. Paul ἐ. τῶν ἀπεριτμήτων *A.*(*Pass.*)*Petr.et Paul.*1(p.118.6); iron., of Novatian ὁ ἐ. ... τοῦ εὐαγγελίου Corn.ap.Eus.*h.e.*6.43.11(M.20.621A); ἐ. κακίας, διάβολον Jo.Carp.*cap.*7(M.85.1840); Jo.D.*imag.*3.10(M.94.1333A); tr. name Jareb, Cyr.*Os.*59(3.92C).

ἔκδικος, ὁ, 1. *champion* τῆς ἀληθείας ἔ. *A.Petr.et Paul.*60(p.205.12); Heracleon ap.Or.*Jo.*20.38(30; p.380.10; M.14.664D); tr. name Jareb, Cyr.*Os.*59(3.92C); **2.** *legal representative, public advocate* εἶδος ἦν δικαστῶν ἐν τῇ Ἀσίᾳ εὐτελῶν οἱ ἀγοραῖοι...ὥσπερ εἰσὶν οἱ ἔ. κατὰ πόλεις τινάς Ammon.*Ac.*19:38(M.85.1577C); Pall.*v.Chrys.*15 (p.91.5; M.47.51); of Church συνεδρεύσαντες ἅμα τοῖς ἀποσταλεῖσιν ἔ. παρὰ τοῦ...Κελεστίνου Jo.Ant.*ep.Xyst.et Cyr.*(p.33.12; M.77.164B); Παῦλος ὁ ἔ. τῆς ἐκκλησίας Thdr.Lect.*h.e.*2.11(M.86.188C); CChalc. *can.*2; *ib.*23.

***ἐκδισκεύω,** *throw out* from τοῦ ζῆν...ἐ. Philost.*h.e.*11.1(M.65.593A).

ἐκδιφρεύ-ω, *throw from a chariot*; pass., met., of Satan διὰ τὸ ὕψος τῆς γνώμης τοῦ ὕψους τῆς ἀξίας ~θείς Bas.Sel.*or.*23.1(M.85.269D).

ἔκδιψος, *very thirsty*, Mac.Aeg.*hom.*18.12(M.34.632B); met. ψυχαὶ ...μηδὲ...ταπεινούμεναι, μηδὲ ἔ. οὖσαι id.*carit.*26(M.34.929A).

***ἐκδιωγμός, ὁ,** *expulsion* ἐ. ... πυρετοῦ Serap.*euch.*29.1.

ἐκδίωξις, ἡ, *expulsion*, Sophr.H.*ep.syn.*(M.87.3176B).

ἐκδορά, ἡ, *flaying*, Thdt.*Dan.*7:5(2.1192); id.*affect.*9(p.229.8; 4.935); Tim.CP *haer.*(M.86.21A).

ἔκδοσις, ἡ, 1. *putting forth, spreading out* αἱ τῶν ὀρπήκων ἐ. Cyr.*Os.*163(3.193B); **2.** *interpretation*; **a.** *exegesis* ἔχει...ἄλλας ἐ. τὰ προειρημένα Clem.*str.*2.18(p.159.14; M.8.1028A); *ib.*6.14(p.489.17; M.9.337C); Jo.D.*hom.*1.7(M.96.557A); **b.** *version* of scriptures ἐ. τῶν Ἑβδομήκοντα Or.*hom.*15.5 *in Jer.*(p.129.12; M.13.433D); id.*Jo.*6.6(3; p.115.7; M.14.212B); †Ath.*exp.fid.*3(M.25.205A); Thdt.*qu.*33 *in 1Reg.*(1.378); **c.** *translation, rendering*; of a word or passage, Epiph.*haer.*19.1(p.218.1; M.41.261A); Cyr.*Jo.*3.4(4.282E); Thdt.*qu.*10 *in 1Reg.*(1.363); **d.** *exposition* ἔ. ἀκριβὴς τῆς ὀρθοδόξου πίστεως Jo.D.*f.o.*tit.(M.94.789).

ἐκδότης, ὁ, *translator*, Epiph.*haer.*65.4(p.6.26; M.42.17B).

ἔκδοτος, *given over, surrendered* ἑαυτὸν ἔ. δέδωκα τῷ θανάτῳ Ign. *Smyrn.*4.2; to the Lord, *A.Thom.*A 13(p.118.12); to eternal punishment, *ib.*58(p.175.8); esp. to passions and vice, Clem.*paed.*2.10(p.210.4; M.8.501B); id.*str.*3.4(p.210.8; ἔνδοτον M.8.1136B); τῇ ἁμαρτίᾳ Mac.Aeg.*or.*6(M.34.857B); Gr.Nyss.*v.Mos.*(M.44.348A).

***ἐκδότως,** ἐ. ἔχω *be inclined* to, c. πρός, Just.*dial.*89.1(M.6.688C).

***ἐκδουλεύω,** *be enslaved*, †Jo.D.*B.J.*15(M.96.992A).

ἐκδοχεῖον, τό, *receptacle*, Clem.*paed.*2.3(p.181.1; M.8.437C); met. Μάρκος μήτραν καὶ ἐ. τῆς Κολορβάσου Σιγῆς αὐτὸν...γεγονέναι λέγων Iren.*haer.*1.14.1(M.7.593A).

[*]**ἐκδόχειος,** *receiving* ἐ. κόλπος Dion.Ar.*c.h.*15.6(M.3.336B).

ἐκδοχή, ἡ, 1. *understanding in a certain sense, interpretation*, of scripture οὕτως ὀνομαζόντων ἡμῶν τὴν πρόχειρον ἐ. Or.*princ.*4.2.4 (11; p.312.10; M.11.364B); id.*Jo.*1.15(p.19.6; M.14.48C); ὁ υἱός... κατὰ ταύτην τὴν ἐ. ἀγένητος ἂν λεχθείη Ath.*Ar.*1.31(M.26.76B); τὴν δὲ σωματικὴν ἐ. ... παραιτούμεθα Proc.G.*Is.*8:16ff.(M.87.1989B); **2.** *expectation* (cf. Heb.10:27), *A.Jo.*88(p.194.2); κατ' ἐ. κολάσεως Max. *qu.Thal.*10(M.90.289B).

ἐκδρομή, ἡ, 1. *coming forth, advance*, of Christ ἐκδρομὴν ὥσπερ τινὰ ἀπὸ τῆς τοῦ τεκόντος οὐσίας σημαίνει Cyr.*Jo.*5(4.447D; εἰσδρομὴν Aubert); met. ἐκ τῶν μερικῶν...ὁ λόγος...ὁ προφητικὸς...ἐπὶ τὰ καθόλου...ποιεῖται τὴν ἐ. Cyr.*Ag.*19(3.649A); **2.** *departure, death*, Sophr.H.*ep.syn.*(M.87.3184B); **3.** *offshoot*, fig. ὥσπερ τινὰς περιττωμάτων ἐ. Cyr.*hom.pasch.*6(5².72A).

ἐκδυναμόω, *deprive of power*, Oecum.*1Cor.*6:15ff.(p.435.15).

ἐκδυσωπ-έω, 1. *put to shame* τὰς τῶν Ἰουδαίων ἀπειθείας ~ῶν Cyr. *ador.*1(1.5B); *ib.*3(100C); hence **2.** *persist in asking, importune, prevail upon*, ref. prayer; of Christ in Gethsemane, Mac.Mgn. *apocr.*3.9(p.72.5); ‡Chrys.*hom.*5(13.213C); Μωυσῆς ἐξεδυσώπει θεόν Cyr.*Os.*40(3.71E); id.*Zach.*6(3.661B); Acac.Mel.*hom.*(p.90.17; M.77.1468A); Jo.Eub.*concept.BMV* 4(M.96.1465A); **3.** *persuade, convince* ἐξεδυσωπεῖτο ὑπὸ τῶν αὐτῆς...συμβουλευόντων Just.*2apol.*2.5(M.6.444B); Thdr.Heracl.*Is.*45:14(M.18.1340D); Cyr.*ador.*1(1.39B); id. *Mal.*38(3.857E); Bas.Sel.*or.*30.1(M.85.336A).

ἐκδύω, med., *strip oneself of, put off*; met., *Hom.Clem.*8.23; ref. 2Cor.5:2(cf.15:53) ἐκδύσασθαι τὴν φθοράν Clem.*ecl.*12(p.140.9; M.9.704B); ref. Eph.4:22 τῆς κακίας ἐκδυσάμενοι τὸν χιτῶνα id.*paed.*1.6(p.109.15; M.8.289A); ἐκδεδυμένος τὸν παλαιὸν ἄνθρωπον Cyr.H. *catech.*19.10.

***ἐκδωματόω,** *build up*, Agath.*v.Gr.Ill.*120(p.61).

***ἐκδωμάτωσις, ἡ,** *construction, building up*, Agath.*v.Gr.Ill.*120 (p.61).

ἐκεῖ, *there*; esp. *in the world to come*, opp. ἐνταῦθα, Athenag.*leg.*12.1(M.6.913A); ἐνταῦθα μικρὰ λαβὼν ἐ. ... σύνοικόν σε ποιήσεται Clem.*q.d.s.*32(p.181.15; M.9.637C); opp. ἐνθένδε, id.*str.*7.7(p.30.32; M.9.456C); ἐ. ... ὅλον δι' ὅλου τὸ θεῖον ὅρασίς ἐστι Gr.Nyss.*Eun.*12 (1 p.274.24; M.45.981A).

ἔκζεσις, ἡ, *breaking out, boiling over* φυσικῆς ἰκμάδος ἔ. προσλαβόμενον Melet.*nat.hom.*synops.(M.64.1084C); met. ἀντιφάρμακον τῆς ἐ. Clem.*paed.*2.2(p.168.28; M.8.413A).

ἐκζητ-έω, 1. *seek out* ~ῶμεν τὰ εὐάρεστα...αὐτῷ [sc. θεῷ] *1Clem.*35.5; *Did.*4.2; *Barn.*2.1; ~εῖτε τοὺς πεινῶντας Herm.*vis.*3.9.5; τὴν ἀγαθὴν ~οῦντες μονάδα Clem.*prot.*9(p.65.30; M.8.200C); ~οῦντες, τί ζητεῖ κύριος ἀφ' ὑμῶν *Barn.*21.6; **2.** *seek*, c. infin., Philox.*ep.*17 (p.168); **3.** *demand an account of, require* οὗ [sc. Christ] τὸ αἷμα ~ήσει ὁ θεός Polyc.*ep.*2.1; Just.*dial.*95.4(M.6.701D); *Dial.Tim.et Aquil.*138 v°; hence **4.** *avenge*, Thphn.*chron.*p.150(M.108.408A).

ἐκζήτησις, ἡ, 1. *inquiry*, Bas.*hom.in Ps.*33(1.146D; M.29.357D); of final judgement, Didym.*Ps.*9:4(M.39.1201B); **2.** *search*, Agath. *v.Gr.Ill.*159(p.81).

ἐκζητητής, ὁ, *investigator*, Thphl.Ant.*Autol.*3.4(M.6.1125C).

***ἐκζητικός,** *investigating*, Max.*qu.Thal.*59(M.90.604B, v.l. ζητητικάς).

ἐκθαμβ-έω, 1. *amaze, stupefy*, Gr.Thaum.*pan.Or.*8(p.22.2; M.10.1077B); Epiph.*haer.*76.33(p.382.12; M.42.584A); **2.** *terrify* δράκων... τοὺς ἀναβαίνοντας...~ῶν ὅπως μὴ τολμῶσιν ἀναβαίνειν *M.Perp.*4 (p.67.16).

***ἐκθαμβητής, ὁ,** *one who terrifies* οἱ ἐ. τῶν προβάτων Epiph.*haer.*77.16(p.429.20; M.42.661D).

***ἐκθάμβωσις, ἡ,** *discomfiture* σταυρέ, ἐ. τῆς φλογίνης ῥομφαίας Sophr.H.*or.*5(M.87.3313B).

ἐκθειάζ-ω, 1. *make into a god, divinize*; **a.** ref. pagan practice of deifying creatures, abstract concepts etc., Clem.*prot.*2(p.19.14; M.8.96A); *ib.*5(p.49.9; 165B); Eus.*l.C.*13(p.236.5; M.20.1397C); Epiph. *haer.*33.8(p.459.1; M.41.569C); **b.** pass., of Adam ὁ δοκῶν ~εσθαι τῇ συμβουλίᾳ τοῦ δράκοντος ‡Caes.Naz.*dial.*30(M.38.892); **c.** met. ~εις τὰ βρώματα...; θεός σού ἐστιν ἡ κοιλία Or.*hom.*7.3 *in Jer.*(p.53.26; M.13.332D); **2.** *confess* or *worship as God* ἡ...ἀκόλουθος Χριστῷ διδασκαλία τὸν δημιουργὸν ~ει Clem.*str.*1.11(p.34.10; M.8.749C); τὸ τῆς ἀρρήτου σοφίας ἐξεθείαζον [sc. angels] πέλαγος [i.e. Christ] ‡Gr. Nyss.*occurs.*(M.46.1156C); **3.** *extol, revere, admire*, Clem.*str.*5.11 (p.372.24; M.9.105B); ‡Just.*coh.Gr.*13(M.6.265D); ~ων...ἀποστολικοὺς ἄνδρας Eus.*h.e.*2.17.2(M.20.176A); Cyr.*Juln.*5(6².155D).

ἐκθε-όω, 1. *make into a god*, of pagans οἱ δὲ ἐξ αὐτῶν ὁρμώμενοι τῶν πραγμάτων ~οῦνται Clem.*prot.*2(p.19.27; M.8.96B); id.*str.*1.21 (p.67.21; M.8.829A); Or.*hom.*5.2 *in Jer.*(p.33.2; M.13.300A); Geo. Pis.*hex.*992(M.92.1511); **2.** *deify* τὴν ἐπουράνιον μελετῶντες πολιτείαν, καθ' ἣν ~ούμεθα Clem.*paed.*1.12(p.149.4; M.8.368B); τῶν ~ουμένων νοῶν πρὸς τὸ ὑπέρθεον φῶς ἕνωσις Dion.Ar.*d.n.*1.5(M.3.593C); *ib.*8.5(893A).

ἐκθερίζω, *reap fully*; met., Cyr.*Os.*122(3.154B); in form ἐξεθέρησεν Jo.Eub.*innoc.*1(M.96.1501A).

***ἐκθεριστικός,** *capable of cutting off completely* ἐ. ... κακίας...ὁ τοῦ θεοῦ λόγος Max.*qu.Thal.*62(M.90.649C).

ἔκθεσις, ἡ, 1. *exposition*; **a.** of writings κεφαλαίων συστηματικὴν ἔ. Clem.*str.*1.1(p.10.26; M.8.704A); esp. of scripture, *exegesis*, *ib.*4.1 (p.248.12; 1216A); σφαλλόμενον ἐν τῇ τοῦ ἀποστολικοῦ ῥητοῦ ἐ. Eus. *Marcell.*1.2(p.11.22; M.24.737B); Diod.*proem.Pss.*(p.82.28); **b.** of teaching ἡ τῆς ἑτεροδόξου διδασκαλίας ἔ. Clem.*ecl.*29(p.146.8; M.9.713B); Epiph.*haer.*72.1(p.256.3; M.42.384A); Thdt.*Ps.*48:4f.(1.916); **c.** in gen., *explanation*, Eus.*Marcell.*2.1(p.31.23; M.24.776B);

2. *citation* τὸν εὐαγγελιστὴν πεποιῆσθαι αὐτοῦ τὴν ἔ. Eus.d.e.9.4(p.413.24; M.22.665D); ‡Just.confut.12(M.6.1516D); **3.** *setting forth, publication*; **a.** in gen. ἡ τοῦδε τοῦ δόγματος ἔ. Eus.v.C.2.23(p.50.26; M.20.1001A); Ματθαῖος μόνος Ἑβραϊστὶ...ἐποιήσατο τὴν τοῦ εὐαγγελίου ἔ. Epiph.haer.30.3(p.338.3; M.41.409B); **b.** esp. of doctrinal statements, *creed* ὑπογράφεις οὖν τῇ ἐ. Λουκιανοῦ ‡Ath.dial.Trin.3.1 (M.28.1204A); ἡ τῶν...Ἀρειανῶν ἔ. Epiph.haer.73.26(p.301.15; M.42.453C); Thdt.h.e.2.22.1(3.881); **4.** title of edict of Heracl. on monothelite controversy, Martin.ap.CLater.act.3(H.3.792D); Max.Pyrr.(M.91.288C); Anast.Ap.a.Max.1.6(M.90.120D).

ἔκθεσμος, *unlawful*, hence *monstrous, depraved* ἐ. σποράν Athenag.res.1(p.48.6; M.6.976A); of idolatry, Eus.v.C.1.13(p.14.10; M.20.928B); Philost.h.e.8.4(M.65.560A); neut. as subst., *unlawful action*, ib.6.3(p.71.18; 533C).

***ἐκθέσμως**, *unlawfully*, Eus.p.e.1.4(11C; M.21.40A); *uncanonically*; ref. election of bishop, Synes.ep.67(M.66.1413D).

***ἐκθεωρέομαι**, *be visible*, Gr.Nyss.v.Mos.(M.44.317D).

ἐκθέωσις, ἡ, *making into a god, deification*; **1.** in paganism τὰς τῶν ἀλόγων ζῴων ἐ. Eus.p.e.2.6(74C; M.21.141B); **2.** myst. ὁ θεὸς... ἑαυτὸν ἐπιδιδοὺς...πρὸς ἐκθέωσιν τῶν ἐπεστραμμένων Dion.Ar.d.n.9.5 (M.3.912D); ib.12.3(972A); ἡ κατὰ χάριν τῶν ἁγίων ἐ. Max.opusc.(M.91.33B); ἡ δοθεῖσα πρὸς ἐκθέωσιν αὐτοῖς [sc. angels] κατὰ χάριν φυσικὴ δυναστεία cat.Judae 6(p.156.2); **3.** Christol. ὥστε γενέσθαι τῷ μὲν κυριακῷ ἀνθρώπῳ...τὸν πλοῦτον τῆς ἐ., ἐκ τῆς πρὸς θεὸν συμφυΐας Leont.H.Nest.1.18(M.86.1468C).

ἐκθεωτικός, *deifying*, myst. δυνάμεις ἐ. Dion.Ar.d.n.2.7(M.3.645A); ἐ. ... χάριν Max.qu.Thal.2(M.90.272B); id.myst.22 tit.(M.91.697D); in next world μίαν ἐνέργειαν τοῦ θεοῦ καὶ τῶν ἁγίων, τὴν πάντων ἐ. τῶν ἁγίων, τῆς ἐλπιζομένης μακαριότητος id.opusc.(M.91.33A).

***ἐκθήγομαι**, *be roused to frenzy*, Cyr.Jo.3.4(4.272D).

ἐκθηλάζ-ω, *caress, flatter* εἰ καὶ ἐκολακεύετο...τὴν ψυχὴν ~ων Gr.Mag.dial.(tr.Zach.)3.38(M.PL.77.318A).

ἐκθηλύν-ω, *make effeminate*, †Bas.Is.48(1.417C; M.30.209B); Gr.Nyss.res.3(M.46.677D); Nil.exerc.34(M.79.761D); met., *deprive* bread *of its goodness*, Clem.paed.2.1(p.155.22; M.8.384A); pass., *be effeminate* ἀπᾴδει γὰρ τοῦ λόγου καὶ τὸ ~εσθαι ib.2.7(p.191.21; 460C); ἡμᾶς βούλεται [sc. ὁ νόμος] μήτε κατὰ τὸ σῶμα καὶ τὰ ἔργα, μήτε κατὰ τὴν διάνοιαν καὶ τὸν λόγον ~ομένους id.str.2.18(p.155.23; M.8.1020C); ~ονται...εἰς ἀνάνδρους ἐπιθυμίας Cyr.Jo.3.6(4.321A); ptcpl. pass., *enfeebled, silly* Ἄρειος...ἔγραψε θαλίαν ἐκτεθηλυμένοις καὶ γελοίοις ἤθεσι Ath.Dion.6(p.50.1; M.25.488B); ἐκτεθηλυμένα ῥήματα id.Ar.1.22(M.26.57C); ψυχὰς...κραταιῶς ἐπιτελούσας τὰ δόγματα, ἀλλ᾽ οὐχὶ...ἐκτεθηλυμένας ὁ λόγος ἐπιζητεῖ †Bas.Is.26(1.400C; M.30.172A); τὸ ἐκτεθηλυμένον *womanish behaviour*, Or.Apoc.16(p.28).

ἐκθηρι-όω, *turn into a beast, make savage*, pass.; **1.** *become like a beast*; through idolatry, Clem.prot.10(p.67.12; M.8.204B); through giving way to passions, Chrys.hom.15.10 in Mt.(7.201C); through sin, id.hom.11.1 in Phil.(11.284A); **2.** *be enraged* Φαρισαῖοι...οὕτως ἐξεθηριώθησαν, ὡς καὶ περὶ σφαγῆς αὐτοὺς βουλεύεσθαι Chrys.hom.39.1 in Mt.(7.432B); ib.29.3(345D); ib.62.1(619D); **3.** *be savagely bent on, crave wildly* τὸ ἄλογον μέρος τῆς ψυχῆς τὸ περὶ ἡδονὰς... ~ούμενον Clem.paed.3.11(p.266.34; M.8.628A).

***ἐκθηρίωσις, ἡ**, *savagery*, Const.Diac.laud.26(M.88.509A).

ἐκθλίβ-ω, **1.** *squeeze out*, Gr.Naz.ep.57(M.37.112B); δάκρυον τῶν ὀμμάτων ~οντι Cyr.Ps.37:1(M.69.952D); id.Mal.38(3.858E); **2.** *squeeze, crush, oppress*, Jerusalem συνάξω τὴν ἐκτεθλιμμένην Mich.4:6 cit.ap.Just.dial.109.3(M.6.728C); Tat.orat.10(p.11.16; M.6.828C); τοὺς πειρασμούς, καθ᾽ οὓς ἐκθλιβέντες...ἐδοκιμάσθησαν Meth.res.1.56(p.316.14; M.41.1149B); ὁ πατήρ μου...ὕβρεσιν αὐτὴν [sc. μητέρα]...ἐξέθλιβεν M.Ner.et Ach.3(p.2.26); **3.** reflex., *squeeze* oneself *out, extricate* oneself τῶν ἀγγέλων τινὰς...μηδέπω τέλειον εἰς τὴν μίαν ἐκείνην ἕξιν ἐκ τῆς εἰς τὴν διπλὴν ἐπιτηδειότητος ἐκθλίψαντας ἑαυτούς Clem.str.7.7(p.35.4; M.9.465C); **4.** ἄγγελος ~ων *destroyer angel* (ref. Ex.12:12), Mel.pass.22 p.4.8; **5.** (Lat. *infligo*) *inflict*, Gr.Mag.dial.(tr.Zach.)1 proem.(M.PL.77.150B).

***ἐκθριαμβεύω**, *publish abroad*, Bas.Spir.66(3.55B; M.32.189A).

ἐκθροέω, *trouble, perturb, terrify*, Apoc.Dan.C(p.121.26); pass., T.Sym.4.9; T.Dan.4.5.

ἐκθρυλέω, *noise abroad, publish*, Cyr.Jo.5.1(4.459C); id.ador.10(1.343A); Socr.h.e.2.29.1(M.67.276C).

***ἐκθρύπτω**, *enervate*, Cyr.ador.5(1.149D).

***ἐκθυλακόομαι**, *come forth from* the womb, ‡Caes.Naz.dial.140 (M.38.1052).

***ἐκθυσιάζω**, *sacrifice*, Orac.Sib.5.355.

***ἐκθωρακίζ-ω**, *disarm* ὁ κριτὴς [sc. Christ] ἰδιωτικὸν ἱμάτιον περιέθετο, ἵνα τὸν κλέπτην διάβολον...~ῃ ὁπλούμενον Procl.CP or.4.2 (M.65.712C).

***ἐκκαής**, *ardent*, Jo.D.imag.1(M.94.1281C); id.hom.4.33(M.96.636B).

ἐκκακ-έω, *be fainthearted, lose heart, grow weary*, Ev.Thom.A 7 (p.148); T.Job 24(p.118.4); Ath.v.Anton.16(M.26.868A); Jo.D.f.o.4.17(M.94.1177A); c. infin. μὴ ~ήσῃς ἀγαθοποιεῖν ἐν τῷ ποιοῦντί σε κακόν A.Phil.95(p.37.20).

***ἐκκακύνω**, *revile*, Isid.Pel.epp.2.128(M.78.573A).

ἐκκαλ-έω, med.; **1.** *call out* δαίμων...ἐνεργῶν ἐν τοῖς ἐνθουσιαζομένοις ὑπ᾽ αὐτοῦ ἀνθρώποις, Εὐὰν ~εῖται Thphl.Ant.Autol.2.28(M.6.1097A); **2.** *call, incite, invite*; to love of wisdom, Clem.paed.1.10 (p.145.7; M.8.360C); εἰς σωτηρίαν ib.1.8(p.129.1; 329B); to sin, ib.2.2 (p.168.24; 412B); Meth.symp.2.5(p.22.15; M.18.56B); εἰς ἁγιασμόν ib.3.10(p.38.8; 76C); πρὸς τὸ πιστεῦσαι Chrys.hom.49.1 in Mt.(7.505B); **3.** in law, *appeal* (*to*), exeg. Ac.25:10 ἐν τῇ Ῥώμῃ θέλω ἀπελθεῖν...κἀκεῖ δικάσασθαι ~οῦμαί σε Ammon.Ac.25:10(M.85.1593B); αἱρετοὺς δικαστὰς μὴ ἐξὸν ~εῖσθαι Cod.Afr.96; ref. African clergy ἐὰν δὲ ἀπ᾽ αὐτῶν [sc. τῶν ἰδίων αὐτῶν ἐπισκόπων] ~έσασθαι θελήσωσι, μὴ ~έσωνται, εἰ μὴ πρὸς τὰς τῆς Ἀφρικῆς συνόδους ib.125; Jo.Mal.chron.13 p.340(M.97.508A).

***ἐκκάλυπτος**, *stripped*, Agath.v.Gr.Ill.50(p.28).

***ἐκκάλυψις, ἡ**, *unfolding, discovery*, Clem.str.1.2(p.13.20; M.8.709A).

***ἐκκάμπτω**, *bend down, submit*, Amph.hom.4.5(M.39.76C).

ἐκκαπηλεύω, **1.** *sell*, Cyr.Joel.38(3.235A); **2.** *adulterate, pervert*, id.Is.1.6(2.170C); ib.5.4(825C); id.ep.40(p.29.7; 5^2.218E).

***ἐκκατάλειψις, ἡ**, *leaving alone, dereliction*, of church without bishop τῆς ἐκκλησίας τῆς ἐν Ἱππῶνι...ἡ ἐ. Cod.Afr.78 (Lat. *destitutio*).

ἔκκαυσις, ἡ, **1.** *kindling, heat*, met. μετ᾽ εὐνοίας, οὐκ ἐ. ‡Pion.v.Polyc.18; Cyr.Ps.9:25(M.69.781A); **2.** *passion* τὰ πρὸς μῖξιν καὶ ἐ. ἁμαρτήματα Meth.res.1.61(p.326.3; M.41.1160A); **3.** *ardour* ἐ. ... καὶ κόλλησις τῆς ψυχῆς πρὸς τὸ θεῖον Diad.perf.16(p.20.13).

ἔκκειμαι, *be cast out*; hence *be excluded* θεὸς...ἐκ θεοῦ κατὰ φύσιν ὑπάρχων ὁ υἱός, τῆς ἐπὶ τούτῳ λαμπρότητος οὐκ ἐκκείσεται Cyr.Jo.2.2 (4.162B).

***ἐκκεκαλυμμένως**, *undisguisedly, openly*, Chrys.hom.77.3 in Mt.(7.744B); id.hom.43.3 in 1Cor.(10.403D); Cyr.Jo.5.3(4.498B).

***ἐκκέλευστος**, *aroused to action*, Synes.ep.73(M.66.1440B).

ἐκκενόω, *empty out, pour out*; ref. Cant.1:2, applied to Christ as Word incarnate τοῦ ὀνόματος τοῦ Χριστοῦ τὴν τὸν κόσμον πληρώσασαν δύναμιν, κατὰ τὴν αὐτοῦ παρουσίαν...'ἐξεκενώθη' δέ, ὡς μηκέτι σιωπᾶσθαι κατακεκλεισμένον ἐν ἀπορρήτοις Or.schol.in Cant.1:2(M.17.253B); cf. *'exinanivit' autem 'de plenitudine'...in qua erat. ... nisi enim exinanisset unguentum, hoc est plenitudinem divini spiritus, et 'humiliasset se usque ad formam servi', capere eum nullus in illa deitatis 'plenitudine' potuisset*, id.Cant.1(p.107.20ff.; M.13.98A); ib.(p.102.4; 93C); cf. δηλοῖ...τὴν εἰς πάντα τὰ ἔθνη τοῦ μονογενοῦς κληθεῖσαν ἐπωνυμίαν, καθ᾽ ὃ πάντα τὰ ἔθνη εὐωδιάζουσι πρὸς αὐτὸν τὴν αὐτοῦ φέροντα προσηγορίαν Cyr.Cant.1:1f.(M.69.1277); v. μύρον.

ἐκκεντέω, *pierce, stab*, ref. side of Christ δύο παρουσίας αὐτοῦ... μίαν μὲν ἐν ᾗ ἐξεκεντήθη ὑφ᾽ ὑμῶν, δευτέραν δὲ ὅτε ἐπιγνώσεσθε εἰς ὃν ἐξεκεντήσατε Just.dial.32.2(M.6.544A); ib.64.7(625A); ib.118.1 (749A); Gnost. exeg. ἐξεκέντησαν δὲ τὸ φαινόμενον, ὃ ἦν σὰρξ τοῦ ψυχικοῦ Clem.exc.Thdot.62(p.128.3; M.9.689A); Marcell.fr.103 ap. Eus.Marcell.2.4(p.53.6f.; M.24.813B); Thdr.Heracl.ap.cat.Jo.12:8 (p.323.25).

***ἐκκέντησις, ἡ**, *putting out* of the eyes, Eus.h.e.8.12(M.20.773A; p.770.17 not.).

***ἐκκένωσις, ἡ**, *complete emptying*; of Christ, Eus.d.e.5.1(p.214.8; M.22.356B); ἐ. τῆς ἐλπίδος ‡Ath.fr.Ps.140:8(p.41).

ἐκκεραΐζ-ω, *overthrow* ~ομένης τοῦ δράκοντος τῆς ἰσχύος Meth.symp.8.13(p.98.5; M.18.160B); Cyr.Zach.10(3.664E).

***ἐκκεχειρία, ἡ**, *respite, intermission* τῶν πολεμίων ἐ. Nil.exerc.32 (M.79.760D); id.Magn.1(M.79.969C); ‡Nil.perist.12.12(M.79.964D).

***ἐκκηρυκτέον**, *one must proscribe, excommunicate*, Isid.Pel.epp.2.114(M.78.556B).

ἐκκήρυκτος, **1.** *excommunicated* ἐκκήρυκτος ἐκκλησίας θεοῦ Gr.Thaum.ep.can.2(M.10.1025D); abs., CAnc.(314)can.18; ἐ. διὰ τὴν ἀσέβειαν γενόμενοι Ath.ep.encycl.5(p.174.12; M.25.233A); Epiph.haer.69.3(p.155.15; M.42.208C); **2.** *rejected, repudiated* ἐ. τῇ θεολογίᾳ πᾶς ὁ ἀλλοτριοεπίσκοπος Dion.Ar.ep.8(M.3.1089C); cf.Ant.Mon.hom.123(M.89.1817D).

ἐκκηρύσσ-ω, **1.** *exclude from civil rights* ὡς ἀθεωτάτους ἡμᾶς [sc. Christians] ~ετε Tat.orat.27(p.28.30; M.6.865A); **2.** *exclude from* μήτε ἑαυτὸν τῶν ἄθλων τοῦ σωτῆρος ~έτω Clem.*q.d.s.*3(p.161.29; M.9.608B); οὓς δεῖ ἐκκηρύξαι τῶν εὐχῶν Gr.Thaum.*ep.can.*5(M.10.1037C); ὃν ἡμεῖς συνόδου Χριστιανῶν ~ομεν Synes.*ep.*5(M.66.1344A); abs., Cyr.*Jo.*3.6(4.328A); **3.** *excommunicate*, Malch.*ep.*ap.Eus.*h.e.*7.30.17(M.20.717C); Gr.Thaum.*ep.can.*2(M.10.1028A); Philost.*h.e.*2.11 (M.65.476B).

ἐκκλησία, ἡ, *church*;

A. as an institution; **1.** def. and descriptions τὸ βούλημα αὐτοῦ [sc. θεοῦ] ἀνθρώπων ἐστὶ σωτηρία καὶ τοῦτο ἐ. κέκληται Clem.*paed.*1.6 (p.106.11; M.8.281B); id.*str.*7.5(p.21.25; M.9.437C) cit. s. ἄθροισμα; ἐ. παρὰ τὸ ἐκκεκλικέναι τὰς ἡδονὰς λέγεσθαι Meth.*creat.*8(p.498.22; M.18.340C); ἐ. δὲ καλεῖται φερωνύμως, διὰ τὸ πάντας ἐκκαλεῖσθαι καὶ ὁμοῦ συνάγειν Cyr.H.*catech.*18.24; ἐ. ... ἡ διὰ τῶν ἡμετέρων ψυχῶν ᾠκοδομημένη οἰκία id.*hom.10.2 in Eph.*(11.78A); τὸ ἄθροισμα τῶν ἁγίων τὸ ἐξ ὀρθῆς πίστεως καὶ πολιτείας ἀρίστης συγκεκροτημένον ἐ. ἐστί Isid.Pel.*epp.*2.246(M.78.685A); Cyr.*glaph.Gen.*4(1.139A); v. σύστημα; Arian οἱ πλήθει τὴν ἐ. ὁρίζοντες, καὶ τὸ βραχὺ διαπτύοντες ποίμνιον Gr.Naz.*or.*33.1(M.36.216A); **2.** characteristics; **a.** unity μετανοήσαντες ἔλθωσιν ἐπὶ τὴν ἑνότητα τῆς ἐ. Ign.*Philad.*3.2; πιστοὺς αὐτοῦ, εἴτε ἐν Ἰουδαίοις εἴτε ἐν ἔθνεσιν, ἐν ἑνὶ σώματι τῆς ἐ. αὐτοῦ id.*Smyrn.*1.2; μία ἐ. Clem.*paed.*1.4(p.96.3; M.8.260C); id.*str.*3.10 (p.227.28; M.8.1172A); opp. multiplicity of heresies φανερὸν οἶμαι γεγενῆσθαι μίαν εἶναι τὴν ἀληθῆ ἐ. τὴν τῷ ὄντι ἀρχαίαν, εἰς ἣν οἱ κατὰ πρόθεσιν δίκαιοι ἐγκαταλέγονται. ἑνὸς γὰρ ὄντος τοῦ θεοῦ...διὰ τοῦτο καὶ τὸ ἄκρως τίμιον κατὰ τὴν μόνωσιν ἐπαινεῖται...τῇ γοῦν τοῦ ἑνὸς φύσει συγκληροῦται ἐ. ἡ μία, ἣν εἰς πολλὰς κατατέμνειν βιάζονται αἱρέσεις. κατά τε οὖν ὑπόστασιν κατά τε ἐπίνοιαν κατά τε ἀρχὴν κατά τε ἐξοχὴν μόνην εἶναί φαμεν τὴν ἀρχαίαν καὶ καθολικὴν ἐ. ... ἡ ἐξοχὴ τῆς ἐ., καθάπερ ἡ ἀρχὴ τῆς συστάσεως, κατὰ τὴν μονάδα ἐστίν, πάντα τὰ ἄλλα ὑπερβάλλουσα καὶ μηδὲν ἔχουσα ὅμοιον ἢ ἴσον ἑαυτῇ *ib.*7.17 (p.76.5ff.; M.9.552A,B); Bas.*ep.*161.1(3.252B; M.32.629B); ἐ. γάρ ἐστιν ἀπὸ μιᾶς πίστεως γεγεννημένη, τεχθεῖσα δὲ διὰ πνεύματος ἁγίου, μία τῇ μόνῃ καὶ μία τῇ γεγεννηκυίᾳ Epiph.*exp.fid.*6(p.501.21; M.42.781D); τὸ γὰρ τῆς ἐ. ὄνομα οὐ χωρισμοῦ, ἀλλὰ ἑνώσεώς ἐστι καὶ συμφωνίας ὄνομα...τὴν ἐπὶ τῆς οἰκουμένης μίαν δεῖ εἶναι ἐ., καίτοι τόποις πολλοῖς κεχωρισμένην Chrys.*hom.1.1 in 1Cor.*(10.4B,D); τὰς κατὰ πᾶσαν τὴν οἰκουμένην ἐ., μίαν νῦν ὀνομάζει, διὰ τὸ ἑνὸς εἶναι δεσπότου καὶ μίαν εἶναι τὴν πίστιν ἐν αὐταῖς...ὥστε καὶ ἀναριθμήτους οὔσας, μίαν εἶναι Cyr.*Ps.*44:10(M.69.1041B); typified by one tabernacle and one Temple, id.*glaph.Lev.*1(1.351C); Olymp.*fr.Jer.*4:6 (M.93.636B); **b.** holiness, *M.Polyc.*proem.; τὴν εἰς τιμὴν τοῦ θεοῦ κατ' ἐπίγνωσιν ἁγίαν γενομένην ἐ. Clem.*str.*7.5(p.21.22; M.9.437C); Bas.*ep.*114(3.207C; 529A); Max.*qu.Thal.*63(M.90.665C); **c.** catholicity ἡ καθολικὴ ἐ. Ign.*Smyrn.*8.2; τῆς κατὰ τὴν οἰκουμένην καθολικῆς ἐ. *M.Polyc.*19.2; ἐ. ... καθ' ὅλης τῆς οἰκουμένης ἕως περάτων τῆς γῆς διεσπαρμένη Iren.*haer.*1.10.1(M.7.549A); *ib.*3.11.8(885A); Clem.*str.*7.17(p.75.8; M.9.548A); ἐκκλησίαι Χριστοῦ δι' αὐτῶν ἐν ὅλοις τοῖς ἔθνεσι συστήσονται Eus.*d.e.*1.1(p.5.7; M.22.20A); Cyr.H.*catech.*18.23 cit. s. ἁμαρτία; opp. heret. assemblies ἐπειδὴ δὲ τὸ τῆς ἐ. ὄνομα περὶ διαφόρων λέγεται πραγμάτων...κυρίως δὲ ἄν τις εἴποι καὶ ἀληθῶς ἐ. εἶναι πονηρευομένων τὰ συστήματα τῶν αἱρετικῶν...διὰ τοῦτό σοι νῦν... παρέδωκεν ἡ πίστις τό, καὶ εἰς μίαν, ἁγίαν, καθολικὴν ἐ.· ἵνα ἐκείνων μὲν τὰ μιαρὰ συστήματα φεύγῃς, παραμένῃς δὲ τῇ ἁγίᾳ καθολικῇ ἐ. ... κἂν ποτε ἐπιδημῇς ἐν πόλεσι, μὴ ἁπλῶς ἐξέταζε...ποῦ ἔστιν ἁπλῶς ἡ ἐ.· ἀλλά, ποῦ ἔστιν ἡ καθολικὴ ἐ. τοῦτο γὰρ ἰδικὸν ὄνομα τυγχάνει τῆς ἁγίας ταύτης *ib.*18.26; *ib.*18.27; ἡ οἰκουμενικὴ ἐ. *Const.App.*7.30.2; ἀπὸ τοιούτων ἡ ἐ. συνείλεκτο, Ἑλλήνων, μάγων, ἀνδροφόνων, γοήτων, ψευστῶν, ὑπούλων Chrys.*exp.in Ps.*5:7(5.34C); id.*Is.interp.*2.3(6.22A); id.*hom.54.2 in Mt.*(7.548D) cit. s. 4.a infra; †Chrys.*Jud.et gent.*1(1.558D); ‡Chrys.*pent.*1(3.789E); Nil.*epp.*3.29(M.79.385B); δέχεται γὰρ ἡ ἐ. κατὰ πάντα καιρὸν τοὺς πιστεύειν ἐθέλοντας, ἐκκλείει δὲ ὅλως οὐδενὶ τὴν εἰς τοῦτο σπουδήν Cyr.*Is.*5.4(2.848C); τὴν... ἐ. κατὰ πρώτην θεωρίας ἐπιβολήν, τύπον καὶ εἰκόνα θεοῦ φέρειν... ὥσπερ γὰρ ὁ θεὸς πάντα τῇ ἀπείρῳ δυνάμει ποιήσας...συνάγει καὶ περιγράφει...κατὰ τὸν αὐτὸν τρόπον καὶ ἡ...ἐ., τὰ αὐτὰ τῷ θεῷ περὶ ἡμᾶς ὡς ἀρχετύπῳ εἰκὼν ἐνεργοῦσα δειχθήσεται. πολλῶν γὰρ ὄντων... ἀνδρῶν τε καὶ γυναικῶν...μίαν πᾶσι κατὰ τὸ ἴσον δίδωσι...θείαν μορφήν Max.*myst.*1(M.91.664D–665C); **d.** apostolicity, v. ἀποστολικός; **e.** credal affirmations of some or all of the above notes, cf. *credis in...sanctam ecclesiam...?* Hipp.*trad.ap.*21.17; Marcell.*ep.*(p.258.12; M.42.385D); πιστεύω...εἰς...ἁγίαν ἐ. καθολικήν *Symb.App.* (Hahn p.30); εἰς μίαν ἁγίαν καθολικὴν ἐ. *Symb.Hier.*ap.Cyr.H.*catech.*18.22(M.33.1044A); εἰς μίαν ἁγίαν καθολικὴν καὶ ἀποστολικὴν ἐ. *Symb.*ap.Epiph.*anc.*118(p.147.14; M.43.232D); *Symb.Nic.–CP*(p.8c.15; H.2.288B); πιστεύομεν εἰς μίαν μόνην ταύτην καθολικὴν καὶ ἀποστολικὴν ἐ. ‡Ath.*interpr.*(p.66.26; M.26.1232B); **f.** indestructibility οὐδὲν ἐκκλησίας δυνατώτερον,...ἄνθρωπον ἐὰν πολεμῇς, ἢ ἐνίκησας, ἢ ἐνικήθης· ἐ. δὲ ἐὰν πολεμῇς, νικῆσαί σε ἀμήχανον...ἡ ἐ. οὐρανοῦ ἰσχυροτέρα Chrys.*a.exil.*1.1(3.415C,D); ref. Mt.16:18 οἱ θεμέλιοι τῆς ἐ. οὐδὲ οὕτως [sc. through persecutions] ἐσαλεύθησαν... ὁ τοίνυν διὰ ῥήματος τὸν οὐρανὸν στερεώσας...τί θαυμάζεις, εἰ τὴν οὐρανοῦ καὶ γῆς...τιμιωτέραν ἐ. διὰ τοῦ ῥήματος τούτου πάλιν ἐτείχισεν; id.*hom.2.1 in Ac.princ.*(3.62B,C); hence ἐ. called a mountain (Is. 2:2) id.*Is.interp.*2.2(6.20C); χειμάζεται ἡ ἐ., ἀλλ' οὐ καταποντίζεται... τὴν βελοθήκην αὐτοῦ ἐξεκένωσεν ὁ διάβολος, τὴν δὲ ἐ. οὐκ ἔβλαψε ‡Chrys.*pent.*1(3.791A,B); **g.** summary, cf. *eorum autem qui ab ecclesia sunt semita, circumiens mundum universum, quippe firmam habens ab apostolis traditionem, et videre nobis donans omnium unam et eandem esse fidem...et eandem figuram ejus quae est erga ecclesiam ordinationis custodientibus...*, Iren.*haer.*5.20.1(M.7.1177A, B); τὸ ἀρχαῖον τῆς ἐ. σύστημα κατὰ παντὸς τοῦ κόσμου linked with apostolic teaching as part of true *gnosis*, *ib.*4.33.8(1077B); **3.** teaching office; **a.** in gen., cf.Iren.*haer.*4.32.1(M.7.1071A); διδασκαλεῖον δὲ ἡ ἐ. Clem.*paed.*3.12(p.289.27; εἰς καλὸν δὲ ἡ ἐ. M.8.677A); Chrys.*exp.in Ps.*48:1(5.204D); **b.** as teacher of truth, cf. *pro sola vera... fide, quam ab apostolis ecclesia percepit, et distribuit filiis suis*, Iren.*haer.*3 proem.(M.7.843B); *non oportet adhuc quaerere apud alios veritatem, quam facile est ab ecclesia sumere*, *ib.*3.4.1(855A); *qui sunt extra veritatem, id est qui sunt extra ecclesiam*, *ib.*4.33.7(1076C); *ubique enim ecclesia praedicat veritatem: et haec est* ἑπτάμυχος *lucerna, Christi bajulans lumen...oportet...confugere autem ad ecclesiam, et in ejus sinu educari*, *ib.*5.20.1,2(1177B–1178A); cf.Or.*princ.*1 proem.2(p.8.27; M.11.116B); id.*hom.5.14 in Jer.*(p.43.29; M.13.317A); **c.** hence uniformity in doctrine, cf. *praedicationem vero ecclesiae undique constantem, et aequalitu perseverantem, et testimonium habentem a prophetis et ab apostolis*, Iren.*haer.*3.24.1 (M.7.966A,B); οὐκ ὀφείλει ἐ. ἐκκλησίας διαφορὰν ἔχειν ἐν γνώσει, ἐπεὶ οὐκ ἐστὲ ἐ. ἡ ψευδομένη Or.*dial.*1(p.120.5f.); **d.** avoiding extremes, ref. Valentinus and Marcion, Chrys.*sac.*4.4(p.114.4; 1.409C) cit. s. ἀμετρία; ref. Nestorians and monophysites τῆς ἐ. παρωσαμένης τὰς ἐφ' ἑκάτερα...παρατροπάς, μέσην τε καὶ ἀληθεστάτην τεμνούσης ὁδόν Thdr.Raith.*praep.*(p.196.3; M.91.1497B); *ib.*(p.199.27; 1501D); **e.** ref. scripture, Iren.*haer.*3.11.8(M.7.885A) cit. s. στήριγμα; φιλομαθῶς ἐπίγνωθι, καὶ παρὰ τῆς ἐ., ποῖαι μέν εἰσιν αἱ τῆς παλαιᾶς διαθήκης βίβλοι, ποῖαι δὲ τῆς καινῆς Cyr.H.*catech.*4.33; ταύτας μόνας μελέτα σπουδαίως, ἃς καὶ ἐν ἐ. ... ἀναγινώσκομεν *ib.*4.35; Chrys.*hom. in 2Tim.3:1*(6.282B) cit. s. γράμμα; ref. Zach.4:3 αἱ δύο...ἐλαῖαι τῆς χρυσῆς λυχνίας, τουτέστι, τῆς ἁγίας καθολικῆς ἐ., αἱ δύο διαθῆκαι τυγχάνουσιν Max.*qu.Thal.*63(M.90.676D); **f.** for Church and faith v. πίστις; and tradition v. παράδοσις; **4.** organization; **a.** founded on S. Peter Πέτρος, χωρήσας τὴν τῆς ἐ. ἐν αὐτῷ οἰκοδομὴν ἀπὸ τοῦ λόγου Or.*Cels.*6.77(p.147.18; M.11.1416B); Πέτρον...τὸν διὰ πίστεως ὑπεροχὴν ἐφ' ἑαυτὸν τὴν οἰκοδομὴν τῆς ἐ. δεξάμενον Bas.*Eun.*2.4(1.240E; M.29.580A); ὁ μὲν Πέτρα καλεῖται, καὶ τοὺς θεμελίους τῆς ἐ. πιστεύεται Gr.Naz.*or.*32.18(M.36.193C); Χριστὸς...λέγει αὐτοῖς· χαῖρε Πέτρε ἐπίσκοπε ὅλης τῆς ἐ. μου *A.Petr.et Andr.*2(p.117.20); ὁ πατὴρ ...τῷ Πέτρῳ τὴν ἀποκάλυψιν τοῦ υἱοῦ ἐχαρίσατο· ὁ δὲ υἱὸς...ἀνθρώπῳ θνητῷ πάντων τῶν ἐν τῷ οὐρανῷ τὴν ἐξουσίαν ἐνεχείρισε, τὰς κλεῖς αὐτῷ δούς, ὃς τὴν ἐ. πανταχοῦ τῆς οἰκουμένης ἐξέτεινε Chrys.*hom. 54.2 in Mt.*(7.548D); ἐκ τοῦ Χριστοῦ σὺ [sc. S. Peter] παραλαβὼν τὴν ἐ. ... καλῶς ἐκυβέρνησας...ἀπόστολε Jo.Mon.*hymn.Petr.*4(M.96.1392D); *ib.*5(1393A); **b.** different orders χρὴ οὖν τὴν ἐ. ... φιλόθεον ἔχειν τάξιν...πρὸ πάντων ὁ ἐπίσκοπος ὡς ἄρχων περὶ ὧν λέγει ἀκουέσθω· οἱ πρεσβύτεροι τὰ κελευόμενα γίνεσθαι σπουδαζέτωσαν· οἱ διάκονοι ἐκπεριερχόμενοι τῶν ἀδελφῶν τὰ σώματα καὶ τὰς ψυχὰς ἐπισκεπτέσθωσαν...οἱ λοιποὶ πάντες ἀδελφοὶ τὸ ἀδικεῖσθαι ἀναδεχέσθωσαν *Hom. Clem.*3.67; relationship between bishop and his church as between husband and wife, Ath.*apol.sec.*6(p.93.12; M.25.260C); τάξις κἂν ταῖς ἐ., τὸ μὲν εἶναι τὸ ποίμνιον, τὸ δὲ ποιμένας διώρισε· καὶ τὸ μὲν ἄρχειν, τὸ δὲ ἄρχεσθαι· καὶ τὸ μὲν οἷον εἶναι κεφαλήν, τὸ δὲ πόδας... τὸ δὲ ἄλλοτι τῶν μελῶν τοῦ σώματος Gr.Naz.*or.*32.10(M.36.185B); Chrys.*hom.30.4 in 1Cor.*(10.274D) cit. s. χήρα; cf.id.*hom.3.3 in Ac.princ.*(3.75Cff.); formed on heavenly hierarchies, Clem.*str.*6.13 (p.485.28; M.9.328C); for allegorical application of Cant.3:9f. to various eccl. offices v. Gr.Nyss.*hom.7 in Cant.*(M.44.913B,C); cf. id.*v.Mos.*(M.44.385A); **c.** requirements for Church rulers, Herm.*vis.*2.2.6 cit. s. προηγέομαι; τοὺς δυνατοὺς λόγῳ καὶ βίῳ ὑγιεῖ χρωμένους ἄρχειν ἐπὶ τὸ ἄρχειν ἐκκλησιῶν παρακαλοῦμεν,...καὶ εἰ ἄρχουσιν οἱ καλῶς ἄρχοντες ἐν τῇ ἐ. τῆς κατὰ θεὸν πατρίδος (λέγω δὲ τῆς ἐ.)... ἄρχουσι κατὰ τὰ ὑπὸ τοῦ θεοῦ προστεταγμένα Or.*Cels.*8.75(p.292.5ff.; M.11.1629B,C); οἱ τῶν ἐ. προεστῶτες τῆς οἰκείας ἀρχῆς ὑφέξουσι τὸν λόγον· καὶ μάλιστα οὗτοί εἰσιν οἱ ἐπὶ πλέον τὰς πικρὰς...εὐθύνας ὑπέχοντες Chrys.*hom.in Mt.18*:*23*(3.7C); learning needed, id.*hom.15.2 in 1Tim.*(11.636F); **d.** remuneration δεῖ γὰρ τοὺς τῇ ἐ. προσεδρεύοντας ἐκ τῆς ἐ. διατρέφεσθαι *Const.App.*2.25.14; **e.** importance of churches founded by apostles, and pre-eminently that of Rome, as source and criterion of doctrinal tradition, Iren.*haer.*3.3.2(M.7.848B–849A); **5.** Church and state πότε κρίσις ἐκκλησίας παρὰ βασιλέως ἔσχε τὸ κῦρος ἢ ὅλως ἐγνώσθη τοῦτο τὸ κρῖμα;...πολλὰ κρίματα τῆς ἐ. γέγονεν, ἀλλ' οὔτε οἱ πατέρες ἔπεισάν ποτε περὶ τούτων βασιλέα οὔτε βασιλεὺς τὰ τῆς ἐ. περιειργάσατο Ath.*h.Ar.*52(p.213.9f.; M.25.756C); church government superior to civil government, Chrys.*hom.15.4 in 2Cor.*(10.548B); **6.** reasons for removal from Church: idolatry, avarice, gluttony, Or.*hom.7.3 in Jer.*(p.54.2f.; M.13.333A); sin in gen., Meth.*lepr.*7(p.461.3); *Const.App.*2.16.1; *ib.*2.17.4; **7.** Church and Israel; **a.** Church continuation of synagogue; cf. ref. Ps.44:7–12 τοῖς εἰς αὐτὸν πιστεύουσιν, ὡς οὖσι μιᾷ ψυχῇ καὶ μιᾷ συναγωγῇ καὶ μιᾷ ἐ., ὁ λόγος τοῦ θεοῦ λέγει ὡς θυγατρί, τῇ ἐ. τῇ ἐξ ὀνόματος αὐτοῦ γενομένῃ καὶ μετασχούσῃ τοῦ ὀνόματος αὐτοῦ Just.*dial.*63.5(M.6.621D); cf. *Abraham, et semen ejus quod est ecclesia*, Iren.*haer.*4.8.1(M.7.993C); cf.*ib.*4.18.2(1025A); cf. *disseminaverunt enim sermonem de Christo patriarchae et prophetae; demessa est autem ecclesia, hoc est, fructum percepit*, *ib.*4.25.3(1051C); ἥτις [sc. ἡ ἐ.] ἐστὶ θυγάτηρ τῆς πάλαι συναγωγῆς Or.*fr.118 in Lam.*(p.278.11; M.13.661B); οἱ γὰρ παλαιότεροι καὶ ὁ νόμος τοὺς τῆς ἐ. προεξήγγειλαν ἡμῖν προφητεύοντες χαρακτῆρας, ἡ δὲ ἐ. τοὺς τῶν καινῶν αἰώνων Meth.*symp.*9.2(p.115.29; M.18.180C); τὴν ἐ. τοῦ θεοῦ, πολλοῖς ἱδρῶσι... συνειλεγμένην, τοῖς πρὸ Χριστοῦ τε καὶ μετὰ Χριστόν Gr.Naz.*or.*21.24(M.35.1109A); Gr.Nyss.*hom.5 in Cant.*(M.44.868A); ἱερὰ καθολικὴ ἐ., ἡ τὴν δεκάπληγον ἐκπεφευγυῖα καὶ τὴν δεκάλογον εἰληφυῖα καὶ τὸν νόμον μεμαθηκυῖα καὶ τὴν πίστιν κεκρατηκυῖα...καὶ τὴν δεκάδα ἐγνωκυῖα καὶ ἐπὶ τὸ ἰῶτα *Const.App.*2.26.2; οὗτος γάρ ἐστιν ὁ χαρακτὴρ τῆς ἐ., ἀπὸ νόμου καὶ προφητῶν καὶ ἀποστόλων καὶ εὐαγγελιστῶν συνηγμένος...τοῖς χρωμένοις εἰς σωτηρίαν κατεσκευασμένη Epiph.*exp.fid.*25(p.525.25; M.42.832B); Chrys.*hom.2.2 in Ac.princ.*(3.62D,E); παραδεξαμένη γὰρ ὥσπερ ἡ ἐ. τὸ Χριστοῦ μυστήριον διὰ τῶν...ἀποστόλων, ὡς ἐξ ὁμοίας μὲν ἀδελφῆς τῆς τῶν Ἰουδαίων συναγωγῆς, μήτηρ πέφηνε λαοῦ τοῦ ἐν προσθήκαις ἀεί,...προστέθειται δὲ ταῖς ἐξ Ἰσραὴλ ἀγέλαις ἡ ἐξ ἐθνῶν ἐ. Cyr.*glaph.Gen.*4(1.137D,E); **b.** Church opp. synagogue (v. συναγωγή); ref. Ps.9:18, Clem.*str.*1.19(p.62.2; M.8.813A); εἰ δέ ἐστί τις διαφορὰ ἐ. καὶ συναγωγῆς, τῆς μὲν κυρίως ἐ. ... ἁγίας καὶ ἀμώμου τυγχανούσης, εἰς ἣν οὔτε ὁ ἐκ πόρνης εἰσέρχεται...ἀλλ' οὐδὲ Αἰγύπτιος ἢ Ἰδουμαῖος, ἐὰν μὴ υἱῶν γεννηθέντων αὐτοῖς διὰ τὴν τρίτην γενεὰν μόλις δυνηθῶσιν ἐφαρμόσαι τῇ ἐ. ... τῆς δὲ συναγωγῆς ὑπὸ ἑκατοντάρχου οἰκοδομουμένης, ἐν τοῖς πρὸ τῆς Ἰησοῦ ἐπιδημίας χρόνοις τοῦτο ποιοῦντος,...ὁ φιλῶν δὴ προσεύχεσθαι ἐν ταῖς συναγωγαῖς οὐ μακράν ἐστι τῶν γωνιῶν τῶν πλατειῶν. ἀλλ' οὐχ ὁ ἅγιος τοιοῦτος· οὐ φιλεῖ γὰρ προσεύχεσθαι ἀλλὰ ἀγαπᾷ, καὶ οὐκ ἐν συναγωγαῖς ἀλλ' ἐν ἐ. Or.*or.*20.1(pp.343.13–344.3; M.11.477C–480A); id.*Cels.*2.6(p.132.22; M.11.804D); ἐπειδὴ δὲ ὁ ἀπόστολος εἰς τὸν Χριστὸν ἐκλαμβάνει καὶ τὴν ἐ. τό, 'καὶ ἔσονται οἱ δύο εἰς σάρκα μίαν', λεκτέον ὅτι οὐκ ἀπέλυσεν ὁ Χριστὸς τὴν προτέραν (ἵν' οὕτως ὀνομάσω) γυναῖκα αὐτοῦ (τὴν προτέραν συναγωγήν) κατ' ἄλλην αἰτίαν...ἢ ὅτε ἐπόρνευσεν ἐκείνη ἡ γυνή id.*comm.14.17 in Mt.*(p.325.7; M.13.1229C); id.*hom.14.15 in Jer.*(p.122.1; M.13.424C); τὰ...τῶν Ἰουδαίων λέλυται· σκιὰ γὰρ ἦν· τὰ δὲ τῆς ἐ. ἥδρασται ‡Ath.*Ar.*4.34(p.83.17; M.26.520D); δευτέραν ᾠκοδόμησεν ἐξ ἐθνῶν ὁ σωτὴρ τὴν τῶν Χριστιανῶν ἡμῶν ἁγίαν ἐ. ... τῆς γὰρ ἐν τῇ Ἰουδαίᾳ μιᾶς ἀποβληθείσης κατὰ πάσης τῆς οἰκουμένης λοιπὸν αἱ τοῦ Χριστοῦ πληθύνουσιν ἐ. Cyr.H.*catech.*18.25; *ib.*18.27; Church more glorious than Temple, Cyr.*glaph.Gen.*2(1.56C); ref. Mt.5:15 μόδιον...κέκληκε τὴν συναγωγὴν τῶν Ἰουδαίων ...ὑφ' ὃν μόδιον κρατεῖσθαι...ὁ λόγος οὐ βούλεται· τὸ ὕψει ἐπικεῖσθαι θέλων, καὶ τῷ μεγέθει τοῦ κάλλους τῆς ἐ. πάντας γὰρ ἄν, τῷ γράμματι τοῦ νόμου καθάπερ μοδίῳ κρατούμενος ὁ λόγος, ἐστέρησε φωτὸς ἀϊδίου, μὴ διδοὺς θεωρίαν πνευματικὴν...ἀλλ' ἐπὶ τὴν λυχνίαν, λέγω τὴν ἐ., ἤγουν τὴν ἐν πνεύματι λογικὴν λατρείαν, ἵνα πάντας φωτίσῃ Max.*qu.Thal.*63(M.90.669A); **8.** Church opp. heresy, cf. *apud eos* [sc. heretics] *quidem error, et seductio, et magica phantasia...in ecclesia autem miseratio, et misericordia, et firmitas, et veritas*, Iren.*haer.*2.31.3(M.7.825B); ἄλλο δέ τι ἔριν, ἣν [ἐν] ταῖς αἱρέσεσι προσκριτέον, ἄλλο χάριν, ἣν τῇ ἐ. προσοικειωτέον Clem.*str.*7.16(p.71.12; M.9.540B); *ib.*(p.74.23; 545B); Church judging heretics, Hipp.*Noët.*1(p.235.12; M.10.804B); προφάσει γνώσεως ἐπανισταμένων τῶν ἑτεροδόξων τῇ...ἐ. Or.*Jo.*5.8(p.105.5; M.14.196A); opp. Valentinians, id.*Cels.*5.61(p.64.24; M.11.1277B); μόνη...ἡ καθολικὴ τοῦ θεοῦ ἐ. εἰς ἑαυτὴν συνεστραμμένη διέλαμπεν, μηδαμοῦ γῆς αἱρετικοῦ συστήματος μηδὲ σχισματικοῦ λειπομένου Eus.*v.C.*3.66(p.113.25; M.20.1144B); ref. Arianism πῶς τῆς καθολικῆς ἐ. εἰσὶν οἱ τὴν ἀποστολικὴν ἀποτιναξάμενοι πίστιν; Ath.*Ar.*1.4(M.26.20A); id.*ep.encycl.*6(p.175.9; M.25.236A); id.*apol.sec.*60(p.140.12; M.25.357C); ref. Manicheans, Cyr.H.*catech.*6.35; τίς οὐκ οἶδεν ὅτι τὸ χωρίζον ἀπὸ τῆς αἱρέσεως τὴν ἐ. ἡ τοῦ κτίσματός ἐστι φωνὴ ἐπὶ τοῦ υἱοῦ λεγομένη; Gr.Nyss.*Eun.*4(2 p.77.11; M.45.652A); opp. dualist heresies, *Const.App.*6.12.1; οἱ ἐξ Εὐτυχέος καὶ Διοσκόρου... πολεμοῦσι τὴν μόνην καθολικὴν καὶ ἀποστολικὴν τοῦ θεοῦ ἐ. Thdr.Raith.*praep.*(p.185.10; M.91.1484A); *ib.*(p.194.29; 1496C); opp. schism, Chrys.*hom.11.5 in Eph.*(11.88A) cit. s. σχίζω; **9.** opp. Judaism, paganism, and heresy, cf. *hanc oblationem ecclesia sola puram offert fabricatori...Judaei autem jam non offerunt...non enim receperunt verbum, [per] quod offertur deo. sed neque omnes haereticorum synagogae*, Iren.*haer.*4.18.4(M.7.1027A); οἱ μὲν ἐν τῇ ἀγνοίᾳ τὰ ἔθνη, οἱ δὲ ἐν τῇ ἐπιστήμῃ ἡ ἐ. ἡ ἀληθής, οἱ δὲ ἐν οἰήσει οἱ κατὰ τὰς αἱρέσεις Clem.*str.*7.16(p.71.5; M.9.540A); ἐκ τοῦ κατὰ τὰς θυσίας νόμου περί τε Ἰουδαίων τῶν χυδαίων περί τε τῶν αἱρέσεων μυστικῶς διακρινομένων, ὡς ἀκαθάρτων, ἀπὸ τῆς...θείας ἐ., καταπαύσωμεν τὸν λόγον *ib.*7.18(p.77.4; 553B); cf.*A.Andr.et Mt.*14(p.81.11); **10.** Christian communities in cities also called ἐ., *1Clem.*proem.; Iren.*haer.*3.3.4(M.7.854B); Clem.*str.*7.12(p.53.16; M.9.501C); *Const.App.*6.12.3.

B. Christ and Church; **1.** Church as belonging to him, Ign.*Philad.*proem.; id.*Smyrn.*8.2; οἱ ἀπὸ τῆς ἐπωνύμου Χριστοῦ ἐ. Or.*Cels.*8.16(p.233.29; M.11.1540B); Ph.Carp.ap.Cosm.Ind.*top.*10(M.88.433C); ᾠκοδόμησε [sc. Χριστός] τὴν ἁγίαν πόλιν, τοῦτ' ἔστι, τὴν ἐ. ... τεθεμελίωκε τοίνυν τὴν ἐ. αὐτὸς ὢν ὁ θεμέλιος, ἐφ' ᾧ καὶ ἡμεῖς ἐποικοδομούμεθα Cyr.*Is.*4.2(2.612B); id.*ador.*3(1.100B); Leont.H.*Nest.*1.18(M.86.1468B); **2.** as bride (v. νύμφη), and wife: as Adam and Eve are parents of all men, so Christ and Church of all good works, Or.*fr.45 in Jo.*(p.520.21); ἐκ τῶν ὀστῶν αὐτοῦ [sc. Χριστοῦ] καὶ τῆς σαρκὸς τὴν ἐ. συμφωνῆσαι γεγονέναι, ἧς δὴ χάριν καταλείψας τὸν πατέρα...κατῆλθεν ὁ λόγος προσκολληθησόμενος τῇ γυναικὶ καὶ ὕπνωσε τὴν ἔκστασιν τοῦ πάθους...ὅπως αὐτὸς ἑαυτῷ παραστήσῃ τὴν ἐ. ἔνδοξον...πρὸς ὑποδοχὴν τοῦ νοητοῦ...σπέρματος, ὃ σπείρει...ἐν τῷ βάθει τοῦ νοός, ὑποδέχεται δὲ καὶ μορφοῖ δίκην γυναικὸς ἡ ἐ. εἰς τὸ γεννᾶν τὴν ἀρετήν...οὐ γὰρ ἂν ἄλλως ἡ ἐ. συλλαβεῖν τοὺς πιστεύοντας... δύναιτο...ἐὰν μὴ καὶ δι' αὐτοὺς ὁ Χριστὸς κενώσας ἑαυτόν...πάλιν ἀποθάνῃ καταβὰς ἐξ οὐρανῶν καὶ προσκολληθεὶς τῇ ἑαυτοῦ γυναικί τῇ ἐ. Meth.*symp.*3.8(pp.35.11–36.3; M.18.73A,B); τῶν οὖν γάμων ἤδη τετελεσμένων, καὶ νυμφευθείσης ὑπὸ τοῦ λόγου τῆς ἐ.,...καὶ εἰς τὸν τῶν μυστηρίων θάλαμον αὐτῆς παραδεχθείσης, ἀνέμενον οἱ ἄγγελοι τὴν ἐπάνοδον τοῦ βασιλέως, τῆς ἐ. ἐπαναχθείσης ἐπὶ τὴν κατὰ φύσιν μακαριότητα Gr.Nyss.*hom.11 in Cant.*(M.44.997A); Χριστὸς εἰσῆλθε ...ἐν παραδείσῳ...καὶ ἐξέστη...τὴν σωτήριον αὐτοῦ ἔκστασιν, δι' ἧς τὴν οἰκείαν σύμβιον ἐ. τέτοκε καὶ προσεκολλήθη ταύτῃ Anast.S.*hex.*12(M.89.1064A); ξύλον δὲ νόησον τὸν λαὸν τοῦ Χριστοῦ· ζωὴν δὲ τὴν ἐ.· αὐτὴ γάρ ἐστι ἣν ἐκάλεσε ζωήν, ὡς μητέρα οὖσαν πάντων τῶν ἐν θεῷ ζώντων· ἣν εἰς τὸν αἰῶνα φυλάττουσιν ἐκ τοῦ ὄφεως τὰ χερουβίμ... ὥσπερ γὰρ ὁ υἱὸς ὁδὸς ἡμῖν ἐστι πρὸς τὸν πατέρα...οὕτως καὶ ἡ ἐ. ὁδὸς ζωῆς ἡμῖν ἐστι πρὸς τὸν υἱόν...καὶ διὰ τοῦτο ζωὴν ὠνόμασε καὶ τὴν αὐτοῦ γυναῖκα, ὡς τὰ ζῷα ὑμᾶς ζωοποιοῦσαν...διὸ τὸ ξύλον ἑαυτὸν τῆς ζωῆς, τοῦτ' ἔστι τῆς ἐ., ταύτης αὐτῷ ἀρθείσης ὑπὸ τοῦ πατρός, καὶ συνενδυθείσης τὸν ἐκ ζῴων τοῦ παραδείσου δερμάτινον χιτῶνα. ὅταν μὲν οὖν ὁ Χριστὸς οἰκεῖ ἐν ἡμῖν...δερμάτινον χιτῶνα ἐνδύεται· ὅταν δὲ πάλιν τὴν λεγομένην ζωὴν γυναῖκα αὐτοῦ ἐ. ὥσπερ τινὰ δίσκηνον θεάσῃς· ὅθεν μὲν ἔχουσαν τὸ ἱερὸν ἱλαστήριον, ἔμψυχον σάρκα περιφέρουσαν τὴν τοῦ ἀμνοῦ *ib.*(1064C–1065A); **3.** operating through and for him, cf.Iren.*haer.*4.37.7(M.7.1104C); Clem.*paed.*3.12(p.291.13; M.8.681A); ἡ ἐ. γὰρ ὑπηρετεῖ τῇ τοῦ κυρίου ἐνεργείᾳ id.*ecl.*23(p.143.6; M.9.708D); Or.*or.*26.3(p.360.24ff.; M.11.501A); *ib.*23.4(p.353.3; 492A); τῆς δυνάμεως τοῦ κυρίου συμπαρούσης τῇ ἐ. *ib.*31.5(p.399.5; 553D); περὶ τῆς ἀνθρωπότητος αὐτοῦ [sc. Χριστοῦ], ἥτις ἐστὶ πᾶσα ἡ ἐ., ἡ ἐν αὐτῷ κυριεύσουσα...μετὰ τὸ αὐτὸν σταυρωθῆναι Ath.*inc.et c.Ar.*21(M.26.1021B); Max.*qu.Thal.*63(M.90.668A); **4.** as his body (v. σῶμα); **a.** in gen., Ign.*Smyrn.*1.2 cit. s. ἀνάστασις; σῶμα δὲ λέγουσιν...τὴν τῶν πιστῶν ἐ. Clem.*ecl.*56(p.152.28; M.9.724C); τὸ σῶμα τοῦ Ἰησοῦ...τύπος...τῆς ἐ. Or.*Jo.*10.35(20; p.209.18; M.14.369D); *ib.*10.43(27; p.222.18; 393B); ὁ κτίσας γε ἀπ' ἀρχῆς τὸν κατ' εἰκόνα...ἄρρεν αὐτὸν ἐποίησε καὶ θῆλυ τὴν ἐ. ... καὶ καταλέλοιπέ γε διὰ τὴν ἐ. κύριος ὁ ἀνὴρ πρὸς ὃν ἦν πατέρα...καὶ ἐκολλήθη τῇ ἐνταῦθα καταπεσούσῃ γυναικὶ αὐτοῦ...καὶ οὐκέτι γέ εἰσι δύο, ἀλλὰ νῦν μία γέ ἐστι σάρξ, ἐπεὶ τῇ γυναικὶ ⟨ἐ.⟩ λέγεται τὸ 'ὑμεῖς δέ ἐστε σῶμα Χριστοῦ ...' οὐ γάρ ἐστί τι ἴδιά σῶμα Χριστοῦ ἕτερον παρὰ τὴν ἐ. οὖσαν σῶμα αὐτοῦ...καὶ ὁ θεός γε τούτους τοὺς μὴ δύο, ἀλλὰ γενομένους σάρκα μίαν συνέζευξεν, ἐντελλόμενος ἵνα ἄνθρωπος μὴ χωρίζῃ τὴν ἐ. ἀπὸ τοῦ κυρίου id.*comm.14.17 in Mt.*(pp.325.31–326.26; M.13.1252A,B); Ath.*inc.et c.Ar.*5(M.26.992B) cit. s. μέλος; cf.*ib.*12(1004B); πᾶσαν τὴν ἐ.

ἓν σῶμα τοῦ νυμφίου Gr.Nyss.*hom.13 in Cant.*(M.44.1052A); *Const. App.*2.8.3; **b.** as his flesh ἐ. ζῶσα 'σῶμά ἐστιν Χριστοῦ'. λέγει γὰρ ἡ γραφή· 'ἐποίησεν ὁ θεὸς τὸν ἄνθρωπον ἄρσεν καὶ θῆλυ'· τὸ ἄρσεν ἐστὶν ὁ Χριστός, τὸ θῆλυ ἡ ἐ. ... ἦν γὰρ πνευματική, ὡς καὶ ὁ Ἰησοῦς ἡμῶν...ἡ ἐ. δὲ πνευματικὴ οὖσα ἐφανερώθη ἐν τῇ σαρκὶ Χριστοῦ, δηλοῦσα ἡμῖν, ὅτι ἐάν τις ἡμῶν τηρήσῃ αὐτὴν ἐν τῇ σαρκὶ καὶ μὴ φθείρῃ, ἀπολήψεται αὐτὴν ἐν τῷ πνεύματι τῷ ἁγίῳ· ἡ γὰρ σὰρξ αὕτη ἀντίτυπός ἐστιν τοῦ πνεύματος...εἰ δὲ λέγομεν εἶναι τὴν σάρκα τὴν ἐ. καὶ τὸ πνεῦμα Χριστόν, ἄρα οὖν ὁ ὑβρίσας τὴν σάρκα ὕβρισεν τὴν ἐ. *2Clem.*14.2–4; **c.** Christ the head, Clem.*paed.*1.5(p.103.21f.; M.8.277A); πάντα γὰρ ταῦτα [sc. Christian doctrines]...διὰ τῆς ἐ. οἱ φίλοι τοῦ νυμφίου μαθόντες, ἐκαρδιώθησαν, ἄλλον χαρακτῆρα τῆς θείας σοφίας ἐν τῷ μυστηρίῳ κατανοήσαντες...ὃν γὰρ οὐδεὶς ἑώρακε πώποτε...οὗτος σῶμα ἑαυτοῦ τὴν ἐ. ἐποίησε, καὶ διὰ τῆς προσθήκης τῶν σωζομένων, οἰκοδομεῖ αὐτὴν ἐν ἀγάπῃ...εἰ οὖν σῶμα τοῦ Χριστοῦ ἡ ἐ., κεφαλὴ δὲ τοῦ σώματος ὁ Χριστός, τῷ ἰδίῳ χαρακτῆρι μορφῶν τῆς ἐ. τὸ πρόσωπον· τάχα διὰ τούτων πρὸς ταῦτα βλέποντες οἱ φίλοι τοῦ νυμφίου, ἐκαρδιώθησαν... κἀκεῖνοι ὡς ἐν κατόπτρῳ καθορῶντες καθαρῷ, τῷ προσώπῳ τῆς ἐ., τὸν τῆς δικαιοσύνης ἥλιον βλέπουσι Gr.Nyss.*hom.8 in Cant.*(M.44.949A, B); *ib.13*(1056A,B); τὸ πλήρωμα τοῦ Χριστοῦ ἡ ἐ., καὶ γὰρ πλήρωμα κεφαλῆς σῶμα, καὶ πλήρωμα σώματος κεφαλή Chrys.*hom.3.2 in Eph.*(11.19F); exeg. 1Cor.12:12, Chrys.*hom.30.1 in 1Cor.*(10.270A) cit. s. σῶμα; v. κεφαλή; **d.** Christ animating Church ὥσπερ ψυχή...κινεῖ τὸ σῶμα οὐ πεφυκὸς ἀφ' ἑαυτοῦ κινεῖσθαι ζωτικῶς, οὕτως ὁ λόγος κινῶν ἐπὶ τὰ δέοντα καὶ ἐνεργῶν τὸ ὅλον σῶμα τὴν ἐ. κινεῖ καὶ ἕκαστον μέλος τῶν ἀπὸ τῆς ἐ. Or.*Cels.*6.48(pp.119.29–120.5; M.11.1373B); *ib.*6.79(p.151.2f.; 1417D); **e.** Christians his members, v. μέλος; **f.** myst. interprn. of various members ἡ ὡραία λαλιά, δι' ἧς τὰ χείλη τῆς ἐ. κατὰ τὸ κόκκινον ἐκεῖνο σπαρτίον εὐπρεπῶς ἐπανθίζεται Gr.Nyss.*hom.7 in Cant.*(M.44.929A); apostles its neck, *ib.*(932Cff.); πρόδηλον, εἰς ποῖα μέλη τῆς ἐ. ὁ τῶν ὀφθαλμῶν ἔπαινος βλέπει. ὀφθαλμὸς ἦν Σαμουὴλ ὁ βλέπων· ὀφθαλμὸς ὁ Ἰεζεκιήλ...καὶ νῦν οἱ τὸν ἐκεῖνον τόπον ἀναπληροῦντες τῷ σώματι τῆς ἐ., καὶ ἐπισκοπεῖν τεταγμένοι, ὀφθαλμοὶ κυρίως κατονομάζονται *ib.*(917D–920A); ὀδόντων χρεία τῇ ἐ., πληρούντων ἐν τῷ διαλεπτύνειν τὴν τῶν δογμάτων σαφήνειαν *ib.*(925D); τῇ γὰρ [sc. ὑπηρεσίᾳ] τῶν ὀδόντων, τουτέστι τῶν διδασκαλικῶν ὑφηγημάτων τὸ στόμα τῆς ἐ. συμφθέγγεται. διὰ τοῦτο πρῶτον οἱ ὀδόντες...λούονται, καὶ οὐκ ἀτεκνοῦσι...καὶ τότε τῷ κοκκίνῳ εἴδει τὰ χείλη περιανθίζεται, ὅταν πᾶσα ἡ ἐ. κατὰ τὴν τοῦ ἀγαθοῦ συμφωνίαν χεῖλος ἓν καὶ φωνὴ μία *ib.*(928B); ἀτελὴς ἐστιν ἐπὶ τοῦ σώματος τῆς ἐ. ἡ τοῦ ὀφθαλμοῦ χάρις τῆς τῶν χειρῶν ὑπουργίας διεζευγμένη...χεῖρα δὲ νοοῦμεν πάντως τὴν τὰ κοινὰ τῆς ἐ. εἰς τὰς τῶν ἐντολῶν χρείας διαχειρίζουσαν *ib.14*(1068C–1069A); αἱ κνῆμαι τοῦ σώματος οἱ μαρμάρινοι στῦλοι, τουτέστιν οἱ τῷ λαμπρῷ βίῳ καὶ τῷ ὑγιαίνοντι λόγῳ τὸ κοινὸν σῶμα τῆς ἐ. βαστάζοντες *ib.*(1077A); Chrys.*hom.10.1 in Eph.*(11.75D); χάρις καὶ δύναμις, οἱ δίδυμοι τῆς ἐ. μασθοί Procl.CP *or.*17.3(M.65.812C); **g.** individual perfection necessary for full membership of body, Clem.*str.*7.14(p.62.19ff.; M.9.521A); ἔστι γὰρ ὅτε πολλαχῶς αὐτὸ τὸ ἄθροισμα...τῶν πεπιστευκότων ἐ. οὕτως ὀνομάζουσιν αἱ γραφαί, τῶν τελειοτέρων κατὰ προκοπὴν εἰς ἓν πρόσωπον καὶ σῶμα τὸ τῆς ἐ. ἀναγομένων. οἱ μὲν κρείττονες...οὗτοι διὰ τὴν τελείαν κάθαρσιν καὶ πίστιν ἀποστερωθέντες τῶν τῆς σαρκὸς ἀτοπημάτων ἐ. γίνονται καὶ βοηθὸς τοῦ Χριστοῦ Meth.*symp.*3.8(p.37.1ff.; M.18.73D); **h.** contemplative and active qualities δι' ἀμφοτέρων προσήκει τῷ σώματι τῆς ἐ. πράττειν καλῶς, τοῦ διορατικοῦ τῆς ἀληθείας συγκεκραμμένου πρὸς τὸ δραστήριον Gr.Nyss.*hom.13 in Cant.*(M.44.1057B); **i.** body of Christ opp. 'church' of Devil σῶμα αὐτοῦ, οἱ ἁμαρτωλοί, καὶ οἱ τὴν ἁμαρτίαν ἐνεργοῦντες δαίμονες, ὥσπερ τοῦ κυρίου ἡ ἐ. οὐκ εἶπε δέ, 'ἥνωνται', ἀλλά, 'κεκόλληνται'· τὸ γὰρ ἓν οὐκ ἔστι παρ' ἐκείνῳ...καὶ ἡ ἐ. αὐτοῦ οὐ μὴν ἥνωται, πρὸς ἑαυτὴν γὰρ διαφέρεται Olymp.*Job* 41:14(M.93.445A).

C. Church and H. Ghost τὸ πνεῦμα τὸ ἅγιον τὸ λαλῆσαν μετὰ σοῦ ἐν μορφῇ τῆς ἐ. Herm.*sim.*9.1.1; ἡ δὲ τῆς ἐ. διακόσμησις...διὰ τοῦ πνεύματος ἐνεργεῖται Bas.*Spir.*39(3.34A; M.32.141A); τῇ ἐ. δεδώρηται ὁ κατὰ φύσιν ἔχων τὸ πνεῦμα [sc. Christ], τὰς ἐνεργείας τοῦ πνεύματος ὡς θεός...τὸ γὰρ πνεῦμα τὸ ἅγιον...τῇ λυχνίᾳ, τουτέστι τῇ ἐ., καθάπερ λύχνους τὰς οἰκείας ἐνεργείας δωρούμενον. λύχνου γὰρ τρόπον τὸ σκότος λύοντος, πᾶσα τοῦ πνεύματος ἐνέργεια τὴν πολύτροπον γένεσιν τῆς ἁμαρτίας ἐξωθεῖσθαι τῆς ἐ. ... πέφυκε Max.*qu.Thal.*63(M.90.672B–D).

D. pre-existent (heavenly) Church; **1.** as first creature, Herm.*vis.*2.4.1; ἡ πρωτότοκος ἐ. Clem.*prot.*9(p.62.25; M.8.193B); τὴν ἐξ ἀρχῆς ἐ. id.*str.*1.19(p.61.23; M.8.812C); *ib.*7.15(p.65.20; M.9.528B); cf. *non...ex adventu salvatoris in carne sponsam dici aut ecclesiam putes, sed ab initio humani generis et ab ipsa constitutione mundi... prima etenim fundamenta congregationis ecclesiae statim ab initio sunt posita, unde et Apostolus dicit aedificari ecclesiam non solum super apostolorum fundamentum, sed etiam prophetarum,* Or.*Cant.*2(p.157.14ff.; M.13.134A,B); Valentinian πρὸ καταβολῆς κόσμου... λέγεται ἡ ἐ. ἐκλελέχθαι Clem.*exc.Thdot.*40(p.119.23; M.9.677C); **2.** ἐ. πρωτοτόκων (Heb.12:23) cf. *apostolorum maximus, qui sciret multas esse non solum in terris, sed et in coelis ecclesias, ex quibus et septem quasdam Johannes enumerat, ipse tamen Paulus ostendere volens esse quandam praeterea etiam primitivorum ecclesiam dicit,* Or.*hom.3.3 in Num.*(p.17.5ff.; M.12.596C); cf. *vos trahit* [sc. *Christus*] *ad salutem, congregat in ecclesiam nunc quidem super terram, si autem dignos fructus feceritis, in ecclesiam primitivorum,* id.*hom. 7 in Lc.*(pp.53.24–54.1; M.13.1819B); Ath.*ep.Aeg.Lib.*19(M.25.584A); Gr.Naz.*or.*8.6(M.35.796B); Dion.Ar.*ep.*9.5(M.3.1112D); **3.** in heaven, as mother (or pattern) of earthly Church ποιοῦντες τὸ θέλημα τοῦ πατρός...ἐσόμεθα ἐκ τῆς ἐ. τῆς πρώτης, τῆς πνευματικῆς. ... τὰ βιβλία καὶ οἱ ἀπόστολοι τὴν ἐ. οὐ νῦν εἶναι, ἀλλὰ ἄνωθεν ⟨λέγουσιν⟩ *2Clem.*14.1,2; εἰκὼν δὲ τῆς οὐρανίου ἐ. ἡ ἐπίγειος Clem.*str.*4.8(p.278.10; M.8.1277B); *ib.*6.14(p.486.4; M.9.329A); *ib.*7.11(p.49.19; 496B); Or.*Ps.*44:9f.(p.42) cit. s. νύμφη; id.*princ.*1.6.2(p.82.16; M.11.168B); χαρακτὴρ τῆς καθολικῆς καὶ ἀποστολικῆς ἐ. τῆς ἀπ' αἰῶνος οὔσης, κατὰ δὲ διαδοχὴν χρόνων...ἐν τῇ τοῦ Χριστοῦ ἐνσάρκῳ παρουσίᾳ ἀποκαλυφθείσης Epiph.*anac.*suppl.(p.415.24; M.42.640C); Cyr.*Is.*5.5(2.885E); Max.*myst.*2(M.91.669A).

E. scriptural types, Eve εἰ δὲ καὶ ἡ Εὔα ἐπιτέτευκται τῷ Παύλῳ εἰς τὴν ἐ. ἀναγομένη, οὐ θαυμαστόν, τοῦ Κάϊν ἐκ τῆς Εὔας γεγενημένου καὶ πάντων τῶν ἑξῆς τὴν ἀναγωγὴν ἐχόντων ἐπὶ τὴν Εὔαν, ἐκτυπώματα τῆς ἐ. τυγχάνειν, πάντων ἀπὸ τῆς ἐ. προηγουμένῳ λόγῳ γεγενημένων Or.*princ.*4.3.7(p.333.25ff.; M.11.388A); Proc.G.*Gen.*3:15(M.87.205C); τῆς ἐ. τύπον ἔχει, μήτηρ εἰκότως ἐστὶ τῶν ζώντων *ib.*3:20(217D); Rebecca, Clem.*paed.*1.5(p.103.13; M.8.276B); Cyr.*glaph. Gen.*4(1.113B); Rachel Λεία μὲν...ἡ συναγωγή, Ῥαχὴλ δὲ ἡ ἐ. ἡμῶν Just.*dial.*134.3(M.6.788A); cf.Iren.*haer.*4.21.3(M.7.1046A); ἑρμηνεύεται ...ἡ Ῥαχήλ, θεοῦ ποίμνιον. ποίμνιον γὰρ τοῦ σωτῆρος ἡ ἐ. Cyr.*glaph. Gen.*6(1.185A); type of gentile Church, *ib.*(207B); Rahab (and Ruth), Chrys.*hom.3.4 in Mt.*(7.38C–39A); Ῥαὰβ 'πλατυσμὸς' ἑρμηνεύεται, ἡ γὰρ τὸ πρῶτον πόρνη, νῦν δὲ σώφρων ἐ. διὰ τῆς πίστεως πλατύνεται ταῖς θεωρίαις, καὶ τοῖς θείοις νοήμασιν Nil.*epp.*1.53(M.79.105D); Thdt.*qu.2 in Jos.*(1.302); bride of Cant., v. νύμφη; 'daughter' of Ps.44:11, Bas.*hom.in Ps.*44(1.167C; M.29.409A); cf. Chrys.*exp.in Ps.*44(5.178C,D); Cyr.*Ps.*44:11(M.69.1041D); Lot's wife, cf.Iren.*haer.*4.31.3(M.7.1070A); wives of Moses and Hosea, cf.*ib.*4.20.12(1042Aff.); Exodus, cf. *a deo typus et imago fuit profectionis ecclesiae quae erat futura ex gentibus,* *ib.*4.30.4(1067C); Judaea and Jerusalem, Chrys.*Is.interp.*2.2(6.20A); holy mountain, ref. Is.63:18, Cyr.*Is.*5.5(2.885C); Mount Carmel, *ib.*3.3(457A); ref. Ps.44:14, Cant. 2:13 διπλοῦς...ὁ τῆς ἐ. χαρακτήρ· ἐν κροσσωτοῖς χρυσοῖς περιβεβλημένη ...πᾶσαν δὲ τὴν τοῦ κάλλους δόξαν...ἔσωθεν ἐπιφερομένη· ἐν μὲν τοῖς βιωτικοῖς ἐκφέρουσα κατὰ τὸν Σολομῶντα, ὡς συκῆ, τῆς σεμνότητος τοὺς ὀλύνθους· ἐν δὲ τοῖς ἱερατικοῖς...προβάλλουσα ὡς ἄμπελος τῆς χρηστότητος τοὺς κυπρίζοντας βότρυας Procl.CP *or.*6.3(M.65.725B); for other types v. Ἱερουσαλήμ; Σιών; παράδεισος; σκηνή; κιβωτός; νῆσος; ἔρημος; περίζωμα; κῆπος; πύργος; λυχνία; πῶλος; δένδρον.

F. metaphors; mother, v. μήτηρ; cf.Iren.*haer.*3.24.1(M.7.966C) cit. s. H infra; exeg. Pr.1:8 πατρὸς μὲν ἀκούομεν λόγους, τῆς γραφῆς· μητρὸς δὲ τὰς ἀγράφους παραδόσεις τῆς ἐ. ... ἔστι δὲ καὶ τοὺς φυσικοὺς νοεῖν πατέρας, ἢ καὶ τοὺς πνευματικοὺς νοεῖν διδασκάλους. καὶ γὰρ τούτων μήτηρ ἡ ἐ. Or.*fr.in Pr.*1:8(M.17.157A); discussion of Is.54:1 as referring to Church of gentiles, Cyr.*Is.*5.2(2.755Eff.); ref. Apoc.12:5, Meth.*symp.*8.7,8(p.89.4ff.; M.18.148B); virgin-mother, v. μήτηρ; BMV = Church ὑμνοῦντας τὴν ἀειπάρθενον Μαρίαν, δηλονότι ἐ. Cyr.*hom.div.*4(p.104.29; 5².358D); Jo.D.*hom.*10.3(M.96.757A); virgin, before rise of heresies, Heges.ap.Eus.*h.e.*3.32.7(M.20.284B); διὰ τοῦτο ἐκάλουν τὴν ἐ. παρθένον, οὔπω γὰρ ἔφθαρτο ἀκοαῖς ματαίαις Eus.*h.e.*4.22.4(380A); ἡ ἐ. ... παρθένος λέγεται, καὶ μὴν πόρνη ἦν πρὸ τούτου· τὸ γὰρ θαυμαστὸν τοῦ νυμφίου, ὅτι ἔλαβε πόρνην, καὶ ἐποίησε παρθένον Chrys.*Eutrop.*2.6(3.392A); Cyr.*Is.*1.2(2.35D); moon, v. σελήνη; ship, Hipp.*antichr.*59(p.39.13; M.10.777B); μέγα πρόκειται τῷ λόγῳ τὸ πέλαγος τῶν θείων ῥητῶν θεωρίας. πολὺς δὲ διὰ τῆς ναυτιλίας ταύτης ὁ τῆς γνώσεως πλοῦτος ἐλπίζεται· ἡ δὲ ἔμψυχος αὕτη ναῦς ἐ., ἐν παντὶ τῷ ἰδίῳ πληρώματι πρὸς τὸν πλοῦτον τῆς ἐξηγήσεως βλέπει μετέωρος Gr.Nyss.*hom.12 in Cant.*(M.44.1016B); Chrys.*hom.2.1 in Ac.princ.*(3.61C); Cyr.*Ps.*103:25(M.69.1264C,D); ship and fold, *Const.App.*2.57.12; other metaphors: fruit (of Christ), Clem.*exc.Thdot.*33(p.117.24; M.9.676B); a man, consisting of body and soul, id.*paed.*1.6(p.113.2; M.8.296B); divine fatherland, Or.*Cels.*8.75(p.292.11f.; M.11.1629C) cit. s. πατρίς; olive-tree, id.*comm.in Mt.*16.17(p.532.28; M.13.1432A) cit. s. ἐλαία; persecuted

Church a widow, Gr.Naz.*or*.4.16(M.35.546B); vineyard, *ib*.35.3(M. 36.260B); crown of bridegroom, Gr.Nyss.*hom.7 in Cant*.(M.44. 916C); bath *βαλανεῖον γάρ ἐστιν ἡ ἐ. πνευματικόν, οὐ ῥυπὸν σώματος, ἀλλὰ ψυχῆς ἀποσμήχον κηλῖδα* Chrys.*hom.15.5 in 2Cor*.(10.551A); house and city, Cyr.*glaph.Gen*.3(1.99C); id.*Is*.1.4(2.123D); v. *γῆ, στῦλος*; list of various metaphors *ὅρα γὰρ τὴν ἐ. ... ὅτι ποτὲ νύμφη ἐστί, ποτὲ θυγάτηρ ἐστί, ποτὲ παρθένος ἐστί, ποτὲ δούλη ἐστί, ποτὲ βασίλισσά ἐστι, ποτὲ στεῖρά ἐστί, ποτὲ ὄρος ἐστί, ποτὲ παράδεισός ἐστι, ποτὲ πολυτόκος ἐστί, ποτὲ κρίνον ἐστί, ποτὲ πηγή ἐστι, πάντα ἐστί. διὰ τοῦτο ἀκούσας ταῦτα, μὴ νόμιζε σωματικὰ εἶναι...ὅτι οὐκ ἐν σώματι ταῦτα, ἀλλ' ἐν ψυχῇ* Chrys.*Eutrop*.2.9(3.393C).

G. Church and world *ὁ θεὸς ὁ...κτίσας ἐκ τοῦ μὴ ὄντος τὰ ὄντα καὶ πληθύνας καὶ αὐξήσας ἕνεκεν τῆς ἁγίας ἐ. αὐτοῦ* Herm.*vis*.1.1.6; *οὐκ ἀγνοοῦμεν δέ τινα κόσμον ἐξειληφέναι τὴν ἐ. μόνην, κόσμον οὖσαν τοῦ κόσμου, ἐπεὶ καὶ φῶς λέγεται τοῦ κόσμου...κόσμος δὲ τοῦ κόσμου ἡ ἐ., κόσμου αὐτῆς γινομένου Χριστοῦ...ὅτε μὲν Χριστὸς φῶς τοῦ κόσμου ἐστίν, τάχα τῆς ἐ. ἐστὶ φῶς· ὅτε δὲ οἱ μαθηταὶ αὐτοῦ φῶς τοῦ κόσμου, μήποτε τῶν παρακαλουμένων εἰσὶ φῶς, ἑτέρων ὄντων παρὰ τὴν ἐ., ὥσπερ τῷ Παύλῳ περὶ τούτων εἴρηται*...[1Cor.1:2]· *ἐὰν ⟨οὖν⟩ τις ὑπονοῇ τοῦ κόσμου φῶς λέγεσθαι τὴν ἐ., οἱονεὶ τοῦ λοιποῦ γένους τῶν ἀνθρώπων καὶ τῶν ἀπίστων...δεικνύτωσαν πῶς τὸ λοιπὸν γένος φωτίζεται ὑπὸ τῆς παρεπιδημούσης τῷ κόσμῳ ἐ. εἰ δὲ τοῦτο δεικνύναι οὐ δύνανται, ἐπιστησάτωσαν μήποτε ὑγιῶς ἐξειλήφαμεν φῶς μὲν εἶναι τὴν ἐ., κόσμον δὲ τοὺς ἐπικαλουμένους...λεγέσθω τοίνυν ἡ ἐ. κόσμος ὅτε ὑπὸ τοῦ σωτῆρος φωτίζεται· ἡμεῖς δὲ ζητοῦμεν εἰ κατὰ τὸ 'ἴδε ὁ ἀμνὸς τοῦ θεοῦ ὁ αἴρων τὴν ἁμαρτίαν τοῦ κόσμου' κόσμον νοητέον ὑγιῶς τὴν ἐ., περικλειομένου τοῦ αἴρεσθαι τὴν ἁμαρτίαν εἰς μόνην τὴν ἐ.* Or.*Jo*.6.49(38; pp.167.22–168.20; M.14.301C–304B); *κόσμου γὰρ κτίσις ἐστὶν ἡ τῆς ἐ. κατασκευή· ἐν ᾗ κατὰ τὴν τοῦ προφήτου φωνὴν καὶ ὁ οὐρανὸς κτίζεται καινός* Gr.Nyss.*hom.13 in Cant*.(M.44.1049B); *διὰ τί οὐρανός; διὰ τὴν ἐ., οὐχ ἡ ἐ. διὰ τὸν οὐρανόν* Chrys.*hom.4.2 in Is.6:1* (6.122E); *τοῦ σύμπαντος κόσμου τοῦ ἐξ ὁρατῶν καὶ ἀοράτων οὐσιῶν ὑφεστῶτος, εἶναι τύπον καὶ εἰκόνα τὴν...ἐ.* Max.*myst*.2(M.91.668C); *ib*.3(672A).

H. Church in human life; **1.** its necessity, cf. *in ecclesiam enim, inquit, posuit deus...universam...operationem spiritus cujus non sunt participes omnes, qui non currunt ad ecclesiam sed semetipsos fraudant a vita...ubi enim ecclesia, ibi et spiritus dei; et ubi spiritus dei, illic ecclesia, et omnis gratia: spiritus autem veritas. quapropter qui non participant eum, neque a mamillis matris nutriuntur in vitam, neque percipiunt de corpore Christi procedentem nitidissimum fontem*, Iren.*haer*.3.24.1(M.7.966B–967A); *ἐν ταύτῃ τῇ ἁγίᾳ ἐ. διδασκόμενοι...τὴν τῶν οὐρανῶν βασιλείαν ἕξομεν* Cyr.H.*catech*.18.28; *σπουδάζετε οὖν μηδέποτε τὴν ἐ. τοῦ θεοῦ καταλιπεῖν· εἰ δέ τις ταύτην ὑπερίδοι ...ὁ τοιοῦτος τί ἀπολογήσεται τῷ θεῷ ἐν ἡμέρᾳ κρίσεως; Const.App*. 2.61.1; Chrys.*Eutrop*.2.6(3.391D); *ib*.2.1(387A); **2.** importance for spiritual life *τελειούμεθα τότε. ὅτε ἐσμὲν ἐκκλησίας τὴν κεφαλήν, τὸν Χριστόν, ἀπειληφότες* Clem.*paed*.1.5(p.101.3; M.8.272A); cf. *οὗτος* [sc. 'gnostic'] *ἑαυτὸν ἐπιδίδωσιν ὑπὲρ τῆς ἐ.* id.*str*.7.9(p.39.28; M.9. 477A); *ἰατρεῖον γάρ ἐστι πνευματικὸν ἡ ἐ., καὶ δεῖ τοὺς ἐνταῦθα παραγενομένους κατάλληλα τὰ φάρμακα λαμβάνοντας, καὶ τοῖς οἰκείοις τραύμασιν ἐπιτιθέντας, οὕτως ἐπανιέναι* Chrys.*hom.1.1 in Gen*.(4.2C); *ib.32.1*(316C); *τρέφει γὰρ ἡ ἐ. ... ἁγίων κεφαλὰς...καύχημα μὲν γὰρ ἐκκλησιῶν οἱ τοῖς τῶν ἀρετῶν ὑψώμασιν ἐμβεβηκότες* Cyr.*Is*.5.4(2. 849A,D); *εἰκὼν...ἐστι τοῦ θεοῦ...ἡ ἁγία ἐ., ὡς τὴν αὐτὴν τῷ θεῷ περὶ τοὺς πιστοὺς ἐνεργοῦσα ἕνωσιν* Max.*myst*.1(M.91.668B); **3.** myst., soul as Church *ἔστι δὲ ἡ νύμφη τοῦ λόγου ψυχή, ἡ τοῦ Χριστοῦ ἐ.* Or.*schol. in Cant*.7:1(M.17.280C); *ib*.8:8(285C); Mac.Aeg.*hom*.12.15(M.34. 565C,D); *εἰ ἐ. κατ' οἶκον ἕκαστος τὴν διάνοιαν ἔχομεν, καὶ τελεῖν ἐν αὐτῇ τοὺς θεσμοὺς τῆς ἐ. ὀφείλομεν* Nil.*paraen*.104(M.79.1260A); cf. *ἄνθρωπον εἶναι τὴν...ἐ. ... ψυχὴν μὲν ἔχουσαν τὸ ἱερατεῖον· καὶ νοῦν, τὸ θεῖον θυσιαστήριον· καὶ σῶμα, τὸν ναόν...καὶ ἔμπαλιν, ἐ. μυστικὴν τὸν ἄνθρωπον, ὡς διὰ ναοῦ μὲν τοῦ σώματος, τὸ πρακτικὸν τῆς ψυχῆς... φαιδρύνοντα· ὡς δι' ἱερατείου δὲ τῆς ψυχῆς τοὺς κατ' αἴσθησιν λόγους... τῷ θεῷ προσκομίζοντα* Max.*myst*.4(M.91.672B); *ib*.5(681C,D); *τῇ κατὰ ἀναγωγὴν θεωρίᾳ τὴν ἐ. ἔλεγεν ἄνθρωπον εἶναι πνευματικόν, μυστικὴν δὲ ἐ. τὸν ἄνθρωπον* *ib*.6(684A); *τὴν ἀρετήν, ἐ. τροπικῶς νοουμένην* *ib*. 9(689B); **4.** and individual perfection, view that Church consists only of perfect *μετὰ τὸ τούτους* [sc. *πονηρούς*] *ἀποβληθῆναι ἔσται ἡ ἐ. τοῦ θεοῦ ἓν σῶμα* Herm.*sim*.9.18.4; cf. *animas scilicet, quae ad perfectionem venerunt, quae omnes simul efficiunt corpus ecclesiae*, Or. *Cant*.3(p.232.22; M.13.191B); cf.*ib*.2(p.113.25ff.; 101D); ref. Ps.91:14 *οἱ πεφυτευμένοι...ἐν τῷ οἴκῳ κυρίου, ἥτις ἐστὶν ἡ ἐ. θεοῦ ζῶντος...ὁ δὲ θεοποιῶν κοιλίαν, ἢ δόξαν, ἢ ἀργύριον...οὔτε ἐν τῇ αὐλῇ ἐστι τῇ ἁγίᾳ, κἂν ἄξιος τῶν αἰσθητῶν συνάξεων εἶναι δοκῇ* Bas.*hom.in Ps*.28(1. 117A; M.29.288C); opposite view *ταῖς παρὰ τῶν δυσσεβῶν τρικυμίαις βαλλομένη ἡ τοῦ θεοῦ ἐ., οὐ μεγαφρονεῖ, ὡς ἀγωνιζομένη, ἀλλὰ ἁμαρτίαις...ἀνατίθησι τὰ γινόμενα, καὶ τῆς παρὰ τοῦ σωτῆρος ἐπικουρίας ἀπολαῦσαι παρακαλεῖ...οὐδὲ ἐκ τελείων πᾶσα συνέστηκεν ἡ... ἐ.· ἀλλ' ἔχει καὶ τοὺς ῥᾳστώνῃ συζῶντας* Thdt.*Ps*.39:13(1.862).

I. various descriptive points: adumbration in pagan literature *Πυθαγόρας...τὴν ἐ. τὴν νῦν οὕτω καλουμένην τὸ παρ' αὐτῷ ὁμακοεῖον αἰνίττεται* Clem.*str*.1.15(p.42.1; M.8.768B); God's special care for it, Chrys.*a.exil*.1.2(3.416A); cf.Herm.*vis*.1.3.4; equality of its members *τοῦτο γὰρ τῆς ἐ. τὸ προτέρημα...ὥστε κἂν δοῦλος ᾖς, κἂν ἐλεύθερος, οὐδέν σοι πλέον, οὐδὲν ἔλαττον* Chrys.*hom.3.2 in Mt*.(7.36B); id.*hom. 1.1 in Philm*.(11.775D); beggars, too, needed for its perfection, id. *hom.30.4 in 1Cor*.(10.274D); laity as *ἡ ἐκλεκτὴ ἐ. Const.App*.2.26.1; *ecclesia* of Gr. citizens compared with Church *δῆμος καὶ ἐ., πολλοὶ τὸν ἀριθμὸν ὄντες ἄνθρωποι, ὡς ἓν ὄντες πρᾶγμα τῇ μιᾷ κλήσει καλοῦνται* Just.*dial*.42.3(M.6.565B); *ἐ. ... τοῦ θεοῦ...ἡ Ἀθήνησι πραεῖά τις καὶ εὐσταθής...ἡ δ' Ἀθηναίων ἐ. στασιώδης καὶ οὐδαμῶς παραβαλλομένη τῇ ἐκεῖ ἐ. τοῦ θεοῦ. τὸ δ' αὐτὸ ἐρεῖς περὶ ἐ. τοῦ θεοῦ τῆς ἐν Κορίνθῳ καὶ τῆς ἐ. τοῦ δήμου Κορινθίων...καὶ ἐὰν εὐγνώμων ᾖ ὁ τούτου ἀκούων...θαυμάσεται τὸν καὶ βουλευσάμενον καὶ ἀνύσαι δυνηθέντα πανταχοῦ συστήσασθαι ἐκκλησίας τοῦ θεοῦ, παροικούσας ἐκκλησίαις τῶν καθ' ἑκάστην πόλιν δήμων. οὕτω δὲ καὶ βουλὴν ἐκκλησίας θεοῦ βουλῇ τῇ καθ' ἑκάστην πόλιν συνεξετάζων εὕροις ἄν, τίνες μὲν τῆς ἐ. βουλευταὶ ἄξιοί εἰσιν...οἱ δὲ πανταχοῦ βουλευταὶ οὐδὲν ἄξιον τῆς ἐκ κατατάξεως ὑπεροχῆς...οὕτω δὲ καὶ ἄρχοντα ἐκκλησίας ἑκάστης πόλεως ἄρχοντι τῶν ἐν τῇ πόλει συγκριτέον* Or.*Cels*. 3.30(p.227.13ff.; M.11.957C–960A); its beauty, Meth.*symp*.8.5(p.87. 12ff.; M.18.145C,D); its predestination, Ign.*Eph*.proem.; not Church, but Christ its head, worshipped, Bas.*hom.in Ps*.44(1. 168A; M.29.409C); dead to world, Cyr.*glaph.Gen*.(1.207C).

J. prayer for Church, *Did*.10.5; *προσευχέσθω ὁ διάκονος ὑπὲρ τῆς ἐ. πάσης Const.App*.2.57.18; *ib*.3.5.2; *ὑπὲρ τῆς ἁγίας καθολικῆς καὶ ἀποστολικῆς ἐ. τῆς ἀπὸ περάτων ἕως περάτων δεηθῶμεν Lit*.ap.*Const. App*.8.10.4.

K. praise of Church *οὐ γὰρ οὕτως ἥλιος φανός, οὐδὲ τὸ ἐκ τούτου φῶς, ὡς τῆς ἐ. τὰ πράγματα* Chrys.*Is.interp*.2.2(6.21B); id.*hom.1.1 in Is.6:1*(6.96B); Cyr.*Is*.5.6(2.901E).

L. of heret. bodies *πάντα μᾶλλον ὑπομένουσι...ὑπὸ φιλοτιμίας τῆς αἱρέσεως καὶ τῆς πολυθρυλήτου κατὰ τὰς ἐ. αὐτῶν πρωτοκαθεδρίας* Clem.*str*.7.16(p.69.20; M.9.536B); *ib*.(p.70.6; 537A); Thdt.*Ps*.47:17 (1.1064); id.*Cant*.2:2(2.54).

M. Gnost.; **1.** distn. bet. heavenly and earthly Church, Iren. *haer*.1.5.6(M.7.501B); acc. Sethians, cf. *esse autem hanc et veram, et sanctam ecclesiam, quae fuerit appellatio, et conventio, et adunatio patris omnium primi hominis, et filii secundi hominis, et Christi filii eorum, et praedictae feminae*, *ib*.1.30.2(693B); acc. Naassenes, Hipp.*haer*.10.9(p.268.20; M.16.3419B); acc. Valentinians *προηνέχθη ὑπὸ τῆς μητρός...σπέρματα τῆς ἐ. μετὰ τὴν τοῦ φωτὸς αἴτησιν* Clem. *exc.Thdot*.40(p.119.14; M.9.677C); *τὸ δ' 'ἀπορροίας ἐκκλησίας ἐπιγείου καὶ περιτομῆς' τάχα ἐλήφθη ἀπὸ τοῦ ὑπό τινων λέγεσθαι ἐ. τινὸς ἐπουρανίου...ἀπόρροιαν εἶναι τὴν ἐπὶ γῆς ἐ.* Or.*Cels*.6.35(p.104.19ff.; M.11.1349B); **2.** Church to be changed into angel, Clem.*exc.Thdot*. 21(p.113.27; M.9.668C); **3.** Valent., relation to body of Jesus *τὸ ὁρατὸν τοῦ Ἰησοῦ ἡ Σοφία καὶ ἡ Ἐ. ἦν τῶν σπερμάτων τῶν διαφερόντων, ἣν ἐστολίσατο διὰ τοῦ σαρκίου* *ib*.26(p.115.15; 672B); *τὸ σῶμα τοῦ Ἰησοῦ, ὅπερ ὁμοούσιον ἦν τῇ ἐ.* *ib*.42(p.120.7; 680A); **4.** an aeon (Valent.) *ἐκ δὴ τοῦ Λόγου καὶ τῆς Ζωῆς προβεβλῆσθαι κατὰ συζυγίαν Ἄνθρωπον καὶ Ἐ.* Iren.*haer*.1.1.1(M.7.448A); Hipp.*haer*.4.51(p.76.2; M.16.3122A); Epiph.*haer*.31.2(p.386.2; M.41.477A).

N. church building; **1.** in gen., Or.*or*.31.7(p.400.20; M.11.556C); *οἰκία κοινὴ πάντων ἐστὶν ἡ ἐ.* Chrys.*hom.32.6 in Mt*.(7.373B); *νόμον τίθημι, ὥστε μηδένα ὀφθῆναι ἔρημον ἐκκλησίας χωρίον ἔχοντα* id.*hom. 18.4 in Ac*.(9.149E); *οἱ πρόγονοι τὰς ἐ. ἡμῖν ᾠκοδόμησαν, οὐχ ἵνα ἐκ τῶν ἰδίων οἴκων συναγαγόντες ἡμᾶς ἀλλήλοις δεικνύωσι...ἀλλ' ἵνα μαθητὰς ὁμοῦ καὶ διδασκάλους συναγαγόντες, βελτίους τούτους δι' ἐκείνων ἐργάσωνται* *ib.29.3*(230A); for interior decoration, v. Nil.*epp*. 4.61(M.79.577Bff.); for distn. bet. *ἐ.* and *ἐκκλησιαστήριον* v. latter; **2.** on going to church *οὐκ ἔστιν ἐν αὐτοῖς οὐδὲν ἀγαθόν...οὐ γὰρ εἴδομεν αὐτοὺς εἰσελθεῖν ἐν ἐ. ποτέ* *Apoc.Bar*.13(p.93.15); *ὦ ἐπίσκοπε, κέλευε...τῷ λαῷ εἰς τὴν ἐ. ἐνδελεχίζειν ὄρθρου καὶ ἑσπέρας ἑκάστης ἡμέρας Const.App*.2.59.1; *αἰσχύνομαι διὰ τοὺς ἅπαξ τοῦ ἐνιαυτοῦ μόλις ἐν ἐ. φαινομένους* Chrys.*hom.2.6 in 2Cor*.(10.437E); prayer in church better than at home, id.*incomprehens*.3.6(1.469C); Nil.*paraen*.105 (M.79.1260A); **3.** behaviour in church *ἐπὶ δὲ τὴν ἐ. ἀκτέον τὴν γυναῖκα καὶ τὸν ἄνδρα ἐστολισμένους κοσμίως, ἀπλάστῳ βαδίσματι* Clem.*paed*.3.11(p.280.4; M.8.657A); cf. *quid de absentibus conqueror? praesentes etiam et in ecclesia positi non estis intenti, sed* *communes ex usu fabulas teritis, verbo dei...terga convertitis*, Or. *hom.10.1 in Gen.*(p.93.7ff.; M.12.215B,C); Cyr.H.*procatech.*14; legislation on sitting or standing in church acc. age etc., *Const.App.* 2.57.12; χρὴ γὰρ ἐν ἐ. ἐπιστημόνως καὶ νηφαλέως...ἑστάναι, ἐκτεταμένην ἔχοντα τὴν ἀκοὴν εἰς τὸν τοῦ κυρίου λόγον *ib.*2.57.13; noisy and ostentatious behaviour castigated, Chrys.*hom.1.2 in Is.6*: *1*(6.97D); id.*hom.19.9 in Mt.*(7.257C); attitude of mind μηδεὶς...ἐν ἐ. τὰ κατὰ τὴν οἰκίαν μελετάτω id.*hom.2.5 in Jo.*(8.14D); τὴν ἐ. ὡς οὐρανὸν πάτει· καὶ μηδὲν ἐν αὐτῇ μηδὲ λέγε, μηδὲ λογίζου γήινον Nil.*paraen.*57 (M.79.1253B); *ib.*65(1253D).

O. *congregation*, *Lit.*ap.*Const.App.*8.5.11; εὐχὴν...ἁπάσης αὐτῷ τῆς ἐ. συμπληρωσάσης Dion.Ar.*e.h.*2.2.6(M.3.396A).

ἐκκλησιάζ-ω, **1.** *attend an assembly*; **a.** *attend a church service*, Eus.*v.C.*4.60(p.142.5); id.*l.C.*1(p.197.12; M.20.1321A); οἶκοι εὐκτήριοι, ἔρημοι τῶν ~όντων Bas.*ep.*90.2(3.182A; M.32.473B); Chrys.*coemet.*1 (2.397A); Soz.*h.e.*7.19.8(M.67.1477B); legislation εἴ τις παρὰ τὴν ἐκκλησίαν ἰδίᾳ ~οι...ἀ. ἔ. CGangr.*can.*6; **b.** *attend a church council*, Eustrat.*v.Eutych.*28(M.86.2308B); pass., *be gathered together*, at CNic.(325), Basilisc.*encycl.*(p.50.6; M.86.2600C); **2.** *address a church meeting, preach*, Bas.*ep.*28.2(3.108B; M.32.308C); Philost.*h.e.*9.14(M.65.580B); **3.** *preach to, teach*, in etym. of Ecclesiastes, ‡Ath.*synops.*23 (M.28.348B) cit. s. ἐκκλησιαστής; πάντας ἀνθρώπους ~ων Olymp.*Eccl.*1 proem.(M.93.480A); **4.** med., *be member of, belong to the Church* ἐν ἐπαίνῳ...παρὰ πᾶσιν ~ομένοις ἐνυπάρχει Epiph.*haer.*59.4 (p.368.16; M.41.1024C); **5.** pass., *be received, approved by Church*, of canonical books ἐκ τῶν...~ομένων γραφῶν Cyr.H.*catech.*15.13; ‡Ath.*synops.*78(M.28.437A); ‡Ath.*dial.Trin.*1.5(M.28.1124C); of πίστις, CEph.(449)*act.*(*ACO* 2.1.1; p.191.12; H.2.257A).

***ἐκκλησιάρχης**, ὁ, *sacristan* περὶ τὸ διάφαυσμα σημαίνει ὁ ἐ. *Const.Stud.*14(M.99.1709B).

***ἐκκλησίασις**, ἡ, *conventicle* ἰδίᾳ συνάξεις ποιούμενοι καὶ ἐ. καὶ διδασκαλίας ἑτέρας CGangr.*ep.*(H.1.530E).

ἐκκλησιαστήριον, τό, *church building*, opp. ἐκκλησία: τὴν μὲν ὄντως ἐκκλησίαν καθαιρεῖ...τὸ δ' ἐ. οἰκοδομεῖ...εἰ δὲ γνοίη ἀκριβῶς, ὅτι ἄλλο ἐστὶν ἐκκλησία καὶ ἄλλο ἐ.· ἡ μὲν γὰρ ἐξ ἀμώμων ψυχῶν συνέστηκε, τὸ δ' ἀπὸ λίθων καὶ ξύλων οἰκοδομεῖται...μανθανέτω, ὅτι ἐπὶ μὲν τῶν ἀποστόλων, ὅτε ἡ ἐκκλησία ἐκόμα...χαρίσμασι πνευματικοῖς...ἐκκλησιαστήρια οὐκ ἦν· ἐπὶ δὲ ἡμῶν τὰ ἐ. πλέον τοῦ δέοντος κεκόσμηται, ἡ δ' ἐκκλησία...κωμῳδεῖται Isid.Pel.*epp.*2.246(M.78.685A–C); *ib.*1.113(257C).

ἐκκλησιαστής, ὁ, **1.** *leader of Church*; of Christ, Gr.Nyss.*hom.6 in Cant.*(M.44.905A); **2.** *preacher* ἐ. καὶ Χριστοῦ κῆρυξ Diad.*ascens.*1(M.65.1141A); author of Eccl. ἐκλήθη [sc. Σολομών]...ἐ., ὅτι αὐτὸς ἐξεκλησίαζε τοὺς λαούς ‡Ath.*synops.*23(M.28.348B); Olymp.*Eccl.*1 proem.(M.93.480A); *ib.*1(480D); Isid.H.*etym.*6.2.19.

ἐκκλησιαστικός, *of the Church, belonging to the Church, ecclesiastical*; **1.** of Church doctrine and institutions ἐ. κανόνα *M.Polyc.*epilog.2; Clem.*str.*6.15(p.495.4f.; M.9.349A); τάξει CLaod.*can.*27; διδασκαλίᾳ Eus.*Marcell.*1.3(p.17.29; M.24.749D); Ath.*ep.Afr.*(M.26.1029B); δόγματος Ath.*apol.sec.*69(p.147.20; M.25.372C); Gr.Nyss.*Eun.*1(1 p.146.20; M.45.385D); δόξης Eus.*h.e.*4.7.5(M.20.317A); which form 'mind' of Church ἐκ τοσούτων ἐτῶν καταγγελλομένου τοῦ ἐ. φρονήματος †Hipp.*Artem.*ap.Eus.*h.e.*5.28.6(M.20.513A); *Symb.Ant.*(345)9(p.254.11; M.26.736A); Thdt.*ep.*82(4.1144); **2.** of persons, gen. as subst. masc.; **a.** of Christians opp. pagans ζητοῦμεν τῆς παρουσίας ἡμέτερον σημεῖον, ἐκκλησιαστικὸν ζητοῦμεν οἱ ἐ. Cyr.H.*catech.*15.7; **b.** of orthodox opp. heretics κατὰ μὲν τὸν Ἡρακλέωνα...κατὰ δὲ τὸν ἐ. Or.*Jo.*13.44(p.270.4; M.14.477C); Eus.*h.e.*2.25.6(M.20.208C); λέγει γὰρ καὶ ὁ ἐ. καὶ ὁ αἱρετικός Gr.Nyss.*Eun.*2(2 p.364.29; M.45.544C); Epiph.*haer.*70.9(p.241.20; M.42.353B); **c.** of clerics opp. laymen ἄρχοντας κοσμικοὺς ὑπὸ τῶν ἐ. ἀγομένους Cyr.H.*catech.*17.10; Bas.*ep.*44.1(3.131C; M.32.361A); Nil.*serm.*8(M.79.1276C); **d.** ἡ ἐ. ψυχή *the Christian soul*, Cyr.*fr.Cant.*3:6(M.69.1285D,1288A); **3.** neut. plur.; **a.** *church property*, *Const.App.*3.7.3; Isid.Pel.*epp.*1.269(M.78.341D); **b.** *ecclesiastical functions* Παῦλος, τὰ μὲν ἐ. διατυπῶν Ath.*decr.*5(p.4.17; M.25.432A); Chrys.*fr.in Jer.*1:8(M.64.749C); Philost.*h.e.*9.4(M.65.572A); **4.** name of Valent. aeon Ἐ. καὶ Μακαριότης Iren.*haer.*1.1.2(M.7.449B); Epiph.*haer.*31.2(p.386.4; M.41.477A).

ἐκκλησιαστικῶς, *in accordance with church principles* δικαίως καὶ ἐ. ποιοῦντες Ath.*apol.sec.*89(p.167.11; M.25.408B); Marcell.*ep.*(p.256.18; M.42.384C); Bas.*ep.*156.2(3.246C; M.32.617A); opp. ἀγοραίως, Gr.Naz.*ep.*23.12(M.35.1164C); τῶν βιούντων ἐ. Didym.*Ps.*23:2(M.39.1296A).

ἐκκλησιέκδικος, ὁ, *legal representative of Church, church syndic*, Nil.*epp.*1.71 tit.(M.79.113B); *ib.*3.6 tit.(368D); CCP(536)*act.*2(*ACO* 3 p.159.32; H.2.1233A); Leont.N.*v.Jo.Eleem.*5(p.11.6); *ib.*(p.11.12,14).

ἔκκλησις, ἡ, **1.** for ἔκκλισις, *turning away*, Diod.*Ex.*6:24(M.33.1583A); **2.** error for ἐπίκλησις, Iren.*haer.*4.18.5(M.7.1028B).

ἐκκλητικός, *provocative, stimulating* ἐπιγάστριον βίον, οὗ πλοῦτός ἐστιν ἐ. Clem.*paed.*2.1(p.164.9; M.8.400C); *ib.*2.4(p.181.20; 440B).

ἔκκλητος, *selected for arbitration*; hence as subst. fem., *appeal*, *Hom.Clem.*19.23(*GCS* p.266.14; ἐκκλήτως M.2.445B); Ammon.*Ac.*25:25(M.85.1596B); Socr.*h.e.*2.40.41(M.67.344B); in case of clerical appeal, both parties to choose judges, *Cod.Afr.*96; rules for appeal against bishop and magistrate, Ath.Scholast.*coll.*1.2(p.10).

ἐκκολάπτω, *hew, carve out*, Herm.*sim.*9.9.7; Zach.Mit.*opif.*(M.85.1024B); *M.Ner.et Ach.*20(p.20.10).

ἐκκόλαψις, ἡ, *hewing out*, Herm.*sim.*9.2.2.

***ἐκκομβόομαι**, v. ἐγκομβόομαι.

ἐκκομιστής, ὁ, *corpse-bearer*, Thdr.Stud.*or.*11.4(M.99.805C).

ἐκκομπάζω, *utter boastfully*, Men.*exc.Rom.*14(p.206.20; M.113.904D).

ἐκκοπή, ἡ, **1.** *amputation*, met. τῆς ἐπιθυμίας ἐ. Clem.*str.*6.9(p.468.31; M.9.296A); Chrys.*hom.16.2 in Eph.*(11.117E); *cutting short* of argument, *Dial.Tim.et Aquil.*81 r°, 84 r°; **2.** *falling short, failure*, Cyr.*Is.*4.3(2.630E); Leont.B.*mesopent.*(M.86.1977B); **3.** *segregation* ἡ ἐ. ἐκ πάντων ἐν τῇ ἑνώσει τῇ ἐν Χριστῷ Philox.*ep.*24(p.175).

ἐκκόπτ-ω, **1.** *cut off*, met.; **a.** *extirpate* evil, *1Clem.*63.2; Clem.*q.d.s.*29(p.179.7; M.9.633D); Thdt.*qu.48 in Gen.*(1.62); **b.** *excommunicate* τὸν πεπορνευκότα...ἐξέκοψαν Chrys.*hom.1.1 in 2Cor.*(10.418A); **2.** pass., *be cut off from*, met. ~έσθω τῆς ἐκκλησίας *Can.App.*28; ~έσθω...τῆς κοινωνίας *ib.*29; Phot.*nomoc.*9.15(M.104.1105C).

ἐκκορακίζω, *peck out eyes like a raven* (but perh. f.l. for ⟨ἐσκορακίζω⟩; σκορακίζω = *bid* someone go ἐς κόρακας) ἵνα...ἐκκορακίσω τοὺς ὀφθαλμοὺς αὐτοῦ Thphn.*chron.*p.249(M.108.625B).

ἐκκορυφόω, *pile up*; met., Mac.Aeg.*elev.*10(M.34.897C).

***ἐκκουσσεύω**, (Lat. *excuso*) *excuse, apologize*, Jo.Mal.*chron.*14 p.356(M.97.532B); ἐξκουσ-, *ib.*ap.*Chron.Pasch.*p.316(M.92.804A).

ἐκκρέμαμαι, *hang*; met., *depend*, Just.*dial.*96.1(M.6.704A); *hang upon, cling to* τῆς ἐνταῦθα ζωῆς ἐ. Clem.*q.d.s.*2(p.160.24; M.9.605C).

***ἔκκρουμα**, τό, *shout* ἡ συλλαβὴ ἡ λεγομένη Κὼφ ἑρμηνεύεται ἔ., τουτέστιν ἀναβόησις Hesych.H.*Ps.tit.*144.38(M.27.1317B, v.l. ἔκρουσμα).

***ἐκκρύπτω**, *reveal, make known*, opp. κρύπτω, Bas.Sel.*or.*17.3(M.85.224C).

***ἔκκτητος**, *acquired* ἔ. τε καὶ ἀργυρώνητον Cyr.*ador.*12(1.425B).

ἐκκυκλέω, *display* on a stage, Clem.*prot.*2(p.11.14, v.l. ἐγκ-; M.8.72A).

***ἐκκύκλησις**, ἡ, *bringing out, producing*, Clem.*str.*3.4(p.208.4, v.l. ἐγκ-; M.8.1132A).

ἐκκυλίομαι, *turn aside*, Sophr.H.*ep.syn.*(M.87.3153C).

ἐκκυμαίνω, *agitate*, Clem.*paed.*1.6(p.114.7; M.8.297B); Meth.*lepr.*5(p.456.1); Gr.Nyss.*v.Mos.*17(M.44.304D); met., of stirring up passions, Clem.*paed.*2.2(p.169.20; M.8.413C); id.*str.*3.14(p.240.17; M.8.1196C); Gr.Naz.*carm.*2.1.11.305(M.37.1050A).

***ἐκκωμῳδέω**, *ridicule*, Isid.Pel.*epp.*2.162(M.78.616C); *ib.*2.178 (629C).

***ἐκκωτίλλω**, *allure*, *V.Const.*35(p.565.23).

ἐκλαλητικός, *capable of divulging, babbling out*, Isid.Pel.*epp.*2.109(M.78.549D).

ἐκλαμβάνω, *take down* λόγοι...ὑπὸ τῶν ὀξυγράφων ἐκληφθέντες Socr.*h.e.*6.4.9(M.67.672C); Jo.Mal.*chron.*18 p.494(M.97.713C); abs., CChalc.*act.*1(*ACO* 2.1.1 p.87.19; H.2.93B).

ἐκλαμπρύνω, **1.** *enlighten*, met. οἱ πίστει τῇ εἰς Χριστὸν ἐκλελαμπρυσμένοι Cyr.*Os.*10(3.31B); Sophr.H.*ep.syn.*(M.87.3161A); **2.** *throw light on*; met., Cyr.*Jo.*3.4(4.279E).

***ἐκλαμπτικός**, *illuminating*, Gr.Nyss.*hom.14 in Cant.*(M.44.1072B); met. ἐ. τοῦ βαπτίσματος χάριν *ib.*2(793D).

ἐκλάμπ-ω, **1.** *shine*; met., Trin., of H. Ghost παρὰ τοῦ λόγου...~ει Ath.*ep.Serap.*1.20(M.26.580A); Thdt.*rect.conf.*9(M.6.1221C); ref. Inc. ἡ ἐπιφάνεια ἡ νῦν ἐκλάμψασα ἐν ἡμῖν τοῦ...λόγου Clem.*prot.*1 (p.7.27; M.8.61C); cf.*ib.*11(p.80.17; 232B); Eus.*d.e.*8 proem.(p.351.20; M.22.572B); of grace in soul, Clem.*prot.*11(p.82.25; M.8.236D); id.*str.*7.7(p.29.13; M.9.453B); **2.** c. acc. cogn., *flash forth*, met. ὁ πατὴρ ἐξέλαμψεν ἐξ ἑαυτοῦ τὸν υἱόν, ἀμερίστως...ὥσπερ...ὁ ἥλιος τὸ ἐξ αὐτοῦ πεμπόμενον ἀπαύγασμα Cyr.*thes.*6(5[1].47A).

ἔκλαμψις, ἡ, *shining*; **1.** in gen., Eus.*d.e.*9.1(p.406.7; M.22.656A); Isid.Pel.*epp.*1.395(M.78.404C); Melet.*nat.hom.*2(M.64.1169C); **2.** of Christ, at Inc. τὴν εἰς ἀνθρώπους ἔ. τοῦ...σωτῆρος Eus.*l.C.*9(p.218.15; M.20.1364A); id.*d.e.*9.1(p.405.22; M.22.653C); Cyr.*Ps.*46:4(M.69.1249A); ἡ...μεταμόρφωσις κατὰ τὴν ἔ. ἣν Vict.*Mc.*9:3(p.353.9); Jo.D.

*hom.*1.13(M.96.565B); of Second Advent τὴν ἐ. τῆς δόξης Chrys.*hom.* *76.3 in Mt.*(7.735D).

ἐκλέγ-ω, *choose*; **1.** of man συγχωρεῖ [sc. H. Ghost]...τὰ πρὸς τὸ χρήσιμον συντελοῦντα τῇ ἀνθρωπείᾳ φύσει ∼ειν ποτὲ τὴν κτίσιν Didym. *Trin.*2.7(M.39.600A); θεοῦ παιδεύοντος...ἐπὶ τῷ ∼εσθαι τὰ βελτίω Cyr.*Ps.*33:8(M.69.977A); **2.** med., of divine election θεὸς...ὁ ἐκλεξάμενος τὸν...Χριστὸν καὶ ἡμᾶς δι' αὐτοῦ εἰς λαὸν περιούσιον *1Clem.* 64; Ign.*Eph.*proem.; Clem.*str.*5.12(p.378.20; M.9.117B); ‡Meth.*Sym. et Ann.*13(M.18.380A); ref. choice of apostles, *Barn.*5.9; Didym. (‡Bas.)*Eun.*5(1.300B; M.29.720D).

ἔκλειψις, ἡ, 1. *eclipse*; **a.** at Crucifixion, Or.*comm.ser.in Mt.* 134(p.274.6; M.13.1783); prophesied in Zach.14:6,7, id.*fr.83 in Lc.* (p.273.2); οὐκ ἦν ἔ., ἀλλ' ὀργή,...τρεῖς γὰρ ὥρας παρέμεινεν Chrys. *hom.88.1 in Mt.*(7.825A); **b.** as argument agst. divinity of moon, Arist.*apol.*6.3; Zach.Mit.*opif.*(M.85.1049A); **2.** *omission*; cf. *eclipsis est defectus dictionis, in quo necessaria verba desunt*, Isid.H.*etym.* 1.34.10.

ἐκλεκτικῶς, *judiciously, with discrimination*, Clem.*str.*7.15(p.64. 16; M.9.525B).

ἐκλεκτός, A. *chosen*; **1.** ref. divine election; **a.** in gen. οἱ ἐ. τοῦ θεοῦ *1Clem.*49.5; ἱκεσίαν ποιούμενοι, ὅπως τὸν ἀριθμὸν...τῶν ἐ. αὐτοῦ ...διαφυλάξῃ ἄθραυστον ὁ δημιουργός *ib.*59.2; *ib.*2.4; τοῖς...δικαίοις· εἰσὶν δὲ οὗτοι ἐ. τοῦ θεοῦ *ib.*46.4; cf.*ib.*1.1; διὰ ταύτης [sc. faith] σῴζονται οἱ ἐ. τοῦ θεοῦ Herm.*vis.*3.8.3; πνευματικὸς καὶ διὰ τοῦτο ἐ. Clem.*str.*4.26(p.323.9; M.8.1377B); *ib.*(p.324.15; 1380B); Or.*engast.* 10(p.294.9; M.12.1028B); ἐγλεκτὸς τοῦ θεοῦ *MAMA* 1.237(Phrygia); **b.** in OT ὁ ἐ. Δαυίδ *1Clem.*52.2; of Abraham, Clem.*str.*5.1(p.328.5; M.9.13A); **c.** of Church ἐ. πόλεως Aberc.*epitaph.*1; ἡ καθολικὴ ἐκκλησία καὶ ἀμπελὼν αὐτοῦ ἐ. *Const.App.*1 proem.; *ib.*2.26.1; ref. Is. 43:20, 1Petr.10:9 τὸ γένος μου τὸ ἐ. Cyr.*Is.*4.1(2.574B); **d.** in heret. systems; **i.** dualist in gen. πᾶς βίος ἀκίνδυνος ἐκλεκτῷ Clem.*str.*3.5 (p.214.15; M.8.1144B); **ii.** Basilides τὴν...ἐ. [sc. ψυχήν] ἐπιτίμως διὰ μαρτυρίαν *ib.*4.11(p.285.5; 1292C); φύσει πιστοῦ καὶ ἐ. ὄντος *ib.*5.1(p.327.27; M.9.13A); **iii.** Valent. πᾶν πνευματικὸν σπέρμα, τοὺς ἐ. id.*exc.Thdot.*1(p.105.10; M.9.653A); τὴν ἐκκλησίαν..., τὸ ἐ. καὶ τὸ κλητόν *ib.*58(p.126.12; 688A); τάχα...ὡς ἐκ τῆς αὐτῆς οὐσίας τῶν ἐ. ... γενομένων *ib.*13(p.111.12; 664B); ὁ Χριστὸς ὡς πρὸς τὰ πληρώματα ἐ. γενόμενος *ib.*33(p.117.20; 676B); τῶν ἐ. τῶν ἀγγελικῶν ὑπὸ τοῦ ἄρρενος ἔτι πρότερον προβεβλημένων *ib.*39(p.119.11; 677C); **iv.** Naassene, of angelic Church ἐκκλησία ἐ. Hipp.*haer.*5.6(p.78.21; M.16.3126B); **v.** Manich. τοῖς ἐ. αὐτοῦ,...οὐ πλέον ἑπτὰ οὖσι τὸν ἀριθμόν Hegem.*Arch.*11(p.19.5; M.10.1445B); *ib.*10(p.16.10; 1444A); **2.** of Christians in gen. τῶν ἀπίστων καὶ τῶν ἐ. *M.Polyc.*16.1; Clem. *q.d.s.*36(p.183.18; M.9.644A); *Const.App.*3.16.3; τὸν Χριστόν, οὗ μέτοχοι γενόμενοι...μέλη ἐστὲ...ἐ. *ib.*2.61.5; τίνας...φησι τοὺς ἐ.; τοὺς πιστούς Chrys.*hom.76.2 in Mt.*(7.733C); **3.** ref. choice by God for a particular function, of Christ ἐ. ... οὐκέθ' ὁμοίως τοῖς ἀποστόλοις· ...ἀλλὰ καὶ τὸ πνεῦμα τοῦ θεοῦ ἐπὶ μόνον αὐτὸν ἐπανεπαύσατο Eus. *Is.*42:1(M.24.385B); of prophets Ἰερεμία, ὁ ἐ. μου *Apoc.Bar.rel.*1. 1; of apostles, Eus.*d.e.*2.3(p.86.9; M.22.153A); οἱ...ἐ. μου,...τουτέστιν, οἱ...μαθηταί, ἤγουν...οἱ τῶν ἐμῶν θεσπισμάτων ἱερουργοί Cyr. *Is.*5.6(2.905D); of BMV, Jo.Mon.*hymn.Geo.*4(M.96.1393A).

B. *choice, excellent*, of Christ τὸ ἐ. φῶς, τὸ ἐξελθὸν ἐκ στόματος αὐτοῦ *Apoc.Bar.rel.*3.9; Proc.G.*Is.*49:1–13(M.87.2472B); of saints, Ign.*Philad.*11.1; of patriarchs, prophets, Or.*Jo.*28.16(21; p.415.33; M.14.725B); of Christians ὅλοι ἐ. καὶ ἅγιοι γενέσθωσαν Serap.*euch.* 5.3; Didym.*Ps.*17:26(M.39.1253D); τῶν ἐ. πατέρων Evagr.*h.e.*1.13 (M.86.2456A).

***ἐκλεπτουργ-έω,** *work out in detail* ὁ θεὸς οὐκ αὐτὸς ∼εῖ τῶν δεῦρο τὰ ἕκαστα, ἀλλὰ χρῆται χειρὶ τῇ φύσει Synes.*regn.*27(p.58.6; M.66. 1104D).

ἐκλεπτύν-ω, 1. *wear down*, Thdr.Mops.*Zach.*1:18–21(M.66.516C); met. αἱ μάστιγες τὴν φλεγμονὴν τῆς παρακοῆς ∼ουσι Const.Diac.*laud.* 29(M.88.512D); **2.** *make subtle*, Gr.Nyss.*hom.opif.*30.24(M.44.249D); pass., of risen body of believer, Isid.Pel.*epp.*2.43(M.78.485B).

ἐκλευκαίν-ω, *make white*; **1.** lit., Clem.*paed.*1.6(p.114.12; M.8. 297C); **2.** met., *make plain*, ‡Ath.*nativ.Chr.*6(M.28.969D); Thdt. *ep.*112(4.1186); γράμματα...τὸ ἦθος τῆς ψυχῆς ∼οντα Sophr.H.*ep. syn.*(M.87.3200B).

ἐκληπτέον, *one must understand*, Clem.*str.*1.28(p.110.5; M.8.925A); Chrys.*hom.26.3 in 1Cor.*(10.231A); Dion.Ar.*d.n.*2.1(M.3.637A).

ἐκλήπτωρ, ὁ, *one who takes up*; met., of one undertaking work, Epiph.*haer.*66.85(p.128.6; M.42.165B); of one co-operating with grace, *cat.Apoc.*3:14–17(p.232.4); *contractor* ἐπίσκοποι καὶ πρεσβύτεροι καὶ διάκονοι ἐ. μὴ γίνωνται *Cod.Afr.*16; ἐ. τῶν δημοσίων φόρων Thphn.*chron.*p.323(M.108.781A).

ἐκληρέω, *speak foolishly*; of heretics, Isid.Pel.*epp.*1.247(M.78. 333A).

ἔκληψις, ἡ, 1. *undertaking*; in commerce, forbidden to bishops, priests, and deacons, *Cod.Afr.*16; **2.** *assumption* τὴν πρὸς αὐτὸν [sc. τὸν Χριστόν] ἔ. τῆς σαρκὸς ὁ λόγος ἔπραξε Leont.H.*Nest.*6.9(M.86. 1757B); **3.** *interpretation* πρὸς...πνευματικὴν ἔ. Cyr.*Ps.*65:3(M.69. 1133A); τὴν...ἀλληγορικὴν ἔ. Areth.*Apoc.*26(M.106.624B); cf.*ib.*29 (648A); in gen., Leont.H.*Nest.*7.6(M.86.1768[d]B).

ἐκλικμάω, *winnow*; met., *scatter like chaff*, Socr.*h.e.*6.6.33(M.67. 680C).

ἐκλιμπάνω, *cease*; hence **1.** *die*, Hipp.*Dan.*4.51.3; **2.** *be eclipsed*; of sun, Jo.D.*hom.*8.10(M.96.716B).

ἐκλογεύς, ὁ, *one who chooses, selector* εἰ δὲ καὶ ἃ βούλει λαμβάνεις ἀπὸ τῆς θείας γραφῆς καὶ ἃ βούλει καταλιμπάνεις,...οὐχ ἑρμηνευτὴς τῶν νόμων ἀλλὰ ἐ. τῶν οὐ κατὰ τὸν νοῦν σου γραφέντων Epiph.*haer.* 44.5(p.196.11; M.41.828C); of H. Ghost ἁγίων ἐ. id.*anc.*73(p.91.27; M.43.153A).

ἐκλογή, ἡ, *choice*; **1.** of divine election; **a.** in gen., ref. denial that circumcision attests election, *Diogn.*4.4; τὸν κύριον τὸν ἐκλογὰς ποιοῦντα ἀπὸ τῶν ἰδίων δούλων *M.Polyc.*20.1 = *M.Sab.*8.3; ἡ ἐ. *the elect*, Clem.*str.*3.9(p.225.14; M.8.1165C); σφόδρα εἰσὶν ὀλίγοι οἱ καταντῶντες ἐπὶ τὴν ἐ. τοῦ θεοῦ Or.*hom.4.3 in Jer.*(p.26.4; M.13. 289A); mystery symbolized in Lc.14:16ff., id.*Jo.*13.34(p.259.28; M. 14.460A); τὴν...ἑτοιμασθεῖσαν ἡμῖν ἐν αὐτῷ τῷ λόγῳ, κατ' ἐ., ζωήν Ath.*Ar.*2.76(M.26.309A); **b.** of covenant with Israel τῇ τῶν πατέρων ἐ. Thdr.Mops.*Rom.*11:28(p.159.20; M.66.860A); of Jews in Christ's time τὸ κατ' ἐ. χάριτος λεῖμμα Or.*Cant.*2(p.131.27; M.17.256C); **c.** messianic μὴ ἀρνεῖσθαι ὅτι οὗτός ἐστιν ὁ Χριστός, ἐὰν...ἐ. γενόμενος εἰς τὸν Χριστὸν εἶναι ἀποδεικνύηται Just.*dial.*48.3(M.6.580C); **d.** of the faithful ἐκλογῆς μέρος ἡμᾶς ἐποίησεν αὐτῷ *1Clem.*29.1; of Jews and Greeks ἡ ἐξ ἀμφοῖν ἐ. μία Clem.*str.*6.13(p.435.24; M. 9.328B); of calling of gentiles, ref. Dt.32:21 προφητικῶς δηλοῦται ἡ διὰ τὰ ἁμαρτήματα τοῦ προτέρου λαοῦ ἐσομένη τῶν...ἐθνῶν ἐ. Or. *princ.*4.1.4(p.298.6; M.11.348B); prophesied in Ps.21, Eus.*d.e.*10.8 (p.491.28; M.22.789B); of Jewish converts ἐ. τοὺς ἐξ αὐτῶν πεπιστευκότας καλεῖ Thdt.*Rom.*11:7(3.119); **e.** of man's part in election τὴν διαφορὰν τῆς ἐ. ἀξία γενομένη ψυχῆς αἵρεσίς τε καὶ συνάσκησις πεποίηκεν Clem.*str.*5.14(p.421.13; M.9.205C); οὐ...ἡ ἐ. [sc. τοῦ θεοῦ] ...βιαστικὴ τῶν καλουμένων ἐστίν, ἀλλὰ προτρεπτική Chrys.*hom.47.4 in Jo.*(8.281C); Thdt.*Cant.*2:3(2.55); **f.** in system of Basilides φυσικὴν ἡγοῦνται τὴν πίστιν... καθὸ καὶ ἐπὶ τῆς ἐ. τάττουσιν αὐτήν Clem.*str.*2.3(p.118.11; M.8.941B); *ib.*(p.118.18; 941B); μὴ βιούντων ὀρθῶς..., ὡς ἤτοι ἐχόντων ἐξουσίαν καὶ τοῦ ἁμαρτεῖν διὰ τὴν τελειότητα, ἢ πάντως γε σωθησομένων φύσει, κἂν νῦν ἁμάρτωσι, διὰ τὴν ἔμφυτον ἐ. *ib.*3.1(p.196.17; 1104A); ξένην τὴν ἐ. τοῦ κόσμου *ib.*4.26(p.321.29; 1376A); denied μαθήσει καὶ καθάρσει καὶ τῇ τῶν ἔργων εὐποιίᾳ, ἀλλ' οὐ φύσει σωζομένης τῆς ἐ. *ib.*5.1(p.328.1; M.9.13A); **g.** Valent. ἑαυτοὺς...ἀποκαλοῦντες...σπέρματα ἐκλογῆς Iren.*haer.*1.6.4(M.7. 509A); ref. Gen.1:27 τὴν προβολὴν τὴν ἀρίστην...τῆς Σοφίας,...ἀφ' ἧς τὰ μὲν ἀρρενικὰ ἡ ἐ., τὰ δὲ θηλυκὰ ἡ κλῆσις, καὶ τὰ μὲν ἀρρενικὰ ἀγγελικὰ καλοῦσι Clem.*exc.Thdot.*21(p.113.20; M.9.668B); **h.** of divine election to functions in Church: of apostles, Iren.*haer.*1.3.2 (M.7.469A); Or.*Jo.*32.18(11; p.457.15; M.14.792C); Eus.*h.e.*2.1.1(M. 20.133A); of clergy ἔξεστιν...κατὰ τὸ εὐαγγέλιον τελείως βιώσαντας... εἰς τὴν ἐ. τῶν ἀποστόλων ἐγγραφῆναι Clem.*str.*6.12(p.485.8; M.9. 328A); ἐκφαντορικός [sc. ordaining bishop] ἐστι τῆς θεαρχικῆς ἐ. Dion.Ar.*e.h.*5.3.5(M.3.512B); **2.** *the elect* (collectively), Clem.*str.*3.9 (p.225.14; M.8.1165C); Or.*Jo.*2.3(p.56.5; M.14.112B); **3.** of human power of choice τὰ ἔργα ἡμῶν ἐν ἐ. ... τῆς ψυχῆς ἡμῶν *Pss.Sal.*9.7; of lay people, opp. monks ἐν ἐκλογαῖς γε μὴν διατριβόντων Eus.*d.e.*6.18 (M.22.460C; conj. μὴ διατριβόντων *not concerning themselves with a choice* (*of the best*), p.279.34).

***ἐκλόγιον, τό,** *elect member* ὦ τιμιώτατα τῆς ἐκκλησίας ἐ., ἱερεῖς καὶ πατέρες ‡Jo.D.*fid.dorm.*1(M.95.248A).

ἐκλογισμός, ὁ, descriptive *account*, Clem.*str.*6.4(p.448.28; M.9. 253A)

***ἐκλόχευσις, ἡ,** *birth*, Sophr.H.*or.*2.31(M.87.3256A).

ἐκλοχίζω, *pick out, choose*, ref. Cant.5:10 ὁ υἱὸς τοῦ ἀνθρώπου, ὡς ἐκλελοχισμένον ἀπὸ μυριάδων ἑαυτὸν κατασημαίνει Cyr.*Jo.*1.4(4.39E).

ἔκλυσις, ἡ, 1. *relaxation*, in laughter τοῦ προσώπου ἔ. Clem.*paed.* 2.5(p.186.2; M.8.448C); *ib.*2.8(p.205.25; 492C); **2.** *weakness*; **a.** physical, a hindrance to prayer, Mac.Aeg.*or.*3(M.34.856A); *fainting*, ref. Christ's delay before raising Lazarus ἵνα μηδεὶς ἔχῃ λέγειν...ὅτι ἔ. ἦν ...καὶ οὐ θάνατος Chrys.*hom.62.1 in Jo.*(8.369C); **b.** moral, Meth. *symp.*8.7(p.90.2; M.18.149B); Bas.*reg.fus.*proem.1(2.327B; M.31. 889B); Gr.Naz.*ep.*95(M.37.169A).

***ἐκλυτέον**, *one must relax*, Clem.*paed*.3.9(p.263.17; M.8.617B).

ἐκλυτρόομαι, *be redeemed*, Cyr.*Nest*.5.2(p.96.42; 6^{1}.128C); id.*ador*. 1(1.41D); id.*Abac*.1(3.518D).

ἐκλύτρωσις, ἡ, *redemption*, *cat.Mt*.27:27(p.234.26).

ἐκλύτως, *unrestrainedly* οὐκ ἀφίησιν [sc. Χριστός] αὐτὴν [sc. τὴν σάρκα] τοῦτο παθεῖν ἐ. Cyr.*Jo*.7(4.685C).

ἐκμαγεῖον, τό, **1.** *eraser, obliterator*; met., of almsgiving ἐ....τῶν ...κακῶν Chrys.*hom.14.2 in 1Tim*.(11.627F); **2.** *impress*, met.; **a.** of Christ ὁ λόγος...τὸ ἐ. τοῦ ἀρχετύπου...κάλλους Gr.Naz.*or*.38.13(M.36. 325B); **b.** of soul τοῦ ἀληθινοῦ φωτὸς ἐ. Gr.Nyss.*hom.2 in Cant*.(M.44. 805D); Nil.*Magn*.44(M.79.1024B); Cyr.*glaph.Gen*.1(1.5E); **c.** of OT types Χριστοῦ...ἐ. ὁ ἱερεύς id.*ador*.13(1.475C); of tabernacle ἐ. τοῦ παντὸς κόσμου Cosm.Ind.*top*.arg.(M.88.56C).

***ἐκμαγεύς, ὁ**, *one who wipes*, in enumeration of servants waiting at meals ῥαντῆρες, ἐ. κύκλων Gr.Naz.*carm*.1.2.8.145(M.37.659A).

ἐκμαγεύω, *bewitch*, ‡Felix III Papa *ep.Petr*.2(p.13.16; H.2.824E).

ἐκμάθησις, ἡ, **1.** *study*, Gr.Thaum.*pan.Or*.6(p.15.23; M.10.1069B); Nil.*epp*.3.43(M.79.413A); Proc.G.*Is*.2:1–11(M.87.1893C); **2.** *teaching*, ref. scriptures τὰς ἐ. καὶ ἐπαγγελίας αὐτῶν Eus.*Is*.3:1–2(M.24.108C); id.*h.e*.6.2.8(M.20.524C).

***ἐκματαιάζω**, *labour in vain*, Gr.Nyss.*hom.1 in Eccl*.(M.44. 628D).

ἐκμεθύσκω, **1.** *give to drink*, Cyr.*inc.unigen*.(5^{1}.711E); **2.** *intoxicate*; met., id.*ador*.1(1.19D).

***ἐκμει-όω**, *destroy* χάριν φωτοφόρον σκότος ~οῦσαν ‡Sophr.H. *triod*.(M.87.3872C).

***ἐκμελέομαι**, *placate*, Chrys.*prod.Jud*.3(2.722A; conj. ἐκμειλίξασθαι M.50.717).

ἐκμελής, *inharmonious*; hence met., *unrestrained*, Clem.*paed*. 2.5(p.186.2; M.8.448C); id.*str*.5.4(p.338.25; M.9.37B); Eun.ap.Gr. Nyss.*Eun*.1(1 p.50.27; M.45.280A); ἐ. ... νοῦς Cyr.*Zach*.71(3.750C); of impious words, Gr.Nyss.*Eun*.1(1 p.38.6, v.l. ἐμμ- M.45.265B).

ἐκμελῶς, **1.** *inharmoniously*; met., Clem.*paed*.2.4(p.185.27; M.8. 448B); hence **2.** *unseasonably*; met., Olymp.*Job* 22 proem.(M.93. 237A); **3.** *carelessly*, Men.*exc.Rom*.20(p.220.16; M.113.925B).

***ἐκμεστόομαι**, *be filled up*, met. ζωῆν...εὐωδίας δὲ τῆς νοητῆς ἐκμεμεστωμένην Cyr.*ador*.16(1.566A); *ib*.17(614D); id.*Juln*.4(6^{2}. 145E).

***ἐκμηκάω**, *bellow, shout*, Nil.*epp*.3.43(M.79.412D).

ἐκμηχανάομαι, *devise, contrive*, Cyr.*Ps*.37:13(M.69.964C); id.*Jo*. 10.2(4.907D).

ἐκμισθόομαι, *hire, engage* services of, ‡Bas.*Lac*.5(2.591B; M.31. 1448A); Gr.Nyss.*Eun*.1(1 p.34.25; M.45.261C).

ἐκμολύνω, *defile*, Bas.*hom.in Ps*.7(1.100C; M.29.236A).

ἐκμοχλεύω, *overthrow*; met., Cyr.*ador*.14(1.490A); id.*hom.pasch*. 10(5.140D); of Christ ἐξεμόχλευε...τὰ τοῦ ᾅδου θεμέλια Bas.Sel.*or*.26.2 (M.85.308A).

***ἐκμυέω**, *exclude, reject*, †Gregent.*disp*.(M.86.673B).

[*]**ἐκμυζαίνω**, *squeeze out*; met., ‡Caes.Naz.*dial*.146(M.38.1128).

ἐκμύζ-ω, **1.** *squeeze*, *T.Dan* 1.8; med., *press upon*, *A.Xanthipp*.8 (p.63.3); **2.** *squeeze out* from ἰὸν...τῆς φύσεως ἡμῶν ~εσθαι ‡Caes. Naz.*dial*.146(M.38.888).

ἐκμυκτηρίζω, *mock*, *T.Jos*.2.3; *Protev*.3(p.7); Nil.*epp*.2.151(M.79. 272B).

ἐκμυκτηρισμός, ὁ, *mockery*, Max.*qu.Thal*.proem.(M.90.256C).

***ἐκμύξησις, ἡ**, *drawing out, extraction* ἐ. μυελῶν Const.Diac.*laud*. 32(M.88.516A).

ἐκμυσάττομαι, *loathe, abominate*, Cyr.*Jo*.3.4(4.271A); *ib*.5.5(553A).

***ἐκνεανιεύομαι**, *act pretentiously, give oneself airs*, Cyr.*Jo*.1.4 (4.37D).

***ἐκνεκρόω**, *mortify, annihilate*, Amph.*hom*.1.5(M.39.44B); Cyr. *hom.pasch*.14(5^{2}.187E); δαιμόνων...ἐκνενέκρωται...ἐνέργεια Sophr.H. *or*.4(M.87.3304D).

ἐκνέμω, *assign*, Cyr.*ador*.13(1.453B); of Church as people assigned to Christ, id.*Is*.2.2(2.236D).

ἐκνευρίζ-ω, *unnerve*; met., *weaken, deprive of strength* τὸ... μυστήριον τῆς Χριστοῦ γενέσεως ἐκνευρίσαντας [sc. Arians] Alex.Al. *ep.Alex*.14(p.29.12; M.18.569C); αἱ τῶν ἀτόπων ἐπιθυμίαι τὸν τόνον τῆς ψυχῆς ~ουσιν Gr.Nyss.*or.dom*.3(p.50.18; M.44.1152B); ὃν [sc. Devil] ὁ Χριστὸς ἐξενεύρισε Proc.G.*Jud*.1:2(M.87.1045A); τὸν ἐχθρὸν ἐξηνεύρισας [sc. S. George] νεῦρον Jo.Mon.*hymn.Geo*.8(M.96.1400A); pass., of human nature at Fall, Gr.Nyss.*or.dom*.4(p.72.12; M.44. 1164C); of soul, Nil.*epp*.2.167(M.79.281A).

ἐκνευρόω, = foreg., met. ἐξενεύρωσεν ὑμᾶς [sc. devils] ὁ κύριος Ath.*v.Anton*.9(M.26.857B); *V.Pach.A* 26(p.153.16).

ἐκνεύ-ω, *turn the head aside*; hence intrans. **1.** *turn aside*, Just. *dial*.9.3(M.6.496A); Pall.*h.Laus*.35(p.106.4; M.34.1131A); **2.** *turn, incline* to, met. ὁ ~ων πρὸς σωφροσύνην Meth.*res*.1.60(p.324.16; M.41.1157B); Cyr.*Ps*.31:1(M.69.865C); Bas.Sel.*or*.5.1(M.85.76C); **3.** trans., *project*, Cyr.*ador*.9(1.310C).

ἐκνήφω, *become sober*; met., *mend one's ways*, Bas.*reg.fus*.proem. 1(2.328A; M.31.892B); Cyr.*Ps*.3:8(M.69.729C); Thphn.*chron*.p.301 (M.108.736A).

***ἐκνίκημα, τό**, *reward of victory, prize*; met., in address to catechumens, ref. theol. controversies ἐμὸς ὁ πόλεμος, ἔστω σὸν τὸ ἐ. Gr.Naz.*or*.40.43(M.36.420C).

ἐκνίκησις, ἡ, *complete victory* τὸ δέ, εἰς νῖκος, τὸ εἰς ἐ. Cyr.*Soph*.33 (3.610C; ἐκδίκησιν Aubert).

ἔκνοος, *not perceiving, not admitting to the mind* στηλώθην, βροτέης ἔκνοος εὐπαθίης Gr.Naz.*carm*.2.1.34.170(M.37.1319A).

ἐκνοτίζω, *make to drip*, Geo.Pis.*hex*.252(M.92.1453A).

***ἐκνυμφεύω**, *deflower*; met., *Hom.Clem*.5.14.

ἐκουσιάζ-ομαι, *offer willingly, spontaneously* ~όμενον δὲ λέγει τῷ κυρίῳ, τὸν οὐχ ὑπὲρ ἁμαρτημάτων προσφέροντα, δῶρα δὲ προσκομίζοντα τῷ θεῷ Proc.G.*2Par*.17:6(M.87.1213A); id.*Cant*.7:1(M.87. 1728B).

ἐκουσιασμός, ὁ, **1.** *voluntary offering*, ref. unworthy widows οὔτε γὰρ οἱ ἱερεῖς τοιαύτης ἐ. δέξονταί ποτε οἷον ἅρπαγος ἢ πόρνης *Const. App*.3.8.2; **2.** *free will*, of divine good pleasure τὰ δὲ καθ' ἐκουσιασμὸν γενόμενα Eus.Nic.*ep.Paulin*.(p.17.6; M.82.916B).

***ἐκουσιαστί**, *voluntarily*, Afric.*chron*.5(M.10.81A).

***ἐκουσιογνώμων**, *having a willing mind*, neut. as subst. εἰς... ἁπλότητα...καὶ ἐ. ... ἐληλακότας Jo.Clim.*scal*.4(M.88.688B).

ἐκούσιος, *voluntary*, ref. God οὔτε γὰρ ὁ θεὸς ἄκων ἀγαθὸς... (ἐκούσιος δὲ ἡ τῶν ἀγαθῶν μετάδοσις αὐτῷ) Clem.*str*.7.7(p.32.1; M.9. 457C); ref. Christ τῷ ἐ. πάθει ‡Ath.*dial.Trin*.4.5(M.28.1257B); τὸν ἐ. ...θάνατον *Lit.Jac*.(p.200.26); of free will in men ἐ. προαιρέσει σωζόμενοι Clem.*paed*.1.6(p.110.4; M.8.289B); of offerings, *Const. App*.2.25.2; *ib*.3.4.2; neut. as subst. ἀρετῆς μὲν ἐὰν ἀνέλῃς τὸ ἐ., ἀνεῖλες αὐτῆς καὶ τὴν οὐσίαν Or.*Cels*.4.3(p.276.18; M.11.1033A); τῷ ἐ. τῆς ἁμαρτίας id.*or*.25.1(p.357.20; M.11.497A).

ἐκουσιότης, ἡ, *willingness* Ἰωναδὰβ γὰρ ἑρμηνεύεται θεοῦ ἐ. Hesych.H.*Ps.tit*.70(M.27.931C); *voluntary choice*, ref. counsels of perfection Χριστὸς...οὐδ' ἐξ ἐπιταγῆς τινα παρθενεύειν βούλεται, ἀλλ' ἐξ ἐ. Mac.Mgn.*apocr*.3.43(p.149.30); ‡Caes.Naz.*dial*.132(M.38. 1036).

ἐκουσίως, *voluntarily* ὁ σωζόμενος...ἐ. ... σπεύσει πρὸς σωτηρίαν Clem.*str*.7.7(p.32.4; M.9.460A); Or.*hom.19.2 in Jer*.(p.178.15; M.13. 501D); ref. Christ's death, Meth.*symp*.3.8(p.35.13; M.18.73A); Didym.*Trin*.3.10(M.39.856A); Anast.S.*hod*.23(M.89.304A) cit. s. γνωμικῶς.

***ἐκπαθαίνομαι**, *indulge one's passions*, Clem.*prot*.4(p.47.16; M. 8.160C); id.*paed*.2.10(p.218.11; M.8.517C).

ἐκπαλαί-ω, *carry through a struggle* πλέξαντα τοῖς ~ουσι στεφάνους Isid.Pel.*epp*.1.302(M.78.357C).

***ἐκπαρέχω**, *surrender, give up*, Mac.Aeg.*elev*.3(M.34.892C).

***ἐκπασσαλεύω**, *unfasten*, ‡Gr.Naz.*Chr.pat*.1264(M.38.237A).

ἐκπατέω, **1.** *tread*, Eus.*Is*.1:24ff.(M.24.100B); **2.** met., *tread under foot, despise*, *A.Andr.fr*.7(p.41.13).

***ἔκπεινος**, *very hungry*; met., Mac.Aeg.*hom*.10.4(M.34.544A); ψυχαί...ἔ. οὖσαι περὶ τὴν δικαιοσύνην id.*carit*.25(M.34.928C).

ἐκπειράζω, *tempt*, Herm.*mand*.4.3.6 al.; Clem.*str*.2.12(p.143.27; M.8.996A); *ib*.3.16(p.242.31; 1204A); *A.Andr.et Mt*.12(p.78.2).

ἐκπέμπ-ω, **1.** *send forth*, of Christ ἀπὸ τοῦ θεοῦ ἐξεπέμφθη *1Clem*. 42.1; τὸ πνεῦμα...ἐξ αὐτῆς [sc. divine essence] φυσικῶς ~όμενον Cyr. *thes*.34(5^{1}.342E); hence **2.** *exclude*; met., of possibilities in argument, Cyr.*thes*.32(5^{1}.301C); id.*Ps*.34:1(M.69.893C).

ἔκπεμψις, ἡ, **1.** *sending forth, procession*, theol. υἱοῦ δέ, ἡ γέννησις· πνεύματος δέ, ἡ ἔ. Gr.Naz.*or*.25.16(M.35.1221B); **2.** *offering*, in pagan ritual οἱ τὴν ἔ. τῶν ἄρτων βαστάζοντες Clem.*str*.6.4(p.449. 22; M.9.256A).

ἐκπερίειμι, *go out and around*; met., of circumventing, Gr. Thaum.*pan.Or*.6(p.16.20; M.10.1072A); of investigating, *ib*.15(p.34. 27; 1096A); Eus.*d.e*.8.5(p.401.28; M.22.648D).

ἐκπεριέρχομαι, **1.** *go out and around*, met. ἐ. ἡ πρόνοια τοῦ θεοῦ Or.*enarr.in Job* 22:14(M.17.84D); **2.** *surround*; met., of fostering pupils' abilities, Gr.Thaum.*pan.Or*.7(p.18.26; M.10.1073B).

***ἐκπεριέχομαι**, *surround completely*, Gr.Nyss.*hex*.14(M.44.77A).

***ἐκπεριζώννυμαι**, *gird*, met. ταύτην [sc. ἱερωσύνην] καὶ ὁ Ἀβραὰμ ἐκπεριζωσάμενος Ephr.3.5D.

***ἐκπεριθέω**, *travel about, traverse, go round*, Cyr.*Abac*.50(3.564A); id.*hom.pasch*.14(5^{2}.187C).

***ἐκπερίιξις, ἡ,** *travelling about,* Synes.*regn.*27(p.57.21; M.66.1104C).

***ἐκπεριλαμβάνω, 1.** *embrace, encompass,* Bas.*hex.*4.4(1.36C; M.29.85C); **2.** *comprise, include,* Or.*Cels.*4.62(p.333.27; M.11.1129B); πάντα...προγνώσει ἐ. ὁ θεός *ib.*6.45(p.116.16; 1368D); Gr.Nyss.*anim. et res.*(M.46.60B, v.l. ἐμπ.).

***ἐκπερινοστέω,** *go round, traverse,* Just.*1apol.*54.9(M.6.412A); of apostles, Eus.*fr.Lc.*9:3(M.24.544D); Synes.*ep.*101(M.66.1472B); met. Ἡρακλῆς...ἐστι νοῦς, ὃς...ἐ. τὸν κόσμον *Hom.Clem.*6.16.

ἐκπερονάω, *pierce,* met. Χριστὲ...σῶμ' ἐμὸν ἐκπερόνησον Eudoc.*Cypr.*1.176(M.85.840A).

ἐκπετάννυμι, *stretch out*; of Moses stretching out his hands in prayer; as type of Cross, Just.*dial.*90.4(M.6.692A) v. σταυρός; of God, ref. Rom.10:21 τὸ...ἐκπετάσαι τὰς χεῖρας, τὸ καλέσαι... δηλοῖ Chrys.*hom.18.3 in Rom.*(9.633D).

ἐκπέτασις, ἡ, *rift,* eschatol. σημεῖον ἐκπετάσεως ἐν οὐρανῷ *Did.* 16.6.

ἐκπιεσμός, ὁ, *squeezing out*; met., *oppression* πενήτων ἐ. Isid.Pel. *epp.*1.37(M.78.205A).

ἐκπίπτ-ω, A. *fall* from; **1.** of original Fall; **a.** of angels ἐκπεσόντες τῶν οὐρανῶν, περὶ τὸν ἀέρα ἔχοντες καὶ τὴν γῆν Athenag.*leg.*25.1(M.6.948C); τῶν...λογικῶν τὰ ἁμαρτήσαντα καὶ διὰ τοῦτο ἐκπεσόντα τῆς ἐν ᾗ ἦσαν καταστάσεως Or.*princ.*2.8.3(p.160.19); who did not all fall to same extent, *ib.*1.6.2(p.81.6; M.11.167A); of the Devil, Ath.*inc.* 25.5(M.25.140B); **b.** of men ὁ ἄνθρωπος ἐξέπεσεν ἐκ τελείου ἐπὶ τὸ ἀτελές Or.*Jo.*13.37(p.262.31; M.14.464C); Eus.*p.e.*7.8(307D; M.21.521B); Nemes.*nat.hom.*1(M.40.516B); abs. πρὸ τοῦ ἐκπεσεῖν Meth. *res.*1.49(p.303.8; M.18.280A); *ib.*1.38(p.283.7; M.41.1108A); id.*symp.* 11(p.136.17; M.18.213A); **c.** Gnost., acc. Heracleon, of Samaritans as fallen spirits, Or.*Jo.*13.25(p.249.7; M.14.441A); (Valent.) of Sophia when dazzled by brightness of First God, Didym.*Trin.*3.42 (M.39.992C); **2.** *lapse*; **a.** intellectually; from orthodoxy, Or. *fr.1 in Jo.*(p.483.12); Eus.*e.th.*1.7(p.65.28; M.24.836C); Chrys.*hom. 24.2 in Jo.*(8.140D); into ἐπὶ Ἰουδαϊσμόν Eus.*d.e.*1.2(p.9.2; M.22.25B); εἰς αἵρεσιν Ath.*Ar.*1.54(M.26.125A); *fall into (the error of) imagining, make the mistake of thinking of* φῶς...ἀκούων οὐκ ἐ. ἐπὶ τὸ σωματικὸν φῶς Eus.*e.th.*2.11(p.112.15; M.24.924A); **b.** morally; of those who deny the faith in persecution τοῖς ἐκπεπτωκόσι Petr. I Al.*ep.can.*8(M.18.480D); *ib.*10(488B); ἐ. τις ἀπὸ τοῦ πνεύματος διά τινα κακίαν Ath.*Ar.*3.25(M.26.376C); esp. of virgins and widows, Bas.*ep.*199 *can.*18(3.291B; M.32.717A); Chrys.*hom.13.2 in 1Tim.*(11.619C); *ib.15.1*(635A); **3.** *be drawn out* εἰς...ἄμετρον μῆκος ἐξέπεσεν ἡ γραφή Eus.*Marcell.*1.1(p.2.9; M.24.713A); **4.** *fail* ∼ει τοῦ Ὠριγένους ἡ ἀλληγορία Epiph.*anc.*62(p.75.15; M.43.129A); μὴ εἴπωσι...ὅτι ἐξέπεσεν ἡ ἐπαγγελία τοῦ θεοῦ Chrys.*hom.16.2 in Rom.*(9.605D); **5.** of persons, *run out* of πάντων [sc. arguments] ∼οντες Ath.*Ar.*1.31(M.26.76B); **6.** ἐς τὸ φανερὸν ἐ. *be made known publicly, become public knowledge,* Men.*exc.gent.*30(p.472.5; M.113.840D).

B. *be excluded* from, ref. excommunication εἰς τὸν ἀφ' οὗ ἐξέπεσον τόπον ἀναλαμβάνονται Bas.*ep.*188.3(3.271C; M.32.672B); of Christ acc. Marcellus ἐκπεσεῖσθαι τῆς βασιλείας Eus.*Marcell.*2.1 (p.33.29; M.24.780C); ref. deposition, Constantius Imp.ap.Ath.*apol. Const.*31(M.25.636C); CChalc.*can.*2.

ἐκπλατύν-ω, *widen out, broaden*; hence met.; **1.** *open* μὴ τοῖς ἑτεροδιδασκαλοῦσιν ὁ κατὰ τῶν ἁπλουστέρων ∼ηται δρόμος Cyr.*Jo.*1 proem.(4.8E); **2.** *explain, ib.*1.7(58B); **3.** *spread, amplify* ∼εσθαι τοῦ σωτῆρος τὴν δόξαν *ib.*10(830A); **4.** reflex., *magnify oneself*; of Pharisees, *ib.*6.1(621B).

ἐκπλέκω, *disentangle,* Herm.*sim.*6.2.6.

***ἐκπλεονεκτ-έω,** *remove greed,* i.e. *satisfy* παραπέφυκε...τοῖς τὴν... ἀλαζονείαν ἠρρωστηκόσι τὸ πλεονεκτεῖν ἐθέλειν· οὓς οὐ δύναται τὸ τυχὸν...∼εῖν Or.*adnot.in Dt.*14:19(M.17.25C).

ἐκπλέω, *disembark,* Marc.Diac.*v.Porph.*61.

***ἔκπληγμα, τό,** *terrifying object, terror* ὁ σταυρός, τρόπαιον κατὰ τῆς ἀδικίας καὶ ἔ. Meth.*Porph.*1(p.504.12; M.18.400B).

ἔκπληκτος, 1. *astonishing,* of the empty tomb ἔ. ... πρᾶγμα Chrys.*hom.89.2 in Mt.*(7.834D); of Inc. ἔ. μυστήριον Epiph.*haer.*79.3(p.477.33; M.42.744B); Gr.Mag.*dial.*(tr.Zach.)3.5(M.*PL.*77.227B); **2.** *astonished, A.Thom.*A 40(p.157.20); **3.** *mad* βουλὴ...ἔ. Herm.*vis.* 1.2.4; οἱ ἔ. Vict.*Mc.*3:24f.(p.309.17).

ἐκπλήκτως, 1. *in an astonishing way,* Trin. ὁ γεννηθεὶς...ἐκ τοῦ ἐ. γεννήσαντος Epiph.*haer.*76.28(p.377.20; M.42.573C); **2.** *in astonishment,* Melet.*nat.hom.*30(M.64.1284C).

ἐκπληξία, ἡ, *unconsciousness, stupor*; of disciples, acc. pagan opinion, Eus.*d.e.*3.5(p.121.29; M.22.208B); contrasted with ἔκπληξις, Geo.Pis.*Pers.*2.313(M.92.1231A).

ἔκπληξις, ἡ, 1. *terror,* ref. Valent. theory of Creation ἐκ τῆς ἐ. ... τὰ στοιχεῖα Clem.*exc.Thdot.*48(p.122.16, v.l. πλήξεως M.9.681C); **2.** *amazement, admiration, A.Paul.et Thecl.*10(p.242.10); ref. wonders of creation ἐπέκεινα...ἐ. Eus.*l.C.*11(p.228.13; M.20.1384A); ref. divine action οὐ κενὴν ἔ. ... κινεῖ Cyr.*Lc.*5:5(M.72.836A); ref. unity of Trin. πάσης γέμον...ἐ. Sophr.H.*ep.syn.*(M.87.3156B); **3.** *trance,* exeg. Ac.10:10 δηλοῖ...τὴν ἐπὶ θαυμασμῷ ἔ. Didym.*Ac.*10:10(M.39.1677A).

***ἐκπληροφορέομαι,** *be fully intent on, persevere in,* Mac.Aeg.*or.*4 (M.34.856B).

ἐκπληρόω, *fulfil*; hence **1.** *accomplish,* Thdt.*Rom.*4:1(3.46); *ib.*8:3 (81); Thphn.*chron.*p.388(M.108.925C); **2.** *celebrate* festival, *ib.*p.234 (590C); **3.** *satisfy,* Clem.*prot.*2(p.24.6; M.8.408A); **4.** *grant* prayer, Or.*or.*11.4(p.323.26; M.11.452A).

ἐκπλήρωσις, ἡ, 1. *fulfilment*; of prophecies, Eus.*d.e.*1.3(p.18.18; M.22.40D); ‡Just.*qu.et resp.*58(M.6.1300C); Pall.*v.Chrys.*12(p.78.24; M.47.44); **2.** *accomplishment,* Bas.*Eun.*2.12(1.247B; M.29.593B); Gr.Nyss.*or.catech.*33(p.125.15; M.45.84D); ref. Father τὴν...διὰ τῶν ἔργων ἐ., διὰ τοῦ Χριστοῦ Chrys.*hom.1.4 in Eph.*(11.8A); **3.** *satisfaction* τὴν τῆς ὀργῆς ἐ. Philost.*h.e.*4.12(M.65.525C); *cat.Mt.*18:22 (p.149.28).

ἐκπληρωτής, ὁ, *one who carries out, fulfils* ὁ τῶν θείων θελημάτων ἐ. Cyr.*Am.*61(3.318A; om. Aubert); Leont.N.*v.Jo.Eleem.*46(p.102.17).

***ἐκπλουτέω,** *be very rich in, abound in*; spiritually, Cyr.*ador.*9 (1.294A); id.*Os.*9(3.30C, conj. πεπλουτηκότες).

ἐκπλύν-ω, 1. *wash away*; met., ref. *forgiveness of sins* τὴν ∼ουσαν δύναμιν [i.e. of Inc.] Gr.Nyss.*or.catech.*27(p.102.4; M.45.69D); of Jo. Bapt., Bas.Sel.*or.*18.1(M.85.228A); **2.** *wash, wash clean,* met. ἑτέρους τῶν μιασμάτων ∼οντα [sc. τὸν ἐπίσκοπον] Synes.*ep.*105(M.66.1484D).

ἔκπλυσις, ἡ, *washing away, ablution*; of OT ablutions foreshadowing Christian dispensation, Cyr.*ador.*11(1.395C); *ib.*15 (548B); id.*Ps.*50:8(M.69.1096A); met. κάθαρσίς ἐστιν ἔ. μολυσμάτων Gr.Naz.*carm.*1.2.34.173(M.37.958).

ἔκπνευσις, ἡ, *expiring, breathing one's last,* of Christ τὴν ἔ. οὐκ ἄν τις εἴποι θεότητος μετάστασιν, ἀλλὰ ψυχῆς ἀποχώρησιν ‡Ath.*Apoll.*1. 18(M.26.1125B); Anast.S.*qu.et resp.*152(M.89.808C).

***ἔκπνοια, ἡ,** *breathing out,* Max.*schol.c.h.*2.3(M.4.41A).

***ἐκπόθητος,** *much desired,* Thdot.Anc.*hom.BMV et Sym.*3(M.77.1393B).

ἐκποιέω, med.; **1.** *exclude*; met., Gr.Thaum.*pan.Or.*13(p.29.7; M.10.1088A); **2.** *alienate* church lands, alienation of which is invalid, CNic.(787)*can.*12.

***ἐκποιητέον,** *one must allow, accept,* Proc.G.*Dt.*24:6(M.87.937A).

ἐκποικίλλω, *adorn,* met. pass., Cyr.*ador.*1(1.4A).

ἐκπολεμέω, *defeat,* Gr.Thaum.*pan.Or.*16(p.38.10; M.10.1100C).

ἐκπολεμόομαι, *defeat* ἐξεπολεμώθησαν Οὐνιγούροις Men.*exc.gent.* 2(p.443.8; ἐξεπολεμήθησαν M.113.793C).

ἔκπομα, τό, 1. *potion* ἔοικεν γὰρ ὁ πονηρὸς τοῖς τὰ θανάσιμα φάρμακα διδοῦσιν γλυκέσιν ἐκπόμασιν ‡Ath.*diab.*2(p.5.27); **2.** = ἔκπωμα, *drinking cup,* Thdr.Stud.*antirr.*2.29(M.99.373B).

ἐκπομπεύ-ω, 1. *lead about,* Chrys.*hom.12.6 in 1Cor.*(10.105C, 106C); **2.** *reveal, expose*; lit., Socr.*h.e.*3.2.6(M.67.381B); Soz.*h.e.*7.15.2 (M.67.1453A); met., of indiscriminate publication of Christian doctrine, Chrys.*hom.7.1 in 1Cor.*(10.51A); id.*hom.70.2 in Mt.*(7.689E); Bas.Sel.*or.*16.1(M.85.205B); θεῖα μυστήρια...πᾶσιν ἔθνεσιν ∼όμενα [i.e. through Passion] Areth.*Apoc.*45(M.106.701A); **3.** *publicly hold up to blame,* Chrys.*hom.11.3 in 1Cor.*(10.91B); id.*hom. 31.3 in Heb.*(12.289D); Isid.Pel.*epp.*2.297(M.78.724D); **4.** *indulge in display,* Chrys.*hom.71.4 in Mt.*(7.699D); ref. use of rhetoric, Bas. Sel.*or.*34.1(M.85.369B).

ἐκπομπή, ἡ, *sending forth,* ref. Creation ἐκπομπῇ...πνεύματος τὰ γενόμενα γίγνεται Didym.(‡Bas.)*Eun.*5(1.307B; M.29.737A); in gen., Andr.Caes.*Apoc.*59(M.106.408B); *emission* of light, Areth.*Apoc.*10 (M.106.568D); met., *announcement* μυστηρίου ἐ. id.ap.*cat.Apoc.*17:7 (p.429.26).

***ἐκπονεστέρως,** *with toil, diligently,* Mac.Aeg.*hom.*29.3(M.34.717B).

***ἐκπονηρεύω,** *corrupt,* Synes.*ep.*114(M.66.1496B).

***ἐκπόρευμα, τό,** *that which proceeds,* †Ath.*exp.fid.*4(M.25.208A) cit. s. ἀεί; πνεῦμα, ἐνυπόστατον ἐ. Jo.D.*trisag.*28(M.95.60D).

***ἐκπορεύσιμος,** *proceeding*; of H. Ghost, Gr.Naz.*carm.*1.2.10.989 (M.37.751A).

***ἐκπόρευσις, ἡ,** *going forth, procession*; **1.** lit., of evacuation τῶν βρωμάτων...ἡ. ἐ. Cyr.ap.†Leont.B.*sect.*10(M.86.1260D); **2.** of procession of H. Ghost from divine substance of Father ἀπὸ τοῦ ἑνὸς πατρὸς καθ' ἕνωσιν τῆς ἑαυτοῦ θεότητός ἐστι...ἐ. Didym.*Trin.*2.2(M.39.460B); *ib.*3.38(976B); οὐδὲ ἐν ἴσῳ τῷ ἁγίῳ πνεύματι τὴν ἐκ τῆς οὐσίας πρόοδον, ἤγουν ἐ. ... δημιουργικῶς δὲ μᾶλλον Cyr.*Is.*5.3(2.809E); as distinctive property of H. Ghost ἀγεννησίαν τοῦ πατρός...γέννησιν τοῦ υἱοῦ...καὶ τὴν ἐ. τοῦ πνεύματος Gr.Naz.*or.*31.8(p.155.3; M.36.141B); διαφορὰ τῆς γεννήσεως καὶ τῆς ἐ. ‡Ath.*dial.Trin.*3.4(M.28.1209A); Didym.*Trin.*2.1(M.39.448C); ἀγεννησία, καὶ ἡ γέννησις καὶ ἡ ἐ., ἅπερ καὶ ἰδιότητας ὀνομάζουσι Max.*opusc.*(M.91.249B); *ib.*(136A) cit. s. πνεῦμα; ‡Caes.Naz.*dial.*3(M.38.861A); Jo.D.*f.o.*1.2(M.94.794C); its mode incomprehensible, *ib.*1.8(820A); Jo.V H.*icon.*4(M.96.1353A); typified ὁ τύπος τῆς ἐ. τοῦ...πνεύματος θεωρεῖται εἰς τὴν ἐκπορευτὴν Εὔαν ‡Ath.*qu.al.*15(M.28.785D).

***ἐκπορευτής, ὁ,** *one who causes procession* πατὴρ...ἐ. πνεύματος Leont.H.*Nest.*1.20(M.86.1485B).

***ἐκπορευτικός, 1.** *causing procession,* of Father ἐ. τοῦ πνεύματος Leont.H.*Nest.*1.29(M.86.1496A); **2.** *sent out, proceeding*; **a.** in gen. ἡ ἐκ τόπου εἰς τόπον ἐ. μετάστασις Anast.S.*hod.*20(M.89.272B); **b.** of H. Ghost πνευματικῶς ἐ. καὶ οὐ δημιουργικῶς Didym.*Trin.*2.2(M.39.464C); ἡ ἐ. ὑπόστασις ‡Gr.Nyss.*hom.5 in Jo.*(p.183.31); cf.*ib.*9(p.289.8); Anast.S.*hod.*17(264C).

***ἐκπορευτικῶς,** *by proceeding* ὁ Ἀδὰμ...προβάλλων ἐκ τῆς ἑαυτοῦ οὐσίας ἐ. μὲν τὴν Εὔαν...καὶ γεννητικῶς τὸν...Σὴθ Cosm.Ind.*top.*5(M.88.309C); of H. Ghost, opp. γεννητικῶς, Didym.*Trin.*1.35(M.39.437C); ‡Ath.*dial.Trin.*1.6(M.28.1125A) cit. s. δημιουργικῶς; Leont.H.*Nest.*2.4(M.86.1537C) cit. s. γεγεννημένως; Zach.Mit.*opif.*(M.85.1116D).

***ἐκπορευτός,** *proceeding*; of H. Ghost, as his distinguishing characteristic τὸ...ἀγέννητον, καὶ τὸ γεννητόν, καὶ τὸ ἐ. Gr.Naz.*or.*42.17(M.36.477C); Leont.H.*Nest.*2.17(M.86.1576B); ἐκ πατρὸς...πνεῦμα ἅγιον οὐ γεννητόν, ἀλλ' ἐ. Jo.D.*haer.*102(M.94.780A); term denotes Person, not divine nature, Thdt.*rect.conf.*3(M.6.1212A); εἰ...τὸ πνεῦμα...καθ' ὃ ἐ., φύσις ἐστί, καὶ οὐ καθ' ὃ θεός, οὐδ' ἔσται φύσει θεός Eulog.*fr.dogm.*(M.86.2945D); Thdr.Stud.*antirr.*3.7(M.99.432A); typology ἡ Εὔα ἐ. ἐκ τῆς πλευρᾶς τοῦ Ἀδὰμ εἰς τύπον τοῦ...πνεύματος ‡Ath.*qu.al.*15(M.28.785C); cf.Meth.*fr.*3(p.521.8); τὸ ἐ. ἐξώρισαν [sc. Arians] τῆς θεότητος Gr.Naz.*or.*21.13(M.35.1096B).

***ἐκπορευτῶς,** *by procession* οὔτε...ὁ θεὸς γεγέννηκε υἱὸν ἐ. Hier.H.*Trin.*(M.40.853A); of H. Ghost πνεῦμα...προϊὸν...ἐκ τοῦ πατρός, οὐχ υἱϊκῶς δέ,...ἀλλ' ἐ. Gr.Naz.*or.*39.12(M.36.348B); Thdt.*rect.conf.*9(M.6.1224A); Thal.*cent.*4.94(M.91.1468D); Jo.D.*hom.*4.4(M.96.605A).

ἐκπορεύ-ω, I. *send out*;

A. in gen.; of export of merchandise, Thphn.*chron.*p.121(M.108.340B).

B. Trin. ὁ πατὴρ...~ει καὶ οὐκ ~εται ‡Ath.*qu.al.*11(M.28.784C); μηδὲ ἀφ' ἑαυτοῦ [sc. the Word] ~ειν πνεῦμα πρώτως, μηδὲ ~εσθαι κατὰ τὸ ἅγιον πνεῦμα Leont.H.*Nest.*2.24(M.86.1585C).

II. med. and pass., *proceed*;

A. of Son before Inc. (cf. Mich.1:2–4) τὸν κύριον τὸν μηδέπω ~όμενον ἐκ τοῦ τόπου ἑαυτοῦ Or.*Jo.*20.18(16; p.350.26; M.14.613B); ἐκ τοῦ πατρὸς ~εται Marcell.*fr.*60 ap.Eus.*e.th.*3.4(p.158.10; M.24.1004B); εἰ...οὐκ ἐκ τοῦ πατρὸς ~εται τουτέστιν, ἐκ τῆς οὐσίας αὐτοῦ, ὁ υἱός..., πῶς οὐκ ἐν ἀμείνοσι νοοῖτ' ἂν τὸ πνεῦμα παρὰ τὸν υἱόν; Cyr.*Jo.*10.2(4.911D).

B. of H. Ghost; **1.** as proceeding from Father; **a.** in gen. τὸ μόνον ἐκ τῆς ὑποστάσεως αὐτοῦ ἀνάρχως...ἐκπορευθέν Didym.*Trin.*2.1(M.39.448A); τῆς...τοῦ πατρὸς αἰτίας ἐξημμένον ἔχει τὸ εἶναι, ὅθεν καὶ ~εται Gr.Nyss.*diff.ess.*4(M.32.329C); **b.** ἐκ τοῦ πατρός: Bas.*ep.*125(3.216E; M.32.549C); *Symb.*ap.Epiph.*anc.*118(p.147.12; M.43.232D); *Symb.Nic.–CP*(*ACO* 2.1.2 p.80.13; H.2.288B); ἐξ αὐτοῦ...τοῦ πατρὸς...τὸ πνεῦμα ~εται ἐνυπόστατον ὄν Epiph.*haer.*57.4(p.349.17; M.41.1001B); **c.** παρὰ τοῦ πατρός: Bas.*Eun.*2.34(1.271B; M.29.652C); ‡Chrys.*Mt.20:1*(8.104C); ἐκ τοῦ θεοῦ καὶ παρὰ τοῦ πατρὸς ~εται Gr.Nyss.*or.dom.*3(p.64.1); **2.** relation of his procession to Son; **a.** proceeds from Father and is of Son ὁ παρὰ τοῦ πατρὸς ~εται, καὶ τοῦ υἱοῦ ἴδιον ὄν Ath.*ep.Serap.*1.2(M.26.533B); cf. ἐκ πατρὸς λέγεται ~εσθαι, ἐπειδὴ παρὰ τοῦ λόγου τοῦ ἐκ πατρὸς ὁμολογουμένου ἐκλάμπει *ib.*1.20(580A); ὁ...υἱός, ὁ τὸ ἐκ τοῦ πατρὸς ~όμενον πνεῦμα δι' ἑαυτοῦ καὶ μεθ' ἑαυτοῦ γνωρίζων Gr.Nyss.*diff.ess.*4(M.32.329C); ref. Jo.15:16 ~εται ἐκ τοῦ θεοῦ καὶ πατρὸς...κατὰ τὴν τοῦ σωτῆρος φωνήν, ἀλλ' οὐκ ἀλλότριόν ἐστιν τοῦ υἱοῦ Cyr.*apol.Thdt.*9(p.135.2; 6[1].229B); **b.** expressions based on Jo.16:14f. ἐκ τοῦ πατρὸς ~όμενον, ἐκ τοῦ υἱοῦ λαμβανόμενον Gr.Nyss.*Maced.*10(M.45.1313B) ∞ *Symb.*ap.Epiph.*anc.*119(p.148.30; M.43.236B) ∞ Epiph.*anc.*7(p.13.15; 28A); id.*haer.*69.63(p.213.1 M.42.305C); et freq.; **c.** procession through Son; **i.** asserted ἐκ τοῦ πατρὸς οὐσιωδῶς, δι' υἱοῦ γεννηθέντος, ἀφράστως ~όμενον Max.*qu.Thal.*63(M.90.672C); δύναμις τοῦ πατρός· ἐκ πατρὸς ...δι' υἱοῦ ~ομένη Jo.D.*f.o.*1.12(M.94.849A); **ii.** denied ἴδιον δὲ τὸ πνεῦμα τοῦ υἱοῦ, εἰ μὲν ὡς ὁμοφυὲς καὶ ἐκ πατρὸς ~όμενον ἔφη, συνομολογήσομεν. ... εἰ δὲ ὡς ἐξ υἱοῦ ἢ δι' υἱοῦ τὴν ὕπαρξιν ἔχον, ὡς βλάσφημον τοῦτο...ἀπορρίψομεν Thdt.ap.Cyr.*apol.Thdt.*9(p.134.10; 6[1].228C); id.*ep.*171(p.163.32; 4.1355); **3.** procession illustrated by similes; **a.** breathing; ref. Ps.32:6 ὃ παρὰ τοῦ πατρὸς ~εται (τουτέστιν, ὃ ἐκ τοῦ στόματος αὐτοῦ) Bas.*hom.in Ps.*32(1.135E; M.29.333B); ‡Ath.*qu.al.*15(M.28.785C); **b.** flowing of water ἡ πηγὴ οὐ γενεσιουργεῖ τὸ ἐξ αὐτῆς ὕδωρ, ἀλλ' ~όμενον ἔχει καὶ ὁμοούσιον Didym.*Trin.*2.22(M.39.553C); ‡Chrys.*Spir.*(3.798C); **c.** creation of Eve ὡς ἡ Εὔα οὔτε γεννητὴ οὔτε ἀγέννητος, ἀλλὰ μέσως, οὕτως καὶ τὸ ...πνεῦμα παρὰ τοῦ πατρὸς ~εται ‡Ath.*qu.al.*15(M.28.785C); Jo.D.*f.o.*1.8(M.94.817A); **4.** heret.; difficulties of Marcellus about bearing of procession on divine unity stated at length, Marcell.*fr.*60 ap.Eus.*e.th.*3.4(p.158.4ff.; M.24.1004B); ? against Sabellians οὔτε τοῦ πνεύματος, ἢ εἰς πατέρα μεταπίπτοντος, ἢ εἰς υἱόν, ὅτι ἐκπεπόρευται Gr.Naz.*or.*39.12(M.36.348C); against Macedonius ὃ παρὰ τοῦ πατρὸς ~εται ὃ καθ' ὅσον μὲν ἐκεῖθεν ~εται, οὐ κτίσμα· καθ' ὅσον δὲ οὐ γεννητόν, οὐχ υἱός *ib.*31.8(p.154.15; 141B).

ἐκπορίζω, *sail out* [sc. from CP, through straits], Marc.Diac.*v.Porph.*27; Thphn.*chron.*p.294(M.108.720B).

ἐκπορνεύ-ω, 1. *fornicate*; **a.** lit. ἐ. ἐν γυναιξίν *T.Dan* 5.5; Tat.*orat.*10(p.11.21; M.6.828C); Or.*mart.*6(p.7.30; M.11.569C); Eus.*Is.*1:22(M.24.97C); Soz.*h.e.*3.14.36(M.67.1080C); of Nicolaitans, Clem.*str.*3.4(p.207.25; M.8.1132A); cf.*Const.App.*6.8.2; *ib.*6.10.3; **b.** met.; **i.** of moral degeneration, Clem.*paed.*2.1(p.154.23; M.8.380A); *ib.*2.12(p.232.30; 549C); **ii.** of intellectual unfaithfulness; pagan philosophy, id.*str.*1.5(p.18.29; M.8.720C); Or.*mart.*9(p.10.7; M.11.576B); Eus.*Is.*25:11(M.24.269D); δι' ἀποστασίαν Χριστοῦ...~σασα [sc. ψυχή] †Bas.*Is.*42(1.413A; M.30.200B); **2.** *prostitute*; met., of corruptors of the faith τῶν τὴν σεμνότητα τῶν μυστηρίων ~σάντων *ib.*46(416B; M.208A).

***ἐκπραγματεύομαι,** *elaborate*, Cyr.*Jo.*1.7(4.60B).

ἔκπραξις, ἡ, 1. *punishment* ἐ. παραπτωμάτων *Hom.Clem.*12.11; Eus.*Is.*63:2(M.24.501C); **2.** *accomplishment* ἐ. δίκης *V.Const.*27(p.559.25).

ἐκπραΰνω, *soothe, subdue*, ‡Paul.Sil.*therm.Pyth.*154(M.86.2266).

***ἐκπροθέω,** *extend, stretch*, Paul.Sil.*ambo.*61(M.86.2254B).

ἐκπροικίζω, *provide with dowry*, Eus.Al.*serm.*21.16(M.86.441C).

***ἐκπροπόρευμα, τό,** *that which proceeds*; of H. Ghost, Anon.ap.Didym.*Trin.*2.27(M.39.753A).

***ἐκπροσωπ-έω,** ? f.l. for εὐπροσωπέω, *be of fine appearance* τῷ ~οῦντι τῷ ἐπιγείῳ βασιλεῖ ἐξομοιωθῆναι ‡Jo.D.*conf.*9(p.118.27; M.95.293B).

***ἔκπτυστος,** *spat out*; met., Sophr.H.*v.Anast.*(M.92.1697B).

ἔκπτωσις, ἡ, 1. *falling out*, Christol. διάκρινον...λοιπὸν τὰς φύσεις ...οὔτε...κατ' ἐ. ἐκ θεοῦ γέγονεν ἄνθρωπος, οὔτε κατὰ προκοπὴν ἐξ ἀνθρώπου θεός Amph.*fr.*(M.39.109A); Max.*ep.*19(M.91.592D); **2.** *fall*; **a.** of Devil, Eus.*d.e.*4.9(p.163.7; M.22.272C); ref. question how if Christ has foreknowledge, he is not cause of fall of Devil and Adam, ‡Just.*qu.et resp.*58(M.6.1300B); τῆς ἐ. τῷ διαβόλῳ τῦφος ἐγένετο πρόξενος Thdt.*haer.*5.8(4.407); **b.** ref. Or.'s doctrine of fall of created spirits, Or.*princ.*4.14(p.319.12; M.11.372B); idea of a perpetual fall refuted in case of spirits in human bodies, Isid.Pel.*epp.*4.163(M.78.1248D); **c.** of man ἐγενόμεθα...ἄδοξοι...διὰ τὴν ἐ. Bas.*hom.in Ps.*114(1.202A; M.29.489B); ἡ τοῦ...σωτῆρος...περὶ τὸν ἄνθρωπον οἰκονομία ἀνάκλησίς ἐστιν ἀπὸ τῆς ἐ. id.*Spir.*35(3.28C; M.32.128C); ἡ. ἐ. τῆς δόξης Chrys.*hom.16.5 in Gen.*(4.130C); ἡ ἐν Ἀδὰμ... ἐ. Sophr.H.*or.*7.4(M.87.3328A); Anast.S.*hod.*13(M.89.220D); **d.** of moral failure ἐ. πίστεως Bas.*fid.*1(2.224D; M.31.680A); Chrys.*hom.13.2 in Eph.*(11.300C); id.*hom.67.5 in Mt.*(7.668B); of defection of Jews, *ib.68.1*(669D); Euthal.Diac.*epp.Paul.*(M.85.752B); **3.** *exclusion*; **a.** of removal from office, suspension, or degradation as clerical penalty ἡ ἐ. τῆς ὑπηρεσίας Bas.*ep.*127.51(3.325C; M.32.796A); ἡ τῆς ἱερωσύνης ἐ. Niceph.Ur.*v.Sym.*151(M.86.3128A); dismissal from magistrate's office ἐ. ... τῆς ἀρχῆς Ath.Scholast.*coll.*4.13(p.58); from military rank ἐ. τῆς ζώνης *ib.*1.2(p.7); deposition from throne, Thphn.*chron.*p.403(M.108.960C); **b.** of exclusion of an idea in argument, Diod.*fat.*(M.103.852C); **4.** *loss*; in gen., ‡Just.*qu.et resp.*98(M.6.1341A); ref. pain of loss in hell τὴν ἐ. τῆς δόξης ἐκείνης πολὺ τῆς γεέννης πικροτέραν Chrys.*hom.23.7 in Mt.*(7.295A); cf.*ib.23.9*(298A); through immoral living, *ib.25.4*(305E); Cyr.*Ps.*36:2(M.69.924D); ἐ. ... κερδῶν Phot.*nomoc.*13.2(M.104.901A); *loss of life*, Or.*Jo.*28.10(9; p.400.26; M.14.700C); **5.** *lack*, Gr.Nyss.*v.Mos.*(M.44.369C).

***ἐκπτωτικός,** *tending to fall away*, Pall.*h.Laus.*47(p.138.6).

ἔκπτωτος, **1.** *fallen*; of sinners, ‡Thdr.Mops.*resp.Chrys.*(M.48. 1063); of man in gen., Thdot.Anc.*hom.*2.11(p.79.5; M.77.1381A); ἐ. γένος Jo.Thess.*dorm.BMV* B 11(p.423.24); **2.** *excluded* from, of man who dies in sin ἐ. τοῦ παντός †Gregent.*disp.*(M.86.645B); Ἀδὰμ ἐ. τοῦ παραδείσου Anast.S.*qu.et resp.*59(M.89.628A); **3.** *rejected*; of men before Inc., Chrys.*cruc.*2.1(2.411C).

***ἐκπυρακτόομαι**, *be made red hot*, Bas.*Eun.*3.2(1.274A; M.29. 660B).

***ἐκπυρεύω**, *inflame*, Jo.D.*hom.*1(M.96.557B).

ἐκπύρωσις, ἡ, *conflagration, burning*;

I. of final conflagration;

A. in gen., prophesied in Dt.32:22, Just.*1apol.*60.8(M.6.420A); renewing and not destroying creation ἔθος ταῖς γραφαῖς...τὴν εἰς τὸ κρεῖττον...ἀπὸ ταύτης τῆς καταστάσεως τοῦ κόσμου μεταβολὴν ἀπώλειαν λέγειν. ... ταραχθήσεσθαι...τὴν κτίσιν, ὥσπερ τεθνηξομένην κατὰ τὴν ἐ., ἵνα καὶ ἀνακτισθῇ Meth.*res.*48(p.301.6; M.18.276A).

B. in non-Christian thought; **1.** Stoic; **a.** resemblances between Stoic and Christian doctrines listed, Just.*1apol.*20.4(M.6.357C); Stoic doctrine derived from prophets, Clem.*str.*5.1(p.332.2; M.9. 21A) cit. s. ἀνάστασις; *ib.*5.14(p.396.23; 160B); **b.** moral aspect; theory incompatible with free will, Just.*2apol.*7.3(M.6.456B); and rejected because it would mean resurrection of evil to continue evil-doing, Tat.*orat.*3(p.3.22; M.6.809B); **c.** ref. denial that all natures will be changed into fire ἡμεῖς τὴν ἐ. φαμεν γενήσεσθαι, ἀλλ' οὐχ, ὡς οἱ Στοϊκοί, κατὰ τὸν τῆς ἄλληλα πάντων μεταβολῆς λόγον Just. *2apol.*7.3(M.6.456B); οἱ μὲν οὖν ἀπὸ τῆς στοᾶς, ἐπικρατήσαντος ὡς οἷόν τε τοῦ ἰσχυροτέρου τῶν ἄλλων στοιχείου, τὴν ἐ. ἔσεσθαι πάντων εἰς πῦρ μεταβαλλόντων, ἡμεῖς δὲ τῆς λογικῆς φύσεώς φαμεν ὅλης κρατῆσαί ποτε τὸν λόγον καὶ μεταποιῆσαι πᾶσαν ψυχὴν εἰς τὴν ἑαυτοῦ τελειότητα Or.*Cels.*8.72(p.288.23; M.11.1624C); **d.** other Christian objections τις...λέγει...ἐ. ἀποβαίνειν κατὰ καιρούς, ἐγὼ δὲ εἰσάπαξ Tat.*orat.*25(p.27.7; M.6.861A); ὁ τῶν Στοϊκῶν θεὸς...ἡ ἐ. [i.e. opp. true concept of God as incorruptible and simple] Or.*Cels.*4.14(p.284. 25; M.11.1045A); **e.** argumentum ad hominem: elements cannot be divine if they perish in ἐ., Athenag.*leg.*22.3(M.6.937B); **2.** in argument of Celsus βουλόμενος ἡμᾶς παραδεῖξαι μηδὲν...καινὸν λέγειν περὶ...ἐ., ἀλλὰ καὶ παρακούσαντας τῶν παρ' Ἕλλησιν ἢ βαρβάροις... λεγομένων ταῖς ἡμετέραις πεπιστευκέναι...γραφαῖς Or.*Cels.*4.11(p.281. 13; M.11.1040C); and reply that Moses wrote of ἐ. first, *ib.*(p.281. 31; 1041A); ἐ. not part of cosmic cycle but due to sin, *ib.*4.12 (p.282.15; 1041C); **3.** ref. idea of Noëtus that world will end by ἐ., taken from Heraclitus, Hipp.*haer.*9.10(p.243.27; M.16.3375C); **4.** of pagan philosophers' relation to biblical eschatology οἱ τὴν ἐ. εἰσάγοντες τοῦ κόσμου Ἑλλήνων σοφοί, τὰ μὲν περὶ ἡλίου καὶ σελήνης εἰρημένα δέχονται, οὐκέτι δὲ καὶ τὴν ἐξ οὐρανοῦ τῶν ἀστέρων πτῶσιν ὁμολογοῦσιν Thdr.Mops.*Mt.*24:29(M.66.712A); **5.** Jewish ἐν...τῷ πολέμῳ πεσεῖν τὸν Χριστὸν ἐν μαχαίρῃ, ἔπειτα μετ' οὐ πολὺ τὴν συντέλειαν καὶ ἐ. τοῦ παντὸς ἐπιστῆναι Hipp.*haer.*9.30(p.264.16; M.16. 3411B); partic., Essene κρίσιν ἔσεσθαι καὶ τοῦ παντὸς ἐ., καὶ τοὺς ἀδίκους κολασθήσεσθαι *ib.*9.27(p.261.11; 3406B); Pharisee, *ib.*9.28 (p.262.10; 3407B).

II. of fire of hell οὐ...μὴ γενέσθαι τὴν ἐ. ἐπὶ κολάσει τῶν ἀσεβῶν οἱ ...δαίμονες πεῖσαι δύνανται Just.*1apol.*57.1(M.6.413B).

III. of lust; ἐ. τοῦ σώματος as ground for second marriage, Meth. *symp.*3.12(p.41.5; M.18.80A).

ἐκπυρωτικός, *burning, consuming*, Dion.Ar.*c.h.*13.3(M.3.301B).

ἐκριζ-όω, **1.** *uproot*; met.; **a.** ref. material things, *destroy*, Cyr.S. *v.Euthym.*17(p.27.23); **b.** moral ∼οῖ [sc. the virtuous soul] τὴν ἁμαρτίαν *T.Aser* 1.7; πολλοὺς ∼οῖ [sc. ἡ διψυχία] ἀπὸ τῆς πίστεως Herm.*mand.*9.9; of true penance as uprooting of sin, Clem.*q.d.s.*39 (p.185.16; M.9.644C); Isid.Pel.*epp.*2.171(M.78.621D); **2.** *overthrow*, met. ἄνθρωποι...ὑψούμενοι ∼οῦσθε *Orac.Sib.fr.*3.21; ζῆλος καὶ ἔρις ...ἔθνη μεγάλα ἐξερίζωσεν *1Clem.*6.4; *A.Jo.*5(p.153.12); *ib.*8(p.155. 17).

***ἐκρίζωμα, τό**, *uprooting*; met., †Nil.*vit.*3(M.79.1141D).

***ἐκρίζωσις, ἡ**, *uprooting, pulling out* ὀδόντων ἐ. Nect.*Thdr.*6(M.39. 1828B); met., Or.*hom.1.9 in Jer.*(p.8.23; M.13.265C); ἐ. τῆς ἁμαρτίας Meth.*res.*1.42(p.288.14); πλάνης ἐ. ‡Just.*qu.et resp.*1(M.6.1249B).

***ἐκριζωτέος**, *to be uprooted* or *eradicated*, CSard.*can.*1.

***ἐκριπτέον**, *one must cast away*, Clem.*paed.*2.10(p.212.16; M.8. 505B).

ἔκριψις, ἡ, *casting out*, Meth.*res.*2.25(p.381.14; M.18.329A).

ἐκρύομαι, *deliver*, Cyr.*glaph.Gen.*1(1.12D); †Gregent.*disp.*(M.86. 645B).

ἔκρυσις, ἡ, *efflux*; met., ref. Christ διὰ δὲ τῶν ἐκρυέντων ἐκ τῆς πλευρᾶς ἐδήλου ταῖς ἐ. τῶν παθῶν ἀπὸ τῶν ἐμπαθῶν ἀπαθεῖς γενομένας τὰς οὐσίας σεσῶσθαι Clem.*exc.Thdot.*61(p.127.9, v.l. τὰς ἐ. M.9. 688C).

ἐκσεί-ω, **1.** *shake*, fig. κατασύρονται [i.e. from true doctrine] τοῦ δράκοντος ∼σθέντες ταῖς πλοκαῖς Meth.*symp.*8.10(p.92.23; M.18. 153B); **2.** reflex.; met., *shake oneself out*, hence *examine one's conscience* ἐπὶ πολὺ οὖν ἐμαυτὸν ∼σας οὐχ εὗρον ἐμαυτὸν πλημμελήσαντα εἰς αὐτήν Jo.Mosch.*prat.*46(M.87.2901B).

***ἐκσελλίζομαι**, *be unseated, be thrown*, Jo.Mal.*chron.*4 p.89(M.97. 173A).

***ἐκσκέπτωρ, ὁ**, (Lat. *exceptor*) *amanuensis, secretary* (cf. Justn. *cod.*12.19.5 al.); charged with promulgating decrees Καλλικράτῃ ἐ. Ῥουφίνου τοῦ ἐπάρχου Epiph.*haer.*71.1(p.250.25; M.42.376C); official assisting at Councils τῶν δεήσεων ἡ ἀνάγνωσις...διὰ τοῦ...ἐ. ἀνεγνώσθη CChalc.*act.*1(*ACO* 2.1.1 p.152.19; H.2.177B); ἐ. τοῦ θείου σκρινίου τῶν λιβέλλων...τὰ ὑπομνήματα ἐξέδωκα *ib.*(p.179.12; 213B); ἐ. ... δι' ὧν δηλοῦσι τοῖς δήμοις οἱ ἄρχοντες τὸ δοκοῦν Proc.G.*Jos.*1:11 (M.87.996B).

***ἐκσκουβίτωρ, ὁ**, (Lat. *excubitor*) *member of imperial palace guard*, Evagr.*h.e.*4.2(p.154.2; M.86.2705A); *Chron.Pasch.*p.323(M.92.825C); Thphn.*chron.*p.116(M.108.328B).

ἐκσμήχω, *wash off*; med., met., moral pollution, Cyr.*ador.*6 (1.195E).

ἐκσοβέω, *drive away*; met., cf. 1Cor.15:24 παραδίδωσι [sc. Christ] τὴν βασιλείαν αὐτῷ [sc. τῷ πατρί]...ἐλευθέραν,...ἐκσεσοβημένων τῶν ἐχθρῶν Cyr.*Juln.*4(6².150B); of Jews τῆς πρὸς αὐτὸν [sc. τὸν Χριστόν]...οἰκειότητος ἐκσεσοβημένοις id.*Ps.*34:6(M.69.897C); id. *ador.*7(1.239E); λόγοις...ἐκτὸς ὁδοῦ τῆς βασιλικῆς...ἐκσεσοβημένοις id. *Jo.*4.1(4.333A).

***ἐκσπελλευτής (ἐκσπηλευτής), ὁ**, **1.** *exactor of money*, official charged with enforcing payment, Cyr.S.*v.Sab.*61(p.163.3); *ib.*70 (p.172.21); **2.** met., *reckoner*; of angels present at hour of death ὅτε οἱ θεῖοι ἐ. καλοῦσιν τὴν ψυχὴν ἐκ τοῦ σώματος ἀποδημῆσαι Ephr.3. 265C; *ib.*266E; οὐ γὰρ ἔχει ἡ ὥρα ἐκσπηλευτῶν μου ἐγγισάντων Anast. S.*Ps.*6(M.89.1112C).

***ἐκστάνω**, v. ἐξιστάνω.

ἔκστασις, ἡ, **A.** various meanings defined (exeg. Ac.10:10) ἐ. ... δηλοῖ...τὴν ἐπὶ θαυμασμῷ ἔκπληξιν, καὶ τὸ ἔξω τῶν αἰσθητῶν γενέσθαι, ποδηγούμενον ἐπὶ τὰ πνευματικά, καὶ τὸ παρακόπτειν Didym.*Ac.* 10:10(M.39.1677A); ἐ. ἐστι νεῦσις πάλιν πρὸς κακίαν λογικῆς ψυχῆς μετὰ τὴν ἀρετὴν καὶ γνῶσιν τὴν τοῦ θεοῦ Evagr.Pont.*cap.*9(M.40. 1265B); ἐ. δὲ κατὰ διαφορὰς πολλὰς ἔχει τὸν τρόπον. ἐ. δι' ὑπερβολὴν θαύματος λέγεται καὶ ἐ. λέγεται ἡ μανία διὰ τὸ ἐκστῆναι τοῦ προκειμένου. ἐκείνη δὲ ἡ τοῦ ὕπνου ἐ. [sc. that of Adam] κατ' ἄλλον τρόπον ἐρρέθη, κατὰ τὴν φυσικὴν ἐνέργειαν Epiph.*haer.*48.4(p.226.7ff.; M.41. 861C); of myst. ecstasy τί ἐστιν ἐ.; πνευματική, φησί, θεωρία γέγονεν αὐτῷ· τοῦ σώματος, ὡς ἂν εἴποι τις, ἐξέστη ἡ ψυχή Chrys.*hom.22.1 in Ac.*(9.178E).

B. *separation*, Christol. οὐδὲ γὰρ κατ' ἐ. θεότητος γέγονεν ἄνθρωπος ‡Chrys.*nativ.*1(6.392B).

C. met., *alienation* or *distraction of mind*; **1.** in gen. ἑωράκαμεν πολλοὺς ἀπαλλαγέντας χαλεπῶν συμπτωμάτων καὶ ἐ. καὶ μανιῶν Or. *Cels.*3.24(p.220.31; M.11.948C); Evagr.Pont.*vit.cog.*9(M.40.1276A); Proc.G.*Is.*8:19ff.(M.87.1996C); of Christianity considered by pagans as frenzy, iron. μενέτω δὲ ἡ ἐ. μέχρι θανάτου Eus.*d.e.*3.4(p.120.12; M.22.205A); **2.** caused by intoxication, Meth.*symp.*5.5(p.58.22; M. 18.105B); *ib.*5.6(p.60.12; 108B); **3.** caused by fear, Epiph.*haer.*48.5 (p.227.11; M.41.864A); of Abraham ἐ. καὶ φόβος μέγας...ἐπιπίπτει αὐτῷ Chrys.*hom.37.2 in Gen.*(4.375C); ref. Second Advent Χριστὸς... τοσαύτην ἐμποιήσει τὴν ἐ., ὡς καὶ αὐτὰς ἐκπλαγῆναι τὰς οὐρανίους δυνάμεις ‡Jo.D.*B.J.*25(M.96.1096C); **4.** by sin ὑπὲρ τῶν διὰ νόσον τῆς ψυχῆς καὶ ἐ. τοῦ κατὰ φύσιν λογισμοῦ ἔτι ἐχθρῶν Or.*Cels.*4.19(p.289. 12; M.11.1052D); exeg. Ps.30(tit. and v. 23) τὸ δέ, 'ἐκστάσεως', οὐδὲν ἕτερον ἢ αὐτὴν τὴν ἁμαρτίαν ἡμῖν κατασημαίνει, δι' ἣν ὥσπερ ἀγαθῶν φρενῶν ἐξίστατο ἡ ψυχή Ath.*exp.Ps.*30(M.27.156D); 'εἰς δὲ τὸ τέλος, ψαλμὸς τῷ Δαβίδ, ἐκστάσεως'...αἰνίττεσθαι δέ μοι τὰ κατὰ τὸν Οὐρίαν δοκεῖ...'ἐγὼ δὲ εἶπον ἐν ἐ. μου, ἀπέρριμαι ἀπὸ προσώπου τῶν ὀφθαλμῶν σου'· τουτέστιν, ᾠήθην ἡμαρτηκώς, τῆς σῆς γεγυμνῶσθαι προνοίας Thdt.*Ps.*30:1(1.792); but cf. ὁ δὲ τῆς ἐ. ψαλμὸς...ἐκστῆναι συμβουλεύων ἐκείνων, ὧν ἐπιβλαβής ἐστιν ἡ συνάφεια Gr.Nyss.*Pss.titt.*B 6(M. 44.509C); **5.** by opinions of heretics, ‡Ath.*haer.*7(M.28.516B); **6.** in attenuated sense; **a.** *distraction* (in prayer), Jo.Clim.*scal.*28(M.88. 1137A); **b.** *surprise*, *A.Phil.*11(p.6.7).

D. myst., *ecstasy*; **1.** exeg.; **a.** of Adam's 'ecstasy'; not an alienation of the mind, Epiph.*haer.*48.6(p.227.23,26; M.41.864C); οὔτε ἐ. μόνον, ἣν τὸ συμβάν, οὔτε ὕπνος ὁ συνήθης· ἀλλ' ἐπειδὴ ὁ σοφὸς...δημιουργὸς ἔμελλεν ἐκ τῆς πλευρᾶς αὐτοῦ μίαν ἀφαιρεῖσθαι, ἵνα μὴ ἡ αἴσθησις ὀδύνην αὐτῷ ἐργάσηται...καὶ μισήσῃ τὸ πλαττόμενον ζῶον...διὰ τοῦτο τοσοῦτον αὐτῷ ὕπνον ἐπήγαγεν, ἔ. ἐπιβαλών Chrys. *hom.15.2 in Gen.*(4.117C); ἔ. δέ, τὸ ἔξω γενέσθαι τῆς συνήθους αἰσθήσεως, οἷα φιλεῖ θεός, οἰκονομίας χάριν ποιεῖν· οὕτω καὶ τῷ Ἀβραὰμ ἐπέπεσεν ἔ. εἰς τὸ δείξασθαι τῶν ἀποκαλυπτομένων τὴν θεωρίαν...τὸ γάρ, ὕπνωσεν, οὐχ ὕπνον, φασίν, ἀκαριαῖον δηλοῖ ἐν ᾧ τὴν γυναῖκα θεὸς ἅμα τῷ θέλειν ἐποίησεν, ἀλλὰ τῆς ἐ. τὸ εἶδος δηλοῖ Proc. G.*Gen.*2:18(M.87.173B); **b.** of Christ's 'ecstasy' on Cross; typified by Adam's, Meth.*symp.*3.8(p.35.13; M.18.73A) cit. s. ἐκκλησία; τοῦτο γὰρ κυρίως ἂν ἡ πλευρὰ λέγοιτο τοῦ λόγου, τὸ πνεῦμα τῆς ἀληθείας... ἀφ' οὗ λαμβάνων ὁ θεὸς μετὰ τὴν ἔ. τοῦ Χριστοῦ, ὃ δή ἐστι μετὰ τὴν ἐνανθρώπησιν καὶ τὸ πάθος, τὴν βοηθὸν αὐτῷ κατασκευάζει, λέγω δὴ τὰς ἡρμοσμένας αὐτῷ καὶ νενυμφευμένας ψυχάς *ib.*(p.36.17; 73C); **c.** prophetic ecstasy, as state distinct from normal consciousness, ref. Zach.2:10–13 τοῦτον [sc. Ἰησοῦν] δὲ αὐτὸν οὐκ ἐν τῇ ἀποκαλύψει αὐτὸν ἑωράκει ὁ προφήτης, ὥσπερ οὐδὲ τὸν διάβολον καὶ τὸν τοῦ κυρίου ἄγγελον οὐκ αὐτοψίᾳ, ἐν καταστάσει ὤν, ἑωράκει, ἀλλ' ἐν ἐ., ἀποκαλύψεως αὐτῷ γεγενημένης Just.*dial.*115.3(M.6.741B); νομίζω...ὑμᾶς... οὐκ ἀνοήτους γεγονέναι...τῶν...προφητῶν, οἳ κατ' ἔ. τῶν ἐν αὐτοῖς λογισμῶν, κινήσαντος αὐτοὺς τοῦ θείου πνεύματος, ἃ ἐνηργοῦντο ἐξεφώνησαν, συγχρησαμένου τοῦ πνεύματος ὡς εἰ καὶ αὐλητὴς αὐλὸν ἐμπνεῦσαι Athenag.*leg.*9.1(M.6.908A); ἐκστάσει μὲν οὖν ἅπαντες ὡς εἰκὸς τῶν ἀπορρητοτέρων ἐδέχοντο τὴν γνῶσιν, ἐπείπερ ἐνῆν αὐτοὺς ταῖς ἐννοίαις πόρρω που τῆς παρούσης καταστάσεως γεγονότας, οὕτω δυνηθῆναι τῇ τῶν δεικνυμένων θεωρίᾳ προσανέχειν μόνῃ Thdr.Mops. *Nah.*1:1(M.66.401C); of David (ref. Ps.115:11) εἶδεν ἐκεῖνο τὸ ἀμήχανον καὶ ἀπερινόητον κάλλος ἐν τῇ μακαρίᾳ...ἐ. Gr.Nyss.*virg.*10 (p.290.5; M.46.361B); id.*hom.10 in Cant.*(M.44.989D); **d.** of ecstasies of apostles: S. Peter, Thdr.Mops.*Nah.*1:1(M.66.401D) cit. s. θεωρία; contrasted with Montanist pseudo-ecstasies (v. infra, 2.d) γεγόνασι δὲ ἐν ἐ. οἱ προφῆται, οὐκ ἐν ἐ. λογισμῶν. γέγονε γὰρ καὶ Πέτρος ἐν ἐ., οὐχὶ μὴ παρακολουθῶν τῷ λόγῳ, ἀλλὰ ὁρῶν ἀντὶ τῆς καθημερινῆς ἀκολουθίας ἕτερα παρὰ τὰ τοῖς ἀνθρώποις ὁρώμενα...ὅρα δὲ ὅτι παρηκολούθει καὶ οὐκ ἦν ἐν ἐ. φρενῶν ὁ ἅγιος Πέτρος. ὅτε γὰρ ἤκουσεν ⟨τό⟩, 'ἀναστὰς θῦσον καὶ φάγε' οὐχ ὡς μὴ τὸν νοῦν ἐρρωμένος ἐπείσθη, ἀλλά φησι πρὸς τὸν κύριον, μηδαμῶς Epiph.*haer.*48.7(p.228.14–23; M. 41.865A); cf.Didym.*Ac.*10:10(M.39.1677A); S. Paul, ref. Ps.67:28 τίς δὲ ὁ Βενιαμὶν ἢ ὁ μακάριος ἀπόστολος Παῦλος, ὁ ἐκ φυλῆς Βενιαμίν; ...ἐν ἐ. δὲ διὰ τὰς ὑπερβολὰς τῶν ἀποκαλύψεων Ath.*exp.Ps.*67:28(M. 27.301B); cf.Cyr.*Ps.*67:28(M.69.1156C); ὥσπερ...Δαβὶδ...ἐν ἐ. γενόμενος, εἶδε τὸ ἀθέατον κάλλος...οὕτως ἐμεθύσθη καὶ ὁ νεώτερος Βενιαμὶν Παῦλος, ὅτε ἐν ἐ. ἐγένετο λέγων, εἴτε γὰρ ἐξέστημεν, θεῷ, πρὸς ἐκεῖνον γὰρ αὐτὸν ἡ ἔ. ἦν Gr.Nyss.*hom.10 in Cant.*(M.44.989D); **2.** as myst. experience of other Christians; **a.** characteristics; ref. Ps.115:11 ἀλλ' ἔκστασίν τινα θείαν οἵαν ὑπέμεινεν ὁ ἐν τῇ ἐκστάσει εἰπών, 'πᾶς ἄνθρωπος ψεύστης', ἐπὶ ταῖς αἰτήσεσι καὶ τοῖς συνδούλοις ἐκ τούτων ἐκστᾶσα, γυμνῷ, φημί, τῷ νῷ τοῦ καθ' ἑαυτὴν ἔρωτος ἐμφορεῖσθαι †Bas.Anc.*virg.*26(M.30.725A); leaves behind the things of sense, Dion.Ar.*myst.*1.1(M.3.100A); ἄσχετον ἔ. φησι τὴν ἀναχώρησιν πάσης σχέσεως, ἀντὶ τοῦ ἵνα μηδεμιᾷ κατέχοιτο σχέσει, μήτε πρὸς αὐτόν, μήτε πρός τι τῶν κτισμάτων Max.*schol.myst.*1.1 (4.417B); senses being closed τοῦ γὰρ σώματος ἡ ἀκοὴ μετὰ τῶν ἄλλων αἰσθητηρίων ἤργει διὰ τὴν ἔ. Nil.*Magn.*27(M.79.1004B); is prayer of the perfect ἔστι μὲν γὰρ προηγουμένη τῶν τελείων προσοχὴ (perh. f.l. for προσευχή) καὶ τῶν κατὰ τὴν αἴσθησιν ἔ. ὁλοσχερὴς *ib.* (1004A); μοναχός ἐστιν ἀδιάστατος ἔ. Jo.Clim.*scal.*23(M.88.969A); experience of martyr Περπετούα...ὡς ἐξ ὕπνου ἐγερθεῖσα οὕτως ἐν πνεύματι γέγονεν ἔ. παθοῦσα *M.Perp.*20(p.91.28); **b.** combined with visions, Mac.Aeg.*hom.*8.3(M.34.529A); Pall.*h.Laus.*1(p.15.25; M.34. 1010A); *ib.*4(p.20.17; 1017B) ∞ Soz.*h.e.*6.2.7(M.67.1296A); *Apophth. Patr.*(M.65.357B); **c.** ecstasy and 'inebriation' πᾶσα μέθη ἔ. εἴωθε ποιεῖν τῆς διανοίας...τοῦτο διὰ τῆς θείας ἐκείνης βρώσεώς τε καὶ πόσεως καὶ τότε ἐγίνετο, καὶ πάντοτε γίνεται, συνεισιούσης τῇ βρώσει τε καὶ τῇ πόσει τῆς ἀπὸ τῶν χειρόνων πρὸς τὰ βελτίω μεταβολῆς καὶ ἐ. Gr.Nyss.*hom.10 in Cant.*(M.44.989C); ref. Cant.5:1 τοιαύτης τοίνυν γινομένης τῆς ἐκ τοῦ οἴνου μέθης, ὃν προτίθησι τοῖς συμπόταις ὁ κύριος, δι' ἧς πρὸς τὰ θειότερα τῆς ψυχῆς ἔ. γίνεται *ib.*(992B); Dion.Ar.*ep.*9.5 (M.3.1112C) cit. s. μέθη; **d.** heret. ecstasy (cf. παρέκστασις) of false prophets ἐν δὲ τοῖς ψεύδεσι καὶ ἀληθῆ τινα ἔλεγον οἱ ψευδοπροφῆται, καὶ τῷ ὄντι οὗτοι ἐν ἐ. προεφήτευον ὡς ἂν ἀποστάτου διάκονοι Clem. *str.*1.17(p.55.11; M.8.800C); of Montanist prophets and prophetesses, who, unlike true prophets, prophesy in ecstatic frenzy, Epiph. *haer.*48.3(p.224.7; M.41.860C); cf.Mont.*fr.*ap.Epiph.*haer.*48.4(p.224. 22ff.; M.41.861A) cit. s. πλῆκτρον; **3.** pagan, of the Pythia τὸ εἰς ἔ. καὶ μανικὴν ἄγειν κατάστασιν τὴν δῆθεν προφητεύουσαν Or.*Cels.*7.3 (p.155.24; M.11.1425A).

ἐκστατικός, **1.** *alienated, mentally deranged*, Epiph.*haer.*48.5 (p.227.12; M.41.864A); **2.** *causing mental derangement* πάσης μέθης θυμὸς καὶ ἁμαρτία ἐκστατικώτερον Chrys.*hom.60.1 in Mt.*(7.607B); *alienating*, in good sense οἶνον, τὸν φύσεως ἐ. κατὰ τὴν τῆς θεώσεως χάριν Proc.G.*fr.Cant.*6:10(M.87.1757B); **3.** myst., *ecstatic*, of God κατ' ἐ. ὑπερούσιον δύναμιν ἀνεκφοίτητον ἑαυτοῦ Dion.Ar.*d.n.*4.13(M.3. 712B); esp. of divine love ἔστι δὲ καὶ ἐ. ὁ θεῖος ἔρως, οὐκ ἐῶν ἑαυτῶν εἶναι τοὺς ἐραστάς, ἀλλὰ τῶν ἐρωμένων *ib.*(l.c.); τὴν ἀγάπην...ἐ. οὖσαν τῶν ἐξ αὐτῆς Max.*ambig.*(M.91.1249B); *ib.*(1088B); of myst. transports ὕπνου...ὥσπερ...ἐ. ... φορᾶς πρὸς θεοειδῆ μεταποιουμένους κατάστασιν παραπέμποντος Andr.Cr.*or.*12(M.97.1052C).

***ἐκστάω**, late form of ἐξίστημι; **1.** *cause* ἔκστασις, *terrify*, Jo.D. *carm.theoph.*87(p.212; M.96.829B); **2.** intrans., *stand outside, be separated from* τὸ γὰρ τῶν κατὰ φύσιν ἐκστᾶν Max.*opusc.*(M.91.96B).

ἐκστηθίζω, **1.** *recite by heart*, Anast.S.*hod.*3(M.89.92A); Thdr. Stud.*poen.*1.55(M.99.1740C); **2.** *prate, babble*, Jo.Clim.*scal.*18(M.88. 932C).

ἐκστραγγίζ-ω, *squeeze out, drain*, *A.Phil.*131(p.61.9); met. πίνει... τὸ ποτήριον...καὶ πίνων ~ει Eus.*Is.*51:18f.(M.24.449D); cf.SM ap. Proc.G.*Is.*52:1ff.(M.87.2500D).

ἐκστρατεία, ἡ, *military expedition*, Cyr.*Is.*2.4(2.303D); Men.*exc. Rom.*3(p.185.11; M.113.873A); †Jo.D.*B.J.*25(M.96.1089B).

ἐκσφενδονάω, *cast out, expel*; met., of Devil expelling man from life, *Barn.*2.10; Bas.*hom.*10.3(2.85C; M.31.357D).

ἐκσφράγισμα, τό, **1.** *impression of a seal* ὡς...κατὰ δακτυλίου χαρακτὴρ ἐντυπούμενος, τὸ...ἐ. μηδὲν ἐν τοῖς κατ' οὐσίαν ἐλλεῖπον ἔχει· οὕτως ὁ υἱὸς τὸν αὐτὸν χαρακτῆρα τοῦ πατρὸς φέρει ‡Ath.*annunt.* 6(M.28.924C); **2.** *image*; met., of death of S. Peter τοῦ θείου πάθους ἐ. Jo.Mon.*hymn.Geo.*5(M.96.1393A); τοῦ σταυρωθέντος Χριστοῦ...τὸ ἐ. διὰ τοῦ σταυροῦ κοσμούμενον ‡Bas.*h.myst.*7(p.259.20); **3.** *seal*; met., of sign of cross at end of τρισάγιον: οἱονεὶ ἐ. τῶν περὶ Χριστοῦ προηγορευμένων προφητικῶν φωνῶν ‡Sophr.H.*liturg.*17(M. 87.3997A).

***ἐκσχετικός**, *depending on, clinging to*, dub. l., Melet.*nat.hom.*27 (M.64.1257B, v.l. ἐκ σχέσεως).

ἔκταξις, ἡ, *office of tax collector*, meton., of one charged with this office ταξεώτην ἤτοι μανδάτορα, ἤ τινα ἑτέραν ἔ. †Gregent.*leg.Hom.*45 (M.86.605B).

***ἐκτάραγμα, τό**, *disturbance*, opp. γαλήνη, Nil.*epp.*4.1(M.79.549D).

ἔκτασις, ἡ, **1.** *stretching out*, of hands; **a.** of Christ's hands on Cross signifying calling of Jews and gentiles, Iren.*haer.*5.17.4(M.7. 1171C); **b.** in prayer τὴν κατάστασιν τὴν μετ' ἐ. τῶν χειρῶν καὶ ἀναστάσεως τῶν ὀφθαλμῶν πάντων προκριτέον· οἱονεὶ τὴν εἰκόνα τῶν πρεπόντων ἰδιωμάτων τῇ ψυχῇ κατὰ τὴν εὐχήν, καὶ ἐπὶ τοῦ σώματος Or.*or.*31(p.396.11; M.11.549D); ἔχοντος...τοῦ σώματος...χεῖρας, εἰς ...ἔ. τῆς πρὸς τὸν θεὸν εὐχῆς Ath.*gent.*4(M.25.9D); example of Moses in battle shows gesture was familiar to saints, †Bas.*Is.*35(1.408B; M.30.189A); οὐκ ἐν...ἐ. τῶν χειρῶν τὸ ἀκούεσθαί ἐστιν Chrys.*hom. 1.4 in 2Tim.*(11.664C); τί βούλεται καὶ τῶν χειρῶν ἡ ἔ. ἐν τῇ εὐχῇ; ἐπειδὴ πολλαῖς πονηρίαις διακονοῦνται αὗται...δι' αὐτὸ...τοῦτο κελευόμεθα αὐτὰς ἀνατείνειν, ἵνα ἡ τῆς εὐχῆς διακονία δεσμὸς αὐταῖς γένηται τῆς κακίας id.*exp.in Ps.*140:2(5.431C); **c.** typifying arms of Cross; of Moses and others, v. σταυρός, σταυροειδής; **2.** *extension*, Trin., ref. eternal generation of Son against Marcellus οὐδὲ σῶμα ἦν, ὡς...ἔ. ἢ μεταβολὴν...ἐπ' αὐτῷ λογίσασθαι Eus.*e.th.*1.12(p.72.17; M. 24.849A); γεγεννῆσθαι παρὰ τοῦ πατρὸς τοῦ υἱοῦ τὴν οὐσίαν, οὐ κατὰ ἔ. προβληθεῖσαν Eun.ap.Gr.Nyss.*Eun.*4(2 p.56.29; M.45.628B); ἀναθεματίζομεν...τοὺς λέγοντας τὸν λόγον τοῦ θεοῦ τῇ ἐ. καὶ τῇ συστολῇ ἀπὸ τοῦ πατρὸς κεχωρίσθαι Dam.Papa *anath.*ap.Thdt.*h.e.*5.11.5(3. 1037); ἔ. δέ τινα τῆς τοῦ πατρὸς θεότητος ἔφησεν εἰς τὸν Χριστὸν ἐληλυθέναι, καὶ ταύτην θεὸν λόγον ἐκάλεσε. ... τὸ δὲ...πνεῦμα παρέκτασιν τῆς ἐ. λέγει Thdt.*haer.*2.10(3.336); **3.** *attaining* to, ref. spiritual 'inebriation' δι' ἧς τοῖς ἀνθρώποις ἐκ τῶν ὑλικῶν πρὸς τὸ θειότερον ἡ ἔ. γίνεται Gr.Nyss.*hom.5 in Cant.*(M.44.873B).

ἐκτάσσ-ω, **1.** *draw up in battle order*; met., ref. Eph.6:14ff. ἡμᾶς ὁ ἀπόστολος εἰρηνικῶς ~ει Clem.*prot.*11(p.82.13; M.8.236C); **2.** *assign*, *T.Job* 32(p.123.3); Meth.*symp.*7.3(p.74.14; M.18.129A); Ath. Scholast.*coll.*20.1(p.172); **3.** *give commands* to θεοῦ...ἴδιον...τοῖς στοιχείοις ~ειν Tim.III Al.*fr.*(p.316.26; M.86.268C); **4.** *fulfil* an office, †Gregent.*leg.Hom.*45(M.86.605B).

ἐκτατέον, *one must stretch out*, Clem.*paed.*2.1(p.163.8; M.8.397C).

***ἐκτατικῶς**, *at great length*, comp., Gr.Nyss.*v.Ephr.*(M.46.849B).

ἐκτείν-ω, **I.** *stretch out*;

A. the hands; **1.** of Christ stretching out both hands on Cross to call both Jew and gentile, Ath.*inc.*25.3(M.25.140A); **2.** of outstretched arms of Moses as type of Crucifixion, v. σταυρός; **3.** of hands stretched out to perform cures; an act of Christ's human nature, Ath.*ep.Serap*.4.14(M.26.657A); id.*Ar*.3.32(M.26.392A) cit. s. θεϊκῶς; **4.** in prayer, *1Clem*.2.3; Eus.*v.C*.4.15(p.123.25; M.20.1164B); Ath.*ep.mort.Ar*.3(p.179.16; M.25.688B); use of gesture illustrated from scripture, †Bas.*Is*.35(1.408B; M.30.188D); **5.** liturg., in blessing ~ω τὴν χεῖρα ἐπὶ τὸν λαὸν τοῦτον Serap.*euch*.15.1; *ib*.4.1; in ordination of priest τὴν χεῖρα ~ομεν...ἐπὶ τὸν ἄνθρωπον τοῦτον *ib*. 27.1; in renunciation of Devil at baptism πρὸς τὰς δυσμὰς ἑστῶτες... προσετάττεσθε ~ειν τὴν χεῖρα· καὶ ὡς παρόντι ἀπετάττεσθε τῷ σατανᾷ Cyr.H.*catech*.19.2.

B. met., of God ἡ χεὶρ τοῦ μονογενοῦς...ἐκταθήτω ἐπὶ τὰς κεφαλὰς τοῦ λαοῦ τούτου Serap.*euch*.6.1; ref. the tension of spiritual exertion in pursuing action or contemplation πρὸς ἣν [sc. πρᾶξις or θεωρία] πέφυκας, ~ου πλέον Gr.Naz.*carm*.1.2.33.4(M.37.928A); of fixing eyes on an object, Gr.Mag.*dial*.(tr.Zach.)2.31(M.*PL*.66.189B); ἐ. τοὺς ὀφθαλμοὺς...κατὰ τὴν χώραν τῆς Αἰθιωπίας *Vaticin*.1(p.48).

II. *stretch along the ground*, hence *prostrate*, of Christ ἐν τῷ ὄρει ...αὐτὸν [sc. διάβολον]...ἐξέτεινεν Chrys.*hom*.78.4 *in Mt*.(7.756A); of animals, pass., *crawl* ὅσα εἰς γῆν ἐκτέταται Dion.Ar.*d.n*.4.2(M.3. 696C).

III. *expand*; **1.** Trin., ref. theory of Marcellus τοῦτο...ἀπὸ τῶν Στωϊκῶν ὑπέλαβε, διαβεβαιουμένων συστέλλεσθαι καὶ πάλιν ~εσθαι τὸν θεὸν μετὰ τῆς κτίσεως, καὶ ἀπείρως παύεσθαι ‡Ath.*Ar*.4.13(p.57. 4; M.26.484C); agst. Sabellius εἰ μὴ ἡ λεγομένη παρ' αὐτῷ μονὰς ἄλλο τί ἐστι παρὰ τὸν πατέρα. οὐκ ἔτι...πλατύνεσθαι ἔδει λέγειν, ἀλλ' ἡ μονὰς τριῶν ποιητική, ὥστε εἶναι μονάδα, εἶτα καὶ πατέρα, καὶ υἱόν, καὶ πνεῦμα. εἰ γὰρ ἐπλατύνθη αὕτη, καὶ ἐξέτεινεν ἑαυτήν, αὐτὴ ἂν εἴη, ὅπερ ἐξετάθη *ib*.(p.57.14; 485A); εἰς πλῆθος ~ειν τὸν ἀριθμὸν τῶν θεοτήτων, μόνων τῶν τὴν πολύθεον πλάνην νενοσηκότων ἐστί Gr.Nyss. *Trin*.4(p.74.14; M.32.688C); **2.** of Christ as reinterpreting content of Law τὴν προτέραν ἐντολὴν...εἰς ἄκρον φιλοσοφίας...ἐκτείνας Chrys. *hom*.17.1 *in Mt*.(7.222A).

IV. *apply, extend*; **1.** in gen. ἐπὶ τὰ τοιαῦτα τὰς...ἐπιθυμίας ἐ. Const.ap.Eus.*v.C*.2.41(p.59.1; M.20.1017B); ‡Ath.*Apoll*.2.9(M.26. 1148B); of laws, Ath.Scholast.*coll*.1.16(p.22); Heracl.*nov*.25(p.46); **2.** of God ἅπασι τὸ φῶς ἐξέτεινεν Const.ap.Eus.*v.C*.2.71(p.70.10; M.20.1045A); Ath.*decr*.16(p.20.16; M.25.457D); ἡ τἀγαθοῦ θεωνυμία... εἰς τὰ ὄντα, καὶ εἰς τὰ οὐκ ὄντα ~εται, καὶ ὑπὲρ τὰ οὐκ ὄντα ἐστίν Dion. Ar.*d.n*.5.1(M.3.816B); similarly with names Being, Life, Wisdom, *ib*.(l.c.); εἰς τὰ οὐκ ὄντα ~εται τὸ ἀγαθόν, ὡς εἰς τὸ εἶναι καλοῦν αὐτά Max.*schol.d.n*.5.1(M.4.309B); **3.** of Christ ἀρχὴν ἔχει τοῦ τὴν κυριότητα ἑαυτοῦ...~ειν...πρὸς τοὺς ἀπειθήσαντας Ath.*Ar*.2.12(M.26. 173A); of gospel εἰς πάντας ἀνθρώπους ἡ τῆς σωτηρίας ἐκτέταται χάρις Cyr.*Ps*.35:8(M.69.920B).

ἐκτελ-έω, **1.** *accomplish*; pass., of fulfilment of prophecies, Or. *hom*.11 *in Lc*.(p.77.6); **2.** *perform*; of celebrating liturg. functions: Jewish, Eus.*d.e*.1.3(p.14.24; M.22.33C); *ib*.1.6(p.28.16; 57A); eucharist, *ib*.1.10(p.47.32; 89D); Eustrat.*v.Eutych*.29(M.86.2309A); Leont.H.*monoph*.(M.86.1900B); baptism and eucharist, Cosm.Ind. *top*.5(M.88.193C); **3.** *make* ὁ κατ' εἰκόνα ~ούμενος τοῦ κυρίου [i.e. the 'gnostic'] Clem.*str*.3.10(p.227.24; M.8.1172A); *ib*.2.18(p.165.22; 1040A); *ib*.7.16(p.71.20; M.9.540B).

ἐκτέμνω, **1.** *cut off*; met., c. genit., *disinherit* from, Chrys.*hom*.11.4 *in 2Cor*.(10.511B); *divorce*, id.*hom*.26.8 *in 1Cor*.(10.239C); *excommunicate*, *ib*.18.1(152B); Thdt.*haer*.4.10(4.365); **2.** *castrate*; of castration of pagan gods as proof that they are not divine, Athenag.*leg*.21.3(M.6.936A); Clem.*prot*.2(p.13.10; M.8.76B); of castration ref. clergy, CNic.(325)*can*.1; a punishment of martyrs, Eus.*m.P*.7(p.923.21; M.20.1484C).

***ἐκτενή**, ἡ, *prolonged, fervent prayer*, Afric.*chron*.10(M.10.72A).

ἐκτενής, **1.** *intensive, concentrated*, Clem.*str*.6.11(p.479.8; M.9. 316A); **2.** *assiduous, earnest, fervent* νηστείαν μετὰ...ἐ. ὀλολυγμοῦ Just.*dial*.107.2(M.6.725A); μισθὸν...ἐ. πίστεως Jo.Mosch.*prat*.171 (M.87.3040B); τὸ ἐ. εἰς ἀρετήν Cyr.*Ps*.62:9(M.69.1121D); esp. of prayer, in gen. ἐ. τὴν δέησιν καὶ ἱκεσίαν ποιούμενοι *1Clem*.59.2; *Ep. Lugd*.ap.Eus.*h.e*.5.2.3(M.20.433B); Chrys.*nativ*.1.7(2.365C); ἐκτενεστέρας...προσευχάς Cyr.*ep*.25(p.119.1; 5².88E); Messalian μόνη ἡ ἐ. προσευχὴ διώκειν δύναται...τὸν δαίμονα Tim.CP *haer*.(M.86.48B); of monks ἀγρυπνίας μετὰ ἐ. προσευχῆς Jo.D.*spir.neq*.4(M.95.80B); liturg., of litany said by deacon while celebrant prays secretly (consisting of nine petitions each answered by choir with threefold *kyrie*) τῆς ἐ. ἱκεσίας cf.*Lit.Chrys*.(p.373.4).

ἐκτενῶς, *fervently, perseveringly*; **1.** ref. prayers βοήσωμεν πρὸς αὐτὸν ἐ. *1Clem*.34.7; Chrys.*hom*.83.1 *in Mt*.(7.791B); Nil.*epp*.1.246 (M.79.173A); ‡Ath.*ep.Cast*.1(M.28.852A); **2.** ref. liturg. prayer said by deacon for catechumens ὁ διάκονος...κηρυττέτω...ὑπὲρ τῶν κατηχουμένων 'πάντες τὸν θεὸν ἐ. παρακαλέσωμεν' *Lit*.ap.*Const.App*. 8.6.5; *ib*.8.6.7; or energumens, *ib*.8.7.2; or penitents, *ib*.8.9.2; *ib*. 8.9.5; Chrys.*hom*.2.5 *in 2Cor*.(10.435B,C); ἔτι ἐκτενέστερον ὑπὲρ αὐτῶν παρακαλέσωμεν *ib*.2.7(438B).

***ἐκτεχνάζομαι**, *invent, devise*, Mac.Mgn.*apocr*.3.27(p.117.33); Sophr.H.*ep.syn*.(M.87.3157B).

ἐκτίθημι, *set out*;

A. act., *expose* children; practice condemned, Just.*1apol*.27.1 (M.6.369B); *ib*.29.1(373A); Athenag.*leg*.35.2(M.6.969B); Clem.*str*.2.18 (p.163.3; M.8.1033A).

B. med. and pass.; **1.** of various ways of diffusing ideas; **a.** *publish*, Eus.*v.C*.4.46(p.136.32; M.20.1197A); Philost.*h.e*.8.2(M.65.556A); abs., of parties in controversy, *set forth one's views* ἔμειναν... μαχόμενοι πρὸς ἀλλήλους καὶ ἐκτιθέμενοι †Leont.B.*sect*.5.4(M.86. 1232A); **b.** *quote*, Or.*Jo*.10.31(18; p.205.23; M.14.364C); *ib*.13.61(59; p.294.6; 517A); **c.** *apply* μαρτυρίαν...εἰς μόνον τὸ πρόσωπον τοῦ υἱοῦ ἐκτεθεῖσαν Gel.Cyz.*h.e*.2.16.11(M.85.1261C); **2.** of various kinds of intellectual formulation; **a.** *state*, Arist.*apol*.8.2; Meth.*res*.3.18 (p.414.20; M.18.325B); *Hom.Clem*.2.1; **b.** *narrate*, Tat.*orat*.36(p.38. 7; M.6.880B); Socr.*h.e*.1.1.1(M.67.33A); Bas.Sel.*v.Thecl*.2 proem. (M.85.561A); **3.** *expound* scripture, Or.*Jo*.10.23(16; p.194.28; M.14. 348A); Meth.*res*.1.54(p.310.15; M.41.1129A); **4.** *define*, pass.; **a.** of formulations of councils, Ath.*decr*.3(p.3.7; M.25.420C); ‡Ath.*dial. Trin*.3.1(M.28.1204A); τοῖς ἐκτεθεῖσι συνέθεντο Thdt.*h.e*.1.8.17(3.763); **b.** of scriptural readings, *be appointed*, Eus.*d.e*.4.16(p.193.33; M.22. 321D).

ἐκτικός, **1.** *retentive, tenacious*, Iren.*haer*.1.4.5(M.7.488A); Clem. *str*.6.9(p.470.17; M.9.297C); **2.** *participating*, Nemes.*nat.hom*.2(M. 40.580B); **3.** *habitual*; Christol. οὐ νομιοῦμεν...προαιρετικὴν καὶ ἐ. ἀρετὴν ἐνδείκνυσθαι τὸν υἱόν...φύσεως δὲ μᾶλλον ἀτρέπτου καρπόν Cyr.*Jo*.5.5(4.530C); ref. Jo.15:2ff. ἐ. μέν ἐστιν ἡμῶν ἡ κόλλησις πρὸς Χριστὸν καὶ προαιρετικὴν ἔχουσα τῆς συναφείας τὴν δύναμιν, τελειοῦσα δὲ ἀγάπῃ καὶ πίστει *ib*.10.2(866D).

ἐκτιναγμός, ὁ, **1.** *shaking, gnashing* Σενναάρ, ὅπερ ἑρμηνεύεται ὀδόντων ἐ. Or.*Cels*.5.30(p.31.23; M.11.1225C); **2.** *shaking off* ἐ. ὕπνου Nil.*epp*.1.26(M.79.93A); ref. Ps.126:4, id.ap.Proc.G.*Cant*.2:15(M.87. 1612B).

ἐκτιστής, ὁ, *one who pays back* μὴ...γένῃ...πονηροῦ δανείου πονηρότερος ἐ. Bas.*hom*.10.3(2.85A; M.31.357B); of God, ‡Nil.*perist*. 4.17(M.79.848D).

ἐκτομεύς, ὁ, *one who cuts out, removes*, Geo.Pis.*Sev*.307(M.92. 1645A).

***ἔκτομος**, **1.** *cut out* φιάλη τις, 'Ιασσίδος ἔ. ἄκρης Paul.Sil.*Soph*.595 (M.86.2142A); **2.** *castrated*, ref. priests of Cybele ἔ. ἠχή Gr.Naz.*carm*. 2.2(poem.)7.262(M.37.1571).

***ἔκτονος**, *out of tune*, Clem.*str*.2.2(p.180.4; M.8.1068B).

ἐκτοπίζω, **1.** *expel*, Jul.Papa *ep.Dian*.(p.113.14; M.25.308B); Ath. *h.Ar*.19(p.192.18; M.25.713C); Gr.Naz.*or*.42.3(M.36.461A); **2.** pass., *be outlandish*; of Christianity regarded by pagans as ἐκτετοπισμένη, Eus.*h.e*.1.2.1(M.20.53B); id.*d.e*.1.2(p.7.20; M.22.24A).

***ἐκτοπιστέον**, *one must send away*, Clem.*paed*.3.3(p.247.29; M.8. 581B).

ἔκτοπος, *inordinate*; esp. of passions, Meth.*symp*.4.5(p.51.24; M.18.96A); Eus.*h.e*.1.12.19(M.20.64A); Cyr.*Is*.1.1(2.20D); Thdt. *haer*.5.20(4.447).

ἐκτόπως, *excessively, intemperately*, Cyr.*Ps*.49:16(M.69.1084B); id.*Nah*.17(3.496C).

ἐκτορεύω, *carve, fashion*; pass., met., of the matter of poetry, Cyr.*Chr.un*.(5¹.714D).

ἐκτορνεύ-ω, *carve, fashion*; lit., Chrys.*hom*.14.6 *in 1Tim*.(11. 632D); of God τῶν δὲ [sc. ὤτων] ἑλικοειδῶς ἐξετόρνευσεν Pall.*v.Chrys*. 4(p.26.23; M.47.17); pass., of the ear, Chrys.*hom*.6.6 *in Phil*.(11. 243E); ‡Caes.Naz.*dial*.140(M.38.1060); of man εἰκόνα τοῦ πλάσαντος ...~θεῖσαν Bas.Sel.*or*.2.1(M.85.37B); of the creed, Cyr.*ep*.40(p.23.23; 5².112E).

ἕκτος, *sixth*, ἕκτη [sc. ὥρα] *sext* ἕ. ... καὶ τὰς ἑσπερινὰς εὐχὰς ἐπιτελοῦσι Chrys.*hom*.14.4 *in 1Tim*.(11.631A).

ἐκτός, **1.** *outside*; **a.** Trin.; **i.** of Son λόγου...ἴδιον ἐργάζεσθαι τὰ τοῦ πατρὸς ἔργα, καὶ μὴ εἶναι ἐ. αὐτοῦ Ath.*Ar*.2.20(M.26.189C); (Arian) εἰ...οὐκ ἔστιν ὁ λόγος πατήρ,...ἐ. ἂν εἴη ὁ λόγος τοῦ πατρός, ὄντος τοῦ υἱοῦ ἐν τοῖς κόλποις τοῦ πατρός ‡Ath.*Ar*.4.16(p.60.20; M.26. 489B); refuted διὰ τί οὖν οὐχὶ καὶ τὸ πνεῦμα [sc. ἐν τῷ τοῦ πατρὸς ὀνόματι περιέχεται]; ἢ ἐ. τοῦ πατρὸς τὸ πνεῦμα; *ib*.4.21(p.67.24; 500A); **ii.** of H. Ghost ἐν τῷ υἱῷ ἐστιν ὁ πατήρ, καὶ τὸ πνεῦμα οὐκ ἔστιν ἐ. τοῦ λόγου Ath.*ep.Serap*.1.14(M.26.565B); ἐν ᾧ...θεοποιεῖται ἡ κτίσις, οὐκ ἂν εἴη ἐ. αὐτὸ τῆς τοῦ πατρὸς θεότητος *ib*.1.25(589B); **b.** Christol. ἐν πάσῃ τῇ κτίσει ὤν, ἐ. μέν ἐστι τοῦ παντὸς κατ' οὐσίαν id.*gent.*33(M.25.68A); οὐκ ὄντος [sc. Christ's body] ἐ. αὐτοῦ τοῦ λόγου id.*Ar.*1.45 (104C); **c.** moral, of the flesh as τὸν ἐ. ἄνθρωπον Clem.*paed.*3.1(p.237.6; M.8.557A); **d.** of non-Christians οἱ ἐ. *ib.*3.11(p.281.21; 661A); ‡Just.*qu.et resp.*33(M.6.1280B); *Const.App.*1.10.3; Epiph.*haer.*66.10 (p.31.8; M.42.44C); **2.** *without* οὐ δακρύων ἐ. Eus.*v.C.*4.71(p.147.5; M.20.1225B); ref. coeternity πατὴρ γὰρ ἐ. υἱοῦ οὐκ ἂν κληθείη Jo.D. *f.o.*1.8(M.94.812A).

ἐκτραγῳδ-έω, 1. *deck out in tragic language,* Gr.Naz.*or.*16.6 (M.35.941B); Ast.Am.*hom.*1(M.40.172A); Proc.G.*Dt.*32:25(M.87.969A); pass., Clem.*prot.*1(p.4.2; M.8.53A); **2.** *dramatize, ib.*2(p.14.7; 77B); **3.** *reveal,* Chrys.*hom.11.3 in 1Cor.*(10.91B); id.*hom.71.4 in Mt.*(7.699D); αὐτῷ ~ήσατε δυσχερείας Isid.Pel.*epp.*1.226(M.78.324C).

ἐκτραν-όω, *make clear*; hence **1.** *say openly,* ref. CSel. φανερῶς τὸ ὁμοιούσιον ἐδογμάτισαν, τὸ πρότερον...οὐκ ~οῦντες αὐτό Socr.*h.e.* 2.45.3(M.67.360A); **2.** *speak clearly*; without accent, *ib.*6.11.3(697A); **3.** *set forth* πρὸς τὸ ~οῦσθαι χαλεπώτατα τὰ τῆς θείας φύσεως ἴδια Cyr. *Jo.*1(4.8D).

ἐκτραχηλίζω, *overthrow*; met., of spiritual downfall: intellectual τοὺς δήμους εἰς τὴν ὁμοίαν πλάνην ἐξετραχήλισαν [sc. Greek philosophers] Eus.*p.e.*4.22(173D; M.21.304A); Bas.*Eun.*1.9(1.221B; M.29.532A); of Adam through Devil's lies, Chrys.*hom.15.2 in Mt.*(7.186B); Isid.Pel.*epp.*2.90(M.78.536A); of Jews by misinterpretation of prophecy, Areth.ap.*cat.Apoc.*11:10(p.343.32); moral: esp. through pursuit of pleasure, Meth.*symp.*5.6(p.61.3; M.18.108C); Cyr.H.*catech.*19.6; Chrys.*hom.39.9 in 1Cor.*(10.376D); id.*hom.13.5 in Heb.*(12.138D); Areth.ap.*cat.Apoc.*17:2(p.428.6); through pride, Chrys.*hom.3.5 in Heb.*(12.33B); Pall.*h.Laus.*26(p.81.3; M.34.1091B); Thdr.Stud.*epp.*2.162(M.99.1505A); through fame, Chrys.*hom.40.4 in Mt.*(7.443B); through riches, id.*hom.66.1 in Jo.*(8.394C).

***ἐκτράχηλος,** *violent, uncontrolled* ἐ. μηδὲν ἐννοεῖν Gr.Naz.*carm.* 2.1.11.1907(M.37.1163).

ἐκτραχύν-ω, *make rough* or *harsh*; **1.** lit.; med., *become rough*; of skin, Bas.*hex.*5.7(1.46E; M.29.109C); **2.** esp. ref. taste, *ib.*5.8(48C; M.113C); Proc.G.*Is.*5:20(M.87.1920C); med., c. dat. βοτάνη τις... ~ομένη τῇ γλώσσῃ Or.*enarr.in Job* 20:18(M.17.73C); **3.** met. ἡ ἀρετὴ...πόνοις ~ει τὸν βίον τῶν ἀσκουμένων †Bas.*Is.*213(1.539A; M.30.488A); pass., Cyr.*Jo.*3.4(4.272B); of persons εἰς θυμοὺς ~όμενοι ‡Chrys.*pasch.*2(8.255B).

***ἐκτρεπτέον,** *one must change,* Clem.*paed.*3.6(p.256.3; M.8.604B).

ἐκτρέπ-ω, 1. *turn from*; med. and pass., of defection from truth or virtue, Ign.*Magn.*11.1; Just.*dial.*8.2(M.6.492D); τῶν ἐκτραπέντων ἀπὸ τῆς ἀληθείας Ath.*ep.Serap.*1.33(M.26.605C); **2.** *avoid*; med. and pass., esp. error and ref. refusal of communion to heretics, Clem. *paed.*3.2(p.241.27; M.8.569B); Ath.*h.Ar.*41(p.206.18; M.25.741C); οὓς [sc. heretics] ἐκτραπεῖσα ἡ ἐκκλησία Eus.*e.th.*1.3(p.64.2; M.24.832D); τοῦτον ~όμενοι Socr.*h.e.*5.3.4(M.67.569B); *ib.*4.28.16(540B); **3.** *turn away* ἔννοιαι...ἡμαρτημέναι...τὸν ἄνθρωπον...οὐρανίου ἐξέτρεψαν διαίτης Clem.*prot.*2(p.19.9; M.8.96A); ‡Ath.*Apoll.*2.18(M.26.1165A).

ἐκτρέφ-ω, 1. *bring up, rear*; met., of Church ἐγὼ ὑμᾶς ἐξέθρεψα ἐν πολλῇ ἁπλότητι Herm.*vis.*3.9.1; ἡ ἐκκλησία εἰς τὸ γεννᾶν τὴν ἀρετὴν καὶ ἐ. Meth.*symp.*3.8(p.35.18; M.18.73A); **2.** *bring forth* συκῇ...τὸν καρπὸν ~ούσῃ Bas.*hex.*5.7(1.47D; M.29.112C).

ἐκτρέχ-ω, *run from*; hence **1.** *proceed,* of Son οὐκ ἂν εἴη τέλειος, μὴ πάντως ἀπό τινος ~ων ἀρχῆς Cyr.*thes.*10(5^1.77E); **2.** *depart*; met., from an opinion, id.*ador.*11(1.400A); **3.** *continue,* Aen.*ep.*25(p.31); met., of gospel as superseding Law μετάστασις τύπων ἐκδεδραμηκότων πρὸς ἀλήθειαν Cyr.*Is.*4.5(2.703D); **4.** *overrun* Οὖννοι...τὴν Ἀρμενίαν ἐξέδραμον Thphn.*chron.*p.138(M.108.376B).

ἐκτρίβω, 1. *wear out,* Ephr.1.205D; Chrys.*hom.8.3 in 1Tim.*(11.592D); met., *spend* time, Just.*dial.*2.5(M.6.477C); **2.** *crush*; met., of effect of sin on soul, Herm.*sim.*6.2.1; cf.id.*mand.*10.2.1ff.; of oppression, Malchus *exc.Rom.*9(p.169.8; M.113.777D); hence med., *beat down* πληγὰς...ἐκτριψάμενος *A.Andr.*B 2(p.59.5).

***ἐκτροπαλίζομαι,** *turn aside*; met., Meth.*symp.*6.4(p.68.14; M.18.117D).

ἐκτροπή, ἡ, *turning from,* hence *divergence* ἑκούσιος...ἡ...τῆς ἀληθείας ἐ. Clem.*str.*1.17(p.57.19, v.l. ἐκλογή M.8.804C); τὸ ψεῦδος μυρίας ἐ. ἔχει *ib.*1.13(p.36.8; 753C); *ib.*2.11(p.141.13; 989A); of distractions in prayer αἱ τῶν λογισμῶν ἐ. Mac.Aeg.*or.*4(M.34.856B); id. *ep.*(M.34.412A); of idolatry, Thdr.Mops.*Os.*4:15–19(M.66.153B); of Jewish rejection of Christ, Cyr.*Is.*1.1(2.4D).

ἔκτροπος, 1. *inharmonious, out of tune,* Gr.Naz.*carm.*1.1.8.92(M.37.453); neut. as subst. ἀνάρμοστον δὲ τὸ ἔ. Gr.Nyss.*Eun.*4(1 p.93.27; M.45.669C); id.*Pss.titt.*A 3(M.44.444B); **2.** met., *unbefitting* ἔ. εἶδος Gr.Naz.*carm.*2.2(poem.)6.73(M.37.1547).

ἐκτρυγ-άω, *gather fully* ἕως ὁ τῶν ἀμπέλων καρπὸς ~ηθῇ Mac.Mgn. *apocr.*4.16(p.186.29).

ἔκτρωμα, τό, *abortion*; **1.** in gen., Olymp.*Job* 3:16(M.93.64A); †Jo. Jej.*serm.*(M.88.1924A); **2.** as expression of humility εἰμι...ἔσχατος αὐτῶν καὶ ἔ. Ign.*Rom.*9.2; κἀγὼ...τὸ ἔ. τῶν μοναχῶν Sym.Styl.*ep.* (p.194.34; M.86.2533A); so meant by S. Paul, Thdt.*1Cor.*15:8(3.266); Jo.D.*1Cor.*15:8(M.95.689D); **3.** Valent., ref. Achamoth after separation from Pleroma ὥσπερ ἔ., διὰ τὸ μηδὲν κατειληφέναι Iren.*haer.* 1.4.1(M.7.480A); cf.*ib.*1.8.2(523B); τῆς ἔξω Σοφίας, τουτέστι τοῦ ἐ. Hipp.*haer.*6.36(p.166.8; M.16.3250C); τῷ γεγεννημένῳ ὑπ' αὐτῆς ἐ. *ib.*6.31(p.158.22; 3239C); in system of Basilides, of human race οἱονεὶ ἔ. *ib.*7.26(p.205.8; 3315C); cf. of men as children of the fem. principle, Clem.*exc.Thdot.*68(p.129.13; M.9.692A).

***ἐκτρώσκω,** *produce abortion, Orac.Sib.*2.282.

ἐκτυπ-έω, for ἐκκτυπέω; **1.** *bang, make a loud noise on* κελεύσας ...ταυρέας ~εῖν πρὸς τὸ ἀποδιωχθῆναι τὰ πνεύματα Jo.Mal.*chron.*11 p.272(M.97.412C); **2.** *deafen* (met.) by a loud noise βρονταῖς αὐτοὺς ~ήσει Thdt.*Zach.*9:15(2.1638).

ἔκτυπος, 1. *express, distinct* τρανὴν καὶ ἔ. ... κατάληψιν Or.*Jo.*13.3 (p.228.19; M.14.404A); τοῦ πρωτοτύπου ἔ. χαρακτήρ Alex.Al.*ep. Alex.*38(p.25.26; M.18.561C); Acac.Caes.*fr.Marcell.*(p.260.15; M.42.389B); comp., *clearer, more distinct,* Gr.Naz.*or.*33.17(M.36.237A); εἰς ἀρραβῶνα τοῦ ἐκτυπωτέρου τε καὶ ἀληθεστέρου πάσχα Sophr.H. *or.*5(M.87.3316B); **2.** *manifest, A.Thom.*A 138(p.245.12).

ἐκτυπ-όω, 1. *impress* a seal etc., hence *work in relief, model, Diogn.*2.3; οἱ τεχνῖται τῶν ἰδιωτῶν καὶ παρὰ τὰς κοινὰς ἐννοίας ~οῦσι τὸ βέλτιον Clem.*str.*7.16(p.68.5; M.9.533A); Or.*Jo.*10.39(23; p.216.25; M.14.384A); fig. τῶν τιμωρητῶν ἀγγέλων ἐντραπησομένων τὴν ἀπὸ τοῦ αἵματος ἐπ' αὐτοῖς ἐκτετυπωμένην σφραγῖδα Meth.*symp.*9.1(p.115.21; M.18.180C); Bas.Sel.*v.Thecl.*1(M.85.513B) cit. s. σταυρός; met. τὸ ἅγιον πνεῦμα...εἰς τὰς λέξεις ὡς εἰπεῖν τὴν αὐτοῦ διάνοιαν ~ωσάμενον Clem.*ecl.*32(p.146.29; M.9.716A); τῆς καθ' ὁμοίωσιν μορφῆς ἐν αὐτοῖς [sc. τοῖς φωτιζομένοις] ~ουμένης τοῦ λόγου Meth.*symp.*8.8 (p.90.10; 149C); *ib.*(p.91.3; 152A); Thdt.*Col.*3:10(3.493); **2.** *form* ἡ ὕλη...~οῦται τὰς ἰδέας ἀπὸ τοῦ υἱοῦ· ~οῦται δὲ ὁ μὲν υἱὸς ἀπὸ τοῦ πατρὸς Hipp.*haer.*5.17(p.114.22; M.16.3175C); *ib.*5.19(p.118.20; 3182C); τὸν ἄνθρωπον ὃν ἀνείληφεν...μορφούμενον κατὰ δικαιοσύνην καὶ ~ούμενον Or.*Jo.*1.28(30; p.36.7; M.14.76C); Didym.(‡Bas.)*Eun.*5 (1.301E; M.29.724C); Gr.Naz.*carm.*1.2.8.82(M.37.655A); ~οῦντες καὶ ὀνομασίας μυρίας βαρβαρικὰς ἀρχόντων Epiph.*haer.*25.3(p.270.12; M.41.324C); *ib.*33.8(p.458.5; 568D); *ib.*73.36(p.311.11; M.42.469C); Chrys.*hom.8.3 in 1Tim.*(11.592E); **3.** *represent* τὸ ἐν τῷ ὕδατι, ὅτε ἐβαπτίζετο, ἀντὶ τῆς σαρκὸς ἐκείνης ἐκτετυπωμένον σῶμα Hipp.*haer.* 8.10(p.230.23; M.16.3355B); ὁ υἱός, εἰκὼν ἀκριβής, φύσει ~οῦσα τὸν ἴδιον πατέρα Epiph.*haer.*65.8(p.11.29; M.42.25C); **4.** *express* τὴν σελήνην...διὰ τῶν ἡμερῶν τὸν ἀριθμὸν τῶν τριάκοντα αἰώνων ~οῦν Iren.*haer.*1.17.1(M.7.640A); θελήσαντά φησι τὸν δημιουργὸν τῆς ἄνω ὀγδοάδος τὸ ἀπέραντον...μιμήσασθαι καὶ μὴ δυνηθέντα τὸ μόνιμον αὐτῆς καὶ ἀΐδιον ~ῶσαι *ib.*1.17.2(641A); **5.** *indite,* cf. διατυπόω; βίβλους τινὰς ἐξετύπωσαν Epiph.*haer.*40.7(p.88.8; M.41.688C); **6.** τοὺς πρεσβευτὰς...δικαιοτάτῃ ἀντιρρήσει ἀντιβεβηκέναι, ὥστε μὴ παραίτησιν ἔχειν τὴν ἐπιχείρησιν, ἥτις ἑαυτὴν οὐδὲ ἐκτυπωθεῖσα ἐπέσχεν Leo Mag.*ep.*104.4(p.60.25; M.*PL.*54.998A; prob. f.l. for ἐπιτιμηθεῖσα ed.).

ἐκτύπωμα, τό, A. *impression* of a seal; **1.** lit. ἐ., ὃ καὶ ἐκσφράγισμα ἑρμηνεύεται ‡Ath.*annunt.*6(M.28.924C); ὥσπερ σφραγῖδος ἐ. πολλὰ μετέχει τῆς ἀρχετύπου σφραγῖδος Dion.Ar.*d.n.*2.5(M.3.644A); Max.*ambig.*(M.91.1076C); **2.** met., of sign of cross as baptismal seal, Serap.*euch.*25.2 cit. s. χρίω; ἐλαίῳ ἔλιπανέ σου τὴν κεφαλὴν...ἵνα γένῃ ἐ. σφραγῖδος, ἁγίασμα θεοῦ Cyr.H.*catech.*22.7; Jo.D.*imag.*1.27(M.94.1264B) cit. s. μυστήριον; **3.** of a die ἐν τοῖς χρυσοῖς νομίσμασι τὴν αὐτὸς αὐτοῦ εἰκόνα ὧδε γράφεσθαι διετύπου...τούτου μὲν οὖν τὰ ἐ. καθ' ὅλης τῆς Ῥωμαίων διέτρεχεν οἰκουμένης Eus.*v.C.*4.15(p.123.22; M.20.1164B); hence **4.** *image* of any kind, Athenag.*leg.*19.3(M.6.929B); Eus.*h.e.*7.18.2(M.20.680B); Thdt.*qu.20 in Gen.*(1.26); Philost.*h.e.*3.11(p.40.15; M.65.496C); ‡Jo.D.*ep.Thphl.*21(M.95.373A); προσκύνει... τὸ σεβάσμιον ἐ. τοῦ δεσποτικοῦ χαρακτῆρος †Jo.D.*B.J.*19(M.96.1032B); (Gnost.) *image* in sense of *representation* of a heavenly reality πασῶν...τῶν ἀπείρων τοῦ τρίτου αἰῶνος ἰδεῶν ἀπειλημμένων ἐν τούτῳ τῷ κατωτάτῳ σκότῳ...ἐναπεσφράγισται μετὰ τῶν λοιπῶν τὸ ἐ. πῦρ ζῶν ἀπὸ φωτὸς γενόμενον Hipp.*haer.*8.9(p.228.25; M.16.3351D); σοὶ λέγω τῷ ἐ. τῷ ἐν τῷ οὐρανῷ *A.Andr.et Mt.*13(p.80.1); τὸν Χριστὸν εἶναί τι ἀνδροείκελον ἐ. Epiph.*haer.*30.17(p.356.19; M.41.433C); **5.** *representation, likeness,* Cyr.*Os.*1(3.9B); id.*Am.*55(3.310C);

τὸ ἀκριβὲς τοῦ εἴδους ἐ. καθάπερ ἡ τοῦ βασιλέως ἐν ξύλῳ γραφή id.*Jo.*2.8(4.230A); εἶχεν δὲ ἡ εἰκὼν τὸ ἐ. τῆς δεσποίνης ἡμῶν Jo.Mosch.*prat.*45(M.87.2900B); **6.** *corresponding likeness*, as of matrix and seal τὰ νοήματα ὁμοιώματα καὶ ἐ. τῶν ὑποκειμένων ὄντα Clem.*str.*8.8(p.94.7; M.9.589A); λέοντες λέοντας οὐκ ἐσθίουσι, διὰ τὸ ἴδιον ἐ. Epiph.*haer.*66.76(p.118.1; M.42.149B); *ib.*76.3(p.343.14; 520C); **7.** *similitude*, ‡Ath.*qu.al.*19(M.28.789C); **8.** *expression* νοῦ δ' ἔργον ἡ νόησις ἐ. τε Gr.Naz.*carm.*1.2.34.28(M.37.947A); **9.** *material form* ἐμμένειν... πρὸς τὸν ἔσω ἡμῶν ἄνθρωπον, ὅπου οὐκ ἔστιν ἐ. τῶν λογισμῶν καὶ οὐδὲ θεωρία τῶν συνθέτων Isaac *ep.*22(p.174).

B. *figure, type* τοῦ Κάιν ἐκ τῆς Εὔας γεγενημένου καὶ πάντων τῶν ἑξῆς τὴν ἀναγωγὴν ἐχόντων ἐπὶ τὴν Εὔαν, ἐ. τῆς ἐκκλησίας τυγχάνειν Or.*princ.*4.3.7(p.333.27; M.11.388A); τὰς αἰσθητὰς εὐωδίας, ἐ. τῆς νοητῆς διαδόσεως Dion.Ar.*c.h.*1.3(M.3.121D); id.*e.h.*2.3.2(M.3.397C); σκηνὴν...ἐ. παντὸς τοῦ κόσμου Cosm.Ind.*top.*arg.(M.88.56C).

C. *pattern* ἡττήθη τελέως ὁ θάνατος, εἰς ἀφθαρσίας ἐ. ἀνασταυρωθείσης τῆς σαρκός Meth.*Porph.*3(p.507.6; M.18.401C); id.*symp.*1.4(p.13.8; M.18.45A).

ἐκτύπως, **1.** *in outline* ταῦτ' ἐστὶν ἡμῖν ἐ. ὁρίσματα Gr.Naz.*carm.*1.2.34.267(M.37.964); **2.** *clearly, distinctly, definitely* εἰκόνα...ἐ. καὶ ἀκριβῶς ὡμοιωμένην πρὸς πατρικὴν ἀγαθότητα Acac.Caes.*fr.Marcell.*(p.261.22; M.42.392A); Cyr.*hom.pasch.*22(5^2.274B); comp., Or.*Jo.*13.36(p.261.17; M.14.461B); Gr.Naz.*or.*41.11(M.36.444B); Jo.D.*carm.pasch.*125(p.221; M.96.844B).

ἐκτύπωσις, ἡ, **1.** *clarification* ἐ. καὶ τράνωσις τούτων...ὑπὸ τοῦ...πνεύματος Or.*comm.in Eph.*1:13(p.243); **2.** *form, expression*, Hipp.*haer.*10.11(p.271.20; M.16.3423C); Max.*schol.e.h.*3.3.7(M.4.144B); **3.** *likeness* τοὺς χαρακτῆρας καὶ τὴν ἐ. τοῦ Χριστοῦ προσλαμβάνουσι οἱ φωτιζόμενοι Meth.*symp.*8.8(p.90.8; M.18.149B).

ἐκφαίν-ω, **1.** *produce*, Trin. θεὸς...ἐ. ... λόγον ἀληθῶς ἐξ ἑαυτοῦ Didym.(‡Bas.)*Eun.*5(1.306E; M.29.736B); **2.** *make clear*; ref. outstretched arms of Moses as type of cross πρῶτος ἐξέφανεν...τὴν δοκοῦσαν κατάραν Just.*dial.*90.3(M.6.689C); of Christ explaining parables, Clem.*paed.*1.8(p.29.7; M.8.329C); Dion.Ar.*c.h.*7.3(M.3.209B); ref. purpose of angelic illumination τὸ ~ειν ἐν ἑαυταῖς τὴν κρυφίαν ἀγαθότητα id.*d.n.*4.2(M.3.696B); id.*myst.*1.3(M.3.1000C); φωναῖς οὐκ ~εται *Hymn.*(*AS* 1 p.547).

***ἐκφανδόν**, *openly*, Cyr.*ador.*4(1.110A; ἐκφάνδην M.68.308A).

ἐκφανής, **1.** *shining out, made manifest*; of Inc. ἀπειρίας τὰς ἐ. διὰ σαρκὸς θεουργίας ἀνθρώποις παρέχειν...μηνύματα Max.*ambig.*(M.91.1168A); neut. as subst., the *open* εἰς τὸ ἐ. προελθεῖν Gr.Nyss.*hex.*10(M.44.72D); **2.** *illustrious*, Socr.*h.e.*6.2.12(M.67.664C).

ἔκφανσις, ἡ, *manifestation*; **1.** of God ὥσπερ ἔ. ὄντα ἑαυτοῦ δι' ἑαυτοῦ Dion.Ar.*d.n.*4.14(M.3.712C); πρὸς τῶν διαπύρων...νοῶν εἰς ἔ. ἀνακινεῖσθαι φιλεῖ id.*e.h.*4.3.10(3.481D); **2.** Trin., of eternal relations τὸ...τῆς ἐ., ἵν' οὕτως εἴπω, ἢ τῆς πρὸς ἄλληλα σχέσεως διάφορον διάφορον αὐτῶν καὶ τὴν κλῆσιν πεποίηκεν Gr.Naz.*or.*31.9(p.155.14; M.36.141C); cf.Cyr.*Jo.*3.5(4.302B); τὰς διακρίσεις...τῆς θεαρχίας, προόδους τε καὶ ἐ. Dion.Ar.*d.n.*2.4(M.3.640D); τὴν τρισυπόστατον τῆς ὑπερουσίου γονιμότητος ἔ. *ib.*1.4(592A); Max.*schol.d.n.*1.4(M.4.196B) cit. s. πρόοδος; ἡ τῆς ἐνεργείας τοῦ υἱοῦ διὰ τοῦ πνεύματος ἔ. *cat.Rom.*8:10(p.228.14); **3.** ref. Inc. ἡ ἔ. ἡ εἰς ἀνθρώπους Chrys.*hom.13.3 in Jo.*(8.76A); κρύφιος...ἐστι καὶ μετὰ τὴν ἔ., ἤ, ἵνα τὸ θειότερον εἴπω, καὶ ἐν τῇ ἐ. Dion.Ar.*ep.*3(M.3.1069B); τῇ καθ' ἡμᾶς ἐ. ἄνθρωπος γέγονε τέλειος Max.*ambig.*(M.91.1280B); of manifestation of divine attributes in Christ's life, Cyr.*Lc.*2:40(M.72.508B); **4.** *explanation*, Dion.Ar.*c.h.*2.5(M.3.144C).

***ἐκφαντεία**, ἡ, *elucidation, explanation*, Dion.Ar.*c.h.*2.1(M.3.136D).

ἐκφαντικός, **1.** *manifesting*, Dion.Ar.*d.n.*4.11(M.3.708C); Max.*ambig.*(M.91.1109B); of Christ ὡς ἄνθρωπος...τῆς οἰκείας ἐκφαντικὸς ὑπῆρχε θεότητος *ib.*(1056A); Trin., of Word τῆς τοῦ πατρὸς οὐσίας ἐ. Eun.ap.Cyr.*Jo.*1.4(4.31A); Cyr.*Jo.*3.5(306E) cit. s. πρόοδος; λόγος τῶν τοῦ πατρὸς θελημάτων ἐ. *ib.*11.7(964B); ref. H. Ghost ἐν τῷ λόγῳ ἀναπαυομένην [sc. δύναμιν], καὶ αὐτοῦ οὖσαν ἐ. Jo.D.*f.o.*1.7(M.94.805B); **2.** *clear*, Areth.*Apoc.*55(M.106.729B).

***ἐκφαντικῶς**, **1.** *by way of manifesting*, Cyr.*Jo.*6.1(4.607D); ἐν τῇ τοῦ πατρὸς νηδύϊ γεννώσῃ...τὸν υἱὸν ἐ., ὡς ἐν ἐκλάμψει *ib.*1.10(105E); **2.** *clearly*, superl., ‡Meth.*Sym.et Ann.*8(M.18.369C).

ἐκφαντορία, ἡ, *manifestation, revelation*; **1.** of God τῇ κρυφιότητι τῶν ἀπορρήτων οἰκειοτέρα μᾶλλόν ἐστιν ἐπὶ τῶν ἀοράτων ἡ διὰ τῶν ἀνομοίων ἀναπλάσεων ἐ. Dion.Ar.*c.h.*2.3(M.3.141A); manifestation transmitted by angels, *ib.*4.2(180B); **2.** of apparitions of angels ὑπερκοσμίους ἐ. *ib.*2.1(137C); ‡Ath.*occurs.*2(M.28.976A); **3.** of revelation in scripture ἡ τῶν προφητῶν ἐ. ‡Sophr.H.*liturg.*(M.87.3997B); ‡Bas.*h.myst.*39(p.387.2); Jo.D.*trisag.*(M.95.25A); description and explanation, Dion.Ar.*c.h.*5(M.3.196B); **4.** = *tradition* ἡ πατρικὴ ἐ. Mod.*dorm.*3(M.86.3285B).

ἐκφαντορικός, **1.** *manifesting, revealing, expressing*; **a.** ref. God τὴν τῶν ὅλων τοῦ θεοῦ προόδων ἐ. ἀγαθωνυμίαν Dion.Ar.*d.n.*3.1(M.3.680B); ὁ Ἰησοῦς κατὰ τὴν σωστικὴν ἀγαθουργίαν, εἰς ἐ. ἐληλυθὼς τάξιν id.*c.h.*4.4(M.3.181D); διὰ λόγου προβολεὺς [sc. Father] ἐ. πνεύματος Jo.D.*f.o.*1.12(M.94.848D); **b.** of angels πρώτως...ἐ. τῆς θεαρχικῆς κρυφιότητος Dion.Ar.*c.h.*4.2(180A); ἐ. ... πάντες εἰσὶ καὶ ἄγγελοι τῶν πρὸ αὐτῶν *ib.*10.2(273A); **c.** ref. scripture αἱ τῶν λογίων ...ἐ. παραδόσεις *ib.*5(196B); cf.id.*e.h.*5.3.7(M.3.513C); **d.** of bishop, in ordaining ἐ. ἐστι τῆς θεαρχικῆς ἐκλογῆς *ib.*5.3.3(512B); in excommunicating ὡς ἐ. τῶν θείων δικαιωμάτων *ib.*7.3.7(564B); **2.** *splendid* ἐκφαντορικώτατον...ὕμνον ‡Ath.*annunt.*15(M.28.940B).

***ἐκφαντορικῶς**, **1.** *by explaining*, Dion.Ar.*e.h.*5.1.6(M.3.505D); id.*d.n.*1.4(M.3.592B); **2.** *clearly*, id.*c.h.*7.1(M.3.205C); Jo.Thess.*dorm.BMV* 2.1(p.406.20).

ἐκφάντωρ, ὁ, *one who declares, expounds*, Dion.Ar.*ep.*7.1(M.3.1077C); οἱ ἱερεῖς ἐ. εἰσι τοῦ θεοῦ *ib.*8.2(1092A).

***ἐκφαραγγόομαι**, *be made into gullies*, Gr.Nyss.*hex.*27(M.44.89B).

***ἐκφεγγής**, *radiant, shining*, Philost.*h.e.*10.9(p.129.13; M.65.589B).

***ἐκφενακίζω**, *deceive*, Didym.*Trin.*3.42(M.39.992B).

ἐκφέρ-ω, *bring out*; **1.** Trin. ὁ πατὴρ...ἐξ ἑαυτοῦ ἐξήνεγκε τὸ πνεῦμα τὸ ἅγιον Epiph.*haer.*76.49(p.403.28; M.42.620C); **2.** of revealing θεοῦ μόνου ἐστὶ τὸ τὰ ἐν τῇ καρδίᾳ ἀπόρρητα ~ειν Chrys.*hom.29.2 in Mt.*(7.344A); of mysteries not to be revealed to non-Christians, id.*hom.40.1 in 1Cor.*(10.379A); cf.*ib.16.3*(139B); **3.** of giving opinion or judgement, Clem.*str.*7.16(p.68.24; M.9.533C); Eus.*h.e.*5.23.4(M.20.493A); τὴν καθαιρετικὴν ψῆφον...ἐξενεχθῆναι Philost.*h.e.*2.11(M.65.476A).

ἐκφεύγω, *escape*, esp. of avoidance of eternal punishment ἵνα πιστεύσαντες εἰς τὸν θάνατον αὐτοῦ τὸ ἀποθανεῖν ἐκφύγητε Ign.*Trall.*2.1; δι' ὕδατος καὶ πίστεως καὶ ξύλου οἱ προπαρασκευαζόμενοι... ἐκφεύξονται τὴν μέλλουσαν ἐπέρχεσθαι τοῦ θεοῦ κρίσιν Just.*dial.*138.3(M.6.793C); id.*1apol.*68.2(M.6.432A).

ἔκφευξις, ἡ, *escape*, Eus.*Ps.*54:7–12(M.23.477C).

***ἐκφλεγμαίνω**, *seethe*, Bas.*hom.in Ps.*32(1.136C; M.29.336A).

ἐκφλέγω, *kindle*; lit., Clem.*str.*6.15(p.490.21; M.9.340C); met. ὁ λόγος...ἐ. ... τὸν ἄνθρωπον *ib.*5.8(p.360.2; 80A); ἐ. τὰς ἐπιθυμίας id.*paed.*2.4(p.183.5; M.8.441C); Meth.*symp.*3.11(p.39.20; M.18.77B).

ἐκφλογ-όω, *inflame* τῇ περισσείᾳ τοῦ αἵματος τὰ ἔνδος [v.l. ἐντὸς] ~οῦσθαι *M.Ner.et Ach.*4(p.3.16).

ἐκφλόγωσις, ἡ, *conflagration*; at end of world, Meth.*res.*1.47(p.299.19; M.18.276A); ref. end of Sodom, Jo.D.*Man.*1.41(M.94.1545A).

ἐκφοίτησις, ἡ, *becoming public, publication*, Clem.*str.*5.10(p.370.9; M.9.100C).

***ἐκφοιτητικῶς**, ἐ. ἔχω *be going out* or *advancing* τῷ μὴ ἐ. ἔχοντα πρὸς τὸν ὄντα, ἀπιέναι...πρὸς τὸ μὴ εἶναι Leont.H.*Nest.*2.30(M.86.1589A).

ἐκφορά, ἡ, *bringing forth*; of Creation, Clem.*str.*6.16(p.506.18; M.9.376B).

ἐκφόρησις, ἡ, *carrying away, removal*, Clem.*str.*1.23(p.99.7; M.8.905A); Melet.*nat.hom.*synops.(M.64.1109A).

ἔκφορος, *to be divulged* μὴ ῥίπτειν εἰς βεβήλους ἀκοὰς τὰ μὴ ἔ. Gr.Naz.*or.*27.5(p.9.7; M.36.17B); ref. S. Paul's rapture εἰ μὲν ἔ. ἦν ἃ παρέσχεν ὁ τρίτος οὐρανός *ib.*28.20(p.51.11; 52C); Dion.Ar.*d.n.*1.8(M.3.597C); Areth.*Apoc.*28(M.106.640B).

ἐκφορτίζομαι, *be relieved, freed* πᾶν εἶδος ἀκαθαρσίας σαρκικῆς... ἐκπεφορτισμένους Cyr.*ador.*11(1.408B).

***ἐκφορτόω**, *unload*, Geo.Pis.*hex.*1123(M.92.1521A).

ἔκφρασις, ἡ, *exposition*, Clem.*str.*1.1(p.9.9; M.8.700A); γένους... τοῦ Χριστοῦ...οὔτις ἂν εἰς ἔ. αὐτάρκης γένοιτο λόγος Eus.*h.e.*1.2.2(M.20.53B).

***ἐκφρενής**, *demented*, Tim.I Al.*resp.*(M.33.1305B).

***ἔκφρικτος**, *dreadful*, Herm.*vis.*1.3.3.

ἐκφρονέω, *deviate from*, Gr.Nyss.*v.Ephr.*(M.46.828A).

ἐκφυάς, ἡ, *offshoot*; met., ref. heresies, Hipp.*haer.*9.6(p.240.15; M.16.3370B).

***ἐκφυή**, ἡ, *production, growth* τῶν πονηρῶν καρπῶν ἐ. Eus.*theoph.fr.*11(6; p.25.15; M.24.636C).

ἐκφυσ-άω, *blow away*, met. τοῦ ἁγίου πνεύματος ~ῶντος τοὺς χείρονας Heracleon ap.Or.*Jo.*10.33(19; p.207.11; M.14.368A).

***ἐκφυσιόω**, *puff up*, Anon.ap.Eus.*h.e.*5.16.9(M.20.468B).

ἔκφυσις, ἡ, *germination, growth*; met., of evil thoughts, Meth.*res.*1.41(p.287.10; M.18.269C).

[*]**ἐκφυτέω,** *spring from, be begotten*; of Christ, Jo.Mon.*hymn.Nic.* 5(M.96.1385C).

***ἐκφώνημα, τό,** *utterance*, Tat.*orat.*22(p.25.13; M.6.857A); *ib.*33 (p.34.23; 873C); of Montanist prophecies ἐν τῇ τῶν νόθων ἐ. ἀκροάσει Anon.ap.Eus.*h.e.*5.16.8(M.20.468A).

ἐκφώνησις, ἡ, 1. *pronunciation*, of emanation of aeons from Father (Marcosian) ἕκαστον...τῶν στοιχείων...ἴδιαν ἐ. ... ἔχειν Iren. *haer.*1.14.1(M.7.596A); τὸν πατέρα ἐπιστάμενον τὸ ἀχώρητον αὐτοῦ, δεδωκέναι τοῖς στοιχείοις, ἃ καὶ αἰῶνας καλεῖ, ἑνὶ ἑκάστῳ αὐτῶν τὴν ἰδίαν ἐ. ἐκβοᾶν, διὰ τὸ μὴ δύνασθαι ἕνα τὸ ὅλον ἐκφωνεῖν *ib.*1.14.2 (601A); τὴν ἀποκατάστασιν τῶν ὅλων ἔφη γενέσθαι, ὅταν τὰ πάντα κατελθόντα εἰς τὸ ἓν γράμμα, μίαν καὶ τὴν αὐτὴν ἐ. ἠχήσῃ· ἧς ἐ. εἰκόνα τὸ ἀμὴν ὁμοῦ λεγόντων ἡμῶν ὑπέθετο εἶναι *ib.*1.14.1(597A); **2.** *expression, designation*; **a.** in gen., Thphl.Ant.*Autol.*2.18(M.6. 1081A); Bas.*Spir.*5(3.5B; M.32.76B); Gel.Cyz.*h.e.*proem.tit.(p.1.24); **b.** ref. theol. terminology ἡμῶν [i.e. opp. pagans]...θειοτέρας... τινος ἐ. λόγοις καταχρωμένων Tat.*orat.*12(p.14.1; M.6.832D); οὐ...τοῦ πνεύματος ἐλευθερίαν δουλεύειν...φάμεν τῇ σμικροπρεπείᾳ τῶν ἔξωθεν, ἀλλὰ...οἰκείως ὑπαλλάττειν τὰς ἐ. Bas.*Spir.*6(3.5E; M.32.77A); Trin. αἱ...τῶν ὀνομάτων διαστολαί...ὡς οὐχὶ ὅσων αἱ ἐ. αἱ αὐταί, ταῦτα καὶ τῷ σημαινομένῳ ἤδη ταὐτά, ἵνα τὸ πατέρα εἶναι τοῦ υἱοῦ τὸν θεὸν διὰ τοὺς ἐπὶ γῆς πατέρας ὀνομαζομένους ἀφέληται id.*Eun.*2.22(1.257E; M. 29.620B); of formula *Gloria patri* etc., Philost.*h.e.*3.13(M.65.501B); **3.** *prayer said aloud*, at conclusion of prayers said silently by priest, *Lit.Jac.*(p.220.18); **4.** *promulgation* of conciliar decree συνοδικὴ ἐ. Tarasius ap.CNic.(787)*act.*1(H.4.73C).

***ἐκφωνητήριον, τό,** *utterance, means of expression*, Const.*or.s.c.*1 (p.154.8; M.20.1233A).

***ἐκφώσκω,** *dim the light, obscure*, met. τῆς θείας εἰκόνος χαρακτῆρας ἐξεφώσκαμεν Jo.D.*f.o.*4.4(M.94.1108B).

***ἐκφωτίζ-ω, 1.** *shed light* (*upon*), met. ὁ λόγος...ὁ...~ων τὸν ἄνθρωπον Clem.*str.*5.8(p.360.2; M.9.80A); **2.** *bring to light, reveal*; met., ref. fathers of CNic. τὸ ἅγιον πνεῦμα τοιούτων...ἀνδρῶν ταῖς διανοίαις ἐγκείμενον τὴν θείαν βούλησιν ἐξεφώτισε Const.*ep.*(Opitz 3 p.54.4)ap.Socr.*h.e.*1.9.40(M.67.85C).

ἐκχαραδρ-όω, pass., *be broken up into streams* or *channels*, Gr. Nyss.*virg.*8(p.285.7; M.46.356C); met. ἀπὸ τῆς τῷ πολλῷ ῥεύματι τῶν παθῶν ~ωθείσης σαρκός ‡Proc.G.*Pr.*30:17(M.87.1529A).

***ἐκχερσόω,** *dry up*, met. ῥύπους...τῆς σῆς προσευχῆς ἐξεχέρσωσας ξίφει Geo.Pis.*hex.*39(M.92.1429A); id.*Heracl.*2.67(M.92.1322A).

ἐκχέ-ω, *pour forth*; **1.** lit.; **a.** in gen., ref. baptism in absence of running water ~ον εἰς τὴν κεφαλὴν τρὶς ὕδωρ *Did.*7.3; of casting figures κηροπλαστοῦσι, καὶ οὕτως ~ουσι καθ' ὁμοιότητα ἐκείνου Mac. Aeg.*hom.*16.7(M.34.617D); **b.** of blood of Christ ἐκχυθὲν παντὶ τῷ κόσμῳ *1Clem.*7.4; Clem.*paed.*1.6(p.116.6; M.8.301B); Or.*hom.14.6 in Jer.*(p.111.26; M.13.412B); **2.** met.; **a.** of H. Ghost, usu. ref. Joel 2:28 πνεῦμα τῆς χάριτος τὸ ἐκχυθὲν ἐφ' ἡμᾶς *1Clem.*46.6; *Barn.* 1.3; Or.*Jo.*19.5(1; p.303.33; M.14.533B); poured out by Father, Ath.*ep.Serap.*3.1(M.26.625B); by Son, id.*Ar.*2.18(M.26.184B); **b.** ref. Inc. ἐκχεῖσθαι...ὁ λόγος Or.*Cels.*6.78(p.150.11; M.11.1417B); **c.** of surrender to passion or emotion ἐκχεῖσθαι πρὸς ἕτερον id.*mart.* 9(p.9.28; M.11.576B); Meth.*symp.*5.6(p.60.19; M.18.108B); Chrys. *hom.9.5 in 1Thess.*(11.492F); of BMV at Annunciation οὐκ...ἑαυτὴν ἐξέχεεν...ἀλλ' 'ἐταράχθη' id.*hom.4.5 in Mt.*(7.54B); **d.** of extension in time, ref. Son πρὸ τῶν αἰώνων καὶ μετὰ τούτους τὸ ἄπειρον αὐτοῦ τῆς ζωῆς...ἐκκέχυται Gr.Nyss.*Eun.*1(1 p.215.3; M.45.464B).

ἐκχοΐζω, *dig away*; **1.** lit., Marc.Diac.*v.Porph.*76; Pall.*h.Laus.*39 (p.125.1; M.34.1195C); Jo.Mal.*chron.*9 p.225(M.97.349B); **2.** met. τὰς ...καρδίας ἐ. †Cyr.*coll.VT*(6⁴.58A; M.77.1261C) = Max.*cap.*2.60(M. 90.1244A).

***ἐκχοΐσις, ἡ,** *digging out, excavation*, Jo.Mal.*chron.*18 p.437(M.97. 645A).

***ἐκχοϊσμός, ὁ,** = foreg., Thphn.*chron.*p.43(M.108.164B); *ib.*p.148 (401B).

***ἔκχυμα, τό,** *pouring out*, *Orac.Sib.*3.320; plur., *ib.*11.106.

ἔκχυσις, ἡ, *pouring out, shedding*, *Apoc.En.*17.7; Isid.Pel.*epp.*1. 297(M.78.356B); met., of H. Ghost πνεύματος ἁγίου ἐ. ἐπὶ πάντας ἐγίνετο *1Clem.*2.2; of divine wisdom (ref. Ecclus.1:9f.), Ath.*Ar.*2.79 (M.26.313C).

ἐκχώρησις, ἡ, *submission, surrender*; of will to God, Max.*ambig.* (M.91.1076B).

***ἐκχωρισμός, ὁ,** *banishment*; met., of evil spirits, Serap.*euch.*29.1.

***ἔκψηγμα, τό,** plur., *scrapings, chips*, Clem.*paed.*2.12(p.227.18; M.8.540B).

***ἐκψοφέω,** *frighten with noise*, Hipp.*haer.*5.16(p.111.19; M.16. 3171B; conj. ἐκφοβοῦν).

ἐκψύχω, 1. *faint*; met., Thphl.Ant.*Autol.*1.6(M.6.1033C); **2.** *die*, Philost.*h.e.*3.26(M.65.513B).

ἑκών, *willing*, i.e. having a deliberate intention; **1.** of Christ, ref. Phil.2:7 ἑ. κενώσας ἑαυτὸν Or.*hom.1.7 in Jer.*(p.6.27; M.13.264B); σωματικὰς ὕβρεις, ἃς ἑ. ... ὑπὲρ ἡμῶν ὑπέμεινεν Ath.*Ar.*1.7(M.26.24C); Chrys.*hom.84.2 in Mt.*(7.899D); **2.** of intellectual and moral life, ref. martyrdom ἑ. ὑπὲρ θεοῦ ἀποθνήσκω Ign.*Rom.*4.1; voluntary martyrs blamed ὁ παραβιασάμενος ἑαυτόν τε καί τινας προσελθεῖν ἑκόντας *M.Polyc.*4; of penance τινὲς ... ἑ. θλίβονται, γινώσκοντες τὰς πράξεις αὐτῶν ἃς ἔπραξαν Herm.*sim.*8.10.4; Thal.*cent.*3.16(M.91. 1449B); of heretics τὰ...τοῖς θεοπνεύστοις λόγοις...παραδιδόμενα ἑκόντες εἶναι σοφίζονται Clem.*str.*7.16(p.73.6; M.9.544A); Ath.*inc.*40. 5(M.25.165C); of Jews rejecting Christ μὴ ἀγνοοῦντες, ἀλλ' ἑ. id.*ep. Serap.*4.20(M.26.669C); Thdt.*Rom.*10:13(3.113).

ἐλαία, ἡ, I. *olive-tree*;

A. lit.; **1.** use of its wood for ancient pagan images, Athenag.*leg.* 17.3(M.6.924B); **2.** of Noah's olive-branch πόθεν εὗρε τὸ φύλλον τῆς ἐ.;...τὸ δένδρον ἀειθαλές ἐστι, καὶ εἰκός, τῶν ὑδάτων ὑπονοστησάντων, ἔτι...τὴν τῶν φύλλων ἔχειν κόμην Chrys.*hom.26.4 in Gen.*(4.250B); **3.** of Mount of Olives; **a.** as abode of ascetics, Pall.*h.Laus.*44 (p.131.12; M.34.1209C); **b.** symbolism of name τὸ ὄρος δὲ τῶν Ἐ. ⟨ἡ ἐκκλησία⟩ ἐστίν,...αἵτινες λέγουσι καρποφοροῦσαι καλλιέλαιος οὖσαι· ἐγὼ δὲ ὡσεὶ ἐ. κατάκαρπος ἐν τῷ οἴκῳ τοῦ θεοῦ· καὶ...εἰσὶν ὡσεὶ νεόφυτα ἐλαιῶν κύκλῳ τῆς Χριστοῦ τραπέζης Or.*comm.in Mt.*16.17 (p.532.28; M.13.1432A); **c.** as place of pilgrimage, Eus.*onomast.* (p.74.17); **d.** scene of vision of Cross before Constantius' victory over Magnentius, Cyr.H.*ep.Const.*4(M.33.1169A); Soz.*h.e.*4.5.2(M.67. 1117B).

B. as symbol; **1.** of peace, ref. Gen.8:11 ἀποστέλλονται...οἱ ἅγιοι παρὰ Χριστοῦ...ὑπονοστοῦσι δὲ ὥσπερ λαλοῦντες εἰρήνην. τουτὶ γὰρ οἶμαι πλαγίως ὑποδηλοῦν τὸ ἐν στόματι κεῖσθαι τῆς περιστερᾶς τὸν τῆς ἐ. θαλλόν Cyr.*glaph.Gen.*(1.40C); **2.** of mercy, Meth.*symp.* 10.2(p.123.11; M.18.193D); καθάπερ οἱ ἄνθρωποι, κλάδους ἐ. ἐκκόψαντες, ἐπισείουσι τοῖς βασιλεῦσι, διὰ τοῦ φυτοῦ αὐτοὺς καὶ φιλανθρωπίας ἀναμιμνήσκοντες, οὕτω...οἱ ἄγγελοι τότε ἀντὶ κλάδων ἐ. αὐτὸ τὸ σῶμα δεσποτικὸν προτεινόμενοι, τὸν δεσπότην παρακαλοῦσιν Chrys.*incomprehens.*3.7(1.470D); **3.** as emblem of priesthood, *T.Lev.* 8.8; **4.** exeg.: Jud.9:8–15, as symbol of Law, Meth.*symp.*10.2 (p.123.22; M.18.196A); Ps.51:10 ὁ καρπὸς τοῦ πνεύματός ἐστι χαρά, εἰρήνη,...τοῦτον τοίνυν τὸν καρπὸν ἔχων ἐν ἑαυτῷ ὁ ἅγιος ἔλεγεν, ἐγὼ δὲ ὡσεὶ ἐ. κατάκαρπος. ἐλαίᾳ...ὁμοιοῖ ἑαυτόν, ἐπειδὴ ἐλεημοσύνης ἐπικρατούσης ἐν αὐτῷ, ἀκολούθως εἵποντο αἱ λοιπαὶ ἀρεταί Or.*sel. in Ps.*51:10(M.12.1460A); μεταφυτεύῃ λοιπὸν εἰς τὰς ἐ. τὰς νοητὰς... ἐγὼ δὲ ὡς ἐ., κτλ. ... ἐ. οὐκ αἰσθητή, ἀλλὰ νοητή, φωτοφόρος Cyr.H. *catech.*1.4; ὁ γὰρ ὡς ἐ. κατάκαρπος ῥιζωθεὶς ἐν τῷ οἴκῳ τοῦ θεοῦ καὶ τὸ ἑδραῖόν τε καὶ ἀμετακίνητον τοῦ κατὰ τὴν πίστιν στερεώματος ἐν ἑαυτῷ βεβαιώσας καὶ τὴν ἐλπίδα τοῦ θείου ἐλαίου δι' εὐχαριστίας τῇ ἀπειρίᾳ τῶν αἰώνων συμπαρατείνας Gr.Nyss.*Pss.titt.*B 13(M.44. 565A); Is.17:6 οἱ δὴ πάντες ἐπ' ἄκρου τῆς ἐ., δηλαδὴ τῆς Ἰουδαίων διαδοχῆς, ἣν καὶ Παῦλος ῥίζαν ἁγίαν καὶ ἀπαρχὴν καὶ καλλιέλαιον εἴρηκε Proc.G.*Is.*17:1–11(M.87.2124D); Zach.4:3, the two olive-trees typifying: kingship and priesthood, Thdr.Mops.*Zach.*4:1–3(M.66. 528D); Thdt.*Zach.*4:1–3(2.1613); synagogue and gentiles (ref. Rom. 11:17), Cyr.*Zach.*23(3.683E); Nil.*epp.*2.15(M.79.205D); Rom.11:17, grafting simile not true to nature, cf.Or.*comm.in Rom.*8.11(M.14. 1195A); bearing of simile on problem of free will; every man, possessing one and same nature, may prove to be either good or wild olive according to his free choice, cf.*ib.*(M.14.1192A); ὅταν καὶ οἱ κατὰ φύσιν τῆς ἐ. κλάδοι δι' ἀπιστίαν ἐν ἀπωλείᾳ μένωσιν, καὶ οἱ ἐκ τῆς ἀγριελαίου παρὰ φύσιν εἰς καλλιέλαιον ἐμφυτευόμενοι σῴζωνται, πῶς οἱ καὶ σωτηρίαν καὶ ἀπώλειαν ἐκ φύσεως εἰσάγοντες οὐκ αἰσχύνονται; Apoll.*Rom.*11:24(p.74.29); μία μὲν φύσις πάντων ὥσπερ καὶ τῆς ἐ., οὐ μία δὲ προαίρεσις ὥσπερ ἐπὶ τοῦ ἀγρίου καὶ ἡμέρου Sever.*Rom.* 11:24(p.223.2); Jo.D.*Rom.*11:24–27(M.95.536A); Pauline simile applied to relationship of faith to philosophy, Clem.*str.*6.15(p.491.7; M.9.341B); and to transformation of catechumen into baptized Christian, Cyr.H.*catech.*1.4; interpretation ἀπαρχὴν καλεῖ...Χριστὸν ...ῥίζαν δὲ...Ἀβραάμ...κλάδους δὲ ἐ. τὸν τῶν Ἰουδαίων λαὸν...πιότητα δὲ ἐ. τὴν τῆς εὐσεβείας διδασκαλίαν Thdt.*Rom.*11:18(3.122); **5.** of BMV αὕτη ἡ ἐν τῷ οἴκῳ τοῦ θεοῦ πεφυτευμένη κατάκαρπος ἐ. Procl. CP *or.*6.17(M.65.757A); τὴν...καλλίκαρπον ἐ. τοῦ πατρικοῦ ἐλαίου (v.l. ἐλέου) Jo.D.*hom.*9.14(M.96.741A).

II. *olive*;

A. lit., recommended as article of temperate diet, Clem.*paed.*2.1 (p.164.23; M.8.401A); part of ascetic's diet, *Hom.Clem.*12.6; *V. Pach.A* 15(p.139.5).

B. met., symbol of peace, cf. *'pacem meam relinquo vobis.' de hac ergo oliva oleum premamus operum nostrorum*, Or.*hom.13.2 in Lev.*(p.470.26; M.12.546C).

III. *naevus, mole* on the skin, Jo.Mal.*chron.*5 p.138(M.97.236C).

***ἐλαιάζω,** *be olive-green*, Gr.Nyss.*hom.14 in Cant.*(M.44.1072C).

ἐλαιόδευτος, *soaked in oil*, of Jewish meal-offering σεμίδαλις ἐ. Cyr.*Ps.*34:28(M.69.912D); id.*Is.*1.1(2.14D); id.*ador.*2(1.55E); id. *glaph.Num.*(1.399A).

ἐλαιόθρεπτος, *oil-fed*; of wise virgins' lamps (Mt.25:1–4), Meth. *symp.*6.3(p.66.14; M.18.116C); Rom.Mel.(*SBBAW* 1899 p.53).

***ἐλαιόκλαδος, ὁ,** *olive twig*, Jo.Mal.*chron.*11 p.272(M.97.412C).

ἐλαιοκομέω, s.v.l., *be filled with oil*, Pall.*v.Chrys.*20(M.47.72; ἐλαίῳ κομούσων p.129.12).

***ἐλαιόμορφος,** *like oil*, *Apoc.Paul.*28(p.54).

ἔλαιον, τό, I. in secular use;

A. *olive-oil*; **1.** in gen.; in use by athletes, Thphl.Ant.*Autol.*1.12 (M.6.1041B); Clem.*paed.*2.8(p.197.11; M.8.473A); for food, *A.Thom.* A 29(p.146.2); Heracleon ap.Or.*Jo.*13.32(p.257.16, v.l. ποτοῦ M.14. 456B); Thdt.*Ps.*103:15(1.1336); used by ascetics at Pentecost only, id.*h.rel.*5(3.1166); abstinence from oil as penance, Thdr.Stud.*conf.*6 (M.99.1724C); used for illumination in churches, *Can.App.*3; **2.** first-fruits of oil offered; **a.** by Jews, Just.*dial.*112.4(M.6.733C); **b.** by Christians; to prophets, *Did.*13.6; to bishop, *Const.App.* 2.34.5; 7.29.3.

B. *fish oil* συμβρέξαντες ἐλαίῳ τῶν δελφίνων *A.Mt.*18(p.240.8).

C. *mineral oil* (= ῥαδινάκη), found in Persia, Hipp.*haer.*5.21 (p.124.22; M.16.3190C).

II. *oil*, in religious use;

A. in OT; **1.** in anointing of **a.** kings, Chrys.*hom.4.4 in Phil.* (11.225B); Thdt.*Ps.*88:20(1.1237); **b.** priests, *T.Lev.*8.4; ‡Germ. CP *contempl.*(M.98.385C); **c.** prophets, Chrys.*hom.4.4 in Phil.*(11. 225B); ‡Germ.CP *contempl.*(M.98.385C); but ποῦ χριστοὺς καλεῖ τοὺς μὴ χρισθέντας ἐλαίῳ; 'μὴ ἅπτεσθε τῶν χριστῶν μου, καὶ ἐν τοῖς προφήταις μου πονηρεύεσθε.' τότε δὲ οὐδὲ ἡ κατασκευὴ...τῆς χρίσεως ἦν Chrys.*hom.1.1 in Rom.*(9.430B); **2.** in sacrifices, symbolizing joy caused by Christ's sacrifice, Cyr.*glaph.Lev.*2(1.345C).

B. of anointing of Christ; **1.** typified by Jacob's pouring of oil on stone which is Christ, Just.*dial.*86.3(M.6.681A); **2.** anointing with oil being symbol of Christ's unction with H. Ghost, Gr.Nyss. *Maced.*16(M.45.1321A); αὐτὸς κεχρίσθαι λέγεται, οὐδαμοῦ χρισάμενος ἐ., ἀλλὰ πνεῦμα δεξάμενος Chrys.*hom.1.5 in Ac.*(9.9D); Χριστὸς δὲ ἀπὸ τοῦ χρισθῆναι λέγεται...καὶ ποίῳ, φησίν, ἐ. ἐχρίσθη; ἐ. μὲν οὐκ ἐχρίσθη, πνεύματι δέ id.*hom.1.1 in Rom.*(9.430B); exeg. Ps.44:8 καλῶς δὲ ἀγαλλιάσεως ἔ. τὸ πνεῦμα προσαγορεύεται, ἐπειδὴ καὶ εἷς τῶν ὑπὸ τοῦ πνεύματος...γεωργουμένων καρπῶν ἐστιν ἡ χαρά Bas. *hom.in Ps.*44(1.165E; M.29.405A); εἰ χρίεται Χριστός, οὐκ ἐν ἐ. γηΐνῳ, ἀλλὰ πνεύματι θεοῦ *Dial.Ath.et Zacch.*58(p.36.3); **3.** ἐ. ἀγαλλιάσεως (Ps.44:8) interpreted of Christ's anointing (cf. supra), Just.*dial.*56.14(M.6.601B); Or.*Cels.*6.79(p.150.33; M.11.1417C); *Const. App.*5.20.8.

C. of baptismal anointing; **1.** oil (for baptismal use), with bread and water, regarded by heathen as apostle's principal magical apparatus, *A.Thom.*A 152(p.261.14) cit. s. γοητεύω; **2.** administered before baptism; **a.** as sign of bestowal of H. Ghost ἄρας τὸ ἔ. κατέχεεν ἐν τῇ κεφαλῇ αὐτῆς, εἰπών, ἔ. ἅγιον εἰς ἁγιασμὸν ἡμῖν δοθέν... ἐλθέτω ἡ δύναμίς σου...ἐπιχυθέντος δὲ τοῦ ἐ. ... ἐβάπτισεν...ὡς δὲ ἐβαπτίσθη...ἄρτον κλάσας...κοινωνὸν ἐποίησεν αὐτὴν τῷ τοῦ Χριστοῦ σώματι *ib.*121(p.230.22); *ib.*132(p.239.25); *ib.*157(p.266.11); cf.*T.Lev.* 8.4; *A.Xanthipp.*2(p.59.6); χρίσεις τὴν κεφαλὴν τῶν βαπτιζομένων... τῷ ἁγίῳ ἐ. εἰς τύπον τοῦ πνευματικοῦ βαπτίσματος...ἔπειτα βαπτίσεις ...καὶ μετὰ τοῦτο ὁ ἐπίσκοπος χριέτω...τῷ μύρῳ. ἔστι...τὸ ἔ. ἀντὶ πνεύματος ἁγίου *Const.App.*3.16.4; *ib.*7.22.2; **b.** as preparatory rite, with 'oil of exorcism', cf.Hipp.*trad.ap.*21; εἶτα ἀποδυθέντες, ἐ. ἠλείφεσθε ἐπορκιστῷ, ἀπ' ἄκρων τριχῶν κορυφῆς ἕως τῶν κάτω· καὶ κοινωνοὶ ἐγίνεσθε τῆς καλλιελαίου, Ἰησοῦ Χριστοῦ Cyr.H.*catech.*20.3; πρῶτον μὲν ἐ. χριόμεθα, ἔπειτα δὲ τὰ προλεχθέντα ἐν τῇ κολυμβήθρᾳ τελέσαντες σύμβολα, τῷ μύρῳ σφραγιζόμεθα ὕστερον ‡Just.*qu.et resp.* 137(M.6.1389C); Dion.Ar.*e.h.*2.2.7(M.3.396C); προσφέρεται ὁ βαπτιζόμενος, καὶ λαμβάνει ὁ ἱερεὺς ἐκ τοῦ ἁγίου ἐ. τῷ δακτύλῳ αὐτοῦ, καὶ ποιεῖ σταυροῦ τύπον ἐπὶ τοῦ μετώπου...καὶ λέγει· χρίεται ὁ δεῖνα ἔ. ἀγαλλιάσεως *Rit.Bapt.*(p.403); its significance τὸ...ἐπορκιστὸν ἔ. σύμβολον ἦν τῆς κοινωνίας τῆς πιότητος τοῦ Χριστοῦ, φυγαδευτήριον τυγχάνον παντὸς ἴχνους ἀντικειμένης ἐνεργείας Cyr.H.*catech.*20.3; **3.** administered after baptism; in symbolical explanation of Susanna's bath, Hipp.*Dan.*1.16.3(M.10.693A) cit. s. χρίω; τὴν Σωσάνναν μιμήσασθε καὶ πάντα ῥύπον ἀποσμήξασθε καὶ ἐ. ἐπουρανίῳ ἁγιάσθητε *ib.*1.33; anointing with oil administered by presbyter immediately after baptism, followed by bishop's unction with oil, cf.Hipp.*trad.ap.*21,22; cf. τὸ ἔ. τὸ χρῖσμα μυστικὸν...λέγει Ath. *exp.in Ps.*22:5(M.27.140D); Bas.*Spir.*66(3.55A; M.32.188B); administered by bishop, *Const.App.*2.32.3; προσεπενήνεκται δὲ καὶ ἡ τοῦ ἐ. χρεία, συντελοῦσα πρὸς τελείωσιν τοὺς δικαιουμένους ἐν Χριστῷ διὰ τοῦ ἁγίου βαπτίσματος Cyr.*Joel.*32(3.224E); δῆλα ταῦτα τοῖς μεμυημένοις,...ἴσασι γὰρ καὶ τὸ πνευματικὸν ἔ. Thdt.*Ps.*22:5(1.749); τὸ ἔ. βαπτίσματι παραλαμβάνεται, μηνύον τὴν χρῖσιν ἡμῶν, καὶ χριστοὺς ἡμᾶς ἐργαζόμενον Jo.D.*f.o.*4.9(M.94.1125B); τὸ χρίεσθαι ἐ. τοὺς βαπτιζομένους ἐστὶ κατὰ τὸ ἔ. ᾧ ἐχρίοντο οἱ βασιλεῖς...καθὼς καὶ ὁ Χριστὸς ἐχρίσθη ‡Germ.CP *contempl.*(M.98.385C); combined with consignation (but for this purpose μύρον q.v. more commonly used), cf.Hipp.*trad.ap.*22; cf. ἐκέλευσεν προσενεγκεῖν αὐτοὺς ἐ., ἵνα διὰ τοῦ ἐ. δέξωνται τὴν σφραγῖδα *A.Thom.*A 26(p.142.4); Cyr.H. *catech.*22.7 cit. s. ἐκτύπωμα; regarded as sacramental medium of bestowal of H. Ghost, Hipp.*Dan.*1.16.3(M.10.693A); Thdt.*Ps.*22:5 (1.749); Jo.D.*f.o.*4.9(M.94.1125B); cf.Hesych.H.*Ps.*104:15(M.93. 1293C); its use warranted not by scripture but by tradition, Bas. *Spir.*66(3.55A; M.32.188B); **4.** in Gnost. initiation, mixture of water and oil poured on initiate's head, Iren.*haer.*1.21.4(M.7.664B).

D. of anointing of sick with oil (cf. Jac.5:14) δεόμεθα, ὥστε ἐκπέμψαι δύναμιν ἰατικὴν...ἐπὶ τὸ ἔ. τοῦτο, ἵνα γένηται τοῖς χριομένοις ...εἰς ἀποβολὴν πάσης νόσου Serap.*euch.*29.1; *PLond.*1928.6; cf.Gr. Naz.*or.*43.37(M.36.545C,548A); Βενιαμὶν...κατηξιώθη χαρίσματος ἰαμάτων, ὡς πάντα ᾧ ἂν χεῖρα ἐπετίθει ἢ ἔ. εὐλογήσας ἐδίδου, πάσης ἀπαλλάττεσθαι ἀρρωστίας Pall.*h.Laus.*12(p.35.4; M.34.1034D); ‡Pall. *h.mon.*1.12(p.7.16; M.34.1113A); *ib.*9.11(p.53.2; 1154B); ‡Jo.D.*fid. dorm.*18(M.95.264B); oil employed being taken from church lamps, Chrys.*hom.22.6 in Mt.*(7.373C); from relics, Eustrat.*v.Eutych.*45 (M.86.2328A) cit. s. εἰκών; *ib.*55(2337A); from martyrs' sanctuaries, Chrys.*pan.mart.*2(2.669E); used with accompaniment of magical formulae ἐάν τις βαλεῖ ἅλας εἰς ἔ. καὶ ἐπαλείψει τὸν ἀσθενῆν λέγων, χερουβίμ, σεραφίμ, βοηθεῖτε, εὐθὺς ἀναχωρῶ [sc. demon] *T.Sal.*18. 34(M.122.1345C); used in curing sick animals, Thdt.*h.rel.*8(3. 1183).

E. in anointing of dead, Iren.*haer.*1.21.5(M.7.665B); ‡Chrys.*pat.*1 (9.808D); by Archontici to obtain invisibility and superiority over heavenly powers, Thdt.*haer.*1.11(4.303); Dion.Ar.*e.h.*7.2(M.3.556D); *ib.*7.3.8(565A).

F. in anointing of holy places τὸ παρὰ πολλῶν γυναίων τῶν ἐν κυρίῳ πεπιστευκότων γινόμενον· εἰώθασι γὰρ ἐν τοῖς θείοις σηκοῖς ἐ. χρίειν τὰς τῶν ἀνακτόρων κιγκλίδας, καὶ τῶν ἁγίων μαρτύρων τὰς θήκας Thdt.*qu.84 in Gen.*(1.94).

G. Manich. ἐὰν παύσησθε ἐσθίοντες [sc. οἱ ἐκλεκτοί] εὔχεσθε καὶ βάλλετε ἐπὶ τῆς κεφαλῆς ἔ. ἐξωρκισμένον ὀνόμασι πολλοῖς, πρὸς στηριγμὸν τῆς πίστεως ταύτης Hegem.*Arch.*11(p.19.7; M.10.1445B).

H. consecration of oil, for baptismal use καὶ ὁ ἄρτος καὶ τὸ ἔ. ἁγιάζεται τῇ δυνάμει τοῦ ὀνόματος, οὐ τὰ αὐτὰ ὄντα κατὰ τὸ φαινόμενον οἷα ἐλήφθη, ἀλλὰ δυνάμει εἰς δύναμιν πνευματικὴν μεταβέβληται Clem.*exc.Thdot.*82(p.132.10; M.9.696C); for purpose not clearly stated Ἰησοῦ ἐλθέτω ἡ νικητικὴ αὐτοῦ δύναμις, καὶ ἐνιδρύσθω τῷ ἐ. τούτῳ...ἐλθέτω δὴ καὶ ἡ δωρεὰ δι' ἧς τοῖς ἐχθροῖς αὐτοῦ ἐμφυσήσας εἰς τὰ ὀπίσω ὑποχωρῆσαι ἐποίησας...καὶ ἐπιδημῆσαι τῷ ἐ. τούτῳ ᾧ ἐπιφημίζομεν τὸ σὸν ἅγιον ὄνομα *A.Thom.*A 157(p.267.6); Bas.*Spir.* 66(3.55A; M.32.188B); Gr.Nyss.*bapt.Chr.*(M.46.581C); *Const.App.* 7.42.3; *Rit.Bapt.*(p.402); v. εὐλογέω, εὐλογία; for unction of sick, Serap.*euch.*17.1; *ib.*29.1; *Const.App.*8.29.2, private offerings of oil and water consecrated for exorcism and healing, cf.*Euchol.* (pp.332–346).

I. of 'oil of tree of life'; sought by Adam as remedy for Fall, *Apoc.Mos.*9(p.5); *A.Pil.*B 19(p.325).

J. in Elchezaite baptismal formula, Hipp.*haer.*9.15(p.253.19; M. 16.3391A) cit. s. μάρτυς; *ib.*(p.254.10; 3391C).

K. met.; **1.** ref. unction with H. Ghost; **a.** of Christ, ref. Ps.22:5 μυρίζει τὴν κεφαλὴν τῷ ἐ. τοῦ πνεύματος Gr.Nyss.*ascens.*(M.46.692B); **b.** of soul αἱ γὰρ εἰς τὴν φύσιν αὐτῶν ἀπομένουσαι ψυχαί...ἄνωθεν... ἐκ τοῦ πνεύματος οὐκ ἐγεννήθησαν, τὸ ἔ. τῆς ἀγαλλιάσεως μὴ δεξάμεναι Mac.Aeg.*hom.*4.6(M.34.477B); **2.** of 'royal unction' of Christians, Thphl.Ant.*Autol.*1.12(M.6.1041C) cit. s. Χριστιανός; Mac.Aeg.*hom.* 15.35(M.34.600B) cit. s. βασιλεύς; *ib.*17.1(624D); **3.** as symbol of God's loving-kindness, Chrys.*hom.4.4 in Phil.*(11.225B); **4.** of divine mercy (with play on ἔλεος, ἐλεέω), Clem.*paed.*2.8(p.195.9; M.8.468B); Chrys.*hom.78.1 in Mt.*(7.752A); τὸ γὰρ ἔ. τοῦτο οὐ νῦν μόνον πολλὴν ἔχει τὴν ἰσχύν· ἀλλ' ὅτε καὶ αἱ θυσίαι ἤνθουν παρευδοκίμησε...τὴν ἐκείνων δύναμιν· ἔλεον (v.l. ἔλαιον) γάρ, φησί, θέλω καὶ οὐ θυσίαν id.*hom.13.4 in Jo.*(8.76D); τὴν ἱερωσύνην ἀπὸ ἐλέους ἐποίησε, καὶ βασιλεῖς ἐλαίῳ ἐχρίοντο· κἂν ἄρχοντά τις ἐπαινῇ, οὐδὲν οὕτως αὐτῷ πρέπον ἐρεῖ, ὡς ἔλεον· τοῦτο γὰρ ἀρχῆς ἴδιον, τὸ ἐλεεῖν id.*hom.4.4 in Phil.*(11.225B); id.*hom.6.3 in 2Tim.*(11.695D); Cyr.*ador.*16(1.585C); Vict.*Mc.*6:12(p.324.11); **5.** of cheerfulness, Bas.*hex.*5.6(1.45C; M.29.108B); Cyr.*Os.*30(3.55E); id.*hom.pasch.*2(5^2.20C); Thdt.*qu.1 in Lev.*(1.184); **6.** of spiritual riches, Cyr.*ador.*17(1.626A); **7.** of tranquillity, Jo.Clim.*scal.*8(M.88.832D); **8.** of Christian doctrine, cf.Or.*hom.7.4 in Ezech.*(p.394.24; M.13.722C); Cyr.*ador.*9(1.321C); **9.** of grace preserved by good living, cf. *quicumque custodit se post acceptam gratiam dei...non contaminavit sanctificationem dei...quia sanctum oleum chrismatis dei super ipsum est. illud oleum de quo in Exodo scriptum est, quomodo potest secundam litteram proprie oleum dei dici, quod ante myrepsica confectum est...?*, Or.*hom. 12.4 in Lev.*(p.462.18; M.12.540C); **10.** of good works, '*...pacem meam relinquo vobis.' de hac ergo oliva oleum premamus operum nostrorum ex quo lucerna domino possit accendi, ut non in tenebris ambulemus*, *ib.13.2*(p.470.26; 546C); οἷόν τι ἔ. τὴν ἀγαθὴν πρᾶξιν τῷ νοερῷ τούτῳ φωτὶ προσενέγκωμεν Thdt.*Gal.*6(3.397); **11.** of BMV αὕτη τὸ ἅγιον τῆς χρίσεως ἔ. Procl.CP *or.*6.17(M.65.753B); **12.** exeg., **a.** Ps.44:8, of object of 'spiritual sense' of smell αἰσθήσεις τοῦ δικαίου, ...γευόμεναι ζῶντος ἄρτου, ὀσφραινόμεναι Χριστοῦ μύρων εὐωδίας, ἔ. ἀγαλλιάσεως Or.*fr.57 in Lc.*(p.261.3; M.17.357A); for Christol. interprn. v. supra II.B; **b.** Ps.140:5, cf. *ungue etiam caput tuum, sed observa ne oleo peccati: oleum enim peccatoris non impinguet caput tuum*, Or.*hom.10.2 in Lev.*(p.444.10; M.12.527C); εἰ δὲ οὕτως ἀποροῦσιν αἱ ἐκκλησίαι, λυσιτελεῖ διαφθαρῆναι, ἢ παρ' ἐχθρῶν τοῦ θεοῦ λαβεῖν τι...περὶ γὰρ τοιούτων καὶ ὁ προφήτης λέγει, ἔ. ἁμαρτωλοῦ μὴ λιπανάτω τὴν κεφαλήν μου *Const.App.*4.8.2; **c.** Mt.25:1–13, cf. *oleum autem caritatis et pacis et reliquarum virtutum in vasis suis condere nescierunt*, Or.*hom.1.5 in Lev.*(p.288.10; M.12.411B); *vendunt...oleum luminibus...prophetae sancti et apostoli qui...consilium dant*, *ib.*4.5(p.322.18; 439C); ἔ. ὁ ἐπιχεόμενος λόγος τοῦ ψυχικοῦ τοῦ τὴν ἀγαθὴν πρᾶξιν ἐργαζομένου id.*fr.in Mt.*25:1(p.147.15; M.13.1700C); τὸ γὰρ ἔ. τῇ σοφίᾳ καὶ τῇ δικαιοσύνῃ παραβλητέον Meth.*symp.* 6.3(p.67.18; M.18.117B); as symbolizing mercy, Chrys.*hom.78.1 in Mt.*(7.752A); id.*hom.6.3 in 2Tim.*(11.695D); τὸ τῆς εὐσεβείας ἔ. *Const.App.*2.13.3; symbolizing grace of H. Ghost, Mac.Aeg.*hom.* 4.6(M.34.476D); **d.** Lc.10:30–37 Ἰησοῦς...τὸ ἔ., τὸν ἐκ σπλάγχνων πατρὸς ἔλεον, προσενεγκών Clem.*q.d.s.*29(p.179.12; M.9.636A); cf. *vulnera peccatorum non solum olei lenitate mitigentur, verum etiam vini austeritate purgentur*, Or.*hom.17.9 in Gen.*(M.12.261C); Sophr. H.*mir.Cyr.et Jo.*67(M.87.3656B); **e.** Lc.12:49 τὸν...βαπτιστὴν...οὐχ ἑτέρωθεν τὴν τοῦ δύνασθαι φωταγωγεῖν κομισάμενον δύναμιν, ἢ διὰ τοῦ ἐ. τοῦ νοητοῦ, δυνατῶς...ἔχοντος εἰς τὸ φῶς καῦσαι τὸ θεῖον ἐν ἡμῖν, ὃ δὴ καὶ...ὁ σωτὴρ κατεμήνυσε λέγων, πῦρ ἦλθον βαλεῖν ἐπὶ τὴν γῆν κτλ. Cyr.*Jo.*3.1(4.250C); **f.** Mt.26:7 τὸ ἔ. αὐτός ἐστιν ὁ κύριος, ἀφ' οὗ τὸ ἔλεος τὸ ἐφ' ἡμᾶς· τὸ δὲ μύρον, δεδολωμένον ἔ., ἐστὶν ὁ Ἰούδας ὁ προδότης Clem.*paed.*2.8(p.194.25; M.8.468A).

ἐλαιοτριβεῖον, τό, *oil-press*; hence (in translation of Hebr. בַּת) a liquid measure, Epiph.*mens.*21(M.43.273A).

***ἐλαιοτρίπτης, ὁ,** *oil-presser*, Epiph.*mens.*21(M.43.273B).

***ἐλαιοφορ-έω,** *bear oil*; of BMV, with play on ἔλαιον, ἔλεος: ἡ ~ήσασα ἡμῖν, ὡς θεογεώργητον χωρίον, τὴν πηγὴν τοῦ ἐλέους Χριστὸν Mod.*dorm.*2(M.86.3285A).

ἐλαιοφόρος, *oil-bearing*; of Samaria, Cyr.*Os.*135(3.167E); of widow's cruse (3Reg.17:14), id.*Jo.*3.4(4.280E).

ἐλαιώδης, *having the nature of oil* εὐκατάπρηστος γὰρ ἡδοναῖς ἡ νεότης, ὡς ἐλαιωδεστέρα πρὸς ἔξαψιν ‡Chrys.*Thecl.*(2.749C).

Ἐλαιών, ὁ, *Olivet, Mount of Olives*, Just.*dial.*99.2(M.6.708C); Or.*comm.in Mt.*16.17(p.532.1; M.13.1429C); ὁ σωτὴρ ἀνελήφθη ἀπὸ τοῦ Ἐ. Epiph.*mens.*14(M.43.261A); serves as witness of Christ's Resurrection ἕστηκε μέχρι σήμερον ὁ Ἐ. τὸν...ἀναβάντα τοῖς τῶν πιστῶν ὀφθαλμοῖς μονονουχὶ δεικνύων...πολλοὺς οὖν ἔχεις τοὺς μάρτυρας· ἔχεις ἀναστάσεως τὸν τόπον τοῦτον Cyr.H.*catech.*14.23; scene of vision of Cross at time of Constantius' victory over Magnentius, ‡Jo.D.*Artem.*10(p.51.18; M.96.1261C); site of monastery Ἰννοκέντιον τὸν πρεσβύτερον τοῦ Ἐ. Pall.*h.Laus.*44(p.131.2; M.34.1209B).

ἐλασία, ἡ, 1. *riding, running*, Ph.Carp.*Cant.*proem.(M.40.28A); Jo.Mal.*chron.*2 p.48(M.97.121B); **2.** met., *expulsion* τῶν δαιμόνων ἐ. ‡Pall.*h.mon.*2.6(p.25.23; M.34.1027C).

ἐλάτη, ἡ, 1. *spathe of date*, or *fruit* enclosed by it, exeg. Cant. 5:11 οἱ βόστρυχοι διὰ τὴν πυκνότητα παραβάλλονται ταῖς τῶν φοινίκων ἐ. Or.*schol.in Cant.*5:11(M.17.273D); ἐ., καρπός εἰσι φοινίκων ἀρσένων, τοῖς θήλεσιν ἐπιβαλλόμενοι, καὶ ὡρίμους γίνεσθαι παρασκευάζοντες τοὺς ἐκείνων καρπούς. ἐπειδὴ τοίνυν τῶν ποικίλων αὐτοῦ χαρισμάτων ἀπολαύοντες οἱ πεπιστευκότες αὐτῷ καρποφοροῦσιν αὐτῷ τὴν εὐσέβειαν, ἐλάταις εἰκότως ἀπεικάζει τοὺς βοστρύχους Thdt.*Cant.*5:1(2.117); *ib.* 7:8f.(148); **2.** *silver fir* ἐ.... γινόμενοι [sc. βόστρυχοι]...προσθήκη τοῦ κάλλους γίνονται τοῦ νυμφίου...καθὼς...ὁ ἀπὸ κόρακος ἐ. γενόμενος [sc. S. Paul], καὶ διὰ τοῦτο βόστρυχος τῆς θείας κεφαλῆς χρηματίσας Gr.Nyss.*hom.13 in Cant.*(M.44.1056C,D).

ἐλατήρ, ὁ, met., *one who expels, exorcizes*, ref. πάθη, Philost.*h.e.* 2.8(M.65.472A); τῶν ἀπαισίων ἐ. Men.*exc.Rom.*8(p.192.32; M.113.885A).

***ἐλαττόνως,** *to a lesser extent* ὁ...πατὴρ...φθάνει εἰς ἕκαστον τῶν ὄντων,...ἐ. δὲ παρὰ τὸν πατέρα ὁ υἱὸς φθάνων ἐπὶ μόνα τὰ λογικά Or.*princ.*1.3.5(p.56.1, v.l. ἐλάττων M.11.150B); ref. H. Ghost τὸ μὴ... ἔχειν...δυνάμει καὶ δόξῃ ἐ. Didym.*Trin.*2.6(M.39.508A).

ἐλαττ-όω, A. *diminish*; **1.** ref. God καθ' ἑκάστην...ἡμέραν ἁμαρτήματα...γίνεται. καὶ...ὁ θεὸς πάρεστι καὶ τὰ τῆς δίκης οὐχ ὑστερίζει. τί οὖν παρὰ τοῦτο ~οῦται; Const.ap.Gel.Cyz.*h.e.*3.19.33 (M.85.1353A); τὰ...κτίσματα κἂν μηδέπω ὑπάρχῃ, οὐκ ~οῖ τὸν ποιητήν Ath.*Ar.*1.29(M.26.73A); of divine gifts οὐκ ~οῦνται ταῖς μετοχαῖς Dion.Ar.*d.n.*9.1(M.3.909C); **2.** Trin., Just.*dial.*61.1(M.6.616A) cit. s. πῦρ; ὥσπερ...ἀπὸ μιᾶς δᾳδὸς ἀνάπτεται μὲν πυρὰ πολλά, τῆς δὲ πρώτης δᾳδὸς διὰ τὴν ἔξαψιν τῶν πολλῶν δᾳδῶν οὐκ ~οῦται τὸ φῶς, οὕτω καὶ ὁ λόγος προελθὼν ἐκ τῆς τοῦ πατρὸς δυνάμεως, οὐκ ἄλογον πεποίηκε τὸν γεγεννηκότα Tat.*orat.*5(p.6.2; M.6.817A); οἱ ~οῦντες τὸν μονογενῆ τοῦ θεοῦ υἱὸν εἰς θεὸν βλασφημοῦσι Ath.*hom.in Mt.11*:27(M.25.220A); τὸν υἱὸν...ἀϊδίως...ὄντα ἐν αὐτῷ [sc. τῷ πατρί],...καὶ κατ' οὐδένα τρόπον ~οῦντα τὴν τοῦ πατρὸς οὐσίαν Cyr.*thes.*16(5^1.176A); **3.** Christol.; **a.** in gen. 'ὁ Χριστός', φησί [sc. Arius], 'δι' ἡμᾶς πέπονθεν.' ἀλλ' ἤδη φθάσας ἔγωγε εἶπον, ὡς μορφῇ σώματος ἀπεστάλη. 'ναί', φησίν, 'ἀλλὰ δέος μὴ δόξωμεν κατά τι ~οῦν' Const.ap.Gel.Cyz.*h.e.*3.19.32(M.85.1352D); Ath.*decr.*14(p.12.29; M.25.440D) cit. s. θεοποιέω; ref. Jo.5:34 οὐδὲν ἐγὼ παρὰ τοῦτο εἰς τὴν φύσιν ἠλάττωμαι τὴν ἐμήν Chrys.*hom. 6.1 in Jo.*(8.43A); ref. Ps.8:6 and Heb.2:7 ὁ βραχὺ παρ' ἀγγέλους ἠλαττωμένος διὰ τὸ τῆς ἀνθρωπότητος μέτρον Cyr.*Heb.*2:7(p.385.9; M.74.961D); **b.** ref. scriptural difficulties, Is.48:16 ἔστι...περὶ τοῦ ἀποστείλαντος τὸν Χριστὸν πνεύματος ἀπολογήσασθαι, οὐχ ὡς φύσει διαφέροντος ἀλλὰ διὰ τὴν γενομένην οἰκονομίαν τῆς ἐνανθρωπήσεως τοῦ υἱοῦ τοῦ θεοῦ, ἐλαττωθέντος παρ' αὐτοῦ τοῦ σωτῆρος Or.*Jo.*2.11(6; p.66.21; M.14.129C); Mt.28:18 τὸ ἐδόθη...καὶ τὸ ὅμοια τούτοις, οὐκ ~οῖ τὴν θεότητα τοῦ υἱοῦ, ἀλλὰ καὶ μᾶλλον δείκνυσιν αὐτὸν ἀληθῶς υἱόν Ath.*Ar.*3.36(M.26.400C); Lc.2:52, *ib.*3.53(433C); Ps.109:1, ‡Ath. *serm.fid.*19(p.13; M.26.1272D); **4.** exeg. Jo.3:30 οὔτε ὁ Χριστὸς αὔξει, οὔτε ὁ Ἰωάννης ~οῦται, ἀλλὰ δίκην ἑωσφόρου ὁ Ἰωάννης ὑπὸ τοῦ νοητοῦ ἡλίου σκέπεται Ammon.*Jo.*3:30(M.85.1416A); Cyr.*Jo.*2.1(4.160E); δεῖ...αὐτὸν μὲν...ταῖς καθ' ἡμέραν τῶν σημείων προσθήκαις ἀεὶ πρὸς τὸ μεῖζον ἀναπηδᾶν,...ἐμὲ δὲ ~οῦσθαι, μένοντα ἐν οἷσπερ ὑπάρχων ὁρῶμαι *ib.*(160C).

B. med., *be less* or *lower than* εἰ...τὸ μὲν πνεῦμα...ἐν τῷ λόγῳ πάρεστιν..., οἱ δὲ ἄγγελοι ~οῦνται τούτῳ...οὐκ ἀμφίβολον οὖν, ὅτι οὔτε τῶν γενητῶν, οὔτε ὅλως ἄγγελός ἐστιν...τὸ πνεῦμα Ath.*ep.Serap.*1.26 (M.26.592C).

ἐλάττωμα, τό, *defect*; **1.** Trin. τὸ...γέννημα, ἐὰν μὴ ἀεὶ συνῇ τῷ πατρί, ἐ. τῆς τελειότητος τῆς οὐσίας αὐτοῦ ἐστιν Ath.*Ar.*1.29(M.26.73A); **2.** Christol. ἐπειδὴ...αὐτὸς λέγεται ὑψῶσθαι, καὶ ὅτι ὁ θεὸς αὐτῷ ἐχαρίσατο, καὶ νομίζουσιν οἱ αἱρετικοὶ ἐ. εἶναι ἢ πάθος τῆς τοῦ λόγου οὐσίας *ib.*1.45(104C); οὐδὲ τοῦτο [sc. ignorance] ἐ. τοῦ λόγου ἐστίν, ἀλλὰ τῆς ἀνθρωπίνης φύσεως ἧς ἐστιν ἴδιον καὶ τὸ ἀγνοεῖν *ib.*3.43 (413B); ὅταν πεινάσῃ μετὰ τὸ νηστεῦσαι, τοῦ σώματος ἐ. ‡Ath.*serm.fid.* 24(p.20; M.26.1277A); **3.** in anti-pagan apologetic, man cannot be divine ἐ. πολλὰ ἔχοντα Arist.*apol.*7.3; ref. pagan gods τοῖς ἀνθρωπίνοις αὐτῶν ἐ. τὰς θεοῦ ἐννοίας μὴ ἁρμόζειν αὐτοῖς διελέγξουσι Ath. *gent.*17(M.25.36C); **4.** moral; **a.** to be corrected ἀποταξάμενοι τοῖς ἐ. [i.e. at baptism] Clem.*paed.*1.6(p.109.3; M.8.288B); φόβος θεοῦ παντοίων ἐ. ψυχῆς περιγίνεται Bas.*reg.fus.*10.2(2.352E; M.31.945B); τὰ ἐ. ἑαυτῶν ἀναλογισάμενοι, διανύσωμεν τῷ χρόνῳ τὴν τούτων διόρθωσιν, τῷ μὲν παρόντι μηνὶ τοῦτο, τῷ δὲ ἐπιόντι τὸ ἕτερον Chrys. *hom.84.5 in Jo.*(8.497E); correction of one's faults to be asked of others, id.*hom.30.3 in Heb.*(12.283C); οἱ...θέλοντες σωθῆναι, οὐδὲ προσέχουσιν ἐ. τοῦ πλησίον, ἀλλ' τοῖς ἰδίοις Dor.*doct.*6.6(M.88.1692B); **b.** to be borne patiently in case of others; superiors, Nil.*exerc.*27 (M.79.756B); ref. Mt.5:32 πάντα φέρειν κελεύει τὰ τῆς γυναικὸς ἐ. Thdt.*affect.*9(p.237.19; 4.944); **c.** and concealed συγκρύπτετε ἀλλήλων τὰ ἐ. *T.Jos.*17.2; Chrys.*hom.21.4 in Heb.*(12.199D); Esaias *or.* 4.1(M.40.1112B).

ἐλάττων, *less*; **1.** Trin.; ref. Arian exegesis of Jo.14:10 λέγοντες ...πῶς...δύναται ὁ πατήρ, μείζων ὤν, ἐν τῷ υἱῷ ἐ. ὄντι χωρεῖν; Ath. *Ar.*3.1(M.26.321B); ref. names λόγος and σοφία: εἰ ὀνόματα μόνον ἐστὶ ταῦτα τοῦ υἱοῦ, ἄλλος αὐτὸς εἴη παρὰ ταῦτα. καὶ εἰ μὲν βελτίων ἐστὶ τῶν ὀνομάτων, οὐχ ὅσιον ἐκ τῶν ἐ. τὸν βελτίονα σημαίνεσθαι· εἰ δὲ ἐ. ἐστὶ τῶν ὀνόματων, πάντως ἔχει καὶ τὴν αἰτίαν τῆς ἐπὶ τὸ κάλλιον προσηγορίας id.*decr.*16(p.13.20; M.25.441C); προειπὼν γάρ, καὶ θεὸς ἦν ὁ λόγος, ἵνα μὴ νομίσῃ τις ἐ. εἶναι τὴν θεότητα τοῦ υἱοῦ, εὐθέως αὐτοῦ καὶ τὰ γνωριστικὰ τῆς γνησίας τίθησι θεότητος Chrys.*4.3 in Jo.*(8.30D); **2.** Christol. οὐ γὰρ ἐξ ἐλαττόνων βελτίον γέγονεν· ἀλλὰ μᾶλλον θεὸς ὑπάρχων τὴν δούλου μορφὴν ἔλαβε Ath.*Ar.*1.40(M.26.93C); ref. Mt.12:28 οὐ παρῃτήσατο διὰ τὸ ἀνθρώπινον ἑαυτοῦ εἰπεῖν ἑαυτὸν καὶ ἐ. τοῦ πνεύματος *ib.*1.50(116A); id.*ep.Serap.*4.20(M.26.669C); ref. Jo. 20:22 τοῖς δὲ μαθηταῖς τὴν θεότητα...δεικνὺς ἑαυτοῦ, οὐκέτι δὲ ἐ. τοῦ πνεύματος ἑαυτόν, ἀλλὰ ἴσον σημαίνων, ἐδίδου μὲν τὸ πνεῦμα id.*Ar.*1.50(116B); ref. Heb.1:4 οὐ μετὰ τὸ σῶμα γέγονε κρείττων τῶν ἀγγέλων, ἵνα μὴ τὸ πρὶν ἐ., ἢ ἴσος αὐτῶν φαίνηται id.*Dion.*11(p.54.10; M.25.496C); **3.** in anti-pagan apologetic; sun cannot be divine ἐ. ὄντα τοῦ οὐρανοῦ πολύ Arist.*apol.*6.2; nor can moon, being less than sun, *ib.*6.3; **4.** superl., of Inc. πῶς ἂν...ἐν ἐ. μέρει γῆς φανείη...; Just.*dial.*127.3(M.6.773A); πολλὴν...τὴν θεολογίαν εἶναι καὶ ἐ. [i.e. because of impossibility of adequate expression] Dion.Ar.*myst.*1.3(M.3.1000B); **5.** neut. as adv., Epiph.*haer.*30.31(p.376.13; M.41.460D); Chrys. *hom.4.4 in 1Cor.*(10.30B); id.*hom.4.3 in 2Cor.*(10.458A).

ἐλάττωσις, ἡ, *diminution*; **1.** Trin., ref. Eunomian theory that Son is of different nature from Father γίνεται αὐτοῖς ἡ τῆς ἐ. κατασκευὴ τῶν Μανιχαϊκῶν δογμάτων ἀρχή Gr.Nyss.*Eun.*1(1 p.165.1; M.45.404D); ref. Jo.1 as proof that there was no diminution of Godhead in Logos, Chrys.*hom.4.3 in Jo.*(8.31A); cf.*ib.*5.3(37C); against Pneumatomachoi; no ἐ. in case of H. Ghost implied by 1Cor.12:8, id.*hom.29.4 in 1Cor.*(10.264E); **2.** Christol. τὸ ἄκτιστον...μήτε αὔξησιν, μήτε ἐ. ἐπιδεχόμενον ‡Ath.*Apoll.*1.4(M.26.1100A); ἔλεγεν ἀπεστάλθαι, οὐχ ἵνα ἐ. τινα αὐτοῦ νομίσῃς εἶναι τὸ ῥῆμα, ἀλλ' ἵνα ἐμφράξῃ τὰ ἐκείνων στόματα Chrys.*hom.39.2 in Jo.*(8.228A); ref. 1Cor.11:3 ἐνταῦθα ἐπιπηδῶσιν ἡμῖν οἱ αἱρετικοὶ ἐ. τινα ἐκ τῶν εἰρημένων ἐπινοοῦντες τῷ υἱῷ id.*hom.26.2 in 1Cor*(10.229B).

ἔλαφος, ὁ, ἡ, *deer*; **1.** of Christ νεβρῷ...ἐλάφων ὁ νυμφίος ἀπείκασται, οὐ μόνον ὡς ἀναλίσκων τοὺς ὄφεις, ἀλλ' ὅτι καὶ παιδίον ἐγεννήθη ἡμῖν...καὶ ὅτι ἐταπείνωσεν ἑαυτόν· ἢ γὰρ ἂν 'ἐ.' ὑπῆρχε τελεία Or.*Cant.*3(p.201.30; M.13.167D); cf. *cervus...inimicus serpentum atque bellator est. ... forsitan salvator...sit...cervus juxta opera. ... interficit ipse serpentes, contrarias fortitudines jugulat,* id.*hom.2.11 in Cant.*(p.56.28; M.13.56C); cf.id.*Cant.*3(p.213.25; M.13.176D); διὰ τοῦτο...ὡμοίωται νεβρῷ...ἐλάφων, ὡς πατῶν...τὴν ἐναντίαν ἐνέργειαν Gr.Nyss. *hom.5 in Cant.*(M.44.861C); Ph.Carp.*Cant.*49(M.40.65C); ἀπόστρεψον ἐπὶ τὰ ἔθνη, ὁμοιούμενος τῷ δόρκωνι ἢ νεβρῷ τῶν ἐ. τῇ ὀξύτητι καὶ τῷ τῆς πίστεως δρόμῳ, ἐπὶ πάντα τὰ πέρατα τῆς οἰκουμένης διατρέχων ἐν ὡραίοις ποσὶ τῶν ἀποστόλων *ib.*71(76B); νεβρῷ...αὐτὸν ἐλάφων ἐοικέναι φησίν, ὡς...συνθλάσαντα τὰς κεφαλὰς τοῦ δράκοντος...καὶ δεδωκότα τοῖς ἑαυτοῦ μαθηταῖς ἐξουσίαν πατεῖν ἐπάνω ὄφεων καὶ σκορπίων, καὶ ἐπὶ πᾶσαν τὴν δύναμιν τοῦ ἐχθροῦ Thdt.*Cant.*2:9(2.62); Cyr.*Ps.*17:34(M.69.825A); **2.** of apostles and preachers of Christianity; in desert of world that does not know God ἐλάφους γάρ,...ὁ κύριος καταρτισάμενος· ζῷον φιλέρημον Eus.*Ps.*28:9(M.23.257B); ὅτε...καὶ αὐτὸς ὁ νυμφίος ἐλάφῳ παραβάλλεται, τίνας δ' ἂν εἴποις ἐνταῦθα ἐ. ἢ τοὺς μαθητὰς καὶ ἀποστόλους; ἔστι δὲ καὶ ὀφιοκτόνον τὸ ζῷον. διδάσκει τοίνυν ὁ παρὼν λόγος, ὡς ἀπὸ τῆς ἐρημίας τοῦ Ἰουδαίων ἔθνους ἐ. τινες παρῆλθον, οἱ μαθηταί id.*Is.*34:15(M.24.337B); Ath.*exp.Ps.*17:34(M.27.117C); ἐ. ... ἐνταῦθα τοὺς...ἀποστόλους ὀνομάζει, ὧν οἱ πόδες ὡραῖοι...ὡς πατοῦντες τοὺς θανατοῦντας ὄφεις, καὶ ταῖς τῶν ἀνθρώπων ψυχαῖς ἐπιβουλεύοντας Thdt.*Cant.*2:9(2.64); id.*Ps.*28:9(1.784); Hesych.H.*Ps.tit.*28.18(M.27.752B); **3.** of converts, ref. Is.35:6, Dt.12:15 μὴ μάτην ἐλάφῳ καθαρῷ ζῴῳ καὶ πολεμίῳ τῶν ὄφεων καὶ μηδὲν βλάπτεσθαι ὑπὸ ἰοῦ αὐτῶν δυναμένῳ παραβεβλῆσθαι τοὺς πρότερον χωλοὺς καὶ διὰ Ἰησοῦν ἁλλομένους ὡς ἐ. Or.*comm. in Mt.*11.18(p.66.10; M.13.968A); id.*Cels.*2.48(p.170.20; M.11.872B); Eus.*Is.*35:5(M.24.340D); Cyr.*Is.*3.3(2.474B); **4.** of the righteous; **a.** as destroying power of serpent, Or.*Cant.*3(p.214.17; M.13.177B); Eus.*Ps.*17:33(M.23.181A); Ath.*exp.Ps.*17:34(M.27.117C); ἔ. ... διψαλέον...γίνεται καὶ ἀπὸ τῆς φύσεως καὶ ἀπὸ τοῦ τοὺς ὄφεις κατεσθίειν...καὶ σὺ τοίνυν τοῦτο ποίησον· τὸν νοητὸν ὄφιν κατάφαγε· ἐδάφισον τὴν ἁμαρτίαν, καὶ δυνήσῃ διψᾶν τὸν τοῦ θεοῦ πόθον Chrys.*exp.in Ps.*41(5.138A); **b.** as seeking heights of spiritual life; ref. Ps.103:18 cf. *ego puto quod scientiam trinitatis montes excelsos appellaverit, ad cujus capacitatem nullus, nisi cervus efficiatur, adscendit,* Or.*Cant.*3(p.214.21; 177B); ref. Ps.103:18 and Ps.41:2 ὄρη...τὰ ὑψηλὰ ταῖς ἐ. καί, ἐπιποθεῖ ἡ ἔ. ἐπὶ τὰς πηγὰς τῶν ὑδάτων. ἐπεὶ οὖν καὶ πᾶς δίκαιος ἐν ὑψηλοῖς ἔχει τὴν διατριβήν,...καὶ πρὸς τὰς ποτίμους πηγὰς ἀνατρέχει, τὰς πρώτας ἀρχὰς τῆς θεολογίας ἀναζητῶν Bas.*hom.in Ps.*28(1.121D; M.29.300B); †Bas.*hom.in Ps.*28(1.361B; M.30.80C); Ath.*exp.Ps.*41:2(M.27.201A); Proc.G.*Cant.*8:14(M.87.1780A); **5.** of OT saints; ref. Ps.28:9, Cant.2:9, cf. *forte possunt cervi accipi sancti quique,...ex quorum semine Christus secundum carnem descendit. quos cervos vox domini perfectos fecit et ipsorum est hinnulus iste,* Or.*Cant.*3(p.214.11; M.13.177A); ἡ ἔ. ... καθαρὸν κατὰ τὸν νόμον, ἤδη δὲ καὶ ὀφιοκτόνον...καὶ τῶν τὰς ἐρήμους μεταδιωκόντων. τοιοῦτος δὲ ἦν ὁ προφητικὸς χορός Eus.*Ps.*41:2(M.23.369A); **6.** (Naassene) τριτάτη ψυχὴ δ' ἔλαβεν ἐργαζομένην (sic) νόμον, διὰ τοῦτο ἔλαφον (sic) μορφὴν περικειμένη Hipp.*haer.*5.10(p.103.1; M.16.3159A).

ἐλαφρία, ἡ, *levity, lightheartedness,* Bas.*reg.fus.*41.2(2.387E; M.31.1024A); Mac.Aeg.*hom.*27.8(M.34.697D); Cyr.*Os.*26(3.49D); Isid.Pel.*epp.*1.430(M.78.420C).

ἐλαφρίζω, *lighten*; met., *alleviate,* Gr.Naz.*carm.*1.2.1.265(M.37.542A); Nonn.*par.Jo.*11:31(M.43.844B).

ἐλαφρός, 1. *light,* ref. Mt.11:30 ἐ. ἔσται τὸ φορτίον...ἂν ταπεινὸς γένῃ καὶ πρᾶος καὶ ἐπιεικής Chrys.*hom.38.2 in Mt.*(7.428B); ἐ. ἐστιν ὁ ζυγὸς τοῦ Χριστοῦ· ἐπεὶ οὐ κολάζει ἡμᾶς καθάπερ ὁ νόμος Cyr.*fr. Mt.*11:30(M.72.405B); **2.** *simple, unintelligent, Const.App.*1.6.2; Mac.Aeg.*hom.*17.5(M.34.628A); Cyr.*ep.*11.4(p.11.16; 5^{2}.38A); **3.** *easy*; of the way to heaven ὁ σωτὴρ...ταύτην ἐ. ... κατεσκεύασεν Ath.*ep. fest.*28(p.296.7; M.26.1433C).

ἐλαφρότης, ἡ, *lightheartedness, freedom from care* ἐ., καὶ ἀγαλλιάσει θείᾳ Mac.Aeg.*hom.*24.6(M.34.665D); ἐν ἀναπαύσει καὶ ἐ. Ammonas *ep.*2(p.437.7).

ἐλαφρύν-ω, *relieve*; of bishop reconciling sinners, *Const.App.* 1.18.7; *ib.*1.20.4; ref. Gal.5:3 ἑνὸς...ὄντος δεσπότου, δυναμένου βαρύνειν καὶ ~ειν Epiph.*haer.*42.11(p.156.25; M.41.776A).

ἐλαφρῶς, *lightly,* Herm.*sim.*7.6.

***ἐλεακατάκαρπος,** *bearing the fruit of mercy* with play on *olive-bearing,* ref. BMV ἐ. τὰς ψυχὰς...ἱλαρύνουσα Ephr.3.529B.

ἐλεγκτικός, 1. *reproving,* of prophecy ψόγος ἐ. Clem.*paed.*1.9(p.134.29; M.8.341B); of Christ reproving sin, Or.*Jo.*13.9(p.233.30; M.14.412D); *ib.*6.23(13; p.133.12; 241B); τὸ...ἐν τῷ πυρὶ βάπτισμα ἐ. ... ἐστι πάσης κακίας †Bas.*bapt.*1.3.1(2.649D; M.31.1573A); ὁ ἐ. [sc. ἀπέχεται] ὑποκρίσεως Marc.Er.*opusc.*2.24(M.65.933C); of scripture ὁ ἐ. λόγος Thdt.*Cant.*3:8(2.86); Euthal.Diac.*Ac.*(M.85.653A); **2.** *argumentative* χρὴ μετεῖναι τὸ ἐ. εἶδος ἕνεκα τοῦ τὰς δόξας ἀπατηλὰς διακρούεσθαι τῶν σοφιστῶν Clem.*str.*1.6(p.23.19; M.8.729C); Or.*Jo.*10.24(16; p.196.26; M.14.349B); **3.** *attracting* ἐ. εἰς ἐπιθυμίαν ἐστὶ τὸ προσηνὲς τῇ ὄψει Gr.Nyss.*hom.6 in Cant.*(M.44.900C).

ἐλεγκτικῶς, 1. *reprovingly,* Clem.*paed.*1.2(p.92.23; M.8.253C); **2.** *by argument,* id.*str.*8.1(p.80.7; M.9.560A).

ἐλεγμός, ὁ, *reproach, Pss.Sal.*10.1; Ammon.*Ac.*18:25(M.85.1572D); exeg. Is.37:3 ἐ. δὲ [sc. καλεῖ] τὴν τοῦ λαοῦ παρανομίαν Thdt. *Is.*37:3(p.145.17); ref. Jo. Bapt. ὑπὲρ ἐλεγμοῦ ἀληθείας...τυμπανισθείς Thdr.Stud.*epp.*2.37(M.99.1228A).

ἔλεγξις, ἡ, 1. *reproach, Apoc.En.*14.1; τὸ ὕδωρ τῆς ἐ. κυρίου *Protev.*16(p.30); **2.** *refutation* τῆς πλάνης ἡ ἔ. ‡Ath.*Apoll.*1.3(M.26.1097A).

ἔλεγχος, ὁ, 1. *examination,* ref. final judgement ἐν καιρῷ τοῦ ἐ. περὶ τῶν ἁμαρτημάτων Meth.*res.*1.24(p.248.20; M.41.1093C); **2.** *proof,* ref. persecution of Christians ἡμῶν...τὸ ὄνομα ὡς ἔ. λαμβάνετε Just. *1apol.*4.4(M.6.333A); of arguments from scripture agst. heretics and Jews, Ath.*Ar.*1.10(M.26.32B); id.*inc.*33.3(M.25.153A); as title of books written by Dion. Al. to refute accusation of heresy, id.*Dion.*13(p.55.20; M.25.500B) al.; of proof given by Christ of his divinity, Chrys.*hom.52.3 in Jo.*(8.308A); **3.** *condemnation,* in writings of S. John ὁ ἔ. τοῦ κόσμου τοῦ διαβόλου τοῦ ἀντιχρίστου Dion.Al. ap.Eus.*h.e.*7.25.21(M.20.701C); **4.** *reproof*; **a.** administered by God ἐλέγχου σκοπὸς ἡ τῶν ἐλεγχομένων σωτηρία Clem.*paed.*1.8(p.132.8; M.8.336C); πάντα ποιήσωμεν εἰς τὸ ⟨μὴ⟩ δεηθῆναι τοιούτων ἐ. Or.*Jo.*6.58(37; p.167.17; M.14.300B); **b.** in Christian life φιλεῖ...πως τὸ μὴ λανθάνον δι' αἰσχύνην τῶν ἐ. ἀφίστασθαι τῶν ἁμαρτημάτων Clem.*paed.*3.2(p.241.17; 569A); ἀφόρητον...ἔ. ... ὅταν μὴ καὶ παράκλησιν ἀναμεμιγμένην ἔχῃ Chrys.*hom.9.1 in 2Tim.*(11.715D); τὸ...ἀταράχως βαστάζειν τὸν...ἔ.,...σημεῖόν ἐστιν, ὅτι ἡττώμενος ἢ ἀγνοῶν ἐνήργησεν αὐτό [sc. τὸ πάθος] Dor.*doct.*19(M.88.1809D); ἔ. πρὸς τοὺς ἐξ ἀπειρίας μὴ εἰδότας βοηθεῖν τοῖς κάμνουσι ἐπίστασις *Schol.*21 in Jo.Clim.*scal.*26(M.88.1041B); ἐάν...φῶς ὦμεν, καὶ φανεροῦν τὸ σκότος δυνάμεθα τῇ τοῦ φωτὸς ἀντιθέσει, ἔ. οὗτος ὁ κάλλιστος Jo.D.*Eph.*5:12–15(M.95.848C); **c.** ref. heretics τὰς προφητείας εἴργουσιν ἑαυτῶν τῆς ἐκκλησίας, ὑφορώμενοι δι' ἔ. Clem. *str.*7.16(p.70.6; M.9.537A); **5.** *catalogue,* Eus.*d.e.*1 proem.(p.3.7; M.22.16B).

ἐλέγχ-ω, A. *reprove*; **1.** of God θυμῷ θεοῦ ἔστιν ~θῆναι Or.*Jo.*6.58

(37; p.167.14; M.14.300B); ὁ ἐνοικῶν εἰς τὰς καρδίας τῶν πιστευόντων εἰς αὐτόν, καὶ διδάσκων αὐτοὺς τὸ θέλημα αὐτοῦ οὐκ ἔχει ἐλέγξαι ὑμᾶς ἐν τῇ ἡμέρᾳ τῆς κρίσεως; Hesych.H.*Ps.tit*.93.18(M.27.1053C); Andr. Caes.*Apoc*.9(M.106.249D); **2.** of Christ at Temptation, rebuking Devil, Just.*dial*.125.4(M.6.768B); cf.Chrys.*hom.13.3 in Mt*.(7.170E); παντὶ σθένει ὁ τῆς ἀνθρωπότητος παιδαγωγὸς...σώζειν ἐπιβέβληται τοὺς νηπίους,...~ων Clem.*paed*.1.9(p.133.30; M.8.341B); reproving Pharisees, Or.*Jo*.6.31(15; p.140.16; M.14.253A) al.; **3.** of scripture τὰ διὰ τοῦ θεοῦ ὑπὸ τοῦ προφητικοῦ πνεύματος ~ονται Just.*dial*.38.2 (M.6.557B) al.; of S. Paul τοιούτου μάρτυρος ~οντος τὴν τῶν ἀνθρώπων ἄνοιαν Clem.*prot*.9(p.63.13; M.8.196A); προφήτου τὴν παρανομίαν ~οντος ‡Nil.*narr*.2(M.79.608A) etc.; **4.** ref. Christian life; **a.** utility of reproving μεῖζον...ἀγαθὸν τὸ ~θῆναι τοῦ ἐλέγξαι νομίζω, ὅσῳ μεῖζόν ἐστι τὸ αὐτὸν ἀπαλλαγῆναι κακοῦ τοῦ ἄλλον ἀπαλλάξαι Meth. *res*.1.30(p.262.13; M.41.1140C); ~ομένη...ἁμαρτία πολλάκις ὑπερυθριᾷ, καὶ ὑπονοστεῖ τρόπον τινά, πρὸς τὸ πρόσω χωρεῖν καὶ ἐπεκτείνεσθαι μηδαμόθεν εὑρίσκουσα· δοκοῦσα δέ πως διαλανθάνειν ἀεὶ πρὸς τὸ μεῖζον αἴρεται Cyr.*Jo*.6(4.565C); id.*Is*.2.1(2.195D); τοὺς ἁμαρτάνοντας ἐνώπιον πάντων ~ε, ἵνα καὶ οἱ λοιποὶ φόβον ἔχωσι Jo.D.*1Tim*.5:16–25 (M.95.1013A); **b.** manner of reproving οὐ λήψῃ πρόσωπον ἐλέγξαι τινὰ ἐπὶ παραπτώματι *Barn*.19.4; *Did*.4.3; ~ετε ἀλλήλους μὴ ἐν ὀργῇ, ἀλλ' ἐν εἰρήνῃ *ib*.15.3; *ib*.2.7; *Const.App*.7.31.3; Chrys.*hom.9.1 in 2Tim*.(11.715E); ref. 1Tim.5:20 ~ε δὲ οὐχ ἁπλῶς, φησίν, ἀλλὰ μετὰ ἀποτομίας· οὕτω γὰρ καὶ οἱ λοιποὶ φόβον ἕξουσι id.*hom.15.2 in 1Tim*. (11.637D); the more serious sins to be reproved sharply, id.*hom.5.3 in Tit*.(11.759F); **c.** of how reproof should be received οὐ...μισῶν τοὺς ~οντας ἀλλὰ καὶ μᾶλλον ἀγαπῶν Or.*Jo*.32.15(9; p.450.23; M.14. 781A); διὰ...τοῦτο...ἐπαχθεῖς ἐσμεν ~οντες, ἐπειδὴ ἐκθηριούμεθα ~όμενοι. εἰ γὰρ ᾔδει ὁ ἀδελφός, ὅτι ἐλέγξας σε ἐπῃνεῖτο παρὰ σοῦ, καὶ αὐτὸς ~όμενος τὴν αὐτὴν ἀμοιβὴν ἀπέδωκεν ἂν Chrys.*hom.3.1 in Ac*. 9:1(3.117E); σημεῖόν ἐστιν ὅτι ἑκουσίως ἐνεργεῖ τις πάθος, ὅτε ~όμενος ...περὶ αὐτοῦ ταράσσεται Dor.*doct*.19(M.86.1809D); of man who practises self-accusation τοὺς ~οντας...ὡς εὐεργέτας ἀγαπᾷ *Schol*.33 in Jo.Clim.*scal*.25(M.88.1009D).

B. *examine* τὸ πνεῦμα...τὰ κρυπτὰ ~ει Ign.*Philad*.7.1.

C. *convict*; **1.** in gen., Just.*dial*.141.1(M.6.797C); ref. command in Gen.2:17 ἵνα γένηται καὶ ~θῇ...ὁ...τέκτων τῆς ἁμαρτίας ἁμαρτωλός Meth.*res*.2.2(p.332.11; M.41.1165A); exeg. Jo.8:46 τὸ δέ, ἐλέγξει περὶ ἁμαρτίας, τοῦτ' ἔστι, πᾶσαν ἀπολογίαν αὐτῶν ἐκκόψει Chrys.*hom. 78.2 in Jo*.(8.459E); Cyr.*Jo*.6(4.564D); cf.Ammon.*Jo*.8:46(M.85. 1453A); **2.** of persecution of Christians τοὺς μὲν ἄλλους αἰτίαν λαβόντας ἀδικημάτων μὴ πρότερον ἢ ~θῆναι κολάζεσθαι, ἐφ' ἡμῶν δὲ μεῖζον ἰσχύειν τὸ ὄνομα τῶν ἐπὶ τῇ δίκῃ ἐλέγχων Athenag.*leg*.2.2(M. 6.893C); Just.*1apol*.4.2(M.6.332B).

D. *test*, martyrs ἵνα τὴν δόξαν παρ' αὐτῷ κτήσωνται μείζονα, διὰ πολλῶν αὐτοὺς ἤλεγξε πόνων Meth.*res*.1.56(p.315.11; M.41.1149B).

E. *prove* ἐλέγξας [sc. God before Inc.]...ἐν...τῷ πρόσθεν χρόνῳ τὸ ἀδύνατον τῆς ἡμετέρας φύσεως εἰς τὸ τυχεῖν ζωῆς *Diogn*.9.6; hence *convince*, *Barn*.12.5.

F. *prove wrong, refute* ἡ...τοῦ ἰσχυροῦ αὐτοῦ λόγου δύναμις, δι' ἧς... ἤλεγξε τοὺς...Φαρισαίους Just.*dial*.102.5(M.6.713C) al.; esp. of confutation of heretics from scripture, Clem.*str*.4.1(p.249.3; M.8. 1216B); Ath.*gent*.6(M.25.13B); Jo.D.*f.o*.1.7(M.94.808A).

G. *overcome* κἂν ἅπαντα ὁμοῦ συνέλθῃ τὰ ἐν ἀνθρώποις κακά, τὴν τοῦ φιλοθέου...ψυχὴν οὐδέποτε ἐλέγξει Chrys.*Laz*.3.7(1.747C).

ἐλεεινότης, ἡ, *pitiable state, misery*, ‡Meth.*Sym.et Ann*.8(M.18. 365C); *Lit.Jac*.(p.218.14); as humble way of referring to oneself, *Rit.Bapt*.(p.399).

ἐλε-έω, A. *have mercy*, of God; **1.** in gen., *2Clem*.1.7; Herm.*vis*. 1.3.2; Clem.*prot*.1(p.6.31; M.8.60B) etc.; **2.** modes of expression; **a.** by creating man in his image, Ath.*inc*.3.3(M.25.101B); *ib*.11.1 (116A); **b.** by saving him, Or.*princ*.3.1.8(p.208.3; M.11.261B); ref. Rom.9:16, *ib*.3.1.18(p.229.10ff.; 288A); hence **c.** through Inc., *Diogn*. 9.2; ἐπεὶ δὲ πλουσίως ~εῖ ἀγαθὸς ὢν ὁ θεός...διὰ τῆς τοῦ υἱοῦ παρουσίας ...~ῶν...τοὺς ἐλεημένους, κυρίως τε ~εῖ ὁ κρείττων τοῦ ἐλάσσω,... κρείττων δὲ ὁ θεὸς τοῦ ἀνθρώπου κατὰ πάντα, εἰ τοίνυν ὁ κρείττων τὸν ἥσσω ~εῖ, μόνος ἡμᾶς ὁ θεὸς ἐλεήσει Clem.*str*.2.16(pp.151.27–152.3; M.8.1012B,C); ὁ θεὸς...~ήσας καὶ θέλων πᾶσι γνωσθῆναι, ποιεῖ τὸν ἑαυτοῦ υἱὸν ἐνδύσασθαι σῶμα ἀνθρώπινον Ath.*Ar*.2.14(M.26.176B); **d.** and Passion, Just.*dial*.106.1(M.6.721C); υἱὸς...ὑπὲρ ἡμῶν προσενέγκας ἑαυτὸν ἠλέησεν ἡμᾶς Ath.*Ar*.2.9(M.26.165B); **3.** Gnost., God having mercy only on πνευματικοί, Or.*princ*.3.1.8(p.207.5; M. 11.261A); **4.** liturg., ref. prayer for catechumens, *Lit*.ap.*Const.App*. 8.6.4; κύριε ~ησον before collect, *Lit.Jac*.(p.166.16); after Alleluia, *ib*.(p.170.19).

B. pass., *receive, find mercy*, with God; **1.** in gen., *1Clem*.56.16; ἵνα ἐν ᾧ κλήρῳ ἠλεήθην ἐπιτύχω Ign.*Philad*.5.1; id.*Rom*.9.2; Clem. *paed*.2.8(p.195.9; M.8.468B); **2.** of Church τῇ ἠλεημένῃ...ἐκκλησίᾳ Ign.*Rom*.proem.; id.*Philad*.proem.; id.*Smyrn*.proem.; ἐγὼ κατάκριτος, ὑμεῖς ἠλεημένοι id.*Eph*.12.1; **3.** of Jews εὐχόμεθα ὑπὲρ ὑμῶν, ἵνα ~ήθητε ὑπὸ τοῦ Χριστοῦ Just.*dial*.96.3(M.6.704B).

C. of men; **1.** *have pity*; on pagans, Just.*1apol*.25.3(M.6.368A); οὓς οὐ μόνον οὐ μισοῦμεν, ἀλλ'...~οῦντες μεταθέσθαι πεῖσαι βουλόμεθα *ib*.57.1(413C); as special activity of 'gnostic' ἔχων...ἔναυλον τὴν φωνὴν τὴν λέγουσαν, ὃν ἐγὼ πατάξω, σὺ ~ησον Clem.*str*.7.12(p.53. 19; M.9.501C); discussion of when showing pity would be inopportune, Or.*hom.12.5 in Jer*.(p.91.25ff.; M.13.385Aff.); **2.** *give alms*, *Did*.5.2 = *Barn*.20.2; to be done in secret, Clem.*str*.4.22(p.309.15; M.8.1348B); indiscriminately, Chrys.*Laz*.2.5(1.734E); not for sake of human praise, id.*hom.65.4 in Mt*.(7.650A); possible also to poor, id.*anom*.8.2(1.516A); ref. Manicheans ἐχθρόν ἐστι παρ' αὐτοῖς τὸ ~εῖν πένητα. ἦν τοίνυν καινὴ μέμψις...ἐπινοηθὲν παρ' αὐτῶν...ὁ μὲν ~ῶν κατηγορεῖτο, ὁ δὲ εὐεργετούμενος ἐτύπτετο· καὶ μᾶλλον ἤθελον πεινᾶν τὸν πένητα ἢ τὸν βουλόμενον ~εῖν παρέχειν Ath.*h.Ar*.61(p.217. 24ff.; M.25.768B).

***ἐλεημονητικός,** *merciful*; neut. as subst., in catalogue of virtues, Jo.D.*virt*.(M.95.85C); = Ephr.3.425D (ἐλεημονιτικόν).

***ἐλεημονικός,** *merciful, compassionate*, Adam.*dial*.3.4(p.118.26; M.11.1796A); *Hom.Clem*.3.26; Olymp.*Eccl*.5:17–19(M.93.549A); neut. as subst., Eus.*fr.Lc*.17:3(M.24.581B).

***ἐλεημονιτικός,** v. *ἐλεημονητικός.

ἐλεημοσύνη, ἡ, I. *mercy*;

A. divine, *Pss.Sal*.9.20; *ib*.15.15; exeg. Ps.32:5 εἰ καθ' ἑαυτὴν ὑπῆρχεν ἡ τοῦ θεοῦ κρίσις,...ποία ἦν ἐλπίς;...νῦν δὲ 'ἀγαπᾷ ἐ. καὶ κρίσιν.' οἱονεὶ πάρεδρον ἑαυτῷ τὴν ἐ. ποιησάμενος,...οὔτε ἡ ἐ. ἄκριτος, οὔτε ἡ κρίσις ἀνελεήμων. πρὸ τῆς κρίσεως οὖν ἀγαπᾷ ἐ., καὶ μετὰ τὴν ἐ. ἔρχεται ἐπὶ τὴν κρίσιν Bas.*hom.in Ps*.32(1.134D,E; M.29.332A); compared with human ἐ. (= *almsgiving*), Chrys.*hom.71.4 in Mt*. (7.699D,E).

B. human, perh. also = *almsgiving* λέγω δὴ τὴν ἐ. τὴν βασιλίδα τῶν ἀρετῶν, τὴν ταχέως ἀνάγουσαν εἰς τὰς ἁψῖδας τῶν οὐρανῶν τοὺς ἀνθρώπους, τὴν συνήγορον τὴν ἀρίστην. μέγα πρᾶγμα ἐ. ... μεγάλα τὰ πτερὰ τῆς ἐ.· τέμνει τὸν ἀέρα, παρέρχεται τὴν σελήνην...παρατρέχει... τὰς ἀνωτέρας πάσας δυνάμεις, καὶ αὐτῷ παρίσταται τῷ θρόνῳ τῷ βασιλικῷ Chrys.*poenit*.3.1(2.295C,D); its superiority over κακία, id.*hom. 1.3 in Ps.48*:17(5.509B); βλέπε πόσον ἐστὶν ἐ. ἑαυτῷ παραβάλλει ὁ θεὸς τὸν ἐλεήμονα ‡Chrys.*eleem*.1(1.819B); ἐ. χωρίς, ἄκαρπος ἡ ψυχή †Max.*loc.comm*.7(M.91.765D); *act of mercy* τὸ οὖν σπεύδειν σωφρονεῖν τοὺς ἀδελφούς, τοῦτο πρώτη ἐ. *Hom.Clem*.3.68.

II. *almsgiving*;

A. def. and scope; **1.** in gen. τέχνη τίς ἐστιν ἡ ἐ., ἐν οὐρανῷ τὸ ἐργαστήριον ἔχουσα Chrys.*hom.52.3 in Mt*.(7.533E); ἐ. δὲ οὐκ ἐν χρήμασι γίνεται μόνον, ἀλλὰ καὶ ἐν πράγμασιν id.*hom.25.3 in Ac*.(9. 205D); cf.*ib*.25.4(l.c.); ἡ μικρὰν ἐ. οἴει εἶναι, ψυχὴν ἀπορουμένην, κινδυνεύουσαν περὶ τῶν ἐσχάτων, ὑπὸ πυρώσεως συνεχομένην, δυνηθῆναι ἀπαλλάξαι τῆς νόσου; *ib*.(206A); **2.** part of service of God, cf. Iren.*haer*.3.12.7(M.7.900B); ὃς καὶ χρήματα διδούς, αἰτεῖ παρά σου τὴν ἐ. διὰ τῆς χειρὸς τῶν πενήτων Bas.*hom*.5.7(1.40E; M.31.253D); τίς ὁ τῆς ἐ. τεχνίτης ἐστίν; ὁ τὸ πρᾶγμα καταδείξας, θεὸς δηλονότι Chrys. *hom.71.3 in Mt*.(7.699A); ref. Lc.16:9, id.*hom.1.4 in Heb*.(12.12A); ‡Nil.*perist*.9.6(M.79.873D); cf.*ib*.12.12(964B); οὐδὲν οὕτως εὐφραίνει τὸν θεόν, ὡς ἐ. †Max.*loc.comm*.7(M.91.768C).

B. necessity and importance τὰ τῆς σωτηρίας δι' ἐλεημοσύνης ἐφόδια ὠνησώμεθα Nect.*Thdr*.18(M.39.1836B); *ib*.22(1837D); μή... ἀμελῶμεν τῆς ἑαυτῶν σωτηρίας, ἀλλ' ἐπιθώμεθα τῇ ἐ. Chrys.*hom. 1.6 in Col*.(11.332D); πολλὴν ἐπιδειξώμεθα περὶ τὴν ἐλεημοσύνης σπουδήν, ἐπειδὴ μηδὲ ἑτέρως ἔστι τῆς βασιλείας τῶν οὐρανῶν ἐπιτυχεῖν id.*hom.1.8 in 2Cor*.4:13(3.266C); ref. Mt.25:35 τέσσαρας ἀνάγκας ἐφίστησιν ἐ.· τὸ ἀξιόπιστον τοῦ αἰτοῦντος, ὅτι δεσπότης ἐστὶν ὁ αἰτῶν· τὸ ἀναγκαῖον τῆς χρείας, ὅτι πεινᾷ· τὸ εὔκολον τῆς δόσεως, ὅτι τραφῆναι ζητεῖ καὶ ἄρτον αἰτεῖ μόνον...τὸ μέγεθος τῆς δωρεᾶς, ὅτι βασιλείαν ἀντὶ τούτων τῶν μικρῶν ἐπαγγέλλεται id.*hom.in 1Tim*.5:9(3.326E); hence can be practised also by the poor, since not quantity but the intention is important, id.*anom*.8.2(1.516B); id.*hom.55.4 in Gen*.(4. 536E); ref. Mt.25:1ff. καὶ αἱ παρθένοι διὰ τοῦτο μόνον ἐξεβλήθησαν τοῦ νυμφῶνος...ἐπειδὴ τῆς ἀπὸ ἐ. ἦσαν ἔρημοι βοηθείας, τῷ νυμφίῳ οὐ συνεισῆλθον id.*hom.4.3 in Eph*.(11.29C not.); ‡Chrys.*eleem*.1(1.820B).

C. conditions of right almsgiving; **1.** two opinions; **a.** should be done with discernment, *Did*.1.6; ἐ. δεῖ ποιεῖν...ἀλλὰ μετὰ κρίσεως καὶ τοῖς ἀξίοις Clem.*fr*.53(p.225.25; M.9.744A); **b.** should be done indiscriminately σὺ τοίνυν, ὅτε ἐ. ποιεῖς, μὴ βίον ἐξετάσῃς, μηδὲ τρόπων εὐθύνας ἀπαίτει. ἐ. γὰρ διὰ τοῦτο λέγεται, ἵνα καὶ τοῖς ἀναξίοις παρέχωμεν Chrys.*hom.2.8 in 2Cor.4:13*(3.276C); id.*Laz.*2.5(1.734E); ὁ γὰρ τοὺς μονάζοντας μόνον ἐπιζητῶν, κἀκείνους μόνους εὖ ποιεῖν θέλων,...καὶ λέγων, ἐὰν μὴ ᾖ ἄξιος...οὐκ ὀρέγω χεῖρα, τὸ πλέον τῆς ἐ. ἐξεῖλε...καίτοιγε ἐ. ἐκείνη ἐστίν, ἡ εἰς τοὺς ἁμαρτωλοὺς...ἐ. γὰρ τοῦτό ἐστιν, οὐ τὸ τοὺς κατωρθωκότας, ἀλλὰ τὸ τοὺς πεπλημμεληκότας ἐλεεῖν id.*hom.10.4 in Heb.*(12.108D); cf.Ant.Mon.*hom.*98(M.89.1732B); **2.** from right motives: not from vainglory, Chrys.*hom.20.6 in 1Cor.*(10.178C); Dor.*doct.*14.5(M.88.1784A); not in order to receive benefits from God in exchange, *ib.*14.6(1784C,D); οὕτως διδόντες, ὡς αὐτοὶ λαμβάνοντες. καὶ αὕτη ἐστὶν ἡ ἐν γνώσει ἐ. *ib.*14.7(1785B); **3.** promptly ὁ ἀπαιτούμενος ἄγχεται· καὶ σὺ τὴν ἐ. εἰς τὴν αὔριον ἀναβάλλῃ; Bas.*hom.*6.6(2.49C; M.31.276A); and joyfully, Chrys. *eleem.*4(3.254D); id.*hom.in 1Cor.11:19*(3.243E); id.*hom.55.4 in Gen.*(4.536E); exeg. Mt.6:1, id.*hom.19.1 in Mt.*(7.245A–D); **4.** acc. one's means, id.*hom.28.4 in Heb.*(12.262B); not from ill-gotten gains, id. *hom.73.3 in Jo.*(8.433E).

D. effects; in gen. μέγα οὖν πρᾶγμα ἐ. ... ταύτην ἀσπασώμεθα, ἧς οὐδὲν ἴσον· ἱκανὴ ἐστι καὶ ἄλλας ἁμαρτίας ἐξαλεῖψαι, καὶ τὴν κρίσιν ἀπελάσαι· σοῦ σιωπῶντος ἕστηκε, καὶ συνηγορεῖ...τοσαῦτα ἀγαθὰ ἐκ τῆς ἐ. Chrys.*poenit.*3.3(2.297C,D); id.*hom.52.3 in Mt.*(7.534A); benefits giver rather than receiver, Chrys.*eleem.*4(3.254C); id.*hom. 15.1 in Phil.*(11.309E); id.*hom.20.2 in Mt.*(7.262D); id.*hom.2.9 in 2Cor.4:13*(3.278D); wipes out sins, *2Clem.*16.4; ἐ., ἡ πάσης ἀπηλλαγμένη ἀδικίας· αὕτη πάντα καθαρὰ ποιεῖ Gr.Naz.ap.†Max.*loc. comm.*7(M.91.765C); οὐκ ἔστιν ἁμάρτημα, ὃ μὴ δύναται καθαρίσαι ἐ. ...πᾶσα ἁμαρτία κατωτέρα ταύτης ἕστηκε Chrys.*hom.25.3 in Ac.*(9.205C); οὐδὲ γὰρ οὕτως ὕδατος φύσις ἀπονίπτει κηλῖδας σώματος, ὡς ἐ. δύναμις ἀποσμήχει ῥύπον ψυχῆς id.*hom.3.12 in 2Cor.4:13*(3.289E); id.*poenit.*3.1(2.295E); πλῦνον τὰς χεῖρας τῆς ψυχῆς τῇ ἐ. *ib.*3.2(297A); ‡Chrys.*eleem.*1(1.819C); αὐτὸ τὸ ἀγαθὸν τῆς ἐ. ... ὅτι δύναται καὶ ἁμαρτίας ἀφιέναι Dor.*doct.*14.6(M.88.1784B); spiritual benefits; makes men like fruitful olive (Ps.51:10), Bas.*hex.*5.6(1.46C; M.29.109A); γενοῦ τοῦ προφήτου δι' ἐλεημοσύνης ἑταῖρος...πολύχους βλαστάνει ὁ τῆς ἐ. καρπός Gr.Nyss.*paup.*1(M.46.460A); τὴν ἐ. κατεργασώμεθα· τὴν ὡς ἀληθῶς οὐκ εἰς τρίτον οὐρανόν, ἀλλ' εἰς αὐτὸν τὸν τῶν οὐρανῶν ποιητὴν ἐπαγαγοῦσαν· ἐ., τὴν ὡσεὶ πυρὸς ἅρμα καὶ ὑπὲρ τὸν οὐρανὸν συστὰν εἰσδέξηται γῆθεν ἀνάγουσαν Nect.*Thdr.*15(M.39.1833B); ἐ. ... βασιλὶς γάρ ἐστιν ὄντως, ὁμοίους ἀνθρώπους ποιοῦσα θεῷ Chrys.*hom.32.3 in Heb.*(12.298D); id.*hom.69.3 in Jo.*(8.411C); ὁ κύριος τὴν ἐ. ὥρισε πρὸς τὴν ὁμοίωσιν τοῦ πατρός, ὡς προσεγγίζουσαν αὐτῷ τοὺς τελειοῦντας αὐτήν Isaac *ep.*8(p.162); preserves from damnation, Chrys.*exp.in Ps.*111:5(5.282B); δυνατὸν σωθῆναι, τὸ τῆς ἐ. κατασκευάζοντας φάρμακον id.*hom.64.5 in Mt.*(7.641C); procures merciful judge, id.*hom.5.2 in Gen.*(4.33C); εἰ ...ἁμαρτωλὸς ὁ τεθνηκὼς...δεῖ...ποιεῖν τὰ δυνάμενα τινὰ παραμυθίαν αὐτῷ περιποιῆσαι, ἐ. καὶ προσφοράς id.*hom.62.5 in Jo.*(8.374D); *ib.* 86.5(511C); ὅσῳ πλειόνων γέγονεν ἁμαρτημάτων ὑπεύθυνος, τοσούτῳ μειζόνως αὐτῷ δεῖ τῆς ἐ. ... δυσωπήσει τοῦτο τὸν θεόν, εἰ καὶ μὴ ὑπ' αὐτοῦ, ἀλλὰ δι' αὐτὸν ἕτερος αἴτιος γίνεται τῆς ἐ. ... πολλοὶ καὶ ἐκ τῶν ὑφ' ἑτέρων δι' αὐτοὺς γεγενημένων ἐ. ἀπώναντο id.*hom.21.3 in Ac.*(9.175B,C); ‡Nil.*perist.*6.1(M.79.856D); hence to be given on behalf of dead, Justn.*ep.Thdr.Mops.*(p.68.4; M.86.1091A); punishment hereafter for refusal to give alms, Chrys.*Laz.*2.4(1.733A); salvation impossible without it, id.*hom.23.3 in Jo.*(8.136E); other effects: cures wrath, Evagr.Pont.*cap.pract.*A 63(M.40.1237B); makes houses immune from demons, Chrys.*eleem.*4(3.254B); keeps lamps burning (Mt.25:1ff.), id.*hom.23.3 in Jo.*(8.136D); overcomes death, id.*hom. 55.4 in Gen.*(4.536B); keeps Devil away, id.*hom.45.4 in Ac.*(9.343E).

E. in relation to other virtues and good works καλὸν οὖν ἐ. ὡς μετάνοια ἁμαρτίας· κρείσσων νηστεία προσευχῆς, ἐ. δὲ ἀμφοτέρων *2Clem.*16.4; cf. μετάνοια, νηστεία; ass. fasting and prayer, Ath. *virg.*6(p.40.1; M.28.257B); better than fasting and sleeping on ground, Gr.Naz.ap.†Max.*loc.comm.*7(M.91.765C); surpasses virginity, Chrys.*eleem.*3.2(2.296A,C); id.*anom.*8.2(1.515E); id.*hom.1.6 in 2Cor.4:13*(3.265D); indispensable for prayer, *ib.3.12*(289E–290A); πτερόν ἐστι τῆς εὐχῆς ἡ ἐ. ... ὥσπερ γὰρ πῦρ ἐὰν μὴ ἔχῃ ἔλαιον ἐπιστάζον, σβέννυται· οὕτως καὶ ἡ εὐχή, ἐὰν μὴ ἔχῃ ἐ. ἀφανίζεται *Schol.*16 in Jo.Clim.*scal.*28(M.88.1444C,D); ass. μακροθυμία and ἀμνησικακία, Evagr.Pont.*cap.pract.*A 63(M.40.1236C); superior to other virtues, Chrys.*hom.6.2 in Tit.*(11.768A,B); id.*El.et vid.*1(3.328B).

F. Sunday most suitable day because free from business, Chrys. *eleem.*3(3.252D).

G. exhortation to women ποίοις δὲ ὀφθαλμοῖς ἀντιβλέψετε ἐ. ἀπαιτοῦσαι τοὺς ἄνδρας, ὅταν τὰ πλείονα εἰς τὴν τοῦ σώματος περιβολὴν ἀναλίσκητε; τότε δυνήσῃ μετὰ παρρησίας διαλέγεσθαι τῷ ἀνδρὶ περὶ ἐλεημοσύνης, ὅταν τὸν κόσμον τῶν χρυσίων ἀποθῇ Chrys.*hom.69.3 in Jo.*(8.412B).

ἐλεήμων, *merciful*; **1.** of God, Just.*dial.*107.2(M.6.725A); *Hom. Clem.*2.45; Gr.Nyss.*beat.*5(M.44.1249B); Son, Clem.*str.*6.15(p.491.14; M.9.341C); †Hipp.*Artem.*ap.Eus.*h.e.*5.28.12(M.20.513D); Dion. Ar.*ep.*8.5(M.3.1096C); gospel ἐγέννησε φόβον ὁ νόμος, ἐ. οὗτος εἰς σωτηρίαν Clem.*str.*1.27(p.108.13; M.8.921B); baptism ἔστι γάρ τι ἐκεῖ ἀπαρχῆς ἐ., ἐπιφερόμενον τῷ ὕδατι *Hom.Clem.*11.26; **2.** virtue demanded from Christians, *Did.*3.8; *2Clem.*4.3; ref. Mt.5:7 ἐ. δ' εἶναι βούλεται οὐ μόνον τοὺς ἔλεον ποιοῦντας, ἀλλὰ καὶ τοὺς ἐθέλοντας ἐλεεῖν, κἂν μὴ δύνωνται Clem.*str.*4.6(p.265.14; M.8.1249B); cf.id.*paed.* 3.12(p.286.25; M.8.672A); ἀγαπᾶτε...τοὺς ἀδελφοὺς...ἐ. ὀφθαλμοῖς *Clem.ep.*8; κἂν ἄνθρωπός τις ὢν ἐ. γένηται, τῆς θείας ἀξιοῦται μακαριότητος Gr.Nyss.*beat.*5(M.44.1249B); Chrys.*hom.14.9 in Rom.*(9.588C); esp. from priests, Polyc.*ep.*6.1; from true prophets, *Hom. Clem.*2.6; ὁ ἐ. loved by all, Chrys.*hom.1.3 in Ps.48:17*(5.509B); both God and men, id.*hom.32.3 in Heb.*(12.300B); as cognomen of Jo. Eleem., Sophr.H.*epigr.*2(M.87.4009B).

***ἐλεητικῶς**, *mercifully*, Ath.*exp.Ps.*118:64(M.27.492B).

***Ἑλενιανοί, οἱ**, *Heleniani*, sect connected with Simon Magus, Cels.ap.Or.*Cels.*5.62(p.65.16; M.11.1280A).

ἔλεος, ὁ, τό, *mercy, pity*;

A. def. (Stoic) ἀποδιδόασι...τὸ δὲ ἔ. λύπην ἐπὶ ἀναξίως κακοπαθοῦντι Clem.*str.*2.16(p.151.9; M.8.1012A); ὁ δὲ ἔ. οὐχ ᾗ τινες τῶν φιλοσόφων ὑπειλήφασι, λύπη ἐπ' ἀλλοτρίαις συμφοραῖς, μᾶλλον δὲ ἀστεῖον τί ἐστιν *ib.*4.6(p.265.11; 1249B); ἔ. ἐστι πάθος ἐπὶ τοὺς παρ' ἀξίαν τεταπεινωμένους, παρὰ τῶν συμπαθῶς διατιθεμένων γινόμενον Bas.*hom.in Ps.*114(1.201E; M.29.489B); ἔστιν ὁ ἔ. ... ἑκούσιος λύπη ἐπ' ἀλλοτρίοις κακοῖς συνισταμένη...ἔ. ἐστιν ἐπὶ τῶν δυσφορούντων ἐπί τισιν ἀνιαροῖς ἀγαπητικὴ συνδιάθεσις...ἐκφύεταί πως τῆς ἀγάπης ὁ ἔ., οὐκ ἂν γενόμενος, εἰ μὴ ἐκ ταύτης. καὶ εἴ τις ἀκριβῶς ἐξετάσειε τὸ τοῦ ἐ. ἰδίωμα, ἐπίτασιν εὑρήσει τῆς ἀγαπητικῆς διαθέσεως, τῷ κατὰ τὴν λύπην πάθει συμμεμιγμένην Gr.Nyss.*beat.*5(M.44.1252B,C); Thdr. Mops.*Os.*6:4–7(M.66.161D); Jo.D.*f.o.*2.14(M.94.932B).

B. divine; **1.** in gen., *1Clem.*9.1; Just.*dial.*8.4(M.6.493B); Clem. *prot.*10(p.67.19; M.8.204B); in greetings χάρις ὑμῖν, ἔ., εἰρήνη Ign. *Smyrn.*12.2; Polyc.*ep.*proem.; *M.Polyc.*proem.; made manifest on Last Day, Herm.*sim.*4.2; called forth by man's weakness, Clem. *str.*7.7(p.32.9; M.9.460A); more congenial to God's nature than wrath, Gr.Naz.*or.*16.14(M.35.953A); to be measure of human mercy, Chrys.*hom.60.4 in Jo.*(8.356E); **2.** scope τῷ ἐ. αὐτοῦ σκεπασθῶμεν ἀπὸ τῶν μελλόντων κριμάτων *1Clem.*28.1; ἐλέους ... σκοπὸς ἡ τῶν ἐλεγχομένων σωτηρία Clem.*paed.*1.8(p.132.7; M.8.336C); ὁ γὰρ ἔ. σου ἄφατος, καὶ λόγον ὑπερβαίνων...οὐ γὰρ ἁμαρτωλοὶ μόνον ἐλέῳ σώζονται, ἀλλὰ καὶ δίκαιοι ἐ. τειχίζονται...καὶ οἱ δίκαιοι ἐλέους χρῄζουσιν, ἵνα καὶ ἐξ ἁμαρτωλῶν δίκαιοι γένωνται, καὶ ἵνα δίκαιοι γενόμενοι, μένωσι δίκαιοι· καὶ γὰρ ὁ ἀπόστολος ἐξ ἐ. ἐγένετο τοιοῦτος ‡Chrys.*hom. 3.2 in Ps.50*(5.584C,D); ὅπου γὰρ ἔ., ἐξέτασις οὐκ ἔστιν· ὅπου ἔ., δικαστήριον οὐ κάθηται· ὅπου ἔ., εὐθῦναι οὐκ ἀπαιτοῦνται· ὅπου ἔ. ἀνεξέταστος ἡ σωτηρία· ὅπου ἔ., συγχωρεῖται ἡ ἀπολογία *ib.*(585C); **3.** shown esp. through Christ ἔ. ποιήσαντος αὐτοῦ εἰς ἡμᾶς...ὅτι... ἔγνωμεν δι' αὐτοῦ τὸν πατέρα *2Clem.*3.1; called ἐλέους πηγή, Clem. *paed.hymn.*37(684A); with play on ἔλαιον q.v., id.*paed.*2.8(p.194.25; 468A) cit. s. ἔλαιον; τοῦ σωτῆρος...τοῦ ποιοῦντος ἐν παντὶ τόπῳ τὸ ἐ. αὐτοῦ τοῖς ἐπικαλουμένοις αὐτόν Ath.*v.Anton.*58(M.25.928A); ref. Inc. ἐγένετο ὅπερ ἧς σύ, ἵνα γίνῃ σύ, ὅπερ οὐκ ἧς· τοῦτο ἐλέους ‡Chrys. *hom.3.2 in Ps.50*(5.585D); exeg. Os.6:6 εἰ δὲ δή τις ἕλοιτο καὶ αὐτὸν εἶναι λέγειν τὸν υἱὸν τὸ ἐ. τοῦ πατρός, τὸ ὑπὲρ θυσίαν καὶ ὁλοκαυτώματα, συνήσει καλῶς...ἐ. γὰρ ἀληθῶς τὸ παρὰ πατρὸς ὁ Χριστός, ὡς ἀφαιρῶν ἁμαρτίας Cyr.*Os.*65(3.99A,B); **4.** conditional upon renunciation of evil desires, *2Clem.*16.2; because it is not ἄκριτος, Bas.*hom.in Ps.*114(1.201E; M.29.489A); Gr.Naz.*or.*16.19(M.35.961B); *ib.*43.63(M.36.580B); **5.** = salvation μηδέποτε τὰ τῆς μοναρχίας προτιμήσαντες οὐπώποτε ἐ. τυχεῖν δυνηθῶσιν *Hom.Clem.*3.3; *Clem. ep.*8.

C. human οὐδενὶ γὰρ οὕτω τῶν πάντων, ὡς ἐ. θεὸς θεραπεύεται, ὅτι μηδὲ οἰκειότερον ἄλλο τούτου θεῷ, οὗ ἐ. καὶ ἀλήθεια προπορεύονται, καὶ ᾧ προσοιστέον τὸν ἔ. πρὸ τῆς κρίσεως Gr.Naz.*or.*14.5(M.35.864B,C); εὔνοι ἅπαντες τῷ ἐλεοῦντι γινόμεθα, φυσικῶς τοῖς μετέχουσι τοῦ ἐ. τὴν ἀγάπην ἐντίκτοντος. οὐκοῦν ἐστιν ὁ ἔ. ... εὐνοίας πατήρ, ἀγάπης ἐνέχυρον, σύνδεσμος πάσης φιλικῆς διαθέσεως Gr.Nyss.*beat.*5(M.44.1253C); id.*paup.*2(M.46.480D); Chrys.*hom.60.6 in Jo.*(8.360B); said to be lacking in Manicheans, Ath.*h.Ar.*61(p.217.23; M.25.768A).

ἐλέπολις, ἡ, *siege engine*, Cyr.*Jo.*4.4(4.389B); met., of machinations of Devil against soul, Eus.*h.e.*10.4.57(M.20.872B); luxuries,

Nil.*exerc.*59(M.79.792B); ἐπιθυμίαι, Isid.Pel.*epp.*1.87(M.78.244A); Gr.Agr.*Eccl.*7.1(M.98.1024C).

ἐλευθερία, ἡ, I. *freedom*;

A. def. τὸ κρατεῖν τούτων [sc. παθῶν] ἐ. μόνη Clem.*str.*2.23(p.192.21; M.8.1096A); defined as poverty by Crates, Epiph.*exp.fid.*9(p.507.30; M.42.796A); ἡ δ' ἐ. ἐστιν ἡ πρὸς τὸ ἀδέσποτόν τε καὶ αὐτοκρατὲς ἐξομοίωσις...πᾶσα δ' ἐ. μία τίς ἐστι τῇ φύσει καὶ πρὸς ἑαυτὴν οἰκείως ἔχει Gr.Nyss.*anim.et res.*(M.46.101C,D); ἀκριβὴς ἐ. τὸ μηδενὸς ὅλως δεῖσθαι Chrys.*hom.80.3 in Jo.*(8.477A); exeg. Gal.2:4 ἐ. δὲ καλεῖ τὴν ἔξω τοῦ νόμου διαγωγήν Thdt.*Gal.*2:4(3.368); *ib.*5:1(3.387); v. παρρησία.

B. human; **1.** in gen., Tat.*orat.*7(p.7.14; M.6.820B); αὐτεξούσιον δὲ τὸν πρῶτον ἄνθρωπον γεγονέναι λέγω, τουτέστιν ἐλεύθερον, ἀφ' οὗ καὶ οἱ διάδοχοι τοῦ γένους τὴν ὁμοίαν ἐ. ἐκληρώσαντο Meth.*arbitr.*16(p.186.11); Chrys.*dimiss.Chan.*2(3.434D); **2.** proved by possibility of sudden change, Chrys.*Is.interp.*1.6(6.12A); id.*hom.41.3 in Ac.*(9.312B); **3.** in relation to God's law αἱ ἐντολαὶ οὐχὶ τὴν ἁμαρτίαν ἐκκόπτουσι..., ἀλλὰ τοὺς ὅρους τῆς δοθείσης ἡμῖν ἐ. φυλάττουσιν Marc.Er.*opusc.*4(M.65.992A); exeg. Mt.18:7 ὅταν δὲ ἀνάγκην εἴπῃ, οὐ τὸ αὐθαίρετον τῆς ἐξουσίας ἀναιρῶν, οὐδὲ τὴν ἐ. τῆς προαιρέσεως Chrys.*hom.59.1 in Mt.*(7.594B); endangered by Devil, id.*Is.interp.*2.2(6.27C).

C. partic. Christian; **1.** in gen., *A.Thom.*A 166(p.280.17); Ath.*ep.Aeg.Lib.*20(M.25.585B); **2.** through Christ, Clem.*prot.*9(p.63.3; M.8.193C); working through apostles, *A.Thom.*A 39(p.156.16); μηδὲ λεγόντων ἐ. τὴν ὑπὸ ἡδονῆς δουλείαν...ἡμεῖς γὰρ ἐ. μεμαθήκαμεν, ἣν ὁ κύριος ἡμᾶς ἐλευθεροῖ μόνος Clem.*str.*3.5(p.216.25f.; M.8.1148C); μορφὴν δούλου ὁ υἱὸς τοῦ θεοῦ ὑπὲρ ἐλευθερίας τῶν δουλευσάντων τῇ ἁμαρτίᾳ λαβὼν Or.*Jo.*1.31(37; p.41.9; M.14.85B); δι' αὐτοῦ τοῦ λόγου καὶ ἐν αὐτῷ ἡ ἐ. Ath.*Ar.*2.67(M.26.292A); id.*v.Anton.*26(M.26.881C); ἡ ἐ. τοῦ παντὸς ἀνθρώπου δι' ἀνθρώπου ὑπάρξῃ, ἐν τῇ καινότητι τῆς εἰκόνος τοῦ υἱοῦ ‡Ath.*Apoll.*1.14(M.26.1117C); by ransoming man from Devil, Bas.*hom.in Ps.*48(1.179D; M.29.437B); exeg. Jo.8:36 ἐὰν ὁ υἱὸς ὑμᾶς ἐλευθερώσῃ οὐδεὶς ἀντιλέγει λοιπόν, ἀλλὰ βεβαίαν ἔχετε τὴν ἐ. ... δείκνυσι καὶ ἁμαρτίας ἑαυτὸν καθαρόν, καὶ τὴν μέχρι προσηγορίας ἐ. αἰνίττεται· ταύτην γὰρ καὶ ἄνθρωποι διδόασιν, ἐκείνην δὲ μόνος ὁ θεός Chrys.*hom.54.2 in Jo.*(8.317B); CEph.(431)*act.*7(p.122.16; H.1.1620E); χάρις διὰ τὴν εἰς τὸν Χριστὸν πίστιν δύο σοι ἐ. δεδώρηται, οὐ μόνον γὰρ τῆς ἁμαρτίας τὴν δυναστείαν κατέλυσεν, ἀλλὰ καὶ τοῦ θανάτου τὴν τυραννίδα κατέπαυσεν Thdt.*Rom.*8:2(3.80); Dion.Ar.*e.h.*2.3.6(M.3.401D); **3.** in baptism, *A.Thom.*A 121(p.231.4, conj. ἐλαιοθεσία); εἰ οὐκ ἐστὶ τέλειον τὸ βάπτισμα, ἀλλ' ἐξ ἀγώνων λέγουσιν ἔχειν τὴν τελειότητα, μάταιος παρ' ἐκείνοις ὁ τῆς ἐ. νόμος...ἄδικον δὲ καὶ τὸν Χριστὸν εἰσάγουσι, τοῖς βαπτισθεῖσιν ἔργα ἐλευθερίας προστάξαντα, ἔτι παρὰ προαίρεσιν δεδουλωμένοις τῇ ἁμαρτίᾳ, καθὼς λέγουσι· καὶ ἡ χάρις τοῦ θεοῦ, οὐκέτι χάρις...· εἰ δὲ χάριτι, τὸ ἔργον οὐκ ἔστιν ἔργον, ἀλλ' ἐντολὴ τοῦ ἐλευθερώσαντος, καὶ ἔργον ἐ. καὶ πίστεως...ὅτι ἐντολαὶ τοῦ Χριστοῦ αἱ μετὰ τὸ βάπτισμα δεδομέναι, νόμος ἐλευθερίας ἐστί Marc.Er.*opusc.*4(M.65.988A,B); **4.** contrasted with slavery of sin, Clem.*prot.*1(p.4.28; M.8.56B); Chrys.*hom.58.5 in Mt.*(7.593B); Nonn.*par.Jo.*8.36(M.43.817C); cf. liberty of πνευματικός contrasted with slavery of ψυχικός in Valent. system, Clem.*exc.Thdot.*57(p.126.7; M.9.685D); **5.** in spiritual life οὐ γὰρ ἄλλως...ἐ. περιγίνεται ἢ διὰ τῆς ἀπαύστου...πρὸς τὰς τῶν παθῶν ἡμῶν ἀντιμαχήσεις <? ὑπομονῆς, ? ἐνστάσεως, edd.> id.*str.*2.20(p.178.14; M.8.1065A); ἐν ἐ. μετεωροπορεῖν τὸν νοῦν, καὶ τὰ ἄνω βλέπειν Gr.Nyss.*virg.*22(M.46.404A); its condition being poverty, whereas riches endanger it, Chrys.*hom.58.4 in Mt.*(7.590B,C); **6.** personified; Rachel its type, Thdt.*Phil.*3:5(3.462).

D. as quality of saints, cf. παρρησία; of OT prophets, Or.*hom.15.1 in Jer.*(p.125.20; M.13.429A); of martyr, Eus.*m.P.*7(p.923.14; M.20.1484C); of Joseph in service of Potiphar, Thdt.*provid.*8(4.611).

E. of eternal life τῆς δουλείας ἀπαλλάττομαι καὶ εἰς τὴν ἐ. ἐκλήθην *A.Thom.*A 142(p.249.8); σήμερον τὴν ἐ. λαμβάνω *ib.*167(p.282.2); ἐν τῷ καιρῷ τῆς ἀποκαταστάσεως ἁπάντων καὶ αὐτὴν τὴν κτίσιν ἐκ τῆς δουλείας εἰς τὴν ἐ. μεταβληθήσεσθαι Marcell.*fr.*104 ap.Eus.*e.th.*3.9(p.165.28; M.24.1017A).

F. as divine quality Χριστὲ...ὦ ἐ. ἄφραστος δουλαγωγηθεῖσα παρ' ἡμῶν *A.Jo.*77(p.189.18); *ib.*109(p.208.5); εἰ δὲ πᾶσα μὲν ἡ κτίσις συστενάζει ἐ. χάριν τῆς ἀπὸ τῆς φθορᾶς τῆς δουλείας, ὁ δὲ υἱὸς οὐκ ἔστι τῶν στεναζόντων, οὐδὲ τῶν δεομένων ἐ., ἀλλ' αὐτὸς ὁ...ἐλευθερῶν τὰ πάντα Ath.*Ar.*2.72(M.26.300C); of Cross as sign of freedom, Meth.*Porph.*1(p.504.31; M.18.400C).

G. political and religious; position of a free woman διὰ τί γὰρ σχῆμα οὐκ ἐποίησας τῆς σῆς ἐ. *A.Thom.*A 89(p.204.16); or a free man, *Clem.epit.*A 46; Roman citizenship, Soz.*h.e.*1.9.6(M.67.884C); of autonomy of a city, *Chron.Pasch.*p.187(M.92.457C); of freedom of worship endangered by Arians, Ath.*h.Ar.*53(p.213.25; M.25.757B); id.*v.Anton.*82(M.26.960B).

II. *setting free*; of souls in Hades, ‡Bas.*h.myst.*60(p.395.6); *manumission*, *Cod.Afr.*82; Soz.*h.e.*1.9.7(M.67.885A).

III. *liberality*, Bas.*ep.*108(3.201C; M.32.517A); Gr.Nyss.*hom.9 in Cant.*(M.44.972A).

IV. *looseness of expression*, Mac.Mgn.*apocr.*3.11(p.76.10).

V. *impertinence*, ref. Eunomius τοῦτο μὲν ὑπὸ τῆς συγγενοῦς ἐ. ὑφείλετο Gr.Nyss.*Eun.*1(1 p.179.20; M.45.424C).

VI. liturg. εὐχὴ τῆς ἐ. *prayer of absolution* before Communion, *Lit.Gr.Naz.*(M.36.728A).

ἐλευθεριάζ-ω, *be free*; from restraint, to do moral wrong τῶν δεσμῶν μὴ ἐώντων ~οντα χρῆσθαι ταῖς ἡδοναῖς Meth.*res.*1.31(p.266.9; M.41.1141C); *ib.*1.32(p.268.12; 1144C); Bas.*hom.*13.1(2.114E; M.31.425C); to give way to passions, Chrys.*hom.23.2 in 1Cor.*(10.202B); from sin, ‡Nil.*perist.*2.2(M.79.820A); Andr.Caes.*Apoc.*61(M.106.412B); of dogmas, from heret. contamination, Sophr.H.*or.*2.6(M.87.3225A).

ἐλευθερικός, 1. *free*; superl., of service of God, Clem.*str.*7.7(p.32.15; M.9.460A); **2.** *making free, liberating*; of Christ, ‡Meth.*Sym.et Ann.*8(M.18.368C); of his teaching ἐ. παραβολῆς Diad.*perf.* proem.(p.5.17) prob. f.l. for εὐαγγελικῆς; **3.** *exempt from taxation* ζυγῶν ἐ. opp. ταμιακά, Thdt.*ep.*42(4.1101).

ἐλευθέριος, *free*; **1.** ἡ ἐ. ἡμέρα *day of freedom*, or *noble day*; of Easter Day, Ath.*ep.encycl.*5(p.174.8; M.25.232C); **2.** τὸ ἐ. *free will*, Tit.Bost.*Man.*2.20(M.18.1176A).

ἐλευθεριότης, ἡ, *free will*, Tit.Bost.*Man.*2.4(M.18.1141A); making man the image of God, *ib.*2.5(1141C).

ἐλευθερόγλωσσος, *free of speech*, Hipp.*haer.*4.21(p.52.9; M.16.3087A).

***ἐλευθεροπρασία, ἡ,** *licence*, *Orac.Sib.*2.13.

ἐλευθεροπρέπεια, ἡ, *disposition of a free man, nobility of character*, *Hom.Clem.*4.7; Isid.Pel.*epp.*5.332(M.78.1528C).

ἐλεύθερος, A. *free*; **1.** ref. arguments of Pneumatomachoi against divinity of H. Ghost 'οὔτε δοῦλον', φησίν, 'οὔτε δεσπότην, ἀλλὰ ἐ.'... τίνα οὖν λέγεις ἐ.;...τὸν μήτε ἄρχειν ἑτέρου δύναμιν ἔχοντα μήτε ἄρχεσθαι καταδεχόμενον; ἀλλ' οὔτε ἔστι τις τοιαύτη φύσις ἐν τοῖς οὖσι, καὶ τοῦτο ἐννοῆσαι κατὰ τοῦ πνεύματος ἀσέβεια Bas.*Spir.*51(3.42E, 43D; M.32.160C,161C); **2.** ref. Christ; **a.** as free in his divine nature, cf.Jo.8:35, Clem.*paed.*1.5(p.105.4; M.8.280B); ὃς ἐ. ὢν γέγονας δοῦλος καὶ πραθεὶς πολλοὺς εἰς ἐλευθερίαν εἰσήγαγες *A.Thom.*A 39(p.156.15); Cyr.*apol.Thdt.*6(p.129.9; 6^1.223C); from this, Arians argue that he is mutable, Ath.*Ar.*1.35(M.26.84B); **b.** as making men free; by Inc., Meth.*Porph.*1(p.503.12; M.18.397D); ἵνα...τὴν τρεπτὴν σάρκα λαβών, τὴν μὲν ἁμαρτίαν ἐν αὐτῇ κατακρίνῃ, ἐ. δὲ αὐτὴν κατασκευάσῃ εἰς τὸ δύνασθαι λοιπὸν τὸ δικαίωμα τοῦ νόμου πληροῦν ἐν αὐτῇ Ath.*Ar.*1.51(M.26.120A); by his death ἵνα τοὺς μὲν πάντας...ἐ. τῆς ἀρχαίας παραβάσεως ποιήσῃ id.*inc.*20.2(M.25.132A); id.*ep.fest.*(p.295.20; M.26.1433A); **c.** exeg. Ps.87:5 ἐν νεκροῖς κατὰ τὸ μόνος ἐκεῖ εἶναι ἐ. Or.*Jo.*1.31(34; p.39.15; M.14.81C); Meth.*fr.Job* 38:16(p.517.8; M.18.405C); νεκρὸς ἂν ἐ. ἦν μόνος· οὐ γὰρ εἶχεν ἁμαρτίαν τὴν κάτοχον αὐτὸν ποιοῦσαν θανάτῳ Ath.*exp.Ps.*87:5(M.27.380C); Thdt.*Rom.*8:3(3.81); **3.** of men in gen., ref. origin of freedom, Meth.*arbitr.*16(p.186.9) cit. s. ἐλευθερία; λογικὸς μὲν ὢν [sc. Adam] τὴν φύσιν, ἐ. δὲ τὸν λογισμόν ‡Ath.*Apoll.*2.6(M.26.1141A); οἶδεν μὲν γὰρ ἐ. τὴν φύσιν ὁ δημιουργός· πεποίηται γὰρ οὕτως παρ' αὐτοῦ Cyr.*1Cor.*7:21(p.273.15; M.74.877B); its degeneration δοῦλοι γεγόναμεν οἱ ἐ., διὰ τὴν ἁμαρτίαν ἐπράθημεν Tat.*orat.*11(p.12.14; M.6.829B); τὸ φρόνημα, ἐπὰν δέον ἄνω φέρεσθαι, τὰ κάτω ζητεῖ τοῖς τῆς σαρκὸς ἐνεχόμενον κακοῖς...τὸ ἐ. κατὰ τοῦ τιμίου ἀπολωλεκὸς Or.*fr.57 in Lc.*(p.261.14; M.17.357A); **4.** of Christians; **a.** Church, Thdt.*Gal.*4:25(3.386); **b.** as free from dominion of sin οὐκ ἐ. γὰρ οἱ υἱοὶ τῶν βασιλέων τῆς γῆς, ἐπεὶ πᾶς ὁ ποιῶν τὴν ἁμαρτίαν δοῦλος τῆς ἁμαρτίας ἐστίν, ἐ. δὲ οἱ μείναντες <ἐν> τῇ ἀληθείᾳ τοῦ λόγου τοῦ θεοῦ Or.*comm. in Mt.*13.11(p.209.27; M.13.1121C); Chrys.*hom.1.1 in Phil.*(11.194D); Thdt.*1Cor.*7:22(3.207); through faith and baptism, Clem.*paed.*1.6(p.106.24; M.8.284A); Marc.Er.*opusc.*4(M.65.989A); ἐκλήθης διὰ τῆς πίστεως εἰς ἐ. υἱότητα Cyr.*1Cor.*7:21(p.273.12; M.74.877A); as free from actual sin οὐ γὰρ τὸ μὴ κολάζεσθαι τοῦτο ἐ. ποιεῖ σῶμα, ἀλλὰ τὸ ζῆν ἐν δικαιοσύνῃ διηνεκῶς Chrys.*stat.*6.5(2.79E); **c.** of freedom from diabolical possession, *A.Thom.*A 44(p.161.9); δούλους δὲ καὶ ἐ. [sc. νοήσεις] τοὺς ἐν τοῖς δαίμοσι προὔχοντάς τε καὶ ὑποτεταγμένους Oecum.*Apoc.*6:15(p.94) = Areth.*Apoc.*18(M.106.601A); **d.** of martyrs ἐκεῖνοι [sc. SS. Peter and Paul] μὲν ἐ., ἐγὼ δὲ μέχρι νῦν δοῦλος, ἀλλ' ἐὰν πάθω,...ἀναστήσομαι...ἐ. Ign.*Rom.*4.3; **5.** of Sunday as ἐ. ἡμέρα CGangr.*ep.*(H.1.531A); **6.** as subst. ἡ ἐ. widow, Bas.*ep.* 129.21(3.292E; M.32.721A); wife, Chrys.*hom.17.3 in Eph.*(11.125B); id.*hom.5.3 in 1Thess.*(11.463D); Pall.*h.Laus.*37(p.112.10; M.34. 1186B); *ib.*66(p.162.12; 1218B); free woman, Jo.Mosch.*prat.*189(M. 87.3068B); ὁ ἐ. free man, *ib.*203(3093A).

B. *bold, confident* τὰ ἐξαίρετα τῶν προφητῶν, τὸ ἐ. αὐτῶν, κτλ. Or.*hom.15.1 in Jer.*(p.125.17; M.13.429A); ἐ. ὀφθαλμοῖς καὶ ὑψηλῷ προσώπῳ κατάδεξαι τὴν ὁμολογίαν [sc. τοῦ ἐσταυρωμένου] Chrys.*hom. 2.6 in Rom.*(9.444E).

ἐλευθεροστομία, ἡ, *freedom of speech,* coupled with παρρησία: τῶν μετὰ παρρησίας καὶ ἐ. ὁμολογούντων αὐτὸν υἱὸν τοῦ θεοῦ Didym. *Trin.*3.9(M.39.853A); Chrys.*hom.62.5 in Gen.*(4.599A); id.*hom.in Gal.2:11*(3.365D); ref. Chrys. ἐ. ... ἀμέτρως ἐκέχρητο Socr.*h.e.*6.3.14 (M.67.669B).

ἐλευθερ-όω, *set free*; **1.** ref. H. Ghost: agst. Pneumatomachoi ποῦ τοίνυν φέροντες αὐτὸ τάξομεν, μετὰ τῆς κτίσεως; ἀλλ' ἡ κτίσις πᾶσα δουλεύει· τὸ δὲ πνεῦμα ~οῖ Bas.*Spir.*55(3.47E; M.32.172B); *ib.*29 (24C; M.120A); **2.** of Christ; **a.** in his own person, cf.Jo.8:36 ἔδειξεν ἀληθῶς ὁ υἱὸς ὁ ~ώσας, ὡς οὐκ ἔστι κτίσμα Ath.*Ar.*2.67(M.26.289C); οἱ διὰ τιμὴν προσποιούμενοι [sc. Nestorians], τῆς συνθέσεως ~οῦν τὸ θεῖον Leont.H.*Nest.*1.10(M.86.1440D); **b.** as setting mankind free ὁ...συμπαθὴς θεὸς αὐτὸς ἠλευθέρωσεν τὴν σάρκα τῆς φθορᾶς Clem. *paed.*3.1(p.237.7; M.8.557A); Meth.*res.*2.8(p.343.13; M.18.305C); θεὸς ὢν γέγονεν ἄνθρωπος δι' ἡμᾶς...ἵνα ~ώσῃ ἡμᾶς ἐκ τῆς δυναστείας τοῦ διαβόλου Ath.*virg.*3(p.38.21; M.28.256C); id.*Ar.*1.48(M.26.112B); ἐκρατήθη σαρκί, ἵνα καὶ ἡ σὰρξ διὰ τῆς πρὸς αὐτὸν ἀτρέπτου ἑνώσεως ~ωθῇ τοῦ θανάτου Gel.Cyz.*h.e.*2.19.25(M.85.1280D); Dor.*doct.*1.4 (M.88.1621B); **3.** of Christianity; **a.** in gen. ὁ νόμος αὐτοῦ [sc. τοῦ Χριστοῦ]...τὸ ἑκούσιον ~ώσας εἰς πίστιν Clem.*paed.*3.12(p.284.5; M.8.655B); Const.ap.Gel.Cyz.*h.e.*2.7.38(M.85.1241A); Ammon.*Jo.* 8:32(M.85.1452A); ref. Jo.8:32 ἡ ἀλήθεια ~ώσει ὑμᾶς·...τίνος ~ώσει; ...ἁμαρτημάτων Chrys.*hom.54.1 in Jo.*(8.315C); **b.** ref. baptism εἰ δὲ βαπτισθέντες οὐκ ἐλευθερώθημεν ἀπὸ τῆς πατρικῆς ἁμαρτίας, δηλονότι οὐδὲ τὰ τῆς ἐλευθερίας ἔργα ποιεῖν δυνάμεθα· εἰ δὲ δυνάμεθα ποιεῖν αὐτά, φανερὸν μέν, ὅτι μυστικῶς τῆς κατὰ τὴν ἁμαρτίαν δουλείας ἠλευθερώθημεν...~οῦσθαι μὲν χάριτι Χριστοῦ Marc.Er. *opusc.*4(M.65.988C,D); εἰ ἠλευθερώθημεν ἐν τῷ βαπτίσματι, διὰ τί οὐκ οἴδαμεν τὸν ἀέρα τῆς ἐλευθερίας;...~οῦται μὲν ὁ ἄνθρωπος κατὰ τὴν δωρεὰν τοῦ Χριστοῦ. κατὰ δὲ τὸ ἴδιον θέλημα, ὅπου ἀγαπᾷ, ἐκεῖ ἐμμένει, κἂν βεβάπτισται, διὰ τὸ αὐτεξούσιον *ib.*(989A,B); **c.** in practice of Christian life, of 'gnostic' τοῦ γὰρ ἐμπαθοῦς παντὸς περιτμηθέντος...ἠλευθερωμένῳ εἰς υἱοθεσίαν Clem.*ecl.*31(p.146.23; M.9.716A); id.*str.*3.4(p.214.28; M.8.1144C); in death τὸ δὲ ἀποθανεῖν καὶ χωρισθῆναι τοῦ σώματος ~ωθῆναι Meth.*res.*1.57(p.319.14; M.41.1153B); **4.** (Carpocratian) of souls after final transmigration when all sin has been atoned for ὅταν δὲ μηδὲν λείπῃ, τότε...~ωθεῖσαν ἀπαλλαγῆναι πρὸς τὸν ὑπεράνω...θεόν Hipp.*haer.*7.32(p.220.4; M.16. 3339B); some souls being released without being incarnate, *ib.* (p.220.8; 3339B); **5.** of freeing of slaves by Const. ἐπ' ὠφελείᾳ τῶν ἐν ταῖς ἐκκλησίαις ~ουμένων Soz.*h.e.*1.9.6(M.67.884C).

ἐλευθερωτής, ὁ, *deliverer*; **1.** τῷ πάντων ἐλευθερωτῇ θεῷ Const. ap.Eus.*v.C.*2.30(p.54.12; M.20.1009C); from sin etc., Serap.*euch.*3.1; **2.** of Christ ἐ. πάσης...κτίσεως Ath.*ep.Adelph.*4(M.26.1077A); †Bas. *Is.*114(1.458E; M.30.304B); ἐ. αὐτὸν οἱ προφῆται προῦλεγον Chrys.*hom. 6.4 in Mt.*(7.93A); ref. Mt.17:5 πολλάκις ὁ πατὴρ υἱὸν ἀπεκάλει τὸν υἱόν,...διὰ τοὺς δουλαγωγοῦντας τὸν ἐ. Gr.Ant.*bapt.*2.8(M.88.1880B); Sophr.H.*mir.Cyr.et Jo.*34(M.87.3540A); as deliverer from all evil and imperfection ὁ ἐ. τῆς ἐμῆς ψυχῆς ἐκ τῆς τῶν πολλῶν δουλείας *A.Thom.*A 142(p.249.1); ὁ τοῦ νόμου ἐ. ‡Meth.*Sym.et Ann.*3(M.18. 353B).

ἔλευσις, ἡ, *advent*; at Inc. ἡ γὰρ ἔ. τοῦ κυρίου πᾶσα διὰ τὸν ἄνθρωπον γεγένηται, τὸν τεθανατωμένον ἐν τάφῳ...ἁμαρτίας...ἵνα... νῦν ἀναστήσῃ καὶ ζωοποιήσῃ τὸν ἄνθρωπον Mac.Aeg.*hom.*34.2(M.34. 745A); *ib.*3.4(469C); τὴν φανέρωσιν...ἔ. καλεῖ Ammon.*Jo.*1:11,12(M. 85.1397B); prophesied in OT, *1Clem.*17.1; Polyc.*ep.*6.3; εἰ ὁ πονηρὸς ...τὸν νόμον ἔγραψεν, ὁ ἀφεγγὴς ἐκεῖνος, καθόλου...σκότος ὤν, πῶς ᾔδει ἔ. Ἰησοῦ; Serap.*Man.*40(p.58; M.18.1221C); Epiph.*haer.*21.5 (p.244.9; M.41.293A); *Chron.Pasch.*p.147(M.92.364B); at second coming ἐν τῇ ἐ. αὐτοῦ καὶ ἐπιφανείᾳ τῇ ὑστέρᾳ, οὐκ ἔχει τις λόγον ἀπολογίας *A.Thom.*A 28(p.145.7); *1Apoc.Jo.*1(p.71); plur., of both advents, Iren.*haer.*1.10.1(M.7.549A).

***ἐλεφαντία, ἡ,** *elephantiasis,* Chrys.*Stag.*3.13(1.223D) perh. f.l. for ἐλέφαντι, cf.id.*hom.25.5 in Rom.*(9.707E, v.l. ἐλεφαντίᾳ).

***ἐλεφαντοκόλλητος,** *inlaid with ivory,* Clem.*paed.*2.3(p.178.10; M.8.433A).

ἑλικοειδής, *spiral, winding,* of serpent πάντων δὲ τῶν θηρίων πνευματικώτατον τυγχάνει...καὶ ποικίλων σχημάτων τύπους ἀποτελεῖ ὁ δράκων ἑ. ‡Eust.*hex.*(M.18.745C); of construction of ear ἡ ἀκοή, οὐκ ἐπ' εὐθείας ἤνοικται, ἀλλ' ἑ. τῷ πόρῳ τῶν ἐν τῷ ἀέρι ψόφων ἀντιλαμβάνεται. σοφίας καὶ τοῦτο...ὥστε τὴν μὲν φωνὴν ἀκωλύτως διϊέναι...περικλωμένην ταῖς σκολιότησι, μηδὲν δὲ τῶν ἔξωθεν παρεμπιπτόντων κώλυμα εἶναι δύνασθαι τῇ αἰσθήσει Bas.*hom.*3.8(2.24C; M. 31.217A), exeg. 3Reg.6:8 ἑ. γὰρ ἐχρῆν εἶναι τὴν ἐν τῷ ναῷ τοῦ θεοῦ ἄνοδον τῆς ἕλικος ἀναβάσει τὸν ἰσαίτατον κύκλον μιμουμένης Or.*Jo.* 10.40(24; p.218.3; M.14.385C); as mode of divine movement (between εὐθύ and κατὰ κύκλον) τὸ δὲ ἑ. τὴν σταθερὰν πρόοδον καὶ τὴν γόνιμον στάσιν Dion.Ar.*d.n.*9.9(M.3.916D), v. κύκλος.

ἑλικοειδῶς, *spirally, obliquely,* of angelic movement (between κυκλικῶς, i.e. in union with God, and κατ' εὐθεῖαν, i.e. action on lower intelligences) κινεῖσθαι μὲν οἱ θεῖοι λέγονται νόες...ἑ. δέ, ὅτι καὶ προνοοῦντες τῶν καταδεεστέρων, ἀνεκφοιτήτως μένουσιν ἐν ταὐτότητι περὶ τὸ τῆς ταὐτότητος αἴτιον καλὸν καὶ ἀγαθόν, ἀκαταλήκτων περιχορεύοντες Dion.Ar.*d.n.*4.8(M.3.704D); of souls, *ib.*4.9(705A) cit. s. ψυχή.

ἑλιξόπορος, *twisting, intertwining,* Paul.Sil.*Soph.*654(M.86. 2144B).

***Ἐλισσαϊκός,** *of Elisha,* Geo.Al.*v.Chrys.*67(p.246.41).

***ἑλκάς, ἡ,** Arabian coin, *M.Areth.*(p.8).

***Ἐλκεσαῖοι, οἱ,** *Elchezaites,* sect basing teaching about forgiveness of postbaptismal sins by new kind of 'baptism' on a book of angelic revelations bearing name of Elchezai, Epiph.*rescr.*5(p.160. 21; M.41.165A); id.*haer.*30.3(p.336.2; M.41.409A); Thdt.*haer.*2.7(4. 332); connected with Σαμψαῖοι q.v., Epiph.*haer.*53.1(p.314.25; 900A); cf.Hipp.*haer.*9.13ff.

***Ἐλκεσαῖται, οἱ,** = foreg., Or.ap.Eus.*h.e.*6.38(M.20.600A); Eus. *ib.*(597C).

ἑλκηθμός, ὁ, 1. *being dragged* ἀπὸ τῶν θηρίων ἑ. *Ep.Lugd.*ap.Eus. *h.e.*5.1.38(M.20.424A); Chrys.*hom.9.6 in Mt.*(7.139B); **2.** met., *being drawn,* of relationship between Father and Son πρὸς ἑαυτὴν ἕλκει, φησίν [sc. Eun.], ἡ τοῦ υἱοῦ κυριεύουσα οὐσία τὴν τοῦ ὄντος ἔννοιαν. τί βούλεται αὐτῷ ὁ ἑ. τοῦ ὄντος...; εἰ μὲν γὰρ τὴν ἑαυτοῦ οὐσίαν ἕλκειν φησὶ τὸν πατέρα, περιττὸς οὗτος ὁ ἑ. Gr.Nyss.*Eun.*11(2 p.249.1,13; M.45.853A).

***ἑλκογένητος,** ? *bred from ulcers* or *corruption, Anaph.Pil.*B 1 (p.444).

ἑλκτικός, 1. *drawing, attracting* ἑλκτικαῖς ἡδονῶν περιαγωγαῖς Meth.*res.*2.1(p.330.2; M.41.1161D); πρὸς ἡδονὰς ὢν ἑλκτικός *ib.*2.6 (p.340.16; 1173A); ἑ. τῆς ἐν τῷ βάθει νοτίδος...ἡ συκῆ Gr.Nyss.*hom.5 in Cant.*(M.44.872C); Mac.Mgn.*apocr.*4.17(p.192.16); παντὸς ἑλκτικὴν εἶναι τοῦ ὑποκειμένου τὴν τοῦ πυρὸς δύναμιν. ... τὸν θεὸν...ἑ. καὶ αὐτὸν εἶναι...πάντων τῶν βουλομένων τοῖς αὐτοῦ πείθεσθαι νόμοις Max.*ep.*30(M.91.624B); **2.** *drawing in, taking in*; of food into the system, Nemes.*nat.hom.*23(M.40.693A) cit. s. ἀλλοιωτικός; Leont.B. *Nest.et Eut.*1(M.86.1296D); ‡Jo.D.*corp.*3(M.95.409A).

***ἑλκτικῶς,** *by way of attraction,* Geo.Pis.*senar.*156(M.92.1749B).

ἕλκυσις, ἡ, *drawing, guiding,* Sophr.H.*ep.syn.*(M.87.3176A).

ἕλκυσμα, τό, *drawing,* of ploughing εἰλιπόδων ἑλκύσμασι tr.Vergil *ecl.*4.33 ap.Const.*or.s.c.*20(p.185.9; M.20.1297B).

ἑλκυσμός, ὁ, *drawing, dragging*; form of torture, Chrys.*hom. 61.3 in Mt.*(7.614B); *M.Thdot.*1 34(p.82.26).

***ἑλκύστρια, ἡ,** *one who draws* or *sheds* blood, of synagogue ἀλλοτρίων αἱμάτων ἑ. Leont.B.*mesopent.*(M.86.1992C).

ἕλκ-ω, ἑλκύ-ω, A. *draw*; **1.** ref. God attracting men to himself; **a.** in gen. οὔτε διὰ φόβον οὔτε διὰ ἡδονὰς ἐπὶ τὴν γνῶσιν ἵεται·... ἀγάπῃ δὲ τοῦ ὄντως ὄντος ἐραστοῦ ~όμενος [sc. the 'gnostic'] Clem. *str.*4.22(p.312.25; M.8.1356A); τῷ ἁγίῳ πνεύματι ~όμενοι οἱ...ἐνάρετοι *ib.*7.2(p.8.24; M.9.413A); εἷλκεν γὰρ αὐτὸν...θείῳ σὺν πνεύματι φύσις ἀγαθὴ πρὸς τὸν εὐσεβῆ...βίον Eus.*v.C.*1.12(p.13.28; M.20.925C); ὁ σωτήρ, ~ων εἰς εὐσέβειαν Ath.*inc.*31.2(M.25.149B); ref. Jo.12:32 πῶς οὖν φησιν, ὅτι ὁ πατὴρ ~ει; ὅτι υἱοῦ ~οντος, πατὴρ ~ει, ἑλκύσω δέ, φησίν, ἅτε ὑπὸ τυράννου κατεχομένους Chrys.*hom.77.2 in Jo.*(8. 403D); ref. Jo.12:32 δείκνυσιν οὖν ἑαυτὸν ὄντα φύσει θεόν, οὐκ ἔξω τιθεὶς τὸν πατέρα. διὰ γὰρ τοῦ υἱοῦ ~εταί τις εἰς τὴν τοῦ πατρὸς γνῶσιν Cyr.*Jo.*8(4.708A); **b.** ref. freedom of will τοὺς κατὰ προαίρεσιν ἀγαθοὺς ~ει ὁ πατήρ, τοὺς δὲ μοχθηροὺς ἐᾷ. οὐ τὸ ἐφ' ἡμῖν αὐτεξούσιον ἀναιρεῖ ὁ λόγος, ἀλλὰ δείκνυσι βοηθείας δεομένους Ammon.*Jo.*6:44 (M.85.1437A); Chrys.*hom.46.1 in Jo.*(8.269E); **2.** of men attracting God into themselves ~ουσι [sc. virtuous souls]...πρὸς ἑαυτὰς τοῦ ἀφθάρτου νυμφίου τὸν πόθον Gr.Nyss.*hom.1 in Cant.*(M.44.784D); πῶς δὲ αὐτὸν εἵλκυσαν; ἀκολουθήσασθαι τοῖς ἴχνεσιν αὐτοῦ, καὶ τῶν εὐαγγελικῶν ἀπολαύσασθαι μύρων Cyr.*fr.Cant.*1:3(M.69.1277); Thdt. *Cant.*1:3(2.31); **3.** of attraction exerted by evil ὁ διάβολος...πρὸς ἑαυτὸν ~ειν πάντας βουλόμενος Just.*dial.*116.1(M.6.744C); τὰς ἔξωθεν αὐτοὺς ~ούσας ἡδονὰς τοῦ βίου Ath.*gent.*30(M.25.61A); Chrys.*hom.* 6.7 *in Mt.*(7.99B).

B. *derive* (Messalian) ~ειν γὰρ ἕκαστον τῶν τικτομένων ἔλεγεν ἐκ τοῦ προπάτορος, ὥσπερ τὴν φύσιν, οὕτω δὲ καὶ τὴν δαιμόνων δουλείαν Thdt.*h.e.*4.11.7(4.966).

***ἐλλαιμαργέω**, *be greedy for*; c. dat., Gr.Nyss.*infant.*(M.46.188A).

ἐλλαμβάνω, 1. med., *seize hold of*, ref. Mt.10:32 ἐν οἷς καὶ αὐτὸς ὁμολογεῖ ἐνειλημμένος αὐτούς Clem.*str.*4.9(p.280.27; M.8.1281C); **2.** pass., *be held* ἐνειλημμένον ὑποδήμασι Gr.Nyss.*v.Mos.*(M.44.356D); τὸ τῆς ἁμαρτίας βρόχοις ἐνειλημμένον Cyr.*Nest.*3.3(p.65.36; 6^1.80C).

ἐλλαμπρύνομαι, *shine forth, distinguish oneself*; by virtue, Clem.*q.d.s.*1(p.160.13; λαμπρ- M.9.605B); Dion.Al.ap.Eus.*h.e.*6.41.20(M.20.612A); Gr.Nyss.*v.Mos.*(M.44.349B); *be notorious* by wickedness, Eus.*h.e.*9.11.4(M.20.840A); id.*p.e.*4.6(143A; M.21.249B).

ἐλλάμπ-ω, 1. *shine upon*, of spiritual illumination by God: of angels ~ει δὲ τοῖς καθ' ἕκαστον δευτέροις διὰ τῶν πρώτων Dion.Ar.*c.h.*13.4(M.3.305B); of men ἐὰν τηλικοῦτος ἦς, ὡς τοὺς ὀφθαλμοὺς κυρίου ~ειν σοι Or.*hom.6.1 in Jer.*(p.48.12; M.13.323B); ἐλλάμψαντος...ταῖς ἁπάντων διανοίαις τοῦ θεοῦ καὶ πατρός Cyr.*ep.*50(p.98.18; 5^2.168B); through teaching of scripture, Gr.Nyss.*hom.5 in Cant.*(M.44.864D); Dion.Ar.*d.n.*1.3(M.3.589B); of bishop illuminating candidates for baptism, id.*e.h.*2.2.3(M.3.400B); **2.** trans., *enlighten*; spiritually οὐ γὰρ ἔξωθεν αὐτὰς [sc. the angels] ὁ θεὸς ἐπὶ τὰ θεῖα κινεῖ, νοητῶς δέ, καὶ ἔνδοθεν ~ομένων αὐτῶν ἐν αὐγῇ καθαρᾷ καὶ ἀΰλῳ, τὴν θειοτάτην βούλησιν *ib.*1.4(376B); οἱ θεοειδεῖς...ὑπερφυῶς ἐλλαμφθέντες ἐκ τῆς πρὸς αὐτὸ [sc. τὸ ὑπέρθεον φῶς] μακαριωτάτης ἑνώσεως id.*d.n.*1.5(M.3.593C); by Christ οἱ ~όμενοι ὑπὸ Χριστοῦ...οὐδέν τινων διακονουμένων ἀποστόλων καὶ προφητῶν δέονται...οὐδὲ ἀγγέλων Or.*Jo.*1.25(24; p.31.21; M.14.68D); by H. Ghost of prophets, id.*Cels.*7.4(p.155.33; M.11.1425B); of a convert to orthodoxy, Gel.Cyz.*h.e.*2.24.2(M.85.1300A); ref. degrees of illumination, Gr.Naz.*or.*28.17(p.48.6; M.36.48C).

ἔλλαμψις, ἡ, *illumination*; **1.** Trin. φωτὸς πατρικοῦ, ἀπαυγάσματος Χριστοῦ, ἔ. ἁγίου πνεύματος Or.*fr.83 in Lc.*(p.273); operations *ad extra* μίαν ἐκ τῆς μιᾶς θεότητος γενέσθαι τὴν ἔ. ἑνικῶς διαιρουμένην, καὶ συναπτομένην διαιρέτως Gr.Naz.*or.*28.1(p.22.3; M.36.25D); Jo.D.*f.o.*1.14(M.94.860C); **2.** ref. Christ, as contrasted with Law and prophets ἡ τελεία ἔ. γίνεται, ὅταν ἐπιφανῇ τὸ φῶς τὸ ἀληθινόν Gr.Nyss.*hom.5 in Cant.*(M.44.864B); τὴν ἔ. τῆς ἀναστάσεως ‡Sophr.H.*liturg.*7(M.87.3988C); ἐπεδείκνυτο, συμπροσόντων τῶν χρόνων τῆς ἡλικίας, τὴν ἔ. τῆς θεότητος *cat.Lc.*2:51(p.27.28); **3.** ref. H. Ghost, at Inc. πυρσὸς...γαμήλιος ἡ τοῦ ἁγίου πνεύματος ἔ. Gr.Nyss.*hom.13 in Cant.*(M.44.1053A); **4.** ref. angels; as lesser lights than God, Gr.Naz.*or.*38.9(M.36.321A); ἐλλαμπομένας τὴν καθαρωτάτην ἔ., ἢ ἄλλως ἄλλην κατὰ τὴν ἀναλογίαν τῆς φύσεως καὶ τῆς τάξεως *ib.*28.31(p.70.17; 72B); Dion.Ar.*c.h.*3.1(M.3.164D); τῶν ἡττόνων εἶναι τοὺς θειοτέρους...χειραγωγοὺς ἐπὶ τὴν θείαν...ἔ. *ib.*4.3(181A); of angels giving men τὰς θεαρχικὰς ἔ. *ib.*9.3(260C); *ib.*13.3(304A); **5.** of illumination in men in gen. ἅπασι...ὁ τοῦ θεοῦ λόγος ἐκλάμπει τοῖς ἐλλάμψεως δεκτικοῖς Cyr.*Jo.*1.7(4.59D); esp. through Christian doctrine ἣν ἐντεῦθεν ἔ. [sc. H. Ghost] ἐδεξάμην Gr.Naz.*or.*31.33(p.190.6; M.36.172A); διδάσκει ὅτι μόνοις τοῖς μαθηταῖς ἐξαιρέτως...ἔσται ἡ ἔ., ὑπὲρ ὧν τηροῦσι τὰς ἐντολάς Ammon.*Jo.*14:24(M.85.1492D); οἱ ἐξ ἐθνῶν κεκλημένοι διὰ τῆς πίστεως, ὡς ἤδη σοφισθέντες διὰ τῆς τοῦ πνεύματος ἔ. Cyr.*Ps.*24:10(M.69.849B); Dion.Ar.*c.h.*1.2(M.3.121A); different degrees belonging to different orders of hierarchy, id.*e.h.*5.1.7(M.3.508D); through scripture ἐπὶ τοῦ παντὸς ἀνθρώπων γένους ἡ τοῦ θείου πνεύματος ἐν αὐτοῖς [sc. prophets] ἔ. μεγίστην ὑπόθεσιν περιέχουσα Eus.*d.e.*5 proem.(p.206.25; M.22.344A); Gr.Nyss.*Pss.titt.*B 10(M.44.536A); through baptism, Dion.Ar.*e.h.*5.1.3(504B); as conditional upon purity of life, Or.*Jo.*10.41(25; p.219.4; M.14.388B); Gr.Naz. *or.*39.8(M.36.344D); ἵνα χωρήσῃς ὅλην τὴν ἔ. τῆς ἁγίας τριάδος, ἐχώρισας τὸν νοῦν σου πάσης ὑλώδους ἐμφάσεως Jo.Mon.*hymn.Bas.*3(M.96.1372B); Jo.D.*hom.*4.1(M.96.601B); of beatific vision τῆς ἔ. καταξιούμενοι τῆς...τριάδος †Jo.D.*B.J.*39(M.96.1232A).

ἐλλειπής, v. ἐλλιπής.

ἐλλειπῶς, = ἐλλιπῶς, *with ellipsis*, Thdt.*Rom.*7:13(3.75); ἐ. τοῦ ἀναφορικοῦ ἄρθρου Areth.*Apoc.*1:5,6(M.106.508D).

ἔλλειψις, ἡ, *defect*; in argument against polytheism εἰ γὰρ ἤρκει εἷς [sc. for creation], οὐκ ἂν οἱ πολλοὶ τὴν ἀλλήλων ἀνεπλήρουν ἔ. Ath.*gent.*39(M.25.77C); in anti-Arian argument ὥστε γενητὴν εἰσάγειν τριάδα,...τῶν γὰρ γενητῶν ἐστιν ἐλλείψεις...καὶ προσθήκας δέχεσθαι id.*Ar.*1.18(M.26.49B); οὐ μίαν...θεότητος φύσιν εἰσάγοντες, ἀλλὰ...τρεῖς...μαχομένας ὑπερβολαῖς καὶ ἔ. Gr.Naz.*or.*23.6(M.35.1157B); ref. negative theology τὸ...ἄνουν καὶ ἀναίσθητον καθ' ὑπεροχήν, οὐ κατ' ἔ. ἐπὶ θεοῦ τακτέον Dion.Ar.*d.n.*7.2(M.3.869A); of man's natural state, Eus.*e.th.*1.13(p.73.5; M.24.849D); Ath.*inc.*11.1(M.25.116A); of evil οὔτε ἐν δαίμοσιν, οὔτε ἐν ἡμῖν τὸ κακόν, ὡς ὂν κακόν, ἀλλ' ὡς ἔ. ... τῆς τῶν...ἀγαθῶν τελειότητος Dion.Ar.*d.n.*4.24(M.3.728A); τὸ ἀγαθὸν ἐκ τῆς μιᾶς καὶ ὅλης αἰτίας· τὸ δὲ κακὸν ἐκ πολλῶν καὶ μερικῶν ἐ. *ib.*4.30(729C); ἐν τῇ παντελεῖ ἐ. τοῦ ἀγαθοῦ τὸ κακόν· τὸ γοῦν ἐλλεῖπον ὀλίγον τοῦ ἀγαθοῦ οὐ κακόν Max.*schol.d.n.*4.20(M.4.284A).

Ἕλλην, ὁ, 1. *gentile*, *Diogn.*1.1; Heges.ap.Eus.*h.e.*2.23.18(M.20.204A); ref. Rom.1:32 Ἕ. καλεῖ τὸν ἀπηλλαγμένον τῆς παρατηρήσεως τῆς Ἰουδαϊκῆς Chrys.*stat.*12.5(2.130D); Cyr.*ador.*2(1.64A); id.*Jo.*8(4.700B); Thdt.*Rom.*1:8,9(3.31); **2.** *pagan*; marriage with such forbidden except on promise of conversion, CChalc.*can.*14; Σευήρου τοῦ...αἱρεσιάρχου, καὶ Ἕ. Jo.D.*jej.*suppl.(M.95.76B).

***Ἑλληνιανοί, οἱ,** ? name of a Jewish sect; mentioned together with Galileans, Pharisees etc., Just.*dial.*80.4(M.6.665B).

Ἑλληνίζ-ω, 1. *speak Greek*; *speak good Greek* ἡμέτεροι...οἱ λόγοι, καὶ τὸ ~ειν, ὧν καὶ τὸ σέβειν θεούς· ὑμῶν δὲ ἡ ἀλογία καὶ ἡ ἀγροικία Juln.Imp.ap.Gr.Naz.*or.*4.102(M.35.636C); of language, *be Greek*, ref. author of Apoc. διάλεκτον...καὶ γλῶσσαν οὐκ ἀκριβῶς ~ουσαν αὐτοῦ βλέπω Dion.Al.ap.Eus.*h.e.*7.25.6(M.20.704A); **2.** *practise paganism*; in gen., Eus.*v.C.*2.44(p.60.1; M.20.1021A); Thdt.*affect.*3(p.90.21; 4.782); Jo.Mal.*chron.*8 p.207(M.97.321C); of Christians sacrificing in time of persecution, Philost.*h.e.*2.14(M.65.477A); **3.** *be pagan* ὁ λέγων δύο [sc. θεούς], ~ει ‡Ath.*Ar.*4.10(p.54.6; M.26.480C); Gr.Naz.*or.*45.4(M.36.628C); of Manicheans αἱ τῶν βίβλων τοίνυν ὑποθέσεις Χριστιανίζουσι μὲν τῇ φωνῇ, τοῖς δὲ δόγμασιν ~ουσι Socr.*h.e.*1.22.8(M.67.137A); *ib.*1.22.1(136A); Sophr.H.*ep.syn.*(M.87.3153C).

Ἑλληνικός, 1. *Greek*; τὸ Ἑ. *Greek language*, Hipp.*haer.*10.3(p.287.17; M.16.3446B); Eus.*h.e.*4.8.8(M.20.325B); Evagr.Pont.*schol.*(p.205); **2.** *gentile, pagan* διὰ τί οὖν οἱ Ἀρειανοὶ...οὐ συναριθμοῦσιν ἑαυτοὺς μετὰ τῶν Ἑλλήνων;...ἀλλὰ τὸ μὲν ὄνομα τὸ Ἑ. φεύγουσι διὰ τὴν τῶν ἀνοήτων ἀπάτην Ath.*Ar.*3.16(M.26.356A); τεθραμμένος [sc. Abraham] ἐν γῇ Χαλδαίων ἔθεσί τε καὶ νόμοις τοῖς Ἑ. Cyr.*glaph.Gen.*4(1.124C); of Persian religion Ἑ. δόγμα *Chron.Pasch.*p.333(M.92.864A); neut. as subst., *the pagans*, Philost.*h.e.*7.2(M.65.537B).

Ἑλληνικῶς, *in a pagan way*, Soz.*h.e.*3.17.2(M.67.1093C); comp., Chrys.*hom.29.1 in 1Cor.*(10.258E).

Ἑλληνίς, *pagan* (fem.), Chrys.*hom.31.3 in Mt.*(7.361A); Philost.*h.e.*1.6(M.65.464B); αὐτὴν ἐποίησε Χριστιανήν· ἦν γὰρ Ἑ. *Chron. Pasch.*p.312(M.92.796A); as subst., *pagan woman*, ‡Jo.D.*fid.dorm.*9(M.95.253D).

***Ἑλληνισοφία, ἡ,** *wisdom of the Greeks*, Anast.S.*hod.*6(M.89.109E).

***Ἑλληνιστάριοι, οἱ,** *those who use Greek* in liturgy, Thdr.Pet.*v.Thds.*(p.46.1); Cyr.S.*v.Sab.*32(p.117.24).

Ἑλληνιστής, ὁ, 1. *Greek-speaking Jew*, Chrys.*hom.14.1 in Ac.*(9.111D); *ib.21.1*(169D); **2.** *pagan*, Philost.*h.e.*7.1(M.65.537B); Soz.*h.e.*6.35.1(M.67.1397B).

Ἑλληνιστί, *rhetorically*, ref. divine threats in gospels μὴ ἀπατῶμεν ἑαυτούς, νομίζοντες ταῦτα Ἑ. ὑμῖν λέγειν Chrys.*hom.19.5 in Ac.*(9.160D).

***Ἑλληνοκοίτης, ὁ,** *husband of a gentile wife*; ref. accusation brought against Moses, *Const.App.*6.1.2.

Ἑλληνόφρων, *inclined to paganism* Μανιχαῖος καὶ Ἑ. Thphn.*chron.*p.68(M.108.220A).

ἐλλιμενίζω, 1. *stay in harbour*, Synes.*ep.*4(M.66.1337A); **2.** *visit the harbour*, *ib.*148(1544C).

***ἐλλιμνάζ-ω, 1.** *form a pool*, hence *overflow*; c. dat., †Bas.*Is.*283(1.595A; M.30.616C); met. ἡ τῆς εἰρήνης χαρὰ...τῇ ὑπομονῇ ~ουσα Nil.*Eulog.*6(M.79.1101C); **2.** *lie* (*stagnant*) like water in a pool; of wine in the mouth, Bas.*hom.*14.5(2.126E; M.31.453E); of wealth, *ib.*6.5(2.47D; M.272A); πηγαῖς ὄφεις τρεφούσαις, αἷς...~ει ὁ λόγος Pall.*h.Laus.*47(p.140.2; M.34.1202A).

***ἐλλιμνασμός, ὁ,** *pool*, met. τὸν ἐναέριον ἐ. διελεύσῃ Germ.CP *or.*1(M.98.240D).

[*]**ἐλλιμπάν-ω**, collateral form of ἐλλείπω; **1.** *omit, leave undone, neglect*, Bas.*reg.fus.*43.2(2.390B; M.31.1028D); Chrys.*hom.32.6 in Mt.*(7.374C); *V.Max.*1(M.90.68C); **2.** intrans., *fail* ὅταν γὰρ τὰ παρ' ἡμῶν ~ῃ, καὶ τὰ παρὰ τοῦ θεοῦ ἵσταται Chrys.*hom.50.2 in Mt.*(7.516A).

ἐλλιπής (ἐλλειπής), *defective*; denied of God; hence also of Christ, Clem.*paed.*1.6(p.105.8; M.8.280C); implied in Arian doctrine ποτὲ μὲν ἐ. τριάς, ποτὲ δὲ πλήρης· ἐ. μὲν πρὶν γένηται ὁ υἱός· πλήρης δέ, ὅτε γέγονε Ath.*Ar.*1.17(M.26.48B); assertion that God is ἐ. a gross impiety, id.*gent.*39(M.25.77C); of man ἄνθρωπος, τέλειος κτισθείς, ἐ. γέγονε διὰ τῆς παραβάσεως id.*Ar.*2.66(M.26.288B); τὸ τοιοῦτον [sc. evil spirit] οὐ κακόν, ἀλλ' ἐ. ἀγαθόν Dion.Ar.*d.n.*4.23 (M.3.725A).

***ἐλλογίζω**, *set down against*, Isidorus (Gnost.)ap.Clem.*str.*3.1 (p.196.13; M.8.1104A).

ἐλλόγιμος, **1.** *special* ἐ. χάριν Cyr.*Jo.*5.1(4.470A); **2.** *elect, chosen* by God τοὺς [sc. presbyter-bishops] οὖν κατασταθέντας...ὑφ' ἑτέρων ἐ. ἀνδρῶν συνευδοκησάσης τῆς ἐκκλησίας πάσης *1Clem.*44.3; ὁ ποιήσας ...τὰ ὑπὸ τοῦ θεοῦ δεδομένα δικαιώματα..., οὗτος...ἐ. ἔσται εἰς τὸν ἀριθμὸν τῶν σωζομένων *ib.*58.2; cf.*ib.*57.2; **3.** *skilled in use of words, learned* ἐ. ἄνδρες opp. ἰδιῶται, Chrys.*sac.*5.6(p.135.1; 1.418D); Thdt. *h.e.*2.3.8(3.827).

ἐλλογιμότης, ἡ, *eloquence*, Sever.*1Cor.*5:1–5(p.243.24); Cyr.*ep. Euopt.*(p.111.14; 6¹.201D); id.*Is.*3.3(2.444B).

ἐλλογίμως, *eloquently*, *Chron.Pasch.*p.312(M.92.793C).

ἔλλυπος, *subject to sorrow* ὁ ἄνθρωπος διὰ τῆς ἁμαρτίας γέγονε...ἔ. Anast.S.*hod.*13(M.89.212B).

***ἐλλυτρώσιμος**, *redeemable*, Cyr.*ador.*13(1.467C).

ἔλξις, ἡ, *draught*; of water, ‡Paul.Sil.*therm.Pyth.*82(M.86.2265).

ἐλπιδηφόρος, *bringing hope, full of hope*, Olymp.*Job* 39:8(M.93. 413A).

***ἐλπιδόπνοος**, *fragrant with hope*, ‡Chrys.*poenit.*4(9.854A).

***ἐλπιδοσκοπέω**, *content oneself with hopes*, opp. acting, Chrys. *fr.in Pr.*13:12(M.64.697A).

***ἐλπιδοφόρος**, *bearing hope* εὐχὴ..., ἐ. ἄνθος ‡Chrys.*hom.in Ps.* 75:12(5.606C); of BMV, Ant.Ptol.*fr.*ap.Cyr.*Arcad.*(p.66.33; 5². 49E).

ἐλπίζ-ω, *hope*, (v. ἐλπίς);

A. God as cause; **1.** in gen., *1Clem.*11.1; *Did.*4.10; Herm.*mand.* 12.5.2; Just.*1apol.*48.4(M.6.400C); id.*dial.*101.1(M.6.712B); Chrys. *stat.*6.5(2.81D); id.*hom.14.6 in Rom.*(9.584D); **2.** as author of redemption in Christ, *1Clem.*12.7 cit. s. λύτρωσις; and giver of all good things βούλεται γὰρ ἡμᾶς ὁ θεὸς ἀεὶ ~ειν ἐπ' αὐτόν, ὃς καὶ τὰ πράγματα οὕτως κατεστήσατο, ὥστε προελπίσασιν ἐλθεῖν ἡμῖν τὴν ἀπόλαυσιν τῶν αἰτηθέντων προσκαίρων τε, καὶ αἰωνίων ἀγαθῶν Nil. *epp.*1.39(M.79.101A).

B. in Christ; **1.** in gen. ὁ κύριος Ἰησοῦς Χριστός, εἰς ὃν ~ουσιν σαρκί, ψυχῇ, πνεύματι, πίστει, ἀγάπῃ, ὁμονοίᾳ Ign.*Philad.*11.2; ἐλπίσατε...ἐπὶ τὸν ἐν σαρκὶ μέλλοντα φανεροῦσθαι ὑμῖν Ἰησοῦν *Barn.* 6.9; Just.*dial.*47.2(M.6.577A); *A.Jo.*76(p.189.8); *A.Thom.*A 88(p.203. 6); Hipp.*antichr.*59(p.39.10; M.10.777B); οὐκ ἐπ' ἄνθρωπον ἔχω τὴν ἐλπίδα, ~ων ἐπὶ Χριστὸν Ἰησοῦν Or.*hom.15.6 in Jer.*(p.130.10; M. 13.436C); Christ called ὁ ~όμενος id.*Jo.*13.59(58; p.290.6; M.14. 509D); leading to eternal life οἱ ~οντες ἐπ' αὐτὸν ζήσονται εἰς τὸν αἰῶνα *Barn.*8.5; **2.** in Cross, *Barn.*11.8; cf.*ib.*12.2; **3.** in name of Christ, *1Clem.*59.3; *Barn.*16.8.

C. effects ὥσπερ γὰρ τὸν πονοῦντα καὶ ταλαιπωρούμενον...οὕτω καὶ τὸν ~οντα ὁ θεὸς στεφανοῖ...ἀλλ' ὅμως ἐχαρίσατο καὶ τοῦτο τῷ ~οντι, ἵνα παραμυθήσηται τὴν ἀποκαμοῦσαν ψυχήν Chrys.*hom.14.6 in Rom.* (9.585B).

D. need for hope παραμένωμεν τοίνυν τῇ ἐλπίδι...καὶ δῶμεν ἑαυτούς, καὶ ἐλπίσωμεν Cyr.H.*procatech.*9; esp. in difficulties, Chrys. *exp.in Ps.*117:9f.(5.321B); *ib.*(5.320E); and in temptation to despair ὁ δαίμων...πλανᾷ...ἀδελφόν, ὅπως ἀποστὰς τοῦ ~ειν ἐπὶ κύριον, εἰς νεκρὰς φροντίδας...διαχυθῇ Nil.*epp.*3.237(M.79.493C).

ἐλπίς, ἡ, *hope*;

A. def. and described; **1.** in gen. ἐ. δὲ προσδοκία ἀγαθῶν ἢ ἀπόντος ἀγαθοῦ εὔελπις Clem.*str.*2.9(p.134.17; M.8.976B); χρόνου... τῷ μὲν παρῳχηκότι ἡ μνήμη, τῷ δὲ μέλλοντι ἐ. ἐστι *ib.*2.12(p.141.27; 989B); ἐ. δὲ ὁμωνύμως καὶ ἡ τῆς ἐ. ἀπόδοσίς τε καὶ ἀποκατάστασις *ib.* 4.22(p.312.20; 1356A); ἐ. δ' ἀπόντος πράγματος συνουσία Gr.Naz.*carm.* 1.2.34.158(M.37.956A); *ib.*1.2.28.73(862A); ἐν τοῖς στενοῖς φάρμακον, ἡ ἐ. id.*or.*17.2(M.35.965C); ἐ. οὐδὲν ἕτερόν ἐστι κατὰ γένος ἢ προσδοκία ἀγαθῶν Didym.*Job* 8:11(M.39.1140C); **2.** more specifically Christian διττὴν δὲ εἰδὼς [sc. Rom.5:4f.] τὴν ἐ., τὴν μὲν προσδοκωμένην, τὴν δὲ ἀπειλημμένην, ἤδη τέλος διδάσκει τὴν τῆς ἐ. ἀποκατάστασιν Clem.*str.* 2.22(p.187.14f.; M.8.1084A); τοῦτο γὰρ μάλιστα ἐ., τὸ καὶ παραυτίκα μὴ λαβόντας μὴ ἀπογινώσκειν, μηδὲ ἀπαγορεύειν Chrys.*exp.in Ps.* 146:10f.(5.482A); id.*hom.14.6 in Rom.*(9.585A); ἐ. ἐστιν ἀδήλου πλούτου πλοῦτος· ἐ. ἐστιν ἀνενδοίαστος πρὸ θησαυροῦ θησαυρός Jo.Clim. *scal.*30(M.88.1157D).

B. of God as cause and goal of hope; **1.** in gen. τὴν πᾶσαν ἐ. ἐπὶ τὸν...ἔχοντες θεόν Clem.*str.*6.16(p.501.13; M.9.364A); ὁρᾷς τὸν... ὄχλον ἀποκρεμάμενον ἐ. τῇ πρὸς τὸν θεόν σου *A.Jo.*44(p.172.25); *ib.*55 (p.179.5); ὁ θεὸς πάντων τῶν ὄντων,...ἐπὶ σοὶ πεποίθασιν ἐλπίδες ὁσίων *Const.App.*7.33.2; κἂν μυρία...ἐπέλθῃ δεινὰ...οὐκ ἀφιστάμεθα τῆς ἱερᾶς ἀγκύρας, ἀλλ' ἐχόμεθα τῆς ἐ. τῆς ἐπὶ τὴν σὴν συμμαχίαν Chrys.*exp.in Ps.*140:7(5.441D); though man's co-operation is also needed παιδεύων μὴ μόνον ἐν τῇ χρηστότητι τοῦ θεοῦ ἀλλὰ καὶ ἐν τῇ τῶν οἰκείων ἔργων ἀρετῇ τὰς ἐ. ἔχειν τῆς σωτηρίας id.*exp.in Ps.*4:4f. (5.16C); εἰς μηδὲν ἕτερον ἔχῃ τὰς ἐ., μετὰ τὸν ἔλεον τοῦ θεοῦ, ἀλλ' εἰς ἀρετὴν οἰκείαν id.*hom.5.4 in Mt.*(7.78C); **2.** characteristics of hope in God μακάριος, ὁ πάσης ἐ. τῶν κατὰ τὸν κόσμον τοῦτον ἑαυτὸν ἀποστήσας, καὶ μόνην ἔχων ἑαυτοῦ ἐ. τὸν θεόν...οὐ γὰρ ἐπιδέχεται ἐπαμφοτερισμὸν ἡ εἰς θεὸν ἐ. †Bas.*Is.*245(1.566C,D; M.30.549C); τῇ γὰρ ἐ., φησίν, ἐσώθημεν. αὕτη...καθάπερ σειρά τις ἰσχυρὰ τῶν οὐρανῶν ἐξαρτηθεῖσα, τὰς ἡμετέρας διαβαστάζει ψυχάς, κατὰ μικρὸν πρὸς τὸ ὕψος ἐκεῖνο ἀνέλκουσα τοὺς σφόδρα ἐχομένους αὐτῆς...ἂν οὖν τις μαλακισθῇ καὶ ἀφῇ τὴν ἄγκυραν ταύτην τὴν ἱεράν, κατέπεσέ τε εὐθέως καὶ ἀπεπνίγη εἰς τὴν ἄβυσσον τῆς κακίας ἐλθών Chrys.*Thdr.*1.2(1.3A); id.*serm.9.4 in Gen.*(4.694A); ἡ δὲ ἐπὶ θεὸν ἐ. ἀθάνατος, ἄτρεπτος, ἀκίνητος, μεταβολὴν οὐ δεχομένη, ἐν ἀσφαλείᾳ πάσῃ καθιστῶσα id. *exp.in Ps.*4:6(5.20E); *ib.*117:8f.(321C); ἡ εἰς τὸ θεῖον ἐ., πύργος ἐστὶν ἀρραγής Isid.Pel.*epp.*2.17(M.78.469A).

C. of Christ as hope of Christians; **1.** common hope and bond of union οἵτινες ἀρχηγοὶ στάσεως...ἐγενήθησαν, ὀφείλουσιν τὸ κοινὸν τῆς ἐ. σκοπεῖν *1Clem.*51.1; ἄμεινον...ὑμῖν ἐν τῷ ποιμνίῳ τοῦ Χριστοῦ μικροὺς...εὑρεθῆναι, ἢ καθ' ὑπεροχὴν δοκοῦντας ἐκριφῆναι ἐκ τῆς ἐ. αὐτοῦ *ib.*57.2; τῇ ἐ. προσδεδέσθωσαν αἱ ψυχαὶ ἡμῶν τῷ πιστῷ ἐν ταῖς ἐπαγγελίαις *ib.*27.1; δεδεμένον...ὑπὲρ τοῦ κοινοῦ ὀνόματος καὶ ἐ. Ign.*Eph.*1.2; ἔρρωσθε ἐν Χριστῷ Ἰησοῦ, 'τῇ' κοινῇ 'ἐ. ἡμῶν' id.*Philad.* 11.2; *ib.*5.2; id.*Magn.*7.1; ἡ τελεία ἐ., Ἰησοῦς Χριστός id.*Smyrn.*10.2 (v.l. πίστις); προσκαρτερῶμεν τῇ ἐ. ἡμῶν...ὅς ἐστι Χριστὸς Ἰησοῦς Polyc.*ep.*8.1; and hope of salvation, *2Clem.*1.7; *A.Thom.*A 66 (pp.182.16,184.6); Χριστέ, ἡ ἐ. τῶν ἀπελπισμένων *M.Thdot.1* 21 (p.74.9); *Const.App.*5.6.7; Cyr.*Is.*3.1(2.357D); **2.** on account of Passion τὸ εἰρημένον [sc. Dt.21:23]...ἡμῶν τονοῖ τὴν ἐ. ἐκκρεμαμένην ἀπὸ τοῦ σταυρωθέντος Χριστοῦ Just.*dial.*96.1(M.6.704A); hence of Cross βεβαιούσης ἐλπίδος ἀσφάλεια ‡Chrys.*ador.*2(11.822B); σταυρὸς Χριστιανῶν ἐ. Alex.Sal.*cruc.*(M.87.4073B); Andr.Cr.*or.*10 (M.97.1020D); of Resurrection Ἰησοῦ Χριστοῦ τῆς ἐ. ἡμῶν ἐν τῇ εἰς αὐτὸν ἀναστάσει Ign.*Trall.*proem.; through baptism εἰς σωτήριον ἐ. διὰ τῆς ἐν Χριστῷ ἀναγεννήσεως Eus.*Marcell.*1.1(p.3.26; M.24. 716C).

D. principal objects of hope; **1.** repentance and forgiveness ἐστὶν ἐν αὐτοῖς [sc. sinners] ἐ. μετανοίας Herm.*sim.*8.7.2; *ib.*8.10.2; ἡ καταφθορὰ οὖν ἐ. ἔχει ἀνανεώσεώς τινος, ὁ δὲ θάνατος ἀπώλειαν ἔχει αἰώνιον *ib.*6.2.4; forgiveness depending on repentance πῶς οἱ ἀκάθαρτοι...ἐὰν μὴ...μετανοήσωσιν, ἐ. ἔχειν δύνανται ὅτι οὐ μὴ λογίσηται αὐτοῖς κύριος ἁμαρτίαν; Just.*dial.*141.3(M.6.800A); τίνα λέγεις ἐ. ἔχειν παρὰ θεῷ; ἆρ' ἐκεῖνον τὸν πορνεύσαντα καὶ μὴ φροντίσαντα ...ἢ τοῦτον τὸν μετὰ μίαν ἁμαρτίαν πενθοῦντα;...οὗτος ἐλπίδων ἐστίν Or.*hom.20.9 in Jer.*(pp.191.31–192.3; M.13.521C); δεινὸν γάρ ἐστι τὸ μὴ πιστεύειν ἐ. μετανοίας ἐ. Cyr.H.*catech.*2.5; μὴ καταπέσῃς, μηδὲ τὰς χρηστὰς ἐ. ἐκκόψῃς Chrys.*Thdr.*1.1(1.2C); χρηστὰς ὑπέφηνεν ἐ. καὶ τοῖς ἐν πονηρίᾳ ζῶσιν, εἴ γε βουληθῶσι μεταβληθῆναι, ὡς ἐλέου δυναμένοις τυχεῖν id.*exp.in Ps.*5(5.35A); hence sinners ought not to be excommunicated too readily, *Const.App.*2.21.3; cf.*ib.*2.10.4, 2.12.3; and non-Christians should constantly be prayed for ὑπὲρ τῶν ἄλλων δὲ ἀνθρώπων 'ἀδιαλείπτως προσεύχεσθε'· ἔστιν γὰρ ἐν αὐτοῖς ἐ. μετανοίας, ἵνα θεοῦ τύχωσιν Ign.*Eph.*10.1; **2.** salvation; **a.** in gen., Clem.*paed.*1.10(p.143.19; M.8.357C); id.*q.d.s.*42(p.188.1; M.9. 648B); ἐ. δὲ ἀγαθῇ σωθησόμενον Cyr.H.*procatech.*5; Chrys.*hom.14.6 in Rom.*(9.585A); **b.** esp. of eternal life, Herm.*sim.*9.15.3; *ib.*9.26.2; ἐ. οὖν ζωῆς αἰωνίου ἔχοντες Athenag.*leg.*33.1(M.6.965A); Clem.*str.*7.11 (p.46.10; M.9.489A); τῆς τρισμακαρίας ἐ. καὶ τῆς ἀτελευτήτου καὶ ἀφθάρτου ζωῆς Eus.*e.th.*3.16(p.174.23; M.24.1033A); ἡ ἐ. τῆς αἰωνίου ζωῆς Cyr.H.*procatech.*9; cf.*ib.*1; τὴν ἐπουράνιον ἐ. *Lit.*ap.*Const.App.* 8.10.5; Tim.Beryt.*ep.Prosd.*3(p.285.3); cf. ἡ ἐ. τῆς τῶν ἁγίων ἀναστάσεως Eus.*Marcell.*2.4(p.57.35; M.24.821C); given through Inc., Thdt.*ep.*18(4.1081); implying reigning with Christ, Eus.*Marcell.*2.1 (p.34.15; M.24.781B); causing men to meet death with hope, Dion. Ar.*e.h.*7.1.1(M.3.553A).

E. role in Christian life; **1.** its tests and temptations ἐὰν γὰρ ἀπολῦσαι...τὴν ψυχὴν ἐθελήσῃς...ἕξεις αὐτὴν ἐν τῇ ἐ. Clem.*str.*2.20 (p.172.19; M.8.1053A); ὑπὸ θλίψεων ὀχληθεῖσαι καὶ πόνων,...μὴ ὀκλάσητε πρὸς τὰς ἐ. Meth.*symp.*8.4(p.85.18; M.18.144C); *ib.*10.6 (p.129.4; 204B); ἐὰν βουλώμεθα...ἵστασθαι πρὸς τοὺς ἐπαγομένους πειρασμούς· ἂν εἰς τὸν θεὸν ἔχωμεν τὰς ἐ., ἐσόμεθα...ἐν εὐρυχωρίᾳ Chrys.*hom.6.4 in Tit.*(11.769E); διὰ γὰρ τοῦτο ὁ διάβολος ἡμᾶς εἰς τοὺς τῆς ἀπογνώσεως ἐμβάλλει λογισμούς· ἵνα ἐκκόψῃ τὴν ἐ. τὴν πρὸς τὸν θεόν Chrys.*Thdr.*1.2(1.3A); ἡ παροῦσα νῦν ἔνδεια τῶν χρησίμων, καὶ τὸ μὴ ῥᾳδίως, μηδὲ ταχέως αὐτῶν ἐπιτυγχάνειν ἡμᾶς, καὶ τὸ μὴ δῆλον εἶναι πότε καὶ πῶς ἐπιτευξώμεθα τῶν αἰτημάτων ἡμῶν, πάντα ταῦτα γυμνάσια τῆς ἐ. ὑπάρχει Nil.*epp.*1.38(M.79.100D); ἀπαραβάτως ἀγωνιεῖται, πρὸς τὴν τῶν καλῶν ἐπάθλων ἐ. βεβαίως ἔχων Dion.Ar.*e.h.*2.3.6(M.3.404A); **2.** its effects μετὰ γὰρ τὰς θλίψεις ἡ ἐ. ἐκ τοῦ σύνεγγυς δὲ πάρεστι τὰ ἐλπιζόμενα. κἂν γὰρ ὅλον τις εἴποι τὸν ἀνθρώπινον βίον, σμικρότατόν ἐστι διάστημα παντελῶς, συγκρίσει ἐκείνου τοῦ ἀπεράντου αἰῶνος τοῦ ἐν ταῖς ἐ. ἀποκειμένου Bas.*ep.*140.1(3.233A,B; M.32.588B); τὸν γὰρ Χριστιανὸν καὶ ἐν τούτῳ τῶν ἀπίστων διαφέρειν χρή, ἐν τῷ φέρειν γενναίως ἅπαντα, καὶ τῇ τῶν μελλόντων ἐ. πτερούμενον ἀνώτερον εἶναι τῆς τῶν ἀνθρωπίνων κακῶν προσβολῆς Chrys.*stat.*2.3(2.24A); ἡ γὰρ ἐ. ἀεὶ τῶν μελλόντων ἀγαθῶν κούφως ποιεῖ φέρειν τὰ παρόντα λυπηρά id.*hom.17.8 in Gen.*(4.144E); ἡ εἰς τὴν ἄμαχον τοῦ τὰ πάντα οἰακίζοντος δεξιὰν ἐ., οὐ μόνον τὴν τῶν μελλόντων ὠδίνει ἀπόλαυσιν, ἀλλὰ καὶ τοὺς παρόντας ἐπικουφίζει πόνους. ῥᾷον γάρ τις φέρει τοὺς ἄθλους τῇ τῶν στεφάνων ἐ. πτερούμενος Isid.Pel. *epp.*5.58(M.78.1361C); *ib.*4.138(1217D); its power μεγάλη τῆς ἐπὶ τὸν κύριον ἐ. ἡ δύναμις, φρούριον ἀχείρωτον, τεῖχος ἄμαχον, συμμαχία ἀκαταγώνιστος...ἡ γὰρ εἰς τὸν θεὸν ἐ. πάντα μεταρρυθμίζει...ἡ εἰς τὸν θεὸν ἐ. χαλινοῦ παντὸς ἰσχυροτέρα Chrys.*exp.in Ps.*10(5.113C,D); producing joy, Bas.*hom.*4.3(2.27D; M.31.224C); leading man to God, Ant.Mon.*hom.*2(M.89.1437B).

F. relation to other virtues; **1.** faith 'ζωῆς ἐ.', ἀρχὴ καὶ τέλος πίστεως ἡμῶν *Barn.*1.6; ἐν ἐ. τῆς πίστεως *ib.*4.8; following faith, Polyc.*ep.*3.3; ἡ ἐ. ἐκ πίστεως συνέστηκεν Clem.*str.*2.6(p.127.18; M.8.961C); αἷμα τῆς πίστεως ἡ ἐ., ὑφ' ἧς συνέχεται, καθάπερ ὑπὸ ψυχῆς, ἡ πίστις. διαπνευσάσης δὲ τῆς ἐ. δίκην ἐκρυέντος αἵματος τὸ ζωτικὸν τῆς πίστεως ὑπεκλύεται id.*paed.*1.6(p.113.6f.; M.8.296B); ἀπὸ τῆς πίστεως προΐωμεν ἐπὶ τὴν δευτερεύουσαν ἐ., ἥτις ἐξ αὐτῆς ἀρδευομένη καρποφορεῖ...ἡ πίστις, ἐὰν ἔχῃ ἐ., ἔχει τὸ ἴδιον ἔργον, καὶ θέρμη ἐστὶ τῷ κεκτημένῳ Ant.Mon.*hom.*2(M.89.1437C); cf. πίστις...ἐν τῷ τὰ αὐτὰ αἱρεῖσθαι, γνῶσις δὲ ἐν τῷ τὰ αὐτὰ μεμαθηκέναι...ἐ. δὲ ἐν τῷ τὰ αὐτὰ ποθεῖν Clem.*str.*7.12(p.55.1; M.9.505B); hope of ordinary Christian dist. from mysteries known to 'gnostic' ὁ διδάσκαλος οὗτος ὁ παιδεύων μυστηρίοις μὲν τὸν γνωστικόν, ἐ. δὲ ἀγαθαῖς τὸν πιστόν *ib.*7.2(p.6.9; 409A); **2.** charity κράτος ἀγάπης ἐ., δι' αὐτῆς γὰρ τὸν τῆς ἀγάπης μισθὸν ἀπεκδεχόμεθα Jo.Clim.*scal.*30(M.88.1157D); ἐ. ἔλλειψις, ἀγάπης ἀφανισμός *ib.*(1160A); v. ἀγάπη.

G. of false hope; of paganism, Clem.*prot.*10(p.73.4; M.8.216B); ἐψευσμένα δοξάζοντες καὶ ἐπ' οὐδενὶ βεβαίῳ ἔχοντες τὴν ἑαυτῶν ἐ. *Const.App.*2.28.9; in worldly things, Bas.*ep.*18(3.96C,D; M.32.281C); πρὸς ἀδυνάτους ἤρτηται...ἐ., ὁ τὰς τῶν ἁγίων ἐξαιτῶν προσευχὰς ...καὶ ἀγαθοδοτίδων ἐντολῶν ἀποφοιτήσει Dion.Ar.*e.h.*7.3.6(M.3.561A).

***ἐλπιστής**, ὁ, *one who hopes*, Nil.*epp.*3.179(M.79.468C).

ἐλπιστικός, *concerned with hope*, Clem.*str.*8.3(p.82.16; M.9.564B).

***Ἐλωείμ**, (Hebr. אֱלֹהִים) *Elohim* (God), as name of Gnost. aeon, Hipp.*haer.*5.26(p.127.7; M.16.3194D); *ib.*(p.127.28; 3195B).

***ἐμαγκηπατίων**, ἡ, (Lat. *emancipatio*) *emancipation*; of sons from paternal authority, *Cod.Afr.*35.

***ἐμαγκήπατος**, (Lat. *emancipatus*) *emancipated, free*, *Cod.Afr.* 35 tit.

***ἔμβαθμος**, *belonging to one of the orders of ministry* ἐ. διακόνους †Jo.Jej.*poenit.*(M.88.1908B).

ἐμβαθύν-ω, **1.** *dig deep*, Chrys.*pan.mart.*3.1(2.713B); pass., ‡Ath. *sem.*3(M.28.148B); met., *deepen* ~αι τὴν πίστιν Chrys.*hom.54.1 in Jo.*(8.315C); **2.** met.; **a.** *plunge* the mind ἑκάστῃ λέξει τοῦ ψαλμοῦ τὸν νοῦν ἐ. Eus.*d.e.*10.8(p.492.17; M.22.789D); Hesych.H.*serm.*7(M.93.1477B); **b.** intrans., *sink* τοὺς ἐν τοῖς κακοῖς ~οντας Thdr.Heracl. *Is.*31:6(M.18.1325B); Bas.*hom.in Ps.*29(1.127B; M.29.313A); Gr.Nyss. *or.dom.*4(p.78.9; M.44.1168C); **3.** *go deeply into* (cf. French *approfondir*); ref. theol. questions, Or.*comm.in Gen.*ap.Eus.*p.e.*6.11 (283D; M.12.56D); Bas.*hom.in Ps.*33(1.145E; M.29.357A); †Cyr.*coll. VT*(6^{4}.44B).

ἐμβακχεύω, *rage against*, c. dat., Tat.*orat.*16(p.17.20, v.l. ἐκβ- M. 6.840C).

ἐμβαπτίζ-ω, *plunge into, immerse*, met. ὁ...τὴν ψυχὴν ~ει μερίμναις πραγμάτων Synes.*ep.*57(M.66.1388B); id.*insomn.*8(p.158.11; M.66.1293D); id.*Dion* 6(p.249.22; M.66.1129B).

***ἐμβαρύνω**, *weigh down, burden*, ‡Chrys.*prodig.*2.3(8.157C); Cyr. *Is.*3.4(2.480E).

***ἐμβασίλευμα**, τό, *palace*, Gr.Naz.*carm.*1.1.4.99(M.37.423A).

***ἐμβατευτικός**, *invading*; met., Leont.H.*Nest.*1.47(M.86.1505C).

ἐμβατεύ-ω, **1.** c. dat., *reach*, met. τὸν λόγον τοῖς ὑψηλοτέροις ~οντα Gr.Nyss.*v.Macr.*(p.390.16; M.46.977C); Max.*ep.*12(M.91.473C); *enter*, met. ὁ δεσπότης...~ων ταῖς καρδίαις...φωτίζει τὴν διάνοιαν Chrys. *hom.35.1 in Gen.*(4.349E); id.*hom.2.2 in Rom.*(9.437D); Vict.*Mc.*2:9 (p.285.22); οὐκ...ἐ. [sc. Devil] καρδίαις Olymp.*Job* 1:12(M.93.28A); **2.** c. acc., *explore, penetrate*, met.; **a.** of God τὸν τὰς καρδίας ~οντα Chrys.*hom.23.3 in Gen.*(4.209B); of Christ, id.*sac.*2.1(p.26.15; 1.371E); c. εἰς, Thdt.*carit.*(3.1307); **b.** divine mysteries impenetrable by man τολμηρὸν ~ειν τὴν ἀπερινόητον φύσιν Ath.*hom.in Mt. 11:27*(M.25.216A); Bas.*Eun.*1.13(1.225E; M.29.541C); Epiph.*haer.*76. 26(p.373.22; cf.M.42.568B); Procl.CP *annunt.*5(M.85.445B); **c.** *broach* a subject, ‡Caes.Naz.*dial.*178(M.38.1148); **3.** *trample* on, met., ref. Manicheans and gospels οὐ μὲν καὶ ~ουσι [sc. pagans] τοῖς γράμμασι· οἱ δὲ [sc. Manicheans] εἰληφέναι δοκοῦντες, ἐνεβάτευσαν Serap. *Man.*36(p.53; M.18.1213B).

***ἐμβάτη**, ἡ, *cistern, bathing-tub*, Thphn.*chron.*p.50(M.108.181A).

ἐμβάτης, ὁ, *font, cistern*; in which holy water was blessed, *Euchol.*(p.363); cf.*IGC As.Min.*147.

***ἐμβατταρίζω**, *babble*, Gr.Nyss.*Eun.*12(1 p.308.12; M.45.1020D).

***ἔμβαψις**, ἡ, *dipping in*, ref. Jo.13:26, Or.*Jo.*32.22(14; p.465.23; M.14.805B).

ἔμβιος, **1.** *endowed with life*, Synes.*regn.*29(p.62.2; M.66.1108B); **2.** *revived* ἱστορία ἐ. id.*provid.*2.7(p.129.6; M.66.1277C); **3.** *vivid*; of mental images, id.*insomn.*15(p.178.2; M.66.1309D); id.*ep.*146(M.66.1541B).

ἐμβιοτεύ-ω, **1.** *live*, in gen., Or.*princ.*1.8.4(p.102.13); Gr.Nyss. *infant.*(M.46.173B); Thdr.Stud.*epp.*2.186(M.99.1573A); met. ἐ. τῇ ἁπλότητι τῶν ἀπατηθέντων Gr.Nyss.*Eun.*1(1 p.38.12; M.45.265B); **2.** pass., *become part of one's life* οὐκ ἔκ τινος...ἀνάγκης, ἀρετὴν ἢ κακίαν ~εσθαι ‡Caes.Naz.*dial.*111(M.38.989).

ἐμβίωσις, ἡ, *way of life*, Areth.*Apoc.*8(M.106.560B).

ἔμβλητος, *inlaid*, met. τοῖς ἐμβλήτοις τῆς ἀγάπης *Schol.*16 in Jo. Clim.*scal.*22(M.88.961C).

ἐμβοθρεύω, *implant*; pass., of Christ as vine, Cyr.*glaph.Gen.*7 (1.234B); met., of impiety, id.*Os.*102(3.134A).

ἐμβολή, ἡ, **1.** *blast* of wind, Chrys.*hom.50.2 in Mt.*(7.515D); Isid.Pel.*epp.*1.278(M.78.345C); **2.** *receptacle*, of mouth ἡ τῶν ὀδόντων ἐ. Geo.Pis.*carm.*1.94; Leont.N.*v.Sym.*32(M.93.1709B).

***ἐμβολιμεύω**, *intercalate*, Epiph.*haer.*70.13(p.246.17; M.42.368B); *ib.*(p.246.22; M.l.c.).

***ἐμβολισμός**, *intercalary*, Isid.H.*etym.*6.17.22,23.

ἔμβολος, ὁ, [fem., *Apoc.Dan.*C(p.117.58)] *colonnade*; Pall.*h. Laus.*40(p.127.4; M.34.1204D); *Chron.Pasch.*p.284(M.92.709A); eccl. ἐν τῷ ἀριστερῷ ἐ. τοῦ κατηχουμενίου τοῦ ἐν τῷ ἐξαέρῳ *Mir.Cosm. Dam.*12(p.129); of burial in δεξιὸς ἔ. of an oratory, Jo.Mosch. *prat.*92(M.87.2952A); ref. relics of S. Anastasia ἐν τῷ μαρτυρίῳ αὐτῆς τῷ ὄντι ἐν τοῖς Δομνίου ἐ. Thdr.Lect.*h.e.*2.64(M.86.216B); ref. hanging of *ex-voto* ἐν τῷ ἐ. τοῦ τετραστόου τοῦ...εὐκτηρίου id. *fr.*(M.86.224C).

ἐμβομβέω, *buzz, sound in* one's ears, c. dat., Serap.*Man.*33(p.50; M.18.1128B); Synes.*ep.*123(M.66.1504B); *ib.*137(1525B).

ἐμβράσσω, *boil, burn*, Hipp.*haer.*4.33(p.59.13; M.16.3095C); met., of desire, *A.Andr.fr.*3(p.39.8).

ἐμβρίθεια, ἡ, **1.** *heaviness* of soul, Jo.D.*virt.*(M.95.93C); **2.** *firmness* ἡ τοῦ νοὸς ἐ. Jo.Clim.*scal.*15(M.87.900C); **3.** *dignity* τὴν βασιλικὴν ...ἐ. Epiph.*exp.fid.*4(p.499.31; M.42.780B); Chrys.*hom.20.8 in Eph.* (11.144E); **4.** *severity*, Tit.Bost.*Man.*2.38(M.18.1208A); *Const.App.* 4.11.2; Philost.*h.e.*11.6(M.65.600B).

***ἐμβρίθημα**, τό, *severity*, †Gregent.*disp.*(M.86.636B) perh. f.l. for ἐμβριμήματι.

ἐμβριμ-άομαι, -έομαι, **1.** *be deeply moved*, exeg. Jo.11:33 ἐ. δὲ τῷ πνεύματι, τουτέστι τῇ δυνάμει τοῦ ἁγίου πνεύματος ἐπιπλήττει τρόπον τινὰ τῇ ἰδίᾳ σαρκί· ἡ δέ, τὸ τῆς ἑνωθείσης αὐτῇ θεότητος οὐκ ἐνεγκοῦσα κίνημα, τρέμει τε καὶ θορύβου πλάττεται σχῆμα Cyr.*Jo.*7(4.685C); Ammon.*Jo.*11:33(M.85.1468C); **2.** *be enraged, rage* ~ούμενοι *A.Pil.* A 5(p.236); ἐνεβριμοῦντο *Ep.Lugd.*ap.Eus.*h.e.*5.1.60(M.20.432A); ~ούμενοι Men.*exc.Rom.*8(p.193.6; M.113.885A); **3.** *rebuke*, c. dat., *A.Mt.*14(p.233.4); of God rebuking unbelievers and Devil, Eus.*Is.* 17:13(M.24.212C); of Christ, cf.Jo.11:33, Chrys.*hom.63.1 in Jo.*(8. 377A); at death of Lazarus τῷ ᾅδῃ ~ησάμενος Diad.*perf.*62(p.72. 7); **4.** *rush at*, c. dat. ἐνεβριμεῖτο Epiph.*haer.*66.11(p.32.26; M.42. 45C).

ἐμβρίμημα, τό, **1.** *snort*; of fiery breathing of cherubim σὲ [sc. Father] τρέμουσιν...τὰ ἐ. τῶν χερουβικῶν ζῴων πυρίπνοα *A.Phil.* 132(p.63.8); **2.** *rebuke, indignation*, *A.Phil.*131(p.61.8); Jo.D.*hom.* 11.18(M.96.780D).

ἐμβρίμησις, ἡ, *indignation*; **1.** def. ἐ. ἐστι ψυχῆς λογικῆς τοῦ θυμικοῦ μέρους ἐνέργεια Anast.S.*hod.*2(M.89.77D); **2.** in God ἡ ἀπὸ τῶν θείων γραφῶν ἐ. †Bas.*hom.in Ps.*37(1.365D; M.30.89D); *ib.*(366E; M.93B); **3.** in Christ, esp. ref. Jo.11:38, Or.*fr.84 in Jo.*(p.549.19); proving reality of his human nature, Epiph.*haer.*69.9(p.169.8; M.42.232B); agst. Apollinarius, not unworthy of his divinity, *ib.* 77.26(p.439.20; 630B); τὴν κατὰ τοῦ θανάτου δριμεῖαν ἀπειλὴν ἐ. ἔφη Cyr.*Jo.*9(4.734D); ἐνταῦθα τὴν ἐ. νοοῦμεν, τὴν οἱονεὶ μετὰ κινήσεως τῆς κατ' ἐξουσίαν θέλησιν *ib.*7(686E).

***ἐμβρίμιον, τό,** *pillow, cushion, Apophth.Patr.*(M.65.157C); *ib.* (228B); *ib.*(268D).

ἐμβροντάω, pass., *be perverse*; **1.** of heretics, *be wrong-headed* τὰς φρένας ἐμβεβροντημένοι Ath.*ep.Aeg.Lib.*17(M.25.576C); Epiph. *haer.*31.3(p.387.22; M.41.480A); *ib.*66.1(p.15.5; M.42.29B); **2.** of heresies, *be crack-brained, ib.*75.4(p.335.30; M.42.508C); *ib.*9.1(p.197.15; M.41.224B).

ἐμβροντησία, ἡ, *folly*; esp. of paganism and heresy, Just.*1apol.* 9.5(M.6.340B); Cyr.*Chr.un.*(5¹.740B); ἡ τῶν Σεθιανῶν ἐ. Thdt.*haer.*5.9 (4.409); Jo.D.*hom.*12.13(M.96.797D).

***ἐμβρόντησις, ἡ,** *madness,* Epiph.*haer.*65.8(p.12.18; M.42.28B); id.*ep.Arab.*(p.473.8; M.42.736B).

ἔμβροχος, *moistened*; by tears, Bas.*ep.*45.1(3.134A; M.32.368A); abs. ἔ. στεναγμοί ‡Max.*cap.al.*210(M.90.1452A).

***ἐμβρυοκτόνος,** *killing the foetus* in the womb, Bas.*ep.*188 *can.*8 (3.273D; M.32.677A) ∞ CTrull.*can.*91.

***ἐμβρύομαι,** *abound in,* pass. ἐνεβρύθημεν Sophr.H.*or.*7.1(M.87.3324A).

ἐμβρυοτομέω, c. acc., *perform Caesarian operation on,* Marc.Diac. *v.Porph.*28.

***ἔμβως,** v. *ἔνβως.

ἔμετος, ὁ, *vomit,* cf.Pr.26:11; met., of heresy, Ath.*h.Ar.*29(p.198.18; M.25.725B); id.*Ar.*2.30(M.26.212A); Cyr.*inc.unigen.*(5¹.682D).

ἐμέω, *vomit*; met., ref. sins, passions etc., Or.*princ.*3.1.13(p.218.7; M.11.273A); θυμὸν...κατὰ τῆς...διαθήκης ἐμέσει Thdt.*Dan.*11:30(2.1283); ref. heresy, Ath.*syn.*16(p.244.21; M.26.712A); Thdt.*h.e.*1.5.6 (3.751).

[*]ἔμμαλος, *woolly, fleecy* παρέσχεν εἰς τὰ τέσσαρα μέρη Κωνσταντινουπόλεως ὀρχηστὰς ἐ. μικροὺς τέσσαρας...ἔδωκε δὲ τοῖς πρασίνοις ἐ. τὸν Αὐτοκύονα Jo.Mal.*chron.*15 p.386(M.97.573A).

***Ἐμμανουήλ, ὁ,** (Hebr. עִמָּנוּ אֵל) *Emmanuel, God with us,* name of incarnate Word; **1.** in gen., Iren.*haer.*4.33.11(M.7.1080B) cit. s. ἕνωσις; cf.*ib.*3.21.4(951B); Epiph.*haer.*54.3(p.320.9; M.41.965B); Cyr.*Is.*1.5(2.122D); Thdt.*Is.*7:14(p.39.2; 2.218); Sophr.H.*or.*2.42(M.87.3273A,B); **2.** Is.7:14 fulfilled although Christ was not called Ἐ.: cf. *et prophetatur, quia si quis est domus David, vocabit nomen ejus E. in adventu enim Christi sola ecclesia nostra de Christo dicit nobiscum deus,* Or.*hom.*2.2 *in Is.*(M.13.226A); οὐ διέλιπε δὴ ἡ ἁγία τοῦ θεοῦ ἐκκλησία...Ἐ. ὀνομάζειν τὸν κύριον. ἔχομεν δὲ ἐν τῇ ὀνομασίᾳ τοῦ Χριστοῦ πάσας τὰς λοιπὰς ὀνομασίας τοῦ Χριστοῦ περιεχομένας, εἰ καὶ μὴ πάσαις κεχρήμεθα ‡Just.*qu.et resp.*135(M.6.1388B); ἐνταῦθα γὰρ τῷ συμβαίνοντι ὄνομα τίθησι·...οὐδὲν οὖν ἄλλο δηλοῖ τὸ 'καλέσουσιν Ἐ.' ἢ ὅτι ὄψονται θεὸν μετὰ ἀνθρώπων· ἀεὶ μὲν γὰρ γέγονε μετὰ ἀνθρώπων, οὐδέποτε δὲ οὕτω σαφῶς Chrys.*hom.*5.2 *in Mt.*(7.74C); id. *Is.interp.*1.9(6.16D); **3.** bearing of name on virgin birth τίνι μᾶλλον ἁρμόζει γεννῆσαι Ἐ., τουτέστι μεθ' ἡμῶν ὁ θεός, ἆρα γυναικὶ συνουσιασθείσῃ...ἢ...παρθένῳ; Or.*Cels.*1.35(p.86.23; M.11.728B); †Bas.*Is.*201 (1.529A; M.30.464B); **4.** Ἐ. (God with man) typified by Law in ark of covenant, Cyr.*Jo.*4.4(4.387E); **5.** freq. used by Cyr., prob. with anti-Nestorian implications, e.g. *hom.pasch.*17.3(5².231C).

***ἐμμαραίνομαι,** *decay*; of plants, ‡Bas.*const.*4.6(2.549D; M.31.1357C).

***ἐμμαρτυρέω,** *bear witness to, attest,* Germ.CP *or.*1(M.98.229B); med., Hipp.*haer.*proem.(p.3.13; conj. ἐμμάρτυρα ποιούμενοι M.16.3020D).

ἐμμάρτυρος, 1. *witnessed, seen* ἐ. ἔδει γενέσθαι τὸν τούτου [sc. of Christ] θάνατον, ἵνα καὶ ὁ τῆς ἀναστάσεως πιστευθῇ λόγος Ath.*inc.* 24.1(M.25.137A); ἐ. γὰρ εἶναι προσήκει τὸν τοιοῦτον [i.e. of monks] βίον, ὡς ἂν ἐκτὸς εἶναι πονηρᾶς ὑποψίας Bas.*ascet.*1.3(2.320C; M.31.873C); **2.** *testified, attested,* Thphl.Ant.*Autol.*2.14(M.6.1045A); Thdot. Anc.*hom.BMV et Sym.*(M.77.1392C); **3.** *witnessing, testifying,* Epiph.*haer.*42.11(p.125.17; M.41.728C); *ib.*51.7(p.257.5; 900C); of martyrdom ἡ ἐ. ἄθλησις Sophr.H.*v.Cyr.et Jo.*proem.5(M.87.3388A).

***ἔμμαρτυς,** *bearing witness,* Epiph.*haer.*51.7(p.257.5; M.41.900C).

ἐμματαιάζω, *be idly occupied, dally with,* c. dat., Gr.Nyss.*hom.* *8 in Cant.*(M.44.952A); id.*or.dom.*1(p.14.21; M.44.1128C); ‡Proc.G. *Pr.*13:17(M.87.1353C); Gr.Agr.*Eccl.*3.27(M.98.905A).

***ἐμματίζω,** *instruct,* Anast.S.*hod.*1 tit.(M.89.40A).

ἐμμέλεια, ἡ, 1. *harmony, grace,* met. τῆς σῆς ἐ. καὶ πραότητος Bas. *ep.*73.3(3.168A; M.32.444A); as title of respect, *Your Grace* ἡ ἐ. ἡ σή *ib.*243.3(3.374B; M.905C); Chrys.*ep.*2.1(3.535A); **2.** *diligence,* Hipp. *haer.*5.13(p.108.9; M.16.3166C); Eus.*v.C.*4.8(p.121.4); Bas.*Spir.*1(3.2A; M.32.68A); Gr.Naz.*carm.*2.1.11.537(M.37.1066A).

ἐμμελέτημα, τό, *fiction, invention*; derisively of Baal, Eust.*engast.* 8(p.26.4; M.18.625D); of heresy, Gr.Nyss.*Eun.*1(1 p.99.16; M.45.332D).

§ἐμμελής, *diligent,* Ephr.1.1D; *ib.*2B.

***ἐμμελῳδ-έω,** *make music in,* Gr.Nyss.*hom.opif.*9(M.44.149C); met. ἐν ταῖς ῥήσεσι τῶν θεολόγων...∼οῦντας παιδεύεσθαι ‡Chrys. *hom.in Mt.12:14*(10.761C).

ἐμμελῶς, *diligently,* Iren.*haer.*1.23.4(M.7.673A *studiose*).

***ἐμμέρεια, ἡ,** *compositeness,* Leont.H.*Nest.*1.1(M.86.1408A).

***ἐμμερής,** *made up of parts, composite*; ref. unity of Christ in Nestorian controversy, Leont.H.*Nest.*1.1(M.86.1404B,C,D et passim).

ἐμμερίζ-ω, *divide,* Gr.Nyss.*hom.15 in Cant.*(M.44.1113C); Trin. οὐκ ∼ει τὴν ἀμέριστον ἀξίαν Sever.*serp.*6(M.56.508).

ἐμμέριμνος, 1. *anxious* νοῦς ἐ. σὴς βιβρώσκων ὀστέα Gr.Naz.*carm.* 1.2.32.101(M.37.924A); ‡Chrys.*hom.2.4 in Ps.50*(5.577C); through love of visible things ἐ. ἀναφύονται ἔννοιαι τῇ ψυχῇ ‡Proc.G.*Pr.* 26:9(M.87.1481C); *ib.*26:14(1484D); **2.** *diligent* δείξωμεν θεῷ μετάνοιαν ἐ. Ephr.3.312B; ‡Chrys.*anim.*(9.821C); †Jo.D.*B.J.*14(M.96.981C); **3.** *occupied, Schol.Clem.paed.*(p.328.22; M.9.788D).

***ἐμμεσιτεύω,** *mediate,* Clem.*str.*7.9(p.38.31; M.9.473B).

[*]ἐμμίγνυμι, = ἐμμείγνυμι, *mingle, mix with*; **1.** Christol. Χριστὸς ...ὁ λόγος ἦν, τοῦτο καὶ ὁ ἐμμιχθεὶς...ἐν τῇ θεότητι γίνεται Gr.Nyss. *Apoll.*53(M.45.1252C); **2.** eucharistic ἔκλασεν, 'ἐμμίξας ἑαυτὸν τῷ ἀντιτύπῳ' Eutych.*pasch.*2(M.86.2393B); **3.** Gnost., of divine power mingled with elements, Hipp.*haer.*6.13(p.139.10; M.16.3214A).

***ἔμμιξις, ἡ,** *immixture* ἅπας τὸ ἅγιον σῶμα...τοῦ κυρίου δέχεται... μερίζεται γὰρ ἀμερίστως ἐν ἅπασι, διὰ τὴν ἔ. Eutych.*pasch.*2(M.86.2393C).

ἔμμισθος, 1. *given, promised as a reward*; of eternal life, *Const. App.*7.34.8; **2.** *bringing a reward, profitable,* Gr.Naz.*ep.*135(M.37.232A).

***ἐμμίσθως,** *for hire, for pay,* Synes.*ep.*67(M.66.1413A).

ἐμμολύνω, *befoul, pollute...with*; intellectually and morally, Gr.Nyss.*Eun.*7(2 p.172.25; M.45.764C); pass., Bas.*ascet.*1.2(2.319E; M.31.873A); *ib.*(320B; M.873B); Gr.Nyss.*Pss.titt.*A 7(M.44.461B).

ἔμμονος, *enduring, continuing,* of God εἰ δὲ ἐνθυμεῖται καὶ μεταμελεῖται, καὶ τίς νῷ τέλειος καὶ γνώμῃ ἔ.; *Hom.Clem.*2.43; of Son πῶς...εἰ κτίσμα...ἐστι, δύναται μόνος καὶ πρῶτος κτίζεσθαι,...δήλου ὄντος...ὅτι ἐν τοῖς κτίσμασιν οὐδέν ἐστιν ἔ. καθ' ἑαυτὸ καὶ πρῶτον γενόμενον...; Ath.*Ar.*2.48(M.26.249B); ref. function of angels τάχα δὲ καὶ εὐχῇ ἔ. ὑπὲρ σωτηρίας ἡμῶν ‡Ath.*comm.essent.*52(M.28.77B).

ἐμμόνως, *permanently,* of H. Ghost given by Christ ἵνα καὶ ἐν ἡμῖν κατοικήσῃ λοιπὸν ἐ. Cyr.*Joel.*35(3.228C).

ἔμμορφος, *endowed with form,* Trin. τρία ἔ., τρία σύμμορφα Epiph. *anc.*67(p.82.3; M.43.137C) ∞ ‡Caes.Naz.*dial.*3(M.38.861).

***ἐμμορφ-όω,** *shape*; **1.** lit., Mac.Aeg.*hom.*43.7(M.34.776D); **2.** met. κατά τε καρδίαν, καὶ λόγον, καὶ πρᾶξιν...∼ωθεὶς...τῇ διδασκαλίᾳ τοῦ κυρίου †Bas.*bapt.*1.2.10(2.636D; M.31.1541D); Gr.Nyss.*ep.* 3(M.46.1016B); διὰ τὸν τῆς ἀρετῆς τύπον ∼οῖ [sc. H. Ghost] ἡμῖν τὸν Χριστόν id.*Pss.titt.*B 11(M.44.544B); cf.id.*hom.9 in Cant.*(M.44.965B); ref.Inc. ἡ τοῦ ὑψίστου δύναμις, διὰ τοῦ ἁγίου πνεύματος ἐν τῇ ἀνθρωπίνῃ φύσει ἐνεσκιάσθη, τουτέστιν, ἐνεμορφώθη id.*Apoll.*6(M.45.1136C).

***ἐμμοχθέω,** *toil over,* Gr.Nyss.*bapt.diff.*(M.46.428C).

***ἔμμυρος,** *embalmed, fragrant*; met., Gr.Nyss.*hom.3 in Cant.*(M.44.824B).

***ἐμμυστήριος,** *mystical, Lit.Gr.Naz.*(M.36.725A).

***ἐμπαγίως,** *firmly, integrally,* Christol. ἐ. μένειν τὴν δυάδα ἠρνήσατο [sc. Sev. Ant.] Eust.Mon.*ep.*(M.86.912C).

ἐμπάθεια, ἡ, 1. *passibility*; Christol., Clem.*str.*7.2(M.9.412B; εὐπάθεια p.7.24); **2.** *passion, passionateness,* of God οὐδὲ διὰ νομιζομένην συμπάθειαν, τὴν ὄντως ἐ., τὸν τοῦ δικαίου λόγον προδίδωσι Jo.D.*Man.*1.36(M.94.1544A); in moral life, esp. with sexual connotation, Ephr.1.261A; τοῦτο ἐμπαθείας τεκμήριον, τὸ πᾶσι τοῖς ὑπὸ δαιμόνων ὑποσπειρομένοις σχεδὸν ὀξέως ὑπείκειν Jo.Clim.*scal.*29(M.88.1149B); πάντα διαλογισμὸν ἐμπαθείας ἀπαλείψας τῆς ψυχῆς,...ναὸν σεαυτὸν ποιῶν τοῦ ἁγίου πνεύματος †Jo.D.*B.J.*19(M.96.1037A); in scripture τῆς περὶ τὸ γράμμα δοκούσης ἐ., εὐμηχάνως ἐπὶ τὴν τῶν σημαινομένων δογμάτων ὁδηγούσης μυσταγωγίαν Nil.ap.Proc.G.*Cant.* 1:1(M.87.1548B).

ἐμπαθής, *subject to passion, passionate*; **1.** of Godhead τὸ ἐ. τῆς ὀργῆς, εἰ δὴ ὀργὴν τὴν νουθεσίαν αὐτοῦ χρὴ καλεῖν, φιλάνθρωπόν ἐστιν εἰς πάθη καταβαίνοντος τοῦ θεοῦ διὰ τὸν ἄνθρωπον, δι' ὃν καὶ γέγονεν ἄνθρωπος ὁ λόγος τοῦ θεοῦ Clem.*paed*.1.8(p.133.22; M.8.340A); οὐ... θέμις ἐ. νοεῖν τὸν θεόν id.*str*.2.8(p.134.10; M.8.976A); ὕπνοῖ τῇ γραφῇ θεός,...καίτοι τότε γέγονεν ἐ.; Gr.Naz.*or*.31.22(p.172.6; M.36.157A); **2.** Trin., ref. Eunomius and term 'Father' ὁ δὲ ἐπὶ τῆς ἐ. φύσεως τῇ προσηγορίᾳ ταύτῃ συνεθισθείς,...ὡς ἀδύνατον ἀπαρνεῖται Bas.*Eun*. 2.23(1.258E; M.29.621B); *ib*.2.24(260D; M.625C); πῶς οὖν οὐκ ἐ. ἡ γέννησις; ὅτι ἀσώματος Gr.Naz.*or*.29.4(p.77.13; M.36.77C); τῆς ἐ. ἐκ πατρὸς γεννήσεως...καθάπερ ὁ ἡμέτερος λόγος ἐκ τοῦ νοῦ πρόεισιν Areth.*Apoc*.58(M.106.741D) prob. f.l. for ἀπαθοῦς cf.Andr.Caes. *Apoc*.58(M.106.401C); **3.** Christol. τὴν σάρκα τὴν ἐ. φύσει γενομένην ἀναλαβὼν εἰς ἕξιν ἀπαθείας ἐπαίδευσεν Clem.*str*.7.2(p.7.15; M.9.412A); Gr.Nyss.*ep*.3(M.46.1021A); Sophr.H.*ep.syn*.(M.87.3161D); of limits of Christ's passibility οὐκ ἐ. ἦν τὸ δάκρυον τοῦ κυρίου, ἀλλὰ διδασκαλικόν Bas.*hom*.4.5(2.29A; M.31.228B); τὸ σαρκικὸν θέλημα ἀλλότριον...τοῦ Χριστοῦ οἱ ἅγιοι πατέρες ὁρίζουσι, καὶ τὴν σαρκικὴν καὶ ἐ. τῆς ἁμαρτίας ἐνέργειαν Anast.S.*serm.imag*.3(M.89.1160A); in controversies; **a.** Apollinarian τὴν θεότητα ἐν τῷ πάσχοντι εἶναι ὁμολογοῦμεν, οὐ μὲν τὴν ἀπαθῆ φύσιν, ἐ. γενέσθαι Gr.Nyss.*Apoll*.54 (M.45.1253C); τὸ ἐ. τῇ φύσει τὸν θάνατον δέχεται, τὸ δὲ ἀπαράδεκτον πάθους ἐν τῷ παθητῷ τὴν ἀπάθειαν ἐνήργησεν *ib*.5(1133C); **b.** Eunomian κατασκευάζειν τῆς ἐ. αὐτὸν εἶναι φύσεως, μὴ ἂν ἐλθόντα πρὸς τὴν τῶν παθημάτων πεῖραν, εἰ μὴ δεκτικὴν εἶχε τῶν τοιούτων τὴν φύσιν id.*Eun*.5(2 p.113.9; M.45.693A); **c.** monothelite εἰ δὲ τῆς αὐτοῦ μόνης θεότητος [sc. τὸ θέλημα], ἐ. ἔσται θεότης, παρὰ φύσιν βρώσεως καὶ πόσεως ἀφιεμένη Max.*opusc*.(M.91.53C); Jo.D.*f.o*.3.14(M.94.1041A); **4.** in moral order; **a.** of spirits δαιμόνων...ἐ. Clem.*str*.2.8(p.134.10; M.8.976A); angels ἄδεκτοι...εἰσι τῆς καθ' ἡμᾶς ἐ. ἡδονῆς Dion.Ar.*c.h*. 15.9(M.3.340A); **b.** of pagan gods; ἐ. because imagined in human likeness, Clem.*str*.7.4(p.16.9; M.9.428B); Gr.Naz.*or*.28.15(p.44.17; M.36.45A); τοῖς...αὐτῶν ἁλίσκονται θεολόγοις, ὡς μὲν ἐ., ὡς δὲ στασιώδεις *ib*.31.16(p.164.13; 149C); **c.** of men; **i.** origin of susceptibility to passion, law of the flesh (cf. Rom.7:22) οὗτός ἐστιν ὁ τοὺς ἐ. ἀναφύων...περισπασμούς Meth.*res*.2.6(p.340.15; M.18.304C); *ib*.2.7(p.341.4; 305A); ἡ...ἁμαρτία...εἰς τὰς ἐ. ἐπιθυμίας τὴν ψυχὴν καθέλκουσα Bas.*ascet*.1.1(2.318D; M.31.869D); ἐκ τῶν ὑποκειμένων ἐν τῇ ψυχῇ παθῶν λαμβάνοντες οἱ δαίμονες τὰς ἀφορμάς, τοῦ κινεῖν ἐν ἡμῖν τοὺς ἐ. λογισμούς Thal.ap.*cat.Mt*.24:15(p.197.18); *ib*.(p.197.31); ἐ. ἡδονὴν τὴν ἀνθρωπίνην φησίν, ὡς τῇ περὶ τὸ σῶμα εὐαλλοιώτῳ ἐμπαθείᾳ συνισταμένην Max.*schol.c.h*.15.9(M.4.113B); id.*ambig*.(M.91. 1297D); **ii.** characteristic of this life, Or.*princ*.1.8.4(p.103.19); Nil. *epp*.3.20(M.79.380B); **iii.** esp. in those who do not aim at perfection, Clem.*str*.7.11(p.47.2; M.9.489C); id.*ecl*.31(p.146.31; M.9.716A); ref. ordinary life, opp. ascetic τοῖς ἔτι τὰς ψυχὰς ἐ. Eus.*d.e*.1.8(p.39. 8; M.22.76B); ref. life under Law τοῖς ἐ. κατάλληλα διετάττετο *ib*.1. 6(p.34.11; 65D); ἡ ἀπὸ γηΐνης καὶ ἐ. ζωῆς...μεταβολὴ Bas.*Spir*.49(3. 41D; M.32.157C); **iv.** sexual connotation often present; ref. Devil persuading solitaries to visit women καὶ οὕτω...ἐμπαθεῖς τοὺς ἀθλίους ἀπέδειξεν Arsen.*doct*.(M.66.1620C); ἔρωτα ἐ. †Jo.D.*B.J*.31 (M.96.1144B); **v.** results: spiritual torpor from ἐ. προσπάθεια, Ephr. 3.427B; τῶν ἐ. λογισμῶν, δι' ὧν πᾶσα ἁμαρτία τελεῖται *ib*.3.429A; knowledge of highest truth hindered by ἐ. διάθεσις, Max.*ambig*. (M.91.1204B); **vi.** remedies ἡ...τοῦ ἀνθρώπου ἀνδρεία ἐμπαθοῦς... κατὰ τὴν οὐσίαν ἄφοβον...τὸν μετέχοντα αὐτῆς ποιεῖ Clem.*str*.4.23 (p.315.13; M.8.1360B); *ib*.2.18(p.155.15; 1020B) cit. s. ἐγκράτεια; ἡ γνῶσις ἡ τοῦ θεοῦ...πάντα λογισμὸν ἐ. ... ἀπωθεῖται Or.*exp.in Pr*.4:9 (M.17.172A); Meth.*lepr*.6(p.457.12); ref. Mt.19:12 ἀγνεύειν ἐξ αὐτοῦ τοῦ τῆς διανοίας βάθους, τὰς ἐ. ὀρέξεις ἀποτέμνοντας, ἐδίδασκεν [sc. ὁ σωτήρ] Eus.*d.e*.3.6(p.132.31; M.22.224D); καθαρεῦον πάσης ἐ. διαθέσεως, πρὸς τὸν ἀρχηγὸν τῆς ἀπαθείας βλέπει, ὅς ἐστιν ὁ Χριστός Gr.Nyss.*perf*.(p.212.4; M.46.284D); Jo.Clim.*scal*.28(M.88.1133D); **5.** (Valent.) δύο οὐσίας, τὴν φαύλην ⟨ἐκ⟩ τῶν παθῶν, τήν τε ⟨ἐκ⟩ τῆς ἐπιστροφῆς ἐ. Iren.*haer*.1.4.5(M.7.489A); Christol., ref. Lc.9:22 etc. ὅταν λέγῃ δεῖ τὸν υἱὸν τοῦ ἀνθρώπου...σταυρωθῆναι, ὡς περὶ ἄλλου φαίνεται λέγων, δηλονότι τοῦ ἐ. Clem.*exc.Thdot*.61(p.127.12; M.9. 688C); **6.** of physical illness or mutilation, Socr.*h.e*.6.4.6(M.67. 672B); πότε γίνεται ἐπίσκοπος ἢ κληρικὸς εὐνοῦχος, ἢ ἄλλως ἐ. τὸ σῶμα; Phot.*nomoc*.1.14(M.104.997A).

ἐμπαθῶς, **1.** *passionately, with great eagerness*, *T.Benj*.6.4; οὐ δεῖ τὸν μοναχὸν νίπτεσθαι τὸ σῶμα... ἐ. Ephr.1.326C; **2.** *by passion, out of passion*, of those who pray for temporal benefits ἐ. φερόμενοι Nil.*epp*.1.50(M.79.104D); of the possessed ἡ τῶν ἐ. ἐνεργουμένων πληθύς Dion.Ar.*e.h*.3.3.7(M.3.436B); *Schol*. in Jo.Clim.*past*.10(M.88. 1185D).

ἔμπαιγμα, τό, *mockery, delusion*, Diad.*perf*.38(p.44.10); Leo Mag. *ep*.35(p.41.3; M.*PL*.54.806B).

ἐμπαιγμός, ὁ, *mockery, derision*; **1.** in gen., *Pss.Sal*.2.13; *ib*.17. 14; Isid.Pel.*epp*.1.135(M.78.272B); **2.** of Christ, Or.*Jo*.1.11(12; p.17. 4; M.14.44D); **3.** *delusion* ἐ. γάρ ἐστι καὶ ψεῦδος ἡ ἐπιθυμία Chrys. *hom*.5.5 *in Heb*.(12.60B).

ἐμπαιδεύ-ω, pass., *be disciplined in* τὸν ~όμενον τοῖς πειρασμοῖς Nil.*epp*.3.147(M.79.452C).

ἐμπανηγυρίζω, *celebrate*, c. dat.; a person, Chrys.*pan.Laz*.(2. 649C); an anniversary, Synes.*ep*.79(M.66.1449C).

***ἐμπαραμένω**, **1.** c. dat., *persevere in*, Mac.Aeg.*or*.9(M.34.860C); **2.** *endure*, Epiph.*haer*.39.1(p.72.3; M.41.665D).

ἐμπαράσκευος, *prepared*, Hipp.*haer*.4.28(p.56.15; M.16.3091C); τὸ πάντα τὸν βίον ἀεὶ ἐ. εἶναι Chrys.*hom*.23.2 *in Eph*.(11.177A); Nil. *exerc*.60(M.79.793A); †Bas.Sel.*or*.41(M.85.472A).

***ἐμπαραχωρέω**, *yield*, Bas.Sel.*or*.29.2(M.85.332B).

***ἐμπάρειμι**, *coexist in*, c. εἰς, Diad.*perf*.78(p.98.17).

ἐμπαρέχω, *surrender*; of self-surrender to God, Or.*or*.25.1(p.357. 15; M.11.496D); id.*Jo*.6.17(33; p.142.29; M.14.257A).

***ἐμπαρῆναι**, prob. f.l. for ἐμπαγῆναι, Cyr.H.*catech*.23.17.

***ἐμπαρίημι**, **1.** *affix*, *A.(Pass.)Andr*.10(p.24.9); **2.** *fall, slip into*, c. dat., Cyr.*Is*.5.2(2.763E).

ἐμπαροιν-έω, **1.** *be drunk, get drunk*, Or.*or*.19.3(p.343.8; M.11. 478B); Chrys.*hom*.45.4 *in Jo*.(8.268A); **2.** *behave as though drunk*, hence *behave insultingly*; of sinners in gen., Const.*or.s.c*.15(p.176. 13; M.20.1280B); Eus.*l.C*.13(p.240.8; M.20.1405C); Cyr.*Is*.2.1(2.192A); id.*Os*.26(3.66C); of unorthodox ταῖς γραφαῖς ~οῦντες Alex.Al.*ep. Alex*.3(p.21.24; M.18.552D); Epiph.*haer*.30.21(p.361.22; M.41.441A); Chrys.*hom*.23.3 *in Mt*.(7.288A); *ib*. 60.3(7.601C); τὸν...δεσπότην... ὑπὸ τῶν Ἰουδαίων ~ούμενον Cyr.*Arcad*.(p.90.1; 5².84A); **3.** *rage* in, of diabolical possession Λαμίαν ἐμπεπαρῳνηκέναι τῷ Μενίππῳ Eus. *Hierocl*.35(534C; M.22.848B).

ἐμπαρρησιάζομαι, c. dat.; **1.** *profess boldly*; Christianity, Eus. *v.C*.3.2 tit.(p.72.4; M.20.1056B); Gr.Nyss.*ep*.29(p.86.11; M.45.240C); **2.** *speak insolently about*, †Bas.*Is*.174(1.506A; M.30.412A); Gr.Nyss. *Eun*.4(2 p.91.9; M.45.668B).

***ἐμπεδόκυκλος**, *ever-circling*, Nonn.*par.Jo*.8:29(M.43.817B).

ἐμπεδόμητις, *steadfast of purpose, stable-minded*, Nonn.*par.Jo*. 10:18(M.43.836A); *ib*.15:5(873A).

ἐμπεδόμοχθος, *ever-suffering*, Nonn.*par.Jo*.5:5(M.43.785A).

ἐμπεδόμυθος, *steadfast to one's word, faithful* θεὸς ἐ. Gr.Naz.*carm*. 2.2(poem.)7.179(M.37.1565A); of Jo. Bapt., Nonn.*par.Jo*.1:7(M.43. 749B); *ib*.5:33(789C).

ἐμπεδ-όω, **1.** *confirm*, hence *inform* πρὸς τοῦτο ἡμᾶς ὁ σωτὴρ ~οῖ λέγων... Cyr.*Am*.81(3.345C); id.*Os*.23(3.46B); **2.** *accomplish*, Synes.*ep*.143(M.66.1536A); Nil.*Magn*.44(M.79.1024D); Thdt.*ep*.40 (4.1099).

***ἐμπειρόγαμος**, *having experience of marriage*, Cyr.*ador*.4(1. 121E).

ἐμπειροπόλεμος, *experienced in war*; met., of those experienced in spiritual combat, Nil.*epp*.3.176(M.79.464A); Cyr.*Ag*.19(3.650A); Jo.Carp.*cap*.85(M.85.1854) ∞ †Jo.D.*B.J*.11(M.96.960B).

***ἐμπερατόω**, *limit*, Gr.Nyss.*Eun*.12(1 p.345.14; M.45.1065A).

ἐμπεριάγω, *go about in*, c. ἐν, Bas.*renunt*.2(2.203E; M.31.629C).

***ἐμπερίακτος, ὁ**, *vagabond*, Thphn.*chron*.p.421(M.108.996C).

***ἐμπερίγραπτος**, *circumscribed* ὕλη ἐ. ‡Bas.*const*.18.2(2.561E; M. 31.1384C); denied of God, Max.*ambig*.(M.91.1089C).

***ἐμπερίγραφος**, *circumscribed*; Epiph.*haer*.66.15(p.39.4; ἐμπερίγραπτον M.42.52C); ‡Ath.*comm.essent*.9(M.28.45A).

ἐμπεριγράφ-ω, *circumscribe*, Bas.*hex*.2.8(1.20E; M.29.49B); of God as uncircumscribed, Gr.Nyss.*Eun*.1(1 p.95.12; M.45.328C); id. *Apoll*.47(M.45.1240A); ref. Inc. τῇ τοῦ ἀνθρωπίνου βραχύτητι ἑαυτὸν ἐμπεριγράψας *ib*.56(1260D); μητρικαῖς ὠλέναις ~εται ‡Ath.*occurs*.2 (M.28.976C).

***ἐμπεριδράττομαι**, *comprehend, grasp*, Ar.ap.Ath.*syn*.15(p.243. 23; M.26.708C).

***ἐμπεριείργ-ομαι**, *be enclosed, encompassed* τῇ φύσει τῆς σαρκὸς τὴν θεότητα...~εσθαι Gr.Nyss.*or.catech*.10(p.55.11; M.45.41C); id. *Eun*.12(1 p.240.8; M.45.937D).

ἐμπεριεκτικός, *embracing*, of Gnost. Propator ἡ...δύναμις...ἐ. τῶν πάντων Iren.*haer*.1.12.4(M.7.577A); ᾆσματα ᾀσμάτων [sc. καλεῖται] (ἐμπεριεκτικώτερα γάρ ἐστι) Gr.Naz.*or*.40.3(M.36.361C); of God ἡ... τῶν ὄντων ἐ. φύσις οὔτ' ἐν τόπῳ ἐστὶν οὔτε ἐν χρόνῳ Gr.Nyss.*Eun*.1(1 p.130.2; M.45.368A).

ἐμπεριέρχ-ομαι, *go about*, Iren.*haer*.1.17.1(M.7.640A); Hipp.*haer*. 5.26(p.128.19,23; M.16.3195Df.); ἡ ψυχὴ...τοῦ Ἰησοῦ...πάντα αὐτὸν [sc. τὸν κόσμον] ~ομένη Or.*Jo*.19.22(5; p.324.15; M.14.568A); Eus. *v.C*.3.44(p.96.18; M.20.1105A).

ἐμπεριέχ-ω, *encompass*; **1.** of Father ὁ πατὴρ ~ει τὰ πάντα Or. *princ*.4.4(p.360.1; M.11.410A); Heraclides ap.eund.*dial*.2(p.122.10); Gr.Nyss.*or.catech*.25(p.95.5, v.l. περιέχον M.45.65D); Cyr.*Juln*.1(6². 31E f.); **2.** ref. Son οὐδὲ ὑπό τινος ὅλως ~όμενον id.*Jo*.1.9(4.77A); **3.** Trin. οὐσιωδῶς...ὁ υἱὸς ~ει τὸν πατέρα, καὶ ἔστιν ἐν αὐτῷ Ammon. *Jo*.14:11(M.85.1488D); καθάπερ ἐπὶ σωμάτων ἀνθρωπίνων ~εσθαί τι λέγοντες [sc. Eunomians] τῇ τοῦ πατρὸς οὐσίᾳ Cyr.*thes*.7(5¹.58A).

***ἐμπεριήχητος**, *celebrated*, Max.*ambig*.(M.91.1064D).

ἐμπερικλείω, *enclose on all sides*, Geo.Pis.*Heracl*.2.24(M.92.1331A).

***ἐμπερικρατέω**, *rule over*, Gr.Nyss.*or.catech*.8(p.49.14; M.45. 37B).

ἐμπεριλαμβάν-ω, *include*; of power of God in gen. τοῦ νοῦ τοῦ θεοῦ πᾶσαν γνῶσιν τὴν περὶ ἑκάστου τῶν ὄντων ἐμπεριειληφότος Or. *comm.in Gen*.ap.*philoc*.23.20(p.208.28; M.12.81D); ἡ γῆ...τῇ δρακὶ αὐτοῦ [sc. τοῦ θεοῦ] ἐμπεριειλημμένη id.*comm.in Eph*.1:20–23(p.400); Gr.Nyss.*hom.1 in Cant*.(M.44.765D); θεὸς καὶ λόγος, πᾶσαν δύναμιν ποιητικὴν ἐμπεριειληφώς id.*or.catech*.8(p.50.21; M.45.40A); of anthropomorphisms in scripture τῶν διὰ τὸν ἰδιωτισμὸν τὸ ὅσον ἐπ' αὐτοῖς μικρῷ καὶ βραχεῖ τόπῳ ~όντων τὸν...θεόν Or.*or*.23.3(p.351.14; M.11.489A).

ἐμπερινο-έω, *comprehend* τὸ ἀρχὴν ἔχον [sc. Son] τὸν ἄναρχον... ~ῆσαι...οὐχ οἷόν τέ ἐστιν Ar.ap.Ath.*syn*.15(p.243.23; M.26.708C).

***ἐμπερινοστέω**, *inspect, search out, investigate*, Pall.*v.Chrys*.5(p.32. 19; M.47.20); *ib*.12(p.77.31; M.47.44); *ib*.16(p.99.15; M.47.56).

***ἐμπεριορίζομαι**, *be included* in, c. dat., Leont.H.*Nest*.2.33(M.86. 1592A).

ἐμπεριπατ-έω, **1.** *walk on, trample on* ~ήσας [sc. Christ] τὴν ἀντικειμένην ἅπασαν δύναμιν Eus.*d.e*.9.7(p.419.24; M.22.676D); cf.*ib*. 9.12(p.431.8; 696A); **2.** *dwell*; in prayer for divine indwelling in catechumens, cf.Lev.26:12, *Lit*.ap.*Const.App*.8.6.6; of gifts of H. Ghost, Proc.G.*Gen*.4:15(M.87.249C); ref. Lev.26:12 ὁ κύριος ἐπαγγέλλεται ἐνοικήσειν καὶ ἐ. ταῖς τῶν δεξαμένων αὐτὸν ψυχαῖς Oecum.*Apoc*.1:13(p.40); Jo.D.*hom*.2.7(M.96.588C).

***ἐμπερίσπαστος**, *distracted*, v. *ἐμπερίστατος.

***ἐμπεριστατέω**, *surround, encompass*, Nil.*Magn*.2(M.79.972C).

***ἐμπερίστατος**, *involved in business* μετὰ ἀνθρώπων ὑλικῶν καὶ ἐ. Evagr.Pont.*rer.mon*.5(M.40.1256D); *ib*.(1257A) ∞ ‡Ath.*inst.mon*.2 (M.28.848B ἐμπερίσπαστος).

***ἐμπεριστρέφομαι**, *live among, be involved in*, ‡Proc.G.*Pr*.20:1 (M.87.1421B); *ib*.26:14(1484D).

***ἐμπερίτομος**, *circumcised*, *Clem.contest*.1(M.2.29A); of Cerinthus attacking non-circumcised διὰ...τὸ εἶναι αὐτὸν ἐ. Epiph.*haer*.28.2 (p.315.10; M.41.380C); ref. paschal controversy μετὰ τὸν χρόνον τῶν ἐ. ἐπισκόπων *ib*.70.9(p.242.20; M.42.356B); in gen., Chrys.*hom.6.3 in Rom*.(9.476A); Pall.*v.Chrys*.9(p.124.20; M.47.70); Hier.H.*Trin*.(M. 40.848A).

***ἐμπεριχαρής**, *rejoicing in*; ref. Abraham and Sarah at birth of Isaac, Gr.Nyss.*deit*.(M.46.565D); Ephr.2.313C.

ἐμπερονάω, pass.; **1.** *be transfixed*, Gr.Thaum.*Eccl*.12:11(M.10. 1017B); **2.** *be fixed in*, Chrys.*hom.3.5 in 1Cor*.(10.21D).

ἐμπήγνυμι, *implant*, pass., of H. Ghost φυσικῶς ἐνυπάρχον αὐτῷ [sc. θεῷ], καὶ οὐσιωδῶς ἐμπεπηγός Cyr.*thes*.33(5¹.333D).

***ἐμπηλόομαι**, *be immersed in mud*; met., Jo.Clim.*scal*.26(M.88. 1016B).

ἔμπηλος, *of clay*, Mac.Mgn.*apocr*.4.28(p.216.26).

***ἔμπηξ, ἡ**, ? *hook*; instrument of torture, Const.Diac.*laud*.6(M. 88.485B).

***ἐμπηρία, ἡ**, *deformity, maimed condition*, Cyr.*ador*.15(1.520D); id.*glaph.Lev*.(1.374C); id.*Mal*.9(3.826C).

***ἐμπηρόω**, *inflict damage on, slight*, †Gregent.*disp*.(M.86.681D).

ἐμπήσσω, *stick into*, Just.*dial*.97.3(M.6.705A); Sophr.H.*v.Cyr.et Jo*.17(M.87.3400B).

***ἐμπιαίνομαι**, *grow fat upon*, Gr.Nyss.*v.Mos*.(M.44.417D).

***ἐμπίζεως**, ? perh. error for ἐπιζέσεως from ⟨ἐπίζεσις⟩ *zeal* ἐ. καὶ σπουδῆς Ephr.3.341E.

ἐμπιπράσκω, *sell*, met. ὁ νοῦς ἐμπέπραται τῇ ἐνύλῳ ζωῇ Or.*fr. 13 in Jo*.(p.495.19).

ἐμπλατύν-ω, *extend*, Gr.Nyss.*or.dom*.1(p.6.2; ἐκπλ- M.44.1121B); Chrys.*hom.54.3 in Mt*.(7.550A); id.*hom.14.3 in Rom*.(9.580A); ref. Mt.7:13 ὁ...~ων ἑαυτόν, οὔτε εἰσέρχεται id.*hom.33.4 in Heb*.(12. 309C); ὁ ἁμαρτωλὸς ~εται τρυφαῖς Cyr.*Ps*.36:16(M.69.933C).

ἔμπλεγμα, τό, *plait, curl*, *Const.App*.1.8.17; Chrys.*hom.12.7 in Col*.(11.422E); id.*hom.8.1 in 1Tim*.(11.590E).

ἐμπληθής, *plethoric*, Jo.Mal.*chron*.10 p.239(M.97.368B).

***ἐμπληροφορέομαι**, *be filled, satisfied, content*, Mac.Aeg.*or*.12(M. 34.861C); id.*libert.ment*.14(M.34.948A); Ephr.3.336D; *ib*.355A.

***ἐμπληρόω**, *fulfil*, Jo.Mon.*hymn.Geo*.8(M.96.1400B).

***ἐμπλήσκομαι**, *fill, satiate*, *T.Job* 24(p.117.23).

***ἐμπλύνω**, *wash in, use as a basin*, Clem.*paed*.2.2(p.175.12; M.8. 428A).

***ἐμπλωΐζω**, *embark*, Thphn.*chron*.p.378(M.108.904C).

ἐμπνείω, v. ἐμπνέω.

ἔμπνευσις, ἡ, *inbreathing, inspiration*; **1.** lit., Gr.Naz.*or*.40.43 (M.36.420D); **2.** met., of sanctification ἡ θεία ἔ. Or.*schol.in Lc*. 13:20(M.17.357D); ref. Const. in battle ὥσπερ θειοτέρᾳ κινηθεὶς ἐ. Eus.*v.C*.2.12(p.46.15; M.20.992A); cf.*ib*.3.3(p.78.21; 1057B); of gift of H. Ghost to apostles (Jo.20:22), Gr.Naz.*or*.41.11(M.36.444B); of scripture τῆς θείας ἐ. ... διδασκαλίαν Gr.Nyss.*Eun*.7(2 p.156.11; M. 45.744D); ref. prophets κατ' ἔ. θείαν ἢ ἔλλαμψιν Areth.ap.*cat.Apoc*. 16:2(p.410.20); ref. soul created by God διὰ τῆς ζωτικῆς ἐ. Max. *ambig*.(M.91.1324C); *ib*.(1317A).

ἐμπν-έω (ἐμπν-είω), **1.** *breathe in*; med., ref. anthropomorphisms πότερον διαπνεῖται [sc. God]; ἢ ~εῖται μόνον; Clem.*str*.7.6(p.24.5; M.9.444B); hence, met., *imbibe* ~έων θεοῦ σοφίας Eus.*v.C*.3.48(p.98. 5; M.20.1108C); **2.** *breathe into* ~εύσας...ἐν στόματι τοῦ ὄφεως ψευδῆ πάντα λελάληκεν ὁ διάβολος Epiph.*haer*.40.6(p.87.18; M.41.688B); hence *inspire*, c. dat. pers., Clem.*paed*.1.2(p.94.4; M.8.257A); id. *str*.4.1(p.249.17; M.8.1216B); ref. Jo.20:22 πνεύματος αὐτοῖς ~εῦσαι λέγεται θείου Eus.*d.e*.3.7(p.144.21; M.22.244A); Ath.*Ar*.2.44(M.26. 241B); βοήθειά τις...~έουσα τοῖς ἀγωνιζομένοις, καθάπερ ἐπὶ τοῦ βαπτίσματος Chrys.*hom.7.1 in 2Cor*.(10.480D); ref. diabolical suggestion ἔνιοι δὲ δυνάμεις τινὰς ὑποβεβηκυίας ἐμπνεῦσαι τὴν πᾶσαν φιλοσοφίαν ὑπειλήφασιν Clem.*str*.1.16(p.52.18; M.8.796A); *ib*.1.17 (p.53.8; 797A); ἐνέπνευσεν αὐτοῖς [i.e. Arians] ὁ διάβολος Ath.*ep. Aeg.Lib*.5(M.25.548C); **3.** pass., of persons, *be inspired*; ref. inspiration of scripture, of prophets τῶν ἐμπεπνευσμένων Just.*1apol*. 36.1(M.6.385A); ἐκ θείας ἀποκαλύψεως ~ευσθέντες Cosm.Ind.*top*. arg.(M.88.56B); of S. Paul, Chrys.*hom.38.3 in 1Cor*.(10.354A); of Ath. as inspired in his doctrine of H. Ghost, Gr.Naz.*or*.21.33(M. 35.1124A); of a saint foretelling future ὡς ἔκ τινος θείας χάριτος ~ευσθείς Eustrat.*v.Eutych*.46(M.86.2328B); *ib*.9(2284C); by Satan Ἐλιοὺς ~ευσθεὶς ἐν τῷ σατανᾷ *T.Job* 41(p.130.20).

***ἐμπνίγ-ομαι**, *be drowned in*, Cyr.*glaph.Gen*.2(1.39E); met., of baptism ὑλικὸν πνεῦμα...~εται τῇ καθάρσει Gr.Naz.*or*.40.35(M.36. 409A).

ἔμπνοια, ἡ, *inspiration*, Chrys.*hom.7.8 in 1Cor*.(10.63A); Diad. *perf*.75(p.94.1).

ἐμποδίζ-ω, *hinder*, in moral and spiritual life ~οντες [sc. unorthodox] τοῖς ἀρξαμένοις τρέχειν καλῶς Or.*Cant*.3(p.237.28; M.13. 193D); Meth.*symp*.4.2(p.47.8; M.18.88D); id.*res*.1.30(p.263.13; M.41. 1140D); *cat.Lc*.3:2(p.28.33); ἐὰν ~ωσιν [sc. οἱ περιπόθητοι ἀδελφοί] ἀπ' ἐκείνης τῆς ἀγάπης, ὥσπερ εἰπεῖν, ἀποστρέφεται [sc. God] Mac. Aeg.*hom*.4.15(M.34.484B).

ἐμπόδιος, *hindering*, neut. as subst., *hindrance*, Bas.*hom.in Ps*. 28(1.123B; M.29.304A); of body as ἐ. to vision of God: in animals, Just.*dial*.4.4(M.6.484C); in men, Meth.*res*.1.29(p.258.13; conj. ἐμποδὼν M.41.1136C); of sensual pleasures as hindrance to spiritual life, id.*symp*.5.6(p.61.2; M.18.108C); of temptations, Gr.Nyss.*hom. 3 in Cant*.(M.44.816C).

ἐμποδιστής, ὁ, *hinderer*, Pall.*h.Laus*.38(p.119.15; M.34.1193D).

ἐμπολιτεύ-ομαι, **1.** *be engaged on public business*, Clem.*paed*.3.11 (p.269.22; M.8.632C); **2.** *dwell in*; Trin., acc. Beryllus of Bostra τὸν σωτῆρα...μηδὲ μὲν θεότητα ἰδίαν ἔχειν, ἀλλ' ~ομένην αὐτῷ μόνην τὴν πατρικήν Eus.*h.e*.6.33.1(M.20.593A); of Christ ἡ ψυχὴ...τοῦ Ἰησοῦ ~ομένη τῷ ὅλῳ κόσμῳ ἐκείνῳ Or.*Jo*.19.22(5; p.324.14; M.14.568C); cf.*Lit.Bas*.(p.326.20); of indwelling of H. Ghost ἐν καθαρᾷ...ψυχῇ Μωυσέως...ἐμπεπολιτεῦσθαι πνεῦμα θεῖον Or.*Cels*.1.19(p.71.3; M.11. 696A); of evil and imperfection in men, ref. slavery to Devil τὸ κακὸν...~εται ἐν τῇ σαρκί μου Meth.*res*.2.2(p.333.5; M.41.1165B); τῆς ~ομένης τῇ φύσει κακίας Gr.Nyss.*or.dom*.1(p.18.27; M.44.1132A); Nil.*exerc*.47(M.79.777B).

***ἐμπολίτευσις, ἡ**, *sojourn* Χριστοῦ...ἐ. τὴν ἐν κόσμῳ ‡Bas.*h.myst*. 60(p.395.5).

ἐμπομπεύω, **1.** *lord it over*, c. dat., esp. ref. behaviour of evil spirits, †Bas.*Is*.109(1.454D; M.30.293B); *Const.App*.3.12.2; Proc.G. *Is*.3:1–11(M.87.1901B); **2.** *make a spectacle of*, c. acc.; ref. martyrs, *Ep.Lugd*.ap.Eus.*h.e*.5.1.47(M.20.425C); *parade* unorthodox views, Ath.*Ar*.2.82(M.26.321A).

ἐμπόνημα, τό, *labour*, Gr.Mag.*dial*.(tr.Zach.)3.1(M.*PL*.77.215D).

***ἐμπόνησις, ἡ**, *toil*, Mac.Aeg.*cust.cor*.9(M.34.828C).

***ἐμπόνως**, *diligently*, Hipp.*Dan.*4.18(p.230.11); Mac.Aeg.*cust. cor.*13(M.34.837D); Call.*v.Hyp.*(p.10).

ἐμπόρευμα, τό, *gain*, met. νήψεως...ἐ. Isid.Pel.*epp.*1.209(M.78. 316A, v.l. ἐμπύρευμα).

ἐμπορεύ-ομαι, **1.** *traffic in*, of those who defer baptism μὴ ∼ου τὴν χάριν Bas.*hom.*13.5(2.118C; M.31.436A); Gr.Nyss.*bapt.diff.*(M. 46.420B); id.*hom.9 in Cant.*(M.44.960B); hence **2.** *procure* by purchase, Gr.Nyss.*v.Ephr.*(M.46.829A); ref. reward of works of mercy τὰ μικρὰ δῶμεν, ἵνα ∼σώμεθα τὰ μεγάλα Chrys.*hom.25.3 in Jo.*(8. 148A); *ib.77.5*(747E); †Jo.D.*B.J.*4(M.96.881A); **3.** *exploit, make a profit out of*, Epiph.*haer.*59.7(p.372.11; M.41.1029A); Thdt.*provid.*6 (4.565); **4.** *lead* ἐ. βίον ‡Chrys.*hom.suppl.*5(M.64.460D).

ἐμπορία, ἡ, **1.** *merchandise*, met. ἐ. μαθημάτων Eus.*d.e.*5 proem. (p.205.6; M.22.340C); **2.** *usury*, Chrys.*hom.66.5 in Mt.*(7.759E); **3.** *profit* τὴν πνευματικὴν ἐ. Chrys.*hom.in Rom.8:28*(3.156A).

ἔμπρακτος, **1.** *active*, Trin. τρία ἔ. ‡Caes.Naz.*dial.*3(M.38.860); ref. Christ; τὸ ἔ. signified by the lion, Iren.*haer.*3.11.8(M.7.886A); ref. pagan gods μέλλομεν ὑπὲρ ἐ. προσώπου ἐλέγχεσθαι ὡς ψευδεῖς *Pers.* (p.15.1; M.10.104B); **2.** *efficacious*, of Christian doctrine ἔ. ... τῶν ἰδιωτῶν...τὴν διδασκαλίαν Ephr.1.279F; Chrys.*hom.18.4 in Ac.*(9. 149C); Sever.ap.*cat.Ac.*2:4(p.24.15); ref. spiritual life ἀγάλματά τινα...ἔ. τοὺς βίους τῶν ἁγίων Bas.*epp.*2.3(3.73C; M.31.229A); μετανοίας ἐ. Anast.S.*synax.*(M.89.848B); Jo.Mon.*hymn.Chrys.*3(M.96. 1380A); γνῶσις ἔ. Max.*ambig.*(M.91.1032A); of fear of God ἔ. τῆς γνώσεως θύραν id.*ep.*20(M.91.600A); of hearing scripture ἐ. ... ἀκοῇ Areth.*Apoc.*1:3(M.106.504A).

ἐμπρησμός, ὁ, *conflagration* at end of world, *Orac.Sib.*4.161; ἐ. ἀδόκητοι ‡Hipp.*consumm.*8(p.292.10; M.10.912B); final conflagration prophesied, Eus.*Is.*6:4(M.24.128A); of hell, Chrys.*hom.11.4 in Mt.*(7.153E); met. τὸν ἐκ τῆς αἱρέσεως ἐ. Bas.*epp.*164.2(3.255B; M.32. 636D); of persecution, *ib.*248(384A; M.928C); of anger, Chrys.*sac.* 3.14(1.390D).

ἐμπρηστής, ὁ, *burning one*; of seraphim (cf.AQ Dt.8:15; Is.30:6), Dion.Ar.*c.h.*7.1(M.3.205B); *ib.*15.2(329A); id.*e.h.*4.3.10(M.3.481C); ‡Ath.*annunt.*15(M.28.940A); Proc.G.*Is.*6:1ff.(M.87.1932D).

***ἐμπροαίρετος**, *endowed with free will*, Gr.Nyss.*Apoll.*47(M.45. 1240B).

ἐμπρόθεσμος, **1.** *preordained*, *Hom.Clem.*3.15; ἐ. ἀναδύσομαι στέφανον Bas.Sel.*or.*31.2(M.85.345A); **2.** *coming at its due time* νόμος ὁ διὰ Μωυσέως...δόγμα ἐ. ‡Chrys.*pasch.*6.2(8.267B).

***ἐμπρόθετος**, *deliberate, determined* ἐ. πρὸς ἁμαρτίαν ὁρμή Max.*ep.* 32(M.91.628A).

***ἐμπροθέτως**, *deliberately, of set purpose*, Max.*opusc.*(M.91.92B).

***ἐμπρός**, *forwards*; opp. ὀπίσω, Max.*ambig.*(M.91.1232A).

***ἐμπροσθόπους**, *going before, overtaking*, Evagr.*h.e.*3.26(p.123. 14; M.86.2652A).

***ἐμπροσποι-έω**, *make in front of oneself* πηλὸν ∼οῦσι...ἐξ ἰδίων δακρύων Ephr.1.179D.

ἐμπρόσωπος, *in a person, personal* τῇ ἐμπροσώπῳ θεοῦ φύσει θεὸς ἦν ὁ λόγος Leont.H.*Nest.*2.35(M.86.1593B).

ἔμπτυσμα, τό, *spitting*; ref. Passion, *A.Pil.*A 16.7(p.282); ‡Dion.Al.*fr.in Lc.22:42*(p.239.1; M.10.1600A); Mac.Aeg.*hom.*12.4 (M.34.560B); in gen., Pall.*v.Chrys.*16(p.97.23; M.47.55).

***ἐμπτυσμός, ὁ**, = foreg., Andr.Cr.*triod.*(M.97.1400B).

ἐμπύρευμα, τό, *live coal*; met., *fuel*, Clem.*str.*6.16(p.508.28; M.9. 380C); Socr.*h.e.*4.26.3(M.67.528C); Jo.D.*imag.*1.22(M.94.1256A).

ἐμπύριος, *of fire, fiery*, property of first angelic hierarchy of seraphim ἡ ἐ. ἰδιότης Dion.Ar.*c.h.*13.3(M.3.304A); τῆς...αὐτῶν ἐπωνυμίας τὸ ἐ. σημαινούσης...ὑφηγήσασθαι τὰς ἐπὶ τὸ θεοειδὲς τῆς ἐ. δυνάμεως ἀναγωγάς *ib.*13.4(304D); *ib.*15.2(328C); ἐ. ... τυποπλαστία *ib.*(329A).

ἐμπυριστής, ὁ, *incendiary*, †Jo.Jej.*serm.*(M.88.1924B).

***ἐμπυρίως**, *in a fiery manner, by fire* τὴν ἐ. καθαρτικὴν ἰδιότητα τοῖς σεραφὶμ...ἀνατέθεικεν Dion.Ar.*c.h.*13.4(M.3.305C).

***ἐμπυρόμαντις, ὁ**, *fire-diviner*, Cyr.*Juln.*6(6^2.198D).

ἔμπυρος, **1.** lit., *of fire, fiery*; of eternal punishments, Meth.*symp.* 11(p.135.13; M.18.212B); **2.** met., *ardent*; of faith, Gel.Cyz.*h.e.*2.1.1 (M.85.1224C); Thphn.*chron.*p.141(M.108.384A); of zeal, ‡Chrys. *pasch.*2(8.255B); of eye of God, *Orac.Sib.*6.28; in interpretation of name of seraphim, Chrys.*Is.interp.*6(6.66A) cit. s. σεραφίμ.

***ἐμπυρριχίζω**, *entangle oneself in* πυρρίχη (a war dance with elaborate figures); hence, met., *contort oneself* in arguments; of heretics, Gr.Nyss.*Eun.*12(1 p.234.13; M.45.932A).

***ἔμπυρσον, τό**, *spark*, met. ἔ. τοῦ πόθου †Jo.D.*creat.*6(p.136).

ἐμπύρως, *ardently* ἐ. ... τὴν ἀγάπην...ἔχουσαι Mac.Aeg.*hom.*10.2 (M.34.541B); *ib.*44.7(784B).

ἐμπύρωσις, ἡ, *enkindling, conflagration*, met. δυσμενείας ἐ. Men. *exc.Rom.*3(p.183.32; M.113.872A).

[*]**ἐμπωλή**, = ἐμπολή, *sale*, Cyr.*ador.*12(1.467D).

***ἐμφαιδρύνομαι**, *rejoice, glory in*, Gr.Nyss.*Eun.*12(1 p.314.17; M.45.1028C); id.*Spir.*(M.46.701B); id.*v.Gr.Thaum.*(M.46.953C); *M. Thdot.*3(p.132.18).

ἐμφαίν-ω, *manifest*, ref. Jo.14:10 ἐν αὐτῷ [sc. τῷ υἱῷ] δὲ καὶ δι' αὐτοῦ, καὶ ἑαυτὸν ∼ει [sc. ὁ πατήρ] Ath.*gent.*47(M.25.93D); ἀφανὴς ὢν [sc. Christ]...διὰ τῶν ἔργων ἐνέφαινε...ἑαυτόν id.*inc.*16.5(M.25. 125A); Chrys.*hom.15.1 in Jo.*(8.85B); ref. evidence of existence of God εὐτάκτως τοῖς ὅλοις ∼ομένης σοφίας Max.*ambig.*(M.91.1361B).

ἐμφανίζ-ω, *manifest*; **1.** ref. divine appearances in OT to patriarchs θεοῦ ⟨ἑαυτὸν⟩ ∼οντος τοῖς ἀξίοις Or.*Cels.*6.4(p.74.14; M.11. 1296A); ref. Ex.3:2 ∼όμενον τῷ προφήτῃ ‡Meth.*Sym.et Ann.*9(M.18. 369B); **2.** ref. Christ; after Resurrection ὥσπερ ὁ πατὴρ ∼ει ἑαυτόν, οὕτω καὶ ἐγὼ ἐν ἀληθείᾳ καὶ οὐ κατὰ φαντασίαν Ammon.*Jo.*14:22 (M.85.1492B); Mac.Mgn.*apocr.*1.14(p.23.8); Nil.*epp.*3.120(M.79.437D); Gel.Cyz.*h.e.*2.24.28(M.85.1364D); exeg. Heb.9:24 ∼εται δὲ νῦν ὑπὲρ ἡμῶν τῷ προσώπῳ τοῦ θεοῦ τίνα τρόπον; ἆρα οὐκ ἀεὶ...ὑπάρχων ἐμφανής;...∼εται δὲ νῦν...ἐν μορφῇ...τῇ καθ' ἡμᾶς Cyr.*Heb.*9:24(M. 74.985C); Thdt.*Heb.*9:24(3.603); Jo.D.*Heb.*9:24(M.95.973A); **3.** of God in spiritual life κατὰ καιρὸν ἑαυτὸν ∼ει τῇ καμούσῃ πλεῖστα παρὰ τὴν ζήτησιν τὴν αὐτοῦ Or.*schol.in Cant.*3:1–4(M.17.268D); *ib.* 2:16(265C); θεὸς...ἡμῖν πέμψαι αὐτὸν τὸν λόγον, ἑαυτὸν ∼οντα id. *Jo.*20.1(p.327.10; M.14.573A); κατὰ...τὴν προκοπὴν τῆς ψυχῆς καὶ τὸ θεῖον δῶρον τὴν ἑαυτοῦ ἐν τῷ νοῒ ∼ει χρηστότητα Diad.*perf.*78(p.96. 22).

ἐμφανιστικός, *making manifest, revealing*, ‡Chrys.*pasch.*2(8. 255C); Max.*qu.Theop.*(M.90.1393B).

ἐμφαντάζ-ω, **1.** *urge in imagination* λογισμῶν ἀνοικείων...∼όντων ἡμᾶς πρὸς ἃ μὴ θέλομεν Meth.*res.*2.2(p.333.12; M.41.1165C); Gr.Nyss. *Eun.*10(2 p.238.19; M.45.840D); **2.** *present to the imagination, present*, pass. παρὼν δὲ καὶ ∼όμενος ὁ λόγος, ἐπὰν παραδεχθῇ, ἀπειλεῖ τὸ ὑπάγειν Or.*Jo.*19.12(3; p.311.33; M.14.548B); †Bas.*Is.*254(1.573D; M.30.568A); Gr.Nyss.*virg.*10(p.290.17; M.46.361C).

ἔμφασις, ἡ, **1.** *image, reflection*; **a.** Trin., ref. Jo.12:50 etc. θεοπρεπῶς νοῶμεν θελήματος διάδοσιν οἱόν τινος μορφῆς ἔ. ἐν κατόπτρῳ, ἐκ πατρὸς εἰς υἱὸν ἀχρόνως διϊκνουμένην Bas.*Spir.*20(3.17E; M.32.104C, v.l. ἔνδοσιν); **b.** ref. divine names τὸν [sc. τρόπον] κατ' οὐσίαν, τὸν κατὰ κίνησιν, τὸν κατὰ διαφορὰν δι' ὧν ὁ θεὸς γνωστὸς τοῖς ἀνθρώποις γίνεται ἐκ τῶν ὄντων τὰς περὶ αὐτοῦ ἐμφάσεις συλλεγομένοις ὡς δημιουργοῦ καὶ προνοητοῦ καὶ κριτοῦ Max.*ambig.*(M.91.1133B); **c.** ref. OT types, Proc.G.*Is.*19:1–15(M.87.2145A); πᾶσαι αἱ διὰ τοῦ νόμου ἐ. πεπλήρωνται· ὅτι πλήρωμα νόμου Χριστός Eutych.*pasch.*4 (M.86.2396D); Max.*ambig.*(M.91.1141C); **d.** of thoughts, imaginings, Gr.Naz.*carm.*2.1.12.755(M.37.1221A); id.*ep.*215(M.37.352A); Jo.Mon. *hymn.Bas.*3(M.96.1372B) cit. s. ἔλλαμψις; **e.** as mere appearance κατ' ἔμφασιν...οἱ...παρ' Ἕλλησι φιλοσοφήσαντες διορῶσι τὸν θεόν Clem.*str.*1.19(p.61.2; M.8.812A); **2.** *meaning*; **a.** ref. divine names εὑρίσκομεν ἑκάστου τῶν ὀνομάτων ἰδιάζουσαν ἔ., πρέπουσαν περὶ τῆς θείας φύσεως νοεῖσθαι...οὐ μὲν ἐκεῖνο σημαίνουσαν, ὅ ἐστι κατ' οὐσίαν ἡ φύσις Gr.Nyss.*tres dii*(M.45.121B); εἰ δὲ πάντα τὰ ὀνόματα τῇ θείᾳ φύσει ἐπιλεγόμενα ἰσοδυναμεῖ ἀλλήλοις...ἄλλα κατὰ ἄλλην ἔ. ἐπὶ τὸ αὐτὸ τὴν διάνοιαν ἡμῶν ὁδηγοῦντα id.*Trin.*5(p.76.9; M.32.689C); ἐν ἀνθρώποις τὸ τοῦ πατρὸς ὄνομα συνεζευγμένας ἔχει τινὰς ἐ., ὧν ἡ ἀκήρατος ἠλλοτρίωται φύσις id.*Eun.*3(2 p.27.31; M.45.593A); *ib.*(p.43. 4; 609D); **b.** of senses of scripture τῆς προχείρου κατὰ τὴν λέξιν ἐ. id.*hom.1 in Cant.*(M.44.756A); *ib.*(757C); πνευματικὴ ἔ. Ammon.*Ac.* 15:7(M.85.1549A); **c.** *concrete expression, word*, Bas.*Eun.*2.7(1.243D; M.29.585A); *ib.*2.24(1.260C; M.625B); **3.** *manifestation* θεοῦ...ἔ. ἑνὸς ἦν τοῦ παντοκράτορος παρὰ πᾶσι τοῖς εὖ φρονοῦσι πάντοτε φυσική Clem.*str.*5.18(p.383.21; M.9.128C); [sc. patriarchs and prophets] οἱ μὴ δι' ἀνθρώπων πρότερον μαθητευθέντες θεῷ, ἄρχῆθεν δεδύνηνται, ὡς καθαροί, χωρῆσαι τὰς ἐ. τοῦ πνεύματος †Bas.*Is.*198(1.526E; M.30. 460A); *ib.*proem.3(379D; M.121C); τὴν...τριάδα,...ἧς νῦν μετρίως δεδέγμεθα τὰς ἐ. Gr.Naz.*or.*43.82(M.36.605A); Eustrat.*v.Eutych.*102 (M.86.2389A); of visions, apparitions, id.*stat.anim.*20(p.501); χωρητικοῖς οὖσι [sc. saints] τῶν θείων ἐ. Areth.*Apoc.*10(M.106.568B).

***ἐμφεγγής**, *shining, bright*, ‡Chrys.*poenit.*4(9.852A).

ἐμφέρεια, ἡ, *likeness*; **1.** Trin.; **a.** of relation of Father and Son, cf.Jo.10:30 ὅπερ φησὶν ὁ κύριος, οὐ πατέρα ἑαυτὸν ἀναγορεύων...ἀλλ' ὅτι τὴν πατρικὴν ἐ. ἀκριβῶς πέφυκε σώζειν ὁ υἱὸς τοῦ πατρός, τὴν πάντα ὁμοιότητα αὐτοῦ ἐκ φύσεως ἀπομαξάμενος Alex.Al.*ep.Alex.*9 (p.25.24; M.18.561B); τὴν ἐ. ὡς υἱός Ath.*syn.*52(p.276.8; M.26.785D); δεῖξαι θέλων ὁ Παῦλος τὴν πολλὴν ἐ., ἀπαύγασμα καλεῖ τοῦ πατρὸς τὸν υἱόν Ammon.*Jo.*12:46(M.85.1480A); Cyr.*Jo.*8(4.712D); **b.** of Son having no likeness to creatures in Arian sense, Eus.*ep.Caes.*7(p.46.1; M.20.1541C); *ποία γὰρ ἐ. τῶν ἐξ οὐκ ὄντων πρὸς τὸν κτίσαντα, τὰ οὐκ ὄντα εἰς τὸ εἶναι;* Ath.*Ar.*1.21(M.26.56A); *ib.*1.31(76A); **2.** of divine likeness in creatures' knowledge of God; human terms applied to God *ἀποδεόντων...τῆς θεαρχικῆς πρὸς ἀλήθειαν ἐ.* Dion.Ar.*c.h.*2.3(M.3.140C); of angels in gen. *πρὸς τὴν θεαρχικὴν ἐ. ὑπερκοσμίως ὁρῶσαι ib.*4.2(180A); dominations *πρὸς τὴν αὐτῆς* [sc. *τῆς ὄντως κυριότητος*] *κυρίαν ἐ., ὡς ἐφικτόν, ἑαυτήν τε καὶ τὰ μετ' αὐτὴν ἀγαθοειδῶς διαπλάττουσαν ib.*8.1(237C).

ἐμφερής, *like*; **1.** ref. divine transcendence *οὐδεμίαν...οὐσίαν, ἥτις ἀκριβῶς ἐ. ἐστι τῇ πάντων...αἰτίᾳ* Dion.Ar.*d.n.*2.7(M.3.645B); of theol. allegories which are not like God, id.*c.h.*2.3(M.3.141B); **2.** Trin.; **a.** of relation of Son to Father *τέλειον υἱόν, ἐ. τῷ πατρί* Alex.Al.*ep.Alex.*47(p.27.14; M.18.565C); *τὸ τῆς εἰκόνος ἐ. τῷ πατρὶ... κατά τε τὴν ἀρετήν, κατά τε τὴν δύναμιν καὶ τὴν οὐσίαν, κατά τε τὸν τῆς μονάδος καὶ ἑνάδος ἀριθμόν* Eus.*d.e.*4.6(p.158.19; M.22.264C); *τῆς οὐσίας αὐτοῦ...εἰκὼν ἐ.* Cyr.*Jo.*9.14(4.779D); **b.** ref. difference of Son from creatures *μὴ εἶναι αὐτὸν ποίημα τοῖς δι' αὐτοῦ γενομένοις ἐ.* Eus.*ep.Caes.*6(p.45.18; M.20.1141B); id.*e.th.*1.8(p.66.24; M.24.837C); **3.** ref. Christ, of aspects of Word known before Inc. *πάλαι μὲν εἰκόνες, οὐ πᾶσα δὲ ἐ.* Clem.*prot.*12(p.85.8; M.8.41B); *λέγοντες* [sc. Eunomians] *ἕτερον μὲν εἶναι τὸν ἐνδιάθετον ἐν τῷ θεῷ καὶ πατρὶ λόγον, ἕτερον δέ τινα καὶ τῷ ἐνδιαθέτῳ λίαν ἐμφερέστατον...τὸν υἱὸν καὶ λόγον, δι' οὗ θεὸς τὰ πάντα ἐργάζεται* Cyr.*Jo.*1.4(4.29E).

ἐμφέρ-ω, *bring in*, pass.; **1.** in books, Didym.*Trin.*2.5(M.39.504B); of theol. terms not mentioned in scripture, Bas.*fid.*1(2.224C; M.31.677C); ⟨*τὸ*⟩ *ἀγέννητον...οὐκ ἀρνούμεθα, κἂν τε ἐν θείᾳ γραφῇ μὴ ~εται,* ⟨*ὅτι*⟩ *εὐσεβῶς* [*δὲ*] *ἐπινενόηται* Epiph.*haer.*76.29(p.378.3; M.42.576A); Socr.*h.e.*1.19.8(M.67.225C); **2.** *be accepted* as canonical, of epistles of James and Jude *μετὰ τῶν ἄλλων καθολικῶν ἐν ταῖς ἐκκλησίαις ~ομένας cat.Jac.*1:1(p.2.7); **3.** *be in circulation παρ' ὑμῖν ~ονται βίβλοι προφητῶν* Epiph.*mens.*10(M.43.253A).

***ἔμφθαρτος,** *corruptible*, ‡Just.*qu.Gr.*15.20(M.6.1484C).

ἐμφθέγγομαι, *speak then* or *there*; of God at Creation, Bas.*hex.*2.7(1.19C; M.29.45B).

***ἐμφθείρομαι,** *perish in*, c. dat., Max.*ambig.*(M.91.1113D).

***ἐμφιβλόομαι,** *have fastened round one, wear*, Pall.*h.Laus.*21(p.66.8; M.34.1074C).

ἐμφιλόνεικος, *contentious, querulous ἐ. ζητήσεις* ‡Ath.*synops.*69(M.28.425C); Bas.*moral.*25(2.255E; M.31.744B); Gr.Nyss.*ep.can.*(M.45.225B); *ἐ. ... ζῶον ὁ ἄνθρωπος* Anast.S.*qu.et resp.*89(M.89.716B).

ἐμφιλονείκως, *querulously*, Justn.*conf.*(M.86.1029B; *ἐνφ-* p.104.36); Jo.D.*haer.*97(M.94.760A).

***ἐμφιλόπονος,** *well-worked, well-cultivated*, Ephr.2.6F.

ἐμφιλοσοφ-έω, 1. *practise ascetical life in, meditate in ἐπιτήδειον ~ῆσαι διὰ τὴν ἐκ τῆς ἐρημίας ἡσυχίαν* Bas.*ep.*210.1(3.313E; M.32.769A); Gr.Naz.*or.*26.7(M.35.1237A); Gr.Nyss.*hom.7 in Cant.*(M.44.924A); id.*v.Mos.*(M.44.333A); id.*v.Macr.*(p.395.25; M.46.981D); Chrys.*hom.15.4 in 1Tim.*(11.640A); **2.** *philosophize, speculate about Εὐκλείδης...γραμμαῖς ~ῶν ταῖς οὐκ οὔσαις* Gr.Naz.*or.*28.25(p.60.7; M.36.60D); **3.** *bear philosophically ἐ. τοῖς πάθεσιν τοῦ σώματος* Gr.Naz.*ep.*92(M.37.165C).

***ἐμφιλοσόφημα, τό,** *subject of study*, Gr.Naz.*or.*43.61(M.36.576C).

ἐμφιλόσοφος, 1. *worthy of a philosopher*, i.e. *virtuous εἰς βίον ἐ. τε καὶ ἐλεύθερον* Gr.Nyss.*v.Mos.*(M.44.344B); *ἐ. πράξεις* Nil.*epp.*2.83(M.79.240B); *ib.*3.293(528D); Eustrat.*stat.anim.*1(p.338); neut. as subst., Chrys.*hom.83.1 in Mt.*(7.791C); Thdr.Mops.*fr.inc.*(p.307.14; M.66.988D); **2.** *ascetical*, also *contemplative ἡ τῆς παρθένου ζωὴ πρὸς τὴν ἐ. ... καὶ ἄυλον τοῦ βίου διαγωγήν* Gr.Nyss.*v.Macr.*(p.381.20; M.46.969B); *ἐ. ... μελέτην* Euthal.Diac.*Ac.*proem.(M.85.632A); **3.** *pertaining to* (*Christian*) *teaching, theological ἐ. δόγματα* Chrys.*hom.9.2 in Col.*(11.393D).

ἐμφιλοσόφως, superl., *most eruditely*, Jo.VI H.*v.Jo.D.*14(M.94.453A).

***ἐμφιλοτιμέομαι,** *take pride in, glory in*, Gr.Nyss.*Eun.*5(2 p.115.25; M.45.696C).

ἐμφιλοχωρ-έω, 1. *frequent by preference*, Eus.*p.e.*5.2(181B, v.l. *φιλοχωροῦντες* M.21.313C); Didym.*Trin.*1.27(M.39.396C); **2.** *resort to, study*; scripture, †Gregent.*disp.*(M.86.624C); **3.** *dwell in*; **a.** Trin. *~εῖν δὲ τῷ θεῷ...δεῖ τὸ ἅγιον πνεῦμα* Dion.R.ap.Ath.*decr.*26(p.22.9; M.25.464A); *~εῖ μὲν γὰρ τῇ τοῦ πατρὸς φύσει μονονουχὶ ῥίζαν ἔχων αὐτὴν ὁ υἱός* Cyr.*dial.Trin.*5(5[1].558E); id.*Heb.*1:3(p.367.16); id.ap.*cat.Heb.*1:3(p.301.24); **b.** of divine indwelling in creatures; **i.** in heaven *τὸ δὲ ἐναναπαύεσθαι ταῖς ἁγίαις δυνάμεσι, καὶ οἷον ~εῖν* Gr.Naz.*or.*31.5(p.172.17; M.36.157B); in heaven and Church (Sion) *οἷον ~ῶν ἐν αὐτῇ* Cyr.*Ps.*9:12(M.69.769A); Oecum.*Apoc.*4:6–8(p.73); **ii.** on earth *τὸ μὲν οὖν ἅγιον πνεῦμα μόνοις ἁγίοις ~εῖν πέφυκεν* Eus.*e.th.*3.6(p.163.30; M.24.1013B); of Christ as light *οὐκ ~οῦν ταῖς μὴ φωτισθῆναι βουλομέναις ψυχαῖς* Chrys.*hom.5.3 in Jo.*(8.40A); Cyr.*Jo.*2.4(4.177E); *ἔδει γενόμενον ἄνθρωπον τὸ πνεῦμα λαβεῖν ἵν' ἐπείπερ ἐστὶν οὐκ εἰδὼς ἁμαρτίαν, ~οίη λοιπὸν ἐν αὐτῷ τὸ πνεῦμα* id.ap.*cat.Heb.*2:11(p.402.22); *τὸ πνεῦμα τὸ ἅγιον, ~οῦν ἐν δικαίων ψυχαῖς* Jo.D.*hom.*11.13(M.96.776B); **c.** ref. spiritual life in gen. *ὁ δὲ τούτοις* [sc. knowledge and virtue] *~ῶν...σύνοικος γενήσεται αὐτῷ* [sc. *τῷ θεῷ*] Or.*exp.in Pr.*7:19(M.17.176C); cf.Mt.21:13, of soul as den of thieves *ὅταν ἀνελευθέρους...ἐπιθυμίας...~ῆσαι ταῖς ψυχαῖς τῶν νέων ἐάσωμεν* Chrys.*Anna* 3.4(4.728A); **d.** diabolical, †Bas.*Is.*90(1.442A; M.30.265C); *τῶν δαιμόνων τῶν τοῖς γηΐνοις ~ούντων* Oecum.*Apoc.*6:10(p.92); **4.** *dwell on, linger over*, Gr.Naz.*or.*35.4(M.36.261C); Chrys.*Jud.*8.5(1.682A); ‡Chrys.*pasch.*6(8.272D); Pall.*h.Laus.*54(p.147.12; M.34.1227B); Cyr.*ador.*3(1.86C); *κατὰ διάνοιάν τε ~οῦντες τοῖς ὑπὲρ αἴσθησιν* ‡Proc.G.*Pr.*10:13(M.87.1316C); **5.** *follow* an opinion *τοὺς τοῖς τῆς ἀληθείας ~ούντας δόγμασιν* Cyr.*Arcad.*2(p.63.1; 5[2].43D); id.*Juln.*2(6[2].47D); Oecum.*Apoc.*4:6–8(p.73); CCP(681) *ep.Agath.*(M.*PL.*87.1247D).

***ἐμφιλοχώρησις, ἡ,** *intimate indwelling μηδὲ...τὰς πρώτας τῆς ζωοπλαστίας ἀρχὰς ἐσχηκέναι τὴν προσληφθεῖσαν φύσιν ἄνευ τῆς... φυσικῆς ἐ. τῆς προσλαβομένης αὐτὴν θεοῦ λόγου φύσεως* Thdr.Raith.*praep.*(p.192.14; M.91.1492D).

***ἐμφλεγμαίνω,** *wax warm, grow excited over*, Gr.Nyss.*Eun.*1(1 p.47.8; M.45.276A).

ἐμφόβως, *with* (reverent) *fear γραφαῖς...ἐ. ἀκολουθεῖν* Eus.*e.th.*2.19(p.125.13; M.24.945D); *Symb.Ant.*(345)8(p.253.28; M.26.733A); *ἐ. ...πιστεύομεν* Ath.*syn.*23(p.250.3; M.26.724B).

ἐμφορ-έω, 1. *bring in*; hence *affirm*, Just.*1apol.*53.12(M.6.408B); **2.** *fill*; **a.** Christol. *εἰ δὲ τὸν ἴδιον ἔχοντες* ⟨*ἦσαν*⟩ *σὺν τῷ τοῦ Χριστοῦ νῷ, ἀμφοτέρων ἐνεφοροῦντο...τὸ δ' αὐτὸ καὶ ἐπὶ Χριστοῦ γινωσκέτωσαν* Epiph.*anc.*76(p.95.18; M.43.160A); **b.** ref. grace through union with God *τὸ σῶμα αὐτοῦ πρόκειται νῦν ἡμῖν* [i.e. at eucharist]...*ὥστε καὶ φαγεῖν καὶ ~ηθῆναι* Chrys.*hom.50.2 in Mt.*(7.516E); *πάσης ~εῖς θυμηδίας τοὺς τῶν ἀγαθῶν ἀπολαύοντας* Thdt.*Ps.*103:29(1.1340); *ἕκαστος...τῷ ἰδίῳ τάγματι...~εῖται τοῦ Ἰησοῦ* Max.*ambig.*(M.91.1360D); **c.** ref. divine truth, ‡Meth.*Sym.et Ann.*2(M.18.349C); Cyr.*glaph.Ex.*2(1.291B); id.*Mich.*60(4.453C); *ψυχῆς δὲ τροφή,...τὸ τῶν θείων ~εῖσθαι διηγημάτων* Bas.Sel.*or.*16.1(M.85.204C); Max.*ambig.*(M.91.1364D); **d.** ref. sin and evil *ὅσοι ὑπὸ ἀκαθάρτου πνεύματος ἐμπεφορημένοι* Just.*dial.*93.1(M.6.697A); *τῷ κακῷ...~ηθῆναι* Or.*or.*29.13(p.388.9; M.11.540B); id.*princ.*3.1.17(p.226.14; M.11.284A); *ἁμαρτήμασιν...ἐνεφόρησαν* Ath.*inc.*12.6(M.25.118C); hence **3.** *gain satisfaction*, ref. perversion of human powers by evil spirits *μὴ... ~ηθῶσιν οἱ δαίμονες* ‡Proc.G.*Pr.*5:10(M.87.1264A).

ἔμφορος, ὁ, *one who satisfies*, Eus.Al.*serm.*21.3(M.86.425D).

***ἐμφορτικεύομαι,** *lay a burden upon*, Germ.CP *or.*2(M.98.245B).

***ἐμφορύνομαι,** *defile*, Gr.Nyss.*Eun.*12(1 p.375.28; M.45.1101C).

***ἐμφραγή, ἡ,** *obstacle*, Geo.Pis.*Heracl.*2.186(M.92.1330A).

ἔμφραξις, ἡ, *obstruction, stoppage*; medic. *τῷ τῆς ἐ. νοσήματι* Socr.*h.e.*3.26.5(M.67.457A); met., *barrier*, of blood of paschal lamb *ἐ. ... ἀπωλείας* Chrys.*hom.27.1 in Heb.*(12.245D); of psychological depression *πνεύματο ἐ. ib.*29.4(276C).

***ἔμφρενος,** *sane*, Jo.Mal.*chron.*5 p.120(M.97.213C).

***ἔμφρικτος,** *terrifying, awful*, Andr.Cr.*or.*9(M.97.997A); *ib.*14(1108A).

***ἐμφρούριος,** *imprisoned*, Evagr.*h.e.*5.18(p.213.23; M.86.2828C).

***ἐμφυβλάστημα, τό,** s.v.l., *parasitic growth*, Cyr.*ador.*16(1.579A; *ἐμφύτων βλαστημάτων* M.68.1044D).

ἐμφύρ-ω, -άω, 1. *mix up*, hence *defile τὴν ἑαυτοῦ ψυχὴν δικαίων... ἐνέφυρεν αἵμασι* Eus.*v.C.*1.57(p.34.9; M.20.972A); Ath.*gentl.*7(M.25.16B); **2.** pass., *be involved in οἱ ἐν ταῖς πραγματείαις ἐμπεφυρμένοι* Herm.*sim.*8.8.1; *ib.*9.20.1; *ἐ. μοιχείαις* Thphl.Ant.*Autol.*1.14(M.6.1045B); Or.*Jo.*13.42(p.268.10; M.14.473B); Chrys.*oppugn.*3.17(1.107A); ref. sexual intercourse, Clem.*prot.*4(v.l. *συνεφύρετο* p.42.29; M.8.149C); *τῶν γυναικῶν σώμασιν ~όμενος* Chrys.*hom.13.1 in Eph.*(11.95F).

ἐμφυσ-άω, 1. *breathe into, infuse*; **a.** ref. Creation; **i.** in gen. *τὸν δὲ ἄνθρωπον δι' αὐτοῦ ἐχειρούργησεν καί τε αὐτῷ ἴδιον ἐνεφύσησεν* Clem.*paed.*1.3(p.94.11; M.8.257A); Meth.*symp.*2.7(p.24.13; M.18.57C); Proc.G.*Lev.*17:3(M.87.752A); **ii.** Valent. *πεποιηκέναι* [sc. demiurge] *καὶ τὸν ἄνθρωπον τὸν χοϊκόν...καὶ εἰς τοῦτον ~ῆσαι τὸν ψυχικὸν διορίζονται* Iren.*haer.*1.5.5(M.7.500A); Clem.*str.*4.13(p.288.17; M.8.1300A) cit. s. *ζωή*; **b.** ref. Jo.20:22 *μετὰ τὴν ἀνάστασιν ~ῶν τὸ πνεῦμα τοῖς ἀποστόλοις* id.*exc.Thdot.*3(p.106.11; M.9.656A); Ath.*inc.et c.Ar.*

9(M.26.997A); **c.** *breathe* a soul *into*, ref. Creation ἄνθρωπόν τινα ὑπὸ χειρῶν θεοῦ πλασσόμενόν τε καὶ ~ώμενον Cels.ap.Or.*Cels*.4.36(p.306. 24; M.11.1084B); Epiph.*haer*.30.3(p.336.6; M.41.409A); cf. ψυχή; **2.** *breathe* (*on*) in exorcism; **a.** in gen., Ath.*v.Anton*.40(M.26.901A); ref. evil spirits ἡνίκα ~ήσω αὐτοῖς ἀφανεῖς γενήσονται Hesych.H. *Ps.tit*.17.94(M.27.79D); *Pers*.228ª(p.26.3); **b.** before baptism, Ephr. 2.195E; Cyr.H.*procatech*.9; Dion.Ar.*e.h*.2.2.6(M.3.396B); ἐξορκίζομεν αὐτοὺς μετὰ τοῦ ~ᾶν τρίτον εἰς τὸ πρόσωπον καὶ εἰς τὰ ὦτα CCP(381) ‡*can*.7; **c.** ref. an evil spirit, *Contrad*.2(p.9).

ἐμφύσημα, τό, *inbreathing, infusion*; **1.** divine; of divine indwelling, Or.*Jo*.4.24(p.247.30; M.14.440A); ἡ γραφή...τὸ ἅγιον πνεῦμα ἐ. τοῦ θεοῦ λέγει Ath.*inc.et c.Ar*.19(M.26.1020A); ref. H. Ghost and agst. existence of three Gods ὅσα δὲ κἀνταῦθα λέγεται ταπεινότερον, τὸ δίδοσθαι,...τὸ ἐ.,...ἐπὶ τὴν πρώτην αἰτίαν ἀνενεκτέον Gr.Naz.*or*.31.30(p.186.4; M.36.168C); **2.** ref. Gen.2:7; **a.** as cause of human soul ἐπειδὴ γὰρ πνεῦμα ἡ ψυχή, φύσις ἀόρατος, ἐ. θεῖον δημιουργικὸν αὐτῆς εἶναί φησιν Diod.*Gen*.2:7(M.33.1565B); Gr.Nyss. *hom.opif*.28(M.44.129C); Epiph.*haer*.1(p.172.7,13; M.41.177D,180A); εἰ ἐκ τοῦ θείου ἐ. γέγονεν ἡ ψυχή, ἐκ τῆς οὐσίας ἄρα τοῦ θεοῦ ἐστιν ἡ ψυχή; ἀσεβείας ἐσχάτης...ἡ τοιαύτη ἔννοια. τῆς γὰρ δημιουργίας τὴν εὐκολίαν ἔδειξε διὰ τοῦτο ἡ θεία γραφή Thdt.*qu.23 in Gen*.(1.39); οὐ τὸ ἐ. ψυχή, ἀλλὰ ἀθανάτου ψυχῆς ποιητικόν Proc.G.*Gen*.1:27(M.87. 133A); **b.** as soul itself ἡ μὲν ψυχή ἐστιν ἄφθαρτον, μέρος οὖσα τοῦ θεοῦ καὶ ἐ. †Just.*fr.res*.8(p.46; M.6.1588A); ὡς ἐ. θεῖον Nil.*epp*.2.82 (M.79.237B); **c.** effects; **i.** production of image of God, Gr.Naz.*or*. 33.12(M.36.229A); Didym.*Trin*.2.12(M.39.680A) cit. s. εἰκών; **ii.** immortality, Justn.*Or*.(p.192.37; M.86.953B); ἀθάνατον αὐτὴν...κατασκευάσας τῷ ἀπ' ἀρχῆς πνεύματι θείῳ καὶ ἐ. ‡Jo.D.*Artem*.30(p.161. 25; M.96.1280A); **iii.** sanctification, Clem.*str*.5.13(p.384.1; M.9. 129A); Meth.*res*.2.6(p.339.15; M.41.1172C); τὴν γῆν ἣν ἰδίαις χερσὶν ἔπλασεν καὶ ἡγίασεν τῷ θείῳ ἐ.‡Eust.*Laz*.6(p.31.2); τὸ δοθὲν τοιγαροῦν ἐ. θεῖον τῷ πεπλασμένῳ...εἶναί φαμεν...τὴν τοῦ ἁγίου πνεύματος μετουσίαν ἐντεθεῖσαν ἐξ ἀρχῆς τῇ ἀνθρωπείᾳ ψυχῇ Cyr.*thes*.34(5^1. 344E); **d.** heret.; **i.** Valent. ἔλαθεν οὖν, ὥς φασι, τὸν δημιουργὸν ὁ συγκατασπαρεὶς τῷ ἐ. αὐτοῦ ὑπὸ τῆς Σοφίας πνευματικὸς ἀνθρώπων ἀρρήτῳ προνοίᾳ Iren.*haer*.1.5.6(M.7.501A); οὔτ' οὖν ἀπὸ τοῦ πνεύματος οὔτ' οὖν ἀπὸ τοῦ ἐ. σπείρει ὁ Ἀδάμ· θεῖα γὰρ ἄμφω Clem.*exc.Thdot*. 55(p.125.10; M.9.685B); ἐπεὶ δὲ τὸ φαινόμενον αὐτοῦ οὐκ ἔστιν ἡ ἐξ μεσότητος ψυχή, ἔρχεται τὸ διαφέρον, καὶ τοῦτ' ἔστι τὸ ἐ. τοῦ διαφέροντος πνεύματος id.*str*.4.13(p.288.3; M.8.1297B); **ii.** Marcionite τοῦ δημιουργοῦ ἐστιν ἡ ψυχὴ ἐ. Adam.*dial*.2.7(p.70.12; M.11.1769A); consequent difficulties discussed, *ib*.(p.70.21ff.; 1769B); *ib*.(p.72.14, 19; 1769D,1772A); **3.** ref. Jo.20:22; **a.** means of conferring H. Ghost, Ammon.*Jo*.20:24(M.85.1520A); τὸ ἴδιον αὐτοῖς πνεῦμα διδοὺς δι' ἐμφανοῦς ἐ. Cyr.*Jo*.12.1(4.1095B); Max.*schol.e.h*.7.3.7(M.4.181B); **b.** preparation for that gift τὸ μὲν ἐ. καθαρτικόν πως ἦν τῆς τῶν ἀποστόλων ψυχῆς, ἐπιτηδείους αὐτοὺς παρασκευάζον τῆς τοῦ ἁγίου πνεύματος ὑποδοχῆς Eus.*e.th*.3.5(p.160.7; M.24.1008A); **c.** restoration of state of man before Fall, Ammon.*Jo*.20:22(M.85.1520A); πάλιν ἡμῖν ὁ σωτὴρ ὡς ἐν ἀπαρχῇ τῆς ἀνακαινιζομένης φύσεως τοῖς ἁγίοις μαθηταῖς δι' ἐ. ἐναργοῦς τὸ πνεῦμα χαρίζεται Cyr.*Jo*.12.1(4.1097E); Hesych.H.*fr.Ps*.52:3(M.93.1209D); **4.** in exorcisms τὸ ἁπλοῦν ἐ. τοῦ ἐπορκίζοντος, πῦρ γίνεται τῷ μὴ φαινομένῳ Cyr.H.*catech*.16.19; *ib*. 20.3.

ἐμφύσησις, ἡ, *inbreathing, insufflation*, ref. Jo.20:22 δίδωσι δέ [sc. Moses], οὐκ ἐμφυσήσει, καθάπερ ὁ Χριστός· οὐ μὴ ἔστι πηγὴ τοῦ πνεύματος Iren.*fr*.19(M.7.1241A); πνεῦμα ζωοποιὸν ἔχοντες ἀπὸ τῆς ἐ. τοῦ κυρίου Or.*adnot.in Dt*.3:27(M.17.25A); Ammon.*Jo*.20:24(M.85. 1520A); ref. Jo.20:22 and Gen.2:7 καὶ θεία φύσις [sc. τὸ πνεῦμα]... κατὰ τὴν ἐ. εἰς τὸν ἄνθρωπον ἀπεσταλμένη, καὶ κατὰ τὸν σωματικῶς ὑπὸ τοῦ κυρίου διδαχθέντα τύπον, αὖθις ὑπ' αὐτοῦ δι' ἐμφυσήσεως ἀποκαθισταμένη Didym.(‡Bas.)*Eun*.5(1.303E; M.29.729A); ref. Gen. 2:7 τὴν ζωτικὴν...ἐ. Max.*ambig*.(M.91.1316D).

***ἐμφυσίωσις, ἡ,** *inflation, conceit*, Hipp.*haer*.4.7(p.39.17; M.16. 3067D).

ἐμφυτεύ-ω, *implant*; met., ref. Sap.4:11 μεγαλοπρέπειαν τῆς σοφίας τοῖς κατὰ τὴν μάθησιν τέκνοις ~σάσης Clem.*str*.7.16(p.74.11; M.9.545A); of God at Creation τὴν ζωὴν ἐνεφύτευσεν Gr.Nyss.*or. catech*.6(p.31.8; M.45.28A); ref. Christ's miracles ἡ ἁγία σάρξ, ἣν αὐτὸς ἰδίαν ἐποιήσατο, θεοπρεπῆ τὴν δύναμιν ~σας αὐτῇ Cyr.*Lc*.4:38 (M.72.552C); ref. Inc. ἑαυτὸν ἡμῖν ~σας Petr.Laod.*fr.in Lc*.22:19 (M.86.3328D).

ἔμφυτος, 1. *inborn, natural*; **a.** theol.: agst. Marcell. μακρῷ διεστάναι...τὸν ἐ. ἐν ψυχῇ λόγον παρὰ τὸν ἔκ τινος γεννηθέντα...υἱόν Eus.*e.th*.2.16(p.120.7; M.24.937A); of second Person τὴν ἰδίαν αὐτοῦ τοῦ θεοῦ δύναμιν, τὴν ἐ. αὐτοῦ Ast.Soph. *fr*.1(M.26.77B); ἣν ἐν ἀρχῇ πρὸς τὸν θεόν,...ὡς ἐ. Cyr.*Jo*.1.4(4.30A); *ib*.(31E); ref. Father τοῦ ἐ. πνεύματος αὐτοῦ *Hom.Clem*.20.6; ref. Christ., *ib*.3.15; ὡς...θεός, ἔ. ἔχει τὴν βασιλείαν Thdt.*Ps*.2:6(1.620); **b.** of innate knowledge of God, *Lit*.ap.*Const.App*.8.12.18; ὁ δὲ νόμος ὁ ἐν ἡμῖν τῆς ἐ. θεογνωσίας Proc.G.*Gen*.4:2(M.87.236A); **c.** of knowledge of moral law, Just. *2apol*.8.1(M.6.457A); cf.*ib*.13.5(468A); Meth.*res*.2.6(p.340.8; M.18. 304C); *ib*.2.7(p.341.2; 304D); ‡Ath.*synops*.59(M.28.413A); ὁ...νόμον δοὺς αὐτῷ [sc. τῷ ἀνθρώπῳ] ἔ. καὶ γραπτὸν πρὸς τὸ ζῆν αὐτὸν...ὡς λογικόν *Lit*.ap.*Const.App*.8.9.8; **d.** of moral faculties and tendencies τὴν ἔ. ἐκλογήν Clem.*str*.3.1(p.196.20; M.8.1104A); ὑπὸ τῆς ἐ. κακίας ἠναγκασμένος Eus.*h.e*.10.8.8(M.20.896D); cf.id.*m.P*.4.1(p.911.21; M. 20.1472C); **2.** *implanted, engrafted*, met. ὁ...προφητείαν ἔ. ψυχῆς ἰδίαν ἔχων *Hom.Clem*.3.26; τὸ πηγάσαν [sc. body of BMV] τὴν ἔ. ἀθανασίαν...ἐν τῇ θνητῇ...ἡμῶν φύσει Mod.*dorm*.12(M.86.3308C); hence **3.** *deeply-rooted* ἔ. τῆς δωρεᾶς πνευματικῆς χάριν *Barn*.1.2; τὴν ἔ. σου ἀγάπην Ar.*ep.Eus*.2(p.1.5; M.42.209D); ref. S. Peter's confession ἔ. ... τῆς ἀληθείας τὴν εἴδησιν Isid.Pel.*epp*.1.57(M.78.220B); ἔ. τὴν εἰς τὸν...θεὸν...εὐσέβειαν Gel.Cyz.*h.e*.2.1.1(M.85.1224C).

***ἐμφώλευμα, τό,** *lurking-place, haunt*, Andr.Cr.*or*.19(M.97.1220C).

ἐμφωλεύ-ω, 1. *lurk, hide*; met.; **a.** of Inc. δυνάμεώς τινος ~ούσης τῇ ἀδυναμίᾳ τῆς ἡμετέρας φύσεως ἐδεόμεθα Leont.H.*Nest*.1.47(M.86. 1505C); **b.** of natural endowments ἔνεστι γάρ τις ἔρως ~ων τῇ φύσει Chrys.*hom.20.1 in Eph*.(11.142E); τὴν φθορὰν...τὴν πᾶσι κτιστῆς φύσεως ~ουσαν Sophr.H.*ep.syn*.(M.87.3181A); **c.** of sin and evil tendencies ~οντας...λογισμοὺς πονηρούς Or.*hom.2 in Lc*.(p.16.16; M.17.316B); id.*comm.in Ex*.10:27(p.251.25; M.12.277A); τὸν νόμον τῆς ἁμαρτίας τὸν ἐν τοῖς μέλεσι ⟨τοῦ σώματος⟩ διὰ τῆς παραβάσεως ἐν ἡμῖν ~οντα Meth.*res*.2.8(p.343.5; M.18.305B); Bas.*jud*.3(2.215B; M.31.655D); ‡Gr.Nyss.*or.1 in Gen.1:26*(M.44.276D); **d.** ref. diabolical infestation; **i.** of places τοῖς ~ουσι τοῖς ξοάνοις...δαίμοσι πονηροῖς Eus.*l.C*.13(p.236.15; M.20.1397D); Socr.*h.e*.1.18.11(M.67. 124B); Jo.D.*hom*.4.22(M.96.621A); id.*disp*.(M.96.1348B); **ii.** of persons, before baptism τοῖς μέλεσι τοῖς ὑμετέροις ἐνεφώλευον αἱ ἀντικείμεναι δυνάμεις Cyr.H.*catech*.20.2; of souls, Mac.Aeg.*hom*.11.11 (M.34.553A); Chrys.*hom.10.6 in Rom*.(9.529C); Diad.*perf*.79(p.100. 16) cit. s. ἐνάλλομαι; of Judas, Cyr.*Jo*.11.12(4.1012A); **2.** *enter stealthily*, met. μηδὲ πώποτε κἂν ἔννοιά τις ~ῃ τὸ σύνολον Serap.*ep. mon*.15(M.40.941A).

ἐμφωνέω, 1. *call out* to; in paraphrase of Jo.21:4f., Clem.*paed*.1.5 (p.96.30; M.8.261B); **2.** *proclaim, pronounce*, ‡Sophr.H.*liturg*.13 (M.87.3993B); **3.** met., *call forth, evoke*, Or.*fr.in Pr*.1:1(M.17.152B).

***ἐμφώτειος,** *baptismal* ἐ. ἐσθής Gr.Naz.*or*.40.25(M.36.393C).

***ἐμφώτια, τά,** *baptismal garments*, Germ.CP *syn.haer*.15(M.98. 53C).

***ἐμφωτίζομαι,** *be set alight*, Clem.*str*.6.15(p.490.21; M.9.340C).

ἔμφωτον, τό, *interval, empty space* admitting light, Evagr.*h.e*. 4.31(p.181.7; M.86.2761A).

ἔμψηφος, *being a supporter* of χαρὰ...ἀγάπης ἔ. †Nil.*vit*.3(M.79. 1144A).

ἔμψυχος, 1. *animated, living*; **a.** of Christ ἔ. δὲ τυγχάνον τὸ ἀληθινὸν φῶς Or.*Cels*.6.67(p.137.18; M.11.1400C); ἔ. σοφία id.*Jo*.1.19 (22; p.24.8; M.14.56C); λόγος ἔ. id.*Cels*.3.81(p.272.5; 1028B); Gr. Thaum.*pan.Or*.4(p.9.15; M.10.1061B); ἔ. ... εἰκὼν τοῦ ἰδίου πατρὸς ...ἐπειδὰν ᾖ τῷ πατρὶ ὁμοιότατος Eus.*Marcell*.1.4(p.25.16; M.24. 764C); as νόμος ἔ. v. νόμος; **b.** of men as instruments of God's glory ἄγαλμα ἔ. ἡμᾶς τὸν ἄνθρωπον ἔπλασεν Clem.*prot*.10(p.71.22; M.8. 212C); esp. 'gnostic', id.*str*.7.8(p.39.9; M.9.473C); Meth.*symp*.2.6 (p.23.6; M.18.56D); of widows θεοῦ γάρ εἰσιν ἔ. βωμός *ib*.5.8(p.62. 21; 1112A); BMV ἔ. ναὲ τοῦ...ὑψίστου Mod.*dorm*.10(M.86.3301B); **c.** heret., Naassene καὶ γὰρ οἱ λίθοι, φησίν, εἰσὶν ἔ. Hipp.*haer*.5.7 (p.81.11; M.16.3130C); Manich. πάντα δὲ νομίζουσιν ἔ., καὶ τὸ πῦρ, καὶ τὸ ὕδωρ Thdt.*haer*.1.26(4.321); **d.** neut. plur. as subst.; ref. abstinence from animal foods οἶνον...οὐκ ἔπιεν οὐδὲ ἔ. ἔφαγεν [sc. S. James] Heges.ap.Eus.*h.e*.2.23.5(M.20.197A); ὅρα δὲ καὶ τὴν διαφορὰν τοῦ αἰτίου τῆς τῶν ἐ. ἀποχῆς τῶν ἀπὸ τοῦ Πυθαγόρου καὶ τῶν ἐν ἡμῖν ἀσκητῶν· ἐκεῖνοι μὲν γὰρ διὰ τὸν περὶ ψυχῆς μετενσωματουμένης μῦθον ἐ. ἀπέχονται·...ἡμεῖς δὲ κἂν τὸ τοιοῦτο πράττωμεν, ποιοῦμεν αὐτό, ἐπεὶ ὑπωπιάζομεν τὸ σῶμα Or.*Cels*.5.49(p.53.27; 1257C); by Gnostics and Marcionites τῶν λεγομένων παρ' αὐτοῖς ἐ. ἀποχὴν εἰσηγήσαντο, ἀχαριστοῦντες τῷ πάντα πεποιηκότι θεῷ Iren.*haer*.1. 28.1(M.7.690B); *ib*.1.24.2(675D); Ebionites ὅταν δὲ ἐρωτήσῃς ἕνα τῶν αὐτῶν, τίνος ἕνεκεν ἐ. οὐ μεταλαμβάνουσι,...λέγουσι διὰ τὸ ἐκ συνουσίας ...εἶναι αὐτὰ οὐ μεταλαμβάνομεν Epiph.*haer*.30.15(p.353.4; M.41. 432B); Valesians, to avoid sexual stimulation, *ib*.58.1(p.358.16; 1012B); **2.** *having* a rational *soul*; **a.** of Christ, agst. Apoll. ἀδύνατον τὸν τῇ φύσει ἀπαθῆ παθεῖν...μὴ ἑνωθέντα σώματι ἐ., τῷ δυναμένῳ παθεῖν ἑκουσίως ‡Ath.*dial.Trin.*4.2(M.28.1252C); θεότης σαρκὶ ἐ. κεχρημένη Bas.*ep.*236.1(3.361D; M.32.877C); εἰ δὲ ἔ. [sc. ὁ ἄνθρωπος], εἰ μὲν οὐ νοερός, πῶς καὶ ἄνθρωπος; Gr.Naz.*ep.*101(M.37.184A); Cyr.*Pulch.*(p.27.12; 5^{2}.129E) cit. s. θεοτόκος; Mod.*dorm.*5 (M.86.3289C) cit. s. ἔννοος; Jo.D.*disp.*(M.96.1345A); Jo.V H.*icon.*7 (M.96.1356A); witness of tradition that Christ is ἔ., Socr.*h.e.*3.7.5ff. (M.67.392A); **b.** ref. evil οὐχὶ οὐσία ζῶσα καὶ ἔ. Bas.*hex.*2.4(1.16C; M.29.37D).

***ἐμψυχοφαγία, ἡ,** *eating of animal food* Ἐγκρατῖται...πᾶσαν δὲ ἀπαγορεύοντες ἐ. Epiph.*anac.*47(p.211.6; M.41.845D); Jo.D.*haer.*47 (M.94.705B).

ἐμψυχ-όω, perf. ptcpl. pass., *animate*; *possessed of a soul*; Christol.; **1.** usual formula τῆς σαρκός, ἧς ἥνωσεν ἑαυτῷ, τῆς ~ωμένης ψυχῇ λογικῇ Diod.*Ps.*71:8(M.33.1611B); Cyr.*ep.*4(p.26.27; 5^{2}.23B); Just.Imp.*edict.*(p.200.14; M.86.2800A); **2.** ref. Arian and Apollinarian controversies, ref. Mt.26:38, Lc.23:46 γέγονεν ἄνθρωπος ὁ μονογενής, οὐκ ἄψυχόν τε καὶ ἄνουν σῶμα λαβών, ~ωμένον δὲ μᾶλλον ψυχῇ λογικῇ Cyr.*Pulch.*(p.58.34; 5^{2}.176C); ref. Heb.2:14, id.*Heb.*2:14 (p.463.14; M.74.964C); τὸν ἐνανθρωπήσαντα οὐ μόνον ἔνσαρκον ἀλλὰ καὶ ~ωμένον Socr.*h.e.*3.7.2(M.67.392A, v.l. ἐψυχωμένον); τῶν γὰρ Ἀρειανῶν παντάπασιν ἄψυχον λεγόντων τὴν τοῦ κυρίου σάρκα αὐτὸς ὁ Ἀπολινάριος ἔφη, ὅτι σάρκα μὲν ~ωμένην ψυχῇ ζωτικῇ ἀνέλαβεν ὁ κύριος, νοῦν δὲ τὸν ἡμέτερον οὐ προσήκατο Thdr.Raith.*praep.*(p.188.2; M.91.1488A).

ἐν, A. *in*; **1.** *in* a book ἐν τῷ νόμῳ φησίν Ath.*decr.*6(p.6.4; M.25.'433'(425)B); ἐν τῷ Ποιμένι γέγραπται *ib.*18(p.15.19; '456'(448)A); id.*syn.*38(p.264.23; M.26.760B); *in* [i.e. occupied by, immersed in] affairs, Thdt.*ep.*96(4.1167); **2.** *in* a spiritual condition ἐν γνώσει γενόμενος Clem.*ecl.*15(p.141.6; M.9.705A); ἐν τῇ τελειώσει τοῦ βαπτίσματος Ath.*Ar.*2.41(M.26.233A); τῶν ἐν πίστει opp. catechumens, Chrys.*hom.4.4 in Phil.*(11.218A); hence of union with God in Christian life ἵνα ὠφεληθῶσιν οἱ παρόντες λαοὶ...διὰ τοῦ μονογενοῦς... ἐν ἁγίῳ πνεύματι Serap.*euch.*1.4; ἐν τῷ υἱῷ καὶ ἐν πατρὶ ἐσόμεθα, καὶ νομισθησόμεθα ἐν υἱῷ καὶ ἐν πατρὶ ἓν γεγενῆσθαι διὰ τὸ ἐν ἡμῖν εἶναι πνεῦμα, ὅπερ ἐστὶν ἐν τῷ λόγῳ τῷ ὄντι ἐν τῷ πατρί Ath.*Ar.*3.25(M.26.376C); Bas.*Spir.*63(3.53B; M.32.184C) cit. s. μετά; exeg. Jo.17:11 ἐν τῷ ὀνόματί σου· τουτέστι διὰ τῆς σῆς βοηθείας Chrys.*hom.51.2 in Jo.*(8.480C); exeg. Jo.17:22 γίνεται...ἐν ἡμῖν ὁ υἱός, σωματικῶς μὲν ὡς ἄνθρωπος...πνευματικῶς δὲ...ὡς θεός, τῇ τοῦ ἰδίου πνεύματος ἐνεργείᾳ Cyr.*Jo.*11.12(4.1001E); but ἐν Χριστῷ used also to mean simply *Christian* τῆς ἐν Χριστῷ παιδείας *1Clem.*21.8; οἱ ἐν Χριστῷ πιστοί Ath.*inc.*21.1(M.25.132C); id.*h.Ar.*25(p.196.28; M.25.721C); and ἐν κυρίῳ used as epistolary formula of greetings, id.*ep.encycl.*(p.169.2; M.25.221A); Jul.Papa *ep.Dian.*ap.eund.*apol.sec.*35(p.113.25; M.25.308C); **3.** theol.; **a.** ref. relation of Persons of Trin.; **i.** abs. ἐν μόνῳ τῷ...πατρὶ ὅλος ὤν [sc. ὁ λόγος] Ath.*inc.*17.1(M.25.125B); μίαν...θεότητα, ἐμπεριέχουσαν δι' υἱοῦ ἐν πνεύματι ἁγίῳ τὰ πάντα Geo. Laod.*ep.dogm.*ap.Epiph.*haer.*73.16(p.289.1; M.42.433A); τριάς... πατὴρ ἐν υἱῷ, υἱὸς ἐν πατρί, σὺν ἁγίῳ πνεύματι CIllyr.*ep.*ap.Thdt.*h.e.*4.9.6(3.962); εἷς θεὸς ὁ πατὴρ ὁ ἐν υἱῷ καὶ...πνεύματι γνωριζόμενος, εἷς θεὸς ὁ υἱὸς ὁ ἐν πατρὶ καὶ...πνεύματι δοξαζόμενος, εἷς θεὸς τὸ πνεῦμα...ὁ ἐν πατρὶ καὶ υἱῷ προσκυνούμενος *A.Barth.*7(p.144.25); ὁ πατὴρ...ἔστιν ἐν υἱῷ καὶ υἱὸς ἐν πατρί· οὐχ ὡς ταὐτὸν δὲ ὄντες, οὐδὲ ὡς ἓν ἀριθμῷ Cyr.ap.*cat.Heb.*1:8(p.354.6); ref. H. Ghost as in Father and Son, v. πνεῦμα; (Arian) ὁ υἱὸς μετοχῇ τοῦ πνεύματος καὶ βελτιώσει πράξεως γέγονε καὶ αὐτὸς ἐν τῷ πατρί Ath.*Ar.*3.24(M.26.376A); (Sabellian) ὡς ποιότητα εἶναι ἐν τῷ πατρὶ τὴν σοφίαν ‡Ath.*Ar.*4.4(p.48.12; M.26.473A); **ii.** in creation and preservation ἐν αὐτῷ [sc. τῷ λόγῳ] τὸν πατέρα δεδημιουργηκέναι τὴν κτίσιν Ath.*inc.*41.4 (M.25.168C); πάντα ἐκ θεοῦ εἶναι, καὶ πάντα διὰ τοῦ μονογενοῦς καὶ ἐν αὐτῷ συνεστάναι Gr.Nyss.*ep.*24(M.46.1093B); ref. Col.1:16 (Eunomian) Παῦλος οὐ 'δι' αὐτοῦ' φησὶν ἀλλ' 'ἐν αὐτῷ' ἵνα τοῖς δι' αὐτοῦ γενομένοις καὶ αὐτὸς συμπαραληφθείς, πᾶσι γνωρίζῃ...τὴν τοῦ πατρὸς ἐνέργειαν Eun.*apol.*24(M.30.860D); **iii.** Father revealed in Son Χριστός...τὸ ἀψευδὲς στόμα ἐν ᾧ ὁ πατὴρ ἀληθῶς ἐλάλησεν Ign.*Rom.*8.2; τὸν λόγον ἰδών, ὁρᾷ ἐν αὐτῷ καὶ τὸν τοῦ λόγου πατέρα Ath.*gent.*2(M.25.8A); Sever.*Heb.*1:2(p.346.12); **iv.** in redemption δι' οὗ ταύτην [sc. κτίσιν] ἐδημιούργησεν ὁ πατήρ, ἐν αὐτῷ καὶ τὴν ταύτης σωτηρίαν εἰργάσατο Ath.*inc.*1.4(M.25.97C); ἐν αὐτῷ τὰ πάντα ἀνακαινισθῆναι id.*hom.in Mt.11*:27(M.25.212B); id.*Ar.*1.49(M.26.113C); δι' αὐτοῦ καὶ ἐν αὐτῷ ἐνεργεῖσθαι ἡμῖν τὴν χάριν ταύτην Bas.*Spir.*16(3.13C; M.32.93C); **b.** in doxologies; **i.** *in* the Son, *A.Thom.*A 132(p.239.26) cit. s. δόξα; δοξάζειν ἡμῶν τὸν κύριον ἐν Χριστῷ Ἰησοῦ τῷ κυρίῳ ἡμῶν CHier.(350)*ep.*(p.137.15; M.25.352C); ὥσπερ οὖν δι' αὐτοῦ ἀποκαλύπτεται ὁ θεὸς τοῖς γινώσκουσιν, οὕτως...ἡ δόξα καὶ τὸ κράτος ὁμολογεῖται τῷ πατρὶ δι' αὐτοῦ καὶ ἐν αὐτῷ Ath.*ep.Serap.*2.6(M.26.617C); δόξα πατρὶ ἐν υἱῷ σὺν ἁγίῳ πνεύματι Epiph.*haer.*76.53(p.409.10; M.42.629B); but this later regarded as heret. οἱ μὲν πατέρα καὶ υἱὸν ὡς ὁμότιμον ἐδόξαζον· οἱ δὲ πατέρα ἐν υἱῷ, τῇ παρενθέσει τῆς προθέσεως, δευτερεύειν τὸν υἱὸν ἀποφαίνοντες Soz.*h.e.*3.20.8(M.67.1101A); **ii.** *in* H. Ghost τὴν εὐχὴν εἰς δοξολογίαν θεοῦ διὰ Χριστοῦ ἐν ἁγίῳ πνεύματι καταπαυστέον Or.*or.*33.1(p.401.25; M.11.560A); *ib.*33.6 (p.402.34; 562A) cit. s. δοξάζω; Serap.*euch.*5.11 cit. s. δόξα; Ath.*ep.Aeg.Lib.*23(M.25.593A); δοξασθήσεται ὁ θεὸς διὰ Χριστοῦ ἐν τῷ ἁγίῳ πνεύματι *Can.App.*34; δόξα τῷ θεῷ ἐν πνεύματι καὶ ἀληθείᾳ *Const.App.*4.5.4; Bas.*Spir.*3(3.3D; M.32.72C) cit. s. μετά; explanation ἡ...δοξολογία...'ἐν τῷ πνεύματι' οὐχὶ τῆς ἐκείνου ἀξίας ὁμολογίαν ἔχει, ἀλλὰ τῆς ἡμετέρας αὐτῶν ἀσθενείας ἐξομολόγησιν, δεικνύντων ὅτι οὔτε δοξάσαι ἀφ' ἑαυτῶν ἱκανοί ἐσμεν, ἀλλ' ἡ ἱκανότης ἡμῶν ἐν τῷ πνεύματι *ib.*63(53B; M.184C); ὥσπερ ἐν τῷ υἱῷ ὁρᾶται ὁ πατήρ, οὕτως ὁ υἱὸς ἐν τῷ πνεύματι...ὥσπερ οὖν ἐν τῷ υἱῷ προσκύνησιν λέγομεν τὴν ὡς ἐν εἰκόνι τοῦ θεοῦ καὶ πατρός, οὕτω καὶ ἐν τῷ πνεύματι ὡς ἐν ἑαυτῷ δεικνύντι τὴν τοῦ κυρίου θεότητα *ib.*64(53D; M.185A); formula not found in scripture, *ib.*58(49C; M.176A); adopted by Arius δοξολογεῖν...διδάξας τὸν πατέρα διὰ τοῦ υἱοῦ ἐν ἁγίῳ πνεύματι... δοξάζειν δὲ κατὰ τὸν τοῦ βαπτίσματος διεκώλυσε νόμον Thdt.*haer.*4.1 (4.350); by Eunomians τῷ δὲ υἱῷ...ἀφώρισαν τὸ 'δι' οὗ', τῷ δὲ ἁγίῳ πνεύματι, τὸ 'ἐν ᾧ'· καί φασι μηδέποτε τὴν χρῆσιν ταύτην τῶν συλλαβῶν ἐπαμείβεσθαι. τὸ μὲν γὰρ 'ἐξ οὗ' τὸν δημιουργὸν σημαίνειν βούλονται· τὸ δὲ 'δι' οὗ' τὸν ὑπουργόν, ἢ τὸ ὄργανον· τὸ δὲ 'ἐν ᾧ' τὸν χρόνον δηλοῦν ἢ τὸν τόπον, ἵνα μηδὲν...τῆς ἀπὸ τόπου ἢ χρόνου συνεισφορᾶς εἰς τὰ ὄντα πλεῖον φαίνηται τὸ πνεῦμα...περιεχόμενον Bas.*Spir.*4(3.4C; M.73Bf.); οἱ λέγοντες 'δόξα πατρὶ δι' υἱοῦ ἐν ἁγίῳ πνεύματι' οὐ δοξάζουσι τὸν υἱὸν ἢ τὸ πνεῦμα τοῦ θεοῦ Didym.*Trin.*1.34 (M.39.436B); οἱ λέγοντες δόξα πατρὶ δι' υἱοῦ ἐν...ἁγίῳ πνεύματι οἱ καὶ κτίσμα αὐτὸν εἶναι...δοξάζοντες *ib.*1.32(428B); τὸν Ἀντιοχείας Φλαβιανὸν...πρῶτον ἀναβοῆσαι 'δόξα πατρὶ καὶ υἱῷ καὶ ἁγίῳ πνεύματι'. τῶν γὰρ πρὸ αὐτοῦ τοὺς μὲν 'δόξα πατρὶ δι' υἱοῦ ἐν ἁγίῳ πνεύματι' λέγειν...τοὺς δὲ 'δόξα πατρὶ καὶ υἱῷ ἐν ἁγίῳ πνεύματι' Philost.*h.e.*3.13(M.65.501B); and by Macedonians οἱ μὲν λέγοντες, 'δόξα πατρὶ δι' υἱοῦ ἐν ἁγίῳ πνεύματι'· οἱ δὲ 'δόξα πατρὶ καὶ υἱῷ ἐν ἁγίῳ πνεύματι'· καὶ οὕτως τὴν ἀδιαίρετον...θεότητα εἰς τριθεΐαν παραλαμβάνουσιν, μᾶλλον δὲ παραδιδόασι μέγαν καὶ σμικρὸν καὶ σμικρότερον Thdt.*Ps.*57:6(1.985); τοὺς μὲν τὸν 'καί' σύνδεσμον ἐπὶ τῆς τοῦ υἱοῦ δοξολογίας τιθέντας, τοὺς δὲ τὴν μὲν 'δι' οὗ' πρόθεσιν ἐπὶ τοῦ υἱοῦ, τὴν δὲ 'ἐν' ἐπὶ τοῦ πνεύματος προσαρμόζοντας id.*h.e.*2.24.3(3.888); for comparison with σύν v.s.v.; **iii.** *in* Church αὐτῷ ἡ δόξα...ἅμα πατρὶ καὶ ἁγίῳ πνεύματι ἐν τῇ ἁγίᾳ ἐκκλησίᾳ Hipp.*Noët.*18(p.265.30; M.10.829B); cf.id.*trad.ap.*4.13; **4.** Christol. ἀνέστη οὐχ ὁ θεὸς ἐν τῷ ἀνθρώπῳ, ἀλλ' ὁ ἄνθρωπος ἐν τῷ θεῷ CSard.*ep.cath.*ap.Thdt.*h.e.*2.8.49 (3.847); (Apollinarian) οὐκ ἐγένετο ἄνθρωπος ὁ υἱός...ἀλλ' ἐν ἀνθρώπῳ ‡Ath.*dial.Trin.*4.8(M.28.1261C); for controversy over ἐκ δύο φύσεων and ἐν δυσὶ φύσεσι v. φύσις.

B. in pregnant constr., *into, on to*, phrase ἐν ἔργῳ χωρεῖν put *into* effect, Eus.*h.e.*10.8.19(M.20.901A); τὸν ἔλαιον κατέχεεν ἐν τῇ κεφαλῇ αὐτῆς *A.Thom.*A 121(p.230.22); or simply *to* ἦλθεν ἐν αὐτῷ [sc. τῷ σταυρῷ] *A.Andr.*B 4(p.60.12).

C. *in the form of* ἐν τετραγώνῳ ᾠκοδομεῖτο Herm.*vis.*3.2.5; Ath.*gent.*8(M.25.17A); *ib.*29(60A).

D. *by reason of* δέδεμαι ἐν τῷ ὀνόματι Ign.*Eph.*3.1; ἐν τούτῳ...ἀποροῦμαι Herm.*sim.*8.3.1; *as a result of* ἐκκλησίᾳ...ἀγαλλιωμένῃ ἐν τῷ πάθει τοῦ κυρίου ἡμῶν Ign.*Philad.*proem.; τὰ ὦτά σου κωφὰ ἐν ἀλγήσει *A.Phil.*73(p.29.7); c. infin., *in that, inasmuch as* πιστὸς εὑρέθη ἐν τῷ αὐτὸν ὑπήκοον γενέσθαι *1Clem.*10.1; *ib.*3.4; κύριος ἦν...ἐν τῷ ποιεῖν αὐτά Ath.*hom.in Mt.11*:27(M.25.209B); id.*inc.*5.4(M.25.105B).

E. *for the purpose of* τί...οὐκ ἀπέδωκας ἡμᾶς ἐν ἄλλῃ παιδείᾳ; *Apoc.Bar.*1(p.85.13); *A.Thom.*A 32(p.149.15); hence simply *for* τὸν περὶ τῆς οἰκονομίας λόγον ἐν τῷ μετὰ τοῦτον φυλάξομεν λόγῳ Thdt.*haer.*4.8 (4.363); also in expressions of time ἐν καιρῷ τῷ προσήκοντι... τηρῆσαι διδασκαλίαν Chrys.*hom.17.1 in Mt.*(7.222C).

F. *by means of, by* (cf. Hebr. בְּ) ἀδικήσουσιν ἐν ῥομφαίᾳ *T.Sym.*5.4; ἡγιασμένοις ἐν θελήματι θεοῦ *1Clem.*proem.; ἀναζωπυρήσαντες ἐν αἵματι θεοῦ Ign.*Eph.*1.1; *A.Mt.*18(p.240.7); ἐν λίθῳ...ὤλεσεν τὸν Γολιάθ ‡Petr.I Al.*phys.*22(p.54); 'ἐν ἁγιασμῷ πνεύματος...' ἰδοὺ τό, ἐν, πάλαι, διά, ἐστι Chrys.*hom.4.2 in 2Thess.*(11.531E); τό, ἐν υἱῷ, διὰ τοῦ υἱοῦ, φησι id.*hom.1.1 in Heb.*(12.6B).

G. *at* a time, *Pss.Sal.*16.3; ἐν τῷ τῆς νυκτὸς παρελθεῖν *A.Barth.*4 (p.134.25).

ἐναβρύν-ομαι (*ἐναμβρύνομαι), 1. *be conceited, plume oneself* ὑποκριτῶν...ἔργον ἐστὶ τὸ ~εσθαι ἐπ' εὐσεβείᾳ θέλειν Or.*or.*19(p.341.30; M.11.476C); τὴν εὐχὴν προφέρω μὴ ~όμενος μηδὲ ἐγκαυχώμενος, ἀλλ' ὡς ταπεινοφρονῶν Eus.*d.e.*10.8(p.479.21; M.22.772A); Μωσῆς καὶ Ἠλίας...ἐφ' οἷς ἀναπαύεσθε καὶ ~εσθε Leont.B *mesopent.*(M.86. 1981C); †Jo.D.*B.J.*33(M.96.480C); ἐναμβρύνομαι Or.*adnot.in Dt.* 14:19(M.17.25B); Ephr.3.283B; **2.** *glory, exult,* Afric.*ep.Arist.*5 (p.66.19; M.10.61A); Eus.*v.C.*1.9(p.11.10; M.20.921A); Chrys.*hom. 1.5 in Rom.16:3*(3.179D); Δαυὶδ...τῇ κοινωνίᾳ τῶν παθημάτων [sc. of Christ] ~όμενος Thdr.Mops.*Ps.*54(M.66.677B); of S. Paul glorying in tribulations, Chrys.*comm.in Gal.*6:17(10.729D); Thdt.*Eph.* 4:1(3.421); of glorying in Cross ~όμενος τῷ νικητικῷ τροπαίῳ Eus. *v.C.*3.2(p.78.6; 1056C); Cyr.H.*catech.*13.41; of Christ ὃς τοῖς τῆς... θεότητος ~εται θώκοις Cyr.*Nest.*4.6(p.89.24; 6^1.116D); id.*hom.pasch.* 19(5^2.256E); ἐπὶ τὸ θεοπρεπὲς αὐτοῦ ἀνατρέχει ἀξίωμα ~όμενος τοῖς φυσικοῖς αὐτοῦ πλεονεκτήμασι διὰ τὸ χρήσιμον τῶν πιστῶν id.*Jo.*7 (4.666E); οὐ...σωματικοῖς...καὶ τοπικοῖς ὑψώμασιν ~εσθαι τὸν υἱὸν ἐροῦμεν id.*thes.*32(5^1.320D); τοῖς φυσικοῖς ἀξιώμασι τοῦ γεννήσαντος ~εται *ib.*(328E).

***ἐναγαλλιάομαι,** *rejoice in,* Bas.*reg.fus.*6(2.345A; M.31.928A); †Bas.*Is.*166(1.498B; M.30.393B); †Diad.*Ar.*8(M.65.1164B).

***ἐναγάλλομαι,** = foreg., Eus.*e.th.*3.16(p.174.26; M.24.1033A); Nil. *Eulog.*17(M.79.1116B); ‡Proc.G.*Pr.*8:30(M.87.1297C).

ἐναγελάζ-ομαι, *assemble like a flock in* λαοὺς...μυριάνδρους ταῖς Χριστοῦ ποίμναις ~εσθαι Eus.*v.C.*4.8(p.120.32; M.20.1157A).

ἐναγής, 1. *polluted, accursed,* opp. holy θεὸς ἅγιον μόνον οἶδεν τὸ τοῦ δικαίου ἦθος, ὥσπερ ἐ. τὸ ἄδικον καὶ μοχθηρόν Clem.*str.*7.4(p.19. 8; M.9.433B); of bloodshed, Chrys.*hom.33.3 in Mt.*(7.381A); id. *hom.85.3 in Jo.*(8.507D); of crime of Christ's death, Or.*Jo.*28. 25(20; p.422.15; M.14.736B); *ib.*(p.422.21; 736C); Eus.*theoph.fr.*12 (p.26*.23; M.24.644A); of Judas ὦ μιαρὲ...ἐ. καὶ βέβηλε Chrys.*hom. 81.2 in Mt.*(775B); of impiety in gen., Eus.*v.C.*1.13(p.14.6; M.20. 928A); esp. of pagan sacrifices, Const.*or.s.c.*16(p.176.28; M.20. 1280C); Eus.*v.C.*3.26(p.89.34; 1085C); Thdt.*h.e.*1.16.5(3.791); of sin of Korah and similar contempt for priesthood, Chrys.*sac.*3.6(p.56. 14; 1.384B); of heresy and schism, Const.ap.Eus.*v.C.*3.65(p.112.21; 1141B); Eust.*fr.in Pr.8:22*(M.18.681C); †Cyr.*hom.div.*10(5^2.378D); of the excommunicated, Synes.*ep.*72(M.66.1436D); cf.Dion.Ar.*d.n.* 4.22(M.3.724C); of persecutors, Const.ap.Eus.*v.C.*3.52(p.99.24; 1113A); **2.** in gen.; *foul, abominable,* Chrys.*hom.7.5 in Rom.*(9. 490C); *ib.4.3*(458C); id.*hom.42.4 in Jo.*(8.254A); Isid.Pel.*epp.*2.127 (M.78.568C); Philost.*h.e.*2.11(p.24.6; M.65.476A); of Constantine in heathen polemic, ‡Jo.D.*Artem.*43(p.15.28; M.96.1292B); **3.** *impure, sinful* οὐ τολμῶ ὀφθαλμοῖς ἐ. ὁρᾶν τῶν ἁγίων τὰ ἅγια *cat.Lc.*15:20 (p.119.25); of corruptible things of sense opp. things of the spirit, Dion.Ar.*myst.*1.3(M.3.1000C); id.*e.h.*6.3.6(M.3.537A); of passions, *ib.*3.3.11(441B); of prayers offered by unworthy priest, id.*ep.*8.2 (M.3.1092C).

***ἐναγιάζω, 1.** *bind under a curse* τὸ καθ' ἡμῶν χειρόγραφον, ὃ ἐνηγιάσμεθα ἀποτιννύναι Diod.*Ps.*68:5(M.33.1604A); **2.** *sanctify* οὐχὶ ἐνηγιάσθαι παρὰ τοῦ...πατρὸς ἑαυτὸν ἔφη...ὁ Ἐμμανουήλ Cyr.*ador.*11 (1.388B); *ib.*(388C).

ἐναγκαλίζ-ομαι, 1. *take in one's arms, embrace;* in gen., *A. Xanthipp.*7(p.62.20); Bas.*hom.*21.9(2.170E; M.31.557B); Nil.*epp.*4.60 (M.79.577A); of Symeon, Cyr.H.*catech.*12.32; Gr.Naz.*or.*39.14(M.36. 349C); ἐ. κράτος ἀνεκδιήγητον ‡Meth.*Sym.et Ann.*7(M.18.364B); as gesture of reverence, Jo.D.*hom.*9.5(M.96.729D); of God πᾶσαν ἐγκόσμιόν τε καὶ ὑπερκόσμιον ἐνηγκάλισται κτίσιν Gr.Nyss.*or.dom.*3 (p.52.3; M.44.1152C); **2.** met., *embrace, welcome* τὸν ἐναγκαλισάμενόν σου τὰς εὐχὰς καὶ...ὑπακούσαντα *A.Xanthipp.*13(p.66.34); τὴν μακροθυμίαν τῆς ἀγάπης ~ου Nil.*Eulog.*7(M.79.1104A); *Apophth. Patr.*(M.65.105B); †Bas.Sel.*or.*41(M.85.468A); **3.** *embrace, contain, ib.*(461D).

ἐναγλαΐζ-ω, 1. *adorn, illumine, glorify,* Gr.Nyss.*hom.4 in Cant.* (M.44.840A); ‡Nil.*fr.pasch.*2(M.79.1496D); ‡Meth.*Sym.et Ann.*7(M. 18.364C); **2.** med.; **a.** *adorn oneself with,* met. ἀλλοτρίοις ~εσθαι πόνοις Isid.Pel.*epp.*3.183(M.78.873B); **b.** *glory in,* Cyr.*glaph.Gen.*1 (1.18A); id.*Jo.*1.9(4.74B).

ἐναγρυπνέω, 1. *be vigilant in, devote oneself to,* Andr.Cr.*or.*19(M. 97.1216A); **2.** *watch, be awake* καθεύδων...ἡ καρδία τούτου ἐνηγρύπνει Germ.CP *or.*1(M.98.241A).

***ἐνάγχω,** *strangle;* met., *press,* Chrys.*hom.1.3 in Rom.16:3*(3. 176C).

ἐνάγ-ω, 1. *impel, urge* τοιαῦτα...φρονεῖν...ἡ αὐτοῦ περὶ τὸν θεὸν ἐνῆγεν ὁσία Eus.*v.C.*2.45(p.60.15; M.20.1021C); **2.** *lead into some habit* or *belief, initiate, instruct* Ἰουδαΐζοντας ἀνθρώπους ~ειν εἰς πίστιν Chrys.*comm.in Gal.*1:1(10.660E); αὐτός με ὁ νόμος ἐνήγαγεν εἰς τὸ μηκέτι προσέχειν αὐτῷ *ib.*2:19(692A); id.*hom.54.4 in Mt.*(7. 551C); ἐδίδασκε ὁ Παῦλος, ἀλλ' ἐνάξει ὁ θεός. καὶ οὐκ εἶπεν 'ἐνάξει', ἀλλ' 'ἀποκαλύψει' id.*hom.12.2 in Phil.*(11.293B); of Christ οὐκ ἀγνοοῦντος ἡ ἐρώτησις, ἀλλ' ἐπὶ τὴν αἴσθησιν τῆς ἑαυτοῦ δυνάμεως ~οντος Thdr.Mops.*Mt.*15:34(M.66.709D); of education, Chrys. *hom.9.3 in Col.*(11.392E); **3.** *bring into court, prosecute, T.Jos.*13.4; οἱ...~οντες μὲν ἦσαν Ἰουδαῖοι, οἱ δὲ κρίνοντες Ῥωμαῖοι Mac.Mgn. *apocr.*2.17(p.29.12); μητροπολίτης...~όμενος παρὰ τῷ ἰδίῳ κρινέσθω πατριάρχῃ Ath.Scholast.*coll.*1.2(p.10); *accuse,* Eus.Nic.*libell.*(p.65. 15; M.67.113A); Leo Mag.*ep.*44(p.26.5; M.*PL.*54.830A).

ἐναγωγή, ἡ, 1. *introduction, inception,* Cyr.*Joel.*15(3.214C, v.l. ἐπαγωγαῖς); **2.** *accusation, charge,* Dioscorus ap.CChalc.*act.*2(*ACO* 2.1.2 p.14.11; H.2.320C); Eus.Dor.*ib.*(p.14.37; H.321A); of Christ δέχεσθαί τε ἐ. ὑπὸ τῶν ἰδίων κτισμάτων Cosm.Ind.*top.*5(M.88.252D).

***ἐναγωγός, ὁ,** *litigant, opponent in law-suit,* Diad.*perf.*63(p.74. 17) = Ant.Mon.*hom.*12(M.89.1465C).

***ἐναγωνιάω,** *be agonized,* Gr.Nyss.*v.Gr.Thaum.*(M.46.949A).

ἐναγώνιος, A. from ἀγών; **1.** *full of conflicts* or *labours* ἐ. ἀρεταῖς καθαρθέντες Didym.*Trin.*3.34(M.39.960Cn.); Mac.Mgn.*apocr.*2.7 (p.4.3); ἐ. εἶναι χρὴ τὸν βίον τὸν ἡμέτερον Chrys.*hom.2.3 in 2Cor.*(10. 432A); id.*comm.in Gal.*1:17(10.677A); id.*hom.5.4 in Heb.*(12.58C); **2.** *in conflict, struggling,* id.*hom.41.4 in 1Cor.*(10.392D); πάθος ἐ. Mac.Mgn.*apocr.*2.7(p.5.23); Nil.*exerc.*51(M.79.781C); **3.** *strenuous, ready for action,* Chrys.*hom.15.7 in Mt.*(7.195A); id.*hom.21.1 in Rom.*(9.664B); id.*stat.*16.5(2.168A); Diad.*perf.*62(p.72.19); **4.** *ready for fighting,* Synes.*ep.*67(M.66.1413A); *pugnacious;* of style, Isid. Pel.*epp.*2.146(M.78.592A).

B. from ἀγωνία; **1.** *in agony,* ref. Judgement πᾶσα ἡ κτίσις ἐ. ... καὶ οἱ δίκαιοι ἐ. ‡Gr.Nyss.*or.2 in Gen.1:26*(M.44.289A); of Christ in Gethsemane, Chrys.*hom.63.2 in Jo.*(8.377D); in gen., id.*hom.45.4 in Gen.*(4.462C); id.*hom.9.5 in Heb.*(12.99D); id.*hom.8.1 in Phil.* (11.257B); **2.** *anxious, careful,* id.*hom.11.3 in Mt.*(7.152E); id.*hom. 4.4 in 2Cor.*(10.460B); ἄδηλον...τὸ μέλλον, ἵνα ἐ. διηνεκῶς ὦμεν id. *Laz.*2.3(1.730C); Soz.*h.e.*4.9.7(M.67.1129C); Rom.Mel.(*AS* 1 p.213).

***ἐναγῶς,** *impurely* τῶν ἐ. ἐνεργουμένων Dion.Ar.*e.h.*4.3.3(M.3. 477A).

***ἐναδεφένδευτος,** *undefended,* Ath.Scholast.*coll.*13.3(p.146) prob. error for ἐὰν ἀδεφενδεύτους.

ἐναδιαφορέω, 1. *be indifferent* to, πρὸς τὴν εἰδωλολατρείαν Or. *Cels.*6.11(p.81.22; M.11.1308A); c. dat., Bas.*hom.*5.8(2.41D; M.31. 257A); id.*ep.*289(3.428A; M.32.1028A); **2.** *use indifferently* ἐ. τοῖς ὀνόμασιν Leont.B.*arg.Sev.*(M.86.1925B).

ἐναδικός, *single* τὴν ἐ. οὐσίαν τῆς ἁπλῆς καὶ μοναδικῆς...θεότητος ‡Gr.Nyss.*hom.6.79 in Jo.*(p.226.2); neut. as subst. τὸ ἐ. ... τῆς πατρικῆς θεότητος Didym.*Trin.*1.15(M.39.313B).

***ἐναδρύν-ομαι,** *mature;* of embryo Melet.*nat.hom.*synops.(M.64. 1084C); met., *mature in* ψυχῇ...τῇ θεωρίᾳ τοῦ ὄντος ~θεῖσα Gr.Nyss. *infant.*(M.46.180D).

ἐνάερος, *borne through the air,* Germ.CP *or.*8(M.98.368D).

[*]**ἐναθλεύω,** *struggle with,* c. dat., Gr.Naz.*or.*4.122(M.35.661B).

ἐναθλέω, *struggle bravely in* ἀγῶνα Eus.*p.e.*11.6(519A; M.21.860D); c. dat., id.*Ps.*127:2(M.24.21B); esp. under martyrdom, *bear up, suffer bravely,* id.*Is.*62:1–3(M24.497C); Bas.*hom.*18.2(2.143B; M.31. 493B); Gr.Nyss.*v.Gr.Thaum.*(M.46.949A); id.*v.Macr.*(p.371.27; M. 46.961A); Proc.G.*Is.*19:16–25(M.87.2153B).

ἔναθλος, *of the contest,* i.e. martyrdom, Andr.Cr.*or.*17(M.97. 1192C).

ἐναθύρ-ω, *play with, make game of* τοῖς τῆς ἀληθείας ~οντες λόγοις Cyr.*hom.pasch.*16.5(5^2.219B); id.*glaph.Gen.*6(1.203E).

ἔναι, = ἐστί, εἰσί: ὁ θεῖός σου ἔναι πλούσιος Barth.Edess.*Agar.* (M.104.1421D); *ib.*(1440B); τί ἔν' ἀδελφοί; Dam.*troph.*3.4(p.243.1).

ἔναιμος, neut. as subst., *vigour* τὸ ἔ. καὶ ζωτικόν Or.*schol.in Cant.* 4:3(M.17.269D).

***ἐναίσθητος,** *endowed with sense* or *intelligence,* Thdr.Stud.*epp.* 2.94(M.99.1345C).

***ἐνακολουθέω,** *follow, observe,* Anast.S.*haer.*(p.267).

***ἐνακροάομαι,** *listen to,* Bas.*renunt.*8(2.209B; M.31.641C).

ἐναλίσκομαι, 1. *be entangled, caught;* met., Gr.Nyss.*hom.opif.*21 (M.44.201C); Cyr.*Abac.*24(3.538B); id.*glaph.Ex.*2(1.294A); θεὸς... μόνος ἐξέλοιτο ἂν ἐκ τῆς τοῦ διαβόλου χειρὸς τὸν ἐναλόντα νοῦν id. *ador.*1(1.13E); **2.** *be convicted in* ἰσορρόποις ἐναλῶναι δίκαις Cyr. *ador.*14(1.486D).

***ἐναλλάγεια, ἡ,** *change,* Sophr.H.*mir.Cyr.et Jo.*22(M.87.3485A).

ἐναλλαγή, ἡ, 1. *interchange; crossing* of hands, ref. Gen.48:14 as type of Cross, Isid.Pel.*epp.*1.362(M.78.388B); **2.** *change;* of life, Clem. *str.*4.11(p.283.25; M.8.1288C); ὅταν...ἀκούσῃς καινὴν ζωήν, πολλὴν ζήτει τὴν ἐ. Chrys.*hom.10.4 in Rom.*(9.526B); ref. Transfiguration οὐ...τοῦ χαρακτῆρος μεταβολήν τινα προσδοκητέον ἐν τῇ βασιλείᾳ...

ἀλλὰ φωτὸς προσθήκην...καὶ ταύτην εἶναι τὴν ἐ., ἥν ὁ Παῦλός φησι Vict.*Mc.*9:3(p.353.15); of change of priesthood from Aaronic to that of Christ, Thdt.*Heb.*7:11(3.588); **3.** *perversion*, Bas.*hom.*1.9(2.9A; M.31.181A).

ἐνάλλαγμα, τό, *change, alteration*, ‡Hipp.*fr.13 in Pss.*(p.143.2; M.10.720A).

ἐναλλάκτης, ὁ, ? *cross-beam*; part of a bedstead, *Ev.Thom.*A 13 (p.152).

ἐναλλάσσω, 1. *alternate, vary*, Eus.*h.e.*8.3.1(M.20.748B); Chrys.*hom.49.3 in Mt.*(7.508B); id.*hom.29.3 in Rom.*(9.733E); pass., Eus.*m.P.*11(p.931.26; M.20.1441A); *cat.Jo.*6:35(p.249.29); **2.** *exchange*, Thdt.*eran.*1(4.26); *change* horses, id.*h.e.*2.32.2(3.911); **3.** *change, alter*, Clem.*paed.*2.7(p.190.26; M.8.457C); *Χαλδαίων...μυστήρια τοῖς ὀνόμασιν ἐναλλάξαντες* [sc. Gnostics] *αἵρεσιν ἔνθεν συνεστήσαντο* Hipp.*haer.*4.2(p.33.17; M.16.3059C); Meth.*arbitr.*15(p.185.5); Ath.*gent.*35(M.25.72A); **4.** *pervert* ἐνήλλαξαν τάξιν φύσεως αὐτῶν *T.Neph.*3.5; pass., Gr.Nyss.*ep.can.*(M.45.224D); **5.** pass., *be different*, Chrys.*hom.69.4 in Mt.*(7.685D); id.*hom.1.1 in 1Tim.*(11.550A); *V.Zos.*12(p.104.22); perf. ptcpl. pass., *preposterous* ἐνηλλαγμένῳ τρόπῳ ἀπὸ τῆς προεδρίας τῶν ἰδίων ἐκκλησιῶν ἐξωθοῦνται ἀθῷοι ἱερεῖς Innoc.*ep.cler.*(M.52.537); **6.** intrans., *alternate*, Eus.*h.e.*8.9.3(M.20.760B); id.*l.C.*11(p.229.8; M.20.1385A).

ἐναλλοιόω, *alter, change*, of Transfiguration τὴν δὲ θέαν εἴδομεν ἐνηλλοιωμένην *A.Thom.*A 143(p.250.8); Gr.Nyss.*virg.*11(p.295.7; M.46.365D).

ἐνάλλ-ομαι, 1. *leap on, into* τὰ...πονηρὰ πνεύματα...ταῖς αἰσθήσεσι τοῦ σώματος ~ονταί τε καὶ ἐμφωλεύουσι Diad.*perf.*79(p.100.16); **2.** *leap, trample upon*, Chrys.*hom.11.5 in Rom.*(9.537B); Synes.*ep.*73(M.66.1440A); id.*Dion* 10(p.261.6; M.66.1141C); **3.** *exult in* or *over* θανάτῳ...~όμενος διάβολος Ath.*inc.*27.3(M.25.144A); Chrys.*hom.23.3 in Mt.*(7.287B); **4.** *burst into, intrude upon*, Synes.*provid.*2.5 (p.123.5; M.66.1272C).

***ἐναμαρεύομαι,** *follow*, as water in a conduit, ‡Caes.Naz.*dial.*191 (M.38.1169).

***ἐναμάρτητος, 1.** *liable to sin, peccable* τὸν κύριον...τὴν ἐ. φύσιν ἀναμαρτήτως δεξάμενον Isid.Pel.*epp.*1.193(M.78.305C); *Disp.Phot.*(M.88.572C); **2.** *sinful* ἐ. ἡδονή Mod.*occurs.*(M.86.3276C).

ἐνάμαρτος, *sinful*, ‡Nil.*perist.*9.1(M.79.864D); ἐ. ψυχή Marc.Er.*opusc.*2.75(M.65.941A); Ant.Mon.*hom.*25(M.89.1509D); neut. as subst., Tat.*orat.*19(p.22.7; M.6.849C).

ἐναμβλύνω, *deaden*; pass., *grow dull, become complacent* in τῷ ἀλλοτρίῳ ἐ. ὡς σῷ Nil.*spir.mal.*18(M.79.1164A).

***ἐναμβλυωπέω,** *be dim-sighted*, Gr.Nyss.*hom.7 in Cant.*(M.44.920A).

[*]**ἐναμβρύνομαι,** variant of ἐναβρύνομαι q.v.

ἐναμείβω, *change*, Didym.*Trin.*2.24(M.39.745A).

***ἐναμηχαν-έω,** *be at a loss, lose one's way in* ταῖς πολυοδίαις τοῦ βίου τούτου ~οῦντες Gr.Nyss.*hom.6 in Eccl.*(M.44.701C).

ἐναμιλλάομαι, *contend in*; met., c. dat., of moral struggle, Jo. D.*f.o.*4.4(M.94.1109B).

***ἐνανακλίνομαι,** *lie down, rest in*, c. dat.; met., of God in soul, Gr.Nyss.*hom.3 in Cant.*(M.44.821B).

***ἐνανακρύπτω,** *hide oneself from*, c. dat., *A.Thadd.*4(p.275.2 not.).

***ἐναναπαύ-ομαι,** *rest, repose in*, met., ref. Jo.13:23 Ἰωάννης... τοῖς μυστικωτέροις ~όμενος Or.*fr.77 in Lc.*(p.271.14); Mac.Aeg.*elev.*13(M.34.901C); Bas.*hom.in Ps.*14(1.352B; M.29.252B).

ἐνανθρωπ-έω, A. *become man, become incarnate*, ref. Inc. as **1.** of θεός, ref. goats of day of atonement οἱ δὲ δύο τὴν μίαν περιεῖχον τοῦ ~ήσαντος θεοῦ οἰκονομίαν ‡Just.*fr.*(M.6.1596B); θεὸς ὁ ὑπὲρ πάντα τὰ γένητα ἐνηνθρώπησεν Or.*Jo.*2.34(28; p.92.2; M.14.173C); id.*princ.*4.1.2(p.296.4; M.11.345B); Petr.I Al.*fr.*(M.18.521C)ap.Justn.*monoph.*(p.29.22); θεὸς ὢν ἐνηνθρώπησα δι' ὑμᾶς *A.Thom.*B 52(p.40.35); ὁ θεὸς οὖν ὁ ~ήσας...ἄκτιστος θεὸς κτιστῇ περιβολῇ φανερούμενος Apoll.*corp.et div.*6(p.187.15; M.*PL.*8.873D); Gr.Naz.*or.*7.23(M.35.785C) cit. s. ἀνασώζω; αὐτὸς γὰρ ὁμολογεῖ ἀληθὴς θεὸς...ὅταν δὲ περὶ ψυχῆς διηγεῖται, δείκνυσιν ἑαυτὸν ἀληθινῶς ~ήσαντα καὶ μὴ δοκήσει Epiph.*haer.*69.49(p.196.8; M.42.277B); τέλειος ἄνωθεν θεός, οὐκ ἐλθὼν κατοικῆσαι ἐν ἀνθρώπῳ, ἀλλ' αὐτὸς ὅλος ~ήσας...συμπεριειληφὼς...ἅμα τῇ θεότητι τὴν ἰδίαν ἐνανθρώπησιν id.*exp.fid.*15 (p.516.5; M.42.812A); οὔτε θεότητος ὄργανον οὔτε μὴν ἄνθρωπον ἁπλῶς θεοφοροῦντα..., θεὸν δὲ μᾶλλον μετὰ σαρκὸς ἢ γοῦν ἐνηνθρωπηκότα Cyr.*ep.*1(p.19.30; 5^2.14D); id.*Pulch.*(p.43.31; 5^2.154A); Max.*opusc.*(M.91.36A); **2.** of υἱός [θεοῦ]: ὁ γὰρ τοῦ θεοῦ υἱὸς...εἰ καὶ νεωστὶ ἐνηνθρωπηκέναι ἔδοξεν, ἀλλ' οὔτι γε διὰ τοῦτο νέος ἐστί Or.*Cels.*5.37 (p.41.21; M.11.1240A); υἱὸν...ἀποσταλέντα...καὶ σαρκωθέντα ἐνηνθρωπηκέναι Hymen.*ep.*(p.329.1); Eus.*d.e.*9.4(p.413.8; M.22.665C); Cyr.H.*catech.*11.17; *Const.App.*7.43.2; Chrys.*hom.8 in Phil.*(11.349E); ‡Chrys.*Trin.*4(1.840A); ‡Cyr.*Trin.*28(6^3.34A; M.77.1173A) cit. s. ἐνάρετος; καὶ ὁ τὸ πρὶν ἁπλοῦς ὢν καὶ εἷς τῆς ἁγίας τριάδος, καὶ νῦν ὁ αὐτὸς εἷς ἐστι τῆς ἁγίας τριάδος σεσαρκωμένος, καὶ ~ήσας Jo.V H.*icon.*10(M.96.1357A); **3.** of λόγος [θεὸς λόγος, λόγος θεοῦ]: Hipp.*Noët.*4 (p.241.24; M.10.809A); Or.*Apoc.*7(p.24); μονογενοῦς παιδὸς αὐτοῦ, τοῦ πρωτοτόκου πάσης κτίσεως, τοῦ ~ήσαντος λόγου Dion.Al.ap.Eus.*h.e.*7.6.6(M.20.648A); Meth.*symp.*1.5(p.13.17; M.18.45B); Eus.*Ps.*134:8(M.24.32B); αὐτὸς ὁ τοῦ θεοῦ λόγος...ἐνηνθρώπησεν, ἵνα ἡμεῖς θεοποιηθῶμεν Ath.*inc.*54.3(M.25.192B); ‡Ath.*Ar.*4.6(p.50.19; M.26.476C); Cyr.H.*catech.*12.3; εἰ γὰρ ἐνηνθρώπησεν [sc. ὁ λόγος], οὐ μόνον σάρκα εἴληφεν ἀλλὰ καὶ ψυχήν Epiph.*haer.*44.4(p.195.33; M.41.828B); *ib.*62.5(p.394.16; 1057A); Cyr.*Jo.*4.4(4.388B); Χριστὸς...οὐ καθ' ἑαυτὸν ἄνθρωπος κοινῶς τε καὶ ἰδικῶς νοεῖται...~ήσας δὲ μᾶλλον ὁ ἐκ θεοῦ λόγος id.*Heb.*2:9(p.387.11); id.*thes.*15(5^1.171D); ὁ θεὸς λόγος...τῇ φύσει τὴν προτέραν εὐγένειαν ἀπέδωκεν, διὰ τοῦ τιμῆσαι τῷ ~ῆσαι τὴν ἐκ γῆς...διαπλασθεῖσαν φύσιν Procl.CP *Arm.*7(p.190.23; M.65.861D); Justn.*ep.Thdr.Mops.*(p.51.10; M.86.1051D); **4.** of Χριστός, Meth.*symp.*10.1(p.122.12; M.18.193A); Eus.*d.e.*4.16(p.185.28; M.22.309B); πιστεύομεν εἰς Ἰησοῦν Χριστὸν ἐν σαρκὶ παραγενόμενον καὶ ~ήσαντα Cyr.H.*catech.*12.13; Epiph.*haer.*24.9(p.265.23; M.41.317C); *ib.*(p.265.27; 317D); Cyr.*Ps.*9:13(M.69.769B); **5.** of Ἰησοῦς, Or.*Cels.*3.14(p.213.24; M.11.937A) cit. s. ἐνανθρώπησις; **6.** of ὁ κύριος: νύμφην...τὴν σάρκα...τοῦ κυρίου, ἧς χάριν καταλείψας τὸν πατέρα κατῆλθεν...καὶ προσεκολλήθη...~ήσας εἰς αὐτήν Meth.*symp.*7.8(p.78.19; M.18.136A); **7.** of the μία φύσις of Christ, Flav.CP *ep.Thds.*(p.35.21; M.65.892C) cit. s. φύσις; ἐὰν μίαν φύσιν εἴπῃς ἀπολελυμένως μετὰ τὴν ἕνωσιν, σύγχυσιν λέγεις καὶ σύγκρασιν· ἐὰν μέντοιγε προσθῇς σεσαρκωμένην καὶ ἐνανθρωπήσασαν καὶ νοήσῃς παραπλησίως τῷ...Κυρίλλῳ τὴν σάρκωσιν καὶ τὴν ἐνανθρώπησιν, τὰ αὐτὰ λέγεις [sc. Eutyches] ἡμῖν Bas.Sel.ap.CChalc.*act.*1(*ACO* 2.1.1 p.93.36; H.2.101C); **8.** in credal affirmations κατελθόντα καὶ σαρκωθέντα, ~ήσαντα, παθόντα *Symb.Nic.*(325)(p.51; M.20.1540C); *Symb.Ant.*(341)3(p.250.13; M.26.724C); *ib.*4(p.251.6; M.26.725C); *Symb.Ant.*(345)1(p.251.27; M.26.728B); *ib.*6(p.253.10; 732B); cf. ἐκ παρθένου καὶ πνεύματος ἁγίου, κατὰ τὸ εὐαγγέλιον ~ήσαντα Cyr.H.*catech.*12.3; *ib.*15.11; *Symb.Sirm.*1(p.254.22; M.26.736B); *Symb.Sel.*(p.258.12; M.26.745B); Photinus et al.ap.Epiph.*haer.*72.12(p.266.27; M.42.400A); *Symb.Nic.-CP*(p.80.8; H.2.288B); Cyr.*ep.*4(p.26.24; 5^2.23A); τῷ δέ, ~ήσαντα, τὴν ἐκ ψυχῆς λογικῆς καὶ σώματος ἐν αὐτῷ τῆς ἡμετέρας φύσεως συμπλήρωσιν παρεχόμενα CChalc.*ep.*(*ACO* 2.1.3 p.111.37; H.2.648A); εἴ τις οὐχ ὁμολογεῖ τὸν ἕνα τῆς ἁγίας τριάδος...σαρκωθέντα ἐκ πνεύματος ἁγίου καὶ...Μαρίας, καὶ ~ήσαντα Cyrus Al.*cap.*2(H.3.1340E); **9.** of Inc. by H. Ghost and BMV; **a.** in credal definitions v.supra 8; **b.** in gen., Epiph.*haer.*62.5(p.394.16; M.41.1057A); cf.Jo.Mon.*hymn.Nic.*8(M.96.1389A); **10.** abs. μή τις ὑπολάβῃ ἕτερον εἶναι τὸν ἀόρατον...παρὰ τὸν ~ήσαντα Or.*Jo.*6.30(15; p.140.19; M.14.253A); Εἰρηναῖός τε καὶ Κλήμης, Ἀπολινάριός τε ὁ Ἱεραπολίτης καὶ Σαραπίων...ἔμψυχον τὸν ~ήσαντα...φάσκουσιν Socr.*h.e.*3.7.5(M.67.392A).

B. *be man, be incarnate*; **1.** of Christ's incarnate life in gen. τῆς θείας φύσεως ἀπαύγασμα...~ούσῃ ψυχῇ ἱερᾷ τῇ τοῦ Ἰησοῦ συνεπιδημήσει τῷ βίῳ Or.*Cels.*7.17(p.168.16; M.11.1445A); id.*Jo.*6.11(6; p.66.30; M.14.132A); Eus.*p.e.*1.3(7D; M.21.32D); τοῦ καθ' ὃ ἐνηνθρώπει σώματος id.*d.e.*4.13(p.171.4; M.22.285A); ἐδεῖ αὐτὸν ~οῦντα ταπεινόφροσι λόγοις ἐμφαίνειν τὸ ἑαυτοῦ μέγεθος ‡Gr.Nyss.*Ar.et Sab.*11(M.45.1296C); **2.** ref. unauthorized or heret. doctrines of Inc.; **a.** Christ's dwelling in first Adam ἥρμοζε γὰρ τὸ πρωτόγονον τοῦ θεοῦ...τὴν σοφίαν τῷ πρωτοπλάστῳ...καὶ πρωτογόνῳ τῶν ἀνθρώπων ἀνθρώπῳ κερασθεῖσαν ἐνηνθρωπηκέναι. τοῦτο γὰρ εἶναι τὸ Χριστόν, ἄνθρωπον ἀκράτῳ θεότητι καὶ τελείᾳ πεπληρωμένον καὶ θεὸν ἐν ἀνθρώπῳ κεχωρημένον Meth.*symp.*3.4(p.30.22; M.18.68A); **b.** apparent incarnation of Father (Sabellian) ἀρχὴν μὲν ἔχων τοῦ γίνεσθαι υἱός, παυόμενος δὲ τοῦ λέγεσθαι πατήρ· καὶ ~ήσας μὲν ὀνόματι, τῇ δὲ ἀληθείᾳ μηδὲ ἐπιδημήσας ‡Ath.*Ar.*4.25(p.73.8; M.26.505D); (Marcellan) τί τοίνυν ἦν τὸ κατελθὸν τοῦτο πρὸ τοῦ ~ῆσαι; πάντως πού φησιν· πνεῦμα· εἰ γάρ τι παρὰ τοῦτο ἐθέλοι λέγειν, οὐ συγχωρήσει αὐτῷ ὁ πρὸς τὴν παρθένον εἰρηκὼς ἄγγελος, πνεῦμα ἅγιον ἐπελεύσεται ἐπί σε. εἰ δὲ πνεῦμα εἶναι φήσει, ἄκουε τοῦ σωτῆρος λέγοντος, πνεῦμα ὁ θεός. (Marcell.*fr.*49) σαφῶς ἐντεῦθεν τοῦ σωτῆρος περὶ τοῦ πατρὸς εἰρηκότος, πνεῦμα ὁ θεός, ἐλέγχεται Μάρκελλος αὐτὸν τὸν πατέρα ἐνηνθρωπηκέναι εἰπὼν Eus.*Marcell.*2.2(p.35.21; M.24.784C); cf.id.*e.th.*2.1(p.99.17; M.24.900B); εἰ δὴ οὖν ἓν καὶ ταὐτὸν ἦν ὁ θεὸς καὶ ὁ ἐν αὐτῷ λόγος, ὡς δοκεῖ Μαρκέλλῳ, ὁ ἐν τῇ...παρθένῳ γενόμενος καὶ...~ήσας...αὐτὸς ἦν ὁ ἐπὶ πάντων θεός· ὁ δὴ τολμήσαντα φάναι τὸν Σαβέλλιον ἡ ἐκκλησία...ἐν ἀθέοις κατέλεξεν *ib.*2.4(p.102.33;

905A); **c.** Logos not becoming Son until Inc. (Sabellian) αὐτὸν τὸν λόγον υἱὸν τότε γεγενῆσθαι, ὅτε ἐνηνθρώπησεν. ἀπὸ γὰρ λόγου... γέγονεν υἱός, οὐκ ὢν πρότερον υἱός, ἀλλὰ λόγος μόνον ‡Ath.*Ar*.4.15 (p.59.22; M.26.488C); *ib*.4.22(p.69.15; 501B); **d.** living among men but not truly man, cf. τὸν διὰ τὴν ἡμετέραν σωτηρίαν σαρκωθέντα καὶ ἐν ἀνθρώποις πολιτευσάμενον καὶ παθόντα *Symb.Caes*.(p.43.13; M.20.1537B); (Apollinarian) τὸ δ' αὐτὸ καὶ περὶ τῆς ἐνανθρωπήσεως κακουργοῦσι φωνήν, τὸ ἐνηνθρώπησεν, οὐκ, ἐν ἀνθρώπῳ γέγονεν, ὃν ἑαυτῷ περιέπηξεν, ἐξηγούμενοι...ἀλλ', ἀνθρώποις ὡμίλησε, καὶ συνεπολιτεύσατο, λέγοντες Gr.Naz.*ep*.102(M.37.197B); Gr.Nyss.*Apoll*.22 (M.45.1167C); **e.** indwelling man, but not becoming man (Nestorian) καὶ τῆς συνεργίας ἡ ἀπόδειξις πρόδηλος· ὁ υἱὸς ἐνηνθρώπησεν, ὁ πατὴρ συνέστησεν, τὸ πνεῦμα σημείοις ἐσέμνυνε Nest.*fr*.D 6(p.355.8) ap.Cyr.*Nest*.4.2(p.78.39; 6^{1}.100C); Cyr.*ib*.(p.79.2; 6^{1}.100C); **f.** ref. monoph. view ἢ ἄνθρωπον ψιλὸν εἶναι τὸν κύριον,...ἢ θεὸν γυμνὸν καὶ μὴ ἀνηνθρωπηκότα εἶναι τὸν Χριστόν Thdr.Raith.*praep*.(p.199.12; M.91.1501B).

***ἐνανθρώπησις, ἡ,** *incarnation*;

A. of Inc. as an event; **1.** in gen., Hipp.*Dan*.4.39.4; Ἰησοῦς υἱὸς ὢν θεοῦ καὶ πρὶν ἐνανθρωπῆσαι καὶ ἐνανθρωπήσας ἀποδείκνυται. ἐγὼ δέ φημι ὅτι καὶ μετὰ τὴν ἐ. ἀεὶ εὑρίσκεται...πρὸς ἡμᾶς κατελθὼν Or.*Cels*.3.14(p.213.25; M.11.937A); ἐ., ὅτε σάρκα καὶ ὀστέα ἀναλαμβάνει ὁ τοῦ θεοῦ υἱός id.*Jo*.6.35(19; p.144.6; M.14.260A); ἔστι ...περὶ τοῦ ἀποστείλαντος τὸν Χριστὸν πνεύματος ἀπολογήσασθαι, οὐχ ὡς φύσει διαφέροντος ἀλλὰ διὰ τὴν γενομένην οἰκονομίαν τῆς ἐ. τοῦ υἱοῦ τοῦ θεοῦ, ἐλαττωθέντος παρ' αὐτὸ τοῦ σωτῆρος *ib*.2.11(6; p.66.20; 129D); exeg. Jo.1:1 (ἦν), ἦν μὲν κυριώτερον...τὸ ἔστιν εἰπεῖν· ἀλλ' ἐπεὶ πρὸς διαφορὰν τῆς ἐ. γενομένης ἔν τινι καιρῷ ἐδήλου τὴν ὕπαρξιν τοῦ λόγου, ἀντὶ τοῦ ἔστιν τῷ ἦν...κέχρηται id.*fr.1 in Jo*.(p.483.17); ἀγνοῶν [sc. Devil] ὅτι ὁ υἱὸς τοῦ θεοῦ ἐνηνθρώπησεν—ἔλαθε γὰρ αὐτὸν ἡ ἀπόρρητος ἐ.—ὑπέλαβεν, ὅτι ἄνθρωπος ὢν ηὐδοκήθη τῷ θεῷ διὰ τὰς ἀρετὰς αὐτοῦ id.*hom.29 in Lc*.(p.182.27); id.*Ps*.2:4(p.448); ὁ δοὺς ὕπνον ἀνεπαίσθητον τῷ δράκοντι πρὸς τὸ μὴ ἐπιγνῶναι αὐτὸν τὴν ἐ. σου *A.Xanthipp*.12(p.65.38); Meth.*symp*.3.8(p.36.18; M.18.73C); τὸ μυστήριον τῆς ἐ. τοῦ λόγου *ib*.8.7(p.89.8; 149A); σωτῆρα, τὸν ἐν ἀρχῇ πρὸς τὸν θεὸν θεὸν λόγον,...υἱὸν ἀνθρώπου διὰ τὴν ὑστάτην ἐ. αὐτοῦ Eus.*h.e*.1.2.26(M.20.68B); id.*d.e*.4.16(p.187.11; M.22.312C); τῇ τοῦ Χριστοῦ ἐ. *ib*.6.11(p.260.21; 428D); id.*Is*.49:3(M.24.429C); ἐ. τοῦ σωτῆρος id.*e.th*.2.1(p.99.26; M.24.900C); ἐπειδὴ γὰρ ἐξ ἀνθρώπων εἰς ἀνθρώπους ὁ θάνατος ἐκράτησε, διὰ τοῦτο πάλιν διὰ τῆς ἐ. τοῦ θεοῦ λόγου ἡ τοῦ θανάτου κατάλυσις γέγονε Ath.*inc*.10.5(M.25.113C); id.*Ar*.1.44(M.26.101C); οὐ χρὴ ἕτερον μὲν τὸν λόγον, ἕτερον δὲ Χριστὸν νοεῖν, ἀλλ' ἕνα καὶ τὸν αὐτὸν διὰ τὴν ἕνωσιν τὴν πρὸς τὴν θείαν αὐτοῦ καὶ φιλάνθρωπον συγκατάβασίν τε καὶ ἐ. ‡Ath.*Ar*.4.31(p.80.10; M.26.516C); οὐ δοκήσει καὶ φαντασίᾳ τῆς ἐ. γενομένης, ἀλλὰ τῇ ἀληθείᾳ Cyr.H.*catech*.4.9; εἰ γὰρ φάντασμα ἦν ἡ ἐ., φάντασμα καὶ ἡ σωτηρία *ib*.; ἐ. ... τοῦ κυρίου Bas.*hom.in Ps*.32(1.133D; M.29.328C); Δανιὴλ...ἐ. θεοῦ προαγορευτής id.*renunt*.7(2.208D; M.31.641A); ref. 1Cor.2:12 περὶ τοῦ μυστηρίου τῆς ἐ. λέγων id.*Spir*.57(3.48D; M.32.173B); ἐν βραχεῖ τὴν χάριν παρασχόμενος τῆς ἐ., ταχεῖαν, καὶ οἱονεὶ παροδικὴν ποιεῖται τὴν ἐπιδημίαν †Bas.*Is*.247(1.567E; M.30.553B); Gr.Naz.*or*.30.14(p.131.2; M.36.121C); id.*carm*.1.2.34.189(M.37.959A); μέγα μυστήριον τῆς θείας ἐ. as source of redemption, Gr.Nyss.*or.catech*.26(p.101.2; M.45.69C); τὴν διὰ τῆς παρθένου ἐ. id.*ep*.2(M.46.1013B); ref. Arian argument from 'ἐν ᾧ εὐδόκησα': πρὸς τὴν ἐ. αὐτοῦ ὅλον νένευκε τὸ νόημα. ... ἐν τούτῳ, φησίν, εὐδόκησα διὰ τῆς ἐ. αὐτοῦ τὴν σωτηρίαν ὑμῖν πορισθῆναι Didym.*Trin*.1.9(M.39.289A); *Const.App*.2.55.1; *ib*.7.43.2; ἡμεῖς δὲ καὶ θεὸν αὐτὸν λέγομεν...καὶ ἐν μήτρᾳ ...τὸν χρόνον...παραμεμενηκότα, ὅπως τελείως...τὴν ἔνσαρκον ἐ. ἑαυτῷ καὶ οἰκονομίαν οἰκονομήσῃ Epiph.*haer*.30.27(p.370.8; M.41.452C); ref. Christ's human weakness ταῦτα γὰρ οὐχ ἁμαρτίας εἶδος, ἀλλ' ἐ. ἀληθεστάτης γνώρισμα id.*inc*.3(p.230.20; M.41.277A); ἡ γὰρ τοῦ ψυχικοῦ...παράβασις τῆς τε ἐ. πρόφασις γέγονεν, καὶ τοῦ ἡνωθῆναι σώματι τὸν θεὸν λόγον Chrys.ap.*cat.1Cor*.15:46(p.324.16); Thdr.Mops.*Gen*.32:27(M.66.645A); σῶμα τοῦ κυριακοῦ...ἀνθρώπου, κρύπτοντος τοῦ θεοῦ λόγου τὴν ἐ. Nil.ap.Proc.G.*Cant*.2:9(M.87.1600B); τὰ οἰκονομικῶς εἰρημένα περὶ αὐτοῦ διὰ τὴν ἐ. Cyr.*glaph.Ex*.2 (1.272D); τὸν ἀποκεκρυμμένον καὶ οἱονεὶ μέσον τῆς ἐ. λόγον *ib*.(273A); id.*Is*.1.4(2.104B); ἐ. τοῦ μονογενοῦς *ib*.2.1(191C); *ib*.3.1(350A); id.*Os*.26(3.49C); εἴ τις θελήσει τὰ τῆς ἀνθρωπότητος ῥήματα...γυμνῷ προσάπτειν τῷ θεῷ λόγῳ πρὸ τῆς ἐ., ἀσεβήσει μεγάλως id.*thes*.10(5^{1}.72E); δουλοπρεπῆ ῥήματα, οὐκ ἀναβαίνοντα μὲν πρὸς τὴν οὐσίαν αὐτοῦ, ἀλλὰ τῷ τῆς ἐ. προσώπῳ περικείμενα *ib*.9(72A); τὴν τοῦ μονογενοῦς σάρκωσίν τε καὶ ἐ. Thdt.*qu.19 in Gen*.(1.23); ἐ. τοῦ Χριστοῦ Philox.*ep*.20(p.171); ἐν τῇ ἡμέρᾳ ἐκείνῃ λέγει κύριος...ἐν ποίᾳ ἡμέρᾳ...; τῇ τῆς ἐ., ὅτε παρθένος οὐρανὸν ἐμιμήσατο· ὅτε ἐκ γαστρὸς ἐξεπήδησαν ἀκτῖνες Procl.CP *or*.2.6(M.65.700B); λόγου...φιλάνθρωπον ἐ. ‡Gr.Nyss.*hom.1.4 in Jo*.(p.94.17); *ib.1.35*(p.105.36); σωτηρίου ἐ. Oecum.*Apoc*.11(p.224); Call.*v.Hyp*.(p.78); ὡρισμένος ἦν ὁ καιρὸς καὶ τῆς θείας ἐ. δι' ἧς...κατέκρινε σατανᾶν Gr.Agr.*Eccl*.3.20(M.98.884D); αὔξειν λέγεται τῇ ἰδίᾳ σαρκί,...ὅπως δείξῃ κυρίως καὶ κατὰ ἀλήθειαν εἶναι τὴν ἐ. Jo.V H.*icon*.8(M.96.1356C); **2.** heret. opinions τὸν θεὸν ὁμολογοῦντες ἀναίνονται πάλιν τὸν ἄνθρωπον...ἀλλὰ δόκησίν τινα φασματώδη μᾶλλον γεγονέναι, οἷον ὥσπερ Μαρκίων καὶ Οὐαλεντῖνος καὶ οἱ γνωστικοί, τῆς σαρκὸς ἀποδιασπῶντες τὸν λόγον, τὸ ἓν τάλαντον ἀποβάλλονται, τὴν ἐ. Hipp.*fr.in Mt*.25:24(p.209.11; M.10.868B); Sabellian τὸν...ἀπαθῆ πατέρα χωρητὸν ἅμα καὶ παθητὸν διὰ τῆς ἐ. ὑποτίθενται *Symb.Ant*.(345)7(p.253.17; M.26.732C); Marcellan οὐ τοίνυν οὗτος ὁ ἁγιώτατος λόγος πρὸ τῆς ἐ. πρωτότοκος ἁπάσης κτίσεως ὠνόμαστο...ἀλλὰ τὸν πρῶτον καινὸν ἄνθρωπον...αἱ...γραφαὶ πρωτότοκον...ὀνομάζουσιν Marcell.*fr*.6 ap.Eus.*Marcell*.2.3(p.45.18; M.24.801A); εἰ δὲ διὰ τὴν ἐ. ἐπλατύνθη, καὶ γέγονε τότε τριάς, ἄρα πρὸ τῆς ἐ. οὔπω ἦν τριάς. φανήσεται δὲ ὁ πατὴρ καὶ γεγονὼς σάρξ ‡Ath.*Ar*.4.14 (p.58.20; M.26.488A); adoptionist, *Symb.Ant*.(345)4(p.252.29; 729C) cit. s. θεοποιέω; Apollinarian οἱ μὴ τελείαν τὴν Χριστοῦ ἐ. ὁμολογοῦντες Epiph.*anac*.77(p.415.6; M.42.873C); Jo.D.*haer*.77(M.94.728A); orthodox assertion against Nestorians εἶναί τε μετὰ τὴν ἐ. τὸν αὐτὸν θεόν τε ὁμοῦ καὶ ἄνθρωπον id.*haer.Nest*.38(M.95.209D); Arian ὡς ἐν ἐσχάτοις καὶ μόλις τοῖς τῆς ἐ. καιροῖς, πατέρα...γενέσθαι τὸν θεόν Cyr.*inc.unigen*.(5^{1}.685A); Christol. heresies contrasted with Arianism ἐκεῖναι μὲν γὰρ ἢ περὶ τὸ σῶμα καὶ τὴν ἐ. τοῦ κυρίου πλανῶνται...ἢ μηδόλως ἐπιδεδημηκέναι τὸν κύριον...νομίζοντες ἐπλανήθησαν· αὕτη δὲ...εἰς αὐτὴν τὴν θεότητα κατατετόλμηκε Ath.*ep.Aeg.Lib*.17(M.25.577C).

B. Christ's *incarnate life* as a whole τὰ ἐν τῇ ἐ. συμβησόμενα αὐτῷ Or.*sel.in Ps*.2:2(M.12.1104D); id.*fr.66 in Lc*.(p.265); μάρτυρες αὐτοῦ τῆς ἐ. καὶ τῶν παθημάτων *Const.App*.6.19.4; τῷ τέλει τῆς τοῦ σωτῆρος ἡμῶν ἐ. Hesych.H.*fr.Ps*.108:1(M.93.1313C).

C. *incarnate nature, humanity*, of Christ τὸ ἐδόθη μοι πᾶσα ἐξουσία...εἰς τὴν ἐ. νόει Or.*fr.in Mt*.28:18–20(p.235; M.17.309C); τῷ ...μαθητῇ οὐκ εὐθὺς τὰ περὶ τῆς θεότητος τοῦ υἱοῦ...ἀνακοινοῦται, ἀλλὰ τὰ περὶ τῆς ἐ. αὐτοῦ id.*fr.27 in Jo*.(p.504.15); τὰ δὲ περὶ τῆς θεότητος αὐτοῦ καὶ τῆς ἐ. εἰρημένα ῥήματα ἰδίαν καὶ κατάλληλον ἔχει πρὸς ἕκαστον τῶν λεγομένων τὴν ἑρμηνείαν Ath.*Dion*.9(p.52.16; M.25.493A); τῆς ἐ. αὐτοῦ διὰ τῆς ἀρχιερωσύνης μνημονεύει γράφων ὁ ἀπόστολος id.*Ar*.2.10(M.26.168B); ‡Ath.*Apoll*.2.19(M.26.1165A); μίμησις Χριστοῦ ἐν τῷ μέτρῳ τῆς ἐ. Bas.*reg.fus*.43.1(2.389E; M.31.1028B); ἐδόθη μοι πᾶσα ἐξουσία. ... εἰς τὴν ἐ. οὖν, καὶ οὐκ εἰς τὴν θεότητα ταῦτα νοεῖν δεῖ Didym.(‡Bas.)*Eun*.4(1.289B; M.29.693C); οὐχ ἡ θεότης ἡλικίαν ἐπιδεχομένη..., σοφίᾳ δὲ προέκοπτεν ἡ τοῦ σωτῆρος ἐ. Epiph.*anc*.78(p.98.23; M.43.165A); τῆς θεότητος συνούσης τῇ ἐ. id.*inc*.3(p.230.21; M.41.277A); ref. Lc.1:35 ἐν τῷ γὰρ εἰπεῖν, τὸ γεννώμενον, ἔδειξε μὲν τὴν σάρκα ἀπ' αὐτῆς ⟨εἶναι⟩ καὶ τὴν ἄλλην ἐ. id.*haer*.30.20(p.361.8; M.41.440C); *ib*.44.2(p.193.4; 824C); *ib*.44.4 (p.195.27; 828B); συνηνωμένη ἡ ἐ. αὐτοῦ εἰς μίαν ἀπάθειαν *ib*.69.42 (p.190.28; M.42.269A); συνηνωμένης τῆς ἐ. τῇ θεότητι *ib*.69.64(p.213.11; 305D); Eus.Al.*serm*.10(M.86.369B); ὁ υἱός...τῇ ἰδίᾳ ἐ. ἀνελήφθη εἰς τοὺς οὐρανοὺς Jo.V H.*icon*.10(M.96.1357A).

***ἐνανθρωπίζω,** *become man, be incarnate* μὴ ἄλλον ἀλλ' αὐτὸν τὸν θεὸν λόγον ἐνανθρωπίσαι (s.v.l.) Ath.ap.*cat.Heb*.2:11 suppl.(p.400.8); Mac.Mgn.*apocr*.2.9(p.12.13); Thdt.*Bar*.3:28(2.639); *Dial.Christ.et Jud*.18(p.82.36).

***ἐνανθρωπικός,** *manlike, human*, of Inc. τὰ μὲν τῆς πρώτης ἀφίξεως τῆς ἐνανθρωπικωτέρας Eus.*d.e*.9.17(p.440.14; M.22.709A).

***ἐνανθρωπότης, ἡ,** *adoption of human nature*; of Inc., Cyr.*ador*.11 (1.396A).

***ἐνανοῖξαι,** ἐ. τοῦ στόματος prob. for ἐν ἀνοίξει Sophr.H.*v.Cyr.et Jo*.7(M.87.3388D).

***ἐναντιάζομαι,** *oppose oneself to*, c. πρός et acc., Ephr.1.9F.

***ἐναντιοδοκῆται, οἱ,** *contradictory Docetists*, name applied to Nestorians and Eutychians οἱ μὲν γὰρ τὴν θεότητα, οἱ δὲ τὴν ἀνθρωπότητα δοκήσει λέγουσιν εἶναι ἐν τῷ σωτῆρι Leont.B.*Nest.et Eut*.1(M.86.1276A); id.*arg.Sev*.(M.86.1936C).

***ἐναντιοθελής,** *contrary to the will*, Thdr.Stud.*epp*.2.172(M.99.1540B).

ἐναντιολογ-έω, 1. c. dat., *contradict* one's own statement, Cyr.H.*catech*.5.12; **2.** *contradict oneself*, Chrys.*hom.50.1 in Jo*.(8.294D); *ib*.73.2(432C); med., id.*hom.19.2 in 2Cor*.(10.572D); **3.** *speak in contradictions, nonsensically* τάχα ἐξεστηκέναι ὑμῖν δοκῶ οὕτως ~ῶν *ib*.2.6(451C).

ἐναντιολογία, ἡ, *contradiction, contradictory statement*, Chrys.*hom.4.1 in 2Cor*.(10.454D); id.*hom.68.2 in Mt*.(7.671B); Isid.Pel.

epp.4.216(M.78.1309B); *nonsense* ὦ τῆς ἐ. Chrys.*hom.50.1 in Jo.*(8.294B).

ἐναντίος, *opposing, hostile*; **1.** adj., of evil passions, *T.Jud.*18.6; of powers of evil ἐ. ἄγγελοι Or.*Cels*.8.36(p.252.9; M.11.1572D); ἐ. ἀρχῆς καὶ ἐξουσίας *A.Phil.*144(p.86.1); ἡ ὑπερβολὴ τῆς ἐναντίας δυνάμεως τὰς διανοίας τῶν ἀνθρώπων κατέλαβε Const.ap.Gel.Cyz.*h.e.*2.7.37(M.85.1241A); Mac.Aeg.*hom*.21.1(M.34.656B); Thdt.*qu.3 in Gen.*(1.31); **2.** as subst., of Devil βασανίζομαι ὑπὸ τοῦ ἐ. *A.Thom.*A 42(p.160.1); *ib*.157(p.267.15); Cels.ap.Or.*Cels*.6.42(p.110.22; M.11.1360B); Thdt.*Ezech*.32:31(2.953); ‡Ath.*v.Syncl.*85(M.28.1540A); plur. masc., of pagans, ‡Just.*qu.et resp.*55(M.6.1297B); neut., of false teaching ὁ τὰ ἐ. διδάσκων προφήτης Thdt.*qu.12 in Dt.*(1.270).

ἐναντιότης, ἡ, *opposition; contrariety, inconsistency*, Ath.*gent*.10(M.25.21C); id.*Ar*.3.7(M.26.336B); *power of adversary* [i.e. *Devil*] ἡ ἐ. ἐν τοῖς φανεροῖς καὶ ἐν τοῖς κρυπτοῖς ἀπὸ τῆς παραβάσεως τοῦ πρώτου ἀνθρώπου εἰς ἡμᾶς κατήντησεν Mac.Aeg.*hom*.21.2(M.34.656D); *ib*.21.4(657A).

ἐναντιοφανής, *appearing contradictory*, Max.*schol.c.h.*13.1(M.4.96A).

***ἐναντιοφορέω**, *move in opposite direction*, Or.*comm.in Gen.*ap. Eus.*p.e.*6.11(286B; M.12.61A).

***ἐναντιωματάρης, ὁ**, *bellicose opponent*; of Sev. Ant., Eust.Mon. *ep*.(M.86.912C).

ἐναντλ-έω, *pour into*, met. θεῷ...πᾶσι τὸ ζῆν...~οῦντι *M.Apollon.*15(p.31.29).

***ἐναπαλάσσομαι**, prob. f.l. for ⟨ἐναποπλάσσομαι⟩, *portray* to, Nil.*epp*.1.26(M.79.93B).

***ἐναπατάομαι**, *be deceived by*, Jo.VI CP *ep*.(M.96.1428C).

***ἐνάπειρος**, = ἄπειρος, *infinite*, Or.*Ps*.18:8(p.474).

***ἐναπεμέω**, *spit upon*, met. κακίαν ἐ. ‡Proc.G.*Pr*.5:19(M.87.1265C).

ἐναπερείδ-ω, **1.** act.; **a.** *impress, set upon* Gr.Nyss.*virg*.3(p.256.17; M.46.325B); οἱ ἅγιοι...τὸν αἰῶνα τοῦτον διέβησαν, οὐδενὶ τῶν ἐν αὐτῷ τερπνῶν τὸ τῆς ψυχῆς ἴχνος ἐναπερείσαντες Max.*ambig*.(M.91.1204D); **b.** *rest upon*, Or.*Cels*.4.38(p.309.7; M.11.1088B); **c.** *inflict upon*, Chrys.*stat*.5.4(2.65A); **2.** med.; **a.** *impress oneself upon* ἀπάτη ...~ομένη τῇ ψυχῇ Clem.*str*.2.20(p.174.2; M.8.1056B); Thdt.*eran*.(4.187); **b.** *stick into* καταλύεται τοῦ θανάτου τὸ κράτος, οὐκ ἔχοντος τίσι τὸ ἑαυτοῦ κέντρον ἐναπερείσηται Gr.Nyss.*virg*.14(p.307.1; M.46.380A).

***ἐναπέρεισμα, τό**, *impression*, Clem.*str*.2.20(p.173.7; M.8.1053C).

***ἐναπέρχομαι**, *depart, go*, implying *from* one place *to* another, *A.Thom.*B 46(p.39.21); Thdt.*provid*.6(4.579); ‡Jo.D.*Artem*.60(M.96.1308B).

***ἐναποβιόω**, *die in* ἐ. ταῖς ἁμαρτίαις Cyr.*Is*.4.5(2.698E).

ἐναποβλέπω, *have regard to, consider*, c. dat., Eus.*h.e.*4.15.14(M.20.348A); Ath.*gent*.45(M.25.89C).

***ἐναποβλύζω**, *spit, sputter into*, c. dat., Clem.*prot*.10(p.66.9; M.8.201A).

***ἐναπογράφομαι**, **1.** *be enrolled*, Bas.*hom*.13.7(2.120B; M.31.440A); in paraphrase of Heb.12:13, Clem.*prot*.9(p.62.27; M.8.193B); Tim.Ant.*descr.BMV* 6(M.28.952C); ref. book of life, Niceph.Ur.*v.Sym*.146(M.86.3124A); **2.** *be inscribed*; met., of law in the heart, Clem.*paed*.3.12(p.287.25; M.8.673A); Or.*exp.in Pr*.22:56(M.17.221A).

ἐναπόγραφος, **1.** *registered, enrolled*; of BMV, Tim.Ant.*descr. BMV* 1(M.28.945A); *ib*.6(953B); Geo.Pis.*hex*.1463(M.92.1546A); sc. in book of life, Areth.*Apoc*.28(M.106.644B); **2.** masc. as subst., *serf, colonus* δοῦλος ἢ ἐ. CChalc.*can*.4.

ἐναποδείκνυμι, *point out, indicate*, Clem.*str*.5.11(p.377.7; M.9.113B).

***ἐναπόδεικτος**, *explicit* τὰς ἐ. τοῦ δεσπότου φωνάς ‡Ath.*Apoll*.1.1(M.26.1093B); *ib*.1.3(1097A).

***ἐναπόθετος**, *stored up*, †Ath.*fr.Mt*.6:1(M.27.1372C); met. τὸ κάλλος...τὸ ἐ. Jo.D.*hom*.11.12(M.96.773D); neut. plur., †Nil.*vit*.3(M.79.1141D).

ἐναποθησαυρίζω, *store up*; met., Or.*mart*.13(p.13.25; M.11.581A); id.*or*.20.2(p.344.20; M.11.480B); Mac.Aeg.*hom*.5.8(M.34.513B).

ἐναποθλίβω, *impress*; met., divine image on soul, Cyr.*hom.pasch.*10(5².133B).

ἐναποθνήσκω, *die in* or *with* ὁ γὰρ μὴ βουλόμενος αὐτὸν [sc. 'old man'] θανατῶσαι διὰ τῆς πίστεως...ἐναποθανεῖται αὐτῷ Chrys.*hom.53.1 in Jo.*(8.311A); of Israel dying in the Mosaic types and shadows, Cyr.*Jo*.6.1(4.621D).

***ἐναποκαλύπτω**, *make a revelation*, Cyr.*Jo*.1 proem.(4.7B).

ἐναπόκει-μαι, **1.** *be stored up in, laid up in*, Tat.*orat*.6(p.7.2; M.6.820A); Or.*fr.26 in Lam.*(p.247.10; M.13.621C); λόγον...τὸν σπερματικὸν...καθ' ὃν δυνάμει τὰ μηδέπω φύντα ~ται τοῖς σπέρμασιν Eus.*e.th.*2.13(p.114.17; M.24.925D); οὐ...~μένη τῇ γῇ ἡ ψυχὴ τῶν ἀλόγων ἐξεφάνη, ἀλλ' ὁμοῦ τῷ προστάγματι συνυπέστη Bas.*hex*.9.3(1.82A; M.29.192B); Chrys.*hom.40.1 in Jo.*(8.236B); met. αἱ πρόδρομοι...φωναὶ ...αἰνίσσονται...τὴν ~μένην σωτηρίαν Clem.*prot*.1(p.9.26; M.8.65B); ἡ πίστις τοῦ λήψεσθαι εἶδος εὐχῆς ~μένης γνωστικῶς id.*str*.7.7(p.31.25; M.9.457B); τὸν ~μενον τῆς πίστεως θησαυρὸν τῇ...ψυχῇ Sev.Ant. ap.*cat.Mt*.8:8(p.59.3); **2.** *be contained in* θεοῦ...γραφὴ ~μένη τῇ πλακί Clem.*str*.6.16(p.499.18; ἐνυποκειμένη M.9.357C); Or.*princ*.4.17(p.304.6; M.11.356A); Chrys.*hom.7.2 in 1Cor.*(10.51E); θεὸν...τὸν ἀποκαλύπτοντα...τὴν ~μένην τῇ...γραφῇ γνῶσιν δοξάσωμεν Proc.G.*Gen*.50:19(M.87.512B); theol. Χριστὸς...θεοῦ δύναμις...ὅλης τῆς πατρικῆς δυνάμεως ~μένης αὐτῷ δηλονότι Bas.*Eun*.1.23(1.234D; M.29.564B); Eun.*apol*.26(M.30.860C).

ἐναπόκλειστος, *imprisoned*, Jo.Eub.*innoc*.2(M.96.1504A); Thphn.*chron*.p.330(M.108.796C); Thdr.Stud.*epp*.1.48(M.99.1073A).

ἐναποκλεί-ω, **1.** *shut up in, enclose in*, Chrys.*hom.5.4 in Col.*(11.363C); *Dial.Tim.et Aquil.*117 r°(p.90); of spirits in Hades, Cyr.*thes*.24(5¹.229E); met., Eus.*p.e.*7.10(314D; M.21.532C); Gr.Nyss.*or.catech*.10(p.57.1; M.45.41D); Chrys.*hom.3.2 in Ac.princ.*(3.73A); **2.** *limit, confine* τῶν ἐν ἀψύχῳ ὕλῃ ~όντων τὸ θεῖον Eus.*d.e.*5 proem.(p.208.18; M.22.345C); Gr.Nyss.*Steph*.1(M.46.705A); of souls τῷ σπηλαίῳ τοῦ βίου ~εσθε id.*hom.7 in Cant.*(M.44.916A); Cyr.*Jo*.2.4(4.184C); **3.** *comprise, include* τελευταῖον...κριτήριον...πάντας ἑαυτῷ ...τοὺς αἰῶνας ~ον Max.*ep*.1(M.91.384A); ~ειν γνώσει τινὶ τὸ ζητούμενον id.*ambig*.(M.91.1229D); **4.** s.v.l., *exclude* ἀπὸ τοῦ ξύλου τοῦ σταυροῦ τὸ ξύλον τῆς ἐπιθυμίας ἐναποκλεῖσαι *A.(Pass.)Andr.*(p.12.19).

ἐναποκλίνω, *sink down into*, met. εἰς...μέθας ἐ. ‡Jo.D.*Artem*.10(p.49.24; M.96.1261A).

ἐναποκλύζω, med., *wash...in* πρόσωπον Clem.*paed*.2.2(p.175.12; M.8.428A).

***ἐναποκρατέομαι**, *be contained within*, c. dat., Melet.*nat.hom.* synops.(M.64.1121B).

***ἐναποκρεμάννυμι**, *hang upon*, met. Ἕλληνες...πρὸς αὐτὰ [sc. stars] τὰς ἑαυτῶν ἐλπίδας ἐναπεκρέμασαν ‡Jo.D.*Artem*.42(p.163.6; M.96.1289C).

ἐναποκρύπτω, *conceal*, met. τὸ ἐνυπάρχον δὲ φῶς τῷ Μωσέως νόμῳ, καλύμματι ἐναποκεκρυμμένον συνέλαμψε τῇ Ἰησοῦ ἐπιδημίᾳ Or.*princ*.4.1.6(p.302.7; M.11.353A); cf.id.*Jo*.32.2(p.426.17; M.14.741B); Bas.*renunt*.2(2.204B; M.31.632A); Anast.S.*synax*.(M.89.840C).

***ἐναπόκρυφος**, **1.** *hidden*, *A.Thom.*A 123(p.232.11); **2.** *apocryphal* βιβλία ἐ. Epiph.*haer*.8.6(p.192.9; M.41.213B).

***ἐναποκτείνω**, *kill* (*within*), ‡Jo.D.*Artem*.69(p.101.27; M.96.1317B); met. ἁμαρτίαν...ἐ. τῇ ψυχῇ...νηστείᾳ Bas.*hom*.1.1(2.2B; M.31.165A).

ἐναπολαμβάν-ω, *confine*; met., ἐν μέσῳ δυοῖν ἐναπείλημμαι πραγμάτων ἀπορῶν Chrys.*hom.1.4 in Phil.*(11.200B); τὸν τῇ μνήμῃ ~όμενον ἰὸν τῆς κακίας †Cyr.*coll.VT*(6⁴.64E; M.77.1272C); pass., of being in straitened circumstances, *A.Thom.*B 54(p.41.17).

ἐναπολαύω, *enjoy*, c. genit., Thdt.*h.rel*.21(3.1238); Proc.G.*Is*.9:1–7(M.87.2001C); Jo.D.*hom*.1.14(M.96.568B).

***ἐναπολήγω**, *issue, end in*, c. dat., Gr.Nyss.*virg*.13(p.307.15; M.46.380B); id.*hom.5 in Cant.*(M.44.873D); id.*Eun*.1(1 p.72.26; M.45.301D).

ἐναπόλλυμαι, *perish in*, c. dat., Thdr.Mops.*Ps*.15:10(p.99.5; M.66.660A).

ἐναπομάσσ-ομαι, **1.** *impress*; **a.** lit., ref. Abgar's image of Christ ἐναπεμάξατο τῷ ἱματίῳ τὸ ἑαυτοῦ ἀπεικόνισμα Jo.D.*f.o.*4.16(M.94.1173A); ‡Jo.D.*ep.Thphl.*5(M.95.352B); **b.** met.; **i.** ref. divine activity; of Word in Creation τὰς ἀσωμάτους ἰδέας ταῖς τῶν σωμάτων ποιότησιν ~όμενος Eus.*d.e.*4.13(p.171.8; M.22.285B); in baptism τὴν διὰ λουτροῦ σφραγῖδα...ἐναπομάξασθαι ‡Pion.*v.Polyc.*19; ref. Inc. ἐναπομάξασθαί τι τῶν ἰδίων αὐτῇ [sc. τῇ ἀνθρώπου φύσει] Cyr.*hom.pasch*.15(5².205A); **ii.** ref. Fall κηλῖδας ἐναπεμάξατο [sc. Adam] κακίας Meth.*res*.1.38(p.281.8; M.41.1105B); Proc.G.*Gen*.2:8–9(M.87.164C); and gen. diffusion of evil, of Simonians preaching heresy to Christians οἷς ἐναπομάξασθαι...ἰόν Eus.*h.e.*2.1.12(M.20.137C); of wicked soul τὴν κακίαν εἰς τὸ σῶμα ἐ. Chrys.*Laz*.1.8(1.718E); **2.** *express* ἐναπομέμακται...τὰ εἴδη τῶν ἀγαλμάτων τὴν διάθεσιν τῶν δαιμόνων Clem.*prot*.4(p.44.24; M.8.156A).

ἐναπομέν-ω, **1.** *dwell* on or in, ref. divine indwelling ὁ ἐν ἁγίῳ βαπτίζων πνεύματι, ᾧπερ ἂν ἐπιφοιτήσαν ἐναπομείνῃ τὸ πνεῦμα Cyr.*Jo*.2.1(4.116D); of H. Ghost δι' οὗ...τῆς ἀγενήτου φύσεως ἐ. τὰ σήμαντρα id.*thes*.34(5¹.360B); ref. avoidance of dwelling on temporal things, Eus.*p.e.*11.6(520B; M.21.864A); μὴ ἐ. τῇ κτίσει, ἀλλὰ διὰ ταύτης τὸν δημιουργὸν θεωρεῖτε Chrys.*hom.5.2 in 1Cor.*(10.35D); id.*hom.43.2 in Jo.*(8.257A); Max.*ep*.12(M.91.505B); and sin ὁ δημιουργὸς

...κολάζει τοῖς πταίσμασιν ∼οντας Bas.Sel.*or.*35.1(M.85.376B); †Jo. Jej.*serm.*(M.88.1964B); **2.** *be content with*, ref. imperfect forms of knowledge οὐκ...∼ειν τῇ κοσμικῇ παιδείᾳ Clem.*str.*1.5(p.19.6; M.8. 721A); εἰ δὲ ἐν τάξει τοῦ πνεύματος ὁ νόμος ἦν..., οὐ μὴν διὰ τοῦτο ∼ειν χρὴ τῷ παιδαγωγῷ Chrys.*comm.in Gal.*5:6(10.721C); Proc.G. *Cant.*7:13(M.87.1768C); Dion.Ar.*c.h.*2.5(3.145A); Max.*cap.*5.27(M.90. 1357C); ref. natural state opp. grace, of foolish virgins τῇ ἰδίᾳ φύσει ἐναπομείνασαι Mac.Aeg.*elev.*4(M.34.892D).

ἐναπομόργνυ-μι, *wipe off upon*; met., *impart* to, *impress* on, Synes.*insomn.*7(p.156.15; M.66.1293A); *ib.*19(p.185.7; 1316D); id.*ep.* 44(M.66.1373C); Dion.Ar.*ep.*9(M.3.1104B); Max.*ambig.*(M.91.1137B); μηδεὶς οὖν ἀμφιβολίαν ἐχέτω τὸ ἄφθαρτον...σῶμα καὶ αἷμα τοῦ κυρίου ...ἔλαττον τῶν...παραδειγμάτων τὰς οἰκείας ∼σθαι δυνάμεις Eutych. *pasch.*3(M.86.2393D).

***ἐναπονεκρ-όομαι,** *be dead*, met. αἱ διὰ τὴν πονηρίαν ∼ωθεῖσαι ψυχαί Bas.*hom.in Ps.*48(1.184B; M.29.448B).

***ἐναποξύομαι,** *be scraped out*; of tree trunk to allow insertion of bud in grafting, Clem.*str.*6.15(p.491.32; M.9.344A).

***ἐναποπήγνυμι,** *fix in*; pass., of thorns, *be stuck in*, Ath.*fug.*7 (p.73.2; M.25.652C); met. μνησικακία, ὥσπερ ἐναποπαγεῖσα τῇ ψυχῇ ‡Ath.*v.Syncl.*63(M.28.1524D); Gr.Nyss.*ep.*1(p.5.5, v.l. ἐναποπλαγεὶς M.46.1004B).

***ἐναποπλήσσομαι,** *be dumbfounded*, v. ἐναποπήγνυμι.

ἐναποπλύνω, *wash away in*; met., ref. Jo.4:10ff. τῶν τῆς ἀρᾶς λόγων ἐναποπλυνθέντων ὕδατι Cyr.*ador.*14(1.496A).

ἐναποπνίγ-ω, *suffocate*, *strangle*, *drown*; **1.** lit., *Ep.Lugd.*ap.Eus. *h.e.*5.1.59(M.20.432A); Philost.*h.e.*2.4(M.65.468B); Cyr.*Am.*49(3. 304A); **2.** met., of demon ∼ειν τὸν νοῦν Evagr.Pont.*cap.pract.*A 25 (M.40.1228C); Cyr.*hom.pasch.*30(5^2.348E); Max.*ambig.*(M.91.1204C); ref. sin etc., Cyr.*Os.*90(3.121A); ∼εσθαι τῷ τῆς ἀγνωσίας βύθῳ id.*Ps.* 68:13(M.69.1165A); Max.*ambig.*(1120C).

ἐναπορέω, *be in doubt*, Or.*Jo.*6.37(21; p.146.6; v.l. for ἐπη- M.14. 264B).

***ἐναπορρήγνυμι,** *sever*, ‡Jo.D.*Artem.*60(M.96.1308B).

ἐναπορρίπτ-ω, *cast aside*; met., lapsed, Eus.*h.e.*8.2.3(M.20.744C); sinners ὡς ἄχρηστον ∼εται ῥάκος Gr.Nyss.*hom.in 1Cor.6:18*(M.46. 493B); Philost.*h.e.*7.15(p.103.11; M.65.553D).

ἐναποσβέννυμι, *quench*; pass., *wither away*; of life, Athenag.*leg.* 36.1(M.6.969C); Gr.Nyss.*Pulch.*(M.46.865B).

***ἐναποσβεστέον,** *one must suppress*, Clem.*paed.*2.7(p.193.19; M.8. 464C).

ἐναποσημαίν-ομαι, *impress*, *inscribe* κάλαμος...ταῖς δέλτοις ∼εται τάς τινων φωνάς Cyr.*Ps.*44:3(M.69.1029C); met. τῇ δικαίᾳ ψυχῇ θεία τις ἀγαθωσύνης δύναμις...∼εταί τι Clem.*str.*6.12(p.484.17; M.9.325B); theol. τῆς ὅλης φύσεως τοῦ πατρὸς ἐναποσημανθείσης τῷ υἱῷ Bas. *Eun.*2.16(1.252A; M.29.605A).

***ἐναποσκιρρόομαι,** *become inveterate in*, c. dat., Chrys.*David* 1. 1(4.748A).

***ἐναποσκοπέω,** *gaze upon*, †Gregent.*disp.*(M.86.776D).

***ἐναποσμήχω,** *wipe off*; met., sin, Chrys.*ecl.*24(12.606B).

***ἐναποστίλβω,** *shine brightly*, Ant.Mon.*hom.*113(M.89.1785C).

***ἐναποστράπτω,** *make to shine out upon*, Cyr.*Lc.*9:41(p.84.18); Thdr.Stud.*cant.*16.3(p.371).

ἐναποσφραγίζω, 1. lit., *stamp...upon*, Clem.*paed.*2.11(p.226.24; M.8.537A); Didym.(‡Bas.)*Eun.*5(1.301E; M.29.724C); Gnost., Hipp. *haer.*8.9(p.228.24; M.16.3351D) cit. s. ἐκτύπωμα; **2.** met., med., *bear the impress of*, c. acc. ὅταν...ψυχὴ...ἐναποσφραγίσηται ψευδεῖς περὶ αὐτῆς δόξας Athenag.*leg.*27.2(M.6.953A); ταύτας τὰς...γραφὰς ἐν- αποσφραγισαμένους...τῇ ψυχῇ Clem.*prot.*10(p.76.27; M.8.224B); id. *str.*7.3(p.12.21; M.9.421A); †Bas.*Is.*233(1.556A; M.30.525D).

***ἐναποσφράγισμα, τό,** *impression* πάθη...οἷον ἐ. τῶν πνευματικῶν δυνάμεων Clem.*str.*2.20(p.173.8; M.8.1053C).

***ἐναποταμιεύω,** *store up in*, c. dat.; met., ‡Proc.G.*Pr.*7:1(M.87. 1280B).

***ἐναποτάσσομαι,** *be appointed*, *fixed*, Or.*sel.in Ezech.*8:12(M.13. 797C).

***ἐναποτείνω,** *stretch*, *strain towards*, met. πρὸς οὐρανὸν τὸν νοῦν ἐ. Jo.D.*hom.*1.1(M.96.545B); hence, med., *exaggerate*, Cels.ap.Or.*Cels.* 7.9(M.11.1433A; ἐπανετείνετο p.161.1).

***ἐναποτέλεσμα, τό,** *achievement*, Cyr.*Is.*4.2(2.596A).

ἐναποτελέω, *make complete*, *perfect*, *establish*, Thdr.Mops.*Os.* 7:1ff.(M.66.165C); †Gregent.*leg.Hom.*(M.86.584C).

***ἐναποτεφρόω,** *reduce to ashes in*, met. τὴν ἁγνείαν χωνείᾳ ἐ. Jo. Mon.*hymn.Chrys.*4(M.96.1380B).

ἐναποτίθεμαι, 1. *put into*; ref. divine instilling of natural and supernatural blessings ἃ...βούλεται ὁ θεὸς ἐ. διανοίᾳ Diod.*Ps.*84:9 (M.33.1617B); Gr.Nyss.*hex.*12(M.44.73D); *ib.*13(76C); ἡ τοῦ πνεύματος χάρις...ταῖς τῶν ἁγίων ἐ. ψυχαῖς Chrys.*hom.68.5 in Mt.*(7.676E); of prophecy ἡ ἀποκάλυψις ἡ κατ' ἐνέργειαν τοῦ θεοῦ ἐναποτεθεῖσα Thdr. Mops.*Eph.*6:18–22(p.194.23; M.66.921A); **2.** *store up in* ἀπλήστοις κόλποις...ἐναποθώμεθα τὰ θεῖα χαρίσματα ‡Meth.*palm.*5(M.18.392D); merit, Gr.Naz.*or.*19.7(M.35.1049D); teachings of scripture, Chrys. *hom.25.1 in Jo*(8.143B).

ἐναποτίκτω, *engender in*; met., Chrys.*hom.11.3 in 1Thess.*(11. 506E); ‡Proc.G.*Pr.*24:21f.(M.87.1468B).

ἐναποτυπ-όω, *impress upon* ∼ωθέντας ἐπὶ...χειρῶν τύλους Heges. ap.Eus.*h.e.*3.20.3(M.20.253A); τῷ μὲν ἀψύχῳ ζωὴν τῷ δὲ ἀμόρφῳ ὄντι καὶ ἀειδεῖ τὴν φύσιν μορφὴν ∼ούμενος Eus.*d.e.*4.13(p.171.8; M.22. 285A); †Bas.*Is.*82(1.436B; M.30.253A); ‡Bas.*const.*4(2.547B; M.31. 1353A); Thdr.Mops.*Zach.*1:9(M.66.509A).

***ἐναποτυπωτέον,** *one must stamp on*, *engrave on*, Clem.*paed.*3.11 (p.270.11; M.8.633A).

***ἐναπουλόομαι,** *be cicatrized*, Cyr.*ador.*15(1.543B).

***ἐναπουρέω,** *pass urine on*, Philost.*h.e.*7.10(p.97.23; M.65.549A).

***ἐναποφράττω,** *block up*, met. ἐ. τῆς πονηρίας εἴσοδον ‡Sophr.H. *triod.*(M.87.3856D).

ἐναποψύχω, 1. *expire*, *die* (*in*), Gr.Naz.*ep.*182(M.37.297A); Eustrat.*v.Eutych.*96(M.86.2381B); ‡Jo.D.*fid.dorm.*25(M.95.272B); ‡Jo.D.*Artem.*68(p.96.26; M.96.1316D); **2.** *chill*; pass., *be cold*, ‡Max. *cap.al.*89(M.90.1420C).

ἐνάργεια, ἡ, *self-evident truth*, Or.*Cels.*2.30(p.157.25; M.11.849B); τῷ Χριστῷ...μαρτυρουμένῳ ὑπὸ τῆς ἐ. καὶ τῆς τῶν πραγμάτων ἐκβάσεως Eus.*d.e.*9.15(p.436.34; M.22.704C).

ἐνάρετος, 1. *virtuous*; **a.** of Christ θεοῦ πρωτότοκον ἐ. φύσιν Eus. *d.e.*5 proem.(p.202.5; M.22.336A); ἐνηνθρώπησε ὁ υἱὸς καὶ λόγος τοῦ θεοῦ ἵνα...διδάξῃ...ἡμᾶς τὴν ἐ. πολιτείαν ‡Cyr.*Trin.*28(6^3.34A; M.77. 1173A); **b.** ὁ ἐ. βίος as implied aim of Christians, *1Clem.*62.1; Christians persecuted διὰ...τὸν ἐ. ... βίον αὐτῶν Eus.*fr.Lc.*6:20(M.24. 537A); not to lead to pride, Anast.S.*qu.et resp.*109(M.89.761C); **c.** causes of virtue ἡ φιλοσοφία ἐναρέτους ποιοῦσα Clem.*str.*6.17(p.513. 32; M.9.392B); τῷ ἁγίῳ πνεύματι ἑλκόμενοι οἱ μὲν ἐ. *ib.*7.2(p.8.24; 413A); ἡμεῖς δὲ κατὰ μίμησιν γινόμεθα ἐ. καὶ υἱοί Ath.*Ar.*3.19(M.26. 364B); free will, producing τὸ...ἐ. γέννημα, Gr.Nyss.*v.Mos.*(M.44. 328C); Chrys.*hom.12.2 in Jo.*(8.69A); grace, *ib.*76.1(447B); reading of scripture, Euthal.Diac.*Ac.*(M.85.628A); **d.** effects τὸ δὲ ἐ. πᾶν ἀπ' ἀρετῆς τέ ἐστι καὶ πρὸς ἀρετὴν ἀναφέρεται Clem.*str.*6.17(p.513.16; M.9.392A); cf.*ib.*7.2(p.9.31; 416B); οὐδεὶς...ἐ. παρὰ κακοῦ βλάπτεται Hipp.*fr.16 in Pr.*(p.162.21; M.10.620C); ὁ ἐ. ... πάντων ἐστὶ συνετώ- τερος Chrys.*hom.41.3 in Jo.*(8.247A); divine indwelling, Thdr.Mops. *fr.inc.*(p.295.40; M.66.976B); **e.** ref. practice of virtue in different states of life; ref. apostate monk πῶς ἐν τῷ πολυαμαρτήτῳ...βίῳ δυνήσεται κατορθῶσαί τι τῶν ἐ.; Bas.*renunt.*1(2.202E; M.31.628B); κοσμικὸν ἐ. ὑπὲρ μοναχὸν ἄπραγον Pall.*v.Chrys.*19(p.122.33; M.47. 69); **f.** ref. virtue like that of angels: through chastity, Clem.*fr.*1 (p.195.5; M.9.744D); in gen., Chrys.*hom.10.2 in Eph.*(11.76E); **g.** as title of CNic. ἐ. ... συνόδῳ Gel.Cyz.*h.e.*1 proem.2(M.85.1193A); *ib.* 1.10.2(1212B); **2.** *strong*, *excellent* τὰ θηρία...ἐ. Clem.*str.*7.11(p.47.23; M.9.492B); *Ev.Thom.*B 2(p.158); Jo.Mal.*chron.*2 p.32(M.97.101B).

ἐναρέτως, *excellently*, Or.*or.*29.15(p.390.1; M.11.541C).

ἔναρθρος, *articulate*; **1.** ref. voice of God in scripture, his words at Creation not ἔ., Bas.*hex.*3.2(1.23A; M.29.56A); on Sinai ἡ δὲ φωνὴ αὕτη ἔ. ἦν, θείᾳ δυνάμει Gr.Nyss.*v.Mos.*45(M.44.316C); of Father's voice in Jo.12:38, Chrys.*hom.67.2 in Jo.*(8.402C); **2.** ref. testimony of creation to God (Ps.18:4) ἵνα δείξῃ ὅτι ἡ ἐν τῇ κτίσει θεωρουμένη σοφία, λόγος ἐστί, κἂν μὴ ἔ. ᾖ Gr.Nyss.*hex.*11(M.44.73C); Cyr.*Ps.* 18:14(M.69.829B); **3.** Trin., of 'procession' of Word, acc. Marcellus κατὰ προφορὰν φωνῆς ἔ. Eus.*e.th.*2.9(p.109.10; M.24.917B).

ἐναρθρόω, 1. *set* dislocated limb; met., Bas.*reg.br.*102(2.451D; M.31.1153B); **2.** *make articulate*, Epiph.*anc.*31(p.40.28; M.43.73B).

ἐνάρθρως, *with the article*, Cyr.*Chr.un.*(5^1.752D); τὸ εἰπεῖν, ὁ υἱὸς τοῦ θεοῦ, καὶ μὴ εἰπεῖν, υἱὸς θεοῦ, ἐ. σημαίνει αὐτόν, τὸν υἱὸν τοῦ θεοῦ, τὸν ἕνα, τὸν μονογενῆ Jo.D.*haer.Nest.*42(M.95.216B).

ἐναρμόνιος, *harmonious*, exeg. Ps.150:4 τὸ σῶμα λέγει τὸ ἡμέτερον, καὶ χορδὰς τὰ νεῦρα..., δι' ὧν ἐ. εἴληφε τὴν τάσιν Clem.*paed.* 2.4(p.182.27; M.8.441B); τὰ ἐ. ... μέλη τῶν ψαλμῶν Bas.*hom.in Ps.*1 (1.90D; M.29.212B); ref. a bed canopy ἐ. σύνθεσις Gr.Nyss.*hom.4 in Cant.*(M.44.840A); ἡ ἐ. τῶν σπονδύλων θέσις as image of Church, *ib.*7 (933B).

ἐναρμονίως, *harmoniously*, *fittingly*; of Creation, Hipp.*haer.* 4.11(p.44.3; M.16.3075A); Dion.Ar.*d.n.*1.7(M.3.597A); of affections of the soul, id.*e.h.*3.3.5(M.3.432A); of grace of contemplation, id. *d.n.*1.2(M.3.589A).

ἔναρξις, ἡ, **1.** *beginning*, Sophr.H.*v.Anast.*(M.92.1700B); Thphn. *chron.*p.243(M.108.612B); **2.** *aggression, breach of the peace, ib.*p.232 (585C); **3.** liturg., *preliminary part of liturgy* after end of *προσκομιδή* characterized by words of celebrant *εὐλογημένη ἡ βασιλεία τοῦ πατρὸς καὶ τοῦ υἱοῦ καὶ τοῦ ἁγίου πνεύματος* during which psalms are sung in accordance with its preparatory character (celebrant representing Jo. Bapt. as forerunner), ‡Germ.CP *contempl.*(M.98. 401A); ‡Sophr.H.*liturg.*11(M.87.3992B); *ib.*(3992C); *εὐχὴ τῆς ἐ.* being said secretly by priest during it, and at censing in course of it *εὐχὴ τοῦ θυμιάματος τῆς εἰσόδου τῆς ἐ. Lit.Jac.*(Brightman p.32.15); *ib.*(p.32.3); **4.** *beginning* of each of three subdivisions of Psalter divided into twenty sections, *Const.Stud.*4(M.99.1705D).

***ἐνάρρησις**, ἡ, error for *ἀνάρρησις*, Isid.Pel.*epp.*3.90(M.78.796B).

***ἐναρχία**, ἡ, *principle of unity*, Dion.Ar.*d.n.*2.4(M.3.641A).

***ἐναρχικός**, *being the principle of unity ἐ. τριάδι* Dion.Ar.*d.n.*2.4 (M.3.641A); *ib.*3.5(641D); *ib.*4.4(700A).

ἔναρχος, **1.** *original αὐτὸς* [sc. God] *ἐν ἑαυτῷ τῶν ἰδίων πλεονεκτημάτων...ἔ. ἀρχή* Cyr.*Jo.*10.2(4.861E); **2.** *having a beginning* opp. *τὸ ἄναρχον*, *Disp.Phot.*(M.88.560A).

ἑνάς, ἡ, *unity, oneness*; **1.** of God, i.e. divine nature in gen., *deus ...ex omni parte μονάς et ut ita dicam ἑ.* Or.*princ.*1.1.6(p.21.13; M.11. 125A); *ἑ. ἑνοποιὸς ἁπάσης ἑ.* Dion.Ar.*d.n.*1.1(M.3.588B); *μονάδα καὶ ἑ., διὰ τὴν ἁπλότητα καὶ ἑνότητα τῆς ὑπερφυοῦς ἀμερίας ib.*1.4 (589D); ‡Gr.Nyss.*hom.6.1 in Jo.*(p.204.10,12); **2.** of Father and Son *εὐχώμεθα διὰ μὲν τοὺς τηροῦντες τὴν δυάδα, διὰ δὲ τοὺς ἐμποιοῦντες τὴν ἑ., καὶ οὕτως οὐδὲ εἰς τὴν γνώμην τῶν ἀποσχισθέντων ἀπὸ τῆς ἐκκλησίας εἰς φαντασίαν μοναρχίας ἐμπίπτομεν...οὔτε εἰς ἄλλην ἀσεβῆ διδασκαλίαν...τὴν ἀρνουμένην τὴν θεότητα τοῦ Χριστοῦ* Or.*dial.*4(p.126. 16); Eus.*d.e.*4.6(p.158.21; M.22.264C); unity of Persons denied, ref. Jo.10:30 *τί μὴ τηρήσας τῇ ἑ. τὸ πρέπον ἔφασκεν 'ἐγὼ καὶ ὁ πατὴρ ἕν εἰμι'*; Cyr.*Jo.*1.2(4.16E); unity of nature affirmed *τὸ τρισυπόστατον τῆς θείας ἑ.* ‡Meth.*Sym.et Ann.*2(M.18.352C); *υἱόν, τὸν ἄνω...τὴν παρθενίαν τῆς φυσικῆς ἑ. ἀμέριστον...φυλάξαντα ib.*3(353C); Jo.D. *trisag.*12(M.95.45B); dist. from *μονάς*: *μονάς ἐστι καὶ ἑ. τρισυπόστατος* Dion.Ar.*c.h.*7.4(M.3.212C); *αὐτός ἐστι μονάς, ἐπειδὴ τὸ θεῖον ἁπλοῦν καὶ ἀδιαίρετόν ἐστι...ἑ. δὲ διὰ τούτου, ἐπειδὴ καὶ πρὸς ἑαυτὴν ἥνωται ἡ ἁγία τριὰς φυσικῶς* Evagr.Pont.ap.Max.*schol.c.h.*7.4(M.4. 77A); **3.** of angels *ἀγγελικῶν ἑνάδων ζωάς* Dion.Ar.*d.n.*8.5(M.3.892C); **4.** Origenist, of unity from which creatures are supposed to have fallen *τὸ ποικίλον τῆς ἀποπτώσεως τῶν οὐχ ὁμοίως τῆς ἑ. ἀπορρεόντων* Or.*princ.*2.1.1(p.107.5; M.11.182B); *ib.*2.8.3(p.159.5,16); *ib.*(p.160. 15); *εἴ τις λέγει, πάντων τῶν λογικῶν τὴν παραγωγὴν νόας ἀσωμάτους ...γεγονέναι διχὰ παντὸς ἀριθμοῦ...ὡς ἑ. πάντων τούτων γενέσθαι τῇ ταυτότητι τῆς οὐσίας...καὶ τῇ πρὸς τὸν θεὸν λόγον ἑνώσει τε καὶ γνώσει πρὸς* [sc. *δὲ*] *τὸ χεῖρον τραπῆναι...καὶ εἰληφέναι σώματα...ἀ. ἔ.* CCP(543)*anath.*2(p.228; H.3.284C); *ib.*3; *ib.*6; *Χριστὸν...ἐλεήσαντα τὴν ὥς φασι γενομένην πολυσχιδῆ κατάπτωσιν τῶν τῆς αὐτῆς ἑ. ib.*7; cf. Origenist teaching on *ἀποκατάστασις*: *εἰς ἑ. μυθικὴν τὰς... διαφορὰς ἀναχέοντες* Sophr.H.*ep.syn.*(M.87.3184A); cf.Max.*ambig.* (M.91.1070A); **5.** Gnostic aeon, Val.Gn.ap.Epiph.*haer.*31.6(p.393. 13f.; M.41.484D).

ἐνασελγέω, *revel in*, c. dat., Nil.*exerc.*8(M.79.728B).

ἐνασθενέω, *be weak through*; met. *ἐ. τῇ διὰ τὸν σταυρὸν ἀπιστίᾳ* †Bas.*Is.*99(1.448B; M.30.280B).

***ἐνάσκησις**, ἡ, *training* in virtue, Niceph.Ur.*v.Sym.*proem.2(M. 86.2989A).

***ἐνάστειος**, *within the town*, Thphn.*chron.*p.355(M.108.853B).

ἐναστράπτ-ω, *shine in, illuminate, flash into*, met.; **1.** of God *ἡ τριὰς...τῷ φωτὶ μιᾶς θεότητος...ψυχαῖς ~ουσα* Gr.Naz.*or.*21.31(M.35. 1120A); Father and Son *τῷ ἑτέρῳ τὸν ἕτερον ~ειν* Cyr.*Jo.*1.2(4.15E); H. Ghost *~οντος αὐτοῖς τὴν γνῶσιν* id.*dogm.*7(p.562.13; 6[2].377B); id. *Os.*131(3.163E); Proc.G.*Gen.*2:2f.(M.87.148A); **2.** of virtue, Isid.Pel. *epp.*2.210(M.78.649C); *ἐ. γὰρ τοῖς τύποις τῆς εὐσεβείας ἡ μόρφωσις* Cyr.*Am.*22(3.272D); id.*hom.pasch.*10(5[2].136C); of grace, Gel.Cyz. *h.e.*2.22.16(M.85.1293B).

***ἐνασφαλίζομαι**, *confirm*, Epiph.*haer.*69.50(p.197.7; M.42.280B).

ἐνασχολ-έω, *occupy*; **1.** act.; in gen., †Bas.*Is.*165(1.496D; M.30. 389B); Gr.Naz.*ep.*33(M.37.75A); **2.** med.; c. *ἐν*, Men.*exc.Rom.*13 (p.201.16; M.113.897C); c. *ἐπί*, Thphn.*chron.*p.216(M.108.552C); of occupation of mind with spiritual sense of scripture *ἵνα τούτοις ~ούμενος τῶν χειρόνων ἀφέλκηται* †Bas.*Is.*6(1.382B; M.30.128C); of mind occupied with bodily things as prey to Devil, ‡Bas.*const.*17.1 (2.559D; M.31.1380B); Marc.Er.*opusc.*2.161(M.65.956B); of veteran monks *οἱ ~ούμενοι* opp. *οἱ μὴ ἀσκούμενοι*, ‡Epiph.*phys.*22(M.43.532D).

ἐνατενίζ-ω, **1.** *contemplate*, c. dat. **a.** Trin. *ἃ ~ων τῷ πατρὶ ἀρχόμενος ὁ υἱὸς γινώσκει* Or.*Jo.*2.18(12; p.75.25; M.14.145D); Eus.*e.th.* 2.2(p.101.10; M.24.901D); *ib.*3.3(p.154.32; 997B); ref. Jo.5:19 *τοῖς τοῦ γεννήσαντος ἔργοις ~ειν ἑαυτὸν εἰρηκὼς ὁ υἱὸς οὐκ ἀσθενοῦντα δεικνύει, ζηλωτὴν δὲ μᾶλλον* Cyr.*Jo.*2.6(4.216C); **b.** ref. spiritual creatures *αὐτῶν* [sc. seraphim] *ζωὴ...κατὰ φύσιν, τῷ κάλλει τοῦ θεοῦ ~ειν* †Bas.*Is.*185(1.515E; M.30.433A); *οὐ δυναμέναις* [sc. demons] *~ειν τῷ κάλλει τοῦ προσώπου* [i.e. *τῆς ἐκκλησίας*] Or.*schol.in Cant.* 6:3(M.17.276C); **c.** of spiritual men *οἱ δὲ οὐκ ἠθέλησαν ἐ. πρὸς αὐτό* [sc. *τὸ φῶς τὸ ἀληθινόν*] Or.*fr.94 in Jo.*(p.557.20); *μὴ τὸ παρὸν ὁρᾶν, ἀλλὰ τοῖς μικρὸν πορρωτέρω ταῖς ἐλπίσιν ~ειν* Bas.*ep.*240.1(3. 369D; M.32.896B); *οὔτε γὰρ ἀποστερεῖ τινα τῶν βουλομένων αὐτῷ* [sc. Christ] *~ειν* †Jo.D.*B.J.*15(M.96.996B); **d.** ref. God's knowledge of human heart, †Bas.*Is.*2(1.379C; M.30.121C); *πᾶσιν ἀκωλύτως ~οντος* Cyr.*thes.*32(5[1].293A); **2.** *examine ἐ. τῷ βουλήματι ἑκάστης ...λέξεως* Or.*Cels.*3.20(p.217.10; M.11.944A); ‡Max.*cap.al.*78(M.90. 1417B).

ἐνατένισις, ἡ, *fixed attention πρὸς τὸν θεὸν...ἐ.* †Bas.*Is.*proem.3 (1.380A; M.30.124A); *ib.*164(1.496B; M.389A); Nil.*epp.*3.283(M.79. 524C); Max.*ambig.*(M.91.1137A); *ἡ πρὸς τὸ...ὂν ἐ. Schol.* in Max. *opusc.*(M.91.37C).

***ἐνατενῶς**, *attentively*, *cat.Apoc.*7:9ff.(p.292.12).

ἔνατος (ἔννατος), *ninth*; **1.** of hour of prayer, v. *ὥρα*; **2.** neut. plur. as subst., *prayers* offered for dead *on the ninth day* after burial *ἐπιτελείσθω...ἔ. εἰς ὑπόμνησιν τῶν περιόντων καὶ τῶν κεκοιμημένων* *Const.App.*8.42.2; ‡Jo.D.*fid.dorm.*15(M.95.261C); **3.** neut. as subst., *ninth ward* of Alexandria, †Leont.B.*sect.*5.3(M.86.1229C); Justn. *monoph.*tit.(p.7.3; M.86.1104A); Jo.Mosch.*prat.*177(M.87.3048A); in CP, Thphn.*chron.*p.86(M.108.424C).

ἐναυγάζω, **1.** *give light*, Gr.Nyss.*virg.*10(p.289.9; M.46.360D); **2.** *shed* light *into ψυχαῖς ἐ.* [sc. *υἱός*] *φέγγος* Eus.*e.th.*2.14(p.118.12; M.24.933B); **3.** pass., *be irradiated τὴν ἀκοὴν ταῖς ἀκτῖσι τοῦ φέγγους ἐναυγασθῆναι* Gr.Nyss.*v.Mos.*20(M.44.305C).

ἐναυγής, *bright*; of sky, Cyr.*glaph.Ex.*3(1.332C).

***ἐναυθεντέω**, *have full power, be master of*, c. dat., Bas.*reg.fus.*41. 2(2.388C; M.31.1024C); Gr.Naz.*or.*18.36(M.35.1033A).

ἐναυλίζομαι, **A.** *spend the night, bivouac*; fig., of those who die young *τοὺς μὲν διὰ πάντων τῶν τοῦ χρόνου διαστημάτων ὁδεύσαντας· τοὺς δὲ οὐδὲ τοῖς πρώτοις ἐναυλισθέντας τοῦ βίου σταθμοῖς* Bas.*hom.* 21.2(2.164E; M.31.544C).

B. *indwell, abide in*; **1.** of God in saints, Cyr.*Is.*5.3(2.809A); id. *Abac.*32(3.547C); **2.** of Logos; in virtuous actions, Nil.*epp.*3.190 (M.79.472D); in BMV, Cyr.*ador.*9(1.293B); in souls of saints, id. *glaph.Gen.*1(1.12B); **3.** of H. Ghost in men through faith, id.*Jo.*5.2 (4.474E).

ἐναύλιον, τό, *abode*; met., of heart as abode of words of God, Cyr.*ador.*14(1.500B).

***ἐναυλισμός**, ὁ, *indwelling*; of Christ in BMV, Cyr.*ador.*9(1. 137E).

ἔναυλος, ὁ, (*αὐλή*) *indwelling ἐκκλησία, Χριστὸν ἔ. ἔχουσα* Cyr. *ador.*10(1.332B); of God in men, id.*Ps.*32:14(M.69.880B).

ἔναυσις, ἡ, *kindling*; met., Clem.*str.*6.17(p.512.28; M.9.388C).

ἔναυσμα, τό, *spark*; met.; **1.** in gen.; of interest in a subject, Clem.*str.*6.17(p.509.9; M.9.381A); *ἐ. ... ἀγάπης* id.*paed.*2.1(p.157. 28; M.8.388B); *ἐ. ... τὰ ῥήματα* Gr.Nyss.*hom.3 in Cant.*(M.44.821B); *ἔ. πόθου* Proc.G.*Gen.*4:16(M.87.253A); **2.** theol.; of spark of H. Ghost in soul, Tat.*orat.*13(p.14.28; M.6.833C); vestige of Word in creatures, Gr.Nyss.*hom.1 in Cant.*(M.44.781D); spark of Word in Gr. philosophy *ἐ. τινα τοῦ λόγου τοῦ θείου λαβόντες Ἕλληνες* Clem. *prot.*7(p.57.8; M.8.184A); id.*paed.*2.1(p.166.24; M.8.405C); Thdt. *affect.*2(4.742); **3.** with neg. = *not even a vestige*, Thphl.Ant.*Autol.* 2.12(M.6.1069B); Cyr.*Jo.*11.2(4.942A).

ἐναφανίζ-ω, **1.** pass., *disappear*, Hipp.*haer.*1.20(p.24.16; M.16. 3048A); *θεὸς...ᾧ ~εται πᾶσα κακίας ὕλη* Gr.Nyss.*Eun.*5(2 p.119.29; M.45.700D); **2.** *lose in*, met. *νεότητα ἐναφανίσας τῇ ματαιοπονίᾳ* Bas. *ep.*223.2(3.337B; M.32.824A); id.*hom.*12.17(2.112E; M.31.421B); Nil. *epp.*3.10(M.79.372C).

ἐναφίημι, **1.** *leave behind*, †Bas.*Is.*136(1.474C; M.30.340B); Chrys. *hom.39.9 in 1Cor.*(10.377C); id.*hom.10.1 in Heb.*(12.103C); **2.** *shed, infuse into*, Or.*fr.94 in Jo.*(p.558.1); met. *ἀκτῖνα...τοῦ νοήματος ἐναφῶ σου τῇ ψυχῇ* Chrys.*hom.34.2 in 1Cor.*(10.311E); **3.** *introduce into μὴ ἐναφῶσι ταῖς ἐκκλησίαις τὰ σχίσματα* Bas.*ep.*69.2(3.163B; M. 32.433A); Philost.*h.e.*11.7(M.65.601B); **4.** *permit θεὸς...ἐναφιεὶς δὲ τοῖς πόνοις ἑτέρους ἐντρύχεσθαι* Cyr.*Nah.*18(3.497D).

***ἐνάφορμος**, *having a starting-point, reasonable*, Cyr.*Is.*5.1(2. 742C).

***ἐναφόρμως**, error for *εὐαφόρμως*, *opportunely*, Cyr.*Juln.*2(6[2]. 38A).

***ἐναφραίνω**, *be foolish in*, c. dat., Cyr.*Jo*.6.1(4.600E).

***ἐνβάσανος**, *excruciating* τὸν ἀπὸ τοῦ μαρτυρίου πόλεμον ἐ. (sic) Ammon.*Ac*.14:6(M.85.1545A) prob. f.l. for ⟨ἐκβάσανος⟩.

***ἔνβως**, s.v.l., *willingly*, Malchus *exc.Rom*.1(p.161.34; ἔμβως M. 113.768A).

***ἐνδαπαν-άω**, *consume, destroy* (*in*) τῆς ὁρατικῆς δυνάμεως... ~ωμένης Bas.*hex*.6.9(1.59C; M.29.140B); *ib*.(59D; M.140C); Gr.Nyss. *hom.4 in Cant*.(M.44.832B); id.*v.Mos*.(M.44.336C); Pall.*v.Chrys*.20 (p.144.25; M.47.80); ‡Caes.Naz.*dial*.146(M.38.1097); theol., in Eunomius' theory of the natures of ἀγέννητος and μονογενής: ὡς ἀσύμβατον αὐτῶν...τὴν φύσιν καὶ ~ᾶσθαι τῷ ἑτέρῳ τὸ ἕτερον Gr.Nyss. *Eun*.7(2 p.167.9; M.45.757A).

ἐνδαψιλεύομαι, *be liberal, generous in*, Gr.Nyss.*Eun*.1(1 p.49.6; M.45.277B); iron., ref. Eun. τίς...τοσοῦτον ἐνεδαψιλεύσατο ταῖς ἀρνητικαῖς τοῦ κυρίου φωναῖς *ib*.10(2 p.239.29; 841C); v.l. for ἐνεστώσης Sev.Ant.*res*.(p.834.12).

ἐνδεής, **A.** *in need*; **1.** c. genit., *lacking, in need* of, ref. OT sacrifices διὰ τῆς ἁμαρτίας τοῦ λαοῦ ὑμῶν...ἀλλ' οὐ διὰ τὸ ἐ. εἶναι τῶν τοιούτων προσφορῶν Just.*dial*.22.1(M.6.521B); ref. Creation οὐχ ὕλης ἦν ἐ. *Const.App*.5.7.18; agst. idolatry ἐ. ἀεί ποτε ἡ ὕλη τῆς τέχνης Clem.*prot*.4(p.44.15; M.8.153B); agst. Arians οὐ γὰρ ἐ. ἦν πλατυσμοῦ ἡ μονάς ‡Ath.*Ar*.4.14(p.59.6; M.26.488B); ref. Christ ταύτας τὰς...τοῦ πνεύματος δυνάμεις [i.e. gifts of Is.11:1–3] οὐχ ὡς ἐνδεοῦς αὐτοῦ τούτων ὄντος...ἀλλ' ὡς ἐπ' ἐκεῖνον ἀνάπαυσιν μελλουσῶν ποιεῖσθαι,...τοῦ μηκέτι ἐν τῷ γένει ὑμῶν κατὰ τὸ παλαιὸν ἔθος προφήτας γενήσεσθαι Just.*dial*.87.3(M.6.684B); *ib*.88.1(685B); ref. his baptism etc. οὐχ ὡς...ἐ. τούτων ὑπέμεινεν, ἀλλ' ὑπὲρ τοῦ γένους τοῦ τῶν ἀνθρώπων *ib*.88.4(685C); ref. Jo.4:32 οὐκ ἄτοπόν γε λέγειν μὴ μόνον ἀνθρώπους καὶ ἀγγέλους ἐ. εἶναι τῶν νοητῶν τροφῶν, ἀλλὰ καὶ τὸν Χριστὸν τοῦ θεοῦ· καὶ αὐτὸς γάρ, ἵν' οὕτως εἴπω, ἐπισκευάζεται ἀεὶ ἀπὸ τοῦ πατρὸς τοῦ μόνου ἀνενδεοῦς...οὐκ ἄτοπον δὲ καὶ τὸ ἅγιον πνεῦμα τρέφεσθαι λέγειν Or.*Jo*.13.34(p.259.18; M.14.457D); ref. the 'gnostic' οὔτε ἐ. ἐστι κατά γε τὴν ψυχὴν τῶν ἄλλων τινός Clem.*str*. 6.9(p.467.32; M.9.293B); of evil spirits θυμάτων καὶ θυμιαμάτων καὶ σπονδῶν, ὧν ἐ. γεγόνασι Just.*2apol*.5.4(M.6.544C); **2.** abs.; **a.** *in want* οὐκ ἐδύναντο δὲ εὐσεβεῖς ἐνταῦθα ἀποτελεσθῆναι, εἰ μὴ ἦσαν οἱ ἐ. οἷς ἐπικουρήσουσιν *Hom.Clem*.19.23; in anti-pagan apologetic ἐπενδεής ἐστιν [sc. Apollo]; ὅπερ οὐκ ἐνδέχεται θεὸν εἶναι ἐ. Arist. *apol*.11.1(M.96.1116C); and anti-Arian ὑπονοεῖν τὸν κύριον ἐνδεᾶ, ὅταν λέγῃ, 'ἐδόθη μοι' ‡Ath.*Ar*.4.6(p.50.5; M.26.476A); **b.** *deficient*, ref. Trin. γέγονεν δὲ [sc. generation of Logos] κατὰ μερισμόν, οὐ κατὰ ἀποκοπήν· τὸ γὰρ ἀποτμηθὲν τοῦ πρώτου κεχώρισται, τὸ δὲ μερισθὲν οἰκονομίας τὴν διαίρεσιν προσλαβὸν οὐκ ἐ. τὸν ὅθεν εἴληπται πεποίηκεν Tat.*orat*.5(p.5.26; M.6.816A); οὐ γὰρ ἐ. ὁ θεός, οὐδὲ διὰ χρείαν προσελάβετο τὸν υἱὸν εἰς βοήθειαν Ath.*hom.in Mt.11*:27(M. 25.209B); id.*Ar*.2.41(M.26.233C); Χριστιανῶν δὲ ἡ πίστις...οὔτε πλέον τι τῇ τριάδι προστίθησιν, οὔτε ἐ. ποτε ταύτην γεγενῆσθαι λογίζεται *ib*.1.18(49B); **c.** *subject to need* ὁ θεὸς λόγος ἔλαβε...τὸ ἐ. [sc. σῶμα], τὸ θνητόν, κτλ.,...ὅπως τούτων πάντων αὐτὸ ἐλευθερώσῃ Anast.S.*hod*. 13(M.89.220D).

B. comp., *inferior*, ref. submission ἐνδεέστερον γίνεσθαι πάντων ἀνθρώπων Herm.*mand*.8.10.

ἔνδεια, ἡ, *want*; **1.** in gen.; caused by evil spirit Beliar, *T.Benj*. 7.2; not experienced by those who seek necessities of life from Father, Clem.*paed*.3.7(p.260.5; M.8.612A); relief of want a sign of charity, id.*str*.7.12(p.55.18; M.9.508A); τοῦ...ἔνδειαν...δι' ἡμᾶς ὑπομείναντος [sc. Christ] *Const.App*.3.19.4; ὁ ἐνδείας πληρωτής [sc. God] *ib*.7.35.10; Dion.Ar.*d.n*.2.10(M.3.648C); **2.** not found in God, ref. OT sacrifices δι' ἔ. ὁ θεὸς ἐνετείλατο ποιεῖν τοὺς πατέρας ὑμῶν, ἢ διὰ τὸ σκληροκάρδιον αὐτῶν...; Just.*dial*.67.8(M.6.632A); ἡ τῶν πάντων αἰτία...οὐδὲ...ἐν ἐ. ἐστὶ φωτός Dion.Ar.*myst*.4(M.3.1040D); **3.** ref. negative character of evil εἰ εἰσί δὲ πονηροί τινες, κατὰ ἔ. φρενῶν εἰσιν οὗτοι πονηροὶ καὶ οὐ κατὰ γένεσιν Meth.*symp*.8.16(p.107.12; M.18.169D); Dion.Ar.*d.n*.4.23(725B); **4.** esp. of hunger πρὸς τὴν τῶν δαιμόνων φυγὴν ἡ ἔ. ... οἰκειότατόν ἐστι βοήθημα *Hom.Clem*. 9.10.

ἐνδείκτης, ὁ, **1.** *one who shows forth* ἀπόστολος...ἐ. τῆς ἀληθείας *A.Thom*.A 79(p.194.11); **2.** *informer*, Synes.*ep*.118(M.66.1497C); *ib*. 119(1500A); *ib*.131(1516A).

***ἐνδεικτιάω**, *make a show of*, Nil.*epp*.2.19(M.79.208C); v. sq.

***ἐνδεικτιῶνες**, Ephr.3.186C, f.l. for ἐνδεικτιῶντες.

***ἔνδεινα**, f.l. for ἔνδεια, Or.*Jo*.13.7(p.232.5; M.14.409B).

ἔνδειξις, ἡ, **1.** *display*, exeg. Rom.3:25 δικαιοσύνης ἔ., τὸ μὴ μόνον αὐτὸν εἶναι δίκαιον, ἀλλὰ καὶ τὸ ἑτέρους...δικαίους ποιεῖν Chrys. *hom.7.2 in Rom*.(9.485D); sign of goodwill, Synes.*ep*.23(M.66. 1356B); hence **2.** *proof*, Clem.*str*.7.4(p.16.19; M.9.428C); ref. Christ's miracles πρὸς ἔ. τῆς ἀνθρωπότητος καὶ φανέρωσιν τῆς θεότητος Or.*fr. 53 in Jo*.(p.527.17); **3.** *accusation*, ref. Christ ᾧ ἔ. καὶ ἔρις πρὸς ἀνθρώπους οὐδέποτε οὐδεμία Didym.*Trin*.3.17(M.39.876B).

ἐνδεκαχῶς, *in eleven ways*, Jo.D.*dialect*.37(M.94.605A).

ἐνδελεχέω, **1.** *continue, persist* (*in*), c. dat., *T.Gad* 5.1; Marc.Er. *opusc*.2.196(M.65.961A); Eustrat.*v.Eutych*.34(M.86.2313D); **2.** *be constantly present*, Ephr.2.104E; διάβολος...τοῖς μὲν γὰρ διὰ τῆς ἀπογνώσεως ἐ. ‡Ath.*v.Syncl*.85(M.28.1540A).

ἐνδελεχίζω, **1.** *persevere, persist in*, *Const.App*.2.36.6; *ib*.2.36.7; †Cyr.*hom.div*.14(5².413B); **2.** *be constantly present*, *Const.App*.2.59.1; Ant.Mon.*hom*.17(M.89.1481D); *ib*.18(1484B).

ἔνδεσις, ἡ, *binding* to, *union* with πρεσβυτέρα ἡ ψυχὴ τοῦ ἡλίου τῆς ἐ. αὐτοῦ τῆς εἰς τὸ σῶμα Or.*princ*.1.7.4(p.91.5; M.11.174A); Christol. τὴν πρώτην αὐτοῦ εἰς σάρκα ἔ. Eus.*d.e*.10.8(p.481.2; M.22. 773B).

ἔνδεσμος, ὁ, **1.** in architecture, *bonding*, cf.3Reg.6:10, Or.*Jo*.10. 40(24; p.218.5; M.14.385C v.l.); Cyr.*Abac*.26(2.540C); Thdt.*qu.24 in 3Reg*.(1.469); **2.** *bog*, Ephr.1.74D.

ἐνδημ-έω, **1.** *reside in, stay at*, *M.Carp*.1(p.11.4); Soz.*h.e*.3.3.2 (M.67.1037C); **2.** *stay in, at home*, Gr.Naz.*ep*.20(M.37.56A); **3.** *live with*, ref. 2Cor.5:8 οἱ ἐκδημοῦντες ἐκ τοῦ σώματος...~οῦσιν...τῷ κυρίῳ Or.*mart*.4(p.5.24; M.11.568B); Chrys.*hom.3.1 in Philm*.(11. 787C); Jo.D.*hom*.8.10(M.96.716C); **4.** of Christ; **a.** *live, dwell* on earth, *Narr.Jos*.4.3; ὅτε ἐνεδήμει τῷ τῶν ἀνθρώπων γένει Epiph. *haer*.27.6(p.311.3; M.41.373C); abs. οὐκ ἄρα ἄνευ σαρκὸς ἐνεδήμησεν ὁ μονογενής *ib*.42.11(p.150.24; 765C); ~ῶν σαρκὶ ἐν ἀληθείᾳ *ib*.77.35 (p.447.25; M.42.693C); **b.** *indwell* φασὶν [sc. Ebionites]...ἐνδημήσαντα δὲ τὸν Χριστὸν ἐν τῷ Ἀδάμ id.*anac*.30(p.236.15; M.42.857C) = Jo.D. *haer*.30(M.94.696A); **5.** *invade*, Thphyl.*exc.Rom*.4(p.224.6; M.113. 932A); **6.** ? *have in mind, be disposed* to Ῥωμαῖοι τέως πρὸς τὸ συνοίσειν μὴ ἐνδημήσαντες *ib*.5(p.225.31; 933B).

ἐνδημία, ἡ, *sojourning, presence*; **1.** in gen., Pall.*v.Chrys*.19 (p.120.3; M.47.67); Nil.*Eulog*.2(M.79.1096C); of BMV in heaven οὐ θάνατον...σου μετάστασιν λέξομαι, ἀλλὰ...ἐ. Jo.D.*hom*.8.10(M.96.716C); **2.** of Christ incarnate on earth, necessitated by man's sin, Thdr. Heracl.*Is*.53:8(M.18.1357B); ἡ ἔνσαρκος ἐ. Ath.*fr.Pss.comm*.(M.27. 588C); Epiph.*haer*.51.25(p.295.13; οἰκονομίας M.41.933B); ἐ. τῆς ἐνσάρκου παρουσίας *ib*.77.24(p.437.9; M.42.676B); ἡ σωματωδῶς...ἐ. Jo.D.*carm.pent*.117(p.217; M.96.837C); abs., *Incarnation*, Epiph. *haer*.42.9(p.105.21; M.41.708D); *ib*.42.11(p.136.5; 744C); Thdr. Raith.*praep*.(p.192.17; M.91.1493A); **3.** *presence, advent*, of H. Ghost πυρὸς δὲ γλῶσσαι, πνεύματος ἐ. Gr.Naz.*carm*.1.2.34.241(M.37. 963); ἀναμένοντες τὴν ἐ. τοῦ πνεύματος Sev.Ant.*res*.(p.856.10; M.46. 652A).

ἐνδιαβάλλω, **1.** *calumniate, detract*, Iren.*haer*.4.20.12(M.7.1042C); Eus.*h.e*.6.19.2(διαβάλλειν M.20.561C); †Bas.*hom.in Ps*.37(1.370E; M.30.101C); **2.** *deride*, in sense of *cast doubt on* ἐκεῖνο ἐ. ὡς οὐδὲ γεγονός Chrys.*hom.63.1 in Jo*.(8.377B); cf.*cat.Jo*.11:36(p.311.15); Cyr.*Ps*.65:3(M.69.1433C); †Jo.D.*B.J*.24(M.96.1085C); **3.** *reprehend*, Maur. ap.CLater.*act*.2(H.3.732C).

ἐνδιάγ-ω, *pass one's life, continue in* τῷ θεῷ...ᾄδοντας [sc. Christians]...~οντας κελεύει Just.*dial*.74.3(M.6.649B).

***ἐνδιαδοχή, ἡ**, *succession*, Areth.*Apoc*.14(M.106.589A).

ἐνδιάθετος, **A.** *internal, immanent*; **1.** ἐ. λόγος *immanent reason*, opp. uttered speech (προφορικὸς λόγος), cf. *impossibile est autem logo praesente Sigen esse...si autem endiatheton Logon dixerint, endiathetos erit et Sige; et nihilominus solvetur ab endiatheto Logo*, Iren. *haer*.2.12.5(M.7.740A); λόγῳ τῷ ἐν ἡμῖν, εἴτε ἐ. εἴτε καὶ προφορικῷ... οὐκ ἔστιν ἐφικτὸς...ὁ θεός Or.*Cels*.6.65(p.135.19; M.11.1397A); τοῦ λόγου διπλῆ τις...ἔννοια. ὁ μὲν...ὁ διὰ τῆς φωνῆς προφερόμενος...ὁ δέ τίς ἐστιν ὁ ἐ., ἐνυπάρχων ἡμῶν ταῖς καρδίαις· ὁ ἐννοηματικός Bas. *hom*.16.3(2.136B; M.31.477A); ἐ. λόγος τὸ κίνημα τῆς ψυχῆς τὸ ἐν τῷ διαλογιστικῷ γινόμενον ἄνευ τινὸς ἐκφωνήσεως...ὁ δὲ προφορικὸς λόγος ἐν τῇ φωνῇ...τὴν ἐνέργειαν ἔχει Nemes.*nat.hom*.14(M.40.668A); for theol. application v. λόγος; **2.** *inward*, of prayer τὴν ἐ. ὁμιλίαν ὁ θεὸς ἀδιαλείπτως ἐπαΐει Clem.*str*.7.7(p.30.17; M.9.456B); of divine law in the soul, Nil.*epp*.1.208(M.79.160C); Marc.Er.*opusc*.4(M.65. 1016B); **3.** *ingrained, deep-seated*, of affection etc. τῇ...τῶν τέκνων πρὸς τὸν πατέρα ἐ. τιμῇ *Hom.Clem*.3.19; φιλαδελφία ἐ. Bas.*reg.br*.242 (2.496E; M.31.1144C); ἡ ἀγάπη, ἡ πρὸς τὸ καταθύμιον ἐ. σχέσις Gr. Nyss.*anim.et res*.(M.46.93C); id.*hom.2 in Cant*.(M.44.800D); Chrys. *pan.Barl*.4(2.687B); Thdr.Mops.*fr.mir*.(p.339.17; M.66.1004D); τὸ μὲν πρόθυμον τὸ περὶ τὴν νύμφην καὶ τὸ ἐ. ἐπιδεικνύμεναι αἱ νεάνιδες Proc.G.*Cant*.8:8(M.87.1745A).

B. *covenanted*, hence, of scripture, *canonical* ποίαις γραφαῖς πείθῃ;...πάσαις ταῖς ἐ. πείθομαι Adam.*dial*.5.19(p.212.27; M.11.

1857D); τὰ ἐ. βιβλία Bas.*ascet.disc.*1(2.212C; M.31.649B); κατὰ τὰς ῥητὰς γραφὰς καὶ ἐ. Epiph.*haer.*55.2(p.326.1; M.41.973A); Pall.*v. Chrys.*7(p.39.20; M.47.24); Jo.D.*f.o.*4.17(M.94.1180A).

ἐνδιάθηκος, *covenantal*, hence of scriptures *canonical* τὰς ἐ. βίβλους, ὡς Ἑβραῖοι παραδιδόασιν, δύο καὶ εἴκοσι Or.ap.Eus.*h.e.* 6.25.1(M.20.580B); id.*or.*14(p.332.4; M.11.461C) cit. s. ἀντιλέγω; 2Petr. regarded by many as not ἐ., Eus.*h.e.*3.3.1(M.20.217A).

ἐνδιαθρύπτομαι, *give oneself airs*, Gr.Nyss.*Eun.*1(1 p.25.20; M. 45.253B); *ib.*(p.53.25; 281D).

ἐνδιαιτάομαι, *live, dwell in*, met. τῷ θεῷ...ἐ. δεῖ τὸ ἅγιον πνεῦμα Dion.Al.ap.Ath.*decr.*26(p.22.10; M.25.464A); of God indwelling men, Chrys.*pan.mart.*3.3(2.716D); Nil.*Magn.*24(M.79.1000C).

ἐνδιαίτημα, τό, A. *dwelling-place*; **1.** of heaven as ἀγγέλων ἐ. Cyr.H.*catech.*3.5; Cyr.*Ps.*64:2(M.69.1128A); id.*Os.*110(3.142E); of Christ, id.*Pulch.*(p.51.10; 5².165B); of paradise as τὸ ἀρχαῖον ἐ. Anast.Ant.*serm.*3.3(M.89.1389B); **2.** met., of parts of body as dwelling-place; **a.** of faculties ἐ. γὰρ ὥσπερ τοῦ ἐν ἡμῖν λογικοῦ, καρδία καὶ σπλάγχνα Cyr.*ador.*11(1.383D); νοῦ γὰρ ἐ. κεφαλή *ib.*15 (546B); *ib.*16(578E); **b.** of spiritual life τοῖς περὶ θεοῦ λόγοις...ἐ. διδοὺς τὴν καρδίαν *ib.*14(500B); ἐ. ... αὐτῷ [sc. Χριστῷ] φίλον τῶν ἁγίων νοῦς id.*Is.*2.1(2.203A); **3.** of BMV τοῦ θεοῦ ἐ. ‡Meth.*Sym.et Ann.*10 (M.18.373B).

B. medic., *regimen*, Bas.Sel.*or.*30.1(M.85.333A).

ἐνδιαμένω, *continue in*, c. dat., *Hom.Clem.*18.21.

ἐνδιάστροφος, *perverted, perverse*; **1.** in gen., Gr.Nyss.*virg.*22 (p.332.18; M.46.404D); **2.** of heresies ἐ. ... ἑτεροδοξία Acac.Caes.*fr. Marcell.*ap.Epiph.*haer.*72.8(p.263.3; M.42.393B); Bas.*hex.*5.7(1.47C; M.29.112B); Epiph.*haer.*73.1(p.268.7; M.42.401A); Jo.VI CP *ep.*(M. 96.1420A); and other contrary opinions, Chrys.*hom.4.1 in 1Tim.* (11.568B); of heretics οἱ τὴν ψυχὴν ἐ. Bas.*Eun.*1.4(1.213D; M.29. 513B); id.*Spir.*65(3.54C; M.32.188A); id.*ep.*20(3.98A; M.32.285B); **3.** morally, Sever.ap.*cat.Ac.*16:18(p.272.2); neut. as subst., Bas. *reg.fus.*27(2.371D; M.31.988B); Gr.Nyss.*hom.2 in Eccl.*(M.44.640C).

***ἐνδιαστρόφως**, *perversely*; ref. heret. dissensions, Const.ap.Eus. *h.e.*10.5.21(M.20.888C); heret. exegesis, Didym.*Trin.*2.8(M.39. 608C); Epiph.*haer.*42.12(p.182.2; διαστρόφως M.41.812A); morally ἐ. ἔχειν πρὸς μειράκιον Ephr.1.278A.

***ἐνδιασφίγγω**, *bind...to* ὁ θεὸς πάντα...ἀλλήλοις καὶ ἑαυτῷ ἐ. Max. *myst.*1(M.91.664D).

***ἐνδιάτακτος**, liturg., *prescribed, regular* τὸ ἐ. κάθισμα Andr.Cr. *can.BMV* suppl.(M.97.1329C).

ἐνδιατάσσω, *place within*, Clem.*str.*4.25(p.320.4; M.8.1372A).

***ἐνδιατελέω**, *continue in*, c. dat., *Hom.Clem.*3.31.

***ἐνδιατριβή, ἡ**, s.v.l., *delay*, Or.*Jo.*10.19(14; p.190.18; M.14. 340C).

***ἐνδιάτριψις, ἡ**, *occupation with*, ‡Proc.G.*Pr.*23:31(M.87.1457D).

***ἐνδιαχέω**, *diffuse in*, c. dat., ‡Gr.Nyss.*Ar.et Sab.*12(M.45. 1297D).

ἐνδιδύσκ-ω, A. *put on*; **1.** in gen., *A.Thom.*A 23(p.136.20); *M. Perp.*20(p.91.14); Clem.*paed.*3.11(p.271.20; M.8.637B); fig. ἐ. τὴν καλάμην ἀμιάντῳ Ath.*inc.*44.7(M.25.176B); **2.** met., Herm.*sim.*9.13. 5; in paraphrase of 1Cor.15:53, Eus.*d.e.*4.13(p.173.11; M.22.288D); οἱ...∼όμενοι τὸν καινὸν ἄνθρωπον ‡Ath.*dial.Trin.*3.16(M.28.1228C); Ant.Mon.*hom.*74(M.89.1649B); **3.** theol. λόγος...ἐ. τὴν...σάρκα Ath. *Ar.*2.65(M.26.285A); *ib.*3.32(392A).

B. *clothe*, c. acc. pers., Chrys.*hom.11.4 in Heb.*(12.119B); Thdr. Stud.*epp.*2.57(M.99.1296A).

***ἐνδικαστήριος**, *taking place in court*; of legal processes, CChalc. *act.*13(*ACO* 2.1.1 p.55.40; H.2.564A).

ἐνδινέω, *revolve*, Gr.Nyss.*fat.*(M.45.149D).

***ἐνδιοδεύω**, *journey, traverse*, Gr.Nyss.*hom.1 in Eccl.*(M.44. 625C); id.*v.Gr.Thaum.*(M.46.933A); met., id.*hex.*14(M.44.77A); of God τῇ φύσει ἐ. id.*hom.2 in Cant.*(M.44.805D).

***ἔνδιψος**, *liable to thirst* τὸ σῶμα κυρίου...ἔ. Anast.S.*hod.*10(M.89. 169D); neut. as subst., *ib.*13(220D).

ἐνδομυχ-έω, *lurk, lie hidden*; met.; **1.** of various dispositions, Epiph.*anc.*74(p.94.3; M.43.156D); Synes.*insomn.*5(p.153.2; M.66. 1289C); ∼οῦσαν διάθεσιν ‡Nil.*narr.*6(M.79.672B); Philox.*ep.*25(p.176); **2.** esp. of all kinds of evil; demons in souls, *Hom.Clem.*9.9; *ib.*9. 12; sin in gen., Hipp.*haer.*9.11(p.246.8; M.16.3379B); Or.*schol.in Lc.* 9:42(M.17.348A); Mac.Aeg.*elev.*13(M.34.901B); Nil.*epp.*2.209(M.79. 352B); special vices: wrath, †Jo.D.*B.J.*4(M.96.885A); envy, ‡Caes. Naz.*dial.*31(M.38.893); wrong beliefs, pagan, *Hom.Clem.*10.16; heret., Eus.*Marcell.*2.1(p.31.25; M.24.776B); ref. pagan gods ὁ τῇδε [sc. in temple] ἐ. οὐ δαίμων...πλάνος δέ τις ψυχῶν id.*v.C.*3.56(p.104. 3 M.20.1121B); insanity, Chrys.*hom.30.5 in 2Cor.*(10.648A); **3.** neut. ptcpl. as subst., of illness, Gr.Nyss.*or.catech.*29(p.108.12; M.45.76A); of sense of scripture, Cyr.*Jo.*12:1(4.1118E).

ἐνδόμυχος, *interior, being within* a house, Nonn.*par.Jo.*11:20(M. 43.841C); *ib.*20:24(912C); fig. τὸ τῆς ψυχῆς ἐ. ἄλγος Eus.*v.C.*4.65(p.144. 29; M.20.1220D); ἐ. ... πίστις Nonn.*par.Jo.*12:42(857B).

ἔνδον, 1. *within*; **a.** met., ref. spiritual life τὸ φίλτρον ἔ. ἐστὶν ἐν τῷ ἀνθρώπῳ Clem.*paed.*1.3(p.94.15; M.8.257B); id.*prot.*6(p.52.15; M. 8.173B); of indwelling of Christ, Or.*hom.5.6 in Jer.*(p.36.22; M.13. 304D); of sinful thoughts, *ib.1.14*(p.13.8; 272C); faith, Ath.*gent.*30 (M.25.60C); ὁ ἔ. ἄνθρωπος = reason, Clem.*paed.*3.1(p.236.5; 556A); = spiritually as opp. materially minded man, Hegem.*Arch.*5 (p.6.13; M.10.1433C); **b.** theol.; of Word ἔ. μένων ἐν ἡσυχάζοντι τῷ πατρί Eus.*Marcell.*1.1(p.4.15; M.24.717B); *ib.*2.1(p.31.32; 777A); id. *e.th.*1.20(p.91.14; M.24.884B); Μάρκελλος...ἀθετεῖ μὲν τὸν υἱόν, λόγον δέ φησιν ἔ. εἶναι ἐν αὐτῷ *ib.*3.3(p.157.4; 1001B), v. s. λόγος; of divine illumination μένει τε ἔ. ἑαυτῆς ἀραρότως Dion.Ar.*c.h.*1.2(M. 3.121B); **2.** τὰ ἔνδον or τἄνδον; **a.** *what are inside the house*, hence *possessions*, Chrys.*hom.13.4 in 2Cor.*(10.536D); **b.** *interior things*; of moral life, Or.*Cels.*8.75(p.292.19; M.11.1629C); **c.** *esoteric things*; Christian mysteries, Clem.*prot.*1(p.10.17; M.8.68A); **3.** comp. ἐνδοτέρω *more within, closer* to; **a.** met. ἐ. τῆς ἀληθείας Hipp.*haer.* 4.43(p.65.8; M.16.3106B); Clem.*q.d.s.*27(p.178.16; M.9.633B); *more deeply* ἐ. ... καταδῦναι Chrys.*hom.13.2 in 1Cor.*(10.111A); *ib.19.6* (167C); id.*comm.in Gal.*3:28(10.704C); **b.** of time, *within*, Tat.*orat.* 31(p.32.2; M.6.869B); **4.** ἐνδοτάτω *quite within*, met. τῆς διανοίας ἐ. Const.ap.Eus.*v.C.*2.29(p.53.20; M.20.1008A).

ἐνδοξάζ-ομαι, *be glorified, honoured*; **1.** in gen., *T.Sym.*6.5; †Jo. D.*B.J.*6(M.96.904C); **2.** of Son ὁ...μονογενὴς λόγος...πρωτείοις μὲν τῆς τῶν ὅλων ἀρχῆς δευτερείοις δὲ τῆς πατρικῆς βασιλείας ∼όμενος Eus.*l.C.*1(p.198.27; M.20.1324A); but τὸν υἱόν τῇ βασιλείᾳ τοῦ πατρὸς ∼εσθαι Gr.Nyss.*Eun.*10(p.247.18; M.45.852A); id.*Maced.*22 (M.45.1329B).

ἔνδοξος, *glorious, wonderful*; **1.** of divine things, e.g. God's name, Herm.*vis.*3.3.5; *ib.*4.1.3; commandments, id.*mand.*12.3.4; id.*sim.*6.1.1; will, *1Clem.*9.1; Herm.*vis.*1.3.4; benefits, Const.ap. Gel.Cyz.*h.e.*2.7.38(M.85.1241A); **2.** of Christ's second advent opp. first, Just.*dial.*36.1(M.6.553A); δύο παρουσίαι τοῦ Χριστοῦ...μία μὲν ἐν ᾗ παθητός...ἡ δὲ ἑτέρα, ἐν ᾗ καὶ ἔ. ... ἐλεύσεται *ib.*49.2(584A); Dion. Al.ap.Eus.*h.e.*7.24.5(M.20.693C); Ath.*inc.*56.3(M.25.196A); and Transfiguration ἔδειξεν ἡμῖν τὴν ἔ. μορφήν Or.*Cels.*6.68(p.138.20; M. 11.1401C); *ib.*6.77(p.146.23; 1413D); **3.** of angels, Herm.*sim.*7.1; **4.** of Christians, Herm.*sim.*8.10.1 al.; *Barn.*1.2; esp. saints, Polyc. *ep.*3.2, etc.; **5.** of virtues, Meth.*symp.*1.1(p.7.9; M.18.36B) etc.; **6.** ref. external appearance ἀνήρ τις ἔ. ὄψει Herm.*vis.*5.1; **7.** neut. plur. as subst., *matters of conjecture* opp. truth, Clem.*str.*7.16(p.71. 1; M.9.540A); *ib.*8.3(p.84.4; 568B).

ἐνδόξως, 1. *gloriously, magnificently*, *Barn.*16.8; Clem.*str.*4.5 (p.257.11; M.8.1233A); Meth.*symp.*8.17(p.111.15; M.18.173C); of celebration of Easter, id.*res.*2.21(p.376.3; M.18.316A); Eus.*d.e.*7.2 (p.335.13; M.22.548A) etc.; ref. Christ's second advent, Chrys.*bapt.*2 (2.369C) cit. s. ἐπιφάνεια; **2.** *conspicuously*, *Barn.*12.6; **3.** ἐ. ἔχω *be marvellous*, Herm.*sim.*5.5.4.

ἐνδόσιμος, 1. neut. as subst., *signal*, hence *starting point, beginning*, e.g. of teaching, Clem.*q.d.s.*6(p.164.10; M.9.612A); Bas. *Spir.*20(3.17D; M.32.104B); Gr.Nyss.*fat.*(M.45.149A); διδόντος τὸ ἐ. τῇ παρὰ θεοῦ ἀφέσει Vict.*Mc.*11:26(p.396.9); Areth.*Apoc.*1(M.106. 513A); **2.** *yielding*; to emotions, Clem.*str.*7.7(p.34.10; M.9.465A); Gnost. πατὴρ...ἐ. ἑαυτὸν παρασχών id.*exc.Thdot.*30(p.116.28; M.9. 673C); neut. as subst., Niceph.Ur.*v.Sym.*44(M.86.3025B); *gentleness*, Gr.Naz.*or.*16.4(M.35.940A); **3.** neut. as subst.; **a.** *permission*, Thdr. Heracl.ap.*cat.Ac.*8:32(p.145.6); Gr.Ant.*exerc.*(p.229.18; M.88.1884B); Niceph.Ur.*v.Sym.*138(M.86.3113D); **b.** *interval, respite*, Evagr.*h.e.* 2.18(p.80.4); *ib.*(p.85.7; M.86.2576A); **4.** *engrafted* τὸ εἰς τὸν Ἰησοῦν ἐ. ἐστι, ὁ...λόγος Leont.H.*Nest.*5.14(M.86.1736D).

ἔνδοσις, ἡ, 1. *imparting*; meton., of *impulse imparted*, Synes. *provid.*9(p.81.1; M.66.1228B); **2.** *interval* of time, CChalc.*can.*30; *Chron.Pasch.*p.299(M.92.752A).

***ἐνδοτέον**, *one must concede*, Clem.*paed.*2.10(p.221.13; M.8.525A).

ἐνδότερος, *inner* ἐ. οἴκῳ *Hom.Clem.*2.26; Chrys.*hom.14.4 in Mt.* (7.183E); id.*hom.8.4 in Eph.*(11.59C); Jo.Mosch.*prat.*78(M.87.2933C); met. ἡ λαμπὰς τοῦ ἐ. ἀνθρώπου Jo.Thess.*dorm.BMV* 2.8(p.418.31); Gnost.; of 'spiritual body', Epiph.*haer.*31.7(p.397.20; M.41.488C); = *more familiar*, Dion.Ar.*ep.*8.1(M.3.1089A); superl., myst., *innermost* φωτισμὸν τοῦ ἐ. ἀνθρώπου Call.*v.Hyp.*(p.102); *most intimate*, ἐκ τῶν ἐ. καὶ μακαρίων διατριβῶν Or.*schol.in Cant.*7:11f.(M.17.284D); τὰ...ἐ. τῶν θεοειδῶν ἀγαλμάτων Dion.Ar.*ep.*9.1(M.3.1108A); neut.

plur., innermost parts, met., of soul, Chrys.hom.17.2 in Mt.(7.224B); id.hom.7.1 in Heb.(12.71D).

*ἐνδότης, ἡ, inwardness οὐδὲ...πώποτε τῆς οἰκείας ἑνικῆς ἐ. ἀπολείπεται [sc. ἡ τοῦ πατρὸς φωτοδοσία] Dion.Ar.c.h.1.2(M.3.121B, v.l. ἑνότητος); τῆς κατὰ νοῦν ἐ. ‡Proc.G.Pr.1:20(M.87.1229C).

ἐνδοτικός, yielding, met. τὴν καρδίαν...ἐ. ... τῷ θεῷ ποιεῖν Mac.Aeg.libert.ment.19(M.34.952D).

ἐνδοτικῶς, gently, softly; comp., Just.dial.79.2(M.6.661B).

*ἔνδοτος, v. ἔκδοτος.

*ἐνδοχή, ἡ, hearing, attention, ‡Chrys.infant.(10.751A).

ἐνδρανής, active, strenuous, Fr.hist.ap.Jo.Mal.chron.13 p.344(M.97.513A); ib.p.349(520C).

*ἔνδρυμος, dwelling in a wood; of animals, ‡Caes.Naz.dial.110 (M.38.985).

ἐνδυάζω, be in doubt, †Dion.Al.fr.Eccl.2:15(p.221.12; M.10.1585A); Pall.v.Chrys.18(p.112.27; M.47.62); Thdt.Abac.proem.(2.1536).

ἐνδυασμός, ὁ, uncertainty, Pall.h.Laus.86(p.119.12; M.34.1193D); Jo.Thess.mul.ung.1(M.59.636).

[*]ἐνδυαστῶς, = ἐνδοι-, in doubt, Ath.ep.Amun.(M.26.1172C) al.

ἔνδυμα, τό, garment; 1. lit., usu. plur., robes, vestments; of Jewish high priest, Or.princ.4.1.3(p.296.13; M.11.345C); A.Phil.14 (p.7.23); myst. significance φασὶ δὲ καὶ τὸ ἔ., τὸν ποδήρη, τὴν κατὰ σάρκα προφητεύειν οἰκονομίαν, δι' ἣν προσεχέστερον εἰς κόσμον ὤφθη [sc. Logos] Clem.str.5.6(p.353.6; M.9.65B); habit of a consecrated virgin, M.Ner.et Ach.9(p.9.2); of garments worn by newly baptized τὰ νεοφωτιστικὰ ἐ. Jo.Mosch.prat.207(M.87.3099B); symbolical interprn., Gr.Nyss.bapt.diff.(M.46.420C); Chrys.hom.39.5 in Gen.(4.403D); of Joseph's coat (exeg. Gen.37:23ff.) κατ' ἄλλο σημαινόμενον εἴη [δ'] ἂν ἐπιθυμία ⟨τὸ⟩ ποικίλον ἔ., εἰς ἀχανὲς ἀπάγουσα βάραθρον Clem.str.5.8(p.362.21; M.9.84C); 2. met.; a. ἄνθρωπος οὐ δύναται εὑρεθῆναι εἰς τὴν βασιλείαν τοῦ θεοῦ ἐὰν μὴ αὗται [sc. virgins, as powers of Son of God] αὐτὸν ἐνδύσωσι τὸ ἔ. αὐτῶν Herm.sim.9.13.2; of a body of Christians ἦν αὐτῶν ἓν πνεῦμα καὶ ἓν σῶμα [καὶ ἓν ἔ.] ib.9.13.7; (cf. μιᾷ χρόᾳ τῶν ἱματίων αὐτῶν ib.9.13.5); of resurrection bodies Ἰησοῦς...ἐνδῦσαι ἡμᾶς τὰ ἡτοιμασμένα ἐ., ἐὰν πράξωμεν αὐτοῦ τὰς ἐντολάς, ὑπέσχετο Just.dial.116.2(M.6.744C); τὰ ἐ. αὐτὰ τὰ ἐν οὐρανοῖς Meth.res.2.15(p.362.14; M.18.309C); b. of persons as ἐ. of H. Ghost, Hom.Clem.8.23 cit. s. πρόλημμα; c. of body as ἔ. of soul; in Brahman philosophy, Hipp.haer.1.24(p.28.5; M.16.3052A); Christian τῷ ἐ. ἐλαττουμένου [sc. τοῦ γνωστικοῦ] παρὰ τοὺς ἀγγέλους Clem.str.4.3(p.251.22; M.8.1221A); ἐπικαλύμματι τῆς γενέσεως ἡμῶν...τὰ ἐ. ταῖς ψυχαῖς ἐργαζομένη [sc. creative power of God at generation of each human being] Meth.symp.2.5(p.21.8; M.18.53C); d. ref. Inc.; of human body of Christ, Clem.str.5.6(p.353.6; M.9.65B); ὁ κύριος...ἔ. ἔχων τὸ ἀνθρώπινον σῶμα †Hipp.theoph.4 (p.259.11; M.10.856A); τὸν ἄνθρωπον ὄργανον γενονότα καὶ ἔ. τοῦ μονογενοῦς Meth.symp.3.7(p.33.17; M.18.69C); Ath.inc.44(M.25.176C); τὸ σῶμα τοῦ κυρίου...τοῦ λόγου γεγονὸς (? γέγονεν) ἔ. id.ep.Adelph.7(M.26.1081B); e. of soul (Gnost.) ref. resurrection τὰ πνευματικὰ...'ἐ. γάμων' τὰς ψυχὰς λαβόντα Clem.exc.Thdot.61(p.127.25; M.9.689A); ἡ...τῶν πνευματικῶν ἀνάπαυσις ἐν κυριακῇ...παρὰ τῇ μητρί, ἔχοντα τὰς ψυχάς, τὰ ἐ. ἄχρι συντελείας ib.63(p.128.10; 689B); f. of baptism, †Bas.bapt.1.2.27(2.648E; M.31.1572B); βάπτισμα...ἔ. φωτεινόν Cyr.H.procatech.16; ἔ. ... ὡς αἰσχύνης κάλυμμα Gr.Naz.or.40.4(M.36.364A); τὸ ἔ. τοῦ Χριστοῦ δι' αἰσχρῶν ἔργων...μὴ μολύναντας (cf. Gal.3:27) Bas.Sel.v.Thecl.1(M.85.485A); of divine power conferred at baptism τοῖς...καθαροῖς...ἐνοικεῖν καὶ τὸ ἅγιον δύναται πνεῦμα καὶ ἡ ὡς ἔ. ἐξ ὕψους δύναμις Or.Jo.32.7(6; p.436.23; M.14.760A); of spiritual regeneration ἅτινα [sc. ἀφθαρσία καὶ ἀθανασία] ὡς ἐ. τῷ ἐνδυσαμένῳ καὶ περιεχομένῳ τῶν τοιούτων ἐ. οὐκ ἐᾷ φθαρῆναι ἢ ἀποθανεῖν τὸν περικείμενον αὐτά (ref. 1Cor.15:53) id.Cels.7.32(p.183.19,20; M.11.1465D); ὃν ἐντὸς γενόμενον [sc. τὸν θεὸν λόγον] ἔ. ποιεῖται ἑαυτῆς ἡ ψυχὴ κατὰ τὴν τοῦ ἀποστόλου ὑφήγησιν [Eph.4:24]...'Ἰησοῦν δὲ λέγει τὸ ἔ. Gr.Nyss.hom.11 in Cant.(M.44.1005A); πάντες...τὸ τῆς ἀφθαρσίας ἔ. περιβαλοῦνται Thdt.2Cor.5:3 (3.313); g. ref. Jo.1:21ff. προφήτην μὲν καὶ Ἠλίαν ὁ σωτὴρ ἐπὰν αὐτὸν [sc. John the Baptist] λέγῃ, οὐκ αὐτὸν ἀλλὰ τὰ περὶ αὐτόν, φησί [sc. Heracleon], διδάσκει...τὰ περὶ αὐτὸν οἱονεὶ ἐ. ἣν ἕτερα αὐτοῦ Heracleon ap.Or.Jo.6.20(12; p.130.12; M.14.236D); πῶς γὰρ ἐνδύματα τὸ εἶναι τὸν Ἠλίαν τὸν μέλλοντα ἔρχεσθαί ἐστιν Ἰωάννου, οὐ πάνυ τι κατ' αὐτὸν [sc. Heracleon] θεωρῶ· τάχα καθ' ἡμᾶς, ὡς δεδυνήμεθα διηγησαμένους τὸ 'ἐν πνεύματι καὶ δυνάμει Ἠλίου' δυναμένου πῶς λέγεσθαι τοῦτο τὸ πνεῦμα Ἠλίου ἔ. εἶναι τῆς Ἰωάννου ψυχῆς Or.ib.(p.130.14,18; 236D,237A); h. of letters or ciphers as transient ἐ. of words or ideas, to which human body of Christ is compared εἰ γὰρ τῷ γράμματι, ὅ ἐστιν ἔ. λόγου, ὁ ἐμὸς λόγος οὐ συναναφανίζεται, ὁ θεὸς λόγος, ἡ πηγὴ τῆς ζωῆς, τῇ σαρκὶ συναπέθνησκε; Sever.ap.Thdt.eran.3(4.254); acc. Origen, of lit. significance of scripture τὸ ἔ. τῶν πνευματικῶν, λέγω δὲ τὸ σωματικὸν τῶν γραφῶν Or.princ.4.2.8 (14; p.320.15; M.11.373A); cf. 'τὰ ἱμάτια' (Mt.17:2) τοῦ λόγου αἱ λέξεις εἰσὶ τῆς γραφῆς, ἔ. τῶν θείων νοημάτων τὰ ῥήματά ἐστι ταῦτα id.Cels.6.77(p.148.4); i. of abstracts, Herm.mand.12.1.2; τὸ τῆς αἰσχύνης ἔ. Clem.str.3.13(p.238.25; M.8.1193A); of calumnies against the Christians ῥυπαρὰ...ἐ., περιτεθέντα ὑφ' ὑμῶν [sc. Ἰουδαίων] πᾶσι τοῖς ἀπὸ τοῦ ὀνόματος τοῦ Ἰησοῦ γενομένοις Χριστιανοῖς Just.dial.117.3(M.6.748A); 3. met., cloak, disguise ἔ. τῆς ἀσεβείας ἐστιν...ἡ φιλία τοῦ γράμματος Gr.Naz.or.31.3(p.147.9; M.36.136A).

[*]ἐνδυμένεια (ἐνδυμενία), ἡ, clothing, Epiph.anac.15(M.42.845C; ἐνδυμενία p.167.15).

*ἐνδυναμία, ἡ, strengthening τὴν πανοπλίαν...προβάλλειν ἑαυτῷ...εἰς θωρακισμὸν ἑαυτοῦ καὶ ἐ. Epiph.haer.66.46(p.83.21; M.42.100A).

ἐνδυναμ-όω, 1. strengthen; a. in gen. τὰ σώματα...ταῖς...τροφαῖς ∼οῦνται †Bas.Is.99(1.448C; M.30.280C); Chrys.hom.4.1 in 2Tim.(11.678E); οἱ πατέρες...∼οῦσι τὸν ἄνθρωπον διὰ τῆς διδασκαλίας αὐτῶν Dor.doct.13.9(M.88.1769D); b. esp. of God, Just.dial.88.5(M.6.685C); ἐν τοῖς ἁγίοις γινόμενος ὁ θεὸς ∼οῖ αὐτούς Ath.Ar.3.1(M.26.324B); Lit.ap.Const.App.8.15.5; ἡ γῆ...ἐνδυναμώθη τῷ θελήματι τοῦ θεοῦ Chrys.hom.25.1 in Jo.(8.144E); of Christ, Ign.Smyrn.4.2; ἡ δύναμις καὶ ἡ βούλησις τοῦ σωτῆρος ἐνεδυνάμωσεν τὴν σάρκα εἰς τὸ θεάσασθαι [i.e. at Transfiguration] Clem.exc.Thdot.5(p.107.7; M.9.656C); M.Ariadn.(p.131); of H. Ghost, Herm.sim.9.1.2; 2. ascribe strength to (ref. 1Par.29:11) ἐνισχύσαντες καὶ ∼ώσαντες θεοῦ τὴν δύναμιν ὡμολογήσαμεν Epiph.haer.69.62(p.211.6; M.42.301C).

*ἐνδυνάμωσις, ἡ, strengthening, invigoration, Serap.euch.13.15; Thdr.Stud.epp.1.42(M.99.1064A).

ἐνδύνω, v. ἐνδύω.

*ἐνδυσία, ἡ, dress σχήματα ἐθελοθρησκευτικὰ τῆς ἐ. Jo.D.haer.15 (M.94.688A).

*ἐνδυσμενία, τά, s.v.l., garments, clothing, ‡Ath.syntag.4.5 (ἐνδυομενυία M.28.840D; v. Batiffol Studia Patristica not. ad loc. p.129).

*ἐνδυτή, ἡ, 1. garment, Thphn.chron.p.379(M.108.908B); 2. altar-cloth, also called ἅπλωμα or τραπεζόφορον laid above the κατασάρκα and beneath the εἰλητόν q.v., Euchol.(p.498).

ἐνδύ-ω (ἐνδύνω), [aor. 3 sg. ἐνέδυ Clem.q.d.s.37(p.184.5; M.9.641C); ptcpl. ἐνδύνας Cyr.H.catech.3.6]; A. usu. med.; 1. put on, clothe oneself in; fig.; a. (Manichean) ref. creation of man τὸν πρῶτον ἄνθρωπον τὰ πέντε στοιχεῖα...∼σάμενον ὡς πρὸς κατασκευὴν πολέμου Hegem.Arch.7(p.10.8; M.10.1437B); b. pass., be clad in (Origenist) ψυχὰς...σώμασι παχυτέροις τοῖς καθ' ἡμᾶς ἐνδυθῆναι καὶ ἀνθρώπους ὀνομασθῆναι Or.princ.2.8.4(p.160.3); view anathematized, CCP(543)anath.4; c. (Basilidean) πνεῦμα ἅγιον...ἡ υἱότης ἐνδυσαμένη Hipp.haer.7.22(p.199.10; M.16.3307A); cf.ib.10.14 (p.275.9; 3430A); d. (Ebionite) ἐνδημήσαντα δὲ τὸν Χριστὸν ἐν τῷ Ἀδὰμ πρῶτον καὶ κατὰ καιρὸν ἐκδυόμενον αὐτὸν τὸν Ἀδὰμ καὶ πάλιν ∼όμενον Epiph.anac.30(p.236.16; M.41.284C); but cf. τὸν Χριστὸν...κατὰ καιρὸν ∼όμενον αὐτὸν τὸν Ἀδὰμ καὶ πάλιν ἐκδυόμενον ib.(M.42.857C); e. of act of Inc.; i. orthodox statements ὁ δι' ἡμᾶς ἄνθρωπον ∼σάμενος Clem.str.4.21(p.305.23; M.8.1340B); ὁ λόγος τοῦ θεοῦ ἄσαρκος ὢν ἐνεδύσατο τὴν ἁγίαν σάρκα ἐκ τῆς ἁγίας παρθένου Hipp.antichr.4(p.6.21; M.10.732B); διὰ τοῦτο εἰκότως ἐνεδύσατο σῶμα ὁ σωτήρ, ἵνα συμπλακέντος τοῦ σώματος τῇ ζωῇ μηκέτι ὡς θνητὸν ἀπομείνῃ ἐν τῷ θανάτῳ, ἀλλ' ὡς ἐνδυσάμενον τὴν ἀθανασίαν λοιπὸν ἀναστὰν ἀθάνατον διαμείνῃ. ἅπαξ γὰρ ∼σάμενον φθορὰν οὐκ ἂν ἀνέστη εἰ μὴ ἐνεδύσατο τὴν ζωήν Ath.inc.44.6(M.25.176A); CSard.ep.cath.ap.Thdt.h.e.2.8.48(3.847) cit. s. ἄνθρωπος; Ath.Ar.2.9(M.26.165A); ib. infra(l.c.); τὸ κτιστὸν ∼σάμενος γέγονεν ἡμῖν ὅμοιος κατὰ τὸ σῶμα ib.61(277A); τὸν γὰρ Ἀδὰμ ∼σάμενος σὺν τοῖς παθήμασι κατὰ πάντα χωρὶς ἁμαρτίας, τὸν κεκλημένον Ἰησοῦν, ἵνα δι' αὐτοῦ τὸ ἀπολόμενον πρόβατον προσάξῃ τῷ πατρί ‡Ath.serm.fid.15(p.10; M.26.1269D); Epiph.haer.62.5(p.394.16; M.41.1057A); ὁ υἱὸς καὶ λόγος τοῦ θεοῦ...σῶμα ∼σάμενος ἔμψυχον, νοερόν, λογικόν, καὶ ἁπλῶς εἰπεῖν ἀνθρώπινον †Leont.B.sect.1.3(M.86.1197B); ἐνεδύσατο [sc. the human body of Christ] τὸν ἀσώματον τοῦ θεοῦ λόγον Ath.inc.44.8(176C); τὸ σῶμα...∼σάμενον δὲ τὸν ὑπὲρ ἄνθρωπον λόγον, γέγονεν ἄφθαρτον id.ep.Adelph.10(M.26.1068A); ii. heret. views: Gnost. σπέρμα...παρὰ τῆς τεκούσης ἐνεδύσατο [sc. Ἰησοῦς Χριστός], οὐ χωρισθείς, ἀλλὰ χωρήσας αὐτὸ δυνάμει...κατὰ δὲ τὸν Τόπον γενόμενος εὗρεν Ἰησοῦς Χριστὸν ∼σασθαι τὸν προκεκηρυγμένον...ἀλλὰ καὶ οὗτος ὁ ψυχικὸς Χριστός, ὃν ἐνεδύσατο, ἀόρατος ἦν, ἔδει δὲ...αἰσθητοῦ σώματος ἀνέχεσθαι Clem.exc.Thdot.59(p.126.17,19,22; M.9.688A); Docetist ἐγεννήθη τὸ ἐξ αὐτῆς [sc. Μαρίας] ὡς γέγραπται. γεννηθὲν δὲ ἐνεδύσατο αὐτό, ἄνωθεν ἐλθὼν [sc. ὁ μονογενὴς παῖς] Hipp.haer.8.10(p.230.15; M.16.3355A); φάσκουσι...

ἐνδεδύσθαι δὲ τὸν Ἰησοῦν τὴν δύναμιν ἐκείνην τὴν μονογενῆ *ib.*10.16 (p.278.12; 3434C); ἐλούσατο εἰς τὸν Ἰορδάνην...τύπον καὶ σφράγισμα λαβὼν ἐν τῷ ὕδατι τοῦ γεγεννημένου σώματος ἀπὸ τῆς παρθένου, ἵν' ὅταν ὁ ἄρχων κατακρίνῃ τὸ ἴδιον πλάσμα θανάτῳ...ψυχὴ ἐκείνη ἐν τῷ σώματι τραφεῖσα, ἀπεκδυσαμένη τὸ σῶμα...~σηται τὸ ἐν τῷ ὕδατι, ὅτε ἐβαπτίζετο, ἀντὶ τῆς σαρκὸς ἐκείνης ἐκτετυπωμένον σῶμα *ib.*8.10(p.230.22; 3355B); Arian ἵνα...τὸ ἑαυτοῦ [sc. τοῦ λόγου] ὁμοούσιον ~σηται Ath.*ep.Epict.*4(p.8.12; M.26.1057A); **f.** ref. Heb.1:1 πάντοτε ἄνθρωπον ὁ φιλάνθρωπος ~εται θεὸς εἰς τὴν ἀνθρώπων σωτηρίαν, πρότερον μὲν τοὺς προφήτας, νῦν δὲ τὴν ἐκκλησίαν Clem.*ecl.*23.3(p.143.9; M.9.708D); **g.** of spiritual gifts or qualities, *1Clem.*30.3; Herm.*vis.*3.12.2; Ath.*gent.*34(M.25.68C); id.*inc.*28.2(M.25.144C); τοὺς βιωτικαῖς ἐνδεδυμένους φροντίσι Chrys.*hom.*55.5 *in Mt.*(Gaume; ἐνδεδεμένους 7.562B); ref. Rom.13:14, Cyr.H.*catech.*19.10; ἵν' οὖν ταῦτα φύγωμεν ἅπαντα [sc. τὰ κακά] τὸν Χριστὸν ~σώμεθα...ἐπεὶ καὶ τοῦτό ἐστιν ~σασθαι, τὸ μηδέποτε αὐτοῦ ἀπολειφθῆναι, τὸ πάντοθεν αὐτὸν φαίνεσθαι ἐν ἡμῖν διὰ τῆς ἁγιωσύνης ἡμῶν, διὰ τῆς ἐπιεικείας...ὁ γὰρ ~σάμενος, ἐκεῖνο φαίνεται ὅπερ ἐνδέδυται Chrys.*hom.*26.4 *in Rom.*(9.699E); cf. οἱ φοροῦντες φῶς Χριστόν εἰσιν ἐνδεδυμένοι· καὶ οἱ ἐνδεδυμένοι Χριστὸν πατέρα ἐνδέδυνται Ath.*inc.et c.Ar.*15(M.26.1009C); ref. Eph.4:24 οὔτε δὲ ὁ Παῦλος κατ' οὐσίαν κτιζομένους ἐν τῷ κυρίῳ δύο τινὰς ἐδήλου, ἀλλ' οὐδὲ ἄλλον τινὰ ~σασθαι ἡμᾶς ἄνθρωπον συνεβούλευεν· ἀλλὰ τὸν μὲν κατὰ θεὸν ἄνθρωπον, τὸν κατ' ἀρετὴν βίον ἔλεγε id.*Ar.*2.46(M.26.245A); **h.** in other contexts, Eus.*v.C.*1.1(p.7.17; M.20.912B); τὸ τῆς ἀρχῆς ~σασθαι ὄνομα *Hom.Clem.*3.63; ὢ καινῆς αἱρέσεως, ὅλον ~σαμένης τὸν διάβολον ἐν ἀσεβείᾳ καὶ πράξει Ath.*h.Ar.*66(p.219.11; M.25.772A); ἐν παντὶ...τὸ θεῖον, καὶ ~όμενον καὶ ἐμπεριέχον καὶ ἐγκαθημένον (cf. Ps.104:1,2) Gr.Nyss.*or.catech.*25(p.95.5, v.l. ἐνδύον μὲν M.45.65D); **2.** abs., *dress oneself*, Chrys.*hom.*25.1 *in Rom.*(9.695A); perf. ptcpl. pass., *be clad* or *dressed* τί γὰρ ἐλύπει ἐνδεδυμένον αὐτὸν νίψαι τοὺς πόδας τῶν μαθητῶν; Or.*Jo.*32.4(p.431.22; M.14.749C); Ath.*h.Ar.*25(p.196.32; M.25.721D); **3.** pass., of objects, *be plated with*, Chrys.*hom.*83.4 *in Mt.*(7.795E); **4.** c. genit., *cling closely to*, met. ὀδυνηρῶν...ὧν μᾶλλον ~εται καὶ ἐντυποῦται μνήμη Aen.*dial.*(M.85.901A); **5.** *enter*, met., ref. Ac.8:9 ~σάμενος ὁ διάβολος ὑπηρέτην αὐτοῦ *Const.App.*6.7.1.

B. causal, *put on* another, *clothe in*; **1.** met. τὰ σώματα...τῶν μὲν ἀξίων ~σει ἀφθαρσίαν [sc. ὁ κύριος] Just.*1apol.*52.3(M.6.405A); Ath.*inc.*9.2(M.25.112B); πάντας...ἐν τῷ ἰδίῳ σώματι ἐνεδύσατο [sc. Son] ‡Ath.*serm.fid.*36(p.30; M.26.1289A); Didym.*Trin.*2.13(M.39.692B); **2.** *invest with authority*, Thphn.*chron.*p.37(M.108.148B); *ib.*p.56 (193C).

ἐνεάζω, *be silent*, Pall.*h.Laus.*1(p.15.24; M.34.1010A).

ἐνεαρίζω, *spend the spring in*, c. dat. loci, Gr.Naz.*or.*44.10(M.36.620A).

***ἐνεγγυάω**, **1.** *promise, guarantee*, Chrys.*hom.*23.4 *in Mt.*(7.289A); *confirm* a statement, *ib.*40.2(440B); **2.** *stand sponsor to* [sc. at baptism], c. acc. pers., Jo.Mosch.*prat.*207(M.87.3100C).

ἐνέδρα, ἡ, *trickery, treachery* τὰς ἐ. τοῦ διαβόλου Ign.*Trall.*8.1; id. *Philad.*6.2; *Ep.Lugd.*ap.Eus.*h.e.*5.1.14(M.20.413B).

[*]**ἐνεδρευστικός**, prob. f.l. for ἐνεδρευτικός, *insidious*, Nil.*epp.*3.265(M.79.516C).

***ἐνεδρευτικῶς**, *insidiously*, Nil.*exerc.*29(M.79.757B).

ἐνεδρεύ-ω, **1.** of a council, *hold a session, meet*, Sophr.H.*ep.syn.*(M.87.3185A); **2.** *lie waiting*, med. ἀπαλλαγήσεσθαι τοῦ νοσήματος προσδοκῶν ἐνηδρεύετο Ammon.*Jo.*5:5(M.85.1429B); in bad sense, *lie in wait for, beset with snares*, met. ~ων [sc. ὁ διάβολος] τὴν ὁδὸν τῆς δικαιοσύνης Hipp.*fr.*35 *in Gen.*(p.64.15); *Hom.Clem.*1.8; Max.*ambig.*(M.91.1124C); pass., *be ensnared* or *deceived*, *Hom.Clem.*2.7; *ib.*11.3; ὑπὸ τῶν προσκαίρων ἡδονῶν...~εσθε *ib.*11.17; Meth.*fr.*6 *in Job*(p.512.10); Ath.*apol.Const.*26(M.25.628A); of Devil, Meth.*symp.*8.10(p.92.7; M.18.153A); **3.** *defraud, deprive*; c. acc. pers., Chrys.*hom.*9.1 *in Heb.*(12.93A,B); **4.** *hinder*, pass. ~εσθαι ἔμελλε τὰ τῶν ἐκκλησιῶν Chrys.*hom.*10.2 *in 1Tim.*(11.600C).

***ἐνεδριοάω**, *occupy a seat*; fig., of bishops, Gr.Naz.*carm.*2.1.13.7(M.37.1228A).

ἐνεθίζω, *accustom to* a thing, Chrys.*hom.*2.4 *in 2Thess.*(11.521B).

***ἐνεῖδος, τό,** *that which has form* or *shape*, Gr.Naz.*carm.*1.1.4.20(M.37.417A).

ἐνειλινδ-έομαι, *be involved* or *immersed in* τὸ ~εῖσθαι συχναῖς...τύχαις καὶ πράξεσι Synes.*ep.*151(M.66.1552B).

ἐνείργω, *shut up in, confine within*; of relation between soul and body τοῦ σώματος ἐν ᾧ ἐνεῖρκται ἡ ψυχή Or.*exc.in Ps.*77:31(M.17.144 'A'); Meth.*res.*1.29(p.258.6; M.41.1136C).

ἐνείρω, *put* or *join together, engraft*; met., Ath.*gent.*9(M.25.20B); τὴν ἐμὴν διάνοιαν οἱόν τινα βραχὺν μόσχον τῇ ἰκμάδι τοῦ μεγάλου δένδρου, τῇ τοῦ διδασκάλου ἡμῶν σοφίᾳ, ἐνείρας Gr.Nyss.*hex.*2(M.44.64B); ‡Meth.*Sym.et Ann.*8(M.18.368D).

***ἐνέκβασις, ἡ,** *fulfilment*, Sophr.H.*or.*7.5(M.87.3328D).

***ἐνεκτικός**, *continuous* προσκαρτερητέον...τῇ ἐ. λατρείᾳ Nil.*epp.*3.274(M.79.520C).

***ἐνεμβατεύω**, *meditate upon* ὁ...νοῦς ἐ. ταῖς ἄνω θεωρίαις Nil.*Alb.*(M.79.708A).

ἐνεμπορεύομαι, *procure* or *gain by trading*, fig. ἀποδοῦναι αὐτῷ [sc. τῷ κυρίῳ] τὴν ἐμπορίαν ἣν ἐνημπορεύσω ἐκ τῶν αὐτοῦ ταλάντων Ephr.3.81D.

***ἐνενηκοντατέσσαρες** (*ἐνν-), *ninety-four*, Clem.*str.*1.21(p.90.17, v.l. ἐννενηκοντατέσσαρα M.8.885A).

***ἐνενηκοστούτης**, s.v.l., *ninety years old*, Hier.*v.Paul.*A 1(p.10.15).

***ἐνεπινοέομαι**, *be conceived in the mind*, Or.*Jo.*1.19(22; p.23.25; M.14.56B).

ἐνέργεια, ἡ, A. in gen.; **1.** *activity, operation*; **a.** defined and explained ἐ. φυσική ἐστιν ἡ πάσης οὐσίας ἔμφυτος κίνησις. ἐ. ἐστι φυσικὴ ἡ δηλωτικὴ πάσης οὐσίας δύναμις Eust.Ant.*fr.*81(p.97); ἐ. εἶναί φαμεν τὴν φυσικὴν ἑκάστης οὐσίας δύναμίν τε καὶ κίνησιν, ἧς χωρὶς οὔτε ἐστὶν οὔτε γινώσκεται φύσις. νοερῶν γάρ ἐστι νόησις, αἰσθητικῶν αἴσθησις... Gr.Nyss.*fr.*(*AP* p.14.4); ἐ. ἐστι κίνησις δραστική id.ap.*Doct.Patr.*33(p.258.6; M.91.281A); cf. ἀεικίνητος; λέγεται γὰρ ἐ. τὸ πρῶτον ἐν ἡμῖν συνιστάμενον νόημα...λέγεται πάλιν ἐ. ἡ διὰ τῆς προφορᾶς τοῦ λόγου φανέρωσις καὶ ἐξάπλωσις τῶν νενοημένων. ... ἐ. τίς ἐστι καὶ αὐτὸ πάλιν τὸ ἀποτελούμενον ὁμοίως Anast.Ant.*fr.*ap.*Doct.Patr.*13.1(p.78.22ff.); various definitions, Max.*opusc.*(M.91.280Bff.); Jo.D.*f.o.*3.15(M.94.1048A); opp. οὐσία and πρᾶξις, Ath.*gent.*16(M.25.33C); opp. οὐσία, Clem.*str.*8.4(p.85.3ff.; M.9.569ff.); argument from identity of ἐνέργεια to identity of οὐσία, Cyr. ap.Max.*opusc.*(M.91.284C); v. B infra; opp. δύναμις: ταῖς φυσικαῖς ...δυνάμεσι καὶ ταῖς ἐκ τούτων ἐ. Athenag.*res.*24(p.77.27; M.6.1021A); Dion.Ar.*c.h.*13.3(M.3.301C); *ib.*15.9(340A); opp. ἕξις, Clem.*str.*7.11(p.47.18; M.9.492A); Dion.Ar.*c.h.*7.4(212B); id.*e.h.*1.1.1(M.3.372B); opp. συγχώρησις, Chrys.*hom.*20.1 *in Rom.*(9.643A); opp. πάθος: ἐ. μὲν γάρ ἐστι κατὰ φύσιν κίνησις, πάθος δὲ παρὰ φύσιν Nemes.*nat.hom.*16(M.40.673C); opp. πρᾶξις, Hipp.*haer.*4.27(p.54.4; M.16.3090A); of mental *process* or *activity*, Dion.Ar.*d.n.*1.4(M.3.592D); ἡ ψυχὴ ταῖς νοεραῖς ἐ. ἐπὶ τὰ νοητὰ κινεῖται *ib.*4.11(708D); of Christian life and faith ὁ βίος ὁ Χριστιανῶν...ἐστι...ἀδιάπτωτος ἐ. ἣν δὴ πίστιν κεκλήκαμεν Clem.*paed.*1.13(p.151.26; M.8.376A); Ath.*v.Anton.*77(M.26.952A); of forces of Nature, id.*gent.*16(M.25.33C); *ib.*29(57C); *ib.*45(89D); of πίστις, φόβος, ἐγκράτεια, Herm.*mand.*6.1.1; c. genit. obj. μετά...ἐνεργείας ἀγαθῶν Clem.*str.*4.17(p.296.16; M.8.1317A); **b.** *use, meaning, significance* of a word, Cyr.H.*catech.*7.7; **c.** *force* of a command, Clem.*str.*3.2(p.199.29; M.8.1109B); **d.** of specific action τῆς εἰς παιδοποιΐαν χρησίμου...ἐ. Or.*or.*8.1(p.316.23; M.11.441A); Const.ap.Thdt.*h.e.*1.20.10(3.800); plur., *acts*, Meth.*arbitr.*8(p.168.2; M.18.256C); **e.** *process, effect* of drugs, *Hom.Clem.*19.15; **2.** *performance, accomplishment*; esp. of miracles, Eus.*l.C.*16(p.252.16); πᾶσα σημείων ἐ. *Const.App.*8.1.17; Thdt.*h.rel.*1(3.1111A); *production* κτίζων δὲ πνεῦμα εἰς ἐ. ὑετῶν Epiph.*anc.*5(p.11.8; M.43.24C); meton. of thing effected ἐ. δὲ τοῦ ἀνθρώπου ἡ οἰκία καὶ τὸ πλοῖον Gr.Nyss.*Eun.*1(1 p.142.10; M.45.381B); **3.** *actuality* (opp. potentiality), Athenag.*leg.*10.3(M.6.909A); of actual *physical form* a thing takes or in which it exists ὁ κρύσταλλος ὑδατώδης...ἡ ὑπόστασις καὶ λιθώδης ἡ ἐ. ... τὸ ὕδωρ...μονοειδὴς ἡ φύσις, καὶ πολυδύναμος ἡ ἐ. Cyr.H.*catech.*9.9; cf.Anast.S.*hod.*2(M.89.65D); esp. κατ' ἐνέργειαν, Or.*fr.*9 *in Jo.*(p.491.4); ἀπὸ τῆς κατ' ἐ. ἁμαρτίας καθαρισθήσομαι, ἥτις μεγάλη ἐστὶν ὡς πρὸς σύγκρισιν τῆς κατὰ διάνοιαν Cyr.*Ps.*19:14(M.69.833B); cf.Leont.B.*Nest.et Eut.*2(M.86.1332C); and ἐνεργείᾳ: ταῦτα ὄψει καὶ ἐ. ὁρῶμεν τελειούμενα Just.*dial.*35.2(M.6.549C); εἰ δὲ χρὴ κατ' ἀλήθειαν ἐ. καὶ πράγματι πατέρα νοεῖσθαι θεόν Cyr.*thes.*32(5^1.330B); opp. δύναμις v.s.v.; ἐνεργείᾳ opp. ἐπινοίᾳ, κατ' ἐνέργειαν opp. κατ' ἐπίνοιαν in Christol. controversy with monophysites v. ἐπίνοια.

B. of divine *activity* or *operation*; **1.** Trin.; **a.** in gen. θέλησις καὶ ἐ. θεοῦ ἐστιν ἡ παντὸς χρόνου καὶ τόπου καὶ αἰῶνος καὶ πάσης φύσεως ποιητική τε καὶ προνοητικὴ αἰτία Iren.*fr.*5(M.7.1232B); θεοπρεπεῖς δὲ ἐ. εἰσι τὸ δημιουργικόν, τὸ προνοητικόν...καὶ τὰ τούτοις ἐοικότα. ἡ τοίνυν ἀθανασία καὶ ἡ ἀφθαρσία καὶ ἡ ἀπάθεια ἐπὶ τοῦ λόγου καὶ ποιότητές εἰσι φυσικαὶ καὶ πάλιν ἐ. ... καθὸ...εἰς τοὺς ἔξω πρόεισι παρ' αὐτοῦ, νοοῖντ' ἂν αὐτοῦ ὡς ἐ. Gr.Nyss.ap.*Doct.Patr.*14.10(p.90.8ff.); οὐσιώδης ἐ. ἐστι θεοῦ, τὸ μηδαμοῦ εἶναι· οὐ τῷ μὴ εἶναι, ἀλλὰ τῷ ὑπερεῖναι τόπου καὶ χρόνου καὶ φύσεως Chrys.ap.Max.*opusc.*(M.91.281B); Cyr.*ib.*(281C); ὁ θεὸς...μένον (l. μένων) ἐφ' ἑαυτοῦ καὶ τῆς οἰκείας ταυτότητος ἀνεκφοιτήτως κατ' ἐ. μίαν Dion.Ar.*d.n.*9.5(M.3.

912D); παρεῖναι [sc. τὸν θεόν] πᾶσι τῇ πάντων ἀσχέτῳ περιοχῇ, καὶ ταῖς ἐπὶ τὰ ὄντα πάντα προνοητικαῖς προόδοις καὶ ἐ. *ib.*9.9(916C); cf. τὴν...πρόοδον τῶν ἐ. *ib.* infra; known from his creatures ὁ ἐπιστήμων γνωρίζει...διὰ τῶν κτισμάτων τὴν ἐ., δι' ἧς αὖθις τὸ θέλημα τοῦ θεοῦ, προσκυνεῖ Clem.*str.*7.14(p.61.25; M.9.520C); Cyr.H.*catech.*9.14; opp. or dist. from οὐσία: τὴν γνῶσιν...ποτὲ μὲν τῆς οὐσίας ψιλῶς ἀγνοουμένων [δὲ] τῶν ἔργων αὐτῆς...ἀμφοτέρων...τῆς τε οὐσίας τῆς τε ἐ., τὰς ἐπινοίας...λαβόντες οὕτως ἐπὶ τὴν ζήτησιν ἐρχόμεθα. ἔστιν δὲ ὧν καὶ τὰς ἐ. εἰδότες ἅμα ταῖς οὐσίαις ἀγνοοῦμεν τὰ παθήματα Clem.*str.* 8.4(p.85.4ff.; M.9.569Bf.); οὔτε γὰρ οὐσία κατὰ φύσιν ἄνευ ἐ. οὔτε ἐ. χωρὶς οὐσίας ποτέ, μᾶλλον δὲ τὴν οὐσίαν διὰ τῆς ἐ. γνωρίζομεν, αὐτὴν τὴν ἐ. δεῖγμα τῆς οὐσίας πρὸς πίστωσιν ἔχοντες. οὐσίαν γὰρ οὐδεπώποτέ τις εἶδε θεοῦ, διὰ δὲ τῆς ἐ. ὅμως τὴν οὐσίαν πιστούμεθα Bas.ap.*Doct.Patr.*14.9(p.88.19ff.); αἱ μὲν ἐ. ποικίλαι, ἡ δὲ οὐσία ἁπλῆ. ἡμεῖς δὲ ἐκ μὲν τῶν ἐ. γνωρίζειν λέγομεν τὸν θεὸν ἡμῶν, τῇ δὲ οὐσίᾳ αὐτῇ προσεγγίζειν οὐχ ὑπισχνούμεθα. αἱ μὲν γὰρ ἐ. αὐτοῦ πρὸς ἡμᾶς καταβαίνουσιν, ἡ δὲ οὐσία αὐτοῦ μένει ἀπρόσιτος id.*ep.*234.1(3.357D; M.32.869A); ταῦτα πάντα [sc. the heavenly powers] οὐκ ἂν ὁ λελογισμένος εἰς οὐσιῶν διαφορὰς ἀπαγάγοι, προδήλως τῆς ἐ. ὑφ' ἑκάστου τῶν ὀνομάτων σημαινομένης Gr.Nyss.*Eun.*7(2 p.173.29; M. 45.765A); οὐκ οὐσίας ἐστὶ ταῦτα παραστατικὰ τὰ ὀνόματα, ἀλλ' ἐνεργείας Chrys.*hom.32.1 in Jo.*(8.183D); id.*hom.6.1 in Phil.*(11. 234D) cit. s. ἐνυπόστατος; τὸ μὲν γὰρ πῦρ φύσεως ὄνομα, τὸ δὲ καῦμα οὐκέτι οὐσία, ἀλλὰ πυρὸς ἐ. Thdt.*Dan.*3:59ff.(2.1124); **b.** one ἐ. of Trin., Ath.*ep.Serap.*1.28(M.26.596A); ἐὰν ἴδωμεν διαφερούσας ἀλλήλων τὰς ἐ. τὰς παρὰ τοῦ πατρὸς καὶ τοῦ υἱοῦ καὶ τοῦ ἁγίου πνεύματος ἐνεργουμένας, διαφόρους εἶναι καὶ τὰς ἐνεργούσας φύσεις ἐκ τῆς ἑτερότητος τῶν ἐ. στοχασόμεθα...ἐὰν δὲ μίαν νοήσωμεν τὴν ἐ. ... ἀνάγκη τῇ ταυτότητι τῆς ἐ. τὸ ἡνωμένον τῆς φύσεως συλλογίζεσθαι Gr. Nyss.*Trin.*6(p.77.22ff.; M.32.692Dff.); μήτε φύσεως μήτε ἐ. ἐνθεωρεῖσθαί τινα διαφορὰν τῇ θεότητι id.*tres dii*(M.45.133A); id.*comm.not.* (M.45.180C); ὧν αἱ αὐταὶ ἐ. τούτων καὶ ἡ οὐσία μία. ἐ. δὲ πατρὸς καὶ υἱοῦ μία [citing Gen.1:26 and Jo.5:19]...ἄρα καὶ οὐσία μία πατρὸς καὶ υἱοῦ Didym.(‡Bas.)*Eun.*4(1.280C; M.29.676A); Sever.*1Cor.*6:11 (p.246.23); οὐκ ἄρα ἐλάττων ἐστὶν ὁ τὴν αὐτὴν ἔχων ἐ. τῷ τελείῳ πατρί Cyr.*Jo.*1.3(4.22B); ὅπου γὰρ φύσεως ταυτότης ἐν ἀπαραλλάκτοις ὁρᾶται λόγοις, ἐκεῖ τὸ τῆς ἐ. οὐ μεμερισμένον, κἂν ποικίλως τε καὶ διαφόρως ἐνεργεῖσθαι τυχὸν νοοῖτό τινι *ib.*10.2(859D); ‡Cyr.*Trin.*10(6³.16B; M. 77.1144C); ἡ θεία ἔλλαμψις καὶ ἐ., μία οὖσα καὶ ἁπλῆ, καὶ ἀμερής, καὶ ἀγαθοειδῶς ἐν τοῖς μεριστοῖς ποικιλλομένη καὶ τοῖς πᾶσι τὰ τῆς οἰκείας φύσεως συστατικὰ νέμουσα, μένει ἁπλῆ Jo.D.*f.o.*1.14(M.94. 860C); ἐκ τῆς ταυτότητος τῆς τε ἐ. καὶ τοῦ θελήματος, τὴν ταυτότητα τῆς φύσεως ἐπιγινώσκομεν *ib.*3.14(1033C); denied by Anomoeans ἕτερον τὴν φύσιν, εἰ δὲ τὴν φύσιν, καὶ τὴν θέλησιν δηλονότι καὶ τὴν ἐ. Aët.*fr.*ap.*Doct.Patr.*41.30(p.311.22); εἰ δὲ φύσει παθητὸς [sc. ὁ υἱός], καὶ τὴν ἐ. ἔχει πάσχουσαν *ib.*(p.311.15); τοῦ μὲν ἀγεννήτου τὸν υἱὸν εὑρίσκων ποίημα, τοῦ δὲ μονογενοῦς τὸν παράκλητον, κἀκ τῆς τοῦ μονογενοῦς ὑπεροχῆς τὴν τῆς ἐ. διαφορὰν πιστούμενος, ἀναμφισβήτητον λαμβάνει καὶ τῆς κατ' οὐσίαν παραλλαγῆς τὴν ἀπόδειξιν Eun.*apol.*20 (M.30.856C); τῶν αὐτῶν ἐ. τὴν ταυτότητα τῶν ἔργων ἀποτελουσῶν, καὶ τῶν παρηλλαγμένων ἔργων, παρηλλαγμένας καὶ τὰς ἐ. ἀποφαινόντων id.ap.Gr.Nyss.*Eun.*1(1 p.133.15,17; M.45.372A,B); doctrine proved self-contradictory by Bas.*Eun.*1.24(1.235B,C; M.29.565A); opposed also by Gr.Nyss.*Eun.*1(1 p.133.22ff.; 372B); ἐπειδὴ οὐδεὶς τρόπος τῆς τῶν ἐ. παραλλαγῆς ἐν πατρὶ καὶ υἱῷ θεωρεῖται, καὶ τὸ μηδεμίαν ἐν ταῖς οὐσίαις τοῦ υἱοῦ καὶ τοῦ πνεύματος εἶναι διάστασιν, ἐν τῇ ταυτότητι τῆς ὑποστησαμένης δυνάμεως ἐπιδείκνυται...ὥστε εἰ ταυτότης ἐπιτελεῖται τῶν ἔργων ἐν τῇ τῶν ἐ. ὁμοιότητι, ἔργον δὲ κατ' αὐτοὺς τοῦ μὲν πατρὸς ὁ υἱός, τούτου δὲ τὸ πνεῦμα τὸ ἅγιον· ἡ ὁμοιοτροπία τῆς τοῦ πατρὸς καὶ τοῦ υἱοῦ ἐ. τὴν ταυτότητα πάντως τῆς ἀποτελεσθείσης οὐσίας ἐνδείξεται *ib.*(p.136.2ff.; 373C,D); εἰ...ταῖς ἐ., ὡς σὺ φῄς, αἱ οὐσίαι καταλαμβάνονται, ἀκατάληπτον εἶναι τὴν τοῦ πνεύματος φύσιν ὁμολογήσεις...εἰ γὰρ ἐκ τῆς προσεχοῦς ἐ. ἡ οὐσία γνωρίζεται κατὰ τὸν ἡμέτερον λόγον, ἐ. δὲ οὐσιώδης τοῦ πνεύματος οὐδεμία...ἀνεπίγνωστος πάντως ἡ τοῦ πνεύματος φύσις *ib.*(p.143.26ff.; 384A,B); likeness to Father predicated of Son πρὸς τὴν ἐ. but not πρὸς τὴν οὐσίαν: γεννήσαντα καὶ ποιήσαντα [sc. Father] πρὸ πάντων μονογενῆ θεόν... εἰκόνα καὶ σφραγῖδα τῆς ἰδίας δυνάμεως καὶ ἐ. Eun.*apol.*26(M.30. 864A); *ib.*28(868A); οὐκοῦν εἰ τὴν μὲν βούλησιν ἀπέδειξεν ὁ λόγος ἐνέργειαν, οὐκ οὐσίαν δὲ τὴν ἐ., ὑπέστη δὲ βουλήσει τοῦ πατρὸς ὁ μονογενής, οὐ πρὸς τὴν οὐσίαν, πρὸς δὲ τὴν ἐ., ἥτις ἐστὶ καὶ βούλησις, ἀποσώζειν τὴν ὁμοιότητα τὸν υἱὸν ἀναγκαῖον. ... [citing Col.1:15–16] ...τὴν δὲ ἐ., δι' ἧς ὁ υἱός, ἐν ᾧ τὰ πάντα, οὐ πρὸς τὴν οὐσίαν φέροι ἂν ἡ εἰκὼν τὴν ὁμοιότητα, πρὸς δὲ τὴν ἐ. ἐναποκειμένην ἀγεννήτως τῇ προγνώσει, καὶ πρὸ τῆς πρωτοτόκου συστάσεως, καὶ τῶν ἐν αὐτῷ κτισθέντων. τίς γὰρ...πάντα τὰ δι' αὐτοῦ [sc. the Son] γενόμενα καταμαθών, οὐκ ἂν ὁμολογήσειεν αὐτῷ θεωρεῖσθαι πᾶσαν τὴν τοῦ πατρὸς δύναμιν; *ib.*24(860B,C); doctrine opposed by Geo.Laod.*ep. dogm.*ap.Epiph.*haer.*73.15(p.288.9ff.; M.42.432ff.); and by Bas. εἰ μὲν κατ' ἐ. λέγουσιν, ἀνάγκη καὶ κατ' οὐσίαν λέγειν· τῶν γὰρ ἑτερουσίων οὐκ ἂν εἴη ἡ ἐ. ὁμοία Didym.(‡Bas.)*Eun.*4(1.282D; M.29.680C); identity of ἐνέργεια bet. Word and intelligent creation denied, CCP (543)*anath.*13 cit. s. δύναμις; cf.Or.*princ.*2.8(p.159.7); **c.** of rel. of Son to Father; **i.** in gen. ἐστὶν ὁ υἱὸς τοῦ θεοῦ λόγος τοῦ πατρὸς ἐν ἰδέᾳ καὶ ἐ. Athenag.*leg.*10.2(M.6.908B); πᾶσα δὲ ἡ τοῦ κυρίου ἐ. ἐπὶ τὸν παντοκράτορα τὴν ἀναφορὰν ἔχει, καὶ ἔστιν ὡς εἰπεῖν πατρική τις ἐ. ὁ υἱός Clem.*str.*7.2(p.7.22; M.9.412B); γεννήσαντος μὲν τοῦ πατρὸς τὸν υἱὸν ὡς ζῶσαν ἐ. καὶ ἐνυπόστατον, ἐνεργοῦντα τὰ πάντα ἐν πᾶσιν Hymen.*ep.*(p.326.10); ζῶσα καὶ οὐσιώδης ἐ. ... τοῦ πατρός Cyr. *thes.*32(5¹.305B); ὁ πατὴρ...οὐσίας ἢ ἐ. ὄνομα;...οὔτε οὐσίας ὄνομα... οὔτε ἐ., σχέσεως δὲ καὶ τοῦ πῶς ἔχει πρὸς τὸν υἱὸν ὁ πατήρ Gr.Naz.*or.* 29.16(p.97.11ff.; M.36.93C); of God's words as ἐ. λεκτικαί, opp. Word as οὐσία, Geo.Laod.*ep.dogm.*ap.Epiph.*haer.*73.12(p.285.22; M.42. 428C); Μάρκελλος καὶ Φωτεινὸς...τὸν λόγον ἐ. εἶναί φασι...οὐκ οὐσίαν ἐνυπόστατον Chrys.*hom.6.1 in Phil.*(11.234D); of Son in creation, ref. Sap.7:25, cf. *sed et 'speculum immaculatum* ἐνεργείας' *(id est inoperationis) dei esse sapientia nominatur. ergo inoperatio virtutis dei quae sit, prius intelligenda est; quae est vigor quidam...per quem inoperatur pater, vel cum creat vel cum providet vel cum judicat,* Or. *princ.*1.2.12(p.45.10; M.11.143A); ref. Jo.1:3 τὴν δι' υἱοῦ ἐ. δηλοῖ Clem.*str.*6.16(p.506.21; M.9.376B); 'πάντα δι' αὐτοῦ ἐγένετο', κατὰ τὴν προσεχῆ ἐ. τοῦ ἐν ταυτότητι λόγου, τά τε πνευματικὰ καὶ νοητὰ καὶ αἰσθητά id.*exc.Thdot.*8(p.108.22; M.9.657C); anti-Arian in gen. εἰ δὲ μὴ καρπογόνος ἐστὶν αὐτὴ ἡ θεία οὐσία, ἀλλ' ἔρημος, κατ' αὐτοὺς... πῶς δημιουργικὴν ἐ. ἔχειν αὐτὸν οὐκ αἰσχύνονται; Ath.*Ar.*2.2(M.26. 149C); αὐτός ἐστιν ἡ τοῦ πατρὸς ζῶσα βουλὴ καὶ ἐνούσιος ἐ. *ib.*(152A); acc. Eunomius τὸ πνεῦμα...ἐποίησεν [sc. Father] ἐξουσίᾳ μὲν ἰδίᾳ καὶ προστάγματι, ἐ. δὲ καὶ δυνάμει τοῦ υἱοῦ Eun.*apol.*28(M.29.868B); cf. ἔργον ὀνομάζει τῆς τῷ υἱῷ παρεπομένης ἐ. [sc. τὸ πνεῦμα] Gr.Nyss. *Eun.*1(1 p.143.15; M.45.384A); **ii.** ref. coming into being of creative Logos, acc. Marcellus τὴν μονάδα φησὶν Μάρκελλος ἐνεργείᾳ πλατύνεσθαι Eus.*e.th.*2.6(p.103.19; M.24.908A); ἐνεργείας ἡ τοῦ κόσμου γένεσις ἐδεῖτο δραστικῆς· καὶ διὰ τοῦτο μηδενὸς ὄντος ἑτέρου πλὴν τοῦ θεοῦ...τότε ὁ λόγος προελθὼν ἐγίνετο τοῦ κόσμου ποιητής Marcell. *fr.*54 ap.eund.*Marcell.*2.2(p.42.27; M.24.796B); προῆλθεν ὁ λόγος δραστικῇ ἐ. *ib.*108(p.42.23; 796A); Eus.*e.th.*2.9(p.109.7; M.24.917C); πόθεν Μαρκέλλῳ ἐπῆλθεν περιορίσαι χρόνον τῇ τοῦ λόγου ἐ. τὸν τῆς συντελείας, καθ' ὃν ἔσεσθαι φάσκει τὸν λόγον ἐν τῷ θεῷ ὥσπερ καὶ πρότερον ἦν; *ib.*(p.109.23; 917C); **d.** of H. Ghost; symbolized by whip fashioned by Christ at cleansing of Temple (Jo.2:15), Heracleon ap.Or.*Jo.*10.33(19; p.207.11; M.14.368A) cit. s. δύναμις; ὡς ἡ δύναμις τοῦ ὁρᾶν ἐν τῷ ὑγιαίνοντι ὀφθαλμῷ, οὕτως ἡ ἐ. τοῦ πνεύματος ἐν τῇ κεκαθαρμένῃ ψυχῇ [cf.Eph.1:17,18] Bas.*Spir.*61(3.51D; M.32.180C); αἱ δὲ ἐ. τίνες; ἄρρητοι μὲν διὰ τὸ μέγεθος, ἀνεξαρίθμητοι διὰ τὸ πλῆθος. ... ἐὰν δὲ τὴν κτίσιν ἐνθυμηθῇς, ἐστερεώθησαν αἱ τῶν οὐρανῶν δυνάμεις παρὰ τοῦ πνεύματος·...Χριστοῦ ἐνδημία· καὶ τὸ πνεῦμα προτρέχει. ἔνσαρκος παρουσία· καὶ τὸ πνεῦμα ἀχώριστον. ... ἡ ἐκ νεκρῶν ἐξανάστασις, τῇ ἐ. τοῦ πνεύματος *ib.*49(41Aff.; M.156ff.); one with Father and Son, *ib.*37(31A; M.133B); one with Son, Gr. Nyss.*or.dom.*3(p.62.24; M.44.1160B); acc. the scriptures (Ps.32:6 Jo.14:26, 1Cor.12:4–6, etc.), Bas.*Eun.*3.4(1.275Aff.; M.29.661Bff.); cf.Gr.Naz.*or.*31.6(p.151.13; M.36.140A); Chrys.*hom.32.1 in Jo.*(8. 183D); exeg. 'μάχαιραν...τοῦ πνεύματος' εἶπε τὴν τιμωρητικὴν ἐ. τοῦ πνεύματος Sever.*Eph.*6:17(p.312.23); cf.Thdt.*Eph.*6:17(3.440); καλῶς τὸ 'ὅ ἐστι ῥῆμα θεοῦ', εἰς παράστασιν τοῦ δυνατοῦ τῆς ἐ. τοῦ πνεύματος· ῥῆμα γὰρ θεοῦ λέγει ἀντὶ τοῦ θεοῦ ἐ. [cf.Ps.32:6]...κἀνταῦθα τοίνυν θεοῦ ῥῆμα τὴν τοῦ πνεύματος ἐκάλεσεν ἐ. Thdr.Mops. *Eph.*6:17(p.193.16ff.; M.66.920D); of H. Ghost as οὐσία ἐνεργητική (opp. ἐνέργεια), Or.*fr.37 in Jo.*(p.513.13); cf.Gr.Naz.*or.*31.6(p.151. 13; M.36.140A); **2.** Christol.; **a.** in gen. τὴν τελευταίαν τοῦ σωτῆρος εἰς ἡμᾶς ἐ., τὴν προσεχῆ, λέγει τὴν διὰ τῆς παρουσίας, ἐπικρυπτομένην τῷ τῆς προφητείας αἰνίγματι Clem.*str.*5.8(p.363.20; M.9.85C); Ἰησοῦν Χριστὸν ἕνα λέγομεν ἵνα μὴ τὸ πολυώνυμον τῆς ἐ. εἰς πολλοὺς υἱοὺς ἐκχέῃς δυσσεβῶς. λέγεται γὰρ θύρα...ὁδὸς...πρόβατον...ποιμήν Cyr. H.*catech.*10.3; **b.** of operation of Logos incarnate τὸ ἀνθρώπινον... ὄργανον αὐτῆς [sc. τῆς σοφίας] πρὸς τὴν ἐ. τῆς θεότητος καὶ τὴν ἔκλαμψιν αὐτῆς γινόμενον καὶ φαινόμενον πᾶσι Ath.*Ar.*3.53(M.26. 436A); ‡Ath.*Ar.*4.36(p.86.20; 524D); **c.** the ἐνέργεια of Christ one with God, ‡Paul.Sam.*fr.*1(p.339.5); *ib.*3(p.339.15) cit. s. προκοπή; σχέσει φιλίας...καθ' ἣν τῷ θεῷ συναφθεὶς ὁ σωτὴρ οὐδέποτε δέχεται μερισμὸν εἰς τοὺς αἰῶνας, μίαν αὐτῷ καὶ τὴν αὐτὴν ἔχων θέλησιν καὶ ἐ. ἀεὶ κινουμένην τῇ φανερώσει τῶν ἀγαθῶν *ib.*5(p.339.27); **d.** Apoll.

condemned orthodox for attribution of ἐ. ἀνθρωπίνη to Christ, *quod un.Chr.*3(p.296.6; M.28.124C) cit. s. σύνθεσις; **e.** in orthodox statements, one *process* or *practical result of action* (sc. of incarnate Word), but two *modes of action* (sc. acc. the divine and human natures) ἐν μὲν τοῖς ἄλλοις τῶν συναφθεισῶν φύσεων διάφορος ἡ ἐ. τῆς ἀνθρωπότητος καὶ τῆς θεότητος...περὶ δὲ τὴν ἐλεημοσύνην συντρέχει τὰ τῆς διπλῆς ἐ.· ὁ γὰρ ἄνωθεν ἐκ τῶν χερουβὶμ βραβεύων τοῖς ἐλεήμοσιν, οὗτος πρὸ τοῦ γαζοφυλακίου καθημένος δοκιμάζει τοὺς φιλανθρώπους Chrys.ap.*Doct.Patr.*15.1(p.92.3ff.; H.3.885A); Thdr.Mops.*ep.Domn.*(p.339.5; M.66.1013A) cit. s. ἕνωσις; acc. Nestorians, Nest.*fr.*B 9 (p.224.7)ap.CLater.*act.*5(H.3.896C) cit. s. συνάπτω; *ib.*B 6(p.219.20) ap.*Doct.Patr.*41.9(p.305.1ff.) cit. s. ἕνωσις; CLater.*act.*4(849E); esp. ref. working of miracles by Christ ἐσπούδασε [sc. ὁ Χριστός]...δεῖξαι καὶ τῆς θεότητος αὐτοῦ καὶ τῆς ἀνθρωπότητος αὐτοῦ τρανὰς τὰς ἐ.· ἵνα μήτε ἡ θεία δύναμις ἀμβλυνθῇ, μήτε ἡ ἀνθρωπίνη φύσις ἀπιστηθῇ Cyr. H.*fr.*1(M.33.1181A); ἐθαυματούργησεν, ἔδειξε τὴν διπλῆν ἐ. πάσχων μὲν ὡς ἄνθρωπος, ἐνεργῶν δὲ ὡς θεὸς ὁ αὐτός *ib.*2(1181B) = Cyr.*fr.* 15(p.474.21); ref. Lc.8:54 ζωοποιῶν μὲν ὡς θεὸς τῷ παντουργῷ προστάγματι, ζωοποιῶν δὲ αὖ πάλιν καὶ διὰ τῆς ἁφῆς τῆς ἁγίας σαρκός, μίαν τε καὶ συγγενῆ δι' ἀμφοῖν ἐπιδείκνυσι τὴν ἐ. Cyr.*Jo.*4.2(4.361D); παρέστησε [sc. Cyr., l.c.] ταύτας [sc. ἐ.] ἡνωμένας διόλου τῇ πρὸς ἀλλήλας συμφυΐᾳ καὶ περιχωρήσει, ὡς μίαν διὰ τὴν ἕνωσιν αὐτοῦ τε τοῦ λόγου καὶ τῆς παναγίας αὐτοῦ σαρκὸς δείκνυσθαι τὴν ἐ., οὐ φυσικήν, οὐχ ὑποστατικήν...ἀλλὰ συγγενῆ τοῖς μέρεσι Max.*opusc.*(M.91.88A); cf.*ib.*(124C–125C); οὐ κατὰ θεὸν τὰ θεῖα δράσας, οὐ τὰ ἀνθρώπεια κατὰ ἄνθρωπον, ἀλλ' ἀνδρωθέντος θεοῦ καινήν τινα τὴν θεανδρικὴν ἐ. ἡμῖν πεπολιτευμένος Dion.Ar.*ep.*4(M.3.1072C); ὥσπερ οὖν ἄλλη μὲν ψυχῆς ἐ. νοερᾶς, ἄλλη δὲ σώματος, τὸ δὲ ἐκ τούτων κοινὸν τοῦ ἐξ ἑκατέρων ἐστὶ συνεστῶτος ἀνθρώπου, τὸν αὐτὸν τρόπον καὶ ἐπὶ σωτῆρος ἡμῶν τοῦ ἐνανθρωπήσαντος θεοῦ· λόγου νοούμεν, θείας μὲν ἐ. τὰς θείας ὁρῶντες...ἀνθρωπείας δέ, τὴν ζωὴν αὐτὴν λέγω τὴν κατὰ ἄνθρωπον. ... ταῦτα θεωρήσαντες ὥσπερ καὶ τὰς φύσεις, ὅθεν προΐασιν αἱ ἐ., καὶ ἑνώσαντες αὐτὰς ἀλλήλαις, ὥσπερ ἐκ τῶν συνελθουσῶν φύσεων μίαν ἐθεωρήσαμεν ὑπόστασιν ἀδιαίρετόν τε καὶ ἀσύγχυτον οὕτω καὶ ἐκ τῶν διαφόρων ἐ. τὸ ἀποτέλεσμα ἕν· καὶ ἑνὸς Χριστοῦ θεωροῦμεν Anast. Ant.*fr.*ap.*Doct.Patr.*13.1(p.79.16ff.); in anti-monophysite writings, two ἐνέργειαι because two φύσεις, Eust.Mon.*ep.*(M.86.909B); ἐ. τε πρὸς τούτοις ἄλλην μὲν σαρκὸς ἑτέραν δὲ θεότητος, πάθος τε περὶ τὸ σῶμα ἀπάθειαν περὶ τὸν λόγον ὁμολογούντων [sc. followers of Julian], ἀντιπεριχωρεῖν ταύτας δεδώκασι, καὶ ἀντικατηγορεῖσθαι θατέρου, διὰ τὴν ἐν θατέρῳ ταὐτοῦ ἐπαλλάττουσαν ἰδιότητα· τὰ δὲ νῦν...τῷ ἀφθάρτῳ προσθεμένων Leont.B.*Nest.et Eut.*2(M.86.1320A,B); σεσαρκωμένον θεὸν λόγον ἐνηργηκέναι τὴν τοιαύτην ἐ. [i.e. walking on water] ὁμολογοῦντες, τὸ μὲν ἀκολούθως φαμὲν πρὸς τὴν τῆς σαρκὸς γεγενῆσθαι φύσιν. τὰ δὲ διὰ τὴν τῆς θεότητος ὑπερφυᾶ φύσιν· ὥστε καὶ ἐνταῦθα δύο ἐνεργείας Ephr.Ant.*fr.*(M.86.2105B); Jo.Scyth.*fr.*ap.*Doct.Patr.* 13.13(p.86.8; H.3.1240B); Eulog.*fr.Trin.*6.8(p.374); τοῦτο [sc. Inc.] τῆς θείας φύσεως καὶ δυνάμεως ἔργον ἤγουν ἐ. εἶτα ηὐξήθη...ἐν τῇ νηδύϊ τὸ θεόπλαστον σῶμα. τοῦτο ἀνθρωπίνη ἐ. ἐν Χριστῷ *ib.*7.1(p.375); *ib.*7.7(p.377); δύο τοῦ αὐτοῦ καὶ ἑνοῦ Χριστοῦ τοῦ θεοῦ τὰς ἐ. συμφυῶς ἡνωμένας, θείαν καὶ ἀνθρωπίνην, διὰ τὸ καθ' ἑκατέραν φύσιν CLater. *can.*11; refutation of monothelite theory of μία θεανδρικὴ ἐ., v. θεανδρικός; τὸ γοῦν ἀποτέλεσμα...αὐτῶν δύο τῶν ἐμφύτων ἐ., ἤγουν τὴν πρᾶξιν, ὡς ἀμφοτέρας καθ' ἕνωσιν αὐτῶν συλλαβοῦσαν, ἐκ τοῦ κατ' αὐτὰς προσαγορεύσας ὀνόματος ὁ διδάσκαλος [sc. Anast. Ant.] μίαν εἶπεν ἐ. διὰ τὸ μηδὲν θεῖον ἢ ἀνθρώπινον κεχωρισμένως ἐπιτελεῖσθαι ἀλλ' ἐξ ἑνὸς καὶ τοῦ αὐτοῦ συμφυῶς ἅμα καὶ ἡνωμένως προάγεσθαι Max. *opusc.*(232A); id.*Pyrr.*(M.91.345D); Jo.D.*volunt.*42(M.95.181C) cit. s. αὐτεξουσίως; repudiation by Max. of accusation [sc. by monothelites] that he was postulating three ἐνέργειαι in Christ, Max.*opusc.*(113Cff.); denial that ἐνέργειαι of Christ are ὑποστατικαί: ἀλλότριον τοῦ πατρὸς κατ' ἐ. αὐτὸν ὁ τοιοῦτος ἀποφαίνει λόγος, εἴπερ ὑποστατικὴν καὶ οὐ φυσικὴν ἔχει παρὰ τὸν πατέρα ἐ. *ib.*(85B); cf.*ib.*(36B,76A); φυσικὰ γὰρ καὶ οὐχ ὑποστατικά φαμεν τὰ θελήματα καὶ τὰς ἐ. Jo.D. *f.o.*3.14(M.94.1036A); two ἐνέργειαι in Christ affirmed, Max.*opusc.*(M.91.36C) cit. s. κίνησις; *Symb.CP*(681)(H.3.1400E); Thdr.Stud. *epp.*2.199(M.99.1601B); *CIG* 8964; corresponding to οὐσίαι: ἐπειδὴ δὲ τῶν οὐσιῶν ἐστιν ὁμολογουμένη ἡ ἐ., ἀνάγκη θεωρεῖν σὺν ταῖς οὐσίαις καὶ τὰς ἐ. Sophr.H.*schol.*ap.*Doct.Patr.*14.9(p.89.15; M.87.4012B); εἰ οὖν καὶ αἱ δύο προσηγορίαι τῶν οὐσιῶν τοῦ Χριστοῦ, λέγω δή, τὸ θεὸς καὶ ἄνθρωπος, ἐκ τῶν φυσικῶν αὐτῶν ἐ. τὰ ὀνόματα ἔχουσι, πῶς οὐκ αἰσχύνονταί τινες, ἀπαρνούμενοι τὰς δύο λέγειν ἐπ' αὐτοῦ ἐ.; Anast.S.*hod.*2(M.89.68B,C); or to φύσεις, Jo.D.*f.o.*3.14(M.94.1033B); two in Christ, the divine remaining even after crucifixion and death, Anast.S.*hod.*1(M.89.45B); **f.** in monoph. and monothelite thought, esp. of one *mode of action* or *initiative or impulse to action,* acc. one composite nature of Christ in monoph. theory, but acc. divine nature (to which his humanity was subordinated) in theories of Apoll. and monothelites τὸ σῶμα σταυρώσαντες τὸν θεὸν ἐσταύρωσαν, καὶ οὐδεμία διαίρεσις τοῦ λόγου καὶ τῆς σαρκὸς αὐτοῦ ἐν ταῖς θείαις προφέρεται γραφαῖς, ἀλλ' ἔστι μία φύσις, μία ὑπόστασις, μία ἐ., ἓν πρόσωπον, ὅλος θεός, ὅλος ἄνθρωπος ὁ αὐτός Apoll.*fid.inc.*6(p.199.17); id.*fr.*2(p.204.6,14)ap.Anast.S.*monoph.*(M.89.1181Dff.) cit. s. θελητικός; μίαν αὐτοῦ τὴν ἐ. ἐν διαφόροις θαύμασι καὶ παθήμασι τῆς μιᾶς αὐτοῦ φύσεως προϊοῦσαν *ib.*108(p.232.30)ap.Max.*opusc.*(M.91.169C); *ib.*151(p.248.7); id.*fid.sec.pt.*30(p.178.14; M.10.1117A); in monoph. teaching ἀναθεματίζομεν δὲ καὶ...τοὺς λέγοντας...ἐν δύο φύσεσι τὸν ἕνα κύριον ἡμῶν Ἰησοῦν Χριστὸν μετὰ τὴν...ἕνωσιν, καὶ τούτων ἀκολούθως ἐ. ἢ ἰδιότητας Sev.Ant.ap.CLater.*act.*5(H.3.893A); id.ap. CCP(681)*act.*10(H.3.1241D); Paul.CP *ep.Thdr.*(M.*PL.*87.91E); εἰ γὰρ μία ἐστὶν ὑπόστασις καὶ μία φύσις τοῦ θεοῦ, ὥσπεροῦν καὶ ἔστιν, ἀναμφιβόλως καὶ ἓν θέλημα καὶ μία ἐ. Anth.CP *fr.*(H.3.1240E); [citing Cyr.*Jo.*4.2(4.361D)] *ib.* infra; *ib.*(1301E); ἀλλ' οὐκ αὐτοῦ δύο γνώσεις...ἢ δύο ἐ. φαμέν· μία γὰρ ὡς ἀληθῶς ἡ τοῦ σαρκωθέντος λόγου ἐ. τε καὶ γνῶσις, καὶ ἑνὸς ἴσμεν τὰ πάντα Χριστοῦ, κἂν τὰ μὲν θεοπρεπῶς γινώσκῃ καὶ ἐνεργῇ διὰ τῆς ἰδίας σαρκός, τὰ δὲ ἀνθρωπίνως Them.*fr.*(H.3.1240C); cf.*ib.*(1241C); *ib.*(893E); divinity of ἐνέργεια of Christ asserted, Coll.*fr.*(H.3.897E); Thdr.Pharan.*fr.*(H.3.768E); v. κίνησις; in terms of reunion between Cyrus and the monophysites v. θεανδρικός; ηὕρομεν δύο ἐ. ἐπὶ Χριστοῦ τοῦ θεοῦ ἡμῶν εἰρηκότας· εἰ δέ τις...δεῖξαι δυνηθείη τινὰς τῶν ἐκκρίτων...πατέρων... δύο ἐ. ἐπὶ Χριστοῦ λέγειν παραδιδόντας, δεῖ πάντως ἀκολουθῆσαι Serg. *ep.*2(H.3.1309D); reply of Sergius to Cyrus(*ep.*2) approving terms of reunion τὸν αὐτὸν ἕνα Χριστὸν ἐνεργεῖν τὰ θεοπρεπῆ καὶ ἀνθρώπινα μιᾷ ἐ.· πᾶσα γὰρ θεία τε καὶ ἀνθρωπίνη ἐ. ἐξ ἑνὸς καὶ τοῦ αὐτοῦ σεσαρκωμένου λόγου προήρχετο *ib.*1(H.3.777D); use of controversial terms to be avoided μηκέτι τοῦ λοιποῦ τινι συγχωρεῖν μίαν ἢ δύο προφέρειν ἐ. ἐπὶ Χριστοῦ...ἀλλὰ μᾶλλον καθάπερ αἱ ἅγιαι καὶ οἰκουμενικαὶ παραδεδώκασι σύνοδοι ἕνα καὶ τὸν αὐτὸν υἱὸν...ἐνεργεῖν τά τε θεῖα καὶ ἀνθρώπινα, καὶ πᾶσαν θεοπρεπῆ καὶ ἀνθρωποπρεπῆ ἐ. ἐξ ἑνὸς καὶ τοῦ αὐτοῦ σεσαρκωμένου θεοῦ λόγου ἀδιαιρέτως προϊέναι·...διὰ τὸ τὴν μὲν μιᾶς ἐ. φωνήν, εἰ καί τισι τῶν ἁγίων εἴρηται πατέρων, ὅμως ξενίζειν καὶ θορυβεῖν τάς τινων ἀκοάς, ὑπολαμβανόντων ἐπ' ἀναιρέσει ταύτην προφέρεσθαι τῶν...δύο φύσεων,...ὡσαύτως δὲ καὶ τὴν τῶν δύο ἐ. ῥῆσιν πολλοὺς σκανδαλίζειν id.*ep.*3(H.3.1316C); *ib.*(1317B); προτρέποντες ὑμᾶς ἵνα τὴν εἰσαχθεῖσαν προσηγορίαν τῆς νέας φωνῆς τῆς μιᾶς ἢ τῶν δύο ἐ. ἐκφεύγοντες, ἕνα μεθ' ἡμῶν τὸν κύριον...ἐν δύο φύσεσιν ἐνεργοῦντα τὰ τῆς θεότητος καὶ τῆς ἀνθρωπότητος ὀρθοδόξῳ πίστει καὶ ἑνότητι καθολικῇ κηρύξητε *ib.*(1324C); οἱ γὰρ ταῦτα [sc. μίαν ἢ διπλῆν ἐ.] λέγοντες τί ἕτερον ὑπονοοῦσιν ἢ καθ' ὁμοιότητα τῆς προσηγορίας τῆς μιᾶς ἢ τῶν δύο φύσεων Χριστοῦ τοῦ θεοῦ ἡμῶν, οὕτω καὶ μίαν ἢ δύο ἐ.; περὶ οὗ λαμπρῶς ἡ θεία γραφὴ διαγορεύει· μιᾶς δὲ ἐ. ἢ δύο εἶναι ἢ γεγονέναι τὸν Χριστὸν νοεῖν ἢ προφέρειν πάνυ μάταιον Honor.*ep.Serg.*2(H.3.1352E); καὶ ἀντὶ τῶν δύο ἐ., ἐξαιρεθείσης τῆς προσηγορίας τῆς διπλῆς ἐ., αὐτὰς μᾶλλον τὰς δύο φύσεις μεθ' ἡμῶν κηρύξωσι...ἀσυγχύτως ἀδιαιρέτως ἀτρέπτως ἐνεργούσας τὰ ἴδια *ib.*(1353B); discussion of problem of one or two ἐ. forbidden, Heracl. *ecth.*(H.3.796A); Constans *typ.*(H.3.824D); this *typus* anathematized, CLater.*can.*18; **g.** ref. act of Inc.; **i.** in gen. γέγονε γὰρ ταῦτα ἐ. μὲν τοῦ γεννήματος, εὐδοκίᾳ δὲ τοῦ γεννήτορος Gr.Naz.*or.*30.3(p.112.9; M.36.108A); **ii.** theory of Marcellus, Word took flesh ἦν [sc. τὴν σάρκα] ἐ. μονῇ φησὶν [sc. Marcellus] ἀνειληφέναι τὸν ἐν τῷ θεῷ λόγον Eus. *Marcell.*2.2(p.43.22; M.24.797A); εἴποι ἂν ἴσως ἐ. μόνῃ οὐχὶ δὲ οὐσίας ὑποστάσει καὶ ἐν σώματι γεγονέναι· δραστικῇ γὰρ ἐ. μόνῃ, φησί, τῇ σαρκὶ συνών...οὐσίᾳ τῷ θεῷ συνῆπτο *ib.*4(p.57.12; 821A); anathematized, Justn.*conf.*4(p.90.29; M.86.1015A).

C. of supernatural, *influence, agency* or *activity*; **1.** of power of pagan god or image, Athenag.*leg.*18.1(M.6.925B); *ib.*23.1(941B); *ib.* 25.3(949B); of Apollo, *M.Thdot.*1 23(p.75); cf.Or.*Cels.*7.6(p.157.27; M.11.1428C); **2.** of angels, Herm.*mand.*6.2.2; τῶν θεομιμήτων ἐ. Dion.Ar.*c.h.*13.4(M.3.305A); *ib.*(305C); **3.** of divine ἐνέργεια in man πᾶσιν αὐτοῦ τῆς ἐ. μεταδιδόντες,...ἅπαντα γὰρ ὑπ' αὐτοῦ δυναμοῦται Thdr.Mops.*fr.inc.*(p.294.24; M.66.973A); μίαν καὶ μόνην διὰ πάντων ἐ. τοῦ θεοῦ καὶ τῶν ἀξίων θεοῦ Max.*ambig.*(M.91.1076C); operating miracles, Or.*Cels.*2.51(p.174.2; M.11.877A); received at baptism τότε Χριστοῦ προσηγορίαν λάβητε καὶ ἐ. θείων πραγμάτων Cyr.H. *procatech.*15; esp. of *inspiration* of prophets, Clem.*str.*6.7(p.462.18; M.9.284A); of Moses, Just.*1apol.*60.3(M.6.417A) cit. s. ἐπίπνοια; of Nicene fathers, Bas.*ep.*114(3.207C; M.32.529A); of apostles at Pentecost, *Const.App.*5.20.4; οὔτε γὰρ τὸ δαίμονας ἐκβάλλειν ἡμέτερον κέρδος, ἀλλὰ τῶν ἐ. Χριστοῦ καθαιρομένων *ib.*8.1.3; Thdt.*Jer.*32:1 (2.553A); **4.** of diabolical *influence* or *possession*, Just.*1apol.*44.12

(M.6.396B); id.*2apol.*7.3(M.6.456B); Clem.*str.*2.20(p.176.4; M.8.1060B); *ib.*6.12(p.481.6; M.9.320A); Or.*Cels.*1.60(p.111.5; M.11.769C); Eus. *l.C.*13(p.239.22; M.20.1405A); *Const.App.*6.9.2; abs. τὸ πρόσωπον αὐτοῦ κατ' ἐ. ἐστράφη ὀπίσω *Apophth.Patr.*(M.65.321A); **5.** of *agency* or *influence* of stars, Clem.*ecl.*55.2(p.152.18; M.9.724B); **6.** of *effect* or *result* of spells or magic, Or.*Cels.*1.22(p.73.1; M.11.700A); **7.** *evil spirit* εἰσὶ γὰρ ἐ. ἐν τῷ ἀέρι κωλύουσαι τοὺς ἀνθρώπους Ammonas *ep.*2(p.436.13).

D. *action characteristic of an office, function* καθέδρας μὲν μετέχειν, τῶν δὲ λοιπῶν ἐ. ἀπέχεσθαι Bas.*ep.*199 *can.*27(3.294A; M.32.724C); Chrys.*hom.86.4 in Jo.*(8.517C); divine ἐνέργειαι reflected in *functions* of three orders of ministry, Dion.Ar.*e.h.*5.1.7(M.3.508C,D; 509A); CChalc.*act.*3 ap.Evagr.*h.e.*2.4(p.47.10; M.86.2505A).

E. *capacity for action* πέντε αἰσθήσεις ἔχον [sc. τὸ σῶμα] καὶ πέντε ἐ. ψυχῆς Ath.*exp.Ps.*143:9(M.27.1238A); ὧν αἱ ἐ. ἐφ' ἡμῖν, τούτων καὶ αἱ πράξεις αἱ κατὰ τὴν ἐ. ἐφ' ἡμῖν Nemes.*nat.hom.*39(M.40.764C).

[*]**ἐνεργετικῶς**, = ἐνεργητικῶς, *actively* τὴν ἐμὴν [sc. θεωρίαν]... τὴν ἐ. διὰ τῆς χάριτος γενομένην Philox.*ep.*40(p.186).

ἐνεργ-έω, I. gen.;

A. intrans.; **1.** *be in action* or *activity, operate,* abs., Clem.*str.* 8.9(p.96.9,10; M.9.593A); of desires or passions, Herm.*mand.*5. 9.1; Clem.*str.*3.9(p.225.21; M.8.1168A); τὰς διὰ σαρκῶν ~ούσας 'πνευματικὰς ἐξουσίας' ἐμπαθῶν παθῶν *ib.*7.3(p.14.28; M.9.425A); of divine or supernatural action; **a.** of images of pagan gods, Athenag. *leg.*23.1(M.6.941A); *ib.*26.4(952C); *Hom.Clem.*9.15; *ib.*10.24; **b.** of demons, Athenag.*leg.*26.2(M.6.952B); Clem.*exc.Thdot.*77.3(p.131.13; M.9.693D); of the Devil διὰ τῶν ἐν Αἰγύπτῳ μάγων ἐνήργησε Just. *dial.*69.1(M.6.636C); **c.** of God πανταχόθεν...~εῖ *Hom.Clem.*17.7; Dion.Ar.*d.n.*9.3(M.3.912A); exeg. οὐκ ἐπειδὴ καὶ ἄκοντας βιάζεται, ἀλλ' ὅτι προθυμίαν εὑρίσκων αὔξει ταύτην διὰ τῆς χάριτος Thdt.*Phil.* 2:13(3.457); ref. divine inspiration of prophets διὰ στόματος ἀνθρωπίνου κύριος ~ῶν Clem.*str.*7.11(p.44.16; M.9.485B); cf.Socr. *h.e.*5.17.11(M.67.609B); τοῦτο τὸ πῦρ ἐνήργησεν ἐν τοῖς ἀποστόλοις [i.e. at Pentecost] Mac.Aeg.*hom.*25.9(M.34.673B); in Valentinian theory καὶ πάλιν σὰρξ ἐγένετο διὰ προφητῶν ~ήσας [sc. ὁ λόγος] Clem.*exc. Thdot.*19(p.112.30; M.9.665D); **2.** c. infin., *contrive, achieve* εἰ... ~εῖς παραλυτικὸν ἀναστῆσαι Epiph.*haer.*30.34(p.381.19; M.41.472B); **3.** c. εἰς; **a.** *be conducive to, result in* τὸ ψεῦδος αὐτὸ...οὐκ ἀργός ἐστι λόγος, ἀλλ' εἰς κακίαν ~εῖ Clem.*str.*7.9(p.40.8; M.9.477A); **b.** *be effective of* δύναμιν...τοῦ σωτῆρος...τὴν ~ήσασαν εἰς τυφλοὺς ἀναβλέψαι Or.*Jo.*13.56(55; p.286.22; M.14.505A); *be effective* as regards τῶν δικαίων αἱ προσευχαί...εἰς τοὺς ἀξίους ~οῦσι μόνον Dion.Ar.*e.h.*7.6 (M.3.561A).

B. trans.; **1.** *effect, contrive, bring to pass* φαύλων δαιμονίων ~ούντων λοιμοὺς Or.*Cels.*1.31(p.82.29; M.11.720A); ἡ Ἰησοῦ δύναμίς ἐστιν ~οῦσα τὴν ἐπιστροφὴν καὶ τὴν βελτίωσιν ἐν τοῖς πιστεύουσι δι' αὐτοῦ τῷ θεῷ *ib.*1.43(p.94.9; 741B); εἰ...τὰς τῶν θνητῶν συμφορὰς... ~εῖ [sc. τὰ ἄστρα] Meth.*symp.*8.15(p.104.7; M.18.168B); τοῦ τὰ πάντα ~ήσαντος [sc. τοῦ θεοῦ] *Hom.Clem.*5.24; c. acc. cogn. ἐνεργείας ~εῖ Or.*Cels.*7.35(p.186.8; M.11.1469D); pass. μαγείαν καὶ γοητείαν ~ουμένην ὑπὸ πονηρῶν δαιμόνων *ib.*2.51(p.174.12; 877B); μετὰ τὴν ~ουμένην κοσμοποιΐαν *ib.*6.61(p.131.8; 1392A); c. acc. et infin., Just.*dial.*27.5(M.6.533C); *ib.*94.1(700B); Or.*Cels.*3.31(p.228. 17; M.11.960B); hence *cause to be fabricated* evil reports, Just. *1apol.*24.3(M.6.364B); c. dat. pers., *bring* disease *upon, strike* with disease, *Hom.Clem.*8.11; **2.** ptcpl. pass. neut. plur. as subst., *operations,* sc. of God at Creation, *1Clem.*60.1; cf. ὧν τὰ καθ' ἕκαστα βλέποντες ~ούμενα [sc. past, present, and future], καθὼς ἐλάλησεν *Barn.*1.7; **3.** c. acc. pers., *influence, inspire, possess*; of demons, Just.*1apol.*62.1(M.6.421B); pass.; **a.** *be possessed* by demons, *ib.* 26.4(368B); Anon.ap.Eus.*h.e.*5.16.8(M.20.468A); ὁ θεῷ ἡνωμένος οὐκ ~ηθήσεται ὑπὸ ἀκαθάρτου πνεύματος Max.*schol.e.h.*3.3.6(M.4.141D); abs. ~ηθεὶς ὁ ἀδελφὸς Jo.Mosch.*prat.*211(M.87.3101D); ptcpl. as subst. τὸν ~ούμενον Ath.*v.Anton.*64(M.26.933A); prayers offered on their behalf, *Lit.*ap.*Const.App.*8.7.2; Chrys.*hom.18.3 in 2Cor.*(10. 568C); excluded from celebration of eucharist, Dion.Ar.*e.h.*3.1.2(M. 3.425C); but present at singing of psalms and reading of scriptures, *ib.*3.3.6(432C); special position assigned in church, *ib.*3.3.7(433B); **b.** *be influenced* or *affected* by passions, Mac.Aeg.*ep.*2(M.34.412B); ὑπὸ τῆς σκοτομήνης ~ούμεθα id.*hom.*25.4(M.34.669B); ὑπὸ τῆς ἁμαρτίας ἐ. Marc.Er.*opusc.*4(M.65.988D); **c.** *be inspired* by God ἀπ' αὐτοῦ ἐ. *Hom.Clem.*11.8; οὐδὲν εἰκῇ καὶ μάτην ὑπὸ τοῦ θείου πνεύματος ~ούμενον λέγεται Thdt.*Cant.*proem.(2.21); Gnost., of human nature controlled or moved by God, Clem.*exc.Thdot.*27(p.116.16; M.9. 673B) cit. s. θεοφόρος; c. acc. rei, of prophets inspired by the H. Ghost ἃ ἐνηργοῦντο ἐξεφώνησαν Athenag.*leg.*9.1(M.6.908A); οἱ τὰ τοιαῦτα [sc. visions] ~ούμενοι Gr.Naz.*or.*28.19(p.51.7; M.36.52B); **4.** *carry out* commands τὴν διδασκαλίαν ἐ. Bas.*moral.*72.4(M.31. 849A); τὴν ἐντολὴν ἐ. Gr.Naz.*or.*14.35(M.35.905A).

II. in certain theol. controversies, *be in action* or *activity, operate*; see also s. ἐνέργεια; **1.** Trin. οὐδὲν δέ ἐστιν ὃ μὴ δι' υἱοῦ ~εῖ ὁ πατὴρ Ath.*Ar.*3.12(M.26.345B); εἷς θεὸς ὁ πατὴρ...ἐν τῷ πνεύματι δὲ κατὰ τὸ ἐν ἅπασι διὰ τοῦ λόγου ἐν αὐτῷ ~εῖν *ib.*3.15 (353B); λόγος ὢν τοῦ θεοῦ, αὐτὸς διὰ τοῦ πνεύματος ~εῖ τὰ πάντα id. *ep.Serap.*4.20(M.26.669C); εἰ δὲ ᾧ τρόπῳ ~εῖ ὁ πατήρ, πάντα καὶ ὁ υἱὸς ὁμοίως ποιεῖ Gr.Nyss.*Eun.*1(1 p.135.15; M.45.373B); ~εῖ...ὁ πατήρ, ἀλλὰ δι' υἱοῦ ἐν πνεύματι· ~εῖ καὶ ὁ υἱός, ἀλλ' ὡς δύναμις τοῦ πατρός, ἐξ αὐτοῦ τε καὶ ἐν αὐτῷ νοούμενος καθ' ὕπαρξιν ἰδικήν. ~εῖ καὶ τὸ πνεῦμα· πνεῦμα γάρ ἐστι τοῦ πατρός, καὶ τοῦ υἱοῦ, τὸ παντουργικόν Cyr.*dial.Trin.*6(5^{1}.618Eff.); of the λόγος acc. Marcellus μηκέτ' εἶναι αὐτόν, οἷος ἦν ἐν τῷ σιωπῶντι τῷ θεῷ πρότερον ἡσυχάζων [sc. ὁ λόγος], ἀλλ' ~εῖν προερχόμενον τοῦ θεοῦ Eus.*e.th.*2.9(p.109.8; M.24. 917B); denied by Eus., *ib.*2.6(p.103.21,22; 908A) cit. s. πλατύνω; **2.** Christol.; **a.** orthodox ~εῖ γὰρ ἑκατέρα μορφὴ μετὰ τῆς θατέρου κοινωνίας ὅπερ ἴδιον ἔσχηκεν Leo.Mag.*ep.*28.4(p.14.27; M.*PL.*54. 768B); ref. the healing of the leper (Lc.5:12–13) θαυμάσεις ἐν τούτοις θεϊκῶς τε ἅμα καὶ σωματικῶς ~οῦντα Χριστόν· θεϊκὸν μὲν οὖν τὸ θέλειν, ἀνθρώπινον δὲ τὸ ἐκτεῖναι τὴν χεῖρα Cyr.*Pulch.*(p.111.34,36; 5^{2}.116D); ὑπὲρ ἄνθρωπον ~εῖ τὰ ἀνθρώπου Max.*ambig.*(M.91.1053B); **b.** in Apollinarian theory θεὸς ἀναλαβὼν ὄργανον καὶ θεός ἐστι καθὸ ~εῖ καὶ ἄνθρωπος κατὰ τὸ ὄργανον Apoll.*fr.*117(p.235.24)ap.CCP(681) *act.*10(H.3.1248D); **c.** in anti-Nestorian statement εἴ τίς φησιν ὡς ἄνθρωπος ἐνηργῆσθαι παρὰ τοῦ θεοῦ λόγου τὸν Ἰησοῦν καὶ τὴν τοῦ μονογενοῦς εὐδοξίαν περιῆφθαι, ὡς ἑτέρῳ παρ' αὐτὸν ὑπάρχοντι, ἀνάθεμα ἔστω Cyr.*ep.*17 *anath.*7(p.41.11; 5^{2}.76D); **d.** in monoph. doctrine μίαν φύσιν...~οῦσαν τὰ θεοπρεπῆ καὶ ἀνθρώπινα· καὶ οὐ κατὰ τὸν Λέοντος τόμον ~ούσας δύο φύσεις...κοινωνούσας ἀλλήλαις κατὰ συνάφειαν σχετικήν Sev.Ant.*ep.*ap.CCP(681)*act.*10(H.3. 1244A).

ἐνέργημα, τό, 1. *action, activity, operation,* opp. ἐνέργεια, Max.*ep.* 19(M.91.596B); = *miracle* πόσα εἰσὶ...τὰ ἐν πνεύματι ἐ.; Ἠλίας ἑπτὰ πεποίηκεν ἐ. Anast.S.*qu.et resp.*47(M.89.601D); of divine or supernatural action ὅπως καταλαμβάνωσι μὲν διὰ τῶν θείων ἐ., ὡς ἐδύναντο, τὴν δύναμιν αὐτου Clem.*str.*6.16(p.501.12; M.9.361B); Christol. ἀνθρώπινον μὲν τὸ τεθνάναι πάθος, ἐ. δὲ θεϊκὸν τὸ ἀναβιῶναι δεικνύς Cyr.*inc.unigen.*(5^{1}.713A); of demons, Or.*Jo.*20.36(29; p.376. 35; M.14.660A); of Devil, *Const.App.*2.18.3; Epiph.*ep.Arab.*(p.473. 16; M.42.736C); **2.** of that which befalls a person, *accident, event* τὰ δὲ συμβαίνοντά σοι ἐ. ὡς ἀγαθὰ προσδέξῃ *Did.*3.10.

ἐνεργής, *active, effective, effectual*; of pagan images, Clem.*prot.*4 (p.39.12; M.8.141C); of God ὁ πατὴρ...πότε οὐκ ἦν ἐ.; εἰ δὲ παρ' αὐτοῦ τὰ πάντα...ἀεὶ ἐ. ‡Gr.Nyss.*Ar.et Sab.*5(M.45.1288A,B); of Son or Logos (cf. Heb.4:12) τὸν τοῦ...θεοῦ...ζῶντα καὶ ἐ. θεὸν αὐτολόγον Ath.*gent.*40(M.25.81A); id.*inc.*31.3(M.25.149C); λόγον δὲ ἐ. ἐξ οὐρανοῦ ...ἐν αὐτῷ [sc. τῷ Χριστῷ] ὁμολογεῖ [sc. Paul. Sam.] ‡Ath.*Apoll.*1.20 (M.26.1128B); of an *active* life, Just.*dial.*88.8(M.6.688B); of faith, Ath.*v.Anton.*78(M.26.952B); of discipline, Clem.*paed.*1.1(p.91.17; M.8.252B); of prayer, *fervent, earnest,* Or.*exc.in Ps.*9:38(M.17. 108A); Pall.*h.Laus.*28(p.73.20; M.34.1083B); of a curse, Just.*dial.* 96.2(704A); fig., *active* or *positive* ὅπως καὶ τὸ διὰ Ἡσαΐου εἰρημένον καρπὸν ἐ. ἔχῃ *ib.*102.5(713D); neut. as subst., *effectual* or *active character,* Chrys.*hom.5.3 in Eph.*(11.35C).

***ἐνεργητέον,** *one must do* or *perform,* Clem.*str.*6.12(p.483.25; M.9.324C).

ἐνεργητικός, *active*; theol., Eus.*e.th.*1.20(p.88.23; M.24.877D) cit. s. ἐνοικέω; συνθησόμεθα...ἐ. εἶναι...τὴν γέννησιν τοῦ υἱοῦ Cyr.*thes.*5 (5^{1}.42A); Χριστὸς γενόμενος...ἐν δύο φύσεσι νοεραῖς, θελητικαῖς τε καὶ ἐ. †Jo.D.*B.J.*19(M.96.1029A); c. genit., *productive* of τὸ ἐμφύσημα... ἐ. τῆς μεταδόσεως τοῦ...πνεύματος Eus.*e.th.*3.5(p.160.17; 1008B); τῇ θείᾳ γραφῇ ὡς...οὐκ ἐ. τῶν ὠφελεῖσθαι δυναμένων †Bas.*Is.*proem.6 (1.381E; M.30.128B); τὸ πνεῦμα...ἐ. γενόμενον τῆς συλλήψεως τῆς ἐνσάρκου Χριστοῦ παρουσίας Epiph.*haer.*30.31(p.376.17; M.41.461A); neut. as subst., *ib.*66.17(p.40.21; M.42.53B).

ἐνεργολαβέω, *toil over*; c. dat., Or.*Cels.*2.55(p.178.11; M.11. 885A).

ἐνεργός, *active, effectual,* met. ἐ. τὴν πίστιν διὰ τῆς ἀγάπης ποιησάμενοι Clem.*str.*1.1(p.4.25; M.8.689C); πιστὸς...ἔργῳ βεβαίῳ καὶ λόγῳ ἐ. *ib.*7.11(p.45.11; M.9.488A); of Word (cf. Heb.4:12) λόγος δὲ θεοῦ καὶ ῥῆμα ζῶν καὶ ἐ. Didym.(‡Bas.)*Eun.*5(1.304E; M.29.732A); Jo.D.*f.o.*1.7(M.94.805A); theol. (acc. Paul. Sam.) λόγον δὲ ἐ. ἐξ οὐρανοῦ [sc. ἐν τῷ Χριστῷ] ‡Ath.*Apoll.*2.3(M.26.1136B); τρία ἐ., τρία συνεργά Epiph.*anc.*67(p.82.3; M.43.137C); c. genit., *productive* τὸν τῆς φύσεως δημιουργὸν τῆς ἁμαρτίας εἶναι ἐ. ‡Ath.*Apoll*.2.9(1145C); c. εἰς, Clem.*exc.Thdot*.55(p.125.12; M.9.685B).

ἐνεργῶς, *practically, actually,* opp. μυστικῶς, Marc.Er.*opusc*.4 (M.65.488C); Chrysipp.*enc.in Thdr*.(p.57.5).

***ἐνερημόω,** *live in as a hermit*; c. dat. loci, Cyr.*ep.Calos*.(6².365D).

***ἐνέρπ-ω,** *creep in,* met. κατὰ ἴχνος ∼οντος τοῦ θανάτου *Hom. Clem*.2.14.

***ἐνευδοκέω,** *acquiesce in*; c. dat., Cyr.*Ps*.36:7(M.69.928B).

ἐνευκαιρ-έω, 1. of persons, *occupy oneself in,* c. dat., Gr.Nyss.*Eun*. 1(1 p.26.21; M.45.253D); *ib*.7(2 p.158.27; 748B); Nil.*Magn*.21(M.79. 997A); **2.** of thoughts or desires, *flourish within* τῶν ὀθνείων ἐνθυμημάτων ∼ούντων ἐν ἡμῖν Meth.*res*.2.3(p.334.5; M.41.1165D).

***ἐνευμενής,** *benignant,* Thdr.Stud.*epp*.2.207(M.99.1628A).

ἐνευπαθέω, *delight,* Gr.Nyss.*Thdr*.(M.46.740A).

***ἐνευρύν-ομαι,** *increase, extend,* Nil.*Eulog*.13(M.79.1109C); Cyr. *Joel*.16(3.214E); met., of persons in time of prosperity, *flourish, prosper* ἡ πληθὺς...∼ομένη ταῖς παρὰ θεοῦ φιλοτιμίαις id.*ador*.1(1.14E); id.*Joel*.9(207E).

***ἐνευτρεπής,** *prepared, held in readiness,* Heracl.*ep*.(M.92.1024D).

ἐνευφραίν-ομαι, *rejoice in* ὁ πατὴρ...∼όμενος τῷ...κάλλει αὐτῆς [sc. τῆς σοφίας] Or.*Jo*.1.9(11; p.14.28; M.14.40D); τῇ Χριστοῦ...ἐνευφράνθημεν εἰρήνῃ Dion.Al.*ep*.ap.Eus.*h.e*.7.22.5(M.20.688B); τὸ...∼εσθαι τῷ θεῷ Bas.*reg.fus*.6.2(2.345A; M.31.928A).

ἐνευωχέομαι, *rejoice* or *delight in*; c. dat., Synes.*ep*.44(M.66. 1369C); Nil.ap.Proc.G.*Cant*.2:3(M.87.1581B); ‡Nil.*perist*.8.1(M.79. 861D).

[*]**ἐνέχειρον, τό,** Serap.*Man*.53(M.18.1256B) prob. f.l. for ἐνέχυρον, *pledge* (p.76).

***ἐνεχυραστέον,** *one must accept as a pledge,* Proc.G.*Dt*.24:5(M. 87.937A).

ἐνεχυριάζω, *take as a pledge,* pass., Synes.*ep*.4(M.66.1336A).

***ἐνεχυρίασμα, τό,** = ἐνεχύρασμα, *pledge, A.Phil*.115(p.46.3).

ἐνεχυριασμός, ὁ, *taking* property *in pledge,* Ath.Scholast.*coll*. 6.1(p.80).

***ἐνεχυρίζω,** *guarantee,* Ast.Am.*hom*.10(M.40.325B).

ἐνέχω, [perf. pass. ἐνισχῆσθε Cyr.*Juln*.5(6².177C)]; **1.** *be at enmity with, attack*; c. dat. pers., *T.Gad* 5.11; Epiph.*haer*.29.9(p.332.5; M. 41.405A); **2.** pass., *be bound by the marriage bond,* Clem.*str*.3.9(p.226. 28; M.8.1169A).

***ἐνζήτησις, ἡ,** *inquiry, investigation*; prob. f.l. for ζήτησις, Or. *Cels*.1.55(p.106.4; M.11.761B).

***ἔνζυμος,** *leavened,* neut. as subst. τὴν ἀναφορὰν τῶν ἐ. ‡Jo.D. *azym*.1(M.95.392C).

ἐνζωγραφ-έω, *paint in* or *on,* fig. αἱ...τῆς...ἀρετῆς ἀκτῖνες...τῷ ἡμετέρῳ κατόπτρῳ ∼οῦσαι τὸν ἥλιον Gr.Nyss.*hom.3 in Cant*.(M.44. 824C); pass., id.*Eun*.2(2 p.302.8; M.45.473A).

***ἐνζώγραφος,** *painted,* Epiph.*haer*.27.6(p.310.14; M.41.373C).

ἔνηβος, *in the prime of youth,* Geo.Pis.*hex*.662(M.92.1487A).

ἐνήδονος, *delightful, pleasurable, A.Andr.fr*.17(p.45.9); Diad. *perf*.52(p.58.1); †Jo.D.*B.J*.25(M.96.1092A).

***ἐνηδόνως,** *with delight* or *pleasure,* Jo.Clim.*scal*.15(M.88.901C); *ib*.22(972A); *ib*.30(1156C).

ἐνηδύνω, 1. pass., *be beguiled,* Ephr.1.15F; Mac.Aeg.*hom*.42.2 (M.34.769D); **2.** med.; *find pleasure in,* c. dat. rei, ‡Nil.*vit.cog*.(M. 79.1437C); †Jo.D.*B.J*.5(M.96.892C); *ib*.19(1037B).

ἐνηδυπαθέω, med., *delight in, luxuriate in*; c. dat., Chrys.*hom.in Mt.7:14*(3.26D).

***ἐνηθρόνησε,** prob. f.l. for ἐνεθρόνισε, Nest.ap.Cyr.*Nest*.4.2(6¹. 100C; συνέστησεν p.78.39) = Nest.*fr*.D 6(conj. ἐνεθρόνισε p.355.9).

ἐνηκόως, *attentively,* Just.*dial*.137.4(v.l. ἀνηκόως M.6.792B).

ἐνηλ-όω, *nail to*; med. met., *cling to* χαμαιζήλοις πράγμασιν ∼ούμενοι ‡Ammon.*Mt*.24:28(M.85.1385C).

***ἐνηνείη, ἡ,** *clemency,* Gr.Naz.*carm*.2.1.50.67(M.37.1390A); *ib*.2.1. 50.114(1393A).

***ἐνηρέμησις, ἡ,** *cessation,* †Bas.*Is*.179(1.510A; M.30.420C).

ἐνηχ-έω, 1. *ring in the ears of, resound*; **a.** fig. θείας φωνῆς ἐμοὶ ...σφοδρῶς ∼ούσης Gr.Naz.*or*.39.2(M.36.336B); Chrys.*hom.11.4 in 1Cor*.(10.92B); **b.** med. ἄνεμος ὁ ἐν ἡμῖν ∼ούμενος Epiph.*haer*.66.46 (p.83.24; M.42.100A); id.*anc*.5(p.11.7; M.43.24C); Chrys.*hom.19.2 in Jo*.(8.113B); **c.** pass.; of persons, *be stunned with sound,* Mac.Mgn. *apocr*.2.17(p.30.13); of the Lesson, *be read,* Chrys.*hom.65.3 in Mt*. (7.647B); id.*hom.2.5 in 2Cor*.(10.436B); id.*hom.12.4 in Heb*.(12. 126A); **2.** *make to resound,* Ath.*gent*.32(M.25.64C); Thdr.Stud.*epp*.1. 22(M.99.976D); **3. a.** *teach* τὰ ἀπὸ τῆς θείας γραφῆς αὐτοῖς ∼οῦντες Chrys.*hom.4.5 in Gen*.(4.28C); id.*hom.4.1 in Jo*.(8.26C); Eus.Al. *serm*.16.3(M.86.417C); pass., with play on κατηχέω: κατηχούμενος ἐλέγου, ἔξωθεν περιηχούμενος...οὐκ ἔτι περιηχῇ, ἀλλ' ἐνηχῇ Cyr.H. *procatech*.6; Chrys.*hom.1.2 in Ac*.(9.3C); τῆς καρδίας διὰ τῆς τῶν λογισμῶν δόξης ∼ουμένης Nil.*Eulog*.34(M.79.1137D); *cat.2Cor*.2:17 (p.364.16); **b.** pass., c. acc., *be informed about,* Epiph.*haer*.26.17 (p.297.17; M.41.360B); *ib*.60.1(p.379.12; 1037D); Sophr.H.*v.Anast*. (M.92.1685B); **4.** *inspire* ἡ τοῦ πνεύματος ∼εῖ χάρις Chrys.*hom.68.4 in Mt*.(7.675B); θεὸς...εἰς νοῦν ∼εῖ τὴν παντὸς εἴδησιν ἀγαθοῦ Cyr. *Ps*.44:2(M.69.1028C); *Lit.Jac*.(p.174.26); pass., *be inspired,* Eust. *fr*.13(M.18.696B); ‡Ath.*haer*.1(M.28.504A); Thdt.*eran*.1(4.48); **5.** pass., of persons, *be urged* ∼ούμενοι καταπολεμῆσαι τὸν ὑπεραιρόμενον Petr.I Al.*ep.can*.11(M.18.496B).

ἐνήχησις, ἡ, 1. *sound, noise,* Chrys.*hom.1.2 in Is.6:1*(6.98A); **2.** *a sounding in* one's ear, esp. of report or rumour ἐ. πονηρᾶς Epiph.*haer*.9.4(p.202.12; M.41.229C); *ib*.31.2(p.384.7; 476A); *ib*.66. 19(p.43.19; M.42.57C).

ἐνθαλαμεύομαι, *be entombed,* Germ.CP *or*.2(M.98.277B).

ἐνθαλασσεύ-ω, *be at sea,* met. ὁ νοῦς...∼ων Clem.*paed*.2.2(p.173. 19; M.8.424A).

ἐνθάλλω, *ripen,* Cyr.*Is*.1.1(2.9A).

***ἐνθανάτιος,** *at the moment of death,* Anast.S.*Ps*.6(M.89.1112C).

ἐνθάπτ-ω, *bury in,* met. ἐν πάσῃ ἀνομίᾳ...τὴν διάνοιαν ἐ. Epiph. *haer*.76.22(p.369.7; M.42.560C); med. μαλακοῖς ∼όμενος στρώμασιν Chrys.*hom.21.5 in 1Cor*.(10.187A, v.l. ἐνθαλπόμενος); ref. Rom.6:4 τῷ μυστικῷ ὕδατι διὰ τοῦ βαπτίσματος ∼όμενοι Gr.Nyss.*Apoll*.55 (M.45.1260B).

ἔνθεμα, τό, *ornament,* cf.Cant.4:9 ἐν τῷ ἐ. τοῦ τραχήλου σου τὸν τοῦ Χριστοῦ ὁρῶμεν ζυγόν Gr.Nyss.*hom.8 in Cant*.(M.44.952C); met. χαρὰ...ἀποταγῆς ἐ. [sc. ἐστιν] †Nil.*vit*.3(M.79.1144A).

ἐνθεματίζω, *plant*; met., Epiph.*haer*.76.26(p.374.19; M.42.569A).

***ἐνθεματισμός, ὁ,** *putting in, insertion,* Clem.*paed*.1.10(p.146.6; M.8.364A).

***ἐνθεμελι-όομαι,** *have the foundations laid in,* met., ref. 1Cor.3:11 Χριστὸς δέ ἐστιν ἡ ἀλήθεια, ᾗ ∼οῦνται αἱ κνῆμαι Gr.Nyss.*hom.14 in Cant*.(M.44.1077B).

ἔνθεος, A. *full of God, godly, pious,* Clem.*str*.7.7(p.34.6; M.9. 465A); *ib*.(p.35.32; 468B); τῶν ἐ. καὶ σωτηρίων λογισμῶν Or.*or*.30.3 (p.395.10; M.11.550A); ἐ. ζωῆς Euthal.Diac.*epp.Paul*.(M.85.765B); Nil.*serm*.2(M.79.1265C); ἐ. πολιτείαν ‡Proc.G.*Pr*.9:18(M.87.1309B); in prayer for catechumens ἵνα αὐτοῖς δοίη νοῦν ἔ. Chrys.*hom.2.6 in 2Cor*.(10.437A); explained as ἵνα ὁ θεὸς οἰκῇ ἐν αὐτῷ *ib*.

B. *inspired, being of divine origin*; **1.** of OT prophecy, Or.*Cels*. 6.46(p.117.27; M.11.1369D); *ib*.7.11(p.162.24; 1436C); ἐ. νομοθεσίᾳ *ib*.3.7(p.208.10; 929A); *ib*.7.10(p.161.24; 1433C); τὸ τῶν προφητικῶν λόγων ἔ. id.*princ*.4.1.6(p.301.14; M.11.352B); id.*fr.12 in Jo*.(p.494. 19); **2.** of NT τὴν ἔ. διδασκαλίαν [sc. of Christ] Clem.*str*.4.4(p.254. 14; M.8.1228A); Ath.*inc*.3.1(M.25.100D); Epiph.*haer*.51.4(p.252.2; M.41.893A); **3.** iron., of pagans οἱ κατὰ Κέλσον ἄνδρες ἔ., Ἡσίοδος καὶ ἄλλοι Or.*Cels*.4.36(p.307.8; M.11.1084C); Celsus censured for calling depraved pagan nations ἔ. and withholding this epithet from Jews, *ib*.6.80(p.151.20ff.; 1420B,C); **4.** of persons: prophets πνεύματι ἐ. ἐκπεφωνήκασι Athenag.*leg*.7.2(M.6.904C); οὐ δύναμαι κατέχειν τὴν ἡδονήν, ἔ. γίνομαι Gr.Naz.*or*.39.14(M.36.349C); of S. Paul, Chrys.*hom.15.3 in Rom*.(9.598B); id.*hom.3.7 in 2Cor*.(10. 454B); of false prophet ὁ ἔνθους καὶ μαινόμενος Cyr.*Os*.99(3.131C); of S. Peter, Jo.D.*hom*.1.16(M.96.569A).

C. *divine*; **1.** in gen. ἐ. λατρείας Eus.*v.C*.4.71(p.147.3; M.20.1225B); πνεύματος ἐ. id.*l.C*.11(p.224.12; M.20.1376B); ἐ. δυνάμεως *ib*.15 (p.247.16; 1417A); ἐ. τρυφῆς id.*h.e*.1.2.18(M.20.61C); ἔ. σωτηρίαν Max.*ep*.20(M.91.600A); neut. as subst. τὸ ἔ. ... τῆς καθ' ἡμᾶς ἀληθείας Eus.*d.e*.1.1(p.6.6; M.22.20D); **2.** of Christ; **a.** in gen. τὴν εἰς οὐρανοὺς ἔ. ἀποκατάστασιν αὐτοῦ προκηρυττούσαις Eus.*h.e*.1.2.23(M. 20.65B); τῆς δ' εἰς αὐτὸν γενομένης...ἐ. χρίσεως *ib*.1.3.19(76A); ἐ. προγνώσει id.*p.e*.1.3(7D; M.21.32D); τῆς τοῦ κυρίου ἡμῶν Ἰησοῦ ἐ. τελειότητος Epiph.*haer*.69.13(p.163.18; M.42.224A); ἵνα μὴ διορίσῃ τὴν ἔνσαρκον τελείωσιν ἀπὸ τῆς ἐ. τελειώσεως *ib*.69.75(p.223.1; 324B); **b.** Apollinarian contention παρὰ τοῖς ἀπίστοις καὶ ταῖς αἱρέσεσι προτεθρύληται τὸ μὴ δυνατὸν εἶναι θεὸν ἄνθρωπον γενέσθαι καὶ πάθεσιν ὁμιλῆσαι, ὃ καὶ παρὰ ταῖς αἱρέσεσιν ἐπὶ σχήματι πίστεως εἰσάγεται ἄνθρωπον ἔ. διὰ τὴν ἐκ γυναικὸς γέννησιν καὶ διὰ τὰ πάθη λεγούσαις τὸν Χριστόν Apoll.*fr*.14(p.209.1)ap.Gr.Nyss.*Apoll*.4(M.45.1129C); rejected τίνας...οἶδεν αἱρέσεις, αἳ τὸν Χριστὸν ἔ. ἄνθρωπον λέγουσιν, αὐτὸς ἂν εἰδείη, καὶ εἴ τις τὰ ἐκείνου πεπαίδευται· ἡμεῖς δὲ πολλοῖς ἐπιδεδημηκότες τόποις, καὶ κατὰ σπουδὴν τοῖς τε κοινωνοῦσι τοῦ δόγματος, τοῖς τε ἀφεστηκόσι περὶ τῶν κατὰ τὸν λόγον ζητουμένων, καθομιλήσαντες, οὔπω τινὸς ἀκηκόαμεν τὴν τοιαύτην ῥήξαντος περὶ τοῦ μυστηρίου φωνήν, ὅτι ἄνθρωπος ἐ. ὁ Χριστὸς ἦν...ἢ τοίνυν δειξάτω τὸν εἰρηκότα μὴ θεὸν ἐν σαρκὶ πεφανερῶσθαι, ἀλλ' ἐ. ἄνθρωπον τὸν Χριστόν, εἶτα καὶ τὸν λόγον αὐτοῦ, ὡς οὐ μάτην πεποιημένον παραδεξόμεθα· ἢ ἕως ἂν ἡ τοιαύτη μὴ εὑρίσκηται νόσος, μάταιον εἶναι πάντες ὁμολογήσουσι τὸ τοῖς μὴ οὖσι συμπλέκεσθαι Gr.Nyss.*ib.*(M.45.1129D–1132A); *ib.*6(1133C); *ib.*25(1177B).

ἔνθεσμος, 1. *lawful, according to law*; of marriage, Cyr.H.*catech.* 4.25; Isid.Pel.*epp.*1.413(M.78.412C); Jo.D.*haer.*80(M.94.733C); hence of persons lawfully married τῶν παλλάκων τούτων...καὶ οὐκ οὐσῶν ἐ. γυναικῶν...τὰ αὐτῶν τέκνα τῶν οὐκ οὐσῶν ἐ. Epiph.*haer.*80.10 (p.495.7,16; M.42.772Bf.); of moral life ἀμήχανον τὴν ἔ. ... διαμεῖναι ζωὴν ἄνευ τοῦ πνεύματος Bas.*Spir.*38(3.33B; M.32.140A); Pall.*h. Laus.*111(p.144.16; M.34.1212C); of worship, Eus.*v.C.*2.2(p.40.19; M.20.980B); Const.ap.Gel.Cyz.*h.e.*3.19.9(M.85.1348A); ‡Jo.D.*ep. Thphl.*21(M.95.372D); of Church ἡ ἔ. ἐκκλησία τὴν προσήκουσαν τάξιν λαβοῦσα CCP(360)*ep.*ap.Thdt.*h.e.*2.28.8(3.901); neut. as subst., *ordinance*, Or.*enarr.in Job* 3:1(M.17.69A); **2.** of a soldier, *regular, professional*, Isid.Pel.*epp.*1.326(M.78.372A); **3.** *skilled in canon law*, Pall.*v.Chrys.*9(p.54.9; M.47.31).

ἐνθέσμως, *lawfully, according to law* or *canon*, Epiph.*haer.*80.4 (p.489.23; M.42.764A); Pall.*v.Chrys.*15(p.91.10; M.47.51); *Chron. Pasch.*p.2(M.92.73A).

***ἐνθεσπίζ-ω,** *prophesy* ~οντος ἐν αὐτῷ θείου πνεύματος Eus.*d.e.* 6.15(p.269.16; M.22.444A).

ἐνθεωρ-έω, *observe in* ἐπίτασίν τινα τῆς ἐλαττώσεως παρὰ τὸν υἱὸν ~εῖν τῷ ἁγίῳ πνεύματι Gr.Nyss.*Eun.*1(1 p.95.25; M.45.328D); usu. pass. πάντα δὲ τὰ τοῦ υἱοῦ ἀγαθὰ ~εῖται τῷ πνεύματι id.*ep.*25(M.46. 1092C); id.*or.catech.*proem.(p.4.9; M.45.12B); Jo.D.*Man.*2(M.96. 1325B); c. dat., *be seen to possess* ἐκεῖνο δὲ ὑγρᾷ τινι ~εῖται ποιότητι Gr.Nyss.*or.catech.*33(p.125.3; 84C).

ἐνθέως, 1. *piously, in saintly fashion* ἐπὶ τὸν ὕπνον ἰέναι ἡμᾶς ἐ. Clem.*paed.*2.4(p.184.7; M.8.445A); Or.*Cels.*7.30(p.181.12; M.11. 1464B); **2.** *by inspiration, divinely*; of Sibyl, Clem.*prot.*8(p.59.26; M. 8.188B); of scripture, id.*str.*1.5(p.18.10; M.8.720A); ἐ. καὶ προφητικῶς *ib.*3.8(p.224.18; 1164C); Or.*Cels.*7.41(p.192.11; M.11.1480C); **3.** *as befits the Godhead* ἀγνοεῖν...πῶς ἡ μονὰς τριάζεθ', ἡ τριὰς πάλιν ἑνίζετ', ἀμφοῖν ἐ. νοουμένη Gr.Naz.*carm.*2.1.11.659(M.37.1074).

ἐνθήκη, ἡ, 1. *cargo*, Epiph.*haer.*61.4(p.384.21; M.41.1045A); **2.** of money, *investment*, †Cyr.*hom.div.*14(5^2.414D); met. οἵας γὰρ ἐ. ἔχει, τοιαύτας καὶ προσθήκας ἐπιζητεῖ Marc.Er.*opusc.*1.278(M.65.928A); **3.** *keepsake*, *M.Perp.*21(p.93.19).

***ἐνθηκιάζω,** *store up*, Mac.Aeg.*hom.*32.2(M.34.736A); ‡Chrys. *Marth.*(10.758A).

***ἐνθηκόω,** *deposit, implant within* τὴν ὀγδοάδα τῆς ἀνοίας τῶν πονηρῶν πνευμάτων εἰς αὐτοὺς ἐνεθήκωσε Iren.*haer.*1.16.3(M.7. 636B).

***ἐνθησαυρίζ-ομαι,** *treasure in*, Chrysipp.*enc.in Thdr.*(p.73.18); id.*enc.in BMV* 2(p.337.19); τῇ μνήμῃ ~εται Jo.D.*imag.*1.11(M.94. 1241B).

ἐνθλίβ-ω, *impress* τοὺς οἰκείους ἡμῖν χαρακτῆρας ~οντος [sc. τοῦ πνεύματος] Cyr.*Jo.*2.1(4.148A); id.*thes.*34(5^1.360B).

ἐνθουσιασταί, οἱ, *persons inspired* or *possessed*; alternative name for Μασσαλιανοί q.v. ἐ. γὰρ καλοῦνται, δαίμονός τινος ἐνέργειαν εἰσδεχόμενοι καὶ πνεύματος ἁγίου παρουσίαν ταύτην ὑπολαμβάνοντες Thdt.*h.e.*4.11.1(3.964); Tim.CP *haer.*(M.86.48A); Thphn.*chron.*p.54 (M.108.189A).

[*]**ἐνθουσίωσις, ἡ,** *religious frenzy*, Epiph.*exp.fid.*11(M.42.801B; ἐνθουσιάσεις p.511.17).

ἐνθρηνέω, *lament*; med., *Apophth.Mac.Aeg.*(M.34.228A).

***ἐνθρονιάζομαι, 1.** *be enthroned*; of a bishop, Leont.N.*v.Jo. Eleem.*2(p.7.18); *ib.*(p.9.5); of a church, *be consecrated* or *dedicated*, Thdr.Stud.*epp.*1.49(M.99.1089D); **2.** *be presided over* by a bishop τῇ ὑπ' αὐτοῦ ἐνθρονιασθείσῃ ἐκκλησίᾳ *ib.*1.40(1057A).

***ἐνθρονίασις, ἡ, 1.** *dedication, consecration* of a church, ‡Jo.D. *ep.Thphl.*4(M.95.352A); **2.** *enthronement* of a bishop, Steph.Diac. *v.Steph.*(M.100.1077A).

***ἐνθρονιασμός, ὁ, 1.** *enthronement* of a bishop, v. ἐνθρονισμός; **2.** *consecration* of a church, *Schol.* in CCarth.*can.*6(*Mon.*2 p.650).

ἐνθρονιαστικός, *inaugural, upon enthronement* τῶν ἐ. αὐτοῦ [sc. τοῦ ἀρχιεπισκόπου] λόγων Jo.D.*jej.*(M.95.76B).

ἐνθρονίζ-ω, 1. *establish*, Pall.*h.Laus.*89(p.136.17; M.34.1196A); Jo. Mal.*chron.*10 p.242(M.97.372B); met. ~εται [sc. ὁ λογισμός] ἐν ἐγκεφάλῳ Clem.*paed.*1.2(p.92.17; M.8.253B); Melet.*nat.hom.*synops. (M.64.1109D); **2.** *enthrone*; **a.** esp. of enthronement of bishop, Pall. *v.Chrys.*15(p.92.6; M.47.52); Socr.*h.e.*2.43.7(M.67.353B); Jo.Mal. *chron.*10 p.252(M.97.383B); pass., Pall.*v.Chrys.*7(p.40.9; M.47.24); **b.** *dedicate* a church, †Jo.D.*B.J.*33(M.96.1177B); **c.** of God ἐν οἷς [sc. τοῖς ἁγίοις] ~εται Areth.*Apoc.*64(M.104.757C); of Christ σκῆνος, εἰς ὃ ἐνθρονισθεὶς ὁ...Χριστὸς εἰσῆλθεν εἰς τὸν βίον Hipp.*fr.in Is.*19:1 (p.180.6; M.10.632A); ἐν οὐρανῷ κριτὴς ~εται Bas.Sel.*ascens.*1(M.28. 1093A); ‡Nil.*fr.ascens.*3(M.79.1501C); of man through Inc. 'ἐκ δεξιῶν' ἐνθρονισθῆναι τοῦ παντοκράτορος Meth.*symp.*7.9(p.79.20; M. 18.136C).

ἐνθρονισμός, ὁ, *enthronement* of a bishop, CBeryt.(449)*act.*(*ACO* 2.1.3 p.30.1, v.l. ἐνθρονιασμόν H.2.525C); CChalc.*act.*11(*ACO* 2.1.3 p.49.22, v.l. ἐνθρονιασμός H.2.553B).

***ἐνθρονιστής, ὁ,** *one who enthrones* a bishop; plur., Gr.Naz.*carm.* 2.1.11.1814(M.37.1156A); *ib.*2.1.11.1933(1164A).

***ἐνθρονιστικός,** *upon enthronement, inaugural* ἐ. συλλαβαῖς Evagr. *h.e.*4.4(p.154.25; M.86.2708A).

***ἔνθρονος,** *on a throne* τὴν πατρὸς ἔ. βασιλείας ἵδρυσιν [sc. of Christ] Eus.*d.e.*1.1(p.4.10; M.22.17B).

ἐνθύμησις, ἡ, *idea, conception*, of God; acc. Marcellus τὸν λόγον... εἶναι...τὸν ἔνδον ἐν τῷ πατρὶ ὡς ἐν διαλογισμῷ καὶ ἐ. τὸν οὐρανὸν ἡτοιμακότα Eus.*e.th.*3.3(p.156.14, v.l. ἐν θυμήσει M.24.1000C); Gnost. ὁ πατὴρ...διὰ τῆς ἐ. τῆς ἑαυτοῦ προέβαλε τὸν μονογενῆ Clem.*exc. Thdot.*7(p.108.2; M.9.657B); οἱ δὲ ἀπὸ Οὐαλεντίνου τὸ πνεῦμα τῆς ἐ. τοῦ πατρός [sc. φασιν τὴν περιστεράν] *ib.*16(p.112.6; 665A); as an aeon χωρισθείσης γὰρ τῆς ἐ. ἀπ' αὐτῆς [sc. τῆς Σοφίας] αὐτὴν μὲν ἐντὸς πληρώματος εἶναι· τὴν δὲ ἐ. αὐτῆς, σὺν τῷ πάθει, ὑπὸ τοῦ Ὅρου ἀφορισθῆναι, καὶ ἐκτὸς αὐτοῦ γενομένην, εἶναι μὲν πνευματικὴν οὐσίαν, φυσικήν τινα Αἰῶνος ὁρμὴν τυγχάνουσαν, ἄμορφον δὲ καὶ ἀνείδεον διὰ τὸ μηδὲν καταλαβεῖν. καὶ διὰ τοῦτο καρπὸν ἀσθενῆ καὶ θῆλυν αὐτὸν λέγουσι Iren.*haer.*1.2.4(M.7.460Af.); *ib.*1.2.2(456A).

***ἐνθυμιάω,** *fumigate*, Synes.*ep.*122(M.66.1500C).

ἐνθύμιος, *conceived in the mind*; neut. as subst., *thought, concept*, Bas.*Spir.*5(3.5B; M.32.76B); Nil.*Magn.*53(M.79.1037D); ‡Nil.*perist.* 11.21(M.79.933D); hence *judgement, conscience* εὐπαρρησίαστος κατὰ τὸ ἴδιον ἐ. πᾶς ὁ προσιὼν τῷ θεῷ Dion.Al.*ep.can.*4(p.104.9; M.10. 1288C).

ἐνθυσιάζω, *sacrifice*, *Orac.Sib.*5.355.

ἐνθωκεύω, v. *ἐνθωπεύω.

***ἐνθωπεύ-ω,** *lurk* or *lie within*, met. 'ῥίζαν' ~ουσαν 'πικρίας' Meth.*res.*1.42(p.288.12; M.41.1112B); τῆς ἐπιθυμίας ~ούσης *ib.*2.6 (p.340.6, v.l. ἐμφωλευούσης M.18.304C); id.*symp.*3.10(p.38.18, v.l. ἐνθωκεύοντα M.18.76D).

ἑνιαῖος, *single, unitary*; **1.** Trin. τῆς τρισσοφαοῦς ἑ. θεότητος Or.*exp.in Pr.*18(M.17.204A); ‡Gr.Nyss.*hom.1 in Jo.*(p.110.3) al.; Sophr.H.*ep.syn.*(M.87.3153D); neut. as subst., *unity*, Didym.*Trin.* 2.5(M.39.496A); ἀχώρητον γάρ ἐστι τῷ πλήθει τὸ ἑ. τοῦ θείου καὶ ἑνὸς ἔρωτος Dion.Ar.*d.n.*4.12(M.3.709C); id.*c.h.*13.4(M.3.305B); Jo.D. *hom.*11.3(M.96.765A) cit. s. ἅμπαξ; **2.** Christol. τὸ ἑ. τῆς ὑποστάσεως ‡Gr.Nyss.*hom.9.47 in Jo.*(p.295.24); *Lit.Jac.*(*NBP* 10^2 p.106).

ἑνιαίως, *singly* τὸ πνεῦμα ἓν καὶ μόνον εἶναι γέγραπται, διά τε τὸ ἑ. καὶ μόνως αὐτὸ ἐκ τῆς ὑποστάσεως τοῦ θεοῦ καὶ πατρὸς ἐκπορευθῆναι Didym.*Trin.*2.5(M.39.492A); οὐδεμία γὰρ ὀφθήσεται ἑτερότης, ἀλλὰ μόνον ταυτότητα αὐτῆς [sc. relation of Father to Son] ἑ. ἴσμεν Leont. H.*Nest.*7.4(M.86.1768D).

ἐνιαυσιαῖος, 1. *of a year, one year old*; of holy Innocents, Jo. Eub.*innoc.*3(M.96.1505B); of Saul (1Reg.13:1, SM) interpreted as signifying τὴν ἁπλότητα τῆς ψυχῆς, ἣν εἶχεν...ἡνίκα τῆς βασιλείας τὴν χειροτονίαν ἐδέξατο Thdt.*qu.26 in 1Reg.*(1.372); **2.** *annual*; of festivals, Thdt.*Gal.*4:1(3.381); **3.** *lasting one year*, Gr.Nyss.*anim.et res.*(M.46.101A); hence *of annual appointment*, of Jewish high priests (cf. Jo.11:49), Chrys.*hom.79.3 in Mt.*(7.761D); v. ἀρχιερεύς; **4.** *comprising a year* ἐ. χρόνον *M.Ner.et Ach.*19(p.18.9); Gr.Nyss. *ep.can.*(M.45.221B); Olymp.*Job* 3:6(M.93.57B).

ἐνιαύσιος, *annual*, neut. plur. as subst., *anniversary observance*, commemorating dead ἐ. ὑπὲρ μνείας αὐτοῦ *Const.App.*8.42.4.

***ἐνιαχόθι,** *here and there*, Philost.*h.e.*11.7(M.65.601B).

***ἐνιάχω,** *shout, cry aloud*, Nonn.*par.Jo.*6:14(M.43.796B); *ib.*11:36 (845A).

***ἔνιδρος,** *liable to sweat* τοῦ Ἀδὰμ τὸ σῶμα ἐνεδύσατο [sc. ὁ λόγος] ...τὸ ἔ. (cf. Gen.3:19) Eulog.*fr.Trin.*3.4(p.366).

ἐνιδρόω, *sweat* or *toil over*; c. dat., Nil.*epp.*2.1(M.79.204A); Cyr. *Ps.*35:5(M.69.916D); Germ.CP *vit.term.*16(M.98.120C).

ἐνίδρυσις, ἡ, *setting up, establishing*, Chrys.*hom.*7.3 *in Eph.* (11.49C).

***ἐνίδρυτος,** *set* or *established* in a place, met. τὸ ἐ. καὶ τὸ ἐνιδρυόμενον Clem.*str.*7.5(p.22.2; M.9.440A).

ἐνιδρύ-ω, 1. *set in, establish in*, of God τὴν ἀλήθειαν...~σε...ταῖς καρδίαις *Diogn.*7.2; Chrys.*hom.*4.3 *in Tit.*(11.753E); ~σάμενος τῇ ψυχῇ τὴν ἀγάπην τοῦ Χριστοῦ Bas.*renunt*.5(2.207A; M.31.637A); δυνάμεως ...~ούσης τὰ καταδεέστερα...τοῖς ὑπερτέροις Dion.Ar.*d.n*.4.12(M.3.709D); pass. ψυχή, ἐν ᾗ ~εται ὁ πάντων ἡγεμών Clem.*str*.7.3(p.12.17; M.9.421A); Dion.Al.ap.Ath.*Dion*.23(p.63.20; M.25.513C); Bas.*hex*.7.4(1.67A; M.29.157A); **2.** *dwell in* δαίμονες ἐνιδρυμένοι τισὶν ἀγάλμασι Or.*Cels*.8.41(p.256.12; M.11.1577C).

ἐνιζάν-ω, 1. intrans.; *settle in* or *on*; esp. of bees, Chrys.*hom.15.1 in Eph*.(11.109D); Cyr.*Os*.49(3.80A); Thdt.*ep*.62(4.1114); met. τὸ κακὸν...~ει...ἐν τῇ σαρκί μου Meth.*res*.2.2(p.333.5; M.41.1165B); Chrys.*hom.68.4 in Mt*.(7.676C); Cyr.*ador*.15(1.536A); of eternal punishment ~ει αὐτῷ διηνεκῶς Chrys.*hom.31.1 in Jo*.(8.175E); **2.** trans., *cause to remain*, Cyr.*Jo*.11.12(4.1013A); met. ἡ τῶν τοιούτων λόγων μνήμη...κακίαν...ὑμῶν ~ουσα τῇ διανοίᾳ Chrys.*hom.8.4 in 1Thess*.(11.485A); Cyr.*Jo*.6(4.565D); Dion.Ar.*c.h*.2.2(M.3.137C).

***ἐνίζημα, τό,** *seat*; met., of relation of body to soul τὰ δὲ σώματα ...ὄργανα δὲ ὧν μὲν ἐ., ὧν δὲ ὀχήματα Clem.*str*.6.18(p.516.13; M.9.396C).

ἐνίζησις, ἡ, *sitting in, resting in*, of Son τῆς ἐν κόλποις τοῖς πατρικοῖς ἐ. Jo.D.*hom*.1.4(M.96.552B).

ἐνίζ-ω, 1. *sit in* or *on*, met. οὐκ ἔδει ταῖς τῶν εἰδωλολατρούντων γλώσσαις ~ῆσαι τὴν ἀλήθειαν Cyr.*Is*.2.3(2.291A); Ἰδουμαίαν τὴν Ἰουδαίαν ἀποκαλεῖ, ὡς οὐκ εἰδυῖαν τὰ ἄνω φρονεῖν, ~ήσασαν δὲ μᾶλλον τοῖς ἐπιγείοις πράγμασιν *ib*.3.3(467E); **2.** *occupy* a country; c. dat., id.*Is*.2.3(2.261C).

ἐνίζ-ω, *unite, make one*, ref. Inc. τὸ φύραμα κατὰ χάριν ἐ. Max.*opusc*.(M.91.76D); *ib*.(96D); pass., of men τῆς ὑπερφυοῦς ἀμερίας ἐξ ἧς ὡς ἑνοποιοῦ δυνάμεως ~όμεθα Dion.Ar.*d.n*.1.4(M.3.589D); Trin. μίαν...μορφὴν...τῷ ἀπαραλλάκτῳ τῆς θεότητος ~ομένην Bas.*Spir*.45(3.38B, v.l. ἐνεικονιζομένην M.32.149B); Gr.Naz.*or*.40.41(M.36.417C); id.*carm*.2.1.11.659(M.37.1074A); *ib*.2.1.12.310(1188A).

ἑνικός, A. in gen.; **1.** *single*, of soul εἰς ἑαυτὴν εἰσιοῦσα καὶ ἑ. νοερότητι κινουμένη Dion.Ar.*d.n*.4.9(M.3.705B); of universe ὁ θεός... μήτε συστελλόμενος...μήτε συστέλλων κατὰ τὴν μίαν πάντων ἑ. ὁλότητα τὰς τῶν ὄντων διαφοράς, ἀλλὰ πάντα ἐν πᾶσίν ἐστιν ἀληθῶς Max.*ambig*.(M.91.1257B); comp., of sentiments, *more truly one* i.e. in agreement, *ib*.(1036A); **2.** *individual* ἐντολαὶ δέ τινες περιεκτικώτεραι τυγχάνουσι, πολλὰ τῶν ἑ. ἐν ἑαυταῖς περιέχουσαι Marc.Er.*opusc*.3.6(M.65.973D); *ib*.4(1004C).

B. theol.; **1.** *single, one*, of God τῶν μὲν πάντη διαιρετῶν ἑνικωτέρα [sc. divine being], τῶν δὲ τελείως μοναδικῶν ἀφθονωτέρα Gr.Naz.*or*.34.8(M.36.249A); ὑμνήσομεν πῶς ἡ θεία...φύσις ἑ. λέγεται, πῶς τριαδική Dion.Ar.*myst*.3(M.3.1033A); τῆς οἰκείας ἑ. ἑνότητος id.*c.h*.1.2(M.3.121B); neut. as subst., *unity* ἵνα μὴ τὸ ἑ. πολυώνυμον ἀποφήνωσι μηδὲ τῶν τριῶν τὸν ἀριθμὸν ἀποκρύψωσιν Epiph.*anc*.10(p.18.5; M.43.36A); διαφεῦγον...τῷ ἑ. τῆς θεότητος τὴν ἀρίθμησιν Sophr.H.*ep.syn*.(M.87.3156B); **2.** Christol., comp., *more strictly single* τὴν μίαν ὑπόστασιν τῶν δύο φύσεων ὧν οὐδὲν ἑνικώτερον ἢ συμφυέστερον Leont.B.*Nest. et Eut*.3.41(M.86.1380B); ἡ τοιαύτη ἕνωσις, τῶν μὲν πάντη διαιρετῶν ἑνικωτέρα, τῶν δὲ πάντη συγχυτικῶν πλουσιωτέρα id.*arg.Sev*.(M.86.1941B); αὐτοῦ γὰρ ἑνὸς ὄντος οὐδὲν ἑνικώτερον, οὐδ' αὐτοῦ πάλιν τῶν ἑαυτοῦ παντελῶς ἑνικώτερον Max.*ambig*.(M.91.1045A); **3.** *unique, sole* πνεῦμα ἅγιον...οὐδενὶ ἐξισούμενον, οὐκ ἀγγέλῳ, οὐ πνεύματι ἑτέρῳ, ἀλλ' ἑ. Epiph.*haer*.74.11(p.329.8; M.42.496C); ὁ θεός...κατὰ τὴν αὐτὴν ἑ. αἰτίαν οἴσεται πάντα ὡς ἐξ ἑαυτοῦ ὄντα Dion.Ar.*d.n*.7.2(M.3.869B); *ib*.9.4(912C).

ἑνικῶς, 1. *individually, separately* τὸ ἕν...ἑ. ἐστι πάντων τῶν πολλῶν καλῶν καὶ ἀγαθῶν αἴτιον Dion.Ar.*d.n*.4.7(M.3.704B); *ib*.13.3(980C); πρὸς πάντων ἑ. μετέχεται *ib*.5.9(825A); ἐν ᾗ [sc. θεϊκῇ ἑνότητι] πάντα ἑ. συνῆκται *ib*.13.3(980B); πᾶν γενικὸν...ὅλον ὅλοις ἀδιαιρέτως τοῖς ὑπ' αὐτὸ ἑ. ἐνυπάρχει Max.*ambig*.(M.91.1312D); **2.** *while remaining a unity* τὴν μίαν θεότητα...ἐν τοῖς τρισὶν εὑρισκομένην ἑ., καὶ τὰ τρία συλλαμβάνουσαν μεριστῶς Gr.Naz.*or*.40.41(M.36.417B); [sc. ἡ διάκρισις θεία] δωρουμένη...πᾶσι τοῖς οὖσι...ἡνωμένως μὲν διακρίνεται, πληθύεται δὲ ἑ. καὶ πολλαπλασιάζεται ἐκ τοῦ ἑνὸς ἀνεκφοιτήτως Dion.Ar.*d.n*.2.11(M.3.649B).

ἐνιλλώπτω, *wink, ogle*, Clem.*paed*.3.11(p.274.25; M.8.645A).

***ἐνισκάζομαι,** *find reflected*, Ast.Am.*hom*.7(M.40.256B).

***ἐνιστορέω,** *examine, investigate*, Hipp.*antichr*.49(p.33.11; M.10.769B).

ἐνισχυρίζομαι, *be confident*, *A.Andr.et Mt*.3(p.67.9).

***ἐνίσχυσις, ἡ,** *strengthening*, Epiph.*haer*.69.62(p.210.26; M.42.301B).

ἐνισχύ-ω, 1. intrans., *gain strength*, Meth.*symp*.10.3(p.124.24; M.18.196D); c. infin., ‡Meth.*Sym.et Ann*.10(M.18.373A); c. ἐκ, *recover* from illness, Gr.Mag.*dial*.(tr.Zach.)1.10(M.*PL*.77.210B); **2.** trans.; **a.** *strengthen* φρόνησις...τὸ γῆρας ~ει Clem.*paed*.3.3(p.247.13; M.8.581A); Gr.Nyss.*or.catech*.32(p.122.2; M.45.81D); *Lit.Jac*.(p.160.17); pass., Chrys.*hom.84.1 in Mt*.(7.789D); Cyr.*Ps*.7:11(M.69.753A); **b.** *urge* ταῦτα ὑποβαλλόντων καὶ ~όντων *M.Polyc*.17.2.

ἐνλ-, v. ἐλλ-

***ἐνλογισμός, ὁ,** error for εὐλογισμός, *A.Mt*.28(p.259.7).

***ἐννάγιος,** *nine times holy, containing trisagion three times* ἵνα μὴ ἐ. τὴν ἁγίαν τριάδα ἀποφηνώμεθα Jo.D.*trisag*.4(M.95.32B).

***ἐννάγραμμος,** *composed of nine letters*, Jo.Mal.*chron*.4 p.85(M.97.168B).

ἐνναέτης, *of nine years*, Gr.Nyss.*ep.can*.(M.45.232A).

ἐνναετία, ἡ, *period of nine years*, Pall.*h.Laus*.18(p.47.24; M.34.1050A).

[*]**ἐννακισχίλιοι,** = ἐνακισχίλιοι, *nine thousand*, Heges.ap.Eus.*h.e*.3.20.2(M.20.253A).

[*]**ἐνναμηνιαῖος,** v. ἐννεαμηνιαῖος.

[*]**ἐννάμηνος,** = ἐννεά-, *of* or *in nine months*; neut. as subst., Clem.*str*.6.11(M.9.308A; ἐννεάμηνα p.474.20).

[*]**ἐννάς, ἡ,** = ἐννεάς, *set* or *group of nine* ἐ. τῶν ἐτῶν Gr.Nyss.*ep.can*.4(M.45.232A); οὕτω γὰρ ἂν ἐ. ἔσται ἡ θεότης καὶ οὐ τριάς Jo.D.*trisag*.2(M.95.25D).

ἔννατος, v. ἔνατος.

***ἐνναυαγέω,** *suffer shipwreck in*, fig. τὴν ψυχὴν...τῷ βυθῷ τῆς κακίας ἐνναυαγήσασαν Gr.Nyss.*v.Mos*.13(M.44.304A).

ἐννεαδικός, *based on* or *calculated by division by nine*, Hipp.*haer*.4.14(p.46.31ff.; M.16.3079Aff.).

***ἐννεακαιεικάς,** *twenty-ninth*, Cyr.*hom.pasch*.21(5^2.269A).

ἐννεαμηνιαῖος ([*]**ἐνναμηνιαῖος**), *of* or *in nine months*, Chrys.*hom.9.2 in 1Thess*.(11.488D); ἐνναμηνιαῖος τόκος ‡Chrys.*nat.Jo.Bapt*.(10.815E); Mod.*dorm*.3(M.86.3285B); *Chron.Pasch*.p.201(M.92.493D).

ἐννεάπηχυς, *nine cubits high*, Clem.*prot*.4(p.36.12; M.8.136B).

***ἐννεαχῇ,** *in nine parts*, Gr.Nyss.*v.Macr*.(p.393.12; M.46.980D).

ἐννεκρόομαι, pass., *be done to death in*, met. ὡς ζησόμενος βαπτισθῆναι καὶ ἐννεκρωθῆναι τῷ ὕδατι Gr.Naz.*or*.33.17(M.36.236C).

***ἐννενηκοντατέσσαρες,** v. *ἐνεν-.

[*]**ἐννενηκοστοτέταρτος,** s.v.l., = ἐνεν-, *ninety-fourth*, Afric.*chron*.3(M.10.92A) conj. ἐννενηκοστὰ τέταρτα.

ἐννεός, = ἐνεός, *dumbfounded, amazed*, Jo.Mosch.*prat*.176(M.87.3045B); *ib*.178(3048C).

§**ἐννέω,** = ἐνναίω, *dwell in, inhabit*, Didym.*Trin*.2.10(M.39.645B,648B).

ἐννοέω, in gen., *think of, form a notion* or *concept of*; of God at Creation, Just.*1apol*.64.3(M.6.425C) cit. s. ἔννοια; Gr.Naz.*or*.45.5(M.36.629A) cit. s. ἐννόημα.

ἐννόημα, τό, *mental concept*, of God at Creation ἐννοεῖ τὰς ἀγγελικὰς δυνάμεις καὶ οὐρανίους· καὶ τὸ ἐ. ἔργον ἦν, λόγῳ συμπληρούμενον καὶ πνεύματι τελειούμενον Gr.Naz.*or*.45.5(M.36.629A).

ἐννοηματικός, *mental, in the mind*, Bas.*hom*.16.3(2.136B; M.31.477A) cit. s. ἐνδιάθετος; ‡Just.*qu.et resp*.76(M.6.1317C); neut. as subst., Leont.B.*Nest.et Eut*.1(M.86.1296C).

ἐννόησις, ἡ, *thought, conceiving in the mind* ἡ ἐ. καὶ ἡ βλασφημία αὐτοῦ ἡ πρὸς τὸν κύριον *A.(Pass.)Petr.et Paul*.57(p.168.1).

ἐννοητέον, *one must consider*, Clem.*str*.5.11(p.374.16; M.9.109A).

***ἐννοητής, ὁ,** *thoughtful person*, Hipp.*haer*.4.20(p.51.25; M.16.3086C).

ἐννοητικός, *in the mind, mental*, Clem.*str*.2.2(p.117.13, v.l. ἐνωτικήν M.8.940A); ‡Just.*qu.et resp*.77(M.6.1317D).

ἔννοια, ἡ, 1. *thought, idea, concept*; in gen.; **a.** of pagan account of birth of Athene ἐννοηθέντα τὸν θεὸν διὰ λόγου τὸν κόσμον ποιῆσαι ἔγνωσαν, ὡς τὴν πρώτην ἔ. ἔφασαν τὴν Ἀθηνᾶν Just.*1apol*.64.3(M.6.425D); **b.** as Valent. aeon Ἔ., ἣν δὴ καὶ Χάριν καὶ Σιγὴν ὀνομάζουσι Iren.*haer*.1.1.1(M.7.445A); *ib*.(448B); οἱ δὲ περὶ τὸν Πτολεμαῖον δύο συζύγους αὐτὸν [sc. τὸν Βυθόν] ἔχειν λέγουσιν,...Ἔ. καὶ Θέλησιν· πρῶτον γὰρ ἐνενοήθη τι προβαλεῖν...ἔπειτα ἠθέλησε Hipp.*haer*.6.38(p.169.14ff.; M.16.3255Aff.); cf.Epiph.*haer*.33.1(p.448.12; M.41.556Bff.); cf.Iren.*haer*.1.12.1(572A); Ath.*Ar*.3.60(M.26.449A); Epiph.*haer*.31.5(p.390.9ff.; 481B); τὸν Χριστὸν ἐξ ἐ. προελθόντα τῆς Σοφίας Clem.*exc.Thdot*.32(p.117.17; M.9.676A); τὸν Ἀδὰμ ὁ Δημιουργὸς Ἐννοίᾳ προσχὼν ἐπὶ τέλει τῆς δημιουργίας αὐτὸν προήγαγεν *ib*.41(p.119.30; 680A); **c.** Christol. τῇ δὲ ἐ. ... εἰ διαιρεῖς...οὐκοῦν λύεις τὴν ἕνωσιν Thdot.Anc.*hom*.1.5(p.84.1; M.77.1356C); *ib*.1.12(p.89.29; 1368C); **2.** *sense* or *meaning* of a word, phrase, or passage, Or.*Jo*.1.26(24; p.33.22; M.14.72C); Ath.*ep.Epict*.8(M.26.1064A, v.l. διάνοιαν p.13.7); Gr.Nyss.*v.Mos*.14(M.44.304B); **3.** *wisdom*; as complimentary address to church of Alexandria, Const.ap.Ath.*apol.sec*.87(p.166.13; M.25.405B).

***ἐννοιάζομαι,** *be worried* or *anxious,* Barth.Edess.*Agar.*(M.104. 1429D).

ἔννομος, 1. *according to law, lawful,* superl. ἐννομώτατος βασιλεὺς Ῥωμαίων Thphn.*chron.*p.426(M.108.1008C); **2.** *subject to the law* (cf. 1Cor.9:21), Didym.*Trin.*1.1(M.39.272A).

ἔννοος, *having mind* or *intellect;* of Christ's humanity, Cyr. *Pulch.*(p.27.12; 5^2.129E) cit. s. θεοτόκος; ὁ ἐκ...τῆς ἀειπαρθένου σάρκα ἐνδυσάμενος ἔμψυχον καὶ ἔ. ἐκ πνεύματος ἁγίου Mod.*dorm.*5 (M.86.3289C); Jo.D.*disp.*(M.96.1345A); Jo.V H.*icon.*7(M.96.1356A).

***ἐννυστάζω,** *sleep in,* c. dat., Cyr.*Juln.*10(6^2.341D).

ἐννυχέω, *pass the night, A.Thom.*A 101(p.213.23).

ἐννύχιος, neut. as adv., *at night,* Nonn.*par.Jo.*21:3(M.43.916A).

***ἐνογκωδής,** *boastful* ἐ. λόγους Geo.Pis.*hex.*562(M.92.1479A).

ἐνόδιος, *for the journey;* neut. as subst., Marc.Diac.*v.Porph.*14.

***ἐνοδύνως,** *sadly, in sorrow;* prob. error for ἐνωδύνως, Jo.Clim. *scal.*7(M.88.813D).

ἐνοειδής, 1. *of single form, one only;* theol. τὴν ἐ. δόσιν [sc. of Father and Son] Ath.*Ar.*3.12(M.26.346B); ἐ. δὲ καὶ θείαν ζωήν Max. *schol.e.h.*1.1(M.4.116B); neut. as subst. τὸ ἐ. τῆς ἐρωτικῆς θεωνυμίας Dion.Ar.*d.n.*4.12(M.3.709B); **2.** *indicating unity* τὴν τοῦ σωτῆρος ἐ. φωνὴν 'ἐγὼ καὶ ὁ πατὴρ ἕν ἐσμεν' Ath.*syn.*45(p.270.12; M.26.773A); *ib.*49(p.273.11; 780B).

***ἐνοικείωσις, ἡ,** *indwelling;* of God in man, Jo.Clim.*scal.*25 (M.88.989A).

ἐνοικ-έω, *indwell;*

A. of God indwelling man, cf. πνεῦμα; **1.** in gen. σχῆμα τοῦτ' ἔστιν ἔξωθεν ἡμῖν περιβεβλημένον...ἀλλ' ἔνδον κρυπτὸς ~εῖ ὁ πατὴρ καὶ ὁ τούτου παῖς Clem.*q.d.s.*33(p.182.15; M.9.640B); of Christ ὃν ~οῦντα ᾔδειμεν, οὐκ οἶδ' ὅπως ἂν αὐτὸν λωβᾶσθαι τετολμήκειμεν id. *paed.*3.3(p.248.4; M.8.581C); Or.*Jo.*2.7(4; p.61.10; M.14.120D); of H. Ghost, *ib.*32.7(6; p.436.22; 757Dff.) cit. s. ἔνδυμα; of Logos, Ath. *inc.*9.2(M.25.112B); id.*Ar.*3.10(M.26.344A); Thdr.Mops.*fr.inc.*7(p.294. 26; M.66.973A); ~ήσαντος τοῦ θεοῦ ἐν τοῖς ἁγίοις Cyr.*deip.BMV* 7 (p.22.5; M.76.264B); **2.** exeg.; **a.** Rom.8:11 ~ήσαντος πνεύματος ἁγίου καὶ τῆς ἁμαρτίας νεκρωθείσης Diod.*Rom.*8:11(p.92.6); οὐδὲ γὰρ ἁπλῶς αὐτὸ εἶπεν οἰκεῖν πρὸς βραχύ, ἀλλ' ~εῖν διηνεκῶς. διὰ τοῦτο οὐκ εἶπε, τὸ ~ῆσαν πνεῦμα, ἀλλά, τὸ ~οῦν, τὴν διόλου μονὴν ἐνδεικνύμενος Chrys.*hom.13.9 in Rom.*(9.571C); **b.** Col.3:16 ~είτω, φησίν, ἐν ὑμῖν πλουσίως, μὴ ἁπλῶς, ἀλλὰ μετὰ πολλῆς τῆς περιουσίας id. *hom.9.1 in Col.*(11.390C); **c.** 2Tim.1:14 εἰ τοίνυν ~εῖ [sc. H. Ghost] ...τίς χρεία παραγγελίας; ἵνα αὐτὸ...κατέχωμεν,...καὶ μὴ διώκωμεν διὰ τῶν φαύλων πράξεων id.*hom.3.1 in 2Tim.*(11.673A); **d.** Apoc.1:13 εἰ γὰρ αὐτὸς ὁ κύριος ἐπαγγέλλεται ~ήσειν...ταῖς τῶν δεξαμένων αὐτὸν ψυχαῖς, πῶς οὐκ ἂν ἐν μέσῳ τῶν λυχνιῶν ἐθεωρήθη; Oecum.*Apoc.*1:13 (p.40).

B. of demons in men, Val.Gn.ap.Clem.*str.*2.20(p.175.4; M.8. 1057B); ‡Just.*qu.et resp.*40(M.6.1285B); of sin, Meth.*res.*2.4(p.337. 16, v.l. οἰκοῦσαν M.41.1169C).

C. Christol. τὸ σῶμα παραθέσει τοῦ ~οῦντος αὐτῷ Heracleon ap. Or.*Jo.*6.60(38; p.168.35; M.14.304C); τὸ ~ῆσαι ἐν αὐτῷ τὴν σοφίαν λέγειν ὡς ἐν οὐδενὶ ἄλλῳ Paul.Sam.*fr.*9(p.332.13; M.86.1393A); οὐκέτι Σαβελλιανός, Παυλιανὸς δ' ἡμῖν ἔσται...εἰ δὲ τὸν ἐν τῷ θεῷ φαίη λόγον ~ῆσαι τῇ σαρκὶ οὐδὲν ἕτερον ὄντα ἢ λόγον καὶ λόγον σημαντικὸν καὶ ἐνεργητικόν Eus.*e.th.*1.20(p.88.22; M.24.887D); οἱ μὲν ψιλὸν ἄνθρωπον...οἱ δ'...~ῆσαι τὸν...θεὸν τῷ σώματι δογματίσαντες *ib.*1.7 (p.65.18; 836B); κατασκευάζει ἑαυτῷ ναὸν τὸ σῶμα...ἐν αὐτῷ...~ῶν Ath.*inc.*8.3(M.25.109C); id.*Ar.*2.56(M.26.265C); οὐδὲ ἄνθρωπον ἁπλῶς πλάσας ἐνῴκησεν ἐν αὐτῷ, ἀλλὰ καὶ τῆς κυήσεως ἠνέσχετο Chrys.*Is. interp.*7.6(6.83B); ὡς 'ἐν υἱῷ...εὐδοκήσας ἐνῴκησεν...ὥστε ~ήσας ὅλον μὲν ἑαυτῷ τὸν λαμβανόμενον ἥνωσεν, παρεσκεύασεν δὲ αὐτὸν συμμετασχεῖν αὐτῷ πάσης τῆς τιμῆς ἧς αὐτὸς ὁ ~ῶν, υἱὸς ὢν φύσει, μετέχει, ὡς συντελεῖν μὲν εἰς ἓν πρόσωπον κτλ. Thdr.Mops.*fr.inc.*7 (p.296.2ff.; M.66.976B); μήτε τὸν ναὸν ἀντ' ~ουμένου τὸν ~οῦντα νομίζωμεν Nest.*hom.in Heb.*3:1(p.242.17; M.64.492B); acc. Nestorius θεὸς γὰρ ἦν ὁ λόγος, ἀνθρώπῳ τε συνημμένος καὶ ~ῶν αὐτῷ Cyr.*Nest.* 1.2(p.20.2; 6^1.12B); βλασφημία μὴ γεγενῆσθαι τὸν λόγον ἄνθρωπον, ἀλλ' ἐν ἀνθρώπῳ γεννηθέντι ἐκ γυναικὸς ἐνῳκηκέναι λέγουσα Cyr.*deip. BMV* 2(p.19.27; M.76.257B); but cf. ναὸς...οὐκ ἂν λέγοιτό τι κυρίως καὶ ἀληθῶς μὴ ~οῦντος ἐν αὐτῷ τοῦ θεοῦ· ὥσπερ οὖν καὶ ἐφ' ἡμῶν... τὸ σῶμα ναὸν τῆς ~ούσης ἐν αὐτῷ ψυχῆς id.*thes.*32(5^1.317D); συνενούμενοι καὶ ἡμεῖς αὐτῇ [sc. τῇ σαρκὶ τοῦ σωτῆρος] καθάπερ οὖν αὐτῇ τῷ ~ήσαντι λόγῳ id.*Jo.*4.2(4.361C); Philost.*h.e.*8.13(M.65.565B).

ἐνοίκησις, ἡ, *indwelling, inhabitation;* **1.** of God in man, esp. of H. Ghost σωτὴρ...τοῖς ἀνθρώποις...τὴν τοῦ πνεύματος ἐ. ... κατασκευάσῃ Ath.*Ar.*1.46(M.26.108B); τὴν τοῦ πνεύματος ἐ. ἀποφαίνοντος Χριστοῦ Didym.(‡Bas.)*Eun.*5(1.302C; M.29.725B); Oecum.*1Cor.*7: 32ff.(p.437.29); but also in gen. εὐχὴ δὲ καλή, ἡ ἐναργῆ ἐμποιοῦσα τοῦ θεοῦ ἔννοιαν τῇ ψυχῇ. καὶ τοῦτό ἐστι θεοῦ ἐ., τὸ διὰ τῆς μνήμης ἐνιδρυμένον ἔχειν ἐν ἑαυτῷ τὸν θεόν Bas.*ep.*2.4(3.73D; M.32.229D); οὔτε οὐσίᾳ λέγειν οὔτε μὴν ἐνεργείᾳ οἷόν τε ποιεῖσθαι τὸν θεὸν τὴν ἐ. ... δῆλον οὖν ὡς εὐδοκίᾳ λέγειν γίνεσθαι τὴν ἐ. προσήκει· εὐδοκία δὲ λέγεται ἡ ἀρίστη...θέλησις τοῦ θεοῦ ἣν ἂν ποιήσηται ἀρεσθεὶς τοῖς ἀνακεῖσθαι αὐτῷ ἐσπουδακόσιν Thdr.Mops.*fr.inc.*7(p.294.29ff.; M.66. 973A); discussion of modes of divine indwelling in creatures, *ib.* (p.293.29ff.; 972Aff.); ἡ γραφὴ...τοὺς μὴ ἐπιγινώσκοντας τὴν ἐ. τοῦ Χριστοῦ, τούτους ἀδοκίμους εἴρηκεν Marc.Er.*opusc.*1.25(M.65.908D); Cyr.*deip.BMV* 7(p.22.3; M.76.264B); **2.** Christol. τοῦτο γὰρ τὸν μὲν τρόπον τῆς ἐ. τὸν αὐτὸν δηλοῖ [sc. as in other men], μέτρῳ δὲ καὶ πλήθει ὑπερφέρειν Paul.Sam.*fr.*9(p.332.14; M.86.1393A); ref. Diodorus, Apoll.*quod un.Chr.*3(p.296.5; M.28.124C) cit. s. σύνθεσις; τὸ δὲ σῶμα τῇ ἐ. τοῦ θεοῦ λόγου πρὸς τὴν θεϊκὴν ἀξίαν μετεποιήθη Gr. Nyss.*or.catech.*37(p.149.1; M.45.96D); καταβέβηκεν μὲν τῇ εἰς τὸν ἄνθρωπον ἐ. ἔστιν δὲ ἐν οὐρανῷ τῷ ἀπεριγράφῳ τῆς φύσεως πᾶσιν παρών Thdr.Mops.*fr.inc.*10(p.301.25; M.66.984C); in Nestorian controversy εἴ τις οὐχ ὁμολογεῖ τὴν τοῦ κυρίου σάρκα...ἰδίαν αὐτοῦ τοῦ ἐκ θεοῦ πατρὸς λόγου, ἀλλ' ὡς...μόνην θείαν ἐ. ἐσχηκότος...ἀ. ἔ. Cyr.*expl.xii cap.*11(p.24.27; 6^1.156B); ἐ. οὐκ ἐπὶ τοῦ Χριστοῦ, ἀλλ' ἐπὶ τῶν...ἁγίων λέγεται id.*deip.BMV* 7(p.22.3; M.76.264B); εἰ ὅλως ἀποδέχῃ...θεοῦ ἐν ἀνθρώπῳ θείαν ἐ., παῦσαι θεοῦ καὶ σαρκὸς δογματίζων τὴν καθ' ὑπόστασιν ἕνωσιν· ἀλλήλων γάρ εἰσιν ἀναιρετικαὶ ἥ ἐ. καὶ ἡ καθ' ὑπόστασιν φυσικὴ ἕνωσις. εἰ ὑποστατικὴ λέγοιτο καὶ ἡ ἐ. ἤγουν ὡς ὑποστάσεως εἰς ὑπόστασιν ἐνοικούσης, ὄντως φῄς...εἰ δὲ οὐσιακῇ ἐνώσει καθορῶμεν τὴν ἐ. ὥσπερ ὁ λέγων περὶ τῆς ἑαυτοῦ ψυχῆς, ὅτι ἐξῆλθε καὶ ἀπῆλθεν ἀπ' ἐμοῦ ὥσπερ ὁ καταλύων σκηνὴν πήξας, πῶς κωλύεται ἡ καθ' ὑπόστασιν ἕνωσις ἐπὶ Ἐζεκίου νοεῖσθαι, φύσεως φύσει ἐνοικούσης; ἄνθρωπος δὲ καὶ σὰρξ ὁ υἱὸς καὶ λόγος τοῦ θεοῦ πῶς λέγεται, τῷ τῆς ἐ. ἁπλῶς λόγῳ; ὁ γὰρ ἐνοικῶν, οὐ τῆς τοῦ ἐνοικουμένου προσηγορίας εὑρίσκεται κύριος Leont.H.*Nest.*1.46(M.86. 1504D–1505A).

***ἐνοικιάζ-ομαι,** *be valued* or *assessed* οἰκήματα...~όμενα καλῶς †Gregent.*leg.Hom.*57(M.86.612B).

ἐνοικίδιος, *domestic,* Clem.*paed.*2.3(p.179.14; M.8.436A).

ἐνοικίζ-ω, 1. *cause to dwell in* σωματικῶς ἡμῖν ~ουσα τὸν Χριστὸν τῇ μεθέξει καὶ κοινωνίᾳ τῆς ἁγίας αὐτοῦ σαρκός Cyr.*Jo.*10.2(4.862D); **2.** *house, receive in a house* ὅτι οὐ δεῖ αἱρετικὸν ~ειν Euthal.Diac. *epp.cath.*(M.85.688B); **3.** *inhabit, take up one's abode in,* Christol. τὴν ἡμετέραν ἐνεδύσατο φύσιν καὶ ἐνῴκισεν ἐν ἡμῖν Nest.*fr.*C 14(p.287. 19); usu. med. and pass., in gen. ἤτησεν γὰρ ἐπανελθεῖν τὴν ψυχὴν [sc. of Lazarus] καὶ ἐνοικισθῆναι πάλιν τῷ σώματι Or.*Jo.*28.6(5; p.396.10; M.14.692A); τὸ πνεῦμα τὸ ἅγιον...ἀχράντοις καὶ καθαραῖς ψυχαῖς ~εται id.*fr.20 in Jo.*(p.501.9); οὐδὲν κτίσμα μεθεκτόν ἐστι τῇ λογικῇ ψυχῇ, ὡς ~εσθαι αὐτῇ οὐσιωδῶς Didym.(‡Bas.)*Eun.*5(1. 297A; M.29.713A) ∞ id.*Trin.*2.7(M.39.529A); Cyr.*thes.*32(5^1.317D).

ἔνοικος, *indwelling;* of God in men, Platonic τὸν θεὸν τὸν ἔ. αὐτοῖς, τὸν λόγον Clem.*paed.*2.10(p.217.22; M.8.517B); Christian ἐπολέμουν...πρὸς τὸν ἔ. αὐτῶν [sc. martyrs] θεόν Chrys.*pan.Aeg.*1 (2.701A); ref. Holy Communion, Thdt.*1Cor.*11:33(3.240); of Devil, id.*h.e.*4.11.7(3.966); Christol., view attributed to Marcellus τὴν σάρκα μόνον εἰσάγειν δίχα παντὸς ἐ. Eus.*e.th.*1.20(p.88.10; M.24. 877C); ναὸς ἦν θεὸν ἔ. ἔχων Thdt.ap.Cyr.*apol.Thdt.*1(p.109.26; 6^1. 205A).

ἐνολισθαίν-ω, 1. *move unsteadily upon* τοῖς σπονδύλοις ~ουσα [sc. ἡ κεφαλή] Bas.*hom.*14.4(2.126C; M.31.453A); **2.** *slip, walk unsteadily in* τυφλὸς...βόθροις ~ων Chrys.*ecl.*23(12.591A); **3.** *skid, slide* ἐν... τῷ πηλῷ τοῦ τρόχου...~οντος Gr.Nyss.*ep.*6(M.46.1033B); c. dat., id. *Eun.*12(1 p.238.10; M.45.936C); **4.** *slip* or *fall into,* met. ψευδολατρείαις ἐνωλισθηκότες οἱ ἐξ Ἰσραὴλ Cyr.*glaph.Ex.*3(1.317A).

***ἐνόλισθος,** *prone to slip,* met., neut. as subst. τὸ ἐ. ... πρὸς ἁμαρτίαν Cyr.*inc.unigen.*(5^1.692A).

***ἐνολκέομαι,** *be hauled up on the beach;* of a vessel, *M.Areth.* (p.45, v.l. ἐνολκισθῆναι).

***ἐνολολύζ-ω,** *utter a cry within* βαρύ τι καὶ δυσαχθὲς ~ειν τῇ καρδίᾳ Cyr.*Nah.*21(3.500B).

ἔνομβρος, *of rain* ἔ. ... ὕδωρ *rain-water,* Geo.Pis.*hex.*268(M.92. 1455A).

ἐνομιλ-έω, 1. *associate with,* Meth.*res.*1.37(p.278.12, v.l. ὁμιλήσαντες M.18.293B); met., Bas.Sel.*or.*30.2(M.85.337A); **2.** *be well-acquainted with* οἱ ψιλοῖς καὶ μόνοις ~οῦντες τοῖς τύποις Cyr.*Juln.*10 (6^2.326A).

ἐνομόργνυμι, *inject,* Gr.Naz.*carm.*2.1.1.238(M.37.988A).

***ἐνομότως,** *with an oath,* Thphn.*chron.*p.312(M.108.757C).

***ἐνοξίζω,** *turn sour,* Ign.*Magn.*10.2.

ἐνοποι-έω, *unite, make one* ἑαυτὸν ∼εῖ τῷ 'θείῳ χορῷ' Clem.*str*.7.7(p.37.6; M.9.469B); id.*exc.Thdot*.1(p.105.14; M.9.653A); τοῦ θεοῦ... τὴν γενομένην παρ' ἐμοῦ τούτων ∼οῦντος...διάστασιν Max.*ambig*.(M.91.1348D); theol. ἵνα τὸν θεὸν ἕνα τὰ τρία νοήσῃς πρόσωπα· οὐ τὰς ὑποστάσεις ∼ῶν ‡Bas.*struct.hom*.1.3(1.325D; M.30.13C).

***ἐνοποιητικός**, *uniting*, Max.*ambig*.(M.91.1249B).

***ἐνοπτεύ-ω**, *gaze upon* τῆς...δόξης τὸ φῶς ∼οντες ‡Bas.*h.myst*.62(p.397.16).

ἐνοπτρίζ-ω, **1.** act.; *reflect* as a mirror, met. ψυχὴ...προβάλλει... τὰ προσήκοντα καὶ ∼ει τὴν προστασίαν δι' ἧς τὴν ἀντίληψιν τῶν ἐκεῖ μενόντων ἔχει τὸ ζῷον Synes.*insomn*.3(p.150.6; M.66.1288B); **2.** usu. med.; *see as in a mirror, look* or *gaze upon, contemplate* διὰ τούτου [sc. Ἰησοῦ] ∼όμεθα τὴν ἄμωμον ὄψιν αὐτοῦ *1Clem*.36.2; Or.*fr.103 in Jo*.(p.560.9); †Bas.*parad*.3.12(1.351E; M.30.72B); τὰ αἰώνια ἀγαθὰ ∼εσθαι διὰ τὴν μετουσίαν τοῦ πνεύματος Mac.Aeg.*hom*.5.4(M.34.497B); †Jo.D.*B.J*.20(M.96.1040C); c. dat., Clem.*paed*.3.3(p.250.3; M.8.588A); abs., *A.Phil*.124(p.53.21); theol. ἔχαιρέν τε ὁ πατὴρ...εἰς αὐτὸν ἀφορῶν τὸν υἱὸν καὶ ὥσπερ ἐν εἰκόνι ἑαυτὸν ∼όμενος ἐν αὐτῷ Eus.*e.th*.3.3(p.156.1; M.24.1000B).

ἐνόρασις, ἡ, *observing*, Clem.*str*.6.17(p.512.23; M.9.388C).

***ἐνορατικός**, *observing, of observation* τὴν ἐ. δύναμιν τοῦ θεοῦ Or. *sel.in Ezech*.8:18(M.13.800B).

***ἐνόρδινος**, (Lat. *in ordine*) *regular, in order*, Thphn.*chron*.p.303(M.108.740B).

***ἐνορδίνως**, *in succession*, Leont.N.*v.Sym*.54(M.93.1736D); *Didasc.Jac*.4.7(p.69.23).

ἐνορία, ἡ, *district, region*, Gr.Nyss.*ep*.1(M.46.1001A); Epiph.*haer*.40.1(p.81.4; M.41.677C); Cyr.*ep*.77(p.67.14; 5^{2}.209C).

ἐνορκίζω, *adjure*, *A.Jo*.25(p.164.31); *ib*.68(p.185.6); *A.(Pass.) Andr*.14(p.32.16, v.l. ἐνορκωσάμενος M.2.1244B); med., *A.Phil*.23(p.12.21).

***ἐνορκισμός, ὁ**, *adjuration*, Synes.*ep*.68(M.66.1413B).

ἐνορκόω, *adjure*, Jo.Mosch.*prat*.176(M.87.3045A); med., *A.(Pass.) Andr*.14(M.2.1244B; p.32.13 ὁρκίσας).

ἐνορμάομαι, ? error for ἐνορμοῦσθαι, *be placed* or *fixed* τὸ 'ἔνθεμα' εἴρηται παρὰ τὸ ἐντίθεσθαι καὶ ἐνορμᾶσθαι τῷ τραχήλῳ τῆς νύμφης Or. *schol.in Cant*.4:9(M.17.272C).

ἐνορύσσω, *engrave in*; pass., Cyr.*ador*.11(1.380C).

ἑνότης, ἡ, *unity, union*; **1.** in gen.; **a.** *unity*; of any being, Tit. Bost.*Man*.2.38(M.18.1205C); of Christ who can appear as an old or young man πολυπρόσωπον ἑ. *A.Jo*.91(p.196.8); of individuals forming one species ἡ ἑ. τῶν ἀτόμων ἤγουν ταυτότης τῆς φύσεως τὸ καθόλου ποιεῖ Pamph.H.*panopl*.1.2(p.598); **b.** *union*; of moral union, of Christians one with another ἡ δὲ ἑ. γίνεται δι' ἀγάπης καὶ ἀληθείας καὶ προαιρέσεως ἀγαθῆς Or.*fr.28 in Jer*.27:17(p.212.28; M.13.596B); **c.** *uniformity*, Iren.*haer*.1.9.1(M.7.540A); **2.** Gnost.; **a.** as characteristic of first-created angels ἡ ὁμοιότης τῶν πραγμάτων ἑ. καὶ ἰσότητα καὶ ὁμοιότητα ἐνδείκνυνται Clem.*exc. Thdot*.10(p.109.28; M.9.660C); **b.** as name of an aeon, Iren.*haer*.1.11.3(M.7.565A); Epiph.*haer*.31.2(p.386.5; M.41.477A); **3.** of unity of Christians; **a.** one with another as children of God ἐν τῇ ἀνθρωπήσει υἱὸς καὶ οἱ μαθηταὶ ἕν, προσαγομένων τῶν...μαθητῶν ...εἰς μίαν ἑ. υἱοθεσίας διὰ τὴν τοῦ πατρὸς καὶ υἱοῦ καὶ τοῦ ἁγίου πνεύματος εὐδοκίαν Epiph.*haer*.69.69(p.218.6; M.42.313D); *ib*.(p.217.22; 313B); in unity of Christ ἐσώθησαν, ἐν ἑ. Ἰησοῦ Χριστοῦ ὄντες Ign.*Philad*.5.2; **b.** of unity of Jews and gentiles in Christ (ref. Eph.2:14), Cyr.*Mich*.48(3.438A); *ib*.72(473B) cit. s. ἀνακίρνημι; **c.** of union with God in Christ ἵνα γεννήσῃ τὸν λαὸν ἡ νοητὴ Σιὼν... εἰς τὴν ἑ. τοῦ κυρίου καταντήσαντα Meth.*symp*.8.7(p.90.2; M.18.149B); τὸ πνεῦμα...τὸ τοὺς ἁγίους ἀναγεννῶν εἰς ἑ. τὴν πρὸς θεὸν Cyr. *thes*.34(5^{1}.349B); μενοῦμεν...ἐν Χριστῷ...δι' αὐτοῦ τῷ θεῷ πρὸς ἑ. τὴν πνευματικὴν συνδούμενοι id.*Nah*.13(3.491D); **4.** of divine unity; **a.** in Trin. ὄντος δὲ τοῦ υἱοῦ ἐν πατρὶ καὶ πατρὸς ἐν υἱῷ ἑ. καὶ δυνάμει πνεύματος Athenag.*leg*.10.2(M.6.909A); *ib*.12.2(913B); Gr.Naz.*or*.21.2(M.35.1084C); ἵνα εἰς μίαν ἑ. ἀγάγῃ τὴν τριάδος ὀνομασίαν Epiph.*haer*.62.7(p.397.14; M.41.1061A); ἑνότητος ἑνὰς ἁγνά, μονάδων μονάς τε πρώτη Synes.*hymn*.1.58(p.60; M.66.1589); ‡Gr.Nyss.*hom.1.6 in Jo*.(p.95.7); its nature ἀμιγῆ μὲν αὐτὴν [sc. τὴν τριάδα]...τῶν γενητῶν, ἀδιαίρετον δὲ τὴν ἑ. τῆς θεότητος αὐτῆς Ath.*Ar*.1.18(M.26.49B); διαφορὰ...δι' ἧς τὸ ἑκατέρου πρόσωπον εἰσφέρεται ἐν ἰδιαζούσῃ μὲν ὑποστάσει κείμενον, εἰς ἑ. δὲ θεότητος διὰ ταυτότητος φυσικῆς σφιγγόμενον Cyr.*thes*.11(5^{1}.85C); as ground of Christians' mutual unity, Epiph.*haer*.57.10(p.356.15; 1009B); **b.** of Word with Father ἀχώριστον ἔχων [sc. ὁ υἱὸς] πρὸς τὸν πατέρα ἑαυτοῦ τὴν ἑ. τῆς θεότητος Ath.*Ar*.2.41(233A); exeg. Heb.1:3 τὴν ἑ. ἡμῖν παρίστησι τῆς θεότητος Bas.*hom*.24.4(2.193A; M.31.608B); τῆς φυσικῆς ἑ. τῆς ἐν πατρὶ καὶ υἱῷ νοουμένης Cyr.*Jo*.11.9(4.972B); *ib*.1.3(21C); Euthal.Diac.*epp. cath*.(M.85.685A); ref. Jo.10:30 ἀνάγκη...κατὰ τὴν οὐσίαν νοεῖν καὶ τὴν υἱοῦ καὶ πατρὸς ἑ. Ath.*syn*.48(p.273.7; M.26.780A); τήν τε τῆς ὁμοιώσεως ἑ. τοῦ υἱοῦ πρὸς τὸν πατέρα οὐκ ἔλεγον [sc. Arians] κατὰ τὴν οὐσίαν...ἀλλὰ διὰ τὴν συμφωνίαν τῶν δογμάτων *ib*.45(p.270.30; 773C); *ib*.52(p.275.32; 785C); ἔδειξε διὰ τῶν εἰρημένων [Jo.1:1] καὶ τὴν διαίρεσιν τῶν...ὑποστάσεων καὶ τῆς φύσεως τὴν ἑ. ‡Gr.Nyss. *hom.1.6 in Jo*.(p.95.7); τῆς κατὰ φύσιν ἑ. Jo.D.*f.o*.1.7(M.94.805C); cf. περὶ...τοῦ κυρίου ἡμῶν Ἰησοῦ Χριστοῦ καὶ...τῆς πρὸς τὸν πατέρα ἑ. αὐτοῦ Ath.*Ar*.2.39(229B); **c.** of H. Ghost with Son and Father τὸ πνεῦμα τὸ ἅγιον τὸ τὴν αὐτὴν ἔχον ἑ. πρὸς τὸν υἱόν, ἣν αὐτὸς ἔχει πρὸς τὸν πατέρα id.*ep.Serap*.1.2(M.26.533A); **5.** Christol.; ἀνέστη... καὶ συνήνωσεν αὐτὸ [sc. τὸ πνεῦμα] εἰς ἑαυτὸν...εἰς μίαν ἑ. ... εἰς μίαν ἑαυτοῦ θεότητα Epiph.*exp.fid*.17(p.518.15; M.42.817A); αὐτὸ τὸ σῶμα...ἐνδυναμώσας καὶ ἑνώσας εἰς μίαν ἑ. εἰς μίαν θεότητα id.*inc*.3(p.230.10; M.41.276D); exeg. Ps.92:1 τὸ 'διεζώσατο' συνενώσας τὴν αὐτοῦ σάρκα εἰς μίαν θεότητα, εἰς μίαν ἑ. id.*haer*.69.67(p.215.21; M.42.309C); οὐδὲ Χριστοὺς ἐροῦμεν δύο κἂν ἐξ ἀνθρώπου τελείου καὶ ἐκ θεοῦ λόγου τὴν εἰς ἑ. συνδρομὴν πέπραχθαι πιστεύωμεν τοῦ Ἐμμανουὴλ Cyr.*inc.unigen*.(5^{1}.690B); id.*ep*.1(p.15.32; 5^{2}.9B) cit. s. ἀνακίρνημι; *ib*.4(p.27.5; 5^{2}.23C) cit. s. ἀνθρωπότης; τὸ ἐργαστήριον τῆς ἑ. τῶν φύσεων Procl.CP *or.laud.BMV* 1(p.103.13, v.l. ἑνώσεως M.65 681A); Apollinarian τὰ ἔνδοξα τῷ σώματι προσάπτομεν ἐκ τῆς θείας συλλήψεως καὶ τῆς πρὸς θεὸν ἑ. Apoll.*corp.et div*.3(p.186.9; M.*PL*.8.873B); πρὸς ἑνότητα θεῷ συνῆπται *ib*.2(p.186.6; 873B); *ib*.5(p.187.7; 873C) cit. s. ἄκτιστος; δοκεῖ δὲ μὴν ἑτέροις...μὴ...ἔτι καὶ ἐμψυχῶσθαι ...τὴν ἀναληφθεῖσαν σάρκα ψυχῇ λογικῇ καὶ νοῦν ἐχούσῃ τὸν καθ' ἡμᾶς, εἰς ἑ. δὲ τὴν εἰσάπαν...κατασφίγγοντες τόν τε ἐκ θεοῦ λόγον, καὶ τὸν ἐκ τῆς ἁγίας παρθένου ναόν Cyr.*inc.unigen*.(5^{1}.679D); ἀλλ' ἴσως ἐροῦσιν οὐκ ἀποφοιτῆσαι μὲν ὁλοτρόπως τὴν σάρκα τοῦ εἶναι ὃ ἦν, ἀνακραθῆναι δὲ ὥσπερ τῷ θεῷ λόγῳ πρὸς ἑ. φυσικὴν id.*synous*.10(p.485.26; cf.M.76.1432D).

***ἑνοτήσιος**, *uniting*, Synes.*hymn*.2.31(p.44; M.66.1592).

***ἐνουλισμός, ὁ**, *curling*, Clem.*paed*.3.2(p.238.16; M.8.560C).

ἐνουράνιος, *heavenly* λόγον ἐ. Iren.*fr*.29(M.7.1245A).

***ἐνουσία, ἡ**, *existence in another, inherence* οὐ γὰρ ἐνέργεια θεότητος, ἣν ἐ. τίκτει, τὸν ναὸν ἐκεῖνον ἐκυβέρνα τὸν ἄχραντον, ἀλλ' οὐσία μυρίας ἐνεργείας ἔχουσα Isid.Pel.*epp*.4.166(M.78.1256B).

ἐνούσιος, *essential, substantial*; **1.** = ἐνυπόστατος opp. ἀνούσιος, *existing as a substance, really existing* φύσις ἐστὶν ἡ τῶν πραγμάτων ἀλήθεια ἢ τούτων τὸ ἐ. Clem.*fr*.37(p.219.20; M.9.752A); Didym.(‡Bas.)*Eun*.5(1.312D; M.29.749B) cit. s. ἀνυπόστατος; τὸ τοιῶσδε εἶναι, καὶ τοιοῦδέ τινος μετειληφέναι τινά, πολλάκις μὲν ἐ., πολλάκις δὲ καὶ ἀνυποστάτου τινός, υἱὸν τοῦδε ἀληθῶς εἶναι καὶ λέγεσθαι αὐτὸν ποιεῖ Leont.H.*Nest*.4.16(M.86.1681B); implying existence as an entity, *substantive*, esp. of Persons of Trin.; opp. προφορικός, ‡Ath.*disp*.25(M.28.469A) cit. s. λόγος; // ζῶν: αὐτός ἐστιν ἡ τοῦ πατρὸς ζῶσα βουλή, καὶ ἐ. ἐνέργεια, καὶ λόγος ἀληθινός Ath.*Ar*.2.2(M.26.152A); ζῶντα λόγον καὶ ἐ. σοφίαν id.*syn*.41(p.267.26; M.26.768A); αὐτὸς [sc. ὁ υἱός] ἄρα ἐστὶν ἡ ἐ. καὶ ζῶσα τοῦ πατρὸς βούλησις Cyr.*thes*.15(5^{1}.153B); οὐκ ἀνυπόστατος [sc. ὁ λόγος] ὥσπερ ὁ ἀνθρώπινος, ἀλλ' ἐ. τε καὶ ζῶν ὡς ἰδίαν ἔχων...μετὰ πατρὸς τὴν ὕπαρξιν id.*Jo*.5.5(4.527D); with intrans. ptcpls. of ὑφίστημι: τριάδα...ἀληθῶς οὖσαν καὶ ὑφεστῶσαν, πατέρα τε ἀληθῶς ὄντα καὶ ὑφεστῶτα, καὶ υἱὸν ἀληθῶς ἐ. ὄντα καὶ ὑφεστῶτα, καὶ πνεῦμα ἅγιον ὑφεστὸς καὶ ὑπάρχον οἴδαμεν Ath.*tom*.5(M.26.801B); ἐ. δύναμιν ὁμολογεῖ τὸν υἱὸν ὁπωσοῦν ὑποστάντα Gr.Nyss.*Eun*.1(1 p.76.4; M.45.305D); // οὐσιώδης, ‡Ath.*Ar*.4.1(p.45.4; M.26.469A); opp. ἁπλῶς, *ib*.4.2(p.45.5; 469A) citt. s. οὐσιώδης; // ἐνυπόστατος: ὥσπερ οὐ προφορικὸς λόγος ἐν τῷ θεῷ, ἀλλὰ ζῶν καὶ ὑφεστηκὼς...οὕτως ἐν τῷ θεῷ οὐ πνεῦμα διαχεόμενον...ἀλλὰ δύναμις ἁγιαστική, ἐ., ἐνύπαρκτος, ἐνυπόστατος Didym.(‡Bas.)*Eun*.5(1.297C; M.29.713B); ἐ. λόγον καὶ ἐνυπόστατον πνεῦμα...ἐν τῷ πατρί Thdt.*affect*.2(p.65.22; 4.757); also of divine Word in Christ ψιλὸν οὐ λέγει [sc. ὁ Νεστόριος] ἄνθρωπον τὸν Χριστὸν...ὡς οὐδαμοῦ τὴν τοῦ θεοῦ λόγου ὑπόστασιν ἀναιρεῖ, ἀλλὰ πανταχοῦ ἐνυπόστατον αὐτὸν ὁμολογεῖ καὶ ἐ. Socr.*h.e*.7.32.19(M.67.812B); **2.** opp. ἑτερογενής, *of the same substance* τοῖς ἐν οὐσίᾳ καὶ ὑποστάσει πρὸς τὰ ἐ. τε καὶ ἐνυπόστατα ἡ ὁμοιότης ἡ κατὰ τοῦτο σῴζεται, οὐ πρὸς τὰ ἑτερογενῆ, καὶ ἐν ἑτέροις ἔχοντα τὸ εἶναι Cyr.*thes*.8(5^{1}.62A); **3.** opp. ὑπερούσιος, *cosmic, in created form*, πᾶν ἐ. opp. τὸ θεῖον, ‡Just.*qu.Gr*.2(M.6.1469C); Synes.*hymn*.2.37(p.44; M.66.1592); **4.** *being in essence, having a nature*; of attributes, qualities, *inherent in the nature, proper to the essence*, not as // ἐνυπόστατος (except in this sense only); neut. as subst., opp. οὐσία, *that which manifests abstract essence in a concrete instance*; **a.** defined and described οὐ ταὐτὸν...ὑπόστασις καὶ ἐνυπόστατον, ὥσπερ ἕτερον οὐσία καὶ ἐ. Leont.B.*Nest.et Eut*.1(M.86.1277D); ἐ. ἐστι τὸ μὴ μόνον ἐνθεωρούμενον ἔχον ἐφ' ἑαυτοῦ τὸ τῶν ἰδιωμάτων ἄθροισμα ...ἀλλὰ καὶ τὸ κοινὸν τῆς οὐσίας πραγματικῶς κεκτημένον Max.*opusc.*(M.91.152A); ἐ. λέγομεν ἢ αὐτὸ τὸ ὄν, ἢ τὸ ἐν τῇ οὐσίᾳ γνωριζόμενον ἰδίωμα· οἷον, ἐ. ἐστι τοῦ ἀνθρώπου τὸ λογιστικὸν καὶ τὸ φθαρτόν Anast.S.*hod.*2(M.89.61B); οὐ ταὐτὸν οὐσία τε καὶ ἐ. ... ἕτερον γάρ ἐστι τὸ ἔν τινι, καὶ ἕτερον τὸ ἐν ᾧ· ἐ. μὲν γάρ ἐστι τὸ ἐν τῇ οὐσίᾳ θεωρούμενον, τουτέστι τὸ τῶν συμβεβηκότων ἄθροισμα, ὃ δηλοῖ τὴν ὑπόστασιν, οὐκ αὐτὴν τὴν οὐσίαν Jo.D.*Jacob.*11(M.94.1441B); **b.** theol. πάντοτε...ἐνεργόν καὶ ἐ. καὶ ἐνυπόστατον τῇ ἀϊδίῳ φύσει τὸ...ἀΐδιον ἐνθεωρεῖται θέλημα Gr.Nyss.*Eun.*8(2 p.181.26; M.45.776A); esp. of Persons of Trin. μία οὐσία ἡ αὐτή· εἰ καὶ ἕκαστον τῶν προσώπων λέγεται, καὶ ἐ. καὶ θεὸς Gr.Nyss.*comm.not.*(M.45.177A,B); οἱ Ἀρειανοί...ταῖς ὑποστάσεσιν ἐ. οὔσαις, τὰς οὐσίας ἐπεφήμιζον Leont.B.*arg.Sev.*(M.86.1921A); οὐ λέγομεν πρὸς ταῖς τρισὶν ὑποστάσεσι, καὶ τρεῖς οὐσίας· καίπερ ἐ. ἐπιστάμενοι...ἑκάστην Leont.H.*Nest.*2.13(M.86.1560A); ἡ θεοφόρος σάρξ, ἢ ἐ. ἐστιν ἤτοι ἔχει φύσιν, ἢ φύσεως ἄμοιρος Pamph.H.*panopl.*6.2(p.616); ὁ ἐ. λόγος τοῦ πατρός, ἑνωθεὶς τῇ...οὐσίᾳ τῆς μητρός Eulog.*palm.*7(M.86.2924C); τὸ μὴ ἀνούσιον, οὐκ οὐσίαν ποιεῖ τὴν ὑπόστασιν, ἀλλ' ἐ. παριστᾷ, ἵνα μὴ ψιλὸν ἰδίωμα ταύτην, ἀλλὰ μετὰ τοῦ ἐν ᾧ τὸ ἰδίωμα κυρίως γνωρίζωμεν Max.*opusc.*(M.91.205B); ἡ τριάς...ἐ. ὕπαρξις τρισυποστάτου μονάδος id.*ambig.*(M.91.1036C); ἐ. προσώπου θεοῦ παρουσίαν καταγγέλλουσι [sc. οἱ προφῆται] i.e. opp. incarnation of whole Deity, Anast.S.*hod.*8(M.89.133D); οὐ ταὐτόν φαμεν ἐνυπόστατον καὶ ὑπόστασιν, οὔτε μὴν οὐσίαν τε καὶ ἐ.· ἀλλ' ἐ. μέν, τὴν ὑπόστασιν, ἐνυπόστατον δέ, τὴν οὐσίαν. τὴν...οὐσίαν τῆς...θεότητος ἐνυπόστατον ἴσμεν· ἐν ταῖς τρισὶ γάρ ἐστιν ὑποστάσεσι· καὶ ἑκάστην τῶν ὑποστάσεων ὡσαύτως ἐ. Jo.D.*Jacob.*12(M.94.1441D); **c.** Christol. εἰ μὲν ἀνούσια [sc. τὰ μέρη τῆς Χριστοῦ ὑποστάσεως ὁμοουσίου τῷ πατρὶ καὶ τῇ μητρί], πῶς ὁμοούσια τοῖς ἐ.; εἰ δὲ ἐ., πῶς οὐκ οὐσίας μέρη καθέστηκε; πᾶν γὰρ μέρος ἐ., οὐσίας μέρος κυρίως, καὶ οὐχ ὑποστάσεως...μέρη φαμὲν ὑποστάσεως, ὡς ἐκ πλειόνων οὔσης οὐσιῶν, τὰς οὐσίας, καὶ ἐ. ταῦτα, ἤγουν οὐσίας, λέγομεν ἐπὶ Χριστῷ Leont.H.*Nest.*2.4(M.86.1537Bf.); ἡ ὑπόστασις...οὐχ ὡς ὑπόστασις, ἀλλ' ὡς ἐ. λέγεται οἷς λέγεται ὁμοούσιος ἢ ἑτεροούσιος *ib.*2.5(1544B); **5.** of persons, *wealthy*, Thphn.*chron.*p.273(M.108.676A); of things, *sumptuous, costly*, *ib.*p.320(776A).

ἐνουσιόω, *bring into being, give substance to*, ‡Hipp.*Ber.Hel.*8 ap. *Doct.Patr.*44.8(p.326.1; M.10.840A).

ἐνουσίως, *from the point of view of substance, essentially*, opp. personally ἐ. τε κατὰ τὸ κοινόν, καὶ ἐνυποστάτως κατὰ τὸ ἰδικόν Leont.H.*Nest.*7.1(M.86.1760B).

***ἐνοφθάλμισμα, τό**, *grafting*, Synes.*ep.*159(M.66.1560C).

ἐνοχοποιέω, *pledge*, Ath.Scholast.*coll.*15.14(p.158).

ἑνόω, *unite*;

A. in gen.; **1.** *unify*, pass. intrans.; **a.** of solids, *form one solid block, consist of one piece* ἡ...οἰκοδομὴ ⟨τοῦ⟩ διαβόλου...ἐπ' οὐδενὶ...ἐστήρικται ἑδραίῳ...καὶ ἡνωμένῳ Or.*hom.*1.15 *in Jer.*(p.13.27; M.13.273A); τὰ ἡνωμένα opp. τὰ ἐκ πλειόνων συγκείμενα, Bas.*hom. in Ps.*61(1.195B; M.29.473C); **b.** of liquids, *commingle, mix*, of commixtio ἥνωται...εἰς τὸ ὄνομα τοῦ πατρὸς καὶ τοῦ υἱοῦ καὶ τοῦ ἁγίου πνεύματος *Lit.Jac.*(p.230.1); **c.** met., *unite* so as to become identified with αἱ...ἐκ παίδων μαθήσεις συναύξουσαι τῇ ψυχῇ ἑνοῦνται αὐτῇ Iren.*ep.Flor.* ap.Eus.*h.e.*5.20.6(M.20.483A); ἡ γὰρ καθόλου καὶ γεώδης ψυχή...αὐτὴ μὲν ὡς συγγενεῖ ἑνοῦται τῷ πνεύματι, ὅπερ ἐστὶν ἀνθρώπου ψυχή, τὸ δὲ τῆς τροφῆς ὑλῶδες τῷ σώματι ἑνωθὲν ὡς δεινὸς αὐτοῦ ὑπολείπεται ἰός *Hom.Clem.*9.12; of God and matter εἰ μὲν οὖν ἡνῶσθαί τις αὐτὸν εἰπεῖν ἐθέλοι, ἓν τὸ ἀγένητον λέξει. ἕκαστον γὰρ τούτων μέρος ἔσται τοῦ πλησίον Meth.*arbitr.*5(p.157.10; M.18.249B); *be unified* hence *be one, simple*; of divine truth, Dion.Ar.*d.n.*1.4(M.3.592C); **2.** *unite*; **a.** pass., *be joined* or *combine* so as to form a unity τὸ γὰρ εἶναι ἢ μὴ εἶναι σῶμα ἐκ τοῦ ἡνῶσθαι ἢ μὴ ἡνῶσθαι γίνεται Chrys.*hom.30.2 in 1Cor.*(10.271D); ὁ ἄρτος ἐκ πολλῶν συγκείμενος κόκκων ἥνωται *ib.*24.2(213E); ἡνῶσθαι δεῖ τῇ πίστει, ὡς τὸ κλῆμα τῇ ἀμπέλῳ id.*hom.76.1 in Jo.*(8.447A); Dion.Ar.*d.n.*2.4(M.3.641B); **b.** human body, soul, and spirit in Christ τὰ τρία ταῦτα παρὰ τὸν καιρὸν τοῦ πάθους διηρέθη, τὰ τρία ταῦτα παρὰ τὸν καιρὸν τῆς ἀναστάσεως ἡνώθη Or.*dial.*7(p.138.3); soul and body in man ἀσυγχύτως ἥνωται τῷ σώματι ἡ ψυχή Nemes.*nat.hom.*3(M.40.596A); act. trans., ref. creation of man τῷ γηΐνῳ...τὴν ψυχὴν ἥνωσε Meth.*res.*2.24(p.380.5; M.18.329C); **c.** met., in possession of a common nature, Tit.Bost.*Man.*1.16(M.18.1089B); of a study in still life, *form a unity, compose* into a picture, Gr.Nyss.*hom.4 in Cant.*(M.44.849A); **d.** pass., *be united* in marriage, Cyr.*Mal.*28(3.846B); ‡Nil.*narr.*2(M.79.604A); Petr.Laod.*fr.in Mt.*19:11(M.86.3324B); Anast.S.*qu.et resp.*96(M.89.748B); **e.** of union of thing known with knower as symbolic of union of believer with God, Didym.*Ps.*17:45(M.39.1264B), Max.*schol.d.n.*7.4 (M.4.353Cf.) citt. s. γινώσκω; **3. a.** act., *join, add* ἑνώσας τὴν γνῶσιν, πίστιν, ἀγάπην Clem.*str.*3.10(p.227.20; M.8.1172A); ἵνα...ἑνώσῃ καὶ ἐγκαταριθμήσῃ αὐτοὺς τῷ ἁγίῳ αὐτοῦ ποιμνίῳ *Lit.*ap.*Const.App.*8.6.6; **b.** pass., *be joined to, form one group with, associate with* Ἀβραὰμ μετὰ τῶν πατριαρχῶν καὶ τῶν προφητῶν ἑνωθείς [i.e. in Hades] *A.Pil.*B 18.1(p.324); exeg. Ps.1:5 οἱ ἤδη κατεγνωσμένοι εἰς τὸ μὴ ἑνωθῆναι τοῖς ἀπταίστως βεβιωκόσιν Clem.*str.*2.15(p.149.27; M.8.1008B); Chrys.*hom.57.2 in Jo.*(8.335C); ἑνωθῆτε τοῖς πολεμοῦσιν ὑμῖν id.*hom.46.2 in Mt.*(7.483C); of souls of saints ὅσοι τῷ τῶν ἀγγέλων ἡνώθησαν χορῷ Eustrat.*stat.anim.*15(p.445); *be sociable, lead one's life in society* or *community* opp. isolation τὸ...ἀπεσχισμένον καὶ ἰδιάζον τοῦ κοινωνικοῦ καὶ ἡνωμένου τοῖς πολλοῖς προτιμότερον Bas.*hex.*8.7(1.77D; M.29.181B); τὸ ἡνωμένον τῆς ζωῆς τῶν ἀδελφῶν id.*reg.fus.*38(2.385B; M.31.1017B); **4.** of moral union, *unite*; **a.** act. πνεῦμα καὶ ψυχὴν ἑνώσει κατὰ τὴν τοῦ λόγου ὑπακοήν Clem.*str.*3.13(p.239.2; M.8.1193A); **b.** pass., in obedience κατὰ σάρκα καὶ πνεῦμα ἡνωμένοις πάσῃ ἐντολῇ αὐτοῦ Ign.*Rom.*proem.; in suffering κοινῷ στεναγμῷ ἑνωθέντες *M.Perp.*15(p.85.7); in self-identification, Or.*mart.*10(p.10.21; M.11.576C) cit. s. ἀνακιρνάω; τῷ συνδέσμῳ τῆς ἀγάπης τῆς πρὸς αὐτὸν καὶ ἡμᾶς ἡνῶσθαι Ath.*apol.sec.*57.4(p.137.10; M.25.352C); θεῷ περισπούδαστον...τὸ ἡνῶσθαι...ἡμᾶς ἀλλήλοις Chrys.*hom.16.8 in Mt.*(7.216A); ἵνα...ἑνωθῶμεν ἀλλήλοις τῷ τῆς εἰρήνης καὶ τῆς ἀγάπης συνδέσμῳ *Lit.Jac.*(p.182.24); of a bishop and his flock τῷ συνδέσμῳ τῆς ἀγάπης ἑνωθησόμεθα Bas.*ep.*28.3(3.108E; M.32.309C); **c.** *be in concord (with)*; of nations, Eus.*d.e.*9.17(p.441.25; M.22.712A); of individuals σπουδάσατε ἑνωθῆναι ἀλλήλοις· ὅσος γὰρ ἑνοῦταί τι τῷ πλησίον, τοσοῦτον ἑνοῦται τῷ θεῷ Dor.*doct.*6.8(M.88.1696B); exeg. Gen.2:23 ἥνωσεν ἡμῖν τὰς ψυχὰς ὁ διαστήσας τὰ σώματα Bas.Sel.*or.*2.4(M.85.48B); **5.** *bring into* or *restore to communion with (one another)*; **a.** act. ἕνωσον [sc. τοὺς κατηχουμένους] τῇ ἁγίᾳ σου ἐκκλησίᾳ *Lit.*ap.*Const.App.*8.6.13; τὸ ἑνῶσαι τὰς τοῦ Χριστοῦ ἐκκλησίας Jo.Ant.*ep.Cyr.*2(p.8.5; M.77.172A); ἵνα τῆς συνόδου παραγενομένης τὴν...ἐκκλησίαν ὁ Χριστὸς ἑνώσῃ Thal.CP *Thds.*4(p.9.10; M.91.1476C); ἕνωσον αὐτὸν τῇ ἁγίᾳ ἐκκλησίᾳ †Jo.Jej.*poenit.*(M.88.1897C); **b.** pass., Arsen.Hyps.*ep.*(p.148.2; M.25.372D); περὶ τῆς ἑνωθείσης τῷ ἀποστολικῷ θρόνῳ τῆς Κωνσταντινουπόλεως ἐκκλησίας Horm.*ep.Epiph.*(p.57.16; M.*PL.*63.518B); ἡνώθη...τούτῳ ὁ τῆς Κωνσταντινουπόλεως πρόεδρος Ἀκάκιος Evagr.*h.e.*3.16(p.114.28; M.86.2628A).

B. theol.; **1.** act.; **a.** in human thought, *unite, conceive as a unity* μὴ σχίζων τὴν προσκύνησιν, ἀλλ' ἑνῶν τὴν θεότητα ‡Bas.*struct.hom.*1.2(1.325C; M.30.13B); θεός, ὁ τοὺς ἑνοῦντας αὐτὸν ἑνῶν Gr.Naz.*or.*23.4(M.35.1153D); τὰ θεῖα καὶ ἑνοῦν τῷ λόγῳ καὶ διακρίνειν σπεύδομεν, ὡς αὐτὰ τὰ θεῖα καὶ ἥνωται καὶ διακέκριται Dion.Ar.*d.n.*2.6(M.3.644C); **b.** heret. (Gnost.) πρότερον διαστείλας [sc. 'Ιωάννης] τὰ τρία, θεόν, καὶ ἀρχήν, καὶ λόγον, πάλιν αὐτὰ ἑνοῖ Iren.*haer.*1.8.5(M.7.533A); Eunomian ἑνούντων [sc. Greeks] τῇ οὐσίᾳ τὴν ἐνέργειαν, καὶ διὰ τοῦθ' ἅμα μὲν τῷ θεῷ τὸν κόσμον ἀποφαινομένων Eun.*apol.*22(M.30.857C); *ib.*23(860A); **2.** pass., *be one*; Trin. τίς ἡ τῶν τοσούτων ἕνωσις καὶ διαίρεσις ἑνουμένων; Athenag.*leg.*12.2(M.6.913C); Didym.(‡Bas.) *Eun.*5(1.310E; M.29.745B) cit. s. ἀχώριστος; ἑνοῦνται...οὐχ ὥστε συγχεῖσθαι, ἀλλ' ὥστε ἔχεσθαι ἀλλήλων ‡Cyr.*Trin.*10(6³.16A; M.77.1144B); in power θεὸν...καὶ υἱὸν...καὶ πνεῦμα ἅγιον, ἑνούμενα μὲν κατὰ δύναμιν...ὅτι νοῦς, λόγος, σοφία ὁ υἱὸς τοῦ πατρὸς καὶ ἀπόρροια ὡς φῶς...τὸ πνεῦμα...οὐχ ὡς μέρους ὄντος, ἀλλ' ὡς κατ' ἀνάγκην συνόντος παρακολουθήματος, ἡνωμένου καὶ συγκεχρωσμένου Athenag.*leg.*24.1,2(M.6.945B); in nature ἑνούσης τῆς προσηγορίας τὰ ἡνωμένα ἐκ φύσεως Gr.Naz.*or.*23.10(M.35.1161C); ἡ δὲ φύσις μία ἐστίν, αὐτὴ πρὸς ἑαυτὴν ἡνωμένη Gr.Nyss.*tres dii*(M.45.120B); id.*Trin.*6(p.78.8; M.32.693A); ὁ...υἱὸς τῇ τοῦ πατρὸς θεότητι κατὰ φύσιν ἑνούμενος Cyr.*thes.*7(5¹.55D); in substance ἡνωμένον μέν ἐστι τῇ ἐναρχικῇ τριάδι, καὶ κοινὸν ἡ...ὕπαρξις, ἡ...θεότης... Dion.Ar.*d.n.*2.4(M.3.641A); *ib.*2.5(644A); in attributes, *ib.*2.2(640A); τὰ μὲν ἡνωμένα τῆς ὅλης θεότητός ἐστιν *ib.*2.3(640B); of Son with Father ἑνοῦται τὰ δύο, τῷ μὴ διαλλάττειν, μηδὲ καθ' ἕτερον εἶδος...νοεῖσθαι τὸν υἱόν Bas.*hom.*24.4(2.193A; M.31.608B); οὐχὶ συγκρίνοντος ἑαυτόν ἐστι τὸ ῥῆμα...ἑνοῦντος μὲν οὖν...καὶ τὸ τῆς φύσεως ἀπαράλλακτον παριστῶντος ἐντεῦθεν Bas.*Eun.*1.2(1.237E; M.29.572A); after Inc. μετὰ...τὴν ἀνάστασιν συνέφαγεν αὐτοῖς...ὡς σαρκικός, καίπερ πνευματικῶς ἡνωμένος τῷ πατρί Ign.*Smyrn.*3.3; not to be conceived ὡς μέρος ἢ μέλος, ἀγενήτως ἡνωμένον ἀεὶ πρότερον, ἔπειτα δὲ διαστὰν...τὸν υἱὸν ἀπὸ τοῦ πατρός Eus.*d.e.*5.1(p.212.18; M.22.352D); heret. ἡ...σοφία ᾗ ὥσπερ ἰδίῳ πνεύματι αὐτὸς ἀεὶ συνέχαιρεν, ἥνωται μὲν ὡς ψυχὴ τῷ θεῷ *Hom.Clem.*16.12.

C. Christol.; **1.** act., of act of Word; **a.** in uniting human nature to himself δι' ἡμᾶς ἥνωσεν ἑαυτῷ τὴν κτιστὴν σάρκα Didym.*Heb.*

1:6(p.45.5); in 'Nestorian' interpretation ὅλον μὲν ἑαυτῷ τὸν λαμβανόμενον ἥνωσεν Thdr.Mops.*fr.inc.*7(p.296.3; M.66.976B); εἶχέν τε καὶ ῥοπὴν οὐ τὴν τυχοῦσαν πρὸς τὰ κρείττω τῇ πρὸς τὸν θεὸν λόγον ἑνώσει, ἧς ἠξίωτο κατὰ πρόγνωσιν τοῦ θεοῦ λόγου ἄνωθεν ·αὐτὸν ἑνώσαντος ἑαυτῷ *ib.*(p.296.33; 977B); *ib.*(p.298.3; 980B); Apollinarian τὸν...θεὸν λόγον...σάρκα ἐξ ἁγίας παρθένου ἑνώσαντα ἑαυτῷ... ὑπόστασιν μίαν σύνθετον Job.Ep.*symb.*(p.286.21; M.86.3320C); ἀσύγκριτα...ὑπῆρχε τὰ πράγματα πρὶν [ᾖ] ἑνώσει αὐτὰ ἐν ἑαυτῷ ὁ τεχνίτης Isid.Pel.*epp.*1.248(M.78.333B); ἑνώσας ἑαυτῷ καθ' ὑπόστασιν τὸ ἀνθρώπινον Cyr.*ep.*4(p.27.10; 5^{2}.23D); id.*Nest.*2.8(p.44.33; 6^{1}.48D); εἷς ...Χριστὸς ὡς ἑνώσαντος μὲν ἑαυτῷ τοῦ...λόγου τὸ ἀνθρώπινον, μεμενηκότος δὲ καὶ οὕτως ὅπερ ἦν id.*Pulch.*(p.30.24; 5^{2}.134D); id. *Arcad.*(p.81.2; 5^{2}.70E); Bas.Sel.ap.CCP(448)ap.CChalc.*act.*1(*ACO* 2.1.1 p.117.24; H.2.132E) cit. s. φύσις; ὁ...λόγος ἑαυτῷ ἥνωσε τὴν ἡμετέραν σωματέμψυχον φύσιν, οὐκ ἄψυχον κατὰ τοὺς αἱρετικούς Eulog.*fr.Trin.*3.1(p.365); **b.** in uniting himself to human nature ὁ... λόγος ἥνωσεν ἑαυτὸν τῇ γηΐνῃ...σαρκί Cyr.ap.*cat.Heb.*2:15(p.159.11); *ib.*suppl.2:15(p.408:4); cf.Thdot.Anc.*exp.symb.*7(M.77.1324C) cit. s. διαιρέω; **2.** *unite* in human thought on Person of Christ χωρίζω τὰς φύσεις, ἀλλ' ἑνῶ τὴν προσκύνησιν Nest.*fr.*C 9(p.262.6)ap. CEph.(341)(H.1.1413D); id.ap.Cyr.*ep.*50(p.100.5; 5^{2}.170C) cit. s. διαιρέω; **3.** pass.; **a.** of human nature of Christ as being united in him to Godhead, Or.*or.*26(p.362.3; M.11.504A) cit. s. ἀνακίρνημι; ἐχρῆν γὰρ [i.e. if what Apollinarius says is true] ἐπειδὴ θεότης ἥνωται διαιρεῖσθαι τὴν ἀνθρωπότητα Gr.Naz.*or.*22.13(M.35.1145B); Gr.Nyss.*Eun.*5(2 p.117.6; M.45.697B) cit. s. δεξιός; ἀνελήφθη μετὰ τῆς ἑνωθείσης αὐτῷ σαρκός Cyr.*resp.*6(p.587.7; 6^{2}.391A); Ammon. *Jo.*1:4(M.85.1393C); not pre-existent, Marc.Er.*opusc.*10.4(M.65.1121D); not divinized, Cyr.*resp.*(p.591.11; 6^{2}.392C); but united hypostatically, Max.*ambig.*(M.91.1048D); Apollinarian εἰ πρὸς τὸν πατέρα, φησίν, ἥνωται Χριστὸς πρὸ ἀναστάσεως, πῶς πρὸς τὸν ἐν αὐτῷ θεὸν οὐχ ἥνωται; Apoll.*fr.*100(p.230.27f.)ap.Gr.Nyss.*Apoll.*58 (M.45.1265C); οὐδὲν οὕτως ἥνωται πρὸς θεὸν ὡς ἡ σὰρξ ἡ προσληφθεῖσα· τὰ μὴ οὕτως ἡνωμένα οὐδ' οὕτως προσκυνητὰ *ib.*84(p.225.1f.; M.45.1228A); εἰ ἄνθρωπον οἴεταί τις ἑνοῦσθαι θεῷ παρὰ πάντας ἀνθρώπους... ποιήσει μὴ αὐτεξουσίους...τοὺς ἀνθρώπους...οὐκ ἄρα ἑνοῦται ὁ ἄνθρωπος θεῷ *ib.*87(p.226.1ff.; M.45.1232A,B); ὁμοούσιον θεῷ κατὰ τὴν... θεότητα, καὶ ὁμοούσιον ἀνθρώποις κατὰ τὴν...ἡνωμένην αὐτῷ σάρκα... ἄκρως γὰρ ἡνωμένη ἡ σὰρξ τῷ λόγῳ Job.Ep.*symb.*(p.286.26ff; M.86.3320B); *ib.*(p.287.3; 3320C); Apoll.*inc.*3(p.305.23; M.28.93B); in teaching of Thdr.Mops.*fr.mir.*(p.339.14; M.66.1004D) cit. s. ἄνθρωπος; **b.** of divine and human natures as mutually united in Christ, Cyr.*ep.*44(p.36.11; 5^{2}.134A) cit. s. φύσις; Leont.B.*Nest.et Eut.*1(M.87.1305B) cit. s. συγχέω; ὁ ἕτερος [sc. Nestorius] μὴ θέλων τὴν παρθένον...θεοῦ εἶναι γεννητρίαν, ἅπερ ἐν τῷ κυρίῳ ἡμῶν εἰσιν ἡνωμένα, διαιρεῖ Horm.*ep.cler.*(p.55.6; M.*PL.*63.419B); Thdr.Raith.*praep.*(p.191.8; M.91.1492A) cit. s. οὐσιωδῶς; μίαν ὑπόστασιν Χριστοῦ ὁμολογοῦμεν ἐν δύο φύσεσιν ἡνωμέναις ἀδιαιρέτως Thal.*cent.*2.96(M.91.1448A); compared with unity in Trin., Max.*opusc.*(M.91.265C); not of two persons δύο...φύσεις ἡμεῖς ἐν Χριστῷ ἀδιαιρέτους τὰ δύο αὐτοῦ γένη ἤγουν τὰ ἑνωθέντα δύο πράγματα ὁμολογοῦμεν καὶ οὐδὲ εἰς δύο πρόσωπα τὸν Χριστὸν μερίζομεν Eulog.*fr.Trin.*4.3(p.370); Max. *ambig.*(M.91.1060A); *Lit.Jac.*(*NBP* 10^{2} p.37) cit. s. διαιρέω; cf. εἰ δέ τις...λέγει...δύο πρόσωπα ⟨τέλεια⟩ ἑνωθέντα, γινωσκέτω τῆς θείας ἐλπίδος ἀλλότριος ὤν Tim.Beryt.*ep.Prosd.*3(p.285.3); Apollinarian ἑνοῦται ἄρα τὰ τοῦ θεοῦ καὶ σώματος Apoll.*fr.*125(p.238.1)ap.Thdt. *eran.*2(4.170); θεῷ ὁμοούσιος κατὰ τὸ πνεῦμα τὸ ἀόρατον, συμπεριλαμβανομένης τῷ ὀνόματι καὶ τῆς σαρκός, ὅτι πρὸς τὸν θεῷ ὁμοούσιον ἥνωται, καὶ πάλιν ἀνθρώποις ὁμοούσιος, συμπεριλαμβανομένης καὶ τῆς θεότητος τῷ σώματι, ὅτι πρὸς τὸ ἡμῖν ὁμοούσιον ἡνώθη id.*corp.et div.*8(p.188.12ff.; M.*PL.*8.874A); *ib.*17(p.192.16; 875D); Eunomian λέγεται...παρὰ...τοῖς Εὐνομιανοῖς, ἡνῶσθαι τὸν θεὸν λόγον τῷ σώματι, οὐ κατ' οὐσίαν, ἀλλὰ κατὰ τὰς ἑκατέρου δυνάμεις. οὐ γὰρ εἶναι τὰς οὐσίας τὰς ἑνωθείσας ἢ κραθείσας, ἀλλὰ τὰς δυνάμεις...συγκεκρᾶσθαι Nemes.*nat.hom.*3(M.40.605A); **c.** of Word as united to man in Christ οὐ τραπεὶς [sc. ὁ λόγος] εἰς ἄνθρωπον ἀλλ' ἑνωθεὶς καθ' ὑπόστασιν Marc.Er.*Nest.*21(p.104.18); *ib.*10(p.96.15); ὁ ἡνωμένος θεὸς τῇ εὐτελείᾳ τῆς...σαρκός Isid.Pel.*epp.*1.59(M.78.221A); *ib.*1.124(265A); ἡνῶσθαι...σαρκὶ καθ' ὑπόστασιν...τὸν λόγον Cyr.*ep.*17(p.35.26; 5^{2}.70B); id.*apol.Thdt.*anath.2(p.114.6; 6^{1}.208A); id.*Arcad.*(p.110.28; 5^{2}.115A); id.*Ps.*49:2(M.69.1076A); ποῦ γὰρ...ψιλὸς ἄνθρωπος ὁ Χριστός; πότε δὲ δίχα τοῦ ἑνωθέντος αὐτῷ νοεῖται λόγου; id.*Heb.*2:9 (p.390.3); ἄπιστόν σοι φαίνεται εἰ ὁ ἀθάνατος θεὸς...ἑνοῦται σώματι; Procl.CP *or.*6.13(M.65.745C); ἐπιπλήσσει τῇ σαρκὶ...ἥτις μὴ ἐνεγκοῦσα τὸ τῆς ἑνωθείσης αὐτῷ θεότητος κίνημα Ammon.*Jo.*11:33(M.85.1468C); †Leont.B.*sect.*1.3(M.86.1197B); Oecum.*Apoc.*19:16(p.210); *ib.*3:12(p.62); Eulog.*palm.*7(M.86.2924C); ἡ ἀνθρωπότης τοῦ Χριστοῦ ὑπὸ τῆς ἡνωμένης αὐτῇ...θεότητος ἐπιτρέπεται Cosm.Ind.*top.*5(M.88.265A); ἐκ τῶν...θεομήτορος...αἱμάτων οἷς...ἑνωθεὶς ὁ λόγος γέγονε σὰρξ μὴ ἐκστὰς τοῦ εἶναι κατ' οὐσίαν θεός Max.*opusc.*(M.91.60A); ‡Caes.Naz.*dial.*25(M.38.885); *ib.*29(888); οὐχ ὑπάρχειν, ἀλλὰ γίνεσθαι ...ἡνωμένον ψυχῇ τε καὶ σώματι τοῖς ἡμετέροις...δι' ἐμὲ...τοῖς ἐμοῖς ὁ λόγος ἥνωται *ib.*169(1132f.); οὐ μὲν δὲ λέγειν ἀναγκασθησόμεθα πάσας τὰς ὑποστάσεις τῆς ἁγίας θεότητος...καθ' ὑπόστασιν ἡνῶσθαι... πάσῃ...τῇ ἀνθρωπίνῃ φύσει φαμὲν ἑνωθῆναι πᾶσαν τὴν τῆς θεότητος οὐσίαν...ὅλος ὅλῳ ἡνώθη, ἵνα ὅλῳ τὴν σωτηρίαν χαρίσηται Jo.D.*f.o.*3.6 (M.94.1005A); id.*Jacob.*53(M.94.1464C); equated with σαρκοῦμαι, id.*f.o.*3.11(M.94.1025B); its correct interpretation ἑνωθεὶς [sc. ὁ λόγος] κατὰ φύσιν καὶ οὐκ εἰς σάρκα τραπείς Cyr.*ep.*17(p.36.11; 5^{2}.70E); ἡνῶσθαι...σαρκὶ καθ' ὑπόστασιν ὁμολογοῦντες τὸν λόγον, ἕνα προσκυνοῦμεν υἱόν *ib.*(p.35.26; 70B); οὐκ ἔξωθεν ἡ δόξα τῷ σώματι... ἀλλ' ἔνδοθεν ἐκ τῆς...ἡνωμένης αὐτοῦ καθ' ὑπόστασιν...θεότητος Jo.D. *hom.*1.2(M.96.548D); Apollinarian ὁ προϋπάρχων υἱὸς ἑνωθεὶς σαρκὶ ἐκ Μαρίας κατέστη, τέλειον...ἄνθρωπον συνιστὰς ἑαυτόν Apoll.*fid.sec. pt.*36(p.181.11; M.10.1120A); οὐ κατὰ τὴν σάρκα ὁμοούσιος τῷ θεῷ, ἀλλὰ κατὰ τὸ πνεῦμα τὸ ἡνωμένον τῇ σαρκί id.*fr.*41(p.213.35)ap.Gr. Nyss.*Apoll.*19(M.45.1161C); **4.** ? of Ascension πῶς πρὶν ἑνωθῆναι καὶ ἀποθεωθῆναι λέγει 'ἐγὼ καὶ ὁ πατὴρ ἕν ἐσμεν'; *ib.*98(p.230.5; M.45.1261C); **5.** ref. will of Christ, Max.*opusc.*(M.91.53C) cit. s. θέλημα; **6.** of eucharistic bread ὁ...ζωοποιὸς...λόγος ἑνώσας αὐτὸν τῇ ἰδίᾳ σαρκὶ...ζωοποιὸν ἀπέφηνεν αὐτήν Petr.Laod.*Mc.*14:22(M.86.3328A).

D. of union of God with creation; **1.** act. and pass., *unite*, of God's action on the world εἷς...ὢν ὁ θεός, ἐν ἑκάστῳ γινόμενος ἑνοῖ τοὺς πάντας Evagr.Pont.*ep.*7(M.32.260B); τῇ...τριάδι τῇ ἑνούσῃ καὶ ἁγιαζούσῃ ἡμᾶς δι' ἑαυτῆς *Lit.Jac.*(p.160.7); of work of Christ ἑνῶν ἑαυτὸν ἡμῖν, ἡμᾶς τε αὐτῷ Eus.*d.e.*10.1(p.450.26; M.22.725A); τοὺς... κτισθέντας ἐν ἑαυτῷ ἥνωσε Ath.*Ar.*2.55(M.26.265A); τότε κατ' εἰκόνα θεοῦ ἐποίησε τὸν ἄνθρωπον, νῦν αὐτῷ τῷ θεῷ ἥνωσε Chrys. *hom.25.2 in Jo.*(8.145C); id.*hom.8.4 in 1Cor.*(10.70C); ὁ θεὸς... σαρκωθείς, πάσῃ τῇ κτίσει διὰ τῆς σαρκὸς ἡνώθη Thal.*cent.*1.97(M.91.1436D); as Good Shepherd ἄρνα ἐπ' ὤμου λαβὼν σῇ ποίμνῃ ἕνωσας *Pap.Chr.*(p.497); of work of H. Ghost διὰ...τοῦτο τὸ πνεῦμα ἐδόθη ἵνα τοὺς...διεστηκότας ἑνώσῃ Chrys.*hom.9.3 in Eph.*(11.71E); εἰ...ἓν πνεῦμα ἡμᾶς...διεστῶτας ἥνωσε id.*hom.30.2 in 1Cor.*(10.271B); ἑνούμεθα...τῷ θεῷ ἐν πνεύματι Cyr.*Os.*28(3.52D); apprehended by faith (exeg. 1Cor.1:28) οἱ τῷ θεῷ τῷ ὄντι μὴ ἡνωμένοι κατὰ τὴν πίστιν...'μὴ ὄντες' προσηγορεύθησαν Bas.*Eun.*2.19(1.254E; M.29.612C); οὕτω...ἡ τοῦ νόμου δικαίωσις ἐν ἡμῖν κατορθοῦται διὰ πίστεως ἡμῶν ἑνουμένων αὐτῷ, καὶ 'πνευματικῶν' ἀντὶ 'σαρκικῶν' γινομένων Gennad.*fr.Rom.*8:3 (p.375.30; M.85.1689B); **2.** pass., *unite together, be mutually united*; **a.** of prayers in God ἐπιδέομαι...τῆς ἡνωμένης ὑμῶν ἐν θεῷ προσευχῆς καὶ ἀγάπης Ign.*Magn.*14.1; **b.** of powers in Son κύκλος γὰρ [sc. ὁ υἱός]...πασῶν τῶν δυνάμεων εἰς ἓν...ἑνουμένων...διὸ δὴ καὶ τὸ εἰς αὐτὸν...πιστεῦσαι μοναδικόν ἐστι γενέσθαι, ἀπερισπάστως ἑνούμενον ἐν αὐτῷ Clem.*str.*4.25(p.318.2ff.; M.8.1365B) = Or.*Apoc.*5(p.22); **c.** of all created things in God τῷ καλῷ τὰ πάντα ἥνωται Dion.Ar. *d.n.*4.7(M.3.704A); *ib.*8.5(892C); ἐν τῷ θεῷ...ἑνοῦται πᾶσα ἡ κτίσις ‡Caes.Naz.*dial.*160(M.38.1120); from seraphim downwards, united in themselves, to each other, and to God, Dion.Ar.*d.n.*11.1(949A); broken by sin ἡ ἔχθρα τὸ μεσότοιχον...κωλύον τοῦ ἑνοῦσθαι τὴν ἀνθρώπων φύσιν τῇ μακαριότητι τῶν κρειττόνων [sc. δυνάμεων] Or. *Eph.*2:14(p.406); **d.** of Christians ἡνωμένην καὶ ἐκλεγμένην [sc. ἐκκλησίαν] ἐν πάθει ἀληθινῷ Ign.*Eph.*proem.; ἑνώθητε τῷ ἐπισκόπῳ id. *Magn.*6.2; ἐν τελείῳ σώματι ἡνωμένοι καὶ ὑπ' αὐτοῦ τοῦ λόγου βασταζόμενοι Hipp.*Dan.*4.37.2; σὺ δὲ οὐδὲ τῷ ἀδελφῷ ἀξιοῖς ἡνῶσθαι Chrys.*hom.24.2 in 1Cor.*(10.214A); of Jews and gentiles, *ib.30.2* (270D); in fellowship of H. Ghost; of Church of East and West, Bas.*ep.*90.1(3.181E; M.32.474B); in eucharist, Chrys.*hom.24.2 in 1Cor.*(213C); **3.** of union of individual with God, in Church ἵνα... ἑνωθῶσι τῷ...θεῷ διὰ τοῦ ἑνοῦντος αὐτῷ υἱοῦ Or.*Cels.*8.75(p.292.23; M.11.1632A); rendered impossible by sin, ‡Ath.*serm.Ant.*4(M.28.596A); τὸ ἀπαλλαγῆναι τῶν πονηρῶν, τὸ ἑνωθῆναι θεῷ Chrys.*hom.13.3 in 2Cor.*(10.534C); ἑνοῖ τῷ θεῷ...τὰ δάκρυα id.*hom.6.5 in Mt.*(7.95A); Nil.*epp.*2.327(M.79.360D); ἑνῶσαι ἑαυτοὺς τῷ θεῷ Dor.*doct.*1.9(M.88.1628C); in eucharist ὁ...Χριστὸς...σε...ἑαυτῷ ἥνωσε Chrys. *hom.24.2 in 1Cor.*(10.214A); *Lit.Praesanct.*(p.349.15); ἑνωθεὶς ἑαυτῷ τε καὶ σοί. τῇ...μετουσίᾳ τοῦ παναγίου αὐτοῦ σώματος...τὰς σάρκας τὰς ἑνωθείσας σοι *Lit.Jac.*(*NBP* 10^{2} p.109); myst., of prophets οὗτοι...πνεύματι προφητικῷ...κατηρτισμένοι...ὀργάνων δίκην ἑαυτοῖς ἡνωμένοι ἔχοντες ἐν ἑαυτοῖς ἀεὶ τὸν λόγον ὡς πλῆκτρον Hipp.*antichr.*2 (p.4.23; M.10.729A); in gen., Mac.Aeg.*hom.*19.10(M.34.641A) cit. s. ἀνακεράννυμι; διψήσαντες ἑνωθῆναι καὶ εὐαρεστῆσαι τῇ θείᾳ...οὐσίᾳ

‡Tit.Bost.*palm*.4(M.18.1269C); of soul as bride ἀπὸ δὲ ἀμαθοῦς ἔμφρων...ὡς ἐκεῖνος ᾧ ἥνωται, τοῖς πᾶσιν ἀναδειχθῇ †Bas.Anc.*virg*.50 (M.30.769A); perfect detachment as condition for union with God, Dion.Ar.*d.n*.7.3(M.3.872B); τῷ παντελῶς...ἀγνώστῳ τῆς πάσης γνώσεως ἀνενεργησίᾳ, κατὰ τὸ κρεῖττον ἑνούμενος, καὶ τὸ μηδὲν γινώσκειν, ὑπὲρ νοῦν γινώσκων id.*myst*.1.3(M.3.1001A); ὁ θεῷ τελείως τὰς αἰσθήσεις ἑνώσας τοὺς λόγους αὐτοῦ μυσταγωγεῖται ὑπ' αὐτοῦ Jo. Clim.*scal*.30(M.88.1157C).

***ἐνσαββατίζω**, *keep sabbath*, Gr.Nyss.*res*.4(M.46.681B).

***ἐνσαλεύομαι**, *be shaken to and fro*, Gr.Nyss.*laud.Bas*.13(M.46. 801B).

ἔνσαρκος, *of flesh, incarnate*; **1.** in gen. τῆς ἐ. ζωῆς Eus.*p.e*.7.2 (299D; M.21.509A); ταῖς ἐ. ἡμῶν σκηναῖς Meth.*Porph*.1(p.503.10; M.18.397C); περιτομὴν...τὴν ἔ. (opp. τὴν ἐν πνεύματι) Epiph.*haer*. 30.27(p.371.5; M.41.453B); *ib*.30.28(p.372.9; 456A); *ib*.30.33(p.379.24; 469A); Mac.Mgn.*apocr*.4.2(p.159.10); ὁ ἐπὶ γῆς ἔ. ἄγγελος [i.e. Symeon Stylites] Evagr.*h.e*.1.14(p.24.12; M.86.2461A); τὸν ἔ. ᾅδην [i.e. Chosroes] Sophr.H.*v.Anast*.(M.92.1685A); **2.** of Inc. τῆς ἐ. οἰκονομίας Or.*exp.in Pr*.12(M.17.192D); Nil.*epp*.1.259(M.79.177D); Cyr.*thes*.15(5^1.172C); esp. τὴν ἔ. παρουσίαν Or.*hom.1 in Lc*.(p.7.8; M.17.313D); Ath.*Ar*.1.8(M.26.28B); Cyr.H.*catech*.3.11; Chrys.*hom. 36.4 in Mt*.(7.412A); τῆς ἐ. πολιτείας Eus.*h.e*.1.4.1(M.20.76C); τὴν ἔ. ἐπιδημίαν τοῦ λόγου Ath.*Ar*.1.59(133C); id.*fr.Pss.comm*.(M.27.588C); τὴν ἔ. ἐνανθρώπησιν Epiph.*haer*.30.27(p.370.7; M.41.452C); *ib*.69.24 (p.174.1; M.42.240A); εἰ κατὰ τὴν ἄσαρκον ὑπόστασιν ὁμοούσιος ὁ λόγος τῷ πατρί, δῆλον ὅτι κατὰ τὴν ἔ. ὑπόστασιν ἑτερούσιος ὁ λόγος τῷ πατρί Leont.H.*Nest*.1.34(M.86.1497C); τὴν...ἔ. φύσιν Geo.Pis. *carm*.61^c.1; τῆς ἐ. ... μορφώσεως Jo.V H.*icon*.2(M.96.1352A); of events of Inc. τῆς ἐ. γενέσεως Eus.*v.C*.3.41(p.95.7; M.20.1101A) al.; Epiph.*haer*.26.12(p.292.3; M.41.352B); Jo.V H.*icon*.5(1353C); τὸ ἔ. πάθος Epiph.*haer*.9.4(p.201.5; 228D); τὴν ἔ. εἰς τοὺς οὐρανοὺς ἀνάληψιν Iren.*haer*.1.10.1(M.7.549A); Mac.Mgn.*apocr*.4.18(p.197.11); in other contexts τὴν γενεαλογίαν τὴν ἔ. Epiph.*haer*.28.5(p.317.11; 384A); ἵνα μὴ διορίσῃ τὴν ἔ. τελείωσιν ἀπὸ τῆς ἐνθέου τελειώσεως *ib*.69.75 (p.223.1; M.42.324A); τὴν τοῦ θεοῦ λόγου ἔ. δοξολογίαν καὶ τελείαν θεότητα *ib*.69.36(p.184.12; 257B); abs. καὶ πάλιν [i.e. after Resurrection] αὐτὸς ἔ. ... δείκνυσιν †Hipp.*theoph*.3(p.5*.14); πᾶσι μὲν οὖν ὁμοίως ἔ. ὢν ἐσταυρώθη Cyr.H.*catech*.13.4; Apoll. οὐ γὰρ ἂν ἐν ὁμοιώματι ἀνθρώπου γεγονὼς εἴη, εἰ μὴ τυγχάνοι καθάπερ ἄνθρωπος νοῦς ἔ. ὢν Apoll.*fr*.69(p.220.24)ap.Gr.Nyss.*Apoll*.35(M.45.1201B); *ib*.70(p.220.28; M.45.1204D) cit. s. ἐπιδημία; θεὸς ἔ. πρὸ αἰώνων, ὀστώδης καὶ δέρματι...διειλημμένος Gr.Nyss.*ib*.15(1152C); νοῦν ἔ. ὄντα τὸν υἱὸν ἐκ γυναικὸς τεχθῆναι *ib*.23(1173B).

***ἐνσάρκωσις**, ἡ, *incarnation*, Epiph.*haer*.51.23(M.41.932A, v.l. for ἐνσάρκου p.292.6); Chrys.*hom.75.1 in Jo*.(8.439E).

***ἐνσατυρίζω**, *sport in*; met., Gr.Nyss.*Eun*.12(1 p.269.21; M.45. 976A).

ἐνσεμνύνομαι, *be proud of*, Eus.*d.e*.3.6(p.135.2; M.22.228C).

***ἐνσηκάζω (*ἐνσηκέω)**, *shut up in a pen* or *fold*, met. τὰ πρόβατα ταῖς ἰδίαις αὐλαῖς ἐνσηκεῖ [sc. ὁ σωτήρ] Cyr.*Jo*.6.1(4.656E); med., id.*glaph.Gen*.5(1.151E); pass., *ib*.4(124A); id.*ador*.8(1.253C); id.*Ps*. 22:2(M.69.840C).

***ἐνσημάντρως**, *significantly*, ‡Meth.*Sym.et Ann*.11(M.18.376B).

ἐνσήπ-ομαι, *putrefy within*, met. αὐτῇ ~εσθαι τῇ ἁμαρτίᾳ Chrys. *hom.42.3 in 1Cor*.(10.399A).

***ἐνσιελίζω**, *spit into*; c. dat., Gr.Nyss.*Eun*.12(1 p.390.19; M.45. 1120D).

***ἐνσκάζω**, *limp in*, met. ἐ. τῇ ἀσαφείᾳ τῶν θείων λόγων Max.*qu. Thal*.22(M.90.320B); id.*ambig*.(M.91.1141B).

***ἐνσκαίρ-ω**, *leap* or *frisk in*, ‡Caes.Naz.*dial*.70(M.38.937); τὰ μὲν [sc. βρέφη] διαφθείρεται...τὰ δὲ ζωογονεῖται, καὶ περιέπεται ἐν τοῖς ἀνόμοις κόλποις τὰ κακὰ ~οντα *ib*.109(981).

***ἐνσκεδάννυμι**, *scatter in*, met. τοῖς ἀποστόλοις ταύτης ἐνσκεδασθείσης τῆς χάριτος Gr.Nyss.*Steph*.1(M.46.705A).

ἐνσκην-όω, *encamp*, met. ἵνα...ὁ λόγος τοῦ θεοῦ...ἐν αὐτοῖς ~ώσῃ *A.Thom*.A 88(p.203.8).

ἐνσκήπτ-ω, **1.** trans.; **a.** *hurl* or *make to fall in* or *on*, met. φιλίας ἡμῖν κέντρον ἐνέσκηψεν Gr.Thaum.*pan.Or*.6(p.16.16; M.10.1069D); theol. οὔτε ἐν τῷ κτίζειν εἰς τὸν υἱὸν πάθος ἐνσκήψει [sc. ὁ ἀπαθὴς θεός] Epiph.*haer*.69.26(p.176.18; M.42.244D); ἀπὸ τῆς ἰδίας [sc. κεφαλῆς] εἰς Χριστὸν ~ει τὸ τῆς χλεύης ἔργον *ib*.80.7(p.492.21; 768A); **b.** *utter*, *ib*.78.11(p.462.23; 716C); *ib*.78.5(p.455.32; 706C); **2.** intrans.; **a.** *fall in* or *on* φόβος ἐνέσκηψε τοῖς τῆς διανοίας κόλποις Bas.*ep*.45.1(3. 133A; M.32.365A); Gr.Thaum.*pan.Or*.6(p.17.1; M.10.1072A); **b.** *fall upon, affect, do harm to*, c. prep. οὐδὲν...~ουσιν εἰς τοὺς υἱοὺς τῆς ἀληθείας Epiph.*haer*.69.33(p.182.15; M.42.253D); *ib*.69.35(p.183.22; 256D); *ib*.77.28(p.440.31; 681C); c. dat. τὸ πάθος τῇ θεότητι...οὐκ ἐνέσκηψεν *ib*.77.33(p.444.21; 689C); *ib*.69.24(p.174.16; 240D); abs., *ib*. 76.48(p.402.19; 612C); **c.** *attack* ὅλος ὁ διάβολος ἐνέσκηψεν αὐτῷ Meth. *fr.Job* 14(p.515.6); Eus.*h.e*.5.1.5(M.20.409A); hence *find fault with*, Thdt.*rect.conf*.7(M.6.1217C).

***ἐνσκιάζω**, *overshadow*, Gr.Nyss.*Apoll*.6(M.45.1136C) cit. s. ἐμμορφόω.

***ἐνσκιρτάω**, **1.** *dance upon*, Bas.Sel.*v.Thecl*.2.10(M.85.581B); **2.** *leap within*, ‡Chrys.*praecurs*.1.2(2.807C); **3.** *exult* or *rejoice in*; c. dat., Bas.*hom*.18.2(2.140B; M.31.485C).

***ἐνσκοτίζομαι**, *be in darkness*; met., Gr.Nyss.*hom.2 in Eccl*.(M. 44.636C).

ἐνσπαργανόω, *wrap in swaddling clothes*; pass., of Christ, ‡Gr. Naz.*Chr.pat*.1464(M.38.253A).

***ἐνσπαταλ-άω (-έω)**, *luxuriate in* θείοις ~ῶντες λόγοις Cyr.*hom. pasch*.15.1(5^2.198E); id.*Joel*.12(3.311E); id.*ador*.1(1.14E); τὰ θρέμματα τοῖς τῆς γραφῆς ~οῦντα λόγοις id.*Ps*.67:16(M.69.1152B).

ἐνσπείρ-ω, *sow in, implant, impregnate*; ‡Meth.*Sym.et Ann*.4 (M.18.356B); met., *T.Reub*.5.3; ἡ τῶν ἀγγέλων πρὸς τὸ ~εσθαι ψυχὰς σώμασιν λειτουργία Or.*Jo*.13.50(49; p.277.23; M.14.489A); τοῖς ἀνηκόοις ~ων τὸ θεῖον κήρυγμα Isid.Pel.*epp*.3.176(M.78.865D); ἡδονὰς ~ων αἰσχράς Cyr.*Ps*.36:32(M.69.948A); of Christ, *A.Thom*.A 144 (p.251.4); τοῖς πεπιστευκόσι τῇ οἰκονομίᾳ τῆς χάριτος ἑαυτὸν ~ει διὰ τῆς σαρκός Gr.Nyss.*or.catech*.37(p.152.3; M.45.97B); ὡς ἀγαθὰς γεννῶσα πράξεις [i.e. the Church as bride]...διὰ τοῦ ~οντος ἐν αὐτῇ Χριστοῦ Ammon.*Jo*.3:25(M.85.1413D); Gnost. ἐν τοῖς τρισὶ στοιχείοις τὸ πῦρ...ἐνέσπαρται καὶ ἐμφωλεύει Clem.*exc.Thdot*.48(p.122.17; M.9.681C); οὗτος ⟨ὁ⟩ 'κατ' εἰκόνα' ἄνθρωπος. ὁ δὲ 'καθ' ὁμοίωσιν' τὴν αὐτοῦ τοῦ δημιουργοῦ ἐκεῖνός ἐστιν, ὃν εἰς τοῦτον 'ἐνεφύσησέν' τε καὶ ἐνέσπειρεν *ib*.50(p.123.13; 684A); ἔσχεν δὲ ὁ Ἀδὰμ ἀδήλως αὐτῷ ὑπὸ τῆς Σοφίας ἐνσπαρὲν τὸ σπέρμα τὸ πνευματικὸν εἰς τὴν ψυχήν *ib*.53 (p.124.18; 684C).

***ἐνσπερματίζω**, *sow in*, Epiph.*haer*.76.26(p.374.20; M.42.569A).

ἔνστασις, ἡ, **1.** *constancy, resolution*, Just.*dial*.112.5(M.6.736A); τὴν ἀκίνητον ἔ. τῆς ψυχῆς Meth.*symp*.11(p.139.27; M.18.217C); ἐνστάσεις πρὸς τὰς ἀλγηδόνας Eus.*h.e*.4.15.4(M.20.344A); **2.** *bearing, mien* βλέμματος ἔ. Bas.*ascet*.1.5(2.323B; M.31.880C); φοβερὸς ἦν τὴν ἔ. *cat.Lc*.7:24(p.59.21); **3.** *opposition, hostility* πολέμων...ἔ. Epiph. *haer*.8.9(p.197.2; M.41.224A); Thdt.*Dan*.8:25(2.1223); Anast.S.*Ps*. 6(M.89.1089C).

ἐνστατικῶς, *stubbornly, obstinately*, Const.ap.Eus.*h.e*.10.5.21(M. 20.889A); comp., Ephr.1.261C.

***ἐνσταυρόω**, *crucify upon*, c. dat., Alex.Lyc.*Man*.4(p.7.19; M.18. 416D); *ib*.24(p.35.22; 444D).

ἐνστέλλω, med. ἐ. τὴν πορείαν *make a journey*, Epiph.*haer*.78.11 (M.42.716B; στειλαμένου p.462.5).

***ἐνστενόομαι**, *be confined within*, ‡Caes.Naz.*dial*.140(M.38.1048).

***ἐνστενοχωρ-έω**, *be confined within* ὅλος σοι χωρητὸς γίνεται [sc. ὁ θεός],...καὶ οὐκ ~εῖ πάσῃ τῇ φύσει ἐνδιοδεύων Gr.Nyss.*hom.2 in Cant*. (M.44.805D).

***ἐνστερνίζομαι**, **1.** *draw to one's breast, embrace*, Bas.*renunt*.5(2. 206D; M.31.636C); met. τὸν σωτῆρα ἐ. Clem.*paed*.1.6(p.115.28; M.8. 301A); ‡Ath.*qu.script*.30(M.28.720D); Chrys.*hom.12.2 in Eph*.(11. 179E); theol. ὅλου μὲν τοῦ πατρὸς ἐνεστερνισμένου τὸν υἱόν *Symb.Ant*. (345)9(p.253.38; M.26.733B); **2.** *lie on one's breast*, of S. John at Last Supper (cf. Jo.13:23), *Const.App*.5.14.3; **3.** *bear* or *cherish in one's heart* τοὺς λόγους...ἐ. *1Clem*.2.1; Eus.*l.C*.5(p.205.2; M.20.1337A); *Const.App*.1 proem.

***ἐνστερνισμένως**, *with an embrace*, Thdr.Stud.*epp*.2.90(M.99. 1341A).

***ἐνστηθίζω**, *commit to memory*, ‡Ath.*def*.1(M.28.533A).

***ἐνστηλιτεύ-ομαι**, **1.** *be engraved upon*, Gr.Nyss.*Pss.titt*.A 14 (M.44.576B); met. ἐνεστηλιτευμένα τῇ ψυχῇ Bas.*hom.in Ps*.59(1. 191A; M.29.464C); Gr.Nyss.*Pss.titt*.A 4(501C); *ib*.16(597D); **2.** *record* τὸ ἀμαθὲς αὐτοῦ...διὰ μέσου τῶν ἐμῶν λόγων ~εσθαι id.*Eun*.7(2 p.159.3; M.45.748B).

ἐνστίζ-ω, *imprint, impress* τὰ φάλαρα, οἷς ~ουσι καὶ τοῦ ἀργυρίου τὴν καθαρότητα Gr.Nyss.*hom.3 in Cant*.(M.44.817D); met. οὐχ ἥλιον ἔχοντες ἐνεστιγμένον τῷ σώματι...ἀλλὰ τὸ ἡλίου...δεσπότην Chrys. *hom.8.7 in Rom*.(9.508A).

***ἐνστίλβω**, *shine in*, c. dat., Gr.Nyss.*hom.3 in Eccl*.(M.44.657A).

ἐνστομίζομαι, *devour*, Sophr.H.*v.Anast*.(M.92.1728B).

***ἐνστράπτω**, *flash upon*, fig. ἐνέστραψεν ταῖς ἁπάντων καρδίαις τῆς ἀληθοῦς θεογνωσίας τὸ φῶς Cyr.*Ps*.49:4(M.69.1077C).

ἐνστρέφ-ω, *turn in*; **1.** act., *sift* or *riddle in* τοῦ ἐχθροῦ...ψυχὴν... ὡς σῖτόν τινι σινίῳ ~οντος Mac.Aeg.*pat*.20(M.34.881B); **2.** med.;

a. of words, *be in use*, Bas.*fid*.2(2.225D; M.31.681A); **b.** of persons, *be addicted to* τῶν τούτοις [sc. τοῖς βιωτικοῖς] ~ομένων Chrys.*hom*.9.3 *in 2Tim*.(11.718D); Hadr.*introd*.47.

***ἐνστρογγυλόομαι**, *be rounded*, Philost.*h.e*.3.11(M.65.497B).

***ἐνσυμφυΐα, ἡ,** *affinity* or *unity of nature within* [sc. Trin.], Melet.*nat.hom*.1(M.64.1149D).

***ἐνσυνέχομαι,** *heap together*; met., Gr.Nyss.*Apoll*.59(M.45.1269A).

ἐνσφηκόω, *inlay*, Paul.Sil.*ambo*.264(M.86.2261B).

ἐνσφραγίζ-ω, *stamp, impress as with a seal, confirm* ἐπὶ δύο... μαρτύρων ~ει τὰ ἑαυτοῦ κακά Hipp.*haer*.9.15(p.253.22; M.16.3391A).

***ἐνσχεδιάζομαι,** *arise suddenly*, Gr.Nyss.*Eun*.12(1 p.288.12; M.45.997A).

ἐνσώματος, 1. *incarnate*; **a.** of Jo. Bapt. as ἐ. ἄγγελος Sophr.H.*or*.7.19(M.87.3352B); **b.** in gen. οὐκ ἐ., εἰ πνεῦμά ἐστιν [sc. ὁ θεός] Cyr.*ep.Calos*.(6^2.364A); esp. ref. Inc. τὴν ἐ. παρουσίαν Ath.*Ar*.1.53 (M.26.124A); *ib*.2.66(285C); τοῦ...υἱοῦ ἐ. ⟨γενομένου⟩ Epiph.*haer*.69.64(p.213.32; M.42.308B); πρὸ μὲν τῆς ἐνανθρωπήσεως ὡς ἄσαρκος ἔτι λόγος, μετὰ δὲ τὴν ἐνανθρώπησιν ἔτι ὁ αὐτὸς ἐ. Cyr.*expl.xii cap*.2(p.18.6; 6^1.148C); id.*inc.unigen*.(5^1.707E); παρῆλθεν ἐ. id.*Chr.un*.(5^1.769B); id.*ep.Calos*.(364A); **2.** *corporeal*, in title of work by Melito περὶ τοῦ ἐ. εἶναι τὸν θεόν. μέλη γὰρ θεοῦ ὀνομαζόμενα εὑρίσκοντες... Or.*sel.in Gen*.1:26(M.12.93A); ὁ 'περὶ ἐ. θεοῦ' Eus.*h.e*.4.26.2(M.20.392B); Hier.*vir.ill*.24(p.24.13; M.*PL*.23.644B); **3.** *characteristic of* or *belonging to the body*; of sin, Clem.*str*.4.25(p.318.18; M.8.1368A); ἴδιον... τῆς ἐ. φύσεως τὸ διὰ ῥημάτων ἐξαγγέλλειν τὰ...νοήματα Gr.Nyss.*Eun*.12(2 p.273.10; M.45.980B); τῆς παχυτέρας...καὶ ἐ. ζωῆς Cyr.*ador*.16 (1.562A).

ἐνσωματ-όω, *set in a body* τὴν ψυχήν Hermias *irris*.2(M.6.1169B); pass., ref. Inc. τοῦ πρωτοτόκου πάσης κτίσεως ~ουμένου Or.*Jo*.2.31 (25; p.88.13; M.14.168C).

ἐνσωμάτωσις, ἡ, *incarnation, embodiment*, of Inc. τὸ μυστήριον τῆς τοῦ υἱοῦ τοῦ θεοῦ ἐ. Or.*Jo*.6.5(2; p.112.29; M.14.208B); τῆς... ἐκείνου ἐ. ἡμεῖς γεγόναμεν ὑπόθεσις Ath.*inc*.4.3(M.25.104A); Bas.*hom. in Ps*.29(1.124D; M.29.305C) cit. s. ἐγκαινισμός; ἡ δι' ἡμᾶς ἐ. τοῦ θεοῦ Nemes.*nat.hom*.42(M.40.781B); τῆς ταπεινώσεως, τουτέστι τῆς ἐ. Cyr.*Jo*.1.9(4.78C); βούλεται...ἀεὶ καὶ ἐν πᾶσιν ὁ τοῦ θεοῦ λόγος τῆς αὐτοῦ ἐ. ἐνεργεῖσθαι τὸ μυστήριον Max.*ambig*.(M.91.1084D).

ἔνσωμος, *possessing a body, embodied*; of Christ after Resurrection, Eus.*d.e*.3.4(p.115.8; M.22.197A); id.*theoph.fr*.3(p.5*.14).

ἐνσωρεύ-ω, *heap on* or *in*; pass., Cyr.*Is*.4.4(2.709A); met., id.*Nest*.1 (p.14.34; 6^1.4A); δογματικῆς ἀκριβείας ~εται γνῶσις id.*Juln*.7(6^2.233E); *ib*.10(330A).

ἐνταλαιπωρέομαι, *pass one's life wretchedly in*, Chrys.*ep*.3.13(3.568D).

***ἐνταλαμένος,** s.v.l., ? *in a frenzy*, Barth.Edess.*Agar*.(M.104.1428B).

ἔνταλμα, τό, *command, precept* τῶν τοῦ κυρίου ἐ. *2Clem*.17.3; Just.*dial*.46.5(M.6.576A); ἐ. ἀνθρώπων Clem.*str*.3.12(p.237.25; M.8.1192A).

***ἔνταλσις, ἡ,** *order, command*, Thdr.Stud.*epp*.1.10(M.99.941B).

***ἐνταλτικῶς,** *by way of command*, ‡Just.*qu.et resp*.92(M.6.1333B).

***ἐντάραχος,** *agitated, disturbed*; of persons, *A.Thom*.A 43(p.160.8); *ib*.105(p.218.7).

***ἐνταράχως,** *with much disturbance*, Arc.C.*v.Sym*.(M.94.1396A).

ἐντάσσ-ω, 1. *insert, include*, Const.*or.s.c*.19(p.181.17; M.20.1292A); Gel.Cyz.*h.e*.2.29.4(M.85.1313A); *ib*.2.31.10(1319C); pass., Epiph.*haer*.76.22(p.369.26; M.42.561A); *ib*.77.14(p.428.1; 660C); Chrys.*hom.in Philm*.proem.(11.774B); **2.** *store away* gifts, Eus.*v.C*.4.7(p.120.22; M.20.1156C); **3.** pass.; **a.** of persons, *be entered* or *enrolled* in εἰς Λευιτικὴν ~όμενος φυλήν Clem.*str*.5.6(p.353.18; M.9.65C); met. ἐντεταγμένος...εἰς τὸν ἀριθμὸν τῶν σωζομένων *1Clem*.58.2; Clem.*str*.7.7(p.37.7; 469B); **b.** *be mentioned* in οὐκ ἐντέτακται τὸ πνεῦμα...ἐν τοῖς προοιμίοις τῶν ἐπιστολῶν Chrys.*hom*.30.2 *in 2Cor*.(10.651C); **c.** *be assigned* to ἑκάστῳ ἐντετάχθαι τὴν αὐτῷ πρέπουσαν λειτουργίαν Cyr.*ador*.13(1.455D).

ἐνταφιάζω, *bury*, *A.Andr.et Mt*.23(p.98.14); *A.Pil*.B 11.5(p.314); Jo.Thess.*dorm.BMV* 2.14(p.435.39).

ἐνταφίασις, ἡ, *burial*, Steph.Diac.*v.Steph*.(M.100.1093C).

ἐνταφιασμός, ὁ, *laying out for burial*, Gr.Nyss.*hom*.6 *in Cant*.(M.44.897C); of Christ, ‡Just.*qu.et resp*.117(M.6.1368A); ‡Bas.*h.myst*.50(p.391.9); Eutych.*pasch*.1(M.86.2392B).

***ἐντειλίσσω,** ? *roll up, fold*, *Exorc*.(p.345).

ἐντεκταίνομαι, *build* or *fix in* τῶν τῆς ψυχῆς δυνάμεων, ἃς...ὁ δημιουργὸς ἡμῖν ἐνετεκτήνατο Gr.Nyss.*virg*.18(p.318.2; M.46.389C); id.*hom*.7 *in Cant*.(M.44.933A); id.*beat*.5(M.44.1256B).

ἐντέλεια, ἡ, *completeness, perfection*, Max.*opusc*.(M.91.93A); Areth.*Apoc*.2(M.106.516C).

***ἐντελειόομαι,** *be completed*, Pall.*h.Laus*.43(M.34.1210D; τελειωθέντος p.130.22).

[*]**ἐντελεχέω,** = ἐνδελεχέω, *continue* or *persist in*, †Bas.Sel.*or*.41(M.85.464B).

[*]**ἐντελεχισμός, ὁ,** = ἐνδελεχισμός, *persistence, continual desire* or *urge* ὁ ἐ. τῆς σαρκός Ant.Mon.*hom*.17(M.89.1481B).

ἐντελεχῶς, *continually*, Nil.*epp*.2.161(M.79.277A).

ἐντέλλομαι, *enjoin* upon, *urge*, τί τινι; of God, *Barn*.14.6; Just.*dial*.22.1(M.6.521B); Hegem.*Arch*.11(p.19.5; M.10.1445B); of Christ, Just.*1apol*.66.3(M.6.429A); Clem.*exc.Thdot*.76(p.131.5; M.9.693C); †Jo.D.*B.J*.8(M.96.920A); pass., of commands, *be enjoined* upon ἐντέταλται τῷ Ἰσραὴλ προσφέρειν δάμαλιν τοὺς ἄνδρας *Barn*.8.1; φύλακες τῶν ἐντεταλμένων Just.*1apol*.65.1(M.6.428A); Cosm.Ind.*top*.proem.2(M.88.53D).

ἐντεροειδής, *like intestines*, Melet.*nat.hom*.10(M.64.1197C).

***ἐντερόμαντις, ὁ,** *haruspex*, Thdt.*qu*.29 *in Lev*.(1.207).

***ἐντευκτέον, 1.** *one must appeal to*; God in prayer, Or.*or*.14.6 (p.333.21; M.11.464C); a doctor, Bas.*ep*.84(3.177A; M.32.461D); **2.** *one must read*, Clem.*str*.5.14(p.420.27; M.9.205A).

ἐντευκτικός, *petitionary*, Pall.*v.Chrys*.2(p.7.24; M.47.8); *ib*.7(p.42.7; M.47.25); CSyr.*act*.(*ACO* 3 p.102.20; H.2.1381B).

ἔντευξις, ἡ, 1. *appeal, entreaty*; **a.** in gen., *1Clem*.63.2; Just.*1apol*.1(M.6.329A); Chrys.*sac*.3.16(p.86.6; 1.396E); **b.** of appeal to God in prayer, def. ἡγοῦμαι...ἔ. δὲ τὴν ὑπὸ παρρησίαν τινὰ πλείονα ἔχοντος περί τινων ἀξίωσιν πρὸς θεόν Or.*or*.14.2(p.331.7; M.11.461A); ἔ. δὲ [sc. ἐστί] κατηγορία τῶν ἀδικούντων Thdt.*1Tim*.2:1(3.646); ἔ. ἐστι παράκλησις ὑπὸ μείζονος προσαγομένη θεῷ περὶ σωτηρίας ἑτέρων Evagr.ap.*Doct.Patr*.33(p.258.10); its conditions ἐὰν...μιγῇ ἡ ὀξυχολία τῇ μακροθυμίᾳ...οὐκ εὔχρηστος τῷ θεῷ ἡ ἔ. αὐτοῦ Herm.*mand*.5.1.6; *ib*.10.3.2; πᾶσαν...ἔ. ἀναπεμπτέον τῷ...θεῷ διὰ τοῦ ἐπὶ πάντων ἀγγέλων ἀρχιερέως Or.*Cels*.5.4(p.4.24; M.11.1185B); in eucharist, of prayer of consecration ὁ ἄρτος...ἁγιάζεται διὰ θεοῦ λόγου καὶ ἐ. Gr.Nyss.*or.catech*.37(p.150.1; M.45.97A); through baptism εἰς τὸ ἀρχαῖον ἐπανάγεσθαι ἀξίωμα, δι' ἐ. δηλαδὴ καὶ τῆς σωτηρίου ἐπικλήσεως ἐπιφοιτῶντος τοῦ πνεύματος †Jo.D.*B.J*.8(M.96.920A); **2.** *reading* ἐντεύξεις τῶν γραφῶν Clem.*str*.7.7(p.37.4; M.9.469B); Eus.*h.e*.2.15.2(M.20.172C); *ib*.6.2.9(525A); **3.** *discourse, treatise*, id.*p.e*.11.5(514A; M.21.852D); **4.** *character*, sc. of a person, Thphn.*chron*.p.240(M.108.605A); **5.** *outer covering* or *shell* καρυΐνου... ἡ πρώτη ἔ. πικρά Gr.Nyss.*v.Mos*.(M.44.428D).

ἐντεχνής, *skilled*, neut. as subst., Cyr.*Juln*.7(6^2.231C).

***ἐντεχνία, ἡ,** *skill*, Cyr.*Os*.127(3.160A).

ἔντεχνος, *artistic*; neut. as subst.; **1.** *elaboration*, Clem.*paed*.3.10 (p.266.1; M.8.624B); **2.** *skill* τὸ ἔ. τῆς δημιουργίας *Hom.Clem*.6.19; Bas.*ep*.139(3.230D; M.32.581B).

ἐντέχνως, *skilfully*, Tat.*orat*.34(p.36.18; M.6.877A); *Orac.Sib*.1.58; Clem.*str*.1.2(p.14.9; M.8.709C).

***ἐντιθασσεύομαι,** *become* or *be made gentle*, Cyr.*hom.pasch*.9(5^2.115B).

ἐντίναγμα, τό, *shaking*, Serap.*euch*.29.2; Gr.Naz.*carm*.1.2.25.18 (M.37.814A).

ἐντινάσσω, 1. *hurl against*; pass., *be slammed against* ἐντιναχθήσονταί σοι αἱ θύραι ‡Nil.*Epict*.49(M.79.1304D); **2.** *drive* τὰ πρόβατα...ἐ. εἰς τοὺς ἀλώπεκας *Apoc.En*.89.43; **3.** pass., *be thrust into* ξύλῳ ἐντιναγῆναι Just.ap.Eus.*h.e*.4.16.3(M.20.365A) but *2apol*.3.1(M.6.448A) reads ἐμπαγῆναι.

ἐντοίχιος, *within the walls* ἐ. πόλεμος ‡Chrys.*meretr*.2(10.762A).

ἔντοκος, *bearing interest*, Ast.Am.*hom*.4(M.40.220C); Gr.Nyss.*usur*.(M.46.436C); *ib*.(452C).

ἐντολεύς, ὁ, 1. *representative, delegate, attorney*, Eus.Dor.ap.CChalc.*act*.4(*ACO* 2.1.2 p.113.15; H.2.420A); μηδεὶς ἐπίσκοπος...ἐ. δίκης...γινέσθω Ath.Scholast.*coll*.1.2(p.6); Jo.D.*parall*.tit.16(M.95.1053); **2.** *one who gives commands*, of God τὸν ἐ. τοῦ νόμου κύριον *T.Aser* 2.6.

ἐντολή, ἡ, 1. *injunction, command, commandment*; divine; **a.** in gen., esp. of moral precepts ἐὰν...πορευώμεθα ἐν ταῖς ἐ. αὐτοῦ Polyc.*ep*.2.2; Or.*princ*.3.1.19(p.233.10; M.11.292B); Meth.*res*.1.29 (p.260.1; M.41.1137B); Chrys.*hom*.60.6 *in Jo*.(8.360C); **b.** at Creation τὴν πρὸ τῆς ἐ. ἡμῶν ἐν τῷ πρωτοπλάστῳ διαγωγὴν πρὸ σώματος Meth.*res*.1.57(p.317.18; M.41.1152C); ἡμεῖς οἱ ἐξ οὐκ ὄντων κατ' ἐντολὴν ὑπάρχοντες ‡Ath.*dial.Trin*.2.23(M.28.1193A); φῶς μὲν ἦν καὶ ἡ τῷ πρωτογόνῳ δοθεῖσα πρωτόγονος ἐ., ἐπειδὴ λύχνος ἐ. νόμου καὶ φῶς (Ps.117:105) Gr.Naz.*or*.40.6(M.36.364D); opp. generation of Son ὑποστάσει γεννᾷ [sc. Father] καὶ ἐ. κτίζει. ἡ γὰρ ἐ., σύνδρομον ἔχουσα τὴν δύναμιν, παρίστησιν ὃ βούλεται ὁ ἐντειλάμενος· ὑποστάσει δὲ γεννῶν, οὐκ ἀνέχεται ἐντολήν, ἵνα μηδὲν μέσον ᾖ τοῦ γεννῶντος πατρὸς καὶ τοῦ γεννωμένου υἱοῦ ‡Ath.*dial.Trin.*1.4(1121C); *ib.*1.6(1125A) cit. s. δημιουργικῶς; acc. Macedonians ὁ ἐνυπόστατος λόγος ἐστὶν ὁ τὸν οὐρανὸν στερεώσας ἢ ὁ προφορικός; [Macedonius]: τὸν προφορικὸν λέγω, τὴν ἐ. αὐτοῦ [Ps.148:5] εἶπε δὲ καὶ ἐνετείλατο τῷ υἱῷ, ἐνυποστάτῳ λόγῳ· ὁ δὲ τὴν ἐ. λαβὼν υἱὸς ἔκτισεν *ib.*3.23(1240A); **c.** given to Adam, Eus.*h.e.*1.2.18(M.20.61C); μὴ διὰ φωνῆς αἰσθητικῆς δέδωκε τῷ Ἀδὰμ τὴν ἐ. ὁ θεός, ἀλλ' ὥστε ἐντυπῶσαι μὲν αὐτῷ κατὰ τὴν οἰκείαν ἐνέργειαν τήν τε γνῶσιν τοῦ νόμου καὶ τὴν ἀκοήν Diod.*Gen.*2:7(M.33.1567C); νόμῳ τῷ τῆς ἐ. μόνῳ κρατούμενον [sc. Adam] Gr.Naz.*or.*14.25(M.35.892A); *Hom.Clem.*16.6; τὸ δοῦναι τὴν ἐ. μείζονος κηδεμονίας ἐστὶν ἢ τὸ μὴ δοῦναι Chrys.*Stag.*1.5(1.166A); Gel.Cyz.*h.e.*2.24.5(M.85.1300B); Proc.G.*Gen.*3:7(M.87.197A,B); ref. Rom.7:12 δοθείσης γὰρ τῆς ἐ. ἔσχε λαβὴν διὰ τῆς ἐ. ὁ διάβολος κατεργάσασθαι ἐν ἐμοὶ τὴν ἐπιθυμίαν Meth.*res.*2.2(p.331.7; M.41.1164B); νόμον τὸν Μωσαϊκὸν καλεῖ, ἐ. δὲ τὴν τῷ Ἀδὰμ δεδομένην Thdt.*Rom.*7:12(3.73) but v. νόμος; οἱ γὰρ ῥαθυμίᾳ συζῶντες...τοῦ θεοῦ...κατηγοροῦσιν, ὡς τεθεικότος τὴν ἐ. ... εἰ...προορῶν τὴν παράβασιν, τέθεικε τὴν ἐ., αὐτὸς τῆς παραβάσεως αἴτιος·...διά τοι τοῦτο τέθεικε τὴν ἐ. ὁ θεός, ἵνα καὶ τὴν οἰκείαν φύσιν ἐπιγινώσκῃ, καὶ τὸν νομοθέτην δειμαίνῃ *ib.*(l.c.); **d.** given to Moses, Just.*dial.*92.2(M.6.696A); αἱ ἐ. κατὰ νόμον opp. ⟨αἱ⟩ πρὸ τοῦ νόμου Clem.*str.*7.2(p.8.29; M.9.413B); τὰς ἐ. [ἃς] ἔδωκεν τάς τε προτέρας τάς τε δευτέρας ἐκ μιᾶς ἀρυτόμενος πηγῆς ὁ κύριος, οὔτε τοὺς πρὸ τοῦ νόμου ἀνόμους εἶναι ὑπεριδὼν οὔτ' αὖ τοὺς μὴ ἐπαΐοντας τῆς βαρβάρου φιλοσοφίας ἀφηνιάσαι συγχωρήσας *ib.*(p.9.11; 413C); Cyr.*Jo.*9(4.749E); of one of decalogue τὴν ἐν τῷ νόμῳ κειμένην ἐ. Chrys.*hom.21.1 in Eph.*(11.158E); exeg. Eph.6:2 οὐ τῇ τάξει εἶπεν αὐτὴν πρώτην, ἀλλὰ τῇ ἐπαγγελίᾳ *ib.*(159A); εἰσὶν ἄλλαι πρὸ ταύτης ἐ., ἀλλ' ἐκείναις οὐ συνέζευξεν ἐπαγγελίαν ὁ νομοθέτης. ... ἔδειξεν ὁ...ἀπόστολος, ὡς τὰ περιττὰ τοῦ νόμου μετὰ τὴν τοῦ νομοθέτου παρουσίαν ἐπαύσατο, τὰ δέ γε φυσικῶς προηγορευμένα καὶ μετὰ τὴν καινὴν διαθήκην κρατεῖ Thdt.*Eph.*6:2(3.436); **e.** in both OT and NT, Clem.*str.*5.1(p.327.25; M.9.12C); **f.** of Father to Christ, exeg. Jo.12:50 ὥσπερ γὰρ τοὺς ἐ. δεχομένους ἀδύνατον ἄλλο τι ποιεῖν ἢ λέγειν, ἢ ὅσα οἱ πέμψαντες βούλονται, ἕως ἂν ἐ. πληρῶσι...οὕτως οὐδὲ ἐμὲ ἄλλο τι πρᾶξαι ἢ εἰπεῖν δυνατόν, ἀλλ' ἢ ἅπερ ὁ πατὴρ βούλεται Chrys.*hom.69.2 in Jo.*(8.411A); αὐτὸς γὰρ ὢν ὁ...λόγος τοῦ θεοῦ...ἀναγκαίως διερμηνεύει τὰ ἐν αὐτῷ, καὶ τὸ ὡς ἐν θελήσει δοκοῦν τῷ ἰδίῳ γεννήτορι ἐξάγων εἰς φῶς ὡς ἐντολῆς δύναμιν εἰληφέναι φησίν·...οὐδὲν...εἰς τὸν τῆς οὐσίας λόγον, ἤτοι τῆς ἀξίας ὑπομενεῖ τὸ βλάβος ὁ μονογενής, κἂν ἐ. εἰληφέναι λέγεται παρὰ τοῦ θεοῦ καὶ πατρός Cyr.*Jo.*9(4.718A,C); exeg. Jo.12:49–50,14:31 τὴν λεγομένην 'ἐ.' μὴ λόγον προστατικὸν διὰ τῶν φωνητικῶν ὀργάνων ἐξαγγελλόμενον ἐκδεχώμεθα περὶ τῶν ποιητέων τῷ υἱῷ ὡς ὑπηκόῳ νομοθετοῦντα, ἀλλὰ θεοπρεπῶς νοῶμεν θελήματος διάδοσιν Bas.*Spir.*20(3.17E; M.32.104B); **g.** of Christ κεκοσμημένοι ἐν ταῖς ἐ. Ἰησοῦ Χριστοῦ Ign.*Eph.*9.2; ἔχουσι τὰς ἐ. ... τοῦ...Χριστοῦ ἐν ταῖς καρδίαις κεχαραγμένας Arist.*apol.*15.3(p.111.1); Clem.*paed.*1.3(p.95.22; M.8.260B); *ib.*1.13(p.151.27; 376A); προσέχωμεν...ταῖς ἐ. ταύταις, ἵνα 'τέκνα φωτὸς' εὑρεθῶμεν πράσσοντες αὐτάς *Const.App.*1.2.4; κατ' ἐντολὴν Χριστοῦ ζῶν *ib.*2.46.2; of the counsels τῶν ἐ. αἱ μέν εἰσιν ἐπιτεταγμέναι, αἱ δὲ οὐκ ἐπιτεταγμέναι ἀλλ' αὐτεξούσιοι καὶ τῇ προαιρέσει ἐπιτετραμμέναι ὑπὸ τοῦ θεοῦ. αἱ μὲν γὰρ αὐτῶν ὧν οὐκ ἔστιν ἄνευ σωθῆναι, αὗται εἰσὶν αἱ προστεταγμέναι· αἱ δὲ μείζονες τῶν προστεταγμένων, ἃς κἂν μὴ ποιήσωμεν σωζόμεθα, οὐκ εἰσὶν ἐπίταγμα τοῦ θεοῦ Or.*comm.in 1Cor.*7:25(*JTS* 9 p.508); opp. νόμος: ἐν τῇ χάριτί εἰσιν τοῦ σωτῆρος αἱ ἐ.—οὐ νόμοι—ἀλλὰ τῇ προαιρέσει καταλιμπανόμεναι Sever.*1Tim.*1:8–9(p.336.14); exeg. Jo.13:34 πῶς δὲ αὐτὴν [sc. τὴν ἐ.] λέγει καινὴν καὶ ἐν τῇ παλαιᾷ [sc. διαθήκῃ] κειμένην; αὐτὸς αὐτὴν ἐποίησε καινὴν τῷ τρόπῳ· ἐπήγαγε γοῦν, καθὼς ἠγάπησα ὑμᾶς Chrys.*hom.72.3 in Jo.*(8.427A); Cyr.*Jo.*9(4.751A); καινόν ἐστι τὸ εἶδος τῆς ἐ. ταύτης καὶ ὑπὲρ νόμον τὸ ἀγαπᾶν τὸν πλησίον ὑπὲρ ἑαυτόν. οὐ θέλω ὑμᾶς ἀγαπᾶν ἐκείνους οὓς χρεωστεῖτε, ἀλλ' οἷς οὐκ ὀφείλετε· καὶ γὰρ κἀγὼ ὑπὲρ ὑμῶν ἀποθνήσκω, οἷς οὐδὲν ἐποφείλω Ammon.*Jo.*13:34(M.85.1485A); but cf. *quoniam 'caritas numquam cadit' nec mandatum caritatis aliquando veterascit, hoc ...semper novum esse pronuntiat,* Or.*hom.9.4 in Num.*(p.59.18; M.12.629A); of Christ's promise to apostles τὴν δεσποτικὴν ἐ. πληροῦντες τὴν λέγουσαν· 'ἰδοὺ δέδωκα ὑμῖν ἐξουσίαν πατεῖν ἐπάνω ὄφεων κτλ.' Thdt.*Ezech.*31:12(2.940); **2.** *alms*, *Const.App.*8.43 tit.(M.1.1060D); χεῖρας...κέκτησο...εἰς ἐ. καὶ εὐποιΐας Chrys.*hom.11.5 in Phil.*(11.281B); Call.*v.Hyp.*(p.20); ἔλαβες...ἐκ τοῦ οἴκου ἐκείνου ἐντολήν; Leont.N.*v.Jo.Eleem.*22(p.41.5).

ἐντολικάριος, ὁ, *mandatory, delegate,* CEph.(431)*act.*(*ACO* 1.1.3 p.35 not.; H.1.1612B); Thphn.*chron.*p.236(M.108.593B).

ἐντολικός, *of* or *for a command*; neut. as subst., *Cod.Afr.*85, 92; CEph.Orient.*ep.*(*ACO* 1.1.3 p.37.15; H.1.1561D); Thdt.*ep.*170(4.1354).

***ἔντολμος,** *bold* εἰς τὸ...ἔργον ἔντολμοι Epiph.*haer.*58.3(M.41.1013A; εὔτολμοι p.359.25).

***ἐντολοποιέω,** *keep the commandments,* Thdr.Stud.*epp.*2.122(M.99.1400D).

ἐντομή, ἡ, *groove, notch,* Clem.*paed.*2.9(p.205.23; M.8.492C).

ἐντομίς, ἡ, *cut, gash*; ref. pagan rites of mourning, Chrys.*fr. in Jer.*16:5(M.64.912A); Cyr.*Is.*2.3(2.249D).

ἔντονος, *vigorous, eager*; neut. as subst., Cyr.*Ps.*27:2(M.69.853D).

ἐντορεύω, *engrave,* ‡Caes.Naz.*dial.*47(M.38.917).

ἐντορνεύ-ω, *turn by the lathe*; pass., Cyr.*Is.*4.2(2.588A); met., *shape, produce* ἐκ τῆς περιττῆς...φροντίδος ὅτι καὶ λύπας ~ουσιν ὑποταράττοντες τὸ ἡγεμονικόν Nil.*Eulog.*30(M.79.1133B); τὸ τῆς ἀληθείας ἐντετόρνευται κάλλος Cyr.*Is.*5.5(872B).

ἐντοσθίδιον, τό, *inside, inner part*; opp. ἡ δορά, Gr.Nyss.*Apoll.*16(M.45.1153A).

ἐντρεπτικός, *fit to put to shame, shaming*; esp. of words, Chrys.*hom.45.2 in Jo.*(8.264B); *ib.72.1*(423E); σφόδρα ταῦτα ἐ. πρὸς τὸ ποιεῖν αὐτό id.*hom.6.1 in 1Thess.*(11.466D); Cyr.*Mich.*53(3.444D); comp., Chrys.*hom.14.1 in Eph.*(11.103C); id.*hom.14.2 in Phil.*(11.299A).

ἐντρεπτικῶς, *so as to put to shame, reproachfully,* Or.*hom.3.2 in Jer.*(p.21 not.); Chrys.*hom.84.1 in Jo.*(8.499A); Thdt.*Ezech.*36:32(2.992); comp., †Bas.*bapt.*1.1.2(2.625E; M.31.1517B); Chrys.*hom. 18.6 in Mt.*(7.242C); Cosm.Ind.*top.*2(M.88.133B).

ἐντρέπ-ω, med. and pass.; **1.** *reverence* τὸν κύριον Ἰησοῦν... ἐντραπῶμεν *1Clem.*21.6; τὴν δὲ Ἀχαμὼθ ἐντραπεῖσαν αὐτόν [sc. τὸν θεόν] Iren.*haer.*1.4.5(M.7.488); clergy, Ign.*Smyrn.*8.1; id.*Trall.* 3.1,2; Clem.*str.*4.17(p.295.27; M.8.1316A); met. ~όμενός τε αὐτὸν [sc. τὸν Χριστόν] μετὰ αἰδοῦς ὁ τῶν λουτρῶν πάροχος Ἰορδάνης Const.*or. s.c.*11(p.169.1; M.20.1265B); **2.** *feel respect* or *regard for,* Chrys.*hom. 45.4 in Ac.*(9.344D); **3.** *feel shame, be ashamed*; abs., Ign.*Magn.* 12.1; Cyr.*Ps.*17:46(M.69.820B); Proc.G.*Is.*16:7(M.87.2113A); c. dat. ἐντραπῆναι τοῖς ἁμαρτήμασι id.*Gen.*4:2(273D); c. ἐπί, Jo.Mosch.*prat.* 118(M.87.2981D); **4.** *show modesty,* Chrys.*hom.26.5 in 1Cor.*(10.234B); **5.** pass., *be turned about*; met., of one worsted, Meth.*fr.Job* 25(p.519.6); οἱ Σαδδουκαῖοι...ἐνετράπησαν παρὰ τοῦ σωτῆρος Ath.*ep. Aeg.Lib.*9(M.25.568A); **6.** *be influenced* or *persuaded,* Meth.*symp.*11(p.134.14; M.18.209D).

***ἐντρεχεστέρως,** v. ἐντρεχής.

ἐντρεχής, **1.** *quick witted, ready of mind*; comp. ἐντρεχέστερος ...ποιεῖν γενόμενος Dion.Al.*fr.*(p.164.1) v.l. ἐντρεχεστέρως ap.Leont. et Jo.*sacr.*2(M.86.2097C); **2.** *ready, willing* ἐ. πρὸς τὴν τοῦ διαβόλου ὑπουργίαν *M.Seb.*1(p.170.7); **3.** *nimble, swift,* Nil.*exerc.*64(M.79.797C); neut. as subst. τὴν τοῦ ἀετοῦ [sc. μορφήν]...τὸ πρὸς τὴν τροφὴν ὀξὺ καὶ...ἐ. Dion.Ar.*c.h.*15.8(M.3.337A).

ἐντρεχῶς, **1.** *intelligently,* Or.*Cels.*1.50(p.101.31; M.11.753C); **2.** *skilfully,* Isid.Pel.*epp.*2.213(M.78.656A).

ἐντριβής, **1.** of persons, *skilled, practised in*; comp., Clem.*str.* 6.17(p.514.28; M.9.393A); neut. as subst. τὸ ἐν λόγοις...ἐ. Cyr.*Is.* 3.4(2.478A); **2.** *established, familiar*; of a custom, id.*ador.*8(1.255C); id.*Os.*4(3.19E); id.*Abac.*17(3.532C); of a word or phrase, id.*apol. orient.*3(p.37.19; 6^{1}.163C); id.*Lc.*24:36(M.72.945C).

ἐντρίβω, **1.** act., *reprove,* Mac.Mgn.*apocr.*3.27(p.118.5); **2.** med., *come into contact with,* c. dat. pers., Epiph.*haer.*42.7(p.102.23; M.41.704C); **3.** pass., *be conquered,* Gr.Nyss.*v.Mos.*(M.44.325C).

***ἐντριπτέον,** *one must smear,* Clem.*paed.*3.11(p.272.1; M.8.640A).

ἔντριτος, **1.** *of three strands,* met. βαβαὶ τῆς ἐ. ἀγαπῆς [i.e. of Mary, Martha, Lazarus for Christ] τὸ ἀρραγὲς σπαρτίον ‡Eust.*Laz.* 16(p.40.6); of faith, hope, love, Sophr.H.*ep.syn.*(M.87.3149C); **2.** *threefold* ἐ. ἐπιξενωθεὶς τῷ πατριάρχῃ (ref. Gen.18:2) ‡Caes.Naz.*dial.*31(M.38.896).

***ἐντρίχινος,** *made of hair* ἐ. στιχάριον †Gregent.*leg.Hom.*(M.86.572B).

***ἐντρομή, ἡ,** *trembling* Gr.Nyss.*anim.et res.*(M.46.137C).

***ἐντρόμως,** *tremblingly, with trembling,* Thdot.Anc.*hom.BMV et Sym.*8(M.77.1401A); ‡Meth.*palm.*5(M.18.393B).

ἐντροπαλίζομαι, *turn round,* Nonn.*par.Jo.*1:38(M.43.756C); met. ἀπὸ τῆς πίστεως εἰς ἀκολασίαν...ἐ. Meth.*symp.*6.4(p.68.14; M.18.117D).

ἐντροπή, ἡ, **1.** *respect, reverence* πᾶσαν ἐ. αὐτῷ [sc. τῷ ἐπισκόπῳ] ἀπονέμειν Ign.*Magn.*3.1; Iren.*ep.Vict.*ap.Eus.*h.e.*5.24.17(M.20.508A); Clem.*str.*7.7(p.27.19; M.9.449C); **2.** *putting to shame, reproach*;

c. genit., *ib.*1.14(p.38.1; M.8.757C); *ib.*3.12(p.237.4; 1189B); c. adj. εἰς...ἐ. ἡμετέραν Bas.*jud.*3(2.215E; M.31.657C); abs., Clem.*str.*4.16 (p.293.7; 1308B); Chrys.*hom.26.5 in 1Cor.*(10.235D); Jo.Mosch.*prat.* 118(M.87.2981D).

***ἐντροπίας**, οἶνος *turned* (i.e. *sour*) *wine*, ‡Dion.Al.*fr.in Lc.22:42* (p.240.5; M.10.1592B).

***ἐντροπικῶς**, v. ἐπιστρεπτικῶς.

***ἐντρόχιος, ὁ,** vox nihili, Germ.CP *or.*2(M.98.252D), perh. for ⟨ἐντρόχιον⟩, ? *drag.*

ἐντρύφημα, τό, 1. *choice thing* ἀπαρχὰς...προσφέρειν ἐντρυφημάτων *T.Jud.*21.5; **2.** *delight, thing to take pleasure in* ἡ...δημιουργηθεῖσα κτίσις, τὸ κοινὸν ἐ. Gr.Naz.*or.*16.5(M.35.940B); ταῦτά σοι τῆς ἐνταῦθα πανδαισίας [i.e. eucharist] τὰ ἐ. †Cyr.*hom.div.*10(5^{2}.371E); hence, of persons, *joy, pride* οὗτοι...τὸ ἐμὸν ἀγαθὸν ἐ. Gr.Naz.*or.*6.3(724C).

ἐντρύχομαι, *waste away,* Cyr.*Nah.*18(3.497D) cit. s. ἐναφίημι.

[*]ἐντύβιον, τό, = ἔντυβον, *endive,* Cosm.Ind.*top.*tab.4(M.88.469).

ἐντυγχάν-ω, A. *converse;* **1.** with God θεῷ...ἐντευξόμεθα, νῦν μὲν ὀλίγα, μικρὸν δὲ ὕστερον ἴσως τελεώτερον ἐν...Χριστῷ Gr.Naz.*or.*27.10(p.20.9; M.36.25A); **2.** *intercede, make appeal;* **a.** abs., to men, Epiph.*haer.*68.5(p.145.18; M.42.192B); to God βοῶσιν αἱ ψυχαὶ τῶν τετελευτηκότων καὶ ~ουσιν *Apoc.En.*9.10; of Christ (Rom.8:34) τὸ ~ειν μὴ ἐλαττώσεως ἀλλ' ἀγάπης φαίνεται μόνης ὄν Chrys.*hom.16.3 in Rom.*(9.597D); ‡Chrys.*inc.*6(8.224C); of H. Ghost (Rom.8:27) ὑπερεντυγχάνει καὶ ~ει τὸ πνεῦμα, ἡμεῖς δὲ προσευχόμεθα Or.*or.*14.5 (p.332.24; M.11.464A); **b.** c. dat., *intercede with, appeal to, M.Polyc.* 17.2; *Pet.Ar.*3(M.26.821C); in prayer to God, Herm.*mand.*10.3.2; Clem.*paed.*1.6(p.118.19; M.8.305C); τοῦ Ἄβελ...τὸ αἷμα ~ον τῷ θεῷ Meth.*res.*2.3(p.335.2; M.18.301A); τὴν ψυχὴν τὴν ~ουσαν τῷ θεῷ καὶ στενάζουσαν Chrys.*exp.in Ps.*4(5.9B); **c.** c. περί, ὑπέρ *intercede for* or *on behalf of* ἐ. περὶ τῶν ἔν τινι παραπτώματι ὑπαρχόντων *1Clem.*56.1; τὰς χήρας ~ούσας...περὶ πάντων Polyc.*ep.*4.3; of Christ ὃς καὶ ~ει ὑπὲρ ἡμῶν ‡Ath.*serm.fid.*3(p.5; M.26.1265C); ref. Heb.7:25 τὸ... ~ειν οὐχ, ὡς ἡ τῶν πολλῶν συνήθεια, τὸ ζητεῖν ἐκδίκησιν ἔχει...ἀλλὰ τὸ πρεσβεύειν ὑπὲρ ἡμῶν τῷ λόγῳ τῆς μεσιτείας· ὡς καὶ τὸ πνεῦμα ὑπὲρ ἡμῶν ~ειν λέγεται Gr.Naz.*or.*30.14(p.130.10; M.36.121C); c. dat. ὁ πένης...ἐπιχορηγούμενος ὑπὸ τοῦ πλουσίου ~ει αὐτῷ Herm.*sim.*2.6; **d.** c. κατά, *plead against* τότε ἡ γῆ ἐνέτυχεν κατὰ τῶν ἀνόμων *Apoc. En.*7.6; μὴ ἄρα...ἐντύχωσιν καθ' ἡμῶν ὡς τυραννούντων *T.Job* 17 (p.114.4); οὐ κατ' αὐτῶν ἐνέτυχε τῷ θεῷ Bas.*mor.*17.3(3.565B; M.32.1332B); but id.*hom.*10.3(2.85E; M.31.360B) reads κατενέτυχε; med. μὴ θλῖβε τὸ πνεῦμα τὸ ἅγιον...μήποτε ἐντεύξηται [κατὰ σοῦ] τῷ θεῷ Herm.*mand.*10.2.5; **e.** pass., *be appealed to,* of emperor, Eus.*h.e.* 4.12(M.20.333A); *ib.*7.30.19(720A); **3.** *appeal to, call to witness;* c. dat., Chrys.*hom.6.6 in Rom.*(9.470B).

B. *read, peruse* a letter or book, c. dat. rei, Just.*1apol.*26.8(M.6.369B); Tat.*orat.*29(p.30.5; M.6.868A); Clem.*str.*7.16(p.69.7; M.9.536A); abs., Arist.*apol.*15(p.110.23); Dion.Al.ap.Eus.*h.e.*7.7.1(M.20.648B); Ath.*decr.*32(p.28.20; M.25.476B); ἐκεῖσε...ἐντευξόμεθα ταῖς ἐπιστολαῖς Synes.*ep.*55(M.66.1381A); ptcpl. act. as subst., *reader,* Hipp.*haer.*1 proem.(p.3.22; M.16.3021A); Eus.*h.e.*2.5.6(M.20.149A); Gr.Nyss.*v.Mos.*(M.44.424D); also ptcpl. med., Clem.*ecl.*27(p.145.4; M.9.712C); Or.*Cels.*1.42(p.93.6; M.11.737C); Cyr.*Jo.*proem.(4.5D).

***ἐντύμβευσις, ἡ,** *entombment, sepulture,* Andr.Cr.*or.*13(M.97.1088A).

ἔντυπος, esp. ἔ. ἀρχή, applied to initial letter of a proper name ὥστε τριηκοσίης κεραίης λάχεν ἔ. ἀρχήν [sc. Trajan] *Orac.Sib.*5.42; *ib.*12.148; *ib.*14.227; = either 'initial *the same as the sign of* the number 300' or 'the *stamped* initial of the number 300'.

ἐντυπ-όω, A. *impress, imprint, engrave;* **1.** *stamp;* **a.** of a die or seal βασιλέως ἐντετυπωμένην εἰκόνα τοῦ δηναρίου τὸ χάραγμα σημαίνει Or.*schol.in Lc.*13:29(M.17.360C); id.*Jo.*19.7(2; p.307.2; M.14.537D); αἵτινές εἰσιν ἐντετυπωμέναι τῇ ἐπιστολῇ ταυτῇ ἑπτὰ σφραγῖσιν *Ep. Chr.*(p.281.16); Gr.Naz.*or.*40.26(M.36.396C); **b.** fig., *A.Thadd.*3 (p.274.17); of making sign of cross οὐδὲ γὰρ ἁπλῶς τῷ δακτύλῳ ἐγχαράττειν αὐτὸν δεῖ, ἀλλὰ πρότερον τῇ προαιρέσει μετὰ πολλῆς τῆς πίστεως. κἂν οὕτως ἐντυπώσῃς αὐτὸν τῇ ὄψει Chrys.*hom.54.4 in Mt.*(7.551D); cf.id.*ecl.*38(12.720B); τῇ χειρὶ παιδεύετε σφραγίζειν τὸ μέτωπον· καὶ πρὶν ἢ δυνηθῆναι τῇ χειρὶ τοῦτο ποιεῖν, αὐτοὶ ~οῦτε αὐτοῖς τὸν σταυρόν id.*hom.12.7 in 1Cor.*(10.108B); **2.** *engrave* πλαξὶν ~ουμένου νόμου Gr.Naz.*carm.*1.2.6.45(M.37.646A); Gr.Nyss.*hom.14 in Cant.*(M.44.1073A); fig. πάντων τῶν ἀπ' αἰῶνος ἕως συντελείας ἐντετυπωμένων τῇ ἀξίᾳ βίβλῳ τοῦ θεοῦ τῷ οὐρανῷ Or.*comm.in Gen.* ap.*philoc.*23.20(p.209.15; M.12.84B); **3.** met., *impress* on, of image of Father stamped on Son τὴν μόρφωσιν δηλοῖ τοῦ θεοῦ, ἣν ἐνετύπωσεν τῷ σώμα⟨τι⟩ ἐν τῷ παρθένῳ Clem.*exc.Thdot.*60(p.127.3; M.9.688B); τοῦτον ὁ πατὴρ ἐσφράγισεν ὁ θεὸς ὅλον αὐτῷ ἑαυτὸν ἐντυπώσας Bas.*Spir.*15(3.12A; M.32.92A); of gifts impressed on first man, Diod. *Gen.*2:7(M.33.1567C) cit. s. ἐντολή; τοῦ πρωτοκτίστου ἀνθρώπου...ἐν ᾧ τὴν εἰλικρινῆ αὐτοῦ ἀγάπην ἐνετύπωσεν ὁ θεός Gel.Cyz.*h.e.*2.17.27 (M.85.1272A); of resurrection body τὴν...ἑκάστου μορφὴν...ἐν ἑτέρῳ πνευματικῷ ἐντετυπωμένην ἀναστήσεσθαι σώματι Meth.*res.*3.3(p.391.3; M.18.317B); τὸ δὲ σῶμα, ἐν ᾧ ἦν τὸ εἶδος ἐντετυπωμένον διαφθείρεσθαι *ib.*3.6(p.397.21; 321C); on the mind, *inculcate* ἡ αὐτοαλήθεια...ἀφ' ἧς ἀληθείας οἱονεὶ εἰκόνες ἐκείνης ἐντετύπωνται τοῖς φρονοῦσι τὴν ἀλήθειαν Or.*Jo.*6.6(3; p.114.24; M.14.212A); id.*sel.in Ps.*1 ap. *philoc.*2.3(p.41.2; M.12.1084A); id.*princ.*4.1.7(p.305.5; M.11.356B); Gr.Thaum.*pan.Or.*8(p.22.19; M.10.1077C); Meth.*symp.*1.4(p.13.5; M.18.45A); Gr.Nyss.*v.Mos.*(M.44.340B); χαράγματα ἅπερ ὁ διάβολος ἐνετύπωσέ σου τῇ ψυχῇ Chrys.*hom.11.7 in Mt.*(7.158C); λύπης ἴχνος ~ῶν τῇ ψυχῇ Max.*or.dom.*(M.90.893C); **4.** *give form to, form* τὰ ὑποκείμενα πράγματα, ἀφ' ὧν ἡμῖν τὰ νοήματα ~οῦνται Clem.*str.*8.8 (p.94.12; M.9.589A); τοὺς πονηροὺς δαίμονας ἐν σχήμασι πλείοσιν ~ουμένους Eus.*p.e.*4.21(171A; M.21.297C); *ib.*3.3(90D; M.168B); τῶν ἰδιωμάτων ἃ περὶ αὐτὸν θεωρεῖται τὴν ἔννοιαν ~ούμεθα Bas.*Eun.*2.4 (1.240D; M.29.577C); *ib.*2.15(250E; M.601C); ἡ γὰρ ἔννοια οὐδὲν ἐδέξατο οὐδὲ ἐνετύπωσεν ἑαυτῇ· κἂν γὰρ ἀνατυπώσῃ εἰς φύσιν ἔρχεται Chrys. *hom.5.3 in Col.*(11.362A); ταῖς ἰδέαις καὶ τῷ ποικίλῳ τῶν εἰδῶν κάλλει χώραν διδοὺς ὥστε τῇ φθορᾷ καὶ τῇ γενέσει πολλάκις ~οῦσθαι Aen. *dial.*(M.85.969A); **5.** met., med., *impress oneself on,* hence *loiter* ἐντετύπωται δὲ ἀεὶ ἐν ταῖς τῶν δυνατῶν θύραις καὶ προέστηκεν αὐταῖς πλείω καιρὸν ἢ οἱ θυρωροί Hierocles ap.Eus.*Hierocl.*33(532C; M.22.844A); **6.** pass., ? *conform to* οἵδε τοῖς Ἰακώβου φρονήμασι προκατειλημμένοι ἐνετυπώθησαν ἀβασανίστως Leont.H.*monoph.*(M.86.1901A).

B. *appoint,* hence οἱ ἐντετυπωμένοι *praepositi* of a monastery εἴ τις εὑρεθῇ εἰς τὸν κῆπον λαλῶν μετά τινος...ἐκτὸς τῶν ἐργαζομένων ἢ τῶν ἐντετυπωμένων, γενέσθω ἀπευλογίας ‡Bas.*poen.mon.*47(2.529D; M.31.1312C); *ib.*50(530A; M.1313A).

ἐντύπωμα, τό, *intaglio* ὁ τῶν ἐν ταῖς σφραγῖσιν ἐ. τορευτικός Clem. *str.*1.4(p.17.10; M.8.717A); prob. f.l. for ἐκτύπωμα, Meth.*symp.*1.4 (p.13.8; M.18.45A).

***ἔντυφος,** *proud, arrogant,* Tat.*orat.*3(p.3.10; M.6.812A); Ast.Am. *hom.*7(M.40.257D).

ἐντύφω, pass., *smoulder,* Meth.*symp.*3.10(p.38.17; M.18.76D); id. *res.*2.23(p.378.3; M.18.288A); Chrys.*hom.10.3 in Eph.*(11.78D).

ἐντυχία, ἡ, 1. *petition, appeal;* to God, Eus.*Ps.*25:1(M.23.232C); Ath.*ep.Marcell.*14(M.27.25D); ἡ τοῦ σωτῆρος...οἰκονομία ἐ. ὑπὲρ ἡμῶν ὑπάρχει Nil.*epp.*1.114(M.79.132D); **2.** *accusation* or *charge;* **a.** before a court etc., Alex.Al.*ep.Alex.*1(p.20.14; M.18.549B); ἐ. γενομένη ἐν Ἀντιοχείᾳ Ἰωβιανῷ βασιλεῖ, παρὰ Λουκίου...κατὰ Ἀθανασίου *Pet.Ar.*1 tit.(M.26.820A); Pall.*v.Chrys.*7(p.39.4; M.47.24); before God at Judgement, Areth.ap.*cat.Apoc.*10:3(p.327.33); **b.** of appeal to God against a person, Chrys.*exp.in Ps.*48(5.220D); ἐ. λέγεται, ὅταν τις κατὰ τῶν ἀδικούντων ἐντυγχάνῃ τῷ θεῷ προκαλούμενος αὐτὸν εἰς ἐκδίκησιν ‡Chrys.*inc.*6(8.224D); **3.** = Lat. *libellus, written appeal* or *petition,* met., of an appeal to God ὥσπερ ἡμεῖς ἐ. τῷ δικαστῇ ἀναπτύξαντες, ἐὰν ἐν τῷ χάρτῃ πολλὰ ἐμφέρεται τὰ κεφάλαια...οὕτως ὁ προφήτης [Ps.5:1] Ast.Soph.*hom.1 in Ps.5*(M.40.400B).

***ἐντυχῖται, οἱ,** heret. sect, offshoot of Simonians, so-called because of common belief that promiscuous sexual intercourse was practised at nightly meetings of Carpocratians and other heretics, Clem.*str.*7.17(p.76.29, v.l. ἐντυχιταί M.9.554A); also called εὐτυχῖται.

ἔνυγρος, 1. *watery, of the nature of water* ἀπὸ...τῶν δακρύων αὐτῆς [i.e. Sophia] γεγονέναι πᾶσαν ἔ. οὐσίαν Iren.*haer.*1.4.2(M.7.484A); **2.** *full of water;* comp., of clouds, Hipp.*haer.*1.7(p.12.25; M.16.3032B); **3.** *vaporous* ἀστραπὴν...ἐκ τῶν ἐνύγρων ἐκτρέχειν πυρεκβόλων Geo.Pis.*hex.*516(M.92.1475A).

***ἐνυδρόχερσος,** *amphibious,* Cosm.Mel.*schol.*(M.38.635) in Gr. Naz.*carm.*1.2.1.538–9.

***ἐνύπαρξις, ἡ,** *real existence, existence as a substance* ὁ τρόπος τῆς ἑκουσίου ἑνώσεως τὴν ἐ. οὐκ ἀναιρεῖ· εἰ μὴ γὰρ ἐνυπάρχει, οὐδὲ ἥνωται. ἀλλὰ ἡ κατὰ τὴν τῶν φύσεων εἰς ἀλλήλας ἑκούσιον ἕνωσιν ἐ., ἐν δυάδι ὑποστάσεων ποτὲ οὐχ ὑπάρχει, ὡς ἐνοικοῦντος καὶ ἐνοικουμένου Leont. H.*Nest.*7.3(M.86.1756A); (s.v.l.) Clem.*str.*3.4(M.8.1140B; ἐν ὑπάρξει p.212.6).

ἐνυπάρχ-ω, 1. *exist in* τὰς τοῦ ~οντος πνεύματος συμβουλίας Or. *Jo.*2.11(6; p.66.16; M.14.129C); τοῖς ὑπηκόοις θεοῦ...εἷς νόμος ~ει *Const.App.*1.1.7; Trin. τὸν ἐνδιάθετον καὶ ~οντα τῷ θεῷ κατὰ φύσιν λόγον Cyr.*thes.*19(5^{1}.187D); **2.** *inhere* τοῖς φύσει σωζομένοις...~ειν βούλονται [sc. τὴν γνῶσιν, opp. πίστιν] Clem.*str.*2.3(p.118.16; M.8.941B); Didym.(‡Bas.)*Eun.*5(1.312D; M.29.749B) cit. s. ἀνυπόστατος;

hence *exist as attributes only* δέος...μὴ τὸν πατέρα μὲν οὐσιώσωμεν, τἆλλα δὲ [sc. Persons] μὴ ὑποστήσωμεν, ἀλλὰ δυνάμεις θεοῦ ποιήσωμεν ∼ούσας, οὐχ ὑφεστώσας Gr.Naz.*or*.31.32(p.188.2; M.36.169B); opp. συνυπάρχω, of that which is not native to and inseparable from another thing but transient, Bas.*Spir*.63(3.53A; M.32.184B) cit. s. συνυπάρχω; **3.** *be surrounded by* ἐν ἐπαίνῳ μείζονι καὶ τιμῇ παρὰ πᾶσιν ...∼ει Epiph.*haer*.59.4(p.368.16; M.41.1024C); **4.** *be, exist really* ὁ ὑπὲρ τοὺς...ἀγγέλους ∼ων σωτὴρ τοῦ γένους τῶν ἀνθρώπων Or.*Cels*. 1.60(p.111.25; M.11.772B); Bas.*ep*.204.1(3.303A; M.32.745A); ἀμφότεροί τε λέγοντες ἐνυπόστατόν τε καὶ ∼οντα τὸν υἱὸν εἶναι τοῦ θεοῦ... ἀλλήλοις οὐκ οἶδ' ὅπως συμφωνῆσαι οὐκ ἴσχυον Socr.*h.e*.1.23.8(M.67. 144A).

***ἐνυπνία, ἡ,** *dream*, *Exorc*.(p.333).

ἐνυπνιάζ-ομαι, 1. *dream*; met., *be deluded*, Ath.*ep.Serap*.1.30(M. 26.600A); **2.** *be incontinent during sleep*, Epiph.*haer*.26.13(p.293.7; M.41.353A); ‡Pall.*h.mon*.22(p.82.9; M.34.1172B); Anast.S.*qu.et resp*. 98(M.89.752C); exeg. Judae 8 οὐκ εἶπεν...'Ιούδας...περὶ ∼ομένων ἐν σώμασιν'...περὶ τῶν ∼ομένων λέγει τῶν λαλούντων ὡς δι' ὀνειράτων τὰ αὐτῶν ῥήματα Epiph.*haer*.26.13(p.293.18ff.; 353B).

***ἐνυπνίασις, ἡ,** *incontinence during sleep*, Epiph.*haer*.26.13(p.293. 26; M.41.353C).

***ἐνυπνιασμός, ὁ,** = foreg., Cyr.H.*catech*.6.33; Nil.*epp*.2.216(M. 79.312D); Anast.S.*qu.et resp*.8(M.89.389D).

ἐνυπνιαστής, ὁ, *dreamer, visionary*, of monks οἱ ἐ. οἱ τὰς ἐκ τῶν ὀνείρων ἀπάτας πιστοτέρας τῶν εὐαγγελικῶν διδαγμάτων ποιούμενοι Gr.Nyss.*virg*.21(p.337.14; M.46.409B); iron., of Eunomius, id.*Eun*.1 (1 p.139.6; M.45.377C).

ἔνυπνος, *sleeping*; of persons, Geo.Pis.*hex*.1109(M.92.1519A).

***ἐνυπογράφομαι,** *append one's signature to, sign*, c. dat., *V.Chrys*. 97(p.351.15).

ἐνυπόγραφος, *executed and signed*, Leont.N.*v.Jo.Eleem*.3(p.9.13); Agath.Diac.*epilog*.(H.3.1833B).

***ἐνυπόθηκος,** *secured by bail* ἐ. ὁμολογίαν Ath.Scholast.*coll*.1.2 (p.10); Phot.*nomoc*.9.1(M.104.709B).

ἐνυπόκειμαι, 1. *be set out in* θεοῦ...γραφὴ καὶ εἰδοποιία ἐνυποκειμένη τῇ πλακὶ δημιουργία τοῦ κόσμου τυγχάνει Clem.*str*.6.16(M.9. 357C; ἐναποκειμένη p.499.18); **2.** *lie upon*, Germ.CP *or*.2(M.98. 257A).

ἐνυπόκριτος, *interrogative*, Areth.ap.*cat.Apoc*.13:2(pp.369.29, 371.1).

***ἐνυπομάζιος,** *at the breast* βρέφος ἐ. Gr.Nyss.*v.Gr.Thaum*.(M.46. 928B) perh. for ἐν ὑπομαζίον.

***ἐνυπομυχεύ-ω,** *lurk in the inmost parts*, met. τὴν ∼ουσαν ἁμαρτίαν ‡Chrys.*serm.jej*.1(10.846C).

***ἐνυποστατικός,** *conceived as real* or *concrete, objectified* τὰς 'Εβραϊστὶ καλῶς εἰρημένας λέξεις καὶ 'Ελληνιστὶ καλῶς ἑρμηνευθείσας ...εἰς εἰδωλοποιΐας τε καὶ εἰς μορφὰς καὶ εἰς ἐ. ἀρχὰς...ἀνατυποῦσιν Epiph.*haer*.25.4(p.271.16; M.41.325A).

ἐνυπόστατος, *subsistent, substantial* or simply, *existent*; def. τὸ ἐ. ἤτοι ὑπόστασις δύο σημαίνει. σημαίνει γὰρ τὸ ἁπλῶς ὄν· καθ' ὃ σημαινόμενον λέγομεν καὶ τὰ συμβεβηκότα ἐ., εἰ καὶ ἐν ἑτέροις ἔχουσι τὸ εἶναι. σημαίνει καὶ τὸ καθ' ἑαυτὸ ὄν, ὡς τὰ ἄτομα τῶν οὐσιῶν· ὥστε συμβαίνει τὸ καθ' ἑαυτὸ ἐ. διχῶς λέγεσθαι ἐ. †Leont.B.*sect*.7.2 (M.86.1240Cf.) ∾ †Leont.B.*fr*.(M.86.2009Df.); cf. τὸ...ἐ., τὸ μὴ εἶναι αὐτὸ συμβεβηκὸς δηλοῖ Leont.B.*Nest.et Eut*.1(M.86.1277D); ἀνυπόστατος φύσις τουτέστιν οὐσία, οὐκ ἂν εἴη ποτέ, ἀλλ' ἐ., τουτέστι πρᾶγμα ὑφεστὼς ἐν ἑαυτῷ θεωρούμενον Pamph.H.*panopl*.7.1(p.623); cf.Leont.B.*Nest.et Eut*.1(M.86.1280A); ἐ., ἤτοι ἐν ἰδίᾳ ὑποστάσει ὑπάρχον ‡Cyr.*Trin*.9(6^2.13D; M.77.1140C); ἐ. ἐστι, τὸ κατὰ τὴν οὐσίαν κοινόν, ἤγουν τὸ εἶδος, τὸ ἐν τοῖς ὑπ' αὐτὸ ἀτόμοις πραγματικῶς ὑφιστάμενον, καὶ οὐκ ἐπινοίᾳ ψιλῇ θεωρούμενον. ἄλλως, ἢ πάλιν ἐ. ἐστι, τὸ ἄλλῳ διαφόρῳ κατὰ τὴν οὐσίαν εἰς ἑνὸς σύστασιν προσώπου καὶ μιᾶς γένεσιν ὑποστάσεως, συγκείμενόν τε καὶ συνυφιστάμενον, καὶ οὐδαμῶς καθ' αὐτὸ γνωριζόμενον Max.*opusc*.(M.91.149Bf.); τὸ ἐ. κατὰ δύο τρόπους λέγεται, ἢ τὸ κατ' ἀλήθειαν ὑπάρχον, ἢ τὸ ἐν τῇ ὑποστάσει ἰδίωμα, ὡς ἐν τῷ θεῷ καὶ πατρὶ τὸ ἀγέννητον ἐν δὲ τῷ υἱῷ τὸ γεννητόν Anast.S.*hod*.2(M.89.61B); τὸ ἐ. ... ποτὲ μὲν τὴν ἁπλῶς ὕπαρξιν σημαίνει· καθ' ὃ σημαινόμενον, οὐ μόνον τὴν ἁπλῶς οὐσίαν ἐ. λέγομεν, ἀλλὰ καὶ τὸ συμβεβηκός· ὅπερ κυρίως οὐκ ἐ. ἐστι, ἀλλ' ἑτεροϋπόστατον· ποτὲ δὲ καὶ τὴν καθ' ἑαυτὸ ὑπόστασιν, ἤγουν τὸ ἄτομον δηλοῖ· ὅπερ κυρίως οὐκ ἐ., ἀλλ' ὑπόστασίς ἐστί τε καὶ λέγεται. κυρίως...ἐ. ἐστιν, ἢ τὸ καθ' ἑαυτὸ μὲν μὴ ὑφιστάμενον, ἀλλ' ἐν ταῖς ὑποστάσεσι θεωρούμενον...ἢ τὸ σὺν ἄλλῳ διαφόρῳ κατὰ τὴν οὐσίαν εἰς ὅλου τινὸς γένεσιν συντιθέμενον, καὶ μίαν ἀποτελοῦν ὑπόστασιν σύνθετον Jo.D.*dialect*.44 (M.94.616A), latter half ap.Melet.*nat.hom*.31(M.64.1309B); τὸ...ἐ., ποτὲ μὲν τὴν οὐσίαν σημαίνει, ὡς ἐν ὑποστάσεσι θεωρουμένην· ποτὲ δὲ ἕκαστον τῶν εἰς σύνθεσιν μιᾶς ὑποστάσεως συνερχομένων· ὡς ἐπὶ ψυχῆς καὶ σώματος Jo.D.*nat*.6(M.95.120C).

A. 1. *being a hypostasis, having independent existence, substantive* οὐδεμία...ἐνέργεια ἐ. Didym.(‡Bas.)*Eun*.4(1.287B; M.29.689C); οὐκέτι δύο ὑποστάσεις ἐν τῷ ἀνθρώπῳ ἐν μιᾷ συναγόμεναι ὑποστάσει, οὐκέτι ἐ. μόνη ψυχὴ καὶ ἐ. τὸ σῶμα, ἀλλ' εὑρήκαμεν λοιπὸν τέσσαρα Epiph.*anc*.77(p.97.3f.; M.43.161C); εἰ ἄλλο τὸ ἐ., καὶ ἄλλο τὸ ἀνυπόστατον· καὶ θεὸς μὲν ἐκεῖνο, τὸ βούλεσθαι δὲ τοῦτο ‡Just.*qu. Chr*.3.1(M.6.1432D); οὐκ ἐ. τι καὶ ὑπάρχον ἰδίως οἰόμεθά ποτε τὴν οὕτω νοουμένην εἰρήνην, ἀλλ' ἐν ἕξει τῇ τῶν ἀγαπώντων Cyr.*Jo*.10(4.840A); Thdt.*Is*.14:9(p.71.4; 2.267); †Leont.B.*sect*.7.2(M.86.1241Af.); opp. ἀνυπόστατος, *Disp.Phot*.(M.88.548A); Eulog.*fr.dogm*.(M.86.2953Bf.) cit. infra 7; met., *self-contained* ἕν τι γίνεται ὁ σατανᾶς μετὰ τῆς ψυχῆς...πλὴν ἐν ἄλλῃ ὥρᾳ καθ' ἑαυτήν ἐστιν ἡ ψυχὴ ἐ., μεταμελουμένη ἐφ' οἷς ἔπραξε Mac.Aeg.*hom*.16.2(M.34.613C) cf. A.6; **2.** *real, concrete, actual* οὐδὲ ἐ. θεὸς ἄλλος, μὴ γένοιτο Epiph.*haer*.66.68(p.109.15; M.42.137A); ἡ...τοῦ θεοῦ τέχνη ἔκτισεν ἐκ μὴ ὄντων παχύτερα καὶ λεπτότερα καὶ ἁπαλώτερα σώματα ἐ. τῷ θελήματι αὐτοῦ Mac.Aeg. *hom*.4.11(M.34.840D); Chrys.*hom.9.3 in 1Cor*.(10.77B); Marc.Er. *opusc*.1.65(M.65.913B); οὐδὲν ἐ. ἔλαβεν 'Ιακὼβ ἐν μισθῷ, ἀλλ' ἐλπίδα Proc.G.*Gen*.30:32(M.87.441B); ξύλον ἔτι ἄχρυσον τὴν φύσιν, τὸ τὴν ἐ. φύσιν αὐτοῦ κεχρυσωμένον· καὶ ἀνὴρ ἔτι ἀσίδηρος ἢ μᾶλλον εἰπεῖν ἐκ ψιλοῦ τετριχωμένος τὴν φύσιν, ὁ τὴν φυσικὴν ὑπόστασιν αὐτοῦ σεσιδηρωμένος ὁπλίτης, ἢ ἐν ἀκμῇ λασιούμενος Leont.H.*Nest*.4.36(M.86. 1704D); Pamph.H.*panopl*.16.2(p.643); ὁ κόσμος πρεσβύτερα τῆς ὑπάρξεως αὐτοῦ στοιχεῖα ἔχων ἐ. CCP(543)*anath*.6(p.228; H.3.285A); ἡ...ἐπίκλησις τῆς δοθησομένης ἐ. τε καὶ ἐνυπάρκτου κατὰ...χάριν τοῦ ἁγίου πνεύματος υἱοθεσίας ἐστὶ σύμβολον ‡Bas.*h.myst*.61(p.397.1); opp. φαντασιώδης etc., Chrys.*hom.4.7 in Ac.princ*.(3.91D); and // οὐσιώδης κατὰ ἀλήθειαν, Eust.Mon.*ep*.(M.86.909D); οὐκ ἐπὶ φαντασίας ἀλλ' ἐπὶ ἐ. πραγμάτων Eustrat.*stat.anim*.13(p.418); not of evil οὐ γάρ ἐστιν ὑφεστὼς...ἡ πονηρία· οὔτε οὐσίαν αὐτῆς ἐ. παραστῆσαι ἔχομεν Bas.*hom*.9.5(2.78A; M.31.341B); οὐκ ἔστιν ἐκ θεοῦ τὸ κακὸν κατὰ τοὺς λέγοντας ἐ. τὴν κακίαν Didym.*Ps*.5:6(M.39.1169C); Epiph. *haer*.24.6(p.263.6; M.41.316A); Mac.Aeg.*hom*.16.1(613B); **3.** *being the embodiment of*, '*incarnate*' τὴν μὲν ψυχὴν...ὀνομάζοντες...ἁμαρτίαν ἐ. ‡Ath.*Apoll*.1.21(M.26.1129B); **4.** *being, existing in an hypostasis, enhypostatic* τὸ ἐ. opp. ὑπόστασις: ἡ μὲν γὰρ ὑπόστασις τὸν τινὰ δηλοῖ, τὸ δὲ ἐ. τὴν οὐσίαν· καὶ ἡ μὲν ὑπόστασις, πρόσωπον ἀφορίζει τοῖς χαρακτηριστικοῖς ἰδιώμασι· τὸ δὲ ἐ., τὸ μὴ εἶναι αὐτὸ συμβεβηκὸς δηλοῖ, ὃ ἐν ἑτέρῳ ἔχει τὸ εἶναι, καὶ οὐκ ἐν ἑαυτῷ θεωρεῖται Leont.B. *Nest.et Eut*.1(M.86.1277Cf.) ∾ Jo.D.*Jacob*.11(M.94.1441B); Leont.H. *Nest*.5.28(M.86.1748D); Pamph.H.*panopl*.7.1(p.623); κατὰ τὴν τῶν ἁγίων παράδοσιν, καθ' ἣν τὸ μὴ ἀνυπόστατον, οὐχ ὑπόστασιν εἶναι τὴν φύσιν ποιεῖ, ἀλλ' ἐ. ... τὸ ἐ. δηλοῖ τὸ ἐνύπαρκτον, ἐνύπαρκτον δέ ἐστι τὸ οὐσιώδους καὶ φυσικῆς μετέχον ὑπάρξεως Max.*opusc*.(M.91.205Af.); ἐν ὑποστάσεσι μὲν ἡ οὐσία θεωρεῖται, διὸ καὶ ἐ. ἐστιν, ἀλλ' οὐχ ὑπόστασις. οὐκ ἀνάγκη τοίνυν τὸ ἐ. ὑπόστασιν λέγεσθαι Jo.D.*nat*.6(M.95.120C); **5.** *subsistent in, established in the very nature, inherent*, Gr.Nyss. *Eun*.8(2 p.181.26; M.45.776A) cit. s. ἐνούσιος; ἐκ τῶν ἐντός σου...δι' ἐ. πραγμάτων ‡Gr.Nyss.*imag*.(M.44.1340C); εἰ γὰρ φύσει τὸ κακὸν καὶ ἐ. ἐστιν [sc. τῷ ἀνθρώπῳ] Cyr.*Is*.1.1(2.23A); ἐ. σημεῖα Leont.H.*Nest*. 2.1(M.86.1528D); Hier.H.*bapt*.(M.40.865B); Anast.S.*hod*.2(M.89.61B); **6.** *interior* ἀναχωρεῖ μὲν ὁ πλάνος τοῦ δόλου, εἰς πόλεμον δὲ λοιπὸν ἐ. ἐξάπτεται τῆς ψυχῆς Diad.*perf*.31(p.34.26); **7.** *existent* πῶς λέγετε... τὸ ἐ.;...περὶ τοῦ σημαίνοντος τὸ ὂν ἁπλῶς...[ἢ] περὶ τοῦ καθ' ἑαυτὸ ὑπάρχοντος †Leont.B.*sect*.7.2(M.86.1241Af.); εἰ οὖν τις ἐ. κατὰ τοῦτον τὸν λόγον εἴποι τὰς οὐσίας, ὅ ἐστιν ὑπαρχούσας, οὐδὲ ἡμεῖς ἀρνηθείημεν ...οὐ κατὰ τοῦτο οὖν φαμεν τὴν ἡμετέραν ἐν Χριστῷ οὐσίαν ἐ. εἶναι, οἷον ὑπόστασιν καθ' ἑαυτὴν χαρακτηριστικὴν καὶ πρόσωπον οὖσαν Eulog.*fr.dogm*.(M.86.2953Bf.).

B. Trin.; **1.** of Persons; *being an hypostasis* or *Person*; **a.** of second Person τὸν μὲν Μωυσῆν ὡς νόμον...λαμβάνειν, 'Ιησοῦν [i.e. Joshua] δὲ ὡς λόγον, καὶ τοῦ ἐ. λόγου τύπον Iren.*fr*.19(M.7.1240C); Or.*exp.in Pr*.9:1(M.17.185B); τὴν σοφίαν θεοῦ καὶ τὴν δύναμιν, καὶ τὴν δικαιοσύνην ἐ. Cyr.H.*catech*.4.7; τῆς δόξης αὐτοῦ ἐ. αὔγασμα Didym. *Trin*.1.26(M.39.384C); *ib*.2.2(461D); Epiph.*haer*.69.21(p.171.3; M.42. 236A); *ib*.76.35(p.385.22; 588D) cit. s. διαστολή; ‡Ath.*dial.Trin*.2.2 (M.28.1160C); [Mt.7:24] εἰ...ὁ λόγος λόγους ἔχει, οὐκ ἔστιν ἀνυπόστατος· ἀλλ' ἐ. Isid.Pel.*epp*.3.141(M.78.837C); Cyr.*thes*.8(5^1.61Df.) cit. s. βούλησις; id.*ep*.31(p.72.15; 5^2.95E); *ib*.1(p.15.9; 8B) cit. s. ἄναρχος; id.*Jo*.5.5(4.527D) cit. s. βουλή; id.*Juln*.7(6^2.241D); τῆς ἐ. καὶ θεαρχικῆς σοφίας Gr.Agr.*Eccl*.2.12(M.98.837B); Jo.D.*f.o*.1.8(M.94. 816C); of Christ, Or.*adnot.in Dt*.16:19f.(M.17.28B); [1Cor.1:24] δύναμις οὐκ ἀνυπόστατος, ἀλλ' ἐ. Isid.Pel.*epp*.2.143(M.78.585D); ‡Gr. Nyss.*hom.5.5 in Jo*.(p.175.22) cit. s. οὐσιώδης; esp. agst. Paul.

Sam., Hymen.*ep*.(p.326.10) cit. s. *ἐνέργεια*; *λόγος...ἀνθρώπου καὶ σοφία καὶ δύναμις καὶ μορφὴ ἀνυπόστατα μέρη τοῦ ἑνὸς ἀνθρώπου θεωρεῖται...ἡ δὲ μορφὴ τοῦ θεοῦ καὶ ὁ λόγος μετ' αὐτοῦ θεὸς καὶ υἱὸς θεοῦ ἐ. λόγος ἐστὶν τοῦ πατρός* ‡Dion.Al.*ep.Paul.Sam*.(p.5); *φάσκει... μὴ εἶναι τὸν υἱὸν τοῦ θεοῦ ἐ. ἀλλὰ ἐν αὐτῷ τῷ θεῷ* Epiph.*haer*.65.1 (p.3.11; M.42.13A); and Marcellus *τὸν λόγον ἐνέργειαν εἶναί φασι* [sc. Marcellans]...*οὐκ οὐσίαν ἐ.* Chrys.*hom.6.1 in Phil*.(11.234D); hence in repudiation *τρία πρόσωπα ἀπερίγραφα καὶ ἐ. καὶ ὁμοούσια* Photinus et al.*ep*.ap.Epiph.*haer*.72.11(p.266.4; 397B); opp. *προφορικός*: *λόγον οὐ προφορικὸν ἀλλὰ λόγον ἐ. ... καὶ ἐν ὑποστάσει γεννηθέντα* Cyr.H. *catech*.11.10; ‡Ath.*dial.Trin*.3.23(M.28.1240A); *οὐκ ἦν προφορικός, ἀλλ' ἐ.· καὶ οὐ μόνον ἐ., ἀλλὰ καὶ θεός* Ammon.*Jo*.1:1(M.85.1392C); *πατὴρ λόγον γεννήσας, οὐ προφορικόν, οὐδ' αὖ ἐνδιάθετον, ἀλλ' οὐσιώδη τε καὶ ἐ.* Zach.Mit.*opif*.(M.85.1116C); **b.** of H. Ghost *τὸ... πνεῦμα τὸ ἅγιον οὐκ ἀπὸ στόματος...πατρὸς ἢ υἱοῦ λαλούμενον...ἀλλ' ἐ.* Cyr.H.*catech*.17.5; Didym.*Trin*.2.1,10(M.39.452B,648A); id.(‡Bas.) *Eun*.5(1.297C,322C; M.29.713B,772C); *πνεῦμα...ἐξ αὐτοῦ προϊόν, ἐ. τε καὶ ζῶν καὶ ἀεὶ ὄν, ὅτι τοῦ ΟΝΤΟΣ ἐστί* Cyr.*Juln*.8(6^2.275C); Thdt. *affect*.2(p.65.22; 4.757) cit. s. *ἐνούσιος*; ‡Cyr.*Trin*.9(6^2.13D; M.77. 1140C); **c.** of all three Persons, Photinus et al.*ep*.ap.Epiph.*haer*.72. 11(p.266.4; M.42.397B) cit. s. a; *ἐ. ὁ πατήρ, ἐ. ὁ υἱός, ἐ. τὸ ἅγιον πνεῦμα* Epiph.*haer*.62.3,6(pp.392.2,394.28; M.41.1053B,1057B); cf. *tres hypostases ut tria enhypostata, hoc est, tres subsistentes personas*, Hier.*ep*.15.3(M.*PL*.22.356); Sophr.H.*or*.2.2(M.87.3220A); Jo.D. *trisag*.28(M.95.60D); **2.** of the divine being, *being, existing in hypostases, enhypostatic* *μονὰς...ἀληθῶς ἡ μονάς· οὐ γάρ ἐστιν ἀρχὴ τῶν μετ' αὐτήν, κατὰ διαστολῆς συστολήν...ἀλλ' ἐ. ὀντότης ὁμοουσίου τριάδος* Max.*ambig*.(M.91.1036B); Jo.D.*Jacob*.12(M.94.1441C) cit. s. *ἐνούσιος*.

C. Christol.; **1.** *subsisting, having independent existence, being an hypostasis* or *person* *οὐδεὶς...εἴποι ἄν, ὅτι, ὥσπερ ὁ λόγος τέλειος ὢν καὶ ἐ., οὐ προσέδειτο σαρκός, ἵνα θεὸς τέλειος γένηται, οὕτως οὐδὲ τὸ σῶμα τοῦ λόγου ἔχρῃζεν, ἵνα τέλειος καὶ ἐ. ἄνθρωπος γένηται* Apoll. *quod un.Chr*.10(p.301.4,6; M.28.129B); *τὸ γὰρ αὐτὸ ἓν πρόσωπον αὐτοῦ* [sc. *Χριστοῦ*] *ἐ., ἐν ὑποστάτοις δύο προσώποις* [sc. Father and David] *ὁμοούσιον κατὰ θάτερον λόγον καὶ ἑτεροούσιον αὐτὸν ἀπαγγέλλειν δύναται* Leont.H.*Nest*.2.5(M.86.1544B); **2.** *being, existing in an hypostasis* or *Person, enhypostatic*; **a.** of natures of Christ *τὰς...δύο φύσεις ἐν μιᾷ καὶ τῇ αὐτῇ ὑποστάσει λέγομεν ὑφίστασθαι...οὕτως κατὰ τὴν αὐτὴν καὶ μίαν ὑπόστασιν ἑκατέρας ἐ. οὔσης* Leont.H.*Nest*.2.13 (M.86.1561B); *εἰ τοίνυν ἔστι λέγειν, φαμέν, τρεῖς ὑποστάσεις ἐνουσίους ἐν μιᾷ οὐσίᾳ, ἐνδέχεται δηλονότι καὶ φύσεις λέγειν ἐ. δύο ἐν μιᾷ ὑποστάσει* *ib*.(1560B); Eust.Mon.*ep*.(M.86.908B); *ἐπὶ τῆς...τοῦ κυρίου οἰκονομίας, ἐνούσιον μέν φαμεν τὴν ὑπόστασιν...ἐ. δὲ ἑκάστην τῶν οὐσιῶν αὐτοῦ* Jo.D.*Jacob*.12(M.94.1441D); id.*nat*.6(M.95.120C); cf. Socr.*h.e*.7.32.19(M.67.812B) cit. s. *ἐνούσιος*; esp. of human nature as *ἐ.* in second Person of Trin. *ὁ θεὸς λόγος...ναὸν ἑαυτῷ τέλειον ἄνθρωπον ἐδημιούργησε, τουτέστιν οὐσίαν, ἐ. τι μέρος λαβὼν τῆς ἐκείνης φύσεως καὶ εἰς τὴν ἰδίαν ὑπόστασιν οὐσιώσας, καὶ οὕτως ἡμῖν ἐξ αὐτῆς προῆλθε, θεὸς ὢν ὁ αὐτὸς φύσει, καὶ ἄνθρωπος φύσει· εἰ οὖν μὴ ὑπόστασιν ἀνέλαβεν, ἀλλ' οὐσίαν ἀνθρωπίνην ἐ.· οὐδὲ γὰρ...πρὸ τῆς ἑνώσεως τὸ ἀνθρώπινον τοῦ κυρίου ἰδιοσυστάτως καὶ καθ' ἑαυτὸ ὑπῆρχεν* Pamph.H.*panopl*.7.3(p.625); Eulog.*fr.dogm*.(M.86.2953C) cit. s. A.7; Anast.S.*hod*.2(M.89.71B); *οὐ γὰρ ἰδιοσυστάτως ὑπέστη ἡ τοῦ θεοῦ λόγου σάρξ, οὐδὲ ἑτέρα ὑπόστασις γέγονε παρὰ τὴν τοῦ θεοῦ λόγου ὑπόστασιν, ἀλλ' ἐν αὐτῇ ὑποστᾶσα, ἐ. μᾶλλον* Jo.D.*f.o*.3.9(M.94.1017B); **b.** of the union *ἡ κατ' οὐσίαν τε καὶ οὐσιώδης καὶ ἐ. ἕνωσις* Leont.B. *Nest.et Eut*.1(M.86.1300A) = id.*fr*.(M.86.2005D); *αὐτοῦ μὲν γὰρ τῇ φύσει τὰ θεῖα, αὐτοῦ δὲ διὰ τὴν ἐ. ἕνωσιν τὰ ἀνθρώπινα, οὐ γὰρ ἐν ἑτέρῳ ἀλλ' ἐν αὐτῷ ἡ ἰδικὴ αὐτοῦ ὑπέστη σάρξ* Eulog.*fr.dogm*.(2953A).

***ἐνυποστάτως**, **1.** *personally, as a Person* *ἐ. εἶναι τὴν σοφίαν αὐτοῦ* Didym.*Trin*.3.37(M.39.972B); *τὸ πνεῦμα...ἐκ τῆς πατρικῆς ἐ. ἐκλάμψαν πηγῆς* *ib*.2.1(452A); *ἐνουσίως τε κατὰ τὸ κοινόν, καὶ ἐ. κατὰ τὸ ἰδικόν* Leont.H.*Nest*.7.1(M.86.1760B); (Messalian) *συνοικεῖ τῷ ἀνθρώπῳ ἐ. ὁ σατανᾶς* Jo.D.*haer*.80(M.94.729A); **2.** *in virtue of the person* *σῶμα...ἔμψυχον λέγεται ἐφ' ᾧ ἐ. τὸ τῆς ψυχῆς φέρεται ὄνομα. σῶμα δὲ ἀνθρώπου σῶμα λέγεται, καὶ οὐ ψυχή· καὶ ψυχὴ...οὐ σῶμα, ἕτερον πρὸς ἕτερον ὄν* ‡Ath.*Apoll*.1.20(M.26.1128B); **3.** *really, substantially* *ὢν...ἐνταῦθα κατὰ τὴν παροῦσαν ζωήν, διὰ τῆς ἐν πίστει χάριτος, πιστεύομεν μετειληφέναι δωρεῶν τοῦ ἁγίου πνεύματος, τούτων ἐν τῷ μέλλοντι αἰῶνι κατὰ ἀλήθειαν ἐ. αὐτῷ τῷ πράγματι... πιστεύομεν καταλήψεσθαι* Max.*myst*.(M.91.704D).

ἔνυστρον, τό, *fourth stomach of ruminating animals*, Cyr.*ador*.13 (1.464C).

***ἐνυφήκουρας**, prob. f.l. for *ἐν ὕφει κουρᾶς* Proc.G.*1Reg*.6:6(M.87. 1089B).

***ἐνυφιζάνω**, *sink to a lower level among*, Cyr.*ador*.17(1.625D); *ib*. (628B).

ἐνυφίστημι, **1.** act. trans., *give subsistence to* something *within* or *in relation to* *ἵνα...γένηται τὰ πάντα ἐν πᾶσιν...ὁ θεός, πάντα περιλαβὼν καὶ ἐνυποστήσας ἑαυτῷ* Max.*ambig*.(M.91.1092C); Christol. *ὁ λόγος...ἑαυτῷ σάρκα περιβαλὼν αὐτῇ τῇ ἰδίᾳ ὑποστάσει οὐκ ἀνθρώπου ψιλοῦ τὴν ἀνθρωπείαν φύσιν ἐνυπέστησεν* Leont.H.*Nest*.5.28(M.86. 1748D); **2.** act. intrans. and pass., *subsist in* *εἰ καὶ μὴ ἀΐδιον...ἔχειν ὑπόστασιν τὴν ὑπόχρονον φύσιν δυνατόν, ἀλλὰ ὑπὸ χρόνον κτήσασθαι, καὶ ἐνυποστῆναι τῇ ἀιδίῳ ὑποστάσει τὴν ὑπὸ χρόνον φύσιν, δυνατόν... οὕτω...καὶ πᾶς ὁ κόσμος γενητὸς ὢν τῷ ἀγενήτῳ κοσμοποιῷ θεῷ ἐνυφέστηκεν* *ib*.2.23(1585A); *ἡ πρόθεσις τῆς σαρκὸς αὐτῷ προσείληπται, ἐνυποστᾶσα τῷ ἀπαθεῖ αὐτῷ ἡ παθητὴ* *ib*.7.6(1768^{d}C).

***ἐνωδυνηρός**, *sad*; comp., Jo.Clim.*scal*.5(M.88.773A).

***ἐνώδυνος**, **1.** *suffering pain*, Jo.Clim.*scal*.7(M.88.801C); *ib*.(813B); Thdr.Stud.*epp*.2.109(M.99.1369D); **2.** *painful* *τὴν ἐ. σαρκὸς ἡδονήν* Andr.Cr.*can.mag*.(M.97.1357A).

***ἐνωδύνως**, *sadly, in sorrow*, Jo.Clim.*scal*.5(M.88.773A,C); v. *ἐνοδύνως*.

ἑνωθ-έω, *unite*; **1.** theol. *τὸ ὑποταγήσεσθαι τῷ πατρὶ τὸν υἱὸν ἀντὶ τοῦ ~ήσεσθαι τῷ θεῷ τὸν λόγον* Eus.*e.th*.3.14(p.171.27; M.24.1028B); **2.** Christol. *τὴν θείαν τοῦ μονογενοῦς ὑπόστασιν ~ησομένην καὶ συμπλακησομένην τῇ ἀνθρωπίνῃ φύσει* ‡Gr.Nyss.*hom.9.21 in Jo*.(p.288.27).

ἐνώμοτος, *confirmed by an oath*, ‡Just.*qu.et resp*.58(M.6.1300B); Cyr.*Lc*.22:61(M.72.928B).

ἐνωμότως, **1.** *according to oath*, Dion.Al.ap.Eus.*p.e*.14.25(777C; M.21.1280A); **2.** *on oath*, Soz.*h.e*.2.17.4(M.67.977A); Gel.Cyz.*h.e*. 3.13.17; Heracl.*ep*.(M.92.993B).

ἐνωπαδόν, **1.** adv., *face to face, openly*, †Apoll.*met.Ps*.21:28(M. 33.1341A); **2.** prep. c. genit., *in the presence of*, *ib*.40:13(1369B).

ἐνωπίως, *face to face*, ‡Thdt.*nativ.Jo.Bapt*.(5.88); *ἐ. ἐνωπίῳ λαλοῦσιν* Jo.Clim.*scal*.27(M.88.1100B).

ἐνωραΐζομαι, *glory in*; c. dat. rei, Ath.ap.Leont.et Jo.*sacr*.2(M. 86.2041B); Gr.Nyss.*virg*.2(p.253.24; M.46.321D); id.*hom.4 in Cant*. (M.44.849A); abs., Areth.*Apoc*.6(M.106.540B); in bad sense, Gr. Nyss.*Eun*.12(1 p.259.24; M.45.964A).

ἕνωσις, ἡ, *union, unity*, etym. *ἕ. ... εἴρηται διὰ τὸ εἰς ἓν ὦσαι* Anast.S.*hod*.2(M.89.69C); its different modes *τὸ τῆς ἑ. χρῆμα κατὰ πολλοὺς ἐπιτελεῖται τρόπους...κατὰ σύμβασιν φιλικήν, ἐκ μέσου τιθέντες τὰς διαφοράς...τὰ ἀλλήλοις κολλώμενα ἤγουν συνηγμένα καθ' ἑτέρους τρόπους, ἢ κατὰ παράθεσιν, ἢ μίξιν, ἢ κρᾶσιν* Cyr.*schol.inc*.8 (p.220.13; 5^1.782A,B); *ἕ. μέν ἐστι διεστώτων πραγμάτων κοινωνικὴ συνδρομή...πενταχῶς δὲ λέγεται ἡ ἕ. συγχυτική, ὡς ἡ τοῦ οἴνου καὶ τοῦ ὕδατος· διαιρετική, ὡς ἡ ἀνθρώπου πρὸς ἄνθρωπον· σχετική, ὡς χρυσὸς πρὸς χρυσόν. ἡ δὲ τοῦ Χριστοῦ ἕ. ὑπὲρ πάσας ταύτας καθ' ὑπόστασιν εἴρηται. καθ' ὑπόστασιν δὲ ἕ. ἐστιν ἡ ἀμφύπαρκτος...τῶν δύο φύσεων συνδρομή* Anast.S.*hod*.2(M.89.69C) ∞ ‡Ath.*def*.5(M.28. 544Cf. reading *αὐθύπαρκτος*); *ἡ κατὰ...φυρμὸν γίνεται...ἢ κατὰ κόλλησιν...ἢ κατὰ ἁρμονίαν...ἢ κατὰ σύγχυσιν...ἢ κατὰ ἀνάκρασιν... κατὰ συναλοιφήν...ἡ δὲ κατὰ σύνθεσιν ἕ. ἐστιν ἡ εἰς ἄλληλα τῶν μερῶν χωρὶς ἀφανισμοῦ περιχώρησις...ἥντινα ἕ. τινες σύγκρασιν ἐκάλεσαν, ἤγουν συμφυΐαν...αὕτη δέ ἐστιν ἡ καθ' ὑπόστασιν ἕ., ἡ κατὰ σύνθεσιν... ἔστιν ἕ. καὶ ἡ κατὰ παράθεσιν· ἔοικε δὲ τῇ κατὰ ἁρμονίαν. πάλιν ἕ. λέγεται προσωπικὴ...καὶ...σχετικὴ...ὁ δὲ Νεστόριος ἄλλας ἐπενόει ἑ., κατὰ τὴν ἀξίαν φημί, καὶ ὁμοτιμίαν, καὶ ταυτοβουλίαν, καὶ εὐδοκίαν, καὶ ὁμωνυμίαν* Jo.D.*dialect*.65(M.94.661B–664B); Christol. *τοῦτο γάρ ἐστιν ἕ., τὸ τὰ ἴδια τῶν ἑνωθέντων εἰς ἓν ξυνελθεῖν* Thdot.Anc.*exp.symb*.13 (M.77.1332D); *ἕ. ... δύο τινῶν σύνοδος, καὶ εἰς ταὐτὸν συνέλευσις* Jo.D. *Jacob*.53(M.94.1464C); opp. *ἑνότης*, Max.*schol.d.n*.11.3(M.4.396C).

A. in gen.; **1.** *unity* *ἐκ πάντων ἕνωσιν εἰσηγεῖται...τῆς...θείας ἑνότητος τὴν ὁμοίωσιν ἐν ἡμῖν καταυγάζεσθαι βουλόμενος* Jo.D.*Eph*. 4:5f.(M.95.840D); **a.** in material sphere *τὸ σῶμα τοῦ ἀνθρώπου πολυμερὲς ὂν...πρὸς πάντα τὰ μέλη ἀδιάρρηκτον ἕ. ἔχον* Arist.*apol*. 13.5; *μνημείῳ...οὐκ ἐκ λογάδων λίθων οἰκοδομηθέντι καὶ τὴν ἕ. οὐ φυσικὴν ἔχοντι, ἀλλ' ἐν μιᾷ καὶ δι' ὅλων ἡνωμένῃ πέτρᾳ λατομητῇ* Or. *Cels*.2.69(p.191.15; M.11.905A); Gr.Nyss.*or.catech*.16(p.71.4; M.45. 52B); **b.** philos., *unity, simplicity*, of essence *κατὰ τὴν τῆς μοναδικῆς οὐσίας ἕ.* Clem.*prot*.9(p.65.29; M.8.200B); not to be found in matter *οὐδὲν γὰρ ἓν τῆς ὕλης καὶ τῶν σωμάτων, ἀλλ' ἕκαστον...διῄρηται εἰς πλείονα, τὴν ἕ. ἀπολωλεκός· ἓν γὰρ τὸ ἀγαθόν, πολλὰ δὲ τὰ αἰσχρά* Or. *or*.21.2(p.345.19; M.11.481A); **c.** logical *coherence*, systematic *unity*, e.g. of a school of thought *ἐπειδὰν ἔν τινι τῶν ἀποφάσεων μέρει διαφωνῶσιν* [sc. *οἱ φιλόσοφοι*]...*τῇ μέντοι τοῦ δόγματος ἑ. πάλιν εἰς ἀλλήλους συμπνέουσιν* Const.ap.Eus.*v.C*.2.71(p.69.29; M.20.1044C); **d.** corporate *unity*, of [members of] Church *τὴν ἕ. ἀγαπᾶτε· τοὺς μερισμοὺς φεύγετε* Ign.*Philad*.7.2; *ἐμέρισαν τὴν ἕ. τῆς ἐκκλησίας*

Heges.ap.Eus.*h.e.*4.22.6(M.20.381A); ὁ...Βίκτωρ...τῆς Ἀσίας πάσης ...τὰς παροικίας ἀποτέμνειν...τῆς κοινῆς ἑ. πειρᾶται Eus.*h.e.*5.24.9 (M.20.497B); [1Cor.15:28] συνάφειάν τινα πάντων καὶ ἕ. σημαίνειν, εἰ πάντα μέλλοι ὁ θεὸς ἐν πᾶσιν εἶναι id.*e.th.*3.15(p.172.5; M.24.1028C); Thds.Imp.*ep.Jo.Ant.*(p.5.3; M.77.1461C); ἕ. ⟨γενι.σθαι⟩ τῆς...ἐκκλησίας συναφθῆναί τε τὰ μέλη τοῖς μέλεσιν Zeno *henot.*(p.53.11; M. 86.2621B); **2.** *union, coming together*; **a.** in gen. ὡς...ἡ γωνία δύο τοίχων ἕ. γίνεται...οὕτως...ἡ ἁγία ἐκκλησία τῶν δύο λαῶν γέγονεν ἕ. καθ' ἕνα πίστεως λόγον ‡Ammon.*Mt.*23:42(M.85.1385A,B); τὴν γοῦν ἕ. τῶν θείων νοημάτων καὶ τῶν ἐπιγείων λόγων κρᾶσιν οὐκ ἀπεικότως ἐκάλεσε Isid.Pel.*epp.*2.3(M.78.460A); Sophr.H.*mir.Cyr.et Jo.*21(M. 87.3481D); **b.** marriage union μετὰ γνώμης τοῦ ἐπισκόπου τὴν ἕ. ποιεῖσθαι, ἵνα ὁ γάμος ᾖ κατὰ κύριον καὶ μὴ κατ' ἐπιθυμίαν Ign.*Polyc.* 5.2; Athenag.*leg.*33.2(M.6.968A); **c.** of body and soul in man, ‡Just. *qu.et resp.*75(M.6.1317A); Nemes.*nat.hom.*3(M.40.592A) et passim; **d.** moral union αἱ διάφοροι φύσεις...ἕνα καὶ μόνον ἑνώσεως ἔχουσι τρόπον τὴν κατ' ἐνέργειαν ‡Paul.Sam.*fr.*2(p.339.9); Proc.G.*Lev.*19:28 (M.87.761B); of married persons ὑπόλειμμα τοίνυν πνεύματος τοῦ ἀνδρὸς τὴν γυναῖκα καλεῖ, καὶ οἱονεὶ μέρος τῆς αὐτοῦ ψυχῆς, διά τε τὴν ἕ., τὴν ὡς ἕν γε φημὶ τῇ κατὰ τὴν ἀγάπην ὁμοψυχίᾳ Cyr.*Mal.*28(3. 846A); of Christians in a common obedience ἡ...ἐκ πολλῶν ἕ. ... μία γίνεται συμφωνία ἑνὶ χορευτῇ καὶ διδασκάλῳ τῷ λόγῳ ἑπομένη Clem. *prot.*9(p.65.31; M.8.200C); id.*str.*3.13(p.239.5; M.8.1193B); in love, Bas.*ep.*204.1(3.303A; M.32.745A); Chrys.*hom.1.1 in 1Cor.*(10.4B) cit. s. ἐκκλησία; Cyr.*Mal.*25(3.841D); as work of Pentecost ὧδε δὲ ἀποκατάστασις καὶ ἕ. τῶν γνωμῶν Cyr.H.*catech.*17.17; of pre-existent rational beings with Logos ὡς ἑνάδα πάντων τούτων γενέσθαι τῇ ταυτότητι τῆς οὐσίας...καὶ τῇ πρὸς τὸν θεὸν λόγον ἑ. τε καὶ γνώσει CCP(543)*anath.*2(p.228; H.3.284C); **e.** *concord, agreement,* hence *state of being in communion with* ἱκανὸν δὲ γνώρισμα τῆς ἑκάστου ὀρθῆς προαιρέσεως ἔσται ἡ πρὸς τοῦτον [sc. Athanasius] ἕ. Constantius Imp.ap.Ath.*apol.sec.*54.5(p.135.14; M.25.348C); *ib.*70.2 (p.148.19; 373B); πρὸς δὲ τελείαν τῶν...ἐκκλησιῶν ἕ. καὶ κοινὴν ὁμόνοιαν Constans *typ.*(H.3.825A); **3.** *mixture, commingling,* of mixed chalice εὐλόγησον δέσποτα τὴν ἁγίαν ἕ. *Lit.Chrys.*(p.357.23); of *commixtio* ἕ. τοῦ παναγίου σώματος καὶ τοῦ τιμίου αἵματος τοῦ κυρίου *Lit.Jac.*(p.228.25).

B. theol., *unity* of divine Persons, Athenag.*leg.*10.3(M.6.909B) cit. s. διαίρεσις; *ib.*12.2(913B); ref. 1Cor.15:28 τὴν...'ὑποταγὴν' τοῦ υἱοῦ ἕ. ἑρμηνεύει τοῦ λόγου, ἓν καὶ ταὐτὸν γενησομένου τῷ πατρὶ καθ' ἃ καὶ πρότερον ἦν Eus.*e.th.*3.15(p.172.6; M.24.1028C); τὰ γὰρ ὅμοια πρὸς τὰ ὅμοια πέφυκε τὴν ἕ. ἔχειν...διὰ τοῦτο ἐκεῖνος [sc. ὁ λόγος] μέν ἐστι...ἓν μετὰ τοῦ ἑαυτοῦ πατρὸς Ath.*Ar.*3.20(M.26.365A); ὃ οὖν ἐστιν ἐνταῦθα μιμητικῶς ἡ εἰκών, τοῦτο ἐκεῖ φυσικῶς ὁ υἱός. καὶ ὥσπερ ἐπὶ τῶν τεχνικῶν κατὰ τὴν μορφὴν ἡ ὁμοίωσις, οὕτως ἐπὶ τῆς θείας καὶ ἀσυνθέτου φύσεως ἐν τῇ κοινωνίᾳ τῆς θεότητός ἐστιν ἡ ἕ. Bas.*Spir.*45 (3.38C; M.32.149C); τὸ ἓν ἕκαστον αὐτῶν ἔχει πρὸς τὸ συγκείμενον οὐχ ἧττον ἢ πρὸς ἑαυτό, τῷ ταὐτῷ τῆς οὐσίας καὶ τῆς δυνάμεως. καὶ οὗτος ὁ τῆς ἑ. λόγος Gr.Naz.*or.*31.16(p.165.12; M.36.152B); *ib.*39.11(348A) cit. s. διαίρεσις; *ib.*42.15(476B); τὴν τοῦ νοητοῦ πρὸς τὸ νοητὸν διὰ τῆς ταυτότητος τῶν θελημάτων ἕ. τε καὶ ἀνάκρασιν Gr.Nyss.*Eun.*12(1 p.275.20; M.45.981C); περὶ τοῦ πνεύματος οἴεται [sc. Eunomius] ὡς ἀπεξενωμένου τῆς τε πρὸς τὸν υἱὸν καὶ τὸν πατέρα ἑ. *ib.*1(1 p.140.31; 380C); *ib.*6(2 p.147.24; 733B) cit. s. ἐξομοίωσις; οὐ...τρεῖς θεούς... ἀλλὰ τῆς τριάδος τὴν ἕ. ἐν τῇ κοινωνίᾳ τῶν ὀνομάτων ἐπιγνωστέον Didym.(‡Bas.)*Eun.*5(3.310D; M.29.744D); ὅταν ἀκούσωμεν ἕ. πατρὸς καὶ υἱοῦ, τὴν φυσικὴν νοοῦμεν Ammon.*Jo.*14:23(M.85.1492C); ἐπὶ τῆς ἑ. τῆς θείας...ἡνωμένον μέν ἐστι τῇ ἐναρχικῇ τριάδι, καὶ κοινὸν ἡ ὑπερούσιος ὕπαρξις Dion.Ar.*d.n.*2.4(M.3.641A); *ib.*2.11(652A); transcending unity of all creatures ὅπου γε καὶ τὴν ὑπερούσιον ἕ. ὑπεριδρῦσθαί φαμεν, οὐ τῶν ἐν σώμασι μόνον ἑ., ἀλλὰ καὶ τῶν ἐν ψυχαῖς αὐταῖς καὶ ἐν αὐτοῖς νόοις *ib.*2.4(641C); καλῶς οὖν ἡμῖν εἴρηται, ἕ. μὲν ὑποστάσεων ἐν μιᾷ φύσει ἐπὶ τῆς ἁγίας καὶ ὑπερουσίου τριάδος, ἕ. δὲ τῶν φύσεων ἐν μιᾷ ὑποστάσει ἐπὶ τῆς ἁγίας καὶ ἀφράστου σαρκώσεως τοῦ λόγου Leont.H.*monoph.*18(M.86.1780C,D); Max.*opusc.*(M.91. 148A) cit. s. διαφορά; heret. ἵνα καὶ τὴν προβολὴν ἑκατέρων αὐτῶν δείξῃ, τοῦ τε υἱοῦ καὶ τοῦ λόγου, καὶ τὴν πρὸς ἀλλήλους ἅμα καὶ τὴν πρὸς τὸν πατέρα ἕ. Val.Gn.ap.Iren.*haer.*1.8.5(M.7.533A).

C. Christol.; **1.** *union* (term denotes both *act of union* in Inc. and the state of *being in union* of two natures in Christ) οἱ τὸν ἐκ τῆς παρθένου Ἐμμανουὴλ κηρύττοντες, τὴν ἕ. τοῦ λόγου τοῦ θεοῦ πρὸς τὸ πλάσμα αὐτοῦ ἐδήλουν Iren.*haer.*4.33.11(M.7.1080B); οὕτω τοῦ θεοῦ λόγου ἑνώσει, τῇ καθ' ὑπόστασιν φυσικῇ, ἑνωθέντος τῇ σαρκί id.*fr.*26 (M.7.1244C) but cf. *haer.*5.17.4(1171Cf.) where Christol. passage is absent; μονογενῆ...τὴν ἰδίαν ψυχὴν εἶπεν, ὡς...μόνη...εἶχε τοῦ θεοῦ λόγου τὴν ἕ. Or.*Ps.*21:21(p.477); id.*Cels.*3.41(p.237.8; M.11.973A) cit. infra C.3.a; αὐτῷ τῷ ἀνθρωπίνῳ σώματι προσθήκη μεγάλη γέγονεν ἐκ τῆς τοῦ λόγου πρὸς αὐτὸ κοινωνίας τε καὶ ἑ. Ath.*ep.Epict.*9(p.15.8; M. 26.1065B); exeg. Jo.3:13 etc. νομιστέον λέγεσθαι διὰ τὴν πρὸς τὸν οὐράνιον ἕ. Gr.Naz.*ep.*101(M.37.181C); *ib.*102(201B); θείας φύσεως ἕ. τίνα...κατανοήσαντας πρὸς τὸ ἀνθρώπινον Gr.Nyss.*or.catech.*10 (p.57.2; M.45.41D); τὸν τῆς ἑ. οὐκ ἐπιγινώσκομεν τρόπον *ib.*11(p.57. 13; 44B); id.*Eun.*5(2 p.126.5; M.45.708C); *ib.*(2 p.123.17; 705A); εἰ... καὶ διττὴ ἡ φύσις, ἀλλ' οὖν ἀδιαίρετος καὶ ἀδιάσπαστος ἡ ἕ. ‡Chrys.*ep. Caes.*(3.746A); συνῆλθον αἱ φύσεις, καὶ ἀσύγχυτος ἔμεινεν ἡ ἕ. Procl. CP *or.laud.BMV* 8(p.107.4; M.65.689B); ἀνθότου δὲ δὴ παρέντες τὴν ἕ., καίτοι...ἐκ τῶν ἁγίων πατέρων καταβαίνουσιν εἰς ἡμᾶς, συνάφειαν ὀνομάζουσι; καίτοι συγχεῖ μὲν ἡ ἕ. οὐδαμῶς τὰ καθ' ὧν ἂν λέγοιτο, διαδείκνυσι δὲ μᾶλλον τὴν εἰς ἕν τι συνδρομὴν τῶν ἡνῶσθαι νοουμένων Cyr.*Chr.un.*(5[1].733A); καθ' ἕ. ἀπερινόητον καὶ ἀσύγχυτον καὶ ἄφραστον id.*ep.*50(p.91.23; 5[2].159E); in 'formula of concord' ὁμοούσιον τῷ πατρὶ τὸν αὐτὸν κατὰ τὴν θεότητα καὶ ὁμοούσιον ἡμῖν κατὰ τὴν ἀνθρωπότητα· δύο γὰρ φύσεων ἕ. γέγονεν· δι' ὃ ἕνα Χριστὸν...ὁμολογοῦμεν. κατὰ ταύτην τῆς ἀσυγχύτου ἑ. ἔννοιαν ὁμολογοῦμεν... *ib.*39(p.17.14; 106B); *Symb.Chalc.*(p.129.32; H.2.456C) cit. s. φύσις; Leont.H.*Nest.*3.1(M. 86.1604B) cit. s. υἱότης; τὴν τοίνυν ἰδιότητα τοῦ σώματος οὐκ ἐκ τῆς τοῦ λόγου γνωρίζειν ἔστιν ἑ. ἀλλ' ἐκ τῆς τοῦ πνεύματος δυνάμεως...τὴν δὲ ἀναμαρτησίαν...ἡ τοῦ λόγου συμφυὴς ἕ. κατειργάσατο...ὥστε τὴν μὲν σύστασιν καὶ τὴν ἰδιότητα τοῦ σώματος, ἐκ τῆς ἐνεργείας γενέσθαι τοῦ πνεύματος ἔγνωμεν· τὴν δὲ ἕ. οὐκ ἐκ τῆς τοῦ λόγου ψιλῆς ἐνεργείας, ἀλλ' αὐτοῦ τοῦ λόγου οὐσιώδους ἀνακράσεως Leont.B.*Nest.et Eut.*2(M.86. 1353Af.); οὐδενὶ...ᾧ πέφυκεν εἶναι διὰ τὴν μίαν οὐσίαν πατρὶ καὶ πνεύματι ταὐτὸν ὁ υἱός, γέγονε ταὐτὸν τῇ σαρκὶ διὰ τὴν ἕ., κἂν πεποίηκεν αὐτὴν ζωοποιὸν ἑνώσει τῇ πρὸς αὐτόν Max.*ambig.*(M.91.1057C); **2.** the issue, μετὰ τὴν ἕ. and kindred expressions; **a.** pre-Chalcedonian: ἕτερον γάρ ἐστιν ἰδιότης καὶ ἕτερον ἕ. ἕ. δὲ λέγομεν μυστικὴν καὶ ἀσύγχυτον Marc.Er.*Nest.*30(p.113.4); οὐκέτι οὖν μετὰ τὴν ἕ. θεὸν πρὸς ἄνθρωπον δύο πράγματα νοήσαντες οἱ πατέρες, εἰκότως Ἰησοῦν λέγοντες, τὸν θεὸν λόγον σημαίνουσι, καὶ μετὰ τοῦ θεολόγου φράζοντες λόγον τὸν ὁρώμενον Ἰησοῦν ἑρμηνεύουσιν Thdot.Anc.*exp.symb.*13(M.77.1332C); ὡς ἕν τι νοῇ...καὶ τὸν...λόγον καὶ τὸν...ληφθέντα ναόν, οὐχ ὅτι τῆς αὐτῆς οὐσίας εἰσίν, ἀλλ' ὅτι μετὰ τὴν...ἕ. ὁ τοῦ διακόπτειν λόγος οὐκ εὐσεβής Cyr.*Jo.*9(4.747E); id.*ep.*40(p.26.8; 5[2].115D) cit. s. φύσις; cf. ταὐτὸ μὲν πρᾶγμα σημαίνουσι σάρκωσίς τε καὶ ἕ.· μία δὲ ἄρα φύσις πρὸ τῆς ἑ. ἤγουν σαρκώσεως ἦν, μετὰ δέ γε τὴν ἕ. δύο λέγειν προσήκει, τήν τε λαβοῦσαν καὶ τὴν ληφθεῖσαν Thdt.*eran.*2(4.101A); **b.** CChalc. and after: ὥσπερ γὰρ μετὰ τὴν ἕ. ... εἷς ἥλιος τὸ φῶς μετὰ τοῦ σώματος λέγεται· οὕτως ἐπὶ τοῦ ἀληθινοῦ φωτός, καὶ τοῦ παναγίου σώματος, οὐκ ἄν τις εἴποι μετὰ τὴν ἕ., τὸν μὲν κεχωρισμένως υἱὸν τὸν θεῖον λόγον, τὸν δὲ υἱὸν τὸν ἄνθρωπον· ἀλλ' ἕνα καὶ τὸν αὐτὸν ἑκάτερα νοήσει Thdt.*rect. conf.*12(M.6.1229C); μένει ἡ δυὰς καὶ μετὰ τὴν ἕ. Eust.Mon.*ep.*(M.86. 912C); εἴ τις λέγει κατὰ χάριν ἢ κατὰ ἐνέργειαν...ἢ σχέσιν ἢ δύναμιν τὴν ἕ. ... ἢ κατὰ εὐδοκίαν...ἢ κατὰ ὁμωνυμίαν...ἀλλ' οὐχ ὁμολογεῖ τὴν ἕ. ... κατὰ σύνθεσιν ἤγουν καθ' ὑπόστασιν γεγενῆσθαι...ἀ. ἕ. CCP(553) *anath.*4(pp.168f.; H.3.196Aff.); εἷς...ὁ Χριστὸς...μετὰ τὴν σάρκωσιν... ἀδιαίρετον...λόγου καὶ σαρκὸς δοξάζομεν ἕ., ἀδιαίρετον ὑπὲρ ἕνωσιν ψυχῆς καὶ σώματος, πυρὸς καὶ σιδήρου, πορφύρας βαφῆς καὶ βύσσου Eulog.*fr.Trin.*4.7(p.371); οὔτε τὴν αὐτὴν...ἐνέργειαν μετὰ τὴν ἕ. τὴν φυσικὴν καὶ ἀσύγχυτον, τουτέστι τὴν...καθ' ὑπόστασιν ἔχουσιν Sophr. H.*ep.syn.*(M.87.3172A); CLater.*can.*7, having reference to unity of person, not of nature, Max.*ep.*15(M.91.556B,C) citt. s. διαφορά; ὁ... ὁμολογῶν τὴν καθ' ὑπόστασιν ἕ. κἂν λέγῃ δύο φύσεις ἐπὶ Χριστοῦ μετὰ τὴν ἕ. ἡνωμένας διαιρέτως...τῆς ἀληθείας...οὐ διαμαρτάνει *ib.*12 (484A); relation to διαφορά discussed, id.*opusc.*(M.91.253C–256B); v. φύσις; **c.** in view of Apoll. (with whom ἕ. is a favourite word) διαπαίζεις τὴν ἄκραν ἕ. καὶ λέγεις [sc. Diod.] οὐκέτι μένει τὰ ἴδια τοῦ θεοῦ καὶ τὰ ἴδια τῆς σαρκὸς ἐὰν ἕ. ᾖ Apoll.*fr.*140(p.241.10)ap.Leont.B. *Apoll.*(M.86.1965C); id.*quod un.Chr.*3(p.296.6; M.28.124C) cit. s. σύνθεσις; ἓν...καὶ ταὐτὸν τὸ σῶμα καὶ ὁ θεὸς οὗ τὸ σῶμα, οὐ μεταβληθείσης τῆς σαρκὸς εἰς τὸ ἀσώματον, ἀλλ' ἐχούσης καὶ τὸ ἴδιον τὸ ἐξ ἡμῶν κατὰ τὴν ἐκ παρθένου γέννησιν καὶ τὸ ὑπὲρ ἡμᾶς κατὰ τὴν τοῦ θεοῦ λόγου [σύγκρασιν ἤτοι] ἕ. id.*fid.inc.*7(p.199.27; M.*PL.*8.877D); πνεῦμα ὤν, εἰ καὶ σὰρξ κατὰ τὴν ἕ. τῆς σαρκὸς ἀποδέδεικται id.*corp.et div.*6(p.187. 18; M.*PL.*8.873D); ἐν τῇ πρὸς τὸν θεῷ ὁμοούσιον ἑνώσει *ib.*(p.188.15; 874B); ὁ δὲ καὶ τὰ ἴδια γινώσκων καὶ τὴν ἕ. φυλάσσων οὔτε τὴν φύσιν ψεύσεται οὔτε τὴν ἕ. ἀγνοήσει *ib.*17(p.193.1; 875D); εἰ ὁ λόγος σὰρξ ὀνόμασται διὰ τὴν ἕ., ἕπεται καὶ τὴν σάρκα λόγον ὀνομάζεσθαι διὰ τὴν ἕ. id. *fr.*145(p.242.14f.)ap.Leont.B.*Apoll.*(1968C); *ib.*161(p.254.26; 1960C); *ib.*140(p.241.7; 1965C); *ib.*148(p.247.1; 1965B); cf.id.*ep.Dion.*8,9 (pp.259f.; M.*PL.*8.934B); **d.** of Thdr. Mops. ἔσχεν μὲν γὰρ εὐθὺς ἐξ ἀρχῆς ἐν τῇ κατὰ τὴν μήτραν διαπλάσει τὴν πρὸς αὐτὸν [sc. τὸν λόγον] ἕ. Thdr.Mops.*fr.inc.*7(p.296.20; M.66.976D); οὐ φυσικῶς ἐκ τοῦ πατρὸς γεγεννημένος, ἔχων μέντοι παρὰ τοὺς λοιποὺς τὴν ὑπεροχήν, ὅτι τῇ πρὸς αὐτὸν ἕ. κέκτηται τὴν υἱότητα *ib.*12.7(p.306.6; 988A); cf.*ib.*7(p.296.5,32; 976C,977B); *ib.*12.2(p.304.4; 985B) cit. s. διαίρεσις; cf.*ib.*8(p.299.18; 981B); ὁ τῆς κατ' οὐσίαν ἕ. ἐπὶ μόνων τῶν ὁμοουσίων ἠλήθευται λόγος... ὁ δὲ τῆς κατ' εὐδοκίαν ἕ. τρόπος ἀσυγχύτους φυλάττων τὰς φύσεις καὶ ἀδιαιρέτως ἐν ἀμφοτέρων τὸ πρόσωπον δείκνυσιν, καὶ μίαν τὴν θέλησιν καὶ μίαν τὴν ἐνέργειαν id.*ep.Domn.*(p.339.1ff.; M.66.1013A); **e.** to Nest. ἕ. φυσική bears a force // ἕ. καθ' ὑπόστασιν and means a union into one φύσις, si donc Dieu le Verbe...est uni dans une union naturelle...en dehors d'elle (de la nature) il n'existe pas, puisque c'est en elle et par elle qu'il est uni et qu'il s'unit...ainsi...le corps et l'âme, Nest.*Heracl.*45(p.34); ἡ δὲ κατὰ τὴν θέλησιν ἕ. καὶ τὴν ἐνέργειαν, ἀτρέπτους αὐτὰς [sc. τὰς φύσεις] τηρεῖ καὶ ἀδιαιρέτους...ἡ καθ' ὑπόστασιν καὶ φύσιν ἕ. ξένον ἐπάγεται πρὸς τὸ τοῦ Χριστοῦ μυστήριον τὸν λόγον...ἡ δὲ κατ' εὐδοκίαν ἕ. μίαν τῶν ἡνωμένων ἀποσώζουσα θέλησιν καὶ ἐνέργειαν ἀντενδεικνύν τι τοῦ μὴ φαινομένου ποιεῖ τὸ φαινόμενον id.*fr.*B 6(p.219.20ff.)ap.*Doct.Patr.*41.9f.(p.305.1,6); τὰ τῶν φύσεων χωρίζοντες ἴδια, τὴν τῆς ἕ. ἀξίαν συνάπτωμεν *ib.*C 5(p.242.15); interpreted as equivalent of συνάφεια, Jo.Ant.*hom.*(p.84.20), Cyr.*ep.* 17 *anath.*3(p.40.30; 5^{2}.76B) citt. s. συνάφεια; Cyril has no objection κἂν λέγῃ δύο φύσεις τὴν διαφορὰν σημαίνων τῆς σαρκὸς καὶ τοῦ θεοῦ λόγου...ἀλλ' οὐκέτι τὴν ἕ. ὁμολογεῖ μεθ' ἡμῶν *ib.*44(p.35.12; 5^{2}.133A); *ib.*11a(p.171.16; M.77.85C) cit. s. συνάφεια; Leont.B.*Nest.et Eut.*1 (M.86.1297D,1300B); Νεστόριος λέγει δύο φύσεις, οὐκ ἔλεγε δὲ αὐτὰς δέξασθαι ἕνωσιν, ἀλλὰ σχέσιν πολλὴν ἔχειν τὸν ἐκεῖνον πρὸς τὸν υἱόν †Leont.B.*sect.*1(M.86.1200A); cf. Paul the Nestorian ap.Max.*opusc.* (M.91.173Bf.); **f.** of Sev. Ant. καί ἐστι μία φύσις τε καὶ ὑπόστασις ἡ τοῦ λόγου σεσαρκωμένη· καὶ οὐκ ἐκ τούτου περικλειόμεθα, πρὸς τὸ καὶ ἐκ δύο προσώπων λέγειν τὴν ἕ. Sev.Ant.ap.Eust.Mon.*ep.*(M.86.921A); cf. ἡμῶν...οὐχ ὑποστάσεων ἕνωσιν ἀλλὰ φύσεων πρεσβευόντων Leont. B.*arg.Sev.*(M.86.1933D); μήτις ἐγράψατο τὴν ἐν Χαλκηδόνι σύνοδον δύο φύσεις εἰποῦσαν τὸν Χριστόν; μὴ γένοιτο· ἀλλ' ὅτι τὴν καθ' ὑπόστασιν ἕ. καὶ τὴν 'ἐκ δύο' φωνὴν εἰπεῖν παρῃτήσατο Sev.Ant.ap.Eust.Mon. *ep.*(908D); id.ap.Leont.H.*monoph.*(M.86.1848A) cit. s. σύνθεσις; *ib.* (1848C) cit. s. δυάς; ὥστε τὰ δύο τὰ ἐξ ὧν ἡ ἕ. ἐν τῷ συντεθεῖσθαι τῷ νῷ μόνον ἀπ' ἀλλήλων συνθέτως διακρινόμενα id.ap.Eust.Mon.*ep.*(936D); entailing a *communicatio idiomatum* πᾶν γάρ, ὅπερ ὑπάρξαι τῇ σαρκί φαμεν, εἴτε τὸ ἰᾶσθαι τοὺς ἐν ἀρρωστίαις...εἴτε τὸ ὑπὲρ φύσιν ἀναστῆναι, διὰ τὴν πρὸς αὐτὸν τὸν λόγον ἕ. αὐτῇ τοῦτο ὑπάρξαι φαμέν id.*fr.*ap. *Doct.Patr.*20.9(p.128.26); Max.*opusc.*(M.91.40A) cit. s. διαίρεσις; *ib.* (41A,B,44B); **g.** of Julianists Γαιανῖται, ἤτοι Ἰουλιανισταί· οἵτινες λέγουσιν, ἐξ αὐτῆς τῆς ἕ. τὸ τοῦ κυρίου σῶμα κατὰ πάντα τρόπον ἄφθαρτον εἶναι Tim.CP *haer.*(M.86.44B); **3.** in combination with other words, *Schol.* in *Max.opusc.*(M.91.213f.); **a.** ἀνάκρασις and κρᾶσις: τὸ δὲ θνητὸν αὐτοῦ σῶμα καὶ τὴν ἀνθρωπίνην ἐν αὐτῷ ψυχὴν τῇ πρὸς ἐκεῖνον οὐ μόνον κοινωνίᾳ ἀλλὰ καὶ ἕ. καὶ ἀνακράσει τὰ μέγιστά φαμεν προσειληφέναι Or.*Cels.*3.41(p.237.8; M.11.973A); Gr. Nyss.*or.catech.*11(p.57.13,16; M.45.44A,B); Leont.B.*Nest.et Eut.*2(M. 86.1353B) cit. s. C.1; cf.Gr.Nyss.*Eun.*5(2 p.123.17ff.; M.45.705A,B); *ib.*(2 p.117.6f.; 697B); with κρᾶσις, Nemes.*nat.hom.*3(M.40.601B) cit. s. κρᾶσις; cf.*ib.*(605A); **b.** // σύγκρασις, Jo.D.*dialect.*65(M. 94.664A) cit. s.v.; **c.** with σύμβασις v.s.v.; cf. συμβῆναι δέ φαμεν καθ' ἕ. ἀδιάσπαστον...τῇ ἰδίᾳ σαρκὶ τὸν ἐκ θεοῦ λόγον Cyr.*Nest.*1.3(p.22.11; 6^{1}.15C); **d.** with συνάφεια, rare in orthodox sense, v.s.v.; opp. συνάφεια v.s.v.; **e.** ἕ. κατὰ σύνθεσιν v.s.v.; **f.** with σύνοδος v.s.v.; cf.Cyr.*ep.*44(p.36.8; 5^{2}.133E) cit. s. σύνοδος; Sophr.H.*ep.syn.*(M.87. 3165B) cit. s. φυσικός; Max.*ep.*12(M.91.484A) cit. s. k infra; **g.** ἕ. φυσική: δεδόξασται [sc. τὸ σῶμα] τῇ πρὸς ἄκτιστον ἕ. φυσικῇ Apoll.*fr.* 148(p.247.1)ap.Leont.B.*Apoll.*(M.86.1965B); for meaning in Apoll. v. eund.*ep.Dion.*8,9(pp.259f.; M.*PL.*8.934B); τῇ ἀσυγχύτῳ φυσικῇ ἕ. τοῦ λόγου πρὸς τὴν ἰδίαν αὐτοῦ γενομένην σάρκα ‡Ath.*Apoll.*1.10(M.26. 1109B); cf. ἰδία οὐχ ὁμοούσιος οὖσα ἡ σὰρξ τῆς τοῦ λόγου θεότητος... ἀλλ' ἰδία κατὰ φύσιν γενομένη, καὶ ἀδιαίρετος κατὰ ἕ. *ib.*1.12(1113B); variously explained συνῆφθαί φασιν αὐτὸν τῷ ἐκ θεοῦ πατρὸς φύντι λόγῳ κατὰ μόνην τὴν ἀξίαν...οὐ καθ' ἕ. φυσικήν, τουτέστιν ἀληθῆ...οὕτω γάρ πού φησιν καὶ ἡ θεία γραφή [Eph.2:3] τὸ φύσει ἀντὶ τοῦ ἀληθῶς λαμβάνουσα Cyr.*expl.xii cap.*3(p.19.2f.; 6^{1}.149D); id.*apol.orient.*3 (p.40.20; 6^{1}.167B); id.*ep.*17 *anath.*3(p.40.30; 5^{2}.76B) cit. s. συνάφεια; φυσικὴ λέγεσθαι παρ' ἡμῶν ἡ ἕ., τὴν οὐκ ἀληθῆ καὶ σχετικὴν ἐκβάλλουσα ...ἀλλ' οὐχ ὑποτίθησιν ἀνάγκαις καὶ πλεονεξίαις φυσικαῖς τὸν ἀπαθῆ καὶ ἐλεύθερον τοῦ θεοῦ λόγον id.*apol.Thdt.*3(p.120.2; 6^{1}.213C); *ib.*(p.118. 24ff.; 212C); λέγεται [sc. ἕ.]...φυσική, ἡ ὡς κατὰ λόγον φύσεως οὖσα τῷδέ τινι...λέγεται φυσικὴ καὶ ἡ ὡς φύσεών τινων ἁπλῶς ἢ φύσεως οὖσα καὶ οὐ συμβεβηκότων...φυσικὴν μὲν οὖν φαμεν ἡμεῖς τὴν ἕ. ἐπὶ Χριστοῦ, ὡς φύσεων ἡνωμένων κατ' αὐτόν...καὶ ὑποστατικὴν δέ φαμεν τὴν ἕ. ἐπὶ Χριστοῦ· ἀνάπαλιν μέντοι τῷ σημαινομένῳ ἡμῖν κατὰ τὴν φυσικήν· οὐ γὰρ ὡς ὑποστάσεων, ἀλλ' ὡς τοῦ λόγου οὖσαν τῆς ὑποστάσεως αὐτοῦ Leont.H.*Nest.*1.50(M.86.1512Cff.); ἑτέρα...λέγεται φυσικὴ ἕ., ἡ κατὰ τὸ φυσικὸν εἶδος τῶν διαφόρων ὑποστάσεων ὁμοίωσις ...ἑτέρα δέ ἐστι φυσικὴ ἕ., ἡ διαφόρων φύσεων εἰς φύσεως γέννησιν καινοτέρας συνέλευσις...ἥτις καὶ λέγεται δημιουργική. ἄλλη δὲ λέγεται φυσικὴ ἕ., ἡ καθ' ὑπόστασιν μίαν πλειόνων φύσεων συνδρομὴ καὶ εἰς φύσιν μίαν ...καὶ τοῦ πυρὸς καὶ σιδήρου ἕ. φυσικὴ λεγομένη, ὡς κατὰ τὰς φύσεις αὐτῶν καὶ οὐ κατά τινα συμβεβηκότα αὐτοῖς οὖσα ἕ. αὐτῶν *ib.*1.22 (1488Df.); οὐδεμία...πρόφασις ἔνεστιν, ὡς ὑπέστη ποτὲ καθ' ἑαυτὴν [sc. σὰρξ Χριστοῦ] καὶ...οὕτως τῷ λόγῳ καὶ θεῷ πρὸς ἕ. φυσικὴν συνελήλυθε. τὰ γὰρ ἀνὰ μέρος ὄντα, καὶ ἀπ' ἀλλήλων ἐν χωρισμῷ θεωρούμενα, οὐδέποτε φυσικὴν ἢ τὴν καθ' ὑπόστασιν ἕ. δέχεται. ὅπου δὲ ἕ. φυσικὴ μὴ προέρχεται, μηδ' ἡ καθ' ὑπόστασιν γίνεται σύνθεσις Sophr.H.*or.*2.46 (M.87.3280A); Max.*ep.*15(M.91.556C); as understood by Nest. v. 3.e supra; used by Thdt. of union of soul and body in man, Thdt. *eran.*2(4.77) so understood as forming one nature τὴν καθ' ὑπόστασιν ἕ. εἰσάγει [sc. Cyr.] καὶ σύνοδον καθ' ἕ. φυσικήν, κρᾶσίν τινα καὶ σύγχυσιν διὰ τούτων τῶν ὀνομάτων γεγενῆσθαι διδάσκων id.*ep.*151(4. 1292); and as implying physical necessity εἰ τοίνυν φυσικὴ γέγονεν... ἡ ἕ., ὑπ' ἀνάγκης τινὸς βιαζόμενος, ἀλλ' οὐ φιλανθρωπίᾳ κεχρημένος ὁ θεὸς λόγος συνήφθη τῇ τοῦ δούλου μορφῇ Thdt.ap.Cyr.*apol.Thdt.*3 (p.117.4; 6^{1}.210D); **h.** ἕ. οἰκονομική v. s. οἰκονομικός; **i.** οὐσιώδης ἕ. and ἡ κατ' οὐσίαν ἕ.; in Apoll. denotes a union into one οὐσία: τὸ δὲ ἀχωρίστως θεῷ συναφθὲν καὶ ταὐτὸν ἐκείνῳ διὰ τὴν ἕ. τὴν οὐσιώδη γενόμενον Apoll.*fr.*12(p.208.6)ap.Leont.B.*Apoll.*(M.86.1964A) cf. s. οὐσία; in this sense, but not in Christol. context οὐσιώδης...ἕ. ἐστιν, ἡ τὰς διαφόρους κατ' ἀριθμὸν καὶ πολλὰς ὑποστάσεις εἰς μίαν καὶ τὴν αὐτὴν οὐσίαν συνάγουσα Max.*opusc.*(M.91.149D); opp. moral or accidental, *involving essence, substantial, real*, rejected by Eunomius, cf.Nemes.*nat.hom.*3(M.40.605A) cit. s. ἑνόω; and by Thdr. Mops.*ep.Domn.*(p.339.1ff.; M.66.1013A) cit. supra 2.d; οἱ τὴν ἕ. μὴ κατ' οὐσίαν, ἀλλὰ κατ' ἐνέργειαν, ἢ εὐδοκίαν, ἢ ἄλλην...σχέσιν δογματίσαντες Leont.B.*Nest.et Eut.*1(M.86.1300B); opp. κατὰ γνώμην, *ib.* (1297D); *ib.*(1300A) cit. s. ἐνυπόστατος; *ib.*2(1352D); *ib.*3(1380B) = id.*fr.* (M.86.2009B); id.*arg.Sev.*(M.86.1941A); Pamph.H.*panopl.*6.5(p.618) cit. s. ἐπίνοια; ‡Gr.Nyss.*hom.1.15 in Jo.*(p.98.12); *ib.*2.4(p.112.24); v. s. οὐσιώδης, οὐσιωδῶς; **j.** other expressions ἕ. πνευματική, Epiph. *haer.*69.67(p.215.28; M.42.309D); ἕ. ὑποστατική, v. ὑποστατικός; **k.** ἕ. καθ' ὑπόστασιν: ἐὰν δὲ τὴν καθ' ὑπόστασιν ἕ. ... παραιτώμεθα ...ἐμπίπτομεν εἰς τὸ δύο λέγειν υἱούς Cyr.*ep.*4(p.28.7; 5^{2}.24C); CCP (553)*anath.*4(p.169; H.3.196B) cit. supra s. 2.b; ἐνανθρωπῆσαι τὴν καθ' ὑπόστασιν ἕ. *CIG* 8961.15; rejected by Nestorius, Nest.*fr.*B 6 (pp.219.20,220.1)ap.*Doct.Patr.*41.9f.(p.305.1,6) cit. supra 2.e; and by Theodoret περιττὴ τοίνυν ἡ καθ' ὑπόστασιν ἕ. ἣν ἀντὶ κράσεως ἡμῖν... προβάλλεται· ἀρκεῖ δὲ λέγειν τὴν ἕ. Thdt.ap.Cyr.*apol.Thdt.*2(p.115. 1ff.; 6^{1}.208E); *ib.*(p.114.11ff.; 208Bf.); explained and defined τοῖς ἐκείνου [sc. Νεστορίου] μαχόμενοι τὴν καθ' ὑπόστασιν ἕ. γενέσθαι φαμέν, τοῦ καθ' ὑπόστασιν οὐδὲν ἕτερον ὑποφαίνοντος πλὴν ὅτι μόνον ἡ τοῦ λόγου φύσις ἢ γοῦν ὑπόστασις ὅ ἐστιν...ὁ λόγος...ἀνθρωπείᾳ φύσει κατὰ ἀλήθειαν ἑνωθεὶς τροπῆς τινος δίχα καὶ συγχύσεως...εἷς νοεῖται καὶ ἔστι Χριστός, ὁ αὐτὸς θεὸς καὶ ἄνθρωπος Cyr.*ib.*(p.115.12ff.; 209B); why favoured by Cyril, †Leont.B.*sect.*8(M.86.1152Bf.); ἐκ τῆς θείας φύσεως καὶ τῆς ἀνθρωπίνης, τῆς ἕ. καθ' ὑπόστασιν γενομένης, εἷς Χριστὸς ἀπετελέσθη...οὐκ ἀνάχυσίν τινα τὴν εἰς ἀλλήλους τῶν φύσεων πεπρᾶχθαί φαμεν CCP(553)*anath.*8(p.170; H.3.197B); ἡ δὲ καθ' ὑπόστασιν ἕ. δηλοῖ, ὅτι ὁ θεὸς λόγος...οὐ προϋποστάντι ἀνθρώπῳ ἡνώθη, ἀλλ' ἐν τῇ γαστρὶ τῆς...παρθένου ἐδημιούργησεν ἑαυτῷ ἐξ αὐτῆς ἐν τῇ ἰδίᾳ ὑποστάσει σάρκα ἐμψυχωμένην...ὅπερ ἐστὶ φύσις ἀνθρωπίνη Justn.*conf.*(p.74.24; M.86.997B); καθ' ὑπόστασιν μὲν οὖν ἕ. ἐστι...ἡ τῶν ἑτέρων οὐσιῶν εἰς μίαν ὑπόστασιν σύνοδος, θατέρου τῶν κατ' αὐτὴν συγκειμένων, πρὸς τὸν ἕτερον τὴν φυσικὴν ἰδιότητα ἀνόθευτόν τε καὶ ἀμετάβλητον ἔχουσα καὶ ἀδιαίρετον Max.*ep.*12(M.91. 484A); ‡Cyr.*Trin.*18(6^{3}.24B; M.77.1157A); Jo.D.*dialect.*65(M.94. 664A); *ib.*66(665–9); as test of orthodoxy εἴ τις λέγει κατὰ χάριν, ἢ κατ' ἐνέργειαν, ἢ κατ' ἀξίαν...ἢ σχέσιν, ἢ δύναμιν, τὴν ἕ. τοῦ θεοῦ λόγου πρὸς ἄνθρωπον γεγενῆσθαι...ἢ εἴ τις λέγει κατ' εὐδοκίαν τὴν ἕ. ... ὡς ἀρεσθέντος τοῦ θεοῦ λόγου τῷ ἀνθρώπῳ...οὐχὶ καθ' ὑπόστασιν τοῦ θεοῦ λόγου πρὸς τὴν σάρκα...τὴν ἕ. ὁμολογεῖ καὶ διὰ τοῦτο μίαν αὐτοῦ τὴν ὑπόστασιν σύνθετον, ὁ τοιοῦτος ἀ. ἔ. Justn.*conf.anath.*4(p.90. 30ff.; M.86.1015A,B); CLater.*can.*8 cit. s. σύνθεσις; contrasted with ἕ. σχετική, Max.*ep.*12(484A,B); ref. BMV ἡ...νυμφῶν τῆς καθ' ὑπόστασιν ἕ. τῶν φύσεων Χριστοῦ Mod.*dorm.*3(M.86.3288A); **4.** *union* of ἐνέργειαι in Christ τὴν...τῶν φυσικῶν ἐνεργειῶν...συμφυΐαν καὶ ἕ. Max.*opusc.*(M.91.101A); id.*ambig.*(M.91.1052C).

D. spiritual *union*; **1.** of Christ with Church ᾄδω τὰς ἐκκλησίας, ἐν αἷς ἕ. εὔχομαι σαρκὸς καὶ πνεύματος Ἰησοῦ Χριστοῦ Ign.*Magn.*1.2;

οὐ δύναται οὖν κεφαλὴ χωρὶς γεννηθῆναι ἄνευ μελῶν, τοῦ θεοῦ ἕνωσιν ἐπαγγελλομένου, ὅ ἐστιν αὐτός id.*Trall.*11.2; and of Christians with one another, modelled on that between Christ and Father and effected by obedience to bishop, id.*Magn.*13.2; bishop being focus of union, id.*Philad.*8.1; ref. Eph.5:32 τὸ μέγα μυστήριον εἶναι λέγει τῆς τοῦ Χριστοῦ πρὸς τὴν ἐκκλησίαν ἑ. Gr.Nyss.*hom.4 in Cant.*(M.44.836D); κεφαλὴ τῆς ἐκκλησίας ὁ Χριστὸς...λαβεῖν δὲ ἕ. ἀκριβῆ...καὶ γὰρ ἡ ἕ. ἀσφαλεστέρα Chrys.*hom.26.3 in 1Cor.*(10.231B); id.*hom.1.4 in Eph.*(11.8E); perfected only in next life, Max.*myst.*21(M.91.696D) cit. s. συναγωγή; of members with one another τοὺς τοσούτῳ τῷ πλήθει τῶν τόπων διῃρημένους τῇ διὰ τῆς ἀγάπης ἑ. καθορᾶν εἰς μίαν μελῶν ἁρμονίαν ἐν σώματι Χριστοῦ δεδέσθαι Bas.*ep.*70(3.163E; M.32.433C); Chrys.*hom.30.2 in 1Cor.*(10.270E); which is effected by faith, id.*hom.15.3 in Jo.*(8.88E); τηρεῖσθαι γεμὴν ἐν τῇ καθ' ὁμόνοιάν τε καὶ ταυτοβουλίαν ἑ. βούλεται τοὺς μαθητὰς ἀνακιρναμένους ὥσπερ ἀλλήλοις ψυχῇ καὶ πνεύματι καὶ τῷ τῆς εἰρήνης καὶ φιλαλληλίας θεσμῷ...ὡς μέχρι τοσούτου προελθεῖν τὴν ἕ., ὥστε καὶ εἰκόνα τῆς φυσικῆς ἑνότητος, τῆς ἐν πατρὶ και υἱῷ νοουμένης Cyr.*Jo.*11.9(4.972A,B); **2.** eucharistic, Ign.*Philad.*4.1 cit. s. εὐχαριστία; ‡Bas.*h.myst.*63(p.397.25) cit. s. κοινωνία; leading to immortality διὰ τοῦτο κατέμιξεν ἑαυτὸν τῇ ἐπικήρῳ φύσει, ἵνα τῇ τῆς θεότητος κοινωνίᾳ συναποθεωθῇ τὸ ἀνθρώπινον, τούτου χάριν πᾶσι τοῖς πεπιστευκόσι τῇ οἰκονομίᾳ τῆς χάριτος ἑαυτὸν ἐνσπείρει διὰ τῆς σαρκός, ἧς ἡ σύστασις ἐξ οἴνου τε καὶ ἄρτου ἐστί, τοῖς σώμασι τῶν πεπιστευκότων κατακιρνάμενος, ὡς ἂν τῇ πρὸς τὸ ἀθάνατον ἑ. καὶ ὁ ἄνθρωπος τῆς ἀφθαρσίας μέτοχος γένοιτο Gr.Nyss.*or.catech.*37(p.152.5; M.45.97B); signifying mystic union ἐπιτεθέντων τῷ θυσιαστηρίῳ τῶν συμβόλων...πάρεστιν ...ἡ τῶν ἁγίων ἀπογραφή, τὸ συνεζευγμένον αὐτῶν ἀδιαιρέτως ἐμφαίνουσα τῆς πρὸς αὐτὸν ἑ. Dion.Ar.*e.h.*3.3.9(M.3.437C); cf.*ib.*3.3.13(444C); *Lit.Jac.*(*NBP* 10^2 p.109) cit. s. σύγκρασις; **3.** mystical; **a.** typified by matrimonial union, †Bas.Anc.*virg.*50(3.633E; M.30.768C); **b.** its essence, prayer, v. εὐχή, προσευχή; 'deification', Dion.Ar.*e.h.*1.3 (M.3.376A); **c.** means to it, on side of God οὐ γὰρ ἱκανὸς ὁ νόμος συνάψαι θεῷ τελείως τε καὶ καθαρῶς· πρόσιμεν δὲ αὐτῷ δι' υἱοῦ, καὶ τῶν δι' αὐτοῦ θεσπισμάτων, τουτέστι τῶν εὐαγγελικῶν, ἃ καὶ πνευματικὴν ἔχει τὴν ἕ. ἤτοι συνάφειαν Cyr.*Os.*28(3.52D); εὐπρέπεια τοῖς νεάζουσι τῇ καινοποιῷ τοῦ πνεύματος χάριτι, ἡ τοῦ νοῦ ἐστι πρὸς θεὸν ἄτμητος ἕ. ‡Proc.G.*Pr.*20:29(M.87.1429A); on side of man: prayer and recollection, Dion.Ar.*d.n.*3.1(M.3.680B) ∞ Ant.Mon.*hom.*106 (M.89.1756B); Jo.D.*hom.*1.10(M.96.561B) cit. s. ἐκδημία; following Christ Χριστῷ...συνακολουθοῦντες κερδαίνομεν τὴν συνάφειαν τὴν πρὸς θεόν, καὶ τὴν ἕ. τὴν σωτήριον καθ' ὁμοίωσιν αὐτοῦ, καθ' ὁμοίωσιν τῆς θείας ἑ. [sc. within Trin.] †Ath.*fr.*(M.26.1244C); immaterial knowledge αἱ ψυχαὶ...προβαίνουσιν...διὰ τῆς ἀΰλου καὶ ἀμεροῦς νοήσεως ἐπὶ τὴν ὑπὲρ νόησιν ἕ. Dion.Ar.*d.n.*11.2(949D); ἡ θειοτάτη τοῦ θεοῦ γνῶσις, ἡ δι' ἀγνωσίας γινωσκομένη, κατὰ τὴν ὑπὲρ νοῦν ἕ. *ib.*7.3 (872B); οὐ μόνον μαθών, ἀλλὰ καὶ παθὼν τὰ θεῖα· κἀκ τῆς πρὸς αὐτὰ συμπαθείας...πρὸς τὴν ἀδίδακτον αὐτῶν καὶ μυστικὴν ἀποτελεσθεὶς ἕ. καὶ πίστιν *ib.*2.9(648B); charity ἡ ἐρωτικὴ κίνησις τοῦ ἀγαθοῦ προϋπάρχουσα ἐν τῷ ἀγαθῷ...αὖθις ἐπὶ τὸ αὐτὸ ἐπιστρέφει...ὅπερ δηλοῖ τὴν ἡμῶν ἀεικίνητον ἔφεσιν πρὸς τὸ θεῖον καὶ ἕ. ἡ γὰρ πρὸς θεὸν ἀγαπητικὴ ἕ., πάσης ἐξῄρηται καὶ ὑπέρκειται ἑ. Max.*cap.*5.89(M.90.1385C–1388A); cf.id.*schol.d.n.*4.14(M.4.268A); **d.** effects; illumination, Cyr.*Ps.*17:9(M.69.821D); αἱ νοεραὶ δυνάμεις, ὅταν ἡ ψυχὴ θεοειδὴς γινομένη, δι' ἑ. ἀγνώστου ταῖς τοῦ ἀπροσίτου φωτὸς ἀκτῖσιν ἐπιβάλλῃ, ταῖς ἀνομμάτοις ἐπιβολαῖς Dion.Ar.*d.n.*4.11(M.3.708D); **e.** diabolic attempts to disturb it, Andr.Caes.*Apoc.*72(M.106.456C) cit. s. σπέρμα; **4.** angelic σκοπὸς οὖν ἱεραρχίας ἐστίν, ἡ πρὸς θεόν, ὡς ἐφικτόν, ἀφομοίωσίς τε καὶ ἕ. Dion.Ar.*c.h.*3.2(M.3.165A); *ib.*9.2(260B); ἀγγελοπρεπεῖς ἑ. id.*d.n.*1.5(M.3.593B); ref. fallen angels ἀποστάντες δὲ [sc. ἄγγελοι] κατὰ τὴν γενομένην νέαν γραφὴν τῆς τοῦ θεοῦ ἑ. Or.*princ.*1.8.1(p.97.12); **5.** of blessed in heaven ὅταν ἄφθαρτοι καὶ ἀθάνατοι γενώμεθα...μετέχοντες...τῆς ὑπὲρ νοῦν ἑ. Dion.Ar.*d.n.*1.4(592C); **6.** Gnost., in baptismal formula εἰς ὄνομα ἀγνώστου πατρὸς...εἰς ἕ. καὶ ἀπολύτρωσιν καὶ κοινωνίαν τῶν δυνάμεων Iren.*haer.*1.21.3(M.7.661A); ἐγειρόμεθα οὖν ἡμεῖς, ἰσάγγελοι τοῖς ἄρρεσιν ἀποκατασταθέντες, τοῖς μέλεσι τὰ μέλη, εἰς ἕ. Clem.*exc.Thdot.*22(p.114.5; M.9.669A).

E. Valent. aeon, Iren.*haer.*1.1.2(M.7.449A); Epiph.*haer.*31.2 (p.386.5; M.41.477A).

ἐνωτίζομαι, *give ear (to), listen attentively (to)*; c. acc. rei or abs., *T.Jos.*1.2; Arist.*apol.*17.1(not.); τὸ 'ἐνωτίζου' (Is.1:2) ἀπὸ τῶν ὀργάνων τῆς ἀκοῆς τῶν ὤτων προσηγόρευσεν, τὰ σαρκικὰ τοῖς προσανέχουσι τοῖς αἰσθητοῖς ἀπονείμας Clem.*str.*4.26(p.323.17; M.8.1377B); def., Chrys.*exp.in Ps.*48(5.203E); Cyr.*Is.*4.1(2.555D); opp. ἀκούω, †Bas.*Is.*23(1.397C; M.30.164B); Proc.G.*Gen.*4:23–24(M.87.256B).

ἑνωτικός, *serving to unite; unifying*; **1.** ref. created things δύο... ἀρχικὰς δυνάμεις, φιλίαν τε καὶ νεῖκος, ὧν ἡ μέν ἐστιν ἑ., τὸ δὲ διαιρετικόν ‡Just.*coh.Gr.*4(M.6.249A); of tendency of all created things to unite in God πάντα...ἀδιαιρέτως ἡνωμένα...οὐδὲ ἀπαμβλύνοντά τι τῆς ἑ. ἀκριβείας καὶ καθαρότητος Dion.Ar.*d.n.*11.2(M.3.949C); of knowledge, *ib.*7.4(872C) = Max.*cap.*5.91(M.90.1388A) cit. s. γνῶσις; Max.*ambig.*(M.91.1223D); of love τὸν ἔρωτα εἴτε θεῖον εἴτε...νοερὸν...εἴτε φυσικὸν...ἑ. τινα id.*cap.*5.90(M.90.1388A); Clem.*str.*2.2 v. s. ἐννοητικός; **2.** ref. God; **a.** of God τὴν ἑ. φύσιν Serap.*Man.*34(p.51; M.18.1129C); τὴν θείαν...εἰρήνην...ἡ πάντων ἑ. Dion.Ar.*d.n.*11.1(M.3.948D); ἡ τοῦ νοητοῦ φωτὸς παρουσία, συναγωγὸς καὶ ἑ. τῶν φωτιζομένων ἐστὶ *ib.*4.6(701B) = Max.*cap.*5.82(M.90.1384A); **b.** of relation between divine Persons ὅσας γὰρ ἂν ἑνώσεις εἴπῃς τοῦ κτιστοῦ πρὸς τὸ ἄκτιστον, οὐκ οἶμαι εἶναι ταύτας ἑνωτικωτέρας τῆς σὺν ἀλλήλοις ὑπάρξεως τῶν ὁμοφυῶν καὶ ἀΰλων ὑποστάσεων τοῦ θεοῦ Anast.S.*hod.*20(M.89.273C); **3.** Christol. τρεῖς...αἱ...δόξαι περὶ τῆς ἑνώσεως τῶν Χριστῷ φύσεων κατεβλήθησαν· διαιρετική, συγχυτική, καὶ ἡ κυρίως ἑ. λεγομένη Leont.B.*arg.Sev.*(M.86.1940C); **4.** partic., the *Henoticon* of Zeno, †Leont.B.*sect.*5.2(M.86.1228D); Evagr.*h.e.*3.12,14 tit.(pp.110.13,111.1; M.86.2620A,B); ἀκέφαλοι...τῷ ἑ. Ζήνωνος...μὴ ἀρεσθέντες Tim.CP *haer.*(M.86.45A); τὸ ἑ. γράμμα Paul.CP *fr.ep.Jac.*(H.3.1245B); Thdr.Pharan.*fr.*(H.3.1245E).

***ἐνώτιος**, *of ear-rings*, Gr.Nyss.*v.Mos.*(M.44.396C); ‡Proc.G.*Pr.*11:22(M.87.1332A).

ἐνώτισις, ἡ, *observation, attention*, ‡Proc.G.*Pr.*11:22(M.87.1332A).

ἕξ, *six*; **1.** as number of perfection, Or.*Jo.*28.1(p.389.1; M.14.680B) cit. s. τέλειος; *ib.*10.39(23; p.216.28; 384A); θεῖος ὁ ὕμνος τυγχάνων, τῷ δὲ καὶ πράξεις δηλοῦν τοῦ σωτῆρος καὶ θεωρίαν αὐτῶν μεγίστην, ἐν ϛʹ τέτακται ἀριθμῷ, τελείῳ τυγχάνοντι καὶ ἐν μονάσι καὶ ἐν δεκάσι id.*sel.in Ps.*66:2(M.12.1504B); **2.** as number of Creation, ref. Jo.2:6 ἓξ ὑδρίαι εὐλόγως εἰσὶ τοῖς ἐν κόσμῳ καθαριζομένοις, γεγενημένῳ ἐν ἓξ ἡμέραις, ἀριθμῷ τελείῳ id.*princ.*4.2.5(p.315.1; M.11.368A); cf.Epiph.*exp.fid.*4(p.500.14; M.42.780C); τὸν ϛʹ ἀριθμὸν...τὴν ὕλην, τουτέστιν τὸ πλάσμα Heracleon ap.Or.*Jo.*10.38(22; p.214.32; M.14.380B); ἔοικεν οὖν ὁ μὲν ἓξ ἀριθμὸς ἐργαστικός τις εἶναι καὶ ἐπίπονος, ὁ δὲ ἑπτὰ περιέχειν ἀνάπαυσιν Or.*comm.in Mt.*14.5(p.283.4; M.13.1193A); Max.*qu.Thal.*49(M.90.456D).

***ἐξαγγελεύς, ὁ**, *messenger*, Cyr.*Is.*5.2(2.776A); υἱὸς ὡς ἑ. id.*thes.*25 (5^1.240C); Andr.Caes.*Apoc.*58(M.106.401C).

ἐξαγγελία, ἡ, **1.** *report, announcement*, Just.*dial.*114.2(M.6.740A); **2.** *confession* of sins, Ephr.3.406B; οἱ τὰς ἑ. δεχόμενοι Sophr.H.*conf.*(M.87.3365B); *Const.Stud.*22(M.99.1712B).

ἐξαγγέλλ-ω, *confess* φορτικὸν...ὡς ἐν θεάτρῳ ὑπὸ μάρτυρι τῷ πλήθει τῆς ἐκκλησίας, τὰς ἁμαρτίας ∼ειν Soz.*h.e.*7.16.2(M.67.1460A); †Jo.Jej.*poenit.*(M.88.1896C,1912A); usu. abs., *make confession* μὴ θέλοντα ὁμολογῆσαι...μὴ ἔχοντα συνήθειαν τοῦ ∼ειν Dor.*doct.*5.3 (M.88.1680B); Sophr.H.*conf.*(M.87.3368A); ἐνδέχεται εἰς μοναχὸν ἱερωσύνην μὴ ἔχοντα ∼ειν ἡμᾶς ‡Jo.D.*conf.*11(M.95.296A); ἐάν τις ἔχῃ ἀνεξάγγελτόν τι, ἢ καὶ ἄνευ τῶν ὡρισμένων ∼ῃ τινί Thdr.Stud.*poen.*1.25(M.99.1736C).

***ἐξάγγελμα, τό**, *message*, Sophr.H.*or.*7(M.87.3329D).

***ἐξαγγελόω**, *make angelic*, ‡Chrys.*pasch.*6.4(p.167.4; 8.270C).

ἐξάγγελσις, ἡ, *expression*, Max.*schol.c.h.*2.1(M.4.36B).

ἐξαγγελτικός, *expressive*, Gr.Nyss.*hom.13 in Cant.*(M.44.1056A); εἶναι ἀγγέλους ὥσπερ ἑ. τῆς θείας σιγῆς Dion.Ar.*d.n.*4.2(M.3.696B); Max.*schol.c.h.*4.2(M.4.53D); of Son ἑ. τῶν παρ' αὐτοῦ [sc. πατρός] λαλουμένων Cyr.*thes.*19(5^1.189D); neut. as subst. λόγος δὲ ὅτι οὕτως ἔχει πρὸς τὸν πατέρα ὡς πρὸς νοῦν λόγος...διὰ...τὸ ἑ. Gr.Naz.*or.*30.20 (p.139.6; M.36.129A).

ἐξαγιάζω, *test*, Pall.*v.Chrys.*4(p.27.28; M.47.18).

***ἐξάγκωνα**, *with hands behind* one's *back* ἄλλους...ἑ. δήσαντες Thphn.*chron.*p.316(M.108.768B).

***ἐξαγνίζω**, *dedicate*, Gr.Naz.*carm.*2.1.11.196(M.37.1043).

ἐξαγοράζ-ω, **1.** *buy, bribe* a person, *A.Thom.*A 32(p.149.17); Leont.N.*v.Jo.Eleem.*4(p.10.13); **2.** *buy back, redeem*, Arist.*apol.*11.3; ἐννόησόν μοι τινα οἰκίαν ἔχοντα λαμπράν, εἶτά τινας ἐπεισερχομένους ὥστε αὐτὸν ἀνελεῖν, κἀκεῖνον πολλὰ διδόντα...τότε λέγομεν ὅτι ἐξηγόρασεν ἑαυτόν Chrys.*hom.19.1 in Eph.*(11.134C); fig., Jo.Mal.*chron.*10 p.233(M.97.360C); of Christ ὁ τὰς ἀσθενείας ἡμῶν φέρων...ἵνα ἐξαγοράσῃ ἡμᾶς...ὡς καὶ ἀπὸ τῆς κατάρας τοῦ νόμου Or.*schol.in Cant.*2:17(M.17.268A); Gr.Nyss.*Eun.*4(2 p.98.19; M.45.676B); πωλεῖται...ἀλλ' ∼ει κόσμον...τοῦ ἰδίου αἵματος Gr.Naz.*or.*29.20(p.105.7; M.36.101A); med. with act. sense ἀληθῶς σάρκα καὶ αἷμα ἐσχηκώς, δι' ὧν ἡμᾶς ἐξηγοράσατο Iren.*haer.*5.1.2(M.7.1122C); **3.** med., *buy up* time, ref. Eph.5:16, Or.*comm. in Eph.*5:16(p.564); οὐκ ἔστιν ὑμέτερος ὁ καιρός· νῦν πάροικοί ἐστε...μὴ ζητεῖτε τιμάς...πάντα φέρετε, καὶ τούτῳ τὸν καιρὸν ∼εσθε Chrys.*hom.19.1 in Eph.*(11.134B); ὁ ∼όμενος τὸν ἀλλότριον δοῦλον ~εται καὶ κτᾶται αὐτόν. ἐπεὶ οὖν ὁ καιρὸς ὁ παρὼν δουλεύει τοῖς πονηροῖς, ἐξαγοράσασθε αὐτόν, ὥστε καταχρήσασθαι αὐτῷ πρὸς εὐσέβειαν Sever.*Eph.*5:16(p.311.21); **4.** med., *buy oneself off from* τῶν κοσμικῶν κατεφρόνουν βασάνων, διὰ μιᾶς ὥρας τὴν αἰώνιον κόλασιν ~όμενοι *M.Polyc.*2.3.

***ἐξαγόρασις, ἡ,** *redemption*, Tit.Bost.*Lc.*2:21(F. Ducaeus, *Bibl. Patr.Vett.*2.775A); Dam.*troph.*1.1(p.194.5).

ἐξαγορεία (-ία), ἡ, *confession*, †Cyr.*coll.VT*(6⁴.75B; M.77.1288C); Max.*ep.*38(M.91.632C).

ἐξαγόρευσις, ἡ, A. *declaration, public statement* τότε καιρὸς...τῆς σιωπῆς...νῦν τῆς ἐ. Gr.Naz.*or.*8.16(M.35.809A); Anast.Ant.*redit.*(p.256).

B. *confession*; **1.** in gen., Gr.Naz.*or.*5.2(M.35.665B); ἐ. ἁμαρτάδος ἄνδρ' ἐσάωσε μούνη id.*carm.*2.2(poem.)3.118(M.37.1488A); ἐ. ... ἐστὶ χρεῶν ὁμολογία εἴτουν ἐπίγνωσις σφαλμάτων καὶ ἀφροσύνης ἰδίας ἤγουν πτωχείας κατάγνωσις ‡Jo.D.*conf.*3(M.95.285A); **2.** to God συμπληρωθείσης...τῆς ἡμέρας...τῶν παρεθέντων ἡ ἐ. Bas.*reg.fus.*37.4(2.384A; M.31.1016A); Gr.Naz.*or.*40.9(M.36.369A); εἰπεῖν τῷ θεῷ ὅτι, γενηθήτω καὶ ἐν ἐμοὶ τὸ θέλημά σου, ἀνάγκη πᾶσα πρότερον κατειπεῖν ἐκεῖνον τοῦ βίου ὃς ἔξω τοῦ θείου βουλήματος ἦν, καὶ ταῦτα ἐν τῇ ἐ. διεξελθεῖν Gr.Nyss.*or.dom.*4(p.70.19; M.44.1164A); cf.Oecum.*Apoc.*3:18(p.66); προσάγειν αὐτῷ [sc. τῷ θεῷ] ὀφείλομεν...ἐ. τῶν ἁμαρτημάτων ἄπαυστον Diad.*perf.*87(p.120.15); τὴν χάριν ἀνανεοῦσθαι τοῦ βαπτίσματος δι' ἐ., διὰ βίου καθαρότητος, διὰ δακρύων χύσεων, καὶ διὰ μετανοίας *Euchol.*(p.405); in OT ἡ λύσις δι' ἐ. τε καὶ μὴν τῆς ἀμνάδος ἤ τοι προβάτου σφαγῆς Cyr.*ador.*15(1.531C); public, among the brethren οἱ...ἐλέγχοντες καὶ φρατριοῦντες δι' ἐξαγορεύσεως τὰς ἑαυτῶν πράξεις καὶ τὰς τοῦ βελτίονος νοῦ ἐνθυμήσεις Or.*exp.in Pr.*24(M.17.232A); private (sacramental) ἡ ἐ. τῶν ἁμαρτημάτων γίνεσθαι ὀφείλει ἐπὶ τῶν δυναμένων θεραπεύειν Bas.*reg.br.*229(2.492C; M.31.1236A); εὐσχημονέστερον...μετὰ τῆς πρεσβυτέρας πρὸς τὸν πρεσβύτερον ἡ ἐ. γενήσεται *ib.*110(453C; M.1157A); Gr.Nyss.*Eun.*11(2 p.271.2; M.45.880C); id.*ep.can.*4(M.45.229A); ὁ...δι' ἐξαγορεύσεως τὸ πλημμέλημα ...τῷ ἱερεῖ φανερώσας *ib.*6(233C); οἱ τὴν ἐ. δεχόμενοι †Jo.Jej.*serm.*(M.88.1929D); οὐκ ἔρχονται πρὸς τὸ φῶς τῆς ἐ., ἵνα μὴ ἐλεγχθῇ τὰ ἔργα αὐτῶν Anast.S.*qu.et resp.*6(M.89.372D); οἱ ἀμύητοι, οἱ ἀβάπτιστοι καὶ οἱ ἐν ἐπιτιμίοις δι' ἐξαγορεύσεως ‡Germ.CP *contempl.*(M.98.417B).

ἐξαγορεύ-ω, *confess* Χριστιανῶν ἀνθωμολογεῖτο θεῷ καὶ τὰς οἰκείας ἐξηγόρευε θεομαχίας Eus.*v.C.*1.59(p.35.25; M.20.973B); to God, Ath.*exp.Ps.*85:12(M.27.376B); Chrys.*ecl.*35(12.708D) etc.; publicly ἐὰν ...μὴ ~σωσιν ἑαυτῶν τὰς ἁμαρτίας, φοβηθέντες καὶ αἰσχυνθέντες ἀνθρώπους, ὑποσκελισθήσονται Or.*exp.in Pr.*30(M.17.249B); εἴ τις... ἀνεπαισχύντως ~ει τὰ κρυπτὰ τῆς αἰσχύνης Bas.*reg.fus.*10.2(2.353A; M.31.945B); id.*ep.*217 *can.*56(3.326B; M.32.797A) cit. s. προσκλαίω; cf.id.*reg.br.*229 cit. infra; privately ~σαι μὴ αἰδεσθήτω τὸ ἀληθές [sc. τῷ ἐπισκόπῳ τῷ ἱερεῖ] Meth.*lepr.*6(p.459.8); εἰ χρὴ τὰς ἀπηγορευμένας πράξεις...~ειν πᾶσιν ἢ τισί Bas.*reg.br.*229 tit.(2.492B; M.31.1236A); τὰς μοιχευθείσας γυναῖκας καὶ ~ούσας δι' εὐλάβειαν id.*ep.*199 *can.*34(3.295B; M.32.728A); at baptism μὴ...ἀπαξιώσῃς ~εῦσαί σου τὴν ἁμαρτίαν Gr.Naz.*or.*40.27(M.36.397A); μὴ ἀναμάρτητόν τινα ὁ Χριστός σοι ἐπηγγείλατο τοῦ ~ειν, ἢ ἄγγελον ἢ δίκαιον καὶ ἀνέπαφον, ἵνα τὴν ἑαυτοῦ ἀποτομίαν δειλιάσῃς, ἀλλὰ ἄνθρωπον ἁμαρτωλὸν καὶ ὁμοιοπαθῆ σου †Jo.Jej.*serm.*(M.88.1921B); ‡Germ.CP *contempl.*(M.98.417B); med., †Jo.Jej.*serm.*(1921C) cit. s. μετάνοια.

***ἐξαγράμματος,** *composed of six letters*, of name Ἰησοῦς, Iren.*haer.*1.15.2(M.7.620A).

***ἐξάγραμμος,** *containing six grammes* or *scruples*, *Chron.Pasch.*p.386(M.92.989B).

ἐξαγριαίνω, 1. *enrage, make savage*, Cyr.*Rom.*14:20(p.246.25); **2.** intrans., *rage*, Or.*Cels.*8.64(p.280.17; M.11.1613A).

ἐξάγ-ω, 1. *bring out of, release* τρυφῆς...καὶ πάσης ἀκοσμίας ἡμᾶς ὁ νόμος ~ειν προῄρηται Clem.*str.*3.6(p.217.11; M.8.1149A); πρέπει... τῷ θεῷ...~ειν ἐκ τῶν μνημείων ἡμᾶς ἐζωοποιημένους Meth.*res.*1.23(p.248.6; M.41.1093B); soul from life, *Ep.Lugd.*ap.Eus.*h.e.*5.1.18(M.20.416B); of suicide ~ειν ἑαυτοὺς [i.e. those who court martyrdom] ἀμαρτύρως λέγομεν, κἂν δημοσίᾳ κολάζωνται Clem.*str.*4.4(p.256.14; M.8.1229C); **2.** *draw off* moisture; of sun, Bas.*hex.*7.4(1.67A; M.29.157B); **3.** *prolong* a discussion, Meth.*symp.*8.17(p.110.17; M.18.173B); **4.** *extend* the application of an idea προσέθηκε δὲ 'τῷ εὐαγγελίῳ'...κωλύων πανταχοῦ τὸ πρᾶγμα ~ειν Chrys.*hom.22.2 in 1Cor.*(10.194C); **5.** *bring forth, produce* ὁ θεὸς ἄτηκτον καὶ ἄθραυστον [sc. the Second Adam] ἐξήγαγεν εἰς τὸν βίον Meth.*symp.*3.5(p.31.21; M.18.68B); Thdt.*qu.12 in Dt.*(1.270); οὐσίας...οὔσης τῆς ἀγεννησίας... καὶ ἐξ αὐτῆς ἐξαγαγούσης τὸ ἅγιον πνεῦμα, ἀλλ' οὐκ ἐξ οὐκ ὄντων Epiph.*haer.*76.45(p.399.12; M.42.612D); **6.** *set forth*, Chrys.*hom.65.4 in Mt.*(7.649A); ἐξήγαγον τὴν ἀντίρρησιν Thdt.*ep.*150(4.1290); **7.** c. infin., *drive, compel*; pass., Const.ap.Gel.Cyz.*h.e.*3.19.24(M.85.1352A); *bring about that*, Areth.*Apoc.*51(M.106.709B).

ἐξαγωγή, ἡ, 1. *leading forth*, in Empedocles' philosophy τῆς...ἐκ τοῦ κόσμου τῶν γεγονότων ἐξαγωγῆς ... καὶ εἰς τὸ ἓν ἀποκαταστάσεως Hipp.*haer.*7.29(p.211.19; M.16.3326B); **2.** *bringing to light, exposure, exhibition* εἰς ἀποτροπὴν μὲν τῶν ἀκουόντων, εἰς ἐ. δὲ τῶν πραττόντων Epiph.*haer.*26.14(p.294.25; αἰσχύνην M.41.356B); διὰ τί...ἐξαγωγὴν ἡμᾶς ποιεῖς ἔμπροσθεν τῶν ξένων; Jo.Mosch.*prat.*126(M.87.2988C); **3.** *casting forth*, hence *rejected body* (a play on words) τὴν ἀχάριστον συναγωγήν, μᾶλλον δὲ ἐ. τῶν Ἰουδαίων ‡Ath.*nativ.Chr.*3(M.28.964D); **4.** *spending* of one's life, hence *life, existence* τὸ...ἀμετάθετον τῆς τοῦ θεοῦ ἐ. Bas.ap.*cat.Ac.*7:55–56(p.129.7).

***ἐξαγωνιαῖος,** *hexagonal*; neut. as subst., *hexagon*, Epiph.*exp.fid.*4(p.500.22,23; M.42.781A).

ἐξαγωνίζομαι, 1. *struggle*; c. infin., *V.Pach.Φ* 9(p.7.9); **2.** trans., *overcome*, Euthal.Diac.*epp.Paul.*proem.(M.85.700A).

ἐξαγώνιος, *who has abandoned the contest*, Nil.*exerc.*65(M.79.800B).

ἑξάγωνος, *hexagonal*, neut. as subst., of cell of honeycomb τὰ ἑ. καὶ ⟨τὰ⟩ τῶν μελισσῶν ἔργα Or.*Cels.*4.82(p.352.13; τὰ ἑ. τῶν M.11.1156A).

ἐξάδελφος, ὁ, 1. *first cousin*, *Chron.Pasch.*p.340(M.92.885B); **2.** fem. ἐξαδέλφη; **a.** *first cousin*, †Jo.Jej.*poenit.*(M.88.1893D); CTrull.*can.*54; **b.** *niece*, Just.*dial.*49.4(M.6.584C).

ἑξαδικός, *consisting of six* or *sixes*, Max.*qu.Thal.*49(M.90.456C); διὰ τῶν ἐν σοὶ [i.e. τῷ σταυρῷ] ἑξαδικῶν διαστάσεων τὸ παντοκρατορικὸν ὑπέφηνε [sc. Χριστός] παραδόξως, ὅτι κυριεύει τῶν ἄνω καὶ οὐρανίων, τῶν κάτω καὶ ἐπιγείων,...καὶ ὑποχθονίων..., τῶν δεξιῶν, τῶν ἀριστερῶν, τῶν δικαίων καὶ τῶν ἁμαρτωλῶν Germ.CP *or.*1(M.98.244A).

ἐξᾴδω, *sing over and over again, repeat*, Const.ap.Gel.Cyz.*h.e.*3.19.15(M.85.1348D).

***ἐξάερον, τό, 1.** *open air*, Jo.Mal.*chron.*12 p.286(M.97.432C); plur., Thphn.*chron.*p.392(M.108.933C); **2.** *narthex*, *Mir.Cosm.Dam.*12(p.129); *ib.*12(p.131).

ἐξαέρωσις, ἡ, *evaporation*, Anast.Ant.*serm.*1.7(M.89.1372D).

ἑξαήμερος, *of six days*; ref. Creation, Cyr.H.*catech.*3.5; τῆς ἑ. δημιουργίας Cosm.Ind.*top.*10(M.88.428B); τὸν ἐν ἓξ ἡμέραις τὸν ἑ. κόσμον τευξάμενον Sophr.H.*or.*7.13(M.87.3341C); as fem. subst. (sc. περίοδος) the *six days* of Creation, Thphl.Ant.*Autol.*2.12(M.6.1069B); Hipp.*Dan.*2.27.8; Meth.*symp.*7.5(p.76.11; M.18.132A).

***ἐξαθετέω,** *annul*, ‡Jo.D.*Artem.*43(p.14.28; M.96.1292A).

ἔξαθλος, 1. *who has abandoned the contest*; fig., Clem.*q.d.s.*40(p.186.16; M.9.645B); **2.** *disqualified*, ‡Just.*ep.Zen.et Ser.*14(M.6.1200B).

***ἐξαθώωσις, ἡ,** ἐ. ἑαυτοῦ *clearing* oneself *from a charge*, Areth.*Apoc.*1(M.106.501D bis).

***ἔξαιμα, τό,** *descendant* τοῖς ἐ. τοῦ Λευὶ Cyr.*Is.*2.4(2.293C).

ἐξαιμάσσ-ω, *make bloody*, esp. with spurs; fig., *spur on* ὅταν... ~ηται [sc. ἡ ψυχή] πρὸς σπουδὰς μανιώδεις Clem.*q.d.s.*25(p.176.12; M.9.629C).

ἐξαιματ-όω, 1. *turn into blood*; fig., pass., of moon, Eus.Al.*serm.*22.2(M.86.456A); **2.** *make bloody* ~ῶν τὸν ἵππον...κέντρῳ παντὶ χρώμενος Synes.*ep.*104(M.66.1480D) conj. ἐξαιμάττων.

ἐξαίνυμαι, *take out* or *away*, Synes.*hymn.*8.44(p.52; M.66.1613).

ἐξαίρεσις, ἡ, 1. *expulsion*, Gr.Naz.*carm.*1.2.34.236(M.37.962A); **2.** *exception* οὐδενὸς ὑπολειπομένου κατὰ ἐξαίρεσιν Clem.*str.*6.17(p.509.29; M.9.381C).

ἐξαιρετέον, *one must remove, detach* ἐ. τὸν γνωστικὸν...ἀπὸ παντὸς ψυχικοῦ πάθους Clem.*str.*6.9(p.468.27; M.9.296A).

ἐξαίρετος, A. *picked out, selected, chosen* σέβειν δὲ δεῖν...τὸν λόγον ...οὐκ ἐν ἐ. ἡμέραις...ἀλλὰ συνεχῶς τὸν ὅλον βίον Clem.*str.*7.7(p.27.11; M.9.449B); Meth.*res.*1.55(p.313.7; M.41.1148B) cit. s. παράδεισος; τὸ μὲν ἐ. μου ὄνομα Χριστιανός εἰμι, τὸ δὲ ἐκ γονέων ἐπιτεθέν μοι Δάσιος καλοῦμαι *M.Das.*6(p.93.26); Cyr.*Os.*4(3.21A); προαίρεσις ἐ. *deliberate* choice, id.*Jo.*5.5(4.530D).

B. *remarkable* συνάγοντες ἀπὸ τῶν λόγων τῶν προφητικῶν τὰ ἐ. τῆς προφητείας αὐτῶν Or.*hom.15.1 in Jer.*(p.125.13; M.13.428D); καταφρονεῖται...τὰ ἐ. τῶν πραγμάτων, ὅταν μὴ σπανίζῃ παρά τισιν Cyr.*Lc.*4:23(M.72.444B); hence, **1.** of persons, *distinguished*, Or.*fr.116 in Lam.*(p.276.4; M.13.657C); Const.*or.s.c.*22(p.188.33; M.20.1305B); **2.** *special* ἐ. τι ἔχει τὸ εὐαγγέλιον, τὴν παρουσίαν τοῦ σωτῆρος ...τὸ πάθος αὐτοῦ καὶ τὴν ἀνάστασιν Ign.*Philad.*9.2; ὃ κατὰ εἷς τῶν προφητῶν ἔσχεν πνεῦμα ἐ. εἰς διακονίαν, τοῦτο ἐπὶ πάντας τοὺς τῆς ἐκκλησίας ἐξεχύθη Clem.*exc.Thdot.*24(p.115.4; M.9.672A); Or.*Jo.*32.

20(13; p.461.25; M.14.800A); Const.*or.s.c.*22(p.188.30; M.20.1305A); μόνῳ τῷ μονογενεῖ...τὴν ἐ. καὶ πατρικὴν...δόξαν Eus.*e.th.*3.16(p.175.32; M.24.1036B); *ib.*1.12(p.72.28; 849B); τὸ θεὸς ὀνομάζεσθαι, ὥς τι ἐ. καὶ πρέπον τῇ ἑαυτοῦ μεγαλειότητι Bas.*Eun.*1.13(1.225E; M.29.541C); κατ' ἐ. λόγον *in a special sense*, Gennad.*fr.Gen.*6:3(M.85.1641A); *private* property ζητῶν τὰ ἀλλότρια ὡς ἐ. Ast.Am.*hom.*2(M.40.184A); **3.** c. genit., *peculiar to* τὴν πρὸς τὸ νεκροῦσθαι δύναμιν, ἣ τῆς ἀλόγου φύσεως ἐ. ἦν Gr.Nyss.*or.catech.*8(p.43.11; M.45.33C); Didym.*Trin.*1.8(M.39.276C); ἃ ἦν τῶν πιστῶν ἐ. μόνον...τὸν σταυρὸν καὶ τὸ βάπτισμα καὶ τὰ ἐκ τούτων ἀγαθὰ Chrys.*hom.3.2 in 1Cor.*(10.17B); id.*hom.1.3 in 2Cor.*(10.421B); τὸ ἐ. τῆς θείας φύσεως ἀξίωμα λαχὼν [sc. Son] Cyr.*Jo.*5.5(4.531B); **4.** *distinct from*, c. παρά et acc. ἐ. [sc. τὸν λόγον τοῦ κυρίου] παρὰ τὸ εἰρημένον πρὸς λοιποὺς προφήτας Or.*hom.1.5 in Jer.*(p.3.27; M.13.260A); id.*Jo.*13.48(46; p.275.32; M.14.485C); c. genit. διὰ τοῦ ἄρθρου τὸν ἕνα σημαίνει τῶν ἄλλων ἐ. Vict.*Mc.*1:24(p.276.1); **5.** neut. as subst.; **a.** *distinguishing mark* τὸ ἐ. τῆς γνώσεως ἔχων...δι' αὐτὸ τὸ εἶναι γνωστικός Clem.*str.*7.13(p.58.17; M.9.513A); Or.*Jo.*2.26(21; p.83.2; M.14.160B); Bas.*hex.*6.7(1.57B; M.29.133C); of circumcision τὸ τῶν Ἰουδαίων ἐ. Diod.*Gen.*17:14(M.33.1574A); Chrys.*hom.30.2 in 1Cor.*(10.271B); **b.** *distinctive character* παραστῆσαι βουλόμενον [sc. Ἰησοῦν] τοῖς μαθηταῖς τὸ ἐ. τῆς ἐντεῦθεν αὐτοῦ ἀπαλλαγῆς Or.*Jo.*19.16(4; p.316.15; M.14.556B); τὸ ἐ. καὶ ἰδιάζον τῆς τοῦ πατρὸς ἀγενήτου καὶ θεϊκῆς ζωῆς Eus.*e.th.*1.20(p.86.20; M.24.876A); *ib.*2.14(p.117.26; 932D); **c.** κατ' ἐξαίρετον *specially, in particular* ἰδίως πρὸς τὸν Ἰσραὴλ κατ' ἐ. λεχθῆναι Or.*hom.3.1 in Jer.*(p.20.22; M.13.281D); τῶν τοῦ θεοῦ δωρημάτων τὰ μὲν...ἴδια κατ' ἐ. δεδομένα οἷς δέδοται Pall.*v.Chrys.*1(p.3.13; M.47.5); Proc.G.*Dt.*18:11(M.87.917A); τὴν ἑκάστης φύσεως κατ' ἐ. ἰδιότητα Max.*Pyrr.*(M.91.345A); *by way of distinction*, Vict.*Mc.*14:54(p.430.14); *as one's own*, Ast.Am.*hom.*2(M.40.184B); c. genit., *in distinction from* οὐ γὰρ φύσει καὶ κατ' ἐ. τῶν ἄλλων υἱῶν ἔχοντά τι Alex.Al.*ep.Alex.*3(p.21.20; M.18.552C); **d.** ἐν ἐ. *in particular*, Thphn.*chron.*p.196(M.108.505C).

ἐξαιρέτως, **1.** *specially, in a special degree*, Ign.*Trall.*12.2; Clem.*str.*7.2(p.7.1; M.9.409C); Meth.*symp.*9.4(p.119.16; M.18.188A); ἐ. ὅτι Const.*or.s.c.*1(p.155.1; M.20.1236A); **2.** *exclusively*, Clem.*str.*8.6(p.93.12; M.9.388A); Or.*Jo.*10.1(p.171.3; M.14.308A); Bas.*hex.*2.6(1.18B; M.29.44A); ref. Jo.5:18, Chrys.*hom.49.2 in Jo.*(8.290C).

ἐξαιρ-έω, **1.** *remove*; pass., *be removed from*, hence *transcend* οὐσίας ὁ θεὸς ἐξῄρηται, καὶ ἔστιν ὑπερουσίως Dion.Ar.*d.n.*4.20(M.3.720B); perf. ptcpl. pass., *transcendent*, Cyr.*ador.*1(1.27E); τῇ πάντων ἐξῃρημένῃ κατὰ πᾶσαν ὑπεροχὴν αἰτίᾳ Dion.Ar.*d.n.*2.7(M.3.645B); *ib.*4.14(712C); ‡Cyr.*Trin.*7(6^3.8C; M.77.1132B) = Jo.D.*f.o.*1.8(M.94.808D); neut. as subst., *transcendence* ἐθέλει ὁ θεὸς πατὴρ τὸ πνεῦμα αὐτοῦ συντάττεσθαι αὐτῷ...καὶ τὸ ἐ. αὐτοῦ ἀπὸ τῆς κτίσεως καὶ ὑπερέχον ἀσφαλίζεται Didym.*Trin.*2.4(M.39.481A); *detachment* from things of this life, Jo.Mosch.*prat.*171(M.87.3040B); **2.** med., *set free, deliver*, from eternal punishment τὸ βάπτισμα αὐτοῦ πυρὸς ἡμᾶς ἐξείλετο, καὶ τὸ πάθος πάθους Clem.*exc.Thdot.*76(p.131.1; M.9.693B); ὑμᾶς...οὐδεὶς ἐξαιρήσεται τῆς γεέννης Chrys.*hom.27.3 in Jo.*(8.158A); of Christ's redemptive work τοῦ δι' ἀγαθότητα πάλιν ἡμᾶς εἰς ἐλευθερίαν ~ουμένου Gr.Nyss.*or.catech.*22(23; p.85.16; M.45.61A); Cyr.*Ps.*7:7(M.69.749C).

ἐξαίρ-ω, **1.** *exalt* τῶν Ἰουδαϊκῶν ἐθῶν...τὰ τῆς Σαμαρείτιδος δόξης ~ειν Or.*fr.54 in Jo.*(p.527.27); **2.** *root out, get rid of*, *Apoc.En.*1; *1Clem.*48.1; ἡ διορθωσάσθω ἢ ἐξαρθήτω Bas.*reg.br.*281(2.514B; M.31.1280B); ~ειν τὸ νόσημα Chrys.*hom.29.3 in Mt.*(7.346B); *erase* from diptychs, Thphn.*chron.*p.114(M.108.324B); **3.** *except* πάντες· οὐκ ἔνι γὰρ εἰπεῖν ὅτι ἐξῃρτό τις Chrys.*hom.4.1 in Eph.*(11.26D); senses 2 and 3 prob. by confusion with ἐξαιρέω.

ἐξαίσιος, *extraordinary, remarkable* νεώς, ἔργον ἐ. Eus.*v.C.*3.36(p.93.29; M.20.1096B); ἐ. ἀρετάς [i.e. of Daniel] Const.*or.s.c.*17(p.178.19; M.20.1284C); *ib.*11(p.167.25); τὴν...ἐ. τε καὶ ὑπερφυᾶ...τοῦ τεκόντος βουλὴν Cyr.*Jo.*9.7(4.964C); neut. as subst., *extraordinary quality* or *property* τῶν παραγγελμάτων τὸ ἐ. [i.e. of Jewish scriptures] Tat.*orat.*29(p.30.10; M.6.868A); ref. Job 9:8 τὸ ἐ. θεοῦ τοῦτ' εἶναι Mac.Mgn.*apocr.*3.13(p.87.17).

ἐξαισίως, *exceedingly*, Const.*or.s.c.*14(p.174.6; M.20.1276B).

ἐξαΐσσω, *rush forth*; met., *rush* into a course of action, Chrys.*hom.15.5 in Phil.*(11.318A, v.l. ἐξέβη Gaume).

ἐξαιτ-έω, **1.** *ask*; c. ἵνα CNic.(787)*act.*4(H.4.321C); **2.** *beg off* τῆς κολάσεως αὐτοὺς...ἐξῄτησε Chrys.*hom.14.4 in Ac.*(9.117D); **3.** med., *ask for oneself*; *demand the surrender of* ὁ διάβολος...τοὺς ἐχθροὺς ~ούμενος Didym.*Job* 1:7(M.39.1121C).

ἐξαιχμαλωτεύω, *make captive*, Cyr.H.*catech.*2.17.

*__ἐξαιχμαλωτίζω__, *make captive, enslave*, Chrys.*hom.22.4 in Eph.*(11.171D); id.*hom.5.5 in 2Cor.*(10.471E); id.*kal.*1(1.698D); of S. Paul and altar of unknown God ἐξῃχμαλώτισε τὸ ἐπίγραμμα, οὐκ ἐπὶ κακῷ τῶν γραψάντων, ἀλλ' ἐπὶ σωτηρίᾳ αὐτῶν καὶ προνοίᾳ id.*hom.1.4 in Ac.princ.*(3.56B).

*__ἐξακανθέω__, *put out thorns* ἐξακανθησάσῃ ‡Ath.*qu.Ant.*59(M.28.632D, vv.ll. ἀκανθώδους, ἀκανθησάσῃ).

ἐξακανθόομαι, *become prickly*, Gr.Nyss.*ep.*28(p.83.10; M.32.1088B).

*__Ἐξακιονίτης__, *__Ἐξωκιονίτης__, **ὁ**, (perh. corruption of ἐξουκόντιος) name given to Arians Ἐ. προσαγορεύονται ἀπὸ τοῦ τόπου τὴν ὀνομασίαν δεξάμενοι, ἐν ᾧ ποιεῖσθαι εἰώθασι τὴν συνέλευσιν Thdt.*haer.*4.3(4.358); Jo.Mal.*chron.*13 p.325(M.97.485B); *ib.*14 p.372(553B); *ib.*15 p.385(572A); *Chron.Pasch.*p.323(M.92.828A), *ib.*p.327(845A) reading Ἐξωκιονίτης in corresponding passages.

*__ἐξακισχιλιοστός__, *six-thousandth*, in interprn. of days of Creation as epochs of history ἐ. ἄρ' ἔτος φασὶν ἀπὸ Ἀδὰμ εἰς δεῦρο συντείνειν· τῇ γὰρ ἑβδομάδι τῷ ἑπτακισχιλιοστῷ ἔτει κρίσιν ἀφίξεσθαί φασιν Meth.*creat.*12(p.499.28; M.18.344B); as year of Christ's birth, ‡Amph.*v.Bas.*2(p.164B); Jo.Mal.*chron.*10 p.229(M.97.353C); neut. as subst., *six-thousandth part*, *cat.Mt.*10:29(p.80.10).

*__ἐξακολούθησις__, **ἡ**, **1.** c. dat., *following after, pursuit of*, Clem.*str.*2.15(p.149.13; M.8.1008A); **2.** abs.; *putting into effect, carrying out* of a resolution, *Cod.Afr.*53(Lat. *prosecutio*).

ἐξακοντίζ-ω, **1.** *hurl forth*; pass., of Satan cast from heaven, Nil.*epp.*2.172(M.79.288B); *thrust forth* οὐκ ἔχων...ὁ παράλυτος τὸν εἰς τὸ ὕδωρ ~οντα Cyr.*Jo.*2.5(4.208B); **2.** met., *drive out beyond*, Isid.Pel.*epp.*2.190(M.78.640C); *hurry* someone *on* in thought, Chrys.*hom.7.2 in 2Cor.*(10.482A); intrans., *burst out* ἐ. εἰς ἔριν καὶ στάσεις *1Clem.*14.2.

ἐξακουστέον, *one must understand*, Clem.*paed.*1.5(p.101.28; M.8.273A); id.*str.*1.29(p.110.23; M.8.928A); *ib.*5.14(p.420.19; M.9.205A).

ἐξάκουστος, **1.** *heard; audible*, neut. as subst. εἰς ἐ. πᾶσιν *in the hearing* of all, *for* all *to hear*, Eus.*l.C.*10(p.222.24; M.20.1373A); id.*theoph.fr.*7(p.21*.11; M.24.629B); Bas.*ep.*46.5(3.138C; M.32.380B); **2.** *heard of, noised abroad* ἐ. ... ἐν πάσῃ τῇ περιχώρῳ τὸ θαῦμα Vict.*Mc.*1:29(p.277.16); *ib.*3:8(p.296.1); of persons, *famous*, Bas.*hom.*9.5(2.77C; M.31.341A); ‡Jo.D.*fid.dorm.*16(M.95.261D); *notorious* ἐπὶ πονηρίαν...ἐ. Nil.*epp.*1.33(M.79.97D).

ἐξακού-ω, **1.** *understand* in a certain sense ὅσα...περὶ ὕπνου λέγουσιν τὰ αὐτὰ χρὴ καὶ περὶ θανάτου ~ειν Clem.*str.*4.22(p.310.19; M.8.1352A); ἐ. καθολικώτερον *ib.*1.17(p.52.1; 796B); μαργαρίτας τὰ...θεῖα μαθήματα...~ειν Meth.*creat.*1(p.493.10; M.18.332A); Eus.*d.e.*6.15(p.270.6; M.22.444C); c. genit., Or.*Jo.*2.14(8; p.70.25; M.14.137C); τὴν τῶν πολλῶν ἄγνοιαν ἀνθρωπικῶς ~όντων τῆς γεννήσεως τοῦ υἱοῦ Bas.*Eun.*2.14(1.249A; M.29.597B); **2.** *understand* a word needed to complete the sense, Eus.*d.e.*8.2(p.369.1; M.22.600B); μὴ γὰρ οὕτως ~ομένου [sc. τοῦ 'ὅς']...ἡ φράσις ἀχρειωθήσεται Areth.*Apoc.*1(M.106.508D).

ἐξακριβάζ-ομαι, **1.** *inquire accurately*, Herm.*mand.*4.2.3; *ib.*4.3.3; **2.** *examine accurately* εἰ...τις ἐξακριβάσαιτο τὸν ἀληθῆ νοῦν τῆς...γραφῆς Eus.*e.th.*3.2(p.141.31, v.l. -βώσαιτο M.24.976C); abs., Hipp.*antichr.*43(p.27.14; ἐξηκριβωμένους M.10.760D); **3.** *know exactly*, Eus.*d.e.*8.1(p.354.24; M.22.577A); *ib.*(p.364.33; 592D).

ἐξακριβ-όω, **1.** *state accurately, express definitely*, Eus.*Marcell.*1.1(p.6.23; M.24.724B); τοῦ ναὶ...τὸ ἀμετάπτωτον τῶν εἰρημένων ~οῦντος Areth.*Apoc.*1(M.106.512B); med., Eus.*d.e.*1.3(p.16.26; M.22.37B); **2.** *study carefully*, Eus.*v.C.*4.43(p.135.23; M.20.1193B); v. foreg.; **3.** *understand clearly*, Eus.*Marcell.*1.1(p.8.33; M.24.729A).

ἑξάκυκλος, *sixfold*, of Creation τὴν τῆς ἑξακύκλου ἕλικος πραγματείαν Hipp.*haer.*4.43(p.66.2; M.16.3106C).

ἐξαλαόω, *blind, put in darkness*; fig., Eus.*d.e.*5 proem.(p.208.2; cod. ἐξήπλου M.22.345A); met., *extinguish*, †Apoll.*met.Ps.*151:7(M.33.1537C).

*__ἐξαλειπτήριος__, *which wipes out*, ‡Chrys.*poenit.*4(9.852C); Evagr.*h.e.*4.26(p.173.16; M.86.2745B).

ἐξαλείπτης, **ὁ**, *destroyer*, *A.Thom.*A 80(p.196.12).

ἐξάλειπτρον, **τό**, *that which wipes away*; fig., of BMV μόνον τῆς λύπης ἐ. Jo.D.*hom.*9.16(M.96.745A).

ἐξάλειψις, **ἡ**, *blotting out, destruction*, Eus.*h.e.*9.8.5(M.20.816C); Thdr.Heracl.*Is.*28:5(M.18.1316D); Cyr.*Os.*130(3.163B); met., of sin, Iren.*haer.*5.29.2(M.7.1202A); ὧν ἠδικήκαμεν γάρ, οὐχ ὧν πταίομεν, τὸ λουτρὸν ἐ. Gr.Naz.*carm.*2.1.12.475(M.37.1200A); *Lit.Jac.*(p.192.20).

*__ἑξάλιθος__, *of six stones*, Ephr.3.464A.

ἐξαλλαγή, **ἡ**, **1.** *difference*, Didym.*Trin.*1.15(M.39.328B); *ib.*2.19(549A); **2.** *change*; denied of natures of Christ, Leont.B.*Nest.et Eut.*2(M.86.1557C); **3.** *exchange* of gifts, *Const.App.*2.42.1.

ἐξαλλάσσ-ω, **1.** *change*; perf. ptcpl. pass., *different*, Eus.*d.e.*1.6 (p.34.12; M.22.65D); Didym.*Trin.*2.4(M.39.517C); Chrys.*hom.1.4 in Mt.*(7.9C); neut. as subst., *difference*, Cyr.*thes.*32(5^{1}.287B); **2.** *differ from* ἡ...ἄνω γέννησις ἀκατάληπτος...καὶ πᾶσαν ~ουσα γέννησιν Didym.*Trin.*1.15(M.39.309C); **3.** *withdraw* μὴ ~ειν τῆς τοῦ πατρὸς θεότητος...τὸν ἀληθινὸν υἱὸν καὶ τὸ ἅγιον πνεῦμα *ib.*1.34(437A).

ἐξάλλ-ομαι, **1.** *leap forth*; fig., of dreams darting out of the future, Synes.*insomn.*15(p.178.5; M.66.1309D); *leap up*, of a wrestler from a throw; fig., of S. Peter after his denial, Rom.Mel.(*AS* 1 p.113); **2.** met., *dart away*; of foolish thoughts, Rom.Mel.(*ib.*p.90); c. genit., *elude*, Cyr.*Jo.*5.4(4.510A); c. acc., *transcend*, *ib.*3.4(277D); θεός, ὁ...πάντα...νοῦν καὶ σοφίαν ~όμενος id.*thes.*32(5^{1}.287D); οὐκ ἴσος ἄρα ἐκεῖνος τῷ τοσοῦτον ~ομένῳ καὶ ἀναβαίνοντι *ib.*11(97B).

ἔξαλλος, **1.** *special*, *distinguishing*; of clothes, Hipp.*haer.*5.9 (p.99.9; M.16.3154C); hence *distinguished*, *specially beautiful*, Ephr. 1.205B; στολὴν ἔ., τουτέστι ποικίλην ἐνδεδυμένος Proc.G.*2Reg.*5:14(M. 87.1128B); **2.** *strange*, *outrageous*, Just.*dial.*110.2(M.6.729B).

ἔξαλμα, τό, **1.** *leaping*, Gr.Naz.*or.*43.16(M.36.516C); Andr.Cr.*or.* 19(M.97.1225C); **2.** met., *burst*, *outburst*, Trin. τὸ ἓν ἔ. τῆς λαμπρότητος Gr.Naz.*or.*40.5(M.36.364B); ‡Ath.*Trin.*(M.28.1604C); ἓν...ἔ. καὶ μία κίνησις τῶν τριῶν ὑποστάσεων Jo.D.*f.o.*1.14(M.94.860B); ‡Cyr. *Trin.*10(6^{3}.15C; M.77.1141D).

ἐξαλμίζω, *make completely salt*; pass., ‡Chrys.*decoll.*2(8.4B).

***ἕξαμα**, *at one and the same time*, *Mir.Geo.*4(p.34.18).

ἐξαμαρτάνω, *sin*, aor. act. ἐξαμάρτοσαν Meth.*res.*1.54(p.311.2; M.41.1145A).

ἐξαμβλίσκω, *cause to miscarry*, Clem.*paed.*2.10(p.215.5; conj. for ἐξαναλίσκουσιν M.8.512B).

ἐξάμβλωσις, ἡ, **1.** *miscarriage*, met. φρενῶν ἐ. Andr.Cr.*or.*15(M. 97.1124D); **2.** *woman who suffers a miscarriage*, Diod.*Ex.*21:22(M.33. 1584A).

ἐξαμέλγω, *suck out*, met. τῆς γραφῆς...ἐ. ... τὰ ῥήματα Geo.Pis. *Sev.*173(M.92.1636A).

***ἐξαμφωτίζω**, *enlighten*, *Contrad.*2(p.8).

ἐξαναβαίνω, *go up to the top*, *Orac.Sib.*5.408.

***ἐξαναβαπτίζομαι**, *be rebaptized*; fig., of reception of monastic habit, Leont.N.*v.Sym.*12(M.93.1685B).

***ἐξαναδίδωμι**, *make restoration*, Thphn.*chron.*p.412(M.108.977C).

ἐξαναλύω, *loosen* or *remove completely*, Didym.*Trin.*2.14(M.39. 700C).

ἐξανάπτω, *join* battle, Geo.Pis.*Pers.*3.62(M.92.1239A).

***ἐξανάρπαστος**, *arrested*, Isch.*libell.*(p.215.1; H.2.328E).

ἐξανάστασις, ἡ, **1.** arrogant *setting up* of oneself against others, Chrys.*hom.10.1 in Eph.*(11.76B); **2.** *raising up* of a new generation, ref. Gen.4:25, Or.*Jo.*6.11(7; p.121.3; M.14.221B); **3.** *resurrection* τῶν σπερμάτων καὶ καρπῶν...ἐ. Thphl.Ant.*Autol.*1.13(M.6.1044A); of dead, Meth.*symp.*4.5(p.51.15; M.18.93C); Isid.Pel.*epp.*1.239(M.78. 329B); Thdt.*Trin.*28(M.75.1189A).

***ἐξανάστροφα**, *back to front*, *facing backwards*, Thphn.*chron.* p.342(M.108.824B); *ib.*p.372(889B).

ἐξαναφύω, *spring up*, *Orac.Sib.*11.105; *ib.*11.246; *ib.*14.281.

ἐξαναχωρ-έω, *withdraw*, *recede*, met. ἡ τούτων μάθησις...δυσάλωτόν τι χρῆμα...~οῦν ἀεὶ καὶ πόρρω ἀφιστάμενον τοῦ διώκοντος Clem. *str.*2.2(p.115.20; M.8.936A); *ib.*5.6(p.349.2; M.9.60A).

ἐξανδραποδίζω, **1.** *reduce to utter slavery*; met., *enslave* to one's own views Ἄρειος...ἐξηνδραπόδιζεν ὅσους ἴσχυεν Thdt.*h.e.*1.2.11(3. 726); **2.** *carry off as a prisoner*, Dion.Al.ap.Eus.*h.e.*6.40.4(M.20. 604A).

***ἐξάνεσις, ἡ**, *setting forth*, Max.*opusc.*(M.91.112A).

ἐξανθίζω, **1.** *make to blossom* or *deck as with blossoms*; met., pass., *Schol.Clem.paed.*(p.338.34); **2.** med., *gather flowers*; met., *select*, *compile an anthology*, Clem.*str.*6.1(p.423.2; M.9.209A); Eus.*d.e.*5 proem.(p.209.25; M.22.348B); of Marcion, Epiph.*haer.*42.10(p.106. 12; M.41.709A); perf. ptcpl. pass., *choice* ὡραῖον...τὸ χωρίον καὶ τῇ φράσει ἐξηνθισμένον *Schol.Clem.paed.*(p.331.4).

***ἐξανθιστέον**, *one must deck with bright colours*, Clem.*paed.*2.10 (p.223.28; M.8.529C).

ἐξανθρωπίζω, *bring down to human level* μή τις υἱὸν ἀκούσας ἐξανθρωπίσῃ τὸ θεῖον δι' ἐμπαθοῦς ὑπολήψεως Gr.Nyss.*Eun.*4(2 p.54. 9; M.45.624C); id.*or.catech.*4(p.18.13; M.45.20B); *regard* a king *as an ordinary man*, Synes.*regn.*14(p.29.16; M.66.1076D).

ἐξανίστημι, **A.** trans.; **1.** *raise up* from a sick bed, *1Clem.*59.4; **2.** *drive away*, *remove*, Thdt.*h.e.*4.11.4(3.965).

B. intrans.; **1.** *rise* from the dead ἐξαναστάντων αὐτοῖς [sc. τοῖς ἁγίοις] τῶν σωμάτων Meth.*symp.*6.4(p.68.26; M.18.120A); **2.** *rise up* in hostility, *Apoc.En.*15; δείσας μή τις αὐτῷ...ἐπαναστταίη τύραννος κατὰ τῆς αὐτοῦ βασιλείας ἐξανιστάμενος ‡Jo.D.*Artem.*12(p.51.25; M. 96.1261C); **3.** *set oneself up* in arrogance, Chrys.*hom.4.6 in 2Cor.* (10.464B).

ἐξανοίγω, *open*; of doors etc., Diad.*perf.*70(p.86.10); Geo.Pis.*hex.* 172(M.92.1445A).

ἐξάντης, **1.** *healed*; morally *reformed*, Eus.*p.e.*4.16(161D; M.21. 284B); **2.** *harmless* ὕπνος...ἐ. τὴν νόσον ἐποίησεν Synes.*insomn.*4 (p.151.5; M.66.1288B).

ἐξαντλ-έω, **1.** *draw out*, *drain off*, fig. and met. ἀπὸ τῆς ψυχῆς ἐ. τὴν πονηρίαν Chrys.*hom.15.2 in Eph.*(11.111D); id.*hom.28.1 in 1Cor.*(10.250D); Sev.Ant.ap.*cat.Mt.*8:8(p.59.7); τούτου σῶμα...θαυμάτων ὑπολέλειπται...ταμιεῖον, ἀεὶ μὲν ~ούμενον, οὐδέ ποτε δὲ κενούμενον Niceph.Ur.*v.Sym.*250(M.86.3216A); *draw from*, fig. πηγὴν ἀγαθῶν ~οῦντες Thdt.*Is.*1:3(p.4.8; 2.169); **2.** *empty out* contents of a store, Chrys.*hom.39.8 in 1Cor.*(10.375C); met., *lavish* πλοῦτον... τοῖς μοναχοῖς ἐ. Nil.*epp.*2.157(M.79.273D); Diad.*perf.*66(p.80.12).

ἐξάνυσις, ἡ, *full accomplishment*, Isid.Pel.*epp.*1.92(M.78.245C).

***ἐξανυστέος**, *to be fully dealt with*, *Cod.Afr.*56(Lat. *peragendus*).

***ἐξαπάγω**, *lead away*; met., Gr.Nyss.*Eun.*6(2 p.127.3, v.l. ἐπαναγούσης M.45.709A); pass., Gel.Cyz.*h.e.*2.14.1(M.85.1256B).

***ἐξαπαίτησις, ἡ**, *exaction*, Thdr.Stud.*epp.*1.7(M.99.932D).

ἐξάπαντος, **1.** *in every way*, *altogether*, Didym.*Trin.*2.6(M.39. 520C); **2.** *assuredly*, *certainly*, CNic.(325)*can.*12; *ib.*15,19; **3.** *at any rate*, *ib.*4.

ἐξαπατάω, *deceive*; c. genit., *seduce*, *lead away* from, Meth. *symp.*8.13(p.99.7; M.18.161B).

ἐξαπάτη, ἡ, *deception*, of paganism ἐ. δαιμόνων Thdt.*Is.*10:34 (p.59.7; 2.249); id.*h.e.*4.24.3(3.1001); *ib.*5.21.2(1055); of heresy τῆς ...Ἀρειανικῆς ἐ. *ib.*4.12.4(968); *ib.*5.13.1(1041); of Judaism, id.*Phil.* proem.(3.444).

ἐξαπάτησις, ἡ, = foreg. πρὸς ἐ. καὶ ἀπώλειαν τῶν μὴ εὔτονον τὴν πίστιν...φυλασσόντων Iren.*haer.*1.13.4(M.7.585B).

ἐξάπινα, = ἐξαπίνης, *suddenly*, *Pss.Sal.*1.2; Herm.*mand.*9.7.6; Ephr.1.26F.

***ἐξαπινέως**, = foreg., Thdt.*h.e.*2.30.5(3.904).

***ἐξαπλάζω**, *multiply by six*, Jo.Mosch.*prat.*185(M.87.3061C).

***ἐξάπλοκος**, = ἑξαπλοῦς, ref. Eccl.4:12, Oecum.*Apoc.*proem. (p.30).

ἑξαπλοῦς, *sixfold*; neut. as subst., of Origen's *six-column* edition of OT; sing., Didym.*Ps.*23:1(M.39.1293D); *ib.*26:1(1304B) = Thdt. *Ps.*26:1(1.767); *Schol.* in Cyr.*Ps.*13:3(M.69.801D); plur., Eus.*h.e.* 6.16.4(M.20.557A); Epiph.*haer.*64.3(p.408.7; M.41.1076A); id.*mens.*7 (M.43.248A).

ἐξαπλ-όω, **1.** *unfold*; **a.** *stretch out* μὴ ~οῦν τῷ κόσμῳ τὰ μέλη τῶν αὐτῆς [sc. καρδίας] λογισμῶν Mac.Aeg.*elev.*3(M.34.892C); **b.** *extend* τὴν ἐξ ἐθνῶν ἐκκλησίαν καθ' ὅλης τῆς οἰκουμένης ἐξηπλωμένην Eus. *d.e.*3.2(p.107.31; M.22.185B); τὰς τοῦ πατρὸς χάριτας...ἐ. εἰς πάντας id.*l.C.*3(p.202.10; M.20.1332B); Cyr.*Jo.*2.5(4.193B); **c.** *extend* into ἐκεῖνοι [sc. Stoics]...αὐτὸν τὸν θεὸν ~οῦσιν εἰς τὰ πάντα Ath.*Ar.*2.11 (M.26.169C); **d.** pass., of teaching, *be disseminated*, Chrys.*hom.46.2 in Mt.*(7.483B); **e.** *shed* light *upon*, c. dat., Bas.Sel.*or.*9.3(M.85. 136D); Dion.Ar.*d.n.*4.4(M.3.697D); **f.** med., *extend*, *increase*, Thdr. Heracl.*Is.*61:11(M.18.1365D); **2.** met., *explain*; hence *express*, ref. Jo.10:50 εἰς πληθυντικὸν ἀριθμὸν τὸ σημαινόμενον ~οῖ Cyr.*Jo.*1.2(4. 16E); *display* wide knowledge, Eus.*h.e.*6.13.5(M.20.548B).

ἑξαπλόω, *multiply by six*, Max.*comput.*16(M.19.1233A); *ib.*11 tit. (1228B).

ἐξάπλωσις, ἡ, **1.** *unfolding*; **a.** *flattening out* σφαιρικῆς ἐπιφανείας ἐ., ταυτότητα λόγων ἐν ἑτερότητι τῶν σχημάτων τηροῦσαν Synes. *astrolab.*5(p.138.18; M.66.1584B); *ib.*(p.140.1; 1584D); **b.** *extension* τὴν καθ' ὅλης τῆς...οἰκουμένης ἐ. τῆς ἐκκλησίας Eus.*d.e.*6.18(p.279. 17; M.22.460A); Thdr.Mops.*Rom.*5:16(p.120.4; M.66.797D); ἐ. τῆς διδασκαλίας ἐν πάσῃ τῇ γῇ Cosm.Ind.*top.*5(M.88.272C); **2.** *explanation*, Eun.*apol.*6(M.30.841A); Andr.Cr.*or.*15(M.97.1116A); Jo.D.*f.o.* 3.15(M.94.1048C); **3.** *expansion* of an idea, Gr.Naz.*or.*20.9(M.35. 1076B); κατ' ἐ. *in expanded form*, Areth.ap.*cat.Apoc.*7:10(p.293.3).

***ἑξάπλωσις, ἡ**, *multiplication by six*, Max.*comput.*11(M.19.1228B).

ἐξαπορ-έω, *be in great doubt* or *difficulty*; trans., *disconcert*, *put to confusion*, ref. Mt.15:24 οὐκ ἂν ἐξηπόρησε τοῦτο τὸ τότε ῥηθέν; Chrys. *hom.52.2 in Mt.*(7.531A); *ib.26.1*(313E); pass., *ib.32.6*(373C); ref. Mt.26:8 οὐδὲ...ἔδει ὑπὲρ τοσαύτης σπουδῆς ~ηθῆναι τὴν γυναῖκα *ib.80.2*(767C).

***ἐξαπόρησις, ἡ**, *perplexity*, *confusion*, Or.*engast.*2(p.284.25; M.12. 1016A); Chrys.*hom.52.2 in Mt.*(7.531C).

***ἐξαπόριμα, τό**, *puzzle*, Dam.*troph.*suppl.(p.283.13).

***ἐξάπορος**, *helpless*, Jo.Clim.*scal.*7(M.88.809B).

*__ἐξαποστειλάριον__, τό, troparion sung at end of matins, perh. so called from ἐξαπόστειλον, a word occurring in many of them, Andr. Cr.*can.Ann.*(M.97.1316C); id.*can.BMV*(M.97.1329A); *Const.Stud.*8 (M.99.1708A); τὸ ἀναστάσιμον ἐ. *Euchol.*(p.43).

ἐξαποστέλλ-ω, 1. *send, send forth* τῷ θεῷ...τῷ ἐξαποστείλαντι ἡμῖν τὸν σωτῆρα *2Clem.*20.5; Herm.*sim.*9.14.3; Or.*hom.1.3 in Jer.*(p.2.24); ἔξεστιν...τινα εἶναι ἀπόστολον Ἰησοῦ Χριστοῦ ἑνὶ μόνῳ ἐξαποσταλέντα id.*Jo.*32.17(10; p.454.2; M.14.788A); τὸ ἅγιον πνεῦμα ἐξαποστεῖλαι ἐπὶ τὰ προκείμενα, ἵνα ποιήσῃ τὸν ἄρτον σῶμα Χριστοῦ Cyr.H.*catech.*23.7; *Lit.Jac.*(p.204.22); ‡Meth.*Sym.et Ann.*8(M.18.365C); with non-personal object ὅταν ἐξαποσταλῇ λιμὸς ἐπὶ τὴν γῆν Or.*hom.28 in Lc.*(p.176.12); 2. *send away, divorce*; fig., of Israel, id. *hom.4.1 in Jer.*(p.23.19; M.13.285C); *allow to depart*, ref. Ex.5:1, id.*princ.*3.1.8(7; p.206.11; M.11.261A); 3. intrans., *proceed from* φαντασίαν ~ουσαν τοῦ πρὸς τὸν Ἰησοῦν τιμητικοῦ id.*Jo.*32.8(6; p.438.10; M.14.761A).

ἐξαποτίνω, abs., *pay the full penalty*, *Orac.Sib.*1.102,180.

ἑξαπτέρυγος, *six-winged*; of seraphim, Clem.*str.*5.6(p.350.2; M.9.61A); Or.*princ.*1.3.4(p.52.17; M.11.143C); Gr.Naz.*or.*28.19(p.50.16; M.36.52A); as subst., Rom.Mel.(*AS* 1 p.26).

*__ἐξαπτικός__, *exciting*, Max.*qu.Thal.*46(M.90.424D).

ἐξάπτ-ω, A. *fasten*; 1. act., met. μηδ' ἀλκῇ σωμάτων τὰς ἑαυτῶν ~ειν ἐλπίδας Eus.*v.C.*4.19(p.124.27; M.20.1168A); 2. med., *be attached to, cleave to* ἐξημμένην τοῦ ὑποκειμένου τὴν φλόγα Gr.Nyss.*or.catech.* 10(p.56.10; M.45.41D); fig. and met. σφᾶς αὐτοὺς ἐπιδῶμεν κυρίῳ, τὸν βεβαιότατον τῆς πίστεως αὐτοῦ ἐξαψάμενοι κάλων Clem.*paed.*1.4 (p.95.27; M.8.260C); εὐθύμους καὶ ἱλαροὺς τῆς ἐν Χριστῷ πολιτείας ἐξῆφθαι πρέπει Cyr.*ador.*11(1.403D); *take up, be interested in* τῆς ἰατρικῆς ἐ. Philost.*h.e.*3.15(M.65.508B); 3. *have attached to oneself*; hence, met., *be endowed with, possess* θεὸς...τοῦ παντὸς ἐξημμένος τὸ κράτος Gr.Nyss.*fat.*(M.45.152A); 4. pass., *be dependent on* ὁ... λόγος...μόνος μὲν τῆς τοῦ πατρὸς θεότητος ἐξημμένος Eus.*l.C.*4(p.202.33; M.20.1333A); Gr.Nyss.*tres dii*(M.45.125D) cit. s. ζωή.

B. *set fire to*; of combustible material feeding the flame τὴν τὸ πῦρ ~ουσαν ὕλην Gr.Nyss.*or.catech.*10(p.56.4; M.45.41D); fig. and met., *kindle*, Athenag.*res.*12(p.62.12; M.6.997B); ἄσβεστον ἐν τῇ καρδίᾳ τῆς πίστεως ἐξάψαντας τὸν λύχνον Meth.*symp.*5.3(p.55.17; M. 18.100C); ref. Rom.8:4 ἵνα τὸ δικαίωμα τοῦ...νόμου φανερωθῇ ἐξαφθὲν id.*res.*2.8(p.344.14; M.18.308A); τῆς πονηρίας αὐτοῖς ἡ δεινότης...ἐξήπτετο Eus.*v.C.*2.49(p.62.12; M.20.1028A); τῆς χάριτος μυστήριον ἐξήφθη *A.Andr.fr.*18(p.45.14); med. and pass., *blaze up* in anger, *be inflamed*, *A.Andr.*B 3(p.59.28); Ephr.1.4B; *be upset* οἱ ὀλιγόψυχοι ὑπὸ μικρᾶς ὀλιγωρίας ταχέως ~ονται Jo.Mosch.*prat.*164 (M.87.3032B).

ἐξαργυρίζ-ω, 1. *turn into money, sell up*, Clem.*q.d.s.*19(p.172.9; M.9.624B); Chrys.*hom.in 1Cor.11:19*(3.244B); Socr.*h.e.*2.17.2(M.67. 217C); 2. *calculate the cash value of*, ‡Just.*qu.et resp.*108(M.6.1356C); ἀδωροδόκητον...κριτήν, οὐκ ~οντα δώροις τὰ πταίσματα Bas.Sel.*or.* 40.2(M.85.456A); Socr.*h.e.*4.34.5(M.67.553C); 3. med., *plunder*, Iren. *haer.*2.32.4(M.7.830A).

ἐξαρεσκεύομαι, *tempt, allure*, Clem.*paed.*3.1(p.236.10; M.8.556B).

ἐξάρθρημα, τό, *dislocation*, Gr.Naz.*carm.*1.2.8.127(M.37.658A).

ἐξαρθρόω, *dislocate*, Cyr.*Ps.*6:3(M.69.744C); fig., Bas.*reg.br.*102 (2.451D; M.31.1153B); τὴν ψυχὴν ταῖς ἁμαρτίαις ἐξήρθρωτο Amph. *mesopent.*(M.39.124D).

ἐξάρθρωμα, τό, = ἐξάρθρημα, Gr.Naz.*carm.*1.2.10.716(M.37.732A).

ἐξάρθρωσις, ἡ, = foreg., Melet.*nat.hom.*28(M.64.1260C).

ἐξαριθμ-έω, *enumerate, give an account of* τίς ~ήσειε τὸν πατέρα; Ath.*gent.*47(M.25.93C).

ἐξαρκέω, 1. *suffice*; abs., *be strong*, Meth.*symp.*8.15(p.103.17; M. 18.168A); 2. pass., *be satisfied*, *Hom.Clem.*19.25; 3. c. dat., *assist, supply the needs of*, *T.Zab.*6.7.

ἐξαρμόζω, *dislocate*; pass., Cyr.*Ps.*37:4(M.69.656B).

ἐξαρνέομαι, *deny utterly, repudiate*, Thdt.*affect.*9(p.229.18; 3.935); id.*ep.*147(3.1276).

ἐξάρνησις, ἡ, *denial*, Iren.*haer.*1.21.1(M.7.657B); *Ep.Lugd.*ap. Eus.*h.e.*5.1.33(M.20.421A).

ἐξαρπάζω, *snatch away*, ptcpl. pass., *bereft of* τὸν νοῦν ἐξαρπασθέντες Hegem.*Arch.*9(p.14.6; M.10.1441A).

*__ἐξαρπάκτωρ__, ὁ, *plunderer*, of Jo. Bapt. τὸν τῆς γεέννης ἐ. Chrysipp.*enc.in Jo.Bapt.*3(p.33.16).

ἔξαρσις, ἡ, *destruction*, Clem.*str.*6.14(p.507.18; M.9.377B).

ἐξάρτημα, τό, *attachment, appendage*; plur., Tat.*orat.*17(p.18.24; M.6.844A).

ἐξάρτησις, ἡ, 1. *stretching out* of Christ's body on Cross, *A.Jo.* 101(p.201.25); 2. *fitting out, equipping* of ships, Thphn.*chron.*p.287 (M.108.704C) conj. ἐξάρτισις or ἐξάρτυσις; hence a place of this name in Constantinople, ‡Jo.D.*ep.Thphl.*18(M.95.368D).

ἐξαρτίζω, *equip*; *furnish with information, inform*, *A.*(*Pass.*) *Andr.*3(p.7.21).

ἐξαρύω, *drain dry of*; fig., *Orac.Sib.*3.640.

*__ἐξαρχῆθεν__, *from the earliest times*, Ph.Carp.*Cant.*177(M.40. 117A).

*__ἐξαρχία__, ἡ, *province*, ‡Jo.D.*Const.*21(M.95.337C).

ἔξαρχος, ὁ, A. subst.; 1. *originator, founder, author*; of a festival, Gr.Naz.*or.*39.14(M.36.349B); of a heresy, Ath.*ep.Aeg.Lib.*18(M.25. 580C); ἐ. τῆς ἀταξίας καὶ παρανομίας Thdt.*ep.*155(4.1320); Sophr.H. *ep.syn.*(M.87.3196B); ref. old covenant; of Moses, Jo.D.*hom.*1.2(M. 96.548A); of God ἐ. τῶν τῆς ἀριστείας ἔργων ἁπάντων *Pap.Chr.*(p.447); *precentor* τοὺς κληρικοὺς ψάλλειν κελεύομεν· καὶ καταζητεῖσθαι αὐτοὺς παρὰ τῶν κατὰ καιρὸν...ἐπισκόπων καὶ δύο πρωτοπρεσβυτέρων ἑκάστης ἐκκλησίας καὶ τοῦ καλουμένου ἄρχοντος ἤτοι ἐ. καὶ τοῦ ἐκδίκου ἑκάστης...ἐκκλησίας Justn.*cod.*1.3.41(p.28); 2. *leader, chief* ἐγὼ καὶ οἱ ἀδελφοί μου ἐ. σκήπτρων ἐν Ἰσραὴλ ἐσόμεθα *T.Jud.*25.1; Ath.*apol.sec.*46(p.122.14; M.25.333A); of thirty 'apostles' of Simon Magus, *Hom.Clem.*2.23; S. Peter, Isid.Pel.*epp.*1.356(M.78.385B); ταύτης τῆς ὑπουλίας ἐ. ὁ Νικομηδείας Εὐσέβιος Gel.Cyz.*h.e.*2.27.13 (M.85.1309B); τὸν τῆς πρώτης καθέδρας ἐπίσκοπον μὴ λέγεσθαι ἐ. τῶν ἱερέων *Cod.Afr.*39, v. infra 4; of Devil, *T.Sal.*3.6(M.122.1320D); hence *president, moderator*, Thdt.*ep.*147(4.1277); ἐ. [sc. τῆς συνόδου] Evagr.*h.e.*1.10(p.17.19; M.86.2443B); 3. *exarch, viceroy*, with civil and military powers, *Chron.Pasch.*p.386(M.92.989C); *ib.*p.396 (1013B); Thphn.*chron.*p.193(M.108.501B); 4. eccl., *primate* τοῦ ἐ. τῆς ἐπαρχίας, λέγω δὲ τοῦ ἐπισκόπου τῆς μητροπόλεως CSard.*can.*6; CChalc.*can.*9 cit. s. διοίκησις; CChalc.*act.*10(*ACO* 2.1.3; p.30.33; H. 2.528A); οὐδὲν ἔτι διερρωγὸς μεῖναι, ἀλλὰ τούς τε ἑκάστης διοικήσεως πατριάρχας ἀλλήλοις συμβαίνειν, τούς τε τῶν πόλεων ἐπισκόπους τοῖς ἰδίοις ἐ. ἕπεσθαι Evagr.*h.e.*4.11(p.161.30; M.86.2724A); ἐ. διοικήσεως καλεῖ τὸν πατριάρχην ἑκάστης διοικήσεως, ὑφ' ὃν οἱ τῆς ἐκείνης ἐπαρχίας τελοῦσι μητροπολῖται *Schol.* in CChalc.*can.*9(*Mon.*2 p.645); 5. *senior* of a number of heads of religious houses τῶν χωρεπισκόπων καὶ...τοῦ ἐ. τῶν παρ' ἡμῖν μοναζόντων Thdt.*ep.*113(4.1192); ἐ. τῆς... ταύτης πόλεως εὐαγῶν μοναστηρίων CCP(536)*act.*1(*ACO* 3 p.128.3; H.2.1189C); Cyr.S.*v.Sab.*30(p.115.17); Justn.*nov.*133.4(p.671.30); Thdr.Stud.*ep.*140,205(pp.125,177); 6. *archdeacon* Θεοφύλακτος... διάκονος καὶ ἐ. καὶ τὸν τόπον ἐπέχων τοῦ θρόνου Σταυροπόλεως CNic. (787)*act.*7(H.4.457E); 7. an official in S. Sophia ὁ ἐ. ἵσταται πλησίον τοῦ δευτερεύοντος ἐν τῇ ἐκκλησίᾳ. γυρεύει δὲ καὶ πᾶν σκεῦος, καὶ ἀλλαγὰς τῆς περιοχῆς τῆς ἐπισκοπῆς· ἀναθεωρεῖ δὲ καὶ τὰς κρίσεις τῆς ἁγίας ἐκκλησίας, εἰ ἐκρίθησαν δικαίως, καὶ γράφει τὰ ἀντιμίνσια· ἀναγυρεύει δὲ καὶ τῶν ἀνδρογύνων τὰ κωλύματα *Euchol.*(p.225).

B. as adj., *that takes the lead* τῆς ἐ. θείας ἱερωσύνης Max.*ep.*19(M. 91.592B).

ἐξάρχω, *take the lead in, initiate*; *excel*, c. genit., Clem.*str.*4.19 (p.301.1; M.8.1329A).

ἑξάς, ἡ, the number *six*; *group of six*, ref. Mt.25:35–36 τὴν ἑ. τῶν ἐντολῶν Gr.Nyss.*hom.15 in Cant.*(M.44.1113C); μόνη τελέως ἡ ἀγάπη διὰ τῆς ἑ. τῶν οἰκείων μερῶν κατορθωθεῖσα συνίστησι Andr.Cr.*or.*7 (M.97.941B); of a group of aeons, Val.Gn.ap.Epiph.*haer.*31.6(p.393. 7; M.41.484C).

ἐξασθεν-έω, 1. *be utterly weak*; met., Ign.*Philad.*6.2; ἐν τοῖς ἔργοις ἐ. Clem.*str.*7.16(p.72.2; M.9.541A); *be incapable* of ἐ. εἰς τὸ... ἐφαρμόσαι Eus.*d.e.*1.3(p.18.17; M.22.40D); *be ineffective* ἵνα...τοῦ ὄφεως ἡ ἀπάτη ~ήσῃ Ath.*Ar.*1.51(M.26.117C); 2. trans., *weaken*, Chrys.*hom.7.4 in Heb.*(12.79C); pass., *ib.22.1*(201C).

ἐξασκ-έω, A. *adorn, equip* δέλεαρ ἡδονῆς ἐξησκημέναι [sc. γυναῖκες] Clem.*paed.*3.11(p.274.1; M.8.644A); ref. tricks of speech ἄττα...μάλα ἀκριβῶς ἐξησκημένα Const.ap.Gel.Cyz.*h.e.*3.19.8(M.85.1345D); *prepare, dress* stone, Gr.Nyss.*v.Mos.*(M.44.322B); *construct* as adornments προπύλαια...καὶ προτεμενίσματα ἐξήσκηται Clem.*paed.*3.2 (p.238.1; M.8.560A).

B. *train*; 1. of education πάσης Ἑλληνικῆς παιδείας ἐξησκημένος *Hom.Clem.*4.7; Ἑλληνικῇ παιδείᾳ πάνυ ἐξασκήσας ἑαυτόν *ib.*2.22; ἐξησκήθη τοῖς λόγοις πρὸς διακονίαν τῶν θείων λογίων Pall.*v.Chrys.*5 (p.28.4; M.47.18); στόμα ἐξησκημένον ἐν θείοις λογίοις *ib.*13(p.80.28; M.47.46); *ib.*(p.79.20; M.47.45); τῇ ῥητορικῇ τὴν γλῶσσαν ἐξήσκημαι Jo.VI H.*v.Jo.D.*9(M.94.441C); 2. *practise*, Isid.Pel.*epp.*4.16(M.78. 1064C); Cyr.*Am.*17(3.267C); Socr.*h.e.*7.41.4(M.67.832A); Jo.VI H.*v. Jo.D.*8(M.94.441B); abs., *practise asceticism*, Pall.*v.Chrys.*20(p.125. 26; M.47.70); med., Epiph.*haer.*13.1(p.206.5; M.41.237A); perf. ptcpl. pass., *disciplined* ἐξησκημένον βίον Cyr.*Jo.*3.4(4.294D); 3. *put into practice* τὰς ἀπειλὰς καὶ τὰς τιμωρίας...ἐ. Pall.*v.Chrys.*16(p.97.25;

M.47.55); **4.** *study, learn,* Gr.Naz.*or.*7.7(M.35.761C); Ὑπατίαν...παρὰ ...τοῦ πατρὸς ~ῆσαι...τὰ μαθήματα Philost.*h.e.*8.9(M.65.504B); **5.** *profess, hold* a belief τὴν πολυκοιρανίην μᾶλλον ἤπερ τὴν μοναρχίαν ἐξησκήσατε Tat.*orat.*14(p.15.9; M.6.836B).

***ἔξασπρος**, *white, shining white, snow-white, A.Barth.*2(p.131. 23); ‡Chrys.*hom.suppl.*3.5(M.64.437C); Procl.CP *or.*9.2(M.65.773C).

ἐξάστερος (***ἔξαστρος**), *having six stars* ὁ Μαζουρὼθ ὁ λεγόμενος ἐ. Eus.Al.*serm.*22.1(M.86.453B); τῆς ἐξάστρου φωταυγίας Steph.Diac. *v.Steph.*(M.100.1097B).

ἐξαστράπτ-ω, **1.** *flash like lightning, be brilliant, dazzle*; of gold and jewels, Eus.*v.C.*3.36(p.94.10; M.20.1096C); *ib.*4.50(p.137.31; 1200C); *T.Sal.*21.2(M.122.1352A); of a statue, ‡Jo.D.*Artem.*52(p.87. 26; M.96.1300B); at Transfiguration ἐξαστράψαι τὸ πρόσωπον αὐτοῦ Eus.*e.th.*3.10(p.166.5; M.24.1017B); Ἰησοῦς...ἐμφανισθείς μοι [i.e. in a vision] ὅλος ~ων *A.Mt.*17(p.238.5); τὸ τοῦ σταυροῦ σημεῖον μεσούσης ἡμέρας, ὑπὲρ τὸν ἥλιον ~ον ‡Jo.D.*Artem.*45(p.7.18; 1293B); in heaven τοὺς...ἱερουμένους...τοῖς τῆς ἀναστάσεως ἀφθάρτοις σώμασιν ~οντας Eus.*e.th.*3.16(p.175.13; 1033C); ψυχὴν...φωτὸς ~ούσῃ στολῇ καταλαμπομένην id.*v.C.*1.2(p.8.1; M.20.912C); c. acc. cogn. φῶς ~ων ὁ καταβὰς οὐρανόθεν ἄγγελος *ib.*3.26(p.89.21; 1085B); fig. ἔχουσα [sc. ἡ ἐκκλησία]...Χριστὸν...διάδημα περικείμενον τῇ χρυσαυγεῖ ~ων (l. ~ον) λαμπρότητι *M.Ner.et Ach.*8(p.7.24); met. ὁ βίῳ καὶ λόγῳ ~ων Jo.D.*imag.*2.12(M.94.1297A); **2.** trans., *make to flash, shine forth*; fig., Meth.*symp.*6.4(p.68.15; M.18.117D); *ib.*7.2(p.73.4; 128A); of BMV ἐξαστράψασα τὴν τελείαν αὐτοῦ θεότητα ἐν σώματι Mod. *dorm.*3(M.86.3285A).

***ἔξαστρος**, v. ἐξάστερος.

***ἐξάτμημα, τό**, *exhalation,* Jo.D.*hom.*9.1(M.96.724A).

***ἐξάτμησις, ἡ**, *exhalation,* Const.Diac.*laud.*24(M.88.508B).

ἐξατμίζ-ω, *draw out like vapour,* met. τὴν ψυχὴν...χωριζομένην τοῦ σώματος ἐν τῷ ὕπνῳ...~ουσαν αὐτῷ τὴν ζωήν Nemes.*nat.hom.*3 (M.40.596B).

ἐξατον-έω, **1.** *be tired out, flag* ὁδοιποροῦντες...~οῦσαν τὴν ψυχὴν... ἔχομεν Anast.S.*qu.et resp.*127(M.89.777D); **2.** *be weakened* οὐκ ἔστιν ἡμᾶς ὑποπτεῦσαι τὴν αὐτοῦ [sc. τοῦ θεοῦ] ~ῆσαι δύναμιν Cyr.*Ps.*43:5 (M.69.1020C); morally and spiritually, †Bas.*hom.in Ps.*37(1.368C; M.30.97A); Nil.*epp.*3.243(M.79.501A); **3.** *become powerless, lose one's power,* *A.(Pass.)Andr.*14(p.32.7); Ath.*v.Anton.*39(M.26.991A); ‡Meth.*Sym.et Ann.*13(M.18.380C); **4.** c. genit., *be weary of,* Cosm. Mel.*schol.*(M.38.352).

***ἐξαυγάζομαι**, *shine brilliantly,* Philost.*h.e.*10.9(M.65.589B).

***ἐξαυγεία, ἡ**, *brilliance*; plur., *brilliant beams,* Andr.Cr.*or.*17(M. 97.1172A); fig., ‡Meth.*Sym.et Ann.*6(M.18.361C).

***ἐξαυθεντέω**, *arrogate authority,* Thdr.Stud.*epp.*1.33(M.99.1020C).

***ἐξαυθέντησις, ἡ**, *exercise of full authority,* Thdr.Stud.*test.*(M.99. 1820A); τὰ πάντα τὰ ἐν τῇ ἀδελφότητι κοινὰ εἶναι...καὶ μηδὲν κατὰ μέρος τοῦ καθέκαστον εἰς ἐ. id.*epp.*1.10(M.99.941A).

ἐξαυλέομαι, *hear the sound of the flute,* Synes.*Dion* 18(p.278.8; M.66.1161C).

ἐξαυλίζομαι, *go out of camp,* fig. ἀλλογενεῖς καὶ τῆς ἐξ Ἰσραὴλ ἀγέλης ἐξηυλισμένοι Cyr.*glaph.Num.*(1.380E).

ἐξαφανίζ-ω, **1.** *cause to disappear utterly* τὸν εὐχόμενον...τὸ τῆς ὀργῆς πάθος ἐξαφανίσαντα ἀπὸ τῆς ψυχῆς Or.*or.*9.1(p.318.1; M.11. 444A); Gr.Nyss.*or.dom.*4(p.88.18; M.44.1176B); **2.** *destroy, obliterate* ὁ λόγος...ἀπαθὴς...διαμένει, μὴ βλαπτόμενος ἀπὸ τούτων [i.e. τῶν ἰδίων τῆς σαρκός] ἀλλὰ μᾶλλον ~ων καὶ ἀπολλύων αὐτά Ath.*Ar.*3.34 (M.26.396C); id.*ep.Epict.*6(M.26.1061A, v.l. ἀφ- p.11.1); Pall.*v.Chrys.* 12(p.72.14; M.47.41); ἀχαριστίᾳ τὰς εὐεργεσίας ἐ. Isid.Pel.*epp.*1.105 (M.78.253C); hence **3.** *kill, Orac.Sib.*8.103; πρόρριζος ἐξηφανίσθη Dion.Al.ap.Eus.*h.e.*7.23.1(M.20.692A); **4.** *destroy* morally, *corrupt* τὴν ἀστρολογικὴν μάθησιν...~ειν ψυχήν Hipp.*haer.*4.2(p.33.13; M.16. 3059B); *ib.*6.41(p.172.17; 3259B); γυναῖκας ἐ. *A.Thom.*A 79(p.194.18); **5.** *rout, drive right away* τὸν διάβολον...ἐ. *V.Pach.Α* 4(p.127.11).

***ἐξαφανισμός, ὁ**, *destruction,* Or.*Jo.*20.4(p.332.1; M.14.581C); met., of passions, Nil.*epp.*3.142(M.79.449A).

ἐξαφίημι, **1.** *send forth*; *dispatch, kill*; aor. subj. in form ἐξαφήσωμεν Barth.Edess.*Agar.*(M.104.1436A); met., *reject* ἐ. τὰς προφητείας τῶν προφητῶν *Ascens.Is.*A 3.31(p.95); **2.** *let loose* οἱ πυλωροὶ τοῦ ᾅδου...ἐξαφῆκαν τὸν ᾅδην Ath.*Ar.*3.56(M.26.441A).

***ἐξαφορίζω**, *separate,* Iren.*haer.*4.21.12(M.7.1043A).

ἐξαφρίζω, *remove as foam,* †Bas.Anc.*virg.*61(M.30.796A); pass., Bas.*hex.*3.8(1.30D; M.29.73B).

***ἐξαφρισμός, ὁ**, *frothing up,* Clem.*paed.*1.6(p.114.8; M.8.297B).

ἐξαφρόομαι, *become foam,* Clem.*paed.*1.6(p.119.5; M.8.308A).

***ἐξαχνίζω**, *cover with foam,* Gr.Naz.*carm.*1.2.25.114(M.37.821A).

***ἐξαχρει-όω**, **1.** *render useless,* Areth.*Apoc.*51(M.106.709B); τὸν νοερὸν ὀφθαλμὸν ἐξηχρειωμένοι id.ap.*cat.Apoc.*5:4(p.251.10); **2.** *reckon as useless, valueless* τὴν πρόσκαιρον...~ῶν ζωήν Diad.*perf.*58 (p.64.16).

***ἑξάψαλμος, ὁ**, *six psalms* read at matins [3, 37, 42, 87, 102, and 142], Andr.Cr.*can.mag.*rubric(M.97.1329C); not on Easter Day, *Const.Stud.*2(M.99.1705B); *Euchol.*(p.6); τὸ ἑ. *Const.Stud.*3(1705B).

ἔξαψις, ἡ, *kindling*; *fire,* Chrysipp.*enc.in Thdr.*12(p.76.2); plur., *bonfires,* Jo.Mal.*chron.*8 p.206(M.97.321B).

***ἑξαωρία, ἡ**, *first six hours* of the day, Pall.*h.Laus.*108(M.34. 1211D; ἑκτὴν ὥραν p.143.12).

***ἐξεάω**, *let go, let drop, A.Petr.et Paul.*77(p.211.8); *Vaticin.*2(p.57).

ἐξεγείρ-ω, *awaken*; met., *arouse, uplift* τὸ...ταπεινὸν τῆς ψυχῆς... ~ων καὶ ἀνορθῶν μαθήμασιν ἑτέροις Gr.Thaum.*pan.Or.*8(p.22.5; M. 10.1077B); Meth.*res.*2.4(p.336.5; M.41.1168D); *ib.*2.6(p.340.9; M.18. 304C).

***ἐξεγερτικός**, *capable of raising* ἐ. ... νεκρῶν...ἡ δύναμις τοῦ κυρίου Leont.H.*Nest.*5.2(M.86.1725B).

ἐξεδαφίζω, **1.** *beat flat and hard,* Or.*exp.in Pr.*28(M.17.241D); *level* one's enemies *with the ground,* Thphn.*chron.*p.316(M.108.765C); pass., of a city, *Orac.Sib.*8.39; **2.** *dash to the ground,* Jo.Eub.*innoc.*3 (M.96.1505A).

***ἐξεικόνησις**, v. ἐξεικόνισις.

ἐξεικονίζ-ω, **1.** *shape* or *form fully* Χριστὸν τὸν...ἐξεικονίσαντα καὶ ἐκτυπώσαντα ἑαυτὸν εἰς τὸ πλάσμα τῶν χειρῶν αὐτοῦ Agath.*v.Gr.Ill.* 42(p.24); pass. ὁ καρπὸς τοῦ δένδρου ἐὰν ἐξεικονισθῇ καὶ τὴν ἑαυτοῦ μορφὴν ἀπολάβῃ Hipp.*haer.*6.9(p.137.12; M.16.3210C); Bas.*Eun.*2.8 (1.244A; M.29.585C); *Const.App.*7.3.2; Thdt.*qu.48 in Ex.*(1.156); **2.** *express the image of, represent* τὰ τέσσαρα στοιχεῖα...ἀκριβῶς ~ειν τὴν ὀγδοάδα Iren.*haer.*1.17.1(M.7.637A); ὥσπερ ἡ σκιὰ τῷ σώματι, οὕτω ταῖς ψυχαῖς αἱ ἁμαρτίαι παρέπονται, ἐναργῶς τὰς πράξεις ~ουσαι Bas.*hom.*7.6(2.58C; M.31.296C); Cyr.*thes.*6(5^1.48B); Trin. οὐ τῆς οὐσίας τῆς αὐτοσοφίας καὶ μονογενοῦς...ἀλλὰ τῆς ἐν τῷ κόσμῳ ἐξεικονισθείσης Ath.*Ar.*2.79(M.26.313C); ~ει [sc. τὸ πνεῦμα]...ἐν πᾶσιν τὸν θεόν Didym.*Trin.*1.15(M.39.317A); ὁ πατήρ, ἐν ἰδίᾳ ὑποστάσει ὤν, ~εται ἐν τῷ μονογενεῖ *ib.*2.5(504B); εἰκὼν ἀληθὴς... θεοῦ...τὸ πνεῦμα...οὐκ ἐξ εἰκόνος θείας, καθάπερ ἡμεῖς. διὰ τοῦτο γὰρ ~ον οὐκ ~εται Didym.(‡Bas.)*Eun.*5(1.302D; M.29.725B) v. infra 3; Cyr.*Jo.*1.3(4.27B); ref. Mt.3:17 οὗτός ἐστιν ὁ τὴν ἐμὴν ὑπόστασιν ~ων σαφῶς Gr.Ant.*bapt.*2.2(M.88.1873A); **3.** *form in the image of*; pass., ref. Gen.1:26 εἰκών ἐστι τὸ πνεῦμα τὸ ἐπιφερόμενον ἐπάνω τοῦ ὕδατος, ὃ ἐὰν μὴ ἐξεικονισθῇ [sc. ἄνθρωπος] μετὰ τοῦ κόσμου ἀπολεῖται Hipp. *haer.*6.14(p.140.1; M.16.3214C); Didym.(‡Bas.)*Eun.*5, v. supra 2; συμμορφούμεθα τῷ θανάτῳ αὐτοῦ· ὡς ἂν εἰ ἔλεγεν, ~όμεθα Chrys.*hom. 11.2 in Phil.*(11.286D); **4.** *image forth, portray in a picture* συνερείσας τοὺς πόδας καὶ συγκολλήσας καὶ τὰς χεῖρας ἑκατέρωθεν πετάσας εἰς τὸν ἀέρα, τοῦ σταυροῦ τὸ πάθος ἀκριβῶς ~ει τῷ σχήματι ἀκίνητος μένων Ast.Am.*phar.*(p.117.19); Anast.S.ap.Jo.D.*imag.*3 suppl.(M.94. 1416C); πῶς...πιστευθήσεται ἐκ τῆς ἁγίας παρθένου ἀνειληφέναι [sc. τὸν Χριστόν] τὴν σάρκα, εἰ μὴ ἐπ' ἴσης ἡμῖν ~οιτο; Thdr.Stud.*ref.*4 (M.99.445A); **5.** met., *represent, typify,* of threefold immersion in baptism τὴν τριήμερον...τῆς ἀναστάσεως χάριν ~ομεν Gr.Nyss.*bapt. Chr.*(M.46.585B); ~εται...ἡμῖν ὡς ἐν τοῖς κατὰ τὸν θεσπέσιον Ἰωνᾶν τὸ Χριστοῦ μυστήριον Cyr.*Jon.*proem.(3.365C); id.*glaph.Gen.*3(1. 97A); Jo.D.*hom.*1.17(M.96.572C); **6.** *imagine,* pass. αἱ παλαιαὶ ἁμαρτίαι...ἀλύπως ἐξεικονισθεῖσαι τὸν παλαιὸν μολυσμὸν ἐναποτίθενται Marc.Er.*opusc.*2.139(M.65.952B).

***ἐξεικόνισις (-ησις), ἡ**, **1.** *exact portrayal,* Jo.D.*haer.Nest.*37(M. 95.209C); **2.** *pictorial representation,* Thdr.Stud.*ref.*6(M.99.449C); in form ἐξεικόνησις *ib.*4(445B).

***ἐξεικόνισμα, τό**, *image* τὰ τῶν Ἑλλήνων γλυπτὰ...δαιμόνων ἐ. Jo. D.*f.o.*4.16(M.94.1169B).

***ἐξεικονισμός, ὁ**, **1.** *complete formation*; ref. Ex.21:22, Max. *ambig.*(M.91.1340D); **2.** *image, likeness* προσδοκῶντες τὴν θείαν ἐπαμφιέννυσθαι δόξαν, ἧς τύπος μὲν ἐν Μωυσεῖ, ἀλήθεια δὲ ἐν Χριστῷ, ἐ. δὲ εἰς ἡμᾶς Apoll.*Rom.*5:2(p.62.20); γενόμενος [sc. ὁ Χριστός] καθ' ἡμᾶς, ἵνα καὶ ἡμεῖς κατ' αὐτόν, εἰς τὸν διὰ χάριτος ἐ. ... ἀναμορφούμενοι Cyr.*hom.pasch.*10(5^2.138E); τὸν θεῖον ἐ. *ib.*(133B); id.*resp.*14 (p.599.17; 6^2.371B); **3.** *type,* id.*Abac.*33(3.548A); **4.** *imagining* γαστριμαργία...ἐ. βρωμάτων †Nil.*vit.*2(M.79.1141B).

ἐξειλεγμένως, **1.** *with discrimination,* Bas.*reg.fus.*45.2(2.392D; M. 31.1033B); **2.** *by special choice,* Cyr.*Joel.*35(3.226D).

ἐξειλ-έω, **1.** *wriggle out,* fig. ἡ γνώμη τούτων ἔκδηλος ἔσται πᾶσι, κἂν μυριάκις ὡς ἐγχέλυες ~εῖν ἐπιχειρῶσι Ath.*ep.Aeg.Lib.*8(M.25. 556A); **2.** *escape,* Ephr.1.180E; id.2.331A; Dor.*doct.*12.7(M.88.1760D); *Chron.Pasch.*p.396(M.92.1013D); ἐξηλῆσαι prob. error for ἐξειλῆσαι Dor.*doct.*8.3(1709C).

ἔξειμι (A) 1. *go forth, depart* this life ἐ. τὸν βίον Gel.Cyz.*h.e.*2.17.17(M.85.1269A); **2.** *come about, come to pass* εἰ...μὴ ἐξῄει τὰ λεγόμενα Chrys.*hom.24.2 in Jo.*(8.139D).

ἔξειμι (B), only in impers. forms, ἔξεστι *it is possible, lawful,* etc., *LS*; tautologous form ἐξόν ἐστι Ign.*Smyrn.*8.2; *M.Polyc.*12.2; Just.*1apol.*66.1(M.6.428B).

ἐξεῖπον, aor. of ἐξαγορεύω; **1.** *tell out, declare*; hence *confess*, Dor.*doct.*5.3(M.88.1680C); **2.** reflex., *denounce oneself*, Gr.Thaum. *ep.can.*9(p.565; M.10.1044D).

ἐξείρω, *put forth, expel*, Ast.Am.*hom.*2(M.40.184A).

***ἐξεισήγησις, ἡ,** *proposal, motion*, CLater.*act.*4(H.3.816B).

ἐξεκκλησιάζω, *call out to an assembly*, Gr.Nyss.*laud.Bas.*(M.46.793B).

[*]**ἐξελαστέον**, *one must expel*, Clem.*paed.*2.5(p.184.29; M.8.445C).

***ἐξελαστικός**, *that can be rowed*, Thphn.*chron.*p.333(M.108.804C).

ἐξελαύν-ω, 1. *drive out, expel* τοῦ βιοῦ ἐ. Philost.*h.e.*11.7(M.65.601C); met., *exclude*, ref. 1Cor.6:10 τοὺς λοιδορίᾳ χρωμένους ὁ ἀπόστολος ~ει τῆς βασιλείας Thdt.*eran.*1(4.31); **2.** *drive forward, urge on*, fig. μάστιγι δαιμόνων...~όμενοι Just.*1apol.*5.1(M.6.336A).

***ἐξελαφρύνω**, *make light*, Gr.Nyss.*ep.*3.2(M.46.1016C).

***ἐξελεγκτέον**, *one must refute*, Euther.*confut.*2(M.28.1314A).

ἐξέλευσις, ἡ, *going forth* κατάβασιν καὶ ἐ. τοῦ ἀγαπητοῦ ἐκ τοῦ ἑβδόμου οὐρανοῦ *Ascens.Is.*B 1.2(p.341) ∞ *Ascens.Is.*A 3.13(p.92); hence *decease*, *A.Phil.*137(p.69.14); met., *expression, utterance*, ‡Proc.G.*Pr.*1:20(M.87.1229C).

ἐξελίσσ-ω, *follow* a course; of heavenly bodies, *1Clem.*20.3; met. οὐδὲ οἱ ἄγγελοι παρὰ τὸ διατεταγμένον αὐτοῖς οὐδὲν ἕτερον ~ουσιν *Sent.App.*2(p.85).

ἐξέλκ-ω, 1. lit., *drag out*; **a.** *rescue* from slavery, Or.*Jo.*6.2(p.107.28; M.14.200B); **b.** *drag off, flay off* τῶν δερμάτων τῶν ἀπὸ τῶν... ἱερείων ~ομένων Chrys.*hom.7.1 in Heb.*(12.72B); **2.** met., *drag out* τὴν ἐμὴν πίστιν ἀπὸ τῆς ἐμῆς ~ειν ψυχῆς Const.ap.Gel.Cyz.*h.e.*2.7.29(M.85.1237D); *draw forth, attract, entice* τοὺς ~οντας ἡμᾶς εἰς πάθη Meth.*res.*2.5(p.338.4; M.18.301C); *ib.*2.7(p.341.4; 305A); Chrys.*hom.9.4 in Eph.*(11.74C).

***ἐξέλκωμα, τό,** *ulcer*, Isid.Pel.*epp.*1.391(M.78.404A).

ἐξελληνίζω, 1. *turn into Greek*, Gr.Nyss.*hom.13 in Cant.*(M.44.1056A); *cat.Apoc.*8:3(p.300.21); **2.** *put into a Greek form* ὀνόματα Or.*Jo.*2.33(27; p.90.20; M.14.172C); Thdt.*qu.61 in Gen.*(1.74); Proc.G.*Ex.*12:2(M.87.561B); **3.** *call by a Greek name* ἐξελληνισθέντα τὸν τόπον id.*Is.*6:13(M.87.1948D).

***ἐξέμεσις, ἡ,** *vomiting*; of heresy, Epiph.*haer.*76.2(p.342.12; M.42.517D).

ἐξεμ-έω, *vomit forth*; fig., of teaching heresy, Ath.*Ar.*1.10(M.26.32A); Epiph.*haer.*64.5(p.413.13; M.41.1077C); Cyr.*Jo.*9.1(4.798C); μὴ πέραν τῆς [ἑαυτῶν] ~οῦντες, τὰς ὑγιαινούσας...χώρας τοῖς λοιμικοῖς τρόποις αὐτῶν διαφθείρειν Isid.Pel.*epp.*1.484(M.78.445C); *disgorge*, fig. ἵνα ἀποπνιχθεὶς ὁ θὴρ...ζῶντας ἐξεμέσῃ *Ep.Lugd.*ap.Eus.*h.e.*5.2.6(M.20.436B).

***ἐξέμημα, τό,** *vomit*; fig., ref. 2Petr.2:22 ἐ. τῆς ἀσεβείας CLater.*act.*1(H.3.700C).

***ἐξεμπλάριον, τό,** (Lat. *exemplarium*) **1.** *sample, token* τὸ ἐ. ἀγάπης ὑμῶν ἔλαβον...ἐν τῷ ἐπισκόπῳ ὑμῶν Ign.*Trall.*3.2; id.*Eph.*2.1; **2.** *example, pattern* ὄφελον πάντες αὐτὸν ἐμιμοῦντο, ὄντα ἐ. θεοῦ διακονίας id.*Smyrn.*12.1; of Christ ἑαυτὸν ἑτοιμάσας τοῖς πιστοῖς λαοῖς ἀγαθὸν ἀρετῆς ἐ. Max.*qu.Thal.*65(M.90.769A); of Christians τὸν οἰκεῖον βίον πρὸς μίμησιν παρέχοντες...ἐξαίρετον ἀρετῆς ἐ. id.*cap.*4.86(M.90.1341C); **3.** *type* πῶλος, τὸ τῶν ἀλογίστων ἐθνῶν τὸ πρὶν ἀλόγιστον ἐξεμβλάριον (sic) ‡Meth.*palm.*2(M.18.388A).

***ἔξεμπλον, τό,** *copy of a document*, *Cod.Afr.*134(Lat. *exemplum*).

***ἐξενδύομαι**, *take off*, *Mir.Geo.*6(p.69.19).

ἐξεόω, v. ἐξωθέω.

***ἐξεπίγονος**, *born, produced later*, ‡Chrys.*pasch.*6.3(8.268B; conj. ἐπίγονα p.147.6).

***ἐξέπροσεν**, (cf. modern Greek ξέσπροξε from ξεσπρόχνω) *thrust away*, *Dial.Tim.et Aquil.*97 r°.

***ἐξεπωθέω**, *drive out*, met. ἀκηδίαν ἐξεπώσωμεν †Cyr.*hom.div.*14(5^2.415C).

ἐξέραμα, τό, *vomit*; of Arianism, Ath.*h.Ar.*80(p.228.13; M.25.792A); id.*decr.*4(p.3.29; M.25.421B); id.*Ar.*2.1(M.26.148A).

***ἐξεράνησις, ἡ,** v. ἐξερεύνησις.

ἐξεράω, 1. *vomit forth*; fig., of heretics, Ath.*apol.sec.*59(p.139.17; M.25.357A); **2.** *take out*, Synes.*ep.*130(M.66.1513B).

ἐξεργάζ-ομαι, 1. *make* ἀγαθὸν...ἑαυτὸν ἐ. Clem.*str.*7.7(p.36.29; M.9.469A); Meth.*symp.*8.17(p.111.1; M.18.173B); id.*res.*1.42(p.289.8; M.41.1112C); pass. αἰγὸς...εἰς ἀσκὸν ἐξεργασθέντος ‡Caes.Naz.*dial.*103(M.38.969); **2.** pass., *be worked* or *developed*, of a building site τόπου ~εσθαι μέλλοντος Didym.*Trin.*3.1(M.39.781C).

ἐξεργασία, ἡ, 1. *execution, performance* ἐ. τῶν πρὸς ἀρετὴν... συντεινόντων Clem.*str.*6.17(p.513.14; M.9.392A); **2.** *production* τῆς τροφῆς ἐ. ‡Caes.Naz.*dial.*139(M.38.1045); **3.** *operation, activity*, Clem.*str.*6.17(p.511.32; M.9.388A); **4.** *working* χρυσίου ἐ. *wrought gold*, id.*paed.*2.10(p.219.21; M.8.521A); **5.** *elaboration* of a theme, Bas.*ep.*125.2(3.216B; M.32.549A).

ἐξεργαστικός, *productive* ἡ πολυαρχία...πολέμων ἐ. *Hom.Clem.*9.2; Gr.Nyss.*hex.*7(M.44.69A).

ἐξερεύγ-ομαι, *vomit forth, belch forth*; fig., of Devil θάνατον ~ομένου Eus.*h.e.*10.4.14(M.20.853B); met., *utter*; of emission of Logos, Thphl.Ant.*Autol.*2.10(M.6.1064C); Const.*ep.*ap.Gel.Cyz.*h.e.*3.19.4(M.85.1345B); Jo.VI H.*v.Jo.D.*32(M.94.473B).

ἐξερευνάω, *seek*, Thphyl.*exc.gent.*14(p.487.27; M.113.949D).

ἐξερεύνησις, ἡ, *investigation*, Bas.*Eun.*1.14(1.227A; M.29.545A); in form ἐξεράνησις, Jo.D.*haer.*suppl.(M.94.780A).

ἐξέρευξις, ἡ, *belching forth*; fig., Epiph.*haer.*25.4(p.271.7; M.41.325A).

ἐξερημόω, *lay waste*, Philost.*h.e.*11.8(M.65.604A,C).

***ἐξέρκετον, τό,** (Lat. *exercitus*) *army*, Jo.Mal.*chron.*16 p.394(M.97.581C); Maur.*ep.*(M.*PL.*87.103B); *Chron.Pasch.*p.306(M.92.777A).

ἐξέρπ-ω, 1. *creep forth*; hence, of H. Ghost, *proceed* τὸ πνεῦμα... τῆς ἀνωτάτω πασῶν ~ον οὐσίας Cyr.*thes.*34(5^1.353E); **2.** *swarm*, SM Ex.1:7 ap.Proc.G.ad loc.(M.87.513A); trans., *swarm with*, Epiph. *haer.*13.1(p.206.15; M.41.237B).

ἐξέρχομαι, 1. *go* or *come out*; from secular life τῷ βίῳ ἀποταξάμενος ἐξέλθῃ εἰς τοὺς ἀδελφούς Ephr.1.315F; from church during liturgy μετ' αὐτῶν [sc. τῶν ἀκροωμένων ὁ ἀκοινώνητος] ἐξελεύσεται Bas.*ep.*217 *can.*56(3.326B; M.32.797A); *depart* this life ἐ. τοῦ βίου Marc.Diac.*v.Porph.*11; or world, *2Clem.*5.1; ἐ. ἐκ τοῦ σκηνώματος αὐτοῦ Hegem.*Arch.*10(p.16.4; M.10.1444A); τὸν βίον ἐ. Or.*Cels.*5.27(p.28.7; M.11.1221B); Meth.*fr.14 in Job*(p.515.13); Chrys.*hom.4.5 in Heb.*(12.47D); abs. τῇ κεφαλῇ τοῦ ἐξελθόντος Iren.*haer.*1.21.5(M.7.165B); Or.*hom.2.3 in Jer.*(p.20.7; M.13.281B); ἐὰν ἐξέλθῃ ἡ ψυχὴ μὴ γνοῦσα τὴν ἀλήθειαν Hegem.*Arch.*11(p.18.10; 1445A); **2.** *issue forth*, Or.*Jo.*1.36(41; p.46.16; M.14.96A); of procession of H. Ghost, Epiph.*haer.*76.3(p.343.19; M.42.520D); **3.** *burst forth* εἰς ἑτέραν κακίαν ἐ. Chrys.*hom.60.1 in Mt.*(7.605E); *transgress*, Meth.*symp.*4.4(p.50.3; M.18.92B); **4.** *digress*, Thdt.*Dan.*11:37(2.1289); **5.** trans., *go through, describe, recount*, Gr.Thaum.*pan.Or.*13(p.29.1; M.10.1088A); Men. *exc.Rom.*3(p.177.12; M.113.860D); **6.** of speech, *proceed forth*, *Barn.*11.8; *ib.*19.4.

ἐξετάζ-ω, 1. *scrutinize*; pass., *be under scrutiny* ἐν τρισὶν ἔτεσιν ἐξετασθήσονται ἐν μετανοίᾳ Petr.I Al.*ep.can.*7(M.18.480A); **2.** *examine, approve* τὸν ἐν...εὐσεβείᾳ ~όμενον Clem.*str.*7.8(p.37.19; M.9.472A); Const.*or.s.c.*4(p.157.29; M.20.1241C); *try* a criminal; of judgement after death, Anast.*mort.*(*Mon.*2 p.287); **3.** *question* ἐ. τί τινος Const.*ep.*ap.Gel.Cyz.*h.e.*3.19.5(M.85.1345B); ἐ. τινά τι Chrys. *hom.2.5 in Mt.*(7.29C); abs., *conduct an inquiry* περὶ τοῦ Φαραὼ ἐ. Or.*princ.*3.1.17(p.225.14; M.11.284A); **4.** pass., *be counted among*; hence *be found*, Meth.*arbitr.*13(p.179.3; M.18.261C); Const.ap.Eus. *v.C.*3.18(p.86.14; M.20.1077A); τοὺς τῶν ἀποστόλων ἐξετασθέντας ἐν συζυγίαις Eus.*h.e.*3.30.1(M.20.277C); τοὺς πρὸ σοῦ ἐν ταῖς ὁμοίαις περιφανείαις ἐξετασθέντας Bas.*hom.*3.5(2.21D; M.31.209D); Thdt.*Is.*53:8(2.360).

ἐξέτασις, ἡ, 1. *test* διὰ πυρὸς ἐ. Thdr.Mops.*1Cor.*3:14–15(p.175.24; M.66.880C); **2.** *insight* τὸν προφήτην πάσῃ τῇ προφητικῇ ἐ. δοκιμάσαντα *Hom.Clem.*1.19; **3.** *exactitude, precision*, *Ev.Thom.*A 6(p.145).

ἐξεταστήριον, τό, *test*, Or.*mart.*6(p.8.1; M.11.572A).

ἐξεταστής, ὁ, *examiner, investigator* ἀκροαταὶ καὶ ἐ. [sc. παραδοξοτέρων λόγων] Just.*dial.*38.2(M.6.557B); τῶν ἁμαρτημάτων τοῦ πλησίον ...ἐ. Chrys.*hom.11.1 in 1Cor.*(10.87B); id.*hom.9.5 in Phil.*(11.272D); of God ὁ τῆς ἀληθείας ἐ. Euthal.Diac.*Ac.*proem.(M.85.697A); of Christ ὁ τῶν ἡμετέρων διανοιῶν ἐ. Sev.Ant.*cat.Lc.*23:43(p.170.13).

ἐξεταστικός, 1. *capable of investigating* κρίσις ἐ. τῶν πράξεων καὶ τοῦ φρονήματος ⟨ἐξ⟩ ἑκάστου Or.*fr.42 in Jo.*(p.516.26); θεῖον δικαστήριον οὐ μόνον πραγμάτων οὐδὲ ῥημάτων ἀλλὰ καὶ ἐννοιῶν ἐ. Isid. Pel.*epp.*5.186(M.78.1444A); abs., *given to inquiry, inquisitive*, Gr. Naz.*or.*23.6(M.35.1157C); Max.*ambig.*(M.91.1077C); comp., Areth. *Apoc.*71(M.106.784A); superl., Gr.Thaum.*pan.Or.*14(p.31.10; M.10.1089C); **2.** *investigatory* κατὰ τὸν ἀκριβῆ καὶ ἐ. λόγον τὴν κρίσιν ποιήσασθαι Just.*1apol.*2.3(M.6.329B); *Hom.Clem.*1.20; **3.** neut. as subst., *investigation*, Or.*princ*.3.1.17(p.227.13; M.11.285A); Gr.Naz. *or*.43.11(M.36.508C).

ἐξεταστικῶς, 1. *with diligent search*, Or.*Jo*.13.46(p.272.30; M.14. 481A); **2.** *by the method of inquiry* Σωκράτης...ἐ. ταῦτα εἰς φανερὸν ἐπειρᾶτο φέρειν Just.*1apol*.5.3(M.6.336B).

***ἐξετεροτροπέω,** *be thoroughly different in disposition*, Cyr.*Jo*.5.5 (4.550B).

ἐξέτορε, for ἐξέθορε (ἐκθρώσκω, *come forth*), Cyr.*glaph.Gen*.2(1.31E).

ἐξευγενίζ-ω, 1. *make free*, ‡Ath.*diab*.6(p.7.26) cit. s. ἀνεκτίθημι; **2.** *make noble, ennoble*, Jo.Mal.*chron*.4 p.71(M.97.152A); morally and spiritually, Or.*Cels*.3.54(p.249.17; M.11.992A); id.*or*.16.1(p.336. 17; M.11.468C); Ῥοὺθ...ἐπὶ τοσοῦτον ~ομένης ὡς...τὸν κύριον ἡμῶν ἀπ' αὐτῆς ἀνατεῖλαι †Bas.*Is*.290(1.601A; M.30.629C); τοῦ ~οντος ἡμᾶς Χριστοῦ Pall.*h.Laus*.49(p.143.20; M.34.1212A); of things ἐπίφθονος γλῶττα, ἣν ἐν τοῖς ἔξωθεν παιδευθεῖσαν λόγοις, τοῖς θείοις ἐξηυγενίσαμεν Gr.Naz.*or*.36.4(M.36.269B); *ib*.36.11(277D); *Schol*.11 in Max.*qu. Thal*.25(M.90.337D); fig. ἡ ταῖς ἀκάνθαις χερσωθεῖσα γῆ διὰ τῆς τοῦ λόγου ἐπιδημίας ~εται Abr.Eph.*annunt*.3(p.444.26).

ἐξευμενίζ-ω, more often med.; **1.** *propitiate* ἀγαθοεργίαις ~ειν τὸ θεῖον Bas.*renunt*.1(2.202D; M.31.628B); *Const.App*.2.12.3; ~οντες τὸν δίκαιον Chrys.*hom.52.4 in Gen*.(4.511E); τῇ φιλανθρωπίᾳ μίαν ἔχοντας θρησκείαν οὕτως ~εσθαι τὸ θεῖον *M.Ariadn*.4(p.125.5); by a church formerly a pagan temple νῦν θεὸς ~εται *CIG* 8627; ref. Lc. 23:34 Ἰησοῦν...τὸν πατέρα ὑπὲρ αὐτῶν ~όμενον Nil.*epp*.3.108(M.79. 436A); διὰ σωματικῆς ᾤοντο νηστείας ~εσθαι τὸν θεόν Proc.G.*Is*.58:3 (M.87.2587D); Jo.Jej.*poenit.cont.virg*.(M.88.1957C); **2.** *make peace between* two parties, Or.*Cels*.8.63(p.279.26; M.11.1611C); *Lit*.ap. *Const.App*.8.12.31; abs., *make propitiation*, *Pers.capt*.(M.86.3257C); **3.** *offer as propitiation*, Or.*comm.in 1Cor*.7:23(*JTS* 9 p.508); **4.** *make propitious* τῆς χάριτος τοῦ θεοῦ...πάντα ~ούσης αὐτῷ Chrys. *hom.4.6 in Ac*.9:1(3.140A).

ἐξευμενισμός, ὁ, *propitiation*, Or.*Cels*.8.65(p.280.23; M.11.1613B).

ἐξευμενιστέον, *one must propitiate*, Or.*Cels*.8.64(p.280.1; M.11. 1612C).

[*]**ἐξεύρεμα, τό,** *invention*, Ath.*Ar*.2.39(M.26.229C) conj. -ημα.

ἐξευρετέον, *one ought to find out*, Clem.*str*.4.2(p.250.2, v.l. ἐξευρητέον M.8.1217B).

***ἐξευρύνομαι,** *extend*, Cyr.*Os*.114(3.145B).

ἐξευτελίζω, *undervalue, depreciate*, Meth.*res*.2.24(p.379.15; M.18. 289B); met., *disparage, despise*, Or.*hom.19.12 in Jer*.(p.168.14; M. 13.488B); †Bas.*Is*.122(1.464A; M.30.316C); Gr.Nyss.*bapt.Chr*.(M.46. 581C); Aug.ap.Thdt.*eran*.2(4.165); Isid.Pel.*epp*.2.52(M.78.496A); ἑαυτὸν ἐξηυτέλιζεν τοσαύτην ταπεινοφροσύνην...κεκτημένος ‡Pall.*h. mon*.26(p.86.3; M.65.450B); med., *cheapen oneself*, Chrys.*hom.23.3 in Rom*.(9.689D).

***ἐξεφημερία, ἡ,** *turn for daily duty*, Tim.Ant.*nativ.Jo.Bapt*.1(M. 28.908C).

***ἐξεχθρός,** *utterly hateful* ἐ. θεῷ...τὸ ἄτακτον Sophr.H.*or*.8.2(M. 87.3357A).

ἔξηβος, *past one's youth*; met., *on the wane* ἐ. ... ὀργαῖς Cyr.*Jo*. 3.4(4.271B).

ἐξηγ-έομαι, A. *rule*; **1.** in gen., pres. ptcpl., *superior* in a monastery, Mac.Aeg.*perf*.9(M.34.848B); *ib*.8(848A); **2.** *lead the way*, met. τῷ πρὸς τὴν σωτηρίαν ἡμῶν ~ουμένῳ Gr.Nyss.*or.catech*.35(p.131.11; M.45.88A).

B. *expound*, esp. scripture; *interpret as (referring to)* ὅπου ὁ νόμος τοῦ κυρίου ἄμωμος εἴρηται, οὐχὶ τὸν μετ' ἐκεῖνον μέλλοντα ἀλλὰ τὸν διὰ Μωυσέως ~εῖσθε Just.*dial*.34.1(M.6.548A); τοῦτον τὸν ψαλμὸν ὅτι εἰς τὸν Ἑζεκίαν...εἰρῆσθαι ~εῖσθαι τολμᾶτε *ib*.33.1(545B); abs., *compile a commentary*, Vict.*Mc*.proem.(p.263.6); *teach*, Jo.Mosch. *prat*.171(M.87.3040A); *preach*, Thphn.*chron*.p.76(M.108.236B).

C. *tell, narrate*, Chrys.*hom.85.3 in Jo*.(8.508A).

ἐξήγησις, ἡ, 1. *statement*; *telling, expression* τῆς τελειότητος αὐτῆς [sc. ἀγάπης] οὐκ ἔστιν ἐ. *1Clem*.50.1; **2.** *interpretation, exposition*; hence *version* ἐν τῇ τῶν ἑβδομήκοντα ἐ. Just.*dial*.124.3(M.6. 765A); *commentary*, Eus.*h.e*.4.23.6(M.20.385B); Ἐφραὶμ...ἐν ταῖς αὐτοῦ ἐ. Epiph.*haer*.51.22(p.284.19).

ἐξηγητικός, 1. *given to exposition*, †Bas.*ep*.42(3.127A; M.32.352A); **2.** neut. plur. as subst., *expository works, commentaries*, Clem.*str*.4. 12(p.284.5; M.8.1289A); Or.*Jo*.20.44(33; p.388.31; M.14.677D); Vict. *Mc*.1:1(p.266.13).

ἐξηγορία, ἡ, *confession*, *Pss.Sal*.9:12; Olymp.*Job* 22:22(M.93. 249A).

ἐξηκοστός, *sixtieth*; neut. as subst., *minute* or *second* κατὰ ποίου ἐ. ... καὶ κατὰ ποίου ἐ. τοῦ ἐ. Or.*comm.in Gen*.ap.Eus.*p.e*.6.11(294A; M.12.77B); τὸ πρῶτον ἢ τὸ δεύτερον ἐ. *ib*.(294B; M.80A).

ἐξηλιάζω, *hang up in the sun*, ref. 2Reg.21:9, †Cyr.*coll.VT*(6[4]. 54A; M.77.1256C); Thdt.*qu.42 in 2Reg*.(1.445).

***ἐξηλιασμός, ὁ,** *exposure to, hanging up in the sun*, †Cyr.*coll.VT* (6[4].54B; M.77.1256C).

***ἐξῆλιξ,** prob. *beyond youth, elderly* πρωτοτόκους καὶ ἀρτιτόκους, ...ἐ. καὶ ἀφήλικας Didym.*Trin*.2.14(M.39.708B).

ἐξηλλαγμένως, *quite differently*, Chrys.*hom.26.3 in 1Cor*.(10. 231A); Cyr.*hom.pasch*.6(5[2].63C).

ἐξηλόω, *unfasten, detach*; met., Gr.Agr.*Eccl*.9.5(M.98.1092A); τῶν παθῶν ἐ. ... τὰς αἰσθήσεις Max.*qu.Thal*.48(M.90.441A); *ib*.6(280D).

ἐξημαρτημένως, *wrongly, perversely*, Clem.*str*.7.17(p.74.30; M.9. 545C).

ἐξημερ-όω, 1. *tame, humanize*; med., Clem.*str*.7.3(p.12.13; M.9. 420C); **2.** *placate, pacify* ἐ. ἐφ' ἑαυτοῖς τὸν λυτρωτήν Cyr.*Os*.72(3. 107C); *ib*.105(Pusey p.198.21; Aubert om.); ~οῖ [sc. νηστεία] τὸν δεσπότην, κατευνάζει τὴν ὀργήν id.*Joel*.27(3.219A).

ἐξήνιος, *unbridled*; met., *unrestrained, headstrong* τὴν ἀπειθῆ καὶ ἐ. καὶ κυριοκτόνον τῶν Ἰουδαίων πληθύν Cyr.*Os*.5(3.25B); ἐ. καὶ τῶν θείων ἐνταλμάτων καταφρονηταί *ib*.24(47A); cf.id.*Jo*.2.5(4.209A); masc. as subst., id.*Nah*.3(3.478D); neut. as subst., *unruliness, lawlessness, lack of restraint*, id.*glaph.Num*.(1.393E); id.*Is*.1.4(2.110B); *ib*.(120A); id.*Ps*.94:1(M.69.1240B).

ἐξηπλωμένως, *fully, largely*, Olymp.*Job* 22:4(M.93.240A).

ἐξῃρημένως, *transcendently* υἱὸς...ὁμοούσιος ἐ. παρὰ πάντα καὶ ἰδιαζόντως Apoll.*ep.Bas*.1(M.32.1104D); Dion.Ar.*d.n*.4.1(M.3.693B).

***ἐξησκημένως,** *after training*, Cyr.*ador*.4(1.107C).

ἐξηχ-έω, 1. *sound forth, utter*, intrans. τὸ κήρυγμα...τὸ εὐαγγελικὸν εἰς πᾶσαν ~ῆσαν τὴν οἰκουμένην Eus.*d.e*.6.1(p.253.32; M.22.417A); **2.** *deafen*, Clem.*paed*.2.4(p.181.24; M.8.440B); *ib*.2.7(p.193.13; 464C); fig., *stupefy, bewilder* ~εῖ με, οὐ παρακολουθήσω τῇ διανοίᾳ αὐτοῦ *Ev.Thom*.A 7(p.147); pass., Hipp.*haer*.5.23(p.125.16; M.16.3191B); *make to resound*, pass. τὰς ἐκκλησίας ἁπάσας τῆς Μακεδονίας... ~εῖσθαι μαθούσας τὰ κατὰ τὴν πίστιν αὐτῶν Chrys.*hom.2.2 in 2Thess*. (11.516E); **3.** *utter senseless sounds*; med., *V.Dan*.3(p.60.12).

ἐξήχησις, ἡ, *loud sound* γέλωτος ἐ. Olymp.*Eccl*.7:7(M.93.561C).

ἐξηχία, ἡ, *madness, insanity*, *T.Sal*.10.3(M.122.1332A); Mac.Mgn. *apocr*.4.2(p.160.4); Jo.Mal.*chron*.5 p.134(M.97.229D).

***ἐξηχόομαι,** *be made mad, driven insane*, Leont.N.*v.Sym*.48(M. 93.1729B).

ἔξηχος, *stupefied*, Jo.Mal.*chron*.5 p.95(M.97.181B); *stupid, foolish*, Jo.Clim.*scal*.4(M.88.721C); Leont.N.*v.Sym*.33(M.93.1712B).

ἐξι-άομαι, *heal completely*; of spiritual healing, by Christ, Gr. Nyss.*ep*.1(M.46.1005A); Max.*ambig*.(M.91.1317A,1321A); of man by sorrow for sins of others, Bas.*hom*.5.9(2.42D; M.31.257D); ἡ... Ματθαίου ψυχὴ...~ωμένη διὰ τοῦ εὐαγγελίου τοὺς τῇ καρδίᾳ τυφλώττοντας Andr.Caes.*Apoc*.67(M.106.436D).

***ἐξιατρεύω,** = foreg., Isid.Pel.*epp*.1.437(M.78.424A).

ἐξιδιάζ-ω, *be peculiar* to κατατολμῶν εἰς ~ουσαν ἑαυτῇ θείαν ἐνέργειαν ἑκάστην ὑπόστασιν τῶν τριῶν μεταχωροῦσαν παραληρεῖν Areth.*Apoc*.1(M.106.508B); οὐδὲν ἐπὶ τῆς...τριάδος ~όμενον ὁρᾶται, πλὴν τῆς ἰδιοποιούσης ἐν αὐτῇ προσώπου ὑπάρξεως *ib*.7(548D); *ib*. (553A).

ἐξιδιόομαι, 1. *appropriate to oneself*, ‡Eust.*hex*.(M.18.756B); **2.** *be peculiar* to, Areth.*Apoc*.1(M.106.508A).

***ἐξιδίωσις, ἡ,** *peculiar characteristic*, Areth.ap.*cat.Apoc*.13:8 (p.377.6).

ἐξίημι, perf. intrans., *have departed*, Epiph.*haer*.59.10(p.376.2; M. 41.1033B); met., *have diverged* from a pattern, Cyr.*ador*.2(1.61B).

ἐξικνέομαι, *reach, attain*; c. infin., *be able*, Thdt.*provid*.3(4.520).

ἐξιλάσκ-ομαι, *propitiate*; *atone for*, Gr.Nyss.*ep.can*.6(M.45.233C); ‡Chrys.*eleem*.3(9.835C); *make atonement* οἱ ἄγγελοι...~όμενοι πρὸς κύριον ἐπὶ πάσαις ταῖς ἀγνοίαις τῶν δικαίων *T.Lev*.3.5.

ἐξίλασμα, τό, *atonement, propitiatory offering*, Gr.Naz.*carm*.1.2. 34.140(M.37.955A); Isid.Pel.*epp*.1.411(M.78.412A); Jo.D.*imag*.2.1(M. 94.1284B); of eucharist ἐ. τῶν ἡμετέρων πλημμελημάτων *Lit.Jac*. (p.194.15).

ἐξιλασμός, ὁ, *atonement, propitiation*, Afric.*chron*.15(M.10.80B); of Christ's baptism τοῦ σώματος ὑπὲρ ἡμῶν ἐ. ‡Ath.*serm.fid*.24(p.20; M.26.1277C); ἐ. τῶν ἡμαρτημένων Bas.*hom.in Ps*.29(1.127C; M.29. 313A); Gr.Nyss.*mart*.1.2(M.46.765C).

***ἐξιλαστέον,** *one must avert by propitiation* ἐ. τῇ παραυτίκα τίσει τὰς κάτω ποινάς Synes.*ep*.44(M.66.1369D).

ἐξιλε-όω, A. act., *propitiate*, Chrys.*hom.14.3 in 2Cor*.(10.541E); id.*hom.13.4 in Jo*.(8.77B).

B. med.; **1.** *propitiate*, Or.*enarr.in Job* 2:9(M.17.61B); εὐχαῖς καὶ λιτανείαις...~οῦσθαι τὸν Χριστὸν ἡμῖν Const.*or.s.c*.26(p.192.29;

M.20.1316B); διὰ μετανοίας καὶ ἐξομολογήσεως ἐξιλεωθείη [sc. ὁ κύριος] παρ' ἡμῶν ‡Bas.*struct.hom.*2.8(1.342D; M.30.52A); ὁ νηστεύων ἐ. τὸν θεόν Chrys.*hom.57.4 in Mt.*(7.581B); ἐ. τὸν κριτὴν τῇ τῶν ἐντολῶν αὐτοῦ φυλακῇ Thdt.*Is.*16:14(p.78.27; 2.278); Max.*ambig.*(M.91.1152B); **2.** *expiate* φόνῳ τὸν φόνον ἐ. Ammon.*1Petr.3:19–20* (M.85.1609A); Chrys.*hom.52.5 in Mt.*(7.536E); Dor.*doct.*15.1(M.88. 1788B); **3.** *purge from guilt* τὸν 'Ισραὴλ διὰ τοῦ αἵματος ~ούμενος Chrysipp.*enc.in Jo.Bapt.*2(p.32.4); Jo.Mal.*chron.*5 p.135(M.97. 232A); in form ἐξιλευόμενοι Cyr.H.*catech.*23.10(p.386; ed. and M. ~ούμενοι).

***ἐξιλεύω,** v. foreg.

***ἐξιλεωτικός,** *appeasable*; neut. as subst., *readiness to be propitiated,* Hadr.*introd.*20(M.98.1280A); ὦτα καὶ ἀκοὴν τὸ ἐ. αὐτοῦ καὶ τῆς ἡμετέρας δεκτικὸν δεήσεως ‡Cyr.*Trin.*12(6².18B; M.77.1148A) = Jo.D.*f.o.*1.11(M.94.841B).

ἐξιππάζομαι, *ride out,* Synes.*ep.*132(M.66.1516D); s.v.l., *gallop forth* ἐξιππάσονται οἱ ἵπποι Abac.1:8 cit. by Thdr.Mops.ad loc.(M. 66.429C; LXX ἱππεῖς).

ἐξίπτ-αμαι, *fly out* or *away,* met. κακία...τὸ εἶδος ἔχουσα πορνικόν, ἡ ποιεῖ τὰς νέων ~ασθαι καρδίας Or.*exp.in Pr.*7:6(M.17.181A); [sc. παρθενίᾳ] τὸ τῆς ψυχῆς...πτέρωμα τῶν ἀνθρωπίνων ~ασθαι...ἐθιζόμενον σπουδασμάτων Meth.*symp.*8.1(p.81.9; M.18.140A).

ἕξις, ἡ, *having*; *habit*; def., Jo.D.*dialect.*58(M.94.646B); **1.** *having, being in possession*; ? met., *tenacity* πρόσεσχέ μοι ὁ γέρων μετὰ ἕ. καὶ λύπης *Apophth.Patr.*(M.65.192D); **2.** *being in a certain state, permanent condition*; **a.** *state* of body, *estate,* ref. Jo.21:5 τοὺς ἤδη ἐν ἕ. τῶν γνωρίμων παῖδας προσειπών Clem.*paed.*1.5(p.97.1; M.8. 261B); ref. 1Cor.13:11 νήπιον μὲν ἕξει τὴν παροῦσαν γνῶσιν, ἀνδρὸς δὲ τελείου γνῶσιν τὴν μέλλουσαν παραβάλλων Chrys.*incomprehens.*1.3 (1.447A); hence abs., *developed state, maturity* τὴν πρώτην τῶν ἄρτι στοιχειουμένων εἰσαγωγὴν...τὴν τῶν ἐν ἕ. ... ἀκρόασιν Eus.*h.e.*6.15 (M.20.553B); id.*d.e.*1.8(p.39.6; M.22.76B); ὅταν ἐν ἑ. γένηται, ἀφίσταται ὁ παιδαγωγός Chrys.*comm.in Gal.*3:24(10.703D); id.*hom.12.7 in 1Cor.*(10.107D); **b.** natural *state* ἀνατρεπτικὴ τοῦ ταῦτα [sc. θεὸν καὶ ὕλην] συνυπάρχειν...ἡ τῆς ἐναντίας ἕ. διαφορά Dion.Al.ap.Eus.*p.e.*7.19 (334A; M.21.564B); ἐν τῷ ἰδίῳ τῆς ἕ. αὐτοῦ τύπῳ τῶν γενητῶν ἕκαστον μένειν Meth.*res.*1.49(p.303.9; M.18.280A); Chrys.*hom.46.2 in Mt.*(7. 483D); *system* γῆς ἀναρπαζομένης ἀεὶ εἰς τὴν ἕ. τοῦ ξύλου Meth.*res.* 2.9(p.347.20; M.18.308C); **3.** *state* or *habit of mind,* ref. 1Cor.7:34 λέγει...τὴν μὲν ἕ. 'πνεῦμα', τὴν δὲ πρακτικὴν ἐνέργειαν 'σῶμα' Didym. *Trin.*2.6(M.39.528A); Eus.*e.th.*3.2(p.139.19; M.24.972D); Bas.*Eun.* 2.17(1.252B; M.29.605B) cit. s. ἐπιτηδειότης; *good state of mind, state of intelligence* μὴ πρὸς τὴν ἀρχὴν ἀποκάμωμεν τοῦ διηγήματος...ἂν ἐν ἕ. γενώμεθα, ταχέως πρὸς τὸ τέλος ἥξομεν Chrys.*hom.8.2 in Ac.* (9.66A); **4.** *acquired habit, skill, ability, capacity* πολλῶν...θαυμαζόντων μὲν τὸν 'Ιησοῦν ἐπὰν ἐνορῶσιν τῇ περὶ αὐτοῦ ἱστορίᾳ, μηκέτι δὲ πιστευόντων ἐπὰν βαθύτερος καὶ μείζων τῆς ἕ. αὐτῶν αὐτοῖς ἀναπτύσσηται λόγος Or.*Jo.*20.30(24; p.368.6; M.14.644C); *ib.*5.8(4; p.105.22; 196B); 'Ωριγένην...μεγίστην ἤδη συλλεξάμενον ἐκ τῆς μακρᾶς παρασκευῆς ἕξιν Eus.*h.e.*6.36.1(M.20.596C); fig. τοῦ πρακτικοῦ γυναῖκά φησιν εἶναι τὴν ἕ. ὡς τῶν κατ' ἀρετὴν τρόπων γεννητικήν *Schol.*11 in Max.*qu.Thal.*25(M.90.337D).

ἐξισάζ-ω, 1. trans., *make equal,* Chrys.*ecl.*30(12.667D); *make the same for both* ἐ. τὸ ἔγκλημα id.*hom.35.3 in 1Cor.*(10.324C); abs., *put oneself on the same level, ib.39.1*(362B); med., *make oneself equal* τοῖς κατὰ σοφίαν ~εσθαι κρείττοσι Meth.*symp.*6.1(p.64.5; M.18.113A); **2.** intrans., *be equal to* περὶ τῆς τοῦ πνεύματος γνώσεως...εἰπών, καὶ διδάξας ὅτι οὕτως ~ει πρὸς τὴν τοῦ θεοῦ γνῶσιν ὡς ἡ ἀνθρώπου γνῶσις αὐτὴ πρὸς ἑαυτήν Chrys.*hom.7.4 in 1Cor.*(10.55B); *correspond, be equivalent,* ref. Pr.8:12ff., Col.1:15ff. πάντων πρὸς λέξιν ~όντων ⟨τῶν⟩ ἀποστολικῶν πρὸς τὰ παρὰ τῆς σοφίας CAnc.(358)*ep.syn.*ap. Epiph.*haer.*73.7(p.277.16; M.42.416C); Gennad.*fr.Gen.*33:8(M.85. 1653A); med., Melet.*nat.hom.*epit.(M.64.1077A).

ἐξισ-όω, 1. *make equal, put on a level with,* Athenag.*leg.*15.3(M.6. 920B); πρωτότοκος τῆς κτίσεως...οὐχ ὡς ~ούμενος τοῖς κτίσμασι Ath.*Ar.*2.62(M.26.277C); *ib.*3.19(364A); τὸ λέγειν ἑαυτὸν ἀνάστασιν εἶναι καὶ ζωήν,...~οῦντός ἐστι τῷ γεγεννηκότι ἑαυτόν Chrys.*hom.64.1 in Jo.*(8.383C); med., *rival* μάγοι...~οῦσθαι τῇ δυνάμει τῇ ἐνεργουμένῃ διὰ...Μωϋσέως Just.*dial.*79.4(M.6.664A); pass., *be on an equality* ὁ θεῖος λόγος...ὁ τῷ δεσπότῃ τῶν ὅλων ἐξισωθεὶς Clem.*prot.*10 (p.78.13; M.8.228A); ἐάν τις εἴπῃ κελευόμενον διὰ τοῦ λόγου τὸν Χριστὸν ἐργάσασθαι τὰ πάντα...οὐκ ἐξισωθήσεται τῷ κτίσαντι [v.l. κτίσματι] αὐτό Apoll.*fid.sec.pt.*(p.170.2; M.10.1108B); id.*fr.*11(p.207. 26); c. genit., Agath.*v.Gr.Ill.*85(p.44); *match* ἐξισωθήσεσθαι τὴν εὐχαριστίαν ταῖς εὐεργεσίαις Gr.Thaum.*pan.Or.*3(p.7.6; M.10.1057D); **2.** *bring to the level of,* Meth.*Porph.*3(p.506.25; M.18.401B); **3.** *make level* γῆ...ἐξισώθη καὶ πέδιον γέγονε Agath.*v.Gr.Ill.*112(p.57); **4.** *apportion equally,* hence *assess* tribute, Bas.*ep.*98.1(3.191E; M.32. 496A).

ἐξιστάν-ω, (= ἐξίστημι) *amaze, throw into ecstasy* κύριός ἐστιν ὁ ~ων καρδίας ἀνθρώπων Mont.*fr.*ap.Epiph.*haer.*48.4(p.225.1; ἐκστάνων (v.l. ἐτάζων) M.41.861A); med., *change, degenerate* τὸ ἀθάνατον...μὴ...~όμενον εἰς τὴν...θνητὴν φύσιν Meth.*res.*1.36(p.275.16, v.l. ἐξανιστανόμενον; ἐξανιστάμενον M.41.1101A).

ἐξιστάω, = foreg., Epiph.*haer.*48.4(p.225.8; M.41.861A).

ἐξίστη-μι, A. trans.; **1.** *remove, drive away,* met. ~σι τὴν ὀργὴν ἡ χάρις, λύουσα τὰ ἐγκλήματα Cyr.*Abac.*19(3.534C); *drive* from the right path, Hipp.*haer.*9.11(p.245.21; M.16.3379A); *dislodge* from one's opinion, Just.*dial.*67.3(M.6.629B); **2.** *change utterly* οὔτε γὰρ πάθος ὅλως αὐτὸν ἐξέστησεν, οὔτε θάνατος ἐλυμήνατο Meth.*Porph.*3 (p.507.3; M.18.401C); χαλεπὴ τῆς φιλαργυρίας ἡ τυραννίς, δεινὴ ψυχὴν ἐκστῆσαι Chrys.*hom.6.5 in Phil.*(11.241B).

B. intrans.; **1.** *cease from, abandon, let slip, Pers.*(p.31.24); **2.** *be amazed at,* Petr.II Al.*encycl.*(M.33.1277B)ap.Thdt.*h.e.*4.22.6; *be taken out of oneself,* Dion.Ar.*d.n.*4.13(M.3.712A) cit. s. ἐραστής; *fall into a trance,* ref. Gen.2:21, Meth.*symp.*2.2(p.16.14; M.18.49A); τοῦ λόγου συγκαταβαίνοντος ἡμῖν καὶ...ἐξισταμένου κατὰ τὴν ἀνάμνησιν τοῦ πάθους *ib.*3.8(p.35.22; 73B); **3.** *change one's position,* met. οὐ γὰρ ἐξίσταταί ποτε τῆς αὐτοῦ περιωπῆς ὁ υἱὸς τοῦ θεοῦ Clem.*str.*7.2(p.5.26; M.9.408B); abs., Cyr.*Jo.*3.4(4.271B).

***ἐξιστορητέον,** *one must investigate,* Clem.*str.*4.1(p.248.18; M.8. 1216B).

ἐξισχναίν-ω, *cause to wither away, refine away,* met. πᾶν... ἀμβλὺ καὶ νόθον τῆς ψυχῆς...παροξύνων καὶ ~ων τοῖς λεπτοῖς...λόγοις Gr.Thaum.*pan.Or.*7(p.20.17; M.10.1076B).

ἐξισχύω, *put forth strength, be very strong,* Meth.*symp.*8.13(p.98. 13, v.l. ὑπερισχύω M.18.160C).

ἐξίσωσις, ἡ, 1. *equalization, equating* γενητῶν μὲν ἐ. πρὸς τὸ ἀγένητον Ath.*Ar.*1.31(M.26.76C); **2.** *equality* ὁ υἱός...οὐ πρὸς τὰ κτίσματα ἐ. ἔχει *ib.*2.27(304C); ref. Jo.17:21 τὸ 'καθὼς' οὐκ ἀκριβοῦς ἐξισώσεως ἐπ' αὐτῶν Chrys.*hom.82.2 in Jo.*(8.484E); **3.** (Lat. *peraequatio*) *assessment* for taxes, Eus.*v.C.*4.3 tit.(p.114.4; M.20.1152B); Bas.*ep.*36(3.114D; M.32.324A); *ib.*281(423E; M.1017B).

ἐξισωτής, ὁ, 1. *one who makes equal, equalizer* τὰ ἔθνη...μέλλοντα ἐξισοῦσθαι τῷ 'Ισραὴλ διὰ τὸν πάντων ἐ., Χριστόν Proc.G.*Lev.*19:32 (M.87.764B); **2.** (Lat. *peraequator*) *assessor* of taxes, Eus.*v.C.*4.3 (p.119.3; M.20.1152C); Bas.*ep.*198(3.289C; M.32.713B); v.l. ap.Gr. Naz.*carm.*2.2(poem.)1 tit.,2 tit.(M.37.1451A,1477A); cf.Cosm.Mel. *schol.*ad loc.(M.38.469,473).

ἐξιτηλία, ἡ, 1. *vanity, folly*; of worldly pride and pleasure, Cyr. *Ps.*36:35(M.69.949B); id.*Is.*1.3(2.68A); Olymp.*Job* 38 proem.(M.93. 393B); of idolatry, Cyr.*Is.*4.3(2.640D); id.*Mal.*proem.(3.817E); of heresy, id.*Nest.*5.1(p.93.25; 6¹.122E); **2.** c. εἰς, *wasting one's energies* on, *abandonment* to worthless activities, id.*ador.*14(1.496E).

ἐξίτηλος, 1. *evanescent, ready to vanish away* τοῦτο τὸ σαρκίον [sc. σῶμα] νεκροῦντας ἤδη καὶ ἐ. ἀποφαίνοντας ἀποχῇ τῆς πονηρίας Clem.*exc.Thdot.*52(p.124.12; M.9.684C); Cyr.*ador.*12(1.434A); *temporary,* Meth.*symp.*9.1(p.114.3; M.18.177A); of light *that fades,* Bas. *Eun.*2.28(1.264E; M.29.636C); of persons, *ready to die,* id.*ep.*162(3. 253B; M.32.632C); **2.** *lacking* or *having lost power* or *value, feeble,* Ast.Am.*hom.*14(M.40.381B); βαλανεῖα...καὶ δεῖπνα...συνεχῶς γιγνόμενα τὸ σῶμα ἐ. ἐργάζεται Chrys.*hom.18.4 in Jo.*(8.109A); id.*hom. 29.3 in Heb.*(12.276A); of crops, *poor, meagre,* Thdt.*qu.23 in Dt.*(1. 276); of a distant view, *faint* ἐνδαπανηθεῖσα τῷ ἀέρι ἡ ὄψις, καὶ ἐ. γενομένη ‡Eust.*hex.*(M.18.724A); esp. *vain, worthless, foolish*; of heret. opinions, Isid.Pel.*epp.*1.159(M.78.293B); Cyr.*ador.*2(1.54C); *ib.*7(251A); id.*apol.orient.*(p.60.4; 6¹.193E); of Pharisaic tradition, ref. Mt.15:3 εἰς ἐ. τινα καὶ οὐχὶ τῷ νόμῳ διεγνωσμένον μεθορμισάμενοι βίον id.*ador.*16(572E); of idolatry, id.*Is.*4.3(2.651B); *ib.*5.6(895C); of worldly pleasures τὴν θεομισῆ καὶ ἐ. βδελυρίαν, κώμους δὴ λέγω id.*hom.pasch.*11(5².150B); id.*Am.*34(3.287D); id.*Is.*3.2(428A); cf. τὸ ἐ. εἰς τρυφάς *vain pursuit* of, *abandonment* to pleasure, *ib.*1.3(87C); **3.** *vain, proud, boastful* ὁ θρασὺς καὶ ὑπέροπτος καὶ τὸ μέγα καὶ ἐ. ἐκεῖνο βοῶν *ib.*2.1(2.188A); ἐ. ὀφρύν *ib.*3.3(470A); ἐ. ... καὶ ὑβριστής id.*Os.*139(3.172A).

***ἐξιτήλως, 1.** *lightly, cursorily* ἐπιπόνως ἀλλὰ μὴ ἐ. ταῖς θείαις ἐντετυχηκὼς γραφαῖς Eus.*e.th.*3.3(p.148.30; M.24.988B); **2.** *for vain worldly ends,* ref. Is.3:18 ἐν ἐνδείᾳ καὶ ἀποβολῇ πάντων ἔσονται τῶν ἐ. ἐξηυρημένων Cyr.*Is.*1.3(2.69D); id.*Am.*59(3.316B); id.*Os.*21(3.44C); **3.** *foolishly* ἀποσκιρτήσαντα ἐ. τὸν ἄνθρωπον δουλείας τῆς ὑπὸ θεοῦ Or. *sel.in Ps.*2:8(M.12.1108B).

ἐξιτήριος, *at parting* ἐ. δῶρον Bas.*ep.*203.1(3.299E; M.32.737B); ἐ.

λόγος Gr.Naz.*or*.43.24(M.36.529A); ἐ. εὐλογίαις Thdt.*h.e.*1.18.9(3.796); Jo.D.*hom*.9.9(M.96.730B); as subst., *parting gift*, Mac.Mgn. *apocr*.4.14(p.182.7); Bas.*Spir*.73(p.145.7, v.l. ἀλεξητήριον 3.62C; M.32.205A); *parting message*, Anast.Ant.*redit*.(p.251).

ἐξιχνευτέον, *one must trace, search out*, Clem.*prot*.6(p.51.28; M.8.172C); met., *one must examine, discover the meaning of* ἐ. τοῦ ἀποστόλου τὴν φωνήν Meth.*symp*.3.12(p.40.21; M.18.80A).

ἐξιχνεύω, *trace*; met., *trace out the meaning of, examine*, Meth.*symp*.9.1(p.115.2; M.18.180A).

ἐξιχνιάζω, *search out*, Eus.*Ps*.138:1(M.24.40C); ἀδύνατα γὰρ αὐτῷ [sc. τῷ υἱῷ] τὸν πατέρα τε ἐξιχνιάσαι, ὅς ἐστιν ἐφ' ἑαυτοῦ Ar.*Thal.fr*.2(p.257; M.26.708B); Bas.*hex*.6.1(1.50E; M.29.120A); ref. Rom.11:33, Gr.Nyss.*Eun*.3(2 p.36.18; M.45.604B).

ἐξκαιδέκατος, *sixteenth*, Eutych.*pasch*.4(M.86.2396B).

***ἐξκουσεύω**, v. *ἐκκουσσεύω.

ἐξογκόω, *cause to swell up*, Chrys.*hom.7.4 in Col*.(11.376B); met., *exaggerate* συμφορὰν...ἐ. id.*hom.28.4 in 1Cor*.(10.285B); id.*hom.76.1 in Mt*.(7.732E); pass., Isid.Pel.*epp*.5.77(M.78.1372C).

ἐξοδεύω, **1.** *depart* ἐ. τοῦ βίου Gr.Nyss.*ep.can*.5(M.45.232C); abs., *depart this life*, CNic.(325)*can*.13; Bas.*ep*.243.4(3.375D; M.32.909B); Epiph.*haer*.76.1(p.341.17; M.42.517A); in form ἐξωδηκυῖαν τὴν Ἑλλήνων θρησκείαν ‡Jo.D.*Artem*.48(M.96.1296D); **2.** trans., *lead out*; met., *lead away, seduce*, *Clem.ep.Petr*.1(M.2.25B); τὴν ἰδίαν ἐ. ζωήν *lead* one's life, Gr.Nyss.*anim.et res*.(M.46.92A); **3.** = ἐξηγέομαι, *expound, interpret*, Proc.G.*Lev*.proem.(M.87.692A).

ἐξοδιάζ-ω, **1.** *expend* λόγον...τῶν ~ομένων Chrys.*hom.14.4 in 1Tim*.(11.630E); Gr.Mag.*dial*.(tr. Zach.)4.22(M.*PL*.77.354C); **2.** *carry out* for burial; pass., Jo.Clim.*scal*.5(M.88.772C).

***ἐξοδιακός**, adj., *funeral* ἐ. κραββάτῳ CCP(681)*act*.14(H.3.1376D).

***ἐξοδίασις**, ἡ, *expedition* στρατιωτῶν ἐ. Thdt.*h.e*.2.16.28(3.869).

***ἐξοδιαστικός**, *funeral*; neut. as subst., Jo.D.*hymn.exod*.tit.(M.96.1368B); *Euchol*.(p.423).

***ἐξοδίζω**, s.v.l., = ἐξοδιάζω 2, pass., Jo.Mosch.*prat*.77(M.87.2932B).

ἐξοδικός, *expressive* τὸν ἐγκείμενον τῇ φύσει τῆς κτίσεως λόγον διὰ τῆς ἐ. ταύτης ἐνδείκνυται ῥήσεως Gr.Nyss.*hex*.26(M.44.888D); Max.*schol.c.h*.1.3(M.4.36A).

ἐξόδιος, **1.** *belonging to an exit* or *departure*; **a.** *parting* ἐ. ῥήματα Gr.Naz.*or*.8.22(M.35.816A); *ib*.40.11(M.36.373A); Niceph.Ur.*v.Sym*.45(M.86.3028B); **b.** *funeral* ᾠδὴν ἐ. Germ.CP *or*.2(M.98.284A); Jo.D.*carm.dorm.BMV* 8,156(pp.229,232; M.96.1364A,1368A); ref. Holy Saturday κυρίῳ...ἑορτὴν ἐ. Jo.D.*hom*.4.39(M.96.644A); of the Dormition ἑορτὴν ἐ. τῇ μητρὶ τοῦ θεοῦ ἑορτάσωμεν *ib*.9.15(741C); **2.** neut. as subst.; **a.** *going out* τὴν ἑορτὴν τῆς σκηνοπηγίας...ἐ. ὀνομάζει, ὡς ἤδη τῶν ἔργων τῶν ἐν ἀγροῖς ἐκκεχωρηκότων εἰς πέρας Cyr.*Zach*.111(3.810B); τῆς ὀγδόης· ἣν ἐπίσχεσιν ὀνομάζει, μὴ ἔχουσαν ἐ. ἀλλὰ ἀνάπαυσιν παντελῆ Proc.G.*Num*.28:18(M.87.877C); **b.** *death* παρεστῶτος τοῦ ἐ. Gr.Naz.*or*.40.12(M.36.373B); **c.** *funeral* τὴν ἐκκομιδὴν ἤτοι τὸ ἐ. *Schol*. in CCarth.*can*.41(*Mon*.2 p.650); πάντες οἱ ἀδελφοὶ τῆς μονῆς ψάλλοντες ἐν τῷ ἐ. *V.Pach.Γ*(p.437); Jo.Mosch.*prat*.77(M.87.2932B); Jo.Clim.*scal*.26(M.88.1065D); **d.** of the feast of Tabernacles, *commemoration of Exodus*, ref. Ps.28, Gr.Nyss.*Pss.titt*. B 1(M.44.488B); τὸ ἐ. τὸ τέλος σημαίνει τῶν ἑορτῶν...τοῦτο γὰρ ὁ νομοθετῶν ἔφη ὅτι ἐν σκηναῖς κατῴκισα τοὺς υἱοὺς Ἰσραὴλ ἐν τῷ ἐξαγαγεῖν με αὐτοὺς ἐκ γῆς Αἰγύπτου Thdt.*qu.32 in Lev*.(1.210); but cf.Cyr.*Zach*.111 supra.

ἔξοδος, ἡ, **1.** *going out* τὴν τῶν κατηχουμένων καὶ τὴν τῶν μετανοούντων ἔ. *Const.App*.2.57.14; *exile*, Thdt.*h.e*.1.22.2(3.803); *going forth*, of Son αὐτοῦ τοῦ Χριστοῦ δύο ἔ., ἤγουν πρόοδοι· ἡ μὲν πρωΐας, πρὸ πάντων τῶν αἰώνων ἐκ πατρὸς γενομένη...ἡ δὲ ἑσπέρας, ἡ ἐκ παρθένου Ath.*fr.Pss.comm*.64:9(M.27.580A); ὁ...Χριστὸς ἔ. τὴν ἑαυτοῦ παρουσίαν εἰκότως καλεῖ. ἔξω γὰρ ἦμεν τοῦ θεοῦ *cat.Heb*.1:4 suppl.(p.319.32); τὸν τῆς οἰκονομίας λόγον...καὶ τὴν ἔ. τοῦ θεοῦ λόγου τὴν τοῦ πατρός...ἰδιαίτερον τῆς ἑαυτοῦ μόνης ὑποστάσεως ἐποιήσατο ἔ. Anast.S.*hod*.24(M.89.308B); ref. Mt.26:13 τὴν εἰς τὰ ἔθνη ἔ. Chrys.*hom.80.1 in Mt*.(7.767A); **2.** *Exodus* τῷ κακῷ θεῷ ἀνατιθέασιν [sc. Manicheans]...τὴν ἀπὸ Αἰγύπτου ἔ. τῶν Ἰσραηλιτῶν. οὐκ ἔστι γάρ, φασί, τοῦ ἀγαθοῦ θεοῦ τὸ ἐκβαλεῖν αὐτοὺς ἀπὸ Αἰγύπτου †Leont.B.*sect*.3.2(M.86.1213B); hence *Book of Exodus*, freq.; **3.** *departure*; of death, Clem.*str*.3.9(p.226.9; M.8.1168B); τὴν τῆς σαρκὸς ἔ. id.*exc.Thdot*.4(p.106.17; M.9.656A); ἔ. ἀπὸ τοῦ βίου Meth.*symp*.6.4(p.68.22; M.18.120A); id.*res*.2.8(p.343.16; M.41.1176A); *Const.App*.2.13.2; ἐ. ψυχῆς *Poen.App*.2.14(p.156); abs., *decease*, *Ep.Lugd*.ap.Eus.*h.e*.5.1.36(M.20.421B); Or.*hom.2.3 in Jer*.(p.20.6; M.13.281A); **4.** *end, outcome*, Herm.*vis*.3.4.3; **5.** *issue, dispensing* καταγραφὴ τῆς ἐ. τοῦ σίτου Eustrat.*v.Eutych*.17(M.86.2293D).

ἐξόζ-ω, *smell* of; met., c. genit. ἀβελτερίας τῆς...ἐσχάτης ~οντας ...λόγους Cyr.*ep*.50(p.97.31; 5^2.167D); c. acc. ἐ. μοιχείαν Meth.*symp*.1.1(p.9.1; M.18.37C).

ἐξοιδαίνω, *swell up*; met., †Bas.*Is*.118(1.461C; M.30.309B).

ἐξοιδέω = foreg., met. τὸ φλεγμαῖνον τῶν παθῶν καὶ ἐξῳδηκὸς ‡Nil.*perist*.2.5(M.79.821B).

ἐξοικει-όω, **1.** *make like, assimilate* to; pass., Clem.*ecl*.50(p.151.4; M.9.721A); χρὴ ~οῦσθαι ἡμᾶς αὐτῷ [sc. τῷ θεῷ] δι' ἀγάπης τῆς θείας id.*str*.5.1(p.334.19; M.9.28B); Eus.*Is*.13:16(M.24.188D); *adapt*, Dion.Al.ap.Eus.*p.e*.7.19(334B; M.21.564B); **2.** med.; **a.** *appropriate* τῆς Ἑβραίων γραφῆς...ὁ Πλάτων ~οῦται τὸ δόγμα Eus.*p.e*.11.9(524B; M.869A); τὰς ἡμετέρας ἁμαρτίας ~ούμενος [sc. Χριστός] διὰ τὴν πρὸς ἡμᾶς ἀγάπην id.*d.e*.10.1(p.450.3; M.22.724C); *ib*.10.8(p.478.9; M.769A); **b.** *win as a friend, make a friend of*, Clem.*str*.2.19(p.166.16; M.8.1041A); οὐ μόνον τοὺς δώδεκα ἀποστόλους οὐδὲ τοὺς ἑβδομήκοντα μαθητὰς ἐξῳκειωμένος Eus.*d.e*.3.5(p.131.4; M.22.721B); τίνος δ' ἂν ὑστεροῖτο ⟨ὁ τὸν τῶν ὄντως ἀγαθῶν⟩ δημιουργὸν ἐξῳκειωμένος; id.*p.e*.1.1(2D; ὁ τῶν ἀγαθῶν τὸν δημιουργὸν ἐξοικειούμενος M.21.24C); Nil.*epp*.4.22(M.79.560D); **3.** med., *alienate* from τὸ κεφάλαιον τῆς συμφορᾶς ἡμῶν...τὸ ἐξῳκειωθῆναι τοῦ ἀγαθοῦ πατρὸς τὸ ἀνθρώπινον Gr.Nyss.*Eun*.12(2 p.278.11; M.45.889A).

ἐξοικίζ-ω, *remove from home, banish*, met. θρόμβοι ἱδρῶτος αὐτοῦ παραδόξως οἷα σταγόνες αἵματος ἀπέρρεον, ἵνα τῆς ἡμετέρας φύσεως... ἐξοικίσῃ τὴν τῆς δειλίας πηγήν ‡Dion.Al.*fr.in Lc.22:44*(p.243.7; M.10.1593A); Gr.Nyss.*hom.4 in Eccl*.(M.44.676C); φιλοσοφίας ἐξῳκισμένης Synes.*ep*.136(M.66.1524C); hence *remove, separate*, Cyr.*ador*.10(1.360E); ἐν ἠθῶν καταστάσει, τῆς τοῦ διαβόλου τυραννίδος ἐξῳκισμένη *ib*.1(46E); id.*Jo*.2.5(4.192A); med., *go from home, depart*; of migrating birds, Synes.*ep*.138(1528C); ὅπου δὲ ὀργὴ καὶ θυμὸς...τὸ πνεῦμα τὸ ἅγιον...~εται *ib*.67(1421B).

ἐξοικισμός, ὁ, *expulsion, banishment*, Cyr.*Zach*.78(3.760A).

***ἐξοικιστέον**, *one must banish*, Clem.*paed*.2.5(p.185.5; M.8.445C).

ἔξοικος, *homeless, turned out of doors*, Cyr.*Is*.5.2(2.761E); id.*Nah*.13 (ἔ. ὁ 3.491B, v.l. ἐξ οἴκου Aubert); met. τὴν ἀδελφοκτόνον ὀργὴν ἔ. τῆς ἑαυτῶν διανοίας ποιησώμεθα id.*hom.pasch*.7(5^2.86E); *ib*.6(72B).

ἐξοιστρέω (-άω), **1.** *goad on*; fig.; **a.** *infuriate, madden*, Eus.*d.e*.6.10(p.164.29; M.22.270A); Bas.*hom*.14.4(2.125C; M.31.452A); Nemes.*nat.hom*.30(M.40.724A); Pall.*v.Chrys*.20(p.145.10; M.47.81); **b.** *make mad, silly*, Iren.*haer*.1.13.2(M.7.581A); **2.** intrans., *rush madly forth* οὐχ...οἷός τε ὑπάρχει εἰς οὐρανοὺς ἀναβαίνειν ὁ ἐκεῖθεν ἐξοιστρήσας διάβολος ‡Caes.Naz.*dial*.49(M.38.920); in form ἐξοιστράω, Synes.*provid*.15(p.97.9; M.66.1245C).

***ἐξοιστριάζω**, *be mad* ἐξοιστριάσας ἐν ἐπιθυμίᾳ τῆς Ἡρῳδίαδος *A.Jo.Bapt*.8(p.536.2, v.l. ἐξοιστρήσας).

ἐξοίχομαι, *be gone out*, met. εἰς πλατὺ ζητημάτων ἐ. πέλαγος Cyr.*ador*.1(1.3D).

ἐξοκέλλω, **1.** *run aground*; met.; **a.** *drift* into; c. εἰς, *LS*; ἐ. πρὸς κακίαν Clem.*q.d.s*.40(p.186.14; M.9.645B); ἐπὶ τὸ χεῖρον ἐ. Rhod.ap.Eus.*h.e*.5.13.4(M.20.460C); ποῦ οὐκ ἂν ἐξώκειλαν ἀσεβείας; Chrys.*hom.5.4 in Mt*.(7.80A); **b.** c. gen., *drift away, stray* from, *miss* οἱ Ἰουδαῖοι τῆς ἐλπίδος τῶν μελλόντων ἐξώκειλαν ἀγαθῶν Meth.*symp*.9.2(p.115.24; M.18.180C); ἐ. τῇ ἀληθείᾳ [conj. τῆς ἀληθείας] Epiph.*haer*.80.7(p.493.3; M.42.768C); Sophr.H.*ep.syn*.(M.87.3153C); ἐ. τοῦ φρονεῖν καὶ κηρύττειν ὀρθῶς τὸ τῆς εὐσεβείας μυστήριον Anast.S.*haer*.(p.265); **c.** abs., *suffer shipwreck, come to grief*, Meth.*symp*.7.5(p.76.14; M.18.132B); Ammon.*1Petr.3:19–20*(M.85.1608D); Epiph.*anc*.105(p.127.2; M.43.208B); Chrys.*hom.1.1 in Mt*.(7.2B); **2.** trans., *drive on the rocks*; met., *drive headlong* δεινὴ γὰρ ἡ τρυφὴ εἰς κόρον ἐξοκείλασα Clem.*paed*.3.11(p.266.29; M.8.625C); reflex., *get off one's course* παρ' ὀλίγου αὐτὸν ἐξώκειλε τῆς προθέσεως Pall.*h.Laus*.16(p.41.13; M.34.1042A).

ἐξολεθρεύω, = ἐξολοθρεύω, *Pap.Chr*.(p.440); *CG–CI* 1.15.

ἐξολιγωρέω, *value lightly*, Meth.*res*.2.24(p.379.12; M.18.289A).

ἐξολισθαίνω, **1.** *slip away*, met. ἐ. τῆς ἀληθείας Meth.*symp*.5.2(p.54.11; M.18.100A); *ib*.8.3(p.84.17; 144A); εἰ ἐν ψιλῷ καὶ μόνῳ τῷ ὀνόματι διακέκριται θεὸς ὁ υἱός...ἐξολισθήσειεν αὐτοῦ...τὸ χάρισμα Didym.*Trin*.3.10(M.39.856C); εἰς πονηρίαν ἐ. Chrys.*hom.63.4 in Jo*.(8.380A); id.*hom.7.3 in Mt*.(7.107C); Cyr.*Ps*.36:19(M.69.936B); **2.** *slip, stumble*, fig. ὁ...ἐχθρὸς ἀεὶ...προσεδρεύει, καταπιεῖν ἕτοιμος εἴ πού τις ἐξολισθήσειε Chrys.*sac*.3.17(p.89.10; 1.398C); **3.** *slip down, sink down* τῷ βόθρῳ ὑπεκλίθη τοῦ ᾅδου ὁ ποιμὴν ὁ καλός, διὰ τὸ ἐξωλισθηκὸς ἐκεῖ πρόβατον Germ.CP *or*.2(M.98.285A); Men.*exc.Rom*.20(p.220.19; M.113.925C).

***ἐξολίσθησις**, ἡ, *falling away*, Const.ap.Eus.*h.e*.10.7.2(M.20.893B).

***ἐξόλισθος**, *slippery* ἐ. ἡ κατάβασις †Anast.S.*relat*.8(p.65.12).

***ἐξολοθρεύσιον**, τό, *utter destruction*, *A.Xanthipp.*9(p.64.18).

***ἐξολοθρευτής**, ὁ, *destroyer*, Ath.*exp.Ps.*78:50(M.27.356A); †Cyr.*hom.div.*11(5^2.380B).

ἐξολοθρεύ-ω, *destroy utterly*, *exterminate*, Just.*dial.*131.5(M.6.781B); Eus.*h.e.*1.6.11(M.20.89A); *ἐλέει θεοῦ ∼θήσονται οἱ ἐχθροί, οὐ κατ' οὐσίαν φθειρόμενοι...ἀλλὰ τὴν ἕξιν ἀποβαλόντες δι' ἣν ἐχθροὶ τοῦ δικαίου...τυγχάνουσιν* id.*Ps.*142:11(M.24.52B); Gr.Nyss.*Eun.*1(1 p.48.22; M.45.277A); ref. Gen.17:14 *περιτεμνώμεθα πᾶν σαρκικὸν φρόνημα καὶ λόγον καὶ ἔργον παράνομον, ἵνα μὴ ∼θῶμεν* Nil.*epp.*1.13 (M.79.88B).

***ἐξολοκλήρου**, *fully*, *completely*, *Cod.Afr.*93(Lat. *ex integro*).

***ἐξόλου**, *at all τὸ ἐ. μὴ εἶναι θεούς* Thphl.Ant.*Autol.*3.7(M.6.1129C).

***ἐξομαλέω**, = ἐξομαλίζω 1, Nil.ap.Proc.G.*Cant.*2:1(M.87.1577A).

ἐξομαλίζ-ω, **1.** *make quite smooth*, *smooth out*, fig. and met. *ἐ.* [*τῷ λαῷ θεοῦ*] *τὴν ὁδὸν τῆς θεοσεβείας* Eus.*Is.*57:14(M.24.476C); *ἐ. τὴν ἐπιδημίαν τῷ κυρίῳ* †Bas.*hom.in Ps.*28(1.360B; M.30.77C); *ἀρετῆς...τὰς ἀνωμαλίας τῶν πραγμάτων διὰ τῆς ἑαυτῆς φιλοσοφίας ∼ούσης* Isid.Pel.*epp.*2.89(M.78.533B); *Lit.Chrys.*(p.340.25); esp. *smooth out* difficulties of interpretation, *explain*, Or.*sel.in Ps.*50 proem.ap. *philoc.*1.29(p.34.22; M.17.453B); id.*Jo.*20.12(p.342.28; M.14.328C); Eus.*d.e.*10.2(p.456.22; M.22.733D); ‡Ath.*dial.Trin.*3.26(M.28.1244C); Max.*schol.d.n.*7.1(M.4.341C); medic., *smooth away*, *reduce*, fig. *ὁ ὀνειδισμὸς...τὰς ὑπερσαρκώσεις τοῦ τύφου ἐ.* Clem.*paed.*1.8(p.128.11; M.8.328C); *Const.App.*2.41.6; **2.** *make even*, *maintain consistently*, Bas.*reg.br.*16(2.420B; M.31.1092D); *τοὺς προκόπτοντας μὴ ∼ειν τὰς πράξεις* †Bas.*Is.*35(1.408C; M.30.189A); Diod.*fat.*(M.103.860D); **3.** *make to agree ταῖς θεωρίαις τὰς ἱστορίας ἐ.* Didym.*Job* 5:18(M.39.1133C).

***ἐξομαλισμός**, ὁ, *smoothing out of difficulties*, *explanation*, †Bas.*Is.*256(1.574E; M.30.569B) ∞ Proc.G.*Is.*13:2(M.87.2069D); *harmonization κινεῖν...τὰ δόγματα τοῦ χρόνου πολλοῦ...χρῄζοντα πρὸς ἐ. πρέποντα τῇ δικαιοσύνῃ θεοῦ* ‡Nil.*narr.*2(M.79.609C).

ἐξομβρ-έω, *pour out like rain*, ref. 1Cor.10:4 *τὸ ἀποστολικὸν πόμα...∼εῖ* Eus.*Is.*48:20(M.24.428C); Cosm.Ind.*top.*12(M.88.456D).

***ἐξομβρίζω**, = foreg. *ὦ μετάνοια...σὺ...τοῖς...Νινευίταις πηγὰς ζωῆς...ἐξώμβρισας* ‡Chrys.*poenit.*4(9.852C).

ἐξομιλέω, *be familiar with*, ‡Jo.D.*Artem.*34(p.162.15; M.96.1281D).

ἐξόμνυμι, **1.** *deny upon oath*; fig., Synes.*ep.*154(M.66.1556A); **2.** *forswear*, *renounce*, Clem.*paed.*2.1(p.155.4; M.8.380B); Ath.*inc.*37.5(M.25.161A); **3.** *swear a solemn oath*, *Dorm.BMV* 10(p.98).

ἐξομοι-όω, **1.** *make quite like θεοσέβεια ∼οῦσα τῷ θεῷ κατὰ τὸ δυνατὸν τὸν ἄνθρωπον* Clem.*prot.*9(p.64.31; M.8.197C); id.*paed.*1.2 (p.91.26; M.8.252C); *ὁ δὲ θεὸς ταύτην* [sc. *τὴν ψυχήν*] *δι' ὅλου περιλαβὼν μετὰ τοῦ συμπεφυκότος αὐτῇ σώματος ἀναλόγως αὐτὰ ∼οῖ ἑαυτῷ* Max.*ambig.*(M.91.1249C); pass., *become* or *be like*; c. genit., Or.*exp. in Pr.*7:22(M.17.184A); **2.** *imitate*, Gr.Thaum.*pan.Or.*11 (p.26.11; M.10.1084A).

ἐξομοίωσις, ἡ, **1.** *assimilation*, ref. Phil.2:9 *τὴν τοῦ ἀναληφθέντος ἀνθρώπου πρὸς τὸ ὕψος τῆς θείας φύσεως ἐ. τε καὶ ἕνωσιν* Gr.Nyss.*Eun.*6(2 p.147.24; M.45.733B); **2.** *becoming like ἡ πρὸς τὸν ὀρθὸν λόγον ...ἐ.* Clem.*str.*2.22(p.187.8; M.8.1084A); *ἐ. ... τῷ θεῷ ib.*(p.188.20; 1085B); Gr.Nyss.*hom.1 in Cant.*(M.44.776B); *imitation τὴν ἐν παισὶν ἁπλότητα εἰς ἐ. παρακατατιθέμενος ἡμῖν* Clem.*paed.*1.5(p.97.8; M.8.264A); **3.** *likeness ἀνερμήνευτος οὐσία καὶ φύσις, οὐκ ἔχουσα παρὰ βροτοῖς ἐξομοίωσιν* ‡Jo.D.*Artem.*28(p.160.20; M.96.1277B).

ἐξομοιωτικός, *able to make like*, Clem.*str.*1.11(p.34.12; M.8.749C).

ἐξομολογ-έομαι, **1.** *confess*; **a.** in gen. *ὁ δεσπότης...οὐδὲν οὐδενὸς χρῄζει εἰ μὴ τὸ ∼εῖσθαι αὐτῷ 1Clem.*52.1; *περὶ παραπτωμάτων ib.*51.3; *ἐπὶ ἁμαρτίαις Barn.*19.12; *τῶν ἐν μετανοίᾳ ∼ουμένων* Clem.*str.*2.13 (p.144.27; M.8.997A); Or.*hom.1.4 in Jer.*(p.12.3; M.13.272A); *ἐνάτῃ ὥρᾳ...∼ουμένη τὰ παραπτώματά σου...ὅτι ἐν αὐτῇ τῇ ὥρᾳ ὁ κύριος... ἀπέδωκε τὸ πνεῦμα* Ath.*virg.*12(p.46.13; M.28.265B); *διὰ τί...ὁ Κάϊν καὶ ὁ Λάμεχ φόνον δράσαντες οὐχ ὁμοίως ἐκολάσθησαν;...ὁ μὲν ἐλεγχόμενος ἠρνήσατο· ὁ δὲ μὴ ἐλεγχόμενος ἐξωμολογήσατο* Isid.Pel.*epp.*4.8(M.78.1056C); Diad.*perf.*100(p.148.21); *ἔθη πολλάκις τοῖς δαίμοσιν...μὴ ∼εῖσθαι ἡμᾶς ὑποβάλλειν* Jo.Clim.*scal.*4(M.88.709A); *οὐδέποτέ τις εὑρίσκεται...∼ούμενος, εἰ μὴ...σχῇ ἐλπίδα ὅτι ἐὰν ∼ήσωμαι...γενήσεταί μοι ἄφεσις* Thdr.Stud.*resp.*3(M.99.1732C); **b.** in public penance, *Did.*4.14 cit. s. *παράπτωμα*; *αἱ μὲν καὶ εἰς φανερὸν ∼οῦνται, αἱ δὲ...εἰς τὸ παντελὲς ἀπέστησαν* Iren.*haer.*1.13.7(M.7.592A); *ἐπανῆλθεν εἰς τὴν ἐκκλησίαν, ἀποδυρόμενος καὶ ∼ούμενος τὸ ἑαυτοῦ ἁμάρτημα, ᾧ καὶ ἐκοινωνήσαμεν λαϊκῷ* Corn.ap.Eus.*h.e.*6.43.10 (M.20.620B); hence *be a penitent τὸν ἅπαντα χρόνον ∼ουμένη διετέλεσε, πενθοῦσα καὶ θρηνοῦσα* Iren.*haer.*1.13.5(588B); *Κέρδων...εἰς τὴν ἐκκλησίαν ἐλθὼν καὶ ∼ούμενος οὕτως διετέλεσε, ποτὲ μὲν λαθροδιδασκαλῶν, ποτὲ δὲ...∼ούμενος ib.*3.4.3(857A); of emperor Philip, Eus.*h.e.*6.34(M.20.596A); *ὁ γοητείαν καὶ φαρμακείαν ἐξαγορεύων τὸν τοῦ φονέως χρόνον ∼ηθήσεται* †CCP(381)*can.*10; public confession not essential to obtain God's forgiveness, Chrys.*incomprehens.*5.7(1.490C); id.*catech.*5.4(2.240B); v. *μετάνοια*; **c.** sacramentally *ἀναγκαῖον τοὺς πεπιστευμένους τὴν οἰκονομίαν τῶν μυστηρίων τοῦ θεοῦ ∼εῖσθαι τὰ ἁμαρτήματα* Bas.*reg.br.*288(2.516E; M.31.1285A); Socr.*h.e.*5.19.2(M.67.616A) cit. s. *μετάνοια*; regulations, †Jo.Jej.*poenit.*(M.88.1889Aff.); Anast.S.*synax.*(M.89.833C); cf. *ἐὰν οὖν εὕρῃς ἄνδρα πνευματικόν, ἔμπειρον, δυνάμενόν σε ἰατρεῦσαι...∼ησαι αὐτῷ* id.*qu.et resp.*6(M.89.372A); cf. *ἁμαρτία*; **d.** liturg. *∼ούμεθά σοι, φιλάνθρωπε θεέ, καὶ προσπίπτομεν, ἑαυτῶν τὰς ἀσθενείας* Serap.*euch.*5.1; *ἐκ νυκτὸς ὀρθρίζει παρ' ἡμῖν ὁ λαὸς ἐπὶ τὸν οἶκον τῆς προσευχῆς, καὶ ἐν...συνοχῇ δακρύων ∼ούμενοι τῷ θεῷ, τελευταῖον ἐξαναστάντες τῶν προσευχῶν, εἰς τὴν ψαλμῳδίαν καθίστανται* Bas.*ep.*207.3(3.311B; M.32.764A); **e.** of confession of faults in religious communities *ἦλθεν ∼ούμενος ταῦτα πάντα τοῖς πατράσιν* Pall.*h.Laus.*26(p.82.16; M.34.1092A); *ib.*34(p.99.20; 1107B); *ib.*70(p.166.19; 1243A); Jo.Clim.*scal.*4(M.88.681D); **2.** *confess*, *acknowledge*; **a.** one's faults to other men, Or.*Jo.*32.19(12; p.458.29; M.14.793D); *∼οῦμαι ὑμῖν, ἐγὼ μάγος, ἐγὼ πλάνος Hom. Clem.*20.19; **b.** a fact, Clem.*str.*4.8(p.274.5; M.8.1219A); *ib.*7.6(p.7.19; M.9.412B); ref. Phil.2:11 *πᾶσαν...τὴν κτίσιν...∼ουμένην, ὅτι καὶ τὸ γενέσθαι σάρκα τὸν λόγον, καὶ θάνατον ὑπομεῖναι σαρκὶ* Ath.*Ar.*1.42(M.26.100A); Ammonas *opusc.*2.18(p.470.9); **3.** *make grateful acknowledgement*, *give thanks*, *1Clem.*61.3; Or.*hom.17.7 in Jer.*(p.140.4; M.13.449A); Ath.*exp.Ps.*30:24(M.27.161A); *εὐχαριστοῦντες τῷ θεῷ καὶ ∼ούμενοι ἐφ' οἷς εὐηργέτησεν ἡμᾶς ὁ θεός Const.App.*7.30.1; Chrys.*exp.in Ps.*141(5.446B).

ἐξομολόγησις, ἡ, *confession*, def. *διπλοῦν τὸ τῆς ἐ. εἶδός ἐστιν. ἢ γὰρ τῶν οἰκείων ἁμαρτημάτων ἐστὶ κατάγνωσις, ἢ εὐχαριστία εἰς τὸν θεόν* Chrys.*exp.in Ps.*9(5.93B); †Cyr.*coll.VT*(6^4.75B; M.77.1288B); *exomologesis. ...Latine confessio interpretatur, cujus nominis duplex significatio est. aut enim in laude intellegitur confessio sicut est* [cit. Mt.11:25]*; aut dum quisque confitetur sua peccata...cujus indeficiens est misericordia*, Isid.H.*etym.*6.19.75; **1.** *confession* of sins; **a.** to God, cf. *exomologesis est qua delictum domino nostro confitemur; non quidem ut ignaro, sed quatenus satisfactio confessione disponitur, confessione poenitentia nascitur, poenitentia deus mitigatur. itaque exomologesis...humilificandi hominis disciplina est*, Tert.*de poenitentia* 9(M.*PL.*1.1243B); *τὰ μὲν τῶν ἀδελφῶν ἁμαρτήματα μερίσασθαι εὐχόμενος εἰς ἐ. καὶ ἐπιστροφὴν τῶν συγγενῶν* Clem.*str.*7.12(p.57.8; M.9.509C); ref. Ps.50 *τῷ ψαλμῷ τῆς ἐ.* Or.*hom.8.1 in Jer.*(p.56.3; M.13.336C); ref. Novatianist teaching on lapsed *μηκέτι οὔσης αὐτοῖς σωτηρίας ἐλπίδος μηδ' εἰ πάντα τὰ εἰς ἐπιστροφὴν γνησίαν καὶ καθαρὰν ἐ. ἐπιτελοῖεν* Eus.*h.e.*6.43.1(M.20.616B); *ἀρχὴ τῆς σωτηρίας ἡ ἐ.* Ath.*exp.Ps.*118:7(M.27.481A); *πολλάκις δὲ γίνεται τὸν μὲν πολλὰ ἐπταικότα δι' ἐξομολογήσεως ἀπαλλαγῆναι, τὸν δὲ ὀλίγα ἡμαρτηκότα δι' ὑπερηφανίαν μὴ προσελθεῖν τῷ φαρμάκῳ τῆς ἐ. καὶ οὕτως μὴ ὠφεληθῆναι* Tit.Bost.*fr.Lc.*7:39ff.(p.170); ref. Is.13:9 *μὴ οὖν ταμιευώμεθα εἰς ἐκείνην τὴν ἡμέραν τὰς ἐ.* †Bas.*Is.*265(1.581A; M.30.584D); *διὰ πάσης ἐ. τε καὶ ταπεινώσεως τὴν μετάνοιαν ἐπιδειξαμένη* [sc. *ἡ ψυχή*], *τότε καὶ αὖθις τῆς ἐπισκοπῆς ἀξιοῦται τῆς χάριτος* Mac.Aeg.*carit.*28(M.34.932A); Chrys.*Jud.*8.3(1.677B); *ἡ δὲ ἁμαρτία τοσαύτην ἐντίθησι κηλῖδα, ὡς μηδὲ μυρίαις πηγαῖς ἐκκαθᾶραι ταύτην δύνασθαι, ἀλλὰ μόνοις δάκρυσι καὶ...ἐ.* id.*hom.37.6 in Mt.*(7.422C); but cf. *ὃ διὰ νηστείας καὶ ὀδυρμῶν...καὶ μυρίας ἐ. μόλις ἕτεροι κατορθοῦσι, τὸ τὰ ἁμαρτήματα ἐξαλείφειν λέγω τὰ ἑαυτῶν, τοῦτο ἔξεστιν ἡμῖν ῥᾳδίως ποιεῖν ἂν μόνον ἀπὸ τῆς διανοίας ἐξαλείψωμεν τὴν ὀργὴν καὶ μετὰ εἰλικρινείας ἀφῶμεν τοῖς ἠδικηκόσιν ἡμᾶς* id.*hom.in Rom.12:20*(3.171B); *καρδίαν συντετριμμένην καὶ τεταπεινωμένην εἶχεν* [sc. *Δαβίδ*]... *καὶ γὰρ τοῦτο ἐ., τοῦτο μετάνοια* id.*hom.4.6 in 2Cor.*(10.463D); Cyr.*Ps.*37:18(M.69.965D); *δύναται ἐ. καὶ πῦρ αἰώνιον ἀποσβέσαι* Thdr.Stud.*conf.*1(M.99.1721A); cf. *inter litanias vero et exomologesim hoc differt, quod exomologesis pro sola confessione peccatorum agitur; litaniae vero, quae indicantur propter rogandum deum et impetrandam in aliquo misericordiam ejus*, Isid.H.*etym.*6.19.80; necessity before baptism or communion *ἐ. ὁ καιρὸς καὶ τοῖς ἀμυήτοις καὶ τοῖς βαπτισθεῖσι· τοῖς μέν, ἵνα μετανοήσαντες τῶν ἱερῶν τύχωσι μυστηρίων, τοῖς δέ, ἵνα ἀπονιψάμενοι ἐν τῷ βαπτίσματι τὰς κηλῖδας, καθαρῷ συνειδότι τῇ τραπέζῃ προσέλθωσιν* Chrys.*hom.10.5 in Mt.*(7.146A); especially enjoined during Lent, id.*Jud.*3.4(1.611D); and in Holy Week, id.*hom.30.1 in Gen.*(4.294A); but constantly necessary, *ib.* *11.4*(86E); *δεῖ εὐθέως καὶ περὶ τῶν ἀκουσίων πταισμάτων ἐ. σύντονον προσφέρειν τῷ δεσπότῃ...προσέχειν δὲ δεῖ ἀδιαλείπτως τῇ αἰσθήσει τῆς ἐ., μή που ἄρα ἡ συνείδησις ἡμῶν ψεύσηται ἑαυτὴν ὑπονοήσασα ἀρκοῦντας ἐξομολογεῖσθαι τῷ θεῷ Diad.*perf*.100(p.148.12,21); corporate ἡμέρας ἤδη ὑπολαμπούσης, πάντες κοινῇ, ὡς ἐξ ἑνὸς στόματος καὶ μιᾶς καρδίας, τὸν τῆς ἐ. ψαλμὸν ἀναφέρουσι τῷ κυρίῳ, ἴδια ἑαυτῶν ἕκαστος τὰ ῥήματα τῆς μετανοίας ποιούμενοι Bas.*ep*.207.3(3.311C; M.32.764B); cf.‡Hipp.*can*.9; impossible after this life cf. μετάνοια; ἄκαιρος ἡ ἐ., καὶ ἡ παράπλησις οὐκ ἐν καιρῷ τῷ δέοντι γινομένη Chrys.*Laz*.7.4(1.796D); ref. Ps.6:6, *Pers.capt*.(M.86.3257C); except for souls liberated by Christ in Hades, Ammon.*1Petr.3:19–20*(M.85.1608C); ref. name Judah Ἰούδας ἐ. ἑρμηνεύεται, οὗτοι δὲ [sc. οἱ Ἰουδαῖοι] οὐκ εἰσὶν ἐξομολογούμενοι θεῷ τὸ πάθημα τοῦ Χριστοῦ παρανόμως πεποιηκότες, ἵνα καὶ μεταγνόντες σωθῶσιν *Const.App*.2.60.3; Cyr.*Joel*.45(3.245B); †Cyr.*coll.VT*(6⁴.65D; M.77.1273A); regulations for sacramental confession, †Jo.Jej.*poenit*.(M.88.1889Aff.); **b.** to other men, Pall.*v.Chrys*.17(p.104.23; M.47.59); **2.** *penance*, the state of a penitent ⟨τῷ⟩ εἰς τὸ θεραπεύεσθαι, τουτέστιν εἰς τὴν ἐ. ἀφορισθέντι Meth.*lepr*.10(p.464.11); δεῖ μέντοι μὴ μέχρι τῆς ἐξόδου παρατείνειν αὐτῶν τὴν ἐ., ἀλλὰ δέχεσθαι μὲν τὸ μέτρον τῶν δέκα ἐτῶν Bas.*ep*.288 *can*.2(3.271A; M.32.672A); εἰ φιλανθρωπότερος γένοιτο [sc. ὁ θεός] τὸ ὑπερβάλλον τῆς ἐ. ὁρῶν· τοῦ ἡμαρτηκότος †CCP(381)*can*.20; **3.** *confession* of benefits, *thanksgiving*, *Pss.Sal*.3.3; ἡ ἐ. τὴν εὐχαριστίαν καὶ δοξολογίαν σημαίνει Or.*sel.in Ps*.135:2(M.12.1653D); ἐν κιθάρᾳ...αὐτῷ προσφέρειν τὴν ἐ. Ath.*exp.Ps*.42(M.27.204C); *ib*.99 proem.(424A); τίς δέ ἐστιν ἡ τῆς ἐκκλησίας μνήμη; ἡ ἐ. τῶν λαῶν Bas.*hom.in Ps*.44(1.169E; M.29.413D); οὐκ ἀπαιτεῖς σωματικὰς θυσίας, ἐν αἷς πλεονεκτοῦσιν οἱ εὐπορώτεροι,...ἀλλὰ τὴν ἀπὸ διαθέσεως καὶ καρδίας ἀληθινῆς ἐ., ἧς μέτεστι πᾶσιν ἐξ ἴσου τοῖς βουλομένοις †Bas.*hom.in Ps*.115(1.375E; M.30.113B); ἐ. τῆς αὐτοῦ [sc. θεοῦ] φιλανθρωπίας ‡Ath.*Apoll*.1.22(M.26.1132A); τήρει σεαυτὸν ἀκριβῶς,...ὡς ἐνώπιον τοῦ θεοῦ ὢν πάντοτε,...ἵνα ἐν πᾶσι τοῖς λόγοις σου καὶ ἔργοις διδῷς ἐ. Ammonas *opusc*.2.10(p.465.9); Cosm.Ind.*top*.3(M.88.165B); ὁ μὲν αἶνος δόξαν εὐχάριστον ἐμφαίνει θεοῦ, τοῦ ἀπὸ τοῦ μὴ ὄντος εἰς τὸ εἶναι παράγοντος ἡμᾶς...ἐ. δὲ χαριστηρίους φωνὰς ἀνθ' ὧν δυσχερῶν ἐρρύσθη *cat.Apoc*.16:16(p.421.15); **4.** *acknowledgement* of a truth, ref. Ps.75:2 Ἰουδαία γὰρ ἐ. ἑρμηνεύεται Clem.*str*.7.16(p.74.17; M.9.545A).

ἐξομολογητικός, *acknowledging benefits, thankful* ἐ. εὐχαριστίαν †Cyr.*coll.VT*(6⁴.29D; M.77.1249D).

***ἐξομολογία, ἡ,** = ἐξομολόγησις 1, Jo.Mon.*hymn.Chrys*.3(M.96.1380A).

ἐξομόργνυμι, **1.** *wipe off*; met. εἰς ἐκείνους [sc. τοὺς υἱούς] τὴν ἑαυτοῦ κακίαν...ἐ. Dion.Al.ap.Eus.*h.e*.7.10.8(M.20.661B); hence *rid oneself of*, ‡Caes.Naz.*dial*.182(M.38.1157); **2.** *stamp off, imprint* upon εἰς τὰς ἀναγεννωμένων ψυχὰς ἀναγκαῖον ἐξομοργνύμενον ἐκτυποῦσθαι τὸν λόγον τῆς ἀληθείας Meth.*symp*.8.8(p.91.2; M.18.152A); hence ?*produce in large numbers* τὰ ὕδατα...μυρία γένη πλωτῶν ἐμψύχων ...ἐν μιᾷ καιροῦ ῥοπῇ...ἐξωμόρξατο ‡Caes.Naz.*dial*.102(M.38.968).

ἐξόμορξις, ἡ, *impression* of one's likeness on something; hence *assimilation* τὴν...καλουμένην ἐ., ἥτις ἐστὶν ἐκ τῶν διαφόρων σιτίων εἰς αἷμα, κἀκεῖθεν εἰς σῶμα...μεταστοιχείωσις ‡Nil.*perist*.4.12(M.79.837D).

***ἐξονίνημι**, *benefit*, Cyr.*Nah*.20(3.499E).

***ἐξοννοῦται**, *cat.Heb*.5:12 suppl.(p.494.12) f.l. for ἐξορροῦται Clem.*paed*.1.6(p.120.26; M.8.312A).

ἐξονυχίζ-ω, *try* a thing's smoothness *with the finger-nail*; hence, met., *polish to perfection* οὕτως ἀβρύνει...τὸν ἴδιον λόγον, οὕτως ~ει, καθὼς αὐτὸς ὀνομάζει, τὰ ῥήματα Gr.Nyss.*Eun*.1(1 p.158.7; M.45.400A).

ἐξοπλίζω, **1.** *arm fully*, fig. τὴν ἑαυτοῦ γλῶτταν κατὰ τῶν ταῦτα ποιούντων ἐ. Socr.*h.e*.6.18.2(M.67.717A); med., *arm oneself*, Thphn.*chron*.p.61(M.108.204B); fig. and met., Meth.*symp*.8.12(p.97.1; M.18.157C); Epiph.*haer*.33.11(p.463.8); Cyr.*Jo*.1.2(4.15C); c. dat., *ib*.5.1(462A); in gen., *equip, prepare* τινὰ κατά τινος Socr.*h.e*.6.15.1(M.67.708B); **2.** *disarm*; fig., ref. Lev.13:45 τὴν κεφαλὴν ἀκατακάλυπτον οἷον τὸν ἔσω ἄνθρωπον αὐτὸ τὸ ἡγεμονικὸν τῆς σκέπης ἐξωπλισμένον τοῦ θεοῦ Meth.*lepr*.7(p.461.11); Gr.Nyss.*instit*.(p.72.15; M.34.428A).

ἐξόπλισις, ἡ, *getting under arms, arming*, Areth.ap.*cat.Apoc*.19:17(p.464.18; ἐξοπλισθεῖσαν M.106.745A); exeg. Cant.3:8 ἀναιρετικὴ τῶν ῥυπαρῶν ἡδονῶν ἐστιν ἡ τῶν περιστοιχισμένων τὴν κλίνην ἐ. Gr.Nyss.*hom.6 in Cant*.(M.44.901A).

ἐξοπτ-άω, **1.** *bake thoroughly*; fig., ref. Jo.6:35 τὴν ζύμην τοῦ ἀνθρωπείου φυράματος...ὥσπερ ~ήσας τῷ οἰκείῳ πυρὶ τῆς θεότητος Isid.Pel.*epp*.1.360(M.78.388A); **2.** *parch, dry up*, Gr.Nyss.*hex*.42(M.44.101A).

***ἐξόπτησις, ἡ,** *evaporation*, Gr.Nyss.*hex*.43(M.44.101A).

ἐξορίζ-ω, *banish*, from life ὁ πλούσιος ἐξωρίσθη, μὴ συμφθάσας ἆραί τι...ἐφόδιον Eus.Al.*serm*.21.12(M.86.437D); fig. τὴν Μαρκέλλου αἵρεσιν...ὡς...τῆς ὑγιαινούσης πίστεως ἀλλοτρίως ἔχουσαν ἐξορίσαι Bas.*ep*.69.2(3.162D; M.32.432B); μέριμνα γὰρ βιωτικὴ καὶ...μέθη ~ει τὴν σύνεσιν Cyr.*Lc*.21:29(M.72.901A); *exclude* τριετίαν πανοικεὶ τῶν εὐχῶν ἐξόρισον Bas.*ep*.270(417A; M.1004A).

ἐξόριος, **1.** *banished, excluded* ἡ...Ἐπικούρου θεογονία τῶν μὲν ἀπείρων κόσμων ἐ. ἐστιν, εἰς δὲ τὴν ἄπειρον ἀκοσμίαν πεφυγάδευται Dion.Al.ap.Eus.*p.e*.14.26(781A, conj. ἔξορος M.21.1284C); fig. παλαιὰν ζύμην ἀθέου πλάνης τῆς αὐτῆς ψυχῆς ἐξόριον ποιούμενοι Eus.*pasch*.2 (M.24.696C); **2.** ἐξορία [sc. ζωή] *banishment*, Ath.*fug*.8(p.74.8; M.25.656A); Gr.Nyss.*laud.Bas*.(M.46.797A); ἔξω τοῦ παραδείσου τυγχάνεις, ὁ κατηχούμενος, κοινωνῶν τῆς ἐ. τοῦ Ἀδὰμ τῷ προπάτορι id.*bapt.diff*.(M.46.417D); Chrys.*Eutrop*.2.2(3.387D); Socr.*h.e*.4.2.6(M.67.465D); of death, Eus.Al.*serm*.21.12(M.86.437C); fig. χρυσὸς ὁ ἄδικος... πρῶτον ἐ. κατακριθείς, ὡς ἀφανὴς τύραννος Gr.Naz.*ep*.140(M.37.237B); ref. miracles ἦν ἰδεῖν παντοίαν ἐ. παθῶν· λόγος ἀφιεῖτο καὶ νόσος ἠλαύνετο Bas.Sel.*or*.35.1(M.85.373B).

***ἐξόρισις, ἡ,** *banishment, sentence of banishment*, *Pet.Ar*.2(M.26.820C).

ἐξορισμός, ὁ, **1.** *banishment*, Thphl.Ant.*Autol*.2.26(M.6.1093A); Jul.Papa *ep.Dian*.ap.Ath.*apol.sec*.35(p.112.34; M.25.305D); CSard.*ep.Alex*.ap.Ath.*ib*.37(p.115.26; 312B); plur., Eus.*v.C*.1.52 tit.(p.5.28; M.20.965C); **2.** *place of banishment* τινὰς μὲν αὐτῶν ἐν ταῖς ὁδοῖς, τινὰς δὲ ἐν αὐτῷ τῷ ἐ. ἀποθανεῖν Ath.*fug*.7(p.73.14; M.25.653A).

***ἐξοριστέος**, *to be banished, got rid of*, Clem.*paed*.2.3(p.178.22; M.8.433B); Synes.*regn*.13(p.42.3; M.66.1088C).

***ἐξοριστία, ἡ,** = ἐξορισμός, CAlex.*ep*.ap.Ath.*apol.sec*.3,5(pp.90.2, 91.9; M.25.253A,256C).

ἐξόριστος, *banished*, CAlex.*ep*.ap.Ath.*apol.sec*.3,4(p.90.3,21; M.25.253A,C); of Adam, Cyr.H.*catech*.19.9; fig. ἐ. [sc. ἡ ἀδικία] τούτου τοῦ τόπου [i.e. τοῦ κυριακοῦ οἴκου] ἐκκλείεται Const.ap.Gel.Cyz.*h.e*.2.7.6(M.85.1233B); *excluded* from argument, Alex.Lyc.*Man*.7(p.11.11, v.l. ἐξοριστέον M.18.420D).

ἐξορκίζ-ω, **1.** *exorcize*, Just.*dial*.76.6(M.6.653C); κατὰ τοῦ ὀνόματος...τούτου υἱοῦ θεοῦ...πᾶν δαιμόνιον ~όμενον νικᾶται *ib*.85.2 (676C); τοῖς αἱρετικοῖς...οὐδεμία πίστις...ὅπου...~ει δαιμονιζόμενος CCarth.*act*.(H.1.160C); CCP(381)‡*can*.7 cit. s. ἐμφυσάω; (Manich.) ἔλαιον ἐξωρκισμένον Hegem.*Arch*.11(p.19.7; M.10.1445B); pres. ptcpl. pass. neut. as subst. τὸ ὕδωρ, καὶ τὸ ~όμενον καὶ τὸ βάπτισμα Clem.*exc.Thdot*.82(p.132.13; M.9.696C); **2.** *conjure* ἐξώρκιζε λέγουσα, δέομαι, εἰπέ μοι *Hom.Clem*.12.19.

***ἐξόρκισις, ἡ,** *exorcism*, Gr.Naz.*carm*.1.2.34.236(M.37.962A).

ἐξορκισμός, ὁ, *exorcism*, cf. *distribuat panem* ἐξορκισμοῦ *antequam consideant, ut deus agapen eorum praeservet a timore inimici*, ‡Hipp.*can*.179; *ib*.170; Gr.Naz.*or*.40.27(M.36.397A); cf.Iren.*haer*.1.23.4(M.7.672C); *exorcismus Graece, Latine conjuratio, sive sermo increpationis est adversus diabolum ut discedat*, Isid.H.*etym*.6.19.55; *Exorc*.1 tit.(p.332).

ἐξορκιστής, ὁ, *exorcist*, Corn.ap.Eus.*h.e*.6.43.11(M.20.621A); *M.Ner.et Ach*.4(p.3.31).

ἐξορκόω, *invoke*, Bas.*hom*.21.8(2.169E; M.31.556A).

ἐξορμάω, **1.** *send forth*; pass., *leap forth*, Niceph.Ur.*v.Sym*.197 (M.86.3165C); **2.** intrans., *set out*, Gel.Cyz.*h.e*.3.17.32; ‡Jo.D.*Artem*.14(p.56.21; M.96.1264D); *emerge* from a forest, Gr.Thaum.*pan.Or*.14(p.32.8,12; M.10.1092B); *leap forth, burst forth*; of a beast of prey, Alex.Thess.*ep.Dion*.(p.160.26; M.25.393C); of a river, Philost.*h.e*.3.1(M.65.493C); met., *burst out* in angry demands, *ib*.7.6a (636A).

ἐξορμίζω, pass., *come right to land*, Gr.Nyss.*v.Mos*.17(M.44.304D).

ἔξορος, v. ἐξόριος.

***ἐξορρόομαι**, *be curdled*, Clem.*paed*.1.6(p.120.26; M.8.312A).

***ἐξόρυξις, ἡ,** *gouging out* of eyes, Eus.*l.C*.7(p.214.2; M.20.1353D); ‡Ath.*pat*.6(M.26.1304D).

ἐξορύσσω, *dig out*; met., *extract, remove* from ἄλλον...ἐξορύττει [sc. ὁ δαίμων] τῆς θείας σωφροσύνης Nil.*epp*.3.43(M.79.109D); τὴν μὲν οὐσίαν καὶ τὸ ὁμοούσιον ἐξορύξαι τῆς πίστεως Thdt.*h.e*.2.21.1(3.879).

***ἐξορφανίζομαι**, *be deprived* of, Sophr.H.*or*.2.49(M.87.3285C).

ἐξορχ-έομαι, **1.** *dance along*, fig. μὴ τρέχοντα...παριπτάμενον τῶν διδασκομένων τὴν γνῶσιν...τὸν λόγον, ἀλλ' εὐπάρυφόν τε καὶ διαφόρως ~ούμενον Cyr.*Jo*.2.6(4.215A); **2.** *betray* ὅρα ὅπως οὐκ ~ήσῃ τὰ ἅγια τῶν ἁγίων Dion.Ar.*e.h*.1.1.1(M.3.372A); **3.** *dishonour* τῶν ἀρρένων τὴν δόξαν ~ούμενοι Amph.*Seleuc*.91(M.37.1583A); ἄνθρωπος...τοῦ χαρισαμένου τὴν χάριν ἐξωρχήσατο, τὸ δῶρον ἀτιμάσας Mac.Mgn.*apocr*.4.16 (p.186.19); Isid.Pel.*epp*.2.82(M.78.525B); ἐ. τὴν εὐσέβειαν *ib*.2.121 (561A); τὴν ὅλην ἀρχὴν διεπέττευε, τὸ τῆς βασιλείας μέγεθος ~ούμενος ‡Jo.D.*Artem*.10(p.49.25; M.96.1261A); **4.** *mock* τοιούτοις ῥήμασιν

~ούμενοι...τὸν θεὸν ἀνθρώποις ἀπεικάζουσι Ath.*Ar*.1.22(M.26.57C); Synes.*Dion* 3(p.242.19; M.66.1121C).

ἐξοσιόω, med.; **1.** *dedicate*, Gr.Ant.*exerc*.2(p.230.22; M.88.1385B); **2.** *appease* τὸν θεὸν λιταῖς καὶ προσευχαῖς ἐ. Evagr.*h.e*.6.13(p.231.15; M.86.2864C).

***ἐξοσίωσις**, ἡ, *expiation*, Philost.*h.e*.7.8(M.65.545C).

ἐξοστεΐζω, *remove the seeds from*, fig. ἐ. τὴν ἁμαρτίαν Pall.*v.Chrys*. 18(p.119.26; edd. ἐξοστρακίζων M.47.67).

ἐξοστρακίζ-ω, *banish*, Hier.*vir.ill*.(tr.Sophr.Pal.)85(p.50.1; M.*PL*.23.692B); Alex.Sal.*Barn*.3.36(448F); in gen., *exclude, drive out*, Eust.*fr.in Pr.8*:22(M.18.676D); τῆς Ἰουδαίων χώρας ἐξωστρακισμένος...Χριστός Cyr.*Jo*.4.5(4.403C); fig. and met. ὑπερηφανίαν ἐ. *A.Jo.Bapt*.7(p.534.14); τὰ...τοῦ...Ναυάτου βληχήματα, τὴν...μετάνοιαν ~ειν τολμῶντα Nil.*epp*.2.155(M.79.273B); Isid.Pel.*epp*.1.69(M.78.229A); Jo.Carp.*cap*.68(M.85.1851); Jo.D.*hom*.4.19(M.96.617A).

ἐξοστρακισμός, ὁ, *exile*, Philost.*h.e*.1.10(M.65.465B); Evagr.*h.e*.6.7(p.226.31; M.86.2853B); *ib*.1.7(p.14.11; 2437C).

***ἐξοστράκιστος**, *banished, to be banished* τοὺς...ἁγίους πατέρας ἐ. κατεδίκασεν ‡Jo.D.*ep.Thphl*.7(M.95.353D).

***ἐξότονος**, sens. dub., *Chr.sac.A*(p.58).

ἐξουδενέω, = ἐξουδενόω, v.l. for ἐξουθενέω, Bas.*reg.fus*.41.1(2.387C; M.31.1021C); Gr.Nyss.*or.2 in Gen.1*:26(M.44.292C); Diod.*Ps*. 57:7(M.33.1595B).

ἐξουδενίζω, = ἐξουδενόω (LXX Ps.57:8), Diod.ad loc.(M.33.1595B).

ἐξουδεν-όω, **1.** *set at nought, despise*; Christ, ref. Ps.21:6, Just.*dial*.101.2(v.l. ἐξουθενωθείς M.6.712C); ὅσοι...ἠπίστουν αὐτῷ [sc. τῷ ἐπουρανίῳ ἱερεῖ], ὡς ἄνθρωπον αὐτὸν ~οῦντες Hipp.*Dan*.4.32.5(v.l. ἐξουθενοῦντες M.10.653B); ref. Pr.1:7 παντὶ τῷ ~οῦντι σοφίαν λεχθείη ἂν τὸ 'ὑμεῖς ἀτιμάζετέ με' Or.*Jo*.20.37(29; p.378.21; M.14.661B); in gen., ref. virtue of humility, Ephr.1.20D; *Apophth.Patr*.(M.65.405A); Max.*ep*.11(M.91.457A); Jo.D.*spir.neq*.10(M.95.81D); **2.** *bring to nought, destroy* ἐν σοὶ [i.e. Ἰακώβ] ~ώσει κύριος τοὺς Χαναναίους *T.Lev*.7.1.

ἐξουδένωμα, τό, *object of contempt, that which is worth nothing*, Hipp.*Dan*.3.3; paraphrasing Ps.21:6, †Cyr.*coll.VT*(6^{4}.68C; M.77.1277B).

ἐξουδένωσις, ἡ, **1.** *setting no value* on, *disregard* τὴν τοῦ ἁγίου πνεύματος ἐ. ὡς ὁμολογουμένην λαβόντα Bas.*Eun*.2.33(1.270C; M.29.649B); **2.** *contempt*, Gr.Naz.*or*.2.78(M.35.485A); Cyr.*Ps*.14:3(M.69.805C); **3.** *humiliation*, Or.*enarr.in Job* 3(M.17.68B); τίς ἐ. ἀγαπῶν, ἐπὶ ἀτιμίᾳ ταράσσεται; Marc.Er.*opusc*.2.114(M.65.948A); *Apophth.Patr*.(M.65.269D); τίς ἐστιν ἐ.; τὸ εἶναί σε ὑποκάτω τῶν ἀλόγων, καὶ εἰδέναι ὅτι ἀκατάκριτά εἰσιν *ib*.(332C); ἡ ἐ. δύο τρόπους ἔχει, ἕνα τὸν ἀπὸ καρδίας, καὶ ἕτερον ἀπὸ τῶν ἀνθρώπων ἐπιφερόμενον· μείζων δέ ἐστιν ἡ ἀπὸ τῶν ἀνθρώπων ἐ. τῆς ἀπὸ καρδίας Bars.*resp*.(M.88.1816D); Philox.*ep*.38(p.185); of Christ's sufferings, Mac.Aeg.*pat*.18(M.34.880B); †Cyr.*coll.VT*(6^{4}.68C; M.77.1277B).

***ἐξουδενωτέον**, *one ought to despise*, Bas.*hex*.9.1(1.80B; M.29.188B).

ἐξουθεν-έω, **1.** *set no value upon*, Chrys.*hom.23.3 in Eph*.(11.177E); **2.** *set at nought, despise* ὅν [sc. Christ] ποτε ἡμεῖς...~ήσαμεν ἐμπτύσαντες *Barn*.7.9; τῇ...~ημένῃ πρώτῃ παρουσίᾳ αὐτοῦ Just.*dial*.121.3(M.6.757B); *ib*.131.2(780C); id.*1apol*.63.16(M.6.425B); in gen., *Ep.Lugd*.ap.Eus.*h.e*.5.1.53(M.20.429A); Clem.*str*.3.18(p.244.25; M.8.1208C); Or.*hom.14.14 in Jer*.(p.118.24; M.13.420C); οὐ δεῖ...τὸν μὲν ἐκβάλλοντα δαιμόνια θαυμάζειν μόνον, τὸν δὲ μὴ ἐκβάλλοντα ~εῖν Ath.*v.Anton*.38(M.26.897C); Ephr.1.20D; Jo.D.*spir.neq*.10(M.95.84A); ptcpl. pass., *insignificant, despicable*, †Bas.*bapt*.1.2.5(2.633A; M.31.1533C); **3.** *disregard*, Tert.*apologia* 5 ap.Eus.*h.e*.5.5.7(M.20.441A).

***ἐξουθένησις**, ἡ, **1.** *setting no value* on μὴ θελῆσαι πόνους ὑπὲρ αὐτῆς [sc. τῆς γῆς τῆς ἐπιθυμητῆς] ἀναδέξασθαι...τοῦτο ἐ. Chrys.*hom.23.3 in Eph*.(11.177F); **2.** *contempt*, Gr.Mag.*dial*.(tr.Zach.)3.14(M.*PL*.77.243D).

***ἐξουθενητής**, ὁ, *scorner, flippant person*, Hipp.*haer*.4.15,20,22(pp.50.4,51.27,52.18; M.16.3083B,3086C,3087B).

***ἐξουκόντιος**, *Exucontian*, designation of Arians who held that Son was created *out of nothing* (ἐξ οὐκ ὄντων), cf. τῇ ἐξ οὐκ ὄντων ὑποθέσει Alex.Al.*ep.Alex*.2(p.21.12; M.18.552B); οἱ ἐξ οὐκ ὄντων *ib*.9(p.25.14; 561A); esp. of Anomoeans, Ath.*syn*.31(p.260.2; M.26.749A); οἱ...τὰ Ἀετίου φρονοῦντες...ἀνόμοιοι καὶ ἐ. ἐκλήθησαν ὑπὸ τῶν ἐν τῇ Ἀντιοχείᾳ φρονούντων...τὸ ὁμοούσιον Socr.*h.e*.2.45.11(M.67.360C); Soz.*h.e*.4.29.2(M.67.1205A).

ἐξούλη, ἡ, *ejectment*, fig. σε...ἐξούλης γραφὴν ὑπ αὐτῆς [sc. πενίας] φεύγειν Bas.*ep*.4(3.76C; M.32.236C).

ἐξουρέω, *pass urine*; fig., of Nile in flood, Soz.*h.e*.7.20.5(M.67.1481B).

ἐξουσία, ἡ, **A.** *power, authority*; **1.** of God οἰκείαν καὶ ἄναρχον...τῆς μοναρχικῆς ἐ. τὴν θεότητα κεκτημένος Eus.*e.th*.1.11(p.70.2; M.24.844D); τὴν αἰώνιον καὶ σωτηριώδη τοῦ ἀθανάτου θεοῦ ἐ. Const.ap.Gel.Cyz.*h.e*.2.7.34(M.85.1240C); but cf. οὐ γὰρ ἐξουσίᾳ τὴν ἡμετέραν ᾠκονόμησε σωτηρίαν...ἀλλ' ἐκέρασε τῷ δικαίῳ τὸν ἔλεον Thdt.*Rom*.1:17(3.22); ref. Lc.12:4–5, whether of Father or demiurge, Epiph.*haer*.42.11(p.137.20ff.; M.41.745Cff.); word wrongly used of generation of Son εἰ ὅλος ἐστὶν ἀγέννητος [sc. ὁ θεός], οὐκ οὐσιωδῶς εἰς γένεσιν διέστη· ἐξουσίᾳ δὲ ὑπέστησε γέννημα Aët.*synt*.7 ap.Epiph.*haer*.76.11(p.353.21; M.42.537A); refuted τὸ μὲν γεννητόν ἐστι τὸ ἐκ τῆς ὑποστάσεως γεννώμενον, καὶ διὰ τοῦτο ἐκ γαστρὸς λεγόμενον· τὸ δὲ γενητὸν τὸ ἐκ τῆς ἐ. τοῦ γενεσιουργοῦ ‡Ath.*dial.Trin*.1.18(M.28.1145A); εἰ κατ' ἐξουσίαν, ὥς φατε, τὸν υἱὸν ὑπέστησεν ὁ πατήρ, περιττῶς καλεῖται...υἱός Cyr.*thes*.11(5^{1}.81A); **2.** of Father and Son οἱ δαίμονες ...τήν τε τοῦ πατρὸς...καὶ τὴν αὐτοῦ τοῦ Χριστοῦ ἐ. φυγεῖν πειρῶνται Just.*1apol*.40.7(M.6.389B); ref. Jo.16:15 ὄντων γὰρ ἐν τῇ τοῦ πατρὸς ἐ. τούτων, ἔστιν ὁμοίως ἐν τῇ τοῦ υἱοῦ Ath.*hom.in Mt.11*:27(M.25.213C); τὸ ἰσοστάσιον τῆς ἑαυτοῦ καὶ τῆς τοῦ πατρὸς ἐ. *cat.Jo*.14:7(p.346.2); of Son τούτου δὲ ἔχει ἐξουσίαν Ἰησοῦς Χριστός, τὸ ἀληθινὸν ἡμῶν ζῆν Ign.*Smyrn*.4.1; ὁ πῖλος ὁ χρυσοῦς [sc. τοῦ ἀρχιερέως] ὁ ἀνατεταμένος τὴν ἐ. μηνύει τὴν βασιλικὴν τοῦ κυρίου Clem.*str*.5.6(p.351.23; M.9.64B); discussion of Mt.21:23, Or.*comm.in Mt*.17.1(pp.575ff.; M.13.1473ff.); τὸ δὲ [Jo.1:2] τὸ ἐξουσιαστικὸν τοῦ λόγου...ἔοικε σημαίνειν, τὴν ἐ. ἀρχὴν εἰπών Meth.*creat*.11(p.499.13; M.18.344A); τὴν δοθεῖσαν αὐτῷ ἐ. Ἀστέριος δόξαν ὀνομάζει...προκόσμιον Marcell.*fr*.93 ap.Eus.*Marcell*.2.2(p.40.5; M.24.792A); *ib*.97 ap.Eus.*ib*.2.3(p.51.9; 809B); τὴν ἐ. δὲ ἣν ἔλεγε μετὰ τὴν ἀνάστασιν εἰληφέναι, ταύτην εἶχε καὶ πρὸ τοῦ λαβεῖν καὶ πρὸ τῆς ἀναστάσεως Ath.*Ar*.3.40(M.26.408C); καταβέβηκεν ὁ κύριος ἡμῶν εἰς τὸν ᾅδην...ἐν ἐ. καὶ μεγάλῃ δυνάμει id.*virg*.16(p.51.15; M.28.272A); of incarnate Christ ὅτι ἐκβέβηκε τὰ μετὰ τοσαύτης ἐ. εἰρημένα, ἐμφαίνει θεὸν ἀληθῶς ἐνανθρωπήσαντα σωτηρίας δόγματα τοῖς ἀνθρώποις παραδεδωκέναι Or.*princ*.4.1.2(p.296.4; M.14.345B); ἐπ' ἐξουσίας *within one's power* ἀθάνατος...ὤν, σάρκα δὲ θνητὴν ἐπ' ἐξουσίας εἶχεν, ὡς θεός, ἀπὸ τοῦ σώματος χωρισθῆναι καὶ τοῦτο πάλιν ἀναλαβεῖν ὅτε βούλεται Ath.*Ar*.3.57(M.26.444B); κατ' ἐξουσίαν *voluntarily, freely* ἀποθνήσκων ἑκόντι καὶ ἐγειρόμενος κατ' ἐ. id.*inc.et c.Ar*.21(M.26.1024A); τὰ μὲν τῆς ἡμῶν ἐπιτιμίας. ... κατ' ἐ. πάθη δεχόμενος Max.*opusc*.(M.91.32A); **3.** of H. Ghost τῆς αὐτῆς θεότητός ἐστι καὶ τῆς αὐτῆς ἐ. Ath.*inc.et c.Ar*.9(M.26.997A); τοῦ πνεύματος τὴν ἁγιαστικὴν ἐ. Bas.*ep*.189.7(3.280D; M.32.693B); σὺν τῷ πατρὶ καὶ τῷ υἱῷ τῆς μιᾶς καὶ τῆς αὐτῆς οὐσίας τε καὶ ἐ. ὑπάρχειν τὸ ἅγιον πνεῦμα Dam.Papa *anath*.ap.Thdt.*h.e*.5.11.1; **4.** surrendered to God by Christian Χριστιανὸς ἑαυτοῦ ἐ. οὐκ ἔχει, ἀλλὰ θεῷ σχολάζει Ign.*Polyc*.7.3; δεῖ εὐλαβεστέρους ἡμᾶς ὑπάρχοντας τῷ θεῷ τὴν κατὰ πάντων [sc. τῶν μαρτυρίων] ἐ. ἀνατιθέναι *M.Polyc*.2.1; **5.** of authority given to apostles οἱ εὐαγγελισάμενοι ἡμῖν τὴν ἄφεσιν τῶν ἁμαρτιῶν...οἷς ἔδωκεν τοῦ εὐαγγελίου τὴν ἐ. ... εἰς τὸ κηρύσσειν *Barn*.8.3; Παῦλος...ἐ. ἔχων ἀποστολικήν Or.*hom.8.8 in Jer*.(p.62.7; M.13.345A); and prophets, Heracleon ap.eund.*Jo*.2.14(8; p.70.22; M.14.137C); Or.*hom.1.6 in Jer*.(p.4.22; M.13.260D); fig., to the shepherd ἐμοὶ ἡ ἐ. τῆς μετανοίας ταύτης ἐδόθη Herm.*mand*.4.3.5; **6.** of episcopal and pastoral authority τὸν Ἀλεξανδρείας ἐπίσκοπον πάντων τούτων [i.e. τῶν ἐν Αἰγύπτῳ καὶ Λιβύῃ καὶ Πενταπόλει] ἔχειν τὴν ἐ., ἐπειδὴ καὶ τῷ ἐν τῇ Ῥώμῃ ἐπισκόπῳ τοῦτο σύνηθές ἐστιν CNic.(325)*can*.6; αὐτῷ μεταδίδωμι τὴν ἐ. τοῦ δεσμεύειν καὶ λύειν *Clem.ep*.2(M.2.36B); παραιτούμενος τὴν τῆς καθέδρας τιμήν τε καὶ ἐ. *ib*.3(37A); κρῖνε οὖν, ὦ ἐπίσκοπε, μετὰ ἐ. ὡς θεὸς *Const.App*.2.12.1; οὗτοι γὰρ παρὰ θεοῦ ζωῆς καὶ θανάτου ἐ. εἰλήφασιν ἐν τῷ δικάζειν τοὺς ἡμαρτηκότας καὶ...λύειν ἁμαρτιῶν τοὺς ἐπιστρέφοντας *ib*.2.33.3; ἐπειδὴ ὁ ἀρχιερεὺς κεφαλὴ ἦν τοῦ λαοῦ, ἔδει δὲ τὸν πάντων κεφαλὴν γινόμενον ἔχειν κατὰ κεφαλῆς τὴν ἐ. ... τὸ τοίνυν ἔχειν τὸν ἀρχιερέα τὸ εὐαγγέλιον, σημεῖόν ἐστι τὸ ἐπ' ἐξουσίαν εἶναι. ... ἣν οὖν ἡ τιάρα τὸ σχῆμα τῆς ἐ.‡Chrys.*leg*.4(6.410A,C); handed on in ordination ὁ διάκονος...λαβὼν παρὰ τοῦ ἐπισκόπου τὴν ἐ., ὡς ὁ Χριστὸς παρὰ τοῦ πατρὸς τὸ προνοεῖν *Const.App*.2.44.3; τὴν ἐ. διὰ τῆς χειροτονίας Chrys.*stat*.1.1(2.1B); **7.** of authority divinely given; **a.** to secular rulers, *1Clem*.61.1,2; κριτὴς ὢν [sc. Samuel] ἐξίστατο τῆς ἐ. καὶ ταύτην παρεδίδου τῷ βασιλεῖ Thdt.*qu.25 in 1Reg*.(1.372); **b.** to Christians, of forgiving each other, *Const.App*.2.53.7; **8.** of angels ὁ μέν τις ἕξει ἐν τῇ ἐσομένῃ διακοσμήσει τάξιν ἀγγελικὴν ἢ δύναμιν ἀρχικὴν ἢ ἐ. τὴν ἐπί τινων ἢ θρόνον Or.*princ*.1.6.2(p.81.4; M.11.167A); compared with that of demons, ref. Mt.21:23, id.*comm.in Mt*.17.2(p.579.33ff.; M.13.1477Aff.); **9.** of secular power Ἐσθὴρ ῥυομένη τὸν Ἰσραὴλ τυραννικῆς ἐ. καὶ τῆς τοῦ σατράπου ὠμότητος Clem.*str*.4.19(p.300.22; M.8.1329A);

of the emperor μετ᾽ ἐ. πάντας βιάζεται Ath.h.Ar.33(p.201.26; M.25.732B); τῆς τοῦ στρατηλάτου ἐ. ib.75(p.225.3; 784C); of slave owners, Cyr.ador.8(1.263B); **10.** of demonic power ἵνα μήποτε...ὁ πονηρὸς ἄρχων λαβὼν τὴν καθ᾽ ἡμῶν ἐ. ἀπώσηται ἡμᾶς ἀπὸ τῆς βασιλείας τοῦ κυρίου Barn.4.13; Just.dial.105.4(M.6.721B); τῆς διαβολικῆς ἡμᾶς ἐ. ἐρρύσατο Or.fr.54 in Jer.(p.225.17; M.13.580D); οὐ γὰρ ἂν τὴν καθ᾽ ὑμῶν ἔσχον ἐ. οἱ δαίμονες, εἰ μὴ πρότερον τῷ ἄρχοντι αὐτῶν ὁμοδίαιτοι ἐγεγόνειτε Hom.Clem.7.3; ib.8.20; ref. Lc.4:6 'πᾶσα ἡ τρυφὴ τοῦ κόσμου τούτου ὑπὸ ταῖς ἐμαῖς ἐστιν ἐ. ...' ταῦτα δὲ ἔλεγεν εἰδὼς ὅτι μετὰ τὸ προσκυνῆσαι καὶ τὴν κατ᾽ αὐτοῦ εἶχεν ἐ. ib.8.21; V.Aberc.43(p.32.12); ref. Eph.2:2 σαφῶς ἄρχοντα τῆς ἐ. τοῦ κινεῖν τὸν ἀέρα καὶ μεταβάλλειν αὐτὸν εἶναι πρώην διδάξας, νυνὶ δὲ ἐκριφέντα μηκέτι ταύτην ἔχειν τὴν ἀξίαν, ἀλλὰ μᾶλλον ἐνεργεῖν ἐκ κακίας ἐπὶ τοὺς ἁμαρτωλούς Cosm.Ind.top.2(M.88.117D); **11.** of things πληρωθείσης τῆς ἐ. [sc. τοῦ κατὰ τῆς φθορᾶς τῶν ἀνθρώπων νόμου] ἐν τῷ κυριακῷ σώματι Ath.inc.8.4(M.25.109D); ἐν τῇ ἐκκλησίᾳ ὁ ἱερεὺς ἐπιδίδωσι τὴν μερίδα, καὶ κατέχει αὐτὴν ὁ ὑποδεχόμενος μετ᾽ ἐξουσίας ἁπάσης Bas.ep.93(3.187B; M.32.485B); τὸν...συγκληρονόμον σε ἑλόμενον [i.e. Χριστόν], τὸν ἀπὸ σκότους εἰς ἐ. φωτὸς ἀγαγόντα Chrys.hom.23.8 in Mt.(7.296A); *scope* of an argument τὴν εἰς αὐτοὺς γεγενημένην κηδεμονίαν διεξελθών, ἐπὶ τὴν γενικωτέραν ἐ. μετέβη Thdt.Ps.79:2(1.1171).

B. of individuals' *power* of choice παλαιστὴς...οὐκ αὐτὸς ἑαυτῷ τοὺς ἀντιπάλους ἐκλέγεται...ἀλλὰ τῇ τῶν θεωρούντων δίδωσιν ἐ. Ath.inc.24.3(M.25.137B); τῆς ὑμετέρας ἐστὶν ἐ., ὑπείκειν ἢ ἀπειθεῖν Hom.Clem.1.10; ref. free will ὥσπερ οὖν ὁ τῇ ἐ. εἰς τὸ κατ᾽ ἀρετὴν βιῶσαι συγχρησάμενος ἐπαινετός, οὕτω πολὺ μᾶλλον ὁ τὴν ἐ. ἡμῖν δεδωκὼς ἐλευθέραν καὶ κυρίαν...σεμνὸς καὶ προσκυνητός Clem.str.3.5(p.214.21; M.8.1144C); τὴν ἐ. ... ἑλέσθαι τὴν σωτηρίαν ib.4.26(p.324.5; 1380B); φημὶ τὸν θεὸν οὕτω τὸν ἄνθρωπον τιμῆσαι προαιρούμενον καὶ τῶν κρειττόνων ἐπιστήμονα γίνεσθαι, τὴν ἐ. αὐτῷ τοῦ δύνασθαι ποιεῖν ἃ βούλεται δεδωκέναι, καὶ τὴν ἐ. αὐτοῦ εἰς κρεῖττον ⟨τρέπειν⟩ παραινεῖν, οὐκ ἀφαιρούμενον πάλιν τὸ αὐτεξούσιον, ἀλλὰ τὸ κρεῖττον μηνύειν θέλοντα Meth.arbitr.16(p.188.5,6; M.18.264C); οὔτε ἐ. ἐστὶν ἡ προαίρεσις...· ἡ δὲ ἐ., κυριότης ἔννομος τῶν ἐφ᾽ ἡμῖν πρακτῶν. ἢ κυριότης ἀκώλυτος τῆς τῶν ἐφ᾽ ἡμῶν χρήσεως· ἢ ὄρεξις τῶν ἐφ᾽ ἡμῖν ἀδούλωτος. οὐκ ἔστιν οὖν ταὐτὸν ἐ. καὶ προαίρεσις. εἴπερ κατ᾽ ἐ. μὲν προαιρούμεθα· οὐκ ἐξουσιάζομεν δὲ κατὰ προαίρεσιν Max.opusc.(M.91.17C,D); in prepositional phrases: *within the power* of τὰ ἔργα ἡμῶν ἐν ἐκλογῇ καὶ ἐ. τῆς ψυχῆς ἡμῶν Pss.Sal.9.7; ref. emperor worship ὥσπερ ἐπ᾽ ἐξουσίας ἔχοντες τὸ θεοποιεῖν Ath.gent.9(M.25.21A); κατασκευάζων μὴ κατ᾽ ἐξουσίαν προκεῖσθαι τοῖς βουλομένοις τῶν κατὰ γνώμην τὴν αἵρεσιν Gr.Nyss.fat.(M.45.148B); *freely, as one pleases* τὸν μετ᾽ ἐξουσίας ἤδη βιούντων βίον Eus.v.C.2.32(p.55.8; M.20.1009B); μὴ ἐφ᾽ ἡμῖν εἶναι ὅπερ ἂν θέλωμεν κατ᾽ ἐξουσίαν αἱρεῖσθαι Gr.Nyss.fat.(M.45.149A); ἐπ᾽ ἐξουσίας, ἐφ᾽ ὅτῳ ἂν βούλοιτο Cyr.hom.pasch.11(5^{2}.152B); id.ador.6(1.197B); ἐπ᾽ ἐξουσίας αἵρεσιν *free choice*, Eus.v.C.2.20(p.49.23; 997C); Disp.Phot.3.39(M.85.565D).

C. *authority* to receive effects of another's action, *privilege, right* τοὺς μὴ δυναμένους ἐ. υἱοθεσίας φέρειν ὁ φόβος μὴ ἐξυβρίζειν διατηρεῖ Clem.str.3.8(p.262.27; M.8.616C); ἡ ἐ. τοῦ δέξασθαι τὴν ἰατρείαν οὐκ ἐν τῷ προσάγοντι τὸ φάρμακον ἀλλ᾽ ἢ ἐν τῷ κάμνοντι κεῖται Chrys.sac.2.3(p.32.6; 1.374A); Thdt.1Cor.9:18(3.222).

D. abuse of *authority, licence* μὴ δῶμεν τῇ ἑαυτῶν ψυχῇ ἄνεσιν, ὥστε ἔχειν αὐτὴν ἐ. μετὰ ἁμαρτωλῶν καὶ πονηρῶν συντρέχειν Barn.4.2; Βασιλειδιανῶν, ὡς ἤτοι ἐχόντων ἐ. καὶ τοῦ ἁμαρτεῖν διὰ τὴν τελειότητα Clem.str.3.1(p.196.18; M.8.1104A); μὴ τρέφοντας καὶ ῥωννύντας [sc. τὸ σαρκίον ἀντίδικον] τῇ τῶν ἁμαρτημάτων ἐ. id.exc.Thdot.52(p.124.12; M.9.684C); Cyr.H.catech.4.25.

E. *body of magistrates, authorities* τῶν πολιτικῶν ἐ. καὶ παντὸς τοῦ πλήθους Ep.Lugd.ap.Eus.h.e.5.1.30(M.20.420B); ref. Ps.1:1 καθέδρα δὲ λοιμῶν...ἡ ἐξακολούθησις ταῖς πονηραῖς καὶ ταῖς λυμαντικαῖς ἐ. καὶ ἡ κατὰ τὰ ἔργα αὐτῶν κοινωνία Clem.str.2.15(p.149.14; M.8.1008A); Bas.reg.fus.8.1(2.349A; M.31.936C); ἐν τῷ τῆς ὑμετέρας ἐ. ἐργοδοσίῳ ...ἐπὶ ὁλοκλήρῳ τετραμήνῳ...ἐργάζεσθαι †Gregent.leg.Hom.31(M.86.597C); hence as honorary title of a prefect, Thdt.ep.94(4.1164).

F. title of a rank in angelic hierarchy οἱ μὲν διδάξαντες μετατίθενται εἰς ἀρχαγγελικὴν ἐ. Clem.ecl.57(p.154.11; M.9.728A); Or.Jo.1.31(34; p.39.2; M.14.81B); hence, of the angels in this rank, *powers*, Hipp.haer.7.28(p.208.12; M.16.3322A), Or.princ.1.6.2(p.81.4; M.11.167A) citt. s. δύναμις; ἄλλο γὰρ γένος τὸ τῶν ἀγγέλων καὶ ἄλλο τὸ τῶν ἀρχῶν καὶ ἐ. Meth.res.1.49(p.302.16; M.18.277B); ‡Ath.serm.fid.28(p.25; M.26.1284A); ἐ. εἰσὶ δυνάμεις ἐξουσιαστικαὶ κατὰ χάριν θεοῦ Gr.Nyss.ap.Doct.Patr.33(p.257.28); as heavenly bodies, ref. Ps.135:8,9, Thdr.Mops.ap.Thdt.qu.20 in Gen.(1.32); Dion.Ar.c.h.8.1(M.3.240A); ib.11.1(284C); id.e.h.1.1.2(M.3.372C) al.; Jo.Mal.chron.4 p.74(M.97.156A).

G. evil spiritual *powers*, Or.princ.1.6.3(p.83.6); Cainite formula ἡ δεῖνα ἐ., πράττω σοῦ τὴν πρᾶξιν Epiph.haer.38.2(p.64.11; M.41.656C); ὁ πόλεμος πρὸς τὸν διάβολον καὶ τὰς ἐ. τοῦ σκότους Chrys.hom.8.4 in Mt.(7.126C); εἰ γὰρ βίᾳ ἔπασχεν ὑπὸ τῶν ἐ. ὁ ἄνθρωπος, πάντως ἐδύνατο ἐλευθερῶσαι ἡμᾶς ὁ θεός Marc.Er.opusc.4(M.65.989B); Esaias or.1.1(p.1).

H. *pomp* τὴν...σύμπασαν ἑῴαν μεγαλοπρεπείᾳ βασιλικῆς ἐ. ἐμπεριελθοῦσα [sc. Helena] Eus.v.C.3.44(p.96.18; M.20.1105A).

ἐξουσιάζ-ω, **1.** *have power* τὸ πνεῦμα τοῦ ~οντος τὸ ἀπατηλόν Or.exc.in Ps.77:31(M.17.147B); κύριος...~ων ἐκ τοῦ μὴ ὄντος εἰς τὸ εἶναι παράγειν οὐσίας Jo.D.Man.1.9(M.94.1513B); hence *exercise free will*, Max.opusc.(M.91.17D) cit. s. ἐξουσία; **2.** *have power* over; c. acc. A.Barth.6(p.142.17); c. genit., Meth.res.2.1(p.330.15); Ath.inc.25.5(M.25.140B); Didym.(‡Bas.)Eun.5(1.304C; M.29.729B); ὁ τῶν νεκρῶν καὶ τῶν ζώντων ~ων A.Pil.B 22(p.329); c. ἐπί et dat., Thdr.Stud.epp.1.10(M.99.941A); pass., *be under authority*, Pall.v.Chrys.10(p.60.3; M.47.34); Marc.Er.opusc.1.76(M.65.913D).

***ἐξουσιάρχης**, ὁ, *one who rules with power, powerful ruler*, ref. Is.9:6, Andr.Cr.or.5(M.97.905A).

***ἐξουσιαρχία**, ἡ, *supreme authority*, Dion.Ar.c.h.8.1(M.3.240B).

***ἐξουσιαστηκῶς**, v. ἐξουσιαστικῶς.

ἐξουσιαστής, ὁ, *one who wields supreme power, final authority*; of God, Gr.Nyss.Eun.1(1 p.154.11; M.45.396A); ὅ που αὐτὸς ὁ κύριος ...ἡνιοχεῖ τὴν ψυχὴν...αὐθέντης καὶ ἐ. τυγχάνων ἀεί, τὴν νίκην αὐτὸς ἐργάζεται Mac.Aeg.hom.1.9(M.34.460B); ref. 1Reg.17:1 ὁ θεὸς...ὁ ἐπιτάξας...τῷ ὑετῷ...ὁ ἐ. τῷ οὐρανῷ ib.50.1(816D); Jo.D.f.o.1.2(M.94.792C); of Son κύριος στρατῶν καὶ ἐ. Ath.Ar.2.24(M.26.197B); οὗτος ὡς πλάστης καὶ ἐ. τοῦ πράγματος ἑαυτὸν ἀπὸ παρθένου...ἀνεπλάσατο Epiph.haer.79.7(p.481.30; M.42.749D); Procl.CP or.6.11(M.65.741B); of incarnate Christ καὶ ζωῆς καὶ θανάτου...ἐ. Or.fr.155 in Mt.(p.77); Ath.Ar.3.40(M.26.409A); of Manicheans' evil God τοῦ ἀνθρώπου τὴν σάρκα...ὑπὸ τὸν ἄρχοντα τῆς κακίας τάσσων, καὶ ἐ. τοῦτον ἐπιγραφόμενος ‡Ath.Apoll.2.8(M.26.1144C); of Devil τὸν ἐ. τὸν κατ᾽ ἐμοῦ [i.e. τοῦ δαιμόνου] ἔχοντα τὴν ἐξουσίαν A.Thom.A 76(p.190.20); of death, Proc.G.Is.25:7(M.87.2212C); of secular rulers, A.Thom.A 148(p.257.10); of Jewish leaders as authors of Christ's condemnation, Const.App.5.14.12; not of servants of God εὐεργετῶν ὁ θεὸς συμβούλους ἀλλ᾽ οὐχὶ ἐ. δίδωσιν †Bas.Is.57(1.422A; M.30.220C).

ἐξουσιαστικός, **1.** *authoritative* ὁ κύριος τίς; ἐ. ἡ προσηγορία Tit.Bost.fr.Lc.19:31(p.233); ‡Ath.Apoll.2.14(M.26.1156B); cat.Ac.2:13(p.29.8); ref. Ac.7:51, Is.63:10 ἐ. δυνάμεως παραστατικὰ τὰ τοιαῦτα Bas.Spir.50(3.42C; M.32.160B); τὸ ἐ. ... ἀξίωμα τῆς...τοῦ Ἰούδα φυλῆς Eus.d.e.8.1(p.357.36; M.22.581C); neut. as subst., *authority*, Meth.creat.11(p.499.11; M.18.341B); Epiph.haer.69.59(p.207.24; M.42.297A); ib.42.12(p.180.11; M.41.809A); **2.** *free, self-determining*, Max.ambig.(M.91.1076C); id.opusc.(M.91.128C); ref. Inc. οὐκ εἰς δύναμιν ἐ. ἀλλ᾽ εἰς φυσικὴν ἀνάγκην τὸ γεγονὸς ἀναφέρουσιν Gr.Nyss.Eun.12(2 p.290.50; M.45.904B); neut. as subst., *possession of free will* θεοῦ εἰκὼν ὁ ἄνθρωπος...κατὰ τὸ ἐ. Diod.Gen.1:26(M.33.1564D); **3.** *belonging to the* angelic *powers*, Dion.Ar.c.h.8.1(M.3.240A).

ἐξουσιαστικῶς, **1.** *with authority, authoritatively*, ref. generation of Son εἰ οὐκ ἐκ τῆς οὐσίας τοῦ πατρὸς προῆλθεν ὁ υἱός, ὑπέστη δὲ ἐ. Cyr.thes.10(5^{1}.81B); of Son, ref. Jo.1:12 δίδωσι γεμὴν ὁ υἱὸς τὸ μόνῳ καὶ ἰδίως αὐτῷ καὶ κατὰ φύσιν ὑπάρχον ἐ. id.Jo.1.9(4.91A); ref. Christ's miracles τὰ μείζονα ἐ. ποιῶν, ἐν τοῖς ἐλάττοσιν εἰς τὸν οὐρανὸν ἀναβλέπει Chrys.hom.14.1 in Mt.(7.204A); Cyr.hom.pasch.10(5^{2}.139B); ἐνήργει τὰ μὲν θεῖα σαρκικῶς...τὰ δ᾽ ἀνθρώπινα θεϊκῶς, ὅτι κατὰ θέλησιν ἐ. Max.ep.19(M.91.593A); of H. Ghost προσκαλούμενον καὶ ἐ. ἀποστέλλον Cyr.H.catech.16.14; Cyr.thes.34(362A); ref. OT theophany ποῖος ἄγγελος ἐ. οὕτω διαλέγεται; Proc.G.Gen.16:7(M.87.353A); comp., Chrys.hom.27.1 in 2Cor.(10.627B); in form -ηκῶς †Anast.S.relat.7(p.64.22; M.88.608C); **2.** *of one's own free will, freely* τοῦ δὲ λόγου κατὰ θέλησιν ἀνεχομένου καὶ ἐ. τὸ ἴδιον σῶμα εἰς θάνατον προϊεμένου ‡Ath.Apoll.1.6(M.26.1104B); ἡ φύσις ἄγεται... ἐν τῷ ἀνθρώπῳ ἐ. κατὰ θέλησιν κινουμένῳ· ἄρα φύσει θελητικὸς ὁ ἄνθρωπος Max.Pyrr.(M.91.304C); τῆς μὲν νοερᾶς [sc. τῆς ψυχῆς δυνάμεως] ἐ. κατὰ βούλησιν κινουμένης id.myst.5(M.91.672E); Andr.Caes.Apoc.59(M.106.405B); comp., Meth.res.3.9(p.403.7; M.18.324A).

***ἐξουσιοποιός**, *creating authority, who is source of authority*, Dion.Ar.c.h.8.1(M.3.240B).

***ἐξουσιότης**, ἡ, **1.** *free will*, Gr.Naz.carm.1.1.34.37(M.37.948A); *freedom of action*; of God, Disp.Phot.3.39(M.88.565D); **2.** = ἐξουσία: τῆς ὑπερκοσμίου καὶ νοερᾶς ἐ. Dion.Ar.c.h.8.1(M.3.240A).

ἐξοφρυόομαι, *be supercilious, proud*, Cyr.Mich.12(3.402B); perf. ptcpl. pass. as subst., id.ador.14(1.506D); id.Joel.40(3.237E).

***ἐξοφρύσσομαι**, *be haughty*, Or.*adnot.in Dt.*14:19(M.17.25B).

ἐξοχετεύ-ω, *draw off, divert*; met., Synes.*ep.*103(M.66.1476A); τὴν τῶν εἰδώλων φύσιν ἐ. id.*insomn.*15(p.177.13; M.66.1309C); med., *issue forth*, met. ἀπόρροια νοῦ λόγος καὶ...ἀπὸ καρδίας διὰ στόματος ~εται Dion.Al.ap.Ath.*Dion.*23(p.63.8; M.25.513B); Areth.*Apoc.*50 (M.106.709D).

ἐξοχή, ἡ, 1. *prominence, projection*, Geo.Pis.*carm.*1.13(p.1); *summit* of Areopagus, Max.*prol.Dion.*(M.4.17A); plur., *parts* of an engraving *which stand out in relief*, Nemes.*nat.hom.*7(M.40.648B); Thdr.Stud.*antirr.*3.3.5(M.99.421D); **2.** *preeminence, excellence* ἡ ἐ. τῆς ἐκκλησίας Clem.*str.*7.17(p.76.17; M.9.552B); of God, Geo.Pis. *hex.*597(M.92.1481A); plur., *ib.*877(1502A).

***ἐξοχλέω**, *importune*, *Mir.Geo.*9(p.102.3).

***ἐξπαίδειτον, τό**, v. sq.

***ἐξπέδιτον, τό**, cf. Lat. *expeditus*; **1.** *expeditionary force*, Jo.Mal. *chron.*14 p.364(M.97.541B); *Chron.Pasch.*p.335(M.92.869A); **2.** *expedition*, *ib.*p.315(801C); in form ἐξπαιδείτῳ Ath.Scholast.*coll.*20.1 (p.173, v.l. ἐξπεδίτῳ); Phot.*nomoc.*13.3(p.612; M.104.904C).

[*]ἐξπελ(λ)ευτής, ὁ, = ἐξπελευστής, *collector* of arrears, Ath. Scholast.*coll.*20.1(p.171); ἐξπελλευτής Justn.*nov.*128.6.

ἐξυβρίζω, *break out insolently*, Nil.*Magn.*46(M.79.1023B); *call insolently* Αἰθιόπιόν τε τὸν Θεόφιλον ἐ. Philost.*h.e.*9.3(M.65.569A).

***ἐξυδαρεύω**, = ἐξυδαρόω 1; met., Epiph.*haer.*59.2(p.365.27; M.41. 1020C).

ἐξυδαρ-όω, 1. *water down, dilute*, Gr.Nyss.*Pss.titt.*A 8(M.44. 480B); fig. and met. διδάσκαλοι...καπηλεύοντες τὴν διδασκαλίαν... λόγῳ ~οῦντι τὸν ἄκρατον...τῶν...γραφῶν νοῦν Eus.*Is.*1:22(M.24. 97D); †Bas.*Is.*48(1.417B; M.30.209B); ὁ...Σαμοσατεὺς...~ώσας τὸν θεῖον τοῦτον οἶνον ‡Ath.*haer.*6(M.28.512D); καπηλεύοντες τὸν λόγον τοῦ θεοῦ, τοῦτ' ἔστιν ~οῦντες αὐτὸν διὰ ψυχρολογίας καὶ μωρᾶς ἐξηγήσεως Didym.*2Cor.*2:17(p.21.8; M.39.1092D); **2.** pass., met., *weaken* λεπτύνεται καὶ ~οῦται τὸ κακόν Mac.Aeg.*hom.*16.4(M.34.616B); *Const. App.*6.5.6; Bars.*resp.*45; **3.** *make liquid, melt*; pass., of metals, Mac.Aeg.*hom.*26.3(M.34.876D).

ἐξυδατόω, *inundate*, *Chron.Pasch.*p.290(M.92.724C); med., *condense*, Nemes.*nat.hom.*5(M.40.620B).

ἐξυδάτωσις, ἡ, 1. *flood*, Or.*Cels.*1.20(p.70.14; M.11.696A); *M.Pion.* 4.23; **2.** *secretion of fluid*, ‡Caes.Naz.*dial.*140(M.38.1077).

***ἐξύεται**, prob. error in Meth.*symp.*2.2(M.18.49A; conj. ἐξέσσυται p.16.22; v.l. ἐξύσσεται).

***ἐξύμνησις, ἡ**, *praise, laud*, Thdr.Stud.*epp.*1.7(M.99.933A).

ἐξυπηρετ-έω, 1. *act.*; **a.** *serve, obey*, c. dat. τὰ γεγονότα ὑποτέτακται τῷ θεῷ, καὶ τὰ πάντα ~εῖ τῷ βουλήματι αὐτοῦ Iren.*haer.*5.5.3(M.7. 1136B); ὁ τῷ θελήματι τοῦ θεοῦ ~ῶν Clem.*str.*1.1(p.7.33; M.8.696B); *ib.*7.1(p.4.25; M.9.405A); Sophr.H.*v.Anast.*(M.92.1701D); c. acc. ⟨τὰ δὲ⟩ 'θηρία'...δυνάμεις...προσεκαρτέρουν τῷ βασιλεῖ τὰ κελευόμενα ~οῦντες Hipp.*Dan.*3.8.9; **b.** *assist in, minister to* πῶς δὲ ὁ τεθνεὼς οἰκτίστῳ θανάτῳ δυνήσεται πρὸς τιμωρίαν τινὸς ἐξυπηρετῆσαι; Tat. *orat.*17(p.19.22; M.6.845A); Clem.*str.*4.1(p.249.5; M.8.1216B); μὴ περισπώμενοι πρὸς τὰς ἐπιθυμίας ἀπρόθυμοι τῷ πολέμῳ ~ῶμεν *ib.*2.18 (p.156.5; 1021A); *ib.*4.6(p.265.20; 1249C); **2.** med.; **a.** *serve, obey* τὸ σῶμα δοῦλόν ἐστι τῆς ψυχῆς, ἐπὶ πᾶσι ταῖς κρίσεσιν αὐτῆς ~ούμενον †Dion.Al.*fr.Eccl.*4:10(p.227.10); πάσῃ προθυμίᾳ ἐ. τοῖς ὑπὸ τῆς σῆς ὁσιότητος λεγομένοις Const.ap.Eus.*v.C.*2.46(p.61.7; M.20.1024B); Epiph.*haer.*27.5(p.307.7; M.41.369C); Vict.*Mc.*1:31(p.277.30); μία φύσις ἐστὶ πατρὸς καὶ υἱοῦ μία· ὡς οἰκείῳ ~εῖται θελήματι καὶ... καθίσταται ὑπήκοος τῷ πατρὶ μέχρι θανάτου Jo.D.*hom.*2.2(M.96. 580B); *ib.*6.7(672C); **b.** *wait upon, attend*, Eus.*m.P.*10(p.930.25; M. 20.1496C); Epiph.*haer.*30.4(p.339.11; M.41.412B); Jo.VI H.*v.Jo.D.* 26(M.94.468A); of deacons, *Const.App.*8.30.2 cit. s. διάκονος; *assist in*, Eus.*h.e.*2.3.4(M.20.144B); *ib.*3.24.4(264C); *Const.App.*8.28.4 cit. s. διακόνισσα; μήτε...~εῖσθαι τῷ μεγέθει τῶν ζητηθέντων δυνάμενον Max.*ep.*19(M.91.596A); ‡Jo.D.*hom.*6.9(M.96.676B); **c.** *serve, function* τὸ μέγα Σάββατον...οὗ τύπος ἦν τὸ μικρὸν Σάββατον ~ούμενον ἄχρι τῆς αὐτοῦ [sc. Χριστοῦ] παρουσίας Epiph.*haer.*30.32(p.378.24; M.41. 468B); pass., *be made to serve*, *ib.*42.12(p.164.23; 785D).

***ἐξυπνέω**, *awake from sleep*, *A.Xanthipp.*13(p.66.9); Andr.Cr. *or.*19(M.97.1240B); *Mir.Geo.*11(p.110.3); ref. final judgement, ‡Hipp. *consumm.*38(p.304.24; M.10.940C).

***ἐξυπνιασμός, ὁ**, *incitement*, ref. Mt.26:6ff. γύνη πόρνη...ὁ τῶν νέων ἰξός...ἡ τῶν παθῶν ἐ. ‡Chrys.*meretr.*2(10.762A).

***ἐξυπνιαστικός**, v. *ἐξυπνιστικός.

ἐξυπνίζ-ω, *awaken*, met. τὸ τῆς ἐπιθυμίας πάθος ‡Just.*qu.et resp.*8 (M.6.1257C); †Bas.*ep.*42.3(3.127B; M.32.352B); of spiritual awakening, Clem.*exc.Thdot.*3(p.106.8; M.9.653B); *Apoc.Bar.rel.*5.13; ὁ φόβος [i.e. τοῦ θεοῦ]...οὐκ ἐκπλήσσει [sc. τὴν ψυχήν] ἀλλ' ~ει *Hom. Clem.*17.11; to future life, *T.Jud.*25.4; at general resurrection, ‡Sophr.H.*liturg.*5(M.87.3985B).

***ἐξυπνισμός, ὁ**, *watchfulness*, Bas.*reg.fus.*7.3(2.347A; M.31.932B); *Schol.*34 in Jo.Clim.*scal.*4(M.88.741A).

***ἐξυπνιστικός**, *for waking up*, Pall.*h.Laus.*43(p.130.14; ἐξυπνιαστικῷ M.34.1210C).

ἔξυπνος, *awakened from sleep*, *T.Lev.*5.7; Ephr.1.44F; *A.Mt.*28 (p.259.14).

***ἐξυπολύω**, *take off* someone's *shoes*, c. acc. pers., Gr.Mag.*dial.* (tr.Zach.)3.20(M.*PL.*77.270C).

***ἐξυποστρέφω**, *turn back*, Socr.*h.e.*3.17.6(M.67.425A); *ib.*7.24.5 (792C).

ἐξυπτιάζ-ω, 1. *throw back* one's head in derision, hence *mock* ἡ μακρὰ παρενθήκη τῆς ἱστορίας ~εται Gr.Nyss.*Eun.*1(1 p.38.16; M.45. 265C); **2.** *be rigidly upright*, opp. βαθύνω, id.*hom.14 in Cant.*(M.44. 1064C).

***ἐξυστερινός**, *last*, *Exorc.*12(p.336).

ἐξυφαίν-ω, 1. *weave*, fig. μεθ' ἡμέραν μὲν τὰ σωφροσύνης ~οντες δόγματα, νυκτὸς δὲ ἀναλύοντες Clem.*paed.*2.10(p.215.16; M.8.512C); met., *construct* τοίχους ἐ. Chrys.*hom.14.3 in Eph.*(11.106C); *compose* τὴν εὐλογίαν ἐ. Thdt.*haer.*5(4.390); *devise*, Cyr.*Lc.*11:39(M.72. 712D); περὶ τῶν ἐθνῶν ὁ τῆς προφητείας ~εται λόγος id.*Is.*5.2(2.777C); ἀμάρτυρον...κατηγορίαν...ἐ. Gel.Cyz.*h.e.*3.16.19; **2.** *weave together*, Cyr.*Jo.*2.1(4.139E); id.*Ps.*33:1(M.69.884B); συνθεῖσα δὲ ταῦτα [sc. ὀνόματα] καὶ ἐξυφήνασα Thdt.*provid.*4(4.543); **3.** *finish weaving*, fig. ὁ λόγος...ἐνεδύσατο...ὡς νυμφίος ἱμάτιον, ἐξυφήνας ἑαυτῷ ἐν τῷ σταυρικῷ πάθει Hipp.*antichr.*4(p.6.22; M.10.732B).

***ἐξυφαιρέω**, *take away*, Serap.*Man.*36(p.53; M.18.1213A); *ib.*51 (p.72; 1248D).

***ἐξυφαντέον**, *one must weave*, Clem.*paed.*2.10(p.223.27; M.8. 529B).

***ἐξυφάπτω**, *set on fire*; met., of inflaming soul with passions, Eus.*h.e.*10.4.58(M.20.871C).

ἐξύφασμα, τό, *finished web, piece of woven cloth*, Gr.Nyss.*v.Mos.* (M.44.385D).

ἔξω, *outside*; **1.** = outside the church; **a.** adv.; **i.** = pagan τοὺς ἔ. φιλοσόφους Gr.Thaum.*pan.Or.*10(p.25.10; M.10.1081A); τῆς ἔ. σοφίας Gr.Nyss.*Eun.*12(1 p.375.13; M.45.1101B); ref. astrology τῆς ἔ. γεννήσεως Chrys.*hom.*6.2 *in Mt.*(7.89A); οἱ ἔ. συγγραφεῖς Thdt. *Dan.*2:37(2.1089); **ii.** ref. catechumens, Cyr.H.*procatech.*12; **iii.** = excommunicate, *Const.App.*2.20.4; **b.** prep. c. genit. τῶν ἔ. τοῦ μυστηρίου *A.Jo.*100(p.201.11); τοὺς ἔ. τοῦ καθ' ἡμᾶς δόγματος Gr.Nyss.*or.catech.*1(p.7.5; M.45.13A); CAlex.*ep.*ap.Ath.*apol.sec.*6 (p.92.3; M.25.257B); ref. heretics, Ath.*ep.Serap.*4.6(M.26.645A); **2.** = outside the ranks of the clergy, Bas.*ep.*217 *can.*55(3.326A; M. 32.796B); **3.** = outer circle of believers, ref. Mt.13:36 Ἰησοῦ...ἔργον ἦν εἰδέναι χωρίζειν ἐν τοῖς ἀκροαταῖς τοὺς ἔ. ἀπὸ τῶν ἔσω, ἵνα τοῖς μὲν ἔ. ἐν παραβολαῖς λέγῃ...τὸ ἔσω καὶ τὸ ἔ. πνευματικόν ἐστιν Or. *dial.*15(p.152.21); id.*princ.*3.1.17(p.227.3; M.11.285A).

***ἐξωδέω**, *stink*, met. τὴν...ἐξωδηκυῖαν τῶν Ἑλλήνων θρησκείαν ‡Jo.D.*Artem.*48(M.96.1296D).

***ἐξώδης**, *stinking*, met. ἐ. Αἰγυπτιακῆς ζύμης, διδαχῆς τε λέγω Eustrat.*v.Eutych.*10(M.86.2285C).

ἔξωθεν, A. *from outside*; **1.** ref. generation of Son οὐκ ἔ. ἀλλ' ἐκ τοῦ πατρὸς γεννώμενον Ath.*Ar.*2.33(M.26.217B); ἡ κατὰ τοῦ υἱοῦ τόλμα εἰς τὸν πατέρα τὴν βλασφημίαν ἀνάγει εἴγε ἔ. ἐπενόησεν ἑαυτῷ σοφίαν καὶ λόγον *ib.*1.25(64B); εἰ ἔ. ἐστιν, ἐπισυμβέβηκεν ἄρα, καὶ οὐκ ἔστι τῷ πατρὶ συναΐδιος Cyr.*thes.*4(5[1].24A); ref. procession of H. Ghost ὁ θεὸς πηγὴ τοῦ πνεύματός ἐστιν...καὶ χορηγὸς αὐτοῦ, οὐκ ἔ. αὐτὸ προσλαμβάνων, ἀλλ' ἐξ ἑαυτοῦ πηγάζων ‡Ath.*dial.Trin.*2.28(M.28. 1200B); **2.** ref. canon τούτων οὐκ ἔ. ἡμεῖς ἀλλ' ἐκ τῶν γραφῶν ἔχομεν τὴν πίστιν Ath.*decr.*17(p.140.21; M.25.445A); ἔ. ... σοφίας Σιράχ *Can.App.*85; **3.** gramm. ἔ. συνυπακουστέον *cat.2Cor.*1:22(p.357.16).

B. *outside*; **1.** in gen. τοὺς ἔ. ... καλὸν τὰ ἡμέτερα κρύπτειν κακά Chrys.*sac.*1.4(p.13.3; 1.366B); *ib.*5.7(p.136.1; 419B); **2.** *profane, pagan* τοῖς ἔ. αὐτῷ προσιοῦσι φιλάνθρωπον καὶ εὐεργετικὸν παρέχων ἑαυτόν Eus.*v.C.*1.43(p.27.28; M.20.957A); οὐδὲ ἐκ τῆς ἔ. σοφίας...διὰ δὲ μόνην θεοσέβειαν ὁ Ἀντώνιος ἐγνωρίσθη Ath.*v.Anton.*93(M.26. 973B); τοῦ ἔ. βίου Bas.*reg.fus.*20.2(2.364C; M.31.972C); τῆς ἔ. παιδείας Marc.Diac.*v.Porph.*8; τοῖς ἔ. ... καὶ...τοῖς τῆς πίστεως οἰκείοις Chrys.*sac.*5.8(p.138.17; 1.420C); id.*hom.*4.6 *in Jo.*(8.34B); *cat.2Cor.* 11:3(p.420.18); **3.** of officials and institutions, *secular* ἡ ἔ. ἐξουσία CAnt.(341)*can.*5; ταῖς ἔ. προστασίαις Ath.*apol.sec.*18(p.100.14; M.25. 276D); Chrys.*hom.*56.6 *in Mt.*(7.574B).

C. *outward, material* opp. spiritual διαιροῦντες...τὸν ἔ. ἄνθρωπον ἀπὸ τοῦ ἔνδον Hegem.*Arch.*5(p.6.13; M.10.1433C); ‡Ath.*Apoll.*1.17

(M.26.1125A); τῶν ὀφθαλμῶν τῶν ἐ. Chrys.*sac*.6.12(p.162.2; 1.431A); Cyr.*Lc*.11:39(M.72.713A).

D. as prep.; **1.** *outside* οἱ ἐ. τῆς ἡμετέρας θεοσεβείας ‡Just.*coh.Gr.* 10(M.6.261A); ‡Just.*qu.et resp*.55(M.6.1297C); **2.** *apart* from θεϊκῶς ποιοῦντος αὐτοῦ τὰ ἔργα τοῦ πατρός, οὐκ ἦν ἐ. αὐτοῦ ἡ σάρξ Ath.*Ar.* 3.32(M.26.389C).

ἐξωθ-έω, *thrust out*; **1.** *drag out, cause to be disgorged* οὐ καταποθείς, τοὺς προκαταποθέντας θλίψας ἐξέωσεν *Hom.Clem*.6.2; *drive away* clouds, Meth.*symp*.8.4(p.85.16; M.18.144C); **2.** fig., *drive out*, *T. Gad* 5.2; CAlex.*ep*.ap.Ath.*apol.sec*.17(p.99.40; M.25.276B); Cyr.*inc. unigen*.(5^{1}.685E); **3.** met., *reject*; **a.** in gen., Or.*hom.4.5 in Jer.* (p.28.15; M.13.292D); but usu. med. τὴν πίστιν ~ουμένους καὶ τὸν θάνατον τοῦ Χριστοῦ περιττὸν ἀποφαίνοντας Chrys.*comm.in Gal*.3:1 (10.695B); Eus.Al.*serm*.21.4(M.86.428D); ἐξωθησαμένη [sc. the Church] σε ἐπιμανεῖσαν τῷ βασιλεῖ Thdt.*Cant*.1:5(2.38); **b.** *excommunicate*, Anon.ap.Eus.*h.e*.5.16.10(M.20.468C); CNeocaes.*can.2*; **c.** *degrade* αἱ γυναῖκες εἰς τὰ τῶν ἑταιρίδων ἑαυτὰς ἐξώθησαν ἤθη Chrys.*hom.73.3 in Mt*.(7.712C); **d.** *exclude*, Cyr.*Chr.un*.(5^{1}.768E); **4.** med., *repel* suspicions *from oneself*, Eus.Em.*fr.Gal*.1:11–14(p.47. 29); **5.** in form ἐξεόω: ἐξεοῖ Epiph.*haer*.68.4(p.144.14; M.42.189C); ἐξεοῦσι *ib*.70.1(p.233.19; 340C); ἐξεωθῆναι *ib*.70.2(p.234.2; ἐξωσθῆναι 341A); ἐξεῶ Thdr.Mops.*1Cor*.5:5(p.178.14; ἐξῶσαι M.66.881B); ἐξεῶσθαι Socr.*h.e*.2.37.90(M.67.320D).

***Ἐξωκιονίτης,** ὁ, v. *Ἐξακιονίτης.

***ἐξωκοιτέω,** *sleep outside* convent; forbidden to nuns, CTrull. *can*.46.

ἐξώλεια, ἡ, *abomination*; of heresy, Const.ap.Eus.*v.C*.3.65(p.112. 10; M.20.1141A).

[*]**ἔξωλος,** = ἐξώλης, *pernicious*, Clem.*paed*.2.10(p.222.16; M.8. 528A).

***ἐξωμάνδρευτος,** *outside the fold*, fig. μή τις...γένηται...πρόβατον ἐ. καὶ θηριάλωτον Thdr.Stud.*catech.magn*.52(p.145).

ἐξωμίς, ἡ, *tunic with one sleeve*, or *sleeveless tunic*; characteristic of philosophers, Chrys.*hom.10.4 in Ac*.(9.87A); id.*hom.2.5 in Rom.* (9.443B); worn by David χορεύων οὐ τὸ βασιλικὸν περιεβέβλητο ἀλλ' ἐ. μόνην, ἣν νῦν καλοῦσιν Ἀρκαδίκιν Thdt.*qu.1 in Par*.(1.562); Cosm. Mel.*schol*.(M.38.531) in Gr.Naz.*carm*.2.1.44.36; used by THDN of *ephod*, *ib*.(M.38.603) in Gr.Naz.*carm*.2.1.12.653.

ἐξωμοσία, ἡ, *solemn oath*, CChalc.*can*.30.

ἐξων-έομαι, **1.** *buy off* penalties, Chrys.*hom.55.3 in Mt*.(7.559A); Synes.*ep*.44(M.66.1369C); *redeem* τὸν ~ούμενον τῷ...αὐτοῦ αἵματι τὸν κόσμον ‡Meth.*palm*.7(M.18.397A); **2.** *buy up*, fig. ἐ. πολυτίμητον σωτηρίαν...ἀγάπῃ καὶ πίστει ζωῆς Clem.*prot*.9(p.64.24; M.8.197B); id.*paed*.2.1(p.156.17; M.8.385A); Gr.Naz.*or*.4.24(M.35.552B).

***ἐξώνησις,** ἡ, *purchase*, Jo.VI H.*v.Jo.D*.26(M.94.468A).

***ἐξωποιέομαι,** *be opened up*; of earth by ploughing, Ephr.1.64E.

***ἐξώπορτα,** (ἔξω porta) *without the gate*, *Euchol*.(p.640).

***ἐξωπράτης,** ὁ, *foreign merchant*, †Gregent.*leg.Hom*.62(M.86. 616A).

ἐξωραΐζω, *adorn*, Cyr.*Jo*.2.8(4.231D); κῆπος...ποικίλαις ἀνθέων ἰδέαις ἐξωραϊσμένος id.*Is*.5.4(2.822E); id.*Zach*.95(3.784D); fig. and met., id.*Ps*.9:15(M.69.773B); id.*hom.pasch*.12(5^{2}.169A); ἀγενήτου... φύσεως...τῆς τοῖς δεσποτικοῖς ἀξιώμασιν ἐξωραϊσμένης id.*ep*.55(p.52. 18; 5^{2}.178C); id.*Chr.un*.(5^{1}.769A); Χριστὸς...ἐξωράισε τὴν ἀνθρωπείαν φύσιν τῇ ὡραιότητι...τῆς θεότητος αὐτοῦ Mod.*dorm*.8(M.86.3297B); λόγοις ἐ. *describe with flattering* words, Philost.*h.e*.10.6(M.65.588A).

***ἐξωραϊσμός,** ὁ, *adornment*, Cyr.*Chr.un*.(5^{1}.731E).

***ἐξωριγεῖτο,** vox nihili (perh. for ἐξεγείρει), Bas.Sel.*or*.31.2(M.85. 341C).

ἔξωρος, *outside the period* of an historical work, Euthal.Diac. *epp.Paul*.proem.(M.85.713A).

ἐξώτερος, *exterior*, Herm.*sim*.9.9.3 al.; Mac.Aeg.*hom*.4.15(M.34. 484B); Dor.*doct*.19(M.88.1809C); hence, *visible* τὴν ἐ. σκηνὴν τύπον τούτου τοῦ ὁρωμένου κόσμου Cosm.Ind.*top*.2(M.88.92A).

[*]**ἐξωτέρως,** *exteriorly*, Mac.Aeg.*hom*.4.15(M.34.484B).

ἐξωτικός, **1.** *foreign* πολέμους ἐμφυλίους, ἐ. Chrys.*hom.27.1 in 2Cor*.(10.627E); **2.** *who is outside* one's family, of heirs ἐ. τῆς ἰδίας συγγενείας Justn.*ep.Thdr.Mops*.(p.68.22; M.86.1091C); cf.*Cod.Afr.* 81; outside Church; **a.** *secular* ἐ. δικαστοῦ Jul.Papa *ep.Dian*.ap. Ath.*apol.sec*.31(p.110.12; M.25.300D); δικαστηρίων ἐ. Bas.*reg.fus.* 9.2(2.351E; M.31.944A); Chrys.*hom.16.3 in 1Cor*.(10.139B); **b.** *pagan* λόγοι...τῆς ἐ. ... σοφίας Olymp.*Eccl*.1:8(M.93.485C); **c.** *outlying*, of towns outside CP ταῖς ἐ. πόλεσιν Jo.Mal.*chron*.18 p.449(M.97.660B); **3.** masc. as subst., *stranger*, *MAMA* 1.167.

ἐξωφανής, *outward, visible* διπλοῦς ὁ νόμος...καὶ ἔστι μὲν ἐσωτάτω τὸ ἀληθές...καὶ περιττὸν ἐπίβλημα τοῖς κεκρυμμένοις ἐστὶ τὰ ἐ. Cyr. *glaph.Dt*.(1.425C); οὐχὶ μόνον τὴν ἐ. χρηστότητα...καρδίαν δὲ μᾶλλον ἀβέβηλον id.*Soph*.5(3.583E); id.*ador*.8(1.263D); neut. as subst., *outward meaning* τὸ τῆς ἱστορίας ἐ. id.*Is*.2.5(2.338E); *ib*.3.1(356B); τὸ ἐ. τῶν τύπων id.*hom.pasch*.22(5^{2}.273C); *outward manifestation* τῆς νομικῆς λατρείας τὸ ἐ. id.*Is*.3.2(405E).

***ἐξωφανῶς,** *outwardly* χρίεται ..ἐπὶ τὸ ἄκρον, τουτέστιν ἐ. καὶ... τῷ καθ' ἕνωσιν τὴν ἀληθινὴν ἰδίῳ σώματι Cyr.*Nest*.2.2(p.37.29; 6^{1}. 38B).

***ἑονοπυρεῖον,** τό, = αἰωνοπυρεῖον, *place of everlasting fire* (on amulet addressed to demons) Χριστὸς κέλετέ σε φυγεῖν εἰς ἐ. *CIG* 9065.

ἑορτάζ-ω, **1.** *keep* an annual *feast*, of Passover δεῖ τὸν ~οντα τῷ θεῷ 'ἄζυμα ἐπὶ πικρίδων' ἐσθίειν Or.*hom.14.16 in Jer*.(p.122.27; M.13. 425B); hence fig. of eucharist εἴ τις ~ει μετὰ τοῦ Ἰησοῦ, ἄνω ἐστὶ ἐν ἀναγαίῳ μεγάλῳ...ἐὰν ἀναβῇς μετ' αὐτοῦ, ἵνα ἑορτάσῃς τὸ πάσχα, δίδωσί σοι τὸ ποτήριον τῆς διαθήκης τῆς καινῆς *ib.19.13*(p.169.29; 489C); of Easter δεόντως ἐ. Ath.*ep.Drac*.10(M.25.533B); *Const.App*.5.17.1; of Ascension ἐ. τὴν ἑορτὴν τῆς ἀναλήψεως τοῦ κυρίου *ib*.5.20.2; *keep festival*, of Easter eucharist εὐφραινόμενοι καὶ ~οντες, ὅτι ἀρραβὼν τῆς ἀναστάσεως ὑμῶν Ἰησοῦς ὁ Χριστὸς ἐγήγερται ἐκ νεκρῶν *ib*.5.19.7; ref. Second Temple πάντες ἑώρτασαν ἐπὶ τῇ τελεσιουργίᾳ Ath.*apol. Const*.18(M.25.617D); **2.** *celebrate as a feast, celebrate the feast of* οἱ δὲ ἀπὸ Βασιλείδου καὶ τοῦ βαπτίσματος αὐτοῦ τὴν ἡμέραν ~ουσι προδιανυκτερεύοντες ἐν ἀναγνώσεσι Clem.*str*.1.21(p.90.22; M.8.888A); *Const.App*.5.17.3; τὸ σάββατον...καὶ τὴν κυριακὴν ἐ. ὅτι τὸ μὲν δημιουργίας ἐστὶν ὑπόμνημα, τὸ δὲ ἀναστάσεως *ib*.7.23.3; τῇ πρὸ τριῶν καλανδῶν Ἰουλίων...[sc. Παύλου] τὸ μαρτύριον ἐ. Euthal.Diac.*epp. Paul*.proem.(M.85.701A); ‡Nil.*fr.ascens*.3(M.79.1500D); *Chron. Pasch*.p.10(M.92.88B); τελείαν παρουσίαν τοῦ ἁγίου πνεύματος ἐ. Eutych.*pasch*.4(M.86.2396C); Niceph.Ur.*v.Sym*.115(M.86.3093C); τὴν μνήμην τοῦ ζωοποιοῦ σταυροῦ τῇ τεσσαρακαιδεκάτῃ τοῦ Σεπτεμβρίου μηνὸς φαιδρῶς ἐ. Eustrat.*v.Eutych*.70(M.86.2353C); ἀμήχανον μὴ ~ειν τὰ τῶν ἁγίων μνημόσυνα Jo.D.*imag*.1.21(M.94.1253A); fig., of resurrection τότε τὴν ἡμέραν τῆς χαρᾶς ἐ. κυρίῳ εἰλικρινῶς, ὁπότε τὰς σκηνὰς αἰωνίους ἀποληψόμεθα Meth.*symp*.9.2(p.116.9; M.18. 181A); id.*res*.2.21(p.375.4; M.18.285C); **3.** *celebrate by a festival* ταύτην τὴν μυθολογίαν [i.e. ref. Persephone] αἱ γυναῖκες ποικίλως κατὰ πόλιν ~ουσιν Clem.*prot*.2(p.14.5; M.8.77B); ἐνταφιασθεὶς καὶ ἑορτασθείς, καθάπερ ἀθλητὴς νικηφόρος τὸ σωμάτιον Pall.*v.Chrys*.11 (p.69.1; M.47.39); πανήγυριν μεγίστην ἐπιτελέσατε, τὴν οἰκείαν ~οντες σωτηρίαν Thdt.*Ps*.117:27(1.1435); Jo.D.*imag*.1.21(M.94. 1253A); **4.** *rejoice over* ἥδιον τὰς σὰς ἐ. εὐδοκιμήσεις Isid.Pel.*epp*.3.98 (M.78.805B); Eustrat.*v.Eutych*.71(M.86.2353D).

ἑορτάσιος, *festal*, Gr.Naz.*carm*.2.1.45.26(M.37.1355A).

ἑόρτασμα, τό, *festival*, ‡Meth.*Sym.et Ann*.11(M.18.376B).

***ἑορταστέον,** **1.** *one must keep festival* ἐ. πνευματικῶς Gr.Naz. *or*.41.2(M.36.429B); **2.** *one must celebrate* ἐ. τῆς θεοτόκου τὴν κοίμησιν Jo.Thess.*dorm.BMV* 2.1(p.406.10).

ἑορταστικός, *pertaining to a festival*, hence *paschal*; of letters of bishop of Alexandria announcing date of Easter, Eus.*h.e*.7.20(M. 20.681B); *ib*.7.22.11(689B); Cosm.Ind.*top*.10(M.88.416B); Anast.S. *hod*.15 tit.(M.89.257A); τὴν ἐ. πρόσρησιν Thdt.*ep*.72(4.1123); τοῦ ἐ. κύκλου *Chron.Pasch*.p.374(M.92.952D); neut. plur. as subst., *paschal gifts*, CLaod.*can*.37.

***ἑορταστικῶς,** **1.** *as a festival* ἐτήσιον μνήμην ἐ. ἄγουσιν Jo.Thess. *dorm.BMV* 1.1(p.376.6); **2.** *for a festival* μὴ δογματικῶς ἀλλ' ἐ. συνηθροίσθημεν Thdr.Stud.*nativ.BMV* 6(M.96.689A).

ἑορτή, ἡ, **A.** *feast, festival*;

1. Jewish πᾶσα μὲν...ἱλαρὰ ἡμέρα ἐν ᾗ προστέτακται...ποιεῖν ἐξαίρετα, ἐ. καλεῖται· οὐ πᾶσα δέ ἐστι πανήγυρις, ἀλλὰ...ὅτε ἐπὶ τὸ αὐτὸ συναθροίζονται οἱ πανταχόθεν Ἑβραῖοι...οἷον σάββατα καὶ νεομηνίαι ἐ. εἰσιν· ἄζυμα δὲ καὶ αἱ...σκηνοπηγίαι οὐ μόνον αἱ ἐ., ἀλλὰ καὶ πανηγύρεις Or.*sel.in Dt*.16:13(M.12.812B,C); Eus.*qu.Marin. suppl*.7(M.22.996D); τῶν ἐ. αἱ ὑποθέσεις τῆς πρὸς ἀλλήλους ἐπιμιξίας ἀφορμὴ καὶ ὑπόθεσις αὐτοῖς ἐγίνοντο, καὶ πλείων ὁ φόβος, καὶ ἀκμάζουσα ἡ εὐλάβεια, καὶ μυρία κατεσκευάζετο καλὰ ἐκ τοῦ συνεῖναι εἰς τὴν πόλιν αὐτούς Chrys.*exp.in Ps*.121:4(5.340B); Cyr.*glaph.Ex*.3(1. 317C); ref. Christ's presence ἐν...ταῖς ἐ. αὐτὸν εἰς Ἱεροσόλυμα παραγενέσθαι τὰ εὐαγγέλια λέγουσιν, οὐδὲν τῶν ἐν ταύταις ἐπιτελουμένων πεποιηκέναι φασὶν αὐτὸν...ἀλλὰ...διδασκαλίας τοῦ πλήθους ἕνεκα Jo.Philop.*pasch*.(p.211.5); esp. of Passover εἴ τις...κληρικὸς... δέχεται τὰ αὐτῶν [sc. τῶν Ἰουδαίων] τῆς ἐ. ξένια, οἷον ἄζυμα ἤ τι τοιοῦτον, καθαιρείσθω *Can.App*.70; *ib*.71; not to be identified with Last Supper, Jo.Philop.*pasch*.(pp.212.12ff.,214.23); exeg. Mt. 26:5, Mc.14:2, cf. *stetit enim consilium eorum quasi firmum* (*cum ipsi qui consiliabantur staturi non essent*) *ut non in die festo* *occideretur sed in alio die; videlicet ut 'pascha nostrum immolaretur Christus'*, Or.*comm.ser.*76 *in Mt.*(p.178.2; M.13.1721A); Chrys.*hom.* 79.3 *in Mt.*(7.762A); τὴν μὲν ἑ. ὑπερθέσθαι βούλονται· οὐ συγχωροῦνται δέ, ἐπειδὴ τὴν προφητείαν ἔδει πληροῦσθαι Vict.*Mc.*14:2(p.417.13); **2.** Christian εἴ τις ἐπίσκοπος...ἐν ταῖς ἡμέραις τῶν ἑ. οὐ μεταλαμβάνει κρεῶν καὶ οἴνου, καθαιρείσθω *Can.App.*53; ἔνοχος γὰρ ἁμαρτίας... ἡμέραν ἑ. κυρίου κατηφῶν *Const.App.*5.20.19; εὐχῶν ὁ καιρός, οὐ μέθης, ἀεὶ μέν, μάλιστα δὲ ἐν ἑ. ἑ. γὰρ...γίνεται οὐχ ἵνα ἀσχημονῶμεν, οὐχ ἵνα ἁμαρτήματα συνάγωμεν, ἀλλ' ἵνα καὶ τὰ ὄντα ἀνέλωμεν Chrys. *hom.*27.5 *in 1Cor.*(10.249A); τὰς δημοτελεῖς ἑορτάς, ἐν αἷς μάλιστα τῶν ἐκκλησιαστικῶν ἀρχῶν τὰς αἱρέσεις ποιεῖσθαι νόμος id.*sac.*3.15 (p.76.17; 1.392E); Socr.*h.e.*5.22.7(M.67.628A); esp. *Easter*, Dion.Al. ap.Eus.*h.e.*7.22.4(M.20.688B); τὰς τῆς μεγάλης ἑ. παννυχίδας Eus.*h.e.* 2.17.22(M.20.181C); ὡς ὁμόφωνον μὲν κρατῆσαι τὴν πίστιν, τῆς σωτηρίου δ' ἑ. τὸν αὐτὸν παρὰ τοῖς πᾶσιν ὁμολογηθῆναι καιρόν id.*v.C.* 3.14(p.83.26; M.20.1069C); τὴν κυριακὴν τῆς ἁγίας ἑ. Ath.*ep.encycl.*5 (p.174.5; M.25.232C); τύπος τῆς ἄνω χαρᾶς καὶ ἡ νῦν ἐστιν ἑ. id.*ep.fest.* 4.5(p.298.31; M.26.1444A); ἡ καθολικὴ καὶ αὕτη τῆς κτίσεως ἑ. ... ἐν παντὶ πληρουμένη τῷ κόσμῳ, ἐπὶ τῇ ἀναστάσει τοῦ πεπτωκότος ἐπιτελεῖται Gr.Nyss.*ep.can.*(M.45.221B); τὴν ἀναστάσιμον ἑ. πανηγυρίζοντες *Const.App.*7.36.2; εἶδον [sc. ἐν τῇ ἐκκλησίᾳ] φῶτα μεγάλα, ὡς ἐπὶ ἑορτῆς κυρίου *V.Amph.*1(M.39.16B); as ἑ. ἑορτῶν Gr.Naz.*or.*45.2 (M.36.624B); Eustrat.*v.Eutych.*92(M.86.2377B); τὴν τοῦ πάσχα πνευματικὴν ἑ., ἀρχὴν καὶ κεφαλήν, καὶ πρώτην ἡγεμονίαν ἅπαντος τοῦ χρόνου νενομίσθαι ‡Chrys.*pasch.*6.3(p.149.3; 8.268C); of Pentecost τῆς μεγίστης...ἑ., τῆς...πεντηκοστῆς Eus.*v.C.*4.64(p.144.10; M.20. 1220B); ἑ. μέν ἐστιν ἑορτῶν ἡ ἁγία πεντηκοστή Thdr.Stud.*catech. parv.*10(p.24); of Christmas ἑ. μέλλει προσελαύνειν, ἡ πασῶν τῶν ἑ. σεμνοτάτη καὶ φρικωδεστάτη, ἣν οὐκ ἄν τις ἁμάρτοι μητρόπολιν πασῶν τῶν ἑ. προσειπών. ... ἡ κατὰ σάρκα τοῦ Χριστοῦ γέννησις·... ὥσπερ ἀπό τινος πηγῆς ποταμοὶ διάφοροι ῥυέντες, αὗται ἐτέχθησαν ἡμῶν αἱ ἑ. [i.e. τὰ θεοφάνια, τὸ πάσχα, ἡ πεντηκοστή] Chrys.*Philogon.* 3(1.497Bff.); of Annunciation μία τῶν δεσποτικῶν πρώτη τε καὶ πάνσεπτος ἑ.‡Ath.*annunt.*1(M.28.917B); Thdr.Stud.*catech.parv.*64(p.52); of conception of BMV, Jo.Eub.*concept.BMV* 10(M.96.1473C); of a special thanksgiving δευτέραν ταύτην νίκην ἄρασθαι εἰπὼν βασιλεὺς κατὰ τοῦ τῆς ἐκκλησίας ἐχθροῦ ἐπινίκιον ἑ. τῷ θεῷ συνετέλει Eus.*v.C.* 3.14(p.83.30; M.20.1072A); of Passiontide τὰς...ἀσκήσεις ἃς διαφερόντως κατὰ τὴν τοῦ σωτηρίου πάθους ἑ. ἐν ἀσιτίαις καὶ διανυκτερεύσεσιν ἐκτελεῖν εἰώθαμεν id.*h.e.*2.17.21(M.20.181B); **3.** fig., of whole Christian life πάντα τοίνυν τὸν βίον ἑ. ἄγοντες...γεωργοῦμεν αἰνοῦντες Clem.*str.*7. 7(p.27.27; M.9.452A); Eutych.*pasch.*4(M.86.2396D); of righteous man's life ὁ μὲν ἐν δικαιοσύνῃ ζῶν καὶ κατορθώμασι, κἂν μὴ παρούσης ἑ., ἑ. ἄγει, τὴν καθαρὰν ἡδονὴν καρπούμενος τὴν ἀπὸ τοῦ συνειδότος Chrys.*Anna* 5.1(4.740D); id.*pent.*1.2(2.459B); cf.*ib.*1.1(458C); rejoicing of earth for Creation and redemption, Ephr.1.64E; of heaven τὰς ἑ. τὰς οὐρανίους Or.*hom.*5.16 *in Jer.*(p.45.24; M.13.320C); of Resurrection as true Feast of Tabernacles, Meth.*res.*2.21(p.375.5; M.18.285C); ἁρπασθέντες...ἐνδόξως ἑορτάσωμεν αὐτῷ [sc. τῷ κυρίῳ] τὴν φαιδρὰν τῆς ἀναστάσεως ἑ. *ib.*(p.376.4; 316A); **4.** *feasting, festal joy* τὴν ἐπὶ τῇ ἐπανόδῳ ἑκάστου ὑμῶν χαρὰν...καὶ τὸ ἔνδοξον τῆς τῶν συντρεχόντων ἑ. Jul.Papa *ep.Alex.*ap.Ath.*apol.sec.*53(p.134.18; M. 25.345B); *Const.App.*5.18.2.

B. *season* κατανοήσετε...τοὺς φωστῆρας τοὺς ἐν τῷ οὐρανῷ, ὡς... ταῖς ἑ. αὐτῶν φαίνονται καὶ οὐ παραβαίνουσιν τὴν ἰδίαν τάξιν *Apoc. En.*2.1.

ἑορτικός, = ἑορταστικός; neut. plur. as subst., *Easter gifts*, CChalc.*act.*11(*ACO* 2.1.3 p.27.18,20, v.l. ἑορταστικά H.2.521D).

***ἑόρτιος**, *festal*, Gr.Naz.*or.*45.2(M.36.625A); id.*carm.*1.2.1.723(M. 37.577A); Jo.D.*hom.*1.1(M.96.545B); neut. plur. as subst., *festal gifts*, Thdr.Stud.*nativ.BMV* 1(M.96.680D); = *sollemnia* τὰ τῆς λειτουργίας ἑ. ἐπιτελέσαι Gr.Mag.*dial.*(tr.Zach.)3.30(M.*PL.*77.290A).

ἐπαγγελία, ἡ, **1.** *profession, declaration*, Ign.*Eph.*14.2; Clem.*str.* 2.18(p.154.13; M.8.1017A); Or.*Cels.*3.46(p.243.6; M.11.981A); ἀφίσταται σαφῶς τῆς προτέρας ἐ. Marcell.*fr.*29 ap.Eus.*Marcell.*1.4(p.19.13, v.l. ἀπ- M.24.753C); esp. monastic *profession* ἡ παρθενίαν ὁμολογήσασα, καὶ ἐκπεσοῦσα τῆς ἐ. Bas.*ep.*217 *can.*60(3.326E; M.32.797C) = CCP(381)†*can.*5; δεῖ...τὴν ἐπαγγειλαμένην ἄξια τῆς ἐ. ἔργα διαπρασσομένην, δεικνύειν τὸ ἐπάγγελμα αὐτῆς, ὅτι ἐστὶν ἀληθές *Const.App.* 4.14.2; ἡ ἀποταγὴ οὐδὲν ἄλλο ἐστὶν...εἰ μὴ σταυροῦ καὶ θανάτου ἐ. *Euchol.*(p.407); **2.** *promise*, of God to man ἡμεῖς τῇ πίστει τῆς ἐ. καὶ τῷ λόγῳ ζωοποιούμενοι ζήσομεν *Barn.*7.17; κατ' ἐ. τοῦ θεὸν εἶναι...ἐν ἀνθρωπίνῳ φανέντα σώματι Or.*Cels.*1.68(p.123.6; M.11.788D); Χριστιανῶν...οἷς ἡ πᾶσα ὑπόθεσίς ἐστι τῆς πίστεως ὁ θεὸς καὶ αἱ διὰ τοῦ Χριστοῦ περὶ τῶν δικαίων ἐ. καὶ περὶ τῶν ἀδίκων αἱ περὶ κολάσεως διδασκαλίαι *ib.*8.51(p.266.12; 1592C); ref. Mt.5:18 τουτέστιν οὔτε ἡ τοῖς εὐθέσι κατάλληλος ἐ. οὔτε ἡ τοῖς πλαγιάζουσιν ἠπειλημένη κόλασις Clem.*fr.*58(p.227.8; M.9.768A); οὗ δὲ ἡ πίστις, ἐνταῦθα ἡ ἐ., τελείωσις δὲ ἐπαγγελίας ἡ ἀνάπαυσις id.*paed.*1.6(p.107.24; M.8.285B); τοὺς πάντας ἐνέδυσεν ἀφθαρσίαν ἐν τῇ περὶ τῆς ἀναστάσεως ἐ. Ath.*inc.*9.2 (M.25.112B); *Chron.Pasch.*p.52(M.92.180C); of man to God οὐκ ἔστι σά, ἅπερ ἅπαξ διὰ τῆς ἐν ταῖς εὐχαῖς ἐ. ἀνέθηκας Dion.Al.*fr.*(p.251.4) ap.*cat.Ac.*5:4(p.86.2); Ἀνανίας καὶ Σάπφειρα...οἵτινες, ἐ. τῷ θεῷ δεδωκότες, ἀπὸ τῆς ἐ. ἐνοσφίσαντο ‡Ath.*pass.*2(M.28.188C); τῶν ἀπαιδεύτων προσευχῶν καὶ ἐ. ἀπέχεσθαι Bas.*ep.*199 *can.*28(3.294C; M.32. 725A); of land of promise τὴν κατ' ἐ. γῆν Or.*Jo.*6.45(26; p.154.2; M. 14.280A); myst. τὴν γῆν τῆς ἐ., τοὺς οὐρανούς Meth.*symp.*9.5(p.120. 18; M.18.189B); hence *land of promise* οὗτος εἰσήγαγε τὸν λαὸν εἰς τὴν ἐ., ὥσπερ ὁ Ἰησοῦς εἰς τὸν οὐρανόν Chrys.*hom.*27.3 *in Heb.*(12. 250A); id.*hom.*39.4 *in Mt.*(7.435D); **3.** *that which is promised, promised reward* οἵαν τρυφὴν ἔχει ἡ μέλλουσα ἐ. *2Clem.*10.4; οἱ διὰ τὴν ἐ. ὑπακηκοότες τῷ θεῷ Clem.*str.*4.23(p.313.23; M.8.1357A); Meth. *symp.*7.3(p.73.14; M.18.129A); **4.** of things, *promise, likelihood* λαμπάδες τε πυρὸς παρακείμεναι, καθάπερ ἐν ἐ. τοῦ τὸν ναὸν ἐμπρῆσαι Niceph.Ur.*v.Sym.*152(M.86.3128D); **5.** as rhet. figure, *epangelia est promissio...pollicentes nos aliqua magna aut minima dicturos*, Isid. H.*etym.*2.21.44; **6.** in prepositional phrases ἐν ἐ. λέγειν *promise*, Or.*Cels.*8.18(p.236.3; M.11.1545B); ἐξ ἐ. *according to promise*, id. *hom.*1.5 *in Jer.*(p.4.1; M.13.260B).

ἐπαγγέλλ-ω, **1.** *announce, proclaim* τῆς θεότητος τῆς ~ομένης ὑπὸ Ἰησοῦ Χριστοῦ Or.*hom.*9.1 *in Jer.*(p.64.22; M.13.349B); Synes. *Dion* 1(p.234.18; M.66.1113A); *recite* a lesson, Ephr.1.322A; **2.** med., *promise* ἡ...πίστις πάντα ~εται, πάντα τελειοῖ Herm.*mand.*9.10; Gr. Thaum.*pan.Or.*11(p.20.8; M.10.1081D); *put forward, offer* as an excuse, Ath.*Ar.*1.10(M.26.32C); **3.** med., *profess* οἱ ~όμενοι Χριστοῦ εἶναι Ign.*Eph.*14.2; δόγματα...~όμενα τὴν ἀλήθειαν Or.*princ.*4.1.1 (p.293.10; M.11.344A); id.*hom.*17.5 *in Jer.*(p.148.25; M.13.460D); *Const.App.*4.14.1; Chrys.*sac.*3.17(p.89.2; 1.398B); of monastic vows τῶν βίον μοναζόντων ἐπαγγειλαμένων καὶ ἐκπιπτόντων Bas.*ep.*217 *can.*60(3.376E; M.32.800A) = CCP(381)†*can.*5; *Const.App.*4.14.2; **4.** *ask, claim* τῆς εὐλογίας τὴν ἀντίδοσιν ἐ. Thdt.*h.rel.*25(3.1264); id. *affect.*8(p.217.15; 4.922).

ἐπάγγελμα, τό, **1.** *proclamation* πρὸ τῆς Χριστοῦ ἐπιδημίας ὁ νόμος καὶ οἱ προφῆται...οὐκ εἶχον τὸ ἐ. τοῦ περὶ τοῦ εὐαγγελίου ὅρου Or.*Jo.*1.6(8; p.11.4; M.14.33D); *edict, precept, mandate* ἀκόλουθα τῇ ἐπιστημονικῇ θεοσεβείᾳ καὶ τὰ περὶ τὴν ἄλλην πολιτείαν ἐπαγγέλματα Clem.*str.*7.10(p.43.25; M.9.484B); Eus.*d.e.*3.7(p.142.1; M.22. 240A); **2.** *profession*; of religious life, Bas.*ep.*45.2(3.134C; M.32. 368B); *ib.*284(425A; M.1020C); *Const.App.*4.14.2; ἐπιλαθόμενος τοῦ ἱεροῦ ἐ. τε καὶ σχήματος Nil.*epp.*2.77(M.79.236A); ἑκάστου τὸ ἐ. τὸ ἐσθίειν, τουτέστιν οἱ μὲν κοσμικοὶ εἰς πάντα †Jo.Jej.*poenit.*(M.88. 1916C); τὸ μοναδικὸν τοῦτο καὶ ἀγγελοειδὲς ἐ. *Euchol.*(p.409); hence *body of knowledge*, that which a science professes to teach ἑκάστης ἐπιστήμης ἴδιοι λόγοι εἰσί, καθ' οὓς ⟨τῷ⟩ ἀναλαμβάνοντι περιγίνεται τὸ κατ' αὐτοὺς ἐ. Clem.*fr.*68(p.229.5); **3.** *promise* ταῦτα τὰ ἐ. μετὰ τὴν ἐξανάστασιν τελεσιουργηθήσεσθαι Meth.*symp.*4.5(p.51.15; M.18.93C); *ib.*6.5(p.70.6; 121A).

ἐπαγγελτικός, *promising*, c. genit., Clem.*str.*2.7(p.131.18; M.8. 969C).

ἐπαγκαλίζομαι, *embrace*, met. τὸ μῖσος ἐ. Ephr.1.261F.

ἐπαγλαΐζω, *honour, grace*, Cyr.*Jo.*2.2(4.161D); id.*thes.*32(5^1.293A).

ἐπαγορεύω, *dictate*, Jo.Not.*v.Eus.*3(M.86.309C).

ἐπαγορία, ἡ, CCP(448)(H.2.197D) prob. f.l. for ὑπαγορία (conj. *ACO* 2.1.1; p.168.21).

ἐπάγρυπνος, **1.** *wakeful, sleepless*, Eus.*v.C.*4.29(p.128.18, v.l. ἐπαγρύπνως M.20.1177A); **2.** *vigilant* φροντίδος ἐ. †Bas.*bapt.*2.8.9 (2.666A; M.31.1612A); ἐ. σπουδῇ ‡Ath.*v.Syncl.*21(M.28.1500A).

***ἐπαγρύπνως**, **1.** *sleeplessly*, Eus.*v.C.*4.66(p.145.10; M.20.1221B); **2.** *watchfully* ἐ. ἐπισκοποῦντες Olymp.*Job* 20:29(M.93.220D); Gr. Mag.*dial.*(tr.Zach.)2.3(M.*PL.*66.135A); **3.** *carefully* ἐ. ... ὁ προφήτης ἀδελφοὺς ὀνομάσας, ἐπιφέρει χρησίμως 'ὁ οἶκος τοῦ πατρός σου' Cyr. *Jo.*4.5(4.398E).

ἐπάγ-ω, A. act.; **1.** *lay on, apply* ἀντὶ χειρὸς ἐ. τῷ Γρηγορίῳ τὸν λόγον, ἀφιερώσας τῷ θεῷ τὸν σωματικῶς οὐ παρόντα Gr.Nyss.*v.Gr. Thaum.*(M.46.909B); **2.** *bring forward* as a witness ἐ. τὸν προφήτην μαρτυροῦντα τοῖς γενομένοις Chrys.*hom.*27.1 *in Mt.*(7.327C); **3.** *bring into* a discourse, *ib.*37.2(415D); Dam.*troph.*1.7(p.213.11); *add, go on* to say οὕτως γὰρ ἐ. ἡ γραφὴ λέγουσα [Num.11:23] Just.*dial.* 126.6(M.6.772A); εὐθέως μετὰ τὸ εἰπεῖν...ἐπήγαγε... Meth.*symp.*3.13 (p.42.21; M.18.84A); Eus.*d.e.*4.16(p.193.8; M.22.321B); *Hom.Clem.* 17.5; Chrys.*hom.*7.2 *in Mt.*(7.105B); πάντα τὸν λαὸν ~ειν ἀμήν Thdt.*Ezech.*16:59(2.793); τὰ ~όμενα *what follows*, Eus.*d.e.*5.1

(p.211.7; M.22.349D); Cyr.*Ps.*14:1(M.69.805B); Thdt.*Is.*5:8(p.25.18; 2.200).

B. med.; **1.** *bring with one,* Chrys.*hom.28.5 in Heb.*(12.263B); ἐπῆλθε [sc. ὁ διάβολος], τὸν θάνατον ~όμενος Thdt.*Ps.*21:22(1.741); *bring home,* Meth.*symp.*7.4(p.76.1; M.18.129D); **2.** met., *convey* a meaning γέλως ὁ Ἰσαὰκ ἑρμηνεύεται, τὸ τῆς ἐναρέτου χαρᾶς ~όμενος σύμβολον Eus.*p.e.*11.6(519A; M.21.860D); id.*d.e.*7.1(p.305.11; M.22.500B); **3.** *be connected with* τὸν βίον [sc. τοῦ Ἰώβ], Μωσέως μὲν τῆς νομοθεσίας οὐδὲν ~όμενον, τῆς δὲ...εὐαγγελικῆς διδασκαλίας οὐκ ἀλλότριον *ib.*1.6(p.25.18; 52D); ὁ δὲ [sc. λόγος] τῆς ἀιδίου καὶ ἀσωμάτου φύσεως...οὐδὲν ἀνθρώπειον ἐ. ἄν *ib.*5.5(p.228.22; 377A); **4.** *be endowed with, possess, ib.*4.15(p.174.32; 292B); φυσικὴν ἀλλ' οὐκ ἐπίκτητον τὴν εἰκόνα τοῦ πατρὸς ~όμενος *ib.*5.4(p.225.26; 372D); μετακεχειρισμένη σοφιστικῶς,...καὶ πολλὴν τὴν ἀφροδίτην ~ομένη [sc. φιλοσοφία] Synes.*Dion* 1(p.235.8; M.66.1116A); **5.** *win over,* Chrys.*hom.31.1 in Jo.*(8.176A); *ib.40.2*(239A).

§ἐπαγωγεύς, ὁ, *one who introduces,* of the Devil ὀδύνης...ἐ. Anast.S.*qu.et resp.*32(M.89.572A).

ἐπαγωγή, ἡ, 1. *introduction,* Bas.*hom.*21.5(2.167B; M.31.549B); *application* of remedies, Chrys.*serm.4.3 in Gen.*(4.662B); of penalties, Cyr.*ador.*8(1.280E); **2.** *bringing in, addition* τὴν ἐπὶ τέλει τοῦ ψαλμοῦ φήσασαν ἐ. Eus.*d.e.*6.7(p.258.11; M.22.424C); Chrys.*incomprehens.*5.1(1.481B); id.*hom.45.3 in Jo.*(8.266A); τῇ ἐ. τῆς προφητικῆς φωνῆς Vict.*Mc.*4:12(p.306.3); *what follows,* Didym.*Trin.*3.39(M.39.981A); Chrys.*hom.12.2 in Rom.*(9.545A); Thdt.*Joel.*1:8(2.1385); **3.** *bringing up* of enemies *against* βαρύνεσθαι χεῖρά σου ἐπὶ Ἱερουσαλὴμ ἐν ἐ. ἐθνῶν *Pss.Sal.*2.24; abs., *attack, onset* μεγάλων κινδύνων ἐ. Chrys.*hom.1.2 in 2Cor.*(10.420E); ταῖς τῶν δαιμονίων ἐ. Cyr.*ador.*13(1.468C); id.*Os.*16(3.38B); Eustrat.*stat.anim.*25(p.534); Jo.D.*trisag.*6(M.95.37C); plur., *persecutions, afflictions, T.Lev.*3.2; Chrys.*hom.8.8 in Eph.*(11.65D).

ἐπαγωγικός, 1. *persuasive, hortatory* ἐ. καὶ ἠθικὴν διδασκαλίαν Didym.*Ps.*22:5(M.39.1292C); **2.** *convincing*; comp., Thdr.Stud.*epp.*2.36(M.99.1220C).

ἐπαγωνίζ-ομαι, 1. *continue the fight* προηγωνίσατο πατήρ, ἐπαγωνιοῦνται παῖδες Gr.Naz.*or.*15.6(M.35.921B); Chrys.*hom.62.2 in Mt.*(7.621C); *add to the* former *strife* δέον γὰρ κἀντεῦθεν ἡσυχάζειν, οἱ δὲ ~ονται τοῖς προτέροις *ib.71.1*(694C); *ib.9.1*(130A); **2.** *contend* against ἐ. τῇ ἀθέῳ δόξῃ Clem.*str.*3.13(p.238.18; M.8.1192C); Bas.*Eun.*1.17(1.229C; M.29.552A); Chrys.*hom.9.4 in Mt.*(7.134E); **3.** *contend* for, Cyr.H.*catech.*6.17; ὁ τοῖς ἱεροῖς τῆς ἐκκλησίας ~όμενος δόγμασι Cyr.*Jo.*proem.(4.3D); Max.*schol.c.h.*13.4(M.4.100A).

***ἐπαγώνισμα, τό,** *further conflict*; met., of theol. controversy, Thdt.*eran.*proem.(4.4).

***ἐπαδικέω,** *add wrong to wrong,* Ath.*h.Ar.*65(p.218.36; M.25.769D).

***ἐπαδολεσχέω,** *be idle over,* Gel.Cyz.*h.e.*3.9.6.

ἐπᾴδ-ω, 1. *sing to* someone *in order to charm* him ~ωμεν τῇ ψυχῇ τὰς θείας ἐπῳδάς Chrys.*hom.28.2 in Rom.*(9.726D); fig. τῷ... ἐν τῇ...καρδίᾳ...ὄφει ὥσπερ ~οντες *Hom.Clem.*10.5; *ib.*11.11; c. acc. pers., *charm* ἐπᾳσθέντος τοῦ ὄφεως εἰς ἡμερότητα Epiph.*haer.*37.5(p.57.21; M.41.648D); fig. ἐ. τὸ θηρίον Chrys.*hom.7.4 in Heb.*(12.79C); id.*oppugn.*3.6(1.85D); **2.** *utter, chant* θρήνους ἐπαείσετε Nonn.*par.Jo.*16:20(M.43.881A); *sing hymns to* ἄλλος δὲ τοῦ πνεύματος τῇ ἑπτάδι ~ων Clem.*paed.*3.12(p.284.18; M.8.665C); Chrys.*hom.55.5 in Mt.*(7.561D); **3.** *repeat, recite,* Clem.*paed.*3.11(p.281.2; M.8.660B); Or.*hom.20.2 in Jos.*(p.420.29; M.12.922A); ταῦτα ἄνω καὶ κάτω τῆς γραφῆς ~ούσης ἡμῖν Chrys.*hom.29.6 in 1Cor.*(10.267C); id.*hom.1.4 in Jo.*(8.6E).

[*]ἐπαέθλιον, τό, = ἔπαθλον, *Orac.Sib.*2.152.

ἔπαθλον, τό, *prize in a contest,* fig. μέσος ὁ ἄνθρωπος οἷόν τι ἔ. ἀγῶνος τοῖς ἐκ τοῦ ἐναντίου μεταποιουμένοις πρόκειται [sc. οἷον εἰδωλολατρείᾳ καὶ θεοσεβείᾳ] Gr.Nyss.*v.Mos.*(M.44.329D); in gen., *reward* τὸ ἔ. λαβεῖν, τὴν ἐπιστήμην τοῦ ζητουμένου Clem.*str.*8.1(p.80.21; M.9.560B); γνώμης ἐστὶ τὸ ἔ. [sc. παρθενία] *Const.App.*8.24.2; χρὴ...ἀφιέναι τὰ ἁμαρτήματα, εἰ καὶ μὴ ἐκεῖνο ἦν τὸ μέγα ἔ., τὸ ἄφεσιν ἀντὶ τούτων λαμβάνειν Chrys.*hom.51.3 in Jo.*(8.302E); ref. Arian view of Christ's sonship μηδὲ ἐξ ἀρχῆς ἐσχηκὼς τὸ ὄνομα υἱός, εἴ γε τοῦτο τῶν ἔργων ἔ. ἔσχε καὶ προκοπῆς, οὐκ ἄλλης ἢ τῆς ὅτε γέγονεν ἄνθρωπος Ath.*Ar.*1.38(M.26.89C); of reward for evil doing τῆς Ἰουδαϊκῆς ἀπειθείας...τὰ ἔ. ‡Meth.*Sym.et Ann.*12(M.18.377B); esp. of future life, Const.*ep.*(Opitz 3 p.59.7); Eust.*engast.*15(p.40.7; M.18.644D); Ath.*gent.*47(M.25.96B); Thdr.Mops.*Rom.*8:11(M.66.821B).

ἐπαθρέω, *regard*; met., Cyr.*Jo.*5.3(4.501B); Jo.D.*hom.*12.3(M.96.785A).

ἐπαθροίζομαι, *come together,* Meth.*symp.*2.2(p.16.20; M.18.49A).

ἐπαινέτης, ὁ, *one who praises* ἕνα τοῦτον...τὸν σκοπόν, ὥστε τὸν ἀκοίμητον ἐκεῖνον ὀφθαλμὸν ἐ. ἔχειν Chrys.*hom.23.2 in Gen.*(4.207C); hence *one who applauds, supporter,* Soz.*h.e.*3.20.7(M.67.1101A).

ἐπαίρ-ω, A. *lift up*; hence **1.** *elevate*; pass., of an emperor being proclaimed, *Chron.Pasch.*pp.300,320(M.92.753B,816B,817B); fig. πρὸς τὸν ἀκρότατον τῆς ἀνθρωπίνης ἀρετῆς ὅρον ἑαυτὴν διὰ φιλοσοφίας ἐπάρασα Gr.Nyss.*v.Macr.*(p.371.21; M.46.960C); χειρῶν ἔκτασις ἐτροπώσατο τὸν Ἀμαλήκ, καὶ πράξεις ἐπηρμέναι χειροῦνται πάθη σαρκὸς Nil.*spir.mal.*2(M.79.1148A); pass., *rise,* fig. τοὺς μὲν τῆς γῆς μὴ ~εσθαι δυναμένους τοῖς γηΐνοις...προσήλωσαν Just.*1apol.*58.3(M.6.416B); ἂν ἐπαρθῇ τὰ κύματα τῶν πειρασμῶν Chrys.*stat.*2.3(2.24A); λύπης...τὸν νοῦν...οὐκ ἐώσης πρὸς ὕψος ~εσθαι Jo.D.*hom.*1.1(M.96.545B); met., *heighten, exaggerate* οὐχ ἁπλῶς εἶπεν...ἀλλὰ καὶ ἐπῆρε τὸν λόγον εἰπών... Chrys.*comm.in Gal.*5:10(10.715E); *ib.*5:8(715B); id.*hom.3.4 in Rom.*(9.452E); **2.** met.; **a.** *exalt* οἱ...ὑπομένοντες ἐν πεποιθήσει...ἐπήρθησάν τε καὶ ἔγγραφοι ἐγένοντο ἀπὸ τοῦ θεοῦ ἐν τῷ μνημοσύνῳ αὐτοῦ *1Clem.*45.8; ἡ τοῦ λόγου τοῦ θείου ἐπίβασις...ἐν... διανοίαις...ἐπηρμέναις τὸ φρόνημα Eus.*d.e.*6.13(p.263.19; M.22.433A); **b.** *set up, stir up* against ἡ ψιλὴ προφορὰ [i.e. τὸ ἀγέννητον] τὴν ὑπόστασιν ~ει κατὰ πάντων τῶν γεννητῶν ‡Ath.*dial.Trin.*2.25(M.28.1196A); μὴ ἐάσῃς τὴν καρδίαν σου ἐπαρθῆναι κατὰ αὐτοῦ [sc. τοῦ ἀδελφοῦ σου] Dor.*doct.*17.1(M.88.1800D); med., *set oneself up* ταπεινοφρονούντων γάρ ἐστιν ὁ Χριστός, οὐκ ~ομένων ἐπὶ τὸ ποίμνιον αὐτοῦ *1Clem.*16.1; ‡Ath.*dial.Trin.*2.11(1173C); *cat.Rom.*proem.(p.3.5); **c.** *puff up* ταπεινοφροσύνη ~ει ὅταν μὴ γνησία ᾖ Chrys.*hom.2.3 in Philm.*(11.783A); med. or pass., *exalt oneself, be puffed up, 1Clem.*21.5; αὐτῷ ἐπηρμένοι τούτῳ τῷ γινώσκειν τὰς γραφὰς καὶ τὸν διδασκαλικὸν κεκληρῶσθαι θρόνον Meth.*lepr.*12(p.466.9); Const.*or.s.c.*6(p.160.6; M.20.1248A); πεποιθήσει ματαίᾳ τοὺς λογισμοὺς ~όμενοι Eus.*l.C.*9(p.218.33; M.20.1364C); Bas.*hom.*3.5(2.21E; M.31.212A); Chrys.*hom.9.2 in Eph.*(11.71A); perf. ptcpl. pass., in form ἐπαρμένος, *proud,* Gr.Mag.*dial.*(tr.Zach.)1.4(M.*PL.*77.171D).

B. *take off, take away* τοῦ θεάτρου λυθέντος καὶ τῶν προσωπείων ἐπαρθέντων, ἕκαστος, ὅπερ ἐστί, τοῦτο φαίνεται Chrys.*hom.2.4 in Tit.*(11.742E); αὐτὸν...ἔσφαξαν καὶ ἐπῆραν τὴν κεφαλὴν αὐτοῦ *Chron.Pasch.*p.395(M.92.1013A); *carry off* ἐ. αἰχμαλώτους Jo.Mal.*chron.*18 p.462(M.97.676B); *ib.*8 p.198(312B); *ib.*10 p.245(376A); met., *do away with, destroy, kill,* Epiph.*haer.*68.6(p.146.29; M.42.193C); Jo.Mal.*chron.*17 p.417(616D).

ἐπαΐσσω, *rush upon* or *into* πόντον ἐ. Vergil *ecl.*4.32 ap.Const.*or.s.c.*20(p.185.8; M.20.1297B); νῆα ἐ. Nonn.*par.Jo.*6:17(M.43.796B).

ἐπαισχύνομαι, *be ashamed,* Didym.(‡Bas.)*Eun.*4(1.286E; M.29.689A).

***ἐπαισχυντέον,** *one must be ashamed,* Or.*mart.*37(p.34.9; M.11.612B).

ἐπαίτησις, ἡ, *begging,* Or.*comm.in Mt.*16.12(p.514.12; M.13.1413C); Chrys.*hom.11.3 in 1Thess.*(11.506F).

***ἐπαιτικός,** *of a beggar, Apophth.Patr.*(M.65.228B).

***ἐπαιχμαλωτεύω,** (= αἰχμαλωτεύω), *make prisoner,* Thphn.*chron.*p.408(M.108.969C).

ἐπαΐ-ω, c. genit. or abs.; **1.** *hear* ὁ δεόμενος τῆς διὰ λόγου παιδεύσεως καὶ μηδαμῶς ~ων αὐτῆς Or.*Cels.*4.83(p.353.13; M.11.1156C); Gr.Nyss.*v.Macr.*(p.396.25; M.46.984B); χάριν...τοῖς πάλαι κωφοῖς τὸ τῶν θείων λογίων ~ειν παρέχουσαν Thdt.*Pss.*proem.(1.603); **2.** *listen to,* Just.*dial.*67.9(M.6.632B); *ib.*112.4(736A); Gr.Nyss.*or.dom.*2(p.36.20; M.44.1141D); Cyr.*Am.*61(3.317E); **3.** *understand* τοῖς μετρίως ~ειν λόγων θείων δυναμένοις Or.*sel.in Ps.*1(M.12.1077C); βάρβαροι, καὶ τῆς Σύρων οὐκ...~οντες φωνῆς Eus.*d.e.*3.4(p.119.1; M.22.201D); Gr.Nyss.*or.catech.*18(p.77.2; M.45.56B).

ἐπαιωρ-έω, 1. *hold up in the air,* Hipp.*haer.*4.28(p.54.12; M.16.3090B); pass., *be suspended, hang* ἐπὶ τίνι ἄρα ~εῖται ὁ...οὐρανός; *Hom.Clem.*3.35; Evagr.*h.e.*4.8(p.204.8; M.86.2808B); *lean on,* fig. πάντα ...κατασείεται σαθρᾷ τῇ βάσει ~ούμενα Bas.*Spir.*77(3.65D; M.32.213A); met., *threaten* πᾶσι μὲν ἀνθρώποις βαρυτάτας εἰσπράξεις ἐ. Eus.*v.C.*1.13(p.14.14; M.20.928B); usu. pass. intrans. ὀργῆς τοῖς ἀνθρώποις...~ηθείσης id.*d.e.*6.15(p.270.26; M.22.445A); id.*p.e.*4.2(134D; M.21.236D); Synes.*ep.*4(M.66.1336C); **2.** *pile up,* fig. χρεῶν ὄγκον ἀφόρητον ἐ. Chrys.*hom.13.5 in 1Cor.*(10.116C); pass., of a storm, *blow up*; fig., id.*serm.6.1 in Gen.*(4.671A).

ἐπακμάζ-ω, *reach one's prime,* fig. ἐπανθεῖν ἀεὶ καὶ ~ειν πιαινομένη λόγοις πέφυκεν ἡ παρθενία Meth.*symp.*4.3(p.49.10; M.18.92A); met., *reach one's full strength, Hom.Clem.*5.25; ἐ. ταῖς μεγαλοφωνίαις ὁ κῆρυξ Gr.Nyss.*Eun.*4(2 p.55.10; M.45.625B).

***ἐπακοή, ἡ,** *hearing,* ‡Caes.Naz.*dial.*140(M.38.1072); Ath.*ep. Marcell.*25(M.27.37B) prob. error for ὑπακοήν.

ἐπακολουθ-έω, 1. of persons, *follow, succeed, 1Clem.*43.1; Ign. *Smyrn.*10.1; of things, *follow, come next* in speech or writing, Just.*dial.*65.2(M.6.625B); **2.** *follow, result* πίστιν...~ούσης τῆς ἐλπίδος, προαγούσης τῆς ἀγάπης Polyc.*ep.*3.3; ref. Mt.12:44 πληρωθέντων τῶν κενῶν, τότε ἡ σφραγὶς ~εῖ, ἵνα φυλάσσηται τῷ θεῷ τὸ ἅγιον Clem.*ecl.*12(p.140.19; M.9.704C); Or.*hom.17.5 in Jer.*(p.149.4; M.13.460D); Hegem.*Arch.*9(p.15.4; M.10.1441B); τῆς ἐν αὐτῷ σαρκὸς πρώτης ἁγιασθείσης...ἡμεῖς ~οῦσαν ἔχομεν τὴν τοῦ πνεύματος χάριν Ath.*Ar.*1.50(M.26.117B).

ἐπακολούθημα, τό, *secondary consideration* ἦν δὲ ἡ ἀπαγγελία προηγουμένη μὲν περὶ τῆς ἐπιδημίας τοῦ σωτῆρος, ἐ. δὲ περὶ τῶν ἐσομένων τῷ Ἰσραὴλ καὶ τοῖς ἔθνεσι Ath.*syn.*3(p.233.7; M.26.685B).

ἐπακολούθησις, ἡ, 1. *following* in time, *succession,* Just.*dial.*65.3 (M.6.625D); **2.** *consequence,* c. genit. εἰ...μόνον ἦν πλημμέλημα καὶ μὴ φθορᾶς ἐ. καλῶς ἂν ἦν ἡ μετάνοια Ath.*inc.*7.4(M.25.108D); dat. as adv., Gr.Nyss.*v.Mos.*(M.44.333A); **3.** *following* a certain path; hence **a.** *obedience,* id.*hom.15 in Cant.*(M.44.1109C); **b.** *procedure, Cod.Afr.*91(Lat. *prosecutio*).

ἐπακολουθητικός, *consequent, derivative* οὐσίαν...τῶν ἀσωμάτων ...ἐ. εἶναι νομίζουσι Or.*or.*27.8(p.368.1; M.11.512A).

***ἐπακολουθητικῶς,** *consequentially,* Gr.Nyss.*fat.*(M.45.153D).

***ἐπακουσμός, ὁ,** *hearkening* ἑρμηνεύεται γὰρ Ἀναθὼθ ἐ. Or.*hom. 10.4 in Jer.*(p.74.8; M.13.361B).

ἐπακού-ω, *hear;* **1.** *give ear, pay attention,* c. genit., *T.Sym.*7.1; ἐ. τῶν ῥημάτων Chrys.*hom.41.3 in Mt.*(7.448D); abs., id.*hom.8.1 in 1Tim.*(11.590B); esp. of God ἐ. ὁ θεὸς τῶν εὐχῶν ὑμῶν *Pap.Chr.* (p.393); Σαμουὴλ...οὗ ὁ θεὸς ἐ. Or.*engast.*3(p.285.15; M.12.1016C); c. dat., *T.Isach.*2.4; **2.** *understand* πάντας ἀλλήλων ~ειν τῆς διαλέκτου μὴ δύνασθαι Tat.*orat.*30(p.30.29; codd. ὑπ- M.6.868C); *understand* in a certain sense εἰ δὲ θέλεις καὶ νοητῶς τὸν λόγον ~σαι Mac.Mgn. *apocr.*2.7(p.8.2); **3.** *obey,* Ign.*Magn.*3.2; οὐδενὶ ἄλλῳ ἐ. εἰ μὴ μόνον ...θεῷ *M.Das.*8(p.94.3); fig. οὐκ ἐπειδήπερ ἐπίστευσε [sc. ὁ Ἀβραάμ] τὸ γῆρας ἐπήκουσεν; Antip.Bost.*Jo.Bapt.*7(M.85.1769C); **4.** *say in response* to, *A.Jo.*94(p.197.16).

ἐπακροάομαι, *listen,* Bas.*ep.*217 *can.*77(3.329A; M.32.805A).

ἐπακρόασις, ἡ, *hearkening,* Ath.*gent.*4(M.25.9D).

ἐπακτικός, *attractive;* superl., Gr.Thaum.*pan.Or.*6(p.17.3; M.10.1072B).

ἐπακτός, 1. *acquired* οὐκ ἐ. ἔχων τὸ τῆς θεότητος ἀξίωμα, καθάπερ ἡμεῖς Cyr.*hom.pasch.*8(5^{2}.100D); id.*Chr.un.*(5^{1}.769A); id.*Jo.*7(Pusey p.256.15); **2.** αἱ ἐπακταί [sc. ἡμέραι] *intercalary days,* Epiph.*haer.* 70.13(p.246.14; M.42.361B); *Chron.Pasch.*pp.12,14(M.92.89C,93A); Max.*comput.*3(M.19.1221B).

***ἐπακτῶς,** *by acquisition,* Cyr.*Is.*2.1(2.193C).

ἐπαλγέω, *grieve over,* c. dat., Philost.*h.e.*7.3(M.65.540B).

ἐπαλγύνω, *afflict,* pass., Cyr.*Jo.*2.5(4.210D); med., *feel pain at,* id.*Abac.*27(3.541B).

ἐπαλείφ-ω, 1. *paint on,* Cyr.*ador.*1(1.5D); *inlay,* fig. σύμβολον... τῆς ὑπερλάμπρου θεότητος ὁ χρυσός, ἐπαληλειμμένης ὥσπερ τῷ ἁγίῳ σώματι, καὶ τὴν ἰδίαν αὐτοῦ λαμπρότητά τε καὶ ἀφθαρσίαν ἐνιείσης ἀπορρήτως *ib.*9(293E); **2.** *anoint,* fig. τὸ ἀειθαλὲς εὐφροσύνης ⟨καὶ⟩ ἀκήρατον εὐωδίας ~ώμεθα χρῖσμα Clem.*paed.*1.12(p.149.5; M.8.368B); ἀλλήλους...τῷ τῆς χάριτος ἐλαίῳ πρὸς...τελειότητα τοῦ μαρτυρίου ~οντες *M.Pers.*1.2(p.422.15); in gen., *prepare* athletes *for a contest;* fig., Eus.*v.C.*3.59(p.105.24; M.20.1125B); ἐὰν βλέπῃς ἐπιτιθέμενον τὸν ἐχθρὸν...καὶ θέλῃς ~ειν σαυτὸν κατ' αὐτοῦ, ᾆδε τὸν λη' ψαλμὸν Ath.*ep.Marcell.*19(M.27.32B); hence **3.** met., *stir up* against, *encourage* ἐ. ἑαυτοὺς τοῖς τῶν πατέρων...ἀνδραγαθήμασι Petr.II Al. *encycl.*(M.33.1284C)ap.Thdt.*h.e.*4.22.19; ἐ. εἰς προθυμίαν Ath.*v. Anton.*46(M.26.909C); id.*fug.*21(p.82.27; M.25.672A); Gr.Naz.*ep.*18 (M.37.52C); τὸν...εἰς ἔφεσιν ἀρετῆς ~οντα λόγον Cyr.*ador.*5(1.168B); id.*Is.*3.1(2.370C); id.*ep.*1(p.10.15; 5^{2}.2A); ἐ. τοῦ μὴ ἀθυμεῖν Gr.Mag. *dial.*(tr.Zach.)2.1(M.*PL.*66.127B); Thdr.Stud.*epp.*2.71(M.99.1301B).

ἐπαληθεύ-ω, A. trans.; **1.** *substantiate, verify* μὴ ἀληθῶς ἐξ αὐτοῦ τοῦ υἱοῦ τῷ πατρὶ τὴν κλῆσιν ~οντος Gr.Nyss.*ep.*24(M.46.1089B); Max.*ep.*12(M.91.468B); **2.** *say truly,* Eus.*h.e.*10.4.29(M.20.861A); *predicate truly,* Cyr.*thes.*1(5^{1}.12B); τοῖς λογικοῖς κτίσμασιν, οἷς οὐ φύσει τὸ τῆς θεότητος ~εται κάλλος *ib.*4(24E); **3.** *prove one's right to* Θεόδοτος, πράγμασιν αὐτοῖς ἀνὴρ καὶ τὸ κύριον ὄνομα καὶ τὸ ἐπίσκοπον ἐπαληθεύσας Eus.*h.e.*7.32.23(M.20.732A); Cyr.H.*catech.*21.5; Cyr. *Jo.*1.1(4.13D).

B. intrans.; **1.** *be true* τὸν περὶ ψυχῆς ἀθανασίας λόγον...~οντα Eus.*p.e.*1.4(13D; M.21.41C); id.*d.e.*6.20(p.289.2; M.22.473D); *be true* to, *be a true description* of, *tally* with ~ούσης τῇ οὐσίᾳ τῆς προσηγορίας Eun.ap.Bas.*Eun.*2.6(1.242D; M.29.584A); acc. Eunomius οὔτε υἱὸς λεγόμενος, ~ουσαν ἔχει τῇ προσηγορίᾳ τὴν φύσιν Gr.Nyss. *Eun.*12(1 p.230.21; M.45.928A); τῇ προσηγορίᾳ τὴν φύσιν [sc. τοῦ υἱοῦ] ~εσθαι *ib.*1(1 p.160.8; 401B); Euthal.Diac.*epp.Paul.*proem.(M.85.697B); Jo.Ant.*ep.Nest.*3(p.94.9; M.77.1452C); **2.** *speak the truth* about ἐ. τοῖς πράγμασιν Athenag.*res.*6(p.54.6; M.6.984C); ‡Ath. *Apoll.*2.8(M.26.1145A); Chrys.*hom.5.2 in Col.*(11.360B); abs., Isid. Pel.*epp.*1.155(M.78.288A).

ἐπαλλήλως, 1. *in alternate succession, Hom.Clem.*19.24; **2.** *continuously, ib.*20.12; Didym.*Ps.*22:6(M.39.1293C).

***ἐπαλλοτρία, ἡ,** ? *exile, Vaticin.*2(p.58).

ἐπαμάω, *heap up;* med., *have heaped upon* one κόνιν ἐπαμώμενον Epiph.*haer.*64.69(p.514.20, v.l. ἐπαμμένον; M.41.1192C); hence *gather* the harvest, †Apoll.*met.Ps.*125:5(M.33.1509C).

***ἐπαμεριμνέω,** c. dat., *cease from care because of* one's previous achievements, ref. Phil.3:13, †Bas.*ep.*42.1(3.125D; M.32.348C); Bas. *moral.*70.11 tit.(2.295D; M.31.825B).

***ἐπαμφιάζ-ομαι,** *clothe,* of moon πάλιν ~ομένη τὸ φῶς Bas.*hex.* 6.3(1.52D; M.29.124B); pass., of Christ ἐπαμφιασθέντα τῇ ἀφθαρσίᾳ Anast.S.*hex.*12(M.89.1064B).

***ἐπαμφίασις, ἡ,** *putting on,* ref. Inc. ἡ τῆς ἀνθρωπίνης μορφῆς ἐ. ‡Ath.*Sabell.*15(M.28.121A).

ἐπαμφιβάλλω, *be in doubt,* CCP(448)*act.*(*ACO* 2.1.1 p.158.26; H.2. 184E).

***ἐπαμφιβόλως,** *doubtfully, ambiguously,* Epiph.*haer.*69.60(p.208. 29; M.42.300A); Chrys.*proph.obscurit.*1.4(6.175B).

ἐπαμφιέννυμι, 1. *clothe, cover,* Bas.*hex.*6.6(1.55C; M.29.129C); ‡Caes.Naz.*dial.*95(M.38.960); **2.** *put over, use as a covering* τὰς μὲν [sc. ἀτόμους] ἐ. ... δέρμα καὶ σάρκα γενομένας Dion.Al.ap.Eus.*p.e.* 14.26(779A; M.21.1281B); Cyr.*ador.*1(1.14E) prob. f.l. for ἀπαμφ- (M.68.156B).

ἐπαμφίσκω, *put on,* med., Nil.*epp.*1.242(M.79.172B).

ἐπαμφοτεριστής, ὁ, 1. *waverer;* of one who holds contradictory opinions, †Bas.*Is.*153(1.488B; M.30.369D); **2.** *person capable of choosing between two alternatives* ἄνθρωπον τὸν ἐ. τῇ φύσει Proc.G. *Gen.*3:21(M.87.225C).

ἐπαμφότερος, *ambiguous;* neut. plur. as adv., *in two senses,* †Bas. *Is.*62(1.424D; M.30.228A).

ἐπάν, = ἐπεὶ ἄν, *LS;* c. indic., Thphl.Ant.*Autol.*1.12(M.6.1041B); c. opt., Gel.Cyz.*h.e.*2.23.2(M.85.1296B).

ἐπαναβαθμός, ὁ, *step upwards;* met., Dion.Ar.*e.h.*7.3.11(M.3. 568D).

ἐπαναβαίν-ω, 1. *get up upon,* c. dat., Synes.*ep.*67(M.66.1412B); abs., *move up* Ἰωάννης πρότερον ἀνακείμενος ἐν τῷ κόλπῳ τοῦ Ἰησοῦ ἐπαναβέβηκε, καὶ ἐνέπεσεν ἐπὶ τὸ στῆθος Or.*Jo.*32.21(13; p.463.27; M. 801D); **2.** met., *be promoted, rank higher* (*than,* c. acc.) εἶναι θεοῦ δοῦλον μὲν τὰ πρῶτα, ἔπειτα δὲ πιστὸν γενέσθαι θεράποντα...εἰ δέ τις ἐπαναβαίη, τοῖς υἱοῖς ἐγκαταλέγεσθαι Clem.*str.*1.27(p.107.26; M.8. 921A); τὸ [sc. τάγμα] τῶν παντελῶς εἰδωλολατρῶν...καὶ τὸ τῶν ἐκ περιτομῆς διὰ Μωσέως, ἐπὶ τὸν πρῶτον ἀνεληλυθότων τῆς εὐσεβείας βαθμόν, καὶ τρίτον τὸ τῶν ἐπαναβεβηκότων διὰ τῆς εὐαγγελικῆς διδασκαλίας Eus.*d.e.*1.6(p.32.31; M.22.64C); ἄλλην τινὰ ἀξίαν ~ουσαν τοὺς πρεσβυτέρους εἶχον οἱ ἀπόστολοι Ammon.*Ac.*15:6(M.85.1548D); οἱ μὲν καθαρτικοὶ ὑποβεβήκασιν ὡς οἱ ἐπορκισταὶ ὄντες· οἱ δὲ φωτιστικοὶ ἐπαναβεβήκασι τῇ διδασκαλίᾳ οἷον οἱ πρεσβύτεροι καὶ οἱ διάκονοι Max. *schol.c.h.*3.3(M.4.52B); of things τὴν ἐγκύκλιον...τὴν ἐπαναβεβηκυῖαν ...φιλοσοφίαν Clem.*str.*6.11(p.479.13; M.9.316A); **3.** *mount upwards* in thought, *advance* ὁ μὲν ἐξ ἐθνῶν ἐπιστρέφων τὴν πίστιν, ὁ δὲ εἰς γνῶσιν ~ων τῆς ἀγάπης τὴν τελειότητα αἰτήσεται Clem.*str.*7.7(p.34.25; M.9.465B); Or.*princ.*3.1.23(p.242.3; M.11.300C); ἐ. τῇ διανοίᾳ Ath. *Ar.*2.80(M.26.316C); *ib.*3.44(416A); of raising dead contrasted with healing sick τοῖς ὑψηλοτέροις ~ει θαύμασι Gr.Nyss.*hom.opif.*25.9(M. 44.217C); hence *search for higher principles* ἐ. καὶ διερευνῶν τῷ λογισμῷ, εὑρήσει πολὺν ὄχλον ἐπιρρεόντων μεσιτῶν Ath.*Ar.*2.26(201C); **4.** *transcend* τὴν γνῶσιν τοῦ θεοῦ...ἐπαναβεβηκυῖαν τῆς πίστεως δι' ἀγάπην εἰς γνῶσιν Clem.*str.*4.22(p.308.32; M.8.1348A); καινὸν τρόπον τὸν τῆς ψαλμῳδίας...τῆς τοῦ θεοῦ λατρείας εἰσάγει καὶ ἄλλα δὲ πλεῖστα τὸν Μωσέως νόμον ἐπαναβεβηκότα...διδάσκει Hipp.*fr.in Ps.*6 (p.136.10); Eus.*p.e.*4.1(130B; M.21.229B); ‡Pion.*v.Polyc.*16; *be too high for* θειοτέρᾳ τινὶ καὶ τοὺς πολλοὺς ἐπαναβεβηκυίᾳ φιλοσοφίᾳ Eus. *p.e.*8.10(378C; M.640C); Ath.*gent.*27(M.25.52C); **5.** perf. ptcpl. as adj., *transcendent* τῆς ἐ. καὶ προσεχοῦς τοῦ κυρίου ἐν ἀϊδιότητι θεωρίας Clem.*str.*7.2(p.9.8; M.9.413C); *lofty, exalted* γνώσεως ἀκρότητα καὶ τὸ ἐ. ὕψος ἀνδρὸς ἐντελοῦς *ib.*7.7(p.35.5; 465C); Or.*hom.16.3 in Jer.* (p.134.25; M.13.441B); of spiritual interprn. of scripture, id.*comm. in Mt.*14.6(p.287.8; M.13.1196B); id.*schol.in Lc.*9:31(M.17.344B).

ἐπαναβάλλω, *lift up,* Clem.*paed.*3.11(p.275.3; M.8.645B).

ἐπανάβασις, ἡ, 1. *rising above* κατ' ἐπανάβασιν τῶν ἄλλων ἱερέων σπεύδοντα [sc. τὸν ἀρχιερέα] ἐπὶ τὴν τοῦ νοητοῦ δίοδον Clem.*str*.5.6(p.353.14; M.9.65B); **2.** *ascent* γνώσομαι τὴν ἱερωσύνην οὐκ ἀπόβασιν οὖσαν φιλοσοφίας ἀλλ' ἐ. Synes.*ep*.11(M.66.1348D); *ib*.96(M.1465A); κατ' ἐ. *by an ascending scale* ἐνεργεσίαν δὲ ἀγάπη ἐπαγγέλλεται ἡ κυριεύουσα τοῦ σαββάτου κατ' ἐ. Clem.*str*.4.6(p.261.10; M.8.1241A); ἅγια ἁγίων καὶ ἔτι τούτων κατ' ἐ. τὰ ἁγιώτερα ἀποκαλύψαντος *ib*.6.8(p.466.4; M.9.289B); *ib*.7.7(p.28.6; 452B); *one above another* ἑπτὰ οὐρανοί, οὕς τινες ἀριθμοῦσι κατ' ἐ. *ib*.4.25(p.318.31; M.8.1368B); *progression* αἱ ἡμέραι μόριον βίου τοῦ κατ' ἐ. *ib*.2.12(p.142.6; 992A); *advance* κατ' ἐ. ἐκ τῶν εἰρημένων νοητέον καὶ τό [Num.14:28] Or.*Jo*.2.17(11; p.74.29; M.14.145A).

***ἐπαναβεβηκότως**, *in a lofty sense*; ref. spiritual sense of scripture, Or.*comm.in Mt*.10.14(p.17.21; M.13.868D); Bas.*hom.in Ps*.28(1.117A; M.29.288C).

ἐπαναβιβάζω, *raise* rent, †Gregent.*leg.Hom*.57(M.86.612C).

***ἐπαναβλύζω**, *well up, spring up*, Thdr.Stud.*cant*.14.3(p.368).

***ἐπανάγκασμα, τό**, *means of compulsion*, Nemes.*nat.hom*.1(M.40.521B); Gennad.*fr.Gen*.42:24(M.85.1656C).

ἐπάναγκος, *compelling* ἐ. ᾠδαῖς Eus.*l.C*.13(p.236.19; M.20.1400A).

***ἐπαναγνωστικός**, *able to be read out*; neut. as subst., *prepared statement*, Thphn.*chron*.p.213(M.108.545A).

ἐπαναγωγή, ἡ, *restoration* γενόμενος ἄνθρωπος...ἐπ'...ἐπαναγωγῇ τοῦ ἀνθρωπείου γένους Just.*1apol*.23.2(M.6.364B); Max.*ambig*.(M.91.1133D).

ἐπαναδίπλωσις, ἡ, *repetition*, Clem.*paed*.1.9(p.136.23; M.8.345A).

***ἐπαναδρομή, ἡ**, *return* τὴν διὰ πίστεως δικαιοσύνην ἐ. ... εἰς τὸ ἀπ' ἀρχῆς Cyr.*Jo*.4.7(4.430C); *ib*.9.1(814D); *restoration* τῇ πρὸς τὸ ὑγιὲς ἐ. Jo.VI CP *ep*.(M.96.1417B).

ἐπαναζεύγνυμι, *return*, Evagr.*h.e*.1.7(p.13.8; M.86.2436B); *ib*.2.4(p.50.22; 2509B); Heracl.*ep*.(M.92.993A); Jo.D.*hom*.12.9(M.96.793A).

ἐπανάζευξις, ἡ, *return*, Evagr.*h.e*.4.21(p.170.10; M.86.2740A); Thphyl.*exc.gent*.12(p.487.5; M.113.949B); ‡Meth.*Sym.et Ann*.8(M.18.368A).

***ἐπανάθημα, τό**, *superstructure*, Clem.*str*.5.4(p.342.14; M.9.45B).

***ἐπαναιρετέον**, *one ought to adopt* a mode of life, Clem.*paed*.3.11(p.270.3, conj. for codd. ἐπανηιρητέον; ἐπαναρητέον M.8.633A).

ἐπαναιρ-έω, med.; **1.** *take upon one, profess, practise* a mode of life or course of conduct ἀργίαν...ἐ. Tat.*orat*.23(p.25.22; M.6.857B); *ib*.29(p.30.1; 865D); αἱ γυναῖκες τὸ εὔσχημον ~ούμεναι Clem.*paed*.2.2(p.176.14; M.8.429A); id.*str*.1.1(p.5.28; M.8.692C); id.*ecl*.29(p.146.4; M.9.713B); Gr.Thaum.*pan.Or*.13(p.29.16; M.10.1088B); θηριώδη τινὰ τρόπον καὶ βίον ἀβίωτον ἐ. Eus.*h.e*.1.2.18(M.20.61C); esp. of religious life τὸν μονήρη καὶ ἰδιάζοντα βίον ἐ. Gr.Nyss.*ep*.2(M.46.1009B); τὴν παρθενίαν ἐ. Chrys.*virg*.29(1.289A); μοναχὸς ἐπὶ γῆς ἀγγελικὸν ἐπανῃρημένος βίον Hyper.*mon*.87(M.79.1481C); and of Christian life, *cat.Apoc*.14:5(p.388.28); **2.** *choose, undertake* to do something, Meth.*arbitr*.13(p.180.7); *Hom.Clem*.11.21; τῷ εὐλαβεῖ καὶ ἀγαθῷ διδάσκειν ~ουμένῳ...παραδώσω *Clem.contest*.2(M.2.29B); **3.** *profess, hold* a belief or mental attitude τί λόγους ~εῖσθε, τῶν ἔργων μακρὰν ἀφεστῶτες; Tat.*orat*.26(p.28.9; M.6.864A); ἡμᾶς...μαθητὰς θεοῦ γεγονότας, τὴν ὄντως ἀληθῆ σοφίαν ἐπανῃρημένους Clem.*prot*.11(p.79.15; M.8.229A); Meth.*symp*.5.2(p.54.14; M.18.100A).

ἐπανακαινίζω, *renew*, Mac.Mgn.*apocr*.4.16(p.87.26).

ἐπανακάμπτ-ω, **1.** *come back again*, lit. ἐ. εἰς τὴν πόλιν σου Herm.*sim*.1.5; *ib*.9.14.1; Pall.*h.Laus*.2(p.16.23; M.34.1011A); Hesych.S.*temp*.2.32(M.93.1521B); of time, Anast.S.*qu.et resp*.30(M.89.565B); met. τοῖς Ἑβραίοις...τοῖς ~ουσιν εἰς νόμον ἐκ πίστεως Clem.*str*.6.8(p.463.6; M.9.284B); τῶν...~όντων εἰς μετάνοιαν Epiph.*haer*.54.2(p.319.12; M.41.964C); *ib*.51.11(p.263.5; 908D); *M.Ner.et Ach*.5(p.4.16); **2.** *bring back again*, v.l. for ἀνα-, *T.Job* 4(p.106.10).

ἐπανάκαμψις, ἡ, *return*, Hesych.S.*temp*.2.31(M.93.1521A).

ἐπανάκειμαι, *depend upon*, Petr.II Al.*encycl*.(M.33.1281B)ap. Thdt.*h.e*.4.22.13; Cyr.*Is*.3.4(2.480B).

ἐπανακεφαλαιόομαι, *sum up again*, Chrys.ap.*cat.1Cor*.14:40(p.281.19).

***ἐπανακιρνάομαι**, *be mixed up again, combine again*; of bodies at resurrection, Gr.Nyss.*hom.opif*.28.6(M.44.228C).

***ἐπανακλάομαι**, *be reflected back again*, Gr.Nyss.*diff.ess*.5(M.32.333C).

ἐπανάκλησις, ἡ, *recall, restoration* ὁ Χριστὸς...τοῦ Ἀδὰμ ἐ., τῆς Μωσαϊκῆς διδασκαλίας τελείωσις Bas.Sel.*or*.34.1(M.85.368D); τὴν ἐξ ᾅδου τῆς ζωῆς ἐ. *ib*.26.2(308A).

***ἐπανακλητικός**, *restorative*, Max.*ambig*.(M.91.1337A).

ἐπανακλίν-ω, **1.** *make to lie down, rest*; pass., Gr.Nyss.*v.Macr*.(p.309.20; M.46.985C); †Gregent.*disp*.(M.86.745B); **2.** *incline, direct back* ἀποστερεῖ τὸν υἱόν, τὸ δοθὲν ὥσπερ εἰς ἑαυτὸν αὖθις ~ων Eun.ap Cyr.*thes*.6(5^{1}.49B).

ἐπανακομίζω, *bring back*; pass., *return*, Cyr.*Abac*.11(3.526C).

***ἐπανακρίνω**, *inquire*, *Hom.Clem*.13.10; *interrogate*, Thphn.*chron*.p.326(M.108.788B).

ἐπανακτάομαι, *recover, win back* erring souls, Geo.Al.*v.Chrys*.35(p.316.41).

ἐπανακτέον, **1.** *one must raise* ἐ. μοι μικρὸν ἄνω τὸν λόγον Synes.*ep*.57(M.66.1385D); **2.** intrans., *one must return*, ‡Gr.Nyss.*occurs*.(M.46.1157D); Synes.*calv*.6(p.201.10; M.66.1177B).

ἐπανακυκλ-έω, *repeat* ταῦτα...τοῖς αὐτοῖς ~εῖν λόγοις Dion.Ar.*e.h*.4.3.4(M.3.477C); id.*ep*.9.6(M.3.1113B); Thdr.Stud.*epp*.2.40(M.99.1237D).

ἐπανακύκλησις, ἡ, *cycle, revolution*; of transmigration, ‡Jo.D.*Artem*.30(p.161.22; M.96.1280A).

***ἐπανακυκλόω**, = ἐπανακυκλέω, *repeat*, Gr.Nyss.*Eun*.1(1 p.51.4; M.45.280B).

ἐπανακύπτω, *rise up in rebellion*, Marc.Er.*opusc*.2.196(M.65.961A).

ἐπαναλαμβάνω, **1.** *receive back* εἰς πρόσωπον ἐ. ἡμᾶς Eus.Nic.*libell*.(p.65.14; M.67.113A); **2.** *repeat* τὸ ὀφεῖλον πρὸς ἅπαξ δίδοσθαι [sc. βάπτισμα], ἐπαναληφθῆναι οὐκ ἔξεστιν *Cod.Afr*.57(Lat. *iterari*); **3.** med., *take upon oneself, undertake*, Sever.ap.*cat.Ac*.2:15(p.31.22).

[*]**ἐπανάλημψις**, v. ἐπανάληψις.

ἐπαναληπτέον, *one ought to resume*, Gr.Nyss.*hom.opif*.16.5(M.44.180D); id.*Eun*.6(2 p.127.5; M.45.709A).

***ἐπαναληπτέος**, *to be resumed*, Gr.Nyss.*tres dii*(M.45.125A).

ἐπανάληψις ([*]**ἐπανάλημψις**), **ἡ**, **1.** *repetition*, -ημψις, Or.*dial*.12(p.146.16); αἱ τῆς γραφῆς ἐ. οὐκ ἐναντίωσιν ἔχουσιν, ἀλλὰ μόνον σαφήνειαν Proc.G.*Gen*.1:6(M.87.64D); *repetition* of first word of a line at its end, -ημψις, Isid.H.*etym*.1.36.11; **2.** *recovery, restoration*, Gr.Nyss.*hom.4 in Cant*.(M.44.832C); ὁ...δακτύλιος [i.e. given to prodigal son]...τὴν τῆς εἰκόνος ἐ. ὑποσημαίνει id.*or.dom*.2(p.40.2; M.44.1145A); ὁ σωτὴρ...ἐλευθέραν τὴν φύσιν ἡμῶν πρὸς τὴν τῆς μακαριότητος ἐ. ἀπειργάσατο ‡Chrys.*pasch*.7.4(8.281B); τῶν τῆς φύσεως ἀγαθῶν ἐ. ἔσται διὰ Χριστοῦ Cyr.*ador*.13(1.469C); id.*Jo*.5.1(4.468C); Gel.Cyz.*h.e*.2.24.10(M.85.1300D).

ἐπαναλύω, *return*, Marc.Diac.*v.Porph*.25; *M.Ner.et Ach*.19(p.18.9); Heracl.*ep*.(M.92.993); of novices εἰς τὸν κόσμον ἐ. Jo.Clim.*scal*.1(M.88.641A); μέγας ὁ τότε φόβος...ὅτι ὑπάγομεν ὅθεν οὐδεὶς ἐπανέλυσεν Anast.S.*defunct*.(M.89.1196B); ref. Dormition πρὸς αὐτὸν [sc. Χριστόν] ἡδέως ἐπαναλύσω Germ.CP *or*.8(M.98.365B); of resurrection of body, Gr.Nyss.*hom.opif*.27.5(M.44.228B).

ἐπανανέωσις, ἡ, *restoration, renewal* οὐ δόξης ἀρχήν, ἀλλ' ἐ. τὴν εἰς τὸ ἀρχαῖον αἰτεῖ [sc. Christ] Cyr.*Jo*.2.4(4.172B); τὴν ἐκ θανάτου...εἰς ζωὴν...ἐ. τῆς ἀνθρωπείας φύσεως *ib*.4.4(387D).

***ἐπανανtλέω**, med., *endure to the end*, Eus.*fr.Lc*.6:20(M.24.537A).

***ἐπαναπαλαίω**, *return to conflict*, CAnc.(314)*can*.1.

ἐπανάπαυσις, ἡ, *descent* so as to rest upon ἡ πρὸς τὴν ἀνθρωπότητα ἐ. σου συνεσκίασε τῇ σαρκὶ τὴν θεότητα Gr.Nyss.ap. Proc.G.*Cant*.1:15(M.87.1573A); τῆς ἐ. τῆς θείας ἄξιοι Thdt.*rect.conf*.16(M.6.1237A).

ἐπαναπαύ-ω, [in form ἐπαναπαήσομαι *Evangelium Hebraicum* ap. Clem.*str*.5.14(p.389.16; -παύσεται M.9.141B); Mac.Aeg.*hom*.15.33(M.34.597C)]; **1.** *set, make to rest, upon*, ref. Lc.10:34 ἐπὶ τοῦ ἰδίου αὐτὸν κτήνους ἐ. Gr.Nyss.*hom.14 in Cant*.(M.44.1085C); met. ὑμῖν ἐ. τὸν πόθον id.*ordin*.(M.46.552A); *make to rest* ἡ ἁγία παρθενεία μετὰ τῶν ἁγίων σε πάντων ἐ. ἐν τῇ αἰωνίᾳ παρακλήσει *M.Ner.et Ach*.8(p.7.30); **2.** med.; **a.** *rest upon*, ‡Gr.Nyss.*or.2 in Gen.1*:26(M.44.289D); fig., ref. Mt.8:20 μόνῳ...πιστεύοντι...~εται τὸ κεφάλαιον τῶν ὄντων, ὁ χρηστὸς καὶ ἥμερος λόγος Clem.*str*.1.3(p.15.16; M.8.713A); Trin. τοῦ υἱοῦ...μόνου τοῖς πατρῴοις κόλποις ~ομένου διηνεκῶς *Symb.Ant*.(345)9(p.253.39, v.l. ἀνα- M.26.733B); **b.** *ride upon*, ref. triumphal entry, Or.*Jo*.10.28(18; p.202.4; M.14.357C); hence fig. ἐ. ὁ Χριστὸς τῷ νέῳ λαῷ Cyr.*Zach*.57(3.736C); **c.** of God's presence, *abide upon* ὁ κύριος ἐλεύσεται πρὸς τοὺς δικαίους τοὺς πιστούς, οἷς ἐ. καθάπερ σκηνῇ Clem.*ecl*.56(p.153.7; M.9.725A); μὴ εὐδοκιμοῦντος ~εσθαι ὑμῖν διὰ τὰ μοχθηρὰ ὑμῶν ἤθη Thdr.Heracl.*Is*.52:6(M.18.1353D); Mac.Aeg.*carit*.3(M.34.909B); τὸ παλάτιον τοῦ Χριστοῦ ἡ καρδία ἐστί. ... ἐκεῖ ὁ βασιλεὺς Χριστὸς...ἔρχεται ἐπαναπαῆναι id.*hom*.15.33(M.34.597C); ἅγιος εἶ, κύριε...καὶ ἐν ἁγίοις κατοικεῖς καὶ ἐ. *Lit.Jac*.(p.168.15); cf. ἐν ᾧ [sc. tree of knowledge] ἐ. τὸ πνεῦμα τὸ ἅγιον *Apoc.Paul*.45(p.64); **d.** *rely upon*, Bas.*hex*.5.6(1.46A; M.29.108C); εἰς αὐτὴν ἐ. τὴν ἀλήθειαν Chrys.*hom.23.2 in Eph*.(11.176A); **e.** *rest* ὁ θεὸς...ἐ. τερπόμενος τῇ δημιουργίᾳ Clem.*str*.2.2(p.116.8; M.8.937A); Ἰησοῦ ὁ

~όμενος ἀπὸ τῆς ὁδοιπορίας τοῦ καμάτου ὡς ἄνθρωπος *A.Thom.*A 47 (p.164.9); met. ἵνα μήποτε ~όμενοι ὡς κλητοὶ ἐπικαθυπνώσωμεν ταῖς ἁμαρτίαις ἡμῶν *Barn.*4.13; **f.** *rest* under, Gr.Nyss.*hom.11 in Cant.* (M.44.1001B); fig. οἱ ὑπὸ τὴν τοῦ πνεύματος προσφυγόντες καὶ ~σάμενοι καὶ τὴν τοῦ λόγου σκέπην Meth.*symp.*10.5(p.128.10; M.18.201C); Max. *opusc.*(M.91.245C); **3.** med., *come to rest upon, cast oneself upon* ἡ μήτηρ...ἐ. ἐπὶ τὸν τράχηλον τοῦ υἱοῦ αὐτῆς *M.Eleuth.*11(p.161.1).

ἐπαναπίπτω, *lie upon* Ἰωάννου τοῦ...εἰς τὸ τῆς σοφίας στῆθος πιστῶς ἐπαναπεσόντος Geo.Al.*v.Chrys.*63(p.239.36).

***ἐπαναποδισμός, ὁ,** *retracing,* Hipp.*haer.*6.23(p.150.6; M.16. 3227C).

***ἐπαναρρώννυμι,** *strengthen again;* pass., Mat.*ep.*(p.2.19; M.43. 13B).

***ἐπαναρτάω,** *fix upon, attach to,* met. ἐπ' αὐτὸν τὰς ἐλπίδας...ἐ. Germ.CP *or.*1(M.98.229D).

***ἐπαναστασίη, ἡ,** *resurrection,* conj. for ἐπανάστασις, *Orac.Sib.*1. 378.

ἐπανάστασις, ἡ, 1. *standing up again* γονάτων...κλίσεις ἐ. τε Evagr.*h.e.*1.21(p.32.7; M.86.2481C); **2.** *resurrection* νεκρῶν ἐ. *Orac. Sib.*8.205; **3.** met., *rise, appearance* προειπὼν περὶ τῆς τῶν αἱρεσιωτῶν ἐ. Euthal.Diac.*epp.Paul.*proem.(M.85.705B); **4.** *rising up against;* **a.** *rebellion* ἐ. τῆς ἀρχῆς Gr.Nyss.*v.Mos.*(M.44.328B); Gel. Cyz.*h.e.*1.4.2(M.85.1201C); fig. πᾶσα δουλοπρεπὴς τῶν παθῶν ἐ. Max. *ambig.*(M.91.1157D); id.*ep.*19(M.91.596A); **b.** *setting oneself up, opposition* ἐπὶ γῆς...ὤν, οὐκ ἂν ἦν ἱερεύς...πῶς γάρ; οὐκ ἐ. ἦν, φησίν Chrys.*hom.14.1 in Heb.*(12.141A); **c.** *attack* ἐπιστολῇ μυρίων μὲν ὕβρεων...γεμουσῇ καθ' ἡμῶν καὶ ἐ. Bas.*ep.*131.1(3.223D; M.32.565B); *Const.App.*5.20.10; Ammon.*Ac.*19:32(M.85.1577B); Chrys.*stat.*11.1 (2.115D); of demons or temptation, Tat.*orat.*12(p.13.26; M.6. 832C); σοφίᾳ...δι' ἧς κατεκράτησα τῆς ἐ. τῶν ἡδονῶν Gr.Nyss.*hom.2 in Eccl.*(M.44.648C); φόβων ἐ. id.*mart.*1.2(M.46.761C); Diad.*perf.*94 (p.136.18); κόσμῳ τε καὶ σώματι καὶ ταῖς ἐξ αὐτῶν ἐ. γενναίως μαχόμενοι Max.*ambig.*(M.91.1157D); **5.** *rising, piling up* τὴν... ὀχθώδη τῆς εὐνῆς ἐ. Clem.*paed.*2.9(p.204.28; M.8.492A); Bas.*hom.*1.4 (2.3E; M.31.168C); Isid.Pel.*epp.*1.183(M.78.301B); fig. διεβίβασε ἡμᾶς...καθάπερ τινὰ θάλασσαν, τοῦ παρόντος βίου τὸν κλύδωνα, τὰς ἐ. Cyr.*Ps.*77:13(M.69.1193D).

ἐπαναστέλλω, *draw back,* Clem.*paed.*3.2(p.238.10; M.8.560B); med., id.*str.*4.19(p.301.7; M.8.1329A).

ἐπανάστημα, τό, *swelling, rising,* Philost.*h.e.*3.11(M.65.497B).

ἐπαναστρέφ-ω, *turn back again;* of time, ref. 4Reg.20:11, Dion. Ar.*ep.*7.2(M.3.1080D); met. ὕδωρ ἐξ οὗ πάλιν ὁ πίνων εἰς τὴν αὐτὴν ~ει δίψαν Or.*fr.54 in Jo.*(p.528.21); Bas.*hom.*6.3(2.45D; M.31.265C); ἐπὶ τὸ ὁμοούσιον παλιντραπέλως ἐ. Philost.*h.e.*2.7(M.65.469C); *be converted back;* of cedar beams carved in shape of branches, Gr.Nyss. *hom.3 in Eccl.*(M.44.656A).

***ἐπανασώζω, 1.** *restore to salvation* ἄνθρωπος ὁ θεός, ἵν' ἐπανασώσῃ τὸν ἄνθρωπον Nil.ap.*Schol.*in Max.*opusc.*(M.91.89C); **2.** *preserve* τὸ ὀστράκινον σκεῦος, κενὸν τοῦ πλούτου...ἐ. Gr.Nyss.*Melet.*(M.46. 853B).

ἐπανατέλλω, *rise,* Gr.Nyss.*hom.3 in Cant.*(M.44.809B); of plants, *spring up,* Just.*dial.*107.3(M.6.725B); Bas.*hex.*2.1(1.12D; M.29.29A); met. ἐ. ⟨ἐν τῇ ψυχῇ ἡμῶν⟩ τὸ ἀγαθόν Meth.*res.*2.3(p.334.5; M.41. 1165D).

ἐπανατρέπω, *overturn;* met., *refute,* Thphn.*chron.*p.44(M.108. 164C).

ἐπανατρέχω, *return, LS;* pass οἱ ἀπὸ τῆς τῶν ἄστρων σεβήσεως μὴ ἐπαναδραμόντες ἐπὶ τὸν τούτων ποιητήν Clem.*str.*6.14(p.487.19; M.9. 333A).

ἐπαναφέρ-ω, 1. *throw back again,* pass. τὸ πνεῦμα ἀπόρροιαν εἶναί φαμεν τοῦ θεοῦ, ἀπορρέον καὶ ~όμενον ὡς ἀκτῖνα ἡλίου Athenag.*leg.* 10.3(M.6.909B); **2.** *ascribe, refer,* Meth.*lepr.*12(p.467.4); *refer back* to a higher authority, c. dat., Bas.*ep.*54(3.148C; M.32.400B); id. *hom.*4.7(2.32B; M.31.236A); **3.** *direct* one's thoughts *on* πρὸς τὸ τέλος...ἐ. τὴν ἔννοιαν id.*hex.*3.10.(1.32B; M.29.77A).

ἐπαναφορά, ἡ, 1. *regression, Hom.Clem.*5.21; **2.** *rising* of a star, Bas.*hex.*1.4(1.5A; M.29.12B).

ἐπαναχέω, 1. *pour in again, in addition,* Hipp.*haer.*6.40(p.172.6; M.16.3259A); **2.** *pour over repeatedly, Hom.Clem.*6.4.

***ἐπανδρίζομαι,** *show a manly spirit,* hence *show no mercy* ταῖς τῶν πασχόντων ἐ. συμφοραῖς Cyr.*Jo.*12(4.1062C).

ἐπανέρχομαι, 1. *come back again, come to oneself,* ref. Lc.15:17, Gr.Nyss.*or.dom.*5(p.102.29; M.44.1184D); Chrys.*hom.4.5 in Jo.*(8. 33A); *return, be restored,* Synes.*ep.*67(M.66.1420A); **2.** *come up against, attack, T.Jud.*9.2; of Satan's rebellion against God, Didym.*Man.*14(M.39.1104B).

ἐπανθ-έω, 1. *bloom;* εἰς ἀκμὴν ἐ. *come to* full *bloom;* fig., Bas.*hom.* 1.2(2.2E; M.31.165C); τὰ τῶν Ἑβραίων [sc. μαθήματα] ἔχει...τὴν ἀλήθειαν ~οῦσαν τῷ χρόνῳ Thdt.*affect.*1(p.18.22; 4.708); met., *flourish* τὸ πρὶν ὅτε τὰ δαιμόνων ἐπήνθει Eus.*l.C.*8(p.217.29; M.20. 1361B); **2.** *appear on the surface, manifest itself in* οὐκ αὔταρκες εἶναι τὸ λεγόμενον...ἐὰν μὴ καὶ δύναμίς τις θεόθεν δοθῇ τῷ λέγοντι καὶ χάρις ἐ. τοῖς λεγομένοις Or.*Cels.*6.2(p.72.2; M.11.1289D); εὐσέβειαν τὴν πίστει ἀγαθῇ καὶ λογισμοῖς ἀκιβδήλοις...~οῦσαν Zach.Mit.*opif.* (M.85.1036A); **3.** *become bright,* Meth.*symp.*8.17(p.112.2; M.18.173D); trans., *shine with* αἱ κόμαι...τὸν χρυσὸν ἀναμὶξ ἐπήνθουν ‡Jo.D. *Artem.*52(p.87.25; M.96.1300B).

***ἐπανθής,** *of cheerful countenance,* Gr.Naz.*carm.*1.2.29.179(M.37. 897A).

ἐπανίημι, intrans., *revert,* Phot.*nomoc.*2.1(M.104.576C).

ἐπανισόω, *share equally,* Bas.*hom.*8.6(2.68E; M.31.320C).

ἐπανίστημι, aor. 2 and med., *rise up against, attack,* fig. and met. τὰ ἄτοπα ἡμῖν ἐ. πάθη Gr.Thaum.*pan.Or.*9(p.23.15; M.10.1080A); abs., ref. Gal.5:17, Clem.*str.*6.16(p.500.30; M.9.361A); τὴν...ἐπαναστᾶσαν αὐτῷ συμφοράν Gel.Cyz.*h.e.*3.12.7; c. κατά et genit., Gr. Nyss.*v.Mos.*(M.44.428D).

ἐπανίσωσις, ἡ, *assessment,* Gr.Naz.*ep.*68(M.37.133A).

ἐπάνοδος, ἡ, *return,* of the books of Esdras ἀναγινωσκέτω...τὰ τῶν Παραλειπομένων καὶ τὰ τῆς ἐ. *Const.App.*2.57.5; of Resurrection ἡ ἐκείνου ἀπὸ τοῦ θανάτου ἐ. ἀρχὴ τῷ θνητῷ γένει τῆς εἰς τὴν ἀθάνατον ζωὴν ἐ. γίγνεται Gr.Nyss.*or.catech.*25(p.96.8,9; M.45.68A); of Ascension μεμνημένοι...τῆς ἐκ νεκρῶν ἀναστάσεως καὶ τῆς εἰς οὐρανοὺς ἐ. *Lit.*ap.*Const.App.*8.12.38; in moral or spiritual sense ἡ...ψυχὴ οὖσα δεκτικὴ τῆς ἐ. τῆς ἐφ' ὅπερ ἦν ἀρχῇ Or.*princ.*2.8.3(p.161.4; M. 11.223B); τελείωσις καὶ ἀνάπλασις, καὶ πρὸς τὸν πρῶτον Ἀδὰμ ἐ. Gr. Naz.*or.*38.16(M.36.329C); ἐ. τίς ἐστιν ἐπὶ τὴν πρώτην ζωὴν ἡ προσδοκωμένη χάρις Gr.Nyss.*hom.opif.*17.2(M.44.188C); τὴν πρὸς τὴν πίστιν ἐ. Chrys.*hom.19.2 in Rom.*(9.644E); ἐ. πρὸς τὸ καλὸν διὰ τῆς μετανοίας Nil.*epp.*3.171(M.79.464C); εἰς ἀφθαρσίαν ἐ. Cyr.*thes.*15(5^{1}. 174C); τὴν ἐκ τοῦ θανάτου εἰς τὴν ζωὴν ἐ. Oecum.*Apoc.*6:12(p.93); abs., *restoration,* Cyr.*Ps.*65:18(M.69.1140B); id.*Pulch.*(p.38.9; 5^{2}. 145D) cit. s. ἀνακεφαλαιόω.

ἐπανοίγω, *open;* met., *A.Jo.*113(p.212.13); v.l. for ἀνοίγω, Chrys. *hom.2.8 in 2Cor.*(10.440A).

***ἐπανορθοσία, ἡ,** *recovery;* of amendment of life, Cyr.*glaph.Dt.* (1.424A).

ἐπανορθόω, 1. *set up against* κλίμακας...τῷ τείχει ἐ. Jo.Mal.*chron.* 18 p.470(M.97.684C); **2.** med., *supply* τὰς τοῦ βίου χρείας ἐ. Bas.*hex.* 4.7(1.39D; M.29.93B); pass., *have supplied* ὁ τὴν χρείαν αὐτοῦ ἐπανορθωθῆναι ζητῶν ‡Bas.*Lac.*2(2.588B; M.31.1440D).

ἐπανόρθωμα, τό, 1. *correction, improvement,* Clem.*paed.*3.2(p.242. 31; M.8.572B); **2.** *correcting upon* or *according to* a model, id.*str.*4.5 (p.257.6; M.8.1233A); **3.** *corrective effect* ἐξελάσαι τῆς ἐκκλησίας; πρόχειρον μέν, ἐ. δὲ οὐκ ἔχον Isid.Pel.*epp.*3.259(M.78.937C).

ἐπανόρθωσις, ἡ, 1. *upright position,* Gennad.*fr.Gen.*47:31(M.85. 1656C); **2.** *setting right, correction* τὸν Χριστὸν εἰς ἐ. τοῦ πληρώματος προβεβλημένον Iren.*haer.*1.9.2(M.7.540B); παθῶν ἐ. Bas.*hom.*3.3(2. 19A; M.31.204C); τὴν τῶν ἐκκλησιῶν ἐ. CCP(381)*ep.*(H.1.821D)ap. Thdt.*h.e.*5.9.6; plur., Cyr.*Os.*159(3.192C); c. genit. of means used, Gr.Nyss.*or.catech.*8(p.47.5; correction for ἐπανάστασις, M.45.36D); *restoration, re-forming* τοῦ ἐν τῇ χειρὶ τοῦ κεραμέως πηλίνου σκεύους, ὅπερ ἐπιδέχεται μετὰ τὴν συντριβὴν ἐ. Or.*hom.18.1 in Jer.*(p.150.24; M.13.464A); τὸ φώτισμα...πλάσματος ἐ. Gr.Naz.*or.*40.3(M.36.361B); *improving* oneself, Gr.Naz.ap.*cat.Lc.*13:8(p.107.29); **3.** *correctness* of belief or practice πλανωμένους ἀντὶ τῆς προσηκούσης ἐ. ἐν τῷ αὐτῷ ἔτει δεύτερον τὸ πάσχα ἐπιτελεῖν Const.ap.Eus.*v.C.*3.18(p.85. 26; M.20.1076B); **4.** *supply* ἐ. τοῦ λείποντος χαριζομένη τοῖς ἐνδεέσι Bas.*hex.*4.7(1.39D; M.29.93B).

ἐπανορθωτής, ὁ, 1. *corrector,* Gr.Naz.*ep.*140(M.37.237B); **2.** *restorer;* of Christ, *A.Thom.*A 81(p.196.16).

***ἐπανότης, ἡ,** *upper position,* Epiph.*haer.*66.49(p.86.17; M.42. 104B).

ἐπαντιάζω, *oppose* δικαζομένῳ μοι ἐ. ἀγῶνος (v.l. ἀγῶνας) †Apoll. *met.Ps.*142:2(M.33.1525D).

ἐπαντλέω, 1. *pour on* or *over,* fig. and met. ἐ. ... τῆς ἁμαρτίας τὸν βόρβορον Ast.Am.*hom.*2(M.40.185C); Chrys.*hom.30.5 in Mt.*(7. 354E); Synes.*ep.*154(M.66.1553B); ταῖς ἑαυτῶν κεφαλαῖς τὸν ἐκ τῆς ἀσεβείας ἐ. ὄλεθρον Cyr.*Is.*3.2(2.395E); id.*hom.pasch.*8(5^{2}.93C); Bas. Sel.*v.Thecl.*1(M.85.560A); **2.** *pour* food or drink *into* oneself, Bas. *hom.*21.4(2.166C; M.31.548B); **3.** *irrigate,* Ath.*h.Ar.*56(p.215.4; M.25. 761A); **4.** *draw, foment* wounds, Chrys.*stat.*6.1(2.73A); fig. τῇ πυκνότητι τῆς...προσηγορίας [sc. τοῦ Χριστοῦ] τὴν φλεγμονὴν αὐτῶν ἐ.

id.*hom.2.2 in 1Cor.*(10.11A, v.l. ἀπαν-); *ib.26.1*(228A); Geo.Pis. *carm.*1.28(p.2).

ἐπάντλησις, ἡ, *fomentation,* Olymp.*Job* 41:14(M.93.445A); fig. τὴν βαρεῖαν ταύτην φλεγμονὴν τῆς καρδίας ἡμῶν τῇ ἐ. τῶν παρηγορικῶν σου λόγων διαφορήσας Gr.Nyss.*Trin.*1(p.71.17; M.32.685A).

ἐπάνω, *above* τὰς ἐ. φέρω *win the upper hand,* Jo.Mal.*chron.*8 p.210(M.97.328B); *ib.*6 p.167(271B); as prep. c. acc., of place, *upon, on top of,* Herm.*vis.*5.3.4; c. genit., of motion, *upon* πατεῖν ἐ. ὄφεων Gr.Nyss.*hom.2 in Eccl.*(M.44.637B); ἦλθόν ποτε ἐ. αὐτοῦ τρεῖς λῃσταί *Apophth.Patr.*(M.65.196A); *ib.*(377C); *down upon* ἐ. αὐτῶν ἔβαλον πῦρ *Chron.Pasch.*p.337(M.92.879A); *ib.*p.329(852A); of time, *beyond, longer than* ἐ. αὐτοῦ ζῆσαι οὐκ ἤθελεν Gr.Mag.*dial.*(tr.Zach.) 1.8(M.*PL*.77.187A); of relation, *over, in charge of* σακελλάριος τοῦ πατριάρχου καὶ ἐ. τῶν χειροτονιῶν *Chron.Pasch.*p.381(976C); *on behalf of, PLond.*1926; of number, *above, more than,* Cosm.Ind.*top.*2 (M.88.100B).

***ἐπανώτερος,** *above, superior to,* Bas.*hom.in Ps.*29(1.125C; M.29. 309B).

***ἐπανωφόριον, τό,** *outer garment, Const.Stud.*38(M.99.1720A).

ἐπάξιος, *deserved;* neut. plur. as adv., *worthily,* Thdr.Stud.*epp.* 2.41(M.99.1240D).

ἐπαοιδία, ἡ, 1. *use of incantations,* Cyr.H.*catech.*4.37; **2.** plur., *incantations,* Epiph.*exp.fid.*24(M.42.832A; conj. ἐπαοιδάς p.525.10); Leont.N.*v.Sym.*53(M.93.1736C); ‡Caes.Naz.*dial.*117(M.38.1001); Jo. D.*hom.*2.6(M.96.585D).

***ἐπαοιδιστής, ὁ,** = ἐπαοιδός, Barth.Edess.*Agar.*(M.104.1409D).

ἐπαοιδός, ὁ, *enchanter,* hence in gen. of one possessing occult powers, Gr.Nyss.*Apoll.*38(M.45.1209C).

ἐπαπειλέω, *threaten,* pass. ὁ φόβος...ὁ ἐπηπειλημένος Clem.*str.* 4.22(p.313.9; M.8.1356B); med., ‡Jo.D.*Artem.*24(p.83.25; M.96. 1273B).

***ἐπάπειρος,** *boundless, immense,* ‡Caes.Naz.*dial.*146(M.38.1096).

***ἐπαποδύρομαι,** *lament bitterly* ἐ. τῇ ἀπωλείᾳ ἡμῶν Nil.*epp.*3.24 (M.79.381B).

***ἐπαποδυτέον,** *one must strip for;* met., of preparation for study, Clem.*str.*7.15(p.64.28; M.9.525C).

ἐπαποδύ-ω, med.; **1.** *strip* for ὁ ἀθλητής...~εται τῇ διδασκαλίᾳ καὶ ἀγωνίζεται καὶ νικηφόρος γίνεται Clem.*ecl.*28(p.145.23; M.9.713A); **2.** met., *prepare to attack* ἐ. τοῖς μιάσμασιν Chrys.*hom.68.1 in Mt.* (7.670D); id.*hom.16.4 in 1Cor.*(10.140A); ἐ. κατὰ τοῦ πονηροῦ Olymp. *Eccl.*11:9f.(M.93.612B); **3.** *prepare for* τῷ καθ' ἡμῶν ἐ. διωγμῷ Eus. *m.P.*4(p.911.23; M.20.1472C); id.*h.e.*8.4.2(M.20.749A); ἐ. τῇ θεωρίᾳ Nil.*epp.*2.68(M.79.232A); cf. ἐ. τὴν θεωρίαν id.*exerc.*47(M.79.777A); **4.** abs., *prepare for contest;* fig., of martyrs, Bas.*ep.*164.1(3.254D; M.32.636B).

ἐπαποθνήσκω, 1. c. dat., *die with,* Clem.*exc.Thdot.*48(p.122.18; M.9.681C); Chrys.*hom.10.2 in 1Thess.*(11.497E); **2.** abs., *die afterwards, next, A.Jo.*24(p.164.18).

***ἐπαποκρίνομαι,** *answer,* Meth.*res.*2.18(p.369.3; M.18.313A).

ἐπαπορέω, 1. *raise a fresh difficulty* or *objection;* hence gen. *raise difficulties,* Or.*Jo.*10.27(17; p.201.23; M.14.356C); Chrys.*hom. 1.6 in Mt.*(7.13B); perf. or aor. ptcpl. pass. neut. as subst., *difficulty,* Or.*comm.in Mt.*17.35(p.197.23; M.13.1593D); id.*fr.41 in Jo.* (p.516.7); id.*Cels.*2.37(p.162.21; M.11.857C); **2.** c. dat., *raise an objection against, criticize* ἐ. τῇ γραφῇ *ib.*2.32(p.159.12; 852C); ‡Ath. *Apoll.*2.18(M.26.1164A); abs., *object,* Or.*Jo.*13.28(p.252.28; M.14. 448C); Chrys.*hom.39.1 in 1Cor.*(10.363A); Thdt.*Abac.*proem.(2. 1536); Sev.Ant.*res.*(p.796.9; M.46.628D); **3.** *question* ἐ. πρὸς ἀλλήλους, εἰ ἐλεύσεται...'Ιησοῦς Or.*Jo.*28.26(20; p.423.28; M.14.737C); Chrys.*hom.11.4 in Heb.*(12.119A); **4.** = ἀπορέω, *be in a difficulty,* †Bas.*hom. in Ps.*115(1.374A; M.30.109B); pass., *be put to silence, nonplussed, M.Con.*2.7(p.65.4).

***ἐπαπόρημα, τό,** *difficulty, problem,* Or.*Jo.*2.24(19; p.81.9; M.14. 156D); id.*ep.*1.11(M.11.73C); ref. ambiguity in text ὁ θεῖος Γρηγόριος ἐπάγει τὸ γεγραμμένον ὡς ἐ. Cosm.Mel.*schol.*(M.38.600) in Gr.Naz. *carm.*1.2.24 tit.; ref. moral teaching ἐν τοῖς ἐ. περὶ τῆς τῶν ἀρχαίων πολυγαμίας Bas.*Spir.*72(3.61C; M.32.204A).

ἐπαπόρησις, ἡ, 1. *further difficulty,* Or.*engast.*2(p.284.25; M.12. 1016A); id.*Jo.*2.11(6; p.66.1; M.14.129B); Tit.Bost.*Man.*2.1(M.18. 1132D); Gr.Nyss.*anim.et res.*(M.46.145B); **2.** *difficulty* or *objection,* Or.*Cels.*8.2(p.221.19; M.11.1521B); ἐ. τῶν δογμάτων id.*Jo.*10.16(13; p.186.8; M.14.332D); Gr.Nyss.*Eun.*1(1 p.201.15; M.45.448D); δύο... ἐ. τοῦ τρόπου τῆς ἀναστάσεως καὶ τῆς ποιότητος τῶν σωμάτων Chrys. *hom.41.1 in 1Cor.*(10.386C); id.*hom.24.2 in Jo.*(8.140D); Cyr.*thes.*4 (5^1.23C); **3.** *perplexity,* Or.*Jo.*13.32(31; p.256.6; M.14.453B); **4.** *question,* id.*mart.*28(p.24.14); id.*hom.19 in Lc.*(p.130.9); εἰς ἐ. καὶ λύσιν σχηματίζει τὴν προφητείαν Thdt.*Abac.*proem.(2.1538); **5.** *asking of questions* ῥίζα τῆς ἐπί τισιν ἀγνοουμένοις συνέσεως ἡ περὶ αὐτῶν ἐ. Cyr. *Jo.*4.9(4.180A); id.*dogm.*2(p.551.13; 6^2.367D); **6.** *mystery, obscure interpretation,* ref. Eph.5:32 τὸ κατὰ τὸν πρωτόπλαστον καὶ τὴν Εὔαν κατὰ δευτέραν ἐ. εἰς Χριστὸν ἀνηκόντισε καὶ τὴν ἐκκλησίαν Meth. *symp.*3.10(p.38.10; καὶ δευτέραν ἐ. M.18.76C).

***ἐπαπορητέον,** *one must raise a further question,* Or.*princ.*3.1.9 (p.208.9; M.11.264A); id.*Jo.*13.39(p.264.1; M.14.465C); Meth.*symp.* 7.5(p.76.3; M.18.132A).

ἐπαπορητικῶς, 1. *dubitatively, in order to raise doubts,* ref. Mt. 16:26 ἐ. εἰρημένον...καὶ ἀποφαντικῶς Or.*comm.in Mt.*12.27(p.131.3; M.13.1044B); **2.** *expressing doubts,* Nil.ap.Proc.G.*Cant.*7:8f.(M.87. 1733C); **3.** *raising difficulties* ἐ. καὶ δυσωπητικῶς [Jo.13:6] φάσκων Or.*Jo.*32.7(6; p.436.26; M.14.760A); **4.** *interrogatively,* id.*sel.in Ps.* 48:8(M.12.1444D); id.*hom.2.1 in Jer.*(p.17.1; M.13.277B); id.*fr.64 in Lc.*(p.264).

ἐπαποστέλλω, *send upon* or *into,* ref. Mc.5:13 τοῖς χοίροις αὐτοὺς [sc. τοὺς δαίμονας] ἐ. Mac.Mgn.*apocr.*3.4(p.55.15).

***ἐπαποφαίνομαι,** *declare in addition,* Meth.*res.*2.18(p.368.9; M.18. 312C).

ἐπαράομαι, *imprecate,* Synes.*ep.*67(M.66.1413A); aor. ptcpl. in act. form, Chrysipp.*enc.in Thdr.*9(p.72.14).

ἐπαράσσω, *dash against;* pass., *fling oneself upon* a sword, Philost.*h.e.*3.26(ed. for ἐπηρράχθη M.65.513B); intrans., of wind, *whip up,* Synes.*ep.*4(M.66.1332A).

ἐπάρατος, 1. *accursed;* superl., of a person, Synes.*ep.*96(M.66. 1465B); **2.** *invoked as a curse* τὰς ἐκείνων συμφορὰς...ἐ. τοῖς τὰ ὅμοια ζηλοῦσι τίθεσθαι Const.ap.Thdt.*h.e.*1.25.6(3.810).

ἐπαρδεύω, *irrigate;* of rivers, *Orac.Sib.*5.58; Cyr.H.*catech.*16.12; of cultivators, Clem.*str.*1.1(p.8.6; M.8.697A); *M.Con.*2.2(p.64.27); fig., of Christ τὴν καθ' ἕκαστον ἄνδρα [sc. ψυχήν] καὶ κοινῇ τὴν ἐκκλησίαν ἴσα ποτάμοις ἐπαρδεύετο τοῖς θείοις διδάγμασιν Thdr. Heracl.*Is.*43:19(M.18.1337B); *supply* the body *with moisture;* pass., Melet.*nat.hom.*epit.(M.64.1077B); *ib.*synops.(M.64.1104A).

ἐπάρδ-ω, 1. *water, irrigate;* fig. and met., of God as vinedresser ἐ. τοῖς μαθήμασιν τὴν ψυχήν Gr.Nyss.*hom.3 in Eccl.*(M.44.661A); of Son ἐν τῷ οὐρανῷ τὰς ἀγγελικὰς δυνάμεις ~ων καὶ τρέφων τῇ τῆς θεότητος αὐτοῦ δυνάμει Eus.*e.th.*1.20(p.86.18; M.24.876A); of H. Ghost οὗ πάντα ἐφίεται τὰ κατ' ἀρετὴν ζῶντα, οἷον ~όμενα τῇ ἐπιπνοίᾳ Bas.*Spir.*22(3.19C; M.32.108B); of the Christian ~ει [sc. τὴν ψυχήν] ἔργοις τε ἀγαθοῖς καὶ εὐχῇ διαρκεῖ Gr.Nyss.*instit.*(p.71. 22; M.34.425D); **2.** *pour forth upon;* met., Eus.*l.C.*5(p.204.22; M.20. 1336C); ἡ πατρικὴ φιλανθρωπία τὸν...παῖδα ἐπὶ πᾶσιν καθίστη...τὰς ἐξ αὐτοῦ χορηγίας ~οντα id.*e.th.*1.13(p.73.10; M.24.852A); *ib.*2.17(p.121. 13; 940A); of Church τοῖς ἑαυτῆς νηπίοις ~ουσα τὸ λογικὸν καὶ ἄδολον γάλα id.*Is.*66:10f.(M.24.520A).

***ἐπαρηγός, ὁ,** *helper,* Cyr.*Jo.*11.2(4.943E).

ἐπαριθμ-έω, *number with, among* ἐ. αὐτῷ [sc. τῷ θεῷ] παντελῶς οὐδένα Cyr.*Is.*3.1(2.365D); ~ουμένου...τοῦ ἁγίου πνεύματος [i.e. with Father and Son] id.*Jo.*1.2(4.16B); *ib.*6.1(646B).

***ἐπαρίθμησις, ἡ,** *enumeration,* Cyr.*ador.*4(1.115A).

ἐπάρκεια, ἡ, *succour;* in form ἐπαρκία, of work of Christ, Leont. H.*Nest.*1.12(M.86.1449B); *relief* ἐ. τοῦ λιμοῦ *Chron.Pasch.*p.97(M.92. 265D).

ἐπαρκέω (*ἐπαρκείω), 1. *help, assist;* c. infin., Meth.*symp.*7.1 (p.71.5; M.18.124A); **2.** *supply,* -κείω, *Orac.Sib.*3.243; **3.** *be sufficient,* c. πρός et acc., Gr.Nyss.*v.Macr.*(p.380.1; M.46.968C); Alex. Sal.*Barn.*proem.2(437A); abs., of God ὁ διδοὺς καὶ δι' αἰώνων ἐπαρκεῖ Didym.*Trin.*2.8(M.39.616B); **4.** med. c. dat., *be satisfied with, A.Thom.*A 79(p.195.1, v.l. ἀρκ-); v.l. for ἀρκ-, *ib.*45(p.162. 13).

ἔπαρμα, τό, 1. *something lifted up in addition* or *as a protection;* a kind of bulwark, Pall.*v.Chrys.*14(p.89.1; M.47.50); **2.** *something to be lifted, load,* Epiph.*mens.*21(M.43.273A); **3.** *elevation, exaltation* τὸ ἀνάστημα τοῦ ἀπὸ τοῦ λόγου ἐ. Or.*Jo.*6.35(19; p.144.32; M.14.261B); id.*Ps.*3:4(p.250); θεῷ...μόνῳ πρέπει τὸ ἔ. καὶ ἡ δόξα Jo.D.*Man.*1.14(M.94.1520C); id.*hom.*11.12(M.96.776A); **4.** *elation, vanity* ἔ. καρδίας καὶ φυσίωμα πνεύματος ἀλλοτρίου Hipp.*Noët.*1 (p.235.6; M.10.804A); ὁ μηδὲν ἔχων ἔ. ... ἐστι...ταπεινὸς τῷ πνεύματι Bas.*hom.in Ps.*33(1.155D; M.29.380C); †Bas.*Is.*86(1.438E; M. 30.260A).

***ἐπαρνησιθεΐα, ἡ,** for ἀπαρνησιθεΐα, *denial of* the true *God* ἡ... ἐκκλησία...οὐ δέχεται ἐ. Epiph.*haer.*61.4(p.384.16, v.l. ἀπαρνησίαν; M.41.1044D); *ib.*66.64(p.104.15; M.42.129B); id.*mens.*16(M.43.264C); of paganism ἐ. καὶ ἀθεμιτουργίαν 'Ελληνισμοῦ id.*haer.*68.2(p.142.5; 185C); of Judaism, *ib.*50.2(p.247.26; M.41.888B); of heresy ταῦτα [sc.

errors of Paul. Sam.]...ἐ. πάσης ἔχοντα τοὺς χαρακτῆρας *ib.*65.8 (p.12.19; M.42.28B); of Judas, with whom Aëtius is compared, *ib.* 76.25(p.372.13; 565A).

***ἐπαρνησίθεος**, (for *ἀπαρνησίθεος), *denying* the true *God*; of Jews, Epiph.*haer.*54.5(p.322.20; M.41.969A); of heretics, *ib.*65.2,8 (pp.5.4,11.28; M.42.13D,25C).

ἐπάρουρος, *earthly, mortal*, Nonn.*par.Jo.*6:58(M.43.801B).

ἔπαρσις, ἡ, **1.** *lifting up*, Clem.*exc.Thdot.*84(conj. p.132.20); ref. Lc.24:50 σύμβολον...ἡ ἔ. τῶν χειρῶν τοῦ σωτῆρος· ταῖς γὰρ ὑπὲρ ἄνθρωπον πράξεσιν ὕψωσεν αὐτοῦ τὰς χεῖρας καὶ ἔσωσε τοὺς πιστεύοντας Or.*fr.87 in Lc.*(p.275); ἡ ἔ. τῶν ἀποστολικῶν ὀφθαλμῶν id.*Jo.*13. 46(p.272.16; M.14.480C); Gr.Nyss.*v.Macr.*(p.409.20; M.46.996A); ἡ εἰς τὸ ὕψος τῶν τοιούτων κυμάτων ἔ., λέγω δὴ τὰ τῶν παθῶν κυματα id.*Pss.titt.*A 8(M.44.476A); βουνεύρων τε...τὰς ἐ. *Hymn.*(*AS* 1 p.634); **2.** *promotion, elevation* to high office, Gr.Naz.*carm.*2.1.12.80 (M.37.1122A); **3.** *exaltation* of spirit τὴν...χαρὰν εὔλογον ἐ. Clem.*str.* 2.16(p.151.8; M.8.1012A); Gr.Nyss.*hom.opif.*19.5(p.218; M.44.193C); **4.** *elation, pride*, Or.*comm.in Rom.*7:15(*JTS* 14 p.16); †Bas.*Is.*6(1. 390D; M.30.148C); Gr.Naz.*or.*36.5(M.36.269C); Epiph.*haer.*69.29 (p.178.25; M.42.248D); Chrys.*hom.2.4 in Philm.*(11.784D); λογισμὸς ἐπὶ τοῖς ἀγαθοῖς ἔργοις πρὸς ἔ. κινηθεὶς ἀφανίζει τὰ κεκτημένα Nil. *Magn.*6(M.79.977B); †Jo.D.*B.J.*12(M.96.968A); **5.** *expression of pride, pomp* τοῦ πλουσίου ἡ ἔ. καὶ ἡ φαντασία Eus.Al.*serm.*21.17(M. 86.444D); **6.** *rising against, rebellion*, Bas.*reg.fus.*2.4(2.340A; M.31. 916C); ὁ θάνατος τοῦ Χριστοῦ...κατέβαλε τὴν τῶν ἐπιβουλευσάντων ἔ. *M.Thdot.*3(p.131.15).

ἐπαρτ-άω, **1.** *suspend, make to hang over*, lit., Cyr.*Is.*1.3(2.77A); id.*ador.*6(1.194E); *ib.*9(294D); fig. αὐτὴν [sc. ἁμαρτίαν] ταῖς σφῶν αὐτῶν ~ήσαντες κεφαλαῖς *ib.*3(104A); met. ἐντολὴ...ἀπαγορεύει, τὸν φόβον ~ῶσα Clem.*str.*2.7(p.130.10; M.8.968B); **2.** *hold out as a threat* to βίον ἀβίωτον αὐτοῖς...ἐ. Eus.*v.C.*1.13(p.14.15; M.20.928B); τοῖς Ἱεροσολύμοις ὀργὴν ἐ. Cyr.*Os.*7(3.27C); **3.** pass. intrans., *threaten* ὁ κίνδυνος ὁ ἐπηρτημένος Clem.*str.*4.22(p.313.9; M.8.1356C); Const. *or.s.c.*20(p.184.3; M.20.1296A); Bas.*hom.*5.2(2.34A; M.31.240B); **4.** *attach, assign*, Cyr.*Zach.*29(3.696C); Eudoc.*Cypr.*2.334(M.85. 857C); perf. ptcpl. pass., *accompanied* by, *associated* with ἀὴρ... οὔτε ἀπηνότητι ψυχρίας τετονωμένος, οὔτε...ἐκπυρώσει καύσωνος ἐπηρτημένος Epiph.*haer.*52.2(p.313.19; M.41.957A).

ἐπαρτύνω, *season*, fig. τῷ θείῳ τῆς γραφῆς ἅλατι τὸν περὶ μυστηρίου λόγον ἐ. Gr.Nyss.*Apoll.*34(M.45.1197D).

ἐπαρυστρίς, ἡ, *vessel for pouring* oil into a lamp, ref. Zach.4:2 ἑπτὰ ἐ. καὶ ἑπτὰ λύχνους...ὅτι ἑπτὰ πνεύματα παρὰ θεοῦ †Epiph. *num.myst.*5(M.43.516A); αἱ ἐ. τὰς τῶν θείων χαρισμάτων χορηγίας σημαίνουσι Cyr.*Jo.*4.4(4.390D); Anast.S.*qu.et resp.*49(M.89.609B).

ἐπαρχεία, ἡ, v. ἐπαρχία.

ἐπαρχεώτης, ὁ, v. ἐπαρχιώτης.

ἐπαρχία, ἡ, **1.** *province* of the empire, being sphere of eccl. jurisdiction of a metropolitan ἐπίσκοπον προσήκει μάλιστα μὲν ὑπὸ πάντων τῶν ἐν τῇ ἐ. καθίστασθαι. ...τὸ δὲ κῦρος τῶν γινομένων δίδοσθαι καθ' ἑκάστην ἐ. τῷ μητροπολίτῃ CNic.(325)*can.*4; τὰ ἀρχαῖα ἔθη κρατείτω...ὥστε τὸν Ἀλεξανδρείας ἐπίσκοπον πάντων τούτων ἔχειν τὴν ἐξουσίαν, ἐπειδὴ καὶ τῷ ἐν τῇ Ῥώμῃ ἐπισκόπῳ τοῦτο σύνηθές ἐστιν· ὁμοίως δὲ καὶ κατὰ Ἀντιόχειαν καὶ ἐν ταῖς ἄλλαις ἐ. τὰ πρεσβεῖα σώζεσθαι ταῖς ἐκκλησίαις *ib.*6; τοὺς καθ' ἑκάστην ἐ. ἐπισκόπους εἰδέναι χρή, τὸν ἐν τῇ μητροπόλει προεστῶτα ἐπίσκοπον καὶ τὴν φροντίδα ἀναδέχεσθαι πάσης τῆς ἐ. διὰ τὸ ἐν τῇ μητροπόλει πανταχόθεν συντρέχειν πάντας τοὺς τὰ πράγματα ἔχοντας· ὅθεν ἔδοξε καὶ τῇ τιμῇ προηγεῖσθαι αὐτόν, μηδέν τε πράττειν περιττὸν τοὺς λοιποὺς ἐπισκόπους ἄνευ αὐτοῦ...ἢ ταῦτα μόνα, ὅσα τῇ ἑκάστου ἐπιβάλλει παροικίᾳ καὶ ταῖς ὑπ' αὐτὴν χώραις CAnt.(341)*can.*9; ἐπίσκοπον μὴ χειροτονεῖσθαι δίχα συνόδου καὶ παρουσίας τοῦ ἐν τῇ μητροπόλει τῆς ἐ. *ib.*19; τὰ καθ' ἑκάστην ἐ. ἡ τῆς ἐ. σύνοδος διοικήσει, κατὰ τὰ ἐν Νικαίᾳ ὡρισμένα CCP(381)*can.*2; εἰ...τινὲς...λέγοιεν...ἔχειν τινὰ...κατὰ τοῦ ἐπισκόπου κατηγορίαν· τούτους κελεύει ἡ...σύνοδος πρῶτον μὲν ἐπὶ τῶν τῆς ἐ. πάντων ἐπισκόπων ἐνίστασθαι τὰς κατηγορίας. ... εἰ δὲ συμβαίη ἀδυνατῆσαι τοὺς ἐπαρχιώτας πρὸς διόρθωσιν τῶν...ἐγκλημάτων..., τότε αὐτοὺς προσιέναι μείζονι συνόδῳ τῶν τῆς διοικήσεως ἐπισκόπων ἐκείνης *ib.*6; μὴ δεῖν ὑπερορίας ἕλκεσθαι τὰς δίκας· ἐν ταῖς ἰδίαις ἐ. τὰ τῆς ἐ. γυμνάζεσθαι Chrys.*ep.Innoc.*1.1(p.9.22; 3.516D); εἴτε ὁ μητροπολίτης τῆς ἐ. ἀποστατήσας τῆς...οἰκουμενικῆς συνόδου προσέθετο τῷ τῆς ἀποστασίας συνεδρίῳ [i.e. CEph.Orient.]...οὗτος κατὰ τῶν τῆς ἐ. ἐπισκόπων διαπράττεσθαί τι οὐδαμῶς δύναται...ἀλλὰ καὶ αὐτοῖς τοῖς τῆς ἐ. ἐπισκόποις καὶ τοῖς πέριξ μητροπολίταις τοῖς τὰ τῆς ὀρθοδοξίας φρονοῦσιν ὑποκείσεται, εἰς τὸ...τοῦ βαθμοῦ τῆς ἐπισκοπῆς ἐκβληθῆναι CEph.(431)*can.*1; τινες παρὰ τοὺς ἐκκλησιαστικοὺς θεσμοὺς προσδραμόντες δυναστείαις, διὰ πραγματικῶν βασιλικῶν τὴν μίαν ἐ. εἰς δύο κατέτεμον, ὡς ἐκ τούτου δύο μητροπολίτας εἶναι ἐν τῇ αὐτῇ ἐ. ὥρισε τοίνυν ἡ...σύνοδος...μηδὲν τοιοῦτον τολμᾶσθαι παρὰ ἐπισκόπῳ...ὅσαι δὲ ἤδη πόλεις διὰ γραμμάτων βασιλικῶν τῷ τῆς μητροπόλεως ἐτιμήθησαν ὀνόματι, μόνης ἀπολαυέτωσαν τῆς τιμῆς...σωζομένων δηλονότι τῇ κατ' ἀλήθειαν μητροπόλει τῶν οἰκείων δικαίων CChalc.*can.*12; τῇ συνόδῳ τῆς ἐ. *ib.*17; Thdt.*h.e.*5.23.3(3.1061); ref. jurisdiction of apostles and others who were later equated with bishops οἱ δὴ τὴν τοῦ χειροτονεῖν ἐξουσίαν ἔχοντες, οἱ νῦν ὀνομαζόμενοι ἐπίσκοποι, οὐ μιᾶς ἐκκλησίας γινόμενοι, ἀλλ' ἐπαρχίας ὅλης ἐφεστῶτες, τῇ τῶν ἀποστόλων ἐκαλοῦντο προσηγορίᾳ. οὕτως ἁπάσῃ τῇ Ἀσίᾳ τὸν Τιμόθεον ἐπέστησεν ὁ...Παῦλος, καὶ τῇ Κρήτῃ τὸν Τίτον. δῆλον δὲ ὅτι καὶ ἑτέρους ἐ. ἑτέραις κατὰ μέρος ἐπέστησεν Thdr.Mops.*1Tim.*3:8(p.121. 13); **2.** in gen., of a ruler's *dominion* οὐ μόνον ἐκ τῆς σῆς ἐ. [sc. Nero's empire] στρατολογοῦμεν, ἀλλὰ καὶ ἐκ τῆς οἰκουμένης πάσης *A. Paul.*(*LB* p.110.12; ἐπαρχείας *PHamb.*p.9.3).

ἐπαρχικός, *of a prefect* ἐ. τάξεως Const.ap.Eus.*v.C.*2.46(p.61.6; M.20.1024B); as subst., *member of the prefect's guard* or *suite* (unless from ἐπαρχία, *provincial*), Nil.*epp.*1.103 tit.(M.79.128P); *ib.*2.5 tit. (204C); plur. as subst., *prefect's guard*, Chrys.*ep.*11(3.591C); Pall. *v.Chrys.*20(p.129.10; M.47.72).

[*]**ἐπάρχιος**, ἡ, = ἐπάρχειος [sc. χώρα], *civil province*, Tert. *apologia* 2 ap.Eus.*h.e.*3.33.3(M.20.285C); Eus.*m.P.*8(M.20.1488A; ἐπαρχίαν p.925.11); *ib.*13(1517B; ἐπαρχίαν p.949.21).

ἐπαρχιώτης, -εώτης, ὁ, *bishop of a province*, CAnt.(341)*can.*20; CCP(381)*can.*6; Leo Mag.*ep.*106.5(M.*PL.*54.1008B; -εωτῶν p.58.9); ἐ. ἐπίσκοποι CEph.(431)*can.*2.

ἔπαρχος, ὁ, **1.** *procurator*, Eus.*h.e.*9.11.4(M.20.837C); **2.** τῷ ἐ. τῆς διοικήσεως CChalc.*can.*17, prob. f.l. for ἐξάρχῳ; **3.** as adj., *prefectorial*, Eus.*v.C.*1.34(p.23.14; M.20.949A); *ib.*2.44(p.60.3; 1021A).

ἐπαρχότης, ἡ, *prefecture, office of a prefect*, Mac.Aeg.*hom.*16.12 (M.34.621C); Chrys.*hom.2.2 in Col.*(11.336B); *M.Bon.*1(p.325).

ἐπάρχω, **1.** *command*, Philost.*h.e.*7.7(M.65.544C); **2.** *lead* a sect, *ib.*12.11(conj. for ὑπ- 620B); **3.** *be appointed* as bishop of a metropolitan see τοῦ τῆς Ἀντιοχείας ἐπάρξας θρόνου *ib.*5.1(529A).

***ἐπάσκεια**, ἡ, *training*, conj. for ἐπιεικείας, Cyr.*hom.pasch.*8(5². 93E).

***ἐπάσκησις**, ἡ, *practice, study*, *Hom.Clem.*2.24.

ἔπασμα, τό, *incantation, enchantment*, Gr.Naz.*or.*40.17(M.36. 381A); plur., *meretricious arts*, Cyr.*Os.*3(3.16C).

***ἐπασμός**, ὁ, *incantation*, Bas.*renunt.*4(2.205C; M.31.633B).

***ἐπαστής**, ὁ, *one who utters incantations, enchanter*, Just.*2apol.* 6.6(M.6.456A).

***ἐπαστοῦται**, Ps.57:6 SM, cited by Thdt. ad loc.(1.985), prob. f.l. for ἐπαστοῦ.

ἐπαστράπτ-ω, *shine in* ἐπευχόμενος τοῦ θεοῦ τὴν λαμπρότητα... τῷ ἡμετέρῳ βίῳ διὰ καθαρᾶς ζωῆς ~ειν Gr.Nyss.*Pss.titt.*A 7(M.44. 465A); id.*Eun.*1(1 p.26.10; M.45.253C); id.*mort.*(M.46.536B).

ἐπασφαλίζ-ω, *make secure* ἀναγκαῖον...~ειν ἑαυτούς, καὶ μὴ διδόναι ἀφορμὴν τοῖς ζητοῦσιν ἀφορμήν Ephr.1.219F; usu. med., lit., Epiph.*haer.*51.2(p.249.22; M.41.889C); *establish, confirm* statements or beliefs, Eus.*d.e.*1.3(p.13.9; M.22.32C); Didym.*Trin.*2.2(M.39. 457A); τοῦ κυρίου μέλλοντος τὰ διὰ τοῦ νόμου...παραδοθέντα τελείως... ~εσθαι Epiph.*haer.*7.3(p.193.12; M.41.216A); *ib.*51.19(p.277.1; 924C); ἐ. τὴν πίστιν *ib.*69.69(p.217.25; M.42.313C); *secure* Christians in the faith ~όμενος...τοὺς ἑαυτοῦ μαθητὰς...ταπεινοφρονεῖν ἐνουθέτει *ib.*42. 11(p.143.22; M.41.753D); τὸ εὐαγγέλιον ~εται ἡμᾶς λέγον... *ib.*79.4 (p.479.20; M.42.748D); *ib.*69.61(p.209.23; 300C); abs., *make sure, take precautions* against future heresies, *ib.*42.12(p.172.1; M.41. 797B); *ib.*54.2(p.319.16; 963C); *ib.*59.5(p.369.26; 1025C).

ἐπασχάλλω, *be vexed, indignant*, Cyr.*Nest.*5 proem.(p.92.29; 6¹. 121D); id.*Jo.*4.5(4.401A); id.*hom.pasch.*8.3(5².98D).

***ἐπασχολέομαι**, *be occupied*, Gr.Nyss.*hom.3 in Eccl.*(M.44.661B).

***ἐπάσχολος**, *fully occupied*, Gr.Mag.*dial.*(tr.Zach.)3.33(M.*PL.* 77.298D); *ib.*1.12(211C).

***ἐπασωτεύομαι**, *lavish, squander*; met., of idolaters τῆς ἀρρήτου οὐσίας τὴν δόξαν ξύλοις...ἐ. Cyr.*hom.pasch.*6.3(5².64A); id.*Jo.*2.1(4. 156D); *ib.*4.3(374C); μυστικὸν ἐ. λόγον εἰς ἀλλογενοῦς ἀκοάς *ib.*12 (1051B).

***ἐπαυθίδα**, vox nihili, Arist.*apol.*11(*TS* p.106.21, vv.ll. ἐπανθίδα, ἐπαυλίδα, conj. πηκτίδα).

***ἐπαυλή**, ἡ, *place for cattle, steading*, *T.Job* 40(p.129.15,19).

ἐπαυλίζομαι, pass., *pass the night*; fig., of those who die young, Bas.*mor.*11.1(3.532C; M.32.1257C); but ἐναυλ-, id.*hom.*21.2(2.164E; M.31.544C).

ἔπαυλις, ἡ, **1.** *steading, sheepfold* ἡ ἐκκλησία βοοστασίου οὐδὲν διενήνοχε, καὶ ἐ. ὄνων καὶ καμήλων Chrys.*hom.88.4 in Mt.*(7

830D); fig., of a monastery ὁ ἀγελάρχης τῶν θείων ἐ. *Hymn.*(*AS* I p.610); **2.** *cottage*, *A.Jo.*49(p.175.18); Or.*Cels.*7.59(p.208.31; M.11.1505B).

ἐπαυξάνω, **1.** trans., *increase, add to* Ἀέτιος...τὴν Ἀρείου βλασφημίαν ταῖς ἐπινοίαις ἐ. Thdt.*h.e.*2.24.6(3.888); *increase the effect of, emphasize* a statement, Thdr.Mops.*Gal.*1:8(p.10.26; M.66.901C); **2.** intrans., *increase, grow*, Hipp.*haer.*9.7(p.240.27; M.16.3371A); ἐ. ἀεὶ τὴν ἀγάπην Gr.Nyss.*hom.4 in Cant.*(M.44.853A); Const.*or.s.c.*ap.Gel.Cyz.*h.e.*2.7.36(M.85.1240D).

ἐπαύξημα, **τό**, *increase, increment*; plur., Ath.Scholast.*coll.*2.3 (p.36).

ἐπαύξησις, **ἡ**, *increase, growth* διὰ τῆς ἐνεργείας τοῦ ἁγίου πνεύματος ὁ ἄρτος καὶ ὁ οἶνος εἰς ἐ. τοῦ σώματος τοῦ Χριστοῦ γίνεται ἓν σῶμα ‡Jo.D.*corp.*proem.(M.95.401A).

ἐπαύριον, τῇ ἐ. [sc. ἡμέρᾳ] *on the morrow*, *A.Jo.*31(p.167.27); *A.Petr.et Paul.*26(p.189.14); Philost.*h.e.*9.5(M.65.572B); c. genit., *on the day after* τῇ ἐ. τοῦ διαφθαρῆναι τὸν ἀποστάτην *ib.*8.1(533D).

***ἐπαύσσω**, *stamp, beat* τὰς ὁπλάς Gr.Nyss.*infant.*(M.46.161B) perh. f.l. for ἐπαΐσσω.

ἐπαυτομολέω, *approach*, ‡Caes.Naz.*dial.*148(M.38.1100).

ἐπαυχένιος, *on* or *for the neck*, fig. ζεῦγος ἱερὸν εἶναι καὶ ὑπὸ τὸν ζυγὸν τρέχειν τοῦ Χριστοῦ, ὡς ἂν ἄρωνται αὐτὸν ἐ. Jo.VI H.*v.Jo.D.*22 (M.94.461C).

ἐπαφ-άω, med.; **1.** *touch lightly*; of the sun's rays, Eus.*d.e.*7.1 (p.302.19; M.22.496B); ὡς οὐδ' ἡλίου...πάθοιεν ⟨ἂν⟩ τι ἀκτῖνες...σωμάτων νεκρῶν...ἐφαπτόμεναι...πολὺ πλέον ἡ ἀσώματος τοῦ θεοῦ λόγου δύναμις οὔτ' ἂν πάθοι ⟨τι⟩...σώματος ἀσωμάτως ∼ωμένη *ib.*4.13(p.171.3; 285A) = id.*l.C.*14(p.242.14; M.20.1409B); **2.** met., *touch* ἡ τοῦ συνειδότος ∼ωμένη τῆς ψυχῆς δύναμις Clem.*str.*7.7(p.29.3; M.9.453A); *touch upon* ἐ. τῆς ἀληθείας id.*prot.*6(p.52.1; M.8.173A); Or.*Cels.*5.63(p.66.11; M.11.1284A); Synes.*ep.*139(M.66.1529A).

ἐπαφή, **ἡ**, *touch, caress*, †Jo.Jej.*poenit.*(M.88.1896A); myst., Gr.Nyss.*hom.1 in Cant.*(M.44.780D) cit. s. ἀφή.

ἐπάφησις, **ἡ**, *touching*, Clem.*paed.*2.12(p.227.23; M.8.540B).

ἐπαφίημι, **1.** *throw, discharge at*; fig., Gr.Naz.*or.*4.118(M.35.657B); καθάπερ τι βέλος τὸ τῆς γαστριμαργίας πάθος ἐ. τῷ λαῷ Gr.Nyss.*v.Mos.*(M.44.412C); χεῖρας ἐπαφεῖναι τῷ παροξύναντι *strike at*, Bas.*hex.*2.5(1.16E; M.29.40A); id.*hom.*3.7(2.23A; M.31.213B); Chrys.*stat.*5.3(2.64C); med., *throw oneself into* τοῖς ὕδασιν ἐ. Mac.Aeg.*pat.*26 (M.34.888A); met., *throw oneself upon, attack* in argument, *cat.Gal.*2:15(p.38.28); **2.** *let loose upon* ἐ. αὐτῷ πλῆθος Chrys.*hom.60.2 in Mt.*(7.607C); Philost.*h.e.*2.11(M.65.473B); fig. and met. τοῖς ἁμαρτάνουσιν θεὸς ἐ. τὰς τιμωρίας Didym.*Ps.*17:16(M.39.1248D); ἐ. τὴν γλῶτταν τοῖς ἁμαρτάνουσιν Chrys.*hom.61.2 in Mt.*(7.612E); πάσας τῇ ψυχῇ ἐ. τὰς ἡδονάς id.*hom.5.4 in Tit.*(11.763A, v.l. τῆς ψυχῆς); id.*hom.6.1 in Heb.*(12.61D); Isid.Pel.*epp.*1.73(M.78.232D); ὁ δαίμων τῆς ὑπερηφανείας ἤρξατο ἐπάρσεως λογισμοὺς αὐτῷ ἐπαφίειν (sic) Gr.Mag.*dial.*(tr.Zach.)2.20(M.*PL.*66.171A); *let loose to, let run before* ναῦν...ἐ. τῷ πελάγει Synes.*ep.*4(M.66.1329C); **3.** *let in upon* τὴν θάλασσαν ἡμῖν ἐ. Chrys.*hom.11.6 in Rom.*(9.539E); ἐπαφῶμεν...τὸ πῦρ τοῦ πνεύματος, καὶ κατακαύσωμεν τὰς...ἐπιθυμίας id.*hom.49.8 in Mt.*(7.513A); **4.** *pour forth upon*, Bas.*hex.*6.10(1.60B; M.29.141B); ref. seventy elders as types of seventy disciples ἑβδομήκοντα ἐπελέξατο [sc. Μωϋσῆς], ἐπηφίει δὲ τοῖς ἐξειλεγμένοις τὸ πνεῦμα Cyr.*Lc.*10:1(M.72.665B); **5.** *shed* tears, Petr.II Al.*encycl.*(M.33.1276C)ap.Thdt.*h.e.*4.22.1; **6.** *utter*, *ib.*6(1285A)ap.Thdt.*h.e.*4.22.21; **7.** *leave behind for* ὑπόδειγμα καλοῦ βίου ἐπαφήσασαν ἡμῖν Thdr.Stud.*epp.*2.144(M.99.1453C).

ἐπαφρίζω, *foam up*; met., *foam with anger*, Petr.II Al.*encycl.*5(M.33.1284A)ap.Thdt.*h.e.*4.22.17.

ἐπάχθεια, **ἡ**, *burden, annoyance, trouble*, Bas.*ep.*30(3.110A; M.32.313A); *ib.*73.3(168A; M.444A); αἱρεῖσθαι τὰς ἀπὸ τῶν νοσημάτων φέρειν ὀδύνας ἢ τὴν ἀπὸ τῶν βοηθημάτων ὑπομένειν ἐ. Chrys.*paralyt.*5 (3.41A); Pall.*v.Chrys.*13(p.79.25; M.47.45); *ib.*17(p.103.8; M.47.58); *ib.*8(46.9; M.47.27); of married life, Nil.*Magn.*36(M.79.1012C); esp. of importunate pleaders, Bas.*ep.*37(3.114D; M.324B); Chrys.*ep.*14.3 (3.597E); id.*hom.36.2 in Mt.*(7.316C).

ἐπαχλύω, *shed darkness upon*; fig., Gr.Naz.*carm.*2.1.13.158(M.37.1239A).

ἐπεγείρω, **1.** intrans., *rise*; **a.** *rise up against*, med. c. dat., Gr.Nyss.*Pss.titt.*B 14(M.44.576A); id.*laud.Bas.*(p.42.13; M.46.809B); act., *take an opposite position* καθ' ἑαυτοῦ ἐ. Epiph.*haer.*54.6 (p.323.6; M.41.969C); **b.** *rise* as mark of respect *for* someone, abs. or c. dat., Thphn.*chron.*p.290(M.108.712B,C,D); **2.** *raise* πόδας ἐ. *stand on tiptoe* πόδας ἐ. κατὰ τὴν τελευταίαν τῆς εὐχῆς συνεκφώνησιν Clem.*str.*7.7(p.30.20; M.9.456B).

***ἐπεγερμός**, **ὁ**, *excitement, applause*, Clem.*paed.*2.8(M.8.481B; περιαγερμός p.201.14).

***ἐπεγερτέον**, *one must wake up*, Clem.*paed.*2.9(p.207.11; M.8.496B).

***ἐπεγερτικῶς**, *wakefully, so as to wake easily*, Clem.*paed.*2.9 (p.205.27; M.8.492C).

***ἐπεγκυλίομαι**, *be involved, entangled in*, Clem.*str.*7.12(p.54.2; M.9.504A).

***ἐπεγχείρημα**, **τό**, *undertaking*, ‡Pion.*v.Polyc.*17.

ἐπεί, ἐπειδάν, ἐπειδή, **1.** *when*; ἐπειδάν c. indic. (s.v.l.) ἐπειδὰν παρῆλθες τὸν βίον, καὶ κατολίσθης ἐν τῇ τοῦ θανάτου μάνδρᾳ Gr.Nyss.*hom.2 in Cant.*(M.44.805B); id.*or.dom.*3(M.44.1148D; εἰσάγῃ p.44.37); Cyr.*Is.*3.2(2.409B); **2.** *since* ἐπειδὴ γὰρ = ἐπειδήπερ, *A.Thom.*A 57 (p.174.2); Epiph.*haer.*66.69(p.110.20; M.42.140B) al.

***ἐπειγμένως**, **1.** *hurriedly hastily*, Gr.Nyss.*bapt.diff.*(M.46.420A); **2.** *eagerly*, Thdr.Stud.*epp.*2.46(M.99.1249C).

ἐπείγ-ω, **1.** act., *drive* ἤπειγεν ἑαυτόν *hastened*, Ath.*v.Anton.*91(M.26.969B); met., *urge* γυναῖκα...∼ουσάν με παρανομεῖν *T.Jos.*2.2; Or.*Jo.*10.26(17; p.199.15; M.14.353C); Gel.Cyz.*h.e.*2.7.4(M.85.1233A); **2.** med., *drive on, sweep forward*; of a storm, Nonn.*par.Jo.*6:16 (M.43.796C); met., *press on* εἰς τὴν πατρῴαν αὐλὴν...∼εται Clem.*str.*7.10(p.42.14; M.9.481B); Or.*or.*8.2(p.317.6; M.11.441B); Chrys.*hom.9.1 in 1Tim.*(11.594D); **3.** pass., *be driven, forced* ἐπὶ τὴν τῆς ἐπιστολῆς ταύτης ἀνάγκην ἐπειχθείς Const.ap.Eus.*v.C.*2.60(p.68.8; M.20.1040B); c. infin., Ath.*ep.encycl.*1(pp.169.19,170.19; M.25.224B, 225A); **4.** impers., *there is pressing need*, Eus.*h.e.*4.18.3(M.20.373C).

ἐπείκτης, **ὁ**, **1.** *one who urges on*, Thphn.*chron.*p.306(M.108.745A); **2.** as adj., *urgent, pressing, persuasive* ὑφέξει τοῖς ἐ. ἀγγέλοις τοὺς συλλογισμοὺς τῶν χρεῶν καὶ τῶν τόκων Geo.Pis.*hex.*1465(M.92.1546A); τοὺς στεναγμοὺς ἐκ βάθους, πρέσβεις ἐ. κοσμικῆς σωτηρίας id.*carm.*4.123(p.14).

ἐπειλίσσω, v. ἐπελίσσω.

ἔπειμι (*ibo*), **1.** *come upon* μαλάσσεται κηρὸς...ἵνα τὸν ἐπίοντα χαρακτῆρα παραδέξηται Clem.*str.*7.12(p.51.17; M.9.500A); θεία...δύναμις ἣν ἡ πάντα ἐπιοῦσα καὶ κατορθοῦσα Chrys.*hom.1.4 in Mt.*(7.9A); **2.** of time, *elapse*, Eus.*v.C.*1.12(p.13.11; M.20.925A); **3.** *go over, traverse*, Philost.*h.e.*3.9(M.65.492B); met., Clem.*str.*7.16(p.68.32; M.9.533D); hence *enumerate*, Chrys.*scand.*7(3.479E); *read*, id.*hom.68.4 in Mt.*(7.676D).

ἐπεῖπον, aor.; **1.** *call, name, describe as*, Synes.*ep.*4(M.66.1340B); **2.** *call upon, invoke*, Gr.Naz.*or.*4.84(M.35.612A).

ἐπεισάγ-ω, *bring in, introduce* οὐκ ἔξωθέν τίς ἐστιν ἐφευρεθεῖσα ἡ τοῦ υἱοῦ οὐσία, οὐδὲ ἐκ μὴ ὄντων ἐπεισήχθη Thgn.*hypot.fr.*2(p.76; M.10.240A); (Arian) ἔξωθεν ∼όμενός [sc. ὁ λόγος] ἐστι καὶ ξένος αὐτοῦ [sc. τοῦ θεοῦ] Ath.*Ar.*1.17(M.26.48A).

ἐπεισαγωγή, **ἡ**, **1.** *bringing in besides, introduction*, Clem.*paed.*3.2(p.239.15; M.8.561B); ἄγνοια τοῦ θεοῦ καὶ πολλῶν θεῶν ἐ. *Const.App.*7.18; τὸν ἀκροατὴν καταπλήξει τῇ τοῦ παραδόξου πράγματος ἐ. Chrys.ap.*cat.Mt.*1:18(p.10.26) for ἐπαγ- id.*hom.4.2 in Mt.*(7.49C); **2.** *means of bringing in* ὁ φόβος ἐκεῖνος...ἐ. τινα εἶχεν καλλίονος...νοῦ Vict.*Mc.*9:3(p.355.10).

ἐπείσακτος, *brought in from outside* ἐ. καὶ δοτὸν τῷ λύχνῳ τὸ φῶς Cyr.*Jo.*1.8(4.66E); τοῖς ἐν κλήρῳ τεταγμένοις ἀπαγορεύομεν...γυναῖκά τινα ἐν τῷ ἰδίῳ οἴκῳ ἐ. ἔχειν Justn.*nov.*123.29(p.615.30); cf. Theodorus Balsamon *schol.in CNic.*(*325*)*can.*3(M.137.232B); *alien*; of heret. doctrines, Didym.*Trin.*3.3(M.39.825A); Thdot.Anc.*exp.symb.*2(M.77.1316D); of Fall φυσικὴ μὲν ἔστιν ἡ τῆς ζωῆς ὁδός, ἐ. δὲ ἡ τοῦ θανάτου *Const.App.*7.1.3; τῆς ἐ. φθορᾶς Cyr.*Jo.*5.3(4.497A); hence of God's punishments, Thdt.*Ps.*77:66(1.1163); Trin., *alien, adventitious* οὔτε οὖν κτιστόν τι, ἢ δοῦλον ἐν τῇ τριάδι, οὔτε ἐ. τι, ὡς πρότερον μὲν οὐχ ὑπάρχον, ὕστερον δὲ ἐπεισελθόν Gr.Nyss.*v.Gr.Thaum.*(M.46.913A); τῆς...μακαρίας...οὐσίας, τῆς ἐ. ἐχούσης οὐδέν Chrys.*hom.11.1 in Jo.*(8.63E); εἰ...τέλειος...ἐστι [sc. ὁ πατήρ] καὶ δίχα τοῦ δύνασθαι γεννᾶν, περιττὸν ἄρα καὶ ἐ. ἐγγέγονεν αὐτῷ τοῦτο Cyr.*thes.*5(5^1.37E); ‡Caes.Naz.*dial.*3(M.38.861); applied by Arius to Logos, Const.ap.Gel.Cyz.*h.e.*3.19.30(M.85.1352C); τὸν υἱόν...ἔκφυλόν τινα τῆς πατρῴας οὐσίας, καὶ ἐ. φαντάζεσθαι Cyr.*thes.*32(282A); and to his attributes εἰ μὴ κατὰ φύσιν ἔχει τὸ εἶναι ζωὴ ὁ...λόγος, ἐ. δὲ ...κεκτημένος αὐτό *ib.*14(141D); neut. plur. as subst., *things brought in as an addition* γινώσκειν τί νόμος φυσικὸς καὶ τί τὰ τῆς δευτερώσεως· τά τε ἐν τῇ ἐρήμῳ τοῖς μοσχοποιήσασι δοθέντα ἐ. *Const.App.*1.6.8; *ib.*6.22.5.

***ἐπεισάκτως**, *from outside, adventitiously*, ref. Inc. οὐ...ἐ. οὐδ' ἀλλογενῶς ἀλλ' οὐσιωδῶς ‡Gr.Nyss.*imag.*(M.44.1340A); ἡ ἁμαρτία οὐκ ἔχουσα ἀρχὴν ῥίζης..., ἐν ἡμῖν δὲ ἐ. γινομένη Epiph.*haer.*36.6(p.49.24; M.41.640C); αὐτὸς [sc. ὁ θεός] μὲν φύσει...ἔχει [sc. τὴν ἀφθαρσίαν], ἡμεῖς δὲ ἐ. Chrys *hom.4.2 in 1Tim.*(11.570B); Jo.D.*dialect.*51(M.94.637A).

***ἐπείσαξις**, ἡ, *means of bringing in besides, entrance for* an *additional* class of people, Just.*dial.*135.5(M.6.789A).

ἐπεισβαίνω, *come in against*, Chrys.*fr.in Jer.*2:17(M.64.764D).

ἐπείσειμι (*ibo*), **1.** *come in to, approach*, Clem.*str.*4.25(p.318.16,19; M.8.1368A); **2.** *come in against*, Chrys.*hom.51.5 in Mt.*(7.527B); id.*hom.29.1 in 1Cor.*(10.259A); **3.** ptcpl. as subst. τὸ ἐπεισιόν *what occurs to one*, Eus.*d.e.*8.2(p.377.24; M.22.612C); τὰ ἐπεισιόντα *income*, Chrys.*hom.63.2 in Mt.*(7.630A).

ἐπεισκρίν-ω, *admit, introduce as an addition from outside*, Gr.Nyss.*hom.opif.*30.11(M.44.240B); ‡Caes.Naz.*dial.*140(M.38.1052); of soul into body, Clem.*str.*6.16(p.500.9; M.9.360B); Gr.Nyss.*hom.opif.*29.1(229C); id.*anim.et res.*(M.46.117A); διὰ τῆς πίστεως ἡ κατὰ φύσιν ἡμῖν ~εται ζωή Cyr.*Jo.*2.4(4.173D); *ib.*4.2(360D); τῇ φύσει τὸ παθητὸν ἐπεισεκρίθη Max.*ambig.*(M.91.1340B); id.*opusc.*(M.91.252D); Trin. εἶναι...τοῦ υἱοῦ...τὸ πνεῦμα τὸ ἅγιον, καὶ οὐκ ~εται ἔξωθεν Cyr.*Jo.*10.2(4.911B).

ἐπεισκυκλέω, *bring on* the stage *one after another*; fig., Athenag.*res.*20(p.73.14; M.6.1013C); met., *bring on in addition* Ναυατιανῷ... περὶ τοῦ θεοῦ διδασκαλίαν ἀνοσιωτάτην ἐπεισκυκλήσαντι Dion.Al.ap.Eus.*h.e.*7.8(M.20.652B); Bas.*ep.*135.1(3.226D; M.32.572C); Cyr.*hom.pasch.*5(5^2.50B).

ἐπεισκωμάζω, *make inroads upon*, met. τὰ...τῆς εἰδωλολατρείας κακὰ...ἐπεισκωμάσαντα τῷ βίῳ τούτῳ Bas.Sel.*v.Thecl.*1(M.85.497A).

ἐπεισόδιος, neut. as subst., *interlude*, Ast.Am.*hom.*14(M.40.388A).

***ἐπεισουσιώδης**, *consequent upon, additional to the essence*, Jo.D.*dialect.*14(M.94.577B).

***ἐπεισπελάζω**, *sweep down upon*, ‡Nil.*narr.*2(M.79.604B).

ἐπεισπηδάω, **1.** *leap in upon*; fig., *burst in upon*, Dion.Ar.*ep.*8.1(M.3.1089A); **2.** *fall upon, usurp power over* ἐ. τῇ Ἀντιοχέων ἐκκλησίᾳ Ath.*syn.*12(p.239.16; M.26.701B).

ἐπεισπνέω, *inspire again and again*, Meth.*symp.*4.1(p.46.2; M.18.88A).

ἐπεισρέ-ω, **1.** *flow in upon*, met. οὐρανόθεν ~οντος ἡμῖν τοῦ ἁγίου πνεύματος Clem.*paed.*1.6(p.106.25; M.8.284A); ~ουσαν...τὴν ἐπιθυμίαν...εἰς τὴν καρδίαν Meth.*symp.*11(p.138.17; M.18.216C); of invaders, *rush in upon*, c. dat., Philost.*h.e.*11.8(M.65.601D); **2.** trans., *pour in upon*, fig. αἱ ἀκοαί...τὸν τῆς ταραχῆς...βόρβορον τοῖς λογισμοῖς ἐ. Gr.Nyss.*res.*3(M.46.677D).

ἐπεισφέρ-ω, **1.** *bring in besides* οἴεσθαι μὴ εἶναι θεὸν τὸν ἐκ θεοῦ... ἀλλὰ νόθον...τινὰ καὶ ψευδώνυμον ἡμῖν ~εσθαι Cyr.*Jo.*1.3(4.19D); **2.** *ascribe* writings to τὰ εἰς αὐτὸν ~όμενα Tat.ap.Eus.*p.e.*10.11(495D; M.21.825A); for ἐπιφερόμενα id.*orat.*41(p.42.5; M.6.885B).

***ἐπεισφθείρομαι**, *creep in to do harm*, Bas.Sel.*v.Thecl.*1(M.85.489B, v.l. ἐπιφθαρέντι).

***ἐπεισφορά**, ἡ, **1.** *bringing in, introduction* ἀλλεπάλληλον τῶν νοημάτων ἐ. Cyr.*Jo.*1 proem.(4.8B); id.*Os.*proem.(3.2C); **2.** *bringing in instead* ἀθέτησις...τῆς ἀρχαίας...ἐντολῆς καὶ τῆς δευτέρας ἐ. id.*ador.*1(1.3C); ἐ. ποιεῖσθαι *introduce instead*, id.*hom.pasch.*16(5^2.219B).

ἐπεισφρέω, **1.** *bring in besides* ποῖον...συναίτιον τῷ θεῷ ἐπεισφρήσουσιν; Zach.Mit.*opif.*(M.85.1080B); *ib.*(1052B); *intrude* ἐ. ἑαυτοὺς τῇ [sc. συνόδῳ] Pulch.*ep.Strat.*(p.29.18; H.2.48); **2.** *come in upon*; in hostile sense, ‡Just.*qu.et resp.*100(M.6.1344D); ἐ. ταῖς διανοίαις τῶν ἀνοήτων Pall.*h.Laus.*proem.(p.9.9; M.34.1001); Geo.Pis.*hex.*995(M.92.1511A); ‡Caes.Naz.*dial.*137(M.38.1041).

***ἐπεκβολή**, ἡ, *additional, late product*, Cyr.*Mich.*61(3.454B).

ἐπεκδιηγέομαι, *explain further*, Clem.*str.*4.7(p.268.24; M.8.1257A).

***ἐπεκδιήγησις**, ἡ, *additional narrative*; of words found in LXX of Gen.1:9, but not in Hebr., Bas.*hex.*4.5(1.37C; M.29.89A).

ἐπεκδικ-έω, **1.** *avenge* injuries, Dor.*doct.*1.13(M.88.1633D); *ib.*10.6(1732C); **2.** *fully satisfy* passions ὁ ἐνεργῶν τὸ πάθος ἐστὶν ὁ πράττων αὐτό, ὁ ~ῶν αὐτό *ib.*10.5(1729B) al.

***ἐπεκδίκησις**, ἡ, *vengeance, retribution*, Geo.Al.*v.Chrys.*(p.250.6).

***ἐπεκδικία**, ἡ, *vindication*, Geo.Al.*v.Chrys.*(p.203.14).

***ἐπεκδύω**, *strip further*, Gr.Nyss.*usur.*(M.46.436C).

ἐπέκεινα, **1.** c. genit., *beyond, above* τῆς τελείας ὄντως ἐπιστήμης ἐ. κόσμου περὶ τὰ νοητὰ καὶ ἔτι τούτων τὰ πνευματικώτερα ἀναστρεφομένης Clem.*str.*6.8(p.465.35; M.9.289B); ἐ. πάσης καταλήψεως Eus.*l.C.*12(p.229.20; M.20.1385B); ref. Mt.10:34 οὐ ξίφος λέγων, ἀλλὰ τὴν εἰρήνης ἐ. τμητικὴν...τοῦ...πνεύματος...σοφίαν Didym.*Trin.*2.5(M.39.505C); πάσης ἱερωσύνης ἐ. ... μυστήριον, τὸ τοῦ δεσπότου μου βάπτισμα Jo.VI H.*v.Jo.D.*6(M.94.437C); of God τὸν ἐ. ὅλων θεόν Eus.*e.th.*1.7(p.65.34; M.24.836D); τὸν ἀνωτάτω καὶ ἐ. τῶν ὅλων id.*p.e.*3.6(96D; M.21.177B); τοῦ πατρὸς...τῶν ὁρωμένων ἁπάντων ἀνωτάτω ἐ. τε οὐρανοῦ καὶ πάσης γενητῆς οὐσίας id.*d.e.*4.7(p.161.16; M.22.269A); ἐ. πάσης εἰκόνος τε καὶ παραδείγματος ὁ τοῦ...θεοῦ τέλειος λόγος id.*l.C.*12(p.230.17; 1388B); ἐ. ... ἐστιν ὁ θεός...ὥσπερ τοῦ σώματος, οὕτω καὶ τοῦ ἀσωμάτου ‡Just.*qu.Gr.*2(M.6.1469C); τὴν ἐ. πάσης ἀρχῆς... ὕπαρξιν Chrys.*hom.7.1 in Jo.*(8.44E); ἵνα...ὁ πάντων αἴτιος ἐ. ᾖ πάντων Dion.Ar.*d.n.*11.6(M.3.956B); *ib.*4.16(713C); ‡Gr.Nyss.*hom.2.1 in Jo.*(p.111.4); *beyond, worse than* πάσης συμφορᾶς ἐ. Eus.*v.C.*4.42(p.134.9; M.20.1192A); Bas.*hex.*6.7(1.56D; M.29.132D); πάσης ἀτοπίας καὶ βλασφημίας ἐ. Gr.Nyss.*Maced.*7(M.45.1309B); **2.** abs.; **a.** *afar off* τοῖς ἐ. ἀδελφοῖς τὴν ἐπιστολὴν διαπέμψασθε *M.Polyc.*20.1; **b.** = *transcendent* τὸ ἐ. αἴτιον, τὸν πατέρα τῶν ὅλων Clem.*str.*7.1(p.4.7; M.9.404C); τῶν ἐ. θείων καὶ ὑπερκοσμίων δυνάμεων Eus.*e.th.*3.3(p.151.27; M.24.992C); τὸν ἐ. θεόν id.*d.e.*1.5(p.22.26; M.22.48B); *ib.*5 proem.(p.202.3; 336A).

ἐπέκτασις, ἡ, **1.** *extension, extent*; in time, Epiph.*haer.*42.11(p.139.23; M.41.749A); met. ἡ φύσις ἐνδυναμωθεῖσα τοῦ ἀδυνάτως ἔχοντος πρὸς ἐ. τοῦ δυνατοῦ *ib.*70.7(p.239.29; M.42.352A); **2.** ref. Phil.3:13, *stretching out, reaching forth* ἡ τοῦ πλείονος ἐ. ‡Bas.*struct.hom.*2.2(1.338E; M.30.44A); τῶν ἔμπροσθεν ἐ. Gr.Nyss.*hom.6 in Cant.*(M.44.888A); ἐ. ἐπὶ τὰ ἔμπροσθεν †Cyr.*coll.VT*(6^4.33C; M.77.1225A); **3.** *sending out* τῇ πτερωτῇ τοῦ τάχους ἐ. Geo.Pis.*hex.*1478(M.92.1548A); *bestowal*, *ib.*1772(1571A).

ἐπεκτείν-ω, **1.** *extend, increase*, met. πλεῖον ἑαυτῶν ἐ. τὴν ἀσέβειαν Ath.*gent.*8(M.25.17C); med., *extend, apply* more widely πᾶσι τὴν νουθεσίαν ἐ. Epiph.*haer.*64.71(p.518.5; M.41.1196A); **2.** *stretch forward* ἡ νύμφη τοῖς ὑψηλοτέροις ἑαυτὴν ἐ. Gr.Nyss.*hom.9 in Cant.*(M.44.997A); id.*v.Gr.Thaum.*(M.46.901C); id.*hex.*75(M.44.121A); Chrys.*hom.12.1 in Phil.*(v. infra); usu. pass. intrans., *stretch forward to, reach out after* τοῦ ἄνω Χριστοῦ, ἐκείνου τοῦ ἐπεκταθέντος τῷ σταυρῷ Iren.*haer.*1.7.2(M.7.516A); *ib.*1.4.1(480A); *ib.*1.8.2(524A); Clem.*q.d.s.*1(p.160.17; M.9.605B); ψυχὴν...κατὰ προκοπὴν ἑκάστην ~ομένην εἰς ἕξιν ἀπαθείας id.*str.*7.2(p.9.4; M.9.413B); ὅτῳ...ἀσθενεῖ ~εσθαι ἡ ψυχὴ πρὸς τὴν πολυμαθῆ ἐμπειρίαν *ib.*6.18(p.515.26; 396A); ὁ γὰρ ~όμενος οὗτός ἐστιν ὁ τοὺς πόδας...τῷ λοιπῷ σώματι προλαβεῖν σπουδάζων, ~ων ἑαυτὸν εἰς τὸ ἔμπροσθεν καὶ τὰς χεῖρας ἐκτείνων, ἵνα καὶ τοῦ δρόμου πλέον τι ἐργάσηται Chrys.*hom.12.1 in Phil.*(11.291E); τὸ συμπαθὲς ἑαυτοῦ δεικνὺς κἂν τοῖς τοιούτοις ~όμενον Olymp.*Job* 30:25–6(M.93.317A); ‡Meth.*Sym.et Ann.*1(M.18.549B); abs., *reach out farther, advance*, Ath.*inc.*5.3(M.25.105A); **3.** *direct towards* τοῖς ἀφεστηκόσι τὸν ὀφθαλμὸν ἐ. Gr.Nyss.*Pss.titt.*A 6(M.44.453A); met., *promote* πρὸς βασιλείαν ~όμενος Bas.Sel.*or.*14.2(M.85.188C); **4.** *direct against* κατ' ἀνθρώπων τὰ τῆς ἐπιβουλῆς ἐ. ‡Just.*qu.et resp.*127(M.6.1377A); **5.** *expand, explain*, Ath.*Ar.*3.21(M.26.368B).

ἐπελαύν-ω, **1.** *drive against*, met. καταφορικῶς ἡμῖν ἐ. τὴν γλῶσσαν Gr.Nyss.*Eun.*6(2 p.134.17; M.45.717D); **2.** intrans., *draw on* τῆς τοῦ σωτηρίου πάθους ἑορτῆς ~ούσης Eus.*h.e.*8.2.4(M.20.745A); id.*d.e.*10.8(p.474.22; M.22.764A).

ἐπελαφρίζω, *lighten, make easy to bear*, Or.*Cels.*6.20(p.90.20; M.11.1321A); Eus.*m.P.*2(p.909.22; M.20.1468A); Cyr.*hom.pasch.*6(5^2.81A).

ἐπελαφρύνω, *lighten*, Ast.Am.*hom.*1(M.40.177D).

ἐπελέγχω, *refute cumulatively*, Sophr.H.*ep.syn.*(M.87.3176A).

***ἐπελεέω**, *pity*, Chrys.*prod.Jud.*2(2.386C); Sophr.H.*mir.Cyr.et Jo.*13(M.87.3464C).

ἐπέλευσις, ἡ, **1.** *coming upon*, of H. Ghost; on BMV, Gr.Nyss.*ep.*3(M.46.1021A); id.*Apoll.*27(M.45.1181B); id.*nativ.*(M.46.1141B); *Chron.Pasch.*p.198(M.92.489A); at Pentecost, Jo.Nic.*nativ.*(M.96.1440B); in eucharist, *Lit.Jac.*(p.186.1); **2.** *coming, arrival*, *Chron.Pasch.*p.392(M.92.1005B); of God in judgement, *cat.Apoc.*3:3(p.221.2); **3.** *coming against, attack*, Geo.Pis.*Pers.*2.366(M.92.1235A).

ἐπελευστικός, *ready to attack, impetuous, violent*, Cyr.*glaph.Gen.*7(1.214C); id.*Os.*36(3.66E).

ἐπελίσσ-ω, ἐπειλίσσω, for ἐφελίσσω; **1.** *wriggle up to* τούτοις ὁ ὄφις ἑαυτὸν ἐπειλίξῃ Gr.Nyss.*or.dom.*4(p.84.23; ἐπελλίζῃ M.44.1172D); med. intrans., *wriggle up*, Clem.*paed.*2.9, v.l. for ἐφελ- (M.8.492C; περιελ- p.205.23); **2.** *wind round*, ἐπειλ-, Paul.Sil.*Soph.*368,561(M.86.2133B,2141A); **3.** met., *roll on after* ἑπτὰ τοῖς ὀφλήμασιν ~ομένων ἐνιαυτῶν Cyr.*ador.*8(1.273C).

ἐπελπίζω, *pin one's hopes upon, hope in*, Gr.Nyss.*Pss.titt.*B 10(M.44.540A); τοὺς ἐπηλπικότας ἐπὶ τῷ ἐσταυρωμένῳ Socr.*h.e.*7.16.3(M.67.772A).

ἐπεμβαίν-ω, **1.** *tread upon*, hence *trespass upon*, Bas.*hex.*7.3(1.66B; M.29.156A); Chrys.*hom.16.2 in 1Tim.*(11.646A); **2.** *trample upon*; met., *insult, exult over*, Gr.Nyss.*v.Mos.*(M.44.409C); abs., Const.*or.s.c.*11(p.167.2; M.20.1261A); Ath.*ep.Aeg.Lib.*19(M.25.581A); **3.** *come up over* τοῦ ποταμοῦ τοῖς ἀγροῖς ~οντος Gr.Nyss.*v.Gr.Thaum.*(M.46.929B); met., *enter upon* τῇ τέχνῃ Aen.*dial.*(M.85.

929B); *come in upon*, *T.Benj.*11.2; **4.** *attack*; in argument, CAlex. (338)*ep*.ap.Ath.*apol.sec*.4(p.90.34; M.25.256A); Vict.*Mc*.10:3(p.372.13).

ἐπεμβάλλ-ω, 1. *throw in afterwards*, Hipp.*haer*.9.25(p.260.2; M.16.3403A); **2.** *pile one upon another*, met. πολλῶν...ἀλλήλοις ~ομένων Gr.Nyss.*hom.opif*.10.3(M.44.152C).

***ἐπεμβάς, ὁ, 1.** *rising, elevation*, Paul.Sil.*Soph*.308(M.86.2131B); **2.** *increase*, *ib*.935(2154B).

***ἐπεμέω,** *vomit over*, Gr.Nyss.*Eun*.4(2 p.86.13; M.45.661C).

***ἐπεμφύρω,** *dip deeply into*, Clem.*paed*.2.1(p.162.1; M.8.396C).

***ἐπενδεής,** *in need*, Arist.*apol*.10.2; *ib*.11.1.

***ἐπενδημέω,** *dwell in*, Meth.*symp*.8.2(p.83.16; M.18.141A).

***ἐπενδιδύσκομαι,** *put on besides*, Ath.*Ar*.2.7(M.26.161B); *ib*.2.52 (257A).

ἐπένδυμα, τό, *upper garment*, something *put on on top*, Hipp. *haer*.9.28(p.261.23; M.16.3407A); fig. πνεῦμα τὸ οὐράνιον ἐ. τῆς θνητότητος τὴν ἀθανασίαν κεκτήσεται Tat.*orat*.20(p.23.1; M.6.852B).

ἐπενδύτης, ὁ, *upper garment, short upper tunic*, *Ev.Thom*.B 10 (p.162); ῥάψασα τὸν χιτῶνα εἰς ἐ. σχήματι ἀνδρικῷ *A.Paul.et Thecl*.40 (p.266.4); ref. Mt.10:10 τὸ...ἔνδυμα ὅπερ ἔδωκεν τοῖς ἀποστόλοις...ἐ. μόνον ἦν καὶ λέντιον *A.Phil*.6(p.4.6); Ath.*v.Anton*.46(M.26.912A); of a nun's upper garment ὁ ἐ. σου μέλας, μὴ βεβάμμενος ἐν βαφῇ id. *virg*.11(p.44.23; M.28.264B); of ephod, Gr.Nyss.*or.dom*.3(p.40.8; M.44.1148D); id.*v.Mos*.(M.44.388B); Thdt.*qu.60 in Ex*.(1.166); fig. γένοιτο...ἐπιτεθῆναι τῷ λόγῳ τὸν ἐ., ᾧ ὄνομά ἐστι Λόγιον...καὶ Ἀλήθεια Gr.Nyss.*hex*.78(M.44.124C).

ἐπενδύ-ω, 1. *put on besides*; fig. and met., Clem.*exc.Thdot*.55 (p.125.8; M.9.685B); ἵν' οὖν, φασὶν οἱ δοκηταί,...τὸ σκότος ~σηται [sc. Christ] τὸ ἐξώτερον, τὴν σάρκα Hipp.*haer*.8.10(p.230.12; M.16.3355A); *ib*.(p.230.8; 3355A); μηκέτι ἐ. τὴν σῆς ἁμαρτίας χιτῶνα Gr.Nyss.*hom.11 in Cant*.(M.44.1005B); ‡Meth.*Sym.et Ann*.6(M.18.360C); esp. ref. 2Cor.5:2–4 χρὴ τοὺς...ἀναληφθησομένους τῷ...Χριστῷ ...~σαντι τὴν ἀφθαρσίαν καθαροὺς προσιέναι Meth.*lepr*.10(p.464.16); med. οἱ...τῆς κακίας ἐκδυσάμενοι τὸν χιτῶνα, ἐ. δὲ τὴν ἀφθαρσίαν τοῦ Χριστοῦ Clem.*paed*.1.6(p.109.16; M.8.289A); τὴν ἀκήρατον τῆς ψυχῆς ἐσθῆτα, τὴν σάρκα, ἁγιάζονται, καὶ ταύτῃ ἐ. ἀφθαρσίαν *ib*.2.10 (p.223.1; 528B); id.*str*.4.22(p.309.12; M.8.1348B); ὁ...πιστεύσας ἀποδύεταί τε καὶ ἐ.... τὴν ἁγιασμένην στολὴν *ib*.5.6(p.345.1; M.9.68A); μὴ θέλοντες τὸ σῶμα ἀπεκδύσασθαι ἀλλ' ἐπ' αὐτῷ τὴν ἄλυπον ἐ. ζωὴν Meth.*res*.2.15(p.363.15; M.18.312B); Nil.*epp*.1.111(M.79.132A); **2.** *put on again*, Clem.*str*.4.19(p.301.9; M.8.1329B).

***ἐπενεκτέον, 1.** *one must add*, Thdt.*Ps*.9:4(1.666); **2.** *one must lay* a charge, Epiph.*haer*.26.7(p.283.20; M.41.341B).

ἐπένεξις, ἡ, *application* of a remedy, Jo.Clim.*past*.2(M.88.1169A).

ἐπενθήκη, ἡ, *addition*; plur., Thphyl.*exc.gent*.13(p.487.21; M.113.949C).

***ἐπενθουσιάω,** *use the language of enthusiasm*, i.e. *emotional* or *ecstatic religious language*, abs., Chrys.*hom.20.2 in Ac*.(9.164E).

ἐπενθυμέομαι, *consider*, Jo.Jej.*doct*.1(p.228).

ἐπενθύμησις, ἡ, *reflection* following sense experience, Bas.*Eun*. 1.6(1.217E; M.29.524B), Leont.B.*arg.Sev*.(M.86.1932A) citt. s. ἐπίνοια.

***ἐπέννοια, ἡ,** = foreg., Leont.B.*arg.Sev*.(M.86.1932A).

***ἐπεντρανίζω,** *fix the eyes upon*, c. dat., Germ.CP *or*.1(M.98.232B); *ib*.2(257B).

***ἐπεντριβή, ἡ,** *annoyance*, Epiph.*haer*.26.1(p.275.11; M.41.332A); *ib*.61.7(p.389.2; 1049D).

ἐπεντρίβω, 1. *inflict further, in addition* καινότερα...ταῖς τοῦ διωγμοῦ συμφοραῖς ἐ. Eus.*m.P*.12(p.947.4; M.20.1513A); αὐτῷ...διαβολὴν ἐ. id.*Hierocl*.48(545C; M.22.868B); *afflict* λύκοι...τὴν Χριστοῦ ποίμνην ἐ. id.*h.e*.1.1.1(M.20.49A); **2.** *spend time upon*, Epiph.*haer*.1.2(p.170.21; M.41.176C); med., *occupy oneself with*, c. dat., Eus.*d.e*. 1.1(p.6.10; M.22.20D); Epiph.*haer*.58.4(p.361.5; M.41.1013D); *ib*.66.58(p.95.17; M.42.117B).

ἐπεξαμαρτητέον, *one ought to sin yet more*, Gennad.*fr.Rom*. 6:1(p.365.14; M.85.1673B).

***ἐπεξανάστασις, ἡ,** *assault*, *A.Andr.fr*.18(p.45.20).

ἐπέξειμι (*ibo*), **1.** *break out*, Gr.Naz.*or*.28.27(p.64.10; M.36.65A); **2.** trans., *depart from, quit* ἐ. τὸν βίον Bas.Sel.*v.Thecl*.2.20(M.85.601C); **3.** *go over in detail*, c. dat., Gr.Nyss.*hex*.77(M.44.124A); id. *Pss.titt*.B 10(M.44.541B); Synes.*Dion* 4(p.245.3; M.66.1124D).

ἐπεξέλευσις, ἡ, *visitation, punishment*, Isid.Pel.*epp*.3.154(M.78.848B); Evagr.*h.e*.1.7(p.13.28; M.86.2437A); Eustrat.*v.Eutych*.35(M.86.2316B); plur., Isid.Pel.*epp*.3.216(897B).

ἐπεξεργάζομαι, 1. *create in addition, make also* ἑαυτοῖς κίνδυνον ἐ. *1Clem*.47.7; Ath.*ep.Max*.5(M.26.1089C); **2.** *complete*, Bas.*hex*.4.3 (1.35D; M.29.84C); **3.** *work out further, elaborate* a point, Just.*dial*. 137.4(M.6.793A); Or.*Cels*.5.29(p.31.15; M.11.1225C); id.*sel.in Ps*.3:1 (M.12.1120A); Eus.*Marcell*.2.4(p.52.23; M.24.812C); Ath.*ep.encycl*.1 (p.167.18; M.25.224B); ἐ. χρησίμως τὸ εἰρημένον ὁ εὐαγγελιστής Cyr. *Jo*.1.9(4.96B); hence *explain, interpret* τὰ ῥήματα τῆς γραφῆς ἐ. Meth.*symp*.3.2(p.29.5; M.18.64A); Eus.*d.e*.9.14(p.434.22; M.22.700D); τινὰ μὲν ἀγράφως διὰ λόγων ἐ. *Cod.Afr*.134(Lat. *prosecuti sunt*); pass. οὐδέπω τῶν κεφαλαίων ἱκανῶς ἐπεξειργασμένων Meth.*symp*.7.4 (p.75.4; 129B); *be fully defined*, *Cod.Afr*.128(Lat. *expressum est*); **4.** *investigate fully*, Or.*Jo*.32.19(12; p.459.1; M.14.793D); Dion.Al. ap.Eus.*p.e*.14.26(779D; M.21.1281D); id.ap.Ath.*Dion*.20(p.61.24; M.25.569C).

ἐπεξεργασία, ἡ, 1. *working out, fuller treatment, elaboration* of a theme, Clem.*str*.7.1(p.3.21; M.9.404B); Chrys.*hom.4.1 in 1Tim*.(11.568C); Thdt.*Jer*.proem.(2.403); Leont.B.*cap.Sev*.30(M.86.1916B); **2.** *accomplishment, perfecting* τὴν ἐ. ... τοῦ κεκρυμμένου μυστηρίου Or.*Jo*.13.46(p.273.2; M.14.481B); ἐ. τῆς ἀρετῆς Vict.*Mc*.4:24–25 (p.310.1).

***ἐπεξέργασις, ἡ,** *working out in detail*, ‡Eust.*hex*.(M.18.712A).

***ἐπεξεργαστέον,** *one must work out, investigate*, Cyr.*Jo*.6.1(4.652C).

***ἐπεξεργαστής, ὁ,** *executor, one who carries out a decree*, *Cod. Afr*.123(Lat. *exsecutor*).

ἐπεξεργαστικῶς, comp., *in greater detail*, Bas.*hex*.3.3(1.24E; M.29.60A); Pall.*v.Chrys*.13(p.81.8; M.47.47); Cosm.Ind.*top*.1(M.88.65C).

ἐπεξέρχ-ομαι, 1. *attack*, Eus.*h.e*.5.16.2(M.20.464B); **2.** *punish* πάσης τῆς κτίσεως ἐπὶ τούτῳ [sc. τῷ ἀσεβήσαντι]...ἀγανακτούσης καὶ φυσικῶς ~ομένης *Hom.Clem*.11.10; **3.** *exact the penalty, take vengeance for* ἐ. τοῖς ἀδικήμασι Athenag.*leg*.3.1(M.6.896C); Gr.Naz. *ep*.125(M.37.220B); Chrys.*Jud*.8.2(1.676C); ἐ. τὰ ἁμαρτήματα *Hom. Clem*.16.20; *ib*.18.18; Chrys.*hom.69.1 in Mt*.(7.680B); **4.** *go out*, Or. *Jo*.20.10(p.338.6; M.14.592D); **5.** *go through*, Evagr.*h.e*.3.1(p.99.7; M.86.2593D); met., *examine*, c. dat., Or.*princ*.4.2.1(p.305.11; M.11.356C); ἐ. τῷ παρόντι χωρίῳ Chrys.*hom.6.1 in Mt*.(7.84A); Synes.*ep*. 67(M.66.1424C); *go through, enumerate* τοῖς ἐκείνων ἐγκωμίοις ἐ. Chrys.*hom.1.2 in 1Thess*.(11.427F); Philost.*h.e*.11.7(M.65.601C); **6.** *proceed*, c. infin., *Const.App*.2.17.1; c. ptcpl., Sever.*1Cor*.1:18–20 (p.228.22).

***ἐπεξεύρεσις, ἡ,** *invention*, Ath.*ep.Serap*.1.30(M.26.600A).

ἐπεξηγέομαι, *explain further*, Iren.*haer*.1.9.2(M.7.541A); Clem. *str*.3.15(p.240.13; M.8.1196C); Chrys.*hom.81.1 in Jo*.(8.477E).

ἐπεξήγησις, ἡ, 1. *additional explanation*, Chrys.*hom.22.3 in 1Cor*.(10.195B); id.*hom.9.2 in Col*.(11.393E); ref. Mt.3:11 τῇ ἐ. τοῦ πυρός *additional detail, additional mention*, id.*hom.11.4 in Mt*.(7.154C); **2.** *detailed account*, Bas.*hex*.3.3(1.24E; M.29.60A); Proc.G. *Gen*.1:6(M.87.64C).

ἐπεξηγητέον, *one ought also to explain*, Clem.*paed*.1.6(p.110.27; M.8.292A).

***ἐπέραιστος,** prob. f.l. for ἐπήρατος, Jo.Mal.*chron*.13 p.326(M.97.488A).

ἐπέραστος, 1. of things, *lovely* τὴν θεοείκελον αὐτῆς [sc. τῆς ψυχῆς] καὶ ἐ. ἰδέαν Meth.*symp*.6.1(p.64.22; M.18.113C); ἐ. τι τὸ τῆς παρθενίας ἐστίν...καὶ τριπόθητον κλέος *ib*.7.9(p.80.3; 136C); *ib*.9.1 (p.113.1; 176B); τὴν ἐ. προσηγορίαν ἣν ἔχομεν...Χριστιανοὶ γὰρ ὀνομαζόμεθα Thdt.*ep*.146(4.1269); παρθενία...ποθητὴ...θεῷ καὶ ἀγγέλοις ἐ. *M.Ner.et Ach*.5(p.4.3); **2.** *beloved, dear*, Chrys.*hom.2.1 in Ac.princ*.(3.61C); of the beloved disciple, id.*scand*.3(3.470B); of Christian as dear to God, ‡Bas.*const*.proem.2(2.534D; M.31.1324D); Chrys.*hom.1.3 in Eph*.(11.6B); νυμφικῶς τὰς ψυχὰς ἡμῶν κοσμήσαντες, ἐ. ἑαυτοὺς τῷ βασιλεῖ παραστήσομεν Andr.Caes.*Apoc*.9(M.106.252D); of Church, ref. Ps.44:11–12, Chrys.*hom.3.4 in Mt*.(7.39A); of God, Dion.Ar.*d.n*.10.1(M.3.937A); of Christ, *A.Thom*.A 160 (p.272.12); **3.** *welcome, acceptable*, of things ἐ. ἡμῖν τὸν ἀγῶνα τῆς πρὸς ἐκεῖνον [sc. τὸν θεόν] ποιούσης ἀγαπῆς Gr.Nyss.*instit*.(p.75.21; M.46.429C); Chrys.*hom.16.11 in Mt*.(7.221B); id.*hom.33.3 in Jo*.(8.194B); of persons, id.*hom.32.5 in Mt*.(7.372A); id.*hom.1.2 in 1Cor*. (10.6A).

ἐπεργάζομαι, 1. *work upon*, Ath.*Ar*.1.24(M.26.61A); Gr.Nyss. *hom.opif*.30.30(M.44.253C); Chrys.ap.*cat.Mt*.25:24(p.209.17) for ἐργασώμεθα id.*hom.78.3 in Mt*.(7.754D); **2.** *work out in detail*, *Symb.Ant*.(345)10(p.254.8; M.26.733C); c. πῶς, Epiph.*haer*.29.8 (p.331.15; M.41.404B); **3.** *do in addition*, Philost.*h.e*.3.22(M.65.512A).

***ἐπεργασία, ἡ,** *making, manufacture*, Gr.Nyss.*hom.2 in Eccl*.(M.44.640C).

***ἐπέργιον, τό,** *additional work*, *Const.App*.2.60.6; *ib*.2.63.1.

ἐπεργός, ὁ, *one who works upon, perfecter*, †Nil.*vit*.2(M.79.1141C).

ἐπερείδ-ω, 1. act., *press upon, against*, Clem.*str*.8.9(p.98.20; M.9.596C); *make to lean upon*, met. τὸ νόημα ἐ. τῇ Χριστοῦ δυνάμει id.*fr*.44(p.222.15); **2.** med. or pass.; **a.** *rest* or *lean upon*; met., *depend* or *rely upon*, id.*str*.8.8(p.94.15; M.9.589A); δωροδοκίᾳ τῶν δικαζόντων ἐ. Bas.*hom*.5.1(2.33D); Jo.D.*hom*.1.5(M.96.553B); esp. upon authorities for one's opinions, Ath.*v.Anton*.78(M.26.952B); id.*Ar*. 1.32(M.26.77B); τινὲς διὰ τοῦ ῥητοῦ [Jo.1:14] ~όμενοι Epiph.*anac*.77 (p.415.8; M.42.640B); οἱ…καθαροὶ…ταῖς λεγομέναις Πράξεσιν Ἀνδρέου τε καὶ Θωμᾶ τὸ πλεῖστον ~ονται id.*haer*.61.1(p.381.3; M.41.1040D); **b.** *cleave to* ἡ παρθένος…τῇ σωφροσύνῃ ~ομένη ἔφυγεν ‡Ath.*diab*.7 (p.8.19); Chrys.*a.exil*.1.4(3.418D) sens. dub., passage apptly. corrupt.

***ἐπερμηνεύω**, *expound*, Abr.Eph.*occurs*.3(p.450.23).

***ἐπερυθριάω**, *blush at, be ashamed of*, c. dat., Gr.Nyss.*Eun*.1(1 p.55.15; M.45.284B); id.*Apoll*.22(M.45.1168B); ἐ. … τῷ σταυρῷ Cyr. *Nest*.5 proem.(p.91.17; 6^1.119C); abs., id.*ador*.6(1.209D).

ἐπέρχ-ομαι, 1. *come upon* τὸ ἐπελθὸν τῇ παρθένῳ πνεῦμα Eus.*e.th*. 2.1(p.99.24; M.24.900B); in punishment ὀργὴν ~ομένην ἐπὶ σέ Ath. *v.Anton*.86(M.26.964A); of passions ἐὰν δὲ ὀξυχολία τις ἐπέλθῃ, εὐθὺς τὸ πνεῦμα τὸ ἅγιον…στενοχωρεῖται Herm.*mand*.5.1.3; μή ποτε ἡμᾶς…δόξῃς ἐπέλθῃ πόθος, ὅσος αὐτοῦ τοῦ τῆς ἀληθείας λόγου Clem. *prot*.12(p.85.26; M.8.244A); **2.** *attack*, abs. τὸ σκότος ἐπελθὸν ἐκ τῶν ὁρίων αὐτοῦ προσεμαχήσατο τῷ φωτί Hegem.*Arch*.7(p.10.3; M.10. 1437A); c. acc., Meth.*fr.24 in Job*(p.518.13); τοὺς εἰς τὰς ἐκκλησίας αὐτῶν ἐπελθόντας CSard.*ep.cath*.ap.Ath.*apol.sec*.49(p.123.4; M.25. 336A); Ath.*apol.Const*.27(M.26.629C); id.*h.Ar*.55(p.214.29; M.26. 760C); **3.** *put oneself forward* ὁ κατὰ θεὸν πολιτευόμενος ἐὰν πᾶσαν ἀρετὴν κατορθώσῃ, οὐ φυσιοῦται, οὐκ ~εται Ephr.1.316F; **4.** *come after* Ἰωάννης μὲν προελήλυθε…Χριστὸς…ἐπελθὼν ἔπαυσέ τε αὐτὸν τοῦ προφητεύειν Just.*dial*.31.2(M.6.583D); *come in succession*, id.*2apol*.2. 20(M.6.448A); Ath.*inc*.54.4(M.25.192C); τὰ νοήματα ~όμενα id.*Ar*.2. 36(M.26.224C); **5.** *go through, traverse*, fig. ἡ ψυχὴ…τῷ πλάτει τῆς οἰκουμένης ~ομένη Gr.Nyss.*or.catech*.10(p.55.5; M.45.41C); met., *examine*, c. dat., id.*Pss.titt*.B 14(M.44.573B); **6.** *practise* ἀρκεῖ… ταύτην τὴν ἀρετὴν ἐπελθόντα μόνον μηδὲν ἔλαττον ἐκείνων ἔχειν Chrys. *hom.46.4 in Mt*.(7.486C); πᾶσαν ἐ. κακίαν id.*hom.2.6 in Rom*.(9. 445B); *ib.19.1*(643E).

ἐπερωτάω, 1. *ask a question*; pass. ptcpl. neut., *question*, *Ep. Lugd*.ap.Eus.*h.e*.5.1.20(M.20.416C); Meth.*symp*.10.1(p.121.20; M.18. 192C); **2.** *ask, demand*, ref. Ps.136:3f. ἐπηρωτῆσθαι πρὸς τῶν αἰχμαλωτιστῶν…τὴν ᾠδὴν ἐπὶ γῆς ἀλλοτρίας ᾆσαι κυρίου *ib*.4.4(p.49. 24; 92B); **3.** in law, *stipulate*, Phot.*nomoc*.13.4(M.104.909D,912A).

ἐπερώτημα, τό, 1. *inquiry*, Herm.*mand*.11.2; **2.** *pledge* given in response to a formal demand, ref. 1 Petr.3:21 τί τὸ ἐκ συνειδήσεως ἀγαθῆς ἐ.; τῆς εἰς Χριστὸν πίστεως ὁμολογία Cyr.*hom. pasch*.30.3(5^2.346D).

***ἐπερωτηματικῶς**, *in the form of a question*, Diod.ap.*cat.Rom*. 7:18(p.109.7); Cyr.H.*catech*.13.19.

ἐπερώτησις, ἡ, 1. *questioning, interrogation*; κατ' ἐπερώτησιν *interrogatively*, Cyr.*Os*.155(3.188A); **2.** Lat. *stipulatio*, Phot.*nomoc*. 13.4(M.104.909D).

***ἐπερωτητέον**, *one must further ask*, Gel.Cyz.*h.e*.2.16.1(M.85. 1260C).

ἐπεσθίω, *eat at* or *with*, Gr.Nyss.*v.Mos*.(M.44.364B).

ἐπεσκεμμένως, *carefully*, Gr.Nyss.*Eun*.10(2 p.234.21, v.l. -ος M. 45.836C); ἐ. ἔχω *be accurate, correct*, Gr.Naz.*or*.6.1(M.35.721B).

***ἐπεσκιασμένως, 1.** *obscurely, in parables* ταῦτ' οὐκέτ' ἐ. ἀλλ' ἄντικρυς ἤδη γυμνῇ τῇ κεφαλῇ μεταπεφρασμένα Eus.*p.e*.11.19(540D; M.21.900B); id.*theoph.fr*.6(p.24*.23; M.24.633C); Chrys.*hom.1.2 in 1Thess*.(11.427F); Cyr.*Jo*.5.5(4.534E); **2.** *secretly*, Marc.Er.*opusc*.7.14 (M.65.1092A).

***ἐπέτος**, = ἐπ' ἔτος, *every year*, Petr.I Al.*ep.can*.2(M.18.516A).

ἐπευδοκέω, *approve*, Niceph.Ur.*v.Sym*.156(M.86.3132C).

ἐπευκτός, *blessed*, *Pss.Sal*.8.18.

ἐπευνάζ-ω, *rest upon*; τὰ ~όμενα *resting places*, ‡Caes.Naz.*dial*.92 (M.38.956).

***ἐπευρύνομαι**, *extend*, Cyr.*Ps*.61:9(M.69.1117C); met., *be puffed up*, id.*Is*.1.3(2.67D).

ἐπευφημ-έω, 1. *assent* ὁ προεστὼς…εὐχαριστίας…ἀναπέμπει, καὶ ὁ λαὸς ~εῖ λέγων τὸ 'ἀμήν' Just.*1apol*.67.5(M.6.429C); *ib*.65.3,5(428B); **2.** *applaud* ὁρᾷ ἐν ἀποκαλύψει…τάγματα…ἀγγέλων…τινι κινήσει χειρῶν ἐξαισίᾳ οἷον ~οῦντα Niceph.Ur.*v.Sym*.156(M.86.3132C).

***ἐπευφημίζω**, s.v.l., *call after an honourable name* τοῦ Χριστοῦ ἑαυτοὺς ἐπευφήμιζον Chrys.ap.*cat.1Cor*.1:12(p.16.9), cf. ὅτι τὸν Χριστὸν ἑαυτοῖς ἐπεφήμιζον Chrys.*hom.3.2 in 1Cor*.(10.16E).

***ἐπευφραίνω**, *rejoice in* ἐπὶ τούτοις…ἐ. ‡Jo.D.*Artem*.59(M.96. 1308A); usu. med., Cyr.H.*catech*.13.23; Gr.Nyss.*ordin*.(M.46.544B); abs., Bas.*ep*.15(3.94E; M.32.280A); Gr.Nyss.*Eun*.12(1 p.259.4; M.45. 961C); *Hymn*.(*AS* 1 p.660).

***ἐπευχαριστέω**, *give thanks* ἐπευχαριστήσας τῷ θεῷ ἐπὶ τῷ εὐφρανθῆναι *Hom.Clem*.10.26.

***ἐπεύχη, ἡ**, = ἐπεύχιον, *kneeler*, *Euchol*.(p.655).

ἐπεύχ-ομαι, A. *pray*; **1.** trans.; **a.** *invoke* something *upon* another; usu. blessings, Hipp.*fr.49 in Gen*.(p.70.1); Eus.*v.C*.4.63 (p.144.2; M.20.1220A); ἐ. τοῖς πεπιστευκόσι τὴν εἰς τὸ τέλειον αὔξησιν Gr.Nyss.*v.Gr.Thaum*.(M.46.953D); Euthal.Diac.*epp.cath*.(M.85. 689B); *Const.App*.2.54.2; Chrys.*hom.30.4 in 1Cor*.(10.274E); also of invoking destruction upon evil thoughts, †Nil.*mal.cog*.2.3(M.79. 1225D); **b.** *pray for* a thing τὸ περιττὸν οὐκ ἐ. Chrys.*hom.19.3 in 2Cor*.(10.574B); a person, *A.Phil*.32(p.16.29); **c.** *pray over* a person, Eus.*h.e*.3.39.10(M.20.297D); **d.** *offer* prayer, *say in prayer* ταῦτα ἐ. *Lit*.ap.*Const.App*.8.5.8; Dion.Ar.*e.h*.7.3.6(M.3.562C); **e.** *pray to*, Thdt.*Ps*.53:6(1.956); **2.** c. dat., *pray for* another, Or.*Cels*.7.7 (p.159.25; M.11.1432B); *A.Phil*.28(p.15.17); κλάσας τὸν ἄρτον ἐπέδωκεν πᾶσιν ἡμῖν, ἑκάστῳ τῶν ἀδελφῶν ~όμενος ἄξιον ἔσεσθαι αὐτὸν τῆς τοῦ κυρίου χάριτος *A.Jo*.110(p.208.12); Chrys.*hom.18.3 in 2Cor*.(10.568D); **3.** *pray over* a meal, *say grace* οὐ γεύεταί τις, εἰ μὴ ἐπεύξεται εὐλογῶν ὁ ἱερεύς Hipp.*haer*.9.21(p.257.18; M.16.3398B); **4.** abs., Ath.*ep.Serap*. 1.7(M.26.548C); Chrys.*hom.32.2 in Rom*.(9.756A); perh. in sense *pray further, go on praying*, *Lit*.ap.*Const.App*.8.7.4; *ib*.8.9.7; *make request* ἐ. ὑπὲρ τῆς παραχωρήσεως…τῶν τόκων Jo.Mosch.*prat*.193 (M.87.3076B).

B. *exult*, abs. τὸν διάβολον καταργήσας εἰκότως ~όμενος εἴρηκεν [1Cor.15:55] Clem.*paed*.2.8(p.203.9; M.8.488A).

ἐπέχ-ω, 1. *hold out*; met., *offer* βλασφημίας ‡Ath.*dial.Trin*.2.16 (M.28.1184A); **2.** *hold* ἡ τοῦ θεοῦ σοφία τὸ ὅλον ὡς λύραν ~ων Ath. *gent*.42(M.25.85A); *keep, maintain* ὁ τοῦ κόσμου ποιητὴς ἀνωτέρω τῶν γεγονότων ~ων αὐτὸν τῇ τούτων προνοίᾳ Athenag.*leg*.8.2(M.6.905A); **3.** *have also, sustain in addition*, Epiph.*haer*.76.31(p.380.33; M.42. 580B); **4.** *appoint, put in charge* τοὺς…ἐφισταμένους…καὶ ~ομένους ἐπιτρέπειν τοῖς ἔθνεσιν εἰς πόλεμον *ib*.51.34(p.310.1; M.41.952B); **5.** *hold in check, hinder*, Meth.*lepr*.7(p.40.4); εἴ τις ἐν πταίσματι ἐξετασθείς, ἐπεσχέθη τῆς λειτουργίας Bas.*ep*.188 *can*.1(3.269A; M.32. 665A); *ib*.217 *can*.70(3.327E; M.32.665A) = CCP(381)†*can*.15; *stop, conclude* ἐ. τὸν λόγον Meth.*symp*.8.17(p.111.8; M.18.173B); *keep a check on*, c. dat., *Hom.Clem*.16.6; med., *be a hindrance* ἐπέσχετο τὸν ἄνδρα κακῶς τεθνάναι *A.Jo*.81(p.191.10); abs., *refrain*; ptcpl. pres., *in silence*, Eus.*l.C*.16(p.250.3; M.20.1425B); **6.** *occupy*; met., *assume, possess*, *A.Jo*.39(p.170.7); τὴν σκηνὴν…τύπον ~ουσαν τοῦ κόσμου παντός Thdt.*Heb*.9:1(3.597); id.*Ezech*.3:17(2.704); **7.** *predominate, have power* τοῦ ~οντος ἄρχοντος Athenag.*leg*.25.4(M.6.949C); c. infin., *be strong enough* πρὸς τὴν μόρφωσιν ἀναδραμεῖν καὶ τὸν φωτισμὸν ἐπίσχωσιν τοῦ λόγου Meth.*Porph*.1(p.504.8; M.18.400A).

[*]**ἐπεωρέω**, = ἐπαιωρέω (*LS*), *A.Andr.fr*.18(p.45.31).

ἐπήβολος, 1. *acquainted with* ἄνθρωπον ἑαυτόν τε γινώσκειν…καὶ τοῦ θεοῦ ἐ. καθίστασθαι Clem.*str*.3.5(p.216.22; M.8.1148B); hence, as subst., *student of* ἐ. ἀκριβὴς τῶν…γραφῶν Soz.*h.e*.3.14.26(M.67. 1077A); abs., *complete, having attained* ἐ. … πίστεως Clem.*str*.6.9 (p.470.6; M.9.297B); **2.** *befitting, worthy* πρόφασιν…ἐ. [i.e. of death] Nonn.*par.Jo*.18:38(M.43.897A).

[*]**ἐπηβόλως**, *shrewdly*, Thdt.*affect*.3(p.72.16, v.l. εὐεπιβόλως 4.763).

ἐπηγορία, ἡ, *appellative, name* τῆς σωτηρίου ἐ. Eus.*v.C*.1.31(p.22. 2; M.20.945A); τὸν ἕνα θεὸν συκοφαντοῦντες διτταῖς ἐ. id.*e.th*.1.4(p.64. 14; M.24.833A); *ib*.1.20(p.82.8; 868B); *appellation, calling* τινες…τὴν οὐσίαν ὁμοῦ τῇ τῶν ὀνομάτων ἐ. πάθος διαιρέσεως ὑπομένειν δοξάζοντες †Gr.Thaum.*ep.Philagr*.(M.46.1104A).

ἐπήκοος, *hearing*; as a place name, tr. Hebr. מָעוֹן (as though מַעֲנֶה) ὁ Ἀκύλας ἡρμήνευσεν…τὸ ἐν τῇ ἐρήμῳ τῇ ἐπηκόῳ, ἐν τοῖς ὁμαλοῖς Thdt.*qu.55 in 1Reg*.23:24(1.391).

***ἐπηκόως**, *so as to be heard* ἐ. εὔχεσθε· εὐχαὶ δὲ ἐπήκοοι γίνονται ταῖς εὐπραγίαις *Clem.ep*.14(M.2.49B).

ἐπηλλαγμένως, *interchangeably, alternately*, Max.*ambig*.(M.91. 1269C).

ἐπηλυγάζω, *obscure*, Dion.Al.ap.Eus.*h.e*.7.23.2(M.20.692B); abs., *cast a shade*, id.ap.eund.*p.e*.14.25(777A; M.21.1277C); met., med., *conceal, obscure*, Synes.*ep*.154(M.66.1556D); ‡Jo.D.*Artem*.3(p.153. 16; M.96.1256A).

ἔπηλυς, *strange, foreign*; fig., of cosmetics, Clem.*paed*.3.11(p.273. 2; M.8.641A).

ἐπηλυσίη, ἡ, *entrance*, Nonn.*par.Jo*.10:1(M.43.832B).

ἐπηλύτης, ὁ, *foreigner*, Cyr.*Os.*110(3.142C, v.l. ἐπήλυδες).

ἐπημάτιος, *ephemeral*, Eudoc.*Cypr.*2.420(M.85.861B).

ἐπηρεάζ-ω, 1. *abuse, misuse* τὴν μέθοδον ᾗ οἱ χρώμενοι φρεναπατοῦσιν ἑαυτούς, ~οντες τὰς γραφάς Iren.*haer.*1.9.1(M.7.537A); *insult, blaspheme against*, Hipp.*haer.*5.13(p.105.25; M.16.3152A); **2.** *cast in one's teeth* τοὺς ~οντας ἡμῶν τὸ τρίθεον Evagr.Pont.*ep.*2(M.32.248C); Gr.Naz.*or.*22.11(M.35.1144A); **3.** *injure*; pass., *come off worse, have the worst of it*, Chrys.*sac.*4.7(p.121.5; 1.412C); id.*Stag.*1.4(1.163A); id.*Laz.*3.8(1.748A); *be vexed, take it hardly*, id.*oppugn.*2.9(1.72E); id. *hom.10.2 in Ac.*(9.83C).

ἐπηρεαστής, ὁ, *one who insults, calumniator* τοῖς ἐ. θεότητος Gr.Naz.*or.*42.17(M.36.477C); Max.*ambig.*(M.91.1325C); abs., Gr.Nyss.*Eun.*11(2 p.251.7; M.45.857A).

ἐπηρεαστικός, 1. *insolent*; neut. as subst., *insolent behaviour*, Chrys.*hom.4.5 in 2Cor.*(10.462C); **2.** in controversy, *perverse, captious* ἐ. ἐρώτησις Bas.*ep.*234.1(3.357B; M.32.868C).

ἐπηρεαστικῶς, *perversely, captiously*, Bas.*hom.*24.7(2.196B; M.31.616B); Gr.Nyss.*Eun.*4(2 p.57.14; M.45.628C); *ib.*6(2 p.134.5; 717C); comp., *ib.*12(1 p.384.28; 1113B).

ἐπήρεια, ἡ, 1. *abuse, ill-treatment* τὴν πᾶσαν ἐ. τοῦ ἄρχοντος τοῦ αἰῶνος τούτου Ign.*Magn.*1.3; ἔργον τῶν μεγίστων...βασιλέων ἀποσκευάσαι ἡμῶν νόμῳ τὴν ἐ. Athenag.*leg.*2.1(M.6.893C); c. genit. subjective or objective αἱ τῶν ἀδικούντων ἐ. Chrys.*sac.*3.17(p.90.16; 1.399A); Isid.Pel.*epp.*1.149(M.78.284A); ἐ. τῆς χήρας Chrys.*hom.in 1Tim.5:9*(3.311B); ἐ. τῶν πενήτων Thdr.Mops.*Abac.*proem.(M.66.425C); physical *injury*, Gr.Nyss.*beat.*3(M.44.1220D,1224D); *Lit.*ap.*Const.App.*8.11.2; ὀφθαλμῶν ἐ. Cyr.*Os.*37(3.68E); *wrong*, of marital infidelity πολλὴ ἀνάγκη θατέρῳ τῷ μέρει γενέσθαι τὴν ἐ. Chrys.*virg.*32(1.291D); *damage* to property, Ath.Scholast.*coll.*4.2(p.53); **2.** *attack, assault*, Eus.*v.C.*1.51(p.31.24; M.20.965B); Gr.Nyss.*v.Ephr.*(M.46.849B); τὰς παρὰ τῆς λεγομένης τύχης ἐ. Bas.*ep.*1(3.69A; M.32.220A); *Can.App.*21; ὁ πνευματικὸς πλοῦτος...πάσης ἐ. ἐστὶν ἀνώτερος Chrys.*paralyt.*1(3.33A); esp. demonic, Bas.*hom.*2.2(2.11B; M.31.185C); *Lit.*ap.*Const.App.*8.9.2; Chrys.*hom.7.6 in 2Cor.*(10.488C); id.*res.Chr.*2(2.439B); Cyr.*Am.*74(3.335C); **3.** in argument, *captiousness, cavilling* εἰ...τις ἐριστικῶς καὶ πρὸς ἐπήρειαν ἀκούοι τοῦ λόγου Gr.Nyss.*diff.ess.*4(M.32.333A); id.*anim.et res.*(M.46.57C); *misuse* of terms, misrepresentation ἵνα σπαράξῃ τοὺς ὑγιαίνοντας λόγους ταῖς ἐ. Gr.Naz.*or.*28.2(p.23.5; M.36.28B); **4.** *indignation* ἐβούλετο μέν τι καὶ εἰπεῖν, ὑπὸ δὲ τῆς ἐ. κατεχόμενος Chrys.*sac.*1.3(p.11.12, v.l. ἀπορίας 1.365D).

ἐπηρεμέω, 1. *rest*, Gr.Nyss.*Pss.titt.*B 10(M.44.537D); **2.** *remain unmoved* by, c. dat., Clem.*paed.*3.8(p.262.8; M.8.616A).

ἐπηρέμησις, ἡ, *pause*, Bas.*Spir.*35(p.74.11; 3.29A); Gr.Nyss.*Pss.titt.*B 10(M.44.536B); cf.Isid.Pel.*epp.*3.144(M.78.840B).

***ἐπηρμένως, 1.** *with exaltation*, Didym.*Ps.*9:2–5(M.39.1189A); **2.** *proudly*, ‡Chrys.*ascet.facet.*(1.811A).

ἐπηχέω, *resound*; trans., *make to sound*, Clem.*prot.*2(p.18.4; M.8.89C).

ἐπί, I. c. genit.;

A. of place; **1.** *in* or *on*; **a.** lit. παίζουσιν ὡς ἐπὶ σκηνῆς Ath.*v.Anton.*28(M.26.888A); πετεινὸν...ὁλόκληρον ἄρτον ἔχον ἐ. τοῦ στόματος Hier.*v.Paul.*B(p.21.16); ἐ. τῶν χειρῶν λαβέτω Mac.Mgn.*apocr.*2.7(p.4.3); **b.** met. ὁ μὲν [sc. νοῦς] ἐν τῇ καρδίᾳ, ὁ δὲ [sc. λόγος] ἐ. τῆς γλώττης καὶ τοῦ στόματος Dion.Al.ap.Ath.*Dion.*23(p.62.15; M.25.513C); ἵνα ἐ. εἰκόνος αὐτὸ θεωρήσωμεν Ath.*gent.*31(M.25.61D); Gel.Cyz.*h.e.*1 proem.3(M.85.1193A); **2.** ἐφ' ἑαυτοῦ *by oneself*, of celibacy ἐφ' ἑαυτοῦ μείνας ὁ νεανίσκος Just.*1apol.*29.3(M.6.373A); δόξαν αὐτῷ οὐράνιον περιποιεῖ ⟨ὁ⟩ μείνας ἐφ' ἑαυτοῦ Clem.*str.*3.12(p.234.1; M.8.1184A); εἰ...μείνῃ ἐφ' ἑαυτῆς δῶρον ἔχουσα χηρείας, μακαρία εὑρεθήσεται *Const.App.*3.1.4; met., *in itself* οὐδὲν ὄνομα ἐφ' ἑαυτοῦ καὶ δι' αὐτοῦ οὐ πονηρὸν οὐδὲ χρηστὸν νομίζεται Athenag.*leg.*2.2(M.6.893C); **3.** *upon*, with sense of motion βάλλεται ἐ. τῆς κεφαλῆς ἔλαιον ἐξωρκισμένον Hegem.*Arch.*11(p.19.6; M.10.1445B).

B. of time, *at* or *on*, Chrys.*sac.*4.2(p.107.25; 1.407A); ἐ. τῆς ἕκτης συμπεπλήρωκε πάντα Thdr.Mops.*fr.Gen.*2:2(M.66.636C); ἐφ' ἑκάστης [sc. ἡμέρας] *daily*, Didym.*Trin.*3.1(M.39.780D); Mac.Mgn.*apocr.*3.12(p.82.7); Evagr.*h.e.*4.4(p.154.24; M.86.2708A).

C. of relation; **1.** *in dependence on*, Didym.*Trin.*3.20(M.39.893C); **2.** *for, over, on account of* διὰ τί οὕτως...ἐ. τοῦ κυρίου οὐκ ἐφοβήθης, ἐ. τοῦ κυρίου οὐκ ἐκώκυκας; Mel.*pass.*99 p.16.33; *ib.*27 p.5.3; Clem.*prot.*1(p.7.1; M.8.60C); ἐ. τοῦ ἑαυτοῦ παιδὸς λέγοντα 'ὤμοι ἐγών' ‡Just.*coh.Gr.*2(M.6.244B); Thdt.*Ezech.*20:9(2.823); **3.** *with reference to* πολλὰ...ἔπραξαν...φρικωδέστατα..., πα[τὴρ ἐ. π]αιδός, υἱὸς ἐ. μητρός, καὶ ἀδελφὸ[ς ἐ. ἀ]δελφῆς, καὶ ἄρρην ἐ. ἄρρενος Mel.*pass.*53 p.9.4; Ath.*Ar.*3.60(M.26.449A); ‡Ath.*Ar.*4.24(p.71.18; M.26.504C); μὴ δεῖν ἐ. τῆς ἁγίας τριάδος νοεῖν διαφορεῖν Gel.Cyz.*h.e.*2.22.6(M.85.1292B); *ib.*2.16.3(1260D); hence apply *to*, predicate *of* οὐκ ἐ. ἀφρόνων τάττεται τὸ νήπιον Clem.*paed.*1.5(p.101.6; M.8.272A); Or.*Jo.*1.38(42; p.49.15; M.14.100B); Ath.*Ar.*1.62(M.26.141A); ἐ. δὲ τῆς ἁγίας τριάδος τρεῖς νοοῦμεν τὰς ὑποστάσεις Thdt.*qu.20 in Gen.*(1.28); cf. κοινόν ἐστιν ἐ. τῆς τῶν στοιχείων φύσεως τὸ ὑλῶδες Gr.Nyss.*anim.et res.*(M.46.33C); **4.** *according to* ὅσα...ἐ. Σαβελλίου ἄτοπα ἀπαντᾷ ‡Ath.*Ar.*4.25(p.73.10; M.26.508A); *ib.*4.3(p.46.22; 472A); *after the manner of* ἐ. τῆς σοφωτάτης μελίσσης τὰ ψυχωφελῆ τῶν πατέρων ἀρυσάμενος κατορθώματα Jo.Mosch.*prat.*proem.(M.87.2852C); **5.** adv. phrases ἐπὶ λέξεως *word for word*, Gr.Nyss.*Eun.*1(1 p.28.8; M.45.256C); Didym.*Trin.*1.26(M.39.389C); Evagr.*h.e.*1.7(p.13.9; M.86.2436B); ἐ. ῥήματος *ib.*1.6(p.10.34; 2432C); ἐ. χάριτος *graciously*, Thdt.*h.rel.*26(p.16.27; 3.1281).

II. c. dat.;

A. *at*, CAlex.*ep.*ap.Ath.*apol.sec.*4(p.90.38; M.25.256B); ἐ. τέλει Hegem.*Arch.*13(p.21.4; M.10.1448B).

B. *in* εἰπὼν...ἐφ' ἡμετέραις ἀκοαῖς Eus.*v.C.*4.24(p.126.9; M.20.1172A); ἐπ' ὄψει πάντων Ath.*inc.*22.5(M.25.136B); *ib.*23.2(136D); ἐφ' ἡμῖν *in our presence*, id.*Ar.*2.16(M.26.180B); τὸ ἀλληλούϊα...'αἰνεῖτε τὸν κύριον' ἐ. τῇ Ἑλλάδι φωνῇ Thdt.*Ps.*110:1(1.1399); met., *based upon* ἐπ' ἄλλαις ἱστορίαις τὴν ἔκδοσιν νῦν ποιησόμεθα Gel.Cyz.*h.e.*2.17.4(M.85.1265C); *in the name of* δύο ἢ τρεῖς συνηγμένοι...ἐ. τῷ ὀνόματι τοῦ κυρίου CAlex.*ep.*ap.Ath.*apol.sec.*6(p.93.9; M.25.260C); Cosm.Ind.*top.*3(M.88.140A).

C. *to* ὁρᾶν ἐπ' αὐτῷ Eus.*v.C.*2.16(p.47.24; M.20.993B); διδάσκων...ἐ. τίσιν ἀπελευσόμεθα Chrys.*hom.15.5 in 2Cor.*(10.550C); ἐ. τούτοις ὑπογράφειν Ath.*h.Ar.*54(p.214.8; M.25.760A); τί...γέγονεν ἐπ' αὐτῷ; Evagr.*h.e.*1.7(p.12.14; M.86.2436A); *ib.*1.10(p.18.13; 2449A).

D. *against* τῶν λαῶν...συναχθέντων ἐ. τῇ τοιαύτῃ καινοτομίᾳ Ath.*ep.encycl.*3(p.171.25; M.25.228B).

E. of time; **1.** *for, during* ἐ. τῇ ἀπουσίᾳ τοῦ ἐπισκόπου CSard.*ep.Alex.*ap.Ath.*apol.sec.*37(p.116.18; M.25.313B); Chrys.*hom.3.1 in Eph.*(11.17A); id.*anom.*12.2(1.550E); Thdt.*Ps.*135:16(1.1523); εὐλόγησεν τὴν Μαρίαν ἐ. τρισὶν ὥραις Jo.Thess.*dorm.BMV* 8.13(p.430.12); **2.** *in* the time of τὴν σταυρωθέντα...ἐ. χρόνοις Τιβερίου Καίσαρος Just.*1apol.*13.3(M.6.348A); τὸ γενόμενον ἐφ' ἡμῖν Ath.*ep.Aeg.Lib.*21(M.25.588B).

F. *according to* εἰ κοινὴν...ἐπ' εὐχαῖς ταῖς ἐμαῖς ὁμόνοιαν καταστήσαιμι Eus.*v.C.*2.65(p.67.15; M.20.1037C); Ath.*gent.*11(M.25.24D); ἐ. μάρτυρι τῇ ἀληθείᾳ id.*fug.*24(p.84.25; M.25.676B); Evagr.*h.e.*2.1(p.38.6; M.86.2489A).

G. *causal*: *because of* ἀποδυρόμενοι...ἐφ' οἷς πεισθέντες τῷ...κακοήθει θηρίῳ...τῆς ἐκκλησίας ἀπελείφθησαν Corn.ap.Eus.*h.e.*6.43.6(M.20.617C); *Lit.*ap.*Const.App.*8.12.38; Socr.*h.e.*3.1.44,45(M.67.376B,C); *on the basis of* ἐ. τούτοις ἀρκεσθήσομαι Hegem.*Arch.*5(p.7.14; M.10.1436B).

H. ἐφ' ᾧ *with a view to* τὴν πρὸς ἐκείνους ὑποκρινόμενος ὁμοδοξίαν ἐφ' ᾧ τοὺς περὶ βασίλειον ἀντιλυπῆσαι Philost.*h.e.*4.12(M.65.525B); *ib.*4.1(516C).

I. *in respect of* ἐ. ὀρθοδοξίᾳ μαρτυρούμενον Jul.Papa *ep.Dian.*ap.Ath.*apol.sec.*32(p.111.1; M.25.301B).

III. c. acc.;

A. of place; **1.** *upon*; **a.** met. = *multiplied by* γενόμενος ὁ δύο ἐ. τὸν τρία πεποίηκεν τὸν ἕξ Or.*Jo.*28.1(p.389.5; M.14.680B); **b.** with verbs of rest τῆς θείας τραπέζης καὶ τοῦ ἐπ' αὐτὴν μυστηρίου Gel.Cyz.*h.e.*2.31.6(M.85.1317A); Evagr.*h.e.*1.13(p.22.27; M.86.2456C); εἶχεν...στέφανον...ἐ. τὴν κεφαλήν Leont.N.*v.Jo.Eleem.*8(p.15.18); *ib.*46(p.100.10); met. ἐπ' αὐτὴν τὴν ἀλήθειαν ἀναπαυομένη Clem.*prot.*9.(p.65.33; M.8.200C); hence creep *upon*, *ib.*11(p.78.27; 228C); ὁ ἐ. γαστέρα αὐτῷ βίος id.*paed.*3.7(p.258.8; M.8.608B); **2.** *to* τὸν ψαλμὸν οὐδ' ἐφ' ἕτερον ἢ ἐ. μόνον αὐτὸν [sc. τὸν σωτῆρα] ἀναφέρειν Eus.*d.e.*10.8(p.472.32; M.22.760D); *ib.*7.3(p.341.11; 556D); Hegem.*Arch.*5(p.7.2; M.10.1436A); ‡Ath.*Apoll.*1.15(M.26.1121A); **3.** *in* κρατοῦντες ἐ. χεῖρα τὰ...ὄργανα Eus.*Pss.*proem.(M.23.76B); of H. Ghost τὸ...εἰδὸς τὰ τοῦ θεοῦ καὶ ὃν ἐ. τὸν υἱόν, οἶδεν καὶ τὰ τοῦ υἱοῦ Didym.*Trin.*3.37(M.39.969B); believe *in*, Mel.*pass.*61 p.10.18; hope *in*, Hegem.*Arch.*12(p.20.17; M.10.1448B); Ath.*v.Anton.*8(M.26.856A); **4.** *at* table, Leont.N.*v.Jo.Eleem.*27(p.58.8); **5.** ἐ. πόδας *feet uppermost* ἐ. πόδας σταυροῦται Pall.*v.Chrys.*18(p.118.14; M.47.66).

B. of time; **1.** *after*, Jo.Mal.*chron.*18 p.482(M.97.697C); ἀπέθανον, ἓν ἐ. τὸ ἕν, τὰ τέσσαρα [sc. παιδία] Thphn.*chron.*p.58(M.108.200A); **2.** *on* ἐ. τὴν αὔριον Leont.N.*v.Jo.Eleem.*21(p.39.24).

C. of relation; **1.** *for, on account of* ἐ. τὴν τοῦ παιδὸς προθυμίαν *T.Sal.*1.2; Nil.*paraen.*38(M.79.1252D); **2.** *for, on behalf of* αὐτὸν ὁ πατριάρχης ἐπεκαλεῖτο ἐ. τοὺς ἐκγόνους Ath.*Ar.*3.13(M.26.349A);

3. *for the purpose of, with a view to*, Diod.*Ps.*67:4(M.33.1601D); ὁ ἐ. τὸ σῶσαι καλέσας Thdt.*1Thess.*5:24(3.525); **4.** *about, concerning* ἐπιστήμην ἐ. ἀγῶνας καὶ ἄθλους id.*provid.*9(4.639).

***ἐπιανακαινισθείς**, Clem.*str.*1.21(M.8.837B) f.l. for ἐπεὶ ἀνακαινισθεὶς (p.71.21).

***ἐπιαυγάζομαι**, = ἐπαυγάζω, *shine*, ‡Barth.Edess.*Muham.*(M.104.1456A).

***ἐπιβαβύζ-ω**, *bark near* τὸ κυνάριον...τῇ κέλλῃ τῆς ἡγουμένης ~ον Steph.Diac.*v.Steph.*(M.100.1093A).

ἐπιβαίν-ω, A. c. acc., *enter upon* τὸ τριακοστὸν δεύτερον ἔτος ~οντος τῆς βασιλείας τοῦ Κωνσταντίνου Philost.*h.e.*2.16(M.65.477B).

B. c. genit.; **1.** *go upon, set foot upon*; fig. γῆς ~ειν κεκώλυκεν αὐτήν [sc. τὴν θάλατταν] Clem.*prot.*1(p.6.2; M.8.57C); **2.** *enter* τοὺς πολεμίους πεζῇ τῆς πόλεως ἐπιβήσεσθαι Evagr.*h.e.*4.27(p.174.31; M.86.2748B); **3.** *be in, occupy* τοῦ βασιλικοῦ ἐ. ἄστεος Thphyl.*exc.Rom.*3(p.223.10; M.113.929C).

C. c. dat.; **1.** *enter*; **a.** ἐ. τοῖς ἱεροῖς Just.*1apol.*62.2(M.6.421C); Ath.*ep.Aeg.Lib.*9(M.25.557B); Chrys.*hom.*73.4 *in Mt.*(7.711C); ἐ. τῇ Κωνσταντινουπόλει Philost.*h.e.*8.8(M.65.564A); cf. ἐν Κωνσταντινουπόλει ἐ. *Chron.Pasch.*p.296(M.92.741B); **b.** *go up to, go to* ἐ. ἀλλοτρίᾳ κοίτῃ Clem.*str.*3.17(p.243.14; M.8.1205A); Chrys.*hom.*8.2 *in Mt.*(7.121C); **c.** *mount*, fig. μοχθηροὶ ἄνθρωποι ~οντες τῇ ἰδιωτείᾳ τῶν εὐεξαπατήτων ἄγουσιν αὐτοὺς ᾗ βούλονται Or.*Cels.*1.9(p.61.15; M.11.672A); **2.** *walk upon, walk in*, Meth.*res.*2.23(p.378.13; M.18.316B); Ath.*Ar.*2.80(M.26.316C); ἐ. τοῖς θείοις ἴχνεσι τοῦ ἀθλητῶν πρώτου Dion.Ar.*e.h.*2.3.6(M.3.404A); fig. μελλόντων ὑμῶν εὐαγγελίζεσθαι τὰ ἀγαθὰ καὶ καθαροῖς τοῖς ποσὶν ἐ. ταῖς τῶν ἀνθρώπων ψυχαῖς Or.*Jo.*32.8(6; p.438.4; M.14.761A); met., *insult, trample upon* ἐ. τῇ ἁπλότητι τῶν ἡμετέρων id.*comm.in Ex.*10:27(p.245.9; M.12.273D); Chrys.*hom.*48.4 *in Mt.*(7.498C); **3.** *stand upon* μὴ δύνασθαι ἐλευθέροις ~ειν τοῖς ποσίν Or.*Jo.*28.7(6; p.398.10; M.14.696B); met., *depend on* ὀνόματι μὲν πατρὸς καὶ υἱοῦ ἐπιβεβηκότας Clem.*str.*7.18(p.78.7; M.9.556B); Or.*hom.*12.5 *in Jer.*(p.91.20; M.13.385A); τῶν ὡς σαφεῖ τῇ λέξει ~όντων id.*comm.in Rom.*1:1(*JTS* 13 p.210); **4.** *come upon*, of Inc. ἐπιβὰς...τῇ ἡμετέρᾳ φύσει πάρεισιν εἰς ἀνθρώπους Eus.*d.e.*4.10(p.168.18; M.22.280D); ~οντος αὐτῷ [sc. τῷ σώματι] τοῦ λόγου Ath.*inc.*31.4(M.25.149D); τὴν νηδὺν ἐκείνην ᾗ ὁ πάντων δημιουργὸς ἐπέβη Chrys.*hom.*4.5 *in Mt.*(7.54C); **5.** *go above* or *beyond, transcend* ὁ λόγος...τοῖς γενομένοις ἐπιβέβηκεν Ath.*gent.*41(M.25.81C); ἐπέβη τοῖς ἀγγέλοις, ἀναβαίνων ὡς ἄνθρωπος id.*Ar.*3.48(M.26.425B); τῆς τοῖς χερουβὶμ ἐπιβεβηκυίας ὑπερενδόξου θεότητος Dion.Ar.*c.h.*8.2(M.3.241B); τὴν μίαν...τῆς πάντων εἰρήνης ἀρχὴν καὶ αἰτίαν, ἥτις, ἀμερῶς ἐπιβεβηκυῖα τοῖς ὅλοις...τὰ πάντα...ἀσφαλίζεται id.*d.n.*11.1(M.3.949A).

D. c. prep. or abs.; **1.** *go to, enter* ἐ. εἰς τὴν Ἱερουσαλὴμ Just.*dial.*16.2(M.6.509B); εἰς τὰ ἱερὰ ἐ. id.*1apol.*62.1(M.6.421B); Clem.*str.*5.4(p.339.1; M.9.37C); Meth.*res.*2.24(p.381.6; M.18.328C); **2.** *approach* μελλούσης ἐπιβήσεσθαι τῆς μεγάλης...ἑορτῆς Thphyl.*exc.gent.*15(p.488.8; M.113.952A); **3.** *enter upon* πάντες...εἰς αὐτὴν [sc. τὴν ὁδόν] ἐ. Ath.*gent.*30(M.25.60D); Dion.Ar.*e.h.*7.1.3(M.3.556B); **4.** *walk*, fig. διὰ πίστεως ἐ. Meth.*res.*2.16(p.365.10; M.18.312B) = περιπατοῦμεν 2Cor.5:7; met., *trample upon* οἱ ἰσοσθενεῖς οὐδέτερος πρὸς τὸν ἕτερον ἐπιβῆναι δύνανται Adam.*dial.*3.8(p.126.10; M.11.1800B); ἐ. κατ᾽ αὐτοῦ [sc. τοῦ θανάτου] Ath.*inc.*27.1(M.25.141C); **5.** *go* μέχρι τάφου καὶ ᾅδου ἐ. ‡Ath.*Apoll.*1.12(M.26.1113D); **6.** *attack*, Meth.*res.*2.3(p.334.12; M.41.1168A); id.*Porph.*11(p.507.11; M.18.345A); λογισμοῖς ἐ. Ath.*v.Anton.*6(M.26.849A); **7.** *descend upon*, *Pap.Chr.*(p.440); ~ων ὁ λόγος εἰς τὴν ἡμετέραν σάρκα Ath.*Ar.*2.76(M.26.309A).

ἐπιβάλλ-ω, 1. *throw* or *cast upon*, met. ὀφθαλμὸν εἰς αὐτὴν ἐ. Meth.*symp.*9.5(p.121.7; M.18.192A); ἐν τοῖς...μυστηρίοις τὸν τοῦ νοὸς αὐτῆς [sc. τῆς ψυχῆς] ἀσώματον ὀφθαλμὸν ἐ. Gr.Mag.*dial.*(tr.Zach.)4.26(M.*PL.*77.358D); *spread as a covering* τὰ χερουβὶμ τὰς πτέρυγας ἐ. ... ἐν φόβῳ Chrys.*Eutrop.*2.8(3.393E); **2.** *assign* a name, Clem.*ecl.*6(p.138.25; M.9.701A); med., *assign* one's property by will, Gr.Naz.*or.*7.20(M.35.781B); **3.** *impose*, Const.ap.Ath.*apol.sec.*60(p.140.18; M.26.357C); ἵνα λήθῃ τὴν ἰδίαν ~ων αἵρεσιν Ath.*Ar.*1.8(M.26.28A); ὁ τὴν ἀνάγκην ~ων αὐτῷ [sc. τῷ θεῷ] *ib.*3.62(453B); αὐτοῖς [sc. τοῖς θεοῖς] γλύφοντες ἐ. μορφὴν id.*gent.*19(M.25.40A); **4.** *apply* one's mind to, c. εἰς, Clem.*str.*5.14(p.417.31; M.9.200A); Eus.*p.e.*11.9(525B; M.21.872A); Dion.Ar.*d.n.*1.4(M.3.592D); abs., Clem.*str.*1.4(p.17.14; M.8.717A); hence *consider, treat* ποιηταὶ...καὶ φιλόσοφοι...ἐ. στοχαστικῶς Athenag.*leg.*7.1(p.8.9; M.6.904B); Or.*exp.in Pr.*1:7(M.17.164A); ἐ. υἱῷ, τίς ἦν ὁ βασιλικός...ἐπώνυμος id.*Jo.*13.58(57; p.288.13; M.14.508B); id.*sel.in Ps.*4(p.238.16; M.12.1160A); Bas.*Eun.*2.13(1.248B; M.29.596C); †Bas.*Is.*237(1.559E; M.30.536A); *understand* in a certain way τοῖς προκειμένοις θεωρήμασιν ἐ. ἑτέρως Cyr.*ador.*7(1.223D); id.*Ps.*47:13(M.69.1065B); *undertake* ἐ. τὴν ζήτησιν ταύτην Adam.*dial.*5.16(p.202.34; M.11.1853B); **5.** *conjecture* ἐ. Γαΐον τοῦτον εἶναι Max.*schol.epp.Dion.Ar.*(M.4.528A); **6.** impers., *be proper, incumbent*; pres. ptcpl., *duty*, Clem.*str.*2.20(p.180.8; M.8.1068B) cit. s. ἀκροδίκαιος; Or.*Apoc.*30B(p.7); συμπληρώσας τὰ ~οντα Bas.*hom.in Ps.*1(1.93A; M.29.217A).

ἐπιβαπτίζ-ω, *sink, overwhelm*, fig. κύματά με...~οντα ὑπερσχεῖν Bas.*ep.*162(3.253C; M.32.633A).

ἐπιβαρέω, *weigh down*; of serpents, *drag down*, Dion.Ar.*ep.*8(M.3.1100B).

ἐπιβαρής, *burdensome*, c. dat., *T.Abr.*B 2(p.106.11); *ib.*4(p.108.13); c. genit., *ib.*11(p.116.5).

ἐπίβασις, ἡ, 1. *entering upon, entrance*; of Inc., Eus.*d.e.*6.13(p.263.17; M.22.433A); τῇ...τοῦ λόγου εἰς αὐτὸ [sc. τὸ σῶμα] ἐ. Ath.*inc.*20.4(M.25.132B); αὐτὸς ὑπὲρ πάντων πάσχων διὰ τὴν πρὸς αὐτὸ ἐ. *ib.*20.6(132C); of descent into hell, ‡Ath.*Apoll.*1.7(M.26.1105A); τοῦ μὲν τάφου σωματικὴν ἐπιδεχομένου τὴν ἐ.,...τοῦ δὲ ᾅδου ἀσώματον *ib.*1.13(1117A); of divine presence in soul οἱ τῆς θείας ἐ. ἄξιοι διὰ τὴν τῆς ψυχῆς καθαρότητα, ὧν ἐν ταῖς καρδίαις αἱ τοῦ θεοῦ ἀναβάσεις Thdt.*Ezech.*28:16(2.916); id.*Ps.*67:18(1.1064); **2.** *attack*, Valent.Imp.*ep.episc.*ap.Thdt.*h.e.*4.8.3(3.957); Thphn.*chron.*p.424(M.108.1004B).

ἐπιβατεύ-ω, 1. *set foot upon*; *range over*, c. genit. ἡ ψυχὴ...μέχρις οὐρανῶν ἀνιοῦσα καὶ τῶν ἀβύσσων ~ουσα Gr.Nyss.*or.catech.*10(p.55.4; M.45.41C); id.*Eun.*1(1 p.63.17; M.45.292C); c. dat. τὸ θεῖον τῆς σοφίας πνεῦμα...τοῖς οὐρανίοις ἐ. Eust.*fr.in Pr.*8:22(M.18.684A); met., *transcend* οὐσίᾳ ταῖς ὅλαις οὐσίαις ἀχράντως ἐ. Dion.Ar.*d.n.*2.10(M.3.648C); id.*myst.*1(M.3.1001A); **2.** *come upon, invade, occupy*, Clem.*exc.Thdot.*73(p.130.8; M.9.692D); of Inc. τῆς παρθενικῆς ἐ. μήτρας Eust.*fr.in Pr.*8:22(M.18.684A); c. dat., Athenag.*leg.*27.2(M.6.953A); **3.** *usurp* ἐ. τοῖς ὀνόμασιν *ib.*26.1(952A); *ib.*23.1(941B); **4.** *mount* a horse, fig. τῶν προκειμένων ἐ. καὶ κρατύνειν αὐτὰ πειρώμενοι Dion.Al.ap.Eus.*h.e.*7.24.8(M.20.696B); **5.** *be a passenger* on a ship; fig., of Satan τῇ ψυχῇ ὥσπερ ~ων Didym.*Trin.*1.2(M.39.372B).

ἐπιβατήρια, τά, 1. *words* or *ceremonies of welcome*, Gr.Naz.*ep.*195(M.37.317C); Jo.Mon.*hymn.Chrys.*5(M.96.1381A); fig. πικροῖς ἡμᾶς ἡ πόλις ἐ. ἐξένισεν Synes.*ep.*57(M.66.1392B); id.*calv.*7(p.204.5; M.66.1180C); **2.** *dedication* of a church, Socr.*h.e.*1.28.1(M.67.160A).

ἐπιβάτης, ὁ, 1. *passenger* on board ship; fig., of laity παρεικάσθω ὁ κυβερνήτης Χριστῷ,...οἱ ναῦται πρεσβυτέροις, τοῖς ἐ. τὸ τῶν ἀδελφῶν πλῆθος *Clem.ep.*14(M.2.49A); *ib.*15(49C); *Const.App.*2.57.2; any *one on board*, Chrys.*hom.*57.5 *in Mt.*(7.584A); id.*hom.*39.1 *in 1Cor.*(10.376E); **2.** *rider*, fig. τὸν ἐ. καθαραῖς φρεσὶν ἐποχούμενον Meth.*symp.*5.3(p.56.4; M.18.101A); ἡ ψυχὴ...ἡνιοχουμένη ὑπὸ τοῦ ἐ. Χριστοῦ Mac.Aeg.*hom.*23.2(M.34.661B); Gr.Naz.*or.*27.5(p.7.15; M.36.17A).

ἐπίβατος, *accessible*, met. μηδὲ ἐ. ... ταῖς ὑπὸ γαστρὶ ὀρέξεσιν Areth.*Apoc.*2(M.106.517C).

ἐπιβεβαιόω, *confirm further*; med., *assert further, add as further proof*, Epiph.*ep.Arab.*ap.*haer.*78.21(p.471.11; M.42.732D).

***ἐπιβελτιόω**, *make better*; pass., *Const.App.*2.39.6; Thphn.*chron.*p.111(M.108.317B).

ἐπιβήτωρ, ὁ, 1. *one who sets foot on*, Nonn.*par.Jo.*4:7(M.43.773C); **2.** *one who rules over*, *Orac.Sib.*3.168; **3.** *one who ascends*, Nonn.*par.Jo.*6:62(M.43.801B); **4.** as adj., *springing, leaping*, *ib.*21:11(817A).

ἐπιβιβάζω, *put upon* ἐ. τῷ θρόνῳ (i.e. a bishop) Philost.*h.e.*4.4(M.65.520A); *establish* ἐ. τῇ βασιλείᾳ *ib.*8.8(564B).

ἐπιβιόω, *live after, survive*, Eus.*h.e.*3.32.5(M.20.284A); Evagr.*h.e.*3.44(p.146.31; M.86.2700B); *ib.*3.41(p.141.16; 2685C).

ἐπιβλαβῶς, *hurtfully, with harmful consequences*, Or.*Jo.*32.5(p.433.22; M.14.753B); Bas.*reg.br.*159(2.468D; M.31.1185C); id.*hom.in Ps.*28(1.123C; M.29.304B).

***ἐπιβλεπτικός**, *able to see*, †Bas.*Is.*8(1.383E; M.30.132B).

ἐπιβλέπ-ω, 1. *look favourably*, Just.*dial.*19.3(M.6.516C); met., *consider, pay attention to* τῷ ~οντι τὴν σωτηρίαν Clem.*q.d.s.*42(p.191.7; M.9.652B); **2.** *supervise*, Phot.*nomoc.*11.3(M.104.845D).

***ἐπιβλεφαρίδιος**, *on the eyelids*, Synes.*calv.*7(p.204.11, v.l. ἐπιβλεφαρίδων; M.66.1180D).

ἐπίβλεψις, ἡ, *looking upon, visitation* ἡ ἐνανθρώπησις τοῦ λόγου νοοῖτ᾽ ἂν εἰκότως ἐπίσκεψις εἶναι τοῦ θεοῦ...ἤγουν ἐ. ἐνθάδε λεγομένη Cyr.*Ps.*32:13(M.69.877D).

ἐπίβλημα, τό, 1. *something thrown over, covering*; of an altar-cloth, Chrys.*hom.*50.4 *in Mt.*(7.518E); **2.** *something put on*; of grave clothes, *ib.*27.4(332B); met., ref. heret. notion of Christ's sonship, Cyr.*Chr.un.*(5^1.774D).

ἐπιβλητικός, *of* or *pertaining to* mental *application* κατὰ τὴν ἐ. δύναμιν ἐνεργεῖν Synes.*insomn.*10(p.164.16; M.66.1300B).

ἐπιβλύζω, *pour forth*; met., Gr.Naz.*carm*.1.2.8.31(M.37.651A).

ἐπιβοάω, **A.** act.; **1.** *utter sounds*, Hipp.*haer*.6.48(p.180.17; M.16.3275A); *say*, Clem.*str*.3.11(p.230.24; M.8.1177A); ἐ. ἅπαντες τὸ ἀμήν Chrys.*hom.2.7 in 2Cor*.(10.440D); **2.** *invoke* H. Ghost at baptism, Dion.Ar.*e.h*.2.2.7(M.3.396D); *ib*.6.3.2(533B); **3.** c. dat., *cry out against*, Clem.*str*.2.20(p.171.15; M.8.1049C); **4.** abs., *shout, cheer*, Chrys.*hom.11.3 in Col*.(11.409A).

B. med.; **1.** *say loudly, proclaim*, Clem.*str*.2.23(p.190.5; M.8.1089A); Bas.*Spir*.25(3.21C; M.32.112C); Gr.Nyss.*or.catech*.22(p.85.8; M.45.60D); **2.** *call to witness*, Clem.*str*.2.7(p.131.7; M.8.909B); *ib*.4.4(p.256.21; 1232A); **3.** *appeal to* ἐ. τὸν Καίσαρα Euthal.Diac.*epp.Paul*.(M.85.700B).

ἐπιβόησις, ἡ, *shouting against, hostile shouting*; plur., *Ep.Lugd*. ap.Eus.*h.e*.5.1.7(M.20.409B).

ἐπιβολή, ἡ, **1.** *casting* of lots, Just.*dial*.97.3(M.6.705A); **2.** *application* ταῖς τοῦ μύρου πανιέροις ἐ. Dion.Ar.*e.h*.2.2.7(M.3.396C); met. κατ' ἐπιβολὴν ὄψεως ὁρᾶν...τὰ ὁρατά Or.*fr.14 in Jo*.1:18(p.496.11); **3.** *apprehension* of sense of a passage; hence *reading, interpretation*, id.*hom.1.7 in Jer*.(p.6.9; M.13.261D); Bas.*Eun*.1.7(1.218E; M.32.525C); Max.*ambig*.(M.91.1297D); **4.** *darting forth* ταῖς τῶν ὑπερφανῶν ἀκτίνων ἀγνώστοις καὶ μακαρίαις ἐ. Dion.Ar.*d.n*.1.4(M.3.592C); *attack*, met. ὁ...Χριστὸς...ἀμυδρώσας τῶν ἡδονῶν τὰς ἐ. Meth.*Porph*.1(p.503.11; M.18.397D).

ἐπιβομβέω, *cry out, shout out*, Nonn.*par.Jo*.8:13(M.43.813B).

ἐπιβουλευτικῶς, *treacherously*, Or.*comm.in Mt*.14.6(p.286.33; M.13.1196A).

ἐπιβουλεύω, *plot against*; trans., Or.*adnot.in Dt*.14:19(M.17.25C); Ath.*h.Ar*.71(p.222.6; M.25.777C); Chrys.ap.*cat.Mt*.4:23(p.30.6) (Chrys.*hom.15.3 in Mt*.(7.181B) om.); med., Chrys.*hom.13.3 in Rom*.(9.561C); abs., id.*hom.34.1 in 1Cor*.(10.310D); *plot* to do something ἐ. ὑπὲρ τοῦ καταβαλεῖν πτωχόν Or.*or*.29.6(p.384.11; M.11.533C); pass., *be plotted against*, Eus.*h.e*.3.5.2(M.20.221C); ‡Bas.*Lac*.6(2.592B; M.31.1449B).

ἐπιβουλή, ἡ, **1.** *plot* τὰς εἰς ἀλλήλους τῶν ἀδελφῶν ἐ. Cels.ap.Or.*Cels*.5.59(p.63.12; M.11.1276B); c. objective genit., *Hom.Clem*.11.15; Thdt.*Ps*.118:10(1.1440); τὰς ἐκ τῶν ὁμοίων ἐ. *plots* hatched by one's equals, *Hom.Clem*.17.11; result of a plot, *injury*, Chrys.*hom.56.6 in Mt*.(7.574A); hence, gen., *harm, damage*, id.*hom.20.5 in 1Cor*.(10.176A); **2.** *attitude towards* οἱ ἐν τῇ πλάνῃ μένοντες...τῆς τούτων ἐ. δώσουσι δίκην id.*hom.34.4 in Mt*.(7.394A).

ἐπίβουλος, **1.** *insidious, harmful*, Clem.*paed*.2.3(p.178.13; M.8.433A); Thdt.*2Cor*.2:15(3.300); **2.** as subst., *enemy* τῶν ἐ. σωτηρίας Clem.*prot*.3(p.32.14; M.8.128A); Hipp.*haer*.9.22(p.258.2; M.16.3399A); *Const.App*.2.14.1; *ib*.6.14.4; of heretics ἐ. τῆς ἐκκλησίας *ib*.6.18.2; τῆς τριάδος ἐ. Evagr.*h.e*.3.44(p.146.20; M.86.2700A).

***ἐπιβραβεύω**, *grant*, †Jo.Jej.*poenit*.(M.88.1892A); †Jo.D.*B.J*.34(M.96.1185C); Areth.*Apoc*.6(M.106.544C).

ἐπιβραδύνω, *linger in*, Bas.*ep*.101(3.197C; M.32.508A); abs., Mac.Mgn.*apocr*.4.13(p.180.11).

***ἐπίβραχυς**, *shallow*, *Chron.Pasch*.p.394(M.92.1009C).

ἐπιβρέμω, *roar out, utter loudly*; c. cogn. acc., Nonn.*par.Jo*.19:6(M.43.897C).

ἐπιβρέχω, **1.** *water, moisten*, Evagr.*h.e*.4.7(p.157.8; M.86.2713B); **2.** met., *rain down, shed*, *ib*.2.6(p.53.31; 2516C).

ἐπιβρίθω, trans., *weigh down*, fig., Chrys.*sac*.1.1(p.3.12; 1.363A).

ἐπιβρύχω, *gnash* the teeth, Cyr.*Ps*.34:16(M.69.905B).

ἐπιγαμβρεία (-ία), ἡ, **1.** *connexion by marriage*, Clem.*str*.1.21(p.77.26; M.8.853A); Eus.*v.C*.1.49(p.30.25; M.20.964C); μηδέν σοι κοινὸν πρὸς αὐτοὺς...μὴ ἐπιγαμίαι, μὴ ἐπιγαμβρίαι Chrys.*dimiss.Chan*.7(3.438D); **2.** *marriage*, Cyr.S.*v.Sab*.2(p.88.4); **3.** *wife* αὐτῷ δοῦναι τὴν θυγατέρα ἐπιγαμβρίαν ‡Ath.*sem*.12(M.28.160B).

ἐπιγαμβρεύω, *give* a younger son *as a second husband* to a widowed daughter-in-law, ref. Gen.38:8, *T.Jud*.10.4.

ἐπιγαμέω, *marry a second time*, ref. Mc.10:11, Athenag.*leg*.33.2(M.6.968A); μοιχείαν ἡγεῖται τὸ ἐπιγῆμαι ζῶντος θατέρου τῶν κεχωρισμένων Clem.*str*.2.23(p.193.8; M.8.1096B).

ἐπιγαμία, ἡ, **1.** *connexion by marriage* οὐ δεῖ πρὸς πάντας αἱρετικοὺς ἐ. ποιεῖν CLaod.*c*.10.31; **2.** *marriage as well*, as an additional bond μὴ τὴν ἑτέρωθεν ὁμόνοιαν σφίγγεσθαι ταῖς ἐ.· μήτε ἔχειν τὴν αὐτὴν ἀδελφὴν καὶ γαμετήν Diod.*Gen*.5:4(M.33.1569D).

***ἐπιγαννύσκομαι**, *exult over, rejoice in*, c. dat., Zach.Mit.*opif*.(M.85.1036A).

ἐπιγάν(ν)υμαι, = foreg.; c. dat., Gr.Nyss.*beat*.3(M.44.1224B); Didym.*Trin*.3.3(M.39.812A); Cyr.*ador*.14(1.492C); c. ἐπί, id.*Is*.3.5(2.529B).

ἐπιγάστριος, *devoted to the belly*, Clem.*paed*.2.1(p.164.9; M.8.400C).

***ἐπιγαυρίασις**, ἡ, *arrogance*, *Cod.Afr*.79(Lat. *insultatio*).

***ἐπιγαυριάω**, *exult in*, †Bas.*Is*.284(1.595C; M.30.617B); abs., of God, Gr.Nyss.*Eun*.12(1 p.259.17; M.45.961D).

ἐπιγαυρ-όω, pass., *be a source of pride* πόλις...πᾶσιν ~ουμένη Bas.Sel.*v.Thecl*.2.13(M.85.588D).

ἐπίγειος, *of* or *on the earth, earthly*; τὸν ἐ. λέγει κόσμον· οὐ γὰρ νομιστέον τὰ ἀντικείμενα αὐτὸν λέγειν φάσκοντα [Jo.17:11b] Or.*comm.in Mt*.13.20(p.236.13; M.13.1152A); contrasted explicitly or implicitly with ἐπουράνιος: οὐ γὰρ ἐ. ... εὕρημα...οὐδὲ θνητὴν ἐπίνοιαν...οὐδὲ ἀνθρωπίνων οἰκονομίαν μυστηρίων *Diogn*.7.1; βίον ἕτερον βιώσεσθαι ἀμείνονα ἢ κατὰ τὸν ἐνθάδε καὶ ἐπουράνιον, οὐκ ἐ. Athenag.*leg*.31.3(M.6.961C); Tat.*orat*.32(p.33.3; M.6.872A); ἐν οὐρανοῖς ἐστιν αὐτὴ ἡ ἐπουράνιος εὐωχία, ἡ δὲ ἐ. δεῖπνον κέκληται Clem.*paed*.2.1(p.157.17; M.8.388A); id.*str*.3.6(p.222.4; M.8.1160B); εἰκὼν δὲ τῆς οὐρανίου ἐκκλησίας ἡ ἐ. *ib*.4.8(p.278.11; 1277B); ἐ. εἰκὼν θείας δυνάμεως ἡ γνωστικὴ ψυχή *ib*.7.11(p.46.18; M.9.489A); τὰ δοκοῦντα εἶναι τῆς ἐ. φιλοσοφίας δόγματα Hipp.*haer*.4.51(p.76.31; M.16.3122D); τὸ αὐτοῦ [sc. Κηρίνθου] δόγμα, ἐ. ἔσεσθαι τὴν τοῦ Χριστοῦ βασιλείαν Dion.Al.ap.Eus.*h.e*.7.25.3(M.20.697A); of persons οὐ στρατεύομαι ἐ. βασιλεῖ *M.Das*.7.2; ὁ ἐπίσκοπος...ὑμῶν ἐ. θεὸς μετὰ θεόν *Const.App*.2.26.4; contrasted with γήϊνος, ref. Jo.3:12 οὐκ εἶπεν ὁ Ἰησοῦς 'εἰ τὰ γήϊνα εἶπον ὑμῖν' ἀλλὰ 'τὰ ἐ.', ἐ. λέγων ἃ τοῖς ἐπὶ γῆς ἔτι διατρίβουσιν ἀνθρώποις δύναται ὑπάρξαι τε καὶ νοηθῆναι. οὐ γὰρ παρὰ τὴν ἑαυτῶν φύσιν ἐ. ἀλλ' ἐπουράνια ὄντα δωρεᾷ θεοῦ τοῖς ἀνθρώποις δέδοται Or.*fr.38 in Jo*.(p.514.13); as subst. ἀληθῶς ἐσταυρώθη καὶ ἀπέθανεν, βλεπόντων τῶν ἐπουρανίων καὶ ἐ. καὶ ὑποχθονίων Ign.*Trall*.9.1; τὰ ἐ. *worldly goods*, Clem.*paed*.3.6(p.256.14; M.8.604C); *worldly matters*, Or.*or*.8.1(p.316.27; M.11.441B).

***ἐπιγειόφρων**, *earthly-minded, worldly-wise*, ‡Jo.D.*ep.Thphl*.25(M.95.377C).

***ἐπιγέλαστος**, *ridiculous*, Gr.Nyss.*Eun*.12(1 p.286.1; M.45.1116A); id.*or.catech*.28(p.105.13; M.45.73A); id.*v.Gr.Thaum*.(M.46.936C).

***ἐπιγελάστως**, *ridiculously*, Gr.Nyss.*Eun*.4(2 p.69.23; M.45.641D).

ἐπιγελάω, *mock at*; c. genit., *A.Andr.et Mt*.26(p.103.16); *A.Phil*.40(p.19.1); c. ἐπί and dat., *M.Pion*.4.3; ptcpl. abs., *mocking*, Clem.*paed*.1.8(p.128.29; M.8.329B); ‡Jo.D.*Artem*.33(M.96.1281B); med., Clem.*prot*.2(p.12.19; M.8.73B).

***ἐπιγένειος**, *up to the chin*, Gr.Naz.*or*.5.38(M.35.713C); Cosm.Mel.*schol*.(M.38.538) in Gr.Naz.*carm*.2.2(epitaph.)40.3.

***ἐπιγενεσιουργός**, *creative*, Clem.*str*.5.6(p.351.16; M.9.64A).

ἐπιγένημα, τό, *something added*, *Hom.Clem*.9.15(*GCS* p.137.29, v.l. ἐπιγεννήματα M.2.252D); ἐξ ἐ. *additionally, adventitiously*, Or.*Cels*.6.44(p.114.19; M.11.1365B).

***ἐπιγενηματικός**, *adventitious*; neut. as subst., Gr.Nyss.*Apoll*.43(M.45.1228A); for τοῦτο ἐπὶ γενηματικὸν ἐπισυμβέβηκεν Proc.G.*Gen*.1:27(M.87.128D).

***ἐπιγενητός**, *added later, adventitious*; of aeon Thelema in Valent. system, Hipp.*haer*.6.38(p.170.5, v.l. ἐπιγεννητοῦ M.16.3255B); ἄρ' οὖν ἐ. ἐστιν ἡ τοῦ υἱοῦ βασιλεία Or.*Jo*.1.28(30; p.35.21; M.14.76B); οὐδὲν...ἐν τριάδι κτιστὸν ἢ ἐ. Epiph.*anc*.7(p.14.13; M.43.28C); τὸ δὲ ὁμοούσιον τῷ πατρὶ ἐ. οὐκ ἔστι Cyr.*thes*.9(5[1].67C); εἰ οὐδὲν ἐ. ἐν θεῷ...οὐκ ἐπιγέγονεν ὁ υἱός, ἀλλ' ἦν τῷ πατρὶ συναΐδιος *ib*.4(26A).

ἐπιγενν-άω, *produce in addition, further*, Iren.*haer*.1.18.1(M.7.641B); Hipp.*haer*.10.33(p.290.14; M.16.3450B); ἐπαύσατο γεννῶν ὁ πατὴρ ἢ ~ᾷ; Dion.Al.*fr*.(p.259); pass., *be produced afterwards* ἑτέρας ~ηθείσης Χριστῷ φύσεως Leont.H.*monoph*.33(M.86.1789B).

ἐπιγεννηματικός, *produced later*, Bas.*Eun*.3(1.275A; M.29.661B); Gr.Nyss.*hom.opif*.16.9(v.l. ἐπιγενηματικήν M.44.181C); εἰ ἐ. τῷ θεῷ τὴν ἀφθαρσίαν...ὥς ποτε περὶ αὐτὸν μὴ οὖσαν id.*Eun*.12(1 p.341.29; M.45.1061A); ἐ. ... τὴν πρὸς ἀνθρώπους τοῦ υἱοῦ ὁμοιότητα id.*Apoll*.22(M.45.1168C).

***ἐπιγεννητικός**, = foreg., Gr.Nyss.*Apoll*.22(M.45.1168B).

ἐπιγεννητός, v.l. for ἐπιγενητός, Iren.*haer*.1.12.1 ap.Hipp.*haer*.6.38(p.170.5; M.16.3255B); Epiph.*haer*.74.12(p.330.11; M.42.497C); *ib*.76.46(p.400.7; 613C).

ἐπιγηράσκω, *grow old*, Pall.*h.Laus*.30(p.86.7; M.34.1098C).

ἐπιγί(γ)ν-ομαι. **1.** *become* or *come into being afterwards*; Trin. (Arian) ἦν ὅτε ὁ θεὸς μόνος ἦν, καὶ οὔπω πατὴρ ἦν· ὕστερον δὲ ἐπιγέγονε πατήρ Ar.*Thal.fr*.3 ap.Ath.*Ar*.1.5(M.26.21A); cf. φασκόντων...φρονεῖν τὸν Διονύσιον...'ὁ υἱὸς οὐκ ἦν πρὶν γεννηθῇ...οὐ γὰρ ἀΐδιός ἐστιν, ἀλλ' ὕστερον ἐπιγέγονεν' Ath.*Dion*.14(p.56.24; M.25.501B); orthodox denial υἱὸς ὑπάρχων...καὶ σοφία, καὶ λόγος, οὐκ ἔξωθεν ~ομένων τούτων αὐτῷ id.*gent.*46(M.25.93B); ἀδιαίρετόν ἐστι τὸ ἀπαύγασμα πρὸς τὸ φῶς...καὶ οὐκ ἐπιγέγονεν ὕστερον id.*ep.Aeg.Lib.*13(M.25.568C); οὔτε ὁ λόγος ἐπιγέγονεν οὐκ ὢν πρότερον id.*Ar.*1.25(M.26.64B); *ib.*3.6 (333A); Cyr.*thes.*4(5¹.26C); Christol. ἡ πρὸς πατέρα ἰσότης προϋπάρχουσα, καὶ ἡ πρὸς ἀνθρώπους ὁμοιότης ~ομένη Gr.Nyss.*Apoll.*22(M. 45.1168C); **2.** *come in besides*, Or.*Jo.*2.18(12; p.76.3; M.14.148A); **3.** *come as a fulfilment, at the end* μετὰ τὴν παρουσίαν τοῦ Χριστοῦ οὐκέτι καιρός ἐστιν ἐνεστώς· πῶς γάρ, ~όμενος καὶ τέλος ἔχων; Chrys. *hom.15.2 in Heb.*(12.151A); **4.** ἀπογίνομαι καὶ ἐ. *go and come back, come and go*, Meth.*res.*2.3(p.391.7; M.18.317B); Chrys.*hom.12.6 in Rom.*(9.522A).

ἐπιγι(γ)νώσκω, **1.** *get to know further, more fully* ὁ θεὸν ἐπιγνοὺς... ἐὰν οὖν...ὀφείλων ἀγαθοποιεῖν πονηρεύηται, οὐ δοκεῖ πλείονα πονηρίαν ποιεῖν παρὰ τὸν μὴ γινώσκοντα τὸν θεόν; Herm.*sim.*9.18.1; πάρεστιν ἐπιγνόντι σοι τὸν Χριστὸν τοῦ θεοῦ καὶ τελείῳ γινομένῳ εὐδαιμονεῖν Just.*dial.*8.2(M.6.493A); ἵνα...τὰς γραφὰς ἐπιγνόντες πολιτευσώμεθα καθ' ὑπακοήν Clem.*str.*1.10(p.30.21; M.8.744A); ἐπιγνωσθήσεται δὲ πάλιν ἐκ τοῦ υἱοῦ ἡ περὶ τοῦ πνεύματος γνῶσις Ath.*ep.Serap.*3.4(M.26. 632A); hence **2.** *recognize* a thing for what it is ἵνα...οἱ...εἰληφότες τὴν σφραγῖδα καὶ τεθλακότες αὐτὴν καὶ μὴ τηρήσαντες ὑγιῆ ἐπιγνόντες τὰ ἑαυτῶν ἔργα μετανοήσωσι Herm.*sim.*8.6.3; ἐπιγινώσκει δέ τις ἑαυτόν, ἐπάγων ταῖς πράξεσι τὴν διάνοιαν Or.*fr.81 in Lam.*(p.266. 19; M.13.645D); ὁ τὴν ταπεινοφροσύνην κτησάμενος, ἀποκαλύπτει αὐτῷ ὁ θεὸς τὰς ἁμαρτίας αὐτοῦ εἰς τὸ ἐπιγνῶναι αὐτάς Esaias *or.*17.2 (p.103; cf.M.40.1143B); *recognize* a fact ἐ. τίς ἐστιν ὁ Χριστός Just. *dial.*88.6(M.6.688A); εἰ μὴ ποιηταὶ καὶ φιλόσοφοι ἕνα μὲν εἶναι ἐπεγίνωσκον θεόν Athenag.*leg.*24.1(M.6.945A); Ath.*ep.Drac.*10(M. 25.533C); Didym.(‡Bas.)*Eun.*5(1.310D; M.29.744D); id.*Trin.*2.20(M. 39.752A); c. dupl. acc., *recognize as* Ἰησοῦν ὂν...ἐπέγνωμεν Χριστὸν υἱὸν θεοῦ Just.*dial.*132.1(781D); Ath.*Ar.*1.39(M.26.93A); ἐ. ἅπαντα ὡς ἐγένοντο γνώμῃ τῶν σὺν αὐτῷ κληρικῶν Gel.Cyz.*h.e.*3.15.12; *recognize* fraternally, *greet* ἀλλήλους ἐπίγνωτε *Lit.Jac.*(p.176.16); cf. Iren.*haer.*3.3.4(M.7.853B); **3.** *recognize, acknowledge* τὴν πρὸς τοὺς πτωχοὺς κοινωνίαν ἐ. Ath.*ep.fest.*45(p.298.19; M.26.1441C); ἀλήθειαν ἐπιγνῶσι id.*Dion.*27(p.67.3; M.25.521B); **4.** *get to know later* οἱ προκεκοιμημένοι νεκροὶ...διὰ τούτων οὖν ἐζωοποιήθησαν καὶ ἐπέγνωσαν τὸ ὄνομα τοῦ υἱοῦ τοῦ θεοῦ Herm.*sim.*9.16.7; **5.** *make good, repay* οἴκοθεν τὰς ζημίας τῷ ἠδικημένῳ κατὰ τὸ διπλάσιον ἐπιγνώσεται Ath. Scholast.*coll.*4.22(p.62).

[*]**ἐπιγκέρνης, ὁ,** = ἐπικέρνης, *cup-bearer*, Gr.Mag.*dial.*(tr.Zach.) 3.5(M.*PL.*77.227A).

***ἐπιγλίχομαι,** *long for more*, Clem.*paed.*2.7(p.191.2; M.8.460A).

***ἐπιγνόφω,** *cloud, darken*; met., Geo.Pis.*Pers.*2.291(M.92.1229A).

ἐπιγνωμοσύνη, ἡ, **1.** *knowledge, consciousness*, Dion.Ar.*e.h.*4.3.8 (M.3.481B); Max.*ep.*4(M.91.417A); τῆς τῶν οἰκείων πταισμάτων ἐ. Andr.Caes.*Apoc.*49(M.106.364B); **2.** *conscience*, Dion.Ar.*e.h.*7.3.6(M. 3.561B).

ἐπιγνώμων, **1.** as subst., *judge, appraiser*, ironically ὁ τῶν πράξεων τοῦ θεοῦ βασανιστὴς καὶ ἐ. Gr.Nyss.*res.*3(M.46.672A); **2.** *conscious of* τῆς οἰκείας ἐ. βραχύτητος Dion.Ar.*e.h.*7.3.6(M.3.561B); Max.*ep.*19(M. 91.593D); *acknowledging* ἐ. ... καὶ ὑπήκοα τοῦ πεποιηκότος Jo.D.*Man.* 1.31(M.94.1537C); **3.** abs., *understanding, intelligent* ὁ οὐράνιος τοῦ θεοῦ λόγος...νοῦν ἐπὶ πᾶσιν ἀνθρώποις ἐ. καὶ θεωρητικὸν τῆς αὐτοῦ σοφίας δωρούμενος Eus.*d.e.*4.5(p.157.31; M.22.264A); Pall.*h.Laus.*32 (p.93.5; M.34.1100C); Evagr.Pont.*or.*144(M.79.1197B); Max.*carit.* 3.81(M.90.1041B).

***ἐπιγνωρισμός, ὁ,** *recognition*, ‡Ath.*qu.Ant.*22(M.28.612A); Anast. S.*qu.et resp.*89(M.89.720B).

ἐπίγνωσις, ἡ, *knowledge*, esp. of divine truth, cf. γνῶσις; **1.** in rel. to γνῶσις: τῶν ἀνθρωπίνων καὶ τῶν θείων γνῶσιν, ἔπειτα τῆς τούτων θεότητος καὶ δικαιοσύνης ἐ. Just.*dial.*3.5(M.6.481B); εἰ γὰρ μὴ ταὐτόν ἐστι γνῶσις θεοῦ καὶ ἐ. θεοῦ, ἀλλ' ὁ ἐπιγινώσκων οἱονεὶ ἀναγνωρίζει ὃ πάλαι εἰδὼς ἐπελέληστο, ὅσοι ἐν ἐ. γίνονται θεοῦ πάλαι ᾔδεσαν αὐτόν Or.*comm.in Eph.*1:15ff.(p.399); ἕτερόν ἐστι γνῶσις πραγμάτων, καὶ ἕτερόν ἐστιν ἀληθείας ἐ. ... ἡ τῶν πραγμάτων γνῶσις κατ' ἀναλογίαν τῆς ἐργασίας τῶν ἐντολῶν προσγίνεται· ἡ δὲ ἀληθείας ἐ., κατὰ τὸ μέτρον τῆς εἰς Χριστὸν ἐλπίδος Marc.Er.*opusc.*2.85(M.65. 949C); ἄλλο γάρ ἐστι γνῶσις,...καὶ ἄλλο ἐ. ... γνῶσις μὲν γάρ ἐστι, τὸ εἰδέναι τὰ ὄντα...ἐ. δέ ἐστιν, ἡ μετὰ ψευδῆ ἐπιγινομένη ἀληθὴς γνῶσις Jo.D.*Man.*1.78(M.94.1577A); **2.** source: Christ, *M.Polyc.*14.1; Iren. *haer.*1.2.5(M.7.461B); grace, Clem.*str.*6.18(p.517.25; M.9.400A); baptism, Or.*Jo.*28.7(6; p.397.30; M.14.696A); scripture, Chrys.*hom.in Mt.7:14*(3.25A); **3.** in gen. τὸ μέγιστον, ἡ πατρός, καὶ υἱοῦ, καὶ ἁγίου πνεύματος, ἐ. Gr.Naz.*or.*32.23(M.36.201A); Cyr.*Abac.*16(3.531D); Παῦλος, μετὰ τὴν ἐ.,...ὑπέστρεψεν εἰς Ἱερουσαλὴμ Proc.G.*Is.*1:11ff. (M.87.1845D); **4.** in rel. to faith ἐ. πατρὸς as foundation of faith in Christ, *Diogn.*10.1; opp. to it, Gr.Nyss.*Eun.*10(2 p.230.22; M.45. 832B); **5.** opp. ignorance, *1Clem.*59.2; ref. Socrates πρὸς θεοῦ δὲ τοῦ ἀγνώστου αὐτοῖς διὰ λόγου ζητήσεως ἐ. προὐτρέπετο Just.*2apol.*10.6 (M.6.461A); ἃ γὰρ ἡ ἄγνοια συνέδησεν κακῶς, ταῦτα διὰ τῆς ἐ. ἀναλύεται καλῶς Clem.*paed.*1.6(p.107.33; M.8.285B); τῶν ἀγνοουμένων καὶ προσαγωγῆς εἰς ἐ. δεομένων Dion.Al.ap.Ath.*Dion.*18 (p.60.7; M.25.508A); Ath.*ep.Max.*5(M.26.1089C); τυφλώττων περὶ τὴν τῶν θείων μυστηρίων ἐ. ‡Ath.*serm.fid.*39(p.31; M.26.1289D); sin αἰτεῖται...ἐπικουφισμὸν περὶ ὧν ἡμαρτήσαμεν ἡμεῖς καὶ ἐπιστροφὴν εἰς ἐ. Clem.*str.*7.12(p.56.23; M.9.509B); pagan errors ἐπὶ τὴν τῆς ἱερᾶς θρησκείας ἐ. ... σπεύδοιεν Constantius Imp.ap.Ath.*apol.sec.*55 (p.135.32; M.25.349A); **6.** effects: eternal life, Tat.*orat.*13(p.14.16; M.6.833B); salvation, Clem.*str.*7.1(p.4.30; M.9.405B); εὐχόμενος [sc. 'gnostic'] δὲ ὡς πλείστους ὅσους ἐν ἐ. γενέσθαι, ἵν' ἐν τοῖς σῳζομένοις διὰ τῆς σωτηρίας κατ' ἐπίγνωσιν ὁ θεὸς δοξάζηται *ib.*7.7(p.31.22f.; 457B); id.*fr.*44(p.223.18); cf.Dion.Ar.*e.h.*2.2.1(M.3.593A); enlightenment, †Bas.*Is.*135(1.473D; M.30.337B); *ib.*159(492C; M.380C); power over demons, *Hom.Clem.*10.25; purification, Gr.Naz.*or.*39.10(M.36. 344D); fear, ref. Zacharias, women at empty tomb etc. ὁ φόβος ἐκείνων...κατ' ἐπίγνωσιν τῆς τῶν κρειττόνων παρουσίας Ath.*v.Anton.* 35(M.26.896B); (Gnost.) salvation, ref. Simon Magus τοῖς ἀνθρώποις σωτηρίαν παρέσχε διὰ τῆς ἰδίας ἐ. Hipp.*haer.*6.19(p.147.1; M.16. 3223B); **7.** special kinds of ἐ.: angelic, Clem.*str.*5.6(p.360.5; M.9. 61A); prophetic, *Hom.Clem.*3.12; **8.** exeg. Mt.25:1ff. ἔλαιον δὲ εἰς τὰς λαμπάδας ἡ ἐν ἐ. σπουδή Or.*fr.in Mt.*25:1–9(p.204; M.17.304D).

ἐπιγογγύζω, *complain*, *Const.App.*3.19.6.

ἐπίγραμμα, τό, *commemorative inscription*, Evagr.*h.e.*4.18(p.168. 15; M.86.2736B).

ἐπιγραφή, ἡ, **1.** *superscription* on a coin, ref. Mt.22:20 ὁ πιστὸς ἐ. μὲν ἔχει διὰ Χριστοῦ τὸ ὄνομα τοῦ θεοῦ, τὸ δὲ πνεῦμα ὡς εἰκόνα Clem.*exc.Thdot.*86(p.133.3; M.9.697B); ‡Ath.*serm.fid.*24(p.20; M.26. 1276D); on outside of a letter, giving addressee and sender, Chrys. *hom.1.3 in Ac.princ.*(3.55A); **2.** *title, heading*, Epiph.*haer.*42.11 (p.124.25; M.41.728A); id.*rescr.*5(p.161.19; M.41.165C); **3.** *delineation, painting*, Gr.Nyss.*hom.3 in Eccl.*(M.44.656C); **4.** cosmetic *painting*, Gr.Naz.*or.*37.8(M.36.292C); Chrys.*Eutrop.*1.3(3.384B).

ἐπίγραφος, *entitled*, Nemes.*nat.hom.*2(M.40.584A unless ἐπιγράφον, cf. ἐπιγράφω); *inscribed* with the name of, *signed by* ἡ ἐ. πίστις τῶν Μαρκέλλου Epiph.*haer.*72.11 tit.(p.265.6; ἡ ἐπιγραφὴ πίστεως M.42.396D).

ἐπιγράφ-ω, **1.** *inscribe* ῥάβδους ἐπιγεγραμμένας ἑκάστης φυλῆς κατ' ὄνομα *1Clem.*43.2; ἐ. ἐπὶ δίσκου Evagr.*h.e.*6.21(p.236.18; M.86. 2872D); *address* a letter, *ib.*2.2(p.39.14; 2492A); *write upon* a person, i.e. *tattoo* ὧν ἐπιγράψας τὰ πρόσωπα μέλανι κεντητῷ 'Ἀρμενιακὸς ἐπίβουλος' Thphn.*chron.*p.396(M.108.941C); **2.** *entitle* ἐν τῇ βίβλῳ ἣ ~εται Ἔξοδος Just.*dial.*59.2(M.6.612A); Eus.*h.e.*2.18.1(M.20.184C); Hier.*vir.ill.*(tr.Sophr.Pal.)18(p.20.17; M.*PL.*23.638A); abs. in pass. sense Ἑρμᾶς...λέγεται αὐθέντης γεγενῆσθαι βίβλου ~ούσης Ποιμήν *ib.* 10(p.13.13; 626B); *ib.*38(p.29.20; 654A); Leont.N.*v.Jo.Eleem.*12(p.23. 22); Thdr.Stud.*epp.*2.162(M.99.1504D); med., *name, call* τὴν γέννησιν ὑπὸ τὸν ἄρχοντα τῆς κακίας τάσσων, καὶ Ἐξουσιαστὴν τοῦτον ~όμενος ‡Ath.*Apoll.*2.8(M.26.1144C); Bas.*ep.*218(3.331C; M.32. 809C); **3.** *write as well, in addition*, Epiph.*haer.*30.22(p.363.10; M.41. 444A); **4.** *charge* οὐκ ἔπρεπεν...σε φιλόχριστον ὄντα βασιλέα ἐπὶ φόνοις Χριστιανῶν...~εσθαι Ath.*apol.Const.*34(M.25.641B); med., id.*h.Ar.* 67(p.220.4; M.25.773B); c. dupl. acc., *prefer* a charge of...*against* Εὐστάθιον...παιδίσκης μῖξιν...αἰτίαν ἐπιγραψαμένους Philost.*h.e.*2.7 (M.65.469C); **5.** med., *enrol under* τοῖς τὸ σωτήριον ~ομένοις ὄνομα Eus.*v.C.*1.52(p.32.13; M.20.968A); τὴν σωτήριον ἐ. θεοσέβειαν [i.e. Christianity] *ib.*4.38(p.132.15; 1188A); fig. abs. Ἰωσήφ, οὐ...ἡ γραφὴ ...τοὺς ὑπὲρ ἀρετῆς ἱδρῶτας ἀνέγραψεν, ἵνα πρὸς τοῦτον ὁρῶντες ~ωνται Bas.Sel.*or.*8.1(M.85.113A); **6.** med., *enrol oneself as a citizen of*, met. ἕξιν τὴν κοσμικήν, ἣν ὥσπερ τινὰ χώραν ἐπιγραψάμενοι Cyr.*Jo.*3.6(4. 313C); πατρίδα...ἐ. τὸν οὐρανόν id.*Abac.*33(3.548B); **7.** med., *register* or *be registered as* ἐπιγεγραμμένος εἰς τὰς βίβλους τῶν ζώντων Herm. *sim.*2.9; Clem.*str.*6.8(p.466.13; M.9.289C); ἐπιγραψαμένου κυρίου τῆς οἰκοδομῆς τοῦ θεοῦ, καὶ ἄρχοντος τῆς φρουρᾶς τῆς πόλεως τοῦ τῶν ὅλων δεσπότου Or.*princ.*3.1.19(p.231.7; M.11.289A); **8.** med., *claim* as a father, *register* as a patron [sc. διὰ τῆς δεισιδαιμονίας] ~όμενον ψευδωνύμους θεοὺς ἀντὶ τοῦ...θεοῦ, ὥσπερ ὁ ἐκ τῆς πόρνης τοὺς πολλοὺς ~εται πατέρας ἀγνοίᾳ τοῦ πρὸς ἀλήθειαν πατρὸς Clem.*prot.*2 (p.18.27; M.8.93B); hence, gen., *acknowledge* as a superior or ruler ἐπεγράφετο [sc. ὁ κόσμος]...βασιλέα τὸν σατανᾶν Cyr.*glaph.Gen.*5(1. 143C); freq. of Christian's relationship to God οἱ ἐξ ἐθνῶν δι' αὐτοῦ τὸν ἕνα καὶ μόνον ἀληθῆ πατέρα θεὸν ἐπιγραψάμενοι Eus.*d.e.*8.1(p.363.

32; M.22.592A); *ib.*(p.365.11; 593A); ὁ καὶ πατρὸς ἐν χώρᾳ καὶ κηδεμόνος τὸν μέγαν προστάτην καὶ παμβασιλέα τῶν ὅλων ~όμενος id. *p.e.* 1.1(2D; M.21.24C); Ath.*syn*.4(p.233.26; M.26.688A); μετὰ καθαρᾶς συνειδήσεως πατέρα ~όμενοι τὸν θεόν Cyr.H.*catech*.23.11; Epiph. *haer*.35.3(p.43.19; M.41.632C); Nil.*Magn*.50(M.79.1033D); Cyr.*Is*.2.2 (2.228A,B); of Son τὴν οἰκείαν δούλην ἐ. μητέρα Procl.CP *or.laud. BMV* 4(p.104.24; M.65.685A); met., things, *claim derivation from* οὐχ οἷόν τε τὴν τοῦ σύμπαντος κόσμου διάταξιν...αὐτόματον ~εσθαι τὴν αἰτίαν Eus.*p.e*.7.3(301D; M.21.512C); τὰ Ἑβραίων λόγια...θεόν τε αὐθέντην ~όμενα *ib*.13.14(691D; M.1140B); cf. θεὸς...ὁ ἐπέκεινα... αὐτὸς ἀνώτερον αἴτιον οὐκ ~εται id.*l.C*.12(p.232.30; M.20.1392B); Gr.Nyss.*or.catech*.5(p.27.7; M.45.24D); **9.** *ascribe* εὐχαριστία Χριστῷ τὰς νίκας καὶ τὰ λοιπὰ ἀγαθὰ τοῦ βασιλέως ~ουσα Const.*or.s.c*.22 tit. (p.153.2, v.l. γραφ- M.20.1305B); Eus.*l.C*.11(p.226.7; M.20.1380B); τῷ λόγῳ τῆς σαρκώσεως ~ομένης Didym.(‡Bas.)*Eun*.5(1.311B; M. 29.748A); τῇ τοῦ θεοῦ βοηθείᾳ τὸ πᾶν ~ειν Thdt.*qu*.7 *in Dt*.(1.266); *ascribe* to an author λόγους ἐπιγεγραμμένους εἰς Σολομῶνα Just. *dial*.64.5(M.6.624C); **10.** *assign* οἱ προσεκύνησαν τῇ κτίσει παρὰ τὸν κτίσαντα ξύλοις καὶ λίθοις ἐπεγράφοντο θεούς Cyr.*Is*.5.2(2.776E); med., *have assigned to one*, Sev.Ant.*res*.(p.832.8); *assign as cause* κεχρηματίσθαι τὴν θεραπείαν λέγουσιν ἵνα τὸ ἀναίσθητον ἐπιγράψωσι σέβασμα *Hom.Clem*.9.18; *ib*.12.11; **11.** med., *claim, assume* a name φιλοσοφίας ὄνομα καὶ σχῆμα ἐ. τινες οἱ οὐδὲν ἄξιον τῆς ὑποσχέσεως πράττουσι Just.*1apol*.4.8(M.6.333B); Eus.*m.P*.11(p.973.3; M.20.1504A); εὐσέβεια οὐχ ἡ ψευδώνυμος...ἀλλ' ἡ σὺν ἀληθείᾳ τὴν προσηγορίαν ~ομένη id.*p.e*.1.1(2B; M.21.24B); pass., *be called by*, ref. Ex.23:20 ἐμοῦ...τοὔνομα ἐπιγέγραπται ὁ μέλλων εἰσάξειν τὸν λαὸν εἰς τὴν γῆν τῆς ἐπαγγελίας id.*d.e*.4.17(p.197.3; M.22.328C); μὴ ἰδιοϋποστάτως ὑπάρξαν ποτέ, οὐκ ἂν ἴδιον ἐπιγράψεται πρόσωπον Eust.Mon.*ep*.(M. 86.912A); **12.** med. abs., *claim credit* ἐὰν δὲ αὐτοῦ [sc. τοῦ θεοῦ] θεραπεύοντος, ἄλλος ἐπιγράφηται *Hom.Clem*.11.9.

ἐπιγώνιος, *at the corner*, ref. Mc.12:10 τῇ ἐ. κεφαλῇ Gr.Nyss.*hom. in Cant*.proem.(M.44.760D).

ἐπιδάκν-ω, *sting*, fig. πίστιν τὴν ὡς κόκκον σινάπεως ~ουσαν ὠφελίμως τὴν ψυχήν Clem.*str*.5.1(p.327.18; M.9.12B).

ἐπίδακρυς, *tearful* ἀκούσασα καὶ ἐ. γενομένη *Hom.Clem*.13.1; ἐγενόμην...ἐ., οἷον λόγον εἶπεν ἀνήρ *ib*.12.7.

ἐπιδακρύω, *weep over*, ? c. acc. ἐ. τοὺς λόγους τοῖς τοῦ ἱκέτου *A.Andr*.A 5(p.48.17 conj. τοῖς λόγοις).

***ἐπιδανειστής, ὁ**, *creditor*, Anast.S.*qu.et resp*.20(M.89.524A).

ἐπιδαπανάω, *consume*, Chrys.*Laz*.1.1(1.708E).

ἐπιδαψιλεύομαι, [in form -έομαι, Gr.Nyss.*engast*.(p.63.9; M.45. 108A)]; **1.** *abound in* μείζοσιν ἐ. τερατολογίαις Eus.*h.e*.3.26.1(M.20. 272B); ἐ. τῇ κακίᾳ Jo.D.*hom*.2.4(M.96.584C); ἐ. τὴν ἀρετήν id.*jej*.6 (M.95.72A); abs., *abound*, Cyr.H.*catech*.6.10; **2.** *flourish upon*, Bas. *hom*.10.3(2.85E; M.31.360B); ἐ. τῷ πάθει Chrys.*hom.18.3 in Mt*.(7. 237E); id.*hom.22.1 in Eph*.(11.166C); **3.** *lavish, bestow freely*, c. acc. τὸν ἐκ σπλάγχνων πατρὸς ἔλεον...ἐ. Clem.*q.d.s*.29(p.179.13; M.9. 636A); Eus.*v.C*.3.53(p.101.2; M.20.1116B); Chrys.*hom.in Mt.18:23* (3.3B); c. dat. πλείστοις ἐ. χαρίσμασιν Eus.*v.C*.3.1(p.76.17; 1053B); Gr.Nyss.*engast*.(p.63.9; M.45.108A); Chrys.*hom.6.2 in Rom*.(9. 473D); c. infin., Or.*Cels*.4.98(p.372.4; M.11.1177C); abs., *be generous* ἐ. ἔτι μᾶλλον τὴν αὐτοῦ διάνοιαν ἐμφαίνων Eus.*Marcell*.2.2(p.40.25; M.24.792C); Chrys.*hom.16.6 in 1Cor*.(10.144C); **4.** *respond generously* to ἐ. τῇ αἰτήσει Chrys.*hom.48.4 in Gen*.(4.485E); **5.** *overflow* ἡ δύναμις τοῦ σταυροῦ ἐ. μου τῇ διανοίᾳ Germ.CP *or*.1(M.98.232D).

ἐπιδεής, *in need* of, c. genit., Clem.*str*.7.13(p.58.7; M.9.513A); Meth.*symp*.proem.(p.6.17; M.18.36A); Ath.*gent*.28(M.25.56B); abs., *defective*; neut. as subst., Clem.*str*.7.7(p.35.24; 468B).

ἐπιδείκνυμι, **1.** *display, demonstrate*, Meth.*arbitr*.22(p.204.8); **2.** *parade, make a show of*, Herm.*mand*.3.3; **3.** *introduce, bring on the scene*, Aen.*dial*.(M.85.889A); med. ὁ σωτὴρ...ὁ τὸν θάνατον καταργήσας, καὶ κατ' αὐτοῦ τρόπαια καθ' ἡμέραν ἐν τοῖς ἑαυτοῦ μαθηταῖς ἐπιδεικνύμενος Ath.*inc*.29.3(M.25.145C); **4.** *reveal, make manifest* ἀνθρώπων οὐδεὶς οὔτε εἶδεν οὔτε ἐγνώρισεν [sc. τὸν θεόν], αὐτὸς δὲ ἑαυτὸν ἐπέδειξεν. ἐπέδειξε δὲ διὰ πίστεως *Diogn*.8.5; *M.Polyc*.1.1; ἅμα τε ἠβουλήθη καὶ ἀχρόνως καὶ ἀπαθῶς ἐξ ἑαυτοῦ αὐτὸν γεννήσας ἐπέδειξεν *Symb.Sirm*.1 *anath*.25; **5.** *show* an answer to a sum, *make* the answer συντιθέντες μέχρι τοῦ η τὸν τριάκοντα ἀριθμὸν ἐπιδεικνύουσιν Hipp.*haer*.6.52(p.185.16; M.16.3286A); *ib*.6.50(p.183.4; 3279A); cf. *make* a beginning ἂν εἰς ἓν ἀρχὴν ἐπιδείξηται Chrys.*hom.9.5 in Heb*.(12.100B); **6.** *show to be* ἡ περὶ τῆς θεοσεβείας...γνῶσις...ἡλίου λαμπροτέραν ἑαυτὴν...ἐπιδείκνυται Ath.*gent*.1(M.25.4A); ‡Ath.*Apoll*. 1.7(M.26.1105B); **7.** *expound* ἐπιδείξασθαι τὸν λόγον Bas.Sel.*v.Thecl*. 2.27(M.85.612C).

ἐπιδεικτι-άω, **1.** trans.; *expose to insult*, Alex.Al.*ep.Alex*.14(p.29. 10; M.18.509C); **2.** intrans., *wish to display oneself*, Cels.ap.Or.*Cels*. 4.6(p.278.20; M.11.1036B); Or.*ib*.(p.278.32; 1036C); εἰς κενοδοξίαν προκαλέσαι οὐκ ~ῶντα ‡Ign.*Phil*.10; Chrys.*hom.7.1 in Ac*.(9.56C).

ἐπιδεικτικός, *showy, ostentatious*, Clem.*paed*.3.10(p.266.2; M.8. 624B); of persons, Gr.Naz.*or*.8.9(M.35.800A); *of outward show* τῷ ἐ. κόσμῳ †Bas.*Is*.21(1.394B; M.30.156B); neut. as subst., *ostentation*, Or.*fr.in Mt*.9:30,31(p.91); ref. Mt.6:2 τὸ ἐ. ὡς ἐπιβλαβὲς παραιτεῖσθαι κελεύων Nil.*Magn*.6(M.79.977A).

ἐπιδεικτικῶς, *ostentatiously, for mere show*, Bas.*ep*.2.5(3.73E; M.32. 229C); οἱ ἐ. εὐποιοῦντες Isid.Pel.*epp*.1.187(M.78.304B); ref. the gift of tongues λίαν αὐτῷ ἐ. καὶ οὐκ ἀναγκαίως ἐχρῶντο Thdt.*1Cor*.12:28(3. 250); c. genit., *so as to display, show off* τῶν μὲν Ἑλληνικῶν λόγων ἐ. Eus.*Marcell*.1.3(p.16.5; M.24.748B).

ἐπίδειξις, ἡ, **1.** *showing forth, manifestation*, ref. Jo.1:14 μαρτυρίαν ποιεῖται ὁ...Ἰωάννης τῆς ὀργανικῆς τοῦ σώματος ἐ. ‡Ath. *Apoll*.2.1(M.26.1133B); κατὰ τὴν τῆς σαρκὸς ἐ. καὶ κατὰ τὴν μορφὴν τοῦ δούλου *ib*.1.5(1100C); **2.** *display, exposing*, Clem.*paed*.2.6(p.188.8, v.l. ἀποδειξ- M.8.453A); **3.** *show, ostentation*, Or.*hom.2 in Lc*.(p.19.5); Const.*or.s.c*.21(p.187.16); Jo.D.*hom*.2.6(M.96.585D); **4.** *demonstration*, ‡Ath.*Apoll*.1.6(M.26.1104A); *ib*.1.5(1100D); *ib*.2.10(1148C); *ib*. 2.18(1164C); **5.** *proof* εἰς ἐ. ὅτι καὶ θεὸς καὶ κύριος τῶν δυνάμεων...ὁ Χριστὸς...καλεῖται Just.*dial*.36.2(M.6.553B); ‡Ath.*Apoll*.2.13(M.26. 1153B); **6.** *example, piece of evidence* τῆς ἀναμαρτησίας ἡ ἐ. *ib*.1.7 (1104D); *ib*.2.12(1152B).

ἐπιδέκατος, *for a tenth, tithe* ἀπαρχή μοι ἡ πρωτότοκος αὕτη καὶ ἐ. οὗτος, ἡ τελευταία ὠδίς Gr.Nyss.*v.Macr*.(p.385.5; M.46.973A); neut. as subst. τὸ ἐ. τοῦτο, δείξασα...τὸν παῖδα *ib*.(p.385.8; 973B).

ἐπίδεκτος, *receptive*, c. genit., Or.*or*.27.8(p.368.14; M.11.512B).

***ἐπίδεμα, τό**, *bandage*, fig., Epiph.*haer*.61.7(p.388.5; M.41.1049B).

ἐπιδέξιος, *favourable*; of winds, fig., Gr.Nyss.*hom.10 in Cant*.(M. 44.984B); *suitable* πεδίον ἐ. πρὸς πόλεμον Thphn.*chron*.p.265(M.108. 660A).

***ἐπιδέομαι**, abs., *be in need*, *Diogn*.10.6; Mac.Aeg.*cust.cor*.12(M. 34.832D); in form ἐπιδέεται, ‡Just.*confut*.25(M.6.1524A); ‡Just.*qu. Chr*.2.8(M.6.1428A).

ἐπίδεσμα, τό, *amulet*, Cyr.H.*catech*.4.37.

ἐπιδεσμεύω, *tie up, bind*; reflex., of bondage to sin, Thdr.Heracl. *Is*.28:22(M.18.1320B).

ἐπιδεσμέω, = foreg., fig. ἐ. διὰ παρακλητικῆς νουθεσίας *Const. App*.2.20.4(vv.ll. ἐπιδέμμων, ἐπιδέννων); *ib*.2.41.5; Chrys.*hom.27.2 in 2Cor*.(10.628E).

ἐπίδεσμος, ὁ, *bandage*, fig., Chrys.*sac*.2.4(p.34.2: 1.374D).

ἐπιδευτερόω, *repeat*, Epiph.*haer*.69.66(p.215.9; M.42.508B); ‡Epiph.*v.proph.Mal*.3(p.30; M.43.419C).

***ἐπιδέχνυμαι**, = ἐπιδέχομαι, Nonn.*par.Jo*.3:32(M.43.772C).

ἐπιδέχ-ομαι, **A.** *admit afterwards*, Clem.*paed*.2.10(p.213.5; M.8. 508A); hence **1.** *welcome, take pleasure in*, *T.Isach*.4.4; *ib*.4.6; *entertain* περὶ ἡμᾶς τοῦ θεοῦ...ἐπιδεξαμένου φιλοστοργίαν Thdt.*Ps*. 29:11–13(1.791 s.v.l.); **2.** *receive, accept* ἐ. νουθετεῖσθαι Clem.*str*.2.7 (p.130.11; M.8.968B); *ib*.3.4(p.209.28; 1136A); ‡Ath.*Apoll*.1.13(M.26. 1117A) cit. s. ἐπίβασις.

B. *admit of*; **1.** in gen. οὐδὲ γὰρ ὁ λόγος ~εται θάνατον, ἀλλὰ τὸ ἀνθρώπινόν ἐστι τὸ τοῦτο ἐπιδεξάμενον Or.*hom.14.6 in Jer*.(p.112.12; M.13.412C); ‡Ath.*serm.fid*.18(p.11; M.26.1272C); ‡Ath.*Apoll*.2.7(M. 26.1144B); **2.** ~ονται τὸ δεῖσθαι as periphrasis for δέονται, Or.*Jo*. 32.10(7; p.442.25; M.14.768B); cf.*ib*.13.59(58; p.291.1; 512B); **3.** *be capable of, liable to*, Clem.*str*.1.3(p.17.1; M.8.716C); ref. Jo.11:51 μοχθηρὰ ψυχὴ ~εταί ποτε τὸ προφητεύειν Or.*Jo*.28.13(12; p.405.20; M.14.708C); id.*princ*.3.1.8(p.208.6; M.11.261C); ἐν ταύτῃ [sc. τῇ ζωῇ] ἁμαρτάνειν ~όμεθα, ὅθεν καὶ νομίμων ἡμῖν χρεία Thdr.Mops.*Gal*. 1:4(p.7.26; M.66.900B); id.*Col*.2:15(p.291.15).

ἐπιδηλόω, *indicate*; hence *tell, be decisive, critical* ἐν νόσοις ἐ. ἡ ἑβδομάς Anat.Laod.*decad*.(p.35).

***ἐπιδήλωσις, ἡ**, *declaration, statement*, Gr.Nyss.*comm.not*.(M.45. 176B).

ἐπιδημ-έω, **A.** *go home to, go to dwell permanently* in τῇ πατρίδι ἐ. ἀπὸ τῆς Αἰγύπτου Synes.*ep*.123(M.66.1504B); fig., in heaven, Herm. *sim*.1.9; ὃς ἂν ἁγνείας μὴ εὑρεθῇ κλάδοις κεκοσμημένος, οὐ τεύξεται τῆς ἀναπαύσεως...οὐδὲ εἰς τὴν γῆν ἐπιδημήσει τῆς ἐπαγγελίας Meth. *symp*.9.5(p.120.2; M.18.88C); abs., of Ascension ὅτε ἐπιδεδήμηκεν ὁ σωτήρ Or.*hom.9.3 in Jer*.(p.67.7; M.13.352D).

B. *come to reside in* a place; **1.** in gen. Πολυκάρπου ἐπιδημήσαντος τῇ Ῥώμῃ Iren.*ep.Vict*.ap.Eus.*h.e*.5.24.16(M.20.565A); ἐ. ἐν τῇ Ῥώμῃ Iren.*haer*.1.27.1(M.7.687B); τῆς Ῥώμης ἐ. Hipp.*haer*.6.20 (M.16.3226B; conj. τῇ Ῥώμῃ p.148.11); Or.*Jo*.10.11(p.162.2; M.14. 325B); *call* at a house σκέπης ἕνεκεν ἐ. Bas.*reg.fus*.14(2.355B; M.

31.952A); **2.** of Inc. ἐπιδημεῖ δὲ δύναμις καὶ θειότης δι' οὗ βούλεται καὶ ἐν ᾧ εὑρίσκει χώραν, οὐκ ἀμείβοντος τόπον οὐδ' ἐκλείποντος χώραν αὐτοῦ κενήν Or.*Cels*.4.5(p.277.30; M.11.1033D); Procl.CP *or*.2.6(M.65.701A); of angels τῶν ἐπιδημησάντων τῷ περιγείῳ τόπῳ ἀγγέλων διὰ τὴν Ἰησοῦ γένεσιν Or.*Cels*.1.60(p.111.5; 769C); **3.** fig. and met. ἀρετὴ ἐ. αὐτῶν ταῖς ψυχαῖς *ib*.3.71(p.263.16; 1013B); ref. Ex.15:25 ἐὰν...ἡ διδασκαλία τοῦ σωτῆρός μου ἐπιδημήσῃ, γλυκάζεται...ὁ Μωσέως νόμος id.*hom.10.2 in Jer*.(p.73.6; M.13.360C); *ib*.8.8(p.62.10; 345B); *Hom.Clem*.5.11; ἡμῖν ἀεὶ καὶ ἀπιὼν ~εῖς τῇ μνήμῃ Synes.*ep*.149(M.66.1549C); **4.** myst., of God dwelling in soul θεοῦ διδόντος καὶ τῆς Χριστοῦ δυνάμεως τῇ ψυχῇ ἡμῶν ~ούσης Or.*Cels*.2.79(p.202.7; M.11.920C); ~οῦντος ἡμῶν τῷ φανταστικῷ πνεύματος θεοῦ καὶ φαντάζοντος ἡμᾶς τὰ τοῦ θεοῦ *ib*.4.95(p.368.20; 1173C); τοῦτο μὲν θεοῦ ἔργον ἐστίν, ἀοράτως ~εῖν κατὰ τὸ ἑαυτοῦ πνεῦμα μετὰ τοῦ πνεύματος Χριστοῦ οἷς κρίνει δεῖν ~εῖν *ib*.5.11(p.1.12; 1181B); *ib*.8.18(p.235.30; 1545B); id.*hom.9.1 in Jer*.(p.63.24; M.13.348C); πῶς δύνανται ἐκεῖνοι [sc. Moses and Isaiah] λόγον θεοῦ λελαληκέναι τοῦ λόγου τοῦ θεοῦ μὴ ἐπιδημήσαντος αὐτοῖς; *ib*.(p.64.17; 349A); exeg. Jo.13:20 ὁ μὲν λαμβάνων ὃν ἐὰν ἐγὼ πέμψω, ἐμὲ λαμβάνει...ὁ δὲ μὴ διά τινός μου ἀποστόλου ἐμὲ λαμβάνων...~οῦντα ταῖς τῶν εὐτρεπισάντων ἑαυτοὺς πρὸς τὴν ἐμὴν παραδοχὴν ψυχαῖς, τὸν πέμψαντά με λαμβάνει πατέρα id.*Jo*.32.17(10; p.454.22; M.14.788B); Gr.Thaum.*pan.Or*.5(p.11.6; M.10.1064B); Eus.*h.e*.2.15.1(M.20.172B); c. cogn. acc., Or.*Jo*.13.56(55; p.287.21; M.14.505D); cf. Ἡρακλῆς ὁ γνήσιος καὶ φιλόσοφός ἐστι νοῦς, ὃς...ἐκπεριονοστεῖ τὸν κόσμον, ~ῶν ταῖς ψυχαῖς καὶ σωφρονίζων τοὺς ἐντυγχάνοντας *Hom.Clem*.6.16.

C. *dwell* among or with; **1.** in gen., of Christ in Egypt αὐτομάτως σεισθῆναι...πάντα τὰ ξόανα τῶν Αἰγυπτίων ἐπιδημήσαντος...τότε τοῦ Χριστοῦ Soz.*h.e*.5.21.10(M.67.1281B); **2.** esp. of Inc., Or.*Cels*.4.6(p.278.26; M.11.1036C); ὁ Ἰησοῦς ἡμῶν ἐπιδεδήμηκεν *ib*.5.33(p.35.5; 1229D); ἐπιδεδημηκέναι τὸν Ἰησοῦν ἀπὸ τοῦ θεοῦ τοῖς ἀνθρώποις *ib*.5.54(p.58.6; 1265A); Ἰουδαίοις ἐ. *ib*.2.57(p.181.12; 888C); τῇ ἐπιδεδημηκυίᾳ τῷ γένει τῶν ἀνθρώπων ζωῇ *ib*.2.75(p.196.22; 912C); ὁ ἡμῖν ~ῶν ἀληθείας λόγος id.*Jo*.1.38(42; p.49.14; M.14.100B); ref. Lc.10:9 'ἤγγικεν', φησίν, καὶ ἤδη ἐπιδημῆσαι ὑμῖν id.*fr.32 in Lc*.(p.248); id.*princ*.4.3.8(p.334.4; M.11.389A); Χριστὸν...ἐπιδημήσειν ποτὲ εἰς ἀνθρώπους ἔφασαν Eus.*d.e*.1.1(p.3.13; M.22.16C); ὁ κύριος ἡμῶν...ἐπιδημήσας πρὸς ἡμᾶς Dor.*doct*.22.3(M.88.1825B).

D. *come into* human life, the world of men; of human beings, Or.*Jo*.20.2(p.328.17; M.14.573C); of human soul, id.*Cels*.1.32(p.84.24; M.11.724A); of Christ τὸ φιλάνθρωπον τοῦ λόγου...τῷ βίῳ τῶν ἀνθρώπων ἐ. *ib*.1.9(p.62.13; 673B); Eus.*h.e*.1.2.23(M.20.65B).

E. abs., *appear*; **1.** in gen., of Jo. Bapt., Or.*Jo*.2.37(30; p.96.13; M.14.181B); of antichrist, id.*Cels*.6.45(p.116.32; M.11.1369A); of angels ἐ. ἐπ' εὐεργεσίᾳ καὶ σωτηρίᾳ τῶν εὐχομένων θεῷ *ib*.8.34(p.249.25; 1568A); **2.** esp. ref. Inc. οὐδὲ ~οῦντος μόνον τοῦ σωτῆρος, ἀλλὰ καὶ ἀπαλλαγέντος Quad.ap.Eus.*h.e*.4.3.2(M.20.308B); τῆς περὶ τοῦ ἐλπιζομένου ἐπιδημήσειν προσδοκίας Or.*Cels*.3.28(p.225.29; 956B); ὁ ἐν τῷ Ἰησοῦ ἐπιδημήσας λόγος *ib*.8.54(p.270.23; 1597C); id.*fr.28 in Jer*.(p.212.23); ~οῦντος τοῦ λόγου αὐτοῦ εἰς τὸ παραστῆσαι τὴν δόξαν τοῦ θεοῦ id.*Jo*.32.29(18; p.415.29; 821B); Ath.*inc*.14.8(M.25.121B); id.*Ar*.3.39(M.26.408A); id.*ep.Epict*.11(p.17.4; M.26.1068B); μάταιοι οἱ λέγοντες ὡς ἐπὶ ἕνα τῶν προφητῶν ἐπιδεδημηκέναι τὸν λόγον ‡Ath.*Apoll*.1.21(M.26.1129A); ἡμεῖς ὁμολογοῦμεν οὐκ εἰς ἄνθρωπον ἅγιον ἐπιδεδημηκέναι τὸν τοῦ θεοῦ λόγον...ἀλλ' αὐτὸν τὸν λόγον σάρκα γεγενῆσθαι μὴ ἀνειληφότα νοῦν ἀνθρώπινον...ἀλλὰ θεῖον Apoll.*ep.Diocaes*.(p.256.5; M.86.1969D); **3.** ref. mode of Inc. ἐπὶ τὴν ἁγίαν παρθένον Μαρίαν ~οῦντος τοῦ λόγου Ath.*ep.Serap*.1.31(M.26.605A); id.*Ar*.3.31(M.26.388C); προφητεύεσθαι τίνα τρόπον ἐ. διὰ τῆς ἀμιάντου παρθένου ὁ Ἐμμανουήλ †Bas.*Is*.198(1.527A; M.30.460A); Μαρκίων καὶ Μανιχαῖος, θεὸν ἐπιδημήσαντα ἐν παρθένῳ καὶ ἀθίγως προεληλυθότα, καὶ ἀνεπιδέκτως ἔχοντα κοινωνῆσαι φύσει ἀνθρωπίνῃ, τῇ ὑποπεπτωκυίᾳ τῇ ἁμαρτίᾳ ‡Ath.*Apoll*.2.3(M.26.1136C); ref. second advent φοβερὸς ὁ ἐν φωνῇ σάλπιγγος μετὰ ἁγίων ἀγγέλων ~εῖν μέλλων ἐξ οὐρανῶν †Bas.*Is*.214(539E; M.489A); *ib*.232(555D; M.525B).

F. *come upon, visit, descend upon*; **1.** of H. Ghost on disciples μετὰ τὴν οἰκονομίαν...τοῦ ἁγίου πνεύματος ἐπιδημήσαντος τοῖς μαθηταῖς...γενομένοις καθαροῖς καὶ νιψαμένοις τοὺς πόδας Or.*Jo*.32.8(6; p.437.31; M.14.760D); Gr.Naz.*or*.31.26(p.179.3; M.36.164A); on converts ἐ. τοῖς περὶ Κορνήλιον πρὸ τοῦ βαπτίσματος, ἄλλοις μετὰ τὸ βάπτισμα διὰ τῶν ἀποστόλων *ib*.34.14(253C); at baptism, Or.*Jo*.6.33(17; p.143.4; M.14.257A); at ordination, Serap.*euch*.27.1; on chrism Ἰησοῦ ἐλθέτω ἡ νικητικὴ αὐτοῦ δύναμις...καὶ ~ησάτω τῷ ἐλαίῳ τούτῳ ᾧ ἐπιφημίζομεν τὸ σὸν ἅγιον ὄνομα *A.Thom*.A 157(p.267.10); of Logos on eucharistic elements ~ησάτω...ὁ ἅγιός σου λόγος ἐπὶ τὸν ἄρτον τοῦτον, ἵνα γένηται ὁ ἄρτος σῶμα τοῦ λόγου Serap.*euch*.13.15; **2.** of Christ as judge, ref. Mal.3:2 ὡς πῦρ χωνευτηρίου...ἑκάστῳ τῶν δεομένων ~ήσειν Or.*Cels*.5.15(p.16.13; M.11.1204A); **3.** abs., *appear, happen*, Epiph.*inc*.1(p.227.12; M.41.273B); πάθος ἐ. λοιμῶδες Evagr.*h.e*.4.29(p.177.7; M.86.2752C); of a festival, Sophr.H.*v.Anast*.(M.92.1713A).

ἐπιδημία, ἡ, **1.** *sojourn, stay* δύο...ἐ. ἐν Κανᾷ...σημαίνουσιν τὰς δύο τοῦ σωτῆρος εἰς τὸν κόσμον ἐ. Or.*Jo*.13.57(56; p.287.28; M.14.505D); on earth, *life* τῇ τῆς σαρκὸς ἐ. Clem.*str*.6.9(p.471.17; M.9.300B); Or.*hom.9 in Lc*.(p.63.19); αἱ...ἡμέραι...ἃς ἐνθάδε ἐσμὲν εἰς ἐ. Meth.*symp*.8.11(p.94.5; M.18.156A); **2.** *coming* among people, *visit*; **a.** in gen. τῇ τῶν ἀποστόλων πανταχόσε ἐ. τῶν ὑπὸ τοῦ Ἰησοῦ ἐπὶ τὸ καταγγεῖλαι τὸ εὐαγγέλιον πεμφθέντων Or.*princ*.4.1.5(p.300.15; M.11.352A); id.*Jo*.10.8(6; p.178.19; M.14.320B); ἑορτὴν...ἱλαρωτέραν τῇ ἑαυτοῦ ποιῶν ἐ. *ib*.13.54(53; p.284.29; 501B); *ib*.13.62(60; p.294.12; 517B); c. objective genit. τὸ τῆς ἐ. τῆς ἐμαυτοῦ...χρέος, *visit* to, Bas.*ep*.162(3.253A; M.32.632B); †Bas.*hom.in Ps*.28(1.361B; M.30.80C); Chrys.*hom.28.2 in 1Cor*.(10.253A); of an invader, †Bas.*Is*.240(1.561E; M.30.540B); **b.** *visitation, appearance*: of angels τοὺς πρώτους...ὁρῶντας ἔσθ' ὅτε ἀγγέλων θεοῦ ἐ. γεγενημένας πρὸς αὐτούς Or.*Cels*.4.80(p.350.3; M.11.1152C); μηδέπω κεκαθαρμένοι οὐκ ἐχώρουν ἀγγέλων παρ' αὐτοῖς ἐπιδημίαν id.*Jo*.6.57(37; p.165.32; M.14.300A); τὴν τοῦ Γαβριὴλ πρὸς αὐτὴν [sc. τὴν Μαρίαν] ἐ. id.*hom.7 in Lc*.(p.46.6); Ath.*Ar*.2.73(M.26.301C); of a vision of Christ attended by angels τὸ φρικτὸν τῆς ἐ. Niceph.Ur.*v.Sym*.115(M.86.3093C); of Jo. Bapt. ὑπόθεσιν οὐκ ἄλλην τῆς εἰς τὸν βίον ἐ. ἔχοντα ἢ τὴν περὶ τοῦ φωτὸς μαρτυρίαν Or.*Jo*.2.30(24; p.87.1; M.14.165B); of return of Elijah ἄνδρες ἀνεγνωκότες ἀντειλῆφθαι αὐτὸν ὡς εἰς τὸν οὐρανὸν καὶ προσδοκῶντες ἐ. αὐτοῦ *ib*.6.13(7; p.122.21; 224C); of demons and heathen gods, Hipp.*haer*.9.4(p.240.4; M.16.3370A); Maximinus Daia ap.Eus.*h.e*.9.7.5(M.20.812A); of antichrist, *cat.Apoc*.9:1(p.311.30); fig. νικᾶται νόσος τῇ τῆς ὑγείας ἐ. †Bas.*Is*.211(1.537D; M.30.484B); **3.** of Christ; **a.** of Inc. either as *coming* or as *dwelling* τῆς εἰς ἀνθρώπους ἐ. Clem.*paed*.2.8(p.203.18; M.8.488A); τὸν προνοούμενον τῆς ὡς ἀνθρώπου ἑαυτοῦ εἰς τὸν βίον ἐ. Or.*Cels*.1.66(p.119.23; M.11.784B); *ib*.4.1(p.274.8; 1029B); ref. Ex.32:22 ἐὰν ἴδῃς τὴν Ἰησοῦ ἐ., ὅλον αὐτὸν νοήσας πέτραν, ὄψει τὴν ὀπὴν κατὰ τὴν ἐ. αὐτοῦ, δι' ἧς ὀπῆς θεωρεῖται τὰ μετὰ τὸν θεόν id.*hom.16.2 in Jer*.(p.134.18; M.13.441A); id.*Jo*.1.5(7; p.10.5; M.14.33A); τὴν τοῦ σωτῆρος ἡμῶν ἐν ἀνθρώποις ἐ. *ib*.2.30(24; p.87.4; 165C); Ath.*inc*.29.2(M.25.145B); id.*Ar*.1.59(M.26.133C) cit. s. ἔνσαρκος; *ib*.(136C); ref. Jo.17:22 ἡ τούτων τελείωσις δείκνυσιν ἐ. γεγενῆσθαι τοῦ σοῦ λόγου *ib*.3.23(373B); †Bas.*Is*.247(1.567E; M.30.553B); ἑορτάζομεν...ἐ. θεοῦ πρὸς ἀνθρώπους, ἵνα πρὸς θεὸν ἐνδημήσωμεν Gr.Naz.*or*.38.4(M.36.316A); τῇ τοῦ σώματος ἐ. τοῦ πάσχα ‡Chrys.*pasch*.6.3(p.151.10; 8.268E); Euther.*confut*.12(M.28.1376A); πάντα τὰ σωματικῶς εἰρημένα ἐπὶ θεοῦ, κεκρυμμένην ἔχει τινὰ ἔννοιαν, εἰ μή τι περὶ τῆς σωματικῆς τοῦ θεοῦ λόγου ἐ. εἴρηται Jo.D.*f.o*.1.11(M.94.844B); ref. Trin. or Christol. errors cited or refuted τὸ τοῦ Σαβελλίου κακόν...ἀρνεῖται τὴν οἰκονομικὴν αὐτοῦ πρὸς ἀνθρώπους ἐ. Bas.*ep*.210.3(3.315A; M.32.772B); οἱ ἀσώματον αὐτοῦ τὴν ἐ. γεγενῆσθαι διοριζόμενοι *ib*.260.8(400C; M.965B); οἱ νομίσαντες πρὸ τῆς Μαρίας...τινὰ ἐσχηκέναι ψυχὴν ἀνθρωπίνην τὸν λόγον, καὶ ἐν αὐτῇ πρὸ τῆς ἐ. ἀεὶ γεγενῆσθαι Ath.*ep.Epict*.8(p.13.9; M.26.1064B); οὐ προϋπάρξασαν τῆς τοῦ λόγου ἐ. [sc. τὴν τῆς σαρκὸς ἕνωσιν] ‡Ath.*Apoll*.1.4(M.26.1097C); εἰ μὴ νοῦς ἔνσαρκός ἐστιν ὁ κύριος...οὐκ ἦν ἐ. θεοῦ ἡ Χριστοῦ παρουσία, ἀλλ' ἀνθρώπου γέννησις Apoll.*fr*.70(p.220.30)ap.Gr.Nyss.*Apoll*.36(M.45.1204D); μὴ ὀνομάσας μήτε σάρκα μήτε ἐ. μήτε ἐνανθρώπησιν, εἰ μὴ μόνον γυμνὴν τὴν θεότητα τοῦ θεοῦ λόγου Anast.S.*hod*.10(M.89.188B); loosely used both of Christ's coming and that of Christian missionaries τῷ ἀσυνέτῳ ἔθνει ὅπερ ὁ θεὸς ἐξελέξατο διὰ τῆς ἐ. Χριστοῦ Ἰησοῦ καὶ τῶν μαθητῶν αὐτοῦ Or.*princ*.4.1.4(p.298.13; M.11.349A); **b.** of second advent αἱ προφητεῖαι δύο λέγουσιν εἶναι τὰς Χριστοῦ ἐ., τὴν μὲν προτέραν ἀνθρωποπαθεστέραν καὶ ταπεινοτέραν...τὴν δ' ἑτέραν ἔνδοξον καὶ μόνον θειοτέραν id.*Cels*.1.56(p.107.8; M.11.764A); id.*Jo*.6.5(2; p.113.3; M.14.208C); *ib*.6.60(38; p.168.14; 304B); ἡ σάλπιγξ ἡ τὴν τοῦ βασιλέως ἐ. σημαίνουσα Bas.*hom*.21.12(2.173B; M.31.564B); Didym.*Ps*.3:5(M.39.1164B); also of Inc. and descent into hades ἀμφοτέρων τῶν ἐ. Or.*Jo*.6.35(19; p.144.16; 260B); **4.** of H. Ghost: on prophets, Or.*Cels*.7.4(p.156.2; M.11.1425B); οὐ κατὰ ἔκστασιν διανοίας...τοῦ ἀνθρωπίνου νοῦ καλυπτομένου παρὰ τοῦ πνεύματος, ὃ δὴ θείας ἐ. ἀνάξιον Proc.G.*Is*.proem.(M.87.1817A): on Christ ἐχρίσθη τῷ ἀληθινῷ χρίσματι ἡ σὰρξ τοῦ κυρίου τῇ τοῦ...πνεύματος εἰς αὐτὴν ἐ. Bas.*hom.in Ps*.44(1.165E; M.29.405A); on apostles γλώσσαις λαλοῦντες...πᾶσι φανερὰν ἐποίησαν τὴν ἐ. τοῦ πνεύματος †Bas.*Is*.217(1.541E; M.30.493B); **5.** spiritually; **a.** in OT Χριστοῦ ἐ. καὶ πρὸ τῆς κατὰ σῶμα ἐ. τὴν νοητὴν γεγονέναι τοῖς τελειοτέροις Or.*Jo*.1.7(9; p.11.26; M.14.36B); εἰ μὴ ἄρα ἡ νοητὴ αὐτοῖς γεγένηται ἐ. Χριστοῦ καὶ ἔσχον ποτὲ τελειωθέντες τὸ τῆς υἱοθεσίας πνεῦμα *ib.*19.5(p.304.1; 533B); οὐ προκριτέον ποιεῖ τῶν τὴν νοητὴν ἐ. ἐσχηκότων τὸν ἑωρακότα τὴν κατὰ σάρκα *cat.1Petr.*1:12(p.45.25); fig., of Law Μωυσῆς νόμον ἔλαβε· τοῦτο...ἀνομίας κατάλυσις, δικαιοσύνης εἴσοδος, θεοῦ ἐ. ‡Bas.*struct.hom.*2.7(1.341E; M.30.49A); **b.** to Christians δυνατὸν τῇ εἰς τὴν ψυχὴν ἡμῶν ἐ. τοῦ λόγου τοῦ θεοῦ... γενέσθαι ἡμᾶς τέκνα τοῦ θεοῦ Or.*or.*22.4(p.349.13; M.11.485C); τὴν τοῦ ἀγαθοῦ πατρὸς ἐν υἱῷ τοῖς βουλομένοις παραδέξασθαι ἐ. id.*Jo.*1.5(7; p.10.7; M.14.33A); *ib.*13.56(55; p.287.22; 505D); ref. Jo.4:46 δύνανται ...δύο τοῦ λόγου εἶναι ἐ. ἐν τῇ ψυχῇ, ἡ μὲν προτέρα τὸν ἐξ ὕδατος γινόμενον οἶνον χορηγοῦσα εἰς εὐφροσύνην τῶν συνεστιωμένων, ἡ δὲ δευτέρα πᾶσαν τὴν καταλειπομένην ἀσθένειαν καὶ τὸ πρὸς θάνατον κινδυνῶδες περιαιροῦσα *ib.*13.57(56; p.288.2; 508A); ref. Lc.1:30 παντὸς φόβου ἀφαίρεσις ἡ τοῦ σωτῆρος ἐ. id.*hom.6 in Lc.*(p.40.20); ref. Lc.3:5 ἕκαστος ἡμῶν σκολιὸς ἦν· ἐν...τῇ Χριστοῦ ἐ. τῇ γενομένῃ εἰς τὴν ψυχὴν γίνεται τὰ σκολιὰ εἰς εὐθεῖαν *ib.22*(p.144.9); ref. Is.6:7 δεξώμεθα...θείου λόγου ἐ., ἵνα καθαρίσῃ ἡμῶν τὰ χείλη καὶ ἀφέλῃ τὰς ἁμαρτίας ἡμῶν †Bas.*Is.*186(1.517A; M.30.436B); ref. Jo.17:21 εἷς ὢν ὁ θεός, ἐν ἑκάστῳ γινόμενος, ἑνοῖ τοὺς πάντας· καὶ ἀπόλλυται ὁ ἀριθμὸς τῇ τῆς μονάδος ἐ. Evagr.Pont.*ep.*7(M.32.260B); ‡Epiph.*hom.*1(M.43.433C); Zach.Mit.*opif.*(M.85.1141C).

ἐπιδήμιος, 1. *dwelling among* or *coming to dwell among* ἐπὴν...ἐ. ἔλθῃ πνεῦμα Nonn.*par.Jo.*15:26(M.43.877A); cf.*ib.*7:39(812A); *visiting, sojourning* τῶν Πέτρου ἐπιδημίων κηρυγμάτων [i.e. *delivered on his visits*] *Clem.ep.*20(M.2.56B); **2.** *prevalent, epidemic*; fig., of heresy, Gr.Nyss.*deit.*(M.46.557C); hence, s.v.l., met., *tainting* νοῦς ...χωρίζεται ῥᾳδίως...ὧν ἐ. ἡ συνάφεια Anast.Ant.*redit.*(p.252).

ἐπίδημος, *dwelling* among, c. dat., Synes.*hymn.*9.8(p.53; M.66.1613).

***ἐπιδήν,** *for long* οὐκ ἐπιδήν Gr.Naz.*carm.*2.2(epitaph.)31.4(M.38.26).

***ἐπιδηρόν,** = foreg., Gr.Naz.*carm.*2.2(epitaph.)88.3(M.38.56).

ἐπιδιαγιγνώσκω, *consider afresh*, Synes.*ep.*67(M.66.1421B).

ἐπιδιαίρεσις, ἡ, *re-division*, i.e. *different division*; opp. subdivision, Jo.D.*dialect.*6(M.94.549B).

ἐπιδιαιρέω, *subdivide, divide further*, Meth.*symp.*8.14(p.101.18; M.18.164C).

***ἐπιδιαμαρτύρομαι,** *make solemn protest against* someone, or perh. *persist in making solemn protest*, Ephr.3.417F.

ἐπιδιαμέν-ω, 1. *continue to exist* τὴν...φύσιν [sc. τῆς ψυχῆς] οἱ μὲν ἀθάνατόν φασιν, οἱ δὲ θνητήν, οἱ δὲ πρὸς ὀλίγον ~ουσαν Hermias *irris.*2 (M.6.1169B); μὴ νόμιζε [sc. ψυχὴν κτηνῶν] ~ουσαν μετὰ τὴν τῆς σαρκὸς διάλυσιν Bas.*hex.*8.2(1.71D; M.29.168A); τῆς ~ούσης εἰσαεὶ φύσεως τῶν ἀγγέλων Gr.Nyss.*hom.4 in Cant.*(M.44.856C); **2.** *continue for a time*; opp. eternally, Hipp.*haer.*1.20(p.24.16; M.16.3048A); ~ειν ἢ ἀθάνατον [sc. τὴν ψυχὴν] εἶναι Or.*Cels.*3.22(p.218.27; M.11.945A).

ἐπιδιανέμω, *assign* εὐηθέστερον...ἡμέρας...ἐπιδιανεῖμαι τῇ κοσμογονίᾳ πρὶν εἶναι ἡμέρας Cels.ap.Or.*Cels.*6.60(p.130.10; M.11.1380B).

***ἐπιδιασκέπτομαι,** *consider further*, Nemes.*nat.hom.*1(M.40.529A).

***ἐπιδιαστρέφω,** *alter, distort afterwards*, pass., †Hipp.*Artem.*ap. Eus.*h.e.*5.28.17(M.20.517).

ἐπιδιατάσσ-ομαι, 1. *make further dispositions in, add to* a will; hence *add to* NT, Anon.ap.Eus.*h.e.*5.16.3(M.20.465A); **2.** *think further* εἴ τις...ταῖς...δύο θελήσεσι...θείᾳ καὶ ἀνθρωπίνῃ ~εται συνομολογεῖν αὐταῖς...μίαν θέλησιν CLater.*can.*13; Max.*ep.*19(M.91.596B); **3.** *lay commands* upon, *give orders* οὔτε πηλὸς ἐπιδιατάξεται τῷ πλάστῃ... οὐδ' ὑμεῖς, φησί, τῷ θεῷ ἐπιδιατάξεσθε Thdr.Heracl.*Is.*45:9(M.18.1340A).

***ἐπιδιατριπτέον,** *one must spend more time on*, Or.*Jo.*2.14(8; p.70.17; M.14.137B).

ἐπιδίδ-ωμι, 1. *give afterwards, give in turn* πρεσβύτερος...εὐλογίας δέχεται παρὰ ἐπισκόπου καὶ συμπρεσβυτέρου, ὡσαύτως ἐπιδίδωσιν συμπρεσβυτέρῳ *Const.App.*8.28.3; hence *fulfil* a promise, Ath.*ep. encycl.*3(p.172.3; M.25.228C); *administer* Communion, Chrys.*hom. 50.3 in Mt.*(7.517A); **2.** *give* ὁ θεὸς...ἑαυτὸν ἐπιδιδοὺς ἀκλίτῳ δυνάμει πρὸς ἐκθέωσιν τῶν ἐπεστραμμένων Dion.Ar.*d.n.*9.5(3.912D); cf. ἐ. πρὸς ἕνα ἄρτον τοὺς ἀγρυπνοῦντας Jo.Not.*v.Eus.*3(M.86.308A); fig. ἐπίδος σου τὴν χεῖρα τῇ σοφίᾳ Meth.*fr.11 in Job*(p.514.10); **3.** *hand over, deliver*, Herm.*sim.*8.1.10; *hand on* to a successor, pass., Jo.Mosch. *prat.*195(M.87.3080D); hence **4.** *entrust* ἐ. ἑαυτοὺς τῷ θεραπεύοντι θεῷ *2Clem.*9.7; ἐπ' ἀδήλῳ τύχῃ τὴν ἰδίαν ἐ. ἐλπίδα *Hom.Clem.*4.11; *put* oneself *under* a teacher, Just.*dial.*2.3(M.6.477A); *put* oneself *in the hands of* Ἰουδὶθ...ὑπὲρ τῆς πατρίδος ἑαυτὴν ἐπίδοσιν τοῖς πολεμίοις Clem.*str.*4.19(p.300.18; M.8.1328B); Synes.*regn.*17(p.38.10; M.66.1085A); **5.** *give up, surrender, abandon*; in bad sense, *T.Jos.*3.2; ἐ. τὴν προαίρεσιν εἰς ἡδονάς Clem.*paed.*2.2(p.176.26; M.8.429B); Or. *fr.incert.in Jer.*(p.195.13; M.14.1309C); *lay down* one's life ὑπὲρ ἀληθείας ἀόκνως...τὰς ψυχὰς ~οντες Athenag.*leg.*3.2(M.6.897A); τὸν κύριον ὑπὲρ οὗ καὶ τὸ σῶμα ἑκὼν ἐπιδέδωκεν, πρὸς δὲ καὶ τὴν ψυχήν Clem.*str.*4.4(p.254.28; M.8.1228B); *ib.*(p.256.17; ἀποδιδ- 1232A); abs., *ib.*7.11(p.48.4; M.9.492C); ἐ. αὐτοὺς τῷ ἀναιρεῖσθαι Or.*Jo.*28.23(p.418.6; M.14.720A); of Christ's sacrifice, Clem.*paed.*1.11(p.148.7; M.8.365C); id.*exc.Thdot.*73(p.130.12; M.9.693A); Or.*hom.14.6 in Jer.* (p.112.2; M.13.412B); **6.** *devote* oneself, Or.*Jo.*5.1(p.100.5; M.14.185D); ἐπὶ τὰ ἀλλότρια ἑαυτὸν ἐ. Epiph.*haer.*42.6(p.101.14; M.41.701C); Chrys.*hom.22.4 in 1Cor.*(10.197B); abs., *dedicate* oneself, Gr.Thaum.*pan.Or.*3(p.7.26; M.10.1060B); **7.** *subscribe* to a letter, *Pap.Chr.*(p.371); *Ep.Alex.*(p.153.3; M.25.380D).

ἐπιδιηγέομαι, *narrate in addition*, Hipp.*haer.*9.14(p.253.7; M.16.3390C); Synes.*ep.*127(M.66.1508B).

ἐπιδικάζ-ω, 1. *adjudge worthy*, Or.*comm.in 1Cor.*4:9(*JTS* 9 p.360); **2.** med., *claim at law*; hence **a.** *claim* in gen., Clem.*fr.*10(p.198.22; M.9.745C); Hipp.*haer.*6.19(p.145.14; M.16.3222D); Or.*comm.in Mt.*11.17(p.62.20; M.13.960C); οὐκ ~εται ὁ θεὸς τιμῆς *Hom.Clem.*11.8; **b.** *seek earnestly, strive after* τοὺς ὄχλους τοὺς τῆς σοφίας αὐτοῦ ~ομένους Or.*Cels.*3.46(p.242.18, v.l. ἐπιθυμοῦντας M.11.980C); *Clem. ep.*18; ἀρετῆς ἐ. ‡Just.*or.Gr.*1(M.6.232A); **3.** pass., *be liable to prosecution under, be guilty of breaking* the commandments, Or. *sel.in Ps.*118:98(M.12.1605D).

***ἐπιδίκησις, ἡ,** *sentence, punishment*, Ephr.1.76C.

***ἐπιδίμοιρος,** = ἐπιδιμερής, *in the ratio of 5 to 3*, Clem.*str.*6.11 (p.475.11; M.9.308C).

ἐπιδιορθ-όομαι, *correct afterwards, revise*, Gr.Nyss.*Eun.*12(1 p.342.12; M.45.1061B); opp. προδιορθ-, Chrys.*hom.3.2 in Heb.*(12.26D); ἃ πεπόνηκε πρότερον...~ούμενος πρὸς ἀκρίβειαν Jo.VI H.*v.Jo. D.*36(M.94.484B); often simply *correct*, Eus.*p.e.*7.5(303D; M.21.516A); id.*h.e.*4.29.6(M.20.401A); ὀλέθριον παραλογίσασθαι μὲν τὰς θείας ταύτας φωνάς...ὥσπερ ~ουμένους τὸν θεὸν λόγον Gr.Nyss.*Eun.*2 (2 p.298.15, v.l. -ουμένας 469A); pass., *accept correction* διὰ ποίων ῥημάτων ~οῦσθαι δύναται καὶ εὐχαριστεῖν τῷ κυρίῳ; †Thdt.*Pss. proem.*(5.73).

ἐπιδιόρθωσις, ἡ, *correction of a previous expression*, Bas.*Eun.*1.5 (1.215D; M.29.517C); Chrys.*hom.4.1 in 2Cor.*(10.455C); simply *correction*, Bas.*Eun.*1.4(213B; M.513A).

***ἐπιδιπλασιασμός, ὁ,** *repetition*, Didym.*Ps.*56:2(M.39.1413A).

ἐπιδιστάζω, *be in doubt about*; c. πρός et acc., Gr.Nyss.*tres dii* (M.45.117B); c. dat., id.*Eun.*1(1 p.150.14; M.45.389D); ‡Nil.*fr. ascens.*3(M.79.1501C).

***ἐπιδιφρεύ-ω,** *drive, ride*, fig. ἀρετῶν ὀχήματι ~ων Jo.Mon.*hymn. Chrys.*8(M.96.1376A); id.*hymn.Petr.*8(1388D).

ἐπιδίφριος, *sedentary*, of consultants who sit in their surgeries ὑπηγόρευσε τὸ φάρμακον...καθάπερ...τις τῶν ἐ. ἰατρῶν Cyr.*Juln.*7 (6^4.237B); as subst. plur., *artisans* as a class ἐξ ἐπιδιφρίων ἐπίσημον ἄνδρα Evagr.*h.e.*3.28(p.124.20; M.86.2653A); *ib.*5.18(p.212.27; 2828A).

***ἐπιδιψάω,** *thirst*, Rom.Mel.(*AS* 1 p.122).

ἐπιδιώκω, *pursue, follow in pursuit*; abs., Clem.*str.*1.24(p.101.6, 13; M.8.908C,D); Thphn.*chron.*p.223(M.108.344B).

***ἐπιδογματίζω,** *teach in addition*, Epiph.*haer.*62.1(p.389.8; M.41.1052A).

ἐπιδοιάζω, c. ptcpl., *hesitate* to, Mac.Aeg.*carit.*18(M.34.924B).

ἐπίδοξος, 1. *glorious*; of second advent, Or.*fr.in Mt.*12:23(p.98); ὄνομα ἐ. Ἰησοῦν *A.Phil.*12(p.6.20); of chastity, Meth.*symp.*9.5 (p.119.29; M.18.188C); neut. as subst., *glory*, Cyr.*ador.*15(1.530A); Max.*myst.*(M.91.705C); **2.** of persons, *famous, distinguished* ἐ. καὶ οὐχ οἱ τυχόντες ἀκροαταί Adam.*dial.*1.1(p.4.1; M.11.1717A); οἰκετῶν τε καὶ ἐλευθέρων, ἀδόξων τε καὶ ἐ. Eus.*p.e.*1.4(12D; M.21.41A); ἀνὴρ κατὰ παιδείαν ἐπιδοξότατος id.*h.e.*5.10.1(M.20.453C); *approved* πᾶσιν ἐ. δι' ἀρετήν Alex.Sal.*Barn.*11(p.439C).

ἐπιδόξως, *gloriously*; of martyrs dying, Eus.*h.e.*4.15.48(M.20.364A).

ἐπιδόρπιος, *for dinner* ἐ. ὥρην Nonn.*par.Jo.*4:8(M.43.773C).

ἐπίδοσις, ἡ, A. *giving, bestowal*; **1.** in gen. ἐ. καὶ δογμάτων καὶ χρημάτων Clem.*str.*7.7(p.37.8; M.9.469B); plur., *acts of generosity*, id.*paed.*3.6(p.257.13; M.8.605B); Gr.Nyss.*or.dom.*4(p.86.30; M.44.1173C); **2.** *giving more* than might be expected, *lavishness* τῆς ἄνωθεν...εὐμενείας...τὴν ἐ. Cyr.*Jo.*11.9(4.980A); plur., Dion.Ar.*d.n.*13.1(M.3.977B); **3.** *free gift, donation*, Gr.Naz.*ep.*211(M.37.348C); **4.** *additional endowment*, Thdt.*ep.*8(4.1067); **5.** *giving* of one's *views on* a passage, *exposition*, Cyr.*Is.*1.1(3.3E).

B. *increase, advance*; **1.** in gen. ἡ δεισιδαιμονία...μὴ ἀνακοπεῖσα ἀλλ' εἰς ἐ. ἐλθοῦσα Clem.*prot*.3(p.34.2; M.8.129C); τῆς πρὸς ἐπίδοσιν τοῦ γένους εὐλογίας Gennad.*fr.Gen*.49:4(M.85.1657C); **2.** moral *progress, improvement* δικαιοῦντες ἑαυτοὺς...οὐ προκοπὴν οὐκ ἐ. ὁσημέραι δέχονται Mac.Aeg.*or*.12(M.34.861D); ἀρετῆς ἐ. Chrys.*sac*.6.3(p.145.19; 1.423D); c. objective genit., *ib*.3.12(p.69.8; 389D); **3.** theol. εἰ...τρεπτὸς καὶ ἀλλοιούμενός ἐστιν ὁ λόγος,...ποῖον αὐτοῦ τὸ τέλος ἔσται τῆς ἐ.; Ath.*Ar*.1.35(M.26.84C); Cyr.*Arcad*.11(p.69.14; 5^2.53C); **4.** self-*surrender*, self-*abandonment*, Clem.*paed*.2.8(p.201.15; M.8.481B).

***ἐπιδραμητέον**, *one must run over*; met., *one must touch upon*, Clem.*str*.2.1(p.114.5; M.8.932C).

ἐπιδράττομαι, *lay hold of*; met. τίς ἐ. τῆς...ἀχωρήτου θεότητος; Didym.*Trin*.2.7(M.39.576B); ἐ. τῆς αἰωνίου ζωῆς Cyr.*Zach*.112(3.811C); ἐ. ... τοῦ θέλειν ἀγαθουργεῖν id.*Is*.5.4(2.825A); ἡ ἀκηδία πασῶν τῶν τῆς ψυχῆς δυνάμεων ἐ. ‡Ammon.*Mt*.24:13(M.85.1385B); c. ἀπό, Cyr.*glaph.Ex*.2(1.299C).

ἐπιδρέπω, *gather*, med. τιμήν Clem.*prot*.2(p.30.18; M.8.121B).

***ἐπιδρομεύς, ὁ**, *attacking* λέοντος ἐ. τῷ παρατυχόντι Nil.*epp*.3.265 (M.79.516D).

ἐπίδρομος, 1. *that can be run over, level*; fig., Gr.Nyss.*beat*.6(M.44.1273B); ἐπὶ τὰ...ἐ. τὸν λόγον εὐθύνωμεν id.*Eun*.12(1 p.311.19; M.45.1024D); **2.** *running smoothly*; met., Gr.Naz.*ep*.176(M.37.283C).

***ἐπιδροσίζω**, *bedew*, Gr.Nyss.*hom.6 in Cant*.(M.44.897A).

ἐπιδύω (-δύνω), of the sun, *set upon* μὴ ἐπιδύνειν ἥλιον ἐπὶ τῷ παροργισμῷ Epiph.*haer*.61.1(p.381.23, v.l. -δύειν M.41.1041A); cf. Jul. Papa *ep.Dian*.ap.Ath.*apol.sec*.21(p.103.16; M.26.284C); met. τῆς ζωῆς ἡμῶν ἐπιδυείσης Gr.Nyss.*hom.1 in Eccl*.(M.44.625C).

***ἐπιδωμάτιος**, *on the house top* ἐ. χόρτος Gr.Nyss.*Pss.titt*.B 14 (M.44.588B).

ἐπιείκεια (ἐπιεικία), ἡ, A. *forbearance, gentleness*; **1.** def. τοῦτο γὰρ ἀληθῶς ἐ., οὐχ ὅταν τις παρὰ τῶν ἐν δυναστείᾳ ἀδικούμενος φέρῃ πρᾴως, ἀλλ' ὅταν καὶ ὑπὸ τῶν νομιζομένων ὑποδεεστέρων εἶναι ἐπηρεαζόμενος παραχωρῇ Chrys.*hom.52.2 in Gen*.(4.508B); **2.** in gen. *1Clem*.30.8; *ib*.56.1; Ign.*Philad*.1.1f.; CAlex.*ep*.ap.Ath.*apol.sec*.3 (p.90.7; M.25.253B); **3.** taught and exemplified by Christ, *1Clem*. 13.1; and saints τοιούτους ἡγεμόνας ἐπιεικείας ἔχομεν, παρακαλέσωμεν ἑαυτοὺς καὶ ἀλλήλους τοῖς ἐκείνων ἴχνεσιν ἕπεσθαι ‡Chrys.*mans*.(12.427A); Dion.Ar.*ep*.8(M.3.1085C); implying fortitude, Chrys.*hom.48.3 in Ac*.(9.362C); **4.** opp. vices: θυμός, Gr.Nyss.*beat*.2(M.44.1213D); χολή, Chrys.*hom.6.4 in Ac*.(9.54A); dist. from ἀνανδρεία: τί οὖν ἐστιν ἐ., καὶ τί ἀνανδρία; ὅταν ἑτέροις μὲν ἀδικουμένοις μὴ ἀμύνωμεν, ἀλλὰ σιγῶμεν αὐτοί, τοῦτο ἀνανδρίας ἐστίν· ὅταν δὲ αὐτοὶ κακῶς πάσχοντες φέρωμεν τοῦτο ἐ. *ib.48.3*(362A,B); **5.** its power and effects: making men brethren, Ign.*Eph*.10.3; οὐδὲν ἐπιεικείας ἰσχυρότερον, καὶ οὐδὲν ταύτης δυνατώτερον Chrys.*hom.57.1 in Gen*. (4.548D); οὐδὲν γὰρ ἐ. σφοδρότερον. ὥσπερ γὰρ τὴν πυρὰν σφοδρῶς πολλάκις ἐκκαιομένην ὕδωρ ἐπιβληθὲν κατέσβεσεν, οὕτω καὶ τὸν θυμὸν καμίνου σφοδρότερον ἐξαπτόμενον λόγος μετ' ἐπιεικείας προϊὼν κατασβέννυσι· καὶ διπλοῦν ἡμῖν τὸ κέρδος γίνεται, ὑπὲρ ὧν τε αὐτοὶ τὴν ἐ. ἐπιδεικνύμεθα, καὶ ὑπὲρ ὧν τοῦ ἀδελφοῦ τὸν θυμὸν καταπαύσαντες *ib.58.5*(568D); οὐδὲν γὰρ ἴσον ἐπιεικείας, ἣ καὶ τοῖς κεκτημένοις, καὶ τοῖς χρωμένοις σφόδρα ἐστὶ χρησίμη id.*hom.29.4 in Ac*.(9.233B); defeating wrath, *ib.7.1*(55B); σφοδρὸς ἔλεγχος, ὅταν μετ' ἐπιεικείας γένηται, ὁ μάλιστα δυνάμενος δακεῖν οὗτός ἐστιν id.*hom.6.2 in 2Tim*. (11.694A); **6.** as style of address ἡ σὴ ἐ. CArim.*ep.Const*.1(p.238.9; M.26.697C); *ib*.(p.238.16; 700A).

B. *modesty* ὁ Ματθαῖος δι' ὑπερβολὴν ἐ. ... τελώνην ἑαυτὸν ἀπεκάλει Eus.*d.e*.3.5(p.126.14; M.22.216A); in sense of 'want of ambition' γένος...δυσγενὲς δέ, τὸ πενήτων πατέρων, ἢ διὰ συμφοράν, ἢ δι' ἐ. Gr.Naz.*or*.33.12(M.36.229B); *condescension*; of Const., Gel. Cyz.*h.e*.3.13.15.

C. *virtue* in gen. τὸ...μεῖζον ἢ μεῖον ἐν ἐπιεικείαις Cyr.*ador*.8(1.253E); *virtuousness* τοῖς τῆς...ἐ. ... τρόποις *ib*.16(576E); *ib*.17(625C); plur. also *virtuous acts* ταῖς δὲ εἰς μετάγνωσιν σπουδαῖς καὶ ἐ. ἐκμειλίσσεσθαι θεόν id.*Nah*.31(3.508E); id.*resp*.11(6^2.379C).

D. *reasonable opinion, fair teaching* κατά γε τὸ τοῖς ἱεροῖς γράμμασιν δοκοῦν καὶ ταῖς τῶν ἁγίων πατέρων ἐ. Cyr.*apol.Thdt*.8(p.132.11; 6^1.226C).

ἐπιεικής, 1. *gentle, mild*, in gen. ἐ. ... εὐσέβειαν *1Clem*.1.2; Herm. *mand*.12.4.2; Arist.*apol*.15.5; Athenag.*leg*.12.1(M.6.913B); Bas.*hom*. 10.6(2.89D; M.31.368C); of God ἀγαπῶντες τὸν ἐ. ... πατέρα ἡμῶν *1Clem*.29.1; subst. masc., *honest, just man* τὰς εὐχὰς...μετ' ἐπιεικῶν ποιεῖσθαι πρέπον ἐστίν Clem.*str*.7.7(p.36.31; M.9.469A); ἀψευδεῖν χρὴ τὸν ἐ. *ib*.7.15(p.64.3; 525A); **2.** *moderate, restrained*; of language, Gr.Thaum.*pan.Or*.5(p.12.1; M.10.1065A); neut. as subst. τὸ ἐ. τῆς γλώσσης *1Clem*.21.7.

ἐπιεικτός, *accessible to, within the power of*, c. dat., Eudoc.*Cypr*. 1.197(M.85.840B).

ἐπιζεύγνυμι, 1. pass., *be yoked together* for καταπαύσαντος θεοῦ... ἐπὶ τῶν...χερουβὶμ ἐπεζευγμένων αὐτῷ Proc.G.*Dt*.33:12(M.87.985C); **2.** of a bridge, *span*; c. dat., Malch.*exc.Rom*.1(p.162.28; M.113.768C, v.l. ὑπέζευκτο).

***ἐπιζητητής, ὁ**, *seeker* ἀπολωλότων ἐ. *A.Xanthipp*.9(p.63.25); ἐ. τῶν ἁμαρτωλῶν *ib*.14(p.67.18).

***ἐπιζοφόω**, *put in darkness*, Gr.Naz.*carm*.2.1.12.52(M.37.1170); Olymp.*Job* 3:1(M.93.53A).

ἐπιζυγόω, *bolt, bar*, Synes.*ep*.29(M.66.1357C); Germ.CP *or*.2(M.98.276D).

***ἐπιζωγραφέω**, *paint in outline*, Diad.*perf*.89(p.124.14).

ἐπίηρα, *on account of* ἀμπλακίης ἐ. Nonn.*par.Jo*.8:46(M.43.820C).

ἐπιθάλπω, *cherish, show favour to*, *T.Jos*.5.4.

ἐπιθειάζω, 1. *address as God* πολλὰ γὰρ κατὰ μέρος ἐπιθειάσας αὐτόν †Dion.Al.*fr.2 in Job*(p.204.1); Gel.Cyz.*h.e*.1.5.5(M.85.1204D); **2.** *be inspired* προφήτης...τῷ...ἁγίῳ πνεύματι ἐπιθειάσας Eus.*d.e*.7.1 (p.299.3; M.22.489B); id.*p.e*.7.11(317D; M.21.537A); id.*v.C*.3.27(p.90.27; M.20.1088A); **3.** *declare by inspiration*, Gr.Naz.*or*.5.3(M.35.668B).

ἐπίθεσις, ἡ, 1. *laying on* of hands for healing of sick, Iren.*haer*. 2.32.4(M.7.829B); Eustrat.*v.Eutych*.5(M.86.2280C); v. χείρ; **2.** *application*, medic., *M.Tar*.6(p.462); **3.** *imposture* (cf. Eng. *put on*), Clem.*paed*.3.2(p.239.9; M.8.561B); Chrys.*hom.14.9 in Rom*.(9.588D); *Chron.Pasch*.p.296(M.92.744A); **4.** *trick*, *A.Petr.et Paul*.2(p.179.4); *A.(Pass.)Petr.et Paul*.17(p.134.9).

ἐπιθεωρ-έω, 1. *observe, consider*; *consider in, consider as being in* εἰ ἔξωθεν ~εῖται τῷ θεῷ τὸ ἀγέννητον, οἱ ἐπιθεωρήσαντες τοῦ ἐπιθεωρηθέντος εἰσὶν ἀμείνους, κρεῖττον ὄνομα τῆς φύσεως αὐτῷ πορισάμενοι Aët.*synt*.13(p.354.24; M.42.537D); περὶ τῆς ἀγεννησίας... καὶ πῶς ~εῖται τῷ θεῷ Bas.*Eun*.1.14(1.227A; M.29.545A); εἰ δὲ... γνωριστικάς τινας ἰδιότητας ~ουμένας τῇ οὐσίᾳ δέχοιτό τις εἶναι τὸ γεννητὸν καὶ τὸ ἀγέννητον *ib*.2.28(265B; M.637B); οὐκ ἔστι τὰ τῆς σαρκὸς ἰδιώματα τῷ ἐν ἀρχῇ ὄντι ἐπιθεωρηθῆναι λόγῳ Gr.Nyss.*Eun*.6 (2 p.129.12; M.45.712D); ἕξεις τῇ...οὐσίᾳ ~ούμεναι Max.*ambig*.(M.91.1177B); **2.** *interpret* scripture *spiritually* σεμνῶς ~εῖν, καὶ εἰς ἀναγωγὴν ὑψηλοτέραν ἀποφέρειν τὰ νοήματα Diod.*proem.Pss*. (p.88.16); *ib*.(p.90.27); **3.** *consider subsequently*, Max.*ambig*.(M.91.1072B).

ἐπιθεωρία, ἡ, *contemplation*, hence *spiritual interpretation* of scripture ὁ ἀπόστολος ἀλληγορίαν τὴν ἐ. καλεῖ [Gal.4:24] Diod.*proem. Pss*.(p.90.30).

ἐπιθήγ-ω, *stimulate, incite* ταῦτα τὰ φρονήματα...πᾶν...νόημα μανικὸν...~ει Gr.Nyss.*res*.3(M.46.676B); Ast.Am.*hom*.5(M.40.237B); Cyr.*ador*.1(1.24A).

***ἐπιθηριόομαι, 1.** *become like a wild beast*, Cyr.H.*catech*.2.18; **2.** v. ἀποθηριόω.

***ἐπιθησαυριστέον**, v. ἀπο-.

ἐπιθολ-όω, *make turbid*, met.; **1.** *confuse, disturb, becloud* ἐπεθόλωσεν τὸ μὴ ἀπίθανον παρατήρημα Or.*Jo*.13.16(p.239.31; M.14.421C); ~οῦσθαι τὸν νοῦν ὑπὸ ἑτέρων λογισμῶν id.*or*.9.1(p.318.2; M.11.444A); ταράσσεσθαι τὸ ἡγεμονικόν, ~ούμενον ταῖς ἐξαλλαγαῖς τοῦ βίου Meth.*symp*.5.2(p.55.11; M.18.100C); Ath.*gent*.34(M.25.69A); Gr.Nyss.*hom.9 in Cant*.(M.44.965A); τὸ διειδὲς...τῆς εὐσεβείας...τῇ τῶν εἰδώλων ~οῦντες ἐπιμιξίᾳ Thdr.Mops.*Os*.6:8–11(M.66.164A); Isid.Pel.*epp*.1.432(M.78.421A); Thdr.Stud.*epp*.1.30(M.99.1005C); **2.** *defile*, Meth.*symp*.8.12(p.96.19; M.18.157C); ψυχὴ...πολλοῖς ~ωθεῖσα πάθεσιν Chrys.*hom.2.4 in Jo*.(8.13E); Dion.Ar.*d.n*.11.2(M.3.949C).

***ἐπιθόλως**, *with uneasy mind*, Pall.*v.Chrys*.14(p.85.10; M.47.48).

***ἐπιθόλωσις, ἡ**, *clouding of mind*, Cyr.*ador*.1(1.37A).

***ἐπιθορόω**, *impregnate*, Clem.*paed*.2.10(p.210.13; M.8.502B).

ἐπιθορυβέω, 1. *wail*, Gr.Nyss.*v.Macr*.(pp.401.10,407.4; M.46.988B,992D); **2.** pass., *be disturbed* ἐπεθορυβεῖτο πάθεσι τοῖς σωματικοῖς Gr.Nyss.*Apoll*.46(M.45.1237B).

ἐπιθρυλ(λ)-έω, *make a noise about*, Gr.Naz.*ep*.202(M.37.332A); ~ῶν ἑαυτῷ διὰ τοῦ βαπτίσματος τὴν πρὸς τὸ κρεῖττον μεταβολήν Gr.Nyss.*or.catech*.40(p.161.18; M.45.104B); *declaim noisily against* πῶς δέ τις ἐπιθρυλλήσει τὴν ἀσωτίαν τῷ ἀνακεχωρημένῳ; id.*v.Mos*.(M.44.141C); id.*Trin*.2(p.72.27; M.32.685C).

ἐπιθυμ-έω, *set one's heart upon* a thing, *long for, desire*; **1.** explained ἐκ γὰρ τοῦ ὑστερεῖν τὸ ἐ. ἐστιν, ἐκ δὲ τοῦ πάντα ἔχειν τὸ μηδενὸς ἐ. Clem.*fr*.46(p.223.33); **2.** ref. evil: worldly things, *2Clem*. 5.6f.; Ign.*Rom*.7.1; ἀεί τι ἐργάσασθαι ~οῦντες κακόν Athenag.*leg*.11.2 (M.6.912B); worldly glory, Clem.*str*.7.16(p.73.4; M.9.544A); Const.

ap.Gel.Cyz.*h.e.*2.7.24(M.85.1237A); δοκοῦσαν εὐπάθειαν ἐ. Dion.Ar. *e.h.*3.3.7(M.3.436A); **3.** ref. good: heaven, Polyc.*ep.*1.3; Clem.*prot.* 10(p.75.14; M.8.221A); martyrdom, *M.Polyc.*19.1; τὸ φίλον γενέσθαι...θεῷ...~οῦντες Gr.Thaum.*pan.Or.*12(p.28.22; M.10.1085C); **4.** sexually, Just.*dial.*134.1(M.6.785C).

ἐπιθύμησις, ἡ, *desire*, *A.Thadd.*3(p.274.14 n.); *A.Thom.*A 58 (p.175.1).

***ἐπιθυμητέον**, *one must desire*, ‡Just.*ep.Zen.et Ser.*5(M.6.1188C).

ἐπιθυμητικός, *desiring, endowed with desire*, Max.*ambig.*(M.91.1248B); τὸ ἐ. *seat of desires and affections* in soul, dist. from λογιστικόν and θυμικόν: πολύμορφον δὲ τὸ ἐ. Clem.*paed.*3.1(p.236.7; M.8.556B); νεφροὶ δὲ ἐν τῇ γραφῇ τὸ ἐ. Or.*fr.73 in Lam.*(p.264.11; M.13.644C); cf.Thdt.*Jer.*11:20(2.473); *Hom.Clem.*5.21; τὸ ἐ. τετάσθω σοι πᾶν πρὸς θεόν Gr.Naz.*or.*44.7(M.36.613C); should be detached from material things, Gr.Nyss.*hom.1 in Cant.*(M.44.768C); Chrys.*hom.18.4 in Jo.*(8.109B); Max.*ambig.*(1196C).

ἐπιθυμητικῶς, *eagerly, full of desire* εἰ μὴ ἐ. ἔρχεται ἐπὶ τὸ ψάλλειν Bas.*reg.br.*281(2.514B; M.31.1280B).

ἐπιθυμητός, *to be desired, desirable*; in gen., *T.Lev.*8.16; Clem.*str.*4.13(p.289.27; M.8.1301A); Bas.*hom.*1.8(2.7A; M.31.176C); τὰ ἐ. Chrys.*hom.43.3 in Mt.*(7.632C); ἐ. γὰρ ἡμῖν πληροφορῆσαί σε Gel.Cyz.*h.e.*2.24.2(M.85.1297D); spiritually εὐδοξία ἐ. Meth.*symp.*10.6(p.129.1; M.18.204A); Gr.Nyss.*v.Mos.*7(M.44.301A); id.*hom.1 in Cant.*(M.44.777B); sexually, Hegem.*Arch.*9(p.14.3; M.10.1441A); fig. ἐὰν ...ἀπαλείψῃς τοὺς σπίλους τῶν πονηρῶν μαθημάτων...ἐπιθυμητὴ φανήσῃ τῷ νυμφίῳ Bas.*hom.in Ps.*44(1.167E; M.29.409B).

ἐπιθυμία, ἡ, **A.** *desire, lust, 'concupiscence'*; **1.** def. and properties πάντων προέχουσα ἐ. γυναικὸς ἀλλοτρίας ἢ ἀνδρός, καὶ πολυτελείας πλούτου καὶ ἐδεσμάτων πολλῶν ματαίων καὶ μεθυσμάτων, καὶ ἑτέρων τρυφῶν πολλῶν καὶ μωρῶν...αὗται οὖν αἱ ἐ. πονηραί εἰσι Herm.*mand.*12.2.1,2; cf.*ib.*6.2.5; πάντα γὰρ ἡ ἐ. γίνεταί τε καὶ πλάττεται καὶ φενακίζειν βούλεται, ἵνα κατακρύψῃ τὸν ἄνθρωπον Clem.*paed.*3.1(p.236.20; M.8.556C); in rel. to ὄρεξις: ὁρίζεσθαι ἀξιοῦσιν...τὴν μὲν ἐ. ὄρεξιν ἀπειθῆ λόγῳ *ib.*1.13(p.150.23; 372B); id.*str.*2.20(p.177.21; M.8.1064A); ὄρεξιν οὖν ἐπιθυμίας διακρίνουσιν...καὶ τὴν μὲν ἐπὶ ἡδοναῖς καὶ ἀκολασίᾳ τάττουσιν ἄλογον οὖσαν, τὴν δὲ ὄρεξιν ἐπὶ τῶν κατὰ φύσιν ἀναγκαίων λογικὴν ὑπάρχουσαν κίνησιν *ib.*4.18(p.300.1; 1325B); κατὰ τὰς θείας γραφὰς ἡ ἐ. τῶν μέσων ἐστίν, οὐκ εἰδυίας τὴν Ἑλληνικὴν τὴν σημαινομένων παρὰ τοῖς τὰ τοιαῦτα διαρθροῦσιν ἀκρίβειαν, ὥστ' ἂν τὸ μὲν ἀστεῖον βούλησιν ὀνομάσαι, ἣν ὁρίζονται εὔλογον ὄρεξιν, τὸ δὲ φαῦλον ἐ., ἥν φασιν εἶναι ἄλογον ὄρεξιν Or.*Jo.*20.22(20; p.355.18ff.; M.14.621B,C); id.*comm.in Rom.*7:8(*JTS* 14 pp.13f.); cf. ἐ. δὲ τὴν ὀργὴν ἐκάλεσεν· ἐκ ταύτης γὰρ καὶ ἡ ὀργὴ τὴν ἐτυμολογίαν ἔχει· ὀρέγεται γὰρ ὁ ὀργιζόμενος ἀμύνασθαι τὸν ἐχθρόν Thdt.*qu.110 in Gen.*(1.112); ἐ. ἐστὶ δύναμις ψυχῆς ὀργῆς ἀφανιστική *Doct.Patr.*33(p.258.12); ἐ. ἐστὶ παντὸς ἐμψύχου πρώτη ὁρμὴ πρός τι τῶν φιλουμένων *ib.*(p.260.19); ἔχει γὰρ ἴδιον ἡ ἐ. πῦρ Nil.*praest.*7(M.79.1068D); **2.** in gen. τῶν ἐ. τῶν ματαίων *2Clem.*19.2; Polyc.*ep.*5.3; ἡ ἐ. τῆς πονηρίας Herm.*vis.*1.1.8; id.*mand.*6.2.5; id.*sim.*5.1.5; equated with sin, Clem.*str.*7.12(p.53.6; M.9.501B); Meth.*res.*2.7(p.341.6; M.18.305A); *ib.*2.8(p.344.7; 308A); **3.** and other vices πάθη ὀργῆς καὶ ἐ. Athenag.*leg.*21.1(M.6.933A); πάσης γὰρ ἡδονῆς ἐ. κατάρχει, ἐ. δὲ λύπη τις καὶ φροντὶς δι' ἔνδειαν ὀρεγομένη τινός Clem.*str.*3.5(p.215.7; M.8.1145A); and θυμός v.s.v.; ὕβρις, id.*paed.*2.10(p.211.13; M.8.504B); πάθος, Meth.*symp.*8.2(p.82.8; M.18.140B); lesser evil than wrath, Chrys.*hom.17.1 in Eph.*(11.122E); εἰ δέ ποτε συμβαίη πέρα τοῦ μέτρου τὴν ἐ. προκύψαι, νύττειν ἐκέλευσε [sc. God] τὸν θυμόν· ἵνα ὁρμήσας οὗτος, ἴσον πάλιν ἐργάσηται τὸν ζυγόν. εἰ δὲ οὗτος δέξαιτο τῆς ἀμετρίας τὸ πάθος, τὴν ἐ. πάλιν κινεῖσθαι παρεγγυᾷ, καὶ τοῦ θυμοῦ τὴν ἀμετρίαν κολάζειν Thdt.*Rom.*7:17(3.77); στῆθος δὲ θυμόν, γαστέρα δὲ τὴν ἐ. ... ἐλέγομεν Dion.Ar.*d.n.*9.5(M.3.913A); cure of both ἀλλόφυλος δὲ παῖς καὶ παιδίσκη, ὁ θυμός καὶ ἡ ἐ., οὓς ὑποζεύγνυσι...τῇ δεσποτείᾳ τοῦ λόγου πρὸς ὑπηρεσίαν τῶν ἀρετῶν δι' ἀνδρείας καὶ σωφροσύνης ὁ θεωρητικὸς νοῦς, οὐ διδοὺς αὐτοῖς παντελῶς τὴν πρὸς ἐλευθερίαν ἄφεσιν, ἕως ἂν καταποθῇ τῷ νόμῳ τοῦ πνεύματος τελείως ὁ τῆς φύσεως νόμος...καὶ πᾶσα δειχθῇ καθαρῶς ἡ τῆς ἀνάρχου βασιλείας εἰκών...καθ' ἣν γενόμενος ὁ θεωρητικὸς νοῦς, ἐλευθέρους ποιεῖται τόν τε θυμὸν καὶ τὴν ἐ.· τὴν μέν, πρὸς τὴν ἀκήρατον τοῦ θείου ἔρωτος ἡδονήν,...τὸν δέ, πρὸς ζέσιν πνευματικήν Max.*qu.Thal.*55(M.90.548C,D); **4.** connected with demons; as 'Devil's daughter', Herm.*mand.*12.2.2; id.*sim.*6.2.3; *ib.*6.3.3; demons, Just.*1apol.*10.6(M.6.341B); Hipp.*haer.*5.9(p.102.17; M.16.3160A); τῶν ἐν παντὶ υἱῷ διαβόλου ἐ. ἀπὸ τῶν ἐν τῷ διαβόλῳ ἐ. γεννωμένων, σαφὲς ὅτι αἱ ἐκείνου ἐ. φρόνημα ὕλης εἰσίν Or.*Jo.*20.22(20; p.354.7ff.; M.14.620B); Meth.*res.*2.2(p.331.4; M.41.1164B); Ath.*inc.*11.5(M.25.116C); Dion.Ar.*d.n.*4.23(M.3.725B); hence **5.** absent from paradise, Meth.*res.*2.1(pp.329.15–330.1; M.18.297A); but (Manich.) trees in paradise = ἐ. καὶ ἄλλαι ἀπάται διαφθείρουσαι τοὺς λογισμούς Hegem.*Arch.*11(p.18.2; M.10.1445A); **6.** with or without πονηρά, opp. good things, e.g. τὰ λόγια τοῦ κυρίου Polyc.*ep.*7.1; justice and truth, Herm.*sim.*9.25.2; sanctification, *1Clem.*30.1; cf. ὁ γάμος... κατὰ κύριον, καὶ μὴ κατ' ἐπιθυμίαν Ign.*Polyc.*5.2; repentance, Herm.*vis.*3.7.2; id.*sim.*9.14.1; H. Ghost and things of spirit τὸ...πνεῦμα ἰδίως [l. τοῖς] καταπατοῦσι τὰς γεώδεις ἐ. Iren.*haer.*5.12.2(M.7.1152B); ἀποθέμενοι...τὰς ἐ. τῆς σαρκός, καὶ προσλαβόντες τὸ πνεῦμα τὸ ἅγιον *ib.*5.12.3(1154A); πόρρω γὰρ ἐ. ... τὰ πνευματικά Meth.*res.*2.2(p.332.15; M.18.300B); σωφροσύνη and φρόνησις, Clem.*str.*4.23(p.315.15; M.8.1360C); virginity, Meth.*symp.*1.1(p.8.17; M.18.37C); *ib.*11(p.131.2; 208A); ὑπομονή, *ib.*(p.140.25; 220C); divine law, id.*res.*2.6(p.340.6ff.; M.18.304B,C); heavenly things, Ath.*gent.*2(M.25.8A); **7.** effects: privation of good, Dion.Ar.*d.n.*4.20(M.3.720B); fornication, *Did.*3.3; Clem.*paed.*2.6(p.188.18; M.8.453B); Chrys.*poenit.*6.2(2.319C); enslavement, Ign.*Polyc.*4.3; Just.*2apol.*5.4(M.6.452C); blindness, Chrys.*hom.20.5 in Mt.*(7.266D); suffering, Clem.*str.*2.15(p.147.13; M.8.1001A); Chrys.*hom.59.2 in Gen.*(4.572D); τοιοῦτον γὰρ ἡ ἐ., τυραννικόν τι πρᾶγμα καὶ ἱκανὸν πεῖσαι τὸν ἁλόντα, ὑπὲρ ὁτουοῦν καὶ παθεῖν καὶ ὑπομεῖναι id.*oppugn.*3.19(1.111D); id.*res.mort.*2(2.425B); and death, Herm.*mand.*12.1.3; *ib.*12.2.2; **8.** cure; **a.** through Christ, Clem.*str.*4.23(p.315.24; M.8.1360C); τὴν ἔνδον ἐ., ἣ οὐ δύναται ὑπὸ ἄλλων θεραπευθῆναι, αὐτὸς θεραπεύει Or.*engast.*6(p.289.24; M.12.1021B); Χριστὸς...μάχαιρα...νεκροῦσα τὰ πρὸς ἐ. κινήματα Bas.*hom. in Ps.*44(1.163C; M.29.400B); Chrys.*hom.18.5 in Mt.*(7.241E); **b.** by human effort, *Did.*1.4; *2Clem.*16.2; ἐὰν ἀφέξηται πάσης ἐ. πονηρᾶς, κληρονομήσει ζωὴν αἰώνιον Herm.*vis.*3.8.4; id.*sim.*5.3.6; *Hom.Clem.*9.19; Nil.*inst.*(M.79.1237B); esp. ascetic practices, Chrys.*hom.15.2 in 1Cor.*(10.127D); Max.*carit.*2.47(M.90.1000C); **9.** incompatible with divinity, ref. pagan gods, Athenag.*leg.*21.4(M.6.936A); κρεῖττον ἐπιθυμίας τὸ θεῖον *ib.*29.2(957C); (Manich.) τὸ παρ' ὑμῖν [sc. Christians] τίμιον...ὄνομα Σαβαὼθ αὐτὸ εἶναι τὴν φύσιν τοῦ ἀνθρώπου καὶ πατέρα τῆς ἐ.· καὶ διὰ τοῦτο ἁπλάριοι προσκυνοῦσι τὴν ἐ., θεὸν αὐτὴν ἡγούμενοι Manes ap.Hegem.*Arch.*11(p.19.11; M.10.1445C); cf. *ib.*12(p.20.5,16; 1448A,B).

B. *desire, longing*, good or indifferent; **1.** opp. evil ἐ.: ἆρον ἀπὸ σεαυτοῦ πᾶσαν ἐ. πονηράν, ἔνδυσαι δὲ τὴν ἐ. τὴν ἀγαθήν...ἐνδεδυμένος γὰρ τὴν ἐ. ταύτην μισήσεις τὴν πονηρὰν ἐ. ... ἀγρία γάρ ἐστιν ἡ ἐ. πονηρὰ καὶ δυσκόλως ἡμεροῦται...λίαν τῇ ἀγριότητι αὐτῆς δαπανᾷ τοὺς ἀνθρώπους...τοὺς μὴ ἔχοντας ἔνδυμα τῆς ἐ. τῆς ἀγαθῆς Herm.*mand.*12.1.1f.; ὁ γὰρ φόβος τοῦ θεοῦ κατοικεῖ ἐν τῇ ἐ. τῇ ἀγαθῇ. ἡ ἐ. ἡ πονηρά, ἐὰν ἴδῃ σε καθωπλισμένον τῷ φόβῳ τοῦ θεοῦ...φεύξεται ἀπὸ σοῦ *ib.*12.2.4; ἐὰν δουλεύσῃς τῇ ἐ. τῇ ἀγαθῇ...δυνήσῃ τῆς ἐ. τῆς πονηρᾶς κατακυριεῦσαι *ib.*12.2.5; δύο γὰρ κινήσεε ἐν ἡμῖν ἐστόν· ἐ. πεφυκότε σαρκὸς καὶ ψυχῆς, διαφέρετον ἀλλήλοιν. ὅθεν καὶ δύο ἐλαβέτην ὀνόματε· ἡ μὲν γὰρ ἀρετῆς, ἡ δὲ κακίας Meth.*symp.*8.17(p.111.4; M.18.173B); τοῖς μὴ κατὰ τὴν ἐ. τῆς σαρκὸς περιπατοῦσιν, ἀλλὰ κατὰ τὴν ἐ. τοῦ πνεύματος id.*res.*2.8(p.345.1f.; M.18.308B); Thdt.*Ps.*52:5(1.1325); **2.** in gen., for salvation, *Barn.*17.1; *ib.*21.7; ἐ. τῆς δικαιοσύνης Herm.*mand.*12.2.4f.; for σοφία and γνῶσις, Clem.*str.*6.15(p.492.27f.; M.9.344C,D); for γνῶσις, Meth.*arbitr.*4(p.156.4; M.18.249A); ἐ. ... ὡς ἄπλαστος οἰκεῖν ἐν τῇ οἰκίᾳ αὐτοῦ Ath.*v.Anton.*1(M.26.841A); ἡ τῆς δόξης ἐ. Gr.Naz.*or.*40.23(M.36.389C); for God, Chrys.*exp.in Ps.*142:6(5.455C); ἡ τῶν κρειττόνων ἐ. *Schol.*2 in Jo.Clim.*scal.*15(M.88.904C); οὗτινος ὁ νοῦς διαπαντός ἐστι πρὸς θεόν, τούτου καὶ ἡ ἐ. εἰς τὸν θεῖον ὑπερηύξησεν ἔρωτα Max.*carit.*2.48(M.90.1000C); combined with λόγος and θυμός, id.*cap.*2.25(M.90.1229C); **3.** necessity occasioned by man's indigence, Meth.*symp.*8.16(p.104.13; M.18.168B); δεῖται γὰρ ἐ., οὐ τροφῆς ἕνεκα μόνον, ἀλλὰ καὶ παιδοποιΐας, καὶ γηπονίας, καὶ τῶν ἄλλων χάριν τεχνῶν. ταύτης γὰρ οὐκ οὔσης, οὐδὲν τούτων συνέστηκεν. αὕτη ἡμῖν καὶ εἰς τὴν τῆς ἀρετῆς κατόρθωσιν συντελεῖ. ὁ γὰρ μὴ ἐφιέμενος ταύτης, τῶν ὑπὲρ ταύτης οὐκ ἀνέχεται πόνων. αὕτη καὶ τὸν θεῖον ἡμῖν ἐξεργάζεται πόθον. ἡ μὲν οὖν συμμετρία τῆς ἐ. τῶν ἀγαθῶν ἐστι συνεργός· ἡ δὲ ταύτης ἀμετρία τὴν ἀκολασίαν εἰσάγει Thdt.*Rom.*7:17(3.76f.); **4.** effects ἤθελον...γνῶναι ποίοις τρόποις με δεῖ δουλεῦσαι τῇ ἐ. τῇ ἀγαθῇ...ἐργάσαι δικαιοσύνην καὶ ἀρετήν, ἀλήθειαν καὶ φόβον κυρίου Herm.*mand.*12.3.1; ἡ τῶν κρειττόνων ἐ. ἐν ἐξουσίᾳ...ἔχουσα τὴν ἀπόλαυσιν τῶν ἐπιθυμουμένων, καταφρονεῖν...ἀναγκάζει τὰ ἐλάττονα Bas.*reg.br.*30(2.425B; M.31.1104A); ἡ γὰρ ἐ. ὅταν στῇ, τότε παρέχει τὴν ἡδονὴν Chrys.*hom.12.8 in Rom.*(9.554A); fulfilled by Christ, Thdt.*Ps.*102(1.1325); τὴν μὲν ἐ., ποιῶν ἔφεσιν τῶν θείων ἀπολαυστικὴν Max.*qu.Thal.*55(M.90.549A); **5.** ἐ. and prayer ὧν...αἱ...ἐ. ... τούτων εἰσὶ καὶ αἱ εὐχαί... τούτων οὖν αἱ εὐχαὶ ὧν καὶ αἰτήσεις, καὶ τούτων αἱ αἰτήσεις ὧν καὶ ἐ. Clem.*str.*7.7(p.29.21ff.; M.9.453C); **6.** two kinds ἐ. μὲν εἶναί φαμεν, ἐπὶ τῶν ἀλόγων ἀπερίσκεπτόν τινα...προσπάθειαν...ὅταν δέ, τὰς ἀνομοίους ὁμοιότητας τοῖς νοεροῖς περιτιθέντες, ἐ. αὐτοῖς περιπλάσωμεν, ἔρωτα θεῖον αὐτὴν ἐννοῆσαι χρή Dion.Ar.*c.h.*2.4(M.3.141D–144A); cf.*ib.*15.8(337B).

C. esp. *sexual desire*; **1.** without connotation of sin ἡμῖν μέτρον ἐπιθυμίας ἡ παιδοποιΐα Athenag.*leg.*33.1(M.6.965A); Clem.*str.*3.12 (p.236.15; M.8.1188C); Meth.*symp.*2.2(p.17.3; M.18.49B); ἡ ἐ. δὲ εἰς μὲν γάμους οὐ κακή *Hom.Clem.*19.18; ἤτε γὰρ ἐ. ἐκ τοῦ πάντα καλῶς δημιουργήσαντος συμβαίνειν τῷ ζώῳ γεγένηται, ἵνα ὑπ' αὐτῆς ἀγόμενον πρὸς κοινωνίαν τὴν ἀνθρωπότητα πληθύνῃ...πλὴν ἄνευ ἐ. τὴν πρὸς γυναῖκα κοινωνίαν οὐδεὶς ἂν ἀνεδέξατο *ib.*19.21; but hindering union with God, unlike virginity, Athenag.*leg.*33.1(M.6.965A); **2.** entering through the eyes, Clem.*paed.*3.11(p.274.27; M.8.645A); thus indulged even in church, Chrys.*David* 3.1(4.769E); *ib.*(770A); **3.** deified by pagans (as Eros), Clem.*prot.*3(p.33.31; M.8.129B); **4.** met., of wrongful desire of a bishop for another see, Ath.*apol. sec.*6(p.93.4; M.25.260B).

***ἐπιθυσία, ἡ,** v. *ἐφηθυσία.

ἐπιθύω, *offer sacrifice* (pagan) τοῦτον ὁ ἀνθύπατος...ἔπεισεν ὀμόσαι καὶ ἐπιθῦσαι *M.Polyc.*4; τί γὰρ κακόν ἐστιν εἰπεῖν· κύριος καῖσαρ, καὶ ἐπιθῦσαι; *ib.*8.2; Clem.*prot.*5(p.49.13; M.8.165B); ἐπίθυσον ὑπὲρ σωτηρίας τῶν αὐτοκρατόρων *M.Perp.*6(p.71.16); Hipp.*antichr.*49 (p.32.23; M.10.769A); *Hom.Clem.*10.23; πρεσβυτέρους τοὺς ἐπιθύσαντας...προσφέρειν...ἢ ὅλως λειτουργεῖν...μὴ ἐξεῖναι CAnc.(314) *can.*1.

ἐπικαγχάζω, *laugh loudly at*, c. dat., Gr.Nyss.*v.Gr.Thaum.*(M.46. 940D).

ἐπικαθέζ-ομαι, *be attached, devoted to*, Epiph.*haer.*66.2(p.17.21; M.42.32C); εἰδώλοις ∼εται [sc. ψυχή] Nil.*exerc.*54(M.79.785D).

ἐπικάθισμα, τό, *seat, saddle*, Chrys.*fr.in Jer.*38:11(M.64.1004A).

***ἐπικαθυπνόω,** *sleep in*, met. ἵνα μήποτε ἐπαναπαυόμενοι ὡς κλητοὶ ἐπικαθυπνώσωμεν ταῖς ἁμαρτίαις ἡμῶν *Barn.*4.13.

***ἐπικαινοτομ-έω,** *refashion, innovate, add to* παράδοσιν ∼εῖν οἰόμενος Eus.*h.e.*7.3(M.20.641A); Cyr.*Jo.*4.4(4.394A); *ib.*9(765B).

ἐπικαλ-έω, 1. act. and med., *call upon, invoke*; **a.** ref. prayer to God in gen. ∼ουμένων σε αὐτῶν ὁσίως *1Clem.*60.4; ∼εῖσθαι δυνάμενος ἐπὶ τῷ ὀνόματι τοῦ κυρίου Or.*Jo.*20.10(p.339.1; M.14.593C); ∼ούμεθα τὸν τῶν ὅλων δεσπότην ἀντιλαβέσθαι τῆς ἡμῶν πτωχείας Epiph.*haer.*proem.1(p.169.18; M.41.173B); ἡμῖν ἐν τῇ ἁγίᾳ ὥρᾳ ταύτῃ ∼ουμένοις σε *Lit.Jac.*(p.182.9); **b.** ref. invocation in Marcosian baptisms, Iren.*haer.*1.21.3(M.7.661A); in Peratic rites τὸν Φρῆν ἤ τινα ἕτερον ∼οῦντες δαίμονα Hipp.*haer.*4.28(p.54.16; M.16. 3090C); in magic spells ἐπὰν...ἐπικαλέσηται ὁ ἐπαοιδὸς τὴν σελήνην *ib.*4.37(p.63.14; 3102D); of invocation of pagan deities for healing, Cels.ap.Or.*Cels.*8.58(p.274.31; M.11.1605A); **c.** in consecration prayer in eucharist σὲ γὰρ τὸν ἀγένητον ἐπεκαλεσάμεθα διὰ τοῦ μονογενοῦς ἐν ἁγίῳ πνεύματι Serap.*euch.*13.16; v. ἐπίκλησις; **d.** in blessing of oil etc., *ib.*29.1,2; **e.** ref. invocation of saints θεῷ προσευξάμενος, τὴν τῶν ἁγίων πρεσβείαν ἐπεκαλέσατο Gr.Nyss.*mart.*3 (M.46.784C); δέχομαι δὲ...τοὺς ἁγίους ἀποστόλους, προφήτας, καὶ μάρτυρας, καὶ εἰς τὴν πρὸς θεὸν ἱκεσίαν τούτους ∼οῦμαι, τοῦ δι' αὐτῶν, ἤγουν διὰ τῆς μεσιτείας αὐτῶν, ἵλεών μοι γενέσθαι τὸν...θεόν †Bas.*ep.*360(3.462E; M.32.1100B); of living saint, Niceph.Ur.*v.Sym.* 74(M.86.3056B); **2.** *name, entitle, surname* πάσῃ ψυχῇ ἐπικεκλημένῃ τὸ...ὄνομα αὐτοῦ *1Clem.*64; Ἑρμῆς ὁ Τρισμέγιστος ∼ούμενος Athenag. *leg.*28.4(M.6.956B); of nominal Christians οἱ τὸ ὄνομα ἐπικεκλημένοι μόνον, βιοῦντες δὲ οὐ κατὰ λόγον Clem.*str.*7.14(p.62.20; M.9.521B); **3.** *object, raise objections*, Just.*1apol.*46.1(M.6.397B); **4.** *allege* against, *charge with* Διαγόρᾳ...ἀθεότητα ἐπεκάλουν Ἀθηναῖοι Athenag. *leg.*4.1(M.6.897A); pass. καθαροὺς ἀπολύει τῶν ἐπικληθέντων Philost. *h.e.*9.6(M.65.573A).

[*]**ἐπικαλινδέομαι,** (= ἐπικυλινδέομαι), *welter*, ‡Nil.*narr.*5(M.79. 648A).

ἐπικαλλωπίζω, med., *adorn oneself*, Chrys.*hom.87.4 in Jo.*(8. 525A); pass., Thphn.*chron.*p.383(M.108.916C).

ἐπικάλυμμα, τό, *veil*; lit., of woman's veil, Isid.Pel.*epp.*5.331(M. 78.1528B); met. πάλαι μὲν ἀνθρώποις σωφρονοῦσιν ἐ. ἡδονῆς νὺξ ἦν σιωπωμένη Clem.*prot.*2(p.17.12; M.8.89A); ἡ ἀτιμία...ἐ. γίνεται τοῦ προσώπου μου Or.*hom.5.8 in Jer.*(p.38.14; M.13.308A); Meth.*symp.* 2.5(p.21.7; M.18.53C) cit. s. ἔνδυμα; τὰ δὲ ἄλλα πάντα...τί ἐνέσκηψε τῇ αὐτοῦ θεότητι; ποῖον ἐ. ἔσχεν, ὡς ἐν ἡμῖν, ἡ σαρκὸς κατοχή; Epiph. *haer.*77.28(p.441.13; M.42.684A); διήγησιν...παντὸς ἀπηλλαγμένη ἐ. Socr.*h.e.*6 proem.9(M.67.660B).

***ἐπικαλυμματίς, ἡ,** *altar-cloth*, Thdr.Stud.*epp.*2.219(M.99.1661B).

***ἐπικάλυψις, ἡ, 1.** *veiling*; of faces of seraphim, Or.*Jo.*4.4(2; p.111.13; M.14.205B); of women, *Const.App.*1.8.23; **2.** in gen., *concealment*, †Bas.*Is.*114(1.458B; M.30.304A); **3.** *covering* (i.e. putting out of the way); of sin, in baptism by H. Ghost, Didym.*Trin.*2.1 (M.39.453A).

***ἐπικαμαρόω,** *put over like a vault* τῷ μαλακῷ τὸ βαρύτατον ἐπεκαμάρωσεν ‡Caes.Naz.*dial.*92(M.38.956).

***ἐπικαμμύ-ω, 1.** *shut the eyes*, Pall.*h.Laus.*22(M.34.1067B; καμμύων p.61.9); **2.** *shut one's eyes to* ∼οντες τῇ θεωρίᾳ τῆς προκειμένης ἡμῖν ἱστορίας Ephr.2.190F.

ἐπίκαμψις, ἡ, *influencing, winning over*, Thdr.Stud.*epp.*2.6(M. 99.1128C).

***ἐπικαπνίζω,** f.l. for καπνίζω, *T.Sal.*5.9(M.122.1324A; καπνιζόμενον p.23.10).

ἐπίκαρπος, *set over the harvest*, Dion.Al.ap.Eus.*p.e.*14.25(777C; M.21.1277D).

***ἐπίκαρρος,** f.l. for ἐπίκαιρος, Nil.*praest.*2(M.79.1064B).

***ἐπικαταγελάω,** *jeer at*, c. dat., *Apoc.Bar.rel.*5.23.

***ἐπικαταγι(γ)νώσκω,** pass., *be under condemnation*, Bas.*epit.can.* 9(2.531B; M.31.1316A).

ἐπικαταλαμβάν-ω, 1. *overtake, come upon* χρὴ οὖν με ταχέως αὐτὸν ἐπικαταλαβεῖν *Hom.Clem.*3.59; *ib.*20.23; Ant.Mon.*ep.Eust.*(M.89. 1424C); **2.** *find in existence* τέταρτον ἤδη πάσχα ἐπικατείληφε τὸν διωγμόν Petr.I Al.*ep.can.*1(M.18.468A); **3.** *find, discover*, Petr.I Al. *fr.*(M.18.513B); **4.** *come on* ἑσπέρας ἐπικαταλαβούσης *Hom.Clem.*8.2; **5.** *come up, arise* εἴ που...ἐπικαταλάβοι χρεία Clem.*str.*2.18(p.155. 26; M.8.1020C); ταῦτα δὴ τῶν ἐπισκόπων διατεθέντων, ∼ει ἕτερα τοῦ βασιλέως γράμματα Socr.*h.e.*1.33.3(M.67.165A); *ib.*4.28.6(537B).

***ἐπικαταλλάσσω,** pass., *be reconciled*, *1Clem.*48.1.

***ἐπικαταπέτομαι,** *fly down*, Niceph.Ur.*v.Sym.*105(M.86.3084D).

ἐπικαταράομαι, *curse*, Clem.*paed.*2.1(p.156.10; M.8.384B); τρὶς τῆς ἡμέρας φάσκοντες [sc. Jews], ὅτι ἐπικαταράσαι ὁ θεὸς τοὺς Ναζωραίους Epiph.*haer.*29.9(p.332.4; M.41.404D); ‡Anast.S.*Jud. disp.*3(M.89.1245A).

ἐπικατάρατος, *accursed*, ref. Dt.21:23, *A.Pil.*A 16(p.283); *Dial. Ath.et Zacch.*41(p.30); in gen., *Barn.*10.5; ἔχουσιν τὸ ἐ. εἶναι· οὐ γὰρ ἤκουσαν τῆς διαθήκης Or.*hom.9.2 in Jer.*(p.66.15; M.13.352B); τὰ ἐπὶ τῆς ἐ. γῆς ἐν τοῖς ἔργοις τοῦ ἐκβληθέντος ἀπὸ τοῦ παραδείσου id.*Jo.*20. 26(21; p.362.34; M.14.633D); ἐ. γὰρ εἴ τις εἰδώλοις λατρεύει *A.Phil.*1 (p.2.10); εἴ τις φάγει αἷμα κτηνῶν, ἐ. ἔστω *Poen.App.*13; ἐ. ἄνθρωπος ὃς τὴν ἐλπίδα ἔχει ἐπ' ἄνθρωπον Cyr.*Ps.*30:2(M.69.857B); as gen. term of abuse, *M.Tar.*8(p.469); *Chron.Pasch.*p.392(M.92.1005A); *ib.* p.393(1008A).

***ἐπικατασκήπτω,** *attack*; of disease, Dion.Al.ap.Eus.*h.e.*7.22.6 (M.20.688B).

***ἐπικατασπάζομαι,** *greet in addition*, *Apophth.Mac.Aeg.*(M.34. 228D).

***ἐπικατονομάζομαι,** *be dedicated* to (through invocation of name), Clem.*paed.*2.1(p.159.20; M.8.392B).

***ἐπικαυχάομαι,** *glory in*, Gr.Nyss.*Pss.titt.*B 8(M.44.524D).

***ἐπικεκαλυμμένως,** *obscurely, in a veiled manner* λόγους, τοὺς ἐ. καὶ ἐν παραβολαῖς...λελεγμένους Just.*dial.*68.6(M.6.636A); Eus.*d.e.*2.3 (p.81.14; M.22.145B); ψαλμὸς...τὸ πάθος ἐ. τοῦ προφητευομένου δηλοῖ *ib.*5.3(p.223.6; 368B); τὰ ἀμφίβολα καὶ ἐ. εἰρῆσθαι δοκοῦντα ἔν τισι τόποις τῆς...γραφῆς ὑπὸ τῶν ἐν ἄλλοις τόποις ὁμολογουμένων σαφηνίζεται Bas.*reg.br.*267(2.506E; M.31.1264C).

ἐπικεκρυμμένως, *in a hidden manner* ὁ νοῦς...τοῦ προφητικοῦ... πνεύματος ἐ. λαλούμενος Clem.*str.*1.9(p.30.3; M.8.741B); ἡ ἰσχὺς τοῦ λόγου...πάντα τὸν καταδεξάμενον...αὐτὴν ἐ. ... πρὸς ἑαυτὴν ἕλκει *ib.*5. 12(p.379.29; M.9.120B); Or.*Cels.*5.32(p.33.28; M.11.1229A); ὡς ἐν χρησμοῖς ἐ. ἐκφαίνειν Eus.*d.e.*8.2(p.368.8; M.22.597C); περὶ τῆς τοῦ σωτῆρος...παρουσίας θεσπίσας...ὁ λόγος...τοτὲ μὲν ἐ. καὶ δι' αἰνιγμάτων, τοτὲ δὲ ἀκαλύπτως ἀναφωνεῖ *ib.*8.4(p.394.22; 637B); τὴν θείαν οὐσίαν...ἐ. ὁ ἀριθμὸς οὗτος ὑποσημαίνει. ... οὐσίαν διὰ τοῦ τρεῖς ἀριθμοῦ δηλουμένην Max.*ambig.*(M.91.1400D).

***ἐπικεκυφότως,** *bending down*, ‡Bas.*h.myst.*60(p.395.28).

ἐπικεντρίζω, *graft in*, Mac.Aeg.*hom.*5.6(M.34.512B); ‡Ath.*sem.*5 (M.28.149D).

***ἐπικερδῶς,** *with advantage*, Socr.*h.e.*3.21.10(M.67.453A).

ἐπικεύθω, *hide* τὸν ἐν ὕδασιν ἐπικεύσαντα τὴν γῆν Eun.*exp.fid.*2 (p.257).

ἐπικέφαλα, *head downwards*, *A.Andr.*B 6(p.61.20).

***ἐπικήλησις, ἡ,** *allurement, bewitchment*, Clem.*str.*2.2(p.118.8 conj. for ἐπιτελέσεις M.8.941A).

***ἐπικήπιος,** *of a garden*, Nonn.*par.Jo.*19:41(M.43.908A).

***ἐπικιναίδισμα, τό,** *lewd suggestion*, Clem.*paed.*3.4(p.253.16; M.8. 596C).

***ἐπικλαγγάζω,** *shout at*, c. dat., Bas.Sel.*v.Thecl.*1(M.85.557B); ‡Caes.Naz.*dial.*1(M.38.856); *ib.*140(1072).

ἐπίκλησις, ἡ, **A.** *naming* διὰ...τοῦ τύπου...τῆς τοῦ Ναυῆ υἱοῦ ἐ. τοῦ ὀνόματος Ἰησοῦ...Ἰσραὴλ...ἐνίκα Just.*dial*.91.3(M.6.693B); ἡ τοιαύτη τοῦ θεοῦ ἐ. [sc. 'of Abraham' etc. as used in magical invocations] Or.*Cels*.4.33(p.304.2; M.11.1080A).

B. *invocation, calling upon by name*; **1.** of prayer in gen. διὰ τῆς εἰς αὐτὸν ἐ. Eus.*l.C*.16(p.253.2; M.20.1425D); in exorcism ποίου σταυρωθέντος ἐ. ἑτέρου ποτὲ τοὺς δαίμονας ἀπήλασεν; Cyr.H.*catech*.4.13; Gr.Nyss.*or.catech*.34(p.127.3; M.45.85A); of prayer at wedding ἡ στεφανικὴ ἐ. Thdr.Stud.*epp*.1.50(M.99.1093A); **2.** of invocation by which baptismal water is consecrated βάπτισμα θεῖον ὀνομάζεται, οὐκέτι μὲν ψιλὸν ὕδωρ· ἁγιάζεται γὰρ μυστικῇ τινι ἐ. Or.*fr.36 in Jo*.(p.512.12); ὕδωρ πνεύματος ἁγίου, καὶ Χριστοῦ καὶ πατρὸς τὴν ἐ. λαβόν, δύναμιν ἁγιότητος ἐπικτᾶται Cyr.H.*catech*.3.3; εὐχὴ καὶ δυνάμεως θείας ἐ. ἐπὶ τοῦ ὕδατος γινομένη ζωῆς ἀρχηγὸς τοῖς μυηθεῖσι γίνεται Gr.Nyss.*or.catech*.33(p.124.5; M.45.84B); ὕδωρ μυστικόν, ἐ. θείας δυνάμεως *ib*.35(p.138.14; 92B); τῇ...ἐ. τῆς ἁγίας τριάδος ἁγιάζεται τῶν ὑδάτων ἡ φύσις Thdt.*1Cor*.6:11(3.196); δι' ὕδατος ἀναγεννᾶσθαι καὶ πνεύματος, δι' ἐντεύξεως καὶ ἐ., τῷ ὕδατι ἐπιφοιτῶντος τοῦ ἁγίου πνεύματος Jo.D.*f.o*.4.9(M.94.1121A); at Epiphany, Thdr.Lect.*h.e*.2.48(M.86.209A) cit. s. θεοφάνεια; and of baptismal invocation of Trin. in its effect on candidate διὰ τοῦ...ὕδατος καὶ τῆς τοῦ κυρίου ἐ. καθαριζόμεθα Iren.*fr*.33(M.7.1248C); τῶν τῆς προσκυνητῆς τριάδος ἐ. Or.*Jo*.6.33(17; p.142.30; M.14.257A); ἐν τρισὶν καταδύσεσι, καὶ ἰσαρίθμοις ταῖς ἐ., τὸ μέγα μυστήριον τοῦ βαπτίσματος τελειοῦται Bas.*Spir*.35(3.29D; M.32.132A); μηδένα παρακρουέσθω τὸ τοῦ ἀποστόλου, ὡς τὸ ὄνομα τοῦ πατρὸς καὶ τοῦ πνεύματος...πολλάκις παραλιμπάνοντος, μηδὲ διὰ τοῦτο ἀπαρατήρητον οἰέσθω τὴν ἐ. εἶναι τῶν ὀνομάτων *ib*.28(23B; M.116C); εὐχὴ...καὶ χάριτος οὐρανίας ἐ. καὶ ὕδωρ καὶ πίστις ἐστὶ δι' ὧν τὸ τῆς ἀναγεννήσεως πληροῦται μυστήριον Gr.Nyss.*or.catech*.33(p.123.11; 84B); Epiph.*anc*.116(p.144.11; M.43.228C); ἢ σὺ ὁ ἐπίσκοπος ἢ ὁ ὑπό σε πρεσβύτερος τὴν ἱερὰν ἐπ' αὐτοῖς εἰπὼν καὶ ἐπονομάσας ἐ. πατρὸς καὶ υἱοῦ καὶ ἁγίου πνεύματος βαπτίσεις αὐτοὺς ἐν τῷ ὕδατι *Const.App*.3.16.4; τὸ πνεῦμα...ἐν τῇ ἐ. τοῦ ἁγίου βαπτίσματος σὺν πατρὶ καὶ υἱῷ...ἐλευθεροῦν τῶν ἁμαρτιῶν Isid.Pel.*epp*.1.109(M.78.256B); **3.** in consecration of chrism μύρον, οὐκ ἔτι ψιλόν, οὐδ' ὡς ἂν εἴποι τις κοινὸν μετ' ἐπίκλησιν Cyr.H.*catech*.21.3; **4.** in eucharist ποτήρια...προσποιούμενος εὐχαριστεῖν [sc. Marcus], καὶ ἐπὶ πλέον ἐκτείνων τὸν λόγον τῆς ἐ. [i.e. apptly. eucharistic prayer as a whole] ...ὡς δοκεῖν τὴν...χάριν τὸ αἷμα τὸ ἑαυτῆς στάζειν ἐν τῷ ἐκείνῳ ποτηρίῳ διὰ τῆς ἐ. αὐτοῦ Iren.*haer*.1.13.8(M.7.580A); ἄρτος προσλαμβανόμενος τὴν ἐ. τοῦ θεοῦ, οὐκέτι κοινὸς ἄρτος ἐστίν, ἀλλ' εὐχαριστία *ib*.4.18.5(1028B); ὁ ἄρτος καὶ ὁ οἶνος...πρὸ τῆς ἐ. τῆς...τριάδος, ἄρτος ἦν καὶ οἶνος λιτός· ἐ. δὲ γενομένης, ὁ μὲν ἄρτος γίνεται σῶμα Χριστοῦ, ὁ δὲ οἶνος αἷμα Χριστοῦ Cyr.H.*catech*.19.7; ἄρτος...μετὰ τὴν ἐ. τοῦ ἁγίου πνεύματος...σῶμα Χριστοῦ *ib*.21.3; τὰ τῆς ἐ. ῥήματα ἐπὶ τῇ ἀναδείξει τοῦ ἄρτου τῆς εὐχαριστίας καὶ τοῦ ποτηρίου τῆς εὐλογίας τίς τῶν ἁγίων ἐγγραφῶς ἡμῖν καταλέλοιπεν; Bas.*Spir*.66(3.54E; M.32.188B); cf.Isid.Pel.*epp*.1.109(M.78.256C) cit. s. σῶμα; τὰ σύμβολα τοῦ δεσποτικοῦ σώματός τε καὶ αἵματος, ἄλλα μέν εἰσι πρὸ τῆς ἱερατικῆς ἐ., μετὰ δέ γε τὴν ἐ. μεταβάλλεται, καὶ ἕτερα γίνεται [monophysite view] Thdt.*eran*.2(4.126); τὰ...μηδέπω τελειωθέντα διὰ τῆς ἀρχιερατικῆς ἐ. Eutych.*pasch*.8(M.86.2401A); ὁ...ἄρτος οἶνός τε...διὰ τῆς ἐ. καὶ ἐπιφοιτήσεως τοῦ...πνεύματος...μεταποιοῦνται εἰς τὸ σῶμα τοῦ Χριστοῦ καὶ τὸ αἷμα Jo.D.*f.o*.4.13(M.94.1145A); **5.** in pagan and magical invocations, Iren.*haer*.1.13.3(M.7.584A)(Marcosian); cf. *invocationibus angelicis*, *ib*.2.32.5(830A); δαιμόνων ἐ. Eus.*d.e*.3.6(p.138.23; M.22.233C); κρέα ἢ ἄρτοι ἢ ἄλλα...μιανθέντα τῇ τῶν...ἐ. δαιμόνων τῇ τοῦ διαβόλου πομπῇ ἐγκαταλέγεται Cyr.H.*catech*.19.7; in Heracleonite initiations, Epiph.*haer*.36.2(p.46.1; M.41.636A); χάρτην τῶν γοητευτικῶν ἐ. CBeryt.*act*.(*ACO* 2.1.3 p.24.35; H.2.517E); **6.** of invocation of a living saint, Niceph.Ur.*v.Sym*.50(M.86.3033A).

***ἐπικλινίδιος**, *of a bed*, Greg.Nyss.*hom.5 in Cant*.(M.44.868B).

***ἐπικοιτωνίτης**, ὁ, *groom of bedchamber*, Socr.*h.e*.2.2.8(M.67.188B); *ib*.5.25.4(652A).

***ἐπικολυμβάω**, *swim* upon, Mac.Aeg.*hom*.5.6(M.34.508A).

***ἐπικορής**, *sated with* τῶν ἀναγκαίων ὄντες ἐ. Gr.Naz.*or*.43.7(M.36.501B).

ἐπικόσμημα, τό, *adornment*, Tat.*orat*.20(p.23.4; M.6.852A).

ἐπικόσμησις, ἡ, *adorning*, *Const.App*.1.8.24.

***Ἐπικουρίζω**, *be a follower of Epicurus*, Or.*Cels*.4.75(p.344.18; M.11.1145B).

ἐπικουφισμός, ὁ, *lightening, relief*, Clem.*str*.7.12(p.56.22; M.9.509B).

***ἐπικράνιος**, *on the head*, †Cyr.*hom.div*.10(5^2.371D).

ἐπίκρανον, τό, *capital* of pillar, ‡Epiph.*v.proph.Abac*.12(p.28; M.43.409D).

***ἐπικρατητέον**, *one must keep in check*, Clem.*paed*.2.10(p.211.26; M.8.505A).

ἐπικρατύνω, *strengthen for*, Meth.*res*.1.25(p.250.15; M.41.1096B).

[*]**ἐπικρεμν-άω**, = ἐπικρεμάννυμι, *hang over* as a threat τοῖς ἄρχουσιν ∼ᾷ τὸν κίνδυνον Chrys.*hom.46.1 in Mt*.(7.481A, v.l. ἐπικρεμᾷ); id.*comm.in Gal*.5:4(10.714B); id.*fr.in Jer*.4:4(M.64.796C).

***ἐπικρυπτέον**, *one must conceal*, Clem.*str*.1.12(p.35.16; M.8.753A).

***ἐπικρυπτομένως**, *obscurely*, Didym.*Trin*.3.31(M.39.957A).

***ἐπίκρυπτος**, *secret*, Thdr.Stud.*epp*.1.41(M.99.1060A).

ἐπίκρυψις, ἡ, *concealment* of meaning ἐπεδείκνυτο γὰρ αὐτοῖς ὁ Νουμᾶς δι' ἐπικρύψεως ὡς οὐκ ἐφάψασθαι τοῦ βελτίστου δυνατὸν ἄλλως ἢ μόνῳ τῷ νῷ Clem.*str*.1.15(p.45.17; M.8.777A); of Pythagorean tradition, *ib*.5.8(p.355.31; M.9.72B); ref. 1Cor.2:6 Παῦλος λέγει, τὴν προφητικὴν καὶ τῷ ὄντι ἀρχαίαν σῴζων ἐ. *ib*.5.10(p.370.5; 100B); τὰ ἀποκεκαλυμμένα δὲ τῷ Ἰωάννῃ τίς οὐκ ἂν ἀναγνοὺς καταπλαγείη τὴν ἐ. ἀπορρήτων μυστηρίων; Or.*princ*.4.2.3(p.310.14; M.11.361B); of allegorical meaning hidden in scripture, †Bas.*Is*.93(1.444B; M.30.272A); Gr.Naz.*or*.4.118(M.35.657B); αἰνίγματα μετ' ἐ. σημαίνοντα τὴν ἀλήθειαν ‡Proc.G.*Pr*.1:6(M.87.1225A).

ἐπίκτητος, *acquired*, opp. φυσικός, theol. ἀπὸ πρώτης ὑπάρξεως φυσικὴν ἀλλ' οὐκ ἐ. τὴν εἰκόνα τοῦ πατρὸς ἐπαγόμενος Eus.*d.e*.5.4(p.225.26; M.22.372D); ἔχθιστοι...οἱ τὸν υἱὸν ἐξ οὐκ ὄντων καὶ ἀποστελλομένης ἀρχῆς εἶναι ἐ. λέγοντες τῷ πατρί Apoll.*fid.sec.pt*.1(p.167.3; M.10.1105A); λεγέσθω τὸ λαμβάνειν αὐτὸν [sc. Christ] ζωήν, ἢ κρίσιν...καὶ τοῦτο τῆς ἀνθρωπότητος. εἰ δὲ καὶ τῷ θεῷ δοίης, οὐκ ἄτοπον, οὐ γὰρ ὡς ἐ. δώσεις, ἀλλ' ὡς ἀπ' ἀρχῆς συνυπάρχοντα, καὶ λόγῳ φύσεως, ἀλλ' οὐ χάριτος Gr.Naz.*or*.30.9(p.121.4; M.36.113C); εἰ κατὰ φύσιν οὐκ ἔστιν ἄτρεπτος ὁ υἱός, συνέβη δὲ αὐτῷ τὸ εἶναι τοῦτο ὅπερ ἐστι, καὶ ἐ. ἔχει τὴν πρὸς τὸν πατέρα ὁμοιότητα, ἣν ἄρα χρόνος ὅτε ἦν μὲν ὁ υἱός, ἀνόμοιος δὲ τῷ πατρί; Cyr.*thes*.13(5^1.127B); *ib*.14(142C); θεὸς ἐκ θεοῦ...κατὰ ἀλήθειαν, οὐ καθάπερ ἡμεῖς ἐ. ἔχων τὴν προσηγορίαν id.*Jo*.1.5(4.44D); Ἰησοῦς οὐκ ἐ. ἔσχε τὸ τῆς δόξης ὡράϊσμα, ἀλλ' ἐκ τῆς ἐμφύτου τῆς θείας δόξης λαμπρότητος Jo.D.*hom*.1.10(M.96.561D); of human properties of Christ τὰς μὲν τοῦ σωτηρίου πάθους ταπεινώσεώς τε...καὶ ὧν ἐ. ὁ σωτὴρ δι' ἡμᾶς ἀνεδέξατο φωνάς Alex.Al.*ep.Alex*.9(p.25.18; M.18.561B); διαβεβαιοῦντο γὰρ [sc. Apollinarians] μὴ ἐ. εἶναι τὴν σάρκα κατ' οἰκονομίαν...προσληφθεῖσαν... ἀλλ' ἐξ ἀρχῆς ἐν τῷ υἱῷ τὴν σαρκώδη ἐκείνην φύσιν εἶναι Gr.Naz.*ep*.102(M.37.332B).

***ἐπικυβιστάω**, *somersault on*, c. dat., †Chrys.ap.Jo.D.*parall*.(M.95.1240B).

***ἐπίκυβος**, ὁ, *integer multiplied by cube*, Thdt.*affect*.6(4.866).

ἐπικυκλέω, *include*, Thdr.Stud.*epp*.2.127(M.99.1412B).

***ἐπικύλισις**, ἡ, *rolling on* ἐπικυλίσεις...ὁμαλαῖς εὐναῖς Clem.*paed*.2.9(p.204.30; conj. for ἐπικλίσεις M.8.492A).

***ἐπικυοφορέομαι**, pass., *be borne in the womb*, Sophr.H.*mir.Cyr.et Jo*.44(M.87.3592D).

***ἐπιλαιμαργέω**, *be greedy for* ἐ. τῷ ὄψῳ Clem.*paed*.2.1(p.161.23; M.8.396B).

***ἐπιλαλία**, ἡ, *incantation, spell* οὐδ' ἔστιν πώποτε Χριστιανὸν περιάμμασι χρώμενον θεάσασθαι, οὐδ' ἐπιλαλιαῖς Eus.*d.e*.3.6(p.134.1; M.22.225C); Leont.N.*v.Sym*.48(M.93.1729A); πολλαῖς ἐ. οἱ φαρμακοὶ χρησάμενοι Gr.Mag.*dial*.(tr.Zach.)1.10(M.*PL*.77.202B); among works of Devil, Jo.D.*hom*.2.6(M.96.585C).

ἐπιλέγ-ω, **1.** *repeat* συνεχῶς ταῦτα ∼ει Chrys.*hom.78.2 in Mt*.(7.753A); id.*hom.39.2 in 1Cor*.(10.365C); Thdt.*h.e*.5.19.4(3.1052); **2.** *recite over, say over*; **a.** incantations in Gnost. rites ἐπὶ γῆς βαλὼν τὸν παῖδα πολλὰ ∼ει αὐτῷ, τοῦτο μὲν Ἑλλάδι φωνῇ, τοῦτο δὲ ὡς Ἑβραΐδι, τὰς συνήθεις τοῖς μάγοις ἐπαοιδάς Hipp.*haer*.4.28(p.55.1; M.16.3090C); Ἡρακλεωνῖται...πρὸς τῇ τελευτῇ τοὺς...τελευτῶντας ὁμοίως τῷ Μάρκῳ λυτροῦνται δι' ἐλαίου, ὀποβαλσάμου καὶ ὕδατος, ἐπικλήσεις τινὰς Ἑβραϊκαῖς λέξεσιν ∼οντες ἐπὶ τῇ κεφαλῇ τοῦ δῆθεν λυτρουμένου Epiph.*anac*.36(p.1.17; M.41.580A); **b.** blessings, Chrys.*hom.32.6 in Mt*.(7.373B); ὁ...προεστώς, εἰρήνη ὑμῖν, ∼ων id.*hom.3.3 in Col*.(11.347D); **c.** eucharistic prayer ἡμεῖς ∼οντες τῷ ποτηρίῳ τὰς ἀφάτους εὐεργεσίας τοῦ θεοῦ id.*hom.24.1 in 1Cor*.(10.212D); **3.** med., *choose, select*, for eccl. office, id.*sac*.3.14(p.73.18; 1.391C); Soz.*h.e*.1.24.2(M.67.928A); of divine election εἰδὼς...ὁποῖον τόνον ἕξει πρὸς τὴν θεοσέβειαν ὁ Παῦλος...πρὶν κτίσαι τὸν κόσμον...αὐτὸν ἐπιλέξομαι Or.*or*.6.5(p.315.13; M.11.440B); pass., Clem.*ecl*.12(p.140.18; M.9.704C); Didym.*Trin*.3.6(M.39.848C).

ἐπίλεκτος, *chosen, elect*; of Christ, Didym.*Trin*.3.6(M.39.848C); cf. ἐλθὲ ἡ ἐπισταμένη [i.e. H. Ghost] τὰ μυστήρια τοῦ ἐ. *A.Thom*.A 50(p.166.9).

ἐπιλεπτύνω, *fine down, subdivide*, Gr.Nyss.*fat*.(M.45.156C).

ἐπιληπτεύομαι, *be epileptic, frenzied*; of madness simulated for evasion of sacrifice in persecution, Petr.I Al.*ep.can.*5(M.18.473D); in gen., Bas.*hom.in Ps.*33(1.143C; M.29.352B); *V.Alex.Acoem.*14 (p.669.4).

[*]**ἐπιληπτιάζω**, *have a fit*, Jo.Clim.*scal.*6(M.88.796C).

***ἐπιλήπτως**, *reprehensibly*, Or.*princ.*3.1.16(p.225.7; M.11.281C).

***ἐπιλησμονέω**, *disregard, forget*, c. genit., Isid.Pel.*epp.*1.45(M.78. 209C).

ἐπιλησμονή, ἡ, *forgetfulness*, Epiph.*haer.*42.15(p.184.18; M.41. 813D); Thdt.*Ps.*12:1(1.677).

ἐπιλιμνάζ-ω (-νίζω), **1.** *inundate* πόλιν ἐπιλιμνίζων ‡Eust.*hex.* (M.18.780B); Eus.*d.e.*4.5(p.156.2; M.22.260D); **2.** intrans., *overflow* with; met., of Son πάντων ἀγαθῶν ἐκ τοῦ οἰκείου πληρώματος τοῖς πᾶσιν ∼ων id.*l.C.*12(p.230.26; M.20.1388C); id.*e.th.*2.17(p.121.15; M. 24.940A).

ἐπιλογή, ἡ, **1.** *choosing, choice*, Socr.*h.e.*5.10.25(M.67.588B); προαίρεσις, εἴτουν ἡ ἐ. τοῦ δόξαντος καλοῦ ‡Cyr.*Trin.*15(6^3.22A; M.77. 1153A); ὁ τρόπος τῆς κατ' ἀρετὴν...ἢ κακίαν ζωῆς...ἐξ ἐ. ἡμῖν πρόσεστιν Max.*Pyrr.*(M.91.308B); Jo.D.*f.o.*2.22(M.94.945B); κατ' ἐπιλογήν *by selection* Γορδιανὸς...ἐποίησεν ἀριθμὸν τῶν...κανδιδάτων, ἐπάρας αὐτοὺς κατ' ἐ., ὡς τελείους καὶ εὐσθενεῖς *Chron.Pasch.*p.269 (M.92.661B); **2.** *election*; of a bishop, Socr.*h.e.*4.29.2(M.67.541B); ref. divine election, Leo Mag.*ep.*72(p.38.1; M.*PL.*898A).

ἐπιλόγιον, τό, medic., *prescription*, *Mir.Artem.*26(p.38.22).

ἐπίλογος, ὁ, *incantation*; in Mithraic rites, Just.*1apol.*66.4(M.6. 429A); linked with ἐπαοιδαί, perh. as being in prose whereas latter are metrical, Hipp.*haer.*9.14(p.253.4; M.16.3390C).

***ἐπίλοχος**, *lying-in* ἐ. ἐστιν [sc. ἡ γυνή] Anast.*liturg.*(p.278).

ἐπίλυσις, ἡ, *release* from, *end* of, a fast, Eus.*h.e.*5.23.1(M.20. 492A); *ib.*5.23.2(492B).

***ἐπιλυσσ-άω**, **1.** *be mad for, be filled with lust for* τῇ ἀθέσμῳ μίξει τῶν ἀλλοφύλων ∼ήσαντας Gr.Nyss.*v.Mos.*(M.44.424A); id.*infant.*(M. 46.188A); ‡Caes.Naz.*dial.*109(M.38.980); **2.** *be furious at* Κάϊν ὁ τῇ εὐδοκιμήσει τοῦ Ἄβελ ∼ήσας Gr.Nyss.*beat.*3(M.44.1221B).

ἐπιλυτέον, *one must solve*, Clem.*str.*6.1(p.422.22; M.9.209A).

***ἐπιλύχνιος**, *of lighting the lamp*, in gen. τὰς ἐ. ὥρας Evagr.*h.e.* 5.14(p.211.5; M.86.2821C); esp. of vesper hymn sung at that hour ὅστις μὲν ὁ πατὴρ τῶν ῥημάτων ἐκείνων τῆς ἐ. εὐχαριστίας, εἰπεῖν οὐκ ἔχομεν· ὁ μέντοι λαὸς ἀρχαίαν ἀφίησι τὴν φωνήν, καὶ οὐδενὶ πώποτε ἀσεβεῖν ἐνομίσθησαν οἱ λέγοντες· αἰνοῦμεν πατέρα καὶ υἱὸν καὶ ἅγιον πνεῦμα θεοῦ Bas.*Spir.*73(3.62B; M.32.205A); ἡ φωνὴ τῶν ψαλλόντων πρὸς τὰς ἐ. εὐχαριστίας ἐξεκαλεῖτο Gr.Nyss.*v.Macr.*(p.395.4; M.46.981C); μετὰ τὸ ῥηθῆναι τὸν ἐ. ψαλμὸν προσφωνήσει ὁ διάκονος ὑπὲρ τῶν κατηχουμένων καὶ χειμαζομένων καὶ τῶν φωτιζομένων καὶ τῶν ἐν μετανοίᾳ *Const.App.*8.35.2; Niceph.Ur.*v.Sym.*250(M.86. 3216A); *Mir.Artem.*39(p.64.20).

***ἐπιλωβάω**, *pollute*, Meth.*symp.*11.2(p.138.14; M.18.216C).

ἐπιμάζιος, *at the breast*, Bas.*hom.*8.3(2.65B; M.31.312B).

***ἐπίμαλος, ὁ**, *woolly caterpillar*, *Euchol.*(p.555).

***ἐπιμανίζω**, *be furious at* ἐπεμάνισεν ὁ κόσμος...Χριστῷ Cyr. *glaph.Gen.*5(1.155B).

***ἐπιμανίκιον, τό**, (cf. Lat. *manicae*) plur., *cuffs* (embroidered), or sometimes *armlets* reaching elbow, confining sleeves of alb, worn by clergy at eucharist, cf. ὁ διάκονος εἰς ἓν μέρος τοῦ ἱερατείου...τὰ ἐ. ἐπιθέμενος ταῖς χερσίν, ἐν μὲν τῇ δεξιᾷ λέγει...ἐν δὲ τῇ ἀριστερᾷ λεγει ...*Lit.Chrys.*(p.355.13; M.63.903); cf. ὁ ἱερεὺς...λαβὼν τὰ ἐ., ὡς ἄνωθεν εἴρηται *ib.*(p.355.35); also worn by priest at baptism, *Euchol.*(p.287); v. ὑπομανίκιον.

ἐπιμέλεια, ἡ, **1.** *care, diligence, attention* ἐκδίκει σου τὸν τόπον ἐν πάσῃ ἐ. σαρκικῇ τε καὶ πνευματικῇ Ign.*Polyc.*1.2; πλέονος ἐ. ... δεόμεθα εἰς τὴν ἐξέτασιν τοῦ πῶς ἀκριβῶς βιωτέον Clem.*str.*7.15(p.64. 21; M.9.525C); ἐ. τὸν ἀκριβῶς ἐντευξόμενον τῇ γραφῇ ποιητέον Or.*Jo.* 6.8(5; p.117.16; M.14.216B); χωρὶς γὰρ Ἰησοῦ οὐδεὶς...καθαρὸς γίνεται, κἂν...νομισθῇ διά τινος ἐ. αὐτὸν καθαρὸν πεποιηκέναι *ib.*32.7(6; p.436.19; 757C); of bishop's pastoral care, *Const.App.*3.15.5; of God's providential care, Clem.*str.*7.2(p.8.2; 412C); Nemes.*nat.hom.* 43(M.40.792B) cit. s. πρόνοια; Thdt.*provid.*7(4.602); Cosm.Ind.*top.* 2(M.88.121A); as title of address, Const.ap.Eus.*h.e.*10.5.7(M.20. 881C); *ib.*10.5.20(888B); **2.** *guard* μετὰ στρατιωτικῆς ἐ. *Ep.Lugd.*ap. Eus.*h.e.*5.1.59(432A).

***ἐπιμεμορφασμένως**, *insincerely*, Meth.*symp.*4.4(p.50.10; M.18. 92C).

ἐπιμένω, **1.** trans., *sustain* σύντομον ἐπέμεινε θάνατον Or.*Ps.*54:21 (p.59); **2.** intrans., *continue, persist*; hence *continue to exist, remain alive*, Thdr.Stud.*epp.*2.147(M.99.1461C).

ἐπιμερισμός, ὁ, **1.** *distribution, apportionment* τὸν λόγον ἐρευνητέον τὸν περὶ τῆς οὐσίας τῆς ψυχῆς...καὶ τῆς εἰς τὸ γήϊνον σῶμα εἰσκρίσεως αὐτῆς, τῶν τε ἐ. τοῦ ἑκάστης βίου καὶ τῆς ἐντεῦθεν ἀπαλλαγῆς Or.*Jo.*6. 14(7; p.123.34; M.14.225C); **2.** *division besides*, or *in addition* ἡ μία φύσις τοῦ...λόγου σεσαρκωμένη, ἢ ταὐτόν ἐστι τῇ μιᾷ, καὶ περιττῶς πρόσκειται τό, σεσαρκωμένη,...ἢ ταῖς δύο φύσεσι ταὐτὸν συνάγει,...ἢ οὔτε μία πάντη ἐστίν, οὔτε δύο, καὶ ἀνάγκη μίαν σὺν ἐ. λέγειν αὐτοὺς ἔσχατα νηπιάζοντας Leont.H.*monoph.*43(M.86.1796B); **3.** *cutting asunder* ἐ. ψυχῆς καὶ πνεύματος οἱ μὲν...διχοτομούμενοι πείσονται *cat.Lc.*12:46(p.104.23).

***ἐπιμέστωμα, τό**, *fulfilment*, Ephr.3.337E.

ἐπιμέτρησις, ἡ, *dispensation* κατὰ τὴν ἄνωθεν ἐ. Soz.*h.e.*1.9.3(M.67. 884A).

ἐπιμετρίως, *at due length*, Cyr.*Zach.*proem.(3.653B; Aubert om.).

***ἐπιμηνιάω**, *be angry*, Cyr.*ador.*8(1.270C); id.*Am.*13(3.264A).

ἐπιμιξία, ἡ, **1.** *intercourse*, of social relations in gen., *LS*; sexual, Clem.*str.*2.23(p.190.7; M.8.1089A); Meth.*symp.*3.12(p.41.21; M.18. 81A); id.*arbitr.*3(p.152.4; ἐπιθυμίᾳ M.18.245C); **2.** *communion, fellowship*, between heretics and orthodox δειξάτωσαν ἢ κανονικὰ γράμματα παρ' ἐμοῦ πρὸς αὐτὸν διαπεμπόμενα [sc. Bas. to Apoll.],...ἢ τῶν κληρικῶν τὰς πρὸς ἡμᾶς ἐ. Bas.*ep.*224.2(3.343B; M.32.837A); μὴ καθαρῶς αὐτοὺς [sc. Secundus and Serras] ἱερᾶσθαι διὰ τὴν ἐ. πρὸς τὸ ὁμοούσιον θρησκεύοντας ἀποφαινόμενος [sc. Aët.] Philost.*h.e.*3.19(M. 65.509B); **3.** *intermingling, mixture*, in gen., Diad.*perf.*50(p.56.10); of divine and human ἀναγκαῖον ἦν ζώπυρα τοῦ γένους τῶν ἀνθρώπων ἀρξάμενα ὑπό τινα γεγονέναι φρουρὰν τὴν ἀπὸ κρειττόνων, ὥστε κατ' ἀρχὰς ἐ. γεγονέναι τῆς θείας φύσεως πρὸς τοὺς ἀνθρώπους Or.*Cels.*4. 78(p.349.24; M.11.1152C); as result of Inc. κατεμίχθη πρὸς τὸ ἡμέτερον, ἵνα τὸ ἡμέτερον τῇ πρὸς τὸ θεῖον ἐ. γένηται θεῖον Gr.Nyss. *or.catech.*25(p.96.5; M.45.65D); *ib.*27(p.103.5, v.l. ἐπιδημίαν 72B); Christol. τῷ λύθρῳ τῆς ἀνθρωπίνης φύσεως καταμίγνυνταί, ὡς καὶ τὰς ὑψηλὰς ἐνεργείας αὐτοῦ τῇ πρὸς τὸ ταπεινὸν ἐ. συνευτελίζεσθαι *ib.*14 (p.62.14; 48A); μεταποιήσας διὰ τῆς πρὸς τὸ κρεῖττον ἐ. τὸ γήϊνον id. *Apoll.*48(M.45.1240C); δέχεται τὴν πρὸς τὸ ταπεινὸν ἡμῶν τῆς φύσεως ἐ., καὶ τὸν ἄνθρωπον ἐν ἑαυτῷ λαβών, καὶ αὐτὸς ἐν τῷ ἀνθρώπῳ γενόμενος *ib.*53(1252B); term later discouraged κατ' οὐδεμίαν ἐ. συγχέομεν Leo Mag.*ep.*165.6(p.59.38; M.*PL.*54.1166A).

ἐπιμνημονεύω, *mention also*, Epiph.*haer.*69.28(p.177.31; M.41. 248A); *Chron.Pasch.*p.25(M.92.113C).

ἐπιμοιράω, *receive as one's share*, Eus.Al.*serm.*21.16(M.86.444A).

ἐπιμολύνω, *pollute*, Gr.Nyss.*virg.*17(p.317.5; M.46.389A); *ib.*21 (p.328.21; 401A); Epiph.*haer.*63.1(p.399.20; M.41.1064C).

ἐπιμονή, ἡ, **1.** *steadfastness*; hence *obduracy* ἐ. τῶν αἱρετικῶν Leo Mag.*ep.*165.7(p.60.10; M.*PL.*54.1166C); **2.** *continuance, permanence*, Tat.*orat.*32(p.33.12; M.6.872B); *Ep.Lugd.*ap.Eus.*h.e.*5.1. 20(M.20.416C); **3.** rhet., *dwelling on a point*, hence *inculcation*, ‡Pion.*v.Polyc.*19.

ἐπιμορφάζ-ω, **1.** *simulate, pretend to* ἀγάλματα...οἷς ∼ετε εὐσέβειαν Clem.*prot.*4(p.35.28; M.8.136A); οἱ ∼οντες τῷ δοκεῖν τὴν τοῦ καλοῦ φαντασίαν...ὑποκριταί εἰσι δικαιοσύνης Or.*or.*20.2(p.344.14; M.11.480B); of Maxentius εὐσέβειαν ∼ων Eus.*h.e.*8.14.1(M.20.781A); ‡Chrys.*fug.spec.*(1.815C); med., Meth.*symp.*1.1(p.9.15; M.18.40B); Πυθαγόρειον ∼όμενος ἀγωγήν Eus.*Hierocl.*5(514D; M.22.804B); Nil. *serm.*7(M.79.1276A); Proc.G.*Gen.*3:15(M.87.204C); **2.** *fictitiously, falsely ascribe* to οὐδὲ συναναμιγνυμένης τῆς ἐπιθεωρουμένης αὐτοῖς ἰδιότητος, ὡς ἢ τῷ πατρὶ τὴν γέννησιν, ἢ τῷ υἱῷ τὴν ἀγεννησίαν ∼ειν Gr.Nyss.*diff.ess.*7(M.32.340A).

***ἐπιμορφίζ-ω**, *simulate*; pass., Gr.Nyss.*beat.*7(M.44.1288D); med. ∼όμενος τὴν ἀρετήν Didym.*fr.Job* 8:21(M.39.1141D); Max.*cap.theol.* 1.19(M.90.1089D).

ἐπιμορφόω, *form, fashion*, Gr.Nyss.*hom.2 in Cant.*(M.44.789D); Philost.*h.e.*3.15(M.65.504A); pass., *be transformed into* Λαμία ἐπεμορφώθη [sc. Zeus] ἔποψ *Hom.Clem.*5.13.

***ἐπιμόρφωσις, ἡ**, *counterfeiting*, Leont.B.*Nest.et Eut.*1(M.86. 1276B).

ἐπίμοχθος, **1.** of persons, *laborious, hard-working*, Tat.*orat.*9 (p.10.1; M.6.825B); δοῦλος ἐ. Gr.Nyss.*usur.*(M.46.437C); Chrys.*hom.* *1.3 in 2Tim.*(11.663C); **2.** *toilsome, full of toil, laborious* τὴν ἐ. ταύτην ζωήν Or.*schol.in Cant.*6:10–11(M.17.280A); Chrys.*hom.68.3 in Mt.*(7.674E); εἰς γῆν ἐ. ... ἐρρίφημεν [i.e. at expulsion from Paradise] Isid.Pel.*epp.*1.282(M.78.348C); of virtue as achieved only by toil, Chrys.*hom.7.5 in 1Cor.*(10.57B); **3.** *painful, troublesome*; of S. Paul's tribulations, *ib.14.4*(122B); **4.** neut. as subst., *laboriousness*, Heracleon ap.Or.*Jo.*13.10(p.235.13; M.14.416A).

ἐπίμυσις, ἡ, *closing* of eyes, Clem.*paed.*2.9(p.206.24; M.8.493C); Gr.Nyss.*virg.*12(p.298.26; M.46.369D); id.*res.*3(M.46.660C); of lips, id.*hom.opif.*9(M.44.152A); id.*beat.*7(M.44.1285B).

ἐπιμύσσω, f.l. for ἐπιμύω, *close*, Melet.*nat.hom.*10(M.64.1196C).

ἐπιμυχθίζω, *sneer at*, Gr.Naz.*carm*.2.1.1.548(M.37.1011).

ἐπίμωμος, *blemished*, *maimed*; physically, *Orac.Sib*.1.351; Or. *comm.in Mt*.10.7(p.8.13; M.13.849C); Mac.Aeg.*hom*.32.6(M.34.737B); spiritually τὸν σὸν ἐ. βίον Or.*exc.in Ps*.36:6(M.17.124A); *Const.App*. 2.37.2; ἡ φύσις τῆς ἀνθρωπότητος, ἐὰν καθ' ἑαυτὴν γυμνὴ ἀπομείνῃ, καὶ μὴ λάβῃ τὴν...κοινωνίαν τῆς ἐπουρανίου φύσεως...ἔμεινε...ἐ. εἰς τὴν φύσιν αὐτῆς ἐν ῥυπαρίᾳ πολλῇ Mac.Aeg.*hom*.32.6(737B).

ἐπινεανιεύομαι, **1.** *rage* against, CAlex.*ep*.ap.Ath.*apol.sec*.3(p.89. 14; M.25.252C); **2.** *add a further outrage* to ἐπενεανιεύσατο δὲ τούτοις Bas.*ep*.130.2(3.222D; M.32.564B).

ἐπινέμησις, ἡ, **1.** *spreading*, *extension* εἰδωλολατρεία ἐκ τοῦ ἑνὸς εἰς τοὺς πολλοὺς ἐ. ἐστι θεούς Clem.*str*.3.12(p.237.11; M.8.1189B); **2.** = ἰνδικτίων, Bas.*ep*.54(3.149A; M.32.401B); Pall.*v.Chrys*.13(p.83. 10; M.47.47); series beginning at 2nd year of reign of Augustus, *anno mundi* 5460, Max.*comput*.33(M.19.1249C).

***ἐπινεωτερίζω**, *make further innovations*, Eus.*m.P*.12(p.947.3; M. 20.1513A).

***ἐπινηστεύω**, *fast after* someone, ‡Chrys.*serm.jej*.2(11.806C); *fast in addition*, Thphn.*chron*.p.376(M.108.901A).

ἐπινήχ-ομαι, **1.** *swim*, *float on*, Bas.*hex*.7.1(1.63B; M.29.148C); **2.** *rest upon* τὸ...λόγιον...ἐπενήχετο τῷ στέρνῳ Cyr.*ador*.11(1.383B); of a shallow skin-disease, opp. leprosy ~εται...ὥσπερ ἄκρῳ *ib*.15 (537E); **3.** met., *rest on*, *be buoyed up by*, †Bas.Anc.*virg*.4(M.30. 677C); ἀθλίοις ~εσθαι λογισμοῖς Cyr.*ador*.6(1.200D); *ib*.(206E); id. *Am*.57(3.313E); id.*Jo*.9.1(4.796E).

ἐπινίκιος, *of triumph*, of songs ἐ. ᾠδή ἐστιν ὁ ψαλμός Ath.*exp.Ps*. 46:1(M.27.217A); ἐ. ... εἶναι τὸν λόγον τῆς ψαλμῳδίας ἡ ἐπιγραφὴ σημαίνει...'εἰς τὸ τέλος' γάρ, φησίν,...καὶ ἀντὶ τοῦ 'εἰς τὸ τέλος', ἕτεροι τῶν ἑρμηνέων 'ἐ.' ἐκδεδώκασιν Gr.Nyss.*Pss.titt*.B 13(M.44.568A); ἐν ἑκάστῳ ψαλμῷ ἐν ᾧ οἱ ἑβδομήκοντα 'εἰς τὸ τέλος' τεθείκασιν...ὁ... Σύμμαχος 'ἐ.' Thdt.*Ps*.8:1(1.649); ἀλληλούϊα ἐ. καὶ οὗτος ὁ ὕμνος *ib*. 150:1(1583); of Tersanctus, *Lit.Jac*.(p.200.2); *Lit.Chrys*.(p.313.24).

***ἐπινίπτω**, *let fall upon like snow* τροφὴν αὐτοῖς...ὤμβρησεν οὐρανός, ποτὲ μὲν μάννα, ποτὲ δὲ ὀρτυγομήτραν ἐπινίψας ‡Nil.*perist*.11. 9(M.79.916C).

ἐπινοητής, ὁ, *deviser* ἀγαθῶν ἐπινοητάς Jo.Mal.*chron*.2 p.54(M.97. 129A).

***ἐπινοητικῶς**, *conceptually*, *in thought*, opp. φυσικῶς, Or.*sel.in Gen*.2:16–17(M.12.100D); Marc.Er.*opusc*.8.3(M.65.1105D).

ἐπίνοια, ἡ, **A.** *thought*, *conception*; **1.** in distinguishing various aspects of Christ's redemptive activity μηδεὶς δὲ προσκοπτέτω διακρινόντων ἡμῶν τὰς ἐν τῷ σωτῆρι ἐ., οἰόμενος καὶ τῇ οὐσίᾳ ταὐτὸν ἡμᾶς ποιεῖν Or.*Jo*.1.28(30; p.36.25; M.14.77B); **2.** Trin., ref. Sabellian view ᾤοντο...μὴ διαφέρειν τῷ ἀριθμῷ τὸν υἱὸν τοῦ πατρός, ἀλλ' ἓν οὐ μόνον οὐσίᾳ ἀλλὰ καὶ ὑποκειμένῳ τυγχάνοντας ἀμφοτέρους, κατά τινας ἐ. διαφόρους, οὐ κατὰ ὑπόστασιν λέγεσθαι πατέρα καὶ υἱόν *ib*.10.37 (21; p.212.15; 376B); ref. Arian doctrine οὐχ ὁ μὲν Ἄρειος κατ' ἐπίνοιαν λέγει τὸν λόγον, ὁ δὲ Διονύσιος ἀληθινὸν καὶ φύσει λόγον τοῦ θεοῦ; Ath.*Dion*.24(p.64.15; M.25.516B); Ar.*ib*.23(p.63.1; 513A) cit. s. ξένος; ὁ κύριος κατ' ἐπίνοιαν λέγεται λόγος διὰ τὰ λογικά, καὶ κατ' ἐ. λέγεται σοφία διὰ τὰ σοφιζόμενα id.ap.Ath.*ep.Aeg.Lib*.12(M.25.565A); Ath.*ib*.14(569A); εἰ γάρ...διὰ τὰ λογικὰ λόγος...καὶ τάχα διὰ τὰ ὄντα ἔχει καὶ τὸ εἶναι κατ' ἐπίνοιαν id.*Ar*.2.38(M.26.228A); in orthodox teaching θεοῦ μίαν οὐσίαν εἶναι...κἂν ἐ. τισὶ διαιρουμέναις συνδιαιρῆται καὶ τὰ ὀνόματα Gr.Naz.*or*.29.13(p.93.1; M.36.92A); *ib*.30.8(p.120.7; 113B) cit. s. συνδιαιρέω; in controversy of Basil and Gr. Nyss. agst. Eunomius, used by former to denote *reflection* on concept already formed, opp. direct conception or perception ὥστε μετὰ τὸ πρῶτον ἡμῖν ἀπὸ τῆς αἰσθήσεως ἐγγινόμενον νόημα τὴν λεπτοτέραν καὶ ἀκριβεστέραν τοῦ νοηθέντος ἐπενθύμησιν ἐ. ὀνομάζεσθαι Bas.*Eun*.1.6(1. 217E; M.29.524B); πάντα τὰ τῇ αἰσθήσει γνώριμα, καὶ ἁπλᾶ μὲν εἶναι τῷ ὑποκειμένῳ δοκοῦντα, ποικίλον δὲ λόγον κατὰ τὴν θεωρίαν ἐπιδεχόμενα, ἐπινοίᾳ θεωρητὰ λέγεται *ib*.(218B; M.524C); εἶπε...ὁ Βασίλειος μετὰ τὸ πρῶτον ἐγγενόμενον ἡμῖν περὶ τοῦ πράγματος νόημα τὴν λεπτοτέραν...τοῦ νοηθέντος ἐξέτασιν ἐ. λέγεσθαι. καὶ...ἐν οἷς οὐκ ἔστι πρῶτον καὶ δεύτερον νόημα οὔτε λεπτότερον ἕτερον ἑτέρου...οὐκ ἂν ἔχοι ...χώραν τὸ κατ' ἐ. Eun.ap.Gr.Nyss.*Eun*.12(1 p.312.18; M.45.1025C); ἄφθαρτον γὰρ καὶ ἀγέννητον εἶναι τὸν θεὸν τῶν ὅλων λέγομεν, κατὰ διαφόρους ἐπιβολὰς τοῖς ὀνόμασι τούτοις προσαγορεύοντες...ὡς οὖν τὸ ἀτελεύτητον τῆς ζωῆς ἄφθαρτον, οὕτω τὸ ἄναρχον αὐτῆς ἀγέννητον ὠνομάσθη, τῇ ἐ. θεωρούντων ἡμῶν ἑκάτερα. τίς οὖν ἀντερεῖ λόγος καὶ ἐπινοεῖσθαι τῶν ὀνομάτων τούτων ἑκάτερον, καὶ ὁμολογίαν εἶναι τοῦ κατ' ἀλήθειαν τῷ θεῷ προσόντος; Bas.*Eun*.1.7(219A; M.525C); ἔστι γὰρ κατά γε τὸν ἐμὸν λόγον ἡ ἐ. ἔφοδος εὑρετικὴ τῶν ἀγνοουμένων, διὰ τῶν προσεχῶν τε καὶ ἀκολούθων τῇ πρώτῃ περὶ τὸ σπουδαζόμενον νοήσει τὸ ἐφεξῆς ἐξευρίσκουσα Gr.Nyss.*Eun*.12(1 p.265.22; 969C); hence Basil οὐδαμῶς ἄλλως τὴν προσηγορίαν τῆς ἀγεννησίας ἢ κατ' ἐπίνοιάν φησιν ἐπιλέγεσθαι τῷ θεῷ *ib*.(p.220.1; 913B); Eunomius maintains that οὐσία of God can be known and named and that ἀγεννησία constitutes it, cf. Eun.*ib*.(1 p.264.11; 968D); and uses ἐ. in sense of *invention*, *fancy* τῶν γὰρ οὕτω κατ' ἐπίνοιαν λεγομένων...τὰ μὲν κατὰ τὴν προφορὰν ἔχειν μόνην τὴν ὕπαρξιν ὡς τὰ μηδὲν σημαίνοντα, τὰ δὲ κατ' ἰδίαν διάνοιαν Eun.*ib*.(p.264.25; 969A); cf.Gr.Nyss.*ib*.(p.292.15; 1001C); κατὰ πάντα ἕν εἰσιν ὁ πατήρ, καὶ ὁ υἱός, καὶ τὸ ἅγιον πνεῦμα· πλὴν τῆς ἀγεννησίας καὶ τῆς γεννήσεως καὶ τῆς ἐκπορεύσεως. ἐπινοίᾳ δὲ τὸ διῃρημένον ‡Cyr.*Trin*.10(6^3.15D; M.77.1144A); **3.** Christol. καθὸ Χριστός, ἕν...καὶ τὸ αὐτὸ ὢν τῇ οὐσίᾳ, εἰ καὶ τὰ μάλιστα πολλαῖς ἐ. ἐπινοεῖται Hymen.*ep*.9(p.330.3); οὐ δύο λέγομεν, θεὸν ἰδίᾳ, καὶ ἄνθρωπον ἰδίᾳ (εἷς γὰρ ἦν), ἀλλὰ κατ' ἐ. τὴν ἑκάστου φύσιν λογιζόμενοι Didym.(‡Bas.)*Eun*.4(1.293D; M.29.704C); monophysite view πῶς οἱ...δύο λέγοντες φύσεις φασὶ μὴ λέγειν δύο ὑποστάσεις;...καὶ ἐν τῇ ἐ. διαιρουμέναις ταῖς φύσεσιν ἤγουν ὑποστάσεσιν, συνεπινοεῖται τὰ πρόσωπα...ἐν συνθέσει δὲ ὑφισταμέναις ταῖς φύσεσιν ἐξ ὧν ὁ εἷς Χριστὸς...συναπολήγει καὶ ἡ φαντασθεῖσα τῇ ἐ. τῶν ὑποστάσεων καὶ προσώπων δυάς Sev.Ant.*fr*.(M.86.908A); τὰς φύσεις μόνῃ τῇ ἐ. καὶ ἡμεῖς θεωροῦμεν...ᾧ γὰρ λόγῳ ὑμεῖς τὰς ὑποστάσεις τῇ ἐ. λαμβάνοντες, καὶ ταύτας ἑνώσαντες, εἰς μίαν ὑπόστασιν αὐτὰς συντίθετε, τούτῳ τῷ λόγῳ καὶ ἡμῖν αἱ φύσεις, εἰς μίαν φύσιν συντιθέμεναι συγχεόμεναι καὶ τὴν διαίρεσιν ἐκκλίνουσι καὶ τὴν ἕνωσιν γνωρίζουσιν Leont.B.*arg.Sev*. (M.86.1929D); orthodox reply τὴν ἐ. οἱ πατέρες...διττὴν ἀπεφήναντο εἶναι· ἡ μὲν γὰρ οἷον ἐπέννοιά τίς ἐστι καὶ ἐπενθύμησις, τὴν ὁλοσχερῆ καὶ ἀδιάρθρωτον τῶν πραγμάτων ἐξαπλοῦσά τε καὶ διασαφοῦσα θεωρίαν...ἡ δὲ ἀνάπλασμα διανοίας τυγχάνει...ἐκ τῶν ὄντων τὰ μηδαμῶς ὄντα συντιθεῖσα, καὶ εἶναι δόξαντα. ... κατὰ ποίαν τοίνυν... τῶν ἐ. τούτων θεωρίαν τὰς δύο φύσεις λαμβάνεις; εἰ μὲν οὖν κατὰ τὴν πρώτην, θεωρημάτων ἄθροισμα, ἀλλ' οὐ φύσεων σύνοδον, τὸν Χριστὸν εἶναι ὁρίσῃ·...εἰ δὲ κατὰ τὴν δευτέραν,...ψευδῶν...ἀναπλασμῶν τὴν σαυτοῦ διάνοιαν πλήρη πεποίηκας *ib*.(1932A,B); *ib*.(1933B); ἐπινοίᾳ καὶ οὐκ ἐνεργείᾳ ἡ ἀνθρωπότης ἀπὸ τῆς θεότητος ἑνωθεῖσα χωρίζεται *ib*. (1937C); εἰ μὲν οὖν τὴν ἐπινοίᾳ λέγουσι μίαν εἶναι τῶν ἐξ ὧν [sc. φύσεων] ὁ σωτὴρ σύνθετός ἐστι κατὰ μίαν φύσιν ὑφεστώς, σαφὲς ὡς τὸ ἥμισυ τοῦ κατ' αὐτὸν φυσικοῦ λόγου, ἐπινοίᾳ ἔσται ἔχων καὶ οὐ πράγματι, ἤγουν τὸ ἀνθρώπινον μέρος τῆς συνθέσεως αὐτοῦ Leont.H. *monoph*.58(M.86.1800D); διὰ δὲ τὴν οὐσιώδη σύγκρασίν τε καὶ ἕνωσιν αὐτῶν, τὴν τούτων διαίρεσιν κατ' ἐπίνοιαν λέγομεν Pamph.H.*panopl*. 6.5(p.618); τὰς μὲν φύσεις τῇ ἐνεργείᾳ εἶναι πιστεύομεν, τὴν δὲ τούτων διαίρεσιν τῇ ἐ. θεωρουμένην, μὴ πραγματικὴν τούτων...διαίρεσιν δογματίζοντες *ib*.9.4(p.634); οὗτος [sc. Severus] ψιλὴν τὴν διαφορὰν πρεσβεύων μετὰ τὴν ἕνωσιν, κατὰ μὲν τὴν ἐ. εἶναι φρονεῖ τῶν διαφερόντων τὴν ὕπαρξιν· κατὰ δὲ τὴν ἐνέργειαν, τὴν αὐτῶν ἐπιδιατίθεται σύγχυσιν Max.*opusc*.(M.91.41B); *Lit.Jac*.(*NBP* 10^2 p.37) cit. s. διαιρέω; **4.** name of second aeon in Simonian system, Hipp.*haer*.6. 20(p.148.22; M.16.3226C); Ἐ. μεγάλη Simon Magus *ib*.6.18(p.144.15; 3222A); indwelling Helena, *ib*.6.19(p.145.14; 3222D).

B. *meaning*, *sense* of a word, Serap.*Man*.32(p.49).

ἐπινομή, ἡ, *spread* of fire, poison, etc.; ? = ἐπινομίς, *addition to a law*, *codicil*, or *assignment*, ref. appointment of ministers in primitive Church διὰ ταύτην...τὴν αἰτίαν πρόγνωσιν εἰληφότες [sc. apostles] τελείαν κατέστησαν τοὺς προειρημένους καὶ μεταξὺ ἐ. δεδώκασιν, ὅπως, ἐὰν κοιμηθῶσιν διαδέξωνται ἕτεροι δεδοκιμασμένοι ἄνδρες τὴν λειτουργίαν αὐτῶν *1Clem*.44.2(vv.ll. ἐπιδομήν, ἐπὶ δοκιμήν).

ἐπινοστέω, *return*, Cyr.*ador*.1(1.23C).

ἐπινυκτίς, ἡ, *night-journal* corresponding to ἐφημερίς (*diary*), Synes.*insomn*.18(p.183.11; M.66.1316B).

***ἐπινυσταγμός**, ὁ, *greater drowsiness*, Or.*exp.in Pr*.6(M.17.177A).

ἐπιξαίνω, *scratch*, *lacerate*; met., *exacerbate*, Bas.*hom*.6.3(2.46C; M. 31.268B); Ast.Am.*prod*.(p.115.21); id.*phar*.(p.119.33).

***ἐπιξενίζομαι**, *be entertained as guest*, *T.Abr*.A 4(p.80.18); *ib*.B 6 (p.110.18).

ἐπιξεν-όομαι, **1.** *live abroad*, *be a sojourner*, met. ἡ τοῦ σοφοῦ τε καὶ γνωστικοῦ ψυχή, οἷον ~ουμένη τῷ σώματι Clem.*str*.4.26(p.321.25; M.8.1376A); **2.** *perform episcopal duties in vacancy of see* μὴ ὀφείλειν ἐπίσκοπον ~ούμενον καθέζεσθαι ἐν ᾗ καθέδρᾳ ~οῦται *Cod.Afr*.74(Lat. *interventor...ubi interventor est*).

ἐπίξενος, ὁ, *guest*, *T.Abr*.A 2(p.78.20); *ib*.3(p.80.2); in scale ξένοι, ἐ., φίλοι, ἀδελφοί Clem.*str*.2.9(p.135.2; M.8.977A).

***ἐπιξύστης**, ὁ, *polisher*, *Chron.Pasch*.p.48(M.92.173A).

ἐπιορκίζω, v. *ἐπορκίζω.

***ἐπιορκισμός**, ὁ, *conjuration*, *spell*; of Jewish magical incantations, Epiph.*haer*.30.8(p.343.12; ἐφορκισμούς M.41.417B).

***ἐπίουρεν**, ἐπίουρεν...κονιορτόν, ? f.l. for ἐπῆρεν, Jo.Mosch.*prat*.60 (M.87.2912D).

***ἐπιουσία, ἡ,** prob. *coming after, succession,* of Elisha ὅλος...τῆς ἐπιθυμίας γενόμενος τῆς ἑλκούσης αὐτὸν πρὸς τὴν τοῦ διδασκάλου ἐπιουσίαν, κατεφρόνησε τῶν ὁρωμένων Nil.*exerc*.43(M.79.773A), but poss. *presence*.

ἐπιούσιος, exeg. ἄρτος ἐ. Mt.6:11; alternative derivations ἐ. δὲ ἄρτον, ἢ τὸν συνιστῶντα τὸ σῶμα ἡμῶν φησι, τουτέστι τὸν ἐφήμερον, εἴτε τὸν ἐπιόντα, τὸν μέλλοντα...ἢ παρὰ τὸ ἐπιέναι..., ἵνα ᾖ·...τὸν ἀποδοθησόμενον ἐν τῷ μέλλοντι τοῖς ἁγίοις, δὸς ἡμῖν ἤδη· ἢ...οἷα ἡ τῆς ψυχῆς ἡμῶν φύσις Petr.Laod.*or.dom.*(p.110.11; M.86.3333A); **1.** derived from εἶμι; **a.** *pertaining to the future,* i.e. *of the world to come* ἐρεῖ δέ τις τὸ ἐ. παρὰ τὸ ἐπιέναι κατεσχηματίσθαι, ὥστε τὸ οἱονεὶ αὔριον δοθησόμενον 'σήμερον' ἡμῖν δοθῆναι, 'σήμερον' μὲν τοῦ ἐνεστῶτος αἰῶνος λαμβανομένου αὔριον δὲ τοῦ μέλλοντος Or.*or*.27.13 (p.372.3ff.; M.11.517A); τὸν ἐ. ἄρτον, τουτέστι τὸν μέλλοντα, οὗ ἀπαρχὴν ἔχομεν, ἐν τῇ νῦν ζωῇ Ath.*inc.et c.Ar*.16(M.26.1012B); τὸν ἄρτον...τὸν ἐ. ... τὴν μέλλουσαν δόξαν τὴν ἐν Χριστῷ Ἰησοῦ Thdt. *Phil*.4:19(3.470); τὸ...ἐ. δηλοῖ, ἢ τὸν μέλλοντα, τουτέστι τὸν τοῦ μέλλοντος αἰῶνος, ἢ τὸν πρὸς συντήρησιν τῆς οὐσίας ἡμῶν λαμβανόμενον Jo.D.*f.o*.4.13(M.94.1152B); **b.** *for the day, daily* τὸν ἐ. ἄρτον, τουτέστι τὸν πρὸς τὴν ἐφήμερον ζωὴν τῇ οὐσίᾳ ἡμῶν χρησιμεύοντα Bas.*reg.br*.252(2.500C; M.31.1252B); τὸν ἐφήμερον ἄρτον Gr.Nyss.*or. dom*.4(p.78.13; M.44.1168D); τὸν ἄρτον...τὸν ἐ. ... ἀντὶ τοῦ, τὴν τῆς ἡμέρας τροφήν Chrys.*hom.54.5 in Gen*.(4.530A); τὸν ἐφήμερον id. *hom.19.5 in Mt*.(7.251D); τοῦ καθημερινοῦ id.*hom.43.2 in Jo*.(8. 257C); cf. *petendo panem quotidianum, perpetuitatem postulamus in Christo, et individuitatem a corpore ejus,* Tert.*de oratione* 6(M.*PL*.1. 1263A); cf. *hunc...panem dari nobis quotidie postulamus,* Cypr.*de or. dominica* 18(M.*PL*.4.549A); in gen. τὴν ἐ. ἐδέχετο μᾶζαν Pall.*v. Chrys*.12(p.76.12; M.47.43); ἔργῳ χειρῶν κοπιῶντας τὸν ἐ. πορίζεσθαι ἄρτον Niceph.Ur.*v.Sym*.116(M.86.3096A); **2.** from εἰμί; **a.** substantialis, *suited to one's nature* ἡ λέξις ἡ ἐ. παρ' οὐδενὶ τῶν Ἑλλήνων οὔτε σοφῶν ὠνόμασται οὔτε ἐν τῇ τῶν ἰδιωτῶν συνηθείᾳ τέτριπται, ἀλλ' ἔοικε πεπλάσθαι ὑπὸ τῶν εὐαγγελιστῶν...δοκεῖ μοι...παρὰ τὴν οὐσίαν πεποιῆσθαι, ἡ...τὸν εἰς τὴν οὐσίαν συμβαλλόμενον ἄρτον δηλοῦσα Or. *or*.27.7(p.366.34ff.; M.11.509C,D); ἐ. τοίνυν ἄρτος ὁ τῇ φύσει τῇ λογικῇ καταλληλότατος καὶ τῇ οὐσίᾳ αὐτῇ συγγενής *ib*.27.9(p.369. 18ff.; 513A); Bas.*reg.br*.252 v. 1.b supra; ἐ. τουτέστιν, ἢ τὸν τῇ ψυχῇ ἁρμόδιον, ἢ τὸν τῇ σαρκὶ αὐτάρκη Isid.Pel.*epp*.4.24(M.78.1073C); ἄρτον...ἐ. ... τὰ εἰς ζωὴν ἐπιτήδεια Cyr.*glaph.Ex*.2(1.286E); Jo.D.*f.o*. 4.13 v. 1.a supra; esp. to soul τὸν ἐ. ἄρτον...τὸν ἀναδιδόμενον εἰς τὴν οὐσίαν τῆς ψυχῆς Or.*exc.in Ps*.77:30f.(M.17.145A); ὁ ἄρτος οὗτος ὁ κοινὸς οὐκ ἔστιν ἐ. ἄρτος δὲ οὗτος ὁ ἅγιος ἐ. ἐστιν, ἀντὶ τοῦ ἐπὶ τὴν οὐσίαν τῆς ψυχῆς κατατασσόμενος...εἰς πᾶσαν σοῦ τὴν σύστασιν ἀναδίδοται εἰς ὠφέλειαν σώματος καὶ ψυχῆς Cyr.H.*catech*.23.15; cf. (ref. Mt.6:9ff.) ζητητέον...σαρκικὸν μὲν οὐδέν, θεῖα δὲ πάντα καὶ πνευματικά Cyr.*ador*.13(1.471E); **b.** supersubstantialis, *supernatural* ἄρτον...ἐ., οὐ τρυφήν, ἀλλὰ τροφήν, τὴν τὸ ἐλλεῖπον ἀναπληροῦσαν τοῦ σώματος...ἐπὶ τὴν οὐσίαν τοῦ σώματος διαβαίνοντα, καὶ συγκροτῆσαι ταύτην δυνάμενον Chrys.*hom.in Mt*.7:14(3.30E); cf. *pasti sumus pane...quem oratio dominica nominat supersubstantialem,* Proc.G. *Lev*.22:3(M.87.773); *panem quidem dixit, sed* ἐ., *hoc est supersubstantialem. non iste panis est, qui vadit in corpus, sed ille panis vitae aeternae, qui animae nostrae substantiam fulcit. ideo Graece* ἐ. *dicitur; Latinus autem hunc panem quotidianum dixit, quem Graeci dicunt advenientem...Graecus utrumque uno sermone significavit,* Ambr.*de sacramentis* 5.4.24(M.*PL*.16.452A).

ἐπιπαράγω, *produce in addition,* †Proc.G.*Procl*.(M.87.2792[h]B).

ἐπιπείθω, *lay an obligation on, bind* with an oath, Thdt.*h.rel*.6 (3.1171).

***ἐπιπειθῶς,** *obediently,* Gr.Nyss.*Apoll*.7(M.45.1137C).

ἐπίπεμπτος (A), as subst. neut., *a fifth part besides;* cf. exeg. Lev.5:16, *simpliciores...aestimant ita dictum ut, verbi causa, si quinque nummi subtracti sunt, unus addatur, ut pro quinque sex reddere videatur. sed qui in disciplina numerorum peritiam gerunt, longe aliter istius vocabuli numerum supportant. nam et in Graeco non habet* πέμπτον, *quod simpliciter 'quintas' facit, sed habet* ἐ., *quod...possumus dicere 'supra quintas'...ut verbi gratia intelligatur, qui furatus sit quinque nummos, ipsos quidem quinque restituere et alios quinque uno superaddito,* Or.*hom.3.6 in Lev*.(p.311. 11; M.12.431B).

§**ἐπίπεμπτος (B), 1.** *sent to;* of Manes as sent into world by Devil, Epiph.*haer*.66.20(p.48.9; M.42.65A); **2.** as subst., *emissary* εἷς τις ἐ. τοῦ σατανᾶ *A.Jo*.63(p.181.22).

***ἐπίπερ,** ἵν' ὃ ἐ. prob. f.l. for ἵνα ἐπείπερ Cyr.*hom.pasch*.15(5[2]. 208D).

ἐπιπέτομαι [also pres. ἐφίπταμαι, aor. ἐπέπτην], *fly to, light upon,* of H. Ghost ὡς περιστερὰν τὸ...πνεῦμα ἐπιπτῆναι ἐπ' αὐτόν [sc. Christ] Just.*dial*.88.3(M.6.685B); τῆς ἐπιπτάσης τῷ σωτῆρι βαπτιζομένῳ...περιστερᾶς Or.*Cels*.1.40(p.90.23; M.11.736A); abs., Mont.*fr*. ap.Epiph.*haer*.48.4(p.224.23, v.l. ἵπταμαι M.41.861A) cit. s. πλῆκτρον; τὸ ἐπιπτῆναι τὴν τοῦ πνεύματος χάριν Chrys.*hom.23.3 in Jo*.(8. 136C).

***ἐπιπηγάζ-ω,** *make to gush forth* ὁ ~ων καὶ τὸν νοῦν καὶ τὸν λόγον Clem.*str*.1.1(p.9.22; M.8.701A).

ἐπιπήγνυμι, *fix upon,* Paul.Sil.*Soph*.497(M.86.2138B).

ἐπιπηδ-άω, 1. *rush upon, rush into,* lit. and met. ἐπεπήδησεν τῇ διδασκαλίᾳ Clem.*str*.1.1(p.5.29; M.8.692C); ἐπιπηδήσας τῇ γραφῇ Eus.*Marcell*.1.4(p.28.2; M.24.769A); Bas.*Eun*.2.7(1.243B; M.29. 584D); of rashly rushing into martyrdom ψέγομεν...τοὺς ἐπιπηδήσαντας τῷ θανάτῳ· εἰσὶ γάρ τινες οὐχ ἡμέτεροι, μόνου τοῦ ὀνόματος κοινωνοί, οἳ δὴ αὑτοὺς παραδιδόναι σπεύδουσι τῇ πρὸς τὸν δημιουργὸν ἀπεχθείᾳ Clem.*str*.4.4(p.256.11; 1229B); Or.*Jo*.28.23(18; p.417.28; M.14.728C); Chrys.*hom.25.2 in 2Cor*.(10.615B); into temptation, id.*hom.13.1 in Mt*.(7.168C); **2.** *invade, usurp,* of bishops ἐπίσκοπον μὴ ἐξεῖναι καταλείψαντα τὴν ἑαυτοῦ παροικίαν ἑτέρᾳ ~ᾶν *Can.App*. 14; τίνος ἕνεκεν ἕτερος ἄρχων ἑτέρᾳ ἐκκλησίᾳ ~ᾷ; Chrys.*hom.11.5 in Eph*.(11.87C); μὴ δεῖν ἐπίσκοπον ἀφιέναι τὴν ἑαυτοῦ πόλιν καὶ θρόνοις ἀλλοτρίοις ἢ καὶ τοῖς εὐκαιροῦσιν ~ᾶν Jo.Scholast.*nomoc*. 12(p.13.19); in gen. ὥσπερ γὰρ ὁ ~ῶν μὴ δεδομένῃ παρὰ θεοῦ τιμῇ, μέμψεως ἄξιος...οὕτως ὁ...ἀποπηδῶν...ὑπεύθυνος παρακοῆς Chrys.*hom.1.1 in 1Tim*.(11.548E); **3.** *leap, dance,* †Thdt.*Pss.proem*. (5.75).

***ἐπιπιστεύω,** *trust in,* c. dat., †Apoll.*met.Ps*.24:2(M.33.1344A).

ἐπίπλαστος, *feigned, fictitious, sham,* Tat.*orat*.40(p.41.9; M.6. 884C); Clem.*paed*.3.11(p.272.9; M.8.640A); τὴν ἐ. ἀρετήν Or.*hom.29 in Lc*.(p.182.9); Eus.*p.e*.14.4(726C; M.21.1193A); of Arian Christ ἐ. καὶ νόθον ἔχων τὸ μονογενὴς υἱὸς καὶ θεὸς ὄνομα Didym.*Trin*.3.4(M. 39.828C); Ἰακὼβ ἄνθρωπος ἄπλαστος οἰκῶν οἰκίαν, τουτέστι μηδὲν ἔχων ἐ. ἢ ἐπείσακτον κακόν Proc.G.*Gen*.25:27(M.87.409A).

ἐπιπλάστως, *feignedly, falsely,* Or.*sel.in Ps*.25:3(M.12.1273B); Eus.*h.e*.9.9.13(M.20.824C); id.*v.C*.3.66(p.113.13; M.20.1144A); τοὺς λόγον μὲν μόνον αὐτὸν ψιλὸν τοῦ θεοῦ...ἐ. καλοῦντας *Symb.Ant*.(345)5 (p.252.35; M.26.729D).

ἐπιπλατύνω, *extend;* time, Epiph.*haer*.70.12(p.245.12; M.42.364B); *broaden out, spread,* opp. λεπτύνω, Gr.Nyss.*mort*.(M.46.513B).

***ἐπιπλεῖον (ἐπιπλέον),** (ἐπὶ πλεῖον), adv., *further, at greater length* ἐ. περὶ τούτων διαλαβεῖν Or.*Jo*.6.58(37; p.167.13; M.14.301B); εἰ καὶ ἐ. τῆς λέξεως παρεθέμην τῶν εὐαγγελιστῶν *ib*.10.22(15; p.194. 12; 345C); τὴν ἐ. διατριβήν *ib*.10.9(7; p.179.7; 320B); plur. form ἐπιπλείονά σε βασανίζων *M.Tar*.3(p.456); *ib*.7(p.464); ἐπιπλέον Or. *Jo*.6.6(3; p.113.14; 208D).

ἐπιπληθύν-ω, *increase* ~ομένης αὐτῷ τῆς τῶν λόγων ἐπικαρπίας Jo.VI H.*v.Jo.D*.12(M.94.448B); intrans. ~οντι τῷ καρπῷ *ib*.

ἐπιπληκτικός, *of rebuke, rebuking* ἐπίπληξίς δέ ἐστιν ἐπιτίμησις ἐ. ἢ ψόγος πληκτικός Clem.*paed*.1.9(p.135.21; M.8.344A); τὸ ἐ. ... εἶδος τῆς παιδαγωγίας *ib*.1.10(p.145.23; 361A); Or.*or*.29.8(p.385.7; M.11.536A); Chrys.*hom.in Phil*.proem.2(11.191D); neut. as subst., Clem.*paed*.1.9(p.136.5; ἐπιδεικτικόν 344B).

ἐπιπληκτικῶς, 1. *so as to rebuke,* Or.*Jo*.6.22(13; p.132.5; M.14. 240A); comp., Chrys.*hom.4.6 in Mt*.(7.56B); ἐ. τῷ λόγῳ χρώμενος id.*hom.10.4 in Rom*.(9.525D); **2.** c. genit., *in rebuke of,* Or.*hom.15.1 in Jer*.(p.125.21; M.13.429A).

***ἐπιπλημμυρίζω,** *overflow,* Gr.Nyss.*mort*.(M.46.505A).

***ἐπίπλοκος,** *complicated;* neut. as subst., *intricacy,* Bas.*hom*.12.7 (2.103D; M.31.400C).

***ἐπιπλωτής, ὁ,** *passenger or soldier carried on board ship,* opp. crew, Geo.Pis.*bell.Avar*.182(M.92.1275B).

ἐπίπνοια, ἡ, *inspiration;* **1.** in scripture, of LXX translation κατ' ἐπίπνοιαν τοῦ θεοῦ εἰσὶν ἡρμηνευμέναι αἱ γραφαί Iren.*haer*.3.21. 2(M.7.948B); of Moses κατ' ἐπίπνοιαν καὶ ἐνέργειαν τὴν παρὰ τοῦ θεοῦ ...λαβεῖν...χαλκὸν καὶ ποιῆσαι τύπον σταυροῦ Just.*1apol*.60.3(M.6. 417A); of prophets, Clem.*str*.1.21(p.84.6; M.8.869B); Or.*ep*.1.10(M. 11.72B); *ib*.(73B,C); †Bas.*Is*.proem.1(1.378B; M.30.120B); of scripture in gen., Or.*Jo*.1.3(5; p.7.2; M.14.28C) cit. s. θεόπνευστος; ἐξ ἐ. ἁγίου πνεύματος *ib*.2.34(28; p.92.32; 176B); μὴ ἀνθρώπων εἶναι συγγράμματα τὰς ἱερὰς βίβλους, ἀλλ' ἐξ ἐ. τοῦ...πνεύματος βουλήματι τοῦ πατρὸς...διὰ Ἰησοῦ Χριστοῦ ταύτας ἀναγεγράφθαι καὶ εἰς ἡμᾶς ἐληλυθέναι id.*princ*.4.2.2(p.308.12; M.11.360B); Const.*or.s.c*.1(p.154. 16; M.20.1236A); Eus.*p.e*.11.7(521B; M.21.864C); λογίων δὲ χρησμοί, οὐκ ἐκ μαντείας...φωτὸς δ' ἐπιπνοίαις ἐνθέου προσπεφωνημένοι id.*l.C*. proem.(p.196.7; M.20.1317C); γραφὴν...διὰ τῆς ἐ. τοῦ ἁγίου πνεύματος συγγραφεῖσαν Bas.*Spir*.52(3.45C; M.32.165C); τοῦτον [sc. Νεῖλον] ἐκεῖθεν ῥεῖν ἢ Μωσέως ἐ. λέγει Philost.*h.e.*3.10(M.65.493C); **2.** of pentecostal inspiration ὁμόγλωσσοι...οἱ διακονοῦντες τὸν λόγον ἐκ θείας ἐ. ... ἐγένοντο Gr.Nyss.*or.catech.*30(p.112.5; M.45.77A); of S. Peter's inspiration by H. Ghost at Transfiguration οὐ λογισμῷ... ἐφθέγγετο, ἐ. δὲ τοῦ τὰ μέλλοντα προθεσπίζοντος πνεύματος Jo.D.*hom.* 1.16(M.96.572A); **3.** of inspiration of Constantine, Const.*or.s.c.*2 (p.156.2; M.20.1237B); Eus.*l.C.*11(p.225.9; M.20.1377C); of a Christian teacher, Dion.Ar.*d.n.*2.9(M.3.673A); **4.** of divine inspiration by which Greek philosophers proclaim belief in one God, Clem.*prot.*6 (p.53.28; M.8.176C); cf.Or.*Cels.*4.30(p.300.19; M.11.1073B); also of Egyptian sages ἐξ ἐ. θειοτάτης ἔφασαν τὸν θεὸν εἶναι μονάδα ἀδιαίρετον Hipp.*haer.*4.43(p.65.14; M.16.3106B); of Erythraean Sibyl in prophesying Christ, Const.*or.s.c.*18(p.179.15; M.20.1288B); of poets, *ib.*10(p.165.7; 1257C); **5.** of evil inspiration [sc. ἐπιθυμία] ἥτις ἐξ ἐ. ...ἐγενήθη τοῦ ὑλικοῦ πνεύματος Meth.*res.*6(p.340.7; M.18.304C); τί δὲ βούλει μετασχεῖν τῶν Ἑλληνικῶν λογίων, ὄντων νεκρῶν ἀνθρώπων ἐξ ἐ. διαβόλου ἀποφανθέντων; *Const.App.*2.61.3.

***ἐπιπνόως**, *by inspiration*, Clem.*q.d.s.*37(p.184.15 conj. for ἐπιπόνως M.9.641D).

ἐπιποι-έω, **1.** *add*, abs. φῶς...οὐδὲ οἱονεί τινος ~οῦντος δεόμενον [i.e. *to add to it*] Hipp.*haer.*8.9(p.228.9; M.16.3351B); *add to*, with sense of making artificial or false addition, Synes.*Dion* 3(p.241.15; M.66.1121A); id.*provid.*13(p.92.19; M.66.1241A); med., *add for oneself*, Jo.VI H.*v.Jo.D.*35(M.94.481A); **2.** *make one's abode* in συνηθῆναι ἡμᾶς τοσαύτας ἡμέρας ἐν ἑνὶ τόπῳ ~ῆσαι Heracl.*ep.*(M.92.1024B); ~ησάντων δὲ ἡμῶν...ἕως τῆς τρίτης τοῦ Ἀπριλίου μηνὸς *ib.*(1025A).

***ἐπιποίητος**, *made up*, *artificial* κάλλος Synes.*calv.*19(p.224.9; M. 66.1200A); τὸ φαινόμενόν τε καὶ ἐ. id.*regn.*16(p.35.11; M.66.1081B); id. *ep.*44(M.66.1373B).

***ἐπιποιήτως**, *artificially*, ref. Marcion's text of epistles ἔν τισι λέξεσιν ἐ. προσθήκην ἔχουσαν Epiph.*haer.*42.11(p.124.5; M.41.725C).

ἐπιπολαιόρριζος, *with roots along the surface*, Isid.Pel.*epp.*2.111 (M.78.552C).

ἐπιπόλαιος, *on the surface*; met., *superficial, obvious* λόγοι...ἐ. Clem.*str.*7.3(p.14.19; M.9.424C); Gr.Nyss.*or.catech.*7(p.38.13; M.45. 32A); esp. of literal interprn. of scripture, Or.*princ.*4.3.11(p.340. 4; M.11.396A); τοῦ νόμου τὸ μὲν αἰσθητὸν καὶ ἐ. Thdt.*qu.1 in Lev.* (1.179); of persons, Or.*hom.18.4 in Jer.*(p.154.21; M.13.469A); τελεταί, πρεσβευόμενοι μὲν λογικῶς ὑπὸ τῶν...λογίων, συμβολικῶς δὲ γινόμεναι ὑπὸ τῶν...πολλῶν καὶ ἐπιπολαιοτέρων id.*Cels.*1.12(p.65.14; M.11.677C); Gr.Nyss.*or.dom.*1(p.22.37; M.44.1133C).

***ἐπιπολαιοτέρως**, *more shallowly*, Or.*princ.*3.1.14(p.219.12; M. 11.276B).

***ἐπιπολαιόφυτος**, *planted near the surface*, Isid.Pel.*epp.*2.111(M. 78.552C).

ἐπιπολαίως, *on the surface*; met., *in a shallow, superficial manner* ἄρχεται μὲν ἐπιπολαιότερον, προχεῖται δὲ εἰς τὸ ὑψηλότερον Meth. *symp.*3.2(p.28.20; M.18.61D); οἱ τῷ λόγῳ προσελθόντες ἐ. Gr.Naz.*or.* 4.11(M.35.541A); Gr.Nyss.*hom.2 in Cant.*(M.44.796B); Diod.*proem. Pss.*(p.82.22); ref. literal interpretation of scripture, Clem.*q.d.s.*5 (p.163.29; M.9.609D); Or.*hom.18.4 in Jer.*(p.154.14; M.13.468C).

ἐπιπολή, ἡ, **1.** *surface*, Or.*princ.*3.1.13(p.218.7; M.11.273A); plur. εἰς τὰς ἐ. τῆς ἐγρηγόρσεως Clem.*paed.*2.9(p.206.22; ἐπιβολάς M.8. 493C); **2.** genit., also ἐξ ἐ., *superficially, on the surface*; hence **a.** *lightly, so as merely to touch*, ‡Dion.Al.*fr.in Lc.22:42*(p.232.10; M.10.1597B); **b.** *in a shallow* or *superficial way*, Clem.*str.*7.16(p.69. 11; M.9.536B); Or.*fr.33 in Jo.*2:23(p.508.21); **c.** of translation, *literally*, Epiph.*mens.*2(M.43.240B, v.l. ἐπιστολῆς); ref. interprn. of scripture ἡ δὲ ἐξ ἐ. τοῦ γράμματος διάνοια Thdt.*qu.3 in Jos.*(1.306); id.*Ps.*64:14(1.1040); **d.** *to outward appearance*, Or.*hom.19.12 in Jer.* (p.167.22; M.13.488A).

***ἐπιπολιτεύομαι**, *conduct oneself* πῶς χρὴ ἐπιπολιτεύεσθαι εἰς τὸν λαόν; Eus.Al.*serm.*5(M.86.348D).

ἐπιπολύ, *largely, to a great extent*, *Barn.*4.1; Or.*Jo.*6.58(37; p.166. 21; M.14.300C).

***ἐπιπόνηρος**, Proc.G.*ep.*67(M.87.2725A), error for ἐστι πονηρός *EG.*

***ἐπιπόντιος**, *maritime*, Ath.Scholast.*coll.*17.1(p.161).

***ἐπιπορίζω**, *gain more*, Mac.Aeg.*hom.*15.37(M.34.601B).

ἐπιποτάμιος, *beside the river* ὁδὸς...ἐ. Gr.Nyss.*ep.*6(M.46.1033B); as subst. masc., *one who works on* or *by the river*, Synes.*provid.*16 (p.103.4; M.66.1252B).

ἐπιπράσσω, *do in addition*, Thdr.Stud.*epp.*2.157(M.99.1493A).

ἐπιπρίω, *gnash* teeth, Gel.Cyz.*h.e.*3.19.3(M.85.1345B).

ἐπιπροβάλλ-ω, *project, bring forth, in addition*, of emanations brought about through fall of Sophia in Valent. system ἐπιπροβληθεὶς οὖν ὁ Χριστὸς καὶ τὸ ἅγιον Πνεῦμα ὑπὸ τοῦ Νοῦ καὶ τῆς Ἀληθείας...τὸ ἔκτρωμα...τῆς Σοφίας μονογενὲς...ἀποχωρίζει τῶν ὅλων αἰώνων...πάλιν καὶ ὁ Πατὴρ ~ει αἰῶνα ἕνα τὸν Σταυρόν,...εἰς φρουρὰν καὶ χαράκωμα τῶν αἰώνων προβεβλημένος Hipp.*haer.*6.31(p.159.2; M.16.3239D); τοὺς ἐντὸς πληρώματος αἰῶνας τριάκοντα πάλιν ἐπιπροβεβληκέναι αὐτοῖς κατὰ ἀναλογίαν αἰῶνας ἄλλους *ib.*6.34(p.162.16; 3246B); *ib.*6.36(p.166.10; 3250C).

***ἐπιπροπίν-ω**, *bestow freely* (from custom of giving wine-cup to person pledged) τοῖς ἀξίοις ἀπωλείας σωτηρίαν ~ει ‡Chrys.*disc. benign.*(1.814D).

ἐπιπρόσθεσις, ἡ, *interposition, placing in front* διὰ τὴν ἐ. τοῦ ἐπικειμένου αὐτῷ σώματος Bas.*hex.*2.1(1.13A; M.29.29C).

ἐπίπτησις, ἡ, *alighting*, ‡Chrys.*praecurs.*1(2.805B).

ἐπίπτυξις, ἡ, *folding in*, hence *contraction*, Bas.*hex.*7.1(1.63E; M.29.149B).

***ἐπιπύλιος**, ὁ, ? *gate-house*, Gr.Nyss.*hom.3 in Eccl.*(M.46.656B).

***ἐπιραγολογ-έω**, **1.** *glean grapes*, Evagr.Pont.*cap.pract.*B 100 (M.40.1252C); Jo.Clim.*scal.*10(M.88.848D); **2.** trans., *glean grapes from* ~ουμένοις τὴν ἄμπελον Leont.N.*v.Jo.Eleem.*proem.(p.2.19).

***ἐπιρέμβομαι**, *roam about*, c. dat., Nil.*praest.*7(M.79.1068D).

***ἐπιρρέπεια**, ἡ, **1.** *propensity*, towards c. πρός and acc., Or.*comm. in Mt.*10.12(p.13.26; M.13.861C); **2.** *partiality* μετὰ πολλῆς τῆς προσκλίσεως καὶ ἐ. Chrys.*hom.14.2 in Eph.*(11.105B).

ἐπίρρημα, τό, **1.** *something added*; gram., of adverbs, Clem. *str.*7.8(p.38.3; M.9.472B); Ath.*Ar.*1.11(M.26.33B); conjunctions, *ib.* 3.22(369B); Chrys.*hom.56.1 in Jo.*(8.327D); interjections, id.*virg.*21 (1.283E); **2.** = ἐπίρρησις (*LS*), *incantation*, Epiph.*haer.*31.7(p.397. 11; M.41.488B).

ἐπίρρινος, *with prominent nose*; of human appearance of Christ, ‡Jo.D.*ep.Thphl.*3(M.95.349C); of S. Paul μικρῶς ἐ. *A.Paul. et Thecl.*3(p.237.8).

***ἐπιρριπτάριον**, τό, monk's *cowl*, *V.Dan.*7(p.70.18); Jo.Mosch. *prat.*92(M.87.2949C).

ἐπιρρίπτ-ω, **1.** *ascribe, lay to the charge of* δεῖ ~ειν τὰς ἁμαρτίας [sc. τῷ διαβόλῳ] ὡς αἰτίῳ...τοῦ ἁμαρτάνειν Or.*hom.23 in Lc.*(p.153.22); Proc.G.*Gen.*2:17(M.87.169B); pass., *be predicated* υἱὸς ἀληθῶς, οὐκ ἀνυπόστατος χαρακτὴρ οὐδὲ ἀνυπάρκτως ἐπερριμμένος ἢ ἀσυμβεβηκὼς ὡς εἶδος ἐν σώματι Cyr.*dial.Trin.*5(5^1.558E); **2.** intrans., *rush upon*, Sever.*Eph.*3:2–3(p.310.8); *attack*, abs., Jo.Mosch.*prat.*212(M.87. 3105A); c. dat., *Chron.Pasch.*p.42(M.92.160C); c. κατά and genit., Thphn.*chron.*p.278(M.108.688C); c. acc., *ib.*p.299(729B).

ἐπίσαθρος, *rotten, weak*, Ephr.2.66A; met. πνεύματα Iren.*haer.*1. 13.4(M.7.585B).

ἐπισαλεύω, *stir up against* τινὲς...τοῖς Ἰουδαίοις ἐπεσάλευον τοῦ πολέμου τὴν ἔφοδον Cyr.*hom.pasch.*18(5^2.238D).

ἐπίσαλος, **1.** *rough*; of the sea, ‡Chrys.*cruc.*(2.821C); **2.** *unstable* τὰ βιωτικὰ...ἐ. *V.Alex.Acoem.*5(p.661.2).

***ἐπισαφηνίζω**, *make still more plain*, Clem.*str.*3.11(p.230.24; M.8. 1176D).

ἐπισεμνύνω, **1.** act., *make grave, reduce to sobriety*, Jo.VI H.*v.Jo. D.*36(M.94.484B); **2.** med., *take pride in, glory in*, Cyr.*Abac.*30(3. 545A); *ib.*51(565D); id.*Jo.*9(4.753A).

ἐπισημειόομαι, **1.** *signify, indicate*, Iren.*haer.*1.8.2(M.7.525A); Gr.Nyss.*Eun.*9(2 p.218.6; M.45.816D); **2.** *note, remark*, Afric.*chron.* 13.1(M.10.73B); Or.*Cels.*4.12(p.282.9; M.11.1041B); Eus.*d.e.*8 proem. (p.351.23; M.22.572B); *take note of* a person's face ἐπισημειώσασθε τὰ πρόσωπα ἡμῶν ἐπιμελῶς ἵνα καὶ ἐπιγνῶτε ἡμᾶς [sc. martyrs] ἐν ἐκείνῃ τῇ ἡμέρᾳ [i.e. of Judgement] *M.Perp.*17(p.87.16); **3.** *take down notes*, Eus.*h.e.*7.29.2(M.20.709A); **4.** pass., *be distinguished, set out distinctively*, ‡Hipp.*fr.26 in Ps.*57:12(p.150.12; M.10.721C).

ἐπισημείωσις, ἡ, **1.** *designation, indication*, Hipp.*haer.*4.50(p.74. 8; M.16.3118C); Or.*Jo.*10.40(24; p.217.24; M.14.385A); Eus.*d.e.*5.11 (p.234.21; M.22.388A); **2.** *note*, Eus.*h.e.*6.24.3(M.20.580A); **3.** *comment*, Bas.*ep.*125.3(3.216D; M.32.549B).

***ἐπισημειωτέον**, *one must note*, Or.*Jo.*6.60(38; p.169.5; M.14. 304D).

ἐπίσημον, τό, **1.** *symbol*, esp. of sign ϛ′, *six*, as symbol of Ἰησοῦς (name of 6 letters), Iren.*haer.*1.15.2(M.7.617B); ἡ δυὰς ἀπ' αὐτῆς [sc. μονάδος] προελθοῦσα ἕως τοῦ ἐ., οἷον δύο καὶ τέσσαρες καὶ ἕξ, τὴν δωδεκάδα ἀπέδειξε...τὴν οὖν δωδεκάδα, διὰ τὸ ἐ. συνεσχηκέναι, διὰ τὸ συνεπακολουθῆσαν αὐτῇ τὸ ἐ., πάθος λέγουσι [i.e. 6 is connected with man, created on sixth day, Christ's passion on sixth day at sixth hour] *ib.*1.16.1(629A); τὸ γὰρ στοιχεῖον τὸ η′ σὺν μὲν τῷ ἐ. ὀγδοάδα εἶναι θέλουσι *ib.*1.16.2(632A); Clem.*str.*6.16(p.503.19; M. 9.368B); ἐν τῇ ἕκτῃ ὁ ἄνθρωπος λέγεται πεποιῆσθαι ὁ τῷ ἐ. [i.e. Ἰησοῦς] πιστὸς γενόμενος ὡς εὐθέως κυριακῆς κληρονομίας ἀνάπαυσιν ἀπολαβεῖν *ib.*(p.503.25; 369A); difference between Marcan (third hour) and Johannine (sixth hour) accounts of Passion ascribed to scribal confusion between *Γ* and *ϛ*, Eus.*qu.Marin.suppl.*2.4(M. 22.1009B); **2.** plur., *insignia* τῶν τῆς βασιλείας ἐ. Philost.*h.e.*10.8(M. 65.589A).

ἐπίσημος, 1. of money, *stamped*, Thdt.*affect.*9(p.220.9; 4.925); ref. Gen.30:42, of cattle, *marked, spotted*; prob. with baptismal symbolism, of believers marked as Christ's property τοῦ πίνειν τὰ πρόβατα, ἀφ' ὧν ἔμελλεν γενέσθαι τὰ ἐ. καὶ ἡ μερὶς τοῦ Ἰακὼβ Or.*Jo.*28.2(p.390. 25; M.14.681C); with play on sense of *stamped coin* ὁ ἐξ ἐ. πλοῦτος, οἷος ἦν ὁ τοῦ Ἰακώβ, ἀληθινός ἐστι πλοῦτος· ὁ δὲ ἐξ ἀσήμου, οἷος ἦν ὁ τοῦ Λαβάν,...οὐ κυρίως ἐστὶ πλοῦτος Proc.G.*Gen.*30:39(M.87.445A); **2.** *notable*; in gen., *LS*; comp., Hadr.*introd.*31; of numbers, *significant, symbolical*, of number six (v. ἐπίσημον) Ἰησοῦς μὲν γὰρ ἐστιν ἐ. ὄνομα, ἓξ ὧν γράμματα Iren.1.14.4(M.7.604A); τὸν [sc. Christ] μετὰ τὰς ἓξ ἡμέρας τέταρτον ἀναβάντα εἰς τὸ ὄρος, καὶ γενόμενον ἕκτον, τὸν...καταβάντα ἐν τῇ ἑβδομάδι, ἐ. ὀγδοάδα ὑπάρχοντα *ib.*1.14. 6(608A).

ἐπισημότης, ἡ, *conspicuous position*, Cyr.*Jo.*2.1(4.152A).

***ἐπισικρίτῳ,** (Lat. *a secretis*) *secretary*, ‡Caes.Naz.*dial.*tit.(M.38. 852).

***ἐπισκαλίζ-ω,** *stir up, incite* ~ων ἀσεβῶν ὁρμάς, Μάνην καὶ Οὐαλεντῖνον καὶ Εὐτυχῆ ὁπλίζων τοῦ φάσκειν παθητὸν τὸ θεῖον ‡Justic.*ep.*(p.12.18; H.2.840E).

[*]**ἐπισκεδάζω,** = ἐπισκεδάννυμι, *scatter, sprinkle over*, c. dat., Gr. Nyss.*Eun.*12(1 p.389.15; M.45.1120A); id.*infant.*(M.46.188A).

***ἐπισκελιζω,** *spring upon*, Cosm.Mel.*schol.*(M.38.474) in Gr.Naz. *carm.*2.2(poem.)2.3.

ἐπισκέλλω, perf. intrans., *be dried up, withered*, Jo.Clim.*scal.*5 (M.88.772A).

ἐπισκεπάζω, *cover, shelter*, Hipp.*haer.*4.37(p.63.17; M.16.3103A); ‡Just.*monarch.*6(M.6.325C).

ἐπισκέπτης, ὁ, *visitor*, Ephr.2.197E; χηρῶν καὶ ἀδυνάτων οἱ ἐ. Eus.Al.*serm.*21.3(M.86.425D).

***ἐπισκεπτητής, ὁ,** = foreg. (s.v.l.), ‡Chrys.*poenit.*1(9.768A) = Eus.Al.*serm.*21.3(M.86.425D ἐπισκέπται).

***ἐπισκεπτήτρια, ἡ,** *visitor*, Steph.Diac.*v.Steph.*(M.100.1168D).

ἐπισκέπτ-ω, A. act., *consider, examine* κύριος ~ει τὴν ψυχὴν αὐτοῦ *T.Benj.*6.6; Thphn.*chron.*p.230(M.108.581C).

B. med.; **1.** *look to, have regard to*; c. prep. εἰς αὐτὴν δὴ ταύτην ~όμενος τὴν περικοπὴν Meth.*symp.*3.1(p.27.15; M.18.61B); **2.** *consider* ἐπισκεψώμεθα, πῶς...ἀνήγαγε *ib.*3.4(p.30.16; 65A); id.*res.*3.6 (p.397.5; M.18.321A); **3.** *care for* ~εσθε ἀλλήλους Herm.*vis.*3.9.2; Ἰωάννης ἐστὶν ὁ ~όμενός σε Jo.Thess.*dorm.BMV* A 6(p.384.3); **4.** *visit*; **a.** of divine visitation: in gen. ἐν τοῖς μανδραγόροις ἐπεσκέψατο αὐτὴν [sc. Rachel] ὁ κύριος *T.Isach.*2.2; δοξάσωμεν τὸν θεόν,...ὅτι καὶ ἡμᾶς ἐπεσκέψατο Just.*dial.*29.1(M.6.537A); in providential care, Cyr.*Ps.*93:5(M.69.1232D); in judgement, *Pss.Sal.*9. 8; ἐπισκέψεται γὰρ ὁ θεὸς ἐν ῥάβδῳ, τῷ Χριστῷ, τὰς ἀνομίας αὐτῶν, ὧν ἐπισκέψεται Or.*Jo.*1.36(41; p.46.20; M.14.96A); οὐκ ~όμενος ἡμᾶς ἐπὶ ταῖς ἁμαρτίαις id.*princ.*3.1.12(p.215.3; M.11.269B); †Bas.*Is.* 18(1.389D; M.30.145B); in mercy ἕως ἂν ἐπισκέψηται κύριος ὑμῖν *T. Jud.*23.5; Herm.*sim.*9.10.4; **b.** pastoral, esp. of visiting the sick πρεσβύτεροι...~όμενοι πάντας ἀσθενεῖς Polyc.*ep.*6.1; ὀρφανοὺς καὶ ὑστερουμένους ~εσθαι Herm.*mand.*8.10; as task of deacons οἱ διάκονοι...τῶν ἀδελφῶν τὰ σώματα καὶ τὰς ψυχὰς ~έσθωσαν *Hom. Clem.*3.67; perh. also of special order of sick-visitors πολλοὺς δὲ χωρὶς τῶν ~ομένων νοσεῖν καὶ ὀδύρεσθαι. ... τῶν...λειτουργῶν τῆς ἐκκλησίας διωκομένων Ath.*ep.encycl.*5(p.175.3; M.25.233C); χρὴ... τοὺς διακόνους ~εσθαι πάντας τοὺς δεομένους ἐπισκέψεως *Const.App.* 3.19.7; of a Novatianist bishop τοὺς ἐν φυλακαῖς ἀόκνως ἐπεσκέπτετο Socr.*h.e.*7.17.5(M.67.772C); ἀσθενοῦντα ~ου Eus.Al.*serm.*1(M.86. 324C); ὁ οὖν ~όμενος τοὺς ἐν ἀρρωστίαις, ἢ ἐν φυλακαῖς, ἢ ἐν ἀνάγκαις, τὸν δι' ἡμᾶς πτωχεύσαντα θεὸν λόγον ~εται. ὅτι δὲ καλὸν τὸ ~εσθαι ὀρφανοὺς καὶ χήρας...καὶ πολυτέκνους πένητας, μάλιστα δὲ πρῶτον καὶ τοὺς οἰκείους τῆς πίστεως, πᾶσιν πρόδηλα...ἐστιν Ant.Mon.*hom.*99 (M.89.1732D); **c.** of visiting carried on between monks τὸ μὲν ~εσθαι ἀρεστὸν θεῷ· δεῖ δὲ τὸν ~όμενον συνετὸν εἶναι ἀκροατήν, καὶ φρόνιμον ἐν ταῖς ἀποκρίσεσι Bas.*reg.br.*311(2.526A; M.31.1304C); εἰ χρὴ τοὺς ~ομένους λαϊκοὺς προτρέπεσθαι εἰς εὐχὴν...εἰ φίλοι εἰσὶ θεοῦ, ἀκόλουθον *ib.*312(526B; M.1305A); εἰ χρὴ ἐργάζεσθαι, ~ομένων τινῶν...οὐδὲν τῶν κατ' ἐντολὴν γινομένων ἐκκόπτεσθαι χρὴ *ib.*313 (526C; M.1305A); **d.** of visit of a council to a place for its session ὀφείλομεν ἑκάστην ἐπαρχίαν ἐν τῷ καιρῷ τῆς συνόδου ~εσθαι *Cod.Afr.* 52; **e.** theol., of Inc. as visitation ζωὴ...ἐπισκεψαμένη τὴν θνητὴν φύσιν ‡Ath.*serm.fid.*27(p.24; M.26.1281A).

***ἐπισκεύασμα, τό,** *device*, Eus.*Is.*54:14(M.24.465D).

ἐπισκευαστός, *adventitious*, ref. H. Ghost οὐκ ἐ. ἔχον τὴν ἀγαθότητα, ἀλλ' ἐκ φύσεως αὐτῷ συνυπάρχουσαν Bas.*Eun.*3.3(1.274E; M.29.661B); τισὶ μὲν ἐκ φύσεως, τισὶ δὲ ἐ. ... προσηγορίαν Gr.Nyss. *Eun.*3(2 p.39.12; M.45.605D); ἐ. ἀθανασίαν ὁ ποιητὴς τῷ θνητῷ ζώῳ τὴν παιδοποιΐαν ἐμηχανήσατο Thdt.*affect.*3(p.93.25; 4.785); φύσει μὲν οὐκ ἦν ἀθάνατος [sc. Ἀδάμ], ἐ. δὲ ἀθανασίαν δευτέρῳ λόγῳ καρπούμενος Proc.G.*Gen.*3:18(M.87.217A).

***ἐπισκευαστῶς,** *adventitiously, by outside support*, ref. H. Ghost οὐκ ἐ. ζῶν, ἀλλὰ ζωῆς χορηγόν Bas.*Spir.*22(3.19C; M.32.108B).

ἐπισκευή, ἡ, *device* τῶν ἀσεβῶν ταῖς ἐ. πειραθῆναι Leo Mag.*ep.*51 (p.51.24; M.*PL.*54.846A).

ἐπίσκεψις, ἡ, *visitation, inspection, inquiry*, of divine providence ἐ. τινα τοῦ πατρὸς εἶναι τοιαύτην, ὥστε ἀεὶ νικᾶν τοὺς μεγαλοψύχως φέροντας τὰ προσπίπτοντα Const.*or.s.c.*15(p.174.21; ἐπίσκηψιν M.20. 1277A); θείας προνοίας ἐμφανὴς ἐ. Eus.*h.e.*8.16.2(M.20.789A); Cyr. *Zach.*88(3.775E); of episcopal visitations, Chrys.*hom.1.4 in Tit.*(11. 736D); of visiting of monks by superior, Ath.*v.Anton.*15(M.26. 865B); in gen. of monks τὸ δὲ ἢ διὰ συγγένειαν ἢ διὰ φιλίαν ἐ. ποιεῖσθαι ἀλλότριον τοῦ ἡμετέρου ἐπαγγέλματος Bas.*reg.br.*311(2.526B; M. 31.1304C); Esaias *or.*4.4(p.19); of visitation of sick, Ephr.1.320D; *Const.App.*3.19.7; ἀσθενούντων ἐ. προβάλλεται ὁ ἀκηδιαστής, πληροφορεῖ δὲ τὸν ἴδιον σκοπόν Nil.*spir.mal.*13(M.79.1157D); in gen., of visitation of sick and needy ἡ ἐ. ὁμόσκηνος καὶ ὁμοδίαιτός ἐστιν τῆς φιλοξενίας καὶ τῆς φιλοπτωχίας Ant.Mon.*hom.*99(M.89.1732C).

***ἐπισκήνωσις, ἡ,** *tabernacling in, indwelling* ἐκεῖνο τὸ σῶμα ἄρτος τῇ δυνάμει ἦν, ἡγιάσθη δὲ τῇ ἐ. τοῦ λόγου τοῦ σκηνώσαντος ἐν τῇ σαρκί Gr.Nyss.*or.catech.*37(p.149.5; M.45.96D); of Apollinarian view of redemption ἐὰν πᾶσα ἡ ἀνθρωπίνη φύσις τῇ ἐ. τῆς θείας δυνάμεως σώζηται, ἀνθρωπόθεος ὁ θεὸς λόγος ὀνομασθήσεται id.*Apoll.* 49(M.45.1241C).

ἐπισκιάζ-ω, *overshadow*, of tabernacling of divine presence (cf. ἐπισκίασις) τὸ πνεῦμα οὖν καὶ τὴν δύναμιν τὴν παρὰ τοῦ θεοῦ οὐδὲν ἄλλο νοῆσαι θέμις ἢ τὸν λόγον...καὶ τοῦτο ἐλθὸν ἐπὶ τὴν παρθένον καὶ ἐπισκιάσαν οὐ διὰ συνουσίας, ἀλλὰ διὰ δυνάμεως ἐγκύμονα κατέστησε Just.*1apol.*33.6(M.6.381C); μία γὰρ οὐσία θεότητος τοῦ μαρτυροῦντος, καὶ τοῦ μαρτυρουμένου υἱοῦ, καὶ τοῦ ~οντος πνεύματος Jo.D.*hom.*1.15 (M.96.568D).

***ἐπισκίασις, ἡ,** *overshadowing*, of divine presence tabernacling in Temple ποῦ τὸ θυσιαστήριον...ποῦ ἡ ἐ. τοῦ ναοῦ; *Dial.Christ.et Jud.*9 (p.59.16) = ‡Anast.S.*Jud.disp.*1(M.89.1221B); τὴν κατὰ νόμον... μεταξὺ τῶν τυπικῶν χερουβὶμ ἐ. τῆς θείας...δόξης ‡Meth.*Sym.et Ann.* 4(M.18.357A); ref. Lc.1:35 Ἰησοῦν...ἐπισκιάσει πατρὸς καὶ πνεύματος θεοῦ παρθένος ἔτεκεν Domit.*Jo.Bapt.*3(p.321); διὰ τῆς ἐπιφοιτήσεως καὶ ἐνεργείας τοῦ...πνεύματος καὶ τῆς τοῦ...λόγου σκηνώσεως ἔσται ἡ σύλληψις, ὥστε πρῶτον γενέσθαι τὴν τῆς δυνάμεως τοῦ ὑψίστου ἐ., ἤτοι τοῦ λόγου τὴν σύλληψιν, καὶ τότε τὴν τῆς σαρκὸς ὕπαρξιν ἐν αὐτῷ τῷ λόγῳ ὑφισταμένης Jo.D.*haer.Nest.*1(M.95.189A); *Chron.Pasch.* p.198(M.92.489A); of protective 'overshadowing' of suppliants by BMV θεοπρεπεῖ αὐτῆς μνήμῃ, ἐ. τε καὶ ἐπιστασίᾳ πρὸς τοὺς ἀξίους τῶν αὐτῆς οἰκτιρμῶν, ἐλέους...ἀξιωθῶμεν Jo.Thess.*dorm.BMV* A 14 (p.403.32); of overshadowing by Christ when healing ἰσχὺν λαβοῦσα [sc. woman with issue of blood] διὰ τῆς ἐ. αὐτοῦ *Anaph.Pil.*A 4 (p.438); of shadowy apparitions αἱ ἐν τοῖς ναοῖς καὶ σωροῖς τῶν ἁγίων γινόμεναι ἐ. ... οὐ διὰ τῶν ψυχῶν τῶν ἁγίων γίνονται, ἀλλὰ δι' ἀγγέλων ἁγίων μετασχηματιζομένων εἰς τὸ εἶδος τῶν ἁγίων ‡Ath.*qu. Ant.*26(M.28.613B).

ἐπισκιασμός, ὁ, *overshadowing*, ref. Lc.1:35 ἐκ...δυνάμεως ἐ. τὸ ἅγιον ἐκ τῆς παρθένου συνίσταται βρέφος Apoll.*corp.et div.*13(p.191.8; M.*PL.*8.875B); ἐν ἐ. δυνάμεως θεοῦ Cyr.*ep.*50(p.98.4; 5².167E).

***ἐπισκιώδης,** *in shadow*, ‡Ath.*qu.al.*4(M.28.776B).

***ἐπισκοπεῖον, τό, 1.** *bishop's residence* ποῦ θέλεις οἰκοδομήσωμεν συναγωγὴν καὶ ἐ.; *A.Phil.*88(p.34.18); ἐν τῷ τρικλίνῳ τοῦ ἐ. Pall. *v.Chrys.*(p.45.26; M.47.27); id.*h.Laus.*63(p.158.11; M.34.1235B); Thphn.*chron.*p.30(M.108.133C); of property pertaining to bishop's establishment εἴ τις ἐπίσκοπος εὑρεθείη...ἐκ τῶν αὐτουργιῶν τοῦ ἐ. ... ἐκδιδοὺς CNic.(787)*can.*12; hence **2.** *bishop's household* ἀποστέλλει ἕνα παῖδα τοῦ ἐ. Jo.Mosch.*prat.*108(M.87.2972A); **3.** *bishop's throne*, Thdr.Stud.*epp.*2.119(M.99.1393A).

***ἐπισκοπευτικός,** *watchful* τῶν...ἐ. σου [sc. God] δυνάμεων Didym. *Ps.*30:22–23(M.39.1317C).

ἐπισκοπεύ-ω, A. *supervise, exercise oversight of*; of God, *T.Benj.* 6.6 (v.l. for ἐπισκέπτει).

B. *be a bishop*; **1.** abs., Heges.ap.Eus.*h.e.*4.22.2(M.20.377C); Ἀνέγκλητον...~σαντα...διαδέχεται Κλήμης Eus.*h.e.*3.15(249A); of James at Jerusalem, Epiph.*haer.*66.19(p.44.6; M.42.57D); Procl.CP *ep.*13(M.65.881C); **2.** c. dat., *supervise as bishop* ~ειν τῇ ἐκκλησίᾳ

A.Jo.14(p.160.3); **3.** c. genit., *be bishop of* ~σαντα τῆς Τυρίων Eus. *Marcell*.1.4(p.18.3; M.24.752A); Epiph.*haer*.66.20(p.46.1; M.42.61A); Anast.S.*haer*.(p.267); **4.** met., of reason's exercise of control over heart and its offering of reasonable service to Christ, Jo.Clim. *scal*.28(M.88.1137B).

ἐπισκοπ-έω, I. *observe, regard, consider* τὴν ἑαυτῶν ~οῦντες φύσιν Athenag.*res*.13(p.63.12; M.6.1000B); Clem.*prot*.2(p.19.19; M.8.96A); ~οῦμεν πῶς ὁ λόγος ἦν πρὸς τὸν θεόν Or.*Jo*.2.1(p.52.5; M.14.104C); τὸν νοῦν ~εῖν χρὴ τοῦ λόγου Eus.*e.th*.1.10(p.68.24; M.24.841C); ~ῆσαι τὸ ἀληθές Meth.*res*.1.30(p.264.1; M.41.1140D); ~εῖν ὡς ἔχει πολλὴν διάπτωσιν *ib*.1.49(p.302.3; M.18.277A).

II. *direct, superintend, exercise oversight*;

A. in gen. τὰ καθ' ἑαυτὸν ~ούμενος Philost.*h.e*.3.12(M.65.500D); of control exercised by spiritual powers over men's lives and revealed by the stars, Clem.*exc.Thdot*.70(p.129.21; M.9.692B); καταλιπούσης...τὸν τόπον ἐφορώσης καὶ ~ούσης δυνάμεως Eus.*d.e*.8.2 (p.388.11; M.22.628A); ὁ διάκονος ~είτω τὸν λαόν, ἵνα μή τις ψιθυρίσῃ *Const.App*.2.57.13; ~ησον...τὰ τῆς ἐμπορίας σου Ephr.1.50C; pass. ὁ ~ούμενος...φησίν Or.*Jo*.6.19(11; p.128.6; M.14.233A).

B. of God's oversight and providential care κύριος ~εῖ τὴν ψυχὴν αὐτοῦ *T.Gad* 5.3(v.l. ἐπισκέπει); θείας δυνάμεως ~ούσης αὐτούς Or. *princ*.4.1.5(p.301.5; M.11.352A); τῆς...~ούσης...προνοίας Eus.*theoph*. 12(p.27*.21; M.24.644C); Ath.*exp.Ps*.113:1(M.27.468D); Bas.*ep*.101 (3.197A; M.32.505C); and of Christ; **1.** exercising divine oversight of all creation conjointly with Father, Eus.*d.e*.4.10(p.167.28; M.22. 280B); **2.** exercising care and supervision over disciples until end of world (cf. Mt.28:20), id.*e.th*.3.14(p.170.34; M.24.1025C).

C. in Christian ministry, *exercise supervision over Church, be a bishop*; **1.** *be bishop of* ἀντὶ ἐμοῦ...μόνος αὐτὴν [sc. τὴν ἐν Συρίᾳ ἐκκλησίαν] Ἰησοῦς Χριστὸς ~ήσει Ign.*Rom*.9.1; παροικιῶν ἃς Εἰρηναῖος ἐπεσκόπει Eus.*h.e*.5.23.4(M.20.493A); of Constantine (v. ἐπίσκοπος) id.*v.C*.4.24(p.126.12; M.20.1172B); c. genit. τῆς Ἀντιοχείας ~ήσας Philost.*h.e*.4.12(M.65.525A); *ib*.8.2(556B); *ib*.9.18(581C); Thphn.*chron*.p.51(M.108.184A); c. dat. ἐπίσκοποι...οἱ...διαφόροις τόποις ἐπεσκόπησαν Agath.*v.Gr.Ill*.157(p.80); **2.** abs., *be a bishop*, Herm.*vis*.3.5.1 cit. s. διακονέω; χαίρων οὖν ~ησον *Clem.ep*.4(M.2. 40A); Constantius ap.Ath.*apol.sec*.55(p.135.21; M.25.348C); med. κοινωνὸς τῶν ~ουμένων ἐγίνετο Eus.*v.C*.1.44(p.28.22; M.20.960A); **3.** pass., *be made a bishop* Πολυκάρπῳ ἐπισκόπῳ ἐκκλησίας...μᾶλλον ἐπεσκοπημένῳ ὑπὸ θεοῦ (with play on general sense of *superintend*) Ign.*Polyc*.proem.

III. *visit* (cf. ἐπισκοπή B); **1.** of visiting sick νοσήσαντες... παρακαλοῦμεν τοὺς ~οῦντας ἡμᾶς Or.*hom.17.6 in Jer*.(p.150.11; M. 13.461C); Dion.Al.ap.Eus.*h.e*.7.22.7(M.20.688C); **2.** ref. divine visitation, of Christ ἐχαρίσατο...τὸ ἐμβλέψαι αὐτῷ, ὅπερ ἐστὶ διὰ τοῦ ἐμβλέψαι ~ῆσαι καὶ φωτίσαι αὐτοῦ τὸ ἡγεμονικόν Or.*Jo*.2.36(29; p.95. 30; M.14.181A); τί...τὸν ἔμπροσθεν ἐποίει χρόνον ὁ Χριστός, τὸ τῶν ἀνθρώπων οὐκ ~ούμενος γένος; Chrys.*hom.8.1 in Jo*.(8.50A).

IV. *review, take a census* προσέταξε μὲν ὁ θεὸς ~ηθῆναι τὸν λαόν †Cyr.*coll.VT*(6^{4}.36E; M.77.1229C).

ἐπισκοπή, ἡ, A. *care, oversight, supervision*; **1.** in gen.; **a.** *oversight* μάλιστα τούτοις σύνεστι προσεχεστέρα ἡ ἐ., ὅσοι διαπρεπεῖς τὰς φύσεις τε καὶ δυνατοὶ τὰ πλήθη συνωφελεῖν ὑπάρχουσιν Clem.*str*.6.17 (p.513.9; M.9.389B); πεπιστευμένοι δὲ τῶν ἐνδεῶν τὴν ἐ. Proc.G.*Is*. 1:21(M.87.1857C); **b.** *attention, study* νηφάλιον ἐφιστῶντας τὴν τῆς διανοίας ἐ. ‡Bas.*const*.2.1(2.541A; M.31.1340A); **c.** *inspection*, Or. *schol.in Cant*.7:11,12(M.17.284D); **2.** of God, *providential care* διαμείνητε ἐν ἑνότητι θεοῦ καὶ ἐ. Ign.*Polyc*.8.3; Clem.*str*.2.19(p.167.5; M.8.1041B); Or.*Jo*.6.19(11; p.128.2; M.14.233A); πᾶσα ἡ γῆ...ἀπολαύει τῆς ἐ. αὐτοῦ Ath.*exp.Ps*.112:1(M.27.468A); Cyr.*Jo*.3.4(4.288C); of Christ, ref. Ps.8:5, id.*Heb*.2:9(p.386.20); of BMV ἐ. θείας καὶ προνοίας τῆς παρὰ σοῦ ἀξίωσον,...θεομῆτορ *Euchol*.(p.673).

B. divine *visitation*; **1.** of manifestation of divine activity, revelation of God's power and glory in his dealings with man ἵνα παρέλθῃ Ἰσραὴλ ἐν ἐ. δόξης θεοῦ αὐτῶν *Pss.Sal*.11.7; τῶν ἐν βραχίονι ὑψηλῷ καὶ ἐ. μεγάλης δόξης λυτρωθέντων ἀπὸ τῆς Αἰγύπτου Just.*dial*. 131.3(M.6.780C); ἐ. τῆς ἀγαθότητος τοῦ κυρίου Bas.*ep*.90.1(3.181E; M. 32.473A); ἐ. θείου φωτός *cat.Mt*.25:32(p.211.14); partic. of Inc. ἐν ἐ. μονογενοῦς προφήτου *T.Benj*.9.2; and ultimate manifestation of kingdom of God, *1Clem*.50.3; **2.** partic. of God's *visitation in wrath* τίς γὰρ οὐκ ἂν φοβηθείη, ἐ. ἐκ θεοῦ ὁρῶν γινομένην κατὰ τῶν ἀσεβῶν; Ath.*exp.Ps*.63:10(M.27.281D); φοβερωτάτη...ἡ ἐπὶ τοῖς πλημμελήμασι τοῖς ἡμετέροις ἐ. τοῦ θεοῦ Cyr.*glaph.Lev*.(1.362C); ἡμέραν γὰρ ἐπισκοπῆς ἐκάλεσε τὸν τῆς τιμωρίας καιρόν...τὴν τιμωρίαν ἐ. ὀνομάζει Thdt.*Is*.10:3(p.53.20f.; 2.241).

C. of an office or function exercised in Church; **1.** *oversight, superintendence*, *1Clem*.44.1 cit. s. ἀπόστολος; ἁμαρτία...ἔσται, ἐὰν τοὺς ἀμέμπτως καὶ ὁσίως προσενεγκόντας τὰ δῶρα τῆς ἐ. ἀποβάλωμεν *ib*.44.4; apparently exercised by πρεσβύτεροι, *ib*.44.5; of rule and priesthood exercised by apostles τὴν ἐ. αὐτοῦ λαβέτω ἕτερος· τουτέστι τὴν ἀρχήν, τὴν ἱερωσύνην Chrys.*hom.3.2 in Ac*.(9.24E); **2.** in fully developed threefold ministry, *bishop's office* τρίτῳ τόπῳ ἀπὸ τῶν ἀποστόλων τὴν ἐ. κληροῦται Κλήμης Iren.*haer*.3.3.3(M.7.849B); Ath.*apol.sec*.6(p.93.12; M.25.260C); Eus.*e.th*.3.22(p.132.31; M.24. 960B); of S. James at Jerusalem, Chrys.*hom.5.3 in Mt*.(7.78A); v. διέπω; partic. uses: of episcopate as a κλῆρος, Iren.*haer*.3.3.3(M.7. 851B); as a διακονία, *Ep.Lugd*.ap.Eus.*h.e*.5.1.29(M.20.420A); of καθέδρα as symbol of bishop's office, Epiph.*ep.Arab*.ap.*haer*.78.6 (p.457.21; M.42.709A); of priesthood of bishop's office, Socr.*h.e*.4. 29.1(M.67.541B); of episcopal succession ἡ τῆς ἐ. ... διαδοχή Cyr. *hom.pasch*.1.2(5^{2}.4B); of grace of episcopate πρὶν μὲν λάβῃς τὴν τῆς ἐ. χάριν Ath.*ep.Drac*.2(M.25.525B); of rank, or honour, of bishop's office τὸ τῆς ἐ. ἀξίωμα Const.ap.Eus.*v.C*.3.62(p.110.24; M.20.1137B); Chrys.*hom.1.2 in Tit*.(11.732E); of honorary rank of bishop, involving no tenure of see, Philost.*h.e*.4.3(M.65.520A); of 'episcopal' office held by women among Montanists, Epiph.*haer*.49.3(p.243. 19; M.41.881B); of nominal ἐ. held by ἀπόλιδες, CEph.(431)*ep*.(*ACO* 1.1.3 p.7.24; H.1.1508B) cit. s. ἄπολις.

[*]**ἐπισκοπία, ἡ,** *office of bishop* παραιτουμένη τὴν ἐ. τῆς κατὰ τὴν Ἀντιόχειαν ἐκκλησίας Const.ap.Eus.*v.C*.3.61(p.109.15; M.20.1136A); παρήγγειλεν ἀποδοθῆναι τὴν ἐ. Epiph.*haer*.69.11(M.42.220B; ἐπισκοπήν p.161.12).

ἐπισκοπικός, A. *surveying, directing, controlling* τῆς...ἐ. αὐτοῦ [sc. θεοῦ] δυνάμεως Or.*Ps*.12:2(p.467); ἔθος τῇ θείᾳ γραφῇ πτέρυγας καλεῖν τὴν ἐ. δύναμιν τοῦ θεοῦ Ath.*exp.Ps*.56:2(M.27.257D); ὑπὸ τῆς ἐ. δυνάμεως τοῦ θεοῦ σκεπόμενος Olymp.*Eccl*.2:26(M.93.505D).

B. *pertaining to bishop's office*; **1.** of things: throne, Socr.*h.e*. 4.29.5(M.67.541B); house ἐν τοῖς ἐ. οἴκοις συμμένειν αὐτῷ *ib*.6.14.1 (705A); **2.** of qualities, conditions, etc., e.g. bishop's appointment ὁ...ἀπόστολος περὶ τῆς ἐ. χειροτονίας νομοθετῶν Thdt.*haer*.5.8(4.407); id.*h.e*.2.29.1(3.902); succession of bishops ἐπὶ Ὑγίνου, ἔνατον κλῆρον τῆς ἐ. διαδοχῆς ἀπὸ τῶν ἀποστόλων ἔχοντος Iren.*haer*.1.27.1(M.7. 687B); bishop's rank τοῦ...ἐ. ἀξιώματος CEph.(431)*act*.1(*ACO* 1.1.2 p.54.27; H.1.1421E); function of ruling ὡς τὴν ἐ. οἰκονομίαν αὐτὸς ἐπεπιστεύετο Thdt.*Phil*.1:2(3.446); of regulations concerning bishop's office μετὰ...τοὺς ἐ. νόμους id.*1Tim*.3:1(3.652); outward adornments of episcopal office, Gr.Nyss.*ep*.17(M.46.1061A).

C. pertaining to bishop's work and administration, of *episcopal* letters of commendation, admired by Julian ζηλῶσαι λέγεται τὰ συνθήματα τῶν ἐ. γραμμάτων Soz.*h.e*.5.16.3(M.67.1261B).

D. consisting *of bishops* συνόδους ἐ. συναθροίζω Thdt.*ep*.81(4. 1139).

***ἐπισκοπικῶς,** *episcopally, in the manner of a bishop* τὸν θρόνον τὸν ἐστολισμένον ἐ. Ath.*apol.sec*.17(p.100.8; M.25.276C); ἐ. κινούμεθα Gr.Naz.*ep*.49(M.37.101A).

***ἐπισκοπομάρτυς, ὁ,** *martyr-bishop*, Didym.*Trin*.3.41(M.39.988C).

ἐπίσκοπος, I. as adj.; **A.** *well-aimed, directed at a mark* τὸ βέλεμνον ἐ. ἐν χερὶ κείσθω Gr.Naz.*carm*.1.2.9.121(M.37.677A); Evagr.*h.e*.6.14 (p.232.12; M.86.2865C).

B. *having the oversight, directing* ὁ ἐπιστάτης καὶ ἐ. νοῦς ‡Pion.*v. Polyc*.9; of eye of God, Gr.Naz.*carm*.1.1.27.73(M.37.504A); comp., Pall.*v.Chrys*.9(p.55.8; M.47.32) cit. s. II.B.3 infra.

II. as subst., *overseer, superintendent*;

A. denoting function rather than status, of anyone who exercises supervision or control; **1.** in gen., of secular officials, controllers, inspectors, etc., cf.SM Gen.41:34(LXX τοπάρχας); Or. *Apoc*.30(p.36.30); Gr.Naz.*carm*.1.2.8.146(M.37.659A); **2.** of God (cf. pagan usage) τὸν παντὸς πνεύματος κτίστην καὶ ἐ. *1Clem*.59.3; *Orac.Sib.fr*.ap.Thphl.Ant.*Autol*.2.36(p.190; M.6.1109C); *Lit.Marc*. (*PDêr-Baliz*.1 v° 11); ὁ ἐ. πάντων *A.Phil*.132(p.64.3); Olymp.*Job* 20:29(M.93.221A); **3.** of Christ τὸν κύριον Ἰησοῦν...τὸν...ἐ. τῆς καρδίας ἡμῶν Clem.*str*.4.17(p.295.26; M.8.1316A); ‡Gr.Naz.*Chr.pat*. 1736(M.38.275A); **4.** of apostles, *A.Petr.et Andr*.2(p.117.19); *M.Ner. et Ach*.2(p.1.19); **5.** of Constantine, as overseer of Church's external affairs or perh. as 'bishop' of non-Christians δεξιούμενος ἐπισκόπους λόγον ἀφῆκεν...ὑμεῖς μὲν τῶν εἴσω τῆς ἐκκλησίας, ἐγὼ δὲ τῶν ἐκτὸς ὑπὸ θεοῦ καθεσταμένος ἐ. ἂν εἴην Eus.*v.C*.4.24(p.126.7ff.; M.20.1172B); and as convener of councils οἷά τις κοινὸς ἐ. ἐκ θεοῦ καθεσταμένος συνόδους τῶν τοῦ θεοῦ λειτουργῶν συνεκρότει *ib*.1.44 (p.28.20; 957D).

B. in Christian ministry, *overseer of Church, bishop*; **1.** of member of body exercising oversight and government in a church, equivalent to πρεσβύτερος as in Ac.20:28, cf.Phil.1:1,; **a.** in contexts which imply a two-fold ministry of ἐπίσκοποι and διάκονοι, and virtual identity of ἐπίσκοποι and πρεσβύτεροι: ὁ Χριστὸς οὖν ἀπὸ τοῦ θεοῦ, καὶ οἱ ἀπόστολοι ἀπὸ τοῦ Χριστοῦ...καθίστανον τὰς ἀπαρχὰς αὐτῶν...εἰς ἐ. καὶ διακόνους τῶν μελλόντων πιστεύειν *1Clem*.42.2,4 (where ἐπίσκοποι perform functions of rule and oversight assigned (*ib*.44.5,57.1) to πρεσβύτεροι q.v.); so, prob. *Did*.15.1 cit. s. 3.b infra; Herm.*vis*.3.5.1 cit. s. διακονέω; **b.** in commentaries on NT passages in which such a ministry appears to be indicated, **i.** some commentators allow that ἐ. and πρεσβύτερος are equivalent terms in these passages, v. πρεσβύτερος; but **ii.** some add that at first τοὺς δὲ νῦν καλουμένους ἐ. ἀποστόλους ὠνόμαζον· τοῦ δὲ χρόνου προϊόντος, τὸ μὲν τῆς ἀποστολῆς ὄνομα τοῖς ἀληθῶς ἀποστόλοις κατέλιπον τὴν δὲ τῆς ἐπισκοπῆς προσηγορίαν τοῖς πάλαι καλουμένοις ἀποστόλοις ἐπέθεσαν Thdt.*1Tim*.3:1(3.652); **iii.** others account for or deny apparent identity, v. πρεσβύτερος; **iv.** Aërius inferred total identity of episcopal and presbyteral orders, v. πρεσβύτερος; **c.** ἐπίσκοποι are sometimes loosely termed πρεσβύτεροι after universal establishment of threefold ministry, v. πρεσβύτερος; **2.** in threefold ministry (ἐπίσκοποι, πρεσβύτεροι, διάκονοι) of a single bishop exercising ἐπισκοπή over a church; **a.** early instances Πολυκάρπῳ ἐ. ἐκκλησίας Σμυρναίων Ign.*Polyc*.proem.; ὑποτασσόμενοι τῷ ἐ. καὶ τῷ πρεσβυτερίῳ id.*Eph*.2.2; Polycr.ap.Eus.*h.e*.5.24.4(M.20.496A); of S. James at Jerusalem εὐλόγηται ὁ σε...καλῶς ἡμῖν καταστήσας ἐ. *Clem.contest*.5(M.2.32C); Πέτρος Ἰακώβῳ τῷ κυρίῳ καὶ ἐ. τῆς ἁγίας ἐκκλησίας *Clem.ep.Petr*.proem.; τῷ κυρίῳ καὶ ἐπισκόπων ἐπισκόπῳ *Clem.ep*.proem.(M.2.32Df.); appointed bishop of Jerusalem by SS. Peter and John, Clem.*fr*.10(p.198.23; M.9.745C); **b.** appointed by apostles; **i.** in twofold ministry, *1Clem*.42.4 cit. s. B.1 supra; **ii.** in threefold ministry Πολύκαρπος...ὑπὸ ἀποστόλων κατασταθεὶς ...ἐ. Iren.*haer*.3.3.4(M.7.852A); Clem.*q.d.s*.42(p.188.5; M.9.648B); Πέτρος...ἀπὸ τῶν ἑπομένων αὐτῷ πρεσβυτέρων ἐ. ... καταστήσας *Hom. Clem*.7.5; *ib*.11.36; **c.** regarded as successor of apostles, exercising functions of apostolate, *M.Polyc*.16.2; cf. *episcopi quibus apostoli tradiderunt ecclesias*, Iren.*haer*.5.20.1(M.7.1177A); cf.Firmilianus *ep.* int. opp. Cypr.*ep*.75.16(M.*PL*.3.1216C); Serap.*euch*.28.1 cit. s. διαδοχή; Thdt.*1Tim*.3:1(3.652); **d.** and as deputy of Christ, occupying καθέδρα Χριστοῦ, *Hom.Clem*.3.60; *ib*.3.70; **e.** typifies God the Father, Ign.*Magn*.6.1 cit. s. πρεσβύτερος; id.*Trall*.3.1 cit. s. διάκονος; ὁ γὰρ ἐ. προκαθεζέσθω ὑμῶν ὡς θεοῦ ἀξίᾳ τετιμημένος *Const.App*.2.26.4; cf.*Hom.Clem*.3.62; comparison of bishop, priest, and deacon with three Persons of Trin.,‡Ath.*dial.Trin*.1.27(M.28.1156C); and Christ, Ign.*Eph*.6.1; ὁ γὰρ ἐ. εἰς τύπον ὢν τοῦ Χριστοῦ, τὸ ἔργον ἐκείνου πληροῖ Isid.Pel.*epp*.1.136(M.78.272C); to be regarded by congregation as ἐπίγειος θεός, *Const.App*.2.26.4; hence Ps.81:6 [θεοί ἐστε καὶ υἱοὶ ὑψίστου] applied to bishops, *ib.*; cf. τὸν ἰσάγγελον...ἐ. *Dial.Tim. et Aquil*.138 r°(p.104; M.86.253A); **f.** compared with OT priest, Meth.*lepr*.6(p.459.6); hence freq. termed ἱερεύς (q.v.); and OT high priest, *Const.App*.2.26.3; cf.*1Clem*.40.5; hence ἀρχιερεύς freq. used of Christian ἐ., v. ἀρχιερεύς; typified by Aaron's son, as Christ is by Aaron, Meth.*lepr*.7(p.459.25); **g.** ass. 'angel' of a church (Apoc.1:20), Or.*hom.13 in Lc*.(p.92.12; M.13.1832A); cf.Bas.*ep*.238 (3.367A; M.32.889B); Andr.Caes.*Apoc*.2(M.106.232A); **3.** functions; **a.** summed up σκοπὸς...ὁ κατασταθεὶς τῇ ἐκκλησίᾳ ἐ. *Const.App*.2.6.11; hence office reflects character of God οὐδὲν πρεσβύτερον θεοῦ, οὐδὲ ἐπισκοπώτερον. θεὸς γὰρ ὁ ἐπισκοπῶν...τὰ πάντα. ὁ τοίνυν ἐ. ἢ πρεσβύτερος, ὡς κοινωνὸς τῶν ὀνομάτων, οὕτω καὶ τῶν πραγμάτων ὀφείλει εἶναι Pall.*v.Chrys*.(p.55.10; M.47.32); Olymp. *Job* 20:29(M.93.221A); **b.** include exercise of prophetic ministry χειροτονήσατε οὖν ἑαυτοῖς ἐπισκόπους καὶ διακόνους ἀξίους τοῦ κυρίου ...ὑμῖν γὰρ λειτουργοῦσι καὶ αὐτοὶ τὴν λειτουργίαν τῶν προφητῶν καὶ διδασκάλων *Did*.15.1; Πολύκαρπος...διδάσκαλος ἀποστολικὸς καὶ προφητικὸς γενόμενος, ἐ. *M.Polyc*.16; cf.Ign.*Philad*.7.1 cit. s. διάκονος; **c.** chiefly: ruling Church, Ign.*Eph*.5.3; id.*Magn*.13.2; id.*Trall*.13.2; ὁ ἐπίσκοπος ὡς ἄρχων περὶ ὧν λέγει ἀκουέσθω *Hom. Clem*.3.67; as ruler, bishop leads men to God through Christ, *ib*.3.70; endowed with προεδρία in virtue of his liturgical and administrative offices, Bas.*ep*.188 *can*.1(3.269A; M.32.665A); Epiph. *haer*.42.1(p.95.4; M.41.696D); Chrys.*hom.3.4 in Col*.(11.349D); and with πρωτοκαθεδρία, Clem.*str*.7.16(p.69.21; M.9.536B); Thdr.Lect. *h.e*.2.34(M.86.201C); and described as προεστώς, v. προΐστημι; and προηγούμενος, v. προηγέομαι; represented as ὁ πρωρεύς in comparison of Church with a ship, *Clem.ep*.14(M.2.49A) cit. s. πρεσβύτερος; by Philost. (alone) termed ἔφορος q.v.; hence **d.** as president of assembled church, occupies θρόνος, Hipp.*haer*.9.11(p.245.14; M.16.3378C); Eus.*h.e*.7.19(M.20.681A); Chrys.*hom.2.1 in Tit*.(11.738A); regarded as Χριστοῦ θρόνος, id.*hom.3.4 in Col*.(11.349E); or occupies καθέδρα, CSard.*can*.4; Epiph.*ep.Arab*.ap.*haer*.78.7(p.457.21; M.42.709A); *Cod.Afr*.23; which belongs to him also by virtue of his office as teacher Κλήμεντα...ἐπίσκοπον...χειροτονῶ, ᾧ τὴν ἐμὴν τῶν λόγων πιστεύω καθέδραν *Clem.ep*.2(M.2.36A); **e.** forms centre of Church's unity, Ign.*Eph*.4.1; id.*Philad*.proem. cit. s. πρεσβύτερος; **f.** as exercising pastoral oversight, is described as ποιμήν q.v.; and as watchman (cf. Ezech.33:1–6), *Const.App*.2.6.7; *ib*.2.6.11; cf.Isid.Pel.*epp*.1.151(M.78.284C); exercises ministry of reconciliation as spiritual physician, Meth.*lepr*.7(p.460.3); **g.** is normal celebrant of eucharist, *Did*.15.1; cf.*ib*.10.7; Ign.*Smyrn*.8.1 al.; and very freq. thereafter; **h.** exercises teaching office, *M.Polyc*.16; Hipp.*haer*.proem.(p.3.4; M.16.3020C) v. διάδοχος; *Clem.ep*.2(M.2.36A); Isid.Pel.*epp*.2.208(M.78.648D); cf. δεῖ τοὺς τῶν ἐκκλησιῶν προεστῶτας ἐν πάσαις μὲν ἡμέραις, ἐξαιρέτως δὲ ταῖς κυριακαῖς, πάντα τὸν κλῆρον καὶ τὸν λαὸν ἐκδιδάσκειν CTrull.*can*.19; and as guardian of Church's teaching possesses divine gift of truth, cf. *cum episcopatus successione charisma veritatis certum...acceperunt*, Iren.*haer*.4.26.2(M.7.1053C); but, at Rome οὔτε...ὁ ἐ., οὔτε ἄλλος τις ἐπ' ἐκκλησίας...διδάσκει Soz.*h.e*.7.19.5(M.67.1476B); **i.** and preaches, cf. Chrys.*sac*.4.5(p.116.5f.; 1.415Af.); after disturbance caused by Arius' preaching, bishop alone preached at Alexandria, Soz.*h.e*.7.19.5(M.67.1476B); **j.** and alone possesses power of ordination, v. πρεσβύτερος; **k.** and of confirmation, at least as regards blessing of chrism, Didym.*Trin*.2.15(M.39.721A); **l.** acts as reader of scriptures τεσσάρων οὐσῶν περικοπῶν...ὅ τί ποτε βούλεται ὁ ἐ. προτεινάτω τῶν τεσσάρων Or.*engast*.1(p.283.21; M.12.1013B); ὁ ἐ. ἀνέγνω τὸ εὐαγγέλιον *A.Mt*.25(p.254.2); except at Alexandria, where bishop remains seated during reading of Gospel, Soz.*h.e*.7.19.6(M.67.1477A); bishop reads Gospel at festivals, e.g. at CP at Easter, *ib.*; **m.** bishop's ministry is that of ambassador, Chrys.*hom.3.4 in Col*.(11.350B); of mediator between God and faithful, *Const.App*.2.25.8; **n.** bishop administers reconciliation of penitents (Marcosian), Hipp.*haer*.6.41(p.173.5; M.16.3259C); at Rome, Soz.*h.e*.7.16.10(M.67.1460B); **o.** is in charge of church property and funds, cf.Clem. *q.d.s*.42(p.189.10; M.9.649A); πάντων τῶν ἐκκλησιαστικῶν πραγμάτων ὁ ἐ. ἐχέτω τὴν φροντίδα, καὶ διοικείτω αὐτὰ ὡς θεοῦ ἐφορῶντος *Can. App*.38; *ib*.41; CAnt.(341)*can*.25; *Const.App*.2.25.2; but is ordered to administer church property through agency of clerical οἰκονόμος, CChalc.*can*.26; **p.** supervises care of widows, orphans, and poor, and controls Church's social work, Herm.*sim*.9.27.2; cf.Ign.*Smyrn*.6,13; *Can.App*.41; cf.Chrys.*sac*.3.16(p.83.23; 1.396A); *Const.App*.2.25.2; Soz.*h.e*.5.15.5(M.67.1256B); *ib*.6.34.9(1397A); **q.** exercises personal hospitality ἐ. φιλόξενοι, οἵτινες ἡδέως εἰς τοὺς οἴκους ἑαυτῶν πάντοτε ὑπεδέξαντο τοὺς δούλους τοῦ θεοῦ Herm.*sim*.9.27.2; *Const.App*.2.4.1; *ib*.2.50.1; Chrys.*hom.2.2 in Tit*.(11.739D); **r.** exercises arbitral jurisdiction; **i.** bishop supervises arbitration exercised by presbyters between Christian litigants, *Hom.Clem*.3.67 cit. s. πρεσβύτερος; **ii.** bishop's own decisions given legal force by Const., Eus.*v.C*.4.27(p.127.31; M.20.1176B); τῶν δὲ ἐ. ἐπικαλεῖσθαι τὴν κρίσιν ἐπέτρεψε τοῖς δικαζομένοις, ἢν βούλωνται τοὺς πολιτικοὺς ἄρχοντας παραιτεῖσθαι· κυρίαν δὲ εἶναι τὴν αὐτῶν ψῆφον, καὶ κρείττω τῆς τῶν ἄλλων δικαστῶν, ὡσανεὶ παρὰ τοῦ βασιλέως ἐξενεχθεῖσαν Soz.*h.e*.1.9.5(M.67.884B); and bishop's jurisdiction subsequently extended in scope, Justn.*nov*.123.21(pp.609ff.); **iii.** bishop deals with offences committed in and against Church, without recourse to secular judges, Bas.*ep*.286(3.425D; M.32.1021B); **iv.** clergy may litigate with each other only before bishop, and cleric proceeding against bishop must do so before provincial synod, CChalc.*can*.9; bishop condemned by synod may appeal to larger council, but not to emperor's jurisdiction, CAnt.(341)*can*.12; *ib*.15; **v.** bishop must exercise sound judgement, *Const.App*.2.37.1; and follow well-defined judicial procedure, *ib*.2.49–51; judicial functions occupy much of bishop's time and present much difficulty, cf.Chrys.*sac*.3.18(p.92.14f.; 1.399E); **s.** bishop, assisted by presbyters, fills up ecclesiastical vacancies, cf.Chrys.*sac*.3.15(p.77.1f.; 1.392E); and approves appointments made by private patrons, cf. Justn.*nov*.57.2(pp.313f.); **t.** bishop must not engage in secular business, *Can.App*.7; **4.** appointment; **a.** popular election prescribed, *Did*.15.1 cit. s. II.B.3.b supra; cf.Hipp.*trad.ap*.1.1; ἐὰν ὀλιγανδρία ὑπάρχῃ καὶ μήπου πλῆθος τυγχάνῃ τῶν δυναμένων ψηφίσασθαι περὶ ἐπισκόπου ἐντὸς δεκαδύο ἀνδρῶν, εἰς τὰς πλησίον ἐκκλησίας... γραφέτωσαν, ὅπως ἐκεῖθεν ἐκλεκτοὶ τρεῖς ἄνδρες παραγενόμενοι δοκιμῇ δοκιμάσαντες τὸν ἄξιον ὄντα *Ordo Eccl.App*.16; *Const.App*.8.4.2; Soz.*h.e*.6.8.5(M.67.1316A); Gel.Cyz.*h.e*.2.33.5(M.85.1337B); restricted, CLaod.*can*.13; **b.** selection by emperor, Soz.*h.e*.7.8.3(M.67.

1433B); approval by emperor of bishop's election, Philost.*h.e.*2.11 (M.65.473Af.); appointment by civil authority forbidden, *Can.App.* 30; CNic.(787)*can.*3; **c.** consecration by all bishops of province, or at least three, with authority of metropolitan, CNic.(325)*can.* 4; CAnt.(341)*can.*19; CLaod.*can.*12; *Const.App.*8.27.2; consecration by one bishop only is cause for deposition, *ib.*; as is also repetition of ordination, *Can.App.*68; **d.** bishop normally not to be appointed before death of his predecessor, CAnt.(341)*can.*23; but to be appointed within three months of vacancy of see, CChalc.*can.*25; **e.** prayers for use at bishop's consecration, Serap. *euch.*28; *Const.App.*8.4.6ff.; **5.** qualifications; **a.** gen. moral requirements, *Ordo Eccl.App.*16; *Const.App.*2.1; *ib.*2.57.1; Chrys.*hom.10.1 in 1Tim.*(11.599C); **b.** minimum age: fifty, *Const.App.*2.1.1; thirty-five, Phot.*nomoc.*1.27(p.476; M.104.552C); **c.** promotion through regular grades of ministry required; ordination *per saltum* forbidden, CSard.*can.*10; Phot.*nomoc.*1.11(p.469; 497Dff.); hence neophyte disqualified, CNic.(325)*can.2*; CSard.*can.*10; Chrys.*hom.10.2 in 1Tim.*(11.601A); Thdt.*1Tim.*3:6(3.655); **d.** bishop must be unmarried or once-married (cf. 1Tim.3:4), *Ordo Eccl.App.*16; *Const. App.*2.2.3; Chrys.*hom.2.1 in Tit.*(11.738A); is to be separated from wife after consecration, CTrull.*can.*48; **6.** bishop's diocese; **a.** varies greatly in size, e.g. in Arabia and Cyprus καὶ ἐν κώμαις ἐ. ἱεροῦνται Soz.*h.e.*7.19.2(M.67.1476A) (but consecration of bishops for villages where one presbyter suffices is forbidden ἵνα μὴ κατευτελίζηται τὸ τοῦ ἐ. ὄνομα CSard.*can.*6); but in Scythia many cities share one bishop, Soz.*h.e.*7.19.2(1476A); there is one bishop of Goths, *ib.*7.17.11(1468A); **b.** diocese may be administered by not more than one bishop ἵνα μὴ ἐν τῇ πόλει δύο ἐ. ὦσιν CNic.(325)*can.*8; Bas.*ep.*244.6(3.380C; M.32.920C); but cf. Soz.*h.e.*7.2.6(M.67.1420C); **c.** bishop may not leave own diocese to interfere in another, *Can. App.*14; CAnc.(314)*can.*18; **d.** translation forbidden, CNic.(325) *can.*15; CAnt.(341)*can.*21; CSard.*can.*1; cf.Dam.Papa *anath.*ap. Thdt.*h.e.*5.11.5,6(3.1037f.); Socr.*h.e.*7.35.2(M.67.817A); CChalc.*can.* 5; **7.** bishop's dignity in relation to that of secular power; bishop's office superior to that of secular ruler, as soul is to body, *Const.App.*2.34.4; bishops buried with emperors in Church of Apostles at CP τῆς ἱερωσύνης ὁμοτίμου τῆς βασιλείας οὔσης, μᾶλλον μὲν οὖν ἐν τοῖς ἱεροῖς τόποις καὶ τὰ πρῶτα ἐχούσης Soz.*h.e.*2.34.6(M.67. 1032C).

C. *watcher over*, of Erinyes in a curse ἐπισκόπους δὲ ἔχοι Ἐρεινύας *CG–CI* I p.33 = *IG* 12.9.1179(Euboea saec.iii (?), ? Christian).

***ἐπισκότισμα, τό,** *obscurity, clouding* of one's judgement, Leont. H.*monoph.*testimonia(M.86.1892B).

ἐπίσκοτος, ὁ, *darkener* (play on ἐπίσκοπος) Σέβηρον τὸν ἐπίσκοπον, μᾶλλον δὲ ἐ. Ἀντιοχείας Anast.S.*haer.*(p.262); term of abuse for iconoclast bishops, Steph.Diac.*v.Steph.*(M.100.1140B).

***ἐπισκότωσις, ἡ,** *darkness, obscurity*, Ephr.3.324E; ἐ. τῇ ψυχῇ Call.*v.Hyp.*(p.42); Thdr.Stud.*epp.*2.131(M.99.1424C).

***ἐπισκωμματίζω,** *mock*, Epiph.*rescr.*2(p.156.16; M.41.160B); id. *haer.*64.63(M.41.1177B; ἐπισκώπτων p.500.19).

***ἐπισκωμματικῶς,** *mockingly*, Epiph.*anc.*103(p.124.13; M.43. 204A); id.*haer.*76.54(p.412.25; M.42.636B).

[*]**ἐπισκωτέω,** = ἐπισκοτέω, *darken*, ‡Nil.*perist.*9.4(M.79.869D).

***ἐπισοβαρεύομαι,** *plume oneself upon*, c. dat., Gr.Nyss.*Eun.*1(1 p.26.28; M.45.256A); Cyr.*Jo.*6.1(4.616E).

ἐπισπαίρ-ω, *strive in, take part in* contests ∼ειν γυμνασιαρχικοῖς ...ἀγῶσι *PLond.*1912.92.

***ἐπισπάσσω,** *sprinkle upon* ἐπέσπαττον τῷ τάφῳ μύρα Gr.Ant. *mul.ung.*6(M.88.1856A).

***ἐπισπάστρα, ἡ,** *covering cloth* for protection of sacred vessels, Thdr.Stud.*poen.*1.107(M.99.1748B).

ἐπισπείρ-ω, 1. *sow as a second crop*, ref. Mt.13:25f. ὥσπερ ἐν τῇ βαρβάρῳ φιλοσοφίᾳ, οὕτως καὶ ἐν τῇ Ἑλληνικῇ ἐπεσπάρη τὰ ζιζάνια πρὸς τοῦ τῶν ζιζανίων οἰκείου γεωργοῦ Clem.*str.*6.8(p.465.25; M.9. 289A); Or.*hom.1.14 in Jer.*(p.13.13; M.13.272D); id.*Cels.*5.62(p.65. 24; M.11.1281A) cit. s. γεωργός; Devil's action compared with introduction of heresies into Church, Chrys.*hom.46.1 in Mt.*(7. 481D); ζιζάνια...τὰ ∼όμενα τῆς ἀπιστίας διδάγματα Thdot.Anc.*exp. symb.*1(M.77.1316A); in gen. τὰ πνεύματα τὰ ἀκάθαρτα εἰς τὴν τοῦ ἁμαρτωλοῦ ψυχὴν ∼ειν Clem.*str.*2.20(p.176.5; M.8.1060B); ἐπισπαρήσεσθαι τὰς αἱρέσεις τῇ ἀληθείᾳ *ib.*7.15(p.63.31; M.9.525A); Ath.*Ar.*1.8 (M.26.25D); **2.** *scatter, disperse*, Or.*Cels.*1.55(p.106.7; M.11.761B); Eus.*d.e.*6.18(p.277.1; M.22.456B); Proc.G.*Jos.*18:4(M.87.1025C).

ἐπισπλαγχνίζομαι, *have compassion on*, Clem.*fr.*12(p.199.12).

***ἐπισπορεύς, ὁ,** *one who makes a second sowing* in existing crop; of Devil, ref. Mt.13:25f. σπέρμα ἐπιθυμίας ὑπὸ τοῦ ἐ. ἐχθροῦ δεξάμενος Bas.*renunt.*5(2.207C; M.31.637C); τὸν...ἐ. διάβολον Olymp. *Eccl.*3:8(M.93.513D); ὁ τῶν ζιζανίων ἐ. Jo.D.*fid.Nest.*1(p.560).

***ἐπισπόριον, τό,** *second crop*, Germ.CP *or.*2(M.98.265C).

ἐπισπουδαστής, *zealous* ὁ ἐ. βασιλεύς ‡Jo.D.*ep.Thphl.*20(M.95. 372B); as subst., *partisan* οἱ κακοὶ ἐ. τοῦ νοητοῦ Φαραώ Nil.*epp.*2.52 (M.79.224A).

***ἐπίσπουδος,** *urgent, important*, ‡Jo.D.*fid.dorm.*20(M.95.268A).

ἐπιστάζω, *drip into*, Geo Pis.*carm.vit.*35.

ἐπίσταμαι, *believe, assume* τοῖς ἀγένητον αὐτὴν [sc. ὕλην] ἐπισταμένοις Or.*Jo.*1.16(18; p.22.15; M.14.53B).

***ἐπιστάνω,** *know*, Hipp.*Noët.*7(p.247.11; M.10.813A); Didym. *Trin.*1.20(M.39.372A).

ἐπιστασία, ἡ, 1. *control, authority*; **a.** in gen. ὁ λόγος ὁ παιδαγωγὸς τὴν ἐ. εἴληχεν εἰς τὴν ἀλόγου κώλυσιν ἁμαρτίας Clem.*paed.*1.2(p.92.21; M.8.253B); Gr.Naz.*carm.*1.1.7.24(M.37.440A); of man's status in regard to women, Chrys.*hom.30.5 in Mt.*(7.354B); **b.** esp. of divine government; in pagan beliefs, Or.*sel.in Pss.*proem.(M.12.1053C); of God's providential care, Bas.*jud.*3(2.215D; M.31.657B); πᾶσα πρόνοια...καὶ τοῦ παντὸς ἐ. Gr.Nyss.*tres dii*(M.46.128D); Chrys.*hom. 83.5 in Jo.*(8.496A); of Christ τοὺς προσπεφευγότας τῇ ἐ. αὐτοῦ Bas. *Spir.*17(3.14D; M.32.97A); of H. Ghost, Thdr.Mops.*Ag.*2:1–5(M.66. 485A); **c.** of office of angels in caring for created order, Meth.*res.*2.10 (p.351.14); ἀρχαγγέλων ἐπιστασίαι Bas.*hex.*1.5(1.5D; M.29.13A); *Lit.* ap.*Const.App.*8.12.30; **d.** of BMV for suppliants, Jo.Thess.*dorm. BMV* A 14(p.403.32) cit. s. ἐπισκίασις; **e.** of a bishop's office ἐν τῇ ἐ. τοῦ μακαρίου ἀνδρός Jo.Not.*v.Eus.*2(M.86.304A); **f.** of pastoral care in gen., Chrys.*hom.85.4 in Mt.*(7.809E); **2.** *attack*, Chrys.*hom. 25.3 in 2Cor.*(10.616E); ‡Nil.*perist.*7.1(M.79.860A).

***ἐπιστέφιος,** *celebrating victory*, Gr.Naz.*carm.*2.1.38.48(M.37. 1329A).

***ἐπιστήθιος, ὁ,** *bosom-friend*, Thphn.*chron.*p.394(M.108.937B); of S. John, Eus.Al.*serm.*19(M.64.47A); *Hymn.*(*AS* 1 p.506); Jo.D. *imag.*1.19(M.94.1249C); ‡Gr.Naz.*Chr.pat.*187(M.38.152A).

[*]**ἐπιστήκω,** = ἐφίσταμαι, *be present*, †Polyb.*v.Epiph.*48(M.41. 84D).

ἐπιστήμη, ἡ, I. *knowledge*, cf. γνῶσις, νοῦς, σοφία, φιλοσοφία;

A. def. and scope, etym. τὴν ἐ. ἐτυμολογεῖν χρὴ καὶ ἀπὸ τῆς στάσεως τὴν ἐπιβολὴν αὐτῆς ληπτέον, ὅτι ἵστησιν ἡμῶν ἐν τοῖς πράγμασι τὴν ψυχήν, ἄλλοτε ἄλλως πρότερον φερομένην Clem.*str.*4.22 (p.311.17; M.8.1353A); τὴν...ἐ. ὁρίζονται φιλοσόφων παῖδες ἕξιν ἀμετάπτωτον ὑπὸ λόγου *ib.*2.2(p.117.22; 940B); *ib.*2.17(p.152.29; 1013C); ἴδιον δὲ ἐπιστήμης καθολικοῖς ἐπερείδεσθαι θεωρήμασι καὶ ὡρισμένοις *ib.*8.8(p.94.14; M.9.589A).

B. origin; **1.** gift of God, in enumerations combined with other intellectual endowments, e.g. σοφία, σύνεσις, etc., *Barn.*2.3; *ib.*21.5; personified, as offspring of faith, Herm.*vis.*3.8.5; being daughter of σεμνότης and mother of ἀγάπη, *ib.*3.8.7; ἐπαγγέλλεται ὁ λόγος τοῦ θεοῦ ἐμποιήσειν ἐ. τοῖς προσιοῦσιν Or.*princ.*3.1.15(p.223.7; M.11. 280C); id.*hom.16.1 in Jer.*(p.132.9; M.13.437D); **2.** obtained through careful inquiry, Clem.*str.*8.1(p.80.21; M.9.560B); τὴν ἐ. τῶν θείων καὶ ἀνθρωπίνων ἐντίθησιν ἡ διδασκαλία *ib.*1.6(p.23.11; M.8.729B); ἐκ δὲ αἰσθήσεως καὶ τοῦ νοῦ ἡ τῆς ἐ. συνίσταται οὐσία *ib.*2.4(p.119.23; 944C).

C. man's knowledge of God, cf. πίστις, αἴσθησις; **1.** possibility discussed, Just.*dial.*3.5–7(M.6.481B,C); ἐπὶ δὲ τοῦ κατ' ἐπιστήμην νοητοῦ ὡς ἔστιν θεὸς δογματίζων [sc. Euripides] Athenag.*leg.*5.1(M. 6.900A); οὐδὲ ἐ. λαμβάνεται [sc. θεός] τῇ ἀποδεικτικῇ· αὕτη γὰρ ἐκ προτέρων καὶ γνωριμωτέρων συνίσταται, τοῦ δὲ ἀγεννήτου οὐδὲν προϋπάρχει Clem.*str.*5.12(p.381.5; M.9.124A); id.*q.d.s.*7(p.164.19; M.9.612B); **2.** characteristic of believers, opp. ἄγνοια, Just.*1apol.*61.10(M.6. 421A); Clem.*str.*7.16(p.71.4; M.9.540A) cit. s. ἐκκλησία; τῆς τελείας ὄντως ἐ. ἐπέκεινα κόσμου περὶ τὰ νοητὰ καὶ ἐπὶ τούτων τὰ πνευματικώτερα ἀναστρεφομένης *ib.*6.8(p.465.35; 289B); *ib.*4.6(p.266.17; M.8. 1252B); esp. of 'gnostic' τῷδε ἡ ἐ. ἀναπόβλητος οὐκ ἀκουσίως, ἀλλ' ἑκουσίως...καθίσταται *ib.*7.7(p.35.11; M.9.468A); *ib.*7.14(p.60.4; 516D); ὅσοι δὲ μετ' ἐπιστήμης εὐλαβοῦνται,...οὗτοί εἰσιν οἱ ἀπὸ προσώπου τοῦ θεοῦ εὐλαβόμενοι Or.*hom.5.11 in Jer.*(p.40.25; M.13.309D); of which Moses was worthy, but not the Egyptians, *ib.1.10*(p.9.21; 268B); hence Christians do not consider ἐ. evil in itself, as Celsus alleges, id.*Cels.*3.75(p.267.23; M.11.1020B); ref. Plato's division εἰ δὲ καὶ ἀνάλογόν ἐστι τῷ τετάρτῳ ὄντι ἐ. ἢ ἐν τοῖς καθ' ἡμᾶς τελείοις σοφία ὁ Χριστός, ἐπιστήσει ὁ δυνάμενος *ib.*6.9(p.79.24; 1304C); τὰ ῥήματα τοῦ θεοῦ ἀκούει...ἐ. αὐτῶν ἀναλαμβάνων id.*Jo.*20.33(27; p.371.12; M.14. 649B); κατ' ἐπιστήμην τοῦ ἀληθοῦς φοβηθῆναι τὸν θεόν Meth.*arbitr.* 4(p.155.13; M.18.248C); opp. beatific vision μέχριπερ ἂν...μηκέτι δι' ἐπιστήμης κατασκέψηται τὸ ὄν, ἀλλὰ τρανῶς ἐποπτεύσῃ Χριστῷ συνεισβᾶσα id.*symp*.8.11(p.94.10; M.18.156A); two kinds τετελεσμένας...οὐχ ὡς ποικιλίας ἱερᾶς ἀναλυτικὴν ἐ. ἐλλαμπομένας, ἀλλ' ὡς ...κατὰ τὴν ὑπερτάτην ὡς ἐν ἀγγέλοις τῶν θεουργιῶν ἐ. Dion.Ar.*c.h.* 7.2(M.3.208C); ἡ ὑπερκόσμιος ἐ. *ib*.15.9(340B); μυστικὴ ἐ. id.*e.h*.1.1 (M.3.372B); leading to perfection, *ib*.6.1.3(532D), ὑπερούσιος ἐ. called an ἀγνωσία, id.*d.n*.1.1(M.3.588A); καθ' ἕξιν ἐ. ἐστὶν ἡ...τῆς ἐλλαμφθείσης γνώσεως κατάληψις Max.*schol.c.h*.7.3(M.4.73A); **3.** effects: right choice, Clem.*str*.4.5(p.258.5; M.8.1233C); ὁ τὸ πάντων ἀγαθώτατον κατὰ τὴν ἐ. κεκτημένος *ib*.7.7(p.33.21; M.9.464B); purification, Dion.Ar.*c.h*.7.3(M.3.209C); *ib*.13.4(305C).

D. divine knowledge, in relation to human free will οὔτε τὸ ἐφ' ἡμῖν χωρὶς τῆς ἐ. τοῦ θεοῦ, οὔτε ἡ ἐ. τοῦ θεοῦ προκόπτειν ἡμᾶς ἀναγκάζει Or.*princ*.3.1.24(p.243.10f.; M.11.301B); as leading God to create, Meth.*arbitr*.22(p.203.2ff.); *ib*.(p.205.15); θείᾳ ἐ. τὰ ὄντα... γεγονέναι id.*creat*.6(p.497.9; M.18.337A); in argument against Arians εἰ γὰρ διδακτόν ἐστι τὸ δημιουργεῖν, σκοπείτωσαν μὴ καὶ αὐτὸν τὸν θεὸν εἴπωσι μὴ φύσει, ἀλλ' ἐ. δημιουργὸν εἶναι Ath.*Ar*.2.28(M.26.208A); (Arian) καὶ πρὶν τῆς γενέσεως τοῦ υἱοῦ ὁ πατὴρ προϋπάρχουσαν εἶχε τὴν τοῦ γεννᾶν ἐ. Ast.Soph.*fr*.4(p.343)ap.Ath.*syn*.19(M.26.716B).

II. *discipline*; tr. *disciplina*, Tert.ap.Eus.*h.e*.3.33.3(M.20.285C); ἐκκλησιαστικὴ ἐ. Corn.*ib*.6.43.8(620A); δημοσίαν ἐ. Galerius *ib*.8.17.6 (792B); θεωρεῖς μοι τάξιν καὶ ἐ.; Cyr.H.*procatech*.4; CEph.(431)*act*.3 (*ACO* 1.1.3 p.59.25; H.1.1476B); τῶν ἱερῶν ἡ πάνσοφος ἐ. Dion.Ar.*e.h.* 3.3.6(M.3.433A); *ib*.5.1.6(505D); λειτουργικὴ ἐ. *ib*.7.3.3(560A); perh. also in def. of hierarchy as τάξις ἱερά, καὶ ἐ. id.*c.h*.3.1(M.3.164D); id. *e.h*.1.1(369D); τὴν ἱεραρχικὴν ἐ. ἐκ παραδόσεως παρέλαβεν Max.*schol. e.h*.1.1(M.4.116A).

***ἐπιστημονάρχης**, ὁ, *disciplinary officer* in monastery, Thdr. Stud.*iamb*.8 tit.(M.99.1781D); *Const.Stud*.18(M.99.1709D).

ἐπιστημονικός, **1.** *concerned with, relating to knowledge* σώφρονός τε, οὐκ ἐ. καθηγήσασθαι βίου Clem.*paed*.1.1(p.90.21; M.8.249B); πιστὴ ἡ γνῶσις ἥτις ἂν εἴη ἐ. ἀπόδειξις τῶν κατὰ τὴν ἀληθῆ φιλοσοφίαν παραδιδομένων. ... πίστεως δ' οὔσης διττῆς, τῆς μὲν ἐ., τῆς δὲ δοξαστικῆς, οὐδὲν κωλύει ἀπόδειξιν ὀνομάζειν διττήν, τὴν μὲν ἐ., τὴν δὲ δοξαστικήν id.*str*.2.11(p.138.17; M.8.984B); οὐδὲ...οἱ λόγοι οἱ πειστικοὶ...ἐ. τῆς ἀληθείας διαμονὴν παράσχοιεν ἂν *ib*.7.3(p.14.20; M.9.424C); ἐγγυμναζόμενος τῇ ἐ. θεωρίᾳ *ib*.7.11(p.44.13; 485B); τέλος... τοῦ γνωστικοῦ τό γε ἐνταῦθα διττόν, ἐφ' ὧν μὲν ἡ θεωρία ἡ ἐ., ἐφ' ὧν δὲ πρᾶξις *ib*.7.16(p.72.8; 541A); Eus.*p.e*.1.1(2D; M.21.24C); **2.** *intelligent, having understanding* ἀποκρίνεται οὐκ ἐ. ἀπόκρισιν Or.*Jo*. 32.8(6; p.438.10; M.14.761A); πανσόφους καὶ ἐ. τῶν ὅλων θεωρίας τε καὶ δυνάμεις Eus.*d.e*.5.1(p.215.16; M.22.357A); *having knowledge* of ὡς ἐ. τῆς τελεστικῆς μεταδόσεως Dion.Ar.*c.h*.3.3(M.3.168A); **3.** *being the object of knowledge* θεὸς ἀναπόδεικτος ὢν οὐκ ἔστιν ἐ., ὁ δὲ υἱὸς σοφία τέ ἐστι καὶ ἐπιστήμη, καὶ...ἀπόδειξιν ἔχει Clem.*str*.4.25(p.317.22; M.8.1365A).

ἐπιστημονικῶς, *with knowledge*, Clem.*str*.7.10(p.41.31; M.9.481A) cit. s. ἐποπτεύω; Or.*Ps*.48:5(p.49); Eus.*d.e*.10.8(p.487.9; M.22.781D); τῶν αὐτῶν πραγμάτων τοὺς τύπους ἐνσημαίνεται μὲν ὁ πατήρ, ἐπιτελεῖ δὲ ὁ λόγος, οὐ δουλικῶς, οὐδὲ ἀμαθῶς, ἀλλ' ἐ. Gr.Naz.*or*.30.11(p.124.16; M.36.117A); ἀκρόασιν πρότερον κατὰ τὴν εἰσαγωγικὴν διδασκαλίαν δεξάμενός τις, ἔρχεται εἰς τὸ ἰδεῖν αὐτὸν ἐ. μετὰ πολλὴν γυμνασίαν Sev.Ant.ap.*cat.1Jo*.1:1(p.107.5); *ib*.2:27ff.(p.120.30).

ἐπιστημοσύνη, ἡ, *knowledge*, Christol. οὐκ ἄρα σώζεται τὸ ἀνθρώπινον γένος δι' ἀναλήψεως νοῦ καὶ ὅλου ἀνθρώπου ἀλλὰ διὰ προσλήψεως σαρκός...ἐδεῖτο δὲ ἀτρέπτου νοῦ μὴ ὑποπίπτοντος αὐτῇ διὰ ἐπιστημοσύνης ἀσθένειαν, ἀλλὰ συναρμόζοντος αὐτὴν ἀβιάστως ἑαυτῷ Apoll.*fr*.76 (p.222.23)ap.Gr.Nyss.*Apoll*.40(M.45.1213C).

ἐπιστήριγμα, τό, *support*, Melet.*nat.hom*.synops.(M.64.1120C).

ἐπιστηρίζω, *stablish, confirm*; *fix* the eyes upon, Thphn.*chron*. p.230(M.108.581C).

***ἐπιστητικός**, *scientific*, Clem.*str*.2.17(p.152.29; M.8.1013C).

***ἐπιστιβάζω**, *press closely upon*, ‡Eust.*hex*.(M.18.725A).

***ἐπιστιχάομαι**, *approach*, Nonn.*par.Jo*.4:45(M.43.781C).

ἐπιστοιβάζω, *heap upon*, Chrys.*fr.in Pr*.6:24(M.64.676C); id.*pan. Dros*.6(2.697B).

ἐπιστοιχειόω, *inform concerning principles, ground in*; pass., CEph.(449)*act*.(*ACO* 2.1.1 p.189.23; H.2.237C).

ἐπιστολεύς, ὁ, *letter-carrier*, *Pap.Chr*.(p.384) saec. iii; Thphyl.*exc. gent*.3(p.480.20; M.113.940B).

ἐπιστοληφόρος ([*]**ἐπιστολοφόρος**), ὁ, = foreg., Eus.*h.e*.1.13.2 (M.20.120B); Jo.D.*jej*.7(M.95.72B); -λοφόρος, of S. Paul, †Cyr.*hom. div*.11(5^2.383B).

ἐπιστολίδιον, τό, *brief note*, Bas.*ep*.199 *can*.23(3.293C; M.32.724A).

[*]**ἐπιστολοφόρος**, ὁ, v. ἐπιστοληφόρος.

ἐπιστοματίζω, *put to silence*, *cat.Ac*.7:60(p.131.19).

ἐπιστομίζ-ω, **1.** *bridle, curb*; evil thoughts, Meth.*res*.2.3(p.334.4; M.41.1165D); passion, Bas.Sel.*or*.8.2(M.85.121B); *overcome* ~ουσι ...προποσίαι...τὸν λογισμόν Meth.*symp*.5.6(p.60.9; M.18.108B); **2.** *impose silence on* ὅταν...ὁ διάκονος ἑστὼς ~ῃ πάντας Chrys.*hom. 3.4 in 2Thess*.(11.527E); Cyr.*Am*.62(3.320A); **3.** *put to silence, refute*, Gr.Thaum.*pan.Or*.1(p.1.10; M.10.1052A); ψευδηγόρων γλώττας ~ουσα Eus.*d.e*.1.1(p.6.7; M.22.20D); Ath.*Ar*.1.7(M.26.25C); Chrys.*hom.28. 1 in Jo*.(8.158C); ~ων ἀντιλογίαν *ib.31.4*(180B); ‡Pall.*h.mon*.27.1 (p.86.12; M.65.448C); εἰ δὲ ἀντιλέγοι ὁ Ἰουδαῖος...ὑπὸ τῆς...γραφῆς ~έσθω Jo.D.*f.o*.1.7(M.94.808A).

***ἐπιστομιστέον**, *one must put a muzzle on*, Clem.*paed*.2.5(p.185.19; M.8.448B); *ib*.2.6(p.187.8; 452B); *ib*.2.7(p.192.23; 464A).

***ἐπιστοχάζομαι**, *conjecture*, Ammon.*Ac*.15:6(M.85.1548D); †Leont.B.*sect*.8.5(M.86.1256D).

ἐπιστρεπτικός, **1.** *corrective* προσέχων λόγοις ἐ. καὶ παιδευτικοῖς Or.*comm.in Gen*.(M.12.68A); id.*Ps*.37:3(p.14); ἐ. τὸ τοιοῦτον τῶν ἁμαρτανόντων id.*Cels*.3.63(p.257.16; M.11.1004A); ἐπιστρεπτικώτατος λόγος Eus.*h.e*.4.28(M.20.397C); γραφὴ ἐ. *ib*.6.46.2(633D); of laws, id.*d.e*.3.6(p.138.10; ἀποτρεπτικοί M.22.233A); Cyr.*Os*.133(3.166C); **2.** *chastising* ἐ. πληγαῖς Eus.*Ps*.38:8–12(M.23.349B); id.*Is*.10:24(M.24.168A); †Bas.*Is*.18(1.389E; M.30.145B); **3.** *responding to attraction* τῆς τῶν λογίων ἐ. ἐπὶ τὰ κρείττω διδασκαλίας Dion.Ar.*e.h*.3.3.7(M.3.436A); id.*d.n*.4.6(M.3.701B); Max.*ambig*.(M.91.1081C); **4.** *able to reprove* or *correct*; of bishops, *Const.App*.2.24.7.

ἐπιστρεπτικῶς, **1.** *by way of correction*, Dion.Ar.*c.h*.8.2(M.3.240D); Sev.Ant.*res*.(p.824.11; ἐντροπικῶς M.46.640A); **2.** *by way of response to attraction*, Dion.Ar.*c.h*.15.1(328B); τὰ ἥττω τῶν κρειττόνων ἐ. ἐρῶσι id.*d.n*.4.10(M.3.708A).

ἐπιστρέφεια, ἡ, **1.** *diligence, attention*, Eus.*v.C*.4.8(p.121.5); as title of honour ἡ σὴ ἐ. Sabinus ap.Eus.*h.e*.9.1.6(M.20.801A); **2.** *correction, punishment*, Dion.Al.*ib*.7.11.11(665B); **3.** *reformation, amending*, Tit.Bost.*Man*.2.16(M.18.1165A); *ib*.(1168A); **4.** *repentance, turning* to God, Thdr.Mops.*Os*.12:5–8(M.66.196C); CNic.(325)*can*. 12 ap.Gel.Cyz.*h.e*.2.32.12(M.85.1330) for ἐπιστροφήν.

ἐπιστρέφ-ω, **A.** trans.; **1.** *turn back* ἡ γὰρ παράβασις τῆς ἐντολῆς εἰς τὸ κατὰ φύσιν αὐτοὺς [sc. mankind] ἐπέστρεφεν Ath.*inc*.4.4(M.25.104B); ἐπέστρεψεν τὴν πέτραν, ὡς ἦν ἀπ' ἀρχῆς *Mir.Geo*.13(p.133.16); **2.** *make to return* Ἰησοῦς...τὴν διασπορὰν τοῦ λαοῦ ἐπιστρέψει Just. *dial*.113.3(M.6.736C); *Clem.ep*.12(M.2.48A); **3.** *win over, persuade* τὰ ῥήματα ταῦτα ~ει πάντας μᾶλλον τῶν ἱματίων τῶν χρυσῶν Chrys.*hom. 10.4 in 1Cor*.(10.86C); τὰ δεσμὰ ταῦτα πολλοὺς ἐπέστρεψε id.*hom. 2.1 in 2Tim*.(11.665F); id.*hom.2.3 in Ac*.(9.18B); **4.** *convert* μετανοίας τόπον ἔδωκεν...τοῖς βουλομένοις ἐπιστραφῆναι ἐπ' αὐτόν *1Clem*.7.5; τοὺς ἐκ φόβου εἰς πίστιν ἐπιστραφέντας Clem.*ecl*.60(p.154.24; M.9.728B); ἐὰν καὶ τοὺς ἀγροικοτάτους...οἷός τέ τις γένηται ~ειν Or.*Cels*. 6.1(p.70.13; M.11.1289A); Eus.*theoph*.12(p.27*.15; M.24.644B); Chrys. *hom.43.2 in Mt*.(7.460C); id.*hom.9.2 in Col*.(11.395A); **5.** *reform, restore to righteousness* τοὺς πλανωμένους τοῦ λαοῦ σου ἐπίστρεψον *1Clem*.59.4; πρεσβύτεροι...~οντες τὰ ἀποπεπλανημένα Polyc.*ep*.6.1; ἐσκανδαλισμένους ἀπὸ τῆς πίστεως μὴ ἀποβάλλεσθαι ἀλλ' ~ειν Herm. *mand*.8.9; Or.*Jo*.28.23(18; p.417.27; M.14.728C); Chrys.*hom.41.2 in Ac*.(9.310D); id.*hom.15.3 in Eph*.(11.113D); *Exorc*.22(p.340); **6.** *correct*, hence *chastise* υἱὸν κολάζεις ἵνα τοῖς πόνοις αὐτὸν ἐπιστρέψῃς Or.*hom.12.3 in Jer*.(p.91.1; M.13.384C); διὰ τῶν περιστάσεων κατὰ καιρὸν ~οντα τὸν αὐτοῦ λαὸν Eus.*h.e*.9.8.15(M.20.820A); id.*d.e*. 1.3(p.15.5; M.22.36A); ῥαθυμοῦντας ~ωμεν Chrys.*hom.16.7 in Mt*. (7.214A); id.*hom.8.1 in Phil*.(11.256C).

B. intrans. act. and med.; **1.** *return*; of return of Israel from exile in Media prevented by wickedness of Dan and Gad, ‡Epiph. *v.proph.Ezech*.19(p.24; M.43.401D); of Adam returning to the dust, Gr.Thaum.*pan.Or*.16(p.35.28; M.10.1097A); of reverting to evil, Herm.*sim*.8.7.5; of response to attraction πᾶν ὂν ἐκ τοῦ καλοῦ...εἰς τὸ καλὸν ~εται Dion.Ar.*d.n*.4.10(M.3.705D); cf. ἐπιστρεπτικός; **2.** esp. *be converted, turn to God*, *T.Dan*.6.4; ὅποτε ἐπέστρεψαν καὶ ἐπίστευσαν Meth.*symp*.8.9(p.91.18; M.18.152B); τοῖς τῶν ἀποστόλων κηρύγμασιν ἐξ ἀσεβείας αὐτῶν τῆς προτέρας ἐπιστρέψαι id.*creat*.1 (p.493.14; M.18.332B); Chrys.*hom.43.2 in Mt*.(7.460C); id.*hom.41.2 in Ac*.(9.311E); τὴν πίστιν δέξασθαι...καὶ ἐ. id.*hom.43.3 in 1Cor*.(10.403E); ἐπιστρέψαντες προσέλθωμεν πρὸς αὐτόν Mac.Aeg.*hom*.4.16 (M.34.485A); Gr.Mag.*dial*.(tr.Zach.)2.18(M.*PL*.66.169A); **3.** *return to right conduct, reform* ἐπιστρέψει ἀπὸ τῆς ἐπιθυμίας τῆς πονηρᾶς *T. Jos*.3.10; of repentance, *1Clem*.9.1; *2Clem*.16.1; *ib*.19.2; ἐπὶ τὸν ἐξ ἀρχῆς ἡμῖν παραδοθέντα λόγον ἐπιστρέψωμεν Polyc.*ep*.7.2; Herm. *sim*.9.26.2; οὕτως ~ουσιν, ὥστε ἀξίους αὐτοὺς γενέσθαι ἀφέσεως ἁμαρτημάτων Or.*princ*.3.1.16(p.223.15; M.11.281A); εἰ μὴ ἐπιστρέψαιεν μετὰ τὴν ἁμαρτίαν id.*Jo*.10.23(16; p.195.6; M.14.348B).

ἐπιστροφεύς, ὁ, *one who corrects* or *amends* σὺ δέ, ὁ ἐπίσκοπος, ἔσο...ἐ., διδακτικός *Const.App*.2.57.1.

ἐπιστροφή, ἡ, *turning about*; hence **1.** *conversion* (religious) πᾶν ῥῆμα, ὃ ἐὰν ἐξελεύσεται ἐξ ὑμῶν διὰ τοῦ στόματος ὑμῶν ἐν πίστει καὶ ἀγάπῃ, ἔσται εἰς ἐ. ... πολλοῖς *Barn*.11.8; λαὸν...εἰς ἐ. καὶ μετάνοιαν τοῦ πνεύματος κέκληκε Just.*dial*.30.1(M.6.537C); ἐ. τῆς μηδέπω πιστευούσης ψυχῆς Clem.*str*.6.3(p.448.10; M.9.252C); *ib*.6.6(p.454.20; 268B); τὴν...πρὸς τὸν θεὸν ἐ. *ib*.7.7(p.32.32; 461A); διδοὺς...τόπον μετανοίας καὶ ἐ. Or.*hom.1.1 in Jer*.(p.1.12; M.13.256B); id.*princ*.3.1.17(p.226.6; M.11.284A); ἐ. μετὰ ψιλῆς πίστεως id.*Cels*.1.9(p.62.9; M.11.673A); ἡ περὶ τὸ ἄφθαρτόν τε καὶ θεῖον ἐ. καὶ πίστις Meth.*Porph*.5(p.507.16; M.18.345B); Eus.*d.e*.8.2(p.370.24; M.22.601C); εἰς ἐ. καὶ μετάνοιαν ἀγαγεῖν μυρία πλήθη τῶν πρότερον ἐν πολυθέῳ πλάνῃ...βιούντων id.*theoph*.9(p.23*.28; M.24.633A); Gr.Nyss.*ep.can*.1(M.45.221B); τὴν ἐν ὑστέροις καιροῖς ἐσομένην τοῦ Ἰσραὴλ ἐ. καὶ κλῆσιν Cyr.*Ps*.43:27(M.69.1025B); id.*Os*.68(3.102E); ἡ βασιλικὴ ναῦς [sc. BMV], ἡ...ἐκ τῆς ἐθνικῆς προσφέρουσα χώρας τῶν ἐθνῶν τὴν ἐ. τῷ βασιλεῖ τῆς ἄνω Ἱερουσαλήμ Procl.CP *or*.6.17(M.65.756B); τῶν ἐθνῶν τὴν πρὸς τὸν θεὸν διὰ τοῦ Χριστοῦ ἐ. Cosm.Ind.*top*.5(M.88.269D); **2.** *reform, amendment* (Gnost.) γενέσθαι δύο οὐσίας, τὴν φαύλην τῶν παθῶν, τήν τε τῆς ἐ. ἐμπαθῆ Iren.*haer*.1.4.5(M.7.489A); in gen., Clem.*str*.4.5(p.257.11; M.8.1233A); linked with ἐξομολόγησις, *ib*.7.12(p.57.8; M.9.512A); ἀρχὴν ἔχοντες ἐπιστροφῆς λέγουσιν τό, 'ἡμάρτομεν' Or.*hom.5.10 in Jer*.(p.39.32; M.13.309A); ἐ. μετὰ τὸ ἡμαρτηκέναι id.*Jo*.28.7(6; p.398.20; M.14.696C); τὰ...διὰ τῆς κακώσεως εἰς ἐ. ἄγοντα, γίνεται εἰς ἀγαθόν Bas.*reg.br*.276(2.512A; M.31.1273D); Gr.Naz.*or*.39.17(M.36.356A); ἐν πᾶσίν εἰσι λῃσταί...ἀλλ' ὅμως ὑπὲρ πάντων εὐχόμεθα· ἴσως ἔσται τις αὐτῶν ἐ. Chrys.*hom.3.4 in Phil*.(11.218B); ἡ ἐ. πολλῆς δεῖται τῆς ταπεινώσεως Jo.Clim.*scal*.8(M.88.829B); Anast.S.*Ps*.6(M.89.1080A); ref. penitential discipline ἐπισκόπους ἐξουσίαν ἔχειν τὸν τρόπον τῆς ἐ. δοκιμάσαντας φιλανθρωπεύεσθαι ἢ πλείονα προστιθέναι χρόνον CAnc.(314)*can*.5; ὁ δὲ φωραθεὶς ἐπὶ τῷ κακῷ...ἐν ἐπιτεταμένῃ γίνεται τῇ ἐ. Gr.Nyss.*ep.can*.4(M.45.229A); **3.** *correction*, *A.Jo*.41(p.171.1); ποίοις ἐπιτιμίοις κεχρῆσθαι δεῖ...πρὸς τὴν τῶν ἁμαρτανόντων ἐ.; Bas.*reg.br*.106 tit.(2.452C; M.31.1156A); οὐδεμίαν ἐ. δεχόμενος Chrys.*hom.1.3 in 2Tim*.(11.663A); πρὸς ἐ. καὶ διόρθωσιν τῶν ἁμαρτανόντων Philost.*h.e*.12.10(M.65.620A); **4.** *conversion*, i.e. response of inferior being to attraction of superior αἱ πρόνοιαι τῶν ὑπερτέρων...αἱ ἐ. τῶν καταδεεστέρων Dion.Ar.*d.n*.4.7(M.3.704B); *ib*.4.12(709D).

***ἐπιστυγής,** *hateful*, Clem.*prot*.10(p.72.5; M.8.213A).

***ἐπιστυγνάζ-ω,** *be distressed* at εὐλάβειαν ~ουσαν τοῖς συμβεβηκόσι Bas.*ep*.184(3.266D; M.32.661A); Ast.Am.*hom*.13(M.40.360C); Nil.*Magn*.58(M.79.1045D); Cyr.*ador*.5(1.160E); Thdr.Stud.*epp*.2.56(M.99.1269A); abs., Cyr.*apol.Thdt*.10(p.137.22; 6[1].231E).

***ἐπιστυπτικός,** *astringent, dry*, Eus.*Is*.1:22(M.24.97D).

***ἐπιστωμύλλ-ομαι,** *rival in nonsense* κωμῳδίαις ~ομαι πρὸς τὸν πόνον ἑκάστου τοῦ γράψαντος Synes.*Dion* 18(p.278.11; M.66.1161D).

***ἐπισυγγράφω,** *add new writing*, Anon.ap.Eus.*h.e*.5.16.3(M.20.465A).

***ἐπισυγκεράννυμι,** pass., *become mixed with*, Athenag.*leg*.27.1(M.6.952D).

ἐπισυλλέγω, pass., *assemble, be gathered together*, *A.Jo*.66(p.183.8).

ἐπισυμβαίν-ω, 1. *supervene, be added* εἰ δέ ἐστιν ἐν τοῖς φυομένοις δηλητήριον, τοῦτο διὰ τὸ ἐνάμαρτον ἡμῶν ἐπισυμβέβηκεν Tat.*orat*.19(p.22.7; M.6.849C); Clem.*paed*.2.10(p.213.18; M.8.508B); τήρησις τῶν...ἐντολῶν...δι' ἣν ἡ ἀφθαρσία ~ει id.*str*.6.15(p.492.31; M.9.344D); Eus.*d.e*.5.4(p.224.3; M.22.369A); theol. οὐ γὰρ ἀτελὴς οὐσία τοῦ πατρὸς ἦν ποτε, ἵνα καὶ τὸ ἴδιον αὐτῆς ~ῃ ταύτῃ Ath.*Ar*.1.14(M.26.41B); οὐδὲν ~ειν τῇ οὐσίᾳ τοῦ θεοῦ φάσκοντες, οὐκ εἶναι δώσουσι συμβεβηκός [sc. τὸ πατὴρ ὄνομα] Cyr.*thes*.31(5[1].263E); of Son φύσει θεὸς...ὢν...οὐχὶ δὲ ὁμοίως τοῖς ἔξωθεν εἰσποιουμένοις, ἐπισυμβεβηκός γε τὸ ἀξίωμα τῆς τοῦ θεοῦ προσηγορίας ἐπέχουσιν Eus.*d.e*.5.4(p.225.28; M.22.372D); in Arian doctrine ὅτι τὸ ἐκ τοῦ θεοῦ ἐπισυμβέβηκεν αὐτῷ Ath.*decr*.12(p.10.25; M.25.436C); in Nestorian Christology ~ούσης ταῖς φύσεσι τῆς θείας φύσεως Leont.H.*Nest*.3.8(M.86.1632B); **2.** in gen., *be adventitious*; of evil as not being an ultimate principle, Or.*Ps*.36:1–2(p.10); Adam.*dial*.3.9(p.126.21; M.11.1800B); Tit.Bost.*Man*.1.9(M.18.1080C); **3.** *befall, occur* εἰ ~ει πάθος τι τῷ λόγῳ τοῦ θεοῦ, αἰδεῖται τὸ θεῖον Adam.*dial*.4.14(p.170.14; M.11.1829A); perf. ptcpl. neut. plur. as subst., *accidents, accidental properties*, Athenag.*leg*.23.4(M.6.944B); of misfortunes, *happen accidentally* ἐπισυμβάντος δέ τινος μὴ ἀγανακτεῖν Clem.*ecl*.47(p.150.4; M.9.720B); Max.*ambig*.(M.91.1193A).

***ἐπισυμβατός,** *adventitious* εἰ λάχανον...ἐπισυμβαίνει τῇ γῇ,...καὶ λαχάνῳ ὁμοιοῦται ἡ κακία, ἐ. ἄρα ἡ κακία Or.*Ps*.36:1–2(p.10).

ἐπισυμπλέκ-ω, *conjoin, add* ἑτέρα ταῖς προτέραις ~εται ταραχή Socr.*h.e*.2.6.3(M.67.192B); *ib*.5 proem.6(565B); gram. εἰ δέ τις αὐτὸ ~ειν φιλονεικοίη ὡσὰν καὶ τοῦ θεὸς καὶ τοῦ πατὴρ ἐπὶ τοῦ προσώπου νοεῖσθαι ὀφείλοντος τοῦ Χριστοῦ, οὐδὲ πρὸς τοῦτο μαχόμεθα Thdr.Mops.*Eph*.1:3(p.121.20; M.66.912C).

ἐπισυνάγ-ω, 1. *collect together, assemble*; things, Or.*Jo*.20.2(p.328.3; M.14.573B); ἀγύρτην...μύθους...~οντα ‡Jo.D.*Artem*.47(p.164.15; M.96.1296A); *collect oneself* in preparation for death ἐπισυνάξαι ἑαυτὴν καὶ πρὸς τὴν ἔξοδον ἑτοιμασθῆναι Cyr.S.*v.Euthym*.35(p.53.21); **2.** *congregate, gather together*; persons, Or.*exp.in Pr*.28:22(M.17.245A); of a congregation brought together and re-invigorated by a zealous bishop, Eus.*h.e*.4.23.3(M.20.385A); ~εῖν αὐτῷ τὰ τέκνα ὑπὸ τὸν τῆς θεοσεβείας ζυγόν id.*theoph*.12(p.27*.12; M.24.644B); esp. of final gathering in of the elect, *T.Neph*.8.3; *T.Aser* 7.7; ἐπισυναχθήτω σου ἡ ἐκκλησία ἀπὸ τῶν περάτων τῆς γῆς εἰς τὴν βασιλείαν σου Ath.*virg*.13(p.47.6; M.28.265C); cf. (συνάγω) *Did*.10.5; **3.** *add, introduce besides*, Leont.H.*monoph*.(M.86.1808C); ‡Jo.D.*hom*.5(M.96.653B).

ἐπισυναγωγή, ἡ, 1. *assembling, collection*, Or.*hom.2.2 in Gen*.(p.29.23; M.12.168A); Max.*ambig*.(M.91.1281A); **2.** *assemblage, gathering* of persons; of Christian congregations, Eus.*h.e*.8.1.5(M.20.741A); cf. τὰς ἐ. ἡμῶν κύριε εὐλόγησον *Lit.Marc*.(p.121.26); esp. (eschatological) of gathering in of faithful to Christ τῆς...ἐκ νεκρῶν ἀναστάσεως καὶ τῆς πρὸς αὐτὸν ἐ. καὶ ὁμοιώσεως Dion.Al.ap.Eus.*h.e*.7.24.5(M.20.693C); Eus.*d.e*.2.3(p.87.2; M.22.153D); τὴν ἁπάντων τῶν ἁγίων ἐ. εἰς Χριστόν Cyr.*Jo*.3.4(4.270B).

ἐπισυναθροίζω, *collect together in addition*, Philost.*h.e*.2.11(M.65.476A).

ἐπισυνάπτ-ω, 1. *conjoin, couple together*; **a.** in gen., Athenag.*leg*.22.2(M.6.937A); παραστήσας δὲ τὰ...αὐτῷ εἰρημένα...~ει ταῦτα Or.*Jo*.10.2(1; p.172.17; M.14.309A); ἄλλην ~ων ἱστορίαν Eus.*h.e*.1.5.3(M.20.81B); id.*d.e*.1.7(p.37.24; M.22.73A); id.*Marcell*.1.4(p.19.22; M.24.756A); Bas.*reg.br*.66(2.439A; M.31.1129B); γελοῖον εἶναι...τὸ ἀσώματον...σώματι...~ειν Aen.*dial*.(M.85.976A); **b.** sexually, Epiph.*haer*.77.36(p.448.27; M.42.696B); Max.*ambig*.(M.91.1200A); **c.** theol. πεπιστεύκαμεν γὰρ ἀμεσιτεύτως αὐτοὺς...ἀλλήλοις [sc. Persons of Trin.] ἐπισυνῆφθαι *Symb.Ant*.(345)9(p.253.37; M.26.733B); **d.** of adding one prayer to another in liturgy, *Lit.Jac*.(p.192.13,24); of running psalms together in recitation μὴ δεῖν ~ειν ἐν ταῖς συνάξεσι τοὺς ψαλμούς, ἀλλὰ διὰ μέσου καθ' ἕκαστον ψαλμὸν γίνεσθαι ἀνάγνωσιν CLaod.*can*.17; **2.** *prolong, continue* ~ειν τὴν νηστείαν Soz.*h.e*.1.11.10(M.67.889B); **3.** *continue* an appointment ~έσθω αὐτῷ καὶ ἐπὶ ἄλλην διετίαν τὸ ὀφφίκιον Ath.Scholast.*coll*.4.24(p.67).

***ἐπισυνεισφέρομαι,** *introduce besides*, Epiph.*haer*.40.2(p.82.12; M.41.680B).

***ἐπισυνεισφορά, ἡ,** *additional contribution*, Epiph.*haer*.76.38(p.391.16; M.42.597D).

***ἐπισυνέρχομαι,** *be multiplied with*, c. dat., Iren.*haer*.1.15.2(M.7.616A).

***ἐπισυνηγορέω,** *join in advocating*, Isid.Pel.*epp*.1.39(M.78.208A).

ἐπισύνθετος, *compound*, Clem.*str*.5.6(p.351.3; M.9.61C).

***ἐπισύνοδος, ἡ,** *combined attack*, Meth.*symp*.8.10(p.92.19; M.18.153B).

ἐπισυντρέχω, *run together*, *A.Thadd*.7(p.277.23).

***ἐπισυρράπτω,** *patch together*, met. ἐ. διαβολήν Gel.Cyz.*h.e*.3.15.17.

***ἐπισυχνάζω,** *attend to frequently*, Thal.*cent*.2.36(M.91.1441A).

***ἐπίσφηνον, τό,** *sucker, shoot*, Clem.*str*.6.15(p.491.28; ἐπίσφινον M.9.344A).

ἐπισφραγίζ-ω, *seal, set seal on*; hence **1.** *complete, finish off*, Chrys.*hom.3.1 in Philm*.(11.787B); Pall.*v.Chrys*.11(p.68.11; M.47.38); *consummate* ἐπισφραγίσας [sc. Polycarp] διὰ τῆς μαρτυρίας αὐτοῦ κατέπαυσεν τὸν διωγμόν *M.Polyc*.1.1; **2.** *confirm, attest*, *Ep.Lugd*.ap.Eus.*h.e*.5.2.3(M.20.433B); Clem.*str*.5.12(p.379.17; M.9.120A); Eus.*d.e*.1.3(p.13.28; M.22.33A); *ib*.1.10(p.46.1; 88B); τῶν εὐαγγελικῶν τὰς τῶν προφητικῶν μαρτυρίας ~ομένων *ib*.4.15(p.173.29; 289C); τοὺς τῶν ἐπισκόπων δὲ ὅρους τοὺς ἐν συνόδοις ἀποφανθέντας ἐπεσφραγίζετο, ὡς μὴ ἐξεῖναι τοῖς τῶν ἐθνῶν ἄρχουσι τὰ δόξαντα παραλύειν id.*v.C*.4.27(p.127.32; M.20.1176B); φωναὶ μεθ' ὅρκου ~ουσιν, ὅτι εἷς ἐστιν ὁ θεός *Hom.Clem*.16.7; Ath.*fug*.14(p.78.15; M.25.661C); *Const.App*.2.14.15; ἀπόστολοι ταῦτα γράφουσιν, αὐτοῦ...τοῦ σωτῆρος ταῦτα ~ομένου Didym.*Pss*.proem.(M.39.1157A); τῇ μαρτυρίᾳ ~ει τὸ εἰρημένον Chrys.*hom.8.4 in Rom*.(9.503B); Cyr.*Soph*.16(3.597A); σημείοις τε καὶ τέρασιν ~οντες τοὺς...λόγους id.*Zach*.89(3.776E); of baptism confirming or sealing candidate's credal profession of belief in Trin., Bas.*Spir*.28(3.24A; M.32.117C); id.*Eun*.3.5(1.276E; M.29.665C); **3.** *set seal upon* as one's possession; of action of H. Ghost in baptismal anointing, *A.Thom.*A 27(p.143.3); in consecration of eucharistic elements ~ει καὶ τελειοῖ τὰ προκείμενα ἅγια δῶρα εἰς σῶμα καὶ αἷμα τοῦ Χριστοῦ ‡Bas.*h.myst*.60(p.395.18); **4.** *impress*, Clem.*str*.1.24(p.100.18; M.8.908A); **5.** *seal up*, Ath.*fug*.6(p.72.7; M.25.652A); id.*h.Ar*.58(p.216.3; M.25.764B).

***ἐπισφραγίς, ἡ,** *seal* ἐ. τῆς ὁμολογίας Epiph.*haer*.62.4(p.392.28; M.41.1056A); *ib*.74.11(p.329.23; M.42.497A).

ἐπισφράγισμα, τό, 1. *seal*, fig. προσθήσωμεν τῷ...λόγῳ ὡς χρυσοῦν ἐ. Ephr.3.433A; **2.** *completion, consummation* ὥσπερ ἐ. σε τῆς ὅλης ὑποθέσεως ἀναβοώμενοι Eus.*h.e*.10.1.2(M.20.841B); of a martyr as παντὸς τοῦ κατὰ Παλαιστίνην ἀγῶνος ἐ. id.*m.P*.13(p.948.8; M.20.1516B); of baptism under Mosaic Law as ἐ. τοῦ καθαρισμοῦ †Bas.*bapt*.1.2.5(2.632D; M.31.1533B); of unction with oil and prayer for descent of H. Ghost as ἐ. τῆς σφραγῖδος [i.e. initiation] *A.Thom.*A 27(p.142.10); **3.** *confirmation, attestation* ἐ. τοῦ λόγου γένοιτ' ἂν ἡμῖν ὁ Πλάτων...φάσκων Eus.*p.e*.1.9(29B; M.21.68B); τῶν εἰρημένων ἐ. ... ἡ Διοδώρου μαρτυρία *ib*.10.7(480A; M.797C); of *amen* (ref. Dt.27:26), Sever.*appar*.9(M.65.21D); Thdr.Stud.*epp*.2.12(M.99.1153B).

***ἐπισχυρίζω,** *strengthen*, *A.Andr.et Mt*.28(p.108.6, v.l. ἐνισχ-).

***ἐπισωζομένη, ἡ, 1.** *Ascension Day* εἰς τὴν...ἀνάληψιν τὴν λεγομένην τῷ ἐπιχωρίῳ τῶν Καππαδόκων ἔθει τὴν ἐ. Gr.Nyss.*ascens*.tit.(M.46.689); **2.** ? *Sunday preceding Ascension*, or ? *Passion Sunday*, Chrys.*stat*.19 tit.(2.188D).

[*]**ἐπιτάκτης, ὁ,** as adj., *domineering*; of character of those born under Aquarius, Hipp.*haer*.4.25(p.53.7; M.16.3087C).

ἐπιτακτικῶς, prob. f.l. for ἐπιτατικῶς, Chrys.*hom.6.3 in Ac*.(9.51D).

ἐπιτατικός, *emphatic*, Chrys.*hom.19.7 in Rom*.(9.653B); Isid.Pel.*epp*.5.245(M.78.1480D); Gr.Agr.*Eccl*.1.2(M.98.756B).

ἐπιτατικῶς, *emphatically*, Thdt.*Ps*.8:2(1.651); *ib*.91:6(1265); comp., Thphl.Ant.*Autol*.3.13(M.6.1140B); v. ἐπιτακτικῶς.

***ἐπίτατις, ἡ,** f.l. for ἐπίτασις = *increase*, Thdr.Mops.*Am*.1:3(M.66.249A).

ἐπιταχύνω, trans., *hasten on*; intrans., *make haste*, Dion.Al.*ep.can*.1(p.100.11; M.10.1276D); Jo.Ant.*relat.imp*.(p.125.15; M.83.1441C).

ἐπιτείν-ω, *direct*; a letter, *PLond*.1915.29 [saec.iv]; a wish for something, hence συντυχίαν ~ειν πρός τινα *wish* someone good fortune, *Mir.Artem*.35(p.56.17).

ἐπιτειχίζ-ω, 1. *fortify a position against*; met., *attack, assault* τῶν λογισμῶν τῶν ἀτόπων...[sc. τὴν διάνοιαν] ~όντων Chrys.*hom.11.4 in 1Cor*.(10.92A); **2.** *set up against*, ref. Christ's healings οὐκ ἂν δὲ εἰ ἐχθρὰ ἡ σὰρξ ἦν τῆς ψυχῆς, ἐπετείχισεν αὐτῇ τὴν ἐχθρὰν δι' ὑγείας ἐπισκευάζων Clem.*str*.3.17(p.244.15; M.8.1208B); Chrys.*hom.17.4 in Mt*.(7.228B); *ib.23.4*(289D); *ib.37.7*(423D); οἱ τῆς γενέσεως τὴν τυραννίδα ~οντες...τοῖς τῆς ἐκκλησίας δόγμασι *ib.75.4*(728C); πολλοὶ καὶ γένεσιν ἑαυτοῖς ~ουσι id.*hom.4.6 in 1Cor*.(10.32A); *ib.12.6*(106A); ἀνάγκην ~οντες τῇ τῆς προαιρέσεως ἐλευθερίᾳ *ib.22.4*(197C); *ib.26.2*(230D); ἐπιτειχίσωμεν εὐθυμίαν κατὰ τῆς...λύπης *ib.38.7*(361E); πολλὰ ἐπιτειχίσαντος τοῦ θεοῦ γίνεσθαι πρὸς τοῦτο id.*hom.4.5 in Heb*.(12.46B).

ἐπιτέλεια, ἡ, s.v.l., *perfection*, Chrys.ap.*cat.Mt*.5:19(p.469.9) for ἐπιμέλειαν id.*hom.16.4 in Mt*.(7.208D).

***ἐπιτελεύτιος,** *concluding*, Evagr.*h.e*.1.20(p.28.33; M.86.2476A).

ἐπιτελ-έω, A. *complete, fulfil* a prophecy, *1Clem*.3.1 etc.

B. *perform* religious rites; **1.** in gen. οἱ...τούτου [sc. Simon] μαθηταὶ μαγείας ~οῦσι καὶ ἐπαοιδάς Hipp.*haer*.6.20(p.148.1; M.16.3226A); ἀποτροπαίους ἱκετηρίας τῶν δεινῶν ~εῖν τοὺς Χριστιανοὺς κατηγορεῖ Philost.*h.e*.2.17(M.65.480A); of offering of sacrifice, Epiph.*ep.Arab*.ap.*haer*.78.23(p.473.11; M.42.736B); **2.** of Jewish worship προσφορὰς καὶ λειτουργίας ~εῖσθαι *1Clem*.40.2; θυσίας αὐτῷ δι' αἵματος...~εῖν *Diogn*.3.5; τὰ τῆς λατρείας ἐπετελεῖτο Eus.*d.e*.1.3(p.11.7; M.22.29A); *ib*.1.7(p.38.22; 73D); *ib*.1.10(p.49.17; 93A); **3.** *observe, celebrate* a festival (pagan), Pall.*v.Chrys*.16(p.96.8; M.47.54); (Christian) ~εῖν τὴν τοῦ μαρτυρίου αὐτοῦ ἡμέραν γενέθλιον *M.Polyc*.18.2; Eus.*h.e*.5.24.11(M.20.500A); CLaod.*can*.51; μνήμην τοῦ μακαριωτάτου Πέτρου παρὰ Σεβαστηνοῖς πρώτως ἀγομένην ἐπιτελέσας, καὶ τὰς συνήθεις παρ' αὐτῶν ~ουμένας τῶν...μαρτύρων μνήμας...συνδιαγαγὼν ἐκείνοις Gr.Nyss.*ep*.1(M.46.1001A); μὴ μετὰ τῶν Ἰουδαίων χρὴ τὸ πάσχα ~εῖν Epiph.*haer*.70.10(p.243.11; M.42.357A); Cyr.*ep*.76(p.27.20; 5².207B); ~εῖν ἑορτήν id.*Ps*.60:5(M.69.1113C); Dor.*doct*.23.1(M.88.1829B); **4.** *hold* a service συνάξεις ~ει Ath.*virg*.12(p.46.9; M.28.265A); Epiph.*exp.fid*.24(p.525.18; M.42.832A); **5.** *offer* prayer, CLaod.*can*.19; ~ούντων...τὴν εὐχήν Gr.Naz.*ep*.86(M.37.160A); *Const.App*.2.59.4; Eutych.*pasch*.8(M.86.2401A); **6.** *celebrate* eucharist τὴν τούτου μνήμην τοῦ τε σώματος αὐτοῦ καὶ τοῦ αἵματος τὴν ὑπόμνησιν ὁσημέραι ~οῦντες Eus.*d.e*.1.10(p.46.14; M.22.88C); τὴν ἁγίαν προσφορὰν ~εῖσθαι CLaod.*can*.19; οὔτε διάκονοι ἐν τῇ ἐκκλησιαστικῇ τάξει ἐπιστεύθησάν τι μυστήριον ~εῖν, ἀλλὰ μόνον διακονεῖν τὰ ~ούμενα Epiph.*haer*.79.4(p.478.31; M.42.745A); ὅταν... τὴν φρικωδεστάτην ἐπιτελῇ θυσίαν Chrys.*sac*.6.4(p.147.10; 1.424B); id.*Jud*.3.5(1.612B); Eustrat.*v.Eutych*.78(M.86.2364B); **7.** *perform* reading of liturg. lessons, *ib*.

ἐπιτέρπ-ω, 1. act., *give delight*, Synes.*Dion* 3(p.242.14; M.66.1121B); **2.** med., *rejoice in* μαρτύρων τιμαῖς ~ομαι Gr.Naz.*or*.24.3(M.35.1173B); ~εσθαι εἰς τὰς ὀρχήσεις Chrysipp.*enc.in Jo.Bapt*.(p.46.22).

***ἐπιτεταγμένως,** *in due order*, Bas.*hom.in Ps*.28(1.115C; M.29.284C, v.l. ἐπιτετευγμένως); cf.†Bas.*Is*.252(1.572B; M.30.564B).

***ἐπιτετηρημένως,** *of set purpose, carefully*, Bas.*reg.br*.222(2.489C; M.31.1229B); id.*reg.fus*.37.5(2.384C; M.31.1016C); †Bas.*bapt*.1.2.6(2.633D; M.31.1536B).

***ἐπιτέχνασμα, τό,** *device*, *Schol.* in *Can.App*.42(*Mon*.2 p.643).

ἐπιτηδειότης, ἡ, 1. *aptitude, fitness*; *propensity*, Aët.*synt*.32(p.358.25; M.42.544B); **2.** *faculty* ὁ υἱὸς...σοφία καὶ δύναμις καὶ δικαιοσύνη θεοῦ οὐχ ὡς ἕξις οὐδὲ ὡς ἐ., ἀλλ' οὐσία ζῶσα καὶ ἐνεργὴς Bas.*Eun*.2.17(1.252B; M.29.605B); ταῦτα [sc. σοφία κτλ.] ὑπάρχει ὁ μονογενής, οὐ καθάπερ...ἐ., ἀλλ' οὐσιωδῶς Didym.*Trin*.1.15(M.39.309B).

ἐπιτηδευτός, *artificial*, *manufactured*, *Can.App*.2; hence *designed, brought about by special provision* θεὸν φύσει ὄντα τεκεῖν [sc. BMV] ἀψευδῶς γεννήσει οὐ φυσικῇ οὔσῃ θεοῦ ἀλλ' ἐ. Leont.H.*Nest*.4.37(M.86.1709D).

***ἐπιτήμησις, ἡ,** v. ἐπιτίμησις.

***ἐπιτηρήσιμος,** *to be observed* ἐ. ἡμέραι *Hom.Clem*.19.22.

ἐπιτήρησις, ἡ, 1. *observation, investigation*, Eus.*h.e*.1.10.6(M.20.113A); Cyr.*Os*.44(3.75A); ἔθος τοῖς...προφήταις τὴν εἰς καρδίαν καὶ νοῦν ἐ., ἣν ἂν ποιοῖντο τυχόν,...φυλακὴν ἀποκαλεῖν, ἤγουν ἀκοήν id.*Abac*.59(3.574A); **2.** *observance* of, *careful attention* to ὁ...νόμος πλείστην ἔχει τὴν ἐ. περὶ θυσιῶν id.*Soph*.32(3.609C); λεπτὴν ἐφ' ἅπασι τοῖς ἀναγκαίοις ποιοῦνται τὴν ἐ. id.*ador*.13(1.454C); **3.** *carefulness, exactitude*, id.*Ps*.67:5(M.69.1144C); id.*Is*.4.4(2.673A); **4.** *observance*, Eus.*v.C*.3.18(p.85.14; M.20.1076A); σαββάτου ἡμέρας ἐ. id.*d.e*.1.6(p.25.13; M.22.52C); ἐ. τῶν...ἑορτῶν Cyr.*Am*.36(3.290D); **5.** *notice* ἀπόδειξις ἐξ ἐ. γραφικῶν, ὅτι ὡς θεὸς οὐδὲν τῶν κτισμάτων προσκυνεῖται id.*thes*.15(5¹.149B).

ἐπιτίθημι, [infin. ἐπιτίθειν, Thphn.*chron*.p.355(M.108.853B)]; **1.** *set upon, place on*, c. dat., sacrificial offerings on altar, Philost.*h.e*.7.4(M.65.541A); of ceremonial imposition of hands: by Moses on Joshua, Just.*dial*.49.6(M.6.584D); by offerers on sin-offerings; explained, Thdt.*qu.61 in Ex*.(1.168); in healing, confirmation of baptized, ordination, etc., v. χείρ; of making sign of cross, Chrys.*hom.87.2 in Mt*.(7.820B); *ib.87.3*(822A); **2.** *apply, instil* fear πᾶσιν ἐπιθεῖναι φόβον Thdt.*Ezech*.32:28(2.951); *ib*.32:32(952); **3.** med., *attack*; medic. πυρετὸς...ἐπετίθετο τῷ γέροντι Jo.Mosch.*prat*.1(M.87.2853A); **4.** *inflict* blows *on* πληγὰς τὰ σώματα...ἐπιθέμενοι Malchus *exc.gent*.4(p.572.31; M.113.788A).

ἐπιτίκτω, 1. *bear* children *in addition*, Philost.*h.e*.11.6(M.65.600B); **2.** pass., *be fulfilled, come to pass subsequently*, Gr.Nyss.*fat*.(M.45.172D).

***ἐπιτιμάζω,** *subject to penance*, †Jo.Jej.*poenit*.(M.88.1905B).

ἐπιτιμ-άω, *rebuke, censure, punish*; hence *subject to penitential discipline* σκεῦος...ἁγιασθὲν μηδεὶς...εἰς οἰκείαν χρῆσιν σφετεριζέσθω ...εἰ δέ τις φωραθείη, ~άσθω ἀφορισμῷ *Can.App*.73; ~ηθήσονται τρία ἔτη Bas.*ep*.199 *can*.38(3.295D; M.32.728C); ἕως χρόνου, ἢ καὶ ἥμισυ ~ᾶσθαι †Jo.Jej.*poenit*.(M.88.1905A).

ἐπιτίμησις, ἡ, 1. *rebuke, censure* ἐ. δέ ἐστι ψόγος ἐπ' αἰσχροῖς οἰκειῶν πρὸς τὰ καλά Clem.*paed*.1.9(p.134.33; M.8.341B); *ib*.1.11(p.147.6; 365A); δεῖ...τὴν ἐ. οὕτως δέχεσθαι, ὡς φάρμακον ἀναιρετικὸν πάθους Bas.*moral*.72.5(2.307D; M.31.849B); Chrys.*paralyt*.3(3.36D); **2.** *penance* ἐν τέσσαρσιν ἔτεσιν ὡρισμένη τοῖς πορνεύουσιν ἡ ἐ. Bas.*ep*.199 *can*.22(3.293B; M.32.724A); †Jo.Jej.*poenit*.(M.88.1905A) al.; **3.** *valuation*, ἐπιτήμ-, Ath.Scholast.*coll*.4.24(p.66).

***ἐπιτιμητικῶς,** *by way of reproof, chidingly*, Clem.*paed*.3.11(p.276.7; M.8.649A); Chrys.*hom.51.4 in Mt*.(7.525D); Cyr.*Lc*.9:61(*TU* p.98.14).

ἐπιτιμία, ἡ, 1. *punishment*, Clem.*paed*.3.2(p.244.28; M.8.576B); ὥσπερ...ἄψυχα θρησκεύουσιν, οὕτω καὶ τὴν ψυχὴν οὐκ ἔχειν λογικὴν νομίζοντες, αὐτόθεν ἔχουσι τῆς παραφροσύνης τὴν ἐ. ἐν ἀλόγοις καταριθμούμενοι Ath.*gent*.34(M.25.68B); id.*Ar*.2.42(M.26.236C); Max.

opusc.(M.91.29D); **2.** *penance* οὐ γὰρ ἁπλῶς πρὸς τὸ τῶν ἁμαρτημάτων μέτρον δεῖ καὶ τὴν ἐ. ἐπάγειν, ἀλλὰ καὶ τῆς τῶν ἁμαρτανόντων στοχάζεσθαι προαιρέσεως Chrys.*sac.*2.4(p.34.7; 1.374E); Niceph.Ur. *v.Sym.*221(M.86.3189C); **3.** *rebuke, censure*; ref. Mc.8:33, Epiph. *haer.*42.11(p.129.16; M.41.733C); Mac.Mgn.*apocr.*3.27(p.116.14); in gen., Epiph.*haer.*68.2(p.142.4; M.42.185C); **4.** *dignity, honour*, Athenag.*leg.*1.4(M.6.893A); of civic status, Bas.*ep.*148(3.238A; M.32.597C); of episcopal rank, *MAMA* 1.170(Laodicea, c. 340); CChalc. *act.*4(*ACO* 2.1.3 p.108.26; H.2.444A).

***ἐπιτιμιάζω**, *censure, place under discipline*, CChalc.*act.*4(*ACO* 2.1.2 p.115.9; H.2.421C).

ἐπιτίμιον, τό, *penalty*; in eccl. discipline, *Can.App.*74; Bas.*ep.* 199 *can.*21(3.292E; M.32.721A); *ib.*199 *can.*22(293B; M.724A); ὁ συνεγνωκὼς ἑκάστῳ τῶν προειρημένων ἁμαρτημάτων, καὶ μὴ ὁμολογήσας, ἀλλ' ἐλεγχθείς, τοῦ τοσούτου χρόνου, εἰς ὃν ἐργάτης τῶν κακῶν ἐπιτετίμηται, καὶ αὐτὸς ἔσται ἐν ἐ. *ib.*217 *can.*71(328A; M.801A); *ib.* 217 *can.*74(328C; M.804A); ὑποκεῖσθαι αὐτὸν κανονικῷ ἐ. CChalc.*can.* 25; εἰ θέλεις ἰατρείας τυχεῖν, εἰπέ μοι εἰς ἀλήθειαν τὰς πράξεις σου, ὅπως κἀγὼ ταύταις ἁρμόζοντα προσάγω τὰ ἐ. Jo.Mosch.*prat.*78(M.87. 2933A); μὴ κατὰ τὴν ἀκρίβειαν τῶν...κανόνων διορίζειν τὰ ἐ., ἀλλὰ κατὰ τὴν ποιότητα τοῦ προσώπου †Jo.Jej.*poenit.*(M.88.1904A); ἐὰν ...τὰ ἐ. αὐτῶν πληρώσωσιν, ὅσα ἂν ἔτη ἔλαβον παρὰ τοῦ δεσμεύσαντος αὐτούς *ib.*(1905C); ἐνδέχεται γὰρ τὸν ὀλιγαμάρτητον καὶ πρόθυμον μέγα λαβεῖν ἐ., ὅπως μὴ μόνον ἄφεσιν κακῶν, ἀλλὰ καὶ στέφανον λάβῃ †Jo.Jej.*serm.*(M.88.1925D).

***ἐπιτίμως**, *honourably*, Clem.*str.*4.12(p.285.5; M.8.1292C).

***ἐπιτινάσσω**, *overthrow*, Bas.*hom.*21.10(2.171C; M.31.560A).

***ἐπιτοπίως**, *on the spot*, Thphn.*chron.*p.332(M.108.801B).

***ἐπιτράνωσις, ἡ,** *clearness*, Or.*hom.8.3 in Jer.*(p.58.14; M.13.340B).

***ἐπιτραχήλιον, τό,** *stole* worn by bishops and priests, a broad strip of silk with aperture at one end for neck, hanging in front like a scapular, symbolizing rope on neck of Christ when taken to Calvary, ‡Bas.*h.myst.*19(p.262.10); cf. περιτραχήλιον, ‡Germ.CP *contempl.*(M.98.393C); right part representing reed in right hand of Christ, left part the carrying of Cross, *ib.*(393D); cf. ὁ ἱερεὺς... λαβὼν τὸ ἐ. καὶ σφραγίσας περιτίθεται αὐτὸ λέγων εὐλογητὸς ὁ θεὸς ὁ ἐκχέων τὴν χάριν αὐτοῦ ἐπὶ τοὺς ἱερεῖς αὐτοῦ *Lit.Chrys.*(p.355.28); λαβὼν τὸ ἐ. καὶ εὐλογήσας ἀσπάζεται *Lit.Chrys.*(M.63.903); ἱερεὺς λειτουργῶν χωρὶς ἐ. αἱρετικός ἐστιν· ἐπιτιμάσθω χρόνοις γ', μετανοίαις ρ' *Nomoc.*129.

***ἐπιτρεπίζω**, *prepare*, Thdt.*Is.*62:11(p.244.31; 2.387).

ἐπιτριβή, ἡ, 1. *vexatiousness, provocation* τοὺς ἐπὶ τῆς Ἄφρων χώρας διαστασιάζοντας εἰς τοσοῦτον συνέβαινεν ἐπιτριβῆς ἐλαύνειν Eus.*v.C.*1.45(p.29.3; M.20.960B); *ib.*4.54(p.139.27; 1205A); ἔσται...ἐ. τοῦ πονηροῦ πρὸς τὸ ἐπιστρέψαι πάλιν καὶ πόλεμον ἐνστήσασθαι Epiph. *haer.*66.58(p.94.31; M.42.116D); **2.** *evil conduct*; in gen., Or.*Cels.*4.70 (p.339.23; M.11.1140A); id.*comm.in Mt.*13.30(p.262.28; M.13.1173B); Mac.Mgn.*apocr.*4.25(p.208.11); **3.** *injury* to, c. genit., Or.*comm.in Gen.*ap.Eus.*p.e.*6.11(286C; M.12.61A); **4.** *oppression* τὴν παρὰ τοῦ δουκὸς ἐ. καὶ ἐξουσίαν Ath.*h.Ar.*62(p.218.5; M.25.768D).

ἐπιτρίβ-ω, 1. *aggravate*; poverty, Chrys.*hom.15.8 in Mt.*(7.198E); στάσιν ἐ. id.*hom.11.1 in 1Cor.*(10.87C); ἀλλοτρίας συμφορὰς...ἐ. Isid.Pel.*epp.*5.210(M.78.1457B); **2.** *stir up, incite*, Or.*comm.in Gen.* ap.Eus.*p.e.*6.11(289D; ἐπέτρεψεν M.12.68C); of poets 'expelled' by Plato ὡς ∼οντας τοὺς νέους id.*Cels.*4.36(p.307.14; M.11.1085A); ἐ. εἰς τὴν ἀσέβειαν Ath.*h.Ar.ep.*2(p.181.20; M.25.693A); Chrys.*hom.87.4 in Mt.*(7.823C); **3.** *annoy, provoke*, Or.*hom.12.5 in Jer.*(p.92.8; M. 13.385B); id.*Jo.*13.32(31; p.256.15; ἐπιθορυβηθείσης M.14.453C).

***ἐπιτρίζ-ω**, *grind* teeth, Cyr.*ador.*3(1.86A); σατανᾶς τοὺς ὀδόντας ∼ων τοῖς ἁγίοις *ib.*4(109D); id.*Jo.*5.3(4.498B); abs. Παύλῳ τοσοῦτον ἐπέτριζον τῶν Ἰουδαίων τινές *ib.*10.2(913E); id.*Mich.*34(3.420D).

***ἐπίτριμμα, τό,** *cosmetic*, Ephr.3.426F; Chrys.*hom.6.5 in Mt.*(7. 96A); τῶν παρειῶν τὰ ἐ. id.*hom.18.4 in Jo.*(8.110A); Isid.Pel.*epp.*3. 133(M.78.833A).

ἐπιτροπία, ἡ, *governance*, Clem.*str.*1.21(p.85.23; M.8.873A).

***ἐπιτρούλλιον, τό,** *skull-cap* worn by deacon, ‡Sophr.H.*liturg.* 8(M.87.3988C).

ἐπιτροχάδην, 1. *cursorily*, Cyr.*ador.*4(1.134D); id.*glaph.Gen.*5(1. 155A); **2.** *glibly, fluently*, Men.*exc.Rom.*8(p.195.5; M.113.888C).

***ἐπιτρυγάω**, *glean* grapes, Or.*fr.44 in Jer.*1:22(p.255.3; M.13. 632C).

ἐπιτυγχάνω, *attain, gain one's end*; of receiving answer to prayer, Or.*or.*13.2(p.326.13; M.11.453C); *Hom.Clem.*11.13; *CIG* 8874(Syria).

***ἐπίφ (ἐπιφί),** an Egyptian month approximating to late June and early July, CEph.(431)*act.*2(*ACO* 1.1.3 p.53.9, v.l. ἐπιφί H.1. 1465A).

ἐπιφαίν-ω, 1. *reveal, make manifest* ὁ θεὸς λόγος ἐπέφανεν ἑαυτὸν κατὰ τὸν ὑπογραφέντα τῆς ἐνανθρωπήσεως αὐτοῦ χρόνον Eus.*d.e.*8 proem.(p.351.12; M.22.572B); pass., *appear, be manifest*; of God, *1Clem.*59.4; of Christ, Or.*hom.19.10 in Jer.*(p.165.13; M.13.484B); in Inc. ὁ κάτω ἐπιφανεὶς καὶ τῶν πατρῴων κόλπων μὴ χωρισθεὶς †Hipp.*theoph.*7(p.261.8; M.10.857C); *V.Aberc.*16; Meth.*Porph.*1 (p.503.10; M.18.397D); **2.** med., *appear* σώματα ἐν οἷς ∼ονται πρὸ τῆς ἀναστάσεως Meth.*res.*3.18(p.416.4); δαίμονες καθ' ἃς βούλονται μορφὰς ∼όμενοι *Hom.Clem.*9.14; ref. images τίς ἡ χρεία τῆς μορφῆς, καὶ μή, πρὶν πλασθῆναι ταῦτα, διὰ πάσης...ὕλης ∼εσθαι τὸν θεόν; Ath. *gent.*20(M.25.41A); **3.** act. intrans., *appear*, Iren.*haer.*1.8.2(M.7. 524B); of Inc., Hipp.*haer.*7.28(p.209.5; M.16.3322B) cit. s. δόκησις; Eus.*d.e.*8.2(p.383.4; M.22.620C); Cyr.*Ps.*1:3(M.69.720A); id.*Abac.* 36(3.552B).

ἐπιφάνεια, ἡ, I. *appearance, manifestation*;

A. of God in OT; **1.** a proof of divine election τῆς τοῦ θεοῦ ἐ. ... συστήσαντος πρότερον μὲν τὸν Ἰουδαϊσμὸν μετὰ δ' αὐτὸν τὸν Χριστιανισμόν Or.*Cels.*3.14(p.213.28; M.11.937B); ref. Dt.24:3; no further appearance of God to Jews because they are rejected, id.*hom.4.2 in Jer.*(p.24.30; M.13.288C); **2.** appearances of second Person, to prophets ἐ. οὐ μόνον ἀγγέλων ἀλλὰ καὶ θεοῦ ἐν Χριστῷ id.*Jo.*6.4(2; p.110.20; M.14.204D); ref. Gen.18:1ff. ὁ σωτὴρ αὐτὸς μετὰ τῶν δύο ἀγγέλων τὴν ἑαυτοῦ ἐ. τῷ Ἀβραὰμ ἐπεδαψιλεύσατο Const.*ep.*ap.Eus. *v.C.*3.43(p.101.1; M.20.1116B); miraculous element should lead pagans to accept manifestation of God in Ex.3:2; 19:18; 20:18, Clem.*str.*6.3(p.447.6; M.9.249B).

B. of Christ's first coming; **1.** in gen., Clem.*prot.*1(p.7.27; M.8. 61C); id.*str.*6.17(p.515.1; M.9.393B); ἡ ἐ. τοῦ σωτηρίου λόγου Afric. *chron.*1(M.10.65A); Or.*Cels.*8.12(p.229.31; M.11.1533B); ἡ θεία αὐτοῦ πρὸς ἡμᾶς ἐ. Ath.*inc.*1.1(M.25.97A); Cyr.*Is.*5.5(2.879B); Thdt.*Ps.* 89:16(1.1255); **2.** prophesied in OT; **a.** specific texts: Ps.18:3–6, Just.*1apol.*40.1(M.6.388C); announced by bells on high priest's tunic, ref. Ex.28:29 etc., Clem.*str.*5.6(p.351.19; M.9.64B); Ps.109:3, ‡Ath.*Ar.*4.28(p.77.9; M.26.512C) cit. s. ἑωσφόρος; Ps.79:3, Sever. *appar.*5(M.65.20A); Pr.8:22, Gel.Cyz.*h.e.*2.17.3(M.85.1265C); Is., Proc.G.*Is.*40:1–8(M.87.2332B); *ib.*49:1–13(2461C); **b.** interprn. μετὰ ...τὴν δεσποτικὴν ἐ., ἀφαιρεθεισῶν τῶν σφραγίδων, τὰ γὰρ πράγματα μαρτυρεῖ τοῖς λόγοις, καὶ πλεῖστοι ἐξ Ἰουδαίων τῶν προρρήσεων ἔμαθον τὴν διάνοιαν, καὶ τὰ ἔθνη...ἀναγινώσκουσι τὸ βιβλίον, ὃ τοῖς ἀπίστοις Ἰουδαίοις ἐσφραγισμένον ἔτι μεμένηκε Thdt.*Is.*29:11(p.117. 16; 2.303); ref. Dt.18:18 ὡς γὰρ ἀσθενεστέροις τῆς κρείττονος θεωρίας τὴν ἀνθρωπίνην αὐτοῖς ἐ. ἐπηγγείλατο Proc.G.*Dt.*18:11(M.87. 920A); **3.** effects: destruction of the passions, Bas.*ep.*260.7(3.400A; M.32.964D); and sin, Isid.Pel.*epp.*1.436(M.78.421D); and death τὴν ...αἰτίαν τῆς σωματικῆς ἐ. αὐτοῦ...τὸ φθαρτὸν εἰς ἀφθαρσίαν μεταβαλεῖν Ath.*inc.*20.1(M.25.129C); *ib.*29.3(145C); end of the Law οὐ γὰρ ἔτι μετὰ τὴν Χριστοῦ ἐ. ἐκ τῶν ἐθνῶν ἔλαβε προσηλύτους ὡς τὸ πρίν Oecum.*Apoc.*12:1–2(p.136); end of power of paganism, Eus. *d.e.*1.6(p.31.12; M.22.61B); Ath.*inc.*55.3(193B); destruction of magic, *ib.*47.2(180D); ref. idols, etc. μετὰ δὲ τὴν τοῦ σωτῆρος ἡμῶν ἐ., τὸ μὲν ἐκείνων διελήλεγκται ψεῦδος, δέδεικται δὲ τῆς ἀληθείας τὸ κάλλος Thdt.*Is.*2:2(p.12.32; 2.183); supreme revelation of God's counsel (cf. Rom.16:25) μυστήριον χρόνοις αἰωνίοις σεσιγημένον φανερωθὲν δὲ νῦν ἐν ταῖς προφητικαῖς φωναῖς καὶ τῇ τοῦ κυρίου ἡμῶν Ἰησοῦ Χριστοῦ ἐ. Or.*Cels.*2.4(p.131.3; M.11.801D); ref. Gal.5:6 διδάσκειν μὲν οὖν βούληται, ὡς ἡ Χριστοῦ ἐ. καινήν τινα καὶ τὴν μόνην πίστιν ἅπασιν ἀνθρώποις ἐξεύρετο Didym.*Trin.*1.7(M.39.276A); moral change μετὰ τὴν ἐ. τοῦ Χριστοῦ ὁμοδίαιτοι γινόμενοι, καὶ ὑπὲρ τῶν ἐχθρῶν εὐχόμενοι Just.*1apol.*14.3(M.6.348C); *A.Thom.*A 39(p.156.20); τὴν... νύμφην τὴν...ἐκκλησίαν...ἐξήγειρεν καὶ ἐξανέστησεν θεοῦ...νεύματι καὶ τῆς Ἰησοῦ Χριστοῦ δυνάμεως ἐπιφανείᾳ Eus.*h.e.*10.4.54(M.20. 869D); **4.** Gnost. διὰ τῆς τοῦ σωτῆρος ἐ. ἡ σοφία ⟨ἀπαθὴς⟩ γίνεται καὶ τὰ ἔξω κτίζεται Clem.*exc.Thdot.*45(p.121.10; M.9.680C).

C. *incarnate life, humanity* of Christ, ref. Mt.8:29 αἱ πονηραὶ δυνάμεις...αἱροῦνται γενέσθαι πυρίκαυστοι μᾶλλον, ἢ ὑπὸ τῆς ἐν σαρκὶ Χριστοῦ ἐ. κατακρίνεσθαι †Bas.*Is.*225(1.549E; M.30.512B); τοῦ τριακοστοῦ ἔτους τῆς κατὰ σάρκα ἐ. τοῦ...σωτῆρος *Chron.Pasch.*p.203(M. 92.500A).

D. of partic. manifestations of incarnate Christ: to apostles after Resurrection ἐβεβαιώθησαν διὰ τῆς ἐ. αὐτοῦ πρὸς τὸ πιστεύειν ἔτι μᾶλλον καὶ βεβαιότερον παρὰ τὸ πρότερον ὅτι υἱὸς ἦν τοῦ θεοῦ Or.*Cels.* 2.39(p.164.8; M.11.861A); to S. Paul διὰ τῆς τεραστίου ἐ. πεπίστευκεν Or.*Jo.*13.61(59; p.293.27; M.14.516D); cf.id.*Cels.*5.8(p.8.23; M.11. 1192C); at his baptism σήμερον τὰ ἁλμυρὰ ὕδατα τῆς θαλάσσης γλυκέα μεταβλήσκονται τῇ ἐ. τοῦ ἰδίου δεσπότου *Rit.Epiph.*(p.418).

E. of second coming; in gen. οὐδεὶς ἄνθρωπος γνώσεται τὴν ἡμέραν ἐκείνην τὴν μεγάλην καὶ ἐ. τὴν κατέχουσαν κρῖναι τὸν κόσμον *Apoc.Esd.*(p.27); ἐν τῇ...ἐ. τῇ ὑστέρᾳ *A.Thom.*A 28(p.145.7); ἡ ἐ. τῆς παρουσίας Χριστοῦ Or.*Jo.*2.7(4; p.61.22; M.14.121A); *ib.*20.11 (p.340.26; 597A); τὴν δευτέραν αὐτοῦ πάλιν πρὸς ἡμᾶς ἔνδοξον...ἐ. Ath.*inc.*56.3(M.25.196A); in prophecy, ref. Is.66:18 τοῦτο δὲ λέγει τὴν ἡμέραν τῆς ἐ. αὐτοῦ *2Clem.*17.4; Thdt.*Ps.*9:18(1.671); ἡ ἀνθρωπεία φύσις ὁδηγηθῆναι πρὸς τὴν ἀλήθειαν παρακαλεῖ τοὺς εὑρισκομένους ἀνθρώπους ἐν τῇ τοῦ σωτῆρος ἡμῶν ἐ. *ib.*89:16(1255); contrasted with first coming, ref. feast of Christ's baptism οὐ μία τίς ἐστιν ἐ., ἀλλὰ δύο. μία μὲν ἡ παροῦσα αὕτη καὶ γενομένη, δευτέρα δὲ ἡ μέλλουσα, καὶ κατὰ τὴν συντέλειαν ἐνδόξως γενησομένη Chrys.*bapt.*2(2.369C); δύο δείκνυσιν ἐνταῦθα ἐ.·...ἡ μὲν προτέρα χάριτος, ἡ δὲ δευτέρα ἀνταποδόσεως καὶ τοῦ δικαίου id.*hom.5.1 in Tit.*(11.757E); inspiring fear τὴν ἐπὶ τῷ τέλει τῶν αἰώνων φοβερὰν αὐτοῦ ἐ. Gr.Nyss.*Eun.*4(2 p.63.10; M.45.633D); ‡Gr.Nyss.*or.2 in Gen.1:26*(M.44.289B); †Bas.Sel.*or.* 40.1(M.85.453B); to be prepared for by practice of virtue, Chrys. *hom.9.3 in 2Tim.*(11.718B); χαλεπῶς μὲν ἡμᾶς ἡ ἀθυμία διέθηκεν. ... τῆς δὲ δεσποτικῆς ἐ. ἡ μνήμη φάρμακον ἀλεξίκακόν μοι γεγένηται Thdt. *ep.*55(4.111); ref. millenarianism of followers of Nepos τινων διδασκάλων τοὺς ἁπλουστέρους ἀδελφοὺς ἡμῶν οὐδὲν ἐώντων ὑψηλὸν καὶ μεγαλεῖον φρονεῖν περὶ τῆς ἐνδόξου καὶ ἀληθῶς ἐνθέου τοῦ κυρίου ἡμῶν ἐ. ... ἀλλὰ μικρὰ καὶ θνητὰ καὶ οἷα τὰ νῦν Dion.Al.ap.Eus.*h.e.* 7.24.5(M.20.693C); also of individual judgement, exeg. 1Tim.6:14 'μέχρι τῆς ἐ. τοῦ κυρίου...'Ιησοῦ Χριστοῦ'· τουτέστι, μέχρι τῆς σῆς τελευτῆς, μέχρι τῆς ἐξόδου Chrys.*hom.18.1 in 1Tim.*(11.654A).

F. of manifestation of H. Ghost at Christ's baptism οὐκ ἀνθρωπίνην ὁμοίωσιν ἐνταῦθα τοῦ θεοῦ παρειληφότος, ἀλλὰ τῆς περιστερᾶς, ὅτι τὴν ἀφέλειαν καὶ τὸ πρᾶον τῆς νέας ἐ. τοῦ πνεύματος ἐβούλετο δεῖξαι τῷ τῆς περιστερᾶς ὁμοιώματι Clem.*fr.*57(p.226.24; M.9.765C).

G. of Christ's spiritual presence φρόνιμοι ψυχαί,...τὴν ἄγνοιαν ἐξελαύνουσι καὶ ζητοῦσι τὴν ἀλήθειαν καὶ τοῦ διδασκάλου τὴν ἐ. ἀναμένουσι Clem.*str.*5.3(p.337.8; M.9.36A); ref. interpretation of scripture ὁμολογῶ κατ' ἐμαυτὸν μὴ δύνασθαι αὐτὰ [sc. τὰ γράμματα] διηγήσασθαι, ἀλλὰ δεῖσθαι, ὡς προεῖπον, ἐπιφανείας τῆς δυνάμεως 'Ιησοῦ...ἵνα ἡ ἐ. αὐτοῦ ποιήσῃ φῶς ἐπὶ τοῦ προσώπου τῆς ψυχῆς μου Or.*hom.19.11 in Jer.*(p.167.1; M.13.485C); of illumination by grace, †Bas.*Is.*138(1.476A; M.30.344A); to be prepared for by practice of virtue, ref. 2Tim.4:8 ὁ ἀγαπῶν αὐτοῦ τὴν ἐ. πάντα πράξει ὥστε καὶ πρὸ ἐκείνης τῆς καθολικῆς γενέσθαι αὐτῷ τὴν μερικήν Chrys.*hom.9.3 in 2Tim.*(11.718B).

H. of appearances of spirits; **1.** of good angels, Afric.*ep.Or.*1 (p.79.6; M.11.44A); Clem.*str.*1.21(p.77.15; M.8.852B); Celsus rejects biblical accounts of angelic appearances after Resurrection but accepts their appearance to pagans, Or.*Cels.*5.57(p.60.18; M.11. 1272B); of a vision before birth of Macrina ἔκ τινος ἐ. ἐπωνομάσθη Gr.Nyss.*v.Macr.*(p.372.4; M.46.961A); ref. vision of Cornelius, Eus. *h.e.*2.3.3(M.20.144B); *Chron.Pasch.*p.229(M.92.556B); **2.** of devils; leading to sin, Just.*1apol.*5.2(M.6.336A); *ib.*14.1(348B); produced by idols, Ath.*gent.*19(M.25.40C); εἰ δὲ ἡ ἐπικειμένη μορφὴ αἰτία γίνεται τῆς θείας ἐ. τίς ἡ χρεία τῆς ὕλης,...καὶ μὴ μᾶλλον δι' αὐτῶν τῶν φύσει ζώων, ὧν εἰσι μορφαὶ τὰ γλύμματα, τὸν θεὸν ἐπιφαίνεσθαι; *ib.*20(41A); *ib.*21(41C).

I. of miracles οὐκ ὀλίγαι θεραπεῖαι τῷ 'Ιησοῦ ὀνόματι καὶ ἄλλαι τινὲς ἐ. οὐκ εὐκαταφρόνητοι ἐπιτελοῦνται Or.*Cels.*3.28(p.225.14; M.11. 956A).

J. as name of festival; **1.** of Christ's baptism taken as a manifestation of Trin. δευτέρα δὲ ἑορτή, ἡ ἐ. Χριστοῦ...καθ' ἣν ἐν τῷ 'Ιορδάνῃ παραγινόμενος ἔδειξε πᾶσιν ἀνθρώποις τῆς...αὐτοῦ εὐσπλαγχνίας τὴν συγκατάβασιν· ἐν ᾗ καὶ φωνὴ πατρὸς ἐξ οὐρανοῦ ἦλθε...ἀλλὰ καὶ τὸ πνεῦμα...ἐλθὸν ἔμεινεν ἐπ' αὐτόν, τῆς ὁμοουσίου τριάδος... ἐπιφανείσης ‡Chrys.*ascens.*4(3.783D); as greatest of feasts, ref. Tit. 2:11, *ib.*; Gr.Ant.*bapt.*1(M.10.1177C); rel. to Nativity τίνος ἕνεκεν οὐχὶ ἡ ἡμέρα καθ' ἣν ἐτέχθη, ἀλλ' ἡ ἡμέρα καθ' ἣν ἐβαπτίσθη, ἐ. λέγεται;...ἐπειδὴ οὐχ ὅτε ἐτέχθη, τότε πᾶσιν ἐγένετο κατάδηλος, ἀλλ' ὅτε ἐβαπτίσατο Chrys.*bapt.*2(2.369D,E); **2.** indeterminate τῆς... δεσποτικῆς ἐ. ἡ μνήμη Thdt.*ep.*54(4.111).

II. *outward appearance, aspect,* of literal sense of scripture ἡ τοῦ γράμματος ἐ. Thdt.*Ps.*95:1(1.1289); of appearances from which mind rises to God, ‡Proc.G.*Pr.*30:17(M.87.1528D).

III. *splendour,* in soul, through imitation of saints, Gr.Naz.*or.* 7.14(M.35.772C); of worshippers, Proc.G.*Num.*7:1(M.87.809A).

***ἐπιφάνιος**, **A.** *of Epiphany* ἡ ἐ. [sc. ἡμέρα] *Const.App.*5.13.2.

B. τὰ ἐ. *Epiphany*; feast; **1.** of Nativity τὰ ἐ. καλῶς εἴρηται ἡ ἔνσαρκος γέννησις τοῦ σωτῆρος..., ἐπιφανέντος τοῖς ποιμέσι καὶ τῷ κόσμῳ διὰ τῆς τῶν ἀγγέλων μαρτυρίας· ἐπεφάνη δὲ καὶ τῇ Μαρίᾳ καὶ τῷ 'Ιωσήφ. ἐν ἐκείνῃ δὲ τῇ ὥρᾳ καὶ ὁ ἀστὴρ ἐφάνη ἐν τῇ ἀνατολῇ τοῖς μάγοις. ... καὶ αὐτὸ τὸ ῥῆμα τῶν ἐ. ἐποιεῖτο τὴν ἐπωνυμίαν ἐκ τοῦ τὸν 'Ηρῴδην λέγειν 'τοῦ φανέντος ἀστέρος' Epiph.*haer.*51.22 (p.287.5); *ib.*(p.288.8); date calculated as 6 Jan. from Lc.3:23 τῆς τῶν γενεθλίων αὐτοῦ ἡμέρας τουτέστιν ἐ., ἥτις τυγχάνει πέμπτῃ εἰς ἕκτην ἐπιφώσκουσα 'Ιανουαρίου μηνός *ib.*51.27(p.298.19; M.41.936C); *ib.*51.16(p.270.16; 920A); as feast even if falling on Wednesday or Saturday, id.*exp.fid.*22(p.523.11; M.42.828B); **2.** of Christ's baptism; in gen., CChalc.*act.*1(*ACO* 2.1.1 p.187.12; H.2.233E); *Chron. Pasch.*p.209(M.92.512C); a manifestation of all three Persons of Trin. (v. ἐπιφάνεια), *Const.App.*8.33.7; οἱ δὲ 'Ιεροσολυμῖται ὡς ἐκ τοῦ μακαρίου Λουκᾶ λέγοντος περὶ τοῦ βαπτισθῆναι τὸν κύριον ἀρχόμενος ὡς ἐτῶν λ', τοῖς ἐ. ποιοῦσι τὴν γένναν. ... ἐξ ἀρχαιόθεν δὲ ἡ ἐκκλησία, ἵνα μὴ τὰς δύο ἑορτὰς ὁμοῦ ποιοῦσα λήθην ποιήσῃ μιᾶς ἐξ αὐτῶν, ἐνομοθέτησε μεσάζειν δώδεκα ἡμέρας...καὶ οὕτως γίνεσθαι τὴν ἑορτὴν τῶν ἐ. Cosm.Ind.*top.*5(M.88.197B); **3.** indefinite, context not showing to which mystery it refers, Chrys.*Jud.*4.3(1.620B); a day of gen. Communion, id.*hom.3.4 in Eph.*(11.22B); prob. Christmas ἑορτὴ πρώτη τὰ ἐ. id.*pent.*1.1(2.458D); ‡Pall.*h.mon.*34.10(M.34.1257C; -ειῶν p.97.3).

ἐπίφασις, ἡ, *becoming visible*; *appearance* of something high in the field of vision, ref. a perspective drawing ἐντεῦθεν ἐπιφάσεις καὶ ὑποφάσεις καὶ φάσεις σώζονται Clem.*str.*6.7(p.460.10; M.9.277C).

***ἐπίφαυσις**, ἡ, *daybreak*, Epiph.*haer.*70.12(p.245.28; M.42.365A); τοῦ φωτὸς τῆς ζωῆς τὴν ἐ. Isid.Pel.*epp.*1.357(M.78.385C).

***ἐπιφαύ-ω**, *dawn* ἡμέρας ~ούσης *A.Jo.*61(p.180.25); *A.Thom.*A 34 (p.151.11); οἱ ~σαι τὸν ἥλιον αὐτοῖς εὐχόμενοι Gr.Nyss.*or.catech.*34 (p.128.14; ἐπιφᾶναι M.45.85C) (last two instances perh. from ἐπιφαύσκω *LS*).

ἐπιφάω, in form ἐπιφέειν, *dawn*, *A.Thom.*A 29(p.146.4, vv.ll. ἐπιφαίνειν, ἐπιφαίειν).

ἐπιφήμισμα, τό, *acclamation*, ‡Epiph.*hom.*1(M.43.432D).

ἐπιφθάνω, **1.** *anticipate, forestall*, Malchus *exc.gent.*1(p.571.17; M. 113.784D); **2.** *rush upon*, Agath.*v.Gr.Ill.*20.

***ἐπιφιλανθρωπεύομαι**, *relax one's harshness*, *M.Pion.*11.4.

***ἐπιφιλονεικέω**, *oppose*, Chrys.*stat.*14.1(2.142C).

***ἐπιφλύζω**, *burst out*, ‡Sophr.H.*v.m.Cyr.et Jo.*8(M.87.3681C).

ἐπιφοιτ-άω, *visit, be present at*; **1.** in gen. ἄνθρωπος καθεύδων... ψυχῆς ἀκοιμήτῳ λόγῳ τοῖς πᾶσιν ~ᾷ Mac.Mgn.*apocr.*3.14(p.92.3); of mediated presence τοῖς...τῶν ἐθνῶν ἄρχουσιν αὐθεντίᾳ βασιλικῇ διὰ τῶν...γραμμάτων ~ᾷ Eus.*v.C.*3.51(p.99.13; M.20.1112B); **2.** *come* to mind, *frequent* the soul; of evil thoughts, Meth.*res.*2.3(p.334.11; M. 41.1168A); σωτήριον λόγον πολλοῖς μὲν ~ῶντα Gr.Thaum.*pan.Or.*6 (p.16.26; M.10.1072A); Ammonas *ep.*3(p.440.2); **3.** with hostile intent, *attack*, Const.*or.s.c.*15(p.175.16; M.20.1277B); *ib.*17(p.179.2; 1285B); **4.** of divine visitation; **a.** pagan οἱ νομιζόμενοι θεοὶ τοῖς τινων ~ῶντες μέλεσιν Tat.*orat.*18(p.20.19; M.6.848A); Clem.*str.*4.25 (p.317.15; M.8.1364C); ref. presence of the divine in images εἰ διὰ τὴν ἐπιστήμην ~ᾷ τὸ θεῖον τοῖς γλύμμασι, τίς πάλιν ἡ χρεία τῆς ὕλης, οὔσης τῆς ἐπιστήμης ἐν τοῖς ἀνθρώποις; Ath.*gent.*20(M.25.41B); **b.** of Inc. υἱός...θεοῦ δεῦρο ἐπιφοιτήσας σεσάρκωται καταλιπὼν τὰ οὐράνια Isid.Pel.*epp.*1.139(M.78.273D); **c.** of grace τοῖς μὲν ~ᾷ καὶ παραμένει· τῶν δὲ ἀποφοιτᾷ· εἰς δὲ τοὺς οὐδὲ τὴν ἀρχὴν καθίεται *ib.*3.271 (952A); **d.** of H. Ghost's descent at Pentecost, Evagr.*h.e.*1.3(p.8.18; M.86.2428A); in consecration of eucharistic elements ὁ ἄρτος διὰ τὸ ~ῶν αὐτῷ πνεῦμα ἄρτος οὐράνιος γίνεται Chrys.*hom.45.2 in Jo.*(8. 264A); ἵνα ἐπιφοιτῆσαν τῇ...αὐτοῦ παρουσίᾳ ἁγιάσῃ καὶ ποιήσῃ τὸν μὲν ἄρτον τοῦτον σῶμα ἅγιον Χριστοῦ *Lit.Jac.*(p.206.9); Jo.D.*f.o.*4.13 (M.94.1141A); *ib.*(1145A).

ἐπιφοίτησις, ἡ, *visitation*; **1.** of demonic possession δαιμόνων εἰσὶν ἐ. Tat.*orat.*17(p.18.25; M.6.844A); as cause of pagan prophesying (ref. oracles), Eus.*d.e.*5 proem.(p.208.1; ἐμφοιτήσεως M.22.345A); **2.** of divine visitation; **a.** of providential guidance κατὰ πρόνοιαν καὶ ἐ. θεοῦ Hier.(tr.Sophr.Pal.)*vir.ill.*38(p.30.10; M.*PL.*23.688B); **b.** of advent of Christ παρουσίαν λέγει οὐ τὴν ἐπιφανῆ...τὴν... συντέλειαν, ἀλλὰ τὴν κατὰ διαφόρους καιροὺς ἐ., δι' ἧς ὀπτανόμενος τὴν παρ' αὐτοῦ βοήθειαν παρέξει Or.*fr.in Mt.*10:23(p.98); of physical presence of incarnate Christ in earthly ministry, Gr.Naz.*or.*37.1 (M.36.281A); of Inc., Hesych.H.*fr.Ac.*13:33(M.93.1388C); Oecum. *Apoc.*5:1(p.77); heret., of descent of Logos on man Jesus, Cyr.*deip. BMV* 3(p.20.11; M.76.257D); **c.** of visitation of H. Ghost, in inspiring prophets, ‡Hipp.*consumm.*1(p.289.3; M.10.905A); on baptized through imposition of hands, †Ath.*fr.*(M.26.1221C); on exorcists, *Const.App.*8.26.2 cit. s. ἐπορκιστής; upon Christ at his baptism, symbolized by chrismation of those baptized, Cyr.H. *catech.*21.1; as cause of prophesying, renewal, and heavenly blessings, Didym.*Trin.*2.6(M.39.533A); on Christ, Chrys.*hom.29.2 in*

Jo.(8.166B); bestowed on believers, id.*hom.7.9 in 1Cor.*(10.64E); in baptism τὴν ἐ., τὴν ἀπὸ τοῦ βαπτίσματος καὶ πρὸ τῶν μυστηρίων ἐγγινομένην ἡμῖν *ib.30.2*(271A); on apostles at Pentecost, Isid.Pel. *epp.*1.169(M.78.293B); giving them τὴν τοῦ βαπτίσματος αὐτοῦ χάριν Anast.S.*qu.et resp.*148(M.89.801D); ref. conception of Christ, Procl. CP *annunt.*5(M.85.444D); Jo.D.*haer.Nest.*1(M.95.189A) cit. s. ἐπισκίασις; in consecration of eucharistic elements τὴν ἐ. τοῦ ἁγίου πνεύματος προσεδόκων, ὅπως τῇ αὐτοῦ...παρουσίᾳ τὸν...ἄρτον καὶ οἶνον...τὸ σῶμα καὶ αἷμα τοῦ...Χριστοῦ ἀποφήνῃ τε καὶ ἀναδείξῃ ‡Procl.CP *tract.*(M.65.852A); Eus.Al.*serm.*16.3(M.86.417C); visible to a holy man, Jo.Mosch.*prat.*25(M.87.2872A); in response to epiclesis, *Lit.Jac.*(p.224.5); on deacon at ordination, *Euchol.*(p.209); **3.** of angelic visitations, Meth.*fr.9 in Job*(p.513n.; M.18.405A); **4.** *visitation, unexpected turn* of fortune, Thphyl.*exc.Rom.*3(p.223.27; M.113. 929D); **5.** *appearance* of stars in sky, Tat.*orat.*26(p.28.1; M.6.861C).

ἐπιφορά, ἡ, *impact, attack*; hence divine *visitation*, of H. Ghost upon men in prophecy, Eus.*d.e.*5 proem.(p.207.11; M.22.344C); of a calamity, Marc.Er.*opusc.*2.58(M.65.940A); *ib.*7.19(1097D).

ἐπιφορέω, *put upon*; *make pregnant*, CAnc.(325)*can.*25.

***ἐπιφροντίζω,** f.l. οὐκ ἐπεφρόντιζον Eust.*engast.*9(M.18.629A) for οὐκέτι ἐφρόντιζον (p.27.33).

[*]**ἐπιφυλλάς, ἡ,** = ἐπιφυλλίς, *grapes left for gleaning*, ‡Max.*cap. al.*167(M.90.1440C).

***ἐπιφυτικός,** *innate*, Gr.Nyss.*hom.1 in Cant.*(M.44.769D).

ἐπιφώνησις, ἡ, *utterance of spells, incantation*; to be eschewed by Christians, *Const.App.*2.62.2; *ib.*8.32.11; among works of Satan renounced at baptism, Ephr.3.215D.

***ἐπιφωνητέον,** *one must repeat*, Epiph.*haer.*16.4(p.213.9; M.41. 253B).

***ἐπιφωράω,** *discover by research*, Sophr.H.*or.*9(M.87.3364B); *discover, catch* in guilty action, Philost.*h.e.*11.3(M.65.597A).

ἐπιφώσκ-ω, *dawn, begin to grow light*, *Hom.Clem.*3.1; Eus.*qu. Marin.*2.1(M.22.941A); ref. pre-Easter fast ὅλην τὴν ἑβδομάδα τινὲς ἀχρὶ ἀλεκτρυόνων κλαγγῆς τῆς κυριακῆς ~ούσης. ... ἔν τισι δὲ τόποις τὴν μετὰ τὴν πέμπτην ἀγρυπνοῦσιν ~ουσαν εἰς τὸ προσάββατον καὶ τὴν κυριακὴν μόνας Epiph.*fid.*22(p.523.23; M.42.828C); id.*haer.*50.2 (p.247.11; M.41.888A); ref. date of Nativity πέμπτῃ Ἰανουαρίου ἑσπέρᾳ εἰς ἕκτην ~ουσα *ib.*51.24(p.293.2); *ib.*68.6(p.146.28; M.42. 193C); so of beginning of day including period from previous sunset to dawn, Cyr.*hom.pasch.*1(5^2.16C); ref. Christ's burial ἐπεὶ καὶ σάββατον ~ει *Ev.Petr.*2(p.214); τῇ νυκτὶ ᾗ ἐπέφωσκεν ἡ κυριακή *ib.*9 (p.292); of Easter vigil ~ούσης μιᾶς σαββάτων, ἥτις ἐστὶ κυριακή, ἀπὸ ἑσπέρας ἕως ἀλεκτοροφωνίας ἀγρυπνοῦντες *Const.App.*5.19.3; *Chron.Pasch.*p.218(M.92.532D).

[*]**ἐπιχαιρεσίκακος,** *rejoicing in* another's *ills, malignantly pleased* κάτω δυνάμεις αἱ ἐ. Or.*mart.*18(p.17.9; M.11.588A); τοῦ σατανᾶ τὸ ἐ. id.*or.*2.2(p.300.23; M.11.420A); ἐ. δαίμονα Eus.*h.e.*4.7.10 (M.20.320A); id.*Is.*30:29–32(M.24.313A); *Const.App.*2.21.2; τὸ ἐ. τῶν αἱρέσεων Pall.*h.Laus.*28(p.117.13; χαιρέκακον M.34.1188D).

***ἐπιχαιρεσικάκως,** *with malignant joy*, Didym.*Ps.*6:9(M.39. 1177D).

***ἐπιχαρμός, ὁ,** *ridicule, disgrace*, *Dial.Tim.et Aquil.*132 r° (p.99).

***ἐπιχάσκω,** *gape at greedily* τοῖς ὄψοις ἐπικεχήνασιν Clem.*paed.*2.1 (p.155.16; M.8.384A).

ἐπιχηρεύω, *spend one's widowhood with*; c. dat., Bas.Sel.*v.Thecl.* 2.4(M.85.572C).

***ἐπιχιονέομαι,** *be covered with snow*, Thphn.*chron.*p.365(M.108. 876A).

ἐπιχορηγ-έω, *supply, furnish*; of divine gift of chastity, *1Clem.* 38.2; of God's gifts to men in answer to prayer, Or.*or.*14.1(p.330.19; M.11.460C); id.*princ.*3.1.12(p.216.6; M.11.272A); id.*Cels.*5.1(p.2.16; M.11.1181C); ὁ θεὸς...τοῖς ἐπ' αὐτὸν ἐλπίζουσιν ἑτοιμάζει τὰς ἐκ πνεύματος ἁγίου δωρεὰς ~ούμενος Epiph.*haer.*66.11(p.32.9; M.42. 45B); of Son, Eus.*p.e.*7.15(325C; M.21.549C); δευτερεύοντος δὲ καὶ ὡς ἂν ἀπὸ πρώτης καὶ ἡγουμένης οὐσίας ~ουμένου τοῦ υἱοῦ id.*d.e.*5.1 (p.214.17; M.22.356B); of God as giver of gifts of H. Ghost, *Lit.Jac.* (p.208.2); of gift of H. Ghost, in gen., *Hom.Clem.*3.17; and of gifts of power by H. Ghost, Eus.*p.e.*7.15(325C; M.549C); of Law and prophets supplying light of divine γνῶσις to men, Meth.*symp.*10.6 (p.128.25; M.18.204A); abs. ὁ πλούσιος ~είτω τῷ πτωχῷ *1Clem.*38.2; Arist.*apol.*15.7; of activity of Roman church in sending supplies to brethren in mines, Dion.Cor.ap.Eus.*h.e.*4.23.10(M.20.388B).

ἐπιχορηγία, ἡ, *supply*; of God's grace in revelation, Cyr.*Jo.*4.7 (4.429D); of activity of Son in giving life in creation and in sustaining order of nature, Eus.*l.C.*11(p.229.5; M.20.1384C); id.*d.e.*4.5 (p.157.10; M.22.261C); πάντα...τῆς ζωῆς μέτοχα ἐξ ἐ. τοῦ υἱοῦ ζῇ id. *e.th.*1.20(p.86.31; M.24.876B); esp. of grace of H. Ghost in rel. to men, Or.*schol.in Lc.*13:20(M.17.357C,D); εὐξώμεθα ἔχειν τὴν ἐκκλησίαν τὴν ἐ. τοῦ πνεύματος †Bas.*Is.*107(1.453C; M.30.292A); Cyr. *inc.unigen.*(5^1.678C); of baptismal gift of H. Ghost as antitype of Aaron's anointing, id.*ador.*11(1.391D).

***ἐπιχορηγός, ὁ,** *one who supplies*; of God, Epiph.*haer.*76.26 (p.374.21; M.42.569A).

***ἐπιχρεμετίζω,** *neigh*, Leont.B.*mesopent.*(M.86.1980C).

ἐπίχρισις, ἡ, *anointing*, of post-baptismal unction τοῦ αἱρετικοῦ ἐπὶ τὴν ὀρθοδοξίαν ἐρχομένου τὸ σφάλμα διορθοῦται,...τοῦ...βαπτίσματος τῇ ἐ. τοῦ ἁγίου μύρου ‡Just.*qu.et resp.*14(M.6.1261D); of Christ's anointing of blind with clay, Cyr.H.*hom.*13(M.33.1145C).

ἐπίχρισμα, τό, *unguent, cosmetic*, Melet.*nat.hom.*synops.(M.64. 1141A).

ἐπιχρίω, *anoint, smear*; **1.** in gen., Chrys.*hom.17.2 in Heb.*(12. 167A); Nonn.*par.Jo.*9:6(M.43.824C); **2.** of sealing of Christ's tomb with seven seals, *Ev.Petr.*8(p.286); **3.** of Christians' unction with blood of Christ, compared with paschal anointing of door-posts, Chrys.*hom.27.1 in Heb.*(12.245C); τὸ αἷμα τὸ ταῖς φλιαῖς ἐπιχριόμενον Thdt.*1Cor.*2:13(3.178).

***ἐπίχροια, ἡ,** *sheen*, Clem.*str.*6.12(p.484.14; M.9.325A); Or.*comm. in Mt.*10.7(p.9.2; M.13.852B).

ἐπιχρυσόω, *gild*, Paul.Sil.*Soph.*672(M.86.2145A).

ἐπιχώννυμι, 1. *bury under* or *in*, Clem.*prot.*4(p.44.4; M.8.153A); met., id.*paed.*2.1(p.157.7; M.8.385B); *ib.*2.2(p.173.17; 424A); Meth. *res.*2.8(p.344.16; M.41.1176C); **2.** *heap up*, Gr.Nyss.*v.Mos.*(M.44. 428B).

ἐπιχώρησις, ἡ, 1. *possession, entry upon*, Clem.*str.*4.18(p.299.21; M.8.1325A); **2.** *going over, yielding* to τῇ πρὸς Ἀθανάσιον ἐ. Philost. *h.e.*3.12(M.65.501A).

ἐπιψάλλω, *make response*, Clem.*str.*5.8(p.359.6; M.9.77A); Pall.*v. Chrys.*20(p.138.16; M.47.77).

ἐπιψοφέω, *make a clamour*, Clem.*paed.*3.4(p.253.15; M.8.596C); Pall.*v.Chrys.*6(p.38.1; M.47.23).

ἐπόγδοος, 1. *one eighth more* πρῶτος [sc. ἐννάς] ἐστιν ἐ. Anat. Laod.*decad.*(p.39); **2.** *next to the eighth*, of second string in octave of lyre ὁ τὴν ὑπάτην ψήλας οὐ τὴν παρ' αὐτήν, τὴν ἐ., ἀλλὰ τὴν ἐπιτρίτην καὶ τὴν νήτην ἐκίνησεν Synes.*insomn.*2(p.147.14; M.66.1285B).

***ἐποδυνάομαι,** *be grieved at*, Gr.Nyss.*v.Mos.*(M.44.409C).

ἐποδύρομαι, *lament over*, Epiph.*haer.*49.2(p.243.8; M.41.881A).

ἐπόζω, *become stinking*, Dion.Al.ap.Eus.*h.e.*7.21.6(M.20.685A); *V.Pach.Σ* 66(p.238.4); met., of corrupt soul, Meth.*symp.*1.1(p.8.19; M.18.37C).

ἐποικοδομή, ἡ, *superstructure*, Clem.*str.*7.10(p.41.2; M.9.480A).

***ἐποικοδόμημα, τό,** = foreg., Clem.*str.*5.4(p.342.13; M.9.45B).

ἐποκλάζω, *bend the knee*, hence *succumb*, Gr.Nyss.*v.Mos.*(M.44. 341C); id.*mart.*1(M.46.752C); id.*v.Macr.*(p.389.21; M.46.977A); Max. *cap.theol.*1.99(M.90.1124B).

***ἐπολέθριος,** *pernicious*, Const.*ep.*ap.Gel.Cyz.*h.e.*2.7.22(M.85. 1236D).

[*]**ἐπολισθαίνω,** = ἐπολισθάνω, *slip, fall*, Chrys.*hom.9.3 in 1Thess.* (11.490D).

ἐπολολύζ-ω, *bewail, lament over* θυγατέρες...νεκρῷ...~ουσαι Cyr. *Juln.*10(6^2.342C).

ἐπομβρίζω, trans., *rain down* μάννα...θεὸς ἐ. *Hom.Clem.*8.15; met., Clem.*str.*1.7(p.24.19; M.8.732B).

***ἐπομόργνυμι,** *wipe on*, hence *apply to* μοι πικρὴν ἐπομόρξατο ποινήν Gr.Naz.*carm.*1.2.14.57(M.37.760A, v.l. ἐνομόρξατο).

ἐπονειδίζ-ω, *cast reproach on, reproach* τὴν Ἰουδαίων ~ων σκληροκαρδίαν Clem.*paed.*2.2(p.176.10; M.8.429A); Eus.*v.C.*1.14(p.14.27; M.20.928C); Thdr.Heracl.*Is.*45:14(M.18.1340C); τῇ πόλει...τὴν τῶν οἰκητόρων ἐρημίαν ~ειν Gr.Nyss.*hom.2 in Cant.*(M.44.792C); id.*Eun.* 9(2 p.206.26; M.45.804C); Oecum.*Apoc.*3:18(p.66); τὸν Δαυὶδ ~ειν Jo.Eub.*concept.BMV* 6(M.96.1469A).

***ἐπονειδιστικός,** *worthy of reproach*, comp., Chrys.*hom.7.3 in Phil.*(11.249A).

ἐπονομάζ-ω, 1. *invoke, name over*, in eucharistic anaphora τίνα αἶνον ἢ ποίαν προσφορὰν ἢ τίνα εὐχαριστίαν κλῶντες τὸν ἄρτον τοῦτον ἐπονομάσωμεν ἀλλ' ἢ σὲ μόνον κύριε Ἰησοῦ; δοξάζομέν σου τὸ λεχθὲν ὑπὸ τοῦ πατρὸς ὄνομα *A.Jo.*109(p.207.9); in blessings in gen., *A.Phil.* 93(p.36.5); τὸν...σταυρὸν ~ων [i.e. in working a miracle] *A.Mt.*19 (p.243.2); of invocation of divine name as apotropaic spell, *Hymn. Gnost.*ap.*A.Thom.*A 111(p.222.14); **2.** *consecrate, dedicate*, Or.*Jo.*6. 45(26; p.154.15; M.14.277C); ‡Pion.*v.Polyc.*27; **3.** *pronounce* to be, *determine* ἐξότε ἐπωνομάσθη τὸ ὑποτελεῖς εἶναι τοὺς ἀνθρώπους τοῖς βασιλεῦσιν Jo.Mal.*chron.*2 p.24(M.97.89A).

***ἐπονομασία**, ἡ, **1.** *naming over, invocation,* of baptismal formula ἀπολουσάμενοι ἐπὶ τῇ τρισμακαρίᾳ ἐ. *Hom.Clem.*9.19; τρισμακαρίᾳ ἐ. εἰς ἄφεσιν ἁμαρτιῶν βαπτισάμενοι *ib.*9.23; *ib.*11.26; **2.** *surnaming, adopting of distinctive name*; ref. parties of Paul, Cephas, etc., at Corinth, Sever.*1Cor.*1:1f.(p.225.17).

ἐποξύνω, med., *irritate, exasperate,* Gr.Nyss.*beat.*2(M.44.1216C).

***ἐποξυσμός**, ὁ, *irritation, exasperation,* Ephr.3.448F.

***ἐποποιέω**, *write in hexameters,* Nil.*epp.*2.49(M.79.221B).

ἐποπτεία, ἡ, **1.** *contemplation*; **a.** of full initiation into mysteries, esp. of Eleusis, *LS*; v. ἐποπτεύω, ἐποπτικός; **b.** Christian; of contemplation of God and divine things ἔστι δὲ ἡ κατὰ τὸν θεὸν παιδαγωγία κατευθυσμὸς ἀληθείας εἰς ἐ. θεοῦ Clem.*paed.*1.7(p.122.9; M.8.313B); ἡ...κατὰ Μωυσέα φιλοσοφία τετραχῇ τέμνεται, εἴς τε τὸ ἱστορικὸν καὶ τὸ...νομοθετικόν,...τὸ τρίτον δὲ εἰς τὸ ἱερουργικόν,...καὶ τέταρτον...τὸ θεολογικὸν εἶδος, ἡ ἐ., ἥν φησιν ὁ Πλάτων τῶν μεγάλων ὄντως εἶναι μυστηρίων, Ἀριστοτέλης δὲ τὸ εἶδος τοῦτο μετὰ τὰ φυσικὰ καλεῖ id.*str.*1.28(p.108.28; M.8.924A); *ib.*4.1(p.249.12; 1216C); οἱ καθαροὶ τὴν καρδίαν...ἀκορέστου θεωρίας εἰλικρινεῖ ἐ. προσανέχοντες *ib.*6.14(p.486.9; M.9.329B); τὴν τοῦ θεοῦ ἐ., ἣν κορυφαιοτάτην προκοπὴν ἡ γνωστικὴ ψυχὴ λαμβάνει *ib.*7.11(p.49.15; 496A); τῆς τῶν ἀληθῶν ἐ. Eus.*d.e.*4.15(p.176.15; M.22.293B); μόνῳ δὲ τῷ Ἑβραίων γένει τὴν ἐ. ἀνατεθεῖσθαι [sc. τῆς θεωρίας] τοῦ τῶν ὅλων ποιητοῦ τε καὶ δημιουργοῦ θεοῦ id.*p.e.*1.9(30B; M.21.70B); τὸ τρίτον μέρος τῆς καθ' Ἑβραίους φιλοσοφίας (τοῦτο δ' ἦν τὸ φυσικόν), διαιρούμενον καὶ παρ' αὐτοῖς εἴς τε τὴν τῶν νοητῶν καὶ ἀσωμάτων ἐ., καὶ εἰς τὴν τῶν αἰσθητῶν φυσιολογίαν *ib.*11.7(521A; M.864C); *ib.*(523A; M.868A); Cyr.*ador.*16(1.561B); of prophetic insight, Proc.G.*Is.*proem.(M.87.1817B); **2.** *oversight, providential care,* of God, Thdr.Heracl.*Is.*28:6(M.18.1317A); Cyr.*Os.*46(3.77C); id.*Nah.*32(3.510B).

***ἐπόπτευσις**, ἡ, *inspection* of entrails for purpose of divination, Just.*1apol.*18.3(M.6.356A).

***ἐποπτευτέον**, *one must survey,* Dion.Ar.*c.h.*4.1(M.3.177C).

ἐποπτεύ-ω, **1.** *superintend, watch over*; **a.** of God τὸν δημιουργὸν θεὸν συνέχοντα καὶ ~οντα ἐπιστήμῃ καὶ τέχνῃ καθ' ἣν ἄγει τὰ πάντα Athenag.*leg.*13.2(M.6.916B); ψυχῆς...ῥυθμιζούσης ἑαυτὴν ἀρέσκειν ὡς παρόντι καὶ ~οντι...τῷ ἐτάζοντι καρδίας Or.*or.*8.2(p.317.15; M.11.441C); Chrys.*hom.51.2 in Jo.*(8.300E); **b.** of Christ τὴν ἐκκλησίαν ~ει τὴν ἑαυτοῦ Clem.*paed.*1.5(p.103.21; ἀποπτεύει M.8.277A); **c.** of deities in gen. ἔοικεν οὖν δηλοῦν ὅτι καὶ τὴν Ἰουδαίων χώραν...~ει τις ἤ τινες, ὑφ' οὗ ἢ ὑφ' ὧν οἱ Ἰουδαίων νόμοι συνεργοῦντος ἢ συνεργούντων Μωϋσεῖ ἐτέθησαν Cels.ap.Or.*Cels.*5.25(p.26.23; M.11.1220B); **d.** of Christian pastors τοὺς πρεσβυτέρους ἀνάγκην ἔχειν ~ειν τὰ τῆς ἐκκλησίας λογικὰ ποίμνια Ammon.*Ac.*20:28(M.85.1581B); **2.** *behold, contemplate*; esp. **a.** of initiate's full participation in mysteries of Eleusis Ἀθηναῖοι...ἐπιδεικνύντες τοῖς ~ουσι τὸ...μέγα...μυστήριον Hipp.*haer.*5.8(p.96.11; M.16.3150C); v. ἐποπτικός; of Corybantic rites, Clem.*prot.*2(p.15.1; M.8.80B); **b.** of Christian contemplation as highest degree in Christian mystery, often of vision of God δι' οὗ μόνου [sc. Χριστοῦ] θεὸς ~εται *ib.*1(p.10.19; 68A); δᾳδουχοῦμαι τοὺς οὐρανοὺς καὶ τὸν θεὸν ~σαι ἅγιος γίνομαι μυούμενος, ἱεροφαντεῖ δὲ ὁ κύριος καὶ τὸν μύστην σφραγίζεται φωταγωγῶν *ib.*12(p.84.24; 241A); φώτισμα [sc. baptism] δι' οὗ τὸ ἅγιον ἐκεῖνο φῶς τὸ σωτήριον ~εται id.*paed.*1.6(p.105.26; M.8.281A); φωτεινὸν ὄμμα τοῦ πνεύματος...ᾧ δὴ μόνῳ τὸ θεῖον ~ομεν *ib.*(p.106.25; 284A); id.*str.*5.11(p.374.3; M.9.108B); διαβιβάζει [sc. γνῶσις] τὰς προκοπὰς τὰς μυστικὰς τὸν ἄνθρωπον, ἄχρις ἂν εἰς τὸν κορυφαῖον ἀποκαταστήσῃ τῆς ἀναπαύσεως τόπον, τὸν καθαρὸν τῇ καρδίᾳ πρόσωπον πρὸς πρόσωπον ἐπιστημονικῶς καὶ καταληπτικῶς τὸν θεὸν ~ειν διδάξασα *ib.*7.10(p.41.31; 481A); τὸ γὰρ ἀληθὲς ἀκριβῶς μετ' ἀνάστασιν δηλωθήσεται, ὁπότε πρόσωπον κατὰ πρόσωπον τὴν ἁγίαν σκηνήν, τὴν πόλιν τὴν ἐν τοῖς οὐρανοῖς ~σομεν Meth.*symp.*5.7(p.62.14; M.18.112A); *ib.*8.11(p.94.10; 156A); Eus.*d.e.*3.2(p.108.23; M.22.188A); in liturgy, Hesych.S.*temp.*1.9(M.93.1484C); in future life καθαρῷ νῷ καθαρὰν τὴν ἀλήθειαν ~οντες Gr.Naz.*or.*7.17(M.35.776C); of Logos τοῖς τοῦ πατρὸς λογισμοῖς ἐνατενίζων καὶ μόνος ~ων τὰ ἐν αὐτῷ βάθη Eus.*e.th.*3.3(p.154.33; M.24.997B); **c.** of philosophical contemplation of the divine τοῦτο ἄρα βούλεται καὶ τῷ Πυθαγόρᾳ ἡ τῆς πενταετίας σιωπή, ἣν τοῖς γνωρίμοις παρεγγυᾷ, ὡς δὴ ἀποστραφέντες τῶν αἰσθητῶν ψιλῷ τῷ νῷ τὸ θεῖον ~οιεν Clem.*str.*5.11(p.371.5; M.9.104A); Hipp.*haer.*6.24(p.151.4; M.16.3230B); **d.** of contemplation in gen. τὴν ἐναργῆ τῶν ἀρετῶν ~σαντες πίστιν Clem.*prot.*10(p.70.15; M.8.209B); ὁ ἔσω...ἄνθρωπος καθαρῶς...τὴν ἀλήθειαν ~ει Meth.*symp.*7.2(p.72.22; M.18.128A); of prophetic insight, Eus.*d.e.*7.1(p.319.19; M.22.521C); Dion.Ar.*c.h.*3.3(M.3.165D); **3.** *consider, regard,* Dion.Al.ap.Eus.*p.e.*14.25(777A; ὑποπτεύειν M.21.1277C); Eus.*Marcell.*1.2(p.13.1; M.24.740B); Gr.Naz.*or.*26.5(M.35.1233B); **4.** *see* μὴ τὸν ὁρώμενον τοῖς πολλοῖς ἄνθρωπον τὸν δ' ἐν ἑκάστῳ τιμώμενον ~ειν ἐδόκει θεόν Eus.*v.C.*1.42(p.27.21; M.20.956D); ἀναβεβιωκότα [sc. Marcellus] τὸν νέον Σαβέλλιον ~σωμεν id.*e.th.*1.20(p.98.11; M.24.896C); **5.** *have in mind,* Cyr.*Lc.*21:1(M.72.896A); **6.** *inspect, make a survey of,* Cyr.S.*v.Sab.*73(p.176.27).

ἐπόπτης, ὁ, **1.** *overseer, one who watches over,* of God ἐ. τῶν ἀνθρωπίνων ἔργων *1Clem.*59.3; Just.*2apol.*12.6(M.6.465A); Const.*or.s.c.*6(p.160.12; M.20.1248B); Gr.Nyss.*Eun.*12(2 p.277.24; M.45.888D); of Christ τὸν ἐν σαρκὶ ἐ. ὀφθαλμόν Clem.*paed.*2.12(p.228.7; M.8.540C); ref. Ps.83:10 Χριστὸς ὀνομαστὶ τὸν θεὸν ἐ. ἐπιγραφόμενος Eus.*d.e.*4.16(p.187n.; M.22.313B prob. *Schol.*); of pagan gods, Cels.ap.Or.*Cels.*5.25(p.26.9; M.11.1220A); id.*ib.*5.27(p.27.26; 1221A); **2.** *judge,* Const.*or.s.c.*10(p.164.31; M.20.1257B); ‡Thdt.*nativ.Jo.Bapt.*(5.99); **3.** *contemplator* ὀφθαλμοὶ δὲ ὑπαληλιμμένοι λόγῳ...ἁγίων ἐπόπτην παρασκευάζουσιν Clem.*paed.*2.12(p.234.9; M.8.553A).

[*]**ἐποπτία**, ἡ, = ἐποπτεία, *watchful care,* Cyr.*Ps.*12:2(M.69.800A).

ἐποπτικός, **A.** *of* or *belonging to vision*; hence **1.** of Eleusinian mysteries, *connected with third* or *highest degree* τελειότατον ἐ. ... μυστήριον, τεθερισμένον στάχυν Hipp.*haer.*5.8(p.96.12; M.16.3150C); **2.** Christian, *belonging to full participation*; *consisting in contemplation,* Clem.*paed.*1.3(p.95.6; M.8.260A); θεωρία μεγίστη, ἡ ἐ., ἡ τῷ ὄντι ἐπιστήμη...αὕτη ἂν εἴη μόνη ἡ τῆς σοφίας γνῶσις, ἧς οὐδέποτε χωρίζεται ἡ δικαιοπραγία id.*str.*2.10(p.138.12; M.8.984B); *ib.*5.11(p.374.5; M.9.108B); τινὲς μὲν διὰ τὴν πολλὴν ἁπλότητα μὴ εἰδότες μὲν δοῦναι λόγον περὶ ὧν ποιοῦσιν...ἕτεροι δὲ μετ' οὐκ εὐκαταφρονήτων λόγων ἀλλὰ καὶ βαθυτέρων καί, ὡς ἂν εἴποι τις Ἕλλην, ἐσωτερικῶν καὶ ἐ., ἐν οἷς πολύς ἐστι λόγος περὶ θεοῦ καὶ τῶν τετιμημένων ἀπὸ θεοῦ διὰ τοῦ...θεοῦ λόγου Or.*Cels.*3.37(p.236.2; M.11.968C); οἱ μὲν οὖν προφῆται ὅσα ἦν...νοηθῆναι τοῖς ἀκούουσι χρήσιμα...χωρὶς πάσης ἐπικρύψεως...εἰρήκασιν, ὅσα δὲ μυστικώτερα ἦν καὶ ἐποπτικώτερα καὶ ἐχόμενα θεωρίας τῆς ὑπὲρ τὴν πάνδημον ἀκοήν, ταῦτα δι' αἰνιγμάτων καὶ ἀλληγοριῶν...ἀπεφήναντο *ib.*7.10(p.162.4; 1436A); id.*fr.73 in Lc.*15:23(p.269; M.17.365A); οὐ μονοειδῆ τὰ δόγματα, ἀλλὰ ποικίλα..., ἠθικούς τε καὶ φυσικοὺς καὶ τοὺς ἐ. λεγομένους περιέχοντα λόγους Bas.*hom.in Ps.*44(1.167B; M.29.408C); ἐ. βίος contrasted with πρακτικός, †Bas.*Is.*6(1.382E; M.30.129A).

B. *capable of contemplation* ψυχὴ...ἐ. Clem.*paed.*2.2(p.174.14; M.8.425A); Bas.*Spir.*47(3.39C; M.32.153A); ἐπὶ τὰ τῆς φυσιολογίας ἀνώτερα προκόψας, τὰ καλούμενα παρά τισι μεταφυσικά, ἐ. γενέσθαι δύναται †Bas.*Is.*162(1.494D; M.30.385A); φαμὲν...τῆς ψυχῆς τὴν...τῶν ὄντων ἐ. δύναμιν οἰκείαν εἶναι, καὶ διὰ τῆς θεοειδοῦς χάριτος, διὰ τοῦτο σώζειν ἐν αὐτῇ τὴν εἰκόνα Gr.Nyss.*anim.et res.*(M.46.57B).

C. *connected with, belonging to, oversight, care, providence* πάρεστιν ἀεὶ τῇ τε ἐ. τῇ τε εὐεργετικῇ...ἡμῶν δυνάμει δύναμις τοῦ θεοῦ Clem.*str.*2.2(p.115.25; M.8.936B); of God's providence (τὸ ἐ.) symbolized by 'eye' of God, Or.*fr.4 in Reg.*(p.295.27; M.17.44B); τὸ τῆς θεότητος ὄνομα...τὴν ἐ. ... ἐξουσίαν σημαίνει Gr.Nyss.*Eun.*12(2 p.277.21; M.45.888D); Cyr.*Ps.*10:3(M.69.793A).

***ἐπορθρίζω**, *rise early,* Gr.Nyss.*or.dom.*1(p.2.19; M.44.1120C); id.*res.*1(M.46.613B).

***ἐπορκίζ-ω**, **1.** *exorcize*; of Jewish exorcisms, Chrys.*hom.in 1Cor.*proem.(10.1C); of Christian exorcizing of the possessed; in gen., Just.*dial.*85.2(M.6.676C); id.*2apol.*6.6(M.6.453B); of pre-baptismal exorcisms of catechumens, Cyr.H.*procatech.*9, *ib.*14 cit. s. ἐπορκισμός; τὸ ἁπλοῦν ἐμφύσημα τοῦ ~οντος, πῦρ γίνεται τῷ μὴ φαινομένῳ [sc. demon] id.*catech.*16.19; οὐ δεῖ ~ειν τοὺς μὴ προαχθέντας ὑπὸ ἐπισκόπων CLaod.*can.*26; administered by deacons, ἐφορκ-, CSyr.*act.*(*ACO* 3 p.99.31, v.l. ἐπιορκ- H.2.1577A); ἐφορκ-, Jo.D.*imag.*1.24(M.94.1257A); ἐπιορκ-, Phot.*nomoc.*4.2 tit.(M.104.1056B); v. s. ἀφορκίζω; **2.** *adjure* ~οντές σε κατὰ τοῦ...θεοῦ...ταῦτα εἰς γνῶσιν ἀνενεγκεῖν *Ep.Mareot.*2(p.156.12; M.25.385C).

***ἐπορκισμός**, ὁ, *exorcism*; of pre-baptismal exorcisms administered to catechumens during period of preparation for baptism τοὺς ἐ. δέχου μετὰ σπουδῆς· κἂν ἐμφυσηθῇς, κἂν ἐπορκισθῇς, σωτηρία σοι τὸ πρᾶγμα Cyr.H.*procatech.*9; ὅταν ἐ. γένηται, ἕως ὅτου οἱ ἄλλοι ἐπορκιζόμενοι παραγένωνται, ἄνδρες μετὰ ἀνδρῶν, καὶ γυναῖκες μετὰ γυναικῶν *ib.*14; cf. ἐπιορκισμός.

ἐπορκιστής, ὁ, *exorcist,* as one of a minor order in Church, concerned with exorcism of those demoniacally possessed, Corn.ap.Eus.*h.e.*6.43.14(M.20.621B); as fifth order after bishop, presbyter, deacon, and reader, Eus.*h.e.*8.6.9(756A); function might be included in that of deacon Παλαιστινὸς γὰρ οὗτος ὢν διάκονός τε καὶ ἐ. τῆς ἐν Καισαρείᾳ παροικίας id.*m.P.*2(p.909.7; M.20.1465A); as third minor order after readers and subdeacons, CAnt.(341)*can.*10(in form ἐφορκιστής); οὐ δεῖ ἱερατικοὺς ἀπὸ πρεσβυτέρων ἕως διακόνων καὶ ἑξῆς τῆς ἐκκλησιαστικῆς τάξεως ἕως ὑπηρετῶν ἢ ἀναγνωστῶν ἢ ψαλτῶν ἢ ἐ. ἢ θυρωρῶν...εἰς καπηλεῖον εἰσιέναι CLaod.*can.*24; ἐ. οὐ χειροτονεῖται. εὐνοίας γὰρ ἑκουσίου τὸ ἔπαθλον καὶ χάριτος θεοῦ... ἐπιφοιτήσει τοῦ ἁγίου...πνεύματος· ὁ γὰρ λαβὼν χάρισμα ἰαμάτων, δι' ἀποκαλύψεως ὑπὸ θεοῦ ἀναδείκνυται, φανερᾶς οὔσης πᾶσιν τῆς ἐν αὐτῷ χάριτος *Const.App.*8.26.2; as minor order after reader and deaconess and before interpreters of tongues, κοπιαταί, and door-keepers, Epiph.*exp.fid.*21(p.522.22; M.42.825A); in fifth rank below bishop, *Lit.Jac.*(p.218.16); in gen., of Christians who succeed in exorcizing in name of Jesus Christ 'crucified under Pontius Pilate' when other exorcists have failed, Just.*2apol.*6.6(M.6.453B,C); of Jewish exorcists οἱ ἐξ ὑμῶν ἐ. τῇ τέχνῃ, ὥσπερ καὶ τὰ ἔθνη, χρώμενοι ἐξορκίζουσι καὶ θυμιάμασι καὶ καταδέσμοις χρῶνται id.*dial.*85.3(M.6.676C); οἱ τοῦ Σκευᾶ υἱοὶ περιῄεσαν ἐν ἐπορκιστῶν σχήματι Thdr.Mops. *1Cor.*13:10(M.66.892A).

***ἐπορκιστός**, *exorcized*; of oil hallowed so as to be free from all taint of evil and used in pre-baptismal anointing of candidates for baptism to expel evil spirits from them, Cyr.H.*catech.*20.3 cit. s. ἔλαιον.

ἔπος, τό, *word*; in phrase πρὸς ἔπος, *literally*, Or.*Jo.*20.16(14; p.347.8; M.14.608B).

***ἐποσφραίνομαι**, *catch the scent of*, *Schol.*8 in Jo.Clim.*scal.*26(M.88.1037C).

***ἐπουλή, ἡ**, *scar*, fig. τὴν ἐ. τῆς κακίας Mac.Aeg.*hom.*50.4(M.34.820A).

ἐπουλωτικός, *promoting cicatrization*, *Const.App.*2.41.5.

ἐπουράνιος, *heavenly*; **1.** in sense of *divine* δέσποτα ἐ. *1Clem.*61.2; τοῦ ἐ. ἀρχιερέως...Χριστοῦ *M.Polyc.*14.3; λόγος γὰρ ὁ ἐ. πνεῦμα γεγονὼς ἀπὸ τοῦ πνεύματος Tat.*orat.*7(p.7.6; M.6.820A); *ib.*16(p.18.5; 841A); Mac.Aeg.*hom.*44.5(M.34.781C); **2.** *celestial*, of angels τὰ ἐ. καὶ ἡ δόξα τῶν ἀγγέλων Ign.*Smyrn.*6.1; ἐ. καλεῖ τὰς ἀοράτους δυνάμεις Thdt.*Phil.*2:10(3.455); dist. from τῶν ἐν τοῖς ἐ. πνευματικῶν τῆς πονηρίας ἀντιπαλαιόντων τοῖς ἐπὶ γῆς Or.*or.*26.5(p.362.5; M.11.504A); **3.** of archetypal man in Simonian system, Hipp.*haer.*6.17(p.143.5; M.16.3219A); of Valentinian aeons as ἄγγελοι ἐ. *ib.*6.34(p.163.2; 3246B); of πλήρωμα: τὴν ἐ. κτίσιν,...αὐτὸς εἰργάσατο ὁ δημιουργὸς ὁ μέγας σοφός (Basilidian) *ib.*7.23(p.201.16; 3310D); **4.** in Eleusinian mysteries ἡ γένεσις ἡ...ἐ., ἡ ἄνω *ib.*5.8(p.96.19; 3151A); μυεῖσθαι τὰ μεγάλα τὰ ἐ. *ib.*(p.97.11; 3151B); **5.** in gen. of heavenly opp. earthly persons and things; **a.** ref. Apollinarian Christology ἐ. ἄνθρωπος καὶ πνεῦμα ζωοποιόν Apoll.*fr.*89(p.227.24)ap.Gr.Nyss. *Apoll.*48(M.45.1240C); εἰ ἐκ πάντων...τῶν ἴσων ἡμῖν ἐστι τοῖς χοϊκοῖς ὁ ἐ. ἄνθρωπος, ὥστε καὶ τὸ πνεῦμα ἴσον ἔχειν τοῖς χοϊκοῖς, οὐκ ἐ. ἀλλ' ἐ. θεοῦ δοχεῖον Apoll.*fr.*90(p.228.1; 1240D); οὐδὲ κατῳκηκέναι τὸν ἐξ οὐρανοῦ ἐν ἀνθρώπῳ...χοϊκῷ, ἀλλ' αὐτὸν τὸν δεύτερον Ἀδὰμ ἐ. εἶναι. ἐ. ἐστιν ὁ λόγος ὁ τὴν σάρκα ἔχων τὴν ἐκ Μαρίας καὶ ἡμᾶς...διὰ τοῦ ἐ. ἐπουρανίους καθ' ὁμοίωσιν ποιῶν, ὄντας χοϊκούς Tim.Beryt.*ep. Prosd.*3(p.285.9f.; M.*PL.*8.958B); agreement that ὁ...ἀνακραθεὶς τῷ ἐ., καὶ μεταποιήσας διὰ τῆς πρὸς τὸ κρεῖττον ἐπιμιξίας τὸ γήϊνον, οὐκ ἂν χοϊκός, ἀλλ' ἐ. λέγοιτο Gr.Nyss.*Apoll.*48(1240C), and refutation of implications of Apollinarius' further statements, *ib.*(1241A,B); in Apollinarius' alleged teaching τὴν σάρκα ποτὲ μὲν ἄκτιστον, ποτὲ δὲ ἐ., ποτὲ δὲ ὁμοούσιον τῷ λόγῳ ‡Ath.*Apoll.*1.21(M.26.1129B); **b.** of heavenly beings and states in gen. ἐσταυρώθη...βλεπόντων τῶν ἐ. καὶ ἐπιγείων Ign.*Trall.*9.1; ᾧ [sc. Χριστῷ] ὑπετάγη τὰ πάντα ἐ. καὶ ἐπίγεια Polyc.*ep.*2.1; ἔχοιτε ἀφ' ἑαυτῶν καὶ τὴν ἐ. βασιλείαν ἐξετάζειν Athenag.*leg.*18.1(M.6.925B); (Gnost.) ἐκκλησίας τινὸς ἐ. καὶ κρείττονος αἰῶνος ἀπόρροιαν εἶναι τὴν ἐπὶ γῆς ἐκκλησίαν Or.*Cels.*6.35(p.104.20; M.11.1349B); ἀναλαμβάνοντες εἰς θείαν τινὰ καὶ ἐ. πόλιν τοὺς ἐν ταῖς ἐλαχίσταις πόλεσι καλῶς βιώσαντας *ib.*8.74(p.291.24; 1629A); of heavenly Jerusalem, id.*princ.*4.3.8(p.334.8; M.11.389A); ὑπὲρ τῶν... προσφερόντων κυρίῳ...δεηθῶμεν, ὅπως ὁ...θεὸς ἀμείψηται αὐτοὺς ταῖς ἐ. αὐτοῦ δωρεαῖς *Lit.*ap.*Const.App.*8.10.12; δεῖ γὰρ τὴν ψυχὴν... μετατεθῆναι...καὶ οὕτως δύναται χρησιμεῦσαι εἰς τὴν ἐ. βασιλείαν Mac. Aeg.*hom.*44.5(M.34.781C); of heavenly realities opp. earthly types, Thdt.*Ezech.*43:7(2.1028); of heavenly altar ὑπὲρ τοῦ δώρου... δεηθῶμεν, ὅπως ὁ...θεὸς προσδέξηται αὐτὸ...εἰς τὸ ἐ. αὐτοῦ θυσιαστήριον *Lit.*ap.*Const.App.*8.13.3; v. θυσιαστήριον; esp. of eternal life ἐφανέρωσεν ἡμῖν τὴν...ἐ. ζωήν *2Clem.*20.5; v.l. for αἰώνιον *M.Polyc.* 20.2; τὴν ἐ. αὐτοῦ ἐλπίδα *Lit.*ap.*Const.App.*8.10.5; cf. τι τῶν ἐ. αὐτοῦ θαυμάτων ὁρᾶν Diad.*perf.*36(p.42.6); of heavenly realities in gen. νοεῖν τὰ ἐ. Ign.*Trall.*5.2; of angels προσάγοντας τὰς τῶν ἀνθρώπων ἐντεύξεις ἐν τοῖς καθαρωτάτοις τοῦ κόσμου χωρίοις ἐ. Or.*Cels.*5.4(p.4.16; M.11.1185B); exeg. Eph.1:3 τὸ δέ, ἐν τοῖς ἐ., ἀντὶ τοῦ περὶ τῶν ἐ., οὐχ ἵνα γῆν κληρονομήσωμεν κατὰ νόμον, οὐδ' ἵνα κατὰ γῆν πολιτευσώμεθα Thdr.Mops.*Eph.*1:3(M.66.913A); προστέθεικεν ἐν τοῖς ἐ.· ἐ. γὰρ τὰ δῶρα ταῦτα Thdt.*Eph.*1:3(3.402); **c.** of celestial (resurrection and angelic) bodies σώματα γοῦν ἐ. εὔμορφα καὶ νοερὰ οἶδεν ὁ ἀπόστολος Clem.*exc.Thdot.*11(p.110.13; M.9.661B); Or.*Cels.*4.60(p.332.1; M.11.1128A); ἐσχηματίσθαι γὰρ τῶν ἐ. τὰ σώματα, ὡς καὶ γόνατα σωματικὰ ἔχειν αὐτά, ὑπολαμβάνειν οὐ πάνυ τι χρή, σφαιροειδῶν... ἀποδεδειγμένων αὐτῶν τῶν σωμάτων id.*or.*31.3(p.397.4; M.11.552B); **6.** in sense of *spiritual* opp. material οὐδὲ φαντασίαν...ἔχοντες...ἐ. αἰτημάτων, πᾶσαν εὐχὴν περὶ τῶν σωματικῶν...ἀναπέμποντες Or.*or.* 21.1(p.345.13; M.11.480D–481A); id.*mart.*37(p.35.4; M.11.612C); of spiritual ascent μέλλων διδάσκεσθαι περὶ τῶν ἐ., ἀναβαίνω id.*hom. 18.2 in Jer.*(p.152.27; M.13.465A); Chrys.*hom.42.1 in 1Cor.*(10.395D); **7.** of spiritual realities effected in sacraments δεῖ τοὺς φωτιζομένους μετὰ τὸ βάπτισμα χρίεσθαι χρίσματι ἐ. CLaod.*can.* 48; hence of sacraments πνευματικῶν...καὶ ἐπουρανίων...μυστηρίων Cyr.H.*catech.*19.1; and of altar τῆς ἐ. τραπέζης *Lit.Jac.*(p.238.10).

§**ἐπουρίζ-ω**, *water* Νεῖλος...πᾶσαν ~ων Λιβύην ἠδ' Αἰθιοπίαν *Orac. Sib.*14.286.

ἐπουσιώδης, *non-essential, adventitious, additional to substance* ἐ. δὲ καλοῦσιν οἱ φιλόσοφοι τὰ ἀχώριστα συμβεβηκότα *Doct.Patr.*33(p.260.7); τῆς γὰρ ὑποστάσεως ἡ ὑπογραφή, ἐξ ἰδιοτήτων τινῶν παρὰ τὰ ὁμοούσια ἔν τινι ἐπουσιωδῶν ἢ ἐπιουσιωδῶν καὶ συμβεβηκότων τινῶν, ἀχωρίστως ὄντων ἢ ἐπιγενομένων, συνίσταται Leont.H.*Nest.* 1.6(M.86.1421A); τὸ 'ἄλλο' καὶ κατ' ἐναλλαγὴν φύσεως νοεῖται, καὶ κατ' ἐπίκτησιν καὶ κατὰ παραβολήν τινα τῶν ἐ. *ib.*1.30(1496B); *ib.*2.16(1572D); αἱ ποιότητες, αἵ τε οὐσιώδεις καὶ ἐ. καλούμεναι Leont.B. *Nest.et Eut.*1(M.86.1277D); τὸ δὲ ἴδιον καὶ τὸ συμβεβηκός, ἐ., ἐπειδὴ ὑπάρχει τινί id.*fr.*(M.86.2009C); ἐ. ... λέγουσι τὰ ἀχώριστα συμβεβηκότα· οὐδὲν δὲ τούτων ἁπάντων κυρίως καὶ προηγουμένως, καὶ καθ' ἑαυτό ἐστιν οὐσία Pamph.H.*panopl.*2.2(p.602); Eulog.*fr.dogm.*(M.86.2948A); αἱ ποιότητες, αἵ τε οὐσιώδεις καὶ ἐ. ... αἵτινες οὐκ εἰσὶν οὐσία, οὐδὲ καθ' ἑαυτά, ἀλλὰ ἐν τῇ οὐσίᾳ τυγχάνουσι, καὶ δίχα ταύτης τὸ εἶναι οὐκ ἔχουσιν Max.*opusc.*(M.91.261B); ὑπογραφὴ ἐκ τῶν ἐ. σύγκειται Jo.D.*dialect.*8(M.94.553B).

***ἐπουσιωδῶς**, *in respect of that which is adventitious* or *non-essential* τὰ γὰρ διαφέροντα ἢ οὐσιωδῶς διαφέρει, ἢ ἐ. ἀλλ' εἰ μὲν ἐ., ὑποστάσεις ἂν εἶεν, καὶ οὐ φύσεις· εἰ δὲ οὐσιωδῶς, φύσεις Jo.D.*Jacob.* 21(M.94.1448B).

***ἐπουσίωσις, ἡ**, *addition to substance*, Leont.H.*Nest.*4.47(M.86.1720C).

***ἐποφειλή, ἡ**, *debt*, Or.*exp.in Pr.*11:27(M.17.192C).

ἐποφείλ-ω, **1.** *owe* τὰ θεῷ ~όμενα Or.*exp.in Pr.*11:27(M.17.192C); τὰ τοῖς γονεῦσιν ~όμενα ἐκ τῶν υἱῶν id.ap.*cat.Mt.*15:5(p.121.20); Cyr.*Lc.*9:26(M.72.652B); τὸ παρ' ἡμῶν...~όμενόν σοι σέβας ‡Meth. *Sym.et Ann.*5(M.18.360A); πάντες μὲν θεῷ ~ομεν, σοὶ δὲ ~εται *ib.*10(373A); liturg. ἄξιόν ἐστι...καὶ ~όμενον σὲ αἰνεῖν *Lit.Jac.*(p.198.20); *ib.*(p.240.5); **2.** pass., *be owed* a debt ἐξ ὧν ὕβρισμαι, τροφὴν ~ομαι Sev.Ant.ap.*cat.Mt.*15:30(p.125.11); **3.** pass., *be due to* ἀτιμίας ἡμῖν ~ομένας εἰς ἑαυτὸν μετατιθεὶς [sc. Χριστός] Eus.*d.e.*10.1(p.450.21; M. 22.724D).

ἐποφθαλμι-άω, **1.** *cast envious eyes upon*, of Eus. Nic. seeking translation from one see to another πανταχοῦ ταῖς ἀλλοτρίαις ~ῶν πόλεσι CAlex.*ep.*ap.Ath.*apol.sec.*6(p.93.6; M.25.260B); ὁ πλεονέκτης ...~ῶν...τοῖς ἀλλοτρίοις Ast.Am.*hom.*3(M.40.201A); **2.** *be envious*, Ath.*h.Ar.*7(p.186.13; M.25.701A); **3.** *envy*; c. dat., *Libell.*ap.CCP(536)*act.*5(p.38.34; H.2.1284D); c. acc., Or.*sel.in Gen.*31:7(M.12.125C).

ἐποφλισκάνω, *owe*, i.e. **1.** *be bound to render*, Cyr.*ador.*7(1.233A); *ib.*8(274D); **2.** *owe* a debt, id.*Zach.*82(3.766C); id.*Lc.*16:1(M.72.809D).

***ἔποφρυς**, *supercilious*, Gr.Naz.*carm.*2.1.30.201(M.37.1298A).

ἐποψία, ἡ, **A.** *vision*; **1.** of Moses' vision of God αὐτὸν...ὁ θεὸς τῆς ἐ. ἠξίωσε τῆς αὐτοῦ Jo.Philop.*opif.*2.13(p.79.23); of Apoc. τὴν... μυστικὴν ἐ. τοῦ τῶν μαθητῶν ἀγαπητοῦ Dion.Ar.*e.h.*3.3.4(M.3.429D); οἱ δὲ τῆς ὑψηλῆς θεολογίας, ὡς υἱοὶ βροντῆς, τὴν μυστικὴν ἐ. παρὰ τοῦ λόγου πιστεύονται Andr.Cr.*or.*7(M.97.948D); τοῦ λόγου τὴν ἐ. ἀναπετάσαντες *ib.*13(1076C); **2.** esp. of admission to highest degree in Christian mysteries, hence of contemplation of divine things, partic. of participation in eucharist, cf. οἱ κατειληφότες τὰ πόρρω τῆς ἡμετέρας ἐ., οἱ μεμυημένοι παρ' αὐτοῦ τὴν ἐσωτερικήν τε καὶ ἀπόρρητον μύησιν Gr.Nyss.*Eun.*12(2 p.304.25; M.45.1016D); ὕπνος... ὅταν εἰς τὰς τελεωτάτας τῶν ὄντων ἐ. ὁδὸν ἀνοίξῃ τῇ ψυχῇ Synes. *insomn.*3(p.151.6; M.66.1288D); ἱεραρχίας τὸ πέρας...ἡ τῆς ἐ. ἑστίασις, τρέφουσα νοητῶς καὶ θεοῦσα πάντα τὸν εἰς αὐτὴν ἀνατεινόμενον Dion. Ar.*e.h.*1.3(M.3.376A); διὰ τοῦ ταύτης [sc. baptism] ἀρχικωτάτου φωτὸς ἐπὶ τὴν τῶν ἄλλων ἱερῶν ἐ. φωταγωγοῦμαι *ib.*3.1(425B); ref.

dismissal of catechumens μένουσι δὲ οἱ τῆς θείων ἐ. καὶ κοινωνίας ἄξιοι ib.3.2(425C); ἡ τῶν...ἐνεργουμένων πληθὺς...πάσης ἀλλοτρία τῆς τῶν ἱερῶν ἐ. καὶ κοινωνίας ib.3.3.7(436B); ib.4.3.3(477A); ἡ δὲ τῶν ἱερέων φωταγωγικὴ τάξις ἐπὶ τὰς θείας τῶν τελετῶν ἐ. χειραγωγεῖ τοὺς τελουμένους ib.5.1.6(505D); ib.(508A); ib.6.1.2(532C); καθαιρομένη δὲ τάξις ἡ τῆς ἱερᾶς ἐ. καὶ κοινωνίας ἀμέτοχος ib.6.3.5(536D); ib.7.3.3 (557C).

B. *inspection*, hence imperial *commission* of assessment, Thdt. *ep*.42(4.1100); *ib*.(1101); *ib*.43(1102).

C. *oversight*; in gen., Areth.*Apoc*.45(M.106.697A); of God's providential care, Thdt.*Ezech*.39:29(2.1018); Geo.Pis.*hex*.1498(M.92.1550A).

D. *visible part*, hence *surface* of skin, Andr.Cr.*or*.21(M.97.1277A).

ἑπτά, *seven*; **1.** as indefinite number signifying *many*, cf.*T.Benj*.7.4; ὁ γὰρ ἑ. ἀριθμὸς παρὰ τῇ γραφῇ ἀδιορίστου πλήθους ἐστὶ σημαντικός Chrys.*Jud*.8.2(1.676C); ref. Mt.18:22 οὐκ ἀριθμὸν τιθεὶς...ἀλλὰ τὸ ἄπειρον καὶ διηνεκὲς...καὶ γὰρ τό, 'στεῖρα ἔτεκεν ἑ.', τὸ πολλά φησιν ἡ γραφή. ὥστε οὐκ ἀριθμῷ συνέκλεισε τὴν ἄφεσιν id.*hom.61.1 in Mt.*(7.611A); exeg. 1Reg.2:5 στεῖρα ἔτεκεν ἑ., τὴν τῆς ἐκκλησίας προκηρύττει πολυγονίαν. ὁ γὰρ ἑ. ἀριθμὸς τοῦ πλήθους δηλωτικός. ἐν ἑ. γὰρ ἡμέραις ἅπας χρόνος ἀνακυκλεῖται, καὶ τῆς ἐκκλησίας οἱ παῖδες τὴν οἰκουμένην ἐπλήρωσαν Thdt.*qu.3 in 1Reg.*(1.357); **2.** as indicating perfection, or completeness, *T.Zab*.7.4; cf. list of seven virtues, Herm.*vis*.3.8.2ff.; τῶν ἑ. φωνηέντων τὴν ἐπὶ τὸ αὐτὸ σύνθεσιν μιᾶς τινος ἀπορρήτου προσηγορίας περιέχειν φασὶν ἐκφώνησιν, ἣν διὰ τεσσάρων στοιχείων παῖδες Ἑβραίων σημειούμενοι ἐπὶ τῆς ἀνωτάτω τοῦ θεοῦ δυνάμεως κατατάττουσιν...καὶ τῶν παρ' Ἕλλησι δὲ σοφῶν... τις τοῦτο μαθὼν ᾐνίξατο...φήσας· ἑ. με φωνήεντα θεὸν μέγαν ἄφθιτον αἰνεῖ γράμματα [i.e. divine name is contained in combination of seven vowels, cf.*Liber Mosis* 17.13 ap. A. Dieterich *Abraxas* (Leipzig 1891) p.195.3] Eus.*p.e*.11.6(519D; M.21.861B); τῆς δὲ τοῦ ἑ. τιμῆς, πολλὰ μὲν τὰ μαρτύρια...ὡς ἑ. μὲν ὀνομαζόμενα τίμια πνεύματα. τὰς γὰρ ἐνεργείας ...τοῦ πνεύματος, πνεύματα φίλον τῷ Ἠσαΐᾳ καλεῖν Gr.Naz.*or*.41.3(M.36.432C); other examples from scripture include seven trumpets of Joshua at Jericho, ἐν ἑ. μὲν ἡμέραις ὁ ἱερεὺς τελειούμενος, ἐν ἑ. δὲ ὁ λεπρὸς καθαιρόμενος, ἐν τοσαύταις δὲ ὁ ναὸς ἐγκαινιζόμενος...Ἰησοῦς ...οἶδε τρέφειν...ἑ. [sc. ἄρτοις] τετρακισχιλίους. καὶ τὰ...λείψανα... σπυρίδες ἑ.· οὐδέτερον ἀλόγως...οὐδὲ ἀναξίως τοῦ πνεύματος *ib*.41.4 (433C); ‡Gr.Nyss.*hom.2 in Gen.1:26*(M.44.288B); ref. Naaman's sevenfold washing ἢ ἵνα εἰδέναι ἔχοι...ὡς πληρωματικός ἐστι καὶ τέλειος ὁ ἀριθμὸς ὁ ἑ. ἢ μᾶλλον, ὅτι τὸ...πνεῦμα ᾐνίξατο, Ἠσαΐας γὰρ τὸ παντελὲς καὶ πρὸς τὸν υἱὸν ἀπαράλλακτον τῆς φύσεως αὐτοῦ τῇ πίστει ἐγχωρούντως θεωρήσας, ἑ. σημασίας περὶ αὐτοῦ κατέλεξεν Didym.*Trin*.2.14(M.39.700C); ref. Zach.4:2 ἑ. λύχνους, ἀντὶ τοῦ τῆς πνευματικῆς δωρεᾶς τὴν...τελειότητα *ib*.(704B); question discussed why number seven admits of mutation exhibited in such natural phenomena as growth of teeth in 7th month, second teeth in 7th year, etc.; answer given that potency of the number causes the natural developments αἰδεσιμώτερος δὲ ἐν τῇ...γραφῇ ὁ ἑ. ἀριθμὸς [number esp. to be honoured in memory of Creation] παρὰ τοὺς λοιποὺς...ὅτι ἐν αὐτῷ ὁ πᾶς χρόνος τῆς τε τοῦ κόσμου ποιήσεως καὶ τῆς τοῦ πεποιηκότος...καταπαύσεως ‡Just.*qu.et resp*.69(M.6.1309C–1312A); ὁ ἑ. παρὰ τῇ γραφῇ τίμιος καὶ τέλειος ἀριθμός· τέλεια τοιγαροῦν θύματα κελεύονται προσφέρειν Olymp.*Job* 42:8(M.93.456A); ὁ ἑ. κατὰ τὴν...γραφήν, ὡς μὲν ἀριθμὸς μόνον λαμβανόμενος, πολλὴν ἔχει φυσικῶς τὴν ἐπ' αὐτῷ κειμένην τῶν φιλοπονούντων τὰ θεῖα μυστικὴν θεωρίαν. σημαίνει γὰρ καὶ χρόνον, καὶ αἰῶνα, καὶ αἰῶνας, κίνησίν τε καὶ περιοχὴν καὶ μέτρον, καὶ ὅρον καὶ πρόνοιαν, καὶ ἕτερα πολλά [discussion of seven (or sabbath) as signifying mystical rest follows] Max. *ambig*.(M.91.1389D); φασὶ δὲ καὶ συγγένειάν τινα πνευματικὴν κατὰ μυστικὴν θεωρίαν πρὸς τὸν ζʹ ἀριθμὸν ἔχειν τὸν γʹ...τῷ τὴν...τριάδα διὰ τοῦ γʹ σημαίνεσθαι, καὶ πάλιν τὴν αὐτὴν διὰ τοῦ ζʹ τῷ τὸν ζʹ ἀριθμὸν παρθένον εἶναι. τῶν γὰρ ἐντὸς δεκάδος ἀριθμῶν μόνος οὗτος οὔτε γεννᾷ, οὔτε γεννᾶται. τοῦτο δὲ...ἐνδείκνυται διεξιὼν ἐν τῇ βίβλῳ τῶν ἐπῶν 'περὶ παρθενίας' οὑτωσὶ λέγων, 'πρώτη παρθένος ἐστὶν ἁγνὴ τριάς *ib*.(1393C); representing completeness of evil or of divine punishment, *T.Sym*.2.12; μάχαιρά ἐστι ἑ. κακῶν μήτηρ *T.Benj*.7.2; Gr.Naz.*or*.41.3(M.36.432C); Mod.*mul.ung*.(M.86.3273); **3.** of seven angels ἑ. ἄνδρας ἐν ἐσθῆτι λευκῇ *T.Lev*.8.2; ref. Apoc.1:4 τινὲς τὰ ἑ. πνεύματα τὰς ἐνεργείας τοῦ ἁγίου ὑπέλαβον πνεύματος. δοκιμώτερον δὲ ἀγγέλους ταῦτα νοεῖν Areth.*Apoc*.1(M.106.505B); the seven archangels, Clem.*str*.6.16(p.504.18; M.9.369C); seven ἄγγελοι πρωτόκτιστοι id.*exc.Thdot*.10(p.109.29; M.9.660C); 'seven spirits of God', id.*str*. 5.6(p.349.13; M.9.61A) interpreting Zach.4:2; Gr.Naz.*or*.41.3(M.36.432C); **4.** of heavens; description, *T.Lev*.3.1ff.; of seven heavenly powers in Marcosian system, Iren.*haer*.1.14.7(M.7.608B); Hipp. *haer*.6.48(p.179.19ff.; M.16.3274A); as 'seven houses', i.e. spheres occupied by seven planetary powers ἐλθὲ ἡ μήτηρ τῶν ἑ. οἴκων, ἵνα ἡ ἀνάπαυσίς σου εἰς τὸν ὄγδοον οἶκον γένηται *A.Thom*.A 27(p.142.17); **5.** of seven Manichean prophets ἐνετείλατο δὲ τοῖς ἐκλεκτοῖς αὐτοῦ μόνοις, οὐ πλέον ἑ. οὖσι τὸν ἀριθμόν Hegem.*Arch*.11(p.19.5; M.10.1445B); **6.** of seven loaves and seven baskets (Mc.8:6,8), interpreted as denoting superiority of spiritual capacity of the 4000 as compared with the 5000, Or.*comm.in Mt*.11.19(p.68.28ff.; M.13.972C); number to be interpreted spiritually, Gr.Naz.*or*.41.4(M.36.433C) cit. supra 2; **7.** of the Seven of Ac.6:1ff. and bearing of their number on that of deacons in church, v. διάκονος.

[*]**ἑπτάαστρος**, = ἑπτάστερος, *of seven stars*, i.e. Great Bear τὴν ἑ. ἄρκτον *M.Areth*.(p.36).

***ἑπταδύναμος**, *consisting of seven powers* (i.e. cosmic powers of seven heavens), Hipp.*haer*.6.48(p.180.4; M.16.3274A).

***ἑπταετέω**, *spend seven years*, Thdr.Stud.*epp*.2.147(M.99.1461A).

***ἑπταετήριος**, *lasting seven years* μόχθῳ ἑπτα[ετη]ρίῳ *CIG* 8664 (Nicaea, saec. viii).

***ἑπταετηρίς**, ἡ, *period of seven years*, Dion.Al.ap.Eus.*h.e*.7.23.4 (M.20.692C).

***ἑπτακαιδεκαετηρίς**, ἡ, *period of seventeen years*, *Chron.Pasch*. p.288(M.92.720 diagram).

ἑπτάκαυλος, *with seven branches*; met., of Gr. Naz. ἑ. ... λαμπάδιον...πυρσούμενον Cosm.Mel.*schol*.proem.(M.38.342).

ἑπτάκις, *seven times*; **1.** ref. Ps.118:164 πρὸ ἡλίου...τὸν πρῶτον ἀνέπεμπεν ὕμνον· εἶτα...κατὰ τὴν πρώτην ὥραν...καὶ κατὰ τὴν τρίτην ...τὸν τρίτον καὶ...κατὰ τὴν ἕκτην τὸν τέταρτον, κατὰ δὲ τὴν ἐνάτην ὥραν τὸν πέμπτον, κατὰ δὲ τὴν δωδεκάτην τὸν ἕκτον, εἶθ' ἑσπέρας...ἐπὶ κοίτην μέλλων τρέπεσθαι τὸν ἕβδομον ὕμνον...καὶ οὕτως ἐπλήρου τό· 'ἑ. τῆς ἡμέρας ᾔνεσά σε' Eus.*Ps*.118:164(M.23.1392A); αἰνεῖ τὸν θεὸν [sc. ὁ δίκαιος] ἑ. ὑπερκόσμιος γεγονώς, τοῦ ἄνω κεχωρηκέναι τοῦ ἐν ἓξ ἡμέραις γενομένου κόσμου· ἅτε καὶ ἐν τῷ παραδείσῳ τοῦ θεοῦ γεγενημένος Ath.*exp.Ps*.118:164(M.27.508A); τινὲς τὸ ἑ. πλειστάκις ἡρμήνευσαν Thdt.*Ps*.118:164(1.1478); **2.** as number of perfection (v. ἑπτά) ἁμαρτωλός, οὐχ ἑ. μόνον, ἀλλὰ καὶ ἑβδομηκοντάκις ἑπτὰ συγχωρούμενος καὶ...ἐκ τῶν ἐναντίων...Κάϊν μὲν ἐκδικούμενος ἑ. Gr. Naz.*or*.41.3(M.36.432C); ref. Naaman's washing, interpreted either as denoting perfection, or as instructing him as a gentile that God rested from Creation on seventh day, Didym.*Trin*.2.14(M.39.700C).

***ἑπτακισχιλιοστός**, *seven thousandth*, Meth.*creat*.12(p.499.30; M.18.344B) cit. s. ἑξακισχιλιοστός.

***ἑπτακοστός**, = ἑβδομηκοστός, *seventieth*, Epiph.*haer*.70 tit.(M.42.340A; οʹ p.232.16).

***ἑπτάκυκλος**, **1.** *with seven cycles* (*spheres*); of heaven, fig., ref. BMV ὦ γαστὴρ ἑ. οὐρανός ‡Epiph.*hom*.5(M.43.497B); **2.** *of sevenfold cycle* of days of week, Geo.Pis.*hex*.337(M.92.1460A).

***ἑπτάλογος**, ἡ, *Book of Seven* (cf. decalogue), title of Manich. work καινοτομοῦσιν ἑαυτοῖς δαιμονιώδη βιβλία ἅπερ εἰσὶ τάδε...εʹ. ἡ ἑ. Ἀλογίου Tim.CP *haer*.(M.86.21C); but cf. ἠριθμοῦντο δὲ τῷ χορῷ τῶν μαθητευθέντων αὐτῷ [sc. Manes] καὶ Ἀγάπιος, ὁ τὴν ἑ. καλουμένην συντάξας Phot.*contra Manichaeos* 1.14(M.102.41B).

ἑπτάλοφος (**-λωφος**), *with seven hills*; of Rome, *Orac.Sib*.2.18; *ib*.13.45; *ib*.14.108; of CP, *Apoc.Dan*.C(p.119); *ib*.(p.116); a part of CP (in form ἑπτάλωφος), *V.Amph*.5(M.39.25C).

***ἑπτάμετρος**, *sevenfold*, Jo.D.*carm.theog*.88(p.207; M.96.824A).

[*]**ἑπταμηναῖος**, v.l. for ἑπταμηνιαῖος, *born in the seventh month*, Thphn.*chron*.p.45(M.108.169A).

***ἑπτάμορφος**, *in seven forms*, ref. Is.11:2 of H. Ghost τὸ πνεῦμα τῆς ἀληθείας τὸ ἑ. Meth.*symp*.3.8(p.36.16; M.18.73C).

ἑπτάμυξος, *with seven wicks*; of seven-branched candlestick as representing sabbath-rest of God, Didym.*Trin*.2.14(M.39.700C); as part of cult apparatus added to Israelite system after covenant and adduced in refutation of Aërius' appeal to primitive simplicity of church order, Epiph.*haer*.75.5(p.337.10; M.42.509D); καιρὸν...καθ' ὃν ἡ συναγωγὴ διελύετο, καὶ ἡ ἐκκλησία ἐσφίγγετο...καθ' ὃν ἡ ἑ. λυχνία ἐσβέννυτο, καὶ ὁ δωδεκάκτινος σταυρὸς ἀνήπτετο Leont. B.*mesopent*.(M.86.1992A).

§**ἑπτάμυχος**, *with seven lamps* (cf. Ex.25:37, Apoc.1:20); of Church, cf. *ubique enim ecclesia praedicat veritatem: et haec est* ἑ. *lucerna, Christi bajulans lumen*, Iren.*haer*.5.20.1(ἑπτάμυξος M.7.1177C).

ἑπταπλασίων, *sevenfold* ὁ θρόνος ἑπταπλασίων φωτὸς ἡλίου ἀνατέλλοντος *Apocalypsis Sophoniae* ap.Clem.*str*.5.11(p.377.23; M.9.116A); 'ἀπόδος τοῖς γείτοσιν...ἑ. ...' πολλαπλασίαν...τὴν τιμωρίαν ἐπάγαγε. οὐ γὰρ ὡρισμένον ἀριθμὸν διὰ τῶν εἰρημένων ἐδήλωσεν Thdt.*Ps*.78:12 (1.1170); signifying completeness ἑπταπλασίονα τοίνυν τὴν ἀντίδοσιν ἡμῖν χρεωστουμένην τοῖς ἁμαρτωλοῖς συγχωρήσει ὁ κύριος ἐνταῦθα ‡Bas.*struct.hom.*2.8(1.342D; M.30.52A); Sever.*Abr.*1(M.56.554) cit. s. ἑπτάφωτος.

ἑπταπλασίως, *sevenfold, seven times,* as denoting an indefinitely large number of times ἔδει...τοὺς οὕτω τρυφῶντας...ἑ. βασανίζεσθαι Herm.*sim.*6.4.2; ὥστε τὸν οὐρανὸν γενέσθαι φωταγωγὸν ἑ. ὑπὲρ πάσας τὰς ἡμέρας *Anaph.Pil.*A 9(p.440); Or.*Jo.*19.9(2; p.309.11; M.14.544A); τὸ ἑ. ἀντὶ τοῦ πολλαπλασίως τέθεικε. τοῦτο γὰρ σύνηθες τῇ θείᾳ γραφῇ Thdt.*Ps.*11:7(1.676).

***ἑπτάπληγος,** *of seven* [i.e. an indefinite number of] *plagues* ἔπεμψεν ὁ θεὸς...ἑ. ὀργήν Jo.Mal.*chron.*3 p.65(M.97.144A).

***ἑπταπλόω,** *multiply by seven,* ‡Germ.CP *contempl.*(M.98.392C).

***ἑπταπλωμένως,** *by being multiplied by seven,* ‡Sophr.H.*liturg.*5 (M.87.3985C) cit. s. κρατέω.

ἑπτάς, ἡ, *group of seven*; of gifts of H. Ghost, Clem.*paed.*3.12 (p.284.18; M.8.665C) cit. s. ἐπᾴδω.

ἑπτάστολος, *seven-robed,* i.e. with seven planets; of Isis, Hipp. *haer.*5.7(p.84.4; M.16.3134B).

***ἑπτασύλλαβος,** *of seven syllables*; λόγος ἑ. as title of sermon; ? *consisting of seven headings* or poss. connected with theme of seven gifts of H. Ghost, contrasted with four-syllable theme [cf. τετρασύλλαβος] of preceding sermon which deals with διάβολος, Ephr.1.182B.

***ἑπτασύνθετος,** *multiplied by seven,* Geo.Pis.*Sev.*119(M.92. 1632A).

***ἑπτάτομος,** *in seven books* ἡ...τῆς ἑ. [sc. ἱστορίας] ὑπόθεσις Socr. *h.e.*7.48.8(M.67.841A).

***ἑπτάφωτος,** *with seven lights,* exeg. Zach.4:2 ἑ. εἰσάγει λυχνίαν διὰ τὴν τοῦ κυρίου ἔνσαρκον οἰκονομίαν. λυχνία γὰρ ἦν ἀληθὴς ἡ σὰρξ δεσποτική, ἡ τοῦ ἁγίου πνεύματος τὰς ἐλλάμψεις ἑπταπλασίονι χάριτι δείξασα Sever.*Abr.*1(M.56.554); ref. Samson ὅς γε ἑπτὰ βοστρύχους ἐπὶ τῆς κεφαλῆς ἔφερε τῆς ἑ. χάριτος τὴν εἰκόνα βαστάζων Ephr.3.72C = ‡Chrys.*decoll.*(8.3C); ref. BMV ὦ γαστὴρ ἑ. χάριτος τὸ ἄσβεστον ἔχουσα φῶς ‡Epiph.*hom.*5(M.43.497B); τῆς ἑ. λυχνίας τῶν δογμάτων πυρσοὺς ἀνάπτων αἱρέσεις καταφλέγει Geo.Pis.*carm.* 11.1.

ἐπῳδή, ἡ, A. *charm, spell*; **1.** in good sense ἐ. τὰς ὑγιεῖς παρὰ Θρᾳκῶν λαμβάνεις [sc. Plato] Clem.*prot.*6(p.53.14; M.8.176B); ἀναιρῶν τὸ ἰοβόλον τῷ κατακοιμίζων ἐπῳδῇ ἢ δυνάμει τινὶ κενῶν αὐτὸ τοῦ ἰοῦ Or.*Jo.*6.54(36; p.163.24; M.14.296A); εἴ ποτέ τις ὑμῶν ἑώρακεν ἀπὸ ἐπῳδῶν ἀσπίδα κοιμιζομένην id.*hom.20.2 in Jos.* (p.418.31; M.12.920B); *ib.20.1*(p.416.21; 920A); fig., *ib.*(p.418.30; 920B); ἐπὰν δὲ οὓς φησιν εἶναι ἰδιωτικοὺς λόγους ὁ Κέλσος κατανοήσωμεν, ὡσπερεὶ ἐ. δυνάμεως πεπληρωμένους καὶ τοὺς λόγους θεωρῶμεν id.*Cels.*3.68(p.260.25; M.11.1009B); in comparison of Logos with Orpheus μουσικὸν ὄργανον χερσὶ λαβών...τὸν ἄνθρωπον, ᾠδὰς καὶ ἐ. διὰ τούτου λογικοῖς ἀλλ' οὐκ ἀλόγοις θηρσὶν ἀνεκρούετο, πάντα τρόπον ἀνήμερον...τοῖς τῆς ἐνθέου διδασκαλίας φαρμάκοις ἐξιώμενος Eus.*l.C.* 14(p.242.26; 1409C); προσευχῇ καὶ σφραγῖδι τὴν θεραπείαν ἐδέξατο, καὶ τῇ τῆς θείας προσηγορίας ἐ. τὰς ὀδύνας ἐκοίμισε Thdt.*h.rel.*22(3. 1255); προσενεγκεῖν τῇ ψυχῇ τῶν θείων λόγων τὴν ἐ. id.*ep.*14(4.1072); **2.** in gen.; effectiveness dependent on use of original language οἱ περὶ τὴν χρῆσιν τῶν ἐ. δεινοὶ ἱστοροῦσιν, ὅτι τὴν αὐτὴν ἐ. εἰπόντα μὲν τῇ οἰκείᾳ διαλέκτῳ ἔστιν ἐνεργῆσαι ὅπερ ἐπαγγέλλεται ἡ ἐ.· μεταλαβόντα δὲ εἰς ἄλλην...φωνὴν ἔστιν ἰδεῖν ἄτονον καὶ οὐδὲν δυναμένην Or. *Cels.*1.25(p.76.17; M.11.708A); *ib.*5.45(p.49.1; 1252A); βαρβάρων δέ τινες ἐπὶ ταῖς παραδόξοις ἐξ ἐπῳδῶν δυνάμεσι...ἔνδοξοι γεγένηνται *ib.* 1.30(p.81.20; 717A); δαιμόνων καὶ τῆς καλούσης αὐτοὺς ἐ. *ib.*1.60 (p.110.26; 769B); used by Magi until Inc. when power of demons was broken and magic became ineffective, *ib.*(p.111.9; 769C); ref. release of SS. Peter, Paul, and Silas from prison ἔδοξε [sc. Celsus] γὰρ ἂν λέγειν...ὅτι καὶ γόητές τινες ἐπῳδαῖς δεσμοὺς λύουσι *ib.*2.34 (p.160.22; 856A); *ib.*5.9(p.9.4; 1192D); ἀετὸν ἐν ὕψει πετόμενον δι' ἐπῳδῆς καταπεσεῖν ἐπὶ γῆς πεποίηκε [sc. Pythagoras] ‡Jo.D.*Artem.* 29(p.161.5; M.96.1277C).

B. *canticle* (OT), Eus.*p.e.*11.5(513B; M.21.852B).

ἐπωδίν-ω, *suffer birth-pangs*; met., *be grieved at* φθόνος ὁ τοῖς ἀγαθοῖς ἀεὶ ~ων Isid.Pel.*epp.*2.54(M.78.497C).

ἐπωμάδιος, *on the shoulders* ἐ. ... ἔχων τὸν...σταυρὸν ἔξω τῆς πύλης ἔπαθεν ὁ Ἰησοῦς Or.*sel.in Gen.*22:6(M.12.117B) = Cyr.*glaph. Gen.*3(1.86A); Cyr.*ador.*7(1.229A); id.*Jo.*2.5(4.208D).

ἐπώμιος, *on the shoulders*; neut. as subst., *cape* worn by women, Ath.*virg.*11(p.45.3; M.28.264B); monastic *scapular,* ‡Jo.D.*ep.Thphl.* 28(M.95.380D).

ἐπωμίς, ἡ, A. *shoulder*; hence *garment worn on shoulder*; **1.** *ephod,* priestly garment made of two pieces joined on shoulder (Ex.28:6–7), Ath.*Ar.*2.7(M.26.161B); Gr.Nyss.*v.Mos.*(M.44.320B); Epiph.*gemm.* proem.(M.43.293B); Chrys.*sac.*3.4(p.51.11; 1.382C); Thdt.*qu.*60 *in Ex.* (1.166); Cosm.Ind.*top.*5(M.88.212D); v. ἐφούδ; **2.** *stole,* indicative of priesthood ἐγένετο κληρικός, καὶ ἐπέθηκαν αὐτῷ τὴν ἐ. *Apophth.Patr.* (M.65.284B).

B. plur., *flanks* of a door, Thdt.*Ezech.*40:47–49(2.1023).

[*]**ἐπωμώτης, ὁ,** = ἐπωμότης, *perjurer,* ‡Caes.Naz.*dial.*109(M.38. 977).

***ἐπωνυμικῶς,** *in accordance with* one's *name* πραγμάτων τὴν ἀνέγερσιν ἡμῖν ἐ. προοιμιάζεται [sc. Anastasius II] Jo.VI CP *ep.*(M. 96.1429A).

ἐπωρύω, med., *roar*; of the sea, Gr.Nyss.*hom.5 in Cant.*(M.44. 869C); of enemies of Christ, Cyr.*Zach.*76(3.757C).

ἐπωτίς, ἡ, *handle* of a cup, *Schol.Clem.paed.*2.3(p.328.6; M.9. 788C).

***ἐραία, ἡ,** *fleece, wool,* Ephr.2.176C.

***ἐρανάριος, ὁ,** (? from Lat. *arenarius*) ? *sandstone weapon, stone club* ὄχλον ἄτακτον μετὰ ξιφῶν καὶ ἄλλων τινῶν ἐ. CChalc.*act.*11(*ACO* 2.1.3 pp.46.13,47.20; H.2.548E,549E).

ἐρανίζ-ω, 1. med., *collect for oneself*; **a.** *gather, learn* ~ονται...τὸ ἐν γνώσει τέλειον Cyr.*Jo.*2.1(4.140D); *ib.*(132D); τῶν ὁρωμένων τὴν ἀποκάλυψιν διὰ τῆς τῶν ἀγγέλων ~εται φωνῆς *ib.*1.9(73C); **b.** *acquire* τὴν ἐπὶ τῷδε πίστιν ~ομένους id.*glaph.Gen.*2.1(1.46B); οὐδὲ ἀπὸ τῆς τέχνης τὸ ἐνεργεῖν ἠρανισμένους Thdt.*Dan.*5:4(2.1160); **c.** *earn* one's living τὸν βίον ἐκ τούτων ~ομένων ἀφ' ὧνπερ καὶ τὸ πρότερον ἐποιεῖτο Bas.Sel.*v.Thecl.*2.7(M.85.576C); **d.** *beg,* Cyr.*Juln.*8(6[2].265A); ἑστᾶσιν ἀναιδῶς ~όμενοι ‡Nil.*perist.*9.9(M.79.881B); Philost.*h.e.*11.3(M.65. 597B); **e.** *borrow* τὸ δύνασθαι συντρίβειν σατανᾶν ὡς δοτὸν παρ' ἑτέρου καὶ μόλις ~όμενον; Cyr.*Nest.*4.3(p.81.26; 6[1].104D); ἆρα ἑτέρωθεν ~εται [sc. Christ] τῆς εὐεργεσίας τὴν δύναμιν; Bas.Sel.*or.*33.2(M.85. 361C); **2.** pass.; **a.** *be produced* τὸ ἐξ ὕλης καὶ τέχνης ἐρανισθέν, θεὸς ὀνομάζεται Thdt.*affect.*3(p.90.78; 4.782); **b.** *be assisted by public contributions* ἑταίρας καὶ ὀρχηστρίδας...καὶ πλῆθος ~ομένων *Ep.*ap. CSyr.(518)*act.*(*ACO* 3 p.96.23; H.2.1372B); τοὺς ἐρανισθέντας ὑπ' αὐτοῦ Epiph.Tyr.*ep.*(p.82.13; H.2.1349A).

ἐρανισμός, ὁ, *collection,* ‡Chrys.*pasch.*6.8(p.135.6; 8.266E).

***ἐρανιστέον,** *one must contribute,* Clem.*str.*6.11(p.476.22; M.9. 309C).

ἐρανιστής, ὁ, *collector* ὄνομα δὲ συγγράμματι, ἐ., ἢ πολύμορφος. ἐκ πολλῶν γὰρ ἀνοσίων ἀνθρώπων ἐρανισάμενοι τὰ δύστηνα δόγματα, τὸ ποικίλον τοῦτο καὶ πολύμορφον προφέρουσι φρόνημα Thdt.*eran.* proem.(4.2).

ἔρανος, ὁ, (**ἔρανον, τό**), **1.** *free gift* οὐκ ἔ. τὴν ἀπαλλαγὴν τῆς κολάσεως ἀξιοῦντες λαβεῖν ‡Nil.*perist.*4.17(M.79.848D); **2.** *collection* of waters, Thdt.*Is.*7:12(p.110.11); **3.** *public contributions,* Ephr.3. 440A; τοῖς ἐκ τῶν ἐ. σιτιζομένοις Epiph.Tyr.*ep.*(p.82.17; H.2.1349B); neut. plur. ἔρανα, Sophr.Al.*libell.*(p.24.9; H.2.337B); CSyr.*act.*(*ACO* 3 p.102.33, v.l. ἔρανον H.2.1381D).

***ἐρασιχρηματία, ἡ,** *love of money,* Olymp.*Job* 31:27(M.93.329D).

***ἐράσκομαι,** variant of ἔραμαι *love, Pers.*(p.6.2).

***ἐρασμιότης, ἡ,** *loveliness,* Epiph.*haer.*1.23(p.248.17; M.41.300A).

***ἐρασμίως,** *lovingly,* Nil.*epp.*2.282(M.79.341A); ἐ. ἔχω *want,* ἐ. τε ἔχοντα μονάσαι *Mir.Artem.*39(p.64.2); ὡς ἐ. ἔχεις ποίει Thphn.*chron.* p.290(M.108.712C).

ἐραστής, ὁ, A. *lover*; **1.** of God as lover of souls ἀπειλεῖται νῦν ἡ ψυχὴ παρὰ τοῦ ἐ. Or.*Cant.*(p.141.31; M.17.257A); φίλει γάρ, φησὶ [sc. God], μετ' ἐμοῦ, καὶ τότε σε καὶ ἐγὼ φιλήσω μειζόνως. ὁρᾷς ἐ. σφοδροῦ ῥήματα; Chrys.*hom.*23.4 *in Rom.*(9.691B); ref. Cain οὐδὲ... ὁ θεὸς ἀφίσταται, ἀλλὰ...ἐραστοῦ φθέγγεται ῥήματα ὑβρισμένου *ib.*23.5 (692D); ἵνα...τὸν ἁπάντων δεσπότην θεὸν ἔχητε ἐ. id.*hom.*28.7 *in Heb.* (12.268B); ζηλωτὴς ὁ θεός, ὡς ἐ. τῆς πάντων σωτηρίας Max.*schol. d.n.*4.13(M.4.265C); **2.** of Christ; as lover of chastity, Meth.*symp.* 7.1(p.71.20; M.18.125A); μάθε ὅτι τῷ Χριστῷ ἡρμόσθης,...ἐπιζητεῖ κάλλος οὗ καὶ σφοδρός ἐστιν ἐ., τὸ ἐν τῇ ψυχῇ λέγω Chrys.*hom.*30.6 *in Mt.*(7.355E); ἁπάντων μεῖζον τὸ τὸν Χριστὸν ἐρώμενον ἔχειν ὁμοῦ καὶ ἐ. id.*hom.*9.4 *in Rom.*(9.519B); exeg. Mt.23:37 πρὸς ἐρωμένην... καταφρονήσασαν δὲ τοῦ ἐ. ... ἀπολογεῖται λοιπὸν μέλλων ἐπάγειν τὴν κόλασιν id.*hom.*74.3 *in Mt.*(718C); *ib.*(718E); **3.** of lovers of God and Christ, †Bas.Anc.*virg.*25(M.30.721C); χρὴ περὶ τὸ θεῖον ἔχειν τοὺς ἐ. τοῦ ὑπερκοσμίου κάλλους Gr.Nyss.*hom.*6 *in Cant.*(M.44.885B); ἔστι δὲ καὶ ἐκστατικὸς ὁ θεῖος ἔρως, οὐκ ἐῶν ἑαυτῶν εἶναι τοὺς ἐ., ἀλλὰ τῶν ἐρωμένων Dion.Ar.*d.n.*4.13(M.3.712A); of S. Paul Παῦλος... ὡς ἀληθὴς ἐ. καὶ ἐξεστηκώς *ib.*; of S. Peter σφοδρὸς ἦν ἐ. τοῦ Χριστοῦ Chrys.*hom.*54.2 *in Mt.*(7.547C); *ib.*56.3(568D); **4.** of lovers of virtue, Chrys.*hom.*62.5 *in Mt.*(7.627C); charity, id.*hom.*17.1 *in Eph.*(11.122C); truth, Clem.*str.*7.16(p.67.3; M.9.532A); *ib.*8.1(p.81.5;

561A); Or.*fr.42 in Jo.*3:19(p.517.18); Epiph.*haer.*28.2(p.314.14; M.41.380B); justice, Clem.*prot.*10(p.68.19; M.8.205B); Meth.*symp.*7.5(p.77.1; M.18.132B); ref. Christ as unicorn οἱ κεράτων μονοκερώτων ἐρασταί Clem.*paed.*1.5(p.100.4; M.8.269A); τῶν θείων οἱ ἐ. Thdt.*h.e.*2.15.10(3.863); *ib.*2.24.9(889); ἐ. ... τῆς ἐνθένδε ἀπαναστάσεως Gr.Naz.*or.*7.22(M.35.785B); **5.** of lovers of evil, pagans τῶν πρὶν κακῶν ἐ. τῆς πορνευούσης ἐκ θεοῦ ψυχῆς Or.*hom.8.4 in Ex.*(p.224.26); τῶν ἐθνικῶν ψυχῶν ἀσυγκρίτως ἀμείνους πορευομένων ὀπίσω τῶν ἐ. τῶν ἀντικειμένων δυνάμεων id.*Cant.*2(p.145.28; M.17.257B); devils ἐὰν ἴδῃς ψυχὴν ἐγκειμένην τοῖς βουλομένοις ἐ., ὄψει ὅτι 'πεποίηκεν οἴκημα πορνικόν' καὶ ἐπιδέχεται πάντας τοὺς προαιρουμένους πορνεύειν μετ' αὐτῆς, δηλονότι τὰς ἀκαθάρτους δυνάμεις id.*hom.7 in Ezech.*(p.396.27; M.13.723n.); ἐ. γάρ εἰσιν ὁ διάβολος καὶ οἱ περὶ αὐτὸν ἄγγελοι, οἱ τὸ λογικὸν ἡμῶν...κάλλος μιαίνειν...τεχναζόμενοι καὶ μοιχοὶ γενέσθαι πάσης τῆς τῷ κυρίῳ νενυμφευμένης ἐπιθυμοῦντες ψυχῆς Meth.*symp.*6.1(p.65.3; M.18.113C).

B. *friend, follower, adherent* δέκα τις μόνον, ἢ εἴκοσι ἔχων ἐραστὰς ἐν δήμῳ τοσούτῳ Chrys.*serm.2.1 in Gen.*(4.651D); Thdt.*h.rel.*2(3.1124); τῶν Χριστιανῶν...ἐραστής ‡Jo.D.*Artem.*9(M.96.1260B); of adherents of heretics, Philost.*h.e.*2.5(M.65.469B); *ib.*5.1(528C); *ib.*8.3(557B).

ἐραστός, *beloved, desirable*; **1.** esp. of God συνὼν [sc. ὁ γνωστικός] ἤδη δι' ἀγάπης τῷ ἐ. Clem.*str.*6.9(p.468.1; M.9.293B); ἀγάπῃ δὲ τοῦ ὄντως ὄντος ἐ. ἑλκόμενος *ib.*4.22(p.312.25; M.8.1356A); *ib.*3.5(p.216.4; 1148A); οἱ θεολόγοι...αὐτόν [sc. θεόν] φασι...ἐ. ... ὡς καλὸν καὶ ἀγαθόν Dion.Ar.*d.n.*4.14(M.3.712C); τὸ δὲ ἀγαπητὸν καὶ ὄντως ἐ. αὐτός [sc. θεός] ἐστι...τῷ δὲ αὐτὸν εἶναι τὸ ἀληθῶς ἐ. ... κινεῖ τὰ πρὸς τοῦτο ὁρῶντα Max.*schol.d.n.*4.14(M.4.265C); of καλὸν καὶ ἀγαθόν used as synonym of God, Dion.Ar.*d.n.*4.10(M.3.708A); *ib.*4.13(712B); τὰ ὄντως ἐ. καὶ θεῖα *ib.*8.8(896C); **2.** in gen., of the beautiful that is desirable to God, Meth.*Porph.*3(p.506.14; M.18.401A); πρὸς εὐδοξίαν ...ἐραστήν id.*symp.*10.6(p.129.1; M.18.204A); ἐ. θεωρία Dion.Ar.*c.h.*13.4(M.3.308B); id.*e.h.*5.3.6(M.3.513B).

[*]**ἐρατόχρως,** *with lovely colours*, Gr.Naz.*carm.*1.2.2.624(M.37.627A).

[*]**ἐρατωπός,** *of splendid appearance*, *Orac.Sib.*11.84.

ἐράω, *love*, used in act. only in pres. and imperf.; other tenses supplied by ἔραμαι (freq. used interchangeably with φιλέω and ἀγαπάω, though also of sexual love and passionate desire, *LS*); **1.** of God loving creatures ὁ τῆς γῆς δεσπότης...σφόδρα ἡμῶν ἐρᾷ Chrys.*hom.76.4 in Mt.*(7.738C); οὐδενὸς δεῖται ἐκεῖνος ἡμετέρων, καὶ οὐδὲ οὕτω παύεται ἡμῶν ἐρῶν id.*hom.6.7 in Rom.*(9.471E); ὁ πάντων αἴτιος δι' ἀγαθότητος ὑπερβολὴν πάντων ἐρᾷ Dion.Ar.*d.n.*4.10(M.3.708A); ὁ θεὸς πάντων ἐρᾷ, ἵνα τὰ πάντα ἀγαθὰ ποιήσῃ Max.*schol.d.n.*4.10(M.4.261A); cf.id.*schol.epp.Dion.Ar.*8.1(M.4.545B); of Christ loving virgin souls ἐρᾶσθαι τοῦ κάλλους τῆς ἀκμῆς αὐτῆς ὁμολογεῖν οὐκ ἐπαισχύνεται [sc. ὁ Χριστός] Meth.*symp.*7.1(p.72.1; M.18.125A); **2.** of creatures loving God ὁ ἐρῶν ὄντως θεοῦ, καὶ μεριμνῶν πῶς τῷ ἐρωμένῳ ἀρέσῃ †Bas.Anc.*virg.*25(M.30.721B); χρὴ τὴν ψυχὴν πρὸς τὸ ἀπρόσιτον τῆς θείας φύσεως κάλλος ἐνατενίζουσαν, τοσοῦτον ἐρᾶν ἐκεῖνον, ὅσον ἔχει τὸ σῶμα τὴν σχέσιν πρὸς τὸ συγγενές Gr.Nyss.*hom. 1 in Cant.*(M.44.773D); cf.*ib.*(772A); κινητικὸν πρὸς ἐρωτικὴν συνάφειαν τὴν ἐν πνεύματι τὸν θεὸν εἶναί μοι νόει...καὶ πρὸς ἑαυτὸν συναρμοστὴν τοῦ ἐρᾶσθαι αὐτὸν ὑπὸ τῶν αὐτοῦ ποιημάτων Max.*schol.d.n.*4.14(M.3.265D); and Christ ἁπάντων μεῖζον τὸ τὸν Χριστὸν ἐρώμενον ἔχειν ὁμοῦ καὶ ἐραστήν Chrys.*hom.10.4 in Rom.*(9.519B); τοῦ Χριστοῦ ...ἀγάπης...ἐρῶν Gr.Nyss.*instit.*(p.65.18; M.34.421B); pass. ptcpl. as subst. τοῦτον τὸν ἐραστὴν πρὸς ἑαυτὸν ἐκ τῶν κατὰ γὴν παθῶν ἀνακαλῶν ὁ ἐρώμενος [sc. Christ] †Bas.Anc.*virg.*25(721D); of irrational creatures τῶν ἀψύχων καὶ ἀναισθήτων κατὰ τὴν ἐκτικὴν ἐπιτηδειότητα ἐρώντων τοῦ δημιουργοῦ διὰ τὸ ὑπ' αὐτοῦ συνεστάναι Max.*schol.d.n.*4.15(M.4.269A); cf.Dion.Ar.*d.n.*4.10(M.3.708A); **3.** of men loving spiritual things χρὴ οὖν τὴν παρθένον ἀεὶ τῶν καλῶν ἐρᾶν Meth.*symp.*1.1(p.9.7; M.18.40A); ἀληθείας ἐρῶν *Hom.Clem.*5.2; τῆς ἄνω πατρίδος ἐρᾶν Chrys.*hom.54.5 in Mt.*(7.552D); τῶν ὄντως ὄντων ἐρῶσιν Dion.Ar.*e.h.*4.3.1(M.3.476A); effects of such love οὗτος [sc. ἔρως πνευματικός] καὶ τὸν ὄντα πόλεμον ἐκβάλλει, καὶ ἐν εἰρήνῃ πολλῇ τοὺς ἐρῶντας καθίστησι Chrys.*hom.in 2 Cor.11:1*(3.291B); ὁ γὰρ ψυχῆς ἁγίας ἐρῶν...κἂν αὐτὸς...ἁπάντων ἀνθρώπων αἴσχιστος, ἐμμένων τῷ ἔρωτι τῶν ἁγίων, ταχέως ἔσται τοιοῦτος, οἷος ὁ ἐρώμενος *ib.*(291D); **4.** of perverted love of devils κατ' εἰκόνα...δημιουργηθεῖσα [sc. ἡ ψυχή] τοῦ μονογενοῦς...ἀνυπέρβλητον ἔχει τὸ κάλλος. διὸ δὴ καὶ τὰ πνευματικὰ τῆς πονηρίας ἐρῶσιν αὐτῆς καὶ ἐφεδρεύουσι, χρᾶναι βιαζόμενα τὴν θεοείκελον αὐτῆς ἐκείνην καὶ ἐπέραστον ἰδέαν Meth.*symp.*6.1(p.64.21; M.18.113C).

***ἐργαγαθ-έω,** *perform good* or *worthy actions* νήφειν πρὸς τὰς νυκτερίνας ὑπηρεσίας, καὶ εἴ τις ἑτέρα βούλοιτο ~εῖν *Sent.App.*(p.85).

ἐργάζ-ομαι, 1. *work at, practise* virtue, etc. ἔχετε μεθ' ἑαυτῶν εἰς οὓς ἐργάσεσθε τὸ καλόν *Barn.*21.2; οἱ ~όμενοι τὴν δικαιοσύνην Herm.*vis.*2.2.7; ~εται τὴν εὐποιΐαν Clem.*str.*7.13(p.58.18; M.9.513B); **2.** *digest* εἰ...ἡ γαστὴρ τὸ πᾶν εἰργάζετο Chrys.*hom.13.4 in 1Tim.*(11.624C); pass. τροφή...εἰργασμένη Clem.*str.*7.6(p.25.3; M.9.445B); **3.** *overcome*, cf. κατεργάζομαι: οὐχ ἁπλῶς ἐργάσασθαι εἶπεν ἀλλὰ κατεργάσασθαι, ὥστε οὐκ ἀνελεῖν μόνον, ἀλλὰ καὶ στῆναι μετὰ τὸ ἀνελεῖν Chrys.*hom.22.3 in Eph.*(11.170B); ἐλπίδα ἔχω τοὺς πολεμίους ἐργάσασθαι Thphn.*chron.*p.186(M.108.484B); **4.** *work in* καμήλους...τρισχιλίας ~εσθαι πᾶσαν πόλιν *T.Job* 9(p.108.25); **5.** *cause*, c. infin. τὸ ὄνομα βεβηλωθῆναι...εἰργάσαντο Just.*dial.*117.3(M.6.748A); **6.** theol., *work*, of man opp. God οἱ μὲν λόγοι τῶν ἀνθρώπων οὐδέν εἰσιν εἰς ἐνέργειαν· διὸ οὐδὲ διὰ λόγων ἀλλὰ διὰ χειρῶν ἄνθρωπος ~εται, ὅτι αὗται μὲν ὑπάρχουσιν, ὁ δὲ λόγος αὐτῶν οὐχ ὑφίσταται Ath.*Ar.*2.35(M.26.221C); man not created in order to work Ἀδὰμ γὰρ ἐκτίσθη, οὐχ ἵνα ~ηται, ἀλλ' ἵνα πρῶτον ὑπάρχῃ ἄνθρωπος· μετὰ ταῦτα γὰρ ἔλαβε τὴν ἐντολὴν τοῦ ~εσθαι *ib.*2.51(256A); of Christ ἵν', ὥσπερ ἐν τῇ κτίσει διὰ τῶν ἔργων γνωρίζεται, οὕτως καὶ ἐν ἀνθρώπῳ ἐργάσηται id.*inc.*45.1(M.25.176C); that Father and Son work same work is proof that Son is not a creature, id.*Ar.*2.21(189C); of God sustaining creation, Chrys.*hom.38.2 in Jo.*(8.219B); Ammon.*Jo.*5:17(M.85.1429B).

ἐργαλεῖον, τό, *tool, instrument*; **1.** met.; **a.** in gen. ἐ. ἐστι τὸ σῶμα καὶ ὥσπερ ἱμάτιον καὶ στολὴ ψυχῆς Cyr.H.*catech.*4.23; ταῦτα... τὰ τρία ἐ. εἰσὶ πρὸς κατόρθωσιν ἀρετῶν καὶ τῆς ἐκ θεοῦ ἁγνείας ἐγκράτεια γαστρὸς καὶ γλώσσης, καὶ ὀφθαλμοῦ χαλινός Ephr.1.325E; ἡ νηστεία...ἐ. ... ἐστι ὥσπερ εἰς σωφροσύνην ῥυθμίζον τοὺς θέλοντας Diad.*perf.*47(p.552.19); **b.** of Logos, acc. Arians ὁ δημιουργὸς θεὸς... ὑποστήσας ἑαυτῷ ὡς ἐ. τὸν υἱὸν ἔκτισε δι' αὐτοῦ τὸν κόσμον Gel.Cyz.*h.e.*2.16.3(M.85.1260D); orthodox answer ἐν τῷ γὰρ εἰπεῖν 'ποιήσωμεν ἄνθρωπον' ἀναιρεῖ τὴν τῶν ἐ. ἐπίνοιαν *ib.*2.16.11(1261C); ἐ. ... τῆς ἐνούσης τέχνης ἤτοι σοφίας ἔτεκεν ὁ πατήρ Cyr.*Jo.*9.1(4.789E); μὴ... ὁμολογεῖν ὅτι θεός ἐστιν ὁ Χριστός, ὄργανον δὲ μᾶλλον καὶ ἐ. θεότητος id.*ep.*2(*ACO* 1.1.1 p.24.8; 5².20B); **2.** *organ* of body, †Gregent.*leg. Hom.*7(M.86.565B); *ib.*50(608B).

ἐργάνη, ἡ, *work*, Clem.*paed.*3.4(p.252.12; M.8.593B).

ἐργασία, ἡ, 1. *operation, work*; of God in Creation, Just.*dial.*114.3(M.6.740B); Ath.*decr.*8(p.7.19; M.25.429A); id.*Ar.*2.24(M.26.197C); *ib.*2.25(200B); of God sustaining creation, ref. Jo.5:17 ἐ. λέγει τὸ διακρατεῖν τὰ γεγενημένα, καὶ τὴν διαμονὴν αὐτοῖς χαρίζεσθαι, καὶ ἡνιοχεῖν τὰ σύμπαντα Chrys.*hom.10.7 in Gen.*(4.80D); τίς οὖν ὁ τρόπος τῆς ἐ.; προνοεῖ, συγκροτεῖ τὰ γενόμενα πάντα id.*hom.38.2 in Jo.*(8.219B); ποίαν ἐ. λέγεις;...τὴν καθημερινὴν πρόνοιαν id.*anom.*12.4(1.555E); **2.** *action* μύρον εὐωδίας καὶ τὴν οἰκίαν ἐπλήρωσαν, ἡ μὲν Μαρία διὰ τῆς ὁμολογίας, ἡ δὲ Μάρθα διὰ τῆς ἐ. ‡Eust.*Laz.*12(p.37.3); *ib.*27(p.49.7); **3.** *keeping, fulfilling* of commandments, Thdt.*Cant.* 8:12(2.163); Philox.*ep.*31(p.179); **4.** *way of life*, Jo.Mosch.*prat.*54(M.87.2909A); **5.** *function*, Eustrat.*stat.anim.*1(p.338); **6.** *profit, interest* τὸ μὲν τάλαντον ἔχεις, τὴν δὲ ἐ. οὐκ ἐπιφέρῃ Bas.*hom.*13.5(2.119B; M.31.437A); Chrys.*stat.*12.6(2.132B); Thdt.*affect.*12(p.302.9; 4.1015); **7.** plur., ? *manual assaults*, CAlex.*ep.*ap.Ath.*apol.sec.*15(p.98.33; M.25.273A); **8.** prob. error for ἐργάτης, Ath.*h.Ar.*55(p.214.14; M.25.760A).

ἔργασις, ἡ, *labour, work*, Bars.*resp.*(M.86.896B).

ἐργαστηριακός, ὁ, *workman, working man*, Leont.N.*v.Jo.Eleem.* 1(p.6.15); *ib.*16(p.33.18); id.*v.Sym.*43(M.93.1724A); *Chron.Pasch.* p.391(M.92.1000B).

ἐργαστηριάρχης, ὁ, *foreman of workshop*, Mac.Aeg.*hom.*27.18(M.34.705D).

ἐργαστήριον, τό, 1. lit., any place in which work is done; *surgery*, Chrys.*hom.88.3 in Mt.*(7.829B); met. ἐ. τῆς σωτηρίας Pall.*v.Chrys.*5(p.31.22; M.47.20); **2.** met.; **a.** in gen., *workshop, laboratory* Ἀλεξάνδρου πόλιν...παντοίας παιδεύσεως...οὖσαν...ἐ. Gr.Naz.*or.*7.6(M.35.761A); ὁ γάμος ζωῆς ἐστι ἐ. Ephr.3.210F; ἐν τῷ κρυπτῷ τῆς καρδίας ἐ. Call.*v.Hyp.*(p.102); **b.** of the womb; in phrase τὸ τῆς φύσεως ἐ. Clem.*str.*3.12(p.234.13; M.8.1184C); Eus.*v.C.*11.15(p.229.1; M.20.1384C); Gr.Naz.*or.*28.22(p.55.3; M.36.56A); Thdt.*Ps.*138:15(1.1535); of BMV εἰς ἀνθρωπότητα, τουτέστιν εἰς ἐργαστήριον Μαρίας Epiph.*anc.*40(p.50.9; M.43.88D); *ib.*75(p.94.24; 157B); τὸ θεόθεν ἐ. τῆς παγκοσμίου σωτηρίας Mod.*dorm.*13(M.86.3309A); **c.** of persons, *gang*, esp. of heretics τὸ μυσαρὸν ἐ. τῶν Χριστομάχων Ath.*Dion.*13(p.56.1; M.25.500B); περὶ Μανιχαίων...καὶ παντὸς αὐτῶν τοῦ ἐ. Chrys.*hom.12.1 in 1Tim.*(11.610A); Cyr.*ador.*14(1.486A); τὸ τῶν Φαρισαίων θεομισὲς ἐ. id.*Is.*4.1(2.561D); id.*Mal.*37(3.857B); of publicans, id.*Lc.*5:27(M.72.569A); Thdt.*affect.*8(p.196.24; 4.900); **3.** *work* τὰ τῆς ἀπάτης ἐ. Cyr.*Mich.*52(3.443D).

ἐργατεία, ἡ, *work, labour*; sing. and plur., Jo.Mal.*chron.*3 p.63 (M.97.141B); Jo.Mosch.*prat.*37(M.87.2885D,2888A,C); Leont.N.*v.Jo. Eleem.*36(p.70.2,22).

ἐργατεύ-ω, 1. *make to work* οὐ τῷ θεῷ πονοῦντες, ἀλλὰ τοῖς ἀνθρώποις ἑαυτοὺς ∼οντες ‡Bas.*const.*10.1(2.556C; M.31.1373A); πολλοὺς ∼σον τῶν θλιβομένων εἰς τὴν κοινωνίαν τῆς προσευχῆς Bas.*hom.*14.8(2.130B; M.31.461C); **2.** *work as a labourer*, Leont.N.*v.Jo. Eleem.*20(p.37.23); med., ‡Ath.*syntag.*6.9(p.126; M.28.844A); ‡Chrys. *Mt.20:1*(8.100D).

ἐργατικός, 1. *active* ἡ σωφροσύνη...ἐ. ... καὶ οὐ θεωρητική Clem. *str.*6.15(p.495.12; M.9.349A); *effective*; of a word, Or.*fr.hom.39 in Jer.*(p.197.8); **2.** comp., *more laborious*, *V.Pach.Π* 32(p.276.31).

ἐργατικῶς, 1. *as a working man*, Ephr.1.113C; **2.** *in workmanlike ashion*, Agath.*v.Gr.Ill.*98(p.49).

ἐργατίνης, ὁ, 1. *workman*; of a fisherman, Nonn.*par.Jo.*1:43(M. 43.757B); **2.** *creator*; of Christ, Paul.Sil.*Soph.*711(M.86.2146B).

ἐργάτις, ἡ, as adj., *of labour, working*; of seventh day, Clem.*str.* 6.16(p.502.15; M.9.364C).

ἐργεπείκτης, ὁ, *taskmaster*; of the sun, Geo.Pis.*hex.*229(M.92. 1451); of Satan, Germ.CP *or.*1(M.98.236D).

ἐργοδιωκτέω, *force one to work*, Ephr.1.20D.

ἐργοδιώκτης, ὁ, *taskmaster*, Mac.Aeg.*hom.*47.3,6(M.34.797D,800C); Gr.Naz.*carm.*2.1.22.3(M.37.1281A); Cyr.*Is.*4.1(2.543B); met. μὴ ἀρνούμενος τὸ παρὸν ἀνειληφέναι πρὸς ἡμᾶς ἔργον τῶν τοῦ θεοῦ ἐ. Or. *Jo.*5.1(p.100.2; M.14.185C); ἐ. οἱ δαίμονες Nil.*epp.*3.257(M.79.512D).

***ἐργοδόσιον, τό, 1.** *hard labour establishment*, †Gregent.*leg.Hom.* 31(M.86.597C); *ib.*32(600A); **2.** *workshop* τοῦ βασιλικοῦ ἐ. τῶν χρυσοκλαβαρίων Thphn.*chron.*p.395(M.108.941B).

ἐργοδοτέω, *let out work*, Dion.Al.ap.Eus.*p.e.*14.25(776B; M.21. 1277A); Ephr.1.90C.

ἐργοδότης, ὁ, *one who farms out work*; of Pharaoh, Gr.Naz.*or.*16. 14(M.35.940A); ref. Mt.20:1f., *ib.*40.20(M.36.385B); Ephr.1.311F.

***ἐργοεπιστάτης, ὁ,** *overseer, foreman*, Mac.Aeg.*hom.*47.3(M.34. 797D).

***ἐργοκηδεστής, ὁ,** *overseer*, Cyr.*Is.*5.5(2.884A).

ἐργολαβέω, *busy oneself with*, Nil.*epp.*2.77(M.79.236A).

ἐργολάβος, ὁ, *busybody*, Leont.et Jo.*sacr.*tit.(M.86.2022C,2080D); Jo.D.*parall.*tit.(M.95.1536D).

***ἐργολαμβάνω,** *defend* legally, Ath.Scholast.*coll.*4.1(p.50); *ib.*20.3 (p.179).

***ἐργόμοχθος,** *painstaking*, Geo.Pis.*hex.*1205(M.92.1527A).

ἐργομωκέω, *mock*, *V.Ephr.*(p.xxxiiB).

ἔργον, τό, A. *work*; **1.** of man (often plur.); **a.** in gen. ἡμέτερον ἔ. τὸ βιῶσαι καλῶς ἐστι Or.*princ.*3.1.6(p.201.7; M.11.256B); ἡ τῶν ἀναγκαίων τε καὶ συμφερόντων πρᾶξις, ἔ. παρὰ τῆς γραφῆς ὀνομάζεται Gr.Nyss.*hom.1 in Eccl.*(M.44.621B); ἐν τῷ ἔ. τοῦ κυρίου...τουτέστιν, ἐν τῷ βίῳ τῷ καθαρῷ Chrys.*hom.42.3 in 1Cor.*(10.398B); εἰ δὲ λέγεις μοι χρηματισμοὺς καὶ καπηλείας καὶ τὴν τῶν ὄντων ἐπιμέλειαν καὶ προσθήκην, εἴποιμι ἄν σοι καὶ αὐτός, ὅτι ταῦτα οὐκ ἂν εἴη ἔργα, ἀλλ' ἐλεημοσύνη καὶ εὐχαί, καὶ τῶν ἀδικουμένων προστασίαι, καὶ ὅσα τοιαῦτα, ὧν ἐν ἀργίᾳ ζῶμεν διαπαντός id.*hom.35.3 in Mt.*(7.402B); connexion with prayer τινες προφάσει τῶν εὐχῶν καὶ τῆς ψαλμῳδίας παραιτοῦνται τὰ ἔ. ... τὴν προσευχὴν μεταξὺ τοῦ ἔ. πληροῦν Bas.*reg. fus.*37.2(2.382D,E; M.31.1012B,C); τὰ γὰρ ἔ. ἐστὶ τὰ ἀκουόμενα καὶ τὰ κατορθώματα· οὐχ ἁπλῶς δὲ αἱ εὐχαὶ ἀλλ' αἱ κατὰ νόμον τοῦ θεοῦ γινόμεναι εὐχαί Chrys.*exp.in Ps.*4(5.11E); οὔτε εὐχὴν χωρὶς ἔργων οὔτε ἔ. χωρὶς εὐχῆς τίθησι id.*hom.32.2 in Rom.*(9.756A); **b.** esp. good works ἐν ἔ. ἀγαθοῖς πάντες ἐκοσμήθησαν οἱ δίκαιοι *1Clem.*33.7; ἐάν τις θέλων ὁδὸν [sc. τοῦ φωτός] ὁδεύειν...σπεύσῃ τοῖς ἔ. αὐτοῦ *Barn.* 19.1; Just.*1apol.*10.2(M.6.341A); by which soul is protected after death from powers of darkness, Esaias *or.*16.1(cf.*or.*17.1(Lat.)M. 40.1146C); their witness at Judgement ὅτε ἐλθὼν λυτρώσεται ἡμᾶς ἕκαστον κατὰ τὰ ἔ. αὐτοῦ *2Clem.*17.4; κατὰ τὴν ἀναλογίαν τῶν ἔ. σου κίρναταί σοι ὁ θυμὸς καὶ ἡ κόλασις Or.*hom.12.2 in Jer.*(p.88.27; M.13. 381A); ὁ θεὸς ἑκάστῳ κατὰ τὰ ἔ. καὶ κατὰ τὰ ἐπιτηδεύματα ἀποδίδωσι Meth.*res.*1.57(p.319.11; M.41.1153B); πᾶς ἄνθρωπος...ὑπὸ τῶν ἰδίων ἔ. ἢ βοηθούμενος ἢ κατακρινόμενος *Rit.Bapt.*(p.441); their rel. to faith and grace (v. πίστις); **i.** works do not save οὐ δι' ἑαυτῶν δικαιούμεθα, οὐδὲ διὰ τῆς ἡμετέρας σοφίας...ἢ ἔ. ὧν κατειργασάμεθα ἐν ὁσιότητι καρδίας, ἀλλὰ διὰ τῆς πίστεως *1Clem.*32.4; οὐ...τὸ ἴδιον ἔ. σώζει τὸν ἄνθρωπον, ἀλλ' ὁ χαρισάμενος τὴν δύναμιν Mac.Aeg.*hom.*37.9(M.34. 756C); οὐκ ἔστι μισθὸς ἔργων ἡ βασιλεία τῶν οὐρανῶν, ἀλλὰ χάρις δεσπότου πιστοῖς δούλοις ἡτοιμασμένη Hesych.S.*temp.*1.79(M.93.1504D); **ii.** but are necessary οὔτε τὰ δόγματα χωρὶς ἔ. ἀγαθῶν εὐπρόσδεκτα τῷ θεῷ· οὔτε τὰ μὴ μετ' εὐσεβῶν δογμάτων ἔ. τελούμενα, προσδέχεται ὁ θεός Cyr.H.*catech.*4.2; οὔτε πολιτείας ἀκρίβεια καθ' ἑαυτήν, μὴ διὰ τῆς εἰς θεὸν πίστεως πεφωτισμένη, ὠφέλιμος, οὔτε ὀρθὴ ὁμολογία, ἀγαθῶν ἔ. ἄμοιρος οὖσα, παραστῆσαι ἡμᾶς δυνήσεται τῷ κυρίῳ, ἀλλὰ δεῖ ἀμφότερα συνεῖναι Bas.*ep.*295(3.433D; M.32.1040A); Gr.Naz. *or.*40.45(M.36.424D); Chrys.*hom.11.2 in Phil.*(11.286B); Cyr.*ep.*55 (*ACO* 1.1.4 p.49.13; 5^2.174D); Gnost. ἐπαιδεύθησαν...τὰ ψυχικὰ οἱ ψυχικοὶ ἄνθρωποι, οἱ δι' ἔργων καὶ πίστεως ψιλῆς βεβαιούμενοι, καὶ μὴ τὴν τελείαν γνῶσιν ἔχοντες Iren.*haer.*1.6.2(M.7.505A); **iii.** works of faith τὰ ἔ. τῆς πίστεως Herm.*sim.*8.9.1; ἔ. τὴν πίστιν λέγει Chrys. *hom.66.2 in Jo.*(8.329C); τοῦτο γὰρ ἔ. πίστεως. εἰ πιστεύεις, πάντα πάσχε· εἰ δὲ μὴ πάσχεις, οὐ πιστεύεις Chrys.*hom.1.1 in 1Thess.*(11. 426E); ἔ. τῆς πίστεως, τὸ ἐν κινδύνοις βέβαιον Thdt.*1Thess.*1:3(3. 504); ἔ. ... πίστεως...τὴν ἐν τοῖς παθήμασιν ὑπομονήν id.*2Thess.*1:11 (3.531); **c.** ref. sabbath legislation τὸ πνευματικὸν οὐκ ἀπηγόρευσεν ἔ. ἔφη γάρ, πᾶν ἔ. λατρευτὸν οὐ ποιήσετε, πλὴν ὅσα ποιηθήσεται ἐπὶ τῇ ψυχῇ, οἷον ἀναγνώσεις, θείων λογίων ἀκροάσεις... id.*qu.1 in Dt.*(1. 262); **2.** of Devil φύγωμεν οὖν τελείως ἀπὸ πάντων τῶν ἔ. τῆς ἀνομίας, μήποτε καταλάβῃ ἡμᾶς τὰ ἔ. τῆς ἀνομίας *Barn.*4.1; *1Clem.*28.1; Herm.*mand.*12.6.4; διὰ τὸ...λῦσαι τὰ ἔ. τοῦ διαβόλου ἐλήλυθεν ὁ σωτήρ Ath.*Ar.*2.55(M.26.261D); ἔ. δὲ τοῦ σατανᾶ πᾶσά ἐστιν [ἡ] ἁμαρτία, ᾗ καὶ ἀποτάσσεσθαι ἀναγκαῖον Cyr.H.*catech.*19.5; ἀποτάσσομαι τῷ σατανᾷ καὶ τοῖς ἔ. αὐτοῦ *Symb.*ap.*Const.App.*7.41.2; *Rit.Bapt.*(p.395, p.440); **3.** of angels ἄγγελον δὲ τὸν Ἰωάννην καλεῖ...ὅτι ἀγγέλου ἔ. ἐποίησεν, ἀναγγέλλων τοῦ Χριστοῦ παρουσίαν Cyr.*Lc.*7:25(M.72.617C); ἔ. ... ἔχοντας τὴν ἐν οὐρανῷ χορείαν καὶ τοῦ πεποιηκότος τὴν ὑμνῳδίαν Thdt.*affect.*3(p.94.17; 4.786); **4.** of God; **a.** creation; **i.** in gen. ὁ δημιουργὸς ἐπὶ τοῖς ἔ. αὐτοῦ ἀγαλλιᾶται *1Clem.*33.2; τὸ θέλημα αὐτοῦ ἔ. ἐστί, καὶ τοῦτο κόσμος ὀνομάζεται Clem.*paed.*1.6(p.106.9; M.8. 281B); πρὶν γενέσθαι τὰ ἔ., ἦν μὲν ἀεὶ ὁ υἱός Ath.*Ar.*2.51(M.26.256B); Cyr.*Jo.*2.6(4.221C); **ii.** esp. of man πάντας ἀνθρώπους ἑνὸς ὄντας ἔργα τοῦ θεοῦ Clem.*str.*7.14(p.61.23; M.9.520B); τὸ ἔ. τοῦ θεοῦ, τουτέστιν ὁ ἄνθρωπος Ath.*Ar.*2.66(288B); ἅπαντες...εἰσιν τοῦ θεοῦ ἔργα *Const.App.*7.2.3; **iii.** acc. Arians, of Son ἓν γὰρ τῶν πάντων ἔ. ἐστὶ καὶ αὐτός Ath.*ep.Aeg.Lib.*12(M.25.564B); theory denied οὔτε οὖν κτίσμα ἐστὶν ὁ λόγος, οὔτε ἔ. ταὐτὸν γὰρ ἐστι κτίσμα καὶ ποίημα καὶ ἔ. id.*Ar.*2.71(M.26.297A); exeg. Pr.8:22 εἰ γὰρ εἰς τὰ ἔ. ἐκτίσθη, πρὸ δὲ τῶν ἔ. ἐστί, δῆλον ὅτι καὶ πρὸ τοῦ ἐκτίσθαι ἐστὶν *ib.*2.80(317A); ἔ. ὀνομάζει τῆς οὐσίας τὴν οὐσίαν, τὴν μὲν δευτέραν τῆς πρώτης, τῆς δὲ δευτέρας...τὴν τρίτην Gr.Nyss.*Eun.*1(1 p.83.13; M.45.316A); cf. ὁ δὲ λόγος οὐ κατὰ κενοῦ χωρήσας ἔ. πρωτότοκον τοῦ πατρὸς γίνεται Tat. *orat.*5(p.5.24; M.6.816A); **iv.** acc. Eun., of H. Ghost ἓν ἅγιον πρῶτον καὶ μεῖζον πάντων τῶν τοῦ μονογενοῦς ἔ. Eun.*apol.*28(M.30. 868C); **b.** man's salvation τοῦτο τὸ μέγιστον καὶ βασιλικώτατον ἔ. τοῦ θεοῦ, σώζειν τὴν ἀνθρωπότητα Clem.*paed.*1.12(p.150.4; M.8.369B); Ath.*Ar.*3.23(M.26.372C); Cyr.*Jo.*2.5(4.198A); ἔ. θεοῦ τῶν ἀνθρώπων τὴν σωτηρίαν φησίν Thdr.Mops.*Rom.*14:20(p.167.1); exeg. Pr.8:22 οὐ τὴν οὐσίαν, ἀλλὰ τὸ ἀνθρώπινον τοῦ λόγου σημαίνει· εἰ γὰρ εἰς ἔ. φησὶν ἐκτίσθαι, φαίνεται μὴ τὴν οὐσίαν ἑαυτοῦ σημᾶναι θέλων, ἀλλὰ τὴν εἰς τὰ ἔ. αὐτοῦ οἰκονομίαν γενομένην, ὅπερ δεύτερόν ἐστι τοῦ εἶναι Ath. *Ar.*2.51(M.26.256A); ὁ τέλειος τοῦ θεοῦ λόγος τὸ ἀτελὲς περιτίθεται σῶμα, καὶ λέγεται εἰς τὰ ἔ. κτίζεσθαι *ib.*2.66(288B); ref. Passion ἐκ μακρ[οῦ προ]οικονομεῖ τὸ πίστεως ἔ. [ἐκ] μακροῦ προοραθὲν Mel.*pass.* 57(p.9.34); **c.** Christ's miracles ὦ Ἰσραὴλ...οὐδὲ ἐδυσωπήθης τὰ ἔ. αὐτοῦ *ib.*77 p.12.32; διὰ τῶν ἔ. ἐδυσώπει τοὺς...ἀνθρώπους Just.*dial.* 69.6(M.6.640A); ἐπὶ τῷ πρώτῳ ἔ. Or.*Jo.*10.12(10; p.182.31; M.31. 328A); τὰ τοῦ θεοῦ ἔ. τῷ Βεελζεβοὺλ ἐλογίζοντο Ath.*Ar.*3.55(M.26. 440A); τὸ ἔ. τῶν ἄρτων Chrys.*hom.45.2 in Jo.*(8.264A); **d.** works of Father performed by Son ἅπερ ἐστὶν ἔ. τοῦ πατρός, ταῦτα λέγει ἡ γραφὴ τοῦ υἱοῦ εἶναι καὶ τοῦ ἁγίου πνεύματος Ath.*inc.et c.Ar.*14(M.26. 1008C); ὁ υἱός...οὐκ ἐπειδὴ υἱός, ἀλλ' ὡς θεὸς ἐκ θεοῦ, δύναται καὶ αὐτὸς τὰ τοῦ πατρὸς ἔ. ποιεῖν Cyr.*Jo.*7(4.665B); that Father and Son do same work is proof of consubstantiality, Chrys.*hom.61.2 in Jo.* (8.364C); **e.** connexion of Christ's ἐνέργεια q.v. with his works ἀνάγκη πᾶσα εὐσεβῶς δύο λέγειν καὶ τὰς φυσικὰς ἐνεργείας ἐν Χριστῷ. ἐνεργείας δὲ τὰ ἔ. Χριστοῦ νόησον καὶ μηδὲν ἕτερον, θείαν μὲν ἐνέργειαν τὰς θαυματουργίας, ἀνθρωπίνην δὲ τὰς διὰ τοῦ σώματος πράξεις Eulog. *r.Trin.*6.12(p.375); *ib.*7.1(p.375); πότερον δὲ διὰ τὰ ἔ. τῆς θεότητος καὶ τῆς ἀνθρωπότητος μία ἢ δύο ἐνέργειαι ὤφελον παραγενόμεναι λέγεσθαι ἢ νοεῖσθαι, ταῦτα πρὸς ἡμᾶς ἀνήκειν οὐκ ὤφελον· ἀλλὰ καταλιμπάνομεν ταῦτα τοῖς γραμματικοῖς, ἤγουν τεχνογράφοις Honor. *ep.Serg.*1(H.3.1321D); εἰ οὖν πρὸς τὸ ἀποτέλεσμα τῶν ὑπὸ Χριστοῦ γενομένων ἔ. ἀπιδόντες μίαν ἐνέργειαν ἐδογματίσατε ἢ καὶ μίαν πρᾶξιν ἐδογματίσατε· ἢ διὰ τὰς ἀπείρους πράξεις, ἀπείρους καὶ τὰς ἐνεργείας· πλὴν περὶ τῶν ἔ. ἡμῖν ἐστι τὸ ζητούμενον Max.*Pyrr.*(M.91.341B,C); monothelite view ἔ. θεοῦ ἅπαντα, ὅσα περὶ Χριστοῦ καὶ ἀκούομεν καὶ πιστεύομεν, εἴτε τῇ θείᾳ φύσει προσεοικότα, εἴτε τῇ ἀνθρωπίνῃ. καὶ κατὰ τοῦτο μία ἐνέργεια ταῦτα τῆς θεότητος αὐτοῦ καὶ τῆς ἀνθρωπότητος εὐσεβῶς ὠνόμασται Thdr.Pharan.*fr.*(H.3.1344C).

B. in transferred sense; **1.** *result, fulfilment, fruit* of an action; **a.** in gen. εἰ δὲ καὶ τραυματισθήσεται...καὶ τοῦτ' ἔ. ἔσται τῶν ἡμετέρων ἁμαρτιῶν Eus.*d.e.*3.2(p.105.9; M.22.181B); ἅμα λόγῳ τοὔργον ἐπήγαγεν id.*l.C.*16(p.251.15; M.20.1425C); τὸ δὲ ἔ. μὴ ἐπιθέντα τῷ λόγῳ Thdt.*qu.in Lev.*proem.(1.183); **b.** esp. in phrases with vb. of motion, come to *fulfilment* δι' ἔργων ἐχώρει τὰ πρὸς τοῦ νόμου διηγορευμένα Eus.*v.C.*2.43(p.59.22; M.20.1020B); id.*l.C.*16(p.252.15); τὸν ἡμέτερον κάματον τάχιστα εἰς ἔ. ἐκβῆναι Leo Mag.*ep.*104(*ACO* 2.1.2 p.56.12; M.*PL.*54.992B); **2.** *reality, actuality* ὁ λόγος ἔργον ἐγένετο Thdt.*qu.11 in Gen.*(1.14); ἡ ὄψις ἔργον ἦν Niceph.Ur. *v.Sym.*244(M.86.3209C); **3.** *realization* τὸ ἔ. τῶν λόγων Mac.Aeg.*hom.* 17.9(M.34.629B); **4.** *valid action* εἰ δέ τις ἄνευ τοῦ ἐπισκόπου ποιεῖ τι, εἰς μάτην ποιεῖ αὐτό· οὐ γὰρ αὐτῷ εἰς ἔ. λογισθήσεται *Const.App.*2.27. 2; **5.** *building* πασῶν τῶν ἐκκλησιῶν τὰ ἔ. Const.*ep.*ap.Eus.*v.C.*2.46 (p.60.24; M.20.1024A); Ath.*Ar.*2.79(M.26.316A); of a church ἔλειπε δὲ πολλὰ καὶ τῷ ἔ. id.*apol.Const.*14(M.25.612C); **6.** *material to work on*; met., of a philosophical *maxim* τοῦτο δὴ τὸ ἄριστον φιλοσοφίας ἔ. ... τὸ 'γνῶθι σαυτόν'. τὸ δὲ εἶναι ὄντως ἔ. φρονήσεως Gr.Thaum.*pan.Or.*11(p.27.8,10; M.10.1084B,C).

***ἐργοπαρέκτης, ὁ,** *employer, 1Clem.*34.1.

ἐργοπονέω, *work hard, Const.App.*2.36.7.

ἐργοπόνος, 1. *laborious, hardworking* ἐ. ἐν τοῖς ἀγαθοῖς ἔργοις *Const.App.*2.20.10; of women's arms, Paul.Sil.*Soph.*397(M.86. 2134B); **2.** *creative,* of Logos ἐ. ... μύθου Nonn.*par.Jo.*1.3(M.43. 749A).

***ἐργοπράτιον, τό,** *place for selling work, sale room*; in a monastery, Cyr.S.*v.Sab.*86(p.194.11).

***ἐργοσκόπος, ὁ,** *spy* ἐ. καὶ λογοσκόπους Pall.*v.Chrys.*6(p.35.25; M.47.22).

***ἐργοχειριάστης, ὁ,** *manual worker*; of monks, Thdr.Stud.*poen.* 1.21(M.99.1736C).

ἐργόχειρον, τό, 1. *handiwork*; **a.** of monks, *Apophth.Patr.*(M.65. 436C); Cyr.S.*v.Sab.*10(p.94.11); τὸ ἐ. αὐτοῦ πωλῆσαι Jo.Mosch.*prat.* 114(M.87.2977D); σπυρίδας ἃς εἶχον ἐ. πολλὰς συναγηοχώς Jo.VI H. *v.Jo.D.*26(M.94.465C); **b.** met., of creation τῶν σῶν μεγίστων ἐ. τὴν κτίσιν Geo.Pis.*hex.*351(M.92.1461A); **2.** *handicraft*; of monks, Bas. *renunt.*4(2.205D; M.31.633C); τρεφόμενος ἐκ τοῦ ἐμοῦ ἐ.· εἶχον γὰρ τὴν τοῦ καλλιγράφου τέχνην Marc.Diac.*v.Porph.*5; ‡Ath.*ep.Cast.*2.3(M. 28.881B,C); ἡμᾶς μηδὲ τὴν ἀναγκαίαν χρείαν τοῦ σώματος ἐκ τοῦ ἐ. ἡμῶν ἔχειν Cyr.S.*v.Euthym.*9(p.17.25); only a by-work, *Apophth. Patr.*(M.65.189B); ‡Nil.*vit.cog.*(M.79.1452B); used by Devil to tempt monks from study, ‡Chrys.*pat.et consumm.*(12.818C); practised during prayer, Jo.Mosch.*prat.*73(M.87.2925C).

***ἐργοχειρ-όω,** *fulfil* πᾶς λόγος ~ούμενος Euther.*confut.*11(M.28. 1373A).

***ἐργωδία, ἡ,** *troublesomeness, difficulty, labour,* Gr.Nyss.*hom.opif.* 27.6(M.44.228C); id.*res.*1(M.46.609B); Chrys.*hom.52.4 in Mt.*(7.535C); διὰ ψιλῶν ῥημάτων καὶ πίστεως μόνης, χωρὶς ἐ. πάσης id.*hom.5.1 in Col.*(11.358D).

ἐργωδῶς, comp. ἐργωδέστερον *with more difficulty,* Gr.Naz.*ep.*106 (M.37.341C); *more effectually,* Euthal.Diac.*Ac.*(M.85.633A).

ἐρεβίνθιον, τό, *chickpea, Apophth.Patr.*(M.65.189A).

ἐρεθισμός, ὁ, 1. *stimulation, incitement*; of fleshly lusts, Clem. *paed.*2.2(p.168.30; M.8.413A); Or.*princ.*3.1.4(p.199.8,11; M.11.253A); Meth.*symp.*2.2(p.16.18; M.18.49A); †Bas.*Is.*166(1.498B; M.30.393A); **2.** *provocation* ἐ. κατὰ τῶν τὸ ὁμοούσιον φρονούντων λέγοντες Socr. *h.e.*6.8.4(M.67.689A).

ἐρεθιστής, ὁ, *rebellious* or *perverse person*; of those born under Aries and Taurus, Hipp.*haer.*4.15,16(p.50.2,14; M.16.3083B,C).

ἐρεθιστικός, *provocative, stimulating, enticing*; of fleshly lusts, Clem.*paed.*2.4(p.181.20; M.8.440B); Bas.*renunt.*5(2.206D; M.31. 636C); Nil.*praest.*10(M.79.1072D); neut. as subst. τὸ ἐ. τῶν μύρων Clem.*paed.*2.8(p.199.1; 476B); ἡδοναὶ...τὸ δριμὺ καὶ ἐ. παρεχόμεναι †Bas.*Is.*21(1.394E; M.30.157B).

[*]ἐρ(ε)ικίνη, ἡ, (**[*]ἐρηκινός, ἐρίκινος, ὁ, [*]ἐρίκινα, τά**), *heather*; shrub or tree, perh. *tamarisk* ἐρίκινα λεπτόκλονα *Phys.* A 36(p.116.7); τοὺς κλάδους τῆς ἐρικίνης *ib.*(p.117.1); δένδρον μέγα... ὅμοιον ἐρηκινοῦ *T.Abr.*B 3(p.107.7); ἐρίκινοι φωτόκλονοι ‡Petr.I Al. *phys.*3(p.34); παίζει [sc. ὁ ἀνθόλοψ] ταῖς ἐρεικίναις ‡Eust.*hex.*(M.18. 740C).

***ἐρειοφορέω,** v. *ἐριοφορέω.

***ἐρειπιόομαι,** *be ruined* οἰκοδομημάτων...ἐρειπιωθέντων Gr.Nyss. *v.Gr.Thaum.*(M.46.924C); v. [*]ἐρειπόω.

[*]ἐρειπόω, ἐριπόω, 1. *ruin,* pass. τὸ ἱερὸν...ἠρείπωται Eus.*d.e.* 2.3(p.70.23); ἠρειπίωται M.22.128C); τόπον ἠριπωμένον id.*h.e.*10.2.1 (ἠρειπ- M.20.845B); τὸ ἐρειπωθὲν Gr.Nyss.*Pss.titt.*B 8(M.44.524A); id.*hom.6 in Eccl.*(M.44.708A); ἠριπωμένων οἴκων *Chron.Pasch.*p.281 (M.92.701B); **2.** *fall in ruins* Λαοδίκεια...ἐριποῦσα *Orac.Sib.*3.471.

ἐρεοῦς, *of wool, woollen,* neut. as subst. οὐδὲ γὰρ ἐρεοῦν ἐφόρει [sc. S. James] Heges.ap.Eus.*h.e.*2.23.6(M.20.197A).

ἐρέπτω, *feed on,* Nonn.*par.Jo.*6:58(M.43.801B); *ib.*13:18(864A).

ἐρεσχελέω (**ἐρεσχηλέω**), only in pres.; **1.** *cavil, make objections,* Clem.*str.*4.7(p.269.22; M.8.1260A); μηδεὶς ταῦτα ἀκούων ἐρεσχηλείτω Apoll.*Rom.*7:7(p.63.20; ἐρεσχελ- cod.); Max.*ambig.*(M.91.1069D); c. dat., *cavil* at, Petr.Al.*ep.can.*13(M.18.501C); **2.** *contend* οἱ νόμοι... οὐ πρὸς τὰ πρόσωπα ἐρεσχηλοῦσι Serap.*Man.*49(p.70; M.18.1244C); ἐ. ἑκάτερος πρὸς ἑκάτερον Epiph.*haer.*73.23(p.296.5; M.42.444C); Nil.*Magn.*52(M.79.1036C).

ἐρεσχελία (**[*]ἐρισχελία**), **ἡ, 1.** *idle disputing, sophistry, quibbling*; about theological matters, Gr.Naz.*or.*27.3(p.5.12; M.36.16A); ἐρισχ- Didym.*Trin.*2.3(M.39.477B); Epiph.*haer.*47.1(p.215.4; M.41. 849D); Chrys.*hom.11.1 in 1Cor.*(10.87C); Gr.Agr.*Eccl.*6.2(M.98. 984A); ῥητορικὴν ἐ. Jo.Mon.*hymn.Geo.*4(M.96.1396B); τὴν τῶν Ἑλλήνων ἐ. Melet.*nat.hom.*synops.(M.64.1089B); **2.** *quarrel, dispute, contention*; esp. in religious contexts, Const.ap.Eus.*v.C.*2.69(p.69. 2; M.20.1041C); Eus.*ib.*4.41(p.133.19; 1189A); Bas.*reg.fus.*49(2.394D; M.31.1037A); Epiph.*haer.*73.35(p.310.1; M.42.468C); Chrys.*sac.*4.5 (p.116.5; 1.410B); Marc.Diac.*v.Porph.*22; Socr.*h.e.*3.7.12(M.67. 393A); **3.** ? *insolence,* ‡Jo.D.*ep.Thphl.*13(M.95.361C); τῶν κρατούντων...ἐ. Thdr.Stud.*epp.*2.18(M.99.1173C).

***ἐρεσχελίζομαι,** *sport, trifle* ματαία ἡ τῶν ἀνθρώπων ζωή...εἴπερ πάλιν [i.e. in the future life] ἡ φύσις ἐρεσχελισθήσεται πράγμασιν Max.*qu.Thal.*38(M.90.389D).

***ἐρέσχελος,** *quarrelsome,* Nil.*serm.*2(M.79.1265C).

ἐρεσχηλέω, v. ἐρεσχελέω.

[*]ἐρετίζω, = ἐρεθίζω, *provoke,* Or.*Ps.*54:4(p.56).

ἐρετμόω, *use* hands *as oars,* Nonn.*par.Jo.*21:7(M.43.916C).

***ἔρευγμα, τό,** *belching,* Gr.Naz.*carm.*2.2(epigr.)26.5(M.38.97A).

ἐρεύγ-ομαι, 1. *utter,* ref. Ps.44:2 ὁ πατὴρ ~εται καὶ ποιεῖ τὸν τύπον αὐτῶν ἐν τῷ λόγῳ Or.*Jo.*1.38(42; p.50.7; M.14.100D); **2.** *blurt out* ὁ ἡμέτερος νοῦς ~εται...ἀφ' ἑαυτοῦ τὸν λόγον Dion.Al.ap.Ath. *Dion.*23(p.63.12; M.25.513B); Ath.*ep.Epict.*2(p.5.8; M.26.1053B); Cyr.*Mal.*36(3.855B); Nonn.*par.Jo.*2:19(M.43.764B); c. infin. ποῖος ᾅδης ἠρεύξατο ὁμοούσιον εἰπεῖν τὸ ἐκ Μαρίας σῶμα τῇ τοῦ λόγου θεότητι; Ath.*ep.Epict.*2(p.4.11; M.26.1052C).

***ἐρευματίζω,** *imprison,* Jo.Mal.*chron.*16 p.408(M.97.604A).

ἔρευνα, ἡ, *inquiry, search*; **1.** in gen., *Ep.Aeg.*(p.157.26; M.25. 389A); Ath.*ep.Serap.*1.1(M.26.529A); id.*h.Ar.*36(p.203.27; M.25. 736B); **2.** ref. divine matters διοιχθέντος δὲ τοῦ ἐμποδὼν κατὰ τὴν ἔ. ἐπιστημονικὴ ἐγγίνεται θεωρία Clem.*str.*8.1(p.80.13; M.9.560A); εἰς ἀναγωγὴν...διὰ τῆς ἀκριβοῦς τῶν ἱερῶν ἐ. Dion.Ar.*c.h.*2.5(M.3.145B); ἐκ τῆς ἐπιστημονικῆς τῶν λογίων ἐ. id.*d.n.*2.9(M.3.648A); esp. ref. scriptures τὰ περὶ αὐτοῦ [sc. Christ] μετὰ ἐρεύνης εὑρίσκοντες Or. *Jo.*1.24(23; p.30.15; M.14.65D); πρὸς τὴν ἐκ τῶν γραφῶν ἔ. καὶ γνῶσιν ἀληθῆ, χρεία βίου καλοῦ καὶ ψυχῆς καθαρᾶς καὶ τῆς κατὰ Χριστὸν ἀρετῆς Ath.*inc.*57.1(M.25.196C); χρεία καὶ πολλῆς ἐ. ἐστὶν ἡμῖν, ὥστε μηδὲν ἡμᾶς λαθεῖν τῶν ἐν τῷ βάθει κειμένων Chrys.*hom.* *24.1 in Gen.*(4.216D); ὁ Χριστὸς παραπέμπων τοὺς Ἰουδαίους ταῖς γραφαῖς, οὐκ εἰς ἁπλῆν ἀνάγνωσιν, ἀλλ' εἰς ἔ. ἀκριβῆ...αὐτοὺς παρέπεμπεν id.*hom.41.1 in Jo.*(8.243A); ἡ ἔ. ἐν ταῖς...γραφαῖς λέγεται καὶ ἐπὶ θεοῦ, καὶ ἐπὶ ἀνθρώπων· ἀλλ' ἐπὶ μὲν θεοῦ τὸ ἀκριβὲς τῆς γνώσεως μηνύει· ἐπὶ δ' ἀνθρώπων τὸ μετὰ πόνου...εὑρίσκεσθαι τὸ ζητούμενον Isid.Pel.*epp.*3.92(M.78.796D).

ἐρευν-άω, 1. *search after,* Just.*dial.*56.16(M.6.601C); ἐ. τὸν λόγον, διὰ τί... Or.*hom.11.5 in Jer.*(p.83.13; M.13.373C); ἐ. τὰ ὑπὲρ ἃ γέγραπται id.*Jo.*13.5(p.230.20; M.14.405D); **2.** *search, investigate, examine*; **a.** trans.; **i.** of God ὁ κύριος ὁ τὰ κρυπτὰ ~ῶν Ath.*v.Anton.* 55(M.26.924A); ~ᾷς ἑκάστου τὴν γνώμην *Const.App.*7.23.2; exeg. 1Cor.2:10 οὐ γὰρ ἀγνοίας, ἀλλ' ἀκριβοῦς γνώσεως ἐνταῦθα τὸ ἐ. ἐνδεικτικόν Chrys.*hom.7.4 in 1Cor.*(10.55B); Thdt.*1Cor.*2:10(3.177); **ii.** in gen., act. or med. ἐ. τὴν ἐκείνων διάνοιαν Ath.*syn.*8(p.235.19; M.26.692B); one's own mind, id.*Ar.*2.77(M.26.312A); καθ' ἑσπέραν ~ᾶν ἑαυτὸν πῶς παρῆλθε τὴν ἡμέραν Dor.*doct.*4.5(M.88.1664D); a house, Ath.*h.Ar.*58(p.215.38; M.25.764B); a person ~ήσας δὲ αὐτὸν ηὗρεν ἐν αὐτῷ ῥάκος Call.*v.Hyp.*(p.90); of the wind πάντα τὰ φυτά... ~ᾷ Mac.Aeg.*hom.*2.4(M.34.465B); **iii.** ref. religious matters, esp. scriptures, cf. Jo.5:39 τὸν ἐν αὐτοῖς κεκρυμμένον νοῦν...ἐ. Clem.*q.d.s.*5 (p.163.19; M.9.609C); ἐ. τὴν ἐν αὐτῷ γυμνὴν τύπων ἀλήθειαν Or.*Jo.*1.8 (10; p.13.18; M.14.37C); δὸς ἡμῖν ἐ. ... τὰ θεῖά σου λόγια Serap.*euch.*

12.3; ἡ γλῶσσα ψαλλέτω, ὁ νοῦς ἐ. τὴν διάνοιαν τῶν εἰρημένων Bas.*hom.in Ps.*28(1.123B; M.29.304A); **iv.** ref. inscrutable matters ἐ. τὰ ἀνερεύνητα Ath.*ep.Serap.*4.4(M.26.644A); ἀπόρρητον ἀγαθότητα καὶ οὐδὲ ~ηθῆναι δυναμένην Chrys.*hom.21.1 in Rom.*(9.656B); opp. θεωρία: ὁ τῆς πίστεως βυθὸς ~ώμενος μὲν κυμαίνεται· ἁπλῇ δὲ διαθέσει θεωρούμενος γαληνιᾷ Diad.*perf.*22(p.24.12); **b.** intrans., *Barn.*4.1; ἐ. περὶ θεότητος καὶ ἀληθείας Herm.*mand.*10.1.6; Just. *1apol.*28.1(M.6.372B); **3.** *find out* ἐ. εἴ που γέγραπται Ath.*Ar.*2.11(M. 26.169B); *ib.*2.12(172A); ἐ. δι' ἣν αἰτίαν... Dion.Ar.*c.h.*5(M.3.196B).

ἐρευνητέον, *one must investigate,* Clem.*str.*7.15(p.64.26; M.9. 525C); Or.*Jo.*6.14(7; p.123.32; M.14.225C).

***ἐρευνητέος,** *to be investigated* ἐ. ἂν εἴη, πῶς... Gr.Nyss.*hom.7 in Cant.*(M.44.925B).

ἐρευνητήρ, ὁ, *searcher, explorer,* Nonn.*par.Jo.*1:42(M.43.757A).

ἐρευνητής, ὁ, *one who searches out,* of God ἐ. ... ἐννοιῶν καὶ ἐνθυμήσεων *1Clem.*21.9; of soul, Gr.Nyss.*hom.11 in Cant.*(M.44. 1009B); in derogatory sense *busybody,* Bas.*renunt.*6(2.208B; M.31. 640C).

***ἐρευνητικός,** masc. as subst. ὁ ἐ. *one who searches, investigates* οἱ ἐ. τῶν γραφῶν Leont.H.*Nest.*5.3(M.86.1725D); neut. as subst., *faculty of inquiry,* Meth.*fr.9 in Job*(p.513n.; M.18.404C).

***ἐρευνητικῶς,** *searchingly* ἐ. καὶ οὐ παροδευτικῶς πᾶσι τοῖς γραφικοῖς καὶ πατρικοῖς διδάγμασιν ἐγκύπτοντες Taras.*ep.*4(M.98. 1453A); CNic.(787)*can.*2.

***ἔρευνον, τό,** *search*; plur., Pall.*h.Laus.*63(p.160.2; τὴν ἔρευναν M. 34.1235D).

[*]**ἐρηκινός, ὁ,** v. [*]ἐρεικίνη, ἡ.

***ἐρημάδελφος,** *deprived of a brother,* Thdr.Stud.*epp.*2.214(M.99. 1644C).

ἐρημαῖος, *in the desert,* Nonn.*par.Jo.*6:58(M.43.801A); *ib.*6:32 (800A); *deserted, ib.*20:1(908B).

ἐρημάς, fem. of ἔρημος, *deserted* ἐρημάδος ἀστὸς ἐρίπνης Nonn. *par.Jo.*1:6(M.43.749B); *ib.*6:3(793A); *ib.*12:1(849B).

ἐρημία, ἡ, 1. *solitude,* as state of hermits, freq. combined with ἡσυχία: ἀναχωρῶ ἐπὶ τὴν ἐ. καὶ ἡσυχίαν Or.*hom.20.8 in Jer.*(p.190. 4; M.13.520A); ἐν ἡσυχίᾳ βαθείᾳ, καὶ ἐν ἐ. τῶν ἁγίων ᾀδόντων Chrys. *hom.14.4 in 1Tim.*(11.630B); favourable to union with God εἰς δὲ τὴν ἔρημον τῆς ἐ. γαλήνην θεῷ πεπολιτευμένος [sc. Jo. Bapt.] Clem. *paed.*2.10(p.224.18; M.8.532B); εὔχεται [sc. Christ] διανυκτερεύων ἐν ταῖς ἐ., ἡμᾶς παιδεύων καὶ νουθετῶν, ἐπειδὰν μέλλωμεν ὁμιλεῖν τῷ θεῷ, φεύγειν θορύβους...καὶ πρὸς ἐ. ἀναχωρεῖν Chrys.*anom.*10.2 (1.532A,B); cf.Evagr.Pont.*rer.mon.*6(M.40.1257B); but liable to demonic temptations οἱ δαίμονες...παλαίουσι...μοναχοῖς...διὰ τῶν λογισμῶν· πραγμάτων γὰρ διὰ τὴν ἐ. ἐστέρηνται id.*cap.pract.*B 48 (M.40.1245B); as spiritual condition necessary in order to attain to union with God, not dependent on physical solitude ὃς πόλιν οἰκῶν τῶν κατὰ τὴν πόλιν κατεφρόνησεν...καὶ καθάπερ ἐν ἐ. τῇ πόλει βιοῖ, ἵνα μὴ ὁ τόπος αὐτὸν ἀναγκάζῃ, ἀλλ' ἡ προαίρεσις δεικνύῃ δίκαιον Clem.*str.*7.12(p.55.7; M.9.505B); ἐρημίας ἐπιζητῶμεν, μὴ τὰς ἐκ τόπων μόνον, ἀλλὰ καὶ τὰς ἀπὸ τῆς προαιρέσεως, καὶ πρὸ τῶν ἄλλων ἁπάντων τὴν ψυχὴν εἰς αὐτὴν ἄγωμεν τὴν ἀοίκητον Chrys.*compunct.*2.3 (1.144A); **2.** *desolation,* of spiritual separation from God χρεία δὲ τῆς φωνῆς τοῦ βοῶντος ἐν τῇ ἐρήμῳ, ἵνα καὶ ἡ ἐστερημένη θεοῦ ψυχὴ καὶ ἔρημος ἀληθείας, (τίς γὰρ ἄλλη χαλεπωτέρα ἐ. ψυχῆς θεοῦ καὶ πάσης ἀρετῆς ἐρημωμένης;)...παρακαλῆται Or.*Jo.*6.18(10; p.127.23; M.14. 232C); Chrys.*hom.17.3 in Eph.*(11.125B).

***ἐρημικοειδής,** *suitable to a hermit,* Thdr.Stud.*epp.*2.137(M.99. 1437C).

ἐρημικός, *solitary, eremitical*; **1.** of persons οἱ δὲ νόμον ἀγάπης τῇ κοινωνίᾳ στέργοντες, ἐρημικοί τε ὁμοῦ καὶ μιγάδες Gr.Naz.*or.*21.19 (M.35.1104A); ἐ. βίος ‡Nil.*narr.*1(M.79.589A); Thdt.*h.rel.*1(3.1108); †Jo.D.*B.J.*2(M.96.868C); opp. βίος πολιτικός, Thdt.*h.rel.*25(3.1264); superl. ἐρημικώτατος, Thphn.*chron.*p.276(M.108.684A); **2.** neut. as subst., of places πρὸς τὴν Αἴγυπτον ἐπὶ τὰ ἐ. κατοικήσας ἐν μοναστηρίῳ Epiph.*exp.fid.*13(p.513.17; M.42.895A); ἐξήγαγέ με ἔξω τῆς πόλεως εἰς τὰ λεγόμενα ἐ. Pall.*h.Laus.*1(p.16.18; M.34.1010B).

ἐρημίτης, ὁ, *hermit,* ‡Chrys.*hom.*1(13.204E); *Apophth.Patr.*(M.65. 240A); Cyr.S.*v.Sab.*30(p.115.18); of Jo. Bapt., Max.*ambig.*(M.91. 1292A); legislation concerning hermits living by themselves in towns τοὺς λεγομένους ἐ., οἵτινες μελανειμονοῦντες καὶ τὰς κεφαλὰς κομῶντες περιάγουσι τὰς πόλεις...ὁρίζομεν, εἰ μὲν αἱροῦνται τὰς κόμας ἀποκειράμενοι τὸ τῶν λοιπῶν μοναχῶν ἀναδέξασθαι σχῆμα, τούτους ἐν μοναστηρίῳ ἐγκαθίστασθαι...εἰ δὲ μὴ τοῦτο προέλοιντο, παντάπασιν αὐτοὺς τῶν πόλεων ἀπελαύνεσθαι καὶ τὰς ἐρήμους οἰκεῖν, ἐξ ὧν καὶ τὰς ἐπωνυμίας ἑαυτοῖς ἀνεπλάσαντο CTrull.*can.*42; plur., alternative name for Encratites, Mac.Mgn.*apocr.*3.43(p.151.24).

***ἐρημοβάτευτος, ὁ,** *wanderer in the desert,* †Gregent.*disp.*(M.86. 705C).

ἐρημοδίκιον, τό, *undefended action,* Ath.Scholast.*coll.*4.13(p.57).

ἐρημοποιός, *making desolate,* Eus.*Ps.*119:3(M.24.9B); of demons, †Bas.*Is.*97(1.447A; M.30.277A); of idols, Thdt.*Jer.*2:24(2.418).

***ἐρημοπολίτης, ὁ,** *one who dwells in the wilderness, citizen of the desert* τὸ μοναχικὸν σχῆμά ἐστι κατὰ τὴν μίμησιν τοῦ ἐ. καὶ βαπτιστοῦ Ἰωάννου ‡Bas.*h.myst.*21(p.262.19); ‡Gr.Nyss.*hom.1 in Jo.*(p.108. 11); Nil.*exerc.*21(M.79.748B); as adj. ὁ τῶν μοναχῶν ἐ. βίος †Bas.*ep.* 42.5(3.130A; M.32.357C).

ἔρημος, A. *destitute, bereft*; theol.; **a.** of God and Christ, ref. divine fatherhood, Chrys.*hom.4.1 in Jo.*(8.27E) cit. s. ἀΐδιος; ἀδύνατον γὰρ τὸν θεὸν εἰπεῖν, ἔ. τῆς φυσικῆς γονιμότητος Jo.D.*f.o.*1.8(M. 94.812B); of flesh of Christ which, in Eusebius' interprn. of Marcellus' teaching, would be left destitute of Logos τῷ Χριστῷ... ἀθρόαν γενήσεσθαι στέρησιν,...τῆς δὲ σαρκὸς ἧς ἀνείληφεν καταλειφθησομένης ἐ. Eus.*Marcell.*1.1(p.6.15; M.24.724A); τὴν δὲ σάρκα [sc. Χριστοῦ] θεολογῶν, ἣν μικρὸν ὕστερον ἔ. ἔσεσθαι τοῦ λόγου ὁ ἀνευλαβὴς ὡρίζετο *ib.*2.2(p.43.26; 797B); id.*e.th.*3.11(p.167.23; M.24.1020D); Christol., agst. monothelite teaching μηδεμίαν τούτων ἔ. ἐπιστάμεθα φυσικῆς ὑπάρξεως, θελήσεώς τε καὶ ἐνεργείας Max.*opusc.*(M.91.96A); **b.** abs., of soul without God οἶδα ψυχὴν ἔ. εἰ γὰρ οὐκ ἔχει τὸν θεόν, ⟨εἰ⟩ οὐκ ἔχει τὸν Χριστόν...εἰ οὐκ ἔχει τὸ πνεῦμα τὸ ἅγιον ψυχή, ἔ. ἐστιν Or.*hom.8.1 in Jer.*(p.55.22ff.; M.13.336C).

B. subst. fem. [sc. χώρα], *desert, solitude*; **1.** lit.; **a.** as place loved by Christ ἐν ταύτῃ τῇ ἐ. διάγω,...ἐν ᾗ ὁ κύριος διέτριβεν ...ὁ Χριστὸς ὁ τῆς ἐρήμου φίλος †Bas.*ep.*42.5(3.129D,130A; M.32. 357B,C); διὰ τοῦτο συνεχῶς εἰς ἐρήμους ἄπεισιν [sc. Christ]... παιδεύων ἡμᾶς καὶ τὴν ἀπὸ τοῦ καιροῦ καὶ τὴν ἀπὸ τοῦ τόπου θηρᾶσθαι ἐν ταῖς εὐχαῖς ἀταραξίαν. ἡσυχίας γὰρ μήτηρ ἡ ἐ. Chrys.*hom.50.1 in Mt.*(7.513D); **b.** subject to demons, Jo.Clim.*scal.*15(M.88.893A); **c.** spiritual value ἡ ἔ. πολλάκις ποτὲ μὲν τοῖς φεύγουσι γίνεται ὠφέλιμος, ποτὲ δὲ τοῖς δυνατοῖς· τοῖς φεύγουσι μέν, ἵνα μὴ εὑρεθῇ αὐτοῖς ὕλη αὐξῆσαι τὰ πάθη αὐτῶν· τοῖς δυνατοῖς δὲ τῷ μεσάζειν ἐν ὕλῃ καὶ καταντῆσαι πρὸς τοὺς πολέμους τοῦ πονηροῦ Philox.*ep.*6(p.161); **2.** met., of spiritual life τὸ τοίνυν ἐκ τῆς ἐ. ἀναβαίνειν αὐτὴν (Cant. 3:6) μαρτυρίαν περιέχει τοῦ διὰ προσοχῆς τε καὶ ἐγκρατείας ἐς τοσοῦτον ...ὕψος ἀναδραμεῖν Gr.Nyss.*hom.6 in Cant.*(M.44.897B); καθάπερ ἐξ Αἰγύπτου μετακεχωρήκαμεν εἰς τὴν ἔ. τουτέστιν εἰς πλατεῖαν καὶ καθαρωτάτην ἀληθῶς, καὶ ἀσυμμιγῆ τοῦ χείρονος πολιτείαν, φημὶ δὴ τὴν εὐαγγελικήν Cyr.*Am.*21(3.271D); of pagans τὴν ἔ. ὑπέταξεν ὁ πατὴρ τῷ Χριστῷ Or.*hom.2.4 in Jos.*(p.298.27; M.87.993B).

C. exeg.; **1.** Jer.2:31 ὁ θεὸς ἐν τῷ Ἰσραὴλ οὐ γέγονεν ἔ. ... ἆρα οὖν ἔ. γέγονεν ὁ κύριος τῷ Ἰσραὴλ σήμερον...ὅτε τῷ Ἰσραὴλ ἦν οὐκ ἔ. ... τοῖς ἔθνεσιν ἦν ἔ. ... εἰ γὰρ πᾶσιν ἀεὶ οὐκ ἔ. ἐστι...τίς χρεία τοῦ ἰδίως πρὸς τὸν Ἰσραὴλ κατ' ἐξαίρετον λεχθῆναι· 'μὴ ἔρημος ἐγενόμην τῷ οἴκῳ Ἰσραήλ...;' Or.*hom.3.1 in Jer.*(p.20.16ff.; M.13.281C,D); οὐδενὶ ἔ. ἐστιν ὁ θεός...πῶς ἔ., ἀνατέλλων ἡμέραν καὶ νύκτα...πῶς ἔ. τὴν γῆν ποιῶν καρποφορεῖν; πῶς ἔ. ἕκαστον οἰκονομῶν κατὰ τὴν ψυχὴν ...; ἔστιν οὖν οὐδενὶ ἔ. ὡς πρὸς τὸν καθόλου λόγον ὁ θεός. ὡς δὲ πρὸς τὸν ἰδικόν, ἔρχομαι ἐπὶ τὰ τοῦ Ἰσραὴλ πράγματα καὶ λέγω· οὔτε ἔ. οὔτε γῆ κεχερσωμένη ἦν, ὅτε ἐν Αἰγύπτῳ ἐποίει τὰ σημεῖα...εἰ δέ τις καιρὸς γέγονεν ὅτε ἐγκατελείφθησαν, οἱονεὶ ἔρημος αὐτοῖς, οὐκ ἔ. ὢν αὐτός, ἐγένετο. ὅτε μέντοι ἦν τῷ Ἰσραὴλ οὐκ ἔ. ... τοῖς ἔθνεσι κατὰ τὸν ἰδικὸν λόγον ἔρημος...ὅτε δὲ ἀπεστράφη τὸν Ἰσραὴλ καὶ γέγονε τῷ Ἰσραὴλ ἐκείνῳ ἔρημος...τότε ἐξεχύθη ἡ χάρις ἐπὶ τὰ ἔθνη, καὶ γέγονε νῦν ἡμῖν Χριστὸς Ἰησοῦς οὐκ ἔ. ἀλλὰ πλήρης *ib.*3.2(pp.20.26–21.14; 281D–284A); **2.** Is.54:1 (freq. with play on two senses of 'barren woman' and 'desert'), of Christ and Church ὁ τῆς στείρας ἀνήρ, ὁ τῆς ἐ. γεωργός Clem.*prot.*1(p.9.33; M.8.65B); *ib.*(p.10.1; 65C); ἔ. μὲν ἡ ἐκκλησία· ἔ. αὕτη νόμου, ἔ. αὕτη θεοῦ ἦν Or.*hom.9.3 in Jer.*(p.67. 13f.; M.13.352D,353A); ἔ. δὲ ὀνομάζει τὰ ἔθνη, ὡς ἔ. πάλαι γεγενημένα θεοῦ Thdt.*Ps.*28:8(1.784).

ἐρημόω, *spoil* a garment, Ephr.1.205B; pass., of food, *Apophth. Patr.*(M.65.301A).

***ἐρημώδης,** *desolate, waste* ὄρος...ἐ. Herm.*sim.*9.19; *ib.*9.26.1; met., of men estranged from God, *ib.*9.26.3.

ἐρήμωσις, ἡ, *desolation*; for τὸ βδέλυγμα τῆς ἐ. (Dan.11:31, Mt. 24:15) v. βδέλυγμα.

***ἐρημωτικός,** *devastating,* Epiph.*haer.*52.1(p.311.14; M.41.953D).

***ἐρηρεισμένως,** *fixedly, firmly,* Gr.Nyss.*Eun.*12(1 p.253.33; M.45. 956B); Cyr.*Os.*11(3.32C); Thdr.Stud.*epp.*2.199(M.99.1601B).

[*]**ἐρία, ἡ,** = ἐρέα, *wool,* Isid.Pel.*epp.*1.45(M.78.209C).

ἐριδμαίνω, *contend against,* c. dat., Eudoc.*Cypr.*2.241.

***ἐρίδομος,** *well built, IGC As.Min.*81.4(Smyrna).

ἐρίδωρος, *rich in gifts,* Gr.Naz.*carm.*1.2.9.71(M.37.673A).

ἐρίζωος, *lively*, Gr.Naz.*carm*.2.1.32.18(M.37.1302A).

ἐριηχής, *clear-voiced*, Gr.Naz.*carm*.1.2.1.324(M.37.546A); *ib*.2.2 (poem.)6.103(1550A).

ἐριθεία, ἡ, *selfish* or *factious ambition* μηδὲν κατ' ἐριθείαν πράσσειν, ἀλλὰ κατὰ Χριστομαθίαν Ign.*Philad*.8.2; ‡Just.*or.Gr*.5(M.6.240A); ἐ. ...τὸ ἐξ ὧν ποιεῖ τις, ἐπιδεικτικῶς ἢ κενοδόξως προκαλεῖσθαι, καὶ ἐρεθίζειν ἄλλους εἰς τὰ ὅμοια Bas.*reg.br*.66(2.438E; M.31.1129B).

[*]**ἐρίθηλος**, *very flourishing*, *Orac.Sib*.8.145; *ib*.11.261.

[*]**ἐρικίνη, ἡ, ἐρίκινος, ὁ**, [*]**ἐρίκινα, τά**, v. [*]ἐρεικίνη, ἡ.

***ἐρίκνημις**, *high-shouldered*; of a mountain, Paul.Sil.*Soph*.304 (M.86.2131B).

***ἐρίκνημος**, = foreg.; of a dome, Paul.Sil.*Soph*.274(M.86.2130A).

***ἐρικτήμων**, *wealthy*, Gr.Naz.*carm*.1.2.2.452(M.37.614A).

ἐριλαμπής, *brightly shining*, Gr.Naz.*carm*.1.1.3.79(M.37.414A); *ib*. 1.1.9.72(462A).

[*]**Ἐριννυώδης**, *like the Furies*, Nil.*epp*.3.166(M.79.461B); φάλαγγας Bas.Sel.*v.Thecl*.2.11(M.85.585A).

[*]**ἔρινος**, *woollen* τιάραις ἐ. worn by monks, Soz.*h.e*.3.14.13(M. 67.1072B).

ἐριουργικός, *of wool-working* ἡ τέχνη ἡ ἐ. Adam.*dial*.2.16(p.90. 26; M.11.1785B).

***ἐριοφορέω**, (*ἐρειο-), *bear wool* τὸ ἐρειοφοροῦν Gr.Nyss.*hom.7 in Cant*.(M.44.925B); Cyr.*ep*.41(*ACO* 1.1.4 p.43.8; 5².125A).

ἐριοφόρος, *wool-bearing*; of sheep, Gr.Nyss.*hom.2 in Cant*.(M.44. 808B).

ἐριπόω, v. [*]ἐρειπόω.

***ἐρίπτολις**, *eminent in the city*, Gr.Naz.*carm*.2.2(poem.)6.106(M. 37.1550A).

***ἐρισθενέτης**, *very strong, powerful*, †Apoll.*met.Ps*.151:3(M.33. 1538B); Paul.Sil.*Soph*.535(M.86.2140A).

ἐριστής, ὁ, *wrangler*, *Const.App*.2.37.6.

[*]**ἐρισχελία, ἡ**, v. ἐρεσχελία.

[*]**ἐρίφιος**, = ἐρίφειος, *of a kid*, Or.*Jo*.10.5(4; p.175.23; M.14. 313C).

***ἐριφώδης**, *kid-like*, Isid.Pel.*epp*.1.193(M.78.305C).

ἐρίχρυσος, *rich in gold*, Paul.Sil.*Soph*.1012(M.86.2158A).

ἑρκίον, τό, *fence, enclosure*, hence *defence*; of oyster's shell, Bas. *hex*.7.3(1.65C; M.29.153A); met. ὁ τοιούτων δένδρων κῆπος...τῷ τῶν ἐντολῶν ἑ. ... ἠσφαλισμένος Gr.Nyss.*hom.9.1 in Cant*.(M.44.964B).

ἕρκος, τό, *fence*; of stone tracery guarding edges of steps up to ambo, Paul.Sil.*ambo*.70(M.86.2254B).

ἑρμαῖος, **1.** *advantageous, suitable* ἑ. ... καιρόν ‡Eust.*hex*.(M.18. 785A); **2.** masc. plur. as subst., name given to Valentinus and Basilides Ἑ. προσαγορεύονται ἀπό τινος οὕτω κληθέντος λαχόντες τὸ ὄνομα Tim.CP *haer*.(M.86.17B).

ἑρμηνεία, ἡ, **1.** *interpretation*; esp. of scriptures, Mel.*pass*.41 p.6. 37; ἡ ἑ. τοῦ ψαλμοῦ Just.*dial*.124.4(M.6.765B); Iren.*haer*.1.3.6(M.7. 477A); allegorical κατὰ τὸ γράμμα καὶ οὐ καθ' ἑρμηνείαν Dam.*troph*. 2.4(p.224.1); hence *commentary* τῆς θείας γραφῆς ἑ. Eus.*h.e*.5.27.1(M. 20.512A); ὁ Θεόδωρος...τῶν θείων εὐαγγελίων τὴν ἑ. συνέγραψεν Thdt.*h.e*.2.3.8(3.828); Vict.*Mc*.proem.(p.263.10); **2.** *translation*; esp. of LXX, Clem.*str*.1.22(p.92.10,19,22; M.8.892A,893A); Thdt.*Pss. proem*.(1.606); **3.** *glossary*, id.*qu.54 in 1Reg*.(1.389); τῆς τῶν Ἑβραίων ὀνομάτων ἑ. ἡ βίβλος *ib*.59(394).

ἑρμηνεύς, ὁ, *interpreter, expounder*; **1.** of interpreters of scriptures, Gr.Thaum.*pan.Or*.15(p.34.21; M.10.1096A); Eus.*e.th*.3.3(p.152. 35; M.24.993D); of Moses νόμων...ἑ. Clem.*str*.1.22(p.93.12; M.8.896A); of S. Paul ἑ. τῆς θείας φωνῆς id.*prot*.9(p.65.16; M.8.200A); Ath. *gent*.19(M.25.40A); apptly. of members of eccl. order ranking below readers, Serap.*euch*.11.4; **2.** of 'interpreters' attending on apostles (v. ἑρμηνευτής) μέχρι γε τῆς Ἀντωνίνου τοῦ πρεσβυτέρου διέτειναν [sc. heretics] ἡλικίας, καθάπερ ὁ Βασιλείδης, κἂν Γλαυκίαν ἐπιγράφηται διδάσκαλον, ὡς αὐχοῦσιν αὐτοὶ τοῦ Πέτρου ἑρμηνέα Clem.*str*.7.17(p.75.16; M.9.549A); **3.** of Christ as *revealer* of Father, Dion.Al.ap.Ath.*Dion*.23(p.64.2; M.25.516A); Eus.*e.th*.2.22(p.132. 12; M.24.957D); Ath.*gent*.45(M.25.89A); of Christ's body οἷα μέγας βασιλεὺς δι' ἑρμηνέως τὸν ἀνθρώπειον διεξελθὼν βίον Eus.*theoph.fr*.3 (p.6*.4); *ib*.(p.7*.10).

ἑρμηνευτέον, *one must interpret*, Or.*Jo*.10.16(13; p.186.32; M.14. 333B); id.*fr.6 in Jo*.(p.488.24); *ib*.51(p.526.7).

ἑρμηνευτής, ὁ, **1.** *interpreter, expounder*, in gen. τὸν Ἑρμῆν... λόγων ἑ. Arist.*apol*.10(p.105.24); of an attendant upon S. Peter, acting either as expounder of his teaching (perh. as catechist) or possibly as interpreter in sense 2 infra Μάρκος...ἑ. Πέτρου γενόμενος, ὅσα ἐμνημόνευσεν, ἀκριβῶς ἔγραψεν Papias *fr*.2.15; Μάρκος ὁ μαθητὴς καὶ ἑ. Πέτρου...τὰ ὑπὸ Πέτρου κηρυσσόμενα ἐγγράφως ἡμῖν παραδέδωκεν Iren.*haer*.3.1.1(M.7.845A); cf. ἑρμηνεύς; of Logos as revealer of Father, Isid.Pel.*epp*.3.141(M.78.837B); **2.** *translator, interpreter*, Thdt.*h.e*.5.30.2(3.1070); esp. of translators of OT, Or. *fr.59 in Jer*.(p.227.17); Eus.*e.th*.3.2(p.142.1; M.24.976C); †Ath.*exp. fid*.3(M.25.205A); Chrys.*hom.5.2 in Mt*.(7.75B); Thdt.*Dan*.11:13(2. 1275); apptly. of order in Church, ranked after exorcists ἑ. ἀπὸ γλώσσης εἰς γλῶσσαν ἢ ἐν τοῖς ἀναγνώσεσιν ἢ ἐν ταῖς προσομιλίαις Epiph.*exp.fid*.21(p.522.22; M.42.825A); *Lit.Jac*.(p.214.7).

ἑρμηνευτικός, *explanatory, interpretative*, c. genit., Cyr.*Jo*.1.4 (4.38E); Dion.Ar.*d.n*.4.2(3.696B).

ἑρμηνεύ-ω, **1.** *interpret, expound, comment on* Ματθαῖος Ἑβραΐδι διαλέκτῳ τὰ λόγια συνεγράψατο, ἡρμήνευσε δ' αὐτὰ ὡς ἦν δυνατὸς ἕκαστος Papias *fr*.2.16 (or perh. in sense 3 infra); ἑ. τὴν περὶ τοῦ μάννα ἱστορίαν Or.*Cels*.4.49(p.322.23; M.11.1108D); τὴν τοῦ...Παύλου διδασκαλίαν ἑ. Thdt.*epp.Paul.proem*.(3.1); esp. of allegorical interpretation, Dam.*troph*.2.4(p.223.10); of Father revealed by Son, Serap.*euch*.13.3; c. infin., Iren.*haer*.1.3.5(M.7.476B); Or.*Jo*.13.11 (p.236.4; M.14.416C); Eus.*Marcell*.2.3(p.47.14; M.24.804B); **2.** *denote*, Clem.*str*.7.16(p.74.1; M.9.544C); Thdt.*Os*.4:15(2.1330); id. *Ezech*.1:19–21(2.689); **3.** *translate* προφητείας εἰς τὴν Ἑλλάδα διάλεκτον ἑ. Clem.*str*.1.22(p.92.14; M.8.892A); ~θέντα Ἑλληνιστί Ath.*syn*.9(p.236.34; M.26.696B); ἐκ Ῥωμαϊκοῦ...ἡρμηνεύθη Socr.*h.e*. 2.37.17(M.67.304C); Thdt.*Ps*.1:6(1.615); *ib*.2:1(617); **4.** pass., *have* something *explained* τὴν παραβολὴν ~θῆτι Gr.Naz.*or*.40.20(M.36. 385A); τὰ Ἑλλήνων παιδευθεὶς...τὰ ἱερὰ ἡρμηνεύθη βιβλία Socr.*h.e*.2. 9.3(M.67.197C).

***ἑρμητάριον, τό**, *stake* to which prisoners were tied to be flogged, Ath.*apol.Const*.33(M.25.640B); Ephr.3.220A.

[*]**Ἑρμοδάκτυλος, ἡ**, *Colchicum*, a plant, Evagr.*h.e*.6.24(p.240. 13; M.86.2881B).

ἐρνοκόμος, ὁ, *gardener*, Gr.Naz.*carm*.1.2.1.243(M.37.541A).

ἐροτή, ἡ, v. sq.

ἔροτις (**ἐροτή**), **ἡ**, = ἑορτή, *festival*, Eudoc.*Cypr*.2.53(M.85.848B ἐροτή).

[*]**ἐρουσίβη, ἡ**, = ἐρυσίβη, *rust* in corn, *Euchol*.(p.555).

***ἑρπετόμορφος**, *reptilian*, Epiph.*haer*.35.3(p.44.1; M.41.632D).

ἑρπετοφάγος, *eating animals* αἴλουρον τὸν ἑ. Epiph.*anc*.103(p.124. 4; M.43.201C).

ἑρπετώδης, *snake-like*; met., esp. of heresies, Epiph.*haer*.63.3 (p.401.2; M.41.1065B); *ib*.51.2(p.249.25; 889C).

ἑρπηδών, ἡ, *crawling*; met., *onset* τὴν τῆς ἡδονῆς ἑ. Gr.Nyss.*hom. 4 in Eccl*.(M.44.676C).

ἑρπηστικός, v. ἑρπυστικός.

***ἑρπιστήριον, τό**, *creeping place* ὄφεως ἑ. *Max.invect*.(M.90. 204C).

[*]**ἑρπιστικός**, v. ἑρπυστικός.

ἕρπυσις, ἡ, *creeping*, ‡Ath.*def*.4(M.28.541D).

ἑρπυστήρ, ὁ, **1.** *reptile*, *Orac.Sib*.1.59; Gr.Naz.*carm*.1.1.8.5(M.37. 447A); **2.** as adj., *creeping*, *Orac.Sib*.1.370; *serpentine*, Paul.Sil. *ambo*.272(M.86.2262A).

ἑρπυστής, ὁ, = foreg.; **1.** *reptile*, *Orac.Sib*.13.160; *A.Thom*.A 32(p.148.17); **2.** as adj., *creeping*, *Orac.Sib*.1.18; *A.Thom*.A 32(l.c.); †Apoll.*met.Ps*.148:7(M.33.1536).

ἑρπυστικός (**ἑρπηστ-**, [*]**ἑρπιστ-**), *creeping, crawling* ἑρπιστικῶν θηρίων Thdt.*Ps*.139:4(1.1539); met., of sins ἀνομία ἑρπηστική Diod. *Ps*.56:3(M.33.1594C); Gr.Nyss.*v.Mos*.(M.44.349A); id.*Pss.titt*.A 5 (M.44.452B).

***ἐρρᾳδιουργημένως**, *recklessly*, ref. Marcion's treatment of Lc., Epiph.*haer*.42.11(p.108.3; M.41.712A).

[*]**ἐρρίζω**, cf. ἐνριζόω *LS*; pass., *be rooted, grounded in*, c. dat., Or.*Ps*.1:3(p.445).

[*]**ἐρρωδιός, ὁ**, = ἐρῳδιός, *heron*, Or.*exp.in Ps*.7:22(M.17.181D).

ἐρρωμένος, v. ῥώννυμι.

ἐρρωμένως, **1.** *soundly, rightly* εἰ ἐ. καὶ εἰλικρινῶς πολιτεύοιντο Heracleon ap.Or.*Jo*.13.60(59; p.292.27; M.14.516A); ὑγιῶς καὶ ἐ. φρονεῖν Eus.*p.e*.1.4(13D; M.21.41C); **2.** *firmly, steadfastly* ἵνα ἐρρωμενέστερον μάθω Meth.*symp*.11(p.137.21; M.18.213C).

ἐρυγή, ἡ, **1.** *belching*, exeg. Ps.44:2, Or.*Jo*.1.38(42; p.50.6; M.14. 100D); **2.** theol. Φιλογονίου καὶ Ἑλλανικοῦ καὶ Μακαρίου, ἀνθρώπων αἱρετικῶν ἀκατηχήτων τὸν υἱὸν λεγόντων οἱ μὲν ἐ., οἱ δὲ προβολήν, οἱ δὲ συναγέννητον Ar.*ep.Eus*.(p.2.7; M.42.212A).

***ἐρυγόβιος, ὁ**, *glutton*, Gr.Naz.*carm*.2.2(epigr.)48.7(M.38.108A).

ἐρύθρημα, τό, *rosiness* τὸ ἐπὶ τῆς παρειᾶς ἐ. Gr.Nyss.*ep*.19(M.46. 1072B).

***ἐρυθριασμός, ὁ**, *blushing*, Gr.Nyss.*res*.3(M.46.657C).

ἐρυθροειδής, *red-looking*, Ph.Carp.*Cant*.113(M.40.133D).

ἐρυθρότης, ἡ, *redness,* Jo.Mosch.*prat.*proem.(M.87.2852A).

[*]**ἐρυσίπελος,** *erysipelas,* Pall.*v.Chrys.*17(p.104.19; M.47.58).

ἐρυσίπτολις, *protecting the city* σταυρὸν...ἐ. Paul.Sil.*Soph.*492(M.86.2138B).

ἔρχ-ομαι, *come;* **1.** exeg. Mt.11:3 περὶ δὲ τοῦ, εἰ αὐτὸς μέλλει ~εσθαι ἔχρῃζεν ὁ Ἰωάννης μαθεῖν, ~εσθαι δὲ ἐν τοῖς κάτω, ἔνθα ηὐτρέπιστο πορεύεσθαι ὁ Ἰωάννης Or.*fr.*220 II *in Mt.*11:2f.(p.105); φασί τινες...ὅτι μὲν αὐτὸς ἦν ὁ Χριστός, ᾔδει [sc. ὁ Ἰωαννης]· εἰ δὲ καὶ ὑπὲρ ἀνθρώπων ἔμελλε τελευτᾶν, οὐκ ᾔδει· διὰ τοῦτο εἶπε 'σὺ εἶ ὁ ~όμενος;' τουτέστιν, ὁ εἰς τὸν ᾅδην μέλλων καταβαίνειν· ἀλλ' οὐκ ἂν ἔχοι τοῦτο λόγον· ὁ γὰρ Ἰωάννης οὐδὲ τοῦτο ἠγνόει Chrys.*hom.36.2 in Mt.*(7.406E); exeg. 'thy kingdom come' ἢ τάχα τὸ ἐλθέτω καθαιρετικὸν τῆς ἀξίας νομίζουσιν; εἶτα οὐκ ἀκούουσιν τοῦ μεγάλου Δαυίδ, καὶ τὸν πατέρα πρὸς ἑαυτὸν ἕλκοντος καὶ 'ἐλθὲ εἰς τὸ σῶσαι ἡμᾶς' βοῶντος; εἰ οὖν ἐπὶ τοῦ πατρὸς τὸ ἐλθεῖν σωτήριον, πῶς ἐπὶ τοῦ πνεύματος τὸ ἐλθεῖν ἐπονείδιστον; Gr.Nyss.*or.dom.*3(p.65.35f.; M.44.1160C); **2.** in creeds ~όμενον κρῖναι ζῶντας καὶ νεκρούς *Symb.Nic.*(325)(p.52.1; M.20.1540C); *Symb.Ant.*(341)1(p.249.6; M.26.721A); *Symb.Nic.-CP*(p.80.11; H.2.288B).

ἔρως, ὁ, *love* (v. ἀγάπη);

A. defence of term as synonym of ἀγάπη, cf. *quaecumque de caritate scripta sunt, quasi de amore dicta suscipe nihil de nominibus curans; eadem namque in utroque virtus ostenditur,* Or.*Cant.*proem.(p.70.33; M.13.70B); that *amor* = ἐ. is shown by translation of Ignatius' ὁ ἐμὸς ἐ. ἐσταύρωται, *meus autem amor crucifixus est,* discussed, *ib.*(p.71.26; 70D); ἐπιτεταμένη γὰρ ἀγάπη ἐ. λέγεται· ᾧ οὐδεὶς ἐπαισχύνεται, ὅταν μὴ κατὰ σαρκὸς γένηται παρ' αὐτοῦ ἡ τοξεία Gr.Nyss.*hom.13 in Cant.*(M.44.1048C); μή τις ἡμᾶς οἰέσθω παρὰ τὰ λόγια τὴν τοῦ ἐ. ἐπωνυμίαν πρεσβεύειν...πλὴν ἵνα μὴ ταῦτα εἰπεῖν δοκῶμεν, ὡς τὰ θεῖα λόγια παρακινοῦντες, ἀκουέτωσαν αὐτῶν οἱ τὴν ἔρωτος ἐπωνυμίαν διαβάλλοντες· 'ἐράσθητι αὐτῆς' [Pr.4:6] Dion.Ar.*d.n.*4.11(M.3.708B–709A); θεῖον αὐτὸν [sc. ἐ.] λέγων, ἐπειδὴ καὶ πρῶτον αἴτιον τοῦ οὐρανίου ἐ. ὁ θεός ἐστιν...εἰ γὰρ ὁ ἐ. αὐτός ἐστιν ἡ ἀγάπη...δῆλον ὅτι πάντων ἑνοποιὸς ἐ. ἤτοι ἀγάπη ὁ θεός ἐστιν Max.*schol.d.n.*4.15(M.4.268C); θεοπρεπῶς γὰρ τοῦ ὄντως ἐ., οὐχ ὑφ' ἡμῶν μόνον, ἀλλὰ καὶ πρὸς τῶν λογίων αὐτῶν ὑμνουμένου...ἀχώρητον ...τῷ πλήθει τὸ ἑνιαῖον τοῦ θείου καὶ ἑνὸς ἐ.· διὸ καὶ ὡς δυσχερέστερον ὄνομα τοῖς πολλοῖς δοκοῦν, ἐπὶ τῆς θείας σοφίας τάττεται, πρὸς ἀναγωγὴν αὐτῶν...εἰς τὴν τοῦ ὄντως ἐ. γνῶσιν...ἐπὶ τοῖς ὀρθῶς τῶν θείων ἀκροωμένοις ἐπὶ τῆς αὐτῆς δυνάμεως τάττεται πρὸς τῶν ἱερῶν θεολόγων τὸ τῆς ἀγάπης καὶ τὸ τοῦ ἐ. ὄνομα κατὰ τὰς θείας ἐκφαντορίας Dion.Ar.*d.n.*4.12(709B,C).

B. definitions and qualities; **1.** in gen. ἐκ τῶν ἐναντίων τῆς σωματικῆς ἐπιθυμίας τὸν θεῖον ἐ. γίνεσθαι· ὥστε...ἀκατάπληκτον ἀνδρείαν ὕλην τοῦ θείου ἐ. γίνεσθαι Gr.Nyss.*hom.6 in Cant.*(M.44.900C,D); τὸν ἐ., εἴτε θεῖον, εἴτε ἀγγελικόν, εἴτε νοερόν, εἴτε ψυχικόν, εἴτε φυσικὸν εἴποιμεν, ἑνωτικήν τινα καὶ συγκρατικὴν ἐννοήσωμεν δύναμιν, τὰ μὲν ὑπέρτερα κινοῦσαν ἐπὶ πρόνοιαν τῶν καταδεεστέρων, τὰ δὲ ὁμόστοιχα πάλιν εἰς κοινωνικὴν ἀλληλουχίαν Dion.Ar.*d.n.*4.15(M.3.713A); θεῖον αὐτὸν λέγων, ἐπειδὴ καὶ πρῶτον αἴτιον τοῦ οὐρανίου ἐ. ὁ θεός ἐστιν...ἐκεῖθεν οὖν μεταβατικῶς πρόεισιν ἐπ' ἀγγέλους· ὅθεν καὶ ἀγγελικὸν αὐτόν φησιν, ἔνθα μάλιστα καὶ τὸν τῆς ἑνότητος εὕροι τις ἂν ἐ. θεῖον...εἶτα μετ' ἀγγέλους, καὶ νοερόν φησιν ἐ., τουτέστι παρὰ θεοσόφοις ἀνδράσιν, οἵ εἰσι τῆς ἐκκλησίας...ψυχικὸν δὲ ἐκάλεσεν ἐ. τὸν τῶν ἀλόγων, τὴν αἰσθητικὴν φιλίαν...φυσικὸν δὲ ἐ. φησι τὸν τῶν ἀψύχων καὶ ἀναισθήτων κατὰ τὴν ἑκτικὴν ἐπιτηδειότητα...ἐρώντων τοῦ δημιουργοῦ Max.*schol.d.n.*4.15(M.4.268C–269A); **2.** love as ecstatic κατάστασίς ἐστι προσευχῆς ἕξις ἀπαθής, ἐ. ἀκροτάτῳ εἰς ὕψος νοητὸν ἁρπάζουσα τὸν φιλόσοφον, καὶ πνευματικὸν νοῦν Evagr. Pont.*or.*52(M.79.1177C); Dion.Ar.*d.n.*4.13(M.3.712A) cit. s. ἐκστατικός; μακάριος ὅστις τοιοῦτον πρὸς θεὸν ἐκτήσατο ἐ. οἷον μανικὸς ἐραστὴς πρὸς τὴν ἑαυτοῦ ἐρωμένην κέκτηται Jo.Clim.*scal.*30(M.88.1156C); of individuals καθάπερ γάρ τινα κάρον ὑπὸ τῆς τοῦ ἐ. ἐκείνου δεξάμενος [sc. Moses] μέθης, καὶ τῷ φίλτρῳ λίαν ἐκβακχευθείς, τὴν μὲν οἰκείαν ἠγνόησε φύσιν, ἐπεθύμησε δὲ ἰδεῖν, ἃ μὴ θέμις ἰδεῖν Thdt. *carit.*(3.1301); Παῦλος...ἐν κατοχῇ τοῦ θείου γεγονὼς ἐ., καὶ τῆς ἐκστατικῆς αὐτοῦ δυνάμεως μετειληφὼς Dion.Ar.*d.n.*4.13(M.3.712A).

C. of God's love τοῦ...θεοῦ...τοιαύτη πέφυκεν φύσις, παντὸς ἤδη ποτὲ ἐντὸς ὅρων θεοσεβείας ὄντος...στοργῇ τῇ πρὸς αὐτὸν εἰς αὐτὸν φέρειν τὴν ψυχήν, ὑπ' αὐτοῦ εἰς αὐτὴν ἔρωτος ἰδέᾳ *Hom.Clem.*3.6; τί οὐκ ἐποίησεν ὁ θεός, ὥστε φιληθῆναι παρ' ἡμῶν;...αὐτὸν ἔπεμψε τὸν υἱόν· ἀνῃρέθη καὶ οὗτος ἐλθών, καὶ οὐδὲ οὕτως ἔσβεσε τὸν ἐ., ἀλλ' ἀνῆψε μειζόνως Chrys.*hom.5.6 in Rom.*(9.470C); Thdt.*Cant.*1(2.23); ἐ. signifying its supra-rational and supra-sensible quality, which binds together seeming contradictions ὅταν δέ, τὰς ἀνομοίους ὁμοιότητας τοῖς νοεροῖς περιτιθέντες, ἐπιθυμίαν αὐτοῖς περιπλάσωμεν, ἐ. θεῖον αὐτὴν ἐννοῆσαι χρὴ τῆς ὑπὲρ λόγον καὶ νοῦν ἀυλίας, καὶ τὴν ἀκλινῆ καὶ ἀνένδοτον ἔφεσιν τῆς ὑπερουσίως ἁγνῆς καὶ ἀπαθοῦς θεωρίας Dion.Ar.*c.h.*2.4(M.3.144A); ἔστι καὶ ὁ θεῖος ἐ. ἀγαθὸς ἀγαθοῦ διὰ τὸ ἀγαθόν. αὐτὸς γὰρ ὁ ἀγαθοεργὸς τῶν ὄντων ἐ., ἐν τἀγαθῷ καθ' ὑπερβολὴν προϋπάρχων, οὐκ εἴασεν αὐτὸν ἄγονον ἐν ἑαυτῷ μένειν, ἐκίνησε δὲ αὐτὸν εἰς τὸ πρακτικεύεσθαι κατὰ τὴν ἁπάντων γενητικὴν ὑπερβολήν id.*d.n.*4.10(M.3.708B); τοὺς ἐκ τοῦ ἑνὸς πολλοὺς ἐ. διετάξαμεν...νῦν αὖθις ἀναλαβόντες ἅπαντας εἰς τὸν ἕνα καὶ συνεπτυγμένον ἐ., καὶ πάντων αὐτῶν πατέρα συνελίξωμεν...πρῶτον εἰς δύο συναιροῦντες αὐτῶν τὰς ἐρωτικὰς καθόλου δυνάμεις, ὧν ἐπικρατεῖ...ἡ ἐκ τοῦ πάντων ἐπέκεινα παντὸς ἐ. ἄσχετος αἰτία, καὶ πρὸς ἣν ἀνατείνεται...ὁ ἐκ τῶν ὄντων ἁπάντων ὁλικὸς ἐ. *ib.*4.16(713B,C); comment εἰπὼν ὁλικὸν ἐ., δηλοῖ καὶ μερικούς, λέγων τὸν θεὸν εἶναι τὸν ὁλικὸν καὶ τὸν μερικόν,...τῶν γὰρ εἰδῶν μεταλαμβάνει ἕκαστος πρὸς τὴν οἰκείαν ἐπιτηδειότητα· οὕτω καὶ ὁ θεὸς καὶ ὅλον καὶ μέρη τοῦ ἐ. Max.*schol.d.n.*4.17(M.4.269C,D).

D. of man's love towards God; **1.** towards God and divine beauty in gen. ὅ γέ τοι οὐράνιος καὶ θεῖος ὄντως ἐ. ταύτῃ προσγίνεται τοῖς ἀνθρώποις, ὅταν ἐν αὐτῇ που τῇ ψυχῇ τὸ ὄντως καλὸν ὑπὸ τοῦ θείου λόγου ἀναζωπυρούμενον ἐκλάμπειν δυνηθῇ Clem.*prot.*11(p.82.23; M.8.236D); εἰς ἐ. τὸν τὸ θεῖον κάλλος κατανοοῦντα οὐράνιον προκαλουμένῳ Or.*Jo.*1.9(11; p.14.29; M.14.40D); Gr.Nyss.*hom.1 in Cant.*(M.44.772B); †Bas.Anc.*virg.*48(M.30.765B); Pall.*h.Laus.*46(p.134.5; M.34.1225A); Thdr.Stud.*epp.*1.8(M.99.936D); **2.** towards Christ, freq. as a 'wounding love', esp. in bridal imagery, v. τιτρώσκω, ἀγάπη: ψυχή, ἥτις ἡττηθεῖσα τῷ πνευματικῷ ἐ. ἀξίως ἐνυμφεύθη τῷ θεῷ λόγῳ Mac.Aeg.*ep.*(M.34.417A); id.*hom.*4.6(M.34.477A); ἡ ῥανὶς τοῦ πνεύματος...ἔτρωσε τὴν καρδίαν αὐτῶν ἔρωτι θείῳ πρὸς τὸν ἐπουράνιον βασιλέα Χριστόν *ib.*5.6(500B); οὔπω ἐτρώθημεν τῷ θείῳ ἐ., οὔτε ἐπλήγημεν ὑπὸ τῆς πνευματικῆς ἀγάπης τοῦ νυμφίου *ib.*25.5(669D); τὸ ἄφραστον ὁρᾷ τοῦ νυμφίου κάλλος· καὶ διὰ τοῦτο τρωθεῖσα τῷ ἀσωμάτῳ καὶ διαπύρῳ βέλει τοῦ ἐ. Gr.Nyss.*hom.13 in Cant.*(M.44.1048C); Pall.*h.Laus.*21(p.64.10; M.34.1073B); Isid.Pel.*epp.*1.27(M.78.200B) cit. s. ἀνάγνωσις; **3.** of Christ as beloved of soul ὁ ἐμὸς ἐ. ἐσταύρωται, καὶ οὐκ ἔστιν ἐν ἐμοὶ πῦρ φιλόυλον Ign.*Rom.*7.2 interpreted *memini aliquem sanctorum dixisse, Ignatium nomine, de Christo: meus autem amor crucifixus est; nec reprehendi eum pro hoc dignum judico,* Or.*Cant.*proem.(p.71.26; M.13.70D); ἔδοξέ τισι τῶν καθ' ἡμᾶς ἱερολόγων καὶ θειότερον εἶναι τὸ τοῦ ἐ. ὄνομα τοῦ τῆς ἀγάπης. γράφει δὲ καὶ ὁ θεῖος Ἰγνάτιος· ὁ ἐμὸς ἐ. ἐσταύρωται Dion.Ar.*d.n.*4.12(M.3.709A,B); Ἰγνάτιος ἔφασκεν, ὅτι ὁ ἐμὸς ἐ. ἐσταύρωται· ὄντινα ἐ. θεοῦ, καὶ ἀγάπην θεοῦ...μὴ ἔχοντες, οὗτοι τὸ θέλημα τὸ διαβολικὸν ἔχοντες Anast.S.*serm.imag.*3(M.89.1168D); τοῦτο δηλοῦντες οἱ ἅγιοι, ἠγοῦν τὸ θερμὸν τῆς πρὸς αὐτὸν [sc. Χριστόν] ἀγάπης, ὁ μέν φησιν... ἕτερος δέ· ὁ ἐμὸς ἐ. ἐσταύρωται Χριστός Thdr.Stud.*catech.parv.*3(p.7); cf.id.*iamb.*70(M.99.1797D); esp. of virgins, †Bas.Anc.*virg.*26(M.30.724B); *ib.*49(765C); **4.** its power and effects οὕτω γάρ ἐστι τυραννικὸν ὁ ἐ. ὁ πνευματικός, ὡς μηδενὶ παραχωρεῖν καιρῷ, ἀλλ' ἀεὶ τῆς ψυχῆς ἔχεσθαι τοῦ φιλοῦντος Chrys.*hom.1.3 in Phil.*(11.198D); οὐκ ἔστι γενέσθαι ταπεινόν, ἀλλ' ἢ διὰ τοῦ τῶν θείων ἐ. id.*hom.2.3 in 1Cor.*(10.8A); ἐ. θείῳ καὶ ἀμιγεῖ καθαρθέντες Dion.Ar.*e.h.*3.7(M.3.436B).

E. of love towards saints ἐμοῦ δὲ παραχρῆμα πῦρ ἐν τῇ ψυχῇ ἀνήφθη, καὶ ἐ. ἔχει με τῶν προφητῶν καὶ τῶν ἀνδρῶν ἐκείνων, οἵ εἰσι Χριστοῦ φίλοι Just.*dial.*8.1(M.6.492C); ἅπαντας μὲν φιλῶ τοὺς ἁγίους, μάλιστα δὲ τὸν μακάριον Παῦλον...τοῦτο δὲ εἶπον, καὶ ὃν περὶ αὐτὸν ἐ. ἔχω...ἵνα ὑμᾶς κοινωνοὺς ποιήσω τοῦ φίλτρου. οἱ μὲν γὰρ τὸν σωματικὸν ἐ. ἐρῶντες εἰκότως αἰσχύνονται ὁμολογεῖν...οἱ δὲ τὸν πνευματικόν, μηδέποτε ὁμολογοῦντες παυέσθωσαν...ἐκεῖνος μὲν γὰρ ὁ ἐ. ἔγκλημα, οὗτος δὲ ἐγκώμιον Chrys.*hom.in 2Cor.11:1*(3.291A,B); cf.*ib.*(292A,B).

F. of love for others 'ἀσπάσασθε Ἀμπλίαν τὸν ἀγαπητόν μου'... οὐδὲ γὰρ ἄν, εἰ μὴ πολλὴν ἀρετὴν ἐκέκτητο, εἰς ἐ. αὐτὸν ἐπεσπάσατο Chrys.*hom.31.2 in Rom.*(9.748A); ὁ Ἰὼβ τὸν ἐ. τῶν οἰκετῶν τὸν περὶ αὐτὸν ἐνδεικνύμενος id.*hom.24.4 in 1Cor.*(10.218A); Proc.G.*ep.*94(M.87.2745C).

G. for virtues etc. ὑποδεικνύων...τὸν μισθὸν τῆς γνώσεως εἰς ἐ. αὐτῆς τοὺς συνετοὺς ἐκκαλεῖται Clem.*paed.*1.10(p.145.7; M.8.360C); freedom, id.*str.*2.20(p.180.18; M.8.1069A); wisdom, id.*prot.*11(p.79.26; M.8.229D); virtue, Ath.*v.Anton.*44(M.26.908A); truth, Chrys. *comm.in Gal.*1:14(10.673C); Dion.Ar.*e.h.*2.3.5(M.3.401C); chastity, Meth.*symp.*1.1(p.9.19; M.18.40B); kingdom of heaven, Chrys.*hom.9.4 in 1Cor.*(10.79D); Mac.Mgn.*apocr.*3.12(p.81.28).

ἐρωτάω, 1. *ask for* μυστήριον ἐ. (tr. *interrogavit sacramentum*) CCarth.(256)*act.*(H.1.160D); **2.** *ask,* c. dat., *Ev.Barth.*2.2(*RB* 10 p.321); *Mir.Geo.*11(p.109.5); ἐρωτησάντων ἀλλήλοις Leont.N.*v.Jo. Eleem.*22(p.41.5).

ἐρωτητέον, *one must ask*, Clem.*str*.8.4(p.87.1,3; M.9.576A).

***ἐρωτητικῶς**, *interrogatively*, Epiph.*haer*.76.52(p.406.16,17; M.42.625A).

ἐρωτίζω, *question*; pass., Jo.D.*disp*.(M.96.1336B).

ἐρωτικός, *loving, longing*; **1.** ref. God's love ὁ πάντων αἴτιος...δι' ὑπερβολὴν τῆς ἐ. ἀγαθότητος Dion.Ar.*d.n*.4.13(M.3.712A); God called ἐ. κίνησις, drawing things to himself, *ib*.4.14(712C); ὅτι ἡ ἐ. κίνησις, τοῦ ἀγαθοῦ προϋπάρχουσα, ἐν τῷ ἀγαθῷ ἁπλῆ καὶ αὐτοκίνητος οὖσα, καὶ ἐκ τοῦ ἀγαθοῦ προϊοῦσα, αὖθις ἐπὶ τὸ αὐτὸ ἐπιστρέφει, ἀτελεύτητος καὶ ἄναρχος οὖσα, ὅπερ δηλοῖ τὴν ἡμῶν ἔφεσιν πρὸς τὸ θεῖον Max. *schol.d.n*.4.14(M.4.268B); cf.*ib*.(265D) = id.*cap*.5.88(M.90.1385B); *ib*. 5.89(M.90.1385C); ref. mutual love between God and man δι' ἀμοιβῆς παρ' ἀμφοτέρων ἀλλήλοις τὴν ἐ. ἀντιχαριζομένων διάθεσιν Gr.Nyss.*hom.9 in Cant*.(M.44.956A); **2.** ref. man's love for God ἐγερτικὸν τῆς ἐφέσεως αὐτοῦ [sc. θεοῦ] τῆς ἐ. Dion.Ar.*d.n*.4.13(M.3.712B); of ecstasy, Max.*schol.d.n*.4.13(M.4.265B); τὰ τοῦ νυμφίου Χριστοῦ ἐ. ἰδιώματα Thdr.Stud.*epp*.2.150(M.99.1469B); **3.** justification of use for divine love τὸ σφοδρότατον τῶν καθ' ἡδονὴν ἐνεργουμένων (λέγω δὴ τὸ ἐ. πάθος) τῆς τῶν δογμάτων ὑφηγήσεως αἰνιγματωδῶς προεστήσατο Gr.Nyss.*hom.1 in Cant*.(M.44.773C); **4.** *affectionate*, Chrys.*hom.1.1 in Tit*.(11.730A).

ἐρωτικῶς, **1.** *amorously*, ref. language of Cant. λέξις ἐρωτικότερον ἐσχηματισμένη Nil.ap.Proc.G.*Cant*.1:1(M.87.1548B); **2.** *affectionately, eagerly* οὐδὲ γάρ ἐστιν ἑτέραν πόλιν εὑρεῖν οὕτως ἐ. πρὸς τὴν ἀκρόασιν τῶν πνευματικῶν λογίων διακειμένην Chrys.*prod.Jud*.1.1(2.376A); **3.** *lovingly*, ref. spiritual love πάσης κατασβεσθείσης σωματικῆς διαθέσεως, μόνῳ τῷ πνεύματι ζέειν ἐ. ἐν ἡμῖν τὴν διάνοιαν Gr.Nyss. *hom.1 in Cant*.(M.44.773D); ψυχὴ...ἐ. ... πρὸς τὴν κατὰ Χριστὸν ἀγάπην διακειμένη Mac.Aeg.*carit*.26(M.34.929B); ἐφέσεις τῶν νοῶν, ἐ. ἀεὶ γλιχόμεναι τῆς ἐγχωρούσης τῶν ὑπερφυῶν θεωρίας Dion.Ar. *d.n*.3.3(M.3.684C); **4.** ἐ. ἔχω *behave lovingly, be fond of* τὰς ἐ. ἐχούσας αὐτοῦ [sc. θεοῦ]...ψυχάς Mac.Aeg.*libert.ment*.31(M.34.964D); id.*perf*. 5(M.34.845B).

***ἐρωτισμός, ὁ**, v. *αἱρετισμός.

***ἐρωτοαπόκρισις, ἡ**, *dialogue*, *Nomoc*.254 tit.

ἐρωτομανία, ἡ, *craze for sex*, Nil.*epp*.2.167(M.79.284C).

***ἐρωτοποιέομαι**, *be made in order to allure* ἐρωτοπεποιημένῳ... προσώπῳ Just.*2apol*.11.4(M.6.461C).

ἐσθής, ἡ, *clothing, dress*; of baptismal garment, Gr.Naz.*or*.40.25 (M.36.393C); Dion.Ar.*e.h*.2.2.7(M.3.396D); τὴν μυστικὴν ἐ. Soz.*h.e*. 7.8.7(M.67.1436A); of liturg. vestments οἱ διάκονοι παριστάσθωσαν εὐσταλεῖς τῆς πλείονος ἐ. *Const.App*.2.57.4; εὐξάμενος ὁ ἀρχιερεὺς... λαμπρὰν ἐ. μετενδύς *Lit*.ap.*Const.App*.8.12.4; of monk's habit at clothing ceremony τὴν ἐσθῆτα πᾶσαν ἀπαμφιέσας, ἑτέραν ἀμφιέννυσι Dion.Ar.*e.h*.6.2(M.3.533B); its significance explained ἡ δὲ τῆς προτέρας ἐ. ἀποβολή, καὶ τῆς ἑτέρας λῆψις, τὴν ἀπὸ μέσης ἱερᾶς ζωῆς ἐπὶ τὴν τελειοτέραν μετάταξιν ἐμφαίνει, καθάπερ ἐπὶ τῆς ἱερᾶς θεογενεσίας ἡ τῆς ἐσθῆτος ἄμειψις ἐδήλου τὴν ἀποκαθαιρομένης ζωῆς εἰς θεωρητικὴν καὶ φωτιστικὴν ἕξιν ἀναγωγήν *ib*.6.3.4(536B).

***ἐσθίασις, ἡ**, *clothing*, Eus.Al.*serm*.9(M.86.364A).

***ἐσθλόγαμος**, *well married*, Gr.Naz.*carm*.2.1.16.20(M.37.1255A).

ἐσθλοδότης, ὁ, *giver of good*, Synes.*hymn*.4.270(p.33; M.66.1608).

ἔσθω, = ἐσθίω, *eat*, Epiph.*haer*.26.3(p.279.5; M.41.336B).

***ἐσκεπασμένως**, *in an obscure way*, Or.*Jo*.13.48(46; p.275.22; M. 14.485C).

***ἐσκληκίασαν**, v. σκληριάζω.

***ἐσκοτισμένως**, *obscurely*, ‡Jo.D.*conf*.2(p.111.4; M.95.284B).

[*]**ἐσοπτρίζ-ω**, (variant of εἰσοπτρίζω), **1.** *show as in a mirror, reflect*, ref. Devil tempting monk ἀφ' ἧς ἐξελήλυθε τὸ γένος ~ων Nil. *Eulog*.2(M.79.1096C); *ib*.(1133C); ref. S. Paul ὦ ὀφθαλμοὶ ἐσοπτρισάμενοι τὴν ἁγίαν τριάδα Procl.CP *or*.18.4(M.65.821C); **2.** pass., *be shown* (i.e. have shown to one) *as in a glass*, Nemes.*nat.hom*. (M.40.529B); Ephr.3.1A.

***ἐσόπτρως**, *as in a mirror*, Dan.Raith.*v.Jo.Clim*.(M.88.601A).

[*]**ἐσός**, late form of σός, *thy*, *Contrad*.2(p.8).

[*]**ἐσότι**, = εἰσότι, *against the time when*, Men.*exc.Rom*.13(p.202. 25; M.113.900A); id.*exc.gent*.4(p.444.3; M.113.796B).

***ἐσπάμπαν**, *altogether*, Didym.*Trin*.2.20(M.39.740C).

ἑσπέρα, ἡ, *evening*; **1.** in gen. τὸ μὲν τέλος τοῦ φωτὸς ἑσπέραν καλῶν, τὸ δὲ τέλος τῆς νυκτὸς πρωΐαν, καὶ ἡμέραν τὸ πᾶν προσαγορεύων ...μηδὲ νομίζειν τὴν ἑ. τέλος εἶναι τῆς ἡμέρας, ἀλλ' εἰδέναι σαφῶς ὅτι ἀμφοτέρων τὸ μῆκος μίαν ἡμέραν πληροῖ Chrys.*hom.4.6 in Gen*.(4. 28D); οἱ...Ἰουδαῖοι...τὴν ἑ. ἀρχὴν τῆς ἐπιούσης ἡμέρας εἶναι νομίζουσιν, ἀπατῶντες ἑαυτοὺς *ib*.5.5(4.37C); cf.Cosm.Ind.*top*.2(p.90.3; M.88.125D) cit. s. κυριακός; **2.** as time for; **a.** prayer, CLaod.*can*.18; ἑσπέρᾳ δὲ εὐχαριστοῦντες, ὅτι ἡμῖν ἀνάπαυσιν ἔδωκεν τῶν μεθημερινῶν κόπων τὴν νύκτα *Const.App*.8.34.6; *ib*.2.59.2; *Euchol*.(p.31); **b.** baptism, on Holy Saturday, Cyr.H.*catech*.19.1; εὐχαὶ τοῦ ἁγίου βαπτίσματος...μάλιστα καὶ τῷ ἁγίῳ σαββάτῳ ἑσπέρας *Euchol*.(p.291); **c.** eucharistic celebration, in Egypt πρὸς ἑσπέραν τῷ σαββάτῳ συνιόντες, ἠριστηκότες ἤδη, μυστήριον μετέχουσι Soz.*h.e*.7.19.8(M.67. 1477B); **3.** connexion with fasting τὴν ἑ. ἀναμένεις εἰς μετάληψιν Bas. *hom*.1.10(2.9B; M.31.181B); νηστεύειν ταύτας [sc. ἡμέρας]...ἄχρις ἑ.· ἐν δὲ ταῖς λοιπαῖς ταῖς πρὸ τῆς παρασκευῆς ἐνάτην ὥραν ἢ ἑσπέραν ἕκαστος ἐσθίετο...ἀπὸ δὲ ἑ. πέμπτης μέχρις ἀλεκτοροφωνίας ἀπονηστιζόμενοι *Const.App*.5.19.2; *ib*.5.19.3; μὴ νομίζωμεν τὴν ἀσιτίαν μόνον τὴν μέχρι τῆς ἑ. ἀρκεῖν ἡμῖν πρὸς σωτηρίαν Chrys.*hom.4.7 in Gen*.(4. 29D); μέχρι τῆς ἑ. ἄσιτοι *ib*.8.6(63C).

Ἑσπερία, [sc. χθών], ἡ, **1.** the *western land*; in gen., the *west*, Gr. Naz.*or*.21.34(M.35.1124A); Philost.*h.e*.11.6(M.65.600A); **2.** the *evening star*; dwelling place of Beelzebub, *T.Sal*.6.7.

***ἑσπερίζω**, *spend the evening*, Thdt.*affect*.12(p.314.15; 4.1029); Dor.*doct*.11.7(M.88.1741D).

ἑσπερινός, *of the evening, in the evening, evening* ἑ. εὐχαριστίαν *Const.App*.8.37.2; ἑ. εὐχάς Chrys.*hom.14.4 in 1Tim*.(11.631A); ἑ. λειτουργίας Jo.Ant.*relat.imp*.1(p.124.35; M.83.1441A); Eustrat.*v. Eutych*.94(M.86.2380B); *Euchol*.(p.35); sc. ὕμνος: μετὰ τὸν ἑ. ἐσθίομεν Anast.*temp*.(p.279); τὴν ἐν τῷ σαββάτῳ ἑ. τῶν ἱερωμένων πρὸς τὸ θυσιαστήριον εἴσοδον CTrull.*can*.90; neut. sing. or plur. as subst., *evening service*, Gr.Mag.*dial*.(tr.Zach.)3.15(M.*PL*.77.251D); *Const. Stud*.18(M.99.1709D); *Euchol*.(p.2); *ib*.(p.5).

ἑσπέριος, *western*; of emperor, Philost.*h.e*.3.3(M.65.481B); of bishops, *ib*.5.1(529A).

ἐσσήν, ὁ, *king* (i.e. *queen*) bee, Or.*comm.10.7 in Mt*.(p.7.19; M.13. 849A).

ἐστηριγμένως, *definitively*, †Bas.*bapt*.1.2.9(2.635C; M.31.1540C).

ἑστία, ἡ, = ἑστίασις, Or.*Cels*.4.75(p.345.15; M.11.1145D); Diod. *Ps*.62:6(M.33.1597B); ‡Nil.*perist*.11.17(M.79.928C).

***ἑστιακός**, *vestal* παρθένους Soz.*h.e*.1.9.4(M.67.884B).

ἑστίασις, ἡ, **1.** *banquet, feast*; of eucharist, Dion.Al.ap.Eus.*h.e*. 6.42.5(M.20.613C); Ath.*ep.fest*.27(p.296.1; M.26.1433B); πνευματικὴν ...ἑ. Chrys.*nativ*.7(2.365B); ref. Gen.1:29 τοῦ κατ' εἰκόνα...πλασθησομένου ἑστίασιν Jo.D.*hom*.4.5(M.96.608C); met. ἑ. ...ψυχικῆς Clem. *str*.6.12(p.481.30; M.9.320C); **2.** *eating*, Clem.*paed*.2.1(p.162.15; M.8. 397A).

***ἑστιατικός**, = ἑστιακός, Or.*sel.in Jer*.51:21(M.13.604A).

ἑστιατορία, ἡ, *food, sustenance*, Ant.Mon.*hom*.7(M.89.1453C).

ἑστιάτωρ, ὁ, **1.** *host*, met. οἱ...προφῆται ἑστιάτορες τῶν λογικῶν ὑπάρχουσι ‡Tit.Bost.*palm*.3(M.18.1268A); **2.** *guest* ἡ αὐλήτρια περιερχομένη πάντας τοὺς ἑ. *A.Thom*.A 5(p.108.14).

ἑστι-άω, **1.** *eat*, Pach.*reg*.B 46(p.13.1; M.40.948C); pass. τοῦ δρακοντείου σώματος ὑπὸ τῶν Αἰθιόπων ~ωμένου Or.*or*.27.12(p.371.4; M.11.516B); **2.** med., *be a guest*; met., of Christ ἐν τοῖς κόλποις εἶναι 'τοῦ πατρός', ~ώμενον ἐπὶ γῆς αὐτῷ σώματι Eust.*engast*.18(p.46.7; M.18.652D).

ἐστοχασμένως, *having regard* to; *conformably* to; *in accordance* with ἐ. τοῦ...πλήθους τῶν ἁπλούστερον πιστευόντων Or.*Cels*.4.49(p.322. 2; M.11.1108B); Bas.*reg.br*.152,303(2.466C,522D; M.31.1181C,1297B); τὴν παραλλαγὴν πρὸς τὰ ἑκάστῳ συμπίπτοντα ἐ. γίνεσθαι...ἀφίεμεν id. *reg.fus*.19.1(2.362C; M.31.968A); οὐκ ἐ. τῆς...ἐπιθυμίας Gr.Naz.*ep*.102 (M.37.201B); ἐ. τοῦ ἀποστολικοῦ βουλήματος ἑρμηνεύσει...τὴν λέξιν Gr.Nyss.*Eun*.12(2 p.283.10; M.45.896A); abs., *with due consideration* διὰ βουλῆς λογικῆς ἐ. τε καὶ ὀρθῶς...ὁρισάμενος λόγον Max.*ambig*.(M. 91.1108C); *ib*.(1101A).

[*]**ἐσύ**, = σύ, *thou*, *Mir.Geo*.5(p.47.10).

ἐσφαλμένως, *erringly, amiss*, Or.*Cels*.1.24(p.75.14; M.11.705B); Eus.*Ps*.46:2–3(M.23.413B); Ammon.*Jo*.8:15(M.85.1448C).

ἐσχατιά, ἡ, **1.** *farthest part, extremity* τῶν ἐ. τῆς γῆς Eus.ap.*cat.Ac*. 18:22(p.415.14); abs., with τῆς γῆς understood τῶν τὰς ἐ. οἰκούντων Constantius Imp.ap.Ath.*apol.Const*.30(M.25.633A); Nil.*epp*.2.321 (M.79.357A); *ib*.4.54(576A); **2.** *remote retreat, solitary spot*, sts. *hermitage* τῆς ἐ. ταύτης Bas.*ep*.2.1(3.71A; M.32.224A); *ib*.4.1(76C; M.236C); Gr.Naz.*ep*.4(M.37.25A); Gr.Nyss.*v.Macr*.(p.387.20; M.46. 976B); id.*v.Gr.Thaum*.(M.46.913C); **3.** *lowest state* τὴν ἀνθρωπίνην ἐ., ἐξ ἧς ἀρρήτως ὁ ἁπλοῦς Ἰησοῦς συνετέθη Dion.Ar.*d.n*.1.4(M.3. 592A); of catechumens, id.*e.h*.3.3.7(M.3.433B); *ib*.3.3.11(441A).

ἐσχατίζω, *be last, behind*, Ant.Mon.*hom*.55(M.89.1601D).

ἔσχατος, *last* in time; **1.** in phrase ἐπ' ἐσχάτων τῶν ἡμερῶν; **a.** ref. Inc. ὁ Ἰησοῦς...ἐφανερώθη...ἐπ' ἐ. τῶν ἡμερῶν *2Clem*.14.2; Ath.*Ar*. 1.55(M.26.125C); ἐπ' ἐ. σαρκωθέντα ‡Eust.*Laz*.29(p.50.11); Χριστὸν ...ἐπ' ἐ. τῶν ἡμερῶν κενῶσαι ἑαυτόν CCP(543)*anath*.7(Hahn p.228); in creeds ἐπ' ἐ. τῶν ἡμερῶν...κατελθόντα *Symb.Ant*.(341)1(p.249.3;

M.26.721A); *Symb.Ant.*(345)1(p.251.27; M.26.728B); *Symb.Sirm.*1 (p.254.22; M.26.736C); **b.** ref. end of this age, *Did.*16.3; τοῖς δὲ ἔθνεσιν μετάνοιά ἐστιν ἕως ἐ. ἡμέρας Herm.*vis.*2.2.5; credal ἐλευσόμενον ἐν τῇ ἐ. ἡμέρᾳ τῆς ἀναστάσεως *Symb.Sirm.*3(p.236.5; M.26.693B); *Symb. CP*(360)(p.259.8; M.26.748B); **2.** exeg.; **a.** Mt.19:30, three explanations of οἱ ἔ.: those converted late in life, Or.*comm. in Mt.*15.26 (p.426.28; M.13.1329B); gentiles, *ib.*(p.427.20,24; 1329C); men opp. angels, *ib.*15.27(p.429.31; 1333A); **b.** Jo.6:40 ἐν τῷδε τῷ κόσμῳ, ὃν ἐ. ἡμέραν ἠνίξατο Clem.*paed.*1.6(p.107.13; M.8.255A); **c.** 1Cor.15:26 πῶς ἔ. [sc. ἐχθρὸς ὁ θάνατος]; μετὰ πάντας, μετὰ τὸν διάβολον, μετὰ τὰ ἄλλα πάντα...πρότερον...ἡ συμβολὴ τοῦ διαβόλου, καὶ ἡ παρακοή, καὶ τότε ὁ θάνατος Chrys.*hom.39.4 in 1Cor.*(10.368A); **d.** Apoc.22:13 εἴρηται A ὁ Χριστὸς διὰ τὴν θεότητα. Ω δὲ ἤτοι ἔ. διὰ τὴν ἀνθρωπότητα Andr. Caes.*Apoc.*71(M.106.449A).

ἐσχάτως, *finally,* Thphn.*chron.*p.66(M.108.216B).

ἐσχηματισμένως, 1. *figuratively,* Olymp.*Job* 8:21(M.92.112D); **2.** *in a feigned* or *counterfeit manner, fraudulently,* Bas.*reg.fus.*20.3. (2.364E; M.31.973A); σωματικῶς καὶ ⟨οὐκ⟩ ἐ. Epiph.*haer.*70.2(p.234.21; if οὐκ be omitted ἐ. means *by the possession of form,* as M.42.341C); Cyr.*inc.unigen.*(5^1.693D); **3.** *privily* φανερῶς ἢ ἐ. Ath. Scholast.*coll.*1.1(p.3).

ἔσω, v. εἴσω.

ἐσωτερικός, 1. *inner, esoteric,* of teaching τὰ μὲν ἐ. εἶναι τῶν συγγραμμάτων αὐτοῦ [sc. Ἀριστοτέλους], τὰ δὲ...ἐξωτερικά Clem. *str.*5.9(p.365.12; M.9.89B); οὐ μόνον ἴδιον τοῦ Χριστιανῶν λόγου ἀλλὰ γὰρ καὶ τοῦ φιλοσόφων, παρ' οἷς τινες μὲν ἦσαν ἐξωτερικοὶ λόγοι, ἕτεροι δὲ ἐ. Or.*Cels.*1.7(p.60.10; M.11.668B); *ib.*3.37(p.234.1; 968C); τῆς ἐ. μυσταγωγίας Gr.Nyss.*anim.et res.*(M.46.133B); τὴν ἐ. καὶ ἀπόρρητον μύησιν id.*Eun.*12(1 p.304.26; M.45.1016D); **2.** of persons, *initiated* τοὺς μαθητὰς διεῖλε καὶ τοὺς μὲν ἐ. τοὺς δὲ ἐξωτερικοὺς ἐκάλεσεν [sc. Πυθαγόρας] Hipp.*haer.*1.2(p.5.15; M.16.3024A).

ἐσώτερος, comp. of ἔσω *inner,* Mac.Aeg.*hom.*17.15(M.34.633B); neut. as adv. τὸν ἔσω ἄνθρωπον, ⟨τὸν⟩ ἐσώτερον ψυχῆς καὶ σώματος Epiph.*haer.*36.2(p.46.11; M.41.636B); ᾤκησεν ἐσώτερον τῆς ἐρήμου Hier.*v.Paul.*B(p.11.14).

***ἐσωφόριον, τό,** *undergarment,* Leont.N.*v.Jo.Eleem.*22(pp.42.21, 43.5).

ἑταιρ-έω, 1. *make to fornicate, prostitute,* fig. ἡταίρηκεν ὑμῖν τὰ ὦτα Clem.*prot.*4(p.47.13; M.8.160C); τῇ ἀνθοφορούσῃ καὶ ~ούσῃ μουσικῇ id.*paed.*2.4(p.184.26; M.8.445B); **2.** *commit fornication,* always pres. or perf. ptcpl., *fornicator;* of women, *ib.*2.10(p.220.9; 521C); Chrys.*hom.4.3 in 1Tim.*(11.573C); of men, id.*hom.16.4 in 1Cor.*(10.140C); id.*ep.*3.3(3.568B); Isid.Pel.*epp.*4.42(M.78.1093B); Areth.*Apoc.*71(M.106.784C).

***ἑταιριάζ-ω,** *give a companion to,* cf. sq. φεύγοντες [sc. the Mohammedans] ~ειν τὸν θεὸν ἐκόψατε αὐτόν Jo.D.*haer.*101(M.94.768C).

ἑταιριαστής,** (ἑτεριστής**), **ὁ,** name given to Christians by Mohammedans καλοῦσι δὲ ἡμᾶς ἑ., ὅτι, φησί, ἑταῖρον τῷ θεῷ παρεισάγομεν λέγοντες εἶναι τὸν Χριστὸν υἱὸν θεοῦ καὶ θεόν Jo.D. *haer.*101(M.94.768B); ἀρνητὰς ὀνομάζει καὶ ἑτεριστάς ‡Barth.Edess. *Muham.*(M.104.1456B).

ἑταιρίζ-ω, *treat as fornication* μοιχεύει...τὸν ἑαυτοῦ γάμον ὁ ~όμενος αὐτόν Clem.*paed.*2.10(p.216.18; M.8.516A).

ἑταιρισμός, ὁ, 1. *harlotry, Const.App.*1.3.9; **2.** *meretricious ornament,* Epiph.*haer.*80.7(p.492.12; M.42.768A).

ἔτασις, ἡ, 1. *trial,* Hipp.*Dan.*1.15.6; ὁ...θεὸς...ὥρισεν ἡμέραν ἀναστάσεως καὶ ἐ. †Jo.D.*B.J.*8(M.96.925C); Thdr.Stud.*epp.*2.81(M.99.1321B); **2.** *examination* ἡ...τῆς πράξεως ἔ. *Schol.* in CSard.*can.*14 (*Mon.*2 p.649); Ephr.3.446C.

ἐτασμός, ὁ, 1. *affliction,* Hipp.*antichr.*49(p.33.8; M.10.769B); Thal.*cent.*2.67(M.91.1444C); **2.** *trial* κύριος δὲ μόνος καινὸν ἔχει τρόπον ἐτασμῶν, ἐτάζων γάρ ἐστι καρδίας Or.*hom.*20.9 *in Jer.*(p.193.32; M.13.525A); Thdt.*Ps.*104:15(1.1346); cf.id.*qu.62 in Gen.*(1.74); Anast.S. *serm.imag.*3(M.89.1157C).

ἐταστής, ὁ, 1. *examiner,* Anast.S.*hod.*6(M.89.105C); **2.** *executioner, A.(Pass.)Andr.*10(p.26.8).

***ἐταστικός,** *inquisitorial,* Olymp.*Job* 9:34(M.93.129C); id.*fr.Jer.* 17:17(M.93.665D).

***ἑτεραχθής,** *leaning to one side, favouring one side,* Cyr.*Mal.*4 (3.820C, v.l. ἑτεραλκές Aubert); *ib.*31(847E, v.l. ἑτεραλκῆ Aubert); id.*Juln.*7(6^2.222C).

***ἑτεριστής, ὁ,** v. *ἑταιριαστής.

***ἑτερόβιος,** *living in quite other conditions,* ‡Caes.Naz.*dial.*102 (M.38.968).

***ἑτεροβουλία, ἡ,** *change of counsel,* Cyr.*Abac.*12(3.527B).

***ἑτερόβουλος,** *different in will;* **1.** of H. Ghost ἡ κτίσις ἡ λογικὴ ἀρετῆς τε κακίας τέ ἐστι δεκτική...τὸ δὲ...πνεῦμα...οὐδενός ἐστι τούτων δεκτικὸν ὡς οὐδὲ ὁ πατήρ, οὐδ' ὁ υἱός. εἰ δὲ μὴ δεκτικόν, οὐδ' ἑ. εἰ δὲ τοῦτο...οὐδ' ἑτεροούσιον Didym.*Trin.*2.5(M.39.524A); *ib.*3.19 (892A); **2.** of will of Christ in rel. to his humanity and divinity τοιοῦτον γάρ, ὡς ἔφθην εἰπών, ἡ προαίρεσις· εἰ δὲ τῆς τοῦ Χριστοῦ χαρακτηριστικόν ἐστιν ὑποστάσεως, ἀφώρισαν αὐτὸν κατὰ δὴ τοῦτο τὸ θέλημα τοῦ τε πατρὸς καὶ τοῦ πνεύματος ἑ. τε καὶ ἑτερόγνωμον Max. *opusc.*(M.91.29B); in monothelite theory δειχθήσεται [sc. Χριστός] σαφῶς ἑ. πατρί τε καὶ πνεύματι...καὶ μαχόμενος *ib.*(M.91.53C); εἰ φυσικὸν οὐκ ἔστι τὸ θέλημα, ἢ ὑποστατικὸν ἔσται, ἢ παρὰ φύσιν· ἀλλ' εἰ μὲν ὑποστατικόν, ἑ. οὕτως γε ἔσται ὁ υἱὸς τῷ πατρί Jo.D.*f.o.*3.14(M.94.1040B); id.*volunt.*28(M.95.165B).

***ἑτερογλώσσως,** *in a foreign tongue,* Chrys.*hom.3.4 in 2Thess.* (11.528C).

***ἑτερογνήσιος,** *of a different kind,* Cyr.*defunct.*(p.544.4; M.76.1425B).

***ἑτερογνωμία, ἡ,** *another meaning* πρὸς ἑτερογνωμίαν τὸν λόγον μετήγαγεν Steph.Diac.*v.Steph.*(M.100.1084C).

ἑτερογνωμονέω, *be of different opinion,* Cyr.*ador.*8(1.255E); id. *Zach.*33(3.705B); id.*Juln.*4(6^2.144B).

ἑτερογνώμων, 1. *holding changeable opinions, of inconstant mind, 1Clem.*11.2; opp. μονότροπος, Cyr.*ador.*5(1.147B); διψύχου καὶ ἑ. id. *Ps.*11:1(M.69.796A); **2.** of opinions, *alterable, inconstant,* Synes.*regn.* 9(p.19.7; M.66.1068A); **3.** *different in thought;* of will of Christ in rel. to his humanity and divinity, cf. ἑτερόβουλος, Max.*opusc.*(M.91.29C); ἓν θέλημα...μηδὲν ἑ. Thdr.Stud.*epp.*2.134(M.99.1432D); **4.** *discordant* ἑ. στοιχεῖα Didym.*Trin.*3.16(M.39.865C).

***ἑτερογνώμως,** *with a different purpose,* ref. H. Ghost μὴ...ἑ. τοῦ πατρός Didym.*Trin.*2.2(M.39.461A).

***ἑτερόδεκτος,** *heterodox,* Didym.*Ac.*10:10(M.39.1676B).

***ἑτεροδέσποτος,** *belonging to another master,* Thdr.Stud.*epp.*1.14 (M.99.956D).

ἑτεροδιδασκαλέω, *teach false doctrine,* Ign.*Polyc.*3.1; Dion.Al.ap. Eus.*h.e.*7.7.4(M.20.649A); Cyr.*Jo.*proem.(4.5C); id.*Am.*57(3.314A).

***ἑτεροδιδασκαλία, ἡ,** *teaching of false doctrine;* sing., Or.*fr.in Ezech.*13:31(p.546); Thdr.Stud.*epp.*2.161(M.99.1504D); plur., Or. *Jo.*13.51(50; p.279.25; M.14.493A); Epiph.*haer.*80.9(p.494.5; M.42.769B); Cyr.*Ps.*39:5(M.69.985A).

***ἑτεροδιδάσκαλος,** *one who teaches false doctrine,* Eus.*h.e.*3.32.8 (M.20.284C); Cyr.*ador.*8(1.262C).

ἑτεροδοξ-έω, 1. *hold different opinions* τοὺς ~οῦντας ἡμῖν τῶν παρ' Ἕλλησι φιλοσόφων Eus.*p.e.*15.1(789B; M.21.1295D); **2.** *hold heterodox, false opinions* ἑ. εἰς τὴν χάριν Ign.*Smyrn.*6.2; ἑ. περὶ τὰς... γραφάς Or.*Jo.*13.2(p.227.9; M.14.401A); abs., *be heterodox,* Eus.*h.e.* 5.24.9(M.20.497A); †Bas.*Is.*310(1.613A; M.30.657C); Cyr.*Joel.*6(3.204C); Philost.*h.e.*5.1(p.66.19; M.65.528D).

ἑτεροδοξία, ἡ, *difference of opinion, heterodoxy* μὴ πλανᾶσθε ταῖς ἑ. Ign.*Magn.*8.1; παύσατε, μαντικὴ καὶ ἅπασα ἑ. Or.*Ps.*39:5 (p.35); τὴν ἐν πολυτρόποις δόγμασιν ἑ. Eus.*d.e.*2.1(p.307.24; M.22.504A); Epiph.*haer.*1(p.173.18; M.41.180C); esp. of heresies τὴν Ἀρειανὴν ἑ. Ath.*syn.*6(p.234.24; M.26.689B); id.*ep.Aeg.Lib.*6(M.25.552A); περὶ θεότητος καὶ οὐσίας Χριστοῦ...ἑ. Acac.Caes.*fr.Marcell.* ap.Epiph.*haer.*72.8(p.263.4; M.42.393B); ἀρχόμενος πίστιν τε καὶ ἀπιστίαν, εὐδοξίαν τε καὶ ἑ. ἀναγγέλλειν Epiph.*haer.*proem.1(p.169.3; M.41.173A).

ἑτερόδοξος, 1. *not in accordance with established doctrine, heterodox,* Clem.*ecl.*29(p.146.8; M.9.713B); Or.*Jo.*13.12(p.236.23; M.14.417A); ἑ. αἵρεσιν Ath.*v.Anton.*91(M.26.972A); fig. μεθέξειν τοῦ ἑ. ἄρτου Thdr.Stud.*epp.*2.136(M.99.1436A); **2.** very freq. as subst. ὁ ἑ. *heterodox* or *heretical person,* Clem.*str.*7.7(p.31.4; M.9.457A); Ath. *Ar.*2.33(M.26.217A); *Lit.*ap.*Const.App.*8.12.2; Cyr.*inc.unigen.*(5^1.680C); Jo.Clim.*scal.*25(M.88.996B).

ἑτεροειδής, 1. *of another kind,* Cyr.*ador.*8(1.262B); theol., of Logos οὐ γὰρ ἑ., ἵνα μὴ ξένον καὶ ἀνόμοιον τῇ οὐσίᾳ τοῦ πατρὸς ἐπιμιγνύηται Ath.*decr.*23(p.19.21; M.25.457A); λέγοντες [sc. Arians] ...μὴ ἴδιον...τῆς οὐσίας τοῦ πατρός, πολλοὺς ἂν εἰσάγοιεν διὰ τὸ ἑ. αὐτῶν id.*Ar.*3.15(M.26.353A); of Trin. σχίζοντες [sc. Arians] αὐτὴν καὶ ἐπιμίσγοντες αὐτῇ ἀλλοτρίαν καὶ ἑ. φύσιν id.*ep.Serap.*1.2(M.26.533A); Sophr.H.*ep.syn.*(M.87.3156D); **2.** *of diverse kinds* ὁ ἄνθρωπος ...ἐξ ἑτεροειδῶν συνέστηκεν Leont.B.*Nest.et Eut.*1(M.86.1280B).

***ἑτεροενεργής,** *having a different activity* εἰ...ὑποστατικὰ δῶμεν αὐτὰ [sc. τὰ θελήματα καὶ τὰς ἐνεργείας], ἑτεροθελεῖς καὶ ἑ. τὰς τρεῖς ὑποστάσεις τῆς ἁγίας τριάδος εἰπεῖν ἀναγκασθησόμεθα Jo.D.*f.o.* 3.14(M.94.1036A).

***ἑτεροεργής,** = foreg. (tr. Lat. *alienae...operationis*) εἰ δὲ σύνθετον, ξένον τοῦ πατρὸς τὸν υἱὸν ὑπογράφουσι, ἤγουν ἑ., καὶ ἑτεροούσιον Martin.ap.CLater.*act*.3(H.3.786D).

ἑτεροζυγ-έω, **1.** *be yoked in unequal partnership* οἱ...Δωνατιανοὶ... καὶ οἱ ~οῦντες αὐτοῖς Ναυατιανοί Epiph.*haer*.59.13(p.379.2; M.41.1037B); νόμος ὁ διὰ Μωυσέως...τῶν ~ούντων ἀνάγκης ζυγός ‡Chrys.*pasch*.6.9(p.135.17; 8.267A); hence **2.** *be at variance* ἑ. περὶ τὴν ἀλήθειαν Gr.Naz.*or*.6.11(M.35.736C); Max.*opusc*.(M.91.129A).

ἑτεροζυγία, ἡ, *bias, inclination to the other side* ἑ. τῆς διανοίας Anast.S.*qu.et resp*.30(M.89.565A).

[*]**ἑτεροήμερος**, = ἑτερήμερος, *on alternate days, day and day about*, Tat.*orat*.10(p.11.18; M.6.828C).

***ἑτεροθεΐα**, ἡ, *diversity of deities*, CTrull.*can*.1.

***ἑτεροθελής**, *having a different will*, Jo.D.*f.o*.3.14(M.94.1036A) cit. s. ἑτεροενεργής.

***ἑτεροθρησκεία**, ἡ, *different religion*, Const.Diac.*laud*.40(M.88.525B).

ἑτερόθροος, **1.** *speaking a different language*, Cyr.*Juln*.4(6².147E); **2.** v. ἐτυμόθροος.

ἑτεροίως, *otherwise, differently*, Dion.Al.ap.Eus.*p.e*.14.25(775D; M.21.1276C); Cyr.*ador*.12(1.415B); id.*Nah*.3(3.477D); almost = *wrongly* ἰδίως καὶ ἑ. ἰδίαν δόξαν παρεισηγάγοσαν Heges.ap.Eus.*h.e*.4.22.5(M.20.381A); ἵνα μὴ...τὰ τῆς ἀληθείας ἑ. ... ἀπαγγέλληται Eus.*ep.Caes*.1(p.42; M.20.1537A); *ib*.17(p.47.2; 1544C).

***ἑτεροκαινοδοξέω**, *hold new false opinions*, CIllyr.*ep*.ap.Thdt.*h.e*.4.9.4(v.l. ἑτεροκενοδοξεῖν 3.962).

ἑτεροκλινής, *leaning to one side*, Gr.Naz.*or*.20.5(M.35.1072A); met., *inclining to the other side*; of persons, *1Clem*.11.1; τοὺς ἑ. ὑπάρχοντας ἀφ' ἡμῶν *ib*.47.7; of a battle, Isid.Pel.*epp*.2.107(M.78.548D); of the eye, *squinting* ἑ. ἔχουσι τῆς διανοίας τὸ ὄμμα Thdt.*Ps*.16:11(1.699); neut. as subst. τὸ ἑ. ὡς ἀνόσιον ἀποσειομένους Cyr.*ador*.8(1.278C).

***ἑτεροκλινία**, ἡ, *a leaning over to one side*; of an unevenly weighted boat, *Clem.ep*.15(M.2.49C).

***ἑτεροκνεφής**, *half dark*, Synes.*insomn*.6(p.163.10; M.66.1297D).

***ἑτερολαμπής**, *shining in a different way*, Thdr.Stud.*epp*.1.8(M.99.936C).

***ἑτερόλεκτος**, *commanded by another*, neut. as subst. βάρος...τῷ ταπεινῷ τὸ ἑ. Jo.Clim.*scal*.25(M.88.100C); explained ἤγουν τὸ ὑπ' ἄλλου λεχθὲν αὐτῷ ἐπιτραπέν *Schol*. ad loc.(M.88.1009D).

***ἑτερολέκτως**, c. ἔχω, *be expressed differently*, Thdr.Stud.*or*.11.30(M.99.833B).

***ἑτερολεξία**, ἡ, *difference of expression* κατὰ ἑτερολεξίαν τὸ αὐτὸ νόημα ἔφησε Olymp.*Eccl*.12:6(M.93.620D); Thdr.Stud.*antirr*.2.27(M.99.372A).

***ἑτερομέρησις**, ἡ, *partiality*, Const.Pogon.*sacr*.1(M.*PL*.87.1151A).

***ἑτεροουσία**, ἡ, *difference of substance* αὐτοουσία ἐστὶν ὁ θεὸς πατὴρ καὶ ὁ υἱὸς καὶ ἅγιον πνεῦμα καὶ οὐχ ἑ. Epiph.*haer*.76.46(p.400.6; M.42.613C); Max.*ep*.12(M.91.496A).

***ἑτεροουσιαστής**, ὁ, one who believes that the Son is of a different substance from the Father Εὐσέβιος...τῇ τῶν ἑ. αἱρέσει πάνυ κατισχυμένος *V.Const*.34(p.564.13).

ἑτεροούσιος, sts. ἑτερούσιος, *of a different substance* or *essence*, opp. ὁμοούσιος;

A. in gen.; **1.** def. ἑ. ἐστι τὸ κατὰ πάντα τρόπον τοῦ ἑτέρου ἀνόμοιον, ὡς πῦρ καὶ ὕδωρ, καὶ ἄνθρωπος καὶ θεός Anast.S.*hod*.2(M.89.72B); cf. ‡Ath.*def*.6(M.28.545B); **2.** implications discussed εἰ ἑ. ἐστιν ἄνθρωπός τις παρ' ἕτερον, καὶ ἑτερογενεῖς εἶναι τὰς τῆς ψυχῆς δυνάμεις Or.*Jo*.8.44(20; p.358.7,17; M.14.625C,628A); τὸ μεῖζον οὐ πάντως καὶ ἑ. ...τὰ συγκριτικὰ ἐπὶ τῶν ὁμοουσίων καὶ οὐκ ἐπὶ τῶν ἑ. λέγεται Didym.(‡Bas.)*Eun*.4(1.289C; M.29.696A); ἑ. ... ἀλλήλοις συγκρίνεσθαι οὐ δύναται Isid.Pel.*epp*.1.422(M.78.417B); αἰσθητὰ καὶ νοητὰ ἐναντίωσιν ...ἔχουσιν ὡς ἑ. Max.*opusc*.(M.91.212C); τὰ δὲ κατὰ μίαν καὶ τὴν αὐτὴν ὑπόστασιν ἤγουν πρόσωπον ἡνωμένα, τουτέστιν τὰ μιᾶς καὶ τῆς αὐτῆς ὄντα συμπληρωτικὰ καθ' ἕνωσιν ὑποστάσεως, ὁμοϋπόστατα μὲν ἀλλήλοις εἰσὶ καὶ ἑ. ... ἑ. δέ, τῷ λόγῳ τῆς πρὸς ἄλληλα φυσικῆς ἑτερότητος id.*ep*.15(M.91.552C,D).

B. theol.; **1.** not of Persons of Trin. τοῦτο δὲ πάλιν οὐκέτι ἓν εἶναι δείκνυσι τὴν τριάδα, ἀλλὰ ἐκ δύο καὶ διαφόρων φύσεων συγκειμένην αὐτήν, διὰ τὸ ἑ. τοῦ πνεύματος, ὡς αὐτοὶ ἑαυτοῖς ἀνεπλάσαντο Ath.*ep.Serap*.1.2(M.26.533A); οὐχ ἑ. τῷ μονογενεῖ καὶ τῷ ἁγίῳ πνεύματι ἡ δόξα ἀναπέμπεται Didym.*Trin*.1.19(M.39.369A); τὴν Εὐνομιανῶν καὶ Ἀρειανῶν καὶ πνευματομάχων βλασφημίαν ἰσχύειν,...τῇ ἀκτίστῳ καὶ ὁμοουσίῳ καὶ συναϊδίῳ τριάδι μεταγενεστέρας τινὸς ἢ κτιστῆς ἢ ἑ. φύσεως ἐπαγομένης CCP(382)*ep*.ap.Thdt.*h.e*.5.9.11(3.1032); Sophr.H.*ep.syn*.(M.87.3156D); εἰ μερικὰς φύσεις ἐπὶ τῆς ἁγίας τριάδος ὁμολογεῖτε, ἑ. ταύτην δοξάζετε, καὶ πάλιν ἐγήγερται Ἄρειος Jo.D.*Jacob*.10(M.94.1440A); term repudiated at CCP(360), Thdt.*h.e*.2.27.17(3.897); at CAnt.(363) along with ὁμοούσιος, *ib*.2.31.1(3.907); **2.** esp. ref. Son; **a.** as not ἑ. from Father λέγοντες μὲν ἀνομοιούσιον καὶ ἑ. οὐ σημαίνομεν τὸν ἀληθινὸν υἱόν, ἀλλ' ἕν τι τῶν ποιημάτων καὶ τὸν εἰσποιητὸν καὶ θέσει υἱόν, ὅπερ τοῖς αἱρετικοῖς δοκεῖ Ath.*syn*.54(p.277.11; M.26.789B); οὐχ ἑ. ... τὸν υἱὸν...τοῦ πατρός, ἀλλ' ἐκ τῆς αὐτοῦ οὐσίας Petr.II Al.*encycl*.5(M.33.1284B)ap.Thdt.*h.e*.4.22.18; Gr.Nyss.*Apoll*.19(M.45.1161B); ‡Gr.Nyss.*hom.1.7 in Jo*.(p.95.31); Epiph.*haer*.65.8(p.11.9,10; M.42.25A) cit. s. ταυτοούσιος; Chrys.*hom.15.2 in Jo*.(8.87A); ἑ., ὡς οὐ σύνθετον ἔχοντος τοῦ πατρὸς τὴν οἰκείαν ἐνέργειαν Martin.ap.CLater.*act*.3(H.3.785D); **b.** ref. problem of Christ's suffering εἰ δὲ λέγεις ὅτι ὁ πατὴρ οὐκ ἔπαθεν, ἑ. πεποίηκας τὸν υἱόν objection ascribed to Nest. by Cyr.*dial.Nest*.(M.76.253D); οὕτω λέγοντες, συναινέσομεν αἱρετικοῖς λέγουσιν τὴν θεότητα τοῦ μονογενοῦς παθητήν, τὴν δὲ τοῦ πατρὸς μὴ ἐπιδέχεσθαι πάθος· ὅθεν καὶ τὸ ἑ. λέγουσιν Cyr.*apol.orient*.12(6¹.196A); **c.** of Christ as ὁμοούσιος with Father acc. Godhead and ἑ. in respect of Inc. εἰ κατὰ τὴν ἄσαρκον ὑπόστασιν ὁμοούσιος ὁ λόγος τῷ πατρί, δῆλον ὅτι κατὰ τὴν ἔνσαρκον ὑπόστασιν ἑ. ὁ λόγος τῷ πατρί...δῆλον ὡς καὶ μεμένηκεν ὁμοούσιος ἡ τοῦ λόγου ὑπόστασις πρὸς τὸν πατέρα, γεγένηται δὲ ὄντως καὶ ἑ. πρὸς τὸν αὐτὸν δι' ἑτέρας μέντοι ἐγγενομένης αὐτῇ φύσεως Leont.H.*Nest*.1.34(M.86.1497C); **d.** of Christ as ἑ. from man acc. his Godhead ὁ θεὸς ἀνθρώποις ὁμοούσιος ὢν κατὰ τὴν σάρκα, ἑ. ἐστιν καθὸ λόγος καὶ θεός Apoll.*fr*.126(p.238.10f.)ap.Leont.B.*Apoll*.(M.86.1968C); **e.** but not acc. manhood εἴ τις ἑ. λέγει τῆς ἡμετέρας σαρκὸς τὴν σάρκα τοῦ Χριστοῦ...καθαιρείσθω ‡Quint.*ep*.(p.17.15; M.85.1740B); opp. Eutyches' view τοῦ Χριστοῦ ...τὸ σῶμα καὶ ἑ. ἡμῶν...ὑπάρχον Anast.S.*hod*.7(M.89.113A); hence of BMV as implied by Eutychian doctrine, Oecum.*Apoc*.12:1(p.136); **f.** of Christ's two natures as ἑ. from each other πῶς γὰρ ἐξ ἑ. καὶ διαφόρων, μίαν τὴν φύσιν ἡμῶν ἐδημιούργησε; ‡Caes.Naz.*dial*.140(M.38.1053); ἐκεῖνοι...[sc. Arians and Eunomians] τὸ ἑ. κατασκευάσαι μὴ δυνάμενοι, τὰ παθήματα καὶ τὰς εὐτελεῖς φωνὰς τῇ θεότητι τοῦ Χριστοῦ περιάπτουσιν Jo.Ant.*ep.Ruf*.(p.41.23; M.83.1480B); ἀδύνατον...ἐκ δύο φύσεων ἑτερογενῶν καὶ ἑ. ἓν θέλημα καὶ μίαν ἐνέργειαν εἶναι Gel.Caes.*fr*.13(p.48.6); τῶν δύο φύσεων τῶν ἑ. ἐν ἑνὶ Χριστῷ υἱῷ ὄντι τοῦ θεοῦ σωζομένων Cyr.*hom.div*.21.3(p.540.22; M.77.1113B); εἰ δὲ ἑ. ἡ σὰρξ τοῦ θεοῦ λόγου, πῶς οὐ δύο φύσεων ὁ Χριστός; Eulog.*duab.nat*.3(M.86.2940A); ὁ δὲ τοιοῦτος ὅρος διὰ μὲν τοῦ λέγειν 'δύο φύσεις' σημαίνει τὸ ἑτερογενὲς καὶ ἑ. τῶν συνελθουσῶν δύο φύσεων Thdr.Raith.*praep*.(p.191.15; M.91.1492B); μόνου τε καὶ μόνως ἀπαθῶς τε καὶ ἀληθῶς προσλαβόντος τὸ ἑ., καὶ ἄτρεπτον ἑαυτὸν... φυλάξαντος καὶ ἀπλήθυντον Max.*ep*.13(M.91.532A); **g.** of Christ ἑ. from both God and man acc. iconoclasts' principles, Thdr.Stud.*probl*.1(M.99.477B); **3.** of God, exeg. Dt.32:12 'οὐκ ἦν μετ' αὐτῶν θεὸς ἀλλότριος', τοῦτ' ἔστιν ἑ. Didym.*Trin*.1.19(M.39.368B); **4.** of pagan deities Ἑλλήνων...τὸ πλῆθος δαιμονίων μέγα, καὶ μικρόν, καὶ χρονικόν, καὶ ἑ. *ib*.1.34(M.39.457B).

***ἑτεροουσιότης**, ἡ, *difference of substance* or *essence* μὴ Ἀρειανικὴ ἑ. παράσφαλον ποιήσῃς Chrys.ap.Anast.S.*qu.et resp*.8(M.89.401B); Cyr.*thes*.11(5¹.91D); μερίζειν ἣν αὐτοὶ λέγουσιν μίαν Χριστοῦ φύσιν εἰς τε ὁμοουσιότητα καὶ εἰς ἑ. Leont.B.*cap.Sev*.19(M.86.1908C); id.*arg.Sev*.(M.86.1917D); cf.Jo.D.*Jacob*.80(M.94.1477B).

ἑτεροουσίως, *with a difference of substance*, Didym.*Trin*.2.6(M.39.508A); *ib*.3.2(789D).

***ἑτεροπάρακτος**, *owing one's origin to another*, ‡Just.*qu.Chr*.3.1(M.6.1432B) cit. s. αὐτοπάρακτος; *ib*.3.5(1441D).

***ἑτερόπιστος**, *of a different faith*, Chrys.*hom.24.4 in Eph*.(11.185E); Jo.D.*rect.sent*.8(M.94.1432C).

***ἑτεροπροσκύνητος**, *to be worshipped differently* εἰ ἑ. ἐστιν ἡ εἰκὼν πρὸς τὸ οἰκεῖον πρωτότυπον· πῶς τοῦτο ἐν αὐτῇ ὁρᾶται, καὶ αὐτὴ ἐν τῷ πρωτοτύπῳ;...οὐκ ἄρα ἑ. ἡ εἰκὼν τοῦ Χριστοῦ πρὸς αὐτόν· ἀλλ' ὁμοπροσκύνητος, ὡς ἐμφερής τε καὶ αὐτόμοιος Thdr.Stud.*antirr*.3.3.8(M.99.424B).

ἑτερορρεπής, *inclining to one side or the other*, Ast.Am.*hom*.14(M.40.380B); ‡Proc.G.*Pr*.11:1(M.87.1324A).

***ἑτερόσημος**, *with a different meaning*, Leont.H.*Nest*.1.6(M.86.1420C).

***ἑτεροσκευωρία**, ἡ, ? *wicked intrigue*, CChalc.*ep*.(*ACO* 2.1.3 p.111.30; H.2.645E).

ἑτερόστοιχος, *belonging to another series* ὁμόστοιχον τῷ περιγραπτῷ τὸ ἀπερίγραπτον, ἢ ἑ. ... εἰ δὲ ἑ., πάντως καὶ ὁ λόγος ἑτεροούσιος ὢν παρὰ τὴν σάρκα...καθ' ἑκατέραν οὐσίαν τῆς αὐτοῦ θεότητος καὶ ἀνθρωπότητος...περιγραφόμενος καὶ μὴ περιγραφόμενος Thdr.Stud.*probl*.3(M.99.480A).

ἑτερόσχημος, *of various shapes* σχῆμα πρῶτον τὸ τρίγωνον, εἶθ' οὕτως τὰ λοιπὰ ἑ. Thdr.Stud.*ref*.13(M.99.460B).

***ἑτερότεχνος**, *of a different craft*, Chrys.*hom.16.1 in Eph.*(11.117C).

ἑτερότης, ἡ, **1.** *difference, distinction*; of natures in Christ, Eust.Mon.*ep.*(M.86.936C); κἂν τῇ ταυτότητι τῆς μιᾶς ὑποστάσεως μεμένηκεν, ἡ φυσικὴ τῶν ἡνωμένων ἑ. ἀσύγχυτος Max.*ambig.*(M.91.1040C); **2.** *diversity* τὴν ἑ. τῶν ποικίλων τοῦ θεοῦ κατὰ τὰς πολυειδεῖς ὁράσεις σχημάτων Dion.Ar.*d.n.*9.5(M.3.912D); *ib.*(913A,B).

***ἑτεροτροπέω**, *have different habits*, Cyr.*ador.*8(1.262D); id.*Jo.*10.2(4.897C).

ἑτερότροπος, *of a different character*, Cyr.*Am.*31(3.280E); id.*Is.*4.3(2.642B); Proc.G.*Gen.*9:3(M.87.297D).

***ἑτεροτρόπως**, *in a different way*, Cyr.*Os.*22(3.45B); id.*Am.*24(3.274D); c. ἔχω *be of a different character*, id.*ep.*41(p.40.6; 5^{2}.121B); Thdr.Stud.*epp.*2.36(M.99.1216C).

***ἑτερότροφος**, *differently reared*, Synes.*regn.*19(p.44.4; M.66.1089C).

***ἑτεροϋπόστατος**, *different in person, personally differentiated, objectively distinct*; **1.** in gen. εἴ τι ἑτεροούσιον, τοῦτο πάντως καὶ ἑ. Leont.H.*Nest.*2.13(M.86.1560D); εἰ δὲ ταὐτὸν μὲν οὐσία καὶ φύσις· ταὐτὸν δὲ πρόσωπον καὶ ὑπόστασις, δῆλον ὡς τὰ ἀλλήλοις ὁμοφυῆ καὶ ὁμοούσια, πάντως ἀλλήλοις ἑ. Max.*opusc.*(M.91.549B); τὸ ἐνυπόστατον ...τὴν ἁπλῶς ὕπαρξιν σημαίνει...οὐ μόνον τὴν ἁπλῶς οὐσίαν ἐνυπόστατον λέγομεν, ἀλλὰ καὶ τὸ συμβεβηκός· ὅπερ κυρίως οὐκ ἐνυπόστατόν ἐστι, ἀλλ' ἑ. Jo.D.*dialect.*44(M.94.616A); **2.** Trin. ὥσπερ διὰ τὸ ὁμοούσιον τῆς ἁγίας τριάδος, μίαν οὐσίαν καὶ διὰ τὸ ἑ. τρεῖς ὑποστάσεις λέγεις Max.*opusc.*(M.91.148C); ἑ. ... ὁ υἱὸς πρὸς τὸν πατέρα Jo.D.*haer.Nest.*21(M.95.200A); εἷς...θεὸς ἡ τριάς, διὰ τὸ ὁμοούσιον, εἰ καὶ διῄρηται διὰ τὸ ἑ. Thdr.Stud.*test.*2(M.99.1813C).

***ἑτεροφαής**, *half in light*, Synes.*insomn.*10(p.163.9; M.66.1297D).

ἑτεροφανής, v. ἑτεροφυής.

***ἑτερόφθογγος**, *with a different cry*, Synes.*hymn.*3.340(p.17; M.66.1598).

***ἑτερόφιλος**, v. ἑτερόφυλος.

***ἑτεροφρούρητος**, *guarded by another*, ‡Just.*qu.Chr.*5(M.6.1456B).

ἑτερόφρων, **1.** *differently-minded, thinking differently*, Gr.Naz.*carm.*1.2.14.131(M.37.765A); Cyr.*ador.*6(1.175E); Nonn.*par.Jo.*6:67(M.43.804B); hence **2.** *heterodox*, Didym.*Trin.*3.3(M.39.808A); τοὺς ἑ. καὶ δοκησισόφους καὶ τὰ ὀρθὰ τῆς ἐκκλησίας δόγματα διαστρέφοντας Cyr.*Mich.*69(3.466B); Thdt.*rect.conf.*1(M.6.1208A); Δωροθέου τοῦ ὀρθοδόξου...καὶ οὐ τοῦ ἑ. *Proem.*in Dor.*doct.*(M.88.1612A); *Nomoc.*336.

ἑτεροφυής, *of a different nature*; **1.** in gen. ἄνθρωπος κυνὶ οὐκ ἀνόμοιος λέγεται ἀλλ' ἑ. Ath.*syn.*53(p.276.28; M.26.788C); Gr.Nyss.*anim.et res.*(M.46.620C); Jo.D.*dialect.*41(M.94.608B,609A); **2.** of God and creation ὁ διὰ τοῦ δύνασθαι κτίζειν ἑ. ὡς πρὸς τὴν κτίσιν ἀναδεικνύμενος Cyr.*thes.*32(5^{1}.301B); id.*Jo.*1.7(4.63C); id.*Is.*4.5(2.706E); **3.** Christol., Justn.*conf.*(p.80.20; M.86.1003B); Max.*ep.*13(M.91.532A); monoph. view εἰ δὲ μία φύσις...ἡ τραπεῖσα ἑκατέρα φύσις ἑ. ἐστιν Justn.*conf.*(p.82.6; 1005A); μόνον ὁμωνυμίᾳ ἡνώθησαν τὰ δύο, ἑ. δὲ καὶ ἀσύνθετα ἀλλήλοις ἔτι ἐστὶν Leont.H.*monoph.*61(M.86.1804A); Apollinarian ἀλόγου φύσεώς τινος ἑ. ἡμῖν παριστάνων εἶναι τὴν ἐκ τῆς οἰκονομίας εὐεργεσίαν *ib.*testimonia (M.86.1809C); ‡Hipp.*Ber.Hel.*8 ap.*Doct.Patr.*44(p.325.20; ἑτεροφανοῦς M.10.837D); εἰ ἑ. τι παρὰ τὰς συνελθούσας φύσεις ἀπετελέσθη καθὼς Ἀπολινάριος βλασφημεῖ Pamph.H.*panopl.*6.1(p.615); **4.** Trin. τίς οὕτω τολμηρός, ὡς εἰπεῖν ἀνόμοιον καὶ ἑ. τὴν τριάδα πρὸς ἑαυτήν; Ath.*ep.Serap.*1.20(M.26.577A); Didym.*Trin.*1.26(M.39.388A); ἀνοηταίνουσι...οἱ λέγοντες τὸν υἱὸν ἑ. καὶ ἀλλότριον τῆς τοῦ θεοῦ καὶ πατρὸς οὐσίας Cyr.*Heb.*1:8(p.461.21; M.74.960A); Jo.D.*Jacob.*81(M.94.1477C).

***ἑτεροφυΐα**, ἡ, *difference of nature* τὴν τοῦ ἀκτίστου...πρὸς τὸ κτιστὸν ἑ. Leont.H.*Nest.*1.26(M.86.1493A).

ἑτερόφυλος, *of a different kind* or *sort*, in gen. μὴ ἐνταῦθα ὁμόπιστοι καὶ ἔξω ἑ. ‡Chrys.*hom.*9(13.237D; ἑτερόφιλοι Gr.Ant.*bapt.*2.10(M.88.1884A)); of Christ ἑ. ... καὶ ἑτεροούσιον ἐδόξασαν τοῦ... πατρός ‡Gr.Nyss.*hom.1.7 in Jo.*(p.95.31); Trin. οὔτε τρεῖς...θεότητας ...οὐχ ὁμοφύλους οὐχ ἑ. Sophr.H.*ep.syn.*(M.87.3156D).

***ἑτεροφυῶς**, *with a different nature* τοῦ μὴ νοεῖσθαι ἑ. ἢ ἑτερογνώμως τοῦ πατρὸς οἰκεῖν [sc. τὸ ἅγιον πνεῦμα] ἐν ἡμῖν Didym.*Trin.*2.2(M.39.461A); c. ἔχω, *have* or *be of a different nature*, Gr.Nyss.*v.Mos.*(M.44.404C); id.*anim.et res.*(M.46.21A).

ἑτεροφωνία, ἡ, *difference of tongue* or *language*, Chrys.*hom.30.4 in Gen.*(4.300A).

ἑτεροχροέω, *be of different colour*; pres. ptcpl., Bas.*ascet.*1.2(2.320B; M.31.873B); Gr.Nyss.*anim.et res.*(M.46.73D).

ἑτερωνυμία, ἡ, *difference of name*, Epiph.*haer.*32.6(p.446.13; M.41.553A); Thdr.Stud.*epp.*1.40(M.99.1053C).

ἑτερώνυμος, *having different names, heteronymous*, of a pair of correlatives ἑ. δὲ ὅσα περὶ τὸ αὐτὸ ὑποκείμενον ἐν διαφόροις ἐστὶν ὀνόμασιν, οἷον ἀνάβασις καὶ κατάβασις...τὸ δ' ἄλλο εἶδος τῶν ἑ., οἷον ἵππος καὶ μέλας, καὶ ὄνομα καὶ λόγον ἕτερον ἀλλήλων ἔχοντα μηδὲ τοῦ ὑποκειμένου κοινωνοῦντα, ἕτερα δὴ λεκτέον, οὐχ ἑ. Clem.*str.*8.8(p.95.9f.; M.9.592A); Leont.H.*Nest.*1.6(M.86.1420C); Thdr.Stud.*probl.*10(M.99.481D).

***ἑτερωνύμως**, *by the other name, heteronymously*; ref. two correlative terms, Epiph.*haer.*32.2(p.440.22; M.41.545B); *ib.*69.54(p.201.9; M.42.285D).

ἑτέρως, *in another place, in the other verse*; used in exeg. passages, Cyr.*Ps.*7:9(M.69.752A); Thdt.*2Cor.*3:10(3.304).

ἐτήσιος, neut. as subst., *anniversary*, Gr.Naz.*or.*40.1(M.36.360B).

ἐτησίως, *annually*, *Clem.epit.*A 173(M.2.597C); *V.Chrys.*(p.352.18).

ἑτοιμασία, ἡ, **1.** *readiness* εἰς ἑ. ... τοῦ κατὰ τὸ εὐαγγέλιον δρόμου Eus.*d.e.*9.13(p.432.22; M.22.697B); ἑ. καρδίας...ἡ οἷον ὑπόσχεσις τῶν τῆς ψυχῆς κινημάτων πρὸς συνακολούθησιν θεοῦ Ath.*exp.Ps.*10:17(M.27.92C); Bas.*reg.fus.*23(2.368E; M.31.981B); ἑ. τῆς καρδίας, ἡ ἀπομάθησις τῶν ἐκ πονηρᾶς συνηθείας προκατασχόντων αὐτὴν διδαγμάτων id.*ep.*2.2(3.72A; M.32.225B); θείας τραπέζης ἑ. (ref. Ps.22:5) Gr.Nyss.*hom.12 in Cant.*(M.44.1032B); of preparedness for receiving Communion, Bas.*reg.br.*172(2.473B; M.31.1196C); exeg. Eph.6:15 ὑποδυσάμενοι τοὺς πόδας ἐν ἑ. τοῦ εὐαγγελίου...μὴ εἰς ἀτόπους πράξεις τοὺς πόδας κινεῖτε, ἀλλὰ τοῦ εὐαγγελίου δρόμον πληροῦτε Thdt.*Eph.*6:15(3.440); of God οὐδὲ ἡ ἑ. ... αὐτοῦ βουλῆς ἐπιδέεται Epiph.*haer.*69.70(p.218.20; M.42.316A); **2.** *preparation* εἰς...τὴν...τῶν μελλόντων ἄσκησίν τε καὶ ἑ. *M.Polyc.*18.3; Or.*Jo.*10.38(22; p.213.30; M.14.377C); of God τοὺς κατηρτισμένους εἰς πᾶν ἔργον ἀγαθὸν ἐκ τῆς ἑ. τοῦ ἐφ' ἡμῖν Bas.*Spir.*18(3.15E; M.32.100B); †Gregent.*disp.*2(M.86.652A); of Jo. Bapt. διαδεχόμενος αὐτοῦ τὴν ἑ. ... ὁ κύριος Bas.*hom. in Ps.*28(1.360B; M.30.77C); ἡ ἑ. τῆς ὁδοῦ τοῦ κυρίου Epiph.*haer.*62.5(p.394.2; M.41.1056D); **3.** concretely, of something prepared, *equipment*, Eus.*h.e.*8.15.2(M.20.788B); Thphn.*chron.*p.287(M.108.704B); exeg. Eph.6:15 ἡ...ἑ. τοῦ εὐαγγελίου...βίος ἄριστος Chrys.*hom.24.1 in Eph.*(11.179F).

***ἑτοιμαστής**, ὁ, *one who prepares, makes ready* τοῦ κυρίου... ἑτοιμασταί Clem.*str.*6.18(p.517.31; M.9.400A); of Christ, ref. Jo.14:3, Or.*fr.105 in Jo.*(p.560.25); ἑ. ... ὁ θεὸς ἀγαθῶν Chrys.*hom.23.3 in Heb.*(12.215A).

***ἑτοιμαστικός**, *preparatory*, Epiph.*haer.*69.41(p.189.5,13; M.42.265B,C).

***ἑτοιμόγενος**, *about to calve*, Ephr.3.xxiiiB,xxviE.

ἑτοιμοθάνατος, *ready for death*, i.e. *desperate*, *Const.App.*2.14.10; Thphn.*chron.*p.155(M.108.421A).

***ἑτοιμολογία**, ἡ, *readiness of speech*, Epiph.*haer.*71.1(p.250.5; M.42.376A).

ἑτοιμολόγος, *glib*, Gr.Naz.*carm.*1.2.14.24(M.37.757A).

***ἑτοιμοπαθής**, *ready for passion*, ‡Proc.G.*Pr.*25:20(M.87.1477A).

ἕτοιμος, *ready*, c. genit. ἑ. τοῦ διακονεῖν αὐτοῦ Herm.*sim.*8.4.2; c. dat. ἑ. τοῖς ἐχθροῖς Chrys.*exp.in Ps.*7:5(5.57B); c. πρός: ἑ. ... ὑμῖν πρὸς ἀνάκρισιν Tat.*orat.*42(p.43.13; M.6.888B); Clem.*str.*1.1(p.11.18; M.8.704C); Chrys.*hom.5.4 in Phil.*(11.224F); c. εἰς, Clem.*str.*2.15(p.149.2; 1005A); Ath.*h.Ar.*75(p.225.4; M.25.784C).

***ἑτοιμόσβεστος**, *readily extinguished*, ‡Chrys.*pat.*1(9.808A).

ἑτοιμότης, ἡ, **1.** *readiness* τῶν λόγων ἢ ἑ. Philost.*h.e.*11.3(M.65.596C); **2.** *abundance*, Isid.Pel.*epp.*5.186(M.78.1440D); Vict.*Mc.*8:6(p.341.14).

***ἑτοιμοτρεπής**, *readily turning*, Cyr.*Zach.*99(Aubert; ἑτοιμοτέρα πως 3.790C).

***ἑτοιμότρωτος**, *vulnerable*, Geo.Pis.*hex.*463(M.92.1471A).

***ἑτοιμόφθορος**, *easily destroyed*, ‡Chrys.*hom.in Ps.38*:7(5.567B); ‡Chrys.*pat.*1(9.808A).

***ἐτυμόθροος**, *speaking truth*, Nonn.*par.Jo.*1:19(M.43.752C); *ib.*8:17(ἑτερόθροος 816A).

ἐτυμολογ-έω, **1.** *investigate a word and find its origin, etymologize*; pass., Clem.*paed.*1.10(p.146.5; M.8.361B); Gr.Naz.*or.*30.18(p.136.7; M.36.128A); Melet.*nat.hom.*17(M.64.1216C); **2.** *mean by etymology* τὸ δὲ καταπέτασμα ἐξ ὑπερεχόντων δεσμῶν κατεώρηται, τὴν ἄνωθεν κατάπτησιν τῆς ὀθόνης ~οῦντος τοῦ ὀνόματος Nil.*serm.*8(M.79.1276D).

***ἐτυμολογητέον**, *one must analyse*, Clem.*str.*4.22(p.311.20; M.8.1353A).

ἐτυμόλογος, *studying etymology*; as subst., *etymologist*, †Gregent.*disp.*(M.86.697A).

εὐαγγελίζ-ομαι, **1.** intrans.; **a.** *utter good news* 'ὁ κύριος μετὰ σοῦ' ἰστέον ὅτι ἅμα τῷ εὐ. εὐθὺς συνέλαβεν ἡ παρθένος παραδόξως Or.*hom.6 in Lc.*(p.40.5); ~όμενος λέγει 'γυναῖκες χαίρετε' ‡Chrys.*pasch.*6.7 (p.133.18; 8.266E); **b.** *bring good news, preach the gospel, evangelize,* abs. τοῦ Πέτρου καὶ τοῦ Παύλου ἐν Ῥώμῃ ~ομένων Iren.*haer.*3.1.1 (M.7.845A); Πέτρος...εὐηγγελίζετο Ath.*ep.Drac.*8(M.25.532C); Cyr. H.*catech.*3.13; c. περί: περὶ...τοῦ Χριστοῦ εὐ. Ath.*decr.*13(p.11.38; M.25.440A); c. acc. and infin., *1Clem.*42.3 cit. s. ἀπόστολος; of Christ's preaching εὐ. ἐν σώματι Clem.*str.*4.8(p.278.21; M.8.1277C); ὁ κύριος δι' οὐδὲν ἕτερον εἰς ᾅδου κατῆλθεν εἰ μὴ διὰ τὸ εὐ. *ib.*6.6(p.455.1; M.9. 268C); τὸν εὐ. καὶ διδάξαντα περὶ τοῦ πατρός *ib.*7.10(p.42.27; M.9. 481C); **c.** *write a gospel* τὴν περὶ τοῦ Χριστοῦ γενεαλογίαν διαφόρως ἡμῖν ὅ τε Ματθαῖος καὶ ὁ Λουκᾶς ~όμενοι παραδεδώκασιν Eus.*h.e.* 1.7.1(M.20.89B); ὁ...Ἰωάννης...τελευταῖος...τοῖς χρόνοις εὐ. Epiph. *haer.*51.19(p.276.7; M.41.924B); Vict.*Mc.*2:14(p.288.7); **d.** *read the Gospel* of the day ὁ δὲ διάκονος ὁ ~όμενος τύπος ἦν τοῦ ~ομένου ἀγγέλου Jo.Jej.*liturg.*(p.441); Sophr.H.*mir.Cyr.et Jo.*37(M.87. 3565A); cf. εἰρήνη σοι τῷ ~ομένῳ *Lit.Chrys.*(p.372.39); at morning service, Thdr.Stud.*epp.*2.203(M.99.1617C); **2.** trans.; **a.** *bring good news to, preach the gospel to, evangelize*; **i.** in gen. οἱ εὐαγγελισάμενοι καὶ οἱ προφῆται Polyc.*ep.*6.3; Clem.*str.*6.6(p.455.1; M.9.268C); Meth. *symp.*10.2(p.124.2; M.18.196B); **ii.** ref. Annunciation ὁ...ἄγγελος θεοῦ εὐ. αὐτήν Just.*1apol.*33.5(M.6.381B); Hipp.*haer.*8.10(p.230.13; M.16.3355A); Eus.*Marcell.*2.1(p.32.16; M.24.777B); Gr.Nyss.*Eun.*6 (2 p.145.4; M.45.729D); **b.** *preach as good news, preach as gospel*; **i.** in gen. οἱ εὐ. ἡμῖν τὴν ἄφεσιν τῶν ἁμαρτιῶν καὶ τὸν ἁγνισμὸν τῆς καρδίας *Barn.*8.3; Just.*dial.*29.2(M.6.537A); Ἰησοῦς...τὰ τοῖς ἁγίοις ἀποκείμενα εὐ. τοῖς πτωχοῖς Or.*Jo.*1.8(10; p.13.23; M.14.37D); ζητητέον εἴ που Χριστὸς ἑαυτὸν εὐ. *ib.*13.28(p.251.32; 445D); εὐ. πᾶσι πατέρα Ath.*decr.*1(p.2.8; M.25.417C); εὐ. τὸν λόγον τῆς ἀληθείας id. *fug.*21(p.82.18; M.25.672A); εὐ. πᾶσι τὴν ἀνάστασιν ‡Ath.*Apoll.*1.7 (M.26.1105A); **ii.** of preaching Christ, Just.*dial.*136.3(M.6.789D); Clem.*exc.Thdot.*18(p.112.19; M.9.665C); Or.*Jo.*1.10(11; p.15.25; M. 14.41C); Ath.*decr.*4(p.4.10; M.25.421D); **iii.** followed by text Ἰωάννης...εὐηγγελίζετο 'ἐν ἀρχῇ ἦν ὁ λόγος' *ib.*17(p.14.28; M.25. 445A); **c.** *announce as good news* Γαβριὴλ εὐ. τῷ μὲν Ζαχαρίᾳ τὴν Ἰωάννου γένεσιν, τῇ δὲ Μαριὰμ τὴν τοῦ σωτῆρος ἡμῶν ἐν ἀνθρώποις ἐπιδημίαν Or.*Jo.*2.30(24; p.87.3; M.14.165C); Eus.*e.th.*2.14(p.117. 21; M.24.932C); τοῦ παιδίου τὴν γέννησιν εὐ. Gr.Nyss.*Eun.*5(2 p.104.7; M.45.684A); ταῖς δὲ γυναιξὶ χαρὰν εὐ. Chrys.*hom.86.3 in Jo.*(8.588C); Cyr.ap.*cat.Lc.*3:23(p.32.25); Isid.Pel.*epp.*1.428(M.78.420B); simply *proclaim* βλέμμα μορφοῦσιν ~όμεναι τὸ πάθος ‡Nil.*vit.cog.*4(M.79. 1149A); τὸν υἱὸν εὐ. ζῶντα ‡Nil.*narr.*6(M.79.676A); **d.** c. dupl. acc., *announce* as news *to* ἅπερ ὁ Γαβριὴλ τὴν παρθένον εὐ. Eus.*Marcell.* 2.1(p.33.6; M.24.780A); id.*h.e.*3.4.2(M.20.220A); of bad news εὐ. Σευῆρον καὶ Θεοδόσιον ἀρὰν μεγάλην Anast.S.*hod.*9(M.89.144A); **3.** pass.; **a.** *be given good news* κατὰ ποῖον καιρὸν εὐηγγελίσθη Ζαχαρίας Chrys.*nativ.*4(2.360B); ἡ δὲ Μαρία πανταχόθεν εὐηγγελίζετο Antip.Bost.*annunt.*15(M.85.1785B); εὐηγγελίσθη ἡ παρθένος Μαρία ὑπὸ...Γαβριὴλ *Dorm.BMV* 37(p.107); **b.** hence partic., *be evangelized, 1Clem.*42.1 cit. s. ἀπόστολος; εὐηγγελίσθησαν οἱ ἐν θλίψει ὄντες Clem.*str.*6.6(p.457.30; M.9.273B); ‡Eust.*Laz.*2(p.27.10); **c.** *be given good news about,* Clem.*paed.*1.6(p.116.31; M.8.304A); id.*str.*3. 3(p.201.10; M.8.1116A); τῆς Σάρρας γένεσιν παιδὸς εὐαγγελισθείσης *ib.*6.12(p.482.16; M.9.321B); **d.** *be announced, be preached* τὸν διὰ νόμου καὶ προφητῶν κηρύξαντα, καὶ τὸν δι' αὐτοῦ εὐαγγελισθέντα πατέρα *ib.*3.11(p.230.5; M.8.1176B); ἡ εὐαγγελισθεῖσα ἡμῖν διὰ τῆς γενέσεως Χριστοῦ Ἰησοῦ χαρὰ Or.*Jo.*1.12(13; p.18.3; M.14.45C); Ath. *Ar.*2.39(M.26.229B); id.*ep.fest.*39.10(M.26.1437C); ‡Ath.*Apoll.*2.15 (M.26.1157A).

***εὐαγγελικός**, **1.** *of the gospels* τῆς παρ' αὐτοῖς [sc. Christians] καλουμένης εὐ. ἁγίας γραφῆς Arist.*apol.*15(p.110.22); τῷ κατὰ τὴν ἀλήθειαν εὐ. ... κανόνι Clem.*str.*3.9(p.226.13; M.8.1168C); ἀπὸ τῶν εὐ. γραμμάτων Or.*Cels.*1.70(p.124.6; M.11.789B); ἐπὶ τῶν ἀποστολικῶν καὶ εὐ. ἀναγνωσμάτων id.*or.*29.10(p.386.3; M.11.536D); τῆς εὐ. καὶ ἀποστολικῆς πίστεώς τε καὶ ἀγάπης Bas.*fid.*5(2.229A; M.31.684B); τὴν εὐ. παράδοσιν Gr.Nyss.*Eun.*7(2 p.155.19; M.45.744B); τῆς εὐ. ἱστορίας *ib.*12(1 p.249.23; 949C); **2.** in wider sense, *of the gospel of Christ* τὰ τοῦ Ἀριστοτέλους δόγματα εἰς τὸν εὐ. καὶ σωτήριον ἡμῶν λόγον μεθαρμοζόμενος Hipp.*haer.*7.19(p.195.16; M.16.3302B); οὐκ ἔστι δυνατὸν κατὰ τοὺς εὐ. νόμους αὖθις βαπτίσασθαι Or.*mart.*30(p.26.22; M.11. 600C); Meth.*symp.*8 proem.(p.80.20; M.18.137B); οὐ γὰρ οἷοί τε ἦσαν οἱ συνεχῶς ἀπαγόμενοι τῇ πολυθέῳ πλάνῃ τὴν εὐ. παραδέχεσθαι χάριν Eus.*e.th.*2.20(p.127.24; M.24.949D); τὴν εὐ. νομοθεσίαν πρὸ τῆς νομοθεσίας πεπλήρωκε Thdt.*qu.19 in 4Reg.*(1.523); of Christian, opp. John's, baptism, ‡Chrys.*ascens.Ac.*13(3.770A); **3.** *according to the gospel*; **a.** πολιτεία: ἡμεῖς ἐσμὲν τὸ ἔθνος, οἷς ἐδόθη ἡ βασιλεία τοῦ θεοῦ, ἡ εὐ. πολιτεία Or.*fr.5 in Lc.*(p.257); described, Bas.*hom.*13.7(2. 120C; M.31.440A); Chrys.*hom.4.3 in 1Cor.*(10.28B); Cyr.*inc.unigen.* (5^1.690D); Thdt.*Pss.proem.*(1.603); partic. of monastic life, Cyr. *Am.*21(3.271D); Thdt.*h.rel.*10(3.1195); **b.** ζωή: †Bas.*Is.*38(1.409D; M.30.192C); τῆς οὕτως εὐαγοῦς καὶ καθαρωτάτης ζωῆς, φημὶ δὴ τῆς εὐ. Cyr.*Juln.*9(6^2.307E); **c.** βίος: ἐν γὰρ πρώτῳ Χριστῷ ὁ εὐ. ἀνέλαμψε βίος id.*thes.*15(5^1.157B); Bas.Sel.*or.*17.1(M.85.217A); **4.** *befitting the gospel*; of OT conduct, Proc.G.*Dt.*21:16(M.87.925A); **5.** *of good news, bearing good news* διακονίαν εὐ. Or.*Jo.*1.14(p.18.28; M.14. 48B); τῆς εὐ. διδασκαλίας τοῦ Χριστοῦ Eus.*p.e.*10.9(483B; M.21.804C); τῆς τοῦ Γαβριὴλ εὐ. εἰσόδου Epiph.*haer.*79.6(p.480.28; M.42.748D); **6.** neut. as subst.; **a.** *the gospel* οὐ κατὰ τὸ προφητικὸν...ἀλλὰ κατὰ τὸ εὐ. Or.*Cels.*6.76(p.146.9; M.11.1413C); ἄλλον μὲν τὸ νομικόν, ἄλλον δὲ τὸ εὐ. id.*Jo.*13.49(47; p.276.15; M.14.488A); plur. τῶν εὐ. καὶ τῶν ἀποστολικῶν Iren.*haer.*1.3.6(M.7.477A); Ath.*ep.Amun.*(M.26.1173D); Epiph.*haer.*57.7(p.353.7; M.41.1005C); **b.** *gospel text,* Pall.*v.Chrys.*6 (p.34.24; M.47.21).

***εὐαγγελικῶς**, **1.** *in accordance with the gospels,* ref. texts from gospels, Gr.Nyss.*Eun.*12(1 p.370.5; M.45.1096A); Thdr.Stud.*epp.*1.4 (M.99.1080C); Thphn.*chron.*p.371(M.108.888C); **2.** *in the gospels* οὐδεὶς...θεῷ δουλεύειν δύναται καὶ μαμμωνᾷ, ὡς εὐ. ἐμάθομεν Taras. *ep.*3(M.98.1441C); **3.** *in accordance with the gospel, evangelically* γυναῖκες εὐ. ζῆν προελόμεναι παρθενίαν γάμου προτιμῶσαι Bas.*ep.*207. 2(3.310D; M.32.761B); βιοῦν ὀρθῶς τε καὶ εὐ. Cyr.*ador.*6(1.184D); Hyper.*mon.*(M.79.1473D); Max.*ep.*11(M.91.456A); δύο τὰς οὐσίας εὐ. τε καὶ πατρικῶς ὁμολογοῦμεν Jo.D.*f.o.*3.15(M.94.1052C); ref. behaviour of OT persons εὐ. ἡ Ζωσάννα κατεφρόνησε τῶν ἀποκτεινόντων τὸ σῶμα Hipp.*Dan.*13:24(M.10.696B); εὐ. κινηθεὶς [sc. Elisha] πρὸς τὴν ἴασιν Isid.Pel.*epp.*1.16(M.78.789B); εὐ. φησιν [sc. David] Proc.G.*Dt.*19:21(M.87.921B); **4.** *in the manner of the gospel,* opp. OT εὐ. μᾶλλον καὶ ἀποστολικῶς ἢ προφητικῶς καὶ αἰνιγματωδῶς Thdt. *Dan.*7:14(2.1201).

***εὐαγγελιοειδής**, *resembling the gospels*; neut. as subst., *evangelical character* τοῦ ἀρχιεράρχου τὸ εὐ. καὶ ἔνθεον *V.Chrys.*61 (p.326.1).

***εὐαγγελιολύτης, ὁ**, *one who destroys* or *denies the gospel,* Thdr. Stud.*epp.*1.49(M.99.1088C).

εὐαγγέλιον, τό, *good news of Christ, gospel*;

A. early uses; **1.** prob. without actual ref. to written gospel, Ign.*Smyrn.*5.1; ἤκουσά τινων λεγόντων, ὅτι, ἐὰν μὴ ἐν τοῖς ἀρχείοις εὕρω, ἐν τῷ εὐ. οὐ πιστεύω· καὶ λέγοντός μου αὐτοῖς, ὅτι γέγραπται, ἀπεκρίθησάν μοι, ὅτι πρόκειται id.*Philad.*8.2; ἵνα ἡμῖν ὁ κύριος ἄνωθεν ἐπιδείξῃ τὸ κατὰ τὸ εὐ. μαρτύριον *M.Polyc.*1.1; τὸ μαρτύριον... κατὰ τὸ εὐ. Χριστοῦ γενόμενον *ib.*19.1; cf. *usque ad mortem tradiderunt animas propter evangelium Christi,* Iren.*haer.*3.12.13(M.7.907A); **2.** perh. ref. written gospels περὶ δὲ τῶν ἀποστόλων καὶ προφητῶν, κατὰ τὸ δόγμα τοῦ εὐ. οὕτω ποιήσατε *Did.*11.3; ὡς ἐκέλευσεν ὁ κύριος ἐν τῷ εὐ. αὐτοῦ 'οὕτω προσεύχεσθε· πάτερ ἡμῶν' *ib.*8.2; ἐλέγχετε δὲ ἀλλήλους μὴ ἐν ὀργῇ, ἀλλ' ἐν εἰρήνῃ ὡς ἔχετε ἐν τῷ εὐ. *ib.*15.3,4; προσέχειν...τῷ εὐ., ἐν ᾧ τὸ πάθος ἡμῖν δεδήλωται καὶ ἡ ἀνάστασις τετελείωται Ign.*Smyrn.*7.2; οὐχ οὕτως διδάσκει τὸ εὐ. *M.Polyc.*4; **3.** ref. written gospels τὰ ἐν τῷ λεγομένῳ εὐ. παραγγέλματα Just.*dial.* 10.2(M.6.496C); ἐν τῷ εὐ. δὲ γέγραπται εἰπών· 'πάντα μοι παραδέδοται' *ib.*100.1(709A); Ματθαῖος...γραφὴν ἐξήνεγκεν εὐαγγελίου Iren.*haer.* 3.1.1(M.7.844B); *ib.*(845A) cit. infra B.3.c; Ἰωάννης...ἐξέδωκε τὸ εὐ. *ib.*(845B); **4.** of one specific gospel ἐν...τῷ κατὰ Ματθαῖον εὐ. Clem. *str.*1.21(p.91.28; M.8.889B); Or.*Cels.*1.34(p.85.31; M.11.725B); ἐν τῷ κατὰ Μάρκον εὐ. Clem.*q.d.s.*5(p.163.13; M.9.609B); Or.*Cels.*1.62 (p.113.21; 773C); ἐν τῷ εὐ. τῷ κατὰ Λουκᾶν Clem.*str.*1.21(p.90.6; 884B); Or.*Cels.*1.63(p.115.24; 777B); ἐν τῷ κατὰ Ἰωάννην εὐ. Clem. *paed.*1.6(p.112.29; M.8.296A); Or.*comm.in Mt.*16.19(p.543.5; M.13. 1441A) etc.; **5.** sing., of gospels in gen. ἔνια τῶν ἐν εὐ. κειμένων Iren.*haer.*1.20.2(M.7.653A); Clem.*paed.*1.5(p.96.29; M.8.261B); Or. *mart.*28(p.24.19; M.11.596D); **6.** plur., of the four gospels (cf. B infra) στασιάζειν δοκεῖ κατ' αὐτοὺς τὰ εὐ. Claud.*fr.pasch.*(M.5.1297A); Iren.*haer.*3.11.8(M.7.886B); Clem.*str.*4.6(p.266.26; M.8.1252C); **7.** in wider sense incl. other parts of NT, cf. *eorum qui et evangelium conscripserunt apostolorum,* Iren.*haer.*3.5.1(M.7.857C); *ib.*4.34.1(1083C); incl. Ac., *ib.*3.15.1(917B); εὐ. πως εἰπεῖν τὰ ὑπὸ τῶν ἀποστόλων γεγραμμένα Or.*Jo.*1.3(5; p.7.14; M.14.29A); *ib.*(p.7.23); ἔστι δε προσαχθῆναι ἀπὸ τῶν ὑπὸ Παύλου λεγομένων περὶ τοῦ πᾶσαν τὴν καινὴν εἶναι τὰ εὐ., ὅταν που γράφῃ 'κατὰ τὸ εὐ. μου'· ἐν γράμμασι γὰρ Παύλου οὐκ ἔχομεν βιβλίον εὐ. συνήθως καλούμενον, ἀλλὰ πᾶν, ὃ ἐκήρυσσε καὶ ἔλεγε, τὸ εὐ. ἦν...εἰ δὲ τὰ Παύλου εὐ. ἦν, ἀκόλουθον λέγειν ὅτι καὶ τὰ Πέτρου εὐ. ἦν καὶ ἁπαξαπλῶς τὰ συνιστάντα τὴν Χριστοῦ ἐπιδημίαν καὶ κατασκευάζοντα τὴν παρουσίαν αὐτοῦ ἐμποιοῦντά τε αὐτὴν ταῖς ψυχαῖς τῶν βουλομένων παραδέξασθαι τὸν...εἰσελθεῖν βουλόμενον εἰς τὰς ψυχὰς λόγον θεοῦ ib.1.4(6; p.9.13f.; 32B,C); δύνασθαι εὐ. εἶναι πᾶσαν θείαν γραφήν ib. 1.15(14; p.19.15; 48C).

B. of the four gospels; **1.** traditionally accepted by Church ἐν τοῖς παραδεδομένοις ἡμῖν τέτταρσιν εὐ. Clem.*str*.3.13(p.238.27; M.8.1193A); περὶ τῶν τεσσάρων εὐ., ἃ καὶ μόνα ἀναντίρρητά ἐστιν ἐν τῇ ὑπὸ τὸν οὐρανὸν ἐκκλησίᾳ τοῦ θεοῦ Or.*comm.in Mt*.1(p.3.2; M.13.829A); id.*hom.1 in Lc*.(p.5; M.17.312B); τὰς δηλωθείσας τῆς καινῆς διαθήκης γραφάς...ἐν πρώτοις τὴν ἁγίαν τῶν εὐ. τετρακτύν Eus.*h.e*.3.25.1(M.20.268D); εὐ. τέσσαρα, κατὰ Ματθαῖον, κατὰ Μάρκον, κατὰ Λουκᾶν, κατὰ Ἰωάννην Ath.*ep.fest*.39.7(M.26.1437A); ‡Ath.*synops*.76(M.28.432C); τῆς δὲ καινῆς διαθήκης τὰ τέσσαρα μόνα εὐ.· τὰ δὲ λοιπὰ ψευδεπίγραφα καὶ βλαβερὰ τυγχάνει Cyr.H.*catech*.4.36; **2.** their agreement; **a.** explained ἐπειδὴ τέσσαρα κλίματα τοῦ κόσμου ἐν ᾧ ἐσμεν εἰσί, καὶ τέσσαρα καθολικὰ πνεύματα, κατέσπαρται δὲ ἡ ἐκκλησία ἐπὶ πάσης τῆς γῆς, στῦλος δὲ καὶ στήριγμα ἐκκλησίας τὸ εὐ., καὶ πνεῦμα ζωῆς· εἰκότως τέσσαρας ἔχειν αὐτὴν στύλους...ἐξ ὧν φανερόν, ὅτι ὁ...λόγος...ἔδωκεν ἡμῖν τετράμορφον τὸ εὐ., ἑνὶ δὲ πνεύματι συνεχόμενον Iren.*haer*.3.11.8(M.7.885A,B); ὡς εἷς ἐστιν ὃν εὐαγγελίζονται πλείονες, οὕτως ἕν ἐστι τῇ δυνάμει τὸ ὑπὸ τῶν πολλῶν εὐ. ἀναγεγραμμένον καὶ τὸ ἀληθῶς διὰ τεσσάρων ἕν ἐστιν εὐ. Or.*Jo*.5.7(p.104.30,31; M.14.193D); *ib*.10.3(2; p.172.21; 309A); οὐκέτ' ἂν δόξαι διαφωνεῖν ἀλλήλοις τὰ εὐ. τῷ τὸ μὲν κατὰ Ἰωάννην τὰ πρῶτα τῶν τοῦ Χριστοῦ πράξεων περιέχειν, τὰ δὲ λοιπὰ τὴν ἐπὶ τέλει τοῦ χρόνου αὐτῷ γεγενημένην ἱστορίαν Eus.*h.e*.3.24.13(M.20.268A); cf.*ib*.3.24.12(268A); οὐδεμία σκολιότης οὐδ' ἐναντιότης ἐν τοῖς ἁγίοις εὐ. οὐδὲ παρὰ τοῖς εὐαγγελισταῖς εὑρίσκεται, ἀλλὰ πάντα σαφῆ· χρόνων δέ εἰσι διαστάσεις Epiph.*haer*.51.15(p.270.8; M.41.917D); *ib*.51.6ff.(p.252.19ff.; 896Dff.); Chrys.*comm.in Gal*.1:7(10.667E); Thdt.*Gal*.1:6–7(3.362); **b.** defended, Iren.*haer*.3.11.9(M.7.890A,B); εἰ μὲν οὖν πιστεύεις τοῖς εὐ., καὶ τοῦτο κἀκεῖνο λέγουσι πίστευσον. εἰ δὲ μή, ἀτοπώτατον ποιεῖς, τὸ μὲν ἐγκρίνων, τὸ δὲ εἰσβάλλων Isid.Pel.*epp*.4.31(M.78.1084B); ref. Marcion's treatment of gospels, cf. *rejiciens evangelium imo vero seipsum abscindens ab evangelio, partem gloriatur se habere evangelium*, Iren.*haer*.3.11.9(M.7.890B); τῶν δὲ εὐ. ἢ τοῦ ἀποστόλου τὰ ἀρέσκοντα αὐτῷ αἱρεῖται Hipp.*haer*.7.38(p.224.7; M.16.3346A); ἀθετοῦντα αὐτοῦ τὴν ἐκ Μαρίας γένεσιν κατὰ τὴν θείαν αὐτοῦ φύσιν, ἀποφήνασθαι ὡς ἄρα οὐκ ἐγεννήθη ἐκ Μαρίας, καὶ διὰ τοῦτο τετολμηκέναι περιγράψαι τούτους τοὺς τόπους ἀπὸ τοῦ εὐ. Or.*Jo*.10.6(4; p.176.12; M.14.316B); ref. harmonies of the gospels: Tatian's, Eus.*h.e*.4.29.6(M.20.401A) cit. s. συνάφεια; λέγεται δὲ τὸ διὰ τεσσάρων εὐ. ὑπ' αὐτοῦ γεγενῆσθαι, ὅπερ κατὰ Ἑβραίους τινὲς καλοῦσι Epiph.*haer*.46.1(p.205.1; M.41.840B); οὗτος καὶ τὸ διὰ τεσσάρων καλούμενον συντέθεικεν εὐ., τάς τε γενεαλογίας περικόψας, καὶ τὰ ἄλλα ὅσα ἐκ σπέρματος Δαβὶδ κατὰ σάρκα γεγεννημένον τὸν κύριον δείκνυσιν. ἐχρήσαντο δὲ τούτῳ, οὐ μόνοι οἱ τῆς ἐκείνου συμμορίας, ἀλλὰ καὶ οἱ τοῖς ἀποστολικοῖς ἑπόμενοι δόγμασι, τὴν τῆς συνθήκης κακουργίαν οὐκ ἐγνωκότες, ἀλλ' ἁπλούστερον ὡς συντόμῳ τῷ βιβλίῳ χρησάμενοι. εὗρον δὲ κἀγὼ πλείους ἢ διακοσίας βίβλους τοιαύτας ἐν ταῖς παρ' ἡμῖν ἐκκλησίαις τετιμημένας, καὶ πάσας συναγαγὼν ἀπεθέμην, καὶ τὰ τῶν τεττάρων εὐαγγελιστῶν ἀντεισήγαγον εὐ. Thdt.*haer*.1.20(4.312); by Ammonius Ἀμμώνιος...ὁ Ἀλεξανδρεὺς...τὸ διὰ τεσσάρων ἡμῖν καταλέλοιπεν εὐ. Eus.*ep.Carp*.(M.22.1276C); **3.** individual details; **a.** Mt.: alone accepted by Ebionites, cf.Iren.*haer*.3.11.7(M.7.884B); δέχονται...τὸ κατὰ Ματθαῖον εὐ. ... τούτῳ γὰρ καὶ αὐτοί, ὡς καὶ οἱ κατὰ Κήρινθον καὶ Μήρινθον χρῶνται μόνῳ. καλοῦσι δὲ αὐτὸ κατὰ Ἑβραίους Epiph.*haer*.30.3(p.337.10; M.41.409B); but cf. ἐν τῷ...παρ' αὐτοῖς εὐ. κατὰ Ματθαῖον ὀνομαζομένῳ, οὐχ ὅλῳ δὲ πληρεστάτῳ, ἀλλὰ νενοθευμένῳ καὶ ἠκρωτηριασμένῳ *ib*.30.13(p.349.2; 428C); Thdt.*haer*.2.1(4.328); originally composed in Hebrew, Iren.*haer*.3.1.1(844B); Or.*comm.in Mt*.1(p.3; M.13.829A); Eus.*h.e*.3.24.6(M.20.265A); Cyr.H.*catech*.14.15; Epiph.*haer*.30.3(p.338.3; M.41.409B); *ib*.51.5(p.253.16; 896A); Chrys.*hom.1.3 in Mt*.(7.7B); cf. Ματθαῖος μὲν οὖν Ἑβραΐδι διαλέκτῳ τὰ λόγια συνετάξατο Papias *fr*.15; brought to 'India' by Bartholomew, Eus.*h.e*.5.10.3(M.20.456B); written eight years after Ascension, ‡Jo.D.*ep.Thphl*.3(M.95.349A); **b.** Mc.: ἔλεγεν...τοῦ Πέτρου δημοσίᾳ ἐν Ῥώμῃ κηρύξαντος τὸν λόγον, καὶ πνεύματι τὸ εὐ. ἐξειπόντος, τοὺς παρόντας, πολλοὺς ὄντας, παρακαλέσαι τὸν Μάρκον, ὡς ἂν ἀκολουθήσαντα αὐτῷ πόρρωθεν καὶ μεμνημένον τῶν λεχθέντων, ἀναγράψαι τὰ εἰρημένα· ποιήσαντα δέ, τὸ εὐ. μεταδοῦναι τοῖς δεομένοις αὐτοῦ· ὅπερ ἐπιγνόντα τὸν Πέτρον προτρεπτικῶς μήτε κωλῦσαι μήτε προτρέψασθαι Clem.*fr*.8(p.197.25; M.9.749C); δεύτερον δὲ τὸ κατὰ Μάρκον [sc. εὐ.] ὡς Πέτρος ὑφηγήσατο αὐτῷ, ποιήσαντα Or.*comm.in Mt*.1(p.3; M.13.829A); Eus.*h.e*.2.15.1(M.20.172B); Epiph.*haer*.51.6(p.256.4; M.41.900A); cf.Papias *fr*.15; written ten years after Ascension, ‡Jo.D.*ep.Thphl*.3(M.95.349A); **c.** Lc.: ὁ Λουκᾶς...ὁ ἀκόλουθος Παύλου τὸ ὑπ' ἐκείνου κηρυσσόμενου εὐ. ἐν βιβλίῳ κατέθετο Iren.*haer*.3.1.1(M.7.845A); τρίτον [sc. εὐ.] τὸ κατὰ Λουκᾶν, τὸ ὑπὸ Παύλου ἐπαινόμενον εὐ., τοῖς ἀπὸ τῶν ἐθνῶν πεποιηκότα Or.*comm.in Mt*.1(p.3; M.13.829A); Eus.*h.e*.3.24.15(M.20.268B); cf.Epiph.*haer*.51.7; cf. Λουκᾶς...ἐν τοῖς περὶ τὴν Ἀχαίαν τὸ πᾶν τοῦτο συνεγράψατο εὐ. *Proem.in Ev.Lc*.(*SB Pr.Akad*.Phil.-hist.Kl.1928,p.322); written fifteen years after Ascension, ‡Jo.D.*ep.Thphl*.3(M.95.349A); a revised version made by Marcion, Iren.*haer*.3.11.7(M.7.884B); Thdt.*haer*.1.24(4.316); **d.** Jo.: ἔλεγεν...τὸν μέντοι Ἰωάννην ἔσχατον, συνιδόντα ὅτι τὰ σωματικὰ ἐν τοῖς εὐ. δεδήλωται, προτραπέντα ὑπὸ τῶν γνωρίμων, πνεύματι θεοφορηθέντα πνευματικὸν ποιῆσαι εὐ. Clem.*fr*.8(p.197.29; M.9.749C); a supplement to Lc., Epiph.*haer*.51.12(p.264.2; M.41.909B); written thirty-two years after Ascension in reign of Domitian, ‡Jo.D.*ep.Thphl*.3(M.95.349A); accepted by Valentinians, cf.Iren.*haer*.3.11.7(M.7.884C); rejected by Alogoi, Epiph.*haer*.51.3(p.250.23; M.41.892B); translated into Hebrew, *ib*.30.12(p.348.29; M.41.428B); cf.*ib*.30.3(p.338.5; 409C); its superiority to other three, Or.*comm.in Mt*.1(p.3; M.13.829A); ἀπαρχὴν τῶν εὐ. εἶναι...τὸ κατὰ Ἰωάννην id.*Jo*.1.4(6; p.7.34; M.14.29C); οὐκ ἐν τοῖς προοιμίοις δὲ μόνον, ἀλλὰ καὶ διὰ παντὸς τοῦ εὐ., τῶν ἄλλων ἐστὶν ὑψηλότερος Chrys.*hom.1.3 in Mt*.(7.7A); **4.** their symbolism; **a.** in gen., ref. Apoc.4:7 ὁποία ἡ τῶν ζώων μορφή, τοιοῦτος καὶ ὁ χαρακτὴρ τοῦ εὐ. τετράμορφα γὰρ τὰ ζῶα, τετράμορφον καὶ τὸ εὐ. καὶ ἡ πραγματεία τοῦ κυρίου Iren.*haer*.3.11.8(M.7.889B); ref. Jud.9:8–15 διὰ τοῦτο καὶ εὐ. τέσσαρα παραδέδοται, τετράκις εὐαγγελισαμένου τοῦ θεοῦ τὴν ἀνθρωπότητα καὶ παιδαγωγήσαντος τέσσαρσι νόμοις, ὧν οἱ καιροὶ σαφῶς ἀπὸ τῆς διαφορότητος δηλοῦνται [διὰ] τῶν καρπῶν Meth.*symp*.10.2(p.124.1; M.18.196B); ref. Ezech.47:1–5 ἐπιστῆσαι δὲ προσήκει, ὡς τετράκις ἐμέτρησε, καὶ τοῖς θείοις εὐ. ἰσάριθμον τὸ μέτρον προσήνεγκεν. ἡγοῦμαι δὲ τὸ τέταρτον μέτρον τοῦ θεσπεσίου Ἰωάννου παραδηλοῦν τὸ εὐ., θεολογίαν ἔχον ἄβατον ἀνθρώποις καὶ ἀνυπέρβατον Thdt.*Ezech*.47:3–5(2.1040); γῆς οὖν καὶ δικαιοσύνης μυστικῶς λόγον ἐπέχει, τὸ κατὰ Ματθαῖον εὐ., ὡς φυσικώτερον τὸν λόγον ποιούμενον· ὕδατος δὲ καὶ σωφροσύνης τὸ κατὰ Μάρκον, ὡς ἐκ τοῦ βαπτίσματος Ἰωάννου καὶ τῆς κηρυττομένης ὑπ' αὐτοῦ μετανοίας, καθ' ἣν ἡ σωφροσύνη συνέστηκεν, ἀρχόμενον· ἀέρος δὲ καὶ ἀνδρείας τὸ κατὰ Λουκᾶν, ὡς περιοδικώτερον καὶ πλείοσιν ἱστορίαις πυκνούμενον· αἰθέρος δὲ καὶ φρονήσεως τὸ κατὰ Ἰωάννην, ὡς πάντων ἀνώτατον, καὶ ἁπλῆν μυστικῶς τὴν περὶ θεοῦ πίστιν εἰσάγον, καὶ ἔννοιαν Max.*ambig*.(M.91.1245C); φασὶ δὲ καὶ ἄλλως σύμβολον εἶναι τὴν τῶν ἁγίων εὐ. τετράδα, πίστεως, καὶ πρακτικῆς καὶ φυσικῆς καὶ θεολογικῆς φιλοσοφίας *ib*.(1245D); Ματθαῖος ἑρμηνεύεται μέλι· Μάρκος, οἶνος· Λουκᾶς, γάλα· Ἰωάννης, ἔλαιον. τὰ τέσσαρα εὐ. εἰσι, κατὰ τὰ τέσσαρα πνεύματα καθολικά, ἀπηλιώτην, ζέφυρον, νότον καὶ βορρᾶν. αὐτὰ γάρ εἰσι πρὸς σύστασιν τοῦ παντός. καθολικὰ δὲ λέγονται, διὰ τὰ ἀντιπνέοντα ὀκτώ ‡Germ.CP *contempl*.(M.98.413B); **b.** Mt. symbolized by a man, Iren.*haer*.3.11.8(M.7.888A); ‡Ath.*synops*.76(M.28.432D); **c.** Mc. symbolized by an eagle, Iren.*haer*.3.11.8(M.7.888B); Andr. Caes.*Apoc*.4:7(M.106.257A); by a calf, ‡Ath.*synops*.76(M.28.432D); **d.** Lc. symbolized by a calf, Iren.*haer*.3.11.8(M.7.887B); by a lion, ‡Ath.*synops*.76(M.28.432D); **e.** Jo. symbolized by a lion, Iren.*haer*.3.11.8(M.7.887A); by an eagle, ‡Ath.*synops*.76(M.28.432D); **5.** inspiration ἀκριβῶς πιστεύομεν ἀναγεγράφθαι συνεργοῦντος καὶ τοῦ ἁγίου πνεύματος τὰ εὐ. Or.*comm.in Mt*.16.12(p.510.16; M.13.1409B); **6.** interpretation ἀπὸ δὲ τοῦ εὐ. λαμβάνειν δεῖ τάχα μέν τι καὶ βαθύτερον τάχα δέ τι καὶ ἁπλούστερον, ὅτι χρὴ μὴ ξενίζεσθαι ταῖς περὶ τῶν τροφῶν καὶ ἐνδυμάτων τὴν ψυχὴν φροντίσιν id.*Cels*.7.24(p.176.6; M.11.1456C); id.*comm.in Mt*.10.1(p.2.7; M.13.837B); *ib*.12.11(p.88.11; 1004A); cf.id.*hom.7.5 in Lev*.(p.387.22; M.12.487B); private interpretations condemned, cf.id.*hom.2.1 in Ezech*.(p.342.16f.; M.13.683B); **7.** as means of salvation ὁ σωτὴρ...διδάξας...τοὺς παρόντας διὰ τῆς γλώσσης, σώσας δὲ τὴν οἰκουμένην διὰ τῶν γεγραμμένων εὐ. Pall.*v.Chrys*.12(p.72.24; M.47.41).

C. of apocryphal gospels; **1.** 'of Hebrews', Clem.*str*.2.9(p.137.4; M.8.981A); Or.*Jo*.2.12(6; p.67.19; M.14.132C); ἕτερα δὲ πλεῖστα γράφει [sc. Heges.] ἔκ τε τοῦ καθ' Ἑβραίους εὐ. Eus.*h.e*.4.22.8(M.20.384A); used by Ebionites, *ib*.3.27.4(M.20.273B); Thdt.*haer*.2.1(4.328); identified with altered version of Mt., Epiph.*haer*.30.13(p.349.2; M.41.428C) cit. supra B.3.a; v. Ἑβραῖος; **2.** 'of Peter' τὸ...ὀνόματι Πέτρου εὐ. Serap.Ant.ap.Eus.*h.e*.6.12.6(M.20.545B); where heret. character discussed, Or.*comm.in Mt*.10.17(p.21.28; M.13.876C); τὸ κατ' αὐτὸν ὠνομασμένον εὐ. τό τε λεγόμενον αὐτοῦ κήρυγμα... οὐδ' ὅλως ἐν καθολικοῖς ἴσμεν παραδεδομένα, ὅτι μήτε ἀρχαίων μήτε μὴν καθ' ἡμᾶς τις ἐκκλησιαστικὸς συγγραφεὺς ταῖς ἐξ αὐτῶν συνεχρήσατο μαρτυρίαις Eus.*h.e*.3.3.2(217A); *ib*.3.25.6(269B); οἱ δὲ Ναζωραῖοι

...τῷ καλουμένῳ κατὰ Πέτρον εὐ. κεχρημένοι Thdt.haer.2.2(4.329); **3.** 'of Thomas', Or.hom.1 in Lc.(p.5.14; M.17.312B); Eus.h.e.3.25.6 (M.20.269B); ‡Ath.synops.76(M.28.432B); ἔγραψαν καὶ Μανιχαῖοι κατὰ Θωμᾶν εὐ., ὅπερ εὐωδίᾳ τῆς εὐαγγελικῆς ἐπωνυμίας ἐπικεχρωσμένον, διαφθείρει δὲ τὰς ψυχὰς τῶν ἁπλουστέρων Cyr.H.catech.4.36; ib.6.31; †Leont.B.sect.3(M.86.1213C); Jo.D.imag.3.16(M.94.1301D); **4.** 'of Matthias', Or.hom.1 in Lc.(p.5.14; M.17.312B); Eus.h.e.3.25.6 (M.20.269B); **5.** 'of Philip' οἱ...Λευῖται...προφέρουσι...εἰς ὄνομα Φιλίππου τοῦ ἁγίου μαθητοῦ εὐ. πεπλασμένον Epiph.haer.26.13(p.292.14; M.41.352D); Manichean, †Leont.B.sect.3(M.86.1213C); **6.** 'of Judas', composed by Cainites, Iren.haer.1.31.1(M.7.704B); Epiph. haer.38.1(p.63.13; M.41.656B); Thdt.haer.1.15(4.309); **7.** 'of the Twelve', Or.hom.1 in Lc.(p.5.3; M.17.312B); **8.** Syriac, Eus.h.e. 4.22.8(M.20.384A); **9.** 'of the Egyptians', Clem.str.3.9(p.225.3; M.8.1165B); Or.hom.1 in Lc.(p.5.2; M.17.312B); Epiph.haer.62.2(p.391.6; M.41.1052D); **10.** 'of Eve', ib.26.2(p.277.17; 333C); **11.** 'of perfection' ἐπίπλαστον εἰσάγουσιν [sc. Gnostics] ἀγώγιμόν τι ποίημα...εὐ. τελειώσεως τοῦτο φάσκοντες, καὶ ἀληθῶς οὐκ εὐ. τοῦτο, ἀλλὰ πένθος τῆς τελειώσεως ib.(p.277.15f.; M.41.333C); **12.** of Basilides ἐτόλμησε καὶ Βασιλείδης γράψαι κατὰ Βασιλείδην εὐ. Or.hom.1 in Lc.(p.5.6; M.17.312B); **13.** of Manes μίαν καλουμένην εὐ., οὐ Χριστοῦ πράξεις περιέχουσαν ἀλλ' ἁπλῶς μόνον τὴν προσηγορίαν Cyr.H.catech.6.22; Socr.h.e.1.22.5(M.67.136C); **14.** unidentified λέγει γὰρ ὁ κύριος ἐν τῷ εὐ. 'εἰ τὸ μικρὸν οὐκ ἐτηρήσατε, τὸ μέγα τίς ὑμῖν δώσει;' 2Clem.8.5; τὰ ὑπομνήματα αὐτοῦ περιέχουσιν αὐτοῖς λέγεται εὐ.· 'εὑρίσκωμεν πόθεν ἐστίν, καὶ τοὺς γονεῖς αὐτοῦ σὺν αὐτῷ, καὶ πῶς θεός ἐστιν οὗτος' Dial.Tim.et Aquil.80 r°.

D. in more gen. sense, usu. not referring to written gospel; **1.** described ἔστι τοίνυν τὸ εὐ. λόγος περιέχων ἀπαγγελίαν πραγμάτων κατὰ τὸ εὔλογον διὰ τὸ ὠφελεῖν εὐφραινόντων τὸν ἀκούοντα, ἐπὰν παραδέξηται τὸ ἀπαγγελλόμενον· οὐδὲν δὲ ἧττον ὁ τοιοῦτος λόγος εὐ. ἐστιν, ἂν καὶ πρὸς τὴν σχέσιν τοῦ ἀκούοντος ἐξετάζηται. ἢ εὐ. ἐστι λόγος περιέχων ἀγαθοῦ τῷ πιστεύοντι παρουσίαν ἢ λόγος ἐπαγγελλόμενος παρεῖναι ἀγαθὸν τὸ προσδοκώμενον Or.Jo.1.5(7; p.9.25ff.; M.14.32Cf.); τί βούλεται τοῦτο δηλοῦν ὅ φαμεν εὐ. ... τοῦτο δὴ πᾶσιν ἀνθρώποις τὴν παρουσίαν τῶν ἀνωτάτω καὶ μεγίστων ἀγαθῶν, πάλαι μὲν προηγορευμένων νεωστὶ δὲ τοῖς πᾶσιν ἐπιλαμψάντων, εὐαγγελίζεται Eus.p.e.1.1(2A; M.21.24A); εἰ τοίνυν τις ὁριζόμενος εἴποι τὸ εὐ. εἶναι τοῦ ἐξ ἀναστάσεως βίου προδιατύπωσιν, οὐκ ἄν μοι δοκεῖ τοῦ προσήκοντος ἁμαρτεῖν Bas.Spir.35(3.30E; M.32.131A); τί ἐστιν εὐ.; τοῦ θεοῦ λόγου κυρίου Ἰησοῦ Χριστοῦ παρουσία, πρὸς σωτηρίαν τοῦ γένους τῶν ἀνθρώπων σαρκωθέντος, ἐκ πνεύματος ἁγίου καὶ Μαρίας τῆς ἀειπαρθένου ‡Ath.comm.essent.50(M.28.77A); τὰ...εὐ. ὧν ὁ Χριστὸς ἐποίησε καὶ εἶπεν ἱστορία τίς ἐστιν Chrys.hom.1.5 in Ac.(9.9B); **2.** contents πασῶν τῶν γραφῶν...πρωτογέννημα μὲν τὸν Μωϋσέως νόμον, ἀπαρχὴν δὲ τὸ εὐ. Or.Jo.1.2(4; p.6.13; M.14.28A); of Mt. εὐ. δὲ αὐτοῦ τὴν πραγματείαν εἰκότως ἐκάλεσε. καὶ γὰρ κολάσεως ἀναίρεσιν, καὶ ἁμαρτημάτων λύσιν, καὶ δικαιοσύνην, καὶ ἁγιασμόν, καὶ ἀπολύτρωσιν, καὶ υἱοθεσίαν, καὶ κληρονομίαν τῶν οὐρανῶν, καὶ συγγένειαν πρὸς τὸν υἱὸν τοῦ θεοῦ, πᾶσιν ἦλθεν ἀπαγγέλλων·...τί ποτ' οὖν τῶν εὐ. τούτων ἴσον γένοιτ' ἄν; θεὸς ἐπὶ γῆς, ἄνθρωπος ἐν οὐρανῷ Chrys.hom.1.2 in Mt.(7.4Af.); ἔστι δὲ εὐ. ἑρμηνεία τοῦ πράγματος· εὐαγγελίζεται γὰρ ἡμᾶς τὴν...τοῦ σωτῆρος οἰκονομίαν, ὅτι ὁ θεὸς ἐν ἀνθρώποις ἐγένετο διὰ φιλανθρωπίαν, οὐ τὴν προαιώνιον ἀξίαν προαποθέμενος, ἀλλὰ τὴν σωτήριον οἰκονομίαν ἐνδυσάμενος Sever.sigill.1(M.63.532); ἀνακηρύττει πᾶσι τὰ ὄντως εὐ., θεὸν ἵλεω τοῖς ἐπὶ γῆς ἐξ οἰκείας ὄντα καὶ φυσικῆς ἀγαθότητος, αὐτὸν ὡς ἡμᾶς εὐτόνως ἀφικέσθαι διὰ φιλανθρωπίαν ἀξιώσαντα, καὶ τῇ πρὸς αὐτὸν ἑνώσει δίκην πυρὸς ἀφομοιῶσαι τὰ ἑνωθέντα Dion.Ar.e.h.2.2.1(M.3.393A); εὐ. δὲ τὸ κήρυγμα προσηγόρευσεν, ὡς πολλῶν ἀγαθῶν ὑπισχνούμενον χορηγίαν. εὐαγγελίζεται γὰρ τὰς τοῦ θεοῦ καταλλαγάς, τὴν τοῦ διαβόλου κατάλυσιν, τῶν ἁμαρτημάτων τὴν ἄφεσιν, τοῦ θανάτου τὴν παῦλαν, τῶν νεκρῶν τὴν ἀνάστασιν, τὴν ζωὴν τὴν αἰώνιον, τὴν βασιλείαν τῶν οὐρανῶν Thdt. Rom.1:1(3.13); id.Ezech.39:29(2.1019); **3.** in some sense identified with Christ προσφυγὼν τῷ εὐ. ὡς σαρκὶ Ἰησοῦ Ign.Philad.5.1; τῆς ἀληθείας τὸ φῶς, ὁ λόγος...εὐ. γενόμενος Clem.prot.2(p.10.8; M.8.65C); ὁ...σωτὴρ...τὸ εὐ. σωματοποιηθῆναι θελήσας Or.Jo.1.6(8; p.11.5; M.14.33D); αὐτός ἐστιν τὸ εὐ. τῆς σωτηρίας ἡμῶν Cyr.Arcad.(p.115.20; 5^2.122B); **4.** its essence ἐξαίρετον δέ τι ἔχει τὸ εὐ., τὴν παρουσίαν τοῦ σωτῆρος...τὸ πάθος αὐτοῦ καὶ τὴν ἀνάστασιν Ign.Philad.9.2; cf. *haec quidem sunt principia evangelii, unum deum fabricatorem hujus universitatis*, Iren.haer.3.1.1(M.7.884A); τὴν τοῦ εὐ. ὑπόθεσιν, ὅτι δόσις ἐστὶν αἰωνίου ζωῆς Clem.q.d.s.6(p.164.6; M.9.612A); τῶν γὰρ εὐ. τὸ κεφάλαιον ἐντεῦθεν ἔχει τὴν ἀρχήν, ἀπὸ τοῦ τὸν θεὸν γενέσθαι ἄνθρωπον, καὶ σταυρωθῆναι, καὶ ἀναστῆναι Chrys.hom.38.1 in 1Cor.(10.351B); οὐδὲν...ἄλλο ἐστὶ τὸ κήρυγμα, ἀλλ' ἢ σωτηρίας εὐ., ὅτι τοὺς ἀξίους ἀπόλλυσθαι οὐκέτι ἀπόλλυσιν id.hom.2.1 in Eph.(11.10E); τὸ εὐ. ... τοῦτ' ἔστιν ἡ ἀνάστασις Sever.1Thess.2:4(p.329.8); Thdr. Mops.1Cor.15:1(p.193.24; M.66.892B); Cyr.1Cor.15:1(p.297.3; M.74.893B); Thdt.1Cor.15:11(3.267); ὁ...τοῦ εὐ. σκοπὸς τῶν ἀνθρώπων ἡ σωτηρία ib.9:23(3.224); Jo.D.1Cor.15:1(M.95.688D); **5.** its beginning, cf. infra 14.b.i; ἀρχὴ τοῦ κόσμου τὸ ὕδωρ· καὶ ἀρχὴ τοῦ εὐ. ὁ Ἰορδάνης Cyr.H.catech.3.5; ὁ δὲ Μάρκος ἀρχὴν τοῦ εὐ. τὸ Ἰωάννου πεποίηκε κήρυγμα Bas.Eun.2.15(1.250B; M.29.601A); **6.** as gospel of God, cf. *evangelium patris evangelium filii est*, Or.comm.in Rom.1.3(M.14.847A); Chrys.hom.2.2 in Rom.(9.438E); **7.** its preachers; **a.** Jo. Bapt., Or.hom.21 in Lc.(p.136.17); **b.** apostles τοὺς ἰδίους ἀποστόλους τοὺς μέλλοντας κηρύσσειν τὸ εὐ. αὐτοῦ ἐξελέξατο Barn.5.7; cf.Iren. haer.3.1.1(M.7.844A); A.Paul.et Thecl.40(p.266.9); Clem.paed.2.8 (p.194.16; M.8.465C); cf. *neque enim gentes...credere poterant evangelis, nisi per gratiam quae apostolis fuerat data, per quam praedicantibus apostolis in fidem obedire dicitur*, Or.comm.in Rom.1.7(M.14.853A); Ath.Ar.1.2(M.26.16B); πλουσία καὶ ἄφθονος ἡ χάρις ἐκκέχυται ἐπὶ τοὺς κήρυκας τοῦ εὐ., οὓς καὶ χείλη Χριστοῦ ὠνόμασεν ἡ γραφή Bas.hom.in Ps.44(1.162D; M.29.397A); **c.** priests τοῦτον...πλήρωσον τῆς τοῦ ἁγίου σου πνεύματος δωρεᾶς ἵνα γένηται ἄξιος...κηρύσσειν τὸ εὐ. τῆς βασιλείας σου Euchol.(p.243); **d.** qualities of its preachers, cf. *sacrificale opus esse annuntiare evangelium...qui evangelium sacrificat et verbum dei annuntiat, curare omnimodis debet, ne qua in praedicando macula, ne quod in docendo vitium, ne qua in magisterio culpa nascatur*, Or.comm.in Rom.10.11(M.14.1268B); **8.** extent of its preaching τὸ εὐ. τῆς βασιλείας ἀπὸ τῶν ἡμετέρων τόπων ἀρξάμενον εἰς πᾶσαν ἐξῆλθε τὴν οἰκουμένην Bas.ep.243.3(3.374E; M.32.908B); ib. 165(256C; M.640A); Chrys.hom.75.2 in Mt.(7.725E); **9.** gospel as a way of life τὸ εὐ. εἰ μὴ βούλοιτό τις ἕπεσθαι, ἔξον μὲν αὐτῷ ἐστιν, ἀσύμφερον δέ Iren.haer.4.37.4(cf.M.7.1101C); κατὰ τὸ εὐ. τελείως βιώσαντας καὶ γνωστικῶς Clem.str.6.12(p.485.9; M.9.328A); Or. comm.in Mt.17.4(p.588.30; M.13.1484C); id.mart.12(p.11.26; M.11.577C); Eus.h.e.2.17.15(M.20.180B); Bas.ep.22(3.99A; M.32.288B); πάντες ἄνθρωποι ἀπαιτηθησόμεθα τὴν πρὸς τὸ εὐ. ὑπακοήν, μοναχοί τε καὶ οἱ ἐν συζυγίαις id.renunt.2(2.203C; M.31.629A); **10.** as storehouse of teaching, Hipp.Dan.4.20.3; cf. *secundum evangelii leges*, Or. comm.in Rom.2.13(M.14.912B); ὁμοούσιόν ἐστι [sc. τὸ πνεῦμα] πατρὸς καὶ υἱοῦ, καὶ ἐκ πατρὸς μὲν ἐκπορεύεται κατὰ τὴν τῶν εὐ. διδασκαλίαν Thdt.Rom.8:11(3.84); **11.** its spiritual and literal sense τὸ σωματικὸν κηρύττειν εὐ. Or.Jo.1.7(9; p.13.5; M.14.37B); ib.1.8(10; p.13.12f.; 37C) cit. s. αἰσθητός; **12.** as eternal ὥσπερ ἔστι 'νόμος σκιὰν' περιέχων 'τῶν μελλόντων ἀγαθῶν' ὑπὸ τοῦ κατὰ ἀλήθειαν καταγγελλομένου νόμου δηλουμένων, οὕτω καὶ εὐ. σκιὰν μυστηρίων Χριστοῦ διδάσκει τὸ νομιζόμενον ὑπὸ πάντων τῶν ἐντυγχανόντων νοεῖσθαι. ὃ δέ φησιν Ἰωάννης 'εὐ. αἰώνιον' οἰκείως ἂν λεχθησόμενον πνευματικόν ib.1.7(9; p.12.11f.; M.14.36D); cf. *utrum simpliciter accipi debeat evangelium per scripturas propheticas a deo repromissum; an ad distinctionem alterius evangelii quod aeternum dicit Joannes in Apocalypsi*, Or. comm.in Rom.1.4(M.14.847B); *si ergo cum apparuit nobis hominibus, non sine evangelio apparuit, consequentia videtur ostendere quod etiam angelico ordini non sine evangelio apparuerit, illo fortassis quod aeternum evangelium a Joanne memoratum supra edocuimus*, ib.(848A); ib.1.14(861A); cf. τὸ δὲ αἰώνιον εὐ., τὸ ἐξ αἰῶνος τοῦτο παρὰ τῷ θεῷ προωρίσθαι Andr.Caes.Apoc.40(M.106.344D); **13.** in Gnost. theory ἦλθε τὸ εὐ. εἰς τὸν κόσμον καὶ διῆλθε διὰ πάσης ἀρχῆς καὶ ἐξουσίας <καὶ> κυριότητος <καὶ> παντὸς ὀνόματος ὀνομαζομένου Hipp. haer.7.25(p.203.18; M.16.3314B); ἦλθεν...τὸ εὐ. πρῶτον ἀπὸ τῆς υἱότητος ib.7.26(p.204.1; 3314C); ἔδει λοιπὸν καὶ ἐπὶ τὴν ἑβδομάδα ἐλθεῖν τὸ εὐ. ib.(p.204.19; 3315A); εὐ. ἐστι κατ' αὐτοὺς ἡ τῶν ὑπερκοσμίων γνῶσις ib.7.27(p.207.4; 3319A); **14.** relationship to OT; **a.** in gen. πρὸ τοῦ εὐ., ὃ γέγονε διὰ τὴν Χριστοῦ ἐπιδημίαν, οὐδὲν τῶν πάλαι εὐ. ἦν. τὸ δὲ εὐ., ὅπερ ἐστὶ διαθήκη καινή, ἀποστῆσαν ἡμᾶς παλαιότητος τοῦ γράμματος τὴν μηδέποτε παλαιουμένην καινότητα τοῦ πνεύματος, οἰκείαν τῆς καινῆς διαθήκης τυγχάνουσαν, ἐν πάσαις ἀνακειμένην γραφαῖς τῷ φωτὶ τῆς γνώσεως ἀνέλαμψεν. ἐχρῆν δὲ τὸ ποιητικὸν τοῦ καὶ ἐν τῇ παλαιᾷ διαθήκῃ νομιζομένου εὐαγγελίου εὐαγγέλιον ἐξαιρέτως καλεῖσθαι 'εὐ.' Or.Jo.1.6(7; p.11.18ff.; M.14.36B); ἡ παλαιὰ μὲν οὐκ εὐ., οὐ δεικνύουσα 'τὸν ἐρχόμενον' ἀλλὰ προκηρύσσουσα ib.1.3(5 p.7.4; 28C); **b.** to Law; **i.** as fulfilment τὰ τοῦ εὐ. δόγματα ὑπὸ τοῦ νόμου προεκηρύχθη Mel.pass.39 p.6.30; τί δὲ ἄτοπον τὸ ἀρχὴν τοῦ ἡμετέρου δόγματος, τουτέστι τοῦ εὐ., εἶναι τὸν νόμον;...ὁ Μάρκος φησίν· 'ἀρχὴ τοῦ εὐ. Ἰησοῦ Χριστοῦ κτλ. ...' δεικνὺς ὅτι· ἡ τοῦ εὐ. ἀρχὴ τῶν Ἰουδαϊκῶν γραμμάτων ἤρτηται Or. Cels.2.4(p.131.9f.; M.11.801B); ὡς μὲν πρὸς τὴν μάθησιν, οὐδὲν διέστηκε τὰ εὐ. τοῦ νόμου· ὡς δὲ πρὸς τὴν ἐπαγγελίαν καὶ ἀπόδοσιν, διέστηκε. τί γάρ ἐστι ὁ νόμος; εὐ. προκατηγγελμένον· τί δὲ τὸ εὐ.;

νόμος πεπληρωμένος ‡Just.*qu.et resp.*101(M.6.1345D); **ii.** one God being author of both, cf.Iren.*haer.*4.12.3(M.7.1005B); Clem.*str.*2.23(p.193.23; M.8.1096D); Or.*hom.5 in Lev.*(p.333.24; M.12.421C); cf. id.*Tit.*(M.14.1303C); cf. *haereticis..., qui...dividunt unitatem deitatis, et qui legem ab evangeliis separant,* id.*comm.in Rom.*2.14(M.14.916D); *πόθεν τῷ Μαρκίωνι καὶ Μανιχαίῳ τὸ εὐ., ἀρνουμένοις τὸν νόμον;* Ath.*ep.Aeg.Lib.*4(M.25.544C); **iii.** both needed, Or.*comm.in Mt.*14.18(p.328.11; M.13.1233A); **iv.** difference between them *νομικοῦ μὲν τελείωσις γνωστικὴ εὐαγγελίου πρόσληψις, ἵνα γένηται ὁ κατὰ νόμον τέλειος...ἐν εὐ. δὲ ἤδη προκόπτει ὁ γνωστικός, οὐ βαθμῷ χρησάμενος τῷ νόμῳ μόνον, συνιεὶς δὲ αὐτὸν καὶ νοήσας ὡς παρέδωκε τοῖς ἀποστόλοις ὁ τὰς διαθήκας δεδωκὼς κύριος* Clem.*str.*4.21(p.305.25,28; M.8.1340Cf.); *οὗτος* [sc. one who marries twice] *οὐχ ἁμαρτάνει μὲν κατὰ διαθήκην (οὐ γὰρ κεκώλυται πρὸς τοῦ νόμου), οὐ πληροῖ δὲ τῆς κατὰ τὸ εὐ. πολιτείας τὴν...τελειότητα ib.*3.12(p.233.28; 1184A); *ib.*7.12 (p.54.12; M.9.504B); *περισσεία δὲ τῆς τοῦ νόμου δικαιοσύνης ἡ τοῦ εὐ. ἐστὶν ὑψηλότης* Isid.Pel.*epp.*1.79(M.78.237B); *ib.*3.53(765Df.); Max.*ambig.*(M.91.1244D); gospel as image of truth *ὁ μὲν γὰρ νόμος τῆς εἰκόνος ἐστὶ τόπος καὶ σκιά, τουτέστι τοῦ εὐ., ἡ δὲ εἰκών, τὸ εὐ., αὐτῆς τῆς ἀληθείας* Meth.*symp.*9.2(p.115.27; M.18.180C); *ib.*9.3(p.118.3; 185A); as law *τῶν γὰρ πρώτων ἀδυνατησάντων σῶσαι νομοθετημάτων τὸν ἄνθρωπον...ἡ κατὰ τὸ εὐ. ἔσωσε μόνη νομοθεσία πάντας ib.*10.3 (p.125.3; 197A); id.*res.*2.8(p.345.3; M.18.308B); gospel not exclusive *ὁ...νόμος ἑνὶ ἐκηρύττετο ἔθνει· τὸ δὲ εὐ. εἰς πέρατα τῆς οἰκουμένης διαδέδοται* Jo.D.*Rom.*1:5(M.95.444C); **v.** as opp. Law *εἰ δὲ γελοῖος, ἡλίου λάμποντος, ὁ λύχνον ἑαυτῷ παραφαίνων, πολλῷ γελοιότερος ὁ εὐ. κηρυσσομένου, τῇ σκιᾷ τῇ νομικῇ παραμένων* †Bas.*Is.*76(1.433A; M.30.245C); *ὅρα γοῦν ὁ Παῦλος πῶς τὴν περιτομὴν ἀνατροπὴν τοῦ εὐ. καλεῖ...καίτοι ἡ περιτομὴ παρὰ θεοῦ δεδομένη ἦν, ἀλλ' ὅμως ἐπειδὴ ἐλυμαίνετο τῷ εὐ. οὐκ ἐν καιρῷ τελουμένη, πάντα ἔπραττεν ὁ Παῦλος, ὥστε αὐτὴν περικόψαι* Chrys.*comm.in Gal.*1:7(10.669B,D); **c.** to prophets; **i.** as fulfilment, Ign.*Philad.*9.2; *ib.*5.2; *τὴν μίαν τὴν ἐκ προφητείας εἰς εὐ. τετελειωμένην δι' ἑνὸς καὶ τοῦ αὐτοῦ κυρίου... σωτηρίαν* Clem.*str.*2.6(p.128.28; M.8.964D); *ὁ...θεὸς τὸ εὐ. ἑαυτοῦ προεπηγγείλατο διὰ τῶν προφητῶν* Or.*Jo.*2.10(6; p.64.20; M.14.125B); id.*fr.48 in Jo.*(p.523.16); Eus.*d.e.*3 proem.(p.95.15; M.22.165A); *οὐ γὰρ ἀφ' οὗ ἐφάνη Χριστός, τὸ εὐ. ἤρξατο· ἀλλ' ἐρριζώθη μὲν ἐν ταῖς βίβλοις τῶν προφητῶν, ἐβλάστησε δὲ ἐν τῷ κηρύγματι τῶν ἀποστόλων* ‡Chrys.*leg.*1(6.403D); *σοφία, λόγος, καὶ δύναμις, ὁ ἐν προφήταις ῥηθεὶς καὶ προκηρυχθείς, ἐν εὐ. δὲ φανερωθεὶς* ‡Germ.CP *contempl.*(M.98.413A); **ii.** prophets as part of gospel, Or.*Jo.*1.15 (14; p.19.13; M.14.48C); **iii.** containing same faith, CArim.*ep. Const.*1(p.237.8; M.25.696C); **iv.** superior to prophets *πᾶσα μὲν ἡ τῶν εὐ. φωνή, μεγαλοφυεστέρα τῶν λοιπῶν τοῦ πνεύματος διδαγμάτων, καθ' ὅτι ἐν ἐκείνοις μὲν διὰ τῶν δούλων ἡμῖν ἐλάλησε τῶν προφητῶν, ἐν δὲ τοῖς εὐ. αὐτοπροσώπως διελέχθη ἡμῖν ὁ δεσπότης* Bas.*hom.*16.1 (2.134A; M.31.472B); *οὐ γὰρ ἦλθέ τι σκυθρωπὸν ἀπαγγέλλων, ὥσπερ οἱ προφῆται κατηγορίας καὶ ἐγκλήματα καὶ ἐπιτιμήσεις, ἀλλ' εὐ., καὶ εὐ. θεοῦ, μενόντων καὶ ἀκινήτων ἀγαθῶν θησαυροὺς μυρίους* Chrys.*hom. 1.1 in Rom.*(9.431B); **d.** to both Law and prophets: all preach one God, Clem.*str.*3.2(p.199.18; M.8.1109A); *ib.*3.11(p.228.3; 1172B); Or. *comm.in Mt.*10.10(p.11.26; M.13.857C); id.*fr.24 in Lc.*(p.244); Alex. Al.*ep.Alex.*12(p.27.3; M.18.565A); and are necessary, cf.Or.*comm. in Rom.*1.15(M.14.861B,C).

E. exeg.: Rom.2:16 *φασὶν δὲ ὡς ἄρα τοῦ κατ' αὐτὸν εὐ.* [sc. Lc.] *μνημονεύειν ὁ Παῦλος εἴωθεν, ὁπηνίκα ὡς περὶ ἰδίου τινὸς εὐ. γράφων ἔλεγεν 'κατὰ τὸ εὐ. μου'* Eus.*h.e.*3.4.7(M.20.220C); 1Cor.9:12 *τῷ εὐ. ... τουτέστιν τῇ κατηχήσει ὑμῶν* Chrys.*hom.21.4 in 1Cor.*(10.185D); 1Cor.9:23 *ἵνα δυνηθῶ κοινωνῆσαι τοῖς ἐν τῷ εὐ. πεπιστευκόσιν ib.22.3* (10.196B); 2Cor.4:4 *ἔγνων τινὰς...φάσκοντας κεκαλυμμένον εἶναι τὸ εὐ. οὐ τοῖς πάντῃ ἀπίστοις· οὐδὲ γὰρ κεκαλυμμένου αὐτοῦ ἢ γυμνοῦ πεῖραν ἔχουσιν. ἔλεγον δὲ οὗτοι ἀπολλυμένους εἶναι ἐν οἷς κεκάλυπται τὸ εὐ., τοὺς παραδεξαμένους μὲν αὐτό, μὴ μὴν ἄνευ καλύμματος προσβαλόντας αὐτῷ* Didym.*2Cor.*4:3–4(p.24.6); *κἂν ᾖ κεκαλυμμένον τὸ εὐ., τοῖς ἀπίστοις κεκάλυπται, οὐχ ὡς ἐν τῷ νόμῳ ἀπὸ παντὸς Ἰσραὴλ ἐπεκάλυπτο ἡ δόξα τοῦ προσώπου Μωϋσέως* Sever.*2Cor.*4:3 (p.287.22); 2Cor.8:18 *τινὲς τὸν Λουκᾶν φασι, τινὲς τὸν Βαρνάβαν· καὶ γὰρ τὸ ἄγραφον κήρυγμα τὸ εὐ. ἐστιν* Jo.D.*2Cor.*8:18(M.95.749B); Eph.6:15 *τὸ γὰρ εὐ., εἰρήνης ἐστίν...ἂν τῷ διαβόλῳ πολεμῶμεν, εἰρηνεύομεν τῷ θεῷ* Chrys.*hom.24.1 in Eph.*(11.180A); Phil.1:5 *κοινωνίαν δὲ τοῦ εὐ. τὴν πίστιν ἐκάλεσε* Thdt.*Phil.*1:5(3.446); Phil. 1:7, Chrys.*hom.div.*7.2(12.357D); *βεβαίωσιν δὲ τοῦ εὐ. τὰ παθήματα προσηγόρευσεν* Thdt.*Phil.*1:7(3.446); Phil.1:13 *προκοπὴν γὰρ τοῦ εὐ. τὸ πλῆθος τῶν πιστευόντων ἐκάλεσε ib.*1:13(3.448); Col.1:5 *τὸ εὐ. δὲ τοῦ παρόντος εἰς ὑμᾶς, φησίν, οὐκ ἔστι ψεῦδος, ἵνα παροφθῇ* Sever. *Col.*1:5(p.316.23); Col.1:23 *τίς δέ ἐστιν ἡ ἐλπὶς τοῦ εὐ., ἀλλ' ἢ ὁ Χριστός;* Chrys.*hom.4.1 in Col.*(11.352A); *ἐλπίδα δὲ τοῦ εὐ. τὴν ἀνάστασιν καλεῖ καὶ τὴν ζωὴν τὴν ἀθάνατον καὶ τὴν τῶν οὐρανῶν βασιλείαν* Thdt.*Col.*1:23(3.480); 1Tim.1:11 *εὐ. δὲ δόξης αὐτὸ καλεῖ, δι' οὐδὲν ἕτερον, ἀλλ' ἢ πρὸς τοὺς αἰσχυνομένους ἐπὶ τοῖς διωγμοῖς, καὶ ἐπὶ τῷ πάθει τοῦ Χριστοῦ* Chrys.*hom.2.2 in 1Tim.*(11.558B); *εὐ. δὲ δόξης, τὸ κήρυγμα κέκληκεν, ἐπειδὴ τὴν μέλλουσαν δόξαν ἐπαγγέλλεται τοῖς πιστεύουσιν* Thdt.*1Tim.*1:11(3.642); Jo.D.*1Tim.* 1:11(M.95.1001B); 2Tim.2:8 *πανταχοῦ τοῦτο τίθησι τῶν ἐπιστολῶν λέγων 'κατὰ τὸ εὐ. μου', ἐπειδὴ αὐτῷ πείθεσθαι ἐχρῆν, καὶ ἐπειδὴ καὶ ἕτεροι ἦσαν εὐαγγελιζόμενοι ἕτερα* Chrys.*hom.4.2 in 2Tim.*(11.680E).

F. *gospel-lection, Gospel for the day*; **1.** in gen. *εἰσῆλθεν εἰς τὴν ἐκκλησίαν καὶ συνέβη τότε τὸ εὐ. ἀναγινώσκεσθαι* Ath.*v.Anton.*2(M.26.841C); *μετὰ τὴν ἀνάγνωσιν τοῦ νόμου καὶ τῶν προφητῶν καὶ τοῦ εὐ.* *Const.App.*2.39.6; Jo.Mosch.*prat.*32(M.87.2880C); *τὴν τῆς προφωνῆς ἑβδομάδα ἐν ᾗ ἀναγινώσκεται τὸ ἱερὸν εὐ. τοῦ τελώνου καὶ τοῦ Φαρισαίου* *Catech.Stud.*8(M.99.1697D); *εὐ. τε ἐκφωνεῖν ἐπὶ ὄρθρου* Thdr.Stud. *epp.*2.214(M.99.1652B); *εὐχὴ πρὸ τοῦ εὐ.* *Lit.Jac.*(p.170.23); *Lit. Chrys.*(p.314.27); *ἔπειτα ὁ διάκονος· σοφία· ὀρθοί, ἀκούσωμεν τοῦ ἁγίου εὐ. ὁ ἱερεύς· εἰρήνη πᾶσι, καὶ εὐθὺς ἐπιφέρει· ἐκ τοῦ κατὰ τόνδε ἁγίου εὐ. τὸ ἀνάγνωσμα. καὶ ὁ λαός, δόξα σοι, κύριε, δόξα σοι· ὁ διάκονος· προσχῶμεν, καὶ ἀναγινώσκει ὁ ἱερεὺς τὸ εὐ.* *Euchol.*(p.6); congregation advised to read Gospel carefully at home before service, Chrys.*hom.11.1 in Jo.*(8.62B); **2.** all standing while it is read, *Const.App.*2.57.8(cf.Philost.*h.e.*3.5); *ὀρθοί, ἀκούσωμεν τοῦ ἁγίου εὐ.* *Lit.Jac.*(p.172.20); bishop standing, Isid.Pel.*epp.*1.136(M.78.272D); except in Alexandria, Soz.*h.e.*7.19.6(M.67.1477A); **3.** its exposition *ὁ διδάσκαλος ἑρμηνεύσει τὸ εὐ. ὅταν λειτουργῇ ὁ ἀρχιερεὺς* *Euchol.* (p.224); **4.** its symbolism *τὸ δὲ ἅγιον εὐ. γενικῶς μὲν σύμβολόν ἐστι τῆς συντελείας τοῦ αἰῶνος τούτου· ἰδικῶς δέ, τῶν μὲν πιστευσάντων δηλοῖ τὸν παντελῆ τῆς ἀρχαίας πλάνης ἀφανισμόν* Max.*myst.*24(M.91.708A); cf.*ib.*13,14(692Bf.); *τὸ εὐ. ἐστιν ἡ παρουσία τοῦ υἱοῦ τοῦ θεοῦ, καθ' ἣν ὠράθη ἡμῖν, οὐκέτι διὰ νεφελῶν καὶ αἰνιγμάτων λαλῶν ἡμῖν ὥς ποτε τῷ Μώσῃ...ἀλλ' ἐμφανῶς ὡς ἄνθρωπος ἀληθῶς ἐφάνη* ‡Germ. CP *contempl.*(M.98.412D).

G. *gospel-book*; **1.** in gen. *βαστάσας τὸ εὐ. καὶ τοῦ Δαυὶδ τὸ ψαλτήριον* *A.Mt.*25(p.252.7); Gr.Nyss.*Eun.*2(2 p.304.20; M.45.476C); CLaod.*can.*16; **2.** in private possession *οἱ ἀντὶ τῶν εὐ. τὰς κιθάρας καὶ τὰς λύρας ἐπὶ τῶν οἴκων φυλάσσοντες* †Bas.*Is.*157(2.490D; M.30.376C); *ἐκέκτητό τις τῶν ἀδελφῶν εὐ. μόνον, καὶ τοῦτο πωλήσας ἔδωκεν εἰς τροφὴν τοῖς πεινῶσιν* Evagr.Pont.*cap.pract.*B 97(M.40.1249D); miniature copies worn round the neck by women and children *αἱ γυναῖκες καὶ τὰ μικρὰ παιδία ἀντὶ φυλακῆς μεγάλης εὐαγγέλια ἐξαρτῶσι τοῦ τραχήλου, καὶ πανταχοῦ περιφέρουσιν, ὅπου περ ἂν ἀπίωσιν* Chrys.*stat.*19.4(2.197E); id.*hom.72.2 in Mt.*(7.703B); Isid.Pel.*epp.*2.150(M.78.604B); copy hung beside bed, Chrys.*hom. 43.4 in 1Cor.*(10.405E); **3.** used in swearing oaths, Chrys.*stat.*15.5 (2.159A); *ib.*(2.159B); *εἰς τὰ εὐ. παρορκήσας* Pall.*v.Chrys.*11(p.64.6; M.47.36); *φέρε τὸ εὐ. καὶ ὄμοσόν μοι ἐν αὐτῷ* id.*h.Laus.*38(p.118.21; M.34.1193B); *βαστάζων τὸ ἅγιον εὐ. ... ἐπωμόσατο αὐτοῖς ὁ βασιλεὺς λέγων 'μὰ τὴν δύναμιν ταύτην'* *Chron.Pasch.*p.338(M.92.880B); **4.** placed on throne at councils *ἡ ἁγία σύνοδος συναγήγερτο,... σύνεδρον δὲ ὥσπερ καὶ κεφαλὴν ἐποιεῖτο Χριστόν· ἔκειτο γὰρ ἐν ἁγίῳ θρόνῳ τὸ σεπτὸν εὐ.* Cyr.*apol.Thds.*(p.83.25; 6¹.251C); *τὸ θεῖον προτεθεικὼς εὐ.* Thdt.*h.e.*5.3.15(3.1019); CChalc.*act.*13(*ACO* 2.1.3 p.54.1f.; H.2.560D); CCP(681)*act.*3(H.3.1068C); **5.** placed on head of bishop at his consecration *τῶν δὲ διακόνων τὰ θεῖα εὐ. ἐπὶ τῆς τοῦ χειροτονουμένου κεφαλῆς ἀνεπτυγμένα κατεχόντων* *Const.App.*8.4.6; Pall.*v.Chrys.*16(p.93.13; M.47.53); rubrics describing procedure *ὁ διάκονος...εἰσέρχεται μετὰ τοῦ εὐ. μόνος εἰς τὸ ἅγιον θυσιαστήριον* *Euchol.*(p.252); *εἷς δὲ τῶν ἀρχιερέων, ἤγουν ὁ πρῶτος, λαμβάνει τὸ ἅγιον εὐ., καὶ τοῦτο ἀνανεώξας τίθησιν αὐτὸ ἐξάπινα ἐπὶ τῆς κεφαλῆς αὐτοῦ, ἐπὶ προσώπου κρατοῦντες αὐτὸ οἱ ἕτεροι ἀρχιερεῖς ἔνθεν κἀκεῖθεν ...οἱ δὲ ἀρχιερεῖς κρατοῦντες τὸ εὐ. καὶ ὁ χειροτόνων ἀρχιερεὺς κάμνει ἐπὶ τῆς κεφαλῆς τοῦ χειροτονουμένου σταυροὺς τρεῖς ἐπευλογῶν αὐτὸν ib.*(p.256); *καὶ μετὰ τὸ ἀμὴν ἐφαίρει τὸ εὐ. ὁ πατριάρχης καὶ ἀποτίθησιν αὐτὸ ἐν τῇ ἁγίᾳ τραπέζῃ ib.*(p.252); reason for custom *ἵνα μάθῃ ὁ χειροτονούμενος ὅτι τὴν ἀληθινὴν τοῦ εὐ. τιάραν λαμβάνει, καὶ ἵνα μάθῃ ὅτι εἰ καὶ πάντων ἐστὶ κεφαλή, ἀλλ' ὑπὸ τούτους πράττει τοὺς νόμους, πάντων κρατῶν, καὶ τῷ νόμῳ κρατούμενος, πάντα λογοθετῶν, καὶ ὑπὸ τοῦ λόγου νομοθετούμενος* ‡Chrys.*leg.*4(6.410B); *τὸ...ἔχειν τὸν ἀρχιερέα τὸ εὐ., σημεῖόν ἐστι τὸ ἐπ' ἐξουσίαν εἶναι ib.*(6.410C); **6.** liturg. ceremonies; at Little Entrance folld. by a litany, *Lit.Jac.*(p.172.24); cf. *ἔρχεται ὁ διάκονος εἰς τὸ μέσον καὶ στὰς ἔμπροσθεν τοῦ ἱερέως ἀνυψοῖ μικρὸν τὰς χεῖρας καὶ δεικνύων τὸ ἅγιον εὐ. λέγει μεγαλοφώνως· σοφία· ὀρθοί. εἶτα προσκυνήσας αὐτός τε καὶ ὁ ἱερεὺς κατόπισθεν αὐτοῦ* εἰσέρχονται εἰς τὸ ἅγιον βῆμα καὶ ὁ μὲν διάκονος ἀποτίθησι τὸ ἅγιον εὐ. ἐν τῇ ἁγίᾳ τραπέζῃ *Lit.Chrys.*(p.368.23,26; M.63.909); ὁ δὲ διάκονος ...προσκυνήσας μετ' εὐλαβείας τὸ ἅγιον εὐ. αἴρει αὐτὸ καὶ ἐξελθὼν διὰ τῶν ἁγίων θυρῶν, προπορευομένων αὐτῷ λαμπάδων, ἔρχεται καὶ ἵσταται ἐν τῷ ἄμβωνι ἢ ἐν τῷ τεταγμένῳ τόπῳ *ib.*(p.372.22; M.910); omitted in liturgy of presanctified, Thdr.Stud.*praesanct.*(M.99.1688C); it is kissed, cf. ἀσπάζονται τὸ ἅγιον εὐ. καὶ τὴν ἁγίαν τράπεζαν *Lit.Chrys.*(p.354.38); cf. ὁ διάκονος...ἀσπάζεται τὸ εὐ. εἰ πάρεστιν *ib.*(p.368.20; M.909); γίνεται ὁ ἀσπασμὸς τοῦ ἁγίου εὐ. παρὰ τῶν ἀδελφῶν συνήθως *Euchol.*(p.6); symbolism ἡνίκα γὰρ...ὁ ἀληθινὸς ποιμὴν παραγένηται διὰ τῆς τῶν εὐ. τῶν προσκυνητῶν ἀναπτύξεως, καὶ ὑπανίσταται καὶ ἀποτίθεται τὸ σχῆμα τῆς μιμήσεως ὁ ἐπίσκοπος, αὐτὸν δηλῶν παρεῖναι τὸν κύριον Isid.Pel.*epp.*1.136(M.78.272D); ‡Bas.*h.myst.*33(p.265.12) cit. s. εἴσοδος; *ib.*43(p.388.9); βαστάζει δὲ ὁ διάκονος τὸ ἅγιον εὐ. ὡς θείαν κέλευσιν τοῦ βασιλέως τοῖς στρατηγοῖς τοῦ πιστοῦ λαοῦ προσάγων αὐτῷ ‡Sophr.H.*liturg.*14(M.87.3993D); cf.Cyr.*apol.Thds.* cit. supra 4; **7.** treatment; touched with washed hands, Chrys.*stat.*7.5(2.90B); venerated τί δέ σοι δοκεῖ τὸ εὐ. ἅγιον καλούμενον οὐχὶ καὶ προσκυνητὸν ὑπάρχειν; Thdr.Stud.*antirr.*2.24(M.99.376A).

εὐαγγέλιος, *of good news* τὴν εὐ. καὶ ἡγεμόνιον ἐπιστήσας τοῦ λόγου δύναμιν Clem.*paed.*1.7(p.124.16; M.8.320B); *of the gospels* εὐ. φωνή Thphl.Ant.*Autol.*3.13(M.6.1140B); Clem.*paed.*1.8(p.131.13; 336A); εὐ. ... μαθήματα ‡Just.*qu.et resp.*101(M.6.1345A).

***εὐαγγελισμός**, ὁ, **1.** *glad tidings, preaching of the gospel* μαρτυροῦσιν αἱ θεῖαι γραφαὶ τοῖς ὑπὸ τῶν ἀποστόλων εὐ. καὶ τῷ ὑπὸ τοῦ σωτῆρος ἡμῶν Or.*Jo.*1.8(10; p.13.25; M.14.37D); ὁ περὶ τῆς ἀναστάσεως εὐ. Cyr.H.*catech.*14.1; τὸν μὲν εἰς ὑμᾶς, φησίν, εὐ. ... διὰ τῆς ἐκείνων ἀπαλλοτριώσεως ἔδει γενέσθαι, καὶ διὰ τοῦτο ἠλλοτριώθησαν Apoll.*Rom.*11:28(p.75.6); ὁ εὐ. τοῦ προδρόμου ἐν τῷ ᾅδῃ Eus. Al.*serm.*1(M.86.512A); τὸν τῆς πνευματικῆς χαρμοσύνης εὐ. Thdot. Anc.*hom.BMV et Sym.*1(M.77.1392A); ὅταν ἴδητέ με ἐκ νεκρῶν ἀνιστάμενον...τότε γνώσεσθε...τὸν ἡμέτερον εὐ. Cosm.Ind.*top.*3(M.88. 145A); τῶν ποιμένων τὸν ὑπὸ τοῦ ἀγγέλου μετὰ χαρᾶς εὐ. *ib.*(165B); ὁ λευκὸς ἵππος σύμβολον εὐ. τυγχάνει Oecum.*Apoc.*6:2(p.84); Areth. *Apoc.*14(M.106.588B); ἄλλος δὲ εὐ. ποιεῖται, διὰ λόγων ἢ γραμμάτων, ὡς Φίλιππος μὲν διὰ λόγων, οἱ δὲ γράψαντες τὰ εὐαγγέλια, διὰ γραμμάτων Jo.D.*Eph.*4:11(M.95.841D); met., of God σὺ γὰρ εἶ ὁ εὐ. καὶ φωτισμός *Lit.Jac.*(p.172.17); **2.** *annunciation*; **a.** of Gabriel to BMV; **i.** in gen. τοῦ Γαβριὴλ πρὸς αὐτὴν...τὸν εὐ. Or.*hom.7 in Lc.*(p.46.7); χειραγωγῶν αὐτὴν πρὸς τὸ πιστεῦσαι τῷ εὐ. Chrys.*hom.49.3 in Gen.*(4.494D); τοῦ εὐ. τῆς θεοτόκου ‡Ath.*annunt.*7(M.28.925C); *Chron. Pasch.*p.12(M.92.92C); Jo.Nic.*nativ.*(M.96.1444A); Germ.CP *or.*5(M. 98.321D); **ii.** its date and season ἦν οὖν τὸ τηνικαῦτα ͵εφα' ἔτος...τῶν ἀπὸ Ἀδὰμ ἀριθμουμένων ἐτῶν. ἐν τούτῳ γὰρ ὅτε εὐ. γέγονε τῆς παρθένου...ἔτος δὲ ἦν ἡλίου τὸ ιγ', σελήνης τὸ ι', ἡμέρα δὲ τῆς ἑβδομάδος τοῦ...εὐ. β' Max.*comput.*(M.19.1249B); τοῦ Νεσάν, ἐν ᾧ γέγονεν ὁ εὐ. Jo.Nic.*nativ.*(M.96.1444B); **iii.** its importance πάντων ἡμῖν τῶν ἀγαθῶν ἀρχὴ γέγονε ὁ εὐ. τῆς...Μαρίας ‡Gr.Thaum.*annunt.*2(M.10. 1161A); **iv.** as subject of an icon, ‡Jo.D.*Const.*3(M.95.313D); **b.** of Gabriel to Zacharias, *Chron.Pasch.*p.12(M.92.92B); ἐγένετο ὁ εὐ. τῷ Ζαχαρίᾳ Jo.Nic.*nativ.*(M.96.1444A); **c.** festival of Annunciation; **i.** in gen. προτρέψωμεν καὶ ὑμᾶς τὴν τοῦ εὐ. ἡμέραν ἑορτάζειν Abr. Eph.*annunt.*2(p.443.17); *Chron.Pasch.*p.196(M.92.484B); Thdr.Stud. *epp.*1.3(M.99.917C); **ii.** as subject of sermons ἐν τῇ μεγάλῃ ἡμέρᾳ τοῦ εὐ. οὐδεὶς φαίνεται ἐξ αὐτῶν [sc. Ath., Bas., Gr., Chrys., Cyr., Procl. CP] λόγον συντεταχὼς καθ' ἣν ὀφείλει ἀνυπερθέτως τοῦτο γίνεσθαι Abr.Eph.*annunt.*1(p.442.17); **iii.** date ἡμῖν ἀνεφύη μείζων ἡ ζήτησις, καὶ ὑπέκρουσέ τις τῶν θερμοτέρων, εἰ ἐν τῷ πλάτει, λέγων, τοῦ μηνὸς γεγονέναι φησὶν οὗτος τὸν ἀσπασμόν, ἤτοι τὸν εὐ., τίς ἡ ἀποκλήρωσις τῇ σήμερον αὐτὸν ἐπιτελεῖσθαι, τουτέστι τῇ εἰκάδι πέμπτῃ, καὶ μὴ ἐν ἄλλῃ τοῦ μηνὸς ἡμέρᾳ; Anast.Ant.*serm.*2.4(M.89. 1380C); cf. ταύτην ἄγομεν ἑορτὴν καὶ πανήγυριν τῆς...παρθένου εὐ., παντὸς δὲ τοῦ κόσμου γενέσιον [sc. because, as the Creation began on 20 March at the vernal equinox, man was created on 25 March] *ib.*3.8(M.89.1384D); τινες...περὶ...τὰς ἄλλας ἑορτὰς τὰς τελουμένας ἐν αὐτῇ [sc. τῇ ἐκκλησίᾳ] σφόδρα πεπλάνηνται, οἷον...τὸν εὐ. τῆς... Μαρίας ὃν καὶ αὐτὸν ἀνεπιλήπτως ἐπιτελεῖ ἡ τοῦ θεοῦ ἐκκλησία τῇ εἰκάδι πέμπτῃ τοῦ κατὰ Ῥωμαίους Μαρτίου μηνός *Chron.Pasch.*p.11 (M.92.89A); *ib.*p.198(M.92.488C); **iv.** ref. rules about fasting τὸ δὲ ὀψάριον ἐσθίομεν ἐν...τῇ ἡμέρᾳ τοῦ εὐ. ... εἰ δὲ μέσον ἐν τῇ μεγάλῃ ἑβδομάδι τύχῃ ὁ εὐ., οὐκ ἐσθίομεν ὀψάριον, ἀλλὰ μόνον ἔλαιον καὶ οἶνον Anast.*temp.*(p.280); οἱ δὲ μοναχοὶ ὀψάριον μὴ ἐσθιέτωσαν τὴν ἁγίαν τεσσαρακοστήν· εἰ μὴ μόνον τοῦ εὐ. *Nomoc.*255; ἐὰν δὲ τύχῃ ὁ εὐ. γίνεται...ἀδιακρίτως μετέχειν ἐκ πάντων *ib.*434; **v.** liturgy used ἐν πάσαις τῆς ἁγίας τεσσαρακοστῆς τῶν νηστειῶν ἡμέραις, παρεκτὸς σαββάτου καὶ κυριακῆς καὶ τῆς ἁγίας τοῦ εὐ. ἡμέρας, γινέσθω ἡ τῶν προηγιασμένων ἱερὰ λειτουργία CTrull.*can.*52; τῇ δὲ ἑορτῇ τοῦ εὐ., εἰ θεοτόκος ἔσται ὁ ναός, γενέσθω προσκομιδή, καὶ λειτουργείτω ἡ λειτουργία τοῦ Χρυσοστόμου *Nomoc.*526; **vi.** its importance πρώτην δὲ [sc. ἑορτήν] πάντων, τὸν εὐ. τῆς ἁγίας θεοτόκου ‡Gr.Thaum.*annunt.* 2(M.10.1156B); μία τῶν δεσποτικῶν πρώτη καὶ πάνσεπτος ἑορτή, κατὰ τὴν τῶν πραγμάτων τάξιν καὶ σύνταξιν τῶν ὑποκειμένων ἐν τοῖς κατὰ Χριστὸν κηρύγμασιν ὑπάρχουσα τοῦ θείου εὐ. κλητὴ ἁγία ἡμέρα, περὶ τῆς ἐξ οὐρανοῦ καταβάσεως τοῦ υἱοῦ τοῦ θεοῦ κατασκευάζει τὸ κήρυγμα ‡Ath.*annunt.*1(M.28.917C); εὐ. πάρεστι, καὶ τῶν δεσποτικῶν ἑορτῶν ἐστιν ἡ πρώτη Thdr.Stud.*catech.parv.*64(p.152); τοῦ εὐ. τὴν ἑορτὴν τὸ σέβας ἀπονέμειν· ὅτι σεβασμία πασῶν τῶν ἑορτῶν *Nomoc.*2; **3.** *evangelization* πρὸς εὐαγγελισμὸν τῆς ἐκκλησίας Thdot.Anc.*hom.BMV et Sym.*2(M.77.1392B).

εὐαγγελιστής, ὁ, **1.** *bringer of good tidings*, Chrys.*hom.32.1 in Mt.*(7.365E); **2.** *preacher of the gospel, evangelist*; **a.** of God ὁ αὐτὸς νομοθέτης ἅμα καὶ εὐ. Clem.*str.*3.12(p.234.19; M.8.1184C); **b.** of Christ ὁ τῶν νεκρῶν εὐ. καὶ τῶν ψυχῶν λυτρωτής Hipp.*cant.Mos.*(p.83.5; M.10.609D); **c.** of angels οὐκ ἔδει τοὺς...ἀγγέλους ἐστερῆσθαι τοῦ καὶ αὐτοὺς εἶναι εὐ.; Or.*Jo.*1.12(13; p.17.25; M.14.45B); **d.** of men χαρακτηριζομένου τοῦ εὐ. καὶ ἐν προτρεπτικῷ λόγῳ τῷ εἰς πιστοποίησιν τῶν περὶ Ἰησοῦ *ib.*1.3(5; p.7.8f.; 28D); ἦσαν εἰς ἔτι τότε πλείους εὐ. τοῦ λόγου, ἔνθεον ζῆλον ἀποστολικοῦ μιμήματος συνεισφέρειν ἐπ' αὐξήσει καὶ οἰκοδομῇ τοῦ θείου λόγου προμηθούμενοι· ὧν εἷς γενόμενος καὶ ὁ Πάνταινος Eus.*h.e.*5.10.2(M.20.456A); 'εἰς εὐαγγέλιον τοῦ θεοῦ'· οὐκ ἄρα μόνος Ματθαῖος εὐ. οὐδὲ Μάρκος, ὥσπερ οὐδὲ οὗτος μόνος ἀπόστολος, ἀλλὰ καὶ ἐκεῖνοι, εἰ καὶ κατ' ἐξαίρετον ὁ μὲν τοῦτο, οἱ δὲ ἐκεῖνο λέγονται εἶναι Chrys.*hom.1.1 in Rom.*(9.430E); οὐκέτι...ὡς Ἰουδαίοις προφητεύων τοῖς τὴν Παλαιστίνην οἰκοῦσι διαλέγεται, ἀλλ' ὥσπερ τις ἀπόστολος καὶ εὐ. πρὸς ἅπασαν τὴν τῶν ἀνθρώπων φύσιν ἀποτείνει τὸν λόγον id.*exp.in Ps.*48:1(5.203C); Παῦλον πότε μὲν διώκτην, πότε δὲ εὐ. ‡Ath.*dial.Trin.*1.12(M.28.1136C); exeg. Eph.4:11 'τρίτον εὐ.'· οἱ μὴ περιϊόντες πανταχοῦ, ἀλλ' εὐαγγελιζόμενοι μόνον, ὡς Πρίσκιλλα καὶ Ἀκύλας ... ἢ εὐ. φησι τοὺς τὸ εὐαγγέλιον γράψαντας Chrys.*hom.11.2 in Eph.*(11.83C); ἦσαν δὲ καὶ εὐ., ἐν οἷς ἦν καὶ ὁ μακάριος Φίλιππος, εἷς τῶν ἑπτά. ... ποιμένας δὲ καὶ διδασκάλους... μετὰ τοὺς εὐ. τέθεικεν, ἐπειδὴ ἐκεῖνοι περιϊόντες ἐκήρυττον Thdt.*Eph.* 4:11(3.424); exeg. 2Tim.4:5 ἔργον ἐπετέλουν εὐ., τοῖς ἔτι πάμπαν ἀνηκόοις τοῦ τῆς πίστεως λόγου κηρύττειν φιλοτιμούμενοι καὶ τὴν τῶν θείων εὐ. παραδιδόναι γραφήν Eus.*h.e.*3.37.2(M.20.293A); ἄρα τοῦτο ἔργον εὐ., τὸ κακοπαθεῖν, καὶ παρ' ἑαυτοῦ καὶ παρὰ τῶν ἔξωθεν Chrys. *hom.9.2 in 2Tim.*(11.716C); 'ἔργον ποίησον εὐ.' φέρε μεθ' ἡδονῆς τοὺς ὑπὲρ τῆς εὐσεβείας κινδύνους Thdt.*2Tim.*4:5(3.692); **e.** esp. of the four evangelists: Matthew, ‡Hipp.*consumm.*41(p.305.38; M.10. 944A); Or.*fr.7 in Lc.*(p.235); *A.Mt.*31(p.261.23); with Mark, *A. Thadd.*1(p.273.11); Mark, *Const.App.*7.46.5; Luke, Marcell.*ep.* ap.Epiph.*haer.*72.2(p.257.32; M.42.385C); Ath.*syn.*4(p.233.19; M.26. 688A); Bas.*Eun.*1.15(1.227B; M.29.545B); John, Eus.*p.e.*11.18 (840A; M.21.900A); ‡Eust.*Laz.*1(p.26.8); freq. without name ὁ εὐ. Or.*hom.7 in Lc.*(p.46.9) etc.; ref. agreement of evangelists ἐπίστησον δὲ...ὡς τάς γε ἐναλλαγὰς τῶν γεγραμμένων καὶ τὰς διαφωνίας διαλύεσθαι παρὰ τὸν τῆς ἀναγωγῆς τρόπον, ἑκάστου τῶν εὐ. διαγράφοντος διαφόρους τοῦ λόγου ἐνεργείας ἐν διαφόροις ἤθεσι ψυχῶν οὐ τὰ αὐτὰ ἀλλά τινα παραπλήσια ἐπιτελούσας Or.*Jo.*10.31(18; p.205.8; M.14. 364B); *ib.*10.8(6; p.128.17; 320B); οὐδὲ...τοὺς εὐ. φαίημεν ἂν ὑπεναντία ποιεῖν ἀλλήλοις, ὅτι οἱ μὲν τῷ σαρκικῷ τοῦ Χριστοῦ πλέον ἐνησχολήθησαν, οἱ δὲ τῇ θεολογίᾳ προσέβησαν· καὶ οἱ μὲν ἐκ τῶν καθ' ἡμᾶς, οἱ δὲ ἐκ τῶν ὑπὲρ ἡμᾶς ἐποιήσαντο τὴν ἀρχήν Gr.Naz.*or.*43.69(M.36. 589C); οὐχὶ ἑκάστῳ ἐμέρισεν ὁ θεός, ἵνα οἱ τέσσαρες εὐ. ὀφείλοντες κηρῦξαι εὕρωσιν ἕκαστος τί ἐργάσωνται, καὶ τὰ μὲν συμφώνως καὶ ἴσως κηρύξωσιν, ἵνα δείξωσιν ὅτι ἐκ τῆς αὐτῆς πηγῆς ὥρμηνται, τὰ δὲ ἑκάστῳ παραλειφθέντα ἄλλος διηγήσηται, ὡς ἔλαβε παρὰ τοῦ πνεύματος μέρος τῆς ἀναλογίας Epiph.*haer.*51.6(p.254.23; M.41.896D); οὐκ ἤρκει εἷς εὐ. πάντα εἰπεῖν; ἤρκει μέν· ἀλλὰ κἂν τέσσαρες ὦσιν οἱ γράφοντες, μήτε ἐν τοῖς αὐτοῖς τόποις...μεγίστη τῆς ἀληθείας ἀπόδειξις τοῦτο γίνεται Chrys.*hom.1.2 in Mt.*(7.5B); **3.** *reader* of Epistle and Gospel, cf. εὐλόγησον δέσποτα τὸν εὐ. τοῦ ἁγίου ἀποστόλου καὶ εὐαγγελιστοῦ *Lit.Chrys.*(p.372.10).

***εὐαγγελίστρια**, ἡ, *bearer of the good news, evangelist* (fem.), of the Canaanite woman εὐ. γίνεται Chrys.*dimiss.Chan.*4(3.435D); of the Samaritan woman, id.*hom.div.*7.1(12.356C); of Thecla, Bas.Sel. *v.Thecl.*1(M.85.517B); of the women in Lc.23:55,56, *Hymn.*(*AGC* p.95).

εὐάγγελος, **1.** *bringing good news*, Nonn.*par.Jo.*6:8(M.43.793B); **2.** *who reads the Gospel* at church services εὐ. ἀνὴρ βίβλον ἀερτάζων διανίσσεται Paul.Sil.*ambo*.247(M.86.2261A).

εὐαγέως, εὐαγῶς, *holily, purely, lawfully*, Nonn.*par.Jo.*14:21(M.

43.896C); Gr.Nyss.*Eun.*12(1 p.301.8; M.45.1012D); εὐαγῶς Epiph. *haer.*21.1(p.238.5; εὐαγώγως M.41.285B); Synes.*calv.*6(p.202.9; M.66. 1177D); Dion.Ar.*e.h.*3.3.1(M.3.428B).

εὐαγής, 1. *unpolluted* sexually, of BMV ἡ εὐ. τὸν κατὰ τῶν ἀναγῶν φυλάττει ὁρισμὸν τὸν τετταράκοντα ἡμέρων ‡Meth.*Sym.et Ann.*3(M.18.353B); **2.** *holy, pure*; **a.** of things, Nonn.*par.Jo.*4:20 (M.43.777A); Evagr.*h.e.*1.16(p.26.3; M.86.2465B); *ib.*1.17(p.26.23; 2468D); of buildings, Const.ap.Eus.*v.C.*2.40(p.58.22; M.20.1017B); Evagr.*h.e.*1.20(p.29.23; M.86.2477A); Jo.Mosch.*prat.*197(M.87. 3084A); **b.** of persons, Dion.Ar.*e.h.*7.3.2(M.3.556C); *MAMA* 3.197 (Corycus, saec. v); Marc.Diac.*v.Porph.*75; **c.** of abstracts εὐ. ... θρησκείας Isid.Pel.*epp.*4.144(M.78.1225B); λειτουργίας Thdt.*h.rel.*4 (3.1159); τῆς οὐκ εὐ. χειροτονίας Philost.*h.e.*2.11(M.65.476A); ἁγιότητα Marcian.Imp.*const.Chalc.*(p.119.3; H.2.661B); *ib.*(p.119.9; 661C).

***εὐάγω,** *guide well* ἐπὶ τὸ ἄληπτόν τε καὶ ἀόριστον εὐαχθήσεται ἡμῶν ἡ διάνοια Gr.Nyss.*hom.13 in Cant.*(M.44.1052B) perh. better written *divisim.*

εὐαγώγως, v. εὐαγέως.

εὐαγῶς, v. εὐαγέως.

[*]**εὐαερής,** *well-aired,* Chrys.*hom.56.3 in Jo.*(8.330C).

εὐάζω, *celebrate* εὐ. ... πάσχα Nonn.*par.Jo.*2:23(M.43.765A).

εὐαισθησία, ἡ, *keen perception,* Clem.*paed.*1.12(p.149.30; M.8. 369B); Isid.Pel.*epp.*3.154(M.78.845B); opp. ἀναισθησία, Nil.*epp.*3.136 (M.79.448A).

εὐαισθητέω, *have keen perception, quick sensibility*; of an animal behaving like humans, Pall.*h.Laus.*20(M.34.1060D); Jo.Disc.*v. Epiph.*19(M.41.48A).

εὐαισθήτως, *with keen perception* or *feeling* τὸ χαίρειν ἐδωρήσατο τοῖς εὐ. πενθήσασιν Bas.*hom.*8.3(2.65B; M.31.312B); *ib.*8.5(66E; M. 316B); τοῖς εὐ. δεχομένοις τοὺς λόγους Thdr.Stud.*epp.*1.48(M.99. 1084B); εὐ. ἔχω, c. genit., *have keen perceptions* of, Clem.*str.*6.11 (p.477.11; M.9.312B).

εὐάκουστος, *easily heard,* Heges.ap.Eus.*h.e.*2.23.11(M.20.200B).

***εὐακροάτης, ὁ,** *attentive listener,* Leont.B.*parasc.*(M.86.1997B).

***εὐαλκής,** *sturdy,* Clem.*str.*1.23(p.94.3; M.8.896B).

εὐαλλοίωτος, *easily changed,* Dion.Ar.*c.h.*13.3(M.3.301B); Max. *schol.c.h.*15.8(M.4.113B).

***εὐάμορφος,** v. *εὐάφορμος.

εὐάμπελος, *suitable for growing vines,* Cyr.*ador.*5(1.151C).

εὐανάλωτος, *thoroughly impregnable,* Gr.Nyss.*Eun.*12(1 p.238.29; M.45.936D).

εὐανάτρεπτος, *easily upset, unstable,* †Bas.*Is.*82(1.436A; M.30. 253A); Cyr.*Is.*3.5(2.515C); id.*Soph.*23(3.605A); id.*Jo.*9(4.776A); *easily set aside, repealed* εὐ. ... ὅρον τοῦ ψευδοσυλλόγου CNic.(787)*act.* 6(H.4.325B).

***εὐαναφόρος,** *acceptable*; of sacrifice, *Const.App.*7.30.2.

εὐανδρία, ἡ, *high courage*; as Christian virtue, Cyr.*Chr.un.*(5^1. 754E); id.*Lc.*9:27(p.79.9; M.72.652D); εἰς πνευματικὴν εὐ. ἀλείφει τοὺς ἀγαπῶντας αὐτόν *ib.*12:4(724D); τοῦ θεοῦ οἱ κραταιοί, τουτέστιν οἱ πνευματικὴν ἔχοντες εὐ. id.*Ps.*46:10(M.69.1057C).

εὐάντητος, 1. *easy to withstand,* Cyr.*Juln.*7(6^2.221A); met. οὐκ εὐ. ...ἀρχήν id.*Os.*28(3.53E; Aubert om.); σύνεσις id.*Is.*5.2(2.771B); **2.** *accessible, approachable* νοῦς id.*hom.pasch.*27(5^2.322B); τὸν πατέρα id. *Abac.*35(3.550B); σέλας Paul.Sil.*Soph.*1002(M.86.2157A).

εὐάντυξ, *well-vaulted,* Paul.Sil.*Soph.*254(M.86.2129B).

***εὐαξίωτος,** *ready to pay attention*; of God, ‡Chrys.*prov.*4(2. 767D).

εὐαπάλλακτος, 1. *easily dispelled,* Bas.*ep.*2.6(3.75A; M.32.233A); **2.** *untrammelled, unencumbered,* Cyr.*Zach.*35(3.711C); **3.** *easily dispelling,* c. genit., Isid.Pel.*epp.*1.53(M.78.216B); abs., of an argument, *easily refuting,* Gr.Nyss.*Eun.*12(2 p.291.31; M.45.905A).

εὐαπαλλάκτως, *with easy riddance, summarily,* Chrys.*hom. 23.4 in 2Cor.*(10.601E); Cyr.*ador.*7(1.239E); Max.*schol.d.n.*13.3(M.4. 413B).

εὐαπάντητος, *approachable, courteous*; of persons, Clem.*str.*7.7 (p.34.8; M.9.465A); Thdr.Stud.*epp.*2.149(M.99.1465A); τὸ εὐ. *ib.*2.124 (1405A); of things said, *acceptable,* *ib.*1.48(1084B).

εὐαπάτητος, *easily deceiving* εὐ. λόγον Ammon.*Ac.*17:7(M.85. 1561D).

εὐαπόβλητος, *easily lost, easily discarded,* Didym.*Trin.*3.10(M.39. 856C); Cyr.*Jo.*4.1(4.341E); εὐ. ... τὰ ἐν τῷδε τῷ βίῳ id.*hom.pasch.* 24(5^2.295B); Jo.D.*dialect.*51(M.94.636A).

εὐαπόδεικτος, *easily demonstrated,* Hipp.*haer.*10.33(p.291.2; M. 16.3451A); ‡Ath.*Apoll.*1.10(M.26.1112A); Pall.*v.Chrys.*20(p.133.25; M.47.74).

***εὐαποδεξία, ἡ,** *kindly reception,* Thdr.Stud.*epp.*2.54(M.99. 1265C).

εὐαπολόγητος, 1. *able to make a good defence,* Epiph.*haer.*64.71 (p.519.17; M.41.1196D); neut. as subst., ‡Jo.D.*Artem.*48(M.96. 1296D); **2.** *easily excused*; of a person, Jo.Clim.*scal.*25(M.88. 996C).

***εὐαπόπλυτος,** *easily washed out*; of dyes, †Bas.*Is.*44(1.414C; M.30.204A); ‡Chrys.*hom.suppl.*5(M.64.461A).

***εὐαπόπτυστος,** *easily despised,* Hesych.H.*qu.ev.*1(M.93.1393B).

εὐαρεστέω, 1. *be well pleasing,* c. dat.; of Christ to God, Ign. *Magn.*8.2; Just.*dial.*92.6(M.6.697A); of man to God, *1Clem.*62.2; Polyc.*ep.*5.2; Just.*dial.*15.1(508A); Iren.*haer.*2.33.5(M.7.834A); *satisfy* Law, Herm.*sim.*8.3.5; will of flesh, Or.*fr.8 in Jo.*(p.490.11); abs., *1Clem.*62.2; Chrys.*hom.29.4 in 1Cor.*(10.646C); Marc.Er. *opusc.*3.11(M.65.981A); **2.** *be well pleased, satisfied* εὐηρέστησεν τὴν βουλὴν τοῦ θεοῦ καταγγεῖλαι Hipp.*Dan.*4.6.2; πρὸς τὴν πενίαν εὐ. ‡Just.*ep.Zen.et Ser.*5(M.6.1188C).

εὐαρέστησις, ἡ, 1. state of *being well pleasing,* esp. to God εἰς εὐ. τῷ ὀνόματι αὐτοῦ *1Clem.*64; κατὰ τὴν πρὸς θεὸν εὐ., ὡς Ἄβελ, ὡς Νῶε Clem.*str.*2.9(p.136.8; M.8.980A); Bas.*reg.br.*157(2.467E; M.31. 1185A); c. genit. εὐ. τοῦ θεοῦ Jo.Mosch.*prat.*171(M.87.3040B); plur. νηστείᾳ τε καὶ ξηροφαγίᾳ...καὶ ταῖς ἄλλαις...ἀγαθαῖς θεῷ εὐ. Epiph. *haer.*70.14(p.247.23; M.42.372A); abs. τὸ χρῖσμα τῆς εὐ. Clem.*str.*4.18 (p.299.19; M.8.1325A); *ib.*7.3(p.15.14; M.9.425B); τῆς κυρίως εὐ. ἤτοι ἐν τῇ τάξει τῶν ἁγίων ἢ ἐν τῷ τόπῳ τῶν ἁγίων τυγχανούσης Or.*Jo.* 2.17(11; p.74.6; M.14.144C); Cyr.H.*catech.*5.10; esp. of Noah, Gr. Naz.*or.*28.18(p.48.18; M.36.49A); of Enoch, Chrys.*hom.22.2 in Heb.*(12.205C); Cosm.Ind.*top.*5(M.88.232A); of Christ ἡμῖν ὑποτύπωσιν τελείας εὐ. Max.*ep.*27(M.91.620B); plur., Clem.*str.*3.12(p.235. 1; M.8.1185B); **2.** state of *being well pleased, satisfaction*; in gen., Hipp.*haer.*5.26(p.127.27; M.16.3195B); *ib.*(p.129.2; 3198B); of God εὐφραίνεται ἄφατόν τινα εὐ. καὶ εὐφροσύνην καὶ χαράν Or.*Jo.*32.28(18; p.473.33; M.14.820A); ‡Ath.*qu.Ant.*132(M.28.681A); *Lit.Jac.*(p.192. 20); cf.*Lit.Chrys.*(p.371.33).

εὐαρεστία, ἡ, = foreg. 1, *Hom.Clem.*9.22; Nil.*epp.*3.332(M.79. 364A).

εὐαρεστικός, *well-pleasing* (to God), ‡Proc.G.*Pr.*29:25(M.87. 1521B).

εὐάρεστος, 1. *well-pleasing, acceptable,* usu. to God; **a.** of things τὰ καλὰ καὶ εὐ. ἐνώπιον αὐτοῦ *1Clem.*21.1; Ign.*Smyrn.*9.1; εὐχαὶ καὶ εὐχαριστίαι...εὐ. Just.*dial.*117.2(M.6.745C); πρὸς θεὸν ἡ διακονία εὐ. *Const.App.*2.58.6; superl. τὰ εὐαρέστατά σοι Ephr.1.65C; **b.** of persons εὐ. ... δοῦλος τοῦ θεοῦ Herm.*mand.*12.3.1; δίκαιοι καὶ εὐ. τῷ θεῷ ἐλπίζομεν φανῆναι Just.*dial.*92.4(M.6.696B); Clem.*str.*7.12(p.51. 25; M.9.500B); τὰς πρὸ τοῦ κατακλυσμοῦ ψυχάς, εὐ. τῷ θεῷ γεγενημένας, τουτέστι τὰς ἀμφὶ τὸν Ἄβελ καὶ τὸν Σὴθ καὶ τὸν Ἐνώχ Meth.*symp.*7.4(p.75.11; M.18.129C); Νῶε καὶ Ἐνὼχ...εὐ. γινόμενοι τῷ θεῷ Ath.*decr.*5(p.4.12; M.25.424A); of Caleb, id.*ep.Serap.*1.8 (M.26.549C); of Christ οὐδ' ὅτι πιστεύων, εὐ. γέγονεν, ἀλλ' ὅτι υἱὸς ὢν τοῦ ἀληθινοῦ θεοῦ, πιστός ἐστι id.*Ar.*2.6(M.26.160B); **c.** neut. as subst., Clem.*str.*3.9(p.226.24; M.8.1169A); *ib.*6.15(p.493.24; M. 9.345C); **2.** *well-pleased, satisfied,* ‡Just.*ep.Zen.et Ser.*5(M.6. 1188C).

εὐαρέστως, *so as to be well pleasing, acceptably,* Just.*dial.*45.4 (M.6.573A); Clem.*str.*3.12(p.234.2; M.8.1148B); *Const.App.*1.10.4; *ib.*8.18.3; to God, Bas.*jud.*8(2.223B; M.31.676B); id.*reg.br.*303(2. 522E; M.31.1297B); Chrys.*hom.30.6 in Gen.*(4.304C).

***εὐάρετος,** prob. f.l. for ἐνάρετος, †Thdt.*Ps.fr.*(5.1234).

***εὐάριθμος,** *easy to enumerate,* Evagr.*h.e.*4.28(p.176.19; M.86. 2752A); *ib.*4.40(p.191.24; 2784D); *ib.*5.9(p.206.9; 2812A).

***εὐαρμόνιος,** *very harmonious,* Jo.VI H.*v.Jo.D.*27(M.94.468C; perh. error for ἐναρμόνιος).

εὐάρμοστος, 1. *well fitted together,* Hipp.*haer.*4.28(p.56.7; M.16. 3091C); Ath.*Ar.*2.76(M.26.308C); hence **2.** *well-adapted, suitable,* of man εὐ. ὄργανον Meth.*symp.*3.7(p.34.24; M.18.72B); Isid.Pel.*epp.*1. 108(M.78.256B); ἄνθρωπος...ἀνθρώποις εὐ. *ib.*1.364(389A); in gen. ἡ φιλανθρωπία τοῖς δεσπόταις εὐ. Clem.*paed.*3.11(p.277.6; M.8.649C); Gr.Nyss.*hom.7 in Cant.*(M.44.925B); οἶκον...εὐ. μεγέθους Gr.Mag. *dial.*(tr.Zach.)3.4(M.*PL.*77.223C); **3.** *well-tuned, harmonious*; of character, Bas.*hom.in Ps.*1(1.91D; M.29.213C).

εὐαρμόστως, *in a manner suitable* to, Clem.*paed.*3.7(p.259.8; M. 8.609B); Gel.Cyz.*h.e.*2.17.28(M.85.1272B); c. ἔχω, Eun.*apol.*25(M.30. 861B).

εὐαρχία, ἡ, *good government,* Didym.*Trin.*2.26(M.39.768B); Isid. Pel.*epp.*1.208(M.78.313D); *ib.*2.101(545A).

εὐαυξής, *well-grown,* neut. as subst., met. τὸ μεγαλοπρεπὲς ἅμα καὶ εὐ. τῆς δυνάμεως τῆς λογικῆς Clem.*paed*.1.11(p.147.5; εὐαγές M. 8.365A).

εὐαφαίρετος, *easily dispensed, easily taken away*, Jo.Clim.*scal*.7 (M.88.804A); Thdr.Stud.*probl*.2(M.99.489C).

εὐαφής, **1.** *soft, receptive*; of seeds ready to germinate, hence met. of Eve, Clem.*paed*.3.3(p.247.20; M.8.581B); of the heart, Cyr. *Ps*.50:19(M.69.1101C); of the soul, comp., id.*ador*.3(1.87B); **2.** *easily grasped*, Gr.Nyss.*virg*.13(p.307.15; M.46.380B); met., Cyr.*1Cor*.1:3 (pp.255.15,256.3; M.74.864C,D); id.*Is*.4.2(2.607A); Max.*cap.theol*.67 (M.90.1156A).

***εὐάφορμος**, **1.** *well-founded, excusable* οὐκ εὐ. φθόνος Or.*exc.in Ps*.36:14(M.17.129C); Cyr.*Ag*.2(3.628A); id.*Rom*.7:8(p.199.15; εὐάμορφος M.74.804D) al.; Leont.B.*arg.Sev*.(M.86.1929A); **2.** *gracious, ready to excuse* μία πόλις ἐσώθη, τοῦ εὐ. δεσπότου πρόφασιν λαβόντος παρὰ τοῦ Λώτ Proc.G.*Is*.54:1–17(M.87.2548C).

εὐαφόρμως, **1.** *on a firm foundation, with good reason* εὐ. ὁ Χριστὸς ποιεῖται τὸν ἔλεγχον τῷ προδότῃ Or.ap.*cat.Jo*.13:12(p.338. 14); εὐ. ἔρχεται πρὸς τὸ τοῦ Χριστοῦ μυστήριον Cyr.*Abac*.33(3. 547E); id.*Nest*.3.2(p.59.3; 6[1].10A); id.*glaph.Ex*.2(1.277A); **2.** εὐ. ἔχω *be firmly disposed* μήποτε...ἀρρωστίας αἰτίαν παράσχῃ τῷ σώματι εὐ. ἔχοντι πρὸς τὴν ἀσθένειαν Bas.*ep*.198.1(3.290B; M.32.716A).

εὐβαφής, prob. f.l. for εὐαφής, Olymp.*fr.Bar*.4:26(M.93.772C).

εὔβοτος, *abounding in pasture*; hence, met., *fertile*, *Orac.Sib*. 3.368.

εὐβούλως, *prudently*, Thdr.Stud.*epp*.1.6(M.99.928B).

***εὔγαλε**, (= ἔκβαλλε), *take out* of prison, *release* δὸς καὶ εὔγαλε Jo.Mosch.*prat*.86(M.87.3064A).

εὐγένεια, ἡ, *nobility*, hence *excellence, excellency*; **1.** in gen.: of things τὴν τῶν ἐκκλησιαστικῶν εὐ. Thdt.*haer*.5.4(4.396); τῆς θείας γραφῆς τὴν εὐ. id.*affect*.4(p.114.15; 4.807); τῇ εὐαγγελικῇ εὐ. id.*ep*.171 (p.163.27; 4.1355); of martyrs, *Ep.Lugd*.ap.Eus.*h.e*.5.2.4(M.20. 436A); of man's first state, Thdt.*Ps*.60:8(1.1011); varying in kind, Gr.Naz.*or*.26.10(M.35.124B); of Christ ἡ εὐ. παρίσταται τοῦ υἱοῦ Or. *Jo*.1.28(32; p.37.6; M.14.77C); Alex.Al.*ep.Alex*.9(p.25.21; M.18. 561B); τῆς ἐνούσης αὐτῷ φυσικῆς εὐ. Cyr.*Nest*.4.3(p.83.21; 6[1].107D); of Father manifested in Son, *ib*.4.5(p.85.26; 110E); σαρκὶ κεκαλυμμένος τῆς πατρῴας εὐ. τὰς ἀκτῖνας ἠφίει Thdt.*eran.suppl*.1.7(4.265); id.*haer*.5.2(4.383); of Trin., Ath.*Ar*.1.18(M.26.49A); **2.** as style of address πρὸς τὴν σὴν εὐ. Bas.*ep*.11(3.92D; M.32.273B); Gr.Nyss.*ep*.20 (M.46.1084B); Jo.VI H.*v.Jo.D*.16(M.94.456A).

εὐγενής, *noble, excellent*; of God, Ath.*Ar*.1.43(M.26.101B); of Christ μόνος ὑπὲρ πάντας εὐ. ὢν *Hom.Clem*.12.7; of man πάντες ἐσμὲν εὐ. ἐπ' ἴσης ἐπεὶ κατ' εἰκόνα θεοῦ γεγόναμεν Gr.Naz.*or*.36.10 (M.35.1241B); of a freedman ἐλευθεροῦται καὶ εὐ. γίνεται Phot. *nomoc*.1.36(M.104.560A); of κανών of orthodox faith, Cyr.*Is*.4.2(2. 612E).

εὐγενίζω, *ennoble* πρὸς ἐκείνην τὴν φύσιν τὸ ἅγιον σῶμα ηὐγένισται Marc.Er.*opusc*.10.5(M.65.1124C); Max.*ambig*.(M.91.1113C); *ib*. (1116D).

***εὐγενοπρεπῶς**, *in noble fashion*, Thdr.Stud.*epp*.2.123(M.99. 1401D).

εὐγήρως, *enjoying a green old age*, hence superl. εὐγηρότατος, *venerable*, CSard.*ep.Alex*.ap.Ath.*apol.sec*.42(p.120.5; M.25.325C); Ath.*fug*.5(p.71.7; M.25.649B); id.*narr.fug*.(M.26.981C).

εὔγληνος, *keen-sighted*, Gr.Naz.*carm*.2.2.7.121(M.37.1560A); met., *bright-eyed* φέγγος, εὐγλήνοισι πεπαρμένον ἄμμασιν ἥλων Paul.Sil. *Soph*.883(M.86.2152B).

[*]εὐγλώσσεια, ἡ, *fluency of speech*, †Bas.Sel.*or*.41(M.85.464C).

εὐγλωσσέω, *make eloquent*, ‡Chrys.*nat.Jo.Bapt*.(10.816A).

εὔγλωσσος, *eloquent*, met. εὐ. θερισμοῦ Nonn.*par.Jo*.4:35(M.43. 780C).

***εὐγλώσσως**, *eloquently*, ‡Ath.*sem*.4(M.28.149A).

εὐγνωμον-έω, **1.** *have right disposition* or *feeling* ταῦτα λέγω οὐχ ἵνα ἁμαρτάνωμεν ἀλλ' ἵνα ~ῶμεν· ὁ γὰρ τελώνης ἄνθρωπος...εὐγνωμονήσας μόνον...εὔνοιαν ἀπεσπάσατο παρὰ τοῦ θεοῦ Ephr.3.458A; πρὸς τὰς παρακαταθήκας ~εῖτε *Clem.ep*.10(M.2.45B); εὐ. τοῖς ἰδίοις δεσπόταις Jo.Mal.*chron*.7 p.183(M.97.292B); **2.** *repay* ~οῦντα θεὸν... ἑκατονταπλασίονα παρέχοντα Chrys.*hom.7.7 in Rom*.(9.493D); id. *hom.in Mt.18:24*(3.9A); Euthal.Diac.*epp.cath*.(M.85.668A); *make an offering in token of gratitude*, of Cain's sacrifice εὐ. ἀκάρπῳ ψυχῇ Bas.Sel.*or*.4.3(M.85.69A).

εὐγνωμόνως, *with a right mind*; hence **1.** *rightly, reasonably*, Dion.Al.*ep.can*.(p.96.14; M.10.1273C); Meth.*arbitr*.4(p.156.11; M.18. 249A); Adam.*dial*.4.3(p.142.11; M.11.1809B); Eus.*p.e*.10.4(471D; M. 21.784D); Chrys.*sac*.1.5(p.19.6; 1.368E); **2.** *candidly, frankly*, Or. *hom.11.3 in Jer*.(p.80.14; M.13.369C); Eus.*ep.Caes*.11(p.47.3; M.20. 1544C); εὐ. ὡμολόγησας, ἔλυσας τὴν ἁμαρτίαν Chrys.*poenit*.2.2(2. 289E); εὐ. ἡμῶν εἰπόντων ἄληπτον εἶναι τὴν θείαν οὐσίαν Max.*ambig*. (M.91.1229C); **3.** *in a right spirit* εὐ. ἔφερε τὴν ἄκριτον καταδίκην Socr.*h.e*.2.16.5(M.67.216A); Isid.Pel.*epp*.5.363(M.78.1544C); **4.** *in a friendly spirit*, Clem.*str*.4.10(p.282.13; M.8.1285A); εὐ. ... ἀκούειν Or.*fr.44 in Jo*.(p.579.3); Euthal.Diac.*epp.Paul*.(M.85.713A); comp. εὐγνωμονέστερον, with ἀκούειν, Or.*Jo*.10.34(19; p.208.12; M.14. 652B); *ib*.20.23(20; p.356.10; 624A); **5.** *gladly*, Gr.Thaum.*pan.Or*.18 (p.39.4; M.10.1101B); Bas.*moral*.32(2.259A; M.31.749B); ἃ...αὐτὸς ὁ θεὸς ἡμῶν...ἐδίδαξεν, εὐ. ἡμεῖς μιμησώμεθα Isid.Pel.*epp*.1.48(M.78. 212C).

εὐγνωμοσύνη, ἡ, **1.** *right-mindedness, right feeling, right judgement* (fundamental meaning seems to imply an honest acknowledgment of facts) ἔχειν...χρὴ πρὸς μὲν τοὺς ἔξω τὸν βίον ἀξιόπιστον, ὡς μηδὲ ὅρκον αἰτεῖσθαι, πρὸς ἑαυτὸν δὲ καὶ τοὺς συνιέντας εὐ., ἥτις ἐστὶν ἑκούσιος δικαιοσύνη Clem.*str*.7.8(p.38.9; M.9.472B); τῆς τε συνέσεως καὶ τῆς ἄλλης τοῦ ἀληθοῦς εὐ. Eus.*p.e*.13.13(691A; M.21. 1140A); εὐ. δέ ἐστιν τὸ τὴν πρὸς τὸν τοῦ εἶναι ἡμᾶς αἴτιον ἀποσῴζειν στοργήν *Hom.Clem*.3.10(M.2.117C); Gr.Naz.*or*.31.33(p.190.1; M.36. 172A); *Const.App*.5.16.8; κλητὸν ἑαυτὸν καλεῖ, δεικνὺς τὴν οἰκείαν εὐ., καὶ ὅτι οὐκ αὐτὸς ζητήσας εὗρεν, ἀλλὰ κληθεὶς παρεγένετο καὶ ὑπήκουσε Chrys.*hom.1.1 in Rom*.(9.430C); Isid.Pel.*epp*.3.189(M.78. 877A); Cyr.*Ps*.37:5(M.69.957B); Max.*ambig*.(M.91.1372D); hence **2.** in partic. circumstances; **a.** *candour, frankness, honesty*; **i.** in gen. μὴ πάλιν τὴν εὐ. ἡμῶν ἀδείας λάβῃς ἀρχὴν καὶ συκοφαντίας Gr. Naz.*or*.28.5(p.28.13; M.36.32C); ὅρα εὐ. τῆς παιδός· περὶ τοῦ πατρὸς ἐρωτηθεῖσα οὐ μόνον τοῦτο καταμηνύει, ἀλλὰ καὶ τοῦ πατρὸς τὸν πατέρα Chrys.*hom.48.4 in Gen*.(4.486C); **ii.** esp. ref. recognition of sin τοῦ τελώνου τὴν πολλὴν εὐ. *ib.54.1*(521E); id.*hom.3.4 in Mt*.(7. 39C); Isid.Pel.*epp*.1.330(M.78.373A); τό, ὄντα ἁμαρτωλόν, ἔχειν ἑαυτὸν ἁμαρτωλόν,...εὐ. ‡Nil.*vit.cog*.(M.79.1465C); **b.** *gratitude* τὸ εὐαίσθητον καὶ ⟨τὸ⟩ τῆς εὐ. ἔργον τοῦ ἑνός [i.e. the Samaritan leper] Epiph.*haer*.66.41(p.78.17; M.42.92A); Chrys.*hom.77.3 in Mt*.(7. 745D); id.*hom.2.1 in Rom*.(9.436C); Thdr.Mops.*Am*.11:7(M.66. 300B); Bas.Sel.*or*.9.1(M.85.128B); **c.** *loyalty, fidelity* ἀπὸ τῆς περὶ τὰ ἐλάττονα εὐ. ἡ τοῖς μείζοσι τῆς ἀνταποδόσεως κρίσις δικαιοῦται Bas. *moral*.18.3(2.250A; M.31.732B); ὅρα εὐ. οἰκέτου· οὐδὲν ἑαυτοῦ εἶναι βούλεται, ἀλλὰ πάντα τοῦ δεσπότου Chrys.*hom.1.2 in Rom*.(9.432E); *ib.3.2*(450A); **d.** *generosity, liberality* πολλὰ κειμήλια...ἡ ἐκκλησία ἐκ τῆς εὐ. τῶν προσηκόντων αὐτῇ κέκτηται Socr.*h.e*.7.21.3(M.67.781C); Leont.N.*v.Jo.Eleem*.4(p.93.8); **e.** *affection* τὴν περὶ τὸν πατέρα εὐ. ἐπιδεικνύμενος Chrys.*ep*.141(3.682E); **3.** ? *good conduct* πρὸς τὸ μέλλον εὐ. [sc. of a wrongdoer] Gr.Nyss.*Eun*.1(1 p.43.8; M.45. 269D).

εὐγνώμων, **1.** *right-minded, having right feelings* or *right judgement*, *Hom.Clem*.3.10; στησόμεθα πρὸς τοὺς ἐξ ἡμισείας εὐ. Gr.Naz. *or*.31.24(p.175.14; M.36.160C); Cyr.*Ps*.50:7(M.69.1089D); πολλὰ τὰ πρὸς εὐχαριστίαν τοὺς εὐ. ἄγοντα Bas.Sel.*or*.9.1(M.85.128A); hence **2.** in partic.; **a.** *candid, frank, honest*; **i.** in gen. ἀναγκαῖον γὰρ τὸν πιστεύοντα ὅτι ἀληθεῖς αἱ γραφαὶ καὶ ὅτι ὁ θεὸς δίκαιος, ἐὰν εὐ. ᾖ, ἀγωνίζεσθαι, πῶς ἐν τοιαύταις λέξεσι δίκαιος τρανῶς νοηθῇ Or.*princ*. 3.1.9(p.209.9, v.l. εὐγνωμόνῃ M.11.264A); Eus.*Hierocl*.(521A; M.22. 817C); comp. τοὺς εὐγνωμονεστέρους ἐν ταῖς ζητήσεσι Or.*Jo*.2.24(19; p.81.8; M.14.156C); Gr.Naz.*or*.30.1(p.108.7; M.36.104C); *cat.Jo*.4:25 (p.221.3); Chrys.*hom.9.2 in Eph*.(11.71A); **ii.** esp. ref. recognition of sin κατανόησον ὡς εἰσιν οἱ προφῆται εὐ. ἄνθρωποι, καὶ οὐκ ἀποκρυπτόμενοι τὰ ἴδια ἁμαρτήματα ὡς καὶ ἡμεῖς Or.*hom.20.8 in Jer*.(p.189.19; M.13.517C); †Bas.*jej*.3.1(2.622C; M.31.1509A); Cyr.*Ps*.37:5(M.69. 957B); **b.** *grateful*, Gr.Thaum.*pan.Or*.3(p.6.21; M.10.1057C); Chrys. *hom.16.1 in 2Cor*.(10.552C); ἐν παντὶ ἁμαρτήματι ἐταπείνωσεν ἡμᾶς ὁ διάβολος, καὶ ὀφείλομεν εὐ. γενέσθαι τῆς ταπεινώσεως ἡμῶν· οἱ γὰρ εὐ. γενόμενοι τῆς αὐτῶν ταπεινώσεως συντρίβουσι τὸν διάβολον Zos. *alloquia* 5(M.78.1688A); **c.** *loyal, faithful* αὐτοὺς συνίστησιν εὐ. πρὸς τὸν πατέρα Ath.*ep.Pall*.(M.26.1168D); Chrys.*hom.5.7 in Rom*.(9. 470E); Cyr.*Os*.4(3.23A); Thdt.*Trin*.8(M.75.1157B); comp., Gr.Naz. *or*.30.6(p.116.1; M.36.109C); **d.** *dutiful*, Bas.*mor*.24.2(3.586C; M.32. 1377C); **3.** of things; **a.** *right-minded* ὁ...χιλίαρχος ὁ δὴ μείζονα καὶ εὐγνωμονεστέραν τοῦ 'Ιουδαίων ἔθνους ἐνδειξάμενος τὴν εἰς αὐτὸν ὁμολογίαν Eus.*theoph*.4(p.16*.9; M.24.624A); **b.** *honest, candid* οὐ γὰρ προαιρέσεώς ἐστιν εὐ., ἀλλὰ τῆς τῶν πραγμάτων, ὡς ἂν εἴποι τις, λοιπὸν ἀνάγκης Chrys.*hom.36.3 in Mt*.(7.411D); *Ep.Dor*.(M.88. 1616C); **c.** *faithful* ἡ πρὸς τὸν ὄντως δεσπότην εὐ. δουλεία *Hom.Clem*. 17.12; **4.** neut. as subst. τὸ εὐ. *what is reasonable* or *right*, Ath. Presb.*libell*.(p.21.11; H.2.332E); comp. τὰ εὐγνωμονέστερα *what is more reasonable* or *sensible*, ‡Gr.Nyss.*hom.2 in Gen*.1:26(M.44. 285C).

εὐγονία, ἡ, *fruitfulness*; met., of BMV τὴν εὐ. τεκεῖν καὶ μεῖναι τὴν παρθενίαν Leo Mag.*ep.*35.3(p.42.3; M.*PL*.54.808B).

εὐγράμματος, s.v.l., *highly literate*, Pall.*h.Laus.*37(p.109.5, v.l. ἀγράμματος; M.34.1180D).

***εὔγραφος**, *well-marked, beautifully marked*; of marble, Paul. Sil.*Soph.*605(M.86.2142B); id.*ambo*.97(M.86.2255B).

***εὐγρήγορος**, *wakeful*, Eus.Al.*serm.*8(M.86.361B).

[*]**εὐδαιμον-άω**, = εὐδαιμονέω, *be truly happy* ἡ ∼ῶσα τάξις *Pers.*(p.15.10; ∼οῦσα M.10.104C).

***εὐδαπανητός**, *easily consumed*, ‡Chrys.*hom.in Ps.38*:7(5.567B); Andr.Cr.*or.*21(M.97.1269A); neut. as subst., ‡Chrys.*virg.parab.*1 (8.45C).

εὐδήλως, *very plainly*, Gr.Nyss.*hom.5 in Eccl.*(M.44.689C); ‡Hipp.Th.*fr.*14(p.43.12); εὐδηλότερον f.l. in Meth.*res.*2.23(M.18. 288B for ἐνδηλότερον p.378.10).

εὐδιάβατος, *easily accessible*, fig., ref. man τὸ παντὸς πάθους εὐ. καταγώγιον ‡Chrys.*hom.in Ps.38*:7(5.567C).

εὐδιάγνωστος, **1.** *easily recognized*, Const.*or.s.c.*7(p.161.30; M.20. 1252A); Thdr.Stud.*antirr.*2.1(M.99.353B); **2.** *easily distinguished*, Melet.*nat.hom.*2(M.64.1164A); **3.** of a person, *well-known*, ‡Proc.G. *Pr.*26:26(M.87.1489A).

***εὐδιάγραπτος**, *well-delineated*, Andr.Cr.*or.*14(M.97.1092D); *ib.* 21(1269A).

***εὐδιαδότως**, *by penetrating easily*, Dion.Ar.*c.h.*13.1(M.3.301A).

εὐδιάζω, intrans. in act., *be calm*, Gr.Nyss.*hom.3 in Cant.*(M.44. 816D).

εὐδιάθετος, *well-disposed*, hence *attractive* ἡδὺς...τὴν ὄψιν καὶ εὐ. Gr.Nyss.*hom.9 in Cant.*(M.44.969C); id.*laud.Bas.*26(M.46.817A); neut. as subst., *benevolence*, Thdr.Stud.*epp.*2.189(M.99.1577B).

εὐδιάθρυπτος, **1.** *easily crushed* or *destroyed*; of wrong arguments, Cyr.*Is.*5.4(2.852C); superl., id.*Jo.*6.1(4.641E); hence **a.** *contrite, humble*, id.*Am.*34(3.288E); id.*Is.*5.5(2.858D); **b.** *pliable, easily swayed* εὐ. εἰς τὰ χείρω τὴν διάνοιαν ἔχοντες id.*Juln.*9(6^2.308B); τὸν νοῦν εἰς ἔλεον εὐ. ἔχει id.ap.Jo.D.*parall.*(M.95.1317A) cf.Cyr.*Jo.*12 (4.1064B) where this phrase is omitted; neut. as subst., id.*hom. pasch.*22(5^2.274A); **c.** *easily broken*, neut. as subst. ὀπτωμένη γὰρ ἡ πλίνθος...οὐκ ἂν ἔχοι τὸ εὐ. id.*ador.*12(1.441A); hence *tender* τὸ οἱονεὶ τρύφερόν τε καὶ εὐ. τῆς τῶν ἁγίων καρδίας *ib.*; **2.** *well thrashed out* τὴν εὐανθῆ τε καὶ εὐ. τῶν εὐαγγελικῶν παιδευμάτων...τροφήν id. *Is.*2.1(2.200E).

***εὐδιαιρέτως**, **1.** *articulately*, Marc.Diac.*v.Porph.*68; **2.** *by dividing well*, Geo.Pis.*hex.*1616(M.92.1560A).

***εὐδιάκλαστος**, *easy to break, unsound, rotten*, always joined with σαθρός, Cyr.*Soph.*8(3.588A); γνωμῆς id.*ador.*6(1.215A); id.*Is.*3.4 (2.478B).

εὐδιακόμιστος, *easy to carry through* τὰ...οἰστὰ καὶ εὐ. Cyr.ap. *cat.Ac.*15:28(p.253.16).

εὐδιάκονος, *ready to serve*; of a bishop, *Const.App.*2.4.1.

εὐδιακόσμητος, *well-arranged*, Cyr.*Mich.*54(3.447A; Aubert om.).

εὐδιάκριτος, **1.** *easy to explain* or *understand*, Dion.Ar.*e.h.*5.1. 2(M.3.501B); hence *obvious* ὑπομονῆς Thdr.Stud.*catech.parv.*12 (p.30); **2.** *easily distinguishing, exact* τῆς τῶν χρόνων εὐ. διαστολῆς Cyr.*Mich.*44(3.433C).

***εὐδιακρίτως**, *with exactitude*, Dion.Ar.*d.n.*2.4(M.3.640D).

εὐδιάλεκτος, *eloquent*, Ephr.1.116E; Jo.Disc.*v.Epiph.*13(M.41. 37C).

εὐδιάλλακτος, *easily reconcilable*; of God, *V.Aberc.*13(p.12.7); Ephr.3.533B; of brute creation as given to Adam, *Apoc.Sedr.*6 (p.131.35).

***εὐδιάμονος**, *enduring*, ‡Ath.*corp.*(M.28.1432B) = *Schol.* in Anast.S.*hod.*2(M.89.88B).

***εὐδιάρπαστος**, **1.** *easily seized*, Bas.*hex.*5.3(1.42E; M.29.101A); †Bas.*Is.*215(1.540E; M.30.492A); Sever.*sigill.*4(M.63.538); **2.** *easily plundered, made spoil of*, †Bas.*Is.*122(463E; M.30.316A); met., of doctrine, *easily subverted*, *ib.*92(444A; M.269C).

***εὐδιαρ(ρ)ίπιστος**, *easily blown away*; lit., Cyr.*Is.*2.3(2.271A); id. *Os.*147(3.181B); met. πάντα τὰ ἀνθρώπινα μικρὰ καὶ εὐ. id.*Is.*3.5(2. 515C); id.*ador.*1(1.27B); *ib.*6(1.204B).

***εὐδιαστόλως**, *accurately*, Cyr.*Jo.*5.4(4.505D); *ib.*9(762B).

***εὐδιάτμητος**, *easily cut apart*, Cyr.*Is.*5.4(2.830E).

εὐδιαφόρητος, **1.** *easily digested*; comp., Clem.*paed.*1.6(p.116.25; M.8.304A); **2.** *easily carried away*; met., neut. as subst. τῶν ἁμαρτωλῶν...τὸ εὐ. *ib.*1.10(p.144.15; 360B).

***εὐδιάφυκτος**, *easily avoided*, Cyr.*Is.*5.2(2.783C).

εὐδιάχυτος, **1.** *easily diffused*, Gr.Nyss.*Eun.*3(2 p.15.5; M.45. 580A); τὸ...τῆς τρυφῆς...εὐ. Germ.CP *or.*2(M.98.289A); **2.** *quivering*; of colour of a precious stone, Cyr.*ador.*7(1.219E); **3.** *easily dissolved*, met., ‡Ath.*serm.Ant.*4(M.28.593D); ψυχαὶ...ἡδοναῖς εὐ. Jo.D. *hom.*4.30(M.96.632D).

εὐδίνητος, **1.** *well-rounded*, Nonn.*par.Jo.*20:8(M.43.909A); Paul. Sil.*Soph.*482(M.86.2138A); *ib.*864(2152A); met., *uttering well-rounded words*, Jo.D.*carm.pent.*9(p.217; M.96.940A); **2.** *easily turning*, Paul. Sil.*ambo.*120(M.86.2256B).

εὐδινός, late form of εὐδιεινός, *calm, fine, clear*; of weather, etc., Bas.*hex.*9.3(1.83B; M.29.169A); Chrys.*hom.53.3 in Mt.*(7.540E); id. *hom.34.3 in Heb.*(12.318B).

εὐδιόρθωτος, **1.** *well-corrected*, Epiph.*mens.*6(M.43.245D); **2.** *easily remedied* τὰ ἀπελπισμένα τοῖς ἀνθρώποις παρ' αὐτῷ [sc. Χριστῷ] εὐ. τυγχάνει Marc.Diac.*v.Porph.*7; neut. as subst., Chrys.*comm.in Gal.* 5:10(10.715C).

εὐδοκ-έω, **A.** *be well pleased, be content* with; **1.** in gen. εὐδοκήσας ὁ πατὴρ ἔπεμψε τὸν ἑαυτοῦ υἱόν Ath.*Ar.*3.31(M.26.388D); Mac.Aeg. *hom.*16.7(M.34.617D); εὐδοκήσας...ὁ ἄνθρωπος προσεκύνησε τῷ κυρίῳ Thdt.*qu.74 in Gen.*(1.88); Evagr.*h.e.*4.29(p.179.13; M.86.2756C); exeg. Ps.84:2 εὐ. ἐστι τὸ ἀγαθόν τι θελῆσαι Thdt.ad loc.(1.1202); exeg. Rom.15:26 ηὐδόκησαν γὰρ Μακεδονία καὶ Ἀχαΐα, τουτέστιν, ἐδοκίμασαν, ἐπεθύμησαν Chrys.*hom.30.1 in Rom.*(9.738C); exeg. 2Cor.12:10 εὐδοκῶ, τουτέστι, χαίρω, εὐφραίνομαι, μεθ' εὐθυμίας δέχομαι τὰ προσπίπτοντα Thdt.ad loc.(3.350); pass., *be favoured, approved*, Gr.Naz.*or.*29.1(p.74.2; M.36.73B); Epiph.*exp.fid.*16(p.517. 6; M.42.813A); Thdt.*qu.33 in Dt.*(1.297D); **2.** theol.; **a.** ref. functions of Persons of Trin., Iren.*haer.*4.38.3(M.7.1108B) cit. s. δημιουργέω; τὸν μὲν ∼εῖν, τὸν δὲ συνεργεῖν, τὸ δὲ ἐμπνεῖν Gr.Naz. *or.*28.1(p.22.2; M.36.75D); ref. 1Cor.15:28 τοῦτο γὰρ ἡ ὑποταγὴ Χριστοῦ...ἡ τοῦ πατρικοῦ θελήματος πλήρωσις, ὑποτάσσει δὲ καὶ υἱὸς πατρί, καὶ υἱῷ πατήρ· ὁ μὲν ἐνεργῶν, ὁ δὲ ∼ῶν *ib.*30.5(p.114.17; 109A); **b.** exeg. Mt.3:17,17:5 εὐδόκησεν ὁ πατὴρ ἐν τῷ υἱῷ· ἐὰν μὴ καὶ σὺ εὐδοκήσῃς, ζωὴν οὐκ ἔχεις Cyr.H.*catech.*10.2; ref. theol. implications ἐν τούτῳ, φησίν, εὐδόκησα διὰ τῆς ἐνανθρωπήσεως αὐτοῦ τὴν σωτηρίαν ὑμῖν πορισθῆναι, κἂν περὶ τῆς θεότητος δὲ ἐκλάβῃ τις τό, εὐδόκησα, τὸ σόφισμα αὐτῶν ἀκυροῦται Didym.*Trin.*1.9(M.39.289A); τί δέ ἐστιν, ἐν ᾧ εὐδόκησα; ὡσανεὶ ἔλεγεν, ἐν ᾧ ἀναπαύομαι, ᾧ ἀρέσκομαι· διὰ τὸ κατὰ πάντα ἐξισῶσθαι πρὸς αὐτὸν μετὰ ἀκριβείας, καὶ βούλημα ἓν ἐν αὐτῷ εἶναι καὶ τῷ πατρί, καὶ μένοντα υἱὸν διὰ πάντα ἓν εἶναι πρὸς τὸν γεγεννηκότα Chrys.*hom.56.3 in Mt.*(7.570C); **3.** Christol., ref. ἕνωσις κατ' εὐδοκίαν: ὁ τεχθεὶς ἐκ τῆς παρθένου...οὐ διεκρίθη τοῦ λόγου, ταυτότητι γνώμης αὐτῷ συνημμένος, καθ' ἣν εὐδοκήσας ἥνωσεν αὐτὸν ἑαυτῷ Thdr.Mops.*fr.inc.*(p.311.28)ap.CLater.*act.*5(H.3.896B); ref. wills of Christ ∼ῶν μὲν ὡς θεός, ὑπακούων δὲ ὡς ἄνθρωπος Max.*Pyrr.* (M.91.301D).

B. *be well pleasing*; abs., Hipp.*haer.*9.12(p.250.13; M.16.3386D).

***εὐδοκητής**, ὁ, *approver*; of God, Epiph.*exp.fid.*16(p.517.7; M.42. 843A).

εὐδοκητός, *approved*, of Christ τῷ υἱῷ...ἀγαπητῷ καὶ εὐ. Or. *comm. in Mt.*12.42(p.165.32; M.13.1081A); of Valentinian Saviour εὐ. καλεῖσθαι, ὅτι πᾶν τὸ πλήρωμα ηὐδόκησεν δι' αὐτοῦ δοξάσαι τὸν πατέρα Iren.*haer.*1.12.4 ap.Epiph.*haer.*35.1(M.41.628C).

εὐδοκία, ἡ, **A.** *good will, good pleasure* (towards), *favour*; **1.** of God; **a.** in gen. τὸ τῆς εὐ. ὄνομα οὐ τετριμμένον ἐν τῇ τῶν Ἑλλήνων συνηθείᾳ νομίζω ὄν, ὠνοματοποιῆσθαι δὲ ὑπὸ τῶν ἑρμηνευσάντων... ἡ εὐ. ἐμφαίνει τό, εὖ, καὶ τό, δοκεῖν· ὥστε μὴ ἂν λεχθῆναι ἐπὶ τῶν δοκούντων ἡμῖν οὐ καλῶς, ἀλλ' ἐπὶ μόνων τῶν ἐπαινετῶς δοκούντων Or.*comm.in Eph.*1:5(p.237.29); ἀληθῆ γὰρ εἶναι καὶ βεβαίαν τὴν εὐ. τοῦ κυρίου Dion.Al.*fr.*(p.60.6); εὐ. ἡ θεία γραφὴ καλεῖ τὸ ἀγαθὸν τοῦ θεοῦ θέλημα Thdt.*Ps.*5:13(1.639); φθάσας ἐνταῦθα...κατ' εὐ. τοῦ θεοῦ Gel.Cyz.*h.e.*1 proem.9(M.85.1193D); ἡ δὲ εἰς ψυχὴν πίστις ἐστὶν ἐξ εὐ. θεοῦ Leont.H.*Nest.*2.1(M.86.1531A); Euthal.Diac.*Ac.*(M.85. 657C); **b.** dist. from βούλησις, Or.*fr.*57 *in Lc.*(p.261) cit. s. βούλησις; **c.** dist. from συγχώρησις: πάντα τὰ γινόμενα διαιρεῖται εἰς δύο, εἰς τὴν εὐ. θεοῦ καὶ συγχώρησιν· ὅσα τοίνυν γίνεται κατὰ ἀρετὴν εἰς δόξαν θεοῦ, ταῦτα γίνεται εὐδοκίᾳ θεοῦ· ὅσα δ' αὖ πάλιν ἐπιζήμια...καὶ ἐκπτωτικά, ταῦτα γίνεται κατὰ θεοῦ συγχώρησιν Pall.*h.Laus.*47 (p.138.35; M.34.1201A); πάντα τὰ γενόμενα ἢ κατὰ συγχώρησιν θεοῦ γίνεται, ἢ κατ' εὐ. ... λιμός, σεισμός, ἀβροχία, νόσοι, πόλεμοι...οὐ γίνονται κατ' εὐ. θεοῦ, ἀλλὰ κατὰ συγχώρησιν Dor.*doct.*14.5(M.88. 1781C); τῆς δὲ προνοίας, τὰ μὲν κατ' εὐ. ἐστί, τὰ δὲ κατὰ συγχώρησιν. κατ' εὐ. μὲν ὅσα ἀναντιρρήτως εἰσὶν ἀγαθά Jo.D.*f.o.*2.29(M.94.965A); **d.** of Father towards Son, Bas.*jud.*7(2.221D; M.31.672B); in anti-Arian argument ὁ πατὴρ οὐκ εἶπεν, οὗτός ἐστιν...ὃν κατ' εὐδοκίαν ἔσχον υἱόν, ἀλλ' ἁπλῶς, ὁ υἱός μου, καὶ μᾶλλον, ἐν ᾧ ηὐδόκησα· δεικνὺς ἐκ τούτων ὅτι φύσει μὲν οὗτός ἐστιν υἱός, ἐν αὐτῷ δὲ τῶν ἐμοὶ δοκούντων ἡ βούλησις ἀπόκειται Ath.*Ar.*3.67(M.26.461B); τῇ μὲν οὐσίᾳ γέννημα τοῦ πατρός, τῇ δὲ οἰκονομίᾳ κατ' εὐδοκίαν τοῦ πατρὸς ἐποιήθη δι' ἡμᾶς ἄνθρωπος *ib.*2.11(169A); εἰ ἐπὶ τῷ ἤδη ὄντι υἱῷ ἔλεγεν, ἐν ᾧ ηὐδόκησα, οὐκ αἰτία ἡ εὐ. τῆς ὑπάρξεως εὑρίσκεται Didym.*Trin.*1.9(M.39.289A); διὰ τὴν τοιαύτην οἰκονομίαν τὴν εὐ. πατρὸς σημαίνων ὁ ἀπόστολος ἔφη ὅτι ὁ θεὸς ἤγειρεν αὐτὸν ἐκ νεκρῶν Epiph.*haer.*69.59(p.208.12; M.42.297C); ref. fulfilment by Son of Father's good pleasure τὰ δὲ ὡς πατρικῆς εὐ. διὰ τῆς αὐτοῦ ἐνεργείας πληρουμένης, καὶ οὐχ ὡς δι' ὀργάνου...ἀλλ' ὡς δι' οὐσιώδους καὶ ἐνυποστάτου αὐτοῦ λόγου καὶ σοφίας Jo.D.*f.o.*4.18(M.94.1181C); **e.** ref. Creation ὁ τοῦ θεοῦ υἱός... εὐ. θεοῦ γενόμενος τὰ κτίσματα ὑπάρξαι ἠβουλήθη Or.*fr.1 in Jo.* (p.485.7); τὰ μὲν γενητὰ εὐ. καὶ βουλήσει γέγονεν Ath.*Ar.*3.63(M.26. 457B); τῇ τοῦ πατρὸς εὐ. καὶ ὁ υἱὸς τὰ πάντα ἐποίησε Jo.V H.*icon.*4 (M.96.1353A); **f.** ref. Inc. μονογενὴς υἱός, κατὰ τὴν τοῦ πατρὸς εὐ. σαρκωθεὶς ὑπὲρ ἀνθρώπων Iren.*haer.*1.9.3(M.7.541B); *Symb.Ant.*(341) 1(p.249.3; M.26.721A); et freq.; Gnost. ἐξ εὐ. τῶν αἰώνων Ἰησοῦς προβάλλεται παράκλητος τῷ παρελθόντι αἰῶνι Clem.*exc.Thdot.*23 (p.114.20; M.9.669B); ὁ κατελθὼν εὐ. τοῦ ὅλου ἦν, ἐν αὐτῷ γὰρ πᾶν τὸ πλήρωμα ἦν σωματικῶς *ib.*31(p.117.4; 673C); **g.** ref. divine indwelling in man, Thdr.Mops.*fr.inc.*7(p.294.32; M.66.973A) cit. s. ἐνοίκησις; ἄπειρος μὲν γὰρ ὢν καὶ ἀπερίγραφος τὴν φύσιν πάρεστιν τοῖς πᾶσιν· τῇ δὲ εὐ. τῶν μὲν ἔστιν μακράν, τῶν δὲ ἐγγύς *ib.*(p.295.8; 973B, C); *ib.*(p.295.23; 973D); πανταχοῦ κατὰ τὴν οὐσίαν ἐστίν...κατὰ μέντοι τὴν εὐ., οὐκ ἐν ἅπασίν ἐστιν Thdt.*1Cor.*15:28(3.274); **2.** Christol.; **a.** in Antiochene doctrine, Thdr.Mops.*ep.Domn.* (p.339.3; M.66.1013A) cit. s. ἕνωσις; ὁ σωτὴρ ἔδειξεν μίαν εἶναι τὴν θέλησιν...προαγομένην οὐ λόγῳ φύσεως ἀλλ' εὐδοκίας, καθ' ἣν ἡνώθη τῷ θεῷ λόγῳ ὁ...ἐκ σπέρματος Δαβὶδ γενόμενος ἄνθρωπος id.*fr.mir.* (p.339.14; M.66.1003D); οὔτε θεὸν ἀληθινὸν αὐτὸν εἶναι λέγει [sc. Nestorius], ἀλλ' ὡς ἐν εὐ. τοῦ θεοῦ κεκλημένον οὕτως Cyr.*ep.*11a(p.171. 19; M.77.88A); *ib.*14(p.98.24; 5^{2}.44E); Nest.*fr.*B 6(p.220.4) cit. s. ἕνωσις; ὁ δὲ Νεστόριος ἄλλας ἐπενόει ἑνώσεις, κατὰ τὴν ἀξίαν...καὶ ὁμοτιμίαν, καὶ ταυτοβουλίαν, καὶ εὐ. Jo.D.*dialect.*65(M.94.664B); condemned σάρκα ἐμψυχωμένην ψυχῇ λογικῇ ἑνώσας ὁ λόγος ἑαυτῷ καθ' ὑπόστασιν...γέγονεν ἄνθρωπος, οὐ κατὰ θέλησιν μόνην ἢ εὐ. Cyr.*ep.*4 (p.27.1; 5^{2}.23B); οἱ τὴν ἕνωσιν μὴ κατ' οὐσίαν, ἀλλὰ κατ' ἐνέργειαν, ἢ εὐ., ἢ ἄλλην τινὰ τοιαύτην σχέσιν δογματίσαντες, κατ' οὐδὲν μὲν τῇ ἀληθείᾳ ἐγγίζουσι Leont.B.*Nest.et Eut.*1(M.86.1300B); κατ' εὐδοκίαν τὴν ἕνωσιν γεγενῆσθαι καθὼς Θεόδωρος...λέγει...ὁ τοιοῦτος ἀ. ἔ. Justn.*conf.anath.*4(p.90.33; M.86.1015B) ∞ CCP(553)*anath.*4(Hahn p.168); **b.** ref. problem of Christ's will κατ' εὐδοκίαν ἡ ἕνωσις βουλῆς καὶ γνώμης ταυτότητι κρατουμένη, ἵνα καὶ τὸ διάφορον τῶν φύσεων ἀσύγχυτον δείκνυνται, καὶ τὸ τῆς εὐ. μυστήριον μονάδι βουλήσεως Paul. Pers.*judic.fr.*(H.3.896D); **c.** of Christ in assuming manhood οὐκ εὐ. τοίνυν ὁ τρόπος τῆς ἑνώσεως, ἀλλ' ἡ φύσις αἰτία. τὸ μὲν γὰρ ἀναλαβεῖν σῶμα κατ' εὐδοκίαν εἴποι τις ἂν εὐλόγως γεγενῆσθαι· τὸ δὲ ἑνούμενον μὴ συγχυθῆναι, κατὰ τὴν οἰκείαν τοῦ θεοῦ φύσιν οὐ κατ' εὐ. γίνεται Nemes.*nat.hom.*3(M.40.608A); ὁ...λόγος ἥνωσεν ἑαυτῷ σῶμα ἐμψυχωμένον ψυχῇ νοερᾷ καὶ προῆλθεν ἄνθρωπος ἐκ γυναικός, οὐ μεταβολῇ φύσεως καθ' ἡμᾶς γεγονώς, ἀλλ' εὐ. μᾶλλον οἰκονομικῇ Cyr.*ep.*45 (p.153.4; 5^{2}.137A); **3.** exeg. Eph.1:5 κατὰ τὴν εὐ. ... τοῦ θελήματος αὐτοῦ, τουτέστιν διὰ τὸ σφοδρῶς θελῆσαι· ἡ ἐπιθυμία αὐτοῦ...αὐτὴ ἐστί· πανταχοῦ γὰρ εὐδοκία τὸ θέλημά ἐστι τὸ προηγούμενον Chrys. *hom.1.2 in Eph.*(11.5C); εἰ κατὰ τὸν νόμον ἡ θέλησις ἐνέργειά ἐστιν, τίς ἡ εὐ. ἡ ταύτης τῆς θελήσεως; οὐ γὰρ ἂν εἶπε, θέλησιν θελήματος Sever.*Eph.*1:5(p.305.22); εὐ. γὰρ τὴν ἐπ' εὐεργεσίᾳ βούλησιν ἔθος τῇ θείᾳ καλεῖν γραφῇ Thdt.*Eph.*1:5(3.403); exeg. Lc.2:14 τί ἐστιν εὐ.; καταλλαγή· οὐκέτι μεσότοιχόν ἐστιν ὁ οὐρανός Chrys.*hom.3.3 in Col.* (11.347B); λέγων οὖν, εὐ., τὸ ἑκούσιον αὐτῆς [sc. the soul] ἔδειξε καὶ τὴν πρὸς αὐτὸν νυμφίον εὐ. Ph.Carp.*Cant.*167(M.40.113C).

B. *object of good pleasure, delight* σώφρων γυνή...θεοῦ εὐ. *Hom. Clem.*13.21.

[*]**εὐδοκιάω**, metr. gr. for εὐδοκέω, †Apoll.*met.Ps.*2:7(M.33. 1316A; *Teub.* om., v. not.).

εὐδοκιμάζω, *choose*, Or.*adnot.in Gen.*7:4(M.17.13A).

εὐδοκίμησις, ἡ, *good repute, reputation, credit*, Eus.*p.e.*10.1 (461B; M.21.768B); Chrys.*hom.*5.2 *in 1Tim.*(11.577B); Cyr.*glaph. Gen.*6(1.191B).

*__εὐδοκίμητος__, *giving satisfaction*, *Orac.Sib.*3.824.

εὐδοξία, ἡ, **1.** *virtue, excellence*, Meth.*symp.*10.6(p.129.1; M.18. 204A); **2.** *glory* τοῦ μονογενοῦς Nest.*fr.*C 1(p.225.14)ap.Cyr.*Nest.*2.6 (p.43.3; 6^{1}.46A); **3.** *right opinion, right judgement*, Meth.*symp.*8.8 (p.90.6; M.18.149B); εὐ. τε καὶ ἑτεροδοξίαν Epiph.*haer.*1.1(p.169.3; M.41.173A).

*__εὐδούλευτος__, *being a good servant*, ‡Chrys.*Petr.et Paul.*(8.10C).

εὐδρανής, **1.** *powerful, vigorous*, Cyr.*apol.Thds.*(p.81.30; 6^{1}.249A); id.*glaph.Ex.*3(1.316B); id.*Ps.*37:20(M.69.968C); neut. as subst. τὸ τῆς διανοίας εὐ. id.*glaph.Ex.*3(332A); **2.** of persons, *sturdy, buxom* παρθένον id.*glaph.Gen.*3(1.90A).

εὐδρομέω, **1.** *run well* or *fast* εἰς μάχην μὴ εὐ. Eus.Al.*serm.*1 (M.86.321A) perh. read ἐνδρομήσῃς; Thdr.Stud.*catech.parv.*9(p.22); hence **2.** met.; **a.** *do well*, Thdr.Stud.*epp.*1.2(M.99.912D); **b.** *live honestly*, Gr.Naz.*carm.*1.2.2.367(M.37.607A); *ib.*1.2.9.102(675A); *ib.* 2.1.12.788(1223A); **c.** εὐ. τὴν γλῶτταν *be glib*, id.*or.*14.33(M.35. 901C).

εὐδρομία, ἡ, *honest living, righteous living*, Thdr.Stud.*catech. parv.*9(M.99.520C).

εὔδρομος, **1.** *running well*; hence **a.** *swift*, Clem.*paed.*1.5(p.98.30; M.8.268A); *Pet.Ar.*4(M.26.824A); superl., Cyr.*Ps.*17:34(M.69.824D); id.*ador.*4(1.503E); neut. as subst., Gr.Nyss.*hom.11 in Cant.*(M.44. 1001B); **b.** *effective*; of arguments, ‡Hipp.Th.*fr.*14(p.43.11); Jo.D. *volunt.*8(M.95.140B); Thdr.Stud.*iamb.*58(M.99.1796D); neut. as subst., Gr.Naz.*carm.*1.1.6.83(M.87.436A); **2.** *easy to attack*; of persons, Cyr.*Is.*5.5(2.853C).

*__εὐδωρία__, ἡ, *liberality*, Const.*or.s.c.*8.1(p.162.13; M.20.1252C).

εὔδωρος, *generous*, *Orac.Sib.*8.497; Paul.Sil.*Soph.*920(M.86. 2154A).

εὐείδεια, ἡ, *good looks, beauty of form*, Cyr.*Soph.*24(3.605C); Melet.*nat.hom.*4(M.64.1181A).

εὐειδής, *well-shaped, comely*, of physical beauty; of things ὄρη ...εὐ. *Apoc.En.*24.2(p.54.20); ἄγαλμα ‡Eust.*Laz.*4(p.29.9); comp. καρποί Herm.*sim.*9.28.3; hence *beautiful*; of language, Gr.Thaum. *pan.Or.*1(p.2.11; M.10.1052B); *ib.*2(p.3.22; 1053B); of persons in respect of character, *A.Thom.*A 44(p.161.14); *ib.*157(p.267.2).

εὔεικτος, **1.** *pliant, tractable*, Dion.Ar.*c.h.*13.3(3.301B); neut. as subst., Gr.Nyss.*hex.*25(M.44.88A,B); id.*hom.opif.*30.8(M.44.244A); **2.** *yielding, complaisant, obedient* τὴν ψυχὴν...ὡς κηρὸν εὐ. Bas.*reg. fus.*15.4(2.357B; M.31.956A); καρδίαν Cyr.*Is.*4.2(2.610D); υἱοί Nil. *epp.*4.28(M.79.564A); προαίρεσιν Max.*qu.Thal.*15(M.90.297B); neut. as subst., Thdt.*h.e.*5.13.1(3.1041); τὸ εὐ. τῆς ἀκοῆς CChalc.*act.*2 (*ACO* 2.1.2 p.82.38; H.2.308C); **3.** *easily turned* λόγον εὐ. εἰς σαφήνειαν Max.*opusc.*(M.91.112A).

εὐείκτως, *obediently*, Max.*ep.*21(M.91.604C).

*__εὐειμονέω__, *be well dressed*, Cyr.*hom.pasch.*5(5^{2}.45A).

εὐεκτικός, **1.** *of sound constitution*, *A.Paul.et Thecl.*3(p.237.8); **2.** *receptive* εὐεκτικὸν τῆς κατὰ νοῦν ἀντιληπτικῆς δυνάμεως Dion. Ar.*e.h.*4.3.5(M.3.480B).

εὔελπις, *hopeful*; as subst. εὔ., ἡ, *good hope*, Clem.*str.*2.9(p.134. 17; M.8.976C); ἀσφαλεῖς αἱ...τῶν ἀνθρώπων εὐ. Procl.CP *hom.*1.4(M. 65.837A).

*__εὐελπίστως__, *hopefully*, Jo.Clim.*scal.*5(M.88.765D).

εὐεμπτωσία, ἡ, *proclivity*, Clem.*str.*7.16(p.72.23; M.9.541B); id. *paed.*1.2(p.92.2; M.8.253A); Isid.Pel.*epp.*1.158(M.78.433D).

εὐέντευκτος, *approachable*, superl. Χριστὸν...τὸν εὐεντευκτότατον Or.*comm.in Mt.*16.8(p.497.8; M.13.1396C).

εὐεξέλεγκτος, *easy to refute*, Athenag.*res.*2(p.50.4; M.6.977B); neut. as subst., Clem.*paed.*3.11(p.271.1; M.8.636B).

εὐεξία, ἡ, *good health, good condition*; of Church as body of Christ, Chrys.*sac.*4.2(p.108.23; 1.407C); met., of God διὰ τὴν ὑπερπλήρη...τῆς εὐωχίας, ἢ κυριώτερον εἰπεῖν, εὐ. τοῦ θεοῦ παντελῆ καὶ ἄφατον ἀμετρίαν Dion.Ar.*ep.*9.6(M.3.1112C).

εὐεπήκοος, *listening readily, responsive*, Andr.Cr.*or.*16(M.97. 1160B).

*__εὐεπηκόως__, *responsively, obediently*, Thdr.Stud.*iamb.*5(M.99. 1781B).

εὐεπής, *eloquent* λόγον...εὐ. Gr.Thaum.*pan.Or.*1(p.2.13; M.10. 1052B); Cyr.*glaph.Ex.*2(1.305D).

εὐεπίβατος, **1.** *easy to ascend* εὐ. τῷ λόγῳ...τὴν ἄνοδον Gr.Nyss. *beat.*2(M.44.1208D); **2.** *easy to traverse* ἔρημος...εὐ. Meth.*symp.*8.11 (p.93.15; M.18.153D); *rightly traversed* εἴσοδον...τοῖς ἱερεῦσιν οὖσαν εὐ. ‡Bas.*h.myst.*8(p.259.26); **3.** *easy to attack, easily attacked* πύργον Gr.Nyss.*hom.7 in Cant.*(M.44.933D); τοῖχος Chrys.*hom.7.4 in Phil.*(11.239); met. τὸ ἐμὸν πρόσωπον εὐ. ταῖς συκοφαντίαις εὑρών †Bas.*calumn.Trin.*3(2.610D; M.31.1492B); †Bas.*Is.*42(1.412E; M.30.200A) = Olymp.*Job* 22:7(M.93.244C); **4.** *easily attainable* τὴν ἐνάρετον πολιτείαν...ποιήσας...εὐ. ‡Cyr.*Trin.*28(6^{3}.34A; M.77.1173A); **5.** *easily approachable* ἦθος Evagr.*h.e.*4.40(p.190.33; M.86.2784B); neut. as subst., Max.*ambig.*(M.91.1261B).

εὐεπιβούλευτος, *very vulnerable* πένητα...εὐ. †Bas.*Is.*122(1.463E; M.30.316A); ‡Proc.G.*Pr.*25:28(M.87.1480B).

εὐεπίστροφος, *easily converted*, Isid.Pel.*epp.*1.121(M.78.264B).

*__εὐεπιτήδειος__, *suitable*; comp., Chrys.*hom.12.3 in Phil.*(11. 294D).

εὐεπιφορία, ἡ, *superabundance*, Clem.*str*.2.23(p.193.19; M.8.1096C).

εὐεπιχείρητος ([*]-ρωτος), **1.** *easily attacked* or *harmed*, †Bas.*Is*.4.138(1.476D; M.30.344C); *ib*.4.142(479A; M.349B); of the pupil of an eye, ‡Gr.Nyss.*or.2 in Gen.1*:26(M.44.296C); ‡Proc.G.*Pr*.25:28(M.87.1480B); fig. λέξεως Bas.*Spir*.59(3.49D; M.32.176B); of persons ἵνα ...εὐ. ᾖς τοῖς θηρίοις id.*hom*.13.2(2.114E; M.31.425C); οἱ χοιρώδεις... εὐ. ταῖς τῶν δαιμόνων ἐνεργείαις εἰσί Chrys.*hom.28.4 in Mt*.(7.338C); id.*hom.13.3 in Rom*.(9.330B); -ρωτος, Thdt.*qu.36 in 3 Reg*.(1.481); **2.** *easily attempted*, hence neut. as subst., *suitability* τὸ εὐ. τοῦ καιροῦ Socr.*h.e*.4.21.2(M.67.508A).

***εὐεπίχειρος**, ? *very rewarding*, *Hymn*.(*AS* 1 p.547).

[*]**εὐεπιχείρωτος**, v. εὐεπιχείρητος.

***εὐέργαστος**, *easily worked*, Meth.*symp*.2.5(p.22.5; M.18.56B); met., of persons εὐ. πρὸς ἀγαθωσύνην Clem.*paed*.1.5(p.101.17; M.8.272B).

εὐεργεσία, ἡ, *benefit*, *advantage*; **1.** given by God to man ὁρᾶτε... μὴ αἱ εὐ. αὐτοῦ αἱ πολλαὶ γένωνται εἰς.κρίμα ἡμῖν *1Clem*.21.1; *Diogn*.8.11; οὐδὲ μὴν ἤρξατό ποτε ἡ εὐ. αὐτοῦ, ἀλλ' οὐδὲ περιορίζεται τόποις ἢ ἀνθρώποις τισίν Clem.*str*.6.7(p.463.32; M.9.285B); partic. of existence, *ib*.6.17(p.510.18; 384B); of baptism, Or.*Jo*.20.12(p.341.33; M.14.600A); of Inc., Ath.*Ar*.1.64(M.26.145C); as evidence of the divine, Gr.Nyss.*or.catech*.15(p.63.4; M.45.48A); **2.** given by man to man as each has received from God, Iren.*haer*.2.32.4(M.7.829A); such εὐ. returning to God, Clem.*str*.7.8(p.39.4; M.9.473C); **3.** of Christ τὴν παντὸς τοῦ κοσμοῦ εὐ. ἐκ Μαρίας ‡Ath.*serm.fid*.21(p.18; M.26.1273C).

εὐεργετ-έω, *do good to*, *benefit*; **1.** of God, *1Clem*.20.11; τῆς αὐτῆς εἶναι δυνάμεως...καὶ κρίνειν καὶ εὐ. Clem.*paed*.1.9(p.141.16; M.8.353C); οὐ γὰρ ἡμῶν εὕρεμα τὸ εὐ., ἀλλὰ τοῦ θεοῦ Ath.*Ar*.3.19(M.26.364A); *Const.App*.5.7.23; **2.** Christol. εἰ...φατε, ὅτι τίς...χρεία ἦν συντεθῆναι τὸν μηδὲν ~ηθέντα θεὸν τῇ εὐεργετηθείσῃ φύσει...ἐροῦμεν... ὡς ἡ τῶν ~ουμένων θέωσις...μᾶλλον δοξάζεταί τε καὶ ἀγαπᾶται παρὰ πάντων ὁ συντεθεὶς ἡμῖν δι' ἡμᾶς θεὸς ἡμῶν Leont.H.*Nest*.1.18(M.86.1468D); Θεόδωρος...ἄλλον εἶναι λέγων τὸν...λόγον, καὶ ἄλλον Ἰησοῦν τὸν Χριστόν· καὶ τὸν μὲν ~οῦντα, τὸν δὲ ~ούμενον Leont.B.*Nest.et Eut*.3(M.86.1385C); **3.** Basilidean, v. υἱότης; **4.** of man τῷ γὰρ ὄντι εἰκὼν τοῦ θεοῦ ἄνθρωπος ~ῶν, ἐν ᾧ καὶ αὐτὸς ~εῖται Clem.*str*.2.19(p.169.2; M.8.1045B); χρὴ...μιμητὴν εἶναι τοῦ θεοῦ, ~οῦντα δικαίους καὶ ἀδίκους *Hom.Clem*.12.26.

εὐεργέτης, ὁ, *benefactor*; of God, *1Clem*.59.3; Hipp.*haer*.1 proem.(p.3.7; M.16.3020C); Meth.*creat*.3(p.495.33; M.18.336A); Serap.*euch*.5.11; of Christ, Or.*Cels*.5.55(p.59.3; M.11.1269A); Thdt.*Is*.65:4(p.252.21; 2.394); *Lit.Jac*.(p.180.16); of his divine nature opp. human, Leont.B.*Nest.et Eut*.3(M.86.1385C); fig., of Devil ὁ δὲ τὴν ἀδικίαν γεωργῶν παρὰ τοῦ εὐ. τῆς ἀδικίας σιτίζεται Gr.Nyss.*or.dom*.4(p.86.24; M.44.1173C).

εὐεργετητικός, *tending to do good*; neut. as subst., Clem.*str*.4.22(p.309.17; M.8.1348B).

εὐεργετικός, *beneficent*; of God, *1Clem*.23.1; εὐ. ... μόνον εἶναι τὸν μόνον θεόν Clem.*str*.7.4(p.16.13; M.9.428B); Isid.Pel.*epp*.4.47(M.78.1097C); Max.*ambig*.(M.91.1189A); Arian εὐ. φιλοτιμίᾳ ἐκτίσθη ὁ υἱός Ast.Soph.*fr*.5 ap.Ath.*syn*.19(p.246.29; M.26.716B); superl. εὐεργετικωτάτη ἡ υἱοῦ φύσις Clem.*str*.7.2(p.5.21; 408B); *ib*.7.1(p.4.8; 404C).

εὐεργετικῶς, *beneficently*, Isid.Pel.*epp*.1.112(M.78.257B); *Ep*.ap.*Chron.Pasch*.p.402(M.92.1025C).

εὐεργέτις, ἡ, *benefactress* Δημήτηρ Tat.*orat*.9(p.10.13; M.6.825C); of providence, Clem.*str*.1.27(p.107.23; M.8.920C); *Hom.Clem*.12.25; *ib*.13.10; of BMV τὴν εὐ. τοῦ κόσμου Jo.Thess.*dorm.BMV* A 1(p.377.18).

εὐεργής, **1.** *efficient*, Clem.*paed*.3.11(p.270.5; M.8.633A); **2.** *doing good*; of persons, id.*str*.1.7(p.25.9; εὐεργῶς M.8.733A).

εὐεργός, **1.** *working efficiently*; of persons, Clem.*str*.1.1(p.7.30; M.8.696B); neut. as subst. τὸ εὐ. τῆς ὕλης id.*paed*.2.3(p.179.12; M.8.436A); *suitable* ἔργων *ib*.2.10(p.215.9; 512B); *capable* ἵνα εὐ. γένηται [sc. ἡ ψυχή] πρὸς τὴν τῆς γνώσεως παραδοχήν id.*str*.7.12(p.51.16; M.9.500A); **2.** *well-wrought*; of firmament, Dion.Al.ap.Eus.*p.e*.14.26(780C; M.21.1284B).

***εὐερμήνευτος**, *easily interpreted*, ‡Jo.D.*Const*.7(M.95.324C).

***εὐερνέω**, *have abundant shoots*, ‡Nil.*perist*.1.4(M.79.813D).

εὐερνής, *rich in plants*; superl., Cyr.*ador*.8(1.285C); id.*glaph.Gen*.1(1.14E).

***εὐζήλωτος**, *very emulous*, CLater.*act*.4(H.3.845A); Thdr.Stud.*catech.parv*.13(p.32); neut. as subst., *cat.Jo*.1:49(p.195.7); Martin.ap.CLater.*act*.2(737A); Thdr.Stud.*epp*.2.192(M.99.1584A); as adv., Cyr.S.*v.Sab*.35(p.120.17).

***εὐζηλώτως**, *with great enthusiasm*, CLater.*act*.2(H.3.760A); c. ἔχω, *ib*.(728A).

[*]**εὐζυγής**, *happily married*, Gr.Naz.*carm*.2.2(epitaph.)67.8(M.38.45A).

εὐζωέω, *live well*, Thdr.Stud.*epp*.1.7(M.99.932D).

εὐζωΐα, ἡ, *well-being*, physical; Clem.*str*.4.4(p.256.29; M.8.1232B); in gen., id.*paed*.1.12(p.149.11; M.8.368C); Eus.*l.C*.13(p.237.15); Cyr.*ep*.55(p.49.18; 5^2.174E); in garden of Eden., Epiph.*haer*.52.2(p.313.20; M.41.957B); Isid.Pel.*epp*.1.282(M.78.348C).

εὔζωνος, **1.** *active*, hence *unencumbered*; of a bachelor, Clem.*str*.3.10(p.226.34; M.8.1169B); ἡμῖν...πρὸς ἀλήθειαν ὁδοιποροῦσιν εὐ. id.*paed*.3.7(p.258.28; M.8.609A); Or.*hom.3.1 in Jos*.(p.300.27; M.87.997A); κούφους αὐτοὺς καὶ εὐ. ἡ νηστεία παρασκευάζει Bas.*hom*.2.2(2.11E; M.31.188B); of things, Clem.*paed*.1.12(p.149.10; 368C); *ib*.3.3(p.251.10; 592A); **2.** *swift*, *speedy*, *ib*.2.1(p.158.5; 388B); Chrys.*hom.1.3 in Jo*.(8.5E); comp., Clem.*paed*.3.3(p.250.27; 589B).

εὔζωος, *vital*, *of life*, †Apoll.*met.Ps*.35:10(M.33.1360C).

εὔζωστος, = εὔζωνος, *girt up* for exercise, *active*, ‡Nil.*narr*.3(M.79.621B).

εὐηγορία, ἡ, *noble language*, Cyr.*Juln*.6(6^2.210C).

εὐηκοΐα, ἡ, *ready obedience*, Clem.*paed*.1.11(p.147.20; M.8.365B); Cyr.*glaph.Gen*.3(1.92A); Gr.Ant.*exerc*.(p.230.7; M.88.1885A).

εὐήκοος, **1.** *hearing willingly*, *obedient*, ‡Meth.*palm*.1(M.18.384A); *Const.App*.3.19.7; Thdr.Stud.*catech.parv*.12(p.30); neut. as subst., Cyr.*glaph.Gen*.3(1.92A); id.*Ps*.44:11(M.69.1041D); Thdr.Stud.*epp*.1.49(M.99.1084D); **2.** *inclined to give ear*; of emperor, Isid.Pel.*epp*.1.275(M.78.345A); Thdr.Stud.*epp*.1.23(M.99.981C); of Christ, *Lit.Jac*.(p.180.4); **3.** *readily heard*, i.e. by God in prayer, Soz.*h.e*.3.14.19(M.67.1076A); neut. as subst., ‡Meth.*Sym.et Ann*.7(M.18.364C).

εὐηκόως, *obediently*, Thdr.Stud.*epp*.2.109(M.99.1369B).

εὐήλατος, **1.** *easily managed*, Cyr.*Chr.un*.(5^1.760B); **2.** *easy to pass over* λείαν καὶ εὐ. πᾶσαν ἡμῖν ὁδὸν ἀπέφηνεν ὁ σωτήρ id.*Is*.4.4(2.671D); *ib*.4.5(700D).

εὐήροτος, *well-tilled*, Cyr.*Os*.31(3.56E).

***εὐήφωνος**, s.v.l., *eloquent*, ‡Jo.D.*ep.Thphl*.3(M.95.349C).

εὐηχία, ἡ, *melody*, Cyr.*Am*.54(3.308A).

εὐήχως, *melodiously*, Meth.*symp*.3.7(p.34.25; M.18.72B); †Bas.*Is*.274(1.587E; M.30.600C).

εὐθαρσέω, *be of good courage*, Clem.*str*.4.4(p.254.27; M.8.1228B); id.*fr*.44(p.223.8).

εὐθαρσία, ἡ, *good courage*, Cyr.*Jo*.3.4(4.291D).

[*]**εὔθαρσος**, = εὐθαρσής, *of good courage*, Thdr.Stud.*epp*.2.154(M.99.1481B); neut. as subst., *ib*.2.27(1193D).

εὐθαρσῶς, *boldly*, *courageously*, Clem.*str*.7.11(p.46.18; M.9.489A) al.; Meth.*res*.2.4(p.337.4); Eus.*p.e*.12.10(583A; M.21.968C).

***εὐθειάζω**, ? *equip well* ῥισὶ τῶν ὀσφραντῶν ἀντιλαμβάνειν οὐκ ηὐθείασται Thdr.Stud.*epp*.2.33(M.99.1205D).

***εὐθεμελίωτος**, *well-founded* πίστις Epiph.*haer*.59.8(p.373.16; -ώτατος M.41.1029D).

εὐθετ-έω, *be skilled*, of persons οἱ εἰς τὴν οἰκοδομὴν ~οῦντες Meth.*Porph*.1(p.504.25; M.18.400C).

εὔθετος, *well-arranged*, *well-fitted*, hence *good*, *virtuous* ἐργάτης Clem.*str*.7.12(p.54.1; M.9.504A); of personal appearance, ? *compact*, Jo.Mal.*chron*.5 p.104(M.97.192B); *ib*.10 p.243(372C).

εὐθέτως, *suitably*, *aptly*, Didym.*Trin*.3.31(M.39.952B); Evagr.*h.e*.5.19(p.215.4; M.86.2832B).

εὐθημοσύνη, ἡ, *good disposition*, Max.*prol.Dion*.(M.4.17D); Thdr.Stud.*epp*.2.82(M.99.1324A).

εὐθηνός, *abundant*, ‡Chrys.*poenit*.1.4(9.769C).

[*]**εὐθηπορέω**, v. εὐθυπορέω.

εὐθήρατος, *easily catching*, Thdt.*Ps*.141:4(1.1547).

εὐθής, late form of εὐθύς, Gr.Nyss.*Eun*.1(1 p.195.28; M.45.441C); *Const.App*.6.11.1; Chrys.*hom.20.2 in Rom*.(9.658D).

εὔθικτος, *easily perceptible* ἴχνεσι Paul.Sil.*Soph*.1005(M.86.2157B).

***εὐθνητος**, *easily killed*, Anast.S.*hod*.2(M.89.88A).

εὔθραυστος, *easily injured*; met., *weak*, *Ep.Lugd*.ap.Eus.*h.e*.5.1.25(M.20.417B); Jo.D.*hom*.4.30(M.96.632D); Areth.ap.*cat.Apoc*.15:1(p.404.4; εὐθράστου cod.).

εὐθύβολος, *throwing straight*, Thdr.Stud.*epp*.1.49(M.99.1084C); of wind, *blowing in a direct course*, ‡Chrys.*hom*.6(13.213D); hence, met., *hitting the mark*, *accurate*, Eus.*p.e*.4.5(142A; M.21.248C); ‡Eust.*Laz*.13(p.37.7); Nil.ap.Proc.G.*Cant*.2:9(M.87.1500D).

εὐθυβόλως, **1.** *in a direct course*, ‡Ath.*occurs*.13(M.28.989C); hence **2.** met.; **a.** *appositely*, *to the point*, *skilfully*, Meth.*symp*.3.8(p.35.9; M.18.73A); Gr.Nyss.*Eun*.12(1 p.301.5; M.45.1012C); Euthal.

Diac.*Ac.*(M.85.660C); Nil.*praest.*6(M.79.1092B); superl., Or.*fr.57 in Jo.*(p.531.9); Meth.*symp.*9.4(p.118.23; 185C); **b.** *correctly, wisely,* Bas.*hom.*12.9(2.105C; M.31.404D); †Bas.*Is.*proem.1(2.378C; M.30.120B); Evagr.*h.e.*4.40(p.191.3; M.86.2784B); Thdr.Stud.*epp.*1.23 (M.99.981A); c. ἔχω, Bas.Sel.*v.Thecl.*2 proem.(M.85.564A).

***εὐθύβουλος**, *upright in counsel,* Thdr.Stud.*or.*11.22(M.99.824C).

εὐθυγενής, **1.** *first-born,* Thdt.*qu.31 in Lev.*(1.209); **2.** *growing straight* ὄρπηκας Gr.Nyss.*v.Gr.Thaum.*(M.46.900B); perh. f.l. for εὐθυτενής, cf. s.v.; **3.** *recently born,* Thdt.*qu.28 in Gen.*(1.42, conj. for εὐγενεῖς); id.*qu.38 in Lev.*(1.216) cit. s. ἀντιταλαντεύω; ‡Ath.*qu. script.*58(M.28.736D).

***εὐθυγεννής**, *newly-born,* Philox.*ep.*33(p.181).

εὐθυδίκη, ἡ, v. ἰθυδίκη.

εὐθυδρομέω, *run a straight course;* of persons, *go directly,* Cyr. *ep.*37(p.154.35; 5^2.153B); met., Meth.*res.*2.25(p.381.13; M.18.329A); ‡Nil.*perist.*4.6(M.79.829D); of descent, Thdr.Stud.*nativ.BMV* 5(M. 96.685A).

***εὐθυδρόμως**, *going direct,* Mac.Aeg.*hom.*44.6(M.34.784A).

***εὐθυέλεγκτος**, *easily refuted,* Epiph.*haer.*26.12(p.291.14; M.41. 352A); *ib.*43.2(p.188.16; 820B); of persons, *ib.*29.9(p.331.25; 404C).

***εὐθυμοποιέω**, *make of good cheer,* Bas.*hom.in Ps.*33(1.155C; M. 29.380C); Diod.*Ps.*67:6(M.33.1602C).

***εὐθυμοσύνη**, ἡ, *directness, uprightness,* Thdr.Heracl.*Is.*45:26(M. 18.1344A); Dion.Ar.*d.n.*8.5(M.3.892C); εὐ. φησὶ τὰς εὖ ἐχούσας θέσεις καὶ τάξεις εὐθέτους καὶ εὐσχήμους δημιουργίας Max.*schol.d.n.* 8.5(M.4.360A).

εὔθυνα, εὐθύνη, ἡ, usu. plur.; **1.** *rendering of account, public examination,* ref. Judgement ἡ κτίσις...τὰς εὐ. τῶν πεπραγμένων ἀποδιδοῦσα Bas.*ep.*174(3.262A; M.32.649D); Chrys.*sac.*4.2(p.107.26; 1.407A); **2.** *showing of proof,* Antip.Bost.*Jo.Bapt.*7(M.85.1769B); **3.** *accusation,* Eus.*h.e.*3.10.8(M.20.244C); Chrys.*hom.13.2 in Ac.*(9. 105A); **4.** *punishment, Hom.Clem.*3.13; Thdt.*Ps.*50:2(1.933); *ib.* 105:3(1355); Jo.D.*hom.*1.6(M.96.556C); Thdr.Stud.*epp.*2.88(M.99. 1336A).

εὐθύνω, **1.** *refute,* Clem.*str.*5.13(p.383.5; M.9.128B); Or.*Jo.*20.9 (p.336.24; M.14.589C); *Const.App.*2.47.1; **2.** *convict,* Eus.*p.e.*10.2 (462B; M.21.769B); **3.** act. with pass. meaning, *be governed, T.Sal.* 19.1(M.122.1348B).

εὐθύπλοος, *sailing straight,* Gr.Naz.*carm.*2.1.11.203(M.37.1043A).

εὐθυπορέω ([*]εὐθηπ-), *go straight forward,* met. πρὸς θεόν Isid.Pel.*epp.*1.386(M.78.400D); πρὸς οὐρανόν Bas.Sel.*v.Thecl.*1(M. 85.485B); Max.*ambig.*(M.91.1085D,1128C); Thdr.Stud.*epp.*2.209(M. 99.1632C); οἱ εὐθηποροῦντες τῇ μοναδικῇ πολιτείᾳ id.*catech.parv.*13 (p.32).

εὐθυρ(ρ)ημόνως, *in a plain-spoken way,* Clem.*str.*2.20(p.179.7; εὐθυρρη- M.8.1065C); *ib.*5.14(p.401.10; M.9.168B).

εὐθυρ(ρ)ήμων, *plain spoken;* of Christ, Cyr.*glaph.Gen.*7(1.224D); id.*hom.pasch.*19(5^2.249B).

εὐθύρρις, *straight-nosed,* Soz.*h.e.*9.17.6(M.67.1629B).

εὐθυτενής, **1.** *straight;* hence of ears, *pricked up,* Max.*ambig.*(M. 91.1209D); **2.** met., *upright;* of Const., Eus.*l.C.*6(cj. p.206.32, codd. εὐθυγενής M.20.1341B); καρδίαν Cyr.*Jo.*11.12(4.1005B); πίστις id.*ep.* 55(p.60.28; 5^2.190B); neut. as subst., id.*Ps.*36:37(M.69.949C).

εὐθύτης, ἡ, **1.** *straightness* τῆς πορείας Or.*Jo.*6.19(11; p.128.4; M. 14.233A); **2.** *direction, order* τῶν πραγμάτων Chrys.*hom.in Rom. 12:20*(3.161E); **3.** *righteousness;* of men, *A.Phil.*140(p.75.8); Bas. *hom.*12.10(2.106D; M.31.408B); *Lit.*ap.*Const.App.*8.15.2; of dogma, Thdt.*h.e.*2.2.5(3.826); of God, Herm.*vis.*3.5.3; τὸ πνεῦμα τὸ ἅγιον... πάντα ἔχον καὶ αὐτὸ συνουσιωμένως κατὰ τὴν φύσιν, τὴν ἀγαθότητα, τὴν εὐ. Bas.*hom.*15.3(2.132E; M.31.468D); Ἰησοῦς δέ ἐστιν ἡ εὐ. Gr. Nyss.*hom.1 in Cant.*(M.44.785D).

εὐθύτοκος, *new-born,* Gr.Nyss.*bapt.Chr.*(M.46.580D).

εὐθυτομέω, *make straight* τῆς σῆς εὐσεβείας ἡμῖν τὴν ὁδὸν εὐ. *Lit. Gr.Naz.*(M.36.713B).

***εὐθυφλόγιστος**, *inflammable,* Epiph.*anc.*47.2(p.57.2; M.43.100C).

εὐθύφρων, *thinking rightly,* Sophr.H.*ep.syn.*(M.87.3149C).

[*]**εὐθώραξ**, *broad-chested,* Jo.Mal.*chron.*5 p.104(M.97.193A).

εὐίερος, *very holy,* Paul.Sil.*ambo.*175(M.86.2258B); id.*Soph.*143(M. 86.2125A).

***εὔικμος**, *well-watered;* met., Geo.Pis.*hex.*1403(M.92.1542A).

***εὐιλατεύω**, *be very merciful;* of God, Jo.Thess.*dorm.BMV* B 6 (p.416.23).

εὐίλατος, *very merciful;* of man, *A.Petr.et Paul.*71(p.208.6); of Christ, Cyr.*hom.pasch.*18(5^2.240D); Nil.*epp.*2.52(M.79.224A).

***εὐιματία**, ἡ, *fine clothes;* plur., Cyr.*ador.*1(1.19C).

***εὐισχία**, ἡ, *fine haunches;* of a horse, *Mir.Geo.*8(p.99.12).

εὐκαθοσίωτος, *consecrated,* Epiph.*haer.*42.11(p.148.25; M.41. 764A); Chrys.*hom.3.1 in Tit.*(11.745A); neut. as subst., Pall.*v.Chrys.* 9(p.56.1; M.47.32).

εὐκαιρ-έω, **1.** *have leisure, opportunity* εἰς τὸ ἁγιάζειν Liber. ap.Thdt.*h.e.*2.16.22(3.838); ἔργοις Nil.*praest.*8(M.79.1069D); pass., *be at leisure* ~ηθείς Pall.*h.Laus.*18(p.56.11; ~ούμενος M.34.1065C); *devote time* ἐπὶ πραγματείαν *Pers.*(p.24.8); med., *enjoy* ἐὰν εὐκαιρίσῃ (sic) ποτήριον οἴνου Ephr.1.94D; **2.** *happen to be* somewhere, Tim.I Al.*resp.*1(M.33.1296B); *Apophth.Patr.*(M.65.96D); εὐ. ἐπὶ τὴν ἐκκλησίαν *ib.*(233B); Dor.*doct.*11.3(M.88.1737A); impers., *happen* εὐ. δέ τινι γέροντι ἐξελθεῖν *Apophth.Patr.*(321A); **3.** *be vacant,* of sees θρόνοις ἀλλοτρίοις ἢ καὶ τοῖς ~οῦσιν Jo.Scholast.*nomoc.*12(p.13. 19).

***εὐκαίριμος**, *in due season* ἐν τῇ τοῦ πάσχα εὐκαιριμωτάτῃ παραφυλακῇ Petr.I Al.*fr.*(M.18.516D).

εὔκαιρος, **1.** neut. as adv., *opportunely,* Just.*2apol.*11.2(M.6. 461B); *Const.App.*3.13.1; **2.** *ready* ἔφιππος φαινόμενος, ἕλκων τε καὶ ἄλλον ἵππον εὐ. Nil.*epp.*4.62(M.79.580D).

εὐκάματος, *made with toil,* Paul.Sil.*Soph.*452(M.86.2137A); *ib.*496 (2138B).

***εὐκανόνιστος**, *well-regulated,* Ephr.1.71D; id.1.107A.

εὐκάρδιος, *sturdy;* of plants, Cyr.*Lc.*10:1(p.100.6; M.72.665C); id.*Ps.*91:13(M.69.1228D).

εὐκαρπία, ἡ, **1.** *good crop,* Clem.*str.*4.2(p.251.1; M.8.1220A); *ib.*6.3 (p.444.24; M.9.245A); **2.** *fruitfulness,* plur., Cyr.*Os.*20(3.42B); id. *Joel.*14(3.212D).

***εὐκαρποφόρος**, *fruitful,* Ephr.2.108F.

εὐκατάβλητος, *easily thrown down,* Chrys.*hom.7.1 in Jo.*(8. 44D).

εὐκατάγνωστος, *easily condemned,* Ath.*gent.*27(M.25.52C).

εὐκαταγώνιστος, **1.** *easily conquered,* Gr.Thaum.*pan.Or.*6(p.16. 17; M.10.1069D); Chrys.*hom.34.3 in Mt.*(7.392C); ‡Nil.*narr.*3(M.79. 621B); **2.** *easily destroyed* οἰκίαν Cyr.*hom.pasch.*12(5^2.163E).

***εὐκατάδρομος**, *easily overrun,* Cyr.*ador.*3(1.89D).

εὐκατακόμιστος, *easily carried away,* met. πρὸς τὸ ἀδικοῦν Cyr. *ador.*5(1.152C); neut. as subst., id.*hom.pasch.*19(5^2.256A).

εὐκατάλυτος, *easy to dissolve,* ‡Chrys.*hom.suppl.*5(M.64.453A).

εὐκαταμάχητος, *easily conquered,* ‡Chrys.*hom.*10(13.238C); Cyr. *Zach.*4(3.656D; εὐκαταγώνιστος Aubert).

εὐκατάμικτος, *companionable,* ‡Ath.*ep.Cast.*2.5(M.28.896D) = Ant.Mon.*hom.*25(M.89.1509B).

***εὐκατάνυκτος**, **1.** *thoroughly repentant,* Jo.Clim.*scal.*4(M.88. 788B); Anast.S.*qu.et resp.*105(M.89.757D); Thdr.Stud.*epp.*2.88(M.99. 1333B); neut. as subst., *M.Pers.*12.2(p.534.37); Thdr.Stud.*epp.*1.49 (1084D); **2.** *compassionate, tender, Mir.Artem.*37(p.61.26).

***εὐκατανύκτως**, *with true repentance,* Anast.S.*qu.et resp.*64(M.89. 661B).

εὐκατάπληκτος, *easily scared,* Bas.*hom.*19.4(2.152B; M.31.513C); Nest.*hom.in Heb.3:1*(p.238.15; M.64.485D).

εὐκατάπρηστος, *easily kindled* or *set on fire,* Bas.*hom.in Ps.*1(1. 96D; M.29.225C); Isid.Pel.*epp.*5.181(M.78.1432D); Cyr.*Zach.*91(3. 777D); met. ψυχαῖς Bas.*hom.in Ps.*7(1.105D; M.29.248A); ζωή †Bas. *Is.*64(1.426A; M.30.229B); νεότης ‡Chrys.*Thecl.*(2.749C).

***εὐκαταπτόητος**, *easily startled,* Cyr.*ador.*3(1.87D); id.*Is.*3.4 (2.479B).

***εὐκατάπτωτος**, *ready to collapse;* neut. as subst., Chrys.*exp.in Ps.*128:8(5.366C).

***εὐκατάσβεστος**, *easily extinguished,* ‡Chrys.*hom.in Ps.38:*7(5. 567A).

εὐκατάσειστος, *easily shaken* or *thrown down;* met., Cyr.*glaph. Num.*(1.408D); id.*ador.*6(1.178A); id.*hom.pasch.*11(5^2.144B).

εὐκατάστατος, *firmly established;* of persons, *in good standing,* Ephr.3.138A; Gr.Mag.*dial.*(tr.Zach.)4.31(M.*PL*.77.370B); of a fountain, *unfailing, A.Thom.*A 39(p.157.6).

***εὐκαταστάτως**, *very steadily,* Mac.Aeg.*hom.*6(M.34.517D).

***εὐκατατόλμητος**, *easily undertaken,* Jo.VI H.*v.Jo.D.*7(M.94. 440B).

εὐκατάτροχος, **1.** *easily running* into πρὸς πλεονεξίαν Cyr.*ador.*8 (1.280A); **2.** *easily overtaken* εὐ. τοῖς πάθεσι Cyr.*Abac.*9(3.525B); εὐ. τοῖς διώκειν ᾑρημένοις id.*ador.*5(1.142A).

***εὐκατάφθαρτος**, *readily corruptible,* Andr.Cr.*or.*17(M.97.1188A).

***εὐκατάφλεκτος**, *inflammable,* Evagr.*h.e.*4.27(p.175.21; M.86. 2749A); fig. ὁ θρόνος σου φλέγεται τῇ αἴγλῃ περιλαμπόμενος, καὶ δύναταί σε φέρειν ἡ εὐ. παρθένος; ‡Gr.Thaum.*annunt.*3(M.10.1176D).

εὐκαταφρονήτως, *with scorn,* Or.*Cels.*1.29(p.80.26; M.11.716B); *ib.* 5.15(p.16.2; 1201C); id.*Jo.*10.27(17; p.199.37; M.14.356A).

εὐκάτοπτος, *easily understood*, Cyr.*glaph.Gen.*5(1.150B); id.*Jo.*6 (4.558C); *ib.*6.1(639B).

***εὐκάτοχος**, *easily grasped*; met., Cyr.*Jo.*5.1(4.465A); *ib.*9(4. 724D); Cosm.Ind.*top.*5(M.88.260A).

εὔκαυστος, *easily burning*, Meth.*res.*2.23(p.378.2; M.18.316A); superl., Or.*mart.*36(p.33.27; M.11.612A).

[*]**εὐκεράως**, = εὐκέραος, *with beautiful horns*, *Orac.Sib.*167.

***εὐκερδία, ἡ**, *profit, gain*, *Mir.Artem.*27(p.40.16).

εὐκίνητος, *moving smoothly*; of the firmament, Dion.Al.ap.Eus. *p.e.*14.26(780C; M.21.1284B); ‡Just.*confut.*60(M.6.1561A); neut. as subst., Or.*princ.*1.8.4(p.103.7; p.102.13); met. τὸ...εὐ. τοῦ ἡγεμονικοῦ id.*Jo.*20.5(p.333.11; M.14.584C); σημαίνει δὲ ἡ γλῶσσα ἡ πυρίνη τὸν εὐ. καὶ διάπυρον λόγον Didym.ap.*cat.Ac.*2:3(p.21.27).

εὐκινήτως, *with agility*, Gr.Nyss.*hom.7 in Cant.*(M.44.933C).

εὐκίων, *with beautiful pillars*; fig., Nonn.*par.Jo.*10:22(M.43. 836B).

***εὐκλεέω**, = εὐκλεΐζω, pass., *receive honour*, Thdr.Stud.*epp.*2.82 (M.99.1324C).

εὔκλεια, ἡ, **1.** *glory*; of man from God, Clem.*str.*4.22(p.309.4; M. 8.1348A); Isid.Pel.*epp.*2.79(M.78.521A); **2.** *honour*, in polite form of address τῆς σῆς...θεοφρουρήτου εὐ. Jo.D.*jej.*1(M.95.65B).

***εὐκλήματος**, *with many branches*, ‡Ath.*disp.*34(M.28.484A).

εὐκληρία, ἡ, *good inheritance, prosperity*, Or.*fr.72 in Lc.*(p.269); Gr.Nyss.*beat.*7(M.44.1277B); †Cyr.*hom.div.*10(5^2.376D).

***εὔκλητος**, *worthy of one's calling*, Thdr.Stud.*epp.*2.140(M.99. 1445B).

***εὐκλόνητος**, *easily confused*, neut. as subst. τὸ...εὐ. τῆς σῆς γνωμῆς Nil.*epp.*2.58(M.79.275A).

εὔκλωνος, *with fine twigs*, Diad.*perf.*55(p.60.20).

εὔκνιστος, *easily provoked*, Dor.*doct.*4.8(M.88.1668D).

εὐκολία, ἡ, **1.** *pliability, docility*, Gr.Naz.*or.*6.20(M.35.748B); Chrys.*hom.87.1 in Jo.*(8.519B); *ib.19.1*(111D); *proneness*, Gr.Nyss. *Eun.*1(1 p.37.19; M.45.265A); τὴν περὶ τὸ ἁμαρτάνειν ἡμῶν εὐ. Thdr. Mops.*Rom.*6:6(p.122.3; M.66.801B); Thdt.*Jer.*22:27(2.514); **2.** *levity, fickleness*, Gr.Naz.*ep.*79(M.37.152B); Chrys.*hom.37.1 in Mt.*(7. 415B); Isid.Pel.*epp.*1.173(M.78.296C); *instability* τοῦ πλούτου Bas. *hom.in Ps.*61(1.198A; M.29.481A); **3.** *ease*, in moving, Clem.*paed.*2. 11(p.227.8; M.8.537B); met. εὐ. τοῦ κηρύγματος Thdt.*Is.*40:4(p.155. 17; 2.326); *facility*, Gr.Nyss.*hom.7 in Cant.*(M.44.913C); Chrys. *hom.7.9 in Rom.*(9.496A); Thdt.*Rom.*6:13(3.65); hence **4.** *good condition* τῆς ὁδοῦ Gr.Nyss.*ep.*2(M.46.1013A); id.*v.Mos.*(M.44.324A); **5.** *simplicity, intelligibility* of teaching, Chrys.*hom.2.3 in Jo.*(8. 10D); **6.** *convenience*, cf.*Lit.Chrys.*(p.396.10).

εὔκολος, **1.** *contented, good-natured*; in bad sense, *easily led, prone* πρὸς τὸ ἁμαρτάνειν Hipp.*haer.*6.41(p.172.19; M.16.3256B); Bas. *hom.*3.1(2.17A; M.31.200B); Cyr.*Nah.*27(3.505D); neut. as subst., Serap.*Man.*24(p.40; M.40.920D); **2.** *unstable* τὴν τοῦ βίου εὐ. δόξαν Diad.*perf.*4(p.8.4); neut. as subst. τὸ εὐ. τῆς καρδίας ἡμῶν *ib.*81 (p.106.14); **3.** *able to content*; hence *simple, plain*; of food, Clem.*paed.* 2.1(p.155.22; M.8.384A); *ib.*(p.163.19; 400A); neut. as subst., *ib.*(p.154. 18; 380A); of dress, *ib.*3.11(p.268.14; 629A); **4.** *agile, quick*; of persons, Gr.Naz.*or.*27.4(p.6.8; M.36.16B).

εὔκομος, *well-fleeced* δοράν Ast.Am.*hom.*1(M.40.165A); met., *fruitful*; of crops, Thdt.*Rom.*15:20(3.152).

εὔκομπος, *loud-sounding*; met., *bombastic*, Cyr.*Is.*3.3(2.445E).

εὐκοσμία, ἡ, **1.** *adornment*, Clem.*paed.*2.12(p.234.4; M.8.553A); **2.** *beauty*, Dion.Ar.*c.h.*2.5(M.3.145C); Thdt.*Cant.*4:10(2.100); Evagr. *h.e.*3.28(p.124.32; M.86.2653B); Thphn.*chron.*p.22(M.108.116B); **3.** *good order, harmony*; of universe, Meth.*arbitr.*2(p.150.7; M. 18.244D); Const.*ep.*ap.Gel.Cyz.*h.e.*3(p.195.16; M.85.1357C); Gr.Naz. *carm.*1.1.32.12(M.37.512A); Dion.Ar.*c.h.*8.2(M.3.241C); in worship, id.*e.h.*3.3.6(M.3.433B); *ib.*7.7.6(561C).

εὔκοσμος, *in good order, harmonious*, Dion.Ar.*c.h.*8.1(M.3.240A) cit. s. ἀσύμφυρτος; *ib.*11.2(257C); Max.*opusc.*(M.91.112A).

εὐκράς, τό, = εὔκρατον, Cyr.S.*v.Sab.*44(p.135.2); Jo.Mosch.*prat.* 84(M.87.3057B,C).

εὐκρασία, ἡ, *proper mixing* τῶν ποτῶν Clem.*paed.*3.11(p.272.11; M.8.640A); τῶν στοιχείων Or.*schol.in Cant.*7:6–7(M.17.284A); of good weather ὑπὲρ εὐκρασίας ἀέρων *Lit.Jac.*(p.188.14); cf.*Lit.Chrys.* (p.363.13).

***εὐκράτιον, τό**, = sq., Cyr.S.*v.Jo.Hes.*19(p.216.1).

εὔκρατον, τό, a *mixed drink*, Cyr.S.*v.Sab.*59(p.161.25); id.*v. Cyriac.*5(p.225.7); Jo.Mosch.*prat.*184(M.87.3057C); πᾶσαν...τὴν ἁγίαν μʹ εὐ. πίνομεν...τὸ δὲ εὐ. συνίσταται ἔκ τε πιπέρεως καὶ κυμίνου καὶ ἀνίσου θερμοῦ *Const.Stud.*30(M.99.1716B).

εὐκρατ-όω, **1.** *temper*, Thdr.Stud.*or.*5.5(M.99.729A); pass., Melet. *nat.hom.*synops.(M.64.1133D); **2.** *make sober* ὕδωρ...∼οῖ φρένας Gr. Naz.*carm.*1.2.32.31(M.37.918A).

ἐυκρήπις, *well-based*, Paul.Sil.*Soph.*275(M.86.2130A).

εὐκρίνεια, (-ία), **ἡ**, *clear distinction* τῶν ὑποστάσεων Didym.*Trin.* 1.36(M.39.440B); τῶν διαφερόντων Max.*ambig.*(M.91.1137A).

εὐκρινέω, *explain clearly*; pass., Gr.Nyss.*hom.12 in Cant.*(M.44. 1020B).

***εὐκρισία, ἡ**, *discernment*, Thdr.Stud.*epp.*1.11(M.99.948A).

εὔκριτος, **1.** *rightly judged*, Thdr.Stud.*epp.*2.101(M.99.1356D); **2.** *distinguished* στρατεύμασιν Pamph.Mon.*Soter.*2(p.115.26).

εὔκροτος, *well-sounding*, Gr.Nyss.*Eun.*12(1 p.252.28; M.45.956B); Eustrat.*v.Eutych.*101(M.86.2388C).

εὐκταῖος, *prayed for*; of a person, Mel.*fr.*1.3(p.308; M.5.1212A) cit. s. διάδοχος; fem. as subst., *Hymn.*(*AS* 1 p.559); neut. plur. as subst., Agap.Papa *ep.syn.*(p.153.24; M.*PL.*66.49C).

εὐκταίως, *as one would desire*, Dion.Ar.*e.h.*7.3.1(M.3.556B); Thdr. Stud.*epp.*2.188(M.99.1577A); *ib.*2.185(1569B).

εὐκτήριος, **A.** *of* or *for prayer*; **1.** esp. with οἶκος *house of prayer, chapel*; **a.** in gen., Eus.*v.C.*1.13(p.14.5; M.20.928A); πρὸ τῶν θυρῶν τῶν οἴκων τῶν εὐ. ἔστησαν τοὺς πένητας οἱ πατέρες οἱ ἡμέτεροι... κρῆνας εἶναι ἐν ταῖς αὐλαῖς τῶν εὐ. οἴκων νενόμισται, ἵνα οἱ μέλλοντες εὔχεσθαι τῷ θεῷ, πρότερον ἀπονιψάμενοι τὰς χεῖρας, οὕτως αὐτὰς εἰς εὐχὴν ἀνατείνωσιν Chrys.*hom.3.11 in 2Cor.*4:*13*(3.289C,D); id.*hom. 6.4 in 2Tim.*(11.698A); Thdt.*Is.*53:2(p.214.38; 2.361); ᾠκοδόμησεν ὁ μακάριος Παχούμιος εὐ. οἶκον καὶ ἐποίησεν αὐτῷ στοάς *V.Pach.Λ* 32 (p.157.29); **b.** of church of Anastasis at Jerusalem, Eus.*v.C.*3.25 (p.89.16; M.20.1085A); of church built by Helena at Jerusalem, Socr.*h.e.*1.17.7(M.67.120B); *ib.*1.18.6(124A); **c.** dist. from a church τῶν εὐ. οἴκων τὰς οἰκοδομὰς ὑψοῦν αὔξειν τε εἰς πλάτος καὶ μῆκος τὰς ἐκκλησίας τοῦ θεοῦ Eus.*v.C.*2.45(p.60.10; 1021B); Didym.*Trin.* 2.7(M.39.589B); μήτε μοναστήριον μήτε ἐκκλησίαν μήτε εὐ. οἶκον Justn.*nov.*67.1; **d.** of heret. places of worship τῶν αἱρετικῶν τοὺς εὐ., εἴ γε εὐ. ὀνομάζειν οἴκους προσήκει Const.ap.Eus.*v.C.*3.65(p.112. 29; 1141C); τοὺς μὲν ἄλλους ἔξω τῶν πόλεων συνεχώρησε εὐ. οἴκους κατασκευάζειν· Ναυατιανοὺς δὲ...ἐντὸς τῶν πόλεων τὰς ἑαυτῶν ἐκκλησίας θαρροῦντας ἔχειν ἐκέλευσεν Socr.*h.e.*5.20.6(M.67.620C); οἱ μὲν καθαιρεθέντες, οἱ δὲ ἀκοινώνητοι γενόμενοι, ἐν τοῖς εὐ. ἑορτάζουσιν οἴκοις συνάξεις ἐπιτελοῦντες Jo.Ant.*relat.imp.*4(p.131.15; M.83. 1456A); Thdt.*h.e.*5.32.5(3.1072); **e.** of a martyr's chapel, Eus.*v.C.* 4.61(p.142.25; 1212B); ⟨ἐν⟩ ἀριστερᾷ μὲν εἰσιόντων ὁ εὐ. οἶκος τοῖς μάρτυσιν ἡτοιμασμένος Gr.Nyss.*ep.*2(M.46.1081B); Chrys.*hom.11.4 in 1Thess.*(11.507D); ἔν τινι εὐ. οἴκῳ τοῦ ἁγίου θαυματούργου Τύχωνος where Jo. Eleem. was buried, Leont.N.*v.Jo.Eleem.*45(p.94.14); *Chron.Pasch.*p.276(M.92.685B); **f.** of a monastery chapel, Pall.*h. Laus.*43(p.130.10; M.40.1210C); CChalc.*can.*4; CNic.(787)*can.*17; **g.** of a chapel in a house τοὺς ἐν εὐ. οἴκοις ἔνδον οἰκίας τυγχάνουσι λειτουργοῦντας ἢ βαπτίζοντας κληρικοὺς ὑπὸ γνώμης τοῦτο πράττειν τοῦ κατὰ τόπον ἐπισκόπου ὁρίζομεν CTrull.*can.*31; μηδαμῶς ἐν εὐ. οἴκῳ ἔνδον οἰκίας τυγχάνοντι βάπτισμα ἐπιτελείσθω *ib.*59; **h.** conditions regulating foundation, Justn.*nov.*120.6; *ib.*123.18; **2.** with other words: νεώς Thdt.*h.e.*2.12.2(3.853); also a place of burial, Anton.Hag.*v.Sym.Styl.*32(p.76.10); δόμος Marc.Diad.*perf.*97(p.144. 10); σηκός Thdt.*h.rel.*3(3.1147); χωρίον *ib.*2(1130); τόπος, of a church, Jo.Ant.*relat.imp.*3(p.130.12; M.83.1452C); Thdt.*Ezech.*48(2.1050); Socr.*h.e.*5.10.1(M.67.584A); οἰκίσκος Thdt.*h.e.*5.24.4(1064).

B. neut. as subst., *house of prayer, oratory, chapel*; **1.** in gen., Gr.Thaum.*ep.can.*11(M.10.1048A); Eus.*v.C.*3.50(p.98.27; M.20.1109C); Gr.Nyss.*or.dom.*5(p.108.27; M.44.1188C); as place of sanctuary, *Cod. Thds.*9.45.4(p.63.3); **2.** including churches, Marc.Diac.*v.Porph.*5; **3.** dist. from a church, Didym.*Trin.*2.7(M.39.589C); Gel.Cyz.*h.e.*3. 9.10; Jo.D.*hom.*12.19(M.96.808B); ? part of a church τοῦ εὐ. τῆς ἐπίκλην Ὁμονοίας ἐκκλησίας Evagr.*h.e.*2.13(p.65.8; M.86.2541A); **4.** of various places; **a.** a portable tent, Socr.*h.e.*1.18.12(M.67. 124C); **b.** chapels or churches dedicated to angels, Thdt.*Col.*2:18 (3.490); **c.** memorials to martyrs, Gr.Nyss.*ep.*25(M.46.1096A); but cf.Eus.*v.C.*3.48(p.98.2; M.20.1108C); **d.** chapels or churches dedicated to saints εὐ. μικρὸν τοῦ θεολόγου *A.Jo.*17*(p.160.30); Anton. Hag.*v.Sym.Styl.*32(p.76.12); Leont.N.*v.Jo.Eleem.*42(p.85.6); ἐν τῇ πόλει Ῥώμῃ...ἐν τῷ εὐ. τοῦ ἀποστόλου Πέτρου Valent.Imp.*ep.Thds.* (p.5.9; M.*PL.*54.858A); **e.** chapels or churches in monasteries, ‡Pall. *h.mon.*5(p.29.9; M.65.448A); Jo.D.*haer.*80(M.94.732D); **f.** private chapels, Leont.N.*v.Jo.Eleem.*39(p.77.21); τὸ κατ' οἶκον αὐτοῦ εὐ. Jo. VI H.*v.Jo.D.*18(M.94.457A); ἀναγινώσκουσι τὸ εὐαγγέλιον ἐν τῷ εὐ. τοῦ Παλατίου Alex.Sal.*Barn.*44(451B); **g.** chapels or churches used by heretics μὴ...τοῖς τοιούτοις εὐ. προσψαύσητε κοινωνίας ἕνεκεν Leont.N.*v.Jo.Eleem.*42(p.86.15); **h.** a whole monastery εἴ τις τῶν ὑγιαινόντων κοιμᾶται ἔξω τοῦ εὐ., ἔστω ἀφορισμένος ‡Bas.*poen.mon.* 27(2.528D; M.31.1309B); **5.** conditions regulating foundation, Justn. *nov.*131.7.

εὐκτικός, *of prayer, consisting in prayer,* Nil.*epp.*3.282(M.79.524A); *ib.*3.320(537D); Diad.*perf.*61(p.70.13).

εὐκτικῶς, 1. *in the optative mood,* Or.*or.*24.5(p.356.21; M.11.496B); Eus.*Ps.*137:4(M.24.40A); Olymp.*Job* 5:3(M.93.81A); **2.** *prayerfully, in accordance with prayer,* Meth.*symp.*2.2(p.17.11; M.18.49B); Thdr. Mops.*Ps.*71:19(p.477.10); Thdr.Stud.*catech.parv.*106(p.246).

***εὐκτῖται, οἱ,** = *εὐχῖται, *Apophth.Patr.*(M.65.253B).

***εὐκτῶς,** *in accordance with prayer,* Jo.D.*carm.theoph.*8(p.212; M.96.832A).

εὐλάβεια, ἡ, 1. *cautious fear*; **a.** *discretion* εὐ. καλούντων οἱ φιλόσοφοι τὸν τοῦ νόμου φόβον, εὔλογον οὖσαν ἔκκλισιν...ἡ οὖν εὐ. λογικὴ δείκνυται, τοῦ βλάπτοντος ἔκκλισις οὖσα, ἐξ ἧς ἡ μετάνοια τῶν προημαρτημένων φύεται Clem.*str.*2.7(p.130.14,18; M.8.968B,C); not shared by 'gnostic', *ib.*6.9(p.469.2; M.9.296B); **b.** hence simply *fear, ib.*4.25(p.319.3; M.8.368B); Or.*fr.17 in Lc.*(p.241); Gr.Thaum. *pan.Or.*2(p.4.6,14; M.10.1053C,1056A); **c.** *godly fear, reverence*; **i.** dist. from servile fear τὸν φόβον μεταληπτέον εἰς τὴν παρά τισιν εὐ. ὠνομασμένην, ἥτις οὐδαμῶς κόλασιν ἔχει Or.*sel.in Ps.*2:11(M.12.1116A); **ii.** towards God δουλεύσωμεν αὐτῷ μετὰ φόβου καὶ πάσης εὐ. Polyc.*ep.*6.3; in prayer, Evagr.Pont.*or.*42(M.79.1176B); ἐν εὐ. προσκυνήσω σοι ἐν πνεύματι καὶ ἀληθείᾳ Cyr.*Ps.*5:8(M.69.741D); in church, Chrys.*hom.53.3 in Jo.*(8.313E); in seeking the divine, Gr. Thaum.*pan.Or.*13(p.28.29; M.10.1088A); Ath.*ep.Serap.*1.20(M.26.577B); Dion.Ar.*d.n.*1.2(M.3.589A); of seraphim, id.*c.h.*13.4(M.3.305A); ref. receiving Communion ἐν τάξει μετὰ αἰδοῦς καὶ εὐ. ὡς βασιλέως προσερχόμενοι ὀνόματι *Const.App.*2.57.21; *Lit.ib.*8.13.4; Chrys.*prod.Jud.*1.1(2.377A); πόσην δὲ αὐτὸν ἀπαιτήσομεν καθαρότητα, καὶ πόσην εὐ.; id.*sac.*6.4(p.147.12; 1.424B); in touching the gospel-book, cf.*Lit.Chrys.*(p.372.21); excessive εὐ. as source of doctrinal error ἐκ πολλῆς ἄγαν εὐ. ἐπερυθριᾷ κατὰ τὸ εἰκὸς τοῖς τῆς κενώσεως μέτροις Cyr.*Nest.*4.5(p.85.6; 6[1].110A); **iii.** of God χεὶρ εὐλαβείας καὶ δυνάμεως...εὐλογησάτω τὸν λαὸν τοῦτον Serap.*Euch.*15.2; **d.** *reverence, respect*; for bishops, Gel.Cyz.*h.e.*2.6.1(M.85.1232B); for emperor, Ath.*apol.Const.*13(M.25.612A); of servant for master, Bas. *jud.*7(2.221C; M.31.672A); towards strangers, ‡Pall.*h.mon.*5(p.29.20; M.65.448B); **e.** *reverence,* as a title of honour, esp. for bishops, Alex.Al.*ep.Alex.*1(p.19.7; M.18.548B); Ath.*ep.Serap.*1.33(M.26.605C); Chrys.*ep.*85(3.638C); for a priest, Gr.Naz.*ep.*102(M.37.193B); for a prefect, *ib.*84(157B); for emperor, Ath.*ep.Jov.*1(M.26.816C), v. εὐσέβεια; used of one's self τὴν ἐμὴν...εὐ. Const.ap.Gel.Cyz.*h.e.*3.18.3; *ib.*3.18.7; **f.** *religious scruple* οὐκ ἀνεξέταστον ⟨τὸν⟩ λόγον ἐατέον διὰ τὴν περὶ τοῦ ἁγίου πνεύματος εὐ. Or.*Jo.*2.17(12; p.75.22; M.14.145D); **2.** *piety, Ep.Lugd.*ap.Eus.*h.e.*4.15.8(M.20.345B); Clem. *str.*6.17(p.511.30; M.9.388A); Hipp.*Dan.*3.22.1; ἐπίσκοπος ἢ πρεσβύτερος ἢ διάκονος τὴν ἑαυτοῦ γυναῖκα μὴ ἐκβαλλέτω προφάσει εὐλαβείας *Can.App.*5; Chrys.*bapt.Chr.*1(2.368D); as insufficient qualification for a bishop μηδὲ τοῦτον...εἰ μὴ μετὰ τῆς εὐ. πολλὴν καὶ τὴν σύνεσιν ἔχων τύχοι id.*sac.*3.15(p.77.16; 1.390B); of false piety εὐ. ἐπίπλαστον Or.*adnot.in Dt.*27:15(M.17.33B); Cyr.H.*catech.*11.12; ‡Just.*qu.et resp.*28(M.6.1276A); also *rule of piety*; plur., Cyr.*Jo.*2.5(4.193B); **3.** *religion,* Hier.*vir.ill.*(tr.Sophr.Pal.)54(p.36.22; M.*PL.*23.668A); Chrys.*stat.*1.3(2.5A); *Lit.Jac.*(p.208.23); **4.** the *religious life* ὑπὲρ τῶν ἐν ἐγκρατείᾳ καὶ εὐ. διηνεκῶς ... *Lit.*ap.*Const.App.*8.10.11; perh. also γυνή...τις ἐπίσημος ἐν εὐ. καὶ τοῦ τῆς διακονίας ἠξιωμένη χαρίσματος Thdt.*h.e.*3.14.1(3.927); **5.** *right doctrine* ἡ τῶν συλλειτουργῶν σύμφωνος περὶ Χριστοῦ εὐ. Alex.Al.*ep.Alex.*10(p.26.17; M.18.564B).

εὐλαβ-έομαι, 1. *fear,* of prophets μήτ' εὐλαβηθέντες μήτε δυσωπηθέντες τινά Just.*dial.*7.1(M.6.492B); μὴ ~εῖσθαι τὰ μείζονα Clem. *paed.*3.11(p.276.15; M.8.649B); εὐλαβηθεὶς μὴ...διαφύγωσιν Hipp. *Dan.*1.8.3; ~ούμενος ἀφαιρεθῆναι ἀπ' αὐτοῦ τὸ ἅγιον πνεῦμα Or.*Jo.* 28.15(13; p.408.7; M.14.712C); *Hom.Clem.*3.63; Cyr.*glaph.Ex.*2(1.297E); abs., Jo.Thess.*dorm.BMV* A 5(p.382.1); esp. of fearing God, Const.ap.Eus.*v.C.*2.55(p.63.34; M.20.1029D); id.ap.Gel.Cyz.*h.e.*3.18.10; Ath.*ep.Drac.*5(M.25.528D); **2.** *reverence, honour,* a bishop, *Const. App.*2.2.3; clergy, *ib.*2.33.3; in gen., Dor.*doct.*4.10(M.88.1672B); *be reverent, Const.App.*3.8.1; Dion.Ar.*e.h.*1.1.1(M.3.372A).

εὐλαβής, 1. *devout, pious, good*; **a.** of things χρῆμα Eus.*m.P.*13.4 (p.948.3; M.20.1516A); ψυχῆς Chrys.*ep.*2.1(3.535D); ἐπιγνωμοσύνης Dion.Ar.*e.h.*7.3.6(M.3.561B); **b.** of persons, esp. of women, Clem. *paed.*3.11(p.280.18; M.8.657C); Dion.Al.*ep.can.*2(p.103.3; M.10.1281A); Chrys.*hom.61.3 in Jo.*(8.366A); of virgins, Ath.*virg.*13(p.88.6; M. 28.268A); of a widow, *Const.App.*3.7.7; of men, Hipp.*haer.*9.12 (p.247.6; M.16.3382A); *A.Barn.*5(p.293.20); ὁ...εὐ. ἀφ' ἑαυτοῦ τὸ χρίσμα ἔχει Hesych.H.*serm.*6(M.93.1473A); **c.** as title, superl.; of emperor, Ar.*ep.Const.*(p.64)ap.Socr.*h.e.*1.26.2(M.67.149B); CSard. *can.*7; Ath.*apol.sec.*44(p.119.11; M.25.324B); of monks, Eustrat. *v.Eutych.*62(M.86.2344D); of archimandrites, CCP(449)*act.*(*ACO* 2. 1.1 p.168.1; H.2.197B); of deacons, *Const.App.*7.31.1; CCP(449)ap. CChalc.*act.*1(*ACO* 2.1.1 p.167.10; H.2.197B); of priests, Bas.*ep.*156 (3.246B; M.32.616C); Chrys.*ep.*13(3.594B); Nest.*ep.Cyr.*1(p.25.8; M. 77.44A); of bishops, Bas.*ep.*119(3.210C; M.32.536B); Synes.*ep.*67(M. 66.1412B); CCP(449)*act.*(*ACO* 2.1.1 p.167.27; 197B); **d.** c. περί: ἡ τάξις [sc. of seraphim] εὐ. ἐστι περὶ τὰ τῶν νοήσεων αὐτῆς ὑψηλότερα καὶ βαθύτερα Dion.Ar.*e.h.*4.3.8(M.3.481B); **2.** *religious,* opp. secular τῶν λεγομένων εὐ. ἀνδρῶν τε καὶ γυναικῶν CNic.(787)*can.*19; περὶ τοῦ μὴ ἐξεῖναι κληρικὸν ἢ ἕτερον εὐ. σχήματος αἰτιᾶσθαι πρὸ κρίσεως ἐπισκόπου παρὰ ἄρχοντι Jo.Schol.*coll.cap.*54 tit.; **3.** neut. as subst.; **a.** *devotion, piety,* Just.*dial.*79.2(M.6.661B); of martyrs, Clem.*str.*2.20(p.181.4; M.8.1069B); of virginity, Meth.*symp.*4.5(p.50.20; M.18.93A); τὸ...εὐ. τῆς περὶ τὸν θεῖον φόβον διαθέσεως Eus.*h.e.*6.34(M.20.596B); **b.** *holy fear, godly fear,* id.*d.e.*1.3(p.16.32; M.22.37C); of Christ in his human nature (cf. Heb.5:7), Gr.Naz.*or.*30.6(p.115.15; M.36.109B); **c.** *caution,* caveat, Clem.*str.*5.10(p.370.9; M.9.100C); Or.*Jo.*6.9(6; p.118.12; M.14.217A).

***εὐλαβοειδής,** *pious, reverential,* Thdr.Stud.*epp.*2.88(M.99.1333B).

***εὐλαβοφανής,** *pious-looking, prim,* Didym.*Trin.*2.8(M.39.605A).

εὐλαβῶς, 1. *cautiously,* c. ἔχω, Clem.*str.*1.12(p.35.21; M.8.753A); Or.*ep.*1.6(M.11.61C); **2.** *respectfully, reverently,* Eus.*v.C.*3.24 tit.(p.73.13; M.20.1084D); Gel.Cyz.*h.e.*3.13.10; *with godly fear, reverently,* Clem.*str.*3.10(p.229.24; M.8.1176A); Hipp.*Dan.*3.4.7; Dion.Ar.*c.h.* 7.3(M.3.209B); *Lit.Jac.*(p.196.19); **3.** *piously,* Eus.*v.C.*3.45(p.74.13; 1105B); Soz.*h.e.*2.1.2(M.67.929B).

εὔλαλος, 1. *eloquent,* Gr.Thaum.*pan.Or.*1(p.2.17; M.10.1052B); ‡Chrys.*hom.in Ps.83*(5.607C); Procl.CP *or.*16(M.65.805B); met., *chattering*; of swallows, Anast.S.*defunct.*(M.89.1193B); **2.** *able to speak*; opp. dumb, Eus.*d.e.*9.13(p.432.9; M.22.696D); ‡Chrys.*nat. Jo.Bapt.*(10.815C).

εὐλείμων, *of a fair meadow*; fig., Paul.Sil.*ambo*.288(M.86.2262B).

***εὐλεξία, ἡ,** *fine speech,* Pall.*ep.Laus.*(p.7.15; M.34.1002).

***εὐληθάργητος,** *quickly forgotten,* ‡Chrys.*pat.*1(9.808A); Anast. *mort.*13(p.245).

***εὐληπτικός,** *easily overtaking* or *overcoming* εὐ. καὶ ἐπώδυνα τὰ παριστάμενα Thdr.Stud.*nativ.BMV* 5(M.96.685B).

εὔληπτος, 1. *easily taken*; of food, Clem.*paed.*1.6(p.114.23; M.8.300A); met., *easily grasped* or *understood,* Gr.Nyss.*or.catech.*27 (p.104.19; M.45.72D); Chrys.*hom.25.2 in 2Cor.*(10.613E); Isid.Pel. *epp.*1.115(M.78.413A); comp., Or.*Ps.*1:1–2(p.445); Chrys.*hom.6.1 in Jo.*(8.43A); **2.** *easily captured*; of soul, Meth.*res.*1.57(p.319.1; M.41.1153A); **3.** *easily carried away, transient,* Gr.Naz.*carm.*1.2.40.3 (M.37.968A); **4.** *easily refuted* τὸ εὐ. τοῦ λόγου Epiph.*haer.*64.9(p.418.18; M.41.1084D).

εὐλήπτως, *so as to be easily apprehended*; comp., Nest.*fr.*C 10 ap. Cyr.*Nest.*2.1(p.34.24; 6[1].33C).

εὐλογ-έω, *bless*;

I. in gen.;

A. *speak well of, praise*; **1.** men in gen. ~εῖ ὡς εὖ πεποιηκότας οὓς ἐπαινεῖ Or.*princ.*3.1.21(p.236.10; M.11.296A); id.*Cels.*7.57(p.207.9; M.11.1504A); ~οῦσι, τουτέστι, ἐγκωμιάζουσιν Chrys.*exp.in Ps.*113:22 (5.300E); (ref. Lc.6:28) τοὺς προκατάρξαντας λοιδορίας, ~εῖν Athenag. *leg.*11.2(M.6.912B); καταρᾶταί σοί τις; σὺ εὐλόγησον αὐτόν *Const. App.*1.2.1; *ib.*3.15.4; ‡Pall.*h.mon.*21.4(p.80.20; M.34.1171C); ref. 1Cor. 4:12 λοιδορούμενοι, καὶ ~οῦσιν *Diogn.*5.15; **2.** saints and martyrs ἐν παντὶ τῷ κόσμῳ...ἀνυμνεῖται καὶ εὐ. [sc. ἡ ἁγία Μαρία] Nil.*epp.*2.180 (M.79.293A); cf.Chrys.*incomprehens.*2.1(1.453B).

B. *show favour to, favour* ~ῶν ἡμᾶς διὰ γραμμάτων μὴ κατόκνει Gr.Naz.*ep.*65(M.37.129A); *ib.*67(129C).

II. addressed to God;

A. *bless, praise*; **1.** God ἔσονται πάντες λατρεύοντες οἱ λαοὶ καὶ ~οῦντες πάντες ἐμοὶ καὶ προσκυνοῦντες *Apoc.En.*10.21; but usu. c. acc. ~ήσω τὸν ὕψιστον ἐπὶ τοῖς θαυμασίοις αὐτοῦ *T.Sym.*6.7; ~ῶ σε ὅτι ἠξίωσάς με τῆς ἡμέρας...ταύτης *M.Polyc.*14.2; ~οῦμεν τὸν ποιητὴν τῶν πάντων διὰ τοῦ υἱοῦ αὐτοῦ Ἰησοῦ Χριστοῦ καὶ διὰ πνεύματος τοῦ ἁγίου Just.*1apol.*67.2(M.6.429B); ref. Job ὅστις τοσαῦτα παθὼν...ἐπιμένει ~ῶν τὸν κύριον Or.*or.*30(p.394.12; M.11.548B); αἱ χεῖρες πρὸς τὸν θεὸν ἐκτεινόμεναι τὸν κύριον ἑαυτῶν ~οῦσιν Bas. Sel.*or.*10.1(M.85.141A); in *Gloria in excelsis* αἰνοῦμέν σε, ὑμνοῦμέν σε, ~οῦμέν σε *Const.App.*7.47.1; at anaphora, *Lit.Bas.*(p.322.4); *Lit.Jac.*(p.198.21); of man's praise compared with God's blessing upon men, cf. *sciendum tamen est quod sermo hic benedictionis in* *scripturis diverse positus invenitur. nam et deus benedicere vel homines, vel cetera quae creaverat, invenitur; et homines, vel ceterae creaturae deum benedicere jubentur. sed dei quidem benedictio aliquid muneris semper his qui ab eo benedicuntur impertit: homines vero deum benedicere, pro eo quod est laudare, et gratias referre, dicuntur,* Or.*comm.in Rom.*9.14(M.14.1221A); *ὁ...θεὸς ~εῖται μὲν ὑπὸ τῶν ἔργων αὐτοῦ, τοῦτ' ἔστιν δοξάζεται· ~εῖ δὲ αὐτὸς τὰ οἰκεῖα κτίσματα, τοῦτ' ἔστιν ἁγιάζει* Didym.*Trin.*1.32(M.39.425B,C); *ὁ τὸν θεὸν ~ῶν, αὐτὸς κερδαίνει, λαμπρότερον ἑαυτὸν καθιστάς...ὁ δὲ θεὸς ~ῶν, ἡμᾶς λαμπροτέρους ποιεῖ* Chrys.*exp.in Ps.*113:20,21(5.299B,C); *ib.*134:19ff.(5.396A); Thdt.*Ps.*66:8(1.1053); *~ούμενος ὁ θεὸς ~εῖ, ἀλλ' ~εῖ μὲν ἔργῳ, ~εῖται δὲ λόγῳ ib.*134:21(1519); pass. *~ημένη ἡ δόξα κυρίου Pss.Sal.*5.22; *εὐωχούμενοι ἐν τοῖς ἔργοις αὐτοῦ τοῖς ~ημένοις A.Thom.*A 59(p.175.20); as Jewish mode of reference to God (Hebr. בָּרוּךְ) *οὐκοῦν μείζων ἐστὶν ὁ Χριστὸς τοῦ ~ημένου; Dial. Ath.et Zacch.*85(p.46); *~ημένος ὤν, ~ημένου ἐστὶν υἱός* Thdt.*Ps.* 117:26(1.1435); **2.** Christ *δοξάζει τὸν...πατέρα...καὶ ~εῖ...'Ιησοῦν Χριστόν M.Polyc.*19.2; *δοξάζομέν σε καὶ αἰνοῦμέν σε καὶ ~οῦμεν καὶ εὐχαριστοῦμεν τὴν πολλήν σου χρηστότητα...ἅγιε 'Ιησοῦ A.Jo.*77 (p.189.23); *ἐὰν ~ήσῃς 'Ιησοῦν καὶ παραδέξῃ αὐτόν* Or.*hom.14.10 in Jer.*(p.115.7; M.13.416B); *A.Phil.*25(p.14.2).

B. *begin* office, liturgy, etc., *by reciting opening ascription* *~ήσαντος τοῦ ἱερέως, ἀρχόμεθα τοῦ τρισαγίου Euchol.*(p.39); other rites, *ib.*(pp.332,358); *~εῖ κατὰ τὸ ἔθος ib.*(p.328); cf. VI infra.

C. euphemism for *curse* (3Reg.20:10, Job 1:11), Or.*or.*30(p.394. 12; M.11.548B); Didym.*Job* 1:11(M.39.1124B); Thdt.*qu.61 in 3Reg.* 20:10(1.506); Olymp.*Job* 1:11(M.93.28A); *γέγραπται...ἐν...Λευϊτικῷ ὅτι τινὲς...ἐμαχέσαντο...ὧν ὁ ἕτερος τοῦ θείου...ὀνόματος ἐπιμνησθεὶς ηὐλόγησε, ἀντὶ τοῦ κατηράσατο* Cyr.*Jo.*12(4.1047D).

III. as divine act;

A. upon Christ *τὸ ἀρνίον τὸ ~ημένον Pap.Chr.*(p.406).

B. upon men; **1.** in gen. *πάντας ~ήσει Apoc.En.*1.8; *οἱ ~οῦντες αὐτὸν ~ημένοι ἔσονται T.Lev.*4.6; *ὡς τοὺς...~οῦντας ἡμᾶς ~εῖσθαι ὑπὸ τοῦ θεοῦ* Or.*Jo.*20.10(p.338.15; M.14.593A); *τί ἐστιν, ~ησε; μυρίων, φησίν, ἐνέπλησε ἀγαθῶν* Chrys.*exp.in Ps.*113:20f.(5.299B); *διδασκόμεθα...ὡς χρὴ πρότερον τοῖς εὐλογημένοις τὰς θείας αἰτεῖν δωρεάς* Thdt.*qu.11 in Num.*6:27(1.227); id.*Ps.*134:21(1.1519) cit. s. II.A.1; in eucharist *τὴν ἀναίμακτον θυσίαν δι' ἧς ~ούμεθα τὸν ἄρτον ἐσθίοντες* Cyr.*ador.*13(1.457E); **2.** upon Church *'Ιγνάτιος...τῇ ~ημένῃ ἐν μεγέθει θεοῦ πατρὸς πληρώματι...τῇ ἐκκλησίᾳ...ἐν 'Εφέσῳ* Ign. *Eph.*tit.; id.*Magn.*tit.; Herm.*vis.*1.3.4; **3.** upon individuals, *1Clem.* 31.2; Ign.*Eph.*2.1; *τὸν μακάριον 'Ιακὼβ ~ῶν τῷ ἑαυτοῦ ὀνόματι* Just. *dial.*125.5(M.6.768B); **4.** title of BMV *ἡ παναγία, ἄχραντος, ~ημένη ...θεοτόκος Μαρία Chron.Pasch.*p.198(M.92.488C); *Lit.Chrys.*(p.331. 23).

C. upon things *ταῦτα...πάντα τελειώσας ἐπῄνεσεν αὐτὰ καὶ ηὐλόγησεν 1Clem.*33.6; cf.Or.*comm.in Rom.*9.14(M.14.1221A) cit. s. II.A.1; *~ησον τὴν γῆν πᾶσαν* Serap.*euch.*9.3; by Christ *τὸν* [sc. *ἄρτον*] *...~ῶν διεμέριζεν ἡμῖν A.Jo.*93(p.197.2); *ὁ οὐρανὸς καινός, ὃν ὁ καταβὰς τῇ ἀνόδῳ ηὐλόγησε* Procl.CP *or.*13.2(M.65.792B); *ἕως τριακοσταετοῦς χρόνου διανύσας, ἵνα πᾶσαν ἡλικίαν ~ήσῃ* Gel.Cyz.*h.e.*2.24.23 (M.85.1304B); *Lit.Bas.*(p.328.11); v. s. V infra and cf. *εὐλογία*; *ταύτην* [sc. *τὴν τοῦ Πέτρου κάραν*] *ὁ διδάσκαλος Χριστὸς ~ησε* ‡Bas.*h.myst.*13 (p.261.1).

IV. mediated by a representative of God;

A. God the source *~ησον τὸν δοῦλόν σου τοῦτον εὐλογίᾳ τῇ σῇ* Serap.*euch.*24.1; *τὸ ὄνομα κυρίου τὰς εὐλογίας ἐνεργεῖ, οὐ τὸ στόμα τοῦ λέγοντος· ὅθεν κἂν ἁμαρτωλὸς ~ῇ, ὁμοίως ἐνεργεῖται παρὰ τῷ πιστῶς δεχομένῳ ἡ εὐλογία* Proc.G.*Num.*6:27(M.87.808A); cf. *de caelo benedictionem proferunt sacerdotes,* Hesych.H.*Lev.*9:23(M.93. 894A); bestowed upon creatures in Christ (2Cor.1:3) *ἐν τῷ Χριστῷ ~εῖται τὰ ἔθνη πάντα* Just.*dial.*121.1(M.6.757A); *~ησον τὸν λαὸν τοῦτον* [sc. the catechumens]...*εἰς εὐλογίαν τῶν σῶν μυστηρίων διὰ... 'Ιησοῦ Χριστοῦ* Serap.*euch.*4.2; *ib.*17.1; *Lit.*ap.*Const.App.*8.15.6; *~ησον αὐτοὺς διὰ Χριστοῦ Const.App.*8.37.6; cf. *non propria virtute sacerdotes benedictionem praestant, sed quia figuram ferunt Christi, possunt propter eum qui in ipsis est, praestare benedictionis plenitudinem,* Hesych.H.*Lev.*9:23(894B); effected by H. Ghost *~εῖ* [sc. *τὸ πνεῦμα*] *τὸ σῶμα τὸ βαπτιζόμενον, καὶ τὸ ὕδωρ τὸ βαπτίζον* Gr. Nyss.*bapt.Chr.*(M.46.581B); by divine grace *τὸ ὕδωρ οὐδὲν ἄλλο τυγχάνον ἢ ὕδωρ, ἀνακαινίζει τὸν ἄνθρωπον...τῆς ἄνωθεν χάριτος ~ούσης αὐτό ib.*(584B).

B. its agent; under old covenant, the priest, cf.Just.*dial.*33.2 (M.6.545C); Church tracing its authority to Aaronic priesthood *ὁ ἀρχιερεὺς...~είτω τοῦτον, ὡς καὶ Μωσῆς ἐνετείλατο τοῖς ἱερεῦσιν ~εῖν τὸν λαόν Const.App.*2.57.19; Thdt.*qu.11 in Num.*6:23ff.(1.227); cf. Hesych.H.*Lev.*9:22(M.93.893f.); authority vested in Christian priesthood *ἐπίσκοπος ~εῖ, οὐκ ~εῖται...εὐλογίαν παρὰ ἐπισκόπων λαμβάνει, παρὰ δὲ πρεσβυτέρων οὐδαμῶς...πρεσβύτερος ~εῖ, οὐκ ~εῖται, εὐλογίας δέχεται παρὰ ἐπισκόπου καὶ συμπρεσβυτέρου... διάκονος οὐκ ~εῖ· οὐ δίδωσιν εὐλογίαν, λαμβάνει δὲ παρὰ ἐπισκόπου καὶ πρεσβυτέρου Const.App.*8.28.2ff.; *ib.*3.20.2; in individuals by virtue of office *~εῖν...ἕτερον, τὸν τὰ οἰκεῖα τημελεῖν ὀφείλοντα τραύματα, ἀνακόλουθον· εὐλογία γὰρ ἁγιασμοῦ μετάδοσίς ἐστιν. ὁ δὲ τοῦτο μὴ ἔχων, διὰ τὸ ἐκ τῆς ἀγνοίας παράπτωμα, πῶς ἑτέρῳ μεταδώσει; μήτε τοίνυν δημοσίᾳ μήτε ἰδίᾳ ~είτω* Bas.*ep.*199 *can.*27(3. 294A; M.32.724C).

C. recipients; **1.** man; **a.** liturg. at baptism, Serap.*euch.*24.1 cit. s. IV.A supra; *κατασφραγισάμενοι...κλίναντες εὐλογείσθωσαν παρὰ τοῦ ἐπισκόπου τήνδε τὴν εὐλογίαν...~ησον αὐτοὺς καὶ ἁγίασον Lit.*ap. *Const.App.*8.8.4f.; *αὐτοῦ τρὶς ὁμολογήσαντος, ἐπευξάμενος ~εῖ καὶ χειροθετεῖ* Dion.Ar.*e.h.*2.2.7(M.3.396B); at eucharist, before dismissal of catechumens, Serap.*euch.*4.2; *Lit.*ap.*Const.App.*8.6.8,10; of energoumens, *ib.*8.7.3; of penitents, *ib.*8.9.6; cf.*Schol.* in *Cod. Afr.*103(*Mon.*2 p.650); other blessings of the people, Serap.*euch.* 6.2; *ib.*13.19; *ib.*16.3; cf.*Lit.Chrys.*(p.390.9); the final blessing, *Lit.*ap.*Const.App.*8.15.6,8; cf.Serap.*euch.*18.2; *Const.App.*2.58.3; *Nomoc.*135; cf.*Lit.Chrys.*(p.398.18); at evening prayers, *Const.App.* 8.37.6; at morning prayers, *ib.*8.39.4; upon the dead *τὴν...ἔξοδον αὐτοῦ εἰρηνικὴν καὶ εὐλογημένην εἶναι ποίησον* Serap.*euch.*30.3; of the nuptial blessing *φωνουμένου...ἱερέως...~ούμενοι ἀπολυέσθωσαν* †Gregent.*leg.Hom.*(M.86.585A); *Nomoc.*212; cf. *αὕτη* [Gen.1:27]...*ἡ εὐλογία τῆς γαμικῆς συναφείας* Thdr.Stud.*epp.*1.50(M.99.1093A); cf. at ordination, *A.Mt.*28(p.259.13); ? at reception of a novice *ποῖος δὲ ἀββᾶς τὴν χεῖρα τῆς εὐλογίας ἐπέθηκε;* Nil.*epp.*2.96(M.79.244B); **b.** extra-liturg.; before food, *A.Thom.*A 29(p.146.1); *Didasc.Jac.* 5.17(p.87.20); in private blessings *ἐπέθηκεν αὐτοὺς τὰς χεῖρας... καὶ ~ησεν αὐτούς A.Thom.*A 29(p.146.6,17); *παρεκάλουν αὐτὸν ~ῆσαι αὐτάς· καὶ λέγει ὁ Φίλιππος...εὐλογία ἐν ταῖς ψυχαῖς ὑμῶν A.Phil.*87 (p.34.14); cf. *τὴν ἀποστολικὴν ὑμῖν εὐλογίαν προσφέρω* Thdt.*ep.*97 (4.1167); *ὁ...τῶν ἀποστολικῶν ὑπερμαχῶν δογμάτων, δῆλον ὅτι τὴν ἀποστολικὴν εὐλογίαν τρυγήσει ib.*106(4.1176); on entry of a bishop, Philost.*h.e.*7.6(M.65.633D); **2.** things; **a.** liturg., water for baptism and oil for chrism *~οῦμεν διὰ τοῦ ὀνόματος...'Ιησοῦ Χριστοῦ τὰ κτίσμα⟨τα⟩ ταῦτα* Serap.*euch.*17.1; cf.*ib.*18 tit.; *~εῖται...τοῦτο* [sc. *τὸ ἔλαιον*] *παρὰ τοῦ ἱερέως εἰς ἄφεσιν ἁμαρτιῶν καὶ προκατασκευὴν τοῦ βαπτίσματος Const.App.*7.42.2; *~οῦμεν...τό τε ὕδωρ τοῦ βαπτίσματος, καὶ τὸ ἔλαιον τῆς χρίσεως* Bas.*Spir.*66(3.55A; M.32.188B); practice attributed to Jo. Bapt. *~ῶν ὁ 'Ιωάννης τὰ ὕδατα εἶπεν· φωνὴ κυρίου ἐπὶ τῶν ὑδάτων Chron.Pasch.*p.210(M.92.513A); holy water *~είτω ὁ ἐπίσκοπος τὸ ὕδωρ ἢ τὸ ἔλαιον· ἐὰν δὲ μὴ παρῇ ~είτω ὁ πρεσβύτερος Const.App.*8.29.2; cf. *καθ' ἑκάστην ἀρχιμηνίαν...ὕδασιν εὐλογίας... χριόμεθα* Thdr.Balsamon *schol.*in CTrull.*can.*65(M.137.741A); at eucharist, elements prior to consecration *αὐτὸς* [sc. *ὁ θεός*] *~ησον τὴν πρόθεσιν ταύτην καὶ προσδέξαι αὐτήν Lit.Jac.*(*NBP* 10² p.53); vestments, cf.*Lit.Chrys.*(p.355.3,37); *ib.*(p.356.1); fruits, cf.Hipp. *trad.ap.*28.6; cf.‡Hipp.*can.*29; *ib.*194; cf. *ἀπαρχὴ δὲ...προσφερέσθω ...ὅμως ἰδίαν ἐχέτω κυρίως εὐλογίαν ὡς ἐξ ἁγιάσματος τοῦ κυριακοῦ σώματος καὶ αἵματος διΐστασθαι Cod.Afr.*37; *ὡς ἀπαρχὴν...τὴν τῆς σταφυλῆς λογιζομένους προσένεξιν ἰδικῶς τοὺς ἱερεῖς ~οῦντας τοῖς αἰτοῦσι ταύτης μεταδιδόναι* CTrull.*can.*28; **b.** extra-liturg.; upon seed-sowing, *A.Petr.et Andr.*4(p.119.12); among Essenes upon food, Hipp.*haer.*9.21(p.257.18; M.16.3398B); ref. partic. blessings; upon an animal, *A.Thom.*A 40(p.158.14); wine *~ήθη δὲ ὁ...οἶνος τοσοῦτον ὥστε ἐπὶ τρεῖς ἡμέρας ἅπαντας πλουσίως πίνειν ἀπ' αὐτοῦ* Cyr.S.*v.Sab.*46(p.137.9).

V. eucharistic;

A. *consecrate* the eucharist; **1.** at institution *τῶν ὑπὸ 'Ιησοῦ ~ηθέντων ἄρτων* Or.*or.*27(p.364.7; M.11.505B); **2.** as action of H. Ghost *ἐλθεῖν τὸ πνεῦμα σου...ἐφ' ἡμᾶς καὶ ἐπὶ τὰ προκείμενα δῶρα ταῦτα καὶ ~ῆσαι αὐτὰ καὶ ἁγιάσαι Lit.Bas.*(p.329.31); of Christ *κύριε 'Ιησοῦ...~ησον τὸν ἄρτον τοῦτον καὶ ἡμᾶς δι' αὐτοῦ A.Jo.*109 (p.208.10n.); **3.** as act of Church *λαβὼν ἄρτον καὶ ποτήριον ~ησεν καὶ εἶπεν· τὸ σῶμά σου τὸ ἅγιον κτλ. A.Thom.*A 158(p.268.2); *ib.*133 (p.240.6); cf. *~ησον δέσποτα τὸν ἅγιον ἄρτον...τὸ ἅγιον ποτήριον καὶ ὁ ἱερεὺς ~ῶν λέγει Lit.Chrys.*(p.387.3,9f.,15f.); *αἴρων τὴν δεξιὰν αὐτοῦ μετὰ εὐλαβείας ~εῖ τὸν ἅγιον ἄρτον, ἐκφώνως λέγων· λάβετε, φάγετε κτλ. Euchol.*(p.61).

B. *administer* chalice *οὐ δεῖ ὑπηρέτας ἄρτον διδόναι οὐδὲ ποτήριον ~εῖν* CLaod.*can.*25.

VI. gen. uses; power to bless shared by all righteous believers, cf. *non solum is qui sacerdotium sortitus est, sed et omnis justus*

Christum habens in semetipso...idoneus est ad donandam benedictionem, Hesych.H.*Lev*.9:23(M.93.894C); in this sense a blessing may be bestowed by any representative of God, e.g. Messiah ∼ήσει λαὸν κυρίου ἐν σοφίᾳ μετ' εὐφροσύνης *Pss.Sal*.17.40; *T.Neph*.8.2; by powers of heaven and earth, *T.Jud*.25.2; ∼ήσουσιν ὑμᾶς οἱ ἄνθρωποι καὶ οἱ ἄγγελοι *T.Neph*.8.4; cf. ὡς...παρ' ἀγγέλων τὴν εὐλογίαν ἐδέξατο [sc. Lot] Thdt.*Heb*.13:2(3.632); by patriarchs ∼ησέν με ὁ πατὴρ τοῦ πατρός μου κατὰ τῶν ὁραμάτων ὧν εἶδον *T.Lev*.9.2; Ἀβραάμ...∼ησέ με βασιλεύειν ἐν Ἰσραήλ *T.Jud*.17.5; *Barn*.13.5; Or.*Jo*.10.5(4; p.175.27; M.14.313D); a prophet or OT saint λόγος εὐλογίας Ἐνώχ, καθὼς ∼ησεν ἐκλεκτοὺς δικαίους *Apoc.En*.1.1; cf. (ref. Balaam) διὰ μάντεως εὐλογίας πνευματικὰς ἐχαρίσατο Chrys. *hom.86.4 in Jo*.(8.518D); a parent, Just.*dial*.139.1(M.6.793C); cf. Thdt.*h.e*.1.18.9(3.796); a saint upon his disciples, Gr.Nyss.*v.Ephr*. (M.46.844C); other ascetics, ‡Pall.*h.mon*.1.64(p.24.3; M.34.1130D); hence any may pray for a blessing upon another, e.g. a widow, and so become agent ∼ησον, κύριε...τὸν διακονήσαντα αὐτῇ *Const.App*. 3.13.1; a form of greeting ὁ βασιλεὺς Ἰηοῦ ∼ησεν αὐτὸν τουτέστι προσεῖπεν αὐτῷ Thdt.*qu.33 in 4Reg*.10:15(1.532); customary between ecclesiastics, Niceph.Ur.*v.Sym*.155(M.86.3129D); Leont.N. *v.Sym*.41(M.93.1721A); a mark of honour, *Apophth.Patr*.(M.65. 317D); καὶ ἔκειντο ἀμφότεροι ἐπὶ τὴν γῆν, ἕκαστος ἐξαιτῶν ∼ῆσαι τὸν ἕτερον, καὶ οὐδὲν ἦν ἀκοῦσαι παρὰ ἀμφοτέρων λεγόμενον, εἰ μὴ τό, ∼ησον ‡Sophr.H.*v.Mar.Aeg*.13(M.87.3708A); πάτερ (or κύριε), εὐλόγησον, or simply εὐλόγησον, at beginning of homilies and lives of saints originates in request for a blessing from presiding minister on one who is about to preach or to read from scripture or lives of saints, *M.Perp*.tit.(p.61.2); *M.Ner.et Ach*.tit.(p.1.4); ‡Epiph.*hom*.1 tit. (M.43.428B).

VII. ptcpl. as iron. or slang term (cf. Eng. 'blessed') ἄρχεται λέγειν μεμφόμενος τὸ ἔργον· τοσαῦτα ἔτη ἐργάζομαι ἐν τῷ ∼ημένῳ ἔργῳ τούτῳ, καὶ οὔτε μισθωμάτιον ἔχω Ephr.2.101C.

VIII. *grant permission, excuse*, a form of excuse from table ∼ήσατε, πατέρες, ἐρεῖς Niceph.Ur.*v.Sym*.36(M.86.3020A); cf. εὐλογία.

***εὐλόγημα, τό,** *object of blessing*, formed on analogy of ἐπιθύμημα: φήσεις ὅτι τὰ ἐπιθυμήματα τοῦ ἐπιθυμῆσαί τινα αὐτῶν ἄξιά ἐστιν, ὡς τὰ εὐλογητὰ τοῦ εὐλογεῖσθαι...ὥσπερ...τὰ εὐ. μᾶλλον ὑπὸ θεοῦ εὐλογεῖται...οὕτω καὶ τὰ ἐπιθυμήματα...ἂν ὑπὸ θεοῦ...ἐπιθυμηθείη Or. *Jo*.20.23(20; p.356.7; εὐλογητά M.14.624A).

***εὐλόγησις, ἡ,** *blessing*, *Rit.Epiph*.(p.416).

***εὐλογητάριον, τό,** troparion or *short hymn*, so called because it follows recitation of versicle εὐλογητὸς εἶ, κύριε, *Euchol*.(p.43); *ib*. (p.451).

***εὐλογητέον,** *one must bless*, Clem.*paed*.2.9(p.206.1; M.8.493A).

εὐλογητός, *blessed*; **1.** usu. of God εὐ. εἶ, κύριε *Apoc.En*.22.14; *T.Sal*.proem.(p.5.2; M.122.1316A); *Const.App*.7.34.1; σε...τὸν εὐ. καὶ χορηγὸν πάσης εὐλογίας Serap.*euch*.11.1; διὰ...τοῦ μονογενοῦς σου υἱοῦ μεθ' οὗ εὐ. εἶ *Lit.Bas*.(p.320.18); and his name, *Apoc.En*. 9.4; Just.*dial*.64.6(M.6.624D); **a.** freq. followed by specification of occasion for praise εὐ. κύριος ὁ ποιῶν ἔλεον *Pss.Sal*.6.9; εὐ. ... ὁ χαρισάμενος ὑμῖν ἀξίοις οὖσιν τοιοῦτον ἐπίσκοπον κεκτῆσθαι Ign.*Eph*. 1.3; εὐ. ὁ κύριος ἡμῶν...ὁ σοφίαν καὶ νοῦν θέμενος ἐν ἡμῖν τῶν κρυφίων αὐτοῦ *Barn*.6.10; εὐ. κύριος...ὁ ποιῶν θαυμάσια μόνος Just.*dial*.34.6 (M.6.548D); *MAMA* 3.520(Corycus); Cosm.Ind.*top*.prec.(p.37.12; M.88.52A); εὐ. ὁ θεὸς ὁ ὁδηγήσας ὑμᾶς εἰς τὴν ἀλήθειαν CNic.(787)*act*.1 (H.4.49B); **b.** of God as blessed in himself ἔστι...καὶ αὐτὸς εὐ., ἐν τῇ φύσει ἔχων τὴν εὐλογίαν Chrys.*exp.in Ps*.134:19ff.(5.396A); or as bestowing blessing εὐ. τὸν θεόν φασιν οἱ θεῖοι λόγοι, οὐ τῷ εὐλογίαν δεδέχθαι, ἀλλὰ τῷ παρέχειν αὐτήν Didym.*2Cor*.1:3(p.15.1; M.39. 1681C); **c.** of Christ ὁ τοῦ...εὐ. παιδός σου Ἰησοῦ Χριστοῦ πατήρ *M.Polyc*.14.1; *Lit*.ap.*Const.App*.8.15.2; εὐ. εἶ, κύριε Ἰησοῦ Χριστέ *M.Carp*.41(p.13.7); **d.** εὐ. κύριος in form of blessing, Jo.Mosch.*prat*. 118(M.87.2981C); **e.** liturg. εὐ. ὁ θεός in *antiphona benedictionis* or ascription with which many offices began, *Lit.Praesanct*.(p.345.8); cf.*Lit.Chrys*.(p.353.11); τὸ εὐλογητὸς ὁ θεὸς ἤκουσεν καὶ τὸ Χριστὸς ὁ ἀληθινὸς οὐκ ἤκουσεν *Nomoc*.408; **2.** of creatures; **a.** of persons as blessed by God εὐλογησόμεθα...γινόμενοι εὐ. ἐπὶ τοσοῦτον Or.*Jo*.20. 10(p.338.14; M.14.593A); **b.** of things *ib*.20.23(20; p.356.6; 624A) cit. s. εὐλόγημα; **3.** liturg., neut. as subst., *antiphona benedictionis, opening antiphon*, so called from first words ποιεῖ εὐλογητόν, τρισάγιον *Nomoc*.458; cf.*Lit.Chrys*.(p.353.10); and various rites, *Euchol*.(pp.195,271,378,451).

εὐλογία, ἡ, *blessing*; various uses in scripture, cf. *sciendum tamen est quod sermo hic benedictionis in scripturis diverse positus invenitur...dei quidem benedictio aliquid muneris semper his qui ab eo benedicuntur impertit: homines vero deum benedicere, pro eo quod est laudare et gratias referre, dicuntur*, Or.*comm.in Rom*.9.14(M.14. 1221A);

A. *praise*; usu. with God as object; **1.** *blessedness* of God in himself ἔστι...καὶ αὐτὸς εὐλογητός, ἐν τῇ φύσει ἔχων τὴν εὐ., οὐ δεόμενος τῆς παρ' ἑτέρων εὐφημίας Chrys.*exp.in Ps*.134:19ff.(5.396A); ἔχει... τὴν εὐ. καὶ τὴν εὐφημίαν ἄναρχον καὶ ἀήττητον Thdt.*Ps*.112:2(1. 1407); **2.** recognition of this by man in *blessing, praise* of God διὰ ταύτην [sc. τὴν ἀκήρατον οὐσίαν] ὀφείλεται αὐτῷ παρ' ἡμῶν...εὐλογία. ...οὐ χρείαν ἔχει τῶν παρ' ἡμῶν...εὐ., οὐδὲ προστίθεται αὐτοῦ τι τῇ δόξῃ παρὰ τῆς τῶν διακονουμένων εὐφημίας Chrys.*exp.in Ps*.144:3 (5.468B); τοῦτο...μάλιστά ἐστιν εὐ. ἠκριβωμένη, ὅταν μετὰ τῶν ῥημάτων καὶ ὁ βίος σύμφωνα φθέγγηται *ib*.133:2(382C); **3.** *praise* of martyrs which marked observance of their festivals, Chrys.*incomprehens*. 2.1(1.453B); **4.** between men, *good-will, favour* ἡ ἀγαθὴ διάνοια οὐκ ἔχει δύο γλώσσας εὐ. καὶ κατάρας *T.Ben*.6.5.

B. *blessing* as a mark of favour bestowed by God, defined εὐ. ἐστὶ πληθυσμὸς ἀγαθῶν ἐξ ἑκουσιότητος διδόμενος *Doct.Patr*.33(p.260. 21); **1.** upon Christ κατὰ τὸν σωτῆρα, ὅς...σὺν εὐλογίᾳ θεοῦ παρεῖχε τὸν στάχυν Eus.*v.C*.4.72(p.147.23; M.20.1228A); **2.** upon man ἐν τούτῳ ἡ εὐ. κυρίου εἰς πλησμονὴν ἐν δικαιοσύνῃ *Pss.Sal*.5.20; ἵνα δῷ ὁ θεὸς χάριν καὶ δόξαν καὶ εὐ. *T.Sym*.4.5; κολληθῶμεν...τῇ εὐ. αὐτοῦ, καὶ ἴδωμεν τίνες αἱ ὁδοὶ τῆς εὐ. *1Clem*.31.1; τῆς τοῦ θεοφιλοῦς μεταςχεῖν...εὐ. Eus.*d.e*.1.2(p.10.4; M.22.28A); ref. 1Petr.3:9 μήτε οὖν ἐπίσκοπος...μήτε ἄλλος τις ἐκ τοῦ καταλόγου τοῦ ἱερατικοῦ λοιδορίᾳ τὴν γλῶσσαν μολυνέτω, ἵνα μὴ ἀντὶ εὐ. κατάραν κληρονομήσῃ *Const.App*.3.15.5; ταῖς εὐ. κατὰ τὰς σωματικάς τε καὶ ψυχικάς Epiph.*anac*.(M.42.852B) cf. πρὸς τοὺς εὐλόγους χρείας σωματικὰς κτλ. id.*inc*.3(p.230.16; M.41.277A); τὰ χείλη τοῖς τραύμασι [sc. of confessors] προσενήνοχεν, ἑλκύσειν ἐκεῖθεν τῷ φιλήματι τὴν εὐ. πιστεύων Thdt.*h.e*.1.11.1(3.774); esp. at Creation ὁ θεὸς...παρασιωπᾷ, τηρῶν τῷ ἀνθρώπῳ τὴν εὐ. Thphl.Ant.*Autol*.2.17(M.6.1080A); ὁ ἀντικείμενος σβέσιν τινὰ...τῆς εὐ. ἐποίησεν Gr.Nyss.*or.catech*.6 (p.37.4; M.45.29C); bestowed on man in Christ who is called νυμφίος εὐλογίας, Or.*comm.in 1Cor*.7:28(*JTS* 9 p.510); ἔχοντες τὴν... ἑτοιμασθεῖσαν ἡμῖν ἐν αὐτῷ τῷ λόγῳ...ζωήν τε καὶ εὐ. πνευματικήν Ath.*Ar*.2.76(M.26.309A); ἦν...τοὺς τεθέντας φυλάττωμεν νόμους, καὶ τοῦ νομοθέτου τὴν εὐ. τρυγήσομεν ἐν Χριστῷ Ἰησοῦ Thdt.*1Thess*. 5:28(3.526); id.*Ps*.117:29(1.1436); through Cross εὐλογίας...οὐ κατάρας ὄργανον ὁ σταυρός Germ.CP *or*.1(M.98.237C); *ib*.(229C); cf. θεὸς...ὁ τὸν...Χριστὸν ἐξαποστείλας...εὐλογοῦντα καὶ ἁγιάζοντα ἡμᾶς *Lit.Jac*.(p.180.16); bestowed by Christ ἐπαίρει τὰς χεῖρας ὁ κύριος, δύναμιν...τοῖς μαθηταῖς ἐντιθεὶς διὰ τῆς εὐ. Or.*fr.87 in Lc*.24:50(p.275); through eucharist, ref. 1Cor.11:27f. ἔσται τοίνυν πρὸς εὐλογίας, φησί, τῶν ἁγίων μυστηρίων ἡ μέθεξις, τοῖς γε ὡς ἀληθῶς φιλοθεωτάτοις Cyr.*ador*.6(1.177E); Thdt.*Ps*.105:48(1.1365) cit. s. ἀμήν; **3.** upon things πᾶσα ἡ γῆ...πλησθήσεται εὐλογίας *Apoc.En*.10.18; θεία...εὐ. τὴν κέλλαν ἐπλήρωσεν ἕως ἄνω...ἐπὶ οἴνου καὶ ἐλαίου ἡ αὐτὴ γέγονεν εὐ. Cyr.S.*v.Euthym*.17(p.27.21,24); **4.** concrete *blessing, gift, benefit* from God κύριον...τὸν εὐλογητὸν καὶ χορηγὸν πάσης εὐ. Serap.*euch*. 11.1; πολλὰς οὖν εὐ. πέμπει αὐτῷ ὁ θεός Leont.N.*v.Jo.Eleem*.1(p.6.7); ὁ θεὸς...παρέσχεν ἡμῖν τὴν εὐ. τοῦ ὕδατος Jo.Mosch.*prat*.80(M.87. 2937D); bestowed through Christ τῶν...καλούντων αὐτὸν ἕκαστος νῦν εἰς τὴν οἰκίαν τὴν ἑαυτοῦ...εὐ. ἀπολαύσεται μεγάλης Chrys.*hom.59.4 in Jo*.(8.351A); ἁπάσης εὐ. ἀπολαύειν τῆς παρ' αὐτοῦ Cyr.*Jo*.12(4. 1085C); of grace of ordination to Jewish priesthood Λευί, σοὶ ἔδωκα τὰς εὐ. τῆς ἱερατείας *T.Lev*.5.2; εὐ. ... ἱερατικαί Or.*hom.12.3 in Jer*.(p.89.24; M.13.381D); among Jews often taking a material form ἐν εὐ. τῆς γῆς καὶ ἀπαρχῶν καρπῶν *T.Isach*.5.6; καθάρσια σωμάτων, σωματικάς τε εὐ. Eus.*e.th*.2.20(p.127.15; M.24.949C); under Christian dispensation its spiritual character stressed νοητὴν εὐ. Or.*or*.16(p.337.21; M.11.469C); id.*Cels*.7.24(p.176.1; M.11.1456B); πνευματικῇ εὐ. id.*hom.39 in Lc*.(p.228.8); Cyr.*Jo*.11.2(4.939D); cf. διδασκόμεθα...ὡς χρὴ πρότερον τοῖς εὐλογημένοις τὰς θείας αἰτεῖν δωρεάς Thdt.*qu.11 in Num*.6:27(1.227).

C. *blessing* of God bestowed by man, v. εὐλογέω; **1.** eccl., *benediction, blessing* defined εὐ. ... ἁγιασμοῦ μετάδοσίς ἐστιν Bas.*ep*. 199 *can*.27(3.294B; M.32.724C); opp. εὐχαριστία, Eutych.*pasch*.7(M. 86.2400B) cit. s. εὐχαριστέω; conferred by priests alone, *Const.App*. 3.10.1 cit. s. λαϊκός; οὔτε γὰρ διακόνῳ προσφέρειν θυσίαν θεμιτὸν ἢ βαπτίζειν ἢ εὐ. μικρὰν ἢ μεγάλην ποιεῖσθαι *ib*.8.46.11; εἰ...μηδὲν ἐνεργεῖ ὁ θεὸς δι' αὐτοῦ [sc. τοῦ ἱερέως], οὔτε λουτρὸν ἔχεις, οὔτε μυστηρίων μετέχεις, οὔτε εὐλογιῶν ἀπολαύεις Chrys.*hom.2.2 in 2Tim*. (11.668F); accompanied by gesture of hand ποῦ ἡ εὐπροσήγορος δεξιά, τῇ τοῦ στόματος εὐ. τοὺς δακτύλους συνεπισείουσα; Gr.Nyss. *Melet*.(M.46.856B); cf.Hesych.H.*Lev*.9:22(M.93.893Df.); cf. τίνι...ὁ πρεσβύτερος ἐπιθήσει χεῖρα; τίνα δὲ εὐλογήσει; Clem.*paed*.3.11(p.271.

21; M.8.637B); ἐπέθηκεν αὐτοὺς τὰς χεῖρας...καὶ εὐλόγησεν αὐτούς *A.Thom.*A 29(p.146.6,17); *ib.*10f.(pp.115.10f.,116.3); by monastic superiors εἰ δὲ μόνης τῆς εὐ. ἀνάξιός τις ἐκρίθη, συγχωρηθεὶς δὲ φαγεῖν οὐκ ἀνέχεται, ὡς...φιλόνεικος κρινέσθω Bas.*reg.br.*122(2.457D; M.31.1165B) or perh. s. D.3 infra; **2.** *consecration, dedication* τὸ θυσιαστήριον τοῦτο...λίθος ἐστὶ κατὰ τὴν φύσιν κοινὸς...ἐπειδὴ δὲ καθιερώθη τῇ τοῦ θεοῦ θεραπείᾳ, κατὰ τὴν εὐ. ἐδέξατο, ἔστι τράπεζα ἁγία Gr.Nyss.*bapt.Chr.*(M.46.581C); **3.** in non-eccl. sense, v. εὐλογέω.

D. eucharistic; **1.** *consecration* ἐλθάτω δύναμις εὐλογίας καὶ ἐνιδρύσθω ὁ ἄρτος *A.Thom.*A 133(p.240.13); οὕτως τὸ μυστικὸν ἔλαιον, οὕτως ὁ οἶνος· ὀλίγου τινὸς ἄξια ὄντα πρὸ τῆς εὐ., μετὰ τὸν ἁγιασμὸν τὸν τοῦ πνεύματος, ἑκάτερον αὐτῶν ἐνεργεῖ διαφόρως Gr.Nyss.*bapt.Chr.*(M.46.581C); ταῦτα...δίδωσι τῇ τῆς εὐ. δυνάμει πρὸς ἐκεῖνο μεταστοιχειώσας τῶν φαινομένων τὴν φύσιν id.*or.catech.*37(p.152.7; M.45.97B); Cyr.*ep.Calos.*(6².365B) cit. s. μεταβάλλω; and perh. μανθάνειν ἐπείγεσθαι μᾶλλον τῆς εὐ. τὸν τρόπον, οὐκ ἀπερισκέπτως...λέγοντας [Jo.6:52] id.*Jo.*4.2(4.360A); πληρῶσον...ταύτην θυσίαν τῆς παρά σ[ου εὐ. διὰ τοῦ ἁγίου σου] πνεύματος *Lit.Marc.*(*PRyl.* 465.3); **2.** of eucharist in gen. (1Cor.10:16) δίδωσί σοι τὸ ποτήριον τῆς διαθήκης τῆς καινῆς, δίδωσί σοι καὶ τὸν ἄρτον τῆς εὐ., τὸ σῶμα ἑαυτοῦ καὶ τὸ αἷμα ἑαυτοῦ χαρίζεται Or.*hom.19.13 in Jer.*(p.269.32; M.13.489C); ἁπλώσας σινδόνα ἐπ' αὐτὸ ἐπέθηκεν ἄρτον τῆς εὐ. *A.Thom.*A 49(p.166.1); κοινωνῆσαί μοι εἰς τὴν εὐχαριστίαν ταύτην καὶ εὐ. τοῦ κυρίου *ib.*26(p.142.1); *A.Mt.*27(p.258.13); Bas.*Spir.*66(3.54E; M.32.188B) cit. s. ἐπίκλησις; εὐ. ... ὅταν εἴπω, εὐχαριστίαν λέγω Chrys.*hom.24.1 in 1Cor.*(10.212D); ποτήριον...εὐλογίας ἐκάλεσεν, ἐπειδὴ αὐτὸ μετὰ χεῖρας ἔχοντες, οὕτως αὐτὸν ἀνυμνοῦμεν...εὐλογοῦντες ὅτι καὶ αὐτὸ τοῦτο ἐξέχεεν *ib.*(10.213A); διὰ δέ γε τοῦ οἴνου τὴν μυστικὴν εὐ. ὑποδηλοῦν, καὶ τῆς ἀναιμάκτου θυσίας τὸν τρόπον, ἣν ἐν ταῖς ἁγίαις ἐκκλησίαις ἀποπληροῦν εἰθίσμεθα Cyr.*Is.*3.1(2.353D); plur. ὁμολογοῦντες αὐτοῦ τὸ πάθος, καὶ τὴν...ἀναβίωσιν, ταῖς μυστικαῖς προσίεμεν εὐ. id.*glaph.Dt.*(1.414E); **3.** of consecrated gifts ἀρτίως αἱ χεῖρες [sc. of Judas] τὰς εὐ. ἐδέχοντο Cyr.H.*catech.*13.6; Cyr.*glaph.Dt.*(1.428B); τὴν ἀναίμακτον...τελοῦμεν λατρείαν πρόσιμέν τε οὕτω ταῖς μυστικαῖς εὐ. καὶ ἁγιαζόμεθα id.*ep.*17(p.37.25; 5².72D); usu. sing. οὐδὲν ἐκ τῆς εὐ. ὠφελημένον id.*Jo.*9(4.743A); καὶ σῶμα καὶ μέλη Χριστοῦ χρηματίζομεν, ὡς διὰ τῆς εὐ. αὐτὸν ἐν ἑαυτοῖς δεχόμενοι τὸν υἱόν *ib.*4.2(364D); freq. with μυστική: τὴν μυστικὴν εὐ., εἰ ἀπομείνοι λείψανον αὐτῆς εἰς ἑτέραν ἡμέραν id.*ep.Calos.*(6².365B); id.*glaph.Lev.*(1.351D); *ib.*(367C); id.*ador.*2(1.80A); id.*Abac.*48(3.561E); id.*hom.pasch.*9.6(5².123C); μετασχεῖν τῆς εὐ. τῆς μυστικῆς ἓν πρὸς αὐτὸν γέγονε σῶμα id.*Jo.*10.2(4.862E); *ib.*11.12(1001E); Proc.G.*Jos.*5:11(M.87.1012A); κουφίζων ὁ ἱεράρχης τὸν ἅγιον ἄρτον, ἐδείκνυ τὴν εὐ. Max.*schol.e.h.*3.3.10(M.4.148B); *ib.*3.2(137A); v. ζωοποιός; **4.** of eucharistic elements before consecration ἐπὶ τοῦ θείου θυσιαστηρίου προτιθέασι τὸν ἱερὸν ἄρτον καὶ τὸ τῆς εὐ. ποτήριον Dion.Ar.*e.h.*3.2(M.3.425C); *ib.*3.3.8(437A); ἐπέμφθη ἐνέγκαι εὐλογίας...καὶ τὰς αὐτὰς εὐ. προέθηκεν ἐν τῷ δίσκῳ ἐν τῷ...θυσιαστηρίῳ Jo.Mosch.*prat.*25(M.87.2869D); τὸ...προσαγόμενον πολλοῖς ὀνόμασιν ὀνομάζεται· καλεῖται γὰρ εὐ., προσφορά, ἀπαρχή, ἄρτος· εὐ. μὲν ὡς τῆς ἀρᾶς τῶν πρωτοπλάστων ἀναίρεσις ‡Sophr.H.*liturg.*9(M.87.3989A); ὁ τὸ σῶμα διατέμνων ἀπὸ τῆς εὐ. *ib.*10(3989D); ‡Germ.CP *contempl.*(M.98.397C); *Nomoc.*284; of bread offered for eucharist ὑπέθετο τῷ βασιλεῖ...δηλῶσαι τῷ πατριάρχῃ ἀποστεῖλαι τὰς ὑπὲρ τῆς χειροτονίας εὐ. ὁ δὲ...καθαροὺς ἄρτους ἀπέστειλεν εὐλογίας Thphn.*chron.*p.84(M.108.256B).

E. *gift of blessed bread*; in early times eucharist itself sent to absent members and to bishops in other parts as a pledge of unity, cf.Just.*1apol.*67.5(M.6.429C); Iren.*ep.Vict.*ap.Eus.*h.e.*5.24.15(M.20.505A); but this practice forbidden μὴ τὰ ἅγια εἰς λόγον εὐλογιῶν κατὰ τὴν ἑορτὴν τοῦ πάσχα εἰς ἑτέρας παροικίας διαπέμπεσθαι CLaod.*can.*14; (absence of precise terminology impeded appreciation of difference between a sacrament and a sacramental, cf. *quamvis non sit corpus Christi, sanctum tamen est, et sanctius quam cibi quibus alimur, quoniam sacramentum est*, Aug. *de peccatorum meritis* 2.42(M.*PL.*44.176); λειτουργημένας εὐ. ... θυσία προσφερομένη τῷ θεῷ ἐστίν *Nomoc.*112); **1.** of bread offered, but not required for eucharist and given to clergy τὰς περισσευούσας ἐν τοῖς μυστικοῖς εὐ. ... διανεμέτωσαν τῷ κλήρῳ *Const.App.*8.31.2; ἀπὸ...τῶν ἐκκλησιῶν οὐδὲν ἐδέξατο [sc. Novatianist bishop Chrysanthus], πλὴν κατὰ κυριακὴν δύο ἄρτους τῶν εὐ. ἐλάμβανεν Socr.*h.e.*7.12.9(M.67.760B); **2.** or instead of being consecrated, blessed separately and distributed in church as *panis benedictus, pain bénit*, cf. ἀντίδωρον; τὰς προσφερομένας εὐ. τῇ ἐκκλησίᾳ τοῦ θεοῦ, οὐ μόνον τοῖς ἱερεῦσιν προετάσσομεν εἶναι, ἀλλὰ καὶ τοῖς διακόνοις, πᾶσι τοῖς κοπιῶσιν ἐν τῷ ἁγίῳ ἔργῳ τοῦ θεοῦ *Nomoc.*11; to coenobites in form of a collation πίε τὴν εὐ. ταύτην (οἴνου γὰρ οὔτε ὅλως μετελάμβανεν) Call.*v.Hyp.*(p.15); καὶ ἐλθούσης τῆς ἐνάτης ὥρας...εὐ. ... οὐκ ἔλαβεν *ib.*(p.30); πολλάκις...ἐδίδοτο τοῖς ἀδελφοῖς ἀπὸ συνάξεως, παξαμάτην καὶ ποτήριον οἴνου· αὐτὸς δὲ οὐκ ἐλάμβανεν· οὐκ ἀπωθούμενος τὴν εὐ. τῶν ἀδελφῶν, ἀλλὰ τὴν τῆς συνάξεως ἐπικρατῶν ἡσυχίαν *Apophth.Patr.*(M.65.241A); πεντήκοντα ἔτη...ἀρκούμενος τῇ εὐ. τῆς ἐκκλησίας Jo.Mosch.*prat.*41(M.87.2896B); to those who had not communicated including penitents, Sophr.H.*mir.Cyr.et Jo.*38(M.87.356D); *Nomoc.*224,231; in religious houses ἐν τῇ ὥρᾳ τῆς δόσεως τῆς εὐ. Thdr.Stud.*poen.mon.*2.18(M.99.1752B); μετὰ τὸ ἀπολῦσαι τὴν θείαν λειτουργίαν, λαμβάνομεν τὴν εὐ.· εἶτα διακλυζόμεθα μὲν οἱ κοινωνήσαντες, τὴν δὲ εὐ. οὐκ ἐσθίομεν *Const.Stud.*37(M.99.1717C); cf. τοὺς ὄντας ἐν ἐπιτιμίοις μοναχούς, χρὴ...τοῖς λοιποῖς...μετέχειν...εὐ., ἤτοι κατακλαστοῦ Niceph.I CP *can.*19(M.100.857A); **3.** of blessed bread sent as a gift, Call.*v.Hyp.*(p.76); οἱ ἀδελφοὶ...κομιοῦσίν σοι εὐλογίας, ἃς ὑποδεξάμενος μεταλήψῃ σὺν αὐτοῖς καὶ τῷ θεῷ...εὐχαριστήσεις ‡Pall.*h.mon.*1.58(p.22.11; M.34.1129C); ἄλλοτε εὐλογίας τοῖς ἀρρώστοις ἀπέστειλε καὶ ἀπηλλάγησαν εὐθέως τῆς νόσου *ib.*15.7(p.70.18; 1163D); ἕνα...τῶν τῆς εὐ. ἄρτων λαβών, ἄπιθι Niceph.Ur.*v.Sym.*121(M.86.3100A); δίδωσιν αὐτῷ τρεῖς εὐ. ζεστὰς...καὶ λέγει· δὸς τῷ Σαλῷ Leont.N.*v.Sym.*49(M.93.1729D); not to be received from heretics οὐ δεῖ αἱρετικῶν εὐ. λαμβάνειν, αἵτινές εἰσιν ἀλογίαι μᾶλλον ἢ εὐ. CLaod.*can.*32; **4.** in a general distribution of food to poor, Jo.Mosch.*prat.*85(M.87.2941B,D).

F. any *gift*; esp. **1.** an alms (2Cor.9:5f.) τοὺς καρποὺς ὑμῶν καὶ τὰ ἔργα τῶν χειρῶν ὑμῶν εἰς εὐ. ὑμῶν προσφέροντες αὐτῷ [sc. τῷ ἐπισκόπῳ] *Const.App.*2.34.5; ref. Rom.15:29 τί ἐστιν, ἐν πληρώματι εὐλογίας; ἤτοι περὶ χρημάτων φησίν, ἢ περὶ πάντων ἁπλῶς τῶν κατορθωμάτων. εὐ. γὰρ...τὴν ἐλεημοσύνην εἴωθε λέγειν· ὡς ὅταν λέγῃ [2Cor.9:5] Chrys.*hom.30.1 in Rom.*(9.739B); ὠνόμασε τὴν μετάδοσιν ...χάριν, καὶ κοινωνίαν, καὶ εὐ. Thdt.*2Cor.*9:5(3.334); [2Cor.9:6] τουτέστιν δαψιλῶς καὶ μεγαλοψυχῶς Leont.N.*v.Jo.Eleem.*22(p.47.17); cf. σύνες...ὅτι...ἡ βασιλεία τῶν ἐπισκόπων ἐγώ, ἡ δόξα τῶν πρεσβυτέρων ἐγώ, ἡ εὐ. τῶν διακόνων ἐγώ *A.Mt.*2(p.219.7); **2.** other kinds of gift; as a bribe, Gr.Nyss.*v.Ephr.*(M.46.840C); from a bishop, CBeryt.*act.*(*ACO* 2.1.3 p.388.2; H.2.524D); ἑτέρων μοι πεμψάντων θεοφιλεστάτων ἐπισκόπων εὐ. οὐκ ἐδεξάμην Thdt.*ep.*123(4.1207); between monks εἴ τις πέμπει τινὶ εὐ. ... παρεκτὸς τοῦ ἀρχιμανδρίτου, γενέσθω ἀπευλογίας ‡Bas.*poen.mon.*60(2.530D; M.31.1313C); Jo.Mosch.*prat.*42(M.87.2896C); usu. of eatables, to bestow such a gift a sign of seniority οὐκ εἰμί σου χείρων, ἵνα σὺ ἐμοὶ εὐ. πέμψῃς Pall.*h.Laus.*25(p.79.18; M.34.1090C); not to be given to excommunicates, *Apophth.Patr.*(M.65.92B); to monks ταύτης οὖν τυχὼν τῆς εὐεργεσίας πολλὴν μὲν προσήνεγκεν εὐ., ἑτέραν δὲ ὑπέσχετο διδόναι καθ' ἕκαστον ἐνιαυτόν Cyr.S.*v.Euthym.*47(p.68.17); id.*v.Sab.*39(p.130.26); †Jo.D.*B.J.*18(M.96.1020A).

G. *dispensation* or *permission* of superior to monks εἴ τις ἐξέλθοι τοῦ μοναστηρίου, μὴ λαβὼν εὐ., ἔστω ἀκοινώνητος ‡Bas.*poen.mon.*12(2.527E; M.31.1308C); *ib.*21(2.528B; 1309A); Thdr.Stud.*poen.*1.24(M.99.1736C); *ib.*2.1(1748C).

H. name of a kind of plague τὰ μηνύοντα θάνατον παραπλήσια λοιμικῆς, τὰ λεγόμενα μαῦρα· οἱ πολλοὶ δὲ καλοῦσιν αὐτὰ εὐ. *Mir.Artem.*34(p.51.14).

***εὐλογισμός, ὁ,** v. *ἐνλογισμός.

***εὐλογιστικός,** *of blessing*, Thdr.Stud.*epp.*1.50(M.99.1093A).

εὐλόγιστος, 1. *prudent*; neut. as subst., Or.*Jo.*28.23(18; p.418.27; M.14.729C); **2.** *approved, acceptable* ὅπως ὑπὲρ τῶν ἡμῶν ἁμαρτιῶν αἱ νηστεῖαι ἡμῖν εὐ. θεῷ γένωνται Epiph.*exp.fid.*22(p.523.3; M.42.828A).

εὔλογος, 1. *rational*, opp. ἄλογος, Tat.*orat.*9(p.9.29; M.6.825B); **2.** *fair, right*, Clem.*fr.*48(p.224.23)ap.Max.*ambig.*(M.91.1085B); Or.*hom.16.5 in Jer.*(p.138.15; M.13.445C); id.*Jo.*1.5(7; p.9.26; M.14.32D); *ib.*2.11(6; p.66.14; 129C); ref. Atonement ἔδει τοὺς ἀνθρώπους μὴ ἀφιέναι φέρεσθαι τῇ φθορᾷ...ἀλλ'...ἐκ τῶν ἐναντίων πάλιν ἀντίκειται τὸ πρὸς τὸν θεὸν εὐ., ὥστε ἀληθῆ φανῆναι τὸν θεὸν ἐν τῇ περὶ τοῦ θανάτου νομοθεσίᾳ...ἀλλ' ἡ μετάνοια οὔτε τὸ εὐ. τὸ πρὸς τὸν θεὸν ἐφύλαττεν...οὔτε...ἀπὸ τῶν κατὰ φύσιν ἀνακαλεῖται ἀλλὰ μόνον παύει τῶν ἁμαρτημάτων...αὐτοῦ [sc. τοῦ θεοῦ λόγου] γὰρ ἦν πάλιν καὶ τὸ φθαρτὸν εἰς ἀφθαρσίαν ἐνεγκεῖν, καὶ τὸ ὑπὲρ πάντων εὐ. ἀποσῶσαι πρὸς τὸν πατέρα Ath.*inc.*7.1ff.; M.25.108C–109A); Epiph.*haer.*76.52(p.406.7; M.42.625B); Evagr.*h.e.*4.25(p.171.33; M.86.2744A); *in due order, legitimate* τῇ...ψήφῳ εὐ. οὔσῃ καὶ κατὰ κανόνα ἐκκλησιαστικόν CNic.(325)*can.*6.

***εὐλογοφάνεια, ἡ,** *false appearance, plausibility*, Mac.Aeg.*hom.*4.7(M.34.477C); of Devil's wiles, Nil.*epp.*2.62(M.79.228D); Dor.*doct.*5.1(M.88.1676D).

εὐλογοφανής, **1.** *seeming probable*, *specious*, †Bas.*ep*.42.4(3.128D; M.32.356A); Mac.Aeg.*hom*.26.12(M.34.681D); Dor.*doct*.4.11(M.88.1673C); **2.** *plausible*, †Bas.*bapt*.1.1.2(2.625C; M.31.1516D); Gennad.*fr.Gen*.1:1(M.85.1615A).

***εὐλογοφανῶς**, *in a way that seems probable* or *reasonable*, Bas.*renunt*.9(2.210B; M.31.645A); Max.*qu.Thal*.38(M.90.389C); id.*carit*.2.59(M.90.1004B).

εὐλόγως, *with a blessing*, Didym.*Ps*.17:47(M.39.1266C).

εὐλοιδόρητος, of persons, *very blameworthy*, Ant.Mon.*hom*.17(M.89.1480A).

εὔλυσία, ἡ, *release*, Ephr.1.73E.

εὔλυτος, *free*, *unimpeded* ἑτοιμότητα Clem.*paed*.1.12(p.149.10; M.8.368C); βίον Gr.Naz.*carm*.1.2.10.516(M.37.717A); Dion.Ar.*c.h*.15.4(M.3.332D); of persons, Clem.*str*.4.15(p.291.19; M.8.1304C); Chrys.*hom.12.3 in Eph*.(11.94E); id.*hom.54.4 in Jo*.(8.321A); *free from bonds*; of Lazarus, †Hipp.*Laz*.(p.226.30; M.62.778).

εὐλυτ-όω, *deliver*, *free* ∼ώθη τῆς δίκης Jo.Mal.*chron*.15 p.384(M.97.572A); ∼ωσόν με *Chron.Pasch*.p.327(M.92.844A); *ib*.(844B); *V.Dan*.9(p.256.6).

***εὐλύτωσις**, ἡ, *payment*, *settlement* of a debt, Ath.Scholast.*coll*.2.2(p.31).

εὐμάραντος, *soon withering*, Gr.Naz.*carm*.2.2(epit.)129.10(M.37.80A); Diod.*Ps*.70:16(M.33.1613A); Cyr.*Ps*.36:2(M.69.924D); met., of man, Or.*sel.in Ps*.102:15(M.12.1560B); of worldly concerns, Cyr.*hom.pasch*.24(5^2.295B); θνητῇ φύσει καὶ εὐ. Germ.CP *or*.1(M.98.232A).

***εὐμαρίζω**, *ease*, *mitigate*, Chrys.*hom.in Rom.12:20*(3.161C); Thdr.Stud.*epp*.1.40(M.99.1052B); id.*or*.11.33(M.99.836C).

***εὔμασθος**, *fair-breasted*, Jo.Mal.*chron*.5 p.91(M.97.176B).

εὐμέθοδος, *scientific*, *efficient* ἰατρικῆς Nil.*praest*.2(M.79.1064A); ἀθλητής Marc.Er.*opusc*.2.148(M.65.953B).

εὐμείλικτος, *easily appeased*, Thdr.Stud.*epp*.1.23(M.99.980D); *ib*.2.180(1556D).

***εὐμειρέω**, *have a good part in*, c. genit., ‡Amph.*non desp*.(p.273).

εὐμένεια, ἡ, *goodwill*, *favour*; of God, Clem.*str*.2.6(p.128.9; M.8.964B); Const.*ep*.ap.Ath.*apol.sec*.86(p.165.27; M.25.404C); plur., Cyr.*Mich*.8(3.398D); of emperor, Ath.*apol.Const*.12(M.25.609B); plur., Thdr.Stud.*epp*.1.56(M.99.1112B); as complimentary title of emperor, *A.(Pass.)Petr.et Paul*.46(p.158.15); CArim.*ep.Const.2* ap. Thdt.*h.e*.2.20.1,2,3(3.878).

εὐμενέτης, poet. form of εὐμενής, *gracious*, Eudoc.*Cypr*.2.435(M.85.861C).

εὐμενίζω, *propitiate* τὸν θεόν Eus.*h.e*.9.9.12(M.20.824B); ἥρωάς τε καὶ θεούς id.*l.C*.11(p.224.20; M.20.1377A); Max.*ambig*.(M.91.1124A); ὡς ἂν ὁ θεὸς εὐμενισθείη Thdr.Stud.*epp*.2.89(M.99.1337D); med., c. dat., Marc.Er.*opusc*.3.3(M.65.969A).

***εὐμενισμός**, ὁ, *favour*, *benevolence* τοῦ παρὰ τοῦ θεοῦ εὐ. Or.*Cels*.8.64(p.280.8; M.11.1612D).

εὐμενῶς, *graciously*, ref. God εὐ. ἐπιβλέψης ἐπὶ τὰ προκείμενα δῶρα ταῦτα *Lit*.ap.*Const.App*.8.12.39; εὐ. προσδέξαι τὴν ἑσπερινὴν εὐχαριστίαν ἡμῶν ταύτην *Const.App*.8.37.2; superl., Thdr.Stud.*epp*.2.56(M.99.1269A); irreg. superl. εὐμενεστάτως ‡Jo.D.*ep.Thphl*.30(M.95.384B).

εὐμετάγωγος, *easily influenced*, Marc.Diac.*v.Porph*.64.

εὐμετακίνητος, **1.** *easily changed*, Gr.Naz.*or*.40.44(M.36.421B); **2.** *easily removed* or *scattered* γένοιντο...εὐ. ὥσπερ ἐστὶν ὁ χνοῦς τῷ ἀνέμῳ *cat.Ps*.34:5(1.624).

εὐμετακόμιστος, **1.** *easily carried*, Const.ap.Eus.*v.C*.4.36(p.131.25; M.20.1185A), but εὐπαρακόμιστος, ap.Thdt.*h.e*.1.16.2; **2.** *easily moved*, *prompt* θεὸς...εὐ. ... πρὸς τὸ καταλῆξαι θυμοῦ Cyr.*Juln*.5(6^2.162E).

***εὐμετάλλακτος**, *easily changed*, Chrys.*ecl*.40(12.735B), cf. εὐκατάλλακτος *easily appeased*, id.*hom.1.3 in Philm*.(11.778C).

***εὐμεταμέλητος**, *quick to repent*, *changeable*, ‡Chrys.*hom*.13(13.255D) cit. s. ἀντιταλάντευσις.

***εὐμετάμελος**, *ready to change one's mind*, of emperor τὸ φιλάνθρωπον καὶ εὐ. Thdr.Stud.*epp*.1.12(M.99.952C).

***εὐμεταρρίπιστος**, *turbulent*, Oecum.*Apoc*.16:20(p.182).

εὐμετάτρεπτος, *changeable*; neut. plur. as adv., ‡Bas.*const*.8.1(2.554C; M.31.1369A).

εὐμετάφορος, *changeable*, *fickle*, Thdr.Heracl.*fr.Mt*.11:3(p.84.11).

***εὐμετρέω**, *measure carefully*, Cyr.*ador*.1(1.25C; prob. for εὖ μεμέτρηται).

εὐμετρία, ἡ, *skill in metre*, Gr.Naz.*carm*.2.1.39.100(M.37.1336A); Geo.Pis.*bell.Avar*.48(M.92.1267A).

εὐμέτρως, *in due measure* or *proportion*, Eus.*Hierocl*.19(524D; M.22.825C).

εὐμήκης, *long* δάκτυλοι Chrys.*Eutrop*.2.17(3.403B); ὄνυχας Cyr.*glaph.Dt*.(1.418A); *well-proportioned in height* εἰκόνας...αἱ μὲν τῶν προσώπων εἰσὶν εὐ. καὶ εὐμεγεθεῖς καὶ περικαλλεῖς Jo.Jej.*poenit.cont.virg*.(M.88.1972C).

εὐμηχανία, ἡ, *skill in devising means*; of God's power in bringing good out of evil, Chrys.*hom.81.2 in Mt*.(7.775D); id.*hom.12.3 in 2Cor*.(10.524C); id.*exp.in Ps*.7:16(5.73D) = Cyr.*Ps*.7:15(M.69.756C).

εὔμικτος, *kindly*; of God, Didym.*Trin*.3.25(M.39.940D).

***εὐμιμήτως**, *with successful imitation*, Max.*opusc*.(M.91.12A); id.*ambig*.(M.91.1205A); CLater.*act*.1(H.3.692D).

***εὔμισθος**, *profitable*, comp., Thdr.Stud.*epp*.1.11(M.99.945D).

εὔμνηστος, *well-remembered*, *A.Thom*.A 108(p.220.9).

εὐμοιρέω, *be well off for*, *be in happy possession* (*of*), c. acc., Ephr.3.532D; Synes.*calv*.5(p.199.16; M.66.1176C); Jo.D.*hom*.4.23(M.96.621C); abs., Ephr.3.440A.

***εὐμορφοποικιλοκαθαρόμορφος**, *of faultless varied beauty of form*, †Juln.*ep*.205(p.282.5; M.32.344A).

***εὐμορφόχροος**, *beautifully coloured*, *Phys*.B 11(p.204.6).

***εὐμόρφως**, *beautifully*, *A.Xanthipp*.7(p.62.22).

εὐνάζω, *put to rest*, hence *stay*, *stop* πόδας εὔνασεν Nonn.*par.Jo*.20:1(M.43.908B).

εὐνο-έω, *be at peace with*, *in agreement with*, exeg. Mt.5:25 τί δέ ἐστιν ∼εῖν; ἢ τοῦτό φησιν, ὅτι καταδέχου μᾶλλον ἀδικεῖσθαι· ἢ οὕτως, δίκασον τῇ δίκῃ, ὡσανεὶ τὴν ἐκείνου τάξιν ἔχων, ἵνα μὴ τῇ φιλαυτίᾳ τὸ δίκαιον διαφθείρῃς Chrys.*hom.16.10 in Mt*.(7.219B); τινὲς μὲν οὖν τὸν διάβολον αὐτὸν αἰνίττεσθαί φασι τῇ τοῦ ἀντιδίκου προσηγορίᾳ, καὶ κελεύειν μηδὲν ἔχειν τῶν ἐκείνου· τοῦτο γὰρ εἶναι τὸ ∼εῖν αὐτῷ *ib.16.11*(219C); f.l. for ἐννοέω, Cyr.*Mal*.7(3.824A).

εὐνοητικός, *kindly disposed*, Gr.Thaum.*pan.Or*.6(p.16.18; M.10.1069D).

***εὐνοήτωρ**, ὁ, *well-wisher*, Thphn.*chron*.p.404(M.108.961B).

εὔνοια, ἡ, *affection*, *love*; of parents for children, Clem.*str*.1.23(p.94.5; M.8.896B); id.*paed*.1.6(p.119.16; M.8.308B); of man for God, *M.Polyc*.17.3; Clem.*str*.7.7(p.21.31; M.9.457C); Or.*princ*.1.8.1(p.98.4); καταλαμβανόμενος ὑπὸ τῶν ἐν εὐ. ἐπιζητούντων σε *Lit*.ap.*Const.App*.8.15.7.

***εὐνοϊτής**, ὁ, s.v.l., = εὐνοήτωρ, *Didasc.Jac*.1.53(p.777.5).

***Εὐνομιανοί**, οἱ, followers of Eunomius ἀναθεματισθῆναι πᾶσαν αἵρεσιν· καὶ ἰδικῶς τὴν τῶν Εὐ., εἴτουν ἀνομοίων CCP(381)*can*.1; Εὐ. ...τοὺς εἰς μίαν κατάδυσιν βαπτιζομένους CCP(381)‡*can*.7; Εὐ. ..., διὰ τὸ μίαν κατάδυσιν ποιεῖσθαι, λέγοντες μόνον εἰς τὸν θάνατον τοῦ κυρίου βαπτίζεσθαι Didym.*Trin*.2.15(M.39.720A); Ἀετιανοὶ...οἱ καὶ ἀνόμοιοι καλούμενοι, παρά τισι δὲ Εὐ., δι' Εὐνόμιόν τινα μαθητὴν τοῦ Ἀετίου γενόμενον καὶ ἔτι περιόντα...Εὐ. ... ἀναβαπτίζουσι πάντας τοὺς πρὸς αὐτοὺς ἐρχομένους, οὐ μόνον δέ, ἀλλὰ καὶ τοὺς ἀπὸ Ἀρειανῶν· βαπτίζουσι δὲ κατὰ κεφαλῆς ἄνω τοὺς πόδας στρέφοντες τῶν βαπτιζομένων, ὡς πολὺς ᾄδεται λόγος Epiph.*anac*.76(p.231.23ff.; M.42.337B,C); νῦν εἰσιν ἐξ ἐκείνου [sc. Aët.] οἱ τότε μὲν Ἀετιανοὶ νῦν δὲ Εὐ. προσαγορευόμενοι Socr.*h.e*.2.35.14(M.67.300B); Thdt.*haer*.4.3(4.356).

***Εὐνομιοευτυχιανοί**, οἱ, members of a Eunomian sect led by Eutychius of CP, Socr.*h.e*.5.24.5(M.67.618D).

***Εὐνομιοθεοφρονιανοί**, οἱ, members of a Eunomian sect led by Theophronius, Socr.*h.e*.5.24.5(M.67.618D).

***Εὐνόμιοι**, οἱ, followers of Eunomius, Ath.*ep.Serap*.4.5(M.26.645A).

***εὐνοστία**, ἡ, *good flavour*, *relish*, Jo.Disc.*v.Epiph*.17(M.41.44A).

***εὐνουχία**, ἡ, **1.** *abstention from sexual intercourse*, *state of* such *abstention*; used of men only, corresponding to παρθενία of women, Athenag.*leg*.33.1(M.6.965A); οὐδὲ ἡ εὐ. ἐνάρετον, εἰ μὴ δι' ἀγάπην γίνοιτο τὴν πρὸς τὸν θεόν Clem.*str*.3.6(p.219.26; M.8.1153B); ἐξὸν ἑλέσθαι τὴν εὐ. κατὰ τὸν ὑγιῆ κανόνα μετ' εὐσεβείας...οὐ...ἐξουθενοῦντα τοὺς γεγαμηκότας *ib*.3.18(p.244.27; 1208C); ἡμεῖς εὐ. μὲν καὶ οἷς τοῦτο δεδώρηται ὑπὸ θεοῦ μακαρίζομεν, μονογαμίαν δὲ...θαυμάζομεν *ib*.3.1(p.197.10; 1104B); τὸ μὲν ὄνομα τῆς εὐ. ἔνθεν εἰληφέναι ἐκ τοῦ εὔνοιαν ἔχειν πολλὴν πρὸς τὸν δεσπότην ‡Pion.*v.Polyc*.14; †Bas.Anc.*virg*.57(M.30.785A); ἀναίτιοι [sc. congenital eunuchs]...τῆς αὐτῶν εὐ. ... οὔτε μισθὸν ἔχουσιν εὐ. βασιλείαν οὐρανῶν Epiph.*haer*.58.3(p.360.4, 8; M.41.1013B); **2.** state of *being a eunuch* τὸν περὶ εὐνουχίας λόγον ref. Mt.19:12, Or.*comm.in Mt*.15.5(p.361.17; M.13.1265B); τῆς κατὰ σῶμα εὐ. †Bas.Anc.*virg*.60(M.30.792C); met. τῆς μυστικῆς εὐ. *ib*.(794A); τὴν πνευματικὴν εὐ. Cyr.*hom.div*.19(M.77.1108B).

εὐνουχίζω, *castrate*; **1.** lit., Or.*comm.in Mt*.15.1(p.351.23; M.13.

1256B); εἴ τινες ὑπὸ βαρβάρων ἢ δεσποτῶν εὐνουχίσθησαν...τοὺς τοιούτους εἰς κλῆρον προσίεται ὁ κανών CNic.(325)*can.*1; Epiph.*haer.* 58.4(p.361.1; M.41.1013D); Chrys.*hom.5.2 in Tit.*(11.759B); *Chron. Pasch.*p.249(M.92.600B); **2.** met.; **a.** *keep from sexual intercourse,* Clem.*str.*3.11(p.231.23; M.8.1177D); εὐ. τὸν ἔσω ἄνθρωπον Nil.*epp.* 1.323(M.79.200A); ἑαυτοὺς ἐγκρατείᾳ εὐ. ‡Caes.Naz.*dial.*140(M.38. 1048); exeg. Mt.19:12, Basilides ap.Clem.*str.*3.1(p.195.15; 1100A); Gr.Naz.*or.*37.20(M.36.305B); τὸν σπινθῆρα τοῦ καλοῦ διὰ τῆς προαιρέσεως ἀνάψας σαυτὸν εὐνουχίσας, τὴν ῥίζαν ἐξέτεμες, τὰ ὄργανα τῆς κακίας ἐξώρισας *ib.*37.21(305D); ὁ μοναχὸς ὁ εὐνουχίσας ἑαυτόν Chrys. *hom.in Jo.5:19*(6.288C); **b.** *emasculate* οὐκ ἀποκεκομμένος μέν, ὡς ὁ Ἄττις, εὐνουχισμένος δὲ διὰ κωνείου Hipp.*haer.*5.8(p.96.15; M.16. 3150C).

εὐνουχισμός, ὁ, *castration,* state of *being castrated* or *being a eunuch*; **1.** lit., Afric.*ep.Or.*2(p.79.21; M.11.45A); Or.*comm.in Mt.* 15.1(p.349.3; M.13.1253A); Epiph.*haer.*66.77(p.118.20; M.42.149D); **2.** met., †Bas.Anc.*virg.*60(M.30.792D); τὸν ἑκούσιον τῆς ψυχῆς εὐ. σώφρονι λογισμῷ ἑαυτοὺς εὐνουχίσαντες *ib.*64(801A); esp. exeg. Mt. 19:12 τοὺς προτέρους δύο εὐ.· ὁμοίως τῷ τρίτῳ ἀλληγορῆσαι Or.*comm. in Mt.*15.1(p.351.4; M.13.1256A); μεγάλη δὲ δύναμις τὸ χωρῆσαι τὸν ἀπὸ λόγου τῆς ψυχῆς εὐ. *ib.*15.5(p.359.10; M.13.1264B); περὶ διαφορᾶς εὐ. ἐν εὐαγγελίοις παρεγγυᾷ Meth.*symp.*1.1(p.7.15; M.18.37A); ἐπαινῶ καὶ τοῦτον τὸν εὐ. Gr.Naz.*or.*37.20(M.36.305C); *ib.*37.21 (305D); ὁ Χριστὸς τρεῖς τρόπους εὐνουχισμοῦ λέγων τοὺς μὲν δύο ἀφίησιν ἀστεφανώτους, τὸν δὲ ἕνα εἰς τὴν βασιλείαν εἰσάγει Chrys. *hom.36.2 in Jo.*(8.209D).

εὐνοῦχος, ὁ, *eunuch*; **1.** lit., derivation τὸ εὐ. καλεῖσθαι, ἀπὸ τοῦ εὐνοεῖν δύνασθαι ἀφαιρουμένων τῶν μελῶν Epiph.*haer.*58.4(p.361.3; M.41.1013D); unless self-castrated can hold office in Church εἰ μὲν ἐξ ἐπηρείας ἀνθρώπων ἐγένετό τις, ἢ ἐν διωγμῷ ἀφῃρέθη τὰ ἀνδρῶν ἢ οὕτως ἔφυ, καὶ ἔστιν ἄξιος ἐπισκοπῆς, γινέσθω *Can.App.*21; Δωρόθεον, πρεσβείου τοῦ κατὰ Ἀντιόχειαν ἠξιωμένον...τὴν φύσιν δὲ ἄλλως εὐ., οὕτω πεφυκὼς ἐξ αὐτῆς γενέσεως Eus.*h.e.*7.32.3(M.20. 721B); Socr.*h.e.*6.15.15(M.67.709C); *Τίγριος* πρεσβύτερος...οὐκ ἐκ γενετῆς εὐ. Soz.*h.e.*8.24.9(M.67.1580A); can be married οὐδὲν δὲ ἦν ἀπεικός, καὶ εὐ. ὄντα γυναῖκα ἔχειν ἐν τῇ οἰκίᾳ, τῶν ἔνδον ἐπιμελουμένην πραγμάτων Thdt.*qu.98 in Gen.*(1.104); ref. Is.56:4 μηδὲν ἐμποδὼν ἔσεσθαι τοῖς εὐ. φάσκων πρὸς τὸ τυχεῖν τῶν παρὰ θεοῦ ἀγαθῶν, εἰ ζῆν κατὰ θεὸν προέλοιντο Eus.*Is.*56:4(M.24.472A); **2.** met., of those who have no sexual intercourse with women; **a.** in gen. κακίζοντες οἱ μοιχοὶ καὶ παιδερασταὶ τοὺς εὐ. καὶ μονογάμους Athenag. *leg.*34.1(M.6.968B); εὐ. δὲ ἀληθὴς οὐχ ὁ μὴ δυνάμενος ἀλλ' ὁ μὴ βουλόμενος φιληδεῖν Clem.*paed.*3.4(p.252.3; M.8.593A); εἰσὶ δὲ καὶ τοῦ θεοῦ ἄνθρωποι διὰ τοῦτο εὐ. ⟨ἄγονοι παντὸς κακοῦ⟩ ἵν' οἰκοδομήσωσι πεσοῦσαν τὴν Ἱερουσαλήμ Or.*comm.in Mt.*15.5(p.359.20; M.13. 1264B); τοιούτων μὲν οὖν ἄξιοι γέρων εὑρεθήσονται ἐν τῇ βασιλείᾳ οἱ κατὰ νοῦν θεῖοι εὐ. †Bas.Anc.*virg.*60(M.30.792C); ὑπὲρ εὐνούχων ὁσίως πορευομένων δεηθῶμεν *Lit.*ap.*Const.App.*8.10.11; Chrys.*hom. 17.5 in Heb.*(12.171D); **b.** exeg. Mt.19:12; acc. Basilides φυσικήν τινες ἔχουσι πρὸς γυναῖκα ἀποστροφὴν ἐκ γενετῆς, οἵτινες τῇ φυσικῇ ταύτῃ συγκράσει χρώμενοι καλῶς ποιοῦσι μὴ γαμοῦντες· οὗτοι, φασίν, εἰσὶν οἱ ἐκ γενετῆς εὐ.· οἱ δὲ ἐξ ἀνάγκης, ἐκεῖνοι οἱ θεατρικοὶ ἀσκηταί, οἵ τινες διὰ τὴν ἀνθολκὴν τῆς εὐδοξίας κρατοῦσιν ἑαυτῶν, οἱ δὲ ἐκτετμημένοι κατὰ συμφορὰν εὐ. γεγόνασι κατὰ ἀνάγκην. οἱ τοίνυν κατὰ ἀνάγκην οὐ κατὰ λόγον εὐ. γίνονται Clem.*str.*3.1(p.195.11f.; M.8. 1100A); τὸ μὲν γὰρ μέχρι τῶν σωματικῶν εὐ. στῆσαι τὸν λόγον, τυχὸν μικρόν τε καὶ λίαν ἀσθενὲς καὶ ἀνάξιον λόγου· δεῖ δὲ ἡμᾶς ἐπινοῆσαί τι τοῦ πνεύματος ἄξιον Gr.Naz.*or.*37.20(M.36.305B); εἰπὼν τοίνυν τοὺς εὐ., τοὺς εἰκῇ καὶ μάτην εὐ., εἰ μὴ τῷ λογισμῷ καὶ αὐτοὶ σωφρονοῖεν, καὶ τοὺς ὑπὲρ τῶν οὐρανῶν παρθενεύοντας, πάλιν ἐπάγει λέγων· 'ὁ δυνάμενος χωρεῖν, χωρείτω' Chrys.*hom.52.3 in Mt.*(7.624A); τί βούλεται ὁ περὶ τῶν ἄλλων εὐ. λόγος αὐτῷ;...τῶν πονηρῶν λογισμῶν τὴν ἀναίρεσιν *ib.*(623C); εὐ. ἐνταῦθά φησιν οὐ τοὺς τὰ μέλη κόψαντας, ἀλλὰ τοὺς τὸν πονηρὸν λογισμὸν καὶ ἀσελγείας γέμοντα ἀποτεμόντας id.*hom.in Jo.5:19*(6.258B); **c.** exeg. Is.56:3 οὐ γὰρ μόνον ἡ εὐνουχία δικαιοῖ οὐδὲ μὴν τὸ τοῦ εὐ. σάββατον, ἐὰν μὴ ποιήσῃ τὰς ἐντολάς Clem.*str.*3.15(p.241.10; M.8.1197B); εὐ. τοίνυν οὐχ ὁ κατηναγκασμένος τὰ μόρια οὐδὲ μὴν ὁ ἄγαμος εἴρηται, ἀλλ' ὁ ἄγονος ἀληθείας *ib.*(p.241. 20; 1200A); οὐχὶ τοῖς κατὰ περίστασιν καὶ ἁπλῶς εὐ. τὰ εἰρημένα ἀγαθὰ ὑπισχνεῖται, ἀλλὰ τοῖς φυλασσομένοις, φησί, τὰ σάββατά μου καὶ ἐκλεγομένοις ἃ ἐγὼ θέλω †Bas.Anc.*virg.*57(M.30.785A); Cyr.*Is.* 5.3(2.790B).

εὔξυλος, *well-wooded,* Cyr.*glaph.Gen.*1(1.14E); id.*Joel.*9(3.208D).

εὐοδία, ἡ, **1.** *straight path, way of righteousness,* Gr.Naz.*carm.* 2.1.1.246(M.37.988A); **2.** *prosperity,* Or.*exc.in Ps.*36:7(M.17.124D); Bas.*hex.*3.1(1.22D; M.29.53B); Gr.Naz.*carm.*2.2(poem.)1.168(M.37. 1463A); Gr.Nyss.*or.dom.*1(p.6.30; M.44.1124A); **3.** *efficient service,* †Bas.*bapt.*2.2(2.653D; M.31.1581D).

εὐοδμία, ἡ, v. εὐοσμία.

εὔοδος, **1.** *favourable,* †Nil.*vit.*4(M.79.1144D); **2.** fem. as subst., personal *approach,* social *intercourse* τὴν καταφιλικὴν εὔοδον, ἣν ποιοῦνται καὶ ἐν συμποσίοις, καὶ ἐπὶ πένθει πρὸς παράκλησιν Chrys. *fr.in Jer.*16:5(M.64.912C).

εὐοδ-όω, **1.** *guide aright*; c. dat. pers., *Pss.Sal.*2.5; Marc.Diac.*v. Porph.*36; c. acc. pers., Serap.*Euch.*11.1; Cyr.*Ps.*16:3(M.69.820A); c. acc. rei, Gr.Naz.*or.*21.18(M.35.1101B); *ib.*39.2(M.36.336C); Chrys. *stat.*3.2(2.37B); abs., Just.*2apol.*7.8(M.6.456C); θεοῦ ∼οῦντος Thdr. Stud.*epp.*1.15(M.99.957B); **2.** pass., *be prosperously guided, prosper*; of persons, Herm.*sim.*3.3.6; ἀπὸ θεοῦ διὰ Ἰησοῦ Χριστοῦ ∼ούμενοι Or.*Jo.*32.1(p.425.1; M.14.740B); Cyr.*Ps.*9:23(M.69.777D); of things, Bas.*ep.*246(3.383B; M.32.925C); Gr.Nyss.*or.catech.*16(p.72.2; M.45. 52C); Isid.Pel.*epp.*1.14(M.78.189A); c. infin., *be successful in,* Thdr. Stud.*epp.*2.110(M.99.1369D); *ib.*2.127(1409D).

***εὐόδωμα**, τό, *prosperity* ὁ Ζαβουλών, εὐ. τε καὶ εὐλογία Cyr. *glaph.Gen.*4(1.136C).

εὐοικονόμητος, *well-arranged,* Ign.*Rom.*1.2.

εὐολίσθητος, *easily slipping*; met., Clem.*paed.*2.11(p.227.4, v.l. εὐαίσθητον M.8.537B); τοὺς πρὸς ἁμαρτίαν εὐ. Bas.*hom.*9.5(2.77A; M. 31.340A); id.*hom.in Ps.*16(1.97A; M.29.228A); ‡Chrys.*hom.*10(13. 238B).

εὐόλισθος, **1.** *unstable, easily slipping* εὐ. τεῖχος Proc.G.*Is.*16:1–5 (M.87.2101D); met. τὸ τῆς ἡλικίας εὐ. Or.*sel.in Gen.*9:11(M.12.109B); γυναικῶν...τὸ γένος εὐ. Epiph.*haer.*79.1(p.476.12; M.42.740D); εὐ. νεότης Isid.Pel.*epp.*1.316(M.78.365B); Cyr.*Jo.*2.8(4.235D); εὐ. εἰς ἁμαρτίαν τὴν φύσιν id.*Os.*71(3.106D); c. πρός, Chrys.*sac.*6.8(p.156.13; 1.428C); **2.** *smoothly gliding* στόλον Geo.Pis.*hex.*999(M.92.1511A).

***εὐολίσθως**, *with a tendency to slip,* Marc.Er.*opusc.*5.8(M.65. 1041B).

εὐόμματος, *having both eyes,* opp. μονόφθαλμος, Cyr.S.*v.Sab.*47 (p.137.29).

εὐόργητος, *easily roused to anger,* Clem.*str.*7.4(p.17.6; M.9.429A).

***εὐόρθωσις**, ἡ, *building, construction,* Gr.Thaum.*Eccl.*3:3(M.10. 996A).

εὐοσμία (εὐωσμία, εὐοδμία), ἡ, *fragrance, perfume,* met. εὐοδμίας Gr.Nyss.*hom.3 in Cant.*(M.44.824B); τῶν ἁγίων ὁ βίος...ἄπαυστον ἔχει τὴν εὐωσμίαν Cyr.*ador.*12(1.438B); id.*Ps.*24:10(M.69.849C).

εὐόφθαλμος, **1.** *with beautiful eyes,* Isid.Pel.*epp.*4.114(M.78. 1188A); **2.** *with vigilant eyes* ψαλμῳδία Nil.*epp.*3.126(M.79.441D).

εὔοχος, *holding firmly* τὸ...⟨εὔ⟩οχον ἐν λόγῳ Gr.Thaum.*pan.Or.*7 (conj. p.2.18; εὔηχον M.10.1052C).

***εὔοψις**, *clear-sighted* νοῦ *A.Andr.*9(p.41.37).

εὐπάθεια, ἡ, **1.** *happiness, spiritual well-being,* Or.*Jo.*13.45 (p.271.34; M.14.479B); Cyr.*Am.*2(3.249A); Dion.Ar.*c.h.*15.9(M.3. 340A); **2.** *benefit,* ‡Just.*qu.et resp.*104(M.6.1352A); Jo.D.*carm.theoph.* 7(p.212; M.96.829E); **3.** *passibility* διὰ τὴν...φιλανθρωπίαν σαρκὸς ἀνθρωπίνης εὐ. ... ἐνδυσάμενος Clem.*str.*7.2(p.7.24; M.9.412B).

εὐπαθέω, **1.** *be in good condition* physically, Gr.Nyss.*paup.*2(M. 46.481D); Chrys.*hom.38.7 in 1Cor.*(10.361B); **2.** *receive benefits,* Cyr. *Is.*3.4(2.498D).

***εὐπαθῶς**, *delightfully*; ref. spiritual happiness, Dion.Ar.*e.h.* 4.3.4(M.3.480A).

εὐπαιδεύτως, *in the manner of an instructed person,* Cyr.*Jo.*1.10 (4.106C); id.*thes.*32(5[1].319A).

εὐπαλῶς, *with skill,* Cyr.*Is.*1.6(2.157D).

***εὐπαράβλητος**, *appropriately compared,* Isid.Pel.*epp.*4.196(M. 78.1285A).

εὐπαραγωγός, *seductive, alluring,* Nil.*exerc.*54(M.79.785D); ‡Nil. *perist.*9.9(M.79.881B).

εὐπαράδεκτος, **1.** *acceptable,* freq. of things and persons πάντα ὅσα ἔλεγον εὐ. ἦν Or.*schol.in Lc.*9:42(M.17.345B); εἰ μὴ τὴν τοῦ δούλου μορφὴν ἔλαβεν, οὐκ ἂν εὐ. γέγονεν Chrys.*hom.13.2 in Jo.*(8. 73C); ἐσόμεθα εὐ. τῷ θεῷ Cyr.*ador.*16(1.561A); **2.** *receiving readily,* Gr.Nyss.*hom.14 in Cant.*(M.44.1061D).

***εὐπαραδέκτως**, *acceptably,* c. ἔχω, Leont.H.*monoph.*testimonia (M.86.1877D).

***εὐπαράδοχος**, *ready to receive,* Cyr.*Is.*4.2(2.607E).

εὐπαράκλητος, *ready to be comforted,* Thdr.Stud.*epp.*2.76(M.99. 1313C).

***εὐπαρακολουθησία**, ἡ, *readiness to follow,* †Bas.*Is.*176(1.507C; M.30.413C).

εὐπαρακολούθητος, *quick at following, eager to follow,* Clem.*str.* 6.15(p.491.11; M.9.341B); Dion.Al.ap.Eus.*h.e.*7.24.8(M.20.696A).

εὐπαρακολουθήτως, *with ready apprehension*, †Bas.*Is*.176(1.507C; M.30.413C).

εὐπαρακόμιστος, **1.** *easily led*, Cyr.*Is*.1.2(2.42B); id.*Zach*.56(3.735A); neut. as subst., id.*hom.pasch*.24(5^2.290D); **2.** *easy to bear*; of punishment, Or.*Ps*.72:3–4(p.94); Ath.*exp.Ps*.72:3–5; **3.** *easy to carry, portable*, Const.*ep*.ap.Thdt.*h.e*.1.16.2(3.789), but εὐμετακόμιστος, ap.Eus.*v.C*.4.36.

***εὐπαράσκευος**, *well-prepared*, Sophr.H.*v.Anast*.(M.92.1697A).

εὐπαρατήρητος, *easy to keep in mind*, †Bas.*Is*.246(1.567C; M.30.553A).

εὐπαράφορος, *easily led astray*, Cyr.*glaph.Ex*.3(1.337A); id.*dial.Trin*.1(5^1.394A); Proc.G.*Lev*.24:19(M.87.784B); c. πρός, Cyr.*ador*.1(1.7B); c. ἐπί, *ib*.15(1.519C); neut. as subst., id.*Jo*.10.2(4.886C).

***εὐπαραφόρως**, *so as to be easily led astray*, c. ἔχω, Cyr.*Is*.5.3(2.791B).

εὐπάρεδρος, *very attentive, assiduous*, Mac.Aeg.*elev*.13(M.34.901C); Dor.*doct*.1.12(M.88.1633A).

***εὐπαρέδρως**, *very assiduously, attentively*, Cyr.*Jo*.2.1(4.130B); id.*Lc*.16:1(M.72.812B); ‡Jo.D.*ep.Thphl*.30(M.95.384C).

εὐπαρόδευτος, *easy to pass over*, Max.*ambig*.(M.91.1117A).

εὐπάροιστος, *easily carried away*, Cyr.*glaph.Ex*.2(1.286B); met., id.*glaph.Gen*.2(1.35C); id.*Jo*.7(4.678B); id.*hom.pasch*.19(5^2.250D); c. πρός, id.*ador*.7(1.240E); c. ἐπί, id.*glaph.Ex*.3(1.337C); neut. as subst., Sophr.H.*ep.syn*.(M.87.3181A).

εὐπαρόξυντος, *easily provoked, irritated*, Bas.*hom*.14.3(2.125A; M.31.449C); Bas.Sel.*v.Thecl*.2.13(M.85.589A).

εὐπάροχος, *bountiful, generous*, ‡Jo.D.*fid.dorm*.17(M.95.264B).

εὐπαρρησίαστος, *speaking freely and boldly, confident*, Gr.Nyss.*Thdr*.(M.46.744B); Didym.*Job* 6:29(M.39.1140A); Ast.Am.*hom*.3(M.40.192A); of Christians towards God ἔστω...εὐ. κατὰ τὸ ἴδιον ἐνθύμιον πᾶς ὁ προσιὼν τῷ θεῷ Dion.Al.*ep.can*.4(p.104.8; M.10.1288C); εὐ. πρὸς θεόν Jo.Not.*v.Eus*.1(M.86.297B); Thdr.Stud.*epp*.2.27(M.99.1193D); cf. εὐπαρρησιαστότεροι γίνονται [sc. Christians] πρὸς τὸν θεόν †Marcus Aurelius ap.Eus.*h.e*.4.13.5(M.20.336A).

***εὐπαρρησιάστως**, *confidently, with complete freedom*; before God, Meth.*symp*.2.6(p.24.2; M.18.57A); Cyr.H.*catech*.15.33; Ephr.116D.

εὐπάρυφος, met., *stately* λόγον Cyr.*Jo*.2.6(4.214E).

***εὐπαρύφως**, *pompously*, Gr.Nyss.*Eun*.1(1 p.41.11; M.45.269A).

εὐπείθεια, ἡ, *ready obedience*; esp. to God, Clem.*str*.7.3(p.15.13; M.9.425B); †Bas.*bapt*.1.1.2(2.625C; M.31.1516D); Cyr.*Mich*.49(3.441C); of Christ, Cyr.H.*catech*.15.30.

***εὐπειθήνιος**, *docile*, Thdot.Anc.*hom.BMV et Sym*.2(M.77.1392B).

εὐπειθής, *readily obedient*; of Son, Cyr.H.*catech*.10.9; of BMV, ‡Chrys.*annunt.et Ar*.(11.841E).

εὐπειθῶς, *with ready obedience*, †Bas.*Is*.98(1.526E; M.30.457D); αὐτὸς Ἰησοῦς...εὐ. ὑποτάττεται ταῖς τοῦ πατρὸς καὶ θεοῦ δι᾽ ἀγγέλων διατυπώσεσιν Dion.Ar.*c.h*.4.4(M.3.181C); Max.*ambig*.(M.91.1161C, 1221C).

εὐπερίβλεπτος, *with much experience* εὐ. εἰς τὰ τοῦ κόσμου πράγματα Bas.*hom.in Ps*.7(1.103C; M.29.241B).

εὐπερίγραπτος, **1.** *easily circumscribed* μικρόν...καὶ εὐ. ἡ ἀνθρωπίνη φύσις Gr.Nyss.*or.catech*.10(p.54.8; M.45.41B); †Gregent.*disp*.(M.86.737C); met., *limited, moderate*, Tit.Bost.*Man*.1.3(M.18.1073A); †Bas.*Is*.67(1.427E; M.30.233C); **2.** *clearly defined* τὴν ὑπὸ αἴσθησιν ...φύσιν ὀρθῷ λόγῳ εἶναι θεατὴν καὶ εὐ. Max.*ambig*.(M.91.1117A); **3.** *well-chosen* ῥήμασιν Gr.Nyss.*hex*.1(M.44.64A); λόγον id.*v.Gr.Thaum*.(M.46.912C).

εὐπερίγραφος, **1.** *easy to trace out* κύκλον Const.*ep*.ap.Gel.Cyz.*h.e*.3.19.24(M.85.1349D); **2.** *well-defined* ἕξιν *Hom.Clem*.6.24.

***εὐπερίδρακτος**, *easily grasped* λόγου Epiph.*haer*.76.16(p.362.19; M.42.548D); id.*metr*.8(M.43.248D); neut. as subst., Aët.*synt*.proem.(p.352.11; M.42.536A).

***εὐπερίδρομος**, *running round energetically*, Andr.Cr.*or*.19(M.97.1225C); met. εὐ. σε...τῆς εὐσεβείας †Bas.*hom.in Pr*.6:4(2.618D; M.31.1501A).

εὐπερινόητος, *easy to understand*, Or.*comm.in Mt*.17.1(p.576.14; M.13.1473B).

***εὐπερίπτωτος**, *thoroughly come to grief*, Max.*ep*.15(M.91.569B).

εὐπερίσπαστος, *easily distracting* τροφῶν...ἀντέχου...μὴ...εὐ. Evagr.Pont.*rer.mon*.3(M.40.1253C).

εὐπερίστατος, **1.** *admired, unusual*, ‡Ath.*inst.mon*.1(M.28.845D); ἐὰν...τὸ κελλίον ἐν ᾧ καθέζῃ εὐ. ᾖ, φεῦγε, καὶ αὐτοῦ μὴ φείσῃ Evagr.Pont.*rer.mon*.5(M.40.1257A) = ‡Ath.*inst.mon*.3(M.28.848C); **2.** *readily provided* τὴν εὐ. καὶ ἀναγκαίαν τοῦ σώματος τροφήν Eus.Al.*serm*.21.2(M.86.424D); **3.** *readily besetting*, exeg. Heb.12:1, Chrys.*hom.28.2 in Heb*.(12.256D) cit. infra; εὐ. ... ἡ ἁμαρτία, πάντοθεν ἱσταμένη, ἔμπροσθεν, ὄπισθεν, καὶ οὕτως ἡμᾶς καταβάλλουσα id.*hom.2.7 in 2Cor*.(10.438C); id.*exp.in Ps*.48:6(5.208E); Sever.*Heb*.12:1(p.351.10,11); Nil.*epp*.3.261(M.79.516A); Thdt.*Heb*.12:1(3.624); Max.*ep*.6(M.91.432D); Jo.Carp.*cap*.5(M.85.1839); **4.** *easy to be put off, avoided, removed*, exeg. Heb.12:1 εὐ. ... εἶπε τὴν ἁμαρτίαν, ἐπειδὴ μόνιμον στάσιν οὐκ ἔχει, ἀλλὰ ἐκ ταχείας τρέπεται καὶ καταλύεται ‡Ath.*qu.script*.130(M.28.772D); εὐ., ἤ τοι τὴν εὐκόλως περιϊσταμένη ἡμᾶς, ἢ τὴν εὐκόλως περίστασιν δυναμένην παθεῖν, μᾶλλον δὲ τοῦτο· ῥᾴδιον γάρ, ἐὰν θέλωμεν, περιγενέσθαι τῆς ἁμαρτίας Chrys.*hom.28.2 in Heb*.(12.256D).

***εὐπεριστόλως**, *succinctly*, Cyr.*Jo*.9(4.755D); *ib*.11.2(943B).

εὐπερίστρεπτος, *easily turned about*, met. τὸ εὐ. τῆς ἀνθρώπου γνώμης †Or.*fr.4 in 1Reg*.15:9ff.(p.296.25; M.17.44D).

εὐπερίστροφος, *swiftly-turning, quick-glancing* ὄμμα Chrys.*hom.17.5 in Heb*.(12.172A).

εὐπερίτρεπτος, *easy to turn over*; met., *changeable, fickle* δόξα Bas.*ep*.277(3.422A; M.32.1013B); †Bas.*Is*.214(1.540B; M.30.489B); Chrys.*prod.Jud*.2.2(2.389D); *liable to be overturned, upset*, Max.*ep*.15(M.91.569B).

εὐπέτης, *flying well, light*; of a ship, comp., Cyr.*Jon*.4(3.371B).

εὐπήληξ, **1.** *with beautiful helmet*, Paul.Sil.*Soph*.140(M.86.2125A); **2.** *with a beautiful top* οἴκου *ib*.299(2131A); καλύπτρη *ib*.530(2140A).

εὔπηχυς, *with beautiful tributaries*; of the Nile, Paul.Sil.*Soph*.625(M.86.2143A).

***εὐπίθανος**, *convincing*; neut. as subst., Cyr.*Is*.4.4(2.668C).

***εὐπιθάνως**, f.l. for ἀπιθάνως, *not persuasively*, Pall.*v.Chrys*.1(M.47.5; ἀπιθάνως p.3.15).

εὐπιστία (εὐπίστεια), ἡ, *pious belief*, Evagr.*h.e*.1.14(p.24.24; M.86.2461B); Thdr.Stud.*catech.parv*.9(M.99.520C; -εια *NBP* p.21).

εὔπιστος, **1.** *trustworthy, trusty* ὁ δημιουργός Heracleon ap.Or.*Jo*.4.60(59; p.292.20; M.14.513C); of things, *credible*, Or.*Jo*.1.3(5; p.6.22; πιστός M.14.28B); comp., Thdr.Mops.*fr.inc*.10(p.302.7; M.66.954C); neut. as subst., Gr.Mag.*dial*.(tr.Zach.)3.14(M.*PL*.77.243C); **2.** *willing to believe*; neut. as subst., Sophr.H.*v.Anast*.(M.92.1681A).

***εὔπλαγκτος**, *easily deceived*, ‡Gr.Naz.*Chr.pat*.75(M.38.143A).

***εὐπλόησις**, ἡ, *good sailing*, Thdr.Stud.*epp*.2.75(M.99.1312B).

εὔπλωτος, *easy to sail on*, *Orac.Sib*.3.779.

εὐπνοέω, *smell sweetly*, Gr.Nyss.*hom.3 in Cant*.(M.44.824A).

εὔπνοια, ἡ, *fragrance*, *A.Xanthipp*.22(p.74.13); Gr.Nyss.*Eun*.8(2 p.191.15; M.45.785D).

εὐποιέω, *do good, be a benefactor*, better written *divisim*, *T.Job* 44,45(p.133.1,3,9); *Clem.epit*.B 112(p.190).

εὐποιΐα, ἡ, **1.** *beneficence, doing good*; **a.** of man, Clem.*str*.7.12(p.51.20; M.9.500A); *ib*.2.6(p.129.10; M.8.965B) cit. s. ἀντεπάγω; ἐν εὐ. δόξασον τὸν θεόν Or.*hom.12.11 in Jer*.(p.97.17; M.13.393A); τῆς εἰς τοὺς ὀρφανοὺς εὐ. Gr.Naz.*ep*.208(M.37.345A); **b.** of God, Clem.*str*.5.14(p.421.8; M.9.205B); **2.** *benefit*, Iren.*haer*.1.2.6(M.7.465A); τὰς τοῦ θεοῦ εὐ. Clem.*str*.2.18(p.165.20; M.8.1040A); Or.*princ*.3.1.14(p.219.14; M.11.276B); ἡ ἐπὶ τὸ βάπτισμα εὐ. *Hom.Clem*.11.27; **3.** *good work, good deed, beneficent act* ἕτοιμοί ἐστε εἰς εὐ. θεῷ ἀνήκουσαν Ign.*Polyc*.7.3; opp. ἁμαρτία, Or.*Jo*.13.43(p.269.24, cj. for εὐπορία M.14.476B); κατὰ τὸ δυνατὸν ἐκτείνειν τὰς εὐ. id.*Cels*.4.28(p.297.16; M.11.1068D); **4.** *alms*, CGangr.*can*.8; τῶν εὐσεβῶς δόντων εὐ. *Const.Cap*.30; Bas.*hom*.1.2(2.2D; M.31.165B); δοθῆναί τινι αἰτήσαντι εὐ. δέκα φόλλεις μόνον Leont.N.*v.Jo.Eleem*.37(p.76.1); Thphn.*chron*.p.41(M.108.157C); **5.** *good performance* ταῖς τῶν δεομένων εὐ. ‡Hipp.Th.*fr*.16(p.49.4).

εὐποίκιλος, *variegated*, Hipp.*haer*.7.21(p.197.11; M.16.3303C).

***εὐπολίτευτος**, *well-conducted, well-ordered*; of persons, Bas.*hom*.18.1(2.142B; M.31.492A); †Bas.*Is*.110(1.455D; M.30.296D); of life, Gr.Nyss.*usur*.(M.46.433A); Ast.Am.*hom*.1(M.40.164C,167C); ‡Chrys.*hom.suppl*.5(M.64.460D).

εὔπονος, *laborious* τὸ ἐν ἐγκρατείᾳ εὔ. Jo.Jej.*poenit.cont.virg*.(M.88.1972D).

***εὐπόνως**, *with careful labour*, *Schol*.15 in Jo.Clim.*scal*.3(M.88.676B).

εὐπόρευτος, *easy to travel* ὁδός Cyr.*Jo*.3.4(4.272B); id.*Abac*.43(3.558B).

εὐπόρως, *in abundance*, Hipp.*haer*.4.28(p.56.23; M.16.3094A).

εὔπους, *with good feet*, of verse ὕμνους Paul.Sil.*Soph*.172(M.86.2126A); met., *fleeting* ὥρης Nonn.*par.Jo*.19:27(M.43.904B); ἠοῦς Paul.Sil.*Soph*.331(M.86.2132B).

εὐπραγέω, *do right*, *2Clem*.17.7; Chrys.*hom.42.3 in Mt*.(7.456A); ‡Gr.Naz.*Chr.pat*.1892(εὐπραγῶς M.38.287A).

*__εὐπράττω__, *do right*, *Clem.epit.*B 96(p.178), better written *divisim*.

__εὔπρεμνος__, __1.__ *with good stems*, Cyr.*hom.pasch.*16(5^2.212C); Eudoc. *Cypr.*2.47(M.85.848A); v. ἐϋπρήων; __2.__ *well-wooded*, Cyr.*glaph.Gen.*1 (1.4C); id.*Am.*3(3.252B).

__εὐπρέπεια__, ἡ, __1.__ *comeliness, well-ordered beauty* περιθεὶς τὴν εὐ. τῇ κτίσει αὐτοῦ Herm.*vis.*1.3.4; τῶν ἀστρῴων τάξεων καὶ εὐ. Dion.Ar. *d.n.*4.4(M.3.697B); id.*e.h.*4.3.2(M.3.476B); τὰ μὲν φαινόμενα κάλλη, τῆς ἀφανοῦς εὐ. ἀπεικονίσματα λογιζόμενος id.*c.h.*1.3(M.3.121D); *ib.*2.4 (144A); __2.__ *dignity* εὐ. δὲ ὁ πώγων τῷ φιλοσόφῳ Dion.Al.ap.Eus.*p.e.* 14.26(779B; M.21.1281C); τὴν εὐ. τοῦ πράγματος [sc. baptism] *Const.App.*3.9.4; of divine *majesty*, ‡Eust.*Laz.*19(p.42.12); *Const. App.*7.35.9; Dion.Ar.*c.h.*3.2(M.3.165A).

__εὐπρεπῶς__, *attractively*, Herm.*sim.*9.2.4; *ib.*5.2.5; Hipp.*haer.*5.26 (p.129.22; M.16.3198D); Ath.*virg.*1(p.35.15; M.28.252A).

__εὔπρηστος__, *easily inflammable*, Chrys.*pan.Barl.*1(2.682B).

*__ἐϋπρήων__, ? *stony* ἐ. ... Κεδρῶν Nonn.*par.Jo.*18:1(ἐϋπρέμνων... κέδρων M.43.888C); ἐ. ἐρίπνης Paul.Sil.*ambo.*276(M.86.2262A).

__εὐπροαίρετος__, *rightly intentioned*, Clem.*str.*7.7(p.32.18; M.9. 460B); Or.*mart.*28(p.24.12; M.11.596D); ‡Chrys.*Sus.*(6.608A).

*__εὐπρόθυμος__, *very eager*, Call.*v.Hyp.*(p.62); Rom.Mel.(*AS* 1 p.49); Thdr.Stud.*epp.*2.27(M.99.1193D).

*__εὐπροθύμως__, *very eagerly*, Ephr.3.141E; id.1.144C; id.1.146C.

*__εὐπρόοπτος__, f.l. for ἀπρόπτωτος Or.*princ.*4.2.9(M.11.361A; ἀπρόπτωτος p.310.4).

*__εὐπροσάγωγος__, *readily attracted*; comp., Cyr.H.*catech.*19.1.

*__εὐπρόσβατος__, *accessible*, Evagr.*h.e.*6.4(p.224.20; M.86.2848C).

*__εὐπροσδέκτως__, *acceptably*, Epiph.*haer.*42.12(p.166.26; M.41. 789B).

__εὐπρόσεδρος__, *devout*; of virgins (cf. 1Cor.7:35), Chrys.*hom.13.2 in 1Tim.*(11.619D).

__εὐπροσήγορος__, *well-expressed*, Bas.*ep.*2.5(3.74A; M.32.229C); Euthal.Diac.*Ac.*(M.85.832A).

__εὐπρόσιτος__, __1.__ *accessible*, of things εὐνοίᾳ Clem.*prot.*11(p.78.8; M. 8.225C); παραδοχῇ Thdr.Stud.*epp.*2.207(M.99.1628B); neut. as subst., *ib.*2.76(1313A); neut. plur. as adv., *ib.*2.56(1269A); __2.__ *acceptable*; of persons, Jo.D.*hom.*4.34(M.96.637B); of things, Thdr. Stud.*epp.*2.36(1213D); *ib.*2.147(1460C).

__εὐπροσίτως__, *with easy access*, ‡Meth.*Sym.et Ann.*10(M.18.373A) cit. s. ἀντωπέω.

*__εὐπρόσκρουστος__, *assailable*, Gr.Nyss.*castig.*(M.46.316B).

*__εὐπροσκύνητος__, *full of reverence*, ‡Hipp.Th.*fr.*17(p.50.5).

*__εὐπρόστακτος__, *well able to command*; of bishops, *Const.App.* 2.6.4.

*__εὐπροσωπεύομαι__, *appear attractive*, Thdot.Anc.*hom.BMV et Sym.*8(M.77.1401B).

__εὐπροσωπέω__, __1.__ *make a good show*, Chrys.*hom.23.5 in Eph.*(11. 173C, v.l. εὐγνωμονοῦντας); c. acc., Nil.*epp.*2.42(M.79.216C); __2.__ *show a glad face*, Marc.Er.*opusc.*7.14(M.65.1092C); Dam.*troph.*3.4(p.242. 13); *ib.*4.4(p.266.13); __3.__ *have the face to, presume*, Anast.S.*Ps.6*(M.89. 1080C).

__εὐπροσώπως__, __1.__ *in a friendly way*, Thdr.Mops.*fr.in Jo.*6:12(p.328. 3; M.66.745C); Cyr.*Lc.*6:41(M.72.604A); __2.__ *appropriately*, ‡Chrys. *annunt.et Ar.*(11.839C); __3.__ *speciously*, Bas.*Eun.*1.4(1.212A; M.29. 509C).

__εὐπροχώρητος__, *making good progress*, ‡Ath.*Apoll.*1.21(M.26. 1129C).

__εὔπτερος__, *well-winged*; met., of virgins ref. wings of soul, Meth. *symp.*8.2(p.82.12; M.18.140C).

__εὐπτέρυγος__, = foreg.; of angels, Paul.Sil.*Soph.*695(M.86.2146A).

__εὐπτόητος__, *easily scared*, Bas.*hom.in Ps.*33(1.151C; M.29.369C); Cyr.*ador.*5(1.151C); Diad.*perf.*87(p.120.4).

*__εὔπτωτος__, *unstable*, Areth.*Apoc.*52(M.106.713C).

*__εὑρεσιεπέω__, *invent words, chatter*, Cyr.*Juln.*3(6^2.96E).

*__εὑρεσικομπία__, ἡ, *verbal embellishment*, Cyr.*Juln.*4(6^2.114A).

*__εὑρεσιμαῖος__, *found*, Pall.*h.Laus.*6(p.23.12).

__εὕρεσις__, ἡ, *finding, discovery*; hence of conclusion of an inquiry τῆς...περὶ θεοῦ ζητήσεως εὐ. Clem.*str.*6.15(p.493.6; M.9.345A); of intellectual *conception* in literary work, Gr.Thaum.*pan.Or.*1(p.2. 16; M.10.1052B); of conclusion of an investigation into the meaning of a passage, hence *interpretation*, Or.*Jo.*2.1(p.53.25; M.14. 105D); Chrys.*hom.in Mt.26:39*(3.16B); of result of a computation, hence *list* of books etc., Euthal.Diac.*epp.Paul.*(M.85.708A); *invention*, i.e. *falsehood*, Ath.*gent.*11(M.25.24B); Cyr.*Mich.*30(3.417D); *devising, machination* of a disease considered as an evil force, Sophr.H.*mir.Cyr.et Jo.*61(M.87.3637B).

[*]__εὑρεσσίλογος__, v. εὑρησίλογος.

__εὑρετής__, ὁ, *originator* τῆς φιλοσοφίας καὶ τῆς διαλεκτικῆς Clem. *str.*1.9(p.29.30; M.8.741B); τῆς ἀποστασίας Cyr.*Os.*91(3.122C); τῆς Μανιχαϊκῆς αἱρέσεως Thdt.*eran.*proem.(4.2); esp. of Devil as originator of sin, Meth.*res.*1(p.332.1,12; M.18.300A); Ath.*ep.Aeg. Lib.*1(M.25.540B); Gr.Nyss.*or.catech.*26(p.101.7; M.45.69C).

__εὑρετικός__, __1.__ *finding out*, comp., Gr.Naz.*ep.*34(M.37.76B); __2.__ *concerned with inquiry* or *discovery* δύναμιν εὐ. τῶν καταθυμιῶν Gr. Nyss.*hom.2 in Cant.*(M.44.796C); τῶν εὐ. τῆς ψυχῆς δυνάμεων *ib.12* (1028B).

__εὑρέτις__, ἡ, *originator*, fem. of εὑρετής, Clem.*prot.*2(p.21.1; M.8. 100A); Dion.Ar.*ep.*9.6(M.3.1113C).

__εὕρετρα__, τά, *reward given to finder*, Gr.Thaum.*ep.can.*10(M.10. 1045C).

[*]__εὑρέω__, = εὑρίσκω, ‡Chrys.*hom.suppl.*6(13.215A).

__εὕρημα__, (freq. in later form __εὕρεμα__), __τό__, __1.__ *literary invention*, Cyr. *Jo.*4.5(4.410D); __2.__ *reward*, id.*glaph.Gen.*3(1.102E); id.*Os.*3(3.15E).

__εὐρημοσύνη__, ἡ, *fine diction*, *cat.Apoc.*9:3(p.313.28).

__εὑρησιέπεια__, ἡ, *fluency of words*, Cyr.*Juln.*2(6^2.66E); plur., *ib.*5 (178A); id.*hom.pasch.*23(5^2.279C).

__εὑρησιλογέω__, *invent as ingenious explanations* θεωρίας δή τινας εὐ. Eus.*p.e.*5.3(183A; M.21.317A); εὐ. τοιαῦτά τινα Cyr.*ep.*54(p.165. 16; M.77.289C).

__εὑρησιλογία__, ἡ, *plausible argument*, Clem.*str.*8.1(p.81.5; M.9. 561A); Eus.*p.e.*11.6(518B; M.21.860A); Cyr.*Ag.*2(3.628C).

__εὑρησίλογος__, *inventor of tales*, *Orac.Sib.*1.178; cf.*ib.*8.187 (εὑρεσσί-); Mac.Mgn.*apocr.*4.30(p.225.31).

*__εὐριζόομαι__, *be well rooted*; met., Thdr.Stud.*epp.*1.40(M.99. 1052A) better written *divisim*.

__εὔριζος__, *well-rooted*, Diod.*Ps.*91:13(M.33.1626B) = Cyr.*Ps.*91:13 (M.69.1228D); met. πίστις Nil.*epp.*3.284(M.79.524D).

*__εὐρίζω__, *be well rooted*; met., Or.*Ps.*47:3(p.46) better written *divisim*.

__εὐρίπιστος__, *easily swayed*; met., *unstable, fickle*, Or.*Jo.*10.25 (16; p.197.1; M.14.349C); Chrys.*hom.11.6 in Mt.*(7.156C); Cyr.*Ps.* 34:5(M.69.897A); neut. as subst., Epiph.*haer.*59.1(p.364.8; M.41. 1017B); Chrys.*hom.10.3 in 1Cor.*(10.84C); Thdt.*ep.*29(4.1090).

*__εὐριπίστως__, comp., *in a more unstable way*, Thdr.Stud.*epp.* 2.107(M.99.1365D).

__εὔριπος__, ὁ, __1.__ any *strait* or *narrow sea*, where the flux and reflux is violent, met., esp. in Chrys. τὸν εὐ. τῶν κακῶν Chrys.*hom.19.7 in Mt.*(7.255E); id.*compunct.*1.2(1.125D); Thdt.*ep.*14(4.1072); id.*affect.* 11(p.273.6; 4.983); __2.__ as adj., *troubled, unstable*, cf. εὐρίπιστος; Thdt. *h.e.*2.3.6(3.827); *ib.*2.31.10(909); τοὺς εὐ. βροτῶν ‡Caes.Naz.*dial.*112 (M.38.992).

__εὑρίσκω__, *find*; abs., *achieve one's desire, succeed*, Hipp.*haer.*4.20 (p.53.8; M.16.3087C); ἔθος λέγειν...ὁ δεῖνα εὗρεν, ὅταν πολὺ κέρδος ᾖ τὸ γινόμενον Chrys.*hom.19.1 in Rom.*(9.642D); pass., *be found*, i.e. *be present*, Evagr.*h.e.*2.5(p.51.30; M.86.2512B); Thphn.*chron.*p.19 (M.108.108B).

__εὔροιζος__, *ringing true*; of gold, Jo.Mon.*hymn.Chrys.*4(M.96. 1380B); v. ὄβρυζος.

__εὔροος__, *welling up abundantly* φρέατα Bas.*hom.*6.5(2.48A; M.31. 272B).

__εὐρραθάμιγξ__, *with lovely drops* οἴνου Nonn.*par.Jo.*2:3(M.43. 760D).

__εὐρυβόας__, *far-shouting, loud-shouting*, Gr.Naz.*carm.*1.2.15.64(M. 37.769A).

__εὐρυγένειος__, *broad-bearded*; met., *ancient* αἰών Nonn.*par.Jo.* 3:15(M.43.768C); *ib.*6:35(800B); *ib.*18:19(892C).

*__εὔρυζος__, v. ὄβρυζος.

[*]__εὐρυθέμεθλος__, *with broad foundations*, Gr.Naz.*carm.*1.1.5.1(M. 37.424A); *ib.*1.2.1.531(562A).

__εὐρυθέμειλος__, = foreg., *broad*; of floor, Paul.Sil.*Soph.*620(M.86. 2143A).

*__εὐρυθμέω__, __1.__ *order, regulate*, Jo.Mon.*hymn.Geo.*5(M.96.1397A); __2.__ *harmonize*, Thdr.Stud.*iamb.*10(M.99.1784B).

*__εὐρυκέλευθος__, *having wide ways, expansive*, Paul.Sil.*Soph.*721 (M.86.2147A).

*__εὐρύμυθος__, *of much speech*, Sophr.H.*carm.*7.121(M.87.3772A).

__εὐρύνοος__, *broad-minded*, met. νηδύς Sophr.H.*carm.*1.98(M.87. 3737B).

__εὐρύνω__, __1.__ *broaden, enlarge* τὸ τεῖχος Evagr.*h.e.*1.20(p.29.10,15; M.86.2476A,B); Paul.Sil.*ambo.*134(M.86.2257A); met. τὰς τῆς ψυχῆς ἀποθήκας Nil.*epp.*4.27(M.79.561D); τὸν λόγον Thdt.*haer.*5.10,12(4.419, 428); Max.*ambig.*(M.91.1357C); pass., Meth.*res.*2.3(p.334.4; M.41.

1165D); Dion.Ar.*e.h.*3.3.5(M.3.432B); *εἷς κύριος...εἰς κυρίους τρεῖς εὐρυνόμενος* Sophr.H.*ep.syn.*(M.87.3153A); **2.** pass., *have one's reputation enhanced*, Cyr.*Is.*5.1(2.742E).

***εὐρυόεις**, *wide*, Gr.Naz.*carm.*2.1.1.502(M.37.1007A).

***εὐρυπέλωρ**, *of wide boundaries πόλος* Sophr.H.*carm.*1.97(M.87.3737B).

***εὐρύπιστος**, *over-credulous*, Nil.*Magn.*2(M.79.972A).

εὐρύς, met., *ready εὐρὺν κἀκεῖνον εἰς βλασφημίαν* Eus.Al.*serm.*4(M.86.340A).

***εὐρυτένων**, *over-muscular*, Gr.Naz.*carm.*2.1.13.76(M.37.1233A).

***εὐρύτερον**, comp. adv., *more extensively*, Thdt.*haer.*5.23(4.455).

εὐρύτης, ἡ, *broadness*; met., Chrys.*hom.33.4 in Heb.*(12.309B).

***εὐρυφαής**, *shining abroad*, Synes.*hymn.*9.38(p.55; M.66.1613).

εὐρύφλεβος, *with wide veins*, Melet.*nat.hom.*2(M.64.1161D).

εὐρυχωρέω, *give free play*, Thdr.Stud.*iamb.*104(M.99.1805B); opp. *στενοχωρέω*, id.*epp.*2.180(M.99.1560B); med., *have free play*, opp. *στενοχωροῦμαι*, ‡Gr.Nyss.*Ar.et Sab.*12(M.45.1297C).

εὐρύχωρος, **1.** *wide*; met., of BMV *τὴν ὑψηλοτέραν καὶ εὐ. τοῦ οὐρανοῦ* Mod.*dorm.*8(M.86.3296C); neut. as subst., *open space, free space*, Ath.*apol.Const.*18(M.25.617C); met. *τὸ πνεῦμα τὸ ἅγιον ἐν εὐ. κατοικοῦν ἀγαλλιάσεται* Herm.*mand.*5.1.2; plur. *στενὴν...εἴσοδον... ἥτις τούτους δέχεται οἷς οὐδέποτε τὰ εὐ. ἐβοήθησε* Cael.*ep.CP* 2(p.137.2); **2.** *capable of containing*, Gr.Nyss.*v.Mos.*(M.44.344A); *εὐρυχωρότατον σῶμά σου θεοδόχον* Jo.D.*carm.dorm.BMV* 4(p.229; M.96.1364C).

εὐρώεις, *broad*, Eudoc.*Cypr.*2.156(M.85.852A).

***εὐρώννυμι**, *strengthen greatly ἵνα πάντα τὰ ἑαυτοῦ ταῖς ἡμῶν ἀσθενείαις ἀναμίξας...εὐρώσῃ* [sc. Logos] *τὴν ἀνθρώπου φύσιν* Cyr.*thes.*24(5^1.233A).

εὔρωστος, *big, strong*, superl. *τοὺς ἄγαν εὐ., γίγαντας ἀποκαλεῖν* Cyr.*glaph.Gen.*2(1.30A).

εὐσάλευτος, *prone to upheaval*, Ath.*Dion.*27(p.66.26; M.25.521A).

εὐσαρκέω, *be in good bodily health*, Chrys.*ep.*6(3.582B).

εὐσέβεια, ἡ, **A.** *devotion, sense of duty*; in secular affairs, Just.*1apol.*3.2(M.6.332A); *ib.*11.5(344A); Athenag.*res.*11(p.60.17; M.6.993D).

B. *devotion* to God, *piety*; **1.** explained *εἴη δ' ἂν τούτων τὸ κεφάλαιον εὐ. ... ἡ πρὸς τὸν ἕνα καὶ μόνον ὡς ἀληθῶς ὁμολογούμενόν τε καὶ ὄντα θεὸν ἀνάνευσις, καὶ ἡ κατὰ τοῦτον ζωῆς ἔξαψις* Eus.*p.e.*1.1(2B; M.21.24B); *πρὸς πίστιν καθαρὰν καὶ βίον ὀρθόν· τοῦτο γάρ ἐστιν εὐ.* Chrys.*hom.12.2 in 1Tim.*(11.612A); Isid.Pel.*epp.*4.143(M.78.1224C); **2.** partic.; **a.** in OT, *1Clem.*11.1; Cyr.*Thds.*(p.43.15; 5^2.2B); **b.** of Christians, *1Clem.*1.2; Clem.*str.*3.18(p.244.24; M.8.1208C); *αἱ... κατὰ τὸν νόμον θυσίαι τὴν περὶ ἡμᾶς εὐ. ἀλληγοροῦσι ib.*7.6(p.24.22; M.9.445A); Or.*Jo.*1.29(31; p.36.28; M.14.77B); *κλίμακι...προσεοικέναι... τῆς εὐ. τὴν ἄσκησιν* Bas.*hom.in Ps.*1(1.93C; M.29.217C); *Const.App.*5.6.1; ref. Communion *ἵνα οἱ μεταλαβόντες αὐτοῦ βεβαιωθῶσιν πρὸς εὐσέβειαν Lit.*ap.*Const.App.*8.12.39; *ib.*8.14.2; Euthal.Diac.*Ac.*(M.85.636A); **c.** of Christ to Father, Or.*Cels.*7.55(p.205.18; M.11.1500D); *Const.App.*5.5.3; **3.** as a virtue *ἀνθρώπου δὲ ἀρετὴ δικαιοσύνη καὶ σωφροσύνη καὶ ἀνδρεία καὶ εὐ.* Clem.*paed.*2.12(p.230.14; M.8.544C); *ἐν ἀνδρείᾳ καὶ ὑπομονῇ...ἐν εὐ. καὶ ὁσιότητι καὶ ταῖς λοιπαῖς ἀρεταῖς* Or.*hom.12.11 in Jer.*(p.97.18; M.13.303A); above all virtues, Clem.*str.*2.18(p.153.32; M.8.1016B,C); *ἐπὶ πᾶσιν εὐ., ἣν μητέρα φασὶ τῶν ἀρετῶν..., αὕτη γάρ ἐστιν ἀρχὴ καὶ τελευτὴ πασῶν τῶν ἀρετῶν* Gr.Thaum.*pan.Or.*12(p.28.16; M.10.1085C); *ἐν πληροφορίᾳ τῆς κατ' εὐ. ἀρετῆς διατελοῦντες Lit.*ap.*Const.App.*8.10.3.

C. *religion*; **1.** of pagans, Just.*dial.*14.2(M.6.505A); Chrys.*hom.4.4 in 1Cor.*(10.29A); **2.** of Hebrews, Eus.*p.e.*11.15(534A; M.21.885D); **3.** of Christians, Athenag.*leg.*13.1(M.6.916A); Clem.*prot.*4(p.35.28; M.8.136A); Eus.*h.e.*5 proem.4(M.20.408B); Chrys.*hom.33.4 in Mt.*(7.382C); Isid.Pel.*epp.*1.431(M.78.420D); *εὐ. ἀσεβείας καὶ δεισιδαιμονίας μέση τυγχάνουσα ib.*3.320(M.78.984B); Cyr.*Soph.*41(3.620B); Thdt.*Ps.*24:12(1.760); *τὰ ἔθνη μεμάθηκε τῆς εὐ. τὰ γράμματα καὶ ἀναγινώσκουσι τὸ βιβλίον* id.*Is.*29:11(p.117.18; 2.303).

D. *right belief, orthodox faith*, freq. *ἀρκεῖσθαι τῇ ἐν Νικαίᾳ παρὰ τῶν πατέρων ὁμολογηθείσῃ πίστει, διὰ τὸ μηδὲν αὐτῇ λείπειν, ἀλλὰ πλήρη εὐ. εἶναι* Ath.*tom.*5(M.26.800C); *ἀλυσιτελὲς ἔχουσι καὶ τὸ παρ' αὐτῶν διδόμενον ὕδωρ* [sc. in heret. baptisms], *λειπόμενον εὐσεβείᾳ* id.*Ar.*2.45(M.26.237B); *ἀμφότερα* [sc. written and unwritten tradition] *τὴν αὐτὴν ἰσχὺν ἔχει πρὸς τὴν εὐ.* Bas.*Spir.*66(3.54D; M.32.188A); *τὸν ποιμένα τὸν ἀγαθὸν ὁ λαϊκὸς τιμάτω...ὡς διδάσκαλον εὐσεβείας Const.App.*2.20.1; *ἔστι...τὸ κεφάλαιον τῆς τῶν Χριστιανῶν εὐ. τὸ πιστεύειν τὸν μονογενῆ θεόν* Gr.Nyss.*Eun.*12(1 p.220.19; M.45.913D); Epiph.*haer.*34.21(p.38.5; M.41.625A); *εἰ...προηγούμενόν ἐστι καὶ κεφαλαιωδέστερον ἡ εὐ., ἀλλ' οὖν γε χρείαν ἔχει καὶ τῆς ὀρθῆς πολιτείας* Isid.Pel.*epp.*4.226(M.78.1321A); *τῇ δὲ εὐ. συνέζευξε τὴν σεμνότητα, διδάσκων ὡς δεῖται τῶν ἔργων ἡ πίστις* Thdt.*1Tim.*2:2(3.647); *πολλοὶ καὶ Ἑλλήνων καὶ Ἰουδαίων, καὶ τῶν...αἱρετικῶν, καὶ σωφροσύνην, καὶ δικαιοσύνην ἔστιν ὅτε μετίασιν· ἀλλὰ τῆς εὐ. ἐστερημένοι, καρπὸν ἐντεῦθεν οὐδένα πορίζονται* id.*Ps.*4:6(1.632).

E. *right conduct*, Just.*dial.*4.7(M.6.485C); *κανών ἐστι οὗτος* [sc. 'do as you would be done by'] *καὶ εὐ. καὶ φιλανθρωπίας* Isid.Pel.*epp.*4.53(M.78.1104B); Thdt.*qu.36 in Gen.*(1.47); needed in addition to right belief, Chrys.*hom.8.1 in 2Tim.*(11.707D).

F. *religious observance*; **1.** in pagan religions, Athenag.*leg.*30.3(M.6.960C); Clem.*str.*6.4(p.449.18; M.9.253C); **2.** in Christianity *τὸ θεῖον λιταῖς τε καὶ ἄλλαις εὐ. ἐξωσιοῦτο* Evagr.*h.e.*4.24(p.171.14; M.86.2741B); **3.** *reverent behaviour*, Thdt.*h.e.*5.18.24(3.1051); **4.** *worship*, Clem.*str.*1.24(p.100.20; M.8.908B); *εὐ. ἑνὸς τοῦ ἐπὶ πάντων θεοῦ* Eus.*d.e.*3.7(p.145.19; M.22.244D); *σαββατίζειν ἐνετείλω, οὐ πρόφασιν ἀργίας διδούς, ἀλλ' ἀφορμὴν εὐ. Const.App.*7.36.4; *ὁ τοῦ Χριστοῦ θεὸς καὶ πατήρ...οὐ...ἄπαυστος ἡ εὐ. ib.*7.35.10; ref. virgins *οὐκ ἐπὶ διαβολῇ τοῦ γάμου, ἀλλ' ἐπὶ σχολῇ τῆς εὐ. ib.*8.24.2.

G. *worshipfulness, majesty*; of God, *2Clem.*19.1; Eus.*h.e.*1.2.7(M.20.57A); *reverence, majesty*; as title of honour of a monk, Ath.*h.Ar.ep.*1(p.181.8; M.25.692A); of a bishop, id.*ep.Rufin.*(M.26.1181A); freq. of emperor, *A.Petr.et Paul.*3(p.179.13); CAnt.(341)*can.*1; CSard.*ep.cath.*ap.Ath.*apol.sec.*44(p.119.10; M.25.324B); Ath.*ep.Jov.*1 ap.Thdt.*h.e.*4.3.7(*εὐλαβείᾳ* M.26.816C); Marc.Diac.*v.Porph.*48; used by emperor *ὑπὸ τῆς ἐμῆς εὐ.* Const.ap.Eus.*v.C.*3.31(p.92.19; M.20.1092B); id.ap.Ath.*apol.sec.*51(p.132.15; 341B); Leo I Imp. ap.Evagr.*h.e.*2.9(p.60.1; M.86.2528B).

H. *alms εὐσεβείας παρέχων τοῖς πένησιν A.Thom.*A 19(p.128.6); Hegem.*Arch.*10(p.16.11,12; M.10.1444A,B).

I. *'the fear of the Lord'* (Is.11:2) *ἰσχύος δὲ καὶ εὐ.* [sc. *πνεῦμα ἔσχε*] *Μωυσῆς* Just.*dial.*87.4(M.6.684B).

εὐσεβ-έω, **1.** *live* or *behave reverently, piously*, Just.*dial.*10.2(M.6.496C); *ib.*12.3(500C); *εὐ. εἰς τὸ θεῖον* Clem.*str.*2.18(p.158.16; M.8.1025A); *εὐ. κατὰ τὴν διδασκαλίαν Ἰησοῦ* Or.*Cels.*7.52(p.202.27; M.11.1496C); *ib.*8.44(p.259.4; 1581C); Gr.Thaum.*pan.Or.*13(p.29.12; M.10.1088B); hence *be a Christian*, Gr.Naz.*or.*3.7(M.35.524B); *τί γὰρ ὄφελος ἐν τῇ πίστει ∼οῦντας διὰ τοῦ βίου ἀσεβεῖν;* Chrys.*hom.7.1 in 1Tim.*(11.584E); *τοὺς βουλομένους ∼εῖν ἐδίωκον ib.3.1*(563C); Thdt.*ep.*146(4.1266); **2.** *hold pious opinions, be orthodox εἰς τὸν τῶν ὅλων θεὸν ∼εῖν* Or.*Cels.*7.46(p.197.18; M.11.1488C); Gr.Thaum.*pan.Or.*6(p.16.6; M.10.1069C); *οὔτε γὰρ τὸν ἐπέκεινα τῶν ὅλων θεὸν υἱὸν ἄν τις εἰπὼν εὐσεβήσειεν* Eus.*e.th.*1.7(p.65.34; M.24.836D); *ὑμεῖς μὲν γὰρ ∼οῦντες Χριστιανοί ἐστε· ἐκεῖνοι δέ, κτίσμα λέγοντες τὸν...λόγον, οὐδὲν διαφέρουσιν ἐθνικῶν* Ath.*v.Anton.*69(M.26.941B); Bas.*Spir.*18(3.15E; M.32.100B); Epiph.*haer.*76.3(p.344.12; M.42.521B); ptcpl. as subst., *the orthodox*, Gr.Nyss.*Eun.*1(1 p.87.22; M.45.320B); Thdt.*h.e.*4.19.9(3.981); **3.** *reverence, worship θεόν* Eus.*p.e.*3.6(96D; M.21.177C); Cyr.*Juln.*5(6^2.177D); pass. *τῷ ∼ουμένῳ θεῷ* Or.*Jo.*28.23(18; p.418.15; M.14.729B).

εὐσεβής, **A.** *holy, pious, devout*; **1.** of persons, *1Clem.*50.3; *2Clem.*19.4; Just.*dial.*5.3(M.6.488A); *ib.*136.2(789C); Or.*Jo.*13.1(p.226.1; M.14.400A); of martyrs, *ib.*6.54(36; p.163.31; 296B); of Job, Meth.*fr.14 in Job*(p.515.20); of widows, *Const.App.*3.3.1; *ib.*8.41.2; *τὸ μὲν γὰρ εἶναι εὐ. ἐκ τῆς τοῦ τινος εὐνοίας, τὸ δὲ θαυματοποιεῖν ἐκ τῆς τοῦ ἐνεργοῦντος δυνάμεως ib.*8.1.18; Thdt.*Trin.*18(M.75.1176B); comp., id.*Ps.*65:9(1.1047); applied properly to 'gnostic' alone, Clem.*str.*7.1(p.3.28; M.9.404B); as equivalent to *Christian*, Philost.*h.e.*2.5(M.65.468C); *Γάλλον...εὐ. τε ὄντα καὶ...διαμείναντα* Thdt.*h.e.*3.3.1(3.913); *ib.*3.8.1(921); neut. as subst., *Christianity*, Philost.loc. cit.; iron., of Jews as more pious than Eun. because they saw implications of Christ calling God Father (Jo.5:18) whereas Eunomius did not, Didym.(‡Bas.)*Eun.*4(1.295A; M.29.708B); **2.** of qualities, opinions, states, etc. *εὐ. πεποιθήσεως 1Clem.*2.3; *γνώμης* Just.*dial.*80.2(M.6.664B); *ἐπιστήμης* Clem.*str.*1.7(p.25.1; M.8.732D); CAnc.(358)*ep.syn.*(p.269.21; M.42.405A); *πολιτείαν* Thdt.*qu.53 in 4Reg.*(1.547); id.*Ps.*106:36(1.1375); **3.** of things *ὕμνων τε καὶ εὐχῶν* Eus.*d.e.*1.10(p.49.9; M.22.92D); *πρᾶγμα εὐ.* Chrys.*hom.77.3 in Jo.*(8.454D); **4.** neut. as subst.; **a.** *that which is holy*, *2Clem.*20.4; Just.*dial.*45.3(M.6.572C); **b.** *piety, religious devotion*; of Christ to Father, *ib.*98.1(705B); of men to God, Or.*Jo.*6.54(36; p.163.15; M.14.293D); *τὸ δὲ εὐ. μὴ ἐν τῷ πολλάκις περὶ θεοῦ λαλεῖν, ἀλλ' ἐν τῷ τὰ πλείω σιγᾶν εἶναι τιθέμενοι* Gr.Naz.*or.*3.7(M.35.524A); **5.** with partic. connotation of *orthodox* in theology, Or.*Jo.*6.39(23; p.149.9; M.14.269A); *εὐ. ... ἐστιν φρονεῖν καὶ ὁμολογεῖν τὴν...τριάδα ἐν μιᾷ θεότητι* Paulin.T.*symb.*(p.435.3; M.42.672B); of persons, Ath.*ep.Drac.*27(M.25.521A); (masc. as subst.), id.*h.Ar.*67(p.220.14; M.25.773C); Gr.

Nyss.*bapt.Chr.*(M.46.585B); *Const.App.*8.34.12; of teaching, Ath. *apol.sec.*17(p.100.10; M.25.276C); of faith, id.*h.Ar.*34(p.202.16; M. 25.733A); of dogma, Bas.*Spir.*47(3.39E; M.32.153C); *εὐ. ὑπολήψεις* Gr.Nyss.*Eun.*1(1 p.67.17; M.45.296C); neut. as subst., *orthodoxy*, Gr.Naz.*or.*37.18(M.36.304B); **6.** as imperial title, of Antoninus *Pius*, Just.*1apol.*1.1(M.6.328A); of Constantine and of Licinius, *Edict.*ap.Eus.*h.e.*8.17.4(M.20.792A); superl., of Constantine, Ath. *apol.Const.*33(M.25.640B); Constantius, id.*ep.encycl.*5(p.174.21; M. 25.233B); Honorius, Pall.*v.Chrys.*3(p.20.19; M.47.14); of deceased emperors, Mel.*fr.*1.3(p.308; M.5.1212B); of consorts, Jo.Mal.*chron.* 18 p.441(M.97.649B); superl., Thphn.*chron.*p.59(M.108.201B); *Κωνσταντίνου καὶ Εἰρήνης τῶν εὐ. βασιλέων ib.*p.370(885C); *μνήσθητι, κύριε, τῶν εὐ. καὶ πιστῶν βασιλέων Κωνσταντίνου, Ἑλένης, κτλ. Lit. Jac.*(p.218.19); hence **7.** *sacred* as being *imperial εὐ. γράμματα* Phot.Tyr.*libell.*(p.14.16; H.2.504B); *ὁ τῶν εὐ. προεστὼς κοιτώνων* Anast.Ant.*redit.*(p.254).

B. *right, reasonable τὴν γὰρ αὐτὴν οὐσίαν καὶ γεννητὴν εἶναι καὶ ἀγέννητον οὐδεὶς λόγος εὐ. ἐπιτρέπει* Aët.*synt.*5(p.353.15; M.42. 536D); Thdt.*qu.31 in Dt.*(1.280); Jo.Mal.*chron.*18 p.440(M.97.649A).

***εὐσεβοπρεπῶς**, *as befits the devout*, ‡Jo.D.*hom.*5(M.96.656D).

***εὐσεβοφανής**, *apparently orthodox*, monoph.ap.Leont.H. *monoph.*testimonia(M.86.1876D).

***εὐσεβοφρόνως**, *in accordance with orthodox thought*, ‡Ath.*qu. script.*24(M.28.717B); Barth.Edess.*Agar.*(M.104.1404B).

εὐσεβῶς, **1.** *devoutly, reverently*, *1Clem.*61.2; *ib.*62.1; Clem.*str.*7.9 (p.40.12; M.9.477B); Ath.*Ar.*2.76(M.26.308C); ref. Christ *λελέχθαι δὲ εὐ. καὶ μεθ' ὑποτιμήσεως ὅλον τοῦτο 'πάτερ, εἰ δυνατόν ἐστι' κτλ.* Or.*Cels.*2.25(p.155.4; M.11.845B); **2.** *with the right spirit ἄκουε... εὐ.* Gel.Cyz.*h.e.*2.19.8(M.85.1277A); comp., Thdt.*Jer.*36:11–15(2. 563); **3.** *rightly, correctly τὸ τοὺς καρποὺς πλήρεις γεγονέναι οὐκ ἂν εὐ. λέγοιμεν ἔργον εἶναι τοῦ γεωργοῦ...ἀλλ' ἔργον τοῦ θεοῦ* Or.*princ.* 3.1.19(p.232.9; M.11.289C); Chrys.*hom.24.3 in Jo.*(8.141C); Thdt. *1Tim.*6:13(3.671); comp., Ath.*Ar.*3.15(M.26.353B); **4.** *in accordance with right doctrine* or *orthodoxy*, very freq. *πιστεύοντες εἰς αὐτὸν* [sc. Christ] *εὐ.* Ath.*v.Anton.*94(M.26.976A); *ἑκουσίως αὐτὸν καὶ ἐθελοντὴν τὸν υἱὸν γεγεννηκέναι εὐ. ὑπειλήφαμεν Symb.Ant.*(345)8 (p.253.27; M.26.733A); *εἰς μίαν ἄναρχον τῶν ὅλων ἀρχὴν δι' υἱοῦ εὐ. τὰ πάντα ἀνάγομεν Symb.Sirm.*1 *anath.*26; Bas.*Spir.*44(3.38A; M.32.149A); Didym.(‡Bas.)*Eun.*5(1.312B; M.29.749A); Dion.Ar.*d.n.* 9.9(M.3.916C); *τῶν...εὐ. καὶ πιστῶς βασιλευσάντων Lit.Jac.*(p.218. 21).

εὔσειστος, *easily shaken*, Gr.Thaum.*pan.Or.*6(p.18.5; M.10. 1072D).

εὐσέλαος, *shining brightly*, Paul.Sil.*Soph.*830(M.86.2150B).

εὐσημείωτος, *easily counted*, †Bas.*Is.*244(1.564E; M.30.545D); Max.*comput.*(M.19.1256A).

εὔσημος, **1.** *clear, conspicuous*; hence *famous, honourable*, Gr. Nyss.*Maced.*7(M.45.1309B); **2.** *responding well to signs*, hence, of a servant, *well-trained, obedient*, *A.Jo.*14(p.160.9).

εὐσθένεια, ἡ, *strength*, *Hom.Clem.*19.20; Cyr.*Thds.*(p.42.25; 5^2. 1D); id.*Ps.*32:16(M.69.880C); Thdr.Stud.*epp.*2.19(M.99.1197D).

εὐσθενής, **1.** *strong, powerful, vigorous*; of persons, Cyr.*Joel.*6 (3.204C); *Chron.Pasch.*p.269(M.92.661B); Thdr.Stud.*epp.*2.29(M.99. 1197D); comp., ‡Nil.*perist.*10.7(M.79.897D); of a city, Cyr.*Nah.*29(3. 507A); of sun's course, id.*Ps.*38:6(M.69.829C); **2.** *secure, steady στάσιν* id.*inc.unigen.*(5^1.691E); *διάνοιαν* id.*Lc.*12:41(M.72.748D); comp. *ψυχήν* Melet.*nat.hom.*30(M.64.1272A); neut. as subst., Eus. *Is.*10:17–18(M.24.164C); Cyr.*Lc.*12:41(752D).

εὐσθενῶς, *strongly, vigorously*, Cyr.*Os.*166(3.193D); id.*Nah.*40(3. 515A); Geo.Pis.*Pers.*3.83(M.92.1240A); comp., Cyr.*glaph.Gen.*4(1. 121E); id.*Nest.*4.6(p.90.5; 6^1.117D); superl., id.*glaph.Gen.*2(62A).

***εὐσκανδάλιστος**, **1.** pass., *easily offended*, Or.*fr.in Mt.*17:24,27 (p.160; M.17.297C); neut. as subst., Ammon.*Jo.*7:18(M.85.1444B); **2.** act., *easily causing offence*, Leont.N.*v.Jo.Eleem.*36(p.69.19,22); *ib.*(p.72.22); Anast.S.*hod.*1(M.89.41D); *ib.*14(248B).

***εὐσκελής**, *nimble, active*, Chrys.*hom.12.2 in Phil.*(11.292B).

***εὐσκελῶς**, *strongly*; of a horse running, Eust.*engast.*1(p.17.2; M.18.613B).

εὔσκιος, *well-shaded*; hence met., *obscure*, of Logos *εὐ. ἐπὶ τὴν κλίνην τῆς κάτω ζωῆς καταβαίνει, τῇ ὑλικῇ τοῦ ἀνθρωπίνου σώματος φύσει συσκιαζόμενος* Gr.Nyss.*hom.6 in Cant.*(M.44.888D).

***εὐσκιόφυλλος**, *well provided with leaves affording shade ξύλον εὐ.* fig., of BMV, ‡Serg.*acath.*161(p.144; M.92.1341D); *δένδρῳ Phys.* B 15(p.218.4).

εὔσκυλτος, *active, quick*, *Const.App.*2.4.1; *ib.*3.19.7; Jo.Mal. *chron.*12 p.299(M.97.452C); comp., *Const.App.*3.19.1.

εὐσπλαγχνία, ἡ, **1.** *mercy, compassion*; **a.** of God, *1Clem.*14.3; *Ἰησοῦ Χριστὲ ὁ τῆς εὐ. υἱός A.Thom.*A 10(p.114.17); *τῇ ἰδίᾳ αὐτοῦ εὐ. ἠθέλησεν ἡμᾶς σῶσαι A.Phil.*63(p.63.13); *τὸ πᾶν τῆς οἰκονομίας θεϊκῆς ἴδιόν ἐστιν εὐ.* Didym.*Trin.*3.21(M.39.909A); *συνεχώρησέ σοι ἡ αὐτοῦ εὐ. τὴν ἁμαρτίαν ταύτην* Jo.Mosch.*prat.*118(M.87.2981D); exeg. Mt.3:15 *ἄφες ἄρτι πληρωθῆναι τὴν εὐ.* Isid.Pel.*epp.*1.66(M.78.225C); of God's commandments, Thphl.Ant.*Autol.*2.14(M.6.1076A); **b.** of men, Clem.*q.d.s.*3(p.162.4; M.9.608B); *πᾶσαν εὐ. εἰς τοὺς πένητας ἐπιδειξώμεθα* Chrys.*El.et vid.*8(3.337C); Cyr.*hom.pasch.*27(5^2.321E); **2.** *act of compassion* or *mercy αἱ εὐ. αὐτοῦ* [sc. S. Thomas] *καὶ αἱ ἰάσεις A.Thom.*A 20(p.131.2); **3.** *love, affection ὁ πατήρ μου λόγοις πείθειν με κατὰ τὴν ἑαυτοῦ εὐ.* [tr. *pro sua affectione*] *M.Perp.*3(p.63. 30).

***εὐσπλαγχνίζομαι**, *have compassion*, *A.Jo.*81(p.191.16); *V.Aberc.* 15(p.13.10); Hesych.H.*Ps.tit.*79.29(M.27.993D); Chrys.*poenit.*8.4(2. 347E).

εὔσπλαγχνος, *compassionate, merciful, tender-hearted*; **1.** in gen., *1Clem.*54.1; Polyc.*ep.*5.2 cit. s. διάκονος; Hipp.*haer.*9.12(p.248. 7; M.16.3383A); Gr.Naz.*or.*7.4(M.35.760A); Leont.N.*v.Jo.Eleem.*46 (p.99.15); of Church, †Hipp.*Artem.*ap.Eus.*h.e.*5.28.12(M.20.513D); **2.** of God *εὐ. πατέρα 1Clem.*29.1; Just.*dial.*108.3(M.6.728A); *A.Jo.*33 (p.168.14); Bas.*jud.*8(2.222C; M.31.673B); *ὁ θεὸς ὁ μόνος...εὐ. ... ἔπιδε εὐ. ὄμματι ἐπὶ...τὸν λαόν σου Lit.Praesanct.*(p.350.17); **3.** of H. Ghost in invocation at Gnost. initiation *ἐλθὲ ἡ μήτηρ ἡ εὐ. A.Thom.* A 27(p.142.14).

***εὐσπλάγχνως**, *compassionately*, Nect.*Thdr.*11(M.39.1832A).

εὐστάθεια, ἡ, **1.** *soundness, good estate*, *1Clem.*61.1; *ib.*65.1; *τὴν τῆς ψυχῆς εὐ.* Clem.*str.*4.23(p.314.20; M.8.1357D); Thdr.Mops.*Mal.* 3:3–4(M.66.624B); *τὴν ἐν ἀγγέλοις...πολιτείαν τε καὶ εὐ.* Max.*ambig.* (M.91.1368B); esp. in liturg. prayers *ὑπὲρ τῆς τοῦ κόσμου εὐ.* Cyr.H. *catech.*23.8; *Lit.*ap.*Const.App.*8.10.3; *ὑπὲρ εἰρήνης καὶ εὐ. τοῦ κόσμου* Chrys.*hom.3.4 in Phil.*(11.218A); *Lit.Jac.*(p.218.23); **2.** *steadiness, constancy*, Bas.*ascet.*2.2(2.324C; M.31.884A); id.*Spir.*16(3.13C; M.32. 93C); ‡Bas.*const.*7.2(2.553C; M.31.1365D); opp. *προπέτεια*, Chrys. *hom.15.4 in 2Cor.*(10.549A).

εὐσταθέω, **1.** *stand firm, be steadfast*, *T.Job* 36(p.126.13); Ign. *Polyc.*4.1; Gr.Nyss.*Eun.*1(1 p.205.4; M.45.452D); **2.** *flourish, prosper*, Herm.*mand.*5.2.2; id.*sim.*7.3.

εὐσταθής, *stable, steadfast*; of orders of ministry *ταῖς τῶν διακόσμων εὐ. καὶ ἀσυμφύρτοις τάξεσι* Dion.Ar.*e.h.*1.5(M.3.377A).

***εὐσταθμέω**, pass., *be stable*, Nil.*praest.*23(M.79.1088C).

εὐσταθμία, ἡ, *equal balance*, Geo.Pis.*hex.*1469(M.92.1547A).

εὐστάφυλος, *rich in grapes*, Cyr.*hom.pasch.*27(5^2.321D).

***εὔστηθος**, *broad-chested*, Jo.Mal.*chron.*5 p.106(M.97.196B); *ib.*10 p.259(393A); *Chron.Pasch.*p.375n.(M.92.957n.).

εὐστιβής, *easy to tread*, hence *easy, obvious*, Cyr.*Is.*5.3(2.808B); id.*glaph.Ex.*1(1.245B); *θεωρίαν* id.*Jo.*9(4.775A).

εὔστικτος, *clearly marked out τῶν χρόνων εὔστικτα σημεῖα* Geo.Pis. *hex.*609(M.92.1482A).

***εὐστολία**, ἡ, *fine array*, Germ.CP *or.*3(M.98.292C).

εὔστολος, **1.** *well-equipped*, Melet.*nat.hom.*26(M.64.1245C); **2.** *convenient λιμένα* Thdt.*ep.*118(4.1199); **3.** *compactly built*; of a human frame, Jo.Mal.*chron.*4 p.88(M.97.172C); *ib.*5 p.103(192A).

εὐστόμαχος, *having a good digestion*, Isid.Pel.*epp.*4.49(M.78. 1100B).

***εὐστρογγύλως**, *in an exact circle*, *Mir.Artem.*41(p.69.4).

[*]**ἐΰστροφής**, *well-turned μύθοις* Gr.Naz.*carm.*1.1.3.35(M.37.410A).

εὐστροφία, ἡ, *turn for the better, reformation*, Thdr.Stud.*epp.*2.67 (M.99.1293D).

***εὐσύγγνωστος**, *easily pardoned*, Thdr.Mops.*Gen.*19:31(M.66. 641D); Jo.Jej.*canonar.*2(p.438); hence *slight ἐπιτιμίων* †Jo.Jej. *poenit.*(M.88.1917A).

***εὐσυγκατάβατος**, *readily condescending*; neut. as subst., in polite adress, Thdr.Stud.*epp.*2.181(M.99.1560C).

***εὐσύγκρισις**, ἡ, *discretion*, †Jo.Jej.*serm.*(M.88.1929C).

εὐσυγχώρητος, *readily pardoned*, †Jo.Jej.*serm.*(M.88.1928D).

***εὐσύλητος (εὐσύλατος)**, *falling a ready prey*, Cyr.*Jo.*10.2(4. 906D); -*λατος* Ephr.3.206A.

εὐσύλληπτος, *easily understood*, Chrys.ap.*cat.1Cor.*14:8(p.264. 14).

***εὔσυλος**, *easily lost*, Jo.Clim.*scal.*7(M.88.816B).

***εὐσυμπάθητος**, *compassionate*, †Gregent.*disp.*(M.86.784B); of God, †Jo.Jej.*serm.*(M.88.1921A); *καρδίᾳ* Thphn.*chron.*p.258(M.108. 644B); neut. as subst., ‡Chrys.*prec.*2(12.801D); Thdr.Stud.*epp.*2.121 (M.99.1396C).

***εὐσυμπαθήτως**, *compassionately*, †Gregent.*disp.*(M.86.764D).

εὐσυναλλάκτως, *effectively*, Or.*exp.in Pr.*25:11(M.17.236B).

***εὐσυνάρπαστος**, *easily stolen away*, Cyr.*Is.*5.5(2.875B).

***εὐσυναρπάστως**, *impulsively*, Cyr.*Jo.*4(4.392B).

***εὐσυνάρτητος**, *well-knit*, Max.*Pyrr.*(M.91.296B); id.*ep.*13(M.91.513C).

εὐσυνειδησία, ἡ, *good conscience*, Clem.*str.*6.14(p.488.24; M.9.337A); Or.*or.*27.6(p.366.24; M.11.509B); *Hom.Clem.*17.11.

εὐσυνείδητος, 1. *having a good conscience*, Ign.*Philad.*6.3; Clem.*str.*6.14(p.488.18; M.9.336C); Dion.Al.*ep.can.*4(p.104.8; M.10.1288C); Cyr.H.*catech.*3.3; neut. as subst., *Ep.Lugd.*ap.Eus.*h.e.*5.1.43(M.20.425A); Euthal.Diac.*epp.Paul.*(M.85.757C); **2.** *blameless*, Ign.*Magn.* 4; *Const.App.*2.17.1; ‡Just.*ep.Zen.et Ser.*11(M.6.1196B); **3.** *easily understood*, ref. 1Tim.5:4 οὐ γὰρ ἔθηκεν ἐνταῦθα μέγα τι καὶ ὑψηλόν, ἀλλ' ὅπερ ἐστὶν εὐ. Chrys.*hom.13.2 in 1Tim.*(11.619E).

***εὐσυνειδήτως**, *with a good conscience*, Isid.Gnost.ap.Clem.*str.*3.1(p.196.3; M.8.1101A); Bas.*reg.br.*212(2.486C; M.31.1224B); Chrys.*fr. in Jer.*2:11(M.64.761C).

***εὐσυνειδότως**, *with full awareness* τὴν γραφὴν εὐ. ἐξετάζειν δεῖ Or.*Jo.*5.2(p.101.9; M.14.188B; εὐσυνειδήτως *ib.*ap.*philoc.*5.2).

εὐσυνέτως, *carefully, cautiously*, Gr.Mag.*dial.*(tr.Zach.)3.14(M.*PL.*77.247B).

εὐσύνθετος, *well-organized*, Geo.Pis.*Pers.*2.207(M.92.1224A).

***εὐσυνίημι**, *understand well* εὐσυνιέντας Iren.*haer.*1.19.2(M.7.652C) but [εὖ] συνιέντας *ib.*ap.Epiph.*haer.*34.18(p.33.10).

εὐσυνόπτως, *clearly*, Didym.*Trin.*1.27(M.39.404A); Leont.H.*Nest.*1.18(M.86.1468B); Geo.Pis.*hex.*362(M.92.1462A); superl., Cyr.*glaph.Gen.*3(1.73E).

***εὐσυσταλτικῶς**, *in a short time*, comp., Tim.Ant.*caec.*5(M.28.1008B).

εὐσύστατος, *coherent, consistent* γραφαί *Pers.*(p.9.21); δόξας, opp. μεμερισμένας, *ib.*(p.39.20).

***εὐσυστροφέω, 1.** ? *manage well, do well*, Dor.*doct.*5.2(M.88.1677B); **2.** *be strict*, *ib.*19(1809B) cit. s. ἀσυστροφέω.

εὐσφυξία, ἡ, a *strong pulse*, Clem.*paed.*3.11(p.268.5; M.8.628C).

εὐσχημος, *fair*, *T.Sal.*8.1; fig. τὰ ἔργα Bas.*renunt.*9(2.210C; M.31.645B); ironically ψεύδει ‡Nil.*narr.*6(M.79.672B).

εὔσχολος, *at leisure*; of persons, *Hom.Clem.*8.3; Gr.Nyss.*Eun.* 9(2 p.212.7; M.45.809C); hence *devoted, concerned*, c. prep. εὔ. ἐπὶ τὰ κρείττω τὴν ἐπιθυμίαν Cyr.*Lc.*6:20(M.72.589C); τοὺς...εὐ. εἰς τὰ θεοῦ Proc.G.*Num.*3:45(M.87.800B).

***εὐτάλαντος**, *well-balanced, impartial*, Geo.Pis.*hex.*206(M.92.1449A).

εὐταξία, ἡ, 1. *good order*; **a.** in human conduct, Ign.*Eph.*6.2; Bas.*hex.*5.7(1.47C; M.29.112B); αὐτὸς Ἰησοῦς...οὐκ ἀποπηδᾷ τῆς ὑπ' αὐτοῦ ταχθείσης τε καὶ αἱρεθείσης ἀνθρωποπρεποῦς εὐ. Dion.Ar.*c.h.*4.4(M.3.181C); **b.** in Church, Bas.*ep.*161.1(3.252B; M.32.629B); ἡ γὰρ ἐκκλησία οὐκ ἀταξίας, ἀλλ' εὐ. ἐστὶ διδασκαλεῖον *Const.App.*8.31.3; of ministry εἰς καθαρτικὴν καὶ φωτιστικὴν καὶ τελειωτικὴν εὐ. διαιρουμένην Dion.Ar.*e.h.*5.1.3(M.3.504C); **c.** of visible creation, Athenag.*leg.*10.4(M.6.909B); Chrys.*exp.in Ps.*4:4(5.15C); Max.*ambig.*(M.91.1357B); **d.** of heavenly powers, Dion.Ar.*c.h.*6.1(M.3.200C); **2.** *administration, government*, in a convent ἡ πεπιστευμένη τὴν εὐ. Bas.*ascet.*2.2(2.326C; M.31.888B); Thdt.*ep.*81(4.1139).

***εὐταξίας, ὁ**, a church official, *master of ceremonies* εὐ. τὴν λαμπάδα κατέχοντος *Euchol.*(p.2).

***εὐταπείνωτος**, *easily humbled*, Synes.*ep.*140(M.66.1532C).

***εὐτάραχος**, *menacing* λόγχην ‡Eust.*Laz.*24(p.46.9).

***εὐτειχία, ἡ**, *strong fortification*, Cyr.*Os.*131(3.164C).

εὐτέλεια, ἡ, 1. *low estate, inferiority, state of degradation*; **a.** in gen., of man and human nature, ‡Bas.*struct.hom.*2.11(1.344C; M.30.56A); Chrys.*Eutrop.*1.2(3.382C); τῆς ἀνθρωπείας φύσεως...ἡ εὐ. Cyr.*Ps.*38:1(M.69.969B); id.*Jo.*1.9(4.92A); as assumed by Son, hence also of incarnate Christ ἐκ τῆς δοκούσης εὐ. τοῦ λόγου, μείζονα καὶ πλείονα τὴν εἰς αὐτὸν εὐσέβειαν ἔχῃς Ath.*inc.*1.1(M.25.97A); opp. glory at parousia, *ib.*56.3(196A); τὴν εὐ. καὶ τὴν πτωχείαν ἀνεδέξατο id.*inc.et c.Ar.*5(M.26.992A); Mac.Mgn.*apocr.*4.18(p.196.21); Nil.*epp.*2.36(M.79.404C); Sophr.H.*ep.syn.*(M.87.3161D); **b.** of poverty of understanding, Epiph.*haer.*proem.1(p.169.13; M.41.173A); τί οὖν ὁ Νικόδημος; ἔτι ἐπὶ τῆς Ἰουδαϊκῆς εὐ. μένει Chrys.*hom.26.2 in Jo.*(8.151A); of the inferiority of the 'letter' opp. spiritual exegesis οὐδὲ ἵσταμαι ἐν τῇ εὐ. τῆς λέξεως, ἀλλὰ ἀναβαίνω τῷ πτερῷ τοῦ νοήματος id.*Eutrop.*2.9(3.394B); id.*hom.38.4 in Jo.*(8.223B); **c.** of humble man's opinion of himself, Bas.*hom.in Ps.*71(1.193D; M.29.469C); hence as depreciatory mode of referring to oneself, Gr.Naz.*ep.*9(M.37.36C); Chrys.*ordin.*1(1.437A); Leont.N.*v.Jo.Eleem.*44(p.92.5); **2.** *weakness*, Thdt.*h.e.*5.3.7(3.1017); **3.** *making cheap, scorning* Ὀκταβιανὸς ὡπλίσατο κατ' αὐτῶν [sc. Antony and Cleopatra] καὶ διὰ τὴν εὐ. τῆς αὐτοῦ ἀδελφῆς Jo.Mal.*chron.*9 p.219(M.97.341A); Chrysipp.*enc.in Jo.Bapt.*12(p.42.7).

εὐτελής, 1. *thrifty, frugal, simple*, Clem.*paed.*1.12(p.149.19; M.8.369A); *ib.*2.10(p.224.14; 532B); εὐ. πολιτεύεται [sc. ὁ Σκύθης] *ib.*3.3(p.250.26; 589B); Gr.Naz.*ep.*61(M.37.121B); **2.** *lowly*, Chrys.*sac.*3.14(p.73.5; 1.391B); Nil.*epp.*1.1(M.79.81A); Thdt.*Ps.*8:4(1.653); esp. of scriptural language applied to incarnate Logos τῇ κεκρυμμένῃ λαμπρότητι τῶν δογμάτων ἐν εὐ. καὶ εὐκαταφρονήτῳ λέξει ἀποκειμένῃ Or.*princ.*4.1.7(p.304.3; M.11.356A); id.*Jo.*1.4(6; p.9.4; M.14.32B); πᾶσα δὲ ἀκρίβεια τοῦ Χριστιανισμοῦ ἐν τοῖς εὐ. ῥήμασι καὶ πράγμασιν εὑρίσκεται Ath.*inc.et c.Ar.*1(M.26.985A); *ib.*8(996A); Apoll.*fr.*6(p.205.20)ap.Thdt.*eran.*2(4.173); Nest.*fr.*B 10(p.273.9)ap.Cyr.*apol.orient.*4(p.42.27; 6^1.170B); **3.** *insignificant, slight, unimportant* οἱ ἑτερόδοξοι εὐ. ἀμφιβολίαν διαστείλασθαι μὴ δεδυνημένοι Or.*Jo.*6.21(12; p.130.31; M.14.237B); παραμυθίαν Ath.*v.Anton.*50(M.26.916B); εἰ μικρὰ καὶ εὐ., καὶ οὐ πρὸς θάνατον...σοῦ τὰ ἁμαρτήματα Bas.*hom.*13.4(2.117A; M.31.432B); τοὺς δὲ Ναυατιανοὺς οὐκ ἐπαινῶ, ὅτι περὶ εὐ. πταισμάτων τῆς κοινωνίας τοὺς λαϊκοὺς ἀποκλείουσι Socr.*h.e.*7.25.19(M.67.796C); of persons, Or.*Jo.*10.25(16; p.197.22; M.14.352A); Hipp.*haer.*9.12(p.250.20; M.16.3387A); Eus.*v.C.*1.42(p.27.18; M.20.956C); Gel.Cyz.*h.e.*3.10.13; **4.** *vile* γίνεται...ἡ Λητὼ ζῷον εὐ. Tat.*orat.*10(p.11.1; M.6.828A); superl., Cyr.*Joel.*33(3.225E, Aubert om.).

εὐτελίζ-ω, *interpret in an inferior* (i.e. human) *sense* ∼ουσι τὸ 'ἐκ γαστρὸς πρὸ ἑωσφόρου ἐγέννησά σε' ὡς ἂν ἐπὶ τῆς Μαρίας ἁρμόζοντος τούτου ‡Ath.*Ar.*4.27(p.75.6; M.26.509B).

εὐτελισμός, ὁ, *vilification*, Nil.*epp.*3.161(M.79.460C); Proc.G.*fr. Cant.*8:7(M.87.1773D).

εὐτελῶς, 1. *simply* ἀναδεῖσθαι τὴν κόμην εὐ. Clem.*paed.*3.11(p.271.11; M.8.637A); **2.** *meanly, ingloriously* τὰ εὐ. ὑπὸ τοῦ Ἡρακλέωνος εἰρημένα Or.*Jo.*6.60(38; p.169.4; M.14.304D); τὰ ἀνθρωπίνως καὶ εὐ. περὶ τοῦ σωτῆρος εἰρημένα Ath.*Dion.*9(p.52.1; M.25.492B).

***εὐτεχνής, 1.** *skilful*, superl., Cyr.*Is.*1.1(2.25A); id.*ep.*55(p.50.22; 5^2.176A); **2.** *well-devised* τῆς εὐ. κενώσεως id.*apol.Thdt.*6(p.129.14; 6^1.223C); τὴν καθ' ἡμᾶς εὐ. οἰκονομίαν id.*glaph.Ex.*2(1.302A); τὸ τῆς οἰκονομίας εὐ. id.*Arcad.*(p.82.29; 5^2.73C); id.*Os.*158(3.190C).

εὐτεχνία, ἡ, 1. *skill, art*; in use of words, Gel.Cyz.*h.e.*2.20.1(M.85.1281A); *ib.*3.13.14; in war, Cyr.*Nah.*39(3.514B); Geo.Pis.*Pers.*1.229(M.92.1212A); *ib.*2.39(1215A); in theology δογματικῆς εὐ. Cyr.*Ps.*36:21(M.69.940A); id.*Is.*5.4(2.851B); Thdr.Stud.*epp.*2.151(M.99.1472A); of God ἦν ἀκόλουθον καὶ θεοπρεποῦς εὐ. ἄξιον, τὰς τῶν φονώντων ὑποτρέχειν ὀργάς Cyr.*Nest.*4.3(p.82.3; 6^1.105B); in gen. εἴσω τε γεγόνασιν εὐζωΐας εὐαγγελικῆς εὐ. id.*Is.*4.4(2.689E); **2.** *work of art* ταῖς ἑαυτῶν εὐ. τὸ τῆς θεότητος ὄνομα προσνέμειν Cyr.*Is.*4.3(2.648B).

εὐτέχνως, from εὔτεχνος, *skilfully*, Cyr.*Nah.*8(3.484D); id.*ador.*1(1.11D); id.*glaph.Gen.*4(1.110D).

εὐτεχνῶς, from εὐτεχνής, = foreg.; superl., Cyr.*Ps.*36:16(M.69.933B); id.*glaph.Gen.*5(1.170E); id.*Juln.*3(6^2.94D).

***εὐτηρέμω**, ? f.l. for ἠρεμέω, Gr.Nyss.*anim.et res.*(M.46.96B) cit. s. ἀγάπη.

εὔτοκος, *aiding in childbirth*, ‡Petr.I Al.*phys.*22(p.52).

εὐτον-έω, 1. *have power* to do, Hipp.*haer.*7.29(p.211.8; M.16.3326A); Geo.Pis.*hex.*869(M.92.1501A); **2.** *endure* ∼εῖ μὴ ἁμαρτάνων Serap.*ep.Eudox.*(M.40.924C); Pall.*h.Laus.*18(p.50.17; M.34.1057B); ηὐτόνησε παραμένων νῆστις *ib.*(p.52.13; 1057D); τῇ ∼ούσῃ ψυχῇ Nil.*epp.*1.302(M.79.192D).

εὐτονία, ἡ, *endurance, persistency, perseverance*, Ath.*exp.Ps.*131:1(M.27.521A); Chrys.*hom.52.2 in Mt.*(7.532B); Bas.Sel.*v.Thecl.*1(M.85.504B).

εὔτονος, *vigorous, active*, of persons Χριστιανῷ Just.*dial.*93.5(M.6.700A); φιλοσόφων Gr.Thaum.*pan.Or.*9(p.25.15; M.10.1080C); Chrys.*hom.72.2 in Mt.*(7.702D); of things Ἰησοῦν...[sc. acc. Carpocrates] ὅμοιον τοῖς ἀνθρώποις γεγονότα,...τὴν δὲ ψυχὴν αὐτοῦ εὐ. καὶ καθαρὰν γεγονυῖαν Iren.*haer.*1.25.1 ap.Hipp.*haer.*7.32(M.16.3338A); πίστιν Iren.*haer.*1.13.4(M.7.588A); βίον Or.*fr.35 in Jo.*(p.510.3); σχολῇ Eus.*v.C.*3.13(p.83.18; M.20.1069B); neut. as subst., Or.*hom.15.1 in Jer.*(p.125.18; M.13.429A); Chrys.*hom.56.2 in Mt.*(7.567D); Thdr.Mops.*Ps.*74:9(p.503.22; M.66.696D); comp., fig. τὰ εὐ. καὶ μείζονα τῶν δογμάτων Or.*or.*27.6(p.366.17; M.11.509B).

εὐτραπελεύομαι, *indulge in vain and frivolous talk*, Chrys.*hom.17.2 in Eph.*(11.123cf.).

εὐτραπελία, ἡ, *vain and frivolous talk*, Or.*comm.in Eph.*5:3(p.559.20); †Bas.*ep.*42.4(3.129B; M.32.356C); Chrys.*hom.17.2f. in Eph.*(11.123Bf.); τοῦ ἀπέχεσθαι πάντα Χριστιανὸν εὐ. Pamph.H.*can.*8.

***εὐτρέπεια, ἡ**, *preparedness*, †Bas.*bapt.*2.1.2(2.653D; M.31.1581D) perh. error for εὐπρέπεια.

εὐτρεπίζω, 1. *make ready, prepare*; c. infin., ‡Nil.*narr*.7(M.79.684A); med. ηὐτρέπιστο πορεύεσθαι Or.*fr.in Mt*.11:2,3(p.105); Thphn.*chron*.p.60(M.108.201C); *ib*.p.92(276A); **2.** *make, render* ἡ δίψα ἡδὺ τὸ ποτὸν εὐ. Bas.*hom*.1.8(2.6E; M.31.176B); Epiph.*haer*.69.58(p.206.25; M.42.296B).

εὐτρεπισμός, ὁ, *preparation*, Or.*Jo*.13.44(p.270.35; M.14.477C); Bas.*hom.in Ps*.44(1.164E; M.29.401C); Cyr.*ador*.7(1.227C).

***εὐτρεψία, ἡ,** *readiness to change*, Clem.*str*.2.13(p.144.20; M.8.996C).

εὐτριβής, *well-trodden*, hence of roads *smooth, level*, Cyr.*Ps*.27:2(M.69.856B); fig., *easy* οὔτε...εὐ. τὸ τρέχειν εἰς ἀρετήν id.*Is*.5.2(2.783C); *well-worn, familiar* τὴν ἕνωσιν...φωνὴν εὐ. παρ' ἡμῖν id.*Chr.un*.(5^1.733A); id.*Jo*.10.2(4.913A).

εὔτριπτος, *easily rubbed smooth*, Gr.Nyss.*hom.opif*.7.3(M.44.144A).

εὔτριχος, *very hairy*, Clem.*paed*.3.3(p.25.21; M.8.589B).

***εὐτρόπιος,** *morally good*, with pun on name Eutropia, Ath.*apol.Const*.6(M.25.604C).

εὔτροχος, 1. *easily running*; hence, fig., *readily disposed* φύσιν εὐτροχωτάτην...πρὸς ἀλλοίωσιν Cyr.*Thds*.(p.48.30; 5^2.683E); abs., *moving freely*; of standards, Geo.Pis.*Pers*.2.81(M.92.1217); **2.** *easy of passage*, superl. ὁδός Cyr.*Ps*.93:20(M.69.1237D).

εὔτρωτος, *easily wounded*, fig. ἄνοια Epiph.*haer*.39.10(p.80.9; M.41.676D).

εὐτυχής, *successful, fortunate*; official epithet of the emperor, *Edict*.ap.Eus.*h.e*.8.17.4(M.20.792A).

***εὐτυχῆται, οἱ,** prob. f.l. for ἐντυχῖται, Thdt.*haer*.1.1(4.289).

***Εὐτυχιανικός,** *Eutychian, monophysite* αἱρέσεως Thdr.Stud.*epp*.1.33(M.99.1020C).

***Εὐτυχιανισταί, οἱ,** *followers of Eutyches*, *Libell*.ap.CCP(518)*act*.(*ACO* 3 p.74.27; H.2.1337D); Eust.Mon.*ep*.(M.86.909B); Tim.CP *haer*.(M.86.41A); Anast.S.*haer*.(pp.261f.).

***Εὐτυχιανός,** *Eutychian*, Thdt.*haer*.4.13(4.372); Sophr.H.*or*.2.6(M.87.3225A).

***εὐτυχῖται, οἱ,** v. *εὐχῖται.

***εὐύποιστος,** *easily borne*, Petr.II Al.*encycl*.(M.33.1276D)ap.Thdt.*h.e*.4.22.3.

εὐφαής, *very bright*, Nonn.*par.Jo*.20:11(M.43.909B); Paul.Sil.*Soph*.510(M.86.2139A); *ib*.844(2151A); fig., of a person, Cyr.*Soph*.34(3.611A).

εὐφανής, *fair in appearance*; comp., Gr.Nyss.*ep*.3(M.46.1024B); neut. as subst., id.*or.dom*.4(p.80.22; M.44.1169C).

***εὐφαντάσιος,** *imagining good things*, Ath.*ep.Marcell*.29(M.27.41B).

εὐφημ-έω, 1. *praise*, Clem.*str*.5.1(p.328.13; M.9.13B); Or.*mart*.43(p.40.21; M.11.620C); οὐδὲ...τὸν...ἥλιον προσκυνεῖν ἡμῖν θέμις, κἂν ~ῶμεν αὐτόν id.*Cels*.8.67(p.283.16; M.11.1617B); Gr.Thaum.*pan.Or*.(p.6.13; M.10.1057B); Ath.*v.Anton*.79(M.26.933A); **2.** *applaud, acclaim*, Gr.Naz.*or*.21.29(M.35.1117A); Jo.Mal.*chron*.5 p.111(M.97.204B); *Chron.Pasch*.p.302(M.92.760A); as emperor, Thphn.*chron*.p.317(M.108.768C); **3.** *not be blasphemous*, *Hom.Clem*.11.8; Cyr.*Jo*.4.1(4.337A).

***εὐφήμησις, ἡ,** *triumphant shouting, acclamation*, CNic.(787)*act*.8(H.4.485B).

εὐφημία, ἡ, 1. *use of good words*, opp. βλασφημία, Ath.*gent*.5(M.25.12B); *Hom.Clem*.8.9; as deceptive ἐν...τῇ τῶν ῥημάτων εὐ. πᾶσαν κατάραν ἐπάγουσιν αὐτῶν τῇ ζωῇ Bas.*hom.in Ps*.61(1.195E; M.29.476B); ἡ νομιζομένη εὐ. ‡Ath.*Apoll*.1.9(M.26.1108C); hence *silence* σὺν εὐ. δὲ φέρε καὶ τὸν ὑπερήφανον καὶ ὑβριστήν Clem.*fr*.44(p.222.12); **2.** *reverence* μήτε τὴν θεότητα διαιροῦντες τοῦ σώματος ὡς δι' εὐφημίαν Apoll.*ep.Dion*.10(p.260.19)ap.Leont.B.*Apoll*.(M.86.1949B); **3.** *praise*, Gr.Thaum.*pan.Or*.3(p.6.18; M.10.1057B); Meth.*symp*.7.1(p.71.10; M.18.124A); of God, Eus.*v.C*.3.63(p.110.13; M.20.1140A); **4.** *acclamation*, Bas.*hom*.17.1(2.139B; M.31.484B); Chrys.*sac*.5.7(p.136.8; 1.419B); Thdt.*h.e*.4.20.2(3.983); of emperor εὐφημίαις τε καὶ ὕμνοις οἱ πάντες τὸν τρισμακάριον ἐτίμων Eus.*v.C*.1.22(p.18.28; M.20.937C); τὴν συνήθη τοῖς βασιλεῦσιν εὐ. ἐπιβοῆσαι Socr.*h.e*.3.32.4(M.67.293B); **5.** *blessing* τοὺς ἐν εὐφημίας εἴδει γραφέντας...νόμους· 'μακάριοι οἱ πτωχοὶ κτλ.' Thdt.*affect*.11(p.288.24; 4.1001); **6.** *good repute, fame* τῆς ἑορτῆς τὴν εὐ. ‡Epiph.*hom*.1(M.43.432D).

εὐφημίζω, *praise, acclaim*, Anast.S.*hod*.5(M.89.101A); pass., Thphn.*chron*.p.205(M.108.528B).

***εὐφημικῶς,** *with acclamations*, Eulog.*palm*.3(M.86.2920A).

***εὐφημῖται, οἱ,** another name for Messalians, Epiph.*haer*.80.1(p.485.6; M.42.756B); id.*anc*.13(p.22.11; M.43.41A); Jo.D.*haer*.80(M.94.728A).

εὔφημος, 1. *sounding well, auspicious* τὸ 'ὀνομάσαι τὸ ὄνομα κυρίου', τὸ δυσφημεῖν ἐστιν, εὐ. λέξεσι διὰ τῶν ἱερῶν ἐκπεφωνημένον γραμμάτων Cyr.*Am*.62(3.320A); Dion.Ar.*d.n*.4.12(M.3.709C); neut. comp. as subst. θεῷ τὸ εὐ. πρέπει δοῦναι *Hom.Clem*.19.8; deceptively τῆς εὐ. ἐγκρατείας Clem.*str*.3.9(p.225.1; M.8.1165B); τῇ νομιζομένῃ ὑμῶν εὐ. ἐφευρέσει, ἢ τὴν ἐκ τῆς παρθένου τῆς θεοτόκου σάρκα ἀρνεῖσθε, ἢ τὴν θεότητα βλασφημεῖτε ‡Ath.*Apoll*.1.12(M.26.1113B); hence **2.** *correct, reverent* εὔ. καὶ ἀληθὴς οὗτος ὁ λόγος Dion.Al.ap.Eus.*p.e*.7.19(334C; M.21.564C); πίστεως *Hom.Clem*.2.38; γλῶτταν καὶ διάνοιαν Chrys.*sac*.4.1(p.99.24; 1.403B); neut. as subst., Or.*Jo*.6.4(2; p.111.3; M.14.205A); **3.** *of acclamation* βοαῖς τε εὐ. τὸν νέον βασιλέα...ἐκ πρώτης ἀνηγόρευον φωνῆς Eus.*v.C*.1.22(p.18.31; M.20.937C); *ib*.4.29(p.128.26; 1177B); **4.** *with praise* ἀκοήν *ib*.4.1(p.118.2; 1149B); Const.*ib*.2.72(p.71.21; 1048B); neut. plur. as subst., *praises*; of the dead, Epiph.*haer*.80.2(p.486.20; M.42.760B); **5.** *renowned* μνήμης Synes.*ep*.17(M.66.1353A); *ib*.67(1412B); superl. τὰ εὐ. παλαίσματα Agath.*v.Gr.Ill*.136(p.69).

εὐφήμως, 1. *symbolically*, Clem.*prot*.2(p.17.10; M.8.89A); Meth.*symp*.5.2(p.54.6; M.18.97C); **2.** *speciously*, Clem.*str*.3.6(p.216.30; M.8.1148D); Dion.Al.ap.Eus.*h.e*.3.28.5(M.20.276A); **3.** *euphemistically*, Chrys.*hom.40.3 in 1Cor*.(10.382C); Cyr.*Ps*.38:2(M.69.972A); Sophr.H.*mir.Cyr.et Jo*.47(M.87.3600A); **4.** *without blasphemy*, Dion.Ar.*e.h*.7.3.7(M.3.564B).

εὔφορβος, *well-fed*; hence, met., of ploughed land, *fertile*, Eudoc.*Cypr*.2.56(M.85.848B).

εὐφορ-έω, *be productive of*, c. dat., Meth.*symp*.6.3(p.67.2; M.18.117A); met., c. genit. ὧν ~οῦσιν αἱ ἀρεταί Gr.Nyss.*hom.7 in Cant*.(M.44.937C).

εὐφόρητος, 1. *productive*, of Satan εὐ. εἰς ἀσέβειαν Cyr.*ep*.11(p.10.23; 5^2.36D); **2.** *endurable*; comp., Cyr.*glaph.Num*.(1.389B); Thdr.Stud.*epp*.1.2(M.99.913A).

εὐφορία, ἡ, 1. *abundance*, Clem.*ecl*.55(p.152.16; M.9.724B); Or.*hom.16.3 in Jer*.(p.135.30; M.13.444A); *Hom.Clem*.17.17; freq. in liturg. formulae, Serap.*euch*.9.2; τῆς εὐ. τῶν καρπῶν *Lit*.ap.*Const.App*.8.12.48; *ib*.8.15.4; Zeno *henot*.(p.53.8; M.86.2621A); met. ἀγαθῶν εὐ. Eus.*h.e*.8.13.9(M.20.776C); Socr.*h.e*.1.21(M.67.136A); **2.** *fertility*, Eus.*onomast*.(p.42.5).

***εὐφορίζω,** error for ἀφορίζω, Hesych.H.*fr.Ps*.41:1(M.93.1196A).

εὐφόρμιγξ, *playing beautifully upon the lyre*, Nonn.*par.Jo*.15:25(M.43.877A).

εὔφορος, *favourable* ἄνεμος *Apophth.Patr*.(M.65.357C).

εὐφραδῶς, 1. *clearly*, Or.*comm.in Eph*.3:1–3(p.408.6); **2.** *eloquently*, Hier.*vir.ill*.(tr.Sophr.Pal.)5(p.11.15; M.*PL*.23.649A); comp., *ib*.(p.11.16; M.l.c.).

***εὐφραντήριον, τό,** *joy, delight*, Ph.Carp.*Cant*.45(M.40.64B); of persons, Thdot.Anc.*hom.BMV et Sym*.3(M.77.1393B); Thdr.Stud.*epp*.2.158(M.99.1493C).

***εὐφραντικῶς,** *cheerfully, with joy*, Agath.*v.Gr.Ill*.149(p.76); ‡Chrys.*Marth*.(10.756D).

εὐφρασία, ἡ, 1. *joy, delight, gladness*, Arist.*apol*.15(*PLond*.2486.30); Iren.*haer*.1.2.6(M.7.465A); εἰς εὐ. τῶν πνεύματος ἁγίου καταξιουμένων Epiph.*haer*.74.1(p.314.10; M.42.476A); πνευματικῆς εὐ. Cyr.*ador*.17(1.626A); esp. that given by wine, Epiph.*haer*.51.30(p.303.14; M.41.941C); ‡Chrys.*eleem*.3.2(9.834B); Cyr.*Os*.20(3.43A); **2.** *good cheer, festivity*, *A.Paul.et Thecl*.8(p.241.13); *A.Xanthipp*.21(p.73.17); *T.Abr*.B 3(p.107.15); τῶν κληθέντων εἰς τὴν εὐ. [sc. a marriage] Epiph.*haer*.64.70(p.516.11); met. ἡ...ἐκκλησία...ἡ εὐ. ἡ πνέουσα τὴν 'κύπριν' τῆς ἀμπέλου...καὶ τὸ λυσίπονον...πόμα...χαριζομένη id.*exp.fid*.14(p.515.20; M.42.809D).

***εὐφρον-έω, 1.** *be well disposed* ἵν' ~ῇ πρὸς τὴν ἐκ τούτου ἔξοδον Didym.*Trin*.3.1(M.39.780D); **2.** pres. ptcpl. as subst., *one who thinks rightly*, Ath.*Ar*.1.51(M.26.117C); οὐκ ἄν τις εὐ. εἴποι Dion.Ar.*e.h*.3.3.6(M.3.433A).

εὐφροσύνη, ἡ, *joy, gladness* ἄγομεν τὴν ἡμέραν τὴν ὀγδόην εἰς εὐ. *Barn*.15.9; τὴν...τελείαν εὐ., τὴν γνῶσιν τῆς ἀληθείας Clem.*paed*.1.6(p.111.31; M.8.293B); Dion.Al.*ep.can*.1(p.95.5; M.10.1273A); after death, Clem.*str*.7.11(p.48.13; M.9.493A); Or.*fr.18 in Lc*.(p.261); Thdt.*Is*.25:10(p.103.8; 2.294); enjoyed by angels, Dion.Ar.*c.h*.15.9(M.3.340A); ref. Christ Ἰησοῦς Χριστὸς...εὐ. ἐστὶν προσδοκώντων τὴν κατηγγελμένην ὑπ' αὐτοῦ ἀφθαρσίαν Just.*1apol*.42.4(M.6.392C); Χριστὸς...ἐγήγερται, εὐ. αἰώνιος Jo.D.*carm.pasch*.15(p.218; M.96.840C).

***εὐφυᾶ,** f.l. for εὐφυοῦς, Clem.*paed*.2.10(p.212.22n.; M.8.508A).

εὐφυΐα, ἡ, 1. *shapeliness, beauty*, Chrys.*hom.8.2 in 1Tim*.(11.591E); **2.** *cleverness*, id.*hom.in Rom*.proem.(9.425B); **3.** *real* or *actual nature*, theol. τῆς τοῦ τεκόντος εὐ. ἀνάπλεως Cyr.*Jo*.1.7(4.63D); τὴν πατρῴαν ἐφ' ἑαυτῷ φυσικῶς ἀποσῴζων εὐ. *ib*.2.2(161C); εἰ μὴ διασώζοι τὴν αὐτῷ πρέπουσαν εὐ. ὁ υἱός *ib.*4.1(337B); ἡ ἀνθρωπίνη φύσις γέγονε κατὰ χάριν τοῦτο ὅ ἐστι κατὰ φύσιν ἡ θεότης, ἤγουν κύριος...διὰ τῆς ἄκρας τῆς κατὰ μίαν ὑπόστασιν πρὸς αὐτὴν εὐ., χαρισαμένης αὐτῇ τὰ ἴδια φυσικὰ Leont.H.*Nest.*2.37(M.86.1596B).

[*]**εὐφωνής**, = εὔφωνος, *sweet-voiced*; superl., Procl.CP *hom.*2.3 (M.65.840C).

***εὐφώνησις**, ἡ, *good quality of voice*, Thdr.Stud.*poen.*1.105(M.99.1748A).

εὐφώνως, *eloquently*, Just.*1apol.*4.9(M.6.336A); Thphl.Ant.*Autol.*3.15(M.6.1141B).

εὐχαίτης, *shaggy*, *Orac.Sib.*14.138.

εὐχάλινος, *well-bridled*, Jo.D.*imag.*1.2(M.94.1233A).

εὐχαράκτηρος, *having a fair face* Ἑλένη Jo.Mal.*chron.*5 p.91(M.97.176B).

εὐχαρής, *charming, gracious*, *A.Thom.*A 110(p.220.21).

εὔχαρις, fem. as subst., *grace, charm* ἐπὶ τῇ τῆς γλώττης εὐ. θεοῦ Thdr.Stud.*epp.*1.38(M.99.1041B).

***εὐχαριστέον**, *one must be thankful* εὐ. τῷ θεῷ, ὅτι...μείζων [sc. χάρις] ἐξεχύθη Or.*comm.in Mt.*10.22(p.30.13; M.13.896A); εὐ. τῷ... βασιλεῖ Thdr.Stud.*epp.*2.77(M.99.1316D).

εὐχαριστ-έω, **1.** *thank, express gratitude to*; **a.** in gen. ~εῖ Μάρκῳ τῷ ἐπιδιδόντι τῆς ἰδίας χάριτος αὐτῇ Iren.*haer.*1.13.3(M.7.584B); Καῖσαρ...οὔτε ~ούμενος ὠφελεῖται, ἀλλὰ τοῦ ~οῦντος μὲν γίνεται τὸ ἀκίνδυνον *Hom.Clem.*11.9; ταῖς...τὴν μητέρα παραμυθησαμέναις ~ήσας *ib.*12.24; ‡Ath.*diab.*6(p.7.29); Gr.Naz.*test.*(M.37.392C); ὁ...ἀπελέγχων...~ήσεται...πλέον τοῦ κολακεύοντος ‡Proc.G.*Pr.*28:23(M.87.1509C); Dor.*doct.*9.1(M.88.1716D); Εἰρήνη...μεγάλως ἐπὶ τούτοις... ~ηθεῖσα εὐεργετήμασιν Thphn.*chron.*p.401(M.108.956D); **b.** esp. to God ὁ δὲ πτωχὸς ~είτω τῷ θεῷ, ὅτι ἔδωκεν αὐτῷ *1Clem.*38.2; γράφω ὑμῖν, ~ῶν τῷ κυρίῳ Ign.*Eph.*21.1; ~ῶ δὲ τῷ θεῷ μου, ὅτι εὐσυνείδητός εἰμι ἐν ὑμῖν id.*Philad.*6.3; ~οῦσιν τῷ κυρίῳ ὑπὲρ ὑμῶν id.*Smyrn.*10.1; κατὰ πάντα ~οῦντες ὀφείλομεν αἰνεῖν *Barn.*7.1; γενώμεθα ἐκ τῶν ~ούντων, τῶν δεδουλευκότων τῷ θεῷ *2Clem.*18.1; ~ῶν τῷ κυρίῳ περὶ πάντων Herm.*sim.*5.1.1; ~ει τῷ κυρίῳ ὅτι ἄξιόν σε ἡγήσατο τοῦ προδηλῶσαί σοι τὴν θλῖψιν *ib.*7.5; ἐπὶ τούτοις πᾶσιν ηὐχαρίστησα τῷ κυρίῳ, ὅτι ἐσπλαγχνίσθη *ib.*9.14.3; ~οῦντες αὐτῷ κατὰ πᾶσαν ὥραν ἐν παντὶ βρώματι καὶ ποτῷ καὶ τοῖς λοιποῖς ἀγαθοῖς Arist.*apol.*15.10; τὸ ὄφλημα ἀποδιδόντες ~οῦμεν Just.*2apol.*11.1(M.6.461B); Iren.*haer.*1.2.6(M.7.464A); οὕτω βιοῦντες [i.e. as ascetics] ηὐχαρίστουν τῷ κτίσαντι οἱ...προφῆται Clem.*str.*3.6(p.221.4; M.8.1157B); of martyrs ~οῦσι τὸ 'ἐδοκίμασας ἡμᾶς' λέγοντες Meth.*res.*1.56 (p.315.10; M.41.1149A); Ἀττάλῳ...ἀπεκαλύφθη ὅτι μὴ καλῶς ποιοίη ὁ Ἀλκιβιάδης μὴ χρώμενος τοῖς κτίσμασι τοῦ θεοῦ...πεισθεὶς δὲ... πάντων ἀνέδην μετελάμβανεν καὶ ηὐχαρίστει τῷ θεῷ Eus.*h.e.*5.3.3(M.20.437A); οὔτε ὡς κτίστῃ ηὐχαριστήσατε, οὔτε ὡς πατρὶ ἑαυτοὺς ὡμοιώσατε †Bas.*Is.*13(1.387A; M.30.140B); ~ῶν ὑπὲρ τοῦ πλάσματος *Const.App.*7.39.4; ~ήσωμεν...μὴ διὰ πίστεως μόνον, ἀλλὰ καὶ διὰ τῶν ἔργων αὐτῶν Chrys.*hom.46.4 in Jo.*(8.274D); *ib.48.5*(343D); ἐὰν ~ῶμεν, οὐκ ἀθυμήσομεν *ib.62.5*(375C); δεῖ γὰρ ~εῖν τῷ θεῷ καὶ ὑπὲρ τῶν εἰς ἄλλους γενομένων ἀγαθῶν id.*hom.6.1 in 1Tim.*(11.579E); ἐπὶ παντὶ θλιβερῷ ἐπερχομένῳ ἡμῖν...ἀναγκαῖον τὸ ~εῖν τῷ θεῷ Nil.*epp.*3.118(M.79.437B); Cyr.*Os.*17(3.39A); τῷ ὕπνῳ...~ήσαντες Bas.Sel. *v.Thecl.*2.19(M.85.600D); δοξάζοντες καὶ ~οῦντες Χριστόν *Mir.Geo.*4 (p.38.3); **c.** in thanksgiving for food, *say grace* εὐλογήσας δὲ ἐπὶ τῆς τροφῆς καὶ ~ήσας *Hom.Clem.*1.22; τοὺς τροφῆς ἀρχομένους ~εῖν δεῖ τῷ θεῷ Chrys.*hom.42.2 in Jo.*(8.251B); id.*hom.82.2 in Mt.*(7.784B); τὸ ποτήριον, ὃ ἐκέλευσεν αὐτοὺς εἰς ἀλλήλους διαμερίσαι, τοῦ δείπνου ἦν, οὐ τῶν κοινωνικῶν μυστηρίων...εἰ δὲ καὶ ἐπὶ τῷ ποτηρίῳ τοῦ δείπνου ηὐχαρίστησεν, οὐ θαυμαστόν· καὶ ἡμεῖς γὰρ ~οῦμεν, καὶ ἐπὶ τῆς κοινῆς ἑστιάσεως, καὶ ἐπὶ τῆς μυστικῆς· διάφορος δὲ ὅμως ἡ εὐχαριστία καὶ ἡ εὐλογία. τὸ δὲ καὶ ἐπὶ βρώσει ~εῖν, ἐκ τοῦ εὐαγγελίου ἡμῖν παραδέδοται Eutych.*pasch.*7(M.86.2400B); **d.** esp. of saying thanksgiving over eucharistic oblations, *say eucharistic prayer (over)*, hence *celebrate eucharist* or *consecrate* elements, *Did.*9.1–3 cit. s. ποτήριον; perh. of thanksgiving at *agape*, *ib.*10.1,2,4; τοῖς δὲ προφήταις ἐπιτρέπετε ~εῖν, ὅσα θέλουσιν *ib.*10.7; ~ήσαντος δὲ τοῦ προεστῶτος καὶ ἐπευφημήσαντος παντὸς τοῦ λαοῦ οἱ...διάκονοι διδόασιν ἑκάστῳ...μεταλαβεῖν ἀπὸ τοῦ ~ηθέντος ἄρτου καὶ οἴνου καὶ ὕδατος [i.e. consecrated by having had thanksgiving said over them] Just.*1apol.*65.5(M.6.428B); *ib.*66.2(428C) cit. s. εὐχή; μετάληψις ἀπὸ τῶν ~ηθέντων ἑκάστῳ γίνεται *ib.*67.5(429C); ποτήρια οἴνῳ κεκραμένα προσποιούμενος ~εῖν Iren.*haer.*1.13.2(M.7.580A); εἰσὶ γὰρ οἳ καὶ ὕδωρ ψιλὸν ~οῦσιν Clem.*str.*1.19(p.62.1; M.8.813A); λαμβάνων ποτήριον ὡς ~ῶν καὶ ἐπὶ πλεῖον ἐκτείνων τὸν λόγον τῆς ἐπικλήσεως Hipp.*haer.*6.39(p.171.1; M.16.3258A); ἐβάπτισεν αὐτὴν...καὶ ~ήσας καὶ ἁγιάσας μετέδωκεν αὐτοῖς τῶν...μυστηρίων *A.Thom.*B 28(p.34.17); *Const.App.*7.25.1; *Lit.*ap.*Const.App.*8.12.5; οὐδὲ γὰρ ἐκεῖνος [sc. celebrant] ~εῖ μόνος, ἀλλὰ καὶ ὁ λαὸς ἅπας Chrys.*hom.18.3 in 2Cor.*(10.568D); Dion.Ar.*e.h.*3.3.15(M.3.445B); διδάσκει...~εῖν οἷς ἐδωρήσατο διὰ τοῦ ἰδίου πάθους, δι' οὗ καὶ τὰ σύμβολα γίνεται, σώματος ἐχόντων μνήμην καὶ αἵματος Petr.Laod.*fr.in Mt.*26:26(M.86.3325A); **e.** similarly in prayer for blessing of chrism, *Const.App.*7.27.1,2; **f.** of whole action of eucharist as expressing thanksgiving, Chrys. *hom.25.3 in Mt.*(7.310D) cit. s. εὐχαριστία; **g.** of post-Communion prayer of thanksgiving, Serap.*euch.*16.1,2; *Const.App.*7.26.1,2; *Lit.*ap.*Const.App.*8.15.1; **2.** *offer as thank-offering*, of martyr φθάσαντος ἤδη...τὸ τέλειον ἔργον ἐνδείξασθαι καὶ παραστῆσαι κυρίως δι' ἀγάπης γνωστικῆς εὐχαριστηθέντος αἵματος παραπεμπομένου τὸ πνεῦμα Clem.*str.*4.21(p.306.4; M.8.1341A); **3.** s.v.l., *consider with gratitude* καὶ διὰ τί ὁ λόγος...σὰρξ ἐγένετο, καὶ ἔπαθεν, ~εῖν Iren. *haer.*1.10.3(M.7.556B; conj. Harvey παριστᾶν); **4.** *pray* ~ῶ ἐγὼ... καὶ κλίνω τὴν κεφαλήν [μο]υ *Pap.Chr.*(p.420); c. dat., *pray* for, Dor. *doct.*5.3(M.88.1680B).

εὐχαριστήριος, **A.** adj.; **1.** *expressing thanksgiving, grateful*; **a.** in gen. εὐ. φωνάς *A.Xanthipp.*14(p.67.34); ὕμνον εὐ. ἀναπέμπουσιν ἱλαρῶς αἱ ψυχαὶ τῷ θεῷ Meth.*symp.*4.2(p.47.15; M.18.89A); εὐ. ... εὐχὴν τῷ τῆς νίκης αἰτίῳ Eus.*v.C.*1.39(p.26.14; M.20.953C); CHier. (350)*ep.*(p.137.9; M.25.352C); Ath.*exp.Ps.*7 proem.(M.27.77D); δῶρον εὐ. φέρουσα τῷ ἀνδρί ‡Pall.*h.mon.*28.15(p.89.22); ‡Nil.*narr.*5 (M.79.649A); Ξίσουθρον...μετὰ τὸν κατακλυσμὸν θύσαντα θυσίας εὐ. τοῖς θεοῖς Cosm.Ind.*top.*12(M.88.452D); **b.** of grace after food μετὰ τὸ δεῖπνον...λέγοντές τινας εὐ. ὕμνους εἰς τὸν θεόν Chrys.*hom.55.5 in Mt.*(7.560E); id.*bapt.*4(2.374E); **2.** *graceful* οὐκ ἀνυπαίτιος...ἐὰν τὰ καλὰ μὴ κοσμῇ λόγοις εὐ. Meth.*symp.*4.1(p.46.4; M.18.88A).

B. neut. as subst., *thank-offering, expression of gratitude*; **1.** in gen. εὐχαριστηρίων καιρόν Eus.*v.C.*4.40(p.133.12, v.l. εὐχαριστήριον M.20.1189A); τὴν μὲν ἑορτὴν...εὐ. ἐκτελέσαντες *Mir.Geo.*4(p.39.4); oral, Cyr.*Jon.*15(3.378D); εὐχαριστήρια λέγουσα ‡Epiph.*hom.*1(M.43.433A); ἀποδίδωμί σοι εὐθύμως τὰ εὐ. ‡Meth.*Sym.et Ann.*8(M.18.365B); **2.** of sacrificial offerings ἀπαρχὰς...θυσίας, εὐ. Cyr.*Am.*36(3.290C); **3.** of people's offering at eucharist ἱερεῖς...περὶ μὲν τῶν προσφερόντων οὕτως λέγοντες, τὸ εὐ. τῶν δούλων σου πρόσδεξαι εἰς τὸ οὐράνιον...θυσιαστήριον Cosm.Ind.*top.*7(M.88.385C); cf. τῶν προσφερόντων τὰς θυσίας, τὰς προσφοράς, τὰ εὐ. πρόσδεξαι ὁ θεὸς εἰς τὸ ...νοερόν σου θυσιαστήριον *Lit.Marc.*(p.129.20).

***εὐχαριστηρίως**, *in thanksgiving*, Socr.*h.e.*7.23.12(M.67.792A).

εὐχαριστία (-εία), ἡ, **A.** *thanksgiving*; **1.** *gratitude*, in gen. τὸ μὴ ἐξουδενῶσαί τινα τὴν χάριν τοῦ πλησίον...δεῖ γὰρ καταδέχεσθαι αὐτὴν μετὰ εὐχαριστείας Dor.*doct.*19(M.88.1809B); **2.** *approval* τὴν ἐμὴν εὐ. σιωπῆσαι Leo Mag.*ep.*115.1 [*gratulationem*] (p.63.11; M.*PL.*54.1034B); **3.** *expression of gratitude, thanksgiving, praise*, in worship; **a.** pagan ὅπως...εὐχὰς καὶ εὐ. καὶ νεκρῶν νεκροτέροις προσενέγκητε *Hom.Clem.*11.14; **b.** Christian; **i.** in gen. μὴ...θυσίας ἀφ' αἱμάτων... ἐπὶ τὸ θυσιαστήριον ἀναφέρεσθαι, ἀλλὰ ἀληθινοὺς καὶ πνευματικοὺς αἴνους καὶ εὐ. Just.*dial.*118.2(M.6.749C); ἡ εὐ. δὲ οὐκ ἐπὶ ψυχῆς μόνον καὶ τῶν πνευματικῶν ἀγαθῶν, ἀλλὰ καὶ ἐπὶ τοῦ σώματος γίνεται καὶ τῶν τοῦ σώματος ἀγαθῶν Clem.*str.*5.10(p.367.30; M.9.96A); ὁ συμπαρὼν ἀεὶ διὰ τῆς γνώσεως καὶ τοῦ βίου καὶ τῆς εὐ. ἀδιαλείπτως τῷ θεῷ *ib.*7.7 (p.27.21; 452A); ἥ τε εὐ. ... ἔργον ἐστὶ τοῦ γνωστικοῦ *ib.*(p.31.19; 457B); τὸ δὲ εἶδος αὐτὸ τῆς εὐχῆς εὐ. ἐπί τε τοῖς προγεγονόσιν ἐπί τε τοῖς ἐνεστῶσιν ἐπί τε τοῖς μέλλουσιν, ὡς ἤδη διὰ τὴν πίστιν παροῦσιν *ib.*7.12(p.56.17; 509A); Or.*Jo.*28.6(5; p.395.27; M.14.689C); †Bas.*Is.*23(1.396D; M.30.161B); ἡ εὐ. ἐκείνῳ μὲν [sc. God] οὐδὲν προστίθησιν, ἡμᾶς δὲ οἰκειοτέρους αὐτῷ κατασκευάζει Chrys.*hom.25.3 in Mt.*(7.310D); τὴν ἐφ' οἷς εὖ πεπόνθαμεν εὐ. ἀναπέμπειν θεῷ Cyr.*hom.pasch.*2 (5^2.17D); οἱ πόδες ἐν ἐκκλησίᾳ ἱστάμενοι εὐ. ἀναφέρουσι Bas.Sel.*or.*10.1 (M.85.141A); μὴ οὖν ὁμοιωθῶμεν τοῖς ἀχαρίστοις, ἀλλ' ὡς μαθηταὶ τῆς χάριτος ὑπόδειγμα αὐτῆς διὰ τῆς εὐ. γενώμεθα, ἵνα καὶ αὐτοὶ δυνηθῶσιν, ὁρῶντες τὸ φῶς τῆς εὐ. ἡμῶν, ἀποστῆναι τοῦ κατέχοντος αὐτοὺς σκότους τῆς ἀχαριστίας Ant.Mon.*hom.*117(M.89.1797C); τὴν πρὸς θεολογικὴν εὐ. ἐπιτήδειον ἕξιν Max.*myst.*24(M.91.709A); δῶρον φέροντες ὕμνον εὐχαριστίας Jo.D.*carm.theoph.*120(p.213; M.96.832A); **ii.** at bed-time prayers, Clem.*str.*2.23(p.192.27; M.8.1096A); at 9th hour, *V.Aberc.*17(p.15.3); on rising, Thdr.Heracl.*Is.*26:9(M.18.1312C); in evening συμπληρωθείσης δὲ τῆς ἡμέρας, ἡ εὐ. περὶ τῶν ἐν αὐτῇ δεδομένων ἡμῖν Bas.*reg.fus.*37.4(2.384A; M.31.1016A); after food, id.*ep.*2.6(3.75A; M.32.233A); at lighting of lamp, Gr.Nyss. *v.Macr.*(p.395.4; M.46.981C); τὴν ἑσπερινὴν εὐ. *Const.App.*8.37.2; in morning prayers μέγα εἰς ἁγνείαν καύχημα τὸ ἐκ πρωΐας τῆς αὐτῆς παρίστασθαι τῷ θεῷ, καὶ φθάνειν ἐν εὐ. τὸν ἥλιον Cyr.*Ps.*5:4(M.69.741B); **iii.** in time of sorrow τὸ μὲν γενόμενον κατ' οἰκονομίαν θεοῦ, εὐ., οὐ δακρύων ὑπόθεσίς ἐστι τοῖς γε νοῦν ἔχουσι Gr.Naz.*ep.*238(M.

37.380C); τοῦ γὰρ...ποιεῖν ἐλεημοσύνην, τὸ πάντα ἀφαρπαγέντα γενναίως ἐνεγκεῖν καὶ μετ' εὐχαριστίας πολλῷ μεῖζόν ἐστιν Chrys.*stat.* 1.10(2.16A) ∾ Nil.*epp.*3.13(M.79.376C); ἥρπασεν ὁ δεῖνα· ηὐχαρίστησας ὑπὲρ τῆς ἀδικίας σύ...; μυρίους διὰ τῆς εὐ. ἐκείνης ἐκαρπώσω μισθοὺς Chrys.*hom.71.3 in Jo.*(8.420A); **iv.** plur., *thanksgivings* καὶ εὐχαὶ καὶ εὐ., ὑπὸ τῶν ἀξίων γινόμεναι, τέλειαι μόναι καὶ εὐαρεστοί εἰσι τῷ θεῷ Just.*dial.*117.2(M.6.745B); CAlex.*ep.*ap.Ath.*apol.sec.*7(p.93.31; M.25.261B); αἱ τότε θυσίαι νῦν εὐχαὶ καὶ δεήσεις καὶ εὐ. *Const.App.*2.26.2; Chrys.*hom.25.4 in Mt.*(7.312B).

B. esp. *eucharist* (v. εὐλογία); **1.** of eucharistic prayer as blessing or thanksgiving, *Did.*9.1; ἄθεοι...ὡς οὔκ ἐσμεν, τὸν δημιουργὸν ...ἀνενδεῆ αἱμάτων...λέγοντες, λόγῳ εὐχῆς καὶ εὐ. ἐφ' οἷς προσφερόμεθα πᾶσιν, ὅση δύναμις, αἰνοῦντες, μόνην ἀξίαν αὐτοῦ τιμὴν ταύτην παραλαβόντες, τὸ τὰ ὑπ' ἐκείνου...γενόμενα...ἑαυτοῖς καὶ τοῖς δεομένοις προσφέρειν Just.*1apol.*13.1(M.6.345B); προσφέρεται τῷ προεστῶτι... ἄρτος καὶ ποτήριον...καὶ οὗτος...εὐ. ὑπὲρ τοῦ κατηξιῶσθαι τούτων παρ' αὐτοῦ ἐπὶ πολὺ ποιεῖται· οὗ συντελέσαντος τὰς εὐχὰς καὶ τὴν εὐ. πᾶς ὁ παρὼν λαὸς ἐπευφημεῖ λέγων· ἀμήν *ib.*65.3(428B); ὁ προεστὼς εὐχὰς ὁμοίως καὶ εὐ., ὅση δύναμις αὐτῷ, ἀναπέμπει,...καὶ ἡ διάδοσις ...ἀπὸ τῶν εὐχαριστηθέντων ἑκάστῳ γίνεται *ib.*67.5(429C); *A.Jo.*109 (p.207.8) cit. s. προσφορά; cf. ἡμᾶς ἐπὶ τῆς εὐ. λέγοντας, εἰς τοὺς αἰῶνας τῶν αἰώνων Iren.*haer.*1.3.1(M.7.468B); cf.Or.*Cels.*8.33(p.249.6; M.11.1565C); Chrys.*hom.18.3 in 2Cor.*(10.568D); **2.** of eucharistic action as a whole; **a.** explanation why so called τὰ φρικώδη μυστήρια...εὐ. καλεῖται, ὅτι πολλῶν ἐστιν εὐεργετημάτων ἀνάμνησις, καὶ τὸ κεφάλαιον τῆς τοῦ θεοῦ προνοίας ἐνδείκνυται, καὶ ὅτι διὰ πάντων παρασκευάζει εὐχαριστεῖν Chrys.*hom.25.3 in Mt.*(7.310D); cf. *panis et calicis sacramentum Graeci eucharistiam dicunt, quod Latine 'bona gratia' interpretatur*, Isid.H.*etym.*6.19.38; **b.** in gen. of service of eucharist, considered especially as *thank-offering* συνέρχεσθαι εἰς εὐ. θεοῦ καὶ εἰς δόξαν Ign.*Eph.*13.1; εὐ. καὶ προσευχῆς ἀπέχονται id.*Smyrn.*7.1; ἐκείνη βεβαία εὐ. ἡγείσθω, ἡ ὑπὸ τὸν ἐπίσκοπον οὖσα ἢ ᾧ ἂν αὐτὸς ἐπιτρέψῃ *ib.*8.1; σπουδάσατε οὖν μιᾷ εὐ. χρῆσθαι· μία γὰρ σὰρξ τοῦ κυρίου...καὶ ἓν ποτήριον εἰς ἕνωσιν τοῦ αἵματος αὐτοῦ id.*Philad.*4.1; τοῦ ἄρτου τῆς εὐ., ὃν εἰς ἀνάμνησιν τοῦ πάθους...ὁ κύριος...παρέδωκε ποιεῖν Just.*dial.*41.1(M.6.564B); θυσίας, ἃς παρέδωκεν...ὁ Χριστὸς γίνεσθαι, τοῦτ' ἔστιν ἐπὶ τῇ εὐ. τοῦ ἄρτου καὶ τοῦ ποτηρίου *ib.*117.1 (745B); Iren.*haer.*4.18.5(M.7.1028A); Clem.*str.*4.25(p.320.1; M.8.1369B); ὁ δὲ ἄρτος ὃν ἐγὼ δώσω...ἡ σάρξ μού ἐστιν, ἤτοι ᾧ τρέφεται ἡ σὰρξ διὰ τῆς εὐ. ⟨ἢ⟩, ὅπερ καὶ μᾶλλον, ἡ σὰρξ τὸ σῶμα αὐτοῦ ἐστιν, ὅπερ ἐστὶν ἡ ἐκκλησία id.*exc.Thdot.*13(p.111.10; M.9.664B); νοείσθω δὲ ὁ ἄρτος καὶ τὸ ποτήριον τοῖς μὲν ἁπλουστέροις κατὰ τὴν κοινοτέραν περὶ τῆς εὐ. ἐκδοχήν, τοῖς δὲ βαθύτερον ἀκούειν μεμαθηκόσιν κατὰ τὴν θειοτέραν καὶ περὶ τοῦ τροφίμου τῆς ἀληθείας λόγου ἐπαγγελίαν Or.*Jo.*32.24(16; p.468.14; M.14.809B); οὐκοῦν καὶ θύομεν καὶ θυμιῶμεν· τότε μὲν τὴν μνήμην τοῦ μεγάλου θύματος κατὰ τὰ πρὸς αὐτοῦ παραδοθέντα μυστήρια ἐπιτελοῦντες, καὶ τὴν ὑπὲρ σωτηρίας ἡμῶν εὐ. δι' εὐσεβῶν ὕμνων τε καὶ εὐχῶν τῷ θεῷ προσκομίζοντες, τοτὲ δὲ σφᾶς αὐτοὺς ὅλως καθιεροῦντες αὐτῷ Eus.*d.e.*1.10(p.49.9; M.22.92D); ἐπὶ τῇ ἀναδείξει τοῦ ἄρτου τῆς εὐ. καὶ τοῦ ποτηρίου τῆς εὐλογίας Bas.*Spir.*66(3.54E; M.32.188B); ἡ μυστικὴ...τῆς προσφορᾶς...εὐ. Mac.Aeg.*carit.*29(M.34.932C); **c.** with partic. emphasis on sacrificial aspect, ref. Mal.1:10–12, v. θυσία; **3.** partic. of eucharistic elements μηδεὶς δὲ φαγέτω μηδὲ πιέτω ἀπὸ τῆς εὐ. ὑμῶν, ἀλλ' οἱ βαπτισθέντες *Did.*9.5; τὴν εὐ. σάρκα εἶναι τοῦ σωτῆρος Ign.*Smyrn.*7.1; καὶ ἡ τροφὴ αὕτη [sc. consecrated elements] καλεῖται παρ' ἡμῖν εὐ. Just.*1apol.*66.1(M.6.428B); ὡς γὰρ...ἄρτος...οὐκέτι κοινὸς ἄρτος ἐστίν, ἀλλ' εὐ., ἐκ δύο πραγμάτων συνεστηκυῖα, ἐπιγείου τε καὶ οὐρανίου, οὕτω καὶ τὰ σώματα ἡμῶν μεταλαμβάνοντα τῆς εὐ., μηκέτι εἶναι φθαρτὰ Iren.*haer.*4.18.5(M.7.1028B); ὁπότε οὖν...ὁ γεγονὼς ἄρτος ἐπιδέχεται τὸν λόγον τοῦ θεοῦ, καὶ γίνεται ἡ εὐ. σῶμα Χριστοῦ *ib.*5.2.3(1125B); ref. custom of bishops of Rome of sending portion of their eucharist to congregations in city οἱ πρὸ σοῦ πρεσβύτεροι τοῖς ἀπὸ τῶν παροικιῶν τηροῦσιν [sc. Quartodeciman observance] ἔπεμπον εὐ. id.*ep.Vict.*ap.Eus.*h.e.*5.24.15(M.20.505A); cf.CLaod.*can.*14; κοινωνήσας τοῖς ἀδελφοῖς πᾶσι τῆς τοῦ κυρίου εὐ. *A.Jo.*86(p.193.14); κλάσας τὸν ἄρτον ἐπέδωκεν πᾶσιν...ἑκάστῳ...ἐπευχόμενος ἄξιον ἔσεσθαι αὐτὸν τῆς... χάριτος καὶ τῆς ἁγιωτάτης εὐ. *ib.*110(p.208.13); Clem.*paed.*2.2(p.168.6; M.8.412A); τὴν εὐ. τινὲς διανείμαντες...αὐτὸν δὴ ἕκαστον τοῦ λαοῦ λαβεῖν τὴν μοῖραν ἐπιτρέπουσιν id.*str.*1.1(p.5.18; M.8.692B); ὁ ἀναξίως μεταλαμβάνων εὐ. εἰς κρίμα λήψεται Or.*fr.50 in Jer.*36:21 (p.223.21); in reconciliation of lapsed on death-bed βραχὺ τῆς εὐ. ἔδωκεν [sc. ὁ πρεσβύτερος] τῷ παιδαρίῳ, ἀποβρέξαι κελεύσας καὶ τῷ πρεσβύτῃ κατὰ τοῦ στόματος ἐπιστάξαι Dion.Al.ap.Eus.*h.e.*6.44.4 (M.20.632A); κλάσας τὴν εὐ. ἔδωκεν *A.Thom.*A 158(p.269.2); *Hom.Clem.*11.36; ἐποίησεν αὐτὸν τῆς εὐ. μεταλαβεῖν τοῦ Χριστοῦ *A.Xanthipp.*21(p.73.14); CNic.(325)*can.*13; *ib.*18; Serap.*euch.*13; Cyr.H.*catech.*19.7; τῆς ἁγίας καὶ ἱερᾶς εὐ. μετόχους ποιήσαντας *Const.App.*2.33.2; Chrys.*hom.27.4 in 1Cor.*(10.246C); ἤρεσεν, ἵνα τοῖς σώμασι τῶν τελευτώντων εὐ. μὴ δοθῇ *Cod.Afr.*18; εὐ. dist. from εὐλογία, Eutych.*pasch.*7(M.86.2400B) cit. s. εὐχαριστέω; **4.** of thanksgiving after Communion, Dion.Ar.*e.h.*3.2(M.3.428A); *ib.*3.3.15 (445B); *Lit.Jac.*(p.246.12).

εὐχαριστικός, *of thanksgiving* εὐ. ... φωνήν Bas.*hom.in Ps.*29(1.129B; M.29.317B).

εὐχαριστικῶς, *in thanksgiving,* Germ.CP *or.*6(M.98.345B).

εὐχάριστος, 1. *agreeable, pleasant* ταῦτά σου ταῖς εὐ. τρυφαῖς δεδημιούργηκεν ὁ πατήρ Clem.*prot.*10(p.69.8; M.8.208A); **2.** *congratulatory* εὐ. φωναῖς ‡Nil.*perist.*7.1(M.79.860C); **3.** *thankful, grateful,* esp. to God ἐκείνῳ δὲ εὐ. ὄντας διὰ λόγου πομπὰς καὶ ὕμνους πέμπειν Just.*1apol.*13.2(M.6.345B); Clem.*str.*7.7(p.32.18; M.9.460B); Chrys.*hom.25.2 in Mt.*(7.309A); 'καὶ εὐ. γίνεσθε.' τοῦτο γάρ ἐστιν εὐ. εἶναι...τὸ ὁμοίως κεχρῆσθαι τοῖς ὁμοδούλοις, ὥσπερ αὐτῷ ὁ θεός,...τὸ ὑπὲρ πάντων χάριν ὁμολογεῖν id.*hom.8.3 in Phil.*(11.384A); *Const.App.*7.25.1; ἐν ταῖς θλίψεσι εὐ. ἔσο μάλιστα Nil.*Eulog.*8(M.79.1104B); ‡Nil.*perist.*11.7(M.79.900A); **4.** *expressing gratitude* ἀποδῶμεν καὶ μὴ δεομένῳ μισθὸν εὐ., εὐπείθειαν Clem.*prot.*11(p.81.7; M.8.233A); id.*str.*3.9(p.226.11; M.8.1168B); τὸν...εὐεργετήσαντα εὐ. ἀμείψασθαι φωνῇ *Hom.Clem.*11.8; εὐ. ὕμνον ἀναφέροντα τῷ θεῷ Oecum.*Apoc.*10:3 (p.122).

εὐχαρίστως, 1. *with good grace,* Clem.*str.*4.4(p.254.17; M.8.1228A); Or.*Jo.*13.25(p.249.17; M.14.441B); Chrys.*hom.9.4 in Rom.*(9.518B); **2.** *gratefully,* Clem.*str.*4.4(p.255.27; M.8.1229A); φιλοσόφους παρὰ... τῶν προφητῶν τὰ κυριότατα τῶν δογμάτων οὐκ εὐ. εἰληφότας *ib.*5.1 (p.332.16; M.9.24A); esp. towards God οἱ...δίκαιοι εὐ. τῆς κτίσεως μετελάμβανον *ib.*3.6(p.220.3; M.8.1156A); πάντ' εὐ. δεῖ δέχεσθαι τὰκ θεοῦ Gr.Naz.*carm.*1.2.30.16(M.37.910A); Isid.Pel.*epp.*1.375(M.78.396A); ref. post-Communion thanksgiving τὰς ὑπερουρανίας εὐ. ὑμνήσουσι τῆς θεαρχίας ἀγαθουργίας Dion.Ar.*e.h.*3.3.15(M.3.445C).

εὐχείρωτος, *easily available,* Nil.ap.Proc.G.*Cant.*2:15(M.87.1612B); met. ὡς μήτε τὰ θεῖα τοῖς βεβήλοις εὐ. εἶναι Dion.Ar.*c.h.*2.5 (M.3.145A); id.*ep.*9.1(M.3.1105C).

***εὐχέλαιον, τό,** *sacrament of unction, Euchol.*(pp.335,338,346).

εὐχερής, 1. *ready* εὐ. ἐν καταλαλιᾷ *Barn.*20.2; τὸ εὐ. πρὸς εἰδωλολατρείαν Just.*dial.*67.8(M.6.632A); οἷς εὐ. τὸ ῥιγοῦν *who are inclined to, suffer easily from,* cold, Clem.*paed.*2.2(p.174.9; M.8.424B); c. εἰς, Ath.*decr.*32(p.27.2; M.25.472D); **2.** *easy, obvious,* Or.*hom.16.10 in Jer.*(p.141.21; M.13.452A); Ath.*apol.Const.*21(M.25.621C); Jo.D.*carm.theog.*54(p.206; M.96.821B); of wounds, *slight,* Or.*princ.*3.1.17 (p.226.9; M.11.284B); of disposition, *light-minded,* Ath.*apol.Const.*3 (600A).

εὐχέτης, ὁ, *one who prays*; met., *client,* ‡Jo.D.*Const.*23(M.95.341B).

εὐχή, ἡ, I. *prayer* (treated together with προσευχή, ἡ);

A. εὐ., which can also mean *vow,* contrasted with π.: οὐκ ἄλογον δή μοι ἐφάνη τὸ κατὰ τὰς γραφὰς σημαινόμενον πρῶτον διαστείλασθαι τῆς εὐ. δύο σημαινούσης, ὁμοίως δὲ καὶ τῆς π.· καὶ γὰρ τοῦτο τὸ ὄνομα πρὸς τῷ κοινῷ καὶ συνήθει πολλαχοῦ κειμένῳ τέτακται καὶ ἐπὶ τῆς κατὰ τὸ σύνηθες ἡμῖν σημαινόμενον [τῆς] εὐ. ἐν τοῖς περὶ τῆς Ἄννης λεγομένοις...(cf. 1Reg.1:9–11), Or.*or.*4.1(p.307.5–8; M.11.428B); δύναται μέντοι γέ τις οὐκ ἀπιθάνως ἐνταῦθα, ἐπιστήσας τῷ 'προσηύξατο πρὸς κύριον' 'καὶ ηὔξατο εὐ.' εἰπεῖν ὅτι, εἰ τὰ δύο πεποίηκε, τουτέστι 'προσηύξατο πρὸς κύριον' 'καὶ ηὔξατο εὐ.', μή ποτε τὸ μὲν 'προσηύξατο' ἐπὶ τῆς συνήθως ἡμῖν ὀνομαζομένης τέτακται εὐ. τὸ δὲ 'ηὔξατο εὐ.' ἐπὶ τοῦ ἐν Λευιτικῷ καὶ Ἀριθμοῖς τεταγμένου σημαινομένου *ib.*4.2(p.307.18–21; 428C); ἡγοῦμαι τοίνυν δέησιν μὲν εἶναι τὴν ἐλλείποντός τινι μεθ' ἱκεσίας περὶ τοῦ ἐκείνου τυχεῖν ἀναπεμπομένην εὐ., τὴν δὲ π. τὴν μετὰ δοξολογίας περὶ μειζόνων μεγαλοφυέστερον ἀναπεμπομένην ὑπό του, ἔντευξιν δὲ τὴν ὑπὸ παρρησίαν τινὰ πλείονα ἔχοντος περί τινων ἀξίωσιν πρὸς θεόν, εὐχαριστίαν δὲ τὴν ἐπὶ τῷ τετευχέναι ἀγαθῶν ἀπὸ θεοῦ μετ' εὐχῶν ἀνθομολόγησιν *ib.*14.2(p.331.5; 461A); 'ὅταν προσεύχησθε' φησίν· οὐκ εἶπεν, 'ὅταν εὔχησθε', ἀλλ' 'ὅταν προσεύχησθε'· ὡς τοῦ κατὰ τὴν εὐ. ἤδη προκατορθωθῆναι προσήκοντος, πρὶν διὰ τῆς π. τῷ θεῷ προσεγγίσαι. τίς δὲ τῶν ὀνομάτων τούτων κατὰ τὸ σημαινόμενόν ἐστι διαφορά; ὅτι εὐ. μέν ἐστιν ἐπαγγελία τινὸς τῶν κατ' εὐσέβειαν ἀφιερουμένων· π. δὲ αἴτησις ἀγαθῶν, μετὰ ἱκετηρίας προσαγομένη θεῷ Gr.Nyss.*or.dom.*2(p.30.5ff.; M.44.1137C,D); ὡς οὖν οὐκ ἐσομένης ἐν παρρησίᾳ τῆς ἐντεύξεως, εἰ μὴ ἐπὶ προληφθείσῃ εὐ. τινι καὶ δωροφορίᾳ ἡ πρόσοδος γένοιτο, ἀναγκαίως ἡ εὐ. τῆς π. προηγήσεται *ib.*(p.30.35; 1140A); προσευχή ἐστιν αἴτησις ἀγαθῶν παρὰ θεοῦ· εὐ. δὲ ἡ ἐπαγγελία Olymp.*Eccl.*5:3(M.93.540C); π. δέ ἐστιν αἴτησις ὧν πέφυκε θεὸς ἀνθρώποις δωρεῖσθαι πρὸς σωτηρίαν·...εἰ γὰρ εὐ. ἐστιν, ὑπόσχεσις τῶν ἐξ ἀνθρώπων θεῷ κατ' ἐπαγγελίαν προσαγομένων καλῶν· π. κατὰ τὸν εἰκότα λόγον ἔσται σαφῶς, ἡ τῶν ἐκ θεοῦ πρὸς σωτηρίαν χορηγουμένων τοῖς ἀνθρώποις ἀγαθῶν ἐξαίτησις, ἀντίδοσιν φέρουσα τῆς τῶν προηυγμένων διαθέσεως Max.*qu.Thal.*50(M.90.469A); cf.id. *or.dom.*(M.90.881B,C).

B. nature and characteristics of prayer; **1.** def.; **a.** familiarity with God ὁμιλία πρὸς τὸν θεὸν ἡ εὐ. Clem.*str.*7.7(p.30.16; M.9.456A); Evagr.Pont.*or.*3(M.79.1168C); Gr.Nyss.*or.dom.*1(p.8.17; M.44.1124B); Ant.Mon.*hom.*106(M.89.1756C); **b.** elevation of mind to God, v. ἀνάβασις; **c.** union with God εὐ. ... κοινωνία...ἐστι καὶ ἕνωσις πρὸς θεόν ‡Chrys.*hom.suppl.*6.2(M.64.461D); π. ἐστι...ἕνωσις ἀνθρώπου καὶ θεοῦ Jo.Clim.*scal.*28(M.88.1129A); †Jo.D.*B.J.*20(M.96.1041A); **d.** food of the soul τοῦ νοῦ ἡ πνευματικὴ π. τροφὴ ὑπάρχει Evagr. Pont.*or.*101(M.79.1189B) ∽ Ant.Mon.*hom.*106(M.89.1756C); †Chrys. *hom.prec.*2(2.784D); **e.** summary εὐ. ... ἐστὶν ἀναγκαία τῆς ζωῆς ἡμῶν βοήθεια, ὅπλον κατὰ τὸν διάβολον, ὁμιλία πρὸς θεόν, διάλεξις τοῦ λογικοῦ ζῴου πρὸς τὸν ἀληθινὸν λόγον, ἀναχώρησις καὶ λήθη τῶν γηΐνων πραγμάτων, ἄνοδος πρὸς οὐρανόν, καταφρόνησις τῶν παρόντων, οἰκείωσις πρὸς τὰ μέλλοντα Ast.Am.*phar.*(p.117.7); **2.** necessity εἰ ἀφορμή τις ὁμιλίας τῆς πρὸς τὸν θεὸν γίνεται ἡ εὐ., οὐδεμίαν ἀφορμὴν παραλειπτέον τῆς προσόδου τῆς πρὸς τὸν θεόν Clem. *str.*7.7(p.31.26; M.9.457C); εἰ δὲ Ἰησοῦς προσεύχεται καὶ μὴ μάτην προσεύχεται, τυγχάνων ὧν αἰτεῖ διὰ τοῦ εὔχεσθαι, τάχα οὐκ ἂν αὐτὰ εἰληφὼς χωρὶς εὐ., τίς ἡμῶν ἀμελῇ τοῦ εὔχεσθαι; Or.*or.*13.1(p.325.22; M.11.453B); κύριος...ὑπογραμμὸς ἡμῖν γενόμενος διενυκτέρευεν ἐν τῇ π. τοῦ θεοῦ, θεὸν δεικνὺς ἡμῖν ἀρίστην ὠφέλειαν καὶ πολλὴν πρὸς θεὸν ἐγγύτητα διὰ τῆς ἐπιμόνου π. Ant.Mon.*hom.*106(M.89.1757C); without it a virtuous life is impossible, †Chrys.*hom.prec.*1(2.781A); *ib.* (783A); *ib.*2(784C); and soul becomes a prey to demons, *ib.*(784C); τὸ σχολάζειν τῇ ἀδιαλείπτῳ π., ἀναγκαῖον καὶ ἐπωφελὲς ἡμῖν ὑπάρχει Ant.Mon.*hom.*106(1756B); **3.** *general features*: a bond of union διαμένετε ἐν τῇ ὁμονοίᾳ ὑμῶν καὶ τῇ μετ' ἀλλήλων π. Ign.*Trall.*12.2; a means of obtaining the kingdom τὴν βασιλείαν...ἀδιαλείπτοις...εὐ. ἐκβιάζεσθαι Clem.*str.*5.3(p.336.18; M.9.33A); an act of trust in the goodness of God, *ib.*7.7(p.31.25; 457B); *ib.*7.12(p.56.17; 509A); a weapon μέγα ὅπλον εὐ. βούλει μαθεῖν πῶς μέγα ὅπλον ἡ εὐ.; προστασίας πενήτων παρέδραμον οἱ ἀπόστολοι, ἵνα πλείονα σχολὴν περὶ τὴν εὐ. ἔχωσι Chrys.*hom.*2.4 *in Ac.princ.*(3.68A); id.*pecc.*5(3.348D); πανοπλία γὰρ ὡς ἀληθῶς οὐράνιος ἡ θεία π. †Chrys.*hom.prec.*1(2. 781E); *ib.*(782E); ὁ μὴ κεκτημένος π. καθαράν, οὐκ ἔχει ὅπλον εἰς πόλεμον Nil.*inst.*(M.79.1236C); chief work of ascetic, †Bas.*ep.*42.3 (3.127D; M.32.353A); a secret activity ἡμέρας μὲν σύμβολον ἡ νηστεία, διὰ τὸ ἔκδηλον· νυκτὸς δὲ διὰ τὸ ἄδηλον ἡ εὐ. ‡Max.*cap.al.*84(M.90. 1420A); *ib.*85(1420A); its value μηδὲν τῆς π. εἶναι τῶν κατὰ τὴν ζωὴν τιμίων ἀνώτερον Gr.Nyss.*or.dom.*1(p.8.30; M.44.1124C); οὐ τιμὴ δὲ μόνον, ἀλλὰ καὶ ὠφέλεια μεγίστη γένοιτ' ἂν ἡμῖν ἀπὸ τῆς εὐ., καὶ πρὶν ἢ λαβεῖν, ὅπερ αἰτοῦμεν Chrys.*anom.*7.7(1.512B); ἔστι τῷ ὄντως εὐχομένῳ δικαστήριον καὶ κριτήριον, καὶ βῆμα κυρίου, πρὸ τοῦ βήματος μέλλοντος Jo.Clim.*scal.*28(M.88.1129B); summary π. σωτηρίας ἀφορμή, ἀθανασίας πρόξενος ψυχῆς, τῆς ἐκκλησίας τεῖχος ἀρραγές, φυλακτήριον ἄσειστον, φοβερὸν μὲν τοῖς δαίμοσι, σωτήριον δὲ τοῖς εὐσεβέσιν ἡμῖν †Chrys.*hom.prec.*2(789A); **4.** an angelic activity ἡ εὐ. ... τῶν ἀγγέλων ἡ γλῶττα Chrys.*exp.in Ps.*4:1(5.12C); ἀγγέλων γὰρ ἔργον ἡ π. †Chrys.*hom.prec.*1(2.779B); Jo.Clim.*scal.*28(M.88. 1129A); †Jo.D.*B.J.*20(M.96.1041A); for angels assisting men in prayer v. ἄγγελος; **5.** ideal of prayer εὐ. γὰρ αὐτῷ [sc. γνωστικῷ] ὁ βίος ἅπας καὶ ὁμιλία πρὸς θεόν Clem.*str.*7.12(p.52.22; M.9.501A); πάντα τὸν βίον τοῦ ἁγίου μίαν συναπτομένην μεγάλην εἴπωμεν εὐ. Or.*or.*12.2(p.325.3f.; M.11.452D); ὅταν παριστάμενος εἰς π. ὑπὲρ πᾶσαν ἄλλην χαρὰν γένῃ, τότε ἀληθῶς εὕρηκας π. Evagr.Pont.*or.*153(M.79. 1200C); εὐ. αἱ κάτωθεν ἐκ τοῦ βάθους τῆς διανοίας ἀναπεμπόμεναι, ἐρριζωμέναι μετὰ ἀσφαλείας πρὸς ὕψος ἀνατείνονται, καὶ οὐδεμιᾷ λογισμοῦ προσβολῇ παρατρέπονται Chrys.*incomprehens.*5.7(1.491A); ἀδιάλειπτος γάρ ἐστι π., τὸ τὸν νοῦν ἔχειν ἐν εὐλαβείᾳ πολλῇ καὶ πόθῳ προσκείμενον τῷ θεῷ, καὶ τῆς ἐλπίδος αὐτοῦ ἀεὶ ἀποκρέμασθαι Max. *ascet.*25(M.90.932A); **6.** prayer of Christ, as example διὰ τοῦτο καὶ εὔχεται, ἵνα ἐκεῖνοι μάθωσιν εὔχεσθαι. ἀλλ' οὐκ εὔχεσθαι μόνον, ἀλλὰ καὶ πῶς δεῖ εὔχεσθαι μαθεῖν αὐτοὺς ἐχρῆν· διὰ δὴ τοῦτο καὶ εὐ. παρέδωκεν οὕτως ἔχουσαν· πάτερ ἡμῶν κτλ. Chrys.*hom.in Mt.*26:39(3.23C); Christol. ἐκεῖνοι [sc. Eunomians] μὲν λέγουσιν, ὅτι τῆς θεότητός ἐστιν ἡ εὐ., ἡμεῖς δὲ λέγομεν, ὅτι τῆς οἰκονομίας id.*anom.*7.5(1.508C); οὐκ ἔστι τῆς θεότητος ἡ εὐ.· θεὸς γὰρ οὐκ εὔχεται, θεοῦ γὰρ τὸ προσκυνεῖσθαί ἐστι· θεοῦ τὸ εὐ. δέχεσθαι, οὐ τὸ εὐ. ἀναφέρειν *ib.*(508D); πολλοὶ μὲν γὰρ τῶν αἱρετικῶν λέγουσιν, ὅτι οὐχ ὅμοιος ὁ υἱὸς τῷ πατρί. διὰ τί; ὅτι ἐδεήθη, φησί, π. ὁ Χριστὸς εἰς τὸ ἐγεῖραι τὸν Λάζαρον... βλασφημοῦσι δὲ μὴ νοοῦντες ὅπως συγκαταβάσεως ἦν, καὶ τῆς τῶν παρόντων ἕνεκα ἀσθενείας ἡ π. *ib.*9.1(525A,B); cf.id.*hom.64.3 in Jo.* (8.385D); **7.** God as source of all prayer εἰ προσεύξασθαι βούλει, θεοῦ χρεία τοῦ διδόντος εὐ. τῷ εὐχομένῳ Evagr.Pont.*or.*58(M.79.1180A); χρὴ...αἰτεῖσθαι λαβεῖν χάρισμα εὐχῆς...παρὰ τοῦ διδόντος εὐ. τῷ εὐχομένῳ Ant.Mon.*hom.*106(M.89.1757C); Jo.Clim.*scal.*28(M.88. 1140C); †Jo.D.*B.J.*20(M.96.1041B); esp. H. Ghost τὸ ἅγιον πνεῦμα συμπάσχον τῇ ἡμετέρᾳ ἀσθενείᾳ...ἐπιφοιτᾷ ἡμῖν, καὶ εἰ εὕροι τὸν νοῦν ἡμῶν φιλαλήθως αὐτῷ προσευχόμενον, ἐπιβαίνει αὐτῷ...προτρεπόμενον αὐτὸν εἰς ἔργα πνευματικῆς π. Evagr.Pont.*or.*62(M.79.1180C); Mac. Aeg.*hom.*19.8(M.34.648D).

C. kinds and degrees of prayer; **1.** its principal elements, viz. glorifying Father through Son in H. Ghost, thanksgiving, confession of sins, petition, Or.*or.*33.1(p.401.13ff.; M.11.557B–560A); προσευχῆς διττὸς ὁ τρόπος, ὁ μέν τις πρακτικός, ὁ δὲ θεωρητικός Evagr.Pont.*or.*proem.(M.79.1165B); **2.** mental and vocal prayer; words not necessary for prayer, Clem.*str.*7.7(p.32.30; M.9.461A); ἦθός ἐστι προσευχῆς σύννοια μετ' εὐλαβείας, καὶ κατανύξεως, καὶ ὀδύνης ψυχῆς ἐν ἐξαγορεύσει πταισμάτων μετὰ στεναγμῶν ἀφώνων Evagr.Pont.*or.*42(M.79.1176B); εὐχὴν δὲ λέγω..., οὐ τὴν ἁπλῶς ἐπὶ τοῦ στόματος κειμένην, ἀλλὰ τὴν ἐκ τοῦ βάθους τῆς διανοίας ἀνιοῦσαν Chrys. *incomprehens.*5.7(1.491A); πολλάκις πληρώσαντες τὴν εὐ., μηδὲν ἀκούσαντες ὧν εἰρήκαμεν, ἀπήλθομεν. ἂν οὖν ἐννοήσωμεν τοῦτο, εὐθέως πάλιν αὐτὴν ἀναλάβωμεν...καὶ μὴ πρότερον ἀποστῶμεν εὐχόμενοι, ἕως ἂν ἅπασαν αὐτὴν μετὰ διανοίας νηφούσης εἴπωμεν id.*hom.in Ps.* 145:2(5.534A); οὐκ ἔστι τελεία π. χωρὶς νοητῆς ἐπικλήσεως Marc.Er. *opusc.*2.31(M.65.936A); **3.** degrees of prayer τῆς καθαρᾶς π. δύο εἰσὶν ἀκρόταται καταστάσεις· ἡ μέν, τοῖς πρακτικοῖς· ἡ δέ, τοῖς θεωρητικοῖς ἐπισυμβαίνουσα. καὶ ἡ μέν, ἐκ φόβου θεοῦ καὶ ἐλπίδος ἀγαθῆς τῇ ψυχῇ ἐγγίνεται· ἡ δέ, ἀπὸ θείου ἔρωτος καὶ ἀκροτάτης καθάρσεως. γνωρίσματα δὲ τοῦ μὲν πρώτου μέτρου, τὸ ἐν τῷ συναγαγεῖν τὸν νοῦν ἐκ πάντων τῶν τοῦ κόσμου νοημάτων, καὶ ὡς αὐτῷ αὐτοῦ περιισταμένου τοῦ θεοῦ, ὥσπερ καὶ πάρεστη, ποιεῖσθαι τὰς π. ἀπερισπάστως...τοῦ δὲ δευτέρου, τὸ ἐν αὐτῇ τῇ ὁρμῇ τῆς π. ἁρπαγῆναι τὸν νοῦν ὑπὸ τοῦ θείου καὶ ἀπείρου φωτός Max.*carit.*2.6(M.90.985A,B); ἡ μὲν ψιλὴ εὐ., ὡς ἄρτος ἀρχομένους στηρίζουσα· ἡ δὲ μετά τινος θεωρίας, ὡς ἔλαιον πιαίνουσα· ἡ δὲ ἀνείδεος, ὡς οἶνος εὐώδης, οὗ οἱ ἐμφορούμενοι ἀπλήστως ἐξίστανται ‡Max.*cap.al.*176(M.90.1441B); **4.** relation between work of God and work of men in prayer βιάζεσθαι ἑαυτὸν εἰς τὴν εὐ., μὴ ἔχοντα εὐ. πνευματικήν· καὶ οὕτως ὁ θεός, θεωρῶν τὸν οὕτως ἀγωνιζόμενον,...δίδωσιν εὐ. ἀληθινὴν πνεύματος Mac.Aeg. *hom.*19.3(M.34.645A); στῆθι ἐπὶ τῆς φυλακῆς σου φυλάττων τὸν νοῦν σου ἀπὸ νοημάτων κατὰ τὸν καιρὸν τῆς π.,...ἵνα ὁ συμπάσχων τοῖς ἀγνοοῦσι, καὶ σοὶ ἐπιφοιτήσῃ, καὶ τότε λήψῃ δῶρον προσευχῆς εὐκλεέστατον Evagr.Pont.*or.*69(M.79.1181C); Jo.Clim.*scal.*28(M.88. 1132C).

D. conditions for prayer; **1.** spiritual; **a.** practice of Christian virtues οὐ προσελεύσῃ ἐπὶ π. ἐν συνειδήσει πονηρᾷ *Did.*4.14 = *Barn.* 19.12; δεῖται...ἡ εὐ. ψυχῆς εὐρώστου καὶ λιπαροῦς ἄχρι τῆς ἐσχάτης ἡμέρας τοῦ βίου συμμετρημένης καὶ ⟨ἡ⟩ πολιτεία διαθέσεως χρηστῆς καὶ μονίμου καὶ πάσαις ταῖς ἐντολαῖς τοῦ σωτῆρος ἐπεκτεινομένης Clem.*q.d.s.*1(p.160.14; M.9.605B); καθαρὸς [sc. ὁ γνωστικός] εἰς εὐ. πάντοτε id.*str.*7.12(p.56.5; M.9.508C); εἰ μὴ ἡ ταπεινοφροσύνη καὶ ἀγάπη, ἡ ἁπλότης τε καὶ ἀγαθότης κατακολλῶσιν ἡμῖν τὴν εὐ., ἡ εὐ. αὕτη, μᾶλλον δὲ τὸ πρόσχημα τῆς εὐ., ἥκιστά γε ἡμᾶς ὠφελεῖν δύναται Mac.Aeg.*or.*5(M.34.856C); id.*hom.*19.5(M.34.645C); καθαρὸν ὀργῆς εἶναι τὸν εὐχῇ προσιόντα Chrys.*prod.Jud.*1.1(2.377E); ἑώρακα ἐν ὑπακοῇ ἐξαστράπτοντας...ἀθρόον ἐπὶ προσευχὴν παρασταθέντας, καὶ συντόμως τοῦ ἑαυτῶν νοὸς περιγενομένους, προπαρεσκευασμένοι γὰρ ὑπὸ τῆς ὁσίας ὑπακοῆς ἐτύγχανον Jo.Clim.*scal.*28(M.88.1136B); πᾶσαν μὲν ἀρετήν, ἐπὶ πλείω δὲ τὴν π. αἰσθήσει πολλῇ ποιησώμεθα πάντοτε· τότε ψυχὴ ἐν αἰσθήσει προσεύχεται, ὅταν θυμοῦ κρείττων γένηται *ib.*(1136D); ἀδύνατον εἰρηνικὸν γενέσθαι τὸν νοῦν ἐν εὐ., ἐγκράτειαν καὶ ἀγάπην φίλην τὸν μὴ κτησάμενον ‡Max.*cap.al.*221(M.90.1453A); **b.** recollection δεῖ ὑπὲρ τοῦ μὴ ἐπιθολοῦσθαι τὸν νοῦν ὑπὸ ἑτέρων λογισμῶν πάντων ἐπιλελῆσθαι τῶν ἔξω τῆς εὐ. κατὰ τὸν καιρόν, ἐν ᾧ τις εὔχεται Or.*or.*9.1(p.318.3; M.11.444A); δοκεῖ τοίνυν μοι τὸν μέλλοντα ἥκειν ἐπὶ τὴν εὐ., ὀλίγον ὑποστάντα καὶ ἑαυτὸν εὐτρεπίσαντα, ἐπιστρεφέστερον καὶ εὐτονώτερον πρὸς τὸ ὅλον γενέσθαι τὴν εὐ. *ib.*31.2(p.395.28; 549B); ὁ δὲ ἀληθινὸς θεμέλιος τῆς π. οὗτός ἐστι, τὸ προσέχειν τοῖς λογισμοῖς, καὶ ἐν πολλῇ ἡσυχίᾳ καὶ εἰρήνῃ ποιεῖσθαι τὴν π. Mac.Aeg.*hom.*6.3(M. 34.520B); μὴ ἐν μόνοις τοῖς ἐκτὸς σχήμασι προσεύχου, ἀλλὰ τρέπε τὸν νοῦν σου εἰς συναίσθησιν πνευματικῆς π. μετὰ πολλοῦ φόβου Evagr. Pont.*or.*28(M.79.1173A); ἐν ταῖς εὐ. ἡσυχίαν κατασκευάζειν ἑαυτοῖς καὶ ἠρεμίαν πολλήν Chrys.*hom.83.1 in Mt.*(7.790E); ὅταν σταθῶμεν εἰς π.,...μηδένα λογισμὸν εἰς τὴν καρδίαν ἡμῶν εἰσελθεῖν συγχωρήσωμεν,...πλὴν τῆς πρὸς θεὸν ἱκεσίας Nil.*epp.*3.283(M.79.524C); μακάριος

...ὁ νοῦς, ὃς κατὰ τὸν καιρὸν τῆς π. ἀπερισπάστως τῷ θεῷ προσομιλεῖ Ant.Mon.*hom*.106(M.89.1756D); ἀρχὴ μὲν προσευχῆς προσβολαὶ μονολογίστως διωκόμεναι ἐκ προοιμίων αὐτῶν Jo.Clim.*scal*.28(M.88.1132D); **c.** self-denial, Evagr.Pont.*or*.18(M.79.1172A); *ib*.19(1172B); ἀπόδυσαι τὰ θελήματά σου, καὶ γυμνὸς τούτων πρόσελθε κυρίῳ ἐν π. σου Jo.Clim.*scal*.28(M.88.1133B); φιλίαν πρὸς τὴν εὐ. οὐ δύναται κτήσασθαι, ὁ μὴ πᾶσαν ὕλην ἀπαρνησάμενος, πλὴν τροφῆς καὶ σκέπης. ἔξω τῶν ἄλλων γενοῦ ἐν εὐ., ὁ θέλων μετὰ μόνου γενέσθαι τοῦ νοῦ ‡Max.*cap.al*.91(M.90.1421A); *ib*.184(1444C); **d.** tears, v. δάκρυον; **e.** perfect prayer entailing freedom from activity of imagination ἐπιποθῶν ἰδεῖν τὸ πρόσωπον τοῦ πατρὸς τοῦ ἐν οὐρανοῖς, μὴ ζήτει παντελῶς μορφήν, ἢ σχῆμα δέχεσθαι ἐν τῷ τῆς π. καιρῷ Evagr.Pont.*or*.114(M.79.1192D); μακάριος ὁ νοῦς, ὃς κατὰ τὸν καιρὸν τῆς π. τελείαν ἀμορφίαν ἐκτήσατο *ib*.117(1193A); ἡ δὲ π. παντὸς ἀφίστησι τὸν νοῦν νοήματος αἰσθητοῦ ‡Nil.*perist*.4.4(M.79.829A); Ant.Mon.*hom*.106(M.89.1756C); πᾶσαν αἰσθητὴν φαντασίαν ἐν τῇ π. μὴ προσδέξῃ Jo.Clim.*scal*.28(M.88.1136D); ἆρα ἀπηλλάγημεν τῶν ἐμπαθῶν νοημάτων, καὶ τῆς καθαρᾶς καὶ ἀΰλου ἀπολαύομεν π.; Thal.*cent*.3.26(M.91.1449D); description of perfect prayer ὁ τῆς εὐ. τρόπος· τὸ νηφούσῃ διανοίᾳ, τὸ συντετριμμένῃ ψυχῇ, τὸ μετὰ πηγῶν δακρύων αὐτῷ προσιέναι, τὸ μηδὲν αἰτεῖν βιωτικόν, τὸ τῶν μελλόντων ἐρᾶν, τὸ ὑπὲρ τῶν πνευματικῶν ποιεῖσθαι τὴν ἔντευξιν, τὸ μὴ κατεύχεσθαι τῶν ἐχθρῶν, τὸ μηδενὶ μνησικακεῖν, τὸ πάντα ἐκβάλλειν ἀπὸ τῆς ψυχῆς τὰ πάθη, τὸ συντρίβοντα τὴν καρδίαν οὕτω προσιέναι, τὸ συνεστάλθαι, τὸ πολλὴν τὴν ἐπιείκειαν μελετᾶν, καὶ τὴν γλῶτταν πρὸς εὐφημίαν τρέπειν Chrys.*exp.in Ps*.4:1(5.9C); **f.** conditions for prayer of petition in partic.: choice of right subjects ὁ γνωστικὸς τὴν εὐ. ... τῶν ὄντως ἀγαθῶν τῶν περὶ ψυχὴν ποιεῖται Clem.*str*.7.7(p.29.27; M.9.453C); ἡ δὲ π., ἱκετηρία ἐστί, περί τινος τῶν συμφερόντων προσαγομένη τῷ θεῷ Gr.Nyss.*Pss.titt*.B 3(M.44.493B); μόνην ζήτει ἐν τῇ π. σου τὴν δικαιοσύνην, καὶ τὴν βασιλείαν, τουτέστι τὴν ἀρετήν, καὶ τὴν γνῶσιν Evagr.Pont.*or*.38(M.79.1176A); οὐχ ἁπλῶς δὲ αἱ εὐ., ἀλλ' αἱ κατὰ νόμον τοῦ θεοῦ γινόμεναι εὐ. καὶ τίνες εἰσὶν αὗται; αἱ ταῦτα αἰτοῦσαι, ἃ τῷ θεῷ πρέπει διδόναι, αἱ μὴ τἀναντία τοῖς αὐτοῦ νόμοις αὐτὸν παρακαλοῦσαι Chrys.*exp.in Ps*.4:2(5.11E); ἀξία τοῦ τὸν θεὸν πατέρα καλοῦντος ἡ εὐ., τὸ μηδὲν αἰτεῖν πρὸ τῆς τοῦ πατρὸς δόξης id.*hom.19.4 in Mt*.(7.250C); οὐδαμοῦ ἀρχήν, οὐδαμοῦ πλοῦτον...ἀλλὰ πάντα εἰς ψυχῆς ὠφέλειαν συντελοῦντα ἐνέθηκε τῇ εὐ.· οὐδὲν γήϊνον, ἀλλὰ πάντα οὐράνια id.*hom.43.2 in Jo*.(8.257D); π. μετὰ νήψεως γενέσθω, ἵνα μὴ τὸν θεὸν αἰτοῦμεν, οἷς αὐτὸς οὐκ ἀρέσκεται Nil.*paraen*.42(M.79.1252D); ὅταν εἰς εὐ. στῶμεν, μὴ εὐξώμεθα ἡμῶν θέλημα γενέσθαι... ἀλλὰ τὸ τοῦ θεοῦ Ant.Mon.*hom*.106(M.89.1756D); perseverance μὴ ὡς ἐν δυνάμει κομιζόμενος, εὐθέως τὸ αἴτημα ζήτει· βούλεται γάρ σε ἐπὶ πλέον εὐεργετῆσαι προσκαρτεροῦντα αὐτῷ ἐν τῇ π. Evagr.Pont.*or*.34(1173D); ἃ γὰρ οὐκ ἰσχύομεν πολλάκις ἐξ οἰκείας κατορθῶσαι σπουδῆς, ταῦτα δυνησόμεθα ἀνύσαι εὐμαρῶς δι' εὐχῶν, εὐ. δὲ λέγω τῶν διηνεκῶν Chrys.*hom.in Phil.1:18*(3.308D); discussion of rel. of prayer of petition to immutable will of God, Or.*or*.5–8(pp.311–16; M.11.433–41); **2.** physical and material; **a.** bodily posture μάλιστα μὲν ἡ...εὐ. μειλίσσεται τὸν θεόν...ἢ ἐν πρηνεῖ κατακλίσει καὶ ἐν γόνασιν ὀκλάσαντός τινος Just.*dial*.90.5(M.6.692A); extended hands and raised eyes, Clem.*str*.7.7(p.30.20; M.9.456B); Or.*or*.31.2(p.396.13; M.11.552A) cit. s. ἔκτασις; though circumstances may excuse from this, *ib*.(p.396.19; 552A); signification of extended hands, Chrys.*exp.in Ps*.140:2(5.431C) cit. s. ἔκτασις; cf. description of symbolism, Ast.Am.*phar*.(p.117.11ff.); **b.** eastward direction τοῖς ἐν ἀγνοίᾳ κυλινδουμένοις ἀνέτειλεν γνώσεως ἀληθείας ἡμέρα, κατὰ λόγον τοῦ ἡλίου, πρὸς τὴν ἑωθινὴν ἀνατολὴν αἱ εὐ. Clem.*str*.7.7(p.33.1; M.9.461A); περὶ τοῦ κλίματος, εἰς ὃ ἀφορῶντα εὔχεσθαι δεῖ, ὀλίγα λεκτέον... τίς οὐκ ἂν αὐτόθεν ὁμολογήσαι τὸ πρὸς ἀνατολὴν ἐναργῶς ἐμφαίνειν τὸ δεῖν ἐκεῖ νεύοντας συμβολικῶς, ὡς τῆς ψυχῆς ἐνορώσης τῇ τοῦ ἀληθινοῦ φωτὸς ἀνατολῇ, ποιεῖσθαι τὰς εὐ.; Or.*or*.32(p.400.26; M.11.557A); πάντες μὲν ὁρῶμεν κατ' ἀνατολὰς ἐπὶ τῶν π.· ὀλίγοι δὲ ἴσμεν ὅτι τὴν ἀρχαίαν ἐπιζητοῦμεν πατρίδα, τὸν παράδεισον, ὃν ἐφύτευσεν ὁ θεὸς ἐν Ἐδὲμ κατ' ἀνατολάς Bas.*Spir*.66(3.56A; M.32.189C); cf. *Const.App*.2.57.14; ἐπειδὴ τῶν παρ' ἡμῖν τὰ τιμιώτερα εἰς τιμὴν τοῦ θεοῦ ἀφορίζομεν, κατὰ δὲ τὴν τῶν ἀνθρώπων ὑπόληψιν τιμιωτέρα ἐστὶν ἡ ἀνατολὴ τῶν ἄλλων μερῶν τῆς κτίσεως· διὰ τοῦτο ἐν τῷ καιρῷ τῆς π. νεύομεν πρὸς ἀνατολὴν πάντες. ... οὐκ ἐναντιοῦται δὲ τῇ προφητικῇ τε καὶ ἀποστολικῇ φωνῇ τὸ πρὸς τὴν ἀνατολὴν ποιεῖν ἡμᾶς τὰς εὐ., ἐν παντὶ γὰρ τόπῳ ὑπάρχει ἡ ἀνατολὴ τοῖς εὐχομένοις ‡Just.*qu.et resp*.118(M.6.1368C); cf.†Gregent.*disp*.(M.86.669C); στὰς κατὰ ἀνατολάς, ηὔξατο εὐ. †Jo.D.*B.J*.36(M.96.1204A); **c.** place ἔχει δέ τι ἐπίχαρι εἰς ὠφέλειαν τόπος εὐχῆς, τὸ χωρίον τῆς ἐπὶ τὸ αὐτὸ τῶν πιστευόντων συνελεύσεως Or.*or*.31.5(p.398.14; M.11.553B); *ib*.31.7(p.400.18; 556C); παραινῶ συνεχῶς ταῖς ἐκκλησίαις ἐπιχωριάζειν, καὶ ἐν οἰκίᾳ μετὰ πολλῆς ἡσυχίας εὔχεσθαι...εἰ δὲ ἢ διὰ καιρόν, ἢ διὰ τόπον ἀποληφθείημεν μεταξὺ πολλῶν ἑτέρων, μὴ διὰ τοῦτο τὰς συνήθεις ἀπολιμπάνειν εὐ. Chrys.*Anna* 4.6(4.739A); ὅπου γὰρ ἂν ᾖς, δύνασαι στῆσαι τὸν βωμόν, προαίρεσιν νήφουσαν ἐπιδειξάμενος μόνον, καὶ οὐδὲν κωλύει τόπος, οὐδὲ ἐμποδίζει καιρός, ἀλλὰ κἂν γόνατα μὴ κλίνῃς, κἂν μὴ στῆθος τύψῃ...διάνοιαν δὲ μόνον ἐπιδείξῃς θερμήν, τὸ πᾶν ἀπήρτισας τῆς εὐ. *ib*.(738C); πᾶς τόπος εἰς προσευχὴν ἐπιτήδειος ‡Nil.*perist*.4.5(M.79.829B); by Christ's words in Mt.6:5f. no restriction of place is implied, Chrys.*hom.8.1 in 1Tim*.(11.589E); universality of place corresponds to universality of Christianity, *ib*.(590A); **d.** time and frequency of prayer: to be made thrice in the day, cf. *Did*.8.3, and also at night, Or.*or*.12.2(p.325.4,14; M.11.452D–453A); χρὴ καὶ τῆς κλίνης ἀπανισταμένους φθάνειν ἀεὶ τὸν ἥλιον τῇ τοῦ θεοῦ λατρείᾳ, καὶ τραπέζης ἁπτομένους, καὶ καθεύδειν μέλλοντας· μᾶλλον δὲ καὶ καθ' ἑκάστην ὥραν μίαν π. τῷ θεῷ προσφέροντας, ἴσον τῇ ἡμέρᾳ δρόμον τρέχοντας· ἐν δέ γε τῇ τοῦ χειμῶνος ὥρᾳ, καὶ τῆς νυκτὸς τὸ πλεῖστον μέρος εἰς προσευχὰς ἀναλίσκοντας †Chrys.*hom.prec*.1(2.783A,B); εὐχὰς ἐπιτελεῖτε ὄρθρου καὶ τρίτῃ ὥρᾳ καὶ ἕκτῃ καὶ ἐνάτῃ καὶ ἑσπέρᾳ καὶ ἀλεκτοροφωνίᾳ *Const.App*.8.34.1; four hours of prayer (3rd, 6th, 9th, 12th), Anton.Hag.*v.Sym.Styl*.3(p.22.5); at meals τελεσθέντος δὲ τοῦ δείπνου ἐποίησεν Ἀβραὰμ τὴν κατὰ ἔθος εὐ. *T.Abr*.A 5(p.81.33); εὐ. πρὸ τῆς τροφῆς ἀξίως γενέσθωσαν τῶν τοῦ θεοῦ παροχῶν Bas.*ep*.2.6(3.75A; M.32.232D); Chrys.*bapt*.4(2.375B); τράπεζα γὰρ ἀπὸ εὐχῆς ἀρχομένη, καὶ εἰς εὐχὴν καταλήγουσα, οὐδέποτε ὑστερηθήσεται id.*Anna* 2.5(4.719B); discussion of Christ's apparent prohibition of long prayers δοκεῖ μοι κελεύειν ἐνταῦθα [sc. Mt.6:7f.] μηδὲ μακρὰς ποιεῖσθαι τὰς εὐ.· μακρὰς δὲ οὐχὶ τῷ χρόνῳ, ἀλλὰ τῷ πλήθει καὶ μήκει τῶν λεγομένων...οὐδὲν ἕτερον ἢ τὸ συνεχῶς ἐντυγχάνειν αὐτῷ ἅπαντας ἐνομοθέτησεν, οὐ μὴν μυρίων στίχων εὐχὴν συντιθέντας αὐτῷ προσιέναι καὶ ἀπαγγέλλειν ἁπλῶς κελεύει id.*hom.19.4 in Mt*.(7.249B,C); ὁ Χριστὸς...εἰπὼν γὰρ τοῖς μαθηταῖς, μὴ κατὰ τοὺς ἐθνικοὺς εὔχεσθαι,... καὶ μέτρον ἡμᾶς εὐχῆς ἐδίδαξε· δεικνὺς ὅτι οὐκ ἐν τῷ πλήθει τῶν ῥημάτων, ἀλλ' ἐν τῇ νήψει τῆς διανοίας κεῖται τὸ ἀκουσθῆναι. πῶς οὖν, φησίν, εἰ ὀλίγα δεῖ εὔχεσθαι, παραβολὴν εἶπεν αὐτοῖς πρὸς τὸ δεῖν ἀεὶ προσεύχεσθαι...; πῶς δὲ καὶ ὁ Παῦλος παραινεῖ λέγων, 'τῇ π. προσκαρτεροῦντες', καὶ πάλιν, 'ἀδιαλείπτως προσεύχεσθε'; εἰ γὰρ δεῖ μὴ μακροὺς ἀποτείνειν λόγους, καὶ συνεχῶς εὔχεσθαι, ἐναντίον τοῦτο ἐκείνου. ἀλλ' οὐκ ἔστιν ἐναντίον,...ἀλλὰ καὶ σφόδρα συμβαῖνον. καὶ γὰρ καὶ ὁ Χριστὸς καὶ ὁ Παῦλος βραχείας καὶ πυκνὰς ποιεῖσθαι τὰς εὐ. ἐκέλευσαν ἐξ ὀλίγων διαλειμμάτων id.*Anna* 2.2(714B,C); **3.** impediments to prayer; **a.** natural impediments and imperfections: human sinfulness τοῖς μοχθηροῖς...ἡ εὐ. οὐ μόνον εἰς τοὺς ἄλλους, ἀλλὰ καὶ εἰς σφᾶς αὐτοὺς βλαβερωτάτη Clem.*str*.7.7(p.33.6; M.9.464A); ἡ τοῦ πονηροῦ ἀνδρὸς π., ἕως ἂν ἐν τῇ πονηρίᾳ ᾖ, τοῦ διαβόλου ἐπίκλησις γίνεται Gr.Nyss.*or.dom*.2(p.42.30; M.44.1148A); Chrys.*Is.interp*.1(6.11B); wrath and other passions, Evagr.Pont.*or*.27(M.79.1173A); οὐ δύναται...νοῦς πάθεσι δουλεύων π. πνευματικῆς τόπον ἰδεῖν *ib*.71(1181D); Chrys.*non desp*.2(3.356B); grudges against one's neighbour, Evagr.Pont.*or*.13(1169D); ἡ γὰρ μνησικακία ἀμαυροῖ τὸ ἡγεμονικὸν τοῦ προσευχομένου, καὶ σκοτίζει τούτου τὰς π. *ib*.21(1172B); verbosity πολυλογία μὲν πολλάκις ἐν προσευχῇ τὸν νοῦν καὶ ἐφάντασε καὶ διέχυσε Jo.Clim.*scal*.28(M.88.1132B); preoccupation with material things βαττολογοῦσι...πᾶσαν εὐ. ⟨περὶ⟩ τῶν σωματικῶν καὶ τῶν ἐκτὸς ἀναπέμποντες Or.*or*.21.1(p.345.12; M.11.481A); Gr.Nyss.*or.dom*.1(p.16.3; M.44.1128D); worldliness οὐ καθαρῶς δύναται προσεύξασθαι, ὁ φιλοκάλῳ πάθει καὶ φιλοτίμῳ κρατούμενος. περὶ ταῦτα γὰρ αἱ σχέσεις, καὶ οἱ τῆς ματαιότητος λογισμοὶ τὴν οἰκειότητα ἔχοντες, σχοινίᾳ καθάπερ ἐκείνῳ περιπλεκόμενοι γίνονται, κατασπῶντες ὡς οἷα στρουθίον δεδεμένον ἀναπτῆναι πειρώμενον ἐν τῷ καιρῷ τῆς εὐ. ‡Max.*cap.al*.220(M.90.1453A); description of imperfect prayer ἄλλο ῥύπος προσευχῆς, καὶ ἄλλο ἀφανισμός, καὶ ἄλλο κλοπή, καὶ ἕτερον μῶμος. ῥύπος ἐστὶ θεῷ παρίστασθαι, καὶ ἀτόπους ἐννοίας φαντάζεσθαι· ἀφανισμός ἐστι, τὸ εἰς φροντίδας ἀνωφελεῖς αἰχμαλωτίζεσθαι· κλοπή ἐστι τὸ ἀνεπαισθήτως τὴν ἔννοιαν ῥέμβεσθαι· μωμός ἐστι προβολὴ ἡ οἱαοῦν τότε πρὸς ἡμᾶς ἐγγίζουσα Jo.Clim.*scal*.28(1133A); **b.** diabolic impediments: prayer the special battleground of diabolic temptations πᾶς ὁ συγκροτούμενος πόλεμος μεταξὺ ἡμῶν τε, καὶ τῶν ἀκαθάρτων πνευμάτων, οὐ περὶ ἑτέρου γίνεται, ἢ περὶ πνευματικῆς π. Evagr.Pont.*or*.49(M.79.1177B); ὅταν μὴ δυνηθῇ τὴν μνήμην κινῆσαι ἐν τῇ π. ὁ φθονερὸς δαίμων, τότε τὴν κρᾶσιν τοῦ σώματος ἐκβιάζεται εἰς τὸ ποιῆσαι ξένην καὶ φαντασίαν τῷ νῷ *ib*.68(1181B); Mac.Aeg.*or*.3(M.34.856A); ὁ διάβολος, ἐπειδὰν ἴδῃ τὴν φλόγα τῆς εὐ. ἡμῖν ἀναπτομένην, μυρίας φροντίσιν ἔνθεν καὶ ἔνθεν ῥιπίζων, οὐ πρότερον ἀφίσταται ἕως ἂν σβέσῃ τὸ φῶς Chrys.*pecc*.5(3.348B); οἶδεν ὁ διάβολος ὅσον ἀγαθὸν εὐ.· διὸ βαρὺς ἔγκειται id.*hom.10.2 in Col*.(11.398D); μηδαμῶς θορυβηθῇς, ὅταν ἐν τῷ καιρῷ τῆς π. οἱ φαυλότατοι δαίμονες τὸ στῖφος τῶν ἀτόπων λογισμῶν ὀργιζόμενοι μᾶλλον ἐπάγωσι τῇ ψυχῇ Nil.*epp.* 3.217(M.79.481C); *ib.*3.283(524B).

E. effects; **1.** of prayer; **a.** purification, Clem.*str.*7.7(p.30.12; M.9.456A); Bas.*reg.fus.*6(2.344C; M.31.925B); ψυχὴν ἡμαρτηκυῖαν ἡ π. ῥᾳδίως ἀποκαθαίρει †Chrys.*hom.prec.*1(2.782B); καθάπερ ὕδατι σῶμα, οὕτω δι' εὐχῆς ἡ ψυχὴ καθαίρεται Chrys.*exp.in Ps.*5:4(5.33A); κἂν μυρίοι πνεύσωσιν ἄνεμοι λοιπόν, κἂν πειρασμοί, κἂν ἀθυμίαι, κἂν λογισμοί τινες ἀηδεῖς, κἂν ὁτιοῦν ἐπέλθῃ δεινόν, οὐ δυνήσεται καταβαλεῖν τὴν οἰκίαν ἐκείνην πυκναῖς...εὐ. συνδεδεμένην id.*Anna* 4.5(4.737C); ἄνθρωποι...χρῄζομεν τῶν δι' εὐ. καθαρσίων· ἡ γὰρ εὐχὴ πᾶσαν τὴν ἐπιγινομένην ἡμῖν ἀκαθαρσίαν ἐκπλύνει Nil.*epp.*1.24(M.79.89D, 92A); Jo.Clim.*scal.*28(M.88.1137C); **b.** illumination μετὰ διάρματος ἐνθέου τῆς εὐ. τοῖς νοητοῖς καὶ πνευματικοῖς ὡς ἔνι μάλιστα γνωστικῶς οἰκειούμενος Clem.*str.*7.7(p.34.6; M.9.465A); π. προοίμιόν ἐστι τῆς ἀΰλου, καὶ ποικίλης γνώσεως Evagr.Pont.*or.*85(M.79.1185B); φῶς ἐστι διανοίας καὶ ψυχῆς ἡ μετὰ σπουδῆς εὐ., φῶς ἄσβεστον καὶ διηνεκές Chrys.*pecc.*5(3.348B); ἀνισχούσης...τῆς εὐ., ὥσπερ τινὸς ἀκτῖνος ἀπὸ τοῦ στόματος τοῦ ἡμετέρου...φωτίζεται μὲν ἡ διάνοια id.*anom.*7.7(1.512D); ὥσπερ γὰρ τῷ σώματι φῶς ἥλιος, οὕτω τῇ ψυχῇ ἡ π. ... πόση ζημία Χριστιανῷ τὸ μὴ προσεύχεσθαι συνεχῶς καὶ διὰ τῆς εὐ. τὸ τοῦ Χριστοῦ φῶς εἰς τὴν ψυχὴν εἰσάγειν †Chrys.*hom.prec.*1(2.779A); τινὲς ἐκ π. ἐξιόντες...ὡς ἐκ φωτὸς πεφωτισμένοι, καὶ διπλοΐδα ταπεινώσεως, καὶ ἀγαλλιάσεως ἠμφιεσμένοι Jo.Clim.*scal.*28(M.88.1137C); **c.** union with God δι' εὐχῆς συνεῖναι...θεῷ Clem.*str.*7.7(p.30.30; M.9.456C); εὐχόμενος...ἐπιτηδειότερος γίνεται ἀνακραθῆναι τῷ... τοῦ κυρίου πνεύματι...ἔτι δὲ διά τε τῆς προειρημένης καθαρεύσεως καὶ τῆς εὐ. τοῦ μέσον καὶ τῶν μὴ γινωσκόντων αὐτὸν ἑστηκότος λόγου θεοῦ, οὐδενὸς ἀπολειπομένου τῆς εὐ., μεθέξει, συνευχομένου πρὸς τὸν πατέρα τῷ ὑπ' αὐτοῦ μεσιτευομένῳ Or.*or.*10.2(p.320.17–19; M.11.445C); Bas.*ep.*2.4(3.73C; M.32.229B) cit. s. ἐνοίκησις; κοινωνία τῆς μυστικῆς ἐνεργείας, καὶ συνάφεια διαθέσεως τῆς πρὸς θεὸν ἁγιότητος, καὶ αὐτοῦ τοῦ νοῦ δι' ἀγάπης ἀρρήτου πρὸς κύριον, ἐν τῇ εὐ. τοῖς καταξιουμένοις γίνεται Mac.Aeg.*or.*1(M.34.853A); ἡ δὲ π. ... θεῷ προσομιλεῖν παρασκευάζουσα, καὶ φιλίαν τὴν πρὸς αὐτὸν μνηστευομένη ‡Nil.*perist.*4.2(M.79.828A); Ant.Mon.*hom.*106(M.89.1756B); *ib.*(1757A); Dion.Ar.*d.n.*3.1(M.3.680B); Jo.Clim.*scal.*28(M.88.1133C); ἡ δὲ π. χωρίζει τὸν νοῦν πάντων τῶν νοημάτων, καὶ αὐτῷ αὐτὸν παρίστησι γυμνὸν τῷ θεῷ Max.*ascet.*19(M.90.925D); πρὸς τοῦτο [sc. θεωρίαν τῆς ἁγίας τριάδος] δὲ καὶ ἡ τῆς εὐ. προσεδρεία τὸν νοῦν χειραγωγεῖ, εἰκότως προοίμιον καὶ οἱονεὶ προεικόνισμα ἐκείνης τῆς μακαριότητος κέκληται αὕτη †Jo.D.*B.J.*20(M.96.1041A); **d.** from which results joy π. ἐστι χαρᾶς... πρόβλημα Evagr.Pont.*or.*15(M.79.1169D); ὁ...εὐχόμενος πολλὴν μετὰ τὴν εὐ. εἰς τὴν ψυχὴν τὴν ἑαυτοῦ τὴν ἡδονὴν εἰσοικίσαι δυνήσεται Chrys.*incomprehens.*5.6(1.489A); αἰτίαν τῆς χαρᾶς προσευχὴν ‡Max.*cap.al.*86(M.90.1420B); and physical and spiritual brightness προσευχομένου τοῦ δεσπότου Ἰησοῦ ἐν ὄρει, ἔλαμψεν τὸ πρόσωπον,...ὅπερ συμβαίνειν εἴωθεν τοῖς...τῇ εὐ. προσανέχειν σπουδάζουσι μοναχοῖς· ἐκλάμπει γὰρ τηνικαῦτα τὸ πρόσωπον τῆς ψυχῆς Nil.*epp.*2.74(M.79.233A); **2.** of neglect of prayer: sin διὰ τοῦτο πολλὴ κατὰ τὸν βίον ἡ ἁμαρτία... διότι λήθη τοῦ θεοῦ κατακρατεῖ τῶν πάντων, καὶ τὸ τῆς εὐ. ἀγαθὸν τοῖς ἀνθρώποις τῶν σπουδαζομένων οὐ συνεφάπτεται Gr.Nyss.*or.dom.*1(p.4.33; M.44.1121B); separation from God χωρίζεται δὲ τοῦ θεοῦ, ὁ μὴ συνάπτων ἑαυτὸν διὰ προσευχῆς τῷ θεῷ *ib.*(p.6.35; 1124A); χωρίζεται δὲ ἀπὸ θεοῦ πᾶς ἄνθρωπος, ὁ μὴ βουλόμενος διὰ προσευχῆς τῷ θεῷ συνάπτειν ἑαυτόν Nil.*epp.*3.261(M.79.516A); spiritual death, †Chrys.*hom.prec.*1(2.780C); cf.*ib.*(780D).

F. relation to virtues and other spiritual exercises; **1.** in gen.; **a.** prayer the fount of virtue, Mac.Aeg.*hom.*40.2(M.34.764B); cf.id.*or.*1(M.34.853A); Gr.Nyss.*or.dom.*1(p.8.3; M.44.1124A); κεφάλαιον εἶναι ἀγαθῶν τὴν π. φημι, καὶ κρηπῖδα καὶ ῥίζαν τοῦ λυσιτελοῦντος βίου †Chrys.*hom.prec.*1(2.782C); *ib.*2(783D); ἡ μήτηρ πασῶν τῶν ἀρετῶν π. Nil.*epp.*3.90(M.79.428C); ἡ π., ἀρετὴ λέγεται, κἂν μήτηρ αὐτῶν τυγχάνῃ· ἀπογεννᾷ γὰρ αὐτάς, διὰ τῆς εἰς Χριστὸν συναφείας Marc.Er.*opusc.*2.33(M.65.936B); **b.** prayer above virtues πασῶν τῶν ἀρετῶν π. θειοτέρα Evagr.Pont.*or.*150(M.79.1200A); ἡ π. ὑψηλοτέρα τυγχάνει πασῶν τῶν ἀρετῶν, καθαρὰ οὖσα καὶ θεῷ ἐγγίζουσα Ant.Mon.*hom.*106(M.89.1756C); **2.** in partic.; **a.** humility χωρὶς δὲ ταπεινοφροσύνης οὐκ ἔστιν εὐπρόσδεκτον γενέσθαι προσευχὴν Ant.Mon.*hom.*106(M.89.1757A); **b.** faith τῆς πίστεως τὴν εὐ. ἰσχυροτέραν ἀπέφηνεν ὁ σωτὴρ τοῖς πιστοῖς ἀποστόλοις...εἰπών· 'τὰ τοιαῦτα εὐχῇ κατορθοῦται' Clem.*ecl.*15(p.141.3; M.9.705A); ἡ εὐ. τῆς πίστεως σώσει τὸν κάμνοντα Eustrat.*v.Eutych.*45(M.86.2328A); Jo.Clim.*scal.*27(M.88.1113B) cit. s. πίστις; πίστις προσευχὴν ἐπτέρωσε· χωρὶς γὰρ ταύτης εἰς οὐρανὸν πετασθῆναι οὐ δύναται *ib.*28(1133C); **c.** charity τὴν τελείαν καὶ πνευματικὴν ἀγάπην, ἐν ᾗ ἡ π. ἐνεργεῖται ἐν πνεύματι καὶ ἀληθείᾳ Evagr.Pont.*or.*77(M.79.1184C); οὐ μικρὸς σύνδεσμος τῆς πρὸς θεὸν ἀγάπης ἡ εὐ. συνήθειαν ἡμῖν ἐμποιοῦσα τῆς πρὸς αὐτὸν ὁμιλίας, καὶ εἰς φιλοσοφίαν ἄγουσα Chrys.*exp.in Ps.*4:2(5.8A); ἀγάπην δὲ μοναχοῦ πρὸς θεὸν ἤλεγξε προσευχῆς καιρὸς καὶ παράστασις Jo.Clim.*scal.*28(M.88.1136B); **3.** prayer combined with fasting, almsgiving, etc. *2Clem.*16.4 cit. s. ἐλεημοσύνη; patience and fasting increasing its power, *T.Jos.*10.1; ἀεὶ μὲν οὖν μεγάλη τῆς εὐ. ἡ δύναμις· τὸ δὲ μετὰ νηστείας εἶναι εὐ., δυνατωτέραν ποιεῖ τὴν ψυχήν Chrys.*hom.in Ps.*145:2(5.531B); τοιοῦτον ἡ ἐλεημοσύνη, τοιοῦτον ἡ εὐ., μᾶλλον δὲ καὶ αὕτη παρ' ἐκείνης δυνατή, καὶ ὑπόπτερος γίνεται...οὐκ εὐ. δὲ μόνον, ἀλλὰ καὶ νηστεία ἐντεῦθεν τὰ νεῦρα ἔχει id.*hom.*77.6 *in Mt.*(7.749D,E); πῦρ ἐστιν ἡ εὐ. μάλιστα ὅταν ἀπὸ νηφούσης καὶ διεγηγερμένης ἀναπέμπηται ψυχῆς·...ἔλαιον δὲ τοῦ πυρὸς τούτου οὐδὲν ἕτερόν ἐστιν, ἀλλ' ἡ ἐλεημοσύνη id.*hom.*3.12 *in 2Cor.*4:13(3.290B); prayer and sexual abstinence καιρὸς γὰρ συνουσίας γυναικὸς καὶ καιρὸς ἐγκρατείας εἰς προσευχὴν αὐτοῦ *T.Neph.*8.8; ὅπου...πειρᾶται ἐμποδίζειν ἡμῖν κατὰ τὸν τῆς π. καιρὸν ὁ διάβολος...ὅπερ ἵνα μὴ πάθωμεν,...μηδὲ αὐτῷ προσκρούωμεν διὰ τῆς οὕτω ματαίας εὐ., κελεύει [sc. ὁ θεός] τῆς κοίτης ἀπηλλάχθαι τότε Chrys.*virg.*31(1.290D,E); id.*hom.*51.5 *in Mt.*(7.527A); **4.** prayer and good works 'ἀδιαλείπτως' δὲ προσεύχεται, καὶ τῶν ἔργων τῆς ἀρετῆς ἢ τῶν ἐντολῶν τῶν ἐπιτελουμένων εἰς εὐχῆς ἀναλαμβανομένων μέρος, ὁ συνάπτων τοῖς δέουσιν ἔργοις τὴν εὐ. καὶ τῇ εὐ. τὰς πρεπούσας πράξεις Or.*or.*12.2(p.324.26f.; M.11.452C); ἐὰν εὐ. τῆς σπουδῆς προηγήσηται, ἡ ἁμαρτία πάροδον κατὰ τῆς ψυχῆς οὐχ εὑρήσει Gr.Nyss.*or.dom.*1(p.6.19; M.44.1121D); *ib.*(p.8.3; 1124A); Chrys.*exp. in Ps.*140:5(5.440D); οὔτε εὐ. χωρὶς ἔργων, οὔτε ἔργα χωρὶς εὐ. τίθησι id.*hom.*32.2 *in Rom.*(9.756A); σπούδαζε...προσκαρτερεῖν ταῖς ἁγίαις εὐ. ... κἂν μὴ σχολάζωσιν αἱ χεῖρες, εὔχου τῇ διανοίᾳ ‡Chrys.*pat.et consumm.*(12.818A); **5.** prayer and sacrifice almost identical; discussion of Mal.1:10 interpreted as referring to Christian sacrifices λέγετε [sc. Jews] ὅτι...προσδέχεται ὁ θεός, τὰς...διὰ τῶν ἐν τῇ διασπορᾷ τότε δὴ ὄντων...εὐχὰς προσίεσθαι αὐτὸν εἰρηκέναι, καὶ τὰς εὐ. αὐτῶν θυσίας καλεῖν Just.*dial.*117.2(M.6.745B); δι' εὐχῆς τιμῶμεν τὸν θεόν, καὶ ταύτην τὴν θυσίαν ἀρίστην καὶ ἁγιωτάτην μετὰ δικαιοσύνην ἀναπέμπομεν Clem.*str.*7.6(p.23.24; M.9.444A).

G. corporate and liturg. prayer; **1.** power of corporate prayer in gen. εἰ γὰρ ἑνὸς καὶ δευτέρου προσευχὴ τοσαύτην ἰσχὺν ἔχει, πόσῳ μᾶλλον ἥ τε τοῦ ἐπισκόπου καὶ πάσης τῆς ἐκκλησίας; Ign.*Eph.*5.2; τί γὰρ ἐν τῇ οἰκίᾳ οὐ δύναμαι εὔξασθαι; δύνασαι μὲν εὔξασθαι, οὐ τοσαύτην δὲ δύναμιν ἔχει ἡ εὐ., ὡς ὅταν μετὰ τῶν μελῶν τῶν οἰκείων γίνηται, ὡς ὅταν ὁλόκληρον τὸ σῶμα τῆς ἐκκλησίας ὁμοθυμαδὸν ἀναπέμπῃ τὴν δέησιν μιᾷ φωνῇ, ἱερέων παρόντων, καὶ τὰς εὐ. τοῦ κοινοῦ πλήθους ἀναφερόντων Chrys.*proph.obscurit.*2.4(6.187D); *ib.*2.5(188C); efficacy of Church's prayer for S. Peter in prison a favourite example, *ib.*(187E); †Chrys.*hom.prec.*2(2.788C); **2.** liturg. prayer; **a.** in gen., of prayers said at celebration of eucharist ἀνιστάμεθα κοινῇ πάντες καὶ εὐ. πέμπομεν Just.*1apol.*67.5(M.6.429B); οὗ συντελέσαντος τὰς εὐ. καὶ τὴν εὐχαριστίαν *ib.*65.3(428B); at baptism, for newly baptized μετὰ τὸ οὕτως λοῦσαι τὸν πεπεισμένον...ἐπὶ τοὺς λεγομένους ἀδελφοὺς ἄγομεν...κοινὰς εὐ. ποιησόμενοι ὑπέρ τε ἑαυτῶν καὶ φωτισθέντος *ib.*65.1(428A); for catechumens who have not been taught the Lord's Prayer ὅταν γὰρ ὁ διάκονος λέγῃ, 'ὑπὲρ τῶν κατηχουμένων ἐκτενῶς δεηθῶμεν', οὐδὲν ἄλλο ἢ τὸν δῆμον ἅπαντα τῶν πιστῶν διανίστησιν εἰς τὰς ὑπὲρ ἐκείνων εὐχὰς...οὐδέπω γὰρ εὐχὴν ἔχουσι τὴν νενομισμένην καὶ εἰσενεχθεῖσαν ὑπὸ τοῦ Χριστοῦ...διὰ τοῦτο καὶ ἀπελαύνονται, τῶν φρικτῶν εὐ. ἐκείνων γινομένων Chrys.*hom.*2.5 *in 2Cor.*(10.435B,C); at ordination, Pall.*v.Chrys.*16(p.96.14; M.47.54); **b.** esp. of prayers of synaxis, preceding Mass of Faithful, to which certain categories of penitents were admitted ...ἐὰν μὲν κατηγορηθέντες ἐλεγχθῶσιν, ὁμοίως ἐν τοῖς ὑποπίπτουσιν· ἐὰν δὲ ἑαυτοὺς ἐξείπωσι καὶ ἀποδῶσι, καὶ τῆς εὐ. ἀξιῶσαι Gr.Thaum.*ep.can.*9(M.10.1044D); περὶ τῶν πρὸς βίαν θυσάντων...εὐ. δὲ μόνης κοινωνῆσαι ἔτη δύο, καὶ τότε ἐλθεῖν ἐπὶ τὸ τέλειον CAnc.(314)*can.*4; ὅσοι...ἥμαρτον πέντε καὶ δέκα ἔτεσιν ὑποπεσόντες κοινωνίας τυγχανέτωσαν τῆς εἰς τὰς προσευχάς, εἶτα ἐν τῇ κοινωνίᾳ διατελέσαντες ἔτη πέντε, τότε καὶ τῆς προσφορᾶς ἐφαπτέσθωσαν *ib.*16; *ib.*24; οὗτοι πληρώσαντες τὸν χρόνον τὸν ὡρισμένον τῆς ἀκροάσεως, εἰκότως τῶν εὐ. κοινωνήσουσι, μετὰ τοῦ ἐξεῖναι τῷ ἐπισκόπῳ, καὶ φιλανθρωπότερόν τι περὶ αὐτῶν βουλεύσασθαι CNic.(325)*can.*12; *ib.*13; and from which others were excluded ἐκεῖνον [sc. one who has committed rape] ἐξόρισον τῶν εὐ., καὶ ἐκκήρυκτον ποίησον· καὶ τοὺς συνεπελθόντας αὐτῷ...τριετίαν πανοικεὶ τῶν εὐ. ἐξόρισον. καὶ τὴν κώμην τὴν ὑποδεξαμένην τὴν ἁρπαγεῖσαν...ἔξω τῶν εὐ. πανδημεὶ ποίησον Bas.*ep.*270(3.416E; M.32.1001D–1004A); ὑπὲρ δὲ τοῦ μὴ ὑμᾶς μολύνεσθαι ἐν κοινωνίᾳ τῶν ἁμαρτημάτων, πανοικεὶ τῶν εὐ. κεχωρίσθω *ib.*287(426C; M.1024B); τοὺς ἐν πορνείᾳ μολυνθέντας, ἐν τρισὶ μὲν ἔτεσι καθόλου τῆς εὐ. ἀποβλήτους εἶναι Gr.Nyss.*ep.can.*(M.45.229A); **c.** of three prayers at beginning of Mass of Faithful τῶν ἐν μετανοίᾳ...προσελθόντων ὑπὸ χεῖρα καὶ ὑποχωρησάντων, οὕτως τῶν πιστῶν τὰς εὐ. γίνεσθαι τρεῖς· μίαν μὲν τὴν πρώτην διὰ σιωπῆς, τὴν δὲ δευτέραν καὶ τρίτην διὰ προσφωνήσεως πληροῦσθαι, εἶθ' οὕτως τὴν εἰρήνην δίδοσθαι CLaod.*can*.19; cf. ἐν τῇδε τῇ ἡμέρᾳ...ἐν ᾗ καὶ τρεῖς εὐ. ἑστῶτες ἐπιτελοῦμεν μνήμης χάριν τοῦ διὰ τριῶν ἀναστάντος ἡμερῶν, ἐν ᾗ προφητῶν ἀνάγνωσις καὶ εὐαγγελίου κηρυκία καὶ θυσίας ἀναφορὰ καὶ τροφῆς ἱερᾶς δωρεά *Const.App*.2.59.4; cf.*ib*.7.45.3; οἱ τὴν πρώτην εὐ. εὐχόμενοι προσέλθετε *Lit*.ap.*Const.App*.8.12.2; of all prayers between Lessons and Communion πάντας τοὺς εἰσιόντας πιστοὺς καὶ τῶν γραφῶν ἀκούοντας, μὴ παραμένοντας δὲ τῇ π. καὶ τῇ ἁγίᾳ μεταλήψει, ὡς ἀταξίαν ἐμποιοῦντας τῇ ἐκκλησίᾳ, ἀφορίζεσθαι χρή *Can.App*.10; CAnt.(341)*can*.2; **d.** of consecration prayer δι' εὐχῆς λόγου τοῦ παρ' αὐτοῦ [sc. Χριστοῦ] εὐχαριστηθεῖσαν τροφήν, ἐξ ἧς αἷμα καὶ σάρκες κατὰ μεταβολὴν τρέφονται ἡμῶν Just.*1apol*.66.2(M.6.428C); ἐπ' ἂν δὲ ἐπιτελεσθῶσιν μεγάλαι...εὐ., τότε γίνεται ὁ ἄρτος, σῶμα, καὶ τὸ ποτήριον, αἷμα τοῦ κυρίου ἡμῶν Ἰησοῦ Χριστοῦ...οὗτος ὁ ἄρτος καὶ τοῦτο τὸ ποτήριον, ὅσον οὔπω εὐχαὶ...γεγόνασι, ψιλά εἰσιν· ἐπὰν δὲ αἱ μεγάλαι εὐ. ... ἀναπεμφθῶσι, καταβαίνει ὁ λόγος εἰς τὸν ἄρτον καὶ τὸ ποτήριον, καὶ γίνεται αὐτοῦ σῶμα †Ath.ap.Eutych.*pasch*.8(M.86.2401A,B); **e.** of whole liturgical service ἐπιχώριοι πρεσβύτεροι ἐν τῷ κυριακῷ τῆς πόλεως προσφέρειν οὐ δύνανται, παρόντος ἐπισκόπου ἢ πρεσβυτέρου πόλεως, οὔτε μὲν ἄρτον διδόναι ἐν εὐχῇ, οὐδὲ ποτήριον. ἐὰν δὲ ἀπῶσι, καὶ εἰς εὐχὴν κληθῇ μόνος, δίδωσιν CNeocaes.*can*.13; ὁ μὲν ἱεράρχης, εὐ. ἱερὰν ἐπὶ τοῦ θείου θυσιαστηρίου τελέσας Dion.Ar.*e.h*.3.1.2 (M.3.425B); **f.** of other liturg. prayers: daily offices, CLaod.*can*.18 cit. s. λειτουργία; Bas.*ep*.99.1(3.193B; M.32.497C); at communion of the sick ποιήσας τὴν συνήθη εὐ., μετέδωκεν αὐτῷ τῆς ἀχράντου κοινωνίας Eustrat.*v.Eutych*.48(M.86.2329B); litanies κοινὰς ποιούμεθα τὰς εὐ., λιτανεύοντες ὑπὲρ νοσούντων Chrys.*hom.78.4 in Jo*.(8.464D).

H. prayer for dead ποιήσωμεν εὐ. ὑπὲρ τῆς ψυχῆς ταύτης...καὶ ἐποίησαν δέησιν καὶ εὐ. ὑπὲρ τῆς ψυχῆς· καὶ εἰσήκουσεν αὐτοὺς ὁ θεὸς καὶ ἀναστάντες ἀπὸ τῆς π. οὐκ εἶδον τὴν ψυχὴν ἱσταμένην ἐκεῖσε...καὶ εἶπεν ὁ ἄγγελος· σέσωσται διὰ τῆς εὐ. σου τῆς δικαίας, καὶ ἰδοὺ ἔλαβεν αὐτὴν ἄγγελος φωτοφόρος καὶ ἀνήνεγκεν αὐτὴν ἐν τῷ παραδείσῳ *T.Abr*. A 14(p.94.2–8); ὅτι δὲ καὶ τῶν δικαίων αἱ κατὰ τὸν τῇδε βίον, μήτι γε μετὰ θάνατον, εἰς τοὺς ἀξίους ἱερῶν εὐ. ἐνεργοῦσι μόνον, αἱ τῶν λογίων ἡμᾶς ἐκδιδάσκουσιν ἀληθεῖς παραδόσεις Dion.Ar.*e.h*.7.3.6(M.3.561A); rejection by heretics denounced ⟨εἰ⟩ εὔχεται, γάρ φησιν [sc. Aërius], ὁ ζῶν...τί ὠφεληθήσεται ὁ τεθνεώς; εἰ δὲ ὅλως εὐ. τῶν ἐνταῦθα τοὺς ἐκεῖσε ὤνησεν, ἄρα γοῦν μηδεὶς εὐσεβείτω...ἀλλὰ κτησάσθω φίλους τινὰς...καὶ εὐχέσθωσαν περὶ αὐτοῦ, ἵνα μή τι ἐκεῖ πάθῃ Epiph.*haer*.75.3 (p.335.6; M.42.508A); εἰ δὲ καὶ ἁμαρτωλὸς ἀπῆλθε...δεῖ...βοηθεῖν...εὐ. καὶ ἱκετηρίαις Chrys.*hom.41.4 in 1Cor*.(10.392E); μὴ δὴ ἀποκάμωμεν τοῖς ἀπελθοῦσι βοηθοῦντες, καὶ προσφέροντες ὑπὲρ αὐτῶν, καὶ ἀξιοῦντες εὐ. ὑπὲρ αὐτῶν τελεῖσθαι *ib.41*.5(393B).

I. intercessory prayers; **1.** of living ἐλπίζουσα τῇ π. ὑμῶν ἐπιτυχεῖν ἐν Ῥώμῃ θηριομαχῆσαι Ign.*Eph*.1.2; μνημονεύετέ μου ἐν ταῖς π. ὑμῶν, ἵνα θεοῦ ἐπιτύχω id.*Magn*.14; ἡ π. ὑμῶν εἰς θεόν με ἀπαρτίσει id.*Philad*.5.1; δίδωσι γὰρ οὕτως καὶ τὴν εὐ. τοῖς δεομένοις ὁ γνωστικὸς καὶ τὸ διὰ τῆς εὐ. ἀγνώστως ἅμα καὶ ἀτύφως παρέχεται Clem.*str*.7.13(p.58.12f.; M.9.513A); σκεπόμεθα τῇ χειρὶ τοῦ κυρίου ἐν τῷ κόσμῳ κατά τινα χρείαν διάγοντες, ἴσως ἐξ εὐ. τοῦ πατρὸς [sc. πνευματικοῦ] πολλάκις, ἵνα μὴ καὶ ὁ κύριος βλασφημηθῇ δι' ἡμᾶς Jo.Clim.*scal*.15(M.88.893B); as taught by Christ, Chrys.*hom.19.4 in Mt*.(7.249E); **2.** of saints in heaven εἰς τοὺς ἁγίους τούτους ὁρῶντες... ἵνα ταῖς εὐ. αὐτῶν δυνηθῶμεν...πρὸς τὰς οὐρανίους αὐτῶν καταταχθῆναι σκηνάς Chrys.*pan.Aeg*.2(2.703A); needing men's co-operation οὔτε τὸ πᾶν ταῖς εὐ. τῶν ἁγίων ἐπιτρέψαντας αὐτοὺς ἀργεῖν χρή...μεγάλα ἡ εὐ. ἡ ὑπὲρ ἡμῶν, ἀλλ' ὅταν καὶ ἡμεῖς ἐργαζώμεθα Chrys.*hom.5.1 in 2Thes*.(11.536E); γένοιτο δὲ εὐχαῖς τῶν ἁγίων...οὐ γὰρ δὴ τοσοῦτον ἡμῶν ἰσχύει τὰ ῥήματα, ὅσον τῆς ἐκείνων εὐ. ἡ παρρησία ‡Chrys.*prov*.2(2.760C,D); ὠφέλιμοι...εἰσὶν ἐν τῷδε τῷ βίῳ τῶν ἁγίων αἱ π. Dion.Ar.*e.h*.7.3.6(M.3.561B); ἐνικήσαμεν...εὐχαῖς πάντων τῶν ἁγίων Dor.*doct*.15.4(M.88.1793C); γένοιτο δὲ ἡμᾶς...εὐχαῖς πάντων τῶν ἁγίων πατριαρχῶν, προφητῶν, ἀποστόλων, μαρτύρων, ὁμολογητῶν, διδασκάλων, συναριθμίους τοῖς ἐκ δεξιῶν γενέσθαι Cosm.Ind.*top*.5 (M.88.313D); ὁ εἷς θεός, οὗ καὶ ἡμεῖς τῆς λαμπρᾶς βασιλείας, εὐχαῖς τῆς ὑπεράγνου θεοτόκου τύχοιμεν, καὶ εὐ. τῶν ὁσίων πατέρων ἡμῶν Hesych.S.*temp*.2.100(M.93.1544D); **3.** of angels, ‡Ath.*comm.essent*. 52(M.28.77B).

J. Lord's Prayer, its special power τοῦ κυρίου π., ὅσης δυνάμεως πεπλήρωται Or.*or*.18.1(p.340.8; M.11.473B); τὰ γὰρ τῆς π. ῥήματα θεραπεία ἐστὶ τῆς ἐγγινομένης τῇ ψυχῇ ἀρρωστίας Gr.Nyss.*or.dom*.4 (p.70.10; M.44.1164A); containing divine teaching on prayer, *ib*.1 (p.1.1,5; 1120B); *ib*.2(p.30.4; 1137C); εἰ τῶν ἐπιθυμιῶν ταῖς ἐμπαθεστέραις δουλεύοις, ἔπειτα τὴν τοιαύτην π. διὰ στόματος λάβοις· τί οἴει ἐρεῖν τὸν εἰς τὸν βίον σου βλέποντα, καὶ τῆς π. ἐπαΐοντα; *ib*.(p.36. 19,20; 1141D); ὁρᾷς εἰς ὅσον μέγεθος ὑψοῖ τοὺς ἀκούοντας διὰ τῶν τῆς π. ῥημάτων ὁ κύριος; *ib*.5(p.94.20; 1177D); τοῦτο δὲ ἡλίκον ἐστὶν [sc. to say ἀββᾶ ὁ πατήρ] ἴσασιν οἱ μύσται, καλῶς ἐπὶ τῆς εὐ. τῆς μυστικῆς τοῦτο πρῶτον κελευόμενοι τὸ ῥῆμα λέγειν Chrys.*hom.14.3 in Rom*.(9. 578E).

II. *vow*;

A. in gen. οὐ γὰρ ἄν, πολλὰ πολλῶν κατ' εὐχὰς ἐν τῷ νόμῳ κατεργασαμένων, μόνοι μεγάλην εὐ. ἐλέγοντο πληροῦν οἱ σφᾶς αὐτοὺς αὐθαιρέτῳ βουλῇ προσενέγκαντες θεῷ Meth.*symp*.5.1(p.53.10; M.18. 97A); μεγάλην εὐ. εἶναι παρὰ πάσας εὐ. ἀποδεικνύουσα τὴν ἁγνείαν *ib*. 5.4(p.56.19; M.18.101B); ἀποδίδωμι τὰς εὐ. μου *Const.App*.1.7.6; of vow of virginity, *ib*.4.14.1; εὐ. καλεῖ τὴν ὑπόσχεσιν, ὃ πολλοὶ τάγμα προσαγορεύουσι Thdt.*qu.38 in Lev*.(1.215); Proc.G.*Num*.30:3(M.87. 880A).

B. as formula of adjuration μὰ τὴν εὐ. †Gregent.*leg.Hom*.(M. 86.537B).

III. *permission* ἐξ εὐ. τοῦ πατρός Jo.Clim.*scal*.15(M.88.893B); so perh. also λαβὼν τὴν εὐ. παρ' αὐτῶν, καὶ εὐλογήσας, ἀπῆλθεν *T.Abr*. A 5(p.82.8).

***εὐχῆται, οἱ,** v. sq.

***εὐχῖται, οἱ,** members of a sect, also called Messalians, which over-emphasized importance of prayer to detriment of sacraments and eccl. discipline; teaching described, Thdt.*haer*.4.11(4.366–8); id.*h.e*.4.11.1(3.964); anathematized, CEph.(431)cit.ap.CNic.(787) *act*.1(H.4.56A); mode of reconciliation to Church, Cyr.*ep*.82(p.20. 14; M.77.376A); Μαρκιανισταὶ καὶ Μεσσαλιανοὶ καὶ εὐτυχῖται [perh. for εὐ.] καὶ ἐνθουσιασταὶ καὶ χορευταὶ καὶ Λαμπετιανοὶ καὶ Ἀδελφιανοὶ καὶ Εὐσταθιανοί· οὕτως προσαγορευόμενοι, διὰ τὸ πολυώνυμον εἶναι τὴν αἵρεσιν Tim.CP *haer*.(M.86.45C); εὐχῆται Philox.*ep*.35 (p.182); Thphn.*chron*.p.54(εὐχῖται M.108.189A).

***εὐχολόγιον, τό,** *Euchologion, Ritual*, a book for use of priest containing rites and ceremonies of Church ἔστιν εὐχὴ εἰς αὐτὸ τοῦτο ἐν τῷ εὐ. Anast.S.*qu.et resp*.141(M.89.793B).

εὔχομαι (with προσεύχομαι), *pray, offer prayer*; **1.** necessity of praying τὸ εὔχεσθαι ὑπὲρ πάντων· τοῦτο ἀποδέχεται ὁ θεός, τοῦτο θέλει Chrys.*hom.7.1 in 1Tim*.(11.585A); ὅστις γὰρ οὐ προσεύχεται τῷ θεῷ, οὐδὲ θείας ὁμιλίας ἀπολαύειν ἐπιθυμεῖ συνεχῶς, νεκρός ἐστι καὶ ἄψυχος †Chrys.*hom.prec*.1(2.780B); esp. of praying for all men παρακελεύεται...ὁ ἀπόστολος, ὑπὲρ πάντων ἀνθρώπων προσεύχεσθαι. τὸ δὲ εὔχεσθαι ὑπὲρ πάντων σημαίνει, ὅτι οὐ μόνον ὑπὲρ τῶν φίλων, ἀλλὰ καὶ ὑπὲρ τῶν ἐχθρῶν δεῖ προσεύχεσθαι Ant.Mon.*hom*.72(M.89. 1645A,B); **2.** prayer to be offered to Father through Christ προσεύχεσθαι μόνῳ τῷ θεῷ τῷ τῶν ὅλων πατρί. ἀλλὰ μὴ χωρὶς τοῦ ἀρχιερέως Or.*or*.15.1(p.334.13; M.11.465B); but, acc. Origen, not to Christ μόνῳ τῷ πατρὶ προσεύχεσθαι χρή...ἀρχιερεῖ γὰρ τῷ ὑπὲρ ὑμῶν κατασταθέντι...προσεύχεσθαι ὑμᾶς οὐ δεῖ *ib*.15.4(p.335.18; 468A); *ib*.16.1(p.336. 6; 468C) cit. s. ἁμαρτία; not to angels ἡ ἐν Λαοδικείᾳ σύνοδος... ἐνομοθέτησε μὴ εὔχεσθαι ἀγγέλοις Thdt.*Col*.3:17(3.496); cf.CLaod. *can*.35; **3.** prayer to be made for contrition πρότερον περὶ λήψεως δακρύων προσεύχου Evagr.Pont.*or*.5(M.79.1168D); Ant.Mon.*hom*.106 (M.89.1757A); for purification προσεύχου πρότερον περὶ τοῦ καθαρθῆναι τῶν παθῶν, καὶ δεύτερον περὶ τοῦ ῥυσθῆναι ἀπὸ τῆς ἀγνωσίας, καὶ τρίτον ἀπὸ παντὸς πειρασμοῦ καὶ ἐγκαταλείψεως Evagr.Pont.*or*.37 (1176A); δίκαιον, μὴ μόνον περὶ οἰκείας καθάρσεως προσεύχεσθαι, ἀλλὰ καὶ περὶ παντὸς ὁμοφύλου *ib*.39(1176B); not for transitory things, Chrys.*hom.in Mt*.7:14(3.26E); **4.** conditions for praying well; **a.** moral purity, Or.*or*.9.3(p.319.14; M.11.445A); εἰ δὲ ἐξασθενήσας ὑπὸ τῆς ἁμαρτίας, ἀπερισπάστως οὐ δύνασαι εὔχεσθαι ‡Bas.*const*.1.4 (2.538D; M.31.1333B); Evagr.Pont.*or*.17(M.79.1172A); οὐ μόνον θυμοῦ, καὶ ἐπιθυμίας δεῖ ἄρχειν τὸν ἀληθῶς προσεύξασθαι ἐπειγόμενον, ἀλλὰ καὶ ἐκτὸς ἐμπαθοῦς νοήματος γενέσθαι *ib*.53(1177C); **b.** recollection πάντως ὤνατό τι ὁ πρὸς τὸ εὔξασθαι ταθεὶς κατὰ τὸν νοῦν, δι' αὐτῆς τῆς ἐν τῷ εὔχεσθαι καταστάσεως θεῷ παριστάναι ἑαυτὸν καὶ παρόντι ἐκείνῳ λέγειν σχηματίσας ὡς ἐφορῶντι καὶ παρόντι Or.*or*.8.2(p.317.7f.; M.11.441B); προσεύχου εὐτόνως, καὶ ἀποστρέφου τὰς τῶν φροντίδων καὶ διαλογισμῶν ἐπιτεύξεις Evagr.Pont.*or*.9(1169B); ἐνώπιον γὰρ κυρίου εὔχεται, ὁ πάντοθεν ἑαυτοῦ τὴν ψυχὴν συλλέγων, καὶ μηδὲν ἔχων κοινὸν πρὸς τὴν γῆν...καὶ πάντα ἀνθρώπινον λογισμὸν ἀπὸ τῆς ψυχῆς ἐκβαλὼν Chrys.*Anna* 2.2(4.713E); ὁ γνησίως τὸν θεὸν ἀγαπῶν, οὗτος καὶ ἀπερισπάστως πάντως προσεύχεται· καὶ ὁ ἀπερισπάστως πάντως προσευχόμενος, οὗτος καὶ γνησίως τὸν θεὸν ἀγαπᾷ. οὐκ εὔχεται δὲ ἀπερισπάστως, ὅ τινι ἐπιγείων ἔχων τὸν νοῦν προσηλωμένον· οὐκ ἄρα ἀγαπᾷ τὸν θεόν, ὅ τινι τῶν ἐπιγείων ἔχων τὸν νοῦν δεδεμένον Max. *carit*.2.1(M.90.984B); **5.** effects of praying: prevention of sin, Or.*or*. 8.2(p.317.22; M.11.441D); ἀμήχανον...ἄνθρωπον μετὰ τῆς προσηκούσης προθυμίας εὐχόμενον...ἁμαρτεῖν ποτε Chrys.*Anna* 4.5(4.736D); fuller knowledge of how to pray εἰ μηδὲν ἕτερον ἡμῖν ἐπακολουθήσει εὐχομένοις, ὅτι τὰ κάλλιστα κερδαίνομεν, τὸ καθὸ δεῖ εὔχεσθαι νενοηκότες καὶ κατορθοῦντες Or.*or*.10.1(p.319.19; 445A); purification of soul as by fire, Chrys.*hom*.5.4 *in 2Cor*.(10.470D); **6.** assistance of Christ and angels at prayer ὁ υἱὸς τοῦ θεοῦ, εὐχόμενος ὑπὲρ τῶν εὐχομένων ...οὐκ ἂν ὡς ὑπὲρ οἰκείων εὐξόμενος τῶν μὴ δι' αὐτοῦ συνεχέστερον εὐχομένων Or.*or*.10.2(p.320.21ff.; M.11.445D); οὐ μόνος δὲ ὁ ἀρχιερεὺς τοῖς γνησίως εὐχομένοις συνεύχεται ἀλλὰ καὶ οἱ ἐν οὐρανῷ χαίροντες ἄγγελοι *ib*.11.1(p.321.15; 448D); **7.** temptations when praying ὅταν ἴδωσιν οἱ δαίμονες προθυμούμενόν σε ἀληθῶς προσεύξασθαι, τότε ὑποτίθενται νοήματά τινων πραγμάτων δῆθεν ἀναγκαίων Evagr.Pont. *or*.10(M.79.1169B); λίαν βασκαίνει ὁ δαίμων ἀνθρώπῳ προσευχομένῳ, καὶ πάσῃ χρᾶται μηχανῇ, λυμήνασθαι τὸν τούτου σκοπόν *ib*.46(1176D); **8.** partic. duties of women at prayer τὴν γυναῖκα χρὴ ἔχειν μάλιστα εὐχομένην τὸ κατεσταλμένον καὶ τὸ κόσμιον ψυχῇ καὶ σώματι, πάντων μᾶλλον ἐξαιρέτως καὶ ὅτε εὔχεται αἰδουμένην τὸν θεὸν καὶ πᾶσαν ἀκόλαστον καὶ γυναικείαν ὑπόμνησιν ἐξορίσασαν ἀπὸ τοῦ ἡγεμονικοῦ Or. *or*.9.1(p.318.8; M.11.444A); **9.** προσεύχομαι dist. from εὔχομαι: εὔξασθαι γὰρ χρὴ πρότερον, εἶτα προσεύξασθαι Gr.Nyss.*or.dom*.2(p.30. 27,28; M.44.1140A); cf. εὐχή.

εὔχορτος, *very grassy*, Nonn.*par.Jo*.6:23(M.43.797B).

εὐχροέω, *be of a good colour* βαφῆς Gr.Nyss.*hom*.2 *in Cant*.(M.44. 788C); ὕλην id.*or.dom*.5(p.104.37; M.44.1185C).

εὔχροια, ἡ, *fair colour*; of metals, Bas.*hom*.13.3(2.116A; M.31. 429A); *ib*.6.4(46C; M.264C); Gr.Nyss.*v.Mos*.(M.44.380C); of flowers, id.ap.Proc.G.*Cant*.2:1(M.87.1576C); of garments, Isid.Pel.*epp*.1.74 (M.78.233B); plur., Bas.*hex*.2.1(1.12D; M.29.29A); Zach.Mit.*opif*.(M. 85.1025A); met. τῆς ἀληθείας τὴν εὐ. Cyr.*Jo*.4.6(4.422B).

εὔχροος, *beautifully coloured* χρυσὸς εὐχροώτερος Gr.Nyss.*hom*. 4 *in Cant*.(M.44.832A); Nonn.*par.Jo*.2:10(M.43.761B).

***εὐχρωματίστως**, *with fine colours*, Andr.Cr.*or*.16(M.97.1153B).

***εὔχρωτος**, *of good complexion*, *T.Sal*.4.2(M.122.1320D) = *ib*.C 11.2.

***εὐχυμίζω**, *make palatable*, Sophr.H.*v.Cyr.et Jo*.10(M.87.3392A).

εὔχυμος, 1. *wholesome* τὸ πάντων εὐχυμότερον...ἔδεσμα ‡Chrys. *prov*.1(2.753B); **2.** *in good condition* σῶμα Dor.*doct*.16.3(M.88.1797C).

***εὔψοος**, prob. f.l. for εὔψοφος, *well-sounding*, Ephr.3.44C.

εὐψυχέω, 1. *be of good courage*, Herm.*vis*.1.3.2; *A.Jo*.6(p.154.8); **2.** c. infin., *dare* to εὐ. εἰσελθεῖν Call.*v.Hyp*.(p.26); *have the heart* to μὴ εὐ. καταπιεῖν αὐτὸ [sc. τὸ βρῶμα] διὰ τὴν ἡδονήν Dor.*doct*.15.2(M. 88.1789B).

§εὐψυχία, ἡ, *coolness* μήτε ἐν ἡμέρᾳ μέσῃ...ἀλλὰ...σκιᾶς ἀπολαύοντες καὶ εὐ. Chrys.*hom*.31.5 *in Jo*.(8.182C).

εὐψύχως, *courageously*, Mac.Aeg.*carit*.27(M.34.929C); id.*libert. ment*.13(M.34.945A); Thdr.Stud.*epp*.2.206(M.99.1625B).

εὐωδέω, *be fragrant*, Gr.Naz.*ep*.17(M.37.61C); id.*or*.14.17(M.35. 877C); Thdr.Stud.*epp*.1.54(M.99.1108B).

εὐώδης, *sweet-smelling, fragrant*, met. τὸ εὐαγγέλιον Chrys.*hom*. 5.2 *in 2Cor*.(10.467C); αἱ τοῦ θεοῦ κρύφιαι καὶ ὑπὲρ νοῦν εὐ. εὐπρέπειαι Dion.Ar.*e.h*.4.3.1(M.3.473B); εἶναι...'Ἰησοῦν ὑπερουσίως εὐ. *ib*.4.3.4(477C); neut. as subst. Χριστοῦ τὸ εὐ. ἐν ἐκκλησίᾳ Cyr.*ador*.9 (1.309D); id.*Os*.160(3.193A); Dion.Ar.*e.h*.4.3.1(476A).

εὐωδία, ἡ, 1. *sweet smell, fragrance*; **a.** lit.; of odour of sanctity παρέδωκε τὸ πνεῦμα [sc. Sisoes]...καὶ ἐπλήσθη ὅλος ὁ οἶκος εὐωδίας *Apophth.Patr*.(M.65.396C); ἐκ τοῦ τιμίου αὐτοῦ λειψάνου μύρων ἰαματικὴν εὐ. πᾶσιν ἀναβλύσαι Leont.N.*v.Jo.Eleem*.46(p.102.2,11); cf. πολλάκις εὐ. ἐξέρχεσθαι ἐκ τοῦ στόματος αὐτοῦ id.*v.Sym*.51(M.93. 1733A); its symbolism, exeg. Cant.2:3 εὐ. ἥτις χαρακτηρίζει τὴν πίστιν Ph.Carp.*Cant*.37(M.40.61A); **b.** fig.; in gen. εὐ. πνευματικῆς Or.*schol.in Cant*.7:4–5(M.17.281D); Cyr.*ador*.17(1.624B); τῆς θεαρχικῆς εὐ. Dion.Ar.*e.h*.4.3.4(M.3.477D); of Father οὐ δεῖται...τῆς ἀπὸ τῶν ἀνθῶν καὶ θυμιαμάτων εὐ., αὐτὸς ὢν ἡ τελεία εὐ. Athenag.*leg*.13.1 (M.6.916B); σοὶ τῷ πεπληρωμένῳ πάσης εὐ. καὶ εὐφροσύνης *Lit.Jac*. (p.168.24); of Christ ὥσπερ ἡ σωματικὴ εὐ. τινὰ τῶν ζῴων λέγεται ἀναιρεῖν, οὕτως διὰ τὴν προγενομένην κακίαν καὶ ἡ Χριστοῦ εὐ. γένοιτο ἂν τισιν τοῖς ἐκ θανάτου εἰς θάνατον αὐτῶν Or.*Jo*.20.44(33; p.388.9ff.; M.14.677B); τοῦτο τὸ μύρον δὸς ἐνεργὲς γενέσθαι ἐπὶ τῷ βαπτιζομένῳ, ὥστε βεβαίαν καὶ πάγιον ἐν αὐτῷ τὴν εὐ. μεῖναι τοῦ Χριστοῦ σου *Const.App*.7.44.2; γένοιτο δὲ πάντας ἡμᾶς...τὴν εὐ. τοῦ Χριστοῦ ἔχειν Chrys.*hom*.52.4 *in Jo*.(8.309E); καὶ τὸ 'Χριστοῦ δὲ εὐ.' διπλῆν μοι τὴν ἐξήγησιν ἔχειν δοκεῖ. ἢ γὰρ τοῦτό φησιν, ὅτι ἑαυτοὺς θυσίαν προσέφερον ἀποθνήσκοντες, ἢ ὅτι τῆς τοῦ Χριστοῦ σφαγῆς εὐ. εἰσίν id.*hom*.5.2 *in 2Cor*.(10.467E); πῶς οὖν ὁ ἐκ θεοῦ πατρὸς λόγος ὀσμή τις καὶ εὐ. νοεῖται τοῦ θεοῦ καὶ πατρός, εἴπερ ἐστὶν ἑτεροφυής; Cyr.*2Cor*.2:14(p.329.9n.); of H. Ghost, Cyr.H.*procatech*.1; εἰ δὲ τὸ πνεῦμα εὐ. καὶ μορφὴ τοῦ υἱοῦ ἐστιν, εὔδηλον ὡς οὐκ ἂν εἴη τὸ πνεῦμα κτίσμα Ath.*ep.Serap*.2.3(M.26.629A); Χριστοῦ γάρ ἐστιν εὐ. τὸ πνεῦμα ...καὶ οἱ ἀπόστολοι Χριστοῦ εὐ. ἦσαν, καὶ εἰσίν· ἐπειδὴ καὶ ναοὶ τοῦ πνεύματός εἰσι ‡Ath.*dial.Trin*.1.7(M.28.1128B); ἡ εὐ. τοῦ θυμιάματος μηνύει τὴν εὐ. τοῦ πνεύματος Jo.Jej.*liturg*.(p.441); in Sethian theory ἡ τοῦ πνεύματος εὐ. μέσην ἔχουσα τάξιν ἐκτείνεται καὶ φέρεται πανταχῇ Hipp.*haer*.5.19(p.117.6; M.16.3179B); **2.** *fragrant substance*, Ath.*virg*. 6(p.40.7; M.28.257C); met. καταργήθητι...ἀπὸ εὐ. ἧς κοινωνεῖν μέλλεις *A.Jo*.84(p.192.29).

εὐωδιάζ-ω, 1. abs., *smell sweet, be fragrant* ἀτμὸς ~ων Gr.Nyss. *hom*.5 *in Cant*.(M.44.873B); met. ἐλπίδα...~ουσαν Ant.Ptol.*nativ*.6 (p.57); freq. in Cyr. ~ει Χριστός Cyr.*ador*.9(1.309A); ἡ τὸ ἀμήρυτον ~ουσα Thdr.Stud.*nativ.BMV* 7(M.96.692C); **2.** trans.; **a.** *perfume, make fragrant* ἀτμὶς θυμιάματος ~ει ἀέρα Nil.*spir.mal*.2(M.79.1148A); ‡Jo.D.*Artem*.67(M.96.1316A); met. ᾠδαῖς πνευματικαῖς αὐτὴν [sc. ἑορτὴν] εὐωδιάσωμεν Ast.Soph.*hom*.3 *in Ps*.5(M.40.425B); Dion.Ar. *e.h*.4.3.2(M.3.476B); εὐωδίασον ἡμῶν τὸ δυσῶδες τῆς ψυχῆς *Lit.Jac*. (p.162.12); τὸ τῆς θεοτόκου σῶμα...τῷ τῆς ἁγιαστείας μύρῳ τὴν συμπᾶσαν εὐωδίασε κτίσιν Andr.Cr.*or*.14(M.97.1092A); **b.** *give forth the fragrance of*, freq. in Cyr. Χριστὸν...~ουσι [sc. οἱ ἅγιοι] Cyr. *ador*.12(1.438B); τὴν εἰς αὐτὸν πίστιν ~οντας id.*Ps*.44:8(M.69.1040A); id.*2Cor*.2:15(Pusey p.329.16).

εὐωδίζ-ομαι, *make to smell sweet*, reflex., *be fragrant*, met. ἑαυτὸν ~ου ἐν πίστει Rom.Mel.(*AS* 1 p.146).

***εὐωδοποιός**, *making fragrant*, met. εὐ. ... ἐπιφοίτησιν [sc. of H. Ghost] Dion.Ar.*e.h*.2.3.8(M.3.404C).

§εὐώνιος, *of little worth, humble* εὐώνιοι καὶ αὐτοὶ ἡμεῖς πως γινώμεθα καὶ ἀθέλητοι Hesych.S.*temp*.1.31(M.93.1489C).

εὔωνος, *cheap*; met., *worthless*, Bas.*ep*.210.2(3.314B; M.32.769B); Gr.Naz.*or*.8.1(M.35.792A); Isid.Pel.*epp*.1.390(M.78.401D).

εὐώνυμος, 1. *left, on the left*, of certain angelic powers according to Valentinian division into εὐ. and δεξιαὶ δυνάμεις; produced by Sophia, Clem.*exc.Thdot*.34(p.118.4; M.9.676C); of tetrad of powers combined with δεξιὰ τετράς to form first ogdoad in system of Secundus, Epiph.*haer*.31.1(p.439.24; M.41.544D); neut. plur. as adv., Herm.*sim*.9.13.8; **2.** *evil*, Thdt.*qu*.8 *in Lev*.(1.187); id.*Ps*. 76:11(1.1146).

εὐώνως, *at a low price*, Gr.Naz.*or*.29.3(p.105.6; M.36.101A); ‡Ath. *syntag*.3.10(p.124; M.28.840C).

εὔωρος, ? *in due order* εὐ. πάντα καὶ δῆλα ταῖς τῶν παρόντων τιθεὶς ἀκοαῖς Niceph.Ur.*v.Sym*.221(M.86.3189C).

[*]**εὐωσμία, ἡ**, v. εὐοσμία.

εὐωχία, ἡ, *feasting*; of heavenly or eschatological banquet, Clem. *paed*.2.1(p.157.17; M.8.388A); *A.Thom*.A 7(p.110.12); of eucharist οὐράνιος εὐ. Ath.*ep.fest*.28(p.296.12; M.26.1433C); τῆς εὐ. τῆς πνευματικῆς Chrys.*pasch*.3(3.753D); μυστικὴν καὶ ἀθάνατον εὐ. Thdt.*Ps*. 21:27(1.744); met., of a feast of speech, Meth.*symp*.9.5(p.121 9; M. 18.192B); ‡Meth.*Sym.et Ann*.10(M.18.372C).

***εὐωχικός**, *like a feast*, Areth.*Apoc*.58(M.106.745C).

ἐφάλιος, *on the sea* πόλις...ἐ. Bas.Sel.*v.Thecl*.2.11(M.85.584A).

ἐφάλλ-ομαι, *spring upon, attack*; met., c. dat. ἡ βλασφημία πᾶσιν ~εται τοῖς ἀθέοις νοήμασι Gr.Nyss.*Eun*.10(2 p.239.25; σφάλλεται M. 45.841C); c. acc. 'παρώργιζεν αὐτήν'...τουτέστιν, ὠνείδιζεν, ἐφήλλετο Chrys.*hom*.24.4 *in Eph*.(11.184E); abs., *leap up* ~εταί σου ἡ διάνοια id.*hom*.11.3 *in 1Thess*.(11.506B); of Lazarus raised from the dead, ‡Eust.*Laz*.8(p.33.12).

ἐφαμαρτάνω, *miss, err from* τῆς ἀληθείας ἐ. Cyr.*Is*.4.3(2.640A); abs., *fail*, *ib*.4.4(663C).

ἐφάμαρτος, *sinful*, †Gregent.*leg.Hom*.40(M.86.604B); *ib*.53(609A); Ant.Mon.*hom*.35(M.89.1544C).

ἐφάμιλλος, *being a match* for, *equal* to, *rivalling*, c. genit., Eus. *v.C*.1.2(p.8.8; M.20.913A); Thdt.*Ezech*.21:12(2.841); Thphn.*chron*. p.339(M.108.817A); neut. as subst., *equality* φέρω πρὸς τὸν ἐμαυτοῦ πατέρα τὸ τῆς οὐσίας ἐ. Bas.Sel.*or*.25.4(M.85.297A); πρὸς τὸ ἐ. ... ἀνατείνουσιν Dion.Ar.*c.h*.13.3(M.3.301C); neut. sing. as adv., Gel. Cyz.*h.e*.1.4.7(M.85.1204A); neut. plur. as adv., Didym.*Trin*.2.8(M.39. 588C); Bas.Sel.*or*.15.2(M.85.193A).

ἐφαμίλλως, 1. *in rivalry*, Eus.*h.e*.6.39.5(M.20.601A); **2.** *similarly* to τοῖς ἔργοις ἐ. ἀποδοῦναι τοὺς λόγους *ib*.10.4.24(860A).

ἐφαπλ-όω, 1. *spread out*; **a.** *unfold* wings, *Apoc.Bar*.6(p.88.26); skins, Jo.Mosch.*prat*.174(M.87.3044A); pass., of a seed, Gr.Nyss.*res*. 3(M.46.669B); met., *explain, relate* τὴν περὶ ἑαυτοῦ γνῶσιν Ath.*inc*. 11.7(M.25.116D); ἐ. σοι οἵῳ τρόπῳ *A.(Pass.)Andr*.6(p.15.10); **b.** *stretch out, extend* hands, Eus.*h.e*.8.7.4(M.20.757A); arms, Anast.S.*Ps*.6(M. 89.1120C); feet, Chrys.*hom*.67.4 *in Gen*.(4.640D); †Cyr.*hom.div*.10 (5^2.376D); the tongue, met. βουλόμεθα ἐ. τὴν γλῶσσαν πρὸς τὴν βασιλίδα; Chrys.*a.exil*.2.2(3.422C); pass., *A.Xanthipp*.14(p.68.8); on ground in prayer, Pall.*h.Laus*.(M.34.1243B); reflex., Ephr.1.221A; τῷ νεκρῷ τοῦ παιδὸς ἑαυτὸν ἐφήπλωσεν σώματι [sc. Ἐλισσαῖος] Bas. Sel.*or*.10.1(M.85.140A); on a cross, *M.Carp*.44; **c.** *spread* a table, met. μίαν πᾶσιν ἐ. τῆς εὐφροσύνης τὴν τράπεζαν Mac.Mgn.*apocr*. 4.25(p.210.17); **d.** *spread out* over, *extend* over τί ἐστι τοῦτο... ὥστε γῇ καὶ θαλάσσῃ ἐξαρκεῖν ~ούμενον; Bas.*Eun*.3.6(1.277C; M.29. 668B); ἀνθηρὰν τῇ σαρκὶ τὴν δορὰν ἐφήπλωσε Mac.Mgn.*apocr*.2.8(p.10. 3); Chrys.*hom.6.6 in Gen*.(4.47D); Thdt.*provid*.5(4.552); met. ἡ σαγήνη τῆς χάριτος ~οῦται ἐπὶ πάντας Mac.Aeg.*hom*.16.52(M.34. 612B); τῷ ψιλῷ ἀνθρώπῳ τὰ τῆς πείρας ἐφήπλωσας ἄθεσμα δίκτυα Arsen.*tent*.(M.66.1621A); hence *bestow* gifts τὸ μὲν δῶρον τοῦ θεοῦ πᾶσιν ἐφήπλωται Cosm.Ind.*top*.5(M.88.281C); πᾶσιν ἴσως ~ούντων τὰ δῶρα τῆς αὐτῶν ἀγαθότητος Sophr.H.*mir.Cyr.et Jo*.51(M.87.3612B); **e.** *spread out before*, met. ~οῦται αὐτῇ ἐλπίς *M.Ner.et Ach*.6(p.5.1); ἐφηπλώσατο...οἷόν τι στάδιον τοῖς ἀνταγωνιζομένοις ὁ ἀνθρώπινος βίος Gr.Nyss.*Steph*.1(M.46.704B); **f.** *spread out towards*, Bas.Sel.*or*.37.4 (M.85.397A); τῷ τοῦ ἱεροῦ πρυτάνει τὰς ἱερὰς ὠλένας ἐφήπλωσε ‡Meth. *Sym.et Ann*.6(M.18.361A); **2.** *shed abroad*; **a.** *diffuse* light, Ath. *inc*.29.3(M.25.145C); Thdt.*rect.conf*.17(M.6.1240A); Jo.D.*fr.Mt*.17:5 (M.96.1408D); met. τὰς τοῦ οἰκείου φωτὸς ἐ. ἀκτῖνας [sc. Christ] Eus.*p.e*.2.5(69B; M.21.133D); †Bas.*Is*.224(1.548C; M.30.508D); Ast. Am.*hom*.9(M.40.304C); **b.** *extend*, Eus.*d.e*.3.3(p.109.14; M.22.188C); ὁ...λόγος...πανταχοῦ τὰς ἑαυτοῦ δυνάμεις ἐ. Ath.*gent*.42(M.25.84B); Epiph.*haer*.61.4(p.385.4; M.41.1045B); ἐ. καὶ ἐπ' αὐτοὺς τὴν...ἀγαθότητα Dion.Ar.*ep*.8.1(M.3.1085C); pass. ἡ δὲ ψυχὴ τοῖς τῆς διανοίας κινήμασι πάσῃ κατ' ἐξουσίαν ~οῦται τῇ κτίσει Gr.Nyss.*or.catech*.10 (p.55.3; M.45.41C); Socr.*h.e*.4.26.8(M.67.529B); ~ωθέντος...τοῦ πατρὸς διὰ τῆς χάριτος τοῦ ἁγίου αὐτοῦ παιδὸς καὶ τοῦ ἁγίου πνεύματος εἰς πάντας τοὺς ἁγίους †Diad.*Ar*.8(M.65.1164C).

ἐφάπλωμα, **τό**, *thing spread over, covering*, Jo.Disc.*v.Epiph*.56 (M.41.93C).

***ἐφαπτέον**, *one must engage in* γυναιξὶ...ταλασίας ἐ. Clem.*paed*.2.9 (p.207.13; M.8.496B).

ἐφαπτίς, **ἡ**, *woman's garment*, Clem.*paed*.2.10(p.224.2; M.8. 532A).

ἐφάπτ-ομαι, c. genit. **A.** lit.; **1.** *touch, be in contact* with τὸ φύσει μέσον τινῶν ἑκατέρων τῶν ἄκρων ἐ. Didym.(‡Bas.)*Eun*.4(1.288A; M.29.692C); ᾠὰ θάλπει, ταῖς πτέρυξιν ἁπαλῶς ~ομένη εἰς τὸ ζωογονεῖν Diod.*Gen*.1:2(M.33.1563C); Cyr.*Ps*.76:19(M.69.1193B); τοίχων ἐφαψάμενος Philost.*h.e*.7.14(M.65.552B); *pass through*; a circle, Meth. *symp*.8.14(p.102.4; M.18.165A); **2.** *lay hands on* (violently), ‡Jo.D. *Artem*.40(M.96.1288A); **3.** *touch, partake of* food, *T.Jud*.16.3; Thphl. Ant.*Autol*.3.4(M.6.1125B); *ib*.3.15(1141A); CAnc.(314)*can*.14; of eucharist τῆς προσφορᾶς ἐ. *ib*.16; τῶν μυστηρίων ἐ. Sophr.H.*mir. Cyr.et Jo*.31(M.87.3524A); *Lit.Jac*.(p.178.8).

B. met.; **1.** *lay hands on* τῆς ἀρχῆς ἐ. Eus.*v.C*.1.27(p.20.14; M.20. 941B); **2.** *start, set out upon* ἱστορίας...οἷά τινος ὁδοιπορίας ἐ. id.*h.e*. 1.5.1(M.20.80D); id.*l.C*.proem.(p.196.13; M.20.1317C); *ib*.6(p.211.12; 1439B); **3.** *touch upon, treat of* a subject, id.*p.e*.5.5(475B; M.21. 789C); id.*d.e*.8.1(p.355.20; M.22.577C); ἐ. δόγματος Gr.Nyss.*anim.et res*.(M.46.108B); **4.** *take, partake of*, id.*or.catech*.24(p.94.18; M.45. 65C); κτίσις...ὑψηλῆς φύσεως ~ομένη τε καὶ μετέχουσα id.*Eun*.1(1 p.101.1; M.45.333D); Dion.Ar.*e.h*.1.5(M.3.377B).

ἐφαρμόζ-ω, **ἐφαρμόττ-ω**, **1.** intrans.; *apply* to, *fit* πάντες...οἱ προειρημένοι...ὅροι ~ουσι τοῖς...εὐαγγελίοις Or.*Jo*.1.5(7; p.10.1; M. 14.33A); τίνι...~ει λέγεσθαι τοῦτο; Meth.*fr.15 in Job* 38:2(p.515. 19); σοι τὸ ψαλμικὸν ~ει Isid.Pel.*epp*.1.214(M.78.317C); Dion.Ar.*d.n*. 1.7(M.3.596C); **2.** trans.; **a.** *apply, fit* one thing to another πειθόμενοι τύπους εἶναι τὰ γεγραμμένα ζητοῦσιν ᾧ δυνήσονται ἐφαρμόσαι ἕκαστον τῶν κατὰ τὴν σκηνὴν λεγομένων Or.*princ*.4.2.2(p.309.9; M.11. 361A); id.*Jo*.10.28(18; p.202.27; M.14.360B); τοῦτο δὲ ἐπὶ μὲν τῶν προφητῶν οὐκ ἂν δύναιο ~ειν, ἐπὶ δὲ μόνον τὸν σωτῆρα καὶ κύριον Eus.*d.e*.3.2(p.102.6; M.22.176D); Gr.Naz.*or*.31.3(p.147.14; M.36. 136B); Gr.Nyss.*v.Mos*.(M.44.341A); of the mind οὐ δεῖ πρόχειρον λέξιν ἁπλῶς οὕτως ἐκλαμβάνειν, ἀλλὰ τὸ πρόσωπον ζητεῖν, καὶ οὕτως μετ' εὐσεβείας τὸν νοῦν ~ειν αὐτῷ Ath.*Ar*.2.44(M.26.240D); **b.** *adapt, make appropriate*, pass. ἦρεν καὶ αἴρει καὶ ἀρεῖ, καθ' ἕκαστον καιρὸν ἐφαρμοττομένου τοῦ αἴρειν Or.*fr.19 in Jo*.1:29(p.499.6); ἁρμονίας τινὸς ἀκολούθως ἐφηρμοσμένης *Hom.Clem*.8.11; **c.** *connect* one thing with another ἐφηρμόσαμεν τὴν τῶν Φαρισαίων πεῦσιν...τῷ βαπτισμῷ αὐτῶν παρὰ τῷ Ματθαίῳ κειμένῳ Or.*Jo*.6.26(14; p.136.7; M.14. 245C); Eus.*e.th*.1.16(p.76.22; M.24.857B); **d.** *fit in* εἰ...βουλόμενοι ἄτρεπτα τηρεῖν τὰ...δοθέντα τοῖς ἁγίοις ἀγαθά, οὐκ ἐφαρμόσομεν τὰ τῆς ἱστορίας, δόξομεν ὅμοιόν τι τοῖς ἀπὸ τῶν αἱρέσεων ἐν τούτῳ ποιεῖν Or.*Jo*.10.42(26; p.219.22; M.14.388D); **e.** *add suitably* ἅγιον πνεῦμα προσέθηκα, ἀλλ' ἅμα καὶ πόθεν καὶ διὰ τίνος ἧκεν ἐφήρμοσα Dion.Al. ap.Ath.*Dion*.17(p.58.18; M.25.504C).

ἐφαρμοστέον, **1.** *one must fit, adapt* τὸ ῥητὸν...τῇ διανοίᾳ ἐ. Clem. *paed*.1.6(p.112.20; M.8.296A); Or.*Jo*.1.31(34; p.39.33; M.14.84B); **2.** *one must show to be fitting* ἐ. ... πῶς ὁ υἱὸς τοῦ θεοῦ τοῦτο τὸ ὄνομα εἶναι λέγεται *ib*.1.24(23; p.30.1; 65B).

ἐφαρμόττω, v. ἐφαρμόζω.

ἐφαρπάζω, *snatch, steal*, perh. for ἀφαρπ-, Eus.Al.*serm*.21.6(M.86. 432B).

ἐφέδρα, **ἡ**, *support*, ‡Nil.*perist*.9.7(M.79.877B).

ἐφεδρευτής, **ὁ**, *one who keeps watch on*; c. genit., ‡Chrys.*nat. Jo.Bapt*.(10.813A).

ἐφεδρήσσω, *rest upon*; c. dat., Paul.Sil.*Soph*.559(M.86.2141A).

***ἐφεδρών**, **ἡ**, *privy*, Or.*adnot.in Dt*.23:14(M.17.33A).

ἐφεκτικός, medic., *astringent*, Leont.H.*Nest*.5.20(M.86.1741D); neut. as subst., *ib*.

ἐφεκτικῶς, comp., *somewhat hesitantly*, Anon.ap.Eus.*h.e*.5.16.3 (M.20.464B).

ἐφελίσσω, v. ἐπελίσσω.

ἐφέλκ-ω, **1.** act.; **a.** *draw* after one, hence met. *attract* σφίσιν αὐταῖς ἐφεῖλκον [sc. αἱ ψυχαί] τὸ πνεῦμα συγγενές Tat.*orat*.13(p.15.3; M.6.836A); **b.** *make applicable* εἰς ἑαυτοὺς ἐφελκύσαι τὸ γεγραμμένον Alex.Al.*ep.encycl*.6(p.9.21; M.18.576C); **2.** med.; **a.** *draw, attract* τοὺς ἀκροατὰς εἰς ἐγκράτειαν ~όμενον Meth.*symp*.1.3(p.12.6; M.18.44B); εἰς εὔνοιαν...ἅπαντας ~όμενος Thdt.*h.e*.3.4.1(3.915); Dion.Ar.*d.n*.4.28(M.3.729B); hence *tempt* εἰς πορνείαν με ἐφελκύσατο *T.Jos*.3.8; *ib*.8.2; **b.** *draw forward*, met. ὁ θεὸς...~όμενος τὸ ἐν κρυπτῷ κακὸν ὑπὲρ τοῦ καθᾶραι τὸν...τὰ σπέρματα τῆς ἁμαρτίας κεχωρηκότα Or.*princ*.3.1.13(p.218.5; M.11.273B).

ἔφελξις, **ἡ**, *drawing up*, Clem.*paed*.2.2(conj. for ἐφέπειξις p.176. 31; ἔπειξις M.8.429C).

***ἐφεόρτιος**, *festive*, ‡Epiph.*hom*.1(M.43.433A); *ib*.(M.43.437A).

***ἐφεπομένως**, *in a secondary way*, Max.*ambig*.(M.91.1197A).

ἐφερμηνεύω, *interpret, explain*, Eus.*p.e*.11.10(527C, v.l. ὑφ- M.21. 873C); id.*Hierocl*.27(527C, v.l. ὑφ- M.22.833A); Max.*schol.ep.4Dion. Ar*.(M.4.533A); abs., Gr.Nyss.*Eun*.5(2 p.116.17; M.45.697A); c. ὅτι, *ib*.(p.124.14; 705C).

***Ἐφεσιακός**, *Ephesian*, ‡Pion.*v.Polyc*.20; *ib*.3.

ἐφέσιμος, *accessible*, Gr.Thaum.*pan.Or*.12(p.28.12; M.10.1085B).

ἔφεσις, **ἡ**, **A.** from ἐφίημι, as legal term, *appeal* Παῦλος...ἐ. χρησάμενος Thdr.Mops.*Phil*.1:12(p.205.20; M.66.921D); Thdt.*2Tim*. 4:17(3.695).

B. from ἐφίεμαι, *aiming at a thing*; **1.** *appetite* ἐπιθυμίαν...ἔ. καὶ ὄρεξιν οὖσαν Clem.*str*.2.20(p.177.22; M.8.1064A); ἡ τῆς τροφῆς ἔ. Gr.Naz.*or*.28.22(p.55.4; M.36.56A); τὴν αἰσχρὰν ἔ. τῷ τῆς νηστείας ἱμάντι μαστίξαντες Nil.*epp*.1.168(M.79.149B); Thdt.*carit*.(3.1301); hence *impulse* τῇ ἐμφύτῳ κινήσει τῆς ζωτικῆς ἐ. Dion.Ar.*d.n*.4.4(M. 3.700B); τῆς κατ' ἔ. ... κινήσεως Max.*ambig*.(M.91.1076C); †Proc.G. *Procl*.(M.87.2992^{h}B); **2.** *yearning, longing, desire* ἔ. ... δυναστείας Const.*or.s.c*.15.2(p.173.25; M.20.1273C); πρὸς τὴν τοῦ πλείονος ἔ. Bas.*hom*.14.4(2.126A; M.31.452C); τὴν εἰς πᾶν ὁτιοῦν τῶν ἀγαθῶν ἔ. Cyr.*dogm*.2(p.552.21; 6^{2}.368C); abs. κλέψῃ τὴν ἔ. Gr.Naz.*or*.28.15 (p.46.1; M.36.45C); καθὸ οὐκ ἐφίενται τοῦ ἀγαθοῦ, τοῦ μὴ ὄντος ἐφίενται· καὶ οὐκ ἔστι τοῦτο ἔ., ἀλλὰ τῆς ὄντως ἐ. ἁμαρτία Dion.Ar. *d.n*.4.34(M.3.733D); Jo.D.*hom*.1.3(M.96.552A).

ἐφέστιος, *at one's own fireside, at home, LS*; neut. as subst., *home*, Ath.*h.Ar*.38(p.204.18; M.25.737B); Isch.*libell*.(p.18.42; H.2.328E); fig. σωφροσύνη ἦν αὐτῷ τὸ ἐ. Gr.Nyss.*laud.Bas*.(M.46.816B); plur., animals' *lairs*, Petr.II Al.*encycl*.7(M.33.1288A)ap.Thdt.*h.e*.4.22.26.

ἐφεστρίς (**ἐφιστρίς**), **ἡ**, *upper garment, wrapper* τί ἐστι μανδύας; εἶδός ἐστιν ἐ. Thdt.*qu.44 in 1Reg*.(1.383); ἐκέλευσε δὲ αὐτῷ καὶ ἐ. γενέσθαι, ἣν οἱ ἑβδομήκοντα ἐπωμίδα ἐκάλεσαν· ἐν δὲ ταῖς βασιλείαις εὑρίσκομεν Ἐφοὺδ αὐτὴν κατὰ τὴν τῶν Ἑβραίων γλῶτταν ὠνομασμένην id.*qu.60 in Ex*.(1.166); ἐφιστρίς Cosm.Mel.*schol*.(M.38.603) in Gr. Naz.*carm*.2.1.12.653 cit. s. ἐφούδ.

ἐφέτης, **ὁ**, *judge of appeals* δικαστὴν ἐ. Synes.*Dion* 12(p.265.6; M.66.1148A).

ἐφετικός, **1.** *desirous* θυμὸς...ἀμύνης ἐ. Clem.*str*.5.5(p.343.18; M.9. 49A); **2.** *permissive*, Hipp.*haer*.5.20(p.121.12,17; M.16.3186A,B); **3.** *of appeal* ἐν τῷ ἐ. δικαστηρίῳ Ath.Scholast.*coll*.7.4(p.84); *ib*.4.13(p.57).

ἐφετινός, *of the present year* κατὰ τὸν ἐ. χρόνον Anast.S.*hod*.12 (M.89.196B).

***ἐφετμεύω**, **ἐφετμέω**, *announce* ἐγὼ γὰρ ἐφετμεύω τρισένα ὑψιμέδοντα, οὗ λόγος ἄφθεγκτος ἐν ἀδέτῳ κόρῃ ἔγκυμος ἔσται *Orac*.ap. ‡Ath.*templ*.(p.109.6; M.28.1429A); ἐγὼ δὲ ἐφετμέω τρεῖν ἕνα μοῦνον ὑψιμέδοντα θεόν κτλ. *Orac*.ap.Jo.Mal.*chron*.4 p.77(M.97.157C).

ἐφέτος, = ἐπ' ἔτος, **ἐφέτως**, adv., *this year*, *M.Pers.*4.1(p.445.14, v.l. ἐφέτως); ἐφετῶς Jo.Mosch.*prat.*85(M.87.2941C).

***ἐφετῶς**, *desirously*, Max.*ambig.*(M.91.1077A); v. foreg.

ἐφεύρεμα (ἐφεύρημα), **τό**, *discovery*, *invention*, Bas.*hom.*1.3(2.3A; M.31.165C); *Const.App.*7.27.7; Anast.S.*hod.*13(M.89.217C); Jo.D.*imag.*1(M.94.1277B); -ρήματα Epiph.*haer.*proem.2(p.170.2, v.l. ἐφευρέματα; ὑφευρέματα M.41.176A); Jo.D.*imag.*2.19(M.94.1305B).

ἐφεύρεσις, **ἡ**, *invention*, *discovery*, *theory* ἀστρολογικῆς ἐφευρέσεως καὶ ἀριθμητικῆς Πυθαγορείου Hipp.*haer.*6.52(p.184.13; M.16.3282B); of heret. doctrines, Ath.*ep.Serap.*4.2(M.26.637C); ‡Ath.*Apoll.*1.12 (M.26.1113C); ἀποτάσσομαι τῷ σατανᾷ καὶ...ταῖς ἐ. αὐτοῦ *Const.App.* 7.41.2; Anast.S.*hod.*23(M.89.304B).

ἐφευρετής, **ὁ**, *inventor*, *discoverer* ἐ. καινῆς τέχνης γραμματικῆς Hipp.*haer.*5.8(p.89.6; M.16.3139B); ξένου τινὸς ὀνόματος ἐ. *A.Mt.*13 (p.54.5); τοῦδε τοῦ δόγματος...ἐ. CArim.*ep.Const.*1 ap.Thdt.*h.e.*2.19. 5(3.874) but εὑρ- ap.Ath.*syn.*10(p.237.29; M.26.697B); καινῆς αἱρέσεως ἐ. Ath.*Dion.*6(p.49.29; M.25.488B); used disparagingly of orthodox by Anomoeans νεωτεροποιούς ἡμᾶς...καὶ ἐ. ῥημάτων...ἀποκαλοῦσιν Bas.*Spir.*13(3.10B; M.32.88A).

ἐφεύρημα, **τό**, v. ἐφεύρεμα.

ἐφηβεία, **ἡ**, *youth* νῦν...δεσμῶτις ἡ Πενταπόλεως ἐ. Synes.*catast.* 2.3(p.289.20; M.66.1569B).

ἐφήγησις, **ἡ**, prob. error for ἐξήγησις, Cyr.*glaph.Ex.*3(1.324B).

ἐφηδύνομαι, s.v.l., *add sweetness to*, *sweeten*; c. dat., Thdot.Anc. *hom.BMV et Sym.*3(M.77.1393A) prob. f.l. for ἐφήδομαι.

***ἐφηθυσί[α]**, **ἡ**, for ἐπιθυσία, *sacrifice*, *Lit.Marc.*(*PStrasb.*r° 18).

ἐφημερευτής, **ὁ**, title of *one who takes his turn of serving* in a monastery ἀναστάντες δὲ οἱ ἐ. ὄρθριοι οἱ μὲν περὶ τὸ μαγειρεῖον οἱ δὲ περὶ τὰς τραπέζας γίνονται Pall.*h.Laus.*32(p.95.6; ἐφημερεύοντες M. 34.1105A); in church; fig., of Joseph at Nativity θυσιαστήριον μὲν ἡ φάτνη, ἐ. δὲ ὁ Ἰωσήφ Tim.Ant.*descr.BMV* 7(M.28.953C).

ἐφημερεύω, *take a turn of service* in a monastery, Pall.*h.Laus.* 32(M.34.1105A; f.l. for ἐφημερευτής, q.v.).

ἐφημερία, **ἡ**, **1.** *daily service* rendered by priests in temple, ref. Lc.1:5, Abr.Eph.*annunt.*2(p.443.31,35); ‡Chrys.*nat.Jo.Bapt.*(10. 813A,D); of duties in a monastery, Bas.*renunt.*9(2.210C; M.31. 645A); ‡Bas.*poen.mon.*51(2.530A; M.31.1313A); Pall.*h.Laus.*51(p.157. 2; M.34.1228D); **2.** in adv. phrases, *in turn* κατὰ ἐφημερίας *Hom. Clem.*12.2; τὴν ἐξ ἐ. ὑπηρεσίαν ἐν τῷ μαγειρείῳ Bas.*reg.br.*152 tit.(2. 466B; M.31.1181C); ἐξ ἐ. ἀπάρχεσθαι τῆς ψαλμῳδίας ἢ τῆς προσευχῆς *ib.*307 tit.(524D; M.1301B).

***ἐφηρεμέω**, *acquiesce* in; c. dat., Const.Diac.*laud.*3(M.88.481C).

ἐφησυχάζ-ω, **1.** abs.; **a.** *remain silent*, *quiet*; of persons, †Bas. *Is.*158(1.491B; M.30.377A); Pall.*h.Laus.*21(p.67.18; ἀφ- M.34.1075C); Isid.Pel.*epp.*3.248(M.78.925D); ἐν κελλίῳ ∼οντι *V.Pach.A* 7(p.130. 26); **b.** *remain inoperative*; of law or custom, Eus.*d.e.*1.2(p.9.6; M.22.25B); *ib.*1.6(p.27.20; 56B); **2.** c. dat.; **a.** *remain silent about*, *pass over in silence*, *acquiesce in*, Bas.*reg.br.*47(2.431A; M.31.1113C); id.*ep.*22.3(3.100C; M.32.292B); Chrys.*Is.interp.*5(6.56A); Nil.*praest.* 27(M.79.1093A); Jo.D.*Man.*1.76(M.94.1573D); **b.** *rest satisfied with* τοῖς προκατηγγελμένοις παρὰ τῶν ἁγίων ἐ. Bas.*Eun.*2.8(1.243E; M.29. 585B); Leo Mag.*ep.*28.6(p.19.10; M.*PL.*54.780A).

***ἐφησύχασις**, **ἡ**, *passing over in silence*, Thdr.Stud.*epp.*1.5(M.99. 924B).

ἐφιαλτικός, *demonic* ἀποστῆσαι τῆς βδελυρᾶς τῶν δαιμόνων προσκυνήσεως καὶ τῆς ἐ. ἐνεργείας τὰ βαρβαρικὰ μέρη Agath.*v.Gr.Ill.* 133(p.67).

ἐφιζάν-ω, **1.** *settle*; abs., Gr.Nyss.*hex.*5(M.44.65D); *settle* upon, c. dat., of insects, Chrys.*hom.68.5 in Mt.*(7.676E); ‡Eust.*hex.*(M. 18.788B); fig. ταὐτά μοι καὶ πρότερον ∼οντα πολλάκις ἀνέστρεφε τὴν διάνοιαν Aen.*dial.*(M.85.900C); **2.** *station*, c. acc., Sophr.H.*v.Anast.* (M.92.1697C) cit. s. δερβᾶς.

***ἐφίζησις**, **ἡ**, *settling upon*, *visitation* τῇ ἐ. τοῦ...χαρίσματος τοῦ πνεύματος *cat.Ac.*2:13(p.29.9).

ἐφικτός, **1.** *accessible*, *easy to reach*; hence **a.** *attainable* τελειότητα γνώσεως τὴν ἐ. τῇ ἀνθρωπίνῃ φύσει Gr.Nyss.*hom.6 in Cant.*(M.44. 892B); Nemes.*nat.hom.*36(M.40.748B); τὴν ἐ. τοῖς ἁγίοις χύσιν τῆς σοφίας Max.*ambig.*(M.91.1033A); neut. as subst. τὰ ἐ. τῇ ἀνθρωπίνῃ φύσει Or.*Jo.*10.10(8; p.180.5; M.14.321C); τὸ ἐ. ἀρετῆς Eus.*d.e.*8.2 (p.373.29; M.22.608A); Jo.D.*f.o.*1.1(M.94.789B); **b.** *comprehensible*, of the divine ἐροῦμεν δὲ οὐχ ὅσος ἐστὶν ὁ θεός, ἀλλ' ὅσον ἡμῖν ἐ. Bas.*hom.*15.1(2.131B; M.31.465A); μὴ ἐ. εἶναι τὸν τῆς ἑνώσεως λόγον Thdt.*eran.*2(4.101); εὑρίσκεται γὰρ [sc. in Arian argument] ἀνέφικτος μὲν ὁ υἱός, ὁ δὲ πατὴρ ἐ. id.*Trin.*11(M.75.1161D); τὰς ἐ. ἡμῖν μορφώσεις Dion.Ar.*c.h.*2.2(M.3.140A); Max.*ambig.*(M.91.1077B); **2.** as subst. fem., ? *attack*, ‡Barth.Edess.*Muham.*(M.104.1453A).

ἔφιξις, **ἡ**, error for ἄφιξις, *arrival*, Eus.*d.e.*3.7(M.22.244C).

ἐφίπταμαι, v. ἐπιπέτομαι.

ἐφιστάν-ω, = ἐφίστημι; **1.** *consider carefully* οὐκ ∼οντες οὐδὲ συνιέντες ὅτι... Thphl.Ant.*Autol.*2.2(M.6.1049A); **2.** *understand*; c. genit., Or.*Cels.*5.45(p.48.13; M.11.1249C); **3.** c. νοῦν, *fix* one's mind *upon* γνησίως αὐτοῖς ἐ. τὸν νοῦν Ath.*inc.*56.1(M.25.196A); and without νοῦν, *attend to* γνησίως ἐ. ταῖς γραφαῖς id.*gent.*46(M.25.92D).

ἐφιστάω, = foreg.; **1.** *set over*, Clem.*paed.*1.7(p.123.1; M.8. 316A); **2.** ἐ. τὸν νοῦν *pay* attention, Eus.*l.C.*16(p.250.7; M.20.1424C); intrans., *pay attention* οὐδαμῶς ἐ. τῇ διανοίᾳ Eus.*d.e.*9.16(p.439.5; M.22.708B); **3.** *check*, *restrain*, Max.*ambig.*(M.91.1165C).

ἐφίστη-μι, **A.** trans.; **1.** *bring in*; **a.** *bring in* a charge μηδὲν ὧν ἐπέστησαν καθ' ἡμῶν εἶχεν ἀληθές Ath.*apol.Const.*1(p.279.8; M.25. 596A); **b.** fig., *make as if present* to, *set before* ∼σιν αὐτοῖς ἤδη τὴν ἀνάστασιν Chrys.*hom.24.1 in Rom.*(9.694C); id.*hom.1.1 in Col.*(11. 323D); **2.** *wonder*, *consider*; **a.** in 1st pers., in phrase *I wonder whether* ἐ. δὲ μήπως τοὺς τρεῖς τριδύμους ἐγέννησεν Or.*sel.in Gen.* 11:26(M.12.112B); id.*Jo.*20.27(22; p.363.17; M.14.636B); Eus.*d.e.*7.3 (p.345.28; M.22.564A); **b.** in other persons, usu. imper., with dependent clause ἐπίστησον εἰ ἡ σοφία...οὕτω δύναται νοεῖσθαι ἀρχή Or.*Jo.*1.18(21; p.23.10; 56A); ἐπιστήσας ὡς... Eus.*p.e.*1.4(11B; M.21. 37D); ἐπίστησον δὲ εἰ... Didym.*Ps.*22:5(M.39.1292C); Diod.*Ps.*51:3 (M.33.1594A); ἐπίστησον τοῦ...γεννωμένου *ib.*70:6(1609A); **3.** *perceive*, *observe*, with dependent clause ἐπιστήσεις κἀκεῖ τί ποιεῖ τὸ πνεῦμα Or.*hom.20.4 in Jer.*(p.182.16; M.13.508B); εἰ ἐπέστησας ὅ φησι Thdr.Stud.*antirr.*2.18(M.99.361D); c. acc. and infin., Meth.*res.* 1.23(p.246.15; ∼σαι M.41.1092C); c. ὅτι, Eus.*h.e.*1.2.13(M.20.60B); c. ὡς, Evagr.*h.e.*4.3(p.154.11; M.86.2705B); **4.** *understand*, c. dat. τούτῳ δὲ καὶ αὐτῇ ἐπιστήσαντι τῇ Ἑβραΐᾳ γλώττῃ φανερὸν ἂν γένοιτο Eus.*d.e.*4.15(p.183.6; M.22.305A); δοκεῖ μοι πάνυ θεοσεβῶς ἐπιστῆσαι τῇ λέξει Anast.S.*hex.*11(*GCS* Clem.vol.3 p.224.34); abs. τοῖς ἐφιστάναι δυναμένοις Meth.*res.*1.23(p.246.13, v.l. ἐφιστάνειν M.41. 1092C); οὐδεὶς ἐπιστῆσαι δυνήσεται Chrys.*hom.2.4 in 1Thess.*(11. 439C); **5.** *explain* ἐνδηλότερον δὲ ἐπιστῆσαι βούλομαι Adam.*dial.*2.18 (p.98.9; M.11.1873A); *ib.*5.6(p.184.4; 1840A); abs., *ib.*5.23(p.224.8; 1865A); **6.** reflex., *check* ἴσως μὴ ἐπιστήσαντες ἑαυτοὺς πρὸς τὰ λεχθέντα νῦν..., λέξετε... Meth.*res.*1.36 ap.Epiph.*haer.*64.28(p.445.3; M.41.1101A); unless conj. μὲν for μὴ be read (*GCS* Meth.p.275.13), when ἐ. would mean *recall*.

B. intrans.; **1.** *come*, *arrive*, *appear*; of persons, abs., Meth. *symp.*proem.(p.3.3; M.18.28); Μακάριος ἐπέστη Ath.*apol.sec.*83 (p.162.10; M.25.397A); Jul.Papa *ep.Dian.*ap.Ath.*apol.sec.*24(p.105. 19; 289A); c. **dat.** ἐπέστη τῷ τόπῳ *ib.*28(p.108.11; M.25.296B); Hier. (tr.Sophr.Pall.)*vir.ill.*5(p.10.6; M.*PL.*23.616B); Evagr.*h.e.*1.5(p.10. 13; M.86.2432A); **2.** *stand* upon, fig. ἀληθείᾳ σωζούσῃ ἐπιστῆναι *Hom. Clem.*3.54; **3.** *stop* at δεῖ ἐπιστῆναι τῇ οἰκίᾳ Vict.*Mc.*14:13(p.42.12); **4.** *occur* ταῦτα τῇ παρθένῳ...ἐπέστη προκηρύξαι Const.*or.s.c.*18(p.181. 13; M.20.1289B).

C. med. and 2 aor. act. in trans. sense, *understand* μὴ δυναμένοις τῇ λεπτότητι ταύτῃ τῶν θεωρημάτων ἐφίστασθαι Gr.Nyss.*Eun.*1(1 p.206.21; M.45.453C); ἔστι τούτῳ ἐπιστῆναι Didym.*Trin.*2.19(M.39. 736A).

[*]**ἐφιστρίς**, **ἡ**, v. ἐφεστρίς.

***ἐφοδέομαι**, *investigate*, Areth.ap.*cat.Apoc.*2:22(p.214.24).

ἐφοδεύ-ω, **1.** *pay a visit* ἐ. εἰς ἄλλον τόπον *Apoc.En.*22.1; *visit*, fig. πῶς ὁ νοῦς...ἐν ἡμῖν μένων καὶ πάντα ἐ. τάχει φορᾶς καὶ ῥεύσεως Gr. Naz.*or.*28.22(p.54.14; M.36.56A); **2.** *approach* πῶς δεῖ ἐ. τὰ ἅγια ἀναγνώσματα Or.*princ.*4.2.1(p.306.1; M.11.357A); id.*Jo.*4.21(p.245. 21; M.14.436A); **3.** *examine*, *pass in review* τὸν ἔλεγχον ἐ. Eus.*p.e.*10. 9(485D; M.21.808D); τῶν ὀνομάτων ἕκαστον ἐ. Bas.*Eun.*1.7(1.218E; M. 29.525B); Max.*cap.*4.26(M.90.1313D); **4.** *lie in wait for*, *plot against*, fig. ὑποκριτὰς ∼οντας δικαιοσύνῃ Clem.*prot.*1(p.5.18; M.8.57A).

ἐφοδηγ-έω, *guide*, of spiritual guides ∼ούμενοι ὑπὸ τοῦ παρακλήτου ‡Ign.*Eph.*20; τοῦ φωτὸς τούτου ἡ δύναμις...∼εῖν τοὺς ἑπομένους Chrys.*hom.15.7 in Mt.*(7.198A); ὅσοι τῷ πηλῷ μάχονται, τούτοις ἡ ἡσυχία συντρέχεται εἴπερ καὶ τὸν ∼οῦντα κέκτηνται Jo.Clim.*scal.*27 (M.88.1097D).

ἐφοδιάζ-ω, **1.** *furnish with supplies*, fig. τὰ παρὰ θεοῦ πρὸς σωτηρίαν ∼ειν ἡμᾶς ἰσχύοντα Cyr.*Jo.*3.4(4.298E); pass., Chrys.*prod.Jud.*1.1(2. 377A); ‡Nil.*narr.*7(M.79.693A); **2.** *supply*, *furnish*, *provide*; **a.** in gen., pass.; **i.** with dat. of thing supplied τοῖς...τούτων γράμμασιν ∼εσθαι CAnt.(341)*can.*11; Cyr.*glaph.Gen.*3(1.82A); *ib.*4(113C); Thdt. *2Cor.*3:1(3.301); Gr.Ant.*mul.ung.*4(M.88.1853A); **ii.** with acc. of thing supplied τὴν δι' αἵματος τοῦ τιμίου...ἀσφάλειάν τε καὶ χάριν ∼όμενοι Cyr.*Jo.*3.6(4.313E); Niceph.Ur.*v.Sym.*205(M.86.3173C); **b.** partic., **i.** *supply with encouragement*, *encourage* ἀργίαν δὲ ∼ειν οὐ καλόν Clem.*str*.1.1(p.8.9; M.8.697A); pass. ~εται καὶ θαρσεῖ †Jo.D.*creat*.5(p.139); **ii.** *supply with instruction*, hence *instruct, teach* ἡμᾶς διδάσκων ~ει φάσκων... Eust.*fr.in Pr*.8:22(M.18.677B); *Hom.Clem*.2.37,38; Bas.*hom*.7.7(2.59E; M.31.300A); †Bas.*Is*.288(1.597E; M.30.624A); **c.** med. in act. sense ἐφοδιασάμενος δὲ αὐτὸν... πρὸς τὴν χρείαν ἐφοδίοις Jo.VI H.*v.Jo.D*.13(M.94.449B); **3.** intrans., *make provision for the journey* ἐφοδιάσας ἱκανῶς *Hom.Clem*.12.9; on behalf of another; of one baptizing a dying man, Gr.Naz.*or*.40.11(M.36.373A).

ἐφοδικός, *systematic*, Max.*ep*.6(M.91.425B).

ἐφόδιον, τό, often plur., *supplies for travelling, provisions, resources*; freq. met., of qualities, and practices which assist Christian life, *1Clem*.2.1; Gr.Thaum.*pan.Or*.5(p.12.23; M.10.1065B); τὸ δὲ ἐ. τῆς κυριακῆς ὁδοῦ οἱ μακαρισμοὶ τοῦ κυρίου Clem.*ecl*.12(p.140.1; M.9.704B); of prayer, Bas.*ep*.174(3.262C; M.32.652A); Bas.Sel.*or*.21.2(M.85.256C); of Bible reading, Isid.Pel.*epp*.2.73(M.78.516D); of a relic, Evagr.*h.e*.4.26(p.173.6; M.86.2745A); also of sacraments: baptism, Bas.*hom*.13.5(2.117C; M.31.432C); τῶν τῆς σωτηρίας ἐ. μεταλαχεῖν Thdt.*h.e*.4.21.11(3.986); Communion εἴ τις ἐξοδεύει, τοῦ τελευταίου καὶ ἀναγκαιοτάτου ἐ. μὴ ἀποστερεῖσθαι CNic.(325)*can*.13; Gr.Nyss.*ep.can*.(M.45.232C); δίδου μοι τῆς μακαρίας ἀποδημίας ἐ. Sophr.H.*v.Anast*.(M.92.1696A); ἀξίως ὑποδέχεσθαι τὴν ἐλπίδα τῶν ἁγιασμάτων σου εἰς ἐ. ζωῆς αἰωνίου *Lit.Bas*.(p.339.5); cf.*Lit.Marc*.(p.141.26).

ἐφόδιος, 1. *on the way* ἐ. ἐσμεν *PLond*.1927.50 (saec. iv); **2.** of letters, *for a journey, for travelling*; hence *introductory*, Synes.*ep*.18(M.66.1353B).

ἐφόλκιον, τό, *burdensome appendage* ἡ λέξις...τὸ τῶν πραγμάτων ἐ. Synes.*insomn*.20(p.187.10; M.66.1317D); Isid.Pel.*epp*.1.45(M.78.209C); esp. of body, freq. in Gr. Nyss. οὐκ ἐβαροῦντο τῷ ἐ. τοῦ σώματος Gr.Nyss.*v.Macr*.(p.383.3; M.46.972A); Eustrat.*stat.anim*.16(p.451); Sophr.H.*v.Anast*.(M.92.1704C).

ἐφομαρτέω, *accompany, follow*, c. dat., Nonn.*par.Jo*.1:41(M.43.757A); *ib*.6:66(804B).

ἐφομιλέω, *live in*, of Christ ἐ. τῷ κόσμῳ Nonn.*par.Jo*.16:28(M.43.881C).

***ἐφομοιόω,** *liken, compare* ἐ. ἑαυτοὺς τοῖς...ἀποστόλοις Philox.*ep*.35(p.183).

***ἐφομοσία, ἡ,** *swearing of oaths*, Thdr.Stud.*epp*.1.7(M.99.932B).

ἐφορ-άω, *watch over, observe*, freq. of God πάντα ἐ. Just.*dial*.127.2(M.6.772B); θεοῦ προνοίας ὡς ἐ. τὰ σύμπαντα Eus.*p.e*.1.4(13D; M.21.41C); Χριστοῦ τοῦ πάσας ~ῶντος ἡμῶν τὰς κρυφιωτάτας ἐννοίας Dion.Ar.*e.h*.3.3.10(M.3.440B); of a bishop πόλιν...ἰδίαν ~ᾶν οὐκ ἐκληρώσατο Philost.*h.e*.3.6(M.65.489A).

ἐφορεία, ἡ, 1. *diocese, see* ἐκ τῆς ἐ. Τύρου εἰς τὴν τῆς Ἀντιοχείας μετέστη Philost.*h.e*.3.15(M.65.504A); *Schol*. in Bas.*ep*.188 *can*.10 (*Mon*.2 p.652); **2.** *lordship, dominion* ἄριστον...παρεσκευακέναι τὸ πνεῦμα τὸ θεῖον ὡς ἐ. ἀξιοῦσθαι νοῦ καὶ θεοῦ Synes.*insomn*.16(p.178.12, v.l. ἐφορίας M.66.1312A).

ἐφορεύω, *govern, rule over*; c. genit., Synes.*regn*.7(p.16.6; M.66.1064C) = id.*provid*.11(p.86.7; M.66.1233A); of a bishop Θεόδωρος... τῆς ἐν Θρᾴκῃ ἐ. Ἡρακλείας Philost.*h.e*.8.17(M.65.568A); ‡Jo.D.*Artem*.16(p.156.22; M.96.1265D).

ἐφορία, ἡ, Clem.*str*.6.14(M.9.337B; conj. ἐπιφορά p.489.16).

***ἐφορκ-,** v. ἐπορκ-.

ἔφορμος, *at anchor*, hence, met., *at a standstill* παρασκευὰς...πρὸς πᾶσαν πρᾶξιν εἶχεν ἐ. Malchus *exc.gent*.5(p.573.17; M.113.788C).

ἔφορος, ὁ, 1. *observer, spectator*, Clem.*paed*.1.5(p.103.4; M.8.276A); **2.** *overseer, guardian, ruler*; **a.** of God, esp. in phrase θεὸς ὁ πάντων ἔ. Eus.*h.e*.1.2.20(M.20.64A); Const.ap.Ath.*apol.sec*.86(p.165.9; M.25.404A); CAnt.(341)*can*.24; τὸν ἔ. ἀληθείας θεόν Synes.*ep*.105(M.66.1488C); τριὰς...τῆς Χριστιανῶν ἔ. θεοσοφίας Dion.Ar.*myst*.1.1.(M.3.997A); abs., Mac.Mgn.*apocr*.3.24(p.109.33); of God's providence, Eus.*fr.Lc*.12:22(M.24.557B); **b.** of angels ὁ ἄγγελος ὁ τῆς ἐκκλησίας ἔ. Bas.*ep*.238(3.367A; M.32.889B); ἅμα γὰρ τὸ εἰσαχθῆναι τὴν αἵρεσιν, ἀπέπτη ὁ ἔ. τῶν ἐκεῖσε ἄγγελος Thdr.Stud.*epp*.2.215(M.99.1648B); Areth.*Apoc*.1(M.106.504D); ἀστέρας δὲ τοὺς ἀγγέλους τοὺς τῶν ἐκκλησιῶν ἐ. καλεῖ *ib*.2(524D); **c.** of bishops, Philost.*h.e*.1.9(M.65.465A); *ib*.3.4(484A); *ib*.3.12(500D).

***ἐφούδ, τό,** (Hebr. אֵפוֹד) *ephod*, priestly garment containing in pouch affixed to the front (over the breast) the oracular Urim and Thummim τὸ ἐ. τῆς προφητείας *T.Lev*.8.2,6; Or.*engast*.3(p.285.10; M.12.1016B); τῷ ἐ. μόνοις ἐξῆν κεχρῆσθαι τοῖς ἱερεῦσι· δι' ἐκείνου γὰρ τὸ πρακτέον ἀπεκαλύπτετο Thdt.*qu*.17 *in Jud*.(1.335); its nature explained, Anast.S.*hod*.40(M.89.585A); renderings of Hebr. τὸ ἐ. ἐπένδυμα ὁ Ἀκύλας εἶπεν· ὁ δὲ Σύμμαχος ἐπωμίδα. ἀλλ' ἦν ἐπενδύματα ἱερατικά, ἣν δὲ καὶ κοινά Thdt.*qu*.1 *in 1Par*.(1.561); ἐ. δέ ἐστιν ἐφιστρίς, ὡς Ἀκύλας· ὡς δὲ Θεοδοτίων, ἐπωμὶς ἢ ἐξωμίς Cosm.Mel.*schol*.(M.38.603) in Gr.Naz.*carm*.2.1.12.653; met., ref. Alexander's reception of Athanasius to be brought up under his care Ἀθανάσιον, ᾧπερ...ὁ ἐπίσκοπος τὸ ἱερατικὸν ἐ. περιτίθησι, νέον αὐτὸν Σαμουὴλ τῇ ἐκκλησίᾳ προβιβάζων Gel.Cyz.*h.e*.3.15.13; of BMV αὕτη τὸ ἱερατικὸν ἐ., τὴν τοῦ θεοῦ μηνύουσα βουλήν Procl.CP *or*.6.17(M.65.753B).

ἐφύβριστος, 1. *wanton, insolent*, Clem.*str*.2.18(p.161.1; M.8.1029A); *ib*.2.20(p.174.1; 1056B); Bas.*ep*.32.1(3.112A; M.32.317A); neut. plur. as adv., Petr.Rav.*ep*.1(p.46.3; M.*PL*.54.742A); **2.** pass.; **a.** *dishonoured*, Clem.*str*.2.22(p.187.25; M.8.1084B); **b.** *dishonourable, shameful*, Gr.Nyss.*Eun*.4(2 p.100.18; M.45.677C); ‡Chrys.*hom*.13(13.256A); Isid.Pel.*epp*.1.170(M.78.440B); τὴν οὕτως ἐ. θάνατον [sc. of Cross] Ammon.*Jo*.13:1(M.85.1480D); ὡς ἐ. τοῦτον [sc. Cross] βαστάσαι Hesych.H.*qu.ev*.45(M.93.1429C).

ἐφυβρίστως, *dishonourably, shamefully*, *Chron.Pasch*.p.295(M.92.740B).

***ἐφυγίας, ὁ,** *healer, saviour*; of Christ, Procl.CP *hom*.1.2(M.65.836A).

ἔφυδρος, *in the water*; of divers, Ast.Am.*hom*.13(M.40.353C).

***ἐφυμνία, ἡ,** *hymn of praise*, Or.*sel.in Ps*.135:3(M.12.1656A).

ἐφύμνιον, τό, *eulogy*, Jo.D.*hom*.10.1(M.96.753A).

***ἐφύμνιος,** *of praise, in praise*, Andr.Cr.*or*.12(M.97.1064C); *ib*.16(1153B); ἡ ἐ. θεολογία τῆς θεοτερποῦς ὡραιότητος *ib*.12(1068A); Jo.D.*carm.theog*.43(p.206; M.96.821A).

***ἐφυπνίζω,** error for ἐξ-, Gr.Mag.*dial*.(tr.Zach.)4.36(M.*PL*.77.382D).

***ἐφύπνιος,** *of falling asleep*; hence fig. *of death, funereal* ἐ. τροπολογίας Andr.Cr.*or*.14(M.97.1092B).

ἐφυπνόω, *shut one's eyes* to; c. dat., *V.Const*.36(p.566.5).

***ἐφυστέρησις, ἡ,** *prolongation* of an activity; of eating, Clem.*paed*.2.7(p.191.3; M.8.460A).

ἐφυστερίζ-ω, 1. *come later*, Gr.Nyss.*hex*.7(f.l. ὑφεστ- M.44.69A); id.*hom.6 in Eccl*.(M.44.697D); Jo.D.*hom*.1.18(M.96.572D); **2.** *come after* ~ειν τὰς ψυχὰς τὴν γένεσιν Gr.Nyss.*anim.et res*.(M.46.125A); id.*hom.6 in Eccl*.(M.44.700A); c. genit, Jo.D.*f.o*.3.14(M.94.1041C); c. dat., id.*hom*.1.13(M.96.565B); abs. τῶν ~όντων παρέχει τὴν γνῶσιν Areth.*Apoc*.55(M.106.733A); **3.** *wait until later* τοὺς δὲ ~οντας...καὶ μέχρι τετάρτης φυλακῆς ἐγκαρτεροῦντας Dion.Al.*ep.can*.1(p.101.3; f.l. ὑφ- M.10.1277A).

***ἐφώθ, αἱ,** *crocodiles*, ‡Epiph.*v.proph.Jer*.3(p.21; M.43.400A), νεφώθ ap.*Chron.Pasch*.p.156 (μενεφώθ M.92.385A); perh. by mistaken interpretation of אֶפְעֶה, *viper*.

***ἐφωραΐζω,** *make beautiful, adorn*, Andr.Cr.*or*.7(M.97.932B).

ἐχέγγυος, 1. *able to give security, trustworthy*, of persons ἐ. διδάσκαλοι Clem.*str*.6.18(p.517.12; M.9.397C); ἐ. μάρτυρα Meth.*symp*.2.7(p.25.9; M.18.60A); τοῖς προσιοῦσιν ἐ. [sc. Christ] Cyr.*Nest*.3.3(p.62.13; 6[1].75A); c. infin., *sufficiently reliable* to Παῦλος ἐ. τῷ λόγῳ πιστώσασθαι Areth.*Apoc*.2(M.106.520B); **2.** neut. as subst., *pledge* τῆς μετὰ θάνατον ζωῆς...λαβόντες τὰ ἐ. Eus.*theoph.fr*.8(p.23*.13; M.24.632C); τῆς πραγματείας τὸ ἐ. Epiph.*haer*.5.1(p.184.8; M.41.201C); Thdt.*Heb*.13:5(3.632).

***ἐχεθύμως,** *using self-restraint*, Epiph.*haer*.66.70(p.111.20; M.42.141A).

***ἐχειρῶν,** Leont.et Jo.*sacr*.tit.(M.86.2080C) error for ἐχθρῶν, cf. *ib*.(2022A).

ἐχέμυθος, 1. *keeping silence, discreet*, Gr.Nyss.*bapt.diff*.(M.46.421C); Didym.*Trin*.2.7(M.39.589A); Synes.*insomn*.13(p.171.1; M.66.1305A); τὸ γὰρ ἐπιστολῆς πρᾶγμα οὐκ ἐ. id.*ep*.137(M.66.1525D); **2.** *mythical*, Meth.*symp*.8.14(p.102.7; M.18.165A).

ἐχέφρων, *sensible, intelligent, wise* γάμος...ἐ. Gr.Naz.*carm*.1.2.1.248(M.37.541A); of Christ ἀμνός ἐ. Nonn.*par.Jo*.1:29(M.43.756A); νέκυς...ἐ. *ib*.20:12(909B); ἐ. ἀνήρ Euthal.*epp.Paul*.(M.85.713A); Thdr.Stud.*epp*.2.193(M.99.1588A); freq. masc. as subst. παρά γε τοῖς ἐ. Tit.Bost.*Man*.1.14(M.18.1088A); Cyr.*Am*.73(3.334A); τοῖς ἐ. δήλη Thdt.*Dan*.2:2(2.1079); neut. as subst., Men.*exc.Rom*.19(p.219.16; M.113.924C).

***ἐχθίστως,** *very wickedly*, †Gregent.*disp*.(M.86.729C).

ἐχθοδοπέω, *show enmity* towards, *engage in hostility* with; c. dat., Gr.Naz.*carm*.2.2(poem.)6.80(M.37.1548A).

ἔχθρα, ἡ, *enmity, hatred*; **1.** exeg. Gen.3:15 τὴν ἔ. ταύτην ὁ κύριος εἰς ἑαυτὸν ἀνεκεφαλαιώσατο ἐκ γυναικὸς γενόμενος ἄνθρωπος, καὶ πατήσας αὐτοῦ τὴν κεφαλήν Iren.*haer*.4.40.3(M.7.1114C); ὁ θεὸς ἔ. ποιεῖ τὴν πρὸς τόνδε, ἵνα φιλίαν ποιήσῃ τὴν πρὸς τὸν Χριστόν Or.ap.*cat.Gen*.3:15(93Δ); ἔστι γὰρ καὶ ἔ. καλή...ἡ γὰρ πρὸς τὸν ὄφιν φιλία ἔ.

πρὸς τὸν θεὸν καὶ θάνατον κατεργάζεται Cyr.H.*catech*.16.10; ἀδιάλλακτος ἡ πρὸς τὸν ὄφιν ἔ. Bas.*hom*.9.9(2.81A; M.31.348C); Gr.Nyss. *ep*.3(M.46.1017A); ἐκείνη ἡ ἔ. τὴν φιλίαν ἔλυσε. φιλίαν λέγω, οὐ τὴν λογικήν, ἀλλὰ τὴν ἄλογον γνῶσιν Sever.*creat*.6.2(M.56.485); **2.** met. ἀναχθεὶς ἀνέμων ἔχθραις ἀντὶ τοῦ εἰς Ἰουδαίαν εἰς Ἀλεξάνδρειαν ἠνέχθην *Hom.Clem*.1.8.

***ἐχθραΐζω**, *be at enmity*, Or.*Cels*.1.40(p.91.3; M.11.736A).

ἐχθραίν-ω, freq. as ptcpl.; **1.** *be at enmity*; **a.** abs. τοῖς ἀδίκως ∼ουσι Just.*1apol*.45.6(M.6.397B); συμβιβάζετε...τοὺς ∼οντας εἰς ὁμόνοιαν *Const.App*.2.46.7; ὑπὲρ τῆς εὐσεβείας ∼ειν κατασχηματίζονται Bas.*ep*.92.2(3.185A; M.32.480C); **b.** c. dat. τοὺς ∼οντας αὐτῷ δαίμονας Just.*1apol*.45.1(M.6.396C); Diad.*perf*.95(p.140.4); Arsen. *doct*.2(M.66.1620A); **c.** c. ἐπί, *Hom.Clem*.1.5; **2.** *make hateful* or *hostile* ∼ουσα τέκνοις γονέας καὶ τέκνα γονεῦσιν *Orac.Sib*.8.26.

ἐχθρεύω, *be at enmity with*, *contend with*; c. genit., *M.Ner.et Ach*. 7(p.6.14).

***ἐχθρόθεος**, *hostile to God*, Thdr.Stud.*epp*.2.120(M.99.1396A).

***ἐχθρόκοσμος**, *hostile to the world*, Thdr.Stud.*epp*.2.68(M.99. 1296C).

ἐχθροποιέω, *make hostile*, Iren.*haer*.4.40.3(M.7.1113C); τὴν ἔχθραν ἣν ἐ. πρὸς αὐτόν *ib*.(1114A); *cat.Lc*.2:14(p.20.22) cf. τὴν ἐχθροποιὸν ἁμαρτίαν Cyr.*Lc*.2:7ff.(M.72.493D); Proc.G.*Gen*.3:15(M.87.205C).

ἐχθρός, *hated*, *hostile*; hence masc. as subst., *enemy*, superl. ἔχθιτος Eudoc.*Cypr*.1.209(M.85.840C); **1.** of Devil in gen., abs. ἐγώ, φησίν, ὁ Χριστός, ἐγὼ ὁ...θριαμβεύσας τὸν ἐ. Mel.*pass*.102 p.17.15; ὁ τὸν ἐ. ἀποστρέφων [sc. Χριστέ] *A.Thom*.A 39(p.157.8); ἐπιδημήσαντος τοῦ κυρίου πέπτωκεν ὁ ἐ. Ath.*v.Anton*.28(M.26.884B); as enemy of God, *A.Jo*.84(p.192.33); *A.Andr.et Mt*.20(p.91.14); as enemy of man, Chrysipp.*enc.in Jo.Bapt*.8(p.40.10); as enemy of both ἐπειδὴ δὲ γέγονεν ἀποστάτης, ἐ. μὲν θεοῦ, ἐ. δὲ ἀνθρώπων τῶν κατ' εἰκόνα θεοῦ γεγενημένων Bas.*hom*.9.7(2.81E; M.31.349C); τοῦ πάντων ἐ., φημὶ δὴ τοῦ σατανᾶ Cyr.*Abac*.24(3.538D); **2.** exeg. Ps.109:1 τίνες οὖν οἱ ἐ.; οἱ φαῦλοι καὶ ἀντιτασσόμενοι τῷ θελήματι αὐτοῦ *1Clem*.36.6; ἐ. διαφερόντως μέν ἐστιν ὁ διάβολος καὶ οἱ τούτου διάκονοι δαίμονες, πρὸς δὲ τούτοις καὶ οἱ τοῖς θείοις αὐτοῦ κηρύγμασιν ἀντιπίπτοντες, Ἰουδαῖοι καὶ Ἕλληνες Or.*Ps*.109:1(p.229) = Thdt.*Ps*.109:1(1.1392); ἐχθροὺς δὲ φησὶ τοὺς διὰ τοῦ προτεταγμένου ψαλμοῦ δεδηλωμένους· καὶ...πάσας τὰς ἀντικειμένας δυνάμεις Eus.*Ps*.109:1(M.23.1341B); exeg. Rom.5:10 οὐ διελιμπάνομεν ἐ. ὄντες τοῦ θεοῦ ἐκπεπολεμωμένοι πρὸς τὸν θεῖον λόγον·...ἐ. ἦμεν. ἀπεστάλη νόμος καὶ οὐ διήλλαξεν. ἦλθον προφῆται, καὶ οὐκ ἔπεισαν· ἀλλ' ἔμειναν οἱ ἐ. τοῦ θεοῦ, ἐ. καὶ πολέμιοι·...ἦλθεν ὁ Χριστός..., καὶ τὴν εἰρήνην κατεβράβευσεν Chrys. *hom.2.11 in Ac.princ*.(3.768B); exeg. 1Cor.15:26, v. ἔσχατος.

ἐχθρώδης, *hateful* ἐ. θεῷ δόγμα ‡Jo.D.*Const*.15(M.95.332C).

ἐχθρωδῶς, *in a hostile way*, Eus.*d.e*.10.2(p.455.15; M.22.732D); Chrys.*sac*.2.1(p.27.15; 1.372B); Anast.S.*hod*.10(M.89.180D); c. ἔχω, *treat as hostile* τὸν...Στρατηγὸν οὐκ ἐ. ἔχομεν Thdr.Stud.*epp*.2.205 (M.99.1624B).

ἔχιδνα, ἡ, *viper* καλῶς οὖν παρεπλησίασεν ὁ Ἰωάννης τῇ ἐ. τοὺς Φαρισαίους· ὃν τρόπον γὰρ ἀποκτείνει ἡ ἔ. τὸν πατέρα καὶ τὴν μητέρα, οὕτω καὶ οὗτοι ἀπέκτειναν τοὺς νοεροὺς αὐτῶν πατέρας τοὺς προφήτας, φησί, καὶ τὸν κύριον ἡμῶν Ἰησοῦν Χριστὸν καὶ τὴν ἐκκλησίαν *Phys*.A 10(p.35.1); Chrys.*hom.11.2 in Mt*.(7.150D); Isid.Pel.*epp*.1.105(M.78. 253B); *Phys*.B 22(pp.240–2).

ἐχιδναῖος, *of a viper* ἐ. ... γόνος Gr.Naz.*carm*.2.2(poem.)5.112 (M.37.1529A).

ἐχιδνότοκος, *born of a viper*; met., of children of a wicked mother, Steph.Diac.*v.Steph*.(M.100.1184A).

***ἐχιδνοχαρής**, *delighting in vipers*, *Orac.Sib*.2.169.

***ἐχύρωμα, τό**, *stronghold*, of BMV δικαιοσύνης ἐ. ‡Gr.Thaum. *annunt*.2(M.10.1160B).

ἔχω, *have*, *hold*; **A.** trans.; **1.** folld. by infin. used as subst. εἰ τὸ πάσχειν ᾔδεις, τὸ μὴ παθεῖν ἂν εἶχες. τὸ παθεῖν σύγγνωθι καὶ τὸ μὴ παθεῖν ἕξεις *A.Jo*.96(p.198.22,23); *ib*.84(p.192.23); *A.(Pass.)Andr*.11 (p.27.10,11); cf. *A.Andr*.B 6(p.61.5); εἶχεν...τὸ μὴ φοβεῖσθαι *A.Andr. fr*.18(p.45.24); **2.** in phrase ἔ. χρόνον, ἔ. ἔτος, etc., *have spent* time, etc. ὅτι πολὺν χρόνον εἶχον ἐν τῇ πίστει ἐδήλωσε λέγων... Chrys.*homm. in Heb*.proem.(12.4E); πόσον χρόνον ἔχει μετὰ σοῦ; *Apophth.Patr*. (M.65.232A); Jo.Mosch.*prat*.20(M.87.2868B); folld. by ὅτε: εἰκοστὸν λοιπὸν ἔτος ἔχων ὅτε ταῦτα ἔγραφεν Chrys.*hom.28.4 in Heb*.(12. 261B); by ὅτι, Jo.Mosch.*prat*.154(3024A); by ἀφ' οὗ, Eus.Al.*serm*.4 (M.86.333A); c. ptcpl. pres. ὀγδοήκοντα καὶ ἓξ ἔτη ἔχω δουλεύων αὐτῷ *M.Polyc*.9.3(M.5.1036C, v.l. for δουλεύω p.125.11); πέντε ἔτη ἔχω ὑπ' αὐτοῦ ἐνοχλουμένη *A.Thom*.A 43(p.161.4); *A.Barn*.6(p.294.9); ἡμέρας γὰρ ἔχω τριάκοντα...ὁδεύων Jo.Ant.*ep.Cyr*.1(p.119.11; M.77.132B); Jo.Mosch.*prat*.172(3041A); c. ptcpl. aor. χρόνους ἔχουσι τοσούτους νικήσαντες Chrys.*hom.28.1 in Heb*.(12.255C); Pall.*h.Laus*.17(p.45.19; M.34.1044C); Jo.Mosch.*prat*.87(2945A); Ant.Mon.*hom*.84(M.89.1692B); **3.** in phrase τί ἔχω, what *ails me*? what *is the matter with me*? σὺ γινώσκεις τί ἔχω *Apophth.Patr*.(M.65.432D); τί κλαίεις; τί ἔχεις; Eustrat.*v.Eutych*.54(M.86.2336C); Jo.Mosch.*prat*.50(M.87.2905B); **4.** reflex. μὴ ἔχων ἑαυτόν *is* not *himself*, Tim.I Al.*resp*.(M.33.1296B); **5.** *come to*, *reach* οὗτοι μὲν δὴ τὴν Κωνσταντινούπολιν εἶχον ἄγοντες τὸν νεκρόν ‡Jo.D.*Artem*.21(p.74.16, v.l. διὰ τὴν Κ. M.96.1269D); **6.** c. dat., *hold fast* to μοναχὸς ἡσυχαστὴς Νεστοριανῷ ἔχων δόγματι Barth.Edess.*Agar*.(M.104.1428A); **7.** *hold to be*, *consider as* θεὸν εἶχον τὸν Ἄψεθον Hipp.*haer*.6.8(p.135.25; M.16.3207B); Or.*fr.155 in Mt*.8:8(p.77); ἄνθρωπον κύριον ἔχοντες Ath.*Ar*.2.16(M.26.181B); **8.** *hold*, *think* πεῖσαι ὑμᾶς μὴ ὡς περὶ ἀθέων ἔχειν δυνάμεθα Athenag. *leg*.11.1(M.6.912A); τὸ οὕτως περὶ τῆς ψυχῆς ἔχειν, οὐδὲν ἄλλο ἐστὶν ἢ ἀλλότριον πρὸς τὴν ἀρετὴν ἔχειν Gr.Nyss.*anim.et res*.(M.46.17B); Chrys.*hom.1.1 in 2Tim*.(11.660A); ἐὰν ἀσκῇ τις, ἢ διὰ κενοδοξίαν, ἢ ἔχων ὅτι ἀρετὴν ποιεῖ, οὐκ ἀσκεῖ ὁ τοιοῦτος ἐν γνώσει Dor.*doct*.14.3 (M.88.1777D); εἶχεν ὅτι λέων ἔφαγεν τὸν ὄνον Jo.Mosch.*prat*.107(M. 87.2968D).

B. intrans.; **1.** in phrase τὸ νῦν ἔχον *for the present*, ‡Pion.*v.Polyc*. 3,20; **2.** as auxiliary or modal vb.; **a.** pres., *happen*, c. infin. pres. ποιεῖ αὐτὸν ἀποσκεπάζεσθαι...τὴν τούτου κεφαλήν, εἰ ἔχει εἶναι ὁ τὸ διάδημα φορῶν †Jo.Jej.*poenit*.(M.88.1892D); ἐὰν ἔχωσί τινες καὶ μοναχοί, εἰ καὶ ἅγιοι εἶναι †Jo.Jej.*serm*.(M.88.1932B); **b.** pres., *is going to*, *will*, c. infin. aor., freq. τὸ δὲ καινότερον καὶ φοβερώτατον ἀκοῦσαι ἔχετε Mel.*pass*.23 p.4.10; ὁ θεὸς...οὐκ ἔχει μερίσαι ὑμᾶς [sc. SS. Peter and Paul] ἀπ' ἀλλήλων *A.Petr.et Paul*.5(p.181.6); Epiph. *haer*.69.9(p.159.22; M.42.217A); ποῦ ἀπελθεῖν ἔχει; Chrys.*hom.21.4 in Heb*.(12.200B); **c.** imperf.; **i.** c. infin. pres., *would* εἰ...ἐπίσκοπος πολλάκις καὶ κεφαλὴ πολλῶν εἶχες εἶναι *Apophth.Patr*.(M.65.176A); Jo.Mosch.*prat*.17(M.87.2865A); **ii.** c. infin. aor., *would have* εἰ μὴ Δὰν...συνεμάχησέν με, εἶχόν με ἀνελεῖν *T.Jud*.7.6; εἰ...σὺ τοιαῦτα πράγματα ἑωράκεις, οὐκ εἶχες ταραχθῆναι ἐπὶ τούτοις; *A.Phil*.128 (p.58.15); Epiph.*haer*.44.3(p.194.9; M.41.825B); Dor.*doct*.7.3(M.88. 1700B); εἶχον...τὰς ἡμῶν ναῦς καῦσαι...εἰ μὴ νὺξ ἐπῆλθε Jo.Mal. *chron*.5 p.128(M.97.224A); with ἄν: εἰ ἐθεασάμεθα καὶ ἐγνωρίσαμεν καθὼς τὸν υἱὸν αὐτοῦ, κἀκεῖνον ἂν εἴχομεν ἱστορῆσαι καὶ ζωγραφῆσαι †Gr.II Papa *ep.Leon*.1(H.4.5D); **iii.** c. infin. aor., *ought to have* κατὰ τὴν πρώτην κλῆσιν εὐθὺς ἐλθεῖν εἴχομεν πρὸς τὴν ὑμετέραν ἀγάπην, ἀλλά...*Ep*.ap.CChalc.*act*.4(*ACO* 2.1.2 p.117.4; H.2.425A); τί οὖν εἶχον ποιῆσαι; *Apophth.Patr*.(M.65.229C); Jo.Mosch.*prat*.85 (M.87.2941D); *ib*.76(2929D); **d.** *be able*, *can*; hence opt., *could*, c. infin. aor. τί γὰρ ἕτερον ἔχοιμι πρὸς ὑμᾶς εἰπεῖν *A.Jo*.107(p.205.11); Clem.*prot*.9(p.62.7; M.8.192D); **e.** pres., c. infin. aor. giving perf. sense ἐπεδείκνυον...ὅτι περὶ τὰ ο' ἔτη ἔχει ὁ γέρων μὴ ἐξελθεῖν τοῦ ἁγίου ὄρους Σινὰ Jo.Mosch.*prat*.127(M.87.2989C), cf. A.2 supra; **f.** imperf., c. ptcpl. pres. giving aor. sense οὐκ ἀπεκρύψατο τοῦ θεοῦ πέρι, ὅτι περ εἶχεν φρονῶν Clem.*prot*.6(p.54.17; M.8.177B).

C. med.; **1.** *follow closely*, hence *study* ἐχομένους γὰρ καθήκει οὐ μόνον τῶν γραφῶν τῶν θείων ἀλλὰ καὶ τῶν ἐννοιῶν Clem.*str*.8.1(p.81.8; M.9.561A); **2.** *be close*, *near*, hence ἐχόμενα *near* used adv. ἐστὶ δὲ ὁ τάφος ἐ. τοῦ τάφου τῶν βασιλέων ‡Epiph.*v.proph.Is*.6(p.20; M.43. 397C,420D); *ib*.1(p.20; 397B,420B); Thphyl.*exc.gent*.5(p.481.13; M. 113.941A).

ἕψεμα, τό, = ἕψημα, *mash* Ἠσαῦ τὰ πρωτοτόκια δι' ἐ. πυροῦ ἀπώλεσεν Epiph.*haer*.47.2(p.218.5; M.41.853A); plur., *vegetables fit for kitchen use*, *V.Pach*.Φ 28(p.18.7, v.l. ἑψήματα).

ἑψητήριον, τό, *cook-house* of a monastery, *V.Pach*.Σ 67(p.238.19); ‡Bas.*poen.mon*.52(3.530A; M.31.1313A).

§**ἑψία, ἡ**, *cooking*, Thdr.Stud.*iamb*.14(M.99.1785B).

§⟨**ἑψιάομαι**⟩, *follow* τίς γὰρ ἑψιωμένων βασιλέα...δῶρα...παρ' αὐτῶν οὐκ ἀμείψεται Jo.Eub.*concept.BMV*(M.96.1481B; conj. for MSS ὁ ψικεύων, ὀψικεύων; ? l. ἑψομένων).

ἑωθινός, **1.** *in the morning*, *early*; of prayers, Eus.*Ps*.45:6(M.23. 409B); Bas.*ep*.99(3.193B; M.32.497C); Marc.Diac.*v.Porph*.76; τὰς ἐ. ἡμῶν εὐχαριστίας *Const.App*.8.78.4; τὴν ἐ. λειτουργίαν *V.Pach*.Σ 58 (p.228.1); τὰς ἐ. λειτουργίας Jo.Ant.*relat.imp*.1(p.124.35; M.83. 1441A); τὸ ἐ. τρισάγιον *Const.Stud*.15(M.99.1209C); fem. as subst., *morning-watch*, morning ἀπὸ ἑωθινῆς ἕως ἑσπέρας *Ep.Lugd*.ap.Eus. *h.e*.5.1.18(M.20.416B); neut. plur. as subst., *morning service* κατελθὼν...διὰ τὰ ἐ. εἰς τὴν ἐκκλησίαν Jo.Mal.*chron*.13 p.334(M.97. 500A); **2.** *eastern* τὸ ἐ. ... κλίμα Philost.*h.e*.11.8(M.65.604A).

ἑωλοκρασία, ἡ, *drunkenness*, Clem.*paed*.2.2(p.174.6; M.8.424B); Chrys.*hom.35.3 in Ac*.(9.273B); Evagr.*h.e*.1.11(p.19.31; M.86.2452B).

ἕωλος, *a day old*, *stale*; hence freq. met., *worthless*, *pointless*, *vain* ἐ. τε καὶ ψευδέσι φήμαις Const.*or.s.c*.10(p.164.29; M.20.1257B);

ἡ πρόφασις αὐτοῖς ἑ. δειχθήσεται Ath.*gent*.16(M.25.33A); ἑ. ἡ τοῦ διαβόλου ἐπιβουλὴ γέγονε Chrys.*hom.85.1 in Jo*.(8.504C); ἐπ' αἰτίαις μὲν ἑ. ἀπεκτονότας τὸν Ἰησοῦν Cyr.*Is*.5.1(2.749D).

ἑῷος, 1. *of the morning*; fem. as subst., *morning*, Synes.*ep*.51 (M.66.1380B); **2.** *eastern*; fem. as subst., *east*, esp. = diocese of the Orient, Eus.*v.C*.1.49(p.30.20; M.20.964B); CSard.*ep.Alex*.ap.Ath.*apol.sec*.37(p.116.7; M.25.312D); Thdt.*h.e*.5.34.11(3.1076) al.

ἑωρίζομαι, *take a walk* ἐ. ... ἐπὶ τὸ παράλιον μέρος Jo.Mal.*chron*.2 p.32(M.97.101A); τὸ ἑωρισθῆναι *ib*.5 p.95(180C).

***ἑωροκοπία, ἡ,** v. *ἀεροκοπία.

ἕως, A. conjunction; **1.** *until*; **a.** use in scripture as tr. of Hebr. עַד explained τὸ δὲ 'ἕ.' οὐ χρόνου σημαντικόν, ἀλλ' ἰδίωμα τῆς γραφῆς ἐπὶ τοῦ ἀδιαλείπτως ἀεὶ τίθεσθαι Or.*Ps*.109:1(p.229) = Thdt.*Ps*.109:1(1.1393); misunderstood by Marcell. τὸ γὰρ 'ἕ.' καὶ τὸ 'ἄχρι' περιωρισμένου χρόνου σημαντικὸν εἶναι ὑπέλαβεν Eus.*e.th*.3.13(p.169.35; M.24.1024D); τὸ 'ἕ.' πολλαχοῦ χρόνου μέν τινα δοκεῖ περιορισμὸν ὑποφαίνειν, κατὰ δὲ τὴν ἀλήθειαν τὸ ἀόριστον δείκνυσιν †Bas.*Chr.generat*.5(2.600A; M.31.1468B,C); τὸ 'ἕ.' οὐ πάντως ἀντιδιαιρεῖ τῷ μέλλοντι, ἀλλὰ τὸ μέχρι μὲν τοῦδε τίθησι· τὸ ὑπὲρ τοῦτο δὲ οὐκ ἀναίνεται Gr.Naz.*or*.30.4(p.113.2; M.36.108B); ἀλλ' οὔτε ἐκεῖ τὸ 'ἕ.', οὔτε ἐνταῦθα [sc. 1Cor.15:25] τὸ 'μέχρις' χρόνων ὅροι εἰσίν Chrys.*exp.in Ps*.109:1(5.253A); τὸ 'ἕ.' πολλάκις καὶ ἐπὶ τοῦ 'διηνεκῶς' ἐν τῇ θείᾳ γραφῇ εὑρίσκομεν κείμενον Isid.Pel.*epp*.1.18(M.78.192B); τὸ δὲ 'ἕ.' πολλαχοῦ τῆς γραφῆς τὴν μετὰ τοῦ ὡρισμένου χρόνου προθεσμίαν σημαίνει· οὐκ ἀποφάσκει δὲ τὸ μετὰ ταῦτα Jo.D.*fr.Mt*.28:20(M.95.1413A); **b.** folld. by adv. of time; **i.** ἕ. οὗ c. subj., *Did*.14.2; Hegem.*Arch*.10(p.16.12; M.10.1444B); Ath.*virg*.19(p.54.22; M.28.276A); c. indic., Clem.*str*.1.21(p.90.3; M.8.885A); Hipp.*haer*.9.16(p.254.27; M.16.3394A); **ii.** ἕ. ὅτε c. subj., *A.Thom*.A 73(p.189.3); c. indic., *ib*.99(p.211.23); Gel.Cyz.*h.e*.2.13.13(M.85.1256A); **iii.** ἕ. πότε; Herm.*vis*.3.6.5; **iv.** ἕ. νῦν *T.Reub*.4.3; Hipp.*haer*.6.20(p.148.17; 3226B); Didym.*Trin*.2.14(M.39.713B); **c.** folld. by prep.; **i.** ἕ. ἐπί c. genit., *Pss.Sal*.17.14; c. acc., *T.Sal*.7.2; Didym.*Trin*.3.16(M.39.869C); **ii.** ἕ. εἰς Ath.*Ar*.1.2(M.26.56B); **2.** = ὥστε *so that* ὑδροφοβοῦσαν...ἕ. ἂν λάβῃ ἄρτον *T.Job* 21 (p.116.7); *ib*.22(p.116.17); *ib*.25(p.118.10); **3.** *while, so long as*, c. opt. τὸ δὲ εὐσεβεῖν ὅσιον παρὰ πᾶσιν ὡμολόγηται...ἕ. μόνον ὁ λέγων εὐσεβὲς ἔχοι τὸ φρόνημα Ath.*decr*.18(p.15.29; M.25.448C).

B. preposition; **1.** c. genit.; **a.** *as far as, up to, to* parts of the body κατακεκαλυμμένη ἕ. τοῦ μετώπου Herm.*vis*.4.2.1; Ath.*v.Anton*.53(M.26.920A); *to* places ἀπὸ τῆς Ἀραβικῆς χώρας ἕ. τῆς Αἰγύπτου εἰς τὴν λεγομένην Ἡλιούπολιν *1Clem*.25.3; ἕ. Συρίας Ign.*Smyrn*.11.2; Dor.*doct*.4.10(M.88.1669D); Cyr.S.*v.Euthym*.20(p.33.14); used to indicate conclusion of a citation 'εἴ τις ἀδελφὸς' ἕ. 'νῦν δὲ ἅγιά ἐστι' Clem.*str*.3.18(p.246.14; M.8.1212B); τὰ ἑξῆς ἕ. 'καὶ δυνάμεις ῥιζῶν' *ib*.2.2(p.115.12; 936A); *with reference to* οὐ γὰρ ἕ. τῶν ἀλόγων ζώων ἦν ἡ ἐπαγγελία, ἀλλ' εἰς ἀνθρώπους ἐστίν Ath.*ep.Epict*.8(p.13.5; M.26.1064A); τριὰς δέ ἐστιν οὐχ ἕ. ὀνόματος μόνον ἀλλὰ ἀληθείᾳ id.*ep.Serap*.1.28(M.26.596B); τὰ κατὰ τὸν θεὸν ἕ. ψιλῆς προσηγορίας ὁμολογηθήσεται ‡Ath.*dial.Trin*.2.15(M.28.1181A); †Apoll.*ep.Bas*.1 (M.32.1104C); **b.** *except* μὴ ἔχειν ἄλλο τί ποτε ἕ. κερατίου ἑνός Leont.N.*v.Jo.Eleem*.1(p.5.10); οὐκ ἀφῆκεν αὐτῷ...ὁ πατὴρ αὐτοῦ ἀποθνήσκων ἕ. ἑνὸς νομίσματος *ib*.34(p.66.22); **2.** c. acc.; **a.** *until* ἕ. αἰῶνας αἰώνων *T.Sym*.6.2; ἕ. τὸ ἅγιον πάσχα Thphn.*chron*.p.198(M.108.512B); **b.** *as far as, up to, to* ἕ. τὸ γόνυ τοῦ ἵππου Jo.Mal.*chron*.12 p.309(M.97.465A); Thphn.*chron*.p.392(936A).

ἑωσφόρος, 1. *bringing the dawn* ἦν ὁ διάβολος ἀστὴρ ἑ. Meth.*res*.1.37(p.279.1; M.41.1104B); **2.** as subst., *morning star*; **a.** exeg. Ps. 109:3 τὸν Χριστὸν...τοῦ θεοῦ υἱόν, ὃς καὶ πρὸ ἑ. ... ἦν Just.*dial*.45.4 (M.6.572D); ἐκ γαστρὸς πρὸ ἑ. ἐγέννησά σε...οὐ σημαίνει ὑμῖν ὅτι ἄνωθεν καὶ διὰ γαστρὸς ἀνθρωπείας...ὁ θεὸς...γεννᾶσθαι αὐτὸν ἔμελλε; *ib*.63.3(620C); ποίημα...ὁ ἐκ γαστρὸς πρὸ ἑ. γεννηθείς; Dion.R.ap.Ath.*decr*.26(p.23.6; M.25.464D); πρόδηλον οὖν τό, πρὸ ἑ. ἐγέννησά σε, ὑπὸ τοῦ παντοκράτορος εἰρῆσθαι δεσπότου περὶ τοῦ διὰ τῆς παρθένου γεννηθέντος σὺν τῇ ἀνθρωπίνῃ σαρκὶ λόγου...τοῦτο τοῦ εὐαγγελίου σημαίνοντος, πρότερον μὲν τὸν δεσπότην...τετέχθαι, ὕστερον δὲ τὸν ἀστέρα φανῆναι Marcell.*fr*.26 ap.Eus.*Marcell*.2.3(p.50.11; M.24.808C); εἰ τὸ πρὸ τοῦ ἑ. τούτου...δείκνυσι τὴν ἐκ Μαρίας γέννησιν, πολλοὶ καὶ ἄλλοι πρὸ τῆς τοῦ ἀστέρος ἀνατολῆς ἐγεννήθησαν ‡Ath.*Ar*.4.28(p.76.2; M.26.509D); οὐκ εἶπε, πρὸ ἀνατολῆς ἑ., ἀλλ' ἁπλῶς πρὸ ἑ. ... εἰ τοίνυν τὸ γένος Δαβὶδ ἐστιν ὁ ἀστήρ,...δῆλόν ἐστι τὸ κατὰ σάρκα τοῦ σωτῆρος ἑ. εἰρῆσθαι οὗ προϋπῆρχε τὸ ἐκ τοῦ θεοῦ γέννημα, ὡς...σε γεγέννηκα πρὸ τῆς κατὰ σάρκα ἐπιφανείας. τὸ γὰρ πρὸ ἑ. ἴσον ἐστὶ τῷ, πρὸ τῆς σαρκώσεως τοῦ λόγου *ib*.(pp.76.16–77.10; 512A–C); ἐκ γαστρὸς πρὸ ἑ. γεγέννηκά σε...εἴπωμεν, ὅτι καὶ ἦν καὶ γεγέννηται Bas.*Eun*.2.17(1.252D; M.29.608A); *ib*.2.24(260C; M.625C); Didym.*Ps*.109:3(M.39.1540C); **b.** of Jo. Bapt., precursor of Christ as sun, Or.*fr.45 in Jo*.(p.521.3,6); **c.** of Satan (*Lucifer*), Gr.Naz.*or*.36.5(M.36.269D); id.*carm*.1.1.7.56(M.37.443A); Thdt.*Is*.14:12(p.71.21; 2.268); Sophr.H.*mir.Cyr.et Jo*.36(M.87.3556A), cf. 1 supra.

Z

***ζάβα, ἡ,** *cuirass*, Jo.Mal.*chron*.13 p.332(M.97.496B); *Chron.Pasch*.p.339(M.92.884B).

§ζάβατος, *wearing a cuirass*, *Chron.Pasch*.p.393(M.92.1009A).

***ζαβέρνα, ἡ,** *bag*, Pall.*h.Laus*.19(p.60.2, v.l. σάκκον M.34.1066B).

[*]ζάβορος, *much-devouring*, Eudoc.*Cypr*.2.294(M.85.857A).

ζάθεος, *holy, sacred*; of persons, Gr.Naz.*carm*.2.2(epitaph.)75.3 (M.38.50A); Nonn.*par.Jo*.4:17(M.43.776B); of places, *ib*.2:17(764B).

ζάκορος, ὁ, *priest*, Eudoc.*Cypr*.1.290(M.85.844A).

***Ζακχαῖοι, οἱ,** sect of Gnostic heretics, also called βαρβηλῖται, Epiph.*anac*.26(p.235.20; M.42.857A); id.*haer*.26.3(p.279.25; M.41.336D).

***ζαλοειδής,** *stormy*, Ant.Mon.*hom*.130(M.89.1848C).

***ζαλώδης,** = foreg., ‡Chrys.*hom*.6(13.213F); †Cyr.*hom.div*.11(5^2.379D); Gr.Mag.*dial*.(tr.Zach.)2.17(M.*PL*.66.167C).

***ζάξ, ἡ,** *corner, nook* εἰς τὸν σταῦλον εἰσῆλθεν. ... ὁ δὲ Βαδούριος ἰδὼν τὸν βασιλέα ἔφυγεν ἀπὸ ζακὸς εἰς ζάκα Thphn.*chron*.p.208(M.108.533C).

***Ζάρ, ὁ,** (Hebr. זָר) *stranger* ἐλέησον ἡμᾶς, ὁ θεὸς Ζάρ *Apoc.Bar.rel*.7.25.

ζάω, *live, be alive*;

A. as divine characteristic; **1.** in gen. ζῇ γὰρ ὁ θεὸς καὶ ζῇ ὁ κύριος Ἰησοῦς Χριστὸς καὶ τὸ πνεῦμα τὸ ἅγιον *1Clem*.58.2; αὐτὸς [sc. θεός] γὰρ ἐξ ὅλης τῆς πάσης οὐσίας τε καὶ φύσεως τῷ ἑαυτοῦ τὰ πάντα εἰς τὸ ζῆν ἐφέλκεται λόγῳ Meth.*Porph*.3(p.506.13; M.18.401A); θεῖος δὲ χαρακτὴρ οὐχ οἷος ἀνθρώπινος, ἀλλὰ ζῶν Didym.(‡Bas.)*Eun*.5(1.302A; M.29.724C); **2.** of Christ Χριστὸν...καθ' ἑαυτὸν δὲ ὄντα καὶ ζῶντα Eus.*e.th*.1.8(p.66.19; M.24.837B); Gr.Naz.*carm*.2.2(*epigr*.)11.1 (M.38.87); esp. of Christ living in man Χριστός, τὸ ἀδιάκριτον ἡμῶν ζῆν Ign.*Eph*.3.2; διὰ Ἰησοῦ Χριστοῦ, δι' οὗ ἐὰν μὴ αὐθαιρέτως ἔχωμεν τὸ ἀποθανεῖν εἰς τὸ αὐτοῦ πάθος, τὸ ζῆν αὐτοῦ οὐκ ἔστιν ἐν ἡμῖν id.*Magn*.5.2; and men in Christ ἐν Χριστῷ Ἰησοῦ εὑρεθῆναι εἰς τὸ ἀληθινὸν ζῆν id.*Eph*.11.1; **3.** of H. Ghost πνεῦμα...οὐκ ἐπισκευαστῶς ζῶν, ἀλλὰ ζωῆς χορηγόν Bas.*Spir*.22(3.19C; M.32.108B); πνεῦμα...δύναμιν οὐσιώδη ζῶσαν Jo.D.*f.o*.1.7(M.94.805B).

B. ref. difference between divine and human life οὐ γὰρ ἴδιον αὐτῆς [sc. ψυχῆς] ἐστι τὸ ζῆν ὡς τοῦ θεοῦ Just.*dial*.6.2(M.6.489B); ἀνθρώπῳ τὸ ζῆν καὶ τὸ τεθνάναι, ἀλλὰ τῷ θεῷ οὐ τὸ τεθνάναι ἀλλὰ τὸ ζῆν, καὶ τὸ ζῆν αἰωνίως *Hom.Clem*.19.11; τότε μὲν εἰς ψυχὴν ζῶσαν ἐγένετο ὁ ἄνθρωπος, νῦν δὲ εἰς πνεῦμα ζωοποιοῦν. πολὺ δὲ τὸ μέσον ἑκατέρων, ἡ μὲν γὰρ ψυχὴ οὐχ ἑτέρῳ παρέχει τὸ ζῆν, τὸ δὲ πνεῦμα οὐ καθ' ἑαυτὸ ζῇ μόνον, ἀλλὰ καὶ ἑτέροις παρέχει τοῦτο Chrys.*hom.25.2 in Jo*.(8.145B).

C. ref. spiritual life; distinction between living, living well, and living eternally τῶν ἀναγκαίων τὰ μὲν πρὸς τὸ ζῆν ἐστι τὸ ἐνταῦθα μόνον, τὰ δὲ ἔνθεν πρὸς τὸ εὖ ζῆν ἐκεῖσε ἀναπτεροῖ, ἀναλόγως καὶ τῶν καθηκόντων τὰ μὲν πρὸς τὸ ζῆν, τὰ δὲ πρὸς τὸ εὖ ζῆν διατάττεται. ὅσα μὲν οὖν πρὸς τὸ ἐθνικὸν ζῆν παραγγέλλεται, ταῦτα καὶ παρὰ τοῖς πολλοῖς δεδήμευται, ἃ δὲ πρὸς τὸ εὖ ζῆν ἁρμόττει, ἐξ ὧν τὸ ἀΐδιον ἐκεῖνο περιγίνεται ζῆν, ταῦτα...ἐξέστω σκοπεῖν Clem.*paed*.1.13(p.152.1ff.; M.8.376B); τὸ ζῆν ἐν ἀρχῇ μετὰ τοῦ πλάσαι παρασχὼν ὡς δημιουργός, τὸ εὖ ζῆν ἐδίδαξεν ἐπιφανεὶς ὡς διδάσκαλος, ἵνα τὸ ἀεὶ ζῆν ὕστερον ὡς θεὸς χορηγήσῃ id.*prot*.1(p.7.31f.; M.8.61C); ἐν πολλῷ δὲ τῷ βίῳ μακαριστὸς οὐ διὰ τὸ μακρὸν [γενόμενος] ζῆν, ᾧ γε καὶ διὰ τὸ ζῆσαι εὖ ὑπῆρξεν ἀξίῳ τοῦ ζῆν ἀεὶ γενέσθαι id.*ecl*.31(p.146.17; M.9.713C); id.*prot*.11(p.79.25; M.8.229B); Or.*Cels*.7.50(p.201.5; M.11.1493B); exeg. Mt.22:32 ὁ θεὸς οὐκ ἔστιν νεκρῶν θεὸς ἀλλὰ ζώντων, καὶ οἴδαμεν τίς ἐστιν ὁ ζῶν, ὅτι ὁ πολιτευόμενος κατὰ Χριστόν id.*hom.9.3 in Jer*.(p.68.4; M.13.353B); attained through baptism εἰς τὸ ὕδωρ οὖν καταβαίνουσι νεκροί, καὶ ἀναβαίνουσι ζῶντες Herm.*sim*.9.16.4; *ib*.9.16.6; through repentance ἵνα μετανοήσωσι, καὶ ζήσονται τῷ θεῷ *ib*.8.11.1; *ib*.8.11.3; *ib*.9.21.4; through faith and hope τῇ πίστει τῆς ἐπαγγελίας...ζήσομεν *Barn*.6.17; *ib*.8.5 cit. s. ἐλπίζω; πιστεύσατε...ἵνα ζήσητε Clem.*prot*.10(p.70.14; M.8.209B); through doing God's will and keeping commandments, *2Clem*.10.1; πορεύεσθε οὖν ταῖς ἐντολαῖς μου...καὶ ζήσεσθε τῷ θεῷ Herm.*mand*.6.1.4; φοβήθητι οὖν *τὸν κύριον, καὶ ζήσῃ αὐτῷ· καὶ ὅσοι ἂν φοβηθῶσιν αὐτὸν τῶν φυλασσόντων τὰς ἐντολὰς αὐτοῦ, ζήσονται τῷ θεῷ ib.*7.4; linked with contemplation *τὸ δὲ ἀεὶ νοεῖν, οὐσία τοῦ γινώσκοντος κατὰ ἀνάκρασιν ἀδιάστατον γενομένη καὶ ἀΐδιος θεωρία, ζῶσα ὑπόστασις μένει* Clem. *str.*4.22(p.308.27; M.8.1345C); cf. *ἐν τῇ προσευχῇ...κατὰ νοῦν ζῆθι* Evagr.Pont.*or.*110(M.79.1192B).

D. ref. eternal life *ὅταν τὸ ἀληθῶς ἐν οὐρανῷ ζῆν ἐπιγνῷς, ὅταν τοῦ δοκοῦντος ἐνθάδε θανάτου καταφρονήσῃς Diogn.*10.7; *κληρονομεῖν δὲ τὸ ζῶν λέγει, καὶ ἀποθνήσκειν μὲν σάρκα, ζῆν δὲ τὴν βασιλείαν τῶν οὐρανῶν* Meth.*res.*2.18(p.370.13f.; M.18.313B); *τῶν δὲ ἱερῶν πτυχῶν... ἀνάρρησις...τοὺς δὲ ὡς ζῶντας ἀνακηρύττουσα, καὶ ὡς ἡ θεολογία φησίν, οὐ νεκρωθέντας* Dion.Ar.*e.h.*3.3.9(M.3.437B).

E. of spiritual things *ἐκκλησία ζῶσα σῶμά ἐστιν Χριστοῦ 2Clem.* 14.2; *μαθηταὶ τοῦ Ἰησοῦ, ἵνα ὁδεύσωσιν τὴν ζῶσαν καὶ ἔμψυχον ὁδόν* Or.*Jo.*32.7(6; p.437.15; M.14.760C); *νόμος θεοῦ ἁπλοῦς...ζῶν οὗτος ἐνυπάρχει Const.App.*1.1.7.

F. *ζῶν ὕδωρ*, lit., ref. baptism, v. *ὕδωρ*; met., ref. Jo.4:10ff., v. *ὕδωρ*.

G. *ζώσης φωνῆς*, *viva voce*, Eus.*h.e.*5.10.4(M.20.456B); CHier.(335) *ep.*(p.248.3; M.26.717D).

ζείδωρος, *life-giving*, Synes.*hymn.*5.27(p.36; M.66.1608); Nonn. *par.Jo.*4:11(M.43.776A); *ib.*6:26(797B).

***ζεόντως**, *eagerly*, Jo.Clim.*scal.*1(M.88.641B).

ζέσις, ἡ, 1. *heat*; of food in digestive organs, Bas.*hom.in Ps.*44 (1.161A; M.29.393B); met., of anger, Gr.Nyss.*hom.9 in Cant.*(M.44. 973C); †Nil.*mal.cog.*16(M.79.1217D); Pall.*h.Laus.*33(p.97.9; M.34. 1105D); **2.** *fervour, zeal*, Gr.Naz.*ep.*216(M.37.353A); id.*carm.*1.2.10. 962(M.37.749A); Cyr.*Jo.*4.4(4.385A); cf.*Lit.Chrys.*(p.394.10).

ζεύγλη, ἡ, *yoke*; met., of divine commandment, Gr.Nyss.*or. dom.*2(p.38.33; M.44.1144D); of service of Christ, Bas.*renunt.*9(2. 294A; M.31.648A); id.*hom.*13.1(2.114E; M.31.425C); of marriage, Thdt.*qu.1 in Lev.*(1.182); id.*qu.25 in 4Reg.*(1.529); of priesthood, id.*h.rel.*15(3.1220); Cyr.*Is.*5.5(2.885C).

ζευκτόν, τό, *yoke* of oxen, *A.Thom.*A 146(p.254.15).

ζεῦμα, τό, *fount*, of eyes *τῶν ζ. τοῦ φωτός T.Abr.*B 6(p.110.14).

***ζευξιμοιχεία, ἡ,** *adulterous marriage*, Thdr.Stud.*epp.*1.33(M.99. 1017D).

***ζεφυρώδης**, *with a westerly* or *favourable wind*, Jo.VI H.*v.Jo.D.* 11(M.94.445B).

***ζεφύρωσις, ἡ,** *blowing of the west wind*, Steph.Diac.*v.Steph.*(M. 100.1092A).

ζέω, *be hot, fervent, ardent*; **1.** in gen., Athenag.*leg.*22.2(M.6. 937A); *Hom.Clem.*4.24; of a recent wound, Jo.Clim.*scal.*26(M.88. 1089A); liturg., of water added to chalice before Communion, cf. *Lit.Chrys.*(p.394.7); **2.** met., of youth, Clem.*paed.*2.2(p.168.15; M.8. 412A); the spirit, Chrys.*hom.21.3 in Rom.*(9.675C); Thdt.*Rom.*12:11 (3.133); anger, Clem.*q.d.s.*8(p.165.5; M. om.); Chrys.*scand.*10(3. 490C); lust, *Hom.Clem.*3.68; love, Gr.Nyss.*virg.*3(p.261.1; M.46. 329D); Chrys.*scand.*6(3.475D); faith, Marc.Diac.*v.Porph.*16; *τῷ πνεύματι ζ.* Gr.Naz.*or.*32.6(M.36.180B).

***ζέως**, *ardently*, Jo.Clim.*scal.*2(M.88.656B).

ζηγήμων, *ardent*, Gr.Naz.*carm.*1.1.9.25(M.37.458A); *ib.*2.2(epigr.) 11.2(M.38.87A).

ζῆλος, ὁ and **τό, 1.** *jealousy, envy*; **a.** in gen., as cause of persecution of Christians, *1Clem.*5.2ff.; a cause of anger, *ib.*63.2; of Devil's envy of man, ‡Ign.*Trall.*4; caused by lust, *T.Reub.*6.4; *T.Jud.*13.3; *Κάϊν ὁ ἑρμηνεύεται ζ. Hom.Clem.*3.42; prompting Jews to crucify Christ, Thdt.*Is.*26:11(p.105.18; 2.295); of heret. factions, Alex.Al. *ep.Alex.*9(p.25.11; M.18.561A); **b.** in good sense; of God's jealousy of Devil *ποῖος ζ., ᾗ ὃν ἐζήλωσεν ἀγαθὸν καὶ αὐτῷ πρέποντα, εἰς τὸ σῶσαι πάντας τοὺς ὑπὸ τοῦ διαβόλου καταδυναστευθέντας...;* Eus.*Is.* 9:7(M.24.153C); Cyr.*Is.*1.5(2.157A); ref. Jo.6:59 *εἰπὼν...ζωὴν διδοὺς τῷ κόσμῳ,...εἰς ζ. αὐτοὺς ἐνάγει, ὥστε κἂν ἀλγήσαντας ἐπὶ τῷ ἄλλους ἀπολαύειν τῆς δωρεᾶς, μὴ μεῖναι ἔξω* Chrys.*hom.47.1 in Jo.*(8.276D); hence **2.** *imitation*, of creatures' love reciprocating God's love *ζ. ...τῆς ἐφέσεως αὐτοῦ τῆς ἐρωτικῆς* Dion.Ar.*d.n.*4.13(M.3.712B); **3.** *righteous indignation* of God, against sinner, cf.Dt.13:9, *Pss. Sal.*4.3; *ζ. κατὰ τῶν πολεμίων* Thdt.*Is.*63:15(p.248.37; 2.390).

ζηλοτυπ-έω, 1. *be jealous of*; of God's affection for Israel, Thdt. *Ezech.*16:42(2.788); pass. *δι' αὐτοὺς τοὺς ~ουμένους πάντα ποιεῖ* Chrys.*hom.23.1 in 2Cor.*(10.595D); pass., *be under suspicion*, Clem. *str.*3.4(p.208.3; M.8.1132A); met., *long for*, Gr.Naz.*or.*8.22(M.35. 813C); **2.** *resent ζ. τὸ ἐκείνου μεγαλοφυὲς στρεφόμενον ἐν ταῖς χείροσι ib.*7.15(773B).

ζηλοτυπία, ἡ, 1. in gen., *ardent emotion*, of love *φίλτρου κλαπέντος εἰς ξένον...καλοῦσι...ζ.* Gr.Naz.*carm.*1.2.34.81(M.37.951A); Chrys. *hom.23.1 in 2Cor.*(10.595C); *irritation*, ref. Dt.32:21, Or.*princ.*4.1.4 (p.298.12; M.11.349A); **2.** *jealousy*; Clem.*str.*2.18(p.161.7; M.8.1029B); *ib.*3.4(p.207.21; M.8.1129B); hence name of sacrifice, 'offering of jealousy' (Num.5:15 al.), †Bas.*Is.*29(1.402A; M.30.176A); *emulation*, ref. alms-giving, *cat.2Cor.*11:9(p.423.12).

***ζηλοτυπικός**, *zealous*, Ammon.*Ac.*15:39(M.85.1553B).

***ζηλοτυποειδής**, *seemingly jealous*, Or.*sel.in Ezech.*16:8(M.13. 809D).

ζηλότυπος, 1. *jealous ζ. ... αἱ ψυχαὶ αἱ σφόδρα τῶν ἐρωμένων περικαιόμεναι* Chrys.*hom.23.1 in 2Cor.*(10.595C); of God, id.*fr. in Jer.*2:13(M.64.764A); of a husband, Thdt.*qu.39 in Ex.*(1.150); **2.** *contentious νόμοι, ζ. ἀνθρώποις κείμενοι Hom.Clem.*5.11.

ζηλοτύπως, *with jealousy ζ. ... ἔχοντες ἀεὶ πρὸς τοῦ Χριστοῦ μαθητὰς οἱ μαθηταὶ Ἰωάννου, καὶ πρὸς αὐτὸν...τὸν Χριστόν* Chrys. *hom.29.1 in Jo.*(8.165E); id.*hom.14.1 in Mt.*(7.179C).

ζηλ-όω, 1. *imitate ἵνα...εἰ θέλομεν μετὰ τῶν προφητῶν ἔχειν ἀνάπαυσιν, τὰ ἔργα τῶν προφητῶν ζηλώσωμεν* Or.*hom.14.4 in Jer.* (p.119.10; M.13.421A); *ib.*(p.120.4; 421C); Eus.*h.e.*2.17.5(M.20.177A); Cyr.*ador.*4(1.139C); Chrys.*stat.*1.6(2.9B); of imitation of suffering Christ, id.*hom.83.5 in Jo.*(8.496C); **2.** *be jealous* (*for*) *προσθήσει κύριος τοῦ δεῖξαι τὴν χεῖρα αὐτοῦ, ὑπὲρ τοῦ ~ῶσαι τὸν Ἰσραήλ, καὶ οἷον μὴ μόνοις τοῖς ἔθνεσι παραχωρῆσαι Χριστόν* Cyr.*Is.*2.1(2.204A); *jealously oppose μηθέν με ~ώσαι τῶν ὁρατῶν καὶ τῶν ἀοράτων, ἵνα Ἰησοῦ Χριστοῦ ἐπιτύχω* Ign.*Rom.*5.3; **3.** *be zealous*, of Jews who persecuted Christ *ὡς ὑπὲρ τοῦ θεοῦ ~οῦντες* Chrys.*hom.44.3 in Jo.* (8.319C); of God *~ώσει γὰρ καὶ φείσεται ὑμῶν...εἰ μεταμελομένους τε ἴδοι* Thdr.Mops.*Joel.*2:18(M.66.225C); ref. divine adoption *~ώσατε...τὴν συγγένειαν* Thdt.*Eph.*5:1(3.429).

ζηλωτής, ὁ, 1. *jealous*, adj. and subst.; **a.** ref. divine jealousy, Cyr.*Juln.*5(6[2].157A); Thdt.*qu.39 in Ex.*(1.150); Dion.Ar.*d.n.*4.13 (M.3.776B); **b.** of men, in gen., *Did.*3.2; Arist.*apol.*7.3; *Const.App.* 7.5.5; hence **2.** *object of jealousy, opponent φιλόνεικοι τὸν ζ. καταπεπωκότες* ‡Just.*ep.Zen.et Ser.*6(M.6.1189C); **3.** *zealous follower, emulator, votary*; **a.** in rel. to God, Meth.*symp.*proem.(p.7.4; M. 18.36B); Tit.Bost.*Man.*2.5(M.18.1141C); Chrys.*hom.77.2 in Jo.*(8. 453B); Thdt.*2Cor.*10:1f.(3.337); esp. of OT prophets, etc. *Φινεὲς ζ.* Bas.*Eun.*1.1(1.208C; M.29.501A); *Ἠλίας ὁ ζ. τῶν προφητῶν Const. App.*6.19.4; *τὸν Ἠλίαν ζ. τοῦ κυρίου* ‡Chrys.*hom.suppl.*6(M.64.464C); *ὁ ζ. Ἱερεμίας* Gr.Nyss.*Eun.*10(2 p.233.15; M.45.836A); **b.** in rel. to other men: apostles and others, Eus.*h.e.*3.4.1(M.20.220A); of bishop as *ζ. τῶν μαρτύρων* Chrys.*ascens.*1(2.448A); of holy monk, ‡Pall. *h.mon.*8.17(p.38.2; M.34.1139C); in rel. to ideas and beliefs *ζ. περὶ τῶν ἀνηκόντων εἰς σωτηρίαν 1Clem.*45.1; Or.*princ.*4.1.1(p.294.8; M. 11.344B); *τοὺς Ἑλλήνων σοφοὺς ζ. ... τῶν Ἑβραϊκῶν...δογμάτων* Eus. *p.e.*10.14(505C; M.21.841A); Ath.*Ar.*2.21(M.26.192B).

ζηλωτικός, 1. *jealous*, Hipp.*haer.*4.26(p.53.18; M.16.3090A); **2.** *zealous*, Pall.*h.Laus.*66(p.150.1; M.34.1244D); neut. as subst., Epiph.*haer.*66.8(p.28.26; M.42.41B).

***ζηλωτρία, ἡ,** *zealous woman, zealot*, Thphn.*chron.*p.117(M.108. 332A).

***ζημαρχός, ὁ,** error for *δημαρχός*, Jo.Mosch.*prat.*190(M.87.3069B).

ζημιωτής, ὁ, *he who punishes ὁ ὕπνος τῆς ψυχῆς, ὁ ζ. τῶν χαυνοτέρων* ‡Chrys.*poenit.*1.1(9.764A).

ζητέω, *seek*; **1.** mentally and spiritually; for Christ, Ign.*Rom.* 6.1; *ἐκζητοῦντες τί ζ. κύριος ἀφ' ὑμῶν Barn.*21.6; *ζ. πῶς προσάγωμεν αὐτῷ* [sc. God] *ib.*2.9; *ζ. τὰ ἀνήκοντα ταῖς ψυχαῖς ὑμῶν Did.*16.2; **2.** *inquire, seek*, in scriptures *ζ. ... εἰ ἐμέλησεν τῷ κυρίῳ προφανερῶσαι περὶ τοῦ ὕδατος καὶ περὶ τοῦ σταυροῦ Barn.*11.1; Or.*princ.*4.3.1(p.324. 6; M.11.377A); *ζ. κατὰ τὸν Ἀβραὰμ καὶ Ἰακὼβ παιδοποιΐας* Eus.*d.e.* 1.9(p.42.33; M.22.81C); *ib.*5.6(p.229.22; 380A); hence pass. ptcpl neut., *problem* of exegesis or theology, Or.*Cels.*4.88(p.360.9; M.11. 1165C); *ζ. τι...ἀπὸ τῆς Ἐξόδου* id.*comm.in Gen.*(M.12.69A)ap.Eus. *p.e.*6.11(290B); Eus.*d.e.*5.1(p.214.25; 356C); **3.** of rational inquiry about object of faith, Clem.*fr.*67(p.228.30); *ἵν' οὖν μὴ...τὰ πιστευθέντα ἡμῖν ζ.* Ath.*ep.encycl.*1(p.170.16; M.25.225A); ref. Heb.11:6 *πιστεῦσαι γὰρ δεῖ...οὐχὶ ζ.* †Bas.*hom.in Ps.*115(1.372A; M.30.105B); *οὐ δεῖ ζ. καὶ περιεργάζεσθαι τὰ μὴ παραδεδομένα ἡμῖν ὑπὸ τῶν ἁγίων προφητῶν* Jo.D.*f.o.*1.1(M.94.789A).

ζήτησις, ἡ, *question, inquiry*, in gen. *περὶ θεοῦ ζ.* Just.*1apol.*63.17 (M.6.425B); id.*2apol.*10.6(461A); *νόμων ζ. Const.App.*7.16.5; esp. ref. exegetical problems, Just.*dial.*112.4(M.6.736A); Or.*engast.*2(p.284. 24; M.12.1016A); Meth.*res.*1.27(p.256.7; M.41.1133C); ref. theol. controversies, Clem.*ecl.*36(p.148.6; M.9.717A); *ἀγράφοις τε εἰς πρόσωπον ζ.* Eus.*h.e.*4.24(M.20.389B); *ib.*5.23.1(489C); *ζ.* [such as] *ὁ ἀγέννητος πῶς ἀγέννητος* Gel.Cyz.*h.e.*2.19.13(M.85.1277C); as title of book *Γάϊος...ἐν τῇ φερομένῃ ζ. ... γράφει* Eus.*h.e.*3.28.1(273C).

ζητητέον, *one must inquire* or *investigate*; ref. philos. and theol. method, Clem.*str*.8.2(p.81.22; M.9.561C); *ib*.8.6(p.90.11; 581B); ref. theol. questions, Or.*Jo*.2.12(p.67.30; M.14.145D); *one must seek* ὑγείαν ...τῆς ψυχῆς ζ. id.*sel.in Ps*.4(p.238.3; M.12.1157D).

***ζητητήρ, ὁ**, *seeker*, Mac.Mgn.*apocr*.4.14(p.181.13).

ζητητικός, *inquiring*; ref. exegesis and theology, Clem.*paed*.2.10 (p.219.15; M.8.521A); φύσει...ὁ ἄνθρωπος...ζῷον...τοῦ καλοῦ ζ. *ib*.3.7 (p.258.7; 608B); id.*str*.6.15(p.491.10; M.9.341B); Or.*princ*.4.2.9(p.322. 9; M.11.376A); ref. Jo.5:39 τό, ἐρευνᾶτε τὰς γραφάς, οὐ τοὺς ζ. ἐστιν εἰσάγοντος πόνους Chrys.*hom.1.2 in 1Tim*.(11.551E); λογισμοὶ ζ. *ib*.*7.1*(584C); neut. as subst., *inquiry*, ref. Lc.12:28 μὴ εἰς τρυφὴν τὸ ζ. ἀπολλύωμεν Clem.*paed*.2.10(p.219.15; 521A).

***ζητουμένως**, *questionably*, Chrys.*hom.11.1 in 1Tim*.(11.606A).

ζιβύνη, ἡ, *spear*; met., ref. Is.2:4 τὰς ζ. εἰς γεωργικὰ μεταβάλομεν, καὶ γεωργοῦμεν εὐσέβειαν Just.*dial*.110.3(M.6.729B); ref. submission of heretics μεταχαλκεύσαντες τὰς ζ. εἰς ἄροτρα Bas. *hom*.24.2(2.190E; M.31.604A); as sign of repentance, cf.Joel 3:10 συγκόψωμεν, καθὼς γέγραπται...τὰς ζ. εἰς δρέπανα Cyr.*hom.pasch*.8.4 (5^2.99E).

[*]**ζιγγίβερ, τό**, *ginger*, Thphn.*chron*.p.268(M.108.665A).

ζιζάνιον, τό, *tare*, met.; **1.** of diabolical action or suggestion in general, *A.Thom*.A 145(p.253.17); Or.*hom.1.15 in Jer*.(p.14.14; M. 13.274C); **2.** of ὑλικόν or σαρκικόν element sown in man by Devil, Clem.*exc.Thdot*.53(p.124.16; M.9.684C); id.*str*.3.4(p.211.19; M.8. 1140A); Thdt.*haer*.1.16(4.309); hence *vice* μιμεῖται τὴν ἀρετὴν ἡ κακία, καὶ τὸ ζ. βιάζεται σῖτος νομισθῆναι Cyr.H.*catech*.4.1; **3.** of heresy μὴ οὖν ἐπίσπειρε ζ. τῷ ἀγρῷ τῆς θείας γραφῆς ‡Ath.*dial.Trin*. 2.9(M.28.1169B); ὁ τῶν ζ. σπορεύς Gr.Naz.*or*.21.21(M.35.1105B); Epiph.*haer*.40.1(p.80.28; M.41.677B); *ib*.70.15(p.249.15; M.42.373C); στενοχωρεῖται γὰρ ἡ σοφία ἐν τοῖς τὰ ζ. γεωργοῦσι Pall.*v.Chrys*.14 (p.89.16; M.47.50); Thphn.*chron*.p.79(M.108.241C).

***ζιζανιόσπορος**, *sowing tares*; met., of heresies, Anast.S.*hod*.9 (M.89.140C).

***ζιζανιώδης**, *like tares*; met., of heresy, Gr.Nyss.*Eun*.12(1 p.370. 3; M.45.1096A); id.*Apoll*.51(M.45.1245C); Epiph.*haer*.26.17(p.298.17; M.41.361A).

***ζιζανιωδῶς**, *like tares*; met., ref. errors by Devil, Epiph.*haer*.52. 1(M.41.956B; ζιζανίων p.312.16).

***ζικίον, τό**, error for βικίον, *vessel, box*, Jo.Mosch.*prat*.203(M.87. 3094B).

***ζόμφος**, *flexible*, comp., Steph.Diac.*v.Steph*.(M.100.1140A).

ζοφερός, *dark*; met., ref. sin and error φαντασίαν τὴν ζ. συγχεῖν τῷ τῆς ἀληθείας φωτί Clem.*str*.5.4(p.343.21; M.9.49A); ref. human race before Inc. ἐν νυκτὶ ζ. Eus.*h.e*.10.4.13(M.20.853A); of earthly delights λαβύρινθος ζ. Isid.Pel.*epp*.5.485(M.78.1609B); ref. death ὁ θάνατος...ἐποίησεν ὄψιν ζ. *T.Abr*.A 17(p.99.15, v.l. φοβεράν); Nonn. *par.Jo*.12:35(M.43.856C); of Devil ζ. ἄρχων Cyr.H.*catech*.19.4.

***ζοφηφορία, ἡ**, *gloom*, Gr.Naz.*ep*.4(M.37.25A).

ζοφόεις, *dark*, *Orac.Sib*.2.302; Nonn.*par.Jo*.9:26(M.43.829A); *ib*. 20:15(909C); met., of human hearts, *Orac.Sib*.8.230; of the world, Nonn.*par.Jo*.9:5(824A); *obscure, hidden*, Geo.Pis.*carm.vit*.7.

ζοφώδης, *dark*, met. ἀποβάλλοντες ζ. διάθεσιν Or.*sel.in Jer*.17:21ff. (*AS* 3 p.541); *benighted, unenlightened*, Rom.Mel.(*AS* 1 p.12).

ζόφωσις, ἡ, *darkness*, met. τῇ ζ. τῶν παθῶν Geo.Pis.*carm*.107.31; *gloom* πάντας κατεῖχε ζ. καὶ...ἀθυμία Thphn.*chron*.p.403(M.108.960B).

***ζταγγίον, τό**, a kind of *shoe*, for τζαγγίον, Jo.Mal.*chron*.17 p.413 (M.97.612B).

***ζυγαδικός**, *conjugal*, ref. Creation ἄνευ τῆς ζ. φύσεως συνεστήσατο ἄνθρωπον Ephr.2.277D.

***ζυγαῖος**, *yoked together*, met. ζ. ... φῶς καὶ ἀθανασία ‡Chrys. *circ*.(8.88B).

§**ζυγάς, ἡ**, *pair*; hence met., *union* ὅτι οὐδὲν μεῖζον ἀγάπης· ἐν ᾧ ἀποδείξεις ἔχει τὰς ἀδελφικὰς ζ. Isid.Pel.*epp*.1.10 tit.(M.78.185B).

ζυγή, ἡ, *pair*; **1.** in gen., Epiph.*mens*.3(M.43.241C); κατὰ ζυγὴν ἐν κοιτῶσι...καθεύδοντες [sc. LXX] *ib*.; *Dial.Tim.et Aquil*.117 r°; of couples in ark, Cosm.Ind.*top*.2(M.88.84D); **2.** *yoke*, instrument of torture, *M.Carp*.35; *M.Artem*.(p.168.10).

***ζυγιάζω**, *weigh* ὁ Δοκιὴλ ὁ ἀρχάγγελος ὁ δίκαιος ζυγοστάτης...ζ. τὰς δικαιοσύνας καὶ τὰς ἁμαρτίας ἐν δικαιοσύνῃ θεοῦ *T.Abr*.A 13(p.93. 6); *ib*.12(p.91.14).

***ζυγιανός, ὁ**, *one born under the constellation* Libra, Bas.*hex*.6.6 (1.55C; M.29.129C).

ζύγιον, τό, *scales*, Mac.Aeg.*hom*.5.6(M.34.504A,C); plur., Nil.*epp*. 3.5(M.79.368A).

ζύγιος, *of the yoke*; hence, met.; **1.** *married*, Gr.Naz.*carm*.1.2.2. 328(M.37.604A); ἀζυγέων καὶ ζ. *ib*.1.2.29.260(903A); **2.** *balancing* εὗρεν [sc. recording angel]...ζ. τὰς ἁμαρτίας καὶ τὰς δικαιοσύνας ἐξ ἴσου *T.Abr*.A 12(p.91.24).

ζυγόδεσμος, ὁ, *yoke-band*; met., of bonds of sin, ref. Is.5:18, †Bas.*Is*.171(1.502B; M.30.401C); broken by Christ, Paul.Sil.*Soph*. 948(M.86.2155A).

ζυγοκρούστης, ὁ, *one who uses false weights*, *Const.App*.4.6.5.

ζυγομαχία, ἡ, *internal strife*, Const.ap.Eus.*h.e*.10.5.24(M.20. 892A); Gr.Naz.*or*.22.13(M.35.1145A); Gel.Cyz.*h.e*.2.8.2(M.85.1244B).

ζυγός, ὁ, (ζυγόν, τό), **1.** *yoke, link*; **a.** of material things, *crossbar* of cithara, Clem.*prot*.1(p.3.16; M.8.52A); **b.** of one thing with another, *pair*, Ath.*Ar*.3.60(M.26.449A); **c.** met., of yoke of God, *Pss.Sal*.7.8; *ib*.17.32; ὁ ζ. τῆς χάριτος [sc. Χριστοῦ] *1Clem*.16.17; τὸν ζ. τοῦ κυρίου *Did*.6.2; ὁ τῆς θεοσεβείας...ζ. Eus.*l.C*.17(p.255.30; M.20.1433A); Thdt.*Ps*.2:3(1.619); Dion.Ar.*e.h*.3.3.11(M.3.440C); *ib*. 5.3.8(516A); ἡ θεαρχία...ἐπιβάλλουσα πᾶσι τοὺς ἐθελουσίους ζ. id.*d.n*. 10.1(M.3.937A); of Law ζ. δουλείας Thdt.*Gal*.5:1(3.387); of spiritual government, Chrys.*sac*.2.4(p.34.3; 1.374D); priesthood, *ib*.1.6(p.10. 24; 1.365C); Evagr.*h.e*.1.15(p.25.19; M.86.2464B); ὁ γαμικὸς ζ. Thdt. *qu.2 in Ruth*(1.350); ζ. ἀνάγκης *Barn*.2.6; **2.** *balance*, met. ἐν ζ. στήκεις, ἢ δεχθῆναι ἢ μὴ δεχθῆναι [sc. catechumen] Cyr.H.*procatech*. 13; ref. freedom of choice ζ. ὠνόμασεν ἡ γραφή, διὰ τὸ ἴσην δύνασθαι λαμβάνειν τὴν ῥοπὴν ἐφ' ἑκάτερα Bas.*hom.in Ps*.61(1.197D; M.29. 479B) = Nil.*epp*.3.5(M.79.368A); with idea of equality, of equal desires of two persons ὁ ζ. ... ἴσος Chrys.*sac*.1.1(p.3.9; 1.363A); ἡ... θεία ζωὴ κατ' ἀξίαν ὑπὸ τῶν δικαιοτάτων ζ. ἀντιδίδοται Dion.Ar.*e.h*. 7.3.7(M.3.561D); id.*d.n*.1.3(M.3.616C); ref. gift of spiritual understanding in proportion to capacity of each recipient τὰ θεία ζ. id.*e.h*.1.2(373B); **3.** constellation *Libra*, Bas.*hex*.6.6(1.55D; M.29. 129D).

ζυγοστασία, ἡ, *weighing*, Thdr.Stud.*or*.11.1(M.99.808C).

ζυγοστατ-έω, *weigh*, met.; **1.** of psychological operations, ref. power of judgement to sway will πιστεύοντες...αἰτήσομεν...· τοῦ γὰρ αἰτοῦντος ἡ προσευχὴ...~εῖται...καὶ ταλαντεύεται ὁ νοῦς ὅποι κλίνει ‡Pion.*v.Polyc*.31; ref. freedom of choice λογισμοῦ διάκρισις ~οῦσα τῶν πρακτέων τὴν αἵρεσιν Bas.Sel.*or*.3.2(M.85.52A); ref. sense perception, *distinguish* δικαστῇ δακτύλῳ ζ. τὸ χαῦνον ἐκ τοὐναντίου Geo. Pis.*hex*.696(M.92.1488B); **2.** of theol. speculation τίς ζ. τὰ ἀζυγοστάτιστα; ‡Chrys.*transfig*.(p.339.8); Gr.Ant.*bapt*.2.10(M.88.1881C); ref. Arian speculations on the Trinity, ‡Caes.Naz.*dial*.3(M.38.861); of heretics in gen. τὴν ἄρρητον φύσιν λόγοις ζ. Isid.Pel.*epp*.3.386(M.78. 1028D); **3.** of divine action; ref. God's acceptance of prayer τὰ ῥήματα ζ. Ast.Soph.*hom.3 in Ps.5*(M.40.425B); ref. Christ's judgement of souls ζ. οἶδεν δίκαιον Sophr.H.*v.Cyr.et Jo*.14(M.87.3396B); *measure*, ref. testing of Abraham ἀνδρείαν ζ. Bas.Sel.*or*.7.1(M.85. 104C).

ζυγοστάτης, ὁ, *one who weighs*, met.; ref. judgement of souls, *T.Abr*.A 13(p.93.5) cit. s. ζυγιάζω; ref. keeping balance between ἀσιτία and πολυσιτία, Nil.*epp*.3.247(M.79.496C) = Isid.Pel.*epp*.1.141 (M.78.417C); ref. false reasoning of heretics πονηροὶ τῆς τριάδος ζ. Procl.CP *or*.2.1(M.65.693A).

ζύγωμα, τό, *cross-beam* or *bench* in a boat, Epiph.*haer*.61.3(p.383. 10; M.41.1044A).

***ζυθοποιός, ὁ**, *maker of Egyptian beer*, Eus.*Is*.19:10(M.24.228B).

ζῦθος, ὁ, *Egyptian beer*, met. ποιοῦσι [sc. Sophists] τὸν ζ. ... νόθην τινὰ καὶ ἄχρηστον διδασκαλίαν Cyr.*Is*.2.4(2.287).

ζύμη, ἡ, *ferment, leaven*, met.; **1.** of sin; **a.** in gen. τὰ παλαιὰ τῆς κακῆς ζ. ἔργα Just.*dial*.14.2(M.6.504D); of the wicked ὥσπερ κακὴ ζ. *Hom.Clem*.8.17; Chrys.*hom.15.4 in 1Cor*.(10.129E); ζ. ... ταῖς... γραφαῖς, φαυλότητος καὶ ἁμαρτίας εἰς τύπον παραλαμβάνεται Cyr.*hom. pasch*.19(5^2.249D); id.*Juln*.9(6^2.322A); διὰ...τῆς ζ., τὴν παλαιότητα τῆς πονηρίας αἰνίττεσθαι Thdt.*qu.1 in Lev*.(1.181); ζ. παλαιὰν τὴν πρὸ τοῦ βαπτίσματος καλεῖ id.*1Cor*.5:7(3.193); ἤγουν ζ. καλεῖ τὴν ἐπὶ κακῷ πανουργίαν Proc.G.*Lev*.2:11(M.87.701C); **b.** of partic. sins: heresy, Bas.*ep*.250(3.385E; M.32.932B); greed, Chrys.*hom.15.5 in 1Cor*.(10.131B); ζ. σαρκικῆς ἀκαθαρσίας Cyr.*Juln*.9(6^2.322A); as symbol of pride, ‡Nil.*perist*.12.10(M.79.960D); **2.** of grace, Proc.G. *Lev*.2:11(M.87.701C); τοῦ πνεύματος ζ. Mac.Aeg.*hom*.24.4(M.34.665A); of Christ νέα ζ. Ign.*Magn*.10.2; of Inc., Isid.Pel.*epp*.1.201(M.78. 312B); ζ. ἐπουράνιος ἀγαθότητος Mac.Aeg.*hom*.24.3(664C); of Christ's sacramental body in eucharist, ref. 1Cor.5:6 καθάπερ...μικρὰ ζ. ... ὅλον τὸ φύραμα πρὸς ἑαυτὴν ἐξομοιοῖ Gr.Nyss.*or.catech*.37(p.143.2; M.45.93B); Chrys.*hom.24.2 in 1Cor*.(10.214C) cit. s. ἀνακεράννυμι; ὁ Χριστὸς ζ. τὴν διδασκαλίαν ἐκάλεσε *ib.15.3*(10.128D).

ζυμίτης ἄρτος, *leavened* bread, plur., as sign of Αἰγυπτιακὴ πολιτεία (ref. Lev.2:2), Thdt.*qu.1 in Lev*.(1.181).

ζυμ-όω, *leaven, ferment*; **1.** lit., ref. creation of human body τίς...

ἐζύμωσε χυμὸν δεύσας αἵματι...; Meth.*symp.*2.6(p.23.4; M.18.56D); symbolizing pagan conduct, ref. 1Cor.5:8, Chrys.*hom.15.3 in 1Cor.*(10.129C); **2.** met.; **a.** of sinning, esp. spreading of evil by wicked, cf. 1Cor.5:6 ἡ παλαιὰ ζύμη ἄλευρον ποιεῖ ~ωθῆναι ‡Ath.*qu.script.*99(M.28.757A); of heretics, CAnc.(358)*ep.syn.*ap.Epiph.*haer.*73.2(p.270.7; M.42.405B); κἂν μικρὰ ἐξ ἀδικίας κερδάνῃς, ὁλόκληρόν σου τὴν οὐσίαν ἐζύμωσε Chrys.*hom.15.5 in 1Cor.*(10.131B); **b.** pass., of being fervent ἐν τῇ ζυμωμένῃ ψυχῇ ὅλῃ ἐξ ὅλου τῷ θείῳ πνεύματι Mac.Aeg.*hom.*24.3(M.34.664C); ~ωθῆναι ἐν τῇ χρηστότητι τοῦ κυρίου *ib.*; Cyr.*ador.*17(1.614B); **c.** of σπέρμα in Valent. doctrine, Clem.*exc.Thdot.*2(p.106.2; M.9.653B).

***ζυμώνω**, *leaven* ἐκείνην ἢ ζυμώνει τὴν προσφορὰν μετὰ μάχης ἢ καὶ ἀκαθαρσίας *Ep.Chr.dom.*(p.27).

ζυμωτός, *leavened*, Gr.Nyss.*res.*1(M.46.620B); Thdr.Mops.*Mal.*1:7(M.66.602D).

ζωάγριος, *life-saving*, Nonn.*par.Jo.*16:13(M.43.876A).

ζωαρκής, **1.** *life-preserving* ζ. ... ἔδεσμα ψυχῆς, ὁ τοῦ θεοῦ λόγος Cyr.*glaph.Gen.*(1.121D); neut. plur. as subst., *necessaries of life* τὸν σῖτον καὶ τὸν οἶνον καὶ τὸ ἔλαιον...ὅσα ἐστὶν ἀναγκαῖα καὶ ζ. id.*Os.*30(3.55B); ref. Num.35:1ff., id.*ador.*13(1.465B); of spiritual and bodily necessaries, id.*Jo.*3.4(4.276B); **2.** *life-giving*; ref. creation of man δῶμεν ἔχειν ζ. πνοιήν *Orac.Sib.*8.443; of God's hand in creation of Eve, Gr.Naz.*carm.*1.2.1.106(M.37.530A); of Inc., Nonn.*par.Jo.*16:22(M.43.876C); of baptism τὸ ζ. νᾶμα Cyr.*Is.*2.1(2.213C).

***ζωαρχία**, ἡ, *source of life*; of Christ, ‡Rom.Mel.(*AS* 1 p.233).

***ζωαρχικός**, *life-giving*; **1.** of Trin., *A.Xanthipp.*21(p.73.6); Gr.Nyss.*v.Ephr.*(M.46.849C); Cosm.Ind.*top.*prec.(p.37.6; M.88.52A); Sophr.H.*or.*2.2(M.87.3217B); *Symb.CP*(681)(H.3.1400B); ‡Anast.S.*Jud.al.*(M.89.1277B); Jo.D.*Jacob.*57(M.94.1472C); †Jo.D.*B.J.*8(M.96.921B); Thphn.*chron.*p.350(M.108.840C); **2.** of Father ζ. δεξιὰ τοῦ δεσπότου †Jo.D.*B.J.*18(M.96.1025C); **3.** of Christ ζ. ἀνάστασις ‡Gr.Nyss.*hom.4.36 in Jo.*(p.168.16); Gr.Agr.*Eccl.*4.2(M.98.924C); σταυρὸς ζ. *Lit.Jac.*(*NBP* 10^{2}.p.107); **4.** of H. Ghost, Jo.D.*hom.*12.23(M.96.813D); *ib.*1.18(573B); **5.** of BMV θέαν τοῦ ζ. καὶ θεοδόχου σώματος Dion.Ar.*d.n.*3.2(M.3.681C); ζ. μήτηρ Jo.D.*hom.*8.3(M.96.705B); her body ζ. σκήνωμα *ib.*9.13(740C); id.*carm.dorm.BMV* 87(p.230; M.96.1365A).

ζωγραφ-έω, *paint, depict, represent*; **1.** of material representation, ref. Son πῶς δὲ τῆς οὕτω θαυμαστῆς καὶ ἀλήπτου μορφῆς...εἰκόνα τις ζ.; Eus.*ep.Constant.*(M.20.1548B); faith prompts material representation of the Word ζ. ... πίστις τὸν ἐν μορφῇ τοῦ θεοῦ ὑπάρχοντα λόγον Cyr.*fr.*ap.Hadr.Papa *ep.Const.*(M.*PL*.96.1230A); οἱ θεοσεβεῖς καὶ φιλόχριστοι ἄνθρωποι...ἰδόντες τὸν κύριον, καθὼς εἶδον, ἱστορήσαντες ἐζωγράφησαν †Gr.II Papa *ep.Leon.*1(H.4.5C); of saints ἰδόντες Ἰάκωβον τὸν ἀδελφὸν τοῦ κυρίου,...τὸν πρωτομάρτυρα Στέφανον ...τὰ πρόσωπα τῶν μαρτύρων...ἐζωγράφησαν *ib.*; **2.** met.; **a.** of Son τὴν τοῦ τέκτονος οὐσίαν ἐν τῇ οἰκείᾳ φύσει ζ. Ammon.*Jo.*7:29(M.85.1445A); ἐν ἑαυτῷ τὸν γεννήσαντα ζ. Cyr.*Jo.*1.2(4.16A); **b.** ref. Creation, God working like a painter τὸν κόσμον...ἐργάζεται ~ῶν ὁ θεός Meth.*symp.*2.1(p.15.16; M.18.48C); *ib.*6.2(p.65.9; 116A); **c.** ref. generation ᾧ γραφέως...~οῦντος ‡Nil.*fr.pasch.*2(M.79.1496C); **d.** of representation in words or imagination διὰ τί οἱ οὐράνιοι ῥήτορες πτεροφόροι τῇ γραφῇ ~οῦνται; Nil.*epp.*2.324(M.79.360A); of Devil tempting τὴν ἁμαρτίαν ἀκριβῶς ζ. *ib.*3.43(409C); of heathen poets δύο ἀρχὰς ἀγενήτους ζ. τῷ λόγῳ Thdt.*provid.*1(4.486); ζ. κοσμικὴν φαντασίαν Jo.VI H.*v.Jo.D.*24(M.94.464C); **e.** of symbolism, esp. scriptural ἵνα ...καθάπερ ~ούμενον ἐν τοῖς ὁρατοῖς ἐκφανῇ τὸ ἀόρατον ‡Chrys.*pasch.*1(8.251C); ref. realization of prophecies by Christ τὰ ἐν τῇ βίβλῳ Ἰησοῦ τοῦ Ναυῆ...ἐζωγράφησε †Epiph.*num.myst.*5(M.43.516D); δεκτὸν...τὸ εὐσθενές, ὡς ἐν ἀρσένων φύσει ~ούμενον Cyr.*ador.*15(1.521E); ref. cloud at Transfiguration τὸ σέλας ζ. τοῦ πνεύματος Jo.D.*hom.*1.4(M.96.552D); **f.** reflex., of imitation, ref. following of Christ πρὸς ἐκεῖνον ἑαυτὸν ζ. Meth.*symp.*8.13(p.99.1; M.18.161A).

ζωγραφητός, *depicted*, Tim.Ant.*nativ.Jo.Bapt.*2(M.28.909B).

ζωγραφία, ἡ, *painting* ἐγὼ...προσκυνῶν εἰκόνα λέγω δόξα σοι ὁ θεὸς τῶν ἁγίων, καὶ οὐ λέγω δόξα σοι ξύλον ἢ ζ. *Dial.Christ.et Jud.*(p.74.15).

ζωγράφος, ὁ, *painter*, not to be admitted as catechumen unless he ceases from making idols, cf.Hipp.*trad.ap.*16.11; cf.*Const.App.* 8.32.7 (εἰδωλοποιός); craft approved πῶς...τὰς ἁγίας ἐξ οἰκουμενικὰς συνόδους ἢ τῶν ζ. τέχνη ἀθετεῖ; CNic.(787)*refut.*(H.4.352ff.); use by ζ. of pre-existing colours contrasted with divine Creation *ex nihilo*, Meth.*creat.*6(p.497.14; M.18.337B); complexity of painter's task illustrating that of the search for union with God, Isid.Pel.*epp.*1.403(M.78.408B); met., of God in Creation πάντων...ζ. Eus.*d.e.* 5.4(p.226.5; M.22.373A); of Christ as representing Father to men, id.*ep.Constant.*(M.20.1549A); of God portraying Church in scriptures, Gr.Nyss.*hom.7 in Cant.*(M.44.917A); of Devil tempting through imagination ζ. τῆς κακίας Nil.*epp.*2.140(M.79.261A); (Gnost.) of Sophia as creative principle, Clem.*str.*4.13(p.287.30; M.8.1297B); impersonal ζ. γὰρ τοῦ θανάτου ὁ πόλεμος Thphyl.*exc.gent.* 3(p.479.24; M.113.937B).

***ζωγρευτικός**, *of fishing*; ref. work of disciples, Isid.Pel.*epp.*1.183(M.78.301B).

ζωγρέω, **1.** *take alive, capture*; met.; **a.** capture by sin, Bas.*ep.* 258.4(3.394E; M.32.953A); Proc.G.*Jud.*1:7(M.87.1045A); also lit., of capture by thieves compared with that by devils, Tat.*orat.*18(p.20.17; M.6.848A); **b.** of conversion of sinners, Chrys.*hom.div.*1.2(12.325A); of atheists, ‡Cyr.*Trin.*1(6^{3}.2C; M.77.1121B); of pagans ζ. τοὺς τῷ ζόφῳ τῆς ἀγνοίας κατεχομένους Thdt.*h.e.*5.39.20(3.1085); id.*Rom.*15:19(3.152); Bas.Sel.*v.Thecl.*1(M.85.484B); ἐζωγροῦντο πόλεις id.*or.*29(M.85.332B); **2.** *restore to life*; of power of God to raise from the dead, Nonn.*par.Jo.*5:21(M.43.783C); also *restore to health*, *ib.*7:23(808C).

***ζώγρημα**, τό, *prey* οὐκ ἐγένεσθε ζ. τοῦ διαβόλου Serap.*ep.mon.*8(M.40.933D).

ζώγριον, τό, *cage*, *M.Perp.*19(p.91.7).

ζῶγρος, ὁ, = foreg., Bas.*hex.*9.6(1.87E; M.29.205B); ‡Bas.*struct.hom.*1.12(1.329D; M.30.21D); Mac.Mgn.*apocr.*3.9(p.71.9).

ζῳδιακός, *of the zodiac* ἐγὼ [sc. a devil] δεκανὸς α′ τοῦ ζ. κύκλου *T.Sal.*18.4(M.122.1341C).

***ζῳδιογράφος**, ὁ, *painter of figures* or *signs*, Eust.*engast.*27(p.59.26; M.18.669D).

ζῴδιον, τό, **1.** *figure, image*; **a.** in gen. ποικίλα ἱμάτια ἔχοντα ζ. ἐν τῇ πορφύρᾳ Clem.*paed.*2.10(p.222.20; M.8.528A); τὸ δὲ ζ. γίνεσθαι, ἢ ἐν τοίχοις, ἢ ἐν ἱματίοις, ποῦ χρήσιμον; Chrys.*hom.49.4 in Mt.*(7.509D); of image of Aphrodite erected on site of Calvary, Soz.*h.e.* 2.1.3(M.67.932A); **b.** met., of man λογικὸν ἐκ σταγόνος συντίθεται ζ. ‡Nil.*fr.pasch.*2(M.79.1496C); action of grace and sin on soul compared with that of sculptor making ζ., Mac.Aeg.*hom.*16.7(M.34.617C); **2.** *sign of the zodiac*; influence on genesis of living things, Clem.*ex.Thdot.*71(p.129.25; M.9.692B); signs symbolically interpreted as foundations of world, *Hom.Clem.*6.14; [sc. a devil] ἐν ποίῳ ζ. κεῖσαι; *T.Sal.*2.2(M.122.1320A); Marcosian τὰ γὰρ δώδεκα ζ. ...τὴν τοῦ Ἀνθρώπου καὶ τῆς Ἐκκλησίας θυγατέρα δωδεκάδα σκιαγραφεῖν λέγουσι Iren.*haer.*1.17.1(M.7.637B); Valent. οἱ ἀπόστολοι, φησί, μετετέθησαν τοῖς δεκαδύο ζ. Clem.*exc.Thdot.*25(p.115.12; M.9.672B); **3.** *cage* ζ. χαλκοῦν Anast.S.*Ps.*6(M.89.1104B).

ζῳδιοφόρος, *bearing signs of zodiac* ζ. κύκλον Gr.Nyss.*fat.*(M.45.149C).

[*]**ζῷδον**, τό, = ζῴδιον 1, Dam.*troph.*3.6(p.245.11).

ζωή, ἡ, *life*, esp. *eternal* and *spiritual life*;

I. natural life πηγαὶ...παρέχονται τοὺς πρὸς ζωῆς ἀνθρώποις μαζούς *1Clem.*20.10; οἷς τὴν κατὰ φύσιν συνεξέπλησεν ζ. καὶ τοὺς ἐν τῇ ζ. πόνους Athenag.*res.*7(p.56.11; M.6.988B); τὴν λίχνον διωκάθοντας ζ., τὸ ἀγαθὸν ἐνταῦθά που κατορύξαντας περὶ τὴν οὐκ ἐσομένην ζ. Clem.*paed.*2.1(p.160.11f.; M.8.393A); ἡ ἐν τῷ γεώδει σώματι ζ. Or.*Cels.*7.5(p.157.13; M.11.1428B); ἡ τοῖς πάθεσι τῆς σαρκὸς δεδουλωμένη ζ. Bas.*Spir.*53(3.46A; M.32.168B); Chrys.*hom.31.3 in Mt.*(7.361D); ζ. ἀνιεροῦ Dion.Ar.*c.h.*4.2(M.3.180B).

II. eternal and spiritual life, freq. identified;

A. def. and described θάνατος μὲν εἶναι ἡ ἐν σώματι κοινωνία τῆς ψυχῆς ἁμαρτητικῆς οὔσης, ζ. δὲ ὁ χωρισμὸς τῆς ἁμαρτίας Clem.*str.* 4.3(p.253.18; M.8.1224C); ζ. δὲ αἰώνιός ἐστιν οὐχ ἡ κοινὴ ἥτις καὶ ἑτέροις ζῴοις ὑπάρχει, ἀλλ' ἡ ἐκ τῆς πίστεως καὶ τῆς λοιπῆς ἀρετῆς ἐγγινομένη Or.*fr.39 in Jo.*(p.515.15); δύο γὰρ τὰ εἰς ἄκρον ἀλλήλοις ἐναντία ζ. καὶ θάνατος...ἰσότης μὲν γάρ ἐστιν ἡ ζ., ἀνισότης δὲ ἡ φθορά Meth.*symp.*3.7(p.34.2f.; M.18.69C–72A); ζ. δέ ἐστιν ἡ ἄνωθεν ἐκ τοῦ θεοῦ γέννησις Mac.Aeg.*hom.*30.3(M.34.721D); τὸ δὲ βλέπειν τὸν θεόν, ἐστὶν ἡ ζ. τῆς ψυχῆς...εἴρηται γὰρ τὴν ἀληθῆ ζ. τῆς ψυχῆς ἐν τῇ μετουσίᾳ τοῦ ἀγαθοῦ ἐνεργεῖσθαι, τῆς δὲ ἀγνοίας πρὸς τὴν θείαν κατανόησιν ἐμποδιζούσης ἐκπεσεῖν τῆς ζ. τὴν ψυχὴν τὴν τοῦ θεοῦ μὴ μετέχουσαν Gr.Nyss.*infant.*(M.46.176A); ὅτι πᾶν ἀγαθὸν τῇ ἑαυτοῦ φύσει ὅρον οὐκ ἔχει, τῇ δὲ τοῦ ἐναντίου παραθέσει ὁρίζεται· ὡς ἡ ζ., τῷ θανάτῳ...ὡς γὰρ τὸ τῆς ζ. τέλος ἀρχὴ θανάτου ἐστίν· οὕτω καὶ τοῦ κατ' ἀρετὴν δρόμου ἡ στάσις ἀρχὴ τοῦ κατὰ κακίαν γίνεται δρόμου id.*v.Mos.*5(M.44.300D).

B. dist. from physical life and from life of sin ὥσπερ ἐστίν τις ζ. ἀδιάφορος, ἡ μήτε ἀγαθὸν μήτε κακὸν τυγχάνουσα, καθ' ἣν λέγομεν ζῆν καὶ τοὺς ἀσεβεῖς καὶ τὰ ἄλογα ζῷα· καὶ ἑτέρα διάφορος ἀλλὰ ἀγαθόν, περὶ ἧς φησιν ὁ Παῦλος· 'ἡ ζ. ἡμῶν κέκρυπται σὺν τῷ Χριστῷ ἐν τῷ θεῷ·' καὶ αὐτὸς ὁ κύριος ἡμῶν περὶ ἑαυτοῦ· 'ἐγώ εἰμι ἡ ζ.' οὕτως τὸν μὲν ἐναντίον τῇ ἀδιαφόρῳ ζ. θάνατον ἀδιάφορον ἐρεῖς Or.*Jo.*20.39 (31; p.380.27ff.; M.14.665A,B); cf.Chrys.*hom.3.2 in Phil.*(11.214B–F); διπλῆ τίς ἐστιν ἡμῶν ἡ ζ. ἡ μὲν οἰκεία τῇ σαρκί, ταχὺ παρερχομένη, ἡ δὲ συγγενὴς τῇ ψυχῇ, μὴ δεχομένη περιγραφήν Bas.*hom.*3.3(2.18E; M. 31.204B); δύο σοι νόμισον εἶναι θυγατέρας· τὴν εὐπάθειαν τὴν ἐνθάδε, καὶ τὴν ζ. τὴν ἐν τοῖς οὐρανοῖς...μὴ τὴν ἐνταῦθα διαγωγὴν ὑπέρπλουτον δείξῃς, γυμνὴν δὲ τὴν ἄλλην...ἡνίκα ἂν δέῃ σε τῷ Χριστῷ παραστῆναι... νύμφης ἔχουσαν σχῆμα καὶ κλῆσιν τὴν κατ' ἀρετὴν ζ. *ib.*8.8(71C,D; M.325C,D); τὸ μὴ δεῖν πρὸς τὴν αἰσθητὴν ταύτην βλέπειν ζ.· ἥτις συγκρινομένη πρὸς τὴν ὄντως ζ., ἀνύπαρκτός τις καὶ ἀνυπόστατός ἐστιν ...ὅ γε πεπαιδευμένος τὰ θεῖα μυστήρια, οὐκ ἀγνοεῖ πάντως, ὅτι οἰκεία μὲν καὶ κατὰ φύσιν τοῖς ἀνθρώποις ἐστὶν ἡ ζ. ἡ πρὸς τὴν θείαν φύσιν ὡμοιωμένη· ἡ δὲ αἰσθητικὴ ζ., διὰ τῆς τῶν αἰσθητηρίων ἐνεργείας διεξαγομένη, ἐπὶ τούτῳ φύσει δέδοται, ἐφ' ᾧ τὴν τῶν φαινομένων γνῶσιν ὁδηγὸν γενέσθαι τῆς ψυχῆς πρὸς τὴν τῶν ἀοράτων ἐπίγνωσιν Gr.Nyss. *hom.1 in Eccl.*(M.44.624A,B).

C. in relation to βίος; **1.** opp. βίος; latter designating merely physical or worldly life καθῆκον δὲ ἀκόλουθον ἐν βίῳ θεῷ καὶ Χριστῷ βούλημα ἕν, κατορθούμενον ἀιδίῳ ζ. Clem.*paed.*1.13(p.151.24; M.8. 376A); τὰς ἀκάνθας τοῦ βίου (cf. Mt.13:22) αἳ τὸ σπέρμα τῆς ζ. συμπνίγουσιν id.*q.d.s.*11(p.166.29; M.9.616A); περὶ τῆς ἑξῆς τῷ βίῳ τούτῳ ζ. προφητεύσαντος Or.*Cels.*3.16(p.215.11; M.11.940C); ὅπερ γὰρ ἐστιν ὄναρ ἓν πρὸς ἑκατὸν ἔτη, τοῦτό ἐστιν ὁ παρὼν βίος πρὸς τὴν μέλλουσαν ζ. Chrys.*Laz.*1.11(1.723D); τὸν παρόντα βίον ἅπαντα ἐν πειρασμοῖς...διάγοντας...ἑτέραν ζ., καθ' ἣν μέλλει τοὺς τῆς εὐσεβείας ἀθλητὰς στεφανοῦν id.*stat.*1.9(2.13C); *ib.*(13D); οὐ ζῶμεν μετὰ τῆς προσηκούσης τοῖς Χριστιανοῖς σκληραγωγίας· ἀλλὰ τὸν ὑγρὸν τοῦτον καὶ διαλελυμένον...ἐζηλώσαμεν βίον...ὡς εἴγε ἐν νηστείαις, καὶ παννυχίσι, καὶ εὐτελείᾳ διαίτης τὴν ζ. διηνύομεν ταύτην...ταχέως ἂν τῶν μελλόντων ἐπεθυμήσαμεν *ib.*6.3(77C); θάνατος γὰρ ψυχῆς ἀσέβεια καὶ βίος παράνομος. οὐκοῦν καὶ ζ. ψυχῆς ἡ τοῦ θεοῦ λατρεία, καὶ βίος ὁ ταύτῃ πρέπων †Chrys.*hom.prec.*1(2.779D); **2.** used interchangeably with βίος q.v.

D. in gen., Arist.*apol.*15.3; τὴν ἐπέκεινα τῆς διαλύσεως ζ. ἥτις ἑαυτῇ συνεισάγει τὴν ἀνάστασιν Athenag.*res.*16(p.68.16; M.6.1008A); id.*leg.*32.3(M.6.964D); Tat.*orat.*14(p.15.20; M.6.836B); Clem.*prot.*12 (p.86.27; M.8.245B); Or.*Cels.*2.48(p.170.18; M.11.872B); δέξαι σὺν παιδὶ σῷ, πάρεσμεν, ἔνδον εἰς ζωῆς πύλας, πάτερ, καὶ ἡμέας Meth.*symp.* 11(p.136.29; M.18.213A); exeg. Abac.3:2, v. ζῷον.

E. God as life and giver of life; **1.** without distn. of Persons, *1Clem.*35.2 cit. s. ἀθανασία; ἐκ τῶν ἰδίων ἔργων ἀνάξιοι ζωῆς νῦν ὑπὸ τῆς τοῦ θεοῦ χρηστότητος ἀξιωθῶμεν *Diogn.*9.1; ἐπεὶ ζῆσαι ἄνευ ζ. οὐχ οἷόν τε ἦν· ἡ δὲ ὕπαρξις τῆς ζ. ἐκ τῆς τοῦ θεοῦ περιγίνεται μετοχῆς· μετοχὴ δὲ θεοῦ ἐστι τὸ γινώσκειν θεόν Iren.*haer.*4.20.5(M.7.1036A); ἵνα μὴ ὡς ἐξ ἡμῶν αὐτῶν ἔχοντες τὴν ζ., φυσηθῶμεν καὶ ἀπαρθῶμέν ποτε κατὰ τοῦ θεοῦ...πείρᾳ δὲ μαθόντες, ὅτι ἐκ τῆς ἐκείνου ὑπεροχῆς, οὐκ ἐκ τῆς ἡμετέρας φύσεως, τὴν εἰς ἀεὶ παραμονὴν ἔχομεν *ib.*5.2.3(1127C); θεὸς...ζ. χαρίζεται Clem.*prot.*10(p.67.7; M.8.204A); οὐκ ἔνι γὰρ ἑσπέρα θεοῦ, ἐγὼ δὲ ἡγοῦμαι, ὅτι οὐδὲ πρωΐα, ἀλλὰ ὁ συμπαρεκτείνων τῇ ἀγενήτῳ καὶ ἀιδίῳ αὐτοῦ ζ., ἵν' οὕτως εἴπω, χρόνος ἡμέρα ἐστὶν αὐτῷ σήμερον, ἐν ᾗ γεγέννηται ὁ υἱός Or.*Jo.*1.29(32; p.37.10; M.14.77D); πνεῦμα ὁ θεός· ἐπεὶ γὰρ εἰς τὴν μέσην καὶ καινότερον καλουμένην ζ. σπῶντος τοῦ περὶ ἡμᾶς πνεύματος τὴν καλουμένην σωματικώτερον πνοὴν ζωῆς, ζωοποιούμεθα ἀπὸ τοῦ πνεύματος, ὑπολαμβάνω ἀπ' ἐκείνου εἰλῆφθαι τὸ πνεῦμα λέγεσθαι τὸν θεὸν πρὸς τὴν ἀληθινὴν ζ. ἡμᾶς ἄγοντα *ib.*13.23(p.247.14ff.; 437B); ὁ δὲ θεὸς καὶ ἀθανασία καὶ ζ. καὶ ἀφθαρσία Meth.*res.*1.34(p.272.3; M.41.1097C); παρὰ τοῦ πάντα δυναμένου θεοῦ ζ. αἰώνιον προσδοκᾶν *Hom.Clem.*7.8; ὑμνητέον ἡμῖν τὴν ζ. τὴν αἰώνιον, ὡς ἧς ἡ αὐτοζωή, καὶ πᾶσα ζ., καὶ ὑφ' ἧς εἰς πάντα τὰ ὁπωσοῦν ζωῆς μετέχοντα τὸ ζῆν οἰκείως ἑκάστῳ διασπείρεται. καὶ γοῦν ἡ τῶν ἀθανάτων ἀγγέλων ζ. ... διὸ καὶ ζῶντες ἀεὶ καὶ ἀθάνατοι λέγονται, καὶ οὐκ ἀθάνατοι πάλιν, ὅτι μὴ παρ' ἑαυτῶν ἔχουσι τὸ ἀθάνατοι εἶναι καὶ αἰωνίως ζῆν, ἀλλ' ἐκ τῆς ζωοποιοῦ καὶ πάσης ζ. ... αἰτίας. ... τῆς αὐτοζωῆς ἐστιν ἡ ὑπὲρ ζωὴν ἡ θεία ζ., ζωτική, καὶ ὑποστατική, καὶ πᾶσα ζ., καὶ ζωτικὴ κίνησις ἐκ τῆς ζ., τῆς ὑπὲρ πᾶσαν ζ. καὶ πᾶσαν ἀρχὴν πάσης ζ. ἐξ αὐτῆς καὶ αἱ ψυχαὶ τὸ ἀνώλεθρον ἔχουσι, καὶ ζῷα πάντα καὶ φυτὰ κατ' ἔσχατον ἀπήχημα τῆς ζ. ἔχουσι τὸ ζῆν. ἧς ἀνταναιρουμένης...ἐκλείπει πᾶσα ζ. Dion.Ar.*d.n.*6.1(M.3.856A,B); *ib.*6.2(856C,D); ἐξ αὐτῆς [sc. divine life] ζωοῦται...ζῷα πάντα... καὶ εἴτε νοερὰν εἴποις, εἴτε λογικήν, εἴτε αἰσθητικήν, εἴτε θρεπτικήν, καὶ αὐξητικήν, εἴτε ὁποίαν ποτὲ ζ., ἢ ζωῆς ἀρχήν, ἢ ζωῆς οὐσίαν, ἐξ αὐτῆς καὶ ζῇ καὶ ζωοῖ τῆς ὑπὲρ πᾶσαν ζ. ... ἡ γὰρ ὑπέρζωος καὶ ζωαρχικὴ ζ. καὶ πάσης ζ. ἐστιν αἰτία...καὶ διαιρετικὴ ζωῆς, καὶ ἐκ πάσης ζ. ὑμνητέα, καὶ πάσῃ ζ. θεωρουμένη καὶ ὑμνουμένη...καὶ ὡς ὑπὲρ πᾶσαν ζ. ζωοποιὸς καὶ ὑπερζωός *ib.*6.3(857B); πάσης γὰρ ζ. καὶ ἀθανασίας...δημιουργός ἐστιν ὁ θεὸς Max.*cap.theol.*1.50(M.90.1101B); though God is ὑπὲρ πᾶσαν...ζ. Dion.Ar.*c.h.*2.3(M.3.140C); *ib.*4.1 (177D); as synonym of God, Clem.*paed.*1.10(p.146.15; M.8.364A); who is ἡ τῶν ζώντων ζ. Dion.Ar.*d.n.*1.3(589C); **2.** Father τῷ δὲ ἐπιβλέποντι τὴν σωτηρίαν...παρέξει...τὴν ἄτρεπτον ζ. ὁ πατὴρ...ὁ ἐν τοῖς οὐρανοῖς Clem.*q.d.s.*42(p.191.9; M.9.652B); ἡ...ὄντως ζ. καὶ ἀληθῶς, ἔστιν ὁ πατήρ Cyr.H.*catech.*18.29; Cyr.*Jo.*1.6(4.52D); dispensing life through Son, Clem.*q.d.s.*6(p.164.12; M.9.612A); **3.** Son; **a.** in gen. εἷς ἰατρός ἐστιν...ἐν ἀνθρώπῳ θεός, ἐν θανάτῳ ζ. ἀληθινή Ign.*Eph.*7.2; τὸ ἀδύνατον τῆς ἡμετέρας φύσεως εἰς τὸ τυχεῖν ζωῆς, νῦν δὲ τὸν σωτῆρα δείξας δυνατὸν σώζειν καὶ τὰ ἀδύνατα *Diogn.*9.6; ὁ Χριστὸς...ὁ ζ. χαρισάμενος Clem.*prot.*9(p.63.20; M.8.196B); αὐτὸς γάρ ἐστιν ἡ ζ. ἡμῶν εἰς τοὺς αἰῶνας *A.Phil.*141(p.77.7); ὁ Χριστὸς ζ. καὶ ζωοποιῶν *A.Thom.*A 104(p.217.14); ζωῆς χορηγός, Χριστέ Meth. *symp.*11(p.133.5; M.18.209A); Χριστὸν...τὸν τῆς αἰωνίου ζ. τοῖς πᾶσιν αἴτιον Eus.*Marcell.*2.1(p.33.29; M.24.780C); id.*e.th.*1.8(p.66. 30; M.24.837C) cit. s. ἀκτίς; *ib.*1.20(p.86.30f.; 876B); λόγος, ὡς ζ. νεκροῖς ἐπιφοιτῶσα τοῖς οὖσι Max.*cap.theol.*2.36(M.90.1141C); ὁ κύριος λέγεται...ζ. ... ζ. δέ, ὡς τὴν πρέπουσαν ψυχαῖς ἀγαπώσαις τὸν κύριον ἐν τοῖς θείοις παρεχόμενος κίνησιν *ib.*2.70(1156C); **b.** partic. through Inc., Clem.*prot.*1(p.9.28; M.8.65B); Cross πνεῦμα τοῦ σταυροῦ, ὅ ἐστιν σκάνδαλον τοῖς ἀπιστοῦσιν, ἡμῖν δὲ σωτηρία καὶ ζ. αἰώνιος Ign. *Eph.*18.1; Resurrection, Ign.*Magn.*9.1; **c.** in contrast to Mosaic Law εἰ γοῦν ἱκανὸς ἦν ὁ Μωσέως νόμος ζ. αἰώνιον παρασχεῖν, μάτην μὲν ὁ σωτὴρ αὐτὸς παραγίνεται καὶ πάσχει δι' ἡμᾶς Clem.*q.d.s.*8(p.164. 30; M.9.612C); **d.** exeg.: Jo.1:3f. γέγονεν οὖν ἡ ζ. ἐν τῷ λόγῳ· καὶ οὔτε ὁ λόγος ἕτερός ἐστι τοῦ Χριστοῦ,...οὔτε ἡ ζ. ἑτέρα τοῦ υἱοῦ τοῦ θεοῦ...ὥσπερ οὖν ἡ ζ. γέγονεν ἐν τῷ λόγῳ, οὕτως ὁ λόγος ἦν ἐν ἀρχῇ Or. *Jo.*1.19(22; p.23.27ff.; M.14.56C); αὐτὸς γὰρ ὑπάρχων ἡ κατὰ φύσιν ζ., τὸ εἶναι καὶ ζῆν καὶ κινεῖσθαι πολυτρόπως τοῖς οὖσι χαρίζεται...μία δὲ ἡ πάντων ζ. χωροῦσα πρὸς ἕκαστον Cyr.*Jo.*1.6(4.49E–50A); ὡς ἴδιον ἀγαθὸν ἑαυτῷ περιτίθησι μόνῳ τὸ εἶναι ζ. *ib.*(51E); Jo.1:4 προτάσσει γὰρ τὴν ζ. τοῦ τῶν ἀνθρώπων φωτός, εἰ καὶ ταὐτόν ἐστι 'ζωὴ' καὶ 'ἀνθρώπων φῶς', τῷ προαπαντᾶν ἡμῖν ἐπὶ τῶν μετεχόντων τῆς ζ., τυγχανούσης καὶ φωτὸς ἀνθρώπων, τὸ ζῆν αὐτοὺς τὴν...θείαν ζ. παρὰ τὸ πεφωτίσθαι...εἰ γὰρ καὶ ταὐτόν ἐστιν ἡ ζ. καὶ τὸ φῶς τῶν ἀνθρώπων, ἀλλ' αἵ γε ἐπίνοιαι καθ' ἕτερον καὶ ἕτερον λαμβάνονται Or.*Jo.*2.23(18; p.80.24ff.; M.14.156B); 'ζωὴ' ἐνταῦθα οὐχ ἡ κοινὴ λογικῶν καὶ ἀλόγων λέγεται, ἀλλ' ἡ ἐπιγινομένη τῷ ἐν ἡμῖν συμπληρουμένῳ λόγῳ, τῆς μετοχῆς ἀπὸ τοῦ πρώτου λαμβανομένης λόγου· καὶ κατὰ μὲν τὸ ἀποστραφῆναι τὴν δοκοῦσαν ζ., οὐκ οὖσαν δὲ ἀληθῶς, καὶ ποθεῖν χωρῆσαι τὴν ἀληθῶς ζ. πρῶτον κοινωνοῦμεν αὐτῇ, ἥτις γενομένη ἐν ἡμῖν καὶ φωτὸς γνώσεως ὑπόστασις γίνεται. καὶ τάχα αὕτη ἡ ζ. παρ' οἷς μὲν δυνάμει καὶ οὐκ ἐνεργείᾳ φῶς ἐστι, τοῖς τὰ τῆς γνώσεως ἐξετάζειν μὴ φιλοτιμουμένοις, παρ' ἑτέροις δὲ καὶ ἐνεργείᾳ γινομένη φῶς *ib.*2.24(19; p.81.12ff.; 156D–157A); cf.Clem.*prot.*11(p.80.18,26; M.8. 232B,C); Cyr.*Jo.*1.7(4.54Aff.); Jo.4:14, in subordinationist sense ἡ γενομένη ἐν τῷ πιόντι ἐκ τοῦ ὕδατος, οὗ δίδωσιν ὁ Ἰησοῦς, πηγὴ ἅλλεται εἰς τὴν αἰώνιον ζ. τάχα δὲ καὶ πηδήσει μετὰ τὴν αἰώνιον ζ. εἰς τὸν ὑπὲρ τὴν αἰώνιον ζ. πατέρα· Χριστὸς γὰρ ἡ ζ. ὁ δὲ μείζων τοῦ Χριστοῦ, μείζων τῆς ζωῆς Or.*Jo.*13.3(p.229.7; M.14.404C); similarly, Jo.5:26 ἔχει...ζ. οὐκ ἄναρχον οὐδὲ ἀγένητον, οὐδὲ ἰδιόκτητον ὁμοίως τῷ πατρί, ἀλλὰ παρὰ τοῦ πατρὸς λαβών Eus.*e.th.*1.20(p.86.24; M.24. 876A); but ὅτι...ζ. κατὰ φύσιν ἐστὶν ὁ μονογενής, καὶ οὐ ζ. τῆς παρ' ἑτέρου μέτοχος, ζωογονεῖ τε οὕτως ὥσπερ καὶ ὁ πατήρ Cyr.*Jo.*2.8(4. 235E); Col.3:3f. ἡ ὄντως ζ. ὁ Χριστός, καὶ ἡ ἡμετέρα ἐν αὐτῷ διαγωγὴ ζ. ἐστιν ἀληθινή Bas.*hom.in Ps.*33(1.152B; M.29.372C); οὐκ ἔστιν αὕτη, φησίν, ἡ ζ. ἡ ὑμετέρα· ζ. ἑτέρα τίς ἐστιν...μὴ φαίνεται ὁ Χριστός; οὐδὲ ἡ ζ. ὑμῶν, ἐν τῷ θεῷ ἄνω ἐστί. τί οὖν; πότε ζησόμεθα; 'ὅταν ὁ Χριστὸς φανερωθῇ, ἡ ζ. ὑμῶν', τότε τὴν δόξαν ζητεῖτε, τότε τὴν ζ. Chrys.*hom.7.2 in Col.*(11.373C,D); Gal.2:19f. τὸ τῆς ζ. ὄνομα πολύσημαντόν ἐστιν...ἔστι ζ. αὕτη ἡ τοῦ σώματος, ἔστι ζ. ἡ τῆς ἁμαρτίας... ἄρα ἐστὶ ζωὴν τὴν τῆς ἁμαρτίας ζῆν·...ἔστι ζ. ἡ ἀίδιος καὶ ἀθάνατος, μετὰ ζωῆς αἰωνίου ἡ οὐράνιος· ἔστι ζ. ἡ τοῦ σώματος...οὐ τὴν φυσικὴν οὖν φησι μὴ ζῆν ζ., ἀλλὰ ταύτην τὴν τῶν ἁμαρτημάτων, ἣν ἅπαντες ἄνθρωποι ζῶσιν· ὁ μὴ ἐπιθυμῶν τῆς παρούσης ζ., πῶς ταύτην ζῇ;... οὗτος οὐδὲ τὴν φυσικὴν ζ. ζῇ· ὁ μηδενὸς φροντίζων τῶν βιωτικῶν, οὐ ζῇ...ὅτι γὰρ οὐ τὴν φυσικὴν παραιτεῖται ζ., φησὶν ἀλλαχοῦ· 'ὃ δὲ νῦν ζῶ ἐν σαρκί, ἐν πίστει ζῶ τῇ τοῦ υἱοῦ τοῦ θεοῦ...' τουτέστι, καινήν τινα ζ. ζῶ Chrys.*hom.3.2 in Phil.*(11.214B–F); **e.** Christ as life; denied by Eunomius βούλεται γὰρ ἄλλο τι δεῖξαι παρὰ τὴν αἰωνίαν ζ. τὸν υἱὸν ὄντα, ἥτις εἰ μὴ ἐν τῷ μονογενεῖ θεωροῖτο, ματαία μὲν ἡ πίστις ἀποδειχθήσεται...τί γὰρ κατήγγειλαν τὸν Χριστόν, ἐν ᾧ τῆς αἰωνίας ζ. κατ' Εὐνόμιον οὐκ ἔστιν ἡ δύναμις; εἰς τί δὲ τῷ ὀνόματι Χριστοῦ τοὺς πεπιστευκότας κατονομάζουσιν, εἰ μὴ διὰ τούτου τῆς αἰωνίας μέλλοιεν μετέχειν ζωῆς; Gr.Nyss.*Eun.*10(2 p.231.11,19; M.45.832C,D); διὰ τῆς πολυπραγμοσύνης τοῦ νοῦ τοῖς ὑπερκειμένοις τῆς τοῦ υἱοῦ ζ. ἐμβατεύων, ἐκεῖ τὴν αἰώνιον ζ. ἐρευνώμενος ὅπου ὁ μονογενὴς θεὸς οὐκ ἔστιν. πόθῳ γὰρ τῆς αἰωνίας, φησί, ζ. εἰς τὰ ἐπέκεινα τοῦ υἱοῦ τῷ νῷ φέρεται, ὡς ἐν τῷ υἱῷ πάντως μὴ εὑρὼν τὸ ζητούμενον. εἰ οὖν οὐκ ἔστιν ἐν τῷ υἱῷ ἡ αἰώνιος ζ., ἄρα ψευδὴς ἁλώσεται ὁ εἰπὼν ὅτι, 'ἐγώ εἰμι ἡ ζ.', ἢ ζ. μὲν ἐστίν, οὐκ αἰώνιος δέ; ἀλλὰ τὸ μὴ αἰώνιον πρόσκαιρον πάντως, τὸ δὲ τοιοῦτο τῆς ζ. εἶδος κοινὸν καὶ τῶν ἀλόγων ἐστίν. ποῦ τοίνυν τὸ μεγαλεῖον τῆς ὄντως ζ., εἰ μετέχοι ταύτης καὶ ἡ ἄλογος φύσις; *ib.*(p.232.7ff.; 833A,B); πᾶς ὁ ποθῶν τὴν αἰώνιον ζ., ἐπειδὰν εὕρῃ τὸν υἱόν,...ὅλον εὗρεν ἐν αὐτῷ ὅπερ ἐπόθησε, διότι καὶ αὐτός ἐστιν ἡ ζ. καὶ ἐν ἑαυτῷ τὴν ζ. ἔχει. ἀλλ' ὁ λεπτὸς οὗτος τὸν νοῦν...ὑπὸ πολλῆς ὀξυωπίας τῷ υἱῷ τὴν αἰώνιον οὐκ ἐνευρίσκει ζ., ἀλλ' ὑπερβὰς τοῦτον καὶ καταλιπὼν οἷον ἐμπόδιόν τι πρὸς τὸ ζητούμενον ἐκεῖ διερευνᾶται τὴν αἰώνιον ζ., ὅπου μὴ εἶναι οἴεται τὴν ὄντως ζ. *ib.*(p.234.9ff.; 836B,C); **4.** H. Ghost δύναται ἡ σὰρξ αὕτη μεταλαβεῖν ζ. καὶ ἀθανασίαν, κολληθέντος αὐτῇ τοῦ πνεύματος τοῦ ἁγίου *2Clem.*14.5; ὡς οὖν ὁ εἰς ψυχὴν ζῶσαν γεγονώς, ῥίψας ἐπὶ τὸ χεῖρον, ἀπώλεσε τὴν ζ., οὕτω πάλιν ὁ αὐτὸς ἐκεῖνος ἐπὶ τὸ βέλτιον ἐπανελθών, καὶ προσλαβόμενος τὸ ζωοποιοῦν πνεῦμα, εὑρήσει τὴν ζ. Iren.*haer.*5.12.2(M.7.1153B); cf.*ib.* 5.7.2(1141A); πνεῦμα...ζωῆς χορηγόν Bas.*Spir.*22(2.19C; M.32.108B); τοῦ πνεύματος...πρὸς τὴν πνευματικὴν ἐκείνην ζ. τὰς ψυχὰς ἡμῶν μεταρυθμίζοντος *ib.*49(41D; M.157B); **5.** Trin. ἡ αὐτὴ ζ. καὶ παρὰ τοῦ πατρὸς ἐνεργεῖται, καὶ παρὰ τοῦ υἱοῦ ἑτοιμάζεται, καὶ τῆς τοῦ πνεύματος ἐξῆπται βουλήσεως Gr.Nyss.*tres dii*(M.45.125D); ταύτης ἀρχὴ τῆς ἱεραρχίας ἡ πηγὴ τῆς ζ. ... ἡ μία ὄντων αἰτία τριάς Dion.Ar.*e.h.*1.3 (M.3.373C); τῆς πηγῆς τῆς ὄντως ζ., τῆς ἁγίας τριάδος Gel.Cyz.*h.e.*2. 23.6(M.85.1296D); **6.** divine grace, Eus.*e.th.*1.13(p.74.7; M.24.852D); **7.** discussion whether soul is life in itself or receives it from God, Just.*dial.*6.1(M.6.489B).

F. derived from Church, Sacraments and Word; **1.** Church ἡ ἐκκλησία...βλαστάνουσα ζ. Meth.*symp.*8.11(p.93.16; M.18.153D); **2.** baptism ἡ ζ. ὑμῶν διὰ ὕδατος ἐσώθη καὶ σωθήσεται Herm.*vis.*3.3. 5; τὸ βάπτισμα...τὸ ὕδωρ τῆς ζ. Just.*dial.*14.1(M.6.504C); *ib.*19.2 (516C); †Hipp.*theoph.*2(p.258.6; M.10.853A) cit. s. ἀκατάληπτος; ζ. αἰώνιον σὺν ἔργοις καλοῖς δωρεῖσθαι τὸν θεὸν ἐπὶ τῷ βαπτίσματι *Hom.Clem.*13.10; Cyr.H.*procatech.*9; Dion.Ar.*e.h.*2.2.5(M.3.396A); **3.** eucharist φάγωμεν ἐν τῷ ἀναγαίῳ τὸ πάσχα, ἔχοντες μεθ' ἑαυτῶν τὸν ὑπὲρ ἡμῶν τυθέντα Χριστόν, ὅλον αὐτὸν ὡς ζ. ἐσθίοντες Thphl.Al. *fr.ep.pasch.*1(p.300.7; M.65.53A); exeg. Jo.6:57 ζ. δὲ ἐνταῦθα λέγει, οὐ τὴν ἁπλῶς, ἀλλὰ τὴν εὐδόκιμον. καὶ ὅτι οὐ περὶ τῆς ἁπλῶς ζ. εἶπεν, ἀλλὰ περὶ τῆς ἐνδόξου καὶ ἀπορρήτου ἐκείνης, δῆλον ἐκεῖθεν...πάντες, καὶ οἱ ἄπιστοι ζῶσι...μὴ φαγόντες ἀπὸ τῆς σαρκὸς ἐκείνης. ὁρᾷς ὅτι οὐ περὶ ταύτης ὁ λόγος ἐστὶ τῆς ζ., ἀλλὰ περὶ ἐκείνης; Chrys.*hom.47.1 in Jo.*(8.276B); cf.Dion.Ar.*e.h.*3.3.13(M.3.444C); **4.** word of God ἵνα δείξῃ τὴν τοῦ εὐαγγελίου ὑπόθεσιν, ὅτι δόσις ἐστὶν αἰωνίου ζ. Clem. *q.d.s.*6(p.164.6; M.9.612A); ὁ λόγος τοῦ κυρίου ἡμῶν ζ. ἐστιν ἀληθινή *A.Phil.*142(p.80.24).

G. obtained through human co-operation; **1.** through Christian life; **a.** in gen. ἐὰν ἀφέξηται πάσης ἐπιθυμίας πονηρᾶς, κληρονομήσει ζ. αἰώνιον Herm.*vis.*3.8.4; τῶν οὖν φοβουμένων αὐτὸν καὶ φυλασσόντων τὰς ἐντολὰς αὐτοῦ, ἐκείνων ἡ ζ. ἐστι παρὰ τῷ θεῷ· τῶν δὲ μὴ φυλασσόντων τὰς ἐντολὰς αὐτοῦ οὐδὲ ζ. ἐν αὐτῷ id.*mand.*7.5; id.*sim.*8.7.6; Clem.*prot.*1(p.7.20; M.8.61B); *A.Jo.*76(p.191.11); ἐπ' ἀγῶνος τὸν διὰ πάσης κακουχίας διεληλυθότα καὶ ἄμεμπτον εὑρεθέντα ἐκεῖνον ζ. αἰωνίου καταξιοῦσθαι *Hom.Clem.*12.29; τοὺς...πρὸς ἐναρέτου ζωῆς τελείωσιν...ἀφικομένους...εἰς θειοτάτην ζ. ἐκ θανάτου μεταφοιτήσαντας Dion.Ar.*e.h.*3.3.9(M.3.437B); *ib.*7.37(561D); **b.** repentance, Herm. *sim.*8.6.6; **c.** faith, *A.Jo.*47(p.175.2); Clem.*paed.*1.6(p.107.16; M.8. 285A); τὸ μέγιστον...τῶν πρὸς τὴν ζ. μαθημάτων...γνῶναι τὸν θεὸν τὸν αἰώνιον...καὶ ἕνα καὶ ἀγαθὸν θεόν id.*q.d.s.*7(p.164.14; M.9.612B); Or. *mart.*41(p.38.21; M.11.617A); *Hom.Clem.*10.2; faith and charity ἐὰν ...εἰς Ἰησοῦν Χριστὸν ἔχητε τὴν πίστιν καὶ τὴν ἀγάπην· ἥτις ἐστὶν ἀρχὴ ζωῆς καὶ τέλος· ἀρχὴ μὲν πίστις, τέλος δὲ ἀγάπη Ign.*Eph.*14.1; hope of life as ground and end of faith ζωῆς ἐλπίς, ἀρχὴ καὶ τέλος πίστεως ἡμῶν *Barn.*1.6; cf.*ib.*1.4; **d.** charity ἡ πρὸς αὐτὸν [sc. θεόν] ἀγάπη καὶ ἐξομοίωσις μόνη ζ. Clem.*q.d.s.*7(p.164.23; 612B); ψυχαί, αἱ ἐμπύρως...τὴν ἀγάπην πρὸς κύριον ἔχουσαι, ἄξιαι τῆς αἰωνίου ζ. τυγχάνουσι Mac.Aeg.*hom.*10.2(M.34.541B); ζ. τῆς ἄνω φύσεως ἀγάπη ἐστίν...ἀεὶ ἡ θεία ζ. δι' ἀγάπης ἐνεργηθήσεται Gr.Nyss.*anim.et res.* (M.46.95C); **e.** chastity ποιήσαντες τὸ θέλημα τοῦ πατρὸς...ληψόμεθα ζ. αἰώνιον,...τηρήσατε τὴν σάρκα ἁγνὴν καὶ τὴν σφραγῖδα ἄσπιλον, ἵνα τὴν ζ. ἀναλάβωμεν *2Clem.*8.4,6; τῆς εἰς τὸν παράδεισον ἀποκαταστάσεως καὶ τῆς εἰς ἀφθαρσίαν μεταβολῆς...οὐδὲν αἴτιον οὕτως ἄλλο γέγονε καὶ σωτήριον ἀνθρώποις, τὸ στρατηγῆσαν ἡμᾶς εἰς ζ., ὡς ἁγνεία Meth.*symp.*4.2(p.46.12; M.18.88C); **f.** obedience, Clem.*paed.* 1.1(p.90.1); **g.** good works ποιήσας...ἀγαθὰ ὡς θέλων τὴν ἀληθινὴν ζ. Or.*Cels.*6.54(p.125.25; M.11.1581C); *Hom.Clem.*18.2; Chrys.*Thdr.*1. 12(1.19C); **h.** summary τοῖς δὲ δικαίοις, καὶ ὁσίοις, καὶ τὰς ἐντολὰς αὐτοῦ τετηρηκόσι, καὶ ἐν τῇ ἀγάπῃ αὐτοῦ διαμεμενηκόσι, τοῖς ἀπ' ἀρχῆς, τοῖς δὲ ἐκ μετανοίας, ζ. χαρισάμενος Iren.*haer.*1.10.1(M.7. 552A); **2.** through martyrdom [sc. τὴν δι' αἵματος μαρτυρίαν τοῦ κυρίου] τῆς ὄντως οὔσης ζ. ἀρχὴν εἶναι τὴν τοιαύτην τοῦ θανάτου πύλην Clem.*str.*4.7(p.268.5; M.8.1256B); τὴν ζ. ἑαυτοῖς διὰ τοῦ θανάτου πραγματευσώμεθα...μὴ φείδεσθε ζ. ἧς ἀναγκαία ἡ στέρησις Bas.*hom.* 18.8(2.148D; M.31.505C); **3.** related to γνῶσις: εὐχαριστοῦμεν...ὑπὲρ τῆς ζ. καὶ γνώσεως, ἧς ἐγνώρισας ἡμῖν διὰ Ἰησοῦ *Did.*9.3; ref. Gen. 2:9 οὐδὲ γὰρ ἄσημα τὰ γεγραμμένα, ὡς θεὸς ἀπ' ἀρχῆς ⟨ξύλον γνώσεως καὶ⟩ ξύλον ζ. ἐν μέσῳ παραδείσου ἐφύτευσε, διὰ γνώσεως ζωὴν ἐπιδεικνύς,...οὐδὲ γὰρ ζ. ἄνευ γνώσεως, οὐδὲ γνῶσις ἀσφαλὴς ἄνευ ζ. ἀληθοῦς...ἣν δύναμιν ἐνιδὼν ὁ ἀπόστολος τήν τε ἄνευ ἀληθείας προστάγματος εἰς ζ. ἀσκουμένην γνῶσιν μεμφόμενος λέγει· 'ἡ γνῶσις φυσιοῖ ...' ὁ γὰρ νομίζων εἰδέναι τι ἄνευ γνώσεως...μαρτυρουμένης ὑπὸ τῆς ζ., οὐκ ἔγνω...ὁ δὲ μετὰ φόβου ἐπιγνοὺς καὶ ζ. ἐπιζητῶν ἐπ' ἐλπίδι φυτεύει ...ἤτω σοὶ καρδία γνῶσις, ζ. δὲ λόγος ἀληθής, χωρούμενος ‡*Diogn.*12. 3–7; (cf. Mt.23:3) αὐτῶν δέ, εἶπεν, ὡς τὴν κλεῖδα τῆς βασιλείας πεπιστευμένων, ἥτις ἐστὶ γνῶσις, ἡ μόνη τὴν πύλην τῆς ζ. ἀνοῖξαι δύναται, δι' ἧς μόνης εἰς τὴν αἰωνίαν ζ. εἰσελθεῖν ἔστιν *Hom.Clem.*3.18; **4.** as lost through human free will μονοειδὴς ἦν ἡ τῶν ἀνθρώπων ζ. μονοειδὲς δὲ λέγω τὴν ἐν μόνῳ τῷ ἀγαθῷ ὁρωμένην...ἀλλ' ἑκουσίως ὁ ἄνθρωπος... καταλιπὼν τὴν ἀμιγῆ τοῦ χείρονος μοῖραν, τὴν ἐκ τῶν ἐναντίων σύγκρατον ζ. ἐπεσπάσατο Gr.Nyss.*anim.et res.*(M.46.81B).

H. ref. two ways, of life and death (cf. Dt.30:15) ὁδοὶ δύο εἰσί, μία τῆς ζ. καὶ μία τοῦ θανάτου...ἡ μὲν οὖν ὁδὸς τῆς ζ. ἐστιν αὕτη· πρῶτον, ἀγαπήσεις τὸν θεόν...δεύτερον, τὸν πλησίον σου ὡς σεαυτόν *Did.*1.1,2; εἰ οὖν ὁ θάνατος ἐπικρατήσας τοῦ ἀνθρώπου ἔξωσεν αὐτοῦ τὴν ζ., καὶ νεκρὸν ἀπέδειξε· πολλῷ μᾶλλον ἡ ζ. ἐπικρατήσασα αὐτοῦ ἀπωθεῖται τὸν θάνατον, καὶ ζῶντα τὸν ἄνθρωπον καταστήσει τῷ θεῷ Iren.*haer.*5.12.1(M.7.1151C); Clem.*prot.*10(p.69.26f.; M.8.208C); ζ. γοῦν καὶ θάνατος...πλεῖστον ἀλλήλων διαφέρειν δοκοῦντα, εἰς ἄλληλα περιχωρεῖ πως καὶ ἀντικαθίσταται. ἡ μὲν γὰρ ἐκ φθορᾶς ἀρχομένη τῆς μητρὸς ἡμῶν, καὶ διὰ φθορᾶς ὁδεύουσα τῆς ἀεὶ τοῦ παρόντος ἐκστάσεως, εἰς φθορὰν καταστρέφει τὴν τοῦ βίου τούτου κατάλυσιν· ὁ δὲ τῶν ἐνταῦθα κακῶν ἀπαλλαγὴν ἔχων, καὶ πρὸς τὴν ἄνω πολλάκις μετάγων ζ., οὐκ οἶδα εἰ κυρίως προσαγορεύοιτο θάνατος...μία ζ., πρὸς τὴν ζ. βλέπειν. εἷς θάνατος, ἡ ἁμαρτία...ἂν οὕτως ἔχωμεν...οὔτε τῇ ζ. μέγα φρονήσομεν, οὔτε τῷ θανάτῳ λίαν ἀνιασόμεθα. τί τοίνυν δεινὸν πεπόνθαμεν, εἰ πρὸς τὴν ἀληθινὴν ζ. ἐνθένδε μεταβεβήκαμεν; Gr.Naz. *or.*18.42(M.35.1041A,B).

I. aspects of eternal life and belief in it; **1.** many ways of entry afforded by God, Cyr.H.*catech.*18.31; **2.** comparison with present life ὧδε ζ. ἔχουσα τέλος, ἐκεῖ ζ. οὐκ ἔχουσα τέλος Chrys.*Eutrop.*2.13 (3.398D); βούλει μαθεῖν διὰ τί καλὸν ἡ παροῦσα ζ.; ὅτι τῆς μελλούσης ζ. ἡμῖν ὑπόθεσις γίνεται καὶ ἀφορμή, καὶ σκάμμα καὶ στάδιον τῶν ἐκεῖ στεφάνων ἐστίν id.*stat.*6.4(2.78B); id.*serm.9.4 in Gen.*(4.693B); τὰ γὰρ ἄλογα μόνα τῷ παρόντι χρήσιμα βίῳ· ἡμεῖς δὲ διὰ τοῦτο ψυχὴν ἀθάνατον ἔχομεν, ἵνα πρὸς τὴν ἐκείνης τῆς ζ. παρασκευὴν πάντα πράξωμεν id. *hom.31.5 in Jo.*(8.183A); id.*exp.in Ps.*48:13(5.214A); **3.** freedom of eternal life from matter and physical limitations ἄυλον πάντῃ καὶ ἀσώματον ζ. ζώντων ἐν μακαριότητι τῶν ἁγίων Or.*Jo.*1.17(p.21.13; M. 14.52B); οὐκ ἔνι ἄρσεν καὶ θῆλυ ἐν ἀναστάσει, ἀλλὰ μία τίς ἐστιν ζ. καὶ μονότροπος, εὐαρεστούντων τῷ ἑαυτῶν δεσπότῃ Bas.*hom.in Ps.*114(1. 203B; M.29.492C); τὸ ἀνενδεὲς τῆς ζ. ἐκείνης καὶ ἄυλον, ἐν ᾗ τὸ διακρατοῦν τῆς ψυχῆς τὴν ὑπόστασιν, οὐ ξηροῦ τε καὶ ὑγροῦ τινός ἐστι μετουσία, ἀλλ' ἡ τῆς θείας φύσεως κατανόησις Gr.Nyss.*mort.*(M.46.504D); διὰ τοῦτο μακαρία τίς ἐστιν ἐκείνη ἡ ζ. καὶ ἀκήρατος, μηκέτι ταῖς τῶν αἰσθητηρίων ἡδοναῖς πρὸς τὴν τοῦ καλοῦ κρίσιν ἐμπλανωμένη *ib.*(505A); as life with angels, Chrys.*exp.in Ps.*48:10(5.211E); **4.** description τί οὖν ταύτης μακαριώτερον γένοιτ' ἂν τῆς ζ.; οὐκ ἔστιν ἐκεῖ πενίαν δεῖσαι καὶ νόσον· οὐκ ἔστιν ἀδικοῦντα οὐδὲ ἀδικούμενον ἰδεῖν, οὐ παροξύνοντα καὶ παροξυνόμενον...οὐδὲ γὰρ ἐκεῖ νύξ, οὐδὲ συνδρομῇ κρύπτεται νεφελῶν ...τὸ δὲ τούτων ἁπάντων μεῖζον, τὸ τῆς πρὸς τὸν Χριστὸν ὁμιλίας ἀπολαύειν διηνεκῶς...μετὰ τῶν ἀνωτέρω δυνάμεων Chrys.*Thdr.*1.11(1. 15B); **5.** arguments for body's participation εἰ ἡ δύναμις αὐτοῦ [sc. θεοῦ], ἥτις ἐστὶ ζωῆς παρεκτική, ἐν ἀσθενείᾳ τελειοῦται, τουτέστιν ἐν σαρκί· εἰπάτωσαν ἡμῖν οἱ λέγοντες μὴ εἶναι δεκτικὴν τὴν σάρκα τῆς παρὰ τοῦ θεοῦ δεδομένης ζ., πότερον ζῶντες νῦν, καὶ μετέχοντες τῆς ζ. λέγουσι ταῦτα, ἢ τὸ καθόλου ζ. μετέχοντες μηδέν, νεκροὺς δὲ αὐτοὺς τῷ παρόντι ὁμολογοῦσιν; ἀλλ' εἰ μὲν εἰσὶ νεκροί, πῶς καὶ κινοῦνται... εἰ δὲ ζῶσι νῦν, καὶ ὅλον σῶμα αὐτῶν μετέχει τῆς ζ., πῶς τολμῶσι λέγειν μὴ εἶναι τὴν σάρκα δεκτικήν...τῆς ζ., ὁμολογοῦντες ἔχειν ζ. ἐν τῷ παρόντι;...οὗτοι ζῆν λέγοντες καὶ βαστάζειν ζ. ἐν τοῖς ἰδίοις μέλεσιν, ἔπειτα ἑαυτοῖς ἐναντιούμενοι, τὰ μέλη αὐτῶν ἐπιδεκτικὰ μὴ λέγουσι τῆς ζ. εἰ δὲ τὸ πρόσκαιρον τοῦ ζῆν, πολλῷ ἀσθενέστερον ἐκείνης τῆς αἰωνίας ζ., ὅμως τοιοῦτον δύναται, ὥστε ζωοποιεῖν ἡμῶν τὰ θνητὰ μέλη· ἡ τούτου δραστικωτέρα αἰώνιος ζ. τί ὅτι οὐ ζωοποιεῖ τὴν σάρκα, τὴν ἤδη εἰθισμένην βαστάζειν τὴν ζ.; ὅτι γὰρ ἐπιδεκτικὴ ζωῆς ἐστιν ἡ σάρξ, ἐκ τοῦ ζῆν δείκνυται...ἐκείνου [sc. θεοῦ] γὰρ παρέχοντος ἡμῖν τὴν ζ., καὶ τοῦ θεοῦ οὖν δυνατοῦ ὄντος ζωοποιεῖν τὸ πλάσμα τοῦ ἑαυτοῦ, καὶ τῆς σαρκὸς δυναμένης ζωοποιεῖσθαι, τί λοιπὸν τὸ κωλῦον αὐτὴν μετέχειν τῆς ἀφθαρσίας, ἥτις ἐστὶ μακαρία καὶ ἀτελεύτητος ζ. ὑπὸ θεοῦ διδομένη; Iren.*haer*.5.3.3(M.7.1131A–1132C); exeg. 2Cor.5:1–4 ἐὰν οὖν ἡ νῦν δὴ αὕτη ἡ τοῦ σώματος ζ. δίκην οἰκίας καταλυθῇ, ἕξομεν τὴν ἐν τοῖς οὐρανοῖς ἀχειροποίητον ⟨οἰκίαν, τουτέστι ζ. αἰώνιον⟩. ἀχειροποίητόν φησι διὰ τὸ χειροποιητὸν ταύτην λέγεσθαι τὴν ζ. κατὰ ἀντιδιαστολήν, παρὰ τὸ πάντα ἡμῶν τὰ κοσμήματα καὶ σπουδάσματα τοῦ βίου χερσὶ παλαμᾶσθαι ἀνθρώπων...τίς οὖν ἐστιν ἡ χειροποίητος οἰκία; ἡ βραχύβιος...αὕτη ζ., ἡ ἀπ' ἀνθρωπίνων χειρῶν δραματουργουμένη...ἧς καταλυθείσης ἐκείνην τὴν ἀχειροποίητον ζ. ἔχομεν Meth.*res*.2.15(p.362.5–363.1; M.18.312A); exeg. 1Cor.15:50 διδάσκων οὐ κληρονομεῖσθαι βασιλείαν θεοῦ, αἰώνιον ὑπάρχουσαν ζ., ὑπὸ τοῦ σώματος, ἀλλὰ τὸ σῶμα ὑπὸ τῆς ζ. εἰ γὰρ ἐκληρονομεῖτο ἡ βασιλεία τοῦ θεοῦ ὑπὸ τοῦ σώματος, ζ. ὑπάρχουσα, συνέβαινεν ἂν τὴν ζ. ὑπὸ τῆς φθορᾶς καταπίνεσθαι· νῦν δὲ τὸ τεθνηκὸς ἡ ζ. κληρονομεῖ, ἵνα εἰς νῖκος καταποθῇ ὁ θάνατος ὑπὸ τῆς ζ. *ib*.2.18(p.371.4ff.; M.18.284D–285A); **6.** credal affirmations, *Symb.App*.(p.30); *Symb.Hier*.ap.Cyr.H.*catech*.18; προσδοκῶμεν...ζ. τοῦ μέλλοντος αἰῶνος *Symb*.ap.Epiph.*anc*.118 (p.147.16; M.43.232D); *Symb*.ap.Epiph.*anc*.119(p.149.4; 236B); *Symb.Nic.–CP*(p.80.16; H.2.288B).

J. mystical and angelic life; **1.** mystical and 'deiform' ὅλοι γενοίμεθα τοῦ θεοῦ καὶ τῆς μετ' αὐτοῦ καὶ παρ' αὐτῷ ζ. ὡς κοινωνήσοντες τῷ μονογενεῖ αὐτοῦ καὶ τοῖς μετόχοις αὐτοῦ Or.*mart*.11(p.11.17; M.11.577B); Ἰησοῦς...εἰς ἑνοειδῆ καὶ θείαν ἀποτελειώσας ζ. Dion.Ar.*e.h*.1.1(M.3.372B); expressed liturg. in kiss of peace, *ib*.3.3.8(437A); τὴν δ' αὖ καρδίαν, σύμβολον εἶναι τῆς θεοειδοῦς ζ. id.*c.h*.15.3(M.3.332C); μοναχοὺς ὀνομάζοντες, ἐκ...τῆς ἀμερίστης καὶ ἑνιαίας ζ. id.*e.h*.6.1.3 (533A); exeg. Gal.2:20 ὡς ἀληθὴς ἐραστὴς καὶ ἐξεστηκώς, ὡς αὐτός φησι, τῷ θεῷ, καὶ οὐ τὴν ἑαυτοῦ ζῶν, ἀλλὰ τὴν τοῦ ἐραστοῦ ζ. id.*d.n*.4.13(M.3.712A); ἔζησε τὴν τοῦ θεοῦ μακαρίαν ζ., τοῦ μόνου κατ' ἀλήθειαν κυρίως ζ. καὶ λεγομένου καὶ ὄντος Max.*cap.theol*.1.54(M.90.1104B); ὁ μαθὼν ὀρύσσειν κατὰ τοὺς πατριάρχας διὰ πράξεως καὶ θεωρίας τὰ ἐν αὐτῷ τῆς ἀρετῆς καὶ τῆς γνώσεως φρέατα, τὸν Χριστὸν ἔνδον εὑρήσει τὴν πηγὴν τῆς ζ. *ib*.2.40(1144A); **2.** angelic αἱ...τῶν οὐρανίων οὐσιῶν διακοσμήσεις...νοερὰν ἔχουσαι τὴν πᾶσαν ζ. Dion.Ar.*c.h*.4.2(M.3.180A); τῶν σεραφὶμ οὐσίας, ἐκ τοῦ κατὰ θείαν καὶ ἀκίνητον ζ. διαπύρου id.*e.h*.4.3.9(M.3.481C); id.*d.n*.8.5(M.3.892D).

K. τὸ ξύλον τῆς ζ.; **1.** exeg. Gen.3:22, cf. *ejecit eum de paradiso, et a ligno vitae longe transtulit: non invidens ei lignum vitae, quemadmodum quidam audent dicere, sed miserans ejus, ut non perseveraret semper transgressor*, Iren.*haer*.3.23.6(M.7.964A); οὐ γάρ, ὅτι μὴ θέλων ὁ θεὸς ἀπὸ τοῦ ξύλου δρέψασθαι τῆς ζ. αὐτὸν καὶ φαγεῖν ἐξέβαλεν (ἐδύνατο γὰρ εἰς τὸν αἰῶνα ζῆν, αὖθις φαγὼν ἀπὸ τῆς ζ.), ἀλλ' ἵνα μὴ ἀθάνατον...γενηθῇ τὸ κακόν. ἐπεὶ διὰ τί τὸν Χριστὸν ἀπὸ τῶν οὐρανῶν ἀπέστελλεν εἰς τὴν γῆν, εἰ ὅλως ἤθελε ζωῆς τὸν ἄνθρωπον ἄγευστον ἀποθανεῖν εἰς τὸ παντελές;...ὥστε οὐκ ἄρα διὰ τὸ μὴ σώζεσθαι εἰς τὸν αἰῶνα φαγόντα αὐτὸν ἀπὸ τοῦ ξύλου τῆς ζ. ἐξέβαλεν, ἀλλὰ διὰ τὸ νεκρωθῆναι πρῶτον θανάτῳ τὴν ἁμαρτίαν Meth.*res*.1.39(pp.283.14ff.–284.6; M.41.1108B); met., in souls of faithful εἴσεσθε ὅσα παρέχει ὁ θεὸς τοῖς ἀγαπῶσιν ὀρθῶς, οἱ γενόμενοι παράδεισος τρυφῆς...ἐν γὰρ τούτῳ τῷ χωρίῳ...ξύλον ζωῆς πεφύτευται ‡*Diogn*.12.2; **2.** ref. Christ and Cross ἐπιφερόμενος τὸ ξύλον τῆς ζ. Clem.*paed*.3.3(p.251.13; M.8.592A); ἠδυνθήτω ἡ ζ. τὰ ἐν τῷ ξύλῳ. καὶ πίστευσον τῷ σταυρωθέντι *A.Andr*.A 16(p.56.20); ὁ μὴ πιστεύσας Χριστῷ, μηδὲ τὴν ἀρχὴν αὐτὸν εἶναι, τὸ ξύλον τῆς ζ. ἠσθημένος...πῶς ἑόρτασε; Meth.*symp*.9.3(p.117.27; M.18.184B); in description of Ophite rite τοῦ δὲ σφραγιζομένου ...ἀποκρινομένου· κέχρισμαι χρίσματι λευκῷ ἐκ ξύλου ζωῆς Cels.ap.Or.*Cels*.6.27(p.97.5; M.11.1333A); περὶ δὲ τοῦ τῆς ζ. ξύλου εὐκαιρότερόν τις διηγήσεται ἑρμηνεύων τὰ περὶ τὸν ἐν τῇ Γενέσει ἀναγεγραμμένον παράδεισον...παρακούσας [sc. Celsus] οἶμαι τοῦ συμβολικῶς εἰρημένου, ὅτι διὰ ξύλου ζ., θάνατος μὲν κατὰ τὸν Ἀδὰμ ζ. δὲ κατὰ τὸν Χριστόν Or.*Cels*.6.36(p.105.27ff.; 1352B,C); cf. ὁ...τοῦ κυρίου στέφανος...τῆς πίστεώς ἐστιν τύπος, ζωῆς μὲν διὰ τὴν οὐσίαν τοῦ ξύλου Clem.*paed*.2.8 (p.202.14; M.8.485A); **3.** hence sign of cross signifies life, Dion.Ar.*e.h*.5.3.4(M.3.512A).

L. of monastic life (usu. βίος) τὴν τελειοτάτην αὐτῷ [sc. μοναχῷ] ζ. ὑφηγεῖται Dion.Ar.*e.h*.6.2(M.3.533B); ἡ μοναδικὴ ζ. Thdt.*haer*.5.24 (4.463).

M. Gnost., ref. Valentinians οἱ ἀντίμιμοι τοῦ δημιουργοῦ... ἐμφυσῶντες τὴν ζ. τὴν ἄνωθεν κατὰ τὴν τοῦ δόγματος αἵρεσιν Clem.*str*.4.13(p.288.17; M.8.1300A); as aeon αἰσθόμενόν τε τὸν Μονογενῆ τοῦτον ἐφ' οἷς προεβλήθη, προβαλεῖν καὶ αὐτὸν Λόγον, καὶ Ζωήν,...ἐκ δὴ τοῦ Λόγου καὶ τῆς Ζωῆς προβεβλῆσθαι κατὰ συζυγίαν Ἄνθρωπον καὶ Ἐκκλησίαν Iren.*haer*.1.1.1(M.7.448A); πρὸς δὲ τούς...οἰομένους ὑπὸ νοῦ καὶ ἀληθείας προβεβλῆσθαι λόγον καὶ ζ. οὐκ ἀπίθανον καὶ ταῦτα ἀπορῆσαι. πῶς γὰρ ἡ κατ' αὐτοὺς σύζυγος τοῦ λόγου ζ. τὸ γεγονέναι ἐν τῷ συζύγῳ λαμβάνει; 'ὃ γέγονε', γάρ φησιν, 'ἐν αὐτῷ...ζ. ἦν.' λεγέτωσαν οὖν ἡμῖν, πῶς ἡ σύζυγος τοῦ λόγου ζ. γέγονεν ἐν τῷ λόγῳ, καὶ πῶς μᾶλλον τοῦ λόγου ἡ ζ. φῶς ἐστι τῶν ἀνθρώπων Or.*Jo*.2.24 (19; p.81.3ff.; M.14.156C).

***ζωηπάροχος**, v. *ζωοπάροχος.

ζωηρός, **1.** *living*; *of life*, Thdr.Stud.*nativ.BMV* 4(M.96.684A); ‡Meth.*Sym.et Ann*.8(M.18.368B); neut. as subst., *vital principle* τὸ ζ. τῆς ἀρχαίας εὐζωΐας ‡Nil.*perist*.1.6(M.79.817A); **2.** *life-giving*; of sign of cross, Ephr.3.404B; τοῦ κυρίου ζ. μυστήρια Andr.Cr.*or*.8(M.97.960B); of grace of H. Ghost, Jo.VI H.*v.Jo.D*.3(M.94.433B).

***ζωήρρυτος**, *flowing with life* ζ. πηγὴ τοῦ παρακλήτου ‡Sophr.H.*liturg*.1(M.87.3981C); of heart of Jesus, Andr.Cr.*or*.8(M.97.960B).

ζωητόκος, *life-giving* ζ. μήτηρ τῶν πιστῶν...ἐκκλησία Anast.S.*hex*.12(M.89.1072A); as subst. of BMV, Meth.*symp*.11(p.135.23; M.18.212C).

***ζωηφόριος**, *life-giving* θρόνισόν με, πάτερ, φωτὸς ἐν ἀλκᾷ ζωηφορίου Synes.*hymn*.3.599(p.23; M.66.1602).

ζωηφόρος, *life-bringing*, of God τῷ ζ. ἐμφυσήματι Eus.Al.*serm*.21.4(M.86.428B); of H. Ghost ζ. πνεύσεις †Max.*hymn*.2(M.91.1422C); ref. Christ ἀγκάλαι ζ. Meth.*symp*.11(p.132.8; M.18.208D); ζ. ἀνάστασις Chrys.*hom.4.6 in Ac.princ*.(3.89E); ζ. πάθος ‡Gr.Nyss.*hom.3.82 in Jo*.(p.156.11); Jo.Eub.*concept.BMV* 10(M.96.1476A); ζ. τελευτήν Gr.Ant.*mul.ung*.1(M.88.1848A); ζ. τάφος cf.*Lit.Praesanct*.(p.498.17); τύμβος ‡Gr.Naz.*Chr.pat*.1914(M.38.288A); as γέννημα...ζ. Geo.Pis.*hex*.1818(M.92.1574A); ἄμπελος ζ. Jo.Mon.*hymn.Blas*.(M.96.1401A); of orthodoxy as ζ. ὁδός †Ath.*fr*.(M.26.1257C); of adoptive sonship of Christians, Dion.Ar.*e.h*.4.3.3(M.3.477A); of angels, *Apoc.Dan*.C (p.118, v.l. πυρφόρος Vassiliev p.45); ref. BMV ζ. κοίμησις Jo.Eub.*concept.BMV* 22(1497B).

ζωμάριον, τό, *soup*, *sauce*, ‡Nil.*narr*.3(M.79.616A).

ζωμός, ὁ, *soup*, *sauce* τὴν ἀγάπην τὴν ἡγιασμένην...ζωμοῦ ῥύσει καθυβρίζοντες Clem.*paed*.2.1(p.156.14; M.8.384B); ‡Nil.*narr*.3(M.79.616B); Gr.Naz.*ep*.5(M.37.29A); met., of blood, ref. Is.63:2 πολέμου γὰρ ζ. τὴν ἐσθῆτα τοῦ πολεμοῦντος ἐφοίνιξεν Bas.Sel.*or*.40.1(M.85.453A).

ζωναῖοι, οἱ, supernatural beings inhabiting zones of heaven, Synes.*hymn*.3.281(p.15); cf. Michael Psellus *Expositio brevis dogmatum Chaldaicorum* (M.122.1149).

ζώνη, ἡ, *girdle*, *belt*; **1.** lit.; **a.** of monks; use required by tradition, Bas.*reg.fus*.23(2.368C; M.31.981A); ἡ ζ. ἣν φοροῦμεν, σύμβολόν ἐστι...ὅτι ἐσμὲν εὐτρεπισμένοι εἰς ἔργον...καὶ...ἵνα ὥσπερ ἐστὶν ἀπὸ νεκροῦ σώματος ἡ ζ. οὕτως καὶ ἡμεῖς νεκρώσωμεν τὴν ἐπιθυμίαν ἡμῶν Dor.*doct*.1.13(M.88.1633B); *Apophth.Patr*.(M.65.276D); **b.** of angels, *Apoc.Paul*.12(p.40); τὰς δὲ ζ. τὸ τῶν γονίμων αὐτῶν φρουρητικὸν δυνάμεων, καὶ τὸ τὴν συνάγωγον αὐτῶν ἕξιν [sc. σημαίνειν οἴομαι] Dion.Ar.*c.h*.15.4(M.3.333A); **c.** of soldiers; as badge of service, denotes *military service*, Chrys.*oppugn*.3.12(1.97C); ref. converts τὴν πρώτην ὁρμὴν ἐνδειξάμενοι, καὶ ἀποθέμενοι τὰς ζ. CNic.(325)*can*.12; abandoned by Christians to avoid compulsion to sacrifice, Socr.*h.e*.3.13.3(M.67.413A); Christians deprived of it in persecution, Pall.*v.Chrys*.11(p.65.14; M.47.37); of officers, equivalent to *commission*; forfeited by Christians through refusal to sacrifice, *M.Seb*.1(p.172.10); *ib*.5(p.175.3); **d.** of military or civil officials, equivalent to *office in government service* τὴν ζ. τῆς ἀρχῆς ἀφαιρεθῆναι *M.Artem*.(p.168.27); Chrys.*hom.76.5 in Mt*.(7.739B); ἐκπίπτων τῆς ζ. ἐξορίζεται Ath.Scholast.*coll*.4.22(p.62); forfeited for heresy, Constans *typ*.(H.3.825B); **e.** of priests, cf.*Lit.Chrys*.(p.355.32); **f.** moral symbolism: purity, *Asen*.14(p.60.12); temperance, Gr.Naz.*or*.45.18 (M.36.648C); manliness, *ib*.; **2.** met., of that which surrounds τὴν ὠκεάνιον ζ. Mac.Mgn.*apocr*.3.14(p.93.7); of throng of angels round Michael, Didym.*Trin*.2.8(M.39.589A); *tier* or *row* of seats in theatre, Jo.Mal.*chron*.9 p.222(M.97.345B).

***ζώνησις**, ἡ, *girdle*, v. ζῶσις.

ζώννυμι (**ζωννύω**), **1.** *gird*, *put on*; met., ref. wicked angels in spiritual combat ὁ γὰρ πονηρὸς οὐ παρὰ βασιλέως ἐζώσατο Clem.*exc.Thdot*.72(p.130.5; M.9.692C); τῶν ἀνθρώπων ἡ ψυχή...ζωσαμένη τὴν τῶν θείων λήθην Ath.*gent*.8(M.25.16C); οὐδὲν γὰρ ἕτερόν ἐστι τὸ ἐζῶσθαι, ἢ τὸ δεδέσθαι τὴν ἰσχὺν τῆς ὀσφύος Isid.Pel.*epp*.1.9(M.78.185B); **2.** *invest*, *appoint* Γερμανὸς ζωσθεὶς στρατηλάτης Jo.Mal.*chron*.p.480(M.97.696B); *ib*.p.490(709A); **3.** *go round*, of Devil τὴν σφαῖραν ζωννύων A.Thom.A 32(p.149.2); *surround* ζ. τὴν πόλιν Thphn.chron.p.365(M.108.876C).

ζωογον-έω, *give life (to)*; **A.** ref. natural life; **1.** of God θεοῦ... μόνου...ζ. ... νεκρούς Eus.d.e.9.13(p.432.5; M.22.696D); ἡ τριὰς εἷς θεός ἐστιν...πάντα ~ῶν πνεύματος ἐξ ἰδίου Gr.Naz.carm.1.1.31.3ff.(M.37.511A); **2.** of Son; **a.** in creation and preservation, Eus.l.C.12(p.232.3; M.20.1389C); Ath.gent.42(M.25.84C); Cyr.Juln.10(6^2.339C); ὁ μονογενὴς...λόγος...ἡ πάντα ~οῦσα φύσις id.Arcad.3(p.69.13; 5^2.44C); **b.** giving life to dead οὐδεὶς ἀνθρώπων ~εῖ· οὐ γάρ ἐστι Χριστός. Χριστὸς δὲ ~εῖ· οὐκ ἄρα ἄνθρωπος ὁ Χριστός Apoll.anac.13(p.243.24; M.28.1272C); ἐπειδὴ...ἰδία γέγονε τοῦ λόγου ἡ σὰρξ τοῦ πάντα ~οῦντος, διὰ τοῦτο ζωοποιὸς καὶ αὐτὴ cat.Lc.7:11(p.56.28); as raising his own body, Chrys.hom.29.3 in 2Cor.(10.643E); **3.** of H. Ghost ζ. ... τὰ πάντα τὸ τοῦ θεοῦ πνεῦμα Cyr.Juln.2(6^2.55A); ref. Gen.1:2 τισὶ δοκεῖ τὸ πανάγιον πνεῦμα ~οῦν τῶν ὑδάτων τὴν φύσιν, καὶ διαγράφον τὴν τοῦ βαπτίσματος χάριν Bas.hex.2.6(1.18D; M.29.44B); Thdt.qu.8 in Gen.(1.13); **4.** τὰ ~ούμενα *the living*, Clem.str.5.14(p.397.19; M.9.161B); ib.6.16(p.504.17; 369C).

B. ref. supernatural life; **1.** of Father τὰ πάντα ζ. Bas.Spir.56(3.48B; M.32.172C); in baptism and elsewhere, Gr.Nyss.Maced.19(M.45.1325A); **2.** of Son ζ. τὸν τῶν ἀρετῶν κύκλον Gr.Naz.or.45.13(M.36.641A); ὁ...Χριστὸς...ἐζωοποίησε· καὶ διπλοῦν τὸ θαῦμα δείκνυσιν, ὅτι καὶ τὸν νεκρὸν ἐζωογόνησε, καὶ διὰ θανάτου τὴν ζωὴν ἐχαρίσατο Chrys.comm.in Gal.2:19(10.692C); cat.Jo.6:35(p.249.9); **3.** ref. transmission of spiritual life, by baptism τὸ ὕδωρ τὸ τῷ πνεύματι κοινωνοῦν, δι' οὗ...ἀναγεννώμενος ~εῖται ἄνθρωπος †Hipp.theoph.8(p.262.20; M.10.860B); by practice of virtue, Gr.Nyss.v.Mos.(M.44.328C); by bishops λύειν ἁμαρτιῶν τοὺς ἐπιστρέφοντας καὶ ζ. αὐτούς Const.App.2.33.3.

ζωογόνησις, ἡ, *generation of life* πνεῦμα...ὃ ἔδωκεν ὁ θεὸς εἰς ζ. τῇ κτίσει Thphl.Ant.Autol.2.13(M.6.1072B); Epiph.exp.fid.16(p.516.28; M.42.812D); Sever.1Tim.6:13(p.341.9).

ζωογονία, ἡ, *account of the origin of living things* ἡ...τῶν Φοινίκων καὶ Αἰγυπτίων ζ. Eus.p.e.7.17(329B; M.21.557B).

[*]**ζῳογραφία**, ἡ, poet. for ζωγραφία, *painting, picture*, Orac.Sib.3.589.

***ζωοδοτέω**, *vivify*, Didym.Trin.2.1(M.39.449B).

ζωοδοτήρ, ὁ, *life-giver*; as adj. ζ. ... τοῦ ἁγίου πνεύματος...ζωή Ph.Carp.Cant.209(M.40.132B).

ζωοδότης, ὁ, *life-giver* Ἠλίας...τῇ πενιχρᾷ χήρᾳ ζ. ‡Chrys.hom.2(13.207B); of Christ, Bas.Sel.or.10.2(M.85.148A); Dion.Ar.e.h.2.3.7(M.3.404B); ‡Sophr.H.triod.(M.87.3917D); as adj.; of Christ, Procl.CP or.10.2(M.65.780C); Jo.D.hom.1.18(M.96.572B).

***ζωοδοτικός**, *life-giving* τὸ ζ. as attribute of divine nature, Jo.D.f.o.1.14(M.94.860A).

***ζωοδότος**, *life-giving*, of Son ὡς ζ. ... φῶς...ἐκ τοῦ πατρικοῦ φωτὸς ἐκλάμψαν Didym.Trin.3.3(M.39.808B); ref. raising of Lazarus δύναμις ζ. Sophr.H.carm.6.35(M.87.3761B).

***ζωοδόχος**, *receiving life*; **1.** of BMV ἐν τῷ τάφῳ μὴ παθούσης τῷ ζ. σώματι διαφοράν Mod.dorm.7(M.86.3294A); ib.12(3308C) cit. s. ἀφθαρσία; ὁ τῆς ἐπιθυμίας Δαβὶδ ζ. λάκκος τῆς Βηθλεέμ, ἀφ' οὗ πόμα ἀθανασίας ἐξέβλυσε ‡Meth.Sym.et Ann.10(M.18.372C); **2.** of tomb of Christ, Procl.CP or.13.1(M.65.792A); and BMV, Mod.dorm.13(M.86.3312A); Jo.D.hom.9.3(M.96.728C); **3.** of heaven ζ. χωρίον Thdr.Stud.epp.1.2(M.99.912C).

***ζωόδωρος**, *life-giving* ζ. πλευρὰ τοῦ Χριστοῦ ‡Jo.D.Const.17(M.95.336A); τὸ φερέσβιον καὶ ζ. ... τῆς προνοίας τοῦ Χριστοῦ Areth.Apoc.67(M.106.765D).

***ζωοθαλπέω**, *warm into life* καθάπερ ὄρνις ᾠὰ θάλπει...οὕτω καὶ τὸ πνεῦμα ἐπεφέρετο τοῖς ὕδασι ζωοθαλποῦν Diod.Gen.1:2(M.33.1563C).

***ζωοθυσία**, ἡ, **1.** *animal sacrifice* μὴ τὴν Ἰουδαϊκὴν ζ. πάλιν ἐπαναληφθήσεσθαι λέγομεν Gr.Nyss.hom.9 in Cant.(M.44.957B); id.ep.3(M.46.1024B); fig. ζ. κατασφάζει τὰ πάθη id.res.1(M.46.620B); **2.** *slaughter of animals* for food, etc., Bas.ep.258.4(3.394E; M.32.953A); ref. absence in Eden, id.hom.1.3(2.3C; M.31.168B).

ζωοθυτέω, *sacrifice animals*; in gen., Eus.d.e.1.9(p.43.10; M.22.84A); Isid.Pel.epp.4.57(M.78.1108C); Cyr.Ps.9:12(M.69.769A); met. ὁ Χριστὸς...ζ. ... τὴν σάρκα καὶ τὸ αἷμα αὐτοῦ ‡Bas.h.myst.3(p.258.10); ptcpl. masc. as subst., of Abel ὁ ζωοθυτήσας Eus.d.e.1.9(p.44.1; 84C); pass. ptcpl. neut. as subst., *animals for sacrifice*, ib.(p.45.3; 85C).

***ζωοθύτης**, ὁ, *butcher* βυρσοτόμον ἢ ζ. ὀφείλομεν νοεῖν τὸν θεόν, ἵνα τὸν Ἀδὰμ ἐνδύσῃ τοὺς χιτῶνας δερματίνους; ‡Caes.Naz.dial.142(M.38.1105).

***ζωόκαυστος**, *burnt alive*, Chron.Pasch.p.302(M.92.757B); Thphn.chron.p.311.(v.l. ζωκαύστους; M.108.756B).

***ζωοκοίμητος**, *alive in death*; of BMV, Germ.CP or.6(M.98.340C).

***ζωοκτονία**, ἡ, *slaughter of animals*, Bas.Sel.v.Thecl.1(M.85.540C).

ζῷον, τό, *living being, animal*; **1.** in gen. ζ. πονηρόν ἐστιν ὁ ἐνεστὼς αἰών Or.comm.in Eph.2:1ff.(p.403); of man as λογικὸν ζ. id.schol.in Cant.6:7–8(M.17.277C); ζ. καλεῖται λογικόν, καὶ ὁ ἄνθρωπος, καὶ ὁ ἄγγελος Thdt.Ezech.1:5(2.685); ὁ πονηρός, εἰ ἀπὸ τοῦ θεοῦ ζ. γεγέννηται Hom.Clem.19.9; ref. universality of Christ's preaching μέχρι ζῴων ἑαυτὸν κηρύξας A.Jo.112(p.211.5); **2.** Christol. ἡ σὰρξ τοῦ κυρίου...προσκυνεῖται, καθὸ ἕν ἐστι πρόσωπον καὶ ἓν ζ. μετ' αὐτοῦ Apoll.fr.85(p.225.20)ap.Gr.Nyss.Apoll.44(M.45.1228C); ἓν ζ. ἐκ κινουμένου καὶ κινητικοῦ συνίστατο καὶ οὐ δύο ἢ ἐκ δύο τελείων καὶ αὐτοκινήτων διόπερ ἄνθρωπος μὲν ἕτερόν τι ζ. πρὸς θεὸν καὶ οὐ θεός, ἀλλὰ δοῦλος θεοῦ. ... σὰρξ δὲ θεοῦ σὰρξ γενομένη ζ. ἐστι μετὰ ταῦτα συντεθεῖσα εἰς μίαν φύσιν ib.107(p.232.16)ap.Justn.monoph.(M.86.1124A); δύο μὲν γὰρ...νοοῦμεν τὰς φύσεις [sc. of man], μίαν μὲν τῆς ψυχῆς, ἑτέραν δὲ τοῦ σώματος. ἀλλ' ἐν ψιλαῖς διελόντες ἐννοίαις... οὐκ ἀνὰ μέρος τίθεμεν τὰς φύσεις...ἀλλ' ἑνὸς εἶναι νοοῦμεν, ὥστε τὰς δύο μηκέτι μὲν εἶναι δύο, δι' ἀμφοῖν δὲ τὸ ἓν ἀποτελεῖσθαι ζ. οὐκοῦν κἂν εἰ λέγοιεν ἀνθρωπότητος φύσιν καὶ θεότητος ἐπὶ τοῦ Ἐμμανουήλ, ἀλλ' ἡ ἀνθρωπότης γέγονεν ἰδία τοῦ λόγου καὶ εἷς υἱὸς νοεῖται σὺν αὐτῇ Cyr.ep.46(p.162.9; 5^2.145C); ὡς σύνθετόν τε τὸ τοιόνδε ζ. ... ὡς ἕν εἶναί τι θεανδρικῶς ζῶν πρόσωπον τόδε...ζ. ἄρα τὸ ἓν ὡς ὑφεστὼς πρόσωπόν ἐστιν ἕν Leont.H.monoph.(M.86.1856C–1857A); in anti-Nestorian argument ἀνάγκη λέγειν καὶ τούτοις, τὸν Χριστὸν αὐτῶν, ἢ ἥττονα εἶναι, ἢ κρείττονα κατά τι τῶν οἰκείων μερῶν καθ' ἑαυτά, ἐπινοουμένων· εἰ ὅλως ἓν ζ. ἐστι κατ' αὐτοὺς ὁ Χριστός, ἐκ θεοῦ καὶ ἀνθρώπου ἀποτελεσθέν...εἰ γὰρ τὸ κατ' αὐτοὺς ἐκ θεοῦ λόγου καὶ σαρκὸς ζ. κρεῖττον κατά τι τοῦ θεοῦ λόγου καθ' ἑαυτὸν νοουμένου, τοῦτο αὐτὸ κρεῖττον δηλονότι καὶ τοῦ πατρὸς καὶ τοῦ πνεύματος μὴ συγκειμένων τῇ σαρκί id.Nest.1.51(M.86.1516B); ib.2.1(1533A); **3.** exeg. Abac.3:2 ἐν μέσῳ δύο ζ. interpreted as ζωῶν, not ζῴων, and referred to ζωὴ ἔνθεος and ζωὴ ἀνθρωπίνη Eus.d.e.6.15(p.270.7; M.22.444C); discussion of various renderings of text in LXX and other versions, ib.; interpreted of Israel and Babylonians, Thdr.Mops.Abac.3:2(M.66.441D); δύο κεκλῆσθαι ζ., τὸ πνεῦμα καὶ τὸν υἱόν, ὧν καὶ ἐν μέσῳ γινώσκεσθαι τὸν θεὸν καὶ πατέρα Cyr.Abac.2(3.549D); interprn. which make δύο ζ. represent angels and men, cherubim and seraphim, Jews and Babylonians, rejected ἐμοὶ... δοκεῖ μὴ ζῷα ἀλλὰ ζωὰς εἰρηκέναι τὸν προφήτην, τήν τε παροῦσαν καὶ τὴν μέλλουσαν, ὧν μέσος ὁ δίκαιος κριτὴς ἀναφαίνεται Thdt.Abac.3:2(2.1550); **4.** *animal part of man, body*, Chrys.hom.44.5 in Mt.(7.474D); ib.62.3(623D).

***ζωοπάροχος**, *life-giving*, in spiritual sense; of Christ, Sophr.H.or.2.18(M.87.3237B); of Passion, ib.5(3313C); of eucharist ζ. μυστήριον Jo.D.anacr.(M.96.855B); of brazen serpent, Germ.CP or.1(M.98.232A); of side of Christ, ζωηπ-, Rom.Mel.(AS 1 p.492); of Cross, ‡Chrys.ador.2(11.824B).

***ζωοπλάσσω**, *form as a living being*; pass., ‡Cyr.Trin.14(6^3.20C; M.77.1152A).

ζωοπλαστ-έω, **1.** *give life to*; **a.** of God in creation χωρὶς τοῦ θεοῦ φὴς ~εῖσθαι ἐν τῇ μήτρᾳ ἄνθρωπον; Adam.dial.4.15(p.172.15; M.11.1829C); Eus.l.C.11(p.229.1; M.20.1384C); id.e.th.3.3(p.155.14; M.24.997D); Gr.Nyss.Apoll.54(M.45.1256A); ref. humanity of Christ τὸ δὲ πνεῦμα τὸ ἅγιον τὸν ναὸν ἐζωοπλάστει Procl.CP or.3.3(M.65.708A); **b.** of natural birth ζ. τὸ τικτόμενον ἡ φύσις ἐν ἑαυτῇ Cyr.ador.7(1.235C); **2.** met., *fashion*, ref. imaginary descriptions of Greek god τί γὰρ χρὴν ἀνδρῶν καὶ γυναικῶν σχήματα ζ.; Eus.p.e.3.3(91B; M.21.168C).

ζωοπλάστης, ὁ, *creator*, Meth.res.2.20(p.375.10; M.18.285C); ‡Nil.narr.3(M.79.617A).

ζωοπλαστία, ἡ, *production of life*; of Inc., Thdr.Raith.praep.(p.192.13; M.91.1492D).

ζωοποι-έω, *give life to*; **A.** ref. natural life; **1.** of God giving life to dead εἰ...τὸ θνητὸν οὐ ζ. ... οὐκ ἔστι δυνατὸς ὁ θεός Iren.haer.5.3.2(M.7.1129B); ‡Ath.serm.fid.29(p.26; M.26.1284D); Const.App.5.7.20; Chrys.hom.8.5 in Rom.(9.503E); **2.** of Son; **a.** in gen., A.Thom.A 104(p.217.14); τὰ ὅλα ~ῶν Ath.gent.42(M.25.84B); id.inc.1(M.25.97A); Eun.ap.Gr.Nyss.Eun.2(2 p.342.17); Cyr.Zach.15(3.670D); **b.** giving life to dead, Bas.hom.4.5(2.29B; M.31.228B); Gr.Nyss.hom.11 in Cant.(M.44.1013A); **c.** raising his own body ὁ...πάντας τοὺς νεκροὺς ~ῶν, καὶ τὸν ἐκ Μαρίας ἄνθρωπον Χριστὸν Ἰησοῦν ἐζωοποίησεν, ὃν ἀνείληφεν ‡Ath.serm.fid.2(p.5; M.26.1265B); Cyr.Rom.8:11(p.215.3; M.74.820D); **d.** by virtue of hypostatic union, Gr.Nyss.or.catech.12(p.59.3; M.45.44D); ~ῶν μὲν ὡς θεός, τῷ παντουργῷ προστάγματι· ~ῶν δὲ αὖ πάλιν καὶ διὰ τῆς ἁφῆς τῆς ἁγίας σαρκός, μίαν τε καὶ συγγενῆ δι' ἀμφοῖν ἐπιδείκνυσι τὴν ἐνέργειαν Cyr.Jo.4.2(4.361D); Max.

opusc.(M.91.105B); ib.(109D); **e.** ref. Apollinarianism εἰ ἡ αὐτὴ φύσις Χριστοῦ, οἵα καὶ ἡ ἡμῶν, ὁ παλαιός ἐστιν ἄνθρωπος, ψυχὴ ζῶσα καὶ οὐ πνεῦμα ~οῦν, καὶ ὁ τοιοῦτος οὐδὲ ~ήσει Apoll.anac.23(p.245.1; M.28.1276D); ib.24(p.245.5; 1277A); εἰ μόνον ἄνθρωπος ἦν ὁ Χριστός, οὐκ ἂν ἐζωοποίει τοὺς νεκρούς, καὶ εἰ μόνον θεός, οὐκ ἂν ἰδίᾳ παρὰ τὸν πατέρα ἐζωοποίει τινὰς τῶν νεκρῶν ib.20(p.244.13; 1273D); **3.** of H. Ghost ζωὴν τὸ πνεῦμα δείκνυσι τὸ ζ. Didym.(‡Bas.)Eun.5(1.303D; M.29.728C).

B. ref. supernatural life; **1.** of God ἀποκτέννει ὁ θεὸς τῇ ἁμαρτίᾳ ἵνα μετὰ τοῦτο ζ. τὸν ἀποθάνοντα τῇ ἁμαρτίᾳ Or.comm.in Rom.6:23 (JTS 13 p.368); Meth.res.1.23(p.248.5; M.41.1093B); Hom.Clem.7.3; ζ. ... τοὺς κατὰ γνώμην αὐτοῦ βιοῦντας ib.17.4; Didym.(‡Bas.)Eun.5 (1.317C; M.29.760D); **2.** of Father, acting through Son αὐτὸς [sc. ὁ λόγος] ὢν τὸ θεοποιὸν καὶ φωτιστικὸν τοῦ πατρός, ἐν ᾧ τὰ πάντα θεοποιεῖται καὶ ζ. Ath.syn.51(p.274.28; M.26.784A); acting with H. Ghost, cf.Rom.8:11 οὐκ εἶπεν, ἀναστήσει, ἀλλά, ζ.· ὃ πλέον τῆς ἀναστάσεως ἦν, καὶ τοῖς δικαίοις μόνοις δεδωρημένον Chrys.hom.13.8 in Rom.(9.570D) = Jo.D.Rom.8:11(M.95.501C); **3.** of Son; **a.** in gen., cf.1Petr.2:3 τοὺς γευσαμένους τῆς χρηστότητος αὐτοῦ ἐζωοποίησεν Clem.str.5.11(p.375.2; M.9.109B); Or.fr.547 in Mt.27:12f.(M.17.308B); **b.** giving life to humanity through Inc. ὁ κύριος ἦλθε ~ῶν· ἵνα ὡς ἐν τῷ Ἀδὰμ πάντες ἀποθνήσκομεν, ὅτι ψυχικοί, ἐν τῷ Χριστῷ ζήσωμεν, ὅτι πνευματικοί Iren.haer.5.12.3(M.7.1154A); τὸ διὰ τοῦ λόγου λυτρωθὲν σῶμα καὶ ~ηθέν Ath.ep.Epict.9 (p.15.6; M.26.1065B); ἐδεῖτο τοῦ ~οῦντος ὁ ἀφαμαρτὼν τῆς ζωῆς [i.e. fallen man] Gr.Nyss.or.catech.15(p.63.12; M.45.48B); Cyr.Mich.72 (3.472C); Procl.CP or.7.3(M.65.760C) cit. s. ὕδωρ; through his death ἵνα ἡ πληγὴ αὐτοῦ ζ. ἡμᾶς Barn.7.2; Μωϋσῆς ποιεῖ τύπον τοῦ Ἰησοῦ, ὅτι δεῖ αὐτὸν παθεῖν καὶ αὐτὸς ~ήσει ib.12.5; Ath.Ar.1.42(M.26.100A); Chrys.comm.in Gal.2:19(10.692C); **c.** by forgiving sins, Or. Jo.28.6(5; p.396.35; M.14.693A); γένονας εἴσω δικτύων ἐκκλησιαστικῶν·...ἀγκιστρεύει γάρ σε Ἰησοῦς, οὐχ ἵνα θανατώσῃ, ἀλλ' ἵνα θανατώσας ζ. ... ἀπόθανε τοῖς ἁμαρτήμασιν, καὶ ζῆσον τῇ δικαιοσύνῃ Cyr.H.procatech.5; Gr.Naz.or.38.16(M.36.329B); **4.** of H. Ghost; **a.** in gen., cf.Jo.6:64, Bas.Spir.24(3.48C; M.32.173A); ~ούμεθα...διὰ πνεύματος id.Eun.3.4(1.276B; M.29.666A); Chrys.hom.25.2 in Jo.(8.145B); Eus.Al.serm.19(M.64.45); **b.** in conversion of sinners, Iren. haer.5.12.2(M.7.1153B); πνεῦμα τὴν χάριν [sc. φησί], τὴν διὰ τοῦ βαπτίσματος τοὺς ὑπὸ τῶν ἁμαρτιῶν νεκρωθέντας ~οῦσαν Chrys. hom.6.2 in 2Cor.(10.475E); **5.** ref. means by which this life is transmitted; **a.** preaching of word τῇ πίστει τῆς ἐπαγγελίας καὶ τῷ λόγῳ ~ούμενοι Barn.6.17; Herm.mand.4.3.7; μετὰ τὸ ἀποθανεῖν τῷ κόσμῳ καὶ τῇ ἁμαρτίᾳ, ~εῖται ὑπὸ τοῦ λόγου τοῦ θεοῦ Or.hom.16.1 in Jer.(p.132.18; M.13.440A); λόγια θεοῦ ζῶντος ζῶντα καὶ ~οῦντα Const.App.2.61.1; **b.** sacraments ἀνάγκην...εἶχον δι' ὕδατος ἀναβῆναι, ἵνα ~ηθῶσιν Herm.sim.9.16.2; ib.9.16.7; ἐζητεῖτο...πῶς τὸ...σῶμα τοῦ Χριστοῦ πᾶσαν ζ. τὴν τῶν ἀνθρώπων φύσιν, ἐν ὅσοις ἡ πίστις ἐστί Gr.Nyss.or.catech.37(p.147.3; M.45.96B); τῆς μυστικῆς εὐλογίας, καθ' ἣν...~ούμεθα Cyr.Lc.22:14(M.72.905C); **c.** virtuous living, ref. renunciation of riches, Clem.q.d.s.12(p.167.10; M.9.616B); endurance of persecution and martyrdom, Diogn.5.12; κολαζόμενοι χαίρουσιν ὡς ~ούμενοι ib.5.16; Clem.str.4.8(p.272.34; M.8.1280A); A.Andr. A 14(p.55.14); ref. martyrs converting lapsed while awaiting sentence διὰ τῶν ζώντων ἐζωοποιοῦντο τὰ νεκρά Ep.Lugd.ap.Eus.h.e.5. 1.45(M.20.425A); **6.** (Gnost.) ref. Christ sending Spirit to apostles ἐξῆπτε...τὸν σπινθῆρα καὶ ἐζωοποίει Clem.exc.Thdot.3(M.9.656A; ἐζωπύρει p.106.12); **7.** met., ref. wine at Cana as symbol of blood of Christ τὸ δὲ ὑδαρὲς τοῦ φρονήματος ἐζωοποίησεν, τοῦ νόμου τὴν ἐργάτιν (l. τὸν ἐργάτην) ἐξ Ἀδάμ, τὸν κόσμον ὅλον αἵματι πληρώσας ἀμπέλου Clem.paed.2.2(p.174.2; M.8.424B).

ζωοποίησις, ἡ, *quickening, making alive*; of resurrection typified by trees coming to life in spring, Cyr.H.catech.18.7; ref. work of Christ φωταγωγεῖ τοὺς ἀνθρώπους πρὸς...πᾶν εἶδος ἀρετῆς, δι' ὧν ἡ ζ. γίνεται Ammon.Jo.1:4(M.85.1393C); ἦλθεν ὁ λόγος...γενέσθαι ἄνθρωπος, εἰς ζ. μὲν τοῦ ἀνθρώπου ‡Ath.Apoll.2.10(M.26.1148C); of H. Ghost as source of spiritual life, Or.Jo.13.23(p.247.16; M.14.437B); Didym.(‡Bas.)Eun.5(1.307C; M.29.737A); of spiritual life in gen., Chrys.hom.39.3 in 1Cor.(10.367A); οἱ τὴν ἄνωθεν ἔχοντες ἐν ἑαυτοῖς ζ. Cyr.Is.1.5(2.146D); ref. baptism, id.inc.unigen. (5^1.705D); πρώτη ἀνάστασις ἡ ἐκ νεκρῶν ἔργων ζ. cat.Apoc.20:6 (p.568.1).

ζωοποιητικός, *life-giving*, of Logos ζ. σχέσις Or.fr.2 in Jo.(p.486. 21); δύναμις ζ. Eus.fr.Lc.21:28(M.24.600A); ὁ θεὸς ἔχει δύναμιν ζ. τῶν νεκρῶν ‡Just.qu.Gr.42(M.6.1489A).

ζωοποιΐα, ἡ, *giving of life* ἡ...ζ. καὶ ἡ νέκρωσις, ἑκατέρα λέγεται περὶ Χριστοῦ Leont.H.Nest.5.2(M.86.1725C).

ζωοποιός, *life-giving*; **1.** of God, Cyr.Am.2(3.298E); ἡ ζ. φύσις, τουτέστι ἡ θεία id.Arcad.(p.94.20; 5^2.90E); ref. gift of spiritual life to repentant sinners, Sophr.H.or.5(M.87.3313C); **2.** of Trin. οὐ λέγομεν τρεῖς ζ. τοὺς τὴν μίαν ἐνεργοῦντας ζωήν Gr.Nyss.tres dii(M.45. 128A); ἡ...ζ. τῶν ὅλων τριάς Basilisc.encycl.(p.51.26; M.86.2604A); cat.Lc.11:5(p.91.17); **3.** of Father ὁ ζ. τῶν νεκρῶν διὰ Ἰησοῦ Χριστοῦ Const.App.7.34.8; ref. generation of Son ζ. πηγῆς τῆς πατρικῆς ἀγαθότητος Bas.Eun.2.25(1.261E; M.29.629B); **4.** of Son; **a.** in gen. πηγή ζ. Clem.prot.10(p.78.22; M.8.228B); ζ. πάντων Ath.gent.47(M. 25.93C); ref. eternal generation, Bas.Eun.2.27(1.264B; M.29.636A); **b.** in giving natural life, Eus.e.th.1.4(p.66.33; M.24.837D); τῇ ἀθανάτῳ ζ. θεότητι ‡Ath.serm.fid.27(p.24; M.26.1281A); Cyr.ep.4(p.27. 19; 5^2.24A); **c.** by virtue of hypostatic union οὔτε γὰρ τὸ σῶμα καθ' ἑαυτὸ φύσις [sc. ἐπὶ τοῦ ἑνὸς Χριστοῦ], ἐπεὶ μηδὲ ζ. καθ' ἑαυτὸ μηδὲ διατέμνεσθαι δυνάμενον ἄνευ τοῦ ζ. [sc. λόγου] Apoll.ep.Dion.8(p.259. 15ff.; M.PL.8.934A); ref. his miracles of healing, increase, and resurrection ἵνα ἀποδείξῃ καὶ τὴν σάρκα ζ., ὡς αὐτοῦ κυρίως, καὶ οὐκ ἄλλου ὑπάρχουσαν, τῇ πρὸς αὐτὸν ἀκραιφνεῖ ἑνώσει Max.Pyrr.(M.91. 344C); id.opusc.(M.91.108B); **d.** in giving life to dead ἡ σὰρξ τοῦ πάντα ζωογονοῦντος, διὰ τοῦτο ζ. cat.Lc.7:11ff.(p.56.29); Cyr.Arcad. (p.95.38; 5^2.92E); τὴν ζ. αὐτοῦ φύσει καὶ θείαν ἐνέργειαν, ἀσωμάτως τε προάγειν καὶ διὰ σώματος Max.opusc.(M.91.125B); in raising his own body ἡ δύναμις τοῦ κυρίου...ζ. Leont.H.Nest.5.2(M.86.1725B); **e.** in giving supernatural life ζ. λίθος Or.fr.426 in Mt.21:42(p.178); ζ. τῶν ὅλων ἄρτου id.schol.in Lc.13:20(M.17.360A); ζ. αἷμα Gr.Nyss. hom.3 in Cant.(M.44.824D); ‡Meth.palm.7(M.18.397A); ζ. ἀπαρχῆς ‡Meth.Sym.et Ann.7(M.18.365A); ref. Christ as the Bread of life imparted to the gentiles παρατεθεῖσθαι τράπεζαν τὴν ζ. Cyr.Is.5.3 (2.793D); ref. Is.12:3 ὕδωρ...ἀποκαλεῖ τὸν ζ. τοῦ θεοῦ λόγον ib.2.1(2. 212E); ζ. διδάσκαλος Procl.CP or.10.2(M.65.780C); **f.** in eucharist ζ. σῶμα Cyr.Arcad.(p.95.10; 5^2.91E); ἵνα εἰς μέθεξιν ζ. ἔχωμεν αὐτά, καὶ οἷον σπέρμα ζ. ἐν ἡμῖν εὑρεθῇ τὸ σῶμα τῆς ζωῆς id.Lc.22:19(M.72. 912A); πῶς...ζ. ἡ σάρξ;...καθ' ἕνωσιν...τὴν πρὸς τὸν ζῶντα...λόγον id.inc.unigen.(5^1.708C); τῆς μυστικῆς εὐλογίας τὴν μέθεξιν, δι' ἧς τῷ ζῶντι καὶ ζ. προσοικειούμεθα λόγῳ id.Jo.11.5(4.953C); μετασχεῖν εὐλογίας τῆς ζ. id.ador.7(1.231D); ref. Is.3:2, id.Is.1.2(2.53B); Vict. Mc.14:22(p.438.8); **g.** of Passion, Max.myst.8(M.91.688C); Lit.Jac. (p.204.3); Cross, ‡Hipp.consumm.33(p.303.2; M.10.936D); Dor.doct. 22.5(M.88.1828D); Thphn.chron.p.18(M.108.104B); death, Lit.Jac. (p.200.27); sepulchre, Jo.Mosch.prat.48(M.87.2904A); **5.** of H. Ghost; **a.** in gen., M.Scill.(p.27.5); Ath.decr.32(p.28.26; M.25.476C); Gr. Naz.or.9.6(M.35.825C); Gr.Nyss.Eun.2(2 p.301.1; M.45.472B); τὸ πνεῦμα...τὸ ζ. Symb.Nic.–CP(p.80.12; H.2.288B); Chrys.hom.53.5 in Mt.(7.545D); Jo.V H.icon.16(M.96.1361C); **b.** in giving natural life, Gr.Nyss.virg.13(p.307.2; M.46.377A); δημιουργεῖ θεός,...ἐνεργείᾳ ζῶντος λόγου, καὶ πνεύματος μεταδόσει ζ. Didym.(‡Bas.)Eun.5(1. 304A; M.29.729A); prob. in this sense, Mod.dorm.12(M.86.3308B); **c.** in giving supernatural life: in baptism τὸ...πνεῦμα τὴν ζ. ἐνίησι δύναμιν, ἀπὸ τῆς κατὰ τὴν ἁμαρτίαν νεκρότητος εἰς τὴν ἐξ ἀρχῆς ζωὴν τὰς ψυχὰς ἡμῶν ἀνακαινίζον Bas.Spir.35(3.29C; M.32.129D); in eucharist ἡ ζ. δύναμις τοῦ πνεύματος Gr.Nyss.or.catech.36(M.45.93C; p.144.3 om. τοῦ πνεύματος); ref. NT as contrasted with Law τῆς δυνάμεως τῆς ζ., τουτέστι τοῦ ἁγίου πνεύματος Cosm.Ind.top.7(M.88. 361B); ref. Pentecost, Evagr.h.e.1.3(p.8.18; M.86.2428A); Jo.Eub. concept.BMV 22(M.96.1497C); **6.** of grace, Gr.Nyss.Maced.19(M.45. 1325A); Cyr.ador.4(1.139D); baptism, Cyr.H.catech.19.1; ref. 1Cor. 10:4 ζ. νάματα παρέχεται ὁ Χριστὸς διὰ τῶν μυστηρίων, οὗ τύπος ἦν ἡ πέτρα Cosm.Ind.top.5(M.88.200C); sacraments μυστήρια ζ. ib. (196A); **7.** of Christian doctrine and commandments, Eus.l.C.9 (p.221.6; M.20.1369B); †Bas.Is.166(1.497E; M.30.392C); ζ. μάθημα Cyr.Ps.32:19(M.69.881C); id.Is.5.2(2.776B); τὰς...ζ. ἐντολὰς τοῦ Χριστοῦ ἡ ἀγάπη φυλάττει Philox.ep.27(p.177); message of prophets ζ. κηρύγματα Cyr.Nah.4(3.480A); ref. NT, cf.2Cor.3:6, Cosm.Ind. top.7(M.88.361B); of martyrdom ὁ ζ. θάνατος εἰς Χριστόν Clem.str. 4.8(p.275.3, v.l. ζώπυρος M.8.1272A); of banner of cross ζ. σημεῖον Eus.v.C.2.16(p.47.31; M.20.993C); of a measure of emperor against heretics ζ. διδασκαλία ib.3.62(p.111.10; 1140A); ζ. γνῶσις Cyr.Juln. 5(6^2.159C); ref. fasting τὰ ζ. αὐτῆς [sc. νηστείας] χαρίσματα Sophr.H. or.5(M.87.3313A); ζ. πάσχα Chron.Pasch.p.9(M.92.85A); **8.** ref. natural life of soul ὥσπερ ἔκ τινος πηγῆς ζωῆς ζωὴ καὶ ζ. προελθοῦσα Anast.S.serm.imag.3(M.89.1164C); τῆς ζωτικῆς καὶ ζ. τῆς ψυχῆς ἡμῶν ἐνεργείας ib.(1168B); **9.** as subst.; **a.** *life-giver*; of Christ, prob. as giver of supernatural life, Eus.h.e.10.4.12(M.20.853A); **b.** *vivifying, quickening* τὸ πνεῦμα τὸ ἅγιον καὶ κατὰ τὸ ζ. Gr.Nyss.Maced.22(M. 45.1328D); *vital principle*, of H. Ghost in gift of supernatural life τὸ ἀίδιον καὶ ζ. Diad.perf.28(p.32.3); Gel.Cyz.h.e.2.24.13(v.l. τοῦ ζωτικοῦ

M.85.1301A); Anast.S.*serm.imag.*3(M.89.1165C); **10.** met., of infant Christ ζ. ἄνθραξ ‡Meth.*Sym.et Ann.*7(M.18.364A,B).

***ζωοποιοφόρος**, *life-giving* ὁ...χιτῶνας νεκροῦ ἐνδεδυμένος τὸ πρίν, ἴδε νῦν φορούμενον τὸν ζ. [sc. χιτῶνα which is Christ] †Ephr.*nativ.*130(p.90).

ζωόπυρος, v. ζώπυρος.

ζωοτοκέω, *bring into being*; of Creation, Meth.*res.*1.34(p.271.5; M.41.1097B).

ζωοτόκος, *life-producing*, ref. resurrection ζ. τύμβοι Nonn.*par.Jo.*5:28(M.43.789B); of Christ, Paul.Sil.*Soph.*330(M.86.2132A); as subst., of BMV, Ant.Ptol.*fr.*ap.Cyr.*Arcad.*(p.66.32; 5^{2}.49E); ἡ ζ. ἀνάστασις Sophr.H.*or.*4(M.87.3305D).

[*]**ζωοφαγεία**, ἡ, *eating of animal flesh*, Olymp.*fr.Jer.*5:27(M.93.637D).

***ζωοφθορά**, ἡ, *bestiality*, Gr.Nyss.*ep.can.*4(M.45.228C).

***ζωοφθορία**, ἡ, *abortion*, *Poen.App.*2.14.

***ζωοφθόρος**, *guilty of bestiality*, Bas.*epp.*188 *can.*7(3.272B; M.32.673C).

***ζωοφορία**, ἡ, s.v.l., *production of life* ζωοφορίας διδασκαλία ‡Ath.*sem.*3(M.28.148A) perh. error for ζωοφόρος.

ζωοφόρος, *producing life*; of zodiac, Bas.*hex.*6.5(1.54D; M.29.128C); Gr.Naz.*carm.*1.1.5.46(M.37.427A).

ζωόφυτον, τό, *zoophyte*, Nemes.*nat.hom.*1(M.40.509B).

ζωόφυτος, v. ζώφυτος.

ζω-όω, **1.** *give life to*; **a.** in creation and preservation; by power and wisdom of God, Eus.*d.e.*5.4(p.157.8; M.22.261C); by divine goodness, Dion.Ar.*d.n.*4.2(M.3.696C); *ib.*4.4(697C); by the divine life, *ib.*6.3(857B); **b.** ref. Apollinarianism ἐκ ταύτης τῆς ὕλης ὁ κύριος ἑαυτῷ διαπλασάμενος σῶμα, καὶ τοῦτο ζ. τῇ ἰδίᾳ οὐσίᾳ...ἐποίει ζῷον θεόν ‡Ath.*dial.Trin.*4.9(M.28.1264C); ἔφη...μὴ ~οῦσθαι...ὑπὸ ψυχῆς τὸ σῶμα τοῦ κυρίου Leont.H.*monoph.*(M.86.1865C); **c.** atonement κύριε Ἰησοῦ Χριστέ· ἀπέθανες...ἵνα ζ. *A.Thom.*A 19(p.129.15); **2.** *restore to life*; ref. Resurrection of Christ, Eus.*d.e.*4.13(p.173.10; M.22.288D); Cosm.Ind.*top.*5(M.88.241C).

***ζωπύρησις**, ἡ, *kindling into life*, met. οἷον ψυχούμενος τῇ ζ. τῆς ἐγρηγόρσεως Gr.Nyss.*res.*3(M.46.673A).

ζώπυρον, τό, *spark*, met. συνεξάπτει δὲ ἡ γραφὴ τὸ ζ. τῆς ψυχῆς Clem.*str.*1.1(p.8.11; M.8.697A); τὰ ζ. τῶν τῆς ἀληθοῦς γνώσεως...δογμάτων *ib.*7.18(p.78.21; M.9.556C).

ζώπυρος (**ζωό-**), *kindling*; **1.** in gen. νεκροῦται γὰρ ἐκείνων [sc. serpents] ὥρᾳ χειμῶνος ἡ ζ. δύναμις Gr.Nyss.*res.*3(M.46.672A); ἀνανεωτικὸν τῇ ζωοπύρῳ θερμότητι Dion.Ar.*c.h.*15.2(M.3.329B); **2.** met., of saints εὐσεβείας ζ. σπέρματα Eus.*l.C.*7(p.215.8; M.20.1356C); id.*p.e.*7.8(309A; M.21.524A); id.*d.e.*1.6(p.23.25; M.22.49B); **3.** *stinging* τοῦ ζ. σφηκίου Epiph.*haer.*44.7(p.198.16ff.; M.41.832C,D).

***ζωπυρ-όω**, **1.** *kindle*, Geo.Pis.*hex.*241(M.92.1452A); **2.** met., *bring into being* εἰ λέγειν χρή, καὶ τὰ μήπω πρὸς κτίσιν ἐλθόντα τῇ σῇ ~οῦσθαι προσθέσει *ib.*1704(1567A).

ζῶσις, ἡ, *girdle*, *Apoc.Paul.*35(p.59, v.l. ζώνησις); met., of virginity τὴν τῆς αἰωνίου ζωῆς ζ. ἐν αὐτῇ κατέχουσα *M.Ner.et Ach.*6(p.5.8).

ζῶσμα, τό, *belt*; hence *loins*, Thphn.*chron.*p.207(M.108.532A).

ζωστήρ, ὁ, *girdle, band*, of linen round head of dead Christ κεφαλῆς ζ. Nonn.*par.Jo.*20:7(M.43.909A).

ζωτικός, **1.** *of life, living, vital*; **a.** in gen., of God ζ. δύναμις Gr.Nyss.*or.catech.*36(p.140.4; M.45.92D); of Christ's exercise of vital powers of breathing, etc., as proof of reality of Inc., Max.*Pyrr.*(M.91.345B); Jo.D.*Jacob.*82(M.94.1481B); ref. Ps.1:3, of the righteous as ζ. ξύλον Clem.*str.*4.18(p.299.29; M.8.1325B); met. ζ. εὐωδία Eus.*d.e.*4.3(p.153.30; M.22.256D); *ib.*5.1(p.213.35; 356A); ζ. δικαίωμα Eulog.*fr.dogm.*(M.86.2964A); neut. as subst., *vital force* ἔχει γὰρ αὐτὴ [sc. soul] καὶ τὸ λογικὸν καὶ τὸ ζ. Thdt.*qu.20 in Gen.*(1.28); met. διαπνευσάσης δὲ τῆς ἐλπίδος...τὸ ζ. τῆς πίστεως ὑπεκλύεται Clem.*paed.*1.6(p.113.7; M.8.296B); **b.** name of gate in amphitheatre at Carthage through which combatants entered, opp. *porta Libitinensis* through which dead were carried out, *M.Perp.*10(p.79.11); *ib.*20(p.91.25); **c.** of rhetoric, *lively, vivid*, Isid.Pel.*epp.*5.121(M.78.1396B); of light, *bright*; met., ref. example to be given by priests (cf. Mt.5:14) τὰς ἀκτῖνας τῆς ζ. λαμπηδόνος *ib.*1.32(201C, v.l. ζωῆς λαμπηδόνος); **2.** *life-giving*, in gen. ἡ πνοὴ ζ. [ref. Adam's creation] Diod.*Gen.*2:7(M.33.1565B); of cause of life in human body ζ. αἴτιον Gr.Nyss.*anim.et res.*(M.46.16B); esp. ref. spiritual life, of God as ζ. πηγή Clem.*prot.*10(p.68.5; M.8.205A); of Christ, ref. Jo.4:13, id.*paed.*1.9(p.139.5; M.8.349B); of divine life, Dion.Ar.*d.n.*6.1(M.3.856B); of mystery of salvation, Epiph.*haer.*76.35(p.384.17; M.42.585D); of Resurrection, ‡Dion.Al.*fr.in Lc.*22:42(p.240.14; M.10.1592C); of living water (Jo.4:14), Or.*Jo.*13.3(p.228.23; M.14.404B); of bread of life as contrasted with manna, *ib.*6.45(26; p.155.1; 280A); of grace of H. Ghost, Eus.*d.e.*9.6(p.417.20; M.22.673A); baptism ζ. ἀπότεξις Dion.Ar.*e.h.*6.1.1(M.3.532A); eucharist ἄρτον τὸν ζ. Andr.Cr.*triod.*(M.97.1417C).

ζωύφιον, τό, *insect*; given by providence to other creatures for food, Isid.Pel.*epp.*4.43(M.78.1093D); Jo.Carp.*cap.*48(M.85.1847); prayed for by S. James of Nisibis to infest Persian army ὥστε καὶ διὰ τῶν μικρῶν ζ. τοῦ σφίσιν ἐπαρκοῦντος ἐπιγνῶναι τὴν δύναμιν Thdt.*h.e.*2.30.12(3.907); example of industry, Cyr.*hom.pasch.*29(5^{2}.336E); their capture by spiders like that of men by women, Ant.Mon.*hom.*18(M.89.1484D).

ζώφυτος, *fertilizing*; *generative*, Gr.Nyss.*ep.*12(p.40.23, v.l. ζωόφυτον M.46.1045A).

ζώωσις, ἡ, *giving of life*; **1.** of divine action, in gen. αἱ οὐσιώσεις, αἱ ζ. Dion.Ar.*d.n.*2.5(M.3.664A); ref. Creation ἡ τῶν ὅλων ζ. Eus.*d.e.*4.5(p.155.17; M.22.260B); ref. resurrection of dead ἡ ἐλπὶς τῆς ζ. ἐκείνης Sever.*1Tim.*6:13(p.341.15); Max.*Pyrr.*(M.91.344C); **2.** met., giving to the stars names of living beings, Tat.*orat.*9(p.9.24; M.6.825A).

H

ἡγεμονεύω, *rule* λόγον εἶναι τοῦ θεοῦ τὸν ἐπὶ πάντων ὄντα τε καὶ ἡ. Ath.*ep.Aeg.Lib.*15(M.25.573A); of senses ruled by mind, id.*gent.*31(M.25.64A); of bodily organs ruled by heart, Mac.Aeg.*hom.*15.20(M.34.589A).

ἡγεμον-έω, *rule*; of the head ruling body, Clem.*str.*6.18(p.516.22; M.9.397A); of divine providence, *ib.*7.2(p.8.1; 412C); ~οῦν ἔχων ἐν ἑαυτῷ τὸ πνεῦμα Cyr.*Ps.*50:14(M.69.1101A).

ἡγεμονία, ἡ, **1.** *authority, command*; in gen., of that of earthly rulers as given by God, *1Clem.*61.1; of evil rulers as caused by wickedness of their subjects, Thdt.*provid.*7(4.602); among angels, *ib.*(601); of Roman see ἔχει...τῶν κατὰ τὴν οἰκουμένην ἐκκλησιῶν τὴν ἡ. διὰ πολλά, καὶ πρὸ τῶν ἄλλων ἁπάντων, ὅτι αἱρετικῆς μεμένηκε δυσωδίας ἀμύητος id.*ep.*116(4.1197); of governance of reason in man's constitution, Clem.*str.*5.14(p.417.7; M.9.197A); **2.** *rule, office of a superior*; episcopal, *Const.App.*8.4.4; of superior of convent, Sergia *Olymp.*1(p.44.6); *ib.*4(p.46.8); hence of sphere of bishop's rule, *diocese*, Thdt.*h.e.*1.21.1(3.801); **3.** *pre-eminence* ἡ. παντὸς τοῦ χρόνου...νενομίσθαι [sc. the Passover] ‡Chrys.*pasch.*6.3(p.149.3; 8.268C); of spiritual pre-eminence of saints in heaven, Thdt.*2Tim.*4:22(3.697).

ἡγεμονικός, **I.** in gen.;

A. adj.; **1.** *of a leader, leading, governing*; **a.** ref. Son ἡγεμονικωτάτη...ἡ τοῦ υἱοῦ φύσις Clem.*str.*7.2(p.5.21; M.9.408B); id.*exc.Thdot.*10(p.109.25; M.9.660C); **b.** exeg. Ps.50:14: cf.Hipp.*trad.ap.*3.3; ὁ γοῦν Δαβίδ...αἰτεῖ τὸν πατέρα λέγων· 'πνεύματι ἡ. στήριξόν με'...τὸ ἡ. ὁ πατήρ Or.*hom.8.1 in Jer.*(p.56.6; M.13.336D); cf. *de eodem dicere videtur: quemque principalem spiritum propterea arbitror nominatum, ut ostenderetur esse quidem multos spiritus, sed in his principatum et dominationem hunc spiritum sanctum, qui et principalis appellatur, tenere*, id.*comm.in Rom.*7:1(M.14.1103C); τοὺς δὲ δι' εὐήθειαν ἐνδυαστῶς ἔχοντας, ἡ. πνεύματι κρατυνθῆναι Ath.*ep.Amun.*(M.26.1176A); οὐ τοίνυν ὁμόδουλον ἡμῖν λέγειν αὐτὸ θεμιτόν, τὸ ἡ. τῇ φύσει Bas.*Eun.*3.2(1.273E; M.29.660A); Didym.(‡Bas.)*Eun.*5(1.314C; M.29.753C); ἐστηρίχθημεν τῷ ἡ. πνεύματι, ὅπερ ἐστὶν ἡ διὰ τοῦ ἁγίου πνεύματος εὐανδρία Cyr.*Ps.*50:14(M.69.1101A); ‡Cyr.*Trin.*9(6^{3}.13C; M.77.1140B); **c.** astrol. ὁ δεῖνα οὖλος, φησί, τὴν τρίχα, καὶ χαροπός· κριοῦ γὰρ ἔχει τὴν ὥραν...ἀλλὰ καὶ μεγαλόφρων· ἐπειδὴ ἡ. [sc. ζῷον] ὁ κριός Bas.*hex.*6.6(1.55C; M.29.129C); **2.** *principal* τύπον ...τῶν ἡ. λογισμῶν τῆς ψυχῆς...λέγω δέ, τὸ θέλημα, ἡ συνείδησις, ὁ νοῦς, ἡ ἀγαπητικὴ δύναμις Mac.Aeg.*hom.*1.3(M.34.452C); τεσσάρων δὲ ὄντων τῶν τῆς θεότητος ἡ. ὀνομάτων ‡Chrys.*pasch.*6.4(p.167.16; 8.270D).

B. neut. as subst.; **1.** *governing, principal part* τῇ κεφαλῇ καὶ τῷ ἡ. τοῦ σώματος Clem.*paed.*2.8(p.203.6; M.8.485C); of man in rel. to creation, id.*str.*6.17(p.510.16; M.9.384B); of abstracts ἡ. τῆς γνώσεως *ib.*6.18(p.516.25; 397A); *ib.*7.7(p.28.7; 452B); in Stoic natural philosophy τὴν πυρώδη καὶ θερμὴν οὐσίαν τὸ ἡ. φάσκοντας εἶναι τοῦ κόσμου Eus.*p.e.*3.9(102C; M.21.185D); ref. angelic hierarchies, Dion.Ar.*c.h.*9.1(M.3.257B); **2.** *sovereignty*, Or.*Cant.*1(p.108.30; M.17.253C); of Adam τοῦ ἡ. αὐτοῦ ἐκπεσόντος Proc.G.*Gen.*3:15

(M.87.204D); τῷ Ἀδὰμ τὸ ἡ. σώζων ἐπὶ τοῖς ἀλόγοις ἔδωκε τὴν τῶν ὀνομάτων θέσιν id.*Num.*11:4(M.87.824A).

II. *principal part* of the soul, *intellect*; Stoic term developed by Christians (usu. as subst. neut. with ψυχῆς understood and rarely as adj.);

A. definitions and relation to other parts of soul, cf. *principalitas sensuum...quod hegemonicum appellatur*, Tert. *de resurrectione carnis* 15(M.*PL*.2.814A); *a duobus exorsus titulis, principali, quod aiunt* ἡ., *et a rationali, quod aiunt* λογικόν, id.*de anima* 14(M.*PL*.2.668B); ὁ λογισμὸς καὶ τὸ ἡ. ἄπταιστον μένον καὶ καθηγούμενον τῆς ψυχῆς κυβερνήτης αὐτῆς εἴρηται Clem.*str*.2.11(p.141.5; M.8.988B); ἔστι...δεκάς τις περὶ τὸν ἄνθρωπον αὐτόν, τά τε αἰσθητήρια πέντε καὶ τὸ φωνητικὸν καὶ τὸ σπερματικὸν καὶ τοῦτο δὴ ὄγδοον τὸ κατὰ τὴν πλάσιν πνευματικόν, ἔνατον δὲ τὸ ἡ. τῆς ψυχῆς καὶ δέκατον τὸ διὰ τῆς πίστεως προσγινόμενον ἁγίου πνεύματος...ἰδίωμα *ib*.6.16(p.500.4; M.9.360A); ἐπεισκρίνεται δὲ ἡ ψυχὴ καὶ προσεισκρίνεται τὸ ἡ., ᾧ διαλογιζόμεθα, οὐ κατὰ τὴν τοῦ σπέρματος καταβολὴν γεννώμενον *ib*.(p.500.10; 360B); ἐνταῦθα [sc. in soul] γὰρ τὸ ἡ. ἱδρῦσθαι λέγουσι, τὴν διὰ τῶν αἰσθητηρίων ἐπείσοδον τῆς ψυχῆς ἐπὶ τοῦ πρωτοπλάστου [εἴσοδον] ἑρμηνεύοντες, διὸ καὶ 'κατ' εἰκόνα καὶ ὁμοίωσιν τὸν ἄνθρωπον' γεγονέναι *ib*.5.14(p.388.12; M.9.140A); τὴν ἀσώματον φύσιν καὶ νοητὴν τοῦ ἡ. ἡμῶν Or.*comm.in Eph*.1:15ff.(p.399.30); τὸ διανοητικόν, ὅ τινες ἡ. καλοῦσιν id.*fr.18 in Jo*.(p.497.21); dist. from λόγος and πράξεις, id.*Cels*.4.64(p.334.36; M.11.1132B); παρασύρει...τὴν διάνοιαν, καὶ καροῖ τὸ φρόνημα, καὶ αὐτὸ τὸ ἡ. ἀκρωτηριάζει, καὶ ἐξίστησι τὸν νοῦν †Bas.*contub*.2(M.30.817A); identified with νοῦς, †Bas.*Is*.26(1.399C; M.30.168C); exeg. τὸ ἡ., ὡς ἐπὶ νύμφης μαστοί Or.*schol.in Cant*.4:5f.(M.17.272C); *ib*.6:10f.(280B); term applied to animals as well as to men, id.*Cels*.4.85(p.356.6ff.; M.11.1160B).

B. physical seat; **1.** usu. assumed to be in heart, with which it is sometimes identified, Or.*Jo*.2.35(29; p.94.18; M.14.177C); *ib*.6.38(22; p.146.24; 264D); καρδία ἐστὶν ἔχουσα καθ' ἡμᾶς τὸ ἡ. id.*hom.5.15 in Jer*.(p.44.31; M.13.320A); id.*or*.29(p.382.16; M.11.532B); exeg. 2Cor.3:3 ἀπόστολος, καρδίας ὀνομάζων τὰς πλάκας, τουτέστι, τὸ ἡ. τῆς ψυχῆς Gr.Nyss.*v.Mos*.(M.44.397A); Leont.et Jo.*sacr*.2 tit.(M.86.2024B); **2.** other opinions ἀγνοοῦμεν...ἐν τίνι τοῦ σώματος μορίῳ τὸ ἡ. ἐστι τῆς ψυχῆς Clem.*str*.8.4(p.88.30; M.9.577D); acc. Empedocles τὸ δὲ ἡ. οὔτε ἐν κεφαλῇ οὔτε ἐν θώρακι, ἀλλ' ἐν αἵματι Eus.*p.e*.1.8(24D; M.21.60D).

C. as seat of free choice τὴν προαιρετικὴν δὲ τὸ ἡ. ἔχει δύναμιν, περὶ ἣν ἡ ζήτησις καὶ ἡ μάθησις καὶ ἡ γνῶσις. ἀλλὰ γὰρ ἡ πάντων ἀναφορὰ εἰς ἓν συντέτακται τὸ ἡ. καὶ δι' ἐκεῖνο ζῇ τε ὁ ἄνθρωπος καί πως ζῇ Clem.*str*.6.16(p.500.21f.; M.9.360C); τὸ γὰρ ἑκάστου ἡ. αἴτιον τῆς ὑποστάσης ἐν αὐτῷ κακίας ἐστίν, ἥτις ἐστὶ τὸ κακόν Or.*Cels*.4.66(p.336.29; M.11.1133D).

D. present in demons ἐν καταστάσει δαιμόνων αὐτῶν ὑποστῆναι τὸ ἡ. Or.*Cels*.4.65(p.336.16; M.11.1133C); and accessible to demons and evil οἱ ἐν τῇ εἰδωλολατρείᾳ κατορωρυγμένον ἔχοντες τὸ ἡ. Clem.*str*.6.6(p.453.27; M.9.265A); οὐκ ἔστιν ὁ θεὸς ὁ ἀποκρύπτων αὐτοῦ τὴν δόξαν ἀφ' ἡμῶν, ἀλλ' ἡμεῖς τὸ κάλυμμα ἀπὸ τῆς κακίας ἐπιτιθέντες τῷ ἡ. Or.*hom.5.9 in Jer*.(p.39.11; M.13.308C); μὴ ἐπιβῇ τι τῶν δαιμονίων τῷ ἡ. ἡμῶν id.*Cels*.4.95(p.368.17; 1173C); *ib*.8.63(p.279.10; 1612B); τὸν ἐνιέμενον νοητὸν ἰὸν ἀπὸ τῶν ἀντικειμένων δυνάμεων τῷ ἡ. τῶν ἀμελούντων τοῦ εὔχεσθαι id.*or*.12.1(p.324.18; M.11.452C); *ib*.28.5(p.378.9; 525B); τοῦ δαιμονίου ἡμᾶς νικήσαντος καὶ τὸ ἡ. ἡμῶν θολώσαντος id.*Jo*.20.36(29; p.376.33; M.14.660A); τῆς ἐν τῷ ἡ. ἑαυτοῦ στάσεως τῶν παθῶν *ib*.20.37(29; p.378.29; 661C); Meth.*symp*.5.2(p.55.10; M.18.100C); τὸ ἡ. συγκεχυμένον...ἀπὸ τῶν τῆς ἁμαρτίας σπίλων †Bas.*Is*.proem.3(1.379D; M.30.121C); Gr.Naz.*or*.27.3(p.5.3; M.36.16A); μᾶλλον γὰρ τῷ βάρει τῆς ἀλόγου φύσεως συγκατασπᾶται τὸ ἡ. τῆς ψυχῆς, ἤπερ τῷ ὕψει τῆς διανοίας τὸ βαρύ τε καὶ χοϊκὸν ἀνυψοῦται Gr.Nyss.*hom.opif*.18.6(M.44.193C); ζητητέον δὲ πῶς ἐν ταῖς καθ' ὕπνον φαντασίαις τυποῦσιν ἡμῶν τὸ ἡ. καὶ σχηματίζουσιν οἱ δαίμονες †Nil.*mal.cog*.4(M.79.1204C); Max.*ambig*.(M.91.1112B).

E. consequent necessity of protection and purification of ἡ.; **1.** through divine action, Ath.*exp.Ps*.118:51(M.27.489A); τὸ κουκούλιον σύμβολόν ἐστι τῆς χάριτος τοῦ...θεοῦ, σκεπαζούσης ἡμῶν τὸ ἡ. Dor.*doct*.1.13(M.88.1636A); **2.** and human effort ἡ γνῶσις, ⟨ἡ⟩ τοῦ ἡ. τῆς ψυχῆς κάθαρσίς ἐστι Clem.*str*.4.6(p.265.28; M.8.1249C); τὴν γυναῖκα χρὴ ἔχειν μάλιστα εὐχομένην...πᾶσαν ἀκόλαστον καὶ γυναικείαν ὑπόμνησιν ἐξορίσασαν ἀπὸ τοῦ ἡ. Or.*or*.9(p.318.11; M.11.444A); ἥκειν ἐπὶ τὸ εὔξασθαι...καὶ πρὸ τοῦ στῆναι διεγείραντα χαμόθεν τὸ ἡ. *ib*.31(p.396.5; 549C); id.*Jo*.13.44(p.270.35; M.14.477C); στῆναι μᾶλλόν με πρὸς τὸν ἀγῶνα παρεκάλει ὁ λόγος καὶ τηρῆσαι τὸ ἡ., μήποτε μοχθηροὶ λογισμοὶ ἐξισχύσωσι τὸν χειμῶνα *ib*.6.2(1; p.108.2; 200C); Gr.Nyss.*hom.3 in Cant*.(M.44.809B); ἡ πίστις...ἀντὶ περικεφαλαίας σωτηρίου. ἂν σβέσωμεν αὐτοῦ τὰ βέλη, ταχέως καὶ τοὺς σώζοντας λογισμοὺς δεξόμεθα τοὺς τὸ ἡ. ἡμῶν οὐκ ἐῶντάς τι παθεῖν. ἐὰν γὰρ οὗτοι σβεννύωνται οἱ λογισμοὶ οἱ ἐναντίοι, ταχέως οἱ μὴ τοιοῦτοι, ἀλλὰ σώζοντες ἡμᾶς...ἐν ἡμῖν τεχθήσονται, καὶ καθάπερ περικεφαλαία τῇ κεφαλῇ, τῷ ἡ. ἡμῶν ἐγκείσονται Chrys.*hom.24.2 in Eph*.(11.182F); Jo.Carp.*cap*.82(M.85.1853); ἀπάθεια, ἡ καὶ αὐτῆς τῆς ψιλῆς φαντασίας παντελὴς κάθαρσις, ἐν τοῖς διὰ γνώσεως καὶ θεωρίας καθαρὸν καὶ διειδὲς ἔσοπτρον τοῦ θεοῦ ποιησαμένοις τὸ ἡ. συνισταμένη Max.*cap*.3.51(M.90.1281C) = id.*qu.Thal*.55(M.90.544D); ἡ. educated by contemplation of icons, Steph.Diac.*v.Steph*.(M.100.1157B).

F. seat of contemplative and mystical life; **1.** created *capax dei* and enlightened by God, Or.*fr.27 in Lam*.(p.248.9; M.13.624A); id.*Cels*.3.61(p.255.21; M.11.1000D); χάριτι θεοῦ, φωτίζοντος τὸ ἡ. *ib*.4.66(p.336.33; 1133D); τοῖς ἐλλαμπομένοις τὸ ἡ. ὑπ' αὐτοῦ τοῦ λόγου καὶ θεοῦ *ib*.6.17(p.88.19; 1317A); ἐὰν...διδῶμεν τόπον τῷ θεῷ, χαίρων ὁ θεὸς σπείρει τὰ σπέρματα αὐτοῦ ἐπὶ τὸ ἡ. ἡμῶν id.*hom.1.14 in Jer*.(p.13.18; M.13.273A); Σίμωνι ἐχαρίσατο ὁ Ἰησοῦς τὸ ἐμβλέψαι αὐτῷ, ὅπερ ἐστὶ διὰ τοῦ ἐμβλέψαι ἐπισκοπῆσαι καὶ φωτίσαι αὐτοῦ τὸ ἡ. id.*Jo*.2.36(29; p.95.30; M.14.181A); αὐτὸν τὸν θεὸν ἐντυπώσας [sc. Christ] ἐν τῷ ἡ. λογισμῷ Gr.Nyss.*or.dom*.3(p.48.11; M.44.1149C); also in angels διὰ καθαρότητα τοῦ ἡ., τὸν πρέποντα αἶνον ἀποδιδόναι τῷ κτίσαντι Bas.*hex*.3.9(1.31C; M.29.73D); **2.** apprehending truths of revelation καθαροὺς...τοὺς εἰς ἐπίγνωσιν τοῦ θεοῦ ἀφικνουμένους εἶναι βούλεται, ἵνα μηδὲν ἔχῃ νόθον ἐπιπροσθοῦν τῇ δυνάμει ἑαυτοῦ τὸ ἡ. Clem.*str*.4.6(p.266.5; M.8.1252A); πεπλήρωται ἡμῶν τὸ ἡ. ἁγίων μαθημάτων ἢ τῆς σωτηρίου πίστεως Or.*comm.in Eph*.4:27(p.554); τὸ ἡ. αὐτοῦ καθοραθέν, τῇ τῆς θεολογίας σφραγῖδι τετύπωται id.*schol.in Cant*.4:3(M.17.272D); id.*fr.138.1 in Mt*.(p.69; M.17.292B); id.*Jo*.13.53(52; p.282.1,4; M.14.497A); ἡμᾶς δὲ εὔχεσθαι χρὴ λαβεῖν τὸ τῆς σοφίας, καὶ τὸ τῆς γνώσεως, καὶ τὸ τῆς διδασκαλίας χάρισμα, ὥστε πάντα ὁμοῦ συνδραμόντα τῷ ἡ. ἡμῶν ἐντυπῶσαι τὴν πάσης τῆς προφητευομένης ἀληθείας μόρφωσιν †Bas.*Is*.2(1.379A; M.30.121A); **3.** and visions, prophetic revelations and indwelling of Christ τί ἄτοπον τὸ τυποῦν τὸ ἡ. ἐν ὀνείρῳ δύνασθαι αὐτὸ τυποῦν καὶ ὕπαρ πρὸς τὸ χρήσιμον τῷ ἐν ᾧ τυποῦται ἢ τοῖς παρ' αὐτοῦ ἀκουσομένοις; καὶ ὥσπερ φαντασίαν λαμβάνομεν ὄναρ ἀκούειν καὶ πλήσσεσθαι τὴν αἰσθητὴν ἀκοὴν καὶ ὁρᾶν δι' ὀφθαλμῶν, οὔτε τῶν τοῦ σώματος ὀφθαλμῶν οὔτε τῆς ἀκοῆς πλησσομένης ἀλλὰ τοῦ ἡ. ταῦτα πάσχοντος, οὕτως οὐδὲν ἄτοπον τοιαῦτα γεγονέναι ἐπὶ τῶν προφητῶν Or.*Cels*.1.48(p.97.28,32; M.11.748C); id.*schol.in Cant*.4:3(M.17.272A); τὴν Χριστοῦ μορφὴν ὁρᾶν ἐν τῷ ἡ. Mac.Aeg.*hom*.25.3(M.34.668D); †Bas.*Is*.3(1.380B; M.30.124B); τὸ ἡ. τοῦ προφήτου ἀπὸ τῆς ἐγγινομένης αὐτῷ παρὰ θεοῦ δυνάμεως ἐτυποῦτο †Bas.*hom.in Ps*.28(1.359B; M.30.76B); εἴτε φαντασία τις ἦν ἡμερινή...εἴτε τοῦ ἡ. τύπωσις συγγινομένη τοῖς μέλλουσιν ὡς παροῦσιν Gr.Naz.*or*.2.19(M.36.52B); commented upon τὴν δὲ τοῦ ἡ. τύπωσιν οἶμαι κατ' ἔμφασιν αὐτὸν λέγειν τοὺς μονοτρόπως, ὡς ἐν εἰκόνι, κατὰ τὴν ἁπλῆν καὶ ἀδιάστατον τοῦ νοεροῦ προσβολὴν τοῖς ἁγίοις προσφαινομένους τῶν μελλόντων τύπους Max.*ambig*.(M.91.1236C); Epiph.*haer*.48.5(p.227.7; M.41.864A); ἔοικε τὸ ἡ. τῶν ἁγίων πυξίῳ τινί, ἢ δέλτῳ, ἐν ᾧ καταγράφει ὁ θεὸς ἅπερ λεχθῆναι δέον τῷ λαῷ αὐτοῦ Nil.*epp*.1.108(M.79.129A); οὐ γὰρ δι' ἀκοῆς ἐδέξατο, τῷ δὲ νῷ τυπωθεῖσαν ἐξαγγέλλει διάνοιαν...ταῦτα δὲ θεὸς ἐντυποῖ τοῦ ἡ. τῶν ἀξίων ἀπτόμενος Proc.G.*Is*.1:1(M.87.1824C); *ib*.6:6–13(1944D); Andr.Caes.*Apoc*.1(M.106.220D); **4.** as organ of prayer and worship βωμοὶ μέν εἰσιν ἡμῖν τὸ ἑκάστου τῶν δικαίων ἡ., ἀφ' οὗ ἀναπέμπεται ἀληθῶς καὶ νοητῶς εὐώδη θυμιάματα, προσευχαὶ ἀπὸ συνειδήσεως καθαρᾶς Or.*Cels*.8.17(p.234.18; M.11.1541A); ἐν γὰρ τῷ κρυπτῷ ἡμῶν κατ' αὐτὸ τὸ ἡ. εὐχαί εἰσιν *ib*.8.74(p.291.20; 1629A); Gr.Nyss.*hom.4 in Cant*.(M.44.828B); **5.** in relation to conversion πολλοὶ ὡσπερεὶ ἄκοντες προσεληλύθασι Χριστιανισμῷ, πνεύματός τινος τρέψαντος αὐτῶν τὸ ἡ. αἰφνίδιον ἀπὸ τοῦ μισεῖν τὸν λόγον ἐπὶ τὸ ὑπεραποθανεῖν αὐτοῦ Or.*Cels*.1.46(p.96.10; M.11.745A); martyrdom παρὰ τὸν καιρὸν τῶν θλιβόντων καὶ ὡσπερεὶ πιέζειν τὰς ψυχὰς ἡμῶν ἐθελόντων ἀποστρέψαντες τὸ ἡ. ἡμῶν ἀπὸ τῶν ἐπιπόνων σκοποῖμεν οὐ τὰ ἐνεστηκότα ἐπίπονα ἀλλὰ τὰ διὰ τὴν ἐν τούτοις ὑπομονὴν τοῖς 'νομίμως' ἐν Χριστῷ ἀθλήσασι χάριτι θεοῦ ἀποκείμενα id.*mart*.2(p.4.10; M.11.565B); *ib*.33(p.28.20; 604C); Judgement οὐ μὴν χρόνους γε προσήκει νομίζειν καταναλωθήσεσθαι εἰς τὸ ἕκαστον ἰδεῖν ἑαυτὸν μετὰ τῶν ἑαυτοῦ πράξεων, καὶ τὸν κρίτην καὶ τὰ ἀκόλουθα τῷ θείῳ δικαστηρίῳ ἀφάτῳ δυνάμει ἐν ῥοπῇ καιροῦ φαντασιουμένου τοῦ νοῦ, καὶ πάντα ἀναζωγραφοῦντος ἑαυτῷ, καὶ οἱονεὶ ἐν κατόπτρῳ τῷ ἡ. ἐνορῶντος τοὺς τύπους τῶν πεπραγμένων †Bas.*Is*.120(1.462D; M.30.312D).

G. exeg. Ps.74:5 δηλοῖ δὲ καὶ τὴν ὑπεροψίαν τοῦ ἡ. τὸ κέρας, ὡς ἐν τῷ 'μὴ ἐπαίρετε εἰς ὕψος τὸ κέρας ὑμῶν' Or.*fr.45 in Lam*.(p.255.16; M.13.632D); Lc.8:16 σκεύη μὲν οἰκίας αἱ τῆς ψυχῆς δυνάμεις...λυχνία δὲ τὸ ἡ. id.*fr.11 in Lc.*(p.236); Eph.3:16f. ὁ Χριστὸς...κατοικεῖ δὲ διὰ τῆς πίστεως εἰς τὸν ἔσω ἄνθρωπον, τουτέστι τῷ ἡ. id.*comm.in Eph.* 3:16f.(p.411); κατὰ τὰς καρδίας ὑμῶν, τουτέστιν τὰ ἡ. *ib.*3:17ff.(p.411); Pr.2:14 κάτω νεύων ἀεὶ καὶ ἐσκοτισμένον ἔχων τὸ ἡ. †Dion.Al.*fr.Eccl.* (p.219.13; M.10.1584B); Ps.37:5 κεφαλὴν δὲ λέγει τὸ ἡ. Cyr. ad loc. (M.69.957C).

H. Christol., in Apollinarian controversy σὰρξ καὶ τὸ σαρκὸς ἡ. ἓν πρόσωπον Apoll.*fr.*153(p.248.16)ap.Leont.B.*Apoll.*(M.86.1961B); id. *fr.*107(p.232.13)ap.Justn.*monoph.*(p.17.2; M.86.1124A); ‡Ath.*dial. Trin.*4.5(M.28.1257A) cit. s. ἀποθεόω; ἡ. ἐχωρήθη ὑπὸ ἀνθρώπου σώματος ‡Chrys.*pasch.*6.4(p.171.19; 8.271B).

I. in God ὁ τῶν Στωϊκῶν θεός, ἅτε σῶμα τυγχάνων, ὁτὲ μὲν ἡ. ἔχει τὴν ὅλην οὐσίαν Or.*Cels.*4.14(p.284.24; M.11.1045A); ref. anthropomorphites ἐκεῖνοι μὲν οὐκ αἰδοῦνται λέγειν ὅτι καὶ φθαρτός ἐστιν σῶμα ὢν [sc. θεός], σῶμα δὲ πνευματικὸν καὶ αἰθερῶδες, μάλιστα κατὰ τὸ ἡ. αὐτοῦ id.*Jo.*13.21(p.245.11; M.14.433B).

ἡγεμόνιος, *ruling, commanding*, Clem.*paed.*1.7(p.124.16; M.8. 320B).

***ἡγεμόνισσα**, ἡ, *ruler* ἡ τοῦ θεοῦ σοφία...ἡ. ‡Chrys.*hom.*7(13. 218B).

ἡγεμών, ὁ, **1.** *ruler*; of God and his Word, Clem.*paed.*1.8(p.128. 19; M.8.329A); id.*str.*7.3(p.12.17; M.9.421A); *ib.*7.7(p.27.10; 449B); ref. divine providence θεὸς ἡ. τοῦ παραδόξου Synes.*ep.*137(M.66. 1525C); of angels as sharing in God's providential action, Dion.Ar. *c.h.*13.4(M.3.308A); of apostles, ref. Ps.44:14, Thdt.*Ps.*54:14(1.964); of a ruler of a synagogue, Nonn.*par.Jo.*7:48(M.43.813A); **2.** *guide*, of angels πρὸς τὴν ἱερὰν ταύτην τελείωσιν ἡγεμόνας τὰς περὶ θεὸν πρωτίστας οὐσίας Dion.Ar.*e.h.*5.1.2(M.3.501A); of Joseph and Daniel as interpreters of visions, id.*c.h.*9.4(M.3.261B); **3.** *guide* in the ways of God, i.e. *godfather*, Dion.Ar.*e.h.*2.3.4(M.3.401A); *ib.*2.2.7 (396D).

ἡγ-έομαι, **1.** *precede*; of prayer, preceding and anticipating experience of future blessings, Clem.*str.*7.12(p.56.19; M.9.509A); Trin. ὡς ἂν πρώτης καὶ ~ουμένης οὐσίας ἐπιχορηγουμένου τοῦ υἱοῦ Eus.*d.e.* 5.1(p.214.16; M.22.356B); ἀγγέλων χορούς, τοὺς μὲν ~ουμένους τοῦ δεσπότου Χριστοῦ Thdt.*Ps.*23:6(1.753); neut. ptcpl. as subst., in logic, *premiss*, Or.*Jo.*20.17(15; p.34.28; M.14.609C); met., *excel*, Areth.*Apoc.*67(M.106.768A); **2.** *lead, introduce* τὸν κύριον διά τε τῶν προφητῶν διά τε τοῦ εὐαγγελίου καὶ διὰ τῶν...ἀποστόλων...εἰς τέλος ~ούμενον τῆς γνώσεως Clem.*str.*7.16(p.67.17; M.9.532B); met., *bring to notice*, CSyr.*ep.*(p.92.8; H.2.1364E); *Ep.*ap.CSyr.(p.94.36; H.2. 1369A); **3.** *come from* τῶν εἴκοσι τεσσάρων στοιχείων βούλεται [sc. Marcus] τὰ πάντα ἡγεῖσθαι Jo.D.*haer.*34(M.94.700A); **4.** *rule* ἡ. διδασκαλείου Eus.*h.e.*5.10.4(M.20.456B); τῆς Ῥωμαίων ἐκκλησίας ἐπίσκοπος Σωτὴρ...ἡγησάμενος *ib.*5 proem.1(405D); *ib.*1(48B); ἡγήσασθαι...τῆς μονῆς ‡Ath.*doct.Ant.*18(M.28.581A); v. ἡγούμενος; met., of reason ruling desire, Thdt.*qu.19 in Dt.*(1.275).

ἡγεσία, ἡ, *command, sovereignty*, Gr.Naz.*carm.*1.1.8.91(M.37. 453A).

ἡγητηρία, ἡ, *rule*; of abbot, Ant.Mon.*ep.Eust.*(M.89.1425D).

ἡγήτωρ, ὁ, *governor*, of God τὸν μόνον...ἡ. κόσμου *Orac.Sib.fr.*1. 15; ref. religious superiors (bishops, heads of monasteries of men or women), CNic.(787)*can.*19.

***ἡγουμενεία (ἡγουμενία)**, ἡ, office of a monastic superior, *abbacy, priorship*, Nil.*epp.*4.1(M.79.544C); Eustrat.*v.Eutych.*18(M. 86.2296A); Jo.Mosch.*prat.*95(M.87.2953B); Jo.Clim.*scal.*22(M.88. 952B); CTrull.*can.*46.

***ἡγουμενεῖον**, τό, *superior's cell* in a monastery, Jo.Clim.*scal.* 4(M.88.697D).

ἡγουμένη, ἡ, *superior* of a monastery of women, *abbess, prioress*, *A.Petr.et Paul.*16(p.186.10); Jo.Mosch.*prat.*128(M.87.2992B); Max. *ep.*11(M.91.453A); in double monasteries, her presence necessary for interviews with monks, CNic.(787)*can.*20.

ἡγουμενικός, *abbatial*, Thdr.Stud.*epp.*1.11(M.99.945A).

ἡγούμενος, ὁ, **1.** *ruler*; **a.** in gen.; of queen bee, regarded as male, Philost.*h.e.*10.9(M.65.589B); **b.** of clergy, *1Clem.*1.3 τρία καθ' ἑκάστην ἐκκλησίαν τάγματα, ἐν...τὸ τῶν ἡ. Eus.*d.e.*7.1(p.311.17; M. 22.509B); **c.** of bishops, cf.Lc.22:26 ὁ...ἡ. (οὕτω δὲ οἶμαι ὀνομάζειν τὸν καλούμενον ἐν ταῖς ἐκκλησίαις ἐπίσκοπον) Or.*comm.in Mt.*16.8 (p.493.19; M.13.1393A); *Const.App.*2.25.7; *ib.*2.26.4; hence **2.** *bishop*, Eus.*d.e.*2.3(p.77.33; M.22.140C); *Const.App.*3.5.3; Cyr.*Lc.*5:2(M.72. 553A); ὁ...τῆς Ἀντιοχέων ἐκκλησίας ἡ. Soz.*h.e.*7.8.4(M.67.1433B); Thdt.*h.e.*1.28.4(3.816); **3.** *monastic superior* μηδεὶς πορεύσηται ἔμπροσθεν τοῦ ἡ. Pach.*reg.*B(p.20.25; M.40.952C); *ib.*(p.15.23; 949B); Nil.*epp.*2.33(M.79.213A); *ib.*2.64(229A); *V.Alex.Acoem.*31(p.682.10); ὁ ἡ. τῆς μονῆς Jo.Mosch.*prat.*21(M.87.2868B); Jo.Clim.*scal.*4(M.88. 721A); a monk of one monastery cannot become superior of another, *Cod.Afr.*80.

***ἤδικτον**, τό, (Lat. *edictum*) *edict*, Jo.Mal.*chron.*9 p.216(M.97. 335B); Justn.*conf.*(p.72.10; M.86.993C); Const.Pogon.*edict.*tit.(H.3. 1445C); *Chron.Pasch.*p.378(M.92.969A); in form ἴδικτον, Thdr.Lect. *h.e.*1.34(M.86.181B); Cyr.S.*v.Sab.*85(p.192.1); Evagr.*h.e.*4.39(p.190. 16; M.86.2781B); Anast.S.*serm.imag.*3(M.89.1156A).

ἡδονή, ἡ, *pleasure*; **1.** gen. description οὐκ ἀναγκαῖον τὸ τῆς ἡ. πάθος, ἐπακολούθημα...χρείαις τισὶ φυσικαῖς, πείνῃ, ῥίγει, γάμῳ; Clem. *str.*2.20(p.177.15; M.8.1064A); ἐπιτυγχάνουσα...ἡ ἐπιθυμία, ἡδονὴν ἐμποιεῖ Nemes.*nat.hom.*17(M.40.676B); cf.Melet.*nat.hom.*synops.(M. 64.1112C); ἔστι ἡ λύπη διάθεσις ψυχῆς ἡδονῶν ἐστερημένη *ib.*(1136B); ἡ. ἐστι κίνησις ψυχῆς ὀξεία ἐκ μνήμης γινομένη *Doct.Patr.*33(p.261. 10); αἴσθησις κατ' ἐπιθυμίαν κινηθεῖσα ἡδονὴν ἀπεργάζεται τὸ αἰσθητὸν προσλαβοῦσα Max.*ambig.*(M.91.1112C); **2.** types, bodily and spiritual ἄλλοι δὲ ἄλλως τὸ ὄνομα τῆς ἡ. ἐξέλαβον· οἱ μὲν γὰρ τὴν κατὰ τὰς θνητὰς ἐπιθυμίας, οἱ δὲ τὴν ἐπὶ τῇ ἀρετῇ ἡ. Hipp.*haer.*1.22(p.27.5; M.16.3049C); ψυχικαὶ [sc. ἡ.]...ὅσαι μόνης εἰσὶ τῆς ψυχῆς αὐτῆς καθ' ἑαυτήν, ὡς αἱ περὶ τὰ μαθήματα, καὶ τὴν θεωρίαν. ... σωματικαὶ...αἱ μετὰ κοινωνίας τῆς ψυχῆς καὶ τοῦ σώματος γινόμεναι,...ὡς αἱ περὶ τροφάς, καὶ συνουσίας, καὶ τὰ τοιαῦτα. μόνου δὲ τοῦ σώματος οὐκ ἂν εὕροι τις ἰδίας ἡ. Nemes.*nat.hom.*18(M.40.677B); legitimate and forbidden τῆς ἡ. τὸ μέν ἐστι κτηνῶδες καὶ ἄλογον, τὸ δὲ καθαρόν τε καὶ ἄυλον Gr.Nyss.*mort.*(M.46.536D); μετὰ...τὴν ἡ. χαρὰ ἡ λύπη συνίσταται· εἰ μὲν γὰρ ἀγαθὰ τὰ τῆς ἡ. τέλη, χαρά· εἰ δὲ φαῦλα, λύπη Melet. *nat.hom.*synops.(M.64.1112C); **3.** admissible; **a.** if inevitable οὐδεμίαν χώραν ἀπονέμομεν ἡδονῇ πρὸς οὐδεμίαν συμπεπλεγμένῃ λυσιτελῆ τῷ βίῳ χρείαν Clem.*paed.*2.8(p.198.3; M.8.473C); εἰ δὲ τῇ χρείᾳ καὶ τὸ ἡδὺ πολλάκις συγκαταμέμικται...οὐκ ἀπωστέον τὴν χρείαν διὰ τὴν ἐπακολουθοῦσαν ἀπόλαυσιν· οὔτε μὴν κατὰ προηγούμενον μεταδιωκτέον τὴν ἡ. Gr.Nyss.*virg.*21(p.330.3; M.46.401C); cf.id.*mort.*(M.46.528C); Nemes.*nat.hom.*18(M.40.680A); τὸν κατὰ θεὸν ζῶντα δεῖ μετέρχεσθαι τὰς ἀναγκαίας ἅμα καὶ φυσικάς· ἐν δευτέρᾳ δὲ τάξει τὰς φυσικὰς καὶ οὐκ ἀναγκαίας τίθεσθαι, μετὰ τοῦ προσήκοντος καιροῦ, καὶ τρόπου, καὶ μέτρου γινομένας. τὰς δὲ ἄλλας χρὴ πάντως παραιτεῖσθαι Jo.D.*f.o.*2.13 (M.94.932A); cf.Melet.*nat.hom.*synops.(M.64.1113A); **b.** in moderation ἵνα...ἐγκριθῶμεν εἰς τὴν βασιλείαν τῶν οὐρανῶν, ἐν πάσαις ἡ. καὶ λύπαις δοκιμασθέντες, εἰ μὴ μεταβαλλοίμεθα Meth.*res.*2.4(p.337.7; M. 41.1169B); εἰ...ἡ. ἐπιζητοῦμεν, ἐν αὐταρκείᾳ ταύτην μᾶλλον ἢ ἐν τρυφῇ οὖσαν εὑρήσομεν ‡Chrys.*prov.*6(2.776C); cf.Chrys.*stat.*2.7,8 (2.31B); **c.** when not pursued for its own sake and not contrary to nature or reason ψιλὴ γὰρ ἡ., κἂν ἐν γάμῳ παραληφθῇ, παράνομός ἐστι καὶ ἄδικος καὶ ἄλογος Clem.*paed.*2.10(p.212.24; M.8.508A); πᾶν τὸ παρὰ τὸν λόγον τὸν ὀρθὸν τοῦτο ἁμάρτημά ἐστιν. ... ἡ. δὲ ἔπαρσιν ψυχῆς ἀπειθῆ λόγῳ *ib.*1.13(p.150.24; 372A); Or.*Jo.*2.15(9; p.72.1; M.14.140D); δυσπαράδεκτόν ἐστι τῇ φύσει πᾶν τὸ πρὸς ἡδονὴν ἀλλοτρίως ἔχον (ἡ. δὲ λέγω τὴν τοῦ σώματος φίλην) Gr.Nyss.*Pss.tit.*A 2(M.44. 437A); **4.** in bad sense, Herm.*sim.*8.8.5; *ib.*8.9.4; μισεῖ τὴν ψυχὴν ἡ σὰρξ καὶ πολεμεῖ..., διότι ταῖς ἡ. κωλύεται χρῆσθαι· μισεῖ καὶ Χριστιανοὺς ὁ κόσμος...ὅτι ταῖς ἡ. ἀντιτάσσονται *Diogn.*6.5; πάτερ τοῦ μονογενοῦς...κατάργησον...πᾶσαν ἡ. ... ἀπὸ τοῦ λαοῦ τούτου Serap. *euch.*12.2; Gr.Naz.*carm.*1.2.32.85(M.37.922A); ἡδονῆς...τύπος, ἡ γυνή Cyr.*ador.*1(1.10D); **5.** diabolical instigation αἱ...δυνάμεις...ἡδονὰς... προτείνουσι ταῖς εὐεπιφόροις ψυχαῖς...κατασοφισάμεναι τοὺς μὴ διακρίνειν δυνηθέντας τὴν ἀληθῆ ἀπὸ ψευδοῦς ἡ. Clem.*str.*2.20(p.173.26; M.8. 1056A); in marriage, *ib.*3.15(p.240.16; 1196C); in gen., Meth.*res.*2.6 (p.340.16; M.41.1173A); Ath.*v.Anton.*22(M.26.877A); Ephr.3.494C; ἀναρίθμητα βάλλει [sc. Devil] ἔμπροσθέν μου ὀλισθήματα...ἡ. σαρκικῶν id.3.507A; ἐοίκασιν οὖν πονηραί τινες δυνάμεις διὰ τῆς κατὰ τὴν φωνὴν ἐκκλήσεως, ἡ. ἐμποιοῦσθαι ταῖς ψυχαῖς, ὧν καταμελῳδοῦσιν ἐπ' ὀλέθρῳ, θηρεύειν τοὺς διερχομένους †Bas.*Is.*276(1.589C; M.30.604B); *ib.*(589E; M.604C); Cyr.*Ps.*36:32(M.69.948A); Nil.*epp.*4.24(M.79.561A); Devil using pleasure to counteract the effects of prayer, Evagr.Pont.*or.* 47(M.79.1177A); **6.** life of pleasure incompatible with spiritual life, *T.Benj.*6.3; οὐχ ἥδομαι...ἡδοναῖς τοῦ βίου τούτου· ἄρτον θεοῦ θέλω Ign.*Rom.*7.3; πῶς...ἐστι δυνατὸν ἡττηθέντα τῶν τοῦ σώματος ἡ. ἐξομοιοῦσθαι τῷ κυρίῳ ἢ γνῶσιν ἔχειν θεοῦ; Clem.*str.*3.4(p.215.5; M.8. 1145A); ref. conversion to Christianity μηκέτι μνησθῆναι τῶν προτέρων ἡ. *A.Thom.*A 117(p.227.18); *ib.*126(p.235.10); πᾶς...ὁ κατὰ τὴν ἡ. βιούς, τὸ εὐρύχωρον ἀγαπήσας, ἐκπέπτωκε τῆς στενῆς καὶ τεθλιμμένης ὁδοῦ Ἰησοῦ Χριστοῦ Or.*or.*19(p.343.9; M.11.478B); τὸ ἐπιθυμητικὸν ἡμῶν φύσιν οὐκ ἔχει ὁμοῦ ταῖς σωματικαῖς ὑπηρετεῖν ἡ., καὶ τὸν πνευματικὸν μετιέναι γάμον Gr.Nyss.*virg.*20(p.326.4; M.46.397C); Dion.Ar.*e.h.*3.3.7(M.3.433D); **7.** evil effects of irrational pleasure; **a.** obscuring of judgement ἠμαύρωσέ μου τὴν καρδίαν ἡ ἡ. *T.Jud.* 13.6; μετάγεται...ἡ διάνοια ὑπὸ ἡ. Clem.*paed.*3.2(p.244.21; M.8.576A);

id.*q.d.s.*41(p.187.14; M.9.645D); Cyr.*Ps.*37:11(M.69.964A); Hesych. S.*temp.*1.57(M.93.1497D); **b.** hindrance to knowledge of God, Meth. *creat.*1(p.493.4; M.18.332A); *οἱ ἄνθρωποι, νικώμενοι ταῖς παραυτίκα ἡ., καὶ ταῖς παρὰ δαιμόνων φαντασίαις καὶ ἀπάταις, οὐκ ἀνένευσαν πρὸς τὴν ἀλήθειαν* Ath.*inc.*12.6(M.25.117C); id.*gent.*30(M.25.61A); **c.** psychological unrest *πάσης...ἡ. ἐπιθυμία κατάρχει, ἐπιθυμία δὲ λύπη τις καὶ φροντὶς δι' ἔνδειαν ὀρεγομένη τινός* Clem.*str.*3.4(p.215.7; M.8.1145A); Ephr.3.427E; *τί γὰρ ἕτερόν ἐστιν ἡ., ἢ τὸ φροντίδος ἀπηλλάχθαι καὶ φόβου καὶ ἀθυμίας, καὶ πᾶσιν ἀχείρωτον εἶναι; τίς γὰρ ἐν ἡ., ...ὁ μαινόμενος καὶ σφαδάζων καὶ κεντούμενος ὑπὸ ἐπιθυμιῶν πολλῶν, καὶ οὐδὲ ἐν ἑαυτῷ ὤν;* Chrys.*hom.22.5 in 1Cor.*(10.199E); *ἡ. οὐ τῶν ἱσταμένων καὶ ἠρεμούντων, ἀλλὰ τῶν κινουμένων, καὶ ταραχῆς γεμόντων ἐστί* Nil.*exerc.*58(M.79.789D); **d.** harm to soul *λήθη, ῥαθυμία καὶ ἄγνοια· ταύτας δὲ ἀποτίκτει ἡ., καὶ ἄνεσις* Ephr.3.427B; Ath.*v.Anton.* 14(M.26.865A); *ἡ. λύπης οὐκ ἔλαττον...κακόν, δῆλον ἀφ' ὧν τὴν ψυχὴν διατίθησι· καὶ γὰρ καὶ κούφην ποιεῖ καὶ μετέωρον καὶ ἀνεπτερωμένην* Chrys.*hom.40.5 in Mt.*(7.444A); leading to sin *τίς δ' οὐ τὰς δι' ὤτων, τίς δ' οὐ τὰς διὰ γεύσεως ὀσφρήσεώς τε καὶ ἁφῆς ἡ. ... ἀποδέχεται, τὸν ἡνίοχον μὴ φέρων, σωφροσύνην;* Meth.*symp.*5.3(p.56.8; M.18.101A); *ἡ. ἄγκιστρόν ἐστι τοῦ διαβόλου πρὸς ἀπώλειαν ἕλκον. ἡ. μήτηρ τῆς ἁμαρτίας* Bas.*hom.*13.5(2.118C; M.31.436A); *ἅπασα...ἔκτοπος ἡ. ... τὸν ἀνθρώπινον καταγοητεύουσα νοῦν* Cyr.*Is.*5.3(2.800E); *ἀεὶ...ἡμᾶς κατασείουσι...εἰς ἁμαρτίαν, αἱ σὺν ἡμῖν τε καὶ ἐν ἡμῖν ἡ.* id.*ador.*1(1.10C); *οἱ...φιλήδονοι στερούμενοι τῶν ἡ. ὀργίζονται καὶ πικραίνονται* Nil.*exerc.*55(M.79.788D); **8.** ref. gluttony *πολλὰ βλάβην καὶ λύπην ἐνεγέννησεν ἡ., δυσπάθειαν δὲ καὶ λήθην καὶ ἀφροσύνην ἡ πολυτροφία ἐντίκτει τῇ ψυχῇ* Clem.*paed.*2.1(p.166.18; M.8.405C); *ἀφεκτέον...τοῦ ἐσθίειν κατὰ γαστριμαργίαν ἢ καθὸ ἄγεσθαι ὑφ' ἡ. χωρὶς τῆς εἰς ὑγείαν τοῦ σώματος...προθέσεως* Or.*Cels.*8.30(p.245.21; M.11.1561A); *ἀναγκαίαν πρὸς θεὸν λειτουργίαν μὴ ἐμποδίζεσθαι ὑπὸ τῆς ἡ. τῶν βρωμάτων* Marc.Er.*opusc.*9.1(M.65.1112A); **9.** sexual pleasure; **a.** legitimate; natural *τὴν κατὰ φύσιν...ἡ., ἧς ἐδύναντο μετὰ ἀδείας πλείονος ἀπολαύοντες καὶ μείζονος τῆς εὐφροσύνης, ἀπηλλάχθαι αἰσχύνης* Chrys. *hom.4.1 in Rom.*(9.454E); can lead to sin, *T.Jud.*14.3; Clem.*str.*7.6 (p.25.21; M.9.448A); **b.** illegitimate; **i.** in gen.; ref. pagan gods as evidence that they are not divine, Clem.*prot.*2(p.23.21; M.8.105B); to be renounced by follower of Logos, id.*paed.*2.10(p.223.17; M.8. 529B); ref. 1Cor.15:50 *σάρκα, φησίν, οὐ τὴν σάρκα αὐτὴν ἐδήλωσεν, ἀλλὰ τὴν ἄλογον πρὸς τὰς μαχλώσας τῆς ψυχῆς ὁρμὴν ἡδονάς* Meth.*res.* 2.18(p.368.6; M.18.312C); *ἡ...πορνεία...οὐκ ἐπὶ παιδοποιΐᾳ γινομένη, ἀλλ' ἡδονῇ χαριζομένη τὸ πᾶν* *Const.App.*6.28.3; Chrys.*Thdr.*2.3(1. 39A); **ii.** leading to other sin, Clem.*prot.*12(p.83.21; M.8.240A); *ἡ. ἐστι τὸ μέγα τοῦ κακοῦ δέλεαρ, δι' ἣν εὐέμπτωτοι μάλιστα πρὸς ἁμαρτίαν ἐσμὲν οἱ ἄνθρωποι* Bas.*reg.fus.*17.2(2.360D; M.31.964B); Gr.Nyss.*v. Mos.*(M.44.421A); deterring men from receiving baptism, Bas.*hom.* 13.5(2.117E; M.31.433B); **10.** ref. state of man; **a.** before Inc.; ref. Lc.12:50, applied to man before conversion to Christianity *ὡς ἐν ἑνὶ οἴκῳ τῷ ἀνθρώπῳ αἱ πέντε αἰσθήσεις, πρὶν μὲν ἐλθεῖν αὐταῖς τὸν λόγον, ὁμονοοῦσιν ἐν ταῖς ἡ.* Or.*fr.65 in Lc.*(p.265); ref. Fall *χωρὶς σώματος ὑπὸ ἀλόγου ἡ. οὐ κρατεῖται ἡ ψυχή, ἐκρατήθησαν δὲ οἱ πρωτόπλαστοι ἀλόγῳ δελεασθέντες ἡ. ἦν ἄρα ἡ ψυχὴ μετὰ σώματος καὶ πρὸ τῆς ἁμαρτίας* Meth.*res.*1.54(p.311.17; M.41.1145C); of fallen men turning to bodily pleasures, Ath.*gent.*3(M.25.8C); Ast.Am.*hom.*14(M.40. 373C); ref. Eve *δι' ἐκείνην ἡδονῇ κλαπεῖσαν, ἀπεθάνομεν πάντες* Anast. Ant.*serm.*2.8(M.89.1384C); of BMV *ἡ μόνη ἄνευ ἡ. ὀγκωθεῖσα* Procl.CP *or.*5.3(M.65.720C); **b.** after Inc. *ἐξουσίαν ἔχων* [sc. Christ] *τοῦ κόσμου καὶ τῶν ἐν αὐτῷ ἡ.* *A.Thom.*A 143(p.250.16); *ἕως ὁ κύριος Χριστὸς δι' ἧς ἐπεφάνη σαρκὸς τῷ βίῳ ἀμυδρώσας τῶν ἡ. τὰς ἐπιβολάς, αἷς αἱ κάτω δυνάμεις καθ' ἡμῶν ὡπλίζοντο καταδουλῶσαι τὸ διανοητικόν, ἐλεύθερον πάντων τὸν ἄνθρωπον διέδειξε κακῶν* Meth.*Porph.*1(p.504.10; M.18. 397D); **c.** at resurrection *τότε δὲ μετασχηματισθήσεται* [sc. body] *εἰς σῶμα ἀπαθές,...τῷ μὴ ἐπιθυμεῖν τῶν ὑλικῶν ἡ.* Meth.*res.*3.16(p.412. 22; M.18.317B); **11.** remedies; **a.** divine help, Cyr.*Ps.*93:14(M.69. 1236B); *ib.*93:18(1237B); *τούτων ἁπάντων* [sc. *τῶν ἐκτόπων ἡ.*] *ἡμᾶς ἡ τοῦ ἁγίου πνεύματος ἀπαλλάττει χάρις, ἐνοικισθεῖσα τῷ νῷ* id. *Juln.*10(6².353C); *ὑποδεξώμεθα καὶ ἡμεῖς τὸν Ἰησοῦν* [sc. in eucharist]. *ὅταν γὰρ εἰσβάλῃ καὶ ἐν ἡμῖν, καὶ ἔχωμεν αὐτὸν εἰς νοῦν καὶ καρδίαν, τότε τῶν ἐκτόπων ἡ. τὴν πύρωσιν ἀποσβέσει* id.*Lc.*5:38(M.72.552B); **b.** human action *ὀργίζεσθε...τῇ ἡ., καὶ οὐχ ἁμαρτήσετε* Isid.Pel.*epp.* 2.239(M.78.677A); *ib.*3.238(997D); *ἡμῖν δὲ σπουδὴ αὐτὴν θλάσαι τὴν προσβολὴν τῆς ἡ., ταύτης γὰρ συντριβείσης ἀσθενὴς ἡ ἐνέργεια* Nil. *exerc.*39(M.79.768B); *Schol.*16 in Jo.Clim.*scal.*14(M.88.876C); **c.** practice of virtues *ὡς εἶναι τὸν γνωστικὸν σώφρονα καὶ ἀπαθῆ, ταῖς ἡ. τε καὶ λύπαις ἄτεγκτον* Clem.*str.*7.11(p.49.3; M.9.493C); trust in Christ, Meth.*symp.*11(p.139.15; M.18.217B); cultivation of soul in gen., Ath.*v.Anton.*45(M.26.909B); *ἔστιν ἡ ἐγκράτεια...ἐν ἑαυτῇ τὸ κέντρον τῆς ἡ. ἀφανίζουσα* Bas.*reg.fus.*17.2(2.360D; M.31.964B); ascetic life, Mac.Aeg.*hom.*5.6(M.34.512C); *οἱ τῶν ἡ. καταφρονοῦντες, ἢ φόβῳ καταφρονοῦσι, ἢ ἐλπίδι, ἢ γνώσει, ἢ τῇ εἰς θεὸν ἀγάπῃ* *Schol.*7 in Jo.Clim.*scal.*7(M.88.820D); **d.** sign of cross, Ath.*inc.*31.2(M.25.149B); **e.** renunciation; ref. monk *ἀναχωρήσας τε τοῦ βίου καὶ τῶν κοσμικῶν ἡ.* Ephr.3.337E; †Bas.*ep.*42.2(3.127B; M.32.352B); *κατὰ μικρὸν...κλέπτε τὰς ἡ. τοῦ βίου,...μήποτε ἀθρόως πάσας ὁμοῦ ἐρεθίσας τὰς ἡ., ὄχλον πειρασμῶν σεαυτῷ ἐπαγάγῃς* *ib.*(126E; M.350D); **12.** spiritual pleasures *κυρίως...εἰσὶν ἡ. αἱ τῇ κατανοήσει τοῦ θείου καὶ ταῖς ἐπιστήμαις καὶ ταῖς ἀρεταῖς ἐπιγινόμεναι* Nemes.*nat.hom.*18(M.40.680C); contrasted with vice *οὐχ ἡ παρ' ἡμῖν ἡ. τοιαύτη·...ἀλλὰ διαπαντὸς ἀχείμαστον τηρεῖ τὴν ψυχήν, καὶ θόρυβον οὐδένα, οὐδὲ κλόνον ἐπάγει· καθαρὸν δέ τινα εὐφροσύνην, καὶ εἰλικρινῆ, καὶ ἔνδοξον, καὶ τέλος οὐκ ἔχουσαν* Chrys. *oppugn.*2.10(1.73E); found in union with God *τοιοῦτον...ἔχων δεσπότην, τοῦτό μοι ἡ.* id.*exp.in Ps.*9:3(5.96A); Dion.Ar.*e.h.*4.3.4 (M.3.477C); *τί γὰρ θεώσεως τοῖς ἀξίοις ἐρασμιώτερον, καθ' ἣν ὁ θεὸς θεοῖς γενομένοις ἑνούμενος τὸ πᾶν ἑαυτοῦ ποιεῖται δι' ἀγαθότητα; διὸ καὶ ἡ. ... ὠνόμασαν τὴν τοιαύτην κατάστασιν, τὴν τῇ θείᾳ κατανοήσει καὶ τῇ ἑπομένῃ αὐτῇ τῆς εὐφροσύνης ἀπολαύσει, ἡδονὴν μέν, ὡς τέλος οὖσαν τῶν κατὰ φύσιν ἐνεργειῶν (οὕτω γὰρ τὴν ἡ. ὁρίζονται)* Max.*ambig.*(M.91.1088C); in contemplation *τῆς ἄνω τροφῆς ἐξέχεσθαι τῆς θείας...καὶ τῆς τοῦ ὄντως ὄντος ἀπληρώτου ἐμπίμπλασθαι θέας, τῆς βεβαίου καὶ μονίμου καὶ καθαρᾶς γενομένους ἡ.* Clem.*paed.*2.1(p.160.4; M.8.393A); id.*str.*6.11(p.481.27; M.9.320C); Ephr.3.456B; *τῆς θεωρίας ἡ ἡ., μεγίστη τε οὖσα..., δι' ἀκινησίας γίνεται* Nemes.*nat.hom.*18(M. 40.685A); in virtue *ἐκκλησία παρὰ τὸ ἐκκεκλικέναι τὰς ἡ. λέγεσθαί φησιν* Meth.*creat.*8(p.498.22; M.18.340C); *ἡ...τοῦ πνεύματος ἐν ταῖς ἀρεταῖς καρποφορία, ἀπόλαυσίς ἐστι πνευματικὴ ἐν ἡ. ἀφθάρτῳ ἐν καρδίαις πισταῖς καὶ ταπειναῖς ἀπὸ τοῦ πνεύματος ἐνεργουμένη* Ephr. 3.347D; Chrys.*Anna* 5.1(4.740D); Dion.Ar.*e.h.*7.1.2(M.3.553D); *ib.*7. 1.3(556B); in partic. virtues *μεγίστη...ἡ σωφροσύνης συζυγία καθαρᾶς ἡ. ἀποπνέουσα* Clem.*paed.*3.12(p.282.23; M.8.664A); virginity, Meth. *symp.*8.17(p.112.1; M.18.173C); in victory over temptation, Chrys. *hom.27.4 in 1Cor.*(10.348E); poverty *ὁ ἀκτήμων ἀμέριμνον ἔχει τοῦ βίου τὴν ἡ.* Nil.*Eulog.*11(M.79.1108B); of spiritual pleasures as a spur to virtue, Herm.*sim.*6.5.7; making all torments bearable, Chrys.*hom.1.4 in 2Cor.*(10.424B); of pleasure of heaven; as reward of martyrs, Clem.*str.*4.5(p.258.8; M.8.1233D); cf.*ib.*7.11(p.48.13; M. 9.493A); in gen., *A.Thom.*A 124(p.233.15); *ἔνθα...παναγίας ἡ. ἀπόλαυσις* Eus.*l.C.*6(p.211.19; M.20.1349B); **13.** of evil pleasures of the mind, ref. heretics *πολλοὶ...λύκοι ἀξιόπιστοι ἡ. κακῇ αἰχμαλωτίζουσιν τοὺς θεοδρόμους* Ign.*Philad.*2.2; cf.id.*Trall.*6.2; *πᾶσα αἵρεσις ἀρχὴν ὦτα ἀκούοντα οὐκ ἔχει τὸ σύμφορον, μόνον δὲ τοῖς πρὸς ἡδονὴν ἀνεῳγότα* Clem.*str.*7.16(p.69.26; M.9.536C); Ath.*decr.*30(p.27.6; M. 25.473A); **14.** in argument against Epicureanism *εἴ τινας μὲν αἱρούμεθα τῶν ἡ., τινὰς δὲ φεύγομεν, οὐ πᾶσα ἡ. ἀγαθόν* Clem.*str.*4.5 (p.258.2; M.8.1233C); Or.*Cels.*3.75(p.266.24; M.11.1017B); **15.** as Gnost. aeon *Αὐτοφυὴς καὶ Ἡ.* Iren.*haer.*1.1.2(M.7.449A); Hipp. *haer.*6.30(p.157.15; M.16.3238C); *Ἀκίνητος καὶ Ἡ.* Val.Gn.ap.Epiph. *haer.*31.2(p.386.5,13; M.41.477A,B); id.*ib.*31.5(p.392.17; 484B); id.*ib.* 31.6(p.393.2; 484C); **16.** in Gnost. practice (Nicolaitan) *διὰ τῆς χρήσεως ἔφασκεν τῆς ἡ. ἡδονῇ μάχεσθαι* Clem.*str.*2.20(p.176.23; M.8. 1061A); exeg. Rom.1:27 (Naassene) *ἐν...τούτοις τοῖς λόγοις...ὅλον φασὶ συνέχεσθαι τὸ κρύφιον αὐτῶν καὶ ἄρρητον τῆς μακαρίας μυστήριον ἡδονῆς. ἡ γὰρ ἐπαγγελία τοῦ λουτροῦ οὐκ ἄλλη τίς ἐστι κατ' αὐτούς, ἢ τὸ εἰσαγαγεῖν εἰς τὴν ἀμάραντον ἡ. τὸν λουόμενον κατ' αὐτούς* Hipp. *haer.*5.7(p.83.3; M.16.3131C); **17.** ref. evil spirits *τῶν θυομένων ἀποφορᾶς λίχνως μεταλαμβάνοντες παράνομον ἡ.* Or.*Cels.*7.64(p.214.11; M.11.1512C); **18.** *Ἡ.* not used as name of God, for fear of giving rise to obscene fables (cf. Plato *Philebus* 12C), Or.*Cels.*4.48(p.321.20; M.11.1108A); **19.** of angels *ἄδεκτοι παντελῶς εἰσι τῆς καθ' ἡμᾶς ἐμπαθοῦς ἡ.* Dion.Ar.*c.h.*15.9(M.3.340A).

***ἡδοποιοῦμαι**, *take pleasure in*, Const.Diac.*laud.*27(M.88.509A).

***ἡδυβόρος**, *sweet* or *pleasant to taste*, Gr.Naz.*carm.*1.1.27.96(M. 37.505A); *ib.*1.1.8.114(455A).

ἡδύλαλος, *sweet-singing*, Ephr.3.262A.

***ἡδύληπτος**, *sweet to take*, of a spring of water *ἡ. ἕλξιν* ‡Paul.Sil. *therm.Pyth.*82(M.86.2265).

ἡδυμέλεια, ἡ, *sweet strain*, *harmony*, Leont.N.*v.Sym.*62(M.93. 1745A).

ἡδυμελής, *sweet-sounding*; as name of a Gnostic aeon, Epiph. *haer.*31.3(p.387.6; M.41.477D).

ἡδυντικός, *that gives pleasure*, †Cyr.*coll.VT*(6⁴.23D; M.77.1210D).

ἡδύνω, **1.** *sweeten*; met., of influence of H. Ghost on soul, Diad. *perf.*33(p.36.24); of grace on hearts of those who observe the commandments, *ib.*88(p.122.27); **2.** *delight*, Maximinus Daia ap.Eus.

*h.e.*9.7.11(M.20.813B); *Pers.*(p.3.11); Gr.Nyss.*hom.3 in Cant.*(M.44.829A).

ἡδυπάθεια, ἡ, plur.; **1.** *pleasures, enjoyments, 2Clem.*16.2; οἱ... δίκαιοι...μισήσαντες τὰς ἡ. τῆς ψυχῆς *ib.*17.7; Clem.*paed.*2.27(p.172.12; M.8.420C); Meth.*symp.*1.3(p.11.22; M.18.44A); Eus.*d.e.*3.4(p.118.23; M.22.201D); **2.** *delicacies for the table,* Clem.*paed.*2.1(p.155.6; M.8.380B).

ἡδυπαθέω, *live in luxury,* Marc.Er.*opusc.*1.163(M.65.925A).

ἡδυπαθής, *voluptuous,* Clem.*str.*6.11(p.477.8; M.9.312A); Eus.*d.e.*6.20(p.286.20; M.22.472A); id.*l.C.*7(p.213.9; M.20.1353A); ἡδυπαθέστερος ὁ νοῦς Dor.*doct.*13.4(M.88.1765B); ἡ. ... ὀρχήσεις †Jo.D.*B.J.*31(M.96.1160C); neut. as subst., *voluptuousness,* Cyr.*ador.*1(1.31B).

***ἡδυπληθής**, *full of sweetness,* Meth.*symp.*11(p.133.30; M.18.209C).

ἡδυσμός, ὁ, *sweetness,* met. τῆς ἡσυχίας ὁ ἡ. Nil.*epp.*3.213(M.79.480D).

ἡδύτης, ἡ, *sweetness, M.Ner.et Ach.*2(p.2.8); ‡Pamph.Abyd.*ep. Petr.*(p.9.17; H.2.849C); Melet.*nat.hom.*30(M.64.1276C).

***ἡδυφαγέω**, *feed on dainties,* Cyr.*hom.pasch.*27(5².314C).

***ἡδυφανής**, *seemingly sweet* ὁ σατανᾶς ἐν ἡ. τινι αἰσθήσει...τὴν ψυχὴν παρακαλεῖ Diad.*perf.*31(p.34.19); *ib.*32(p.36.14); neut. as subst. τὸ τοῦ καρποῦ ἡ. *ib.*56(p.62.16).

ἡδύφθογγος, *sweet-voiced, tuneful, A.Xanthipp.*6(p.61.34); Isid. Pel.*epp.*1.108(M.78.256B).

ἡδυφωνία, ἡ, *sweet sound,* Thphl.Ant.*Autol.*2.30(M.6.1100C); Jo. Clim.*scal.*15(M.88.897C).

***ἡδυφώνως**, *sweetly;* of sound, ‡Chrys.*hom.in Ps.100*(5.638B).

***ἠερίηθεν**, *from the misty land,* i.e. *from Egypt,* Ἀερία (Ἠερίη) being an old name for Egypt, †Apoll.*Ps.*113:1(M.33.1488A).

ἠεροφοίτης, ὁ, as adj., *moving in the air;* of angels, Nonn.*par. Jo.*1:52(M.43.760B).

ἠερόφοιτος, = foreg., Nonn.*par.Jo.*8:52(M.43.821B); Eudoc. *Cypr.*2.37(M.86.845C).

ἠθάς, ὁ, ἡ, used adjectivally, *accustomed* ἡ. μηλοβοτῆρα Nonn. *par.Jo.*10:14(M.43.833B); *ib.*20:26(913A).

***ἠθικοπροσκόπται**, οἱ, *Stumblers in Morals,* name given to a heretical sect ἠ.· οἱ ἐν τῇ ἠθικῇ, ἤγουν πρακτικῇ, προσκόπτοντες Jo.D. *haer.*96(M.94.760A).

***ἠθικός**, *moral;* **1.** in gen. ἠ. πραγματεία Clem.*str.*1.28(p.108.26; M.8.921D); ref. philosophy and doctrine, Hipp.*haer.*10.6(p.265.26; M.16.3414C); δόγματα...ἠ. Or.*fr.14 in Lam.*(p.241.2; M.13.613A); of conduct, id.*fr.36 in Jo.*(p.512.20); ἐπὶ κατορθώσει ἀγωγῆς τῆς ἠθικωτέρας Eus.*p.e.*10.4(470C; M.21.784C); τὸ ἠθικώτερον μέρος τῆς φιλοσοφίας Chrys.*oppugn.*1.6(1.53C); ἠ. ... διδασκαλία Thdt.*Ps.*1:1(1.609); id.*haer.*5.2(4.388); Gennad.*fr.Rom.*12:1(p.402.35; M.85.1720B); **2.** in partic. expressions; **a.** system *of morals* ἠ. τόπος Clem. *str.*7.18(p.78.19; M.9.556C); ᾗ μὲν οὖν ἐστιν [sc. God] οὐσία, ἀρχὴ τοῦ φυσικοῦ τόπου· καθ' ὅσον ἐστὶν τἀγαθόν, τοῦ ἠ. *ib.*4.25(p.320.18; M.8.1372B); Or.*hom.11.4 in Jer.*(p.81.23; M.13.372B); id.*Cels.*1.30(p.81.27; M.11.717A); **b.** discourse *about morals* ὁ ἠ. λόγος Clem.*str.*4.1(p.248.8; M.8.1216A); ref. law of Moses, Or.*Cels.*1.18(p.69.30; 692C); Chrys.*hom.17.1 in Mt.*(7.222B); id.*hom.43.1 in 1Cor.*(10.399E); ref. Sermon on Mount, id.*hom.20.3 in Rom.*(9.660D); **3.** neut. as subst., *morals, ethics* τὰ ἠ. Clem.*str.*1.14(p.40.8; M.8.764A); *ib.*4.25(p.320.5; 1372A); τὸ ἠ. Hipp.*haer.*1.17(p.18.22; M.16.3040D); Chrys.*hom.43.1 in 1Cor.*(10.400A); τὰ ἠθικώτερα id.*hom.17.10 in Rom.*(9.620E).

***ἠθικότης**, ἡ, *courtesy,* ‡Chrys.*hom.1.2 in Gen.*(6.534A); Thphn. *chron.*p.363(M.108.872A).

ἠθικῶς, **1.** *morally,* Clem.*str.*4.26(p.321.1; M.8.1373A); ref. exegesis, *in a moral sense,* Nil.*epp.*2.173(M.79.288D); **2.** *gently, mildly,* Chrys. *hom.33.1 in 1Cor.*(10.300A); id.*hom.87.2 in Jo.*(8.453E).

ἠθμός, ὁ, *strainer,* liturg. ἠ. διὰ τὸ μή τι κοινὸν ἐμπεσεῖν εἰς τὸν θεῖον κρατῆρα ‡Sophr.H.*liturg.*5(M.87.3985C).

ἠθοποιέω, **1.** *write in character,* Cyr.*Juln.*2(6².59C); **2.** *express the significance of,* Chrys.*fr.Job* 1:8(M.64.525B).

ἠθοποιΐα, ἡ, in rhetoric, *the attribution of the words or deeds of one person to another,* Or.*sel.in Ps.*41:7(M.12.1417C); ref. Rom.7:9, Nil.*epp.*1.153(M.79.145B); Thdt.*Ps.*41:7(1.873); id.*Ezech.*38:10–12(2.1007); Isid.H.*etym.*2.21.32; ref. vision of Is. ἡ τοῦ ἀγγέλου ἠ. Max. *schol.c.h.*13.4(M.4.101C).

ἦθος, τό, **1.** *character;* **a.** in gen. φιλοξενίας...ἦ. as mark of Christians, *1Clem.*1.2; ἁγνείας ἦ. *ib.*21.7; ref. providence ἀναλόγως τοῖς ἑαυτῶν ἤθεσι διοικεῖται καὶ τὰ μικρότερα Clem.*str.*7.2(p.9.30; M.9.416A); ἀμετάβλητον αὐτοῦ [sc. one newly-baptized] τὸ ἦ. ... διαφύλαξον Serap.*euch.*21; ἦ. ἐστι προσευχῆς σύννοια μετ' εὐλαβείας Evagr.Pont.*or.*42(M.79.1176B); of God τὸν...πατέρα ἐν τῷ οἰκείῳ τῆς ἀναλλοιώτου θεότητος ἤθει μεμενηκέναι *Symb.Ant.*(345)7(p.253.19; M.26.732C); **b.** literary *style,* Dion.Al.ap.Eus.*h.e.*7.25.8(M.20.697C); ἔγραψε Θαλίαν...γελοίοις ἤ. κατὰ τὸν Αἰγύπτιον Σωσάτην Ath.*Dion.*6(p.50.1; M.25.488B); id.*Ar.*1.2(M.26.16A); **c.** prepositional phrases; **i.** μετὰ ἤθους *figuratively,* Or.*comm.in Ex.*(p.252.22; M.12.277C); Eus. *h.e.*2.18.8(M.20.188A); *with emphasis,* Or.*hom.19.12 in Jer.*(p.167.14; μετὰ βρίθους M.13.485D); **ii.** ἐν ἤ. *after the manner, T.Aser.* 4.5; *with emphasis,* Cyr.*Jo.*6(4.569E); *figuratively,* id.*Nah.*39(3.513E); *courteously,* id.*Jo.*6.1(4.618A); *rhetorically,* Olymp.*Job* 34:9(M.93.357C); **2.** *conduct;* **a.** of Christ ἐνιδεῖν...ἔστι...τῷ τοῦ Ἰησοῦ ἤ. πανταχοῦ περιϊσταμένου τὴν περιαυτολογίαν Or.*Cels.*1.48(p.99.27; M.11.752B); as example to men, *ib.*1.68(p.123.3; 788D); (in Ebionite view) κατὰ προκοπὴν ἤθους αὐτὸ μόνον ἄνθρωπον δεδικαιωμένον Eus. *h.e.*3.27.2(M.20.273A); **b.** in gen. τῆς γραφῆς ἀναγινωσκομένης ὃ μὲν εἰς πίστιν, ὃ δὲ εἰς ἦ. ὠφελεῖται Clem.*ecl.*28(p.145.20; M.9.713A); ref. influence of Christianity ὅσων ἄγρια ἤθη ἡμεροῦται προφάσει τοῦ λόγου Or.*Cels.*1.64(p.118.1; M.11.781A); *ib.*3.79(p.270.6; 1024A); **c.** *moral sense* of scripture, id.*princ.*3.1.11(p.213.8; M.11.268B); *ib.* 3.1.12(p.215.2; 269B); **d.** *morals, ethics* κατὰ τὸ ἦ. Bas.*hex.*5.7(1.47C; M.29.112C); **e.** *usages, customs,* ref. Ebionites ἤθεσι Ἰουδαϊκοῖς Hipp.*haer.*7.8(p.190.10; M.16.3294B).

ἠθροισμένως, *all together, in one,* Eus.*Is.*9:3(M.24.149C); Apoll. (‡Gennad.)*Rom.*9:32(p.69.2n.; M.85.1712B).

ἠκριβωμένως, *accurately, scrupulously, Or.fr.57 in Jo.*(p.531.8); Cyr.*Am.*58(3.314E).

ἡλάριον, τό, *small nail,* Dor.*doct.*14.4(M.88.1781A).

***ἠλαττωμένως**, *by way of diminution, so as to disparage,* Epiph. *haer.*69.17(p.166.17; M.42.228A); *ib.*76.16(p.362.8; 548C).

ἠλεκάτη, ἡ, *distaff,* ‡Sophr.H.*v.Mar.Aeg.*20(M.87.3712B).

***ἠλεκτροειδής**, *of amber,* Ammon.*Ac.*7:55(M.85.1529C).

ἤλεκτρον, τό, **1.** *amber;* as symbol of spiritual perfection, ref. Ezech.1:27, Or.*hom.11.5 in Jer.*(p.83.12ff.; M.13.373Cff.); or perh. **2.** *electrum, compound of gold and silver;* as symbol of Christ's humanity, compounded of body and soul, Thdt.*Ezech.*1:27(2.693).

ἡλιακός, *of the sun;* **1.** lit., of vision of burning bush as brighter than light of sun, Gr.Nyss.*v.Mos.*20(M.44.305C); of teachings of S. John τῶν ἡ. ἀκτίνων...φανερώτερα Chrys.*hom.2.3 in Jo.*(8.10C); of brightness of divine indwelling in soul compared with that of sun, *ib.*5.4(40B); ref. eastward posture for worship πρὸς τὸ ἡ. κλίμα...ὡς τιμιώτερον μέρος τῆς κτίσεως ‡Just.*qu.et resp.*118(M.6.1368B); **2.** fig. and met., of Christ τῆς ἡ. ἀκτῖνος Or.*exc.in Ps.*77:31(M.17.141B); as illuminating soul τὰς ἡ. Χριστοῦ ἀκτῖνας id.*Jo.*1.25(24; p.31.26; M.14.69A); of voice of Spouse καθάπερ τις κύκλος ἡ. Gr.Nyss.*hom.3 in Cant.*(M.44.808D); of grace of H. Ghost not diminished when imparted to many καθάπερ αἱ ἡ. ἀκτῖνες Chrys. *hom.36.1 in Jo.*(8.208A); ref. a holy monk ποία ἀκτὶς ἡ. ... ὡς ὁ ἡμέτερος πατὴρ...τὰς καρδίας κατέλαμψεν; Jo.Mosch.*prat.*109(M.87.2972D); **3.** σαύρα ἡ. a kind of lizard; met., of Sampsaean heresy, Epiph.*haer.*53.2(p.316.13; M.41.961A); **4.** masc. as subst., a heretical sect, translation of Σαμψαῖοι, *ib.*(p.316.17; l.c.); **5.** neut. as subst.; *place exposed to the sun,* Eustrat.*v.Eutych.*24(M.86.2301B); Polychr.Mon.*exp.fid.*(H.3.1376B); Steph.Diac.*v.Steph.*(M.100.1156D).

***Ἠλίας** (*Ἡ-), ὁ, *Elijah;* **1.** in gen.; **a.** non-scriptural sources of information, *in nullo...regulari libro...nisi in secretis Eliae prophetae,* Or.*comm.ser.117 in Mt.*(p.250.5; M.13.1769C); ‡Ath.*synops.*75(M.28.432B); βιβλία ἀπόκρυφα...Ἠ. *Const.App.*6.16.2; story of portent before his birth, ‡Epiph.*v.proph.*5(p.32; M.43.396C); **b.** titles: man of God οὐ πάντες μὲν ἄνθρωποι χρηματίζουσιν ἄνθρωποι θεοῦ, μόνοι δὲ οἱ ἄξιοι τοῦ θεοῦ· ὁποῖος ἦν Μωυσῆς καὶ Ἠ. Or.*Cels.*8.25(p.241.28; M.11.1553C); τὸν τῶν προφητῶν πανάριστον· Ἠ. ... οὗτος ἦν Cyr. *hom.div.*9(5².368C); **c.** with epithet μέγας, Eus.*Marcell.*1.2(p.11.6; M.24.737A); Ath.*fug.*10(p.75.18; M.25.657B); Chrys.*hom.2.4 in Rom.16:3*(3.187D); Thdt.*qu.52 in 3Reg.*(1.498); Bas.Sel.*or.*11.1(M.85.148A); Cosm.Ind.*top.*5(M.88.260A); Max.*or.dom.*(M.90.888D); Andr. Cr.*or.*15(M.97.1113B); **d.** as inspired by H. Ghost, Ath.*fug.*17(p.79.31; M.25.665B); *ib.*18(p.81.3; 668B); περὶ...Ἠ. ... καὶ Ἐλισσαίου, τῶν πνευματοφόρων καὶ θαυματοποιῶν, φανερὸν κἂν μὴ λέγωμεν, ὅτι πλήρεις ἦσαν ἁγίου πνεύματος Cyr.H.*catech.*16.28; Anast.S.*qu.et resp.*47(M.89.601D); **e.** as living μετὰ λόγου and hence a Christian, Just.*1apol.*46.3(M.6.397C); **2.** in relation to Jo. Bapt.; **a.** reincarnation asserted by believers in transmigration of souls, Or.*Jo.*6.10(7; p.119.24; M.14.220A); rejected οὐ γὰρ ἐν ψυχῇ Ἠ. φησίν—οὐ γὰρ ἦν μετεμψύχωσις—ἀλλ' ἐν πνεύματι καὶ δυνάμει Ἠ. id.*hom.4 in Lc.*(p.29.8); *ib.*(pp.29.17,30.6); ἐν τούτοις Ἠ. οὐχ ἡ ψυχὴ...δόκει μοι λέγεσθαι, ἵνα μὴ ἐμπίπτω εἰς τὸ ἀλλότριον τῆς ἐκκλησίας τοῦ θεοῦ περὶ τῆς μετενσωματώσεως δόγμα id.*comm.in Mt.*13.1(p.172.27; M.13.1088A); 'καὶ προφήτην μὲν καὶ Ἠ. ὁ σωτὴρ ἐπὰν αὐτὸν λέγῃ, οὐκ αὐτὸν ἀλλὰ τὰ περὶ αὐτόν,' φησι [sc. Heracleon], 'διδάσκει' id.*Jo.*6.20 (12; p.129.30; M.14.236C); **b.** having same χαρίσματα, id.*comm.in Mt.*13.2(p.178.31; 1093A); *ib.*10.20(p.28.3; 888B); id.*hom.4 in Lc.*(p.29.11); ref. Is.35:2 ἐπειδὴ γὰρ Ἠ. μὲν ᾤκει τὸν Κάρμηλον,...ὁ δέ γε Ἰωάννης ὁ βαπτιστὴς ἐν τῷ πνεύματι Ἠ. διαλάμπων, τὸν Ἰορδάνην ἡγίαζε· διὰ τοῦτο ὁ προφήτης ἐθέσπιζε, τὴν τιμὴν τοῦ Καρμήλου τῷ ποταμῷ δοθήσεσθαι Gr.Nyss.*bapt.Chr.*(M.46.593C); κατὰ τὸν τρόπον τῆς διακονίας Ἰωάννην Ἠ. καλεῖ...ὥσπερ γὰρ ἐκεῖνος τῆς δευτέρας ἔσται παρουσίας, οὕτως οὗτος τῆς προτέρας ἐγένετο πρόδρομος Chrys.*hom.57.1 in Mt.*(7.577A); both possessing H. Ghost τὸ ἐν Ἠ. γενόμενον πνεῦμα τοῦ θεοῦ, ἐν Ἰωάννῃ Just.*dial.*49.3(M.6.584B); τοῦ τὸν ζῆλον Ἠ. κατὰ τὴν κοινωνίαν τοῦ ἁγίου πνεύματος ἔχοντος Ἰωάννου Or.*Jo.*6.22(13; p.132.18; M.14.240C); cf.*ib.*6.11(7; p.120.14ff.; 220C); **3.** at Transfiguration; **a.** representing prophets Μωυσῆς μὲν τοῦ νόμου τὸ πρόσωπον δηλῶν, Ἠ. δὲ τῶν προφητῶν Or.*fr.22 in Lc.*(p.243); *Const.App.*6.19.4; Anast.Ant.*serm.*1.5(M.89.1369A); **b.** his presence showing that Christ was not Elijah, Chrys.*hom.56.1 in Mt.*(7.566C); Cyr.*hom.div.*9(5^{2}.368B); Bas.Sel.*or.*40.3(M.85.457C); **c.** as a valid witness to Christ, having seen God (ref. 3Reg.19:13) ἀλλὰ καὶ μάρτυρας δύο παρέχομεν, τοὺς ἐν ὄρει Σινᾶ τῷ κυρίῳ παραστάντας· Μωσῆς ἦν ἐν ὀπῇ τῆς πέτρας, καὶ Ἠ. Cyr.H.*catech.*12.16; ref. 3Reg.19:32 Ἠ. τε ἀντέφησεν· οὗτός ἐστιν, ὃν ὡς ἐν λεπτῇ αὔρᾳ τῷ πνεύματι ἀσωμάτον τὸ πάλαι τεθέαμαι Jo.D.*hom.*1.15(M.96.568D); **d.** his presence refuting Jewish accusation against Christ of blasphemy Ἠ. ... ὑπὲρ τῆς δόξης τοῦ θεοῦ ἐζήλωσε, καὶ οὐκ ἄν, εἰ ἀντίθεος ἦν, καὶ θεὸν ἑαυτὸν ἔλεγεν...μὴ ὢν ὅπερ ἔλεγε, μηδὲ προσηκόντως τοῦτο ποιῶν, παρέστη καὶ αὐτὸς καὶ ὑπήκουσεν Chrys.*hom.56.1 in Mt.*(7.566E); **e.** as preparing apostles for Passion, etc.; Christ speaking of Passion to Elijah, who has himself suffered from Jews, Chrys.*hom.56.2 in Mt.*(7.566E); Tim.Ant.*cruc.*(M.86.261B); Jo.D.*hom.*1.14 (M.96.568A); **f.** as helping to show extent of Christ's power ἵνα μάθωσιν ὅτι καὶ θανάτου καὶ ζωῆς ἐξουσίαν ἔχει...τὸν τετελευτηκότα, καὶ τὸν οὐδέπω τοῦτο παθόντα εἰς μέσον ἄγει Chrys.*hom.56.2 in Mt.*(7.567A); Cyr.*hom.div.*9(5^{2}.369A); *ib.*(368B); ref. Phil.2:10 ἐκ τῶν καταχθονίων ἀνήγαγεν τὸν Μωυσῆν, ἐκ τῶν ἐπουρανίων κατήγαγεν τὸν Ἠ., ἐκ τῶν ἐπιγείων παρέστησεν Πέτρον, καὶ Ἰάκωβον, καὶ Ἰωάννην Tim.Ant.*cruc.*(M.86.261B); Jo.D.*carm.transfig.*(M.96.849C); id.*hom.*1.3,17(M.96.549C,572C); **g.** his vision of Christ in glory being a reward for faithful prophesying, Or.*Jo.*13.47(46; p.273.27; M.14.484A); **h.** recognized as Elijah because he appeared with his chariot, Tim.Ant.*cruc.*(M.86.261B); S. Peter thinking that if anyone attacks Christ, Elijah will rain fire on them, *ib.*(261D); **4.** assumption; **a.** expression of 4Reg.2:1, ὡς εἰς τὸν οὐρανόν, taken to distinguish his ascension from Christ's, Or.*fr.75 in Jo.*(p.542.19); Cyr.H.*catech.*14.25; οὔτε Ἠ., οὔτε ἕτερός τις ἀνέβη εἰς τὸν οὐρανόν, εἰ μὴ μόνος...ὁ...τοῦ θεοῦ υἱός ‡Epiph.*hom.*4(M.43.481B); Chrys.*ascens.*5(2.455B); ‡Chrys.*ascens.*1(3.777B); Bas.Sel.*ascens.*4(M.28.1097B); Thdt.*Ps.*23:7(1.755); but contrast ὁ...ἀὴρ τὸν Ἠ. εἰς οὐρανὸν ἀνεκόμισεν Adam.*dial.*5.18(p.212.10; M.11.1857C); πρὸς οὐρανόν Gr.Naz.*or.*28.19(p.50.3; M.36.49C); εἰς τὸν οὐρανόν ‡Chrys.*circ.*(8.88A); some authors using both kinds of expression; not in heaven, Chrys.*ascens.*5(2.455B); εἰς τὸν οὐρανόν id.*stat.*1.9(2.34A); ὡς εἰς οὐρανούς,... πρὸς τὸν οὐρανόν ‡Chrys.*El.*(6.603C); ὡς... Cosm.Ind.*top.*5(M.88.260C); τὸν οὐρανὸν ἀθρόον διατρέχων *ib.*(260B); **b.** assumption being to paradise, whence Adam was driven, Iren.*haer.*5.5.1(M.7.1135A, B); but Ἠ. εἰς οὐρανὸν μόνον· Παῦλος δὲ καὶ εἰς οὐρανόν, καὶ εἰς παράδεισον Cyr.H.*catech.*14.26; **c.** in the flesh, Iren.*haer.*5.5.1(M.7.1134B); miraculous preservation of Jonah and of the three children as instances to prove its possibility, *ib.*5.5.2(1135Cff.); Chrys.*hom.75.5 in Jo.*(8.445D); **d.** as ground of hope for resurrection of body, *ib.*5.5.1(1134B); Bas.Sel.*ascens.*3(M.28.1096D); ὅτι, εἰ ἐβούλετο [sc. Christ] πάντας ἀνθρώπους εἶναι ἀθανάτους, ἠδύνατο, ἔδειξεν τὸν Ἐνὼχ καὶ τὸν Ἠ. μὴ ἐάσας θανάτου πεῖραν λαβεῖν *Const.App.*5.7.8; ἔχεις...εἰκόνα τῆς ἀναστάσεως· λέγω τὴν Ἠλίου ἁρπαγήν Chrys.*exp.in Ps.*117:17(5.323D); ‡Nil.*fr.ascens.*3(M.79.1501A); Cosm.Ind.*top.*5(M.88.260C); *Chron.Pasch.*p.146(M.92.361A); **e.** as type of Ascension, Or.*hom.4 in Lc.*(p.29.21); Bas.Sel.*ascens.*3(M.28.1097B); making assumption of BMV credible, Andr.Cr.*or.*13(M.97.1081A); **5.** at parousia; **a.** assertion of his presence often based on Mal.4, Just.*dial.*49.2(M.6.581B); Hipp.*antichr.*46(p.29.16; M.10.764C); †Gr.Nyss.*test.*17(M.46.229B); Thdr.Mops.*Mal.*4:5(M.66.632B); τοῦ ἀντιχρίστου ἐκεῖνα τολμῶντος, φανήσεται ὁ μέγας Ἠ., κηρύττων Ἰουδαίοις τὴν τοῦ κυρίου παρουσίαν, καὶ πολλοὺς ἐπιστρέψει Thdt.*Dan.*12:1(2.1294); Cosm.Ind.*top.*5(M.88.273C); **b.** on other texts, or asserted without biblical reference, Hipp.*antichr.*43(p.27.25; 761A); id.*Dan.*4.35.3(M.10.656D); Ephr.3.141F; ref. Mt.17:11, Chrys.*hom.57.1 in Mt.*(7.577A); id.*hom.9.2 in 1Thess.*(11.488C); Rom.11:26–27, Thdt.*Ps.*105:47(1.1364); Cosm.Ind.*top.*5(260B); *ib.*(229D); ὁ θεολόγος Ἰωάννης...ἔδειξεν ὡς Ἠ. ἐλεύσεται Rom.Mel.(*SBBAW* 1898^{2} p.167); destruction by antichrist, *1Apoc.Jo.*8(p.76); Andr.Caes.*Apoc.*30 (M.106.313B); death and resurrection ἐγώ εἰμι Ἐνώχ...καὶ οὗτός ἐστιν Ἠ. ... μέλλομεν ἀποσταλῆναι παρὰ θεοῦ ἐπὶ τῷ ἀντιστῆναι τῷ ἀντιχρίστῳ καὶ ἀποκτανθῆναι παρ' αὐτοῦ, καὶ μετὰ τρεῖς ἡμέρας ἀναστῆναι καὶ ἐν νεφέλαις ἁρπαγῆναι πρὸς τὴν τοῦ κυρίου ὑπάντησιν *A.Pil.*B 25(p.331); cf.Tert.*de anima* 50(M.*PL.*2.735A); **c.** corresponding to Jo. Bapt. in first advent, ‡Hipp.*consumm.*21(p.297.9; M.10.921C); Chrys.*hom.57.1 in Mt.*(7.575E); τῆς δὲ προτέρας ἐλεύσεως τοῦ θεοῦ ἡμῶν Ἰωάννης προέδραμεν, κηρύττων πᾶσιν μετάνοιαν· πρόδρομος Ἠ. τῆς δευτέρας ἐλεύσεται παρουσίας ὁ δίκαιος Rom.Mel.(*SBBAW* 1898^{2} p.166); **d.** opinion of Origen; **i.** traditional view cited ὁ Ἰωάννης...ὡς πρόδρομος γεγονὼς τῆς πρώτης τοῦ Χριστοῦ παρουσίας, ὡς καὶ ὁ Θεσβίτης τῆς δευτέρας Or.*hom.4 in Lc.*(p.28.17); **ii.** not Elijah but Jo. Bapt. will precede Christ (cf. Mal.3:22ff.), id.*comm.in Mt.*13.2(p.182.16ff.; M.13.1096Bff.); id.*Jo.*2.37 (30; p.97.9; M.14.184A); **e.** accompanied by angels, Chrys.*hom.56.4 in Mt.*(7.571B); Thdt.*Dan.*12:1(2.1295); and Enoch, Cosm.Ind.*top.*5(M.88.229D); Rom.Mel.(*SBBAW* 1898^{2} p.167); ὀλίγοι οἱ μέλλοντες στῆναι. διὰ τοῦτο Ἠ. καὶ Ἐνώχ. οὐκ οἴδαμεν εἰ καὶ ὁ θεολόγος καὶ εὐαγγελιστής, ἀρωγοὶ τῆς ἀνθρωπίνης ἀσθενείας Thdr.Stud.*epp.*1.36(M.99.1033B); **f.** not sent before Passion ὅτι καὶ νῦν Χριστὸν νομίζοντες Ἠ. εἶναι, οὐκ ἐπίστευον αὐτῷ Chrys.*hom.57.2 in Mt.*(7.577E); **6.** according to Jews, has yet to come as forerunner of Messiah, to anoint him, Just.*dial.*8.3(M.6.493B); *ib.*49.1(581B); Heracleon agrees with them that Elijah will baptize before coming of Messiah (cf. Jo.1:25), Or.*Jo.*6.23(13; p.134.2ff.; M.14.241D); οὐκ οἶδα πόθεν κινούμενοι οἱ Ἑβραῖοι παραδιδόασι Φινεές...αὐτὸν εἶναι Ἠ. καὶ τὸ ἀθάνατον ἐν τοῖς Ἀριθμοῖς αὐτῷ διὰ τῆς ὀνομαζομένης εἰρήνης ἐπηγγέλθαι *ib.*6.14(7; p.123.20; 225B); δύο...ἥξειν προσδοκωμένων, τοῦ τε κατὰ τὸν νόμον προφήτου φημί, τουτέστι Χριστοῦ, καὶ Ἠλίου Cyr.*Jo.*5.2(4.476D); **7.** considerations arising out of his life; **a.** goodness of nature shown by feeding by ravens, Clem.*str.*3.6(p.220.4; M.8.1156A); ref. Transfiguration τὸν ζῶντα νόμον τῆς φύσεως, τὸν διὰ τοῦ ζῶντος προφήτου δηλούμενον Andr.Cr.*or.*7(M.97.952B); *ib.*(953C); **b.** relation of OT and NT ἔδειξε...πᾶσαν προφητείαν, οὐδὲ μετὰ τὸ ἐνανθρωπῆσαι ἀποθνήσκουσαν ἀλλ' ἀναλαμβανομένην εἰς οὐρανόν, ἧς σύμβολον Ἠ. ἦν Or.*Cels.*6.68(p.138.23; M.11.1401C); cf.id.*comm.in Mt.*12.38(p.155.23; M.13.1072A); Μωσῆς νομοθέτης...καὶ Ἠ. ὁ ζηλωτὴς τῶν προφητῶν συνῆσαν...ὡς φίλοι Χριστοῦ καὶ οἰκεῖοι, ἀλλ' οὐχ ὡς ἐχθροὶ ἢ ἀλλότριοι· ἐξ ὧν δείκνυται, ὅτι καὶ ὁ νόμος καλὸς καὶ ἅγιος καὶ οἱ προφῆται *Const.App.*6.19.4; **c.** possibility of resurrection proved by raising of widow's son, Or.*Cels.*2.57(p.181.8ff.; M.11.888B); Eus.*Marcell.*1.2(p.11.6; M.24.737A); *Const.App.*5.7.8; **d.** feeding by ravens indicates that unworthiness of minister does not invalidate sacraments, Isid.Pel.*epp.*2.37(M.78.481A); **e.** wonders done by his mantle a sign of virtue of relics, Chrys.*stat.*8.2(2.93Af.); **8.** typology; **a.** calling of gentiles signified by mission to widow, Chrys.*El.et vid.*5(3.331D); Proc.G.*3Reg.*17:9(M.87.1169A); **b.** crossing of river as type of baptism, Or.*Jo.*6.46(27; p.155.9ff.; M.14.280B); **c.** sacrifice on Mt. Carmel as type of faith in Trin., Gr.Nyss.*bapt.Chr.*(M.46.592A); *Rit.Epiph.*(p.415); and of baptism, Bas.*hom.*13.3(2.115E; M.31.428D); **d.** as illustration of spiritual life, 3Reg.19:11,12 referred to mystical knowledge of God τάχα...ἐν ὅσοις δεήσει γίνεσθαι πῦρ τῆς καταλήψεως τοῦ κυρίου δηλοῦται διὰ τούτων Or.*Jo.*13.24(p.248.16; M.14.440B); Ἠ. ... κεκλεισμένον...τὸν οὐρανὸν...ἀνοίγει· ὅπερ παντί τῳ κατορθοῦται ἀεί, διὰ τῆς εὐχῆς λαμβάνοντι τὸν ὑετὸν τῆς ψυχῆς, τῶν διὰ τὴν ἁμαρτίαν πρότερον αὐτοῦ ἐστερημένων id.*or.*13(p.330.2; M.11.460A); Gr.Nyss.*engast.*(p.67.28; M.45.113A); **e.** assumption compared with circus performance as figure of spiritual combat, ‡Chrys.*circ.*(8.88A); gift of mantle to Elisha signifies gift of divine grace in conversion of sinners, Nil.*epp.*2.241 (M.79.325A); miraculous gift of food teaches men not to be solicitous about things of the body, ‡Nil.*perist.*11.17(M.79.928ff.); ref. 3Reg.17:9 πᾶσα...ψυχὴ χηρεύουσά τε καλῶν καὶ ἀρετῆς ἔρημος καὶ γνώσεως θεοῦ, ἐπειδὰν τὸν θεῖον καὶ διαγνωστικὸν ὑποδέξεται λόγον Max.*ambig.*(M.91.1125C); ref. his experience of God μετὰ τὸ πῦρ ἐκεῖνο, μετὰ τὸν συσσεισμόν, μετὰ τὸ μέγα καὶ κραταιὸν πνεῦμα..., ἃ δὴ ζῆλον καὶ διάκρισιν εἶναι καὶ τὴν ἐν πληροφορίᾳ πρόθυμον πίστιν ὑπολαμβάνω *ib.*(1121C); πᾶς οὖν κατὰ τὸν μέγαν Ἠ. ζητῶν ἀληθῶς τὸν θεόν, οὐ μόνον ἐν Χωρὴβ γενήσεται· τουτέστιν, ὡς πρακτικὸς ἐν τῇ ἕξει τῶν ἀρετῶν· ἀλλὰ καὶ ἐν τῷ σπηλαίῳ τῷ ἐν Χωρήβ· τουτέστιν, ὡς θεωρητικὸς ἐν τῇ κρυφιότητι τῆς σοφίας τῇ ἐν μόνῃ τυγχανούσῃ τῇ ἕξει τῶν ἀρετῶν id.*cap.theol.*174(M.90.1160A); gift of mantle signifies mortification of flesh: the horses, virtues, id.*or.dom.*(M.90.889A).

ἡλικία, ἡ, 1. *age*, of eternal life τὰς διαφόρους...ἡ. ἐκβάλλει Thdt.*Is.*65:20(p.255.35; 2.396); met., of Christians opp. Jews ὡς τέλειοι τὴν ἡ. ἀκούομεν κολάσεων χαλεπωτέρων Or.*hom.18.15 in Jer.*(p.175.3; M.13.497B); **2.** *youth* μὴ συγχρᾶσθαι τῇ ἡ. τοῦ ἐπισκόπου Ign.*Magn.*3.1; *M.Polyc.*3; met., of Adam before Fall νεάζων τὴν πνευματικὴν ἡ. ‡Proc.G.*Pr.*2:17(M.87.1237D).

***ἡλικιότης, ἡ,** *mature age*, *Ev.Thom.*A 14(p.152).

ἡλικιώτης, ὁ, 1. *one who is of the same age* ἐν τῷ ἴσῳ χρόνῳ, ἡλικιώτην τοῖς ἀγγέλοις συντάσσει [sc. Valentinus]...τὸ πνεῦμα Ath.*ep.Serap.*1.11(M.26.557B); Didym.*Trin.*2.6(M.39.548B); as adj. οἱ ἡ. αὐτοῦ [sc. τοῦ παρακλήτου] ἄγγελοι Ath.*ep.Serap.*1.10(557A); **2.** perh. *old*, Pall.*h.Laus.*22(p.71.15; M.34.1081C).

ἧλιξ, 1. *equal in duration* to; c. genit., Nonn.*par.Jo.*3:5(M.43.765C); **2.** subst., *adult*, Mac.Mgn.*apocr.*3.8(p.67.11); met., *one who is mature in spirit* τοὺς ἀρτιτόκους ἐκτρέφουσα [sc. σοφία] ἥλικας ἀπεργάζεται καὶ μαθητὰς οὐρανίου βασιλείας ἀποτελεῖ *ib.*3.23(p.104.32).

ἡλιοβολ-έω, *emit* as rays of the sun, of Christ indwelling the soul ὡς ἥλιος...δικαιοσύνην ∼ῶν Hesych.S.*temp.*2.64(M.93.1532D).

***ἡλιοβολία, ἡ,** *effusion of the rays of the sun*; met., of divine illumination, Nil.*epp.*3.283(M.79.524C); Dion.Ar.*c.h.*15.8(M.3.337A).

***ἡλιογνῶσται, οἱ,** *sun-worshippers* ἀνατείλαντος τοῦ ἡλίου, προσεύχονται καὶ λέγουσιν, ἐλέησον ἡμᾶς. οὐ μόνον ἡ. καὶ αἱρετικοὶ τοῦτο ποιοῦσιν ἀλλὰ καὶ Χριστιανοί...ἀφέντες τὴν πίστιν Eus.Al.*serm.*22.2(M.86.453D).

ἡλιοειδής, *sunlike*; of garments of Christ at Transfiguration, Gr.Nyss.*hom.11 in Cant.*(M.44.1005C).

***ἡλιοειδῶς,** *like the sun*, Nil.*epp.*3.90(M.79.428C); Dion.Ar.*e.h.*3.3.14(M.3.445A); Melet.*nat.hom.*2(M.64.1169D).

***ἡλιολάτρης, ὁ,** *sun-worshipper*, Geo.Al.*v.Chrys.*59(p.235.42).

ἡλιόμορφος, *shining like the sun*, *T.Abr.*A 7(p.84.5); *ib.*13(p.92.1); *ib.*16(p.97.9); of eternal life τῆς ἡ. στολῆς opp. dark garment of hell, Ephr.3.511F.

***ἡλιόπεμπτος,** *sent by the sun*, *Orac.Sib.*13.151; *ib.*13.164.

***ἡλιόρατος,** *resembling the sun* ἀνὴρ θαύμαστος ἡλιόρατος ὅμοιος υἱῷ θεοῦ *T.Abr.*A 12(p.90.23).

ἥλιος, ὁ, *sun*;

A. lit.; **1.** question whether animated ἀρχοντικὸς ἄγγελος ἐν ἡ. Clem.*ecl.*56(p.153.12; M.9.725A); Or.*hom.10.6 in Jer.*(p.76.22; M.13.365A); πειθόμενοι...ἡ. καὶ σελήνην καὶ ἀστέρας εὔχεσθαι τῷ...θεῷ διὰ τοῦ μονογενοῦς αὐτοῦ id.*Cels.*5.11(p.12.11; M.11.1197B); ἡ. ... οὐκ ἔμψυχος ὤν, οὐδὲ λόγῳ χρώμενος Thdt.*Ps.*103:19(1.1337); cf.*ib.*148:3(1577); **2.** not divine; arguments from reason οἱ...νομίζοντες τὸν ἡ. εἶναι θεὸν πλανῶνται. ὁρῶμεν γὰρ αὐτὸν κινούμενον κατὰ ἀνάγκην Arist.*apol.*6.1,2(M.96.1112A); sun is a part only of universe, Ath.*gent.*27(M.25.53B,C); regularity of its motions argues a creator, *ib.*37(73B); τὸν...ἡ. ἂν αἰσθητὸν ὡς σῶμα καὶ γενητόν· ᾧ ἕπεται τὸ φθαρτὸν εἶναι τοῦτον Zach.Mit.*opif.*(M.85.1049B); sun obeys necessity, Sophr.H.*v.Anast.*(M.92.1705A); ἐκλείπει...ὁ ἡ. καὶ ἡ σελήνη,... ὡς τρεπτά εἰσι καὶ ἀλλοιωτά. πᾶν δὲ τρεπτόν, οὐ θεός Jo.D.*f.o.*2.7(M.94.896B); arguments from scripture and Christian doctrine, Clem.*prot.*4(p.48.23; M.8.164B); οὐδ' αὐτὸς [sc. God] γ' ἂν θέλοι ὁ ἡ. προσκυνεῖσθαι Or.*mart.*7(p.9.3; M.11.573A); divinity disproved by fact of its creation, Chrys.*hom.6.4 in Gen.*(4.44Aff.); argument against Julian, ‡Jo.D.*Artem.*47(p.165.5; M.96.1296B); ref. orientation of tabernacle οἱ τῷ θεῷ μόνῳ λατρεύειν προστεταγμένοι ὄπισθεν τὸν ἡ. ἔχωσι πρὸς τὴν σκηνὴν τετραμμένοι, καὶ μὴ τοῦτον, ἀλλὰ τὸν τούτου ποιητὴν προσκυνῶσι Thdt.*qu.60 in Ex.*(1.165); worship forbidden, Olymp.*Job* 31:27–28(M.93.332B); ref. creation on fourth day ἡ. δὲ οὔπω ἦν..., ἵνα μήτε φωτὸς ἀρχηγὸν καὶ πατέρα τὸν ἡ. ὀνομάσωσι, μήτε τῶν ἐκ τῆς γῆς φυομένων δημιουργὸν οἱ τὸν θεὸν ἀγνοήσαντες ἡγήσωνται Bas.*hex.*6.2(1.51A; M.29.120C); *ib.*5.1(40C; M.96A); Sever.*creat.*3.2(M.56.448f.); cf.Eus.*Ps.*103:19(M.23.1280B); worship allowed to gentiles in OT, ref. Dt.4:19 ἔδωκεν δὲ [sc. ὁ θεός] τὸν ἡ. ... εἰς θρησκείαν ...ἵνα μὴ τέλεον ἄθεοι γενόμενοι τελέως διαφθαρῶσιν Clem.*str.*6.14(p.487.13; M.9.333A); **3.** eclipse at Crucifixion witnessing to divinity of Christ, Ath.*inc.*19.3(M.25.129B); Cyr.H.*catech.*4.10; Gr.Naz.*or.*45.29(M.36.661D); Sever.*creat.*3.7(M.56.455); said to be referred to in other texts: Joel 2:31, Thdr.Mops.ad loc.(M.66.232D); Amos 8:9, Zach.14:6,7, Jo.D.*hom.*4.26(M.96.625C,D); Apoc.6:12, Areth.*Apoc.*18(M.106.597B); **4.** in eschatology; **a.** in gen., ref. times of antichrist πενθεῖ...ὁ ἡ. ‡Hipp.*consumm.*33(p.302.38; M.10.936C); Joel 2:31 referred to second coming, Bas.*hex.*6.4(1.53E; M.29.125D); Thdt.*Joel* 2:31(2.1399); eclipse of Apoc.8:12 prophesied by Joel, Andr.Caes.*Apoc.*25(M.106.293D); τὸ δὲ μέλαν τοῦ ἡ. ... τὸ τοῖς καταλειφθεῖσιν ὑπὸ τῆς θείας ὀργῆς ἀφώτιστον ἐνδείκνυται. οὕτω γὰρ πολλάκις καὶ ὁ μακάριος Κύριλλος ἐξήλειφε Areth.*Apoc.*18(M.106.600A); **b.** question whether eclipse at second coming will be real or figurative, ref. Mt.24:30 εἴ γε ἐκεῖνος μὲν σκοτίζεται..., οὗτος δὲ φαίνεται· οὐκ ἂν φανείς, εἰ μὴ πολλῷ τῶν ἡλιακῶν ἀκτίνων φαιδρότερος ἦν Chrys.*hom.76.3 in Mt.*(7.736B); cf.‡Hipp.*consumm.*36(p.303.39; M.10.940A); ref. Mt.24:29 ὁ ἡ. σκοτισθήσεται, οὐκ ἀφανιζόμενος, ἀλλὰ νικώμενος τῷ φωτὶ τῆς παρουσίας αὐτοῦ Chrys.*hom.76.3 in Mt.*(7.735E); in gen., Eus.*fr.Lc.*21:25(M.24.596B); *ib.*21:28(600B); ὁ...ἡ. καὶ ἡ σελήνη ἀμαυρωθήσονται·...τοῦ δημιουργήσαντος αὐτὰ πάλιν μεταστοιχειοῦντος...ἀνακαινιζομένης γὰρ τῆς ἀνθρωπότητος...συνανακτίζεται καὶ ἡ διὰ τὸν ἄνθρωπον δημιουργηθεῖσα κτίσις Cyr.*fr.Mt.*24:29(M.72.441B); **5.** moral and allegorical applications: its undeviating course an example of obedience, Eus.*Ps.*18:6(M.23.192B); sign of eternity because source of night and day, Thdt.*Ps.*88:37(1.1243); ref. Ps.18:5 ἡλίου...ἐπαινεῖται παρὰ τῷ Δαβὶδ κάλλος, καὶ μέγεθος, καὶ δρόμου τάχος, καὶ δύναμις·...τοῦ δὲ κάλλος μέν, ἡ ἀρετή· μέγεθος δέ, ἡ θεολογία· δρόμος δέ, τὸ ἀεικίνητον, καὶ μέχρι θεοῦ φέρον ταῖς ἀναβάσεσι· δύναμις δέ, ἡ τοῦ λόγου σπορὰ καὶ διάδοσις Gr.Naz.*or.*43.66(M.36.584C); ref. Cant.1:5 πειρασμὸν...διὰ τῆς ἑρμηνείας ὀνομάζει τὸν ἡ. Gr.Nyss.*hom.2 in Cant.*(M.44.793B); cf.Andr.Caes.*Apoc.*20(M.106.285B); Areth.*Apoc.*20(M.106.612A); **6.** heret.; **a.** Hermogenes τὸ σῶμα τοῦ κυρίου ἐν τῷ ἡ. αὐτὸν ἀποτίθεσθαι Clem.*ecl.*56(p.152.26; M.9.724C); **b.** Valentinians φησὶν ὁ Πυθαγόρειος λόγος δημιουργὸν... εἶναι τῶν γενομένων πάντων...τὸν μέγαν γεωμέτρην καὶ ἀριθμητὴν ἡ. καὶ ἐστηρίχθαι τοῦτον ἐν ὅλῳ τῷ κόσμῳ, καθάπερ ἐν τοῖς σώμασι ψυχήν Hipp.*haer.*6.28(p.154.16; M.16.3234D); **c.** Manich., ref. soul of world πέμπει καὶ συλᾷ ἀπ' αὐτῶν [sc. τῶν ἀρχόντων] τὴν ψυχὴν αὐτοῦ καθ' ἡμέραν διὰ τῶν φωστήρων τούτων, ἡ. καὶ σελήνης, ὑφ' ὧν ὅλος ὁ κόσμος καὶ πᾶσα ἡ κτίσις ἁρπάζεται Hegem.*Arch.*12(p.20.11; M.10.1448B); carries souls to eternal life, Epiph.*haer.*66.10(p.30.20; M.42.44B); ref. Joel 2:31 μηδὲ τὸν σκοτισθησόμενον τοῦτον ἡ., τὸν Χριστὸν εἶναι δυσσεβῶς νομιζέτωσαν Cyr.H.*catech.*15.3; ref. identification of sun with Christ τούτου τεκμήριον ἱκανὸν παρέχουσι τὸ τὸν ἡ. ἐκλείπειν ἐν τῷ τοῦ σταυροῦ καιρῷ Thdt.*haer.*1.26(4.320); **d.** ἡλιοτροπῖται, Jo.D.*haer.*89(M.94.757A) cit. s. ἡλιοτροπῖται.

B. met. and fig.; **1.** of God, *Barn.*5.10; ὡς πηλὸς ὑπὸ ἡ. σκληρύνεται, οὕτως ὑπὸ τῶν αὐγῶν τοῦ θεοῦ ἐπισκοπουσῶν τὸν Ἰσραὴλ ἐσκληρύνθη [sc. ἡ καρδία Φαραώ] Or.*Cant.*2(p.128.31; M.13.113B); τοῦτο ἐν αἰσθητοῖς ἡ., ὅπερ ἐν νοητοῖς θεός, ἔφη τις τῶν ἀλλοτρίων [sc. Plato]. αὐτὸς γὰρ ὄψιν φωτίζων, ὥσπερ ἐκεῖνος νοῦν Gr.Naz.*or.*28.30(p.68.8; M.36.69A); εἰ ὁ τῇ φθορᾷ ὑποκείμενος ἡ. οὕτω καλὸς...ποταπὸς τῷ κάλλει ὁ τῆς δικαιοσύνης ἡ.; Bas.*hex.*6.1(1.50E; M.29.120B); τυφλοί...ὁ ἡ. τοὺς ἀμβλυωποῦντας...οὕτω καὶ οἱ ἄπιστοι...οὐ δύνανται ἐνιδεῖν ταῖς τῆς θεότητος ἀκτῖσιν Cyr.H.*catech.*6.29; God said to be the sun as being in it by essence, presence, and power, Dion.Ar.*d.n.*1.6(M.3.596C); diffusion of divine goodness like diffusion of sun's rays, *ib.*4.1(693B); sun an image of God as source of life, *ib.*4.4(697Cff.); and as drawing everything to itself, *ib.*(700B,C); ὁ ἡ. τῆς δόξης Gr.Agr.*Eccl.*1.3(M.98.757B); **2.** Trin., in gen. ὡς ἐκ τοῦ ἡ. μέν ἐστιν ἡ ἀκτίς... οὕτω τὸ συναφές τε καὶ ἀΐδιον τῆς ἐκ τοῦ πατρὸς ὑπάρξεως τοῦ μονογενοῦς παραδιδοὺς ὁ ἀπόστολος ἀπαύγασμα δόξης τὸν υἱὸν κατωνόμασε Gr.Nyss.*Eun.*8(2 p.180.18; M.45.773B); Anast.Ant.*fid.*(M.89.1404C); comparison inadequate, Gr.Naz.*or.*31.32(p.187.10; M.36.169B); as illustrating unity ὁ ἡ. καὶ ἡ θέρμη αὐτοῦ καὶ ἡ ἀκτὶς... τρία μὲν ὀνόματά εἰσι, μία δὲ οὐσία ἡλίου Hier.H.*Trin.*(M.40.852C); and consubstantiality ὡς...μένων ὁ ἡ. ὁ αὐτὸς οὐ μειοῦται ταῖς ἐκχεομέναις ὑπ' αὐτοῦ αὐγαῖς, οὕτως οὐδὲ ἡ οὐσία τοῦ πατρὸς ἀλλοίωσιν ὑπέμεινεν, εἰκόνα ἑαυτῆς ἔχουσα τὸν υἱόν Thgn.*hypot.fr.*2(p.76; M.10.240A); Ath.*hom.in Mt.11:27*(M.25.213D); Cyr.*Jo.*1.4(4.46C); Thdt.*haer.*5.2(4.386); and coeternity, Dion.Al.ap.Ath.*Dion.*15(p.57.7; M.25.501C); Cyr.*thes.*14(5^1.139E); ref. Heb.1:3 τὸ...ἀπαύγασμα τίκτεται...ἐξ ἡ., οὐδαμῶς...νοεῖται τοῦ ἡ. μεταγενέστερον·...τὸ οὖν συνυπάρχειν ἀεὶ τῷ πατρὶ τὸν υἱόν, μηνυέτω σοι τὸ ἀπαύγασμα Thdot.Anc.*hom.*2.6(p.77.6; M.77.1376D); Nil.*Magn.*63(M.79.1053B); and coequality, Cyr.H.*catech.*4.5; in anti-heret. argument οὐδὲ...τρεῖς ἀρχὰς ἢ τρεῖς πατέρας εἰσάγομεν, ὡς οἱ περὶ Μαρκίωνα καὶ Μανιχαῖον· ἐπεὶ μηδὲ τριῶν ἡ. ὑπεθέμεθα τὴν εἰκόνα, ἀλλὰ ἡ. καὶ ἀπαύγασμα, καὶ ἓν τὸ ἐξ ἡ. ἐν τῷ ἀπαυγάσματι φῶς Ath.*Ar.*3.15(M.26.352C); ref. Apollinarianism ὥσπερ...συγγενῶς ἔχει πρὸς τὸν ἡ. ἡ ἀκτίς...οὕτως... εἴπερ τὸ ἡμῖν φανὲν παρὰ τῆς δόξης τοῦ πατρὸς ἀπηυγάσθη, καὶ ὁ χαρακτὴρ αὐτοῦ τῆς ὑποστάσεως σάρξ ἐστι, σαρκώδης...καὶ ἡ τοῦ πατρὸς φύσις Gr.Nyss.*Apoll.*19(M.45.1160C); **3.** of Father ὁ νοητὸς ἥ. Or.*Jo.*6.55(37; p.164.19; M.14.297A); Evagr.Pont.*ep.*7(M.32.260B); Jo.D.*f.o.*1.12(M.94.848C); **4.** of Son; ref. Mal.4:2, Cyr.*Mal.*44(3.866D); Hesych.H.*fr.Ps.*103:19(M.93.1288C); Areth.*Apoc.*2(M.106.521B); as giving spiritual light, Clem.*prot.*12(p.84.20; M.8.240C); *ὁμοίως ἥ. ταῖς αὐγαῖς τῆς αὐτοῦ διδασκαλίας τὸν σύμπαντα καταλάμπων κόσμον* Eus.*Ps.*71:5(M.23.800A); Ath.*hom.in Mt.11:27*(M.25.220B); Mac.Aeg.*hom.*33.4(M.34.774B); Epiph.*anc.*45(p.56.4; M.43.97D); Cyr.*Is.*3.4(2.505E); as enduring for ever, Or.*hom.1.5 in Jos.*(p.293.29; M.87.1021A); Eus.*Ps.*71:5(800B); *συμπαραμενεῖ...τῷ ἥ. τῆς δικαιοσύνης, καὶ ἣν ἥνωσεν ἑαυτῷ σάρκα ἐμψυχωμένην ψυχῇ λογικῇ..., τὴν ἕνωσιν ἀδιαίρετον ἔχουσα* [sc. *σάρξ*] Didym.*Ps.*71:5(M.39.1465C); Thdt.*Ps.*71:5(1.1104); in other respects *ὅνπερ τρόπον...ὁ ἥ. ... πρὸς τοὺς μυχαιτάτους οἴκους ἀποστέλλει τὴν αὐγήν, οὕτως ὁ λόγος...τὰ σμικρότατα τῶν τοῦ βίου πράξεων ἐπιβλέπει* Clem.*str.*7.3(p.15.28; M.9.428A); *ὁ...τὰ πάντα καθιππεύων δικαιοσύνης ἥ. ... τὴν δύσιν εἰς ἀνατολὴν μετήγαγεν καὶ τὸν θάνατον εἰς ζωὴν ἀνεσταύρωσεν* id.*prot.*11(p.80.17; 232B); as being chief of spiritual world, Or.*Jo.*1.25(24; p.31.2; M.14.68B); of Messiah *οὗτος ἀναλάμψει ὡς ὁ ἥ. ἐν τῇ γῇ, καὶ ἐξαρεῖ πᾶν σκότος...ὑπ' οὐρανόν* *T.Lev.*18.4; *ib.*18.3; *T.Jud.*24.1; in Inc.; vanquishes darkness of idolatry, Ath.*inc.*55.3(M.25.193B); cf.*ib.*29.3(145B); bringing spiritual light, Chrys.*exp.in Ps.*111:4(5.281D); ‡Chrys.*transfig.*(10.774A); Cyr.*Is.*4.1(2.542C); Gr.Agr.*Eccl.*10.2(M.98.1140D); ref. his baptism *εἰ...ὁ ἥ. ... λούεται ἐν ὠκεανῷ, διὰ τί καὶ ὁ Χριστὸς ἐν Ἰορδάνῃ οὐ λούεται;...μόνος ἥ. οὗτος* Mel.*bapt.*4(p.311); Ps.18:6 referred to second coming, Clem.*ecl.*56(p.152.21ff.; M.9.724Bff.); ref. Jo.3:30 *τοῦ ἥ. φανερουμένου ὁ ἑωσφόρος ἐλαττοῦται* Or.*fr. 45 in Jo.*(p.521.6); ref. Jo.3:2 *οὐ γὰρ ἀνατετάλκει αὐτῷ ὁ τῆς δικαιοσύνης ἥ.* *ib.34*(p.509.27); ref. Resurrection *ὁ τῆς δικαιοσύνης τριήμερος ἥ. ἀνέτειλε* ‡Epiph.*hom.*3(M.43.465A); Hesych.H.*fr.Ps.*103:22(M.93.1289A); of Passion; likened to setting of sun, *ib.*103:19(1288C); ref. first and second comings, Thdt.*Mal.*4:2(2.1692); ref. Transfiguration *ὥσπερ ὁ ἥ. εἷς μέν ἐστιν, ἔχει δὲ οὐσίας δύο, τοῦ τε φωτὸς...καὶ τοῦ τῇ κτίσει ἐφυστερίζοντος σώματος...οὕτω καὶ ὁ Χριστός...εἷς ἐστιν ἥ. δικαιοσύνης...ἐν δύο ἀδιαιρέτως ταῖς φύσεσι γνωριζόμενος* Jo.D.*hom.*1.13(M.96.565A); in heaven, giving spiritual light to angels, Eus.*l.C.*6(p.211.27; M.20.1349C); and saints, Cyr.*Mal.*44(3.867D); in spiritual life *τὴν ταπεινὴν...τὴν τὸν ἥ. τῆς δικαιοσύνης ἐν τῇ καρδίᾳ ἔχουσαν* *A.Xanthipp.*8(p.63.10); *ὥσπερ...ἡ. φωτίζοντος ἀμαυροῦται τὸ δύνασθαι φωτίζειν σελήνην καὶ ἀστέρας, οὕτως οἱ ἐλλαμπόμενοι ὑπὸ Χριστοῦ...οὐδέν τινων διακονουμένων ἀποστόλων καὶ προφητῶν δέονται...οὐδὲ ἀγγέλων* Or.*Jo.*1.25(24; p.31.20; M.14.68D); of Christ in the saints *ὡς ἥ. νεφέλαις καθαραῖς* Hesych.S.*temp.*1.35(M.93.1492D); *ib.*2.64(1532D); ref. human obstacles to his action *ὁ τῆς δικαιοσύνης ἥ. ... οὐ πᾶσι τὴν ἑαυτοῦ φαιδρότητα χαρίζεται, ἀλλὰ τοῖς ἀξίως αὐτοῦ πολιτευομένοις* Bas.*hom.in Ps.*33(1.147A; M.29.360B); ref. Cant.1:5 *διὰ τὰς τῶν ἁμαρτιῶν μελανίας, ὅτι παρέβλεψέ με Χριστός, τῆς δικαιοσύνης ὁ ἥ.* Ph.Carp.*Cant.*12(M.40.45D); sins preventing man from seeing his light, Thdt.*rect.conf.*17(M.6.1240A); esp. of Jews, Or.*Cant.*2(p.126.30; M.13.111D); Ath.*inc.*40.6(M.25.168A); *τοῖς Ἰουδαίων δήμοις ἐμπαροινήσασι τῷ Χριστῷ κατέδυ λοιπὸν ὁ νοητὸς ἥ., οὐκέτι θεοῦ καταλάμποντος* Cyr.*Mich.*32(3.419B); ref. degrees of communication of his light *ὅθεν ἡ...Ἑλληνικὴ φιλοσοφία τῇ ἐκ τῆς θρυαλλίδος ἔοικεν λαμπηδόνι, ἣν ἀνάπτουσιν ἄνθρωποι, 'παρ' ἡ. κλέπτοντες ἐντέχνως τὸ φῶς'· κηρυχθέντος δὲ τοῦ λόγου πᾶν ἐκεῖνο, τὸ ἅγιον ἐξέλαμψεν φῶς* Clem.*str.*5.5(p.345.6; M.9.52B); ref. Apoc.12:1 *τὴν...γυναῖκα τὴν περιβεβλημένην τὸν ἥ. ... τὴν ἐκκλησίαν ἐδήλωσεν, ἐνδεδυμένην τὸν λόγον...ὑπὲρ ἥ. λάμποντα* Hipp.*antichr.*61(p.41.12; M.10.780C); ‡Epiph.*hom.*3(M.43.465C); ‡Chrys.*transfig.*(10.774A); ref. Is.26:9 *νύκτα καλεῖ, τὸν πρὸ τῆς ἐνανθρωπήσεως τοῦ κυρίου καιρόν· ὄρθρον δὲ τὴν προφητικὴν πρόγνωσιν· φῶς δὲ ἀληθινὸν τὸ εὐαγγέλιον τοῦ ἥ. τῆς δικαιοσύνης* Cyr.*Is.*3.1(2.361B); **5.** of H. Ghost *ὥσπερ ἥ. κεκαθαρμένον ὄμμα παραλαβών, δείξει σοι ἐν ἑαυτῷ τὴν εἰκόνα τοῦ ἀοράτου* Bas.*Spir.*23(3.20B; M.32.109B); **6.** of Church; as enduring for ever, Eus.*Ps.*88:36(M.23.1108C); *πληρουμένου τοῦ ἥ., ἐκλαμψόντων τῶν δικαίων ὡς ὁ ἥ.* Didym.*Ps.*88:36(M.39.1493D); Diod.*Ps.*88:36(M.33.1622C); *ἡ ἐκκλησία...μένουσα διηνεκῶς ὥσπερ ὁ ἥ.* Cyr.*Ps.*88:37(M.69.1213C); **7.** of BMV; ref. Ps.18:6, ‡Epiph.*hom.*5(M.43.489B); *πρὸ τοῦ ἥ. τὸ φῶς σου* Germ.CP *or.*7(M.98.353B); **8.** apostles, Dion.Ar.*d.n.*7.1(M.3.865B); **9.** of spiritual life *ὥσπερ...ὁ ἥ. οὐ μιαίνεται προσέχων ἐπὶ κόπρον καὶ βόρβορον,...οὕτω...ὁ καθαρὸς νοῦς ἐν τοῖς μιασμοῖς τῆς γῆς συνεχόμενος...οὐ μιαίνεται* *T.Benj.*8.3; *ἀπεικάζουσα...τὴν...γνῶσιν ἥ. καὶ φωτὶ τοῦ θεοῦ* Clem.*prot.*8(p.59.26; M.8.188B).

C. *ἡ ἡλίου λεγομένη ἡμέρα*, *Sunday*, Just.*1apol.*67.3(M.6.429B) etc.

***ἡλιότευκτος**, *made by the sun*, Dion.Ar.*e.h.*2.1(M.3.392C).

ἡλιοτρόπιον, τό, *solstice*, hence *S. John Baptist's day*, †Jo.Jej.*poenit.*(M.88.1916A).

***ἡλιοτροπῖται, οἱ,** heretics who worshipped the flower heliotrope, taking it as symbol of soul's turning to God *οἱ τὰς λεγομένας ἡλιοτρόπους βοτάνας ταῖς ἀκτῖσι τοῦ ἡλίου συμπεριφερομένας, λέγοντες δύναμίν τινα θείαν ἔχειν* Jo.D.*haer.*89(M.94.757A).

***ἡλιοφοινίσσομαι**, *be reddened by the sun*, Pall.*v.Chrys.*11(p.67.13; M.47.38).

***ἡλιόφρων**, *of Eastern mind, with Eastern sympathies*, Gr.Naz.*carm.*2.1.11.1803(M.37.1155A).

ἡλιτόμηνος, *untimely born*; neut. plur. as subst., Gr.Naz.*carm.*1.2.1.649(M.37.571A).

***ἡλιωδῶς**, *after the likeness of the sun*, Melet.*nat.hom.*2(M.64.1169D, v.l. *ἡλιοειδοῦς*).

***ἤλμευγε**, imperf. of *ἀμέλγω*, *milk* (tr. Lat. *mulgebat*), *M.Perp.*4(p.69.4,7).

ἧλος, ὁ, *nail, corn, wart*; met., *source of irritation*, Chrys.*hom.4.3 in Eph.*(11.106E).

***ἡλότυπος**, *bearing nail-prints*, Nonn.*par.Jo.*20:20(M.43.912B).

***ἡλουργικός**, *of making nails*, Sophr.H.*mir.Cyr.et Jo.*43(M.87.3588B).

***ἡλουργός, ὁ,** *maker of nails*, Sophr.H.*mir.Cyr.et Jo.*43(M.87.3588C).

ἡλόω, 1. *nail*, Clem.*paed.*2.11(p.227.2; M.8.537B); Isid.Pel.*epp.*1.253(M.78.336B); **2.** *fix*, Anast.S.*hex.*12(M.89.1065B); the mind, Ephr.1.152B.

***ἥλωμα, τό,** *nail, bolt*, Gr.Mag.*dial.*(tr.Zach.)3.36(M.*PL*.77.303C).

***ἡλωτάριον, τό,** *lock*, Pall.*h.Laus.*38(p.122.3; M.34.1194C).

ἡμεδαπός, 1. *our*, Clem.*str.*2.10(p.137.14; M.8.981B); *ib.*2.16(p.151.13; 1012A); Eus.*v.C.*3.56(p.104.7; M.20.1124A); **2.** subst., *native*, Thdt.*provid.*8(4.624).

ἡμέρα, ἡ, *day*; **1.** lit.; **a.** in gen. *Βενιαμίν, ὅ ἐστιν υἱὸς ἡμερῶν* *T.Benj.*1.6; name for books of Chronicles *αἱ τῶν Ἡ.* *Const.App.*2.22.3; *ἡ. μίαν οἶδεν ἡ γραφὴ τὸ ἡμερονύκτιον* Olymp.*Job* 3:1(M.93.52D); **b.** ref. God *ἡμερῶν...παλαιὸς ὁ θεὸς ὑμνεῖται διὰ τὸ...αὐτὸν εἶναι...πρὸ ἡμερῶν...ὡς αἰῶνος καὶ...ἡμερῶν αἴτιον* Dion.Ar.*d.n.*10.2(M.3.937B); **c.** day of Christ's Resurrection identified with that of Ps.117:24, Or.*sel.in Ps.*117:24(M.12.1584B) = Chrys.*exp.in Ps.*117:24(5.326Cff.); Thdt.*Ps.*117:24(1.1434); **d.** of Judgement, *T.Lev.*18.2; *ἡ ἡ. κυρίου* *Const.App.*2.42.1; *τὴν ἡ. ἐκείνην* Chrys.*sac.*6.13(p.173.13; 1.436B); *μεγάλη...ἡ ἡ. Χριστοῦ* Cyr.*Os.*9(3.30E); **e.** of last days *ἐν ταῖς ἐσχάταις ἡ.* *T.Zab.*8.2; *Barn.*4.9, etc.; **f.** of feasts, Easter *ἡ ἁγία ἡ.* Thphl.Caes.ap.Eus.*h.e.*5.25(M.20.509A); *ἡ μεγάλη ἡ.* CAnt.(341)*can.*6; *τῆς μεγίστης ἡμερῶν* Gr.Naz.*or.*45.2(M.36.625B); *ἡ βασιλὶς τῶν ἡ.* *ib.*44.10(617C); *τὴν ἡ.* CBeryt.*act.*(*ACO* 2.1.3 p.20.37; H.2.512E); of saints *αἱ ἡ. τῶν ἀποστόλων* *Const.App.*8.33.8; *ἐν ἡ. μαρτύρων* Chrys.*hom.5.3 in 1Tim.*(11.577E); **g.** exeg. Jo.8:56 *τὴν...ἡ. ἐνταῦθά μοι δοκεῖ λέγειν τὴν τοῦ σταυροῦ* Chrys.*hom.55.2 in Jo.*(8.323E); referred to first or second coming, Cyr.*Jo.*6(4.538Bf.); **h.** ref. superstitious observance; of Devil corrupting moral sense *διὰ παρατηρήσεως ἡμερῶν* Chrys.*Is.interp.*2(6.27C); practice forbidden by Col.2:8, id.*hom.2.1 in Col.*(11.365F); **i.** phrases *ἀφ' ἡμερῶν εἰς ἡμέρας* *for ever*, *Pss.Sal.*19.2; *μέσον ἡμέρας* *at midday*, Clem.*str.*7.12(p.57.15; M.9.512A); **2.** met.; **a.** of Christ, ref. Ps.117:24, Just.*dial.*100.4(M.6.709C); Clem.*str.*6.16(p.506.24; M.9.376C); *'ἐγὼ' γάρ 'εἰμὶ' φησίν 'ἡ ἡ.'* Marcell.*fr.*25 ap.Eus.*Marcell.*1.2(p.12.26; M.24.740B); cf.id.*fr.*37 *ib.*(p.12.29; 740B); ref. Jo.8:56 *ἡ. ὁ κύριος τὸ πάθος προσαγορεύει* Thdt.*eran.*3(4.202); cf.Cosm.Ind.*top.*5(M.88.240D); **b.** of eternity, Or.*Jo.*20.42(p.385.15; M.14.673A); id.*hom.17.6 in Jer.*(p.150.13; M.13.461D; Evagr.Pont.*ep.*7(M.32.257B); *τὴν ἡ. κυρίου τὴν μεγάλην, ἣν...ἀνατολὴ τοῦ τῆς δικαιοσύνης ἡλίου καταφωτίζει* †Bas.*Is.*31(1.404B; M.30.180B); Thdt.*Ps.*24:5(1.757); *ib.*93:13(1280); **c.** of this life, ref. Jo.9:4, Am.5:18 *ἡ. ... ὠνόμασε τὸν αἰῶνα τοῦτον,... νύκτα τὴν συντέλειαν διὰ τὰς κολάσεις* Or.*hom.12.10 in Jer.*(p.96.12; M.13.392B); ref. Eph.6:13 *ἡ. ... πονηράν, τὸν παρόντα βίον...φησί* Chrys.*hom.6.3 in Eph.*(11.170A); *ἀνθρωπίνην...ἡ. ἐκάλεσε τὸ τῆς φύσεως ὀλιγόβιον* Thdt.*1Cor.*4:3(3.186); **d.** of spiritual life *ἐν τῷ βίῳ τούτῳ ἡ. πνευματικῆς* Or.*Jo.*32.2(p.426.13; M.14.741B); ref. Jo.13:30 *ἡ. ... καθαιρομένοις...τοὺς ἐν τοῖς ποσὶν τῆς ψυχῆς αὐτῶν ῥύπους* *ib.*32.24(p.469.1; 809D); *ἡ. λέγει τὴν γνῶσιν τοῦ Χριστοῦ* id.*sel.in Ps.*117:24(M.12.1584B); of divine illumination, id.*Jo.*1.25(24; p.31.5; M.14.68B); id.*fr.34 in Jo.*(p.509.28); †Bas.*Is.*135(1.473C; M.30.337A); **e.** of light of Christianity, Clem.*str.*7.7(p.32.34; M.9.461A); cf.Cyr.*ador.*3(1.84E).

ἡμερήσιος, *of the day, daily*; neut. as adv., *daily*, Pall.*h.Laus.*65

(p.161.12; -ια M.34.1251C); Jo.Mosch.*prat*.163(M.87.3029D); Leont. N.*v.Sym*.42(M.93.1724A).

***ἡμερικῶς,** *by day*, *Lit.Gr.Naz*.(M.36.729A).

ἡμερινός, *of day*; met., *righteous* ἡ. ἔργα *cat.Apoc*.10:1(p.327.2).

***ἡμερινῶς,** *by day* τυπικῶς καὶ νυκτερινῶς τὸ πάσχα ὁ Ἰσραὴλ ἐποίησεν· ἐνταῦθα φωτεινῶς καὶ ἡμερινῶς τὸ πάσχα ἑορτάζομεν ‡Epiph.*hom*.3(M.43.469A).

ἡμέριος, *of the day*, *of the sun*, *Orac.Sib*.3.445; neut. as adv., *daily*, Dor.*doct*.4.10(M.88.1672A).

***ἡμεροβαπτιστής, ὁ, 1.** *one who baptizes daily*; ref. Jo. Bapt., *Hom.Clem*.2.23; **2.** plur., *Hemerobaptists*, a Jewish sect who practised daily ablutions, Epiph.*anac*.17(p.167.25; M.42.845D) ∞ Jo.D. *haer*.17(M.94.688B); αἵρεσις ἡμεροβαπτιστῶν...ἴσα τῶν γραμματέων καὶ Φαρισαίων φρονοῦσα, οὐ μὴν ἐξισουμένη τοῖς Σαδδουκαίοις Epiph. *haer*.1.17(p.214.5; M.41.256A); washing away sins, *ib*.(p.214.13; 256A); cleansing household vessels, *Const.App*.6.6.5; Isid.H.*etym*. 8.4.11.

ἡμεροκαλλές, τό, *Martagon lily*, Isid.Pel.*epp*.5.563(M.78.1640A).

ἡμερολόγιον, τό, *diary*, Cosm.Ind.*top*.5(M.88.276A).

***ἡμερομισθέω,** *work by the day*, Jo.Mosch.*prat*.183(M.87.3056A).

ἡμερονύκτιον, τό, *a day and a night*, Isid.Pel.*epp*.1.114(M.78. 257C); *ib*.2.212(653C).

ἥμερος, 1. *mild, gentle*; **a.** in gen. ῥήματα...ἡ. Herm.*vis*.1.3.3; Clem.*str*.6.16(p.499.23; M.9.357C); Chrys.*hom.7.7 in 2Cor*.(10.491C); **b.** partic. of Christian doctrine οὐδὲν...ἡμερώτερον Herm.*mand*.12. 4.5; of Christian character, Ign.*Eph*.10.2; Clem.*str*.7.7(p.34.7; M.9. 465A); of Christ's judgement of men, Chrys.*hom.48.6 in Mt*.(7. 501E); id.*hom.39.3 in Jo*.(8.230A); **c.** as title, *most clement* ὁ ἡμερώτατος βασιλεὺς Περσῶν Heracl.*ep*.(M.92.1025A); *Ep*.ap.*Chron. Pasch*.p.402(M.92.1025B); neut. as subst., *mildness, gentleness*, Clem. *str*.2.18(p.162.13; M.8.1033B); Or.*princ*.3.1.5(p.200.13; M.11.256A); **2.** *tamed, civilized*; of converts, Chrys.*hom.48.6 in Mt*.(7.501E); *ib.61.3*(615A); ἐπὶ τὸ ἥ. Cyr.*Lc*.19:35(M.72.876C).

ἡμερότης, ἡ, *gentleness, kindness*; in gen., as Christian virtue, Clem.*str*.7.3(p.10.26; M.9.417A); of God ἡ τοῦ δημιουργοῦ ἡ. Cyr. *glaph.Gen*.1(1.7B); id.*Os*.126(3.158A,B); seen in phenomena of nature, id.*Ps*.5:8(M.69.740D); id.*Os*.53(97A); of Christ healing, id. *Lc*.5:12(M.72.557B); as a title, *Clemency*, of emperor ἡ ἡμετέρα ἡ. Const.ap.Eus.*v.C*.3.53(p.100.29; M.20.1116B); Const.*ib*.4.36(p.131. 29; 1185A); id.ap.Ath.*apol.sec*.70(M.25.373B); Ath.*syn*.55(p.278.20; M.26.792C); Pall.*v.Chrys*.9(p.54.11; M.47.31); Leo Mag.*ep*.115(p.62. 29; M.*PL*.54.1032B); of pope, Pall.*v.Chrys*.3(p.21.14; M.47.14); *ib*. (p.22.4; M.47.15); of other prominent men, Bas.*ep*.75(3.171A; M.32. 449C); Greg.Naz.*ep*.104(M.37.204C, v.l. καθαρότητος).

***ἡμεροτρωθέντες,** perh. error for ⟨ἡμεροτροφοῦντες⟩ *feeding daily on*, met. τὸ τῆς ἀγλαοφεγγοῦς καὶ μακαρίας ταύτης ⟨τροφῆς⟩ ἡ. Euthal.Diac.*Ac*.(M.85.628A).

ἡμερούσιος, 1. *daily*, *A.(Pass.)Andr*.7(p.18.22; καθημερινοί M.2. 1232A); Nil.*spir.mal*.2(M.79.1148A); neut. as subst., *daily wage*, Jo. Mosch.*prat*.134(M.87.2997C); **2.** *of a day* τὸ ἡ. διάστημα Nil.*praest*. 24(M.79.1089B); **3.** neut. as adv., *daily*, *Apophth.Patr*.(M.65.305A).

ἡμερουσίως, *daily*, Geo.Al.*v.Chrys*.19(p.182.35).

ἡμεροφαής, 1. *shining by day*, *Dial.Ath.et Zacch*.23(p.19); **2.** *shining in the sunlight*, Jo.Mon.*hymn.Chrys*.7(M.96.1381D).

***ἡμερόφοιτος,** *roaming by day*, Bas.*hex*.8.7(1.77B; M.29.181A).

***ἡμερωσύνη, ἡ,** *gentleness*, Eus.Al.*serm*.21.1(M.86.423B).

ἡμέτερος, *our*, of Christians οἱ ἡ. *M.Polyc*.9.1; Clem.*str*.4.4(p.256. 12; M.8.1229B); *A.Andr.et Mt*.3(p.67.9); of the orthodox, Gel.Cyz. *h.e*.3.16.5; of Christian revelation, ref. OT texts ἐν ἐκείνοις ἐσκιογράφηται τὰ ἡ. Thdt.*Ps*.106(1.1365); id.*Ezech*.34:30(2.975); τὴν... προφητείαν...ἡ. id.*Ps*.28:1(778); of human nature in Christ τὴν ἡ. ἀναλήψεται σάρκα Marcell.*fr*.13 ap.Eus.*e.th*.3.3(p.146.31; M.24.984C); τὸ ἡ. σῶμα *ib*.82 ap.Eus.*Marcell*.1.4(p.24.18; M.24.764A); τῆς...ἡ. φύσεώς ἐστιν ἀπαρχή, καὶ πρώτῳ πρέπει τὰ ἡ. λέγειν Thdt.*Ps*.39:7–8 (860); ἐβαπτίσθη ὑπὸ Ἰωάννου· τοῦτο δείκνυσι τὸ ἡ. id.*ep*.151(4.1300); used for sing. by emperor, Const.ap.Thdt.*h.e*.1.16.3(3.790); Dial. *ib*.2.16.1(864); by Christ ἡ. μύθων Nonn.*par.Jo*.16:4(M.43.877C); = objective genit. ἡ. ... πίστιν faith *in me*, *ib*.6:35(800B).

***ἡμιάγιος,** *half-holy*, ref. τρισάγιον as an expression of equal praise to each Person of Trin. οὐ λέγουσι ἅγιος καὶ ἡ., ἀλλ' ἴσως λέγουσι τὸ ἅγιος Epiph.*anac*.26(p.34.28; M.43.64C).

ἡμιάνθρωπος, *half-man* τελείαν ἔχει τὴν διπλῆν φύσιν ὁ Χριστὸς... οὔτε ἡμίθεος ὤφθη ἐπὶ γῆς, οὔτε ἡ. ἀνέβη εἰς οὐρανούς Ephr.Ant.*fr*. ap.*Doctr.Patr*.4.12(p.32.5; M.86.2108C).

***ἡμιαρείζω,** *be a Semi-Arian* τινες ἡμιαρείζουσιν ἐκείνου [sc. Ἀρείου] μὲν τὸ ὄνομα ἀρνούμενοι, αὐτὸν δὲ καὶ τὴν αὐτοῦ κακοδοξίαν ἐνδεδυμένοι Epiph.*haer*.73.1(conj. ἡμιαρει⟨ανί⟩ζουσιν p.267.28; M.42. 400D).

***ἡμιάρειοι, οἱ,** *Semi-Arians* ἡ., οἱ Χριστὸν μὲν ὁμολογοῦντες,... κτίσμα αὐτὸν φάσκοντες, οὐχ ὡς ἓν τῶν κτισμάτων...καὶ περὶ...τοῦ πνεύματος τοῦ ἁγίου ὡσαύτως κτίσμα...ὁρίζονται, παρεκβάλλοντες υἱοῦ τὸ ὁμοούσιον, ὁμοιούσιον δὲ θέλουσι λέγειν. ἄλλοι δὲ ἐξ αὐτῶν καὶ τὸ ὁμοιούσιον παρεξέβαλον Epiph.*anac*.73(p.230.22; M.42.872A); id.*haer*. 73.1(p.268.7ff.; M.42.401Aff.); anathematized, CCP(381)*can*.1; οἱ δὲ οὔτε κτίσμα οὔτε θεόν, ἀλλ' ἐλεύθερον [ἐδογμάτιζον]· οὓς ἡ. ἐκεῖνος ὠνόμαζε Gr.Presb.*v.Gr.Naz*.(M.35.276A).

ἡμιγενής, *half-complete* εἰ οὖν μία φύσις ὁ Χριστός, πάντως ἡ. ὁ ἄνθρωπος, καθὼς οἱ τῶν Μανιχαίων μῦθοι διδάσκουσιν Anast.S.*hod*.10 (M.89.192A).

***ἡμίγυνος,** *effeminate*, Synes.*ep*.44(M.66.1372C).

***ἡμιδάκτυλος, ὁ,** *half-digit*; a measure of length, Hermias *irris*. 9(M.6.1177D).

***ἡμιδράκων, ὁ,** *half-dragon, half-serpent*, Gr.Naz.*carm*.2.2(poem. 7.104(M.37.1559A).

ἡμιθανής, *half-dead*, *A.Xanthipp*.25(p.75.33); ‡Pall.*h.mon*.9(p.51. 13; M.34.1153D); Jo.Mosch.*prat*.196(M.87.3081C).

ἡμίθεος, ὁ, *half-God*; ref. impossibility of Christ having one nature, Leont.H.*Nest*.3.3(M.86.1609B); Ephr.Ant.*fr*.ap.*Doct.Patr*. 4.12(p.32.5; M.86.2108C) cit. s. ἡμιάνθρωπος; Geo.Pis.*Sev*.611(M.92. 1668A); Anast.S.*hod*.18(M.89.265D) cit. s. ἡμιμερής.

ἡμιθνής, *half-dead*, Eus.*h.e*.8.3.2(v.l. ἡμιθανής M.20.748B); Thdt. *h.rel*.30(3.1292); met., of Arius ὅλος ἡ. ... τὸ βλέμμα Const.ap.Gel. Cyz.*h.e*.3.19.35(M.85.1353B); of men before Inc., Eus.*h.e*.10.4.12(M. 20.853A).

ἡμίιππος, ὁ, *mule*, in Christol. argument εἰ...ἐφ' ὧν μηδὲ κατὰ μέλος οἱαοῦν ὁμοιότης σώζεται πρὸς θάτερον τῶν τικτόντων, υἱοί τε λέγονται ἵππων οἱ ἡμίονοι, καὶ τέκνα ὄνων οἱ ἡ., πῶς διὰ τὸ ἐκ μέρους ἀνόμοιον, οὐ δύνασθαι υἱὸν καλεῖν τὸν μὴ πάντη ὅμοιον τοῖς τεκοῦσιν αὐτὸν εἰρήκατε; Leont.H.*Nest*.3.4(M.86.1612B).

ἡμίκρανον, τό, *half the head, back part of the head*, Steph.Diac. *v.Steph*.(M.100.1177B); Geo.Al.*v.Chrys*.8(p.170.44).

ἡμικύκλιον, τό, *? semi-circular couch* or *table*, Chrys.*hom.1.4 in Col*.(11.327E).

ἡμιμεθής, *half-drunk, semi-intoxicated*, Clem.*paed*.2.2(p.171.24; M.8.420B).

***ἡμιμερής,** *half*, ref. monophysite Christology τοῦτο δὲ οὐδὲν ἕτερόν ἐστιν, ἀλλ' ἢ τὸ ὁμολογεῖν...μὴ εἶναι αὐτὸν τέλειον ἐν θεότητι, ἀλλ' ἡμίθεον θεόν, καὶ ἡ. ἄνθρωπον Anast.S.*hod*.18(M.89.265D).

***ἡμίνθη, ἡ,** *mint*, Proc.G.*Gen*.1:11(M.87.81A).

ἡμίξηρος, *half-withered*; of limbs and persons, *T.Sym*.2.12; *A.Thom*.A 12(p.117.10); of plants, etc., Herm.*sim*.8.1.9; opp. ὁλόξηρος, met., of one who is only outwardly reconciled, Anast.S. *qu.et resp*.109(M.89.761B).

ἡμιούγκιον, τό, *half-an-ounce*, Thdt.*qu.29 in 1Reg*.(1.374); Mac. Aeg.*cust.cor*.12(M.34.833A,B).

***ἡμιούσιος,** *semi-substantial* ἡμιούσιον...εἰρήκασι τὴν σάρκα τὴν νεκρὰν ζωῆς κεχωρισμένην Anast.S.*hod*.2(M.89.72B).

***ἡμιπαίδευτος,** *half-educated*, Synes.*astrolab*.1(p.133.10; M.66. 1580A).

***ἡμίπλαστος,** *half-formed*, i.e. *composed of two forms, neither of which is complete* ἀπὸ τούτων τῶν ἡμιαρείων καὶ ἀπὸ ὀρθοδόξων τινὲς...τεράστιοι γενηθέντες ἄνθρωποι διφυεῖς καὶ ἡ., ὡς τοὺς Κενταύρους...⟨διέγραψαν⟩ οἱ ἀναγράψαντες τοὺς μύθους, ἐπανέστησαν ἡμῖν Epiph.*haer*.74.1(p.313.12; M.42.473C).

***ἡμισημέριον, τό,** *half-day*, Max.*comput*.12(M.19.1229A).

***ἡμισπάρακτος,** *half-mangled*, Amph.*Seleuc*.143(M.37.1586A).

***ἡμίσταμνος, ὁ,** *half-jar* of wine, *1Apoc.Jo*.5(p.73).

ἥμισυς, *half*, ἐξ ἡμισείας used adverbially, *T.Aser* 2.9; Chrys. *hom.2.1 in Col*.(11.366B); id.*sac*.2.5(p.41.5; 1.377E).

[*]**ἡμισχοίνιον, τό,** *two Roman miles*, Hipp.*haer*.9.13(p.251.18; M. 16.3387C).

ἡμιτέλεστος, *half-initiated*, of catechumens ἔξιτε ἐκ νηοῖο θεοῦ, βροτοὶ ἡ. Eudoc.*Cypr*.1.278(M.85.841D).

ἡμιτελής, 1. *half-finished, incomplete*, Gr.Nyss.*or.catech*.32(p.115. 12; M.45.80A); id.*Eun*.1(1 p.211.14; M.45.460B); ref. marriage at Cana ἡ. ... γάμοιο μέθην Nonn.*par.Jo*.2:3(M.43.760C); **2.** *half*, Paul. Sil.*Soph*.383(M.86.2134A).

***ἡμιτίμιον, τό,** *half the regular price*, †Gregent.*leg.Hom*.30(M.86. 597B).

***ἡμιτμής,** *half*, Paul.Sil.*Soph*.378(M.86.2134A).

ἡμίτμητος, *cut in half*, Geo.Pis.*hex*.98(M.92.1439A); *ib*.1201 (1527A); *divided*, ref. Christ οὐκ ἔστιν ἡ. id.*Sev*.607(M.92.1668A).

ἡμίτομος, **1.** *cut in half, divided, separate,* Thdt.*h.e.*5.39.8(3.1083); Eudoc.*Cypr.*1.61(M.85.833D); *ἐκ δύο μερικῶν οὐσιῶν καὶ ὑποστάσεων ἡ. εἶπεν* [sc. *Σευῆρος*] *ἀποτελεῖσθαι μίαν φύσιν τὸν Χριστόν* Anast.S.*hod.*6(M.89.108B); *οὐκ ἀντανῆλθεν* [sc. Christ] *ἡ. πρὸς τοὺς ἄνω* Geo.Pis.*Sev.*612(M.92.1668A); **2.** of one half or part *cut off, cut out*; of the constellation Argo (i.e. the stern only), Tat.*orat.*9(p.10.15; M.6.825C); of Eve cut out of Adam opp. normal birth of Seth, Gr.Naz.*carm.*1.1.3.38(M.37.411A); met., *cut short*; of an incomplete definition, Gr.Nyss.*Eun.*1(1 p.211.15; M.45.460B); neut. as subst., *half, ib.*2(2 p.321.4; 493D); Bas.Sel.*or.*18.2(M.85.232C).

***ἡμιυιός,** **ὁ,** *half-son,* Leont.H.*Nest.*3.1(M.86.1604A).

ἡμιφαής, *in half-light* or *semi-darkness*; met., of heretics, Gr.Naz.*carm.*1.1.1.38(M.37.401A).

***ἡμιφανῶς,** *till (only) half-visible,* Gr.Nyss.*ep.*12(M.46.1045A).

ἡμίφαυλος, *half-bad*; of those who compromise with the world, Const.Diac.*laud.*8(M.88.488C).

ἡμίφλεκτος, *half-burnt,* Cyr.*Am.*39(3.294D).

§**ἡμιφόριον,** **τό,** *short outer garment, A.Thom.*A 106(p.218.19); worn by monks, ‡Ath.*ep.Cast.*1.6(M.28.856D); made of silk, Pall.*h.Laus.*61(p.156.5; M.34.1228B).

***ἡμιφωνία,** **ἡ,** *half-speech, faintness of speech,* Melet.*nat.hom.*11(M.64.1201B).

ἡμίφωνον, **τό,** *semi-vowel*; as interpreted by Gnostics, Hipp.*haer.*4.14(p.48.17; M.16.3082B); in system of Marcus *τὰ...ἡ. ὀκτώ, ὄντα τοῦ Λόγου καὶ τῆς Ζωῆς* Iren.*haer.*1.14.5(M.7.604B); equated with aeons, Thdt.*haer.*1.9(4.301).

ἠναγκασμένως, *perforce,* Gr.Nyss.*usur.*(M.46.436C); Jo.D.*haer.*98(M.94.760B).

ἠνεμόφοιτος, *walking on the wind,* Nonn.*par.Jo.*20:24(M.43.912C).

ἡνία, **ἡ,** *rein*; met., of divine government of the world *σοφίας... δεσμοῖς ὥσπερ τισὶν ἡ.* Eus.*l.C.*6(p.206.28; M.20.1341A); *ὁ ἀνθρώπινος νοῦς...ἔχει...τὰς τῶν θελημάτων ἡ.* Cyr.*Rom.*7:20(p.207.21); *αἱ ἡ. οὐ τῆς τοῦ θεοῦ ἐκκλησίας, ἀλλὰ τοῦ...Ἀρειανῶν ἐργαστηρίου* Gel.Cyz.*h.e.*3.16.7.

ἡνιοχεία, **ἡ,** *control, government*; of Devil's rule over the air, Bas.*Sel.or.*3.3(M.85.53C).

ἡνιοχεύς, **ὁ,** *charioteer,* of Christ *ἅρματος ὑψιπόροιο...ἡ.* Nonn.*par.Jo.*1:36(M.43.756B).

ἡνιοχεύ-ω, *rule ξύμπαντα πατὴρ θεὸς ∼ων* Nonn.*par.Jo.*9:31(M.43.829B); *ib.*17:6(884C); of Christ, *ib.*17:2(884B).

ἡνιοχ-έω, **1.** *hold the reins*; met., of divine action in the soul *∼ῶν ταῖς ἡνίαις τοῦ πνεύματος* Mac.Aeg.*hom.*1.3(M.34.453A); *ib.*1.9(460B); hence *ride,* met. *ἡ ἄνω Ἱερουσαλήμ, εἰς ἣν ἀναβήσεται ὁ κύριος, ∼ῶν τοὺς ἐκ περιτομῆς καὶ ἐθνῶν πιστεύοντας* Or.*Jo.*10.29(18; p.202.32; M.14.360B); **2.** *rule, command,* of God *ἡ. τὸ πᾶν* Meth.*res.*2.10(p.352.13); of Christ, Eus.*l.C.*11(p.227.22; M.20.1381B); *ib.*12(p.234.28; 1396B); of God's governance of the cherubim, Mac.Aeg.*hom.*1.9(M.34.460B); Chrys.*hom.5.3 in Gen.*(4.35A); *Ἠλίαν...τὰ οὐράνια ∼οῦντα* ‡Chrys.*Petr.et El.*2(2.732E); of Christ, Gr.Ant.*mul.ung.*12(M.88.1864D).

ἡνίοχος, **ὁ,** *charioteer*; not to be received into Church, *Const.App.*8.32.9; met., *one who holds the reins of command*; of God, ref. divine providence *ἡνιόχῳ θεοῦ λόγῳ* Eus.*p.e.*11.7(522D; M.21.865D); of God as holding reins of Spirit in soul, Mac.Aeg.*hom.*1.3(M.34.453A); *ὁ θεὸς...ἡ. τῶν χερουβίμ* Anton.Hag.*v.Sym.Styl.*14(p.38.20); of temperance as curbing sensual pleasures, Meth.*symp.*5.3(p.56.9; M.18.101A); of mind as governing senses, *Const.App.*7.34.6; and thoughts, Mac.Aeg.*hom.*40.5(M.34.765B); *σωφροσύνη...ὀφθαλμῶν ἡ.* †Nil.*vit.*2(M.79.1141C); of righteous anger as curbing temptations, Diad.*perf.*62(p.72.18); of bishop, *MAMA* 1.171 (c. 375); of Satan, Bas.Sel.*or.*3.3(M.85.53C).

ἡνωμένως, **1.** *in unity*; **a.** (subjectively) *while remaining one* or *in union,* Bas.*Spir.*20(3.17E; M.32.104B) cit. s. *ἀνόρμητος*; Dion.Ar.*d.n.*2.11(M.3.649B) cit. s. *ἑνικῶς*; **b.** (objectively) *as one,* of human concepts of the divine: Trin. *διακεκριμένως μὲν ἀφορίζεσθαι τοῖς ὑποστατικοῖς ἰδιώμασιν, ἡ. δὲ προσκυνεῖσθαι μιᾷ τῇ φύσει τε καὶ θεότητι* Const.Diac.*laud.*19(M.88.501B); Geo.Pis.*hex.*186(M.92.1447A); Christol. *οἱ ἅγιοι πατέρες...ἡ. τὰς δύο Χριστοῦ φύσεις εἶπον* Anast.S.*hod.*20(M.89.280B); *ἡ. ... διαιρεῖ, μίαν μὲν ὑπόστασιν λέγων, φύσεις δὲ δύο* Thdr.Raith.*praep.*(p.195.5; M.91.1496C); **2.** *in union* opp. singly or simply, opp. *μονοειδῶς*: *θεωρῆσαι πάντα ἐν τῷ πάντων αἰτίῳ, καὶ τὰ ἀλλήλοις ἐναντία, μονοειδῶς καὶ ἡ.* Dion.Ar.*d.n.*5.7(M.3.821B), opp. *μονομερῶς,* ref. Nativity *ὁ Χριστὸς...μονομερῶς οὐχ ὑπέστη, ἀλλ' εὐθὺς ἡ. ἐγεννήθη cat.Heb.*7:1 suppl.(p.538.20) but cf. Marc.Er.*opusc.*10.4(M.65.1121D); **3.** *universally, without distinction,* of predicates of the three divine Persons *τὰ μὲν ἡ. παραδίδωσι τὰ δὲ διακεκριμένως* Dion.Ar.*d.n.*2.2(M.3.640A); *ib.*2.1(637C); *ταῦτα κοινῶς ἐπὶ πάσης θεότητος ἐκληπτέον...καὶ ἡ.* Jo.D.*f.o.*1.10(M.94.837B).

***ἠουοκᾶτος,** **ὁ,** (Lat. *evocatus*) *retired soldier honourably recalled to service,* Heges.ap.Eus.*h.e.*3.20.1(M.20.253A).

***ἠπατημένως,** *falsely,* †Bas.*Is.*76(1.433A; M.30.245B).

ἡπατοσκοπία, **ἡ,** *inspection of liver, vaticination,* Eus.*d.e.*5 proem.(p.208.21; M.22.345C); Gr.Nyss.*fat.*(M.45.172C); Soz.*h.e.*7.22.4(M.67.1485C).

[*]**ἠπεδανής,** *weak,* Eudoc.*Cypr.*2.80(M.85.848C).

ἠπειγμένως, *hastily, with all speed,* Const.ap.Ath.*apol.sec.*86(p.165.2; M.25.401D); Bas.*hom.*5.2(2.34C; M.31.240C); ‡Chrys.*pasch.*5.2(8.263E).

ἠπιόθυμος, *gentle ὁ ἐπίσκοπος, ἔσο...ἠ. Const.App.*2.57.1.

***ἠπιόμητις,** *gentle in counsel,* Gr.Naz.*carm.*1.2.2.402(M.37.610A); *ib.*2.2(poem.)2.29(1479A).

ἠπιότης, **ἡ,** **1.** *gentleness*; of God, Cyr.*Os.*70(3.106E); of angel who freed Daniel *πῶς κατῆλθεν...; ἐν τῇ ἀγγελικῇ φοβερᾷ ἐξουσίᾳ... ἢ ἠ.; Dial.Tim.et Aquil.*96 r°; **2.** *tractability μένει* [sc. baptized person] *ἐν νεότητι καὶ ἠ.* Didym.*Trin.*2.1(M.39.453A); **3.** *mental simplicity* of disciples; causing Christ to speak in parables, Ammon.*Jo.*16:25(M.85.1500C).

ἠπίως, *kindly*; of God giving grace, *1Clem.*23.1; of Christ forgiving sins, Didym.*Trin.*1.29(M.39.416B).

***Ἡρακλεωνῖται,** **οἱ,** *followers of Heracleon,* sect of Valentinian Gnostics, Epiph.*anac.*36(p.1.13; M.42.860C); id.*haer.*35.1(p.44.12; M.41.633A).

ἤρανος, **ὁ,** *keeper, ruler,* Paul.Sil.*Soph.*178(M.86.2126B).

ἠρέμα, **1.** *gently ἠ. καὶ κατὰ μικρὸν δεῖ τὰς ἐπιπλήξεις ποιεῖσθαι* Chrys.*hom.3.1 in 1Cor.*(10.14E); **2.** *indirectly,* ref. Gnostics *ἀγαμίαν ἐκήρυξαν,...ἠ. κατηγοροῦντες τοῦ ἄρρεν καὶ θῆλυ εἰς γένεσιν ἀνθρώπων πεποιηκότος* Iren.*haer.*1.28.1(M.7.690A); **3.** *gradually, Hom.Clem.*1.6; Chrys.*hom.84.1 in Mt.*(7.797E).

ἠρεμ-έω, *be at rest,* as proof of reality of Christ's humanity *ὕπνῳ ἠρέμησε* Hipp.*haer.*10.33(p.292.2; M.16.3451C); of God, *ib.*6.29(p.156.11; 3325D); *τὸ μὲν ∼εῖν αὐτὸν ἀφ' ἡμῶν, καὶ οἷον ἀμελεῖν, δι' ἃς αὐτὸς οἶδεν αἰτίας, ὑπνοῦν* Gr.Naz.*or.*31.22(p.172.8; M.36.157B); *ὅπως...∼εῖ...οὔτε ἐννοῆσαί τινι τῶν ὄντων, οὔτε θεμιτὸν οὔτε ἐφικτόν* Dion.Ar.*d.n.*11(M.3.949A).

ἠρεμία, **ἡ,** *rest, peace, quiet*; ascribed by Valentinians to God, Iren.*haer.*1.1.1(M.7.445A); as mark of Christian, Clem.*paed.*2.7(p.193.30; M.8.465A); ref. Mt.26:36 *παιδεύων ἡμᾶς ἐν ταῖς εὐχαῖς ἡσυχίαν κατασκευάζειν ἑαυτοῖς καὶ ἠ. πολλήν* Chrys.*hom.83.1 in Mt.*(7.790E).

ἠρεμίζω, *keep silent about, A.Petr.c.Sim.*8(p.92.5).

ἤρεμος, *tranquil, unmoved*; of Christ, *A.Thom.*A 80(p.195.17).

***ἠρεμόω,** *live in solitude, as a hermit,* †Jo.D.*B.J.*35(M.96.1193A).

***ἤρρει,** error in 'Thdr.Mops.*fr.in Jo.*12:13'(M.66.768A), properly Chrys.*hom.66.1 in Jo.*(8.395E *διήρει*; B. Corderius *catena in S. Joannem* 12:13 (Antwerp 1630) p.306 *ἀνῄρει*).

***ἠρτημένως,** *with hesitation, hesitantly,* CCP(394) *act.*(M.119.824C).

***Ἡρωδιανοί,** **οἱ,** *Herodians* as Jewish sect, Or.*comm.in Mt.*17.26(p.656.5ff.; M.13.1552Bff.); Gr.Naz.*or.*37.5(M.36.288B) cit. s. *κῆνσος*; *οὗτοι* [sc. *Ἡ.*]...*ὅλοι Ἰουδαῖοι ⟨ἦσαν⟩ ἀργοί...Ἡρώδην...ἡγοῦντο Χριστόν* Epiph.*haer.*20.1(p.224.8; M.41.269B).

***Ἡσαϊανισταί,** **οἱ,** *a sect of the Acephali,* Tim.CP *haer.*(M.86.45A).

***ᾐσθημένως,** *with perception, understanding,* Dion.Al.*ep.can.*(p.95.9; M.10.1273A); Eus.*h.e.*10.9.9(M.20.904C); *cat.Ps.*36:30(1.678).

ἧσις, **ἡ,** *delight,* Cyr.*hom.pasch.*9(5².119B).

ἡσυχάζ-ω, **1.** *be quiet* or *tranquil, keep silence*; **a.** theol., ref. Marcellus' alleged doctrine of Logos as impersonal before Creation *λόγος, ἔνδον μένων ἐν ∼οντι τῷ πατρὶ ἐνεργῶν δὲ ἐν τῷ τὴν κτίσιν δημιουργεῖν ὁμοίως τῷ ἡμετέρῳ ἐν σιωπῶσιν μὲν ∼οντι ἐν δὲ φθεγγομένοις ἐνεργοῦντι* Eus.*Marcell.*1.1(p.4.15f.; M.24.717B,C); *λόγον εἶναι φήσας ἔνδον ἐν αὐτῷ τῷ θεῷ, ποτὲ μὲν ∼οντα, ποτὲ δὲ σημαντικῶς ἐνεργοῦντα ib.*2.1(p.31.33; 777A); of Logos as quiescent in Christ during temptation, Iren.*haer.*3.19.3(M.7.941A) cit. s. *ἄνθρωπος*; **b.** of tranquillity in religious life as conducive to prayer *ποίας οὖν δεῖται καταστάσεως ὁ νοῦς, ἵνα ἡσυχάσῃ ἀμεταστρόφως ἐκσταθῆναι πρὸς τὸν οἰκεῖον δεσπότην*; Evagr.Pont.*or.*3(M.79.1168C); id.*rer.mon.*5(M.40.1257A); *μέγα γὰρ ἀληθῶς παρθένῳ ἢ μοναχῷ ∼ειν· μάλιστα δὲ τοῖς νέοις. ἀλλὰ γίνωσκε, ὅτι προθῆται ἡσυχάσαι, εὐθέως ὁ πονηρὸς ἔρχεται καὶ βαρεῖ τὴν ψυχήν Apophth.Patr.*(M.65.201C); **2.** t.t., *live as a hermit* (cf. *ἡσυχαστής*); **a.** opp. cenobitical life *θέλουσί τινες* [sc.

ἀδελφοί] αὐτῶν οἰκοδομῆσαι κελλία μακρὰν ἵνα ἡσυχάσωσι *ib.*(85D); from which a monk could pass to eremitical state δίδωσιν αὐτῷ ὁ πατὴρ ἡμῶν Σάβας κελλίον πρὸς τὸ ἡσυχάσαι Cyr.S.*v.Jo.Hes.*7(p.206.18); ὁ...Σάβας δέδωκεν αὐτῷ ἐντολὰς ~ειν εἰς τὸ ἴδιον κελλίον id.*v.Sab.*41(p.132.4); **b.** in mountain caves, deserts, or secluded cells τινὶ εὐτόνως εὐχομένῳ ἁγίῳ ἐν ἐρήμῳ ~οντι Evagr.Pont.*or.*111(M.79.1192C); τῶν ἐν ὄρεσι καὶ σπηλαίοις ~όντων μοναχῶν Nil.*praest.*1(M.79.1061A); ἀπελθὼν ~ε ἐν κελλίῳ id.*epp.*4.1(M.79.544C); Cyr.S.*v.Jo.Hes.*10(p.208.23); *ib.*11(p.209.11); Jo.Mosch.*prat.*20(M.87.2868B); **c.** dangers and temptations ὁ Ἰάκωβος εἰς τὸ ἑαυτοῦ κελλίον ~ων ἐπειράσθη δεινῶς ὑπὸ τοῦ δαίμονος τῆς πορνείας Cyr.S.*v.Sab.*41(p.131.19); ὁ ~ων, καὶ ἀκηδίᾳ πολεμῶν ζημιοῦται πολλάκις Jo.Clim.*scal.*27(M.88.1109A); ἔγνων τοὺς δαιμόνας τοῖς λόγῳ ~ουσι τοὺς ἀλόγους τῶν γυρευτῶν παραβάλλειν συχνότερον ἀναπείθοντας *ib.*(1112D); hence necessity of discretion and faith, *ib.*(1113A) cit. s. αἴσθησις; εἰ μὴ γὰρ πιστεύσει, πῶς ἡσυχάσει; *ib.*(1113B).

***ἡσυχαστήριον, τό,** *cell of a solitary, hermitage,* Jo.Clim.*scal.*1(M.88.641B).

ἡσυχαστής, ὁ, *solitary, hesychast,* dist. from cenobite (v. ἡσυχία); **1.** description of perfect hesychast ἡ. ἐστιν ὁ τὸ ἀσώματον ἐν σωματικῷ οἴκῳ περιορίζειν φιλονεικῶν, τὸ παράδοξον Jo.Clim.*scal.*27(M.88.1097B); ἡ. ἐστι τύπος ἀγγέλου ἐπίγειος χάρτῃ πόθου καὶ σπουδῆς γράμμασι τὴν ἑαυτοῦ προσευχὴν ῥᾳθυμίας καὶ ὀλιγωρίας ἐλευθερώσας. ἡ. ἐστιν ὁ βοήσας ἐναργῶς· 'ἑτοίμη ἡ καρδία μου, ὁ θεός.' ἡ. ἐστιν ἐκεῖνος ὁ εἰπών· 'ἐγὼ καθεύδω, καὶ ἡ καρδία μου ἀγρυπνεῖ' *ib.*(1100A); *ib.*(1100D); μηδὲ φωνῆς ὀρνέων ἐπαΐοντα τὸν ἡ. ἠρεμεῖν Thdr.Stud.*or.*12.26(M.99.880D); in acrostic, Thal.*cent.*1.60–68(M.91.1433A–C); life built on faith, Jo.Clim.*scal.*27(1113B); and prayer, Esaias *cap.spir.*11(M.40.1209A); κράτος δὲ ἡσυχαστῇ προσευχῆς πλῆθος Jo.Clim.*scal.*27(1117B); **2.** ref. individual hesychasts τὸν μέγαν ἡ. Ῥουφῖνον Nil.*epp.*4.17(M.79.557D); ὁ ἡ. Ἰσαάκιος Pall.*v.Chrys.*8(p.50.6; M.47.29); Ἰωάννην τὸν ἐπίσκοπον καὶ ἡ. Cyr.S.*v.Sab.*21(p.105.19); Jo.Mosch.*prat.*52(M.87.2908A); **3.** in legislation εἰ μή τινες αὐτῶν [sc. monks] τὸν ἐν θεωρίᾳ τε καὶ τελειότητι διαζῶντες βίον ἰδιάζον ἔχοιεν οἰκημάτιον, οὓς δὴ καλεῖν ἀναχωρητάς τε καὶ ἡ. εἰώθασιν...ἐπείτοιγε τοὺς ἄλλους, ὅσοις εἰς πλῆθος ἡ ἄσκησίς ἐστιν, ἐν τοῖς καλουμένοις κοινοβίοις εἶναι βουλόμεθα Justn.*nov.*5.3(p.32.2).

ἡσυχαστικός, *solitary* τοῖς ἡσυχαστικωτέροις...τῶν μοναστηρίων *V.Chrys.*(p.301.36); ref. life of a ἡσυχαστής: ἐν ἡ. τόπῳ μετὰ πατρὸς ἐν ὑποταγῇ καθεσθῆναι Jo.Clim.*scal.*4(M.88.724A); *ib.*15(893A); ἀναχωρήσας...ἐν τῷ ἡ. βίῳ Thdr.Stud.*or.*12.6(M.99.853C).

ἡσυχάστρια, ἡ, *anchoress,* Jo.Mosch.*prat.*127(M.87.2988C).

ἡσυχία, ἡ, A. *silence,* of God prior to revelation of his mysteries καὶ ἔλαθεν τὸν ἄρχοντα τοῦ αἰῶνος τούτου ἡ παρθενία Μαρίας καὶ ὁ τοκετὸς αὐτῆς ὁμοίως καὶ ὁ θάνατος τοῦ κυρίου· τρία μυστήρια κραυγῆς, ἅτινα ἐν ἡ. θεοῦ ἐπράχθη Ign.*Eph.*19.1; in which Christ speaks to soul ὁ λόγον Ἰησοῦ κεκτημένος ἀληθῶς δύναται καὶ τῆς ἡ. αὐτοῦ ἀκούειν, ἵνα τέλειος ᾖ *ib.*15.2; of silence of the divine life ὅ τί ποτέ ἐστι τῆς θείας εἰρήνης καὶ ἡ. ... ὅπως τε ἠρεμεῖ, καὶ ἡ. ἄγει... οὔτε ἐννοῆσαί τινι τῶν ὄντων, οὔτε θεμιτὸν οὔτε ἐφικτὸν Dion.Ar.*d.n.*11.1(M.3.949A).

B. *tranquillity, quiet,* as a state of soul necessary for contemplation; **1.** def. ἡ. μὲν σώματός ἐστιν ἠθῶν καὶ αἰσθήσεων ἐπιστήμη καὶ κατάστασις· ἡ. δὲ ψυχῆς, λογισμῶν ἐπιστήμη καὶ ἀσύλητος ἔννοια Jo.Clim.*scal.*27(M.88.1097A); **2.** in gen. ἐν ἡ. τὸν νοῦν ἔχειν πειρᾶσθαι προσήκει Bas.*ep.*2.2(3.71B; M.32.224B); παιδεύων ἡμᾶς ἐν ταῖς εὐχαῖς ἡ. κατασκευάζειν ἑαυτοῖς Chrys.*hom.*83.1 *in Mt.*(7.790E); τοῦ ...Χριστοῦ τὰς ἀγαθοποιοὺς ἀκτῖνας ἐν ἡ. παραδεχόμενοι Dion.Ar.*ep.*8.1(M.3.1085C); esp. in religious life τοὺς δὲ καθ' ἑκάστην πόλιν... μονάζοντας ὑποτετάχθαι τῷ ἐπισκόπῳ καὶ τὴν ἡ. ἀσπάζεσθαι CChalc.*can.*4; **3.** means of attaining it: giving up one's own will, Jo.Clim.*scal.*27(M.88.1100A); prayer ἵνα δι' εὐχῆς πρὸς τὴν ἡ. συνδράμωσι *ib.*(1100D); recollection ἡσυχίας φίλος ἀνδρεῖός τις καὶ ἀπότομος λογισμός, ἐν θύρᾳ καρδίας ἀνυστάκτως ἱστάμενος *ib.*(1097A); ἔργον ἡσυχίας ἀμεριμνία προηγουμένη πάντων τῶν πραγμάτων εὐλόγων καὶ ἀλόγων *ib.*(1109B); *ib.*(1112A); suffering with Christ οὐδεὶς εἰς ἡ. τελείαν ἔγκαρπον, καὶ εἰς κατάπαυσιν ἁγίαν τῆς τελειότητος δύναται ἐλθεῖν, ἐὰν μὴ πρῶτον συμπάθῃ τῷ Χριστῷ, καὶ ὑπενέγκῃ ὅλα τὰ παθήματα αὐτοῦ Bars.*resp.*(M.88.1813C); **4.** in rel. to apprehension of divine mysteries ὁ ἡσυχίαν καταλαβὼν ἔγνω βυθὸν μυστηρίων,... κυροῖ τὸ εἰρημένον Παῦλος· εἰ μὴ γὰρ ἐν παραδείσῳ ὡς ἐν ἡ. ἡρπάγη, οὐκ ἂν ἄρρητα ῥήματα ἀκοῦσαι ἠδύνατο. τῆς ἡ. τὸ οὖς δέξεται παρὰ θεοῦ ἐξαίσια Jo.Clim.*scal.*27(M.88.1100C); **5.** effects: contemplation τὴν ἡ. οὐκ εἶναι ἀργήν, ἂν μήτι τῶν θεωρίας ἀξίων τὸν νοῦν κατεῖχε ‡Nil.*perist.*1.1(M.79.812B); constant praise of God, Jo.Clim.*scal.*27(M.88.1101A); κατευνάζοντες ἡσυχίᾳ τὰ πάθη Nil.*praest.*12(M.79.1076A); κτῆσαι δὲ καὶ ἡ., ἀδελφέ, ὥσπερ τεῖχος ὀχυρόν· ἡ γὰρ ἡ. ὑψηλότερόν σε ποιεῖ τῶν παθῶν ‡Chrys.*pat.et consumm.*(12.819C); ἡ. ὠφελεῖ, τῶν κακῶν ἀργήσασα...ἡ οὖν ἡ. ὡς καλὴ οὖσα μήτηρ πασῶν τῶν ἀρετῶν τυγχάνει. ἀπογεννᾷ γὰρ αὐτὰς διὰ τῆς πρὸς θεὸν ἀδιαλείπτου καὶ ἀπερισπάστου ἡ. Ant.Mon.*hom.*103(M.89.1745A); **6.** its perfection ἀρχὴ μὲν ἡσυχίας τὸ ἀποσείεσθαι κτύπους, ὡς τὸν βυθὸν ταράσσοντας· τέλος δὲ ταύτης, τὸ μὴ δεδιέναι θορύβους, ἀλλ' ἀναισθητεῖν ἐν τούτοις Jo.Clim.*scal.*27(M.88.1097B); ὦ ἡ., προκοπὴ μοναζόντων· ὦ ἡ., κλῖμαξ οὐράνιος· ὦ ἡ., ὁδὸς βασιλείας οὐρανῶν· ὦ ἡ., κατανύξεως μήτηρ· ὦ ἡ., ἔσοπτρον ἁμαρτημάτων, ἡ δεικνύουσα ἀνθρώπῳ τὰ πλημμελήματα αὐτοῦ·...ἡ δάκρυα μὴ ἐμποδίζουσα·...πραότητος γεννήτρια·...ταπεινοφροσύνης σύσκηνε·...φόβῳ θεοῦ συνεζευγμένη, διανοίας φωταγωγέ·...λογισμῶν κατάσκοπε, καὶ διακρίσεως σύμπονε·...γεννήτρια παντὸς ἀγαθοῦ·...σχόλασις προσευχῆς καὶ ἀναγνώσεως·... γαλήνη λογισμῶν ‡Chrys.*pat.et consumm.*(12.819C–E); exemplified by Mary of Bethany (Lc.10:42), *ib.*(820A).

C. *tranquillity* as state of separation from world, = *solitude;* **1.** non-technical; **a.** double connotation of silence and solitude ἀναχωρῶ ἐπὶ τὴν ἐρημίαν καὶ ἡ. Or.*hom.20.8 in Jer.*(p.190.4; M.13.520A); ἡ. οὖν ἀρχὴ καθάρσεως τῇ ψυχῇ, μήτε γλώττης λαλούσης τὰ τῶν ἀνθρώπων, μήτε ὀφθαλμῶν εὐχροίας σωμάτων...περισκοπούντων Bas.*ep.*2.2(3.72C; M.32.228A); ἡσυχίας γὰρ μήτηρ ἡ ἔρημος Chrys.*hom.50.1 in Mt.*(7.513D); ἀγαγεῖν σε βούλεται εἰς τὴν ἔρημον, τουτέστιν, εἰς τὴν ἡ. ‡Chrys.*pat.et consumm.*(12.820B); of Moses ὁ τεσσεράκοντα ἔτεσι τῆς μετὰ τῶν ἀνθρώπων ἐπιμιξίας ἑαυτὸν ἀποικίσας, καὶ μόνος μόνῳ συζῶν ἑαυτῷ, καὶ διὰ ἡσυχίας ἀμετεωρίστως τῇ θεωρίᾳ τῶν ἀοράτων ἐνατενίζων Gr.Nyss.*Pss.titt.*A 7(M.44.456C); of Christ τοῦ πλήθους ὑποχωρῶν,...ταῖς ἐρήμοις ἐνδιέτριβε, τὸ χρήσιμον τῆς ἡ. τοῖς ὁρᾶν δυναμένοις ἔργῳ παραδηλῶν Nil.*praest.*12(M.79.1076A); of shepherds at Bethlehem ὡς τῇ τῶν πολλῶν ἀναχωρήσει καὶ ἡ. κεκαθαρμένους Dion.Ar.*c.h.*4.4(M.3.181B); of monks τὰς ἐρήμους διώκοντες,...ἐν πολλῇ ἡ. καὶ ἀμεριμνίᾳ τῷ θεῷ προσομιλοῦντες Ant.Mon.*hom.*103(M.89.1745B); **b.** in monastic life ἡ. δὲ καὶ μονοτροπίαν ἑαυτῷ ἁρμόσας Bas.*ep.*45.1(3.133D; M.32.365C); οὐκ ἔστι μοναχοῦ κατάστασιν ἐπιγνῶναι, ἄνευ ἡ. Nil.*inst.*(M.79.1236B); ἔναγχος τῶν βιωτικῶν ἀποστατήσας θορύβων, μεγάλην ἄγειν ἡ. ὀφείλεις id.*epp.*3.223(M.79.485C); coupled with ἀναχώρησις, ‡Pall.*h.mon.*proem.(p.2.4; M.65.444B); Egyptian monks called ἡσυχίας ἐρῶντες, Soz.*h.e.*6.20.1(M.67.1340C); as monk's principal joy, Evagr.Pont.*rer.mon.*2(M.40.1253B); τὸν μονήρη βίον ὡς ἔστιν ἀναλαβεῖν, καὶ ἐπὶ τὰ τῆς ἡ. ἀποτρέχειν τρόπαια *ib.*3(1253C); φροντίζομεν τῆς ἡσυχίας, ἵνα ἐν τῇ ἀδολεσχίᾳ τοῦ θεοῦ διαμείνωμεν Isaac *ep.*8(p.162); for reasons of charity it may be interrupted, *ib.*9(p.163); *ib.*13(p.166); **2.** as t.t. for solitary life of hesychast, accorded to monks desiring it, either temporarily or permanently, after spending a certain time in community; **a.** description ταῦτά σοι οὕτως παραινεῖν οἶδε τὰ χρήσιμα ὁ τῆς ἡ. τρόπος. φέρε δὴ καὶ τῶν ἑξῆς ἐπιφερομένων ἐν αὐτῇ πραγμάτων παραθήσομαί σοι τὸν νοῦν...καθεζόμενος ἐν τῷ κελλίῳ σου, συνάγαγέ σου τὸν νοῦν· μνήσθητι ἡμέρας θανάτου· ἴδε τότε τοῦ σώματος τὴν νέκρωσιν...κατάγνωθι τῆς ἐν τῷ κόσμῳ τούτῳ ματαιότητος· ἐπιμέλησαι τῆς τε ἐπιεικείας καὶ τῆς σπουδῆς, ἵνα δυνηθῇς διαπαντὸς μένειν ἐν τῇ αὐτῇ προθέσει τῆς ἡ. Evagr.Pont.*rer.mon.*9(M.40.1261A,B); ἡ ἡ. ἐστὶ ἀδιάσπαστος θεῷ λατρεία, καὶ παράστασις· ἡ Ἰησοῦ μνήμη ἑνωθήτω τῇ πνοῇ σου (cf. the Jesus-prayer of later hesychasts) καὶ τότε γνώσῃ ἡσυχίας ὠφέλειαν Jo.Clim.*scal.*27(M.88.1112C); **b.** its dangers τοῖς ἐν ἡ., μάλιστα πολεμεῖ τὸ πάθος τῆς ἀκηδίας ‡Nil.*vit.cog.*(M.79.1460A); τῷ αὐτῷ κανόνι καὶ ἐπὶ τῆς ἡ. χρησώμεθα λέγοντες, πολλοὺς δοκίμους δεξαμένη, ἀπεδοκίμασε διὰ τῆς ἰδιορυθμίας Jo.Clim.*scal.*27(M.88.1108A); ἡ. ἀπείρους ἀποπνίγει *ib.*(1112A); φόβου σοι πολλοῦ καθ' ἡσυχίαν χρὴ...οὐδὲν γὰρ οὕτως ἀκηδίαν ἐκδιώκειν δύναται *ib.*(1113C); **c.** its requirements μηδεὶς ὑπὸ θυμοῦ καὶ οἰήσεως, ὑποκρίσεώς τε καὶ μνησικακίας ὀχλούμενος, ἴχνος ἡσυχίας ἰδεῖν τολμήσαι *ib.*(1108A); τῶν λόγῳ τὴν ἡ. μετερχομένων σημεῖα...ταῦτα· νοῦς ἀκύμαντος, ἔννοια ἡγνισμένη, ἁρπαγὴ πρὸς κύριον, κολάσεων παράστασις, θανάτου ἔπειξις *ib.*(1108A); cf.*ib.*(1116B); ὁ οὔπω θεὸν γνούς, εἰς ἡ. ἀδόκιμος *ib.*(1112A); **d.** its fruits διὰ τοῦτο καλὸν ἡ ἡ., ὅτι τὸ βλαπτὸν οὐχ ὁρᾶται, τὸ δὲ οὐχ ὁραθὲν οὐ δέχεται διάνοια Nil.*praest.*11(M.79.1073B) perh. also ref. contemplative quiet in gen.; ἁπλῆ γὰρ ὅλη καὶ ἄδετος τῆς ἡ. ἡ κατάστασις Jo.Clim.*scal.*27(M.88.1116B); **e.** as preparation for apostolate πολλὴν ἡ. πρότερον ἀσκήσαντες, ἐσχήκασιν ἐν ἑαυτοῖς οἰκοῦσαν τὴν δύναμιν τὴν θεϊκήν, καὶ τότε ὁ θεὸς ἀπέστειλεν αὐτοὺς εἰς τὸ μέσον τῶν ἀνθρώπων Ammonas *ep.*1(p.433.4); οἱ δὲ ἀπὸ θεοῦ πεμπόμενοι, ἀποστῆναι μὲν τῆς ἡ. οὐ βούλονται, εἰδότες ὅτι δι' αὐτῆς ἐκτήσαντο τὰς θείας δυνάμεις, ἵνα δὲ μὴ παρακούσωσι τοῦ δημιουργοῦ, ἔρχονται πρὸς τὴν τῶν ἀνθρώπων οἰκοδομήν *ib.*(p.433.14); **f.** eccl. legislation τοὺς ἐν πόλεσιν ἢ χωρίοις ἐν ἐγκλείστραις βουλομένους ἀναχωρεῖν...πρότερον ἐν μοναστηρίῳ εἰσιέναι δεῖ...ἐπὶ τριετῆ χρόνον τῷ τῆς μονῆς ἐξάρχοντι ἐν φόβῳ θεοῦ ὑποτάττεσθαι...τηνικαῦτα γὰρ πληροφορίαν πράξουσιν, ὡς οὐ κενὴν θηρώμενοι δόξαν, ἀλλὰ δι' αὐτὸ τὸ ὄντως καλὸν τὴν ἡ. ταύτην μεταδιώκουσι CTrull.*can*.41; life of hesychast to be given up if needs of Church require, *Ep*.ap.CNic.(787)*act*.3(M.98.1473A).

ἡσύχιος, *quiet*; hence *solitary, eremitical*, of a hesychast τὸν ἐρημικὸν καὶ ἡ. βίον Jo.Clim.*scal*.7(M.88.812A); †Jo.D.*B.J*.12(M.96.965B); οἷς δὲ ὁ βίος ἐστὶν ἡ. καὶ μονότροπος CNic.(787)*can*.22; masc. as subst. πτῶμα...ἡσυχίῳ...προσευχῆς διάστασις Jo.Clim.*scal*.27(1112C).

ἡσυχιότης, ἡ, *tranquillity*, Clem.*str*.7.3(p.13.23; M.9.424A).

***ἠσφαλισμένως**, **1.** *securely, steadily*, Gr.Nyss.*perf*.(p.192.6; M.46.268C); c. ἔχω, *be trustworthy*, Epiph.*haer*.42.11(p.140.25; M.41.749D); *ib*.51.4(p.251.24; 892D); **2.** *guardedly, for safety's sake, ib*.69.40(p.188.11; M.42.264C); *ib*.76.52(p.407.11; 625C); Cyr.*Jo*.1.7(4.61C); c. ἔχω, *be a safeguard*, Didym.*Trin*.1.18(M.39.356C).

[*]**ἤτριος**, *fibrous, loosely-knit*, Thdt.*provid*.5(4.546); *ib*.9(651).

ἥττημα, τό, **1.** *defeat, failure*; of Fall, Meth.*Porph*.1.6(p.504.14; M.18.400B); Germ.CP *or*.1(M.98.228D); in gen., Areth.*Apoc*.2(M.106.525B); **2.** *defect*, ‡Ath.*Apoll*.2.13(M.26.1153B).

ἡττόνως, *less*, Or.*princ*.1.3.5(p.56.2; M.11.150B).

[*]**ἠϋκέρως**, (= εὐκέρως) *with fine horns*, *Orac.Sib*.13.162.

ἠχέω, **1.** *make a sound*; of the heavens glorifying God by speaking letters of the alphabet (Gnost.), Hipp.*haer*.6.48(p.180.12; M.16.3275A); met., of replying in writing, Afric.*ep.Or*.(p.80.13; M.11.48A); **2.** *make to cause a sound* ἠ. τὰ κύματα Thphl.Ant.*Autol*.1.7(M.6.1033C); **3.** *make resound*, with accusations βασιλικὰς ἠχήσαντες κατ' αὐτῶν ἀκοάς Petr.II Al.*encycl*.9(M.33.1292A)ap.Thdt.*h.e*.4.22.36; **4.** *proclaim, announce*, *Pss.Sal*.8.1; Meth.*symp*.6.5(p.69.25; M.18.121A).

ἤχημα, τό, *sound, roaring*, Cyr.*Jo*.5.1(cj. 4.469E for ἐν σχήμασι Aubert).

***ἤχησις, ἡ**, *sound*; of music of the spheres as agent of Creation (Gnost.), Hipp.*haer*.6.48(p.180.13; M.16.3275A); in gen., Gr.Nyss.*Pss.titt*.B 10(M.44.536A).

ἠχητικῶς, *with a loud noise*, *cat.Apoc*.8:12(p.309.16).

ἦχος, ὁ, **1.** *sound* τί...ἐστιν Χριστὸς ἀλλ' ὁ λόγος, ἠ. τοῦ θεοῦ; ἵνα λόγος ᾖ τοῦτο τὸ ὀρθὸν ξύλον ἐφ' ᾧ ἐσταύρωμαι· ἠ. δὲ τὸ πλάγιόν ἐστιν, ἀνθρώπου φύσις *A.Petr.c.Sim*.9(p.96.8); δυσφημότηρον...ὁ Ἡρακλέων ...φησὶν ὅτι ὁ λόγος μὲν ὁ σωτήρ ἐστιν, φωνὴ δὲ ἡ ἐν τῇ ἐρήμῳ ἡ διὰ Ἰωάννου διανοουμένη, ἠ. δὲ πᾶσα προφητικὴ τάξις Or.*Jo*.6.20(12; p.129.2; M.14.233Dff.); ref. Christ δαίμονος οὐ μεθέπει...ἠ. ἱμάσθλης Nonn.*par.Jo*.8:49(M.43.821A); **2.** musical *mode*, †Jo.Jej.*poenit*.(M.88.1889A); Jo.Mon.*hymn.Bas*.(M.96.1372A); *Const.Stud*.2(M.99.1705A).

ἠχώ, ἡ, *sound* ἑρμηνεύεται [sc. Abraham]...πατὴρ ἐκλεκτὸς ἠχοῦς Clem.*str*.5.1(p.331.9, v.l. ἤχους M.9.20A); Or.*Cels*.5.45(p.49.11; M.11.1252B); of voice of God, Nonn.*par.Jo*.12:29(M.43.856A); of literary style, Synes.*Dion* 3(p.241.15; M.66.1121A).

Θ

***Θαιμάν**, *Teman*; exeg. Abac.3:3, referred to Inc. μεταλαμβάνεται ...Θ. εἰς τὸν νότον...ὡς γὰρ ἐκ θεοῦ εἰς ἀνθρώπους τὴν ἄφιξιν πεποιημένος...λέγεται ὁ θεὸς ἀπὸ Θ. ἥξειν Eus.*d.e*.6.15(p.271.21; M.22.445D); as Inc. of God who was seen on Horeb, which is to the south, Cyr.*Abac*.2(3.553C); to Bethlehem ἐκ ποίου μέρους τοῦ περὶ τὴν Ἱερουσαλὴμ ἔρχεται [sc. ὁ κύριος];...ὁ θεὸς ἀπὸ Θ. ἥξει (Θ. δὲ ἑρμηνεύεται νότος) Cyr.H.*catech*.12.20; Cyr.*Abac*.2(3.553D); Θ. οἱ μὲν Λίβα, οἱ δὲ Νότον ἡρμηνεύκασι. προσθεσπίζει δὲ ὁ προφήτης...τὴν τοῦ θεοῦ...ἐνανθρώπησιν, τὴν ἐν Βηθλεὲμ γενομένην, ἥ τις ἀπὸ Νότου καὶ Λιβὸς τῆς Ἱερουσαλὴμ διάκειται Thdt.*Abac*.3:3(2.1550); to two comings of Christ τὸ δὲ Θ. μεταλαμβάνεται εἰς...'συντέλεια' [both advents being ἐπὶ συντελείᾳ τοῦ αἰῶνος] Eus.*d.e*.6.15(p.270.31; 445A).

***θάκη, ἡ**, *privy*; plur., Ath.*ep.mort.Ar*.3(p.179.26; M.25.688C).

θαλαμεύ-ω, **1.** *admit to the bridal-chamber*; met., of S. Stephen's entry into heaven ἐθαλάμευσε...αὐτὸν ἡ βασιλὶς καὶ παρθένος ‡Chrys.*Steph*.3(12.812A); ὃν πᾶσα ἡ κτίσις...ὕμνησεν, αὕτη [sc. BMV] μόνη...ἐθαλάμευσε Procl.CP *or*.5.2(M.65.720A); ref. a saint τὸν σταυρωθέντα ἐν ψυχῇ ἐθαλάμευσεν *ib*.12.1(788B); hence **2.** *espouse*, Melet.*nat.hom*.2(M.64.1164D); met. τὴν...Ῥωμαϊκὴν ἐλευθερίαν...~ων Thphyl.*exc.Rom*.1(p.221.27; M.113.928C); **3.** *keep at home*; pass., of girls and women, *T.Job* 21(p.116.5 n.); Cyr.H.*ep.Const*.4(M.33.1169B); Chrys.*Anna* 1.6(4.710C); Thdt.*h.rel*.13(3.1210); also τὸν στρατιώτην...~όμενον ‡Nil.*perist*.12.2(M.79.941D); met. εἰρήνη ἐθαλαμεύετο Ast.Soph.*Ps.6*(M.40.457B); **4.** pass. intrans., *stay at home*, Clem.*paed*.3.2(p.239.6; M.8.561B); Synes.*regn*.15(p.33.16; M.66.1080C); *ib*.19(p.43.6; 1089B); met., of Spouse in Cant., Nil.ap.Proc.G.*Cant*.4:13(M.87.1668B).

θάλαμος, ὁ, *wedding-feast*, *T.Jud*.10.4.

θάλασσα, ἡ, *sea*; **1.** in gen. εἰ...ἐκ μερῶν συνέστηκε [sc. God], πάντως αὐτὸς ἑαυτοῦ ἀνόμοιος φανήσεται...εἰ γῆ τυγχάνει, οὐκ ἂν εἴη θ. Ath.*gent*.28(M.25.56C); ὡς δεσπότης ἐπέβαινε...τῇ θ. id.*inc*.18.6(M.25.128D); cf.id.*Ar*.3.56(M.26.441A); id.*ep.Serap*.4.16(M.26.660B); as signifying God's immensity, Cyr.H.*catech*.9.10; its obedience to God an example to men, Geo.Pis.*hex*.380(M.92.1463A); ref. its obedience to providential laws τὸ κύτος τῆς ἀπείρου θ. ... καθὼς διέταξεν αὐτῇ, οὕτως ποιεῖ *1Clem*.20.6; εἰ μὴ κρείττονι προστάξει ἐγεγόνει τούτων μία κρᾶσις, πῶς ἂν...ἡ θ. τῇ γῇ...ἐμίγη καὶ συνῆλθεν, ἀνομοίου οὔσης τῆς ἑκάστου πρὸς τὸ ἕτερον φύσεως; Ath.*gent*.37(73B); *ib*.42(84C); as keeping divinely-fixed limits, Cyr.H.*catech*.9.11; Thdt.*provid*.2(4.508); in Valent. theory formed from tears of Ἐνθύμησις, Iren.*haer*.1.4.3(M.7.484B); of Sophia, Cyr.H.*catech*.6.18; **2.** fig., of this life τὴν θ. τοῦ βίου τούτου Or.*hom.18.5 in Jer*.(p.156.22; M.13.472C); cf.*ib.16.1*(p.132.11; 457D); its instability an image of this life, Bas.*hom*.12.15(2.111A; M.31.417B); θ. ... ἀκουστέον...τὸν τῆς κακώσεως τόπον †Bas.*Is*.250(1.570D; M.30.560B); θ.... λέγει τὴν ὑλώδη ταύτην ζωήν, τὴν πᾶσι τοῖς τῶν πειρασμῶν ἀνέμοις ταρασσομένην, καὶ τοῖς ἐπαλλήλοις πάθεσι κυμαινομένην Gr.Nyss.*Pss.titt*.A 8(M.44.473C); Chrys.*serm.9.2 in Gen*.(4.690B); Cyr.*1Cor*.10:1(M.74.879A); Thdt.*Dan*.7:2–3(2.1190); Areth.*Apoc*.55(M.106.733B); of gentiles ὕδωρ καὶ θ. αἰνιγματωδῶς ὀνομάζει τῶν ἐθνῶν τὴν πληθὺν Cyr.*Is*.2.5(2.342C); ref. monks ὥσπερ τὸν ἰχθὺν εἰς τὴν θ. οὕτως ἡμᾶς εἰς τὸ ὄρος ἐπείγεσθαι Ath.*v.Anton*.85(M.26.961C); τὴν ὑελίνην θ. σημαίνειν φασὶ τό τε πλῆθος τῶν σωζομένων Andr.Caes.*Apoc*.45(M.106.353C); **3.** an extended use in scripture ἔθος...τῇ θείᾳ γραφῇ θ. ἀποκαλεῖν τὰ πρὸς τῇ ἑσπέρᾳ μέρη, διάτοι τὸ σφόδρα πολλὴν καὶ εὐρεῖαν εἶναι τὴν ἐκείνης θ. Cyr.*Is*.2.1(2.207C); **4.** of Red Sea; **a.** twelvefold division at Exodus λόγος ἀρχαῖός φησιν εἰς δώδεκα τμήματα διαιρεθεῖσαν τὴν θ., ἑκάστῃ φυλῇ μίαν ἀποδοῦναι ὁδόν Ath.*exp.Ps*.135:13(M.27.525D); αὕτη...ἡ ἱστορία ἡ γενομένη ἐν τῇ Ἐρυθρᾷ θ. εἰς τύπον ὑπῆρχε τοῦ κόσμου τοῦ μέλλοντος διαιρεῖσθαι τοῖς δύο καὶ δέκα ἀποστόλοις παρὰ κυρίου Hesych.H.*Ps.tit*.135(M.27.1269C); Didym.*Ps*.135:13(M.39.1596A); Chrys.*exp.in Ps*.135:13(5.399C); Thdt.*qu.25 in Ex*.(1.143); tradition rejected as Jewish fable, *ib.27*(144); **b.** as baptismal type, Just.*dial*.138.2(M.6.793B); δεύτερον [sc. βάπτισμα] τὸ τοῦ Μωσέως, ὅτε τὴν Ἐρυθρὰν διεπέρασε· τυπικὸν γὰρ ἦν· ὥσπερ γὰρ ἐκεῖ ἡ θ., οὕτω τὸ ὕδωρ ἐν τῷ βαπτίσματι ‡Ath.*qu.script*.101(M.28.760A); ἡ θ. βάπτισμα τυπικῶς, χωρισμὸν ποιοῦσα τοῦ Φαραώ, ὡς καὶ τὸ λουτρὸν τοῦτο τῆς τυραννίδος τοῦ διαβόλου Bas.*Spir*.31(3.26C; M.32.124B); Didym.*Trin*.2.14(M.39.696B); Chrys.*hom.23.2 in 1Cor*.(10.203D); id.*hom.in 1Cor.10:1*(3.234C); Thdt.*qu.27 in Ex*.(1.144); id.*1Cor*.10:1–4(3.225); **c.** in Peratic theory τοῦτό ἐστι...τὸ ἐξελθεῖν ἐξ Αἰγύπτου, ἐκ τοῦ σώματος...καὶ περᾶσαι τὴν θ. τὴν Ἐρυθρὰν τουτέστι τῆς φθορᾶς τὸ ὕδωρ, ὅ ἐστιν ὁ Κρόνος, καὶ γενέσθαι πέραν τῆς Ἐρυθρᾶς θ. τουτέστι τῆς γενέσεως Hipp.*haer*.5.16(p.111.27; M.16.3171C); **d.** as abode of demon, *T.Sal*.23.2(M.122.1356A).

θαλάσσειος, *of the sea*, *Orac.Sib*.3.479.

θαλασσεύ-ω, **1.** *be at sea*, met. ἐπικουρεῖν ἐμοὶ βιωτικῶς ~οντι Sophr.H.*ep.syn*.(M.87.3149C); **2.** *navigate*, Cyr.*Jo*.4.5(4.408D); **3.** *cover with sea*, *M.Thdot*.1 7(p.65.27).

θαλασσίτης, ὁ, a gem; one of the varieties of the hyacinth stone (identified by Epiph. with the lyncurium or tourmaline), so called prob. because of its sea-like colour, Epiph.*gemm*.7(M.43.300A).

***θαλασσοβαδίζω**, *walk on the sea*; ref. S. Bartholomew, Thdr.Stud.*or*.10.8(M.99.801B).

θαλασσοβαφής, *dipped in the sea*; hence *sea-coloured*; of beryl, Epiph.*gemm*.11(M.43.301A); Andr.Caes.*Apoc*.67(M.106.436D).

***θαλασσοθέα, ἡ**, *goddess of the sea* χαίροις, ὦ Ἐφεσίων πόλις, μᾶλλον δὲ θαλασσοθέα †Cyr.*hom.div*.11(5^2.379E).

***θαλασσοκτονέω**, *kill in the sea*, ‡Jo.D.*hom*.5(M.96.653A).

θαλασσομαχέω, *fight against the sea*, Ephr.2.154A; Jo.Mosch.*prat*.203(M.87.3093B).

***θαλασσομαχία, ἡ**, *fight against the sea*; met., ref. temptation, Petr.I Al.*ep.can*.9(M.18.484A).

***θαλασσοπορία, ἡ**, *sea-voyage*, Cosm.Mel.*schol*.(M.38.349) in Gr.Naz.*carm*.2.1.1.6.

θαλασσοπόρος, *sea-faring*, Paul.Sil.*Soph*.907(M.86.2153B).

θαλασσ-όω, *throw into the sea*, Pall.*v.Chrys.*9(p.51.21; M.47.30); pass., *be surrounded as with the sea* νῆσον καλεῖ Αἴγυπτον, ὡς ∼ουμένην τῷ ποταμῷ Thdt.*Is.*20:6(p.88.27; 2.284).

***θαλαττικός**, *of the sea*, Pall.*h.Laus.*14(p.37.21, v.l. θαλάττιος M. 34.1036A).

θάλεια (-λια), ἡ, *banquet*; **1.** title of Arius' songs expressing his Trin. doctrine Ἄρειος...συνέθηκεν ἑαυτοῦ τὴν αἵρεσιν...ὡς ἐν Θ. ζηλώσας τὸν Αἰγύπτιον Σωσάτην Ath.*syn.*15(p.242.5; M.26.705C); id.*Ar.*1.5(M.26.20C); condemned, Socr.*h.e.*1.9.16(M.67.84B); **2.** of eucharist θ. ζείδωρος Nonn.*par.Jo.*6:26(M.43.797B).

θαλλί(ο)ν, τό, **1.** *palm-leaf, palm-branch*, Procl.CP *or.*9.4(M.65. 776D); *Apophth.Patr.*(M.65.93C,253C); **2.** a dry measure, *ib.*(92B).

θαλλός, ὁ, **1.** *branch*; *stalk*; which a martyr was required to use in pagan cult, *M.Con.*4.4; θ. σίτου *Apophth.Patr.*(M.65.352A); **2.** plur., *palm-leaves*, woven into ropes by solitaries, Pall.*h.Laus.*2 (p.17.11; M.34.1011C).

θάλλ-ω, **1.** *flourish, blossom*; of Christian life ∼οντα πρὸς ἀθανασίαν βίον Meth.*res.*2.2(p.331.16; M.41.1164C); **2.** *exult*, *A.Thom.* A 142(p.249.3); **3.** *make to bloom* τοὺς τὴν πίστιν...τεθηλότας Thdt. *Is.*35:7(p.141.5).

θαμβαλέος, **1.** *astonished*, Nonn.*par.Jo.*4:19(M.43.778A); *ib.*8:45 (812C); **2.** *astonishing, wonderful* θ. φωνή *ib.*2:18(764B); ἀρχή θ. *ib.* 11:44(845C).

θαμβόομαι, *be astonished*, Eus.*h.e.*2.13.7(M.20.169B); Jo.D.*haer.* 100(M.94.761B).

θάμβος, τό, *object of wonder*; hence *miracle*, Nonn.*par.Jo.*4:54 (M.43.784C).

θαμνοειδής, *shrub-like, bushy*, Cyr.*glaph.Ex.*1(1.262B).

θανασίμως, *mortally* τὴν...ψυχὴν καιρός ἐστι τρῶσαι, οὐ θ. ἀλλὰ σωτηρίως Clem.*paed.*1.75(p.133.15; M.8.340A).

θανατ-άω, **1.** *desire to die*, prob. ref. Marcionists τῇ πρὸς τὸν δημιουργὸν ἀπεχθείᾳ οἱ ἄθλιοι ∼ῶντες Clem.*str.*4.4(p.256.13; M.8. 1229C); **2.** *not care about death*, Chrys.*hom.48.2 in Ac.*(9.361C).

θανατηφόρος, *death-bringing, fatal* τὴν ὀργὴν αὐτοῦ [sc. God] τὴν θ. *V.Zos.*7(p.101.27); ref. slavery of mankind before Inc., Clem. *paed.*3.1(p.237.8; M.8.557A); of Easter in rel. to death θανάτου θανατηφόρος πληγή, ἀνθρώπων ἡ ἄφθαρτος τροφή ‡Chrys.*pasch.*6.3(p.123. 3; 8.265B); of tree of knowledge, †Dion.Al.*fr.*(p.200.3); of separation from Logos, Clem.*str.*1.8(p.26.27; M.8.737A); θ. ὁ διάβολος Meth. *symp.*5.5(p.59.7; M.18.105B); of heresy, Malch.*ep.*ap.Eus.*h.e.*7.30.3 (M.20.709C); of theatres, etc. θ. ἡδονή Isid.Pel.*epp.*5.185(M.78.1436B).

θανατιάω, = θανατάω, *M.Pion.*5.

θανατικός, *deadly, mortal*; **1.** θ. ἁμαρτία Or.*fr.in Ps.*50:16(p.85); περὶ ἁμαρτίας θ., καὶ μὴ θ. Euthal.*epp.cath.*(M.85.684D); ref. heresy τὰ θ. νάματα Thdt.*h.e.*4.11.8(3.967); **2.** τὸ θ. *plague*, ‡Ath.*qu.Ant.* 103(M.28.661A); Jo.Mosch.*prat.*131(M.87.2996B); θανατικὸν ἐκ τοῦ βομβῶνος Gr.Syc.*v.Thdr.Syc.*8(p.367); Leont.N.*v.Sym.*38(M.93. 1717A); Anast.S.*qu.et resp.*96(M.89.741A).

***θανατοκτόνος**, *death-destroying* τὸ θ. πάθος Procl.CP *or.*17.4 (M.65.813A).

***θανατολογ-έομαι**, *be said to be dead* ἡ σὰρξ διὰ τὴν πρὸς θεὸν λόγον...ἕνωσιν...∼εῖται Anast.S.*hod.*12(M.89.200D).

***θανατόπνοος**, *breathing death*; of envy, ‡Chrys.*hom.in Ps.*75:12 (5.605B).

θανατοποιός, *deadly, death-dealing*, of devils θ. δυνάμεις Eus.*h.e.* 10.4.14(M.20.853B); ἡ θ. ἁμαρτία Gr.Nyss.*hom.12 in Cant.*(M.44. 1021D); ref. OT οὐκ ἦν θ. ἡ διαθήκη, ἀλλὰ κατὰ τοῦ θανάτου Epiph. *haer.*66.73(p.114.28; M.42.145A); of heretics, *ib.*34.21(p.38.18; M.41. 625B); ref. tree of knowledge οὐ φύσιν εἶχε θανατοποιοῦ γνώσεως ἐργαστικήν, ἀλλ' ἀπὸ τῆς περὶ αὐτὸ γενομένης τῷ Ἀδὰμ τραγῳδίας ἔλαβε τὸ ὄνομα Sever.*creat.*6.4(M.56.488).

θάνατος, ὁ, **I.** *death*;

A. physical; **1.** def.; **a.** (Platonic) ὁ θ. χωρισμὸς ψυχῆς ἀπὸ σώματος Clem.*str.*7.12(p.51.18; M.9.500A); *ib.*3.9(p.225.24; M.8. 1168A); Nemes.*nat.hom.*2(M.40.549A); Isid.Pel.*epp.*3.248(M.78. 928B); Andr.Cr.*or.*12(M.97.1049B); Jo.D.*f.o.*4.27(M.94.1220A); **b.** variants of this λέγεται ἐν τῷ θ. τὸ εἶδος χωρίζεσθαι ἀπὸ τῆς σαρκός Meth.*res.*3.6(p.397.4; M.18.321A); ζωὴ δέ, σώματός τε καὶ ψυχῆς δέσις, ὡς θ. εἶναι, τῶν δὲ τὴν διάστασιν Gr.Naz.*carm.*1.2.34.25 (M.37.947A); ὁ θ. ... διάλυσις ψυχῆς τε καὶ σώματος Gr.Nyss.*Apoll.*17 (M.45.1153D); τῆς ἀνθρωπίνης ψυχῆς ἡ ἀπὸ τοῦ σώματος ἔξοδος Cyr. *Jo.*7(4.679B); θ. ἔστιν ἐφ' ἡμῶν οὐ τῆς οὐσίας ἀνυπαρξία κατὰ τὸ δόξαν ἑτέροις ἀλλ' ἡ τῶν ἡνωμένων διάκρισις Dion.Ar.*e.h.*2.3.7(M.3. 404B); **c.** others, cf. *non...aliud est mors quam a vita discedere*, Or. *princ.*1.2.4(p.31.12; M.11.132C); σώματος...ἐστι θ. ἡ τῶν αἰσθητηρίων σβέσις καὶ ἡ πρὸς τὰ συγγενῆ τῶν στοιχείων διάλυσις Gr.Nyss.*Eun.*2 (2 p.366.4; M.45.545B); **2.** nature and causes; **a.** in gen.; natural to man, Ath.*inc.*3.4(M.25.101C); *ib.*21.4(133B); οὐ γὰρ ὁ θ. κακός, ἀλλ' ὁ πονηρὸς θ. κακός Chrys.*exp.in Ps.*110:2(5.267A); **b.** as caused by sin, *Barn.*12.2; τὸ τέλος εἶναι τοῦ νόμου τὸν θ. εἰρῆσθαι νομίζει [sc. Heracleon] ἀναιροῦντος διὰ τῶν ἁμαρτιῶν Or.*Jo.*13.60(59; p.292.10; M.14.513B); cf. *non ipse* [sc. God] *est causa mortis...sed in nostro peccato consistit*, id.*hom.1.9 in Ezech.*(p.333.11; M.13.676A); θ. ... ῥίζαν ἔχων τὴν ἁμαρτίαν Cyr.*ador.*16(1.554D); **c.** ordained by God κατεδικάζετο θ. καὶ φθορᾷ προαναθροῦντος, οἶμαι, θεοῦ τὸ ὡς ἔν γε τῷ συμβεβηκότι λυσιτελέστερον. ... ᾔδει γὰρ ὅτι πέμψει...τὸν ἴδιον υἱὸν...τοῦ θ. καταλύσοντα κράτος id.*glaph.Gen.*1(1.8D); Thdt.*inc.*6 (M.75.1424D); ἵνα...μισῇ τὴν ἁμαρτίαν τῶν ἀνθρώπων τὸ γένος, ὡς αἰτίαν θ. γεγενημένην, μετὰ τὴν παράβασιν τῆς ἐντολῆς ἐπιφέρει τοῦ θ. τὴν ψῆφον ὁ πάνσοφος id.*qu.37 in Gen.*(1.51); but not caused by him, Thphl.Ant.*Autol.*2.27(M.6.1093B); **d.** scope; devils not subject to death, Clem.*prot.*10(p.74.13; M.8.220A); λάβωμεν Ἐνώχ, ὃς... μετετέθη, καὶ οὐχ εὑρέθη αὐτοῦ θ. *1Clem.*9.3; ref. problem why death began with Abel σαθρὸν ἠβουλήθη ὁ θεὸς γενέσθαι τὸν τοῦ θ. θεμέλιον. εἰ γὰρ Ἀδὰμ πρότερος ἐτελεύτησεν, ἔσχεν ἂν ἐκεῖνος ἰσχυρὰν τὴν κρηπῖδα, πρῶτον νεκρὸν τὸν ἡμαρτηκότα δεξάμενος Thdt.*qu.46 in Gen*(1.58); angels not subject to death, Dion.Ar.*d.n.*4.1(M.3.693C); **3.** of Christ's death; **a.** prophecies and types: Ps.21, Just.*dial.*104.1 (M.6.720A); list of prophecies, Ath.*inc.*34.1(M.25.153C); paschal sacrifice, Cyr.*ador.*2(1.79E); OT sacrifices, *ib.*12(430C); Am.9:11, id. *Am.*84(3.350C); **b.** Christol. οὐδὲ...ὁ λόγος ἐπιδέχεται θ., ἀλλὰ τὸ ἀνθρώπινόν ἐστι τὸ τοῦτο ἐπιδεξάμενον, ὡς πολλάκις παρεστήσαμεν Or.*hom.14.6 in Jer.*(p.112.12; M.13.412C); Ath.*inc.*9.1(M.25.112A) cit. s. ἀνάστασις; cf.id.*Ar.*1.41(M.26.96C); ὅπου κεκράτητο ἡ ψυχὴ ἡ ἀνθρωπίνη ἐν θ., ἐκεῖ ἐπιδείκνυται ὁ Χριστὸς τὴν ἀνθρωπίνην ψυχὴν ἰδίαν οὖσαν, ἵνα καὶ παρῇ ὡς ἄνθρωπος ὁ ἀκράτητος ἐν θ., καὶ λύσῃ τὴν κράτησιν τοῦ θ., ὡς θεός ‡Ath.*Apoll.*1.17(M.26.1124C); **c.** as proof of reality of his humanity, cf.Or.*hom.1.4 in Ezech.*(p.328.2; M.13.672C); Ath.*ep.Serap.*4.20(M.26.669B); Anast.S.*hod.*13(M.89.241D); **d.** its circumstances ἔλαθεν τὸν ἄρχοντα τοῦ αἰῶνος τούτου...ὁ θ. τοῦ κυρίου Ign.*Eph.*19.1; not devised by Christ εἰ καὶ τοῦτο ποιήσας ἦν, ὑπόνοιαν καθ' ἑαυτοῦ παρεῖχεν, ὡς οὐ κατὰ παντὸς θανάτου δυνάμενος, ἀλλὰ μόνου τοῦ περὶ αὐτοῦ ἐπινοηθέντος Ath.*inc.*24.2(M.25.137B); ref. three-day interval before Resurrection τάχα δὲ καὶ ἐν ἴσῳ τοῦ διαστήματος ὄντος τοῦ τε θ. καὶ τῆς ἀναστάσεως, ἄδηλον ἐγίνετο τὸ περὶ τῆς ἀφθαρσίας κλέος *ib.*26.3(141A); taking place in public so as to preclude disbelief in its reality, *ib.*23.3(136D); οὐκ ἔπρεπε τῷ τοῦ θεοῦ λόγῳ, ζωῇ ὄντι, τῷ σώματι ἑαυτοῦ θ. παρ' ἑαυτοῦ διδόναι *ib.*22.1(133D); **e.** ref. Christ's agony, exeg. Ps.21 ἀκούσητε...ὡς αὐτὸς δι' ἐκείνου...σωθῆναι ἀπὸ τοῦ θ. τούτου αἰτῶν Just.*dial.*98.1 (M.6.705B); cf. *in morte conturbari refertur*, Or.*princ.*2.6.2(p.141.2; M.11.210C); δειλία μὲν θ. ἐστὶν ἰδίωμα φύσεως ἐκ παρακοῆς προσγενόμενον, τρόμος δὲ θ. ἐστὶν ἀμετανοήτων πταισμάτων τεκμήριον. δειλιᾷ Χριστὸς θ., οὐ τρέμει, ἵνα τῶν δύο φύσεων τὰ ἰδιώματα σαφῶς ἐμφανίσῃ Jo.Clim.*scal.*6(M.88.793B); denial that Jo.12:27, Mt.26:39, Mc.15:34 imply fear of death, Ath.*Ar.*3.54(M.26.436Bff.); Christ being not afraid but showing pity for men, Didym.*Trin.*3.21(M.39. 904Aff.); **f.** ref. Christ as second Adam παρθένος, καὶ ξύλον, καὶ θ. τῆς ἥττης ἡμῶν ἦν τὰ σύμβολα. ... θ. ἦν τὸ ἐπιτίμιον τοῦ Ἀδάμ. ἀλλ' ἰδού, πάλιν παρθένος, καὶ ξύλον, καὶ θ. ... καὶ τῆς νίκης ἐγένετο σύμβολα. ... ἀντὶ τοῦ θ. τοῦ Ἀδάμ, ὁ θ. τοῦ Χριστοῦ Chrys.*coemet.*2 (2.400A,B); τινές φασιν ἐκεῖ τὸν Ἀδὰμ τετελευτηκέναι καὶ κεῖσθαι· καὶ τὸν Ἰησοῦν ἐν τῷ τόπῳ, ἔνθα ὁ θ. ἐβασίλευσεν, ἐκεῖ καὶ τὸ τρόπαιον στῆσαι. καὶ γὰρ τρόπαιον ἐξῄει βαστάζον τὸν σταυρὸν κατὰ τῆς τοῦ θ. τυραννίδος id.*hom.85.1 in Jo.*(8.504A); ἐν αὐτῇ...ἡμέρᾳ ἐν ᾗ ἐπλάσθη ὁ Ἀδάμ, λέγω δὲ τῇ ἕκτῃ, γέγονεν καὶ ἡ παράβασις...καὶ ἡ ἀπόφασις τοῦ θ. ... οὕτως καὶ...ἐν αὐτῇ τῇ ἡμέρᾳ ἐγένετο διὰ ξύλου σταυροῦ ὁ σωτήριος θ. Cosm.Ind.*top.*2(M.88.124C); **g.** of his death as voluntary; cf. *quamvis...in morte fuerit, sed voluntarie et non, ut nos, necessitate peccati*, Or.*Cant.*3(p.222.25; M.13.184A); Meth.*symp.*9.2 (p.116.15; M.18.181A); Cyr.H.*catech.*13.5; Max.*cap.*4.39(M.90.1321C); **h.** and for all men, Ath.*inc.*22.3(M.25.136A); θ. ὑπὲρ πάντων ἔδει γενέσθαι, ἵνα τὸ παρὰ πάντων ὀφειλόμενον γένηται *ib.*20.5(132B); id.*Ar.* 1.41(M.26.97A); **i.** effects: destruction of death ἵνα καταργήσῃ θανάτῳ τὸν θ. Cyr.H.*catech.*19.4; Gr.Nyss.*Apoll.*17(M.45.1156A); λυτρικὸν γὰρ θ. φάρμακον ὁ Χριστοῦ θ., καὶ φθορᾶς ἀμείνους οἱ τῆς μυστικῆς εὐλογίας μέτοχοι Cyr.*ador.*2(1.80A); id.*Jo.*11(4.1026E); and of sin, Polyc.*ep.*1.2; ἵνα νεκρωθῇ διὰ τοῦ θ. τὸ παράπτωμα Meth.*symp.*9.2 (p.116.16; M.18.181A); and Devil διὰ τοῦ σταυροῦσθαι μέλλοντος θ. γενήσεσθαι ἔκτοτε προεκηρύσσετο τῷ ὄφει Just.*dial.*91.4(M.6.693B); ‡Ath.*serm.fid.*13(p.9; M.26.1269C); Cyr.*Jo.*4.2(4.353C); gift of eternal life, Ign. *Magn.*9.1; Max.*cap.*4.43(M.90.1324C); as participation in life of God θ. γεύεται ὁ υἱὸς τοῦ θεοῦ διὰ τὸν σαρκικὸν αὐτοῦ πατέρα, ἵνα οἱ υἱοὶ τοῦ ἀνθρώπου τῆς ζωῆς τοῦ θεοῦ μεταλάβωσι, διὰ τὸν κατὰ πνεῦμα αὐτῶν πατέρα θεόν Ath.*inc.et c.Ar.*8(M.26.996B); Dion.Ar.*e.h.* 4.3.10(M.3.484B); **j.** fruits of his death communicated; through faith and repentance, Ign.*Trall.*2.1; Just.*dial.*13.1(M.6.501A); through baptism which symbolizes the death of Christ ἔστι...τὸ... βάπτισμα εἰς τὸν θ. τοῦ Ἰησοῦ διδόμενον, τὸ δὲ ὕδωρ ἀντὶ ταφῆς *Const.App.*3.17.1; cf.*ib.*7.43.3; *Can.App.*47; Dion.Ar.*e.h.*4.3.10 (M.3.484B); cf.*ib.*2.3.7(404B); τοῦ...δεσποτικοῦ θ. τύπον ἔχει τὸ βάπτισμα Thdt.*Rom.*6:4(3.61); through eucharist which also symbolizes it, Serap.*euch.*13.13; *Const.App.*7.25.5; commemoration of death in anaphora, *Lit.*ap.*Const.App.*8.12.38; **k.** pagan view; Christ's death an argument against his divinity, Cels.ap. Or.*Cels.*7.53(p.203.27; M.11.1497B); **l.** heret., Manichean ὅλως οὐ γέγονε θ. Ath.*Ar.*2.43(M.26.237C); ref. Apollinarian view εἰ...κατὰ μετάστασιν θεότητος ὁ θ. γέγονε καὶ ἡ τοῦ σώματος νέκρωσις, ἴδιον ἄρα θ. ἀπέθανε, καὶ οὐ τὸν ἡμέτερον ‡Ath.*Apoll.*1.18(M.26.1125B); Docetic τὴν οἰκονομίαν τοῦ πάθους καὶ τοῦ θ. καὶ τῆς ἀναστάσεως δόκησιν λέγειν, κατὰ Μαρκίωνα καὶ τοὺς ἄλλους αἱρετικούς *ib.*2.12 (1152C); Eunomian οἱ περὶ Εὐνόμιον...εἰς τὸν θ., ὡς ἔφασκον, τοῦ κυρίου βαπτίζοντες, ὃν ἅπαξ μὲν ἀλλ' οὐχὶ δὶς ἢ τρὶς ὑπὲρ ἡμῶν ἀνεδέξατο Philost.*h.e.*10.4(M.65.585B); **4.** of death of martyrs; in gen., ref. Jo.12:32 τὸν ἐν μαρτυρίῳ θ. ὕψωσιν καλεῖσθαι Or.*mart.* 50(p.47.1; M.11.636A); ref. Jo.21:19 ὁ μαρτυρῶν τῷ ἑαυτοῦ θ. δοξάσει τὸν θεόν *ib.*(p.47.4; 636A); as gate of eternal life, *A.Andr.* A 14(p.55.15); Or.*mart.*22(p.20.13; M.11.592A); θ. μαρτύρων οὐκ ἔστι θ., ἀλλὰ ζωῆς βελτίονος ἀρχὴ καὶ πολιτείας πνευματικωτέρας προοίμια Chrys.*pan.Bab.*1(2.531D); regarded by martyrs as joyful, id.*hom. 38.4 in Mt.*(7.430B); ref. motive οὐ...τὸν χαρακτῆρα σώζουσι τοῦ μαρτυρίου τοῦ πιστοῦ, τὸν ὄντως θεὸν μὴ γνωρίσαντες, θανάτῳ δὲ ἑαυτοὺς ἐπιδιδόασι κενῷ Clem.*str.*4.4(p.256.16; M.8.1229C); of true martyr ὁ αὐτοπροαιρέτως τὸν θ. ὑπὲρ εὐσεβείας ἀναδεξάμενος Or. *mart.*22(p.19.25; M.11.589C); cf.*ib.*29(p.26.18; 600C); ref. Donatists βίαιον θ. μαρτύριον ὀνομάζουσι Thdt.*haer.*4.6(4.360); **5.** of destruction of death by Christ, *Barn.*5.6; *A.Thom.*A 143(p.250.11); Or.*Jo.* 20.39(31; p.381.13; M.14.665C); prophesied by Os.13:15, Cyr.*Os.*156 (3.189B); by reason of his immortality, Or.*Jo.*20.39(31; p.381.23; 665D); cf.id.*princ.*1.2.4(p.31.12; M.11.132C); ὁ κύριος, ἡ ἀφθαρσία νικήσασα τὸν θ. Meth.*symp.*3.7(p.34.25; M.18.72B); Gel.Cyz.*h.e.* 2.19.25(M.85.1280D); by his dying and rising ἵνα ἀποθανὼν καὶ ἀναστὰς νικήσῃ τὸν θ. Just.*1apol.*63.17(M.6.425B); dying being typified by paschal sacrifice, id.*dial.*111.3(M.6.732C); Chrys.*hom. 6.3 in Col.*(11.369B); by his descent into Hades, Or.*engast.*6(p.289. 2; M.12.1020D); Cyr.H.*catech.*14.17; cf.*ib.*14.19; by Resurrection, Meth.*res.*2.18(p.369.1; M.18.284A); ἵνα διὰ...τῆς ἐκ νεκρῶν ἀναστάσεως τὸν συνεισελθόντα τῇ παρακοῇ θ. ἐξαφανίσῃ. ἀφανισμὸς γάρ ἐστι θανάτου ἡ ἐκ θ. τοῦ ἀνθρώπου ἀνάστασις Gr.Nyss.*Apoll.*21(M.45. 1165B); **6.** of death since Inc. as entry to eternal life, *T.Aser* 5.2; *A.Thom.*A 160(p.271.25); μηδὲ ἀποδειλιάσητε πρὸς τὸν θ.· οὐ γὰρ φθορά ἐστιν, ἀλλὰ ζωῆς ἀφορμή †Bas.*hom.in Ps.*115(1.374C; M.30. 109D); ἀγαθὸν ἂν εἴη ὁ θ., ἀρχὴ καὶ ὁδὸς τῆς πρὸς τὸ κρεῖττον μεταβολῆς ἡμῖν γινόμενος Gr.Nyss.*Pulch.*(M.46.877A); Chrys.*exp.in Ps.* 48:11(5.211E); cf.id.*hom.83.1 in Jo.*(8.489A); Cyr.*glaph.Gen.*4(1. 135E); as end of care and sin, Gr.Nyss.*Pulch.*(876D); ἀνάπαυσίς ἐστι τοῖς ἀνδρείοις καὶ γενναίοις ὁ θ., τέλος μὲν ὧν τῶν ἄθλων, ἀρχὴ δὲ τῶν ἐπάθλων Isid.Pel.*epp.*3.12(M.78.737A); as sleep ὕπνον...λέγομεν καὶ κοίμησιν τῶν Χριστιανῶν τὸν θ. Mac.Aeg.*hom.*15.39(M.34.601D); Chrys.*coemet.*1(2.398C); id.*Laz.*5.1(1.763E); πρῶτος ἐν ἀνθρώποις ὕπνον ἔδειξε τὸν θ. ὁ Χριστός (ζωὴ γὰρ ἦν κατὰ φύσιν) Cyr.*glaph.Gen.*4 (1.135E); as matter for rejoicing, not mourning, Bas.*hom.*17.1(2. 139A; M.31.484A); Chrys.*vid.*1.3(1.341C); id.*pan.Bern.*3(2.638E); Cyr.*ador.*12(1.430C); as εὐεργέτης to the righteous, ‡Chrys.*serm. pasch.*6; as ἐχθρὸς ἐπιτήδειος to Christians, *ib.*12; **7.** Christian contempt of death; as distinguishing mark of Christians, *Diogn.*1.1; πρὶν τὴν θείαν ἐπιδημίαν γενέσθαι τοῦ σωτῆρος, φοβερὸς ἦν καὶ αὐτοῖς τοῖς ἁγίοις ὁ θ. Ath.*inc.*27.2(M.25.141D); due to belief in resurrection, Ign.*Smyrn.*3.2; *Diogn.*10.7; Tat.*orat.*19(p.21.3; M.6.849A); Just.*2apol.*11.8(M.6.464A); Ath.*inc.*27.1(M.25.141C); πῶς...ἐπιδείξῃ διὰ τῶν ἔργων τὴν πίστιν; ἐὰν καταφρονῇς θ., καὶ γὰρ καὶ ταύτῃ διεστήκαμεν τῶν ἀπίστων· ἐκεῖνοι μὲν γὰρ καλῶς φοβοῦνται τὸν θ., ἀναστάσεως γὰρ ἐλπίδα οὐκ ἔχουσι Chrys.*stat.*5.2(2.62B); cf.id.*hom. 34.4 in Mt.*(7.394A); to possession of good conscience, Just.*2apol.* 12.1ff.(464A); cf.id.*dial.*30.2(M.6.540A); Or.*Cels.*3.78(p.269.19; M.11. 1021C); Chrys.*stat.*5.3(2.64A); ref. Mt.5:10, etc. κεφάλαιον δ', οἶμαι, πάσης ἀρετῆς κύριος παιδεύων ἡμᾶς τὸ δεῖν γνωστικώτερον δι' ἀγάπην τὴν πρὸς θεὸν θ. καταφρονεῖν Clem.*str.*4.6(p.266.22; M.8.1252B); Christian contempt of death a sign of free will, Tat.*orat.*11(p.11.29; M.6.829A); **8.** as penalty for Christianity; suggested by devils to deter men from pursuit of truth, Just.*1apol.*44.12(M.6.396B); preventing philosophers from becoming Christians, Clem.*str.*6.8 (p.465.24; M.9.289A); in apologetic; men of all conditions have readily suffered for Christ, but never for Socrates, Just.*2apol.* 10.8(M.6.461A); or for pagan gods, id.*1apol.*25.1(365B); **9.** ref. moral conduct; remembrance of death preventing sin, Chrys.*exp. in Ps.*110:2(5.266E); id.*exp.in Ps.*48:18(5.221Dff.); ‡Nil.*Epict.*28(M. 79.1296A); Isid.Pel.*epp.*3.248(M.78.928A); promoting virtue, Gr.Naz. *carm.*1.2.31.3(M.37.911A); Jo.Clim.*scal.*6(M.88.796Bff.); Thdr.Stud. *epp.*2.134(M.99.1429B); but knowledge of date of death likely to lead to reliance on man instead of on God, Gr.Agr.*Eccl.*8.9(M.98. 1081A); and to delay in reception of baptism, Jo.Clim.*scal.*6(796A); **10.** of death personified as angel, *T.Abr.*B 9(p.114.5); cf.*T.Abr.*A 16(p.96.16); **11.** met., exeg. Apoc.20:13f. θ. [sc. εἶναι] τὴν γῆν παρὰ τὸ ἐν αὐτῇ κλίνεσθαι τὰ θνήσκοντα, ὅθεν καὶ χοῦς ἐκλήθη θανάτου ἐν ψαλμοῖς (Ps.21:15), εἰς χοῦν θ. κατῆχθαι εἰρηκότος Χριστοῦ Meth.*res.* 2.28(p.385.22; M.18.316C); exeg. Apoc.20:14–15 ὥσπερ γὰρ πόλις οἱ ταύτης οἰκήτορες λέγονται οὕτω καὶ θ. καὶ ᾅδης, οἱ τούτων αἴτιοι Andr.Caes.*Apoc.*64(M.106.424A).

B. fig.; **1.** of γνῶσις as λογικὸς θ., ἀπὸ τῶν παθῶν ἀπάγων καὶ χωρίζων τὴν ψυχήν Clem.*str.*7.12(p.51.18; M.9.500A); **2.** of death to sin; in gen. οἱ...συναποθανόντες τῷ Χριστῷ ἐν ἀγαθῷ θ. γεγόνασι· καὶ οἱ ἀποθανόντες τῇ ἁμαρτίᾳ τὸν ἀγαθὸν καὶ σωτήριον ἀποτεθνήκασι θάνατον Bas.*hom.in Ps.*33(1.157D; M.29.385A); Cyr.*ador.*16(1.567B); baptism θ. καὶ τέλος λέγεται τοῦ παλαιοῦ βίου τὸ βάπτισμα ἀποτασσομένων ἡμῶν ταῖς πονηραῖς ἀρχαῖς Clem.*exc.Thdot.*77(p.131.8; M.9. 693D); ref. Col.3:5, cf.Or.*hom.12.3 in Num.*(p.102.24; M.12.663A); symbolized by immersion, Bas.*Spir.*35(3.29C; M.32.129C); Dion.Ar. *e.h.*2.3.7(M.3.404B); **3.** of spiritual death; **a.** in gen., as state of sinners, Herm.*sim.*6.2.3; *ib.*8.7.6; ref. fasting as a remedy, Ath.*virg.*6 (p.40.2; M.28.257B); also continence, *ib.*24(p.59.17; 280D); ὥσπερ γὰρ ἐν σαρκὶ τὸ τῆς αἰσθητῆς χωρισθῆναι ζωῆς προσαγορεύομεν θ., οὕτως καὶ ἐπὶ τῆς ψυχῆς τὸν τῆς ἀληθοῦς ζωῆς χωρισμὸν θ. ὀνομάζομεν Gr. Nyss.*or.catech.*8(p.45.14; M.45.36B); cf.id.*Eun.*3(2 p.201.30; M.45. 797C); Isid.Pel.*epp.*3.252(M.78.932B); †Cyr.*hom.div.*14(5^2.415D); **b.** as state brought about by Fall, Just.*dial.*100.6(M.6.712A); κατὰ τὴν παράβασιν τοῦ Ἀδὰμ θ. αὐτοῦ καταψηφισαμένης τῆς τοῦ θεοῦ ἀγαθότητος, τοῦτο πρῶτον μὲν ὑπέστη κατὰ ψυχήν, τῶν νοερῶν αὐτῆς αἰσθητηρίων τῇ στερήσει τῆς ἐπουρανίου καὶ πνευματικῆς ἀπολαύσεως ἀπεσβηκότων αὐτῷ, καὶ νεκρῶν ὥσπερ γεγενημένων Mac.Aeg.*libert.ment.*26(M.34. 957D); θ. οὐχ ὁ κοινὸς μόνος τῶν μελῶν αὐτοῦ [sc. Adam] ἐκράτησεν, ἀλλὰ καὶ ὁ τῆς παρακοῆς κατὰ τῆς ψυχῆς αὐτοῦ εἰσβαλὼν Didym.*Rom.* 7:18(p.4.25); and ended by Inc., Ign.*Eph.*7.2; *Const.App.*7.39.3; **c.** as error or ignorance about God, Ign.*Smyrn.*5.1; τὸ...ἀγνοεῖν τὸν πατέρα θ. ἐστιν Clem.*str.*5.10(p.368.31; M.9.97A); id.*q.d.s.*7(p.164. 21; M.9.612B); **4.** of sin; **a.** in gen., Clem.*prot.*11(p.81.18; M.8.233B); id.*str.*4.3(p.253.17; M.8.1224C) cit. s. ἁμαρτητικός; cf.Meth.*res.*2.8 (p.344.5; M.18.305C); Gr.Naz.*or.*18.42(M.35.1041A); cf.*ib.*37.23(M.36. 308B); *Schol.*71 in Jo.Clim.*scal.*4(M.88.753C); **b.** ref. 'two ways', *Did.*1.1; δύο ὁδοὶ παρετέθησαν ἐνώπιον σοῦ, ἡ ζωὴ καὶ ὁ θ. ... ὁ οὖν θ. ἐστιν ὁ κόσμος· ἡ δὲ ζωή ἐστιν ἡ δικαιοσύνη Ath.*virg.*18(p.53.15; M. 28.273B); *Const.App.*7.1.2,3; *ib.*7.18.1; v. ζωή; **c.** as diabolically instigated, Or.*comm.in Mt.*13.9(p.203.23ff.; M.13.1116C); ref. demons θανάτου νόμους τοῖς ἀνθρώποις παραδεδώκασιν Tat.*orat.* 15(p.17.4; M.6.840A); *ib.*14(p.15.15; 836B); **d.** as life of unregenerate man ὁ βίος ἡμῶν ὅλος ἄλλο οὐδέν ἦν εἰ μὴ θ. *2Clem.*1.6; Mac.Aeg. *hom.*15.39(M.34.60D); **e.** ref. 'sin unto death' (cf. 1Jo.5:16) def. ἀνάγκη πρὸς θ. ἁμαρτίαν ἐκείνην εἶναι τὴν οὐκέτι δυναμένην συγχωρεῖσθαι, οἷα ἦν ἡ τοῦ Ἰούδα...ὅταν γὰρ ἐπὶ τοῖς διὰ βίου πᾶσιν ἀδικήμασιν ἀμετανόητός τις ἁλοὺς, ἐπαυξήσῃ τὴν κακίαν...τότε καὶ πρὸς θ. ἡ ἁμαρτία *cat.1Jo.*5:16f.(pp.142.31–143A); contrasted with other sins οὐ πᾶσα, ἀλλ' ἣν φησιν Ἰωάννης πρὸς θ. ἅμα δὲ καὶ διαστέλλει ὅτι τις ἁμαρτία θ. ἐστιν ψυχῆς, καί τις ἁμαρτία ἀσθένεια αὐτῆς Or.*Jo.*19. 4(3; p.313.19; M.14.549C); cf.id.*comm.in Mt.*12.35(p.149.3ff.; M.13. 1064A); Bas.*hom.*13.4(2.117A; M.31.432B); δέοντα δὲ αἱ μὲν κατ' ἄγνοιαν ἁμαρτίαι, οἱονεὶ ῥύπος τις οὖσαι...τοῦ ἐκ τῆς πλύσεως καθαρισμοῦ· αἱ δὲ πρὸς θ. ἁμαρτίαι τῶν ἑκουσίως ἐξαμαρτανόντων...δεόμεναι τῆς ἐν τῷ καύματι κρίσεως †Bas.*Is.*137(1.475B; M.30.341A); ἡ ἐν συγγνώσει μεγίστη ἁμαρτία, οἷον φόνος, μοιχεία, ἀνδρομανία, θάνατος ψυχῆς λέγεται Anast.S.*qu.et resp.*54(M.89.617A); μὴ πρὸς θ. μὲν ἁμαρτίαν λέγει τὴν ἐν ἀγνοίᾳ *ib.*(616C); ἢ πάλιν ἁμάρτημα πρὸς θ. ἐστιν ἡ εἰς τὸν θεὸν διαβαίνουσα, καὶ οὐκ εἰς τὸν ὁμοφυῆ ἄνθρωπον *ib.*(616D); ref. partic. sins θ. ... ζητούμενον εἴρηκεν τὴν μοιχείαν Clem.*paed.*2.10 (p.216.6; M.8.513B); unnatural vice, Jo.Clim.*scal.*15(M.88.885C);

*Schol.*17 *ib.*(908D); **5.** of eternal death, *Barn.*20.1; Herm.*sim.*6.3,4; *θ.* ... *ἐν ἀθανασίᾳ* Tat.*orat.*13(p.14.14; M.6.833A); Clem.*prot.*10(p.67. 4; M.8.204A); *θ. παρὰ θεοῦ ἐπελεύσεταί σοι αἰώνιος ἐν αἰσθήσει πικρῶς κολαζομένῳ Const.App.*1.3.3; cf.*ib.*1.33.3; *θ. ἀθάνατος· οὐδὲ γάρ ἐστι τῆς ἐκεῖ κολάσεως τέλος* Chrys.*hom.5.4 in Jo.*(8.41A); cf.id. *exp.in Ps.*48:15(5.218B); Cyr.*Jo.*6(4.573C); *τοῦ...δευτέρου* [sc. *θ.*], *τῆς εἰς γέενναν ἐκπομπῆς* Andr.Caes.*Apoc.*59(M.106.408B); *ἵνα ὁ Χριστὸς ἀπὸ τοῦ νοητοῦ θ. τῆς κατακρίσεως ῥύσηται ἡμᾶς cat.2Cor.*4:11(p.377. 17); **6.** of Devil, cf.Or.*hom.9.11 in Lev.*(p.439.15; M.12.524B); id. *hom.12.3 in Num.*(p.103.3; M.12.663B); opp. God who is life *διὸ καὶ τὸ ἀρχέγονον κακὸν ὁ διάβολος καὶ ὁ θ. λέγεται καὶ εὑρετὴς θ.* Gr. Nyss.*Eun.*8(2 p.202.2; M.45.797C).

II. *pestilence, Pss.Sal.*7.4.

***θανατοφθόρος,** *corrupting by death,* Germ.CP *or.*8(M.98.361C) cit. s. *κατάπτωσις.*

θανατοφόρος, *bringing death, fatal,* Bas.Sel.*v.Thecl.*2.20(M.85. 601D).

θανατ-όω, *put to death*; **1.** physically; ref. divine appointment of time of Christ's death, Just.*dial.*102.2(M.6.713B); ref. purpose of Inc. *ἵνα θανατωθεὶς σαρκί, ζωοποιήσῃ πάντας* Ath.*Ar.*1.44(M.26. 104C); Christol. *σαρκὶ θανατωθέντα...καὶ οὐ...θεότητι* ‡Ath.*serm.fid.* 27(p.24; M.26.1281A); of Christians *∼οῦνται, καὶ ζωοποιοῦνται Diogn.*5.12; *∼ούμενοι χαίρομεν* Just.*dial.*46.7(576C); **2.** spiritually *ἐπιθυμίαι πονηραὶ...θ. τοὺς δούλους τοῦ θεοῦ* Herm.*mand.*12.2.2; Clem.*q.d.s.*18(p.171.23; M.9.624A); *πειράζει* [sc. Devil], *ἵνα τοὺς πειθομένους...θ.* Dion.Al.*fr.*(p.252.7); of sin killing soul, Mac.Aeg. *hom.*1.7(M.34.457B); also preoccupation with temporal things, Max. *ambig.*(M.91.1132B); ref. restoration of spiritually dead through Christ, Ath.*inc.et c.Ar.*5(M.26.992A); by means of penance, Dion. Ar.*ep.*8.1(M.3.1088A); **3.** of destruction of evil; Devil being killed through Cross, Just.*dial.*94.2(M.6.700B, v.l. *σταυροῦσθαι* for *τοῦ σταυροῦ ∼οῦσθαι*); ‡Ath.*serm.fid.*13(p.9; M.26.1269C); ref. slaying of 'old man' in baptism *ἀγκιστρεύει...σε Ἰησοῦς...ἵνα θανατώσας ζωοποιήσῃ* Cyr.H.*procatech.*5.

θανατώδης, *deadly θ. εἰσὶν αἱ ἐπιθυμίαι αὗται* [sc. *αἱ πονηραί*] Herm.*mand.*12.2.3; *θ. διαλύσεις...τὰς ἁμαρτίας εἶναι νομίζετε Clem. ep.Petr.*14(M.2.49B).

θάπτ-ω, *bury οὐ...ἐστιν...τεθαμμένον, ὃ οὐκ ἐγερθήσεται Agraph.* (p.72); ref. Is.57:2, interpreted of Christ's burial, Just.*dial.*118.1 (M.6.749B); ref. Jer.20:6, Rom.6:4 *ὁ ἐναντίως διακείμενος τῷ συνθάπτεσθαι τῷ Χριστῷ οὗτος ἐν Βαβυλῶνι ∼εται. ἔστι γὰρ καὶ ταφῆναι μετὰ Χριστοῦ καλῶς διὰ τοῦ βαπτίσματος* Or.*hom.19.14 in Jer.*(p.172.23; M.13.493C).

θαρραλέως, *confidently οὐ δειλιῶν* [sc. Christ before Passion]... *ἀλλὰ θαρραλεώτατα ἐπὶ τὸν ἀγῶνα, ἵν' οὕτως εἴπω, ἀποδυόμενος* Or. *Jo.*32.33(15; p.466.10; M.14.805C).

θαρσαλέος (θαρραλέος), 1. *confident μόνος θ. ὁ γνωστικός* Clem. *str.*7.11(p.47.11; M.9.492A); ref. Christ's agony *ἵνα...θ. τὸν ἄνθρωπον πάλιν πρὸς τὸν θάνατον κατασκευάσῃ* Ath.*Ar.*3.57(M.26.441C); **2.** *inspiring confidence τὰ θ.* (*τουτέστι τὰ ἀγαθά*) Clem.*str.*7.11(p.46. 29; M.9.489B).

θαρσ-έω (θαρρέω), 1. *have courage*; unnecessary for 'gnostic' who is beyond fearing, Clem.*str.*6.9(p.467.22; M.9.293A); **2.** *have confidence in τῷ παντοκράτορι καὶ τῷ κυρίῳ ∼οῦντες ἀντιπολιτευόμεθα ταῖς ἀρχαῖς ib.*4.7(p.269.24; M.8.1260A); id.*prot.*12(p.85.25; M.8. 244A); Ath.*decr.*2(p.2.22; M.25.420A); *M.Thdot.3*(p.141.21); c. *εἰς*, *M. Artem.*41(p.72.32); Thdt.*Jer.*4:29(2.436); Jo.Mal.*chron.*15 p.379(M. 97.564B); **3.** *trust*; pass., Cyr.*ep.*1(p.12.12; 5^{2}.4C); **4.** *make bold*; of Christians who must live good lives before they can venture to say 'Our Father', Gr.Nyss.*or.dom.*2(p.42.37; M.44.1148A); **5.** *say boldly,* Jo.Clim.*scal.*4(M.88.684C); Jo.Mal.*chron.*18 p.493(M.97.713B); **6.** *confirm, reinforce θ. τὴν βουλήν* Eustrat.*v.Eutych.*24(M.86.2301C); Niceph.Ur.*v.Sym.*108(M.86.3088C); **7.** *entrust*; pass., ref. the secret of the last day *μὴ θαρρηθέντες τὸ μυστήριον* Cyr.*resp.*4(p.585.19; 6^{2}. 382E); id.*ep.*78(5^{2}.211A); Thdt.*qu.52 in 4Reg.*(1.544); c. infin., id. *ador.*13(1.459C); **8.** *confide,* Nil.*epp.*2.158(M.79.276B); Chrys.*hom.2.1 in 2Thess.*(11.516B); ref. Jo.15:15 *πάντα ἃ ἤκουσα παρὰ τοῦ πατρός ἀπήγγειλα ὑμῖν· τουτέστιν, ἐθάρρησα ὑμῖν* id.*hom.7.6 in 1Cor.*(10.58E); Jo.Mosch.*prat.*193(M.87.3073B); *ib.*219(3109D); *Mir.Geo.*8(p.95.4).

θαρσήεις, *confident,* Nonn.*par.Jo.*12:35(M.43.856C); *ib.*7:7(805B).

θαρσηρός, *confident, courageous,* Ephr.3.252B.

***θαρσοποιέω,** *encourage, M.Seb.*5(p.175.16); ‡Ath.*proph.*2(M.28. 1068A); †Gregent.*disp.*(M.86.652A).

θάρσυνος, *confident,* †Apoll.*met.Ps.*7:2(M.33.1320A).

***θατεράληπτος,** *able to be caught by other means ἄλλους δ' ὁ πονηρὸς δαίμων...θατεραλήπτους εὑρὼν ἐσφετερίζετο* Eus.*h.e.*3.27.1(M.20.273A).

θάτερος, 1. *each* of two, Eus.*h.e.*5.15(M.20.464A); **2.** *both οἱ θ.* Gel.Cyz.*h.e.*2.21.26(M.85.1289A); **3.** *the other*; of three, *ib.*2.22.12 (1293A); **4.** prob. f.l. for *θᾶττον*, Sophr.H.*or.*7.9(M.87.3326D).

θατέρως, *in one way or another,* Epiph.*haer.*61.1(p.382.1, v.l. *κατὰ θάτερον* M.41.1041B).

θαῦμα, τό, A. *wonder,* ref. God and his works; of his approach to the soul, Clem.*str.*2.2(p.115.21; M.8.936A); of redemption *ὢ θ. μυστικοῦ* id.*prot.*11(p.79.4; M.8.228C); ref. Christ as spiritual food, id.*paed.*1.6(p.115.10; M.8.300B); regeneration (Gnost.) *θ. θαυμάτων* Hipp.*haer.*5.8(p.92.18; M.16.3143C); ref. a cure, Gr.Naz.*or.*8.18(M. 35.812A).

B. *trick τί θαυμάτων ἀπάτῃ διασκεδάζεις τὸ ἔθνος;* ‡Chrys.*Steph. protomart.*1.1(8.18C); ref. stage performances *μὴ τοῖς διαβολικοῖς θ. τὸν διάβολον θεραπεύοντες, τοῦ διαβόλου γενώμεθα σύγκληροι* Bas.Sel. *or.*27.2(M.85.316A); of magical performances, Ath.*inc.*48.3(M.25. 181D).

C. *admiration ἀπελθόντες ὥστε αὐτὸν δῆσαι, ἀπανῆλθον δεθέντες τῷ θ.* Chrys.*hom.52.1 in Jo.*(8.304B).

D. *miracle*; **1.** in gen., *M.Polyc.*15.1; Or.*fr.61 in Jo.*(p.533.14); Thdr.Heracl.*Is.*1:2(M.18.1309B); Gr.Naz.*or.*18.13(M.35.1001Dff.); Chrys.*hom.2.3 in 1Tim.*(11.560C); Evagr.*h.e.*1.14(p.24.23; M.86. 2461A); Jo.Mosch.*prat.*125(M.87.3108A); as being above the natural order, Gr.Nyss.*or.catech.*24(p.91.7; M.45.64C); *νόμῳ θαύματος, ἀλλ' οὐ λόγῳ φύσεως* Leont.B.*Nest.et Eut.*2(M.86.1321B); **2.** effects; faith and hope, Cyr.*hom.pasch.*18.4(5^{2}.244D); effects being permanent, unlike those of human marvels, Isid.Pel.*epp.*1.397(M.78.405A); **3.** ref. Christian attitude to miracles; not to be expected, Chrys. *hom.35.3 in Jo.*(8.206A); *ἐν τοῖς μακαρισμοῖς...οὐδαμοῦ τοὺς τὰ θ. ποιοῦντας τίθησιν, ἀλλὰ τοὺς βίον ἔχοντας ὀρθόν* id.*compunct.*1.8(1. 137A); *ἐρωτᾷς τὸν τρόπον τῶν τοῦ θεοῦ θ.; εἰ ἐφικτὸν ἦν ἡμῖν τὸ ἀκατάληπτον τοῦ λόγου, οὐκ ἦν θ., ἀλλὰ κατὰ φύσιν πρᾶγμα* Thdot. Anc.*hom.*2.4(p.75.26; M.77.1373B); tales of miracles beneficial to soul, Sophr.H.*mir.Cyr.et Jo.*20(M.87.3480C); **4.** as wrought by God; in OT, Gr.Naz.*or.*13.1(M.35.853A); Chrys.*hom.14.3 in Mt.*(7.181B); of virgin birth, Ath.*inc.*20.4(M.25.132B); cf.*ib.*33.3(153A); Amph. *hom.*1.3(M.39.40C); **5.** as wrought by Christ *τῶν ἔργων τὰ θ.* Eus. *h.e.*1.2.23(M.20.65B); Ath.*inc.*38.5(M.25.161D); by his divinity, *ib.* 49.4(184C); Chrys.*hom.26.2 in Mt.*(7.315C); Isid.Pel.*epp.*1.393(M. 78.404B); Nonn.*par.Jo.*2:7(M.43.761A); as proof of divinity, Or. *fr.94 in Jo.*(p.558.3); Gr.Nyss.*or.catech.*11(p.57.18; M.45.44B), *ἤρκει ...μόνα τὰ θ. ἐκφαίνειν τὴν ἄναρχον καὶ ἀπροσδεῆ αὐτοῦ θεότητα* Didym.*Trin.*3.17(M.39.876B); which did not convince Pilate and Jews, Chrys.*hom.86.2 in Mt.*(7.814A); gospels vary in number of miracles recorded, *ib.1.2*(6A); fact that miracles were wrought instantaneously a proof of their supernatural character, id.*hom. 35.3 in Jo.*(8.205D); *ψευδῆ εἰσι καὶ ἀπόβλητα τὰ λεγόμενα παιδικὰ θ. τοῦ Χριστοῦ Schol.* in Anast.S.*hod.*13(M.89.229B); **6.** of miracles of saints; in gen., Eus.*h.e.*6.9.1(M.20.537C); Ath.*v.Anton.* 83(M.26.960B); Bas.*Spir.*74(3.62D; M.32.205C); Thdt.*h.e.*1.7.4(3.755); *ib.*1.24.7(807); wrought by God in saints, Ath.*v.Anton.*58(928B); *τοιαύτη τοῦ μεγάλου Γρηγορίου ἡ δύναμις, μᾶλλον δὲ τοῦ θεοῦ τοῦ ἐνεργοῦντος ἐν ἐκείνῳ τὰ θ.* Gr.Nyss.*v.Gr.Thaum.*(M.46.932C); of apostles, *A.Mt.*7(p.225.1); *A.Phil.*37(p.18.5); *ib.*74(p.29.10); Eus. *h.e.*2.1.7(M.20.136C); Chrys.*hom.4.2 in Eph.*(11.54E); ref. Ac.3:6 *ἐκ τοῦ θ. ἀναγκαία ἡ παραδοχὴ τῆς θεότητος τοῦ μονογενοῦς τοῖς ὁρῶσιν ἐγίνετο* †Bas.*hom.in Ps.*115(1.371C; M.30.104B); of prophets, Gr. Nyss.*v.Gr.Thaum.*(M.46.932D); **7.** of miracles of Christians in gen.; ref. Heb.6:5 *δυνάμεις τε μέλλοντος αἰῶνος. τίνας...; ἢ τὸ θαύματα ἐπιτελεῖν, ἢ τὸν ἀρραβῶνα τοῦ πνεύματος* Chrys.*hom.9.3 in Heb.*(12. 96B); as done through faith, id.*comm.in Gal.*3:5(10.697C); *θαυμάτων ἐδεξάμεθα χάρισμα, καὶ ἀπιστίαις αὐτὸ παρωσάμεθα* Isid.Pel.*epp.*1. 250(M.78.333C); **8.** ref. miracle-working images; of BMV, Evagr. *h.e.*5.18(p.213.23; M.86.2828C); of Christ, Thdr.Stud.*antirr.*2.19(M. 99.365D); **9.** of miracles wrought by Devil and the wicked, Eus.*h.e.*7.17(M.20.680A); *εἰ δὲ φαίη τις, τί οὖν συνεχώρει ὁ θεὸς τοῖς ἀναξίοις τὰ θ., φαίην ἐγώ· ὅτι διὰ τὴν δόξαν οἰκείου ὀνόματος ἐπλήρου τὰς θεοσημείας ὁ κύριος, καὶ τῶν δαιμόνων κωλύων ἐπιβουλάς, καὶ ὁδὸν τῷ εὐαγγελίῳ ὁμαλίζων ἀπρόσκοπον* Isid.Pel.*epp.*1. 145(M.78.280C); and by heretics, Leont.H.*monoph.*testimonia(M.86. 1896cf.).

***θαυμασία, ἡ,** *wonder,* Jo.Mosch.*prat.*195(M.87.3080C).

θαυμάσιος, *wonderful, admirable*; **1.** of holy persons *ὁ θαυμασιώτατος Πολύκαρπος M.Polyc.*5.1; *ib.*16.2; *τοὺς θ. προφήτας* Or.*Jo.*20.39 (36; p.377.2; M.14.656A); *οἱ θ. ἀπόστολοι* id.*hom.19.13 in Jer.*(p.169. 12; M.13.489A); *ὁ θ. Μωσῆς* Eus.*d.e.*1.3(p.16.25; M.22.37B); *Ἀβδιοῦ τὸν θ.* Thdt.*Abd.*proem.(2.1450); **2.** iron. of heretics, Hipp.*haer.*5.8

(p.89.5; M.16.3139B); **3.** as complimentary title, Bas.*ep*.313(3.444B; M.32.1061B); *ib*.215(323B; M.789D); Marc.Diac.*v.Porph*.63; **4.** neut. as subst., *wonder, marvel*; of works of God, *T.Sym*.6.7; Herm. *vis*.4.1.3; *A.Petr.et Paul*.26(p.190.4); ἡ τοῦ θεοῦ σοφία, ἡ διὰ τῶν ἐναντίων θαυματουργήσασα τὰ μεγάλα θ. Gr.Nyss.*hom.8 in Cant*.(M.44.948C); of divine miracles, *A.(Pass.)Petr.et Paul*.20(p.136.12); τὰ θ. τοῦ Ἰησοῦ *A.Andr.et Mt*.11(p.78.5); Jo.Mosch.*prat*.75(M.87.2928C); of miracles worked by apostles, *A.Jo*.42(p.172.1); *A.Phil*.12(p.6.22); *A.Petr.et Andr*.2(p.118.5).

θαυμασιότης, ἡ, 1. *astonishment*, Clem.*str*.2.8(p.132.26; M.8.973A); **2.** *wonderful nature, wondrousness*; of Christ, Or.*engast*.7(p.290.26; M.12.1024A); *cat.Lc*.22:43(p.159.28); as complimentary title, Chrys.*ep*.20(3.606D); Marc.Er.*opusc*.7.11(M.65.1088A); Firm. *ep*.1(M.77.1481A); Thdt.*ep*.8(4.1067); τῆς ὑμετέρας θ. *ib*.125(1210).

***θαυμασιόω,** *amaze, astound*, Eus.*d.e*.3.5(p.131.26; perh. error for θαυμαστόω M.22.221D).

θαυμασμός, ὁ, *wonder*, Just.*dial*.100.1(M.6.709A); Clem.*str*.1.2(p.13.24; M.8.709A); Or.*Cels*.proem.(p.52.8; M.11.644C); id.*Jo*.2.34(28; p.92.2; M.14.173C); Didym.*Ac*.10:10(M.39.1677A) cit. s. ἔκπληξις; Chrys.*hom.4.4 in Eph*.(11.31A).

θαυμαστικός, 1. *astonishing*, †Bas.*Is*.46(1.415D; M.30.205C); **2.** *expressing astonishment* θ. ... φωνή Gr.Nyss.*hom.8 in Cant*.(M.44.948A).

θαυμαστικῶς, 1. *in astonishment, wonderingly*, Or.*Jo*.32.18(11; p.457.13; M.14.792C); θ. φησι πρὸς αὐτήν Gr.Nyss.*hom.3 in Cant*.(M.44.816A); **2.** *wonderfully* τὸν νόμον θ. ἐξέλαβεν Chrys.*comm.in Gal*.5:23(10.722D).

***θαυμαστοθέατος,** *wonderful to behold*, Jo.D.*hom*.5(M.96.652D).

θαυμαστός, 1. *wonderful*; of God, *1Clem*.60.1; Herm.*mand*.12.4.2; τὸ...θ. ὄνομα αὐτοῦ id.*sim*.9.18.5; of Messiah ὁ θ. *Dial.Ath.et Zacch*.28(p.21); of divine works, *1Clem*.35.1; ἡ ἐπαγγελία τοῦ Χριστοῦ...θ. *2Clem*.5.5; in OT, Chrys.*hom.14.3 in Mt*.(7.181B, v.l. θαύματα Gaume); ἀνάστασις...θ. Cosm.Ind.*top*.2(M.88.121C); πᾶσα... πρᾶξις...τοῦ Χριστοῦ...θ.· ἀλλὰ πάντων ἐστὶ θ. ὁ τίμιος αὐτοῦ σταυρός Jo.D.*f.o*.4.11(M.94.1128D); of virtues θ. ἐστιν ἡ ἀγάπη *1Clem*.50.1; θ. ... ἡ παρθενία Meth.*symp*.1.1(p.7.9; M.18.36B); exeg. Is.5:2 ἡ καλουμένη Σωρήκ, ἐκλεκτή τις οὖσα καὶ θ. Or.*hom.12.1 in Jer*.(p.86.28; M.13.377D); iron., of error τῆς θ. φιλοσοφίας Hipp.*haer*.4.15(p.49.6; M.16.3083A); *ib*.27.1(p.53.20; 3090A); Eus.*Marcell*.1.1(p.9.5; M.24.729B); **2.** *admired*, Chrys.*hom.24.1 in Mt*.(7.300B).

***θαυμαστοτόκος,** *bringing forth marvels*; of body of BMV, Jo.D. *hom*.9.13(M.96.740C).

θαυμαστ-όω, 1. *magnify, make wonderful* or *admirable*, ref. God's action in saints ὑπὸ θεοῦ τεθαυμαστωμένοι οἱ ὅσιοι Eus.*Ps*.4:4(M.23.108A); *ib*.15:3(156C); αἱ κατ' εἶδος ἀρεταί, ἃς θ. ὁ θεὸς ἐν τοῖς ἁγίοις Ath.*exp.Ps*.15:3(M.27.101B); Ephr.3.184F; Gr.Nyss.*or.catech*.40(p.162.21; M. om.); Didym.*Ps*.15:3(M.39.1228B); Chrys.*exp.in Ps*.4(5.16B); Cyr.*Ps*.15:3(M.69.808C); Thdt.*Ps*.4:5(1.631); in Christ πῶς ...οὐκ ἐθαυμάστωσεν ἐν αὐτῷ καὶ δι' αὐτοῦ πληρώσας προφητείας, παραδόξων δυνάμεων γενομένων δι' αὐτοῦ...καὶ ἀναστάντος ἐκ νεκρῶν; Didym.*Ps*.4:4(M.39.1165D); **2.** *declare wonderful* or *admirable*; ref. God as praised by men, †Bas.*bapt*.1.2.5(2.633A; M.31.1533C); ∼ῶν μετ' ἐμοῦ τὸ ἔλεός σου ‡Nil.*narr*.7(M.79.685A); hence **3.** pass., *be admired*, Mac.Aeg.*hom*.45.2(M.34.788A); Chrys.Herm.*2.3 in 1Thess*.(11.437B).

θαυμαστῶς, 1. *wonderfully*, Herm.*vis*.3.4.1; id.*sim*.5.5.4; θαυμαστότατα λέγων ὁ Πέτρος Gr.Naz.*ep*.20(M.37.53C); **2.** *with astonishment*, Herm.*vis*.1.1.3.

***θαυματογραφία, ἡ,** *account of miracles*, Sophr.H.*mir.Cyr.et Jo*.67(M.87.3652D).

***θαυματολογία, ἡ,** *collection of marvels*, Synes.*Dion* 5(p.248.5; M.66.1128B).

***θαυματολόγος, ὁ,** *narrator of marvels*, Eus.*Hierocl*.19(524C; M.22.825C).

θαυματοποι-έω, 1. *juggle*; met., of Eunomius ὥσπερ τις τῶν ἐπὶ σκηνῆς ∼ῶν Gr.Nyss.*Eun*.1(1 p.25.6; M.45.253A); **2.** *perform miracles*, ref. Elijah and the rain τὸν...'Ιωάννην τοιοῦτον μέν τι θαυματοποιῆσαι οὐδὲν ἡ θεία φησὶν ἱστορία id.*virg*.6(p.279.14; M.46.349C).

θαυματοποιΐα, ἡ, 1. *working of miracles* ἡ θ. τῶν ἐν Αἰγύπτῳ σημείων Gr.Nyss.*hex*.11(M.44.73C); **2.** *miracle*, Eus.*Hierocl*.35(534D; M.22.848C); Bas.*hom*.11.4(2.93E; M.31.377C).

θαυματοποιός, 1. *wonder-working* ὁ...θ. τοῦ θεοῦ λόγος Ath.*gent*.44(M.25.88C); **2.** as subst.; **a.** *juggler*, Clem.*str*.7.11(p.47.25; M.9.492B); **b.** *worker of miracles*, Iren.*haer*.1.13.2(M.7.581A); Hipp. *haer*.6.40(p.171.19; M.16.3258C); *Const.App*.8.1.15; μηδεὶς ὑμῶν ἐπαιρέσθω κατὰ τοῦ ἀδελφοῦ, κἂν...θ. *ib*.8.1.17; Anast.S.*hod*.7(M.89.113C).

θαυματουργ-έω, 1. *work wonderfully*; of God in Creation, Gr.Naz. *or*.32.9(M.36.184C); of divine wisdom, Gr.Nyss.*hom.8 in Cant*.(M.44.948C); of Christ ὅσα ὁ σωτὴρ...ἐθαυματούργησε Const.*or.s.c*.15 tit.(p.152.13; M.20.1276B); ὁ θεὸς λόγος γέγονεν ἄνθρωπος, οὐ μεταβληθεὶς τὴν φύσιν, ἀλλὰ ∼ήσας τὴν ἕνωσιν Thdot.Anc.*exp.symb*.2(M.77.1317A); τεθαυματούργηκεν ὡς θεός Cyr.*Is*.3.3(2.458E); **2.** *work miracles*; of God, Diod.*Ps*.82:18(M.33.1616B); Chrys.*hom.18.1 in Rom*.(9.631E); so acting when human resources are at an end, id. *ep*.1.1(3.528D); of Christ, id.*hom.42.2 in Jo*.(8.250D); μὴ νομίσητε ὅτι τότε ἐθαυματούργησε, νῦν δὲ οὐ θ. id.*hom.33.3 in Heb*.(12.306C); Cyr.*Lc*.11:57(M.72.721D); id.*Ps*.46:4(M.69.1053A); ἀπαθεῖ δὲ θεότητι διὰ σαρκὸς ∼ῶν ‡Hipp.*Ber.Hel*.2(p.322.31; M.10.833B); beginning at 30, the age of manhood, Leont.B.*Nest.et Eut*.2(M.86.1336A); Sophr.H.*ep.syn*.(M.87.3177D); of H. Ghost διὰ τοῦτο ἐκεῖνο συγχωρεῖ [sc. ὁ...Χριστός] ∼εῖν, ἵνα μάθωσιν αὐτοῦ τὴν ἀξίαν Chrys.*hom.78.3 in Jo*.(8.461D); of Christians: apostles, *ib.42.3*(251C); id.*hom.4.2 in 2Thess*.(11.453D); πῶς...ἔμελλον ∼εῖν, τὴν τοῦ ἁγίου πνεύματος χάριν οὐδέπω ἔχοντες; id.*hom.4.5 in Ac.princ*.(3.89C); and their successors, Thdt.*Heb*.2:2(3.555); apostles and martyrs, CCP(553) *act*.8 ap.Evagr.*h.e*.4.38(p.189.23; M.86.2780A); of the wicked, Chrys. *hom.24.1 in Mt*.(7.299E); οὐδὲ ἡ τῶν σημείων ἐπίδειξις ὀνίνησί τι τὸν ∼οῦντα ἀρετῆς χωρίς *ib*.(300A); of images μή τις εἴπῃ, τίνος ἕνεκεν αἱ παρ' ἡμῖν εἰκόνες οὐ θ.; πρὸς ὃν ἀποκρινούμεθα, ὅτι...τὰ σημεῖα τοῖς ἀπίστοις οὐ τοῖς πιστεύουσιν CNic.(787)*act*.4(H.4.184A); **3.** *work miraculously*; of God, Diod.*Ps*.92:4(M.33.1626D); ἐπὶ τῶν ἀποστόλων ...τοιαῦτα ἕτερα ἐθαυματούργησε διὰ πάντων Chrys.*hom.15.1 in Rom*.(9.594D); ref. Christ τοσαύτη παρ' ἐμοὶ δυνάμεως περιουσία, ὡς καὶ ἑτέρους δύνασθαι ποιεῖν ταῦτα ∼εῖν id.*hom.57.3 in Mt*.(7.579C); μὴ ...ζήτει λόγον τῶν ὑπὲρ λόγον γενομένων καὶ ∼ηθέντων ἐκ δυνάμεως θεϊκῆς Thdot.Anc.*exp.symb*.4(M.77.1320A); ref. Inc., *ib*.14(1333A); of H. Ghost, Thdt.*Trin*.26(M.75.1185A); id.*h.rel*.proem.(3.1106); of saints, Gr.Naz.*or*.24.17(M.35.1189B); Euthal.Diac.*Ac*.proem.(M.85.636A); Chrys.*hom.26.3 in 2Cor*.(10.621B); Thdt.*h.e*.4.18.12(3.979); Evagr.*h.e*.2.3(p.40.30; M.86.2493B); **4.** pass., *be miraculously changed* into, Proc.G.*Gen*.16:1(M.87.349C); ὕδωρ...νέκταρ ∼εῖται Geo.Pis.*hex*.1795(M.92.1573A).

θαυματούργημα, τό, *miracle, marvel*; wrought by God, Cyr.H.*ep. Const*.3(M.33.1168B); *ib*.6(1172B); in OT, Cyr.*Is*.4.2(2.583E); by Christ, *Anaph.Pil*.A 5(p.439); Chrys.*hom.8.9 in Eph*.(11.68A); Leont.B.*Nest.et Eut*.2(M.86.1336A); ‡Chrys.*hom*.9(13.235D) but cf. Gr.Ant.*bapt*.2.7(M.88.1877C δημιουργήματα); by saints, Elijah and Elisha, Ast.Am.*hom*.10(M.40.328B); S. Nicholas, Jo.Mon.*hymn.Nic. Myr*.8(M.96.1389A).

θαυματουργία, ἡ, 1. *working of wonders*; ref. God in nature, Eus. *l.C*.1(p.197.22; M.20.1321B); λέγε...ἑκάστην ὑπόθεσιν ἐκ θεοῦ γεγονυῖαν, πόσην ἔχει τὴν θ. Epiph.*haer*.64.66(p.508.12; M.41.1185A); **2.** *wonder, marvel* τὰς σὰς θ. ἐν τῇ Ἱερουσαλὴμ ἐξηγοῦμαι Or.*Ps*.72:28(p.97); ref. blessed in heaven τὰς θ. ὁρῶσιν Mac.Aeg.*hom*.17.4(M.34.625C); **3.** *working of miracles*; of God, Epiph.*haer*.66.82(p.124.13; M.42.160A); Ammon.*Ac*.27:24(M.85.1601A); Diod.*Ps*.82:18(M.33.1616B); εὐαγγελικῆς θ. Epiph.*haer*.51.16(p.273.4; M.41.920C); Chrys.*hom.77.2 in Jo*.(8.453E); denial that Christ's θ. is of same order as that of holy men, Leont.H.*Nest*.1.19(M.86.1480D); c. genit. ἡ τῶν σημείων θ. Chrys.*hom.62.1 in Mt*.(7.619C); *ib.37.4*(420B); τὰς...τῶν σημείων ἐργασάμενος θ. Gel.Cyz.*h.e*.2.24.25(M.85.1304C); **4.** *miracle*; of God δυνατὸς ταῖς θ. ‡Ath.*Apoll*.2.18(M.26.1164C); Ammon.*Ac*.16:29(M.85.1560C); Jo.Mosch.*prat*.79(M.87.2937B); of Christ, Eus.*d.e*.1.1(p.3.29; M.22.17A) al.; ὁ Χριστὸς ταῖς ἀναγράπτοις θ. πρὸς πίστιν τῶν ὁρώντων κεχρημένος τὰ καινὰ τῆς εὐαγγελικῆς διδασκαλίας αὐτοῦ μαθήματα συνεστήσατο *ib*.3.2(p.97.26; 169C); ‡Tit.Bost.*palm*.1(M.18.1265B); Chrys.*hom.53.2 in Mt*.(7.540B); τοὺς δὲ λέγοντας, ὅτι οὐ χρὴ κοινοποιεῖν τὴν σάρκα τῇ θεότητι τοῦ μονογενοῦς, οὐδὲ τὴν θεότητα τῇ σαρκὶ ἐν ταῖς θ. ... φαμὲν διημαρτηκέναι τῆς ἀληθείας Cyr.*resp*.20(p.586.2; 6².390A); †Gr.II Papa *ep.Leon*.1(H.4.5C); of Christians, *A.Jo*.16(p.160.20); Thdt. *Rom*.1:4(3.15); id.*h.e*.1.23.9(3.805); of Elijah, Bas.Sel.*or*.10.2(M.85.141B).

***θαυματουργικός,** *miracle-working*, Jo.Clim.*scal*.26(M.88.1033B).

θαυματουργός, 1. *working miracles*; of God, ‡Meth.*palm*.3(M.18.388C); ἡ θ. τοῦ Χριστοῦ δύναμις Eus.*h.e*.3.24.3(M.20.264C); θ. τοῦ Χριστοῦ εἰκόνι *A.Thadd*.5(p.275.18n.); θ. ... τοῦ σωτῆρος ἡ σάρξ Proc.G.*Is*.6:6–13(M.87.1940B); **2.** as subst.; **a.** *worker of miracles*; of Christ, Gr.Naz.*carm*.1.2.24.326(M.37.813A); Chrys.*hom.67.1 in Mt*.(7.662B); Vict.*Mc*.4:1(p.301.25); of Gr. Thaum., Gr.Nyss.*v.Gr.*

Thaum.(M.46.893A); Thdr.Lect.*h.e.*2.54(M.86.209B); †Gr.II Papa *ep.Leon.*2(H.4.13D); of saints, *ib.*; Thphn.*chron.*p.16(M.108.17A); **b.** *conjuror, magician*; ref. accusation that Christ did miracles like a magician, Eus.*d.e.*3.5(p.131.25; M.22.221D); in gen., Geo.Pis. *Pers.*2.310(M.92.1231A).

θέα, ἡ, 1. *contemplation, vision*; **a.** ref. etym. of *θεός*: *ἐκ τῆς θ., τὴν θεότητα παρωνομάσθαι* Gr.Nyss.*tres dii*(M.45.125D); **b.** of angels' contemplation of God according to the capacities of their various orders, Dion.Ar.*e.h.*4.3.5(M.3.480B); **c.** of vision of God by men; as end of human nature, Clem.*prot.*10(p.72.28; M.8.216A); but fully attained by few, id.*str.*5.1(p.330.8; M.9.17A); because transcended by the divine *δι' ἀβλεψίας...ἰδεῖν...τὸ ὑπὲρ θ.* Dion.Ar.*myst.*2(M.3.1025A); ref. divinity of Christ *τῆς ὑπὲρ θέαν...ὄψεως* Jo.D.*hom.*1.7 (M.96.557A); of prophet's vision of Christ through H. Ghost, Or. *Jo.*6.3(2; p.109.23; M.14.204A); prophetic visions of God, Ath.*hom. in Mt.11*:27(M.25.217D); obtained through Son, Clem.*exc.Thdot.* 12(p.110.24; M.9.661C); by prayer, virtue, knowledge of Son, id.*str.* 6.12(p.483.11; M.9.324B); love, Or.*schol.in Cant.*5:6(M.17.273C); vision producing lasting pleasure, Clem.*paed.*2.1(p.160.6; M.8.393A); making soul glorious, Or.*Jo.*32.27(17; p.472.33; 817A); **2.** *appearance, aspect*, of risen Christ *ἐν καινῇ θ.* ‡Gr.Naz.*Chr.pat.*2451(M.38.328A); **3.** *spectacle, show*; of gladiatorial shows forbidden to Christians because of human death involved, Athenag.*leg.*35.2 (M.6.969A); Iren.*haer.*1.6.3(M.7.508B); of theatrical shows forbidden because occasions of sin, Clem.*paed.*3.11(p.278.20ff.; M.8.653Bf.); *ἀπέχεσθε...πάσης θ. δαιμονικῆς Const.App.*2.62.4.

θεαγωγία, ἡ, *evocation of deities ὅσα περὶ μαντείας, θ., ψυχαγωγίας, ἄστρων δυνάμεως, τερατεύονται* Gr.Naz.*or.*27.10(M.36.25A); performed by Apollonius of Tyana, Bas.Sel.*v.Thecl.*1(M.85.540D).

***θεάδελφος, ὁ,** *brother of God*; of S. James, Sophr.H.*nativ.* (p.508.12).

***θεαδής,** *pleasing God τὸ δὲ θεοειδεῖς* [v.l. *θειώδεις*] *τῷ θεῷ αὐτοὺς ἀρέσκειν, οἷον θεαδεῖς* [v.l. *θεοαδεῖς*] *ὄντας, ἅδειν γὰρ τὸ ἀρέσκειν* Oecum.*Apoc.*9:17(p.118).

***θεαθέν,** *by sight*, †Jo.D.*B.J.*9(M.96.929A).

θεαίτητος, *asked of God*, tr. name Samuel, Thdt.*qu.6 in 1Reg.* (1.358).

θέαμα, τό, *spectacle, sight*;

A. in gen.; **1.** *visible object*, exeg. Pr.8:22 *ὁδὸς δὲ σωματικόν τί ἐστι θ., ἥτις ἐστὶν ὁ κυριακὸς ἄνθρωπος* †Ath.*exp.fid.*4(M.25.205C); **2.** *public spectacle φεῦγε καὶ τὰς ἱπποδρομίας, τὸ ἔμμανὲς θ. καὶ ψυχὰς ἐκτραχηλίζον* Cyr.H.*catech.*19.6; *φεύγετε δὴ καὶ τὰ ἀπρεπῆ τῶν θ., τὰ θέατρά φημι καὶ τὰς Ἑλληνικὰς πομπάς Const.App.*2.62.2; *θέατρον... ἔνθα ἀσελγῆ θεάματα καὶ ἀκούσματα* Chrys.*hom.1.1 in Ac.princ.* (3.51D); **3.** *spectacle of horror κοινὸν τῶν ἐθνῶν τῆς ἀπανθρωπίας θ. Ep.Lugd.*ap.Eus.*h.e.*5.1.37(M.20.421C); ‡Gr.Naz.*Chr.pat.*1105(M.38.224A); **4.** *wonder, marvellous spectacle ποικίλον τε ἰδὼν θ.* Gr.Thaum. *pan.Or.*14(p.32.21; M.10.1092C); Philost.*h.e.*3.11(M.65.496B); *ib.*3.26 (513A); of earthly paradise, ‡Caes.Naz.*dial.*147(M.38.1097); of wonders performed in pagan magic, Or.*Cels.*1.68(p.122.23; M.11.788C); of God's wonders *τὰ ὄντως δυνατὰ θ. τῶν θείων ἐξουσιῶν καὶ δυνάμεων* Dion.Ar.*c.h.*8.1(M.3.237B).

B. of objects of mystical contemplation *τὸν Πυθαγόρου καὶ Πλάτωνος...περὶ ψυχῆς λόγον, πεφυκυίας ἀναβαίνειν ἐπὶ τὴν ἁψῖδα τοῦ οὐρανοῦ καὶ ἐν τῷ ὑπερουρανίῳ τόπῳ θεωρεῖν τὰ τῶν εὐδαιμόνων θεατῶν θ.* Or.*Cels.*3.80(p.270.22; M.11.1025A); *ἔστι γὰρ ἐν τῷ θεῷ ἐναποθησαυρισμένα πολλῷ μείζονα τούτων θ., ἅτινα οὐδεμία φύσις τῶν ἐν σώματι μὴ πρότερον ἀπαλλαγεῖσα παντὸς σώματος χωρῆσαι δύναται* id.*mart.*13(p.13.26; M.11.581A); Meth.*symp.*8.2(p.82.16; M.18.140C); *διὰ τῆς δυνάμεως φωτιστικῆς τῷ κάλλει τῆς τοῦ θεοῦ τοῦ ἀοράτου εἰκόνος ἐνατενίζομεν, καὶ δι' αὐτῆς ἀναγόμεθα ἐπὶ τὸ ὑπέρκαλον τοῦ ἀρχετύπου θ.* Bas.*Spir.*47(3.39C; M.32.153A); *οἰκείοις μὲν εἰς τὰ θεῖα συμβόλοις χρώμεθα κἀκ τούτων αὖθις ἐπὶ τὴν ἁπλῆν καὶ ἡνωμένην τῶν νοητῶν θ. ἀλήθειαν ἀναλόγως ἀνατεινόμεθα* Dion.Ar.*d.n.*1.4(M.3.592C); id.*myst.*1(M.3.997B) cit. s. *αἴσθησις*.

C. of spiritual sense of scripture, Andr.Cr.*or.*7(M.97.940B).

D. *idea, conception*, Gr.Thaum.*pan.Or.*15(p.35.3; M.10.1096B).

***θεαματίζομαι,** *be granted a vision of τὴν...δόξαν ὁ...Ἡσαΐας θεαματισθεὶς* Germ.CP *or.*1(M.98.241B).

θεάμων, ὁ, *one who beholds, seer*; met., of theologians and philosophers, Meth.*symp.*7.7(p.78.13; M.18.133C); Synes.*provid.*2.8 (p.129.20; M.66.1280A); Max.*ep.*13(M.91.520A).

***θεανδρία, ἡ,** *God-manhood*, of Christ *μητέρα ἐπίγειον, καὶ υἱὸν οὐράνιον, καινήν φημι θ.* ‡Meth.*Sym.et Ann.*11(M.18.376C).

***θεανδρικός,** *of the God-man*, descriptive of incarnate Christ, and mode of operation of his Person in divine and human natures; **1.** of Christ's incarnate life *τὰ δὲ ἑξῆς τῆς θ. αὐτοῦ πολιτείας, πάλιν ἐκ τοῦ εὐαγγελίου μαθησόμεθα* Thdt.*pental.*(5.122); ‡Caes.Naz.*dial.* 14(M.38.872); birth, *ib.*107(973); Gr.Agr.*Eccl.*4.4(M.98.932B); body, ‡Gr.Nyss.*hom.3.80 in Jo.*(p.155.28); soul, ‡Caes.Naz.*dial.*26(885); victory of Cross *σταυροῦ...ἐν ᾧ τὸ πᾶν τῆς θ. νίκης ἤρτητο ib.*133 (1036); **2.** in phrase *θ. ἐνεργεία*: *οὐ κατὰ θεὸν τὰ θεῖα δράσας, οὐ τὰ ἀνθρώπεια κατὰ ἄνθρωπον, ἀλλ' ἀνδρωθέντος θεοῦ, καινήν τινα τὴν θ. ἐνέργειαν ἡμῖν πεπολιτευμένος* Dion.Ar.*ep.*4(M.3.1072C) cit. ap. CLater.*act.*3(H.3.781A); *ταύτης δέ φαμεν τῆς δυνάμεως καὶ τὴν καινὴν* [v.l. *κοινὴν*] *καὶ θ. λεγομένην ἐνέργειαν, οὐ μίαν ὑπάρχουσαν, ἀλλ' ἑτερογενῆ καὶ διάφορον, ἣν ὁ ἐξ Ἀρείου πάγου Παύλῳ...Διονύσιος ἔφησεν, ὡς τὸ θεοπρεπὲς ἐν ταὐτῷ καὶ ἀνθρώπινον ἔχουσαν καὶ...ἑκάστην ἐντελῶς δηλοῦσαν ἐνέργειαν* Sophr.H.*ep.syn.*(M.87.3177B); not to be understood in monothelite sense *οὐ διὰ τοῦτο...ἐξαρνούμεθα, τήν τε τοῦ...Διονυσίου θ. ἐνέργειαν...αὗται μὲν γὰρ διὰ τὴν ἕνωσιν, καὶ τὴν πρὸς ἀλλήλας διόλου τῶν φυσικῶν ἐνεργειῶν συμφυΐαν, εὐσεβῶς αὐτοῖς ἐκηρύχθησαν...ἡ γὰρ θ. τῆς θείας ὁμοῦ καὶ ἀνδρικῆς ἐνεργείας ὑπάρχει περίληψις* Max.*opusc.*(M.91.100B); Dionysius' phrase misused by monothelites *τοῦ γὰρ...Διονυσίου φήσαντος...καινήν τινα θ. ἐνέργειαν ἡμῖν πεπολιτευμένος, ἑκάτερος...κατεψεύσατο. ὁ μὲν Κῦρος...μίαν ἀντὶ τῆς καινῆς θ. ἐνέργειαν αὐτὸν εἰρηκέναι φήσας. ὁ δὲ Σέργιος... ἀκυρώσας πάντῃ τοῦ διδασκάλου τὴν θ. ῥῆσιν, καὶ μίαν ἁπλῶς ἐπὶ Χριστοῦ τοῦ θεοῦ δογματίσας ἐνέργειαν* Martin.ap.CLater.*act.*3(H.3.781E); Max.*schol.ep.*4*Dion.Ar.*(M.4.536A); in monothelite theology *Σεβῆρος...λέγων ὡς τὰ μὲν θείως, τὰ δὲ ἀνθρωπίνως ὁ αὐτὸς ἐνήργησε, τὸ τῆς ἐνεργείας θεανδρικόν, οὐ μόνον μέντοι θεοπρεπὲς ὁμοίως δεῖξαι προῄρητο καταθεάσασθαι ῥᾷον* Them.*fr.*ap.CLater.*act.*3(784D); *μία νοοῖτο θ. τοῦ Χριστοῦ ἡ ἐνέργεια...ἀλλ' οὐ μία θεοπρεπής ib.*(784E); *μία τοῦ λόγου θ. ... ἐνέργειά τε καὶ γνῶσις ib.*; in terms of union between Cyrus and monophysites *εἴ τις...οὐχ...ὁμολογεῖ...τὸν αὐτὸν ἕνα Χριστὸν καὶ υἱὸν ἐνεργοῦντα τὰ θεοπρεπῆ καὶ ἀνθρώπινα μιᾷ θ. ἐνεργείᾳ κατὰ τὸν ἐν ἁγίοις Διονύσιον, θεωρίᾳ μόνῃ διακρίνων τὰ ἐξ ὧν ἡ ἕνωσις γέγονε, καὶ ταῦτα τῷ νῷ διασκοπῶν ἄτρεπτα καὶ ἀσύγχυτα μετὰ τὴν...ἕνωσιν μένοντα...ἀ. ἐ.* Cyrus Al.*cap.*7(H.3.1341C); commented by Pyrr.*serm.fr.*(H.3.1345Cf.); *Μακάριος... ἀρχιεπίσκοπος Ἀντιοχείας εἶπεν...λέγω...ἓν θέλημα καὶ θ. ἐνέργειαν* CCP(681)*act.*8(H.3.1165B); refutation of monothelite theory of *μία θ. ἐνέργεια* Martin.ap.CLater.*act.*3(785C); in conciliar definition *εἴ τις κατὰ τοὺς...αἱρετικοὺς τὴν θ. ἐνέργειαν, μίαν ἀνοήτως ἐκδέχεται, ἀλλ' οὐχὶ διπλῆν αὐτὴν εἶναι ὁμολογεῖ...τουτέστι θείαν καὶ ἀνθρωπίνην, ἢ τὴν ἐπ' αὐτῇ τῇ θεανδρικῇ καινὴν ῥῆσιν, μιᾶς εἶναι σημαντικὴν ἐνεργείας, ἀλλ' οὐχὶ τῆς ἑκατέρων...ἑνώσεως δηλωτικήν, εἴη κατάκριτος* CLater.*can.*15; orthodox explanation of term *ἡ... 'θ.' ... διπλῆν τοῦ διπλοῦ τὴν φύσιν ἐνέργειαν περιφραστικῶς δηλονότι σημαίνει* Max.*opusc.*(M.91.84D); *ib.*(85A); Anast.S.*hod.*1(M.89.45D); *δηλοῖ ἡ θ. ἐνέργεια, ὅτι ἀνδρωθέντος θεοῦ...ἡ ἀνθρωπίνη αὐτοῦ ἐνέργεια θεία ἦν...καὶ ἡ θεία ἐνέργεια οὐκ ἄμοιρος τῆς θείας αὐτοῦ ἐνεργείας, ἀλλ' ἑκατέρα σὺν τῇ ἑτέρᾳ θεωρουμένη* Jo.D.*f.o.*3.19(M.94.1080C); *οὐδὲ εἶπεν...Διονύσιος μίαν θ. ἐνέργειαν· ἀλλ' ἀπολύτως· καινήν, ἤτοι ξένην. ἑκάστη γὰρ αὐτῶν ξένη ἦν καὶ θ. οὐ γὰρ ἀριθμὸν ἐμφαίνων εἶπεν, ἀλλὰ τὸν ξένον τρόπον* id.*volunt.*44(M.95.184C); **3.** of image of Christ *τὸν μηκέτι πλανᾶσθαι...εἰς τὰ εἴδωλα· ἀλλ' ἀντεικονίζειν τὴν θ., ἄχραντον, χειροποίητον στήλην τοῦ ἀληθινοῦ θεοῦ καὶ σωτῆρος...Χριστοῦ* Pamph.H.*can.*4(p.144.20); *τὸν...θεανδρικὸν Χριστοῦ χαρακτῆρα...ἀνετυπώσατο* ‡Jo.D.*ep.Thphl.*3(M.95.348C).

***θεανδρικῶς,** *in divine-human manner*, of mode of operation of Person of Christ *ὡς ἓν εἶναί τι θ. ζῶν πρόσωπον τόδε* Leont.H.*monoph.* testimonia(M.86.1856D); *θ. ἐκ Μαρίας ἐπιφανείς* ‡Epiph.*hom.*1(M.43.432C); *θ. ἤγουν θεϊκῶς ἅμα καὶ ἀνδρικῶς* Max.*ambig.*(M.91.1056C).

***θεανδρίτης, ὁ,** *theandrite, man-god*, word coined to describe Christ as a compound being, divine and human natures being commingled *μηδεὶς...λεγέτω ὅτι θ. τὸν κύριον Ἰησοῦν φησιν· οὐ γὰρ θεανδριτικὴν εἶπεν ἀπὸ τοῦ ὁ θ. σχηματίσας, ἀλλὰ θεανδρικὴν ἐνέργειαν, οἷον θεοῦ καὶ ἀνδρὸς συμπεπλεγμένην ἐνέργειαν* Max.*schol.ep.*4 *Dion. Ar.*(M.4.536A).

***θεανδριτικός,** *pertaining to a man-god* (i.e. pertaining to a being compounded of commingled divine and human natures); rejected as explanation of operation of divinity and manhood in Christ, Max.*schol.ep.*4 *Dion.Ar.*(M.4.536A) cit. s. *θεανδρίτης*.

***θέανδρος, 1.** subst., *God-man*, of Christ *ὁ ἐκ τῆς ἀειπαιδος τεχθεὶς θ.* ‡Caes.Naz.*dial.*133(M.38.1036); **2.** adj., *wedded to God ἐκκλησία...οὐκέτι χήρανδρος, ἀλλὰ θέανδρος* ‡Epiph.*hom.*1(M.43.432B).

***θεανθρωπία, ἡ,** *God-manhood εἴ τις θ. λέγει, καὶ οὐχὶ θεὸν καὶ ἄνθρωπον μᾶλλον λέγει, ἀναθεματιζέσθω* ‡Quint.*ep.*(p.17.13; M.85.1740B).

***θεανθρωπικός,** *pertaining to God–manhood* θεανθρώπου γὰρ ὑπάρχοντος τοῦ Χριστοῦ, καὶ πᾶσα πρᾶξις αὐτοῦ θ. καὶ θεανδρική. τὸ δὲ οὕτω λέγειν οὐ φέρει σύγχυσιν ταῖς ἐνεργείαις ‡Cyr.*Trin.*19(6³.25D; M.77.1160A).

***θεάνθρωπος, ὁ, 1.** *God–man*, cf. *nascitur...deus–homo*, Or.*princ.* 2.6.3(p.142.13; M.11.211C); Χριστὸς οὖν ὁ ἐκ Μαρίας θεὸς ἄνθρωπος ‡Ath.*Ar.*4.36(p.86.15; M.26.524C); Leont.H.*Nest.*4.37(M.86.1708B); θέλων δὲ καὶ κατ' ἄμφω τὰς θελήσεις, κατ' ἄμφω τε τὰς ἐνεργείας ἐνεργῶν, εἷς ὁ αὐτὸς θ. ‡Cyr.*Trin.*18(6³.24E; M.77.1157B); *ib.*19(25D; M.1160A); ὡς ἡ ψυχὴ λογικὴ καὶ ἡ σὰρξ εἷς ἐστιν ἄνθρωπος, οὕτω καὶ ὁ θ. εἷς ἐστι Χριστός ‡Ath.*symb.*3(M.28.1588B); Olymp.*Job* 41:3 (M.93.437C); ‡Jo.D.*hom.*5(M.96.656A); **2.** as adj. (= θεανθρωπικός) τῷ θ. ... τόκῳ Steph.Diac.*v.Steph.*(M.100.1076C).

***θεανθρωπότης, ἡ,** *God-manhood*, in argument against monophysites εἰ μία φύσις τοῦ Χριστοῦ μετὰ τὴν ἕνωσιν, πῶς ὀνομάζεται; χριστότης· δηλαδὴ ἡ θ.· ποίᾳ φύσει; εἰ μία, δηλονότι τῇ μιᾷ αὐτοῦ φύσει. οὐκοῦν ἡ θ. αὐτοῦ. καὶ ἔσται ἡ ἐν Χριστῷ θεότης παθητή Jo.D. *volunt.*8(M.95.140A).

***θεανθρωπόω,** *make God–man*, of Christ προῆλθες...θεανθρωπωθείς *Lit.Gr.Naz.*(M.36.721C).

***θεαρεσκία, ἡ,** *pleasing God*, *Apophth.Patr.*(M.65.421A, v.l. for θεοῦ ἀρεσκείαν).

θεάρεστος, *pleasing to God*; **1.** of persons ὁ δὲ τὰ θεῷ ἐποφειλόμενα πράττων, ζητεῖ θ. ἄνδρας Or.*exp.in Pr.*11(M.17.192C); ‡Meth.*palm.*5 (M.18.392C); opp. αὐτάρεσκος, ‡Proc.G.*Pr.*17:18(M.87.1400A); **2.** of actions and conduct ὀλίγων ἐστὶ...ἀνδρῶν τὸ ἐν πᾶσιν...ἐπίστασθαι, εἰ θ. ἐστι τὸ γινόμενον ‡Ath.*qu.Ant.*132(M.28.680D); τῆς θ. πολιτείας τὰ κατορθώματα Cyr.*Rom.*14:16(p.246.8); exeg. Rom.8:27 ὑπὲρ ἁγίων φησίν· ἀντὶ τοῦ, ὑπὲρ καθαρῶν καὶ θ. ἔργων τὰς αἰτήσεις ποιεῖται Gennad.*fr.Rom.*8:27(p.382.28n.; M.85.1700C); Mod.*dorm.*1(M.86. 3281A); παραγυμνοῖ τὸν θ. ἔρωτα Sophr.H.*v.Anast.*(M.92.1685D); Jo. D.*f.o.*4.17(M.94.1176B); **3.** of worship λατρεία θ. ‡Hipp.*consumm.*34 (p.303.4; M.10.937A); **4.** of Constantine's legislation θ. κατορθωμάτων *Chron.Pasch.*p.8(M.92.84B).

θεαρέστως, *in a manner pleasing to God*, †Cyr.*hom.div.*14(5². 406E); *Chron.Pasch.*p.84(M.92.240C).

***θεαρχία, ἡ,** *Godhead, source* or *principle of deity* ἐπὶ τῇ παρθένῳ ἡ ἐπέλευσις τοῦ πνεύματος ἐγένετο, ἐν πᾶσι τοῖς οὐσιωδῶς προσοῦσιν αὐτῷ κατὰ τὴν θ. ‡Ath.*annunt.*9(M.28.929B); τὸν λόγον...ὡς ἕνα δηλονότι τῆς τρισυποστάτου καὶ μιᾶς θ. ‡Gr.Nyss.*hom.1.3 in Jo.*(p.94. 14); Dion.Ar.*c.h.*2.1(M.3.137A); τῆς ὑπερουσίου θ. μακαριότητα *ib.*2.3 (140C); *ib.*7.3(212C); id.*d.n.*1.3(M.3.589C); *ib.*2.1(637C); ἐν πρόσωπον καὶ θ. μίαν Geo.Pis.*hex.*190(M.92.1448A); πατὴρ...τῶν θεουμένων θεαρχία Jo.D.*f.o.*1.12(M.94.845A); ὁ τρισσοφεγγὴς τῆς θ. τύπος id. *carm.pent.*102(p.216; M.96.837B).

***θεαρχικός,** *of* or *belonging to the Godhead, divine*; **1.** of Father as ultimate Godhead τὴν ἀρχικὴν καὶ ὑπεράρχιον τοῦ θ. πατρὸς φωτοδοσίαν Dion.Ar.*c.h.*1.2(M.3.121A); Jo.D.*hom.*12.11(M.96.796D); **2.** of Logos, Dion.Ar.*e.h.*3.3.12(M.3.444A); as θεαρχικώτατος νοῦς... καὶ θεαρχικωτάτη δύναμις *ib.*1.2(372A); id.*d.n.*2.1(M.3.637B); Max. *ambig.*(M.91.1385A); ‡Sophr.H.*v.m.Cyr.et Jo.*1(M.87.3677A); τοῦ θ. λόγου καὶ ποιητοῦ Gr.Agr.*Eccl.*3:18(M.98.877C); *ib.*3:20(884B); θεαρχικώτατε λόγε *Lit.Jac.*(*NBP* 10² p.105); of divine wisdom, Gr. Agr.*Eccl.*2:12(837B); of incarnate Christ, Dion.Ar.*e.h.*4.3.4(477C); *ib.*5.3.5(512C); **3.** of H. Ghost, *ib.*2.2.8(397A); *ib.*2.3.8(404C); *ib.*5.3.5 (512C); **4.** of Persons of Trin. ἑκάστης τῶν ἁγίων τριῶν θ. ὑποστάσεων ‡Ath.*annunt.*9(M.28.932); ὁ ἀληθὴς περὶ αὐτοῦ λόγος καὶ τῶν ἄλλων δύο θ. ὑποστάσεων ‡Gr.Nyss.*hom.5.5 in Jo.*(p.175.24); Dion.Ar.*d.n.* 2.5(M.3.641D); *ib.*2.11(652A); τὴν μοναδικὴν θ. ἐκ θ. τριῶν ὑποστάσεων πεφυκυῖαν Gr.Agr.*Eccl.*4:1(M.98.920A); Jo.D.*Jacob.*10(M.94.1440A); **5.** of Trin. as a whole τῇ θεαρχικωτάτῃ καὶ βασιλίδι τριάδι Andr. Caes.*Apoc.*1(M.106.224A); Jo.D.*f.o.*3.10(M.94.1021A); without subst. τελεῖσθε πάντες τῇ θεαρχικωτάτῃ ‡Jo.D.*carm.pent.*46(p.215; M.96. 836A); ἄληπτός ἐστιν ἡ θεαρχικωτάτη *ib.*21(p.214; 833B); **6.** of being or substance of God τὴν...ὑπερουσιότητα τὴν θ. Dion.Ar.*d.n.*1.5(M.3. 593C); cf.*ib.*5.1(816B); τὴν θ. ... ὕπαρξιν *ib.*2.1(636C); θ. ἰδιότητος id. *c.h.*15.2(M.3.329A); ‡Gr.Nyss.*hom.1.42 in Jo.*(p.108.3); ἡ θ. μακαριότης, ἡ φύσει θεότης Dion.Ar.*e.h.*1.4(M.3.376B); *ib.*3.3.3(429A); **7.** of God's attributes: goodness, Dion.Ar.*c.h.*7.4(M.3.212B); id. *e.h.*1.5(M.3.376D); *ib.*3.3.11(441A); beauty, id.*c.h.*3.2(165A); *ib.*7. 1(205C); hiddenness, *ib.*12.3(293B); power, *ib.*13.3(293B); id.*e.h.* 5.1.3(505B); light, id.*c.h.*9.3(M.3.261A); life, id.*d.n.*2.1(M.3.637A); **8.** of Christ's attributes: sinlessness, id.*e.h.*5.3.4(M.3.512B); weakness (in Inc.) τὴν ἀπειροδύναμον τῆς θ. ἀσθενείας id.*d.n.*3.2(M.3.681D); **9.** of divine activity in rel. to man; beneficence, id.*e.h.*3.3.8(M.3. 437A); *ib.*7.3.7(561D); σοφοποιΐα id.*c.h.*14(M.3.321A); judgements, id. *e.h.*7.3.7(561C); *ib.*(564A); revelation, id.*c.h.*1.2(121B); *ib.*3.2(165A); *ib.*4.2(180B); *ib.*9.3(260C); id.*e.h.*6.3.6(537C); of Christ's death, *ib.*2.3.7(404B); of Christ as θ. τῶν θείων νοῶν ἀφιέρωσις *ib.*4.3.12 (484D); of the Inc. as θεαρχικὸν μυστήριον id.*c.h.*4.4(181B); of activity of God in Christian worship, id.*e.h.*4.3.10(484A); *ib.*5.1.7 (509A); and in selection of priests, *ib.*5.3.5(512B); **10.** of man's knowledge of God, id.*c.h.*7.3(M.3.209C); *ib.*7.4(212A); of imagery under which God is apprehended, *ib.*2.3(140C); *ib.*2.5(144C); *ib.*4.2 (180A); of mystical apprehension, id.*e.h.*6.3.6(M.3.537B); of summit of mystical ascent ἐπὶ τὴν ἀκρότητα τὴν θ. ... ἱερῶς ἀναχθήσεται *ib.* 2.3.4(400C); of καταπαῦσις as its goal, id.*c.h.*7.4(212C); **11.** of sacraments θ. ... ἐποψιῶν καὶ κοινωνιῶν id.*e.h.*7.3.3(M.3.557C); of eucharist, *ib.*3.1(425A); as θ. κοινωνία *ib.*3.2(428A); *ib.*6.3.5(536B); *ib.*7.3.9 (565B); of its benefits, *ib.*3.1(424D); **12.** of scriptures as divine promises, *ib.*7.3.2(557B); **13.** of prayer θ. ὁμιλίαν *ib.*7.3.6(561C); **14.** of hymns; **a.** Psalms, id.*d.n.*1.3(M.3.589B); **b.** 'Seraphic hymn', id.*c.h.*13.4(M.3.305A); **15.** of priests, id.*ep.*8.4(M.3.1096A); **16.** of an inspired prophet Ἰωὴλ τοῦ θεαρχικωτάτου ‡Jo.D.*carm.pent.*92(p.216; M.96.837A).

***θεαρχικῶς,** *divinely*, Dion.Ar.*e.h.*4.3.10(M.3.484A).

θεαστικός, *inspired*, Areth.*Apoc.*8(M.106.553B).

θεατής, ὁ, *spectator, observer*; **1.** Tat.*orat.*23(p.26.3; M.6.857C); Chrys.*hom.48.3 in Mt.*(7.497A); met. προβησόμεθα...ὡς ἂν τῶν τῆς μανίας πολέμων θεατὴς γένωμαι Const.ap.Gel.Cyz.*h.e.*3.19.6(M.85. 1345C); **2.** of disciples at Transfiguration τοὺς θ. τοῦ τηλικούτου κάλλους Or.*Cels.*6.77(p.146.24; M.11.1416A); **3.** of witnesses, seen and unseen, of Christian's progress in life, *ib.*8.31(p.247.12; 1564B); cf.Chrys.*hom.2.3 in Tit.*(11.741B); **4.** of God as observer of men's actions ὡς ἐπὶ θεοῦ θ. πᾶν ὅ τί ποτ' οὖν ἐπιτελοῦντας Or.*Cels.*3.57 (p.252.19; M.11.996C); in etym. of word θεός: ἐκ τῆς θέας τὴν θεότητα παρωνομάσθαι, καὶ τὸν θ. ἡμῶν θεόν Gr.Nyss.*tres dii*(M.45.121D); **5.** of one who exercises mental and spiritual perception γνῶσις... ἀξιεντρεπτοτέρους ποιοῦσα τοὺς πιστοὺς καὶ τῶν πραγμάτων ἀκριβεῖς θ. Clem.*ecl.*28(p.145.27; M.9.713B); of those who attain summit of mystical contemplation (Platonic and Pythagorean), Or.*Cels.*3.80 (p.270.22; M.11.1025A) cit. s. θέαμα.

θεατικός, *of seeing* μίαν δὲ καὶ ταύτην εἶναι τὴν ἐνέργειαν τὴν ἐποπτικὴν καὶ ὁρατικὴν καὶ ὡς ἄν τις εἴποι θ., καθ' ἣν τὰ πάντα ἐφορᾷ...ὑπειλήφαμεν, ἐκ τῆς θέας τὴν θεότητα παρωνομάσθαι, καὶ τὸν θεατὴν ἡμῶν θεόν Gr.Nyss.*tres dii*(M.45.121D); τὴν ἐποπτικήν τε καὶ θ. δύναμιν, ἥνπερ δὴ θεότητα λέγομεν *ib.*(128B); τὸ θεὸς ὄνομα... ἀριδηλότερον...τῆς θ. ἐνεργείας ἐστὶ παραστατικόν ‡Cyr.*Trin.*11 (6³.17C; M.77.1145C).

θεατρίζ-ω, 1. *act on stage, be an actor* ἀμφότεροι οὖν βαπτισθέντες ἀπέστησαν τοῦ ~ειν Pall.*h.Laus.*37(p.110.3; M.34.1185A); of an actor baptized in mockery on the stage βαπτισθεὶς...οὐκέτι ἠνέσχετο θεατρίσαι *Chron.Pasch.*p.276(M.92.685A); met. ἐν τῷ βίῳ τούτῳ, ὥσπερ ἐπὶ ὀρχήστρας τῆς ἑαυτῶν ζωῆς οἱ πολλοὶ ~ουσιν Bas.*hom.*1. 2(2.2D; M.31.165B); **2.** *exhibit, show off* ὁ ὄρνις...~ει τὸ κάλλος ταῖς ἐρασταῖς Gr.Naz.*or.*28.24(p.59.6; M.36.60B); Nil.*epp.*2.18(M.79.208B); Bas.Sel.*or.*27.1(M.85.312A); **3.** *make a spectacle of, put to shame* before οἴμοι τῇ...τοῖς δαίμοσιν ~ομένῃ *A.Xanthipp.*26(p.76.38); martyrs ~ων τοὺς μακαρίους *Ep.Lugd.*ap.Eus.*h.e.*5.1.47(M.20.425C); Gr.Nyss.*Eun.*1(1 p.205.12; M.45.452E); οὐκ ἔξεστι λαϊκὸν ὑβρίζειν ἱερέα ἢ ~ειν *Poen.App.*7(p.154.20).

θεατρικός, *theatrical*, Clem.*str.*3.1(p.195.11; M.8.1100A); masc. as subst., *actor*; of actor's life as being no preparation for heaven, Mac.Aeg.*hom.*28.20(M.34.708C); neut. as subst., *theatricality*, Isid. Pel.*epp.*2.228(M.78.665B).

***θεάτρισμα, τό,** *show*, Gr.Naz.*ep.*178(M.37.293A).

θεατρισμός, ὁ, *object of ridicule*, Gr.Nyss.*hom.in 1Cor.6:18*(M.46. 493C).

***θεατροκοπ-έω,** *court applause for* ὅστις [sc. Nero] παμμούσῳ φθόγγῳ μελιηδέας ὕμνους ~ῶν *Orac.Sib.*5.142; Tat.*orat.*19(p.21.13; M.6.849A).

θεατροκοπία, ἡ, *courting of popular favour, publicity* οὐδὲ φιλόσοφος ἐγενόμην δημόσιος, οὐδὲ θεατροκοπίαις ἐπεθέμην Synes.*ep.*57 (M.66.1397B).

***θεατρομανής,** *mad on the theatre*, ‡Ath.*sem.*11(M.28.157A); ὁ θ. ...ἐρωτομανὴς γίνεται Isid.Pel.*epp.*5.463(M.78.1596B).

***θεατρομανία, ἡ,** *folly of the theatre*, Or.*Cels.*3.56(p.251.28; M.11. 996A); πομπὴ δὲ διαβόλου ἐστὶ θεατρομανίαι Cyr.H.*catech.*19.6; θεατρομανίᾳ εἴ τις πρόσκειται...ἢ παυσάσθω ἢ ἀποβαλλέσθω *Const. App.*8.32.15.

θέατρον, τό, A. *theatre*; **1.** in gen.; **a.** *theatre* (the building) εἰ γάρ τις ὥσπερ ἐπὶ θεάτρου κορυφῆς καθίσας, τὸν κόσμον κατοπτεύσειε

Chrys.*hom.82.3 in Jo.*(8.487B); as place of public assembly, ‡Pion. *v.Polyc.*30; **b.** *show, play* performed in theatre, Clem.*prot.*7(p.58.26; M.8.185C); *Chron.Pasch.*p.312(M.92.796B); **2.** of theatre and its spectacles as evil καθέδρα δὲ λοιμῶν καὶ τὰ θ. καὶ τὰ δικαστήρια εἴη ἂν Clem.*str.*2.15(p.149.13; M.8.1008A); τί μὲν γὰρ οὐκ ἐπιδείκνυνται αἰσχρὸν ἔργον ἐν θεάτροις; id.*paed.*3.11(p.278.32; M.8.656A); τὰ ἔθνη ...ἐν τοῖς θ. αὐτῶν ὡς ἐν συναγωγῇ πάντες συνέρχονται *Const.App.*2.60.2; κατατρέχεις εἰς τὸ θ., ἰδεῖν νηχομένας γυναῖκας,...καταλιπὼν τὸν Χριστόν Chrys.*hom.7.6 in Mt.*(7.113C); τὸ θ. ὅλον σατανικόν *ib.48.3*(497A); ταῦτα ὑμᾶς τὰ θ. τῆς ἀσελγείας διδάσκει, ὁ λοιμὸς ὁ δυσκατάλυτος, τὰ δηλητήρια φάρμακα...ἡ μεθ' ἡδονῆς τῶν ἀκολάστων ἀπώλεια *ib.73.6*(712B); prison preferable in its effects to theatre ἐν δὲ θ. ... ἀνάλωμα χρόνου...πορνείας γυμνάσιον, ἀκολασίας διδασκαλεῖον, προτροπὴ αἰσχρότητος...ἀσχημοσύνης παραδείγματα id. *hom.42.4 in Ac.*(9.323B); id.*David* 3.1(4.770A); id.*Laz.*7.1(1.791D); **3.** forbidden to Christians, Clem.*paed.*3.11(p.278.30; M.8.656A); id.*str.*7.7(p.28.11; M.9.452B); *Hom.Clem.*4.19; *Const.App.*2.61.2; Chrys.*hom.6.7 in Mt.*(7.99B); under penalty of excommunication, id.*theatr.*4(6.276D); Χριστιανοὺς αὐτοὺς [sc. μίμους] ἐποίησε καὶ τοῦ θεάτρου ἀπέστησε Pall.*h.Laus.*37(p.109.16; M.34.1185A); **4.** met., of Christian life as contest in theatre, Clem.*str.*7.3(p.15.4; M.9.425A); μέγα θ. συγκροτεῖται ἐφ' ὑμῖν ἀγωνιζομένοις Or.*mart.*18(p.16.24; M.11.585A); Meth.*symp.*8.1(p.81.12; M.18.140A); ὁ γὰρ ὑποκριτὴς μέχρι τότε φαίνεται λαμπρός, ἕως ἂν τὸ θ. κάθηται...πλὴν ἀλλὰ τοῦ θ. λυθέντος, σαφέστερον ἅπασιν ἐκκαλύπτεται. τοῦτο...τοὺς κενοδόξους ὑπομένειν ἀνάγκη Chrys.*hom.20.1 in Mt.*(7.260C); id.*hom.83.4 in Jo.*(8.497A); id.*hom.23.5 in 1Cor.*(10.207E); ἀναχώρησον ἐκ τῆς γῆς, πρὸς ἐκεῖνο ἴδε τὸ θ. τὸ ἐν τοῖς οὐρανοῖς id.*hom.2.3 in Tit.*(11.741B); of life as tight-rope performance in theatre, Or.*Cels.*3.69(p.262.2; M.11.1012B); of the world as a theatre λόγος οὐράνιος, ὁ γνήσιος ἀγωνιστὴς ἐπὶ τῷ παντὸς κόσμου θ. στεφανούμενος Clem.*prot.*1(p.4.16; M.8.53C); Bas.*hex.*6.1(1.50B; M.29.117C); of an author's *setting* or *staging* for his story, Chrys.*hom.1.1 in Jo.*(8.2E).

B. *assembly of spectators, audience*; **1.** *public meeting*, Chrys.*hom.40.5 in Mt.*(7.443E); id.*hom.1.2 in 1Tim.*(11.551A); **2.** *audience* οὐδὲ ...ἀπέστησαν οἱ ἀκροαταί, ἀλλὰ καὶ οὕτω τὸ θ. ἅπαν ἠκολούθησε Chrys. *hom.25.1 in Mt.*(7.306D); id.*hom.76.3 in Jo.*(8.450A); Vict.*Mc.*4:2 (p.301.31); of congregation in church οὐ γάρ ἐστι τὸ θ. τοῦτο γέλωτος, οὐδὲ διὰ τοῦτο συνήλθομεν, ἵνα ἀνακαγχάζωμεν Chrys.*hom.6.6 in Mt.* (7.98A); id.*hom.31.1 in Rom.*(9.746E); μετὰ τὸ λυθῆναι τὸ πνευματικὸν τοῦτο θ. id.*pan.Pelag.Ant.*1.3(2.589B); id.*pan.Juln.*5(2.680C); Bas. Sel.*or.*34.1(M.85.369C); **3.** *spectators*, Chrys.*hom.52.1 in Mt.*(7.530B); *ib.57.4*(582B); esp. of heavenly host as spectators of Christians' activities in this world, *ib.34.4*(394A); id.*hom.9.2 in 2Tim.*(11.717B).

C. *spectacle, sight* θ. αἰσχρὸν καὶ γέλως κεκλημένοις Gr.Naz.*carm.*1.2.10.839(M.37.740A); Chrys.*hom.35.3 in Ac.*(9.273B); id.*hom.21.6 in 1Cor.*(10.188C).

***θεατρονόμιον, τό,** ? *theatre-going* μὴ φέροντος τὴν ἐρημίαν τῆς ἐκκλησίας, ἣν ἀρχαὶ πονηραὶ καὶ ἐξουσίαι εἰργάσαντο, καθάπερ θ. ἀποδείξασαι Pall.*v.Chrys.*10(p.61.22; M.47.35; v.l. θεατρονόμον, conj. θέατρον ἀνομιῶν).

***θεατρόσκοπος, ὁ,** *ardent theatre-goer*, Pall.*v.Chrys.*5(p.33.13; M.47.21).

***θεαφίζω,** *be sulphurous*, †Jo.D.*B.J.*15(M.96.997B).

θεάφι(ο)ν, τό, *sulphur*; part of horrors of hell, †Cyr.*hom.div.*14 (5^2.411C); θεάφιν *A.Barth.*7(p.146.27).

***θεαφώδης,** *sulphurous*, *M.Ner.et Ach.*20(p.19.18).

θε-άω, *see, contemplate*; **1.** of God παρὰ...τὸ...θεᾶσθαι τὰ πάντα ὁ θεὸς ὀνομάζεται Evagr.Pont.*ep.*11(M.32.265A); θεότης...ἡ πάντα ~ωμένη πρόνοια Dion.Ar.*d.n.*12.2(M.3.969C); πηγὴν ζωῆς...ἀεὶ δι' ἑαυτῆς ἑαυτὴν ~ωμένην id.*ep.*9.1(M.3.1104C); this being understood of Trin., Max.*schol.ep.*9 *Dion.Ar.*(M.4.560A); **2.** of man's contemplation of God; as goal of life, Clem.*paed.*1.12(p.150.12; M.8.369C); ἔστι...ὁ θεὸς ἀγάπη καὶ δι' ἀγάπην ἡμῖν ἐθεάθη id.*q.d.s.*37 (p.184.1, v.l. ἐθηράθη M.9.37C); as possible only for pure in heart, Or.*Cels.*7.45(p.196.17; M.11.1485C); ἰδοῦσαι [sc. virgins] μακρόθεν ἃ μὴ ἕτερος ἀνθρώπων ἐθεάσατο Meth.*symp.*8.2(p.82.13; M.18.140C); made possible through Inc., Clem.*str.*5.3(p.336.13; M.9.33A); contemplation of Trin. possible through Christ as the way (ref. Jo. 14:6), Proc.G.*Jos.*2:16(M.87.1001C); in Docetist's view of Christ μὴ δύνασθαι θεαθῆναι...διὰ τὸ μεταβαλλόμενον μέγεθος τῆς δόξης Hipp. *haer.*10.16(p.278.13; M.16.3434C).

θεηγενής, *born of God*; of Christ, Nonn.*par.Jo.*19:23(M.43.901C); *ib.*21:20(920B); met., *divine* θ. ἔργα *ib.*12:42(857B).

θεηγορ-έω, 1. *speak as from God* θεηγορεῖ [sc. Μωσῆς]...περὶ τῆς ἀνωτάτω πασῶν οὐσίας Cyr.*Juln.*1(6^2.14D); *ib.*8(267A); Χριστοῦ ~οῦντος, δωρεὰν εἰληφότας ὁμοίως παρέχειν ‡Caes.Naz.*dial.*1(M.38.856); *ib.*11(868); **2.** *speak of as being divine* ξύλα τε καὶ λίθους ~ῶν οὐκ αἰσχύνεται Cyr.*Juln.*6(6^2.194A); *ib.*10(331D).

***θεηγορία, ἡ,** *divine utterance*; of scriptural texts, Didym.*Trin.* 3.1(M.39.781B); *ib.*3.35(965A); ‡Caes.Naz.*dial.*140(M.38.1060).

θεηγόρος, 1. *speaking of God*; **a.** of persons ὁ θ. ἀνήρ [i.e. S. Paul] Mac.Mgn.*apocr.*3.39(p.136.22); θ. ... προφήτης Nonn.*par.Jo.*1:21(M.43.753A); *ib.*1:25(753B); Ἰησοῦν...θ. *ib.*11:56(849A); Cyr.*hom.div.*2 (5^2.354C); Eudoc.*Cypr.*1.270(M.85.841D); τῶν θεηγόρων πατέρων διδασκαλίας Leont.B.*Nest.et Eut.*1(M.86.1305D); θ. Διονύσιος Sophr.H. *ep.syn.*(M.87.3177C); Max.*opusc.*(M.91.165C); ὁ ἀληθὴς θ. ... Διονύσιος id.*ambig.*(M.91.1312D); ὁ θ. ... Βασίλειος Jo.D.*f.o.*4.16(M.94.1169A); CNic.(787)*act.*4(H.4.168E); **b.** of things θ. ἀνθερεῶνα Nonn.*par.Jo.* 1:8(M.43.752A); θ. χείλεα *ib.*8:28(817A); θ. δήνεα βίβλων Paul.Sil. *ambo.*106(M.86.2256A); θ. στόματι Jo.D.*hom.*1.6(M.96.556C); **2.** as subst., *theologian*, esp. of NT writers σάλπιγγες τῶν σημασιῶν, τουτέστι, τῶν θ. οἱ λόγοι Cyr.*ador.*4(1.121B); *ib.*6(210A); *ib.*17(598A); id.*Rom.*8:3(M.74.817B); τὸν τῶν θ. ἰχνηλατοῦντες σκοπόν id.*Nest.*1 proem.(p.15.20; 6^1.5A); θεηγόροι [i.e. apostles] καταυγάσατε ἡμᾶς *IGC As.Min.*61; †Jo.D.*B.J.*9(M.96.932C).

***θεηδόκος,** *receiving God, being hostess to God*; of Mary of Bethany, Nonn.*par.Jo.*11:2(M.43.840A).

θεηδόχος, =θεοδόχος, *receiving God*; **1.** of altar δώρων δοχεῖον ἁγνόν, ἡ θ. τράπεζα Gr.Naz.*carm.*1.2.34.226(M.37.961A, v.l. θυηδόχος); **2.** of the beach where Christ appeared to disciples (Jo.21:1) θ. ἠόνα Nonn.*par.Jo.*21:7(M.43.916C).

θεηλασία, ἡ, *driving by God*; of exile sent as divine vengeance, *T.Benj.*7.2(v.l. αἰχμαλωσία).

θεήλατος, 1. *driven by God*, *Orac.Sib.*3.713; **2.** *pursued, driven mad by God*; as term of abuse in theological argument, Epiph.*anc.* 15(p.23.18; M.43.44A); ὁ θ. Ὠριγένης *ib.*54(p.63.11; 112B); ὁ βδελυρὸς καὶ θ. Sophr.H.*mir.Cyr.et Jo.*32(M.87.3525A); Jo.D.*f.o.*3.3(M.94.993A); **3.** *sent by God*; of plagues and other punishments, Eus.*d.e.* 3.7(p.146.28; M.22.245D); id.*h.e.*8.16.2(M.20.789B); Ast.Soph.*fr.*2a ap.Ath.*Ar.*2.37(M.26.228A); Chrys.*hom.72.3 in Jo.*(8.426E); Bas. Sel.*or.*9.2(M.85.133A); Jo.D.*f.o.*3.10(M.94.1021A).

***θεηλάτως,** *madly*, Leont.H.*monoph.*(M.86.1845A).

θεημάχος, v. θεομάχος.

***θεητόκος,** = θεοτόκος, Nonn.*par.Jo.*2:2(M.43.760C); *ib.*19:25 (904B).

***θεητός,** *visible*; met., Gr.Naz.*carm.*1.1.4.94(M.37.423A); ref. senses of scripture, *ib.*2.2(poem.)7.140(561A).

θεία, ἡ, *aunt*, Ath.*apol.Const.*6(M.25.604C); id.*h.Ar.*13(p.189.22; M.25.708B); Amph.*Seleuc.*337(M.37.1600A); *Chron.Pasch.*p.311(M.92.793A); ref. aunts of clergy, excepted from prohibition against *subintroductae*, CNic.(325)*can.*3.

θειάζ-ω, 1. *deify, regard as divine*; **a.** ref. Christ μετὰ τὴν τελευτήν, καὶ πολὺ μᾶλλον τότε ἢ πρότερον, αὐτὸν τεθειάκασιν Eus.*d.e.*3.4(p.118.7; τεθνηκότα τετιμήκασιν M.22.201B); **b.** in gen. θ. ... τὸν διάβολον Clem.*str.*4.11(p.285.19; M.8.1293A); ἄθεος...ὁ πάντα ~ων *ib.*7.1(p.5.13; M.9.408A); Eus.*l.C.*15(p.247.17; M.20.1420A); Mac.Mgn.*apocr.* 4.29(p.218.5); Philost.*h.e.*7.12(M.65.549C); **c.** met., *set great store by*, ref. Epicurus θ. ... σαρκὸς εὐσταθὲς κατάστημα Clem.*str.*2.20(p.178.2; M.8.1064A); Eus.*l.C.*5(p.205.17; M.20.1337C); Philost.*h.e.*2.5(M.65.469B); Synes.*provid.*2(p.121.22; M.66.1272A); **2.** *be inspired* ~οντες λόγων ἱερῶν παιδεύμασιν Eus.*l.C.*1(p.96.15; M.20.1320A); of prophets, id.*p.e.*7.11(313C; M.21.537D).

θειασμός, ὁ, *frenzy, inspiration, religious enthusiasm*; **1.** pagan ἔπη δέ, οὐκ ἔκ τινος θ. καὶ κατοχῆς...ἀλλ' ἐκ τῆς Ἐμπεδοκλέους... ποιήσεως Thdt.*affect.*10(p.244.22; 4.952); Bas.Sel.*v.Thecl.*2.12(M.85.585C); **2.** Christian Γρηγόριος...εἶπε θ. τινος εἶναι τὸ χρῆμα Evagr. *h.e.*5.21(p.216.23; M.86.2836B).

θεϊκός, *divine*; **1.** ref. God, in gen. θ. οὐσία Eus.*e.th.*1.12(p.71.11; M.24.848A); φύσις Bas.*ep.*262.2(3.404C; M.32.973C); Epiph.*haer.*76.31(p.381.12; M.42.581A); δύναμις Clem.*prot.*10(p.74.5; M.8.217C); *ib.* 11(p.78.9; 228A); Eus.*v.C.*2.16(p.47.21; M.20.993B); id.*l.C.*15(p.244.19; M.20.1413B); *Lit.Bas.*(p.343.23); ἐξουσία Didym.(‡Bas.)*Eun.*5 (1.316C; M.29.757C); πρόνοια Clem.*paed.*2.10(p.215.2; M.8.512B); σοφία id.*prot.*4(p.48.27; 164B); φωνή id.*paed.*1.12(p.148.22; 368B); **2.** partic., ref. Trin. μὴ διαιρῶν [sc. Marcell.] μὲν τὴν...θ. δύναμιν Eus.*e.th.*1.5(p.64.26; M.24.833B); οὐδὲ τρεῖς θεοὺς ὀνομάζειν δυνάμεθα, τοὺς τὴν θ. ταύτην, ἤτοι ἐποπτικὴν δύναμιν...συνημμένως καὶ ἀδιακρίτως δι' ἀλλήλων ἐφ' ἡμῶν...ἐνεργοῦντας Gr.Nyss.*tres dii*(M.45.128A); τὰ συναφείας τῆς θ. ἑρμηνεύματα...τὸν λόγον, τὸ πνεῦμα Didym. (‡Bas.)*Eun.*5(1.307C; M.29.737A); ἅτε δὴ καὶ τῆς θ. ἐνεργείας δι' αὐτοῦ [sc. H. Ghost] πληρουμένης *ib.*(304D; M.729C); ref. the three

Persons τῶν αὐτῶν θ. ἔργων ib.(307C; M.737A); τριάς Epiph. exp.fid.18(p.520.3; M.42.820A); ἑνότης Dion.Ar.d.n.13.3(M.3.980C); **3.** ref. Father, Eus.e.th.1.20(p.86.21; M.24.876A); **4.** ref. Christ; **a.** Christol. δύο θελήματα...δείκνυσι, τὸ μὲν ἀνθρώπινον...τὸ δὲ θ. Ath.inc.et c.Ar.21(M.26.1021C); τὸ σῶμα φύσει μέν ἐστιν ἀνθρώπινον, τῇ δὲ ἑνώσει τῆς οἰκονομίας θ. ‡Ath.dial.Trin.4.1(M.28.1249D); τῇ μὲν θ. φύσει ἀπαθής ‡Ath.Apoll.1.11(M.26.1112C); τάς τε ἀνθρωπίνας [sc. φωνάς], καὶ...τὰς θ., παρ' ἑνὸς εἰρῆσθαι διακεισόμεθα Cyr.ep.17(p.38.8; 5^2.73B); ὁ Παῦλος ἀναμίξας τὰ θ., ἑκάτερα περὶ ἑνὸς καὶ τοῦ αὐτοῦ λέγει Thdot.Anc.exp.symb.3(M.77.1317D); Arian οὐκοῦν ἔδει καὶ τὰ θ. βλέποντας ἔργα τοῦ λόγου, ἀρνήσασθαι τοῦ σώματος αὐτοῦ τὴν γένεσιν Ath.Ar.3.35(M.26.400A); Apollinarian σῶμα ἀνθρώπινον ἔσχεν ὁ Χριστός, ἢ οὔ;...οὐ...ἀλλ' ὁποῖον;...θ. ‡Ath.dial.Trin.4.1(M.28.1249D); σῶμα μεμορφωμένον, ταῖς θ. καταλαμπόμενον ἐνεργείαις ib.4.9(1264C); φησι [sc. Apoll.] λέγειν ἡμᾶς ὅτι ὁ σταυρωθεὶς οὐδὲν εἶχε θ. ἐν τῇ ἑαυτοῦ φύσει Gr.Nyss.Apoll.27(M.45.1181A); **b.** of Inc. and redemption πρὸς...ἡμᾶς θ. κατάβασις Sophr.H.ep.syn.(M.87.3160B); ἵνα δελεάσῃ αὐτὸν ὥσπερ δράκοντα, αἱμοβόρον, τῷ θ. ἀγκίστρῳ, καταβάλλει Jo.Eub.concept.19(M.96.1492D); ref. works performed by incarnate Christ ἡ θ. δύναμις Or.fr.53 in Jo.(p.527.14); Eus.theoph.fr.6(p.19*.31; M.24.628B); id.fr.Lc.9:1(M.24.544B); διὰ τί μὴ καὶ ἐκ τῶν θ. ἔργων ἐπιγινώσκουσι τὸν ἐν τῷ πατρὶ λόγον; Ath.Ar.3.55(M.26.437C); id.ep.Serap.4.22(M.26.673A); Gr.Nyss.Apoll.45(M.45.1232C); διὰ πάντων ἀχωρίστως τῇ θ. δυνάμει συνεκφαίνων τῆς οἰκείας σαρκὸς τὴν ἐνέργειαν Max.ambig.(M.91.1052C); αὐτὸς...τῇ θ. αὐτοῦ δυνάμει ἀνέστη Jo.V H.icon.16(M.96.1361B); **c.** ref. glorified Christ, Eus.l.C.2(p.199.15; M.20.1325B); ἣν γὰρ αὐτὸν πρὸ τούτου θεωρήσας [sc. Isaiah] ἐν τῇ θ. καὶ ἐνδόξῳ αὐτοῦ μορφῇ Ath.inc.et c.Ar.23(M.26.1025B); ref. Jo.17:5 δόξα ‡Ath.Apoll.2.15(M.26.1157B); **d.** neut. as subst., *divinity*, Iren.haer.3.11.8(M.7.888B); τὸ...θ. αὐτοῦ...φανερῶς ἔστιν ἰδεῖν, ὅτε ὑπ' ἀγγέλων προσκυνεῖται Hipp.fr.18 in Pss.(p.146.12; M.10.609A); ἵν'...ἄγευστος ᾖ πάντη τῆς ἁμαρτίας, κατά γε τὸ θ. ‡Ath.Apoll.1.2(1096B); Epiph.exp.fid.17(p.518.23; M.42.817A); ref. risen Christ τὸ θ. καὶ σωματικὸν εἰς ἓν πνευματικὸν τελούμενον id.haer.69.67(p.215.22; M.42.309C); Jo.D.disp.(M.96.1345B); **5.** ref. H. Ghost, Didym.Trin.1.7(M.39.272A); ἡ θ. τοῦ πνεύματος δόξα id.(‡Bas.)Eun.5(1.309E; M.29.741D); heret. οὐδ' ὅτι καταμόνας ἐν θεοῦ δόξῃ τὸ πνεῦμα κηρύσσεται, συνιεὶς τὴν θ. δόξαν ἐπ' αὐτοῦ ib.(308D; M.740B); Nil.Eulog.2(M.79.1096B); τὸ τοῦ πνεύματος...θ. Cyr.thes.33(5^1.335B); **6.** ref. doctrine and law; ref. law of nature πᾶσιν...ἀνθρώποις...ἐνέστακταί τις ἀπόρροια θ. Clem.prot.6(p.52.2; M.8.173A); ἐντολαὶ κυριακαί, αἳ δὴ δόξαι οὖσαι θ. id.paed.1.12(p.151.28; M.8.376A); ref. teaching of Christ θ. ... διδασκαλία ib.2.8(p.194.10; 465B); θ. σοφίας διδάσκαλος Vict.Mc.3:20(p.297.31); ref. preaching of an apostle, A.Thom.A 39(p.156.21); ref. scriptures, †Hipp.Artem.ap.Eus.h.e.5.28.13(M.20.516A); Gr.Naz.ep.235(M.37.377C); Epiph.haer.9.1(p.197.14; M.41.224B); **7.** ref. grace, Clem.paed.1.6(p.108.1; M.8.285B); ἡ θ. χάρις τοῦ Ἰησοῦ Narr.Jos.3(p.465.2); Gr.Nyss.or.dom.2(p.44.2; M.44.1148B); Jo.Mon.hymn.Nic.Myr.4(M.96.1385A); **8.** ref. worship λειτουργία ἡ θ. Clem.paed.2.4(p.182.19; M.8.441A); and virtues ἡ ταπείνωσις μέγα ἔργον ἐστὶ καὶ θ. Dor.doct.2.8(M.88.1649C); †Jo.D.B.J.30(M.96.1141A); **9.** of kingdom of heaven, Eus.fr.Lc.9:26(M.24.548D); Ath.inc.et c.Ar.20(M.26.1020A); **10.** of angels, A.(Pass.)Petr.et Paul.27(p.142.15); A.Petr.et Paul.48(p.199.19); **11.** ref. men τῷ τῆς θ. ἐπηγορίας ἐπωνύμῳ δυναμούμενος [sc. Const.] Eus.l.C.2(p.199.7; M.20.1325A); ref. soul ἡ θ. εἰκών Gr.Naz.carm.1.2.10.21(M.37.682A); ὅτε...τὴν ῥοπὴν δῶμεν πρὸς τὴν ἐντολὴν τοῦ θεοῦ, θ. ὀνομάζεται ἡμῶν τὸ θέλημα, οὐ κατ' οὐσίαν ἀλλὰ κατὰ τὴν πρᾶξιν Ephr.Ant.fr.(M.86.2105D); **12.** in special senses; **a.** *of God* ἐπιλαμψάσης θ. ὄψεως Eus.l.C.11(p.223.29; M.20.1377A); φρονήσει κινούμενος θ. Pall.h.Laus.6(p.22.20); θείῳ πόθῳ M.34.1018C); **b.** *for God* ζῆλος θ. Epiph.haer.68.3(p.143.2; M.42.188B); ib.68.8(p.148.13; 196B); μέριμνα...θ. Isid.Pel.epp.1.213(M.78.317A); **c.** *about God, godly* παιδαγωγία θ. Clem.paed.1.12(p.151.32; M.8.376B); θ. φροντίδες ib.2.2(p.169.9; 413B); ἐπανελθὼν εἰς φρόνημα θ. Pall.h.Laus.26(p.82.16; M.34.1092A); **d.** *with God*; ref. Son θ. κοινωνία Eus.e.th.3.20(p.181.11; M.24.1045A); ref. saints and angels ἡ θ. ὁμωνυμία Dion.Ar.c.h.12.3(M.3.293B); **e.** *due to God* ἡμᾶς προσήκει μόνον τὸν υἱὸν καὶ μηδένα ἕτερον θ. τιμῇ σέβειν Eus. e.th.2.7(p.106.10; 912C).

***θεϊκῶς**, *as God*; **1.** ref. the Godhead αὐτοεῖναι...ἀρχικῶς...θ. καὶ αἰτιατικῶς Dion.Ar.d.n.11.6(M.3.956A); **2.** Trin. θ. ... ἐν τῷ πατρὶ ὢν λόγος καὶ σοφία Ath.Ar.3.46(M.26.421A); οὐκ ἐγένετο, ἀλλ' ἐγεννήθη θ. [sc. Logos] Didym.Trin.1.15(M.39.300B); τὸ πνεῦμα ἐκπορεύεται παρὰ τοῦ πατρός, καὶ μένει παρὰ τῷ υἱῷ θ. ib.1.31(425A); θ. ... ἐγεννήθη ὁ θεὸς λόγος ἐκ θεοῦ Hier.H.Trin.(M.40.857D); **3.** ref. Christ; **a.** in gen. ἐάν...τις θ. τὰ παρὰ τοῦ λόγου γινόμενα βλέπων, ἀρνήσεται τὸ σῶμα... Ath.Ar.3.35(M.26.397C); ref. his body θ. προσκυνεῖται ‡Ath.Apoll.1.6(M.26.1101C); ref. Phil.2:9 εἰ...[sc. θ. ὁ υἱὸς τῷ πατρί] οὐχ ὑποτέτακτο, ἀλλ' ὕστερον ὑποταγήσεται, ἀνθρωπίνως ὡς ὑπὲρ ἡμῶν, καὶ οὐ θ. ὑπὲρ ἑαυτοῦ Didym.(‡Bas.)Eun.4(1.288E; M.29.693B); ἕνα...ὁμολογοῦμεν υἱόν, γεννηθέντα μὲν θ. ἐκ πατρός ...ἀποτεχθέντα δὲ τὸν αὐτὸν ἐκ γυναικὸς κατὰ σάρκα Cyr.Heb.2:14(p.464.9; M.74.965B); id.Chr.un.(5^1.734B) cit. s. γεννάω; ἀπεστάλη... ἀνθρωπίνως, οὐ θ. Thdt.Zach.2:8(2.1606); Jo.D.f.o.3.7(M.94.1012B) cit. s. συστέλλω; ὢν μὲν θ., γενόμενος ὡς ἄνθρωπος id.hom.1.11(M.96.564A); **b.** ref. miracles πεινῶντα μὲν αὐτὸν...σωματικῶς, θ. δὲ χορτάζοντα...πεντακισχιλίους Ath.Dion.9(p.52.22; M.25.493B); οὐδὲ οἷόν τε ἦν, τοῦ κυρίου δι' ἡμᾶς ἀνθρώπου γενομένου, ἀνόητον εἶναι τὸ σῶμα αὐτοῦ...ὁ αὐτὸς ἦν ἀνθρωπίνως μὲν λέγων 'ποῦ Λάζαρος κεῖται;' θ. δὲ τοῦτον ἀνεγείρων· ὁ αὐτὸς δὲ ἦν σωματικῶς μὲν ὡς ἄνθρωπος πτύων, θ. δὲ...ἀνοίγων τοὺς ὀφθαλμοὺς τοῦ...τυφλοῦ id.tom.7(M.26.805A); ἀνθρωπίνως μὲν ἐξέτεινε τὴν χεῖρα, θ. δὲ ἦν παύων τὴν νόσον id.Ar.3.32(M.26.392A); θ. τε ἅμα καὶ σωματικῶς ἐνεργοῦντα Χριστόν Cyr.Lc.5:12(M.72.556B); δι' ὧν...ἔδει γνωρίζεσθαι θεόν, ταῦτα θ. ἐνεργεῖ id.thes.23(5^1.228A); οὐκ ἀνθρωπίνως...ἔπραττε τὰ ἀνθρώπινα· οὐ γὰρ ἄνθρωπος μόνον...οὐδὲ θ. ἐνήργει τὰ θεῖα· οὐ γὰρ θεὸς μόνον Jo.D.f.o.3.15(M.94.1060B); **c.** ref. his knowledge, exeg. Mt.24:36 οὐκ ἠθέλησε θ. εἰπεῖν, ὅτι οἶδα Ath.Ar.3.48(M.26.425A); cf.ib.3.44(416B); ib.3.46(421B); **d.** ref. his birth θ. μέν, ὅτι χωρὶς ἀνδρός· ἀνθρωπικῶς δὲ ὅτι νόμῳ κυήσεως, ὁμοίως ἄθεος Gr.Naz.ep.101(M.37.177C); ref. Passion τὸ μὴ πάσχειν θ., καὶ τὸ λέγεσθαι παθεῖν ἀνθρωπίνως Cyr.ep.46(p.161.7; 5^2.144C); θ. ἄνθρωπος ὢν διεξήει τὰ πάθη τῆς φύσεως, κατ' ἐξουσίαν ἐπιτελούμενα θεϊκήν Max.ambig.(M.91.1060B); ref. Resurrection ἵνα...ἀναστῇ θ. ‡Ath.Apoll.1.6(M.26.1104B); Cyr. Jo.8(4.720C); Sev.Ant.res.(p.826.4; M.46.640B); ref. earthly life and teaching θ. διδάξει Ath.Ar.3.48(425C); ἔλεγε...θ.· ἐξουσίαν ἔχω θεῖναι τὴν ψυχήν μου ib.3.57(444B); ref. Jo.17:5 θ. καὶ οὐκ ἀνθρωπίνως ᾔτει Didym.(‡Bas.)Eun.4(1.292A; M.29.701A); **4.** ref. men ἔχεις τὰς τοῦ υἱοῦ προσηγορίας· βάδιζε δι' αὐτῶν· ὅσαι τε ὑψηλαί, θ. καὶ ὅσαι σωματικαί, συμπαθῶς Gr.Nyss.or.30.21(p.143.13; M.36.133A).

***θειογαμία**, ἡ, *marriage with an uncle*; forbidden by canons, Tim. I Al.resp.(M.33.1304B).

***θειογένεθλος**, *divinely begotten* θ. λόγος Eulog.fr.Trin.3(p.365).

θειογενής, *born of God*, Orac.Sib.5.261.

***θειοδόχος**, v. *θεοδόχος.

***θειολατρεία**, ἡ, *worship of God*, Gr.Naz.carm.2.1.50.96(M.37.1392A).

θειολόγος, ὁ, *theologian*, Gr.Naz.carm.2.2(poem.)7.130(M.37.1561A).

***θειόνοος**, *of god-like mind*; of martyrs, Sophr.H.v.Cyr.et Jo. suppl.(M.87.3421D).

***θειοποιέω**, *deify*, Orac.Sib.fr.3.22.

θεῖος, **A.** *of God*; **1.** in gen., ref. Jo.4:24 εἰ...πνεῦμα, δῆλον ὅτι θ. Eus.Marcell.1.1(p.5.14; M.24.721A); ἡ θ. οὐσία Gr.Nyss.Eun.1(1 p.73.3; M.45.301D); Isid.Pel.epp.4.211(M.78.1305B); Manich. τὰ κακὰ ἄρα ἐκ τῆς θ. οὐσίας Disp.Phot.(M.88.544A); ἡ θ. οὐσία ἀμέριστός ἐστιν· αἱ δὲ ψυχαὶ μέρη τῆς θ. οὐσίας εἰσὶ καθ' ὑμᾶς ib.(536B); orthodox ἐπὶ...τῆς ἀσωμάτου καὶ θ. οὐσίας, οὐ πάθος, οὐ μερισμὸς...συμβήσεται Cyr.thes.4(5^1.31C); ἡ θ. φύσις in gen., Clem.paed.3.7(p.258.10; M.8.608B); Gr.Nyss.Eun.1(1 p.105.9; 340A); Cyr.thes.4(5^1.23D); οὐδὲν... οὕτως ἴδιον καὶ χαρακτηριστικὸν τῆς θ. φύσεως, ὡς τὸ ἀΐδιον Isid.Pel. epp.3.18(M.78.744C); ἡ φύσις ἡ θ. πάντη ἁπλῆ Leont.H.monoph.41(M.86.1793D); ἡ θ. φύσις ἀσώματός τε καὶ ἀπερίγραπτος Leont.N.serm.1(M.93.1568C); οὔτε ἀρχὴν κινήσεως, οὔτε ἠρεμίαν, ἤγουν τέλος, ὁμολογεῖ ἐπὶ τῆς θ. φύσεως Anast.S.hod.8(M.89.140A); Jo.D.f.o.1.14(M.94.860Aff.); (Messalian) ἡ θ. φύσις τρέπεται καὶ μεταβάλλεται εἰς ὅπερ ἂν ἐθέλῃ..., ἵνα συγκραθῇ ταῖς ἑαυτῆς ἀξίαις ψυχαῖς Tim.CP haer.(M.86.49A); ἡ θ. δύναμις Hipp.haer.1.15(p.18.10; M.16.3040B); Or.Cels.8.70(p.287.1; M.11.1621C); Eus.v.C.2.6(p.43.26; M.20.985B); Gr.Nyss.v.Mos.45(M.44.316A); τὸ θ. βούλημα Or.or.28.8(p.380.14; M.11.528C); Gr.Nyss.or.catech.5(p.27.6; M.45.24D); id.tres dii(M.45.129B); ἡ...θ. θέλησις Cyr.ador.6(1.179C); τὸ θ. θέλημα Jo.D.f.o.2.3(M.94.872A); ib.(872C); ἡ θ. πρόνοια CAlex.ep.8(p.94.27; M.25.264B); Nil.epp.1.1(M.79.81A); Dion.Ar.d.n.4.33(M.3.733B); Areth.Apoc.54(M.106.724D); ἡ θ. ὀργή Cyr.hom.pasch.1(5^2.8E); Bas.Sel.or.27.2(M.85.313C); Proc.G.2Reg.14:11(M.87.1137C); ἡ θ. γνῶσις 1Clem.40.1; σύνεσις Thdt.Ps.118:27(1.1445); ἐπιστήμη Dion.Ar.e.h.1.1(M.3.369); δόξα Or.Cels.5.60(p.64.2; 1276D); ref. anthropomorphic metaphors used of God θ. αἴσθησις ib.8.20(p.238.2; 1548D); ἀγαθότης Isid.Pel. epp.3.117(M.78.821B); μακροθυμία,...ἀνεξικακία ib.5.260(1488B); καλλονή Dion.Ar.c.h.2.4(M.3.144A); μακαριότης ib.3.2(165C); **2.** Trin.;

a. in gen., Dion.R.ap.Ath.*decr*.26(p.22.10; M.25.464A); θ. τριάδος Apoll.*fid.inc*.7(p.199.20; M.*PL*.8.877D); **b.** ref. relations τὰ ψεύδη περὶ τῆς τοῦ κυρίου γεννήσεως ὑπολαμβάνοντες οἱ ποίησιν αὐτοῦ τὴν θ. ... γέννησιν λέγειν τολμῶντες Dion.R.ap.Ath.*decr*.26(p.23.9; M.25.465A); τὴν θ. οὐσίαν τοῦ λόγου ἡνωμένην φύσει τῷ ἑαυτοῦ πατρί Ath. *hom.in Mt.11*:27(M.25.216B); θ. γέννησις Bas.*Eun*.2.5(1.241E; M.29.581A); τὸ μὲν θ. ... γέννημα, ἀπείρξειεν ἂν οἶμαι παντελῶς οὐδὲν τῶν εἰς ἀναγκαίους ἡκόντων λόγους, τῷ ἰδίῳ συνυφεστάναι γεννήτορι, ἀεὶ καὶ ἀνάρχως πατρὸς νοουμένου τε καὶ ὄντος θεοῦ Cyr.*dial.Trin*.2 (5^1.459E); ὑπερβήσεται τὴν καθ' ἡμᾶς γνῶσιν...ὁ τῆς θ. γεννήσεως τρόπος id.*thes*.5(5^1.33D); θ. ἕνωσις Dion.Ar.*d.n*.2.4(M.3.640D); θ. διάκρισις *ib*.2.5(641D); ἡ θ. πατριὰ καὶ υἱότης *ib*.2.8(645C); **3.** ref. Father θ. δύναμις Serap.*euch*.10.2; θ. τοῦ πατρὸς οὐσία, ἀσώματος οὖσα, τομῆς τε καὶ διαιρέσεως ἀνεπίδεκτός ἐστιν Cyr.*thes*.9(5^1.68E); θ. καὶ πατρικὴ φιλανθρωπία Dion.Ar.*c.h*.8.2(M.3.240D); **4.** ref. Son; **a.** in gen. ὁ λόγος θ. Just.*1apol*.10.6(M.6.341A); ὁ λόγος...ἀρχὴ θ. τῶν πάντων Clem.*prot*.1(p.7.15; M.8.61B); ζῷον θ. Eus.*ecl*.1(M.22.1121B); λόγος...θ. Ath.*gent*.40(M.25.81B); Isid.Pel.*epp*.3.18(M.78.744C); ὁ θ. ἱεράρχης Dion.Ar.*e.h*.1.3(M.3.373C); exeg. Ps.109:2 ἡ θ. δύναμις..., τοῦτ' ἔστιν...ὁ λόγος †Gregent.*disp*.2(M.86.653D); θ. λόγος Leont.N. *serm*.1(M.93.1569C); **b.** ref. Inc. μυστήριον θ. Clem.*prot*.11(p.79.1; M.8.228C); οὐκ ἐξ ἀνθρωπείου σπέρματος ἀλλ' ἐκ θ. δυνάμεως Just. *1apol*.32.9(M.6.380B); θ. ... πρὸς ἡμᾶς ἐπιφάνεια Ath.*inc*.1.1(M.25.97A); τὴν σάρκωσιν τὴν θ. ‡Ath.*Ar*.4.31(p.81.5; M.26.517A); τῆς θ. ἐπιδημίας Gr.Nyss.*or.catech*.18(p.74.11; M.45.53C); **c.** Christol. τὴν θ. ἕνωσιν ‡Ath.*Ar*.4.32(p.81.11; 517B); τῆς καθ' ὑπόστασιν θείας ἑνώσεως Max.*opusc*.(M.91.96C); θέλημα κατὰ φύσιν εἶχεν ἀνθρώπινον, ὥσπεροῦν καὶ κατ' οὐσίαν θεῖον *ib*.(80C); ὡς ἐκ δύο μὲν τῆς τε θ. καὶ τῆς κοινῆς ἀνθρωπείας ἄμφω προϋπαρχουσῶν τῆς ἑνώσεως Χριστοῦ φαμεν Leont.H.*monoph*.58(M.86.1801B); δύο θελήματα ἀδιάβλητα, τὸ μὲν φύσει ἀνθρώπινον, τὸ δὲ ὑπὲρ φύσιν καὶ θ. Anast.S.*serm.imag*.3(M.89.1160D); ref. operations ἡ θειοτέρα τοῦ Ἰησοῦ δύναμις Or.*Jo*.10.25(16; p.197.30; M.14.352B); τὰ θ. λόγια Chrys.*hom.47.1 in Jo*.(8.275A); cf.*ib.47.2*(278A); δεικνὺς...τὴν ἐν τοῖς θαύμασι θείαν τοῦ λόγου ...ἐνέργειαν, μὴ τοῦ αὐτοῦ μόνον διὰ τὴν φύσιν ὑπάρχειν, ἀλλὰ καὐτῆς τῆς ἁγίας σαρκός, διὰ τὴν πρὸς αὐτὴν καθ' ὑπόστασιν ἕνωσιν· συνεργάτιν γὰρ ἑαυτοῦ ταύτην ἐν τοῖς θ. παρελάμβανεν, ᾗ φησιν ὁ διδάσκαλος, ὥσπερ καὶ ψυχὴ τὸ ἴδιον σῶμα, πρὸς τὴν τῶν οἰκείων ἔργων ἐκπλήρωσιν Max.*opusc*.(M.91.101C); ref. miracles ἐν τοῖς τοιοῖσδε θ. καὶ ἀνθρωπίνη φύσις συνεργοῦσαι ὁρῶνται Leont.H.*monoph*.6(1773A); ref. Christ's humanity ἡ θ. ... ψυχή Cyr.*inc.unigen*.(5^1.692E); *ib*.(693B); τὴν ἀνδρικὴν Ἰησοῦ θ. ζωήν Dion.Ar.*e.h*.5.3.4(512A); θ. σῶμα Gr.Ant. *mul.ung*.3(M.88.1852A); ὅτι...τῇ πρὸς τὸν θεὸν λόγον ἑνώσει θεῖον τὸ... σῶμα αὐτοῦ τυγχάνει, οὐ δεῖ ἀμφιβάλλειν Anast.S.*hod*.23(M.89.301B); ref. monophysite heresies ποτὲ μὲν τὴν θ. φύσιν εἰς σάρκα τετράφθαι λέγοντας, ποτὲ δὲ τὴν σάρκα εἰς θεότητος μεταβεβλῆσθαι φύσιν Thdt. *ep*.83(p.51.3; 4.1150); θεὸς ἀληθὴς ὁ Χριστός,...καὶ θ. ὄντως αὐτοῦ τὸ ἅγιον σῶμα τῇ θεώσει Anast.S.*hod*.14(244C); Apollinarian θ. οὐσίαν τοῦ γεννηθέντος ἐξ αὐτῆς ἐν μορφώσει σαρκίνῃ Apoll.*quod un.Chr*.11 (p.302.2; M.28.129D); σῶμα τὸ θ. *ib*.12(p.302.16; 132A); θεία ἦν ἐμψυχίᾳ ψυχωθέν ‡Ath.*dial.Trin*.4.1(M.28.1252A); ἡ θ. σάρκωσις, ἡ μήτε ἄνθρωπος οὖσα, μήτε θεός Gr.Nyss.*Apoll*.3(M.45.1128C); Nestorian ὡς μηκέτι καὶ τὴν θ. καὶ τὴν ἀνθρωπίνην ἐν τῷ αὐτῷ φύσιν κατ' αὐτοὺς εἶναι Tim.CP *haer*.(M.86.41A); in anti-monophysite argument ἡμῖν ἀκοινώνητον τὸ θ. ἐν Χριστῷ [i.e. on monoph. principles] Leont.H. *monoph*.34(1792A); ἡ παθητὸν καὶ ῥευστὸν λέγων τὸ θ., ἢ ἀρνούμενος τὸ σῶμα καὶ αἷμα τοῦ...Χριστοῦ Anast.S.*hod*.12(209A); **d.** ref. events of incarnate life: conception, Hesych.H.*serm*.4(M.93.1456B); Procl.CP *annunt*.5(M.85.444A); *ib*.(445B); death, etc. τὸ θ. πάθος Thdr.Lect.*h.e*.2.32(M.86.201A); θ. κάθοδος Dion.Ar.*e.h*.4.3.10(484B); τῆς θ. ἐνεργείας μὴ χωρισθείσης ἐξ αὐτοῦ [sc. Christ's body in death] Anast.S.*hod*.1(45B); Resurrection, Thdt.*ep*.145(4.1253); *ib*.146(1273); ἐκ τῆς κατὰ τὴν ἀνάστασιν τοῦ σώματος αὐτοῦ ἐνεργείας, παραστήσας ὄντως θ. αὐτοῦ εἶναι τὴν δύναμιν, ἐκ δὲ τῆς δυνάμεως, τὴν οὐσίαν Leont.H.*Nest*.5.3(M.86.1728B); **e.** ref. divinization through Christ ἵν' ἡ ἀνθρωπίνη [sc. φύσις] τῇ πρὸς τὸ θειότερον κοινωνίᾳ γένηται θ. οὐκ ἐν μόνῳ τῷ Ἰησοῦ ἀλλὰ καὶ πᾶσι τοῖς μετὰ τοῦ πιστεύειν ἀναλαμβάνουσι βίον, ὃν Ἰησοῦς ἐδίδαξεν Or.*Cels*.3.28(p.226.14; M.11.956D); ὁ μετέχων τοῦ υἱοῦ θ. γίνεται κοινωνὸς φύσεως Cyr.*thes*.4(5^1.25D); **5.** ref. H. Ghost, in gen., Herm.*mand*.11.12; Clem.*paed*.1.6(p.106.23; M.8.284A); Cyr.H.*procatech*.9; Bas.*Eun*.2.5(1.241E; M.29.581A); Leont.H. *Nest*.5.3(1725D); theol. πῶς ἔσται ποίημα τὸ ἔχον ἐν ἑαυτῷ φυσικῶς τῆς θ. οὐσίας τὸ ἴδιον καὶ ἐξαίρετον; Cyr.*thes*.34(357E); πῶς ἔσται γενητὸν τὸ δι' οὗ θ. οὐσίας ἡμῖν ἡ εἰκὼν ἐγχαράττεται; *ib*.(360B); οὐσίας θ. ὑπάρχει Thdt.*Trin*.23(M.75.1177Dff.); *ib*.24(1181C); ἐπὶ...τῆς θ. φύσεως τῆς ἁπλῆς καὶ ἀσυνθέτου, τὸ μὲν εἶναι πνεῦμα θεοῦ...ὁμολογητέον Jo.D.*f.o*.1.7(M.94.805A); ref. his divinizing action τὸ πνεῦμα... δι' οὗ τῷ θεῷ κολλώμεθα, καὶ ἐν ὡς πρὸς αὐτὸν ἀποτελούμεθα, τῆς τε θ. αὐτοῦ φύσεως γινόμεθα κοινωνοί Cyr.*thes*.34(356D); (Gnost.) ἔστι...τὸ πνεῦμα τὸ ἐν τῷ κόσμῳ ὁ ὄρνις ὁ Κύκνος...τοῦ θ. σύμβολον πνεύματος Hipp.*haer*.4.49(p.73.24; M.16.3118B); **6.** neut. as subst.; **a.** *divinity*, as simple ἁπλοῦν...τῇ φύσει τὸ θ. ἐστι καὶ ἀσύνθετον Gr.Nyss.*Apoll*.2 (M.45.1128B); Bas.Sel.*or*.35.4(M.85.297C); Jo.D.*f.o*.1.7(M.94.808A); changeless τὸ...θ. καὶ ἀθάνατον καὶ ἀκίνητον καὶ ἀναλλοίωτον Athenag. *leg*.22.5(M.6.937C); Cyr.*thes*.10(5^1.78D); incorporeal, cf.Athenag. *leg*.29.2(957C); μὴ ἀνθρωπόμορφον τὸ θ. Or.*Cels*.7.66(p.216.6; M.11.1516A); Ath.*gent*.22(M.25.44Bff.); infinite, Isid.Pel.*epp*.3.18(M.78.745A); *ib*.3.149(841B); Cosm.Ind.*top*.2(M.88.132D); one, Athenag. *leg*.7.1(M.6.904A); incomprehensible, Gr.Nyss.*Eun*.8(2 p.177.7; M.45.769B); perfect, Jo.D.*f.o*.1.5(801A); (Arian) ἦν...πρὶν γεννηθῆναι [sc. τὸν υἱόν], κατ' ἐκείνους ἐν μονάδι τὸ θ. Cyr.*thes*.9(5^1.66E); (Manich.) περιγραπτὸν εἰσάγων τὸ θ., ὃν ἀγαθὸν καὶ παντοδύναμον ὁμολογεῖς, καὶ ταῦτα ἀπὸ τῆς κακίστης ὕλης περιγραφόμενον Jo.D. *Man*.2(M.96.1321C); ref. knowledge of the divine, as made possible through baptism, Clem.*paed*.1.5(p.105.27; M.8.281A); of the divine as without physical form μὴ σχηματίζῃς τὸ θ. ἐν ἑαυτῷ προσευχόμενος Evagr.Pont.*or*.66(M.79.1181A); ἄποσον...τὸ θ. καὶ ἀσχημάτιστον *ib*.67(1181B); some understanding of the divine being attainable by virtuous, Isid.Pel.*epp*.2.186(M.78.636C); ref. participation by creatures αὗται [sc. angelic powers]...εἰσὶν αἱ πρώτως καὶ πολλαχῶς ἐν μετουσίᾳ τοῦ θ. γινόμεναι Dion.Ar.*c.h*.4.2(M.3.180A); ref. Christ's divinity, veiled from Satan by the humanity, Gr.Nyss. *or.catech*.24(p.92.16ff.; M.45.64D); as impassible, Isid.Pel.*epp*.4.166 (M.78.1257A); invisible, Cyr.*inc.unigen*.(5^1.693D); monophysite doctrine incompatible with fact that divinity is ἀνελλιπές, Anast.S. *hod*.13(M.89.224C); **b.** as synonymous with *God* οὐκ ὀργίζεται τὸ θ. Clem.*paed*.1.8(p.130.7; M.8.332C); Philost.*h.e*.8.3(M.65.557B); τὸ θ. ὥσπερ φιλάνθρωπόν ἐστιν Isid.Pel.*epp*.5.260(M.78.1488C).

B. *divine* by participation or derivation, *holy*; **1.** of Christian doctrine, creeds τὸ θ. ... τῆς ἁγίας ἐκείνης συνόδου χρησμώδημα Cyr. *dial.Trin*.1(5^1.389C); τοῦ θ. συμβόλου Basilisc.*encycl*.(p.50.10; M.86.2600D); in gen. θ. δόγματα Evagr.Pont.*ep*.1(M.32.248A); Cyr.*thes*.6 (5^1.48B); id.*Nest*.1 proem.(p.14.16; 6^1.1B); Cosm.Ind.*top*.2(M.88.73B); Max.*opusc*.(M.91.72C); διδασκαλία θ. Clem.*prot*.9(p.65.2; M.8.197C); ‡Ath.*Ar*.4.9(p.53.19; M.26.480B); Thdt.*ep*.100(4.1169); θ. λόγος Just.*dial*.23.3(M.6.525C); τὰ τῶν Χριστιανῶν θ. διδάγματα id. *2apol*.13.1(M.6.465B); *ib*.4.3(452A); τὰ θ. μυστήρια Gr.Nyss.*Eun*.8 (2 p.186.22; M.45.780D); θ. κήρυγμα Isid.Pel.*epp*.3.345(M.78.1001D); **2.** of scripture ἡ θ. γραφή, αἱ θ. γραφαί Clem.*paed*.2.3(p.179.3; M.8.433C); τῶν...φερομένων γραφῶν καὶ ἐν πάσαις ἐκκλησίαις θεοῦ πεπιστευμένων εἶναι θ. Or.*Jo*.1.2(4; p.6.11; M.14.28A); *Hom.Clem*. 16.8; Didym.*Trin*.2.10(M.39.644B); Cosm.Ind.*top*.1(M.88.57C); Jo. D.*f.o*.1.5(M.94.801A) v. γραφή; τὰ θ. λόγια Ath.*Ar*.1.10(M.26.33A); Cyr.*thes*.10(5^1.82B); Dion.Ar.*e.h*.2.1(M.3.392A); ὁ θ. λόγος *Const. App*.1.8.19; Nil.*exerc*.14(M.79.736B); Proc.G.*Ex*.3:2(M.87.525A); τὴν...ἕνωσιν τῶν θ. νοημάτων καὶ τῶν ἐπιγείων λόγων Isid.Pel.*epp*.2.3 (M.78.460A); **3.** of divine illumination, Mac.Aeg.*elev*.15(M.34.904B); Cyr.*dial.Trin*.1(5^1.387C); Dion.Ar.*c.h*.7.2(M.3.208A); *ib*.1(120A); **4.** of providential law, Just.*2apol*.5.2(M.6.452B); πολεμούντων ἀλλήλοις τῶν ἐναντίων θ. νόμῳ Athenag.*leg*.3.2(M.6.896C); cf.*ib*.31.1 (961B); Ath.*gent*.42(M.25.85B); Dion.Ar.*c.h*.8.2(M.3.240D); **5.** τὰ θ. *divine truths* τῶν θ. γνῶσις Just.*dial*.3.5(M.6.481B); Hipp.*haer*.4.28 (p.55.20; M.16.3091A); τὰ θεῖα θεωρίας Or.*Cels*.6.23(p.93.21; M.11.1325C); Ath.*gent*.3(M.25.8C); id.*ep.Aeg.Lib*.14(M.25.569B); Gr.Naz. *or*.20.1(M.35.1065A); Cyr.*thes*.4(5^1.30D); τὰ θ. ... διὰ τῶν ἀνομοίων συμβόλων ἐκφαίνεται Dion.Ar.*c.h*.2(M.3.136C); **6.** of inspiration, Eus.*h.e*.1.13.4(M.20.121A); cf.id.*v.C*.2.12(p.46.15; M.20.992A); **7.** of grace, Or.*Cels*.7.44(p.195.1; M.11.1484C); id.*Jo*.10.25(16; p.197.31; M.14.352B); Serap.*euch*.19.2; *Can.App*.80; Isid.Pel.*epp*.4.51(M.78.1101A); Mod.*dorm*.1(M.86.3280A); Jo.D.*f.o*.2.3(M.94.869B); of gifts of grace θ. χαρίσματα Or.*fr.44 in Jo*.(p.519.6); Cyr.*thes*.34(5^1.355C); **8.** of sacraments: baptism, Or.*fr.36 in Jo*.(p.512.14); θ. μυστήριον Serap.*euch*.20.1; θ. ἀναγέννησις *ib*.20.2; Cyr.H.*catech*.19.1; θ. κολυμβήθρα Thdt.*Mich*.7:28(2.1516); Max.*opusc*.(M.91.104B); eucharist θ. ἀναφορά *Can.App*.3; θ. μυστηρίων Thdr.Lect.*h.e*.2.34(M.86.201A); θ. δῶρα Dion.Ar.*e.h*.3.3.7(M.3.436D); *ib*.3.1(424D); id.*c.h*.1.3(M.3.124A); Anast.S.*hod*.24(M.89.836A); *Lit.Jac*.(p.160.11); **9.** of ministry ἱεράρχην ὁ λέγων δηλοῖ τὸν ἔνθεόν τε καὶ θ. ἄνδρα Dion.Ar.*e.h*.1.3(M.3.373C); θ. ἱερουργίας *ib*.5.1.5(505B); θ. ἱερωσύνη Max.*opusc*.(M.91.72B); **10.** of virtue ἡ θ. ἀρετή Just.*2apol*.2.13(M.6.445B); Gr.Thaum. *pan.Or*.9(p.23.1; M.10.1077D); Isid.Pel.*epp*.3.118(M.78.821B); Cyr. *ador*.5(1.143D); Max.*opusc*.(M.91.92C); τὸ τῆς ἀρετῆς...θειότατον

Niceph.Ur.*v.Sym.*proem.2(M.86.2988C); of Christian conduct in gen. ἀγωγὴ ἡ θ. Clem.*paed.*1.7(p.122.25; M.8.313C); of partic. virtues, Herm.*vis.*3.8.7; Ath.*gent.*19(M.25.40A); Isid.Pel.*epp.*3.117 (M.78.821B); of ascetical exercises θ. γυμνάσματα Jo.Clim.*scal.*4(M. 88.685B); **11.** of men; **a.** saints, in gen.; prophets and apostles, Or.*Cels.*7.49(p.200.7; M.11.1492C); ascetics, Thdt.*h.rel.*3(3.1138); Cosm.Ind.*top.*2(M.88.73A); Eustrat.*v.Eutych.*proem.1(M.86.2276B); of partic. saints Ἀθανάσιος Philost.*h.e.*2.11(M.65.473A); Βασίλειος Leont.B.*cap.Sev.*5(M.86.1904A); Γρηγόριος Max.*opusc.*(M.91.65B); Συμεών Niceph.Ur.*v.Sym.*proem.1(M.86.2988A); Διονύσιος Jo.D.*f.o.* 1.12(M.94.844C); of OT saints Μωσῆς *Const.App.*6.24.5; Cyr.*dial. Trin.*5(5^1.579E); οἱ θειότατοι προφῆται Ign.*Magn.*8.2; θ. Ἡσαΐου Thdt.*Jer.*22:7(2.509); †Gregent.*disp.*2(M.86.673B); Δαβίδ Cyr.*dial. Trin.*3(5^1.477E); Thdt.*haer.*5.1(4.379); Jo.D.*f.o.*1.7(M.94.808A); ὁ θειότατος...Ἰώβ *Const.App.*5.7.21; Ἰσαάκ Anast.S.*hod.*19(M.89.269A); esp. of apostles, Jo.D.*carm.dorm.BMV* 107(p.231; M.96.1365B); S. Paul ὁ θ. ἀπόστολος Or.*fr.106 in Lam.*(p.276.10; M.13.657D); Eus. *Marcell.*1.1(p.5.21; M.24.721A); Παῦλος Cyr.*dial.Trin.*1(5^1.407C); Thdt.*haer.*146(4.1249); Παῦλος ὁ θειότατος Jo.D.*haer.Nest.*34(M.95. 205A); Ἰωάννης Thdt.*Eph.*proem.(3.400); ὁ θ. εὐαγγελιστής Leont.B. *Apoll.*(M.86.1956A); Jo.D.*haer.Nest.*32(204C); Πέτρος Thdt.*Gal.*5:1 (3.387); of the fathers, Thdt.ap.*cat.Mt.*24:15(p.197.2); Max.*opusc.* (M.91.80B); **b.** man in image of God τῇ λογικῇ ψυχῇ τὸ θ. ἐξεικονίζοντες Isid.Pel.*epp.*3.95(M.78.800C); θ. ... ἡγούμεθα εἶναι τὴν ψυχήν, οὐ μὴν τῆς θειοτάτης καὶ βασιλικωτάτης φύσεως μοῖραν *ib.*5.187 (1444C); ref. 1Cor.11:7 of soul of the male εἰκόνα θ. *ib.*3.95(801B); through grace; ref. the converted αἱ θειότεραι ψυχαί Or.*Cels.*6.23 (p.93.24; M.11.1325C); id.*hom.16.1 in Jer.*(p.133.3; M.13.440A); ref. an ascetic ἡ θ. ... ψυχή Thdt.*h.rel.*3(3.1139); ref. Christian souls ἀγάλματα θ. Dion.Ar.*c.h.*3.2(M.3.165A); of the perfect οἱ θ. id.*e.h.* 1.5(M.3.377B); **c.** of emperor Κωνσταντίνου τοῦ θ. Thdr.Lect.*h.e.*1.4 (M.86.168B); τοῖς θειοτάτοις...δεσπόταις Thds.Imp.*ep.Diosc.*(p.69. 35; H.2.72B); ὁ θ. *Chron.Pasch.*p.278(M.92.693A); hence *imperial* θ. γράμμα Marc.Diac.*v.Porph.*26; Thds.Imp.*ep.Cyr.*(p.114.26; H.2. 1344A); id.*sacr.*3(p.71.1; H.2.76A); θ. νόμος *Chron.Pasch.*p.323(825B); **12.** of angels θ. ἄγγελος Or.*Cels.*1.66(p.119.24; M.11.784B); ὁ θειότατος Γαβριήλ Dion.Ar.*c.h.*4.4(M.3.181B); θειότατοι σεραφίμ id.*e.h.*4.3.9(M. 3.481C); θ. ζῴων Or.*Jo.*1.39(42; p.51.20; M.14.104A); τῶν θ. δυνάμεων Procl.CP *annunt.*2(M.85.429A); Dion.Ar.*c.h.*8.1(M.3.237B); Areth. *Apoc.*10(M.106.572A); **13.** eccl.; **a.** of feasts, Easter ἡ...θ. ἑορτή Cyr.*hom.pasch.*1(5^2.1A); unspecified, Thdt.*ep.*41(4.1099); Presentation, Leont.N.*serm.*1(M.93.1565A); of BMV, Jo.Eub.*concept.BMV* 22(M.96.1497B); Jo.D.*carm.dorm.BMV* 13(p.229; M.96.1364A); **b.** of churches and altars, Thdr.Lect.*h.e.*1.35(M.86.181C); Dion.Ar.*e.h.*3.2 (M.3.425B); Niceph.Ur.*v.Sym.*1(M.86.2989D); **c.** of eccl. legislation θ. ... διατάξεις *Const.App.*8.4.1; θ. κανόσιν CChalc.*can.*26; ref. CNic. (325) ὁ θ. ... τῶν ἀρχιερέων ὅμιλος Thdt.*h.e.*1.9.14(3.768).

C. in objective sense, *of God* i.e. directed to God ἡ θ. ἐπίγνωσις Thdt.*Ezech.*28:25f.(2.920); θ. γνῶσις id.*Ps.*92:1(1.1272); Dion.Ar. *c.h.*7.3(M.3.209D); Tim.CP *haer.*(M.86.13B); Max.*qu.dub.*27(M.90. 808B); ὁ θ. ἔρως Dion.Ar.*c.h.*15.8(M.3.337B); id.*e.h.*4.13(M.3.712A); ἀγάπη θ. Jo.Clim.*scal.*1(M.88.637A); Leont.N.*serm.*1(M.93.1577B); of fear of God, Clem.*paed.*2.4(p.183.13; M.8.444A); Dor.*doct.*4 tit.(M. 88.1657B); ref. prayer θ. ἐπίκλησις Thdt.*Ps.*77:31(1.1072); id.*h.rel.*8 (3.1183); *representing God* θ. εἰκόνες Or.*Cels.*7.66(p.216.3; M.11. 1513D).

D. of things created *by God* τὰ θ. δημιουργήματα Clem.*paed.*3.12 (p.290.17; M.8.680A); of communion *with God* ἡ θ. κοινωνία Gr. Nyss.*or.catech.*6(p.31.3; M.45.25D); of hope *in God* ἡ θ. ἐλπίς Thdt. *Ps.*90:6(1.1259).

θειότης, ἡ, *divinity*; **1.** ref. God in gen. ἐναντίον...ἐστιν αὐτοῦ τῇ θ. καὶ τῇ κατ' αὐτὴν πάσῃ δυνάμει ἡ τοῦ ἀδικεῖν δύναμις Or.*Cels.*3.70 (p.262.32; M.11.1012D); as omnipresent, *ib.*4.5(p.277.31; 1033D); to be confessed even at price of martyrdom, id.*Jo.*6.54(36; p.163.10; M.14.293C); in valediction ἡ θ. ὑμᾶς τοῦ μεγάλου θεοῦ διαφυλάξει πολλοῖς ἔτεσι Const.ap.Eus.*h.e.*10.5.20(M.20.888B); *ib.*10.6.5(893A); οὐ γάρ ἐστι δυνατὸν ἐν τῇ ἁπλότητι τῆς θ. τὸ ποικίλον τε καὶ πολυειδὲς τῆς ἀντιληπτικῆς ἐνεργείας κατανοῆσαι Gr.Nyss.*hom.opif.*6.1(M.44.137D); **2.** Trin.; (Arian) exeg. Rom.1:20 τὴν εἰρημένην ἐνταῦθα θ. οὐκ ἄν τις φαίη Χριστὸν εἶναι, ἀλλ' αὐτὸν ὑπάρχειν τὸν πατέρα· οὕτως οἶμαι καὶ ἡ ἀΐδιος αὐτοῦ δύναμις καὶ θ., οὐχ ὁ μονογενὴς υἱός, ἀλλὰ ὁ γεννήσας ὑπάρχει πατήρ Ast.Soph.*fr.*1 ap.Ath.*Ar.*2.37(M.26.225C); νοῦς καὶ λόγος ἡ θ. ἐστίν Gr.Nyss.*hom.opif.*5.2(M.44.137B); **3.** of Father τὸ δὲ ἀγνοεῖν τὸν πατέρα θάνατός ἐστιν...καὶ τὸ μὲν μὴ φθείρεσθαι θειότητος μετέχειν ἐστί Clem.*str.*5.10(p.369.2; M.9.97A); **4.** of Christ, reported by the gospels, Or.*Cels.*1.63(p.115.17; M.11.777B); attested by saints, *ib.*1.47(p.97.16; 748B); *ib.*7.35(p.186.10; 1469D); by Jo. Bapt. in the womb, id.*Jo.*2.37(30; p.96.7; M.14.181B); exhibited in miracles τὰ ὑπ' αὐτοῦ γενόμενα παράδοξα οὐ μαγγανείᾳ...ἀλλὰ θ. id. *Cels.*8.9(p.227.24; 1532A); τοσαῦτα σημεῖα ποιήσας, οὐ μικρὸν τοῦτό φησιν αὐτοῦ τῆς θ. εἶναι σημεῖον Chrys.*hom.32.1 in 1Cor.*(10.286E); in Inc. συγκαταβαίνων...ἔσθ' ὅτε τῷ μὴ δυναμένῳ αὐτοῦ τὰς μαρμαρυγὰς καὶ τὴν λαμπρότητα τῆς θ. βλέπειν οἱονεὶ σὰρξ γίνεται Or.*Cels.* 4.15(p.285.19; 1048A); divinity known everywhere in consequence of Inc., Ath.*inc.*45.1(M.25.176C); in relation to his humanity τὸ... θνητὸν αὐτοῦ σῶμα καὶ τὴν ἀνθρωπίνην ἐν αὐτῷ ψυχὴν...ἑνώσει...τὰ μέγιστά φαμεν προσειληφέναι καὶ τῆς ἐκείνου θ. κεκοινωνηκότα εἰς θεὸν μεταβεβληκέναι Or.*Cels.*3.41(p.237.7; 973A); as participated in by Christians ἔγνω κύριος τοὺς ὄντας αὐτοῦ ἀνακραθεὶς αὐτοῖς καὶ μεταδεδωκὼς αὐτοῖς τῆς ἑαυτοῦ θ. id.*Jo.*19.4(1; p.303.5; M.14.532B); Christ's divinity signified by fact that Isaac, as his type, was not sacrificed, Clem.*paed.*1.5(p.104.3; M.8.277B); **5.** ref. H. Ghost διὰ τὴν ἐν αὐτῷ [sc. prophet] τοῦ πνεύματος θ. *Hom.Clem.*2.10; *ib.*8.10; Gr.Nyss.*Maced.*14(M.45.1317D); *ib.*6(1309A); **6.** claimed by Simon Magus, *Hom.Clem.*2.27; **7.** as title of address: imperial, *Ep.*ap. Ath.*apol.sec.*85(p.164.8; M.25.401B); Pulch.*ep.Bass.*(p.135.19; H.2. 680E); Sabinian.*supplic.*1(p.65.9; H.2.573A); †Gregent.*leg.hom.*29 (M.86.597A); ? of a bishop τὴν σὴν θ. Thdt.*ep.*2(4.1061); **8.** as synonymous with *God*, (Gnost.) λέγοντες τὴν τοῦ παντὸς οὐσίαν καὶ δύναμιν καὶ πατρικὴν θ. ἀπὸ τῆς τοῦ ἐγκεφάλου διαθέσεως διδάσκεσθαι Hipp.*haer.*4.51(p.76.7; M.16.3122B); τῆς θεραπείας τῆς τῇ θ. ὀφειλομένης Const.ap.Eus.*h.e.*10.7.2(M.20.893B); ὑπὲρ...εἰρήνης, ἣν ἡ θ. εἰς τὸ διηνεκές σοι χαριεῖται CArim.*ep.Const.*1(p.238.29; M.26.700B); *Const.App.*2.52.1; **9.** *sacred character*, of doctrine τῆς τούτων [sc. θείων] θ. Just.*dial.*3.5(M.6.481B); Or.*hom.20.6 in Jer.*(p.186.8; M. 13.513B); ref. Lc.14:18 οἱ...ἀγρὸν ἀγοράσαντές εἰσιν..., οἱ παραλαβόντες δόγματα ἕτερα τῆς θ. id.*fr.69 in Lc.*(p.267); ἡ τῆς γραφῆς θ. id.*princ.*4.1.7(p.303.14; M.11.353C); ἡ θ. τῆς δυνάμεως τῶν τῆς προσκυνητῆς τριάδος ἐπικλήσεων id.*Jo.*6.33(17; p.142.30; M.14.257A).

***θειόφορος, 1.** *inspired*; ref. authors of scripture, or perh. of theologians, Gr.Naz.*carm.*1.1.3.55(M.37.412A); **2.** *in possession of God*; of the blessed in heaven, *ib.*1.1.4.94(423A).

θειώδης, *godlike* τὸ θ. Just.*dial.*134.2(M.6.785A); of the bearing of the good man, Clem.*fr.*44(p.221.26); of angels θειωδεστέρας ὄντες οὐσίας *Hom.Clem.*8.12; in gen., ‡Just.*qu.Chr.*11.11(M.6.1481A).

θειωδῶς, *divinely*; **1.** ref. scripture τὰ θ. προστεταγμένα Adam. *dial.*1.25(p.50.8; M.11.1753C); Dion.Ar.*c.h.*4.4(M.3.181B); ‡Cyr.*Trin.* 1(6^3.2A; M.77.1121A); †Jo.D.*B.J.*19(M.96.1029A); and divine laws, Max.*ambig.*(M.91.1161D); **2.** *imperially, by the emperor* τὰ θ. προσταχθέντα Ath.*apol.sec.*85(p.164.11; M.25.401B).

θείως, 1. *divinely*, ref. scripture θ. λέλεκται Clem.*str.*2.7(p.131.29; M.8.972A); θ. ἡ δύναμις ἡ τῷ Ἑρμᾷ κατὰ ἀποκάλυψιν *ib.*1.28(p.111.1; 928A); ref. divinization by grace τῆς...ἱερᾶς ἀγαπήσεως ἡ πρὸς τὴν ἱερουργίαν τῶν θειῶν ἐντολῶν ἀρχικωτάτη πρόοδος ἡ τοῦ εἶναι θ. ἀρρητοτάτη δημιουργία Dion.Ar.*e.h.*2.1(M.3.392B); τὸ εἶναι θ. ἐστὶν ἡ θεία γέννησις *ib.*; ἡ...ἁγία τριάς, ἡ...πάντων κτιστῶν...θ. δεσπόζουσα Sophr.H.*or.*3.2(M.87.3217C); **2.** *in a godlike way* ὥστε τὰς...θείας [sc. δυνάμεις] θειοτέρως κινεῖσθαι Ath.*gent.*44(M.25.88D); **3.** *excellently*; of Christian opp. pagan teachers λέγομεν...μειζόνως καὶ θ. Just.*1apol.*20.3(M.6.357C); ref. BMV ἐν...τῇ ταύτης νηδύϊ ὁ λόγος ἑαυτῷ τὸν οἶκον διεπλάσατο, ὃν τρόπον ἐξ ἀρχῆς τὸν Ἀδὰμ ἐκ τῆς γῆς· μᾶλλον δὲ θειοτέρως ‡Ath.*Ar.*4.34(p.83.2; M.26.520B).

***θέλγημα, τό,** *charm, attraction*, Mac.Mgn.*apocr.*4.11(p.171.34).

[*]**θελγηστρον, τό,** prob. f.l. for θέλγητρον, Nil.*spir.mal.*4(M.79. 1149B).

θέλγητρον, τό, *charm* τὰ τῆς ἁμαρτίας...θ. Meth.*Porph.*1(p.504.9; M.18.400B).

θέλημα, τό, I. etym. θ. ... λέγεται κατὰ τὸ 'θέειν λίαν' ἢ 'τοῦ θελητοῦ λῆμμα' ἢ ὡς κράτημα ‡Ath.*def.*2(M.28.540D) = Anast.S.*hod.* 2(M.89.61D); and def.;

A. various senses; **1.** properly, *that which is willed, object of an act of willing*; **2.** *faculty of will*, or *act of willing* τὸ...θ., ποτὲ μὲν σημαίνει τὴν θέλησιν, τουτέστι τὴν θελητικὴν δύναμιν· ποτὲ δὲ τὸ θελητόν, τουτέστι τὸ πρᾶγμα ὅπερ θέλομεν Jo.D.*volunt.*24(M.95.153C); **3.** *result* or *product of will* τὸ θ. αὐτοῦ ἔργον ἐστὶ καὶ τοῦτο κόσμος ὀνομάζεται Clem.*paed.*1.6(p.106.9; M.8.281B); id.*str.*4.26(p.325.1; M. 8.1381A); Max.*ambig.*(M.91.1085B).

B. in sense of *faculty of will*; **1.** defined; **a.** οὐσίας νοερᾶς καὶ λογικῆς ἔφεσις πρὸς τὸ καταθύμιον ‡Ath.*def.*2(M.28.540D) reproduced by Anast.S.*hod.*2(M.89.61C); **b.** ὄρεξις λογικὴ καὶ ζωτική Max.*opusc.* (M.91.13A); **2.** divided into three types of will corresponding to the three orders of beings capable of willing [sc. θ.] θεϊκόν, ἀγγελικόν καὶ ψυχικόν ‡Ath.*def*.2(M.28.540D); and three types dist. in scripture θ. θεῖόν ἐστι τὰ προστάγματα τοῦ θεοῦ. θ. δὲ φυσικὸν ἡ ἐργασία τοῦ θεοῦ θελήματος. θ. δὲ σαρκικὸν ἡ παρακοὴ τοῦ θείου νόμου *ib.*; Anast.S.*hod*.2(M.89.64A).

II. in men;

A. *moral will* οὐ γάρ ἐσμεν ἐπιθυμίας τέκνα, ἀλλὰ θ. Clem.*str*.3.7 (p.222.29; M.8.1161B).

B. θ. φυσικόν *natural will*, as common and necessary attribute of humanity opp. θ. γνωμικόν (*purposive, deliberate will*, i.e. faculty of, or object of, free rational choice): θ. φυσικὸν...κοινὸν πᾶσιν ἀνθρώποις. τοῦτο δέ ἐστι τὸ φιλόζωον. ... εἰσὶ δὲ καὶ ἕτερα θ. ἐν ἡμῖν, ἅπερ καλοῦνται γνωμικά. ἄλλος...θέλει ἰδιάζειν, ἄλλος γεωργεῖν. πολλὰ γνωμικὰ θ. ἔχομεν,...ἓν δὲ φυσικὸν θ. ἔχομεν πάντες ‡Ath.*def*.2 (M.28.540D) = Anast.S.*hod*.2(M.89.64D); θ. φυσικόν ἐστιν οὐσιώδης τῶν κατὰ φύσιν συστατικῶν ἔφεσις. θ. γνωμικόν ἐστιν ἡ ἐφ' ἑκάτερα τοῦ λογισμοῦ αὐθαίρετος ὁρμή τε καὶ κίνησις Max.*opusc*.(M.91.153A); *ib*.(280A).

C. of selfish desire; to be abandoned by those entering upon religious obedience, Ant.Mon.*hom*.113(M.89.1785B); Hesych.S. *temp*.1.31(M.93.1489C) cit. s. ἀθέλητος.

III. in God; **A.** in gen.; **1.** of his positive will, *1Clem*.42.2; Cyr.H.*catech*.23.14; Gr.Nyss.*or.dom*.4(p.70.8; M.44.1164A); abs. ἐάνπερ θ. ᾖ τοῦ ἀξιωθῆναί με Ign.*Rom*.1.1; *Polyc*.8.1; Clem.*str*.6.18 (p.517.25; M.9.400A); **2.** of his permission of evil οὔτε...ὁ κύριος θελήματι ἔπαθεν τοῦ πατρός, οὔθ' οἱ διωκόμενοι βουλήσει τοῦ θεοῦ διώκονται...ἀλλὰ μὴν οὐδὲν ἄνευ θ. τοῦ κυρίου τῶν ὅλων Clem.*str*.4.12 (p.286.8; M.8.1293C); and of distn. bet. his primary will to save, and secondary will to punish 'κατὰ τὴν εὐδοκίαν...τοῦ θ. αὐτοῦ'. ...ἡ ἐπιθυμία αὐτοῦ...αὐτή ἐστι· πανταχοῦ γὰρ εὐδοκία τὸ θ. ἐστι τὸ προηγούμενον. ἔστι γὰρ καὶ ἄλλο θ.· οἷον, θ. πρῶτον, τὸ μὴ ἀπολέσθαι ἡμαρτηκότας· θ. δεύτερον, τὸ γενομένους κακοὺς ἀπολέσθαι Chrys.*hom*. *1.2 in Eph*.(11.5C); hence of distn. bet. God's three θελήματα: κατ' εὐδοκίαν, κατ' οἰκονομίαν, κατὰ συγχώρησιν Max.*qu.dub*.20(M. 90.801B).

B. partic.; **1.** ref. Creation; **a.** of eternal exemplars or ideas, pre-existent in God, according to which Creation was accomplished παραδείγματα δέ φαμεν εἶναι τοὺς ἐν θεῷ...προϋφεστῶτας λόγους... καὶ θεῖα καὶ ἀγαθὰ θ. τῶν ὄντων ἀφοριστικὰ καὶ ποιητικά Dion.Ar. *d.n*.5.8(M.3.824C); **b.** of God's will as cause of Creation, Clem.*fr*.48 (p.224.23)ap.Max.*ambig*.(M.91.1085B); Ath.*Ar*.3.64(M.26.457B); Gr. Nyss.*Eun*.8(2 p.188.8; M.45.781D); administered by Son, Clem. *prot*.12(p.84.34; M.8.241B); **2.** ref. Inc. and redemption, Clem.*str*.7.2 (p.8.15; M.9.413A); Bas.*Spir*.18(3.15E; M.32.100B); Gr.Naz.*or*.19.13 (M.35.1060A); Gr.Nyss.*or.dom*.4(p.70.8; M.44.1164A); Sophr.H.*ep. syn*.(M.87.3161A); **3.** as known and performed by man; **a.** God's will embracing every virtue, Gr.Nyss.*or.dom*.4(p.74.3; M.44.1165A); **b.** learnt through practice ποιοῦντες γὰρ τὸ θ. τοῦ θεοῦ, τὸ θ. γινώσκομεν Clem.*str*.1.7(p.25.17; M.8.733B); **c.** ascertained by 'gnostic' through μάθησις, *ib*.7.11(p.44.7; M.9.485A); **d.** infused into souls of the faithful, *ib*.6.17(p.513.4; 389A); **e.** of man's avoidance of sin through subjection of his θέλησις to God's θέλημα, Jo.D.*volunt*.19 (M.95.149C); **4.** ref. Son's generation; **a.** ref. Son as begotten by Father's will υἱὸν θεοῦ κατὰ θ. καὶ δύναμιν Ign.*Smyrn*.1.1; θελήματι δὲ τῆς ἁπλότητος αὐτοῦ προπηδᾷ λόγος Tat.*orat*.5(p.5.21; M.6.813C); οὗτος δὴ ὁ υἱὸς ἐκ θ. τοῦ πατρὸς ἐγενήθη Or.*princ*.4.4.1(p.349.11); in Arian doctrine, Ath.*Ar*.3.60(M.26.449A); **b.** of Son as θ. of Father, Clem.*str*.5.1(p.329.23; M.9.16B); τὸ θ. τοῦ πατρός ἐστιν Ἰησοῦς Χριστός Hipp.*Noët*.13(p.255.24; M.10.820D); opp. Arian teaching πῶς οὖν δύναται, βουλὴ καὶ θ. τοῦ πατρὸς ὑπάρχων, ὁ λόγος γίνεσθαι καὶ αὐτὸς θελήματι καὶ βουλήσει; Ath.*Ar*.3.64(M.26.457B); Gr.Nyss. *Eun*.12(1 p.276.3; M.45.984A); Cyr.*thes*.7(5^1.54E); **5.** of unity of will between Father and Son ὥστε εἶναι τὸ θ. τοῦ θεοῦ ἐν τῷ θ. τοῦ υἱοῦ, καὶ γενέσθαι τὸ θ. τοῦ υἱοῦ ἀπαράλλακτον τοῦ θ. τοῦ πατρός, εἰς τὸ μηκέτι εἶναι δύο θ., ἀλλὰ ἓν θ. Or.*Jo*.13.36(p.260.33; M.14.461A); ‡Dion.Al.*fr.in Lc*.*22*:*42*(p.233.11; M.10.1597C); ἕν ἐστι θ. τὸ ἐκ πατρὸς ἐν τῷ υἱῷ Ath.*Ar*.3.66(M.26.464A); Bas.*Spir*.21(3.18B; M.32. 105B); οὐχ ἵνα ποιῶ τὸ θ. τὸ ἐμόν (Jo.6:38)· οὐδὲ γάρ ἐστι τὸ ἐμὸν τοῦ σοῦ κεχωρισμένον, ἀλλὰ τὸ κοινὸν ἐμοῦ τε καὶ σοῦ Gr.Naz.*or*.30.12 (p.126.13; M.36.120A); Chrys.*hom.in Mt*.*26*:*39*(3.20C); id.*hom*.*24.1 in Mt*.(7.299A); ἐπειδὴ γὰρ ἓν θ. πατρὸς καὶ υἱοῦ, ἅπερ ὁ υἱὸς ἐβούλετο, ταῦτα καὶ ὁ πατὴρ ἤθελεν id.*comm.in Gal*.1:4(10.663B); Max.*opusc*. (M.91.68C); **6.** of unity of will in Trin., Bas.*Spir*.21(3.18B; M.32. 105B); μία τις γίνεται τοῦ ἀγαθοῦ θ. κίνησίς τε καὶ διακόσμησις, ἐκ πατρός, διὰ υἱοῦ, πρὸς τὸ πνεῦμα διεξαγομένη Gr.Nyss.*tres dii*(M.45. 128A); πᾶσαν τὴν διὰ τῆς κτίσεως ὑποστᾶσαν φύσιν, θελήματος κίνησιν ...καὶ δυνάμεως διάδοσιν, εἰκότως ἄν τις προσαγορεύσειεν ἐκ πατρὸς ἀρχομένην, καὶ δι' υἱοῦ προϊοῦσαν, καὶ ἐν πνεύματι ἁγίῳ τελειουμένην id.*Maced*.13(M.45.1317B); ἐν...θ. πατρὸς καὶ υἱοῦ καὶ ἁγίου πνεύματος Chrys.*hom*.*78.3 in Jo*.(8.463A); Cyr.*Jo*.4.1(4.334B); ‡Cyr.*Trin*.10 (6^3.15C; M.77.1141D) cit. s. κίνησις.

IV. Christol.; **A.** doctrine of two wills in Christ; **1.** in gen. δύο θ. ἐνταῦθα [sc. Mt.26:19] δείκνυσι, τὸ μὲν ἀνθρώπινον, ὅπερ ἐστὶ τῆς σαρκός· τὸ δὲ θεϊκόν, ὅπερ θεοῦ Ath.*inc.et c.Ar*.21(M.26.1021B); denial of Christ's human will by Apollinarius implies circumscription of divine will, Gr.Nyss.*Apoll*.31(M.45.1192B); ref. Mt.26:41 δύο θ. ἐμφαίνει, τὸ μὲν θεῖον, τὸ δὲ ἀνθρώπινον Sever.*fr*.ap.*Doct.Patr*.18 (p.120.3); κατεδέξατο τὰ πάθη, προελόμενος τὸ θεῖον θ. παρὰ τὸ ἀνθρώπινον Cyr.*Ps*.68:18(M.69.1169B); ἐν δύο φύσεσι καὶ θ. ... θέλοντα...ὡς θεόν Mod.*dorm*.10(M.86.3304C); CLater.*can*.10; Max. *Pyrrh*.(M.91.301A); ἀποβαλλόμενοι...τὴν ἀσεβεστάτην...περὶ ἑνὸς θ. ...αἵρεσιν CCP(681)*ep.Agath*.(M.*PL*.87.1251C); Jo.D.*volunt*.27(M.95. 157D); **2.** in orthodox theology; no θ. γνωμικόν predicated of Christ, on ground that to do so would imply ignorance and variability in his will εἰ γὰρ γνώμην τὴν διάθεσιν καλοῦσιν οἱ πατέρες, γίνεται δὲ διάθεσις πρὸς τὸ κρυβὲν ἐμφρόνως ὡς ἀπὸ τῆς βουλεύσεως, πῶς φασί τινες τὸν κύριον, τὸν ὑπὲρ ταῦτα πάντα, θ. φέρειν γνωμικόν; ‡Dion. Al.*fr.in Lc*.*22*:*44*(p.245.3; M.10.1593C); ‡Cyr.*Trin*.21(6^3.26E; M.77. 1161A) cit. s. γνώμη; εἶχεν οὖν θ. φυσικὸν ὡς ἄνθρωπος ὁ σωτήρ, τῷ αὐτοῦ θεϊκῷ θ. τυπούμενον...οὐδὲν γὰρ ἠναντίωται...θεῷ φυσικόν, ὁπόταν οὔτε γνωμικόν Max.*opusc*.(M.91.48D); whereas Nestorius postulated a union in Christ of θ. γνωμικά, resulting in division of his person, v. γνωμικός; **3.** two wills in Christ therefore held to be θ. φυσικά, not γνωμικά (which might imply possibility of mutual opposition): ὁ κύριος...δύο κεκτῆσθαι καὶ θ. πιστεύεται φυσικά, θεῖόν τε καὶ ἀνθρώπινον...ἐπεὶ δὲ μιᾶς ὑποστάσεως ἔγνωσται, σφαλερὸν εἰπεῖν ἐπ' αὐτοῦ διάφορα θ. γνωμικά ‡Cyr.*Trin*.20(6^3.26C; M.77. 1160D); ἐν δὲ Χριστοῦ θ. λέγων...εἰ μὲν ὡς Χριστοῦ φυσικόν... οὐδετέρῳ [sc. of Father or mother] κατ' οὐσίαν ἑνούμενον...εἰ δὲ γνωμικόν, μόνης ἔσται τῆς αὐτοῦ χαρακτηριστικὸν ὑποστάσεως· προσώπου γὰρ ἀφοριστικὸν ὑπάρχει τὸ γνωμικόν...οὐ γὰρ...ἔλεγόν [sc. οἱ πατέρες] ποτε γνωμικῶν ἐπὶ Χριστοῦ θ. διαφοράν, ἵνα μὴ δίγνωμον καὶ δίβουλον...καὶ διὰ τοῦτο διπρόσωπον αὐτὸν κηρύττωσιν Max.*opusc*. (M.91.53C,56B); τοὺς προαιρετικὸν καὶ γνωμικὸν αὐτὸ [sc. τὸ ἓν θ.] λέγοντας προσλαμβανόμενος...οὐ μόνον ψιλὸν ἄνθρωπον εἰσῆγε τὸν κύριον, ἀλλὰ καὶ τρεπτόν id.*Pyrr*.(M.91.329D); *ib*.(300C); δύο φυσικὰς θελήσεις ἤτοι θ. ἐν αὐτῷ...κηρύττομεν· καὶ δύο μὲν φυσικὰ θ. οὐχ ὑπεναντία...ἔδει γὰρ τὸ τῆς σαρκὸς θ. κινηθῆναι, ὑποταγῆναι δὲ τῷ θ. τῷ θεϊκῷ κατὰ τὸν...Ἀθανάσιον *Symb.CP*(681)(H.3.1400C); Jo.D. *volunt*.27(M.95.157D); τὸ γὰρ θελητικὸν...καθ' ἑκατέραν φύσιν λέγειν τὸν Χριστόν, οὐδὲν ἕτερόν ἐστιν ἢ δύο φυσικὰ θ. ... νοεῖν Jo.VI CP *ep*. (M.96.1425A); v. προαιρετικός.

B. of doctrine of one will in Christ; **1.** Apollinarian θεϊκῷ θ. μόνῳ κινούμενος Apoll.*fr*.108(p.232.29)ap.Max.*opusc*.(M.91.169C); id. *fr*.150(p.247.24)ap.*Doct.Patr*.41(p.307.6); ἤρκει...τὸ αὐτοῦ [sc. τοῦ θεοῦ] θ. διὰ τοῦ ἐν σαρκὶ σκηνώσαντος λόγου πρὸς ταύτην ζωοποιεῖν καὶ κινεῖν *ib*.2(p.204.6)ap.Anast.S.*monoph*.(M.89.1181D); ἑαυτῷ...ὅλος... θεὸς ἦν ὁ Χριστὸς...οὐ τὸν τρεπτὸν νοῦν ἑαυτῷ καταμίξας, θ. φυσικῷ ἐπὶ τἀναντία κινούμενον, ἑαυτῷ δὲ μᾶλλον γενόμενος νοῦς ἀτρέπτῳ θ. θεϊκῷ πάντα πεποίηκεν Polem.*fr*.173(p.274.8f.)ap.Max.*opusc*.(M.91. 172A); **2.** in teaching of Nestorius; unity of Person depending on identity of will οὐκ ἄλλος ἦν ὁ θεὸς λόγος καὶ ἄλλος ὁ ἐν ᾧ γέγονεν ἄνθρωπος. ἓν γὰρ ἦν ἀμφοτέρων τὸ πρόσωπον ἀξίᾳ καὶ τιμῇ...μηδενὶ τρόπῳ...ἑτερότητι βουλῆς καὶ θ. διαιρούμενον Nest.*fr*.B 9(p.224.15)ap. CLater.*act*.5(H.3.896C); **3.** in monothelite doctrine ἕν ἐστι τὸ θ. τοῦ Χριστοῦ Coll.*fr*.(p.313.25; H.3.897E); εἰ γὰρ μία ἐστὶ...φύσις τοῦ θεοῦ λόγου σεσαρκωμένη...ἀναμφιβόλως καὶ ἓν θ. Anth.CP*fr*.ap.CCP(681) *act*.10(H.3.1240D); ἓν θ. ὁμολογοῦμεν τοῦ κυρίου Ἰησοῦ Χριστοῦ Honor.*ep.Serg*.1(H.3.1320D); monothelite view caused by failure to distinguish between θ. φυσικόν and θ. γνωμικόν: τοῖς μονοθελήταις τὸ μὴ εἰδέναι τὴν διαφορὰν τοῦ φυσικοῦ καὶ τοῦ ὑποστατικοῦ θ., τουτέστι, τοῦ γνωμικοῦ, αἴτιον γέγονε τοῦ ἓν λέγειν ἐπὶ Χριστοῦ θ. Jo.D.*volunt*. 20(M.95.152A).

V. Devil being without θ. and having only ἐπιθυμία, Heracleon ap.Or.*Jo*.20.24(20; p.359.7; M.14.628C).

VI. as name of aeon in system of Barbeliote and Valentinian Gnostics, Iren.*haer*.1.29.1(M.7.692D); Hipp.*haer*.6.38(p.170.9; M.16. 3258A).

θελήμων, *glad, willing*, Nonn.*par.Jo*.19:16(M.43.901A); met. θ. πότμος *ib*.19:30(904C).

θέλησις, ἡ, I. *exercise of will* ἀποθέμενοι ἐκεῖνο ὃ περικείμεθα νέφος τῇ αὐτοῦ θ. *2Clem*.1.6; *A.Xanthipp*.9(p.64.15); Max.*schol.c.h*.11(M. 4.93C); dat., *voluntarily*, *Disp.Phot*.3(M.88.565C).

II. *object of will* (= θέλημα) αἳ δὲ οὐ συνεδόκησαν τῇ θ. αὐτῶν *A.Thom.*A 169(p.284.6); hence γῆ θελήσεως, *promised land* (rendering THDN, Σαβειρ), Thdt.*Dan.*11:16(2.1276).

III. *faculty of will*; **A.** def. θ. ἐστι τῆς νοερᾶς ψυχῆς ὁ ἐφ' ἡμῖν λόγος, ὡς αὐτεξούσιος αὐτῆς ὑπάρχουσα δύναμις. θ. ἐστι νοῦς ὀρεκτικός, καὶ διανοητικὴ ὄρεξις, πρὸς τὸ θεληθὲν ἐπινεύουσα Iren.*fr.*5(M.7.1272B); θ. ἐστι φυσικὴ δύναμις τοῦ κατὰ φύσιν ὄντος ὀρεκτική. ... φυσικὴ ὄρεξις τῇ τοῦ λογικοῦ φύσει κατάλληλος. ... φυσικὴ αὐτοκράτορος νοῦ αὐτεξούσιος κίνησις, ἢ νοῦς περί τι αὐθαιρέτως κινούμενος Clem.*fr.*40(p.220.13; M.9.752A); dist. from βούλησις, *ib.*41(p.220.22) ap.Max.*Pyrr.*(M.91.317C) cit. s. βούλησις; θ. ἐστι φυσική, παντὸς νοεροῦ αὐθαίρετος δύναμις Alex.Al.*ep.Aegl.*(M.18.584A); Eust.*fr.*52 ap.Max.*opusc.*(M.91.277A); dist. from προαίρεσις: ἡ μὲν θ. ἁπλῆ τις ὄρεξίς ἐστι, λογική τε καὶ ζωτική· ἡ δὲ προαίρεσις, ὀρέξεως καὶ βουλῆς καὶ κρίσεως σύνοδος Max.*opusc.*(13A); in rel. to free will τὸ...αὐτεξούσιον...θ. ἐστιν. ... ἐν τοῖς ἀλόγοις ἄγει μὲν ἡ φύσις· ἄγεται δὲ ἐν τῷ ἀνθρώπῳ ἐξουσιαστικῶς κατὰ θ. κινουμένῳ id.*Pyrr.*(304C); in relation to τὸ θελητόν: θ. ἐστιν αὐτὴ ἡ θελητικὴ τῆς ψυχῆς δύναμις, καθ' ἣν θέλομεν. θελητὸν δὲ αὐτὸ τὸ πρᾶγμα, ὅπερ τις θέλει Jo.D.*volunt.*21(M.95.152B); ἡ μὲν θ. ... καὶ αὐτὸ τὸ ἁπλῶς θέλειν, φυσικόν· τὸ δὲ θελητόν, τουτέστι τὸ τοιῶσδε θέλειν, γνωμικὸν καὶ ὑποστατικόν *ib.*22(152C).

B. of God; **1.** of subjection to God's will of that of man, Jo.D.*volunt.*19(M.95.149C); **2.** ref. Son's generation; **a.** ref. Son as begotten by will of Father, Just.*dial.*61.1(M.6.613C); Or.*Apoc.*26(p.32); in Arian and Semi-Arian theology ὑπῆρξε δὲ θ. πατρῴᾳ...ἡ σοφία· σοφία ὑπῆρξε σοφοῦ θεοῦ θελήσει Ar.*Thal.fr.*2 ap.Ath.*syn.*15(M.26.708A); Ἄρειος...βουλήσεως καὶ θ. υἱόν σε ἀποκαλῶν ‡Jo.D.*Artem.*65(p.155.7n.; M.96.1313A); τοὺς λέγοντας...ὅτι οὐ βουλήσει οὐδὲ θ. ἐγέννησεν ὁ πατὴρ τὸν υἱὸν ἀναθεματίζει ἡ...ἐκκλησία *Symb.Ant.*(345)2(p.252.8; M.26.729A); cf. *quod neque consilio neque voluntate pater genuerit filium, Symb.Sard.Orient.*ap. Hil.Pict.*de synodis* 34(M.*PL.*10.507C) altered in orthodox sense to *aut voluntate aut arbitrio pater genuit filium* (prob. representing ἢ ὅτι γνωμῇ ἢ θελήσει ὁ πατὴρ ἐγέννησε τὸν υἱόν), v. E. Schwartz *Zeitschrift für die neutestamentliche Wissenschaft* 1936 p.3; υἱὸς μὲν πατρὸς θελήσει γεγέννηται μόνου Philost.*h.e.*9.14(M.65.636C); **b.** doctrine denied by orthodox as implying substitution of θέλησις as 'mother' for God the Father, Gr.Naz.*or.*29.6(p.80.11ff.; M.36.80C); since nothing is prior to generation of Son, priority of Father's θ. is excluded, Cyr.*dial.Trin.*2(5^1.457C); id.*thes.*7(5^1.51B); Max.*ambig.*(M.91.1264A); Son himself being θ. of Father, Cyr.*dial.Trin.*2(455A); id.*Jo.*5.5(4.527D) cit. s. βουλή; **c.** ref. Son as not the image of Father's θέλησις, but of his οὐσία, ‡Ath.*dial.Trin.*1.4(M.28.1121D); *ib.*2.9(1169C); **3.** of unity of will between Father and Son μίαν μετὰ τοῦ θεοῦ τὴν θέλησιν ἔσχεν ὁ σωτήρ...ἡ σχέσις τῆς ἀγάπης μίαν τῶν πολλῶν...ἐργάζεται θέλησιν ‡Paul.Sam.*fr.*4(p.339.19ff.); πῶς δύναται ἐμοῦ τε καὶ τοῦ πατρὸς διακριθῆναι τὰ ἔργα, ὅπου θ. καὶ λόγος καὶ...θεότης μία; Amph.*fr.*ap.CLater.*act.*5(H.3.864C); θ. ... ὡς ἄνθρωπος ἔχων...τὴν τοῦ πατρικοῦ θελήματος πλήρωσιν Max.*opusc.*(M.91.68C); θ. μίαν ἔχουσιν ὅ τε πατὴρ καὶ ὁ ἐξ αὐτοῦ ἀνάρχως γεννηθεὶς υἱός id.*ambig.*(M.91.1264B); denied by Anomoeans, v. ἐνέργεια; **4.** of unity of will in Trin. εἴ τις μὴ εἴπῃ τοῦ πατρὸς καὶ τοῦ υἱοῦ καὶ τοῦ ἁγίου πνεύματος μίαν...θ., ἀνάθεμα ἔστω Dam.Papa *anath.*ap.Thdt.*h.e.*5.11.11(3.1039); ‡Cyr.*Trin.*7(6^3.8D; M.77.1132B) = Jo.D.*f.o.*1.8(M.94.809A); *ib.*10(15C; M.1141D) = Jo.D.*ib.*(828C); Sophr.H.*ep.syn.*(M.87.3157A).

C. in Christ; **1.** of reality of Christ's human will, compared with θ. αὐτεξούσιος bestowed on Adam, ‡Ath.*Apoll.*1.15(M.26.1120B); λόγον, θ.,...πάντα τὰ κατὰ φύσιν ἀνθρώπῳ προσόντα, προσείληφε ‡Cyr.*Trin.*14(6^3.20B; M.77.1149D); *ib.*20(6^3.26B; M.1160C); **2.** of union of divine and human natures in Christ, in Nestorian doctrine ἡ δὲ κατὰ τὴν θ. ἕνωσις Nest.*fr.*B 6(p.219.20)ap.*Doct.Patr.*41(p.305.1); **3.** of two wills in Christ δύο τοίνυν θ. ἐν τῷ Χριστῷ· θέλων δὲ καὶ κατ' ἄμφω τὰς θ. ... εἷς ὁ αὐτὸς θεάνθρωπος ‡Cyr.*Trin.*18(6^3.24E; M.77.1157B); *Symb.CP*(681)(H.3.1400C) cit. s. θέλημα; Anast.S.*hod.*2(M.89.65C); τοῦ κυρίου,...ἐπειδὴ δύο φύσεις, δύο καὶ φυσικαὶ θ. Jo.D.*volunt.*26(M.95.157B); **4.** of one will in Christ ἕνα τὸν Χριστὸν ὁμολογοῦμεν καὶ μίαν...τήν τε φύσιν καὶ τὴν θ. καὶ τὴν ἐνέργειαν προσκυνοῦμεν Apoll.*fr.*151(p.248.6)ap.*Doct.Patr.*41(p.307.18); ἡ γὰρ θ. θεότητος μόνης (Apollinarian) ‡Ath.*Apoll.*2.10(M.26.1148C); ἡ κατ' εὐδοκίαν τῶν φύσεων ἕνωσις μίαν ἀμφοτέρων τῷ τῆς ὁμωνυμίας λόγῳ ἐργάζεται τὴν προσηγορίαν, τὴν θ. ... μηδενὶ τρόπῳ διαιρουμένην Thdr.Mops.*ep.Domn.*(p.338.24; M.66.1012C); *ib.*(p.339.4; 1013A) cit. s. ἕνωσις; ἡ κατὰ θ. ἕνωσις...μίαν...δεικνῦσα πεποιημένην τὴν θ. καὶ τὴν ἐνέργειαν Nest.*fr.*B 6(p.219.20)ap.*Doct.Patr.*41(p.305.1); id.*fr.*202(p.220.5)*ib.*(p.305.10); id.*fr.*C 9(p.224.6)ap.CLater.*act.*5(H.3.896C) cit. s. συνάπτω; μίαν αὐτοῦ...τὴν θ. ... κηρύττομεν Eun.Berrh.*fr.*178(p.276.29)ap.*Doct.Patr.*41(p.309.13); μία...ἡ γνῶσις ἐπὶ Χριστοῦ, καθάπερ καὶ ἡ θ. Them.*fr.ib.*(p.314.2); τὴν ὡς ἑνὸς μίαν θ. ... πῇ μὲν ἀνθρωπίνως κινεῖσθαι, πῇ δὲ θεοπρεπῶς id.ap.CCP(681)*act.*10(H.3.1240D).

D. as name of aeon in system of Ptolemaeus, cf.Iren.*haer.*1.29.1(M.7.693A); δύο συζύγους...ἃς καὶ διαθέσεις καλοῦσιν, Ἔννοιαν καὶ Θ. Hipp.*haer.*6.38(p.169.14; M.16.3255B); Ath.*Ar.*3.60(M.26.449A).

E. as equivalent to Manich. 'good principle', *Disp.Phot.*(M.88.536D).

θελητής, ὁ, 1. *one who wills*; **a.** of men, ref. pagan doctrines of fate εἱμαρμένην γὰρ καὶ τύχην...οἰακοστρόφους ὥσπερ τινὰς ἐφίσταντες τῷ βίῳ, ἕκαστον μὲν ἡμῶν οὐκ εἶναί φασι τῶν πρακτέων θ. ἢ κύριον Cyr.*ador.*6(1.192A); **b.** of God; theol., ref. Arian doctrine of Son's generation by Father's will ὥσπερ γὰρ τῆς ἰδίας ὑποστάσεώς ἐστι θ., οὕτω καὶ ὁ υἱός, ἴδιος ὢν αὐτοῦ τῆς οὐσίας, οὐκ ἀθέλητός ἐστιν αὐτῷ Ath.*Ar.*3.66(M.26.461C), reproduced by Cyr.*thes.*7(5^1.56D); ἦν...ἅμα πατὴρ ὁ θεός, καὶ θ. τοῦ εἶναι πατήρ id.*dial.Trin.*2(5^1.457D); **2.** *one who desires*; c. genit., †Bas.*hom.in Ps.*37(1.369E; M.30.100C); Thdr.Mops.*Mich.*7:18(M.66.396C); Cyr.*Ps.*37:14(M.69.964D).

***θελητικός,** *possessing the faculty of will, willing, purposive*;

A. of men as rational beings possessing faculty of will productive of either good or evil desires, being itself morally neutral πᾶν γὰρ νοερὸν...θ. ‡Ath.*def.*2(M.28.540D); ἥτις δύναμις...ἕξις ψυχῆς θ. ταύτης...θελημάτων προβολαὶ γίνονται δύο...θεϊκοῦ τε καὶ πονηροῦ Ephr.Ant.*fr.*(M.86.2105D); πᾶν γὰρ φύσει λογικόν, καὶ φύσει θ. πάντως ἐστί Max.*opusc.*(M.91.77B); *ib.*(221D); τὸ θ. differentiating men from animals, Anast.S.*serm.imag.*3(M.89.1165C); θ. natures comprising the divine, the angelic, and the 'psychic', ‡Ath.*def.*2(540B).

B. of God; **1.** ref. providence φῶς οἰκῶν ἀπρόσιτον διὰ παντὸς μόνῃ τῇ θ. δυνάμει νομοθετεῖ καὶ διατάττεται Eus.*l.C.*12(p.229.30; M.20.1388A); ἕκαστον κατὰ τὴν θ. αὐτοῦ ἄχρονον ἔννοιαν, ἥτις ἐστὶ προορισμός, καὶ εἰκών, καὶ παράδειγμα, ἐν τῷ προορισθέντι καιρῷ γίνεται Jo.D.*f.o.*1.9(M.94.837A); **2.** of God's power of willing, productive of many partic. acts of will ἐν τῇ θ. τοῦ θεοῦ δυνάμει πολλὰ θεοῦ ἐν ταῖς θείαις γραφαῖς λέγονται εἶναι θελήματα Ephr.Ant.*fr.*(M.86.2105C).

C. Christol.; **1.** of doctrine of one will ἀναπληρούσης τῆς θείας ἐνεργείας τὸν τῆς ψυχῆς τόπον καὶ τοῦ ἀνθρωπίνου νοός· ὅθεν οὐ προσέθηκε [sc. Jo.1:14] 'καὶ ψυχή'· ἀδύνατον γὰρ δύο νοερὰ καὶ θ. ἐν τῷ ἅμα κατοικεῖν, ἵνα μὴ τὸ ἕτερον κατὰ τοῦ ἑτέρου ἀντιστρατεύηται διὰ τῆς οἰκείας θελήσεως καὶ ἐνεργείας Apoll.*fr.*2(p.204.12)ap.Anast.S.*monoph.*(M.89.1181Dff.); **2.** of doctrine of two wills κατ' ἄμφω τὰς αὐτοῦ φύσεις...θ. ὑπάρχοντα φύσει...παρίστησι...ὁ λόγος Max.*opusc.*(M.91.160C); οὐ μόνον καθ' ὃ θεὸς καὶ τῷ πατρὶ ὁμοούσιος ἦν θ., ἀλλὰ καθ' ὃ ἄνθρωπος καὶ ἡμῖν ὁμοούσιος id.*Pyrr.*(M.91.324C); ὁ αὐτὸς θεὸς τέλειος...καὶ ἄνθρωπος τέλειος,...ἐν δύο φύσεσι νοεραῖς, θ. τε καὶ ἐνεργητικαῖς Jo.D.*f.o.*1.2(M.94.793A); Jo.VI CP *ep.*(M.96.1425A) cit. s. θέλημα.

θελητός, *wished for, willed*; **1.** in gen. θέλημα...λέγεται, κατὰ τὸ...τοῦ θ. λῆμμα ‡Ath.*def.*2(M.28.540D); **2.** ref. God; **a.** of eternal idea of rational and purposive justice pre-existent in the divine nature κατὰ τὸ πᾶσαν ἰσότητα, νοητὴν...καὶ θελητὴν ἐξῃρημένως καὶ ἑνιαίως ἐν ἑαυτῷ προειληφέναι Dion.Ar.*d.n.*9.10(M.3.917A); this ἰσότης θελητή defined as ἣν ἐθέλοντες καὶ ἐκ προαιρέσεως κατορθοῦσιν οἳ τὸ δίκαιον καὶ τὸ περὶ τὸν βίον ἰσονομικὸν μετίασι Max.*schol.d.n.*9.10(M.4.384D); **b.** in orthodox argument that to deny Son's generation to be ἐκ βουλήσεως does not imply that he is ἀθέλητος: ὡς τὸ εἶναι ἀγαθὸς οὐκ ἐκ βουλήσεως μὲν ἤρξατο, οὐ μὴν...ἀθελήτως ἐστὶν ἀγαθός· ὃ γάρ ἐστι, τοῦτο καὶ θ. ἐστιν αὐτῷ Ath.*Ar.*3.66(M.26.461C); **c.** of identity of will between Father and Son κέκληνται...εἰς ἀποστολὴν διὰ Χριστοῦ...ἀλλ' ἦν...τὸ χρῆμα καὶ αὐτὸ θ. τῷ πατρί. ... ὅτι καὶ βουλὴ καὶ σοφία καὶ θέλησις τοῦ πατρὸς ὁ υἱός Cyr.*ador.*11(1.376D); **3.** ref. Christ οὐκ ἂν ἠθέλησε παθεῖν...ποιεῖται δὲ θ. τὸ ἀνεθέλητον διὰ τὰ ἐκ τοῦ πάθους χρήσιμα...ἀνεθέλητον...Χριστῷ τὸ...πάθος, θ. δὲ δι' ἡμᾶς Cyr.*Jo.*4.1(4.331C); ἀβούλητος...ὁ θάνατος ἦν· θ. δ' οὖν ὅμως *ib.*(332C); τὸ...τεθνάναι θ. μὲν ἔχει, διὰ τὸ βεβουλῆσθαι τὴν θείαν φύσιν· ἀνέθελητον δέ, διὰ τὰ...πάθη id.ap.Max.*opusc.*(M.91.165A); τοῦτο [sc. his humiliation] θ. ἐποιήσατο διὰ σέ id.*apol.Thdt.*10(p.139.18; 6^1.234A); **4.** as subst., Valent. aeon, consort of Sophia Θελητός, ὅ ἐστι Φῶς Val.Gn.ap.Epiph.*haer.*31.5(p.392.10; M.41.484A); Iren.*haer.*1.1.2(M.7.449B); *ib.*1.2.2(453A); Hipp.*haer.*6.30(p.157.22; M.16.3239A).

***θελητῶς,** *voluntarily, in accordance with one's wish*, ref. Son's generation; **1.** Arian εἰ μὴ ἀνεθελήτως τέτοκεν ὁ πατὴρ τὸν υἱὸν θ. ...

πάντως που καὶ προηγήσεται...τῆς τοῦ υἱοῦ γεννήσεως ἡ θέλησις τοῦ πατρός Cyr.*dial.Trin.*2(5^1.454B); **2.** orthodox; **a.** Father possesses all his attributes voluntarily, but his will is not anterior to them *θ. ὁ θεὸς ἀθάνατός ἐστιν..., ἢ ἀνεθελήτως;...οὐ προηγεῖται τῆς... ὑπάρξεως καὶ ἀθανασίας θέλημα* Didym.*Trin.*1.9(M.39.285B); *πότερα θ., ἤγουν ἀνεθελήτως ὑπάρχει τε καὶ ἔστιν ὁ πατήρ. καὶ εἰ μὲν οὐ θ. ... ἐκβεβίασται...εἰ δὲ...θ. ... προηγήσεταί που τῆς ὑπάρξεως...τὸ θέλειν αὐτοῦ* Cyr.*dial.Trin.*2(5^1.454E); *ib.*(455D); **b.** since fatherhood is God's essential attribute, generation of Son is voluntary, but not preceded by deliberation *θ. οὖν ἄρα καὶ ἀβουλήτως ὑπάρχει καὶ ὁ λόγος ἐν τῷ πατρί* id.*thes.*7(5^1.53D); **c.** if fatherhood is not God's essential attribute *διημάρτηκε καὶ λογισμοῦ τοῦ πρέποντος, καὶ εἰσδέδεκται θ. τὸ πεφυκὸς ἀδικεῖν* id.*dial.Trin.*2(5^1.457B).

θελκτήριος, *seductive*, Meth.*symp.*11(p.132.19; M.18.209A).

θελκτικός, *enticing*, Just.*2apol.*11.4(M.6.461C); Isid.Pel.*epp.*1.364 (M.78.389A).

θέλξις, ἡ, *enchantment*, met. *τῆς φιλοτησίας θ.* Meth.*symp.*2.2 (p.16.14; M.18.49A); ref. energumen *θ. ἢ ταραχαῖς ἐνεσχημένον* Dion. Ar.*c.h.*3.7(M.3.433B); cf.*ib.*4.3(477A); ref. BMV *ταῖς ἐναντίαις θ. ἄχαυνος* Thdr.Stud.*nativ.BMV* 7(M.96.693C).

θέλ-ω, I. *will*;

A. of men; **1.** ref. antecedent will required for moral effort *αἱ... λογικαὶ δυνάμεις τοῦ βούλεσθαι διάκονοι πεφύκασι· ~ε, φησί, καὶ δυνήσῃ* Clem.*str.*2.17(p.153.22; M.8.1016B); **2.** importance of moral will for attainment of salvation *μὴ λέγε· πῶς μου ἐξαλείφονται αἱ ἁμαρτίαι; ἐγώ σοι λέγω· τῷ ~ειν, τῷ πιστεύειν* Cyr.H.*procatech.*8; *ἀρκεῖ...τὸ ~ῆσαι, καὶ τὸ πᾶν ἤνυσται* Chrys.*hom.49.4 in Mt.*(7.509B); *ὁδός...ἐστι λύσεως ἁμαρτημάτων, οὐ πόνων δεομένη...ἀλλὰ θελῆσαι μόνον* id.*hom.1.2 in Philm.*(11.777D); *ib.1.3*(778A); **3.** of freedom of moral will *εἰ ~εις βλασφημῆσαι...οὐδείς σοι ἀντίκειται...εἰ ~ει τις, ὑποτάσσεται τῷ θεῷ* Mac.Aeg.*hom.*15.23(M.34.592B); **4.** of relation of man's moral will to grace, ref. Jo.5:6 *διὰ τοῦτο ἤκουσε τὸ '~εις;' ἵνα τὸ ~ειν ἐπαγάγῃ τὴν ἐνέργειαν* Cyr.H.*hom.*4(M.33.1136B); *πολλοὺς...ἠλευθέρωσε, τῷ ~ειν διδοὺς χάριν* Gr.Naz.*carm.*2.1.83.28(M.37. 1430A); *ἂν θελήσῃς, τότε ἐνεργήσει τὸ ~ειν...ὅταν γὰρ θελήσωμεν, αὔξει τὸ ~ειν ἡμῶν λοιπόν* Chrys.*hom.8.1 in Phil.*(11.257D); *ὅτι τεύξῃ τοῦ σπουδαζομένου εὔδηλόν ἐστιν, ἕως ἂν τρέχῃς, ἕως ἂν ~ῃς* id. *hom.12.3 in Heb.*(12.125C).

B. of God; **1.** ref. God's will as inseparable from his nature *~ει γὰρ εἶναι τοῦτο ὅπερ ἔστιν ἀεὶ καὶ ἔσται* Cyr.*thes.*7(5^1.56D); **2.** God's power being coextensive with his will, Eus.*d.e.*4.1(p.151.17; M.22. 252D); *τὸ θελῆσαί σου, πρᾶξίς ἐστι συντετελεσμένη* Gr.Naz.*or.*16.12 (M.35.952A); Gr.Nyss.*anim.et res.*(M.46.93B); **3.** of God's will as sole cause of Creation *ἐν θελήματι τοῦ θελήσαντος τὰ πάντα, ἅ ἐστιν* Ign.*Rom.*proem.; Iren.*haer.*1.12.1(M.7.573A); *εἷς θεός ἐστιν...πάντα ποιῶν ὡς ~ει, καθὼς ~ει, ὅτε ~ει* Hipp.*Noët.*8(p.249.25; M.10.816B); Clem.*str.*7.12(p.50.4; M.9.496D); id.*fr.*48(p.224.26)ap.Max.*ambig.*(M. 91.1085B); Eus.*d.e.*4.1(p.151.13; M.22.252C); **4.** God's will being to save rather than punish, Just.*1apol.*15.8(M.6.349C); this positive will not inconsistent with will to chastise sinners *ὁ θεὸς ~ει...τὰ μὲν ἐν μακροθυμίᾳ...ἅπερ ἀγαθά...λέγεται· τὰ δὲ κατ' ὀργὴν διὰ τὰς ἁμαρτίας...ἅπερ κακὰ ὀνομάζεται* Bas.*reg.br.*276(2.511E; M.31.1273C); **5.** ref. generation of Son; **a.** of Logos by Father's will *ὅτε ἠθέλησεν, καθὼς ἠθέλησεν, ἐγέννα τὸν λόγον αὐτοῦ, δι' οὗ τὰ πάντα ἐποίησεν καιροῖς ὡρισμένοις παρ' αὐτοῦ* Hipp.*Noët.*10(p.251.19; M.10.817B); Arian and Semi-Arian *εἴτε γὰρ ἀνάξιον τοῦ δημιουργοῦ τὸ ~οντα ποιεῖν, ἐπὶ πάντων ὁμοίως ἀνῃρήσθω τὸ ~ειν...εἴτε προσῆκον τῷ θεῷ τὸ βούλεσθαι, καὶ ἐπὶ τοῦ πρώτου γεννήματος ὑπαρχέτω τὸ κρεῖττον. οὐ γὰρ δυνατὸν ἑνί τε καὶ τῷ αὐτῷ θεῷ τὸ ~ειν ἐπὶ τῶν ποιουμένων ἁρμόττειν, καὶ τὸ μὴ βούλεσθαι προσήκειν* Ast.Soph.*fr.*15 ap.Ath.*Ar.* 3.60(M.26.449B); *εἴ τις μὴ θελήσαντος τοῦ πατρὸς γεγεννῆσθαι λέγοι τὸν υἱόν, ἀνάθεμα ἔστω* *Symb.Sirm.*1 *anath.*25(p.256.11; M.26.740B); *εἰ μὲν γὰρ οὐ ~ων, φασί* [sc. *γεγέννηκε τὸν υἱόν*], *τετυράννηται...εἰ δὲ ~ων θελήσεως υἱὸς ὁ υἱός* Gr.Naz.*or.*29.6(p.80.9; M.36.80C); *εἰ μὴ βουλήσει, φησί, γέγονεν ὁ υἱὸς τοῦ θεοῦ, ... μὴ ~ων ἔσχεν υἱὸν ὁ πατήρ* Cyr.*thes.*7(5^1.52E); **b.** this view denied *πῶς...οὐχ ὑπερβάλλει πᾶσαν μανίαν τὸ...ἐνθυμεῖσθαι ὅτι...ὁ θεὸς βουλεύεται καὶ...~ειν ἑαυτὸν προτρέπεται ἵνα...λόγον...ἔχῃ;* Ath.*Ar.*3.63(M.26.456C); *ὁ υἱὸς τῇ θελήσει ἣ ~εται παρὰ τοῦ πατρός, ταύτῃ καὶ αὐτὸς ἀγαπᾷ καὶ ~ει...τὸν πατέρα· καὶ ἕν ἐστι θέλημα τὸ ἐκ πατρὸς ἐν υἱῷ* *ib.*3.66(464A); Arian argument refuted *~ων...ὁ πατήρ, ἢ μὴ ~ων;...εἰ μὲν δὴ ~ων, πότε τοῦ ~ειν ἠργμένος;...εἰ δὲ οὐ ~ων, τί τὸ βιασάμενον εἰς τὸ εἶναι;* Gr. Naz.*or.*29.7(p.82.10f.; M.36.81C); *μηδέποτε τὸ καλὸν ἀεὶ ἀπεῖναι αὐτοῦ, μηδὲ ἄνευ υἱοῦ τὸν πατέρα θελῆσαι· θελήσαντα δὲ μὴ ἀδυνατῆσαι ...ἐν τῷ κατὰ γνώμην εἶναι καὶ ἀεὶ ἔχειν τὸν υἱόν, διὰ τὸ ἀεὶ ~ειν τὸ ἀγαθόν* Gr.Nyss.*Eun.*8(2 p.194.24; M.45.789C); *~ει...τὸν υἱὸν καὶ φιλεῖ,...οὕτω καὶ ὁ υἱὸς...οὐκ ἀθέλητός ἐστιν αὐτῷ, εἰ καὶ βούλησις οὐδαμοῦ τῆς γεννήσεως προδραμοῦσα φαίνεται* Cyr.*thes.*7(5^1.56D); *εἰ ...ἐν σοφίᾳ καὶ λόγῳ τὸ ~ειν τοῦ πατρός,...σοφία δὲ καὶ λόγος ἐστὶ... ὁ υἱός, αὐτὸς ἄρα ἐστὶν ὁ ἐν ᾧ πᾶσα θέλησις τοῦ πατρός* id.*dial.Trin.*2 (5^1.454E); **6.** ref. Father's specific operation in redemption *πατὴρ ...ἠθέλησεν, υἱὸς ἐποίησεν, πνεῦμα ἐφανέρωσεν* Hipp.*Noët.*14(p.257. 17; M.10.821C); **7.** [Valentinian] ref. emanation of aeon *Θέλησις*: *δύο ζυγοὺς ἔχειν τὸν ἀγένητον, Ἔννοιαν καὶ Θέλησιν· καὶ πρῶτον ἐνενόησεν, εἶτα ἠθέλησε* Ath.*Ar.*3.60(M.26.449A) citing Iren.*haer.*1. 12.1(M.7.572A), cf.Hipp.*haer.*6.38(p.169.15; M.16.3255B); Epiph. *haer.*33.1(p.448.15; M.41.556B).

C. of Christ; **1.** ref. identity of will in Father and Son *τοῦτο τὸ ~ειν ἐν ἑαυτῷ ποιῶν ὅπερ ἦν καὶ ἐν τῷ πατρί* Or.*Jo.*13.36(p.260.30; M. 14.461A); *τὸ γὰρ ἐκείνου ~ειν οὐδὲ ὑπεναντίον θεῷ, θεωθὲν ὅλον* Gr. Naz.*or.*30.12(p.126.1; M.36.117C); *ἠθέλησέ τι ὁ πατήρ, καὶ ὁ ἐν τῷ πατρὶ ὢν υἱὸς εἶδε τὸ θέλημα τοῦ πατρός* Gr.Nyss.*Eun.*12(1 p.276.2; M.45.984A); **2.** Christol; **a.** ref. doctrine of one will *ἀδύνατόν ἐστιν ἐν ἑνὶ καὶ τῷ αὐτῷ ὑποκειμένῳ δύο τοὺς τἀναντία ~οντας ἀλλήλοις συνυπάρχειν ἑκατέρου τὸ θεληθὲν ἑαυτῷ καθ' ὁρμὴν αὐτοκίνητον ἐνεργοῦντος* Apoll.*fr.*150(p.247.25)ap.*Doct.Patr.*41(p.307.8); Them. *fr.ib.*(p.314.5); **b.** ref. doctrine of two wills, Ath.*Ar.*3.57(M.26.441C); Chrys.*anom.*7.6(1.511B); Thphl.Al.*poenit.*ap.*Doct.Patr.*18(p.120.14); Cyr.*Jo.*4.1(4.331B); Max.*opusc.*(M.91.68B); *ib.*(160B); **3.** ref. Son's will as cause of Creation, Evagr.Pont.*ep.*9(M.32.261B); **4.** ref. Christ's will to save, *2Clem.*2.7; and to suffer, †Thdt.*prop.*(4.1055); *εἰπεῖν θέλεις πρὸς ἐμέ, ὅτι ὁ Χριστὸς ~ων ἔπαθεν, ἢ μὴ ~ων; καὶ ἐάν σοι εἴπω, ~ων ἔπαθεν, ἵνα μοι εἴπῃς...προσκύνησον τοὺς Ἰουδαίους, ἐπειδὴ τὸ θέλημα τοῦ θεοῦ ἐποίησαν...σὺ λέγεις θέλημα εἶναι, ἐγὼ λέγω ἀνοχὴν καὶ μακροθυμίαν* Jo.D.*disp.*(M.96.1340D).

II. *desire, look upon with favour* *θελήσατε, ἵνα καὶ ὑμεῖς θεληθῆτε* Ign.*Rom.*8.1; *Hom.Clem.*11.25; *θελέσθω καὶ φιλείσθω τοίνυν ὁ υἱὸς παρὰ τοῦ πατρός* Ath.*Ar.*3.66(M.26.461C).

III. *suppose* *~εις γάρ, παρῆλθέ τι τὸν ἄνδρα ἐν τῷ ῥοίζῳ τῆς τῶν λόγων ἐξηγήσεως· οὐκ ἔχω λέγειν· ~εις, κατὰ ἀφέλειαν ἀπ' αὐτοῦ ὁ λόγος προήχθη* Epiph.*haer.*73.35(p.310.6; M.42.468C).

IV. = *μέλλω*, *be about to*, *T.Reub.*1.7; Jo.Mosch.*prat.*19(M.87. 2865C).

θέμα, τό, 1. *prize*, of reward of Christian life *τὸ θ. ἀφθαρσία καὶ ζωὴ αἰώνιος* Ign.*Polyc.*2.3; *Orac.Sib.*2.48ff.; *θ. μάρτυσι δώσει ἀθάνατον* *ib.*2.46; **2.** *horoscope*; its use punished by excommunication, Epiph.*mens.*15(M.43.261C); *πῶς τοῦδέ τινος τὸ θ. περιέχει, τίνες αὐτοῦ γεγόνασιν οἱ γονεῖς, εἰ ἐλεύθεροι, εἰ ἀγαθοί;* Proc.G.*Gen.* 1:15(M.87.96A,B); **3.** military; **a.** *legion*, Thphn.*chron.*p.251(M.108. 629A); *ib.*p.298(728B); **b.** *military district*, *ib.*p.293(717B).

θεματίζω, *assert*, CCP(681)*or.imp.*(H.3.1421D).

θέμεθλα, τά, *foundations*, Nonn.*par.Jo.*4:39(M.43.781A).

θεμέλιος, ὁ (θεμέλιον, τό), *foundation*; **1.** of God's will in rel. to Creation *ἥδρασεν ἐπὶ τὸν...τοῦ ἰδίου βουλήματος θ.* *1Clem.*33.3; **2.** of Christ, ref. saints *αὐτὸς...θ. αὐτοῖς ἐγένετο* Herm.*sim.*9.14.6; as foundation of *γνῶσις*, Clem.*str.*7.9(p.41.1; M.9.480A); *σὰρξ ἁγία θεότητι συμφυής...θ. αἰωνίου ζωῆς* Apoll.*fr.*155(p.249.6)ap.Leont.B. *Apoll.*(M.86.1964B); **3.** of apostles and prophets *ὁ μέν τις ἐν τῷ θ. ἀπόστολος ἢ προφήτης βαστάζων τοὺς ἐπικειμένους* Or.*Jo.*10.39(23; p.216.11; M.14.381C); Const.ap.Gel.Cyz.*h.e.*2.7.2,3(M.85.1232C,D); Chrys.*hom.2.2 in Ac.princ.*(3.63Aff.); **4.** of S. Peter *Σίμων, ὁ διὰ τὴν ἀληθῆ πίστιν καὶ τὴν ἀσφαλεστάτην αὐτοῦ τῆς διδασκαλίας ὑπόθεσιν τῆς ἐκκλησίας θ. εἶναι ὁρισθεὶς καὶ δι' αὐτὸ τοῦτο ὑπ' αὐτοῦ τοῦ Ἰησοῦ...μετονομασθεὶς Πέτρος* *Clem.ep.*1(M.2.33A); cf.*Hom. Clem.*17.19; Chrys.*hom.in Mt.18:23*(3.4E); id.*hom.in 2Tim.3:1*(6. 282E); ref. Mt.16:16 *ὁ μακάριος Πέτρος τέθεικε τὸν θ., μᾶλλον δὲ αὐτὸς ὁ δεσπότης* Thdt.*1Cor.*3:11(3.181); *τὸν πρῶτον τῆς ἐκκλησίας θ. καταμάθωσι κλονούμενον, καὶ ὑπὸ τῆς θείας χάριτος βεβαιούμενον* id. *haer.*5.28(4.478); **5.** of virtues as foundation of spiritual life: continence, Clem.*str.*7.12(p.50.18; M.9.497A); faith, hope, charity, *ib.* 4.7(p.273.5; M.8.1265B); in gen., Mac.Aeg.*hom.*28.23(M.34.709C); *πίστιν τὸ τῆς υἱοθεσίας θ.* Bas.Sel.*or.*20.2(M.85.253B).

θεμελι-όω, 1. *found, establish*; **a.** ref. Creation, Herm.*vis.*1.3.4; (Gnost.) *ἐν τῷ οἰκτηρίῳ, οὗ ἡ ῥίζα τῶν ὅλων τεθεμελίωται* Hipp.*haer.* 5.9(p.98.18; M.16.3154B); *ib.*7.27(p.206.20; 3318C); *ἅπερ διὰ τοῦ λόγου γέγονε, ταῦτα τῇ σοφίᾳ τεθεμελίωται* Ath.*decr.*17(p.14.20; M.25. 444D); **b.** Christol. (orthodox), ref. Col.1:26 *αὐτός ἐστι τὸ πρὸ τῶν αἰώνων θεμελιωθέν* ‡Ath.*dial.Trin.*1.9(M.28.1132B); ‡Ath.*serm.fid.* 31(p.28; M.26.1285C); Pr.8:23 fulfilled of Christ in Inc., Ath.*Ar.*2. 74(M.26.305A); *ib.*2.76(309A); (Arian) *ὁ υἱὸς...πρὸ αἰώνων κτισθεὶς καὶ ~ωθείς* Ar.*ep.Alex.*(p.13.9; M.26.709B); id.*ep.Eus.*(p.3.3; M.42. 212B); **c.** ref. Church, as founded on faith, Ath.*ep.Serap.*3.6(M.

26.633C); *ib.*1.27(596A); Paul.Em.*hom.*1(p.10.32; M.77.1436D); by apostles τοῦ Πέτρου καὶ τοῦ Παύλου ἐν Ῥώμῃ...∼ούντων τὴν ἐκκλησίαν Iren.*haer.*3.1.1(M.7.845A); *ib.*3.3.3(849A); ref. S. Paul ∼οῦν ἐκκλησίαν Or.*hom.12.8 in Jer.*(p.95.11, conj. for θεμένου; M.13.389C θέμενος); **d.** of foundation of spiritual life ∼ώσει [sc. God] σε ἐν τῇ δόξῃ αὐτοῦ Herm.*vis.*1.3.2; *ib.*4.1.4; ὑπακοὴ...∼οῦται ἐντολαῖς Clem.*paed.*1.13(p.151.14; M.8.373A); of wisdom of God as foundation of redemption, Ath.*Ar.*2.73(M.26.301B); ἡ ζωὴ ἡμῶν ἐτεθεμελίωτο ...ἐν Χριστῷ Ἰησοῦ *ib.*2.76(302B); τῇ ψυχῇ τεθεμελιώσθω δόγμα τὸ περὶ θεοῦ Cyr.H.*catech.*4.4; **2.** *confirm*; of faith confirmed by repentance, Clem.*str.*2.13(p.143.20; M.8.993B); τὴν πίστιν, εἴτε ὑπὸ ἀγάπης ἐθεμελιώθη εἴτε καὶ ὑπὸ φόβου *ib.*2.6(p.129.5; 965A).

θεμελίωσις, ἡ, *foundation*, met. τῆς κατὰ τὴν πίστιν θ. †Bas.*Is.*209(1.536B; M.30.480C).

θεμελιωτής, ὁ, *founder*, †Bas.*Is.*291(M.30.629A); *Lit.Marc.* (Brightman p.135.12).

***θεμελιωτικός,** *of founding*; neut. as subst., *power of founding*, Dion.Ar.*c.h.*15.5(M.3.333B).

***θεμελιωτός,** *fashioned*, ref. Arian doctrine of Son κτιστὸν εἶναι καὶ θ. Eus.Nic.*ep.Paulin.*(p.16.9; M.82.913D).

θεμιστεύ-ω, *decree* τοῦ θεοῦ ∼οντος τὸν ἄνθρωπον τῶν τῆς σοφίας ἐργάτην τεθῆναι...φυτῶν Meth.*symp.*8.3(p.84.12; M.18.141C).

***θεμιστονόμος, ὁ,** *adjudicator*, *Orac.Sib.*13.26.

θεμιστοπόλος, *dispensing justice*, *Orac.Sib.*12.174; Nonn.*par.Jo.* 7:52(M.43.813A); met. θ. βίβλου...νόμοις *ib.*18:31(896A).

***θεοαδής,** v. *θεαδής.

***θεοβάστακτος,** *bearing God*, of BMV θρόνος θ. Germ.CP *or.*5(M.98.324D); ῥίπτει Παῦλος ἑαυτὸν εἰς τοὺς θ. αὐτῆς πόδας *ib.*8(368A).

***θεοβδέλυκτος,** *abhorred by God*; of a human sacrifice, Thphn.*chron.*p.327(M.108.789C).

θεοβλαβής, *mad*; met., as subst., ref. heretics τῆς ψυχῆς γνόφον καὶ...τὸ θ. Philost.*h.e.*6.2(M.65.533B); of sinners οἱ θ. Areth.*Apoc.*45 (M.106.761D).

***θεοβούλητος,** *willed by God*, *Hom.Clem.*1.21; *Clem.ep.*1(M.2.36A).

***θεοβουλία, ἡ,** *divine counsel, divine plan*, Anast.S.*hod.*4(M.89.93B).

***θεοβούλως,** *according to the divine will*, Gr.II Papa *ep.Germ.* (M.98.149D).

***θεόβροχος,** *rained from God*; of the flood, Tim.Ant.*Sym.*(M.86.237C).

***θεόβρυτος,** *welling forth from God*, met., of BMV ἡ κρήνη ἡ θ. Thdr.Stud.*nativ.BMV* 7(M.96.689C).

***θεοβύθιστος,** *to be sent by God to the bottom of the sea* ὁ...θ. στόλος Thphn.*chron.*p.294(M.108.720B).

***θεογενεσία, ἡ,** *divine generation, coming into being to God*, hence *baptism*, Dion.Ar.*e.h.*2.1(M.3.392B); ἡ τῆς ἱερᾶς τελετὴ θ. *ib.* 2.3.1(397A); *ib.*2.3.8(404C); *ib.*3.1(425A).

***θεογενικός,** *belonging to the Godbearer*, ref. BMV θ. ἀγκάλαις τὸν κτίστην βαστάσασα ‡Jo.D.*hom.*6.7(M.96.672C).

***θεογεννητρία, ἡ,** *mother of God*, Ephr.3.524E; Jo.Mon.*hymn.Geo.*7(M.96.1397D); ὦ πανολβία τρισάνασσα θ. Andr.Cr.*or.*14(M.97.1108A).

***θεογεννήτωρ, ἡ,** *mother of God*; of BMV, Jo.Mon.*hymn.Chrys.*8 (M.96.1384B); θ. καὶ δᾳδοῦχε τῶν πιστῶν ‡Meth.*Sym.et Ann.*10(M.18.372C).

***θεογεώργητος,** *tilled of God*, of BMV θ. χωρίον Mod.*dorm.*2(M.86.3285A).

***θεόγληνος,** *with divine eyes*, Nonn.*par.Jo.*20:12(M.43.909B).

***θεόγλυπτος,** *carved by God* τὴν θεόγλυπτον πέτραν (perh. ref. S. Peter) *CIG* 8816.

θεόγλωσσος, *divinely speaking* θ. βίβλου Nonn.*par.Jo.*2:22(M.43.764C); *ib.*5:37(792A); *ib.*7:26(809A).

θεογνωσία, ἡ, A. *knowledge of God*; **1.** in gen. ἡ τῆς ἁγίας τριάδος θ. ‡Bas.*h.myst.*59(p.393.21); ref. Rom.1:28, threats against those neglecting it, Bas.*jud.*3(2.215B; M.31.657A); **2.** means of its attainment; from inborn principles κἂν τῷ ποιεῖν νόμον δέδωκας αὐτῷ ἔμφυτον, ὅπως οἴκοθεν...ἔχοι τὰ σπέρματα τῆς θ. *Lit.*ap.*Const.App.* 8.12.19; Cyr.*Juln.*3(6².101A); through consideration of visible creation [sc. ὁ κόσμος]...θεογνωσίας ἐστὶ παιδευτήριον, διὰ τῶν ὁρωμένων...χειραγωγίαν τῷ νῷ παρεχόμενος πρὸς τὴν θ. τῶν ἀοράτων Bas.*hex.*1.6(1.6E; M.29.13B); Chrys.*Anna* 1.2(4.701C); by which means some Greeks obtained limited knowledge of God, Anast.S.*qu.et resp.*96(M.89.737B); through reflection on providence, Chrys.*Is.interp.*7(6.74A); id.*scand.*7(3.477B); as learnt by sinners from the pious and those instructed in religion, Or.*exp.in Pr.*14:9(M.17.193A); **3.** ref. obstacles to its acquisition οὐδὲν...οὕτω πρὸς ἀκριβῆ θ. ἄχρηστον, ὡς ἀπόνοια καὶ τὸ προσηλῶσθαι πλούτῳ Chrys.*hom.*5.1 *in 1Cor.*(10.34C); οὔτε ἱκανῶς...χωροῦμεν...ὅσα τὰ ῥητὰ τῆς θ. ἐξειπεῖν Dion.Ar.*d.n.*3.3(M.3.684B); **4.** ref. OT religion, opp. idolatry κέκληνται...εἰς θ. διὰ Μωυσέως Cyr.*Os.*12(3.34C); Proc.G.*Gen.*proem.(M.87.24C); Jo.Mal.*chron.*3 p.57(M.97.133A); **5.** of revelation through Inc., Eus.*h.e.*10.4.10(M.20.852B); φανεὶς ὁ Χριστὸς λαμπρὰν θεογνωσίας ἡμέραν εἰργάσατο Mac.Mgn.*apocr.*3.13(p.89.3); Procl.CP *or.*6.15(M.65.749A); θεογνωσίας τὴν ἀνθρωπότητα ἔρημον [i.e. before Inc.] Thdr.Stud.*nativ.BMV* 5(M.96.685B); as ἡ ἀληθὴς θ. Eus.*d.e.*1.1(p.3.14; M.22.16C); ἡ σάρκωσις τοῦ μονογενοῦς φωταγωγεῖ τοὺς ἀνθρώπους πρὸς τὴν ἀληθῆ θ. Ammon.*Jo.*1:4(M.85.1393C); Cyr.*Ps.*49:4(M.69.1077C); id.*Jo.*11.6(4.958C); and of revelation through Cross δι' αὐτοῦ τὰ τῆς θ. ἔργα πᾶσι πεφανέρωται Ath.*gent.*1(M.25.4B); Cyr.H.*catech.*13.40; **6.** of Christianity; **a.** in gen., ref. Jews and idolaters μήπω τὸ φῶς τῆς ἀληθείας ἐσχηκότας καὶ θ. Or.*adnot.in Dt.* 27:18(M.17.33C); cf.*ib.*27:17(33C); ref. heretics μὴ παρ' αὐτοῖς ἔνι θ., ἀλλ' ἐν μόνῃ τῇ καθολικῇ ἐκκλησίᾳ Ath.*ep.Marcell.*21(M.27.33C); ἄγονος...ἡ ἔξωθεν παίδευσις...πρὶν εἰς τὸ φῶς ἐλθεῖν τῆς θ. Gr.Nyss.*v.Mos.*(M.44.329B); καλεῖ πρὸς θ. τὴν ἀληθῆ...τὸ κήρυγμα τὸ εὐαγγελικόν Cyr.*Arcad.*(p.74.28; 5².61B); Jo.V H.*icon.*11(M.96.1357D); **b.** as prophesied, Eus.*d.e.*1.1(p.5.1; M.22.17D); †Bas.*Is.*159(1.492A; M.30.380B); τὴν ἐσομένην τοῖς ἔθνεσι θ. προλέγων Thdt.*Jer.*10:7(2.464); id.*Ps.*103:31(1.1341); Proc.G.*Is.*55:1–13(M.87.2553C); *ib.*41:1–7 (2349C); **c.** resting on faith τῆς θ. ... κεφάλαιόν ἐστιν ἡ εἰς τὸν υἱὸν πίστις Gr.Nyss.*Pss.titt.*A 5(M.44.504A); faith playing a larger part than reason in acceptance of Christianity, Chrys.*hom.4.2 in 1Cor.* (10.26C); τοῖς ἐξ ἐθνῶν διὰ πίστεως κεκλημένοις εἰς θ. Cyr.*Nest.*3.3 (p.65.43; 6¹.80D); **d.** transmitted through baptism, Bas.*Spir.*35(3.29D; M.32.132A); *ib.*75(64A; M.209A); τὸ τῆς θ. μυστήριον Gr.Nyss.*Eun.*1(1 p.114.12; M.45.349A); *ib.*4(2 p.83.30; 660A); τὴν διὰ τῆς τοῦ ὕδατος παλιγγενεσίας ἐσομένην τοῖς εὐσεβέσι θ. προδηλῶν Thdt.*Ezech.* 1:3(3.681); and preaching, *Const.App.*2.26.7; Cyr.*Abac.*50(3.564A); Dam.*troph.*suppl.(p.277.10); τὸ τῆς θ. κήρυγμα †Jo.D.*B.J.*16(M.96.997C); *ib.*30(1144B); **e.** ref. apologetic function of miracles τῇ τῶν θαυμάτων σαγήνῃ πρὸς τὸ φῶς τῆς θ., ἐκ τοῦ βυθοῦ τῆς ἀγνωσίας αὐτοὺς...ἀνήγαγον ‡Cyr.*Trin.*1(6³.2C; M.77.1121B) = Jo.D.*f.o.*1.3 (M.94.793C); **f.** witnessed to by martyrdom τοῖς τῶν ἁγίων αἵμασιν ἡ θ. ᾠκοδομήθη Oecum.*Apoc.*6:9(p.91); Dion.Ar.*d.n.*7.4(M.3.873A) cit. s. ἁπλοῦς; **g.** ref. Christian revelation stimulating application of reason to divine mysteries πότε...οὕτω θ. ἐξέλαμψεν...εἰ μὴ ὅτε ὁ σταυρὸς τοῦ Χριστοῦ γέγονε; Ath.*v.Anton.*79(M.26.953A); τὸν ἀκριβῶς τὰ βάθη τοῦ μυστηρίου διασκοπούμενον,...κατὰ τὸ ἀπόρρητον μετρίαν τινὰ κατανόησιν τῆς κατὰ τὴν θ. διδασκαλίας λαβεῖν Gr.Nyss.*or.catech.*3(p.15.10; M.45.17C); **7.** ref. spiritual life, monastic τὸν...βίον τῆς θ. Bas.*reg.fus.*10.1(2.352D; M.31.945A); ref. contemplation τῷ πνευματικῷ τῆς θ. ὄρει Gr.Nyss.*hom.1 in Cant.*(M.44.773A); θεὸς ὁ ἐν ἰδίῳ πνεύματι γράφων ἡμῖν τῆς θ. τὴν ὁδόν Cyr.*Arcad.* (p.77.31; 5².65E); ref. rejoicing in suffering ἡ ἀληθὴς θ. ... δι' ἧς δυνάμεθα παρακαλεῖν τὸν θεόν Marc.Er.*opusc.*8.4(M.65.1108C); by angelic illumination, Dion.Ar.*c.h.*13.3(M.3.301D).

B. *knowledge* of Christ *as God* ἐποίει τὰ θαύματα, ὥστε αὐτοὺς εἰς τὴν ἑαυτοῦ θ. ἐπισπάσασθαι Chrys.*hom.28.3 in Mt.*(7.338A); *ib.*57.1 (619C,D).

C. *God's knowledge* τῶν σωμάτων διάλυσιν...ᾠκονόμησε γίνεσθαι κατὰ τὴν οὐσιώδη αὐτοῦ θ. Clem.*fr.*42(p.221.3; M.9.768B).

θεόγνωστος, *known to God*, Gr.Naz.*ep.*102(M.37.200C).

θεογονία, ἡ, 1. *genealogy of gods, theogony*; composed by Hesiod and other pagan writers, Athenag.*leg.*17.1(M.6.921C); Clem.*prot.*2 (p.19.31; M.8.96C); *Hom.Clem.*6.3; not to be understood as implied in Christian teaching on generation of Son, Ath.*Maced.dial.*1.12 (M.28.1309C); **2.** *divine generation* τῆς πατρικῆς θ. τὴν εἴδησιν Alex.Al.*ep.Alex.*12(p.27.10; M.18.565B); Dion.Ar.*d.n.*2.5(M.3.641D); **3.** *divine birth* (of Christ), Jo.D.*carm.theog.*tit.(M.96.817C).

[*]**θεογόνος,** *begetting God* τῆς θ. θεότητος Dion.Ar.*d.n.*2.1(M.3.637B); *ib.*2.7(645B) cit. s. θεόφυτος.

***θεόγραπτος, 1.** *written by God*, Dion.Ar.*e.h.*4.3.1(M.3.473D); CNic.(787)*act.*4(H.4.160C); **2.** *painted by God* τὴν θ. Χριστοῦ εἰκόνα Thdr.Stud.*epp.*2.108(M.99.1629B).

***θεόγραφος, 1.** *drawn, portrayed by God*; of appearance of Cross at Jerusalem at time of victory of Constantius over Magnentius, Philost.*h.e.*3.26(M.65.513A); of portrait of Christ (perh. that said to have been sent to Abgar of Edessa) carried by Heraclius in Persian campaign, Geo.Pis.*Pers.*1.150(M.92.1208A); **2.** written by God τὴν δεκάδα τῶν θ. ἐντολῶν †Cyr.*coll.VT*(6⁴.74B; M.77.1285C); spiritually interpreted πλάκας γνώσεως θ. σὺν αὐτοῖς μετὰ χεῖρας νοερὰς ἐπιφερόμενοι Jo.Clim.*scal.*25(M.88.988C); ἡ τῶν προφητῶν θ. βίβλος ‡Jo.D.*hom*.5(M.96.648C); met., of BMV θ. πλάξ Ephr.3.529E; βίβλον θ. Taras.*praesent.BMV* 8(M.98.1489A).

***θεογράφος**, *writing about God*, Geo.Pis.*hex*.1800(M.92.1573A).

θεοδέγμων, **1.** *receiving God*, Nonn.*par.Jo*.1:41(M.43.757A); *ib*. 3:32(772C); *ib*.19:38(905C); of Paradise, or of Mount of Olives θ. κῆπον *IGC As.Min*.263; of Christ's tomb, Germ.CP *or*.2(M.98. 248D); **2.** *received from God* Παῦλος, ὅλης σοφίης θεοδέγμονος ἔμπλεος ἀνήρ Paul.Sil.*Soph*.787(M.86.2149B); id.*ambo*.300(M.86.2263).

***θεόδεκτος**, *acceptable to God*, Sophr.H.*ep.syn*.(M.87.3197D); Thdr.Stud.*nativ.BMV* 7(M.96.696A).

***θεόδευτος**, *God-drenched*; of burning bush as type of BMV, Thdr.Stud.*nativ.BMV* 7(M.96.689D).

***θεοδήγητος**, *guided by God*, of emperor τῇ θ. αὐτοῦ...γαληνότητι Serg.*ep*.2(H.3.1317E); as complimentary epithet in polite address, Gr.II Papa *ep.Germ*.(M.98.148A).

***θεοδηγήτως**, *as led by God*, Gr.II Papa *ep.Germ*.(M.98.153D).

***θεόδηλος**, *revealing God*; of ephod, Leont.N.*serm*.3(M.93. 1608A) cit. ap. Jo.D.*imag*.1(M.94.1273B).

***θεόδημος**, *? to the people of God* ἡ θ. τοῦ δεσπότου κατέλαβεν αἰγληφόρος παρουσία ‡Epiph.*hom*.2(M.43.456D).

θεοδίδακτος, *taught by God*; **A.** of persons; **1.** of Christians in gen. γίνεσθε...θ., ἐκζητοῦντες, τί ζητεῖ κύριος ἀφ᾽ ὑμῶν *Barn*.21.6; αὐτοὶ θ. ἐστε Alex.Al.*ep.Alex*.35(p.25.9; M.18.561A); Chrys.*hom.54.2 in Gen*. (4.523E); **2.** of inspired prophets, Thphl.Ant.*Autol*.2.9(M.6.1064A); of Jo. Bapt. ἀληθὴς ὁ μαρτὺς θ. ὤν Cyr.*Jo*.1.7(4.62B); of S. Paul, Gr. Nyss.*Eun*.3(2 p.36.23; M.45.604B); of Antony as recipient of divine revelations, Ath.*v.Anton*.66(M.26.936C); **3.** of soul enlightened by Christian faith, Tat.*orat*.29(p.30.11; M.6.1064A); †Jo.D.*B.J*.29(M. 96.1136D).

B. of doctrine, etc.; Christian doctrine οὐκ ἀνθρωπικοῖς οὖσιν, ἀλλὰ θεοφάτοις καὶ θ. Athenag.*leg*.11.1(M.6.912A); *ib*.32.2(964B); evangelists' conception of Christ, Cyr.*Jo*.proem.(4.7A); Christian beliefs about God, opp. pagan theories, Eus.*p.e*.2.6(72D; M.21.140A); revelation of incarnate Christ θ. περὶ αὐτοῦ μυστήριον Cyr.*Jo*.4.1(4. 345B); Christian wisdom, as source of all wisdom, Clem.*str*.6.18 (p.517.28; M.9.400A); inspired utterances, such as cries of multitude on Palm Sunday, ‡Meth.*palm*.2(M.18.385D) (cf. θεολογέω E.4); a text of scripture, Isid.Pel.*epp*.1.434(M.78.421B); Lord's Prayer as taught by Christ, Cyr.H.*catech*.23.18.

***θεοδίκαστος**, *awarded by divine judgement* ὀργή τις θ. παραλαβοῦσα Thdr.Lect.*fr*.(M.86.225A) cit. ap. Jo.D.*imag*.3(M.94.1392B).

***θεοδινής**, *divinely moved*, Nonn.*par.Jo*.3:8(M.43.768A); *ib*.4:14 (776B); *ib*.6:21(797A).

***θεοδιφής**, *seeking God*, Synes.*hymn*.4.262(p.33; M.66.1608).

***θεοδόκος**, *receiving God*; of BMV, Procl.CP *annunt*.4(M.85. 437C).

***θεόδοξα**, ἡ, *glory of God*, Didym.*Ps*.18:2(M.39.1268C).

***θεοδόξαστος**, *glorified by God*, of BMV τῆς θ. κόρης Germ.CP *or*.9 (M.98.373B).

***θεοδοξία**, ἡ, *appearance of divinity*, Clem.*prot*.4(p.48.1; M.8. 161B).

***Θεοδοσιανοί**, οἱ, *Theodosians*, followers of deposed bishop Theodosius of Alexandria, who denied human ignorance in Christ, †Leont.B.*sect*.5.6(M.86.1232D).

***Θεοδοτιανοί**, οἱ, *Theodotians*, followers of Theodotus of Byzantium Θ. ψιλὸν ἄνθρωπον φάσκοντες εἶναι τὸν Χριστὸν καὶ ἐκ σπέρματος ἀνδρὸς γεγεννῆσθαι Epiph.*haer*.54.1(p.318.15; M.41.964A); Μελχισεδεκιανοὺς πάλιν ἕτεροι ἑαυτοὺς καλοῦσιν, ἀποσπασθέντες τάχα ἀπὸ τῶν Θ. καλουμένων *ib*.55.1(p.324.2; 972A).

***θεοδοχία**, ἡ, *reception of God*, Dion.Ar.*c.h*.13.3(M.3.304A).

***θεοδόχος** (*θειο-), *receiving God*; **1.** of Christ's humanity; **a.** as θ. ἄνθρωπος: Χριστὸν δὲ νῦν λέγομεν οὐ πρὸς τὸ ἀΐδιον τῆς θεότητος ἀναπέμποντες τοῦτο τὸ ὄνομα, ἀλλὰ πρὸς τὸν θ. ἄνθρωπον...ἐν ᾧ κατῴκησε πᾶν τὸ πλήρωμα τῆς θεότητος σωματικῶς Gr.Nyss.*hom. 13 in Cant*.(M.44.1056A); id.*or.catech*.32(p.116.10; M.45.80B); **b.** as θ. σάρξ or σῶμα: τοῦ θ. σώματος ἐκείνου ταύτην δεξαμένου τὴν χάριν *ib*. 37(p.148.12; 93C); ἡ θ. ἐκείνη σάρξ *ib*.(p.151.10; 97B); οὐκ ἔγνω ἡ παρθένος ὅπως ἐν τῷ σώματι αὐτῆς τὸ θ. συνέστη σῶμα id.*hom.13 in Cant*.(M.44.1053B); οὐ γὰρ γάμος αὐτοῦ τὴν θ. ἐδημιούργησε σάρκα Thdt.*eran*.1(4.64); Leont.H.*Nest*.4(M.86.1669C); ἐξ αὐτῆς τῆς νηδύος τὴν θ. σάρκα...διαπλαττόμενος Leont.N.*serm*.1(M.93.1581B); cf.Nest. *fr*.C 9(p.263.12); **2.** of BMV; **a.** as term preferred by Nestorius to θεοτόκος: cf. τὴν θ. τῷ θεῷ λόγῳ συνθεολογῶμεν μορφήν, τὴν θ. τῷ θεῷ μὴ συνθεολογῶμεν παρθένον· θ. *dico, non* θεοτόκον, δ *litteram, non* κ *exprimi volens*, Nest.*fr*.C 10(p.276.4); cf. οἶδα σεβασμίαν τὴν δεξαμένην θεόν *ib*.11(p.277.20)ap.Cyr.*Nest*.1.1(p.18.25; 6.10A); **b.** view of Nest. attacked by Cyril ἐπειδὴ δὲ αἰτιᾶται ὡς λέξιν ἀσυνήθη εἴρηκεν ἡ γραφὴ ἢ γοῦν ἡ ἁγία σύνοδος θεοτόκον ὀνομάσασα τὴν ἁγίαν παρθένον, ἐρωτάσθωσαν αὐτοὶ ποῦ Χριστοτόκον ἢ θ. εὗρον γεγραμμένον. πρὸς τούτῳ ἐνέθηκεν αὐταῖς λέξεσιν οὕτως· τὴν θ. τῷ θεῷ μὴ συνθεολογῶμεν παρθένον, οὐκ εἰδὼς ὃ λέγει. εἰ γὰρ μὴ τέτοκε θεόν...πῶς ἔτι θ. ἐστίν; Cyr.*ep*.10(p.111.35; 5^2.35B); and others εἰ δὲ θεὸς...τὸ ἐκ τῆς παρθένου τεχθέν, πῶς οὐ θεοτόκος ἡ παρθένος, ἀλλὰ θ.; ‡Ath.*nativ.Chr*.4(M.28.965A); **c.** in orthodox use ἐπὶ τὴν θέαν τοῦ ζωαρχικοῦ καὶ θ. σώματος συνεληλύθαμεν Dion.Ar.*d.n*.3.2(M.3.681C); cf. θ. σῶμα τάχα τὸ τῆς ἁγίας θεοτόκου λέγει Max.*schol.d.n*.3.2(M.4. 236C); ἡ θ. κυοφόρος παρθένος Sophr.H.*or*.2.32(M.87.3256C); κύριος... ἁγιάσας αὐτὴν εἶναι θ. χωρίον, ἐν ᾧ ὁ...πατὴρ...γέγονε γεωργός Mod. *dorm*.2(M.86.3284B); ἡ μυστικὴ κλεὶς τῆς θ. πύλης Geo.Pis.*hex*.1785 (M.92.1572A); σῶμά σου θ. Jo.D.*carm.dorm.BMV* 48(p.229; M.96. 1364C); νέος ναὸς ἡ νέα κόρη ἀνίσταται θ. ναός Jo.Eub.*concept.BMV* 15(M.96.1484B); σὲ προετύπου στάμνος ἡ μαννοδόχος, ὑπέραγνε, τὴν θ. τράπεζαν Jo.Mon.*hymn.Nic.Myr*.3(M.96.1384D); **3.** of Simeon, ‡Cyr.H.*occurs*.tit.(M.33.1187); τὸν θ. πρεσβύτην ‡Meth.*Sym.et Ann*. 11(M.18.373D); **4.** of land of Palestine ἐν χθονὶ θειοδόχῳ Sophr.H. *mir.Cyr.et Jo*.(M.87.3421D); esp. Bethlehem, id.*nativ*.(p.513.6); **5.** of the intelligence πρὸς τῶν θ. ... ὑμνεῖσθαι νοῶν Dion.Ar.*c.h*.7.4(M.3. 212C); **6.** of power to attain communion with God τῆς γνωστικῆς, τῆς θ. δυνάμεως μετέχουσι *ib*.13.3(304A); **7.** of grace to know God τῆς θ. χάριτος ἀμοιρήσαντες Gr.Nyss.*v.Mos*.(M.44.321B).

***θεοδρόμος**, **1.** as adj.; **a.** *pursuing divine course* τῶν ἁγίων πατέρων θ. σύνοδος ‡Jo.D.*ep.Thphl*.8(M.94.356A); **b.** *moving to God*; of star of Bethlehem, ‡Serg.*acath*.97(p.142; M.92.1340C); **2.** as subst., *runner in God's race*, Ign.*Philad*.2.2; id.*Polyc*.7.2.

***θεόδροσος**, *bedewed by God*; of Gideon's fleece as typifying BMV, ‡Sophr.H.*triod*.(M.87.3860A).

θεοδώρητος, *God-given*; in gen., of fish of Mt.17:27, Clem.*paed*. 2.1(p.163.18; M.8.400A); id.*str*.6.17(p.513.1; M.9.389A); Jo.Mosch. *prat*.80(M.87.2937C); of emperor θ. κράτος Hadr.Papa *ep.Const*. M.*PL*.96.1218D); of Hebrew tongue as θ. διάλεκτος, Or.*Cels*.3.7 (p.208.15; M.11.929A); of grace, Clem.*str*.6.7(p.459.28; 277B); knowledge, *ib*.8.1(p.80.16; 560A); virginity, Meth.*symp*.3.14(p.44.1; M. 18.84C); wisdom, Eus.*Marcell*.1.3(p.16.29; M.24.748D); works of holy men, Pall.*h.Laus*.61(p.157.14; M.34.1233B); providential signs of vocation, Isid.Pel.*epp*.4.172(M.78.1264C); God's commandments, †Cyr.*coll.VT*(6^4.74C; M.77.1285D); baptism as θ. ἀναγέννησις, *Hom. Clem*.11.35.

θεοείδεια, ἡ, *divine likeness* τὸν...ἁπάσης ἱεραρχίας σκοπὸν τῆς θεομιμήτου θ. ἐξηρτημένον Dion.Ar.*c.h*.7.2(M.3.208A); cf.*ib*.8.1(237C); id.*d.n*.4.22(M.3.724B).

θεοειδής, *Godlike*; **1.** in gen., *like God*, in Gnost. idea of human body τὰ...μέχρις ὀμφαλοῦ θεοειδεστέρας τέχνης εἶναι Clem.*str*.3.4 (p.211.9; M.8.1137B); of the rational soul, Eus.*p.e*.6.6(249B; M.21. 424B); of man ζῷον...θεοειδέστατον Cyr.*glaph.Gen*.1.2(1.5C); of vision of Moses, Clem.*paed*.2.8(p.203.16; M.8.488A); Max.*ambig*.(M. 91.1117C); **2.** ref. Inc. (Marcionite) θ. ... τὸ σῶμα ἐν ὁμοιώσει τῇ καθ᾽ ἡμᾶς μόνῃ ‡Ath.*Apoll*.1.12(M.26.1116A); of man as result of redemption θ. εὑρισκόμενοι Sophr.H.*or*.2.48(M.87.3284C); Max.*ambig*. (M.91.1040D); **3.** ref. sacraments, of effect of baptism ἡ φύσις... ἀνακαινιζομένη κατ᾽ εἰκόνα τοῦ κτίσαντος ἐν ἀρχῇ τὸ θ. ὁμοίωμα Gr. Nyss.*Eun*.2(2 p.297.16; M.45.468C); ref. baptismal renunciation τῇ ...θ. τῶν ἐναντίων ἀπαθείᾳ Dion.Ar.*e.h*.2.3.8(M.3.404C); ref. sacraments in gen. τῇ τῶν διαιρετῶν θ. συμπτύξει τὴν πρὸς τὸ ἓν κοινωνίαν καὶ ἕνωσιν *ib*.3.1(424C); cf.*ib*.3.3.4(429C); ref. liturg. symbolism, *ib*.3.3.3(428D); **4.** ref. virtue σωφροσύνη ἡ θ. Gr.Thaum.*pan. Or*.12(p.28.14; M.10.1085B); σωφροσύνης καὶ δικαιοσύνης ποιούσης ἡμᾶς θ. Euthal.Diac.*epp.Paul*.(M.85.764A); ἡ θ. ἀρετή Dion.Ar.*e.h*. 4.3.1(M.3.473B); οὐδὲν...τῆς θείας ἀγάπης θεοειδέστερον Max.*ambig*. (M.91.393B); **5.** of Christians θ. ... ὁ ἀγαθὸς ἀνὴρ κατὰ ψυχήν Clem. *str*.6.9(p.468.6; M.9.293B); of the perfect, Gr.Thaum.*pan.Or*.9(p.23. 4; M.10.1077D); τὰς νοερὰς φύσεις θ. ἀπεργάζεται [sc. God] Gr. Naz.*or*.21.1(M.35.1084A); in gen., Gr.Nyss.*or.catech*.5(p.25.5; M.45. 24B); οἱ θ. Dion.Ar.*e.h*.7.3.6(M.3.560C); **6.** of angels ἑκάστη τῶν περὶ θεὸν διακόσμησις θεοειδεστέρα τῆς μᾶλλον ἀφεστηκυίας ἐστί id. *ep*.8.2(M.3.1092B); τῆς θ. αὐτῶν ἱερώσεως id.*c.h*.1.3(M.3.124A); θ. νόας *ib*.2.1(137A); **7.** neut. as subst., *likeness to God*, Meth.*res*.1.35 (p.274.4; M.18.292C); τὸ θ. τοῦτο καὶ θεῖον...τὸν ἡμέτερον νοῦν τε καὶ λόγον Gr.Naz.*or*.28.17(p.47.18; M.36.48C); Gr.Nyss.*or.catech*.6 (p.32.7; M.45.28A); ref. angels, Dion.Ar.*c.h*.5(M.3.196C); Max.*schol. c.h*.13.4(M.4.101A).

θεοειδῶς, **1.** *like God*, ref. angels τὸ θ. εἶναι ἔχουσι Dion.Ar.*d.n*.5.8 (M.3.821C); θ. κατὰ τὸ ἐφικτὸν τὰ πάντα εἰσόμεθα Max.*ambig*.(M.91.

1088A); **2.** *by God, divinely* τὰ θ. ἡμῖν ἐκ τῶν ἱερῶν λογίων ἐκπεφασμένα Dion.Ar.*d.n.*1.2(M.3.588C).

θεοείκελος, *Godlike*; **1.** in gen.; of virginity, Gr.Naz.*carm.*1.2.1.51 (M.37.526A); *ib.*1.2.1.728(577A); exeg. Cant.5:16 οὗ τὸ κάλλος... ἐστι...θ. Gr.Nyss.*hom.14 in Cant.*(M.44.1080D); **2.** of man; **a.** in gen., Clem.*prot.*12(p.85.16; M.8.244A); **b.** ref. soul θ. ὁ ἀγαθὸς ἀνὴρ κατὰ ψυχήν id.*str.*6.9(p.468.6; M.9.293B); Meth.*symp.*6.1(p.64.22; M.18.113C); τὸ θ. δεδωρημένος [i.e. Christ to the soul], ἄφθαρτον φύσιν, ἀσώματον, λογικήν Eus.*h.e.*10.4.56(M.20.872A); of soul before Fall, id.*p.e.*7.18(332D; M.21.561B); **c.** of the body, Meth.*res.*3.15 (p.411.28; M.18.317A); **d.** of Adam, ‡Nil.*perist.*10.4(M.79.892D); **e.** of Dion. Ar., Max.*ambig.*(M.91.1289A).

***θεοεπαίνετος**, *praised by God*, ‡Meth.*Sym.et Ann.*10(M.18.373B).

θεοεχθρία, ἡ, *enmity towards God*, Eus.*d.e.*3.3(p.113.20; M.22.193D); id.*h.e.*3.17(M.20.249C).

***θεόζευκτος**, *yoked together by God*, Amph.*hom.*2.7(M.39.53D).

***θεόζηλος**, *zealous for God*, Thdr.Stud.*epp.*1.53(M.99.1101C).

***θεοήφαντος**, v. *θεούφαντος.

***θεοηχής**, *filled with the sound of God's voice* θ. ... ἀκοάς Taras.*ep.*1(M.98.1436B).

***θεοθαρσής**, *confident in God*, Leont.H.*monoph.*testimonia(M.86.1853A).

***θεοθεμελίωτος**, *founded by God*; of empire, Agath.Papa *ep.imp.* (M.*PL.*87.1174A).

***θεοθεράπευτος**, *of divine healing*, ‡Chrys.*hom.*13(13.255E).

***θεόθετος**, *set by God*, of BMV χαῖρε, τράπεζα, τὸ θ. κρᾶμα Thdr. Stud.*nativ.BMV* 7(M.96.689C).

***θεοΐδρυτος**, *established by God*, Mod.*dorm.*10(M.86.3305A).

***θεοκάπηλος**, *trading in divine things*; of Athanasius' opponents, Gr.Naz.*or.*21.31(M.35.1117C); simoniacal priests, Isid.Pel.*epp.*1.106 (M.78.253C); false teachers, Olymp.*fr.Lam.*4:10(M.93.753B).

***θεοκαταγνώστης, ὁ**, *one who condemns God*, of heretics θ., οἱ καὶ βλάσφημοι Jo.D.*haer.*92(M.94.757B).

θεοκατάρατος, *cursed by God*; of Jews, Leont.Abb.*v.Gr.Agr.*73 (M.98.680A).

***θεοκατασκεύαστος**, *divinely wrought*, of BMV θ. κιβωτός Thdr. Stud.*or.*5.1(M.99.721A).

***θεοκατήγορος, ὁ**, *accuser of God*, Thdr.Stud.*epp.*1.49(M.99.1088C).

***θεοκατόρθωτος**, *directed by God*, Agath.Papa *ep.imp.*(M.*PL.*87.1166A).

***θεοκάτοχος**, *held by God*, Tim.Ant.*Sym.*(M.86.237C).

θεοκέλευστος, *ordained by God*, †Gregent.*leg.Hom.*61(M.86.613C); †Gregent.*disp.*(M.86.781D).

***θεοκήρυκτος**, *proclaimed by God*, ‡Jo.D.*ep.Thphl.*30(M.95.384C).

θεοκῆρυξ, ὁ, *herald of God*, Leont.N.*v.Jo.Eleem.*13(p.27.2); *ib.* proem.(in v.l. p.4n.).

θεοκίνητος, *moved by God* τῆς θ. τῶν προφητῶν ὑμνολογίας Dion. Ar.*e.h.*4.3.12(M.3.485B); ref. BMV τὸ τῶν σεραφὶμ ἑξαπτέρυγον ψυχῆς θ. πτεροῖς ὑπερβέβηκας Sophr.H.*or.*2.18(M.87.3237C); of lips, Thdr. Stud.*or.*5.2(M.99.721B); of Christ's human nature, Serg.*ep.*ap. CCP(681)*act.*12(H.3.1317A).

***θεοκλητέω**, v. θεοκλυτέω.

θεόκλητος, **1.** *called by God* λόγου ἡ Βηθλεὲμ πατρὶς θ. ἐλέχθη *Orac. Sib.*8.479; Nonn.*par.Jo.*1:22(M.43.753A); ‡Meth.*Sym.et Ann.*11(M.18.376A); **2.** *called by God's name* θ. δ' ἐνὶ νηῷ Nonn.*par.Jo.*2:14(M.43.764A); *ib.*4:21(777B); *ib.*9:22(828C).

θεοκλυτ-έω, **1.** *call on God*, ‡Gr.Naz.*Chr.pat.*811(M.38.201A); **2.** *call on as divine*, cf. τῶν ἄστρων ποιοῦνται τὴν θεωρίαν...διὰ τῶν εὐχῶν ~οῦντες Porphyry ap.Eus.*p.e.*9.2(404B; M.21.681B); **3.** *be inspired, speak with God's voice*, Cyr.*Is.*2.4(2.289C); -κλητέω *ib.*4.3 (2.648C); id.*ador.*6(1.192A); id.*hom.pasch.*14(5^2.193C); id.*Juln.*1(6^2.25B); *ib.*2(59C); pass. ἃ δεῖ πρὸς ἑκάστην τῶν ἐκκλησιῶν τὸν ταῦτα ~ούμενον διαμαρτύρεσθαι Areth.*Apoc.*2(M.106.525A).

***θεοκλυτία, ἡ**, *word inspired by God, inspiration*, Areth.*Apoc.*5 (M.106.536B); ἀστέρα τοῦτον διδόναι ἡ θ. ἐπαγγέλλεται *ib.*6(548A).

θεόκλυτος, *inspired*, *Orac.Sib.*14.301.

θεόκμητος, *wrought by God*, Nonn.*par.Jo.*20:18(M.43.912A).

***θεοκοίρανος**, *ruling as God*, Synes.*hymn.*1.83(p.61; M.66.1589).

θεόκραντος, *? veiling God*, Paul.Sil.*Soph.*770(M.86.2148B).

***θεοκρισία, ἡ**, *divine judgement*, Dion.Ar.*c.h.*8.2(M.3.241B); *ib.* 15.5(333B).

θεόκριτος, *determined by God*, Dion.Ar.*ep.*8.1(M.3.1085A); Geo. Pis.*Sev.*559(M.92.1664A); Max.*opusc.*(M.91.73B).

***θεοκρίτως**, *by the judgement of God*, *Libell.*ap.CLater.*act.*2(H.3.721B); Gr.Agr.*Eccl.*4.3(M.98.925B).

***θεοκρυφής**, *concealing God*, Geo.Pis.*hex.*1489(M.92.1549A).

***θεόκταντος**, *killed at the divine command*, Thphn.*chron.*p.44(M.108.165C); *ib.*p.414(981C).

θεόκτιστος, *created by God*, Marc.Er.*opusc.*4(M.65.996B); Anast.S. *serm.imag.*3(M.89.1169A).

***θεοκτονία, ἡ**, *slaying of God*, ‡Caes.Naz.*dial.*170(M.38.1133).

***θεοκτόνος**, *slaying God*; **1.** of those responsible for Christ's death, Gr.Naz.*carm.*1.1.10.11(M.37.466A); esp. of Jews, Euther.*confut.*3(M.28.1377A); Isid.Pel.ap.*cat.Mt.*suppl.(p.256.18); Leont.H.*Nest.*7.2(M.86.1764B); ‡Caes.Naz.*dial.*118(M.38.1004); θ. φθόνου Geo.Pis.*res.*61 (M.92.1380A); **2.** as subst.; **a.** of Jews, Gr.Naz.*carm.*1.2.34.250(M.37.963A); Cyr.*Ps.*58:6(M.69.1112C); Leont.B.*Nest.et Eut.*2(M.86.1336B); Max.*ambig.*(M.91.1129D); ‡Ath.*azym.*(M.26.1329B) = ‡Jo.D. *azym.*2(M.95.393B); **b.** of heretics, Gr.Naz.*ep.*101(M.37.180B); Σαμοσατῖται...θ. ... γεγονότες Epiph.*haer.*65.2(p.5.3; M.42.13D).

***θεόκτυπος**, *sounding from God*, Cosm.Mel.*hymn.*10(5.167; M.98.497B).

***θεοκυβέρνητος**, *God-controlled*, ‡Jo.D.*hom.*6.9(M.96.676A).

***θεοκυήτωρ**, *conceiving God*; of BMV, ‡Sophr.H.*triod.*(M.87.3897C); *ib.*(3960D).

***θεοκύμων**, **1.** *conceiving God*; of BMV, Paul.Sil.*Soph.*803(M.86.2150A); **2.** *born of God*, Synes.*hymn.*1.10(p.57; M.66.1588).

***θεοκύρωτος**, *ratified by God*, ‡Jo.D.*ep.Thphl.*30(M.95.384D).

***θεολαμπής**, *shining with divine light*, Gr.Naz.*carm.*2.2(poem.)7.118(M.37.1560A); Thdot.Anc.*hom.BMV et Sym.*3(M.77.1393B).

***θεολάμπω**, *shine with divine light*, Jo.D.*carm.transfig.*(M.96.848C).

***θεολάξευτος**, *carved by God*, of BMV θ. λύχνον Taras.*praesent. BMV* 8(M.98.1489C).

***θεολατρέω**, *worship God*, Meth.*res.*2.4(p.335.19; M.41.1168D).

***θεόλεκτος**, **1.** *uttered by God, inspired* προφῆται, ἀπόστολοι...καὶ τὰς θ. αὐτῶν φωνάς Eulog.*palm.*3(M.86.2920A); Sophr.H.*v.Cyr.et Jo.* 27(M.87.3413B); Germ.CP *or.*2(M.98.264D); θ. εὐαγγελίων ‡Jo.D. *ep.Thphl.*30(M.95.384C); **2.** *chosen by God* τοῦ...Ἄβελ τὴν θ. ... προσφοράν Gr.Nyss.*v.Ephr.*(M.46.841D); Const.Diac.*laud.*1(M.88.480A); Leont.N.*v.Sym.*proem.4(M.93.1673A); Jo.D.*hom.*9.6(M.96.732B).

***θεόλεστος**, *cursed* τὰ θ. πτώματα ‡Jo.D.*Artem.*70(in v.l. p.110.14n.); of heretics, Jo.D.*Man.*1.67(M.94.1561C); in gen., Thphn. *chron.*p.423(M.108.1001B).

θεοληπτέομαι, *be possessed by God*, Nil.*Magn.*23(M.79.1000A).

θεοληπτικός, *inspired*; superl., ‡Thdt.*nativ.Jo.Bapt.*(5.92).

θεόληπτος, **1.** *chosen by God*; of Aaron, Pall.*v.Chrys.*1(p.5.4; M.47.6); of S. Paul, Jo.D.*hymn.dorm.BMV* 76(p.230; M.96.1365A); **2.** *inspired, possessed by God*; of Moses, Cyr.*dogm.*6(6^2.374B; θεσπέσιος p.558.14); David, id.*Joel.*45(Aubert; μακάριος 3.245B); prophets, †Bas.*Is.*proem.5(1.381B; M.30.125B); Dion.Ar.*e.h.*4.3.12(M.3.485A); id.*d.n.*2.1(M.3.637A); prophetesses, Bas.Sel.*v.Thecl.*1(M.85.492A); martyrs, Const.Diac.*laud.*26(M.88.508D); divines, Sophr.H. *ep.syn.*(M.87.3157B); Jo.VI CP *ep.*(M.96.1432D).

θεοληψία, ἡ, *inspiration*; of prophets, Eus.*d.e.*5 proem.(p.202.18; M.22.336B); cf.*ib.*(p.206.33).

θεολογ-έω, *speak of God*;

A. *speculate* or *teach about God*; **1.** ref. scope of this activity, its basis in Christ's teaching ~ῶν ἀπήγγειλε τὰ περὶ θεοῦ τοῖς γνησίοις αὐτοῦ μαθηταῖς· ὧν ἴχνη ἐν τοῖς γεγραμμένοις εὑρίσκοντες ἀφορμὰς ἔχομεν ~εῖν Or.*Cels.*2.71(p.193.16; M.11.908B); such speculation likened to looking at reflections of sun in water, Gr.Naz.*or.*28.3 (p.26.3; M.36.29B); ref. allegorical interpretation of scripture ἀποστρέφει κατὰ τὴν τῶν ὑπὸ φύσιν καὶ χρόνον ἀφαίρεσιν, ἀποφατικῶς ~ούμενος ‡Proc.G.*Pr.*23:5(M.87.1452A); speculation not to be perpetual, ref. Ps.1:2 οὐ τὸ μεμνῆσθαι [sc. θεοῦ] διηνεκῶς κωλύω, τὸ θ. δέ Gr.Naz.*or.*27.4(p.7.2; 16C); **2.** in gen., ref. Trin., Bas.*hom.in Ps.*28 (1.115C; M.29.284C); Gr.Naz.*or.*34.15(M.36.253C); μίαν τῶν τριῶν ὑποστάσεων ὁμοφυῆ θεότητα ἐθεολογήσας Jo.Mon.*hymn.Bas.*(M.96.1372C); Jo.D.*hom.*12.9(M.96.793B); ref. Son, exeg. Jo.1:1 ὁ Ἰωάννης, περὶ τοῦ υἱοῦ ~ῶν Ath.*Ar.*2.58(M.26.269B); Gr.Naz.*ep.*58(M.37.116A); Cyr.*deip.BMV* 7(p.21.41; M.76.264B); Procl.CP ap.Anast.S. *hod.*7(M.89.117B); **3.** in scripture αἱ γραφαὶ θ. τὸν θεὸν καθ' αὐτόν Or.*hom.18.6 in Jer.*(p.158.9; M.13.476A); cf.id.*Cels.*4.99(p.373.25; M.11.1180C); προφῆται καὶ ἀπόστολοι καὶ μᾶλλον αὐτὸν [sc. Son] τῶν ἄλλων θεολογήσαντες ἀνθρώπων Meth.*symp.*7.1(p.71.11; M.18.124A); Eus.*e.th.*1.20(p.96.17; M.24.893A); id.*h.e.*1.2.5(M.20.56B); Gr.Nyss. *Eun.*4(2 p.61.8; M.45.632C); Procl.CP *or.*2.5(M.65.697D); of S. John ὥσπερ ἐν τῷ εὐαγγελίῳ, ἐν ταύτῃ τῇ ἐπιστολῇ ~εῖ περὶ τοῦ λόγου Euthal.Diac.*epp.cath.*(M.85.684C); Cyr.*Arcad.*(p.109.4; 5^2.112D);

Hymn.(*AS* 1 p.506); of S. Paul Τιμοθέῳ δὲ γράψας, εἰς ἄκρον ἐθεολόγησεν περὶ αὐτοῦ [sc. Christ] Didym.*Trin.*1.27(M.39.404A); Chrys. *hom.18.1 in 1Tim.*(11.654D); allegorical, ref. Spouse in Cant. τοῖς πνευματικοῖς τελειωθεῖσα, ~οῦσά σου τὸ μετὰ πατρὸς καὶ πνεύματος ὁμοούσιον Proc.G.*Cant.*7:13(M.87.1769A); **4.** pagan speculation contrasted with Christian μὴ δυνηθέντες δὲ εἰς τὸ μέγεθος τοῦ ὄντως θεοῦ ἐκτεῖναι τὸν νοῦν, ταῦτα ἐθεολόγησαν Hipp.*haer.*4.41(p.65.8; M.16.3106A); ταῦτα...μυθολογοῦσιν [sc. pagans]· οὐ γὰρ θ. Ath.*gent.*19(M.25.40C); **5.** ptcpl. pass. neut. as subst., *doctrine*, Ammon.*Jo.*1:8 (M.85.1396C); Dion.Ar.*d.n.*3.3(M.3.684A); Max.*prol.Dion.*(M.4.20B).

B. *speak of God* in prayer, hence *praise*, Or.*schol.in Cant.*7:1(M.17.280D); προσευχόμενοι μὴ βαττολογήσωμεν ἀλλὰ θ. id.*or.*21.1(p.345.3; M.11.480C); ref. 1Tim.6:15 ὁ ἀπόστολος ~ῶν τὸν πατέρα Eus.*e.th.*2.23(p.133.18; M.24.961A); Procl.CP *annunt.*5(M.85.448A); ref. angels, Eus.*l.C.*1(p.198.17; M.20.1324A); ‡Cyr.H.*occurs.*14(M.33.1201A); Didym.*Ps.*18:2(M.39.1268B); Eulog.*palm.*4(M.86.2920B).

C. *think of, speak of as God* τοῖς τελείοις ~εῖται, καὶ ἐν τῇ τοῦ θεοῦ μορφῇ κατὰ τὴν γνῶσιν αὐτῶν θεωρεῖται Or.*schol.in Lc.*9:31(M.17.344C); ~εῖται μὲν ὁ λόγος, γενεαλογεῖται δὲ ἄνθρωπος ‡Ath.*Apoll.*2.16(M.26.1164B); ref. μεσοπεντηκόστη as being between feasts of Resurrection (declaring Christ to be God) and of H. Ghost (declaring the latter to be Lord) ἐκεῖθεν θ. καὶ ταύτην κυριολεκτεῖ Leont.B.*mesopent.*(M.86.1977A).

D. *speak of, discuss divine truths* Ἰησοῦν ἐν παραβολαῖς ~οῦντα Dion.Ar.*ep.*8.1(M.3.1108A); ὁ...Ἰωάννης...οἷα δὴ μετὰ παρρησίας ~ῶν,...μητέρα τοῦ Ἰησοῦ προσηγόρευσεν Sev.Ant.*res.*(p.848.2; M.46.648B).

E. *acknowledge as divine*; **1.** ref. God in gen., Eus.*l.C.*12(p.234.12; M.20.1393D); τὸν ποιητὴν...τοῦ παντὸς μόνον θεὸν γνωρίζειν...καὶ μόνον διὰ τοῦ Χριστοῦ θ. id.*d.e.*3.6(p.136.15; M.22.229D); id.*Is.*35:6 (M.24.341A); **2.** Trin.; **a.** in gen. εἰ...ἄλλον τινὰ θ. καὶ κυριολογεῖν τὸ πνεῦμα τὸ ἅγιόν φατε ὑμεῖς παρὰ τὸν πατέρα τῶν ὅλων καὶ τὸν Χριστὸν αὐτοῦ, ἀποκρίνασθέ μοι Just.*dial.*56.15(M.6.601B); Ath.*ep.Serap.*1.28 (M.26.596A); ‡Ath.*annunt.*3(M.28.920C); πάντας τοὺς μὴ ~οῦντας τὴν ὁμοούσιον τριάδα κατὰ τὸν ἐν Ἀντιοχείᾳ ἐκτεθέντα τόμον, Πνευματομάχους χρῆσαι καλεῖν CCP(381)†*can.*18; οὐ πασῶν δὲ ~ουμένων τῶν οὐσιῶν, ἀλλὰ μιᾶς παρὰ πάσας, ἥτις ἐστὶ θεότης μία ἐν τριάδι Epiph.*haer.*76.51(p.405.30; M.42.624C); **b.** ref. relations of Father and Son, Or.*or.*29.10(p.386.3; M.11.536D); ὁ...λόγος...σὺν τῷ πατρὶ...ἐστι...~ούμενος Ath.*Ar.*2.71(M.26.300A); Didym.*Trin.*1.27(M.39.393B); *ib.*(405B); εἰ οὐκ ἐστὶ προσκυνητός, πῶς ἄρα ~εῖται; Epiph.*haer.*69.31 (p.180.16; M.42.252B); in anti-Arian argument μωρὸν τὸ κτίσιν ~εῖν *ib.*69.36(p.184.19; 257C); Gennad.*fr.*3(p.77.19); **c.** ref. H. Ghost ~ούμενον μετὰ τοῦ λόγου Ath.*ep.Serap.*1.31(M.26.601A); **3.** of Father τῆς τοῦ Χριστοῦ ἐκκλησίας...ἐν ᾗ μόνος ὁ θεὸς καὶ πατὴρ ἐθεολογεῖτο Didym.*Trin.*1.25(M.39.380B); **4.** of Christ, in gen. ὁ νῦν ~ούμενος υἱὸς λόγος Or.*Jo.*2.1(p.52.17; M.14.105A); id.*fr.3 in Jo.*(p.486.29); cf.*ib.*6(p.488.6); Eus.*l.C.*11(p.226.23; M.20.1380D); of orthodox opp. Arians τῶν τὸν δεσπότην Χριστὸν ~ούντων Thdt.*h.e.*4.25.3(3.1002); cf.*ib.*5.32.3(1071); of his divinity as acknowledged in OT: Gen. 19:24 Μωσῆς...δύο θ. κυρίους Eus.*p.e.*11.14(532A; M.21.884A); Ps. 44:7,8, Cyr.*deip.BMV* 7(p.21.41; M.76.264); in NT ὁ ~ούμενος ὑπὸ τοῦ εὐαγγελιστοῦ [sc. S. John] Eus.*e.th.*2.14(p.116.14; M.24.929C); ref. Col.1:15–17 τὰς ἀποστολικὰς φωνάς, δι' ὧν τὸν υἱὸν τοῦ θεοῦ ~εῖ id.*Marcell.*2.3(p.44.26; M.24.800B); *ib.*3.6(p.164.30; 1016A); Cyr.ap. *cat.Heb.*1:2(p.292.34); by other witnesses: Jo. Bapt., Eus.*e.th.*1.20 (p.83.17; 869B); S. Peter in Ac.2 φανερώτερον αὐτὸν ἐθεολόγει Cyr. *deip.BMV* 21(p.28.41; 281B); ref. Mc.3:12, Dion.Ar.*ep.*8.1(M.3.1089B); children on Palm Sunday, Eulog.*palm.*10(M.86.2932B); Christian writers γράμματα...Ἰουστίνου καὶ Μιλτιάδου καὶ Τατιανοῦ καὶ Κλήμεντος καὶ ἑτέρων πλειόνων, ἐν οἷς ἅπασι ~εῖται ὁ Χριστός †Hipp.*Artem.*ap.Eus.*h.e.*5.28.4(M.20.512C); Christol. of the humanity ἡ σὰρξ αὐτοῦ σὺν αὐτῷ ἐθεολογήθη Ath.*inc.et c.Ar.*3(M.26.989A); Socr.*h.e.*3.23.45(M.67.445B); Anast.S.*hod.*12(M.89.200D) cit. s. ἀνθρωπολογέω; in heret. sense τὴν ἐν ταῖς θείαις γραφαῖς περὶ τοῦ μονογενοῦς υἱοῦ τοῦ θεοῦ φερομένην θεολογίαν ἐπὶ τὴν σάρκα μεταφέρει [sc. Marcellus], αὐτὸν μὲν τὸν ἀληθῶς προόντα τοῦ θεοῦ υἱὸν ἀρνούμενος, τὴν δὲ σάρκα ~ῶν Eus.*Marcell.*2.2(p.43.22; 797A); Apoll.*ep. Dion.*10(p.260.19; M.*PL.*8.935A) cit. s. ἀνθρωπολογέω; ὅτι τῇ ἑνώσει τῇ πρὸς τὸν θεὸν λόγον ~ουμένη...ἡ τοῦ κυρίου σάρξ Val.Apoll.*apol.* 1(p.287.26)ap.Leont.B.*Apoll.*(M.86.1953A); **5.** of H. Ghost ὁ...μὴ ~ῶν τὸ πνεῦμα τὸ ἅγιον, διαλύει τὸ βάπτισμα Or.*exp.in Pr.*22:28(M.17.221B); opp. Pneumatomachoi ~εῖτε καὶ ὑμεῖς, ὡς οἱ Ἀρειανοὶ καὶ Ἕλληνες, τὴν κτίσιν Ath.*ep.Serap.*1.29(M.26.597A); in gen., Gr.Naz. *or.*23.12(M.35.1164C); ref. 1Jo.5:6,10 Ἰωάννης...βοᾷ περὶ τοῦ πνεύματος τοῦ ἁγίου ~ῶν αὐτό Gel.Cyz.*h.e.*2.21.15(M.85.1285C); ref. 2Cor.3:17, 1Cor.12:4,6 σαφεστάτη...ἀπόδειξις ~οῦσα τὸ πνεῦμα *ib.*2.21.25(1288D); **6.** *deify*; of men deified in India, Clem.*str.*1.15(p.42.22; M.8.769B); Eus.*d.e.*3.4(p.118.2; M.22.201B); ref. Rom.1:25 τὴν μέμψιν τὴν...ἐπὶ τοῖς τὴν κτίσιν ~οῦσι Epiph.*haer.*64.8(p.417.22; M.41.1081A); κολάσει τοὺς ~οῦντας αὐτοῦ τὰ ποιήματα Zach.Mit. *opif.*(M.85.1132C); κρήνας καὶ ποταμοὺς θ. ‡Caes.Naz.*dial.*50(M.38.921).

θεολογία, ἡ, A. *teaching about God, about the divinity*; **1.** in gen. ἡ περὶ τοῦ τῶν ὅλων ποιητοῦ τε καὶ δημιουργοῦ θ. Eus.*p.e.*11.7(520C; M.21.864A); Bas.*Spir.*12(3.9C; M.32.85A); Gr.Naz.*or.*23.6(M.35.1157A); ἀνέμιξε [sc. psalmist]...θ. τοῖς λόγοις, καὶ προφητείαν Thdt. *Ps.*35:1(1.829); id.*qu.19 in Gen.*(1.24); **2.** its nature and scope πάνυ κεκρυμμένως εἴρηται [i.e. in scripture] διὰ τοὺς...μὴ δυναμένους παρακολουθῆσαι μεγαλονοίᾳ καὶ σεμνότητι θεολογίας Or.*Cels.*6.18 (p.89.13; M.11.1317C); ὁ θεῖος Βαρθολομαῖός φησι, καὶ πολλὴν τὴν θ. εἶναι καὶ ἐλαχίστην...ἐμοὶ δοκεῖ ἐκεῖνο ὑπερφυῶς ἐννοήσας, ὅτι καὶ πολύλογός ἐστιν ἡ ἀγαθὴ πάντων αἰτία, καὶ βραχύλεκτος ἅμα καὶ ἄλογος Dion.Ar.*myst.*1.3(M.3.1000B); διττὴ γὰρ ἡ θ. ὧν ἡ πρώτη περὶ τῆς ὑπάρξεως αὐτοῦ διαλέγεται·...κατὰ γὰρ τὴν δευτέραν, δυνατὸν αὐτοῦ θεωρεῖσθαι τὸ πρόσωπον Proc.G.*Ex.*33:20(M.87.677C); **3.** Trin. πολλὴν θ. σχέσιν τε πατρὸς πρὸς υἱὸν καὶ υἱοῦ πρὸς πατέρα ἔστι μαθεῖν...ἀπὸ τῶν προφητῶν Or.*Jo.*2.34(28; p.92.15; M.14.176A); Ath. *Ar.*1.18(M.26.49A); ἐπὶ δὲ τῆς θ. μίαν φύσιν ὁμολογοῦμεν τῆς ἁγίας τριάδος, τρεῖς δὲ ὑποστάσεις ‡Ath.*def.*8(M.28.537B); ref. Gen.1:27 τὸ γοῦν προοίμιον τῆς ἡμετέρας γενέσεως, θ. κατανενόηται ἀληθινή ‡Bas.*struct.hom.*1.3(1.325F; M.30.13C); Gr.Naz.*or.*28.1(p.21.11; M.36.25C); of Nicene teaching ἡ θ. *ib.*25.8(M.35.1209B); ἡ περὶ τῆς ἁγίας τριάδος θ. †Cyr.*coll.VT*(6[4].8A; M.77.1185C); Thdt.*h.e.*2.31.8(3.909); περὶ ἑνωμένης καὶ διακεκριμένης θ. Dion.Ar.*d.n.*2 tit.(M.3.636B); **4.** ref. Christ ἡ περὶ τοῦ σωτῆρος θ. Or.*Jo.*1.24(23; p.30.13; M.14.65D); Eus.*h.e.*2 proem.1(M.20.132C); as subject-matter of Heb.1 θ. Χριστοῦ ἐν δόξῃ πατρὸς καὶ ἐξουσίᾳ τῶν παντῶν Euthal.*epp.cath.*(M.85.777A); ἡ ἀποστολικὴ θ. Thdt.*Heb.*proem.(3.542); **5.** ref. H. Ghost, Gr.Naz.*ep.*58(M.37.117B); ἡ...ἁγία...σύνοδος προσέθηκεν...τῷ συμβόλῳ καὶ τὴν θ. τοῦ πνεύματος Thphn.*chron.*p.59(M.108.201A); **6.** of scripture, ref. Gal.3:19 ὁ νόμος, ὡς ἡ θ. φησί, δι' ἀγγέλων ἡμῖν ἐδωρήθη Dion.Ar.*c.h.*4.2(M.3.180B); ἡ θ. τῶν...γραφῶν id.*e.h.*1.2(M.3.372C); **7.** in title of Gr. Naz. ὁ ἐν θ. μέγας Γρηγόριος ‡Nil.*vit.cog.*(M.79.1449C); τὸν τῆς θ. ἐπώνυμον Γρηγόριον Taras.*ep.*5(M.98.1468A); **8.** ref. relation of pagan teaching about God to Christian ἥ τε βάρβαρος ἥ τε Ἑλληνικὴ φιλοσοφία τὴν ἀΐδιον ἀλήθειαν σπαραγμόν τινα...τῆς...τοῦ λόγου τοῦ ὄντος ἀεὶ θεολογίας πεποίηται Clem.*str.*1.13 (p.36.29; M.8.756B); οἱ παρὰ τούτων τῶν προφητῶν τὴν θ. δεδιδαγμένοι ποιηταί *ib.*5.4(p.340.25; M.9.41C); ref. Celsus ὡς ἐπὶ ἐνεργέστερον διδάσκαλον τῶν θεολογίας πραγμάτων ἀναπέμπει ἡμᾶς ἐπὶ τὸν Πλάτωνα Or.*Cels.*7.42(p.192.23; M.11.1480D); **9.** plur., of partic. doctrines τῶν θείων δογμάτων πανηγυρικαῖς θ. Eus.*v.C.*4.45(p.136.14; M.20.1196B); ταῖς δογματικαῖς θ. ἀλήθειαν ἐπεμαρτύρει [sc. Const.] *ib.*4.33(p.130.14; 1181B); of truths about Christ revealed by H. Ghost, Bas.*Eun.*2.16(1.251D; M.29.604C); of proofs of Christ's divinity, Didym.*Trin.*1.26(M.39.385C); and of H. Ghost's divinity, *ib.*2.4(516C); τίνες αἱ καταφατικαὶ θ., τίνες αἱ ἀποφατικαί Dion.Ar. *myst.*3(M.3.1032C).

B. *naming of God* ἐπί τινος θ. ἀπορρήτου Or.*Cels.*1.24(p.75.4; M.11.705A); αὕτη δέ ἐστιν ἡ διὰ τῶν τεσσάρων στοιχείων ἀνεκφώνητος...θ. Eus.*p.e.*11.14(532B; M.21.884A); Trin. πᾶσα θ. ἡνωμένη τέ ἐστι καὶ διακεκριμένη Ant.Mon.*hom.*1(M.89.1436C).

C. *praise*; **1.** by angels αὐτῷ καὶ δυνάμεις ἀφανεῖς...τὴν ὀφειλομένην καὶ πρέπουσαν θ. ἀναπέμπουσιν Eus.*l.C.*1(p.198.13; M.20.1324A); ref. trisagion τὴν παραδοθεῖσαν ἡμῖν ἐκ τῶν σεραφὶμ θ. Cyr. H.*catech.*23.6; *Lit.Marc.*(p.131.29); **2.** by men ᾄδει...τῷ θεῷ ὁ διὰ ὑγιῶν δογμάτων τὴν ψυχὴν παιδευόμενος, ὁ τὰς πρεπούσας αὐτῷ θ. ἐκ διανοίας κεκαθαρμένης ἀναπέμπων Or.*Ps.*67:5(p.80); Eus.*h.e.*10.3.3 (M.20.848A); θυσίας τὰς δι' εὐχῶν καὶ ἀπορρήτου θ. τοῖς αὐτοῦ θιασώταις τίς ἐπιτελεῖν παρέδωκεν ἄλλος ἢ μόνος ὁ ἡμέτερος σωτήρ; id.*l.C.*16(p.253.6; M.20.1425D); of prayer of good thief θ. λῃστοῦ Mod.*dorm.*1(M.86.3281A); αἱ θ. Sophr.H.*v.Anast.*(M.92.1708B).

D. *mystical knowledge of God*; of beatific vision, ref. Spouse in Cant. ὅτε τὸ ἡγεμονικὸν αὐτοῦ καθοραθέν, τῇ τῆς θ. σφραγῖδι τετύπωται Or.*schol.in Cant.*4:12(M.17.273A); ἀγάπη δὲ θύρα γνώσεως φυσικῆς, ἣν διαδέχεται θ. καὶ ἡ ἐσχάτη μακαριότης Evagr.Pont.*cap.pract.* A proem.(M.40.1221C); cf.Pall.*h.Laus.*40(p.126.3ff.; M.34.1204C); ὁ νοῦς ἡμῶν...εἰς...τὴν θ. χαίρων ἑαυτὸν ἐπιδίδωσι διὰ τὸ πλατὺ καὶ ἀπολελυμένον τῶν θείων θεωρημάτων Diad.*perf.*68(p.82.21); οὔτε...τὸ τῆς θ. χάρισμα ἑτοιμάζεται τινι ὑπὸ τοῦ θεοῦ, εἰ μὴ ἑτοιμάσῃ ἑαυτόν *ib.*66(p.80.19); οἱ...τῆς θεωρητικῆς ἤδη μυστικῶς ἀξιωθέντες θ.

...πάσης φαντασίας ὑλικῆς τὸν νοῦν καθαρὸν καταστήσαντες Max.*qu. Thal.*10(M.90.288D).

E. *theology* in wider sense; **1.** in gen., as difficult to study because mind is weighed down by body, Gr.Naz.*or.*20.1(M.35.1068A); πρὸ παντός, καὶ μᾶλλον θ., εὐχῆς ἀπάρχεσθαι χρεών Dion.Ar.*d.n.*3.1(M.3.680D); id.*myst.*1.1(M.3.997A); id.*c.h.*2.1(M.3.137A); **2.** in titles of books ἐν τῇ περὶ ἀρχῶν καὶ θ. ἐξηγήσει Clem.*q.d.s.*26(p.177.25; M.9.632C); ἡ συμβολικὴ θ. Dion.Ar.*c.h.*15.6(M.3.336A).

F. *acknowledgement as God* ἡ τοῦ πατρὸς δοξολογία, τοῦ υἱοῦ ἐστιν θ. Euthal.Diac.*epp.cath.*(M.85.685C); of good thief's acknowledgement of Christ, Isid.Pel.*epp.*1.255(M.78.336C); of S. Peter's confession, Dion.Ar.*e.h.*7.7(M.3.564C).

G. *divinity*; **1.** Trin. ἐν τριάδι ἡ θ. τελεία ἐστί Ath.*Ar.*1.18(M.26.49A); ποία οὖν αὕτη θ. ἐκ δημιουργοῦ καὶ κτίσματος συγκειμένη; id.*ep.Serap.*1.2(M.26.533B); εἰς πλῆθος ἀπεσχισμένον τὴν θ. μὴ σκεδαννύντες Bas.*Spir.*45(3.38A; M.32.149B); cf.*ib.*47(39E; M.153C); πάντα τὰ τῆς θ. ὀνόματα κατὰ τὸ ἴσον ἐπί τε ⟨τοῦ⟩ πατρὸς καὶ τοῦ υἱοῦ λέγεται Gr.Nyss.*Eun.*7(2 p.165.32; M.45.756C); cf.*ib.*8(p.191.27; 785D); ‡Chrys.*fid.*3(1.831E); τρεῖς δὲ μὲν τὰς ὑποστάσεις, μίαν δὲ φύσιν ἐπὶ τῆς θ. ὁμολογοῦμεν Leont.B.*cap.Sev.*11(M.86.1904C); †Leont.B.*sect.*1.2(M.86.1197D); Thdr.Raith.*praep.*(p.195.7; M.91.1496D); **2.** ref. Christ; **a.** as attested by S. John, Eus.*h.e.*3.24.13(M.20.268B); ὁ δὲ Λουκᾶς, καὶ αὐτὸς διὰ τῶν σωματικῶν ἀρχῶν τῇ θ. προσέβη Bas.*Eun.*2.15(1.250B; M.29.601A); τὸ τῆς θ. κηρύσσει [sc. S. John] μυστήριον Gr.Nyss.*Eun.*4(2 p.53.1; M.45.624A); cf.*ib.*8(p.179.2; 772B); S. Peter in Ac.2:24, Cyr.*deip.BMV* 21(p.28.32; M.76.1281A); *ib.*20(p.28.18; 1280C); Is.8:3, Proc.G.*Is.*9:1–7(M.87.2009D); ref. S. Peter ὁ δι' ἀποκαλύψεως τοῦ ἁγίου πνεύματος τὴν τοῦ υἱοῦ θ. δεξάμενος Alex. Sal.*Barn.*14(p.440E); **b.** as contrasted with οἰκονομία, Eus.*h.e.*1.1.7(M.20.52B); διὰ θ. καὶ οἰκονομίας τὸν τὸ μυστήριον ἡμῖν τὸ ἀποκεκρυμμένον γνωρίσαντα ἀνυμνήσωμεν Thdt.*inc.*35(M.75.1477A); Jo.D.*f.o.*1.2(M.94.792B); both to be confessed, Bas.*Eun.*2.3(1.240A; M.29.577A); ἵνα μὴ θατέρῳ προσβαίνοντες, θατέρου ἐκπίπτωμεν· καὶ τῇ θ. προσέχοντες, τῆς οἰκονομίας καταφρονῶμεν Evagr.Pont.*ep.*3(M.32.252C); Thdt.*inc.*35(1477A); ἦσαν γὰρ πάλαι διδαχθέντες θεολογεῖν τὸν Χριστόν, καὶ μηδαμῶς αὐτὸν τῆς οἰκονομίας, ὡς ἄνθρωπον, χωρίζειν ἐκ τῆς θ. Socr.*h.e.*7.32.3(M.67.808D); οὐδὲ φιλαλήθους διανοίας καθέστηκε, τὰ ἐπὶ τῆς θ. αὐτοῖς εἰρημένα, μετάγειν ἐπὶ τῆς οἰκονομίας Max.*Pyrr.*(M.91.348C); types of both ἡ σμύρνα καὶ ὁ λίβανος, τουτέστιν ἡ θ. τε καὶ οἰκονομία Thdt.*Cant.*3:6(2.83); πορφύρα and βύσσος of Pr.31:22, Proc.G.ad loc.(M.87.1540D); **c.** as contrasted with ἐνανθρώπησις, Sever.*Heb.*1:1–2(p.346.18); †Leont.B.*sect.*1.4(M.86.1200C); **3.** heret. εἰς θ. ... λαμβάνουσι...τὸν Μελχισεδέκ Marc. Er.*opusc.*10.6(M.65.1125A).

θεολογικός, 1. *concerning God*; **a.** *about God, of God* πᾶσα θ. φωνὴ ἐλάττων μέν ἐστι τῆς διανοίας τοῦ λέγοντος, ἐλάττων δὲ τῆς τοῦ ἐπιζητοῦντος ἐπιθυμίας Bas.*ep.*7(3.80A; M.32.245A); τὰ θ. ῥήματα id.*Spir.*2(3.3A; M.32.69C); ἡ θ. ἐπιστήμη Dion.Ar.*c.h.*7.4(M.3.212B); id.*d.n.*2.2(M.3.640A); in title of a work αἱ θ. ὑποτυπώσεις *ib.*1.1(585B); ἡ θ. ὑμνολογία Max.*myst.*24(M.91.709B); **b.** *in God, to God* θ. πίστις *ib.*(709B); θ. εὐχαριστία *ib.*; **2.** *speaking about God*; **a.** of theologians; superl., *outstanding in theology*, iron. of Eun. ὦ...θ. Gr.Naz.*or.*28.7(p.31.8; M.36.33B); Γρηγόριε...ἱεραρχῶν ὁ θ. Thdr.Stud.*cant.*8.1(p.351); **b.** of statements about the Godhead, Athenag.*leg.*10.3(M.6.909B); Christol. οὐ χρὴ τὰ οἰκονομικῶς εἰρημένα τοῖς θ. συναρμόττειν Thdt.*eran.*2(4.110); of mystical apprehension as ἡ θ. χάρις Max.*carit.*2.26(M.90.992C).

θεολογικῶς, 1. *so as to speak of* Christ *as God*, ref. 1Cor.1:24 τὸ παρὰ Παύλου θ. εἰρημένον· 'Χριστὸν θεοῦ δύναμιν' Didym.*Trin.*3.7(M.39.849A); τὰ μὲν θ. τὰ δὲ οἰκονομικῶς ἡ θεία λέγει γραφή Thdt.*eran.*2(4.110); *ib.*(113); **2.** *in the manner of the theologian* (i.e. Gr. Naz.) θ. εἰπεῖν Jo.D.*imag.*1.8(M.94.1237C); *ib.*3.8(1328B).

θεολόγος, *speaking of God*; **A.** in gen.; **1.** ref. preaching or teaching about God θ. προφητῶν ἀνδρῶν Eus.*p.e.*10.1(461A; M.21.768B); of David as among οἱ θ. ἄνδρες Ath.*gent.*46(M.25.92B); of S. John, *ib.*42(84D); S. Paul, *ib.*35(69C); cf.id.*inc.*10.2(M.25.113A); ἡ θ. τοῦ μαθητοῦ [sc. S. John]...γλῶσσα Philost.*h.e.*7.14(M.65.552C); of Basil ἡ θ. ... σάλπιγξ Jo.Mon.*hymn.Bas.*8(M.96.1376A); τὰς...θ. ... γλώσσας †Jo.D.*B.J.*23(M.96.1069B); cf.*ib.*39(1229A); **2.** of speaking of God in prayer, *occupied with God in mystical prayer* ἡ θ. ψυχή Diad.*perf.*71(p.86.22).

B. as subst.; **1.** *one who teaches about God*; **a.** in OT ὁ Μωυσῆς θ. Clem.*str.*1.22(p.93.11; M.8.896C); οἱ καθ' Ἑβραίους θ. Eus.*d.e.*1.1(p.5.13; M.22.20A); of prophets, Bas.*Eun.*1.14(1.226D; M.29.544C); Gr.Naz.*or.*31.16(p.165.10; M.36.152A); Dion.Ar.*c.h.*8.2(M.3.241A); **b.** of evangelists, Ath.*inc.*18.1(M.25.128A); esp. S. John, ‡Ath.*serm.fid.*26(p.23; M.26.1280D); Paul.Em.*hom.*2.4(p.13.20; M.77.1441B); Ἰωάννης...ὁ πολὺς ἐν θεολόγοις Didym.*Trin.*1.27(M.39.405B); Dion. Ar.*ep.*10(M.3.1117A); *Chron.Pasch.*p.246(M.92.592B); as the theologian *par excellence* ὁ θ. Or.*fr.1 in Jo.*(p.483.14); *ib.*(p.484.7); *A.Jo.*5(p.153.33); Ephr.3.108E; ὁ τῷ ὄντι θ. ‡Gr.Nyss.*hom.1.3 in Jo.*(p.94.3); Anast.S.*hod.*21(M.89.284A); **c.** of Gr. Naz. μόνον τοῦτον μετὰ τὸν εὐαγγελιστὴν Ἰωάννην θ. ὀνομασθῆναι Gr.Presb.*v.Gr.Naz.*(M.35.288C); ὁ θ. Γρηγόριος Philost.*h.e.*8.11(M.65.564C); Max.*Pyrr.*(M.91.316C); Jo.D.*f.o.*3.15(M.94.1048B); **d.** of others Πέτρος, ἡ κορυφαία καὶ πρεσβυτάτη τῶν θ. ἀκρότης Dion.Ar.*d.n.*3.2(M.3.681D); of theologians enlightened by H. Ghost, *ib.*1(585B); iron. of Eunomius ὦ κενὲ θ. Gr.Naz.*or.*29.10(p.87.13; M.36.88A); ὁ καινὸς θ. Gr.Nyss.*Eun.*1(1 p.94.17; M.45.328A); *ib.*4(2 p.50.14; 620C); **2.** *theologian* in wider sense, Dion.Ar.*c.h.*2.2(M.3.137C); **3.** *one speaking of God in prayer*, hence *one practising mystical prayer* εἰ θ. εἶ, προσεύξῃ ἀληθῶς, καὶ εἰ ἀληθῶς προσεύχῃ, θ. εἶ Evagr.Pont.*or.*60(M.79.1180B); Diad.*perf.*72(p.88.19,25).

***θεολοίδορος,** *reviling God*, Leont.B.*Nest.et Eut.*5(M.86.1752B).

***θεομακάριστος,** *blessed of God* Πολύκαρπε θεομακαριστότατε Ign.*Polyc.*7.2; of Christ's Passion, id.*Smyrn.*1.2; of BMV μακαρία σὺ εἶ ἐν γενεαῖς γενεῶν θεομακάριστε Ephr.3.526F; ‡Meth.*Sym.et Ann.*5(M.18.357C).

θεομαχ-έω, *war against God*; **1.** of Christians, acc. Porphyry and other pagans τί γὰρ ἄλλο ἢ ~οῦντας; Eus.*p.e.*1.2(5A; M.21.28C); **2.** of Julian ~εῖ γὰρ ἐκτόπως Cyr.*Juln.*2(6².61D); **3.** of Jewish opponents, id.*Is.*4.2(2.615E); **4.** of heretics, esp. Gnostic ~εῖ...Καρποκράτης Clem.*str.*3.2(p.199.29; M.8.1109B); Arians, Ath.*decr.*3(M.25.'428'(420)C); id.*Ar.*2.32(M.26.216A); Philost.*h.e.*2.3(M.65.465D); Eunomians, Didym.(‡Bas.)*Eun.*5(1.314B; M.29.753A); id.*Trin.*1.17(M.39.340C); **5.** of gen. attitude of those who rebel against God, Pall.*h.Laus.*21(p.67.21; M.34.1075C); ὁ ζήλῳ θείῳ ποιῶν τι, οὗτος οὐ ~εῖ ‡Just.*qu.et resp.*52(M.6.1296B).

θεομαχία, ἡ, *war against God*; **1.** of battle of gods in pagan mythology compared with Marcion's theology of two conflicting deities, Cels.ap.Or.*Cels.*6.74(p.144.2; M.11.1409B); **2.** of revolt of Satan τὴν ἀπὸ τῶν κρειττόνων δι' οἰκείαν μεγαλαυχίαν καὶ θ. ἀπόπτωσιν μεμαθήκαμεν Eus.*p.e.*7.16(329B; M.21.556C); of fallen man, id.*h.e.*1.2.19(M.20.64A); **3.** of efforts of builders of Babel, *Apoc.Bar.*2(p.85.28); **4.** of Jewish opposition to Christ and apostles, ‡Just.*qu.et resp.*108(M.6.1357A); **5.** of pagan opposition to Christianity Δομετιανὸς...τῆς Νέρωνος...θ. διάδοχον ἑαυτὸν κατεστήσατο Eus.*h.e.*3.17(M.20.249C); by persecutors overthrown by Constantine γιγάντων τρόπον θεομαχίαν ἐνστησάμενοι *ib.*10.4.31(861B); of Licinius' party οἱ τῆς θ. σύμβουλοι id.*v.C.*2.18(p.48.9; M.20.996A); of heresy, esp. Marcion's denial of creator, Clem.*str.*3.3(p.201.5; M.8.1116A); **6.** of final war of antichrist μελλούσης γὰρ τὰ τῆς θ. τέρατα καταργεῖν τῆς ἐπιφανείας τοῦ σωτῆρος Eus.*Lc.*21:28(M.24.600D); **7.** of gen. disposition to rebel against God πλεονεξίαι, μιαιφονίαι, θ. δυσσέβειαι Eus.*l.C.*5(p.204.1; M.20.1336A); Niceph.Ur.*v.Sym.*173(M.86.3145B).

θεομάχος (poet. θεημ-), *fighting against God*;

A. as adj., of evil spirits τὰ μὴ ὄντα ὡς ὄντα δοξάζοντες, ἢ ὑπό τινων...θ. πνευμάτων...τυφλῶν δίκην ὧδε κἀκεῖσε περιηγμένοι Eus.*p.e.*4.4(140B; M.21.245A); ὅτι...τῷ πονηρῷ καὶ θ. πνεύματι κάτοχος ἦν [sc. ὁ Ἰουλιανός], ἀποφήσαιμ' ἂν οὐδαμῶς Cyr.*Juln.*6(6².194E); of building of Babel θ. πυργοποιΐας Cosm.Ind.*top.*3(M.88.136B); of Egypt as home of idolatry, Chrys.*hom.8.5 in Mt.*(7.127A); id.*pan.Aeg.*1(2.699A); of Jews, as idolaters in time of prophets, Cyr.*Os.*30(3.55B); id.*Mich.*41(3.429C); id.*Is.*1.1(2.29A); as enemies of Christ and Church, *Narr.Jos.*1.1(p.459); Procl.CP *or.*14.3(M.65.797D); τὸ τῶν Ἰουδαίων θ. καὶ φιλαίτιον καὶ φιλόψογον ἔθνος Sev.Ant.ap.*cat.Mt.*12:18(p.91.1); Germ.CP *or.*2(M.98.244C) cit. s. γογγυστικός; of tyrants overthrown by Constantine, Eus.*v.C.*1.3(p.8.14; M.20.913B); of Chosroes, Heracl.*ep.*(M.92.1017C); of heresies and heretics; Marcion likened to a Titan as an opponent of creator, Clem.*str.*3.4(p.207.10; M.8.1129A) cit. s. γίγας; Arians and Arianism, Ath.*ep.Aeg.Lib.*22(M.25.589B); Gr.Naz.*or.*42.3(M.36.460C); Gel.Cyz.*h.e.*2.14 tit.(M.85.1256B); †Diad.*Ar.*1(M.65.1149A); Arians, Eunomians, Macedonians, Procl.CP *ep.*2.13(M.65.869B); Eunomianism, Bas.*Eun.*2.27(1.264C; M.29.636B); Manicheism, Sev.Ant.ap.*cat.Mt.*15:5(p.122.31); Nestorius, Evagr.*h.e.*1.2(p.7.1; M.86.2424A); all heresies, θεημ-, Gr.Naz.*carm.*1.1.1.15(M.37.399A); Nest.*ep.Cyr.*2(p.32.16; M.77.57A); Sophr.H.*ep.syn.*(M.87.3189B); and disbelievers, θεημ-, Nonn.*par.Jo.*3:18(M.43.769A); in gen., of rebellious disposition, opposed to God εἰς θ. γνώμην ἀνάγων τοὺς εὐχερεῖς Mac.Mgn.*apocr.*10(p.15.15); τὸν...παλαιὸν ἄνθρωπον...θ. Mac.Aeg.*hom.*2.2(M.

34.464C); θεημ-, Nonn.*par.Jo.*8:40(M.43.820A); θεημ-, *ib.*18:14(892B); Olymp.*Job* 21 proem.(M.93.221C).

B. as subst.; **1.** of heretics; Ophites, Gr.Naz.*or.*45.8(M.36.632C); Arians θ. καὶ φθορέας τῶν ψυχῶν Alex.Al.*ep.encycl.*8(p.10.14; M. 18.577C); Ath.*Ar.*1.13(M.26.40B); id.*ep.Serap.*1.3(M.26.536A); Gr. Nyss.*Eun.*1(1 p.35.4; M.45.261C); ἀνοήτως λέγουσιν οἱ θ. περὶ τοῦ υἱοῦ, ὅτι ἦν ὅτε οὐκ ἦν Cyr.*thes.*4(5^1.19E); Origen ὁ μανιώδης καὶ θ. CAlex.(401)*ep.*ap.Justn.*Or.*(p.203.4; M.86.971A); Justn.*Or.*(p.191.1; 949B); Const.Pogon.*edict.*(H.3.1456D); **2.** in gen. of rebels against God οὐδεὶς θ. καὶ ἀλάζων...ὑποκάτω πίπτει τοῦ θεοῦ, ἀλλ' οἱ τὴν ἐκ πίστεως ὑποταγὴν καταδεξάμενοι Bas.*hom.in Ps.*44(1.165B; M.29. 404A); Cosm.Ind.*top.*3(M.88.164B).

***θεομεγάλυντος**, *magnified by God*; of BMV, ‡Jo.D.*hom.*5(M.96. 648B).

θεομηνία, ἡ, *wrath of God, divine visitation*, Soz.*h.e.*2.4.4(M.67. 944B); Proc.G.*2Reg.*1:19(M.87.1121A); of natural calamities, *Chron. Pasch.*p.246(M.92.592A); *ib.*p.322(821B).

***θεομήνυτος**, *taught by God*, ‡Chrys.*hom.*13(13.251C).

[*]**θεομήτηρ, ἡ**, v. θεομήτωρ.

θεόμητις, *divinely wise*, Nonn.*par.Jo.*8:43(M.43.820B).

***θεομητρικός**, *of the mother of God*, Mod.*dorm.*1(M.86.3280B); *ib.*8 (3297C); *ib.*12(3308A).

θεομήτωρ ([*]**θεομήτηρ**), **ἡ**, *mother of God*, title of BMV τὴν παναγίαν ἔνδοξον θ. Sym.Styl.J.*ep.Just.*(M.86.3217A); τὴν θ. Μαρίαν Anast.Ant.*serm.*3.2(M.89.1388C); ‡Ath.*occurs.*20(M.28.1000B); ‡Gr. Nyss.*occurs.*(M.46.1176B); †Cyr.*coll.VT*(6^4.7D; M.77.1185B); Mod. *dorm.*1(M.86.3277B); Sophr.H.*or.*2.25(M.87.3245A); Max.*opusc.*(M. 91.60A); Leont.N.*serm.*1(M.93.1569A); ‡Jo.D.*hom.*6.11(M.96.677C); id.*carm.dorm.BMV* 80(p.230; M.96.1365C); Thdr.H.*ep.syn.*(H.4. 145D); Jo.Mon.*hymn.Blas.*6(M.96.1404D); -μήτηρ, Jo.Mon.*hymn. Petr.*2(M.96.1392A).

***θεόμιλος**, *holding converse with God*, ‡Jo.D.*hom.*5(M.96.648C).

***θεομιμησία, ἡ**, *imitation of God*; **1.** through spiritual union with God in virtue of which men can be called θεοί: ὅσα τῶν νοερῶν... πρὸς τὴν ἕνωσιν αὐτῆς [sc. τῆς θεαρχικῆς κρυφιότητος]...ὁλικῶς ἐπέστραπται, καὶ πρὸς τὰς θείας αὐτῆς ἐλλάμψεις...ἀνατείνεται, τῇ κατὰ δύναμιν, εἰ θέμις εἰπεῖν, θεομιμησίᾳ, καὶ τῆς θεϊκῆς ὁμωνυμίας ἠξίωται Dion.Ar.*c.h.*12.3(M.3.293B); θεογνωσίας τε καὶ θ. ... εἰς ἡμᾶς τῆς θεαρχικῆς ἐλλάμψεως διαδιδομένης *ib.*13.3(304A); id.*ep.*8(M.3. 1085A); **2.** of imitation of Christ, rendered impossible if his true humanity is denied, Leont.B.*Nest.et Eut.*2(M.86.1327A); *ib.*(1349C).

***θεομίμητος**, *imitating God*; **1.** neut. as subst., of imitation of Christ, rendered impossible by monophysite Christology πῶς γὰρ δὴ τὸ θ. ἕξομεν, μὴ συμπαθόντες τῷ πεπονθότι; Leont.B.*Nest.et Eut.*2 (M.86.1321D); in gen. παρακαλεῖτε [sc. τοὺς ἐχθρούς] ὡς ἀδελφούς, τὸ θ. ἐνδεικνύμενοι Jo.VI CP *ep.*(M.96.1432D); **2.** adj. and neut. as subst., ref. imitation of God as goal of spiritual progress ἱεραρχία... ἐπὶ τὸ θ. ἀναγομένη Dion.Ar.*c.h.*3.1(M.3.164D); τὸν...ἁπάσης ἱεραρχίας σκοπὸν τῆς θ. θεοειδείας ἐξηρτημένον ἀρρεπῶς εἶναι *ib.*7.2(208A); πᾶσαν ...θ. ἐνέργειαν ἐπὶ θεὸν μὲν ὡς αἴτιον ἀναφέρουσιν *ib.*13.3(304A); εἰς θεοειδῆ μονάδα συναγόμεθα, καὶ θ. ἕνωσιν id.*d.n.*1.4(M.3.589D); Max. *opusc.*(M.91.57B); διαθέσεως, ἀλλ' οὐ τάξεως εἶναι τὸ θ. id.*ep.*1(M. 91.364B); expressed in charity, ‡Jo.D.*fid.dorm.*8(M.95.253C); and in conduct which denotes possession of divine ὁμοίωσις, Jo.D. *spir.neq.*(M.95.97A).

***θεομιμήτως**, *in a manner imitating God* ἱεράρχης...τὸν προσιόντα φωτίσαι θ. ἑτοιμότατος ὢν Dion.Ar.*e.h.*2.3.4(M.3.400B); θ. ... ἐπίθες τοῖς ὤμοις τὸ πρόβατον Max.*ep.*11(M.91.457C); Andr.Caes.*Apoc.*34 (M.106.329A); *in imitation of Christ*, *ib.*40(344C).

***θεομίσεια, ἡ**, *hatred of God*, Eus.*h.e.*9.7.2(M.20.809B).

θεομισής, **1.** *hated by God*, Cels.ap.Or.*Cels.*1.71(p.124.24; M.11. 792A); ἀδύνατον ἔσται ἄνθρωπος θ., ἐπεὶ ὁ θεὸς ἀγαπᾷ τὰ ὄντα πάντα Or.*Cels.*1.71(p.124.27; 792A); ψυχῆς...θεομισέστατα πάθη Meth.*lepr.* 12(p.466.13); θ. αἱρέσεων Eus.*h.e.*4.7.3(M.20.316C); θ. γοητείαν Cyr. *Jon.*2(3.368B); Isid.Pel.*epp.*5.215(M.78.1460C); **2.** *hating God*; of the Devil, Didym.*Trin.*3.20(M.39.897B); τὰ...τῶν αἱρετικῶν θ. καὶ ἀνόσια στίφη Cyr.*Os.*16(3.39B); παραιτούμενος τὸν θ. καὶ ἐπιστρέφων τὸν ἀλιτήριον *ib.*130(163C); Ἄχαζ...εἰδωλολάτρης...καὶ θ. (in contrast with Ἐζεχίας...θεοφιλής) id.*Is.*3.4(2.476E); τοῦ θ. Λικιννίου Gel.Cyz. *h.e.*1.11.32(M.85.1221D); τῶν θεομισῶν τυράννων *ib.*3.1.1.

θεομίσητος, *hated by God*, *Chron.Pasch.*p.393(M.92.1608C); Heracl.*ep.*(M.92.1020B).

***θεόμοιος**, *like God*, Anast.S.*serm.imag.*3(M.89.1164C).

θεόμορφος, *in the image of God*, ‡Ath.*annunt.*3(M.28.913B); †Cyr. *hom.div.*11(5^2.379C).

***θεονομικός**, *of divine law*, Dion.Ar.*c.h.*4.3(M.3.181A).

***θεονύμφευτος, ἡ**, *bride of God*; of BMV, Ephr.3.533D.

***θεόνυμφος, ἡ**, *bride of God*; **1.** of Church, Meth.*symp.*11.2(p.136. 3; M.18.212C); **2.** of BMV, Germ.CP *ep.dogm.*3.13(M.98.304D).

***θεοπαγής**, *fixed by God* στήριγμα θ. ... τῆς πίστεως τὴν σὴν ἀποστολικὴν καθέδραν ἱδρύσατο...Χριστός Serg.C.*ep.*(H.3.729A).

***θεοπάθεια, ἡ**, *suffering of God*; **1.** alleged by Nestorians to be implied in Cyril's Christology οἴονται πάλιν ἐκεῖνοι τὴν καλουμένην παρ' αὐτοῖς θ. ἡμᾶς εἰσφέρειν διὰ τούτου· καὶ οὐκ ἐννοοῦσι τὴν οἰκονομίαν, κακουργότατα δὲ πειρῶνται μεθιστᾶν εἰς ἄνθρωπον ἰδικῶς τὸ πάθος· εὐσέβειαν ἐπιζήμιον ἀσυνέτως ἐπιτηδεύοντες, ἵνα μὴ ὁ τοῦ θεοῦ λόγος ὁμολογῆται σωτήρ Cyr.*ep.*46.3(p.161.9; 5^2.144C); **2.** in monophysite Christology τί οὖν πυνθάνεσθε ἡμῶν ὡς ἀμφιβαλλομένου ὄντος ποία φύσις προσήλωτο, εἰ μὴ θ. φυσικὴν καὶ οὐ τὴν κατ' οἰκείωσιν λέγετε; Leont.H.*monoph.*46(M.86.1797A); οὔτε μὴν ἑτερογενῶν οὐσιῶν ὀνομάσαντες ἕνωσιν...τὴν μιαρὰν θ. ἱεροῖς μιγνύναι βουλόμενοι δόγμασιν Sophr.H.*or.*2.6(M.87.3224B).

***θεοπαίδευτος**, *instructed by God*, Gr.Nyss.*Eun.*8(2 p.195.14; M. 45.792D).

θεόπαις, ὁ, as adj.; **1.** *who is divine Son* αὐτὸς ὁ θ. κατ' εἰκόνα ...δημιουργήσας Eus.*h.e.*10.4.56(M.20.872A); **2.** *who bears a divine Son*, of BMV, Nonn.*par.Jo.*19:26(M.43.904B); Andr.Cr.*can.Ann.* (M.97.1308C); Thdr.Stud.*nativ.BMV* 2(M.96.681A).

θεοπαράδοτος, *delivered, handed down by God*, of eucharist τὰ θ. μυστήρια διδάσκοντας †Cyr.*hom.div.*10(5^2.378D); of divine λόγια, Dion.Ar.*e.h.*1.4(M.3.376B); of formula of episcopal consecration, Eustrat.*v.Eutych.*25(M.86.2304A); of the gospels, ‡Jo.D.*ep.Thphl.*3 (M.95.348D); of Christian doctrine and practice, Dion.Ar.*e.h.*2.1 (M.3.392B); of the ministry τὴν θ. ... τάξιν id.*ep.*8(M.3.1088C).

***θεοπάρακτος**, *brought into being by God*, ‡Just.*qu.Chr.*3.5(M.6. 1444A).

***θεοπάροχος**, *furnished by God*, Steph.Diac.*v.Steph.*(M.100. 1081A).

***θεοπασχία, ἡ**, *suffering of God*; hence, *the Theopaschite heresy* which asserts that Godhead suffered in Christ, Anast.S.*hod.*12(M. 89.201D,204A); *ib.*13(244B); ‡Jo.D.*ep.Thphl.*8(M.95.356A).

***θεοπασχίανος, ὁ**, = θεοπασχίτης, epithet applied to Apollinarians, Alex.Sal.*Barn.*34(p.448D).

***θεοπασχίτης, ὁ**, *Theopaschite*, i.e. one who asserts, on the ground of monophysitism, that Godhead suffered; epithet applied to Eutyches, Dioscorus, and monophysites ἡ ἀνθρωπότης μόνη ἔπασχε, ἡ δὲ θεότης ἀπαθὴς διέμεινε. καὶ ταῦτα λέγων, ἀντιστομίζεις θ. ‡Ath.*qu.al.*19(M.28.792C); οἱ δὲ θ. ... τὸ σταυρικὸν πάθος...τῇ θείᾳ φύσει προσγράφειν ‡Gr.Nyss.*hom.7.155 in Jo.*(p.279.21); αἱ...γραφαὶ ...Χριστὸν παραδιδόασι...ἐσταυρωμένον, καὶ οὐ τὸ τρισάγιον...ἀλλὰ καὶ ἀποβλητέους εἶπον αἱ γραφαὶ τοὺς θ. ‡Pamph.Abyd.*ep.Petr.*(p.10.13; H.2.852A); subdivisions of Theopaschite sect enumerated, Tim. CP *haer.*(M.86.41B); Εὐτυχέως καὶ Διοσκόρου τῶν θ. Jo.D.*rect.sent.*7 (M.94.1432B); Χριστοῦ παθόντος σαρκί, ὦ θ., καὶ οὐ θεότητι Anast.S. *hod.*10(M.89.188B); ‡Jo.D.*azym.*1(M.95.392C); as rejecting images of the Crucified, CCP(754)*decr.*(H.4.361A); in gen., Thphn.*chron.* p.97(M.108.288B).

***θεοπατορία, ἡ**, *state of being the father of God*; ref. David as ancestor of Jesus, Cyr.*Ps.*20:4(M.69.836C).

θεοπάτωρ, ὁ, *ancestor of God*; of David as ancestor of Jesus, Dion.Ar.*ep.*8.1(M.3.1085B); †Gregent.*disp.*(M.86.628A); Jo.D.*f.o.*4. 11(M.94.1132A); id.*imag.*1.1(M.94.1232B); Thdr.Stud.*or.*5.1(M.99. 721A); of Joseph ὁ θ. Ἰωσὴφ σὺν τῇ θεοτόκῳ Steph.Diac.*v.Steph.* (M.100.1038A); of Joachim and Anna, *Lit.Chrys.*(p.358.35); *Euchol.* (p.32).

θεοπειθής, *believing, trusting in God*, *Orac.Sib.*8.477; Dion.Al.*ep. can.*(M.10.1272B; θεοπρεπεῖ p.94.2); Nonn.*par.Jo.*5:11(M.43.785C); ἐλπίδες...θ. *ib.*5:45(792C); θ. λαῷ *ib.*18:21(893A); of Abraham, *ib.* 8:53(821B); of prayer, Max.*opusc.*(M.91.92C).

θεόπεμπτος, *sent by God*; **1.** of spiritual and intellectual gifts, Clem.*str.*6.8(p.463.16; M.9.284C); θ. ... πίστις Or.*fr.11 in Jo.*1:16 (p.493.29); Didym.ap.*cat.Ac.*5:14(p.90.19); θ. λογισμοί Diad.*perf.*26 (p.28.9); **2.** of visions and dreams, *Hom.Clem.*17.15; **3.** of afflictions, Nil.*epp.*3.17(M.79.377C); *ib.*3.99(432B).

***θεοπιστία, ἡ**, *faith in God*, Tim.Ant.*caec.*4(M.28.1005C); Thdr. Stud.*ref.*(M.99.436B).

***θεοπλανησία, ἡ**, *state of going astray from God*, Ath.*Ar.*2.14 (M.26.176B).

***θεοπλαστία, ἡ**, **1.** *devising gods*; of pagan idolatry, Ath.*gent.*19 (M.25.40B); of unworthy representations of God, found in scripture, and to be interpreted allegorically, Dion.Ar.*ep.*9.1(M.3. 1105B); **2.** *assumption of form by God* ἡ καθ' ἡμᾶς Ἰησοῦ θ. Dion.Ar.

*d.n.*2.9(M.3.648A); τὸ θεαρχικὸν τῆς ἀφθέγκτου θ. μυστήριον id.*c.h.*4.4 (M.3.181B); Max.*opusc.*(M.91.57C).

***θεόπλαστος**, *formed by God*, of man σκεῦος εἰ θ., παρὰ θεοῦ γενόμενον ‡Bas.*struct.hom.*2.1(1.338D; M.30.41C); cf. ἐπλάσθη μὲν ἡ σάρξ· ἐποιήθη δὲ ἡ ψυχή *ib.*(338B; M.41A); Ἀδὰμ ὡς θ. †Apoll.*ep. Bas.*1(M.32.1104A).

***θεόπλευρος**, *of the side of God*, i.e. *piercing the side of God* λόγχῃ τῇ θ. καρδίαν τοῦ τυράννου τὴν ἄσαρκον διατρήσας ‡Epiph.*hom.*2(M.43.456A); πίστει πίετε τὸ αἷμα κενωθὲν τῆς θ. σφαγῆς Andr.Cr.*triod.*(M.97.1417C).

θεοπληγής, *smitten by God*, Synes.*provid.*2.2(p.115.16; M.66.1264D).

θεόπληκτος, *smitten by God*, Cyr.H.*catech.*6.23.

θεόπληξ, = foreg., Max.*opusc.*(M.91.177D).

θεόπλοκος, *made by God*, ref. Christ σὰρξ θ. Leont.H.*Nest.*4.46 (M.86.1717D); θ. δόγματα Jo.Mon.*hymn.Nic.Myr.*7(M.96.1388B).

***θεόπλουτος**, *made rich by God* ὁ πλοῦτος ἐκείνοις [sc. Abraham and Job] οὐκ ἐν χρυσῷ ἦν, οὐδὲ ἐν ἀργύρῳ, οὐδὲ ἐν οἰκοδομήμασιν, ἀλλ' ἐν θρέμμασιν· ἄλλως δὲ καὶ θ. οὗτος ἦν Chrys.*hom.12.3 in 1Tim.*(11.615A).

***θεοπνευστία, ἡ**, *divine inspiration*, Jo.VI H.*v.Jo.D.*34(M.94.481A).

θεόπνευστος, **A.** *divinely inspired*; **1.** of scripture (cf. 2Tim. 3:16); **a.** as representing voice of H. Ghost, Or.*Jo.*6.48(29; p.157.2; M.14.284A); ὅσα ἡ θεία γραφὴ λέγει, τοῦ πνεύματός εἰσι τοῦ ἁγίου φωναί...οὐκοῦν τῇ δυνάμει τοῦ πνεύματος οἱ θεοφορούμενοι τῶν ἁγίων ἐμπνέονται. καὶ διὰ τοῦτο πᾶσα γραφὴ θ. λέγεται, διὰ τὸ τῆς θείας ἐμπνεύσεως εἶναι διδασκαλίαν Gr.Nyss.*Eun.*7(2 p.155.24,156.10; M.45.744Bff.); **b.** hence as containing hidden significance, Or.*Jo.*10.39 (23; p.215.25; M.14.381A); ἔθος δὲ τῇ θ. γραφῇ ἐκ τῶν καθ' ἡμᾶς πραγμάτων σχηματίζειν ἔσθ' ὅτε τὰ μὴ ἐμφανῆ, ἀλλ' ὡς ἐν κρυπτῷ καὶ νοήσει δρώμενα Cyr.*Ps.*7:13(M.69.753D); and deep mysteries κοινὸς μὲν ὁ λόγος τῆς θ. γραφῆς, διδάσκει δὲ μέγα καὶ βαθὺ μυστήριον Procl. CP *or.*2.1(M.65.837C); **c.** and requiring to be read with faith that they are inspired, †Bas.*Is.*197(1.526D; M.30.457C); **d.** comprising; **i.** Law δι' ὃν [sc. Ezra] γίνεται ἡ ἀπολύτρωσις τοῦ λαοῦ καὶ ὁ τῶν θ. ἀναγνωρισμὸς καὶ ἀνακαινισμὸς λογίων Clem.*str.*1.21(p.77.25; M.8.853A); ὁ νόμος ὁ Μωσαϊκός, ἀγαθὸς δέ, ὅτι θ. μόνος αὐτοῖς, καίτοι πολλῶν ὄντων παρ' ἀνθρώποις νόμων Olymp.*fr.Lam.*4:1(M.93.752A); **ii.** Prophets μαθητεύοντες γὰρ τὰ ἔθνη οἱ ἀπόστολοι, εἶχον μεθ' ἑαυτῶν τὰ θ. τῶν προφητῶν λόγια, τὰ μαρτυροῦντα τῷ Χριστῷ Tit.Bost.*palm.*5(M.18.1272A); **iii.** OT history στηλιτεύει αὐτὴν [sc. Jezebel] ἡ θ. ἱστορία Gr.Naz.*or.*35.3(M.36.260B); **iv.** OT as a whole, Gr.Nyss.*hex.*(M.44.68C); Proc.G.*Is.*22:1–14(M.87.2176C); its inspiration being due to Christ δηλωθεὶς αἴτιος εἶναι πάσης ἐκείνης τῆς θ. γραφῆς, παρελκυσάσης ἕως τοῦ βαπτιστοῦ Ἰωάννου Or.*fr.12 in Jo.* (p.494.21); whose Inc. proves it to be inspired, id.*princ.*4.1.6(p.301.15; M.11.352B); **v.** gospels, Eus.*qu.Marin.*proem.(M.22.937A); τὰ θ. ... λόγια *Chron.Pasch.*p.218(M.92.534C); **vi.** canonical scriptures as a whole, *Proem.*in Dor.*doct.*(M.88.1612B); opp. apocryphal books ἐπειδήπερ τινὲς ἐπεχείρησαν ἀνατάξασθαι ἑαυτοῖς τὰ λεγόμενα ἀπόκρυφα, καὶ ἐπιμῖξαι ταῦτα τῇ θ. γραφῇ, περὶ ἧς ἐπληροφορήθημεν, καθὼς παρέδοσαν τοῖς πατράσιν οἱ ἀπ' ἀρχῆς αὐτόπται καὶ ὑπηρέται γενόμενοι τοῦ λόγου Ath.*ep.fest.*39(M.26.1435B); criterion of inspiration being authenticity and early testimonies to canonicity περὶ μέντοι τοῦ θ. τῆς βίβλου [sc. Apocalypse] περιττὸν μηκύνειν τὸν λόγον ἡγούμεθα, τῶν μακαρίων Γρηγορίου...καὶ Κυρίλλου, προσέτι δὲ καὶ τῶν ἀρχαιοτέρων, Παπίου, Εἰρηναίου, Μεθοδίου καὶ Ἱππολύτου ταύτῃ προσμαρτυρούντων τὸ ἀξιόπιστον Andr.Caes.*Apoc.*proem.(M.106.220B); **vii.** hence θ. as freq. epithet of γραφαί or γραφή applied either to contents of scriptures or to the actual volumes κατὰ τὰς θ. γραφάς Clem.*str.*7.16(p.71.23; M.9.540C); Or.*princ.*4.2.1(p.300.10; M.11.352B); id.*exc.in Ps.*5:3(M.17.120C); Meth.*res.*1.28(p.257.15; M.41.1136B); Eus.*h.e.*3.4.6(M.20.220C); θ. ἀναγνωσμάτων id.*Lc.*14:16(M.24.572C); τὰ θ. ... λόγια ἀφανῆ ποιεῖσθαι πυρὶ φλεχθέντα id.*v.C.*3.1(p.77.1; M.20.1053B); *ib.*4.34(p.130.23; 1181C); ‡Bas.*struct.hom.*1.1(1.324A; M.30.12A); †Bas.*bapt.*2.5.2(2.658E; M.31.1593C); Cyr.H.*catech.*4.33; Gr. Nyss.*anim.et res.*(M.46.52A); Mac.Aeg.*hom.*5.6(M.34.508C); Chrys. *hom.in Jer.10:23*(6.160C) cit. s. γραφή; Cyr.*Is.*1.1(2.25B); id.*Os.*3 (3.17C); **viii.** and of doctrine contained or implied in scripture τὰ προσφυῆ τοῖς θ. λόγοις ὑπὸ τῶν μακαρίων ἀποστόλων τε καὶ διδασκάλων παραδιδόμενα Clem.*str.*7.16(p.73.5; M.9.544A); ἡ θ. ... διδασκαλία Gr.Nyss.*Trin.*4(M.32.688C; om. p.74.9); id.*hom.5 in Cant.*(M.44.873C); ταῦτα [sc. Trinitarian doctrine] φρονεῖν ἐκ τῆς θ. διδασκαλίας ἐμάθομεν id.*Eun.*6(2 p.133.1; M.45.717A); rejected by heretics in favour of their own fancies, Thdt.*Trin.*proem.(M.75.1148A); **e.** sufficiency of inspired scripture for knowledge of truth αὐταρκεῖς μὲν γάρ εἰσιν αἱ...θ. γραφαὶ πρὸς τὴν τῆς ἀληθείας ἀπαγγελίαν· εἰσὶ δὲ καὶ πολλοὶ τῶν μακαρίων ἡμῶν διδασκάλων εἰς ταῦτα συνταχθέντες λόγοι· οἷς ἐάν τις ἐντύχοι, εἴσεται μέν πως τὴν τῶν γραφῶν ἑρμηνείαν, ἧς δὲ ὀρέγεται γνώσεως τυχεῖν δυνήσεται Ath.*gent.*1(M.25.4A); **f.** as basis of credal statements τὸ ἐκκλησιαστικὸν ἐν κυρίῳ φρόνημα, μαρτυρούμενον ἀβιάστως ὑπὸ τῶν θ. γραφῶν *Symb.Ant.*(345)10(p.254.12; M.26.736A); and test of doctrinal truth οὔτε γὰρ ἐξ οὐκ ὄντων τὸν υἱὸν λέγειν ἀσφαλές, ἐπεὶ μηδαμοῦ τοῦτο τῶν θ. γραφῶν φέρεται περὶ αὐτοῦ *ib.*3(p.252.10; 729A); παρὰ τὸ βούλημα τῆς θ. γραφῆς τοιαῦτα τετολμήκασι...διορίσασθαι *ib.*8(p.253.25; 732D); τίς νόμος, ποῖοι προφῆται, τίς θ. λόγος, ποῖον συνόδου δόγμα, τοιοῦτον ἡμῖν παρακατέθετο; Gr.Nyss.*Apoll.*34(M.45.1200A); κριτήριον ἀσφαλὲς τῆς ἀληθείας ἐπὶ παντὸς δόγματος ἡ θ. ἐστι μαρτυρία Gr.Nyss.*Eun.*1 (p.107.23; M.45.341B); **g.** as affording spiritual food, Eus.*Is.*49:9 (M.24.433D); but when hidden significance is not investigated this food is raw and fit for irrational beasts only, Gr.Nyss.*hom.1 in Cant.*(M.44.764A); **h.** inspired character of all scripture consistent with degrees of inspiration in its several parts ἐπίστησον εἰ, ἐπὰν λέγῃ ὁ Παῦλος, πᾶσα γραφὴ θ. ... ἐμπεριλαμβάνει καὶ τὰ ἑαυτοῦ γράμματα, ἢ οὐ τό, κἀγὼ λέγω καὶ οὐχ ὁ κύριος...καὶ τὰ τούτοις παραπλήσια ἐνίοτε ὑπ' αὐτοῦ γραφέντα...οὐ μὴν τὸ εἰλικρινὲς τῶν ἐκ θείας ἐπιπνοίας λόγων· ἢ καὶ τούτῳ παραστατέον ὅτι ἡ παλαιὰ μὲν οὐκ εὐαγγέλιον, οὐ δεικνύουσα τὸν ἐρχόμενον ἀλλὰ προκηρύσσουσα, πᾶσα δὲ ἡ καινὴ τὸ εὐαγγέλιόν ἐστιν Or.*Jo.*1.3(5; p.6.24; M.14.28B); πάσης μὲν θ. γραφῆς ἡ ἀνάγνωσις γίνεται τοῖς προσέχουσιν εὐσεβείας ἐπίγνωσις· ἡ δὲ σεπτὴ τῶν εὐαγγελίων γραφὴ ὑψηλοτέρων ἐστὶ διδαγμάτων ὑπεροχή· τὰ γὰρ ἐν αὐτοῖς ἐμφερόμενα λόγια ὑψίστου βασιλέως ὑπάρχει θεσπίσματα Chrys.*hom.in Mt.7:4*(3.25A); **2.** of non-scriptural writings; epitaph of Abercius θ. ἐπίγραμμα *V.Aberc.*76; Basil's *Hexaemeron*, Gr.Nyss.*hex.*proem.(M.45.61A); **3.** of a conciliar decision (condemnation of Nestorius), CEph.*ep.*(*ACO* 1.1.2 p.70.11; H.1.1444D).

B. *holy* λῦσαι...ἱμάντα θ. πεδίλου Nonn.*par.Jo.*1:27(M.43.753C); θ. ...ἀμφὶ λοετρῶν *ib.*4:1(773A); θειότατόν μοι καὶ θεόπνευστον σύστημα ‡Meth.*Sym.et Ann.*3(M.18.353A).

C. *divinely breathing, sweet-smelling* νάμασι τοῖς θ. *Orac.Sib.*5.308; μυρίσμασι θ. *T.Abr.*A 20(p.103.22).

θεόπνους, *breathed on by God, permeated with God's Spirit* ζῶν δὲ Χριστὸς σῶμα θ. καὶ πνεῦμα ἐν σαρκὶ θεϊκόν, νοῦς οὐράνιος Apoll.*fr.*155 (p.249.3)ap.Leont.B.*Apoll.*(M.86.1964B); τῶν ὑπερτέρων νόων ὑπερβέβηκεν ἡ θεόπνους ἀκρότης Geo.Pis.*hex.*1474(M.92.1547A).

***θεοπόθητος**, *beloved by God*; epithet of BMV, ‡Jo.D.*hom.*6.7(M.96.672B).

θεοποι-έω, **I.** *make into a god*; *deify*; *divinize*;

A. ref. creature-worship; **1.** in gen. τὰ δὲ στοιχεῖα καὶ τὰ μόρια αὐτῶν ~οῦσιν Athenag.*leg.*22.6(M.6.940B); *ib.*22.7(940B); Tat.*orat.* 18(p.20.13; M.6.845B); ~ούμενοι τὰ κωφὰ καὶ ἀναίσθητα εἴδωλα Arist.*apol.*13.1; *ib.*7.4; Clem.*prot.*2(p.19.19; M.8.96A); Or.*hom.5.2 in Jer.*(p.33.2f.; M.13.300A); τὸ μὲν Γαριζεὶν ~οῦσιν οἱ Σαμαρεῖς Or. *Jo.*13.13(p.237.21; M.14.417C); ἐπλανήθησαν τὰ μέρη τοῦ παντὸς ~ήσαντες Eus.*l.C.*12(p.232.10; M.20.1392A); Ath.*gent.*20(M.25.41B); μανία σαφὴς...~εῖν τὰ μὴ ὄντα †Bas.*Is.*304(1.609C; M.30.649C); instigated by Devil, ‡Ath.*diab.*5(p.7.5); of deified men παλαιοῦ νόμου κεκρατηκότος μὴ ἄλλως τινὰ παρὰ Ῥωμαίοις ~εῖσθαι μὴ οὐχὶ ψήφῳ καὶ δόγματι συγκλήτου Eus.*h.e.*2.2.2(M.20.140B); **2.** of antichrist τοῦ ὑπ' αὐτῶν ~ηθέντος ἀντιχρίστου Areth.ap.*cat.Apoc.* 16:10f.(p.416.25); **3.** of worship of material things by sinners ~ήσαντες ἑαυτῶν τὰς ἡδονάς Bas.*reg.fus.*20.2(2.364D; M.31.972C); id.*reg.br.*63(2.436D; M.31.1124D); οὐδεὶς δὲ ~ῶν τι ἄλλο παρὰ τὸν θεὸν δύναται προσκυνῆσαι τῷ θεῷ ἐν αὐλῇ ἁγίᾳ αὐτοῦ. ~οῦσι δέ, οἱ μέν, κοιλίαν...οἱ δέ, ἀργύριον †Bas.*hom.in Ps.*28(1.358C; M.30.73B).

B. Christol.; **1.** of Christ 'deified' by Father, Or.*Jo.*2.2(p.54.33; M.14.109A) cit. s. αὐτόθεος; οὔτε ὑφεστὼς [sc. Χριστός] δίχα τοῦ ~οῦντος αὐτὸν πατρός, οὔτ' ἄνευ τοῦ πατρὸς θεολογούμενος, ἀλλ' ὅλον αὐτὸ τοῦτο ὤν τε καὶ ζῶν καὶ ὑφεστὼς διὰ τὸν ἐν αὐτῷ πατέρα, συνὼν τε τῷ πατρὶ καὶ ἐξ αὐτοῦ καὶ δι' αὐτὸν ~ούμενος, τό τε εἶναι ὁμοῦ καὶ τὸ θεὸς εἶναι οὐκ ἐξ ἑαυτοῦ παρὰ δὲ τοῦ πατρὸς ἐσχηκὼς Eus. *d.e.*5.4(p.225.10,13; M.22.372B); **2.** his humanity deified by union with Logos τὸ ἐκ τῆς παρθένου σῶμα, χωρῆσαν πᾶν τὸ πλήρωμα τῆς θεότητος σωματικῶς, τῇ θεότητι ἀτρέπτως ἥνωται καὶ τεθεοποίηται Hymen.*ep.*8(p.329.3); ὁ λόγος, σὰρξ γενόμενος, τὸν ἐκ σπέρματος Δαβὶδ ἀνείληφέν τε καὶ ἐθεοποίησεν Eus.*d.e.*7.3(p.339.27; M.22.553C); ἐλάμβανε [sc. ὁ λόγος] γὰρ κατὰ τὸ ὑψοῦσθαι τὸν ἄνθρωπον. ὕψωσις δὲ ἦν τὸ ~εῖσθαι αὐτόν. αὐτὸς δὲ ὁ λόγος εἶχεν ἀεὶ τοῦτο κατὰ τὴν πατρικὴν ἑαυτοῦ θεότητα Ath.*Ar.*1.45(M.26.105B); *ib.*2.70(296A) cit. s. ἄνθρωπος; οὐ γὰρ ἠλαττοῦτο τῇ περιβολῇ τοῦ σώματος, ἀλλὰ καὶ μᾶλλον ἐθεοποιεῖτο τοῦτο id.*decr.*14(p.12.30; M.25.'448'(440)D); ἡ τὴν ἀνθρώπου φύσιν ἐνδυσαμένη σοφία, τουτέστιν, ὁ τοῦ θεοῦ λόγος...~οῦσα παρὰ τοῖς ὁρῶσι τὸν ἀναληφθέντα ναόν,...οὕτως ἐν σοφίᾳ προέκοπτεν ἡ ἀνθρωπότης, ~ουμένη δι' αὐτῆς Cyr.*thes.*28(5^1.251E); *ib.*20(197D); Leont.H.*Nest.*5.25(M.86.1748A) cit. s. θεοποιός; **3.** in Callistus' alleged theory that Father, being identical with Son, took flesh which he deified οὐ γάρ, φησίν, ἐρῶ δύο θεούς, πατέρα καὶ υἱόν, ἀλλ' ἕνα. ὁ γὰρ ἐν αὐτῷ γενόμενος πατὴρ προσλαβόμενος τὴν σάρκα ἐθεοποίησεν ἑνώσας ἑαυτῷ καὶ ἐποίησεν ἕν Hipp.*haer.*9.12 (p.249.5; M.16.3386A); **4.** in heresies denying divinity of Christ, in gen. οἱ δόσει καὶ χάριτι ~εῖσθαι λέγοντες τὸν υἱόν Apoll.*fid.sec. pt.*1(p.167.4; M.10.1105A); οἱ ἀπὸ Παύλου τοῦ Σαμοσατέως, ὕστερον αὐτὸν μετὰ τὴν ἐνανθρώπησιν ἐκ προκοπῆς τεθεοποιῆσθαι λέγοντες *Symb.Ant.*(345)4(p.252.29; M.26.729C); Arian οὐκ ἔστιν ἀληθινὸς θεὸς ὁ Χριστός, ἀλλὰ μετοχῇ καὶ αὐτὸς ἐθεοποιήθη Ar.*Thal.fr.*3 ap. Ath.*Ar.*1.9(M.26.29B); ὥστε εἰ θεὸν ὁμολογῶσι [sc. Eunomians] τὸν κύριον, καὶ τὴν λοιπὴν κτίσιν ~ήσουσιν Gr.Nyss.*Eun.*4(2 p.59.25; M. 45.629D); τῇ χάριτι τῆσδε τῆς υἱοθεσίας ἥν φατε [sc. Nestorians] ~ηθέντα Leont.H.*Nest.*3.8(M.86.1632B); **5.** ref. Jewish and pagan contention that Christians deify a man αὐτὸς γὰρ Μωυσῆς εἶπε· 'ἐπικατάρατος πᾶς ὁ κρεμάμενος ἐπὶ ξύλου'· βλέπεις οὖν τίνα ~εῖς *Dial. Tim.et Aquil.*fol.100 v°; οὐχ, ὡς σὺ [sc. Julian] νενόμικας, τεθεοποιήκαμεν ἄνθρωπον Cyr.*Juln.*6(6^2.203A).

C. of Christians; **1.** ref. agents and means of deification; **a.** God ἀπὸ τοῦ θεοῦ ἀρυσά⟨μενος⟩ εἰς τὸ ~ηθῆναι αὐτούς Or.*Jo.*2.2(p.55.1; M.14.109A); θεὸς τοὺς ἐγγίζοντας αὐτῷ λόγῳ τῆς διανοίας ἁγιάζει ~ῶν Mac.Mgn.*apocr.*4.26(p.212.21); σχέσει γὰρ τῇ πρὸς θεὸν υἱοποιηθέντες παρ' αὐτοῦ ~ούμεθα Cyr.*thes.*1(5^1.25A); ὁ θεὸς...ἀξίους ~εῖ Max.*cap.* 1.78(M.90.1212B); **b.** Trin. ὥσπερ ὁ πατὴρ δημιουργεῖ, ἁγιάζει, δικαιοῖ καὶ ~εῖ τοὺς πρὸς οὓς γίνεται, τὸν ἴσον τρόπον καὶ ὁ μονογενής, καὶ τὸ πνεῦμα τοῦ θεοῦ ποιεῖ Didym.*Trin.*3.16(M.39.868C); **c.** Christ τοῖς ἀπὸ τοῦ λόγου ~ηθεῖσι Or.*mart.*25(p.22.27; M.11.593D); τρεφόμενοι τῷ ἐν ἀρχῇ πρὸς θεὸν θεῷ λόγῳ ~ηθῶμεν id.*or.*27.13(p.372.2; M.11. 517A); αὐτὸς γὰρ ἐνανθρώπησεν, ἵνα ἡμεῖς ~ηθῶμεν Ath.*inc.*54.3(M. 25.192B); ὁ γὰρ λόγος σὰρξ ἐγένετο, ἵνα καὶ προσενέγκῃ τοῦτο ὑπὲρ πάντων καὶ ἡμεῖς ἐκ τοῦ πνεύματος αὐτοῦ μεταλαβόντες ~ηθῆναι δυνηθῶμεν ἄλλως οὐκ ἂν τούτου τυχόντες, εἰ μὴ τὸ κτιστὸν ἡμῶν αὐτὸς ἐνεδύσατο σῶμα id.*decr.*14(p.12.25; M.25.'448'(440)D); αὐτὸς υἱοποίησεν ἡμᾶς τῷ πατρί, καὶ ἐθεοποίησε τοὺς ἀνθρώπους γενόμενος αὐτὸς ἄνθρωπος id.*Ar.*1.38(M.26.92B); γέγονεν ἄνθρωπος καὶ ἀπέθανεν, ἵνα ἡμεῖς...~ηθῶμεν ‡Ath.*pass.*11(M.28.205B); ἡμεῖς γὰρ φαμεν ἄνθρωπον γεγενῆσθαι τὸν τοῦ θεοῦ λόγον πρὸς σωτηρίαν ἡμῶν, ἵνα...~ηθῶμεν πρὸς ὁμοιότητα τοῦ κατὰ φύσιν ἀληθινοῦ υἱοῦ τοῦ θεοῦ Apoll.*fid.sec. pt.*31(p.179.8; M.10.1117A); Gr.Nyss.*beat.*5(M.44.1249A); εἰ κτίσμα ἐστι...ὁ τοῦ θεοῦ λόγος,...πῶς θεῷ κολλώμεθα καὶ ~ούμεθα συναφθέντες αὐτῷ; Cyr.*thes.*15(5^1.168A); ὁ γὰρ χωρὶς ἁμαρτίας γενόμενος ἄνθρωπος, δῆλον ὅτι χωρὶς τῆς εἰς θεότητα μεταβολῆς, τὴν φύσιν ~ήσει Max.*cap.*1.62(M.90.1204B); and his doctrine οὐρανίῳ διδασκαλίᾳ ~ῶν [sc. Χριστός] τὸν ἄνθρωπον Clem.*prot.*11 (p.81.1; M.8.233A); denied of angels opp. Christ, Didym.*Trin.*2.4 (M.39.481C); **d.** H. Ghost θεϊκοῦ πνεύματος ὑπεδεξάμεθα, δι' οὗ καὶ ~ούμεθα ‡Ath.*ep.cath.*(M.28.84A); πνεῦμα θεῖον...τοῦ θεοῦ ἡμᾶς υἱοὺς ποιεῖ, καὶ ~εῖ Didym.*Trin.*2.25(M.39.749C); εἰ θεοὺς ὀνομάζομεν τοὺς κατ' ἀρετὴν τελείους, ἡ δὲ τελείωσις διὰ τοῦ πνεύματος, πῶς τὸ ἑτέρους ~οῦν, αὐτὸ τῆς θεότητος ἀπολείπεται; Bas.*Eun.*3.5(1.276D; M.29.665B); τὸ πνεῦμα τὸ ἅγιον...τοῖς ἁγίοις δι' υἱοῦ χορηγούμενον, διά τε τοῦτο ~οῦν Cyr.*thes.*33(5^1.335E); †Jo.D.*B.J.*10(M.96.945A); **e.** grace ὁ γὰρ χάριτι ~ούμενος, τῆς μεταπτωτῆς ἐστι φύσεως, ἐξ ἀπροσεξίας ποτὲ καὶ ἀπορρεούσης τοῦ κρείττονος Bas.*Eun.*3.5(1.276E; 665C); Cyr.*thes.*32(5^1.313B); **f.** baptism, word, and priestly ministry πῶς ἐνδύσῃ [sc. Χριστόν] ὁ μήπω τὸ βάπτισμα εἰληφώς;...ἐπεὶ δὲ βούλομαί σε ὅμοιον θεῷ ποιῆσαι, φεύγεις τὸν λόγον τὸν ~οῦντά σε ‡Bas.*struct.hom.*1.21(1.334F; M.30.33C); τέλος...τῆς ἀληθοῦς ἱερωσύνης, τὸ διὰ τούτων ~εῖσθαί τε καὶ ~εῖν Max.*ep.*31(M.91.625A); **g.** scripture, Clem.*prot.*9(p.65.5; M.8.197C) cit. s. γράμμα; **h.** virginity and other virtues, Gr.Nyss.*virg.*1(p.252.8; M.46.320D); Max. *myst.*7(M.91.685D); **2.** of advanced state in spiritual life εἰρήσθω γὰρ τὴν μὲν φρόνησιν ὑπάρχειν γνῶσιν θείαν καὶ ἐν τοῖς ~ουμένοις Clem. *str.*6.15(p.495.9; M.9.349A); προσευχόμενοι μετὰ διαθέσεως τῷ λόγῳ ~ουμένης λέγωμεν Or.*or.*25.2(p.358.22; M.11.497C); ὁ κεκαθαρμένος καὶ ὑπεραναβὰς πάντα ὑλικὰ νοῦς, ἵνα ἀκριβώσῃ τὴν θεωρίαν τοῦ θεοῦ, ἐν οἷς θεωρεῖ ~εῖται id.*Jo.*32.27(17; p.472.30; M.14.817A); **3.** involving immortality, Hipp.*haer.*10.34(p.293.6; M.16.3454B); **4.** ref. partic. individuals τὸ δεδοξασμένον πρόσωπον Μωυσέως, ~ηθέντος αὐτῷ τοῦ νοῦ Or.*Jo.*32.27(17; p.472.34; M.14.817A); heret. ὁ Σίμων... ~ῆσαι ἑαυτὸν ἐπεχείρησεν Hipp.*haer.*6.7(p.135.4; M.16.3206D); *ib.*6. 14(p.139.15; 3214B); Πεπουζηνοὶ προδήλως εἰσὶν αἱρετικοὶ...Μοντανῷ καὶ Πρισκίλλῃ τὴν τοῦ Παρακλήτου προσηγορίαν ἀθεμίτως...ἐπιφημίσαντες...ὡς ἀνθρώπους ~οῦντες Bas.*ep.*188 *can.*1(3.269C; M.32. 668A); ref. Collyridians, giving divine honours to BMV προφάσει γὰρ δικαίου ἀεὶ ὑπεισδύνων τὴν διάνοιαν ὁ διάβολος τῶν ἀνθρώπων τὴν θνητὴν φύσιν ~ῶν Epiph.*haer.*79.4(p.479.10; M.42.745C).

II. pass., *be made by God*, Const.Diac.*laud.*6(M.88.485C).

***θεοποίησις**, ἡ, *deification, making divine*, ref. Jo.10:35 πῶς δὲ καὶ θ. γένοιτ' ἂν χωρὶς τοῦ λόγου; Ath.*Ar.*1.39(M.26.93A); ἡ παρὰ τῆς σοφίας μεταδιδομένη τοῖς ἀνθρώποις θ. καὶ χάρις *ib.*3.53(433B); διὰ τοῦτο...γέγονεν ἡ συναφή, ἵνα τῷ κατὰ φύσιν τῆς θεότητος συνάψῃ τὸν φύσει ἄνθρωπον, καὶ βεβαία γένηται ἡ σωτηρία καὶ ἡ θ. αὐτοῦ *ib.*2.70 (296B).

θεοποιητικός, *deifying* τὴν ἀγάπην,...ἐπὶ πᾶσι θ. Max.*ambig.*(M. 91.1249B).

θεοποίητος, *wrought by God*, Dion.Al.ap.Eus.*p.e.*7.19(333B; M.21. 564A).

θεοποιΐα, ἡ, **1.** *invention of gods*; of invention of pagan theogonies, Eus.*p.e.*1.6(17B; M.21.48B); τὰς μὲν Ἑλλήνων θ., καὶ ἃς καλοῦσι θεογονίας, Ὀρφεύς τε καὶ Ὅμηρος...ἐδίδαξαν Isid.Pel.*epp.*1. 21(M.78.196B); **2.** *making into gods, deification*, Eus.*p.e.*2.6(74C; M.21.141B); ζῴων ἀλόγων θ. id.*d.e.*1.2(p.9.34; M.22.28A); id.*Is.*19:1 (M.24.221A); **3.** in gen., *idolatry* ἀθέων ἐθνῶν τὴν δαιμονικὴν θ. *ib.*41:15(380C); Ath.*gent.*21(M.25.44A); ἐπαρᾶται κακῇ προλήψει θεοποιΐας λέγων, τὰ βρώματα τῇ κοιλίᾳ Epiph.*haer.*66.69(p.109.31; M.42.137C); **4.** *deification, being made divine* τῆς βρώσεως τοῦ δένδρου ἐρασθεῖσα [sc. Eve] θεοποιΐαν ἐφαντάζετο Procl.CP *or.*6.16(M. 65.752B); [sc. Devil] ἄρχων καὶ θεὸς οὐ κατ' οὐσίαν, ἀλλὰ κατὰ θ. ἐξέπεσε Proc.G.*Gen.*3:22(M.87.224B).

θεοποιός, **A.** of pagans, *devising gods*, as subst. προσκυνοῦσιν δὲ οἱ θ. οὐ θεοὺς καὶ δαίμονας...γῆν δὲ καὶ τέχνην, τὰ ἀγάλματα ὅπερ ἐστίν Clem.*prot.*4(p.40.7; M.8.144C); ὦ θ., νέων πάτερ οὐρανιώνων Gr. Naz.*carm.*2.2(poem.)7.69(M.37.1556A).

B. *deifying*; **1.** of divine nature in Christ ἡ μὲν γὰρ ἐθέωσεν ὡς θ. φύσις· ἡ δὲ ἐθεώθη ὡς θεοποιουμένη Leont.H.*Nest.*5.25(M.86.1748A); **2.** of divine grace and virtues by which men are deified; **a.** God and his attributes τὸ καλὸν δὲ καὶ τὸ σοφὸν ἐπὶ τῆς ὅλης θεότητος ὑμνεῖται, καὶ τὸ φῶς, καὶ τὸ θ. Dion.Ar.*d.n.*2.1(M.3.637B); πᾶσα πατροκινήτου φωτοφανείας πρόοδος, εἰς ἡμᾶς...φοιτῶσα...ἐπιστρέφει πρὸς τὴν τοῦ συναγωγοῦ πατρὸς ἑνότητα, καὶ θ. ἁπλότητα id.*c.h.*1.1 (M.3.121A); **b.** Christ αὐτὸς ὢν τὸ θ. καὶ φωτιστικὸν τοῦ πατρός, ἐν ᾧ τὰ πάντα θεοποιεῖται καὶ ζωοποιεῖται, οὐκ ἀλλοτριοούσιός ἐστι τοῦ πατρὸς ἀλλ' ὁμοούσιος Ath.*syn.*51(p.274.27; M.26.784A); πρὸς τοὺς ἐπιγείους ἡμᾶς θεϊκῆς καὶ θ. καταβάσεως Sophr.H.*ep.syn.*(M.87. 3160B); Christ's blood, Jo.D.*prec.*3(M.96.817B); **c.** H. Ghost τὸ πάντων...θ. Cyr.H.*catech.*4.16; Apoll.*fid.sec.pt.*27(p.177.1; M.10. 1116B); Didym.(‡Bas.)*Eun.*5(1.305B; M.29.732B); τῆς θ. καὶ υἱοποιοῦ τοῦ πνεύματος χάριτος Leont.B.*Nest.et Eut.*1(M.86.1301A); **d.** benefits of Communion, Jo.D.*anacr.*(M.96.855A); **e.** Christ's words, *ib.*(855B); **f.** virtues ἀντεισαγόμενος ἕτερον πλοῦτον θ. καὶ ζωῆς χορηγὸν αἰωνίου Clem.*q.d.s.*19(p.172.11; M.9.624C); πῶς γὰρ εἰς τὴν ἑορτὴν συνεισελεύσονται Χριστῷ, μὴ κοσμήσαντες ἑαυτῶν τὴν σκηνὴν κλάδοις ἁγνείας, τῷ θ. καὶ μακαρίῳ φυτῷ; Meth.*symp.*9.4 (p.119.10; M.18.188A).

***θεοπότιστος**, *watered by God*; of BMV θ. ἐλαίαν, Taras.*praesent. BMV* 8(M.98.1489B).

***θεοπραγία**, ἡ, *divine action*, †Gregent.*disp.*(M.86.720A).

θεοπρέπεια, ἡ, *godliness, reverence towards God* ἡ θ. ἕξις ἐστὶ τὸ πρέπον τῷ θεῷ σώζουσα Clem.*str.*7.1(p.4.31; M.9.405B).

θεοπρεπής, **A.** *befitting God, worthy of God*; **1.** ref. divine attributes ἡ θ. ... φιλανθρωπία Dion.Al.*fr.*(p.60.7); Gr.Nyss.*or.catech.* proem.(p.4.14; M.45.12B); ref. H. Ghost οὐ μὴν ἀλλότριόν τι καθ' ὁμοιότητα τοῦ ἡμετέρου πνεύματος ἔξωθεν ἐπιρρεῖν τῷ θεῷ καὶ ἐν αὐτῷ γίνεσθαι τὸ πνεῦμα θ. ἐστιν οἴεσθαι *ib.*2(p.14.8; 17B); θ. ἡμερότης Cyr.*Os.*154(3.187B); *ib.*126(158A); τὴν θ. λογιότητα καὶ σοφίαν Dion. Ar.*c.h.*2.3(M.3.140C); τὰς θ. θεωνυμίας id.*d.n.*2.1(M.3.636C); τὰ θ. τῇ ὅλῃ θεαρχίᾳ πρόσεστι *ib.*(637C); **2.** ref. incarnate life of Christ; **a.** ref. inseparability of τὰ θ. and τὰ ἀνθρωποπρεπῆ v. s. ἀνθρωποπρεπής; **b.** of partic. events τὰ θ. ... θαύματα Or.*fr.*94 *in Jo.*(p.558. 3); τὸ...θ. τῆς ἐκ νεκρῶν ἀναστάσεως Gr.Nyss.*or.catech.*9(p.53.5; M. 45.40D); ref. Mt.10:29,30 πῶς οὐ θεός, ὁ θ. τὴν ἐξουσίαν...ἀνημμένος ...; Cyr.*Arcad.*(p.87.17; 5^2.80A); ref. command to Lazarus θ. ... τὸ κέλευσμα *cat.Jo.*11:49(p.319.2); **3.** exeg. and theol., ref. spiritual interpretation of scripture θεοπρεπέστερον νοήσαντες τὸν Ἰορδάνην

Or.*Jo.*6.48(29; p.157.22; M.14.285A); *ib.*13.24(p.248.6; 440A); ref. anthropomorphic expressions ἃ δὴ προσήκει μεταφέρειν ἐπὶ θ. ἐννοίας, οὐδὲν θνητὸν οὐδ' ἀνθρώπινον ἐν τῷ θεῷ εἶναι φανταζομένους Eus.*Marcell.*1.1(p.5.10; M.24.720D); τῶν θ. ... συμβόλων Dion.Ar. *ep.*9.1(M.3.1108A); **4.** of saints, etc. ὀνόματος θεοπρεπεστάτου [i.e. that of martyr] Ign.*Magn.*1.2; cf.id.*Smyrn.*11.1; the Church of Smyrna θεοπρεπεστάτη *ib.*proem.; of Polycarp θ. πρεσβύτην *M. Polyc.*7.2; θεοφιλὴς ὁ θ. μόνος Clem.*str.*7.1(p.4.32; M.9.405B); of a confessor ὁ θεοπρεπέστατος...Διόσκορος Dion.Al.ap.Eus.*h.e.*6.41.20 (M.20.612A); οἱ...ὡς ἀληθῶς θ. φημὶ δὲ...ἀποστόλους Eus.*h.e.*3.24.1 (M.20.264B); τοὺς...θ. καὶ [τοὺς] μακαρίους προφήτας id.*d.e.*1 proem. (p.2.10; M.22.16A); **5.** of Christian doctrine θ. ... διδασκαλίας Eus. *v.C.*4.55(p.140.6; M.20.1205B); θ. ... ἀναπτύξεσιν Dion.Ar.*d.n.*9.5(M. 3.913A); **6.** of virtue; virtues as καθαρσία θ. Clem.*prot.*1(p.10.9; M.8.65C); τὰς...θ. ἀρετάς Eus.*l.C.*proem.(p.196.12; θεοφιλεῖς M.20. 1317B); θ. ... ἀπάθεια Gr.Nyss.*ep.*3(M.46.1021D); θ. σεβασμιότης Dion.Ar.*c.h.*4.1(M.3.177D); **7.** of divine gifts to man καὶ ζωῇ καὶ λόγῳ καὶ σοφίᾳ καὶ πᾶσι τοῖς θ. ἀγαθοῖς κατεκοσμήθη Gr.Nyss.*or. catech.*5(p.23.12; M.45.21D); **8.** of Holy Communion, Euthal.Diac. *epp.Paul.*(M.85.756B).

B. *divine*; **1.** of Christ, Eus.*e.th.*1.20(p.81.2; M.24.865B); ref. divine names as applied to Son ὅσαι...τὸ θ. ἑρμηνεύουσι Gr.Nyss. *Eun.*3(2 p.44.4; M.45.612C); θ. ... οἰκονομία Cyr.*inc.unigen.*(5^{1}. 679B); δείκνυσιν ἑαυτοῦ τὸ θ. id.*fr.Mt.*23:37(M.72.439D); ἀπὸ τῶν ταπεινοτέρων γὰρ τῆς οἰκονομίας ἀρξάμενος, ἐπὶ τὰ θεοπρεπέστερα προέβη Areth.*Apoc.*1(M.106.500B); **2.** holy things τὰς θ. τελετάς Eus.*l.C.*proem.(p.196.12; M.20.1317C); θ. παράδεισον id.*h.e.*3.24.4 (M.20.264C); τῆς Χριστιανῶν ἀρχαιότητος τὸ παλαιὸν ὁμοῦ καὶ θ. *ib.* 1.2.1(53B); of divine truths τὰ θ. Cyr.*Jo.*5(4.520D); ref. idols τῶν... δοκούντων θ. Dion.Ar.*c.h.*9.3(M.3.260C).

C. *like God*; ref. Christ's redemptive work εἰς τὸ θεοπρεπέστερον τὴν εἰκόνα ἐπισκευάσας Meth.*res.*2.24(p.380.14; M.18.329D).

θεοπρεπῶς, A. *in a way worthy of God, as befits God*; **1.** exeg. and theol.; **a.** in gen. θ. νοῶμεν Bas.*Spir.*20(3.17E; M.32.104C); Didym. *Trin.*1.27(M.39.397D); ‡Ath.*dial.Trin.*1.6(M.28.1125C) cit. s. ἀνθρωποπαθῶς; Cyr.*Nah.*1(3.479D); θ. ... τὸ ἐμφύσημα νοητέον Thdt.*qu. 23 in Gen.*(1.39); τοῖς θ. νοοῦσι Dion.Ar.*d.n.*5.8(M.3.824A); τὰ θεῖα θ. νοητέον *ib.*7.2(869A); *ib.*9.9(916C); cf.*ib.*10.2(937B); Jo.D.*f.o.*1.7(M. 94.808B); **b.** of Christ ὁ τῆς εἰκόνος λόγος θ. παραδεχθείς, τὴν ἑνότητα ἡμῖν παρίστησι τῆς θεότητος Bas.*hom.*24.4(2.193A; M.31.608B); Chrys. *hom.39.4 in 1Cor.*(10.367C); Diad.*ascens.*5(M.65.1145B) cit. s. ἀνθρωποπρεπῶς; **2.** ref. worship and other human action μόνον τὸν γνωστικὸν...θ. τὸν τῷ ὄντι θεὸν θρησκεύοντα Clem.*str.*7.1(p.3.27; M.9. 404B); cf.*ib.*(p.5.8; 408A); θεοῦ λόγων θ. ἀκηκοότες Or.*Jo.*6.4(2; p.110.23; M.14.204D); ref. BMV δοξάσειε θ. ... μητέρα ‡Meth.*Sym.et Ann.*10(M.18.373B); τὰς χιτῶνας τῶν ψυχῶν θ. ἐξαλλάξωμεν ‡Epiph. *hom.*1(M.43.429A); ref. CNic. θ. ἐκφωνηθείσης τῆς πίστεως Gel.Cyz. *h.e.*2.32.8(M.85.1337D); δοίη ὁ θεὸς θ. ὑμνῆσαι τὰς τῆς...θεότητος... πολυωνυμίας Dion.Ar.*d.n.*1.8(M.3.597C); *ib.*4.12(709B); **3.** of divine action, ref. Christ πολλάκις ἀνθρωπίνως ἐφθέγγετο, καὶ πάλιν...θ. Chrys.*anom.*7.4(1.506A); Nil.*epp.*3.323(M.79.357D); Ἰησοῦς...θ. ... τῆς πάντων προνοῶν σωτηρίας Marc.Er.*opusc.*3.1(M.65.965B); κεκλεισμένον τὸν τάφον...ἀπολιπόντα θ. Sev.Ant.*res.*(p.800.6; M.46. 629B); ἰασάτο (sic)...θ. τὸν ὑπομείναντα τὴν πληγήν Vict.*Mc.*14:50 (p.429.2); hence

B. *divinely*, ‡Chrys.*BMV* 1(8.238D); Dion.Ar.*d.n.*1.1(M.3.588A); id.*c.h.*8.2(M.3.240D); Gr.Ant.*mul.ung.*3(M.88.1852A); ref. BMV οὐ σαρκικῶς γεγέννηκεν...ἀλλὰ θ. Maro ap.Anast.S.*hod.*22(M.89.296B).

C. *as God*; **1.** of Christ τοῦτο λέγων θ. Isid.Pel.*epp.*1.79(M.78. 237A); cf.*ib.*1.80(237C); Sev.Ant.*res.*(p.856.1; M.46.649D); ἔδει γὰρ αὐτὸν διὰ μὲν τοῦ ἁγίου πνεύματος ἐν ἡμῖν γενέσθαι θ., συνανακίρνασθαι δὲ ὥσπερ τοῖς ἡμετέροις σώμασι διὰ τῆς ἁγίας αὐτοῦ σαρκὸς καὶ τοῦ τιμίου αἵματος Vict.*Mc.*14:22(p.423.17); θεωπ-, Jo.D.*Man.*1.20(M.94. 1524C); **2.** ref. H. Ghost λέγει...καὶ τὸ πνεῦμα θ. Thdt.*1Tim.*4:1(3. 659).

***θεοπρεσβύτης, ὁ,** *ambassador of God*, ref. a messenger of the church of Smyrna, Ign.*Smyrn.*11.2.

***θεοπρόβλητος,** *promoted, advanced by God*; title of emperors, Isid.Pel.*epp.*4.144(M.78.1225A); of empire, Sophr.H.*trop.*(M.87. 4009A).

θεοπρόπος, *inspired*, of Caiaphas θ. ἀνήρ Nonn.*par.Jo.*11:51(M. 43.848C); of Christ, *ib.*4:29(780A).

***θεοπροστάτευτος,** *championed by God*, Tim.CP *haer.*(M.86. 237B).

***θεοπρότακτος,** *preferred by God*; of BMV, ‡Jo.D.*hom.*5(M.96. 648B).

θεόπτης, ὁ, *one who sees God*, Ἀβραὰμ τὸν πατριάρχην, τὸν θ. τὸν μέγαν Gr.Naz.*carm.*1.2.10.491(M.37.715A); Μωϋσῆς θ. ἐγένετο Sophr.H.*or.*5(M.87.3313A); τοῖς πάλαι πιστοῖς θ. Geo.Pis.*Sev.*202 (M.92.1637A); ὁ θ. Ἡσαΐας Germ.CP *or.*1(M.98.241B); Jo.D.*carm. transfig.*(M.96.848A); as adj. τῇ καταβάσει τοῦ ἁγίου καὶ θ. ἡλίου [prob. Ἠλίου] Jo.Clim.*scal.*7(M.88.812B); θ. πατράσι Geo.Pis.*van.*3 (M.92.1581A).

θεοπτία (-εία), ἡ, *vision of God*; **1.** of special visions granted to Moses, prophets, etc. Δανιὴλ...τὴν θ. ὑπογράφων Eus.*h.e.*1.2.24(M. 20.65B); Μωσῆς...προστάττεται...σύμβολα καταστήσασθαι τῶν ἐν ταῖς θεοπτείαις νενοημένων id.*d.e.*4.15(p.176.14; M.22.293B); *ib.*7.1(p.298. 2; 488C); Didym.*Trin.*1.19(M.39.364B); Epiph.*haer.*51.7(p.257.27; M. 41.901A); ἐδίδου τὰς θ. τοῖς ἁγίοις προφήταις ὁ...θεός Cyr.*Is.*1.4(2. 101E); *ib.*2.4(306D); Dion.Ar.*ep.*8.1(M.3.1085A); **2.** of special visions seen by partic. individuals in post-biblical times, Cyr.H.*ep.Const.*1 (M.33.1165A); Epiph.*haer.*30.11(p.347.4; M.41.424D); **3.** of vision, or contemplation, of God; granted: to angelic orders ἡ τάξις [sc. τῶν σεραφίμ] μέσοις πτεροῖς ἐν συμμετρίᾳ πρὸς θ. ἀνάγεται Dion.Ar. *e.h.*4.3.7(M.3.481B); to Adam before Fall ὅλος ἦν καὶ διὰ παντὸς ἐν θεοπτίαις ὁ νοῦς Cyr.*Rom.*5:18(p.186.26; M.74.789A); and after Redemption, id.*Os.*62(3.95E); to pure in heart, id.*ador.*4(1.136A); and in gen. as object of mystical ascent εἰς...τὰ ὑπερτενῆ τῆς θ. ἱέντες ὑψώματα id.*hom.pasch.*15(5^{2}.199A); μέχρι γὰρ ἐννοίας μόνης ἐπὶ τὴν θ. ἡ τῶν γενητῶν ἔρχεται φύσις id.*Jo.*5(4.450D); πολλάκις γοῦν ὕψωσά μου τὸν λογισμόν, οὐδὲν δὲ ἧττον τῆς θ. ἀπώλισθον Olymp. *Job* 4:17(M.93.76B); **4.** of divine revelation not fully manifested in OT, Didym.*Trin.*1.18(M.39.348C); τὸ τῆς ἀληθοῦς θ. εἰσδέξασθαι φῶς Cyr.*Is.*3.1(2.382D); id.*Jo.*3.3(4.265E); of revelation in Christ, Ammon.*Jo.*14:22(M.85.1492A).

θεοπτικός, *able to see God, seeing God*, of angels ἡ δὲ τῶν χερουβὶμ [sc. ἐπωνυμία], τὸ γνωστικὸν αὐτῶν καὶ θ. Dion.Ar.*c.h.*7.1(M.3. 205C); τῶν θ. τάξεων id.*e.h.*5.1.5(M.3.505A); τὰ σεραφίμ...διὰ τοῦ πλήθους τῶν ὀφθαλμῶν τὸ πρὸς τὰς θείας αὐγὰς θ. αὐτῶν διδασκόμενος Andr.Caes.*Apoc.*10(M.106.256C); of human understanding θ. διανοίᾳ τὰς θεοειδεῖς ἐποπτεύσωμεν...θεωρίας Dion.Ar.*d.n.*1.8(M.3. 597B).

***θεόπτωτος,** *fallen away from God* τὸν θ. Χοσρόην *Chron.Pasch.* p.386(M.92.992A).

***θεορήμων,** v. *θεορρήμων.

***θεορήτωρ, ὁ,** *one who speaks from God, inspired person*; of children at Christ's entry into Jerusalem, ‡Epiph.*hom.*1(M.43. 437B); of Cyril, Anast.S.*hod.*10(M.89.177B).

***θεορρημοσύνη, ἡ,** *divine doctrine*, Dion.Ar.*e.h.*2.3.1(M.3.397B).

***θεορρήμων (*θεορήμων),** *speaking from God* τὸν τοῖς θεορήμοσιν ἐοικότα νοῦν Cyr.*Chr.un.*(5^{1}.740D); ᾗ φησιν ὁ θ. Leont.H. *Nest.*2.16(M.86.1573B); ὁ θ. Γρηγόριος Jo.D.*imag.*1.11(M.94.1241B); θεορή-, Cosm.Mel.*schol.*34(M.38.445) in Gr.Naz.*carm.*1.1.18.

θεόρρητος, *uttered by God, inspired*, Meth.*symp.*8.17(p.111.13; M. 18.173C); θ. ... βίβλων Nonn.*par.Jo.*5:39(M.43.792B); *CIG* 9267.

θεόρρυτος, *flowing from God*; of blood of Christ, Gr.Naz.*carm.* 1.1.9.93(M.37.464A); of Christ's words, Nonn.*par.Jo.*8:14(M.43. 813C); of divine revelation, Geo.Pis.*Sev.*84(M.92.1628B); of Logos, id.*hex.*184(M.92.1447A); of influence of H. Ghost τοῖς θ. τοῦ πνεύματος νάμασι Jo.D.*hom.*4.28(M.96.629B).

θεός, ὁ, *God*;

A. in gen.; **1.** derivations; **a.** from θέω: ἑνὸς ὄντος τοῦ θ. κατὰ τὴν ἀμετάτρεπτον τοῦ ἀεὶ θεῖν τὰ ἀγαθὰ ἕξιν Clem.*str.*4.23(p.315.22; M.8. 1360C); cf.id.*prot.*2(p.19.15; M.8.96A); Eus.*p.e.*1.9(29D; M.21.70A); Jo.D.*f.o.*1.9(M.94.836B); **b.** from θεάομαι, θεωρέω (derivation being expressed or implied) θ. ... ὁ μέλλων ὁρᾶσθαι Iren.*haer.*4.38.3(M.7. 1108C); διά...τὸ αἰτίους εἶναι τοῦ θεωρεῖν τὰ ὁρώμενα, πρώτους θ. ἀνηγορεύεσθαι Eus.*p.e.*5.3(182D; M.21.316D); θ. λέγοντες, τὸν ἔφορον καὶ ἐπόπτην...ἐπινοοῦντες ἐπικαλούμεθα Gr.Nyss.*Eun.*2(1 p.257.12 M.45.960C); cf.id.*tres dii*(M.45.124A); **c.** from τίθημι: θ. ... παρὰ τὴν θέσιν εἴρηται, καὶ τάξιν Clem.*str.*1.29(p.112.2; M.8.929A); **d.** alternative derivations given together; τίθημι and θέω, Thphl.Ant. *Autol.*1.4(M.6.1029A); Dion.Al.ap.Eus.*p.e.*14.27(782D; M.21.1288A); τοῦ θ., κἂν ἀπὸ τοῦ θέειν, ἢ αἴθειν,...διὰ τὸ ἀεικίνητον καὶ δαπανητικὸν τῶν μοχθηρῶν ἕξεων Gr.Naz.*or.*30.18(p.136.6; M.36.128A); τίθημι, θεάομαι, Evagr.Pont.*ep.*11(M.32.265A); θεωρέω, θέω, αἴθω, Anast.S.*hod.*2(M.89.85C); θέω, αἴθω, θεάομαι, *Schol.*4 in Jo.Clim. *scal.*1(M.88.645A); θῶ, q.v., θέω, or θεάομαι, †Jo.D.*Trin.*5(M.95. 16A); **2.** synonyms, cf. *deus, quod...Hebraice Baruch dicitur*, Iren. *haer.*2.24.2(M.7.791A); *Eloe, secundum Judaicam vocem, deum significat*, *ib.*2.35.3(838B); κἄν τε κύριον ἀκούσωμεν, κἄν τε θ., οὐδεμία ἐν τοῖς ὀνόμασίν ἐστι διαφορά Chrys.*hom.14.2 in Gen.*(4.108A);

3. definitions *τὸ κατὰ τὰ αὐτὰ καὶ ὡσαύτως ἀεὶ ἔχον καὶ τοῦ εἶναι πᾶσι τοῖς ἄλλοις αἴτιον, τοῦτο...ἐστιν ὁ θ.* Just.*dial.*3.5(M.6.481B); *θ. ἐστιν οὐσία νοερά, ἀθεώρητος, καὶ ἀνερμήνευτος· θ. ἐστι πνεῦμα ἄυλον, ὀφθαλμὸς ἀκοίμητος, νοῦς ἀκίνητος, οὐσία δημιουργικὴ πάντων* ‡Ath.*qu.al.*1(M.28.773B).

B. ref. God's existence as inferred; **1.** from motion *ἰδὼν...τὸν κόσμον καὶ τὰ ἐν αὐτῷ πάντα, ὅτι κατὰ ἀνάγκην κινεῖται, συνῆκα τὸν κινοῦντα...εἶναι θ.* Arist.*apol.*1.2; **2.** from existence of mutable things which points to an immutable creator, who is God, Jo.D.*f.o.*1.3 (M.94.796Aff.); **3.** from design *τὸν διακοσμήσαντα τὸ πᾶν τοῦτο, τοῦτον εἶναι τὸν θ.* Athenag.*leg.*7.1(M.6.904B); Thphl.Ant.*Autol.*1.6 (M.6.1033A); Ath.*Ar.*2.32(M.26.216B); Chrys.*diab.*1.8(2.259E); *ἡ τῆς κτίσεως συνοχή, καὶ συντήρησις, καὶ κυβέρνησις, διδάσκει ἡμᾶς ὅτι ἐστὶ θ.* Jo.D.*f.o.*1.3(M.94.796C).

C. ref. attributes; **1.** of divine transcendence as implying that God is unlike creatures, Clem.*str.*2.16(p.152.2ff.; M.8.1012C); Or.*Cels.*3.69(p.261.19; M.11.1009D); Eus.*e.th.*3.5(p.163.6; M.24.1012C); *ἔστιν οὐχ ὡς ἡμεῖς ἐσμεν, ἔστι μέντοι ὡς θ.* Ath.*Ar.*1.23(M.26.60B); hence same terms cannot be used univocally of both *τὸ μέγας ἐπὶ θεοῦ ὅταν λέγῃ, οὐ πρός τι μέγας φησίν, ἀλλ' ἀπολύτως μέγας* Chrys.*hom.5.2 in Tit.*(11.759D); *εἰ πᾶν τὸ ὑπὸ γένος καὶ εἶδος χωρὶς τῶν συμβεβηκότων, τοῦτο οὐσία κυρίως, ὑπ' οὐδὲν δὲ τούτων ἐστὶ θ., οὐκ ἄρα οὐσία κυρίως λέγεται θ.* Cyr.*thes.*3(5[1].18E); Dion.Ar.*d.n.*4.20 (M.3.720B); Max.*schol.d.n.*5.1(M.4.308D); *ὁ θ., ὁ μήτε οὐσία, ἀλλ' ὑπὲρ οὐσίαν· μήτε ἁπλοῦς, ἀλλ' ὑπὲρ ἁπλότητα ib.*1.1(189A); **2.** lists of attributes, Arist.*apol.*1.4; Athenag.*leg.*10.1(M.6.908B); *Hom.Clem.*2.45; Cyr.H.*catech.*6.7; *Doct.Patr.*1.19(p.8.1ff.); Jo.D.*f.o.*1.2(M.94.792C); **3.** being and attributes; **a.** fullness of being *ὁ ὄντως ὢν θ.* Clem.*str.*7.9(p.40.18; M.9.477B); Hipp.*haer.*10.34(p.292.20; M.16.3454B); Or.*fr.47 in Jer.*(p.222.4); Gr.Nyss.*Eun.*2(1 p.257.8; M.45.960C); Dion.Ar.*d.n.*5.4(M.3.817D); **b.** simplicity, Or.*Jo.*1.19(22; p.24.23; M.14.57B); Ath.*gent.*41(M.25.81C); id.*decr.*22(p.18.21; M.25.453C); *εἰ...πνεῦμα ὁ θ. ἁπλοῦς...καὶ ἀσύνθετος, καὶ ἀσχημάτιστος* Thdt.*qu.20 in Gen.*(1.25); id.*Is.*40:12(p.157.22; 2.328); cf.Or.*princ.*1.1.6(p.21.10; M.11.125A); denial that plurality of attributes implies that God is composite, Adam.*dial.*1.10(M.18.1081B); Bas.*ep.*139.5(3.279A; M.32.689C); ‡Ath.*dial.Trin.*1.18(M.28.1144D); Jo.D.*f.o.*1.9(M.94.836A); v. *ἁπλοῦς*; ref. heresies; simplicity of God renders divine emanations impossible, the Thinker and the Thought being identical, Iren.*haer.*2.13.5(M.7.745A); God's simplicity implies that knowledge of attributes is equivalent to knowledge of essence (Anomoean), Bas.*ep.*234.1(3.357B; M.32.868B); **c.** incorporeality; ref. argument that if God were corporeal he would be material and so corruptible, Or.*princ.*2.4.3(p.130.17; 201C); id.*Jo.*13.21 (p.245.5ff.; 433A); but cf.*ib.*(p.244.21; 432C) cit. s. *αἰθερώδης*; *ὅτι... ἀσώματον* [sc. *θ.*], *δῆλον. πῶς γὰρ σῶμα, τὸ ἄπειρον, καὶ...καὶ ἀσχημάτιστον, καὶ ἀναφές...ἁπλοῦν, καὶ ἀσύνθετον;* Jo.D.*f.o.*1.4(M.94.797B); ref. arguments from scripture (e.g. Jer.23:24, Sap.1:7) that he is everywhere and is spirit, Gr.Naz.*or.*28.8(p.32.7; M.36.33D); ref. anthropomorphisms in scriptures as not proving the contrary, Or.*fr.in 1Reg.*(p.296.23); cf.Ath.*Ar.*3.1(M.26.324A); *θ. ἐστιν, ὡς καὶ ὁ κύριος λέγει, πνεῦμα. πνεῦμα δέ ἐστι κυρίως οὐσία ἀσώματος καὶ ἀπερίγραπτος* Clem.*fr.*39(p.220.6; M.9.769B); Or.*princ.*1.1.4(p.19.25ff.; M.11.123C); **d.** impassibility, Just.*1apol.*25.2(M.6.365B); *θ. ... ἀπαθὴς ἄθυμός τε καὶ ἀνεπιθύμητος* Clem.*str.*4.23(p.315.16; M.8.1360C); **e.** incorruptibility, Tat.*orat.*7(p.7.9; M.6.820B); Iren.*haer.*2.13.9(M.7.748A); Clem.*str.*5.11(p.371.14ff.; M.9.104A); *ἀφθαρσία...ὁ θ.* Ath.*inc.et c.Ar.*15(M.26.1012A); ref. teaching of Marcellus *τοῦ θεοῦ...σωματικὸν πάθος, ὅπερ οὐ θέμις ἐπὶ τῆς...ἀσωμάτου φύσεως παραδέχεσθαι* Eus.*e.th.*3.3(p.157.7; M.24.1001B); **f.** perfection *πάντοτε ὁ θ. τέλειος διαμένει, πλήρης ὢν...πάντων τῶν ἀγαθῶν* Thphl.Ant.*Autol.*2.15(M.6.1077A); Clem.*str.*7.14(p.63.12; M.9.524A); Meth.*creat.*3(p.495.13; M.18.336A); Ath.*gent.*39(M.25.77C); his perfection proved from Mt.5:48, Cyr.H.*catech.*6.8; Chrys.*stat.*10.4(2.111D); cf.id.*hom.3.1 in Ac.*9:1(3.117B); †Bas.*Is.*25(1.398D; M.30.165C); **g.** holiness, v. *ἅγιος*; **h.** goodness, cf. *deus non est, cui bonitas desit*, Iren.*haer.*3.25.3(M.7.968C); *ὁ φύσει ἀγαθὸς θ.* Clem.*paed.*1.9(p.138.16; M.8.349A); id.*str.*6.16(p.504.3; M.9.369B); cf.Or.*princ.*4.4.8(p.359.11; M.11.409C); Ath.*gent.*41(M.25.81D); Cyr.*Os.*133(3.166B); Dion.Ar.*e.h.*2.2.1(M.3.393A); *ὁ...θ. ... αὐτοαγαθότης* Max.*carit.*3.27(M.90.1025A); God alone being essentially good, Clem.*str.*3.5(p.216.4; M.8.1148A); Bas.*hom.in Ps.*33(1.150B; M.29.368B); *φύσει ἀγαθὸς μόνος ὁ θ. ἐστιν* Diad.*perf.*2(p.6.8); hence impossibility of sin *τὸ μηδ' ὅλως ἐξαμαρτάνειν..., ὃ δή φαμεν εἶναι θεοῦ* Clem.*paed.*1.2(p.92.3; M.8.253A); *οὐ δύναται αἰσχρὰ ὁ θ., ἐπεὶ ἔσται ὁ θ. δυνάμενος μὴ εἶναι θ.* Or.*Cels.*5.23(p.24.14; M.11.1216D); *τὸ μηδὲν ἁμαρτεῖν...μόνου θ.* Gr.Naz.*or.*16.15(M.35.953B); **i.** infinity, ubiquity *μεῖζον...ἐστι τὸ χωροῦν τοῦ χωρουμένου· θ. γὰρ οὐ χωρεῖται, ἀλλὰ αὐτός ἐστι τόπος τῶν ὅλων* Thphl.Ant.*Autol.*2.3(M.6.1049C); Or.*Cels.*7.34(p.184.15; M.11.1468C); Thdt.*qu.20 in Gen.*(1.27); because of his transcendence, Clem.*str.*2.2(p.116.2; M.8.937A); Cyr.H.*catech.*18.3; *θ. ... πανταχοῦ,...τί γὰρ δύναται χωρῆσαι τὴν ἀσώματον φύσιν;* ‡Chrys.*cruc.*(2.821D); **j.** immutability, eternity *τὸν ἄτρεπτον καὶ ἀεὶ ὄντα θ.* Just.*1apol.*13.4 (M.6.348A); *τὸν θ. τὸν ἀπαθῆ καὶ ἀμετάβλητον* Clem.*ecl.*52(p.151.23; M.9.721C); *θ. ἐστιν ἀΐδιος οὐσία καὶ ἀπαράλλακτος Doct.Patr.*33 (p.261.13); without beginning or end, Tat.*orat.*4(p.4.29; M.6.813A); ‡Ath.*dial.Trin.*1.2(M.28.1117D); ‡Gr.Nyss.*Ar.et Sab.*10(M.45.1296B); because cause of all things, Athenag.*leg.*4.2(M.6.897B); Iren.*haer.*4.11.2(M.7.1002A); Epiph.*haer.*66.14(p.36.17; M.42.49B); being in a continuous present, †Bas.*Is.*119(1.461E; M.30.312A); *θ. ἦν μὲν ἀεί, καὶ ἔστι, καὶ ἔσται· μᾶλλον δέ, ἔστιν ἀεί*, Gr.Naz.*or.*45.3(M.36.625C); **k.** unity (v. *εἷς*); taught by philosophers, Athenag.*leg.*6.1(M.6.901A); by Hebr. tradition and gentile reasoning, Iren.*haer.*2.9.1 (M.7.734A); demonstrated by argument that if there were more than one God, both would be in the same place, Athenag.*leg.*8 (904Cff.); cf. *quemadmodum...poterit super hunc* [sc. *deum*] *alia plenitudo...aut alius deus esse: cum oporteat deum horum omnium pleroma...omnia circumcontinere, et circumcontineri a nemine?* Iren.*haer.*2.1.2(M.7.710A); cf.*ib.*2.1.5(712A); and inferred from harmony of universe, Ath.*gent.*38(M.25.76C); and fact that there can be only one God because God is the perfect being, Jo.D.*f.o.*1.5(M.94.801A); ref. scriptural proof, Ign.*Magn.*8.2; Athenag.*leg.*9 (905Cff.); Iren.*haer.*2.35.2(838A); Thdt.*haer.*5.1(4.377–8); Jo.D.*f.o.*1.5(M.94.800D); hence freq. use of term *τῶν ὅλων θεός*, e.g. Clem.*str.*1.27(p.109.9; M.8.924B); Or.*hom.1.10 in Jer.*(p.9.19; M.13.268B); Cyr.H.*procatech.*9; cf. *εἷς...ὤν, καὶ μόνος ὤν, καὶ ἀεὶ ὁ αὐτὸς ὤν, πάντων ἐστὶ θ.* Eun.*apol.*28(M.30.368A); **l.** knowledge extending to everything, Clem.*str.*5.7(p.354.22; M.9.69A); *τὸ...εἰδέναι τὰ πάντα... πρέποι ἂν μόνῳ τῷ κατὰ φύσιν ὄντι θ.* Cyr.*Is.*4.1(2.564E); incl. future, Clem.*q.d.s.*6(p.164.6; M.9.612A); Or.*or.*4.3(p.309.12; M.11.432A); and secrets of men's hearts, id.*princ.*3.1.13(p.218.3; M.11.275A); Chrys.*hom.4.5 in Mt.*(7.56A); God knowing everything in his own essence, which is cause of all things, Clem.*fr.*48(p.224.24) ap.Max.*ambig.*(M.91.1085B); Dion.Ar.*d.n.*7.2(M.3.869C); Max.*schol.d.n.*7.2(M.4.349A,B); id.*carit.*3.22(M.90.1024A); **m.** wisdom, Clem.*paed.*1.10(p.145.25; M.8.361A); *ὁ...θ. ... αὐτοσοφία* Max.*carit.*3.27(M.90.1025A); **n.** truth, Iren.*haer.*2.13.9(M.7.748A); *θ. ... τῶν ὄντων ἀληθείας τὸ μέτρον* Clem.*prot.*6(p.52.25; M.8.73B); **o.** freedom, Tat.*orat.*7(p.7.14; M.6.820B); Iren.*haer.*2.1.1(M.7.710A); cf.*ib.*2.5.5(723C); Clem.*str.*7.7(p.32.7; M.9.460A); Ath.*Ar.*3.62(M.26.456A); *οὐ...ἔστιν ἀνάγκη παρὰ θεῷ· ἀνώτερος νόμων ἐστί* Chrys.*Dan.*9:1–3(6.246C); **p.** love, *Diogn.*10.2; *ὁ...θ. ἡμῶν ἡ ἀγάπη ἐστί* Gr.Naz.*or.*22.4(M.35.1136A); **q.** justice and mercy *ὁ θ. ... σπλαγχνίζεται ἐπὶ τὴν ποίησιν αὐτοῦ* Herm.*mand.*9.3; cf.id.*sim.*9.23.4; *εἰ ἔστιν ὁ θ.,...ἀκόλουθον εἶναι καὶ δίκαιον* Chrys.*diab.*1.8(2.260A); *δικαιοσύνη ὁ θ.* Dion.Ar.*d.n.*8.7(M.3.893D); **r.** goodness expressed in providence, Jo.D.*f.o.*2.29(M.94.964B); **s.** power, cf. *sapientia, per quam deus omnipotens dicitur*, Or.*princ.*1.2.10(p.43.6; M.11.141A); *τῷ...θ., ἀεὶ κατὰ τὰ αὐτὰ ὄντι, καὶ ἀγεννήτῳ ὑπάρχοντι, ὡς πρὸς ἑαυτόν, πάντα δύνατα* Iren.*haer.*4.38.1(M.7.1105A); *δύναμίς ἐστιν ὁ θ., ὡς πᾶσαν δύναμιν ἐν ἑαυτῷ...ὑπερέχων* Dion.Ar.*d.n.*8.1(M.3.889D); not extending to self-contradiction or evil *δύναται...πάντα ὁ θ., ἅπερ δυνάμενος τοῦ θ. εἶναι καὶ τοῦ ἀγαθὸς εἶναι καὶ σοφὸς εἶναι οὐκ ἐξίσταται* Or.*Cels.*3.70(p.262.24; M.11.1012D); Epiph.*haer.*76.31(p.380.11; M.42.580A); Dion.Ar.*d.n.*8.6(M.3.893B).

D. of divine operations *ad extra*; **1.** creation; **a.** in gen., cf. *proprium est...hoc dei supereminentiae, non indigere aliis organis ad conditionem eorum, quae fiunt*, Iren.*haer.*2.2.5(M.7.715A); *μόνος ὁ θ. ἐποίησεν, ἐπεὶ καὶ μόνος ὄντως ἐστὶ θ.* Clem.*prot.*4(p.48.16; M.8.164A); Chrys.*hom.38.2 in Ac.*(9.289D); **b.** in rel. to his nature, cf. *facere...proprium est benignitatis dei*, Iren.*haer.*4.39.2(M.7.1110C); *διὰ μόνην ἀγαθότητα τὸ πᾶν παραγαγεῖν τὸν θ.* Max.*schol.d.n.*1.5 (M.4.205B); Jo.D.*f.o.*2.2(M.94.864C); cf.*ib.*4.21(1197A); **2.** in rel. to evil *οὐκοῦν ἔξω τῆς τῶν κακῶν αἰτίας ὁ θ., ὁ τῶν ὄντων, οὐχ ὁ τῶν μὴ ὄντων ποιητὴς ὢν* Gr.Nyss.*or.catech.*7(p.40.8; M.45.32D); *θ. ... οὐδὲν κακὸν ἐποίησεν,...ἀγαθὸς ὢν τὴν φύσιν,...πάντα περιέχων, αὐτὸς δὲ ὑπ' οὐδενὸς περιεχόμενος* Epiph.*haer.*66.15(p.38.19; M.42.52B); *τὸ κακὸν οὔτε ἐν φύσει ἐστίν...κακὸν γάρ τι ὁ θ. οὐκ ἐποίησεν* Diad.*perf.*3(p.6.16); evil being incompatible with divine goodness, cf. *si dicamus quia bonus deus in ipsa conditione sua aliquid sibi creavit inimicum, ...absurdum videbitur*, Or.*princ.*3.4.5(p.270.17; M.11.325B); *εἰ... κακῶν αἴτιος* [sc. *ὁ θ.*], *οὐκ ἀγαθὸς δηλονότι· ὥστε...ἐστιν ἄρνησις τοῦ* θ. Bas.*hom*.9.2(2.73D; M.31.332B); Dion.Ar.*d.n*.4.21(M.3.721D); οἶδεν ὁ θ. τὸ κακὸν ἢ ἀγαθόν, καὶ παρ' αὐτῷ αἱ αἰτίαι τῶν κακῶν, δυνάμεις εἰσὶν ἀγαθοποιοί *ib*.4.30(729C); ref. Rom.9:14 θεὸν...κηρυττούσης τῆς γραφῆς...ἀναίτιον κακίας Clem.*str*.4.26(p.323.26; M.8.1380A); ref. God's justice εἰ...ἁμαρτητικοὺς λογισμοὺς ἐδημιούργησεν ὁ θ., πῶς καταδικάζει τὸν ἁμαρτήσαντα; ‡Ath.*Apoll*.2.6(M.26.1140C); **3.** in rel. to human action, sustaining the activity of prophets, teachers, etc. ὥσπερ αἱ θεραπεῖαι καὶ αἱ προφητεῖαι καὶ τὰ σημεῖα, οὕτως καὶ ἡ γνωστικὴ διδασκαλία δι' ἀνθρώπων ἐνεργοῦντος τοῦ θ. ἐπιτελεῖται Clem.*ecl*.16(p.141.9; M.9.705B); ἐπὶ τὴν ἐπισκοπὴν αὐτὸν ὁ θ. ἤγαγε CAlex.*ep*.ap.Ath.*apol.sec*.6(p.92.8; M.25.257C); ὁ Ἡσαΐας (μᾶλλον δὲ ὁ θ. δι' αὐτοῦ) εἰπών Eus.*e.th*.2.22(p.132.20; M.24.960A); Chrys. *stat*.11.5(2.122B); as being prime mover in spiritual life, hence virtues are God's work, Ath.*inc*.53.3(M.25.192A); ὁ...θ. συνεργεῖ τοῖς τῆς ἀρετῆς ἐρασταῖς Thdt.*Ps*.89:17(1.1256); οὐ...ἔξωθεν...ὁ θ. ἐπὶ τὰ θεῖα κινεῖ, νοητῶς δέ Dion.Ar.*e.h*.1.4(M.3.376B); God's knowledge of men not abolishing their freedom, Thdt.*Rom*.8:30(3.93).

E. Trin.; **1.** partic. ref. Father ὁ θ. πατήρ Clem.*str*.6.17(p.515.10; M.9.393C); Or.*Jo*.20.17(15; p.348.32; M.14.609C); Ath.*gent*.6(M.25.13B); cf. ἕνα θ. ἔχομεν καὶ ἕνα Χριστὸν καὶ ἓν πνεῦμα *1Clem*.46.6; Or. *princ*.3.1.17(p.227.14; M.11.285B); Bas.*hom*.24.7(2.196D; M.31.616C); **2.** ref. Son τὸ...θ. ἕνα...εἶναι...υἱὸν ἐν πατρί Clem.*paed*.1.8(p.133.9; M.8.337C); τοῦ κατ' οὐσίαν θ. καὶ πατρὸς τὸν κατ' οὐσίαν θ. καὶ υἱὸν γεγεννηκότος Evagr.Pont.*ep*.3(M.32.249C); Epiph.*haer*.76.35(p.385.18; M.42.588D); v. infra F; **3.** ref. H. Ghost εἰ τοίνυν θ. εἴρηται παρὰ τὸ τεθεικέναι ἢ θεᾶσθαι τὰ πάντα, τὸ δὲ πνεῦμα πάντα γινώσκει τὰ τοῦ θ.,...θ. οὖν τὸ πνεῦμα Evagr.Pont.*ep*.11(M.32.265A); θ. τὸ πνεῦμα; πάνυ γε. ... ὁμοούσιον; εἴπερ θ. Gr.Naz.*or*.31.10(p.156.11; M.36.144A); θ. ἐκ θ. τὸ πνεῦμα Epiph.*haer*.69.27(p.177.24; M.42.248A); **4.** ref. whole Trin. ὅλη...[sc. ἡ τριάς] εἷς θ. ἐστι Ath.*ep.Serap*.1.17(M.26.569C); Jo.Mon.*hymn.Bas*.3(M.96.1372C); **5.** ref. significance of θ. in Trin. contexts μὴ πρόσωπον δηλοῖ ὁ θ., ἀλλὰ τὴν οὐσίαν Gr.Nyss. *comm.not*.(M.45.177C); Thdt.*ep*.146(4.1267); Jo.D.*fid.Nest*.13(p.564); and theol. implications of this significance, Ath.*Ar*.3.15(M.26.352Cff.); οὐ...τρεῖς θ.,...ἀλλὰ τῆς τριάδος τὴν ἕνωσιν ἐν τῇ κοινωνίᾳ τῶν ὀνομάτων ἐπιγινωστέον Didym.(‡Bas.)*Eun*.5(1.310D; M.29.744C); Jo.D.*volunt*.8(M.95.136D); **6.** ref. heresies; **a.** Sabellian λόγον αὐτὸν μόνον...ἡνωμένον τῷ θ.,...ὀνόμασιν μὲν διαφόροις πατρὸς καὶ υἱοῦ χρηματίζοντα οὐσίᾳ δὲ καὶ ὑποστάσει ἓν ὄντα Eus.*Marcell*.1.1(p.4.22; M.24.720A); cf.id.*e.th*.1.5(p.64.21; M.24.833B); **b.** opposite view of some Origenists τρεῖς θ. τρόπον τινὰ κηρύττουσιν, εἰς τρεῖς ὑποστάσεις ξένας ἀλλήλων...κεχωρισμένας Dion.R.ap.Ath.*decr*.26(p.22.7; M.25.464A); **c.** in teaching of Paul. Sam. θ. πατέρα καὶ υἱὸν καὶ ἅγιον πνεῦμα ἕνα θ., ἐν θ. δὲ ἀεὶ ὄντα τὸν αὐτοῦ λόγον καὶ τὸ πνεῦμα αὐτοῦ, ὥσπερ ἐν ἀνθρώπου καρδίᾳ ὁ ἴδιος λόγος Epiph.*haer*.65.1(p.3.9; M.42.13A); **d.** Arian ὡς μόνος καὶ ἀρχὴ πάντων, οὕτως ὁ θ. πρὸ πάντων ἐστί. διὸ καὶ πρὸ τοῦ υἱοῦ ἐστιν Ar.*ep.Alex*.(p.13.12; M.26.709C); refutation εἰ...ἐξ οὐκ ὄντων ἐστὶ κτίσμα...ὁ λόγος· ἢ οὐκ ἔστι θ. ἀληθινός,...ἢ...ἀνάγκη λέγειν αὐτοὺς δύο θ. Ath.*Ar*.3.16(M.26.353C); Bas.*hom*.24.1(2.189E; M.31.600C); ἄνθρωπος ἄνθρωπον γεννᾷ, καὶ θ. θεόν Epiph.*haer*.69.26(p.176.7; M.42.244C); **e.** theory of Pneumatomachoi, some believing H. Ghost to be a creature, Ath.*ep.Serap*.1.29(M.26.597A); others that his divinity was not clearly proved in scripture, Gr.Naz.*or*.31.5(p.150.7ff.; M.36.137C); cf.*ib*.43.68(588A).

F. theol., of Son; **1.** ref. Christ as God, Ign.*Eph*.18.2; id.*Rom*.3.3; Just.*dial*.34.2(M.6.548A); Clem.*prot*.11(p.78.13; M.8.228A); Iren. *haer*.1.10.1(M.7.549B); **2.** his divinity proved; from scripture, Just.*dial*.68.4(M.6.633B); Cyr.H.*catech*.10.6; from Resurrection, Ath. *inc*.45.4(M.25.177B); testimony of demons, *ib*.32.5(152B); witness of elements at Crucifixion, *ib*.19.3(129B); miracles, id.*Ar*.2.12(M.26.172C); Chrys.*hom.29.2 in Mt*.(7.343E); **3.** of Christ as θ. rather than ὁ θ.: ὁ Ἰωάννης...τίθησιν μὲν γὰρ τὸ ἄρθρον, ὅτε ἡ 'θ.' ὀνομασία ἐπὶ τοῦ ἀγενήτου τάσσεται τῶν ὅλων αἰτίου, σιωπᾷ δὲ αὐτό, ὅτε ὁ λόγος 'θ.' ὀνομάζεται Or.*Jo*.2.2(p.54.15; M.14.108B); αὐτόθεος ὁ θ. ἐστι...πᾶν δὲ τὸ παρὰ τὸ αὐτόθεος μετοχῇ τῆς ἐκείνου θεότητος θεοποιούμενον οὐχ 'ὁ θ.' ἀλλὰ 'θ.' κυριώτερον ἂν λέγοιτο, οὗ πάντως ὁ πρωτότοκος πάσης κτίσεως, ἅτε πρῶτος τῷ πρὸς τὸν θ. εἶναι σπάσας τῆς θεότητος εἰς ἑαυτόν, ἐστὶ τιμιώτερος, τοῖς λοιποῖς παρ' αὐτὸν θεοῖς...διακονήσας τὸ γενέσθαι θεοῖς, ἀπὸ τοῦ θ. ἀρυσά⟨μενος⟩ εἰς τὸ θεοποιηθῆναι αὐτοὺς *ib*.(p.54.30; 109A); Marcell.*fr*.76 ap.Eus.*e.th*.2.19(p.126.26; M.24.948D); ref. Jo.1:1 δυνάμενος...εἰπεῖν· καὶ ὁ θ. ἦν ὁ λόγος, μετὰ τῆς τοῦ ἄρθρου προσθήκης, εἴγε...ἡγεῖτο...εἶναι τὸν λόγον τὸν ἐπὶ πάντων θ., οὐχ οὕτως ἐξέδωκε τὴν γραφήν. ... διό φησιν 'καὶ θ. ἦν ὁ λόγος', ἵν' ἴδωμεν θ. τὸν ἐπὶ πάντων πρὸς ὃν ἦν ὁ λόγος. καὶ θ. αὐτὸν τὸν λόγον ἄκουε, ὡς εἰκόνα τοῦ θ. Eus.*e.th*.2.17(p.120.15; M.24.937B); cf.*ib*.2.14(p.114.35; 928B); such doctrine denied, ref. Jo.20:28 οὐ γὰρ ἁπλῶς ἔφη κύριός μου καὶ θ. μου, ἵνα μή τις οἴηται καθ' ὁμοιότητα τὴν ἡμετέραν ἤγουν τῶν...ἀγγέλων κύριον αὐτὸν εἰρῆσθαι καὶ θ. Cyr.*Jo*.12.1(4.1109C); **4.** as δεύτερος θ.; cf. ἐστὶ...θ. ... ἕτερος ὑπὸ τὸν ποιητὴν τῶν ὅλων, ὃς καὶ ἄγγελος καλεῖται Just.*dial*.56.4(M.6.597B); Or.*Cels*.5.39(p.43.22; M.11.1244B); *ib*.6.61(p.132.2; 1392C); ὁ μὲν ἀληθὴς καὶ μόνος θ. εἷς ἂν εἴη, μόνος κυρίως τυγχάνων τῆς προσηγορίας· ὁ δὲ δεύτερος μετουσίᾳ τοῦ ἀληθοῦς τῆς κοινωνίας ἠξίωται Eus.*d.e*.5.4(p.225.7; M.22.372B); this doctrine attacked δεύτερον θ. λέγων τὸν Χριστὸν καὶ τοῦτον ἀνθρωπικώτερον γεγενῆσθαι θ., ποτὲ δὲ κτίσμα αὐτὸν εἶναι διοριζόμενος Marcell.*fr*.40 ap.Eus.*Marcell*.1.4(p.28.9; M.24.769B); from pagan standpoint ὀνομάζει...[sc. Moses] θ. πλειόνας, ἐξαίρετον δὲ τὸν πρῶτον, ἄλλον δὲ οὐχ ὑπείληφε δεύτερον Juln.Imp. ap.Cyr.*Juln*.8(6^2.253B).

G. Christol.; **1.** various expressions of union of God and man ἐν σαρκὶ γενόμενος θ. Ign.*Eph*.7.2; θ. ἐν ἀνθρώπου μορφῇ Tat.*orat*.21(p.23.6; M.6.852C); Clem.*paed*.1.2(p.91.23; M.8.252C); ὁ μόνος ἄμφω, θ. τε καὶ ἄνθρωπος id.*prot*.1(p.7.19; M.8.61B); Hipp.*Noët*.17(p.263.9; M.10.828A); Or.*princ*.1 proem.4(p.10.9; M.11.117B); cf. *deus-homo*, *ib*.2.6.3(p.142.13; 211D); θ. ἄνθρωπος Gr.Naz.*carm*.2.1.11.647(M.37.1073A); Jo.Eub.*concept.BMV* 19(M.96.1492B); θ. καὶ ἄνθρωπον τὸν Χριστὸν ὁμολογῶ υἱὸν τοῦ θ., ἕνα υἱὸν δύο φύσεσιν Amph.*fr*.ap.*Doct. Patr*.2(p.12.13; M.39.113B); τέλειος θ. ... καὶ τέλειος ἄνθρωπος, καὶ μετὰ τὴν καθ' ὑπόστασιν τῶν φύσεων ἕνωσιν Jo.D.*volunt*.8(M.95.137A); **2.** ref. operations of divine and human natures; **a.** considered distinctly, of Christ dying as man θ. γὰρ οὐ θεμιτὸν ἀποθνήσκειν λέγειν Or.*Jo*.20.11(p.341.1; M.14.597B); ἀνέστη...ὅτι θ. ἦν αὐτὸς ἐν σώματι Ath.*Ar*.1.44(M.26.101C); ἄνθρωπος γενόμενος ὁ κύριος, δείκνυσι τὸ μὲν κλαίειν τοῦ ἀνθρωπίνου, ἐγείρει δὲ Λάζαρον ὡς θ. id.*Dion*.9(p.52.21; M.25.493A); **b.** as operating indivisibly τοῦ πάθους τοῦ θ. Ign.*Rom*.6.3; in virtue of hypostatic union ὁ... ἀποθανὼν θ. ἐστιν, οὐ φύσει θεότητος ἀποθνήσκων, ἀλλ' ἑνώσεως οἰκονομίᾳ ‡Ath.*dial.Trin*.4.7(M.28.1261B); Jo.D.*f.o*.3.4(M.94.997D); **3.** in Docetist view ἐφανέρωσεν ἡμῖν ὅτι θ. ἐστιν. μὴ οὖν νομίσῃς ὅτι ἄνθρωπός ἐστιν *A.Andr.et Mt*.10(p.76.14); **4.** acc. Paul. Sam. μὴ... θ. πρὸ τῆς ἐνσάρκου γενέσεως ὄντα τὸν Χριστὸν ὡμολόγει Eus.*Marcell*.1.14(p.74.20; M.24.853B); Ath.*syn*.26(p.252.26; M.26.729C); ‡Ath. *Apoll*.1.20(M.26.1128A); **5.** in Apollinarian view τὸν θ. λόγον...οὐ διαιρούμεν αὐτὸν ἀπὸ τῆς αὐτοῦ σαρκός, ἀλλ' ἐστιν ἓν πρόσωπον,...ὅλος ἄνθρωπος, ὅλος θ. Apoll.*fid.inc*.3(p.194.21; M.*PL*.8.876C); Ἰουδαῖοι τὸ σῶμα σταυρώσαντες τὸν θ. ἐσταύρωσαν *ib*.6(p.198.24; 877C); Gr. Naz.*ep*.102(M.37.200B) cit. s. θεοφόρος; in anti-Apollinarian argument εἰ...ὁμοούσιος τοῦ λόγου ἡ σὰρξ καὶ συναΐδιος, ἐκ τούτου ἐρεῖτε καὶ τὰ πάντα κτίσματα συναΐδια τῷ...θ. ‡Ath.*Apoll*.1.12(M.26.1113B); εἰ...θ. ὁ διὰ σαρκὸς παθών..., παθητὸν ἐρεῖτε καὶ τὸν πατέρα, καὶ τὸν παράκλητον *ib*.2.13(1153B); Nestorian τὸ παρελθεῖν τὸν θ. ἐκ τῆς Χριστοτόκου παρθένου παρὰ τῆς θείας ἐδιδάχθην γραφῆς, τὸ δὲ γεννηθῆναι θ. ἐξ αὐτῆς οὐδαμοῦ ἐδιδάχθην Nest.*fr*.C 11(p.277.25)ap. Cyr.*Nest*.1.1(p.18.28; 6^1.10B); Cyr.*Nest*.1.1(p.18.32; 6^1.10B) cit. s. θεοφόρος; cf. ἡμεῖς [sc. orthodox]...οὔ φαμεν τὸν υἱὸν τῆς παρθένου γενέσθαι υἱὸν θεοῦ,...ἀλλὰ τὸν υἱὸν τοῦ θ. γενέσθαι υἱὸν τῆς παρθένου Jo.D.*fid.Nest*.12(p.564).

H. ref. man's knowledge of God; **1.** God is incomprehensible, Iren.*haer*.4.19.2(M.7.1030B); ὁ...θ. ἀναπόδεικτος ὢν οὐκ ἔστιν ἐπιστημονικός Clem.*str*.4.24(p.317.22; M.8.1365A); θ. καταλαμβανόμενος οὐκ ἔστι θ. ‡Ath.*qu.Ant*.1(M.28.597D); τί...ἐστι θεοῦ οὐσία...καὶ ἀγνοοῦμεν καὶ λέγειν οὐ δυνάμεθα Jo.D.*f.o*.1.2(M.94.793B); **2.** and ineffable, Just.*2apol*.13.3(M.6.465C); Tat.*orat*.4(p.5.13; M.6.813B); because he is not in any category, Clem.*str*.5.12(p.380.15; M.9.121A); θ. ... ᾧ μηδὲν ὄνομα προσκέοιτο ἂν ἰδικῶς Cyr.*glaph.Gen*.5(1.173B); τὸ κατ' οὐσίαν ἀσήμαντον θ. Anast.S.*hod*.2(M.89.53A); **3.** but some knowledge of what he is not is possible, Ath.*h.Ar*.proem.2(p.182.3; M.25.693A); ὁ θ. γινώσκεται...διὰ ἀγνωσίας Dion.Ar.*d.n*.7.3(M.3.869C); Jo.D.*f.o*.1.4(M.94.800B); **4.** and some knowledge of his attributes and operations ἐκ μὲν τῶν ἐνεργειῶν γνωρίζειν λέγομεν τὸν θ. ..., τῇ δὲ οὐσίᾳ αὐτῇ προσεγγίζειν οὐχ ὑπισχνούμεθα Bas.*ep*.234.1(3.357D; M.32.869A); Gr.Naz.*or*.28.21(p.53.10; M.36.53B); Chrys.*exp. in Ps*.143:3(5.461D); hence τὸ...πατὴρ καὶ θ. ... οὐκ ὀνόματά ἐστιν, ἀλλ' ἐκ τῶν εὐποιϊῶν καὶ τῶν ἔργων προσρήσεις Just.*2apol*.6.2(M.6.453A); Clem.*str*.5.12(p.381.1; M.9.121B); Dion.Ar.*d.n*.2.7(M.3.645A); **5.** men having innate knowledge of God, Clem.*prot*.6(p.52.2; M.8.173A); Bas.*Eun*.1.12(1.224D; M.29.540A); θ. ... πρὸς τὴν ἑκάστου τῶν λογικῶν οὐσιῶν δύναμιν τὴν αὐτοῦ γνῶσιν κρυφίως ἐνθέμενος Max. *cap*.5.100(M.90.1392B); Jo.D.*f.o*.1.1(M.94.789B); **6.** knowing God through self-knowledge, Clem.*paed*.3.1(p.235.21; M.8.556A); Ath. *inc*.12.1(M.25.116D); τὸν θ. ἔστιν ἐπιγνῶναι...ἐκ τῆς οἰκείας ἡμῶν κατασκευῆς Bas.*hex*.9.6(1.87A; M.29.204C); **7.** and consideration of effects of his activity in world, Thphl.Ant.*Autol.*1.5(M.6.1032A); Ath.*gent.*34(M.25.69A); Chrys.*stat.*10.5(2.113C); οὐκ ἐκ τῆς οὐσίας αὐτοῦ τὸν θ. γινώσκομεν, ἀλλ' ἐκ τῆς μεγαλουργίας αὐτοῦ Max.*carit.*1.96(M.90.931C); **8.** through living a virtuous life, Thphl.Ant.*Autol.*1.2(M.6.1028A); Ath.*virg.*17(p.52.25; M.28.273A); Gr.Nyss.*beat.*6(M.44.1269A); **9.** through revelation; **a.** through appearances of Logos in OT, Just.*dial.*56.4(M.6.597B); *ib.*86.5(681B); Clem.*paed.*1.7(p.124.3; M.8.320A); Chrys.*Is.interp.*6(6.64B); **b.** through advent of Christ in NT, *Diogn.*8.1; Ath.*inc.*35.6(M.25.156C); Cyr.H.*catech.*6.6; **c.** through scripture, Athenag.*leg.*7.2(M.6.904B); Ath.*decr.*9(p.8.18; M.25.432A); Epiph.*haer.*70.6(p.239.24ff.; M.42.349D); sometimes in anthropomorphic terms, Or.*fr.4 in 1Reg.*(p.295.26; M.12.992A); images being adapted to men's varying capacities, Max.*qu.Thal.*28(M.90.360D); God's simplicity forbidding literal interpretation, Jo.D.*f.o.*1.11(M.94.841B); **10.** through baptism τοῦ λουτροῦ·...τῆς γνώσεως τοῦ θ. Just.*dial.*14.1(M.6.504C); faith ἐπίστευσαν τί θ. πίστει γὰρ μόνῃ θεωρεῖται ἡ...φύσις ἐκείνη Chrys.*hom.4.8 in Ac.princ.*(3.93A); and prayer, Clem.*str.*4.23(p.316.2; M.8.1361A); the most perfect knowledge attainable being in beatific vision, Thphl.Ant.*Autol.*1.7(M.6.1036B); Bas.*fid.*2(2.225D; M.31.681A); Gr.Naz.*or.*28.17(p.47.14ff.; M.36.48C); **11.** ref. obstacles to knowledge of God; the body, Or.*princ.*1.1.5(p.20.15ff.; M.11.124B); μέσος ἡμῶν τε καὶ θ. ὁ σωματικὸς οὗτος ἵσταται γνόφος Gr.Naz.*or.*28.12(p.40.17; M.36.41A); sin, Thphl.Ant.*Autol.*1.2(M.6.1028A); Bas.*hom.in Ps.*45(1.175B; M.29.428A); **12.** of knowledge of God by pagans; **a.** derived by Plato and others from scripture, Just.*1apol.*59.1(M.6.416C); *ib.*60.5ff.(420A); Clem.*prot.*6(p.53.16; M.8.176B); **b.** as expressed in sayings quoted from pagan authors, Thphl.Ant.*Autol.*2.37(M.6.1116B); Clem.*str.*5.12(p.380.3; M.9.120C); Eus.*p.e.*passim.

I. ref. plurality of gods in Gnost., Marcionite, and Manich. systems; **1.** two gods; in gen. (Valent.), Iren.*haer.*3.7.1(M.7.864B); τὸν κτίστην ἄλλον εἶναι παρὰ τὸν πρῶτον θ. Clem.*str.*4.13(p.289.28; M.8.1301A); (Cerinthus), Hipp.*haer.*7.33(p.220.12; M.16.3342A); (Marcion), Just.*1apol.*26.5(M.6.368C); Bas.*hom.*24.4(2.192B; M.31.605C); (Manich.), Hegem.*Arch.*11(p.18.6; M.10.1445A); as good and evil (Marcion), cf. *dividens deum in duo, alterum quidem bonum, et alterum judicialem dicens*, Iren.*haer.*3.25.3(968C); (Manich.) δύο... θ.,...ἕνα τῷ ἑνὶ ἀντικείμενον· καὶ τὸ μὲν ἀγαθόν, τὸν δὲ πονηρὸν εἰσηγεῖται Hegem.*Arch.*7(p.9.12; 1437A); Epiph.*haer.*66.8(p.29.7; M.42.41C); as gods of NT and OT (Marcion) ἕτερον...εἶναι τὸν ἀγαθὸν πατέρα τοῦ κυρίου ἡμῶν παρὰ τὸν τοῦ νόμου θ. Or.*or.*29.12(p.387.7; M.11.537C); (Manich.), Tit.Bost.*Man.*3 proem.(M.18.1208D); **2.** three gods (Simon Magus) ὄντα θ. θεῶν· ὃς δύο ἔπεμψε θ., ἀφ' ὧν ὁ μὲν εἷς ἐστιν ὁ κόσμον κτίσας, ὁ δὲ ἕτερος ὁ τὸν νόμον δοὺς *Hom.Clem.*3.2; Simon claiming to be one of these gods himself, Cyr.H.*catech.*6.15; Epiph.*haer.*21.1(p.238.10; M.41.285B); **3.** four gods (Apelles) εἶναί τινα θ. ἀγαθόν,...τὸν δὲ πάντα κτίσαντα εἶναι δίκαιον,... καὶ τρίτον τὸν Μωσεῖ λαλήσαντα—πύρινον δὲ τοῦτον εἶναι—εἶναι δὲ καὶ τέταρτον ἕτερον, κακῶν αἴτιον Hipp.*haer.*7.38(p.224.1; M.16.3346A); (Naassene), *ib.*5.7(p.86.10; 3135B); **4.** names of God in OT taken by some Gnostics as names of different gods, Iren.*haer.*2.35.3(M.7.838B); Thdt.*haer.*5.3(4.392); **5.** (Peratic) οἱ θ. τῆς ἀπωλείας καὶ ὁ θ. τῆς σωτηρίας. εἰσὶ δὲ...οἱ θ. τῆς ἀπωλείας οἱ ἀστέρες Hipp.*haer.*5.16(p.112.2; M.16.3171C); **6.** these ideas refuted by arguments that infinity can belong to only one God, Iren.*haer.*2.1.2(M.7.710B); Dion.Ar.*d.n.*4.21(M.3.721D); there cannot be equality of good and bad principles: one would neutralize the other, Cyr.H.*catech.*6.13; Jo.D.*Man.*1.9(M.94.1513A); ref. Marcion, cf. *hic...qui judicialis, si non bonus sit, non est deus,...et...qui bonus, si non et judicialis, idem quod hic patietur*, Iren.*haer.*3.25.3(M.7.968C); cf.Or.*princ.*2.5.3(p.136.29; M.11.207C); and from scripture, *ib.*2.4.1ff.(p.127.10ff.; 194D); Adam.*dial.*1.1(p.2.17; M.11.1717A); Cyr.H.*catech.*6.16.

J. in anti-pagan apologetic; **1.** heathen gods said to be false because **a.** material, Athenag.*leg.*22.2(M.6.937A); Ath.*gent.*29(M.25.57B); *ib.*22(44D); Cyr.H.*catech.*6.11; **b.** corruptible, Arist.*apol.*4.1; *ib.*7.1ff.; Tat.*orat.*21(p.23.20ff.; M.6.853A); Ath.*gent.*10(M.25.21D); Cyr.H.*catech.*6.11; **c.** not self-sufficient, Arist.*apol.*3.2; ἐνδεὴς...ἡ ὕλη τῆς τέχνης, ὁ θ. δὲ ἀνενδεής Clem.*prot.*4(p.44.15; M.8.153B); Ath.*gent.*13(M.25.28D); Chrys.*stat.*10.4(2.111D); **d.** demons are not gods, for they themselves acknowledge Christ, Ath.*inc.*15.5(M.25.124A); **e.** gods are evil, Tat.*orat.*21(p.23.23; M.6.853B); and incite to unnatural crimes, Athenag.*leg.*26.2(M.6.952A); τίς...ἀπολογία...περὶ τοῦ εἶναι τούτους θ.;...ἀνθρώπους αὐτούς, καὶ ἀνθρώπους οὐ σεμνοὺς ὄντας, ὁ λόγος ἀπέδειξεν Ath.*gent.*18(M.25.37A); Gr.Naz.*or.*31.16(p.64.10; M.36.149C); **2.** ref. origins of pagan attitude to God; **a.** as projection of human desires, cf. *non...totius gentilitatis error hinc accepit exordium, dum ea, quae multum diligunt homines, deos esse volunt?* Or.*hom.2.3 in Jud.*(p.477.10; M.12.960A); ἦν αὐτοῖς θ. ... τὰ ...πρὸς ἡδυπαθῆ ζωὴν αὐτοῖς συμβαλλόμενα. θ. γοῦν αὐτοῖς ἦν ἡ τῶν σαρκῶν ἡδονή, θ. ἡ τροφή Eus.*theoph.*3(p.12*.21); Ath.*gent.*8(M.25.17A); εἰς...τὴν τῶν παθῶν καὶ ἡδονῶν ἀλογίαν πεσόντες οἱ ἄνθρωποι,...ἐν ἀλόγοις καὶ τὸ θεῖον ἀνεπλάσαντο...καὶ θεοὺς τοσούτους γλύψαντες *ib.*19(40A); **b.** as caused by devils persuading men to worship them as gods, Just.*1apol.*5.2(M.6.336A); Tat.*orat.*21(p.24.4f.; M.6.853B); Ath.*inc.*15.2(M.25.121C); id.*exp.Ps.*95:5(M.27.416C); and promoting worship of other false gods, Just.*1apol.*26.1ff.(368A); being instigators of idolatry, Thdt.*ep.*146(4.1266).

K. of men as 'gods'; **1.** as divinized by grace, cf.Or.*hom.6.5 in Ex.*(p.196.21; M.12.335A); τοῖς κατὰ χάριν...θ. Cyr.*Jo.*1.10(4.105C); Anast.S.*hod.*2(M.89.53C); by participation in God παρὰ...τὸν ἀληθινὸν θ. θεῶν πλειόνων τῇ μετοχῇ τοῦ θ. γινομένων Or.*Jo.*2.3(p.55.9; M.14.109C); Ath.*ep.Serap.*2.4(M.26.613Bf.); cf.id.*Ar.*1.39(M.26.93A); Cyr.*thes.*17(5^{1}.181D); through Christ ὁ λόγος ἄνθρωπος,...ἵνα ὁ ἄνθρωπος...υἱὸς γένηται θ. Iren.*haer.*3.19.1(M.7.939B); ἄνθρωποι τὴν φύσιν ὄντες, θεοὶ χρηματίζομεν, ὡς ὄντες καὶ τοῦτο ἐν Χριστῷ Cyr.*thes.*23(5^{1}.229B); διὰ τοῦτο γέγονεν...ἄνθρωπος ὁ...θ. λόγος, ἵνα ποιήσῃ θ. ... τοὺς ἀνθρώπους Max.*cap.theol.*2.25(M.90.1136B); and by virtue, Hipp.*haer.*10.33(p.290.5; M.16.3450A); θ. ὀνομάζομεν τοὺς κατ' ἀρετὴν τελείους Bas.*Eun.*3.5(1.276D; M.29.665B); Max.*cap.*1.28(M.90.1189C); **2.** in various met. uses; θ. γίνεται [sc. almsgiver] τῶν λαμβανόντων *Diogn.*10.6; cf. *unusquisque, quod prae ceteris colit,...hoc ei deus est*, Or.*hom.2.3 in Jud.*(p.476.2; M.12.959A); of bishop ὑμῶν ἐπίγειος θ. μετὰ θεόν *Const.App.*2.26.4; OT priests, Thdt.*Ps.*135:2(1.1520); judges, Or.*sel.in Ex.*21:6(M.12.293C); Moses, Gr.Nyss.*Trin.*8(p.80.12; M.32.696A); as typifying Christ, Thdt.*eran.*2(4.85); angels, *Hom.Clem.*16.14.

***θεόσαρκος**, *of divine flesh* πῶς χρὴ ὀνομάζειν τὸν Χριστὸν ἄνθρωπον, θ. ἄνθρωπον ἢ ἀνθρωπόσαρκον θεόν; Leont.H.*Nest.*6.5(M.86.1756C); Anast.S.*hod.*23(M.89.301C); ref. eucharist μερίδα λαβεῖν ...τῆς αὐτῆς θ. μερίδος †Anast.S.*relat.*42(p.63.19).

θεόσδοτος, *God-given*; in gen., Cyr.*Os.*170(3.195D); id.*Jo.*1.9(4.74B); Dion.Ar.*c.h.*3.3(M.3.168A); Anast.S.*serm.imag.*3(M.89.1169A); ref. Inc. γέγονεν ἄνθρωπος, ᾧ πάντα θ. Cyr.*thes.*14(5^{1}.146A); id.*Jo.*11.12(1006A); of Law, Thdt.*2Par.*5:17(1.592A); †Gregent.*disp.*(M.86.624A); Max.*ambig.*(M.91.1117C); Christianity ἡ θ. θρησκεία Meth.*creat.*1(p.493.4; M.18.332A); theologians θ. διδασκάλους Leont.B.*Nest.et Eut.*3(M.86.1360D); prophecy, Iren.*haer.*1.13.4(M.7.585A); wisdom, Clem.*str.*5.13(p.381.29; M.9.125A); the working of grace θ. ...χρῆμα Cyr.*Ps.*50:17(M.69.1101B); fasting as θ. ἐργαλεῖον Sophr.H.*or.*5(M.87.3313A); ref. Christmas θ. ἑορτῶν id.*nativ.*(p.503.26); of virtues, Clem.*str.*5.13(p.381.22; M.9.124B); *ib.*4.19(p.303.14; M.8.1336A); virginity, Gr.Naz.*carm.*1.2.1.11(M.37.523A); *ib.*1.2.1.353(549A).

θεοσέβεια, ἡ, I. *worship of God*; ref. demons who turn men from it, Tat.*orat.*17(p.19.11; M.6.844B); θυσία...σώματός τε καὶ τῶν τούτου παθῶν ἀμετανόητος χωρισμός, ἡ ἀληθὴς τῷ ὄντι θ. αὕτη Clem.*str.*5.11(p.370.26; M.9.101B); ref. Rom.12:1, Jo.4:24 ὁ ἀπόστολος διδάσκει λέγων λογικὴν λατρείαν τὴν τοιαύτην θ. Heracleon ap.Or.*Jo.*13.25(p.249.3; M.14.441A); of worship of God as perfect in heaven, Or.*ib.*13.13(p.238.12; 420B); ref. Jo.4:46–53 τὸ Ἰσραηλιτικὸν γένος, ἀσθενῆσαν ἐν τῇ θ. *ib.*13.58(57; p.289.19; 509B).

II. *religion*, consisting of doctrine and practice ὁ...τῆς θ. τρόπος ἐκ δύο τούτων συνέστηκε, δογμάτων εὐσεβῶν, καὶ πράξεων ἀγαθῶν Cyr.H.*catech.*4.2.

A. of right belief; **1.** orthodoxy in gen. ἀσέβειά ἐστι τὸ ἐν τῷ τῆς θ. λόγῳ τελευτᾶν λέγοντα ἄλλον εἶναι θεὸν...παρὰ τὸν ὄντως ὄντα *Hom.Clem.*3.7; *ib.*8.9; in Judaism, Hipp.*haer.*9.30(p.263.6; M.16.3410A); of an interpretation of Christianity, Marcell.*fr.*30 ap.Eus.*Marcell.*1.2(p.12.24; M.24.740B); **2.** Christianity, in gen. ἡ θ. τῶν Χριστιανῶν *Diogn.*1.1; *Hom.Clem.*10.12; Eus.*v.C.*4.71(p.147.3; M.20.1225B); *Const.App.*1 proem.; τὴν πᾶσαν ἀκρίβειαν τῆς θ. καὶ πίστεως τῆς ὀρθῆς Epiph.*haer.*69.13(p.163.14; M.42.224A); its nature ἐπιστήμη τίς ἐστιν ἡ Χριστιανικὴ θ. Clem.*fr.*68(p.229.3); δωρεὰ...ἡ διδασκαλία τῆς θ. id.*str.*1.6(p.25.16; M.8.733A); θ. ἐξομοιοῦσα τῷ θεῷ κατὰ τὸ δυνατὸν τὸν ἄνθρωπον id.*prot.*9(p.64.31; M.8.197C); as revealed to prophets and apostles, Or.*Jo.*6.4(2; p.111.21; M.14.205B); as τὸ θεοσεβείας μυστήριον *Diogn.*4.6; Or.*Jo.*2.34(28; p.93.15; M.14.176D); Eus.*h.e.*3.26.4(M.20.272C); proofs of its divine origin found in its acceptance by all kinds of men, Or.*princ.*4.1.2(p.295.6; M.11.345A); and in practice of virginity by Christians, Ath.*apol.Const.*33(M.25.640B); in relation to reason; principles of Christianity attested by prophets rather than abstract reason, *Hom.Clem.*15.5;

ref. Gnost. speculations *ἐντεῦθεν τὴν θ. συνιστᾶν πειρώμενοι μακρὰν ἀπεμφαίνουσαν τῆς τούτων ὑπολήψεως* Hipp.*haer*.4.50(p.74.4; M.16. 3118B); *ἡ...περὶ τῆς θ. ... γνῶσις οὐ τοσοῦτον τῆς παρὰ τῶν ἀνθρώπων διδασκαλίας δεῖται, ὅσον ἀφ' ἑαυτῆς ἔχει τὸ γνώριμον* Ath.*gent*.1(M.25. 4A); cf. *τοῖς...ὑπὸ φιλοσοφίας δεδικαιωμένοις βοήθεια θησαυρίζεται καὶ ἡ εἰς θ. συναίσθησις* Clem.*str*.1.4(p.17.29; M.8.717C); contrasted with heresy, Iren.*haer*.1.16.3(M.7.633B); Hipp.*haer*.6.52(p.184.12; 3282B); Const.ap.Socr.*h.e*.1.9.30(M.67.88C); *τῶν ἔξωθεν τῆς θ.* †Bas.*Is*.79(1. 435A; M.30.252A); *ἡ πλάνη καὶ ἡ διχόνοια ὑποσπείρειν ἀπὸ τῆς μιᾶς θ. εἰς πολλὰς παραπεποιημένας γνώμας* Epiph.*haer*.8.9(p.197.9; M.41. 224A).

B. of practical piety and right conduct; **1.** nature and scope; not including Jewish observances, *Diogn*.4.5; cf.*ib*.3.3; *εἰ δὲ ἀγάπη ὁ θεός, ἀγάπη καὶ ἡ θ.* Clem.*str*.4.16(p.292.26; M.8.1308A); *τέλος... ἐστιν θεοσεβείας ἡ ἀΐδιος ἀνάπαυσις ἐν τῷ θεῷ* id.*paed*.1.13(p.151.17; M.8.373B); as main business of life, *Const.App*.2.60.6,7; **2.** learned from scripture, Marcell.*fr*.59 ap.Eus.*Marcell*.1.4(p.18.18; M.24. 753A); **3.** practised esp. by ascetics, desert being its homeland, Ath.*v.Anton*.44(M.26.908B); **4.** its apologetic value; its rapid extension a sign of divine origin of Christianity, Or.*princ*.4.1.5(p.299. 11; M.11.349B); *αἱ...γυναῖκες διὰ τῆς αἰδοῦς καὶ πραότητος τὴν θ. ἐνδείκνυσθε εἰς ἐπιστροφὴν καὶ προτροπὴν πίστεως καὶ τοῖς ἐκτὸς πᾶσιν* *Const.App*.1.10.3.

C. as style of address; of pope *ἡ θ. σου* Marcell.*ep*.ap.Epiph. *haer*.72.2(p.256.17; M.42.384C); Ath.*ep.Afr*.10(M.26.1045D); other bishops, id.*apol.sec*.40(p.118.23; M.25.323A); Bas.*ep*.48(3.141C; M.32. 384C); Thdt.*ep*.16(4.1078); a synod *ἡ ὑμετέρα θ.* Pall.*v.Chrys*.15 (p.89.24; M.47.51); a priest, Thdt.*ep*.19(4.1081); clergy, *ib*.75(4.1124); a deaconess, *ib*.17(4.1079); *ib*.101(4.1170); emperor, Ath.*apol. Const*.2(p.280.8; M.25.597B).

θεοσεβ-έω, **1.** *serve God* *οἱ ἐν σωφροσύνῃ ~οῦντες* *T.Jos*.6.7; Clem.*paed*.2.10(p.223.5; M.8.529A); id.*str*.4.22(p.312.24; M.8.1356A); *ἁγνῶς...θ.* *A.Petr.c.Sim*.5(p.86.11); **2.** *be pious, religious*, Athenag. *leg*.4.2(M.6.897B); cf.*ib*.14.2(917B); ref. Christian and pagan ideas of piety, *ib*.12.2,3(913Bff.); of Christians as not religious in Jewish way, *Diogn*.3.1; **3.** *be Christian*, Eus.*l.C*.6(p.206.11; M.20.1340B); Ath.*v.Anton*.77(M.26.949C); *οἱ ~οῦντες* *pious Christians*, *ib*.24 (880A); *ib*.28(885B).

θεοσεβής, **1.** *pious, religious*, *θ. γνώμη* Just.*dial*.93.2(M.6.697B); *μόνον ὄντως εἶναι θ. τὸν γνωστικόν* Clem.*str*.7.1(p.3.4; M.9.401B); *οἱ ...θ. ἀγαθῆς τῆς ἀμοιβῆς τεύξονται* id.*prot*.10(p.66.30; M.8.204A); *θ. ἀγωγή* Ath.*h.Ar*.78(p.226.26; M.25.788B); as imperial title *ἡ σὴ θ. ἀνεξικακία* Ath.*apol.Const*.35(M.25.641B); *θ. βασιλεύς* Epiph.*haer*.69. 13(p.163.11; M.42.221D); superl., Eus.*v.C*.3.43(p.95.25; M.20.1104A); id.*l.C*.6(p.212.2; M.20.1349C); Ath.*h.Ar*.29(p.198.20; 725C); Pall. *v.Chrys*.2(p.11.19; M.47.10); as title of functionaries, Or.*mart*.1 (p.3.6; M.11.564A); id.*or*.2.1(p.298.18; M.11.417A); as eccl. title *θεοσεβεστάτῳ ἐπισκόπῳ* Cyr.*ep*.13(p.92.12; 5[2].43A); *ib*.(p.92.27; 5[2]. 43E); *θ. ... ἀββᾶς* Cosm.Ind.*top*.6(M.88.321B); of Christians in gen. *τὸ...θ. γένος τῶν Χριστιανῶν* *M.Polyc*.3; as deserving name more than the Jews, Just.*dial*.118.4(M.6.749C); *ib*.119.6(753A); Athenag. *leg*.37.1(M.6.972A); hence **2.** *Christian*, Chrys.*hom.6.1 in 1Tim.* (11.579B); *θ. παράδοσις* Clem.*str*.6.15(p.294.25; M.9.348A); as subst. plur., Mel.*fr*.(p.307)ap.Eus.*h.e*.4.26.5(M.20.393A); *Hom.Clem*.12.11; Eus.*h.e*.8.6.6(753A); id.*v.C*.1.17(p.16.30; M.20.933B).

θεοσεβῶς, *piously*, Clem.*str*.4.8(p.279.3; M.8.1280A); id.*fr*.49 (p.224.34); †Hipp.*Laz*.(p.218.5; M.62.776).

θεοσημεία (-μία), ἡ, *miracle*; **1.** in gen., of vision of angels at Christ's birth, Or.*Cels*.1.60(p.111.10; M.11.769C); eclipse at Crucifixion, *ib*.2.35(p.161.23; 857A); *ib*.2.36(p.162.12; 857B); in OT, Eus. *h.e*.10.4.5(M.20.849B); Constantine's vision, id.*v.C*.1.28(p.21.8; M.20. 944B); Soz.*h.e*.1.3.1(M.67.865A); divine healing, Thdt.*qu.10 in Ex.* (1.124); plagues of Egypt, Dion.Ar.*ep*.7(M.3.1081A); virgin birth, Leont.H.*Nest*.5.1(M.86.1724D); **2.** of Christ's miracles, Epiph.*anc*. 27(p.36.8; M.43.65C); Isid.Pel.*epp*.1.54(M.78.217A); Cyr.*Chr.un*.(5[1]. 748D); Proc.G.*Is*.59:1–18(M.87.2608C); Jo.D.*haer.Nest*.20(M.94. 197C); Christol. *τὴν πρὸς τὸ ἴδιον σῶμα ἕνωσιν ἀδιαίρετον, δι' αὐτοῦ... θ. εἰργάζετο* Vict.*Mc*.1:31(p.277.26); *ib*.7:32(p.338.27); *εἷς...ὢν... καθ' ὑπόστασιν...καὶ δύο φύσεις ὁ αὐτὸς γνωριζόμενος, κατ' ἄλλην μὲν τὰς θ. εἰργάζετο, κατ' ἄλλην δὲ τὰ ταπεινὰ παρεδέξατο* Sophr.H.*ep.syn.* (M.87.3176D) ∞ Jo.D.*Jacob*.55(M.94.1465A); *δείκνυται...ὡς θεός, καὶ τὸ κατὰ φύσιν ἄνθρωπος ὤν, θεϊκῶς ἐνεργῶν, καὶ τὰς θ. φυσικῶς προβαλλόμενος* Max.*opusc*.(M.91.84C); as signs of his divinity, Cyr. *Juln*.7(6[2].248B); id.*Jo*.3(4.273C); id.*apol.Thdt*.7(p.131.6; 6[1].225B); *θεοσημείας ἔργα* Thdr.Stud.*epp*.2.162(M.99.1509C); as done by power of H. Ghost, Cyr.*Lc*.4:14(M.72.536A); **3.** of saints' miracles; Moses, Cyr.*Rom*.11:30(M.74.852A); apostles, id.*Nah*.17(3.496A); *cat.Ac*.3:15(p.64.1); in gen., Evagr.*h.e*.1.13(p.61.16; M.86.2453C); as worked by apostles to make converts, Jo.D.*f.o*.1.3(M.94.793C).

***θεοσημεῖον, τό,** *miracle*, Ammon.*Jo*.1:15(M.85.1400B); Epiph. *haer*.30.10(p.345.13; M.41.421B); performed by Christ, *ib*.51.21 (p.278.22; 925B); by apostles, *ib*.29.5(p.327.5; 400A); *ib*.42.11(p.151. 8; 768A); in OT, *ib*.42.11(p.131.32; 757C).

***θεοσθενής,** *strengthened by God*, Thdr.Stud.*epp*.1.51(M.99.1096D).

***θεοσκέπαστος,** *defended by God*, Agath.Papa *ep.imp*.(M.*PL*.87. 1163C).

***θεόσκηνος,** *in which God tabernacles* *θ. σκηνήν* Leont.N.*serm*.3 (M.93.1608A).

***θεόσκιος,** *shrouding God*, Jo.D.*imag*.1(M.94.1273B).

***θεοσκόρπιστος,** *dispersed by God*; of Jews, Hier.H.*Trin*.(M.40. 849B).

θεοσοφία, ἡ, **1.** *knowledge of divine things*, of Christian doctrine *καινὴ καὶ ἀληθὴς θ.* Eus.*p.e*.1.5(16D; M.21.48A); Dion.Ar.*myst*.1.1(M. 3.997A); of scripture *τῶν λογίων...θ.* id.*d.n*.2.2(M.3.640A); ref. theologians *οἱ τῆς καθ' ἡμᾶς θ. ἀρχηγικοί* *ib*.7.4(873A); in gen., Leont.B.*Nest.et Eut*.3(M.86.1368D); **2.** *divine wisdom* *θεοσοφίας θαυματουργία* [i.e. Inc.] Thdot.Anc.*exp.symb*.23(M.77.1345D); **3.** as mode of address *αἰτῶ δὲ παρὰ τῆς σῆς θ. ἐπισκεφθῆναι* Thdr.Stud. *epp*.2.15(M.99.1164D).

θεόσοφος, *full of divine wisdom*, of OT theologians *θ. εὕροντο* Eus.*p.e*.11.5(513B; M.21.852B); of scripture *θ. λόγια* *M.Artem*.28 (p.160.28); *θ. διδασκαλίαι* Max.*opusc*.(M.91.245C); of saints, Soz.*h.e*. 1.13.3(M.67.897A); Leont.B.*mesopent*.(M.86.1977B); as subst., *theologian*, Dion.Ar.*c.h*.2.5(M.3.145A); Leont.B.*Nest.et Eut*.1(M.86. 1280C); Sophr.H.*ep.syn*.(M.87.3152B).

***θεοσόφως,** *with God-given wisdom*, Clem.*str*.1.1(p.12.24; M.8. 708A); ‡Meth.*Sym.et Ann*.12(M.18.377C).

θεόσσυτος, *sent by God*, Nonn.*par.Jo*.6:30(M.43.800A); *ib*.8:20 (816B); *ib*.12:47(857C).

***θεόστεπτος,** *crowned by God* *θ. ἐν ἑορταῖς* Paul.Sil.*Soph*.583(M. 86.2141B); of emperors, Sophr.H.*trop*.(M.87.4009A); *Lit.Jac*.(p.186. 17).

***θεοστεφής,** = foreg., ref. BMV *τὴν ἱεράν σου καὶ θεοστεφῆ ἀνυμνήσω κάραν* ‡Meth.*Sym.et Ann*.9(M.18.369A); of a martyr, Geo.Pis.*Sev*.553(M.92.1664A); of the empire *τῆς ὑμετέρας θ. καὶ Χριστιανικωτάτης βασιλείας* Sym.Styl.J.*ep.Just*.(M.86.3216C); of emperors *ὁ θ. Θεοδόσιος* ‡Sophr.H.*v.m.Cyr.et Jo*.14(M.87.3688A); *Φωκᾷ τῷ θ.* *IGC As.Min*.113; *κράτος...θ. Θεοδώρας* *CIG* 8638; of peace of Church *θ. ... γαληνότης* Anast.Ap.*a.Max*.1.4(M.90.116B).

θεοστήρικτος, *stablished by God* *θ. οἴκῳ* Nil.*epp*.2.204(M.79.308C); esp. of emperors in complimentary address *θ. ὑμῶν καρδία* Sym. Styl.J.*ep.Just*.(M.86.3217B); *θ. ... κράτος* Geo.Pis.*Pers*.2.78(M.92. 1217A); *τοῖς θ. ... βασιλεῦσιν* Max.*ep*.44(M.91.648C); Anast.Ap.*a. Max*.1.4(M.90.116A).

θεοστιβής, *trodden by God*, Gr.Naz.*or*.45.19(M.36.649B); met., of BMV, Thdr.Stud.*nativ.BMV* 7(M.96.689D).

***θεοστοιχής,** *pleasing to God* *τὴν θ. καὶ θεόπλαστον μοναδικὴν ἕξιν* Thdr.Stud.*epp*.2.164(M.99.1521A).

***θεόστολος, ὁ,** *envoy of God*; of apostles, Thdr.Stud.*epp*.2.208 (M.99.1629A).

***θεόστομος,** *divinely breathed* *ἡ τοῦ θ. αὐτοῦ* [sc. Christ] *ἐμφυσήματος μετάδοσις τοῦ πνεύματος* Anast.S.*hod*.1(M.89.45D); id.*serm. imag*.3(M.89.1169A).

***θεόστοργος,** *beloved by God*, Nonn.*par.Jo*.4:45(M.43.781B).

***θεοστράτηγος, ὁ,** *divine captain*; of an angel, *Pers*.(p.19.1; *θεῖε στρατηγέ* M.10.108C).

***θεοστυγέω,** *hate God*, ‡Caes.Naz.*dial*.21(M.38.880).

θεοστυγής, *hateful to God*; **1.** of persons; in gen., *Hom.Clem*.1.12; of Jews *ἡ μὲν πρώτη κληρονομία, τουτέστιν ὁ Ἰσραήλ, οὐ κρατίστη ἦν ἀλλὰ καὶ θ. μᾶλλον* Cyr.*Ps*.15:6(M.69.812A); Nonn.*par.Jo*.21:20 (M.43.920B); of heretics, Ath.*Ar*.3.16(M.26.356B); *ib*.3.41(409B); Philost.*h.e*.6.2(M.65.533B); Taras.*ep*.5(M.98.1464C); of pagan deities, Athenag.*leg*.30.1(M.6.957D); **2.** of things and qualities *θ. ... τολμήματα* Cyr.*Os*.4(3.22E); id.*Am*.17(3.267B); id.*Abac*.27(3.541B); Nonn. *par.Jo*.8:40(M.43.820A).

***θεοστυγία, ἡ,** *hatred of God*, *1Clem*.35.5; Eus.*h.e*.2.18.8(M.20. 188A).

***θεοσύλλεκτος,** *assembled by God*, of councils *ἡ θ. ὁμήγυρις τῆς ἐν Νικαίᾳ συνόδου* Leont.H.*Nest*.7.1(M.86.1760C); CCP(681)*act*.18 (H.3.1397E); CNic.(787)*act*.2(H.4.77D); ‡Jo.D.*ep.Thphl*.8(M.95.356B); of assembled Church, ‡Jo.D.*fid.dorm*.15(M.95.261C); ‡Jo.D.*Artem*. 1(p.151.12; M.96.1252A); *Χριστοῦ λαὸς θ.* *ib*.3(p.153.7; 1253C).

***θεοσύλληπτος**, *having conceived God*; of BMV, Rom.Mel.(*AS* 1 p.32).

***θεοσύναπτος**, **1.** *uniting to God* ἡ θ. ἀγάπησις †Cyr.*hom.div.*10(5^2.377E); **2.** *joined by God* (sc. in matrimony), Thdr.Stud.*epp.*2.51 (M.99.1261B).

***θεοσυνέργητος**, *working together with God*, Thphn.*chron.*p.11(M.108.81B); Areth.*Apoc.*proem.(M.106.493A).

***θεοσυνεσία, ἡ**, *understanding of divine things*, Thdr.Stud.*epp.*1.23(M.99.981A).

***θεοσύνετος**, *divinely wise*, Thdr.Stud.*epp.*2.155(M.99.1484C).

***θεοσύνθετος**, prob. f.l. for θεοσύνετος, Thdr.Stud.*epp.*2.206(M.99.1625B).

***θεοσύστατος**, *commending God*, ‡Chrys.*Jo.theol.*1(8.132C).

***θεοσφαγία, ἡ**, *divine sacrifice*, of eucharist φοβερὰν...ζωοποιὸν θ. ‡Chrys.*poenit.*1.2(9.764B).

***θεόσωμος**, *of the body of God* θ. ταφὴν τοῦ κυρίου ‡Epiph.*hom.*2 tit.(M.43.440A); of Christ's death θ. θυσίαν *ib.*(441C); θ. νεκρώσεως Anast.S.*hod.*13(M.89.241A); θ. πλευρᾷ Thdr.Stud.*or.*2(M.99.693A).

***θεόσωστος**, *divinely protected*, Thdr.Stud.*epp.*2.146(M.99.1457C).

***θεότακτος**, *ordered according to the divine will*, v.l. for θεότευκτος *Orac.Sib.*5.502; Thdr.Stud.*epp.*1.36(M.99.1032A).

***θεοτείχιστος**, *defended by God*, in complimentary address to emperors τὴν θ. ὑμῶν εὐσέβειαν CCP(681)*act.*1(H.3.1057D).

***θεοτελής**, *divinely perfect* λόγων καὶ νόμων οὐρανίων καὶ θ. ‡Amph.*circ.*8(p.20B); τὰ θεοπρεπῆ πάντα τῇ ὅλῃ θεαρχίᾳ πρόσεστι κατὰ τὸν θ. λόγον Dion.Ar.*d.n.*2.1(M.3.637C); ἡ ψυχὴ...ἐνεργοῦσα καθ' ὃν καὶ ἔστι καὶ γεγένηται θ. λόγον Max.*ambig.*(M.91.1249B); *ib.*(1317C); τράπεζα...θεοτελῶν μυστηρίων...πλήθουσα Andr.Cr.*or.*13(M.97.1084B); θ. τὴν μαρτυρίαν ποιούμενον Thdr.Stud.*epp.*2.100(M.99.1353D); *completed in God* θ. βίον *ib.*2.145(1457B).

θεοτερπής, *delighting God*, Nonn.*par.Jo.*6:28(M.43.797C); *ib.*8:32 (817B).

θεότευκτος, **1.** *fashioned by God*; **a.** of things, ref. Law θ. ... πλάκας Gr.Nyss.*v.Gr.Thaum.*(M.46.913A); ταῖς πλαξὶ τῆς καρδίας τὸν θεῖον νόμον ἐγχαράξωμεν, πυξίον γενόμενοι θ. ‡Caes.Naz.*dial.*194(M.38.1184); of Temple, *Orac.Sib.*5.150; of picture of Christ said to have been sent by him to Abgar, Evagr.*h.e.*4.27(p.175.7; M.86.2748C); of Church as θ. σκηνή ‡Gr.Nyss.*occurs.*(M.46.1165A); exeg. Ps.47:9 πόλει...θ. ἥτις ἐστὶν ἐκκλησία Eus.*h.e.*10.4.7(M.20.849C); of BMV θ. οἰκία Mod.*dorm.*3(M.86.3285B); **b.** of people λαὸς θ. *Orac.Sib.*5.502, v.l. θεότακτος; πάντων δ' ἡγητῆρα κατέστησεν θ. *ib.fr.*3.13; **2.** *produced, uttered by God* θεΐαν...φωνὴν καὶ θ. Sophr.H.*or.*7.10 (M.87.3337B); **3.** *divinely wrought*; of arms of Achilles, ‡Just.*coh. Gr.*1(M.6.232A); **4.** *attaining to God* (τυγχάνω); hence, *intercessory* τῇ μεσιτείᾳ τῶν θ. ὑμῶν προσευχῶν Max.*opusc.*(M.91.209D).

***θεοτευξία, ἡ**, *working of God*, ‡Gr.Nyss.*occurs.*(M.46.1153A).

***θεοτευχής**, *of God's fashioning*, Gr.Naz.*carm.*2.2(poem.)7.301(M.37.1575A).

***θεοτήρητος**, *guarded by God*, Leont.Abb.*v.Gr.Agr.*20(M.98.584A).

θεότης, ἡ, *deity*;

A. of God in gen.; **1.** definitions and explanations ἡ μὲν γὰρ ὑπόστασις 'τὸ εἶναι' σημαίνει· ἡ δὲ θ. 'τὸ τί εἶναι' ‡Ath.*dial.Trin.*1.2 (M.28.1120A); τὸ ὑπὲρ πᾶσαν οὐσίαν εἶναι καὶ φύσιν, ὃ μόνου θεοῦ καὶ οἱονεὶ φύσις θ. Gr.Naz.*or.*29.14(p.94.12; M.36.92D); τὸ τῆς θ. ὄνομα, εἴτε τὴν ἐποπτικὴν εἴτε τὴν προνοητικὴν ἐξουσίαν σημαίνει Gr.Nyss. *Eun.*12(2 p.277.21; M.45.888D); **2.** properties; **a.** unity, θ. being one because perfect, Gr.Nyss.*or.catech.*proem.(p.4.6ff.; M.45.12Bff.); proved from Eph.4:6 and 2Petr.1:4, Didym.*Trin.*1.16(M.39.333B); **b.** simplicity, Gr.Naz.*or.*30.2(p.110.12; M.36.105B); οὐ...ἡ ἁπλότης, τούτου κατὰ τὸ ἴσον πάντως καὶ ἡ θ. κεχώρισται Gr.Nyss.*Apoll.*2 (M.45.1128B); Cyr.*thes.*9(5^1.69C); ἁπλουστάτην θ. Dion.Ar.*d.n.*12.3 (M.3.969C); **c.** incorporeality, Ath.*gent.*21(M.25.44A); cf.‡Ath.*Apoll.*1.5(M.26.1100D); ref. Jo.1:14 μὴ κατάπτωσιν τῆς θ. ἐννοήσῃς. οὐ γὰρ μεταβαίνει ἐκ τόπου εἰς τόπον ὡς τὰ σώματα †Bas.*Chr.generat.*2 (2.597A; M.31.1460C); **d.** infinity ἄπειρον...ἡ θ. Gr.Nyss.*or.catech.*10 (p.54.9; 41B); Thdr.Stud.*antirr.*3.4(M.99.392B); **e.** various characteristics τὸ χαρακτηρίζον τὴν **θ.** ἡ περὶ μελλόντων ἐστὶν ἀπαγγελία Or.*Cels.*6.10(p.80.17; M.11.1305A); μυρίας...τῆς θ. ἐνεργείας Cyr.H. *catech.*6.7; τὸ...ἀληθῶς καθαρὸν ἡ θ. ἐστίν Gr.Nyss.*or.catech.*36(p.140.8; 92D); κατ' ἀρχὰς...ἡ...θ. ἦν id.*Apoll.*3(1129A); ἄτρεπτος...ἡ θ. Jo.Nic.*nativ.*(M.96.1449C); **3.** not comprehensible, Gr.Nyss.*tres dii* (M.45.129D); cf.Dion.Ar.*d.n.*1.5(M.3.593B); *ib.*1.8(597C); οὐδὲν τῶν νοητῶν ὁ παντὸς νοητοῦ καθ' ὑπεροχὴν αἴτιος. ... οὐδὲ ἑνότης, οὐδὲ θ. ... id.*myst.*5(M.3.1045D,1048A); τῆς θ. ἐνεργείας νοεῖν ἢ λέγειν ἀδύνατον Jo.D.*f.o.*1.11(M.94.841B); but ἡ...τῆς θ. μαρτυρία διὰ τῶν θαυμάτων ἐστίν Gr.Nyss.*or.catech.*34(p.129.6; M.45.85D); revealed in scripture, Dion.Ar.*d.n.*1.1(588A).

B. Trin.; **1.** in gen., Dion.Ar.*d.n.*2.4(M.3.641A); *ib.*2.1(636C); Jo.D.*f.o.*1.12(M.94.848C); **2.** one divinity common to all three Persons μία θ. ἐστὶν ἐν τριάδι Ath.*Ar.*1.18(M.26.48C); ἐν τῇ κοινωνίᾳ τῆς θ. ἐστὶν ἡ ἕνωσις Bas.*Spir.*45(3.38C; M.32.149C); τρεῖς ὑποστάσεις,...μία θ. Epiph.*haer.*25.6(p.273.24; M.41.328D); τοῦ πατρὸς καὶ τοῦ υἱοῦ καὶ τοῦ ἁγίου πνεύματος, τῆς μιᾶς...θ. Cosm.Ind.*top.*proem.1(M.88.52A); Jo.V H.*icon.*4(M.96.1353A); **3.** of divinity of Father and Son; **a.** in gen., ref. Gen.1:26 τὸ γὰρ ποιήσωμεν τὸ πανάγιον καὶ ἀπαράλλακτον τῆς τοῦ πατρὸς καὶ υἱοῦ θ. παρίστησιν ἡ φωνή Gel.Cyz.*h.e.*2.14.6 (M.85.1257A); ὅλον μὲν τὸ πλήρωμα τῆς θ. ὁ πατήρ, ὡς πατήρ, ὅλον δὲ τὸ πλήρωμα τῆς θ. ὁ υἱός, ὡς υἱός ‡Ath.*Sabell.*8(M.28.109C); ref. Is.62:1,2 βραχίονα...τοῦ πατρὸς...καλεῖ τὸν μονογενῆ...οὐχ ὡς μέρος θ. ...ἀλλ' ὡς τῇ οὐσίᾳ συνημμένον ‡Ath.*comm.essent.*(M.28.64D); φύσει ...οὐκέτι δεύτερος, διότι ἡ θ. ἐν ἑκατέρῳ μία Bas.*Eun.*3.1(1.272B; M.29.656A); θεὸν γεννήσας οὐκ αὐτὸς τῆς θ. ἐστερήθη Cyr.H.*catech.*11.18; ὥσπερ ἐπὶ τοῦ Ἀδὰμ καὶ τοῦ Ἄβελ ἀνθρωπότης μία, οὕτω καὶ ἐπὶ τοῦ πατρὸς καὶ ἐπὶ τοῦ υἱοῦ θ. μία Gr.Nyss.*fid.*(M.45.141C); ref. Jo.1:14 μία θ. Epiph.*haer.*57.4(p.349.16; M.41.1001B); ἔστι...μία θ. πατρὸς καὶ υἱοῦ, κἂν ἑκάτερος τῇ τῶν ὀνομάτων ποικιλίᾳ διαφόρως σημαίνηται Cyr.*thes.*9(5^1.69E); **b.** of Son as image of Father ἡ ἐν αὐτῷ θ. εἰκὼν τῆς ἀληθινῆς θ. Or.*Jo.*13.36(p.261.26; M.14.461C); χαρακτὴρ καὶ εἰκὼν τῆς θ. Gr.Thaum.*symb.*(p.3.4; M.10.985A); εἷς δὲ καὶ μονογενὴς τοῦ θεοῦ υἱός, εἰκὼν τῆς πατρικῆς θ., καὶ διὰ τοῦτο θεός Eus.*e.th.*1.2 (p.63.29; M.24.832C); *Symb.Ant.*341(2)(p.249.17; M.26.721C); Ath. *Ar.*3.5(M.26.332B); *ib.*2.43(240A); εἰκόνα εἶναι τοῦ θεοῦ τοῦ ἀοράτου τὸν μονογενῆ, εἰκόνα δὲ οὐ χαρακτῆρος σωματικοῦ, ἀλλ' αὐτῆς τῆς θ. Bas.*ep.*236.1(3.361B; M.32.877A); id.*Spir.*45(3.38B; M.32.149B); Didym.*Trin.*1.16(M.39.336C); **4.** ref. H. Ghost and other Persons ἀπὸ τῶν...γραφῶν δείκνυται μὴ εἶναι κτίσμα τὸ πνεῦμα τὸ ἅγιον, ἀλλὰ ἴδιον τοῦ λόγου καὶ τῆς τοῦ πατρὸς θ. Ath.*ep.Serap.*1.32(M.26.605A); of H. Ghost and Son ἡ τῆς φύσεως ἑνότης τὸν διαμερισμὸν οὐ προσίεται, ὡς μήτε τὸ τῆς μοναρχίας σχίζεσθαι κράτος εἰς θ. διαφόρους κατατεμνόμενον Gr.Nyss.*or.catech.*3(p.16.8; M.45.17D); Didym.(‡Bas.)*Eun.*5(1.311C; M.29.748A); **5.** ref. heresies; ref. tritheistic reaction against Sabellianism κατατέμνοντας...τὴν μοναρχίαν εἰς τρεῖς...μεμερισμένας...θ. Dion.R.ap.Ath.*decr.*26(p.22.3; M.25.461D); ref. Sabellianism and Arianism ἢ διὰ τὸ ἓν θέλημα τῆς θ., καὶ ἓν λέγειν πρόσωπον...ἢ διὰ τὰ τρία πρόσωπα, καὶ τρία θελήματα Max.*opusc.*(M.91.273B); ref. Sabellianism διαίρεσιν θεότητος, καὶ ἀρχῶν καὶ θεῶν ἀρίθμησιν καταιτιώμενος, τῇ Ἰουδαϊκῇ στηρίζεται γνώμῃ ‡Ath.*Apoll.*1.21(M.26.1129C); δογματίζει...τὸν αὐτὸν εἶναι πατέρα, τὸν αὐτὸν υἱόν, τὸν αὐτὸν εἶναι ἅγιον πνεῦμα,...ὡς ἐν ἀνθρώπῳ σῶμα, καὶ ψυχή, καὶ πνεῦμα, καὶ εἶναι μὲν τὸ σῶμα...τὸν πατέρα, ψυχὴν δὲ...τὸν υἱόν, τὸ πνεῦμα δὲ ὡς ἀνθρώπου, οὕτως καὶ τὸ ἅγιον πνεῦμα ἐν τῇ θ. Epiph.*haer.*62.1(p.389.16; M.41.1052A); ref. condemnation of denial by Paul. Sam. of Son's pre-existence περὶ δὲ τῆς τοῦ υἱοῦ θ. ἁπλούστερον γράφοντες, οὐ κατεγένοντο περὶ τὴν τοῦ ὁμοουσίου ἀκρίβειαν Ath.*syn.*45(p.270.19; M.26.773B); ref. Arianism οὐδὲ...διστάσειεν ἄν τις τὸν πατέρα...θεότητι...μείζονα εἶναι, διαμαρτυρουμένου αὐτοῦ τοῦ υἱοῦ [cf. Jo.14:28] *ib.*28(p.257.10; 741C); οὐ ταὐτόν, φησί, τὸ ἀγέννητον καὶ τὸ γεννητόν. ... ὅτι μὲν φανερῶς ὁ λόγος οὗτος ἐκβάλλει τὸν υἱὸν τῆς θ., ἢ τὸν πατέρα, τί χρὴ λέγειν; Gr.Naz.*or.*27.10(p.87.7; M.36.85D); cf.*ib.*18.16(M.35.1005A); καθέλκοντες [sc. Arians]...τὰ περὶ τῆς ἀρρητοτάτης θ. εἰς τὰ τῆς ἡμετέρας φύσεως ἀποτελέσματα Didym.*Trin.*1.16(M.39.332A); εἰ...ὁ πατὴρ οἶδε καὶ αὐτὸς οὐκ οἶδε [cf. Mt.24:36], πῶς δύναται ἡ αὐτὴ θ. πατρὸς καὶ υἱοῦ ὑπάρχειν; Epiph.*haer.*69.43(p.191.8; M.42.269B); περὶ...τὴν θ. ...ἐσφάλλετο, ὅτι ἔλεγε κτίσμα εἶναι τοῦ θεοῦ τὸν υἱὸν καὶ τὸ ἅγιον πνεῦμα †Leont.B.*sect.*3.4(M.86.1216C); ref. notion that Christ's flesh is consubstantial with Godhead τίς δὲ...ταύτην ἐπενόησεν ἀσέβειαν ὥστε...εἰπεῖν ὅτι ὁ λέγων ἐκ Μαρίας εἶναι τὸ κυριακὸν σῶμα οὐκέτι τριάδα ἀλλὰ τετράδα ἐν τῇ θ. φρονεῖ; Ath.*ep.Epict.*2(p.5.6; M.26.1053A); νομίζουσιν ἀντὶ τριάδος τετράδα λέγεσθαι, ὡς προσθήκης γινομένης διὰ τὸ σῶμα...καὶ ὑπονοοῦντες δύνασθαι τὴν θ. προσθήκην λαμβάνειν *ib.*9(p.15.2; 1065A).

C. ref. Father δέον τῇ ἀφάτῳ δυνάμει τῆς θ. αὐτοῦ πεπεῖσθαι περιέχεσθαι καὶ συνέχεσθαι τὰ πάντα ὑπ' αὐτοῦ Or.*or.*23.1(p.349.28; M.11.485D); Gr.Naz.*or.*31.26(p.178.8; M.36.161C); μόνη...πηγὴ τῆς... θ. ὁ πατήρ Dion.Ar.*d.n.*2.5(M.3.641D).

D. ref. Christ, v. ἀνθρωπότης; **1.** gen., Or.*Jo.*1.18(20; p.22.32; M.14.53D) cit. s. ἀνθρωπότης; τῆς σωτηρίου θ. Eus.*l.C.*18(p.259.4; M.20.1437C); ref. Jo.10:11 ποιμὴν [sc. καλεῖται] διὰ τὴν φιλανθρωπίαν τῆς θ. Cyr.H.*catech.*10.3; τῇ ἑαυτοῦ θ. περιποιεῖ τὸν λαόν Didym.*Trin.*

1.27(M.39.396A); Isid.Pel.*epp*.4.166(M.78.1256B); Cyr.*Nest*.3.1(p.57.14; 6^1.67C); *ἡ πάντων αἰτία...τοῦ Ἰησοῦ θ.* Dion.Ar.*d.n*.2.10(M.3.648C); **2.** ref. union of natures, Or.*or*.26.4(p.361.25; M.11.501D); *τὸν Χριστόν, ἄνθρωπον ἀκράτῳ θ. καὶ τελείᾳ πεπληρωμένον καὶ θεὸν ἐν ἀνθρώπῳ κεχωρημένον* Meth.*symp*.3.4(p.31.1; M.18.68A); Cyr.*Is*.1.4(2.107E); *Παῦλος...θ. τε καὶ ἀνθρωπότητα συλλέγων εἰς ἕν* id.*inc.unigen*.(5^1.695D); Leont.B.*Nest.et Eut*.3 proem.(M.86.1269C); Max.*opusc*.(M.91.36C); as hypostatic *ὁ Χριστὸς τὰς δύο οὐσίας καὶ φύσεις ἔσχεν ἀτρέπτους καὶ ἀκεραίους, τὴν θ. καὶ τὴν ἀνθρωπότητα ἐν μιᾷ ὑποστάσει* ‡Ath.*def*.8(M.28.537B); ‡Proc.G.*Pr*.30:5(M.87.1524B); Jo.D.*f.o*.3.11(M.94.1025C); ref. such analogies as relation of iron to fire *οὕτω καὶ ἡ ἀνθρωπίνη τοῦ κυρίου σάρξ, αὐτὴ μετέσχε τῆς θ., οὐ τῇ θ. μετέδωκε τῆς οἰκείας ἀσθενίας* †Bas.*Chr.generat*.2(2.597A; M.31.1460C); *ὁμολογῶ τὴν πανάμωμον αὐτοῦ ἀνθρωπότητα τῆς ψυχῆς καὶ τοῦ σώματος οὕτω καθ' ὑπόστασιν ἡνωμένην τῇ ἀχράντῳ αὐτοῦ θ., ὥσπερ ὅλη δι' ὅλου ἕνωται ἡ ψυχὴ ἡ ἡμῶν τῷ ἡμετέρῳ σώματι* Anast.S.*hod*.21(M.89.281A); without confusion *εἴ τις...λέγει...τραπεῖσαν τὴν θ. εἰς σάρκα ἢ συγχυθεῖσαν ἢ ἀλλοιωθεῖσαν...ἀνάθεμα ἔστω* Apoll.*ep.Jov*.3(p.253.9; M.28.29A); Cyr.*apol.orient*.(p.49.4; 6^1.178D); *μὴ ὑπομείναντα παραλλαγὴν...κατὰ τὴν θ., ἐν τῷ προσλαβεῖν τὸ ἀνθρώπινον* Max.*schol.e.h*.4.3.10(M.4.157B); Anast.S.*hod*.8(M.89.124A); *μὴ μεταβαλὼν τὴν τῆς θ. αὐτοῦ φύσιν εἰς τὴν τῆς σαρκὸς οὐσίαν, μήτε τὴν οὐσίαν τῆς σαρκὸς αὐτοῦ εἰς τὴν φύσιν τῆς αὐτοῦ θ.* Jo.D.*f.o*.3.2(M.94.988A); **3.** of Christ's divinity as hidden from Devil *κρύπτων...τὸ τῆς θ. ἀξίωμα, ἵνα λάθῃ τοῦ δράκοντος τὸ πανούργευμα* †Hipp.*theoph*.4(p.259.12; M.10.856A); *διὰ τί οὐκ...ἡ θ. μόνον τὸν ἄνθρωπον...ἔσωσεν...ἄνευ σαρκός;...κατ' ἀρχάς, ὅταν ἐποίησεν ὁ θεὸς τὸν ἄνθρωπον...οὐκ ἐνίκησεν ὁ διάβολος τὴν θ. ἀλλὰ τὴν ἀνθρωπότητα. διὸ καὶ ἔπρεπε πάλιν αὐτὴ ἡ...ἀνθρωπότης ἵνα...νικήσῃ τὸν ἐχθρὸν αὐτῆς τὸν διάβολον...εἰ γὰρ γυμνὴ ἡ θ. προσήρχετο,...οὐ θαυμαστόν, εἰ καὶ ἐνικήθη· ὑπὸ τῆς θ. γὰρ προσβαλὼν ἐνικήθη* ‡Ath.*qu.al*.20(M.28.792Cff.); *διὰ τοῦτο περικαλύπτεται τῇ σαρκὶ ἡ θ., ὡς ἄν, πρὸς τὸ σύντροφόν τε καὶ συγγενὲς αὐτῷ βλέπων, μὴ πτοηθείη τὸν προσεγγισμὸν τῆς ὑπερεχούσης δυνάμεως* Gr.Nyss.*or.catech*.23(p.89.6; M.45.64A); **4.** of his divinity in events of incarnate life *ἡ ἐπιφάνιος* [sc. *ἑορτή*]*...καθ' ἣν ὁ κύριος ἀνάδειξιν ὑμῖν τῆς οἰκείας θ. ἐποιήσατο* *Const.App*.5.13.2; *ib*.8.33.7; *πνεῦμα ἅγιον...καθαῖρον αὐτήν* [sc. BMV], *καὶ δύναμιν δεκτικὴν τῆς τοῦ λόγου θ. παρέχον, ἅμα δὲ καὶ γεννητικήν* Jo.D.*f.o*.3.2(M.94.985B); as recognized by Jo. Bapt., ‡Chrys.*praecurs*.1(2.807B); Gr.Ant.*bapt*.1(M.10.1181A); as shown at his baptism, ref. Ps.28:3,4 *ὁ...Δαβὶδ καὶ τὴν φωνὴν προφητεύων, ἣν ἐξ οὐρανῶν ὁ πατὴρ ἐπαφῆκε τῷ υἱῷ βαπτιζομένῳ, ἵνα πρὸς τὸ φυσικὸν τῆς θ. ἀξίωμα τοὺς ἀκούοντας ὁδηγήσῃ* Gr.Nyss.*bapt.Chr*.(M.46.596A); in Transfiguration *ἐμφανίσας αὐτοῖς τὸ ἀπρόσιτον αὐτοῦ τῆς θ. κάλλος, οὐχ ὅσον ἦν, ἀλλ' ὅσον ἠδύνατο βαστάσαι ἀνθρώπων ἀνύστακτα βλέφαρα* Tim.Ant.*cruc*.(M.86.261A); Andr.Cr.*or*.7(M.97.932C); *ib*.(949C); as not leaving him at Passion, ref. Mt.27:46 *φωνῆς...γενομένης καὶ ψυχῆς σημαινομένης, οὐ χωρισμὸν θεότητος δηλούσης, ἀλλὰ νέκρωσιν σώματος σημαινούσης, μήτε τῆς θ. τοῦ σώματος ἐν τῷ τάφῳ ἀπολιμπανομένης μήτε τῆς ψυχῆς ἐν τῷ ᾅδῃ χωριζομένης* ‡Ath.*Apoll*.2.14(M.26.1156C); *ib*.1.18(1125B); against Arians, Epiph.*haer*.69.63(p.212.16; M.42.305A); Nil.*epp*.1.102(M.79.125C); as inseparable from soul and body of dead Christ *κατέρχεται εἰς τὰ καταχθόνια ἐν θ. καὶ ἐν ψυχῇ* Epiph.*inc*.2(p.230.3; M.41.276D); *τῆς θ. αὐτοῦ, καὶ μετὰ τοῦ σώματος οὔσης καὶ μετὰ τῆς ψυχῆς· οὐ γὰρ ἐχωρίσθη μετὰ τὴν ἕνωσιν ἡ θ. τῆς ἀνθρωπότητος οὐδαμῶς οὐδαμοῦ· ἀλλὰ καὶ ἐν τοῖς οὐρανοῖς ἦν· καὶ ἐν τάφῳ παρῆν ἀπαθῶς* Gr.Ant.*mul.ung*.2(M.88.1849B); in opinion of Mars of Edessa *σοφίζονται...οἱ...φάσκοντες* [i.e. followers of Cyril], *ὅτι ἀχώριστος ἦν ἐν τῷ τάφῳ τοῦ σώματος τοῦ Ἰησοῦ ἡ θ.* Anast.S.*hod*.14(M.89.248C); in risen Christ *ἵνα δείξῃ καὶ τῆς θ. τὴν ἐνέργειαν, καὶ τοῦ σώματος τὴν ἀλήθειαν* Gr.Thaum.*fid.cap*.1(p.147.24; M.10.1128A); **5.** of divinity as impassible, Apoll.*ep.Jov*.2f.(p.252.1,253.9; M.28.28B,29A); *ἡ ἀπαθὴς θ.* ‡Ath.*Apoll*.1.15(M.26.1121B); *εἰ γὰρ αὐτὴ τέθνηκε τοῦ μονογενοῦς ἡ θ., συναπέθανε ταύτῃ πάντως καὶ ἡ ζωή, καὶ ἡ ἀλήθεια...ταῦτα γὰρ κατὰ διαφόρους ἐπιβολὰς ὁ μονογενὴς θεὸς...ἐστι* Gr.Nyss.*Apoll*.5(M.45.1132C); ref. Mt.27:46 *εἰ γὰρ τὸ πάσχον ἡ θ.,...πῶς μία οὐσία ἡ θ. ἐν τῷ πάθει μερίζεται, καὶ ἡ μὲν καταλείπει, ἡ δὲ καταλείπεται...;* *ib*.24(1176B); *ἡ θ. οὐ πάσχει...ἀπαθὴς διαμένει ὁ θεός, συμπάσχει δὲ τῇ σαρκί, ἵνα τὸ πάθος εἰς τὴν θ. λογισθῇ, μὴ πασχούσης τῆς θ., εἰς τὸ εἶναι ἡμῖν ἐν θεῷ τὴν σωτηρίαν* Epiph.*haer*.69.24(p.174.23; M.42.241A); id.*inc*.2(p.229.20; M.41.276C); Cyr.*deip.BMV* 4(p.20.20; M.76.260A); *ἴσμεν...παρὰ τῆς θείας διδαχθέντες γραφῆς, ὡς ἀπαθὴς ἡ τῆς θ. φύσις. ἀπάθειαν τοίνυν καὶ πάθος ἀκούοντες, καὶ ἀνθρωπότητος καὶ θ. ἕνωσιν, τοῦ παθητοῦ σώματος τὸ πάθος εἶναί φαμεν, τὴν ἀπαθῆ δὲ φύσιν ἐλευθέραν μεμενηκέναι τοῦ πάθους ὁμολογοῦμεν* Thdt.*eran*.3(4.190); *παθητὸς σαρκί, καὶ ἀπαθὴς ὁ αὐτὸς ἐν θ.* Just.Imp.*edict*.(p.199.11; M.86.2796D); *εἰ φύσιν Χριστοῦ μόνην θ. εἶναι λέγει,...ἢ παθητὸν καὶ ῥευστὸν λέγων τὸ θεῖον, ἢ ἀρνούμενος τὸ σῶμα καὶ αἷμα τοῦ Χριστοῦ, ὅπερ προσάγει καὶ ἐσθίει ἐπὶ τῆς μυστικῆς θυσίας* Anast.S.*hod*.13(M.89.209A); heret. *Οὐαλεντῖνος...κοινὸν τῆς τριάδος τὸ πάθος λέγει, τῆς θ. μέρος τὴν σάρκα φανταζόμενος* ‡Ath.*Apoll*.2.3(M.26.1136C); *τὸ τῇ θ. τοῦ Χριστοῦ προσάπτειν τὸ πάθος, ἐκ τῆς Ἀρείου καὶ Εὐνομίου βλασφημίας κεκλόφασιν* Thdt.*eran*.proem.(4.3); *παθητὴν εἰσάγει τὴν θ. κατὰ τὴν Ἀρείου μανίαν* Justn.*ep.Thdr.Mops*.37(p.57.5; M.86.1065B); (Arian) *ἄψυχον...τοῦ κυρίου τὴν σάρκα, καὶ τὸ πάθος καὶ τὴν ταραχὴν τὴν θ. ἀντὶ τῆς ψυχῆς ὑπομεῖναι* Tim.CP *haer*.(M.86.37B); (Apollinarian) *τὸ πάθος δὲ τῇ ἰδίᾳ αὐτοῦ θ. δέξασθαι· καὶ ἐν τῇ τριημέρῳ ἐκείνῃ νεκρώσει τοῦ σώματος, καὶ τὴν θ. συναπονεκρωθῆναι τῷ σώματι, καὶ οὕτω παρὰ τοῦ πατρὸς πάλιν ἀπὸ τοῦ θανάτου διαναστῆναι* *ib*.(40B); conciliar condemnations *εἴ τις τὸν μονογενῆ υἱὸν τοῦ θεοῦ ἐσταυρωμένον ἀκούων, τὴν θ. αὐτοῦ, φθοράν, ἢ πάθος, ἢ τροπήν, ἢ μείωσιν, ἢ ἀναίρεσιν ὑπομεμενηκέναι λέγοι, ἀ. ἔ.* *Symb.Sirm*.1 *anath*.13(M.26.737B); *τοὺς παθητὴν τοῦ μονογενοῦς λέγειν τολμῶντας τὴν θ., τοῦ τῶν ἱερῶν ἀπωθεῖται* [sc. Leo Mag.] *συλλόγου* *Symb.Chalc*.(p.129.18; H.2.456B); **6.** of heresies denying divinity of Christ *οἱ...τὴν θ. αὐτοῦ περιγράψαντες, τὸν δὲ ἄνθρωπον ὡς ἅγιον καὶ δικαιότατον πάντων ἀνθρώπων ὁμολογήσαντες* Or.*Jo*.10.6(4; p.176.14; M.14.316B); (Beryllus of Bostra) *τὸν σωτῆρα...μηδὲ μὲν θ. ἰδίαν ἔχειν, ἀλλ' ἐμπολιτευομένην αὐτῷ μόνην τὴν πατρικήν* Eus.*h.e*.6.33.1(M.20.593A); (Ebionites) *τὴν...τοῦ υἱοῦ θ. μὴ εἰδότας* id.*e.th*.1.14(p.74.16; M.24.853A); (Artemon, Theodotus, Sabellius, Paul of Samosata, Marcellus, Photinus), Thdt.*eran*.2(4.79); (Photinus) *ἀπὸ Μαρίας ἔχειν τὴν ἀρχὴν τῆς θ. καὶ τῆς σαρκὸς τὸν Χριστόν* Anast.S.*hod*.5(M.89.100B); **7.** in Apollinarian view *ἡ τῆς θ. ἀλήθεια μετὰ τοῦ σώματος ἕν ἐστι καὶ εἰς δύο φύσεις οὐ μερίζεται* Apoll.*ep.Dion*.3(p.258.2; M.*PL*.8.929C); *σὰρξ ἁγία θεότητι συμφυής* id.*fr*.155(p.249.5)ap.Leont.B.*Apoll*.(M.86.1964B); Gr.Nyss.*Apoll*.24(M.45.1177A); refuted *πῶς...ἡ μετὰ χρόνον σὰρξ ὁμοούσιος ἂν λέγοιτο τῆς ἀχρόνου θ.;* †Gr.Thaum.*fid.cap*.2(p.148.1; M.10.1128B); Ath.*ep.Epict*.2(M.26.1052C); *οὐ δύναται...θ. καλεῖσθαι κτιστὸν ὑπάρχον τὸ πανάγιον σῶμα, ἵνα μὴ φανῶμεν ὁμοούσιον λέγοντες κτίσματι τὴν θ. τῆς ἁγίας τριάδος* Anast.S.*hod*.13(M.89.205A); **8.** question whether BMV is mother of divinity (v. supra 5) *οὐ γάρ που θ. γυμνήν, ὡς ἔφην, ἐκτέτοκεν ἡ παρθένος* Cyr.*apol.Thdt*.1.15(p.113.7; 6^1.207A); *ὑπόστασιν...ἐγέννησεν ἡ ἁγία θεοτόκος ἐν δυσὶ γνωριζομένην ταῖς φύσεσι, θ. μέν, ἐκ πατρὸς γεννηθεῖσαν ἀχρόνως* Jo.D.*f.o*.4.7(M.94.1113C); **9.** of Christ's divinity; **a.** as incomprehensible, ref. Jer.17:9 *τῆς αὐτοῦ θ. τῆς ἀκαταλήπτου* Epiph.*haer*.54.4(p.321.23; M.41.968B); Andr.Cr.*or*.7(M.97.933C); **b.** as known by revelation *ἀποκαλύπτει...δι' ἁγίου πνεύματος τοῖς αὐτοῖς δούλοις τὴν αὐτοῦ καὶ τὴν τοῦ πατρὸς θ.* Epiph.*haer*.54.4(p.321.27; M.41.968B); *πίστει μόνῃ τὰ περὶ τῆς θ. πάντα παραδίδονται* Anast.S.*hod*.14(M.89.249C); in scripture *τῶν* [sc. gospels] *συνιστάντων τὴν ἐν Ἰησοῦ θ.* Or.*Cels*.2.33(p.160.2; M.11.853A); *ib*.2.36(p.162.12; 857B); id.*Jo*.1.4(6; p.8.9; M.14.29D); *τοὺς οἰομένους μὴ πάνυ τι τὴν θ. παρίστασθαι τοῦ σωτῆρος ἐκ τοῦ κατὰ Ματθαῖον εὐαγγελίου* id.*comm.in Mt*.12.6(p.77.19; M.13.989A); ‡Bas.*struct.hom*.1.2(1.325C; M.30.13B); *Δαυίδ, ἀνακηρύττοντα αὐτοῦ τὴν θ.* Chrys.*hom.71.2 in Mt*.(7.696B); some texts referring to the divinity, others to the humanity *τὰ μὲν ὑψηλότερα πρόσαγε τῇ θ. καὶ τῇ κρείττονι φύσει παθῶν καὶ σώματος* Gr.Naz.*or*.29.18(p.101.13; M.36.97B); Chrys.*hom.29.4 in 1Cor*.(10.368C,D); specific instances *τὸ...'οὔτε ἐμὲ οἴδατε οὔτε τὸν πατέρα μου' περὶ τῆς θ.* [sc. *διαλέγεται*] Or.*Jo*.19.2(1; p.299.23; 525D); Eus.*e.th*.1.20(p.93.1; M.24.885C); Chrys.*hom.45.2 in Jo*.(8.264A); Thdt.*eran*.3(4.191); cf. *εἰς τὴν ἐνανθρώπησιν οὖν, καὶ οὐκ εἰς τὴν θ. ταῦτα* [Mt.28:18] *νοεῖν δεῖ* Didym.(‡Bas.)*Eun*.4(1.289B; M.29.693C); Chrys.*hom.15.1 in Rom*.(9.595C); id.*hom.67.1 in Jo*.(8.401D); *ἐπὶ τοῦ Χριστοῦ, ἐπὶ τοῦ μονογενοῦς λέγω υἱοῦ, καὶ τὸ Χριστὸς καὶ τὸ υἱὸς ποτὲ μὲν ἐπὶ τῆς θ., ποτὲ δὲ ἐπὶ τῆς ἀνθρωπότητος, ⟨ποτὲ δὲ ἐπὶ τῆς ἀνθρωπότητος⟩ καὶ θ.* Nest.*fr*.C 10(p.273.17)ap.Cyr.*Nest*.2.1(p.34.30f.; 6^1.33E); cf.*ib*.C 3(p.228.1); **c.** proved by miracles, Const.ap.Gel.Cyz.*h.e*.2.7.16(M.85.1236B); †Bas.*hom.in Ps*.115(1.371C; M.30.104B); Bas.*ep*.234.3(3.358C; M.32.869D); *τὸ...σῶμα τὴν ἐν αὐτῷ θ. διὰ τῆς ἀφῆς τὰς ἰάσεις ἐνεργοῦν ἐπεσήμαινε* Gr.Nyss.*res*.1(M.46.616C); Cyr.*fr.Mt*.9:6(M.72.392D); Thdt.*eran*.1(4.20); Ephr.Ant.*fr*.(M.86.2105B); ref. eclipse at Crucifixion *βοᾷ ὁ ἥλιος...ἐγὼ...τὸ φῶς τῆς θ. αὐτοῦ φοβηθείς, συνέστειλα τὰς ἀκτῖνας* Procl.CP *or*.13(M.65.793C); by Father's voice *τῆς μακαρίας ἐκείνης φωνῆς,...μαρτυρούσης ἀψευδῶς τῷ μονογενεῖ τὴν θ.* Andr.Cr.*or*.7(M.97.936C); by character of his teaching, *Hom.Clem*.1.6; **d.** witnessed to by Christians, *A.Andr*.A 16(p.57.1); Leo Mag.*ep*.43(p.4.15; M.*PL*.54.824B); **e.** as symbolized, ref. Dan.2:35 *τοῦ μὲν ὄρους τὴν προϋπαρξιν τῆς θ. αὐτοῦ σημαίνοντος, τοῦ δὲ λίθου τὴν ἀνθρωπότητα* Eus.*e.th*.1.20(p.94.25; M.

24.889B); σύμβολον...τῆς ὑπερλάμπρου θ., ὁ χρυσός Cyr.*ador*.9(1.293E); τὸ...πῦρ σημαίνει τὴν θ. Ephr.2.268D.

E. ref. H. Ghost; in gen., Gr.Naz.*or*.31.26(p.178.6; M.36.161C); ref. Jo.16:12, Jo.14:26, as one of the truths to be taught at his coming, *ib*.31.27(p.180.12; 164C); ref. indwelling of H. Ghost τὸ πῦρ τὸ οὐράνιον τῆς θ. Mac.Aeg.*hom*.11.1(M.34.544D); his divinity proved from scripture, Ath.*ep.Serap*.1.32(M.26.605A); ref. 1Jo.3:24, 1Cor.3:16, Eph.2:21–22 εἰ...ἐν ἡμῖν ὁ θεὸς ἐνοικεῖν λέγεται διὰ τοῦ πνεύματος, πῶς οὐχὶ φανερᾶς ἀσεβείας ἐστὶν αὐτὸ τὸ πνεῦμα λέγειν ἀμέτοχον τῆς θ.; Bas.*Eun*.3.5(1.276D; M.29.665B); list of proof-texts, Gr.Naz.*or*.31.29(p.182.4ff.; M.36.165Aff.); attested by baptism being given in his name, Chrys.*hom.20.3 in 1Cor.*(10.173C); denied by Arians, Eun.*apol*.25(M.30.861D); by Sabellius and Eunomians, Gr.Nyss.*Eun*.10(2 p.234.23; M.45.836D).

F. ref. participation of creatures in the divinity ἐν θ. τυγχάνων [sc. Devil] πέπτωκεν Or.*Jo*.32.18(11; p.457.7; M.14.792B); ἐν ἡμῖν μὲν γὰρ ἀπαρχὴ καὶ ἀρραβὼν θεότητος κατοικεῖ Ath.*inc.et c.Ar*.9(M.26.997B); ref. Trin. εἰς ἣν καὶ βαπτιζόμενοι, καὶ ἐν ταύτῃ συναπτόμενοι τῇ θ. id.*ep.Afr*.11(M.26.1049C); cf.Dion.Ar.*e.h*.1.4(M.3.376B); ref. divinization through Christ; of human nature as made to share in divinity through Inc., Mac.Aeg.*hom*.30.2(M.34.721C); cf.*ib*.4.9(480A); ὁ...φανερωθεὶς θεὸς διὰ τοῦτο κατέμιξεν ἑαυτὸν τῇ ἐπικήρῳ φύσει, ἵνα τῇ τῆς θ. κοινωνίᾳ συναποθεωθῇ τὸ ἀνθρώπινον Gr.Nyss.*or.catech*.37(p.151.11; M.45.97B); Cyr.*inc.unigen*.(5^{1}.680A); of individual participation τῶν τετιμημένων ἀπὸ θεοῦ διὰ τοῦ μονογενοῦς θεοῦ λόγου μετοχῇ θεότητος Or.*Cels*.3.37(p.234.2; M.11.968C); cf.*ib*.7.65(p.215.14; 1513B); ἑνωθέντες αὐτοῦ τῇ θ. ... οὐ κατὰ συναλοιφὴν μιᾶς οὐσίας κατὰ δὲ τελείωσιν τῆς εἰς ἄκρον ἀρετῆς Eus.*e.th*.3.18(p.179.29; M.24.1041B); by baptism, Dion.Ar.*e.h*.4.3.11(M.3.484C); by eucharist λέγεται...μετάληψις ὅτι δι' αὐτῆς μεταλαμβάνομεν τῆς Ἰησοῦ θ. Jo.D.*fr.Mt*.26:27(M.96.1409D); through H. Ghost τῇ...τοῦ πνεύματος μετοχῇ συναπτόμεθα τῇ θ. Ath.*Ar*.3.24(M.26.373C); Didym.(‡Bas.)*Eun*.5(1.314D; M.29.753C); Cyr.*thes*.13(5^{1}.135B); Anast.S.*hod*.14(M.89.256C).

G. in personal sense, of God πνεῦμα θεότητος Herm.*mand*.11.10, 14; *ib*.10.1.4ff.; τῶν διαιρούντων τὴν κατὰ τὸ εὐαγγέλιον θ. ἐκ τῆς νομικῆς θ. Or.*Cels*.7.25(p.176.17; M.11.1456D); ἡ θ. φυλάξειέ σε Constantius ap.Ath.*apol.Const*.23(M.25.624C); Epiph.*haer*.69.30(p.179.28; M.42.249D); ἡ ὑπὲρ τὸ εἶναι θ. Dion.Ar.*c.h*.4.1(M.3.177D); of pagan gods αἱ θ. Isid.Pel.*epp*.1.63(M.78.224B).

***θεοτητοανθρωπότης**, ἡ, *God-manhood*; descriptive of monophysite conception of Christ's nature, to be rejected by orthodox, Jo.D.*Jacob*.35(M.94.1453A).

θεοτίμητος, *honoured by God*, esp. as style of address of bishops, Nil.*epp*.3.13(M.79.373B); Sym.Styl.J.*ep.Just*.(M.86.3217B); Max.*ep*.14(M.91.536A); and other high-ranking clergy, id.*opusc*.(M.91.57A); Jo.D.*trisag*.1(M.95.24C).

***θεοτιμία**, ἡ, *honour from God*, Nil.*epp*.3.134(M.79.445A).

***θεοτίμος**, *honouring God*, *Orac.Sib*.5.268.

***θεοτοκίον**, τό, *hymn addressed to BMV*; of concluding troparion of an ode, Andr.Cr.*can.Ann*.1(M.97.1308A); Jo.D.*poem*.2(p.118); *Hymn.*(*AGC* p.59); Jo.Mon.*hymn.Bas*.(M.96.1372B); *Euchol*.(p.380).

θεοτόκος, *God-bearing, who is mother of God*, title of BMV;

A. before 5th-cent. Christol. controversies, gen. as adj. ἐνταῦθα Ἰωσὴφ τὴν Μαρίαν μνηστεύεται καὶ μάρτυς ἀληθινὸς τῆς θ. γίνεται Hipp.*ben.Jac*.1(p.13.7), passage omitted by Armenian and Georgian versions, and prob. interpolated, cf.id.*fr.Cant*.(Slavonic) 18(p.359.9); οὕτω καὶ ἐπὶ τοῦ Ἰωσὴφ καὶ τῆς θ. ἐλέχθη Or.*sel.in Dt*.22:23(M.12.813C); πρὸς τὴν ἁγίαν θ. ὁ Συμεὼν φησι id.*Ps*.21:21(p.477)(if authentic); id.*hom.7 in Lc*.7(p.50.9); cf. Ὠριγένης δὲ ἐν τῷ πρώτῳ τόμῳ τῶν εἰς τὴν πρὸς τοὺς Ῥωμαίους...ἐπιστολὴν ἑρμηνεύων πῶς θ. λέγεται πλατέως ἐξήτασε Socr.*h.e*.7.32.17(M.67.812B); cf. ὁ δὲ Πιέριος ἐν τῷ πρώτῳ λόγῳ...ἐνέτυχον δὲ αὐτοῦ καὶ ἑτέροις σπουδάσμασι πλείοσιν ἀναγκαίοις καὶ μάλιστα τῷ περὶ τῆς θ. Phil.Sid.*fr*.7(p.171.2); Χριστὸς...κατὰ σάρκα τεχθεὶς ἐκ τῆς ἁγίας ἐνδόξου δεσποίνης ἡμῶν θ. Petr.I Al.*fr*.(M.18.517B); Χριστός, σῶμα φορέσας ἀληθῶς...ἐκ τῆς θεοτόκου Μαρίας Alex.Al.*ep.Alex*.12(p.28.15; M.18.568C); βασιλὶς ἡ θεοσεβεστάτη τῆς θ. τὴν κύησιν μνήμασι θαυμαστοῖς κατεκόσμει Eus.*v.C*.3.43(p.95.26; M.20.1104A); τὴν θ. τὴν αὐτοῦ τοῦ σωτῆρος μητέρα id.*qu.Marin*.2.5(M.22.945B); Γαβριὴλ...εὐαγγελιζομένου τὴν θ. id.*Marcell*.2.1(p.32.16; M.24.777B); cf. Εὐσέβιος ἐν τῷ τρίτῳ λόγῳ τῷ εἰς τὸν βίον Κωνσταντίνου...φησί...ἡ βασίλισσα...τῆς θ. τὴν κύησιν...κατεκόσμει Socr.*h.e*.7.32.14ff.(812A); cf.Eust.*fr*.45(Syriac)(p.85), prob. spurious; ‡Eust.*Laz*.18(p.41); cf. Concilium Antiochense (325)*act*.(Opitz 3.1; p.39.10); ὁ Γαβριήλ, καὶ ἐπὶ τῆς θ. Μαρίας... ὡμολόγησε Ath.*Ar*.3.14(M.26.349C); δι' ἡμᾶς σάρκα λαβὼν ἐκ παρθένου τῆς θ. [some MSS omit] Μαρίας *ib*.3.29(385A); γεννωμένης τῆς σαρκὸς ἐκ τῆς θ. Μαρίας αὐτὸς λέγεται γεγεννῆσθαι *ib*.3.33(393B); Ἰωάννης, γενομένης φωνῆς παρὰ τῆς θ. [v.l. κυριοτόκου] Μαρίας, ἐσκίρτησεν id.*v.Anton*.36(M.26.897A); id.*inc.et c.Ar*.22(M.26.1025A); ‡Ath.*Ar*.4.32(p.81.16; M.26.517B); ‡Ath.*Apoll*.1.4(M.26.1097C some MSS only); Cyr.H.*catech*.10.19; μή τι θεόν φησιν ἐκ τῆς παρθένου τεχθήσεσθαι; θ. δὲ ὑμεῖς οὐ παύεσθε Μαρίαν καλοῦντες Juln.Imp. ap.Cyr.*Juln*.8(6^{2}.262D); θ. ὑμεῖς ἀνθ' ὅτου τὴν παρθένον εἶναί φατε; πῶς γὰρ ἂν τέκοι θεὸν ἄνθρωπος οὖσα καθ' ὑμᾶς; *ib*.(276E); ὁμολογῶ δὲ καὶ τὴν τοῦ υἱοῦ ἔνσαρκον οἰκονομίαν καὶ τὴν θ. τὴν κατὰ σάρκα τεκοῦσαν αὐτὸν ἁγίαν Μαρίαν †Bas.*ep*.360(3.462E; M.32.1100B); †Bas.*Chr.generat*.5(2.600A; M.31.1468B); εἴ τις οὐ θ. τὴν ἁγίαν Μαρίαν ὑπολαμβάνει, χωρίς ἐστι τῆς θεότητος Gr.Naz.*ep*.101(M.37.177C); ἐξ αὐτῆς τῆς παρθενικῆς συλλήψεως, καθ' ἣν καὶ θ. ἀποδέδεικται ἡ παρθένος...ἀχώριστός ἐστι καὶ ἀμέριστος τῆς ἑαυτοῦ σαρκός Apoll.*fid.inc*.4(p.195.15; M.*PL*.8.876C); εἰ δὲ μὴ ἐπικοινωνεῖ [sc. τοῦ λόγου ἡ σάρξ]...οὐδὲ θ. ἡ παρθένος ἔτι πιστευθήσεται, ὅπερ ἀθέμιτον καὶ ἀσεβὲς τὸ τοιοῦτον καὶ ἀλλότριον πάσης θεοσεβοῦς ψυχῆς *ib*.5(p.196.22; 877A); ἡ παρθένος ἀπ' ἀρχῆς σάρκα τεκοῦσα τὸν λόγον ἔτικτεν καὶ ἦν θ. *ib*.6(p.198.24; 877C); Gr.Nyss.*ep*.3(M.46.1024A) cit. s. ἀνθρωποτόκος; Γαβριὴλ εὐαγγελιζόμενος τὴν θ. Didym.*Trin*.1.31(M.39.421B); *ib*.2.4(481C); *ib*.(484A); ἡ θ., ἐξ ἧς τὸ κατὰ σάρκα Χριστός, ἐκ πάντων εἰς τὴν οἰκονομίαν ἐπελέγη *ib*.3.6(848C); τὴν θ. Μαριάμ *ib*.3.41(988C); τέλειον εἰς ἑαυτὸν ἀναπλάσας ἄνθρωπον ἀπὸ Μαρίας τῆς θ. διὰ πνεύματος ἁγίου Epiph.*anc*.75(p.95.2; M.43.157C); ‡Chrys.*occurs*.(2.814E); ‡Chrys.*ador*.1.4(3.823C); Ant.Ptol.ap.Cyr.*Arcad*.12(p.66.33).

B. objections by Nestorians to its use; **1.** protests of Dorotheus of Marcianopolis ἐν συνάξει, καθεζομένου ἐπὶ τοῦ θρόνου τῆς ἐκκλησίας...εὐλαβεστάτου Νεστορίου...τετόλμηκεν εἰπεῖν· εἴ τις λέγει θ. εἶναι τὴν Μαρίαν, οὗτος ἀνάθεμα ἔστω Cyr.*ep*.11(p.11.9; 5^{2}.37D); and Anastasius θ. τὴν Μαρίαν καλείτω μηδείς. Μαρία γὰρ ἄνθρωπος ἦν. ὑπὸ ἀνθρώπου δὲ θεὸν τεχθῆναι, ἀδύνατον Socr.*h.e*.7.32.2(M.67.808C); **2.** objections of Nestorius, on ground that **a.** term is unscriptural, cf.Nest.*fr*.A 1(p.167.10); contradicting Heb.7:3, *ib*.C 9(p.252.5); scriptures referring human experiences to Christ, not to God, id.*ep.Cyr*.2(p.31.3; M.77.53B); cf.id.*fr*.C 11(p.277.25)ap.Cyr.*ep*.40.9(p.24.22; 5^{2}.114A); **b.** not sanctioned by Fathers, cf. *hanc enim theotocon vocantes non perhorrescunt, cum sancti...patres per Nicaean nihil amplius de sancta virgine dixissent, nisi quia dominus noster...incarnatus est ex spiritu sancto et Maria virgine*, Nest.*fr*.A 1(p.167.5); cf. τὴν λέξιν μόνην ὡς τὰ μορμολύκια πεφόβηται ...οὐκ ἀκριβῶς προσεῖχε τοῖς παλαιοῖς,...φαίνεται τοίνυν ὁ Νεστόριος ἀγνοήσας τὰς πραγματείας τῶν παλαιῶν Socr.*h.e*.7.32.9f.,18(M.67.809Bff.); **c.** BMV did not bear the divinity, Nest.*fr*.C 9(p.252.5); nor, being a creature, could she bear the creator, *ib*.(p.252.10); **d.** comparison drawn between relation of Logos and man in Christ's birth and that between soul and body in ordinary birth ὥσπερ οὖν ἡ γυνὴ τίκτει μὲν...σῶμα, ψυχοῖ δὲ θεός, καὶ οὐκ ἂν λέγοιτο γυνὴ ψυχοτόκος, ὅτι ἔμψυχον ἐγέννησεν, ἀνθρωποτόκος δὲ μᾶλλον, οὕτω καὶ ἡ...παρθένος, καὶ εἰ τέτοκεν ἄνθρωπον συμπαρελθόντος αὐτῷ τοῦ θεοῦ λόγου, ἀλλ' οὐ διὰ τοῦτο θ. id.*fr*.D 1(p.352.13)ap.Cyr.*Nest*.1.4(p.23.36; 6^{1}.17E); **e.** comparison drawn between BMV and Elisabeth πνεῦμα ἅγιον ἔχων...ὁ...βαπτιστὴς ἀπετίκτετο. τί οὖν; καλεῖς τὴν Ἐλισάβετ πνευματοτόκον; Nest.(p.352.19)*ib*.1.5(p.25.6; 6^{1}.19D); **f.** Father alone is properly θ., id.*fr*.C 10(p.276.7); **g.** term suggests Apollinarianism or Arianism, *ib*.A 6(p.181.18); cf. *scientes quidem quod sermo, quo dicitur* θεοτόκος, *a multis haereticis assumatur ut suus, retinentes vero, quia nonnulli, qui hic sunt, hanc vocem sumentes incautius, per hoc ipsum in haereticas...cogitationes incidunt, et praecipue Arii et Apollinarii impiorum*, *ib*.A 7(p.184.12); τοῖς Ἀρείου καὶ Εὐνομίου καὶ Ἀπολιναρίου καὶ πάντων τοῖς χοροῖς τῶν τοιαύτης φρατρίας σπουδὴ τὸ θεοτόκος εἰσάγειν *ib*.C 10(p.273.8) ap.Cyr.*Nest*.2.1(p.34.25; 6^{1}.33D); cf. *multa dogmatum ibi experimenta suppeditant, maxime quidem, quae sunt Apollinaris sectae et Arii et Eunomii si investiges, unusquisque eorum θ. appellavit virginem sanctam*, id.*fr*.C 18(p.300.21); *noli eam θ. tantummodo appellare. hoc enim Apollinaris vociferatur, hoc etiam Arius praedicat ac veneratur*, *ib*.(p.303.16); **h.** term has pagan ring, *ib*.C 9(p.252.3); suggesting that BMV is a goddess, *ib*.D 3(p.353.18)ap.Cyr.*Nest*.1.10(p.31.33; 6^{1}.29C); **i.** hence Χριστοτόκος is preferable, id.*ep.Cyr*.2(p.31.3; M.77.53B); id.*fr*.A 6(p.181.21); id.*fr*.ap.CEph.(431)*act*.1(H.1.1412B); *Χριστοτόκος dicat, quod nomen sit duarum significatio naturarum*, id.*fr*.C 18(p.312.20); id.ap.Cyr.*ep*.40.9(p.24.22; 5^{2}.114A); Cyr.*Chr.un*.(5^{1}.716C) cit. s. ἀνθρωποτόκος; Thdt.*haer*.4.12(4.371); †Leont.B.*sect*.4.4(M.86.1221C); **j.** or else θεοδόχος, Nest.*fr*.C 10(p.276.

4); **k.** but *θ.* may be accepted; **i.** on account of union between Logos and his 'temple', cf.*ib.*A 1(p.168.1); cf. *concessi, ut pie genitricem...dei virginem nominarent...propter unitionis rationem, quae facta est ex ipso angeli vocum principio, ib.*A 7(p.185.10); *genitrix...dei propterea quod templum, quod in ea creatum est a spiritu sancto, unitum est deitati, ib.*C 19(p.319.11); **ii.** if confusion of natures is avoided, cf. *ad hanc quidem vocem, quae est θ., nisi secundum Apollinaris et Arii furorem ad confusionem naturarum proferatur, volentibus dicere non resisto, ib.*A 6(p.181.18); *ib.*A 7 (p.185.12); *ib.*C 10(p.273.6); **iii.** if used in conjunction with ἀνθρωποτόκος, cf.*ib.*A 9(p.191.19); *ib.*(p.192.6); *ib.*C 18(p.301.17), *ib.*(p.309.8) citt. s. ἀνθρωποτόκος; *ib.*(p.312.26); *ib.*C 19(p.319.11); thus guarding against both Arianism and Apollinarianism and also heresy of Paul of Samosata and Photinus, *ib.*C 18(p.303.15); **iv.** for sake of avoiding schism, *ib.*(p.302.2); **l.** position of Nest. summarized τὴν μὲν θ. φωνὴν ὑπὸ τοῦ...πνεύματος ἤδη χαλκευθεῖσαν διὰ πολλῶν ἐγκρίτων πατέρων, ἐξώθησέ τε καὶ ἀπεβάλετο· τὴν δὲ Χριστοτόκος παραχαράξας, ἀντεχάλκευσέ τε καὶ ἀνετύπωσε Evagr.*h.e.* 1.2(p.7.7; M.86.2424A); **3.** view of Diodorus of Tarsus, cf. *verumtamen dicatur propter unitionem Maria dei genetrix...fatenda vero et hominis genetrix,* Diod.*fr.*(*ACO* 1.4 p.216.17); **4.** views of Theodore of Mopsuestia, Thdr.Mops.*fr.inc.*15(p.310.11; M.66.992B) cit. s. ἀνθρωποτόκος; Nestorius influenced by his views, Evagr. *h.e.*1.2(p.7.22; M.86.2425A); and **5.** Theodoret *θ.* προσαγορεύομεν, οὐχ ὡς θεὸν φύσει γεννήσασαν, ἀλλ' ὡς ἄνθρωπον τῷ διαπλάσαντι αὐτὸν ἡνωμένον θεῷ Thdt.ap.Cyr.*apol.Thdt.*1(p.109.17; 6^{1}.204E); *ib.*(p.109. 27; 6^{1}.205A), id.*ep.*151(4.1303–4), id.*inc.*35(M.75.1477A) citt. s. ἀνθρωποτόκος; **6.** extremer Nestorians' position (e.g. that of Alexander of Hierapolis) will admit *θ.* as term of popular devotion, but not in dogmatic formulae unless always combined with ἀνθρωποτόκος, cf.Alex.Hierapolitanus *ep.*ap.*Synodicon* 94(M.84.708Cff.).

C. orthodox comment; **1.** by Proclus ὁ αὐτὸς ἐν κόλποις πατρὸς καὶ ἐν γαστρὶ παρθένου, ἐν ἀγκάλαις μητρὸς καὶ ἐπὶ πτερύγων ἀνέμων ...οὕτως ἐτέχθη, ὡς συνελήφθη ἀπαθῶς εἰσῆλθεν, ἀφράστως ἐξῆλθεν ...ἰδοὺ ἀπόδειξις ἐναργὴς [sc. Ezech.44:1–2] τῆς ἁγίας καὶ *θ.* Μαρίας Procl.CP *or.laud.BMV* 9(p.107.10–26; M.65.689C); **2.** by Thalassius τὴν ἀπείθειαν αὐτοῦ [sc. Νεστορίου], τὸ μὴ λέγειν *θ.* τὴν...παρθένον Thal.CP *Thds.*2(M.91.1473B); **3.** by Cyril, insisting upon retention of term on ground that **a.** Christ's divinity necessitates its use θεὸς ἡμῶν ὁ Ἐμμανουήλ, ὃν ἡ ἁγία *θ.* παρθένος ἀπεκύησεν Cyr.*Ps.*61:7 (M.69.1117B); *θ.* ὠνόμαζον τὴν ἁγίαν παρθένον (τέτοκε γὰρ τὸν Ἐμμανουήλ, ὅς ἐστι θεὸς ἀληθῶς) id.*ep.*18(p.114.2; 5^{2}.79C); θεὸν εἶναι πιστεύοντες, ὁμολογοῦντες δὲ *θ.* καὶ τὴν κατὰ σάρκα τεκοῦσαν αὐτόν id. *ep.*31(p.73.17; 5^{2}.97B); θεὸς...ἐστιν ἄρα ἐνανθρωπήσας ὁ ἐκ Μαρίας τεχθεὶς...*θ.* δὲ πάντως καὶ αὐτή id.*deip.BMV* 18(p.27.19; M.76.277B); φύσει μὲν καὶ ἀληθείᾳ θεός ἐστιν...*θ.* δὲ δι' αὐτὸν καὶ ἡ τεκοῦσα παρθένος id.*Arcad.*2(p.63.3; 5^{2}.43E); εἰ γὰρ εἶναι πιστεύουσι θεὸν ἀληθῶς αὐτὸν...ἀνθ' ὅτου καταπεφρίκασι *θ.* εἰπεῖν τὴν τεκοῦσαν αὐτόν, κατά γε φημὶ τὴν σάρκα; id.*Chr.un.*(5^{1}.726B); **b.** it is implied in fact of the one Person of the eternal Son ἕνα καὶ τὸν αὐτόν, φύσει μὲν ὄντα θεόν...ἐν ἐσχάτοις δὲ...καιροῖς γενόμενον ἄνθρωπον, καὶ διὰ τῆς ἁγίας καὶ *θ.* παρθένου γεγεννημένον id.*Thds.*(p.53.29; 5^{2}.16D); id.*Chr. un.*(5^{1}.719A); Nestorian refusal of word implies division of Christ, id.*ep.*45(p.152.12; 5^{2}.136B); ὅτε τοίνυν καὶ θεός ἐστιν ἀληθῶς...πῶς ἂν ἐνδοιάσειέ τις *θ.* εἶναι τὴν...παρθένον; προσκύνησον ὡς ἕνα, μὴ διελὼν εἰς δύο μετὰ τὴν ἕνωσιν· τότε γελάσει μάτην ὁ παράφρων Ἰουδαῖος id. *ep.*1(p.23.12; 5^{2}.19B); οἱ δὲ *θ.* ὀνομάζουσι τὴν ἁγίαν παρθένον ἕνα τε εἶναί φασιν υἱὸν καὶ Χριστὸν καὶ κύριον, τέλειον ἐν θεότητι, τέλειον ἐν ἀνθρωπότητι id.*ep.*40(p.24.28; 5^{2}.114C); id.*Arcad.*6(p.63.35; 5^{2}.45A); **c.** and in assumption of flesh by one Person θεὸς κατὰ φύσιν ἐστὶ καὶ εἰς ἑνότητα συνενηνεγμένος, τὴν πρός γε φημὶ τὴν ἰδίαν σάρκα· οὐ δὴ πεφηνότος ἀληθοῦς, *θ.* ἂν λέγοιτο...εἰκότως ἡ...παρθένος id.*ep.* 1(p.19.2; 5^{2}.13D); *θ.* ... τὴν ἁγίαν παρθένον, οὐχ ὡς τῆς τοῦ λόγου φύσεως...τὴν ἀρχὴν τοῦ εἶναι λαβούσης...ἀλλ' ὡς γεννηθέντος ἐξ αὐτῆς τοῦ ἁγίου σώματος ψυχωθέντος λογικῶς, ᾧ καὶ καθ' ὑπόστασιν ἑνωθεὶς ὁ λόγος γεγεννῆσθαι λέγεται κατὰ σάρκα id.*ep.*4.7(p.28.18; 5^{2}.24E); id.*apol.orient.*7(p.35.3; 6^{1}.160A); ὁ γὰρ ἐκ θεοῦ πατρὸς κατὰ φύσιν υἱός, ἔμψυχόν τε καὶ ἔννουν ἑαυτῷ σῶμα λαβών, γεγέννηται σαρκικῶς διὰ τῆς...*θ.* Μαρίας, καὶ οὐκ εἰς σάρκα τραπεὶς...προσλαβὼν δὲ μᾶλλον αὐτήν, καὶ τοῦ εἶναι θεὸς οὐκ ἠμεληκώς id.*Pulch.*(p.27.12; 5^{2}.129E); σάρκα λαβὼν καὶ ἰδίαν αὐτὴν ποιησάμενος ἐγεννήθη σαρκικῶς διὰ τῆς ...*θ.* Μαρίας id.*Arcad.*4(p.63.24; 5^{2}.44D); γέννησιν σαρκικὴν...ὑπομεῖναι λέγεται, διάτοι τὸ ἐκ τῆς ἁγίας παρθένου λαβεῖν τὸ ἑνωθὲν αὐτῷ σῶμα κατὰ ἀλήθειαν, ὅθεν καὶ *θ.* εἶναί φαμεν...ὡς σαρκικῶς...τεκοῦσαν αὐτὸν καίτοι γέννησιν ἔχοντα τὴν προαιώνιον ἐκ πατρός id.*schol.inc.*28 (p.224.12; cf.M.75.1399D); use of term involved by doctrine of hypostatic union, id.*ep.*4.7(p.28.18; 5^{2}.24E) cit. supra; ἐπειδὴ δὲ θεὸν ἑνωθέντα σαρκὶ καθ' ὑπόστασιν ἡ ἁγία παρθένος ἐκτέτοκε σαρκικῶς, ταύτῃ τοι καὶ *θ.* εἶναι φαμὲν αὐτήν, οὐχ ὡς τῆς τοῦ λόγου φύσεως τῆς ὑπάρξεως τὴν ἀρχὴν ἐχούσης ἀπὸ σαρκός...ἀλλ'...ἐπειδὴ καθ' ὑπόστασιν ἑνώσας ἑαυτῷ τὸ ἀνθρώπινον id.*ep.*17(p.40.4; 5^{2}.75B); **d.** its use does not imply derivation of Christ's divinity from Mary, id.*ep.*4 (p.28.18; 5^{2}.24E), id.*ep.*17(p.40.4; 5^{2}.75B) citt. s. c supra; id.*schol. inc.*28(p.224.21–31; cf.M.75.1400Af.); but **e.** is implied by the miraculous birth θαυμάζω δὲ ὅτι *θ.* ὀκνοῦντες εἰπεῖν τὴν ἁγίαν παρθένον θεοπρεπῶς αὐτὴν γεννῆσαί φασιν· οὐ γὰρ ἄνθρωπος κοινὸς τίκτεται θεοπρεπῶς id.*apol.orient.*1(p.35.31; 6^{1}.161A); **f.** *θ.* is of unique application, whereas Χριστοτόκος could be applied to others besides BMV, id.*ep.*1(p.14.28; 5^{2}.7D); *ib.*(p.15.1; 8A); **g.** on Nestorius' view of union of natures, Mary is no more Χριστοτόκος than *θ.*: εἰ γὰρ Χριστοτόκος, πάντως ὅτι καὶ *θ.*· εἰ δὲ οὐ *θ.*, οὐδὲ Χριστοτόκος id. *deip.BMV* 9(p.22.38; M.76.265B); **h.** term is used by fathers, id. *ep.*4.7(p.28.18; 5^{2}.24E); εἰ δὲ μὴ ἐδόκει φορτικὸν εἶναι τὸ ἐσόμενον, πολλὰς ἂν ἔπεμψα βίβλους πολλῶν ἁγίων πατέρων, ἐν αἷς ἔστιν εὑρεῖν οὐχ ἅπαξ, ἀλλὰ πλειστάκις κειμένην τὴν φωνήν, ἐν ᾗ ὁμολογοῦσιν εἶναι *θ.* τὴν ἁγίαν παρθένον id.*ep.*8(p.109.25; 5^{2}.31A); εὑρίσκω γὰρ ἐν συγγραφαῖς καὶ τὸν...Ἀθανάσιον πλειστάκις αὐτὴν ὀνομάσαντα *θ.* καὶ τὸν ...Θεόφιλον καὶ ἑτέρους πολλοὺς τῶν ἁγίων καὶ...ἐπισκόπων, τοῦτο μὲν Βασίλειον, τοῦτο δὲ Γρηγόριον, καὶ...τὸν...Ἀττικόν id.*ep.*14(p.98. 15; 5^{2}.44C); id.*ep.*18(p.114.2; 5^{2}.79C); ὅτι δὲ ἡ *θ.* φωνὴ καὶ αὐτοῖς γέγονε συνήθης τοῖς πρὸ ἡμῶν ἁγίοις πατράσιν, οἳ καὶ ἐπ' ὀρθῇ θαυμάζονται πίστει, καὶ εἰς δεῦρο παρὰ πᾶσι τοῖς ἀνὰ πᾶσαν...τὴν ὑπ' οὐρανόν, δεῖν ᾠήθην ἀληθὲς ἀποφῆναι id.*Arcad.*9(p.65.17; 5^{2}.47D); cf.id.*apol. orient.*14(p.37.4; 5^{2}.162E); **i.** justified by scripture, id.*deip.BMV* 23 (p.29.22; M.76.284A); Χριστοτόκος being no more a scriptural term than *θ.*, id.*ep.*10(p.111.35; 5^{2}.35B); **j.** and cherished by Christian people, id.*ep.*2(p.24.25; 5^{2}.21A); **k.** being used by Eastern and Western theologians, id.*ep.*8(p.109.23; 5^{2}.30E); **4.** in Cyril's anathema εἴ τις οὐχ ὁμολογεῖ θεὸν εἶναι κατὰ ἀλήθειαν τὸν Ἐμμανουὴλ καὶ διὰ τοῦτο *θ.* τὴν ἁγίαν παρθένον (γεγέννηκε γὰρ σαρκικῶς σάρκα γεγονότα τὸν ἐκ θεοῦ λόγον), ἀνάθεμα ἔστω id.*ep.*17 *anath.*1(p.40.23; 5^{2}.76A); **5.** its vindication at Ephesus (431) σύνοδος *θ.*... κηρύττουσα τὴν...παρθένον Eulog.*fr.*(M.86.2944A); **6.** Cyril's insistence on acceptance of it by Paul of Emesa before his reconciliation, Cyr.*ep.* 37(p.154.19; 5^{2}.152E); **7.** its acceptance by oriental bishops κατὰ ταύτην τὴν τῆς ἀσυγχύτου ἑνώσεως ἔννοιαν ὁμολογοῦμεν τὴν ἁγίαν παρθένον *θ.* διὰ τὸ τὸν θεὸν λόγον σαρκωθῆναι καὶ ἐνανθρωπῆσαι καὶ ἐξ αὐτῆς τῆς συλλήψεως ἑνῶσαι ἑαυτῷ τὸν ἐξ αὐτῆς ληφθέντα ναόν Jo.Ant. *ep.Cyr.*2(p.9.3; M.77.172D); this definition accepted by Cyril as formula of union (433), Cyr.*ep.*39(p.17.15; 5^{2}.106C); having been advanced by oriental bishops at CEph.(431)*relat.orient.*(*ACO* 1.1.7 p.70.21; cf.H.1.1558E); and probably composed by Theodoret, cf. Alex.Hierapolitanus *ep.*ap.*Synodicon* 96(M.84.712Bff.); accepted by Paul of Emesa τίκτει οὖν ἡ *θ.* Μαρία τὸν Ἐμμανουήλ...Ἐμμανουὴλ δὲ θεὸν ἐνανθρωπήσαντα Paul.Em.*hom.*1.1–3(p.10.9,15); προσεπάγουσι δὲ [sc. orientals] ὅτι διὰ τὴν ἄφραστόν τε καὶ ἀσύγχυτον ἕνωσιν καὶ *θ.* εἶναι πιστεύουσι τὴν ἁγίαν παρθένον Cyr.*ep.*40(p.28.30; 5^{2}.118D); γεγράφασι...οἱ ἐκ τῆς ἀνατολῆς...λέγοντες ἐναργῶς καὶ *θ.* τὴν...παρθένον, καὶ ὅτι εἷς ἐστιν υἱός τοῦ θεοῦ id.*ep.*42(p.19.11; M.77.221B); **8.** defended by Theodoret against Nestorians ἕνα προσκυνοῦμεν υἱὸν μονογενῆ τὸν ἐνανθρωπήσαντα θεὸν λόγον, τὴν ἁγίαν δὲ παρθένον *θ.* ἀποκαλοῦμεν, ἐπειδὴ τὸν Ἐμμανουὴλ γεγέννηκεν Thdt.*ep.*151(4.1311); cf.†Thdt.*Nest.*(4.1047); **9.** affirmed at Chalcedon ἀναθεματίζοντες πᾶσαν αἵρεσιν...τῶν λεγόντων ἐξ οὐρανοῦ τὴν σάρκα τοῦ κυρίου ἡμῶν ὑπάρχειν καὶ μὴ ἐκ τῆς ἁγίας καὶ *θ.* Μαρίας τῆς παρθένου *Libell.*ap. CChalc.*act.*4(*ACO* 2.1.2 p.110.37; H.2.416B); πρὸ αἰώνων μὲν ἐκ τοῦ πατρὸς γεννηθέντα κατὰ τὴν θεότητα, ἐπ' ἐσχάτων δὲ τῶν ἡμερῶν τὸν αὐτὸν δι' ἡμᾶς...ἐκ Μαρίας τῆς παρθένου τῆς *θ.* κατὰ τὴν ἀνθρωπότητα *Symb.Chalc.*(p.129.29; H.2.456C); cf. ἐπ' ἐσχάτων δὲ τῶν ἡμερῶν... τῆς *θ.* κατὰ τὴν ἀνθρωπότητα διὰ Φωτεινὸν καὶ Θεόδωρον καὶ Διόδωρον καὶ Νεστόριον τοὺς λέγοντας αὐτὸν ἄνθρωπον ἐξ ἀρετῆς κατὰ προκοπὴν θεοποιηθέντα, καὶ οὐχὶ θεὸν ἐκ θεοῦ ὄντα *Doct.Patr.*24(p.176.21); **10.** affirmed by post-Chalcedonian theologians; e.g. **a.** Leont. B. τὸ τὰς ἀρχὰς ἔχειν ἐκ τῆς *θ.* ἀδελφῆς τε ἡμῶν οὔσης κατὰ τὴν φύσιν *Nest.et Eut.*2(M.86.1325C); Leont. H. τὴν...ὑπόστασιν ἰδικὴν μὲν ὡς πρὸς τὸν πατέρα καὶ τὸ πνεῦμα καὶ πρὸς πάντας τοὺς μὴ ἐκ τῆς ἁγίας παρθένου ἀνθρώπους, μόνον δὲ κοινὴν ὡς πρὸς τὴν ἐκ τῆς *θ.* ληφθεῖσαν τῷ λόγῳ σάρκα *Nest.*2.14(M.86.1568C); μόνον ἰδικώτατον καὶ κυριώτατον καὶ σημαντικώτατόν ἐστι τῇ ἁγίᾳ...παρθένῳ ὄνομα τὸ *θ.* *ib.*4.37 (1708D); **b.** Pamph. H. ἐπεὶ οὖν ὁ κυριακὸς ἄνθρωπος...ἐστὶν ἐκ παρθένου, ὑπομεῖναι λέγεται γέννησιν ὁ λόγος ὡς τὰ τούτου οἰκειούμενος ἴδια· ἴδιον γὰρ σαρκὸς τὸ γεννᾶσθαι, καὶ διὰ τοῦτο κυρίως...*θ.*

ἡ παρθένος ὑπάρχει καὶ οὐ Χριστοτόκος *panopl.*4.1(p.611); **c.** Justn. σαρκωθέντα ἐκ πνεύματος ἁγίου, καὶ τῆς ἁγίας ἐνδόξου θ. καὶ ἀειπαρθένου Μαρίας *conf.*(p.72.32; M.86.995C); τοῦ αὐτοῦ θεοῦ λόγου σαρκωθέντος τὴν ἐκ παρθένου γέννησιν εἶναι, καὶ διὰ τοῦτο θ. εἶναι τὴν...Μαρίαν *ib.*(p.88.14; 1011C); εἴ τις κατ' ἀναφοράν, ἢ καταχρηστικῶς θ. λέγει τὴν ἁγίαν...Μαρίαν, ἢ ἀνθρωποτόκον, ἢ Χριστοτόκον, ὡς τοῦ Χριστοῦ μὴ ὄντος θεοῦ, ἀλλὰ μὴ κυρίως καὶ κατ' ἀλήθειαν θ. αὐτὴν ὁμολογεῖ διὰ τὸ τὸν πρὸ αἰώνων ἐκ τοῦ πατρὸς γεννηθέντα θεὸν λόγον...ἐξ αὐτῆς σαρκωθῆναι καὶ γεννηθῆναι, ὁ τοιοῦτος ἀνάθεμα ἔστω *ib.*(p.92.3; 1015B); σχεδὸν ἅπας ἡμῖν ὁ ὑπὲρ τῆς πίστεως ἀγὼν συνεκεκρότητο διαβεβαιουμένοις, ὅτι θ. ἐστὶν ἡ ἁγία Μαρία id.*typ.Thdr.Mops.*(M.86.1037B); **d.** Eulog. κυρίως καὶ κατ' ἀλήθειαν θεὸς ὁ Χριστός, διὸ καὶ κυρίως καὶ κατ' ἀλήθειαν θ. τὴν ἁγίαν παρθένον φαμέν *fr.dogm.*(M.86.2957A) ap.*Doct.Patr.*29(p.212.9); **e.** Sophr. H. εἰ γὰρ ὁ ἐκ σοῦ τεχθησόμενος, σεσαρκωμένος θεός ἐστι κατ' ἀλήθειαν, θ. σὺ δικαιότατα λέγοιο, ὡς θεὸν κατὰ ἀλήθειαν τίκτουσα *or.*2.22(M.87.3241C); **f.** Cyrus Al. εἴ τις οὐχ ὁμολογεῖ τὴν ἁγίαν δέσποιναν ἡμῶν καὶ ἀειπάρθενον Μαρίαν κυρίως καὶ κατὰ ἀλήθειαν θ. εἶναι, ὡς τὸν θεὸν λόγον...τεκοῦσαν, ἀνάθεμα ἔστω *cap.*5(H.3.1341B); **g.** Max. διὸ καὶ θ. ἀληθῶς ἡ παρθένος...τεκοῦσα τὸν ὑπερούσιον λόγον *ambig.*(M.91.1053A); id.*ep.*12(M.91.504A); **h.** Anast. S. εἰ οὖν Ἰησοῦς ὁ Χριστὸς...αὐτός ἐστιν ὁ ἀληθινὸς θεὸς...πῶς οὐ θ. κυρίως καὶ ἀληθινῶς ἡ παρθένος κληθήσεται; ap.*Doct.Patr.*3(p.27.19); **i.** Mod. σώζει...ἀληθῶς ἐκ πάσης θλίψεως τοὺς ὁμολογοῦντάς σε θ. *dorm.*10(M.86.3301C); **j.** Jo. D. ὡς...θεὸς ἀληθὴς ὁ ἐξ αὐτῆς γεννηθείς, ἀληθὴς θ. ἡ τὸν ἀληθινὸν θεὸν ἐξ αὐτῆς σεσαρκωμένον γεννήσασα *f.o.*3.12(M.94.1028B); δικαίως καὶ ἀληθῶς θ. τὴν ἁγίαν Μαρίαν ὀνομάζομεν· τοῦτο γὰρ τὸ ὄνομα ἅπαν τὸ μυστήριον τῆς οἰκονομίας συνίστησι, εἰ γὰρ θ. ἡ γεννήσασα, πάντως θεὸς ὁ ἐξ αὐτῆς γεννηθείς, πάντως δὲ καὶ ἄνθρωπος *ib.*(1029C); *ib.*4.14(1161A); id.*haer.Nest.*1(M.95.188A); **k.** Thdr. Abuc. ἀποδεικνύων θεὸν τὸν Χριστόν, συναποδείκνυμι, ὅτι καὶ ἡ αὐτὸν τεκοῦσα, θ. ὀφείλει ὀνομάζεσθαι· πῶς γὰρ οὐ θ. ἡ θεὸν υἱὸν ἔχουσα; *opusc.*14(M.97.1537B); **11.** in argument against monophysites; if there is 'confusion' of Christ's natures, BMV is not properly θ., Eust.Mon.*ep.*(M.86.913A); εἰ μὴ δύο φύσεις θεοῦ καὶ ἀνθρώπου, ἀλλὰ μία, τίς ἰδίως Χριστοῦ ἐστι φύσις; ἆρα γε ὄντως καθ' ὑμᾶς Χριστοτόκος ἡ ἁγία παρθένος καὶ οὐ θ. λέγοιτο Leont.H.*monoph.*55(M.86.1800A).

D. non-controversial use (esp. in popular devotion) very freq. ἡ ἁγία Μαρία ἡ θ. ἔστηκε καὶ ἔκλαιεν *Apophth.Patr.*(M.65.357B); Procl. CP *annunt.*4(M.85.437C); τὴν μητέρα τῆς ζωῆς, ζωηφόρον σκηνὴν τῆς ἀκηράτου φύσεως τὴν θ. καὶ θεοδόχον καὶ θεοτρόφον Anast.S.*hex.*12(M.89.1053B); ὤμοσεν...κατὰ τῆς θ. Leont.N.*v.Sym.*37(M.93.1716C); exeg. Apoc.12:1 τὴν θ. ἡμῖν ζωγραφεῖ Oecum.*Apoc.*12:1(p.135); τὴν θεωρίαν τὴν περὶ τῆς κοινῆς δεσποίνης τῆς ἁγίας...θ. Μαρίας *ib.*12:2(p.138); Apoc.14:14 νεφέλην...τοὺς ἀγγέλους καλεῖ...ἢ γοῦν νεφέλην καλεῖ τὴν θ. *ib.*14:14(p.168); ref. oil from holy image of BMV, Eustrat.*v.Eutych.*45(M.86.2328A); of BMV as intercessor γένοιτο δὲ ἡμᾶς...εὐχαῖς τῆς δεσποίνης ἡμῶν θ. ... συναριθμίους τοῖς ἐκ δεξιῶν γενέσθαι Cosm.Ind.*top.*5(M.88.313C); συντέτακται δὲ τῷ τέλει τοῦ πρώτου ἀντιφώνου τό, ταῖς πρεσβείαις τῆς θ. σῶσον ἡμᾶς...ἐπεὶ γὰρ ὑπὲρ τῶν ψυχῶν καὶ συγχωρήσεως πταισμάτων τὴν θείαν τελοῦμεν μυσταγωγίαν, εἰκότως ὡς ὑπερτέραν οὖσαν τὴν θεοῦ μητέρα πάντων τῶν ἁγίων...εἰς ἱκεσίαν προσκαλούμεθα ‡Sophr.H.*liturg.*13(M.87.3993B); θεός, οὗ καὶ ἡμεῖς τῆς λαμπρᾶς βασιλείας, εὐχαῖς τῆς ὑπεράγνου θ. τύχοιμεν Hesych.S.*temp.*100(M.93.1544D).

***θεότολμος**, *bold in God*, *Hymn.*(*AS* 1 p.572).

***θεοτράπεζος**, *of God's table*, Thdr.Stud.*epp.*2.220(M.99.1668B).

***θεοτρόπος**, *turning to God*, Geo.Pis.*Sev.*546(M.92.1661B).

***θεοτρόφος**, *feeding God*; of BMV, Anast.S.*hex.*12(M.89.1053B).

***θεοτυπία**, ἡ, *figure of God*, Dion.Ar.*myst.*3(M.3.1033B).

***θεότυπος**, *engraved by God*; of tablets of Law, Cosm.Mel.*schol.*(M.38.454) in Gr.Naz.*carm.*1.1.1.12; Leont.N.ap.Jo.D.*imag.*1(M.94.1273B).

***θεοτύπωτος**, *bearing divine likeness*; of sacred images, Leont.N. ap.Jo.D.*imag.*3(M.94.1384B).

θεούδεια (-είη), ἡ, *godly fear*, *reverence* θεουδείης ὁδόν Nonn.*par. Jo.*15:22(M.43.876C); plur., *ib.*3:21(769B); *ib.*9:31(829B).

θεουδής, **1.** *God-fearing*, *MAMA* 1.171 (c. 340); Πατρικίου...θ. ἀρχιερῆος *ib.*1.412; Gr.Naz.*carm.*1.2.1.82(M.37.528A); Nonn.*par.Jo.*8:39(M.43.820A); *ib.*9:28(829B); *ib.*21:17(917C); Paul.Sil.*Soph.*963(M.86.2155B); **2.** of things, *holy*, Nonn.*par.Jo.*1:28(M.43.753C); *ib.*4:36(780C); *ib.*7:12(805C); Paul.Sil.*Soph.*979(M.86.2156B); of image of God in man θ. τύπους καὶ χαρακτῆρας Chrys.*fr.Job* 1:1(M.64.509C).

***θεοϋπαίνετος**, *praised by God*, ‡Meth.*Sym.et Ann.*10(M.18.373B).

***θεούπολις**, ἡ, *city of God*, name for Antioch, cf. τῆς πάλαι μὲν Ἀντιόχου, νῦν δὲ θεοῦ πόλεως καλουμένης Leont.B.*Nest.et Eut.*3(M.86.1364D); τῆς μεγάλης καὶ κορυφαιοτάτης ἐκκλησίας θεουπόλεως Ἀντιοχείας *Lit.Jac.*(*NBP* 10[2] p.86).

***θεουπολίτης**, ὁ, *citizen of Theopolis*, i.e. Antioch, Epiph.CP *sent.*(p.111.17; M.86.785C).

***θεοϋπόστατος**, **1.** *of divine hypostasis* θ. δογματίζεται ἡ Χριστοῦ σάρκωσις καὶ οὐδαμῶς ἀνθρωποϋπόστατος ‡Ath.*annunt.*6(M.28.925B); Ἰεσσαὶ ῥάβδος...ἐξ ἧς ἀναβήσεται τῷ κόσμῳ ἄνθος θ. ‡Jo.D.*hom.*6.3(M.96.664C); **2.** *divine* τῷ τοῦ θ. ἄνθρακος ψωμισμῷ Germ.CP *or.*1(M.98.221C).

***θεουργ-έω**, **1.** *deify*, *make divine*; of operation of divine grace through Inc., Max.*opusc.*(M.91.57A); ἐξ ὧν ἢ δι' ὧν [sc. virtues] ἡ τῆς ἀγάπης χάρις δημιουργημένη, πρὸς τὸν θεὸν ἄγει θεουργηθέντα τὸν δημιουργήσαντα ἄνθρωπον id.*ep.*2(M.91.405A); διὰ σαρκὸς παθητῆς τὸ γένος ἅπαν τῇ φθορᾷ γεωθὲν ∼οῦσαν id.*ambig.*(M.91.1044D); ἵνα... ὅλος ἄνθρωπος θεωθῇ τῇ τοῦ ἐνανθρωπήσαντος θεοῦ χάριτι ∼ούμενος *ib.*(1088C); θεουργῆσαι τὴν ἡμετέραν φύσιν διὰ τοῦ σαρκὶ παθεῖν αὐτὸν ἑκουσίως ὑπὲρ ἡμῶν CLater.*act.*5(H.3.908C); **2.** *consecrate* μεταδιδόναι τῶν ἁγιασμάτων ἤδη ∼ηθέντων ὑπὸ σεσωσμένου πρεσβυτέρου Thdr. Stud.*epp.*2.203(M.99.1617C).

θεουργία, ἡ, **1.** *divine work*, Dion.Ar.*c.h.*7.2(M.3.208C,D); ‡Caes. Naz.*dial.*21(M.38.880); as done by Christ, Eust.*fr.*13(p.71; M.18.697A); αὐτὸς Ἰησοῦς...πάσης...θ. ἀρχὴ καὶ οὐσία Dion.Ar.*e.h.*1.1(M.3.372A); Max.*ambig.*(M.91.1168A); attributed to H. Ghost, Dion.Ar.*d.n.*2.1(M.3.637C); **2.** *miracle*, Leont.B.*Nest.et Eut.*2(M.86.1336C).

θεουργικός, **1.** *of the divine operation* θ. ὁμοίωσις Dion.Ar.*c.h.*7.2(M.3.208C); θ. γνῶσις *ib.*7.3(209C); neut. plur. as subst., *divine works*, id.*e.h.*1.5(M.3.377B); id.*c.h.*7.2(208C); **2.** *doing a divine work*; of priests, Juln.Imp.ap.Cyr.*Juln.*10(6[2].354A); of oil at baptism, Dion.Ar.*e.h.*2.7(M.3.396D); of sanctification, *ib.*4.3.11(484D); θ. δύναμις [i.e. of God] *Lit.Marc.*(p.142.13).

θεουργός, **1.** *divinely operating*; of operation of H. Ghost, Geo. Pis.*hex.*1772(M.92.1571A); **2.** *deifying*, *making divine* εὐπάθειαν... ἧς ἐν μεθέξει πολλάκις γεγόνασι καὶ ἄνδρες ἱεροὶ κατὰ τὰς θ. τῶν θείων ἐλλάμψεων ἐπιφοιτήσεις Dion.Ar.*c.h.*15.9(M.3.340A); of baptismal gift of H. Ghost, id.*e.h.*2.3.8(M.3.404D); of mystical illumination θεουργὸν τῆς θεαρχίας ἔλλαμψιν *ib.*5.1.2(501B); of realities expressed in symbols θ. μυστήρια id.*ep.*9.1(M.3.1108A); of grace of Christ in redemption, Max.*opusc.*(M.91.245C).

***θεοΰφαντος**, *divinely woven*, *T.Abr.*A 20(p.103.21); †Jo.D.*B.J.*16(M.96.1001A); Thdr.Stud.*nativ.BMV* 1(M.96.681A); θεοήφαντος Ephr.3.530D.

***θεοφαής**, *divinely shining* τὰ ἱερὰ σώματα τῶν ὁσίων· οἷς ὁ πλοῦτος τῶν ἀρετῶν, ἐν νυκτὶ τοῦ τῆδε βίου ἄστροις ἐοικόσι θ. Thdr. Stud.*epp.*2.16(M.99.1165B).

θεοφάνεια, ἡ, *divine manifestation*;

A. nature and gen. characteristics; **1.** def. ἡ πάνσοφος δὲ θεολογία τὴν ὅρασιν ἐκείνην, ἥ τις ἐν ἑαυτῇ διαγεγραμμένην ἀνέφαινε τὴν θείαν, ὡς ἐν μορφώσει τῶν ἀμορφώτων ὁμοίωσιν, ἐκ τῆς τῶν ὁρώντων ἐπὶ τὸ θεῖον ἀναγωγῆς, εἰκότως καλεῖ θ. Dion.Ar.*c.h.*4.3(M.3.180C); **2.** as never revealing divine essence, *ib.*; θ. εἶναί φησιν οὐ διὰ τὸ φαίνειν τὸν θεὸν καὶ δεικνύειν, ὅ τί ποτέ ἐστι· τοῦτο γὰρ ἀμήχανον· ἀλλ' ὅτι θείας ἐλλάμψεως οἱ ἅγιοι ἀξιοῦνται διά τινων ὁράσεων ἱερῶν καὶ αὐτοῖς ἀναλόγων, ἃς δι' ἀγγέλων γίνεσθαι λέγει Max.*schol.c.h.*4.3(M.4.56C); **3.** as recorded ἁπάσης...θ. καὶ θεουργίας ἐν τῇ ποικίλῃ συνθέσει τῶν ἱεραρχικῶν συμβόλων ἱερογραφουμένης Dion.Ar.*e.h.*4.3.12(M.3.485B); as contained in scripture, *ib.*5.3.7(513C).

B. recipients; angels; highest order receiving greatest visions, Dion.Ar.*c.h.*7.1(M.3.205B); gentiles τοῖς ἔθνεσι πρώτοις, μήπω μηδὲ ὀνόματος ὄντος ἐν ἀνθρώποις Ἰσραηλιτικοῦ, οἱ χρησμοὶ παρείχοντο τοῦ θεοῦ καὶ αἱ θ. Eus.*fr.Lc.*7:29(M.24.540C); OT saints, ref. Gen.12:6 τὸν αὐτὸν σωτῆρα τὸν [τε] ἔναγχος ἐπιφανέντα τῷ βίῳ καὶ πρόπαλαι θεοφανείας πεποιῆσθαι φιλοθέοις ἀνδράσιν id.*v.C.*3.51(p.99.8; M.20.1112A); τὸν μονογενῆ θεόν...ἐν τῇ γενομένῃ Μωυσεῖ θ. Gr.Nyss.*Eun.*2(2 p.307.7; M.45.477D); Jo.D.*f.o.*3.1(M.94.981B); Christians; of Constantine's vision, Eus.*l.C.*18(p.259.7; M.20.1437C); in gen., Leont.H.*Nest.*1.14(M.86.1456A).

C. of first coming of Christ; **1.** in gen. τὴν σωτήριον θ. Or.*fr.397 in Mt.*20:1(p.168; M.17.361A); τῆς πρώτης τοῦ σωτῆρος θ. ἄντρῳ Eus. *v.C.*3.41(p.95.6; M.20.1101A); id.*l.C.*9(p.221.21; M.20.1369C); τὴν ἔνσαρκον Χριστοῦ θ. Epiph.*haer.*51.6(p.254.29, v.l. παρουσίαν M.41.897A); Proc.G.*Is.*9:1–7(M.87.2000B); Max.*opusc.*(M.91.160C); ἡ ἐκ τῆς ἀειπαιδος Μαρίας ἐν σαρκὶ θεανδρικῇ θ. τοῦ μὲν πατρὸς βουληθέντος, τοῦ δὲ υἱοῦ σαρκωθέντος, τοῦ δὲ πνεύματος συνεργήσαντος ‡Caes.Naz.*dial.*167(M.38.1129); *Lit.Jac.*(p.206.25); ἡ θ. τοῦ ἑνὸς τῆς ἁγίας τριάδος ‡Meth.*Sym.et Ann.*2(M.18.352C); **2.** as prophesied in OT τὴν...τοῦ θεοῦ λόγου οἰκονομίαν...τὴν προκαταγγελθεῖσαν μὲν διὰ τῶν προφητῶν, φανερωθεῖσαν δὲ διὰ τῆς κατὰ σάρκα τοῦ υἱοῦ θ. Gr.Nyss. *hom.5 in Cant.*(M.44.860D); Ast.Am.*hom.*14(M.40.389A); Cyr.*Ps.* 52:1(M.69.1108A); **3.** its effects: destruction of power of magic, Ath.*inc.*46.3(M.25.177D); cessation of symbolical character of Jewish rites, Gr.Nyss.*or.catech.*18(p.76.11; M.45.56A); **4.** heret. τῶν ἀντὶ τῆς ἀληθοῦς θ. δόκησίν τινα γεγενῆσθαι δογματιζόντων ἐν σωματικῇ μορφῇ κατεσχηματισμένην Gr.Nyss.*ep.*3(M.46.1020D).

D. of Christ's resurrection appearances, Eus.*qu.Marin.*2.3(M.22. 944C); cf.id.*qu.Marin.suppl.*1.5(M.22.992C).

E. of second coming, ref. Lc.9:26 περὶ τῆς δευτέρας αὐτοῦ θ. παραδιδοὺς αὐτοῖς μυστήρια Eus.*fr.Lc.*9:26(M.24.548B); *ib.*19:12 (589A); *ib.*18:2(588C).

F. in spiritual life, ref. help given by Word to those who pray πρὸς τὴν χρείαν ἑκάστῳ γίνεται τὰ τῆς θ. Ath.*Ar.*2.63(M.26.144B); ref. revelation of God obtainable at liturgy by those whose minds are clear of images, Dion.Ar.*e.h.*3.3.11(M.3.440B).

G. of vision of heavenly Christ, Dion.Ar.*d.n.*1.4(M.3.592C); σημειώσαι ὅτι καὶ τὸ θεῖον αὐτοῦ σῶμα ὁρατὴν θ. φησιν, ὡς κατὰ ταὐτὸν ἁρμόττειν τὸ ῥητὸν καὶ κατὰ Νεστοριανῶν καὶ Ἀκεφάλων, καὶ τῶν ὑπολαμβανόντων μὴ εἶναι καὶ νῦν καὶ ἔσεσθαι μετὰ σαρκὸς τὸν κύριον Max.*schol.d.n.*1.4(M.4.197C).

H. of Constantine's vision of the labarum, Eus.*v.C.*1.32(p.22.29; M.20.948B).

I. *feast of Christmas* ἡ γὰρ ἐπὶ τῇ θ. τοῦ μονογενοῦς υἱοῦ χάρις, ἡ διὰ τῆς ἐκ παρθένου γεννήσεως ἀναδειχθεῖσα τῷ κόσμῳ, οὐχ ἁπλῶς ἐστιν ἁγία πανήγυρις, ἀλλὰ...πανήγυρις πανηγύρεων Gr.Nyss.*laud. Bas.*(M.46.789A); cf.id.*ep.*4(M.46.1025A); Χριστῷ τὸν σωματικὸν ἑορτάζομεν τόκον θεοφανείας ἐντρυφῶντες ἡμέραν Job.Mon.*inc.*2(M.86. 3316C).

J. *feast of Christ's baptism* (*Epiphany*) τοῦ φωτίσματος ἡμέραν θεοφανείας προσηγορίᾳ τιμῶντες Job.Mon.*inc.*2(M.86.3316C).

θεοφάνια, τά, neut. plur.; **1.** *Christmas* ὄνομα θώμεθα τῇ ἑορτῇ ἡμῶν θ.· ἑορτάσωμεν τὰ σωτήρια τοῦ κόσμου, τὴν γενέθλιον ἡμέραν τῆς ἀνθρωπότητος †Bas.*Chr.generat.*6(2.602B; M.31.1473A); τὰ δὲ νῦν θ. ἡ πανήγυρις, εἴτουν γενέθλια Gr.Naz.*or.*38.3(M.36.313C); Ast.Am.*hom.* 4(M.40.217C); celebrated before S. Stephen's day, *ib.*12(340A); ὀκτὼ εἰδῶν Ἰανουαρίων, ὅτε ἀληθῶς τὰ θ. ἐγένετο καὶ ἐγεννήθη Epiph. *haer.*51.29(p.300.15; M.41.940A); in gen., Isid.Pel.*epp.*3.110(M.78. 816D); **2.** *feast of Christ's baptism* (*Epiphany*); **a.** in gen., †Hipp. *theoph.*tit.(p.257.1; M.10.852); Marc.Diac.*v.Porph.*21; -εια *Rit. Epiph.*tit.(p.415); **b.** dist. from Christmas, chief feast being ἡ κατὰ σάρκα τοῦ Χριστοῦ γέννησις· ἀπὸ γὰρ ταύτης τὰ θ., καὶ τὸ πάσχα Chrys.*Philogon.*3(1.497C); τὰ γενέθλια μὲν τοῦ σωτῆρος...τελεῖται... πρὸ ὀκτὼ καλανδῶν Ἰανουαρίων κατὰ Ῥωμαίους· θ. δὲ ὡσαύτως·... τρισκαιδεκάτῃ τετάρτου μηνὸς κατὰ Ἀσιανούς ‡Chrys.*pasch.*7.1(8^2. 275B); ἐν τῇ προλαβούσῃ ἑορτῇ τῶν γενεθλίων τοῦ σωτῆρος...ἐν δὲ τῇ σήμερον ἑορτῇ τῶν θ. Procl.CP *or.*7.1(M.65.757C); **c.** observances Πέτρον φησὶ τὸν Κναφέα ἐπινοῆσαι...τὴν ἐπὶ τῶν ὑδάτων ἐν τοῖς θ. ἐπίκλησιν ἐν τῇ ἑσπέρᾳ γίνεσθαι Thdr.Lect.*h.e.*2.48(M.86.209A); βάπτισμα οὐ ποιοῦσι [sc. Acephali] κατὰ τὸν ἐκκλησιαστικὸν κανόνα· ἀλλ' ἐν τῇ ἑορτῇ τῶν ἁγίων θ., ἤγουν φώτων, ἀρύονται ὕδατα, καὶ ταῦτα φυλάττοντες, ἐν αὐτοῖς βαπτίζουσιν Tim.CP *haer.*(M.86.56C); ref. fasting on eve but not on day itself, *Catech.Stud.*7(M.99.1697B); **3.** it is often uncertain which of the two feasts is meant; e.g. ‡Nil. *narr.*4(M.79.640C); Thphl.Al.*theoph.*(M.65.33B); Philost.*h.e.*6.2(M. 65.533B); Cyr.S.*v.Euthym.*5(p.13.24); *ib.*39(p.57.16).

θεόφαντος, *revealing God*, Isid.Pel.*epp.*1.263(M.78.340C).

θεοφάντωρ, *revealing God*, of theologians θ. Κύριλλος Anast.S.*hod.* 10(M.89.176C); τοῦ θ. Διονυσίου Max.*opusc.*(M.91.84D); id.*ambig.*(M. 91.1260B); id.*Pyrr.*(M.91.348B); ‡Jo.D.*ep.Thphl.*22(M.95.373B).

θεόφατος, *uttered by God*, Athenag.*leg.*11.1(M.6.912A).

***θεοφεγγής,** *shedding divine light*, Eus.*h.e.*10.4.59(M.20.872C); ‡Jo.D.*fid.dorm.*(M.95.252C).

***θεοφερής,** *God-bearing*, of BMV ἡ θ. λογικὴ ὁλκάς Mod.*dorm.*4(M. 86.3288C).

θεόφθεγκτος, *sounded by God* προφῆται καὶ δίκαιοι ἐπεβόων τῇ θ. αὐτῶν σάλπιγγι Mod.*dorm.*7(M.86.3296A).

***θεόφθογγος,** *uttering words of God, inspired*; of apostles, Rom. Mel.(*AS* 1 p.169); θ. λύραν κρούων ὁ Δαβίδ Geo.Pis.*hex.*90(M.92. 1438A); Jo.D.*hom.*1.3(M.96.549B); ref. preaching θ. λόγοι †Jo.D.*B.J.* 33(M.96.1177B); Thdr.Stud.*cant.*7.1(p.349).

θεοφιλής, 1. *loved by God, pleasing to God*; **a.** of doctrine θ. λογισμός *Hom.Clem.*16.14; οὐ θ. ἀλλ' ἀσεβὲς τὸ ἐργαστήριον τῶν Ἀρειομανιτῶν Ath.*ep.mort.Ar.*4(p.180.3; M.25.689A); **b.** of saints, Meth.*symp.*2.2(p.17.18, v.l. θεοφυές M.18.49C); Ath.*fug.*19(M.25. 669A); **c.** of virtues, qualities, etc. τῇ θ. παρρησίᾳ Eus.*h.e.*7.16(M. 20.677B); θ. ἀθανασίας Euthal.Diac.*Ac.*(M.85.628A); of table of abstemious man, ‡Chrys.*provid.*6(2.776D); **d.** as title, usu. superl.; **i.** of bishops, Jov.*ep.*(M.26.813A); Bas.*ep.*52.1(3.144E; M.32.392B); *ib.*33(112D; M.320A); Socr.*h.e.*6 proem.7(M.67.660A); Procl.CP *ep.* (p.67.18; M.65.881A); Thdt.*ep.*101(4.1170); **ii.** other ecclesiastics: deacon, Cyr.*ep.*69(5^2.197A; θεοσεβέστατος p.15.27); priest, *IGC As. Min.*225(p.71) c. 602; **iii.** imperial, Ath.*apol.Const.*(p.279.5; M.25. 596A); Cyr.H.*ep.Const.*1(M.33.1165A); *ib.*2(1168A); *IGC As.Min.* 280(p.94); **iv.** in gen., address τὴν...θ. φιλόσοφον [i.e. Hypatia] Synes.*ep.*4(M.66.1341B); **2.** *loving God*, Clem.*q.d.s.*34(p.182.26; M.9. 640C); ref. Lam.4:20 οἱ γὰρ θ. διὰ παντὸς τὸν Χριστὸν ἀναπνέουσι, πρὸ ὀφθαλμῶν αὐτὸν ἔχοντες Or.*fr.116 in Lam.*(p.276.31; M.13.660A); γράμματα βασιλικὰ...ἐπὶ θ. διανοίας ἁγίῳ πνεύματι τυπωθέντα Chrys. *hom.3.2 in Jo.*(8.17C); οἱ θ. *M.Thdot.1* 36(p.84.21); **3.** *intimate with God*, including both the foreg. senses; **a.** of humanity since Inc. εἰ δὲ κοινὰ τὰ φιλῶν, θ. δὲ ὁ ἄνθρωπος (καὶ γὰρ οὖν φίλος τῷ θεῷ, μεσιτεύοντος τοῦ λόγου) Clem.*prot.*12(p.86.10; M.8.244C); hence **b.** of Christians τοῦ θ. καὶ θεοσεβοῦς γένους τῶν Χριστιανῶν *M.Polyc.*3.2; Clem.*str.*6.1(p.422.20; M.9.208B); **c.** of spiritual life, Tat.*orat.*12 (p.13.14; M.6.832B); goal of life of virtue being τὸ θ., Clem.*str.*4.20 (p.304.26; M.8.1337C); cf.*ib.*7.1(p.4.1; M.9.404B); **d.** of saints ὁ... θεοφιλέστατος μάρτυς Eus.*h.e.*5.21.4(M.20.488A); Ath.*fug.*17(p.79.30; M.25.665B); id.*v.Anton.*4(M.26.845C); **4.** *belonging to God, divine* θ. Πρόνοια *Hom.Clem.*2.35.

θεοφιλία (-εια), ἡ, *love of God*, Jo.VI H.*v.Jo.D.*6(M.94.437B); as title; imperial, Eus.*v.C.*4.74(p.148.10; M.20.1229A); Chrys.*ep.Eud.* (M.64.496A); of a priest, Nil.*epp.*3.30(M.79.385B); of bishops, Cyr. *ep.*76(5^2.204A); CCP(448)*act.*6(p.136.20; H.2.157A); of archimandrite, Thdr.Stud.*epp.*1.35(M.99.1028D); of a prioress, *ib.*2.134 (1432C); of deaconess, Thdt.*ep.*17(4.1079); of monks, Justn.*monoph.* (M.86.1105B); Zos.*alloquia* 8(M.78.1692D).

θεόφιλος, *beloved by God*, Leont.Abb.*v.Gr.Agr.*9(M.98.561B).

***θεοφοβία, ἡ,** *fear of God*, ‡Ath.*synops.*46(M.28.377B).

θεόφοβος, *God-fearing*, Jo.Disc.*v.Epiph.*3(M.41.28D); Cyr.*Jo.*9 (4.788E).

***θεοφόβως,** *with the fear of God*, Thdr.Stud.*epp.*2.180(M.99. 1560A).

θεοφορ-έω, 1. *bear God* ὁ γνωστικὸς...ἤδη ἅγιος, ~ῶν καὶ ~ούμενος Clem.*str.*7.13(p.58.26; M.9.513B); *ib.*6.12(p.484.19; 325B); ref. Christ ἡ σὰρξ ~εῖται ἐν τῷ λόγῳ Ath.*Ar.*3.41(M.26.409C); **2.** *inspire*; **a.** Christol. ἵνα μὴ ὡς ἄνθρωπος ἁπλῶς ~ήσας νοοῖτο Cyr.*hom. pasch.*17.2(5^2.226E); **b.** of prophets οὐδενὶ ἄλλῳ ~οῦνται οἱ προφητεύοντες εἰ μὴ λόγῳ θείῳ Just.*1apol.*33.9(M.6.381C); cf.*ib.*35.3(384B); ψυχαῖς...καθαρωτάταις, ἅστινας ~εῖ καὶ προφήτας ποιεῖ Or.*Cels.*4.95 (p.368.4; M.11.1173B); cf.*ib.*8.54(p.270.24; 1597C); Eus.*fr.Lc.*21:28 (M.24.600A); †Bas.*Is.*proem.3(1.380A; M.30.124A); Gr.Nyss.*res.*3(M. 46.676C); id.*Eun.*8(2 p.177.18; M.45.769C); ptcpl. pass. neut. as subst., *inspiration*, Areth.ap.*cat.Apoc.*16:2(p.410.20); **c.** of writers of scripture, Clem.*fr.*8(p.197.29; M.9.749C); the author of Gen., Mac.Mgn.*apocr.*3.13(p.84.23); **d.** of saints τελείους καὶ ~ουμένους Ath.*Ar.*3.23(M.26.372B, v.l. διαφορουμένους); ‡Ath.*v.Syncl.*11(M.28. 1492D); τῶν ἀληθῶς ἁγίων, τῶν ἐν τῷ ἁγίῳ πνεύματι ~ουμένων Gr. Nyss.*or.dom.*1(p.18.23; M.44.1132A); id.*v.Macr.*(p.390.5; M.46.977B); Jo.D.*hom.*1.6(M.96.556A); **e.** of non-Christians ὁ Πλάτων οἷον ~ούμενος Clem.*str.*1.8(p.28.3; M.8.737C); of a magician ~εῖσθαι δοκῶν Hipp.*haer.*4.28(p.54.14; M.16.3090B).

θεοφόρησις, ἡ, *bearing by God, inspiration*, of prophetic inspiration θεοφορήσει δὲ κρείττονος δυνάμεως...τὴν γνῶσιν ἀνατιθέντες Eus. *p.e.*11.7(521B; M.21.864C).

θεοφόρητος, 1. *borne by God*; *inspired*, of David ὁ θεοφορητότατος ‡Hipp.*fr.17 in Pss.*(p.144.28; M.10.720C); **2.** *borne by* (i.e. assumed by) *God*, of Christ ἀλλ' ἔστιν ἄνθρωπος θ., καὶ οὐ θεοφόρος· οὐ γὰρ ἡ σὰρξ ἐσκήνωσεν ἐν τῷ λόγῳ, ἀλλὰ ὁ λόγος ἐν τῇ σαρκί Leont.H.*Nest.* 6.7(M.86.1757A).

θεοφορία, ἡ, *inspiration*, Or.*Cels.*3.81(p.271.33; M.11.1028A); Eus. *p.e.*4.1(132D; M.21.233B); id.*d.e.*5 proem.(p.206.24; M.22.344A).

θεοφόρος, *bearing God*; **1.** of BMV ἡ θ. Hesych.H.*serm.*5(M.93. 1461A); **2.** Christol.; **a.** of flesh of Christ ἡ σὰρξ ἡ θ. †Bas.*Is.*72(1. 430E; M.30.241A); Bas.*ep.*261.2(3.402B; M.32.969C, v.l. Χριστοφόρος); ref. 1Cor.11:12 ἵνα δείξῃ ὅτι ἐκ τοῦ ἀνθρωπείου φυράματος ἡ θ. σὰρξ συνεπάγη id.*Spir.*12(3.9E; M.32.85C); ὑπόδημα...τῆς θεότητος ἡ σὰρξ ἡ θ. Thdt.*eran.*1(4.61); **b.** Nestorian, ref. Mt.2:13 μὴ θεὸς ἀληθῶς, θ. δὲ μᾶλλον ἄνθρωπος ἦν ὁ Χριστός, ὡς γοῦν οἴεται καταδεικνὺς τὴν τοῦ ἀγγέλου φωνὴν τῷ μακαρίῳ λέγοντος Ἰωσὴφ ἐγερθεὶς παράλαβε τὸ παιδίον Cyr.*Nest.*1.1(p.18.32; 6^1.10B); ‡Ath.*annunt.*11(M.28.932Df.);

Cyr.*ep.*2(p.24.7; 5^2.20B); ref. Jo.8:40 εἰ μὴ θ. ἄνθρωπος ὁ Χριστός, οὐδ' ἄρα ἄνθρωπός ἐστιν ὁ Χριστὸς ὁ ἀκούων τὴν ἀλήθειαν παρὰ τοῦ θεοῦ Leont.H.*Nest.*6.7(M.86.1757A); refutations λέγομεν, ὅτι οὐ θ. ἄνθρωπος ἔστιν ὁ Χριστός, ἀλλὰ σαρκοφόρος θεός ‡Ath.*annunt.*11 (933B); εἴ τις τολμᾷ λέγειν θ. ἄνθρωπον τὸν Χριστὸν καὶ οὐχὶ δὴ μᾶλλον θεὸν εἶναι κατὰ ἀλήθειαν ὡς υἱὸν ἕνα καὶ φύσει, καθὸ γέγονε σὰρξ ὁ λόγος...ἀνάθεμα ἔστω Cyr.*ep.*17 *anath.*5(p.41.5; 5^2.76C); id.*Jo.*9.1 (4.790B); Val.Apoll.*apol.*2(p.288.20)ap.Leont.B.*Apoll.*(M.86.1953C); Jo.D.*f.o.*3.12(M.94.1032B); ref. anti-Nestorian arguments; **i.** from scripture, ref. Is.35:3–6 θεὸν ὀνομάζει καίτοι λαλῶν ἐν πνεύματι, ὅτι μὴ ἄνθρωπον ἁπλῶς θ. ἠπίστατο τὸν Ἐμμανουὴλ...ἀλλὰ θεὸν ἀληθῶς ἐνηνθρωπηκότα Cyr.*ep.*1(p.19.9; 5^2.14A); Jo.8:40 ἔστιν ἄνθρωπος θεοφόρητος, καὶ οὐ θ.· οὐ γὰρ ἡ σὰρξ ἐσκήνωσεν ἐν τῷ λόγῳ, ἀλλὰ ὁ λόγος ἐν τῇ σαρκί Leont.H.*Nest.*6.7(M.86.1757A); Mt.16:16 οὐδ' ἄσαρκον καταθεώμενος λόγον, οὐδὲ ψιλὸν καὶ θ. ἄνθρωπον Jo.D.*haer. Nest.*19(M.95.197B); **ii.** union of natures dist. from divine indwelling in men φαμὲν γὰρ ἡμεῖς τὸ μὴ χρῆναι πρός τινος θ. ἄνθρωπον ὀνομάζεσθαι τὸν Χριστόν, ἵνα μὴ καθ' ἕνα τῶν ἁγίων νοοῖτο Cyr.*apol. Thdt.*5(p.126.25; 6^1.220D); cf.id.*hom.pasch.*20(5^2.259C); id.*ep.*17(p.36. 6; 5^2.70D); **iii.** ref. theol. implications of the term εἰ Χριστὸς αὐτὸς ὁ φορούμενος ἦν καθ' ὑμᾶς ὁ καὶ θ., δύο θεοῖς μεσάζει Χριστός· ἑνὶ τῷ ἔνδον αὐτοῦ χωρουμένῳ, διότι θεὸς ἦν ἐν Χριστῷ· καὶ ἑνὶ τῷ ἔξωθεν φορουμένῳ, διότι θ. ὑμῖν δοκεῖ ὁ Χριστός Leont.H.*Nest.*6.2(M.86. 1753D); **c.** Apollinarian; term rejected τὸ δεῖν προσκυνεῖν μὴ ἄνθρωπον θ., ἀλλὰ θεὸν σαρκοφόρον Gr.Naz.*ep.*102(M.37.200B); Apollinarian conception of orthodox interpretation of Heb.1:6 θ. ἀγγέλους θ. ἀνθρώπῳ καταδουλοῦντες Gr.Nyss.*Apoll.*42(M.45.1224C); **d.** orthodox senses θεὸν ὄντα σαρκοφόρον, καὶ ἄνθρωπον θ. Valent. Imp.*ep.episc.*ap.Thdt.*h.e.*4.8.10 (anti-Nest. interpolation: καὶ οὐκ ἄνθρωπον θ. 3.959); τὸν θ. δὲ ἄνθρωπον ὡς πολλοῖς τῶν ἁγίων πατέρων εἰρημένον παραιτούμεθα...καλοῦμεν δὲ θ. ἄνθρωπον, οὐχ ὡς μερικήν τινα θείαν χάριν δεξάμενον, ἀλλ' ὡς πᾶσαν ἡνωμένην ἔχοντα τοῦ υἱοῦ τὴν θεότητα Thdt.ap.Cyr.*apol.Thdt.*5(p.126.13; 6^1.220B); **3.** of angels, Gr.Nyss.*Apoll.*42(M.45.1224C); name 'throne' signifying τὸ θ., Dion. Ar.*c.h.*7.1(M.3.205D); **4.** of men; **a.** of Christian τὸ θ. γίνεσθαι τὸν ἄνθρωπον προσεχῶς ἐνεργούμενον ὑπὸ τοῦ κυρίου καὶ καθάπερ σῶμα αὐτοῦ γινόμενον Clem.*exc.Thdot.*27(p.116.15; M.9.673B); ἡ θ. συνείδησις Diad.*perf.*50(p.56.8); **b.** of men as inspired, esp. prophets ὁ χορὸς τῶν θ. ‡Gr.Thaum.*annunt.*1(M.10.1149B); τῶν θ. προφητῶν Eus.*d.e.*4.1(p.150.15; M.22.252A); ‡Ath.*hom.in Mt.21*:9(M.28. 1029C); Thdt.*affect.*10(p.259.1; 4.968); Hesych.H.*proem.proph.*(M. 93.1340A); Cosm.Ind.*top.*3(M.88.164A); apostles, †Thdt.*Nest.*(4. 1051); Cosm.Ind.*top.*3(177B); Barnabas ὁ τῶν ἐθνῶν θ. ὁδηγός Alex. Sal.*Barn.*proem.6(p.432D); εἰκὸς καὶ τοὺς τοιούτους θ. καλεῖν, ἵνα τὸ ἐπίκτητον τῇ ὑποστάσει τῇ ἀνθρωπίνῃ, ἡ θεία φύσις νοηθῇ Leont.H. *Nest.*6.1(M.86.1753B); theologians Ἰγνάτιος ὁ καὶ θ. Ign.*Eph.* proem.; in gen., Gr.Nyss.*Eun.*2(1 p.301.4; M.45.1012C); fathers of Nicaea, Eust.Seb.*ep.*ap.Soz.*h.e.*6.11.2(M.67.1320C); Dor.*doct.*23.1(M. 88.1829B); in gen., Max.*ambig.*(M.91.1189A); *Chron.Pasch.*p.198(M. 92.488C); Jo.D.*f.o.*3.6(M.94.1005A); orthodox Christians; in gen., Ign.*Eph.*9.2; οὐδεὶς...τῶν θ. γέννησιν προσηγόρευσε τὴν τοῦ θείου πνεύματος ὕπαρξιν Thdt.*haer.*5.3(4.388); Leont.H.*monoph.*(M.86. 1816C); of partic. persons ὁ θ. πατὴρ ἡμῶν Θεόδωρος ὁ Στουδίων Anast.*temp.*(p.279); emperors, ‡Jo.D.*ep.Thphl.*30(M.95.384D); **c.** of men transmitting divine power by miracles ὁ θ. Ἠλίας... ἐγείρει τὸν υἱὸν τῆς χήρας ‡Ath.*disp.*44(M.28.497D); **d.** of saints, as bearing God in themselves by grace: of desert fathers, ‡Pall. *proem.*(p.4.28; M.34.995); Chrysostom, Isid.Pel.*epp.*1.310(M.78. 361C); an ascetic, Cyr.S.*v.Sab.*20(p.105.3); Leo Mag., Jo.Mosch.*prat.* 148(M.87.3012C); πᾶς θ. ἄνθρωπος Χριστὸς λέγεσθαι δύναται Jo.D.*f.o.* 3.12(M.94.1032B); **5.** of scripture τὰ θ. διδάγματα Isid.Pel.*epp.*1. 90(M.78.244D).

θεοφραδής, *speaking from God, inspired*, Nonn.*par.Jo.*3:2(M.43. 765B); *ib.*3:7(768A); *ib.*12:44(857B).

***θεόφραστος**, **1.** *speaking from God* θ. γλώττῃ Isid.Pel.*epp.*3.402 (M.78.1037C); **2.** *spoken from God* τοῖς αὐτοῦ θ. λόγοις Max.*ambig.* (M.91.1304C).

***θεοφρούρητος**, *guarded, watched over, by God*; of universe, ‡Just.*qu.Chr.*5(M.6.1456B); of Christians τὸ τῶν Χριστιανῶν θ. ... γένος ‡Jo.D.*Artem.*35(M.96.1284C); of Church, Sophr.H.*ep.syn.*(M. 87.3189A); as address or title of honour θ. δέσποτα Max.*comput.*1 (M.19.1217B); τῆς σῆς...θ. εὐκλείας Jo.D.*jej.*1(M.95.65B); of emperors, Cyrus Al.*ep.*3(H.3.1340A).

θεόφρων, *of godly mind*; esp. of scriptural writers and notable theologians, Gr.Naz.*carm.*1.1.1.17(M.37.399A); Isid.Pel.*epp.*1.443 (M.78.425C); Max.*ambig.*(M.91.1033C); Jo.D.*hom.*8.5(M.96.708C).

***θεοφυής**, *begotten by God*, Meth.*symp.*2.2(M.18.49C; θεοφιλές p.17.18).

***θεοφύλακτος**, *guarded by God*; **1.** in gen. τὸν σαυτοῦ θ. πλοῦτον... τοῖς μοναχοῖς ἐξαντλεῖς Nil.*epp.*2.157(M.79.273D); Leont.N.*v.Jo. Eleem.*1(p.7.8); esp. of cities, †Cyr.*hom.div.*10(5^2.378A); Jo.Thess. *dorm.BMV* A 1(p.376.8); Jo.VI CP *ep.*(M.96.1417C); **2.** of Christians in gen., Max.*ep.*2(M.91.392D); *ib.*14(537C); τοῦ θ. σου τέκνου Thdr. Stud.*epp.*1.17(M.99.961B); *ib.*2.137(1437B); **3.** as title of emperors τοῦ θ. Καίσαρος Τιβερίου νέου Κωνσταντίνου *CIG* 8646 (Egypt, 577); *IGC As.Min.*114 (Ephesus, 613); *Chron.Pasch.*p.385(M.92.988A); *IGC As.Min.*79; *ib.*80 (saec. vii); and imperial forces τοῦ θ. στρατοῦ *Chron.Pasch.*p.397(M.92.1016C); in complimentary address ἡ ὑμετέρα θ. γαληνότης Sym.Styl.J.*ep.Just.*(M.86.3216C); *ib.*(3217D).

***θεοφύτευτος**, *planted by God*, of BMV παράδεισος θ. ‡Ath. *occurs.*16(M.28.995C); of good thief θ. φραγμοῦ τυχορύγε Ephr.3. 475F; of a monk, Thdr.Stud.*epp.*1.8(M.99.933D).

***θεόφυτος**, *planted by God* πηγαία θεότης ὁ πατήρ, ὁ δὲ Ἰησοῦς [v.l. υἱός] καὶ τὸ πνεῦμα, τῆς θεογόνου θεότητος...βλαστοὶ θ. Dion.Ar.*d.n.* 2.7(M.3.645B).

***θεοφώτιστος**, *divinely illuminated*, of BMV ἡ νοητὴ καὶ θ. σελήνη Thdr.Stud.*or.*5.1(M.99.721A).

***θεοχάλκευτος**, *forged by God*, of Ephrem's eloquence κλεὶς θ. τοὺς τῶν πλουσίων θησαυροὺς διανοίγων Gr.Nyss.*v.Ephr.*(M.46. 837D); met. of BMV λυχνίαν...θ. Taras.*praesent.BMV* 8(M.98. 1489B).

***θεοχάρακτος**, **A.** *engraven* or *written by God*; **1.** of tables of Law, Gr.Naz.*or.*4.107(M.35.641C); *Lit.Praesanct.*(p.352.16); **2.** of Christian doctrines as new Law, Max.*ep.*19(M.91.592B); χαῖρε, βιβλίον ἐσφραγισμένον [sc. BMV]...ἐξ ἧς ὁ θ. νόμου κύριος...ἀναγινώσκεται Thdr.Stud.*nativ.BMV* 7(M.96.692B); **3.** of gospels, Cyr.S.*v.Sab.*57 (p.155.23); Thdr.Stud.*antirr.*9(M.99.340D); id.*epp.*1.34(M.99.1025D); **4.** of declaration of faith of Pope Agatho, CCP(681)*or.imp.*(H. 3.1421E); **5.** of works of Bas., Thdr.Stud.*epp.*2.164(M.99.1520B); and of Jo. D., Jo.VI H.*v.Jo.D.*33(M.94.476A).

B. portrayed by God τύπος...θ. ... τυγχάνει τοῦ Χριστοῦ ὁ θεῖος Ἰσαάκ Anast.S.*hod.*19(M.89.269A).

***θεοχάριστος**, *granted* or *bestowed by God*, Max.*ep.*44(M.91. 644D); Thdr.Stud.*epp.*2.220.1(M.99.1668A).

***θεοχάριτος**, *graced by God*; of BMV, Ephr.3.524E; ‡Meth.*Sym. et Ann.*10(M.18.372C).

***θεοχαρίτωτος**, *graced by God, full of divine grace*, ‡Jo.D.*fid. dorm.*1(M.95.248B); θ. λείψανον Thphn.*chron.*p.370 (θεοχαριτώτατον M.108.885B); of BMV, ‡Jo.D.*hom.*6.10(M.96.677A); *Lit.Jac.*(*NBP* 10^2 p.84); *Hymn.*(*AS* 1 p.529).

***θεοχολωτέομαι**, *be under divine wrath*, Jo.Mal.*chron.*4 p.76(M. 97.157A).

***θεοχρημάτιστος**, *having received a message from God*, ‡Jo.D. *hom.*5(M.96.648B).

θεόχρηστος, *containing a divine oracle*, Didym.*Trin.*1.18(M.39. 344B).

***θεόχριστος**, *anointed by God*, *Orac.Sib.*5.68; met., of scriptural writers οἱ θ. Dion.Ar.*d.n.*3.2(M.3.681B).

***θεοχώρητος**, *containing God*, of BMV τὸ τοῦ ὑψίστου θ. σκεῦος Tim.Ant.*descr.BMV* 8(M.28.957A); ‡Jo.D.*hom.*5(M.96.648C).

***θεοψήφιστος**, *chosen by God*; title of emperor, CCP(681)*act.*3 (H.3.1065C); *ib.or.imp.*(1424A).

***θεόψηφος**, *decided by God* πᾶν ὁτιοῦν...κανονισθήσεται, καὶ κρίσιν ἕξει θ. Thdr.Stud.*epp.*2.6(M.99.1128D).

θεόω, **I.** *make into a god, deify*;

A. of pagans deifying creatures, Eus.*l.C.*13(p.235.23; M.20. 1397A); *ib.*(p.235.31; 1397B).

B. Christol.; **1.** of Christ's humanity deified by hypostatic union; **a.** in gen. τὰ γὰρ ἀμφότερα ἓν τῇ συγκράσει, θεοῦ μὲν ἐνανθρωπήσαντος ἀνθρώπου δὲ θεωθέντος Gr.Naz.*ep.*101(M.37.180A); id.*or.*38. 13(M.36.325C); τῇ βροτείᾳ φύσει ὁ υἱὸς καὶ λόγος τοῦ θεοῦ καὶ θεὸς ἑνωθείς, ἐθέωσε μὲν αὐτὴν...μένει γὰρ αὕτη βροτεία φύσις καὶ μετὰ τὴν θέωσιν, καὶ τεθεωμένη φύσις βροτεία καὶ λέγεται καὶ ἔστι· τεθεωμένη σάρξ, μετὰ ψυχῆς νοερᾶς ‡Cyr.*Trin.*14(6^3.21B; M.77.1152C); τὴν κάτω φύσιν θεώσας κειμένην, ἐν τοῖς οὐρανοῖς συναγαγών, συνεδριάζειν τῷ θεῷ καὶ πατρὶ πεποίηκε †Gregent.*disp.*(M.86.772A); Χριστὸς ὁ θεὸς ἡμῶν ἐξωράισε τὴν ἀνθρωπείαν φύσιν τῇ ὡραιότητι...τῆς θεότητος αὐτοῦ, θεώσας αὐτὴν ἐν ἑαυτῷ Mod.*dorm.*8(M.86.3297B); τὴν ἡμετέραν οὐσίαν...ἐθέωσε, πυρακτωθέντος δίκην σιδήρου Max.*opusc.*(M.91. 60B); ἡ μὲν φύσις τῆς σαρκὸς θεοῦται, οὐ σαρκοῖ δὲ τὴν φύσιν τοῦ λόγου· θεοῖ μὲν τὸ πρόσλημμα, οὐ σαρκοῦται δέ Jo.D.*Jacob.*52(M.94.1461C); **b.** ref. interrelationship between divine and human natures ἡ μὲν [sc. θεότης] ἐθέωσεν ὡς θεοποιὸς φύσις· ἡ δὲ ἐθεώθη ὡς θεοποιουμένη Leont.H.*Nest.*5.25(M.86.1748A); ἡ μὲν [sc. φύσις] ἐθέωσε δηλονότι ὡς θεία, ἡ δὲ ἐθεώθη ὡμολογημένως ὡς μὴ φύσει θείᾳ πάλαι *ib.*5.10(1733B); *ib.*4.37(1712B); **c.** of his mind and will ὁ νοῦς, θεωθεὶς ἑνώσει θεοῦ λόγου, οὐ τρέπεται ‡Ath.*dial.Trin.*4.5(M.28.1256C); τὸ γὰρ ἐκείνου θέλειν οὐδὲ ὑπεναντίον θεῷ, θεωθὲν ὅλον Gr.Naz.*or.*30.12(p.126.1; M. 36.117C); commented ὅλον δι' ὅλου τῇ πρὸς τὸ πατρικὸν συννεύσει τε καὶ συμφυΐᾳ τεθεωμένον, καὶ θεῖον τῇ ἑνώσει κυρίως, ἀλλ' οὐ τῇ φύσει, καὶ γενόμενον ἀληθῶς καὶ λεγόμενον· μηδαμῶς καὶ θεωθῆναι, τοῦ κατὰ φύσιν ἐκστᾶν. τῷ γοῦν θεωθὲν ὅλον εἰπεῖν, τὴν τοῦ κατ' αὐτὸν ἀνθρωπίνου θελήματος πρὸς τὸ θεῖον αὐτοῦ καὶ πατρικὸν ἕνωσιν ὁ διδάσκαλος παραστήσας, πᾶσαν ἐναντίωσιν...τελείως ἀπήλασε Max.*opusc.*(M.91. 81D); ὁπόταν λέγῃ ὁ ἅγιος Γρηγόριος ὁ Ναζιανζοῦ· τὸ γὰρ ἐκείνου θέλειν τοῦ ἐν τῷ σωτῆρι νοουμένου ἀνθρώπου δείκνυσι τὸ ἀνθρώπινον τοῦ σωτῆρος θέλημα δι' αὐτῆς τῆς ἑνώσεως τῆς πρὸς τὸν λόγον θεωθῆναι...ὡσαύτως ἀποδείκνυσιν, ὅτι καὶ ἀνθρώπινον, εἰ καὶ θεωθέν, ἔσχηκε θέλημα...εἰ οὖν καὶ θεῖον καὶ θεωθὲν ἔσχε, δύο πάντως ἔσχε θελήματα Agath.Papa *ep.imp.*(M.*PL.*87.1187D); Const.Pogon.*edict.* (H.3.1453A); cf.CLater.*act.*5(H.3.909B,C); τὸ ἀνθρώπινον αὐτοῦ θέλημα θεωθὲν οὐκ ἀνῃρέθη *Symb.CP*(681)(H.3.1400E); cf.Jo.D.*f.o.*3.17(M.94. 1069C); **d.** of his flesh προελθὼν δὲ θεὸς μετὰ τῆς προσλήψεως, ἓν ἐκ δύο τῶν ἐναντίων, σαρκὸς καὶ πνεύματος, ὧν τὸ μὲν ἐθέωσε, τὸ δὲ ἐθεώθη Gr.Naz.*or.*45.9(M.36.633D) cit. Jo.D.*f.o.*3.17(M.94.1069A) commenting ἡ σὰρξ τοῦ κυρίου τεθεῶσθαι λέγεται,...οὔτε μὴν ἡ σὰρξ θεωθεῖσα τῆς οἰκείας ἐτράπη φύσεως, ἢ τῶν αὐτῆς φυσικῶν ἰδιωμάτων *ib.*; τῆς καθ' ὑπόστασιν ἑνώσεως...τὴν δύναμιν, καθ' ἣν ὁ λόγος σεσάρκωται, καὶ ἡ σὰρξ ἔμψυχος καὶ ἔννους ἀμεταβλήτως τεθέωται Sophr.H.*ep.syn.*(M.87.3164C); Max.*ambig.*(M.91.1040C); of deification of flesh as consummated after Resurrection, Leont.H.*Nest.*4.37 (M.86.1712A); **2.** in controversy; **a.** Apollinarian θεὸς σεσωματωμένος καὶ σῶμα τεθεωμένον Apoll.*fr.*147(p.246.26)ap.Leont.B.*Apoll.* (M.86.1965B); **b.** agst. Nestorians διὰ τῆς πρὸς τὸν φύσει θεὸν ἑνώσεως αὐτῆς ὑποστατικῆς μεταδιδομένης αὐτῇ [sc. human nature] τῆς τοῦ ὀνόματος τοῦ υἱοῦ τοῦ θεοῦ καὶ θεοῦ τιμῆς· οὕτω γὰρ πραγματιωδῶς χαρίσματα καὶ τιμὴ καὶ ὀνομασία μεγάλη τοῦ θεωθέντος παρὰ τοῦ ἀληθῶς θεώσαντος αὐτὸ θεοῦ ἀληθῶς ἐν δόσει ἑαυτοῦ δείκνυται Leont.H. *Nest.*3.5(M.86.1616A); **c.** in monophysite view μετὰ γὰρ τὴν ἕνωσιν οὐκέτι εἰσὶ δύο φύσεις. ἐθεώθη γὰρ ἡ σάρξ, καὶ ἀνεκράθη ὥσπερ σταγὼν ὄξους ἐν τῷ πελάγει Anast.S.*hod.*10(M.89.192C).

C. of men; **1.** in gen. πέρας τοῦ μυστηρίου, τῇ πρὸς θεὸν νεύσει θεούμενον Gr.Naz.*or.*38.11(M.36.324A) = *ib.*45.7(632B); commented θεούμενον δέ, μετοχῇ τῆς θείας ἐλλάμψεως, καὶ οὐκ εἰς τὴν θείαν μεθιστάμενον οὐσίαν Jo.D.*f.o.*2.12(M.94.924A); ‡Paul.Sil.*therm.Pyth.* (M.86.2268); Melet.*nat.hom.*30(M.64.1284C); **2.** of deification as caused by God; **a.** in gen. ἡ φύσει θεότης, ἡ ἀρχὴ τῆς θεώσεως, ἐξ ἧς τὸ θεοῦσθαι τοῖς θεουμένοις ἀγαθότητι θείᾳ Dion.Ar.*e.h.*1.4(M.3. 376B); ἀρχὴ γίνεται [sc. God] τοῦ θεοῦσθαι καὶ ἀγαθύνεσθαι τοὺς θεουμένους καὶ ἀγαθυνομένους id.*ep.*2(M.3.1069A); id.*d.n.*1.3(M.3.589C); **b.** through Christ, his deifying power being adduced as argument for his divinity, Gr.Naz.*or.*40.42(M.36.420A); ὃ γὰρ ἁρμόττει τῷ σαρκωθέντι θεῷ διὰ τὸ σῶμα [i.e. in Ascension], τοῦτο καὶ τοῖς θεωθησομένοις διὰ τὸν πλοῦτον τῆς χάριτος αὐτοῦ, θεοὺς τοὺς ἀνθρώπους ποιῆσαι φιλοτιμησαμένου θεοῦ Diad.*ascens.*6(M.65.1145D); τὴν ὑλικὴν τῶν ἀνθρώπων φύσιν...τῷ θεῷ καὶ πατρὶ προσαγαγὼν σωθεῖσαν, φιλωθεῖσάν τε καὶ θεωθεῖσαν Max.*ep.*12(M.91.468C); **c.** and H. Ghost εἰ μὴ θεὸς τὸ πνεῦμα τὸ ἅγιον, θεωθήτω πρῶτον, καὶ οὕτω θεούτω με τὸν ὁμότιμον Gr.Naz.*or.*34.12(M.36.252C); *ib.*31.28(p.181.12; 165A); τὸ πνεῦμα τὸ ἅγιον...θεοῦν, οὐ θεούμενον *ib.*41.9(441B); ‡Cyr.*Trin.*9 (6[3].13C; M.77.1140B); **3.** as effected by Christian life; **a.** in gen. ὑψοῦ βίῳ τὸ πλεῖον, ἢ φρονήματι· ὁ μὲν θεοῖ σε, τῷ δὲ καὶ πίπτεις μέγα Gr.Naz.*carm.*1.2.33.90(M.37.934A); ὅσοι καθάρσει σωμάτων θεούμενοι *ib.*1.2.10.630(725A); **b.** monastic or eremitical τίς ἀδελφῶν συμφυΐαν...τῶν ὑπὸ σοῦ [sc. Basil] θεουμένων; id.*ep.*6(M.37.29C); ὄλβιος, ὅστις ἔρημον ἔχει βίον, οὐδ' ἐπίμικτον τοῖς χαμαὶ ἐρχομένοις, ἀλλ' ἐθέωσε νόον id.*carm.*1.2.17.2(M.37.781A); **4.** as connected with various aspects of contemplative life εἰς δὲ τὴν ἀπάθειαν θεούμενος ἄνθρωπος Clem.*str.*4.23(p.315.26; M.8.1361A); ἡ τῆς ἐποψίας ἑστίασις, τρέφουσα νοητῶς καὶ θεοῦσα πάντα τὸν εἰς αὐτὴν ἀνατεινόμενον Dion. Ar.*e.h.*1.3(M.3.376A).

II. = θειόω, *consecrate, dedicate* χρῆσον...εἰς τὴν οἰκονομίαν τοῦ μυστηρίου τὸ οὖς καὶ πρὸς τὴν ἀκρόασιν θέωσον τὴν διάνοιαν Mac.Mgn. *apocr.*3.23(p.105.28).

θεραπεία, ἡ, A. *service, worship*; **1.** of God, its nature θ. ... τοῦ θεοῦ ἡ συνεχὴς ἐπιμέλεια τῆς ψυχῆς τῷ γνωστικῷ καὶ ἡ περὶ τὸ θεῖον αὐτοῦ κατὰ τὴν ἀδιάλειπτον ἀγάπην ἀσχολία Clem.*str.*7.1(p.4.13; M.9. 404C); βασιλικωτάτην θ. ..., τὴν διὰ τῆς θεοσεβοῦς γνώμης τε καὶ γνώσεως *ib.*7.7(p.32.15; 460B); its effects διὰ τὴν τοῦ ἀρίστου...θ. ... φίλον ὁμοῦ καὶ υἱὸν τὸν γνωστικὸν ἀπεργάζεται *ib.*7.11(p.49.7; 496A); αὐτοὶ ἀπὸ τῆς πρὸς τὸν θεὸν θ. ὠφελούμενοι καὶ ἄλυποι καὶ ἀπαθεῖς γινόμενοι Or.*Cels.*8.8(p.227.1; M.11.1529B); **2.** of creatures παρὰ τῶν ἀλόγως βιούντων αἰτοῦσι [sc. evil spirits]...θ. Just.*1apol.*12.5(M.6. 344A); θ. δαιμόνων ἐστὶν ἡ θ. τῶν νομιζομένων θεῶν Or.*Cels.*7.69(p.218. 27; M.11.1517D); of worship of images as irrational, *ib.*1.20(p.71. 17; 696B); **3.** of service of God in ascetic life, Thdt.*affect.*3(p.94. 25; 4.786); Dion.Ar.*e.h.*6.1.3(M.3.533A).

B. *religion, system of belief*, Or.*or.*28.9(p.381.4; M.11.529A); τοῦ Χριστιανισμοῦ...θ. Const.ap.Eus.*v.C.*2.24(p.51.8; M.20.1001B).

C. *healing*, **1.** *miraculous*; **a.** wrought by God through men, Clem.*ecl.*16(p.141.9; M.9.705B); οὐκ ὀλίγαι θ. τῷ Ἰησοῦ ὀνόματι... ἐπιτελοῦνται Or.*Cels.*3.28(p.225.15; M.11.956A); *ib.*3.33(p.229.29; 961C); οὐ θ. ... ἀνθρώπων ἐστὶν ἡ θ. ἀλλὰ μόνον τοῦ θεοῦ τοῦ ποιοῦντος Ath.*v.Anton.*56(M.26.925A); *ib.*58(928A); hence forbidden to glory in miraculous powers of healing, *ib.*37(897B); **b.** in apologetic, Or. *hom.*5.3 *in Jer.*(p.34.7; M.13.301A); id.*Jo.*6.33(17; p.142.24; M.14. 256D); miraculous cures inducing belief in God, *Hom.Clem.*27.2; *ib.*15.4; **2.** spiritual; **a.** by God rebuking men, cf.Is.30:1, Clem. *paed.*1.9(p.135.22; M.8.344A); warning them of consequences of sin, *ib.*1.10(p.143.17; 357B); of Logos healing all ills of the soul, Or.*Cels.* 8.72(p.289.6; M.11.1625A); Eus.*e.th.*3.15(p.172.26; M.24.1029B); **b.** by divine truth; Christian doctrine, Or.*Cels.*3.60(p.255.3; 1000C); ἐπὶ τὴν θ. τῆς ψυχῆς...τὰ γεγραμμένα...ἀλληγοροῦντος id.*Jo.*10.28(18; p.201.26; M.14.357C); **c.** by sacraments, ref. water and Spirit healing body and soul φάρμακα πρὸς θεραπείαν Gr.Nyss.*bapt.Chr.*(M.46. 581B); of eucharist φάρμακον ζωῆς...εἰς θ. παντὸς νοσήματος Serap. *euch.*13.15; **d.** by human means θ. παντὸς πάθους, μάθησίς τε τοῦ αἰτίου καὶ τοῦ πῶς ἂν ἐξαιρεθείη τοῦτο, καὶ...ἡ ἄσκησις τῆς ψυχῆς Clem.*str.*7.16(p.69.27; M.9.536C); Jo.Clim.*past.*2(M.88.1169A); **3.** ref. art of healing; medical art as pattern for spiritual healing, Bas. *reg.fus.*55(2.397C; M.31.1044C); of arts of corporal and spiritual healing ἀμφοτέρων τῶν θ. Gr.Naz.*or.*2.22(M.35.432A); **4.** *remedy*, sometimes prescribed by demons to obtain divine honours for themselves, *Hom.Clem.*9.14; met., of spiritual remedies, Or.*hom.* *14.1 in Jer.*(p.106.15; M.13.405A); Ath.*v.Anton.*56(M.26.925A); τὸν σταυρὸν...θ. τῆς κτίσεως id.*gent.*1(M.25.5A); of truth as remedy against error, Gr.Nyss.*or.catech.*proem.(p.2.11; M.45.10B); ἰατρὸς... ὢν [sc. bishop] τῆς ἐκκλησίας..., πρόσαγε θ. ἑκάστῳ τῶν νοσούντων *Const.App.*2.20.11.

D. *care*, Just.*1apol.*9.3(M.6.340B); Clem.*paed.*3.11(p.271.11; M.8. 637A).

θεραπευτέον, *one must treat medically*, met. διδάσκει...ὁ θεῖος νόμος πῶς θ. τοὺς τὰ μέτρια πλημμελήσαντας Thdt.*qu.*9 *in Num.*(1. 222).

θεραπευτής, ὁ, 1. *servant* or *worshipper of God*; **a.** of Christians in gen. θ. τοῦ θείου οἱ ἐλευθερικωτάτην καὶ βασιλικωτάτην θεραπείαν προσάγοντες, τὴν διὰ τῆς θεοσεβοῦς γνώμης τε καὶ γνώσεως Clem.*str.* 7.7(p.32.14; M.9.460A); Or.*Jo.*6.8(5; p.117.9; M.14.216A); τὸν θ. μου καὶ μάρτυρα Στέφανον id.*or.*6(p.315.17; M.11.440B); Eus.*v.C.*3.1(p.76. 13; M.20.1053A); **b.** ref. ascetic life, of Christians in the world πάλιν ἀγροὶ καὶ πάλιν ἐρημίαι τοὺς τοῦ θεοῦ θ. ὑπεδέχοντο Eus.*v.C.*2.2 (p.41.9; 980C); id.*l.C.*17(p.255.15; M.20.1432C); of monks οἱ μὲν θ., οἱ δὲ μοναχοὺς ὀνομάζοντες, ἐκ τῆς τοῦ θεοῦ καθαρᾶς ὑπηρεσίας καὶ θεραπείας Dion.Ar.*e.h.*6.1.3(M.3.532D); Γαΐῳ θ. id.*ep.*1(M.3.1065A); of Egyptian ascetics, described by Philo in *De Vita Contemplativa* θ. αὐτοὺς καὶ θεραπευτρίδας ἀποκαλεῖσθαί φησιν..., ἤτοι παρὰ τὸ τὰς ψυχὰς τῶν προσιόντων αὐτοῖς τῶν ἀπὸ κακίας παθῶν ἰατρῶν δίκην ἀπαλλάττοντας ἀκεῖσθαι καὶ θεραπεύειν, ἢ τῆς περὶ τὸ θεῖον καθαρᾶς καὶ εἰλικρινοῦς θεραπείας τε καὶ θρησκείας ἕνεκα Eus.*h.e.*2.17.3(M.20. 176A); cf. τῶν παρὰ Ἰουδαίοις φιλοσοφησάντων τήν τε θεωρητικὴν καὶ τὴν πρακτικὴν φιλοσοφίαν βίοι· ὧν οἱ μὲν Ἐσσηνοί, οἱ δὲ θ. ἐκαλοῦντο Phot.*cod.*104(M.103.372B); **2.** *one who attends to something* οἱ θ. τοῦ χρυσίου [i.e. goldsmiths] Gr.Nyss.*or.catech.*26(p.99.6; M.45.69A); **3.** *healer* ὁ ἰατρὸς...ἀνεπιστήμων ἐστὶ θ. πρὶν ἂν...μάθῃ τῶν νοσούντων τὸ θεραπεύειν Ast.Am.*hom.*9(M.40.301B); ἐφημίζετο γὰρ οὗτος παθῶν εἶναι θείᾳ δυνάμει θ. Philost.*h.e.*4.7(M.65.521A); of Christ Ἰησοῦς τοίνυν ἐστὶ κατὰ μὲν Ἑβραίους σωτήρ, κατὰ δὲ τὴν Ἑλλάδα γλῶσσαν, ὁ ἰώμενος, ἐπειδὴ ἰατρός ἐστι ψυχῶν καὶ σωμάτων, καὶ θ. πνευμάτων· τυφλῶν μὲν αἰσθητῶν θ. Cyr.H.*catech.*10.13; Epiph.*haer.*29.4(p.325. 23; M.41.397A).

θεραπευτικός, 1. *inclined to serve*; neut. as subst., of priesthood τὸ θ. τοῦ θεοῦ Or.*Jo.*1.2(3; p.5.19; M.14.25A); *servile*, of prayer τί προσάγεις τοὺς θ. ... λόγους τῷ πρὸς τὰ ἔργα βλέποντι; Gr.Nyss.*or.* *dom.*5(p.94.28; M.44.1180A); **2.** *healing*, *Hom.Clem.*9.18; met., of

Christ forgiving sins, Clem.*paed*.1.2(p.93.8; M.8.256A); Eus.*d.e*.4.4 (p.155.6; M.22.257D); Proc.G.*Is*.1:24–31(M.87.1861B); **3.** *medicinal*, met. ἐδεξάμην τὴν ἐπιστολὴν...ἐπιγράφουσαν, ἐγκύκλιος ἐπιστολή, ἤτοι θ. καὶ εὐθὺς...ἐξέστην Thdr.Stud.*epp*.2.162(M.99.1504D).

θεραπευτικῶς, **1.** *so as to serve*, Dion.Ar.*c.h*.7.1(M.3.205D); **2.** *curatively*, Mac.Aeg.*elev*.11(M.34.900A); Chrys.*hom.2.1 in 2Cor.*(10.429B).

θεραπευτός, *curable*, Eus.*h.e*.1.13.2(M.20.120B).

θεραπεύ-ω, **A.** *worship, serve*; **1.** God; **a.** of Christians worshipping God alone, Athenag.*leg*.16.3(M.6.921A); ἕνα...θεόν,...τὸν πατέρα καὶ τὸν υἱὸν ~ομεν Or.*Cels*.8.12(p.229.24; M.11.1533B); of Christ as God πιστεῦσαι ἔδει καὶ θ. Chrys.*hom.64.3 in Jo*.(8.386D); ref. Jo.16:7 πείθων...ἵνα αὐτὸ [sc. τὸ πνεῦμα] ~σωσιν *ib.78.3*(461D); **b.** ref. nature of worship οὐ...μιμεῖσθαί τις δυνήσεται τὸν θεὸν ἢ δι' ὧν ὁσίως ~ει οὐδ' αὖ ~ειν...ἢ μιμούμενος Clem.*prot*.11(p.82.22; M.8.236C); θεὸν...ὁ ~ων ἑαυτὸν ~ει id.*str*.4.23(p.315.30; M.8.1361A); οὐχ ὡς δεόμενον τὸν θεὸν ~ομεν...ἀλλ' ὡς αὐτοὶ ἀπὸ τῆς πρὸς τὸν θεὸν θεραπείας ὠφελούμενοι Or.*Cels*.8.9(p.226.31; 1529B); ἐλέῳ θεὸς ~εται Gr.Naz.*or*.14.15(M.35.864B); ἔδωκέ σοι βίου προθεσμίαν ὁ θεὸς εἰς τὸ θ. αὐτόν Chrys.*hom.58.5 in Jo*.(8.343A); **2.** creatures; of worship of demons, Or.*Cels*.8.13(p.230.5ff.; M.11.1533C); ref. a statue of Christ τὰ πρέποντα ἐθεράπευον, σέβοντες μὲν ἢ προσκυνοῦντες οὐδαμῶς Philost.*h.e*.7.3(M.65.540A); **3.** met., of time-serving καιροὺς ~ομεν Chrys.*hom.10.3 in 1Tim*.(11.602E); **4.** *suit, please* ἂν ~ηται τὸ κράτος σου Thphn.*chron*.p.156(M.108.424A); **5.** *grant* τὴν ἀξίωσιν ἐθεράπευε Thphyl.*exc.gent*.15(p.488.23; M.113.952B).

B. *heal*; **1.** physical ills; of God curing those sick from diabolical causes, Tat.*orat*.16(p.18.11; M.6.841B); of Christ's cures prophesied in Is.35:5–6, Or.*Cels*.2.45(p.169.19; M.11.869C); ref. cures by Christ as proving his divinity, Quad.ap.Eus.*h.e*.4.3.2(M.20.308B); Or.*Cels*.2.45(p.169.19; M.11.869C); τίς ἀνθρώπων τοιαύτας νόσους ἐθεράπευσεν, οἵας ὁ...κύριος; Ath.*inc*.49.1(M.25.184B); of God healing men through saints, *Hom.Clem*.7.1; Ath.*v.Anton*.14(M.26.865A); *ib*.56(925A); οὐ προστάττων...ἐθεράπευεν ὁ Ἀντώνιος, ἀλλ' εὐχόμενος καὶ τὸν Χριστὸν ὀνομάζων *ib*.84(961A); ref. evil spirits οὐ θ. οἱ δαίμονες, τέχνῃ δὲ τοὺς ἀνθρώπους αἰχμαλωτεύουσι Tat.*orat*.18(p.20.14; M.6.845B); ref. cures by Aesculapius as diabolical imitation of prophecies about Christ's cures, Just.*dial*.69.3(M.6.637A); of evil spirits claiming credit for cures due to natural causes, Athenag.*leg*.27.2(M.6.953A); *Hom.Clem*.16.9; **2.** of spiritual healing; by God, Clem.*paed*.1.8(p.128.4; M.8.328B); Or.*Cels*.8.72(p.289.5; M.11.1625A); id.*engast*.6(p.289.24; M.12.1021B); παρεδόθη...αὐτῷ [sc. Christ]...θεραπεῦσαι τὸ δῆγμα τοῦ ὄφεως Ath.*hom.in Mt.11:27*(M.25.212A); cf.id.*inc*.44.2(M.25.173B); of Christ's desire to heal souls, Dion.Ar.*ep*.8.1(M.3.1088A); of healing of ignorance and error by divine truth; through scripture, Clem.*prot*.8(p.59.14; M.8.188A); prophets πέμπων [sc. ὁ θεός] τοὺς ~οντας, μέχρις οὗ ἔλθῃ ὁ ἀρχιατρός Or.*hom.18.5 in Jer*.(p.156.15; M.13.472C); Christianity, id.*Cels*.3.48(p.245.7; 984B); *ib*.3.54(p.250.9; 992C); orthodox faith, Const.ap.Gel.Cyz.*h.e*.3.19.7(M.85.1345D); *Const.App*.2.20.3; of the soul through baptism, *Hom.Clem*.7.8; pastoral care, esp. of bishops, Meth.*lepr*.6(p.459.25); *Const.App*.2.18.7; love, Meth.*symp*.10.5(p.128.4; M.18.201B); repentance, Gr.Nyss.*ep.can*.8(M.45.236B); Thdt.*Ps*.50:2(1.933); different remedies needed for different wounds of the soul, Or.*hom.2.2 in Jer*.(p.18.22ff.; M.13.280B); *Const.App*.2.41.5; **3.** met.; **a.** of correction; of material things, Meth.*res*.1.43(p.290.5); intellectual θ. τὸ ἀπὸ Κέλσου τραῦμα Or.*Cels*.5.1(p.1.10; M.11.1181A); Ath.*ep.Serap*.1.20(M.26.577B); ὁ...Μελέτιος τὰ...πρῶτα...~ων τὸ ἑτεροούσιον ὑπεκρίνετο Philost.*h.e*.5.1(M.65.529A); Thdt.*1Cor*.8:6(3.215); moral, Ath.*apol.sec*.34(p.112.18; M.25.305A); *ib*.33(p.111.32; 304B); Thdt.*Jer*.38:17–18(2.569); **b.** of reconciliation, *Apophth.Patr*.(M.65.100C); **c.** of restitution τὰς ζημίας...θεραπεῦσαι Ath.Scholast.*coll*.4.13(p.57); Phot.*nomoc*.2.1(M.104.576); **d.** of smoothing out a difficulty in scripture, Just.*dial*.57.3(M.6.605A).

C. *apply a remedy to*, met.; **a.** the soul, Chrys.*hom.68.3 in Jo*.(8.408A); **b.** of treating gently, consoling, *T.Jos*.7.2; Bas.*ep*.228(3.351C; M.32.856B); Chrys.*hom.4.2 in Phil*.(11.221D); Thdt.*Ezech*.9:8(2.740); **c.** of mitigating νεφέλης τὴν ὕπαιθρον ἀηδίαν ~ούσης Gr.Nyss.*v.Mos*.44(M.44.313D); Thdt.*provid*.8(4.611).

D. *care for, look after* οὐ...μικρὸν δύναται τὸ θ. ἁγίους,...κοινωνοὺς γὰρ ἡμᾶς ποιεῖ τῶν ἐκείνοις ἀποκειμένων μισθῶν Chrys.*hom.1.2 in Phil*.(11.196D).

θεράπων, **ὁ**, *servant, worshipper*; of Moses, ref. Num.12:7, Heb.3:5 ὁ θ. Or.*fr.7 in Jo*.(p.538.14); id.*Jo*.20.36(29; p.377.2; M.14.660A); ἦν πρᾶος σφόδρα, καὶ ὑπὲρ τούτου λέγεται θ. θεοῦ Dion.Ar.*ep*.8.1(M.3.1085A); of Christians τοῦ Χριστοῦ...θ. Const.ap.Eus.*v.C*.4.42(p.134.6; M.20.1189C); Ath.*Ar*.3.57(M.26.444A); of orthodox opp. heretics, id.*h.Ar*.79(p.227.21; M.25.789A); of the saints θεράποντες ...τοῦ θείου οἱ...θεραπείαν προσάγοντες, τὴν διὰ τῆς θεοσεβοῦς γνώμης Clem.*str*.7.7(p.32.14; M.9.460A); Ath.*Ar*.2.53(260C); esp. of Const. ἐμὲ τὸν θεοῦ θ. Const.ap.Ath.*apol.sec*.86(p.165.24; M.25.404C) al.; Ath.*apol.Const*.12(M.25.609B).

***θεραφίμ**, **τό**, *teraphim* τὸ...θ. ... οὐ θεϊκὸν δέ, ἀλλ' εἰδωλικόν Or.*sel.in Jud*.17:5(M.12.949C); Thdt.*qu.24 in Jud*.(1.341); διὰ τοῦ θ. αἱ τῶν εἰδώλων ἐδηλοῦντο προρρήσεις id.*qu.33 in 1Reg*.(1.378).

θερειγενής, *that comes with summer*, Paul.Sil.*Soph*.316(M.86.2132A).

θερίζ-ω, **1.** *reap*; **a.** ref. Manich. theory of transmigration of souls μεταγγίζεται ἡ ψυχὴ...ἐὰν...θερίσασα...εἰς μογγιλάλους. ... οἱ δὲ θερισταί, ὅσοι ~ουσιν, ἐοίκασι τοῖς ἄρχουσι τοῖς ἀπ' ἀρχῆς οὖσιν εἰς τὸ σκότος, ὅτε ἔφαγον ἐκ τῆς τοῦ πρώτου ἀνθρώπου πανοπλίας Hegem.*Arch*.10(p.15.6ff.; M.10.1441C); **b.** met., ref. Jo.4:35 οὐκ αὐτοὶ [sc. οἱ προφῆται] ἐθέρισαν, ἀλλ' οἱ ἀπόστολοι Chrys.*hom.34.2 in Jo*.(8.197D); **2.** *cut off*, met., ref. apostles' preaching θ. ... ἐκ νομικῆς λατρείας τοὺς ἔτι νόμῳ δουλεύοντας Cyr.*Jo*.2.5(4.199E).

θερισμός, **ὁ**, **1.** *harvest*, met. οὐδενός ἐστι συνάγειν...πάντα ἀπὸ τοῦ θ. ... εἰ μὴ...Ἰησοῦ Χριστοῦ Or.*hom.15.3 in Jer*.(p.127.23; M.13.432B); **2.** ? *cutting-off, destruction*, as name of the death-principle in Manich. system ὁ θ. ἄρχων Hegem.*Arch*.9(p.14.10, vv.ll. θερισμοῦ, θεριστής; M.10.1441B).

θεριστής, **ὁ**, *reaper*, ref. Manich. theory that a man's soul will enter after death into crops of the kind he reaped, Hegem.*Arch*.10(p.15.11; M.10.1441C).

θέριστρον, **τό**, **1.** *light summer garment*, †Bas.*Is*.129(1.469C; M.30.328B); **2.** *veil* τὸ θ., συγκαλύπτον μετὰ τῆς κεφαλῆς καὶ τὸ πρόσωπον Gr.Nyss.*hom.13 in Cant*.(M.44.1029B); Ph.Carp.*Cant*.140(M.40.105C); Nil.ap.Proc.G.*Cant*.5:4(M.87.1684B).

[*]**θέρμα**, **τά**, *lupins*, Gr.Naz.*carm*.1.2.10.550(M.37.720A); Jo.Mosch.*prat*.134(M.87.2997C).

θερμαίν-ω, **1.** *heat*; **2.** *be fervent, fiery*, of Hebr. *seraphim* as signifying ~οντες, Dion.Ar.*c.h*.7.1(M.3.205B); id.*e.h*.4.3.10(M.3.481C); ~οντες ὀνομάζονται καὶ θρόνοι *ib*.

[*]**θερμανσία**, **ἡ**, v. θερμασία.

θερμαντήρ, **ὁ**, *pot* or *kettle for boiling water*, Thdt.*qu.34 in 3Reg*.(1.472).

θερμασία, **ἡ**, *heat*; **1.** lit. (θερμανσία), Melet.*nat.hom*.30(M.64.1281A); **2.** met., of passion, Cyr.*Os*.76(3.111A).

θέρμη, **ἡ**, *fervour* ἡ...θ. τῆς ἀγάπης τοῦ θεοῦ Diad.*perf*.15(p.18.10); *ib*.58(p.64.22); ἡ κατὰ θεὸν θ. Ammon.*ep*.2(p.437.9); θ. εἰς τὸ μοναχικόν Jo.Mosch.*prat*.105(M.87.2961D); Jo.Clim.*past*.13(M.88.1193D).

***θερμήλατος**, *beaten, hammered*; of metal, Jo.Mal.*chron*.10 p.239 (M.97.368B).

θερμίζω, *take treatment at hot springs*, Thphn.*chron*.p.158(M.108.428B).

θέρμιον, **τό**, *lupin*, Cosm.Ind.*top*.2(M.88.100B,C); Jo.Mosch.*prat*.127(M.87.2992A); Leont.N.*v.Sym*.31(M.93.1709A).

***θερμόβλυστος**, *bubbling out hot*, ‡Paul.Sil.*therm.Pyth*.33(M.86.2263).

***θερμοδοτέω**, *act as* θερμοδότης, Leont.N.*v.Sym*.33(M.93.1712A).

θερμοδότης, **ὁ**, *servant who brings hot water* or perh. *hot drinks*, Leont.N.*v.Jo.Eleem*.6(p.5.6); cf.id.*v.Sym*.33(M.93.1712A).

***θερμοπνοέω**, *be ardent*, Thphn.*chron*.p.394(M.108.940B).

θερμός, **1.** *hot*; of hot water allowed for baptism if cold unavailable, *Did*.7.2; **2.** met., *ardent, intense* θ. περὶ τὴν εὐσέβειαν Didym.(‡Bas.)*Eun*.4(1.290A; M.29.696C); θ. ἐραστὴν τῆς...αἱρέσεως Philost.*h.e*.8.3(M.65.557A); ἡ πίστις θ. Chrys.*hom.80.2 in Mt*.(7.768C); *ib.26.1*(313C); as subst., of fervour of seraphim implied in their name, Dion.Ar.*c.h*.7.1(M.3.205B).

θερμότης, **ἡ**, *fervour*, Chrys.*hom.25.1 in Mt*.(7.307D); ἡ θ. τῆς ἀγάπης id.*hom.9.3 in Eph*.(11.72A); in seraphim, Dion.Ar.*c.h*.7.1(M.3.205C); in monks, cooled by example of the lukewarm, Ammonas *ep*.3(p.440.3); of false fervour in the self-willed, *ib*.5.3(p.448.5); θ. τῆς πίστεως Philox.*ep*.34(p.181); *ib*.22(p.173); τῆς τῶν ἁγίων χάριτος...τῆς...θ. Sophr.H.*mir.Cyr.et Jo*.45(M.87.3593C).

***θερμωτικός**, *heating*, Anast.S.*qu.et resp*.96(M.89.749A).

θέσις, **ἡ**, **A.** *laying down, disposition*; **1.** *arrangement, constitution* of man οὐδὲ τὸ δίκαιον ἐκ μόνης φαίνεσθαι τῆς θ. ῥητέον, ἐκ δὲ τῆς ἐντολῆς Clem.*str*.1.6(p.23.3; M.8.729A); physical *frame* or *structure*, Geo.Pis.*carm*.1.21; *ib*.1.56; id.*hex*.630(M.92.1485A); τὴν...τῶν πτερῶν ἑξαπλῆν θ. [i.e. of seraphim] Dion.Ar.*e.h*.4.3.7(M.3.481A); met., ref. apostles as pillars ἀκίνητοι τῇ θ. τῆς πίστεως Const.ap.

Gel.Cyz.h.e.2.7.3(M.85.1232D); *plan of a church*, Marc.Diac.v.Porph. 75; **2.** *decree, ordinance* τὴν κυριακὴν θ. Const.App.2.44.2; in etym. of θεός: ἔστι...διαθήκη ἣν ὁ...θεὸς τίθεται, θεὸς δὲ παρὰ τὴν θ. εἴρηται, καὶ τάξιν Clem.str.1.29(p.112.2; M.8.929A); τῆς τοῦ σαββάτου φυλακῆς οὐχ ἡ φύσις διδάσκαλος, ἀλλ' ἡ θ. τοῦ νόμου Thdt.Ezech.20:13(2.826); esp. θέσει, κατὰ θέσιν (opp. φύσει, κατὰ φύσιν) *by decree, at will, arbitrarily; accidentally*, always = *not essentially*, ref. view of Simon Magus μηδὲν...εἶναι αἴτιον δίκης εἰ πράξει τις κακῶς, οὐ γάρ ἐστι φύσει κακός, ἀλλὰ θ. Iren.haer.1.23.3(cf.M.7.672B); κατὰ φύσιν ἐστὶν ὁ θεὸς ἀγαθός, ᾧ μηδὲν ἐπισυμβαίνει κακόν, κατὰ δὲ θ. ἄνθρωπος λέγεται ἀγαθός Adam.dial.3.9(p.126.27; M.11.1800C); ἥλιος...τῆς θερμῆς ὑπάρχων οὐσίας, τῇ θ. πυρὸς διαφέρει Tit.Bost.Man.2.31(M.18.1193D); ref. Inc. εἰ θ. ἦν ἐν τῷ σώματι ὁ λόγος,...τὸ δὲ θ. λεγόμενον φαντασία ἐστί, δοκήσει εὑρίσκεται καὶ ἡ σωτηρία...τῶν ἀνθρώπων...κατὰ τὸν...Μανιχαῖον Ath.ep.Epict.7(p.11.9; M.26.1061A); ib.2(p.4.14; 1053A); ref. Pr.8:22 εἰ...ἡμεῖς κατὰ φύσιν ἐσμὲν υἱοί, ἔσται καὶ αὐτὸς κατὰ φύσιν κτίσμα...εἰ δὲ ἡμεῖς θ. ... πρὸς υἱότητα καλούμεθα, καὶ αὐτὸς θέσει κτίσμα διὰ τὴν...οἰκονομίαν, τὸ ἐκ φύσεως οὐκ ἀπολλύων ἀξίωμα Cyr.thes.15(5^1.165D); ref. H. Ghost ἀγαθόν, εὐθές, ἡγεμονικόν, φύσει οὐ θ. Gr.Naz.or.31.29(p.183.9; M.36.165C); ἔστιν...ἅπασι τοῖς φωτιζομένοις ἀρχὴ τοῦ φωτίζεσθαι θεὸς μὲν φύσει,...θ. δὲ ...ἡ κατὰ μέρος ὑπερκειμένη [sc. οὐσία] τῇ μετ' αὐτὴν ἑκάστῃ Dion. Ar.c.h.13.3(M.3.301D); **3.** *affirmation, attribution*, Trin., ref. divine names ὡς...ἐπ' ἐκείνων ἀθέτησίν τινα...τῶν ἀλλοτρίων τοῦ θεοῦ ἐσήμαινον αἱ φωναί, οὕτως ἐνταῦθα θ. καὶ ὕπαρξιν τῶν οἰκείων τῷ θεῷ ...ἀποσημαίνουσιν Bas.Eun.1.10(1.223A; M.29.536B); ref. predication of ἀγέννητος and γέννητος of Father and Son ποῖον τῶν εἰρημένων θ. τινὸς νοήματος καὶ ποῖον τὴν τοῦ τεθέντος ἀναίρεσιν ἐνδείκνυται Gr. Nyss.Eun.1(1 p.203.22; M.45.452A); Didym.(‡Bas.)Eun.4(1.281D; M.29.677B); ref. names Father, Son, Spirit τὰ δ' ἄλλα πάντα θέσει ἢ κλήσει, οὐχ ὅμοια τούτοις ἐνεργείᾳ Epiph.anc.71(p.88.21; M.43. 148B); ἡ πάντων θ. ἡ πάντων ἀφαίρεσις, τὸ ὑπὲρ πᾶσαν καὶ θ. καὶ ἀφαίρεσιν Dion.Ar.d.n.2.4(M.3.641A); **4.** *adoption*; of divine adoption of men, Clem.str.2.17(p.153.17; M.8.1016A); ref. Jo.1:12 τὸ... γενέσθαι, διὰ τὸ μὴ φύσει, ἀλλὰ θ. αὐτοὺς λέγεσθαι υἱούς φησι Ath. Ar.2.59(M.26.272C); κατὰ θέσιν τὴν υἱοθεσίαν λαμβάνεις Cyr.H.catech. 3.14; ref. 1Cor.8:5f. τὸν μὲν οὐσίᾳ θεόν,...τοὺς δὲ τῇ θ. θεούς Mac. Mgn.apocr.4.26(p.211.11); ref. means by which adoption is effected θ. καὶ χάριτι υἱοποιούμεθα δι' αὐτοῦ [sc. τοῦ λόγου], μετέχοντες τοῦ πνεύματος αὐτοῦ Ath.Ar.3.19(M.26.364C); ‡Bas.h.myst.62(p.397.21); through faith in Christ, Cyr.Jo.1(4.91E); through Inc., Jo.Mon. hymn.Geo.6(M.96.1397C); denied of Son, Alex.Al.ep.Alex.(p.24.9; M.18.557C); υἱὸς...τοῦ θεοῦ ἐστι φύσει, καὶ οὐ θ. Cyr.H.catech.11.7; Gr.Nyss.Eun.4(2 p.79.14; M.45.653B); Epiph.anc.71(p.89.6; M.43. 149A); asserted by Arius, Const.ap.Gel.Cyz.h.e.3.19.26(M.85.1352B); Ath.Dion.23(p.63.1; M.25.513A); by Eunomius, Didym.(‡Bas.)Eun. 5(1.314A; M.29.753A); by Marcellus, Acac.Caes.fr.Marcell.ap. Epiph.haer.72.9(p.263.24; M.42.393D); Christol., bearing of divine adoption of men οὐκ ἂν...εἴη τὸ κατὰ θ. καὶ ὁμοίωσιν, μὴ προϋποκειμένου πρότερον τοῦ ἀληθοῦς Cyr.thes.32(5^1.309B); of diabolical adoption; ref. Jo.8:44 as interpreted by Heracleon ταῦτα εἴρηται...πρὸς τοὺς φυσικούς, θέσει υἱοὺς διαβόλου γενομένους, ἀφ' ὧν τῇ φύσει δύνανταί τινες καὶ θ. υἱοὶ θεοῦ χρηματίσαι Or.Jo.20.24(20; p.359.4; M.14.628D); Epiph.anc.72(p.90.19; M.43.152B); **5.** *punctuation, stop* at the end of verse of psalm, Marc.Diac.v.Porph.77; plur., Isid.H.etym.1. 20.1.

B. *that in which something is laid, receptacle*, tombs αἱ...τῶν σωμάτων θ. Gr.Nyss.anim.et res.(M.46.88B); IGC As.Min.12.

θέσκελος, **1.** *divine*; of Christ, Nonn.par.Jo.19:7(M.43.900A); ib. 3:13(768A); θ. ἄρτος ib.6:23(797B); διδάγματα θ. ib.8:20(816B); **2.** *God-inspired*; of Elijah, ib.1:21(753A).

θέσμιος, *of judgement* θ. αὐλή Nonn.par.Jo.18:33(M.43.896B).

***θεσμογράφος**, ὁ, *lawgiver*, †Apoll.met.Ps.9:21(M.33.1324A).

***θεσμοδοσία**, ἡ, *ordinance*, Didym.Trin.1.27(M.39.401C).

***θεσμοδοτέω**, *command, order*, Procl.CP annunt.1(M.85.428C).

θεσμοθεσία, ἡ, *ordinance, law*, Dion.Ar.c.h.4.3(M.3.180D); ib.4.4 (181C); τὴν...τῆς καθ' ἡμᾶς ἱεραρχικῆς παραδόσεως θ. ib.2.5(145C); Const.VI Imp.sacr.(H.4.38A); Thdr.Stud.epp.1.14(M.99.957A).

θεσμοθετέω, *legislate, ordain*, Const.or.s.c.6(p.159.15; M.20.1245B) cit. s. θεσμός, Didym.Trin.2.13(M.39.689C); θεὸς ἐθεσμοθέτει διὰ Μωυσέως Cyr.Am.36(3.290B); ἱερωσύνη ἐθεσμοθετήθη Isid.Pel.epp.3. 249(M.78.928C); of Christ ἀνάστασιν θεσμοθετήσας Lit.Jac.(NBP 10^2 p.106).

***θεσμοθέτημα**, τό, *ordinance*, Jo.D.hom.9.2(M.96.725C).

***θεσμοθέτησις**, ἡ, *legislation*, Didym.Trin.2.27(M.39.768B).

θεσμός, ὁ, *law*; **1.** of natural law, in gen. οἱ...τῆς φύσεως...θ. Meth.symp.3.2(p.29.11; M.18.64B); Const.App.6.14.4; ref. Christ ἀγνοοῦμεν...ὅπως ἐκ παρθενικῶν αἱμάτων ἑτέρῳ παρὰ τὴν φύσιν θεσμῷ διεπλάττετο Dion.Ar.d.n.2.9(M.3.648A); exeg. Pr.6:20 τοὺς τεθέντας ἐν τῇ φύσει τῶν ὅλων παρὰ τῆς πάντων αἰτίας σοφίας λόγους ‡Proc.G.Pr.6:20(M.87.1276A); esp. ref. providence, T.Neph.8.10; Const.ap.Eus.v.C.2.58(p.64.26, v.l. καιρόν M.20.1032C); of law that a higher order of beings enlightens a lower, Dion.Ar.c.h.4.3(M.3. 181A); of providential laws as not fated τὸ λέγειν εἱμαρμένον τινὰ θ. εἶναι δηλοῖ ὅτι θ. πᾶς ἔργον ἔστι τοῦ θεσμοθετήσαντος. ἡ τοίνυν [ἡ] εἱμαρμένη, εἴπερ ἐστὶ θ., θεοῦ ἂν εὕρημα εἴη Const.or.s.c.6(p.159.15; M.20.1245B); **2.** of revealed law, Clem.str.1.26(p.104.14; M.8.916A); of Word as rule of human actions νόμος ὢν ὄντως καὶ θ. ib.7.3(p.12. 18; M.9.421A); in Christianity οἱ περὶ ὁμολογίας καὶ ἀρνήσεως τοῦ σωτῆρος ἡμῶν θ. Eus.h.e.8.9.8(M.20.761B); ref. heret. and simoniacal ordination, Ath.ep.encycl.2(p.171.19; M.25.228A); ref. the orders of bishop, priest, and deacon εἰ μὴ...θ. τις ἦν καὶ τάξεων διαφορά, ἤρκει ἂν δι' ἑνὸς ὀνόματος τὰ ὅλα τελεῖσθαι Const.App.8.46.10; **3.** of law as promulgated or followed by the Church; **a.** in matters of doctrine οὐδὲ...ζητεῖν...εἰ ἦν καὶ προῆν ὁ μονογενὴς υἱὸς τοῦ θεοῦ, ὁ τῆς ἐκκλησίας ἐπιτρέποι ἂν θ. Eus.Marcell.1.1(p.4.28; M.24.720A); of orthodoxy ὁ παλαιὸς τῆς ἐκκλησίας θ. CArim.ep.Const.1(p.237. 29; M.26.697B); τὸν Πέτρου θρόνον μὴ ἀδοξεῖν, ὑπὸ δύο ἡγεμόσιν ἰθυνόμενον· ὁ...ἐστι...ἐκκλησιαστικοῦ θ. ἀλλότριον Soz.h.e.4.15.6(M. 67.1153A); ref. custom of using symbols to guard doctrines from the profane, Dion.Ar.e.h.1.5(M.3.376D); ref. worship of images οὐ... εὐσεβῶν βασιλέων ἀνατρέπειν ἐκκλησιαστικοὺς θ. Jo.D.imag.1(M.94. 1281A); **b.** in morals, Eus.h.e.8.18(M.20.741C); φυλάξωμεν καθαροὺς ἑαυτοὺς τῷ θεῷ—ταῦτα γὰρ κανόνες εἰσὶν καὶ θ. τῆς ἐκκλησίας Meth. lepr.9(p.462.10); εἰρήνην κατὰ τὸν τῆς ἐκκλησίας θ. ... φυλάττειν Constantius Imp.ap.Ath.apol.sec.55(p.135.26; M.25.348D); **c.** liturg., Eus.v.C.4.74(p.147.14; M.20.1225C); Ath.apol.sec.11(p.97.1; M.25. 268D); Bas.Spir.66(3.54D; M.32.188A); Mac.Aeg.carit.29(M.34.932C); ref. sitting for the Gospel καὶ ἄλλα τινὰ ὧν μὴ θεῖος θ. ἐπεστάτει Philost.h.e.3.5(M.65.485B); ref. diptychs, etc. τούτων...καθ' ὃν εἴρηται θ. ἱερουργηθέντων Dion.Ar.e.h.3.3.10(M.3.437D); of funeral rites τὸ κατὰ θεσμόν ib.7.1.3(556B).

***θεσμοτόκος**, ὁ, *legislator*; of Moses, Nonn.par.Jo.9.28(M.43. 829B).

***θεσμοφορέω**, *worship at the* θεσμοφόρια (women's festival in honour of Demeter), Clem.prot.2(p.15.9; M.8.81A).

θεσμοφόρος, *law-giving*; of the prophets, Nonn.par.Jo.7:41(M. 43.812B).

θεσμῳδέω, *speak with authority*, Meth.symp.8.7(p.89.9; M.18. 149A).

θεσπέσιος, *divine, holy*; **1.** of that which pertains to God; divine light in the soul, Didym.Trin.2.4(M.39.435A); cf.†Apoll. met.Ps.118:80(M.33.1497D); God's mercy, ib.118:41(1496B); law, ib. 118:93(1500B); **2.** of inspired men: Moses, Clem.prot.8(p.61.20; M. 8.192B); prophets, Ath.hom.in Mt.11:27(M.25.217D); Jo. Bapt., Cyr.Os.4(3.20E); evangelists, Eus.d.e.1.1(p.3.27; M.22.17A); ‡Ath. Ar.4.31(p.80.12; M.26.516C); Dion.Ar.e.h.3.3.4(M.3.429D); apostles, Clem.prot.1(p.7.21; 61B); Eus.h.e.3.24.3(M.20.264B); Cyr.Lc.9:27(M. 72.653C); fathers, MAMA 1.412; τοῦ θ. Βασιλείου Lit.Jac.(p.178.25); with teachers and ascetics, Thdr.Stud.ap.Proem.in Dor.doct.(M. 88.1612A); **3.** of Christ's tomb, Eus.v.C.3.26(p.89.20; M.20.1085B); ib.3.33(p.93.19; 1096A).

θεσπίζ-ω, **A.** *prophesy*; **1.** of predicting future events; **a.** in gen., by prophets, Or.fr.38 in Jer.(p.218.5; M.13.601C); Δανιὴλ ...ὁ θεσπίσας τὰ μέλλοντα Const.or.s.c.17(p.177.23; M.20.1284A); Eus.p.e.11.7(520B; M.21.864C); **b.** through grace of H. Ghost, Just.dial.7.1(M.6.492A); δι' ἐνθέου πνεύματος ~οντες Eus.v.C.3. 33(p.93.16; M.20.1093B); id.p.e.11.7(520B; M.21.864C); **c.** of Christ as foretold in OT ὁ ~όμενος Clem.str.5.8(p.363.22; M.9.85C); ref. Is.7:9 ἐὰν μὴ πιστεύσητε τῷ...ὑπὸ νόμου θεσπισθέντι, οὐ συνήσετε τὴν διαθήκην τὴν παλαιάν ib.4.21(p.308.2; M.8.1345A); Or.Jo.22.15(9; p.450.10; M.14.780C); Thdt.eran.1(4.36); **d.** of other prophecies; by Sibyl, Clem.prot.6(p.54.10; M.8.177A); of soul in sleep καθ' ἑαυτὴν ἐν τοῖς ὀνείροις ἐνεργεῖν, ~ουσαν τὸ μέλλον Nemes.nat.hom.3(M.40. 596B); **e.** ref. predestination ὁ μὲν Κέλσος οἴεται διὰ τοῦτο γίνεσθαι τὸ ὑπό τινος προγνώσεως θεσπισθέν, ἐπεὶ ἐθεσπίσθη· ἡμεῖς δὲ...φαμὲν οὐχὶ τὸν θεσπίσαντα αἴτιον εἶναι τοῦ ἐσομένου, ἐπεὶ προεῖπεν αὐτὸ γενησόμενον, ἀλλὰ τὸ ἐσόμενον ἂν καὶ μὴ θεσπισθέν, τὴν αἰτίαν τῷ προγινώσκοντι παρεσχηκέναι τοῦ αὐτὸ προειπεῖν Or.Cels.2.20(p.148. 20; M.11.836B); **2.** of uttering a divine message irrespective of prediction; ref. Law and Prophets, Clem.str.5.6(p.346.28; M.9. 56B); of Moses recording God's promise to Abraham, Eus.d.e.1.2

(p.9.9; M.22.25B); coupled with previous sense τὰ λόγια...τὰ παρ' ἡμῖν θ. περί τε τῶν ὄντων ὡς ἔστι, περί τε τῶν μελλόντων ὡς ἔσται, περί τε τῶν γεγονότων ὡς ἐγένετο Clem.*str*.5.9(p.471.2; M.9.300A); Or.*Cels*.7.9(p.161.5; M.11.1433A); μεγάλης βουλῆς ἄγγελον φωτός τε ἀπαύγασμα πατρικοῦ μονογενῆ τε υἱόν...θ. ... θεολόγων φωναί Eus. *l.C*.3(p.202.4; M.20.1332B).

B. *decree*; **1.** of God; **a.** in establishing natural law, Athenag. *res*.23(p.76.11; M.6.1017D); θερμότητα καὶ ψυχρότητα, ἐκ τῆς αὐτῆς ...ῥίζης διηθεῖσθαι θ. Const.*or.s.c*.7(p.161.31; M.20.1252A); **b.** in OT, Didym.*Trin*.3.2(M.39.800A); Isid.Pel.*epp*.1.196(M.78.308D); **c.** under new covenant ἐπικρατήσαντος σχεδὸν ἐν ταῖς πάντων ψυχαῖς τοῦ θεσπισθέντος ὑπὸ τοῦ σωτῆρος νόμου Const.*or.s.c*.16(p.176.25; 1280C); ὁ θεσπίσας συμμνημονεύεσθαι αὐτὸ [sc. τὸ πνεῦμα] ἐν τῇ τοῦ βαπτίσματος ἀναγεννήσει Didym.*Trin*.2.8(616A); cf.*ib*.2.1(448C); Chrys.*hom.72.1 in Mt*.(7.701D); id.*hom.12.6 in Col*.(11.421A); ὁ... τοῦ θεοῦ νόμος ἐλεήμονας εἶναι ἡμᾶς ~εται Gr.Agr.*Eccl*.5.4(M.98.964B); **2.** eccl.; **a.** ref. decrees of apostles on ritual observances and morality, Ammon.*Ac*.16:4(M.85.1556A); τοῖς θεολόγοις τεθέσπισται, μονάδα...ἡμᾶς φρονεῖν μιᾷ καὶ ἑνιαίᾳ θεότητι Sophr.H.*ep.syn*.(M.87.3153D); **b.** *give instruction* in church, Jo.Eleem.*v.Tych*.39 (p.150).

C. *declare*; ref. apostles ἐθέσπισαν ἐκκλησίαν Χριστοῦ...πάντας τοὺς πιστεύοντας εἰς τὸ ὄνομα τοῦ πατρός *A.Petr.et Andr*.23(p.127.4); διὰ τὰς προσβολὰς τῶν...'Ιουδαίων, οὐκ ἠδυνήθησαν τὴν ἀκολουθίαν πάσης τῆς ἐκκλησίας...κατὰ τάξιν...θεσπίσαι Jo.Nic.*nativ*.(M.96.1440B); Sophr.H.*mir.Cyr.et Jo*.33(M.87.3532B); iron., *lay down the law*, Or. *Cels*.3.33(p.230.15; M.11.964A); Max.*ambig*.(M.91.1089C).

D. *declare evil, speak ill of* πᾶς ὃς ἐὰν θ. πάντα ἄνθρωπον δουλεύσαντα τῷ πατρί μου...ἐβλασφήμισεν εἰς τὸ πνεῦμα τὸ ἅγιον *Ev.Barth*. (Vassiliev p.22).

θέσπις, **1.** *inspired*, Nonn.*par.Jo*.13:18(M.43.864A); *ib*.1:23(753B); **2.** *divine* θ. βουλή *ib*.4:20(777A); of Christ θ. μορφή *ib*.14:18(869B); θ. φωνή *ib*.5:15(788A).

θέσπισμα, τό, **1.** *oracle*; **a.** of prophetic teaching τῶν παλαιῶν προφητῶν τὰ θ. ... ἅπερ χρὴ περὶ τοῦ θείου φρονεῖν, ἐκπαιδεύουσι Const.ap.Gel.Cyz.*h.e*.2.7.41(M.85.1241B); of scripture in gen. τὰ... θεῖα θ. Isid.Pel.*epp*.2.208(M.78.649A); *ib*.5.126(1397C); τοῦ νόμου καὶ τῶν προφητῶν θεῖα θ. Max.*ambig*.(M.91.1152B); **b.** of scriptural prediction of future τοῦτο Μωυσέως ἦν αὐτοῦ καὶ τῶν μετέπειτα προφητῶν θ., μὴ πρότερον ἐκλιπεῖν τὰ Μωυσέως νόμιμα...ἢ τὰ τοῦ Χριστοῦ φανῆναι Eus.*p.e*.7.8(313A; M.21.529A); cf.id.*d.e*.(p.9.8; M.22.25B); Isid.Pel.*epp*.2.96(M.78.540C); **2.** *decree*; **a.** divine δίκης θ. †Apoll.*met.Ps*.118:14(M.33.1500D); Didym.*Trin*.3.22(M.39.925A); τῶν νομικῶν θ. τὸ πέρας εἰς τὸ ἐπ' αὐτῷ βλέπει μυστήριον Cyr.*Is*.1.1(2.13E); Sophr.H.*mir.Cyr.et Jo*.17(M.87.3476A); **b.** eccl. τοῖς... ἀποστολικοῖς θ. Cyr.*apol.Thdt*.10(p.142.6; 6[1].236D); **c.** secular, Didym.*Trin*.3.3(M.39.824B); Jo.Ant.*ep.Cyr*.2(p.7.21; M.77.169D); ref. CChalc. κατὰ θεοῦ χάριν καὶ θ. τῶν...βασιλέων...συναχθεῖσα CChalc.(451)*act*.5(*ACO* 2.1.2 p.126.8; H.2.452C); Thdt.*ep*.153(4.1316); Gel.Cyz.*h.e*.proem.1(M.85.1192D); **3.** of magical invocation ἡ μὲν μαγεία ἐπίκλησίς ἐστι δαιμόνων ἀγαθοποιῶν πρὸς ἀγαθοῦ τινος σύστασιν· ὥσπερ τὰ τοῦ Ἀπολωνίου τοῦ Τυανέως θ. Cosm.Mel.*schol*.(M.38.491) in Gr.Naz.*carm*.2.2(poem.)7.241ff.

***θεσπιστικῶς**, *authoritatively*, Leont.H.*Nest*.4.49(M.86.1721B).

θετικός, **1.** *attributed, non-essential*, Epiph.*haer*.76.38(p.390.25; M.42.597B); Max.*ambig*.(M.91.1244C); **2.** *put together, mixed*; of spices, Thdr.Stud.*cant*.14.7(p.369).

θετικῶς, **1.** *affirmatively*, Gr.Naz.*or*.30.12(p.126.16; M.36.120A); **2.** *by adoption* υἱὸς καλεῖται [sc. Christ], οὐ θ. προαχθείς, ἀλλὰ φυσικῶς γεννηθείς Cyr.H.*catech*.10.4.

***θεωθέω**, *make divine*, Diad.*ascens*.6(M.65.1145D).

θεωνᾶ, τά, sens. dub. ἦλθεν...κοινωνῆσαι εἰς τὴν ἁγίαν θεοτόκον τὰ θ. †Anast.S.*relat*.56(p.83.12).

***θεωνυμία, ἡ**, *divine appellation*; of divine names as attributed to three Persons alike, Dion.Ar.*d.n*.2.1(M.3.637C) al.; as applied to saints ἀγγελοπρεπῶς...ἐμπολιτευόμενοι, σὺν ἀπαθείᾳ πάσῃ, καὶ θ. id. *ep*.10(M.3.1117B); of the pope's name τῇ ὑπὸ θείων γλωσσῶν πάλαι μεμακαρισμένῃ ὑμῶν θ. Thdr.Stud.*epp*.2.13(M.99.1156B).

***θεωνυμικός**, *pertaining to the name of God* θ. γνῶσις Dion.Ar.*d.n*. 1.6(M.3.596A); *ib*.13.4(981C).

***θεώνυμος**, *bearing the name of God* τὸ θ. πέταλον Leont.N.ap. Jo.D.*imag*.1(M.94.1273B); Εἰρήνη θεώνυμε Thdr.Stud.*epp*.1.7(M.99.933A).

[*]**θεωπρεπῶς**, v. θεοπρεπῶς.

θεωρ-έω, **1.** *contemplate* mystically, through agency of H. Ghost τῷ ἁγίῳ πνεύματι τὸ ἅγιον πνεῦμα ~εῖν Clem.*str*.6.18(p.517.26; M. 9.400A); through the Word ὁ τὸν λόγον τεθεωρηκὼς τοῦ θεοῦ ~εῖ τὸν θεόν...ἀμήχανον δέ ἐστιν μὴ ἀπὸ τοῦ λόγου θεωρῆσαι τὸν θεόν Or. *Jo*.19.6(1; p.305.8,10; M.14.536B); ἡ ψυχὴ τὸν νυμφίον λόγον ἐπιζητεῖ· καὶ εὑροῦσα πάλιν ἑτέροις ἀποροῦσα ζητεῖ· κἀκεῖνα θεωρήσασα ποθεῖ τὴν ἑτέρων ἀποκάλυψιν id.*schol.in Cant*.5:9(M.17.273D); ὑπερκοσμίοις ὀφθαλμοῖς ~ῆσαι πάντα ἐν τῷ πάντων αἰτίῳ Dion.Ar.*d.n*.5.7(M.3.821B); Father to be contemplated only in Son and H. Ghost, Cosm.Ind.*top*.5(M.88.308D); ἄγγελοι τῶν ἐν ἡμῖν ἐλαχίστων πιστῶν ἐν τῷ οὐρανῷ ἑστήκασι ~οῦντες τὸ πρόσωπον τοῦ πατρός *Hom.Clem*. 17.7; of beatific vision σὺν Χριστῷ 'Ιησοῦ τὴν οἰκείαν τῇ μακαριότητι ἀνάπαυσιν ἀναπαυσώμεθα, τὸν αὐτὸν ὅλον δι' ὅλων ἔμψυχον λόγον ~οῦντες Or.*mart*.47(p.43.13; M.11.632A); **2.** *understand the hidden sense* of scripture, *interpret allegorically* ἔχουσι τὸν νόμον καὶ τοὺς προφήτας τῷ μὴ ~εῖν τὸν ἐν αὐτοῖς νοῦν Or.*hom.14.12 in Jer*.(p.117.4; M.13.417C); ἡ 'Ραχὴλ εἰς τύπον τῆς ἐκκλησίας...τηρεῖται, εἰπεῖν δὲ μᾶλλον ~εῖται Or.*fr.35 in Mt*.2:18(p.29); ἐπὶ τῶν ἀλληγορικῶς κατὰ διάνοιαν ~ουμένων Eus.*e.th*.3.3(p.150.26; M.24.989D); id.*h.e*.6.18.3(M.20.561A); τὴν διήγησιν...μυστικῶς...ἐθεώρησε Chrys.*hom.12.1 in Heb*.(12.121B); *ib.15.1*(150D); Gel.Cyz.*h.e*.2.17.28(M.85.1272B); **3.** *see*, in sense of *receive, give audience to* μὴ δεδυνῆσθαί σε τοὺς ἡμετέρους πρέσβεις θεωρῆσαι CArim.*ep.Const*.2(p.278.14; M.26.792B); **4.** *perceive* a smell οὐδέ ποτε ὀσμὴν...θ. ἢ ἴχνος ‡Petr.I Al.*phys*.29.

θεώρημα, τό, *sight*; *speculation*; *vision*; **1.** lit. and philos., *LS*; **2.** theol., *doctrine*, esp. of higher mysteries of the faith, which belong to sphere of σοφία: ζητητέον δὲ εἰ συστήματος θεωρημάτων ὄντος ἐν αὐτῷ [sc. Christ], καθ' ὃ σοφία ἐστίν, ἐστί τινα θ. ἀχώρητα τῇ λοιπῇ παρ' αὐτὸν γεννητῇ φύσει, ἅτινα οἶδεν ἑαυτῷ Or.*Jo*.2.18(12; p.75.19f.; M.14.145D); τὸ πλῆθος τῶν περὶ θεοῦ θ. ... ἄληπτον τυγχάνον ἀνθρωπίνῃ φύσει *ib*.2.28(23; p.85.5; 161D); id.*or*.13.3(p.327.9; M.11.456B); θεωρήματα σοφίας *ib*.25.2(p.358.7; 497B); σοφίαν...τὴν ἐν τοῖς θ. εἴτε θείοις, εἴτε καὶ ἀνθρωπίνοις Gr.Naz.*or*.28.13(p.42.5; M.36.41C); doctrines of the faith being called θεῖα θ. Cyr.*Jo*.5.3(4.502B); *ib*. (497A); id.*Ps*.48:2(M.69.1068D); τὰ ὑψηλὰ κατανοεῖν οὐ δυνάμενοι τῶν θείων θ. Proc.G.*Is*.8:19ff.(M.87.1997A); also of the Law, Eus. *h.e*.1.2.22(M.20.65A); **3.** myst., *contemplative experience, mystic vision*, opp. mere moral teaching τὰ μὲν ἠθικὰ μαθήματα, ζωὴν περιποιοῦντα τῷ μανθάνοντι καὶ πράττοντι, ἄρτος ἐστὶ τῆς ζωῆς..., τὰ δὲ εὐφραίνοντα καὶ ἐνθουσιᾶν ποιοῦντα ἀπόρρητα καὶ μυστικὰ θ., τοῖς ...οὐ μόνον τρέφεσθαι ἀλλὰ καὶ τρυφᾶν ποθοῦσιν, ἔστιν ἀπὸ τῆς ἀληθινῆς ἀμπέλου ἐρχόμενα, οἶνος καλούμενα Or.*Jo*.1.30(33; p.37.29; M.14.80B); τὴν βαθύτητα τοῦ πλήθους τῶν ἐν τοῖς ὑπεραναβεβηκόσι τὰ αἰσθητὰ τῶν περὶ θεοῦ θ. πάλαι παρέστησεν id.*Cels*.6.19(p.90.1; M.11.1320A); id.*Cant*.3(p.175.28; M.13.147D); of higher walks of spiritual life, not accessible to ordinary faithful τὸν πολὺν καὶ ἁπλούστερον, καὶ μὴ δυνάμενον παρακολουθεῖν τοῖς ποικιλωτάτοις τῆς σοφίας τοῦ θεοῦ θ. id.*Cels*.4.9(p.280.25; 1040A); φωτί...θείῳ, φωτίζοντι ψυχῆς ὀφθαλμοὺς εἰς κατανόησιν τῶν...θείων θ. †Bas.*Is*.76(1.432E; M.30.245B); ἐν ταπεινῶν δὲ ψυχαῖς, οὐράνια θ. Jo.Clim.*scal*.23(M.88.969B); of S. Paul's vision τῶν μέχρις οὐρανοῦ τρίτου θ. Eus.*h.e*.3.24.4(M.20.264C); of Transfiguration τῶν κατὰ τὴν μεταμόρφωσιν τοῦ κυρίου γεγενημένων τὰ μυστικὰ θ. Andr.Cr.*or*.7(M.97.936C); **4.** *object of contemplation*; of scriptural passages, as patient of myst. interpretation εἰ δὲ βούλοιτό τις τοῖς προκειμένοις θ. ἐπιβαλεῖν ἑτέρως Cyr.*ador*.7(1.223D); **5.** gramm., *part of speech* λόγος γὰρ εἷς συνεστὼς ἐκ πλειόνων θ., ὧν ἕκαστον θ. μέρος ἐστὶ τοῦ ὅλου λόγου Or.*Jo*.5.5 (p.102.30; M.14.192A); **6.** *narrative* εἰς τὴν ἐκκλησίαν ἀναφέρεσθαι καὶ τὸν Χριστὸν τὸ κατὰ τὴν Εὔαν θ. καὶ τὸν Ἀδάμ Meth.*symp*.3.9 (p.38.4; M.18.76B).

θεωρητής, ὁ, *spectator, one who contemplates*, of Samuel θ. τῶν μυστηρίων τῶν καταχθονίων Or.*hom.18.2 in Jer*.(p.152.31; M.13.465C); Ath.*gent*.2(M.25.5C).

θεωρητικός, *contemplative, speculative*; **1.** of a faculty of the soul ὁρατικὴ τῆς ψυχῆς δύναμις καὶ θ. Or.*Jo*.20.43(33; p.386.26; M.14.676B); *ib*.28.7(6; p.398.22; 696C); Gr.Naz.*or*.45.12(M.36.637C); Gr.Nyss.*hom.1 in Cant*.(M.44.781A); ἡ δὲ θ. δύναμις ἐν προαιρέσει ἔχει τὴν κίνησιν ‡Bas.*const*.2.2(2.542A; M.31.1341A); τὰς θ. καὶ τὰς ὀρεκτικὰς δυνάμεις Proc.G.*Cant*.7:11(M.87.1765D); **2.** ref. characteristics of contemplative faculty οἷον ἄγγελος ἤδη γενόμενος σὺν Χριστῷ τε ἔσται, θ. ὤν, ἀεὶ τὸ βούλημα τοῦ θεοῦ σκοπῶν Clem.*str*.4.25 (p.317.18; M.8.1365A); ἐν οὖν τῷ θ. βίῳ ἑαυτοῦ τις ἐπιμελεῖται θρησκεύων τὸν θεὸν καὶ διὰ τῆς ἰδίας εἰλικρινοῦς καθάρσεως ἐποπτεύει τὸν θεὸν ἅγιον ἁγίως *ib*.4.23(p.315.31; M.8.1361A); ὡς θ. τοῦ θείου βουλήματος Proc.G.*Is*.1:1(M.87.1824B); enabling the soul to 'see' God ὁ θεὸς καθ' ἡμᾶς τῷ μὲν μὴ εἶναι σῶμα ἀόρατός ἐστιν· τοῖς δὲ θ. καρδίᾳ θεωρητός Or.*Cels*.6.69(p.139.11; M.11.1404A); 'Ισραὴλ δὲ ὁρῶν θεόν, ὁποῖος ἂν εἴη ὁ γνωστικὸς καὶ θ. ἐν ἀνθρώπῳ νοῦς Eus.*p.e.*11.6(519B; M.21.860D); and to receive H. Ghost τοῖς μέντοι μαθηταῖς...ὁ κύριος, τὸ καὶ ἐποπτικοῖς ἤδη εἶναι, καὶ θ. τοῦ πνεύματος ἀποδίδωσιν Bas.*Spir.*53(3.46A; M.32.168B); δείκνυσιν, ἐν μὲν τῇ πρώτῃ [sc. commandment] τὴν θ. ἀρετὴν κατορθουμένην Thdt.*Rom.* 13:10(3.138); **3.** ref. contemplative and active qualities, v. πρακτικός; Clem.*str.*6.11(p.477.25ff.; M.9.312C) cit. s. γνωστικός; διττὴν γὰρ εἶναι τῆς ψυχῆς ἔγωγε οἶμαι τὴν δύναμιν, μιᾶς καὶ τῆς αὐτῆς ὑπαρχούσης· τὴν μέν τινα τοῦ σώματος ζωτικήν, τὴν δὲ ἑτέραν τῶν ὄντων θ., ἣν δὴ καὶ λογιστικὴν ὀνομάζομεν ‡Bas.*const.*2.2(2.542A; M.31.1341A); as subst. ὅτε ἐφύλαξαν τὰς ἐντολὰς τὰς δεομένας μεταξὺ τῶν πολλῶν ἀναστρέφεσθαι...ἔκτοτε...ἐξῆλθον εἰς τὴν ἡσυχίαν τῆς ἐρήμου...ὥστε γενέσθαι αὐτοὺς θ. Philox.*ep.*5(p.161); *ib.*32(p.180); **4.** *allegorical* (v. θεωρία), of mystical sense of scripture, Gr.Naz.*or.*45.12(M.36.637C); of Philo as its representative Φίλων ὁ θεωρητικώτατος, καὶ Ἰώσηππος ὁ ἱστορικώτατος Isid.Pel.*epp.*3.19(M.78.745A).

θεωρητός, *contemplative* τὸν θ. ... βίον Or.*sel.in Ps.*18:3(M.12.1241A).

θεωρία, ἡ, **A.** lit.; **1.** subjective; **a.** *seeing, beholding* τὰ δ' ἐπέκεινα λέγειν οὐκ ἔχοντες διὰ τὸ ἀδύνατον τῆς θ. Tat.*orat.*20(p.22.27; M.6.852B); οὐδὲ γὰρ αὐτοῖς τοῖς ἀποστόλοις...ἀεὶ ἐφαίνετο [sc. risen Christ], μὴ δυναμένοις αὐτοῦ χωρῆσαι τὴν θ. διηνεκῶς Or.*Cels.* 2.65(p.187.3; M.11.897C); *Hom.Clem.*12.12; Thdt.*qu.41 in Num.*(1.247); Proc.G.*Gen.*18:1(M.87.364B); τὴν θ. ἐπὶ τῆς γνώσεως ἔλαβε ‡Ath.*dial.Trin.*1.2(M.28.1117C); opp. ἐπιστήμη, Didym.*Pr.*6:8(M.39.1629B); **b.** *sense of sight* ἡ μὲν τοῦ δαίμονος τούτου πονηρία ἑκατέραν τὴν εἴσοδον τοῦ ἀνθρώπου τούτου ἀπέφραξεν,...θ. τε καὶ ἀκοήν *cat.Mt.* 12:22(p.92.29); cf. ὄψιν καὶ ἀκοήν Chrys.*hom.40.3 in Mt.*(7.440B); Thdt.*Ezech.*1:26(2.691); **c.** concrete, *seer, spectator* ὁ Παῦλος...ἡ τῶν ἀφράστων θαυμάτων θ. Geo.Pis.*carm.*83.3; **2.** objective; *sight, spectacle*; **a.** in gen. ταῖς ἐπιγείοις ἡδοναῖς τε καὶ θ. εὐαρεστεῖσθαι Clem.*str.*7.12(p.53.25; M.9.504A); ref. interpretation of forbidden fruit as ἡ τῆς Εὔας θ. ‡Ath.*qu.Ant.*50(M.28.629B); τὴν ἐν τῇ γυμνώσει τοῦ σώματος θ. Thdr.Mops.*Gen.*3:7(M.66.640A) al.; Thdt.*h.rel.*4(3.1154); of a visit to a shrine βασιλεῖς...πολλάκις ἀποδεδημήκασι ταύτης ἕνεκεν θ. Chrys.*hom.16.5 in 2Cor.*(10.626C); **b.** of theatrical performances, etc. οὐ δεῖ ἱερατικοὺς ἢ κληρικούς τινας θ. θεωρεῖν CLaod.*can.*54.

B. met.; of intellectual perception; **1.** *consideration, investigation, study* τὴν θ. τῶν κατὰ τὸν ἄνθρωπον συμβαινόντων Meth.*symp.*2.7(p.25.4; M.18.60A); εἰς τὴν τῶν θείων γραφῶν θ. Eus.*h.e.*6.18.4(M.20.561A); τὰ θεῖα ῥήματα οὐκ ἀλληγορίας δεῖται...θ. δὲ δεῖται καὶ αἰσθήσεως Epiph.*haer.*61.6(p.386.14; M.41.1048B); τῆς προφητείας τὸν σκοπὸν διττὴν ἐν ἑαυτῷ τὴν θ. ὠδίνοντα κατίδοι τις ἄν, πνευματικήν τε ἅμα καὶ ἱστορικήν Cyr.*Abac.*1(3.517B); Thdt.*Pss.proem.*(1.604); **2.** *intellectual apprehension* τὴν τῶν δογμάτων θ. opp. τὸν βίον τοῦ γνωστικοῦ Clem.*str.*7.10(p.43.27; M.9.484B); of H. Ghost as πρὸς θεωρίαν δυσέφικτον Bas.*Spir.*22 tit.(3.45D; M.32.165C); *supervision* κατὰ τὴν θείαν διάταξιν προνοίας τε καὶ θ. Const.ap.Eus.*v.C.*2.48(p.61.25; M.20.1025B); (for rel. to γνῶσις v.s.v.); opp. πρᾶγμα, Didym. *Pr.*6:12(M.39.1629B); **3.** *theory, speculation, science*; sts. also *philosophical* (Platonic) *contemplation*; defined θ. ἐστίν, οὐ τὸ θεωρεῖν μόνον ὡς ἔχουσι τὰ σώματα φύσεως, ἀλλὰ καὶ τοὺς λόγους αὐτῶν πρὸς τί βλέπουσιν ‡Max.*cap.al.*141(M.90.1433B); ἡ θ. τῶν ἰδεῶν Just. *dial.*2.6(M.6.477C); id.*1apol.*43.9(M.6.396A); id.*2apol.*8.3(M.6.457B); ἐπιστημονικὴ θ. Clem.*str.*7.11(p.44.13; M.9.485B); *ib.*8.1(p.80.13; 560A); θ. τῶν πρώτων αἰτίων *ib.*6.17(p.512.1; 388A); λογικὴ θ. Or.*Cels.* 5.20(p.21.19; M.11.1209C); θ. τῶν ὀνομάτων id.*Jo.*6.41(24; p.151.8; M.14.273A); τῇ τῶν ὁρμῶν καὶ παθῶν τῶν τῆς ψυχῆς θ. καὶ κατανοήσει Gr.Thaum.*pan.Or.*9(p.23.10; M.10.1080A); of pagan speculations on Nature, etc. τὰς σεμνοτέρας δὴ θ. τε καὶ φυσιολογίας Eus.*p.e.*2.1(51D; M.21.104B); ἡ τῶν λογικῶν μαθημάτων θ. Philost.*h.e.*3.15(M.65.504A); opp. γνῶσις: κληρονομία ἐστὶ φύσεως λογικῆς, ἡ θ. τῶν γεγονότων καὶ γενησομένων αἰώνων· κληρονομία δὲ Χριστοῦ ἐστιν ἡ γνῶσις ἐκ τοῦ θεοῦ Cyr.*Ps.*16:6(M.69.812B); also, *department of science* εἰς δέκα γὰρ διῄρηνται θεωρίας αἱ προφητεῖαι Epiph.*mens.*1(M.43.237A)ap. *Doct.Patr.*39(p.295.4 conj. δέκα μέρη; but Syriac supports θεωρίας); also of prophetic contemplation, *ib.*

C. *spiritual contemplation*, not always to be sharply distinguished from philosophical contemplation; **1.** human: different uses illustrated ταῦτα δὲ πάντα διὰ τῆς τῶν προκειμένων ἡμῖν ῥητῶν θ. (= *consideration*) μανθάνομεν·...ἡ σωματικὴ τοῦ λόγου ὑπογραφὴ... δίδωσι τῇ θ. τὰς ὕλας (= matter for *meditation*)...διὰ δὲ τοῦ ὀνόματος τῆς νυκτός, ἐκδείκνυται τῶν ἀοράτων τὴν θ. (= *contemplation* proper) Gr.Nyss.*hom.6 in Cant.*(M.44.892A–C); Philox.*ep.*25(p.175); *ib.*26(p.176); **a.** as the goal of life, Clem.*str.*2.21(p.184.7; M.8.1076C); τέλος γὰρ οἶμαι τοῦ τε πολιτικοῦ τοῦ τε κατὰ νόμον βιοῦντος ἡ θ. *ib.*1.25(p.104.2; 913A); τέλος τοῦ σοφοῦ ἡ θ. *ib.*6.7(p.462.24; M.9.281A); equated with kingdom of God, Evagr.Pont.*ep.*12(M.32.265C); **b.** its essence; knowledge of God ζητεῖν τὸν θεὸν καὶ ὡς οἷόν τε γιγνώσκειν ἐπιχειρεῖν, ἥτις ἂν εἴη θ. μεγίστη Clem.*str.*2.10(p.138.12; M.8.984B); ἐνδιατρίψῃ τῇ θ., τῷ θείῳ καθαρῶς ὁμιλῶν *ib.*4.6(p.266.5; 1252A); προσευχὴ θεοῦ ὁμιλία, τῶν ἀοράτων θ. Gr.Nyss.*or.dom.*1(p.8.17; M.44.1124B); **c.** means of attaining it; purity of heart, cf. Mt.5:8 φημὶ τὰς γνωστικὰς ψυχάς, τῇ μεγαλοπρεπείᾳ τῆς θ. ὑπερβαινούσας ἑκάστης ἁγίας τάξεως τὴν πολιτείαν...οὐκ ἐν κατόπτροις ἢ διὰ κατόπτρων ἔτι τὴν θ. ἀσπαζομένας τὴν θείαν...ταυτότητι τῆς ὑπεροχῆς ἁπάσας τετιμημένας διαμένειν. αὕτη τῶν καθαρῶν τῇ καρδίᾳ ἡ καταληπτικὴ θ. Clem.*str.*7.3(p.10.7ff.; M.9.416C); *ib.*6.14(p.486.8; 329B); καθαροὺς τῇ καρδίᾳ γενομένους...προσμένει τῇ θ. τῇ ἀϊδίῳ ἀποκατάστασις *ib.*7.10(p.41.23; 480B); Meth.*symp.*11(p.138.27; M.18.217A); Gr.Nyss.*v.Mos.*(M.44.373B); purification of spirit, Philox. *ep.*37(p.184); knowledge γνῶσιν εἴτε σοφίαν συνασκηθῆναι χρὴ εἰς ἕξιν θεωρίας ἀΐδιον καὶ ἀναλλοίωτον Clem.*str.*6.7(p.463.1; 284B); with which it is closely connected, Andr.Cr.*or.*7(M.97.945B); detachment from sensible things χρὴ μὲν τῶν αἰσθητῶν καὶ προσκαίρων καὶ βλεπομένων πάντων καταφρονεῖν πάντα δὲ πράττειν ὑπὲρ τοῦ τυχεῖν τῆς τοῦ θεοῦ κοινωνίας καὶ τῆς τῶν νοητῶν καὶ ἀοράτων θ. Or.*Cels.* 3.56(p.251.14; M.11.993C); ἡ δὲ τοῦ θεοῦ θ., οὔτε κατὰ τὸ φαινόμενον, οὔτε κατὰ τὸ ἀκουόμενον ἐνεργεῖται Gr.Nyss.*v.Mos.*(M.44.373D); Thdr.Mops.*Nah.*1:1(M.66.401D); οὐκ ἀσφαλὲς οὖν πρὶν ἔξω γενέσθαι τῶν πολλῶν, ἐπιβάλλειν ταῖς περὶ θεοῦ θ. Max.*cap.theol.*1.83(M.90.1117B); though sensible things may offer a way to it ἡμεῖς δὲ [opp. angels] αἰσθηταῖς εἰκόσιν ἐπὶ τὰς θείας, ὡς δυνατόν, ἀναγόμεθα θ. Dion.Ar.*e.h.*1.2(M.3.373B); ψυχὴ...πρὸς τὰ περὶ ἑαυτὴν προϊοῦσα, καὶ ἀπὸ τῶν ἔξωθεν...ἐπὶ τὰς ἁπλᾶς καὶ ἡνωμένας ἀνάγεται θ. id.*d.n.* 4.9(M.3.705B); study of scripture συνεξάπτει δὲ ἡ γραφὴ τὸ ζώπυρον τῆς ψυχῆς καὶ συντείνει τὸ οἰκεῖον ὄμμα πρὸς θεωρίαν Clem.*str.*1.1(p.8.12; M.8.697A); prayer ὁ γνωστικὸς θεωρίαν εὔχεται αὔξειν τε καὶ παραμένειν *ib.*7.7(p.34.26; M.9.465B); with which contemplation is intimately connected τὸ εἰλικρινὲς τῆς θ. διὰ προσευχῆς εἴωθεν ἐμφανίζεσθαι ‡Max.*cap.al.*136(M.90.1432C); *ib.*156(1437A); physical leisure ἡ θεωρητικὴ δύναμις...τῇ τε περὶ τῶν κρειττόνων καὶ προσφυῶν θ. ᾗ ἀπασχολεῖται, καὶ τῇ ἀταραξίᾳ τοῦ σώματος ἐπισκοποῦσα ‡Bas. *const.*2.2(2.542B; M.31.1341A); **d.** ref. superhuman agents that bestow or produce it ὁ...πατρὸς δόξης χαρακτήρ, ἐναποσφραγιζόμενος τῷ γνωστικῷ τὴν τελείαν θ. κατ' εἰκόνα τὴν ἑαυτοῦ Clem.*str.*7.3(p.12.22; M.9.421A); φιλοτιμησώμεθα...προσκυνεῖν τὸν θεόν...τὸν κατὰ τὴν τάξιν τοῦ Μελχισεδὲκ ἀρχιερέα ὁδηγὸν ἔχοντες τῆς...μυστικῆς καὶ ἀπορρήτου θ. Or.*Jo.*13.24(p.248.27; M.14.410C); ἡ ἔκτασις τῶν χειρῶν τοῦ νομοθέτου γίνεται, ἡ τὸ μυστήριον τοῦ σταυροῦ προδεικνύουσα τότε προσάγεται τῇ τῆς ὑπερκειμένης φύσεως θ. Gr.Nyss.*v.Mos.*(M.44.373B); ὅρασιν...ὑποδειχθῆναι τῷ θεολόγῳ δι' ἑνὸς τῶν ἐπιστατούντων ἡμῖν...ἀγγέλων, καὶ...ἐπὶ τὴν νοερὰν ἐκείνην θ. ἀνατεθῆναι Dion.Ar. *c.h.*13.4(M.3.304C); **e.** degrees ἡ μὲν ψιλὴ εὐχή, ὡς ἄρτος ὀφθήσεται ἀρχομένους στηρίζουσα· ἡ δὲ μετά τινος θεωρίας, ὡς ἔλαιον πιαίνουσα· ἡ δὲ ἀνείδεος, ὡς οἶνος εὐώδης ‡Max.*cap.al.*176(M.90.1441B); mount of Transfiguration a symbol of its highest form, Andr.Cr.*or.*7(M.97.941C); **f.** special features of Christian contemplation; nourished by dogma τούτων φύλαξ μοι διαμένοις τῶν δογμάτων...σοφὸς δ' ἁπάσαις μυστικαῖς θ. Amph.*Seleuc.*216(M.37.1591A); closely connected with Christ's humanity τάχα γὰρ κἂν ὁπωσποτὲ ἐν τῇ τοῦ λόγου ὑψηλοτάτῃ καὶ ἀνωτάτῃ θ. γενώμεθα καὶ τῆς ἀληθείας, οὐ πάντῃ ἐπιλησόμεθα τῆς ἐν σώματι ἡμῶν γενομένης δι' αὐτοῦ εἰσαγωγῆς Or.*Jo.*2.8(4; p.62.25; M.14.121D); revealing truth, Andr.Cr.*or.*7(M.97.956D); accompanied by joy τελειωθέντα δι' ἀγάπης καὶ τὴν ἀπλήρωτον τῆς θ. εὐφροσύνην ἀϊδίως καὶ ἀκορέστως ἑστιώμενον Clem.*str.*6.9(p.469.6; M.9.296B); Max.*exp.Ps.*59(M.90.865B); evoked by the object of love ἀγωγὸν δὲ τὸ ἐραστὸν πρὸς τὴν ἑαυτοῦ θ. Clem.*str.*7.2(p.9.10; M.9.413C); though it does not rule out holy fear, Gr.Naz.*or.*39.8(M.36.344A); and needs safeguards against temptation to pride, Didym.*2Cor.*12:7(p.42.16; M.39.1729A); to be pursued at appropriate times μὴ πρόστρεχε θεωρίᾳ ἐν οὐ καιρῷ θεωρίας, ἵνα σου τοῦ κάλλους τῆς ταπεινώσεως καταδιώξηται Jo.Clim.*scal.*7(M.88.813C); ref. spiritual interpretation of sabbath ἡ τοῦ σαββάτου καὶ τῆς καταπαύσεως τοῦ θεοῦ ἡμέρα, ἐν ᾗ ἑορτάσουσιν ἅμα τῷ θεῷ ...ἀναβαίνοντες ἐπὶ τὴν θ. Or.*Cels.*6.61(p.131.22; M.11.1392B); **g.** its effects: unites men with angels, Clem.*str.*7.7(p.37.7; M.9.469B); confirms faith, *ib.*1.11(p.33.26; M.8.749B); perfects virtue, Or.*Jo.*1.16(p.21.1f.; M.14.52A); ἀποκάλυψις δὲ καὶ λήθη εἰκότως προσγίνονται δικαίῳ· λαμβάνοντι μὲν διὰ θεωρίας τῶν ἀπορρήτων τὴν μύησιν· τῶν δὲ κατ' ἀρετὴν πόνων τὴν λήθην, διὰ τὴν διαδεχομένην τοὺς πόνους τῶν ἀρετῶν εὐφροσύνην τῆς πνευματικῆς θ. Max.*exp.Ps.*59:9(M.90.865B);

leads to realization of divine incomprehensibility, Gr.Nyss.*v.Mos.*(M.44.376D); brings union with Christ ἐν Χριστῷ ὢν [sc. S. Paul] διὰ τὴν θ. Didym.*2Cor.*12:2(p.42.11; M.39.1728C); and with God, Jo.D.*Man.*1.71(M.94.1569C); deification ὑπεραναβὰς πάντα ὑλικὰ νοῦς, ἵνα ἀκριβώσῃ τὴν θ. τοῦ θεοῦ, ἐν οἷς θεωρεῖ θεοποιεῖται Or.*Jo.*32.27(17; p.472.30; M.14.817A); **h.** action to be in conformity with contemplation, Clem.*str.*6.11(p.477.31; M.9.312C); as being complementary δικαιοσύνην...ἔργῳ τε καὶ θ. πεπληρωμένην *ib.*4.16(p.292.10; M.8.1305B); τὸ εὐαγγέλιον δι' ἔργων καὶ θ. ἐπαινῶν *ib.*7.12(p.55.23; M.9.508A); τέλος...τοῦ γνωστικοῦ...διττόν, ἐφ' ὧν μὲν ἡ θ. ἡ ἐπιστημονική, ἐφ' ὧν δὲ ἡ πρᾶξις *ib.*7.16(p.72.8; 541A); διχῶς δὲ ἡ ὁδὸς κυρίου εὐθύνεται, κατὰ δὲ τὸ θεωρητικόν, τρανουμένου ἐν ἀληθείᾳ ἀπαραμίκτως τοῦ ψεύδους, καὶ κατὰ τὸ πρακτικὸν μετὰ τὴν ὑγιῆ θ. τοῦ πρακτέου ἁρμονίου πράξεως ἀποδιδομένης τῷ περὶ τῶν πρακτέων ὑγιεῖ λόγῳ Or.*Jo.*6.19(11; p.127.31; M.14.232D); θ. συνέκδημον πρὸς τὰ ἐκεῖθεν ποιούμεθα, καὶ πρᾶξιν θεωρίας ἐπίβασιν Gr.Naz.*or.*4.113(M.35.649B); καλὸν θ., καὶ καλὸν πρᾶξις· ἡ μέν, ἐντεῦθεν ἐπανιστᾶσα, καὶ εἰς τὰ ἅγια τῶν ἁγίων χωροῦσα...ἡ δέ, Χριστὸν ὑποδεχομένη, καὶ θεραπεύουσα *ib.*14.4(864A); βίῳ μὲν ὁδηγῷ θεωρίας, θεωρίᾳ δὲ σφραγῖδι βίου χρησάμενος *ib.*21.6(1088B); δεῖν συνάπτειν τὴν πρακτικὴν φιλοσοφίαν τῇ κατὰ θεωρίαν ἐνεργουμένῃ· ὥστε τὴν καρδίαν μέν, τῆς θ.· τοὺς δὲ βραχίονας τῶν ἔργων σύμβολα γίνεσθαι Gr.Nyss.*v.Mos.*(M.44.392C,D); Cyr.*Jo.*4.2(4.357A); Andr.Cr.*or.*7(M.97.945B); though contemplation is more perfect than action, Gr.Naz.*carm.*1.2.33.1(M.37.928A); relation of action to contemplation, symbolized by bread and wine of eucharist ἀληθῶς μὲν βρῶσις ἡ πρᾶξις, ἀληθῶς δὲ πόσις ἡ θ. ... διὰ τοῦτο πρῶτον δίδωσι τὸν ἄρτον εὐλογήσας καὶ κλάσας τοῖς μαθηταῖς ἐπεὶ πρώτη ἐστὶν ἡ πρᾶξις, καὶ μετὰ τοῦτο λαβὼν ποτήριον. ...ἐπεὶ δεῖ τὰ τῶν πράξεων ῥυθμίσαντα καὶ τὸ πρακτικὸν κατορθώσαντα οὕτως ὁδεύειν διὰ τῶν πραγμάτων καὶ ἐπὶ θεωρίαν αὐτῶν Or.*comm. in Mt.*16.7(p.487.24ff.; M.13.1388A); id.*hom.1 in Lc.*(p.10.1); τὴν ἀγαθὴν πρᾶξιν ὑποβάθραν εἶναι τῆς θ. Thdt.*qu.60 in Ex.*(1.168); Philox.*ep.*5(p.161); Isaac *ep.*12(p.165); οὐκ ἔστιν οὔτε πρᾶξις ἀσφαλὴς θ. ἐκτός, οὔτε θ. ἀληθὴς πράξεως ἄνευ ‡Max.*cap.al.*142(M.90.1433B); ὡς ὕλη τῷ εἴδει, οὕτω πρᾶξις τῇ θ. καὶ ὡς ὀφθαλμὸς προσώπῳ, οὕτω θ. τῇ πράξει ὀφθήσεται *ib.*144(1433C); ὁ μέσως ἔχων περὶ πρᾶξιν καὶ θ. ...ἡδέως φέρων καὶ τοὺς πόνους τῆς πράξεως, διὰ τὸ μέτριον τῆς θ.· καὶ τοὺς λόγους τῆς ἀτελοῦς θ., διὰ τὸ βοηθεῖσθαι ὑπὸ τῆς πράξεως *ib.*151(1436C); πρᾶξις σὺν θ. μὲν ὡς σῶμα μετὰ πνεύματος ἡγεμονικοῦ· ἄνευ δὲ θ., ὡς σὰρξ μετὰ πνεύματος προαιρετικοῦ λογισθήσεται *ib.*157(1437B); **i.** of contemplation perfected in eternity, Clem.*str.*7.2(p.9.9; M.9.413C); Gr.Naz.*or.*32.33(M.36.212C); ὅταν ἄφθαρτοι καὶ ἀθάνατοι γενώμεθα...ἐσόμεθα...θεωρίαις ἀποπληρούμενοι Dion.Ar.*d.n.*1.4(M.3.592C); id.*e.h.*7.9(M.3.565B); **2.** angelic ἀγγέλους...εἶναι ἐν ἀναπαύσει καὶ πρὸς μόνῃ τῇ θ. τοῦ θεοῦ Clem.*ecl.*56(p.153.22; M.9.725B); οἱ ἄγγελοι...ἀπὸ τῆς κατὰ τὴν ἀλήθειαν μετὰ σοφίας θ. δυναμούμενοι Or.*or.*27.10(p.369.30; M.11.513B); τῆς τοῦ καλλοποιοῦ καὶ ἀρχικοῦ κάλλους ὑπερουσίου καὶ τριφανοῦς θ. ... ἀναπιμπλαμένας [sc. first angelic hierarchy] Dion.Ar.*c.h.*7.2(M.3.208C); *ib.*7.4(212A); Andr.Cr.*or.*7(M.97.933C); **3.** of contemplation within Trin. δοξασθῆναι τὸν θεὸν...ἐπὶ τῇ ἑαυτοῦ γνώσει καὶ τῇ ἑαυτοῦ θ., οὔσῃ μείζονι ⟨τῆς⟩ ἐν υἱῷ θ. Or.*Jo.*32.28(18; p.473.31f.; M.14.817D); οὐκ ἤρκει τῇ ἀγαθότητι τοῦτο, τὸ κινεῖσθαι μόνον τῇ ἑαυτῆς [sc. Godhead] θ. Gr.Naz.*or.*38.9(M.36.320C).

D. exeg.; **1.** of visions of prophets and apostles ἡ τοῦ προφήτου ληφθεῖσα διάνοια πρὸς τὴν θ. Thdr.Mops.*Nah.*1:1(M.66.404D); which can be rightly interpreted only by minds detached from earthly things πού γε τὰς οὕτω φοβεράς τε καὶ ἀπορρήτους θ. δυνατὸν ἦν αὐτοῖς ὑποδέχεσθαι, μὴ τῷ λογισμῷ πρότερον κατὰ τὸν τῆς θ. καιρὸν ἐξισταμένοις τῶν παρόντων; οὕτω τὸν μακάριον λέγει Πέτρον ἐν ἐκστάσει γεγονότα τὴν σινδόνα ἰδεῖν ἐκ τοῦ οὐρανοῦ καταφερομένην· ἐπειδὴ ἡ τοῦ πνεύματος χάρις πρότερον αὐτοῦ τὴν διάνοιαν ἀποσπᾶσα τῶν παρόντων, τότε προσανέχειν τῇ θεωρίᾳ παρεσκεύασε τῶν δεικνυμένων, ἵν' ὥσπερ...καθ' ὕπνους τῶν ἀποκαλυπτομένων δεχόμεθα τὴν θ., οὕτω πως τῇ μεταστάσει τῆς διανοίας ὑπὸ τῆς τοῦ ἁγίου πνεύματος καθιστάμενοι χάριτος, τῶν δεικνυμένων ὑποδέχοιντο τὴν θ. *ib.*(401D–404A); ἔθος τοῖς ἁγίοις προφήταις καὶ ἐν θ. αὐταῖς γίνεσθαι πολλάκις τῶν ὡς ἔσονται κατὰ καιροὺς προαπηγγελμένων Cyr.*Mich.*29(3.415C); ἀνεῳχθῆναι δὲ τοὺς οὐρανοὺς ἔφη, οὐκ ἀληθείᾳ καὶ πράγματι, ἀλλὰ πνευματικῇ θ. Thdt.*Ezech.*1:1(2.680; but perh. to be interpreted in sense D.2.a); θ. τοιαύτην ὑποδείκνυσι τῷ προφήτῃ, τῇ τοῦ θείου πνεύματος ἐνεργείᾳ τῆς διανοίας αὐτοῦ φωτίσας τὸ ὀπτικὸν *ib.*40:2(2.1020); ref. Abraham, Proc.G.*Gen.*2:18(M.87.173B) cit. s. ἔκστασις; **2.** as technical term for *spiritual sense of scripture*; **a.** so esp. Antiochene school Διόδωρος...ψιλῷ τῷ γράμματι τῶν θείων προσέχων γραφῶν, τὰς θ. αὐτῶν ἐκτρεπόμενος Socr.*h.e.*6.3.7(M.67.668A); Διόδωρον...τὰς θ. ἀποφεύγοντα Soz.*h.e.*8.2.6(M.67.1516A); but τὴν ἀγωγὴν καὶ τὴν θ. τὴν ὑψηλοτέραν οὐκ ἀποκωλύσομεν. οὐδὲ γὰρ ἐναντιοῦται ἡ ἱστορία τῇ ὑψηλοτέρᾳ θ., τοὐναντίον δὲ κρηπὶς εὑρίσκεται καὶ ὑποβάθρα τῶν ὑψηλοτέρων νοημάτων Diod.*proem.Pss.*(p.88.2ff.); ἐκεῖνο δὲ μόνον χρὴ φυλάττεσθαι, μή ποτε ἀνατροπὴ τοῦ ὑποκειμένου ἡ θ. ὀφθῇ, ὅπερ οὐκέτι ἂν εἴη θ. ἀλλὰ ἀλληγορία. τὸ γὰρ ἄλλως ἀγορευόμενον παρὰ τὸ κείμενον οὐ θ. ἐστὶν ἀλλὰ ἀλληγορία *ib.*(p.88.5ff.); ἄλλο τὸ ἐκβιάσασθαι εἰς ἀλληγορίαν καὶ ἱστορίαν, ἄλλο δὲ καὶ τὴν ἱστορίαν φυλάξαι καὶ θ. ἐπινοῆσαι Sever.*creat.*4.2(M.56.459); exeg. Gal.4:24 ὁ ἀπόστολος οὐδαμοῦ τὴν ἱστορίαν ἀνέτρεψεν, ἐπεισενέγκων τὴν θ. οὐ κατὰ ἀμαθίαν ὀνομάτων, ἀλλὰ διδάσκων ὅτι, κἂν ὄνομα ἀλληγορίας ἐπικρίνηται τοῖς νοήμασι, κατὰ θεωρίαν αὐτὸ χρὴ λαμβάνειν, οὐδαμοῦ βλάπτοντας τῆς ἱστορίας τὴν φύσιν Diod.*proem.Pss.*(p.88.8ff.); Antiochene conception of θ. being placed bet. literalism and fanciful allegory ταῦτα γὰρ οὐδὲ τὴν ἱστορίαν ἀθετεῖ, οὐδὲ τὴν θ. ἐκβάλλει, ἀλλ' ἡ μεσότης αὕτη καὶ ἡ ἐμπειρία, ἥ, κατὰ τὴν ἱστορίαν καὶ θ. καὶ Ἑλληνισμοῦ ἀπαλλάττει...καὶ πρὸς Ἰουδαϊσμὸν οὐ καθέλκει *ib.*(p.88.23ff.); **b.** θ. equated with ἀλληγορία by Alexandrine, Cappadocian, and other fathers; hence ref. Philo ὑψηλὸς...ἐν ταῖς εἰς τὰς θείας γραφὰς θ. γεγενημένος Eus.*h.e.*2.18.1(M.20.184C); and Origen μηδ' ἐξαρκεῖν αὐτῷ τὰς ἁπλᾶς...τῶν ἱερῶν λόγων ἐντεύξεις, ζητεῖν δέ...βαθυτέρας...θ. *ib.*6.2.9(525A); id.*Marcell.*1.3(p.17.22; M.24.749C); allegorical interpretation of Law by the Jews, called ἀλληγορικὴ θ., id.*p.e.*8.8(370A; M.21.624C); of interpretation of OT by NT μνησθεὶς τῶν δύο τοῦ Ἀβραὰμ τέκνων...ἀλληγορίαν ὀνομάζει τὴν περὶ αὐτῶν θ. Gr.Nyss.*hom.in Cant.*proem.(M.44.757B); of spiritual interpretation of life of Moses θ. εἰς τὸν τοῦ Μώσεως βίον id.*v.Mos.*tit.(M.44.327); μηδεὶς δὲ διόλου τὴν τῆς ἱστορίας ἔκθεσιν παρατεθεῖσθαι τῷ εἱρμῷ τῆς τοιαύτης τοῦ νοῦ θ. νομίζων, εἴ πού τι τῶν γεγραμμένων ἔξω τοιαύτης τῆς διανοίας εὑρίσκοιτο, δι' ἐκείνου καὶ τὸ πᾶν ἀθετείτω *ib.*(340B); τὸ μὴ δεῖν πάντως παραμένειν τῷ πράγματι... ἀλλὰ μεταβαίνειν πρὸς τὴν ἄυλόν τε καὶ νοητὴν θ. id.*hom.in Cant.*proem.(757C); συμβαίνει τῇ ἱστορίᾳ ἡ κατὰ ἀναγωγὴν θ. id.*v.Mos.*(397C); θ. freq. used simply to indicate allegorical exegesis πρὸς δὲ θεωρίαν...τὰ κήτη ἀλληγορικῶς καλούμενα Didym.*Job* 9:13(M.39.1144C); id.*Ps.*118:72(M.39.1572B); Hesych.H.*Ps.tit.*103(M.27.1092B); *ib.*148(1332C); sts. with epithets such as μυστική, Cyr.*ador.*1(1.29A); πνευματική *ib.*(1.3E); ἡ ἐν πνεύματι θ. Hesych.H.*fr.Ps.*6:2(M.93.1181A); its chief object, to show Christ foreshadowed in OT, Cyr.*ador.*10(1.341E); id.*glaph.Gen.*5(1.160E); id.*Is.*2.5(2.324A); its necessity χρῆναι δὲ φημί, τοὺς ἐθέλοντας διατρανοῦν τὰ οὕτως... αἰνιγματώδη τῶν θεωρημάτων πλάτη διανοίας ὄμματι περιαθρεῖν ἐπείγεσθαι, καὶ μάλα εὐφρόνως τοῦτο μέν, τῆς ἱστορίας τὸ ἀκριβές, τοῦτο δέ, τῆς πνευματικῆς θ. τὴν ἀπόδοσιν ἵνα πανταχόθεν τοῖς ἐντευξομένοις ἐκβαίη τὸ ὠφελοῦν *ib.*proem.(2**A); in rel. to lit. sense θ. μὲν γὰρ πνευματικὴ καλή τε καὶ ὀνησιφόρος, καὶ τῆς διανοίας τὸν ὀφθαλμὸν εὖ μάλα καταλαμπρύνουσα νουνεχεστάτους ἀποτελεῖ. ὅταν δέ τι τῶν ἱστορικῶς πεπραγμένων διὰ τῶν ἱερῶν ἡμῖν γραμμάτων εἰσφέρηται, τότε δὴ τότε τὸ ἐκ τῆς ἱστορίας χρήσιμον θηρᾶσθαι πρέπει *ib.*1.4(113E); εἰ μὲν γὰρ ἑκάτερα δέχεται τὸ ῥητὸν ἀβιάστως, καὶ τὴν θ., καὶ τὴν ἱστορίαν, χρηστέον ἀμφοτέροις Olymp.*fr.Job* proem.(M.93.17C); **c.** intermediate position between Antiochene and Alexandrine schools καθ' ἱστορίαν εἰρημένα νοῶμεν, καὶ τὰ κατὰ θ. προφητευθέντα ἐκλαμβάνωμεν, μηδὲ τὰ σαφῶς ἱστορηθέντα εἰς θ. ἐκβιαζόμενοι, μήτε τὰ λαμπρῶς θεωρηθῆναι ὀφείλοντα εἰς ἱστορίαν καταβιβάζοντες Isid.Pel.*epp.*4.203(M.78.1292A); *ib.*3.84(789C); **d.** use of θ. in this sense has prob. influenced Dion. Ar.'s use for mystical meaning of sacraments in *e.h.*2.3 et passim, opp. visible sign ἱερουργία: κατίδωμεν...τὴν καθ' ἕκαστον ἀκριβῆ τῆς ἁγιωτάτης τελετῆς ἱερουργίαν καὶ θ. *ib.*3.1(M.3.425B).

θεωρικός, *wise, learned* in spiritual matters θεωρικωτάτων τὸ πρᾶγμα [sc. praise of BMV] Procl.CP *annunt.*1(M.85.425C); Anast.S.*interr.*(p.275).

θεώριον, τό, *spectacle, show,* Thphn.*chron.*p.195(M.108.505A).

θεωρός, ὁ, *spectator, one who contemplates,* as epithet of bishops, Dion.Ar.*e.h.*4.3.2(M.3.476C); interprn.: θ. δὲ καλεῖ τοὺς ἐπισκόπους, ἐπειδὴ καὶ παρ' Ἕλλησι θ. ἐκαλοῦντο οἱ προβαλλόμενοι παρὰ πάντων ἐπερωτᾶν τὸν θεὸν περὶ μελλόντων, καὶ θυσίας ὑπὲρ αὐτῶν προσφέρειν Max.*schol.e.h.*4.3.2(M.4.153C); of Isaiah contemplating seraphim, Attic.*Trin.fr.*ap.*Doct.Patr.*42(p.317.14).

θέωσις, ἡ, *deification, divinization*;

A. Christol.; **1.** in gen. οὔποτε τοῦ εἶναι υἱὸς ἡγμένος· οὐ γὰρ ἐκ μεταμελείας ἡ θεότης, οὐδὲ ἐκ προκοπῆς ἡ θ. Gr.Naz.*or.*25.16(M.35.1221B); μένει γὰρ αὕτη βροτεία φύσις καὶ μετὰ τὴν θ. καὶ τεθεωμένη φύσις βροτεία καὶ λέγεται καὶ ἔστι ‡Cyr.*Trin.*14(6^3.21B; M.77.1152C); τὴν θ. τῆς σαρκὸς γενέσθαι δοξάζομεν Jo.D.*f.o.*3.17(M.94.1069A);

2. of divinization of Christ's body ἡ ἐξ οὐρανῶν φωνή· ἐκεῖθεν γὰρ ὁ μαρτυρούμενος· καὶ ὡς περιστερά, τιμᾷ γὰρ τὸ σῶμα, ἐπεὶ καὶ τοῦτο τῇ θ. θεός, σωματικῶς ὁρωμένη Gr.Naz.*or*.39.16(M.36.353B); θεὸς ἀληθὴς ὁ Χριστός...καὶ θεῖον ὄντως αὐτοῦ τὸ ἅγιον σῶμα τῇ θ. Anast. S.*hod*.14(M.89.244C); θ. τῆς σαρκός, καὶ λόγωσιν...καὶ τὰ τοιαῦτα, τὸν προσγενόμενον τῇ σαρκὶ πλοῦτον ἐκ τῆς πρὸς τὸν ὕψιστον θεὸν λόγον ἑνώσεώς τε καὶ συμφυΐας ἐμφαίνοντες Jo.D.*f.o*.4.18(M.94. 1184B).

B. of angelic hierarchies πρώτης καὶ ὑπερεχούσης θ. ἀποπληρουμένας Dion.Ar.*c.h*.7.2(M.3.208C).

C. of man; **1.** ref. promise of serpent to Eve, Germ.CP *or*.1(M.98. 229A); ὁ διάβολος...ὡμίλησε τῇ γυναικί, καὶ πείσας αὐτὴν φαγεῖν ἐκ τοῦ ἀπηγορευμένου...ξύλου ἐλπίδι θεώσεως, δι' αὐτῆς ἠπάτησε καὶ τὸν Ἀδάμ †Jo.D.*B.J*.7(M.96.908B); **2.** spiritual and mystical; **a.** definitions ἡ δὲ θ. ἐστιν ἡ πρὸς θεόν, ὡς ἐφικτόν, ἀφομοίωσίς τε καὶ ἕνωσις Dion.Ar.*e.h*.1.3(M.3.376A); θ. ἐστιν, ἡ ἐπὶ τὸ κρεῖττον ὕψωσις, οὐ μὴν φύσεως μείωσις, ἢ μετάστασις Anast.S.*hod*.2(M.89.77B); **b.** its source, God and Christ, Dion.Ar.*d.n*.2.11(M.3.649C); *ib*.8.5(893A); in Inc., id.*e.h*.2.2.1(M.3.393A); εἴ γε οὖν φατε, ὅτι· τίς οὖν χρεία ἦν συντεθῆναι τὸν μηδὲν εὐεργετηθέντα θεὸν τῇ εὐεργετηθείσῃ φύσει...ἐροῦμεν ὑμῖν, ὡς ἡ τῶν εὐεργετουμένων θ., δι' ἧς τοσαύτην ἀγαθότητα καὶ δύναμιν εὐεργετικὴν ἔχειν ἑαυτὸν θριαμβεύσας τῷ κόσμῳ,...δοξάζεται Leont.H. *Nest*.1.18(M.86.1468D); τὴν ἐν Χριστῷ πάντων ἀνακεφαλαίωσιν καὶ θ. ἐν ἑαυτῷ τῶν οὐ θείων φύσεων *ib*.3.1(1605A); ἀγωγὲ Χριστέ, τὸν βροτοῖς ἐναντίον, πρόβλημα τὴν σάρκωσιν ἀρρήτως ἔχων, ἤσχυνας, ὄλβον τῆς θ. φέρων Jo.D.*carm.theog*.93(p.208; M.96.824A); through priesthood ἡ φύσει θεότης, ἡ ἀρχὴ τῆς θ., ἐξ ἧς τὸ θεοῦσθαι τοῖς θεουμένοις ἀγαθότητι θείᾳ τὴν ἱεραρχίαν, ἐπὶ σωτηρίᾳ καὶ θ. πάντων τῶν λογικῶν τε καὶ νοερῶν οὐσιῶν, ἐδωρήσατο Dion.Ar.*e.h*.1.4(M. 3.376B); **c.** as work of grace ἡ...πνεύματος χάρις...τοὺς ταύτης [sc. heavenly city] πολίτας ἀξιοῦσα τῆς κατὰ χάριν θ. ‡Proc.G. *Pr*.18:11(M.87.1408A); θεώσεως γὰρ οὐδὲν γενητὸν κατὰ φύσιν ἐστὶ ποιητικόν, ἐπειδὴ μηδὲ θεοῦ καταληπτικόν· μόνης γὰρ τῆς θείας χάριτος ἴδιον πέφυκεν εἶναι, τὸ ἀναλόγως τοῖς οὖσι χαρίζεσθαι θέωσιν Max.*qu. Thal*.22(M.90.321A) = id.*cap*.1.76(M.90.1212A); id.*cap*.4.32(1317B); ἄρα τῆς ἡμῶν οὐκ ἔστι δυνάμεως πρᾶξις ἡ θ., ἧς οὐκ ἔχομεν κατὰ φύσιν τὴν δύναμιν· ἀλλὰ μόνης τῆς θείας δυνάμεως id.*opusc*.(M.91.33C); θέωσιν ὡς ἀγαθὸς ὑπὲρ φύσιν τῷ ἀγομένῳ δωρούμενος [sc. θεός] id. *ep*.9(M.91.445C); **d.** through instrumentality of sacraments ἑκάστης ἱεροτελεστικῆς πραγματείας καὶ τὰς μεριστὰς ἡμῶν ζωὰς εἰς ἑνοειδῆ θ. συναγούσης Dion.Ar.*e.h*.3.1(M.3.424C); baptism ἐπιβὰς δὲ τοῖς θείοις ἴχνεσι τοῦ ἀθλητῶν πρώτου δι' ἀγαθότητα, ταῖς θεομιμήτοις ἀθλήσεσι τὰς πρὸς θέωσιν ἐναντίας αὐτῷ καταπαλαίσας ἐνεργείας τε καὶ ὑπάρξεις, συναποθνήσκει Χριστῷ, μυστικῶς εἰπεῖν τῇ ἁμαρτίᾳ κατὰ τὸ βάπτισμα *ib*.2.3.6(404A); eucharist δεῦρό μοι στῆθι τῶν ἱερῶν πλησίον, καὶ τῆς μυστικῆς ταύτης τραπέζης, κἀμοῦ τοῦ διὰ τούτων μυσταγωγοῦντος τὴν θ. Gr.Naz.*or*.25.2(M.35.1200B); ταῖς ἱερατικαῖς τάξεσιν...ἡ τῆς ἁγιωτάτης εὐχαριστίας κοινωνία μεταδίδοται πρὸς τοῦ τελέσαντος αὐτὰς ἱεράρχου·...ὅτι καὶ αὐτῆς τῆς κοινωνικῆς καὶ θειοτάτης δωρεᾶς ἀναλόγως αὐταῖς καθ' ἑκάστην αἱ ἱεραὶ πᾶσαι τάξεις μετέχουσι πρὸς τὴν οἰκείαν αὐτῶν τῆς θ. ἀναγωγὴν καὶ τελείωσιν Dion. Ar.*e.h*.6.3.5(536C); τὴν ἱερὰν τῶν τελουμένων θέωσιν ἱερουργοῦσαι *ib*. 3.3.7(436C); ‡Proc.G.*Pr*.9:5(M.87.1301D); through priesthood, Dion. Ar.*e.h*.1.2(372D); **e.** connexion with virtue ἐπὶ τὴν ἑνοειδῆ θ. ἐν συμμετρίᾳ τῇ καθ' ἡμᾶς ἀναγόμεθα, θεόν τε καὶ θείαν ἀρετήν *ib*. (373A); esp. charity, Gr.Naz.*carm*.1.2.34.161(M.37.957A); οὐδὲν... τῆς θείας ἀγάπης θεοειδέστερον...οὐδὲ ἀνθρώποις πρὸς θ. ὑψηλότερον Max.*ep*.2(M.91.393B); θείαν ἐπιστήμην, καὶ γνῶσιν ἄπταιστον, καὶ ἀγάπην καὶ εἰρήνην, ἐν αἷς καὶ δι' ὧν ἡ θ. id.*myst*.(M.91.680C); as state in next world, depending on exercise of virtue in this, id. *cap*.1.75(M.90.1209C); id.*qu.Thal*.9(M.90.285B); **f.** in rel. to scripture πᾶσα...ἁγιόγραφος δέλτος...τὴν ὑπερκόσμιον Ἰησοῦ θεολογίαν τοῖς πρὸς θέωσιν ἐπιτηδείοις ὑφηγήσατο Dion.Ar.*e.h*.3.3.4(M.3.429D); **g.** and to contemplation μακάριος οὗτος, τῆς τε ἐντεῦθεν ἀναβάσεως, καὶ τῆς ἐκεῖσε θ., ἣν τὸ γνησίως φιλοσοφῆσαι χαρίζεται, καὶ τὸ ὑπὲρ τὴν ὑλικὴν δυάδα γενέσθαι, διὰ τὴν ἐν τῇ τριάδι νοουμένην ἑνότητα Gr. Naz.*or*.21.2(M.35.1084C); **h.** of deification as goal of life εἰς τοῦτο ἡμᾶς πεποίηκεν ὁ θεός, ἵνα γενώμεθα θείας κοινωνοὶ φύσεως, καὶ τῆς αὐτοῦ ἀϊδιότητος μέτοχοι, καὶ φανῶμεν αὐτῷ ὅμοιοι κατὰ τὴν ἐκ χάριτος θ. Max.*cap*.1.42(M.90.1193D); **i.** of the man who has attained to it ὁ καθόλου θεῖος ἀνήρ, ὁ τῶν θείων ἄξιος κοινωνός, ὁ πρὸς τὸ τοῦ κατ' αὐτὸν θεοειδοῦς ἄκρον ἐν παντελέσι καὶ τελειωτικαῖς θ. ἀνηγμένος, οὐδὲ τὰ σαρκὸς ἐνεργήσει παρὰ τὴν κατὰ φύσιν ἀναγκαιότητα, καὶ τοῦτο εἰ τύχοι παρέργως, ναὸς δὲ ἅμα καὶ ὀπαδὸς ἐν τῇ κατ' αὐτὸν ἀκροτάτῃ θ. τοῦ θεαρχικοῦ πνεύματος ἔσται, τῷ ὁμοίῳ τὸ ὅμοιον ἐνιδρύων Dion.Ar.*e.h*.3.3.7(M.3.433C).

***θεωτικός**, *divine*, Dion.Ar.*c.h*.3.2(M.3.165A); *ib*.6.1(200C).

***θεωχώρητος**, *God-containing*; of BMV, Jo.Thess.*dorm.BMV*2. 14(p.437.16).

[*]**θήβη**, ἡ, v. θίβη.

[*]**θητήρ**, *seeing*, Nonn.*par.Jo*.14:22(M.43.869C); as subst., *ib*. 15:27(877B).

θηλάζω, *suck*; met., ref. Christ as milk received from Father's breast μακάριοι...ὅσοι τοῦτον θ. τὸν μαστόν Clem.*paed*.1.6(p.116.10; M.8.301B); *draw down*, of Moses οὐρανόθεν...ἐθήλασε μάννα Leont.B. *mesopent*.(M.86.1981C).

***θηλάρσην**, *male and female*; of Gnost. aeons, Gr.Naz.*carm*.2.1. 11.1166(M.37.1109A).

***θηλαυγῶς**, prob. f.l. for τηλαυγῶς *clearly*, Philox.*ep*.22(p.173).

***θηλεύομαι** (-ιεύομαι, -υεύομαι), *behave as a woman*, Epiph.*exp. fid*.10(p.510.7; M.42.800A); αἰσχρὸν...τὸ ἄνδρα θηλιεύεσθαι id.*haer*.66. 33(p.72.26; θηλυεύεσθαι M.42.81B).

θηλή, ἡ, *teat, nipple*, met. θ. βοτρύων Mac.Mgn.*apocr*.4.11(p.171. 31); ref. spiritual nourishment ἡμῖν ἐπέχει τὴν πληρωθεῖσαν ὑπὸ τοῦ λόγου θ. Gr.Nyss.*hom.1 in Cant*.(M.44.785D); *feed, suck* θ. ἐκ παρθενίας as miracle pointing to Christ's divinity, id.*or.catech*.23(p.86. 15; M.45.61B).

***θηλιεύομαι**, v. *θηλεύομαι.

θηλυδρίας, ὁ, *effeminate* or *homosexual person*, ref. 1Reg.20:30 θ. υἱὸς κορασίων αὐτομολούντων προσηγορεύθη Gr.Nyss.*or.dom*.2 (p.34.36; M.44.1141C); Const.Diac.*laud*.24(M.88.505D); as adj., Amph.*Seleuc*.93(M.37.1583A); Gr.Naz.*carm*.2.1.12.425(M.37.1197A); Thdt.*affect*.7(p.183.27; 4.885).

θηλυδριώδης, *feminine* ψυχὴ...ὀνόματι θηλυκῷ προσαγορεύεται, πάσης...θ. φύσεως ἀφέστηκεν †Gr.Thaum.*ep.Philagr*.(M.46.1104C); neut. as subst., *the feminine element*, Diad.*perf*.62(p.72.2).

***θηλυεύομαι**, v. *θηλεύομαι.

***θηλύζωος**, *female*; neut. as subst., *female creature*, *Apoc.Dan*. C(p.122.12).

***θηλυκεύομαι**, *behave like a woman*; ptcpl., *effeminate*, Clem.*str*. 4.4(p.255.8; M.8.1228C).

***θηλυκοειδής**, *woman-like, feminine*, Jo.Clim.*past*.13(M.88. 1193A).

θηλυκός, **1.** *effeminate* τὸ θ. ‡Just.*or.Gr*.2(M.6.233B); **2.** *feminine* τὰ δαιμόνια...θ. *T.Sal*.1.7(p.10.9); in Valent. system τὰ μὲν ἀρρενικὰ ἀγγελικὰ καλοῦσι, τὰ θ. δὲ ἑαυτούς,...ἐπὶ τοῦ Ἀδὰμ...πᾶν...τὸ θ. σπέρμα ἀρθὲν ἀπ' αὐτοῦ Εὔα γέγονεν...τὰ θ. δὲ ἀπανδρωθέντα ἑνοῦται τοῖς ἀγγέλοις καὶ εἰς πλήρωμα χωρεῖ Clem.*exc.Thdot*.21(p.113.20; M.9.668B); ref. masc. and fem. names given to each pair of aeons, Epiph.*haer*.31.2(p.385.1; M.41.476C); Gnost., of earth and water καλεῖται τοῦτο τὸ ἡμισφαίριον...θ. ... καὶ κακοποιόν Hipp.*haer*.4.43 (p.66.13; M.16.3107A); τὰ [sc. ὀνόματα]...εἰς τὸν ἄρτιον ἀριθμὸν λέγοντα...θ. καὶ κακοποιά *ib*.(p.67.9; 3107C).

θηλυμαν-έω, *be mad after women*, ref. Gen.6:2 βλασφημίας... ὑπάρχει τὸ οἴεσθαι ἀγγέλους ~εῖν ‡Caes.Naz.*dial*.48(M.38.917).

θηλυμανής, **1.** *mad for women*, Gr.Naz.*carm*.1.2.29.170(M.37. 896A); ὁ θ. ‡Bas.*struct.hom*.1.24(1.335F; M.30.36C); **2.** *mad*, Or.*Jo*. 10.32(18; p.206.1; M.14.364D).

θηλυμανία, ἡ, *madness about women* διὰ τῶν ἄστρων στρώνω [sc. a demon] [? l. οἰστρῶ] θηλυμανίας *T.Sal*.5.8(p.23.5); reality of Inc. rejected by those addicted to θ. because they regard the body as naturally impure, Anast.S.*hod*.14(M.89.252C).

θηλύνω, *become feminine*; met., of God ἀγαπήσας ὁ πατὴρ ἐθηλύνθη Clem.*q.d.s*.37(p.184.2; M.9.641C).

θῆλυς, *female*; **1.** in gen., ref. controversy with pagans τὰ... ἐνάρετα ἅπαντα ὁμοίως καὶ τὰς θ. δύνασθαι φυλάσσειν ὁ θεὸς ἐποίησεν Just.*dial*.23.4(M.6.528B); Clem.*paed*.1.4(p.96.9; M.8.260D); of homosexuality as ἡ θ. νόσος id.*prot*.2(p.18.6; M.8.92A); Eus.*v.C*.3.55 (p.103.7; M.20.1120C); texts on subjection of women quoted agst. divinity of pagan goddesses, *Const.App*.3.9.3; ref. Fall τὸ θ. τουτέστιν τὴν τῶν ἀνθρώπων ἄγνοιαν Epiph.*haer*.37.2(p.52.28; M.41. 644D); **2.** Gnost.; **a.** of the passive principle in creation Ἀχαμώθ, ἥτις ἐστὶ θ. Iren.*haer*.1.21.5(M.7.668Af.); cf.*ib*.1.2.3(456A); τῆς ἄνω θ. ... ἧς τὰ πάθη κτίσις γέγονεν Clem.*exc.Thdot*.67(p.129.8; M.9. 692A); δύο εἰσὶ παραφυάδες τῶν ὅλων αἰώνων...ὧν...φαίνεται...ἡ... ἑτέρα κάτωθεν, ἐπίνοια μεγάλη, θ., γεννῶσα τὰ πάντα Hipp.*haer*.6.18 (p.144.11ff.; M.16.3222A); **b.** of other female aeons, Valent. series named, Iren.*haer*.1.2.6(M.7.464B); Ophite θ. ... τὸ πνεῦμα καλοῦσι Thdt.*haer*.1.14(4.306); **c.** of numbers and elements, the fem. numbers, 2, 4, 6, and 8 used as names of aeons, Val.Gn.ap.Epiph.*haer*. 31.6(p.393.7; M.41.484C); this derived from Pythagoreanism, Hipp. *haer*.1.2(p.6.1ff.; M.16.3024B); *ib*.4.51(p.75.10ff.; 3119B); earth and air fem. in the same system, *ib.*1.43(p.66.14ff.; 3107A); **d.** Valent., of a principle including both sexes *πατέρα...ὑπὲρ ἄρρεν, καὶ ὑπὲρ θ. θέλουσι* Iren.*haer.*1.2.4(M.7.460A); *ib.*1.14.1(593A); Hipp.*haer.*6.18(p.145.3; M.16.3222D); *οἱ μὲν γὰρ αὐτὸν* [sc. *τὸν Βυθὸν*]...*λέγουσι, μήτε ἄρρενα, μήτε θ. ... εἶναι* Iren.*haer.*1.11.5(569A); *ὁ Βυθὸς...τὸν Ὅρον προβάλλεται οὐ μετὰ συζύγου θηλείας* Thdt.*haer.*1.7(4.298); **e.** ref. orthodox doctrine that there is neither male nor female in angels, elements, and heavenly bodies, Hipp.*haer.*10.33(p.289.12ff.; M.16.3447C,D); Thdt.*haer.*5.7(4.401ff.).

***θήλυσμα, τό,** *effeminacy, effeminate pleasure,* Gr.Naz.*carm.*1.2.33.69(M.37.933A).

θηλύτης, ἡ, *femininity,* Clem.*prot.*4(p.46.32; M.8.160B).

θημωνιά, ἡ, *heap*; **1.** in gen., Gr.Nyss.*usur.*(M.46.441B); Chrys.*fr.Job* 2:8(M.64.552A); id.*hom.63.4 in Mt.*(7.633E); **2.** met., of converts, Just.*dial.*113.6(M.6.757A); *θ. τῶν ἀρετῶν* Procl.CP *or.*18.3(M.65.821B); exeg. Cant.7:2, of the virtues, Or.*schol.in Cant.*7:2(M.17.281B); *θ. σίτου...λέγεται ἡ ἁγία ἐκκλησία* Ph.Carp.*Cant.*197(M.40.124B); *ἡ...τῶν θείων βρωμάτων δεκτικὴ κοιλία...θ. σίτου...λέγεται* Nil. ap.Proc.G.*Cant.*7:2(M.87.1729A); *τάχα...ἡ ἀμέριμνος διάνοια, καὶ τὴν βασιλικὴν μορφὴν αἰτοῦσα, θ. ἐστι ib.*; *θ. ... τουτέστι, μετὰ τὰ ταμιεῖά σου τῆς ψυχῆς τῶν κεκρυμμένων μυστηρίων* Thdt.*Cant.*7:2(2.144).

θῆξις, ἡ, *moment ὑπὸ θῆξιν Protev.*18(p.35); *ἐν δὲ ἀναστάσει...ὑπὸ θῆξιν...τὸ ἔργον* Epiph.*anc.*95(p.116.29; M.43.189D); id.*haer.*77.17(p.431.2; M.42.665A); ref. Num.17:6 *ὑπὸ θῆξιν μιᾶς ὥρας ἐτελεσιούργησε τὸ διὰ δεκαδύο μηνῶν...γινόμενον* id.*anc.*95(p.117.3; 192A); *κατὰ θῆξιν every little while, Didasc.Jac.*3.4(p.54.27); for *θίξις*, Gr.Nyss.*bapt.diff.*(M.46.420D).

θήρ, ὁ, *beast*; of persecutors, Eus.*h.e.*10.4.14(M.20.853C); of Devil, *Ep.Lugd.ib.*5.1.57(429B); ‡Gr.Naz.*Chr.pat.*proem.17(M.38.135A).

θήρα, ἡ, 1. *pursuit*; met., of Christ's call of apostles *θ. τῶν τεθηρευκότων* Cyr.*Lc.*5:2(M.72.553A); **2.** *prey*; met., of converts from sin or error, Chrys.*incomprehens.*1.6(1.450E); f.l. for *θύραν*, Isid.Pel.*epp.*5.569(M.78.1644D).

θήραμα, τό, *prey, spoil*; met., ref. powers of evil or error, of sinner as *θ. ... τοῦ διαβόλου* Bas.*hom.*3.2(2.18C; M.31.204A); *ib.*17.2(139C; M.485A); *τῆς...Ἀρειανικῆς ἐξαπάτης...θ. γενομένη* Thdt.*h.e.*4.12.4(3.968); ref. powers of good; of Christ making Devil his prey through Cross, ‡Meth.*palm.*6(M.18.393C); of continual remembrance of God *τοῦ...σωτηρίου θ.* Diad.*perf.*61(p.70.1).

θηρατέον, *one must hunt after,* Clem.*str.*7.15(p.65.4; M.9.528A).

θηρατής, ὁ, *hunter*; **1.** of a fisherman, Vict.*Mc.*8:25(p.345.7); met., of heretics *λέξεων θ.* Sever.*Abr.*6(M.56.560); **2.** = Lat. *venator, bestiarius,* professional fighter against beasts in the arena, *M.Perp.*19(p.91.4).

θήρατρον, τό, *snare*; met., of God's providential devices for winning souls, Thdt.*qu.50 in 1Reg.*(1.386); of enticement to sin *θ. ἀνθρώπων τὸ κάλλος τοῦ σώματος* Clem.*paed.*2.10(p.225.23; M.8.533B); of riches, id.*q.d.s.*17(p.170.16; M.9.621A); of attention to dress, Chrys.*sac.*6.3(p.143.17; 1.422D); of a temple of Venus *ψυχῶν θ.* Eus.*v.C.*3.55(p.102.30; M.20.1120C); plur., of Eunomian arguments, Cyr.*Jo.*1.4(4.29D); of Julian's devices to pervert Christians, Thdt.*h.e.*3.15.1(3.929).

θηράω, med., *search αὐτὰς* [sc. *γραφάς*]...*θηρώμενος* Geo.Pis.*carm.*3.12.

***θήρεθνα, τά,** *wild peoples τὰ πρὶν θ. ἐν σοὶ τυγχάνοντα πρόβατα* ‡Epiph.*hom.*1(M.43.432D).

θηρεπῳδός, ὁ, *charmer of wild beasts*; not to be baptized, *Const.App.*8.32.11 (v.l. *-αοιδός*); *σοφὸν...καταχρηστικῶς τὸν θ. προσηγόρευσεν* Thdt.*Ps.*57:6 (v.l. *θηριέπῳδον* 1.984).

θήρευμα, τό, 1. *prey, spoil*; plur., *game,* Gr.Nyss.*usur.*(M.46.448A); **2.** *snare,* met., ref. demon of sadness *τὰ θ. αὐτοῦ Schol.*24 in Jo.Clim.*scal.*5(M.88.789D).

θηρευτής, ὁ, *hunter*; met., of angels receiving souls at death, Or.*hom.16.1 in Jer.*(p.133.17; M.13.440C); of demons enticing to sin, id.*hom.16.4 in Jos.*(p.398.25; M.87.1025A); of preachers, S. Peter *λογικῶν...ζῴων...θ.* Eus.*theoph.*6(p.19*.22; M.24.628A); *θ. ... τοὺς...τῶν ἁγίων ἐκκλησιῶν ἡγουμένους τε καὶ μυσταγωγούς* Cyr.*Lc.*5:2(M.72.553A); of readers of scripture *θ. νοημάτων* Pall.*v.Chrys.*20(p.144.11; M.47.80); of an ascetic *ταύτης τῆς ἀρετῆς καὶ θ. καὶ παιδοτρίβης* Thdt.*h.rel.*2(3.1127).

θηρευτικός, *ready to hunt,* met. *Φίλιππος...θ. γέγονε τῶν...ψυχῶν* Or.*fr.27 in Jo.*(p.504.10).

θηρεύτρια, ἡ, *huntress,* Jo.Clim.*scal.*27(M.88.1097C).

θηρεύω, A. trans.; **1.** *hunt*; of demons hunting souls, Or.*hom.16.4 in Jos.*(p.398.26; M.87.1025A); **2.** *search for, seek τὸν ἡμῶν θάνατον θ.* Ath.*apol.Const.*35(M.25.641C); *τὸν ἐμὸν θ. θεόν* Thdt.*h.rel.*13(3.1209); of searching for meaning of scriptural passages, Or.*fr.1 in Jo.*(p.484.7); cf.*ib.36*(p.511.21); Eus.*d.e.*10.8(p.492.17; M.22.789D); Thdt.*Dan.*proem.(2.1053); **3.** *catch,* ref. hair of woman in Lc.7:37ff. *δι' ὧν ἐθήρευσε πρὸς ἁμαρτίαν νεότητα, ἐθήρευσεν ἁγιωσύνην* Tit.Bost.*fr.Lc.*7:44f.(p.170); of men caught by evil powers, Cyr.H.*catech.*4.1; in the toils of Arianism, Thdt.*h.e.*5.30.1(3.1069); of conversion, Eus.*theoph.*6(p.19*.8; M.24.625D); Chrys.*hom.47.2 in Jo.*(8.277A); Thdt.*h.e.*4.18.11(3.979); ref. Gen. 18:5 *ὁ Ἀβραὰμ τραπέζῃ τὸν θεὸν ἐθήρευσεν* Pall.*v.Chrys.*12(p.75.3; M.47.42).

B. intrans., *fish ὡς...ἁλιεῖς ἐθήρευον Mir.Artem.*40(p.67.5).

θηριάλωσις, ἡ, *capture of wild beasts,* ref. Gen.49:9[SM] *ἡ ἐκ νεκρῶν ἀνάστασις καὶ ἡ ἐξ ᾅδου, ὥσπερ ἔκ τινος θ., τοῦ σωτῆρος...ἀποφυγή* Eus.*d.e.*8.1(p.364.25; M.22.592C) = Proc.G.*Gen.*49:9(M.87.500A).

θηριάλωτος, *caught by wild beasts*; of food forbidden to Christians, *Hom.Clem.*7.8; *Can.App.*63; of martyrs killed by beasts, Gr.Nyss.*Steph.*2(M.46.725A); Thdt.*h.e.*4.26.4(3.1004); Bas.Sel.*v.Thecl.*1(M.85.529A); met., of those ensnared by Devil *τὸ Χριστοῦ πρόβατον θ.* Bas.*hom.*19.7(2.154C; M.31.520C); Chrys.*hom.4.5 in 2Cor.*(10.461E); *γίνεται...τὸ νόημα τὸ περὶ τοῦ ἀδελφοῦ θ. εἰ μετὰ μίσους νέμοι τὸ ἐν ἡμῖν* ‡Nil.*mal.cog.*17(M.79.1220C); Isid.Pel.*epp.*5.469(M.78.1600A); Jo.Mosch.*prat.*110(M.87.2973C).

***θηριοβολία, ἡ,** *attack by wild beasts,* Epiph.*haer.*8.8(p.195.23; M.41.221A); met., of heresy, *ib.*67.1(p.132.14; M.42.172C).

***θηριόβολος,** *infested by wild beasts*; met., ref. heresy *θ. τόπους* Epiph.*exp.fid.*1(p.496.24; M.42.773D).

θηριόβρωτος, *eaten by wild beasts,* Adam.*dial.*1.16(p.34.2; M.11.1741C); Gr.Nyss.*hom.in 1Cor.6:18*(M.46.496B); Chrys.*hom.8.6 in Col.*(11.388E).

***θηριογνώμων,** *beastlike*; of Arians, Nil.*epp.*1.206(M.79.160B); of Leo Isaurus, Jo.VI H.*v.Jo.D.*14(M.94.452A).

***θηριοδηκτικός,** v. sq.

θηριόδηκτος, *bitten by a wild beast,* esp. ref. serpent-bites, Bas.*renunt.*4(2.205C; M.31.633B); Epiph.*rescr.*1(p.155.16, v.l. *θηριοδηκτικόν* M.41.157D).

***θηριόεις,** *beastlike, savage*; of anger, Eudoc.*Cypr.*2.126(M.85.849C).

θηριομαχέω, *fight with wild beasts*; lit., of martyrs, Ign.*Eph.*1.2; id.*Trall.*10; *M.Polyc.*3.1; *A.Paul.et Thecl.*27(p.255.2); *M.Perp.*15(p.85.2); met., of suffering torments from captors, Ign.*Rom.*5.1; ‡Ign.*Tars.*1.1; of fighting against evil counsels, Pall.*h.Laus.*54(p.147.9; M.34.1227B).

***θηριομάχησις, ἡ,** *fighting with wild beasts*; as punishment for Christians, *M.Tar.*7(p.466).

θηριομαχία, ἡ, *fight against wild beasts* in arena; as punishment of martyrs, *A.Paul.et Thecl.*31(p.258.1, vv.ll. *-εῖον, -εῖν*); plur., *Ep.Lugd.*ap.Eus.*h.e.*5.1.37(M.20.421C).

θηριομάχος, *fighting with wild beasts,* Chrys.*hom.48.4 in Mt.*(7.499A); as subst., *one who fights with beasts* in arena; not to be watched by Christians, Iren.*haer.*1.6.3(M.7.508B); lowest of men, Chrys.*hom.17.5 in Rom.*(9.629B); of martyrs, *A.Paul.et Thecl.*30(p.257.5) = Bas.Sel.*v.Thecl.*1(M.85.529B).

***θηριομορφία, ἡ,** *animal form, bestial form,* Dion.Ar.*c.h.*2.5(M.3.144D); of heresy, Epiph.*haer.*32.1(p.438.28; M.41.544A); v. *θηρομορφία.*

θηριόμορφος, *having the form of a beast,* of pagan gods *αὐτοὶ...θ.* Athenag.*leg.*20.4(M.6.932C); ref. Ezech.1 *περὶ τῶν θ. τύπων* Max.*schol.c.h.*15.7(M.4.112D); *τὸ θ. ... ὅ περὶ τῶν ἀγγέλων φησὶν ἡ γραφή ib.*2.5(48B); Cosm.*schol.*(M.38.488) in Gr.Naz.*carm.*2.2(poem.)7.105; met., of heresy, Epiph.*haer.*27.8(p.313.4; M.41.377C); of evil, Isid.Pel.*epp.*2.174(M.78.625B); of avarice, Chrys.*hom.90.4 in Mt.*(7.843D); Isid.Pel.*epp.*2.233(668D); of the vicious soul, Chrys.*hom.4.8 in Mt.*(7.61C); cf.id.*hom.9.4 in 1Cor.*(10.78C); Isid.Pel.*epp.*5.555(1636C).

θηρίον, τό, *beast*; **1.** in gen., ref. pagan gods *εἰ...μηδὲν διενηνόχασιν τῶν φαυλοτάτων θ. ... οὐκ εἰσὶν θεοί* Athenag.*leg.*20.4(M.6.932C); of appearance of beasts assumed by devils, Ath.*v.Anton.*9(M.26.857A); ref. gladiatorial fights with beasts condemned as pomp of Devil, Cyr.H.*catech.*19.6; **2.** of man's dominion over beasts, Gen.1:28 applied to millennium *τίς οὖν ὁ δυνάμενος νῦν ἄρχειν θηρίων; Barn.*6.18; of beasts as not wild before Fall, Thphl.Ant.*Autol.*2.17(M.6.1080B); man's disobedience to God causing theirs to man, Chrys.*hom.9.4 in Gen.*(4.68B); **3.** *as instruments of martyrdom,* Ign.*Smyrn.*4.2; id.*Rom.*4.1; Herm.*vis.*5.3.2; *M.Polyc.*2.4; *Diogn.*7.7; Just.*dial.*110.4(M.6.729C); *Const.App.*5.1.1; **4.** symbolism, in gen. *τὸ θ. τοῦτο τύπος ἐστὶν θλίψεως τῆς μελλούσης τῆς* μεγάλης Herm.*vis*.4.2.5; εἰς τύπον ἐγένοντο τὰ...θ. ἐνίων ἀνθρώπων τῶν τὸν θεὸν ἀγνοούντων Thphl.Ant.*Autol*.2.17(M.6.1080B); animal symbolism used of God, Dion.Ar.*ep*.9.1(M.3.1105A); beasts in Dan.7 symbolizing pagan kingdoms, Hipp.*Dan*.4.2.1(M.10.680D); ‡Hipp.*consumm*.14ff.(p.294.19; M.10.916D); Chrys.*Dan*.7(6.237A); Thdt.*Dan*.7:3(2.1190); **5.** met.; **a.** of Devil and his angels; **i.** in gen., Clem.*prot*.1(p.8.3; M.8.61C); ref. gluttons κατ' εἰκόνα τοῦ πατρὸς αὐτῶν τοῦ λίχνου θ. id.*paed*.2.1(p.158.19; M.8.389A); **ii.** ref. Apoc.6 θηρία καλῶν γῆς, τὰς τῶν δαιμόνων καθ' ἡμῶν εἰς φθοροποιὰ πάθη ὀχλήσεις καὶ ἐπαναστάσεις Areth.*Apoc*.16(M.106.593A); **iii.** ref. Apoc.12 τὸ μὲν πρῶτον [sc. θ.]...ἐστιν ὁ ἀρχέκακος δράκων...σατανᾶς Oecum.*Apoc*.13:1(p.149); τινὲς...τὸ θ. τοῦτο δευτερεύουσάν τινα δύναμιν τοῦ σατανᾶ Andr.Caes.*Apoc*.36(M.106.332C); **iv.** ref. Apoc.17, cf. *manifestum est...quoniam ex his tres interficiet ille qui venturus est, et reliqui subjicientur ei, et ipse octavus in eis; et vastabunt Babylonem...et dabunt regnum suum bestiae, et effugabunt ecclesiam*, Iren.*haer*.5.26.1(M.7.1192C); τοῦτο τὸ θ. ὁ σατανᾶς ἐστιν· ὃς ἀποκτανθεὶς τῷ τοῦ Χριστοῦ σταυρῷ, πάλιν ἐπὶ συντελείᾳ ἀναζῆν λέγεται, ἐνεργῶν ἐν σημείοις καὶ τέρασι πλάνης διὰ τοῦ ἀντιχρίστου τὴν τοῦ σταυροῦ ἄρνησιν Andr.Caes.*Apoc*.54(M.106.380A); καθημένην...ἐπὶ θ. κοκκίνου, διὰ τὸ τῷ διαβόλῳ τῷ φονίῳ καὶ αἱμοχαρεῖ ταύτην, διὰ πονηρῶν πράξεων ἐπαναπαύεσθαι *ib*.53(376B); cf.Areth.*Apoc*.53(717A); **b.** of antichrist, Gr.Naz.*carm*.1.2.34.245(M.37.963A) cit. s. ἀντίχριστος; θ. τὸν ἀντίχριστον λέγει, διὰ τὸ ὠμὸν καὶ ἀπάνθρωπον καὶ αἱμοβόρον Oecum.*Apoc*.11:7(p.130) = Areth.*Apoc*.30(M.106.652B); his seal, Ephr.2.224F cit. s. τύραννος; τοῖς...ἁγίοις, Μεθοδίῳ καὶ Ἱππολύτῳ καὶ ἑτέροις, εἰς [αὐτὸν] τὸν ἀντίχριστον τὸ παρὸν θ. ἐξείληπται Andr. Caes.*Apoc*.36(M.106.332C); **c.** of heretics θ. τῶν ἀνθρωπομόρφων Ign. *Smyrn*.4.1; Clem.*str*.7.16(p.67.10; M.9.532B); Alex.Thess.*ep.Dion*. (p.160.26; M.25.393C); of Arianism as μέγα...θ. Ath.*h.Ar*.3(p.184. 18; M.25.697B); **d.** of non-Christians, ref. Is.11:7 ὁ ἐθνικὸς...διὰ τῆς ἄρκτου ἐμφαίνεται, ἀκαθάρτου καὶ ἀγρίου θ. Clem.*str*.6.6(p.457.12; M. 9.272C); of Pharisee θ. ἀνθρωπόμορφον ‡Chrys.*publ*.1.2(8.118B); **e.** moral ὡς θ. μεγάλῳ τῇ ἐπιθυμίᾳ *Hom.Clem*.12.7; exeg. Gen.1:26 ἐγένου...ἄρχων θηρίων, εἰ τῶν ἔξω ἄρχεις, τὰ δὲ ἔνδον ἀβασίλευτα καταλείψεις; ‡Gr.Nyss.*or.2 in Gen.1:26*(M.44.277A); θ., τὴν τῶν πολλῶν δόξαν Chrys.*sac*.5.8(p.139.5; 1.420D).

***θηριοπρεπής**, *bestial*; met., of angry men, Isid.Pel.*epp*.2.15(M. 78.468B); ref. Devil ὠμότης θ. Cyr.*Abac*.20(3.534C); ref. soldiers dividing Christ's garments θ. ἀγριότης id.*Jo*.12(4.1062B).

***θηριοπρεπῶς**, *like a beast, like beasts*, Cyr.*Mich*.27(3.414B); id. *Nah*.25(3.503E); ref. evil spirits deterring Christians from good life, id.*Ps*.30:20(M.69.893A).

***θηριοπρόσωπος**, *with the face of a beast* δαίμονα...θ. *T.Sal*.18.1 (p.51.4).

***θηριοτόκος**, *producing wild beasts*, ‡Eust.*hex*.(M.18.782C).

***θηριότροπος**, *bestial*, Olymp.*fr.Bar*.3:16(M.93.765B); cf.id.*Job* 4:16(M.93.445C).

θηριότροφος, *devoured by wild beasts*, ‡Chrys.*neg*.1(8.136D).

***θηριόφρων**, *with the mind of a beast*, Isid.Pel.*epp*.2.135(M.78. 577C).

θηριόω, *turn into a beast*, Gr.Nyss.*v.Mos*.24(M.44.308B); met., pass. intrans., Hipp.*haer*.6.16(p.142.1; M.16.3219A); of man losing the divine image, Gr.Nyss.*hom.8 in Cant*.(M.44.945A).

θηριώδης, *beastlike, savage*, of the avaricious παρὰ φύσιν εἰς τὸ θ. ἑαυτοὺς ἐξάγειν Chrys.*hom.9.4 in 1Cor*.(10.79E); of Devil ὁ θ. Bas. Sel.*or*.3.3(M.85.53C).

θηριωδία, ἡ, *savagery, brutality*; **1.** in gen.; of the beasts, Chrys. *hom.4.8 in Mt*.(7.62B) ∞ Isid.Pel.*epp*.3.208(M.78.889C); **2.** met.; **a.** of savagery and cruelty in men, Chrys.*hom.71.3 in Jo*.(8.421B); Isid. Pel.*epp*.2.15(M.78.468A); Thdt.*Am*.2:1–3(2.1416); id.*haer*.5.28(4. 473); **b.** of refusal to forgive, Chrys.*hom.19.9 in Mt*.(7.258D); Nil. *epp*.2.312(M.79.353B); Andr.Cr.*Geo*.(p.xxiC); **c.** of avarice, Chrys. *hom.9.4 in 1Cor*.(10.80A); **d.** of sinfulness in gen., Eus.*d.e*.7.3(p.343. 20; M.22.560B); id.*p.e*.1.4(12C; M.21.41B); Chrys.*hom.4.8 in Mt*.(7. 62C) ∞ Isid.Pel.*epp*.3.208(M.78.889C).

θηρίωσις, ἡ, *turning into a beast*, Gr.Nyss.*v.Mos*.21(M.44.308A); met., *bestiality*, id.*hom.4 in Eccl*.(M.44.676C).

***θηρολεκτέω**, *hunt for words*; ref. heretics searching scripture for arguments, Epiph.*haer*.47.2(p.217.13; M.41.852D).

***θηρολεκτής**, ὁ, *hunter*, ? error for θηρολέτης, ‡Caes.Naz.*dial*. 140(M.38.1072).

θηρολετ-έω, med., *destroy* something *as if it were a wild beast* ~εῖσθαι τὴν κακουργίαν θέλεις Geo.Pis.*carm*.3.16.

θηρολέτης, ὁ, *slayer of beasts, hunter*, Gr.Naz.*carm*.1.2.15.18(M. 37.767A); Jo.Mal.*chron*.2 p.40(M.97.112A).

***θηρόλετος**, *killed by wild beasts*, Gr.Naz.*carm*.2.2(epigr.)80.8(M. 38.122A).

***θηρομορφία**, ἡ, *animal form*, Dion.Ar.*c.h*.2.1(M.3.137A, v.l. θηριο-); *ib*.15.7(336C, v.l. θηριο-).

θηροτόκος, *producing wild beasts*, Gr.Naz.*carm*.1.2.29.106(M.37. 894A).

***θηρότροπος**, *having the character of a wild beast*, Isid.Pel.*epp*.1. 351(M.78.381D).

θηροτρόφος, *feeding wild beasts*, met. αἱρέσεις θ. Geo.Pis.*carm*. 13.2.

***θηροφονία**, ἡ, *slaughter of wild beasts*, Gr.Naz.*or*.4.80(M.35. 605C).

***θηρώλεθρος**, *destroying wild beasts*, met., ref. destruction of passions πραότης...θ. Jo.Clim.*past*.15(M.88.1201C).

***θησαύρισις**, ἡ, *store, treasury*, met. θ. ἀγαθῶν ἔργων Thdr.Stud. *epp*.2.191(M.99.1581C).

θησαύρισμα, τό, *treasure*; met., of weekly recitation of Ps.118, ‡Chrys.*hom.1.1 in Ps.118*(5.685A).

***θησαυροδότης**, ὁ, *one who gives from a treasury* ἀνέμων θ. [sc. infant Christ as God] Tim.Ant.*Sym*.(M.86.244C).

***θησαυρομανία**, ἡ, *madness about treasures*, Tat.*orat*.22(M.6.856B; θησαυρὸν μανίας p.24.29).

θησαυρός, ὁ, **1.** *treasure*; of God θ. ... αἰώνιον Clem.*paed*.3.6(p.257. 31; M.8.608A); of sin, *diaboli thesaurus*, Or.*hom.6.9 in Ex*.(p.201.3; M.12.338C); martyrs as Lord's treasure, id.*hom.10.2 in Num*.(p.72. 19; M.13.639A); of relics of Chrys., Thdt.*h.e*.5.36.2(3.1078); of Cross, Andr.Cr.*or*.10(M.97.1020B); of divine truths, Clem.*paed*.3.12(p.284. 15; M.8.665C); of mysteries preached by Christ, Or.*Jo*.2.28(23; p.85. 12; M.14.164A); Law and Prophets as treasures of Israel, id.*hom. 14.12 in Jer*.(p.116.19; M.13.417B); of hidden meaning of scripture, id.*hom.8.1 in Gen*.(p.77.16; M.12.203C); of Christ prefigured in OT, id.*Cant*.1(p.97.11; M.13.90B); θ. ... τὸν πλοῦτον τῆς θείας σοφίας ἐν ταῖς ἱεραῖς γραφαῖς Isid.Pel.*epp*.2.4(M.78.460B); *ib*.4.208(1301C); of redemption and justification ὁ θ. τῆς σωτηρίας Clem.*prot*.10(p.68. 24; M.8.205C); θ. ... πνεύματος χορηγίαν, δικαιοσύνην, ἁγιασμόν, ἀπολύτρωσιν Chrys.*Eutrop*.2.11(3.397A); ref. 2Cor.4:7, Isid.Pel.*epp*.2.4 (M.78.460B); Thdt.*2Cor*.4:7(3.310); of virtues: faith and charity, Clem.*prot*.9(p.64.24; M.8.197B); wisdom, id.*str*.5.4(p.340.23; M.9. 41B); almsgiving, Chrys.*hom.69.3 in Jo*.(8.411D); id.*eleem*.3(3.253D); **2.** *treasury, storehouse*; of God, Or.*hom.10.6 in Jer*.(p.61.12; M.13. 344C); θ. ἀγαθῶν Eus.*e.th*.1.8(p.66.30; M.24.837C); ὁ θ. τῶν αἰωνίων ἀγαθῶν *Lit.Jac*.(p.198.22); of heaven οἱ θ. τοῦ πατρός *Dorm.BMV* 39(p.108); of men; soul as storehouse of God's gifts, Clem.*paed*.3. 6(p.257.25; M.8.608A); ἐκεῖ [sc. in the heart]...εἶναι τοὺς πονηροὺς θ. τῶν...ἁμαρτημάτων Ath.*ep.Amun*.(M.26.1172C); of Adam τῆς... συγγενοῦς φύσεως ὁ θ. Bas.Sel.*or*.1.3(M.85.33C); of BMV, Jo.Thess. *dorm.BMV* A 12(p.426.37); of scripture θ. πνευματικός Chrys.*hom. 60.3 in Gen*.(4.580D); id.*hom.2.1 in 2Cor.4:13*(3.280A); Isid.Pel. *epp*.2.5(M.78.461D); Cyr.*fr.Mt*.13:52(M.72.416A); οἱ ἀποστολικοὶ θ. Thdt.*Heb*.1:3(3.549); of its hidden sense τοὺς εἰς τοὺς θ. τῆς λέξεως ἐλθεῖν μὴ βουλομένους Or.*or*.23.3(p.351.19; M.11.489A); εἰ γὰρ δοκεῖ ...εἶναι σαφής, ἀλλ' ἔχει καὶ ἐναποκεκρυμμένον τινὰ θ. νοημάτων ἄφατον Chrys.*hom.in Mt.18:23*(3.6D); of a cemetery ὁ θ. τῶν νεκρῶν Gr.Ant.*mul.ung*.1(M.88.1848A).

θησαυροφυλακέω, *store up, hoard*, Bas.*reg.fus*.262(2.505A; M.31. 1260D).

θησαυροφυλάκιον (-εῖον), τό, *treasury, storehouse*, met. ταπεινοφροσύνη...θ. ἀρετῶν ‡Bas.*const*.16(2.559B; M.31.1377C); Gr.Nyss. *laud.Bas*.(M.46.817B); of soul as storehouse for divine truths, Chrys. *hom.9.1 in Jo*.(8.52D).

θητεία, ἡ, *slavery*; of spiritual bondage, Cyr.*Am*.74(3.335B).

θιασεύ-ω, **1.** *proceed* ὁ λόγος...~έτω †Gr.Thaum.*ep.Philagr*.(M. 46.1101C); **2.** *sanctify*, ‡Gr.Naz.*Chr.pat*.1141(M.38.227A).

θίασος, ὁ, **1.** *Bacchic orgy*; met., of Christian life as participation in divine mysteries δρόμῳ τὸν θ. διώκουσιν Clem.*prot*.12(p.84.15; M.8.240C); **2.** *religious sect*; of Christians, Eus.*h.e*.10.1.8(M.20.845A); id.*p.e*.6.10(280D; M.21.477A); Bas.*hom*.18.2(2.144A; M.31.496A); ὁ θ. τῆς ἐκκλησίας ‡Caes.Naz.*dial*.119(M.38.1005); *ib*.20(876); Gnostic, Iren.*haer*.1.13.4(M.7.585A); **3.** *company* θ. ἀρχαγγέλων Eus.*l.C*.1 (p.196.25; M.20.1320B); τῶν ἀποστόλων τὸν θ. Thdt.*affect*.5(p.137.9; 4.833); **4.** *banquet*; not to be frequented by virgins, Meth.*symp*.5. 4(p.58.2; M.18.104B); met. θ. πνευματικός Cyr.*Is*.4.1(2.543E).

θιασώτης, ὁ, **1.** *member of a company*; of angels as members of various hierarchies, Dion.Ar.*c.h*.2.1(M.3.136D); *ib*.3.2(165A); **2.** *participant in a banquet*; of Christians in eucharist, Ast.Am.*prod*.(p.111. 1); **3.** *follower, disciple*; of Christians, term not used at first by

Christians of themselves ὁ...'Ιησοῦς ὁ ὀφθεὶς τοῖς ἰδίοις θ. (χρήσομαι γὰρ τῷ παρὰ τῷ Κέλσῳ ὀνόματι) Or.*Cels*.3.23(p.220.1; M.11.945D); βίον οὐράνιον αὐτοῖς ἀληθείας δόγμασιν τοῖς θ. παραδούς [sc. Christ] Eus.*h.e*.1.3.13(M.20.73A); Isid.Pel.*epp*.1.499(M.78.453B); Cyr.*Jo*.4(4. 402A); τοῦ σωτῆρος ἡμῶν τοὺς θ. Thdt.*h.e*.3.8.1(3.921); of students of theology, Dion.Ar.*e.h*.1.1(M.3.372A); disciples of Word, Max. *ambig*.(M.91.1380A); of disciples of saints, Thdt.*h.e*.3.9.2(3.922); *ib*. 4.21.7(985); id.*h.rel*.2(3.1121); of followers of heresies τῆς Ἀρείου μανίας τοὺς θ. id.*h.e*.2.2.5(826); id.*Heb*.5:7–9(3.574).

θίβη ([*]**θήβη**), ἡ, *basket made of papyrus*, ‡Epiph.*hom*.3(M.43. 469A); Sophr.H.*mir.Cyr.et Jo*.35(M.87.3544Df.); Jo.D.*hom*.4.25(M. 96.624D); θήβη Cosm.Mel.*schol*.(M.38.366) in Gr.Naz.*carm*.1.2.1.313.

θίξις, ἡ, *touch* μὴ...ἐπιζητεῖτε 'Ιουδαϊκοὺς...καθαρισμοὺς ἐπὶ θίξει νεκροῦ *Const.App*.6.30.1; ref. angels who ate with Abraham ἀσωμάτῳ θ. τὴν τροφὴν ἀναλώσαντες Mac.Mgn.*apocr*.4.27(p.215.29); written for θῆξις in phrase ὑπὸ θῆξιν, Epiph.*haer*.31.1(p.383.8; M. 41.473B); *ib*.64.66(p.508.17; 1185B); cf.Diad.*perf*.88(p.122.16).

***θίτος**, sens. dub., qualifying one of the three parts of the brain, Jo.D.*ep*.(M.95.244C), perh. error for θυμικός or ἐπιθυμητικός, cf. Plato *Respublica* 440E.

θλαδίας, ὁ, *eunuch*, Ath.*h.Ar*.37(p.204.5; M.25.736D); *ib*.67(p.220. 15; 773C); Cyr.*ador*.14(1.483D).

***θλασμός**, ὁ, *crushing*, Nect.*Thdr*.6(M.39.1828B).

[*]**θλημαθής**, *patient*; for τλημαθής, Cyr.*Is*.3.1(2.370C).

θλιβερός, *afflicting*, Anast.S.*defunct*.(M.89.1193C); met., *wretched* θ. καιρός Didym.*Job* 6:15(M.39.1136B); στενωπὸς θ. Chrys.*hom.9.5 in 1Thess*.(11.493C); ref. earth after Fall θ. παροικία Isid.Pel.*epp*.1. 282(M.78.348C); neut. plur. as subst., *afflictions* ἀγαθότητι ὁ θεὸς πειραθῆναι θ. καὶ κακωτικῶν πρὸς σύμφορόν τι συνεχώρησεν Diod.*Ps*. 70:20(M.33.1610B); *ib*.90:15(1626A).

θλίβ-ω, **1.** *crush*; lit., of threshing corn, Hegem.*Arch*.9(p.14.9; M.10.1441A); *ib*.10(p.17.1; 1444B); met., of Christ as grapes crushed for men, Clem.*paed*.2.2(p.167.25; M.8.409B); ref. Jo.14:6, Mt.7:14 ἡ ὁδὸς...τεθλιμμένη ὑπὸ τῶν βιαζομένων...ἐπεὶ οὐκ εἴρηται '∼ουσα' ἀλλὰ 'τεθλιμμένη' Or.*Jo*.6.19(11; p.128.19; M.14.233B); of humanity oppressed by sin, id.*hom.14.11 in Jer*.(p.115.26; M.13.416D); of soul by body, Hegem.*Arch*.8(p.12.7; 1440A); **2.** *afflict*, Ign.*Philad*.6.2; μὴ θ. τὸ πνεῦμα τὸ ἅγιον τὸ ἐν σοὶ κατοικοῦν Herm.*mand*.10.2.5; τῶν σωματικῶν καὶ ∼όντων πραγμάτων Or.*hom.8.1 in Ex*.(p.217.25); through poverty, *T.Isach*.3.8; *T.Benj*.5.1; Ign.*Smyrn*.6; *Did*.5.2; Clem.*str*.7.12(p.49.25; M.9.496C); *Const.App*.2.31.2; **3.** *cause difficulty* δύναται...τὰ πρῶτα, τὰ ∼οντα ὡς πρὸς τὸν σωτῆρα, ἐφαρμόσαι τῷ 'Ιερεμίᾳ Or.*hom.1.7 in Jer*.(p.5.28; M.13.261C); **4.** *blame*, id.*Jo*. 2.19(13; p.76.16; M.14.148C); *ib*.10.27(17; p.200.1; 356A).

θλιβώδης, *distressing, grievous*, Nil.*epp*.4.16(M.79.557C).

***θλιπτέον**, *pressure must be brought*, Or.*comm.in Ex*.(M.12.265C).

θλιπτικός, *grievous*, Thdr.Stud.*epp*.2.30(M.99.1200D); *ib*.2.66 (1292A).

θλιπτικῶς, *with affliction*, Thdr.Stud.*epp*.2.38(M.99.1232C).

***θλιπτωρία**, ἡ, *oppression, torture*, Thdr.Stud.*cant*.16.7(p.372).

θλῖψις, ἡ, **1.** *affliction*; **a.** origin in sin, *T.Lev*.18.6; Herm.*vis*.2.3. 4; God not its source οὐ τὸ ἐνεργεῖν...αὐτὸν τὰς θ. οἴεσθαι χρή,...ἀλλὰ μὴ κωλύειν τοὺς ἐνεργοῦντας πεπεῖσθαι προσήκεν καταχρῆσθαί τε εἰς καλὸν τοῖς ἐναντίων τολμήμασιν Clem.*str*.4.12(p.286.14; M.8.1293D); inevitable accompaniment of spiritual gifts, Nil.*epp*.1.317(M.79. 197A); **b.** advantages, promotion of charity; to be suffered for love of Christ, Clem.*str*.4.13(p.288.30; M.8.1300B); αἱ θ. ... γίνονται...ἐπὶ δοκιμασίᾳ τῆς ἀληθινῆς πρὸς τὸν...θεὸν ἀγάπης Bas.*ep*.101(3.197A; M. 32.505C); id.*hom.in Ps*.23(1.144A; M.29.353A); Chrys.*hom.15.4 in Phil*.(11.317B); inducement to trust in God, Gr.Naz.*or*.17.5(M.35. 972B); Cyr.*Is*.3.3(2.452E); and to gen. moral improvement, Chrys. *exp.in Ps*.141:4(5.444A); καρτέρει τὰς θ.· ἐν αὐταῖς γὰρ αἱ ἀρεταὶ... φύονται Nil.*paraen*.92(M.79.1257A); Cyr.*Am*.76(3.338D); Diad.*perf*. 94(p.136.24); further knowledge of God, Clem.*str*.2.7(p.131.20; M.8. 969C); ἡ θ. ἀντὶ χαρᾶς ὑμῖν ἔστω· τὰ γὰρ τοιαῦτα παθήματα μέρος ἐστὶ μαρτυρίου ϹSard.*ep.Alex*.ap.Ath.*apol.sec*.38(p.117.15; M.25.316A); an occasion of divine consolation, Bas.*ep*.127(3.218B; M.32.533B); advantages gained only by those who accept wholeheartedly, Chrys.*exp.in Ps*.141(5.444A); οὐδὲ τὸν γενναῖον διαφθείρει θ. Jo. Clim.*scal*.4(M.88.741D); **c.** exeg. 2Cor.12:7 αἱ καθ' ἡμέραν θ. ... σκόλοψ λέγονται εἶναι Nil.*epp*.2.255(M.79.332A); **2.** *mortification* τὴν μετὰ τοῦ κηρύγματος διὰ τὸν κύριον θ. Clem.*paed*.2.8(p.194.21; M.8. 465D); of voluntary mortifications helping people to bear unpleasant necessities when they come, *ib*.3.8(p.260.13; 612B); ἡ βασιλεία...τῶν οὐρανῶν...ἔστι τῶν ἐν θ. πολλῇ...διαξάντων τὸν βίον τοῦτον Ath.*virg*.18(p.53.7; M.28.273A); θ. μικρὰ διὰ τὸν θεὸν γινομένη κρείσσων ἐστὶ μεγάλου ἔργου τοῦ ἀθλίπτως τελουμένου. ἡ ἑκούσιος θ., τὸ δοκίμιον τῆς πίστεως καὶ τῆς ἀγάπης ἀνατέλλει Jo.Clim.*scal*.4(M. 88.740D).

θνησιμαῖος (**θνηξιμαῖος**), *that has died a natural death*; **1.** lit., Or.*hom.10.8 in Jer*.(p.78.8; M.13.368A); Phot.*nomoc*.9.21(M.104. 1108A); met., *corrupt* θ. νόημα Gr.Nyss.*hom.2 in Cant*.(M.44.789A); **2.** neut. as subst.; in gen., Clem.*paed*.2.1(p.166.13; θνηξ- M.8. 405B); Ephr.2.196A; εἴ τις ἐπίσκοπος ἢ...ὅλως ἐκ τοῦ καταλόγου τοῦ ἱερατικοῦ φάγῃ...θ., καθαιρείσθω,...ἐὰν δὲ λαϊκὸς ᾖ, ἀφοριζέσθω *Can. App*.63; Thdt.*qu.7 in Lev*.(1.186); *corpse*, Eus.*Is*.5:25(M.24.121B); †Bas.*hom.in Ps*.115(1.375A; M.30.112C).

θνῆσις, ἡ, *death*, Didym.*Trin*.1.15(M.39.321B); of false beliefs as θνήσεις, Anast.S.*qu.et resp*.113(M.89.765B); of death of sin in the soul, Jo.Clim.*scal*.26(M.88.1016A); of mortification of unchastity as requisite in hermits, *ib*.27(1108B).

θνήσκω, *die*; **a.** lit., ref. divination πῶς...ὁ τεθνεὼς...δυνήσεται πρὸς τιμωρίαν τινὸς ἐξυπηρετῆσαι Tat.*orat*.17(p.19.21; M.6.844C); εἰ ...μὴ...τεθνήκει, ἔμεινεν ἂν μόνος ὁ κόκκος τοῦ σίτου Or.*hom.10.3 in Jer*.(p.73.15; M.13.360D); ἔθανεν [sc. Christ] ἀθανασίαν τῷ θνητῷ πορίζόμενος Meth.*Porph*.2(p.505.22; M.18.404A); **b.** met., of Christ γενόμενος...θάνατος διὰ τοῦ θανεῖν θανάτου *ib*.3(p.507.1; 401B); of ascetics τὸν θνητῶν βίον τεθνάναι δοκοῦντες Eus.*d.e*.1.8(p.39.17; M.22. 76C); of spiritual dying διὰ τὰς ἁμαρτίας ὑμῶν τεθνήκειτε ἂν τῷ θεῷ Herm.*sim*.9.28.6; Clem.*q.d.s*.42(p.189.16; M.9.649A); through heresy, *Const.App*.6.18.10; ended at baptism, Gr.Nyss.*hom.2 in Cant*.(M.44.789A); Nonn.*par.Jo*.8:25(M.43.817A); of eternal punishment as death of soul, Tat.*orat*.13(p.14.12; 833A) cit. s. ἀθανασία.

***θνητάθνητος**, *making death mortal, dealing death to death* θ. ... θυσία ‡Epiph.*hom*.2(M.43.452D).

θνητός, **1.** *mortal, perishable*, see also ἀθάνατος; **a.** of human nature in gen., Tat.*orat*.13(p.14.11; M.6.833A) cit. s. ἀθανασία; οὐδὲ θ. καλέσεις τὸν ἐν ὀλίγῳ χρόνῳ γενόμενον ἐν θανάτῳ Chrys.*hom. 79.3 in Jo*.(8.468D); τοῦ Ἀδὰμ...θ. διὰ τὴν ἁμαρτίαν γεγενημένου Thdt.*Rom*.5:12(3.56); Dion.Ar.*e.h*.3.3.11(M.3.440D); **b.** of Christ's humanity, Just.*dial*.14.8(M.6.505C); ἔλαβε σῶμα θ., ἵνα καὶ ὁ θάνατος ἐν αὐτῷ λοιπὸν ἐξαφανισθῆναι δυνηθῇ Ath.*inc*.13.9(M.25.120B); **c.** in pagan controversy γένεσιν ἂν λέγητε θεῶν, καὶ θ. αὐτοὺς ἀποφανεῖσθε Tat.*orat*.21(p.23.20; M.6.853A); cf.Athenag.*leg*.21.3(M.6.936A); *ib*. 28.5(936B); **d.** met., of the sinful soul, Or.*Jo*.13.61(59; p.293.13; M. 14.516C); **2.** *devised by mortals*, denied of Christianity οὐ...θ. ἐπίνοιαν *Diogn*.7.1.

***θνητοψυχῖται**, οἱ, name of sect holding that human soul perishes with body, Jo.D.*haer*.90(M.94.757B).

***θνητῶς**, *like mortals* οὐκ ἄρα ποτὲ θ. βιωτέον ἁγιαζομένους θεῷ Clem.*paed*.2.10(p.217.23; M.8.517B).

[*]**θοάσσω**, variant of θαάσσω, *sit*, †Apoll.*met.Ps*.28:10(M.33. 1349A; θαάσσω p.59).

θοινήτωρ, *feasting, eating* θ. λαῷ Nonn.*par.Jo*.2:2(M.43.760C); *ib*.6:14(796B).

θολοειδής, *dome-like*, Thdt.*Is*.40:22(p.158.34; 2.329).

***θόλον**, τό, *bathroom*, Jo.Mal.*chron*.14 p.360(M.97.536A).

θόλος, ὁ, **1.** *room*; of hermit's cell, Pall.*h.Laus*.35(p.100.11; M.34. 1107D); *ib*.8(p.28.15; 1025D); **2.** ? *canopy*, ? *tent* θ. βασιλικός Chrys. *hom.69.3 in Mt*.(7.684B).

θολός, ὁ, *mud*, Peratic ἡ δύναμις τοῦ ἀβυσσικοῦ θ. Hipp.*haer*.5.14 (p.108.16; M.16.3167A).

***θολόσοφος**, *wise as mud*; of iconoclasts, Jo.V H.*icon*.3(M.96. 1352A).

***θολότης**, ἡ, *dirt, filth*, fig. οὐ θολοῦται ὑπὸ αἱρετικῆς θ. *Mir. Artem*.34(p.54.24).

***θολοτικός**, v. *θολωτικός.

θολόω, *obscure, disturb*; met. in gen., ref. men as made in image of God κἂν τεθολωμένοι τύχωσιν ἄλλοι ἄλλων μᾶλλον Clem.*str*.7.14 (p.61.24; M.9.520C); οὐ...ἐκεῖνο εἰπεῖν ἔχει, ὅτι τὴν τοῦ πατρὸς οὐσίαν φῶς εἶναι τιθέμενος,...τὴν τοῦ μονογενοῦς φῶς...οἱονεὶ τεθολωμένον ὑπέλαβεν Bas.*Eun*.2.27(1.264C; M.29.636B); of faith of apostles disturbed by prospect of Passion, Chrys.*hom.54.3 in Mt*.(7.549A); of idolatry τεθολωμένην...τινα...διδασκαλίαν Cyr.*Os*.67(3.101E); of reason obscured and soul disturbed by false opinions, Clem. *str*.7.16(p.70.1; M.9.536C); *Mir.Artem*.34(p.54.23) cit. s. θολότης; by idolatry, Ath.*inc*.11.4(M.25.116B); philosophy, Epiph.*haer*. 8.2(p.187.15; M.41.208A); Apollinarianism, *ib*.77.15(p.428.29; M.42. 661A); iconoclasts, Jo.V H.*icon*.1(M.96.1349A); by moral evil, Or. *Jo*.20.32(26; p.369.14; M.14.645A); by sorrow, Meth.*symp*.8.4(p.85. 10; M.18.144B); cares and desires, Chrys.*hom.2.5 in Mt*.(7.28B); anger, id.*hom.16.5 in Ac*.(9.126E); drunkenness, Diad.*perf*.61(p.68.

14); by diabolical action, Or.*Jo*.20.36(29; p.376.33; M.14.660A); Mac.Mgn.*apocr*.2.21(p.44.3).

***θολωνέω**, *disturb, trouble*, Ant.Mon.*hom*.56(M.89.1604B).

θόλωσις, ἡ, **1.** *disturbance, clouding*, met. ἀπέχεσθαι τῶν ἐμποιούντων θ. ἐν τῷ ἡγεμονικῷ †Bas.*Is*.177(1.508B; M.31.416C); Chrysipp.*enc.in Jo.Bapt*.(p.41.22); **2.** *filth, dirt*, Diad.*perf*.27(p.30.3); met. θ. τῆς ἁμαρτίας Cyr.*Jo*.1.9(4.79E); καθαίρωμεν...ἑαυτοὺς...βιωτικῆς θ. Jo.D.*hom*.4.1(M.96.601C).

***θολωτικός**, *disturbing, confusing*, *Hom.Clem*.6.9 (v.l. -οτικόν).

§**θολωτός**, *clouded, disturbed*, met. μὴ θ. νῷ παρακαλεῖν τὸν θεόν Marc.Er.*opusc*.7.5(M.65.1077A).

θορυβάζω, **1.** *disturb, throw into confusion*, *Apoc.En*.14.8(p.38.12); **2.** pass. intrans., *be anxious, bustle about*, Eus.Al.*serm*.21.17 (M.86.444C).

***θορυβιαστής**, ὁ, *turbulent person, maker of trouble*, Hipp.*haer*.4.25(p.53.11; M.16.3087C).

θορώδης, *seminal*, Nemes.*nat.hom*.25(M.40.700A).

θράσος, τό, *temerity*, ref. eagerness for martyrdom ἀλώσιμον διὰ θράσος παρέχων ἑαυτόν Clem.*str*.4.10(p.282.24; M.8.1285C); dist. from θάρσος, Gr.Naz.*or*.5.8(M.35.673A).

[*]**θρασύγλωσσος**, *audacious in speech, insolent*, Geo.Pis.*van*.191 (M.92.1595A); id.*Sev*.458(M.92.1656A).

***θρασυλογία**, ἡ, *rash speaking*, Bas.*epit.can*.8(2.531B; M.31.1316A); Leont H.*Nest*.1.13(M.86.1452A).

θρασύνω, *embolden*; met., *stir up* the sea, *Ev.Barth*.(Vassiliev p.18).

θρασυστομία, ἡ, *impudence*; ref. heresy, Bas.*hom*.23.4(2.188B; M.31.597A).

θραῦσις, ἡ, *breaking, cracking*, Clem.*paed*.2.3(p.178.4; M.8.432C); Geo.Al.*v.Chrys*.49(p.226.26); met. θ. τῆς ψυχῆς Clem.*paed*.2.6 (p.187.16; 452B); *A.Jo*.64(p.182.21); of calamity in gen., Gr.Naz.*ep*.77(M.37.144B); id.*or*.16.10(M.35.948B).

θραυσμός, ὁ, *breaking*; met., *distress*, CSard.*can*.7.

θραύω, **1.** *break*, ptcpl. perf. τεθρασμένος Andr.Cr.*Agath*.(M.97.1440C); met. ὅρκια...θ. *Diogn*.11.5; **2.** *wound, offend* τὰ ὦτα θ. Clem.*paed*.2.6(p.187.14; M.8.452B).

θρέμμα, τό, **1.** *creature, offspring*, met. σπέρμα τοῦ Καΐν, θ. τοῦ διαβόλου Clem.*q.d.s*.37(p.184.17; M.9.461D); **2.** *sheep*; met., of Christians, Eus.*l.C*.2(p.199.16; M.20.1325B); of Christians with emperor as shepherd λογικῶν θ. *ib*.(p.200.18; 1328B); of bishop's flock, Thdt.*h.e*.4.26.4(3.1004); *ib*.5.3.14(1018); τῶν τῆς ἐκκλησίας θ. Euthal. Diac.*epp.Paul*.proem.(M.85.696C).

θρεπτάριον, τό, *young disciple*, *Apophth.Patr*.(M.65.148D).

θρεπτήρ, ὁ, *nourisher*; of Christ, Nonn.*par.Jo*.13:2(M.43.860B); as adj., *fostering*, met. θ. ἀγῶνες *CIG* 8638.

θρεπτήριον, τό, **1.** *nursery*, Andr.Cr.*or*.1(M.97.820B); **2.** plur., *price for rearing a child*, νόμῳ θ. τίνων [sc. Christ] Gr.Naz.*carm*.1.1.9.70(M.37.462A).

θρεπτικός, *nourishing*, met. οἱ τοῦ θεοῦ...οἰκτιρμοὶ...τοῦ τῆς καρδίας φωτὸς θρεπτικοί Meth.*symp*.10.2(p.123.15; M.18.196A); ὄντος θεοῦ λόγου ψυχῶν λογικῶν θρεπτικοῦ Eus.*d.e*.7.2(p.336.5; M.22.548C); cf.‡Chrys.*hom*.13(13.253A); τὸ...κακὸν...οὐδενός ἐστι...θρεπτικόν Dion.Ar.*d.n*.4.28(M.3.729B).

θρεπτικῶς, *by way of nourishment*, Eus.*fr.Lc*.22:30(M.24.604C).

θρηνητέον, *one must bewail*, Gr.Naz.*or*.14.38(M.35.908D); Isid. Pel.*epp*.2.285(M.78.716B).

θρηνήτρια, ἡ, *female professional mourner*, Chrys.*fr.in Jer*.9:17 (M.64.856D).

θρηνῳδέω, *lament*, Bas.Sel.*or*.11.3(M.85.156B); Areth.*Apoc*.55(M.106.733C).

***θρηνῳδῶς**, *in the manner of a dirge*, Thdr.Stud.*epp*.1.6(M.99.928A).

θρησκεία, ἡ, **1.** *worship*; **a.** of worship of God as natural instinct, ‡Just.*monarch*.1(M.6.312C,313B); men diverted from it by devils through the body, Meth.*Porph*.1(p.503.19; M.18.397D); as perfect in orthodox Christianity; laws of acceptable worship being revealed by Christ, Eus.*h.e*.2.3.2(M.20.144A); cf.Const.ap.eund.*v.C*.2.67(p.67.27; M.20.1040A); ὅσοι τῆς ἀληθινῆς...ἐπιμέλεσθε θ., εἰς τὴν καθολικὴν ἐκκλησίαν ἔλθετε Const.*ib*.3.65(p.112.17; 1141B); Ath.*gent*.40(M.25.80C); ref. communion with pagans ἐπιβλαβῆ...τὴν κατὰ τὴν θ. κοινωνίαν *Const.App*.4.10.4; τῆς θ. τὸ σύμβολον Dion.Ar.*e.h*.3.3.7 (M.3.436C); **b.** of worship of creatures, ref. apparition of demons ἵνα...τῆς εἰς αὐτοὺς θ. τοῖς ὁμοίοις αὐτοῖς τὰς ἀφορμὰς παράσχωσιν Tat.*orat*.16(p.17.28; M.6.841A); ref. Dt.4:19 ὁδὸς...ἣν αὕτη δοθεῖσα τοῖς ἔθνεσιν ἀνακῦψαι πρὸς θεὸν διὰ τῆς τῶν ἄστρων θ. Clem.*str*.6.14 (p.487.19; M.9.333B); **2.** *religion, creed*, in gen., Or.*Cels*.8.68(p.285.21; M.11.1620C); of belief in one God τῇ μοναρχικῇ θ. *Hom.Clem*.7.12; κατὰ τὰς τῶν θ. διαφορὰς μεθαρμόζειν προσήκει καὶ τὴν κατήχησιν Gr.Nyss.*or.catech*.proem.(p.2.1; M.45.9A); τῆς...Ἀρειανῆς θ. Socr. *h.e*.4.1.6(M.67.464B); πᾶσαι αἱ οὖσαι ἐπὶ γῆς θ. ‡Just.*qu.Chr*.1.3(M.6.1409C); partic. of Christianity οὐ...τὴν κατὰ τὸν θεὸν ἔγνω [sc. ἡ φιλοσοφία] θ. Clem.*str*.6.15(p.494.5; M.9.348A); ref. Judaic Christianity ἡ...ὑπ' αὐτοῦ [sc. τοῦ θεοῦ] ὁρισθεῖσα θ. *Hom.Clem*.7.8; cf.*ib*.11.28; opp. heresy τὴν ὀρθόδοξον θ. Meth.*symp*.8.10(p.92.24; M.18.153B); ἡ θ. Const.ap.Eus.*v.C*.3.17(p.84.27; M.20.1073B); Soz.*h.e*.1.8.3 (M.67.876D); οὕτως ἐκθέμενος τὴν πίστιν ὁ...Φλαβιανὸς ἔσωσεν τὴν ὀρθόδοξον καὶ καθολικὴν θ. CChalc.*act*.1(*ACO* 2.1.1 p.114.16; H.2.129A).

θρήσκευμα, τό, *religion, creed, tenet* ἐλεγχθήτω τὸ θ. ὑμῶν...ὅπως καὶ ὑμεῖς ἀποστήσησθε τῆς παλαιᾶς ὑμῶν πλάνης *A.Jo*.40(p.170.25); *ib*.39(p.170.12); ‡Felix III Papa *ep.Petr*.1(p.20.29; H.2.820C).

***θρησκεύσιμος**, *of worship* τόπος ὁ θ. Gallienus Imp.ap.Eus.*h.e*.7.13(M.20.673D).

θρησκευτήριον, τό, *place of worship*, ‡Jo.D.*Artem*.17(p.31.25; M.96.1268B).

θρησκευτής, ὁ, **1.** *worshipper* μόνου θεοῦ...καὶ Χριστοῦ...θ. Mel. *fr*.(p.308; M.5.1213); **2.** ?*monk*, Synes.*ep*.4(M.66.1340A).

***θρησκευτικός**, **1.** *pious*; superl., as imperial title, *Cod.Afr*.93 (Lat. *religiosissimus*); **2.** s.v.l., ?*pertaining to worship*, Ath. Scholast.*coll*.4.5(p.49).

θρησκεύ-ω, **1.** *worship*; **a.** supposed etym. πόθεν...τὸ ~ειν; οὐ παρὰ Θρᾳκῶν, καὶ ἡ κλῆσις πειθέτω σε; Gr.Naz.*or*.4.109(M.35.645A); **b.** in paganism θ. ... τὴν θρησκείαν τοῦ ὑψίστου *1Clem*.45.7; *Diogn*.2.8; Just.*1apol*.62.2(M.6.421C); τῷ ~ομένῳ...θεῷ [i.e. Apollo] Const. *or.s.c*.18(p.179.10; M.20.1285C); ref. abolition of idolatry at CP ὡς μηδαμοῦ φαίνεσθαι...τῶν...θεῶν ἀγάλματα...~όμενα Eus.*v.C*.3.48 (p.98.7; M.20.1108C); τὰ ἄψυχα ~οντες ἀντὶ τῆς ἀληθείας Ath.*gent*.14(M.25.32B); ὁ...Βάλης πᾶσι μὲν τοῖς ἄλλοις [sc. pagans] ἐπέτρεψε ~ειν ᾗ βούλονται καὶ τὰ ~όμενα θεραπεύειν Thdt.*h.e*.5.20.3(3.1055); Cyr.*Is*.4.2(2.589B); **c.** in Christianity πυνθανόμενον...πῶς ~οντες αὐτὸν [sc. τὸν θεόν] ⟨τόν⟩ τε κόσμον ὑπερορῶσι *Diogn*.1.1; ἐν...τῷ θεωρητικῷ βίῳ ἑαυτοῦ τις ἐπιμελεῖται ~ων τὸν θεόν Clem.*str*.4.23 (p.315.31; M.8.1361A); ἔστι [sc. gnosis] ⟨τὸ⟩ ~ειν τὸ θεῖον διὰ τῆς ὄντως δικαιοσύνης, ἔργων τε καὶ γνώσεως *ib*.6.9(p.470.11; M.9.297B); cf.*ib*.7.1(p.3.28; 404B); Or.*Cels*.1.26(p.78.23; M.11.712A); οἴεται [sc. Celsus] ἐκ τοῦ θ. ἡμᾶς μετὰ τοῦ θεοῦ τὸν υἱὸν...ἀκολουθεῖν...τὸ καθ' ἡμᾶς...καὶ τοὺς ὑπηρέτας τοῦ θεοῦ θεραπεύεσθαι *ib*.8.13(p.230.5; 1533C); τὸ...πλῆθος τῶν ~όντων Const.*or.s.c*.20(p.184.15; M.20.1296B); οὔ μοι δοκοῦσιν ὑγιαίνειν τὴν διάνοιαν οἱ...τὸν...λόγον μὴ ~οντες Ath.*gent*.47(M.25.96B); δι' αὐτοῦ [sc. τοῦ Χριστοῦ] τὸν πατέρα θ. id.*inc*.51.3(M.25.188B); **2.** *venerate* τῷ πάλαι ~ομένῳ παρ' αὐτοῖς τόπῳ [i.e. Jerusalem] Eus.*theoph*.12(p.31*.12; M.24.649B); ὡς ἱερὸς ~όμενος [sc. Gilgal] id.*onomast*.(p.66.4); **3.** *observe religiously*, ref. Ezech.44:27 τῇ ἑβδόμῃ [sc. ἡμέρᾳ]...ἡ ἀνάπαυσις ~εται Clem.*str*.4.25(p.318.23; M.8.1368A); τὰ πάτρια θ. Or.*Cels*.5.25(p.26.17; M.11.1220A); ἐκρύπτετο [i.e. in time of persecution]...ἡ θεοσέβεια καὶ ἐν ἰδιωτικοῖς οἴκοις κεκρυμμένως ἐθρησκεύετο ἡ ἀλήθεια *M.Thdot*.3 (p.131.12); **4.** *believe in* ἀρχιερεῖς...τὸ ὁμοούσιον ~οντας Philost.*h.e*.5.1(M.65.528D); Thdt.*ep*.126(4.1210); Ἄρειος καὶ Εὐνόμιος...καὶ οἱ τὰ ἐκείνων ~οντες id.*Ps*.30:16(1.1185); τῶν...ὁμοφρόνων δοκούντων...καὶ τῶν τἀναντία ~όντων Phot.*cod*.40(ap.*GCS* Philost.p.64.37; M.103.73A).

***θριαμβεία**, ἡ, *triumph*, Const.ap.Eus.*v.C*.2.67(p.67.32; M.20.1040A).

***θριάμβευσις**, ἡ, **1.** *triumph* θ. ἐν τῷ ξύλῳ Or.*fr.89 in Jo*.(p.553.1); **2.** *publication*, Eustrat.*v.Eutych*.34(M.86.2316A).

θριαμβευτής, ὁ, *one who has triumphed* (= Lat. *triumphator*); as imperial title, Constantius Imp.ap.Ath.*syn*.55(p.277.30; M.26.792A).

θριαμβεύ-ω, **A.** *triumph, lead in triumph*; **1.** *lead* as captive, *triumph over*, of Christ ἵνα...τὸν ὄφιν ~σῃ Gr.Naz.*or*.24.4(M.35.1173C); Bas.Sel.*or*.31.3(M.85.345C); Procl.CP *or*.13.1(M.65.789D); of Devil, †Bas.*Is*.109(1.454D; M.31.293C); ἐθριάμβευον ἐμπαίζοντες οἱ στρατιῶται τὸν τῆς στρατιᾶς τῶν οὐρανῶν δεσπότην [i.e. at Crucifixion] Gr.Nyss.*res*.5(M.46.688A); pass. δι'...σταυροῦ...ἐθριαμβεύθη σατανᾶς Serap.*euch*.25.2; abs., *make a triumph, triumph* τηρουμένης...τῆς ψυχῆς ἐν αὐτῷ [sc. the martyr Pothinus] ἵνα δι' αὐτῆς Χριστὸς ~σῃ *Ep.Lugd*.ap.Eus.*h.e*.5.1.29(M.20.420B); ~οντες μᾶλλον ἤπερ ~όμενοι ἀπαγόμεθα [i.e. as martyrs] Or.*mart*.42(p.39.22; M.11.617C); ~όμενος ἐθριάμβευσε Ammon.*Jo*.14:31(M.85.1493B); **2.** *lead in triumph* (as a general his victorious army) ~οντος αὐτοὺς [sc. martyrs] ἐνδόξως τοῦ θεοῦ Dion.Al.ap.Eus.*h.e*.6.41.23(M.20.612C); exeg. 2Cor.2:14 τουτέστι, τῷ πᾶσι ποιοῦντι περιφανεῖς. ὃ γὰρ δοκεῖ εἶναι ἀτιμίας, τὸ πάντοθεν ἐλαύνεσθαι, τοῦτο τιμῆς ἡμῖν εἶναι φαίνεται μεγίστης. διὸ οὐκ εἶπε, τῷ καταδήλους ποιοῦντι, ἀλλά, 'τῷ ~οντι'· δεικνὺς ὅτι οἱ διωγμοὶ οὗτοι τρόπαια συνεχῆ κατὰ τοῦ διαβόλου πανταχοῦ...ἀνιστῶσιν ...οὐ γὰρ μόνον ὑπὸ τοῦ θεοῦ ~όμεθα, ἀλλὰ καὶ 'ἐν Χριστῷ' τουτέστι, διὰ τὸν Χριστὸν καὶ τὸ κήρυγμα Chrys.*hom.5.1 in 2Cor.*(10.466D); hence *flaunt, parade* ἑαυτὸν ~ων οὐκ αἰσχύνεται [sc. Paul. Sam.] Epiph.*haer.*65.9(p.13.15; M.42.28D); met. παύσασθε λόγους ἀλλοτρίους ~οντες, καὶ ὥσπερ ὁ κολοιὸς οὐκ ἰδίοις ἐπικοσμούμενοι πτεροῖς Tat. *orat.*26(p.27.16; M.6.861A).

B. *show*; **1.** *reveal* material things, ‡Nil.*perist.*9.4(M.79.869A); practices, CNic.(787)*can.*8; **2.** *manifest* power; of Christ, Leont.H. *Nest.*1.18(M.86.1468D); **3.** *blaze abroad,* Dion.Ar.*ep.*7.2(M.3.1081A); Sophr.H.*v.Cyr.et Jo.*7(M.87.3388B); **4.** *expose* as false or evil, Ath. *h.Ar.*28(p.198.16; M.25.725B); *Const.App.*1.8.20; τὴν ἁμαρτίαν παραδειγματίσας...καὶ ~σας Gr.Naz.*or.*40.27(M.36.397A); Thdt.*Cant.*7:2 (2.143).

***θριαμβόνικος,** *triumphant,* Germ.CP *or.*2(M.98.256A).

θρίαμβος, ὁ, 1. *triumph*; met., Eus.*l.C.*6(p.212.5; M.20.1352A); θ. κατὰ Ἀρειανῶν Petr.II Al.*encycl.*6(M.33.1284A)ap.Thdt.*h.e.*4.22.20; ref. Ascension ὡς ἐν θ. νικηφόρος ἀναφερόμενος Cosm.Ind.*top.*2(M.88. 121D); of a martyr's triumph in discussion, Sophr.H.*v.Anast.*(M.92. 1704A); of a heretic's triumph over orthodox, Jo.D.*imag.*3(M.94. 1392A); **2.** *object of triumph* or *derision, A.Paul.et Thecl.*26(p.254.8); *Orac.Sib.*8.130; *ib.*13.129; Eus.Al.*serm.*21.12(M.86.437C); **3.** *publication,* Sophr.H.*mir.Cyr.et Jo.*12(M.87.3461C); ref. secret of confessional ἵνα μὴ τοὺς ἐξωμολογημένους διὰ τοῦ θ. ἀνακόψῃ Jo.Clim.*past.* 13(M.88.1196B).

θριδάκιον, τό, *small lettuce,* Pall.*h.Laus.*38(p.122.8; M.34.1194C).

θρίξ, ἡ, *hair*; **1.** in gen.; of overmuch attention to it as showing or leading to immorality, Clem.*paed.*3.3(p.245.16; M.8.577B); *ib.*3.11 (p.271.10; 637A); *Const.App.*1.3.8–11; of tonsure before ordination as lector, Eustrat.*v.Eutych.*12(M.86.2288D); **2.** as symbol of death, Or.*hom.8.11 in Lev.*(p.412.30; M.87.740C); ἄμοιρος...αἰσθήσεως ἡ θ. (M. τρίξ) τῷ σώματι· διὸ κυρίως νεκρότητος γίνεται σύμβολον Gr.Nyss. *v.Mos.*(M.44.385A); id.*hom.7 in Cant.*(M.44.921C); of impurity, cf. Lev.14:8 τὰς ἐν ἡμῖν...ἐμφύτους ἡδονὰς ὡς ἐν εἴδει τριχῶν νοουμένας Cyr.*glaph.Lev.*(1.358A); ref. tonsure ἡ τῶν τριχῶν ἀπόκαρσις ἐμφαίνει τὴν καθαρὰν...ζωήν Dion.Ar.*e.h.*6.3.3(M.3.536A); ref. 1Cor.11:15, 1Tim.2:9 τὰς...τρίχας...τὴν αἰδῶ καὶ σωφροσύνην διὰ τῆς τοῦ Παύλου σοφίας καταλαμβάνεσθαι Gr.Nyss.*hom.7 in Cant.*(M.44.921B); purity of divine nature and attributes signified by τῆς τριχὸς ἡ καθαρότης Thdt.*Dan.*7:9(2.1198).

θρο-έω, *disturb* μὴ ~είτωσαν τὴν οἰκουμένην Epiph.*haer.*79.8(p.483. 2; M.42.752C).

***θρόησις, ἡ,** *wonder,* Gr.Nyss.*hom.12 in Cant.*(M.44.1012B); *ib.* (1012D).

***θροισμός, ὁ,** *terror, Vaticin.*2 p.52.

θρομβοειδής, *clotted*; of clouds, *cumulus,* Gr.Nyss.*hex.*36(M.44. 96B).

θρομβόω, *coagulate,* Clem.*paed.*1.6(p.118.27; M.8.308A); Meth. *symp.*2.2(p.16.21; M.18.49A).

***θρόμβωμα, τό,** *clot,* Melet.*nat.hom.*20(M.64.1224C).

θρονίζ-ω, *enthrone*; pass., of a bishop, Gr.Naz.*carm.*2.1.11.1849 (M.37.1159A); of God in the angels τὸ...ἐναναπαύεσθαι ταῖς ἁγίαις δυνάμεσι...~εσθαι id.*or.*31.22(p.172.18; M.36.157B).

θρόνιον, τό, *small chair,* Dor.*doct.*10.2(M.88.1725B); Jo.Mosch. *prat.*68(M.87.2917D).

***θρόνιος,** *of a throne,* Dion.Ar.*c.h.*13.4(M.3.304A).

θρονισμός, ὁ, *enthronement*; of a bishop, Synes.*ep.*67(M.66. 1417B).

θρονιστής, ὁ, *enthroner*; at an episcopal enthronement, Synes.*ep.* 67(M.66.1417B).

θρόνος, ὁ, *throne*; **1.** lit., episcopal, specially decorated, Ath. *apol.sec.*17(p.100.8; M.25.276C); placed in centre of priests' seats at east end of church, *Const.App.*2.57.4; bishop formally taking possession of it ὡς εἶχεν εὐθὺς ἀπὸ τῆς νεὼς εἰς τὴν ἐκκλησίαν χωρῆσαι καὶ τὸν θ. ἀναλαβεῖν Philost.*h.e.*2.17(M.65.480B); conceived as teacher's chair ἡμεῖς οἱ ἱερεῖς οἱ ἐπὶ θρόνου καθήμενοι καὶ διδάσκοντες ‡Chrys.*Petr.et El.*(2.732B); bishop preaching from it, Soz.*h.e.*8. 18.7(M.67.1564B); **2.** met.; **a.** *bishop's see* or *jurisdiction* πείσατε καταθέσθαι τοὺς παρανόμως ἐπὶ τὸν θρόνον ἀναβεβηκότας Chrys.*hom. 12.6 in Eph.*(11.89C); of Jerusalem τὸν ἀποστολικὸν θ. Eus.*h.e.*7. 32.29(M.20.733B); of Rome ἀποστολικός ἐστι θ. Ath.*h.Ar.*35(p.202. 29; M.25.733C); ὁ πανάγιος θ. Thdt.*ep.*116(4.1197); τοῦ κορυφαίου θ. Thdr.Stud.*epp.*2.66(M.99.1289D); of Antioch ἡ Ἀντιοχεία θρόνου ἠξιώθη ἀρχοντικοῦ· ἐπειδὴ ἐκεῖ πρῶτον ἐχρημάτισαν οἱ πιστοὶ Χριστιανοί Ammon.*Ac.*11:26(M.85.1540A); Alex.Sal.*Barn.*42(p.450F); of Alexandria τοῦ εὐαγγελικοῦ ἐκείνου θ. Isch.*libell.*(p.17.30; H.2.325D); of CP ἐκεῖνον [sc. τὸν τοῦ Χριστοῦ θ.] ἡμεῖς διεδεξάμεθα Chrys.*hom. 3.4 in Col.*(11.349D); τὸν μέγιστον...θ. Thdt.*haer.*4.12(4.370); Basilisc. *antencycl.*(p.107.21; M.86.2612A); of Cyprus as apostolic see, Alex. Sal.*Barn.*37(p.449A); **b.** of Father's throne, word not implying local presence in God, Clem.*str.*5.11(p.374.15; M.9.109A); of Christ as his throne, cf.Is.66:1, Or.*or.*23.4(p.353.2; M.11.489D); **c.** of Christ's throne θ. ἐκ δεξιῶν αὐτοῦ [sc. τοῦ πατρός] Polyc.*ep.*2.1; Χριστός, καθήμενος ἐπὶ θ. χερουβίμ *Dorm.BMV* 38(p.107); ὡς θεὸς ὁ...Χριστὸς...ἔχει...αἰώνιον τὸν θ. ... ὡς δὲ ἄνθρωπος, καὶ ἀρχιερεύς, καὶ ἀπόστολος τῆς ὁμολογίας ἡμῶν, ἀκούει, κάθου ἐκ δεξιῶν μου Thdt. *Heb.*4:16(3.571); typified by sanctuary or βῆμα, ‡Bas.*h.myst.*3 (p.259.14); and by ἁγία τράπεζα, *ib.*(p.258.11) = ‡Germ.CP *contempl.* (M.98.388C); shared with Father, Ath.*Ar.*1.61(M.26.140A); *ib.*2.43 (240B); signifying equal dignity, Bas.*Eun.*1.25(1.236B; M.29.568B) v. βασιλεία; typified by σύνθρονος in apse, ‡Sophr.H.*liturg.*2(M.87. 3984); signifying his dominion over creatures, †Ath.*serm.fid.* 29(p.26; M.26.1284B); Gr.Nyss.*Apoll.*52(M.45.1249C); **d.** plur., an order of angels; **i.** the highest, Clem.*str.*7.13(p.59.2; M.9.516A); dwelling in highest heaven, Cyr.H.*catech.*11.11; nearest to God, Dion.Ar.*c.h.*6.2(M.3.200D); Max.*schol.c.h.*7.1(M.4.65A); **ii.** but sometimes used of other orders as well; names θ. ἐξουσίαι, etc., signifying differences of function, not nature, Gr.Nyss.*Eun.*7(2 p.173.24; M.45.765A); hence thrones sometimes identified with cherubim or seraphim, v. χερουβίμ; **iii.** characterized by wisdom, *T.Sal.*3.5 (p.17.6, v.l. σοφῶν M.122.1320C); seeing God through Word, Ath. *Ar.*3.51(M.26.432A); βλέπουσιν...οἱ ἄγγελοι...καὶ οἱ ἀρχάγγελοι καθ' ὃ δύνανται· θ. δὲ καὶ κυριότητες, μειζόνως μὲν παρὰ τοὺς πρώτους, ἔλαττον δὲ τῆς ἀξίας Cyr.H.*catech.*6.6; οἱ θ. λογικόν ἐστι...σύστημα Thdt.*Ezech.*1:19(2.688); **iv.** functions: continual praise of God, *T.Lev.*3.5; Dion.Ar.*c.h.*7.1(M.3.205D); *Lit.Jac.*(p.198.27); acting as God's messengers, Ath.*Ar.*2.27(M.26.204B); at baptism θ. δὲ καὶ κυριότητας λειτουργοῦντας Cyr.H.*procatech.*15; **v.** ref. Col.1:15–17 θρόνους...διὰ τῆς σαρκὸς τοῦ σωτῆρος λέγων [sc. Marcellus] τῆς ἐν Χριστῷ κτίσεως ἠξιῶσθαι Eus.*e.th.*3.7(p.165.10; M.24.1016C); **vi.** created nature asserted against Gnostics, Cyr.H.*catech.*11.21; **e.** of men as thrones of God ὁ...γινώσκων ἑαυτὸν...ἐστι...θ. τοῦ κυρίου Clem.*fr.*31(p.217.25); Or.*hom.1.2 in Gen.*(p.3.7ff.; M.12. 117B); Eus.*h.e.*10.4.66(M.20.876B); Gr.Nyss.*Eun.*3(2 p.22.5; M.45. 585D); of BMV θ. τῆς θεότητος ‡Epiph.*hom.*5(M.43.492B); χερουβικὸς θ. ἕτερος *ib.*(493D); Jo.Thess.*dorm.BMV* A 14(pp.402.9,404.17); Germ.CP *hymn.BMV*(M.98.453C); Andr.Cr.*or.*12(M.97.1069A); Jo. Eub.*concept.BMV* 15(M.96.1484B); **f.** exeg. Mt.19:28 τιμὴν καὶ δόξαν ...παρεδήλωσε διὰ τῶν θ. Chrys.*hom.64.2 in Mt.*(7.636D); διὰ...τοῦ θ., ἡ ἀνάπαυσις καὶ ἡ βασιλεία τοῦ μέλλοντος αἰῶνος δείκνυται Andr.Caes. *Apoc.*9(M.106.252B); **g.** *rank*; episcopal, Or.*comm.in Mt.*15.26(p.426. 18; M.13.1329B); of priests τινας τῶν ἐκ τοῦ δευτέρου θ. Const.ap. Eus.*h.e.*10.5.23(M.20.889C); priests and bishops θρόνοι, πρώτων τε δευτέρων τε τάξις Gr.Naz.*carm.*2.1.15.51(M.37.1249A); cf.*ib.*2.1.11. 344(1053A); **h.** *power,* in doxologies αὐτῷ δόξα, τιμή,...θ. αἰώνιος *1Clem.*65.2; *M.Polyc.*21.1; of bishop's powers, considered as coming from Christ, *Hom.Clem.*4.70; θ. ... εἰ λέγοιτο θεοῦ, τὴν ὑπ' αὐτῷ βασιλείαν κατασημαίνοι ἂν Cyr.*Juln.*2(6^2.70B).

θρόνωσις, ἡ, *enthronement, Orac.Sib.*8.49.

θρυΐνος, *made of rushes,* Jo.Mal.*chron.*12 p.286(M.97.432C).

[*]**θρυλλ-έω, 1.** *disturb with talk, Hom.Clem.*2.15; Thphn.*chron.* p.199(M.108.513A); **2.** *dispute, raise objections* against ἱστάμενος ⟨πρός⟩ τινας περὶ τῆς τοιαύτης ~οῦντας συνόδου Anast.S.*haer.*(p.271).

[*]**θρύλλημα, τό,** *common talk* θ. τε καὶ βατταρίσματα Taras.*ep.*5 (M.98.1465B).

[*]**θρυλλίζω,** *repeat,* Thdt.*Mal.*3:16(2.1690).

***θρυλλολέκτης, ὁ,** *babbler*; of heretics, ‡Jo.D.*Const.*18(M.95. 336B); Steph.Diac.*v.Steph.*(M.100.1145A).

θρῦλος, ὁ, *rumour,* Cyr.*Os.*80(3.113D); Soz.*h.e.*5.9.12(M.67.1240B).

***θρύπτος, ὁ,** ? *cake,* †Bas.*contub.*9(M.30.824B).

θρύψις, ἡ, *bending,* Gr.Naz.*or.*18.23(M.35.1012B).

θυγάτηρ, ἡ, [acc. -έραν *Pers.*(p.5.12)], *daughter*; **1.** in gen.; of Christian women, *Barn.*1.1; *Const.App.*1.10.4; of virgins as daughters of God, Clem.*prot.*12(p.84.11; M.8.240C); **2.** exeg. Ps. 44:11; **a.** of Church, Just.*dial.*63.5(M.6.621B); Eus.*Ps.*44:10(M. 23.401D); cf.Ath.*exp.Ps.*44:11(M.27.212C); Didym.*Ps.*44:11(M.39. 1368D); Cyr.*Ps.*44:11(M.69.1041D); Hesych.H.*Ps.tit.*44(M.27.828D); as regenerated through baptism, Chrys.*exp.in Ps.*44:11(5.178C); **b.** of BMV, Jo.Eub.*concept.BMV* 14(M.96.1481B); cf.Thdr.Stud. *nativ.BMV* 7(M.96.693A); **3.** exeg. Gen.6:2 θυγατέρας ἀνθρώπων τροπικώτερον [sc. τινες] τὸ γήϊνον σκῆνος λέγεσθαι ὑπειληφότες Or. *Jo.*6.42(25; p.151.17; M.14.273B); cf.id.*hom.*5.7 *in Jer.*(p.37.10; M. 13.305B); **4.** ref. spiritual relationship τῷ τιμιωτάτῳ πατρὶ Ἄππα Παφνουτ[ίῳ] παρὰ τῆς θ. Οὐαλερίας *PLond.*1926 v°(p.109); συγγενεῖ καὶ πνευματικῇ θ. *V.Olymp.*10(p.416.23).

[*]**θυγατρίδης**, ὁ, *daughter's son, grandson*, Thphn.*chron.*p.8(M. 108.76A); *ib.*p.14 (v.l. θυγατρίδος; -δοῦς 92B).

θυγατρόγαμος, *married to one's own daughter*, Bas.*renunt.*7(2. 208C; M.31.640C).

θυγατρομιξία, ἡ, *incest with a daughter*; that of Lot to be taken figuratively, Or.*princ.*4.2.2(p.309.4; M.11.360B); in gen., Eus.*p.e.* 7.2(301A; M.21.512A); Gr.Nyss.*fat.*(M.45.170B); id.*hom.*3 *in Eccl.* (M.44.660B).

***θυηδόχος**, *sacrificial*, Gr.Naz.*carm.*2.2(epitaph.)66.7(M.38.44A).

θυηλή, ἡ, *sacrifice*, of eucharist ἀναίμακτος θ. Paul.Sil.*Soph.*197 (M.86.2127A); *ib.*683(2144B).

[*]**θύηνος**, = θύϊνος, *of wood of the* θύον *tree*, Alex.Sal.*Barn.*44 (p.451B).

θυηπόλος, **1.** *sacrificing, priestly*, of sanctuary θ. ἕρκος Paul.Sil. *ambo.*243(M.86.2261A); of BMV ἡ θ. νεᾶνις Thdr.Stud.*nativ.BMV* 7 (M.96.693A); μοναχοῦ θ. *MAMA* 1.254; **2.** as subst., *priest*; pagan, Eus.*v.C.*2.51(p.62.26; M.20.1028C); of Christ, Gr.Naz.*carm.*1.1.2.75 (M.37.407A); *IGC As.Min.*215[2] (saec. vii to ix).

θυιάς, *troubled*, Nonn.*par.Jo.*21:8(M.43.916C); *ib.*3:23(765A).

θῦμα, τό, **1.** *sacrifice*; **a.** in gen., as not desired by God, *Hom. Clem.*2.44; as diabolical, Just.*1apol.*12.5(M.6.344A); id.*2apol.*5.4(M. 6.452C); participation in pagan sacrifices enslaving worshipper to Devil, *Hom.Clem.*7.3; **b.** of sacrifice of Cross; in allegorical interpretation of a fr. of Euripides, Clem.*str.*5.11(p.373.12; M.9.108A); as being for salvation of all men, Eus.*d.e.*1.10(p.47.14; M.22.89B); destroying death, Ath.*inc.*9.1(M.25.112A); **c.** of eucharist, as prophesied in Ps.22:5, Eus.*d.e.*1.10(p.48.3; M.22.92A); in gen., Chrys.*hom.*8.8 *in Rom.*(9.509B); Philost.*h.e.*2.13(M.65.476C); τοῦ νοητοῦ θ. ‡Germ.CP *contempl.*(M.98.449D); of unconsecrated elements, *Lit.Jac.*(p.178.7); **d.** met., of sacrifice demanded by avarice, Chrys.*hom.*65.3 *in Jo.*(8.393A); **2.** *meat*, Pall.*h.Laus.*44 (p.132.13; M.34.1210B); not eaten by solitaries, *Apophth.Patr.*(M. 65.164C); Jo.Mosch.*prat.*65(M.87.2916C).

θυμαντικός, *passionate*, Arist.*apol.*8.2.

***Θυμβρίας**, *of the Tiber*, i.e. *Latin*, Nonn.*par.Jo.*13:4(M.43.860C).

Θύμβρις, ἡ, *Tiber*, *Orac.Sib.*8.64.

θυμέλη, ἡ, **1.** *stage*, fig. αὕτη δὲ [sc. ἡ αἵρεσις] ἦν ἡ τῆς Ἀρειανῆς θ. ὀρχήστρα Anast.S.*haer.*(p.259); met., of a pander τριβοῦνος θυμέλης *V.Max.*12(M.90.125C); **2.** *theatricality*, ref. ceremonies of Eunomian baptism τὸ πᾶν...θυμέλης αὐτῶν Epiph.*haer.*76.54(p.414.6; M.42. 637B).

***θυμελής**, *theatrical*, hence *ranting*, of heretics θ. ὀρχῆσται Anast.S.*hod.*14(M.89.248A).

θυμελικός, *theatrical*; ὁ θ., *actor*; prohibition of presence of Christians where actors are playing, CLaod.*can.*54; monks required to avoid actors' shows, CNic.(787)*can.*22; ἡ θ. *actress*; as immodest, Dor.*doct.*6.4(M.88.1689B); Leont.N.*v.Sym.*43(M.93. 1724C).

***θυμέομαι**, **1.** *be* or *become angry*, Nemes.*nat.hom.*21(M.40.692A) = Jo.D.*f.o.*2.16(M.94.933A) cit. s. ὀργή; Barth.Edess.*Agar.*(M.104. 1424A); **2.** *harbour in one's heart, meditate* οὐκ ἐθυμήθη τι κακόν *ib.* (1424B).

θυμηδία, ἡ, *delight, joy*, of God πρόσεστι τῷ θεῷ...τὸ ἀτελεύτητον ἐν θ. Cyr.*Jo.*6.1(4.658D); in presence of Christ ἡ πᾶσα...ἡμῶν θ. Χριστός Cyr.*Joel.*32(3.224D); id.*Lc.*2:28(M.72.504C); ‡Meth.*Sym.et Ann.*12(M.18.377A); of blessed in heaven, Eus.*Is.*62:4–5(M.24. 497D); Isid.Pel.*epp.*2.111(M.78.552D); Thdt.*Ps.*5:12(1.639); id.*Is.* 25:10(p.103.8; 2.294); through divine intervention πλείονα θ. ἡ τοῦ θεοῦ χάρις παρέσχεν CHier.(335)*ep.*(p.247.29; M.26.717C); of visions sent by God to soul in sleep πνευματικῆς αὐτὴν καταγεμίζοντες θ. Diad.*perf.*37(p.42.14); in prayer; of soul praying under influence of H. Ghost, *ib.*73(p.90.16); ref. singing of Psalms διὰ ταύτης τῆς θ. καρπουμένους τὴν ὠφέλειαν Thdt.*Pss.*proem.(1.602); in celebration of feasts, Gr.Naz.*or.*35.1(M.36.257B); Jo.D.*hom.*1.1(M.96.545A); in virtue; through acceptance of providential instruction, Clem.*paed.* 1.5(p.103.16; M.8.276B); ζωὴν...τὴν ἐν Χριστῷ...τὴν ἐν...θ. Cyr.*Jo.* 4.2(4.355A); θ. itself is required of men by God for his praise, id. *Ps.*32:2(M.69.872A).

***θυμηδιάω**, *rejoice*, Thdr.Stud.*epp.*1.35(M.99.1029B).

***θυμηδῶς**, *with delight*, Or.*Ps.*58:11(p.73).

θυμήρης, *well-pleasing*, Thdt.*Is.*30:26(p.124.35).

θυμιάζω, *offer incense to*, *A.Thom.*B 20(p.32.21).

θυμίαμα, τό, **A.** *incense*; **1.** not used in early Church because associated with paganism, devils enslaving men through its use, Just.*2apol.*5.4(M.6.452C); ὁ...τοῦ παντὸς δημιουργὸς...οὐ δεῖται...τῆς ἀπὸ τῶν...θ. εὐωδίας, αὐτὸς ὢν ἡ τελεία εὐωδία Athenag.*leg.*13.1(M. 6.916B); **2.** later used as accompaniment of prayer; **a.** liturg. καπνίσατε...ὑμῶν τὰ θ. ἐν οἴκῳ θεοῦ Ephr.2.237C; in procession to martyr's shrine, Chrys.*pan.Pelag.*4(2.590A); in church, id.*hom.*88.4 *in Mt.*(7.830E); Esaias *or.*5.3(cf.M.40.1122D); Thdr.Stud.*praesanct.* (M.99.1688B); *Lit.Jac.*(p.162.5); σοὶ τῷ πεπληρωμένῳ πάσης εὐωδίας... ἐξ ὧν δέδωκας ἡμῖν προσφέρομεν τὸ θ. τοῦτο *ib.*(p.168.24); *Lit.Marc.* (p.118.26) cit. s. ἀντικαταπέμπω; **b.** private ὀρέγει ξύλον Ἰνδικὸν εὐῶδες αὐτῷ, ἀξιῶν δεχθῆναί τε καὶ θ. παρ' αὐτοῦ θεῷ προσαχθῆναι Niceph.Ur.*v.Sym.*219(M.86.3188B); Anton.Hag.*v.Sym.Styl.*24(p.58. 12); θ. ... λαμβάνων τῇ δεξιᾷ, προσέφερε πολλάκις θεῷ καὶ ὁ καπνὸς... χωρὶς ἀνθράκων ἀνῄει Niceph.Ur.*v.Sym.*46(3029A); **3.** symbolism: Christ εἰς Χριστὸν ἀναφερομένου τοῦ θ. (εὐῶδες γὰρ ἀσυγκρίτως) Cyr. *ador.*9(1.324A); BMV τὸ...τῆς συνθέσεως θ. Procl.CP *or.*6.17(M.65. 753B); θ., τὸ ὑπὲρ κόσμου παντὸς ἐνώπιον κυρίου κατευθυνόμενον προσευκτήριον Thdr.Stud.*nativ.BMV* 7(M.96.693B); prayer θ. τὴν ὁσίαν εὐχήν Clem.*str.*7.6(p.24.18; M.9.445A); *ib.*(p.26.18; 449A); ref. Ps.140:2, Or.*hom.*18.10 *in Jer.*(p.164.19; M.13.484A); ref. Apoc. 5:8, Meth.*symp.*5.8(p.63.9; M.18.112B); ref. Mal.1:11 and Ps.140:2, Eus.*d.e.*1.10(p.49.3; M.22.92D); τὸ διὰ προσευχῆς καὶ λόγων...θ. *Const.App.*7.33.2; chastity; because its ingredients have affinities with elements composing body, †Bas.*Is.*29(1.402C; M.30.176B) = Proc.G.*Is.*1:10(M.87.1848C); Andr.Caes.*Apoc.*11(M.106.261B); love, Clem.*paed.*2.8(p.197.21; M.8.473B); τῶν ἁγίων τὸ στῖφος...ἡ σύνθεσις τοῦ θ. τὴν Χριστοῦ γνῶσιν εὐωδιάζοντες Cyr.*ador.*4(1.133B); incense in liturgy representing perfumes used at Christ's burial, ‡Germ.CP *contempl.*(M.98.400D); God's anger, ref. Apoc.5:8 διὸ καὶ θυμιάματα, οὐχὶ ἀρώματα, εἴρηται Areth.*Apoc.*12(M.106.581C); **4.** ref. secular use by Christians; not to be used merely for pleasure, Clem.*paed.* 2.8(p.198.1; M.8.473C); but may be used medicinally, *ib.*(p.203.28; 488B); forbidden to consecrated virgins, Ath.*virg.*6(p.40.7; M.28. 257C); βασιλέων λαυράτοις καὶ εἰκόσιν ἀποστελλομένοις ἐν πόλεσι... ἀπαντῶσι λαοὶ μετὰ...θυμιαμάτων Thds.Am.*libell.*(H.4.45B); a similar practice perh. giving rise to accusation that Christians offered incense to statue of Const., Philost.*h.e.*2.17(M.65.480A).

B. *sacrifice, offering* ἐν τῇ ὥρᾳ τοῦ θ. τοῦ τιμίου σώματος καὶ αἵματος τοῦ Χριστοῦ *Apoc.Paul.*29(p.56).

[*]**θυμιαστήριον**, τό, *cat.*2 *Cor.*2:14(p.363.5) for θυμιατήριον, Chrys. *hom.*5.2 *in 2Cor.*(10.467A).

***θυμιατήρ**, ὁ, *censer* ὁ θ. ἑρμηνεύεται [sc. εὐωδία ἢ καὶ]...εὐφροσύνη ‡Bas.*h.myst.*42(p.387.21); symbolizing Christ's humanity, *ib.*(p.387. 19); ‡Germ.CP *contempl.*(M.98.400C).

θυμιατήριον, τό, **1.** *censer*; **a.** used in church, Cyr.S.*v.Jo.Hes.* (p.215.25); to purify the air in a pilgrimage-church, Sophr.H.*mir. Cyr.et Jo.*31(M.87.3524A); during liturgy, *Lit.Chrys.*(p.371.16); **b.** in private devotion, ref. a man caught in an earthquake censing the place where he is, Evagr.*h.e.*4.7(p.157.8; M.86.2713B); used by a solitary, Niceph.Ur.*v.Sym.*219(M.86.3188C); **c.** symbolism, womb of BMV and baptismal font signified by ἡ γαστὴρ τοῦ θ. ‡Bas.*h. myst.*42(p.388.1); **d.** in secular usage, to show honour to a great person, e.g. a bishop taken to his lodging by women with censers, Cyr.*ep.*24(p.118.8; 5[2].87D); **e.** met., of tongue of one praising a martyr, Chrys.*pan.Pelag.*4(2.590A); of BMV θ., τὸ σκεῦος τὸ χρυσόνουν, ἡ τὸν θεῖον ἄνθρακα ἔνδον φέρουσα Thdr.Stud.*nativ. BMV* 7(M.96.689C); **2.** *incense-burner*; set out by the Beast for the faithful to use before buying and selling, Hipp.*antichr.*49(p.32.21; πυρεῖα M.10.769A); **3.** *altar of incense* in Temple αἱ παρθένοι...εἰς τύπον τοῦ θ. τετιμήσθωσαν *Const.App.*2.26.8; met., of soul at prayer and the mouth of one praying, Chrys.*exp.in Ps.*140:2(5. 431ff.).

θυμιατός, ὁ, **1.** *censer*; **a.** in gen., ‡Bas.*h.myst.*42(p.387.18); *Lit. Chrys.*(p.36.23,28); cf.*ib.*(p.378.15); to be venerated because consecrated to God, Jo.D.*imag.*3.35(M.94.1353D); **b.** symbolism; with incense, signifying grace of H. Ghost, ‡Sophr.H.*liturg.*18(M.87. 3997C); Christ's humanity, ‡Germ.CP *contempl.*(M.98.412D); ὁ...θ. ἐστιν εὐωδεστάτη εὐφροσύνη *ib.*; **2.** *censing* ἡ εἴσοδος...μετὰ θ. λέγεται Thdr.Stud.*praesanct.*(M.99.1688C); symbolizing natures of Christ, Jo.Jej.*liturg.*(p.441); final censing in liturgy representing Christ's gift of Spirit to apostles before Ascension, ‡Germ.CP *contempl.* (M.98.452B).

θυμιατρίς, ἡ, *censer*, Gr.Nyss.*castig.*(M.46.316B).

θυμιάω, **1.** *cense*; **a.** liturg.; by c. 500 in Byz. liturgy bishop censed altar and sanctuary at introit, Dion Ar.*e.h.*3.1(M.3.425B); in Lit. Praesanct., Thdr.Stud.*praesanct.*(M.99.1688B); **b.** met. *τὸν ναὸν τοῦ θεοῦ θ. τῇ ἁγνείᾳ, καὶ τῇ ὀρθῇ προαιρέσει* Ephr.1.325E; **2.** *burn incense, burn incense before,* Niceph.Ur.*v.Sym.*219(M.86.3188B); of Carpocratian Marcellina burning incense before pictures of Jesus, Paul, Homer, and Pythagoras, Jo.D.*haer.*27(M.94.693B); **3.** *offer*; **a.** in gen. *οὔτε σὺ τοῦ θ. ἐξουσίαν ἔχεις, βασιλεῦ* Hos.*ep.*(p.208.24; M.25.748A); of Christ *ἐθυμιᾶτο...ὡς κριός* Cyr.*ador.*11(1.402D); **b.** of offering prayer; ref. Jer.18:15, Or.*hom.18.10 in Jer.*(p.164.9; M.13.484A); ref. Mal.1:11 and Ps.140:2, Eus.*d.e.*1.10(p.49.2,7; M.22.92D).

θυμικός, *irascible,* of the active principle in the sensitive soul *τὸ θ. μέρος* Max.*carit.*1.66(M.90.973C); *ἡ...ἐλεημοσύνη, τὸ θ. μέρος τῆς ψυχῆς θεραπεύει ib.*1.79(977C); neut. as subst., Clem.*paed.*3.1(p.236.7; M.8.556B); *τὸ παθητικὸν μέρος τῆς ψυχῆς, ὅπερ ἐστὶ τὸ θ. καὶ ἐπιθυμητικόν* Or.*fr.54 in Lc.*(p.260); its motions symbolized by the animals in Ps.65:15, id.*Ps.*65:15(p.77); Nemes.*nat.hom.*16(M.40.672B); *τὸ θ. ... ἐκ καρδίας...καὶ ἐκ...τοῦ θ. ὁ θυμὸς γεννᾶται...καὶ τοῦ...θ. εἰσιν ἀρεταί, ὑπομονή, καὶ ἐγκράτεια καὶ ἀνδρεία· κακίαι δέ, ὀργὴ καὶ μανία, καὶ δειλία, καὶ ἀνανδρία* Melet.*nat.hom.*synops.(M.64.1109Bff.); Max.*ambig.*(M.91.198D).

θυμοειδής, **1.** *passionate,* Clem.*str.*7.10(p.43.12; M.9.484A); **2.** neut. as subst., active principle in the sensitive soul, *spirit, passion*; to be subject to reason, *ib.*1.24(p.100.3; M.8.908A); Thdt.*provid.*6(4.567); *πρὸς πολλὰ τῶν τῆς ἀρετῆς ἔργων ἐπιτήδειον ἡμῶν τῆς ψυχῆς τὸ θ.* Bas.*hom.*10.5(2.88C; M.31.365B); Gr.Nyss.*ep.can.*(M.45.224C); id.*anim.et res.*(M.46.49B).

θυμοκάτοχος, *restraining anger,* Or.*comm.in Eph.*6:12(p.572).

***θυμοκτόνος,** *soul-killing,* Mac.Aeg.*hom.*37.7(M.34.753D).

θυμολέοντες, οἱ, *Thymoleontes (Raging Lions),* name given to iconoclasts (cf. 1Petr.5:8), Jo.D.*haer.*102(M.94.773B).

θυμομαχία, ἡ, *fierce fighting, contention*; met., of self-conflict in the soul of the angry, ‡Just.*ep.Zen.et Ser.*2(M.6.1184B).

θυμός, ὁ, **A.** *vis irascibilis, mettle, temper* the active, non-intellectual principle in the soul; **1.** its non-rational basis *τὸ ἄλογον μέρος, ὃ δὴ δίχα τέμνεται, εἰς θ. καὶ ἐπιθυμίαν* Clem.*str.*5.8(p.362.8; M.9.84B); Nemes.*nat.hom.*16(M.40.673A); Chrys.*exp. in Ps.*123:2(5.345B); found also in non-rational creatures, Dion. Ar.*c.h.*2.4(M.3.141C); **2.** the correlative of *ἐπιθυμία*; the two moderating each other, Clem.*str.*3.13(p.238.29; M.8.1193A); Bas. *hom.*10.5(2.88C; M.31.365B); *ὁ...θ. ξυνεργὸς ἐδόθη τῷ λογισμῷ, ἵνα τῆς ἐπιθυμίας κωλύῃ τὴν ἀμετρίαν* Thdt.*affect.*5(p.146.21; 4.844); id. *Rom.*7:17(3.77); Jo.D.*f.o.*2.16(M.94.933A); **3.** its moral uses; **a.** as good in itself *θ. καὶ ἐπιθυμία,...οὐκ ἔστιν ἁπλῶς τῇ ἑαυτῶν φύσει κακά* Dion.Ar.*d.n.*4.25(M.3.728B); ref. doctrine that the highest power of a lower order has affinities with the lowest of a higher order *τὴν νοερὰν ἀνδρίαν, ἧς ἐστιν ἔσχατον ὁ θ. ἀπήχημα* id.*c.h.*15.8(M.3.337B); hence **b.** usable by the reason for either a good or an evil end, Clem.*str.*1.24(p.100.8; M.8.908A); *φύσις θυμοῦ τὸ τοῖς δαίμοσι μάχεσθαι, καὶ ὑπὲρ ἧστινος...ἡδονῆς ἀγωνίζεσθαι· διόπερ οἱ μὲν ἄγγελοι τὴν πνευματικὴν ἡμῖν ἡδονὴν ὑποβάλλονται· καὶ τὴν ἐκ ταύτης μακαριότητα πρὸς τοὺς δαίμονας τὸν θ. τρέψαι παρακαλοῦσιν· ἐκεῖνοι...πρὸς τὰς κοσμικὰς ἐπιθυμίας ἕλκοντες ἡμᾶς, τὸν θ. τοῖς ἀνθρώποις παρὰ φύσιν βιάζονται μάχεσθαι* Evagr.Pont.*cap.pract.* A 15(M.40.1225B); **c.** as instrument of virtue *ἔστι δορυφόρος τοῦ νοῦ ὁ θ. ἐν ὑπομονῇ καὶ καρτερίᾳ καὶ τοῖς ὁμοίοις* Clem.*str.*4.23(p.315.14; M.8.1360C); *ἀγαθὸν κτῆνός ἐστιν ὁ θ., ὅταν τοῦ λογισμοῦ ὑποζύγιον γένηται* Gr.Nyss.*Pss.titt.*A 8(M.44.477B); used to attain the good, the goal of the active life, Max.*cap.*3.26(M.90.1269C); can be allowed free play by soul advanced in contemplative life, id.*qu.Thal.*55(M.90.548D); **d.** of devils stirring it up for evil ends, *Schol.*26 in Jo. Clim.*scal.*1(M.88.652C); **e.** excess to be avoided, as of *ἐπιθυμία*, Clem.*str.*3.10(p.227.17; M.8.1172A); cf.*ib.*6.9(p.469.1; M.9.296A); because both obscure the reason, *ib.*4.6(p.266.11; M.8.1252B); Dion.Ar.*ep.*8.3(M.3.1093A); Moses an example of their subjugation, Gr.Nyss.*anim.et res.*(M.46.53C).

B. *irritation, impatience*; **1.** its physical basis, †Bas.*Is.*180(1.511B; M.30.424A) cit. s. *ὀργή*; **2.** as incipient *ὀργή*, v. *ὀργή*; **3.** usable for a good end, Gr.Naz.*or.*18.25(M.35.1013C); ref. Ps.4:5 *οὐ...τὸν θ. ἐκκόπτει, καὶ γὰρ ὠφέλιμος κατὰ τῶν ἀδικούντων γινόμενος καὶ κατὰ τῶν ῥαθύμων· ἀλλὰ...τὸν ἄλογον θ.* Chrys.*exp.in Ps.*4:5(5.17D); id.*laud.Paul.*6(2.511E); **4.** in God; **a.** not properly to be ascribed to him, being without passions, Or.*hom.18.6 in Jer.*(p.160.12; M.13.477B); †Bas.*Is.*180(1.511B; M.30.424A); *ὅταν ἀκούσῃς θ., μὴ πάθος νόμιζε* Chrys.*exp.in Ps.*6:2(5.40D); Cyr.*Juln.*5(6^2.172E); **b.** fig., to denote punishment, Isid.Pel.*epp.*3.92(M.78.797A); Thdt.*Is.*66:15(2.400); *διὰ...τοῦ θ., τὸ ταχὺ δεδήλωκε...θ. τοίνυν ὀργῆς, τὴν ὀξεῖαν καὶ ἐπίμονον ἐκάλεσε τιμωρίαν* id.*Ps.*68:25(1.1082); v. *ὀργή*; to convert sinners, Or.*hom.18.6 in Jer.*(p.160.12; M.13.477B); *ib.20.1*(p.177.4; 500D); to denote extent of sin, Areth.*Apoc.*45(M.106.700B); **c.** its real existence in pagan gods disproving their divinity, Athenag. *leg.*21.1(M.6.933A).

C. *anger*; **1.** descriptions; as desire for vengeance, Clem.*str.*4.23(p.315.24; M.8.1361A); *θ. ... εὑρίσκεται ὁρμὴ ἐπιθυμίας ἡμέρου ψυχῆς κατ᾽ ἐξοχὴν ἀμύνης ἐφετικὸς ἀλόγως ib.*5.4(p.343.17; M.9.48B); Or. *sel.in Ps.*6:2(M.12.1173B); Nemes.*nat.hom.*21(M.40.692A) = Jo.D. *f.o.*2.16(M.94.932D) cit. s. *ὀργή*; *θ. ἐστιν ὁρμὴ τοῦ κακῶσαι τὸν παροξύνοντα* Gr.Nyss.*anim.et res.*(M.46.56A); cf.Max.*ambig.*(M.91.1197B); *Schol.*3 in Jo.Clim.*scal.*8(M.88.836D); **2.** causes *ὁ δαίμων τοῦ θ.* Or.*hom.6.11 in Ezech.*(p.390.18); *τὸν...θ. κίνησιν δαιμονιώδη... ἔλεγεν* Nil.*epp.*3.33(M.79.392C); use of wine, Meth.*symp.*5.5(p.59.18; M.18.105C); envy, remembrance of wrongs received, Gr.Nyss.*hom. 6.1 in Eccl.*(M.44.705D); *ἐκ τῆς πικρίας θ.* [*γίνεται*] Ant.Mon.*hom.* 110(M.89.1772C); **3.** possibilities for good and evil *ὁ θ. ... μετέχει τἀγαθοῦ κατ᾽ αὐτὸ τὸ κινεῖσθαι, καὶ ἐφίεσθαι τὰ δοκοῦντα κακὰ πρὸς τὸ δοκοῦν καλὸν ἀνορθοῦν* Dion.Ar.*d.n.*4.20(M.3.720C); cf.*ib.*11.5(953A); morally *ὁ θ., ὅτε δεῖ, καὶ ὡς δεῖ κινούμενος, ἀνδρίαν ποιεῖ καὶ ὑπομονὴν καὶ ἐγκράτειαν· παρὰ δὲ τὸν ὀρθὸν λόγον ἐνεργῶν, μανία γίνεται* Bas.*hom.*10.6(2.89B; M.31.368A); *τὸ εὔκαιρον πολλάκις τῆς τοῦ θ. χρήσεως, ὅταν ἐπὶ κολάσει τῆς ἁμαρτίας ζέσῃ τὸ πάθος* Gr.Nyss.*beat.* 6(M.44.1276A); ref. Ecclus.1:21 *θ. γὰρ ἄδικος, φησίν, οὐκ ἀθῳωθήσεται· οὐχ ἁπλῶς θ., ἀλλ᾽ ὁ ἄδικος* Chrys.*laud.Paul.*6(2.511C); Max. *schol.d.n.*4.23(M.4.292C); **4.** consequences if uncontrolled by reason: darkening of the mind, *T.Dan 2.2*; Gr.Nyss.*hom.6.1 in Eccl.*(M.44.705D); Evagr.Pont.*cap.pract.*A 15(M.40.1225B) cit. A.3.b supra; Chrys.*sac.*3.14(p.70.17; 1.390B); *τὸν θ., τὸν πάντων παθῶν ὀξύτερον, τὸν καὶ τὰς ἐννοίας λανθάνοντα, καὶ τοὺς λογισμοὺς προπηδῶντα* Isid. Pel.*epp.*4.152(M.78.1237A); Jo.Clim.*scal.*8(M.88.832C); brawling, etc., Bas.*hom.*10.1(2.83E; M.31.356A); Gr.Naz.*carm.*1.2.25.315ff.(M.37.836A); Chrys.*hom.2.3 in 2Cor.4:13*(3.272A); id.*hom.16.5 in Mt.*(7.211B); Cyr.*Juln.*6(6^2.185D); prevention of movement of soul towards the beautiful, Meth.*res.*1.30(p.263.11; M.41.1140D); avarice, Mac.Aeg.*hom.*38.9(M.34.756C); timidity, Max.*carit.*2.70(M.90.1005D); exclusion of joy, Andr.Cr.*or.*15(M.97.1121A); **5.** to be avoided in rebuke and controversy, Chrys.*hom.17.3 in Ac.*(9.140A); Cyr.*Juln.* 5(6^2.172E); **6.** remedies: meekness, Evagr.Pont.*cap.pract.*A 11(M.40.1224C) cit. s. *ὀργή*; Nil.*spir.mal.*9(M.79.1153C); †Nil.*mal.cog.*14(M.79.1216B); Jo.Clim.*scal.*8(M.88.833D); Max.*carit.*1.80(M.90.977C); thought of the Judgement, Chrys.*hom.4.4 in Jo.*(8.32A); Ant.Mon. *hom.*24(M.89.1505D); love of God, Jo.Clim.*scal.*8(828C); *ib.*(833D); Max.*carit.*2.48(1000C); virtuous life in gen., Clem.*str.*4.23(p.315.24; M.8.1360C); *καταστεῖλαι τὸν θ. ... διὰ μακροθυμίας, δι᾽ ἐπιεικείας, διὰ προσευχῆς καὶ ταπεινώσεως· καὶ ἐν παντὶ ἔχειν ἑαυτὸν ἀψήφιστον* Ant.Mon.*hom.*23(1504C); Max.*carit.*2.70(1005D); **7.** of anger in evil spirits, Ath.*v.Anton.*9(M.26.857A); *τί τὸ ἐν δαίμοσι κακόν; θ. ἄλογος* Dion.Ar.*d.n.*4.23(M.3.725B).

θυμοφθόρος, *soul-destroying,* Meth.*Porph.*3(p.506.19; M.18.401B).

θυμ-όω, med. and pass., *be angry*; ref. God *~οῦσθαί φησιν, ἵνα ἐπιστρέψῃς καὶ ἀληθῶς οὐκ...~οῦται* Or.*hom.18.6 in Jer.*(p.160.20; M.13.477C); met., of the sea, Meth.*arbitr.*2(p.148.18; M.18.244A); *~ωθεὶς κατ᾽ αὐτῶν Pers.*(p.21.16).

θυμώδης, **1.** *angry, passionate,* ref. diabolical action producing *συντυχίαι θ.* Gr.Nyss.*or.dom.*1(p.20.16; M.44.1132C); *τῆς θ. διαθέσεως κατόρθωμα...ἐστιν ἡ πρὸς τὸ κακὸν ἀπέχθεια,...καὶ τὸ πρὸς ἀνδρείαν ἐστομῶσθαι τὴν ψυχὴν* id.*ep.can.*(M.45.225A); bishops esp. forbidden to be *θ.*, *Const.App.*2.6.1; **2.** neut. as subst., *the active, non-rational principle in the soul, T.Dan 3.2*; *ὁ θυμός, ἐνέργεια...ἐστι τοῦ θ.* Nemes.*nat.hom.*16(M.40.673B); Chrys.*hom.17.1 in Eph.*(11.122F); Diad.*perf.*10(p.12.9).

***θυμωτικός,** *furious,* Or.*sel.in Ps.*34:16(M.12.1313A).

θυννοσκοπεῖον, τό, *look-out place for tunnies,* Synes.*ep.*57(M.66.1393B).

θυοσκόπος, *inspecting the entrails,* Isid.Pel.*epp.*2.228(M.78.665B).

***θυοφόρος,** *offering sacrifice,* Gr.Naz.*ep.*140(M.37.240A).

θύπτης, children's copybook word, interpreted symbolically in pagan mysteries, Clem.*str.*5.8(p.359.7; M.9.77A).

***θύπτω,** *burn with lightning* (verb formed from *θύπτης*), a meaningless word to which Clem. assigns this sense, Clem.*str.*5.8(p.359.9; M.9.77A).

θύρα, ἡ, *door,*

A. lit.; **1.** of church doors; **a.** main doors leading from atrium into narthex *οὐ δεῖ ὑπηρέτην...τὰς θ. ἐγκαταλιμπάνειν* CLaod.*can.22*;

separate doors for men and women, closed before beginning of anaphora *οἱ δὲ διάκονοι ἱστάσθωσαν εἰς τὰς τῶν ἀνδρῶν θ. καὶ οἱ ὑποδιάκονοι εἰς τὰς τῶν γυναικῶν, ὅπως μή τις ἐξέλθοι μήτε ἀνοιχθείη ἡ θ., κἂν πιστός τις ᾖ, κατὰ τὸν καιρὸν τῆς ἀναφορᾶς Lit.*ap.*Const.App.* 8.11.11; *πρὸς τὴν τῶν νοητῶν ἐποψίαν ἐντεῦθεν διὰ τῆς τῶν θ. κλείσεως, καὶ τῆς εἰσόδου τῶν ἁγίων μυστηρίων, αὐτοὺς ἀγαγών* Max.*myst.*13 (M.91.692B); *Lit.Chrys.*(p.316.7); *λέγει ὁ διάκονος, τὰς θ. τὰς θ. ib.* (p.321.3); should not be opened before end of service *πόθεν ὁ θόρυβος ...γίνεται; ὅτι οὐ διὰ παντὸς ὑμῖν τὰς θ. ἀποκλείομεν, ἀλλὰ συγχωροῦμεν πρὸ τῆς ἐσχάτης εὐχαριστίας ἀποπηδᾶν καὶ ἀναχωρεῖν οἴκαδε· ὃ καὶ αὐτὸ πολλῆς ἂν εἴη καταφρονήσεως* Chrys.*bapt.*4(2.374D); **b.** sanctuary doors, the three doors in altar-screen *προσήγαγεν* [sc. Constantius] *...εἰς τὰς θ. τῆς ἐκκλησίας ἀμφίθυρα χρυσᾶ Chron.Pasch.*p.294(M.92. 737B); cf. *εἰσελθὼν δὲ ὁ διάκονος ἔνδον τῶν ἁγίων θ. Lit.Chrys.*(p.379. 2); *Euchol.*(p.383); **2.** of gates of paradise, *T.Lev.*18.10; of heaven, *Apoc.Bar.*2(p.85.12); cf. *ἐν ταῖς θ. τοῦ βασιλικοῦ τοῦ ἐξ ἀρχῆς αὐτοῦ Hymn.*ap.*A.Thom.*A 113(p.224.15); *θ. δὲ οὐρανοῦ ἀνοιγείσας, τὴν ἄνωθεν χορηγίαν ἐκάλεσε* Thdt.*Ps.*77:23(1.1154); of Hades *τὰς θ. ἀνοίξας ἀνήγαγες...τοὺς ἐγκεκλεισμένους A.Thom.*A 10(p.115.5); of death, Or.*mart.*22(p.20.13; M.11.592A).

B. met.; **1.** *entrance, means of access ὁ λόγος τῆς πίστεως... ἀνοίγων ἡμῖν τὴν θ. τοῦ ναοῦ ὅ ἐστι στόμα Barn.*16.9; *ἐπὶ τὰς σωτηρίους ἀφικνεῖσθαι θ.* Clem.*prot.*4(p.48.27; M.8.164B); *θ. τῆς ἀληθείας* id.*str.* 8.1(p.80.12; M.9.560A); *ἀνεῳχθήσεταί σοι ἡ τῆς συγχωρήσεως θ. A. (Pass.)Andr.*13(p.30.6); of the senses *κάθοδον...εἰς ψυχὴν διὰ τῶν αἰσθήσεων, οἱονεὶ διὰ θ.* Clem.*paed.*2.8(p.197.20; M.8.473B); of holy images *θ. δὲ ἡ εἰκὼν λέγεται, ἥτις διανοίγει τὸν κατὰ θεὸν κτισθέντα νοῦν ἡμῶν πρὸς τὴν ἔνδον τοῦ πρωτοτύπου καθομοίωσιν* Steph.Diac.*v. Steph.*(M.100.1113A); **2.** *opportunity for, entrance to ἀποκέκλεισται θ. ἀκολούθου διηγήσεως* Or.*Cels.*4.17(p.286.17; M.11.1048D); id.*or.*23 (p.351.20; M.11.489A); esp. of missionary opportunity (1Cor.16:9, etc.) *θ. πίστεως μεγάλην A.Xanthipp.*38(p.84.23); *τί δέ ἐστιν, θ. μεγάλη; πολλοί εἰσιν οἱ παρεσκευασμένοι τὴν πίστιν δέξασθαι* Chrys. *hom.43.3 in 1Cor.*(10.403E); Thdt.*1Cor.*16:9(3.282); **3.** phrases: *θύρας ἀνοίγω, open gates* of, hence *institute τοῦ σωτηρίου μυστηρίου τὰς θ. ἀνέῳξε* Thdt.*1Cor.*11:25(3.238); *ἐπὶ θύραις τίθημι hold out in near prospect,* Chrys.*comm.in Gal.*6:9f.(10.726C); *ἀπὸ τῶν θ.* of dismissal or retirement from office *ὁ ἀνήρ, ἕως τῶν κ΄ χρόνων συλλειτουργῶν τῷ ἱερεῖ, ἐπέκεινα δέ, ἀπὸ τῶν θ. Nomoc.*136; **4.** as description of a deity (perh. in sense of *power*) *τὴν θ. τὴν Ἀφροδίτην ...ἀπάλλαξον τὸν οἶκον...ἀπὸ παντὸς κακοῦ ἑρπετοῦ...ὁ ἅγιος Φωκᾶς ὧδέ ἐστιν Pap.Chr.*(p.403); **5.** ref. Jo.10:7 *αὐτὸς ὢν θ. τοῦ πατρός* Ign.*Philad.*9.1; cf. *δίκαιε* [i.e. S. James]*...ἀπάγγειλον ἡμῖν τίς ἡ θ. τοῦ Ἰησοῦ* Heges.ap.Eus.*h.e.*2.23.12(M.20.200B) prob. = *the door, that is Jesus,* cf. *τί με ἐπερωτᾶτε περὶ τοῦ υἱοῦ τοῦ ἀνθρώπου; ib.*2. 23.13, *ἐρωτηθεὶς...τίνα περὶ τοῦ Χριστοῦ ἔχοι δόξαν* Eus.*d.e.*3.5(p.122. 20; M.22.209A); *ἐγὼ γάρ εἰμι ἡ θ. ... θ. ... τὴν ἀποκεκλεισμένην τέως ὁ ἀνοιγνὺς ὕστερον ἀποκαλύπτει τἄνδον καὶ δείκνυσιν ἃ μηδὲ γνῶναι οἷόν τε ἦν πρότερον* Clem.*prot.*1(p.10.13; M.8.68A); *θ. εἰμί σοι κρούοντί με A.Jo.*95(p.198.12); *ib.*98(p.200.7); *δοξάζομέν σου τὴν εἴσοδον τῆς θ. ib.*109(p.207.12); *ὁδὸς δέ που καὶ θ. εἶναι ὁμολογῶν, σαφής ἐστιν μηδέπω τυγχάνων θ. ᾧ ἔτι ὁδός ἐστιν, καὶ μηκέτι ὁδὸς ᾧ ἤδη θ.* Or. *Jo.*6.43(25; p.152.25; M.14.276B); *οἱ δὲ δεσμοὶ τοῦ δεδεμένου πώλου, καὶ αἱ ἁμαρτίαι παρὰ τὸν ὑγιῆ γεγενημέναι λόγον ἐλεγχόμεναι ὑπ' αὐτοῦ θ. τυγχάνοντος ζωῆς πρὸς ἐκείνην* [*λέγω δὴ τὴν θ.*] *ἦσαν οὐκ ἔνδον, ἀλλ' ἔξω· τάχα γὰρ ἔνδον τῆς θ. δεσμὸς γενέσθαι τῆς κακίας οὐ δύναται ib.*10.30(15; p.204.14; 361C); *V.Aberc.*16(p.14.16); *ποιμένα, θ. Symb. Ant.*(341)2(p.249.16; M.26.721C); *λέγεται γὰρ θ., ἀλλὰ μὴ ξυλίνην εἶναι νόμιζε...ἀλλὰ θ. λογικήν, ζῶσαν, διακριτικὴν τῶν εἰσερχομένων* Cyr.H.*catech.*10.3; *καλῶς ὁ κύριος θ. ἑαυτὸν προσηγόρευσεν, ὡς φυλάττων τοὺς ἔνδον τῆς πίστεως, ὡς ἀποσοβῶν τοὺς ἔξω περιαθροῦντας, καὶ εἰσάγων εἰς τὴν τοῦ οἰκοδεσπότου πατρὸς συντυχίαν* ‡Ath.*caec.*13 (M.28.1021A); *θ. ... τῷ ἐπὶ τὰς σπουδαίας πράξεις διὰ τῆς ὀρθότητος τῶν προσταγμάτων εἰσάγειν* Bas.*Spir.*17(3.15A; M.32.97A); Gr.Naz. *or.*30.21(p.142.17; M.36.132C); Epiph.*haer.*69.35(p.183.23; M.42.256D); Sever.*sigill.*2(M.63.533); *σὺ...ἀξιαγωγεὺς θ. ἡμῶ(ν) φωτινή Pap.Chr.* (p.446); *οἱ πιστοί, ὡς διὰ θ., διὰ Χριστοῦ εἰς τὴν αἰώνιον ζωὴν παραπέμπονται...θ. ἐστιν ὁ...λόγος, εἰσάγων εἰς θεογνωσίαν, καὶ οἱ δι' αὐτοῦ εἰσελθόντες, ἔξω τοῦ κόσμου γίνονται* Ammon.*Jo.*10:9(M. 85.1461A); *θ. τοῦ δικαίου* [sc. Lot] *ἀληθὴς καὶ ἀφάνταστος...ὑπῆρχεν. εἰ τοίνυν ἡ ἀληθεστάτη θ., τοῖς μὲν ἄλλοις φανερὰ...ἐτύγχανεν, ἄδηλος δὲ...τοῖς Σοδομηνοῖς ἦν· οὐκοῦν καὶ Ἰησοῦς...τισὶ μὲν ἐφαίνετο μετὰ τὴν ἀνάστασιν, τισὶ δὲ ἄδηλος ἦν* Nil.*epp.*3.120(M.79.437D); *αὐτὴ* [sc. BMV] *ἤνοιξε θ., ἀφ' ἧς ἐγεννήθη θ., παιδίον νέον* Rom.Mel.(*BZ* 24 p.5); **6.** ref. Jo.10:12 *διὰ πάντων ὥδευσε τῶν περὶ αὐτοῦ γεγραμμένων, καί, ὥσπερ διὰ θ. εἰσελθὼν εἰς τὸν ἀνθρώπινον βίον, παρεγένετο πρὸς τὰ πρόβατα* Thdr.Heracl.*cat.Jo.*10:1–5 ed. B. Corderius *Catena Patrum Graecorum in S. Joannem.* Antwerp 1630(p.262); *οὐ κατὰ τὰς γραφάς* [sc. *εἰσέρχεται ὁ λῃστής*]*· τοῦτο γάρ ἐστι τό, μὴ διὰ τῆς θ. ...εἰκότως δὲ θ. τὰς γραφὰς ἐκάλεσεν. αὗται γὰρ ἡμᾶς προσάγουσι τῷ θεῷ* Chrys.*hom.59.2 in Jo.*(8.346D).

θύραθεν, *outside; θύραθε,* Geo.Pis.*carm.*63.2(p.59); hence **1.** *outside Christianity, pagan,* Thdt.*h.e.*1.23.2(3.804); *τῶν θ. φιλοσόφων ὁ κορυφαῖος* [sc. Aristotle] Gr.Agr.*Eccl.*6.1; *φιλοσοφίαν...οὐ μόνον τὴν καθ' ἡμᾶς...ἀλλ' ἣν καὶ οἱ θ. σοφοὶ διετάξαντο* Jo.VI H.*v.Jo.D.*8(M. 94.441B); *ib.*10(445A); Areth.*Apoc.*2(M.106.524D); *Schol.* in CNic. (325)*can.*5(*Mon.*2 p.658); **2.** *secular γνῶσιν ἑκατέραν...τὴν θ., καὶ τὴν θείαν* Thdt.*haer.*2.8(4.334); *τῶν θ. τεχνολόγων* Andr.Cr.*or.*19(M.97. 1209A); **3.** *outside creation, divine;* term used by Aristotle and perh. also Neoplatonists and taken as referring to H. Ghost *ὁ θ. νοῦς* Gr.Naz.*or.*31.5(p.150.6; M.36.137C).

θυρανοίκτης, ὁ, *door-opener,* ‡Chrys.*circ.*(8.88C).

θυραυλέω, *wait at the door;* ref. Is.54:14, fig. *θ. καὶ ποδηγεῖν τοὺς εἰσιόντας* Eus.*h.e.*10.4.63(M.20.873C); met., *fail to obtain an entrance εἰ μὴ θ. οἱ λόγοι περὶ τὰ ὦτα* Synes.*regn.*29(p.62.4; M.66.1108B); *idle around, lounge about τίς...γεωργὸν...ἀργοῦντα καὶ θ.* Isid.Pel.*epp.*3. 60(M.78.772A).

θυρεός, ὁ, *shield,* met. [sc. *τὴν ἐγκράτειαν*] *προβαλλόμενος ἀντὶ θ. M.Thdot.1* 2(p.62.15); exeg. Cant.4:4 *ὁμοίως...θ. ... τὰ πεπιστευμένα δόγματα* Or.*schol.in Cant.*4:4(M.17.272B); shields signifying angelic aid, Gr.Nyss.*hom.7 in Cant.*(M.44.933D); *θ. ... πάντες οἱ... ἅγιοι* Ph.Carp.*Cant.*98(M.40.92B); *θ. ... τὰς περικοπὰς τῆς πίστεως* Nil.ap.Proc.G.*Cant.*4:4(M.87.1649B).

θύρετρον, τό, *door-way, entrance* to Christ's tomb, Nonn.*par. Jo.*20:11(M.43.909B); plur., *windows,* Paul.Sil.*Soph.*510(M.86. 2139A).

***θυρεών,** ὁ, *door,* Eudoc.*Cypr.*1.299(M.85.844B).

θυρίδιον, τό, *little door, Apophth.Patr.*(M.65.128B).

θυρίς, ἡ, **1.** *window;* fig., of the eye, ‡Bas.*inc.*(p.245); met., ref. Jer.9:21 *ὁ πονηρὸς...τὸν διὰ τῶν θ. ... εἴτουν αἰσθητηρίων, εἰσάγων θάνατον* Gr.Naz.*or.*27.7(M.36.20C); Gr.Nyss.*or.dom.*5(p.106.3; M.44. 1185C); Diad.*perf.*57(p.64.8); *ib.*93(p.142.11); **2.** *door, A.Mt.*24 (v.l. for *πύλης* p.252.2); met. *ἀνοίγεις αὐτῷ* [sc. Christ] *τὰς θ.* Or.*hom. 14.8 in Jer.*(p.113.12; M.13.413A).

***θυροκροτέω,** *knock at the door,* Gr.Nyss.*hom.11 in Cant.*(M.44. 1000C).

θυροκρουστέω, *knock at the door,* Bas.*hom.in Ps.*14(1.109D; M. 29.272A); Gr.Nyss.*hom.7 in Cant.*(M.44.905A); met. *ἡ ἀλήθεια...ἐν ὑπονοίαις τισὶ καὶ αἰνίγμασι θ. τὴν διάνοιαν ib.11*(1001C); *ib.*(1008D).

θυροφύλαξ, *guarding the gate,* Germ.CP *or.*1(M.98.224C).

θύρσος, ὁ, *thyrsus,* wand carried by devotees of Dionysus; met., of action of grace *τὸν θύρσῳ πεπληγότα* Clem.*str.*1.14(p.10.20; M.8.704A).

***θυρωρεία,** ἡ, *? office* or *duties of porter, ? porter's lodge,* Bars. *resp.*(M.88.1820A).

θυρωρέω, *keep the door,* Nil.*exerc.*16(M.79.740A).

***θυρώριον,** τό, **1.** *order of doorkeeper,* Pall.*v.Chrys.*7(p.38.20; M. 47.23 -είον); **2.** *porter's lodge,* Thdr.Stud.*poen.*1.63(M.99.1741A).

θυρωρός, ὁ, ἡ, *doorkeeper;* **a.** in gen., ‡Pall.*h.mon.*19.1(p.78.16; M.34.1177D); *V.Dan.*(p.68.15); of best man, who guarded the nuptial chamber, Synes.*ep.*3(M.66.1325A); **b.** eccl.; as lowest order, CLaod.*can.*24; Epiph.*exp.fid.*21(p.522.24; M.42.825A); CTrull.*can.* 4; Phot.*nomoc.*1.30(M.104.556B); *MAMA* 3.355; **c.** met., of angels, Cels.ap.Or.*Cels.*7.40(p.191.7; M.11.1477C); of mind as keeper of senses, Nil.*exerc.*16(M.79.740B); exeg. Jo.10:3 *θ. ... νοεῖν Μωϋσέα. ἐκεῖνος γὰρ τὰ λόγια τοῦ θεοῦ ὁ ἐμπιστευθεὶς ἦν* Thdr.Heracl.*fr. Jo.*10:1(p.297.7); Chrys.*hom.59.2 in Jo.*(8.347C); Thdr.Mops.*fr. in Jo.*10:3(p.348.2; M.66.757B).

***θῦς,** ἡ, *beast for slaughter τὴν ὗν θ. εἶναι...ὡς εἰς θύσιν...μόνον ἐπιτήδειον* Clem.*str.*2.20(p.170.23; M.8.1049A).

θυσία, ἡ, *sacrifice;* **1.** dist. from *δῶρον*: *διαφέρει δῶρον θυσίας, ὅτι ὁ μὲν θύων ἐπιδιαιρέσει, τὸ μὲν αἷμα τῷ βωμῷ προσχέων, τὰ δὲ κρέα οἴκαδε κομίζων· ὁ δὲ δωρούμενος, ὅλου ἔοικε παραχωρεῖν τῷ λαμβάνοντι* Proc.G.*Gen.*4:2(M.87.237B); cf.Gennad.*fr.Gen.*4:4(M.85. 1640cf.); **2.** in paganism; **a.** as diabolical, ref. evil spirits *οἷς... χρηματίζουσι καὶ θυσίας ἀπαιτοῦσι καὶ συνεστιᾶσθαι κελεύουσιν, ἵνα αὐτῶν τὰς ψυχὰς συμπίνωσιν Hom.Clem.*9.14; *ἐπαναπαύομαι...θ. ταῖς διὰ οἴνου γινομέναις ἐν τοῖς βωμοῖς A.Thom.*A 76(p.191.15); *A.Andr. et Mt.*26(p.104.13); cf.Or.*Cels.*4.32(p.302.20; M.11.1077A); **b.** forbidden to Christians, *A.Jo.*38–41(p.171.17); *ib.*43(p.172.15); *τίς... λογισμοῦ κύριος τὸν οὐρανοῦ δεσπότην καὶ ποιητὴν τῶν ἁπάντων θελήσει καταλιπεῖν καὶ δαίμοσι θ. προσενεγκεῖν; M.Nest.*2(p.116.11);

Niceph.Ur.*v.Sym.*218(M.86.3188A); **c.** Christians ordered to sacrifice, *A.(Pass.)Andr.*6(p.13.20; M.2.1228A); Eus.*m.P.*1(p.908.15; M.20.1464B); id.*h.e.*8.12.2(M.20.769B); *M.Jan.*1(p.105.7); *οὐδὲν μέγα ἔπραξας, ἄκοντί μοι τῶν ἀκαθάρτων σου θ. ἐκχέας τῇ βίᾳ πως, ἵνα οἶδεν ὁ θεὸς τὴν προαίρεσίν μου* *M.Tar.*8(p.468); cf.*ib.*9(p.471); **3.** Jewish; **a.** allowed as remedy for idolatry, Just.*dial.*67.8(M.6.632A); *ib.* 19.6(517A); Gr.Naz.*or.*31.25(p.177.8; M.36.161B); Epiph.*haer.*66.71 (p.112.18; M.42.141B); Cyr.*Juln.*4(6².126C); *ἐπειδὴ…χρόνον συχνὸν ἐν Αἰγύπτῳ διατετελεκὼς ὁ λαὸς θύειν δαίμοσιν ἐδιδάχθη, συνεχώρησε τὰς θ., ἵνα τῆς δεισιδαιμονίας ἐλευθερώσῃ* Thdt.*qu.1 in Lev.*(1.176); **b.** typological significance *αἱ…κατὰ τὸν νόμον θ. τὴν περὶ ἡμᾶς εὐσέβειαν ἀλληγοροῦσι, καθάπερ ἡ τρυγὼν καὶ ἡ περιστερὰ ὑπὲρ ἁμαρτιῶν προσφερόμεναι τὴν ἀποκάθαρσιν τοῦ ἀλόγου μέρους τῆς ψυχῆς* Clem.*str.*7.6(p.24.22; M.9.445A); Or.*Cels.*4.31(p.302.5; M.11.1076B); ‡Ath.*sabb.*6(M.28.141B); *εἰσῆλθεν ὁ γραπτὸς νόμος, συνάγων ἡμᾶς εἰς Χριστόν, καὶ οὗτος τῶν θ. ὁ λόγος* Gr.Naz.*or.*45.13(M.36.640C); *ποιεῖσθαι…προστεταχὼς* [sc. *Χριστός*] *τῆς ἐν πνεύματι λατρείας τὴν δύναμιν εἰς ἀναιμάκτου θ. τρόπον. μετατέθειται γὰρ ἡ σκιὰ πρὸς ἀλήθειαν* Cyr.*Zach.*79(3.761E); of Christ as sacrifice of first-fruits (cf. Lev.11:14,15) *ἔστι αὐτὸς ἡ ὑπὲρ ἡμῶν θ., τὸ πρωτογέννημα τὸ πνευματικόν, τουτέστιν, ἡ τῆς ἀνθρωπότητος ἀπαρχή, ὁ πρωτότοκος ἐκ νεκρῶν* id.*glaph.Lev.*(1.344Dff.); as typified by animal sacrifices of Aaron, *ib.*(372D); **c.** not to be offered by Christians, cf.Is. 1:11–13, *Barn.*2.4; *Orac.Sib.*2.82; Christ being accused by Jews as *θυσιῶν ἀναιρέτης*, *Const.App.*5.14.9; God having no need of sacrifices, Arist.*apol.*1.5; Athenag.*leg.*13.2(M.6.916C); Clem.*str.*7.2 (p.11.12; M.9.417C); sacrifice of flesh forbidden by Jo.4:24, Or.*Cels.*6.70(p.140.24; M.11.1405A); **4.** of sacrifice of Christ; **a.** in gen. *ὑπὲρ τῶν ἡμετέρων ἁμαρτιῶν ἔμελλεν τὸ σκεῦος τοῦ πνεύματος προσφέρειν θ.* *Barn.*7.3; *οὐχ ὑπὲρ ἀνθρώπων μόνον ἀλλὰ καὶ παντὸς λογικοῦ τὴν ἅπαξ θ. προσενεχθεῖσαν ἑαυτὸν ἀνενεγκών* Or.*Jo.*1.35(40; p.45.17; M.14.93A); *οὐδὲ ἥμαρτεν ὁ τὰς ἄλλων ἁμαρτίας λυτρούμενος λόγος, ἵνα τραπεὶς εἰς σῶμα ἑαυτὸν ὑπὲρ ἑαυτοῦ εἰς θ. προσενέγκῃ* Ath.*ep.Epict.*4(p.8.15; M.26.1057B); *διὰ τὴν περὶ τῶν ὁμοίων σωμάτων θ. σῶμα καὶ αὐτὸς ὁ λόγος ἔλαβεν* id.*inc.*10.4(M.25.113B); cf.id. *decr.*14(p.12.12; M.25.440B); *αὐτὸς ὁ προσφέρων, καὶ αὐτὸς ὁ ὑπὲρ κόσμου θ. προσφερόμενος* ‡Cyr.H.*occurs.*5(M.33.1192B); ref. Jo.17:19 *τί ἐστιν, ἁγιάζω ἐμαυτόν; προσφέρω σοι θ.* Chrys.*hom.82.1 in Jo.*(8.484B); cf. *κατὰ φύσιν ὑπάρχων ὑπὲρ πάντα τὸν κόσμον…εἰσβέβηκεν εἰς αὐτὸν μέρος αὐτοῦ γεγονώς, τουτέστιν ἄνθρωπος, οὕτω τε τὴν ὑπὲρ ἡμῶν προσκομίσας θ.* Cyr.*Arcad.*(p.101.15; 5².101A); **b.** ref. its OT types; offering of high priest once a year, Chrys.*hom.17.3 in Heb.* (12.168D); sacrifice of Abraham, id.*hom.47.3 in Gen.*(4.478A,B); Germ.CP *or.*2(M.98.280A); **c.** sacrifice of Cross ending OT sacrifices, Ath.*Ar.*2.9(M.26.165B); cf.id.*inc.*10.5(M.25.113C); *μία…αὕτη ἡ θ., ἐκεῖναι δὲ πολλαί· διὰ γὰρ τοῦτο οὐκ ἰσχυραί, ἐπειδὴ πολλαί* Chrys. *hom.17.2 in Heb.*(12.167C); *δείξας ἑτέραν εἰσενηνέχθαι θ., οὐδεμίαν λοιπὸν ἐλπίδα ἔδωκε τοῦ πάλιν ἐκείνην ἐπανελθεῖν* id.*Jud.*7.4(1.667D); id.*hom.18.1 in Heb.*(12.173B); Cyr.*Juln.*4(6².127A); Eulog.*fr.Novat.* (M.104.340C); **5.** of Last Supper *ἑαυτὸν προσήνεγκε προσφορὰν καὶ θ. ὑπὲρ ἡμῶν, ὁ ἱερεὺς ἅμα, καὶ ὁ ἀμνὸς τοῦ θεοῦ…πότε τοῦτο; ὅτε βρωτὸν ἑαυτοῦ τὸ σῶμα εἰς βρῶσιν σαφῶς ἐνδείκνυται τῷ ἤδη γεγενῆσθαι ἐντελῆ τοῦ ἀμνοῦ τὴν θ.* Gr.Nyss.*res.*1(M.46.612C); *τὴν πνευματικὴν θ. προσφέρων τῷ θεῷ αὐτοῦ καὶ πατρὶ πρὸ τοῦ πάθους, ἡμῖν διετάξατο μόνοις τοῦτο ποιεῖν* *Const.App.*8.46.14; *θ. φρικτῆς ἱερουργία* †Cyr.*hom.div.*10(5².377D); **6.** of eucharist; in gen., Serap.*euch.*13.11; *Can.App.*2; Ath.ap.‡Jo.D.*fid.dorm.*19(M.95.265A); Chrys.*prod. Jud.*1.6(2.385D); id.*Jud.*3.4(1.611B); ‡Chrys.*Petr.et El.*1(2.872B,C); Thdt.*Is.*19:21(p.87.1; 2.283); *ἡ θ. ὑμῶν* *Did.*14.1; *ib.*14.2; *Const. App.*5.19.7; *ἡ θ. ἡμετέρα* Chrys.*Jud.*5.12(1.647D); epithets: *ἀναίμακτος* Gr.Naz.*or.*5.29(M.35.701A); Nil.*epp.*2.294(M.79.345C); Isid. Pel.*epp.*3.75(M.78.784A); Eustrat.*v.Eutych.*proem.3(M.86.2277B); *ib.* 84(M.86.2372A); Evagr.*h.e.*4.31(p.181.1; M.86.2760B); *Lit.Jac.*(p.228.1) etc.; *ἄναιμος* Eus.*d.e.*1.10(p.48.3; M.22.92A); *καθαρὰ καὶ ἀναίμακτος* (cf. Mal.1:10) Thdt.*Mal.*1:10(2.1675); Jo.D.*f.o.*4.13(M.94.1149C); *λογική* Eus.*d.e.*1.10(p.48.3; M.22.92A); id.*l.C.*16(p.253.10; M.20.1425D); *Const.App.*2.25.7; *Lit.Marc.(PStrasb.*r° 11); Thdr.Mops. *Mal.*3:3–4(M.66.621D); Thdt.*Ps.*95:9(1.1291); id.*Jer.*33:18(2.558); Eustrat.*v.Eutych.*84(M.86.2372A); *μυστική* Chrys.*hom.1.4 in Is.6:1* (6.100E); Philost.*h.e.*3.14(M.65.501B); Thdt.*h.rel.*20(3.1234); Eulog. *fr.Novat.*(M.104.340B); Niceph.Ur.*v.Sym.*242(M.86.3208D); *φρικτή* Chrys.*exp.in Ps.*140:3(5.433D) al.; Philost.*h.e.*2.13(M.65.476C); Areth.*Apoc.*1(M.106.508B); *πνευματική* Cyr.H.*catech.*23.8; *Const. App.*8.46.14; Thdt.*h.rel.*20(3.1234); *νοερά* Eus.*l.C.*16(p.253.8; M.20.1425D); Proc.G.*Jos.*5:11(M.87.1012A); *ζῶσα* Serap.*euch.*13.11; *θεμιτός* *Const.App.*8.46.11; *καθαρά* Chrys.*prod.Jud.*1.6(2.384D); *θεία* Nil. *epp.*2.294(M.79.345C); *θείαν καὶ σωτήριον θ.* Thdt.*h.rel.*20(1234); *φοβερά* *Lit.Jac.*(p.190.22); prophesied by Mal.1:10ff.: *Did.*14.3; *τῶν ἐν παντὶ τόπῳ ὑφ' ἡμῶν τῶν ἐθνῶν προσφερομένων αὐτῷ θ., τοῦτ' ἔστι τοῦ ἄρτου τῆς εὐχαριστίας καὶ τοῦ ποτηρίου* Just.*dial.* 41.3(M.6.564C); *ib.*117.1(745A); cf.Iren.*haer.*4.17.5(M.7.1023C); *ib.*4.18.1(1024B); *Const.App.*7.30.1,2; *εἰ μὴ…προλέγει…τὴν θ. τὴν ἡμετέραν, ἀλλὰ τὴν Ἰουδαϊκήν, παράνομος ἔσται ἡ προφητεία* Chrys.*Jud.* 5.12(1.647D); *αὕτη ἐστὶν ἡ καθαρὰ θ., δηλαδὴ καὶ ἀναίμακτος, ἣν ἀπὸ ἀνατολῶν ἡλίου μέχρι δυσμῶν αὐτῷ προσφέρεσθαι διὰ τοῦ προφήτου ὁ κύριος ἔφησε* Jo.D.*f.o.*4.13(M.94.1149C); typified by OT sacrifices, which it replaces, *Const.App.*6.23.5; cf.*ib.*2.26.2; ‡Chrys. *hom.in Ps.95:1*(5.630E); ref. sacrifice of Abraham *κἀκείνη ἡ θ. χωρὶς αἵματος ἐγένετο, ἐπειδὴ ταύτης ἔμελλεν ἔσεσθαι τύπος* Chrys. *pan.Eust.Ant.*2(2.606C); Cyr.*Abac.*47(3.561A); typified in Is.25:6, id.*Is.*3.1(2.353D); *ὁ Χριστὸς…μεταξὺ τοῦ ἄρτου τῆς εὐχαριστίας καὶ τὸ ποτήριον εὐλογήσας, τὸ νομικὸν πάσχα κατέπαυσεν, ἀρχὴν καὶ πάροδον τῆς καινῆς καὶ νοερᾶς θ. λαβούσης* Proc.G.*Jos.*5:11(M.87.1012A); *κρίσιν ἐσχάτην ἀπειλεῖ τοῖς μετὰ τὴν ἐπίγνωσιν τῆς ἀληθείας καὶ τῆς μυστικῆς θ. τὴν ἀπόλαυσιν εἰς ἐκείνην τὴν νομικήν,…ἐπανιοῦσι* Eulog.*fr.Novat.*(M.104.340B); ref. Christ as priest and victim *ἡ φωνὴ αὕτη* [sc. *τοῦτό μού ἐστι τὸ σῶμα*] *ἅπαξ λεχθεῖσα καθ' ἑκάστην τράπεζαν ἐν ταῖς ἐκκλησίαις ἐξ ἐκείνου μέχρι σήμερον, καὶ μέχρι τῆς αὐτοῦ παρουσίας, τὴν θ. ἀπηρτισμένην ἐργάζεται* Chrys.*prod.Jud.* 1.6(2.384B); *ὁ Χριστὸς…ἐν ἄρτῳ τε καὶ οἴνῳ πνευματικῶς προσκομίσας (αὐτὸς δὲ ἦν ὁ καὶ προσφέρων ἄρα καὶ προσφερόμενος)* Niceph.Ur.*v. Sym.*115(M.86.3093B); *ὁ μονογενής σου υἱὸς…μυστικῶς πρόκειται εἰς θ.* *Lit.Jac.*(p.160.15); ref. the celebrant; bishops, *Const.App.*2.25.7; *Lit.ib.*8.5.7; *οὔτε λαϊκοῖς ἐπιτρέπομεν ποιεῖν τι τῶν ἱερατικῶν ἔργων, οἷον θ. ἢ βάπτισμα* *ib.*3.10.1; *οὔτε…διακόνῳ προσφέρειν θ. θεμιτὸν ἢ βαπτίζειν* *ib.*8.46.11; cf.*ib.*8.46.16; *θ. λέγει τὰς λογικάς, ἃς ὁρῶμεν διηνεκῶς ὑπὸ τῶν ἱερέων προσφερομένας* Thdt.*Ps.*95:9(1.1291); id.*Jer.*33:18(2.558); in rel. to that of Cross *καὶ ἡμεῖς, τὸ ὁμοίωμα τοῦ θανάτου ποιοῦντες τὸν ἄρτον προσηνέγκαμεν, καὶ παρακαλοῦμεν διὰ τῆς θ. ταύτης* Serap.*euch.*13.13; *ἅπαξ…τὴν θ. τοῦ ἱερέως τελειώσαντος* Bas.*ep.*93(3.187A; M.32.485A); *ἀντὶ θ. τῆς δι' αἱμάτων τὴν λογικὴν καὶ ἀναίμακτον καὶ τὴν μυστικήν, ἥτις εἰς τὸν θάνατον τοῦ κυρίου συμβόλων χάριν ἐπιτελεῖται, τοῦ σώματος αὐτοῦ καὶ τοῦ αἵματος* *Const.App.*6.23.5; *οὐκ ἄλλην θ., καθάπερ ὁ ἀρχιερεὺς* [sc. *Χριστός*] *τότε, ἀλλὰ τὴν αὐτὴν ἀεὶ ποιοῦμεν· μᾶλλον δὲ ἀνάμνησιν ἐργαζόμεθα θυσίας* Chrys.*hom.17.3 in Heb.*(12.169A); *θυσίᾳ προσέρχῃ φρικτῇ καὶ ἁγίᾳ· ἐσφαγμένος πρόκειται ὁ Χριστός* id.*prod.Jud.*2.6(2.394D); id.*coemet.*3(2.401E); Thdr.Mops.*Mal.*3:3–4(M.66.621D); *εἰ…ὁ κατὰ τάξιν Μελχισεδὲκ ἀρχιερεὺς τὴν θ. προσήνεγκε, καὶ θ. ἑτέρας ἀνενδεεῖς καθέστηκε, τί τῆς καινῆς διαθήκης οἱ ἱερεῖς τὴν μυστικὴν λειτουργίαν ἐπιτελοῦσιν;…τῆς μιᾶς ἐκείνης καὶ σωτηρίου τὴν μνήμην ἐπιτελοῦμεν* Thdt.*Heb.*8:5(3.594); Eulog.*fr.Novat.*(M.104.340D); reasons for offering; as gen. thanksgiving, Chrys.*hom.25.3 in Mt.* (7.311B); for sins *τῆς θ. ἐκείνης τοῦ ἱλασμοῦ* Cyr.H.*catech.*23.8; for the dead *τὰς ἁμαρτωλῶν ψυχὰς μετέχειν εὐεργεσίας τινὸς ἐκ τῆς ὑπὲρ αὐτῶν γενομένης ἀναιμάκτου θ.* ‡Ath.*qu.Ant.*34(M.28.617B); *τίς …τῶν ἀνθρώπων ἄνευ ἁμαρτίας; ἀλλὰ διὰ τοῦτο θ. καὶ ἐκκλησία* ‡Chrys.*Petr.et El.*1(2.730B); as gen. intercession *μετὰ τὸ ἀπαρτισθῆναι τὴν πνευματικὴν θ. … ἐπὶ τῆς θ. ἐκείνης…παρακαλοῦμεν τὸν θεόν, ὑπὲρ κοινῆς τῶν ἐκκλησιῶν εἰρήνης…καὶ ὑπὲρ πάντων βοηθείας δεομένων δεόμεθα* Cyr.H.*catech.*23.8; *διὰ…τὴν εἰρήνην τὴν εἰς τὸν ἀδελφόν σου καὶ αὕτη ἡ θ. γέγονεν* Chrys.*prod.Jud.*1.6(2.385B); for all men, id.*hom.div.*1.2(12.326A); Eustrat.*v.Eutych.*proem.3(M.86.2277B); circumstances of the offering; nothing to be substituted for bread and wine, *Can.App.*2; offered on Sundays, *Did.*14.1; *Const.App.*7.30.1,2; Easter, *ib.*5.19.7; *πάσχα οὐ νηστεία ἐστίν, ἀλλ' ἡ προσφορά, καὶ ἡ θ. ἡ καθ' ἑκάστην γινομένη σύναξιν* Chrys.*Jud.*3.4 (1.611B); at consecration of a bishop, *Lit.*ap.*Const.App.*8.5.9; *ἐν παρασκευῇ, καὶ ἐν σαββάτῳ, καὶ ἐν κυριακῇ, καὶ ἐν ἡμέρᾳ μαρτύρων ἡ αὐτὴ θ. ἐπιτελεῖται* Chrys.*hom.5.3 in 1Tim.*(11.577E); psalms necessary *οὐ γὰρ ἐξὸν χωρὶς τοῦ Δαυὶδ ἀνενεγκεῖν θ.* *Apoc.Paul.*29(p.56); presence of angels, Nil.*epp.*2.294(M.79.345C); in time of persecution *ἀνακείμενον τὸν μάρτυρα…ἐν τῷ οἰκείῳ στέρνῳ…τὴν φρικτὴν θ. τελεσάμενον* Philost.*h.e.*2.13(M.65.476C); ref. excommunication *πᾶς δὲ ἔχων τὴν ἀμφιβολίαν μετὰ τοῦ ἑταίρου αὐτοῦ μὴ συνελθέτω ὑμῖν, …ἵνα μὴ κοινωθῇ ἡ θ. ὑμῶν* *Did.*14.2; cf.Or.*or.*28(p.381.2; M.11.529A); *ἐπίσκοπον ἢ πρεσβύτερον ἢ διάκονον αἱρετικῶν δεξαμένους βάπτισμα ἢ θ. καθαιρεῖσθαι προστάσσομεν* *Can.App.*46; of Arians separating themselves, Philost.*h.e.*3.14(M.65.501B); Lev.17:3,4 forbidding communion with heretics *ἔξω γὰρ θύουσι τῆς ἁγίας σκηνῆς, τὸ περὶ τῆς ἁμαρτίας, οὐκ ἐν τόποις ἁγίοις τὴν ἱερὰν τελοῦσι θ.* Cyr.*glaph.Lev.*(1.351C); ref. Dt.16:5 *εἷς…τόπος, καὶ μία πόλις, ἡ* *καθολικὴ ἐκκλησία...αὕτη τοίνυν ἡ πόλις ἐπιτηδεία μόνη πρὸς τὴν τοῦ πάσχα θ. αἱ γὰρ τῶν αἱρέσεων μάνδραι κατὰ νόμον ἀπόβλητοι* Proc. G.*Dt*.16:5(M.87.913A); of Ophite eucharist *ἡ παρ' αὐτοῖς λεγομένη θ. ... ὄφεως οὖσα σάρξ, καὶ οὐχὶ τοῦ κυρίου* Epiph.*haer*.26.16(p.296.13; M.41.357C); cf.*ib*.26.4(p.281.3; 337C); restricted senses: of unconsecrated elements *ὑπὲρ τῶν τὰς θ. καὶ τὰς ἀπαρχὰς προσφερόντων κυρίῳ τῷ θεῷ ἡμῶν δεηθῶμεν Lit*.ap.*Const.App*.8.10.2; *Const.App*. 2.27.6; of consecrated elements, *Lit*.ap.*Const.App*.8.12.39; Chrys. *hom.17.4 in Heb*.(12.169B); *τῶν θείων μυστηρίων κοινωνοῦσι, τῆς ἀναιμάκτου φημὶ θ.* †Jo.D.*B.J*.12(M.96.968A); of eucharistic *actio*, *Const.App*.2.57.21; *ib*.2.59.4; **7.** of martyrdom, *M.Polyc*.14.2; *ὥσπερ ὁ ἀρχιερεὺς θ. ἑαυτὸν προσήνεγκεν Ἰησοῦς...οἱ ἱερεῖς ὧν ἐστιν ἀρχιερεὺς θ. ἑαυτοὺς προσφέρουσι* Or.*mart*.30(p.27.6; M.11.601B); Chrys.*hom.9.1 in 2Tim*.(11.714D); *κρεῖττόν μοί ἐστιν οἰκείᾳ προαιρέσει τῷ δεσπότῃ Χριστῷ θ. γενέσθαι ἢ τῷ Κρόνῳ ὑμῶν τῷ εἰδώλῳ ἐπιθῦσαι ἐμαυτόν M.Das*.5(p.93.16); *κύριε Ἰησοῦ Χριστέ,...δός μοι... τὴν τοῦ ἐμοῦ αἵματος ἔκχυσιν ἀντὶ σπονδῆς καὶ θ. προσδέξασθαι ὑπὲρ πάντων τῶν διὰ σὲ θλιβομένων M.Eleuth*.21(p.74.9); **8.** of virtuous living, in gen. *ταύτας φημὶ τὰς ἀρετὰς θ. δεκτὴν εἶναι παρὰ θεῷ* Clem. *str*.7.3(p.10.28; M.9.417A); ref. Const. *τῷ βασιλεῖ τῶν ὅλων προσφιλῆ καὶ χαρίεσσαν θ. αὐτὴν δηλαδὴ τὴν αὐτοῦ βασιλικὴν ψυχὴν καὶ τὸν νοῦν* Eus.*l.C*.2(p.200.5; M.20.1328A); *ib*.3(p.200.20; 1328B); *δικαιοπράττοντες, καὶ τοῦτο ὥσπερ θ. ἀναπέμποντες τῷ θεῷ* Ath.*exp.Ps*.4:6(M.27. 73A); *μόνην ἀπαιτοῦντι παρ' ἡμῶν θ., τὴν κάθαρσιν* Gr.Naz.*or*.16.2(M. 35.936B); *προσοίσει...τῷ θεῷ θ. πνευματικάς, ἑαυτὸν ἀνατιθεὶς εἰς ὀσμὴν εὐωδίας, καὶ πᾶν εἶδος συνεπιτηδεύων ἀρετῆς* Cyr.*Nah*.16(3. 494E); id.*Os*.113(3.124E); as necessary preparation for eucharistic offering, Gr.Naz.*or*.2.95(M.35.497A,B); *Lit*.ap.*Const.App*.8.5.7; cf. Chrys.*prod.Jud*.1.6(2.384E); ref. lists of virtues, ‡Chrys.*hom.in Ps*. *95:1*(5.631Cff.); cf.Chrys.*hom.11.3 in Heb*.(12.114Dff.); Cyr.*ador*.1 (1.41B); ref. partic. virtues: fasting, Herm.*sim*.5.3.8; Cyr.*Joel*.11 (3.209E); almsgiving, Herm.*sim*.5.3.8; Chrys.*hom.30.2 in Rom*.(9. 739E); id.*hom.16.9 in Mt*.(7.217B); charity *ἀγάπην...μεγίστην ἡγεῖται εἶναι τὴν θ. ib*.(216E); *μόνην ἀπαιτοῦντι παρ' ἡμῶν θ. τὴν εἰς ἀλλήλους φιλανθρωπίαν* Max.*ambig*.(M.91.1417C); mercy, Cyr.*Mich*. 56(3.449A); negatively; of sacrifice of anger, Chrys.*David* 2.1(4. 761B); *σβέσωμεν...ἐπιθυμίαν, ἀποκτείνωμεν θυμόν, ἀνέλωμεν φθόνον. τοῦτό ἐστι θ. ζῶσα* id.*hom.74.3 in Jo*.(8.437C); self-offering made possible through Christ's sacrifice, †Bas.*Is*.24(1.398C; M.30.165B); *δεκτὴ...ἡμῶν ἡ θ. ... διὰ τὸ πάθος τοῦ Χριστοῦ* Cyr.*ador*.17(1.626B); *πληροῦμεν...μᾶλλον ἐν ἐκκλησίαις τὴν ἐν Χριστῷ νοουμένην θ...., καὶ αὐτὸν προθέντες εἰς ἁγιασμόν* id.*Mal*.35(3.854A); **9.** of prayer *εὐχαὶ καὶ εὐχαριστίαι, ὑπὸ τῶν ἀξίων γινόμενοι, τέλειαι μόναι καὶ εὐαρεστοί εἰσι τῷ θεῷ θ.* Just.*dial*.117.2(M.6.745B); Clem.*fr*.61(p.227.28); *θ. ἀναίμακτον καὶ καθαρὰν ἀναπέμπω κἀγὼ καὶ πάντες Χριστιανοὶ τῷ παντοκράτορι θεῷ...τὴν δι' εὐχῶν M.Apollon*.8; *ib*.44; ref. Const. *εὐχαρίστους εὐχὰς ὥσπερ τινὰς ἀπύρους καὶ ἀκάπνους θ. ἀνεπέμπετο* Eus.*v.C*.1.48(p.30.12; M.20.964A); id.*d.e*.1.6(p.30.33; M.22.61A); *τίνας...θ.; τὴν αἴνεσιν, τὸν ὕμνον, τὴν θεολογίαν* Ath.*exp.Ps*.49:7(M. 27.236A); praise, Bas.*Spir*.62(3.52D; M.32.181D); Chrys.*exp.in Ps*. 49:14(5.231B); thanksgiving, id.*hom.9.5 in Gen*.(4.70B); prayer of angels, Cyr.*Heb*.5:5(M.74.973B); **10.** of preaching, cf.Rom. 15:16 *ἔστι καὶ ἄλλη καινὴ θ., ἡ διὰ τοῦ εὐαγγελικοῦ κηρύγματος πληρουμένη* ‡Chrys.*hom.in Ps.95:1*(5.631C); Chrys.*hom.29.1 in Rom*.(9.731A); **11.** animal sacrifices expected by Cerinthus in millennial reign of Christ, Dion.Al.ap.Eus.*h.e*.7.25.3(M.20.697B); **12.** met., of a banquet offered to bishops, Eus.*v.C*.3.15(p.84.2; M.20.1072A).

θυσιάζω, *sacrifice*, *Pap.Chr*.(p.365.10).

***θυσίασις, ἡ**, *act of sacrifice*, Thdr.Mops.*Zach*.14:21(M.66.596B).

***θυσιασμός, ὁ**, *victim*, meaning of name *Ζεβεέ* (Zeba), Hesych. H.*Ps.tit*.82(M.27.1004D).

θυσιαστήριον, τό, A. *altar*; **1.** in OT *τὸ...θ. τύπος ἂν εἴη καὶ μάλα σαφῶς τῆς ἐκκλησίας τοῦ Χριστοῦ, τῆς οἱονεί πως ἐστὶ τὸ ὄρος κειμένης* Cyr.*glaph.Ex*.3(1.329E); **2.** Christian; **a.** explanation of term *τῆς... ἀναιμάκτου θυσίας ἐπώνυμα θ.* Gr.Naz.*or*.5.29(M.35.701A); *θ. ἐστι κατὰ τὸ ἅγιον μνῆμα τοῦ Χριστοῦ ἐν ᾧ θυσίαν ἑαυτὸν ὁ Χριστὸς προσήγαγε* ‡Bas.*h.myst*.5(p.258.26); *ib*.50(p.391.12); cf.*A.(Pass.)Andr*.6 (p.13.17); Jo.V H.*icon*.(M.96.1360A); *θ. λέγεται κατὰ τὸ ἐπουράνιον καὶ νοερὸν θ. ἐν ᾧ ἀντιτυποῦσι τὰς νοερὰς καὶ ἀΰλους ἱεραρχίας οἱ ἔνυλοι ἱερεῖς...ἢ κατὰ τὸ ἅγιον μνῆμα Χριστοῦ* ‡Bas.*h.myst*.5(p.259.7); **b.** site, orientated *ἐν Ἀντιοχείᾳ δὲ τῆς Συρίας ἡ ἐκκλησία ἀντίστροφον ἔχει τὴν θέσιν· οὐ γὰρ πρὸς ἀνατολὰς τὸ θ., ἀλλὰ πρὸς δύσιν ὁρᾷ* Socr. *h.e*.5.22.53(M.67.640A); not to be erected in honour of martyrs where there are no relics or close association with the saint; private revelations to be disregarded in the matter, *Cod.Afr*.83; **c.** consecrated; with holy oil, Dion.Ar.*e.h*.4.3.12(M.3.484C); by bishops only, *ib*.5.1.5(505C); **d.** stone altars v. *λίθος*; **e.** ornaments *τὰ σηρικὰ ἡμιφόρια τοῖς θ. ἐδωρήσατο* Pall.*h.Laus*.61(p.156.5; M. 34.1228B); a lamp burning before it, *Fr.hist*.2(M.85.1812B); **f.** in ritual *χρὴ ἀπὸ τοῦ βαπτίσματος πρὸς τὸ ἅγιον τοῦ θεοῦ προσελεύσεσθαι θ., καὶ τῶν...ἐπουρανίων ἀπολαύειν μυστηρίων* Cyr.H.*catech*.18.32; ordinands kneel before it to signify consecration of lives to God, Dion.Ar.*e.h*.5.3.2(509D); *ὁ ἱερεὺς τὸν μέλλοντα ἐξομολογήσασθαι...ἱστᾷ ...ἔμπροσθεν τοῦ θ.* †Jo.Jej.*poenit*.(M.88.1889A); **g.** in popular devotion, ref. burial *μὴ ἐάσητέ με...τεθῆναι...ὑπὸ θυσιαστήριον...οὐ γὰρ καθήκει σκώληκι σαπρίαν ἀποβαλόντι κατατεθῆναι εἰς ναὸν καὶ ἁγίασμα κυρίου* Ephr.2.233B; head of sick person laid on it to obtain a cure, Gr.Naz.*or*.8.18(M.35.809C); ref. non-eucharistic offerings *πλὴν νέων χίδρων ἢ σταφυλῆς μὴ ἐξὸν ἔστω προσάγεσθαί τι πρὸς τὸ θ., καὶ ἔλαιον εἰς τὴν λυχνίαν καὶ θυμίαμα τῷ καιρῷ τῆς θείας ἀναφορᾶς Can.App*.3; cf.*ib*.2 and 4; CTrull.*can*.57; as place of sanctuary, Pall.*v.Chrys*.6 (p.37.7; M.47.23); **h.** as sign of unity *ἁγιάσαι...ἔλαιον οὐ δύναται ὁ αἱρετικὸς ὁ μήτε θ. ἔχων, μήτε ἐκκλησίαν* Cypr.*ep*.(H.1.155A); of schismatics *θυσιαστηρίῳ θ. ἀντηγείρατε* Gr.Naz.*or*.26.18(M.35.1252A); *τί βούλεται ἡ τῶν καινῶν θ. ἀντεξαγωγή;* Gr.Nyss.*ep*.3(M.46.1024A); *εἴ τις πρεσβύτερος, καταφρονήσας τοῦ ἰδίου ἐπισκόπου, χωρὶς συναγάγῃ καὶ θ. ἕτερον πήξῃ,...καθαιρείσθω Can.App*.31; cf.CAnt.(341)*can*.5; *Cod.Afr*.10; **3.** of heavenly altar; **a.** as surrounded by martyrs, Or. *mart*.30(p.27.4; M.11.601B); *εἶδόν φησι τὰς τῶν μαρτύρων ψυχὰς τὸν ἀνωτάτω τόπον ἐχούσας· ἦσαν γὰρ ὑπὲρ τὸ ὑπερουράνιον θ.* Oecum. *Apoc*.6:9(p.91); **b.** as place where worship on earth is ultimately offered *λυπηροῦ ἀνδρὸς ἡ ἔντευξις οὐκ ἔχει δύναμιν τοῦ ἀναβῆναι ἐπὶ τὸ θ. τοῦ θεοῦ* Herm.*mand*.10.3.2; Hesych.H.*fr.Ps*.112:4(M.93. 1329B); *δεηθῶμεν, ὅπως ὁ...θεὸς προσδέξηται αὐτὸ* [sc. eucharistic offering]...*εἰς τὸ ἐπουράνιον αὐτοῦ θ. Lit*.ap.*Const.App*.8.13.3; *Lit. Jac*.(p.180.27); *Lit.Bas*.(p.319.25); **c.** rel. to altars on earth *ἐκεῖνο τὸ θ. τοῦ θ. τούτου τύπος ἐστὶ καὶ εἰκών* Chrys.*hom.6.3 in Is.6:1*(6. 141D); **4.** met.; **a.** of Christ, cf. *πάντες...συντρέχετε...ὡς ἐπὶ ἓν θ., ἐπὶ ἕνα Ἰησοῦν Χριστόν* Ign.*Magn*.7.2; *θ. ... τῆς τοῦ κοινοῦ πάντων ἱερέως [τῆς ψυχῆς] τὸ...ἁγίων ἅγιον* Eus.*h.e*.10.4.68(M.20.877A); ‡Eust.*Laz*.23(p.45.5); ref. Ex.20:24 *γήϊνον...ὀνομάζει θ. τὸν Ἐμμανουήλ. γέγονε γὰρ σὰρξ ὁ λόγος* Cyr.*ador*.9(1.290A); *τὸ θ. τὸ χρυσοῦν, καὶ αὐτὸ δὲ τὸ σύνθετον καὶ λεπτὸν θυμίαμα Χριστόν ib*.(1.324D); as altar on which souls are offered to God, Dion.Ar.*e.h*.4.3.12(M.3. 484D); *θ. δὲ χρυσοῦν ὁ Χριστός ἐστιν· ἐν ᾧ πᾶσα λειτουργικὴ καὶ ἁγία συνέστηκε δύναμις, καὶ αἱ μαρτυρικαὶ θυσίαι προσκομίζονται· οὗ ἦν τύπος τὸ δειχθὲν ἐν τῷ ὄρει τῷ Μωσῇ...θ.* Andr.Caes.*Apoc*.21(M.106. 288B); **b.** of BMV, Procl.CP *or*.6.17(M.65.753B); *τὸ ἔμψυχον θ. τοῦ ἄρτου τῆς ζωῆς* ‡Meth.*Sym.et Ann*.14(M.18.381B); **c.** of Church *ἔστι ...τὸ παρ' ἡμῖν θ. ... ἄθροισμα τῶν ταῖς εὐχαῖς ἀνακειμένων* Clem.*str*. 7.6(p.23.27; M.9.444B); *οὐδὲν ἧττόν ἐσμεν καὶ οἱονεί τι θ., συναγηγερμένοι μὲν καθ' ἕνωσιν τὴν πνευματικήν, καὶ τὴν ἐν Χριστῷ πίστιν εὐωδιάζοντες* Cyr.*glaph.Dt*.(1.427C); **d.** of the poor as altars of sacrificial offering; virgins and widows, Polyc.*ep*.4.3; Meth.*symp*. 5.6(p.61.4; M.18.108C); *ib*.5.8(p.62.23; 112B); *Const.App*.2.26.8; *ib*.4. 3.3; Chrys.*hom.20.3 in 2Cor*.(10.581C); **e.** of rational soul mortifying the passions, Or.*fr.49 in Lam*.(p.257.7; M.13.636A); and offering sacrifice of prayer, Gr.Naz.*or*.26.16(M.35.1248D); Chrys.*hom.13.4 in Jo*.(8.77B).

B. *altar-precincts, sanctuary*; **1.** of OT Temple, *Apoc.Bar.rel*.2. 10; *ib*.9.7; **2.** Christian; **a.** in gen. *ὁ...τοῦ ἱεροῦ τὰ μάλιστα χῶρος ἀβέβηλος, καὶ μόνοις ἱερεῦσι βατός, ὅνπερ καλοῦσι θ.* Proc.G.*Soph*. (M.87.2836C); **b.** ref. access to sanctuary *οὐ δεῖ γυναῖκας ἐν τῷ θ. εἰσέρχεσθαι* CLaod.*can*.44; *μόνοις ἐξὸν εἶναι τοῖς ἱερατικοῖς εἰσιέναι εἰς τὸ θ. καὶ κοινωνεῖν ib*.19; cf.Pall.*v.Chrys*.15(p.90.20; M.47.51); laity normally excluded, CTrull.*can*.69; **c.** ref. extra-eucharistic uses; burial of saints, *A.Andr*.A 11(p.64.8); ref. prohibition of an Armenian practice *ὥς τινες ἔνδον ἐν τοῖς ἱεροῖς θ. μέλη κρεῶν ἕψοντες προσάγουσιν ἀφαιρέματα τοῖς ἱερεῦσιν Ἰουδαϊκῶς ἀπονέμοντες* CTrull.*can*.99; **d.** met., of place or sphere of worship *μία...σὰρξ τοῦ κυρίου..., ἓν θ.* Ign.*Philad*.4; *ἐὰν μή τις ᾖ ἐντὸς τοῦ θ., ὑστερεῖται τοῦ ἄρτου τοῦ θεοῦ* id.*Eph*.5.2; *ὁ...ἐκτὸς θ. ὢν οὐ καθαρός ἐστιν· τοῦτ' ἔστιν, ὁ χωρὶς ἐπισκόπου καὶ πρεσβυτηρίου καὶ διακόνου πράσσων τι* id.*Trall*.7.2; **3.** of sanctuary in heaven *τὸ...βῆμά ἐστι κατὰ μίμησιν τοῦ ἐπουρανίου θ.* ‡Sophr.H.*liturg*.3(M.87.3984C).

***θυσιοπάρεδρος**, *assisting at a sacrifice*, ‡Ath.*nativ.Jo.Bapt*.2(M. 28.909B).

***θυσιοφωσφόρος, ὁ**, ? *light-bearer at the altar*; of Zacharias, Chrysipp.*enc.in Jo.Bapt*.(p.31.17).

θύσις, ἡ, *slaughter*, Clem.*str*.2.20(p.170.23; M.8.1049A); *ἡ Χριστοῦ θ.* Or.*Jo*.10.16(13; p.186.24; M.14.333B).

θύτης, ὁ, *offerer of the sacrifice*, of Christ *αὐτὸς ὁ θ., καὶ αὐτὸς ὁ θυόμενος* ‡Cyr.H.*occurs*.5(M.33.1193A).

***θυτόν**, τό, *meat*, Jo.Mosch.*prat*.65(M.87.2916C).

θύω, A. *sacrifice*; 1. ref. sacrifice of Christ; a. on Cross; ref. Gen.22:13 *ἐκεῖνος σφαγεὶς ἐλυτρώσατο τὸν Ἰσαάκ· οὕτως καὶ ὁ κύριος...τυθεὶς ἐλυτρώσατο* Mel.*fr.Gen*.(p.312; M.5.1216B); ref. Is. 53:7 *ἦν τὸ πάσχα ὁ Χριστός, ὁ τυθεὶς ὕστερον* Just.*dial*.111.3(M.6. 732C); b. in eucharist *ἄμωμον ἀμνὸν καθ' ἡμέραν...θ.* *A.(Pass.)Andr*. 6(p.13.17); *ἐπὶ τραπέζης...ἔνθα ὁ Χριστὸς κεῖται τεθυμένος* Chrys. *stat*.15.5(2.158E); *ὁ θεὸς θυόμενος καὶ διαδιδόμενος εἰς σωμάτων...καὶ ψυχῶν περιποίησιν θεουργεῖ τοὺς μετέχοντας* CTrull.*or.imp*.(H.3. 1652D); 2. ref. Christian attitude to sacrifice; a. no material sacrifices offered to God, because he needs none, Athenag.*leg*.13.1 ff.(M.6.916A); Clem.*str*.7.3(p.11.9; M.9.417B); because Christ has abolished those of OT, *Const.App*.2.35.1; b. refusal to sacrifice to pagan gods, *M.Polyc*.12.2; *ἡμεῖς οἱ ζῶντες τοῖς νεκροῖς θεοῖς οὐ θ.* *2Clem*.3.1; cf.Ath.*gent*.25(M.25.49A); id.*ep.Aeg.Lib*.21(M.25.588A); though some think it an indifferent thing, Or.*mart*.45(p.41.21; M. 11.624A); Christians offered liberty if they will sacrifice, id.*Cels*. 2.13(p.142.21; M.11.821A); Eus.*h.e*.8.6.10(M.20.752B) etc.; ref. arbitrary conduct of magistrates in enforcing laws against Christians who will not sacrifice, *ib*.8.3.2(748B); ref. lapsed in persecution *διακόνους...θύσαντας, μετὰ δὲ ταῦτα ἀναπαλαίσαντας τὴν μὲν ἄλλην τιμὴν ἔχειν, πεπαῦσθαι δὲ αὐτοὺς πάσης τῆς ἱερατικῆς λειτουργίας* CAnc.(314)*can*.2; *τοὺς πρὸ τοῦ βαπτίσματος τεθυκότας καὶ μετὰ ταῦτα βαπτισθέντας ἔδοξεν εἰς τάξιν προάγεσθαι ὡς ἀπολουσαμένους* *ib*.12; reconciliation of those who sacrificed under compulsion or because threatened, *ib*.3–8; Arian Asterius habitually called *Ἀστέριος ὁ θύσας* Ath.*decr*.8(p.7.20; M.25.429A); emperors preceding Diocletian allow Christians to be magistrates without sacrificing, Eus. *h.e*.8.1.2(740C); pagan sacrifice forbidden by Const., Soz.*h.e*.1.8.5 (M.67.877B); by Constantius and Constans, *ib*.3.17.2(1093C); 3. met. *πῶς...θύσω τῷ κυρίῳ; θυσία...τῷ κυρίῳ πνεῦμα συντετριμμένον* Clem. *paed*.3.12(p.286.1; M.8.669B); Jo.VI H.*v.Jo.D*.24(M.94.464B); cf. liturg., of piercing the host *θῦσον δέσποτα. θύει αὐτὸν σταυροειδῶς* *Lit.Chrys*.(p.357.13; M.63.904).

B. *kill* *θ. τὸν ἀδελφόν* Chrys.*stat*.15.5(2.159A); pass., of martyrs, *Ep.Lugd*.ap.Eus.*h.e*.5.1.40(M.20.424B).

[*]**θῶ**, properly aor. subj. of *τίθημι*, proposed as form of pres. indic. to provide etymology for *θεός*: *ἐτυμολογεῖται θεός παρὰ τό, θῶ, τὸ κατασκευάζω, καὶ ποιῶ· ὡς πάντων ποιητής* †Jo.D.*Trin*.5 (M.95.16A).

θωή, ἡ, *penalty*, Gr.Naz.*carm*.1.2.2.426(M.37.614A); Euthal.Diac. *Ac*.proem.(M.85.632B).

***Θώθ**, *Thoth*, name of Coptic month corresponding to September, Ath.*syn*.12(p.239.11; M.26.701A); id.*apol.sec*.76(p.156.18; M.25.385C).

θῶκος, ὁ, *seat*, of bishop's throne *πνεύματι καὶ θ. τεσσαρακονταέτης* Gr.Naz.*carm*.2.2(epitaph.)55.2(M.38.38A); *ὁ μέσος θ.* Thdt.*h.e*.5.3.15 (3.1019); *ἀρχιερατικοὶ...θ.* *ib*.4.6.7(954); *ib*.4.21.1(984); *ἱερατικοὶ...θ.* *ib*.5.4.7(1021); *MAMA* 1.233; *ὁ ἀποστολικὸς θῶκως* *CIG* 8799 (? post 800).

***θώπαξ**, ὁ, *flatterer*, Gel.Cyz.*h.e*.3.13.10.

θωπευτικός, 1. *flattering* *τί προσάγεις τοὺς...θ. λόγους* [i.e. in prayer] *τῷ πρὸς τὰ ἔργα βλέποντι*; Gr.Nyss.*or.dom*.5(p.94.29; M.44. 1180A); Bas.Sel.*v.Thecl*.1(M.88.488D); 2. *clinging* *τῷ μὲν ἀνθρώπῳ ἡδονὴν ἐνέσπειρε* [i.e. after the Fall]*· τὸ δὲ θῆλυ θ. ἐποίησεν* Amph. *hom*.4.4(M.39.72C).

θωπικῶς, *coaxingly*, Cyr.*glaph.Gen*.5(1.159C); in good sense, id. *Rom*.11:1–3(M.74.845A).

θωρακίζω, *arm*, met. *οἱ ἀπόστολοι...τῇ θείᾳ συμμαχίᾳ θωρακισθέντες* Isid.Pel.*epp*.2.54(M.78.497C).

θωρακισμός, ὁ, *arming with a breastplate*, met. *ὁ θ. τῶν στοιχείων* Epiph.*haer*.66.46(p.84.14; M.42.100C); *ib*.(p.83.20; 100A).

θώραξ, ὁ, *breastplate*, met. *θώρακι...τοῦ πνεύματος ἐπουρανίου καθωπλισμένος* Tat.*orat*.16(p.18.4; M.6.841A); of virtuous actions *καθάπερ τις θ.* Chrys.*Thdr*.1.19(1.33D).

θωρήσσω, *give weapons to*; met., *provoke*; ref. Israelites provoking God by lack of trust, †Apoll.*met.Ps*.77:22(M.33.1425A); *ib*.77:40 (1425D).

I

***Ἰακωβίτης**, ὁ, *follower of Jacobus Baradaeus* *τοὺς Ἰ. ... καταξιοῦσι καὶ οὐ βαπτίζουσι* Tim.CP *haer*.(M.86.72C); Ant.Mon.*hom*. 130(M.89.1848C); Anast.S.*hod*.8(M.89.129A); *Ἰάκωβος ὁ Σύρος, ἐξ οὗ Ἰ.* Jo.D.*haer*.6(M.94.744A).

***Ἰαλδαβαώθ**, *Ialdabaoth*, Gnost. aeon in Ophite system, principal creator of material universe, Iren.*haer*.1.30.5(M.7.697B); first deity born of the female principle, the Holy Spirit, *ib*.(697A); the least of the aeons, Epiph.*haer*.37.3(p.54.1; M.41.645B); invocation to him, Or.*Cels*.6.31(p.101.12; M.11.1341C); regarded as *θεὸς πύρινος* and demiurge of this world, Hipp.*haer*.5.7(M.16.3135B; *Ἡσαλδαῖος* p.86.9); regarded as fem. by some Nicolaitans, Epiph. *haer*.25.2(p.269.4; 321C); *βιβλία τινὰ ἐξ ὀνόματος τοῦ Ἰ.* *ib*.25.3(p.270. 11; 324C); *ib*.26.8(p.284.12; 341D); father of Devil (Severians), *ib*.45. 1(p.199.19; 833A).

ἴαμα, τό, *cure*; by Christ, Const.ap.Gel.Cyz.*h.e*.2.7.17(M.85. 1236C); of cures at a saint's shrine, *M.Thdot*.2 4(p.87.27); met., of Christianity, Eus.*v.C*.2.59(p.65.9; M.20.1033B); cf.Const.*or.s.c*.11 (p.165.28); of suffering providentially inflicted, id.ap.Gel.Cyz.*h.e*. 2.7.26(1237B); of remedy for sin, Jo.Mosch.*prat*.78(M.87.2933A).

ἰαματικός, *curative, healing*; 1. of the body, fig. *φαρμάκοις ἰ. θεραπούσῃ αὐτοῦ τὰ τραύματα* Mac.Aeg.*hom*.15.30(M.34.596C); lit. *ἰ. αὐτὸ δύναμιν ἐνετίθει* Thdr.Mops.ap.*cat.Jo*.5:4(p.437.28); *τῶν ἁγίων μαρτύρων τὰ σώματα...ὄντα...ἰ. νοσημάτων τῶν κατὰ τὴν ἰατρικὴν τέχνην ἀνιάτων* ‡Just.*qu.et resp*.28(M.6.1276C); *ib*.55(1297C); Jo.Clim.*scal*.28(M.88.1129C); *ὁ...κύριος...εὐδόκησεν ἐκ τοῦ τιμίου αὐτοῦ* [sc. *Ἰωάννου*] *λειψάνου μύρων ἰ. εὐωδίαν πᾶσιν ἀναβλύσαι* Leont. N.*v.Jo.Eleem*.46(p.102.2); Anast.S.*hod*.2(M.89.68A); 2. of the soul *σπουδάσατε λαβεῖν ἐπουράνιον φάρμακον τὸ ἰ. καὶ ἀντίδοτον τῆς ψυχῆς* Mac.Aeg.*hom*.26.24(M.34.692A); *ib*.26.25(692C).

***ἰαματοποιός**, *healing*; ‡Jo.D.*hom*.5(M.96.656D).

***ἰαμβόζω**, *lampoon*, Isid.H.*etym*.1.17.4.

***Ἰαννῆς**, *Jamnes*, an Egyptian magician, cf.2Tim.3:8, Ex.7:11, 22; as type of heretic who goes astray through vainglory, Gr.Naz. *or*.2.41(M.35.449B); his tomb a haunt of evil spirits; visited by a solitary, Pall.*h.Laus*.18(p.49.9; M.34.1053D); ref. source of 2Tim. 3:8, cf. *non invenitur in libris publicis sed in libro secreto qui supra scribitur Iamnes et Mambres, unde ausi sunt quidam epistolam ad Timotheum repellere*, Or.*comm.ser.117 in Mt*.(p.250.8; M.13.1769C); cf.*ib.28*(p.51.5; 1637A); name taken from unwritten Jewish tradition, Thdt.*2Tim*.3:8(3.689); or from revelation by H. Ghost, Chrys.*hom.8.2 in 2Tim*.(11.708C).

***Ἰανουάριος** (Ἰανν-), *January*, ‡Chrys.*pasch*.7(8.275B); *Calendarium* ap.Epiph.*haer*.51.22(p.284.9; M. om.); Epiph.*ib*.51.24(p.292. 20; M.41.932B); *ib*.51.25(p.295.16; 933C); *Chron.Pasch*.p.15 tabula (M.92.96); Jo.Nic.*nativ*.(M.96.1445A); *Ἰανν-*, Pall.*h.Laus*.27(p.83.1; M.34.1092B); Thphn.*chron*.p.44(M.108.165C).

ἰάομαι, *heal*; 1. physically; a. in Christ's miracles; as signs of divinity, Ath.*inc*.18.4(M.25.128B); ‡Ath.*serm.fid*.24(p.20; M.26. 1277B); as proceeding from both his divinity and his humanity, Ath.*Ar*.3.31(M.26.389B); b. by divine power in Church *ἐπορκίζοντες κατὰ τοῦ ὀνόματος Ἰησοῦ Χριστοῦ...ἰάσαντο καὶ ἔτι νῦν ἰῶνται* Just. *2apol*.6.6(M.6.456A); Or.*Cels*.8.58(p.275.18; M.11.1605B); *A.Andr*. A 6(p.49.14); *A.Petr.et Andr*.12(p.122.32); Sophr.H.*mir.Cyr.et Jo*. 15(M.87.3469B) etc.; 2. spiritually *τοὺς ἀσθενεῖς ἴασαι* [sc. God] *1Clem*.59.4; through prayer, Herm.*vis*.1.1.9; suffering, id.*sim*.9.28. 5; repentance, *ib*.9.23.5; cf.*2Clem*.9.7; Bas.*hom*.1.3(2.3B; M.31.168A); eucharist *τοὺς διὰ πίστεως καὶ ἀγάπης προσιόντας ἴᾶσαι* *A.Thom*.A 51 (p.167.12); ref. error; healing of spiritual sense of hearing required for understanding of scripture, Or.*Jo*.20.20(18; p.352.4; M.14.616B); *τὰ νοερὰ...τῆς διδασκαλίας τοῦ Ἰησοῦ νάματα...ἰᾶται...τὴν ἀπὸ τῆς ἀπιστίας δίψαν* id.*fr.54 in Jo*.(p.258.26); *Hom.Clem*.19.22; *Const. App*.2.20.3; ref. Christ as healer, with play on name *Ἰησοῦς*: *οἱ ἰώμενος ἡμῶν καὶ σῶμα καὶ ψυχήν* Clem.*str*.3.17(p.244.12; M.8.1208B); *ἰᾶται τὴν ψυχὴν ἐντολαῖς καὶ χαρίσμασιν* id.*paed*.1.2(p.93.23; M.8. 256B); healing human nature through Inc., Didym.*Ps*.106:22(M.39. 1529B); *ὁ...θεὸς λόγος ἐνανθρωπήσας...τὰ παντοδαπὰ τῶν ψυχῶν ἰάσατο τραύματα* Thdt.*Ps*.106:20(1.1371); Hesych.H.*fr.Ps*.106:20(M.93. 1304A); and through Passion *οἱ ἐν ἁμαρτίαις γενόμενοι καὶ ἰαθέντες ἐκ τοῦ τὸν σωτῆρα πεπονθέναι* Or.*Cels*.1.55(p.106.17; M.11.761C); Ath. *Ar*.2.67(M.26.289A); Cyr.*Is*.5.1(2.745E); Hesych.H.*Ps.tit*.106(M.27. 1128B).

***Ἰάρ**, (Hebr. אִיָּר) *Iyyar*, a Hebrew month of harvest following Easter, Or.*Jo*.13.39(p.264.8; M.14.465D); Jo.Nic.*nativ*.(M.96.1444A).

***ἰασαφήτης**, ἡ, ? *jasper*, *T.Sal*.1.3.

ἴασις, ἡ, *healing, cure*; **1.** bodily, by God through saints, *A.Jo*. 106(p.203.12); *A.Phil*.39(p.18.28); Or.*Cels*.1.46(p.96.6; M.11.745A); through their relics, Eustrat.*stat.anim*.8(p.371); by saints, *Hom. Clem*.19.25; Sophr.H.*mir.Cyr.et Jo*.18(M.87.3477C); outside Christianity, ref. demons luring people to idolatrous shrines in hope of a cure, Cyr.H.*catech*.19.8; **2.** of human nature by Christ, in Inc. δι' ἡμᾶς ἄνθρωπος γέγονεν, ὅπως...τῶν παθῶν τῶν ἡμετέρων συμμέτοχος γενόμενος καὶ ἴ. ποιήσηται Just.*2apol*.13.4(M.6.468A); Clem.*exc.Thdot*. 45(p.121.6; M.9.680C); Marcell.*fr*.18 ap.Eus.*Marcell*.2.3(p.47.9; M. 24.804B); through Passion (cf. Is.53:5), Just.*dial*.95.3(M.6.701C); Ath.*inc.et c.Ar*.5(M.26.992A); **3.** of forgiveness of sin, Or.*or*.31(p.396. 23; M.11.552A); *ib*.33(p.401.20; 560A); which God alone can give, Herm.*mand*.1.4.11; id.*sim*.5.7.3; for all sins, however great, Chrys. *hom.26.6 in Mt*.(7.322A); obtained by amendment of life, Herm. *mand*.12.6.2; id.*sim*.8.11.3; by accepting suffering, *ib*.7.4; Or.*princ*. 3.1.3(p.218.2; M.11.273A); cure of possessed demanding prayer and purity, *Hom.Clem*.9.10.

ἴασπις, ἡ, *jasper*, symbolism; **1.** life αἰνίττεται...ἡμῖν ἡ ἴ. τὸ φερέσβιον τοῦ θεοῦ...ἐπεὶ...πᾶσα τροφὴ...τὴν ἀρχὴν...ἀπὸ χλόης ἀρχομένην ἔχει Oecum.*Apoc*.4:2(p.68); *ib*.21:10–11(p.237); Andr. Caes.*Apoc*.10(M.106.253B); ἴ. τὴν ἀειθαλῆ...ζωὴν τῶν ἁγίων ἐνδείκνυται *ib*.67(433C); Areth.*Apoc*.10(M.106.568B); hence **2.** anything flourishing; S. Peter, because of his vigorous charity and faith, Andr.Caes.*Apoc*.67(433D); cf.Areth.*Apoc*.67(772C); ἡ...χλωρίζουσα ἴ., τὸν τοῦ εὐαγγελίου δρόμον αἰνίττεται τὸν χλωρίζοντα εἰς ἀεί *ib*. (772A); **3.** its clarity signifying sanctity, Oecum.*Apoc*.21:10–11 (p.238); Andr.Caes.*Apoc*.67(429C).

***ἰατήριος**, *curative, healing* ἰ. ἐνέργειαν *Mir.Artem*.29(p.42.18).

ἰατικός, *curative, healing*; met., of remedies for error etc., Clem. *paed*.4.51(p.41.8; M.8.148A); Meth.*res*.1.31(p.266.16; M.41.1141D); ref. baptismal anointing ὥστε τὸν κύριον...ἐνεργῆσαι αὐτῷ ἰ. ... δύναμιν Serap.*euch*.22.2; in prayer at bishop's consecration πλησθεὶς ἐνεργημάτων ἰ. καὶ λόγου διδακτικοῦ *Const.App*.8.16.5.

***ἰάτραινα**, ἡ, *midwife*, Phot.*nomoc*.9.25(M.104.768B).

ἰατρεία, ἡ, **1.** *medical treatment*; met., ref. sin ἡ...ἰ. κοινή,...ἡ δὲ θεραπεία...οὐ κοινή Chrys.*hom.14.4 in Jo*.(8.83D); **2.** *cure* ὁ μετὰ πίστεως αὐτῷ προσιὼν δέξεται τὴν ἰ. εὐκόλως id.*paralyt*.8(3.45A); met., ref. soul in Apollinarian doctrine οὐκ εἰληφὼς...ταύτην...ὁ θεὸς λόγος, οὔτε ἰατρείας ἠξίωσεν Thdt.*h.e*.5.3.4(3.1016).

ἰατρεῖον, τό, *surgery*; met., of scripture as containing remedies for moral ills, Bas.*ep*.2.3(3.73A; M.32.228C); id.*hom.in Ps*.1(1.90B; M.29.209A); of church building; because of remedies provided in sermons, Chrys.*hom.1.1 in Gen*.(4.2C); *ib.32.1*(316C); of prayer ἰ. τῶν πλημμελημάτων id.*hom.27.5 in Heb*.(12.252A).

ἰάτρευμα, τό, *cure, treatment*; met., ref. sin, Cyr.H.*catech*.3.7.

ἰατρεύω, **1.** *heal, treat medically*; met., ref. sin, Thdt.*h.e*.4.6.5(3. 955); **2.** *practise medicine*, Athenag.*res*.24(p.77.22; M.6.1020D); Ath. *syn*.19(p.246.28; M.26.716B).

ἰατρικός, *healing*; fem. as subst. [sc. τέχνη]; met. τῇ ἀπὸ τοῦ λόγου ἰατρικῇ πᾶσαν λογικὴν φύσιν θεραπεῦσαι Or.*Cels*.3.54(p.250.9; M.11.992C); cf.*ib*.3.61(p.256.1; 1001A); ἰ. παιδεία Thdt.*Jer*.46:28(2. 591); *medical* ἰ. ... θεραπεία id.*h.e*.4.6.7(3.954); τὰ ἰ. *doctor's fee*, ‡Chrys.*hom.jej*.1(9.793E).

***ἰατρίσκος**, ὁ, contemptuously, *poor little doctor*, Sophr.H.*mir. Cyr.et Jo*.67(M.87.3656B).

ἰατρός, ὁ, *doctor*; **1.** in gen. ἀρχιδιακ(όνου) κ(αὶ) ἰητροῦ *MAMA* 3. 167; of doctors' deceits, practised for benefit of patients, to be imitated in pastoral care, Chrys.*sac*.1.5(p.21.18ff.; 1.370A); **2.** of God as healer of sin, *Diogn*.9.6; Meth.*res*.42(p.288.14; M.41.1112B); ἀγαπᾷ ὁ θεὸς τὴν κρίσιν, ὥσπερ ἰ. καταντλήμασι...βούλεται καταστεῖλαι τὸ οἴδημα Nil.*epp*.1.36(M.79.100B); **3.** of Christ εἷς ἰ. ἐστιν, σαρκικός τε καὶ πνευματικός, γεννητὸς καὶ ἀγέννητος...Ἰησοῦς Χριστός Ign. *Eph*.7.2; Clem.*paed*.1.2(p.93.18; M.8.256B); *A.Jo*.108(p.206.10); Ath. *inc*.44.2(M.25.173C); Ἰησοῦς...ἐστὶ κατὰ...τὴν Ἑλλάδα γλῶσσαν, ὁ ἰώμενος. ἐπειδὴ ἰ. ἐστι ψυχῶν καὶ σωμάτων Cyr.H.*catech*.10.13; *ib*.12. 8; Gr.Nyss.*Eun*.3(2 p.44.11; M.45.612C); healing human nature παρεδόθη αὐτῷ, ὡς ἰ., θεραπεῦσαι τὸ δῆγμα τοῦ ὄφεως Ath.*hom. in Mt.11*:27(M.25.212A); healing sins and passions of soul, Clem. *q.d.s*.29(p.179.7; M.9.633D); *A.Thom*.A 10(p.114.9); Or.*Jo*.20.32(26; p.369.18; M.14.645C); Gr.Nyss.*or.dom*.4(p.68.31; M.44.1161D); **4.** of other spiritual healers: angels, Or.*fr.38 in Jer*.(p.217.23); inspired writers whose teaching is a remedy for spiritual ills, id.*hom.14.2 in Jer*.(p.107.5; M.13.405B); Cyr.*Is*.3.1(2.366B); bishops ἐπιστήμων ἰ. ὁ ἐπίσκοπος Meth.*lepr*.7(p.460.2); ἰ. ... τῆς ἐκκλησίας τοῦ κυρίου *Const.App*.2.20.11; *ib*.2.41.5,7; all who help to correct sin, Ath.*v. Anton*.87(M.26.965A); Isid.Pel.*epp*.5.165(M.78.1424A); monastic superiors, Jo.Clim.*past*.4(M.88.1173A); id.*scal*.4(M.88.716A); recipients of alms ἰατροὶ τῶν τραυμάτων εἰσὶ τῶν σῶν Chrys.*hom.14.2 in 1Tim*.(11.672E); **5.** in similes; to explain that as doctors let patients think what is not true, so God allows it to seem that he has been changed by Inc., Or.*Cels*.4.19(p.288.26; M.11.1052B); ἐπεὶ...ὁ ἰ. ... ἀποκρύπτει τὸν ἰατρικὸν σίδηρον ὑπὸ τὸν...σπόγγον, κρύπτει δὲ καὶ ὁ πατὴρ τὴν φιλανθρωπίαν διὰ τῆς ἐμφάσεως τῆς ἀπειλῆς id.*hom.20.3 in Jer*.(p.181.22; M.13.508A).

***ἰατροσοφία**, ἡ, *science of medicine*, Barth.Edess.*Agar*.(M.104. 1408A).

ἰατροσοφιστής, ὁ, **1.** *professer of medicine*, Epiph.*haer*.66.10(p.31. 8; M.42.44D); id.*mens*.9(M.43.252A); **2.** *skilled physician*, Sophr.H. *mir.Cyr.et Jo*.30 tit.(M.87.3513C); id.*carm*.23 tit.(M.87.3835A).

***ἰατροσοφιστικός**, in bad sense, *of the quack physician's art*, Epiph.*haer*.64.67(p.510.1; M. om.).

ἰατταταιάξ, *alas!* ἰ. τῶν κακῶν Jo.D.*Jacob*.1(M.94.1436B).

***Ἰαώ**, **1.** *Iao*, Gnost. aeon (Ophite) generated by Ialdabaoth, Iren.*haer*.1.30.5(M.7.697A); sent certain of the prophets, *ib*.1.30.11 (701A); called Ἰ. ... πρῶτε δέσποτα θανάτου Or.*Cels*.6.31(p.101.12; M.11.1344A); (Valentinian) τὸν Ὅρον κωλύοντα αὐτὴν [sc. Sophia] τοὔμπροσθεν ὁρμῆς εἰπεῖν Ἰ.· ὅθεν τὸ Ἰ. ὄνομα γεγενῆσθαι φάσκουσι Iren.*haer*.1.4.1(481A); cf.Thdt.*haer*.1.7(4.298); ἐν τῷ πρώτῳ οὐρανῷ εἶναι τὸν Ἰ. ἄρχοντα Thdt.*haer*.1.7(4.298); **2.** in various forms as signifying name of God; **a.** Ἰά: τοῦ...ἰ. [sc. δηλοῦντος] τὸν κύριον Eus.*Ps*.134(M.24.29A); *ib*.146(65B); Epiph.*haer*.40.5(p.86.13; M.41. 685B); *Pap.Chr*.(p.403); **b.** Ἰαβέ: τὸ Ἰ. ὃς ἦν καὶ ἔστιν ὁ ἀεὶ ὢν Epiph.*haer*.40.5(p.86.13; 685B); καλοῦσι...αὐτὸ [sc. τὸ τετράγραμμον] Σαμαρεῖται...Ἰ. Thdt.*qu.15 in Ex*.(1.133); **c.** Ἰαή, translated κύριον in Ps.146:1, Or.*sel.in Ps*.2:2(M.12.1104B); **d.** Ἰαουε, ὁ μεθερμηνεύεται ὁ ὢν καὶ ὁ ἐσόμενος Clem.*str*.5.6(p.348.18; M.9.60A).

ἰδιαζόντως, **1.** *privately*, Aët.*synt*.ap.Epiph.*haer*.76.11(p.352.1; M.42.533D); περὶ τοῦ μὴ πιστεύεσθαι τὸν ἐπίσκοπον λέγοντα ἰ. αὐτῷ τὸν κληρικὸν συνομολογῆσαι τὸ ἁμάρτημα Phot.*nomoc*.9.20 tit.(M.104. 1108A); **2.** *separately, independently*, Eus.*qu.Marin*.4.2(M.22.953B); Gr.Nyss.*hom.15 in Cant*.(M.44.1113C); Didym.*Trin*.3.16(M.39. 868B); ποιοῦσι [sc. Audians]...τὸ πάσχα ἰ. Epiph.*anac*.70(p.230.9; M.42.336B); hence *individually* τὸ ἰ. ὥσπερ αὐτῷ δοθησόμενον ἀγαθόν Cyr.*Jo*.10(4.830A); Trin., *ib*.1.2(16C); ‡Caes.Naz.*dial*.3(M.38. 861) cit. s. ἀμετάβλητος; Jo.D.*trisag*.7(M.95.40A); Christol. ἡ... σὰρξ...οὐδὲ κεχωρισμένως οὐδὲ κινεῖται ἰ. ὥσπερ ἄνθρωπος ζῷον αὐτενέργητον Apoll.*fr*.153(p.248.22)ap.Leont.B.*Apoll*.(M.86.1961C); opp. κοινῶς, id.*corp.et div*.14(p.191.16; M.*PL*.8.875B); **3.** *properly, inherently*, Athenag.*res*.21(p.75.6; M.6.1016D); Cyr.*Jo*.2.7(4.225C); Trin. θεοῦ καὶ...υἱοῦ...ἀξίωμα κατὰ τὸ αὐτομάτως καὶ ἰ. καθ' ἑαυτὸ συμπρέπον τῇ ἑαυτοῦ οὐσίᾳ Epiph.*haer*.76.36(p.387.8; M.42.592B); **4.** ref. force of a word, *in the proper sense, strictly* μηδεμιᾶς φωνῆς τὴν τοιαύτην ἔμφασιν ἰ. ἐπ' αὐτοῦ [sc. θεοῦ] παρεχομένης Gr.Nyss.*Eun*. 12(1 p.226.25; M.45.921C); id.*tres dii*(M.45.120D); τὸ ἰ. καλούμενον τὸ πνεῦμα τὸ ἅγιον [i.e. opp. 'spirit of God' in other senses] Cyr.H. *catech*.16.13; διαιροῦντες...τὸ γένος ἰ., τὴν μὲν θήλειαν γυναῖκα καλοῦμεν, τὸν δὲ ἄρρενα ἄνδρα...ὁμωνυμικῶς δὲ ἄνθρωπος καὶ ὁ ἀνὴρ καὶ ἡ γυνὴ καλεῖται Epiph.*haer*.35.2(p.42.26; M.41.632A); τὸ ὁμότιμον δεικνύς, τῷ τε πατέρα εἰπεῖν ἰ., καὶ τῷ τὰ αὐτὰ πράττειν ἐκείνῳ Chrys. *hom.38.2 in Jo*.(8.219A); **5.** *distinctively, particularly*; with ἐξαιρέτως, Bas.*hex*.2.6(1.18B; M.29.44A); Trin. εἰ γὰρ ὑπόστασιν ἀποδεδώκαμεν εἶναι τὴν συνδρομὴν τῶν περὶ ἕκαστον ἰδιωμάτων, ὁμολογεῖται δέ, ὥσπερ ἐπὶ τοῦ πατρὸς εἶναί τι τὸ ἰ. ἐπιθεωρούμενον, δι' οὗ μόνος ἐπιγινώσκεται, κατὰ τὸν αὐτὸν δὲ τρόπον καὶ περὶ τοῦ μονογενοῦς τὸ ἴσον πιστεύεται Gr.Nyss.*diff.ess*.6(M.32.336C); Cyr.*thes*.13(5¹.130D); ἡ...τριὰς συσταλήσεται πρὸς ἑνάδα...εἴπερ τὸ ἑκάστῳ...ἰ. προσόν, τῷ τῆς ὁμοουσιότητος ἀφανισθήσεται λόγῳ id.*Jo*.1.4(4.36B); *ib*.7(673D).

ἰδιάζ-ω, **1.** *be alone*, CSard.*ep.cath*.ap.Ath.*apol.sec*.46(p.122.30; M.25.334B); *be alone* with ἡ σώφρων γύνη...σὺν τοῖς νέοις οὐκ ~ει *Hom.Clem*.13.18; c. dat., CSyr.*act*.(*ACO* 3 p.99.33; H.2.1377A); *ib*. (p.100.13; 1377C); ref. inward solitude in company, Gr.Naz.*or*.25.6 (M.35.1205B); *live alone, be solitary* so as to lead contemplative life συντελεῖ...πρὸς τὸ ἀμετεώριστον τῇ ψυχῇ καὶ τὸ ~ειν κατὰ τὴν οἴκησιν Bas.*reg.fus*.6.1(2.344A; M.31.925A); εἰ χρὴ [sc. τὸν ἀναχωρήσαντα τούτων] ~ειν καθ' ἑαυτόν, ἢ ὁμόφροσιν ἀδελφοῖς συζῆν *ib*.7(345C; M.928C); ὁ ἐρημικὸς βίος καὶ ~ων Gr.Naz.*or*.25.5(M.35.1204B); incompatibility of pilgrimages, Gr.Nyss.*ep*.2(M.46.1009B); **2.** *withdraw*, c. ἀπό, *V.Mac*.A(p.153); so as to be alone ὅταν ἐκ τῶν ἀνθρώπων ~ωμεν Max.*carit*.2.13(M.90.988B); of a group ἀδίκημά ἐστιν ἐν συνοδίᾳ εὑρεθῆναι ~ούσας τινὰς φατρίας Bas.*ascet*.2.2(2.325B; M.31.885A); *go home*, Gr.Mag.*dial*.(tr.Zach.)3.10(M.*PL*.77.235B); **3.** *differ* οἱ λόγοι...αὐτῶν [sc. angels of Resurrection] ~ουσι Eus.*qu.Marin. suppl*.2.6(M.22.993A); *ib*.(993C); ref. Jo.5:19 κατὰ σάρκα, καθ' ἣν ~ει ὁ σαρκωθεὶς παρὰ τὸν μὴ σαρκωθέντα πατέρα Ap.ll.*fr*.131(p.239.13)ap.Thdt.*eran*.2(4.171); *go one's own way* ~ειν καὶ μετὰ τῶν Ἰουδαίων ἐπιτελεῖν τὸ πάσχα CAnt.(341)*can*.1; ptcpl., *separate* οὐδὲν ἐν τῷ υἱῷ...πληροῦται ἀφηνιάζον καὶ ~ον τῆς τοῦ πατρὸς ἑνώσεως Epiph.*haer*.69.75(p.223.30; M.42.325A); **4.** *be private* opp. official; of a house, Const.ap.Eus.*v.C*.3.65(p.112.15; M.20.1141A); of a letter, Thphn.*chron*.p.129(M.108.355B); of a person, *Mir.Geo*.1 (p.5.5); **5.** *be proper, belong essentially* to; of rel. of Son, opp. creatures, to Father, Eus.*e.th*.1.9(p.67.23; M.24.840C); Trin. ἃ δοκεῖ ~οντα εἶναι τοῦ πατρός, ταῦτα καὶ τοῦ υἱοῦ εἶναι φαίνεται, καὶ τοῦ ἁγίου πνεύματος Chrys.*hom.86.3 in Jo*.(8.517B); **6.** in rel. to another, *be distinctive, characteristic* of, esp. ptcpl., *one's own, peculiar, individual*; **a.** in gen., Bas.*Eun*.2.28(1.265B; M.29.638B) cit. s. ἰδιότης; ~ων οὗτος τῆς γραφῆς ἐστιν ὁ τρόπος Chrys.*hom.81.2 in Jo*.(8.481A); **b.** Trin. ἑνουσίου...τῇ ἀιδίῳ φύσει τὸ ἀγαθὸν...ἐνθεωρεῖται θέλημα οὔτε ἀπό τινος ~ούσης ἀρχῆς ἐγγινόμενον Gr.Nyss.*Eun*.8(2 p.181.28; M.45.776A); θεῷ...ἐξ οὗπερ κατ' οὐσίαν ἐστὶ [sc. H. Ghost] ~οντι λόγῳ παρὰ πᾶσαν τὴν κτίσιν Thdr.Mops.*symb*.(p.98.7; M.66.1017A); πῶς...εἴρητο 'ἀπαύγασμα δόξης' ὁ υἱός...εἴπερ ~ουσάν τινα ἀρχὴν οὐσίας εἶχε; †Diad.*Ar*.2(M.65.1152C); denied of essence of any Person vis-à-vis another, Ath.*Ar*.1.36(M.26.88A); but asserted of mode of being (agst. Paul. Sam.) εἰ...τὸν ἐν τῷ θεῷ φαίη [i.e. Paul. Sam. in denying hypostatic existence of Logos] λόγον ἐνοικῆσαι τῇ σαρκὶ οὐδὲν ἕτερον ὄντα ἢ λόγον...πῶς οὗτος εἶπεν ἂν ζῆν ~ουσαν ζωὴν παρὰ τὸν πατέρα; Eus.*e.th*.1.20(p.88.24; M.24.877D); ‡Just.*qu.et resp*.17(M.6.1264C); ref. Heb.1:3 τὸν ~οντα χαρακτῆρα τοῦ πρωτοτύπου, ὡς ἐν ὑποστάσει ἐστὶ καθ' ἑαυτόν Chrys.*hom.2.1 in Heb*.(12.14B); εἰς ...ὁ τῆς φύσεως ὅρος, κἂν ἐν ~ούσαις ὑπάρξεσι νοοῦμεν τὴν ἁγίαν τριάδα Ammon.*Jo*.10:38(M.85.1465A) cf. Bas.*Eun*.2.29(1.266A; 640A) cit. s. ἰδιότης; Cyr.*Jo*.1.10(4.105B); of H. Ghost δύναμιν οὐσιώδη αὐτὴν ἀφ' ἑαυτῆς ἐν ~ούσῃ ὑποστάσει Gr.Nyss.*or.catech*.2(p.15.3; M.45.17C); in homoean argument agst. Western homoousian doctrine τὰς ~ούσας ὑποστάσεις πατρὸς καὶ υἱοῦ συνέπλεκον εἰς ἑνότητα Sophronius Paphlago ap.Socr.*h.e*.3.10.8(M.67.408A); **c.** ptcpl. neut. as subst., *distinctive character* ὁ υἱὸς κατὰ τὸ ἄκτιστον τῷ πατρὶ καὶ τῷ πνεύματι συναπτόμενος ἐν τῷ υἱὸς καὶ μονογενὴς εἶναι...τὸ ~ον ἔχει Gr.Nyss.*Eun*.1(1 p.102.12; M.45.336C); esp. τὸ ἰ. τῶν προσώπων (or ὑποστάσεων) *the distinction of Persons* (i.e. 'the being distinct' without the trans. and subjective sense of 'distinguishing') τὸ τῶν προσώπων ~ον ὁμολογεῖσθαι ἐν τῷ ἀφορισμῷ τῶν περὶ ἕκαστον νοουμένων ἰδιωμάτων Bas.*ep*.236.6(3.364B; M.32.884C); id.*Spir*.45 (3.38A; M.32.149B); εἰδὼς καὶ τὸ τούτων [sc. ὑποστάσεων] ἰ. καὶ διῃρημένον, καὶ τῆς οὐσίας τὴν ἑνότητα Chrys.*hom.30.2 in 2Cor*.(10.652C); τὸ ἑτεροῖον καὶ ἰ. τοῦ προσώπου παριστῶν ‡Caes.Naz.*dial*.3(M.38.860); **d.** Christol. εἰ...ἰδικήν τινα ~ουσάν τε χωρὶς τοῦ λόγου ποτὲ ταύτην [sc. Christ's humanity] οἴονται, δῆλον ὡς Νεστοριανῶς ἀσεβοῦσιν [sc. monophysites] Leont.H.*monoph*.58(M.86.1800D); Thdr.Raith.*praep*.(p.192.18; M.91.1493A) cit. s. ἰδιοσύστατος.

***ἰδιαίρετος**, separately chosen, Jo.Clim.*scal*.22(M.88.948D).

***ἰδιαιρέτως**, *independently*, Jo.Clim.*scal*.26(M.88.1021C); Jo.D. *fid.Nest*.21(p.568); *ib*.47(p.579).

***ἰδίασις**, ἡ, *solitary life*, Jo.Clim.*scal*.27(M.88.1105A).

ἰδιασμός, ὁ, *solitude*, Gr.Naz.*ep*.223(M.37.364C).

ἰδικός, freq. opp. κοινός; **1.** *individual, personal* ἐλθεῖν...μετὰ τὰς καθολικὰς εὐεργεσίας αὐτοῦ [sc. God] ἐπὶ τὰς ἰ. Or.*hom.3.1 in Jer*. (p.20.25; M.13.281D); ref. providential use of evil πρὸς τὴν...ἰ. ἢ κοινὴν ὠφέλειαν Dion.Ar.*d.n*.4.33(M.3.733B); theol., Cyr.*dial.Trin*.5 (5^1.558E) cit. s. ἰδικῶς; id.*Jo*.2.6(4.221D); of visions, *private* καθ' ὅσον...ἰδικά, οὐκ ὀφείλει λαλεῖσθαι Ammon.*Ac*.9:12(M.85.1532D); **2.** *proper, one's own* καθ' αὐτὸν ἕκαστος...νοῦς ἰδικὰς ἔχει...δυνάμεις Dion.Ar.*c.h*.10.3(M.3.273C); ref. eucharist τὸ...πνεῦμα...τὸν ἄρτον τὸν κοινόν, σῶμα ἰ. ... τῆς αὐτοῦ σαρκώσεως ἀποφαίνον Isid.Pel.*epp*.1.119(M.78.256C); Christol., Leont.H.*monoph*.6(M.86.1772Df.); *ib*.58 (1801B) cit. s. κοινός; *ib*.(1800D) cit. s. ἰδιάζω; τὴν μὲν φύσιν...κοινὴν ἔχειν πρὸς πάντας τοὺς ἐξ Ἀδάμ, τὴν δὲ ὑπόστασιν ἰ. πρός τε ἡμᾶς καὶ τὸν πατέρα καὶ τὸ πνεῦμα id.*Nest*.2.14(M.86.1568C); *ib*.2.6(1548cf.); superl. τὴν δευτέραν...ἰδικωτάτην...γέννησιν *ib*.4.9(1669B); **3.** *separate, independent*; Gnost., of material and corruptible world as alien from creative Logos and archetypal Adamas; (Naassene), ref. Jo.1:3 τὸ...οὐδέν [ἐστιν], ὃ χωρὶς αὐτοῦ γέγονεν, ὁ κόσμος ⟨ὁ⟩ ἰ. Hipp.*haer*.5.8(p.90.1; M.16.3142A); as created by aeon Ἡσαλδαῖος, *ib*.5.7(p.86.9; 3135B); (Peratic) as third and lowest element in universe τὸ τρίτον ἰ. ... γεννητόν *ib*.5.12(p.104.21; 3162A); τὸ...τρίτον [sc. μέρος] ἀπόλλυσθαι, ὃν κόσμον ἰ. καλεῖ *ib*.10.10(p.270.3; 3422B); cf. *ib*.5.12(p.105.21; 3162C); τὸν κόσμον τὸν καθ' ἡμᾶς, ὃν ἰ. καλοῦσι *ib*. 5.15(p.110.19; 3170C); cf.Thdt.*haer*.1.17(4.310).

***ἴδικτον, τό,** (Lat. *edictum*) *imperial edict*, Cyr.S.*v.Sab*.74(p.179.6); *ib*.85(p.192.1); Thdr.Lect.*h.e*.1.34(M.86.181B); *V.Max*.12(M.90.80C).

ἰδικῶς, 1. *separately, apart*, Meth.*symp*.8.3(p.84.15; M.18.141C); Cyr.*ador*.13(1.454D); Thdt.*haer*.4.7(4.362); Christol. τὴν τοῦ θεοῦ δύναμίν τε καὶ ἐνέργειαν ἡ ἁγία πεφόρηκε σάρξ· ἰδία γὰρ ἦν αὐτοῦ καὶ οὐχ ἑτέρου τινὸς παρ' αὐτὸν ὄντος υἱοῦ καταμόνας καὶ ἰ. Cyr.*Lc*.13:11 (M.72.768A); μερίζει [sc. Nest.]...τὰς ἐν τοῖς εὐαγγελίοις φωνάς, ὡς ποτὲ μὲν τάσδε τινὰς μόνῳ τε καὶ ἰ. ἀνατιθέναι τῷ λόγῳ, ποτὲ δὲ ἰδίᾳ τῷ ἐκ γυναικός id.*Nest*.2(p.33.2; 6^1.31B); περιΐστησιν [sc. Nest.] ἀνοσίως εἰς ἄνθρωπον ἰ. τοῦ μυστηρίου [i.e. of Christ's Passion and death] τὴν δύναμιν *ib*.5.4(p.100.41; 134D); εἴ τις προσώποις δυσὶν...τὰς ...φωνὰς...ὡς ἀνθρώπῳ παρὰ τὸν ἐκ θεοῦ λόγον ἰ. νοουμένῳ προσάπτει, τὰς δὲ ὡς θεοπρεπεῖς μόνῳ τῷ ἐκ θεοῦ λόγῳ ἀ. ἔ. id.*apol.Thdt*.anath.4 (p.120.26; 6^1.214C); μὴ διαιρούμενος εἰς θεὸν ἰ. καὶ εἰς ἄνθρωπον ἰ. ‡Cyr.*Trin*.18(6^3.24E; M.77.1157B); **2.** *personally*; **a.** *individually* τὸ προστεταγμένον οὐ κοινὸν ἅπασι...ἦν...ἀλλ' ἰ. καὶ πρὸς μόνον εἴρητο τὸν Ὠσηέ Cyr.*Os*.2(3.10D); φυσικῶς τε καὶ ἰ. id.*ador*.6(1.184A); ἐν πᾶσι γενικῶς, καὶ τὸ καθ' ἕκαστον ἰ. χωρήσαντος τοῦ θεοῦ Max.*opusc*.(M.91.25B); **b.** Trin., ref. attributes of each Person ἰ. πλὴν οὐ μεμερισμένως Cyr.*Jo*.3.5(4.302C); as a Person ὑφεστάναι καθ' ἑαυτὴν καὶ εἰς ὕπαρξιν ἰδικήν, ἐμφιλοχωρεῖ μὲν γὰρ τῇ τοῦ πατρὸς φύσει, μονονουχὶ ῥίζαν ἔχων αὐτὴν ὁ υἱός...πλὴν ὑφέστηκεν ἰ. id.*dial.Trin*.5(5^1.558E); *ib*.6(592C); τινες...ἀνύπαρκτόν τε καὶ ἰ. οὐχ ὑφεστηκότα φαντάζονται τὸν μονογενῆ, καὶ οὐκ εἶναι μὲν ἐν ὑποστάσει τῇ καθ' ἑαυτόν id.*inc. unigen*.(5^1.686A); **c.** ref. verbal expression, *peculiarly, idiomatically*, Areth.*Apoc*.31(M.106.656A); **3.** *specifically, in particular* σὺν τῷ υἱῷ καὶ τῷ πνεύματι...συνενεργετεῖ ὁ πατήρ...κἂν ποτε ἰ. μὴ ὀνομασθῇ Didym.*Trin*.2.12(M.39.677C); Chrys.*hom.11.1 in Ac*.(9.89E); ἰ. ὥσπερ αὐτοῖς [sc. Scribes and Pharisees] τὴν ἄμετρον ἀπείθειαν ἀνατιθέντος Χριστοῦ Cyr.*Jo*.6(4.566E); Thdot.Anc.*fr.Ac*.2:17(M.77.1431C); **4.** *properly, inherently, peculiarly*, ‡Ath.*def*.3(M.28.541B) cit. s. ἰδίωμα; ref. God, Cyr.*Jo*.4.5(4.411E); ref. Sonship of Christ ὃς [sc. πατήρ] εἰ καὶ γέγονεν ἡμῶν...χάριτι πατήρ, ἀλλ' οὖν ἐστιν ἰ. καὶ μόνου πατὴρ Ἰησοῦ Χριστοῦ id.*Heb*.2:14(p.392n.); Christol. σαρκὸς ἂν εἴη τὸ δεῖμα καὶ τῆς ἀνθρωπότητος ἰ. τὸ κατορρωδεῖσθαι θάνατον id.*dial.Trin*.5(5^1.571E).

***ἰδικωτάτως**, adv. from superl. of ἰδικός, *in one's own particular way, uniquely*, Leont.H.*monoph*.6(M.86.1773A).

***ἰδιοβούλως**, *in accordance with one's individual wishes*, opp. κοινοβιακῶς, Thdr.Stud.*epp*.2.133(M.99.1428D).

***ἰδιογνωμόνως**, *spontaneously*, Cyr.*ador*.14(1.491D).

***ἰδιογνωμόρυθμος**, ὁ, *self-opinionatedness*, Jo.Clim.*scal*.24(M.88.981C).

***ἰδιογνωμοσύνη**, ἡ, *one's own opinion*, Mac.Aeg.*hom*.9.11(M.34.540A).

ἰδιογνώμων, *having one's own purposive will* εἰμὶ μὲν [sc. Christ] ἰ. οὐδαμῶς, συνθελητὴς δὲ ἀεὶ τῷ...πατρί Cyr.*Jo*.5.5(4.521C).

ἰδιόγραφος, *autograph*, Chrys.*comm.in Gal*.6:12(10.727C); Jo.VI CP *ep*.(M.96.1428C).

***ἰδιοκινδύνως**, *at one's own risk*, Ath.Scholast.*coll*.20.1(p.171); Phot.*nomoc*.12.2(M.104.869D); -κηνδύνως Ath.Scholast.*coll*.4.22 (p.62).

***ἰδιοκτημοσύνη**, ἡ, *private ownership*, Thdr.Stud.*epp*.2.43(M.99.1245C); *ib*.2.180(1556C).

ἰδιόκτητος, *possessed in one's own right* ἡμᾶς μὲν γὰρ ἐν χρήσει τὴν χάριν λαμβάνειν λέγουσι,...αὐτοὺς δὲ [sc. Valentinians] ἰδιόκτητον ...ἔχειν τὴν χάριν Iren.*haer*.1.6.4(M.7.509A); of kingdom of God as Christ's own and not merely given by Father, ‡Meth.*palm*.5 (M.18.393A); *held as private property*, ref. his divinity οὐκ ἰ. καὶ τοῦ πατρὸς ἀφωρισμένην Eus.*e.th*.1.2(p.63.22; M.24.832B); cf.id.*d.e*.5.4 (p.226.9; M.22.373A).

***ἰδιοκτήτωρ**, ὁ, *possessor*, ‡Chrys.*hom.suppl*.5(M.64.456D).

ἰδιολογία, ἡ, *property, peculiar principle* ἕνα μὲν θέλοντα...δύο δὲ θελήματα...κατὰ τὴν τῶν φύσεων ἰ. ‡Ath.*annunt*.6(M.28.925C).

***ἰδιοναύκληρος**, ὁ, *shipowner*, Hipp.Th.*fr*.1.5(p.6.7; M.117.1040A).

ἰδιοπαθέω, *feel a personal concern for, take to heart*, Bas.*ep*.297 (3.434D; M.32.1041A); Socr.*h.e*.2.18.1(M.67.221A).

***ἰδιοπαθῶς**, *from personal motives*, Bas.*ep*.79(3.173A; M.32.453D).

***ἰδιοπεριγράπτως**, *independently circumscribed*, Leont.H.*Nest*.1.46(M.86.1505A).

***ἰδιοπερίγραφος**, *individually defined, circumscribed*, Jo.D.*haer.*7(M.94.752B); Thdr.Stud.*antirr.*3.1.22(M.99.400D).

ἰδιοπεριόριστος, *with its own proper bounds*, Christol. εἰ γὰρ ἐκ δύο φύσεων λέγετε τὸν Χριστόν, οὐκοῦν δύο ὑποστάσεις καὶ δύο πρόσωπα καθ' ἑαυτὰ καὶ ἰ. †Leont.B.*sect.*7.1(M.86.1240A); Thdr.Raith.*praep.*(p.188.23; M.91.1488C).

***ἰδιοπισμός**, *self-confident*, †Gregent.*disp.*(M.86.724C).

ἰδιοποι-έω, usu. med.; **1.** *make one's own*; **a.** in gen.; in argument that body cannot come from Devil πῶς ἡ ψυχὴ μὴ τούτου [sc. Devil] οὖσα...~εῖται τὴν σάρκα...καὶ πρὸς ἀρετὴν αὐτὴν παρασκευάζει; Serap.*Man.*51(p.74; M.18.1252A); κύριός ἐστιν ὁ τὰ τῶν χηρῶν καὶ ὀρφανῶν ~ούμενος Bas.*ep.*109(3.202D; M.32.520A); ~είσθω ὁ ἐπίσκοπος τὸ πλημμέλημα, καὶ λεγέτω [i.e. to the despairing sinner]... κἀγὼ τὸν ὑπὲρ σοῦ θάνατον ἀναδέξομαι, ὡς ὁ κύριος τὸν ὑπὲρ ἐμοῦ καὶ πάντων *Const.App.*2.20.6; *win over, gain* πάντας ~εῖτο [sc. ὁ Ἀβεσσαλώμ] Chrys.*hom.15.2 in Eph.*(11.111C); **b.** of Christ assuming human nature ~εῖται τοῦτο [sc. τὸ σῶμα] ὥσπερ ὄργανον Ath.*inc.*8.3(M.25.109C); μοναδικός ἐστι τὴν ὑπόστασιν, ~εῖται τὰ τῆς ἑκατέρας φύσεως †Ath.*fr.*(M.26.1224B); ‡Ath.*Apoll.*1.12(M.26.1113A); τὴν τοῦ Ἀδὰμ πλάσιν...καινὴν ἀπεστήσατο ~ησάμενος καθ' ἕνωσιν *ib.*1.13(1116B); Petr.Laod.*fr.in Lc.*22:19(M.86.3328D); hence ptcpl. pass. neut., opp. ἴδιον, of Christ's humanity opp. divinity πῶς...οὐ δύο...ὡς λόγος καὶ σάρξ, καὶ ὡς ἴδιον καὶ ~ούμενον, ἔσονται; Leont.H.*monoph.*20(M.86.1781C); incl. human weaknesses and limitations εἰκότως...τὰ ἡμέτερα πάθη ~ούμενος φησίν [Ps.40:5] Eus.*d.e.*10.1(p.450.27; M.22.725A); *ib.*(p.450.15; 724D); ~εῖτο τὰ τοῦ σώματος ἴδια, ὡς ἑαυτοῦ ὁ λόγος ὁ ἀσώματος Ath.*ep.Epict.*6(p.10.9; M.26.1060B); Nil.*epp.*1.219(M.79.164A); Cyr.*Jo.*2.1(4.151A); Thdot. Anc.*exp.symb.*18(M.77.1340C); **2.** *claim as one's own, appropriate*; ref. Mt.28:18 ἄνθρωπος...λαμβάνων δυνατὸν ἔχει καὶ τὸ ἀφαιρεθῆναι... ἵνα δὲ...ἡ χάρις...βεβαία φυλαχθῇ τοῖς ἀνθρώποις, διὰ τοῦτο αὐτὸς ~εῖται τὴν δόσιν καὶ λέγει ἐξουσίαν εἰληφέναι Ath.*Ar.*3.38(M.26.405B); ref. Jo.5:17,16:28, ‡Ath.*Ar.*4.22(p.68.19; M.26.500C); unjustly προσκαλέσεται [sc. antichrist] πρὸς ἑαυτὸν τὴν ἀνθρωπότητα, τὰ ἀλλότρια ~εῖσθαι βουλόμενος Hipp.*antichr.*55(p.37.4; M.10.776A); ref. Mt.6:5 τὰς τοῦ θεοῦ δωρεὰς ~ούμενοι Bas.*reg.br.*247(2.498D; M.31.1248C); μήτις τὰ τῆς ἐκκλησίας ~είσθω Thphl.Al.*common.*10(M.65.44A); **3.** *lay exclusive claim to*; *claim as peculiarly one's own* τι...τὸ κοινὸν ~εῖται; Sever.*Rom.*1:1(p.213.3); ὃ καὶ οἱ προφῆται ποιοῦσι, τὸ κοινὸν ~ούμενοι Chrys.*hom.2.1 in Rom.*(9.436D); εἰ οὐκ οὐσιωδῶς υἱός ἐστιν...πῶς τὸν κοινὸν δὴ καὶ πάντων μόνος ~εῖται πατέρα; Cyr.*thes.*32(5^1.317A); πῶς ἐπὶ πάντων ~εῖται τὸν θεόν Olymp.*Job* 6:10(M.93.91B); Trin. οὐ χωρισθεὶς [sc. the Son] τῆς τοῦ πατρὸς ὑποστάσεως ἀλλ'...~εῖται τὴν ἀνθρώπησιν, ἵνα διευκρινηθῶσιν αἱ ὑποστάσεις ‡Ath.*dial.Trin.*3.15(M.28.1225B); Areth.*Apoc.*7(M.106.548D) cit. s. ἐξιδιάζω.

***ἰδιοποίησις**, ἡ, **1.** *appropriation to oneself*, ref. Christ τῇ τοῦ σώματος ἰ. καὶ τῆς ἀναστάσεως χάριτι τὸν θάνατον ἀπ' αὐτῶν [sc. τῶν ἀνθρώπων]...ἐξαφανίζων Ath.*inc.*8.4(M.25.109D); **2.** *individualism*, Trin., Aët.*synt.*ap.Epiph.*haer.*76.12(M.42.537A; εἰδοποίησιν p.354.2) = Didym.*Trin.*1.10(M.39.292C).

ἰδιοποιός, *particularizing*, ? f.l. for ἰδιοποιοῦν: καὶ τόδε τι τὸ πτηνὸν τό τε χερσαῖον, καὶ τὸ ἔνυδρον, ὡς ἰδιοποιὸν ἀπὸ τοῦ κοινοῦ τῆς οὐσίας Leont.B.*arg.Sev.*(M.86.1928D).

ἰδιοπραγία, ἡ, *individual activity* or *action*, Athenag.*res.*22(p.76.2; M.6.1017C); κατὰ τοὺς ἀπὸ Πλάτωνος ἰδιοπραγίαν τῶν μερῶν τῆς ψυχῆς φάσκοντας εἶναι τὴν δικαιοσύνην Or.*Cels.*5.47(p.51.21; M.11.1256A); Pall.*v.Chrys.*7(p.39.28; M.47.24); ἡ θεία δικαιοσύνη καὶ σωτηρία...αἰτία καθαρῶς οὖσα τῆς ἐν τοῖς ὅλοις ἰ. Dion.Ar.*d.n.*8.9(M.3.896D); id.*ep.*8 tit.(M.3.1084A); in spiritual life τῷ τελείῳ γὰρ οὐκ ἐν συμβολαίοις πολιτικοῖς...ἀλλ' ἐξ ἰ. καὶ τῆς πρὸς θεὸν ἀγαπῆς ἡ δικαιοσύνη Clem.*str.*6.15(p.495.16; M.9.349B); δικαιοπραγεῖν μὲν καὶ ἀναγκάζων, εἰ δεῖ λέγειν, διὰ τὴν ἰ. τῆς ψυχῆς, ᾗ προσθέσθαι ἡμᾶς ἔπεισεν Gr.Thaum.*pan.Or.*11(p.26.19; M.10.1084A); *ib.*(p.26.24; 1084B); ἡ αὐτοπραγία, εἴτουν ἰ., δι' ἧς τὰ καθ' ἑαυτοὺς σκοπεῖν τε καὶ διασκέπτεσθαι μόνους μανθάνοντες Max.*myst.*23(M.91.713C).

***ἰδιοπραγμοσύνη**, ἡ, *cultivation of one's personal* spiritual *life*, †Eus.Em.*fr.1Cor.*4:4(p.52.23); Pall.*h.Laus.*proem.(p.11.27; M.34.1003); *ib.*(p.12.6; 1003); Nil.*epp.*2.77(M.79.233D); *ib.*2.204(308B); Leont.et Jo.*sacr.*(M.86.2024B).

***ἰδιοπροσώπως**, *individually, personally*, Steph.Dor.*ep.*(H.3.713A).

***ἰδιορίστως**, *on one's own account, for oneself*, Thdr.Stud.*epp.*1.10(M.99.940C).

[*]**ἰδιορυθμία**, ἡ, *self-reliance, following one's own devices*; in bad sense, Marc.Er.*opusc.*5.5(M.65.1037A); Jo.Clim.*scal.*4(M.88.680C); *Schol.*12 *ib.*2(661B).

[*]**ἰδιόρυθμος**, *following one's own devices*, Marc.Er.*opusc.*5.5(M.65.1036D); *ib.*5.11(M.1048B).

***ἰδιορύθμως**, *on one's own account*, Jo.Clim.*scal.*26(M.88.1028D).

ἴδιος, **A.** *one's own*; **1.** opp. ἀλλότριος: τὰ ὑστερήματα αὐτῶν [sc. τῶν πλησίον] ἴδια ἐκρίνετε *1Clem.*2.6; τὰ ἔργα ἃ ἐποίουν οἱ ἅγιοι, οὐκ ἴ., ἀλλὰ τοῦ δεδωκότος τὴν δύναμιν θεοῦ Ath.*Ar.*3.2(M.26.325C); of possessions ὁ ἴ. τι ἔχειν ἐσπουδακὼς...χωρισμὸν καὶ ἀποστασίαν μελετᾷ ‡Bas.*const.*34.1(2.581A; M.31.1425A); ref. Gen.2:7, Clem.*paed.*1.3(p.94.10; M.8.257A); ref. Jo.1:11 ἴ. σύμπας ὁ κόσμος ἐστὶ τῷ θεῷ, κατά γε τὸν τοῦ πεποιῆσθαι λόγον...πρεπωδέστερον δέ πως ὁ Ἰσραὴλ τῷ τῆς ἰδιότητος ἀποκεκλήσεται λόγῳ Cyr.*Jo.*1.9(4.89E); (Naassene) ὁ Ἀδάμας...λέγει πρὸς τοὺς ἰ. ἀνθρώπους Hipp.*haer.*5.8(p.92.13; M.16.3143C); Trin. ἀποκρίνεται...τὸ πνεῦμα τὸ ἅγιον ἢ ἀπὸ τοῦ προσώπου τοῦ πατρὸς ἢ ἀπὸ τοῦ ἰδίου Just.*dial.*36.6(M.6.556A); εἰ καὶ ἰδίαν ὑπόστασιν ἑκάτερος ἀπετέμετο, τὸν...διορισμὸν οὐ προσίεται Cyr.*dial.Trin.*6(5^1.592C); **2.** substantivally, *member of one's household*, of Christians as belonging to God τοὺς ἰ. ἀναπαύσει Just.*dial.*121.3(M.6.757C); μὴ νομίσῃς ὅτι ἴ. εἶ τοῦ θεοῦ· ἐὰν ᾖς ἁμαρτωλός, ὁ διάβολος γάρ σε κτᾶται Chrys.*fr.in 1Petr.*1:21(M.64.1053C).

B. *peculiar, individual, personal* οὐ τὰ διὰ θεοῦ ὑπὸ τοῦ προφητικοῦ πνεύματος ἐλέγχονται νοεῖν δυνάμενοι, ἀλλὰ τὰ ἴ. Just.*dial.*38.2(M.6.557B); ἴ. χαρακτῆρα διδασκαλείου συνεστήσατο Iren.*haer.*1.28.1(M.7.690C); εἰ γὰρ κατὰ μετάστασιν θεότητος ὁ θάνατος γέγονε...ἴδιον ἄρα θάνατον ἀπέθανε [sc. Christ] καὶ οὐ τὸν ἡμέτερον ‡Ath.*Apoll.*1.18(M.26.1125B); οὐκ ἄρα ὁ θεὸς ἰδίαν ἔχει τὴν ἑαυτοῦ γνῶσιν, ἑτέραν δὲ τὴν κοινῇ τὰ ὄντα πάντα συλλαμβάνουσαν Dion.Ar.*d.n.*7.2(M.3.869C); ὁ ἱεροτελεστὴς...οὐκ αὐτὸς ἰδίᾳ χάριτι τοὺς τελουμένους ἐπὶ τὴν ἱερατικὴν ἄγων τελείωσιν id.*e.h.*5.3.5(M.3.512B); ref. Logos, Marcell.*fr.*65 ap. Eus.*Marcell.*2.2(p.38.24ff.; M.24.789Aff.).

C. *proper, peculiar, specific*; freq. neut. as subst., *distinctive property* or *character*; of God, *attribute*; **1.** def. ἴ. ... λέγεται ὅ τινι ὑπάρχει, μὴ συμπληροῦν δὲ αὐτοῦ τὴν οὐσίαν ἢ ὅλως εἰς τὸν τῆς φύσεως αὐτοῦ λόγον παραλαμβανόμενον (τὸ δ' αὐτὸ λέγοιτο ἂν ἰδιότης τε καὶ ἰδίωμα), οἷον ἴδιον λέγω τοῦ ἀνθρώπου τὸ ὀρθοπεριπατητικόν...ἀκίνητον ἔχειν τοῦτο τὸ μόριον τοῦ ὠτός. ταῦτα οὖν, εἰ καὶ ἴδια λέγονται τοῦ ἀνθρώπου, ἀλλ' οὐκ εἰς τὸν τῆς οὐσίας αὐτοῦ λόγον παραλαμβάνεται... ταῦτα οὖν ἴ. κυρίως λεγέσθω, ὅσα τῷ ὅρῳ προστιθέμενα οὐ περιττεύουσι, μὴ προστιθέμενα δὲ οὐκ ἐλλείπουσι. διαιρεῖται δὲ τὸ ἴ. τετραχῶς... Thdr.Raith.*praep.*(p.217.30ff.); ἴδιόν ἐστι τὸ παντὶ καὶ μόνῳ καὶ ἀεὶ ὑπάρχον Anast.Ap.ap.*Doct.Patr.*33(p.262.13); Jo.D.*dialect.*14(M.94.576Dff.); compared with συμβεβηκὸς ἀχώριστον, *ib.*28(589A); applicable to the general and to the particular, ‡Ath.*dial.Trin.*1.13(M.28.1137Af.) cit. s. ἰδιότης; **2.** to the nature; **a.** Meth.*creat.*11(p.499.14; M.18.344A); ref. God θεοῦ...ἴδιον μὴ ὁρᾶσθαι Ath.*inc.*32.1(M.25.152A); ταῦτα [sc. anthropomorphisms]...οὐκ ἴ. θεοῦ, ἀλλὰ μᾶλλον τῶν ...σωμάτων id.*gent.*22(M.25.44D); τοῦ λόγου ἑνὸς ὄντος ἴδιον, καὶ τοῦ θεοῦ ἑνὸς ὄντος ἴ. καὶ ὁμοούσιόν ἐστι...αὐτὸ μηδὲν κοινὸν μηδὲ ἴ. ἔχειν τι τῇ φύσει...πρὸς τὰ κτίσματα id.*ep.Serap.*1.27(M.26.593C); Gr.Nyss.*or.catech.*36(p.140.5; M.45.92D) cit. s. κάθαρσις; Cyr.*Jo.*6(4.580A); θεοὺς ὀνομάζουσι τοὺς...κρίνειν πεπιστευμένους, ὅπερ ἴδιον μόνου θεοῦ Thdt.*Ps.*49:1(1.924); in argument to show that Devil was created good οὐ γάρ ἐστιν ἴ. δικαίου θεοῦ, κολάσαι τὸν ἀνάγκῃ γενόμενον πονηρόν id.*haer.*5.8(4.409); ἐστι...τοῦτο τῆς πάντων αἰτίας καὶ ὑπὲρ πάντα ἀγαθότητος ἴ., τὸ πρὸς κοινωνίαν ἑαυτῆς τὰ ὄντα καλεῖν Dion.Ar.*c.h.*4.1(M.3.177C); ἐνεργείας...θεοῦ ἴδιόν ἐστι, τὸ...ἐπέκεινα εἶναι...πάσης οὐσίας Jo.D.*volunt.*34(M.95.169D); **b.** Trin. πῶς...τὸ μὴ ἐκ θεοῦ κατὰ φύσιν φορέσει τὸ ἴ. αὐτοῦ;...ἐστι γάρ...σαφὲς...ὡς ἄβατα παντελῶς τὰ τῆς θεότητος ἴ. τῇ πεπονημένῃ κτίσει Cyr.*Jo.*3.5(4.305B); τὸ...ἴ. αὐτὸ τῆς τοῦ πατρὸς οὐσίας φυσικῶς διῆκον εἰς τὸν υἱόν, ἐν αὐτῷ δείκνυσι τὸν πατέρα *ib.*1.10(105E); τὸ ἄφθαρτόν τε καὶ ἀόρατον, καὶ τοῦ υἱοῦ καὶ τοῦ πνεύματος ἴ. Thdt.*1Tim.*1:17(3.644); **c.** Christol., properties of human nature assumed by Son becoming ἴ. of God by *communicatio idiomatum* οὐ γὰρ τοῦ λόγου, ᾗ λόγος ἐστί, ταῦτα [sc. need, ignorance] τυγχάνει ὄντα, ἀλλὰ τῶν ἀνθρώπων ἴδια ταῦτα...εἰ γὰρ καὶ ὁ λόγος σὰρξ ἐγένετο, ἀλλὰ τῆς σαρκὸς ἴ. τὰ πάθη· καὶ εἰ ἡ σὰρξ θεοφορεῖται ἐν τῷ λόγῳ, ἀλλ' ἡ χάρις καὶ ἡ δύναμίς ἐστι τοῦ λόγου Ath.*Ar.*3.41(M.26.409B); κατῴκησεν ἡ θεότης ἐν τῇ σαρκί· ἴσον τὸ φάναι, θεὸς ὤν, ἴδιον ἔσχε σῶμα, καὶ τούτῳ χρώμενος ὀργάνῳ, γέγονεν ἄνθρωπος δι' ἡμᾶς. καὶ διὰ τοῦτο τὰ μὲν ἴ. ταύτης αὐτοῦ λέγεται, ἐπειδὴ ἐν αὐτῇ ἦν...τὰ δὲ αὐτοῦ τοῦ λόγου ἴ. ἔργα...διὰ τοῦ ἰ. σώματος αὐτὸς ἐποίει *ib.*3.31(389A); ὡς...σῶμα φορῶν, ἐδίψα καὶ ἐκοπία, καὶ ἔπασχεν· οὐ γὰρ ἦν ἴ. ταῦτα τῆς θεότητος...ἐγίνετο δὲ ταῦτα οὐ διῃρημένως κατὰ τὴν τῶν γινομένων ποιότητα...συνημμένως δὲ πάντα ἐγίνετο, καὶ εἷς ἦν ὁ ταῦτα ποιῶν κύριος παραδόξως τῇ ἑαυτοῦ χάριτι id.

ep.Serap.4.14(M.26.656C); σαρκὸς...καὶ ψυχῆς λυπουμένης...ταῦτα δὲ οὐκ ἄν τις εἴποι φύσιν εἶναι θεότητος· ἴδια δὲ θεοῦ κατὰ φύσιν γέγονεν, εὐδοκήσαντος τοῦ λόγου ἀνασχέσθαι γεννήσεως ἀνθρωπίνης ‡Ath.Apoll.1.5(M.26.1100D); εἰ μὲν γὰρ θεότητος ἴδιον τὸ 'Χριστὸς' ὄνομα, δίχα σαρκός, προσακτέον ἄρα καὶ τῷ πατρί, καὶ τῷ πνεύματι ib.2.2(1133C); ὁ μονογενὴς...ψυχὴν...ἰδίαν τὴν ἀνθρωπίνην ποιούμενος,...τῆς ἰ. φύσεως τὸ...ἄτρεπτον...ἐγκαταχρώσας αὐτῇ Cyr.inc.unigen.(5^{1}.691D); id.Jo.5.2(4.485E); id.Lc.13:11(M.72.768A) cit. s. ἰδικῶς; Thdr.Raith.praep.(p.194.11; M.91.1496A); Jo.D.f.o.3.4(M.94.1000A) cit. s. ἰδίωμα; v. ἀντίδοσις; neut. as subst. used collectively in sing. as equivalent of 'nature' ἓν γὰρ καὶ ταὐτὸν τὸ σῶμα καὶ ὁ θεός, οὗ τὸ σῶμα, οὐ μεταβληθείσης τῆς σαρκὸς εἰς τὸ ἀσώματον, ἀλλ' ἐχούσης καὶ τὸ ἴ. τὸ ἐξ ἡμῶν κατὰ τὴν ἐκ παρθένου γέννησιν καὶ τὸ ὑπὲρ ἡμᾶς κατὰ τὴν τοῦ θεοῦ λόγου ἕνωσιν Apoll.fid.inc.(p.199.22; M.PL.8.877D); Word and flesh dist. as ἴ. καὶ ἰδιοποιούμενον, Leont.H.monoph.20(M.86.1781C) cit. s. ἰδιοποιέω; **3.** to individuals or individual classes in rel. to others; **a.** in gen. τῷ ἀρχιερεῖ ἴ. λειτουργίαι δεδόμεναί εἰσιν καὶ τοῖς ἱερεῦσιν ἴ. ὁ τόπος...λευΐταις ἰ. διακονία 1Clem.40.5; Meth.res.1.49(p.303.9; M.18.280A); τὸ...τύπτεσθαι Χριστιανῶν ἴ. ἐστι Ath.h.Ar.41(p.206.8; M.25.741B); **b.** ref. two Manich. principles ἑκάστου τὰ ἴ. ἔχοντος Hegem.Arch.7(p.10.2; M.10.1437A); **c.** ref. Persons in Trin. ἡ...θεότης...ἴδιον μὲν πατρός...πατρῷον δὲ τῷ υἱῷ...καὶ τῷ πνεύματι δὲ παρὸν φυσικῶς τὸ πνεῦμα θεοῦ ὑπάρχειν Apoll.fid.sec.pt.14(p.172.5; M.10.1109C); ‡Ath.dial.Trin.1.14(M.28.1140A); εἰκὼν δὲ [i.e. the Son] ὡς πρὸς ἀρχέτυπον ἐν ἰδίᾳ νοούμενος ὑπάρξει Cyr.Jo.3.5(4.306E); ib.4.1(4.334C); Jo.D.volunt.12(M.95.141C); **4.** neut. as subst., *particular, specific*, opp. τὸ κοινόν, Bas.Eun.2.28(1.265C; M.29.637B) cit. s. ἰδιότης; κοινὸν...ἐστι...ἤγουν γενικόν, κατὰ τοὺς πατέρας, ἡ οὐσία καὶ ἡ φύσις...ἴ. δὲ καὶ μερικόν, ἡ ὑπόστασις καὶ τὸ πρόσωπον Max.ep.15(M.91.545A); Jo.D.dialect.21(M.94.585B); Trin. πενταχῶς...ἡ ὑπόστασις· ὑπόστασις, καὶ πρόσωπον, καὶ χαρακτήρ, καὶ ἴ., καὶ ἄτομον id.Trin.5(M.95.17A).

D. of persons, *properly one's own, belonging properly* to, implying 'having the ἴδια of', esp. ref. relations in Trin. τὴν ἰ. ... ἀρχήν, τὸν πατέρα Meth.creat.11(p.499.14; M.18.344A); ὁ κύριος υἱὸν θεοῦ ἑαυτὸν καὶ πατέρα ἴ. ἔλεγεν ἑαυτοῦ εἶναι τὸν θεόν Ath.Ar.2.73(M.26.301C); διὰ τί...τὰ τοῦ υἱοῦ ἴ. ἐστι τοῦ πατρός, ἢ ὅτι...τῆς οὐσίας αὐτοῦ ἴδιόν ἐστι γέννημα ὁ υἱός; ib.3.5(329C); μόνος ὁ υἱός ἐστι καὶ ἴ. κατ' οὐσίαν τοῦ πατρός ib.3.36(401A); of H. Ghost τὸ μὴ ἁγιαζόμενον παρ' ἑτέρου ...τὰ κτίσματα ἁγιάζεται, πῶς ἂν εἴη ἓν τῶν πάντων, ἴδιον τῶν μετεχόντων αὐτοῦ; id.ep.Serap.1.23(M.26.584B); ἔστιν ἴ. τοῦ υἱοῦ τὸ πνεῦμα τὸ ἅγιον ἀμέλει τοῦ πατρὸς Cyr.dial.Trin.6(5^{1}.592E); id.Jo.5.2(4.472A); ἐκπορευόμενον μὲν ἐκ τοῦ πατρός, ἴ. δὲ ὂν τοῦ υἱοῦ Gel.Cyz.h.e.2.23.5(M.85.1296C); cf. (Sethian) ἀπολυθείη ὁ νοῦς, ἀπὸ τοῦ πατρὸς τοῦ κάτωθεν, ὅ ἐστιν ὁ ἄνεμος...γεννήσας νοῦν τέλειον υἱὸν ἑαυτοῦ, οὐκ ὄντα ἴδιον ἑαυτοῦ κατ' οὐσίαν Hipp.haer.5.19(p.119.18; M.16.3183A); denied by Arians καταχρηστικῶς...λέγεται λόγος καὶ σοφία, γενόμενος καὶ αὐτὸς τῷ ἰ. τοῦ θεοῦ λόγῳ Alex.Al.ep.encycl.7(p.7.23; M.18.573B); τῶν...γενητῶν καὶ κτισμάτων ἴ. καὶ εἷς τυγχάνει Ar.Thal.fr.16 ap.Ath.ep.Aeg.Lib.12(M.25.565A); ref. Jo.4:30,14:10 πῶς ὑμεῖς...ἴ. καὶ ὅμοιον τῆς τοῦ πατρὸς οὐσίας αὐτὸν φάσκετε; ἀνάγκη γὰρ ἢ καὶ ἡμᾶς ἰδίους εἶναι τῆς οὐσίας τοῦ πατρός, ἢ κἀκεῖνον ἀλλότριον εἶναι, ὥσπερ καὶ ἡμεῖς ἐσμεν ἀλλότριοι (Arian argument), Ath.Ar.3.17(M.26.360A); ref. 1Cor.1:24 Ἀρείου λέγοντος ἄλλην μὲν ἰ. σοφίαν εἶναι ἐν τῷ θεῷ, ἄλλην δὲ περὶ ἧς φησιν ὁ ἀπόστολος id.Dion.25(p.64.27; M.25.517A); id.Ar.2.33(217C).

E. ? *self-respecting* τὰ γὰρ ἐξιόντα...ἐκ τοῦ στόματος κοινοῖ τὸν ἄνθρωπον, κοινὸν καὶ...ἀσελγῆ δείκνυσιν αὐτόν, οὐχὶ δὲ ἴ. καὶ κόσμιον καὶ σώφρονα Clem.paed.2.6(p.187.12, v.l. ἥδιον; M.8.452B).

F. ἰδίᾳ as adv.; **1.** *on one's own, by oneself; separately*, Athenag.leg.8.2(M.6.905A); Clem.exc.Thdot.61(p.127.16; M.9.688C); εἰ μόνον θεός, οὐκ ἂν ἰ. παρὰ τὸν πατέρα ἐζωοποίει τινὰς τῶν νεκρῶν Apoll.ap.Thdt.eran.3(4.256); Cyr.Nest.2(p.33.2; 6^{1}.31B) cit. s. ἰδικῶς; Trin., id.Jo.2.6(4.221D); **2.** *in one's own Person* εἰ γὰρ ὑφέστηκεν ἰ. καὶ καθ' ἑαυτὸν ὁ θεὸς καὶ πατήρ, ὁμοίως δὲ καὶ ὁ υἱὸς καὶ τὸ πνεῦμα, ἀλλ' οὖν...εἰς μίαν...θεότητος φύσιν σύμπαν αὐτῆς ἀναβαίνει τὸ πλήρωμα Cyr.Jo.5.5(4.530E); **3.** *in particular* opp. general; *in private* opp. public ἡ πρόνοια ἰ. καὶ δημοσίᾳ καὶ πανταχοῦ Clem.str.7.2(p.6.10; M.9.409A); θεὸς...κολάζει...πρὸς τὸ χρήσιμον καὶ κοινῇ καὶ ἰ. τοῖς κολαζομένοις ib.7.16(p.72.22; 541B); ib.7.3(p.12.19; 421A).

***ἰδιοσήμαντρος**, *with its own characteristics*, ‡Bas.struct.hom.1.19(1.332E; M.30.29B).

***ἰδιοστάτως**, *individually, on its own*, ref. two natures in Christ οὐκ ἐν μονάδι κατ' ἰδίαν ὑπόστασιν, ἕκαστον ἰ. θεωρούμενον Sev.Ant.ap.Leont.H.monoph.(M.86.1845D); ἐπὶ τοῦ καθ' ἑαυτὸ ἰ. ὑφεστῶτος προσώπου Leont.B.fr.(M.86.2012C).

***ἰδιοσύστατος**, **1.** *having individual existence, being a distinct entity*; **a.** in gen. ἐκεῖνο [sc. τὸ ἀπαύγασμα]...οὐκ ἰ. ... ἔχει γὰρ ἐν τῷ ἡλίῳ τὸ εἶναι Cyr.thes.6(5^{1}.47A); τῶν ἐξ ὧν ἕνωσις μενόντων ἀμειώτων ...ἐν συνθέσει δὲ ὑφεστώτων, καὶ οὐκ ἐν μονάσιν ἰ. Sev.Ant.ap.Leont.H.monoph.(M.86.1848A); ἡ ἰ. ὕπαρξις *individual existence*; ὑπόστασιν ...τὴν ἰ. τῆς ἑκάστης φύσεως ὕπαρξιν Jo.D.haer.7(M.94.745B); id.dialect.42(M.94.612B); **b.** Trin., agst. alleged Montanist identification of Persons, ref. Jo.14:18 ὡς σὺν τῷ πνεύματι παρὼν ἰ., καθά ἐστιν ἀεὶ πανταχοῦ καὶ ὁ πατήρ Didym.Trin.3.38(M.39.977A); ἑαυτὸν εἶναί φησιν ἐν αὐτῷ [sc. τῷ πατρί] φυσικῶς, κἂν ἐξ αὐτοῦ νοῆται κατὰ τὸ ἰ. Cyr.Jo.3.5(4.302A); ib.1.2(16D); ref. Rom.8:10 δεικνὺς οὐκ ἀλλότριον αὐτὸ [sc. τὸ πνεῦμα] τῆς τοῦ λόγου φύσεως. ἀλλ' οὕτως ἡνωμένον, εἰ καί ἐστιν ἰ., ὡς αὐτό τε ὑπάρχειν ἐν υἱῷ, καὶ υἱὸν ἐν αὐτῷ διὰ τὴν τῆς οὐσίας ταυτότητα id.thes.33(5^{1}.334E); neut. as subst., Didym.Trin.3.23(925B); **c.** Christol. οὔτε...τὰς φύσεις...εἰς μίαν συναλείφομεν φύσιν ...ἵνα μὴ τροπὴν...εἰσάγωμεν· οὔτε εἰς δύο πάλιν ἰδιοσυστάτους... διαιροῦμεν...ἵνα μὴ τὴν ἡμῶν αὐτῶν ἀρνώμεθα σωτηρίαν Max.ep.12(M.91.493C); πῶς...ἡ ἐν Χριστῷ ἀνθρωπότης ἐν ἰδιαζούσῃ ὑποστάσει καθ' ἑαυτὴν οὔποτε γενομένη...πρόσωπον ἰ. καθ' ἑαυτὸ...ἔχοι; Thdr.Raith.praep.(p.192.18; M.91.1493A); τὸ λέγειν...δύο ἰ. καὶ καθ' ἑαυτὰς θεωρουμένας οὐσίας, πολλῆς βλασφημίας τεκμήριον Dam.troph.suppl.(p.284.5); Jo.D.f.o.3.9(M.94.1017B) cit. s. ἰδιοσυστάτως; ref. Christ's human nature οὐκ ἐν ἰ. καὶ ἰδιοπεριγράφῳ προσώπῳ παρὰ τὴν τοῦ λόγου ὑπόστασιν, ἀλλ' ἐν αὐτῇ τὴν ὕπαρξιν ἐσχηκυῖαν Thdr.Stud.antirr.3.22(M.99.400D); **2.** *of the very being* τὸ πνεῦμα ἰ. ὡς ὁμοούσιον πατρὸς καὶ υἱοῦ Ammon.Jo.16:14(M.85.1497D).

***ἰδιοσυστάτως**, *as existing personally, in one's own entity*, Cyr.Nest.2.1(p.35.6; 6^{1}.34B); σημαίνει [sc. τὸ ἐνυπόστατον]...τὸ καθ' ἑαυτὸ ὂν τοῦτο εἶναι ἰ. Leont.B.fr.(M.86.2012A); Max.ep.11(M.91.496A); ὑπόστασις...τὸ καθ' ἑαυτὸ ἰ. ὑφιστάμενον Jo.D.dialect.44(M.94.616B); of Christ in himself opp. indwelling man's soul αὐτὸς ὢν ἐν πᾶσι... μετὰ καὶ τοῦ ὑπάρχειν ἰ. Cyr.Jo.8(4.702A); Trin. ταῦτα...ἓν καὶ ἓν καὶ ἓν πρόσωπον ἰ. δηλοῖ ἐν μιᾷ θεότητι Didym.Trin.3.41(M.39.984B); Cyr.Jo.1.5(46B); ὑπάρχων ἰ., πλὴν οὐ πάντη διακεκομμένως ib.3.5(307B); ref. Gen.18:1f., in Trin. argument from Abraham addressing three visitors in sing., id.Juln.1(6^{2}.20E); ref. H. Ghost, ib.(35D); ref. Jo.14:16 οὐκ ἔξω τιθεὶς αὐτὸ [sc. τὸ πνεῦμα], τὸν δὲ τῆς ἑτερότητος λόγον ἐν μόνῳ νοεῖσθαι διδοὺς τῷ εἶναι καὶ ὑπάρχειν ἰ. αὐτό. οὐ γὰρ υἱὸς τὸ πνεῦμά ἐστιν, ἀλλ' ὄντως, ἰδίως τε ὂν καὶ ὑπάρχον τοῦθ' ὅπερ ἐστὶν ἐν πίστει παραδεξόμεθα id.Jo.9.1(809D); Christol. οὐ δύο Χριστοί, διὰ τὸ μηδὲ τὰς οὐσίας ἤγουν ὑποστάσεις...ἰ. ὑφεστηκέναι Sev.Ant.ap.Eust.Mon.ep.(M.86.924B); οὐ γὰρ ἰ. ὑπέστη ἡ τοῦ θεοῦ λόγου σάρξ... ἀλλ' ἐν αὐτῇ ὑποστᾶσα, ἐνυπόστατος μᾶλλον, καὶ οὐ καθ' ἑαυτὴν ἰδιοσύστατος ὑπόστασις γέγονε Jo.D.f.o.3.9(M.94.1017B).

[*]**ἰδιοτεύω**, *lead an unofficial life, be a civilian*, Thdr.Lect.h.e.1.37(M.86.181C); ‡Jo.D.Artem.7(M.96.1257C; ἰδιωτεύοντι p.26.12).

ἰδιότης, ἡ, I. *property*;

A. *distinctive property, specific character*; of God, *attribute*; **1.** explained αἱ...ἰ. οἱονεὶ χαρακτῆρές τινες καὶ μορφαὶ ἐπιθεωρούμεναι τῇ οὐσίᾳ, διαιροῦσι μὲν τὸ κοινὸν τοῖς ἰδιάζουσι χαρακτῆρσι· τὸ δὲ ὁμοφυὲς τῆς οὐσίας οὐ διακόπτουσιν. οἷον, κοινὴ μὲν ἡ θεότης· ἰδιώματα δέ τινα πατρότης καὶ υἱότης· ἐκ δὲ τῆς ἑκατέρου συμπλοκῆς, τοῦ τε κοινοῦ καὶ τοῦ ἰδίου, ἡ κατάληψις ἡμῖν τῆς ἀληθείας ἐγγίνεται... αὕτη γὰρ τῶν ἰδιωμάτων ἡ φύσις, ἐν τῇ τῆς οὐσίας ταυτότητι δεικνύναι τὴν ἑτερότητα...τήν γε μὴν ἑνότητα τῆς οὐσίας μὴ διασπᾶν Bas.Eun.2.28(1.265Bf.; M.29.637Bf.); ἡ οὐσία τὴν κοινότητα σημαίνει· καὶ εἴ τί ἐστιν ἴδιον τῆς οὐσίας, τοῦτο κοινόν ἐστι τῶν ὑποστάσεων τῶν ὑπὸ τὴν οὐσίαν· ἡ δὲ ὑπόστασις ἰδιότητα ἔχει ἥτις οὐκ ἔστι κοινὴ τῶν τῆς αὐτῆς οὐσίας ὑποστάσεων...τὸ ἔχον ἰ. ἀριθμὸν ἐπιδέχεται...ἄλλο τῆς ὑποστάσεως τὸ ἴδιον, καὶ ἄλλα τῆς οὐσίας ἰδιώματα ‡Ath.dial.Trin.1.13(M.28.1137A ff.); ‡Ath.def.3(M.28.541B) cit. s. ἰδίωμα; Thdr.Raith.praep.(p.217.32) cit. s. ἴδιος; ἰδίωμα ἤγουν ἰ. ἐστὶ τὸ κυρίως ἔν τινι φύσει ἰδικῶς γνωριζόμενον, ἐν ἑτέρᾳ δὲ μὴ εὑρισκόμενον Anast.S.hod.2(M.89.64B); in what sense ἰ. and kindred terms applicable to God ἐπὶ δὲ τῆς ἀγεννήτου καὶ μοναρχικῆς φύσεως, οὐκ ἂν μὲν ὅλως ἢ κυρίως λεχθείη ποιότης...καταχρηστικῶς δέ...φυσικὴ μὲν ποιότης ἐστὶ τὸ πανάγιον... ὑποστατικὴ δὲ...ἀγεννησία, καὶ ἡ γέννησις καὶ ἡ ἐκπόρευσις, ἅπερ καὶ ἰδιότητας ὀνομάζουσι, διὰ τὸ μόνον αὐτῷ καὶ οὐκ ἄλλῳ προσεῖναι ταῦτα φυσικῶς ἢ ὑποστατικῶς. ἐξ ὧν αἵ τε οὐσιώδεις καὶ ὑποστατικαὶ συνίστανται διαφοραί, καταχρηστικῶς μὲν...ἐπὶ θεοῦ, κατὰ φύσιν δὲ κυρίως ἐπὶ τῶν γενητῶν ἁπάντων. ὅθεν ταυτὸν μὲν ἀλλήλοις ὑπάρχειν ταὐτά φασι, ποιότητά φημι καὶ ἰ. καὶ διαφοράν, καὶ τῶν τε συμβεβηκότων, ἀλλ' οὐχ ὑποκειμένου τινός, ἤγουν οὐσίας λόγον ἐπέχειν. διαφέρειν μὲν τῷ τὴν ποιότητα καθολικωτέραν εἶναι, καὶ ἐπὶ πάντων ἁπλῶς...τὴν ἰ. δὲ μερικήν, ὡς πρὸς ἐκείνην, καὶ μὴ ἁπασῶν...τὴν διαφορὰν ὡς συστατικὴν τῶν ὄντων καὶ ἀφοριστικὴν Max.opusc.(M.91.

249Aff.); **2.** essential ἰ.; **a.** of created things πῶς ποικίλα εἴδη τροφῶν τῇ ἰ. τῶν σωμάτων ἁρμόζοντα ἐπινενόηται Bas.*ep*.2.6(3.74E; M.32.232D); ἀναγκαιοτάτη τοῖς ἰατροῖς...ἡ κατανόησις τῆς τῶν στοιχείων ἰ. ... τριχῇ...τῆς ἰ. τῶν τῆς ψυχῆς κινημάτων...τὸ λογιστικόν τε καὶ ἐπιθυμητικὸν καὶ θυμοειδές Gr.Nyss.*ep.can*.(M.45.224C); ὥσπερ οἱ πρῶτοι [sc. angels] περισσῶς ἔχουσι τὰς τῶν ὑφειμένων...ἰ., οὕτως ἔχουσιν οἱ τελευταῖοι τὰς τῶν προτέρων, οὐ μὴν ὁμοίως, ἀλλ' ὑφειμένως Dion.Ar.*c.h*.12.2(M.3.293A); *ib*.11.1,2(284C,285A); **b.** Trin., Persons being consubstantial possess same essential ἰ.: πῶς οὐκ ἔσται κατ' οὐσίαν ὁ αὐτός, ὁ ταῖς τοῦ πατρὸς ἰ. οὕτω διαπρέπων, ὡς ἂν εἰ καὶ αὐτὸς ὁ πατήρ; Cyr.*thes*.14(5^1.145A); γεγέννηται...οὗτος [sc. ὁ υἱός] τοῦ πατρὸς ἰ. πᾶσαν ἔχων ἐν ἑαυτῷ id.*dial.Trin*.6(5^1.592D); ἀδίδακτόν τινα μάθησιν...ἐκ τῆς τοῦ γεννήσαντος ἰ. ἔχων καὶ φύσεως id.*Jo*.5.5(4.526D); *ib*.(528D); *ib*.1.10(105C); τὸ πνεῦμα...ὅλην ἔχον τοῦ θεοῦ...τὴν φυσικὴν ἰ., καὶ ὁμοίως τοῦ μονογενοῦς *ib*.1.9(93E); **c.** Christol. κατά γε τὸν ἰδιότητος λόγον, εἴη...ἑτεροφυὴς ἡ σὰρξ παρὰ τὸν ἐκ θεοῦ...λόγον, πλὴν αὐτοῦ γέγονε καθ' ἕνωσιν ἀδιάσπαστον Cyr.*Diod*.4(p.494.11); θεόν...καὶ ἄνθρωπον ὄντα...τὴν οὐσίαν ἑκατέρου τελείως ἔχοντα, μετὰ τῆς αὐτῆς ἐνεργείας ἤγουν φυσικῆς ἰ. ‡Hipp.*Ber.Hel*.1(p.322.2; M.10.832B); μεμενήκασι...μετὰ τὴν ἕνωσιν αἵ τε φύσεις ἀσύμφυρτοι καὶ αἱ τούτων ἰ. ἀλώβητοι Thdot.Anc.*fr*.(p.128.14); σωζομένης...τῆς ἰ. ἑκατέρας φύσεως καὶ εἰς ἓν πρόσωπον συνιούσης Leo Mag.*ep*.28.3(p.13.11; M.*PL*.54.764A); *ib*.(p.14.1; 766A); *ib*.28.5(p.17.11; 774B); Leont.B.*cap.Sev*.25(M.86.1909D); συνέθεντο τοῖς συνοδικοῖς Σευήρου, ἀναθεματισμὸν ἔχουσιν...τῶν εἰρηκότων δύο φύσεις ἢ ἰ. ἐπὶ τοῦ κυρίου, τῆς σαρκὸς καὶ τῆς θεότητος *Ep*.ap.Evagr.*h.e*.3.33(p.132.30; M.86.2669C); Thdr.Raith.*praep*.(p.194.4; M.91.1493D); *ib*.(p.196.23; 1497D) cit. s. ἰδίωμα; εἴ τις οὐχ ὁμολογεῖ...τὰς φυσικὰς ἰ. τῆς θεότητος τοῦ Χριστοῦ καὶ τῆς ἀνθρωπότητος...ἐν αὐτῷ...ἀμειώτως σωζομένας...εἴη κατάκριτος CLater.*can*.9; in anti-monophysite argument αἱ ἰ. οὐχ ἑαυτῶν, ἀλλὰ τινῶν εἰσιν ἰ. εἰ δὲ δύο κατ' αὐτοὺς μετὰ τὴν ἕνωσιν αἱ ἰ., τινῶν δύο πάντως εἰσὶν ἰ. Leont.B.*cap.Sev*.22(M.86.1908D); *ib*.10(1904C); anti-monothelite οὐχ ὡς μόνα θέλοντος, ἃ φυσικῶς ὡς θεὸς ἤθελεν...ἀλλὰ καὶ τὰ συστατικὰ τῆς ἀνθρωπίνης φύσεως...ἐν ἰ. τῶν φύσεων Jo.D.*f.o*.3.14(M.94.1036D); **3.** hypostatic ἰ.; **a.** within Trin. ἰ. indicate distn. of Persons only ὅταν δὲ λέγωμεν τρεῖς ὑποστάσεις...τὸ ἀληθὲς εἶναι λέγομεν τῶν ἰ. τὴν διαφορὰν ἐν τῇ ὑποστάσει, οὐχὶ δὲ καὶ ἐν τῇ οὐσίᾳ ‡Ath.*dial.Trin*.1.15(M.28.1140C); θεότης μία...ἀριθμῷ μὲν τὴν διαφορὰν ὑπάρχειν, καὶ ταῖς ἰ. ταῖς χαρακτηριζούσαις ἑκάτερον· ἐν δὲ τῷ λόγῳ τῆς θεότητος τὴν ἑνότητα θεωρεῖσθαι Bas.*Eun*.1.19(1.231C; M.29.556B); ἀναγκαῖον...τὸν ἕνα θεὸν τηρεῖν, καὶ τὰς τρεῖς ὑποστάσεις ὁμολογεῖν, καὶ ἑκάστην μετὰ τῆς ἰ. Gr.Naz.*or*.2.38(M.35.445C); ἓν τὰ τρία τῇ θεότητι, καὶ τὸ ἓν τρία ταῖς ἰ. *ib*.31.9(p.156.9; M.36.144A); τρισὶ μὲν κατὰ τὰς ἰ. εἴτουν ὑποστάσεις...εἴτε πρόσωπα...ἑνὶ δὲ κατὰ τὸν τῆς οὐσίας λόγον εἴτουν θεότητος *ib*.39.11(345C); εἷς καὶ ὁ αὐτὸς τῆς θεότητος λόγος, οὐδεμιᾶς ἰ. ἐν οὐδενὶ...εὑρισκομένης Gr.Nyss.*or.catech*.proem.(p.6.1; M.45.12D); μίαν τῆς τριάδος τὴν φύσιν εἶναι πιστεύομεν, μίαν οὐσίαν ἐν τρισὶν ἰ. γνωριζομένην Thdt.*Trin*.28(M.75.1188B); id.*Ps*.101:28(1.1322); ἄλλον αὐτὸν [sc. υἱόν] παρὰ τὸν πατέρα δεικνὺς κατὰ τὸν τῆς ἰ. λόγον id.*Heb*.1:3(3.548); Taras.*ep*.5(M.98.1461D); by Cappadocian fathers often called γνωριστικαὶ ἰ., Bas.*Eun*.2.28(1.265C; M.637B); ἐν τῇ κοινότητι τῆς οὐσίας τὰς γνωριστικὰς ἰ. ἐπιλάμπειν ἑκάστῳ Gr.Nyss.*diff.ess*.5(M.32.336B); cf. τῆς κτιστῆς φύσεως καὶ τῆς θείας οὐσίας...οὐδεμίαν...ἐπιμειξίαν ἐχούσης κατὰ τὰς γνωστικὰς ἰ. id.*Eun*.8(2 p.198.17; M.45.793C); **b.** in what this ἰ. of Person consists τὸ δὲ γεννητὸν καὶ ἀγέννητον γνωριστικαί τινές εἰσιν ἰ. εἰ γὰρ μηδὲν εἴη τὸ τὴν οὐσίαν χαρακτηρίζον, οὐδενὶ ἂν τρόπῳ πρὸς τὴν σύνεσιν ἡμῶν διϊκνοῖτο. μιᾶς γὰρ οὔσης θεότητος, ἀμήχανον ἰδιάζουσαν ἔννοιαν πατρὸς λαβεῖν, ἢ υἱοῦ, μὴ τῇ τῶν ἰδιωμάτων προσθήκῃ τῆς διανοίας διαρθρουμένης Bas.*Eun*.2.29(1.266A; M.640A); πῶς οὐκ ἀσύνθετος ὁ κατὰ τὴν οὐσίαν ἁπλοῦς; οὐ γὰρ δὴ οἱ δεκτικοὶ τῆς ἰ. αὐτοῦ τρόποι τὸν τῆς ἁπλότητος λόγον παραλυπήσουσιν *ib*.(266B; M.640B); τοῦτο γνωριστικὸν τῆς κατὰ τὴν ὑπόστασιν ἰ. σημεῖον ἔχει, τὸ μετὰ τὸν υἱὸν καὶ σὺν αὐτῷ γνωρίζεσθαι [sc. H. Ghost], καὶ τὸ ἐκ τοῦ πατρὸς ὑφεστάναι Gr.Nyss.*diff.ess*.4(M.32.329C); ἀναχωρήσει μὲν γὰρ οὐκ εἰς ἰ. παντελῶς...κεχωρισμένην, διὰ τὸ ἐν μιᾷ θεότητι τὴν ἁγίαν νοεῖσθαι τριάδα Cyr.*Jo*.3.5(4.306D); ὁ τοῦ πῶς εἶναι λόγος...ἤγουν αἱ ἰ. ‡Cyr.*Trin*.2(6^3.2E; M.77.1121C); τῆς ἀγεννησίας καὶ τῆς γεννήσεως καὶ τῆς ἐκπορεύσεως. ἐν ταύταις γὰρ μόναις ταῖς ὑποστατικαῖς ἰ. διαφέρουσιν ἀλλήλων αἱ...ὑποστάσεις *ib*.9(6^3.14B; M.1140D); *ib*.10(15D; M.1144A); ἐπὶ τῆς θεότητος μίαν...φύσιν ὁμολογοῦμεν...πάντα μὲν τὰ φυσικὰ...ἁπλᾶ φαμεν, τὴν δὲ διαφορὰν τῶν ὑποστάσεων ἐν μόναις ταῖς τρισὶν ἰ., τῇ ἀναιτίῳ καὶ πατρικῇ, καὶ τῇ αἰτιατῇ καὶ υἱϊκῇ, καὶ τῇ αἰτιατῇ καὶ ἐκπορευτῇ ἐπιγινώσκομεν...εἰ γὰρ καὶ ἑκάστη...τελεία ἐστὶν ὑπόστασις, καὶ τὴν οἰκείαν ἰ., ἤτοι τὸν τῆς ὑπάρξεως τρόπον διάφορον κέκτηται, ἀλλ' ἥνωται τῇ τε οὐσίᾳ καὶ τοῖς φυσικοῖς ἰδιώμασι Jo.D.*f.o*.3.5(M.94.1000B,C); **c.** orthodox doctrine of ἰ. a safeguard agst. errors εὐλαβουμένους δύο...θεούς...ἤτοι ἀρνουμένους ἰδιότητα υἱοῦ ἑτέραν παρὰ τὴν τοῦ πατρός...ἢ ἀρνουμένους τὴν θεότητα τοῦ υἱοῦ τιθέντας δὲ αὐτοῦ τὴν ἰ. καὶ τὴν οὐσίαν κατὰ περιγραφὴν τυγχάνουσαν ἑτέραν τοῦ πατρός Or.*Jo*.2.2(p.54.25,28; M.14.108C); ἔδει...τὰς ἰ. μεῖναι πατρὶ καὶ υἱῷ ἵνα μὴ σύγχυσις ᾖ παρὰ θεότητι Gr.Naz.*or*.31.29(p.182.12; M.36.165B); συγχεομένων τῶν ὑποστάσεων εἴτ' οὖν τῶν ἰ. ἀναιρουμένων CCP(381)*ep*.ap.Thdt.*h.e*.5.9.11(3.1031); **d.** ἰ. as eternal and unchangeable ἰ. ἀκινήτου μενούσης Gr.Naz.*or*.29.12(p.90.12; 89B); μενούσης αὐτοῖς τῆς ἐπιθεωρουμένης ἰ. εἰς διάκρισιν ἐναργῆ τῶν ὑποστάσεων Gr.Nyss.*diff.ess*.8(M.32.340C); ἡ...ἰ. ἀκίνητος ‡Cyr.*Trin*.10(6^3.16D; M.77.1144D).

B. gen., *character, nature*; ref. creation, Hipp.*haer*.7.20(p.196.3; M.16.3302C); ref. man ὅπερ συμφέρει ἑκάστῳ ἵνα αἴσθηται τῆς ἰ. τῆς ἑαυτοῦ καὶ τῆς χάριτος τῆς τοῦ θεοῦ Or.*princ*.3.1.12(p.216.3; M.11.272A); πάσης ὑπερνικωμένης τε καὶ καλυπτομένης ἀνθρωπίνης ἰ. τῇ ἐπιφοιτήσει τῆς χάριτος ‡Bas.*h.myst*.61(p.397.3); of Christians πάντα τὸν Χριστοῦ λαόν...ἔχειν τὰς ἰ. μυστικώτερον τῶν φυλῶν Or.*Jo*.1.1(p.3.6; M.14.21A); sacerdotal κατὰ...ἵδρυσιν ἰδιότητος ἀπαραλλάκτως ἑστηκυῖαν Dion.Ar.*e.h*.4.3.3(M.3.476D); of God γνῶσιν τῆς ἰ. τοῦ θεοῦ Or.*or*.24.4(p.355.13; M.11.493B); οὐδὲν τῶν ἐν λέξεσι...δύναται παραστῆσαι τὰς ἰ. τοῦ θεοῦ id.*Cels*.6.65(p.135.27; M.11.1397B); Trin. ἐπεὶ...ὁ υἱὸς εἰκών ἐστι τοῦ πατρός, ἐξ ἀνάγκης ἐστὶ νοεῖν, ὅτι ἡ θεότης καὶ ἡ ἰ. τοῦ πατρὸς τὸ εἶναι τοῦ υἱοῦ ἐστι Ath.*Ar*.3.5(M.26.332B); *ib*.3.11(344B); τὴν πατρὸς ἰ. παροῦσαν υἱῷ τε καὶ πνεύματι Apoll.*fid.sec.pt*.15(p.172.12; M.10.1109D).

II. a *being proper, propriety* (in a now obsolete sense), *ownness* ἴδιος μὲν γὰρ σύμπας ὁ κόσμος ἐστὶ τῷ θεῷ...πρεπωδέστερον δέ πως ὁ Ἰσραὴλ τῷ τῆς ἰ. ἀποκεκλήσεται λόγῳ Cyr.*Jo*.1.9(4.89E); Trin. ὁ υἱὸς...τῆς τοῦ πατρὸς οὐσίας ἴδιος καὶ ὁμοφυὴς τυγχάνει...ἐν τῷ εἰπεῖν 'μείζων ἐστίν' ἔδειξε πάλιν τὴν τῆς οὐσίας ἰ. Ath.*Ar*.1.58(M.26.133B); καθαρᾷ τῇ νοήσει καὶ μόνῳ τῷ νῷ νοῶμεν υἱοῦ πρὸς πατέρα τὸ γνήσιον καὶ λόγου τὴν πρὸς τὸν θεὸν ἰ. ... τὴν...τοιαύτην ἑνότητα καὶ φυσικὴν ἰ. [i.e. of sun and light] πῶς ἂν οἱ πιστεύοντες...ὀρθῶς καλέσαιεν ἢ ὁμοούσιον γέννημα; id.*decr*.24(pp.19.33,20.12; M.25.457B,C); of H. Ghost [Jo.3:8] σημαίνει...οὐσίαν εἶναι τὸ πνεῦμα. οὐ γάρ, ὥς τινες οἴονται, ἐνέργειά ἐστι θεοῦ, οὐκ ἔχον...ὑπάρξεως ἰδιότητα Or.*fr*.37 *in Jo*.(p.513.13); οἵαν...ἔγνωμεν ἰδιότητα τοῦ υἱοῦ πρὸς τὸν πατέρα, ταύτην ἔχειν τὸ πνεῦμα πρὸς τὸν υἱὸν εὑρήσομεν Ath.*ep.Serap*.3.1(M.26.625B); ποία ὁμοιότης ἢ ἰ. τοῦ χρίσματος καὶ τῆς σφραγῖδος πρὸς τὰ χριόμενα καὶ σφραγιζόμενα; *ib*.1.23(585A); Christol., ref. Lc.2:40 λέγεται αὐτὸς προκόπτειν διὰ τὴν πρὸς τὸ σῶμα ἰ. id.*Ar*.3.54(436B).

***ἰδιοτικός**, *of one's own*, Afric.*ep.Arist*.5(p.61.17; M.10.61A).

ἰδιότροπος, **1.** *one's own peculiar, distinctive*, ref. Logos as uncreated τὴν γὰρ ἰ. αὐτοῦ ὑπόστασιν ἐδήλωσεν [Jo.1:1ff.] Alex.Al.*ep.Alex*.4(p.22.10; M.18.553A); of the two natures διεσταλμένοις [sc. in Christ]...ἰ. νοήμασιν Sophr.H.*or*.2.4(M.87.3221C); **2.** *on one's own, solitary*, ‡Eust.*Laz*.24(p.45.11).

***ἰδιοϋποστατικῶς**, *in one's own person*, ‡Sophr.H.*liturg*.10(M.87.3989C).

***ἰδιοϋπόστατος**, *self-subsistent*, Eustrat.*stat.anim*.10(p.386); Trin. ἄλλος μὲν γὰρ ὁ πατήρ, ἄλλος δὲ ὁ υἱός, καὶ ἄλλο τὸ πνεῦμα τὸ ἅγιον, καὶ διὰ τοῦτο ἰ. Anast.*fid*.(p.271); Christol. ὡς κεχωρισμένας καὶ ἰ. εἶναι τὰς φύσεις, καθὼς Θεόδωρος καὶ Νεστόριος βλασφημοῦσιν Justn.*conf.anath*.7(p.92.11; M.86.1015C) = CCP(553)*anath*.7(p.170); Leont.H.*Nest*.2.10(M.86.1556A) cit. s. ἄνθρωπος; *ib*.2.5(1540C).

***ἰδιοϋποστάτως**, *with one's own subsistence* εἷς ἐστι θεὸς ὁ πατήρ, μετὰ τῶν δύο ἑαυτοῦ δυνάμεων, ἀχωρίστως ἐν ἀλλήλοις ὄντες, καὶ ἰ. θεωρούμενοι νῷ Cosm.Ind.*top*.5(M.88.309A); εἰ τὰ ἰ. ὑφεστῶτα, ἴδια ἐπιγράφεται πρόσωπα,...ὁ δὲ Χριστὸς...ἐστιν...ἐκ δύο προσώπων κατὰ Σευῆρον Eust.Mon.*ep*.(M.86.924B); *ib*.(912A); ‡Germ.CP *contempl*.(M.98.397D).

ἰδιόχειρος, **1.** *made with one's own hands*, ‡Jo.D.*ep.Thphl*.22(M.95.373C); met., ref. God [sc. τὸ ἀνθρώπινον] ἰ. αὐτοῦ πλάσμα Anast.S.*qu.et resp*.78(M.89.708B); **2.** neut. as subst., *autograph document* τὸ ἰ. τοῦ εὐαγγελιστοῦ, ὅπερ μέχρι τοῦ νῦν πεφύλακται χάριτι θεοῦ ἐν τῇ Ἐφεσίων...ἐκκλησίᾳ Petr.I.Al.*fr*.(M.18.517D); to be made by those professing celibacy, †Gregent.*leg.Hom*.60(M.86.613B); in gen., †Gregent.*disp*.54(M.86.609B); Jo.Mosch.*prat*.195(M.87.3080C).

ἰδιοχείρως, *with one's own hand*, Eustrat.*v.Eutych*.9(M.86.2284C); CLater.*act*.5(H.3.927A); Leont.N.*serm*.3(M.93.1604B).

***ἰδιοχρυσέω**, *have private property*, Thdr.Stud.*epp*.2.180(M.99.1556C).

ἰδίωμα, τό, A. *characteristic property, distinctive feature*; **1.** etym., def., and descriptions ἰ. λέγεται διὰ τὸ ἴδια εἶναι ἅμα· ἀχώριστοι γὰρ εἰσι τῶν φύσεων καὶ τῶν ὑποστάσεων αἱ αὐτῶν ἰδιότητες. ἰ. ἐστι τὸ ἓν τινι φύσει ἰδικῶς γνωριζόμενον καὶ ἐν ἑτέρᾳ μὴ εὑρισκόμενον...ταῦτα μέν εἰσι φυσικὰ ἰ.· ἕτερα καὶ ὑποστατικά, οἷον λευκότης...εἰσὶ δὲ καὶ ἕτερα, ἅπερ οὐ λέγονται κυρίως ἰ., ἀλλὰ συμβεβηκότα...οἷον ἡ νηπιότης ‡Ath.*def.*3(M.28.541B); Thdr.Raith.*praep.*(p.217.32) cit. s. ἴδιος; ἰ. ἐστι σημαντικὸν πάσης οὐσίας σχῆμά τε καὶ πρᾶγμα *Doct.Patr.*33 (p.262.14); πᾶσα φύσις οὐσιωδῶς οἰκείοις ἰ. διειλημμένη· καὶ ταύτῃ τόν τε τρόπον τῆς οἰκείας ὑπάρξεως καὶ τὴν διαφορὰν καθ' ἣν τῶν ἄλλων ἀμιγῶς διώρισται δεικνύουσα φύσεων. ἐπὰν τῶν συνεκτικῶν τῆς οὐσίας αὐτῆς ἀπογένηται ἰδιωμάτων ἢ οὐδ' ὅλως ἔσται ἢ ὅπερ οὐκ ἦν γέγονεν Max.*ep.*7(M.91.436A); not to be confused with essence τὰς τῶν ποιοτήτων ἢ τὰς τῶν ἰ. διαφοράς...ἄλλο τι παρὰ τὸ ὑποκείμενον Gr. Nyss.*Eun.*1(1 p.74.17; M.45.305B); cf. οὐδὲ διαφέρουσιν ἀλλήλων αἱ ὑποστάσεις κατ' οὐσίαν, ἀλλὰ κατὰ τὰ συμβεβηκότα, ἅτινά εἰσι τὰ χαρακτηριστικὰ ἰ. Jo.D.*f.o.*3.6(M.94.1001C); τὸ ἰ. εἴρηται κατὰ τὸ ἴδιον εἶναι ἅμα τῆς ἰδίας φύσεως ἀμιγὲς τῶν λοιπῶν οὐσιῶν ὑπάρχον Anast.S.*hod.*2(M.89.64A); *ib.*(64B) cit. s. ἰδιότης; *ib.*(56C); Jo.D.*inst. el.*4(M.95.101Df.); φυσικὸν οὖν ἰ. ἐστι τὸ συνιστῶν τὴν φύσιν, καὶ χωρίζον εἶδος ἀπὸ εἴδους, τουτέστι φύσιν ἀπὸ ἄλλης φύσεως, καὶ ἐν ἑκάστῃ ὑποστάσει τοῦ αὐτοῦ εἴδους θεωρούμενον...ὑποστατικὸν δὲ ἰ., τὸ χωρίζον ὑπόστασιν ἀπὸ ἄλλης ὑποστάσεως id.*volunt.*5(M.95.133Cf.); examples ἰ. τοῦ σώματος τὸ φθαρτόν, τὸ θνητόν, τὸ ῥευστόν, ἰ. ψυχῆς ἐστι τὸ λογιστικόν, τὸ θελητικόν *Doct.Patr.*33(p.262.18); **2.** essential ἰ.; **a.** in various contexts; of sex, ‡Caes.Naz.*dial.*156(M.38.1116); things material and things spiritual having no common ἰ., Gr.Nyss. *Eun.*4(2 p.51.3; M.45.620D); nor divine and human ἀκοινώνητος ἡ ἰδιότης τῆς ἀνθρωπίνης τε καὶ τῆς θείας ζωῆς· καὶ παρήλλακται παντάπασι τὰ γνωριστικὰ ἰ., ὡς μήτε ταῦτα ἐπ' ἐκείνης, μήτε τὸ ἔμπαλιν ἐπὶ ταύτης ἐκεῖνα καταλαμβάνεσθαι *ib.*(p.51.16; 621A); *attribute* of divine nature ἐν τῇ βραχύτητι τῆς ἡμετέρας φύσεως τῶν...τῆς θεότητος ἰ. αἱ εἰκόνες ἐκλάμπουσιν id.*anim.et res.*(M.46.41D); †Bas.*Is.*4(1.381A; M. 30.125B); as common to all Persons ἄντικρυς τῆς πατρικῆς μαιώσεως φυσικὴν ἐνδείκνυνται [sc. Ps.109:3] υἱότητα...φύσεως ἰδιώματι ταύτην λαχόντος [sc. υἱοῦ] Alex.Al.*ep.Alex.*8(p.25.2; M.18.560B); Ath.*syn.* 50(p.274.13; M.26.781C); Cyr.*Jo.*2.8(4.228B); τὸ...ἄκτιστον...καὶ τὰ τοιαῦτα, κοινὰ πατρός, καὶ υἱοῦ, καὶ ἁγίου πνεύματος. διὰ τοῦτο καὶ τῆς θείας φύσεως ἰδιώματα λέγονται· τῆς θείας μὲν φύσεως ὅτι φυσικά, καὶ οὐχ ὑποστατικά, ταῖς τρισὶν...προσόντα τῆς θεότητος ὑποστάσεσιν· ἰδιώματα δὲ ὡς ἄλλῃ πάσῃ φύσει...πάμπαν ἀμέθεκτα ‡Cyr.*Trin.*13 (6³.19B; M.77.1148Dff.); ref. impeccability of Christ θεοπρεπὲς τῆς οἰκείας φύσεως ἰ. Cyr.*Jo.*2.9(4.240A); **b.** Christol.; **i.** Christ possessing essential ἰ. of God τὰ τῆς θεολογίας ἰ. ἐν τοῖς ἔμπροσθεν ἀποδέδοται Eus.*d.e.*10 proem.(p.446.13; M.22.717C); πῶς ἔσται γενητὸς ὁ τοῖς τῆς θεότητος ἰ. ἐκλάμπων; Cyr.*thes.*32(5¹.329C); ref. names θεός, σοφία, etc. εἷς μὲν...κατὰ φύσιν ὑπάρχων...τοῖς δὲ τῆς θεότητος διαφόροις ἰ., τὸ οἱονεὶ πολυειδὲς ἔχων ἐφ' ἑαυτῷ id.*ador.*10(1.331A); and ἰ. of man κατεμίχθη τῇ ἀνθρωπότητι διὰ πάντων τῶν τῆς φύσεως ἰ. γενόμενος Gr.Nyss.*or.catech.*26(p.101.3; M.45.69C); with exception of ordinary birth, *ib.*13(p.61.7; 45B); **ii.** both ἰ. remaining distinct ἁγιάζει τοίνυν, ὡς θεός, ἰ. φύσεως τῆς ἑαυτοῦ τὸ ἁγιάζειν δύνασθαι λαχών· ἁγιάζεται δὲ...κατὰ τὸ ἀνθρώπινον Cyr.*Arcad.*(p.107.38; 5¹. 111A); τὴν ἑτερότητα τῶν ἰ. καταδεῖξαι...σαρκός τέ φημι καὶ θεότητος id.*Diod.*2(p.493.21); τοῦ ἑκάστῃ [sc. φύσει] πρέποντος ἰ. νοουμένου τε καὶ σωζομένου Ambr.*fr.*ap.Leont.H.*monoph.*testimonia(M.86. 1837A); Jo.D.*hom.*1.1(M.94.545B); id.*volunt.*1(M.95.128A); excluding possibility of composite nature, Leont.H.*monoph.*6(M.86. 1772D); Ephr.Ant.*fr.*(M.86.2105A); ref. Juln. Hal. and Sev. Ant. ἐξ αὐτῆς τῆς ἑνώσεως ἀπαρνηθῆναι τῆς φθαρτῆς φύσεως τὸ ἰ., ὡς μιᾶς φύσεως γενομένων τῶν δύο...τοῦ τε κρείττονός τε καὶ θείου...πρὸς τὸ ἑαυτοῦ ἰ. τὸ ἧττον...μεθαρμόσαντος τῆς κατ' αὐτὸ φυσικῆς ἰδιότητος Thdr.Raith.*praep.*(p.196.20; M.91.1497D); μετὰ τῶν ἄλλων φυσικῶν ἰ. καὶ τὰ θελήματα ταῖς φύσεσι συνομολογεῖν ἀναγκασθήσεσθε Max. *Pyrr.*(M.91.300C); **iii.** united in Person of Christ διὰ τῆς πρὸς τὸ ἄπειρόν τε καὶ ἀόριστον τοῦ ἀγαθοῦ ἀνακράσεως οὐκέτι ἔμεινεν ἐν τοῖς οἰκείοις...ἰ., ἀλλὰ τῇ δεξιᾷ τοῦ θεοῦ συνεπήρθη καὶ ἐγένετο ἀντὶ δούλου κύριος Gr.Nyss.*Eun.*5(2 p.117.21; M.45.697C); ἡ δὲ σὰρξ...ἀνακραθεῖσα δὲ πρὸς τὸ θεῖον, οὐκέτι ἐν τοῖς ἑαυτῆς ὅροις τε καὶ ἰ. μένει ἀλλὰ πρὸς τὸ ἐπικρατοῦν...ἀναλαμβάνεται *ib.*(p.123.22; 705B); cf. ἐπικοινωνεῖν τὴν σάρκα τοῦ κυρίου τοῖς τοῦ λόγου ὀνόμασί τε καὶ ἰ., μένουσαν καὶ ἐν τῇ ἑνώσει σάρκα...καὶ τὸν λόγον ἐπικοινωνεῖν τοῖς τῆς σαρκὸς ὀνόμασί τε καὶ ἰ. μένοντα καὶ ἐν τῇ σαρκώσει λόγον Apoll.*fr.*180(p.278. 17)ap.Leont.B.*Apoll.*(M.86.1960D); unchanged, Jo.D.*f.o.*3.17(M.94. 1069B); and each predicable of the other nature by *communicatio idiomatum*, v. ἀντίδοσις; Leont.B.*arg.Sev.*(M.86.1945C); explained θεότητα...λέγοντες, οὐ κατονομάζομεν αὐτῆς τὰ τῆς ἀνθρωπότητος ἰ. οὐ γάρ φαμεν θεότητα παθητήν...ἐπὶ δὲ τῆς ὑποστάσεως...ἀμφοτέρων τῶν φύσεων τὰ ἰ. αὐτῇ ἐπιτίθεμεν...καὶ ὅταν ἐξ ἑνὸς τῶν μέρων...θεοῦ ὀνομάζηται, δέχεται τὰ τῆς συνυφεστηκυίας φύσεως ἰ. ... θεὸς παθητὸς ὀνομαζόμενος...οὐ καθὸ θεός, ἀλλὰ καθὸ καὶ ἄνθρωπος ὁ αὐτός· καὶ ὅταν ἄνθρωπος...ὀνομάζηται, δέχεται τὰ τῆς θείας φύσεως ἰ. ... καὶ οὗτός ἐστιν ὁ τρόπος τῆς ἀντιδόσεως, ἑκατέρας φύσεως ἀντιδιδούσης τῇ ἑτέρᾳ τὰ ἴδια διὰ τὴν τῆς ὑποστάσεως ταυτότητα, καὶ τὴν εἰς ἄλληλα αὐτῶν περιχώρησιν Jo.D.*f.o.*3.4(M.94.997Cff.); **3.** *individual attribute*; **a.** of individual things and persons τὸ ἰ. τῶν προσώπων τῆς θείας γραφῆς Or.*comm.min.in Cant.*(M.13.36A); ἕκαστος...ἡμῶν καὶ τῷ κοινῷ τῆς οὐσίας λόγῳ τοῦ εἶναι μετέχει, καὶ τοῖς περὶ αὐτὸν ἰ. ὁ δεῖνά ἐστι καὶ ὁ δεῖνα Bas.*ep.*214.4(3.322E; M.32.789A); τὰ ἰ. τῶν οἰκείων ἐπιδείκνυνται τρόπων οἱ μαθηταί, Πέτρος καὶ Ἰωάννης. ὁ μὲν γὰρ θερμότερος, ὁ δὲ ὑψηλότερος ἦν· καὶ ὁ μὲν ὀξύτερος ἦν, ὁ δὲ διορατικώτερος Chrys.*hom.87.2 in Jo.*(8.522A); ταῦτα καὶ τοῦ σατανᾶ ἰ., τὸ κακίᾳ χαίρειν Cyr.*Ps.*51:5(M.69.1105B); αἱ γὰρ ὑποστάσεις, φύσεις εἰσὶ μετὰ ἰδιωμάτων Leont.H.*Nest.*1.20(M.86.1485B); αἱ ὑποστάσεις...τόπῳ διεστήκασι, καὶ χρόνῳ διαφέρουσι, καὶ γνώμῃ μερίζονται καὶ...καὶ πᾶσι τοῖς χαρακτηριστικοῖς ἰ. ‡Cyr.*Trin.*10(6³.15B; M.77.1141D); οὐδὲ διαφέρουσιν ἀλλήλων αἱ ὑποστάσεις κατ' οὐσίαν, ἀλλὰ κατὰ τὰ συμβεβηκότα, ἅτινά εἰσι τὰ χαρακτηριστικὰ ἰ.· χαρακτηριστικὰ δὲ ὑποστάσεως, καὶ οὐ φύσεως Jo.D.*f.o.*3.6(M.94.1001C); **b.** of divine Persons in Trin. τὸ δὲ ἀγέννητον τῷ πατρὶ μόνον ἰ. παρεῖναι Alex.Al.*ep.Alex.*12(p.28.6; M.18.568B); τοῦ ἁγίου πνεύματος ἑτέρου ὄντος παρὰ τὸν πατέρα καὶ τὸν υἱόν, τὸ ἰ. παριστὰς ὁ σωτὴρ κέκληκεν αὐτὸ παράκλητον Eus.*e.th.*3.5(p.163.13; M.24.1012D); Son possessing ἰ. of being μονογενής in respect of his divinity, but of being πρωτότοκος in respect of his humanity, Ath.*Ar.*2.62(M.26. 280B); τοῦ μὲν πατρὸς ἐν τῷ ἰ. τοῦ πατρός, τοῦ δὲ υἱοῦ ἐν τῷ ἰ. τοῦ υἱοῦ, τοῦ δὲ ἁγίου πνεύματος ἐν τῷ οἰκείῳ ἰ. Bas.*fid.*4(2.227E; M.31.685C); ἡ ὑπόστασις ἐν τῷ ἰ. τῆς πατρότητος, ἢ τῆς υἱότητος, ἢ τῆς ἁγιαστικῆς δυνάμεως θεωρεῖται id.*ep.*214.4(3.322E; M.32.789B); furnishing terms in which distn. of Persons is known, id.*Eun.*2.28(1.265C; M.29. 637B); ἐπὶ πατρὸς καὶ υἱοῦ οὐχὶ οὐσίαν παρίστησι τὰ ὀνόματα, ἀλλὰ τῶν ἰ. ἐστὶ δηλωτικά *ib.*2.5(241C; M.580C); Gr.Nyss.*diff.ess.*6(M.32. 336C) cit. s. ἰδιαζόντως; id.*or.dom.*3(p.64.10; M.46.1109B); τὸ ἰ. τῆς γεννήσεως, ὑπόστασίν τε καὶ υἱὸν κεκλῆσθαι πεποίηκεν· ὥσπερ αὖ ἐπὶ τοῦ πατρός, τὸ ἰ. τῆς ἀγεννησίας καὶ τοῦ αἰτίου, ὑπόστασιν καὶ πατέρα ἀπέφηνε Leont.B.*Nest.et Eut.*1(M.86.1288B); concept of ἰ. of each Person shown to be consonant with essential unity, Leont.H.*Nest.* 1.20(M.86.1485Bf.); ἄναρχον...τὸν πατέρα...σύναρχον ὁμολογοῦμεν... τὸν...υἱὸν καὶ...τὸ πνεῦμα...ταῦτα δὲ μὴ ἄλλως εἶναι δυνάμεις ἐν αὐτῷ διαρρεούσας...ἀλλ' ἐν ὑπάρξει πιστεύεσθαι καὶ διακεκριμένως μὲν ἀφορίζεσθαι τοῖς ὑποστατικοῖς ἰ., ἡνωμένως δὲ προσκυνεῖσθαι μιᾷ φύσει Const.Diac.*laud.*19(M.88.501B); τοῖς γὰρ ὑποστατικοῖς ἰ. τὴν πρὸς αὐτὸν κέκτηται διαφορὰν προδήλως ὁ λόγος Max.*opusc.*(M.91.85B); οὐ τὸ τῆς ὑποστάσεως ἰ. δηλοῖ τὸ 'θεός', ἀλλὰ ποίας ἐστὶ φύσεως, τὸ δὲ πατὴρ τὸ ἰ. τῆς ὑποστάσεως Jo.D.*fid.Nest.*13(p.564); ἰ. of Son as basis of hypostatic union οἷς ἠφορίζετο τοῦ κοινοῦ τῆς θεότητος ἰ. ὡς υἱὸς καὶ λόγος, τούτοις πρὸς τὴν σάρκα τὴν καθ' ὑπόστασιν διέσωζεν ἕνωσιν...καὶ οἷς ὡς θεὸς τὴν πρὸς τὴν σάρκα φυσικὴν ἐτήρει διαφοράν, τούτοις πατρί τε καὶ πνεύματι κατ' οὐσίαν ἑνούμενος ἐπήλλαττε τήν τε πρὸς ἑαυτὸν καὶ τὰ ἄκρα διαφορὰν καὶ ταυτότητα Max.*ep.*15(M.91. 557B).

B. gen., *character, property, nature*; theol., of abstracts τοῦ Σαβελλίου...λέγοντος· ἕνα μὲν εἶναι τῇ ὑποστάσει τὸν θεόν, προσωποποιεῖσθαι δὲ ὑπὸ τῆς γραφῆς διαφόρως, κατὰ τὸ ἰ. τῆς ὑποκειμένης ἑκάστοτε χρείας Bas.*ep.*214.3(3.322C; M.32.788C); καὶ θεὸν μὲν τὸν υἱὸν τῷ ἰ. τοῦ πατρὸς καλοῦντες ὡς εἰκόνα καὶ γέννημα, κύριον δὲ τὸν πατέρα τῷ τοῦ ἑνὸς κυρίου προσαγορεύοντες ὀνόματι ὡς τούτου ἀρχὴν καὶ γεννήτορα Apoll.*fid.sec.pt.*17(p.173.1; M.10.1112A); συνήγαγεν εἰς ἓν ὄνομα τό τε τοῦ πατρὸς ἰ. καὶ τοῦ υἱοῦ καὶ τοῦ...πνεύματος Didym.(‡Bas.)*Eun.*5(1.311C; M.29.748A); οὐ χρὴ λέγειν τὸν Ἐμμανουὴλ μιᾶς οὐσίας τε καὶ ποιότητος καὶ ἑνὸς ἰ. Sev.Ant.ap.Leont.H. *monoph.*(M.86.1848B); of character bestowed on man by H. Ghost τὸ διὰ τῆς πίστεως προσγινόμενον ἁγίου πνεύματος χαρακτηριστικὸν ἰ. Clem.*str.*6.16(p.500.5; M.9.360A); ref. Son πρόσωπον εἴρηται τοῦ πατρὸς ὁ υἱός, αἰσθήσεων πεντάδι σαρκοφόρος γενόμενος, ὁ λόγος ὁ τοῦ πατρῴου μηνυτὴς ἰδιώματος *ib.*5.6(p.348.11; 57B).

C. *peculiarity*; **1.** *unique character* τῆς μονοειδοῦς φύσεως...τὸ ἰ. Mac.Mgn.*apocr.*3.27(p.117.18); **2.** *idiosyncrasy* (e.g. local or racial) ἄνδρας [i.e. suitable for consecration as bishops] εὑρήσειν, διὰ τὸ εἶναι ἐν τῇ παροικίᾳ αὐτοῦ καὶ εὐλαβεῖς, καὶ συνετούς, καὶ τῆς γλώττης ἐμπείρους, καὶ τὰ λοιπὰ ἰ. τοῦ ἔθνους ἐπισταμένους Bas.*ep.*99.4(3. 195B; M.32.501D); **3.** *idiom, peculiar mode of expression* τὸ τῆς γραφῆς ἰ. Ath.*Ar.*2.4(M.26.156A); τὰ...τοῦ ἀποστόλου ἰ. Socr.*h.e.*2.45. 14(M.67.361A); θυσίαν μέν...δῶρον δέ...ἐμοὶ...οὐδέν τι δοκεῖ διαφέρειν, ἀλλὰ συνήθως κατὰ τὸ τῆς γραφῆς ἰ. διωρίσθαι Gennad.*Gen.*4:4(M.85.

1640C); κέχρηται [sc. ἡ γραφή] πολλάκις τῷ ἰ. τούτῳ, ὡς ἀπὸ πατρὸς λέγουσα τὴν δημιουργίαν, καὶ τοῦ υἱοῦ τὴν ἐνανθρώπησιν, καὶ τοῦ πνεύματος τοῦ ἁγίου τὴν ἀνάστασιν Cosm.Ind.*top*.5(M.88.312A). **D.** ? *visible feature, appearance* φόβον ὑποκρίνεται...τὸ τῆς ἀσθενείας ἰ. πλάττεται Mac.Mgn.*apocr*.3.9(p.71.7).

***ἰδιωματικός**, *characteristic*, Clem.*prot*.10(p.72.29; M.8.216A).

ἰδίως, **1.** *in a way peculiar to oneself, uniquely* ἰ. παρὰ τὴν κοινὴν γένεσιν, γεγεννῆσθαι αὐτὸν ἐκ θεοῦ λέγομεν λόγον θεοῦ Just.*1apol*.22.2 (M.6.361A); *ib*.23.2(364A); Ἰησοῦς...ἤσθιεν καὶ ἔπινεν ἰ. οὐκ ἀποδιδοὺς τὰ βρώματα Val.Gn.ap.Clem.*str*.3.7(p.223.14; M.8.1161C); ἰ. γὰρ ἕκαστος γνωρίζει τὸν κύριον καὶ οὐχ ὁμοίως πάντες [Mt.18:10] Clem. *exc.Thdot*.23(p.114.27; M.9.672A); τὸ 'μὴ μοιχεύσῃς, μὴ φονεύσῃς' ἰ. ἐκλαμβάνων [sc. the 'gnostic'] id.*str*.7.11(p.44.11; M.9.485B); φῶς ἑαυτὸν εἶναί φησιν οὐκ ἰ. ἢ ἀφωρισμένως τῶν ἐξ Ἰσραήλ, ἀλλ' ὅλου τοῦ κόσμου Cyr.*Jo*.5.2(4.485A); Dion.Ar.*c.h*.9.4(M.3.261B); ref. private interpretations, Or.*Jo*.2.14(8; p.70.24; M.14.137C); Eus.*h.e*.4.29.5 (M.20.400C); **2.** *properly*; **a.** *inherently* ἰ. ἐξ αὐτοῦ [sc. τοῦ πατρός] λόγος...γεγεννημένος, καὶ ὕστερον ἄνθρωπος...γενόμενος Just.*dial*. 105.1(M.6.721A); Clem.*exc.Thdot*.10(p.109.24; M.9.660C); θεός... ποιῶν...ἰ. ἀγαθά id.*str*.6.12(p.484.25; M.9.325B); Dion.Ar.*d.n*.4.4(M. 3.700C); μέγας...ὁ θεὸς...ὑμνεῖται. οὐ πρὸς ἀντιπαράθεσιν...ἀλλὰ διὰ τὸ ἀπαράθετον καὶ ὄντως ἀκατάληπτον τῆς θείας μεγαλειότητος· τοῦτο γὰρ ἐσήμανε τὸ ἰ., ἤγουν ἰδιότητα εἰπών Max.*schol.d.n*.9.2(M.4.369B); **b.** *strictly* οὐκοῦν ἰ. ... αὐτὸ τὸ πρῶτον Meth.*res*.3.6(p.397.23; M.18. 321C); *ib*.(p.398.2; M. l.c.); ref. Jo.1:14 οὐκ ἔστιν ἰ. κτίσμα τὸ σῶμα [i.e. of Christ] εἰπεῖν Apoll.*corp.et div*.2(p.186.3; M.*PL*.8.874A); **3.** *in one's own Person*, Trin., Cyr.*Jo*.9.1(4.809D) cit. s. ἰδιοσυστάτως; **4.** *individually, specifically*, Or.*hom.3.1 in Jer*.(p.20.21; M.13. 281D); ὁ θεὸς...ἀναπλάσας καὶ ἀνακοσμήσας ἰ. ἕκαστον Meth.*res*.1.44 (p.293.7; ἑκάστου...εἶδος M.41.1113D); **5.** *on one's own, separately* οὐκ ἐπειδὴ τρία ὑποτιθέμεθα πρόσωπά τε καὶ ὀνόματα, τρεῖς καὶ ζωὰς ἰ. μίαν παρ' ἑκάστου...λογιζόμεθα Gr.Nyss.*tres dii*(M.45.125D); πῶς γὰρ ἔτι κατὰ φύσιν νοεῖται θεὸς ὁ ἐν μόνῳ τῷ θέλειν τὴν πρὸς αὐτὸν ἔχων ὁμοίωσιν, ἕτερον δέ τι καθ' ἑαυτὸν ἰ. ὑπάρχων; Cyr.*Jo*.2.8(4. 230E).

ἰδιωτεύ-ω, *be unskilled*, τὴν...γλῶτταν ~οντες Gr.Thaum.*pan.Or*. 10(p.25.6; M.10.1081A); Eus.*h.e*.3.24.3(M.20.264B).

ἰδιώτης, ὁ, 1. *unskilled, uncultivated person*, of Christians ἰ. ... σοφῶν δὲ...τὸν νοῦν ὄντων...ὡς συνεῖναι οὐ σοφίᾳ ἀνθρωπείᾳ ταῦτα γεγονέναι, ἀλλὰ δυνάμει θεοῦ Just.*1apol*.60.11(M.6.420B); id.*2apol*. 10.8(M.6.461B); Athenag.*leg*.11.3(M.6.912C); of apostles as too uneducated to have preached successfully by human means alone, Or.*Cels*.8.47(p.262.16; M.11.1588A); cf.*ib*.6.2(p.72.8; 1292A); ref. converts from paganism as capable of receiving wisdom from God, Clem.*str*.7.2(p.9.20; M.9.416A); as needing instruction proportionate to their capacities, Eus.*p.e*.1.5(14D; M.21.44B); ascetics, Ath. *v.Anton*.85(M.26.964A); *ib*.73(945A); ὅσον εἰσέρχεται εἰς γνῶσιν θεοῦ, τοσοῦτον ἔχει αὐτὸν ἰ. Mac.Aeg.*hom*.16.12(M.34.621B); Leont.N. *v.Sym*.17(M.93.1692B); Marc.Er.*opusc*.1.81(M.65.916A); **2.** *lay person*, Ath.*apol.sec*.12(p.97.13; M.25.269A); ἱερεῖς καὶ ἰ. Chrys.*hom.14.3 in Rom*.(9.578E); ἰ. καλεῖ τὸν ἐν τῷ λαϊκῷ τάγματι τεταγμένον· ἐπειδὴ καὶ τοὺς ἔξω τῆς στρατιᾶς ὄντας ἰ. καλεῖν εἰώθασι Thdt.*1Cor*.14:16(3.259).

ἰδιωτικός, 1. *private* Ἰσχύρας...ἰδιώτης ἄνθρωπος...οἰκίσκον οἰκῶν ἰ. CAlex.*ep*.ap.Ath.*apol.sec*.12(p.97.12; M.25.269A); hence *secular* opp. sacred οὐ δεῖ ἰ. ψαλμοὺς λέγεσθαι ἐν τῇ ἐκκλησίᾳ CLaod.*can*.69; **2.** *unlearned* νομίζει εἶναι...ἰ. ὁ Κέλσος τὰ...Χριστιανῶν βιβλία Or. *Cels*.4.87(p.359.3; M.11.1164A); *ib*.1.27(p.79.10; 713A); *ib*.3.68(p.260. 25; 1009B); καρδίαν ἰ. ‡Bas.*struct.hom*.1.4(1.326A; M.30.13D).

ἰδιωτικῶς, 1. *ineptly, without understanding*, Or.*Cels*.6.55(p.126.8; M.11.1384A); **2.** *in an unpolished way*, ref. S. Paul's preaching βούλημα ἦν [sc. τοῦ Χριστοῦ] τὸ οὕτως ἰ. κηρυχθῆναι τὸν λόγον Chrys. *hom.6.1 in 1Cor*.(10.43C); ἐπὶ τῶν προφητῶν τὸ πνεῦμα τὰ νοήματα μόνον ἔλεγεν,...αὐτοὶ δὲ...ἔφραζον ἰ. id.*frr.in Jer*.proem.(M.64.744B).

ἰδιῶτις, as adj., *private*; of houses, Synes.*ep*.67(M.66.1420C).

ἰδιωτισμός, ὁ, *lack of culture*, Iren.*fr*.3(M.7.1222A); as leading to misinterpretation of scripture, id.*haer*.5.30.1(M.7.1203C); Or.*or*.23. 3(p.351.13; M.11.489A); characterizing style of Apoc., indicating that writer was not S. John the Evangelist, Dion.Al.ap.Eus.*h.e*. 7.25.25(M.20.704A); ref. Christian doctrine ὁ ἰ. ... τοῦ ἁπλουστέρου κηρύγματος Gr.Nyss.*Eun*.1(1 p.96.5; M.45.329A); cf.id.*ep*.(M.46. 1024C).

ἴδμων, *having knowledge of, knowing*, Gr.Naz.*carm*.2.2.1.178(M. 37.1464A); Nonn.*par.Jo*.8:48(M.43.821A); *ib*.9:8(825A).

***ἰδοί, αἱ,** (Lat. *idus*) *Ides*, *Chron.Pasch*.p.285(M.92.709C); *ib*.p.292 (729E); Thphn.*chron*.p.60(M.108.204B).

ἵδρυσις, ἡ, 1. *founding, establishment* Ἐλευσινίων ἵ. Eus.*p.e*.10. 9(484C; M.21.805C); **2.** *foundation, ground* ἡ θεία πίστις, ἡ μόνιμος τῶν πεπιστευμένων ἵ. Dion.Ar.*d.n*.7.4(M.3.872C); πάντα γὰρ τὰ θεῖα ...ὁποῖά ποτέ ἐστι κατὰ τὴν οἰκείαν ἀρχὴν καὶ ἵ., ὑπὲρ νοῦν ἐστι *ib*.2.7 (645A); τὸ θεῖον...τῶν ὄντων...ἵ. id.*c.h*.13.4(M.3.304C); ἡ πάσης... εὐκοσμίας ἀρχὴ καὶ ἵ. [sc. θεαρχία] id.*e.h*.5.1.4(M.3.504D); ἡ δικαιοσύνη ...τῆς οἰκείας ἐν τῷ καλῷ...βάσεως...ἵ. Max.*ambig*.(M.91.1245C); **3.** *abiding*, ref. mutual indwelling of Persons of Trin. τῶν ἐναρχικῶν ὑποστάσεων μονὴ καὶ ἵ. Dion.Ar.*d.n*.2.4(M.3.641A); ref. Inc. ἐκ κόλπων πατρικῶν παραγέγονεν, οὐ μεταβὰς τῆς οἰκείας ἵ. Jo.D.*hom*.1.4(M.96. 552B); τὴν ἐν ἀλλήλοις ἵ. id.*Jacob*.78(M.94.1476B); ref. union with God τὴν ἐν τῷ θεῷ γενομένην αὐτῷ [sc. S. Paul]...ἵ. Max.*ambig*. (M.91.1237D); denial that such union is grounded in natural affinity between men and God, *ib*.(1069A); **4.** *sitting*, ref. anthropomorphic language of scripture ἵ. τε γὰρ αὐτῆς [sc. τῆς θείας φύσεως]...καὶ ἔγερσις...λέγονται Cyr.*Mich*.5(3.394A); οὐχ ἵ. τινα... δηλοῖ τὸ 'ἐκάθισεν', ἀλλ' οἷον ἐξουσίας ἐπίδειξιν id.*Ps*.9:5(M.69.764C); **5.** *seat*; of bishop's throne, Gr.Naz.*carm*.2.1.11.1072(M.37.1105A); **6.** *stabilizing* τῶν...παρακινουμένων ἵ. ἱερά Dion.Ar.*d.n*.1.3(M.3. 589B); **7.** *stability* τὴν ὑπερτάτην ὡς ἐν ἀγγέλοις ἀεικίνητον ἵ. id.*c.h*. 7.4(M.3.212A); *ib*.2.4(141D); τῆς κατ' οὐσίαν ἀκινήτου στάσεως καὶ ἵ. id.*e.h*.3.3.3(M.3.429A); τῇ τῶν ψυχῶν ἀτρέπτῳ...ἵ. *ib*.7.1.1(533A).

ἱδρύ-ω, 1. *establish, set firmly*; of Church, Clem.*fr*.54(p.226.4; M. 9.744B); τὰς [sc. ἐκκλησίας]...θεοῦ προνοίᾳ ἱδρυθείσας *Clem.ep*.proem. (M.2.33A); Eus.*h.e*.3.4.3(M.20.220B); of grace ὁ Χριστὸς ἠθέλησεν ἱδρυθῆναι πρὸς σέ Chrys.*hom.20.2 in Heb*.(12.188A); τοῦ πνεύματος χάρις, ἐπειδὰν...ἱδρυνθῇ, πάσης πηγῆς μᾶλλον ἀναβλύζει id.*hom.51.1 in Jo*.(8.300B); of faith, ‡*Diogn*.11.6; Ath.*ep.Ors*.2(M.26.997C); Cyr. ap.*cat.Lc*.12:17(p.101.34); of order of thrones περὶ τὸν ὄντως ὕψιστον ὁλικαῖς δυνάμεσιν...~μένον Dion.Ar.*c.h*.7.1(M.3.205D); of God αὐτὸ καθ' ἑαυτὸ ἐφ' ἑαυτοῦ σταθερῶς...~μένον id.*d.n*.9.4(M.3. 912B); id.*ep*.9.3(M.3.1109B); **2.** *set up*, statues εἴπερ...ὁ θεὸς ~εται ...ἀνίδρυτός ποτε ἦν καὶ οὐδ' ὅλως ἦν Clem.*str*.7.4(p.21.9; M.9.437B); met. ὁ ἐν ἀνθρώποις οἰκοδομήσας νεὼν [sc. Χριστός], ἵνα ἐν ἀνθρώποις ἱ. τὸν θεόν id.*prot*.11(p.83.1; M.8.237A); **3.** *place, situate*; of God as not situated or confined within material nature, Or.*Cels*.5.42(p.46. 9; M.11.1248B); ὑπὲρ νοῦν καθόλου καὶ οὐσίαν ~εται Dion.Ar.*d.n*.1. 5(M.3.593A); **4.** *posit*, *ib*.2.5(641D); **5.** *sit*; understood symbolically of God, ‡Bas.*struct.hom*.1.4(1.326A; M.30.16A).

ἱδρώς, ὁ, *sweat*; **1.** lit., of Christ's sweat as proof of real humanity, ‡Dion.Al.*fr.in Lc.22:42*(p.242.6); Manich. ὁ...ἱ. αὐτοῦ [sc. the great Archon] ἐστιν ἡ βροχή Hegem.*Arch*.9(p.14.10; M.10.1441A); **2.** met., *labour, hardship*; for sake of kingdom of heaven, Ath.*virg*. 18(p.53.9; M.28.273B); inherent in monastic and priestly lives, Chrys.*sac*.6.5(p.150.5; 1.425C); ref. martyrdom, Nil.*epp*.4.61(M.79. 577C); ἱ. ἁγιοπρεπῶν Cyr.*Ps*.36:34(M.69.948C); θείων νόμων τοὺς ἱ. Thdr.*affect*.7(p.181.7; 4.882).

ἵδρωσις, ἡ, *sweating* παροιμία λέγεται ἐπὶ τῶν σφόδρα λυπουμένων ...αἵματος ἱ. ‡Dion.Al.*fr.in Lc.22:42*(p.241.12).

§**Ἱερακῖται, οἱ,** *Hieracites*, name of sect, denying Inc., resurrection of the body, and one first cause; asserting existence of three principles: God, matter, and evil, *Apophth.Mac.Aeg*.(M.34.209D); Epiph.*haer*.67.1(p.133.1; M.42.172C); Jo.D.*haer*.67(M.94.717B); rejecting marriage, Epiph.*haer*.67.1(p.133.23; 175A); taking Melchizedek for H. Ghost, *ib*.67.3(p.135.13; 176B); thinking children are excluded from heaven, *ib*.67.2(p.134.27; 176A); Jo.D.*haer*.67(720A).

ἱερ-άομαι, 1. *be a priest*, ? of all clergy, Eus.*v.C*.4.71(p.147.5; M.20.1225B); of bishops, *ib*.3.62(p.110.11; 1136C); *ib*.3.58(p.105.15; 1125A); of presbyters, Chrys.*sac*.3.11(p.66.25; 1.388C); id.*hom.6.1 in 1Tim*.(11.578A); **2.** *exercise priesthood*; of Christ, Eus.*d.e*.4.15 (p.179.35; M.22.300B); Chrys.*hom.7.3 in Heb*.(12.134C); of bishops, Synes.*ep*.96(M.66.1465A); Philost.*h.e*.3.19(M.65.509B); of a deposed bishop παυθέντα τοῦ ~ᾶσθαι *ib*.4.12(525B); also of Const. as servant of God, Eus.*v.C*.4.23(p.125.34; M.20.1169B); **3.** *be made a priest*; of episcopal consecration, Synes.*ep*.79(M.66.1449C).

***ἱεραρχ-έω**, *direct in the sphere of the holy*; **1.** ref. angelic illumination, of highest orders πρὸς αὐτῆς τῆς θεαρχίας ~ούμεναι Dion. Ar.*c.h*.7.2(M.3.208D); each order teaching the one below it, c. genit., *ib*.9.2(260A); οἱ καθ' ἕκαστον ἔθνος ~οῦντες ἄγγελοι *ib*.9.3(261A); ~ούμεναι. τουτέστι μυσταγωγούμεναι Max.*schol.c.h*.7.2(M.4.72A); **2.** med., of clergy, Leont.B.*Nest.et Eut*.3(M.86.1369B).

ἱεράρχης, ὁ, *one who directs in the sphere of the holy*; **1.** of angels of first hierarchy in relation to the one below, Dion.Ar. *c.h*.13.4(M.3.308A); **2.** of bishops, Evagr.*h.e*.1.16(p.26.9; M.86.2468A); Max.*schol.c.h*.tit.(M.4.29A); of a patriarch, Leont.N.*v.Jo.Eleem*. 6(p.12.18); *ib*.26(p.54.13); Jo.VI CP *ep*.(M.96.1420B); Jo.Mon. *hymn.Bas*.10(M.96.1376D); nature of office ἡ...τῶν ἱ. τάξις...

ἀκροτάτη...καὶ γὰρ εἰς αὐτὴν ἀποτελεῖται...πᾶσα τῆς καθ' ἡμᾶς ἱεραρχίας ἡ διακόσμησις Dion.Ar.*e.h.*5.1.5(M.3.505A); bishop receiving light from lowest hierarchy of angels, id.*c.h.*5(M.3.196C); functions: teaching, id.*e.h.*2.2.1(393A); baptism, *ib.*2.2.7(396D); celebrating eucharist, *ib.*3.2(425B); ordaining, *ib.*5.2(509B); consecrating oil, *ib.*5.1.5(505C); need for knowledge and virtue to correspond with dignity of office, *ib.*1.3(373C); **3.** of priests, Eus. *v.C.*2.4(p.42.2, v.l. ἱερέας M.20.981C); dist. from bishop and people, *Lit.Bas.*(p.312.12).

ἱεραρχία, ἡ, 1. *administration of holy things* ἱ. ... ἔστι ἡ τῆς διατάξεως αὐτῆς τῶν ἱερῶν ἀρχὴ καὶ οἱονεὶ φροντίς Max.*schol.c.h.*tit. (M.4.29A); by angels, amongst themselves τῆς οὐρανίας ἱ. Dion.Ar. *d.n.*4.2(M.3.696B); id.*e.h.*6.3.6(M.3.537B); ἡ θεολογία τὴν καθ' ἡμᾶς ἱ. ἀγγέλοις ἀπονενέμηκεν, ἄρχοντα τοῦ 'Ιουδαίων λαοῦ τὸν Μιχαὴλ ὀνομάζουσα id.*c.h.*9.2(M.3.260B); **2.** *hierarchy*; **a.** its nature ἔστι... ἱ. ... τάξις ἱερά, καὶ ἐπιστήμη, καὶ ἐνέργεια πρὸς τὸ θεοειδὲς ὡς ἐφικτὸν ἀφομοιουμένη *ib.*3.1(164D); οὐκ ἔστιν ἱ., μὴ καὶ πρώτας, καὶ μέσας, καὶ τελευταίας δυνάμεις ἔχουσα *ib.*9.2(257C); 'Ιησοῦς...πάσης ἱ. ... ἀρχή id.*e.h.*1.1(M.3.372A); **b.** among angels; three hierarchies, composed of seraphim, cherubim, thrones; virtues, dominations, powers; principalities, archangels, angels, id.*c.h.*6.2(M.3.202A); the first illuminated directly by God, *ib.*7.3(209C); and transmitting its light to the next, *ib.*7.4(212B); hierarchies of heaven represented by the terrestrial, *ib.*1.3(124A); cf.‡Sophr.H.*liturg.*3(M.87.3984B); **c.** in OT ἡ κατὰ νόμον ἱ. Dion.Ar.*e.h.*2.1.1(M.3.392C); symbolizing spiritual worship of NT, *ib.*5.1.2(501C); **d.** Christian ἡ καθ' ἡμᾶς... ἱ. ... ἐστιν ἡ περιεκτικὴ τῶν κατ' αὐτὴν ἁπάντων ἱερῶν πραγματεία, καθ' ἣν ὁ...ἱεράρχης τελούμενος, ἁπάντων ἕξει τῶν κατ' αὐτὸν ἱερωτάτων τὴν μέθεξιν *ib.*1.3(373C); οὐσία...τῆς καθ' ἡμᾶς ἱ. ἐστὶ τὰ θεοπαράδοτα λόγια *ib.*1.4(376B); *ib.*6.3.5(536D); **3.** *episcopate, tenure of see,* Cyr.S.*v.Cyriac.*(p.224.10); id.*v.Sab.*11(p.95.5); Alex.Sal. *Barn.*4.43(451A); *see,* Sophr.H.*v.Anast.*(M.92.1688A); *episcopal office,* id.*ep.syn.*(M.87.3149D) = Taras.*ep.*5(M.98.1461B); **4.** *high-priesthood*; of Aaron, Jo.D.*f.o.*4.11(M.94.1133A).

***ἱεραρχικός,** *hierarchical, pertaining to the hierarchy*; in gen., Dion.Ar.*c.h.*2.5(M.3.145B,C); id.*e.h.*3.3.4(M.3.428C); of apostles τῆς ...ἱ. δεκάδος *ib.*5.3.5(512D); cf.*ib.*(513A); of clergy in major orders, *ib.*6.1.2(533A); Max.*schol.e.h.*5.2.5(M.4.164B); of bishops, Dion.Ar. *e.h.*5.1.6(505C); Sophr.H.*ep.syn.*(M.87.3148A); Jo.Eleem.*v.Tych.*20 (p.130).

***ἱεραρχικῶς, 1.** *hierarchically,* Dion.Ar.*c.h.*9.2(M.3.257C); τὰ ἱ. τελούμενα id.*e.h.*2.3.6(M.3.401C); **2.** *according to the laws of the hierarchy, ib.*4.3.2(476B); **3.** *as befits a bishop, ib.*2.3.4(400B); *ib.*3.3.12 (441D); Thdr.Stud.*epp.*2.41(M.99.1241B); *ib.*2.49(1260B).

ἱερατεία, ἡ, 1. *priesthood*; of whole hierarchy, Dion.Ar.*e.h.*1.1(M. 3.372B); *ib.*5.3.5(513C); of episcopate, ‡Pion.*v.Polyc.*23; *Const.App.* 2.28.2 (or perh. of presbyterate); τῆς νέας διαθήκης ἡ ἱ. Pall.*v. Chrys.*20(p.147.12; M.47.82); ref. exercise of episcopal functions, *ib.* (p.145.16; M.47.81); of presbyterate, Epiph.*haer.*79.3(p.477.29; M. 42.744B); of celebrant ἐνδεδυμένον τὴν τῆς ἱ. χάριν *Lit.Bas.*(p.318.25); *Lit.Jac.*(p.180.6); **2.** *priestly function* αὕτη ἐστὶν ἱ. καὶ θυσία ἀληθινὴ ἡ εὐχή Clem.*fr.*60(p.227.28); **3.** *priestly act,* hence *eucharist* καιρὸς τῆς ἱ. Pall.*v.Chrys.*14(p.84.25; M.47.48).

ἱερατεῖον, τό, 1. *sanctuary*; **a.** in gen., CAlex.*ep.*ap.Ath.*apol. sec.*5(p.91.7; M.25.256C); Dion.Ar.*e.h.*7.2.2(M.3.556C); Dor.*doct.*5.5 (M.88.1681D); **b.** ref. decoration; one cross on east wall suffices, Nil.*epp.*4.61(M.79.577D); ex-voto placed there, *Mir.Geo.*4(p.39.8); **c.** symbolizing heaven, Max.*myst.*3(M.91.672A); or soul, *ib.*4(672B); **d.** entry restricted; no laity or clergy to enter without leave of celebrant, *Poen.App.*2.8; ἔθος ἦν τοὺς βασιλεῖς ἐν τῷ ἱ. ἐκκλησιάζειν. ... τόπον εἶναι βασιλέως ἐν ἐκκλησίᾳ τέταχε, τὸν πρὸ τῶν δρυφάκτων τοῦ ἱ. Soz.*h.e.*7.25.9(M.67.1496B); τὸν μόνοις ἱερεῦσί τε καὶ λειτουργοῖς ἀπόκληρον τόπον, ὃν καλοῦσιν ἱ. Max.*myst.*2(M.91.668D); **e.** hence bishops take refuge there during riot, Ath.*fug.*24(p.84. 19; M.25.676A); Eustrat.*v.Eutych.*37(M.86.2317C); **2.** *clergy*; **a.** as common term for all in orders εἴ τις πρεσβύτερος ἢ διάκονος ἢ ὅλως τῶν τοῦ ἱ. CAnt.(341)*can.*2; ref. duty of clergy to earn a living by manual work, Bas.*ep.*198.1(3.289E; M.32.713C); in gen., Epiph. *haer.*64.2(p.405.2; M.41.1072B); *ib.*73.35(p.310.1; M.42.468C); dist. as a body from laity, Ath.*ep.Amun.*(M.26.1181A); *CIG* 9263.3 (Phrygia, saec. iv); **b.** of major orders, Malch.*ep.*ap.Eus.*h.e.*7.30. 13(M.20.716A); ref. duty to choose bishop, Jul.Papa *ep.Dian.*ap. Ath.*apol.sec.*30(p.109.18; M.25.300A); ref. priests' duty to approve ordination of new priest, Thphl.Al.*common.*6(M.65.40A); **3.** *clerical office,* CAnt.(341)*can.*1; Ath.*ep.encycl.*1(p.170.5; M.25.224C).

ἱεράτευμα, τό, *priestly body, priesthood,* Leont.H.*monoph.*(M.86. 1877C); πάντων ὁμοῦ τῶν ἀποστόλων τὸ ἱερὸν ἱ. Alex.Sal.*Barn.*proem. 4(437B); Jo.D.*imag.*1.3(M.94.1233C); τῶν σεραφὶμ ἱ. ‡Meth.*Sym. et Ann.*2(M.18.352C).

ἱερατεύω, 1. *be a priest, exercise the priesthood*; **a.** of Christ, *Dial.Tim.et Aquil.*89 v°; διὰ ταύτης [sc. Church] ἱ. ὡς ἄνθρωπος, δέχεται δὲ τὰ προσφερόμενα ὡς θεός Thdt.*Ps.*109:4(1.1397); Leont.H. *Nest.*5.11(M.86.1733C); **b.** of clergy, Cyr.H.*catech.*12.35; †Bas.*bapt.*2. 2 tit.(2.653C; M.31.1581C); Pall.*h.Laus.*18(p.54.14; M.34.1059B); CCP (681)*or.imp.*(H.3.1421C); not permitted to women, *Const.App.*3. 9.3; Epiph.*haer.*79.3(p.477.27; M.42.744A) cit. s. γυνή; save among Pepuziani, Jo.D.*haer.*49(M.94.708A); **2.** trans.; **a.** *be bishop* of; c. genit., Synes.*ep.*67(M.66.1432A); **b.** *sacrifice* ἱ. τὸ σῶμα τοῦ κυρίου †Bas.*bapt.*2.2(2.653E; M.31.1584A); of Solomon, Thdt.*qu.in 2Par.* proem.(1.569).

ἱερατικός, *belonging to the hierarchy*; **1.** *priestly, sacerdotal* οἱ δίκαιοι...φέροντες καρπὸν διὰ τὴν πρὸς θεὸν θεραπείαν ἱερατικήν Or. *schol.in Cant.*6:10,11(M.17.280A); μήτε...ἐπίσκοπος μήτε πρεσβύτερος μήτε διάκονος μήτε ἄλλος τις ἐκ τοῦ καταλόγου τοῦ ἱ. *Const.App.*3.15. 5; ἱ. χάριτος Gr.Nyss.*ep.can.*5(M.45.232C); τοῦ ἱ. τάγματος CIllyr. *ep.*ap.Thdt.*h.e.*4.9.5(3.962); Gel.Cyz.*h.e.*2.33.1(M.85.1336A); τὴν ἱ. καθέδραν Synes.*ep.*67(M.66.1425A); **2.** masc. as subst., *member of hierarchy, priest* ἱερατικούς, ἀπὸ πρεσβυτέρων ἕως διακόνων CLaod. *can.*24; τῷ τάγματι τῶν ἱ. Bas.*ep.*54(3.148C; M.32.400C); τοὺς ἐπιδημοῦντας ἱ. Pall.*v.Chrys.*17(p.110.17; M.47.61).

ἱερατικῶς, *in a priestly manner, as a priest,* Dion.Ar.*e.h.*5.3.2(M. 3.509D); ἱ. τῆς Χριστοῦ προσηγορίας γεγόνατε κοινωνοί Cyr.H.*catech.* 18.33; τὸν τῷ ἰδίῳ αἵματι περὶ τῶν ἁμαρτιῶν ἡμῶν ἱ. ἱλεωσάμενον [sc. Christ] Gr.Nyss.*Eun.*6(2 p.133.13; M.45.717B); πραγματευτικῶς... πολιτευόμενοι, ἀλλ' οὐκ ἐπισκοπικῶς καὶ ἱ. Thdr.Stud.*epp.*1.11(M. 99.949A).

***ἱερατίς, ἡ,** *priestess, Narr.Jos.*2(p.460).

ἱέρεια, ἡ, *priestess*; not permitted in Church, *Const.App.*3.9.3; Epiph.*haer.*79.7(p.482.4; M.42.749D).

ἱερεῖον, τό, *sacrificial victim*; in gen., as delight of evil spirits, Athenag.*leg.*27.2(M.6.953A); consumed by apostates, *Pap.Chr.* (p.378); of sacrifices of Law revived by Cerinthus, Dion.Al.ap.Eus. *h.e.*3.28.5(M.20.276B); of Christ, in gen. μόνος ὑπὲρ ἡμῶν ἱ. ἑαυτὸν ἐπιδέδωκεν Clem.*paed.*1.11(p.148.7; M.8.365C); typified by Isaac, *ib.* 1.5(p.103.25; 277A); cf.id.*str.*2.5(p.123.13; M.8.952C); Or.ap.*cat.Jo.* 13:12(p.333.21); Chrys.*hom.*5.2 *in 2Cor.*(10.467E); of Christ as both priest and victim, Ath.*inc.*9.1(M.25.112A); *Lit.*ap.*Const.App.*8.12. 30; Gr.Ant.*bapt.*2.7(M.88.1880A); *cat.Heb.*9:26(p.229.3); eucharistic, Dion.Ar.*e.h.*5.3.2(M.3.509D); of martyrs, Or.*mart.*30(p.27.12; M.11. 601B); Gr.Naz.ap.Dor.*doct.*23.1(M.88.1829C); of spiritual sacrifices, Chrys.*hom.*5.3 *in 2Cor.*(10.470D); *cat.2Cor.*2:15(p.363.14).

***ἱέρευμα, τό,** *victim,* Const.*or.s.c.*16(p.176.28; M.20.1280C).

ἱερεύς, ὁ, *priest*;

A. of OT priests as symbolic of spiritual truths, Or.*Cels.*4.31 (p.302.5; M.11.1076C); likened to Christian ministry, id.*Jo.*1.2 (3; p.5.22; M.14.25A); id.*hom.12.3 in Jer.*(p.89.22; M.13.381C); to martyrs in respect of offering of sacrifice, id.*mart.*30(p.27.12; M. 11.601B); to all Christians, in respect of their anointing τὴν κεφαλὴν ...χρίσει ὁ ἐπίσκοπος, ὃν τρόπον οἱ ἱ. ... τὸ πρότερον ἐχρίοντο *Const. App.*3.16.3.

B. of Christ as priest; **1.** as foreshadowed in OT, Just.*dial.*34.2 (M.6.548A); *ib.*36.1(553A); πολλαχοῦ 'Ιησοῦς μέγας ἱ. προφητεύεται Or.*Jo.*1.2(3; p.5.27; M.14.25B); Eus.*e.th.*1.20(p.96.33; M.24.893B); in Ps.109, Just.*dial.*33.1,2(545Bff.); *ib.*83.3(672C); Eus.*e.th.*1.20(p.95.13; 892A); Cyr.*ador.*12(1.432E); typified by Joshua, Just.*dial.*115.4(M. 6.741C); Marcell.*fr.*1 ap.Eus.*Marcell.*1.2(p.10.2; M.24.733A); and Eleazar, cf.Or.*hom.18.1 in Jos.*(p.406.27; M.87.1028A); by high priests, ‡Chrys.*leg.*5(6.411D); by ordinary priests, Cyr.*ador.*13(1. 475C); in respect of function as mediators, *ib.*16(585C); priestly character connected with expectation of Messiah from tribe of Levi, Hipp.*ben.Jac.*15(p.31.26); **2.** as different from other priests, Just.*dial.*118.2(M.6.749B); αὐτὸς ἱ. καὶ ἱερεῖον γενόμενος Thdt.*Heb.*7:27 (3.593); his priesthood derived directly from Father, Just.*dial.*86.3 (M.6.681A); from anointing with H. Ghost πνεύματι ἁγίῳ χρισθείς, ἐστὶν ἱ. εἰς τὸν αἰῶνα *Dial.Ath.et Zacch.*86(p.46); Jo.D.*Heb.*5:1–4 (M.95.952A); **3.** ref. his priesthood in rel. to his humanity ἱ. ἐν τῷ σταυρῷ γέγονεν *A.Petr.et Paul.*30(p.192.13); θεὸς ὢν τῇ φύσει, ἔλαβε σάρκα...ἵνα γενόμενος ἄνθρωπος, καὶ τὴν ὑπὲρ ἡμῶν θυσίαν ἀναδεξάμενος, γένηται ἱ. κατὰ τὴν τάξιν Μελχισεδέκ *Dial.Ath.et Zacch.*86 (p.46); cf.Chrys.*hom.13.1 in Heb.*(12.130A); as made priest in womb of BMV, Procl.CP *or.laud.BMV* 3(p.104.15; M.65.684B); **4.** as source of Christian priesthood τῶν...ἀποστόλων τῶν ἐξαφθέντων ἀπὸ τῆς δυνάμεως τοῦ αἰωνίου ἱ. Χριστοῦ Just.*dial.*42.1(M.6.565A); Or.*or.*28. 9(p.381.2; M.11.529A); οἱ ἐξ αὐτοῦ...ἱ. Eus.*d.e.*5.3(p.222.14; M.22. 365C).

C. Christian; **1.** of major orders of clergy; of a deacon, Gr.Naz. *ep.*98(M.37.172B); οὐκ ἔστιν ἱ. ὁ ἀναγνώστης Epiph.*exp.fid.*21(p.522. 17; M.42.824C); **2.** as common term for bishops and priests τοῖς ἐπισκόποις καὶ λοιποῖς ἱ. *Const.App.*6.18.11; cf.*ib.*8.2.6; Epiph.*haer.* 80.5(p.490.27; M.42.764D); μὴ...ἀποδοκίμαζε τοὺς ἱ., διότι οὐχὶ πάντες καθαροὶ τυγχάνουσιν Nil.*epp.*2.261(M.79.333A); **3.** of bishops; **a.** in gen. ὦ ἐπίσκοποι, ἐστὲ τῷ λαῷ ὑμῶν ἱ. λευῖται *Const.App.*2.25.7; Gr.Naz.*ep.*16(M.37.52A); CCP(381)*can.*6; Chrys.*sac.*3.12(p.68.17; 1.389B); Soz.*h.e.*4.22.22(M.67.1184B); Thdt.*Tit.*1:9(3.701); of pope ἐξάρχοντος ἱερέων ἱερέως *Libell.*ap.CLater.*act.*2(H.3.721B); **b.** functions: sacrifice and care of souls, Gr.Naz.*carm.*2.1.13.1ff.(M.37. 1227A); *ib.*2.1.12.751ff.(1221A); celebration of eucharist, Cyr.H. *catech.*23.2; pastoral care, Cyr.*apol.Thds.*7(p.78.1; 6¹.243E); **c.** to be supported by the people, *Const.App.*2.25.14; **d.** not to marry, Max. *qu.dub.*40(M.90.817C); **4.** of presbyter; **a.** equated with OT priest, *Const.App.*2.26.3; ἱ. synonymous with πρεσβύτερος: πρεσβυτέρων, οὓς καὶ ἱ. καλεῖ Max.*schol.in e.h.*5.5(M.4.164C); cf.*ib.*5.6(164D); Thdr. Stud.*epp.*2.6(M.99.1128C); hence dist. from other clergy ἄλλο λειτουργός, καὶ ἄλλο ἱ. Max.*schol.c.h.*13.4(M.4.101B); ἱ. ... καὶ τῶν ἐπισκόπων ὀλίγοι †Jo.D.*B.J.*33(M.96.1177B); *ib.*35(1193B); **b.** functions; in gen., compared with king's office, Chrys.*hom.4.5 in Is.6:1*(6.127E); μέσος τοῦ θεοῦ καὶ τῆς τῶν ἀνθρώπων φύσεως...ὁ ἱ. *ib.5.1*(6.132E); assisting at baptism, Didym.*Trin.*2.12(M.39.672B); Dion.Ar.*e.h.*2. 2.7(M.3.396C); hearing confessions, Gr.Nyss.*ep.can.*6(M.45.233C); Chrys.*sac.*3.5(p.54.15; 1.383C); Isid.Pel.*epp.*1.338(M.78.377A); †Jo. Jej.*poenit.*(M.88.1889A); celebrating eucharist, Bas.*ep.*93(3.187A,B; M.32.485A); assisting bishop at eucharist, Dion.Ar.*e.h.*3.2(M.3.425C); ‡Sophr.H.*liturg.*11(M.87.3992A); teaching ἡ...τῶν ἱ. [sc. τάξις] φωτιστικὴ καὶ φωταγωγός Dion.Ar.*e.h.*5.1.7(M.3.508C); *ib.*6.3.5(536D); **c.** efficacity; **i.** of priests acting as instruments of God, Chrys. *hom.87.4 in Jo.*(8.518E); id.*prod.Jud.*1.6(2.384B); id.*comm.in Gal.* 4:28(10.711C); **ii.** hence ref. efficacy of their acts as not dependent on their personal holiness, id.*hom.4.5 in Is.6:1*(6.127D); Isid.Pel. *epp.*3.340(M.78.1000C); **d.** holiness requisite in priests, Gr.Naz.*or.* 2.95(M.35.497B); Chrys.*sac.*6.4(p.148.21; 1.424E); τύπος ἱ. τοῦ ποιμνίου Isid.Pel.*epp.*1.319(M.78.368A); their virtue eulogized, Eus.*h.e.*10.4. 2ff.(M.20.849A); Gr.Naz.*or.*19.16(1061D); **e.** subject to bishops, *Const.App.*2.11.1; ὁ...ἱεράρχης διὰ τῶν αὐτοῦ...ἱ. καθαίρων ἢ φωτίζων, αὐτὸς λέγεται καθαίρειν καὶ φωτίζειν Dion.Ar.*c.h.*13.4(M.3.305C); τοὺς ἱ. μιμητὰς γενέσθαι τοῦ ἀρχιερέως..., ὡς κἀκεῖνος τοῦ ἀρχιερέως Χριστοῦ Ant.Mon.*hom.*123(M.89.1817C); Max.*schol.c.h.*13.4(M.4. 101B); Thdr.Stud.*epp.*2.6(M.99.1128C); **f.** relation to others; to be honoured, the honour passing to God himself, Chrys.*hom.2.2 in 2Tim.*(11.668D); cf.id.*hom.65.4 in Gen.*(4.626Cff.); office above that of kings, id.*hom.5.1 in Is.6:1*(6.132E); not to be judged by those below them, id.*hom.2.6 in Rom.16:3*(3.190B); Dion.Ar.*ep.*8.1 (M.3.1088C); Anast.S.*synax.*(M.89.848B); to receive first-fruits from laity, *Const.App.*7.29.1; not exempt from land-tax, unlike OT priests, Thdt.*qu.107 in Gen.*(1.109); **g.** discipline; celibacy implied, Chrys.*Jud.*8.4(1.678D); married, Niceph.Ur.*v.Sym.*220(M.86.3188D); to be suspended from exercise of functions for sexual relations with women other than their wives, †Jo.Jej.*poenit.*(M.88.1908C); **h.** symbolism; priests represent shepherds of Nativity, Or.*hom. 13 in Lc.*(p.93.2); grace of Christ, Mac.Aeg.*carit.*29(M.34.932C); hierarchies of angels, ‡Sophr.H.*liturg.*3(M.87.3984B); *ib.*6(3988A); **5.** of Christians in gen., esp. of 'gnostic', Clem.*str.*7.7(p.28.8; M. 9.452B); as becoming priests through prayer, Esaias *or.*5.3(p.36); ἱερέα φρόνησις, καὶ βίος καὶ εὐγένεια ποιεῖ Nil.*paraen.*9(M.79.1249C); through chastity, ref. Rom.12:1, Isid.Pel.*epp.*3.75(M.78.781C); Oecum.*Apoc.*5:10(p.81); Areth.*Apoc.*12(M.106.584A); **6.** Gnost.; of souls possessing seed of Achamoth (Valent.), Iren.*haer.*1.7.3(M.7. 516A).

ἱερεύ-ω, *sacrifice* τὸν ὑπὲρ ἡμῶν ∼θέντα δοξάζομεν σφᾶς αὐτοὺς ∼οντες Clem.*str.*7.3(p.11.10; M.9.417C); Ἰησοῦς...εἰς τὸν αἰῶνα ∼σεται Jo.Eub.*concept.BMV* 18(M.96.1489C).

ἱέρισσα, ἡ, *priestess* διακονισσῶν μόνον τὸ ἐκκλησιαστικὸν ἐπεδεήθη τάγμα,...οὐδαμοῦ δὲ...ἱ. προσέταξε Epiph.*haer.*79.4(p.478.29; M.42. 745A).

***Ἱεριχούντιος,** *of Jericho,* Chrys.*laud.Paul.*4.1(2.492C); masc. as subst., Bas.*hom.*5.2(2.35A; M.31.241B).

***ἱερογλυφία, ἡ,** *sacred, hieroglyphic writing,* Synes.*provid.*1.18 (p.107.21; M.66.1266C).

ἱερογλύφος, ὁ, *carver of hieroglyphs,* Cyr.*Juln.*9(6².299E).

***ἱερογνωσία, ἡ,** *knowledge of divine things,* Dion.Ar.*c.h.*13.4(M.3. 305A); id.*d.n.*3.3(M.3.684B).

***ἱερογραφέω,** *describe* holy things, Dion.Ar.*e.h.*4.3.7(M.3.481A); *ib.*4.3.12(483A); *ib.*5.1.2(501C).

***ἱερογραφία, ἡ, 1.** *sacred description,* Dion.Ar.*c.h.*2.1(M.3.137A); *ib.*15.2(328C); **2.** *holy scripture* ἱρογραφεία *MAMA* 1.157 (Phrygia, c. 310–320).

ἱερογραφικός, *scriptural,* Dion.Ar.*c.h.*1.3(M.3.124A); *ib.*7.2(208B).

***ἱερογραφικῶς,** *with a description of holy things,* Dion.Ar.*e.h.*3.1 (M.3.424C).

***ἱερογράφος, ὁ,** *sacred writer*; of Moses, ‡Caes.Naz.*dial.*148(M.38. 1100).

***ἱερόγραφος,** *sacredly written*; of scripture, Max.*opusc.*(M.91. 57A).

ἱεροδιδάσκαλος, ὁ, *holy teacher,* Dion.Ar.*d.n.*11.6(M.3.956A).

***ἱεροθαρσαλέως,** *with holy confidence,* Thdot.Anc.*hom.BMV et Sym.*10(M.77.1404C).

***ἱεροθεσία, ἡ,** *legislation about rites and ceremonies,* Dion.Ar.*c.h.* 1.3(M.3.121C); Max.*schol.c.h.*1.3(M.4.32D).

ἱεροθετέω, *make a holy law,* Dion.Ar.*ep.*8.1(M.3.1089A).

***ἱεροθέτης, ὁ,** *ordainer of sacred rites*; of Christ, Thdr.Stud.*epp.* 2.155(M.99.1485A); of a bishop, Steph.Diac.*v.Steph.*(M.100.1112C).

***ἱεροθύω,** *sacrifice*; pass., of Christ in eucharist, ‡Bas.*h.myst.*5 (p.258.30).

***ἱεροκάπηλος, ὁ,** *one who trades in the Temple, Schol.* in *Can. App.*27(*Mon.*2 p.643).

***ἱεροκατήγορος, ὁ,** *accuser of priests,* ‡Jo.D.*ep.Thphl.*15(M.95. 365A).

ἱεροκῆρυξ, ὁ, *one who proclaims holy things*; of inspired writers, Didym.*Trin.*2.22(M.39.553B); Eulog.*palm.*3(M.86.2920A); of preachers, Eust.*engast.*1(p.16.8; M.18.613A); ‡Ath.*annunt.*1(M.28. 917A); ‡Meth.*Sym.et Ann.*1(M.18.348A).

***ἱεροκόρος, ὁ,** *temple servant,* ‡Meth.*Sym.et Ann.*7(M.18.364B).

***ἱεροκτόνος, ὁ,** *slayer of priests,* ‡Jo.D.*ep.Thphl.*22(M.95.373C).

ἱερολογ-έω, *recite* holy things ὕμνον...∼εῖ Dion.Ar.*e.h.*2.2.4(M.3. 393C); ref. composing of legends ∼εῖται τὰ τοῦ Ὀσίριδις Synes. *provid.*2.4(p.121.22; M.66.1272A).

ἱερολογία, ἡ, 1. *speech about the holy*; of words prescribed by the ritual, Dion.Ar.*e.h.*4.3.3(M.3.476D); of praise of God ἡ...τῶν ψαλμῶν ἱ. *ib.*3.3.4(429C); of legends of gods, Synes.*provid.*2.5(p.122.20; M. 66.1272C); **2.** *holy words, holy teaching,* Dion.Ar.*e.h.*5.3.7(M.3.513C); *ib.*2.2.6(396B).

ἱερολόγος, ὁ, *one who speaks of holy things,* Didym.*Trin.*2.12 (M.39.681B); Dion.Ar.*d.n.*4.12(M.3.709A).

***ἱερομάκαρ,** *holy and blessed,* Thdr.Stud.*cant.*10.1(p.355); *Hymn.* (*AS* 1 p.584).

***ἱερομανία, ἡ,** *religious frenzy,* Clem.*prot.*2(p.11.15; M.8.72A).

[*]**ἱερομάντης, ὁ,** *holy seer,* Didym.*Trin.*2.1(M.39.453A).

***ἱερομάρτυς, ὁ,** *holy martyr,* Chrys.*pan.Ign.*tit.(2.592A); Pamph. H.*can.*tit.; Jo.Mon.*hymn.Blas.*1(M.96.1401B); Thdr.Stud.*epp.*2.199 (M.99.1604A).

ἱερομύστης, ὁ, *one initiated in holy things*; of S. Paul, ‡Meth. *Sym.et Ann.*4(M.18.357A); of theologians, Dion.Ar.*d.n.*2.4(M.3. 640D); Max.*schol.d.n.*2.4(M.4.216C); of a saint, Jo.Mon.*hymn.Nic. Myr.*8(M.96.1389A).

ἱερονίκης, ὁ, *winner of the sacred contest*; of a martyr, Eus.*m.P.*3 (p.910.9; M.20.1469B); *ib.*11(p.941.5; 1508A); Euthal.Diac.*epp.Paul.* (M.85.701A).

***ἱεροπλαστία, ἡ,** *representation of holy things*; of figurative descriptions of spiritual entities, Dion.Ar.*c.h.*2.1(M.3.137B); *ib.*2.3 (141A); id.*ep.*9.1(M.3.1104C).

***ἱερόπλαστος,** *divinely formed,* Dion.Ar.*c.h.*1.3(M.3.124A); *ib.*7.2 (208C); id.*myst.*3(M.3.1033B).

***ἱεροπλάστως,** *by divine formation,* Dion.Ar.*c.h.*2.1(M.3.137A).

ἱεροποιέω, 1. *perform sacred functions,* of a pagan priest, Clem. *paed.*3.2(p.238.8; M.8.560B); **2.** *make holy,* Clem.*prot.*9(p.65.5; M.8. 197C) cit. s. γράμμα.

ἱεροποιός, *consecratory* ἱ. ἐπικλήσεσιν ἁγιάζεται Dion.Ar.*e.h.*5.2(M. 3.509B).

***ἱεροπροφήτης, ὁ,** *holy prophet,* ‡Hesych.H.*m.Long.*15(M.93. 1557B).

ἱερός, 1. *holy* ὁ δημιουργὸς...ταῖς ἱ. ... χερσὶν ἔπλασεν τῆς ἑαυτοῦ εἰκόνος χαρακτῆρα *1Clem.*33.4; ἐν τῷ φωτισμῷ ὑμῶν...τὴν ἱ. ἐξέτεινεν [sc. κύριος] φωνὴν λέγων 'υἱός μου εἶ σύ' *Const.App.*2.32.3; of Moses, Clem.*prot.*6(p.52.25; M.8.173C); of apostles, Or.*Jo.*2.29(18; p.202. 28; M.14.360B); Sophr.H.*v.Anast.*(M.92.1689C); ref. clergy τοῦ ἱ.

καταλόγου Constantius Imp.ap.Ath.*apol.sec.*54(p.135.11; M.25.348B); τὸν ἱ. κλῆρον Thdt.*h.rel.*2(3.1130); τῆς ἱ. ... συνόδου CSard.*ep.Alex.* ap.Ath.*apol.sec.*39(p.118.1; M.25.316C); of Christians in general τῷ ἱ. λαῷ Dion.Ar.*ep.*8.1(M.3.1089A); cf.Philost.*h.e.*2.13(M.65.476C); of individual Christians, Or.*Jo.*2.1(p.52.2; M.14.104C); Eus.*h.e.*10.1.2 (M.20.841B); Pall.*v.Chrys.*4(p.24.20; M.47.16); ref. Bible ταῖς ἱ. βίβλοις *1Clem.*43.1; τὰς ἱ. ... γραφάς Eus.*h.e.*2.17.12(180A); of eucharist, *Const.App.*2.33.2; of baptism, Dion.Ar.*e.h.*5.2.6(M.3.508A); **2.** ἱ. νόσος ? *leprosy*, Gr.Nyss.*anim.et res.*(M.46.140A); *elephantiasis*, Sophr.*mir. Cyr.et Jo.*15(M.87.3469C); **3.** neut. as subst.; **a.** *sanctuary*, met., of Church, Clem.*str.*7.4(p.21.22; M.9.437C); Christian bodies, id.*fr.*44 (p.223.4); plur., *monastery buildings*, Sophr.H.*v.Anast.*(M.92.1696A); **b.** *sacred mysteries, sacraments*, *Lit.*ap.*Const.App.*8.9.5; Dion.Ar. *e.h.*5.1.4(M.3.505A).

***'Ιεροσόλυμα, τά, 'Ιερουσαλήμ, ἡ,** *Jerusalem* [genit. 'Ιερουσαλῆς †Apoll.*met.Ps.*50:20(M.33.1384D); dat. 'Ιερουσαλῇ *ib.*64:2(1400C)]; **1.** interpretation 'Ι. ... ὅρασις εἰρήνης ἑρμηνεύεται Clem.*str.*1.5(p.18. 18; M.8.720B); Or.*fr.80 in Jo.*(p.547.19); Eus.*d.e.*6.24(p.293.24; M. 22.481D); 'Ι ... ὅρασις εἰρήνης, ἡ μετέωρος θανάτου Cyr.*glaph.Gen.*2.3 (1.49B); **2.** to be scene of millennium, Just.*dial.*80.5(M.6.668A); as is proved by scripture, *ib.*81.1ff.; *Dial.Ath.et Zacch.*70(p.40); but new Jerusalem to be set up in Egypt, *ib.*54ff.; identified by Montanus with Pepuza and Tymion, Apollon.ap.Eus.*h.e.*5.18.2(M.20.476B); **3.** of heaven; in scripture, symbol of Apoc.21:18ff. explained, Clem.*paed.*2.12(p.228.10; M.8.540C); prefigured by land flowing with milk and honey (Ex.3:8), Or.*Cels.*7.29(p.180.7; M.11.1461B); οὐδὲ περὶ τῆς ἄνω 'Ι. ἀνεκάλυπτον οἱ τοῦ θεοῦ προφῆται Eus.*e.th.*2.20 (p.128.25; M.24.952C); its life described, Gr.Naz.*or.*8.6(M.35.796B); esp. its unchanging quality, Chrys.*exp.in Ps.*47:15(5.202D); Cyr. *Jo.*4.6(4.428A); symbol of paradise in Lc.10:30, Or.*hom.34 in Lc.* (p.201.19); **4.** of Church, in gen. τὰ ἀληθινὰ 'Ι. id.*Jo.*13.13(p.238.8; M.14.420A); Gr.Nyss.*Eun.*10(2 p.233.25; M.45.836A); Nil.*epp.*1.258 (M.79.177D); νοητὴν...'Ι. ... τὴν ἐκκλησίαν Cyr.*Is.*1.2(2.34D,35D); Jo.D.*Gal.*4:26–27(M.95.805D); in scripture: in prophets, Or.*or.*15.3 (p.335.7; M.11.465D); id.*Jo.*10.42(26; p.219.24ff.; 389A); id.*hom. 9.2 in Jer.*(p.65.20; M.13.349D); Meth.*symp.*8.5(p.87.1; M.18.145B); Church attacked by heretics typified by Jerusalem besieged by enemies, Cyr.*Is.*3.4(2.493C); symbolism discussed, Proc.G.*Is.* 49:14–26(M.87.2476Cff.); of individual churches (buildings), Eus. *v.C.*3.33(p.93.15ff.; M.20.1093B); id.*h.e.*10.4.3(M.20.849A); **5.** of the soul, Or.*Jo.*10.28(18; p.201.23,32; M.14.357B,C); id.*hom.38 in Lc.* (p.223.6); οὐ δύναται ψυχὴ καθαρῶς 'Ι. ἐν τῷ παρόντι βίῳ γενέσθαι μόνην εἰρήνην ὁρῶσα καὶ μηδὲν ἁμαρτάνουσα id.*hom.21.2 in Jos.* (p.431.19; cf.M.87.1033C); Eus.*d.e.*6.24(p.293.24; M.22.481D); of holy soul, Meth.*symp.*4.5(p.51.8; M.18.93B); Marc.Er.*opusc.*4(M. 65.1008B); **6.** relation of these senses to one another; prophecies about earthly Jerusalem applicable to the heavenly, Or.*princ.*4.3.8 (p.335.1; M.11.389B); Apoc.21:10–12 wrongly understood of rebuilding of earthly Jerusalem after resurrection, cf.*ib.*2.11.2(p.184. 15; M.241C); of heaven as signifying the soul, because of divine indwelling, Gr.Nyss.*hom.15 in Cant.*(M.44.1097C); of Church as type of heaven, Chrys.*comm.in Gal.*4:26(10.710E); of heaven as already present in soul by way of earnest, Marc.Er.*opusc.*4(M.65. 1009B); of heaven and Church as joined in Christ, Andr.Caes.*Apoc.* 65(M.106.425A); **7.** Gnost. (Naassene) ἡ ἄνω 'Ι. as μήτηρ ζώντων Hipp.*haer.*5.7(p.88.19; M.16.3139A); ref. Jer.17:9 τὴν κάτω 'Ι. ... τὴν κάτω γένησιν τὴν φθαρτήν *ib.*5.8(p.96.2; 3150B); (Valent.) 'Ι. as name of Achamoth, Iren.*haer.*1.5.3(M.7.496B); Hipp.*haer.*6.34 (p.163.4; 3246B); τὴν ⟨εἰς⟩ 'Ι. ἄνοδον σημαίνειν τὴν ἀπὸ τῶν ὑλικῶν εἰς τὸν ψυχικὸν τόπον τυγχάνοντα εἰκόνα τῆς 'Ι. Heracleon ap.Or.*Jo.* 10.33(19; p.206.25; M.14.365C).

***'Ιεροσολυμίτης, ὁ,** *inhabitant of Jerusalem*, Iren.*haer.*3.21.2(M.7. 947A).

ἱεροσυλέω, *commit sacrilege against*; of rape of consecrated virgins, Gr.Naz.*ep.*206(M.37.341B); met. τὸν ναὸν τοῦ θεοῦ ἱ. [sc. one who is not free from passion] ‡Just.*ep.Zen.et Ser.*3(M.6.1185C).

ἱεροσυλία, ἡ, *sacrilege*; of fornication with deaconess, Bas.*ep.*199 *can.*44(3.296C; M.32.729B); idolatry, †Bas.*Is.*124(1.465E; M.30.320C); of stealing eccl. property, Chrys.*hom.3.5 in Ac.princ.*(3.78C); of luxurious living by clergy, Pall.*v.Chrys.*12(p.70.4; M.47.39); of degradation of bishop to priesthood, CChalc.*can.*29; included among σωματικὰ πάθη, Jo.D.*virt.*(M.95.88C); of betrayal of Christ, *cat.1Jo.*5:16–17(p.143.1); penalties fo. ἱ., Gr.Nyss.*ep.can.*8(M.45. 236A).

ἱερόσυλος, ὁ, 1. *plunderer* of sacred things οἱ τοῦ γράμματος ἱ. Gr.Naz.*or.*30.1(p.108.4; M.36.104C); Chrys.*hom.12.2 in Ac.*(9.98E); id.*hom.3.5 in Ac.princ.*(3.78D); Pall.*v.Chrys.*19(p.147.5; M.47.82); **2.** as adj., *sacrilegious*, *Cod.Afr.*92; Vict.Carth.*ep.*(M.*PL.*87.90B ἱεροστύλῳ by misprint).

***ἱεροσύντακτος,** *assembled for sacred purposes*, *Hymn.*(*AS* 1 p.596).

***ἱεροτάφιον, τό,** *holy tomb*, Ephr.3.255A.

***ἱεροτελεστής, ὁ,** *one who initiates into sacred things*; of scriptural writers, Dion.Ar.*e.h.*1.4(M.3.376B); of clergy, *ib.*5.3.8(516A); τοῦ ἱ. ... πατριάρχου Thdr.Stud.*epp.*2.126(M.99.1409D).

ἱεροτελεστία, ἡ, *celebration of sacred rites*, ‡Sophr.H.*liturg.*4(M. 87.3985B).

***ἱεροτελεστικός,** *sanctifying*; superl., of eucharist, Dion.Ar.*e.h.* 2.2.7(M.3.396D).

***ἱερότης, ἡ,** *priesthood*; as title of address, *Pers.*(p.11.1).

***ἱερότυπος,** *representing holy things*, Dion.Ar.*c.h.*2.3(M.3.140C).

***ἱεροτύραννος, ὁ,** *tyrant in sacred matters*, Procl.CP *ep.*(p.67.32; M.65.881C).

ἱερουργ-έω, 1. *perform priestly functions*; ref. denial of priesthood to women, Epiph.*haer.*79.3(p.478.12; M.42.744C); of women sacrificing to BMV, id.*ep.Arab.*ap.*haer.*78.23(p.473.13; 736C); ref. suspension as only penance for clergy, †Jo.Jej.*poenit.*(M.88.1908A); Thdr.Stud.*epp.*2.32(M.99.1205A); pres. ptcpl. as subst., CAlex.*ep.* ap.Ath.*apol.sec.*11(p.96.25; M.25.268C); **2.** trans., *minister* the gospel, Cyr.*Joel.*8(3.207C); Dion.Ar.*c.h.*3.2(M.3.165B); Eustrat.*v. Eutych.*81(M.86.2365C); *offer* sacrifice, of Christ ἑαυτὸν ἱερουργήσας Didym.*Trin.*3.27(M.39.944A); Cyr.*Jo.*5.3(4.496E); cf.id.*Os.*40(3.71C); eucharistic ἀμνὸν...μυστικῶς καθ' ἑκάστην ∼ούμενον Or.*hom.13 in Lc.*(p.93.11; some catenae omit or ascribe to Sev. Ant.); αὐτὸς [sc. Χριστός]...∼ούμενος διὰ τῆς μυστικῆς εὐλογίας Tit.Bost.*fr.Lc.* 22:16(p.241); Gr.Nyss.*bapt.Chr.*(M.46.581C); Cyr.*Zach.*115(3.813C); ref. spiritual sacrifices ἱ. τῷ θεῷ τὴν φιλανθρωπίαν Max.*ambig.*(M.91. 1417B); of apostles sacrificing themselves to God, *cat.2Cor.*2:17 (p.363.12).

ἱερούργημα, τό, *sacrifice*; of eucharist, *A.*(*Pass.*)*Andr.*6(p.14.31; M.2.1228B).

ἱερουργία, ἡ, *holy work*; **1.** of OT sacrifices as typical of Christ's, Eus.*d.e.*1.10(p.45.23; M.22.88A); *ib.*7.1(p.319.17; 521C); Thdt.*eran.*3 (4.205); **2.** of eucharist τὴν πνευματικὴν...ἱ. Eus.*d.e.*5.13(p.222.10; 365D); μυστικὴν ἱ. ‡Procl.CP *tract.*(M.65.849C); *ib.*(852A); Anast.S. *synax.*(M.89.829B); *Lit.Jac.*(p.166.11); *Lit.Chrys.*(p.310.2); as ἡ ἱ., *A.Andr.*B 6(p.15.18); *Const.App.*8.16.5; Philost.*h.e.*9.4(M.65.569B); offered in private houses, Leont.H.*monoph.*(M.86.1892A); **3.** liturg. in gen.; of worship of God, Dion.Ar.*e.h.*1.4(M.3.376C); of liturg. rites αἱ ἱ. *ib.*5.1.1(500D); ἡ ἱ. τοῦ μεγάλου Βασιλείου καὶ 'Ιωάννου ‡Sophr.H.*liturg.*2(M.87.3981D); εὐχὰς μυστηρίων, θείας ἱ. *ib.*(3981B); CTrull.*can.*32; **4.** ref. hierarchy ὁ Χριστὸς...τὰ τῆς ἐν ἀνθρώποις ἱ. ... διὰ τῶν αὐτοῦ θεραπευτῶν ἐπιτελεῖ Eus.*d.e.*5.3(p.222.9; M.22. 365C); of priesthood, Chrys.*hom.29.1 in Rom.*(9.731A); Jewish priesthood, Cyr.*Zach.*33(3.705A); of exercise of clerical functions, suspended for certain sins, †Jo.Jej.*poenit.*(M.88.1908C); **5.** of spiritual sacrifices, prayer as λογικὴν ἱ. Or.*or.*11(p.321.20; M.11. 448B); virtue, Eus.*d.e.*1.8(p.39.26; M.22.76C); τὸ ἑαυτοῦ προσάγειν σῶμα τῇ ἱ. Gr.Nyss.*v.Mos.*(M.44.388C).

ἱερουργικός, 1. *priestly*, Iren.*haer.*3.11.8(M.7.886B); Hipp.*haer.*9. 30(p.263.18; M.16.3410B); ref. episcopal order ἡ ἱ. ἐνέργεια Philost. *h.e.*9.10(M.65.576C); **2.** *pertaining to divine worship*, Pall.*h.Laus.*144 (M.34.1249A).

ἱερουργός, ὁ, 1. *one who discharges a sacred function*; of angels, ref. Is.6 ἱ. τῆς τοῦ προφήτου καθάρσεως Dion.Ar.*c.h.*13.2(M.3.300B); of priests and preachers τῶν εὐαγγελικῶν κηρυγμάτων οἱ ἅγιοι ἱ. Cyr.*Ps.*45:9(M.69.1049C); Dion.Ar.*e.h.*3.3.7(M.3.436C); Jo.Mon. *hymn.Blas.*9(M.96.1405D); abs., Ath.*exp.Ps.*50:20(M.27.244C); Cyr. *Soph.*39(3.617D); Proc.G.*Dt.*15:17(M.87.913A); **2.** as adj., *priestly* πρὸς τῆς ἱ. [sc. δυνάμεως] πεφωτισμένους Dion.Ar.*e.h.*5.3.8(516B); Εὐσεβίου τὰς ἱ. αὐτῷ χεῖρας ἐπιθεμένου Philost.*h.e.*3.4(M.65.484A).

ἱεροφαντέω, *instruct in mysteries*, ref. conversion to Christianity ἱ. ... ὁ κύριος Clem.*prot.*12(p.84.25; M.8.241A).

ἱεροφάντης, ὁ, *teacher of sacred truths*; of Christ, Eus.*Marcell.*1.1 (p.5.27; M.24.721B); of prophets, id.*d.e.*proem.(p.2.11; M.22.16A); of Moses, Clem.*prot.*2(p.18.23; M.8.93A); Eus.*d.e.*4.15(p.174.20; M.22.292A); ‡Caes.Naz.*dial.*20(M.38.876); of David, Jo.D.*f.o.*1.3 (M.94.793C); of S. Paul, Pall.*v.Chrys.*11(p.64.3; M.47.36); ‡Meth. *Sym.et Ann.*2(M.18.352C); of S. Luke, Rom.Mel.(*AS* 1 p.159); of Const., Eus.*l.C.*3(p.200.20; M.20.1328B); of Chrys., Pall.*v.Chrys.*11 (p.64.3; M.47.36).

ἱεροφαντία, ἡ, *teaching about sacred things*; of exegesis, Clem.*str.*

4.1(p.249.9; M.8.1216C); Eus.*v.C.*4.22(p.125.25; M.20.1169A); of scripture αἱ ἱ. id.*p.e.*11.9(523D; M.21.868C).

ἱεροφαντικός, *hierophantic,* Clem.*prot.*2(p.16.3; M.8.84A); Thdt. *affect.*1(p.30.26; 4.721).

ἱεροφάντωρ, ὁ, *teacher of sacred mysteries*; of Moses, Epiph.*haer.* 79.2(p.477.19; M.42.741D).

ἱεροφόρος, *bearing holy things,* Mod.*dorm.*13(M.86.3308D).

***ἱεροφωνία, ἡ,** *sacred utterance,* Eust.*engast.*25(p.56.25; M.18. 665D).

ἱερόφωνος, *uttering holy things*; superl., of Isaiah, Thdr.Stud. *epp.*1.7(M.99.932A).

ἱεροψάλτης, ὁ, *singer of psalms*; Jewish, Bas.*hom.in Ps.*61(1. 193C; M.29.469C); Cyr.*Zach.*33(3.705B); id.*Ps.*38:1(M.69.969B); partic. of David, Serap.*Man.*50(p.71; M.18.1245C); Didym.*Trin.*2.6(M. 39.549A); †Thdt.*Nest.*(4.1050); Leont.B.*Nest.et Eut.*3(M.86.1269C); Christian, CTrull.*can.*33.

ἱερόω, 1. *dedicate, consecrate,* usu. pass. ptcpl.; of monks as consecrated to God, Eus.*d.e.*1.8(p.39.21; M.22.76C); of Christians in gen., id.*e.th.*3.16(p.175.11; M.24.1033C); Dion.Ar.*d.n.*3.2(M.3.681C); Philost.*h.e.*3.5(M.65.485A); of ordaining: Jewish priests, Cyr.*ador.* 2(1.60B); Christian clergy, Soz.*h.e.*1.23.2(M.67.925B); chiefly ref. major orders, Eus.*d.e.*1.9(p.43.4; 81D); ref. immunity from taxation, Bas.*ep.*104(3.198D; M.32.509C); Socr.*h.e.*1.11.3(M.67.101C); also subdeacons, Gel.Cyz.*h.e.*2.33.1(M.85.1336A); priests, deacons, †Jo.Jej.*poenit.*(M.88.1909A); of all clergy opp. οἱ πολλοί, Thdt.*h.e.*1. 22.2(3.803); *ib.*3.6.5(918); ‡Caes.Naz.*dial.*140(M.38.1068); of deaconesses and πρεσβυτέρισσαι, †Jo.Jej.*poenit.*(M.88.1912B); †Jo.Jej.*serm.* (M.88.1921D); **2.** med.; **a.** *offer sacrifice, act as priest*; of Christ, Eus. *d.e.*4.10(p.168.2; M.22.280C); *ib.*10 proem.(p.445.12; 716B); **b.** *consecrate* τὰς ἐκκλησίας ἱερωσάμενος Philost.*h.e.*3.5(M.65.485A).

ἱέρωσις, ἡ, *priesthood,* Dion.Ar.*c.h.*1.3(M.3.124A).

ἱερωσύνη, ἡ, *priesthood*; **1.** of Christ, Eus.*e.th.*3.16(p.175.23; M. 24.1036A); αὐτὸς...μετὰ τῶν μαθητῶν...τὴν ἱ. ἔχει *Dial.Ath.et Zacch.* 71(p.41); διὰ τὸ μένειν αὐτὸν εἰς τὸν αἰῶνα, ἀπαράβατον ἔχει τὴν ἱ. Cyr. *ador.*12(1.432E); **2.** Christian; **a.** of episcopate, *Const.App.*2.34.4; to be received only by those who have passed through lower grades of ministry, CSard.*can.*10; ἀργυρίῳ ἱ. πιπράσκεται, εἴ γε καὶ ἱ. Pall. *v.Chrys.*14(p.84.12; M.47.48); ref. suspension for communion with heretics τῆς ἱ. ἀφαίρεσις Philost.*h.e.*7.6(M.65.544B); χρημάτων...τὰς ἱ. καὶ διδόντας καὶ λαμβάνοντας [sc. Arians] *ib.*10.3(585A); **b.** of presbyterate, Pall.*v.Chrys.*5(p.29.24; M.47.19); δέξαι...τῆς ἱ. τὸ δῶρον, τῆς μὲν ἐμῆς δεξιᾶς ὑπερουργούσης, τῆς δὲ τοῦ παναγίου πνεύματος τοῦτο χάριτος χορηγούσης Thdt.*h.rel.*15(3.1220); ref. confession which may be made to monks who have not priesthood, ‡Jo. D.*conf.*11(p.119.24; M.95.296A); **c.** of major orders in gen., Epiph. *exp.fid.*21(p.522.8ff.; M.42.824B); Thdt.*Phil.*1:1(3.445); Dion.Ar. *e.h.*1.1(M.3.372B); ref. pope κεφαλὴ τῆς κατὰ Χριστὸν ἱ. Jo.VI CP *ep.* (M.96.1417A); **d.** ref. characteristics of Christian priesthood ἱ. ... ἁγνισμὸς φρενῶν, θεῷ φέρων ἄνθρωπον, ἀνθρώπῳ θεόν Gr.Naz.*carm.* 1.2.34.227(M.37.962A); cf.Cyr.*Joel.*8(3.206C); Isid.Pel.*epp.*3.20(M.78. 745B); relation to secular power τῆς ἱ. ὁμοτίμου τῆς βασιλείας οὔσης, μᾶλλον μὲν οὖν ἐν τοῖς ἱεροῖς τόποις καὶ τὰ πρῶτα ἐχούσης Soz.*h.e.*2.34. 6(M.67.1032C); Thdr.Stud.*epp.*1.16(M.99.961A); priesthood being superior, *Const.App.*6.2.1; ἄλλοι ὅροι βασιλείας, καὶ ἄλλοι ὅροι ἱ.· ἀλλ' αὕτη μείζων ἐκείνης Chrys.*hom.4.4 in Is.6:1*(6.127B); more difficult to fulfil than monastic vocation, id.*sac.*6.5(p.150.4; 1.425C); typified by OT priesthood, Cyr.*ador.*11(1.401C); as beginning at Last Supper, Thdt.*Ps.*109:4(1.1396); as being of order of Melchizedek, id.*Jer.*33:18(2.558); Max.*qu.dub.*40(M.90.817C); ἡ ἀληθὴς ἱ. χαρακτὴρ ...τῆς...θεότητος id.*ep.*31(M.91.625A); *ib.*21(604D).

***ἱερωτικός,** *of sacred love,* Dion.Ar.*d.n.*4.11(M.3.709A).

Ἰησοῦς, ὁ, *Jesus, Joshua*;

A. of Joshua, son of Nun; **1.** of book of Joshua as canonical, Ath.*ep.fest.*39.4(M.26.1436B); Gr.Naz.*carm.*1.1.2.13(M.37.473A); as written by author later than Joshua (cf. book mentioned in Jos.10:13), Thdt.*qu.14 in Jos.*(1.312); **2.** of Joshua as type of Jesus Christ; **a.** parallel discussed at length, Cyr.H.*catech.*10.11; Chrys. *hom.1.5 in Is.6:1*(6.103Bff.); **b.** typological value depending on name, *Barn.*12.8; Clem.*paed.*1.7(p.125.29; M.8.324A); holding good in form Ἰωσουέ, because it means θεοῦ σωτήριον, Eus.*d.e.*4.17 (p.200.3; M.22.333A); **c.** other similarities: succeeded Moses, as Christ succeeded Law, Or.*Jo.*6.44(26; p.157.17; M.14.276D); was legislator, like Christ, Eus.*d.e.*4.17(p.196.13ff.; 328A); crossing of Jordan by Joshua as figure of institution of baptism by Christ, Nil.*epp.*1.52(M.79.105C).

B. of Joshua the high priest, as type of Jesus Christ, Just.*dial.* 115.4(M.6.741C); because of his name and because he led the people out of captivity, Eus.*d.e.*4.17(p.198.1ff.; M.22.329B).

C. of Jesus Christ (v. Χριστός); **1.** of the name; **a.** etym.; meaning saviour, Just.*1apol.*33.7(M.6.381C); id.*2apol.*6.4(M.6.453B); ἑρμηνεύεται...Ἰ. πῇ μὲν σωτήρ, πῇ δὲ σωτηρία ‡Ath.*serm.fid.*22(p.18; M.26.1276A); Sophr.H.*or.*2.29(M.87.3253A); other derivations σωτήρ in sense of healer, Eus.*d.e.*4.10(p.168.27ff.; M.22.281A); Ἰ. ... ἐστὶ κατὰ μὲν Ἑβραίους σωτήρ, κατὰ δὲ τὴν Ἑλλάδα γλῶσσαν, ὁ ἰώμενος Cyr.H.*catech.*10.13; Epiph.*haer.*29.4(p.325.23; M.41.397C); **b.** as name of Christ as man, Eus.*d.e.*4.10.19(p.168.27; M.22.281A); ἄνθρωπος γενόμενος, κληθεὶς Ἰ. Ath.*Ar.*1.42(M.26.100A); Cyr.*Arcad.*(p.80.41; 5^2.70E); **c.** ref. invocation of name; to heal sickness, put demons to flight, etc., Or.*Cels.*1.67(p.121.23; M.11.785C); Eus.*d.e.*3.6(p.138. 30ff.; M.22.233Cff.); to prevent evil phantasmata during sleep, Diad.*perf.*31(p.34.23); continual repetition of name producing self-knowledge and love of God, *ib.*59(p.66.5ff.); **d.** symbolism; ref. Ps.32 τὸ δεκάχορδον ψαλτήριον τὸν λόγον Ἰ. μηνύει, τῷ στοιχείῳ τῆς δεκάδος φανερούμενον Clem.*paed.*2.4(p.183.33; M.8.444C); Gnost.; by numerical symbolism Ἰ. signifies Χρειστός (Marcosian), Iren. *haer.*1.15.2(M.7.617B); letters of name adding up to 888, so that Ἰ. represents all letters of alphabet and is therefore called *A* and *Ω*, *ib.*1.15.2(616A); Ἰ. ... ἐστιν ἐπίσημον ὄνομα, ἐξ ὧν γράμματα, ὑπὸ πάντων τῶν τῆς κλήσεως γινωσκόμενον *ib.*1.14.4(604A); of name Χρειστὸς Ἰ. as the λόγος spoken by Ἀλήθεια, *ib.*(601B); cf. *Jesus autem nomen secundum...Hebraeorum linguam...significans dominum eum qui continet coelum et terram* [i.e. composed of initial letters of [יהוה, שמים, וארץ], *ib.*2.24.2(789A); **2.** in Gnost. and other systems; **a.** Ἰ. as aeon τὸν Παράκλητον οἱ ἀπὸ Οὐαλεντίνου τὸν Ἰ. λέγουσιν, ὅτι πλήρης τῶν αἰώνων ἐλήλυθεν Clem.*exc.Thdot.*23 (p.114.16; M.9.669B); Hipp.*haer.*6.32(p.160.8; M.16.3242C); cf.Iren. *haer.*1.15.1(M.7.613Aff.); **b.** his birth; **i.** as son of Joseph and Mary, doctrine held by Carpocrates, Iren.*haer.*1.25.1(680C); Epiph.*haer.* 27.2(p.301.10ff.; M.41.364D); by Cerinthus, Iren.*haer.*1.26.1(685D); Epiph.*haer.*28.1(p.314.4; 380A); Thdt.*haer.*2.3(4.329); cf.Just.Gn. ap.Hipp.*haer.*5.26(p.131.20; 3202B); also by Ebionites, Iren.*haer.*1. 26.2 *ib.*(M.16.3342B); Thdt.*haer.*2.1(4.328); doctrine refuted, Epiph. *haer.*27.8(p.312.24; 377B); **ii.** as born of BMV but generated by Demiurge and Sophia (Valent.), Hipp.*haer.*6.35(p.164.18; 3247C); **iii.** as a man born of a virgin (Ophite), Thdt.*haer.*1.14(4.308); so Artemon, *ib.*2.4(330); **iv.** as descending from heaven without human birth, so as to avoid contact with matter (Marcion), Hipp. *haer.*7.31(p.217.13; 3335B); **c.** as possessing σῶμα ψυχικόν (Heracleon and Ptolemaeus), *ib.*6.35(p.165.7; 3250A); **d.** as redeemer; needing redemption himself (Valent.), Clem.*exc.Thdot.*22(p.114.14; M.9. 669B); but τὰ σπέρματα ὁ Ἰ. ... ἐπὶ τῶν ὤμων βαστάσας εἰσάγει εἰς τὸ πλήρωμα. ὦμοι γὰρ τοῦ σπέρματος ὁ Ἰ. λέγεται, κεφαλὴ δὲ ὁ Χριστός *ib.*42(p.120.3; 680A); as delivering believers from the evil creator of this world (Marcion), Thdt.*haer.*1.24(4.316); **e.** ref. Passion; acc. many systems the Christ, who descended on Jesus at baptism, withdrew before Passion and left Jesus to suffer, e.g. Ophite, cf.Iren.*haer.*1.30.13(M.7.702B); Cerinthian, *ib.*1.26.1(M.16. 3342A); Thdt.*haer.*2.3(4.330); but acc. Basilides Simon of Cyrene suffered in place of Jesus, cf.Iren.*haer.*1.24.4(677A); Epiph.*haer.*24. 3(p.260.5ff.; M.41.312B); **f.** ref. equivalent names in Valent. teaching, Iren.*haer.*1.2.6(M.7.465A); λέγει...Ἰ. Χριστόν...καὶ Σωτῆρα καὶ Χριστὸν καὶ Λόγον καὶ Σταυρὸν καὶ Μεταγωγέα καὶ Ὀροθέτην καὶ Ὅρον Epiph.*haer.*31.7(p.396.7; M.41.485D); **g.** (Manich.) of Jesus as tree of knowledge of good and evil, Hegem.*Arch.*11(p.18.4; M.10. 1445A); **3.** Jesus as divine name; ref. Ex.23:20 regarded as one of names of God, Just.*dial.*75.1ff.(M.6.652A); used of second Person, to whom OT theophanies are attributed, *ib.*113.4(736D); common to Father and Son because of their oneness of nature and perh. because of supposed Hebr. meaning, 'Jehovah Salvation', Iren. *haer.*4.17.6(M.7.1024B).

D. as name of Barabbas παλαιοῖς...πάνυ ἀντιγράφοις ἐντυχὼν εὗρον καὶ αὐτὸν τὸν Βαραββᾶν Ἰ. λεγόμενον Or.*comm.ser.121 in Mt.* (p.255.25); suggestion that name was added to text by heretics *ut habeant aliqua convenientia dicere fabulis suis de similitudine nominis Jesu et Barabbae, ib.*(p.256.9; M.13.1772D).

***ἰθμός, ὁ,** *strainer* ὅταν...ἡ τροφή...οἷον ἰ. τινι διακριθεῖσα, καὶ τὸ ἧπαρ καταλαβοῦσα, τὴν εἰς αἷμα μεταβολὴν ὑπομείνῃ...Thdt.*carit.*(3. 1297).

[*]**ἰθυδίκη, ἡ,** = εὐθυδίκη, *right judgement,* Gr.Naz.*carm.*2.2 (epitaph.)106.2(M.38.66A); †Apoll.*met.Ps.*9:17 (εὐθυδίκην M.33. 1321D).

ἰθύδικος, *righteous,* Gr.Naz.*carm.*2.2(poem.)7.2(M.37.1551A).

***ἰθυδρομέω**, *run* or *hasten directly*, Evagr.*h.e.*1.13(p.22.3; M.86.2456B).

***ἰθυνόος**, *of righteous mind*, †Apoll.*met.Ps.*10:2(M.33.1325A).

ἰθυντής, ὁ, *director*; of bishops, *Cod.Afr.*53(Lat. *rectores*).

ἰθύντωρ, ὁ, = foreg., Gr.Naz.*carm.*2.1.34.141(M.37.1317A); Nonn.*par.Jo.*6:14(M.43.796B).

ἰθυπορέω, *advance straight*, Max.*opusc.*(M.91.185B).

ἰθυπόρος, *going straight on*, Nonn.*par.Jo.*12:35(M.43.856C); *ib.* 19:29(904C).

ἰθύς, *straight*; ἐς τὸ ἰ. to the *point*, Men.*exc.gent.*28(p.471.6; M.113.840A).

***ἰθυτενῶς**, *directly*, †Cyr.*coll.VT*(6^4.64D; M.77.1272B); ‡Proc.G.*Pr.*7:8(M.87.1281B).

***ἰθύτομος**, *cut straight*, Dion.Ar.*c.h.*15.9(M.3.337D).

***ἰθύφρων**, *upright*, †Apoll.*met.Ps.*91:16(M.33.1452B); *ib.*93:15(1453A).

[*]**ἱκαν-έω**, *be sufficient* ~ήσει...ὃ δέδωκα ὑμῖν...πρὸς χρείαν Thdr.Stud.*epp.*2.180(M.99.1557A).

***ἱκανοδότις**, ἡ, *giver of satisfaction*, Ephr.3.180E.

***ἱκανοκόσμητος**, *becomingly adorned*, ‡Chrys.*ador.*2(11.824B).

ἱκανός, *sufficient*; in phrase ἱκανὰ...δούς giving *security*, Chrys.*hom.1.1 in 1Thess.*(11.427B).

ἱκανότης, ἡ, **1.** *sufficiency* ἱ. ... ἕξις ἐστὶν ἐξικνουμένη πρὸς τὸ οἰκεῖον πέρας ἀνελλιπῶς Clem.*paed.*2.12(p.233.22; M.8.552B); **2.** *proficiency* ἐν τοῖς ἱεροῖς λόγοις ἱ. Eus.*h.e.*6.18.20(M.20.560B); cf.id.*d.e.* 3.7(p.142.13; M.22.240B).

ἱκαν-όω, intrans., *be sufficient, qualify* ~οῦσι πρὸς μαρτυρίαν Amph.*hom.*3.3(M.39.61C); pass., *be made complete, brought to perfection* χαρὰν...ἱκανουμένην Thdr.Stud.*epp.*1.35(M.99.1028D).

ἱκεσία, ἡ, *supplication* ἱκεσίας...λέγει τὴν ὅλην λειτουργίαν *Schol.* in *Cod.Afr.*103(*Mon.*2 p.650); written, Thdt.*h.e.*4.32.2(3.1011); Marc.Diac.*v.Porph.*46.

ἱκέται, οἱ, *Hicetae*; monks, perh. Messalians, who used dancing in their worship, Jo.D.*haer.*87(M.94.756C).

ἱκετευτικῶς, *by way of supplication*, Olymp.*Job* 7:21(M.93.104C).

***ἱκετηρικός**, *suppliant*, Eus.*v.C.*4.22(p.125.22, v.l. ἱκετήριος M.20.1169A).

***ἰκριόεις**, *of the Cross*, Eudoc.*Cypr.*2.456(M.85.864A).

ἴκριον, τό, *scaffold, gallows*; of cross, Eus.*d.e.*3.4(p.115.1; M.22.196D); Serap.*Man.*40(p.59; M.18.1224D); Isid.Pel.*epp.*3.130(M.78.829D); in form εἴκριον, *Lit.Jac.*(*NBP* 10^2 p.106).

***ἰκρύπτιος**, *with one's back on a wooden rack* ἰ., δεθείς Jo.Mon.*hymn.Blas.*6(M.96.1404C).

ἰκτερώδης, *jaundiced*, Gr.Nyss.*hom.opif.*12.4(M.44.160A).

ἱλάριος, **1.** *pertaining to the Hilaria*, festival of Magna Mater τῶν ἱ. ἡμερῶν Dion.Ar.*ep.*8.6(M.3.1097C); Max.*schol.ep.8.6 Dion.Ar.*(M.4.556A,B); **2.** *of rejoicing* τὰς ἱ. ἡμέρας [i.e. Lent] Thdr.Stud.*epp.*2.147(M.99.1460C).

***ἱλαροποιός**, *making glad*, Cyr.*ador.*11(1.392D).

***ἱλαροπρόσωπος**, *of cheerful countenance*, *A.Jo.*88(p.194.16).

ἱλαρύν-ω, *gladden, rejoice*, †Hipp.*theoph.*1(p.257.15; M.10.852B); εἰς αὐτὸν ἀναφέρεται τὸν κύριον ἡ ἄμπελος πολλαχῶς...ὡς τοῦ...κυρίου τὰς καρδίας ~οντος τῶν ἀνθρώπων Meth.*symp.*10.5(p.128.1; M.18.201B); μικρὸν ~θεὶς τῷ προσώπῳ ‡Chrys.*hom.*13(13.253A); *A.Barth.*2(p.132.19).

ἱλάσκ-ομαι, **1.** pass., *be merciful, gracious* ἐπὶ καρδίᾳ συντετριμμένῃ θεὸς ~εται †Bas.*Is.*24(1.398B; M.30.165A); ἱλάσθητι, δέσποτα Ath.*Ar.*3.63(M.26.456A); **2.** pass. with active meaning, *forgive* παρακαλεῖ τὸν θεὸν ἱλασθῆναι αὐτῷ τὰς ἀνομίας αὐτοῦ *Didasc.Jac.* 4.3(p.64.9); **3.** med.; *worship*, ref. accusation agst. Christians τὴν Κωνσταντίνου εἰκόνα...θυσίαις...~εσθαι Philost.*h.e.*2.17(M.65.480A); **4.** med., *restore by expiating* ὑπὲρ πάντων ~όμενος τὰ πρὸς τὸν θεόν Ath.*Ar.*2.7(M.26.161A).

ἱλασμός, ὁ, **1.** *favour* of God, obtained by prayer, Jo.Eub.*concept.BMV* 3(M.96.1464B); **2.** *means of atonement* ἱ. ... ἡ δι' ὑπακοῆς... ἁγνεία Clem.*str.*4.25(p.318.26; M.8.1368B); Ath.*ep.Serap.*4.23(M.26.676A); ref. Christ ἀδικιῶν ἱλασμὸν τῶν εἰς αὐτὸν πεπιστευκότων Eus.*d.e.*8.2(p.371.15; M.22.604A); ἐπειδὴ γάρ ἐστιν ἀρχιερεὺς τῶν ἡμετέρων ψυχῶν...τὰς ὑπὲρ ἡμῶν διαλέξεις ποιεῖται πρεπωδέστατα, πιστεύειν ἡμᾶς ἀναπείθων ὅτι καὶ νῦν ἱ. ἐστι περὶ τῶν ἁμαρτιῶν ἡμῶν, καὶ παράκλητος δίκαιος Cyr.*Jo.*11.4(4.949C); *ib.*11.8(967A); ref. Ps.129:4 ὁ δὲ τοῦ 'κύριε' διπλασιασμός, θαυμάζοντός ἐστι τῆς τοῦ θεοῦ φιλανθρωπίας τὸν ὄγκον, παρ' ἧς καὶ τὸν ἱ. εἶναί φησιν, ἀλλ' οὐκ ἐν τοῖς ἡμετέροις κατορθώμασιν Or.*Ps.*129:3(p.327); cf. τί ἐστιν [Ps.129:4a]; οὐκ ἐν τοῖς ἡμετέροις κατορθώμασιν, ἀλλ' ἐν τῇ ἀγαθότητι τῇ σῇ ἐστι τὸ διαφυγεῖν τὴν κόλασιν Chrys.*exp.in Ps.*129:4(5.369D); Thdt.*Ps.*129:4(1.1503); ὁ τοῦ σύμπαντος κόσμου...ἱ. ... Χριστός Mod.*dorm.*10(M.86.3305A).

ἱλαστήριος, **A.** *propitiatory*; **1.** in gen.; of hands raised in prayer, Niceph.Ur.*v.Sym.*74(M.86.3056A); of prayers ἱ. πρὸς τὸν θεόν *ib.*109(3089A); of cup of Christ's agony, ‡Caes.Naz.*dial.*135(M.38.1040); **2.** neut. as subst., *place of propitiation, mercy-seat* in Temple; **a.** exeg. Rom.3:25, as type of Christ in respect of atonement; detailed typology, cf.Or.*Rom.*3.8(M.14.946C–951B); Eus.*d.e.* 8.2(p.371.6; M.22.601D); Chrys.*hom.7.2 in Rom.*(9.485C); τέθειται γὰρ ἱ. διὰ πίστεως...ἐπειδὴ γὰρ πεποίηται τῆς ἁπάντων ζωῆς ἀντάλλαγμα τὸ ἴδιον αἷμα,...ἱλεών τε καὶ εὐμενῆ κατέστησεν ἡμῖν τὸν... πατέρα Cyr.*Rom.*3:21(M.74.780B); ἱ. ὁ υἱός...καθίστησι γὰρ τοῖς ἐπὶ τῆς γῆς εὐμενῆ τὸν πατέρα id.*Pulch.*(p.54.7; 5^2.169C); τὸ ἀληθινὸν ἱ. ...ἐστὶ Χριστός. ἐκεῖνο γὰρ τὸ παλαιὸν τούτου τὸν τύπον ἐπλήρου. ἁρμόττει δὲ αὐτῷ ὡς ἀνθρώπῳ τὸ ὄνομα, οὐχ ὡς θεῷ Thdt.*Rom.*3:25(3.43); Jo.D.*Rom.*3:25(M.95.465A); **b.** fig. of Christ's humanity ὑπὸ τῆς ἐμψύχου κιβωτοῦ, ὡς ἐπὶ ἱ., ἐπὶ γῆς πομπεύει ‡Meth.*Sym. et Ann.*1(M.18.349A); **c.** met. of BMV, *ib.*10(372D), cf.Ephr.3.525D; Mod.*dorm.*10(M.86.3305A); **d.** fig. of sanctuary of church, ‡Bas.*h.myst.*59(p.393.27) = ‡Germ.CP *contempl.*(M.98.429B).

B. *reconciling*, ref. absolution ἐπιθέντος γὰρ τὰς ἱ. χεῖρας τοῦ Θεοφίλου Philost.*h.e.*4.7(M.65.521A).

ἱλατεύ-ω, *be gracious, propitious* ἐρωτήσω τὸν κύριον ἵνα ~σηταί μοι Herm.*vis.*1.2.1; ~ει [sc. God] ταῖς ἁμαρτίαις αὐτῶν Hesych.H.*Ps.tit.*77(M.27.977C).

ἱλε-όομαι, *bring about by propitiation* στῆθι καὶ ~ωσαι μεταστραφῆναι τὴν καταιγίδα εἰς αὔραν τοῦ ἁγίου πνεύματος Thdr.Stud.*epp.*2.9(M.99.1141A).

***ἱλεωποιέομαι**, *propitiate*, Ephr.1.42B; id.3.152C; Ant.Mon.*hom.* 121(M.89.1809B).

ἱλεωτήριον, τό, *propitiatory sacrifice*, Gr.Nyss.*v.Mos.*(M.44.321C).

***ἱλεωτικός**, *propitiatory*, Gr.Nyss.*hom.9 in Cant.*(M.44.957A).

ἵλημι, imper., *be gracious* ἵλαθι δέ, ἁγία τριάς Didym.*Trin.*2.3(M.39.477C).

***ἵλησις**, ἡ, *rejoicing* τῆς ἐν τῷ μυστικῷ γάμῳ ἱλήσεως *cat.Apoc.* 7:6(p.289.7).

***ἰλλούστριος**, (Lat. *illustris*) *illustrious* Μαρκέλλῳ, ἀνδρὶ ἰ. *A.Petr.et Paul.*84(p.216.13); Max.*ep.*44(M.91.644D); ὁ μὴ ὢν ἰ., ἀλλὰ μόνον λαμπρότατος Phot.*nomoc.*9.30(M.104.788A); masc. as subst. τις...ἰλλουστρίου ἀξίωμα ἔχων Cyr.S.*v.Sab.*70(p.172.23); *Mir.Artem.* 29(p.42.7).

ἰλυσπάομαι, *crawl*, met. ὅλῳ τῷ σώματι περὶ τὰς ἀνοήτους ἐπιθυμίας ἰ. Clem.*paed.*1.5(p.99.30; M.8.268C); ‡Bas.*const.*8(2.554D; M.31.1369A); Chrys.*hom.7.4 in Ac.*(9.62D).

***ἰλυσσ-άομαι**, = foreg.; of serpent in Eden, Thdt.*qu.34 in Gen.*(1.46); met. τὰ περὶ γῆν ~ώμενα πάθη Areth.*Apoc.*67(M.106.777B).

ἰλυώδης, *filthy*, met. τὸ...ἰ. τῆς ἀπιστίας Gr.Nyss.*Spir.*(M.46.701A); Cyr.*Os.*67(3.101E); ψυχῆς...ἰλυώδη κατάστασιν Nil.*epp.*2.177(M.79.284C).

***ἱμαντία**, ἡ, *binding, brace*, Thdt.*qu.24 in 3Reg.*(1.469) cf. ἱμαντρίς.

***ἱμαντοτόμος**, ὁ, *strap-cutter*, *A.Thom.*B 38(p.36.32).

***ἱμαντρίς**, ἡ, *binding, brace*, Proc.G.*3Reg.*6:24(M.87.1156D); cf. ἱμαντία.

ἱμάντωμα, τό, = foreg., Proc.G.*3Reg.*6:20(M.87.1157A); Dor.*doct.*14.2(M.88.1776B).

ἱμάντωσις, ἡ, *joist*, Chrys.*hom.8.2 in Col.*(11.383A); id.*Anna* 4(4.737B); id.*stat.*6.1(2.74C).

ἱμάτιον, τό, *garment*, ref. ethics of dress; virgins should wear clothes of cheap stuff, Ath.*virg.*11(p.44.3; M.28.264B); clothes should not be elaborate, Gr.Nyss.*mort.*(M.46.528D); Chrys.*hom.10.3 in Phil.*(11.278Cff.); cheapness exemplified by Christ's garments at Crucifixion, id.*hom.85.2 in Jo.*(8.505D); necessity of wearing clothes as reminder of Fall, id.*hom.18.3 in Gen.*(4.152B); met., of 'old man' put off at baptism, Bas.*hom.*18.6(2.153B; M.31.517A); ref. baptized ἐνδεδυμένος τὸ ἱ. σωτηρίου Ἰησοῦν Χριστόν Cyr.H.*catech.*19.10; of Christ as garment assumed in spiritual life, Mac.Aeg.*hom.*20.3(M.34.652B); τὰ τῆς ἀρετῆς καὶ τῆς κακίας ἱ. Chrys.*hom.25.4 in Ac.*(9.206D).

ἱματιοφύλαξ, ὁ, *keeper of clothes* ἱματιοφύλακες...πρὸς ταῖς θύραις δίκην καμψαρίων ὑπ' αὐτῶν [sc. Adamites] ἐπιτεταγμένοι Epiph.*haer.*52.2(p.313.1; M.41.956D).

***ἱμεροδερκής**, *enchanting to behold*, Paul.Sil.*ambo*.304(M.86.2264).

***ἱμπεράτωρ**, ὁ, (Lat. imperator) *emperor*, *Chron.Pasch.*p.192(M.92.473A).

ἵνα, **1.** *in order that*, c. indic. ἱ. ... φιλομαθὴς...ἔσῃ Thphl.Ant.

*Autol.*3.15(M.6.1141C); ἀπόστειλον τὸν ἄγγελόν σου...ἵ. ἐξάξει αὐτόν *A.Andr.et Mt.*4(p.69.2); ἵ. ὅσα ἂν δήσῃς...ἔσται δεδεμένα Chrys. *hom.*54.2 *in Mt.*(7.548B, v.l. καὶ); εἴθε...ἤ...ἐπίγνωσις...πρός με ἐλήλυθεν, ἵ. μήτε ὄνομα νύμφης προσέλαβον *M.Ner.et Ach.*9(p.8.4); ἵ. ... εἰς τὰς ψυχὰς προσχωροῦμεν *A.Barth.*6(p.141.34); ἵ. ... ἱστάμεθα Vict.*Mc.*4:25(p.309.29); **2.** indicating consequence, ref. Rom.5:20 (ἵ. πλεονάσῃ τὸ παράπτωμα), τὸ δὲ 'ἵ.' ἐνταῦθα οὐκ αἰτιολογίας πάλιν ἀλλ' ἐκβάσεώς ἐστιν, οὐ γὰρ...ἐδόθη ἵ. πλεονάσῃ, ἀλλ' ἐδόθη μὲν ὥστε μειῶσαι...τὸ παράπτωμα· ἐξέβη δὲ τοὐναντίον Chrys.*hom.*10.3 *in Rom.*(9.524A); τὸ γὰρ ἵ. τοῦτο, οὐ πανταχοῦ αἰτιολογίας ἐστίν, ἀλλὰ πολλαχοῦ καὶ τῆς τῶν πραγμάτων ἐκβάσεως. οὕτω καὶ ὁ Χριστὸς αὐτὸ τίθησιν, ὅταν λέγῃ...'ἵ. οἱ μὴ βλέποντες βλέπωσι, καὶ οἱ βλέποντες τυφλοὶ γένωνται'· οὕτω καὶ...ὁ Παῦλος, ὅταν...γράφῃ· 'νόμος δὲ παρεισῆλθεν, ἵ. πλεονάσῃ τὸ παράπτωμα' id.*hom.*27.2 *in 1Cor.*(10.243A); οὐ γάρ ἐστι φύσει ἡ κακία, ἵ. μὴ ἔχῃ χώραν ἡ ἀρετή id.*Laz.*6.9(1.787D); cf. νῦν δὲ ἀκαίρως εἰσῆλθες ἵ. ἀκαίρως ἐκβληθῇς Cyr.H.*procatech.*3; **3.** *supposing that* ἵ. αὐτῷ συγχωρηθῇ Μωυσέα ἀκηκοέναι ἀρχαιοτέρου λόγου Or.*Cels.*1.21(p.72.5; M.11.696C); ἵ. γὰρ καὶ ἐκλείπειν αὐτὸν φῶμεν *ib.*4.5(p.277.33; 1036A); id.*or.*8.2(p.317.16; M.11.441C); introducing illustrations ὥσπερ ἵ. ᾖ παράδεισος ἔχων παντοῖα δένδρα Mac.Aeg.*hom.*15.11(M.34.581D); ὥσπερ ἵ. ᾖ τις πλούσιος...καὶ ᾖ ἐπιδεόμενος id.*cust.cor.*12(M.34.832C); *in a case where* ὅπερ γὰρ συμβαίνει ...ἵ. δύο λίθων προσκρουσάντων πῦρ γενηθῇ Or.*hom.*8.4 *in Jer.*(p.60.4; M.13.341C); **4.** *if, if only* ἵ. χρόνον βραχὺν τὰς ὀφρῦς συναγάγωσι ...καὶ κατήφειαν ὑποκρίνωνται Chrys.*sac.*1.4(p.14.1; 1.366D); ποσάκις ...τὸν ὑπηρετοῦντα οἰκέτην καλέσας, ἵ. σχολαιότερον βαδίσῃ, πάντα ἀνέτρεψας id.*hom.*35.5 *in Mt.*(7.404E); *ib.*48.6(501D); **5.** *even if* τὰ πράγματα δὲ οὐδὲν μᾶλλον δύνανται παύσασθαι ὄντα τοιαῦτα, ἵ. τις τὸ μὴ μεταβάλλεσθαι εἰς τὰ χείρω ἔνια συγχωρήσῃ Alex.Lyc.*Man.*12 (p.18.25; M.18.428B); ἵ. δὲ καὶ δοθῇ *even if, granted that*, Or.*Jo.*19.15(4; p.314.28; M.14.552C); **6.** ἵ. μή *unless*, CSyr.*act.*(*ACO* 3 p.93.5; H.2.1365C); **7.** *whenever* ἵ. τὸ σῶμά μου μικρὸν κακωθῇ...τὴν ἴασιν αἰτοῦμαι Ephr.1.315A; **8.** *since, because* ἵ. ἐν ἁμάρτῃ ἁμάρτημα μόνον, ἐκολάζετο πικρῶς Chrys.*hom.*3.5 *in Ac.*(9.30C); ἵ. στυγνάσῃ μόνον...ἀφῆκα τὰ ἁμαρτήματα id.*hom.*8.5 *in 1Cor.*(10.71D); ὁ τελώνης, ἵ. μόνον εἴπῃ, ἱλάσθητί μοι...κατῆλθε δεδικαιώμενος id.*hom.*1.3 *in Philm.*(11.778D); **9.** *that* a fact should be such and such τί... χεῖρον...ἢ ἵ. λίθος...προσκυνηθῇ; Cyr.H.*catech.*6.11; Chrys.*hom.*5.3 *in Phil.*(11.222C); **10.** after commands and prohibitions, c. subj., *LS*; cf. ὡμόσαμεν γὰρ ἀλλήλοις, ἵ. μὴ μάθωσιν...οὔτε γὰρ ὁ Ἰάκωβος θέλει, ἵ. μάθωσιν *Didasc.Jac.*3.2(p.53.18,19); ἔδοξέ μοι ἵ. αὐτὸς ὁ Καικιλιανὸς...εἰς τὴν Ῥώμην πλῷ ἀπιέναι Const.ap.Eus.*h.e.*10.5.22 (M.20.888A); σοὶ γράψαι ἐνομίσαμεν ἵ. ... ἐπὶ τῷ προειρημένῳ τόπῳ ἀπάντησον *ib.*10.5.23(889C); ἐλάλουν...ἵ. μὴ ἀπομετεωρίζεσθαι Dor. *doct.*22.1(M.88.1821B); **11.** *to think that!* τίνος χάριν...ὑπομένομεν ταύτας τὰς...θλίψεις; οὔπω γὰρ ἐπελαθόμεθα τῶν προτέρων, καὶ ἵ. ὑπομείνωμεν καὶ ἄλλην θλίψιν; Jo.Thess.*dorm.BMV* A 5(p.413.27); **12.** *as* ἵ. γὰρ οἶδέ σου ἡ ὁσιότης, ὅτι... Thdr.Stud.*epp.*2.9(M.99.1140B); **13.** in phrases; **a.** ἵ. εἴπῃ *as much as to say, meaning* τὰ κράσπεδα, ἵ. εἴπῃ κροσσούς· καὶ τὰ φυλακτήρια, ἵ. εἴπῃ τῆς πορφύρας τὰ σήματα Epiph.*haer.*15.1(p.209.20; M.41.245A); Vict.*Mc.*9:14(p.359.10); ὁ υἱὸς τοῦ εὐλογήτου, ἵ. εἴπῃ τοῦ θεοῦ *ib.*14:54(p.430.15); **b.** ἵ. μάθῃς *that you may understand, to illustrate, just to show you* ἵ. μάθῃς αὐτοῦ τὴν πονηρίαν, ἀκούσας ταῦτα...οὐκ εἶπεν Chrys.*hom.*27.2 *in Mt.*(7.329B); ἵ. μάθῃς ὅτι...εἴ σοι γέγονεν ἐπιθυμία...πῶς ἂν ταύτην ἔσβεσας *ib.*63.3(632B); ἵ. μάθῃς πόση τῆς συνηθείας ἐστὶν ἡ ἰσχύς, τῶν τοῦ θεοῦ προσταγμάτων πολλάκις ἐκράτησε id.*hom.*7.7 *in 1Cor.*(10.60C); id. *hom.*9.3 *in 2Cor.*(10.502C); **c.** πῶς οὖν ἵ.; *what is to be done that?* πῶς οὖν, ἵ. μὴ τοῦτο γένηται; id.*hom.*68.5 *in Mt.*(7.677C); πῶς οὖν, ἵ. ταῦτα μὴ γίγνηται; id.*hom.*27.5 *in 1Cor.*(10.248E); πῶς οὖν ἵ. τοῦτο τὸ ἴδιον κοινὸν γένηται; *ib.*44.2(409D, most MSS omitting ἵ.).

***ἰνβεντάριον, τό,** (Lat. *inventarium*) *list*, Ath.Scholast.*coll.*7.7 (p.87); *ib.*2.3(p.37).

ἴνδαλμα, τό, *image*; **1.** ref. knowledge of God τινος ἰ. ... ὥσπερ μετασχόντας Didym.*Trin.*1.9(M.39.281A); Gr.Nyss.*hom.*3 *in Cant.* (M.44.821B); of Ezekiel's visions as ἰ. of spiritual beings, not direct revelation of their essence, Thdt.*Ezech.*10:20(2.744); of ἰ. of God produced in soul by contemplation, Dion.Ar.*e.h.*4.3.1(M.3.473C); Max.*schol.in e.h.*4.3.1(M.4.153A); **2.** of phantoms or apparitions, Eust.*engast.*30(p.61.25; M.18.673A); produced by Simon Magus to support his claims, *Hom.Clem.*4.4; in gen., Olymp. *fr.Job* 33:16–18 (M.93.349D).

***ἰνδαλματικός,** v. *ἰνδαλτικός.

***ἰνδαλματώδης,** *fantastic*, Athenag.*leg.*27.1(M.6.952C).

***ἰνδάλμων, ὁ,** f.l. for ἴνδαλμα, Synes.*hymn.*3.315(M.66.1598; ἴνδαλμα μονὰς p. 16).

***ἰνδαλτικός,** *imaginary, visionary*, Epiph.*haer.*26.12(p.291.13; ἰνδαλματικός M.41.352A).

***ἰνδέβιτος,** (Lat. *indebitus*) *not owed*, Phot.*nomoc.*2.1(M.104.576B).

***ἰνδικτιών, ἡ,** *indiction*, a period of 15 years, Ath.*syn.*25(p.250.23; M.26.725A); Euthal.Diac.*epp.Paul.*(M.85.716A); Thdr.Lect.*h.e.* 2.64(M.86.213B); introduced into calendar at Rome on 12 May in first year of Julius Caesar, *Chron.Pasch.*p.187(M.92.460A); though reckoned at Antioch from 1 Sept., cf.*ib.*(461A); origin assigned to second year of Augustus, Max.*comput.*33(M.19.1249D); of A.D. 313 as ἰ. Κωνσταντινιανῶν ἀρχή *Chron.Pasch.*p.281(700A).

***ἴνδικτος, ἡ,** = foreg., *Chron.Pasch.*p.187(M.92.461A); *ib.*p.374 (956A).

ἰνδογενής, *born in India*, *Orac.Sib.*11.62.

***ἰνδουλγεντία, ἡ,** (Lat. *indulgentia*) *pardon, remission of punishment*, Jo.Mal.*chron.*12 p.293(M.97.444B); *ib.*12 p.309(465B); Thphn. *chron.*p.200(M.108.516C).

***ἰντρόϊτον, τό,** (Lat. *introitus*) *entrance* of a church, *Const.App.* 2.57.13.

***ἰοβολία, ἡ,** *emission of venom*, Epiph.*haer.*37.2(p.52.15; M.41.644B); *ib.*40.8(p.90.2; 692A).

ἰοβόλος, *poisonous*, met. ἰ. ὑποκριτάς Clem.*prot.*1(p.5.17; M.8.57A); ἰ. πνεύματα Eus.*Is.*11:8(M.24.173B); θηρίον...ἰ. ὁ φθόνος Chrys. *hom.*55.3 *in Jo.*(8.325D).

***ἰονόργια, τά,** a mystery rite τὰ τῆς Μεγάλης Φλοιᾶς ἰ. Hipp.*haer.* 5.20(p.122.15; v.l. ὄργια M.16.3187A).

ἰός, ὁ, *poison*; met., of refusal to give alms τὸν ἰ. εἰς τὴν καρδίαν Herm.*vis.*3.9.7; of heresy, Const.*ep.*ap.Gel.Cyz.*h.e.*3.19.8(M.85.1345D); Petr.II Al.*encycl.*ap.Thdt.*h.e.*4.22.34(M.33.1289B).

***ἰουγατίων, ἡ,** (Lat. *jugatio*) *assessment of land for taxation*, Thdt.*ep.*42(4.1101).

***ἰοῦγον, τό,** (Lat. *jugum*) *measure of land*, Jo.Mal.*chron.*16 p.394(M.97.584A).

***Ἰούδα, ὁ,** v. *Ἰούδας.

Ἰουδαΐζω, 1. *embrace, practise Judaism* ἄτοπόν ἐστιν, Ἰησοῦν Χριστὸν λαλεῖν καὶ ἰ. Ign.*Magn.*10.3; Clem.*str.*7.15(p.63.30; M.9.525A); id.*fr.*36(p.218.23); Or.*fr.*8 *in Jo.*(p.490.12); Gr.Nyss.*or.catech.* proem.(p.2.4; M.45.10A); **2.** *imitate the Jews*; **a.** of Christians who observe sabbath, CLaod.*can.*29; **b.** of heretics who deny divinity of Christ, Eus.*e.th.*2.14(p.117.29; M.24.932D); Ath.*decr.*2(p.2.13; M.25.417C); Gr.Naz.*or.*38.8(M.36.320B); Gr.Nyss.*fid.*(M.45.137A); of those who will not go beyond letter of scripture, id.*Eun.*12(1 p.270.30; M.45.976D).

Ἰουδαϊκός, *Jewish*; of exclusively literal exegesis of scripture, cf. *Judaicus...sensus*, Or.*princ.*2.11.2(p.186.2; M.11.242C); of denial of divinity of Christ as 'Ἰ. σμικρολογία, Gr.Naz.*or.*20.6(M.35.1072B); *ib.*2.37(445A); of Judaism (ἡ Ἰ.) compared with Eunomianism, Gr.Nyss.*Eun.*9(2 p.207.2; M.45.804C); of Jewish observances followed by Ebionites, Hipp.*haer.*7.34(p.221.10; M.16.3342B); of Ἰ. ἔθιμα, not to be observed by Christians, *Const.App.*6.27.1; cf. CNic.(787)*can.*8; Jewish practices ceasing with Christ's death, Chrys.*ecl.*38(12.719D); and being typical only, id.*hom.*54.1 *in Jo.* (8.315E); ref. Rom.2:29, of Christian προσκυνῶν τὸν δημιουργόν... κατὰ τοὺς λόγους τοὺς πνευματικοὺς Ἰ. Or.*Jo.*13.17(p.241.11; M.14.424C); Cyr.*ador.*9(1.302A); ἡ Ἰ. *Judaea*, *Dial.Tim.et Aquil.*76 v°.

Ἰουδαϊκῶς, *in the Jewish manner, like Jews*; ref. rabbinical exegesis, Clem.*paed.*1.6(p.110.29; M.8.292B); Or.*Jo.*10.42(26; p.219.25; M.14.389A); Gr.Nyss.*Eun.*3(2 p.12.22; M.45.576D); ref. eschatology of Nepos, Eus.*h.e.*7.24.1(M.20.602C); ref. denial of Son's divinity, *Symb.Sirm.*1 *anath.*11; Ath.*Ar.*3.27(M.26.380C); ref. observance of Law by Ebionites, Eus.*h.e.*6.17(560A); Christians prohibited from practising Jewish rites and so living Ἰ., Cyr.*Is.*1.5 (2.143B); ref. offering meat in sanctuary (as in Armenia), CTrull. *can.*99; ref. observance of Jewish date of Easter prevented in East by Const., Soz.*h.e.*1.16.4(M.67.909C); Thphn.*chron.*p.14(M.108.89A).

Ἰουδαῖος, ὁ, *Jew*; **1.** downfall and sufferings of Jews prophesied, Eus.*d.e.*2.2(p.60.20; M.22.112A); †Bas.*Is.*165(1.496D; M.30.389B); Chrys.*Jud.*5.6(1.638Bff.); as proof of Christ's divinity, Isid.Pel.*epp.* 4.146(M.78.1257A); **2.** treatment by secular power: Jews forbidden by Const. to keep Christian slaves, Eus.*v.C.*4.27(p.127.27; M.20.1176B); Soz.*h.e.*3.17.4(M.67.1093C); miraculous prevention of their proposed re-establishment by Juln. in Jerusalem, Gr.Naz.*or.*5.3f. (M.35.668A); Socr.*h.e.*3.20.3ff.(M.67.429A); Soz.*h.e.*5.22.2ff.(1284A); **3.** eccl. regulations about relations with Jews; faithful not to frequent their assemblies, *Can.App.*65; *ib.*71; *Const.App.*2.62.3; Chrys.*Jud.*5.12(1.649B); not to follow their calendar: for Easter, *Can.App.*7; CAnt.(341)*can.*1; in gen., *Can.App.*70; CLaod.*can.*37;

cf.*ib.*38; fasts, Chrys.*Jud.*1.4(1.593A); *ib.*2.1(601B); conversion required before marriage with Christians, CChalc.*can.*14; all relations forbidden, CTrull.*can.*11; **4.** expectation of ultimate conversion of Jews: apptly. denied; they will repent at second coming but too late, Cyr.H.*catech.*13.41; affirmed, Cyr.*Joel.*14(3.213B); id.*glaph. Gen.*6(1.200E); conversion prefigured by cure of cripple at Bethsaida, id.*Jo.*2.5(4.208D); promised in Apoc., Andr.Caes.*Apoc.*8(M.106.245D); **5.** of orthodox Christians as the true Jews Ἰ. ... (ἀπ' αὐτῶν γὰρ ἡ σωτηρία) εἰκόνες εἰσὶν τῶν τοὺς ὑγιαίνοντας φρονούντων λόγους Or.*Jo.*13.13(p.237.18; M.14.417C); exeg. Rom.2:9, cf. true Jew as the Christian who does in spirit what material practices of Jews really signify, cf.id.*comm.in Rom.*2.7(M.14.886cf.); so Rom.2:17, *ib.*2.11(895C); Rom.2:29, *ib.*2.14(914D); of the Christian, since Ἰούδας means 'confession' οἱ ἀληθεῖς Ἰ. ... οἱ Χριστῷ ἐξομολογούμενοι Oecum.*Apoc.*2:9(p.51); Areth.*Apoc.*4(M.106.533A); **6.** of those who deny divinity of Christ οἱ νῦν...Ἰ. [sc. Arians] Ath.*ep.Serap.*1.28(M.26.596B); Gr.Nyss.*Eun.*9(2 p.206.27; M.45.804C); followers of Paul. Sam. δεύτεροι Ἰ. Epiph.*haer.*65.2(p.4.17; M.42.13C); **7.** Ἰουδαία, ἡ, *Judaea*; Ἰ. ... ἐξομολόγησις ἑρμηνεύεται Clem.*str.*7.16(p.74.17; M.9.545B); Or.*fr.58 in Jer.*(p.227.4; M.13.582D).

***Ἰουδαιόφρων**, *Jewish-minded* τὸν Ἰ. Νεστόριον Cyr.S.*v.Euthym.*26(p.40.21); Jo.D.*f.o.*3.12(M.94.1032A); οἱ Ἰ. Ἀρμένιοι καὶ Ἰακωβῖται ‡Jo.D.*azym.*1(M.95.389C).

Ἰουδαϊσμός, ὁ, *Judaism*, in gen., Or.*Cels.*1.2(p.57.2; M.11.656A); Eus.*d.e.*1.2(p.7.27; M.22.24B); analysed, Epiph.*haer.*14(p.207.8ff.; M.41.240A); in rel. to Christianity ὁ...Χριστιανισμὸς οὐκ εἰς Ἰ. ἐπίστευσεν, ἀλλ' Ἰ. εἰς Χριστιανισμόν Ign.*Magn.*10.3; cf.*ib.*8.1; Or.*Cels.*3.14(p.213.29; M.11.937B); μήτε εἰς...Ἰ. ἐκπέσῃς· ἐλυτρώσατο γάρ σε λοιπὸν Ἰησοῦς Cyr.H.*catech.*4.37; μάχεται Ἰ. Ἑλληνισμῷ, καὶ ἀμφότεροι Χριστιανισμῷ Bas.*hom.*24.1(2.189C; M.31.600B); *M.Thdot.*3(p.131.11); ref. Rom.2:29 ὁ ἐν κρυπτῷ Ἰ. as Christian fulfilment of what Jewish observances signified, Or.*fr.8 in Jo.*(p.490.13); of those who deny divinity of Christ τὸν Ἰ. πάλιν ἀνανεοῦνται Bas.*hom.*24.1(190A; M.601A); of Arianism, Ath.*ep.Serap.*1.21(M.26.580C); Gr.Naz.*or.*2.37(M.35.444C); observances followed by Ebionites, Epiph.*haer.*30.2(p.334.11; 408A).

***Ἰουδαϊστής**, ὁ, *Judaizer*; of Marcionites, Adam.*dial.*2.15(p.88.31; M.11.1784B); of Christians observing Jewish sabbath, CLaod.*can.*29; ? of a Jew, *Const.App.*2.21.2.

***Ἰούδας (*Ἰούδα)**, ὁ, *Judah, Jude, Judas* (first usually written Ἰούδα); **1.** etym. Ἰ. ... ἐξομολόγησις ἑρμηνεύεται †Bas.*Is.*231(1.554E; M.30.524B); Cyr.H.*catech.*13.9; Cyr.*Joel.*45(3.245B); ἑρμηνεύεται...αἶνος δὲ καὶ ὕμνησις, Ἰ. id.*glaph.Gen.*2(1.49B); **2.** of Judah, son of Jacob; **a.** as type of Christ, Or.*hom.16.10 in Jer.*(p.141.23; M.13.452A); esp. ref. Gen.49:8, id.*Jo.*1.23(p.28.8ff.; M.14.64A); as Christ is of tribe of Judah, Inc. is prefigured in Gen.49:8, Cyr.*glaph.Gen.*7(1.220D); and in relations of Judah with Tamar, *ib.*6(193D); **b.** as type of Christians ἄνδρες Ἰ. ἡμεῖς ἐσμεν διὰ τὸν Χριστόν Or.*hom.9.1 in Jer.*(p.64.28; M.13.349B); ἡμεῖς...ὁ Ἰ. *ib.4.5*(p.28.7; 292C); **3.** of apostle Jude; ref. canonicity of epistle; **a.** accepted, cf.Clem.*fr.*24(p.206.26; M.9.731D); cf.Or.*hom.7.1 in Jos.*(p.328.3; M.12.857B); *Can.App.*85; CLaod.*can.*60; Cyr.H.*catech.*4.36; Ath.*ep.fest.*39.8(M.26.1437A); Gr.Naz.*carm.*1.1.12.38(M.37.474A); Didym.*Trin.*2.6(M.39.512C,513A); **b.** doubted or rejected: doubted by some, Or.*comm. in Mt.*17.30(p.672.10; M.13.1569B); prob. because of use of apocryphal *Ascension of Moses*, cf.id.*princ.*3.2.1(p.244.18; M.11.303B); doubted, Eus.*h.e.*3.25.2(M.20.269A); Amph.*Seleuc.*315(M.37.1597A); alleged rejection of all catholic epistles by Thdr. Mops., Leont.B.*Nest.et Eut.*3(M.86.1365C); cf. rejection by Syrians, Cosm.Ind.*top.*7(M.88.373B); **4.** of Judas Iscariot, Gnost.; **a.** betrayal as type of passion of Sophia (Valent.) who was the twelfth aeon, Iren.*haer.*1.3.3(M.7.472A); *ib.*2.20.2(777A); idea that betrayal typified *enthymesis* of Sophia, *ib.*2.20.5(778C); **b.** in Cainite system, Judas honoured for betrayal, cf.*ib.*1.31.1(704B); οἱ μὲν λέγουσι διὰ τὸν πονηρὸν εἶναι τὸν Χριστὸν παραδοθῆναι αὐτὸν ὑπὸ τοῦ Ἰ. ... ἄλλοι δὲ ...φασίν,...ἔγνωσαν...οἱ ἄρχοντες ὅτι ἐὰν ὁ Χριστὸς παραδοθῇ σταυρῷ κενοῦται αὐτῶν ἡ...δύναμις. καὶ τοῦτο, φησί, γνοὺς ὁ Ἰ. ... πάντα ἐκίνησεν ὥστε παραδοῦναι αὐτόν Epiph.*haer.*38.3(p.65.21ff.; M.41.657B); Thdt.*haer.*1.15(4.309); Cainites possessing apocryphal Gospel of Judas, cf.Iren.*haer.*1.31.1(704B); Thdt.*haer.*1.15(309); **5.** of Judas Thomas (the apostle), *A.Thom.*A 11(p.116.2) al.

***Ἰουλιανισταί**, οἱ, *Julianists*, monophysite heretics, also called Γαιανῖται q.v., Tim.CP *haer.*(M.86.44B).

Ἰούλιος, ὁ, **1.** *July*, Epiph.*haer.*51.29(p.300.8; M.41.937C); Thphn.*chron.*p.97(M.108.284A); **2.** a Paphian month approximately equivalent to January, Epiph.*haer.*51.24(p.293.5; M.41.932B).

***Ἰούνιος**, ὁ, *June*, Epiph.*haer.*51.29(p.300.9; M.41.937C); *Chron. Pasch.*p.11(M.92.89A); Thphn.*chron.*p.60(M.108.204B).

***ἰουνίωρ**, ὁ, (Lat. *junior*) *younger, junior*, as title, Eus.*chron.*1.49(M.19.305C,D); *Chron.Pasch.*p.269(M.92.665A); *ib.*p.374(953C).

ἱππήλατος, *fit for horsemanship*, met.; **1.** *easy*, Cyr.*Jo.*5.5(4.551C); id.*Zach.*41(3.718D); **2.** *easily accessible*; of obvious meaning of scripture, id.*Jo.*3.2(4.260A); τὴν καρδίαν...ἱ. τοῖς ἀκαθάρτοις πνεύμασιν id.*Joel.*43(3.242D); Isid.Pel.*epp.*3.80(M.78.785D).

ἱππικός, *equestrian* ἀποκηρύσσει...ἱ. ⟨ἀγῶνας⟩ Epiph.*exp.fid.*24(p.525.11; M.42.832A); neut. as subst., **1.** *racecourse*, *Chron.Pasch.*p.284(M.92.708C); Thphn.*chron.*p.109(M.108.313C); **2.** *race-meeting*, *Apophth.Patr.*(M.65.164A); *Chron.Pasch.*p.310(M.92.789A); *ib.*p.312(796B); **3.** a race-game played with dice τοῖς καλουμένοις ξυλίνοις ἱ. Phot.*nomoc.*13.29(M.104.964A).

***ἱπποδρομέω**, met., *run the race*, Cyr.*Jo.*1(4.8B).

ἱπποδρομία, ἡ, *horse-race* πομπὴ...διαβόλου...ἱπποδρομίαι Cyr.H.*catech.*19.6.

ἱπποδρόμιον, τό, *racecourse, circus*, *M.Perp.*13(p.83.14); *A.Barn.*21(p.300.5); *ib.*23(p.301.3); esp. of hippodrome at CP, Eus.*v.C.*2.54(p.101.25; M.20.1117B); Chrys.*hom.9.2 in 2Cor.*(10.501A); Thdr.Lect.*h.e.*1.27(M.86.150A).

ἱπποθόρος, *covering a mare*, of a tune νόμος ἱ. Clem.*paed.*2.4(p.182.11; M.8.441A).

ἱπποκρατέω, med., *resound with the hooves of horses*, Synes.*ep.*130(ἱπποκροτεῖται M.66.1512D).

***ἱπποκροτέομαι**, *resound with the hooves of horses*, Cyr.*Nah.*27(3.505C); v. foreg.

ἱππομανέω, *be mad about horses*, Bas.*hex.*4.1(1.33C; M.29.80A).

ἱππομανής, *mad on horses* or *racing*, Pall.*v.Chrys.*5(p.33.12; M.47.22).

ἱππομανία, ἡ, *madness about horses*, †Bas.*Is.*82(1.436A; M.30.252D).

ἵππος, ὁ, ἡ, **I.** *horse*;

A. lit.; ref. Gen.49:10–11, horse taken for Pegasus by demons, who therefore invented legend of Bellerophon's ascension into heaven, Just.*1apol.*54.7(M.6.409B).

B. met. and fig.; **1.** of human soul; **a.** in gen., cf. *omnes, qui in carne nati sunt, figuraliter equi sunt. ... sunt equi, quos dominus ascendit...sunt autem equi, qui adscensores habent diabolum et angelos ejus*, Or.*hom.6.2 in Ex.*(p.193.6; M.12.332C); Mac.Aeg.*hom.*23.2(M.34.660D); Gr.Nyss.*hom.4 in Cant.*(M.44.845A); **b.** as subject to Christ φέρει [sc. ὁ παιδαγωγός] πρὸς σωτηρίαν τὸν ἵ. τὸν ἀνθρώπειον Clem.*paed.*3.11(p.266.32; M.8.625C); Or.*Cant.*2(p.151.25; M.13.129D); τίνες...ἂν εἶεν οἱ ἵ.; οἱ...μαθηταὶ ἀπόστολοί τε καὶ εὐαγγελισταί...οἱ Χριστὸν ἔποχον...ἔχοντες Cyr.*Abac.*50(3.564B); **c.** as subject to Devil, ref. Zach.9:9–10, cf.Or.*hom.15.3 in Jos.*(p.384.9; M.12.899A); of the proud, Gr.Nyss.*hom.8 in Eccl.*(M.44.745C); Cyr.*Am.*60(3.317Aff.); exeg. Ps.146:10 ἵππου interpreted as τοῦ ἀσυνέτου, Hesych.H.*Ps.tit.*146(M.27.1328A); **2.** of passions; **a.** in gen. τὴν ἄλογον κίνησιν τῆς ψυχῆς λέγει ἵ. Or.*sel.in Ps.*31:9(M.12.1394A); ref. Jos.11:9–11 and Ps.32:17, cf.id.*hom.15.3 in Jos.*(p.385.2; M.12.899B); ἵ. ... νοῶν τὰ σκιρτητικὰ τῶν παθῶν, οἷς ἐπιβαίνουσιν αἱ ἀντικείμεναι δυνάμεις Didym.*Ps.*19:8(M.39.1273B); Areth.*Apoc.*27(M.106.632C); **b.** esp. lust, Cyr.H.*catech.*9.13; ref. Jer.5:8 and Ps.31:9, Gr.Nyss.*hom.3 in Cant.*(M.44.813D); Didym.*Ps.*31:9(M.39.1321C); Chrys.*hom.70.4 in Mt.*(7.692E); Isid.Pel.*epp.*2.135(M.78.577B); Andr.Caes.*Apoc.*27(M.106.301C); **3.** of angels; **a.** good τὴν...τῶν ἵ. [sc. μορφὴν ἐμφαίνειν οἰητέον] τὸ εὐπειθές Dion.Ar.*c.h.*15.8(M.3.337A); significance of colours explained, *ib.*; ref. Heb.3:8 and Cant.1:8, Andr.Caes.*Apoc.*44(M.106.352D); Oecum.*Apoc.*14:20.(p.168); **b.** bad, cf.Or.*hom.15.3 in Jos.*(p.384.19ff.; M.12.899B); ἵ. ... τοὺς ὑποβεβηκότας καὶ ἀρχομένους ἐν τοῖς δαίμοσιν Andr.Caes.*Apoc.*27(M.106.301C); **4.** exeg. Apoc.6:2 ὁ...λευκὸς ἵ. σύμβολον εὐαγγελισμοῦ Oecum.*Apoc.*6:2(p.84); Areth.*Apoc.*13(M.106.588B); Apoc.6:4 ὁ...πυρρὸς ἵ., ἢ τῆς ἐκχύσεως τῶν μαρτυρικῶν αἱμάτων σύμβολον, ἢ τῆς πυριπνόου περὶ Χριστὸν διαθέσεως τῶν μαρτύρων *ib.*14(589A); cf.Oecum.*Apoc.*6:4(p.85); Andr.Caes.*Apoc.*14(M.106.265D); Apoc.6:8 ὁ ἵ. ὁ χλωρὸς ὀργῆς σύμβολον Oecum.*Apoc.*6:8(p.89); Apoc.6:5, black horse denotes mourning of Christians for those who fall away in time of persecution, Andr.Caes.*Apoc.*15(268B); or Devil's mourning for his overthrow, Oecum.*Apoc.*6:5(p.86); Apoc.19:11, the horse interpreted as Christ's body and soul or the Church, Or.*Cant.*2(p.152.12ff.; M.13.130B); ὁ...λευκὸς ἵ. τὴν τῶν ἁγίων φαιδρότητα τὴν μέλλουσαν [sc. δηλοῖ] Andr.Caes.*Apoc.*58(401A); **5.** Gnost.; for Simon Magus, horse of Troy signified ruin brought about by ignorance of his teaching, Epiph.*haer.*21.3(p.241.19ff.; M.41.289A).

II. collectively, ἡ ἵ.;

A. *troop of horses* τῆς ἀγελαίας ἵππου Thphn.*chron*.p.242(M.108.609A).

B. *cavalry*; met., as symbol of might and power, Gr.Nyss.*hom.3 in Cant*.(M.44.812C); as symbol of angels, ref. Abac.3:8, *ib*.(812B); *ib*.(817B).

***ἱππόσταθμος**, ὁ, *four-wheeled courier-chariot* ἃ ἡ παλαιὰ μὲν φωνὴ ἀγγάρους, ἡ δὲ τῶν Ἑλλήνων δημοσίους ἱ., ἡ δὲ τῶν Ῥωμαίων ῥαίδη Areth.*Apoc*.55(M.106.732B).

ἱπποτροφικός, *of horse rearing*, Clem.*str*.1.7(p.24.27; M.8.732C).

***ἱρογραφεία**, ἡ, v. *ἱερογραφία.

ἴς, ἡ, *fibre, thread*, Gr.Nyss.*Maced*.10(M.45.1313A); Thdt.*provid*.4(4.540); of a seam of gold, Chrys.*Laz*.3.1(1.736D).

***Ἰσαάκ**, ὁ, *Isaac*; **1.** etym. = laughter, joy γέλως...ὁ Ἰ. Clem.*paed*.1.5(p.102.23; M.8.276A); Or.*hom.20.6 in Jer*.(p.185.22; M.13.512D); id.*hom.7.1 in Gen*.(p.70.23; M.12.198C); τέρψις τε καὶ ἀγαλλίασμα· ἑρμηνεύεται...οὕτως ὁ Ἰ. Cyr.*glaph.Gen*.3(1.90E); **2.** as type; **a.** of Christ's sacrifice; **i.** in gen., *Barn*.7.3; Iren.*haer*.4.5.4(M.7.985C); Bas.*Spir*.32(3.26E; M.32.124C); Chrys.*hom.in Mt.26*:*39*(3.20B); Cyr.*Jo*.6(4.584A); **ii.** main parallels ὁ Ἰ. ... τύπος...τοῦ κυρίου, παῖς μὲν ὡς υἱός...ἱερεῖον δὲ ὡς ὁ κύριος. ... ἐβάστασε τὰ ξύλα ...ὡς ὁ κύριος τὸ ξύλον. ἐγέλα δὲ μυστικῶς, ἐμπλῆσαι ἡμᾶς προφητεύων χαρᾶς τὸν κύριον τοὺς αἵματι κυρίου ἐκ φθορᾶς λελυτρωμένους. οὐκ ἔπαθεν δέ, ... ἀλλὰ καὶ τοῦ κυρίου τὴν θειότητα αἰνίττεται μὴ σφαγείς Clem.*paed*.1.5(p.103.25ff.; M.8.277A); Thdt.*eran*.3(4.202); **iii.** partic. points of resemblance; Isaac's rescue foreshadows Resurrection, Chrys.*Laz*.5.5(1.770D); Ἰ. μάρτυρα ζῶντα καὶ οὐ ζῶντα, ἀποθανόντα καὶ οὐκ ἀποθανόντα. ... τύπος γὰρ ἦν τοῦ δεσπότου ‡Chrys.*Abr*.2(2.744D); as type of Christ's divinity, the ram typifying the humanity which suffered, cf. *verbum vero in incorruptione permansit, quod est secundum spiritum Christus, cujus imago est I.*, Or.*hom.8.9 in Gen*.(p.84.27; M.12.209A); Thdt.*qu.73 in Gen*.(1.85); Isaac bearing wood as Christ bore Cross, Or.*hom.8.6 in Gen*.(p.81.5; M.12.206B); Cyr.*glaph.Gen*.3(1.86A); id.*hom.pasch*.5.7(5^2.58C); **b.** of Christ and Church Ἰσραηλιτικὸν...τὸ ἀληθινόν,...καὶ...γένος... Ἰ. ... ἡμεῖς ἐσμεν Just.*dial*.11.5(M.6.500A); Or.*Cels*.4.43(p.316.14; M.11.1100A); Isaac's marriage signifying union of Christ with Church, Gr.Naz.*or*.43.71(M.36.592C); Cyr.*glaph.Gen*.3(1.90Dff.); his birth prefiguring baptism προῆλθεν ἐκεῖνος ἀπὸ μήτρας κατεψυγμένης. ἀνέβης σὺ ἀπὸ ὑδάτων ψυχρῶν Chrys.*hom.2.4 in Ac.9*:*1*(3.115A); **3.** Gnost., Abraham, Isaac, and Jacob as figures of three principles in Sethian system, Hipp.*haer*.5.20(p.121.11; M.16.3186A).

ἰσάγγελος, *equal to the angels*; **1.** ref. future life τὸ πρόσωπον ἰ. ἔχοντες πρόσωπον πρὸς πρόσωπον τὴν ἐπαγγελίαν ὀψόμεθα Clem.*paed*.1.6(p.112.4; M.8.293B); cf.id.*str*.7.14(p.60.7; M.9.517A); ὅταν τραπέντες εἰς φῶς τὰ σώματα ἰ. γένωνται *Hom.Clem*.17.16; Ath.*exp.Ps*.8:8(M.27.84A); ref. Lc.20:36 interpreted of beatific vision, Dion.Ar.*d.n*.1.4(M.3.592C); **2.** ref. present life of men who have faith and charity, Clem.*str*.7.10(p.42.11; M.9.481A); Cyr.H.*catech*.4.1; Dion.Ar.*d.n*.7.2(M.3.868C); of fathers of Nicaea, Anast.S.*hod*.9(M.89.141C); ref. conquest of bodily impulses ὁ...εἰς ἀπάθειαν μελετήσας αὐξήσας τε εἰς εὐποιΐαν γνωστικῆς τελειότητος ἰ. Clem.*str*.6.12(p.484.29; 325D); νηστεία τῆς ἰ. πολιτείας τὸ μίμημα Cyr.*hom.pasch*.1(5^2.8B); Hyper.*mon*.53(M.79.1480A); ἡ ἰ. ἁγνεία Nil.*epp*.1.181(M.79.152C); ref. prayer ὁ...μετ' ἀγγέλων εὔχεται, ὡς ἂν ἤδη καὶ ἰ. Clem.*str*.7.12(p.56.6; 508C); Evagr.Pont.*or*.113(M.79.1192D); Max.*myst*.(M.91.709B); ref. monastic life ἰ. ἐπίσκοπος *Dial.Tim.et Aquil*.138 r° (p.104); ἰ. βίος Cyr.H.*catech*.4.24; τὸν παρθενίας βίον ἰ. †Bas.Anc.*virg*.68(M.30.808D).

ἰσάζ-ω, *make equal*; Christol., Ath.*syn*.49(p.273.11; M.26.780B); εἰ μὲν οὖν ἄλλην ἀρχὴν ἐνθυμεῖταί τις καὶ ἄλλον πατέρα διὰ τὸ ~ον τῶν λεγομένων, μανικὸν τὸ ἐνθύμημα *ib*.50(p.274.9; 781B); Nonn.*par.Jo*.5:18(M.43.788B).

ἰσάμιλλος, **1.** *equal in contest*, Isid.Pel.*epp*.5.351(M.78.1540B); Cyr.*Juln*.1(6^2.2A); **2.** *to be contested on equal terms*, id.*Ps*.34:16(M.69.892C); **3.** *equal in force* or *meaning* ἰ. ... τῷ εἰπεῖν 'κύριος μαρτυρεῖ ...' τὸ γράφειν 'τὸ πνεῦμα τῆς ἀληθείας...μαρτυρήσει' Didym.*Trin*.2.5(M.39.501A).

***ἰσάνθρωπος**, *equal with man*, Sever.*creat*.6.5(M.56.491); cf.Proc.G.*Gen*.3:7(M.87.196A); †Jo.D.*creat*.7(p.137).

***ἰσαπόστολος**, *equal to the apostles*; of Thecla, *A.Paul.et Thecl*.tit.(p.235n.); of a notable preacher, *V.Aberc*.70(p.50.1ff.); *ib*.80(p.55.16); Attic.*ep.Cyr*.1(p.23.12; M.77.349A).

ἰσάριθμος, *equal in number* ἰ. ... καθ' ὑμᾶς [sc. Nestorians] δεῖ εἶναι τὰς φύσεις καὶ τὰς ὑποστάσεις Leont.H.*Nest*.2.13(M.86.1564A).

[*]**ἰσελαστικός**, *of a triumphant entry*, *Orac.Sib*.2.39 (v.l. εἰσελαστικός).

ἰσηγορ-έω, **1.** *speak as an equal* πῶς ~ήσειεν ἂν ἄνθρωπος [i.e. Christ] θεῷ Cyr.*Nest*.2.10(p.48.6; 6^1.53D); **2.** ? *speak in public*, Meth.*symp*.7(p.70.13; M.18.121B).

ἰσημέριος, *equinoctial*, *Const.App*.5.17.3.

***ἰσία**, ἡ, *equality*, ‡Ath.*annunt*.3(M.28.920D).

***ἰσογενής**, *equal*, Cyr.*dial.Trin*.5(5^1.581C).

***ἰσογνωμέω**, *be like-minded with*, Cyr.*Jo*.2.1(4.131E).

***ἰσογνώμων**, **1.** *holding the same beliefs*, Cyr.*apol.orient*.proem.(p.33.29; 6^1.158B); id.*Juln*.3(6^2.84C); **2.** *of the same will* or *intention* ὅτι...ὑπάρχοι κατὰ φύσιν θεός, καὶ ἐκ θεοῦ γεγέννηται πατρός, ἰσοσθενής τε ἐστὶ καὶ ἰ. αὐτῷ id.*Jo*.9.1(4.811E); *ib*.2.9(238B).

***ἰσογραφία**, ἡ, *contemporary record*, Gr.Naz.*carm*.2.2(poem.)2.16(M.37.1478A).

ἰσόδοξος, *equal in glory*, †Ath.*exp.fid*.1(M.25.201A).

***ἰσοδόξως**, *with equal glory, so as to ascribe equal glory*, †Diad.*Ar*.7(M.65.1164A).

[*]**ἰσοδύναμαι**, *be entitled to equality* τίς τῶν...ἁγίων ἰσοδύναται εἶναι τοῦ κυρίου [τῷ κυρίῳ] Hesych.H.*Ps.tit*.88(M.27.1025C cod. ἴσος δύναται).

ἰσοδυναμία, ἡ, *equality of power*, Mac.Aeg.*hom*.3.6(M.34.472C); *ib*.16.1(613B).

ἰσοδύναμος, *equal in power*; **1.** Trin. ἁγίαν τριάδα...ἰ. Cosm.Ind.*top*.6(M.88.333C); *cat.2Cor*.4:6(p.375.26); of Christ, ref. Jo.10:30 τὸ ...ἰ. ὑπερδεικνύων ‡Eust.*Laz*.7(p.33.2); κατὰ πάντα ἰ. τῷ πατρί Ath.*virg*.1(p.35.7; M.28.252A); Didym.*Trin*.2.5(M.39.496C); ‡Cyr.H.*occurs*.8(M.33.1196A); Nil.*epp*.1.79(M.79.117A); Gel.Cyz.*h.e*.2.15.3(M.85.1257D); **2.** (Docetic) ἐγέννησαν...τὸν...σωτῆρα...ἰ. ... τῷ σπέρματι τῷ συκίνῳ [sc. ὁ πρῶτος θεός], πλὴν ὅτι γενητός Hipp.*haer*.8.9(p.227.27; M.16.3351A); **3.** ref. eternity of world οὔτε...ἄναρχος ἡ ὕλη..., οὔτε διὰ τὸ ἄναρχον ἰ. τῷ θεῷ Tat.*orat*.5(p.6.13; M.6.817B); Meth.*creat*.7(p.498.17; M.18.340B); Mac.Aeg.*hom*.16.1(M.34.613B); **4.** εἰ ὁ θεὸς αὐτὴν [sc. ὕλην] ἐνεψύχωσε...οὐκέτι τῷ θεῷ ἐχθρόν τί ἐστιν ...ἢ ἰ. *Hom.Clem*.19.15; cf.*ib*.19.14.

***ἰσοεπής**, *speaking equivalently*, Cyr.*dial.Trin*.7(5^1.657E).

ἰσοζυγ-έω, *be equally balanced* τὰς ἁμαρτίας ~ούσας μετὰ τὰ ἔργα αὐτῆς ἅπαντα *T.Abr*.B 9(p.114.1).

ἰσόζυγος, *equal* (*to*), Hipp.*haer*.6.36(p.166.12; M.16.3250C); Epiph.*haer*.66.2(p.18.14; M.42.33A); Nil.*Eulog*.28(M.79.1129C).

***ἰσόζυξ**, = foreg., Nonn.*par.Jo*.5:27(M.43.789A); *ib*.6:57(801A); *ib*.14:18(809B).

***ἰσοθεΐα**, ἡ, **1.** *equality with God*, Ephr.3.298F; Chrys.*hom.59.2 in Mt*.(7.595B); Isid.Pel.*epp*.2.294(M.78.724B); Proc.G.*Gen*.3:1(M.87.189A); **2.** *equality of gods*, Cosm.Ind.*top*.1(M.88.72B).

***ἰσοθέλυμνος**, *of similar origin*, Eudoc.*Cypr*.2.116(M.85.849B).

ἰσόθεος, *equally divine*, Trin. ἓν φάος ἐν τρισσοῖς ἀμαρύγμασιν ἰ. Gr.Naz.*carm*.2.2(poem.)4.88(M.37.1512A).

***ἰσοθέως**, *as equal to God*, of veneration of Son λόγον...οὐ σέβετ' ἰ. πατρός Gr.Naz.*carm*.1.1.11.2(M.37.470A).

***ἰσόθρονος**, *on equal thrones, of equal majesty*; Trin., Eulog.*fr.Trin*.2.1(p.364).

ἰσοκέλευθος, *following the same path*, Gr.Naz.*carm*.1.2.5.4(M.37.642A).

ἰσοκέφαλος, *ambiguous* ἰ. δὲ ἦν ἡ θέα Tit.Bost.*fr.Lc*.19:29(p.233.13).

ἰσοκλεής, *equal in glory*; of Father and Son, Eus.*h.e*.1.2n.(M.20.60A); Cyr.*Jo*.7(4.670A); id.*Juln*.10(6^2.331B); ‡Caes.Naz.*dial*.127(M.38.1024).

***ἰσολαμπής**, *equal in light*, ‡Caes.Naz.*dial*.3(M.38.860).

ἰσομεγέθης, *equal in greatness* ἡ θεία τριὰς...ἰ. ‡Caes.Naz.*dial*.3(M.38.861); ἰ. τὸ θεῖον πνεῦμα ὑπάρχον γινώσκει τὸν πατέρα καὶ τὸν υἱόν *ib*.20(877).

ἰσομετρία, ἡ, *equality of measure*, Ant.Mon.*hom*.76(M.89.1656D).

ἰσόμετρος, *equal in measurement* or *weight*; met., *commensurate* οἷον ἰσομέτρους ταῖς ἀδικίαις τὰς τιμωρίας Const.ap.Eus.*v.C*.2.27(p.52.24; M.20.1005A); Cyr.*Os*.82(3.114B); ἰσομέτρῳ πρὸς αὐτὸν [sc. Christ] τιμῇ id.*Jo*.1.9(4.103A); Thdt.*h.rel*.14(3.1217).

***ἰσομέτρως**, **1.** *in an equal degree, equally* εἰ πᾶν τὸ γενητὸν ἕτερόν ἐστι...τοῦ ἀγενήτου κατὰ τὴν φύσιν, οὐ δύναται τῆς ἐκείνου δόξης ἰ. κοινωνεῖν Cyr.*thes*.17(5^1.179E); id.*Os*.145(3.178E); ἰ. ἔχω *be equal* ὁ...μονογενὴς υἱός, ὁ κατὰ πᾶν ὁτιοῦν ἰ. ἔχων τῷ γεγεννηκότι id.*apol.Thdt*.6(p.129.4; 6^1.223A); id.*ador*.9(1.317D); id.*ep*.1(p.13.29; 5^2.6B); **2.** *in equality, without subordination* πατὴρ ἀνάρχως καὶ δίχα πάθους ἐξ ὅλου ἑαυτοῦ ὅλον ἰ. τέτοκε τὸν υἱόν Didym.*Trin*.3.20(M.39.793D).

***ἰσονέμητος**, *equally distributed*, Gr.Naz.*carm*.1.1.27.104(M.37.506A).

***ἰσονεφής**, *reaching to the clouds*, Bas.Sel.*v.Thecl*.2.12(M.85.585C).

***ἰσονημία**, ἡ, *even thickness of yarn*, Thdr.Stud.*poen*.110(M.99.1748C).

***ἰσονοέομαι**, *be regarded as equivalent*, Sever.*sigill*.3(M.63.537).

***ἰσονυκτία**, ἡ, *equinox*, Epiph.*haer*.51.27(p.298.25).

***ἰσοπεριμέτρητος**, *of equal circumference*, ‡Just.*qu.et resp*.130(M.6.1381B).

§**ἰσόπετρος**, *equal of S. Peter*; of S. John, Thdr.Stud.*or*.9.12(M.99.788B).

***ἰσοπλασιάζω**, *multiply*, *Schol*.44 in Max.*qu.Thal*.65(M.90.781A).

***ἰσοποιέω**, *make equal*, *Ev.Thom*.A 13(p.152).

***ἰσοπροσήγορος**, *equal in designation*, Gel.Cyz.*h.e*.2.18.9(M.85.1276A).

ἰσόρροπος, **1.** *equally balanced* ἰ. λέγουσι τοῦ κακοῦ τὴν πρὸς τὸ ἀγαθὸν ἐναντίωσιν Bas.*hex*.2.4(1.16B; M.29.37B); Epiph.*haer*.66.2(p.18.15; M.42.33A); **2.** *equivalent* ἰ. τῷ εἰπεῖν... Didym.*Trin*.2.5(M.39.497A); Epiph.*anc*.98(p.119.7; M.43.193D); *ib*.4(p.10.15; 24A); id.*haer*.69.32(p.181.24; M.42.253B); **3.** *equivocal*; of arguments, Leont.H.*Nest*.4.5(M.86.1660D); **4.** *belonging to both alike*; of Christ, ref. Jo.5:19 ὁ ταῖς ἰ. τῷ θεῷ καὶ πατρὶ διαπρεπὴς ἐνεργίαις Cyr.*Jo*.2.6(4.216D); of BMV οὐρανοῦ καὶ γῆς ἰ. οἴκημα ‡Gr.Thaum.*annunt*.3(M.10.1177A).

ἴσος, **A.** *equal*; **1.** ref. equality in creatures; **a.** natural, as sign of existence of God, Ath.*gent*.36(M.25.72C); of all creatures as equally distant from God, Gr.Nyss.*or.catech*.27(p.104.3ff.; M.45.72B); and equally subject to him, *ib*.(p.105.3; 72D); **b.** in spiritual life τὴν ἀγάπην...πᾶσιν τοῖς φοβουμένοις τὸν θεὸν...ἴ. παρεχέτωσαν *1Clem*.21.7; Polyc.*ep*.4.2; ref. conditions of spiritual combat πᾶσι...πάντα ἴ. κεῖται παρὰ τοῦ θεοῦ Clem.*str*.7.3(p.15.6; M.9.425A); **2.** ref. God; **a.** discussion of equality in divine essence and operations, and of God as source of equality in creatures, Dion.Ar.*d.n*.9.10(M.3.917A); **b.** Trin.; **i.** in gen. ἴ. δόξα ‡Ath.*symb*.1(M.28.1581A); *ib*.2(1585A); ἐν ταύτῃ τῇ τριάδι οὐδὲν...μεῖζον ἢ ἔλαττον· ἀλλ' ὅλαι αἱ τρεῖς ὑποστάσεις...ἴ. *ib*.1(1584A); *ib*.2(1586A); *ib*.3(1587C); *ib*.4(1589C); **ii.** of three Persons as equal by nature λόγος...ὢν τοῦ πατρός, ἴ. αὐτοῦ ἐστιν. ... κατὰ φύσιν ἴ. ἐστὶ...τῷ πατρί Ath.*inc.et c.Ar*.4(M.26.989C); ὁ κατὰ μορφὴν...ἴ., καὶ κατ' οὐσίαν ἐστὶν ἴ. Didym.(‡Bas.)*Eun*.4(1.280B; M.29.673B); ref. Jo.5:18 ὡς ἀναγκαίως ἑπομένου τῷ πατέρα ἔχειν τὸν θεὸν τοῦ ἴ. ὑπάρχειν αὐτῷ Bas.*Eun*.1.24(1.235B; M.29.564D); Cyr.*Jo*.2.5(4.214B); cf.*ib*.1.10(105C); εἰσι τῇ...οὐσίᾳ κατὰ πάντα ἴ. τὰ τρία Jo.V H.*icon*.4(M.96.1353A); **iii.** equality proved from scripture; equality of Son and H. Ghost from Jo.20:22 and Jo.16:7,13,14, Ath.*Ar*.1.50(M.26.116C); of H. Ghost, ref. 1Jo.4:13 ἀνάγκη...θεοῦ ἀληθινοῦ ὄντος τοῦ πατρός, θεὸν ἀληθινὸν εἶναι ἴ. αὐτῷ Didym.*Trin*.2.5(M.39.496B); Gr.Nyss.*Eun*.2(2 p.380.1; M.45.561B); **iv.** ref. Arian doctrine ἔμαθον οἱ Ἀρειανοὶ λέγειν...ὅτι οὔτε ἴ. τῷ θεῷ ἐστιν οὔτε πατὴρ ἴδιός ἐστι καὶ φύσει τοῦ λόγου ὁ θεός Ath.*Ar*.3.27(M.26.381B); acc. Eun., in view of Jo.14:28 Son could not be equal with Father, Bas.*Eun*.1.22(1.233D; M.29.561A); τίθεται...τὸ ἴ. ἐν τῷ ὄγκῳ...διὰ τοῦτο οὔτε ἴ. φησίν,...ἐπειδὴ καὶ ἄποσός ἐστι *ib*.1.23(234C; M.564A); against Eun. τὸ ἴ. μὴ ἐν τῇ τῶν ὄγκων παραμετρήσει, ἀλλ' ἐν τῇ ταὐτότητι τῆς δυνάμεως *ib*.(234D; M.564B); τὸ μεῖζον...ᾗ γεννήτωρ, καὶ τὸ ἴ. καθ' ὃ θεός Isid.Pel.*epp*.3.334(M.78.992C); **3.** Christol. μείζων ἐστὶ τοῦ υἱοῦ διὰ τὸ σῶμα...ἴ. δέ, καθότι ὅλος ὅλον τέλειον ἐγέννησεν ὁ πατὴρ ἀϊδίως τὸν υἱόν ‡Ath.*serm.fid*.34(p.29; M.26.1288C); ἴ. εἶναι θεῷ καὶ ἐν τῇ σαρκὶ λέγει Apoll.*corp.et div*.15(p.191.21; M.*PL*.8.875C); οὐκ ἄνθρωπος...ἐστιν ἴ. θεῷ...ἀλλὰ ⟨ὁ⟩...γεγεννημένος ἐκ θεοῦ πατρὸς θεὸς υἱὸς μονογενής Epiph.*haer*.65.7(p.10.23; M.42.24D); ἴ. θεῷ καὶ ἐλάττων ἀγγέλων Gennad.*fr*.3(p.78.29); ‡Ath.*symb*.1(M.28.1584B); *ib*.3(1588A); of his equality with Father, proved: from scripture, Didym.*Trin*.3.2(M.39.792B); by miracles ἦν ἀπὸ τῶν ἔργων μαθεῖν...ὅτι ἴ. ἐστὶ τοῦ γεγεννηκότος Chrys.*hom.40.3 in Jo*.(8.240A); *ib.49.2*(291A); ref. Jo.14:23, *ib.45.3*(266B).

B. *equable, balanced* τὸ...λιτόν...ἴ. Clem.*paed*.2.12(p.233.19; M.8.552B); of 'gnostic' in his ἀπαθεία, id.*str*.7.12(p.49.23; M.9.496C); ὅλος ἦν ἴ. ὡς ὑπὸ τοῦ λόγου κυβερνώμενος, καὶ ἐν τῷ κατὰ φύσιν ἑστώς Ath.*v.Anton*.14(M.26.865A); ὅταν ἐμπέσωσιν εἰς ζημίαν...οὐ λυποῦνται, ἀλλ' ἴ. εἰσίν Mac.Aeg.*hom*.27.6(M.34.697B).

ἰσοσθενής, *equal in power*; Trin., of Son ἰ. ὢν τῷ πατρί Or.*sel.in Ps*.49:2(M.12.1449A); ὁ Χριστὸς τῷ πατρὶ ὑπάρχει κατὰ τὴν θεότητα ἰ. Nil.*epp*.1.79(M.79.117B); Cyr.*hom.pasch*.15.3(5^{2}.204D); id.*apol.orient*.9(p.52.18; 6^{1}.183B); ‡Caes.Naz.*dial*.3(M.38.861); ref. Jo.15:10 τὸ...τῆς θεότητος...ἰ. ἐκ τούτων δηλῶν *ib*.(860); ἰ. σου πνεῦμα ‡Jo.D.*carm.pent*.33(p.214; M.96.833C); Marcionite ἰ. [οὐκ] εἰσιν αἱ τρεῖς ἀρχαί Adam.*dial*.1.4(p.8.3; M.11.1720B).

***ἰσοσταθμία**, ἡ, *just weighing*, Ant.Mon.*hom*.76(M.89.1656D).

***ἰσοστάθμως**, **1.** *in equal proportion, equally*, Cyr.*ador*.17(1.626A); **2.** c. ἔχω, *be in equal proportion*, id.*Os*.41(3.73A).

ἰσοστατ-έω, **1.** *be equal*, Cyr.*Jo*.5.1(4.460C); of Son οὐ μείων...ὢν τοῦ πατρὸς...κατὰ πᾶν ὁτιοῦν τὸ ~οῦν id.*inc.unigen*.(5^{1}.698D); **2.** *be impartial*; of God, Clem.*paed*.1.8(p.132.20; M.8.337A).

ἰσόστοιχος, *in even ranks*, Dion.Al.ap.Eus.*p.e*.14.25(777D; M.21.1280B).

***ἰσοσχέδιος**, *identical*; neut. as subst., Gel.Cyz.*h.e*.2.21.5(M.85.1284C).

***ἰσοσχημάτως**, *so as to correspond in form*, Areth.*Apoc*.27(M.106.629C).

ἰσοτενής, *level*, Paul.Sil.*ambo*.187(M.86.2259A).

ἰσοτετράγωνος, *square*, *V.Aberc*.76(p.53.2); Max.*comput*.3(M.19.1265A).

ἰσότης, ἡ, *equality*; **1.** in gen. παντὶ ἀνθρώπῳ...ἰ. ἐστὶ κατὰ τὴν φύσιν Bas.*ep*.262.1(3.403D; M.32.973A); Cyr.*ador*.6(1.203C); Dion.Ar.*d.n*.8.9(M.3.897B); **2.** ref. Jo.6:40 ὁ κύριος...τῆς σωτηρίας τὴν ἰ. ἀπεκάλυψεν Clem.*paed*.1.6(p.107.8; M.8.284C); ref. Mt.18:3 ὁ κύριος...τὴν ἰ. παρεγγυᾷ id.*str*.5.5(p.345.22; M.9.53A); Cyr.*Ps*.10:7(M.69.793C); **3.** in God, Clem.*str*.5.10(p.371.15; M.9.104A); ῥητέον ἴσον τὸν θεόν...κατὰ τὸ πᾶσαν ἰ., νοητήν, νοεράν, λογικήν, αἰσθητικήν, οὐσιώδη, φυσικήν, θελητὴν...ἑνιαίως ἐν ἑαυτῷ προειληφέναι, κατὰ τὴν...πάσης ἰ. ποιητικὴν δύναμιν Dion.Ar.*d.n*.9.10(M.3.917A); οὔτε ἰ. οὔτε ἀνισότης id.*myst*.5(M.3.1048A); πᾶσα ἑνότης καὶ ἰ. καὶ ταὐτότης ἐν τριάδι ‡Caes.Naz.*dial*.3(M.38.861); of Christ's equality with Father; proved from Jo.16:14, Ammon.*Jo*.16:14(M.85.1497C); from his works, Chrys.*hom.61.2 in Jo*.(8.364C); from Jo.5:19, *ib.38.4*(222B); Cyr.*Jo*.2.6(4.216B); from Phil.2:6, Thdt.*inc*.10(M.75.1432A); id.*Phil*.2:6(3.454); Ambr.*fr*.ap.CLater.*act*.2(H.3.744E); Eunomian μηδὲ ὁμοιούσιον, ἐπείπερ...σημαίνει τῆς οὐσίας...ἰ. Eun.*apol*.26(M.30.864C); **4.** Christol., of humanity of Christ acc. Nest. ὁ ἐν ἰ. γεγονὼς τῷ πρὸς θεὸν λόγον Cyr.*Pulch*.(p.35.27; 5^{2}.142A); cf.id.*Nest*.2.1(p.35.5; 6^{1}.34B).

ἰσοτιμία, ἡ, *equality of honour, equality*, natural (ref. Mt.18:3) τὴν...ἰ. τῆς φύσεως Bas.*reg.br*.216(2.487D; M.31.1225B); ref. wives' subjection to husbands ἡ γὰρ ἰ. μάχην ποιεῖ Chrys.*hom.26.2 in 1Cor*.(10.230B); in Christianity; of equality of members of Church, *ib.30.3*(273B); ἐλπίζειν ἀγγέλων ἰ. Gr.Naz.*or*.14.23(M.35.888A); Trin.; Didym.(‡Bas.)*Eun*.5(1.308C; M.29.740A); equality of Son and H. Ghost proved from Jo.16:14, Chrys.*hom.78.2 in Jo*.(8.461A); from Jo.17:17, *ib.82.1*(461A); Christol., ref. Nest. διαιρεῖν τὰς φύσεις,...καὶ κατὰ μόνην ἰ. συνῆφθαι λέγειν ἄνθρωπον θεῷ Cyr.*ep*.40(p.28.20; 5^{2}.118B); id.*Chr.un*.(5^{1}.768A); *ib*.(762A); εἴ τις λέγει...κατ' ἰσοτιμίαν...τὴν ἕνωσιν τοῦ θεοῦ λόγου πρὸς ἄνθρωπον γεγενῆσθαι...ἀνάθεμα ἔστω Justn.*conf.anath*.4(p.90.29; M.86.1015A); Sophr.H.*ep.syn*.(M.87.3165A).

ἰσότιμος, *equal in honour*; **1.** in gen.; of members of Church, Chrys.*hom.30.3 in 1Cor*.(10.273A); of woman ἰ. ἄνθρωπον Bas.Sel.*or*.2.4(M.85.44A); **2.** Trin. οὐδὲ γὰρ ἰ. αὐτὰς [sc. hypostases of Father and Son] ὁριζόμεθα Eus.*e.th*.2.7(p.104.14; M.24.909A); υἱὸν...τὴν ἀληθινὴν εἰκόνα τοῦ πατρός, ἰ. †Ath.*exp.fid*.1(M.25.201A); τὸ ἰ. τῆς δυνάμεως Chrys.*hom.46.1 in Jo*.(8.270B); ἰ. τῷ πατρί *ib.58.2*(339A); Thdt.*Trin*.14(M.75.1165C); ref. Is.30:1 τὸ...πνεύματος ἰ. ἔδειξεν Proc.G.*Is*.30(M.87.2260A); τριάδα...ἰ. Cosm.Ind.*top*.6(M.88.333C); **3.** Christol., ref. Jo.20:17 as not implying Christ's equality with righteous men, Cyr.H.*catech*.7.7.

***ἰσοτροπέω**, *behave in the same way*, Cyr.*Jo*.6(4.559D).

***ἰσοτροπία**, ἡ, *like behaviour*, Cyr.*Jo*.4.5(4.401B); id.*Ps*.36:1(M.69.924D).

***ἰσότροπος**, *of like character*, Didym.*Trin*.1.27(M.39.408A); Cyr.*glaph.Gen*.1(1.17E); id.*Os*.1(3.6C).

***ἰσοτρόπως**, *in the same way*, Pall.*h.Laus*.57(M.34.1250B; v.l. for ὡς ἐν ἐσόπτρῳ p.150.13); Cyr.*dial.Trin*.7(5^{1}.657A).

***ἰσοτυπία**, ἡ, *likeness in form, similarity*, Cyr.*Jo*.11.2(4.931A).

ἰσότυπος, **1.** *of the same kind* τὰ ἰ. πεποιηκυῖα [sc. ἡ Ἑλένη] Iren.*haer*.1.23.2(M.41.289A); Epiph.*haer*.30.31(p.375.23; M.41.460B); **2.** *identical* σφραγὶς γάρ ἐστιν ἰ. ἐν αὐτῷ δεικνὺς τὸν πατέρα, λόγος ζῶν Ath.*hom.in Mt.11:27*(M.25.217B); cf.*Lit.Bas*.(p.322.29); ἡ ἰ. σφραγίς Bas.*Spir*.64(3.54B; M.32.185C); Didym.*Trin*.1.16(M.39.336A); Thdr.Stud.*antirr*.1.19(M.99.348D); **3.** neut. as subst., *copy*, CHier.(335)*ep*.(p.248.7; M.26.720A); Epiph.*mens*.6(M.43.245B); Justn.*ep.Thdr.Mops*.(p.66.16; M.86.1087A).

***ἰσοτυπ-όω**, *be of the same form*, of icons ~ούσης...τῆς εἰκόνος τῷ πρωτοτύπῳ...οὐ πάντως ~οῦντος...τοῦ εἰκονίσματος τῷ ἀρχετύπῳ Thdr.Stud.*antirr*.3.3.5(M.99.421C,D).

***ἰσοτύπως**, *equally, in the same manner* φωρᾶσθαι καὶ τοῦτον ἀγύρτην...ἰ. ταῖς προειρημέναις Epiph.*haer*.34.21(p.38.18; M.41. 625B); ἑαυτὸν [sc. Χριστόν] πληροῦντα τὰ ἰ. παρ' ἐκείνου [sc. Ἐλισσαίου] προγεγενημένα *ib*.42.11(p.144.2; 756A).

***ἰσουργ-έω**, **1.** *do the same as*, ref. Jo.5:21 τὸ ∼εῖν δύνασθαι τῷ θεῷ...ἕτερον οὐδὲν εἴη ἄν, ἢ θεός Cyr.*dial.Trin*.3(5¹.493E); **2.** *effect equally* ἴσος λέγεται ὁ θεός,...ὡς ὑποστάτης τῆς αὐτοϊσότητος...καθ' ἣν ∼εῖ τὴν δι' ἀλλήλων χώρησιν, ὡς ἐπὶ τῶν στοιχείων Dion.Ar.*d.n*. 9.10(M.3.936A).

***ἰσουργία, ἡ**, *doing of like things*, Cyr.*ador*.10(1.361C).

ἰσουργός, **1.** *equal in operation* ἡ ἁγία τριὰς ἰσοσθενής τε καὶ ἰ. Cyr.*apol.orient*.9(p.52.18; 6¹.183B); id.*Nest*.4(p.76.31; 6¹.97A); θεὸν ἐκ θεοῦ κατὰ φύσιν...ἰ. id.*ep*.1(p.13.28; 5².6B); id.*hom.pasch*.13(5². 184A); of H. Ghost οὐκ ἐγχωρεῖ αὐτὸ ποίημα καθεστάναι, ἀλλὰ συνεργὸν καὶ ἰ. τῷ δημιουργῷ Didym.*Trin*.3.2(M.39.804C); **2.** *doing similar things*, Cyr.*inc.unigen*.(5¹.701A).

***ἰσοφαής**, *equal in splendour*, Gr.Naz.*carm*.2.1.87.16(M.37. 1434A); ‡Caes.Naz.*dial*.117(M.38.1004).

***ἰσοφέριστος**, *of equal excellence*, Gr.Naz.*carm*.1.1.1.32(M.37. 401A); *ib*.1.1.4.65(421A).

ἰσοφυής, *of the same nature*; of things, Nonn.*par.Jo*.13:15 (M.43.861C); of Father and Son, *ib*.1:1(749A); ἰ. καὶ ὁμοούσιον ...τῷ πατρί Cyr.*hom.pasch*.24(5².291A); Leont.H.*Nest*.5.4(M.86. 1729A).

***ἰσοφυΐα, ἡ**, *identity of nature*, Leont.H.*monoph*.(M.86.1812C).

***ἰσοφυῶς**, *with the same nature*, ref. Persons of Trin., Anast.S. *hod*.17(M.89.264C).

ἰσόφωτος, *of equal light*, Rom.Mel.(*SBBAW* 1898² p.160); of Trin., Eulog.*fr.Trin*.2.1(p.364).

ἰσόχειρ, *having the same hand*, i.e. *of equal power*, ref. Jo.10:27f. ὁ δὲ δὴ κατάρχων ἐν ἴσῳ τῶν ὅλων ἰ. [sc. Christ] τε καὶ ἰσοσθενὴς τῷ πατρί Cyr.*dial.Trin*.5(5¹.578A).

ἰσόχρονος, *coeval* (Platonist) τὴν...τῆς ὕλης δύναμιν ἀγέννητον καὶ ἰ.‡Just.*coh.Gr*.23(M.6.284A); (Manich.) τὴν ὕλην ἀγένητον ὑποτίθενται καὶ ἰ. ... τῷ θεῷ Alex.Lyc.*Man*.24(p.35.16; M.18.444D); refutation of this view, Mac.Aeg.*hom*.16.1(M.34.613B).

***Ἰσραήλ, ὁ**, *Israel*; **1.** etym.; **a.** 'seeing'; **i.** ὁ Ἰ. ὁ ὁρῶν τὸν θεόν Clem.*paed*.1.9(p.135.9; M.8.341C); cf.Or.*princ*.4.3.12(p.341.16; M.11. 395B); Eus.*p.e*.11.6(519B; M.21.860D); †Bas.*Is*.15(1.388B; M.30.141C); **ii.** Ἰ. ἑρμηνεύεται νοῦς ὁρῶν τὸν θεόν Mac.Aeg.*hom*.47.5(M.34.800B); Cyr.*glaph.Gen*.2(1.49B); †Leont.B.*sect*.1.2(M.86.1196D); Max.*qu. Thal*.65(M.90.753B); **iii.** Ἰ. ... ἄνθρωπος ὁρῶν τὸν θεόν Hipp.*Noët*. 5(p.244.25; M.10.809D); Eus.*p.e*.7.8(310D; M.525B); v. διορατικός; **b.** 'conquering' τὸ Ἰ. ὄνομα τοῦτο σημαίνει· ἄνθρωπος νικῶν δύναμιν· τὸ γὰρ ἰσρα ἄνθρωπος νικῶν ἐστι, τὸ δὲ ἢλ δύναμις Just.*dial*.125. 3(M.6.765D); **2.** of old Israel; its rejection of Christ prophesied in Os.9:17, Cyr.*Lc*.7:9(M.72.609A); as cause of subsequent sufferings, *ib*.2:34(505B); its responsibility; as God's chosen people, it was necessary that some of Israel should forsake its inheritance before the gentiles could enter into it, Or.*comm.in Rom*.8.12(M.14. 1196A); οὐ γὰρ ἵνα σωθῶσιν οἱ ἐθνικοί, διὰ τοῦτο τοῦ Ἰ. τινες ἐπωρώθησαν, ἀλλὰ πωρωθέντων τούτων ἐκεῖνο ἐπηκολούθησεν Gennad.*fr. Rom*.11:32(p.402.14; M.85.1720A); its conversion, prophesied in Jer.31:37, Or.*comm.in Rom*.8.12(M.14.1196C); and Is.29:22–23, Cyr. *Is*.3.2(2.418B); Rom.11:25 quoted in support, *ib*.1.4(112C); Proc.G. *Is*.29:22–24(M.87.2257D); **3.** of Christ as Israel, Just.*dial*.75.2(M.6. 652B); as ἄνθρωπος νικῶν δύναμιν Christ overcame Devil's power, *ib*.125.3ff.(M.6.765D); πτερνίσας τὴν ἀντικειμένην ἐνέργειαν μόνος τε ὁρῶν τὸν πατέρα καί, ὅτε ἄνθρωπος γεγένηται, Ἰακὼβ ἐστι καὶ Ἰ. Or.*Jo*.1.35(40; p.46.5; M.14.93C); ὁ τέλειος Ἰ. Hipp.*Noët*.5(p.243.24; M.10.809C); **4.** of Church as Israel; in gen., Or.*comm.in Mt*.17.5 (p.590.27; M.13.1485C); τὸν ἀληθινὸν Ἰ. ... τὸν ὁρῶντα θεόν *Const. App*.7.36.2; cf.*ib*.7.35.4; *Lit.ib*.8.15.7; Eus.*fr.Lc*.1:32(M.24.532C); Olymp.*Eccl*.1:1f.(M.93.481A); Areth.*Apoc*.66(M.106.768D); in rel. to old Israel; ref. prophecies about Israel, Or.*comm.in Rom*.8.12(M. 14.1197Cff.); Ἰ. as type of Church, Cyr.*Jo*.1.9(4.92E); Church so called after Christ who gave his own name of Ἰ. to Jacob κηρύσσων καὶ διὰ τούτου ὅτι πάντες οἱ δι' αὐτοῦ τῷ πατρὶ προσφεύγοντες εὐλογημένος Ἰ. ἐστιν Just.*dial*.125.5(M.6.768B); Or.*Jo*.1.35(40; p.46.7; M. 14.93C); faithful remnant of Israel being in Church, †Bas.*Is*.22(1. 396B; M.30.160C); seed of Church, Cyr.*Is*.1.4(2.111E); **5.** Christians as τὸ σπέρμα τῶν υἱῶν Ἰ. Cyr.*Is*.4.3(2.624E); as ὁ νοητὸς Ἰ. because they see God, Proc.G.*Is*.47:1–15(M.87.2444A); esp. of saints, Clem.*exc.Thdot*.56(p.126.3; M.9.685C); Diod.*Ps*.72:1(M.33.1613B); Hesych.H.*Ps.tit*.71(M.27.944B); **6.** of angels, as preeminently seeing God, Or.*hom.11.4 in Num*.(p.83.21; M.12.648B); **7.** acc. Just. Gn., one of names of fem. principle, Hipp.*haer*.5.26(p.127.4; M.16. 3194C); **8.** name, or expression, 'God of Israel'; used by pagans in exorcism, Or.*Cels*.1.22(p.72.32; M.11.700A); *ib*.5.45(p.49.14; 1252B).

***Ἰσραηλιτικός**, *Israelitish*, Clem.*paed*.2.1(p.167.7; M.8.408B); id. *str*.1.5(p.20.8; M.8.724B); Or.*engast*.4(p.287.11; M.12.1017D); τὸ Ἰ. Philost.*h.e*.3.6(M.65.483A); of Christians τὸ Ἰ. γένος Just.*dial*.11.5 (M.6.500A); *ib*.135.3(788A).

***Ἰσραηλῖτις, ἡ**, *Israelite* (fem.), Mel.*pass*.96 p.16.17; Eus.*qu. Steph*.1.8(M.22.889B).

ἰστέον, *one must know*, c. ὅτι, Clem.*str*.7.1(p.3.19; M.9.404B); *ib*. 4.21(p.307.30; M.8.1345A); c. acc. and infin., *ib*.4.24(p.316.28; 1364A); c. acc., Or.*Jo*.13.12(p.236.31; M.14.417A); *ib*.1.13(14; p.18.10; 45C).

ἵστημι, **A.** intrans. tenses; **1.** *stand*; **a.** ref. prayer; of standing as normal posture for able-bodied, *Const.App*.2.57.12; Ath.*v.Anton*. 65(M.26.933C); liturg.; faithful told when to stand, usu. by deacon, at beginning ἐπὶ προσευχὴν στάθητε cf.*Lit.Marc*.(p.113.4); at end of preparation, *Lit.Jac*.(p.160.25); before Gospel, cf.*Lit.Marc*.(p.119. 8); cf.*Const.App*.2.57.8; before anaphora στῶμεν καλῶς *Lit.Jac*. (p.196.19); *Lit.Chrys*.(p.321.9); cf.*Const.App*.2.57.21; symbolism τὸν ἀναστάντα δεῖ ἑστάναι καὶ προσεύχεσθαι διὰ τὸ τὸν ἐγειρόμενον ὄρθιον εἶναι *ib*.7.45.1; τὸν διάκονον...λέγειν, ὀρθοὶ στῶμεν καλῶς,...νενομοθέτηται...ἵνα τοὺς χαμαὶ συρομένους λογισμούς...Chrys.*incomprehens*.4.5 (1.478C); Anast.S.*synax*.(M.89.836D); **b.** in system of Simon Magus; ὁ Ἑστώς as title claimed by him, *A.Petr.c.Sim*.2(p.80.37); Clem.*str*. 2.11(p.141.9; M.8.988C); *Hom.Clem*.18.14; *ib*.2.24; as seventh power of hebdomad ὁ ἑστώς, στάς, στησόμενος Hipp.*haer*.6.18(p.142.26ff.; M.16.3218D); οὐ λέγομεν δύο ἀπεστάλθαι ἀγγέλους, τὸν μὲν ἐπὶ τῷ κτίσαι κόσμον, τὸν δὲ ἐπὶ τῷ θέσθαι τὸν νόμον·...οὐδ' ὁ ἑστὼς στησόμενος ἀντικείμενος *Hom.Clem*.18.12; as identified with Christ, Hipp. *haer*.6.9(p.136.5; M.16.3207C); Χριστὸν ἑαυτὸν αἰνισσόμενος, ἑστῶτα προσαγορεύει *Hom.Clem*.2.22; *ib*.18.6; **2.** *be a prostitute*, Clem.*paed*. 3.3(p.248.34; M.8.584C); Thdt.*haer*.1.1(4.287).

B. trans., *keep* oath ὁ ὀμνύων ἐπὶ παραβάσει τῶν ἐντολῶν τοῦ θεοῦ οὐ τὸν ὅρκον ὀφείλει ἱστᾶν *Schol*. in Bas.*ep*.199 *can*.29(*Mon*.2 p.653).

ἱστίον, τό, *sail*, in phrase ὅλοις τοῖς ἰ. *under full sail*; met., Cyr. *Is*.4.3(2.638D); *ib*.5.2(781A); *ib*.5.3(798A).

ἱστοδόκη, ἡ, *mast-holder*, Thdt.*eran*.2(4.81).

[*]**ἱστοπόδη, ἡ**, *beam of a loom*, Chrys.*subintr*.9(1.242A).

***ἱστοπονία, ἡ**, *weaving*, Clem.*paed*.3.4(p.252.11; M.8.593B).

ἱστορέω, *represent, depict*, Steph.Diac.*v.Steph*.(M.100.1085A); Jo.D.*imag*.2.15(M.94.1301A); Jo.V H.*icon*.2(M.96.1352A).

ἱστορία, ἡ, **A.** *investigation, knowledge*; hence **1.** *sight* ὅσον ἐπ' ἐμῇ ἰ. *as far as I can see*, Or.*Jo*.6.2(12; p.130.30; M.14.237B); τῶν τόπων ἰ. ἕνεκεν Eus.*h.e*.6.11.2(M.20.541C); cf.*ib*.8.3.1(748A); Chrys. *hom.1.5 in Rom*.(9.442E); of visits, id.*comm.in Gal*.1:18(10.677E); *review* of troops, Eus.*v.C*.4.7(p.120.16; M.20.1156B); **2.** *consideration*, Gel.Cyz.*h.e*.2.17.28(M.85.1272B); *ib*.2.17.4(1265C).

B. *fact of history*, Or.*hom.19.15 in Jer*.(p.174.13; M.13.497A); Eus.*Marcell*.1.3(p.17.12; M.24.749B).

C. *narrative, history*; **1.** in gen., of God expressing truth in OT διὰ ἰ. τῆς περὶ πολέμων καὶ νενικηκότων to conceal it from unworthy, Or.*princ*.4.2.8(p.320.10; M.11.373A); of some history in OT containing impossibilities, thus showing that spiritual sense is to be sought, *ib*.4.3.4(p.328.15; 384A); ἡ μὲν ἰ. αὕτη [i.e. of Abraham and his children] οὐ τοῦτο μόνον παραδηλοῖ, ὅπερ φαίνεται, ἀλλὰ καὶ ἄλλα τινὰ ἀναγορεύει Chrys.*comm.in Gal*.4:23(10.710B); ref. Deuteronomy, which should be read, if at all, πρὸς τὴν ἰ. and not for instruction in Jewish observances, *Const.App*.1.6.7; **2.** of historical books of Bible περὶ μὲν τῶν πέντε Μωυσέως ἐπιγεγραμμένων βιβλίων... περὶ δὲ τῆς λοιπῆς ἰ. Or.*princ*.4.2.6(p.318.1; M.11.369B); ᾠκονόμησέ τινα οἱονεὶ σκάνδαλα καὶ...ἀδύνατα διὰ μέσου ἐγκαταταχθῆναι τῷ νόμῳ καὶ τῇ ἰ. ὁ τοῦ θεοῦ λόγος [i.e. to call attention to spiritual sense] *ib*. 4.2.9(p.321.6; 373B); ref. Ex. ἐν παλαιᾷ ἰ. Cyr.H.*catech*.19.2; ἐν ἰ. τε καὶ προφητείᾳ καὶ νόμῳ Gr.Nyss.*Eun*.2(2 p.298.20; M.45.469A); πᾶσαν τὴν παλαιὰν ἀεὶ νόμον καλεῖ καὶ τοὺς προφήτας καὶ τὰς ἰ. Chrys.*hom. 26.1 in 1Cor*.(10.333C); Μωυσῆς...τὴν παλαιὰν ἰ. συγγράψας Thdt. *ep*.146(4.1265); **3.** *literal sense* of scripture (v. ἀναγωγή, θεωρία); in gen., Eus.*Marcell*.1.2(p.10.21; M.24.733B); Diod.*Ps*.57:10(M.33. 1596A); id.*proem.Ps.118*(p.95.38); Nil.*serm*.1(M.79.1264B); Thdt. *Nah*.2:1(2.1525); τὴν ἰ. τὴν γραφικήν Proc.G.*Jud*.5:6(M.87.1052D); dist. from varieties of spiritual sense; **a.** from ἀναγωγή, Or.*hom. 19.14 in Jer*.(p.171.1; M.13.492B) cit. s.v.; Chrys.*hom.28.4 in Mt*.(7. 338B); Thdt.*Ps*.13:1(1.681); **b.** from θεωρία: τὸ καθ' ἰ. γεγενημένον opp. πρὸς τὴν τροπικωτέραν...θεωρίαν, Gr.Nyss.*v.Mos*.(M.44.337C); Isid.Pel.*epp*.4.203(M.78.1292A); **c.** from spiritual sense denoted by other terms ἡ ἀλληγορία,...ἡ ἱ. ‡Hipp.*fr.46 in Pr.*(p.174.7); κατὰ μὲν τὴν ἱ. ... κατὰ δὲ μυστικὸν λόγον Or.*Jo.*2.1(p.52.19; M.14.105A); κατὰ τὸν βαθύτερον λόγον *ib.*2.29(24; p.85.30; 164C); id.*fr.77 in Lc.*(p.271.11); Cyr.*Ps.*35:6(M.69.917B); Thdt.*Is.*15:2(2.274); ἡ πρόρρησις κυρίως μὲν ἁρμόττει τῷ σωτῆρι Χριστῷ· κατὰ δὲ ἱ. Σαδούκ id.*qu.7 in 1Reg.*(1.361); prior to spiritual sense, as not requiring a spiritual approach for its understanding προενοήσατο...ὁ θεῖος λόγος ἱ. καὶ γραφῆς τῆς κατὰ τὸ ῥητόν, ἵνα θρέψῃ τὸν κατὰ σάρκα γεγενημένον τῷ Ἀβραὰμ ἐν τοῖς κατὰ σάρκα πρῶτον λόγοις Or.*hom.5.15 in Jer.*(p.44.22; M.13.317C); cf.id.*engast.*2(p.283.25ff.; M.12.1013B); showing necessity of spiritual interprn.; divergences between the narratives of the four gospels show rel. unimportance of lit. sense, id.*Jo.*10.3(2; p.173.26; M.14.312A); some records would be puerile unless spiritually significant, *ib.*10.26(17; p.199.13; 353C); cf.*ib.*10.40(24; p.217.17ff.; 385A); ref. Jo.8:39 δεῖ πᾶσαν τὴν κατὰ τὸν Ἀβραὰμ ἀλληγοροῦντα ἱ. ἕκαστον πνευματικῶς ποιῆσαι τῶν πεπραγμένων ὑπ' αὐτοῦ *ib.*20.10(p.337.30; 592C); rules for interprn.: not everything has spiritual sense πολλῷ...πλείονά ἐστι τὰ κατὰ τὴν ἱ. ἀληθευόμενα τῶν προσυφανθέντων γυμνῶν πνευματικῶν id.*princ.*4.3.4(p.329.11; M.11.384B); Sever.*creat.*4.2(M.56.459) cit. s. θεωρία; Isid. Pel.*epp.*4.203(M.78.1292A); Olymp.*fr.Job* proem.(M.93.17C); lit. sense is foundation of spiritual, Cyr.*Is.*1.4(2.113E); conditions in which details may be disregarded, Gr.Nyss.*v.Mos.*(M.44.340C); extensions of meaning: in parables, the ἱ. is not the moral but the anecdote itself, Cyr.*Jo.*6(4.642C); in prophecy, the ἱ. is the event prophesied, Thdt.*Zach.*14:8(2.1663); **4.** *picture, representation*, Mac. Aeg.*hom.*7.1(M.34.524A); of pictures of OT and NT which churches may contain for sake of illiterate, Nil.*epp.*4.61(M.79.577D); of patterns on silk, id.*exerc.*70(M.79.804B).

ἱστορικός, *historical*; **1.** ref. literal sense of scripture οὐχ ἱ. διήγησιν ἔχοντα, ἀλλὰ θεωρίαν νοητήν Or.*fr.20 in Jo.*(p.501.16); id. *Jo.*10.18(13; p.189.28; M.14.337D) cit. s. νοητός; id.*adnot.in Num.* 23:7(M.17.21B); **2.** of historical books of OT, Or.*schol.in Mt.*13:44(M.17.296A); *Const.App.*1.6.4; †Chrys.*synops.*(6.315A).

ἱστορικῶς, *literally, according to the literal sense*, Or.*fr.98 in Jer.*(p.270.21; M.13.652B); opp. τροπικῶς, Thdt.*Dan.*11:41(2.1292); opp. τυπικῶς, id.*Abac.*3:18f.(2.1559); Max.*ambig.*(M.91.1372A).

ἱστοριογραφέω, **1.** *write the history of*, Mac.Mgn.*apocr.*3.13(p.84.23); **2.** *write history*, Socr.*h.e.*7.48.7(M.67.841A); Cosm.Ind.*top.*2(M.88.116A).

***ἱστοριοποιός**, ὁ, *historian*, *Chron.Pasch.*p.144(M.92.356B).

ἱστοριώδης, *factual, like a record of facts*, Max.*ambig.*(M.91.1413C).

ἱστός, ὁ, *spider's web*, Gr.Naz.*or.*28.25(p.60.4; M.36.60C).

ἱστουργέω, *weave*; met., *blend* ἱ. ... τὸν λόγον...τῷ νῷ Max.*myst.*5(M.91.677C).

ἱστουργία, ἡ, *weaving*, Clem.*paed.*3.10(p.264.26; M.8.621A); met., ref. Gal.5:22 ἡ τῶν καθαρῶν ἔργων ἱ. Gr.Nyss.*hom.9 in Cant.*(M.44.961A).

ἱστουργός, ὁ, *weaver*, Dion.Al.ap.Eus.*p.e.*14.24(774A; M.21.1273A).

ἰσχάς, ἡ, *dried fig*; used in Manich. eucharist, Cyr.H.*catech.*6.33.

***ἰσχνοεπέω**, **1.** *speak with precision*, Cyr.*Is.*4.3(2.629D); **2.** *split hairs*, id.*dogm.*4(p.558.18; 6^2.374C).

***ἰσχνολέσχης**, *hair-splitting*, Geo.Pis.*Sev.*280(M.92.1643A).

***ἰσχνολογέω**, **1.** *speak minutely, go into detail*, Cyr.*ador.*15(1.545B); id.*Nah.*22(3.501A); id.*Ag.*proem.(3.627C); **2.** *speak allusively*, id.*Is.*1.3(2.71B).

***ἰσχνολόγος**, *subtle*, Cyr.*dial.Trin.*1(5^1.413E).

ἰσχνομυθέω, *argue with precision*, Cyr.*ador.*8(1.260C); *ib.*9(315B); id.*Juln.*2(6^2.50E).

ἰσχνομυθία, ἡ, **1.** *subtlety in argument*, Cyr.*ador.*9(1.292B); id. *glaph.Ex.*1(1.244A); id.*Juln.*3(6^2.110A); *over-subtlety* ἰσχνομυθίας ἀφέμενοι...τὰ ἐξ ἀκριβοῦς ἐρεύνης...συλλέγωμεν id.*Nest.*1.6(p.26.15; 6^1.21C); id.*Is.*2.4(2.288A); id.*ep.*40(p.29.6, v.l. ἰσχνοφωνίας 5^2.118E); *subtlety in expression*, id.*ador.*15(537C); **2.** *deficiency of speech*; of Moses, *ib.*11(1.377E); id.*Nest.*2.4(p.39.28; 6^1.41B).

ἰσχνός, **1.** *subtle* ἱ. ... λίαν ἡ γέννησις [i.e. of Son]...καὶ περὰ σωματικῆς φαντασίας Cyr.*Juln.*8(6^2.264E); cf.id.*ador.*9(1.316D); of angels ἱ. ... δυνάμεις id.*Is.*5.5(2.878A); esp. of argument εἶδος τῶν λόγων, τὸ διδασκαλικόν, ἱ. ... καὶ πνευματικόν Clem.*paed.*1.3(p.95.5; M.8.260A); ἱ. ... αἴνιγμα Cyr.*ador.*9(316A); id.*Is.*2.4(287E); Max.*schol. d.n.*12.4(M.4.405B); ref. spiritual sense of scripture λόγος...ἱ. Cyr. *Is.*3.1(2.353B); Thdt.*Ps.*13:1(1.681); **2.** *detailed* ἰσχνοτάτην...βάσανον Cyr.*ador.*15(1.536D); id.*Am.*2(3.251C); **3.** *careful*; of investigation, Or.*Jo.*2.9(5; p.63.20, v.l. συχνότερον M.14.124C); τὸν ἱ. νομοφύλακα Cyr.*Ps.*19:14(M.69.833A).

***ἰσχνοσύνθετος**, *of fine texture*, Geo.Pis.*van.*151(M.92.1592A).

ἰσχνότης, ἡ, **1.** *fineness, subtlety*, of ἱ. τῆς ἀληθείας opp. ὑλικώτερα ...τῶν νοημάτων, Or.*Jo.*2.7(4; p.62.1; M.14.121B); ἐκ νομικῆς καὶ παχείας ἐντολῆς, εἰς τὴν τῆς εὐαγγελικῆς πολιτείας ἱ. Cyr.*Jo.*11(4.939C); id.*ador.*9(1.315A); ἰσχνότητι σωμάτων, οὐχ ὑπερφέρουσιν ἄγγελοι; *ib.*6(214A); **2.** *weakness*; of voice, Chrys.*hom.10.2 in 2Tim.*(11.723C); Sophr.H.*ep.syn.*(M.87.3196C).

***ἰσχνοφωνέω**, *be hesitant in speech*, ‡Epiph.*hom.*5(M.43.488B).

ἰσχνοφωνία, ἡ, *weakness of expression* τὴν τοῦ γράμματος [i.e. of Law] ἱ. Cyr.*ador.*2(1.74E); v. ἰσχνομυθία.

ἰσχνῶς, **1.** *subtly*; of understanding, Cyr.*Nest.*1 proem.(p.13.38; 6^1.2E); of spiritual interprn. of scripture τοιαύτη μὲν ἡ τοῦ θαύματος ἱστορία. χρὴ δὲ...καὶ ἰσχνότερον αὐτὴν θεωρῆσαι Or.*schol.in Lc.*8:52(M.17.337C); Cyr.*ador.*6(1.208E); of argument, Max.*ambig.*(M.91.1165C); **2.** *in detail*; of investigation, Cyr.*Nest.*4 proem.(p.76.20; 96D).

ἰσχυροποι-έω, **1.** *make strong* ~ῆσαι αὐτοὺς ἐν τῇ πίστει Herm. *mand.*12.6.1; ~ούμενοι...οἱ κατ' ἐκκλησίαν Clem.*str.*4.9(p.281.15; M.8.1284B); ~ηθῶμεν ἀπὸ τῆς ἀσθενείας Ἰησοῦ Or.*hom.8.9 in Jer.*(p.63.5; M.13.348A); Nil.*epp.*2.179(M.79.292D); ὁ Χριστὸς ὡς ~ήσας τὴν ἀνθρώπων φύσιν, καὶ τὰ ὑπὲρ νόμον ἐπιτάσσει Cyr.*fr.Mt.*5:27(M.72.380C); Ammon.*Ac.*18:22f.(M.85.1572B); **2.** *establish*; of arguments, Clem.*str.*1.29(p.111.5; M.8.928B); of truth of Resurrection established by prophets, Chrys.*homm.in Heb.*proem.2(12.4D).

ἰσχυροποίησις, ἡ, *strengthening, fortifying*, Herm.*vis.*3.12.3; Clem.*str.*4.12(p.285.26; M.8.1293B).

***ἰσχυροποιητικός**, *strengthening*, Serap.*euch.*22.2.

ἰσχυρός, *strong*, ref. God τῷ ἱ. ῥήματι πήξας τὸν οὐρανόν Herm.*vis.*1.3.4; ἡ δόξα τοῦ θεοῦ...ἱ. id.*mand.*12.4.2; of Christ, ref. Is.28:16 ὡς λίθος ἱ. *Barn.*6.2; of Son, as θεὸς ἱ. Ath.*hom.in Mt.11:27*(M.25.217A); in *trisagion*: ἅγιος ἱ. *Lit.Jac.*(Brightman p.35.25); *Lit. Marc.*(p.118.9); τό, ἅγιος ἱ., ἐπὶ τοῦ υἱοῦ τίθεμεν, οὐκ ἀπαμφιεννύντες τῆς ἰσχύος τὸν πατέρα καὶ τὸ πνεῦμα τὸ ἅγιον Jo.D.*f.o.*3.10(M.94.1020A); ref. virtues, Herm.*sim.*9.15.1; ἡ μετάνοια ἱ. *ib.*7.6; of Devil, ref. Mt.12:29 ὁ δεθείς, ὁ δήσας τὸν ἱ. Claud.*fr.pasch.*(M.5.1297A); *Lit.*ap.*Const.App.*8.7.5; ἱ. ... αὐτὸν καλεῖ...τὴν ἔμπροσθεν δηλῶν τυραννίδα Chrys.*hom.41.3 in Mt.*(7.447E); Jo.Eub.*concept.BMV* 9(M.96.1473B); met., *established, trustworthy*, Herm.*vis.*3.4.3; *ib.*3.10.8.

ἰσχυρότης, ἡ, *strength*, Herm.*vis.*3.12.3; id.*sim.*9.8.7.

ἰσχυρ-όω, **1.** *strengthen*, *A.Andr.*A 5(p.49.2); ? f.l. for ἰσχύω, Herm.*mand.*5.2.8; **2.** *ratify, confirm* τὸν λόγον τῆς οἰκείας οὐσίας ~ούμενον Mac.Mgn.*apocr.*4.16(p.186.3).

ἰσχύς, ἡ, *strength, force*, of God θαυμαστὸς ἐν ἱ. *1Clem.*60.1; Athenag.*leg.*24.2(M.6.945B); proved from marvels of creation, Eus. *Ps.*28:4(M.23.256B); as strength of believers, *Diogn.*9.6; πρὸς τὴν χρείαν ἑκάστῳ γίνεται τὰ τῆς θεοφανείας· καὶ γίνεται τοῖς μὲν ἀσθενοῦσιν ἱ. Ath.*Ar.*2.63(M.26.144B); Thdt.*Ps.*17:2(1.702); ref. Christ ἐν ἱ. τέθεικεν τὴν σάρκα αὐτοῦ *Barn.*6.3; ref. Cross τὸ μέγιστον σύμβολον τῆς ἱ. ... αὐτοῦ Just.*1apol.*55.2(M.6.412A); cf.id.*dial.*111.2(M.6.732B); ref. Is.53:1 referred to Crucifixion, Or.*hom.14.9 in Jer.*(p.113.25; M.13.413C); in Christian life πίστις...ἱ. εἰς σωτηρίαν Clem.*str.*2.12(p.142.12; M.8.992B); τοῖς εὖ βιοῦν ἐπανῃρημένοις ἱ. πρὸς τὴν λοιπὴν σωτηρίαν ἐμπνεῖ [sc. ὁ θεός] *ib.*1.12(p.36.6; 468C); ἐὰν δὲ ἴδῃς ψυχὴν ἁγίαν...ὄψει τὴν ἱ. τοῦ λόγου...καρποφοροῦσαν Or.*hom.14.10 in Jer.*(p.114.24; 416A); of Christ giving strength to renounce Devil, Ath. *Ar.*1.51(120A); cf. baptismal formula of renunciation οὐκ ἔτι σοῦ [i.e. Satan] δέδοικα...τὴν ἱ. Cyr.H.*catech.*19.4; ref. miracles οὐ τῇ τῶν ἀνθρώπων ἱ. ἀλλὰ τῇ [sc. τοῦ θεοῦ] βουλήσει *Const.App.*8.1.7; *ib.*8.1.16; of name of Christ τὴν τοῦ ὀνόματος ἱ. καὶ τὰ δαιμόνια τρέμει Just.*dial.*30.3(M.6.540B).

ἰσχύω, *be strong*, hence *be able* οὐκ ἱ. μνημονεῦσαι Herm.*vis.*1.3.3; *Barn.*5.10; Chrys.*hom.23.5 in Gen.*(4.214B); Philost.*h.e.*7.7(M.65.544C).

ἰσωνυμία, ἡ, *same name*, ‡Caes.Naz.*dial.*140(M.38.1060).

Ἰταλίδης, ὁ, *Italian*, *Orac.Sib.*4.104.

***Ἰταλιεύς**, ὁ, = foreg., *Orac.Sib.*12.76 al.

Ἰταλιωτικός, *Italian*, of a school of Valentinianism ἡ...Ἰ. [sc. διδασκαλία] Hipp.*haer.*6.35(p.165.5; M.16.3250A).

ἰταμεύομαι, *be audacious, reckless*, Chrys.*hom.5.4 in Jo.*(8.41C).

***ἰτρᾶς**, ὁ, ? = ἴτριον, *cake*, dub. l. ἐκαθέζετο εἰς τὸν ἰτρᾶν τρώγων Leont.N.*v.Sym.*47(M.93.1728A).

***ἴυλξι**, prob. f.l. for ἴυγξι from ἴυγξ, *spell, charm* φθοροποιοῖς ἴυλξι κηλοῦσα Mac.Mgn.*apocr.*3.42(p.145.12, MS ἴνυξι κυλοῦσα).

ἰχθυακός, *of a fish*, Or.*hom.16.1 in Jer.*(p.132.21; ἰχθυϊκός M.13.440A).

ἰχθυβόλος, *of fishing*, Nonn.*par.Jo.*18:15(M.43.892B); as subst., *fisherman*, *ib.*1:41(757A); *ib.*21:7(916C).

***ἰχθυβότος**, *feeding on fish*, Nonn.*par.Jo.*21:14(M.43.917B).

ἰχθυοθήρας, ὁ, *fisherman*, Cyr.*Abac.*16(3.530E); id.*Jo.*12.1(4.1113C); id.*Lc.*6:13(M.72.585D).

***ἰχθυολκός**, ὁ, *fisherman*, Thdt.*ep.*76(4.1125).

***ἰχθυοτόκος**, *producing fish*, Chrys.*hom.in Ps.115:1–3*(p.357.12).

ἰχθυοφαγία, ἡ, *eating of fish*, ‡Just.*qu.et resp.*95(M.6.1337A).

ἰχθυοφόρος, *producing fish*, Gr.Naz.*ep.*4(M.37.25C); ‡Chrys.*hom.jej.*4(9.799B).

ἰχθῦς, ὁ, *fish*; **1.** in gen. αἱ δὲ σφραγῖδες ἡμῖν ἔστων πελειὰς ἢ ἰ. (v. 2 infra) Clem.*paed.*3.11(p.270.8; M.8.633A); ref. stench of fish emitted by a demon-possessed boy, Ath.*v.Anton.*63(M.26.933A); of abstinence from fish on fast-days, Chrys.*stat.*3.5(2.42A); multiplication of fishes a sign of Christ's dominion over sea, id.*hom.49.2 in Mt.*(7.506C); **2.** of Christ ref. acrostic Ἰησοῦς Χρειστὸς θεοῦ υἱὸς σωτὴρ σταυρός *Orac.Sib.*8.217; cf.Tert.*de baptismo* 1(M.*PL.*1.1306A); cf.Const.*or.s.c.*18(p.179.16; M.20.1288A); cf. *Jesus Christus ...a Sibylla* Ἰ. ... *operatus est, eo quod mundi vel saeculi hujus mare ingressus est*, Maximus Tauriensis *tractatus 4 contra paganos* (M.*PL.*57.789C); cf.Aug.*de civitate dei* 18.23.1(M.*PL.*41.580); ref. Mt.17:27, Or.*comm.in Mt.*13.10(p.208.1; M.13.1120C); in gen. πίστις ...παρέθηκε τροφὴν παντὶ ἰθχὺν ἀπὸ πηγῆς...ὃν ἐδράξατο παρθένος... καὶ τοῦτον ἐπέδωκε φίλοις ἐσθίειν...οἶνον χρηστὸν ἔχουσα κέρασμα διδοῦσα μετὰ ἄρτου Aberc.*epitaph.*12; ἰ. οὐρανίου θεῖον γένος, ἤτορι σεμνῷ χρῆσε λαβὼν πηγὴν ἄμβροτον ἐν βροτέοις. ... σωτῆρος ἁγίων μελιηδέα λάμβανε βρῶσιν, ἔσθιε πεινάζων ἰ. ἔχων παλάμαις. ἰχθύι χόρταζ' ἄρα λιλαιῶ, δέσποτα σῶτερ. ... ἰχθύος εἰρήνῃ σου μνήσεο Πεκτορίοιο *Pect.epitaph.*1–11 with acrostic on ἰχθῦς in first five lines; **3.** of Christians ἰ. ἁγνοὺς κύματος ἐχθροῦ...γλυκερῇ ζωῇ δελεάζων Clem.*paed.hymn.*26(p.292.26; M.8.681C); ὁ...[sc. ἰ.]...συλληφθεὶς ὑπὸ τῶν ἁλιέων Ἰησοῦ καὶ ἀνελθὼν ἀπὸ τῆς θαλάσσης, καὶ αὐτὸς μὲν ἀποθνήσκει...τῇ ἁμαρτίᾳ, καὶ ζωοποιεῖται ὑπὸ τοῦ λόγου τοῦ θεοῦ Or.*hom.16.1 in Jer.*(p.132.15; M.13.440A); ἡμεῖς...ἐσμεν οἱ ἰ. θηρευθέντες ἐκ τῶν τοῦ βίου ταραχῶν διὰ τῶν ἀποστολικῶν διδαγμάτων. ἔχομεν δὲ ἐν τοῖς στόμασιν ἡμῶν τὸν στατῆρα, τουτέστι τὸν Χριστόν Cyr.*fr.Mt.*17:27 (M.72.429B); **4.** moral symbolism; **a.** in gen., of those who commit sexual sins οἱ δίκην ἰχθύων ζῶντες, Athenag.*leg.*34.2(M.6.968B); of sins of tongue as signified διὰ τῶν ἰ. ἀναύδων Clem.*str.*2.15(p.149.18; M.8.1008A); ref. Gen.1:26, fish being thoughts and passions which saints master, Or.*hom.1.16 in Gen.*(p.20.5; M.12.159A); **b.** esp. of oppressors, because larger fish devour smaller, Bas.*hex.*7.3(1.65A; M.29.152C); Cyr.*Os.*26(3.67B); ‡Nil.*perist.*10.1(M.79.885A); **c.** temperance, signified by Law's prohibition of certain succulent fish as food, Clem.*str.*2.20(p.170.25; M.8.1049B); cf.id.*paed.*2.1(p.163.16; M.8.400A); of their habits as an example of sexual temperance, Gr.Naz.*carm.*1.2.2.543ff.(M.37.621A); ref. Lc.24:42, fish representing asceticism ὥσπερ ὁ ἰ. γίνεται ἐπιτήδειος εἰς τροφὴν ὀπτηθείς...οὕτως καὶ ὁ ἄνθρωπος, διὰ τῆς θέρμης τοῦ ἁγίου πνεύματος καθαρθείς, γίνεται θυσία...τῷ θεῷ ‡Ath.*qu.script.*44(M.28.728A); **d.** avaricious unbelievers, ref. fish in Mt.17:23 with coin in mouth, Clem.*paed.*2.1 (p.163.20; 400A); Or.*comm.in Mt.*13.12(p.211.19ff.; M.13.1124Bf.); **e.** the worldly; followers of Devil, ref Ezech.29:4, Or.*hom.13.2 in Ezech.*(p.445.30; M.13.761C); ref. Os.4:3 ἔοικε...ἰ. ἀποκαλεῖν τοὺς συρφετώδεις καὶ ἀγελαίους, τοὺς ταῖς τοῦ βίου φροντίσι βεβαπτισμένους, καὶ ὑπερβρύχιον ὥσπερ ἔχοντας νοῦν, τοὺς ἀφώνους καὶ ἀλογωτάτους· ἀφωνότατον γὰρ τῶν ἰ. τὸ χρῆμα Cyr.*Os.*26(3.67A).

ἰχνευτής, ὁ, *hunter*, *tracker*; met., of philosopher τῆς ἀληθείας ἰ. Clem.*str.*1.9(p.29.18; M.8.741A); as adj., of dogs, Or.*princ.*3.1.3 (p.198.5; M.11.252B).

ἰχνηλάτης, ὁ, *follower in the footsteps* of, met. οἱ...ἐπίσκοποι, οἱ ἰ. τῶν...ἀποστόλων Jo.Nic.*nativ.*(M.96.1440C).

***ἰχνοβατέω**, *walk*, ‡Chrys.*sac.*7(1.805A) = Ephr.3.1B.

***ἰχνολογέω**, *track out, hunt down*, *Phys.*B 1(p.152.7) ∾ ‡Epiph.*phys.*1(M.43.520A).

***ἰχνοπατέω**, *tread*, †Cyr.*hom.div.*11(5².380A).

ἰχνοποι-έω, **1.** *leave a trace* or *mark*, Hipp.*fr.22 in Pr.*24:54b (p.165.6; M.10.621C); **2.** *tread* τοῖς...ποσὶ τὴν γῆν ∼ῶν Tim.Ant.*descr.BMV* 7(M.28.953B).

ἴχνος, τό, **1.** *footstep* (Docetic) ἴ. αὐτοῦ [sc. Christ] ἐπὶ τῆς γῆς... οὐδέποτε εἶδον *A.Jo.*93(p.197.5); met. οἱ κατ' ἴχνος τὸ ἀποστολικὸν πορευόμενοι γνωστικοί Clem.*str.*4.9(p.282.3; M.8.1284D); τὰ ἴ. τοῦ θεοῦ διώκοντες id.*paed.*1.12(p.149.7; M.8.368B); **2.** *foot*, *A.Petr.et Paul.*18(p.187.2); Bas.*hom.in Ps.*1(1.93D; M.29.217D); id.*hom.*7.5 (2.57A; M.31.292D).

***ἰχωροστατέω**, *be in a state of putrefaction*, ‡Chrys.*Marth.*(10.754D; prob. f.l. for ⟨ἰχωροστακτέω⟩).

***Ἰωάννης**, ὁ, *John*;

A. etym.; **1.** = θεοῦ χάρις Or.*Jo.*2.33(27; p.90.23; M.14.172C); id.*hom.9 in Lc.*(p.65.15); Sophr.H.*or.*4.15(M.87.3345A); *ib.*4.16(3345C); **2.** ἑρμηνεύεται...Ἰ. ... ὁ δεικνύς Or.*hom.9 in Lc.*(p.66.18).

B. as author; **1.** of fourth gospel; **a.** writing in his old age, Eus.*h.e.*3.24.7(M.20.265A); at age of 100, ‡Chrys.*Jo.theol.*1.1(8.131C); when over 90, Epiph.*haer.*51.12(p.263.18; M.41.909B); thirty-two years after Ascension, in reign of Domitian, ‡Jo.D.*ep.Thphl.*3(M.95.349A); at Ephesus, Iren.*haer.*3.1.1(M.7.845A); ‡Chrys.*Jo.theol.*1.1 (8.130C); *Chron.Pasch.*p.246(M.92.592B); autograph kept there, *ib.* p.5(77B); at Patmos, ‡Hipp.*apost.*(M.10.952B); τὸ...κατὰ Ἰ. εὐαγγέλιον ὑπηγορεύθη τε ὑπ' αὐτοῦ τοῦ Ἰ. ὄντος ἐξορίστου ἐν Πάτμῳ τῷ νήσῳ, καὶ ὑπὸ τοῦ αὐτοῦ ἐξεδόθη ἐν Ἐφέσῳ, διὰ Γαΐου τοῦ ἀγαπητοῦ καὶ ξενοδόχου τῶν ἀποστόλων †Ath.*synops.*76(M.28.433A); **b.** objects, to confute heretics esp. Cerinthians and Nicolaitans, Iren.*haer.*3.11.1(M.7.879C); and Ebionites, Epiph.*haer.*51.12(p.264.7; M.41.909B); cf.*ib.*(p.263.16; 909A); since the other evangelists' preoccupation with Christ's humanity could give rise to heresy, Chrys.*hom.4.1 in Jo.*(8.27A); ‡Chrys.*Jo.theol.*1.1(8.132Dff.); τὸν...Ἰ. ἔσχατον, συνιδόντα ὅτι τὰ σωματικὰ ἐν τοῖς εὐαγγελίοις δεδήλωται, προτραπέντα ὑπὸ τῶν γνωρίμων, πνεύματι θεοφορηθέντα πνευματικὸν ποιῆσαι εὐαγγέλιον Clem.*fr.*8(p.197.27; M.9.749C); Cyr.*Jo.*1(4.8C); Andr.Cr.*or.*8(M.97.960B); to supply historical details omitted from other gospels, Eus.*h.e.*3.24.11(M.20.265C); Cosm.Ind.*top.*5(M.88.292C); **c.** symbolized by lion, Iren.*haer.*3.11.8(M.7.886Aff.) = ‡Sophr.H.*liturg.*19(M.87.4000A,B) ∾ ‡Bas.*h.myst.*44(p.388.29ff.); Anast.S.*qu.et resp.*144(M.89.797C); by eagle, †Ath.*synops.*76(M.28.432D); because eagle signifies giving of H. Ghost, and Jo. begins with eternal generation in Trin., ‡Germ.CP *contempl.*(M.98.413C); **d.** attitude to gospel on the part of **i.** heretics; rejected; Montanists not accepting part dealing with sending of Paraclete, Iren.*haer.*3.11.9 (890B); rejected by Marcionites, Adam.*dial.*2.12(p.82.10; M.11.1780B); and by Alogoi, Epiph.*haer.*51.18(p.275.3; M.41.921C); respected; used by Valentinians in support of their doctrines, Iren.*haer.*3.11.7(884C); **ii.** Jews; Hebrew translation made by Ebionites, Epiph.*haer.*30.12(p.348.29; 428B); kept by Jews in their treasury at Tiberias, *ib.*30.3(p.338.4; 409C); **iii.** Platonists, Eus.*p.e.*11.18,19 (540Aff.; M.21.900Aff.); Thdt.*affect.*2(p.59.19; 4.751); **2.** of Epistles; **a.** first epistle recognized as canonical, Or.*or.*22.2(p.347.12; M.11.484B); Dion.Al.ap.Eus.*h.e.*7.25.7(M.20.697C); Meth.*fr.*10(p.513.12); canonicity never doubted, Eus.*h.e.*3.25.1(268D); Chrys.*synops.*(6.318A); Socr.*h.e.*7.32.11(M.67.809C); **b.** second epistle quoted as his, Iren.*haer.*1.16.3(M.7.633B); cf. *secunda Johannis epistola, quae ad virgines scripta est*, Clem.*fr.*4(p.215.3; M.9.737D); *Johannes per epistolas suas*, Or.*hom.7.1 in Jos.*(p.328.4; M.12.857B); **c.** three epistles accepted, cf.Clem.*str.*2.15(p.148.19; M.8.1004B); *Can.App.* 85; Eus.*d.e.*3.5(p.126.31; M.22.216B); CLaod.*can.*60; Cyr.H.*catech.*4.36; ἐπιστολαὶ καθολικαὶ καλούμεναι...Ἰωάννου γ' Ath.*ep.Amun.*(M.26.1177B); id.*ep.fest.*39(M.26.1437B); †Ath.*synops.*3(M.28.292C); Gr.Naz.*carm.*1.1.12.37(M.37.474A); Jo.D.*f.o.*4.17(M.96.1180C); **d.** canonicity of second and third doubted, Or.*Jo.*5.3(p.101.28ff.; M.14.188Df.); Dion.Al.ap.Eus.*h.e.*7.25.7(697C); some accept one, some three, Amph.*Seleuc.*313ff.(M.37.1597A); τὴν δευτέραν καὶ τρίτην οἱ πατέρες ἀποκανονίζουσι Sever.*hom.in Mt.21:23*(M.56.424); some believing them to be by another John, Eus.*h.e.*3.25.3(269A); hence some ascribed all three to the other John, some accepted all, Cosm.Ind.*top.*7(M.88.373B).

***Ἰωαννῖται**, οἱ, *partisans of John* (Chrysostom), *V.Chrys.*104 (p.355.21); Socr.*h.e.*6.18.5(M.67.721A).

***Ἰωαννοτόκος**, *bearing John* εἰ καὶ Ἰ. ἡ Ἐλιζάβετ λέγοιτο Leont.H.*Nest.*4.37(M.86.1709A).

***Ἰώβ**, τό, *Job*, as book of OT ἐν τῷ Ἰὼβ γέγραπται Just.*dial.*79.4 (M.6.664A); Hipp.*haer.*4.47(p.69.11; M.16.3111B); Or.*or.*10(p.320.5; M.11.445B); authorship: τὸ Ἰ. βιβλίον Μωσέως εἶναι Meth.*creat.*10 (p.498.31; M.18.341A); Job 3:19 quoted as Solomon, Gr.Naz.*or.*19.15(M.35.1061B); by Solomon or Moses, †Chrys.*synops.*(6.367B); in OT canon, Mel.*fr.*(p.309)ap.Eus.*h.e.*4.26.14(M.20.397A); alleged rejection by Thdr. Mops., Leont.B.*Nest.et Eut.*3(M.86.1365B).

***Ἰωβήλ**, *jubilee* (Lev.25:10); as type of Pentecost in Christian year, ‡Hipp.*fr.9 in Pss.*(p.138.15; M.10.713C).

***Ἰωβηλαῖος**, ὁ, *jubilee*, cf.Lev.25:10, Lc.7:41 ὁ πεντηκοστὸς κατὰ τὸ εὐαγγέλιον ἄφεσιν ἔσχεν, μαρτυρῶν τῇ νοήσει τῇ περὶ τοῦ Ἰ. ‡Hipp.*fr.9 in Pss.*(p.139.17; M.10.716A); ἑπτὰ δὲ ἑβδομάδες ἐτῶν τὸν ὀνομαστὸν Ἰ. ... ταῦτα δὲ τύποι τοῦ αἰῶνος τούτου...ἐν ᾧ γίνονται αἱ τῶν μετριωτέρων ἁμαρτημάτων ἐκτίσεις Bas.*ep*.260.3(3.396E; M.32.957A); plur., *Book of Jubilees* ἐν τοῖς Ἰ. ... τῇ καὶ λεπτῇ Γενέσει καλουμένῃ Epiph.*haer*.39.6(p.76.16; M.41.672B).

***ἰώθ, τό,** *jod*, Hebrew letter ἰ. ὃ ἑρμηνεύεται ἀρχή Eus.*p.e*.10.5 (473C; M.21.788C).

Ἰωνίζ-ω, *behave like an Ionian* ἐλέγοντο...οἱ χειριδωτοῖς [sc. στολαῖς] χρώμενοι ~ειν *Schol.Clem.paed*.(p.334.15; M.9.791C).

ἰῶτα, τό, *iota*, as a symbol of name Jesus; **1.** as being its initial letter, *Barn*.9.8; ἡ δεκάλογος διὰ τοῦ ἰ. στοιχείου τὸ ὄνομα τὸ μακάριον δηλοῖ, λόγον ὄντα τὸν Ἰησοῦν παριστῶσα Clem.*str*.6.16(p.506.26; M.8. 377A); Or.*fr.65 in Lc*.(p.270); *Const.App*.2.26.2; in paschal controversy λαμβάνομεν...τὸ πρόβατον ἀπὸ δεκάτης, ⟨τὸ⟩ ὄνομα Ἰησοῦ ἐπιγνόντες διὰ τοῦ ἰ. Epiph.*haer*.50.3(p.248.11; M.41.888C); ref. tithes ἣν ἐκεῖ ἀποδεκάτωσις ἀσφαλιζομένη, ἵνα μὴ λάθῃ ἡμᾶς τὸ ἰ. ἡ δεκάς, τὸ πρῶτον στοιχεῖον τοῦ Ἰησοῦ ὀνόματος *ib*.8.6(p.192.24; 213D); **2.** as symbolizing his rectitude by its shape, Clem.*paed*.1.9 (p.140.9; M.8.352C); id.*fr*.58(p.227.1; M.9.765D); **3.** (Valent.) τοὺς δέκα αἰῶνας...διὰ τοῦ ἰ. ... σημαίνουσι λέγεσθαι Iren.*haer*.1.3.2(M.7. 469A).

K

***καβαλλάρης, ὁ,** (cf. Lat. *caballarius*) *horseman*, Geo.Pis.*carm*. 108.1.

καβαλλαρικός, (cf. Lat. *caballarius*) *equestrian* τὰ κ. θέματα Thphn.*chron*.p.303(M.108.740B); neut. as subst., *cavalry*, *ib*.p.298 (729A).

***καβαλλάρι(ο)ς,** (Lat. *caballarius*); **1.** *on horseback* -άρις *Chron. Pasch*.p.382(M.92.980B); *Mir.Geo*.5(p.57.4); **2.** masc. as subst., *horseman, cavalryman*, Chosroes ap.Evagr.*h.e*.6.21(p.235.21; M.86. 2873B); Jo.Mosch.*prat*.72(M.87.2925B); Leont.N.*v.Sym*.50(M.93. 1732C).

***καβαλ(λ)ικεύω,** *ride* a horse, *Nomoc*.99; Thphn.*chron*.p.324(M. 108.784C); *ib*.p.325(785B).

***καβαλλίνα, ἡ,** *horse-dung*, Thphn.*chron*.p.397(M.108.945C).

***καβάλλιος,** *of horses*, Thphn.*chron*.p.346(M.108.833C).

καβιδάριος, ὁ, (Lat. *cavidarius*) *worker in stone, gem-engraver* λιθουργὸς ὃν λέγουσι κ. Pall.*h.Laus*.6(p.23.11; M.34.1018D); Jo. Mosch.*prat*.203(M.87.3093A); *MAMA* 3.118 (Corasion).

***καβούλιον, τό,** (Lat. *cubiculum*) *bedroom*, Gr.Mag.*dial*.(tr. Zach.)3.1(M.*PL*.77.222A).

***καγκελλάριος, ὁ,** (Lat. *cancellarius*); **1.** civil official attached to some functionary whose rank is often indicated *Εὐπρακτοῦ κ. τάξεως καθολικοῦ IGC As.Min*.13 (saec. v); Justn.*nov*.161.1(p.745. 14); Max.*ep*.12(M.91.460A); **2.** patriarchal official, at Jerusalem Λεόντιον τὸν...διάκονον...καὶ τοῦ Εὐαγοῦς ἡμῶν σεκρέτου κ. τε καὶ πρωτονοτάριον Sophr.H.*ep.syn*.(M.87.3200A); at CP, CCP(681)*act*.8 (H.3.1161C).

[*]**κάγκελλον, τό, 1.** *railing* separating chancel from rest of church καθεσθέντων τῶν...ἀρχόντων...ἐν τῷ μέσῳ πρὸ τῶν κ. τοῦ ἁγιωτάτου θυσιαστηρίου CChalc.*act*.1(*ACO* 2.1.1 p.64.37; H.2.65D); πλησίον ἱστάμενος τοῦ θυσιαστηρίου, ἔχων τὰς χεῖρας ἐπεστηριγμένας τῷ κ. τοῦ ἱερατείου Cyr.S.*v.Euthym*.28(p.45.11); τὰ κυκλοῦντα κ. *ib*. 42(p.61.24); κ. εἰσι τὸν τῆς προσευχῆς τόπον δηλοῦντα ἐν ᾧ σημαίνει τὴν μὲν ἔξωθεν τοῦ λαοῦ εἴσοδον, τὴν δὲ ἔσωθεν τὰ ἅγια τῶν ἁγίων ὑπάρχουσαν καὶ μόνοις τοῖς ἱερεῦσιν οὖσαν εὐεπίβατον. ἔστι δὲ ὡς ἀληθῶς καὶ εἰς τὸ ἅγιον μνῆμα κ. χαλκᾶ διὰ τὸ μηδένα εἰσιέναι ἐν αὐτῷ ἁπλῶς καὶ ὡς ἔτυχεν ‡Bas.*h.myst*.8(p.259.24); ‡Jo.D.*ep.Thphl*. 10(M.95.357B); round a tomb τὰ τοῦ μνήματος ἠνέῳκται κ. Sophr.H. *mir.Cyr.et.Jo*.36(M.87.3553B); τὰ κ. ἀντίτυπα τῶν τοῦ τάφου κ. ‡Sophr.H.*liturg*.4(M.87.3984D); **2.** *guard* of a sword, Chrysipp.*enc. in Thdr*.(p.69.12).

κάγκελλος, ὁ, = foreg. 1 τὰς θύρας καὶ τοὺς καγκέλλους ὡς σκῦλα ἕκαστος ἐλάμβανε Ath.*ep.encycl*.4(p.173.6; M.25.229C).

καγκελωτός, *like a grating, lattice* στεφάνην λέγει τὸ κ. σχῆμα, τὸ περὶ τοὺς κίονας Chrys.*fr.in Jer*.52:18(M.64.1037A).

καγχασμός, ὁ, *immoderate laughter*, Clem.*paed*.2.5(p.186.4; M.8. 448C) cit. s. γέλως; Olymp.*Eccl*.7:7(M.93.561C).

κάδ(δ)ιον, τό, 1. *small bag, wallet*, ref. 1Reg.17:40 ἐκ τοῦ ποιμενικοῦ καδδίου, τουτέστιν ἐκ τῶν ἐκκλησιαστικῶν δογμάτων, τοὺς ἀκατασκεύους ...λόγους εἰς ἀνατροπὴν τῆς βλασφημίας ἀφεὶς Gr.Nyss.*Eun*.12(1 p.218. 29, v.l. κάδου M.45.912D); **2.** *small pitcher* εὗρον κάδιον χαλκοῦν κρεμάμενον καὶ ἅλυσιν σιδηρᾶν κατὰ τὸν φρέατος Pall.*h.Laus*.18(p.50. 6, v.l. κάδδιον; κάδον M.34.1052D).

κάδος (κάδδος), ὁ, 1. *vessel, cup* οἱ ἑπτὰ ἀστέρες...οὓς...ἐνηρμόσθαι φασὶν ἑτέρῳ τὸν ἕτερον, κατὰ τὴν εἰκόνα τῶν κ. τῶν εἰς ἀλλήλους ἐμβεβηκότων Bas.*hex*.3.3(1.24C; M.29.57B); **2.** *well-pitcher, bucket* κάδδος Hipp.*haer*.5.21(p.124.18; M.16.3190C); Marc.Diac.*v.Porph*. 80; Pall.*h.Laus*.2(p.18.3; M.34.1011D); for souls in Manich. system μηχανὴν συνεστήσατο ἔχουσαν δώδεκα κ., ἥ τις ὑπὸ τῆς σφαίρας στρεφομένη ἀνιμᾶται τῶν θνησκόντων τὰς ψυχάς Hegem.*Arch*.8(p.12. 15; M.10.1440B); Epiph.*haer*.66.50(p.88.4; M.42.105B); Jo.D.*Man*.1. 67(M.94.1564A).

καθαγιάζ-ω, 1. *consecrate* τὸ...ὕδωρ...ἐπικλήσεσι καθαγιάσας Dion. Ar.*e.h*.2.2.7(M.3.396C); αὐτοῦ [sc. Christ] τοῦ δι' ἡμᾶς ἀνθρωποπρεπῶς τῷ θεαρχικῷ πνεύματι καθαγιασθέντος *ib*.4.3.11(484C); perf. ptcpl. pass. neut., *sanctuary, shrine* τὰ σέμνα τῶν τῆς ἐκκλησίας καθηγιασμένων Eus.*v.C*.1.42(p.27.26; M.20.957A); **2.** *sanctify* τὴν γλῶσσαν ταῖς τῶν ἄλλων εὐφημίαις ~εσθαι Max.*ep*.4(M.91.417D); ὑπὸ πνεύματος ἁγίου ~ομένῃ παρθένῳ Jo.V H.*icon*.5(M.96.1353C).

καθαγνίζω, *hallow, purify* καθαγνισθέντας βαπτίσματι Gr.Naz.*or*. 5.7(M.35.672C); ξένῳ περιτομῆς εἴδει καθαγνίσας αὐτόν [sc. τὸν λαόν] Max.*ambig*.(M.91.1117D).

καθαίρεσις, ἡ, 1. *destroying, demolition* τὴν τοῦ θανάτου κ. Clem. *str*.4.13(p.287.18; M.8.1297A); Chrys.*res.mort*.6(2.431B); met., of an argument, Meth.*res*.2.8(p.345.11; M.41.1176D); **2.** *overthrow, subjugation* προφητεύει...τὴν κ. ἐκείνου τοῦ λαοῦ Or.*hom.22 in Lc*. (p.148.8); ἐπὶ καθαιρέσει τῆς κακίας id.*Cels*.4.21(p.291.11; M.11. 1056A); *ib*.1.31(p.83.3; 720A); τῆς...πολυθέου πλάνης κ. Eus.*p.e*.1.4 (11A; M.21.37D); κ. ... τοῦ διὰ φθόνον ἀπατήσαντος ἐχθροῦ ‡Ath. *Apoll*.2.9(M.26.1148B); Chrys.*hom.29.2 in Jo*.(8.167A); **3.** *taking away*; **a.** *reduction, diminution* οἶμαι καὶ ἐπὶ καθαιρέσει τῆς δόξης αὐτοῦ [sc. Ἰησοῦ] εἰρηκέναι τὸ 'οὗτος ὁ ἄνθρωπος' Or.*Jo*.28.12(11; p.402.30; M.14.704C); id.*Cels*.1.32(p.83.22; M.11.721A); πέφυρται πάντα παρ' αὐτοῖς, γενητῶν μὲν ἐξίσωσις πρὸς τὸ ἀγένητον, ἀγενήτου δὲ κ. μετρουμένου πρὸς τὰ ποιήματα, ἵνα μόνον τὸν υἱὸν ἐν τοῖς ποιήμασι καταγάγωσιν Ath.*Ar*.1.31(M.26.76C); abs. οὐ κ. τῷ πατρί, ἐπειδὴ δι' αὐτοῦ καλούμεθα εἰς κοινωνίαν τοῦ υἱοῦ αὐτοῦ Sever.*1Cor*.1:8–9 (p.226.34); λογισμῶν κ. Marc.Er.*opusc*.3.11(M.65.981B); ‡Caes.Naz. *dial*.121(M.38.1009); **b.** *deposition* Λικιννίου κ. Soz.*h.e*.1.1.12(M.67. 860A); *degradation* of clergy καθαίρεσιν ὀνειδίζειν αὐτῷ [sc. Ath.] τολμᾷ [sc. Eus. Nic.] καθαιρεθεὶς αὐτὸς καὶ μάρτυρα τῆς κ. ἔχων τὴν ἀντ' αὐτοῦ κατάστασιν CAlex.*ep*.ap.Ath.*apol.sec*.6(p.93.15,16; M.25. 260D); οὐ μόνον τοιούτους καθαιρεῖ τῆς λειτουργίας, ἀλλὰ καὶ τοὺς τολμῶντας τούτοις κοινωνεῖν μετὰ τὴν κ. CAnt.(341)*can*.1; Ath.*ep. Afr*.4(M.26.1053C); Pall.*v.Chrys*.9(p.56.5; M.47.32); Thdr.Lect.*h.e*. 2.12(M.86.189A); χειροτονεῖ εὐθὺς ἐπίσκοπον Ἀπαμείας Ἰωάννην τινὰ ἀπὸ κ. *ib*.1.22(177A); **c.** *sentence of deposition* ὡς αἱ κ. εἶχον Soz. *h.e*.3.10.6(M.67.1060A); **d.** *abolition, removal* αἰτίαν τῆς τούτων [sc. graven images] κ. Ath.*gent*.45(M.25.89B); τῆς μὲν ἁμαρτίας τὴν κατάκρισιν ἐπὶ γῆς ἐποιήσατο, τῆς δὲ κατάρας τὴν κ. ἐπὶ ξύλου ‡Ath. *Apoll*.1.5(M.26.1101A); Anast.S.*hod*.6(M.89.104C).

***καθαιρετέον,** *one must reject*, Didym.(‡Bas.)*Eun*.5 tit.(1.306B; M.29.733C).

καθαιρέτης, ὁ, *destroyer, overthrower*; pagan gods, *M.Polyc*.12. 2; Eus.*l.C*.9(p.218.18; M.20.1364B); ἱεροῦ καθαιρέτην [sc. Christ] ἀποκαλοῦντες *Const.App*.5.14.9.

καθαιρετικός, 1. *destructive* κακίαν...κ. τῶν ἐπὶ τὴν γνῶσιν προσκοπτόντων Clem.*str*.7.11(p.47.13; M.9.492A); ῥήμασι...κ. τῆς δόξης τοῦ μονογενοῦς Bas.*Eun*.2.18(1.253C; M.29.609A); καθαιρετικὴ ...τῶν...παθῶν ἐστιν ἡ τοῦ κυρίου ἐπιφάνεια id.*ep*.260.6(3.400A; M.32. 964D); ref. variant in Lord's Prayer (ἐλθέτω τὸ ἅγιον πνεῦμα κτλ.) ἢ τάχα τό, ἐλθέτω, κ. τῆς ἀξίας νομίζουσιν; Gr.Nyss.*or.dom*.3(p.64.35; M.44.1160C); ἀσέβεια κ. τῆς δόξης τοῦ θεοῦ ‡Just.*qu.et resp*.1(M.6. 1405A); **2.** *of deposition* τὴν κ. ψῆφον Philost.*h.e*.2.11(M.65.476A); neut. as subst., *decree of deposition*, Socr.*h.e*.1.32.2(M.67.164B); *ib*. 2.1.5(185B); *decree of condemnation* τὰ κ. τῶν Ὠριγένους βιβλίων, δι' ὧν...τὰ βιβλία...διέβαλλεν *ib*.6.12.1(701A).

***καθαιρετικῶς,** *as a means of putting an end to*, c. genit., Or.*Cels*. 1.31(p.83.1; M.11.720A).

***καθαιρέτις, ἡ,** *destroyer* κενοδοξίαν...κ. τῶν καλῶν πράξεων ‡Bas. *const*.10.2(2.557A; M.31.1373C).

καθαιρ-έω, *take down, put down*; **1.** *close* the eyes of the dead, Dion.Al.ap.Eus.*h.e*.7.22.9(M.20.689A); Chrys.*Stag*.2.10(1.197A); **2.** *reduce, diminish* τὴν τρίχα σου τῆς κόμης μὴ παρατρέφων, μᾶλλον δὲ συγκόπτων καὶ ~ῶν αὐτήν *Const.App*.1.3.8; 'πᾶσα πικρία' οὐχὶ ~είσθω, ἀλλὰ 'ἀρθήτω ἀφ' ὑμῶν' Chrys.*hom.15.1 in Eph*.(11.110D); met., *lower, degrade* μὴ τοίνυν νομίσῃς ~εῖσθαι δεόμενος ἑτέρου id.

hom.22.2 in Rom.(9.682A); πνεῦμα...οὐ πνοὴν ἀνυπόστατον ἐννοοῦμεν. οὕτω γὰρ ἂν ~εῖται πρὸς ταπεινότητα τὸ μεγαλεῖον τῆς θείας φύσεως Jo.D.*f.o.*1.7(M.94.805B); **3.** *overthrow, defeat* spiritual powers ~οῦνται αἱ δυνάμεις τοῦ σατανᾶ Ign.*Eph.*13.1; αἱ ψυχαὶ τῶν διὰ Χριστιανισμὸν ἀποθνησκόντων...καθῄρουν τὴν δύναμιν τῶν δαιμόνων Or.*Cels.*8.44(p.258.27; M.11.1581C); τοῦ σταυροῦ γενομένου, πᾶσα... εἰδωλολατρεία καθηρέθη Ath.*gent.*1(M.25.5A); **4.** *abolish, annul* customs, laws, etc. πῶς ἔτι οὗτος [sc. Christ]...τὸν νόμον καὶ τὸ εὐαγγέλιον...~ῶν; Clem.*str.*3.2(p.199.15; M.8.1109A); ~εθῆναι...τὰς Δομετιανοῦ τιμάς Eus.*h.e.*3.20.8(M.20.256A); τῶν Ἰουδαίων ~εῖται τὸ δόγμα Jo.D.*f.o.*1.7(M.94.808A); **5.** *degrade* ὅσοι προεχειρίσθησαν τῶν παραπεπτωκότων...γνωσθέντες...~οῦνται CNic.(325)*can.*10; εἴ τις εὑρεθείη μετὰ τὸν ὅρον τοῦτον τόκους λαμβάνων...~εθήσεται τοῦ κλήρου *ib.*17; of clerics leaving their parishes εἰ δὲ καὶ ἐπιμένοι τῇ ἀταξίᾳ...~εῖσθαι τῆς λειτουργίας, ὡς μηκέτι χώραν ἔχειν ἀποκαταστάσεως CAnt.(341)*can.*3; *ib.*13; for heresy, of Arian bishops τούτους...καθεῖλεν ἡ...σύνοδος ἀπὸ τῆς ἐπισκοπῆς καὶ...μὴ μόνον αὐτοὺς ἐπισκόπους μὴ εἶναι, ἀλλὰ μηδὲ κοινωνίας μετὰ τῶν πιστῶν αὐτοὺς καταξιοῦσθαι CSard.*ep.cath.*ap.Ath.*apol.sec.*47(p.123.12; M. 25.336A); Ath.*apol.sec.*2(p.88.21; 249D); of Nestorians εἰ...τινες... τῶν κληρικῶν...τολμήσαιεν...τὰ Νεστορίου ἢ τὰ Κελεστίου φρονῆσαι καὶ τούτους εἶναι καθῃρημένους...δεδικαίωται CEph.(431)*can.*4; for *usury, Can.App.*44; involving suspension of functions εἴ τις ἐπίσκοπος ὑπὸ συνόδου ~εθεὶς ἢ πρεσβύτερος ἢ διάκονος...τολμήσειέν τι πρᾶξαι τῆς λειτουργίας...μηκέτι ἐξὸν εἶναι...ἐλπίδα ἀποκαταστάσεως ἔχειν CAnt.(341)*can.*4; οὐ πρότερον αὐτὸν [sc. a bishop] εἰς τὰς δίκας διδόασι, πρὶν τῆς θείας ἀπορρῆξαι τελετῆς, τὰ ἐκείνης ἀφαιρούμενον σύμβολα καὶ οὕτως ~εθέντα ἕνα τῶν λαϊκῶν ἡγεῖσθαι ‡Caes. Naz.*dial.*140(M.38.1068); but distinct from temporary suspension ἐὰν δὲ ἐκβάλῃ [sc. τὴν ἑαυτοῦ γυναῖκα] ἀφοριζέσθω, ἐπιμένων δέ, ~είσθω *Can.App.*5; to be exercised by bishops, *Const.App.*8.28.2; πρεσβύτερος οὐ ~εῖ, ἀφορίζει δὲ τοὺς ὑποβεβηκότας *ib.*8.28.3; or by a synod, Jo.Mal.*chron.*14 p.365(M.97.545A); Thphn.*chron.*p.78(M. 108.240B); dist. from excommunication, Jo.Ant.*ep.Ruf.*(p.40.32; M.83.1477C); ref. rejection of Paulianist clerics ἀναβαπτισθέντες χειροτονείσθωσαν...εἰ δὲ ἡ ἀνάκρισις ἀνεπιτηδείους αὐτοὺς εὑρίσκοι, ~εῖσθαι αὐτοὺς προσήκει CNic.(325)*can.*19; and of others not ordained εἰ δέ τις ὁμολογητὴς μὴ χειροτονηθεὶς ἁρπάσῃ ἑαυτῷ ἀξίωμά τι τοιοῦτον ὡς διὰ τὴν ὁμολογίαν, οὗτος ~είσθω *Const.App.*8.23.4; of a secular official ἐκεῖνος μὲν καθηρέθη καὶ κατεβλήθησαν αὐτοῦ...αἱ εἰκόνες *Chron.Pasch.*p.391(M.92.1004C); **6.** *condemn* τὸν Τιμόθεον... μετὰ τοῦ ἀσεβοῦς αὐτοῦ δόγματος καθείλομεν Dam.Papa *ep.orient.*ap. Thdt.*h.e.*5.10.2(3.1035).

καθαίρ-ω, καθαρίζω, *purify*;

A. of God; **1.** without distinction of Persons κύριε...καθάρισον ἡμᾶς τὸν καθαρισμὸν τῆς σῆς ἀληθείας *1Clem.*60.2; παρακαλοῦμέν σε... ὑπὲρ τῶν χειμαζομένων ὑπὸ τοῦ ἀλλοτρίου...ὅπως...τοὺς δὲ καθαρίσῃς ἐκ τῆς ἐνεργείας τοῦ πονηροῦ *Lit.*ap.*Const.App.*8.12.47; ἡ θεία μακαριότης...~οῦσα Dion.Ar.*c.h.*3.2(M.3.165C); **2.** of Son; **a.** in gen. αὐτὸς τὰς ἁμαρτίας αὐτῶν ἐκαθάρισε πολλὰ κοπιάσας...αὐτὸς οὖν καθαρίσας τὰς ἁμαρτίας τοῦ λαοῦ ἔδειξεν αὐτοῖς τὰς τρίβους τῆς ζωῆς Herm.*sim.*5.6.2,3; ref. Jo.15:1,2 καθυλομανεῖ γὰρ μὴ κλαδευομένη ἡ ἄμπελος, οὕτως δὲ καὶ ὁ ἄνθρωπος· ~ει δὲ αὐτοῦ τὰς ἐξυβριζούσας παραφυάδας ὁ λόγος ἡ μάχαιρα Clem.*paed.*1.8(p.129.12; M.8.329C); ποταμὸς...ἐφ' ὃν ἐρχόμενον ~εσθαι δεῖ...ὁ σωτήρ Or.*Jo.*6.42(25; p.151. 19; M.14.273B); εἰ...ἥλιος...οὐ ῥυπαίνεται τῶν ἐπὶ γῆς σωμάτων ἁπτόμενος...ἀλλὰ μᾶλλον...ταῦτα φωτίζει καὶ καθαρίζει· πολλῷ πλέον ὁ πανάγιος τοῦ θεοῦ λόγος...τὸ σῶμα θνητὸν τυγχάνον ἐζωοποίει καὶ ἐκαθάριζεν Ath.*inc.*17.7(M.25.125D); ἵνα...τὸν...ἀέρα καθαρίσῃ *ib.* 25.5(140B); ὁ φιλάνθρωπος θεὸς διὰ Χριστοῦ...τὰ ἑαυτοῦ πλάσματα... καθαρίσῃ *Lit.*ap.*Const.App.*8.7.2; *Const.App.*8.1.3; **b.** through Passion, Just.*1apol.*32.7(M.6.380B); τοῦ πάθους, οὗ ἔπαθεν ὑπὲρ τῶν ~ομένων τὰς ψυχὰς ἀπὸ πάσης πονηρίας ἀνθρώπων, Ἰησοῦς Χριστός id.*dial.*41.1(M.6.564B); *ib.*13.1(501A); ἵνα τῷ ἰδίῳ αἵματι πάντας ἡμᾶς ἀπὸ τῶν ἁμαρτιῶν καθαρίσῃ Ath.*Ar.*2.7(M.26.161C); id.*inc.*25.6(M.25. 140C); but apostles fully purified only after Ascension, Or.*Jo.*6.57 (37; p.165.31ff.; 300A); **3.** of H. Ghost ἐλθὲ τὸ ἅγιον πνεῦμα καὶ καθάρισον τοὺς νεφροὺς αὐτῶν καὶ τὴν καρδίαν *A.Thom.*A 27(p.143.2); in text of Lord's Prayer as read by Gr. Nyss. ἐλθέτω τὸ ἅγιον πνεῦμά σου...καὶ καθαρισάτω ἡμᾶς Gr.Nyss.*or.dom.*3(p.60.10; M.44.1157D); καθαρίζοντος τὴν ἁμαρτίαν πνεύματος *ib.*(p.60.37; 1160A); **4.** of God acting through secondary causes; **a.** through divine word in scripture and human reason (cf. Jo.1:9) ὁ λόγος ἔχει παντὸς φαρμάκου δύναμιν καὶ παντὸς τοῦ καθαρίζοντος δύναμίς ἐστι Or.*hom.2.2 in Jer.*(p.18. 11; M.13.280A); ὀχεῖται δὲ καὶ τῷ νέῳ πώλῳ, τῇ καινῇ διαθήκῃ· ἐν ἀμφοτέραις γὰρ ἔστιν εὑρεῖν τὸν ~οντα ἡμᾶς τῆς ἀληθείας λόγον καὶ ἀπελαύνοντα τοὺς πωλοῦντας καὶ ἀγοράζοντας ἐν ἡμῖν πάντας λογισμούς id.*Jo.*10.28(18; p.201.30; M.14.357C); χρεία οὖν ἡμῖν τὸν λόγον παραλαβεῖν τὸν ~οντα τὰ δόγματα id.*hom.5.15 in Jer.*(p.44.28; 317D); **b.** through angels and priests ὡς γὰρ ὁ θεὸς ~ει πάντας τῷ πάσης καθάρσεως εἶναι αἰτίας, μᾶλλον δὲ...καθάπερ ὁ καθ' ἡμᾶς ἱεράρχης διὰ τῶν αὐτοῦ λειτουργῶν ἢ ἱερέων ~ων ἢ φωτίζων, αὐτὸς λέγεται ~ειν καὶ φωτίζειν...οὕτω καὶ τὴν οἰκείαν καθαρτικὴν ἐπιστήμην...ὁ τὴν κάθαρσιν τοῦ θεολόγου τελετουργῶν ἄγγελος [cf. Is.6], ἐπὶ θεὸν μὲν ὡς αἴτιον, ἐπὶ δὲ τῶν σεραφὶμ ὡς πρωτουργὸν ἱεράρχην, ἀνατίθησιν· ὡς ἄν τις φαίη, μετ' εὐλαβείας ἀγγελικῆς τὸν ὑπ' αὐτοῦ ~όμενον ἐκδιδάσκων Dion.Ar.*c.h.*13.4(M.3.305C,D); *ib.*(308A); **c.** through external evils κτίζει γὰρ τὰ σωματικὰ ἢ τὰ ἐκτὸς κακά, ~ων καὶ παιδεύων τοὺς μὴ βουληθέντας παιδευθῆναι λόγῳ καὶ διδασκαλίᾳ ὑγιεῖ Or.*Cels.*6. 56(p.127.17; M.11.1385A); Cels.*ib.*4.69(p.338.28; 1137B); Or.*or.*29.15 (p.390.20; M.11.544A); κολαζομένου γὰρ τοῦ σώματος κατὰ μικρὸν ~εται †Leont.B.*sect.*10.6(M.86.1265C).

B. ref. purifying of Church and its members; **1.** in gen. καθαρισθήσεται ἡ ἐκκλησία τοῦ θεοῦ...καὶ ἔσται ἓν σῶμα τῶν κεκαθαρμένων Herm.*sim.*9.18.2,3; καθαρισθήσῃ δὲ ἀπὸ τῶν ὑστερημάτων σου· καὶ πάντες δὲ οἱ μὴ διψυχοῦντες καθαρισθήσονται ἀπὸ πάντων τῶν ἁμαρτημάτων id.*vis.*3.2.2; ἵνα ὦμεν ναοὶ θεοῦ καθαρισθέντες ἀπὸ παντὸς μολυσμοῦ Clem.*str.*4.21(p.306.20; M.8.1341C); ref. apostles τὸν βίον ἄκρως κεκαθαρμένοι Eus.*h.e.*3.24.3(M.20.264B); ref. bishops, *Const. App.*2.1.8; congregation of faithful from which sinners have been excluded αἰσχυνθεὶς...ἐξελεύσεται,...καὶ μενεῖ κεκαθαρισμένον τὸ ποίμνιον *ib.*2.10.4; ref. Lc.2:9 ἄλλος [sc. ἄγγελος] δὲ τοὺς ποιμένας, ὡς τῇ τῶν πολλῶν ἀναχωρήσει καὶ ἡσυχίᾳ κεκαθαρμένους, εὐηγγελίζετο Dion.Ar.*c.h.*4.4(M.3.181B); **2.** acc. hierarchical order ἐπειδὴ τάξις ἱεραρχίας ἐστὶ τὸ τοὺς μὲν ~εσθαι, τοὺς δὲ ~ειν...ἑκάστῳ τὸ θεομίμητον ἁρμόσει κατὰ τόνδε τὸν τρόπον *ib.*3.2(165B); ref. deacon's office ἡ λειτουργικὴ τάξις, ὡς μόνον καθαρτική, τὴν μίαν ἱερουργεῖ τῶν ~ομένων προσαγωγὴν ὑπὸ τὸ θεῖον αὐτὴν ὑποτιθεῖσα θυσιαστήριον, ὡς ἐν αὐτῷ τῶν ~ομένων νοῶν ὑπερκοσμίως ἱερουμένων id.*e.h.*5.3.8(M.3.516B); ~όμεναι μέν εἰσι τάξεις αἱ τῶν ἱερουργιῶν καὶ τελετουργιῶν ἀποδιαστελλόμεναι πληθύεις *ib.*6.1.1(529D); ~ομένη δὲ τάξις ἡ τῆς ἱερᾶς ἐποψίας καὶ κοινωνίας ἀμέτοχος, ὡς ἔτι ~ομένη *ib.*6.3.5(536D); ref. exclusion from celebration of mysteries οὐ πᾶσαι κατὰ τὸ σύνηθες αἱ ~όμεναι τάξεις ἀπολύονται, μόνοι δὲ τῶν ἱερῶν ἐκβάλλονται χώρων οἱ κατηχούμενοι...αἱ δὲ λοιπαὶ τῶν ~ομένων τάξεις ἐν μυήσει μὲν ἤδη γεγόνασιν ἱερᾶς παραδόσεως...οὐκ ἀπεικότως δὲ πάρεισιν ἐπὶ τοῖς νῦν τελουμένοις *ib.*7.3.3(557C); **3.** through baptism τὸ βάπτισμα, τὸ μόνον καθαρίσαι τοὺς μετανοήσαντας δυνάμενον Just.*dial.*14.1(M.6.504C); ἀναγεννηθέντες ἀμίαντον φυλάξωμεν τὸν ἄνθρωπον καὶ νήπιοι ὦμεν ὡς βρέφος τοῦ θεοῦ κεκαθαρμένον πορνείας καὶ πονηρίας Clem.*paed.*1.6 (p.109.18; M.8.289A); καθαρίσας αὐτοὺς τῷ σῷ λουτρῷ *A.Thom.*A 25 (p.140.10); Dion.Ar.*e.h.*2.3.1(M.3.397B); ref. Christ's baptism, cf. Χριστὸς...ἐβαπτίσθη ἵνα τῷ πάθει τὸ ὕδωρ καθαρίσῃ Ign.*Eph.*18.2; Clem.*ecl.*7(p.138.30; M.9.701B); ἀνθρώποις γὰρ ὑπὸ φωνῆς [sc. Jo. Bapt.] ~εται λόγος [i.e. Christ], τῇ φύσει τοῦ λόγου ~οντος πᾶσαν τὴν σημαίνουσαν φωνήν Or.*Jo.*2.32(26; p.90.7; M.14.172B); ref. Christ's death, in baptismal context διεστάλη...διὰ τοῦ θανάτου τὰ ἡνωμένα καὶ πάλιν συνήχθη τὰ διακεκριμένα, ὡς ἂν καθαρθείσης τῆς φύσεως ἐν τῇ τῶν συμφυῶν διαλύσει, ψυχῆς τε λέγω καὶ σώματος, πάλιν ἡ τῶν κεχωρισμένων ἐπάνοδος τῆς ἀλλοτρίας ἐπιμιξίας καθαρεύουσα γένοιτο Gr.Nyss.*or.catech.*35(p.134.3; M.45.89A); ref. future status of baptized and unbaptized πολὺ τὸ μέσον τῶν τε κεκαθαρμένων καὶ τῶν τοῦ καθαρσίου προσδεομένων ἐστίν. ἐφ' ὧν γὰρ κατὰ τὸν βίον τοῦτον ἡ διὰ τοῦ λουτροῦ προκαθηγήσατο κάθαρσις, πρὸς τὸ συγγενὲς τούτοις ἡ ἀναχώρησις ἔσται,...οἱ δὲ ταύτης [sc. purification by baptism] ἀμύητοι τῆς καθάρσεως ἀναγκαίως τῷ πυρὶ καθαρίζονται *ib.*(p.138.7; 92B,C); ref. Jo. Bapt. ~ων...καὶ ἐπὶ μετάνοιαν παρακαλῶν Or.*Jo.*6.32 (17; p.141.23; 256A); ὁ ~ων *baptizer*, Gr.Naz.*or.*40.26(M.36.396C); ref. martyrdom as equivalent to baptism τὸ κατὰ τὸ μαρτύριον βάπτισμα...ἐπὶ πολλῶν θεραπείᾳ ~ομένων γίνεται Or.*mart.*30(p.26. 29; M.11.601A); **4.** through repentance and virtue ἐκαθάρισαν ἑαυτοὺς καὶ μετενόησαν Herm.*sim.*8.7.5; *ib.*8.11.3; μετανοίᾳ κεκαθαρμένον *Const.App.*2.41.2; Or.*Cels.*7.46(p.198.5; M.11.1489A); of pagans, through acting acc. right reason παρ' ὀλίγοις τὰς ψυχὰς τῷ λόγῳ καὶ ταῖς κατ' αὐτὸν πράξεσι κεκαθαρμένοις *ib.*7.8(p.160.28; 1433A); through teaching as preliminary to baptism, *ib.*3.59(p.254. 12; 1000A); ὁ δὲ κατὰ τὸν Ἰησοῦν μυσταγωγῶν τῷ θεῷ τοῖς κεκαθαρμένοις τὴν ψυχὴν ἐρεῖ *ib.*3.60(p.255.1; 1000B); hence through wisdom, id.*fr.hom.21 in Jer.*(p.195.12; M.14.1309C); Dion.Ar.*c.h.*7.3(M.3. 209D); through prayer, Diad.*perf.*17(p.22.1); through sacrifice, Or. *Jo.*6.54(36; p.162.19; M.14.293A); those purified by virtue being immune from purification by fire, Or.*Cels.*5.16(p.17.29; 1205A);

through divine love ἔρωτι θείῳ...καθαρθέντες Dion.Ar.*e.h.*3.3.7(M.3.436B); **5.** ascet., as first stage of threefold way (purgative, illuminative, unitive), ref. angelic orders ~εται καὶ φωτίζεται καὶ τελεσιουργεῖται Dion.Ar.*c.h.*7.3(M.3.209C); *ib.*8.1(240B); ref. men ἡ ...τῶν τελετῶν ἱερουργία πρώτην μὲν ἔχει θεοειδῆ δύναμιν τὴν ἱερὰν τῶν ἀτελέστων κάθαρσιν, μέσην δέ, τὴν τῶν καθαρθέντων φωτιστικὴν μύησιν· ἐσχάτην δέ,...τὴν τῶν μυηθέντων ἐν ἐπιστήμῃ τῶν οἰκείων μυήσεων τελείωσιν. ἡ δὲ τῶν ἱερουργῶν διακόσμησις ἐν μὲν τῇ δυνάμει τῇ πρώτῃ διὰ τῶν τελετῶν ἀποκαθαίρει τοὺς ἀτελέστους· ἐν τῇ μέσῃ δέ, φωταγωγεῖ τοὺς καθαρθέντας· ἐν ἐσχάτῃ δὲ...ἀποτελειοῖ τοὺς τῷ θείῳ φωτὶ κεκοινωνηκότας id.*e.h.*5.1.3(M.3.504A,B); τῆς ἱεραρχικῆς τάξεως, οὐ τελεσιουργεῖν μόνον, ἀλλὰ καὶ φωτίζειν ἅμα καὶ ~ειν ἐπισταμένης *ib.*5.1.7(508C); **6.** as necessary for union with God ὅσοι ἂν καθαρίσωσιν ἑαυτῶν τὰς καρδίας ἀπὸ τῶν ματαίων ἐπιθυμιῶν τοῦ αἰῶνος τούτου, καὶ ζήσονται τῷ θεῷ Herm.*mand.*12.6.5; ὄψονται...τὸν θεὸν...οὐδὲ γὰρ οἱ πολλοὶ τῶν ἀνθρώπων, εἰ μή τις ἐν δίκῃ βιώσαιτο, καθηράμενος δικαιοσύνῃ καὶ τῇ ἄλλῃ ἀρετῇ πάσῃ Just.*dial.*4.3(M.6.484B); ἀσκήσεσι ~όμενος ὁ νοῦς...ὀξυδερκεῖ πρὸς τὴν ἀλήθειαν Meth.*symp.*9.4(p.118.13; M.18.185B); τὸ σῶμα τοῦτο δύναται...τὴν ἀθανασίαν ὑποδέξασθαι, ἐὰν ~οιτο τῆς ἀκρασίας τῶν ὑπεκκαυμάτων id.*res.*1.61(p.325.20); οὐ γὰρ ἔστι μὴ καθαρθεῖσαν ἀκοὴν ἰδεῖν τῶν λεγομένων τὸ ὕψος Chrys.*hom.1.2 in Jo.*(8.4C); τὴν τοῦ καθαρθέντος ἐπὶ τὴν θείαν ὑπακοὴν ἀναζωπύρησιν Dion.Ar.*c.h.*13.2(M.3.300B); **7.** of cleansing by fire (after death): cleansing by fire and water foreshadowed in pagan philosophy *Πλάτων τὴν γῆν χρόνοις τισὶ διὰ πυρὸς ~εσθαι καὶ ὕδατος ὧδέ πως φησι* Clem.*str.*5.1(p.332.4; M.9.24A); by ark in Temple ἡ κιβωτός, τῶν διὰ πυρὸς ~ομένων καὶ δοκιμαζομένων σύμβολον *ib.*6.11(p.475.6; 308B); τάχα εἴποιμι ἂν ὅτι ἡ γέεννα τῶν ἀκουσίων, τῶν δυναμένων καθαρθῆναί ἐστιν Or.*hom.19.15 in Jer.*(p.175.14; M.13.497C); τῷ φρονίμῳ πυρὶ ~ομένοις καὶ ἐν τῇ φυλακῇ ἐκπρασσομένοις id.*or.*29.15(p.390.7; M.11.541D); **8.** ref. purifying from demons ὁ κύριος δι' αὐτοῦ [sc. S. Anthony]...ἄλλους ἀπὸ δαιμόνων ἐκαθάρισε Ath.*v.Anton.*14(M.26.865A); καθαρισθεῖσαν ἀπὸ τοῦ δαίμονος *ib.*48(913A); ἐὰν δέ τις δαίμονα ἔχῃ...μὴ προσδεχέσθω δὲ εἰς κοινωνίαν, πρὶν ἂν καθαρισθῇ *Const.App.*8.32.6; ἐάν τις δαίμονα ἔχῃ, κληρικὸς μὴ γινέσθω,...καθαρισθεὶς δὲ προσδεχέσθω *Can.App.*79; οἱ λειτουργοῦντες τῷ ἱερῷ καθαρίζουσιν ἑαυτοὺς φοβούμενοι τοὺς δαίμονας *A.Andr.et Mt.*14(p.81.3).

C. Gnost.; denial of purification of body by fire after death τὸ γὰρ φαινόμενον οὐ πυρὶ ~εται, ἀλλ' εἰς γῆν ἀναλύεται Clem.*exc.Thdot.*14(p.111.23; M.9.664C); Manich. ἐρῶ...πῶς μεταγγίζεται ἡ ψυχὴ εἰς πέντε σώματα. πρῶτον καθαρίζεται μικρόν τι ἀπ' αὐτῆς, εἶτα μεταγγίζεται εἰς κυνός Hegem.*Arch.*10(p.15.7; M.10.1441C); ὁ δὲ ἀὴρ οὗτος στῦλος ἐστὶ φωτός, ἐπειδὴ γέμει ψυχῶν τῶν καθαριζομένων *ib.*8(p.13.13; 1440C); τὸ γεμίζον τὴν σελήνην, τὸ καθαριζόμενον καθημερινὸν ἀπὸ τοῦ κόσμου *ib.*11(p.18.9; 1445A).

D. *purify, clear,* from accusation ἐκεῖνος ἐκάθαρεν αὐτόν Or.*dial.*11(p.144.11); ἔχουσιν οἱ περὶ Ἀθανάσιον τὰ ἐν τῷ Μαρεώτῃ ὑπομνήματα, ἐξ ὧν αὐτὸς μὲν καθαρίζεται Ath.*h.Ar.*15(p.191.2; M.25.712A); ὃν... πᾶσα ἡ σύνοδος ἐκαθάρισε *ib.*44(p.208.27; 748A).

καθάπαξ, *once and again, frequently* οὐκ ἀνέβην εἰς τὴν κώμην· ὑμεῖς δὲ καθάπαξ ἀναβαίνετε *Apophth.Patr.*(M.65.349B).

καθάπερ, 1. *inasmuch as*; c. ptcpl., Clem.*paed.*3.4(p.253.20; M.8.597A); **2.** *as if*; c. opt., Chrys.*hom.15.3 in 2Cor.*(10.615E).

καθαπλόω, *spread out,* Marc.Diac.*v.Porph.*98; Thdt.*h.e.*1.24.1(3.806).

***καθάπλωμα, τό,** *kerchief, A.Pil.*A 2(p.217).

καθάπτ-ω, med.; **1.** *upbraid* τινα τῶν ἑταίρων ~όμενος λόγοις κατέστειλεν Const.*or.s.c.*15(p.175.15; M.20.1277B); **2.** *attack,* fig. τῷ μεσημβρινῷ καιρῷ, ἐν ᾧ ὁ ἥλιος ~εται Or.*fr.52 in Jo.*(p.526.15); Philost.*h.e.*3.6(M.65.488B); **3.** *make an impression* τὴν περὶ τοῦ κρίματος πολλάκις γινομένην παραγγελίαν σφοδρότερον ~εσθαι... εἰδώς †Bas.*bapt.*2.8.5(2.663C; M.31.1605A); **4.** *touch, concern* ἐκεῖνο μάλιστά μου καθήπτετο διανοίας Gr.Nyss.*ep.*1(M.46.1004C); καθάψεταί σου τὰ εἰρημένα Chrys.*ep.*127(3.673D); **5.** *touch on, handle* τούτων δὲ ἐν μέρει καθάψασθαι Eus.*p.e.*11 proem.(507D; M.21.844B).

καθάρευσις, ἡ, *purity* οὐδὲ χωρὶς κ. ἔστιν ἐπινοῆσαι γινομένην τῇ προσευχῇ σχολὴν Or.*or.*8(p.317.1; M.11.441B); *ib.*10(p.320.17; 445C); δώσει...τὴν παντελῆ κ. ἐν ἀγαμίᾳ καὶ ἁγνείᾳ ὁ θεὸς τοῖς...αἰτοῦσιν αὐτόν id.*comm.in Mt.*14.25(p.348.5; M.13.1252B).

καθαρευτέον, *one must keep oneself pure,* κ. ... κἂν ταῖς προφοραῖς τῶν φωνῶν Clem.*paed.*2.6(p.188.13; M.8.453B); c. genit., *one must keep oneself pure* from, *free* from ἔργων αἰσχρῶν κ. *ib.*(p.188.8; 453A); *ib.*2.10(p.213.32; 509A).

καθαρεύ-ω, 1. *be pure, free*; **a.** abs., in sense of not remarrying, Or.*hom.20.4 in Jer.*(p.183.1; M.13.508D); *ib.*(p.182.31; 508C); Meth.*symp.*11.1(p.130.12; M.18.205C); **b.** c. ἐπί, Or.*hom.20.3 in Jer.*(p.181.15; M.13.505D); c. ἀπό, *ib.*(p.181.1; 505C); id.*Jo.*20.27(22; p.363.33; M.14.636C); **2.** *be purified* τίς γὰρ Χριστὸν...ἴσχυσε χωρῆσαί ποτε, μὴ ~σας πρῶτον; Meth.*symp.*10.6(p.128.33; M.18.204A); Or.*Jo.*20.36(29; p.376.10; M.14.657B); **3.** *purify* τὴν ~ουσαν διδασκαλίαν τὴν ψυχήν id.*fr.36 in Jo.*(p.511.31); πολλαὶ γὰρ αἱ ὁδοὶ αἱ ~ουσαι Chrys.*hom.1.3 in Philm.*(11.778E, v.l. καθαίρειν δυναμέναι); Niceph.Ur.*v.Sym.*17(M.86.3001C).

καθαριεύω, *keep free from* κ. τῆς τῶν κοσμικῶν μνήμης τὴν διάνοιαν Cyr.S.*v.Sab.*28(p.113.18); *be free from* τούτου παντελῶς κ. τοῦ δόγματος Bars.*resp.*(M.86.897D).

καθαρίζω, v. καθαίρω.

καθάριος, 1. *pure,* lit. τροφὴν κ. Or.*Cels.*4.82(p.352.16; M.11.1156A); ὕλη [sc. ἤλεκτρον] ὡς ἐν κόσμῳ καθαριωτάτη id.*hom.11.5 in Jer.*(p.83.18; M.13.373D); fig. κ. ... ἡ σωφροσύνη Clem.*paed.*3.11(p.268.6; M.8.629A); *ib.*(p.267.12; 628B); ἡ...πρώτη καὶ καθαριωτάτη *Μαρκίωνος* αἵρεσις Hipp.*haer.*7.31(p.216.14; M.16.3334B); neut. as subst. πάντα γὰρ τὰ ἐν γενέσει χρήζει τοῦ κ. τοῦ ἀπὸ τοῦ πυρός Or.*hom.11.5 in Jer.*(p.83.15; 373D); **2.** *delicate, refined*; of rich persons, Or.*Cels.*7.59(p.209.3; M.11.1505B).

καθαριότης (καθαρειότης), ἡ, *purity* ἡ...κ. ἕξις ἐστὶν παρασκευαστικὴ διαίτης καθαρᾶς καὶ ἀμιγοῦς αἰσχροῖς Clem.*paed.*3.11(p.268.7; M.8.629A); καθαρειότης ψυχῆς ἐστιν ἀπάθεια ἐκ χάριτος θεοῦ, προσγινομένης καὶ σπουδῆς τοῦ ἀνθρώπου Or.*sel.in Ps.*17:21(M.12.1232D); τῶν ἀγγέλων...ἡ φυσικὴ κ. Areth.*Apoc.*37(M.106.677D).

καθάρισις, ἡ, *cleansing* of lepers, Or.*comm.in Mt.*16.14(p.519.29; M.13.1420A).

καθαρισμός, ὁ, A. *purification, purging*; **1.** of legal purifications of Jews; **a.** in gen. κ. τὸν διὰ Μωσέως *A.Phil.*15(p.8.15); Or.*princ.*4.2.5(p.314.9; M.11.365B); Μωυσῆς...λέγων ἐν τοῖς κ. Meth.*res.*1.62(p.327.17; M.41.1160D); *Const.App.*2.35.1; forbidden to Christians μὴ παρατηρεῖσθε...καθαρισμοὺς ἐπὶ θίξει νεκροῦ *ib.*6.30.1; **b.** partic. from leprosy καθαρθεὶς γὰρ τῆς λέπρας ὅμως ὑπὲρ τοῦ μολυσμοῦ τοῦ φθάσαντος χρόνου δεῖται τοῦ παρόντος κ., μᾶλλον δὲ καὶ ἄλλων τριῶν. εἷς γὰρ κ. τὸ 'ᾗ ἂν ἡμέρᾳ καθαρισθῇ' καὶ τρεῖς μεταξὺ τῷ 'καὶ καθαρὸς ἔσται' τρίτον λεγομένῳ δηλούμενοι· καὶ πέμπτος καὶ τελευταῖος διὰ τοῦ· 'καὶ καθαρισθήσεται'. εἰσὶ γὰρ οἷον καὶ καθαρισμῶν προκοπαὶ πρὶν εἰς τὴν τελείαν ἐλθεῖν καθαρότητα Or.*hom.8.11 in Lev.*(p.411.33ff.; M.87.740C); **c.** ref. Christ and BMV εἰ δὲ ἔκειτο ὑπὲρ τοῦ κ. Μαρίας μόνης οὐδὲν ἐζητοῦμεν· νυνὶ δὲ 'τοῦ κ. αὐτῶν' φησίν. ἆρ' οὖν καὶ Ἰησοῦς δεῖται κ.; ἀλλ' ὅρα τὸ τόλμημα τοῦ λόγου· μνήσθητι τῶν εἰρημένων ἐν τῷ Ἰὼβ μυστικῶς· οὐδεὶς καθαρὸς ἀπὸ ῥύπου id.*hom.14 in Lc.*(p.96.9ff.); **2.** as divine action, *1Clem.*60.2 cit. s. καθαίρω; through Passion of Christ, Or.*fr.90 in Jo.*(p.553.9); γένηται ὁ κ. ὕδατι καὶ αἵματι ἅπερ ἐξῆλθεν ἀπὸ τῆς πλευρᾶς τοῦ σωτῆρος id.*hom.8.10 in Lev.*(p.411.24); Ath.*Ar.*1.55(M.26.125C); τὸ γὰρ ἀπαύγασμα τῆς δόξης καὶ ὁ χαρακτὴρ τῆς ὑποστάσεως τὸν κ. τῶν ἁμαρτιῶν ἡμῶν ἐποιήσατο Gr.Nyss.*Eun.*2(2 p.385.18; M.45.568A); Cyr.*Ps.*8:2(M.69.757C); **3.** baptismal ὥσπερ οὖν συναπεθάνομεν αὐτῷ ἀποθνήσκοντι τότε, οὕτω περιετμήθημεν αὐτῷ περιτμηθέντι τότε· καὶ μετὰ τὴν περιτομὴν αὐτὴν γέγονεν οἰκονομίᾳ ἡ διὰ τοῦ προτέρου κ. Or.*hom.14 in Lc.*(p.95.4); id.*fr.36 in Jo.*(p.512.2); ἕτοιμον τὸ ὕδωρ πρὸς καθαρισμὸν τῶν προσερχομένων τῷ Χριστῷ *A.Xanthipp.*21(p.73.8); τρεῖς εἰσιν αἱ ἐπίνοιαι τοῦ βαπτίσματος, ὅ τε τοῦ ῥύπου κ., καὶ ἡ διὰ τοῦ πνεύματος ἀναγέννησις, καὶ ἡ ἐν τῷ πυρὶ τῆς κρίσεως βάσανος... δέονται δὲ αἱ μὲν κατ' ἄγνοιαν ἁμαρτίαι, οἱονεὶ ῥύπος τις οὖσαι,...τοῦ ἐκ τῆς πλύσεως κ.†Bas.*Is.*137(1.475A,B; M.30.341A); τὸ ὕδωρ τοῦ ῥαντισμοῦ τὸ ἔχον σποδὸν τῆς δαμάλεως, καθαρισμὸν ἐποίει ἀκουσίων ἁμαρτημάτων...τὸ δὲ Ἰωάννου βάπτισμα τοῖς γνησίως μετανοοῦσι καὶ τῶν ἑκουσίων παρεῖχεν αἵρεσιν. τὸ δὲ τοῦ Χριστοῦ, πάντων τῶν ἁμαρτημάτων Ammon.*Jo.*3:26(M.85.1413B); **4.** moral κ. ἡ διὰ νόμου καὶ προφητῶν εἰς τὸ εὐαγγέλιον πίστις Clem.*str.*4.25(p.318.25; M.8.1368B); ὁ δὲ ἐν τῷ σώματι κ. τῆς ψυχῆς [πρώτης] πρῶτος οὗτός ἐστιν, ἡ ἀποχὴ τῶν κακῶν *ib.*6.7(p.462.9; M.9.281B); ψυχὴ...καθαριζομένη εἰς τὸ τέλειον τοῦ κ. φθάνει, τοσοῦτον τῇ ἀγάπῃ προστιθεῖσα, ὅσον ἐλαττοῦται τῷ φόβῳ Diad.*perf.*17(p.22.4); **5.** exeg. Is.6:6f. πῦρ **λῃφθὲν...εἰς** κ. τῶν χειλέων αὐτοῦ †Bas.*Is.*183(1.513B; M.30.428B); ἐπουράνιόν τι χρὴ νοεῖν θυσιαστήριον· τουτέστι, χωρίον καθαρισμοῦ ψυχῶν *ib.*186(1.516D; M.436A); **6.** of Church from heretics ἐπισκόπους τε καὶ πρεσβυτέρους...[ἀ]παντῆσαι εἰς Καισαρίαν...πρὸς διάκρισιν περ[ὶ] κ[α]θαρισμοῦ ⟨τοῦ⟩ ἁγίου Χρηστιανικοῦ [π]λήθους *PLond.*1913.6 (anno 334); **7.** in Apollinarian Christol. argument ὅπου γὰρ τέλειος ἄνθρωπος, ἐκεῖ καὶ ἁμαρτία· καὶ ἔσται αὐτῷ χρεία τοῦ καθ' ἡμᾶς κ. ‡Ath.*Apoll.*1.2(M.26.1096B); **8.** in pagan mysteries (usu. καθαρμός) μίσησον καὶ τὸν κ., καὶ τὸν ὀρχηθμὸν φεῦγε ‡Ath.*exhort.*2(M.28.1112C); φεύγετε...μαντείας, καθαρισμοὺς *Const.App.*2.62.2.

B. *acquittal* (tr. Lat. *purgatio*) περὶ τοῦ κ. τοῦ αὐτοῦ τὰ παρόντα γράμματα...ἀπεστείλαμεν *Cod.Afr.*138.

***καθαριστικός**, *purifying*, abs. κ. αὔραν...τοῦ ἁγίου πνεύματος Diad.*perf.*75(p.94.6); neut. as subst. τὸ δὲ κ....τῆς τελειώσεως *ib.*51 (p.56.22).

[*]**καθαρίως**, *neatly, tidily*, Dor.*doct.*2.5(M.88.1645B).

καθαρμόζω, *marry, espouse*, ref. 2Cor.11:2 ὥσπερ κατὰ τὸν ἀπόστολον αὐτῷ [sc. Χριστῷ] κ. τε καὶ νενυμφευμένοι Meth.*symp.*3.8 (p.37.7; M.18.73D); *ib.*4.5(p.51.11; 93C).

καθαρμός, ὁ, *purification* (ritual); pagan, Clem.*str.*7.4(p.19.7; M.9.433A); Jewish, Chrys.*hom.73.1 in Mt.*(7.709A); Nonn.*par.Jo.* 3:25(M.43.772A); *cat.Jo.*2:6(p.198.34); of baptism τοῦ μυστικοῦ κ. Chrys.*catech.*1.2(2.228A); spiritual μάκαρ, ὅς...θιασεύεται καθαρμοῖσι ψυχάν ‡Gr.Naz.*Chr.pat.*1141(M.38.227A).

***καθαρογραφέω**, *write out clearly*, Anast.S.*hod.*10(M.89.149D).

καθαροποι-έω, 1. *purify*, ref. baptism, Clem.*str.*5.8(p.363.18; M.9. 85B); **2.** *make clear* ~ουμένου τοῦ σφάλματος αὐτοῦ καὶ φανερωμένου †Gregent.*leg.Hom.*53(M.86.609A); hence *explain* τρανώσας τὴν προφητείαν, μᾶλλον δὲ ~ήσας †Gregent.*disp.*(M.86.689C); *ib.*(692A).

***καθαροποιός**, *making pure*, neut. as subst. τῷ καθαρισμῷ τὸ κ. [sc. H. Ghost] συμπροέρχεται Job.Mon.*inc.*2(M.86.3316C).

***καθαροποτίον, τό**, *shop selling white bread and wine*, †Gregent. *leg.Hom.*1(M.86.581C).

καθαρός, I. *pure*;

A. of God; as being without admixture of matter πνεῦμα ὁ θεὸς ...κ. καὶ ἀόρατος ἡ θεία φύσις αὐτοῦ Heracleon ap.Or.*Jo.*13.25(p.248. 29; M.14.440D); of divine light ἄφετέ με κ. φῶς λαβεῖν Ign.*Rom.*6.2; φῶς ἡμῖν ἐξ οὐρανοῦ...ἐξέλαμψεν ἡλίου καθαρώτερον Clem.*prot.*11 (p.80.18; M.8.232B); of Christ in respect of humanity and divinity κ. Ἰησοῦν id.*paed.*2.12(p.228.6; M.8.540C); ὁ κ. ... θεὸς ἡμῶν Ἰησοῦς Χριστός *A.Jo.*107(p.205.1); ὑπὲρ τοῦ λαοῦ δὲ ἀπέθανεν ὁ ἄνθρωπος, τὸ πάντων ζῴων καθαρώτερον Or.*Jo.*28.18(14; p.413.6; M.14.720D); ἄτρωτός γε ἔμεινεν ἡ σοφία...κἂν τεμνομένῳ συνῆν καὶ προσηλωμένῳ τῷ σώματι...καθαρωτέρα φύσεως πάσης μετὰ τὸν γεννησάμενον αὐτὴν θεὸν ὑπάρχουσα Meth.*Porph.*2(p.506.5; M.18.404B); ἐβαπτίσθη δὲ καὶ ἐνήστευσεν...ὁ τῇ φύσει κ. *Const.App.*7.22.5; of his birth τὴν παρθενικὴν καὶ κ. γέννησιν Or.*Cels.*6.73(p.142.24; M.11.1408C); of his body, *ib.*(p.236.23; 1545D); Ath.*inc.*8.3(M.25.109C).

B. of created spirits in relative sense ψυχὴ...αἷμα καὶ σάρξ, οὐκέτι πνεῦμα κ. γιγνομένη Athenag.*leg.*27.1(M.6.952D); καθαρωτέρας οὐσίας παρὰ τὰ ἄλλα ζῷα μετασχὼν [sc. ἄνθρωπος] Clem.*str.*5.13 (p.384.2; M.9.129A); θεὸν...ἔχειν εἰκόνας ἑαυτοῦ ἀπὸ τῆς πνευματικῆς καθαρωτέρας οὐσίας, οἷον τοὺς ἀγγέλους Meth.*res.*2.24(p.379.20; M.18. 329C); ref. thrones κ. ... αὐτὰς ἡγητέον [sc. τὰς πρώτας οὐσίας], οὐχ ὡς ἀνιέρων κηλίδων καὶ μολυσμῶν ἠλευθερωμένας, οὐδ' ὡς προσύλων ἀνεπιδέκτους φαντασιῶν, ἀλλ' ὡς πάσης ὑφέσεως ἀμιγῶς ὑψηλοτέρας, καὶ παντὸς ὑποβεβηκότος ἱεροῦ Dion.Ar.*c.h.*7.2(M.3.208A); ref. demons, Or.*Jo.*13.59(58; p.291.5; M.14.512C).

C. of heavenly life αἰωνίου καὶ κ. βίου Just.*1apol.*8.2(M.6.337B); ἐν τοῖς καθαρωτάτοις τοῦ κόσμου χωρίοις ἢ καὶ τοῖς τούτων καθαρωτέροις ὑπερουρανίοις Or.*Cels.*5.4(p.4.16f.; M.11.1185A,B); ἡ μὲν κ. [sc. ψυχὴ]...μετέωρος φέρεται ἐπὶ τοὺς τόπους τῶν καθαρωτέρων καὶ αἰθερίων σωμάτων *ib.*7.5(p.156.27; 1425D); *ib.*7.32(p.183.4; 1465C); δράκων...ἀποπεσὼν τῆς κ. ζωῆς id.*Jo.*1.17(p.21.14; M.14.52B); εἰς κ. οἴκησιν ἀδύτων φώτων Meth.*symp.*4.5(p.51.21; M.18.96A); ἵνα...μετὰ τὸ ἀποθανεῖν ἐκτακείσης τῆς ἁμαρτίας ἐγερθεὶς ὁ ἄνθρωπος κ. φάγῃ τῆς ζωῆς id.*res.*1.39(p.284.8; M.41.1108C).

D. of Christians; **1.** of baptized in gen. ἐὰν κ. ὄντες ἀπὸ παντὸς παραπεμφθῶμεν ἀδικήματος Athenag.*leg.*12.3(M.6.913C); φυλάξωμεν κ. ἑαυτοὺς τῷ θεῷ, ταῦτα γὰρ κανόνες εἰσὶν καὶ θεσμοὶ τῆς ἐκκλησίας Meth.*lepr.*9(p.462.10); ὁ δὲ βαπτιζόμενος ὑπαρχέτω...κ. *Const.App.* 3.18.1; defended against pagan attacks φησί [sc. Cels.] δ' ἡμᾶς καὶ μηδὲν κ. βλέπειν, τοὺς πειρωμένους μηδὲ μέχρι τῶν λογισμῶν ὑπὸ τῶν ἐνθυμημάτων τῆς κακίας μολύνεσθαι καὶ ἐν τῇ εὐχῇ λέγοντας· 'καρδίαν κ. κτίσον ἐν ἐμοὶ ὁ θεός...' ἵνα τῇ μόνῃ πεφυκυίᾳ βλέπειν θεὸν καρδίᾳ κ. θεασώμεθα αὐτὸν Or.*Cels.*7.45(p.196.13ff.; M.11.1485C); **2.** esp. of those aiming at perfection, ref. 'gnostic' σύνοικος ὢν τῷ κυρίῳ... καθαρὸς μὲν τὴν σάρκα, καθαρὸς δὲ τὴν καρδίαν Clem.*str.*2.20(p.170. 12f.; M.8.1049A); τοῦ γνωστικοῦ μόνου...ὁ βίος κ. ἀπὸ παντὸς πονηροῦ ἔργου id.*ecl.*30(p.146.12; M.9.713C); of virgins, Meth.*symp.*4.3(p.48. 7; M.18.89D); *ib.*11(p.138.11; 216B); ὦ ἐπίσκοπε, σπούδαζε κ. εἶναι τοῖς ἔργοις, γνωρίζων τὸν τόπον σου καὶ τὴν ἀξίαν, ὡς θεοῦ τύπον ἔχων ἐν ἀνθρώποις *Const.App.*2.11.1; ἡ δὲ τῶν τριχῶν ἀπόκαρσις ἐμφαίνει τὴν κ. ... ζωὴν Dion.Ar.*e.h.*6.3.3(M.3.536A); **3.** ref. causes of purity: martyrdom σῖτός εἰμι θεοῦ καὶ δι' ὀδόντων θηρίων ἀλήθομαι, ἵνα κ. ἄρτος εὑρεθῶ Ign.*Rom.*4.1; observance of precepts of scripture, Or. *hom.2.3 in Jer.*(p.20.6; M.13.281B); chastity τὸ...τὴν ψυχὴν...καθαρὰν ἀπολουθῆναι τοῦ κόσμου, μόνη ποιεῖ...ἁγνεία Meth.*symp.*10.1(p.121.25; M.18.192C); grace ἔρχεται ἡ χάρις, καὶ ἀπεκδύεται ὅλον τὸ σκέπασμα, ὥστε λοιπὸν τὴν ψυχὴν κ. γενομένην καὶ ἀναλαβοῦσαν τὴν ἰδίαν φύσιν τὸ κτίσμα τὸ ἄμωμον καὶ κ., πάντοτε λοιπὸν καθαρῶς ἐν τοῖς κ. ὀφθαλμοῖς τὴν δόξαν τοῦ φωτὸς τοῦ ἀληθινοῦ καθορᾶν Mac.Aeg.*hom.*17.3(M.34. 625B); **4.** ref. relation between purity of body and purity of soul βαπτίσθητε τὴν ψυχὴν ἀπὸ ὀργῆς καὶ ἀπὸ πλεονεξίας, ἀπὸ φθόνου, ἀπὸ μίσους· καὶ ἰδοὺ τὸ σῶμα κ. ἐστι Just.*dial.*14.2(M.6.504D); cf. καταργήσαντες δὲ τὰ τῆς σαρκὸς ἔργα, αὐτῇ κ. τῇ σαρκὶ ἐπενδυσάμενοι τὴν ἀφθαρσίαν Clem.*paed.*2.10(p.217.19; M.8.517B); εἰς δὲ τὰ ἅγια καὶ τὰ ἅγια τῶν ἁγίων [sc. Communion] ὁ μὴ πάντη κ. καὶ ψυχῇ καὶ σώματι προσιέναι κωλυθήσεται Dion.Al.*ep.can.*2(p.103.10; M.10.1281A); ὁ δερμάτινος ἔοικεν εἶναι χιτὼν ἐπιρραφεὶς καὶ ἐπιτεθεὶς τῷ προτέρῳ καὶ κ. σώματι, ὃν ὁ...κύριος ἡμῶν τὸν ἄνθρωπον ἐνέδυσεν †Dion.Al.*fr. Cant.*(p.229.7); τὰ δὲ κ. τῶν ἱερῶν ψυχῶν...σώματα...συναπολήψεται τὴν οἰκείαν ἀνάστασιν Dion.Ar.*e.h.*7.1.1(M.3.553A); **5.** ref. knowledge of God and spiritual life ὁ φόβος αὐτοῦ σώζων πάντας τοὺς...ἀναστρεφομένους ἐν κ. διανοίᾳ *1Clem.*21.8; Clem.*prot.*10(p.72.8; M.8. 213B); κ. πρὸς γνώσεως ἐπιτηδειότητα εὐτρεπίζων τὴν ψυχὴν id.*paed.* 1.1(p.91.14; M.8.252B); καθαρὸς εἰς εὐχὴν πάντοτε id.*str.*7.12(p.56.5; M.9.508C); κύριε...γνωρίζωμέν σου τὸ μέγεθος ἀθεώρητον ἡμῖν ἐπὶ τοῦ παρόντος ὑπάρχον, καθαροῖς δὲ θεωρητὸν *A.Jo.*109(p.208.9); τὰ τοῖς κ. ψυχὴν καὶ σῶμα παραδεικνύντα ἀποκάλυψιν μυστηρίου Or.*Cels.*3.61 (p.255.17; M.11.1000D); Thdt.*Joel.*2:28f.(2.1399); τῇ κ. τοῦ κρυφίου θέᾳ Dion.Ar.*myst.*2(M.3.1025B); κ. ... ὑποδοχὴν τῶν θεαρχικῶν ἐλλάμψεων id.*c.h.*15.3(M.3.332A); id.*e.h.*1.4(M.3.376B); ἐν κ. θεωρίᾳ *ib.* 7.3.9(565B); οἱ γὰρ τέλειοι, τῆς θεωρητικῆς ἤδη μυστικῶς ἀξιωθέντες θεολογίας, καὶ πάσης φαντασίας ὑλικῆς τὸν νοῦν κ. καταστήσαντες Max.*cap.*1.68(M.90.1208A); **6.** exeg.; **a.** Mt.5:8 καθαροὺς τῇ καρδίᾳ γενομένους κατὰ τὸ προσεχὲς τοῦ κυρίου προσμένει τῇ θεωρίᾳ τῇ ἀϊδίῳ ἀποκατάστασις...τὸν κ. τῇ καρδίᾳ πρόσωπον πρὸς πρόσωπον... τὸν θεὸν ἐποπτεύειν Clem.*str.*7.10(p.41.21,30; M.9.480B,C); **b.** Jo.13:10 ἐπεὶ τοίνυν εἶχον καὶ οἱ μαθηταὶ τὸ εἶναι κ., προστίθησιν Ἰησοῦς τῇ καθαρότητι αὐτῶν καὶ τὸ νίπτειν αὐτῶν τοὺς πόδας·...οὔτε τοὺς μὴ ὅλους κ., ἀλλ' οὕτως ὥστ' ἂν εἰπεῖν περὶ τῶν οὕτως κ.· κἂν γάρ τις ᾖ τέλειος ἐν υἱοῖς ἀνθρώπων, τῆς ἀπὸ Ἰησοῦ, ἵν' οὕτως ὀνομάσω, καθαρότητος ἀπούσης, εἰς κ. οὐ λογισθήσεται...διὰ τοῦτ' αὐτῶν ἔνιψεν τοὺς πόδας, ἐπεὶ ἦσαν ὡς ἐν ἀνθρώποις καθαροὶ ἀλλ' οὐχὶ καὶ παρὰ θεῷ· χωρὶς γὰρ Ἰησοῦ οὐδεὶς παρὰ θεῷ κ. γίνεται, κἂν πρὸ τούτου νομισθῇ διά τινος ἐπιμελείας αὐτὸν κ. πεποιηκέναι, τοῖς δ' ὡς ἐν ἀνθρώποις κ. ἤδη γεγενημένοις, καὶ λουσαμένοις τὸ τοῦ Ἰησοῦ βάπτισμα...ἐνοικεῖν καὶ τὸ ἅγιον δύναται πνεῦμα Or.*Jo.*32.7(6; p.436.8ff.; M.14.757B,C).

E. of Christian institutions and activities; **1.** of Church and its teaching and worship τοὺς περὶ τοῦ ἀληθινοῦ φωτὸς καθαροὺς...λόγους Clem.*str.*1.12(p.35.24; M.8.753A); τὴν κ. τῆς διδασκαλίας...σποράν Meth.*symp.*3.8(p.37.7; M.18.73D); *ib.*7.4(p.75.15; 129C); ἡ τῆς καθόλου καὶ μόνης ἀληθοῦς ἐκκλησίας λαμπρότης,...τό τε σῶφρον καὶ κ. τῆς ἐνθέου πολιτείας Eus.*h.e.*4.7.13(M.20.320B); τὸ τῆς καθολικῆς ἐκκλησίας κ. Const.ap.Gel.Cyz.*h.e.*3.18.13; τῆς τοῦ θεοῦ κ. ὑπηρεσίας Dion.Ar. *e.h.*6.1.3(M.3.533A); εὐχῶν κ. *Lit.Marc.*(Brightman p.135.13); **2.** of Christian virtues and states of mind; **a.** conscience τῶν ἐν κ. συνειδήσει λατρευόντων *1Clem.*45.7; ἐργάσησθε αὐτὰς [sc. ἐντολάς] ἐν κ. καρδίᾳ Herm.*vis.*5.7; through repentance, id.*sim.*7.5; id. *mand.*12.3.2; Or.*Jo.*20.31(25; p.368.25; M.14.645A); κ. ἀπὸ ἁμαρτίας μετάνοια *ib.*32.19(12; p.458.18; 793C); Meth.*lepr.*7(p.460.11); ref. catechumens διαφυλαττέσθωσαν...ἐν τῇ κ. φρονήσει Serap.*euch.* 3.3; **b.** faith and charity ἀγάπη...χρῆμα κ. Clem.*paed.*2.1(p.157. 25; M.8.388B); τῇ πρὸς αὐτὸν [sc. θεὸν] καθαρωτάτῃ πίστει πέποιθα Const.ap.Gel.Cyz.*h.e.*2.7.38(M.85.1241A); **c.** spiritual joy τῆς θείας ...ἐμπίμπλασθαι θέας, τῆς...κ. γενομένους ἡδονῆς Clem.*paed.*2.1(p.160. 6; M.8.393A); *ib.*3.12(p.282.23; 664A); Chrys.*hom.12.7 in Rom.*(9. 553D); id.*hom.1.3 in 1Tim.*(11.554B); **d.** spiritual freedom, Meth. *res.*3.9(p.403.6); Chrys.*hom.9.4 in Rom.*(9.517E); **e.** spiritual health, *ib.14.11*(9.593D); id.*hom.15.5 in 2Cor.*(10.551A); **3.** of marriage and childbirth κ. οὖν τὸν γάμον ὥσπερ τι ἱερὸν ἄγαλμα τῶν μιαινόντων φυλακτέον Clem.*str.*2.23(p.192.25; M.8.1096A); ἵνα μείνῃ μονόγαμος καὶ κ. Or.*hom.20.4 in Jer.*(p.182.26; M.13.508C); ἀνὴρ οὖν καὶ γυνή, νομίμῳ γάμῳ συνερχόμενοι καὶ ἀπ' ἀλλήλων ἐγειρόμενοι, ἀπαρατηρήτως προσευχέσθωσαν· καὶ μὴ λουσάμενοι κ. εἰσιν. ὃς δ' ἂν ἀλλοτρίαν γυναῖκα ὑποφθείρας μιάνῃ...ἀναστὰς ἀπ' αὐτῆς, οὐδ' ἂν τὸ πέλαγος ὅλον καὶ τοὺς ποταμοὺς πάντας ἀπολούσηται, κ. εἶναι δυνήσεται *Const.App.*6.29.4; ἡ τῶν παίδων γένεσις κ. *ib.*6.28.6.

F. ref. cult and ritual; **1.** in Jewish food laws τὸ κ. βρῶμα καὶ τὸ ἀκάθαρτον κατὰ τὸν Μωυσέως νόμον Or.*or.*27.12(p.371.22; M.11. 516C); id.*Cels.*2.1(p.127.17; M.11.796B); φύσει μὲν κ. ὑπάρχει πάντα τὰ ζῷα...ἀλλ' ἐπειδὴ ἐβούλετο ὁ θεός, ὥσπερ ἐν πᾶσι, τοῖς ἐσθιομένοις ὑπὸ τὸν ζυγὸν τῆς τοῦ νόμου δουλείας ποιήσασθαι τοὺς Ἰουδαίους, διὰ τοῦτο τῶν ζῴων...τινὰ μὲν ὠνόμασε κ., ὧν...τὴν βρῶσιν τοῖς Ἰουδαίοις ἐπέτρεψε· τινὰ δὲ ἀκάθαρτα ὠνόμασεν, ὧν τὴν βρῶσιν αὐτοὺς ἀπεῖργε. κ. οὖν ταῦτα καὶ ἀκάθαρτα λέγονται· κ. μέν, διὰ τὴν φύσιν· ἀκάθαρτα δέ, διὰ τὸν νόμον ‡Just.*qu.et resp.*35(M.6.1281B,C); *Const.App.*6.20.8; **2.** in Christian eucharist *εὐχαριστήσατε, προεξομολογησάμενοι τὰ παραπτώματα ὑμῶν ὅπως κ. ἡ θυσία ὑμῶν ᾖ Did.*14.1; *ἵνα πάσης μικροψυχίας ἀναιρουμένης τὸ δῶρον κ. προσφέρηται τῷ θεῷ* CNic.(325) *can.*5; v. *θυσία*.

II. neut. plur. as subst., *white loaves* δός μοι ὀλίγα ὠά, καὶ ὀλίγα κ. Jo.Mosch.*prat.*211(M.87.3104B).

III. masc. plur. as subst., name given to themselves by Novatianists, v. *Ναυατιανός*, Eus.*h.e.*6.43.1(M.20.616B); ref. eccl. legislation, CNic.(325)*can.*8; Bas.*ep.*188 *can.*1(3.268C; M.32.664C); ‡CCP(381)*can.*7; name criticized by orthodox *αὐτὸς γὰρ* [sc. *Χριστός*] *μόνος ἐστὶ κ. ... οὗτοι δὲ ἑαυτοὺς φήσαντες κ. ἀπ' αὐτῆς τῆς ὑποθέσεως ἀκαθάρτους ἑαυτοὺς ἀποτελοῦσι· πᾶς γὰρ ὁ κ. ἑαυτὸν ἀποφήνας ἀκάθαρτον ἑαυτὸν τελείως κατέκρινε* Epiph.*haer.*59.6(p.372.2; M.41.1028C); *ποῦ οἱ κ. λεγόμενοι, οἱ παντὸς ῥύπου γέμοντες;* Chrys.*hom.14.2 in Eph.*(11.105F); Leont.B.*Nest.et Eut.*2(M.86.1320C).

***καθαρότευκτος**, *purely wrought τὸ κ. κυρίου δῶμα* [sc. BMV] Thdr.Stud.*nativ.BMV* 7(M.96.689C).

καθαρότης, ἡ, *purity*;

A. divine *ἡ θεία φύσις...κ.* Gr.Nyss.*or.dom.*2(p.32.28; M.44.1140D); of Christ *ἡ ἀπαρχὴ τοῦ φυράματος διὰ κ. τε καὶ ἀπαθείας ᾠκειώθη τῷ ἀληθινῷ πατρὶ καὶ θεῷ* id.*perf.*(p.206.10; M.46.280B); *ὁ κύριος...τῇ δὲ προσθήκῃ τοῦ ὕδατος τὴν ἄχραντον κ. ἐδήλου, καὶ ὅτι τοῦ θεοῦ τὸ σῶμα* ‡Ath.*Apoll.*1.18(M.26.1125B).

B. ref. relationship between divine and human purity, ref. Mt.5:8 *ἱκανὴ δὲ ἡ τῆς ψυχῆς κ. ἐστὶ τὸν θεὸν δι' ἑαυτῆς κατοπτρίζεσθαι* Ath.*gent.*2(M.25.8B); *πόθῳ τῆς ἀφθαρσίας ἀνακραθεῖσαι* [sc. *αἱ ψυχαί*] *τῇ τοῦ θεοῦ κ.* Gr.Nyss.*hom.15 in Cant.*(M.44.1112D); *οὕτω γίνεται μακάριος ὁ καθαρὸς τῇ καρδίᾳ, ὅτι πρὸς τὴν ἰδίαν κ. βλέπων, ἐν τῇ εἰκόνι καθορᾷ τὸ ἀρχέτυπον* id.*beat.*6(M.44.1272B); as part of the image of God, id.*hom.opif.*5.1(M.44.137B); *μία γὰρ τῇ φύσει ἡ κ. ἥ τε ἐν τῷ Χριστῷ καὶ ἡ ἐν τῷ μετέχοντι θεωρουμένη* id.*perf.*(p.212.10; M.46.284D); *ὁ νοῦς ὁ ἀνθρώπινος καταλιπὼν τὸν θολερὸν τοῦτον καὶ αὐχμώδη βίον, ἐπειδὰν καθαρὸς γενόμενος ἐν τῇ δυνάμει τοῦ πνεύματος φωτοειδὴς γένηται καὶ ἐμμιχθῇ τῇ...ὑψηλῇ κ. ... μὴ δυνατὸν ἑτέρως εἶναι συναφθῆναι τὴν ψυχὴν τῷ ἀφθάρτῳ θεῷ, μὴ καὶ αὐτὴν ὡς οἷόν τε καθαρὰν γενομένην διὰ τῆς ἀφθαρσίας, ὡς ἂν διὰ τοῦ ὁμοίου καταλάβοι τὸ ὅμοιον, οἱονεὶ κάτοπτρον τῇ κ. τοῦ θεοῦ ἑαυτὴν ὑποθεῖσαν* id.*virg.*11(p.295.10–p.296.6; M.46.368A,C); gained through baptism *ἴδιον δὲ τῆς θείας ἐνεργείας ἡ τῶν δεομένων ἐστὶ σωτηρία. αὕτη δὲ διὰ τῆς ἐν ὕδατι καθάρσεως ἐνεργὸς γίνεται. ὁ δὲ καθαρθεὶς ἐν μετουσίᾳ τῆς κ. ἔσται, τὸ δὲ ἀληθῶς καθαρὸν ἡ θεότης ἐστίν* id.*or.catech.*36(p.140.7; M.45.92D); cf. *ψυχὴ δὲ διὰ περιπλοκῆς σοφίᾳ ἐνωθεῖσα, ἁγιασμοῦ πληροῦται καὶ κ.* Hipp.*fr.7 in Pr.*(p.159.9).

C. in spiritual life; **1.** in gen. *ἐν κ. καρδίας συνήσετε τὸ θέλημα τοῦ θεοῦ κρατεῖν* *T.Neph.*3.1; Clem.*str.*6.3(p.446.23; M.9.249A); *ib.*6.7(p.459.20; 277A); Thdt.*h.rel.*13(3.1208); *οὐ γὰρ τὸ μηκέτι πρᾶξαι τὰ κακὰ μόνον κ. φέρει, ἀλλὰ τὸ ἐπιμελείᾳ τῶν καλῶν κατὰ κράτος ἀθετῆσαι τὰ κακά* Diad.*perf.*98(p.146.6); Dion.Ar.*d.n.*3.3(M.3.684B); **2.** as necessary for contemplation and union with God *σὺν Χριστῷ γενόμενος, ἄξιον ἑαυτὸν παρασχὼν διὰ καθαρότητα* Clem.*str.*7.12(p.56.26; M.9.509B); *τῷ ἐπιτηδείῳ δι' ὑπερβολὴν καθαρότητος νῷ θεωρούμενα δόξα ἂν λέγοιτο εἶναι θεοῦ ὀφθεῖσα* Or.*Jo.*32.27(17; p.472.28; M.14.816D); Gr.Nyss.*hom.13 in Cant.*(M.44.1037A); *οἱ τῆς θείας ἐπιβάσεως ἄξιοι διὰ τὴν τῆς ψυχῆς κ. ὧν ἐν ταῖς καρδίαις αἱ τοῦ θεοῦ ἀναβάσεις* Thdt.*Ezech.*28:16(2.916); *τῇ τῆς ψυχῆς κ., δι' ἣν καὶ τοῦ θείου κάλλους τὴν φαντασίαν δεχόμενος* id.*h.rel.*4(3.1156); *αἱ ψυχαί... πρὸς μίαν νοερὰν συνάγουσαι κ., προβαίνουσιν...ἐπὶ τὴν ὑπὲρ νόησιν ἕνωσιν* Dion.Ar.*d.n.*11.2(M.3.949D); cf.Max.*schol.d.n.*11.2(M.4.396B); *ἀνὴρ...διὰ πολλὴν κ. νοῦ πρὸς θεοπτείαν ἐπιτηδειότατος* Dion.Ar.*ep.*8.6(M.3.1097B); **3.** in rel. to spiritual knowledge *οἱ...πάντα τὸν χρόνον ἀναθέντες τῇ ἐξετάσει τῶν ἱερῶν γραμμάτων τοῖς ἐπιτηδείοις διὰ βίου καθαρότητα καὶ τὴν περὶ τὰ θεῖα φιλομάθειαν παραστήσουσιν* Or.*Cels.*7.30(p.181.14; M.11.1464B); *ζητεῖν δὲ τὴν τῶν μελλόντων γνῶσιν ἐν ψυχαῖς δι' ἄκραν κ. παραδεξαμέναις πνεῦμα τοῦ ἐπὶ πᾶσι θεοῦ* *ib.*5.42(p.46.21; 1248C); *πᾶσι τοῖς μέλλουσι βλέπειν διὰ τὴν αὐτῶν κ. τὴν ἁμαρτίαν τοῦ ἡμαρτηκότος* id.*hom.16.10 in Jer.*(p.142.24; M.13.452D); *τὴν...προδιορατικὴν...κ., ὅτι τὰ ἐν τῇ διανοίᾳ...φυόμενα...λαθεῖν οὐ δύνανται* Gr.Mag.*dial.*(tr.Zach.)2.20(M.*PL.*66.171B); *κ. δὲ καρδίας ἐδέξατο ἔλλαμψιν* Jo.Clim.*scal.*7(M.88.813B); *γινώσκει ἄνθρωπος ὅτι ἦλθεν εἰς τὴν κ. ἡ καρδία αὐτοῦ, ὅταν πάντας καλοὺς θεωρῇ, καὶ οὐχ ὁρᾶταί τις αὐτῷ ἀκάθαρτος* Isaac ap.Jo.Clim.*scal.*7(M.88.825A); *ἑκάστῳ γὰρ ἡ γνῶσις κατὰ τὴν ἀναλογίαν τῆς κ.* Areth.*Apoc.*39(M.106.684C); **4.** equated with holiness, Or.*or.*25.3(p.359.12; M.11.500A); Dion.Ar.*d.n.*12.2(M.3.969B); **5.** hence requisite in priests and religious and others aiming at perfection *ὥς τινας αὐτῶν διὰ τὸν ἔρωτα τῆς ὑπερβαλλούσης κ. καὶ διὰ τὸ καθαρώτερον θρησκεύειν τὸ θεῖον μηδὲ τῶν συγκεχωρημένων ὑπὸ τοῦ νόμου ἅπτεσθαι ἀφροδισίων* Or.*Cels.*1.26(p.78.27; M.11.712A); as opp. conjugal chastity *εἰσί τινες οἱ... ἀσκοῦσι τὴν ἁγνείαν καὶ τὴν κ., καὶ ἄλλοι οἱ...ἀσκοῦσι τὴν μονογαμίαν* id.*hom.20.4 in Jer.*(p.182.22; M.13.508C); *δεόμεθα ὑπὲρ τῶν μοναζόντων καὶ ὑπὲρ τῶν παρθενευουσῶν...ἵνα δυνηθῶσιν ἐν κ. διατρῖψαι* Serap.*euch.*11.5; *ὁ ἀρχιερεὺς εἰς τὰ ἅγια τῶν ἁγίων εἰσελεύσεται...ἐν πάσῃ τῇ κατὰ νόμον ἱεραρχικῇ κ.* Dion.Ar.*ep.*8.1(M.3.1089C); *αὐτοῦ* [sc. *ἱεράρχου*]*...ἐν κ. τῆς θεοειδοῦς ἕξεως ἀναγομένου* id.*e.h.*3.2(M.3.428A); *μέση δὲ τάξις ἐστὶν ἡ θεωρητικὴ καί τινων ἱερῶν ἀναλόγως ἐν κ. πάσῃ κοινωνός* *ib.*6.1.2(532B); ablution of hands being its symbol *ὑποδιάκονος διδότω ἀπόρρυψιν χειρῶν τοῖς ἱερεῦσιν, σύμβολον καθαρότητος ψυχῶν θεῷ ἀνακειμένων* *Const.App.*8.11.12.

D. as style of address to bishops, Dam.Papa *ep.Illyr.*ap.Thdt. *h.e.*2.22.10(3.884).

***καθαροχειρία, ἡ**, *cleanliness of hands*; in weaving, Thdr.Stud. *poen.*1.110(M.99.1748C).

καθαρπάζω, **1.** *take away, carry off*, Or.*adnot.in Dt.*14:19(M.17.25C); *A.Xanthipp.*23(p.74.24); *ib.*24(p.75.4); **2.** intrans., *steal away, withdraw* from; c. genit., Const.ap.Eus.*v.C.*3.64(p.111.31; M.20.1140C).

καθάρσιος, **I.** *purifying*, freq. neut. as subst., *purification*;

A. in OT; **1.** ref. Babel *ἡ κατὰ τὸν πύργον ἱστορία κειμένη ἐν τῇ Γενέσει ἀλλ', ὡς οἴεται Κέλσος, σαφὴς τυγχάνῃ, οὐ δ' οὕτως φαίνεται ἐπὶ καθαρσίῳ τῆς γῆς τοῦτο συμβεβηκέναι· εἰ μὴ ἄρα καθάρσιον τῆς γῆς οἴεται τὴν καλουμένην τῶν γλωσσῶν σύγχυσιν* Or.*Cels.*4.21(p.290.12; M.11.1053B); and Flood *ἡ δ' ἐν τῷ κατακλυσμῷ διαφθορὰ τῶν ἀνθρώπων καθάρσιόν ἐστι τῆς γῆς* *ib.*6.58(p.129.9; 1388C); **2.** ritual, Gr.Nyss.*v.Mos.*(M.44.321B); Chrys.*hom.53.3 in Mt.*(7.541E); Nonn.*par.Jo.*2:6(M.43.761A); Isid.Pel.*epp.*4.200(M.78.1288C); **3.** ref. Is.6:7 *ἐκπέμπεται ταῖς ἁγιαζομέναις δυνάμεσι τὸ κ. πῦρ* †Bas.*Is.*186(1.516D; M.30.436A).

B. Christ as agent of purification *ὁ κύριος, ὄψει καταφρονούμενος, ἔργῳ προσκυνούμενος, ὁ κ. καὶ σωτήριος...ὁ θεῖος λόγος, ὁ...ὄντως θεός* Clem.*prot.*10(p.78.12; M.8.228C); id.*paed.*3.9(p.264.1; M.8.620A); Or.*Jo.*6.53(35; p.162.5; M.14.292D) cit. s. *ἀμνός*; *ὁ δυνάμενος ὑπὲρ ὅλου ⟨τοῦ⟩ κόσμου...ἀναδέξασθαι ἐπὶ καθαρσίῳ αὐτοῦ ἀπολομένου* *ib.*28.19(14; p.413.26; 721B); id.*mart.*30(p.26.29; M.11.601A); but *κύριος κ. δεόμενος τοῦ ἀπὸ μόνου τοῦ πατρὸς αὐτῷ δοθῆναι...δυναμένου* id.*Jo.*6.55(37; p.164.23; 297A); ref. Passion and death *μέγα ἱερεῖον ...τὸ τοῦ παντὸς κ. κόσμου* Eus.*d.e.*1.10(p.45.19; M.22.85D); *ib.*(p.46.7; 88B); *καταλέλοιπεν οὖν αὐτὸν ὁ ἰσχυρὸς αὐτοῦ, θελήσας αὐτὸν μέχρι θανάτου καὶ θανάτου σταυροῦ κατελθεῖν, καὶ τοῦ κόσμου παντὸς λύτρον καὶ ἀντίψυχον ἀποδειχθῆναι καὶ κ. γενέσθαι τῆς τῶν εἰς αὐτὸν πιστευσάντων ζωῆς* *ib.*10.8(p.477.6; 768A); *ὁ θεῖος Δαβὶδ αὐτὸν εἶναί φησι τὸ...μέγα κ.* Cyr.*Ps.*49:23(M.69.1085A); *τὸ κ. αἷμα τοῦ γένους* ‡Gr.Naz.*Chr.pat.*1113(M.38.225).

C. ref. baptism; **1.** of John *ὁ Ἰώσηπος μαρτυρεῖ τῷ Ἰωάννῃ ὡς βαπτιστῇ γεγενημένῳ καὶ καθάρσιον τοῖς βαπτισαμένοις ἐπαγγελλομένῳ* Or.*Cels.*1.47(p.97.2; M.11.745C); *ῥοαῖς καθαρσίοις λούων πλήθη βροτῶν ὁ σὸς πρόδρομος* Meth.*symp.*11(p.135.17; M.18.212B); **2.** Christian *τὸ διὰ τοῦ ὕδατος λουτρόν, σύμβολον τυγχάνον κ. ψυχῆς* Or.*Jo.*6.33(17; p.142.28; M.14.257A); *λουσάμενος ἐνὶ τύποις, λουτρὸν τὸ κ. ἔχει* *PAmh.*2.11; *τὸν δὲ ποταμὸν τὸν ἐπὶ τῆς ἐρήμου καθαίροντα πάντας τοὺς ἀπολουομένους ἐν αὐτῷ κ. τινὸς εἶναι κατὰ διάνοιαν θεωρουμένου εἰκόνα* Eus.*d.e.*9.5(p.417.14; M.22.672D); *οἱονεὶ κ. ἐστι* [sc. *βάπτισμα*] *ψυχῆς τοῦ ἀπὸ τοῦ σαρκικοῦ φρονήματος αὐτῇ προσγενομένου ῥύπου* Bas.*Spir.*35(3.29B; M.32.129B); *μετάσχωμεν κ. ὑδάτων* Gr.Naz.*or.*40.11(M.36.372B); Gr.Nyss.*or.catech.*35(p.138.14; M.45.92B); *ib.*(p.139.6; 92C); Chrys.*catech.*1.2(2.228B); *τινὲς δέ φασι καὶ αἰνίττεσθαι εὐθὺς ἀπὸ καταβολῆς κόσμου τὴν χάριν τοῦ ἁγίου βαπτίσματος. διὸ καὶ τὸ κ. ἡμῶν ἐν ὕδατι μᾶλλον ἢ ἑτέρῳ στοιχείῳ* Proc.G.*Gen.*1:2(M.87.48B); **3.** ref. baptism and eucharist [Jo.19:34 *αἷμα καὶ ὕδωρ*] *τὰ δύο κ. τοῦ τε βαπτίσματος καὶ τῆς μεταλήψεως τῶν ἀχράντων αὐτοῦ μυστηρίων* *Chron.Pasch.*p.220(M.92.536D).

D. ref. washing of disciples' feet *οἱ μετὰ τοῦ Ἰησοῦ δειπνοῦντες... δέονται μὲν κ. τινός...καὶ τοῦτο τὸ κ. ... ὑπ' οὐδενὸς ἢ τοῦ Ἰησοῦ μόνου γενέσθαι δύναται* Or.*Jo.*32.2(p.426.22,25; M.14.741B,C); Nonn.*par.Jo.*13:10(M.43.861A).

E. of the purifying fire, at end of world *τὸ κ. πῦρ καὶ τὴν τοῦ κόσμου φθοράν* Or.*Cels.*4.21(p.291.10; M.11.1056A); *ib.*5.15(p.16.6; 1201D); *ἡνίκα πῦρ κρίνῃσι κ. ἔργματα πάντων* Gr.Naz.*carm.*2.1.1.524

(M.37.1009A); ref. other purification by fire *πάντα γὰρ τὰ ἐν γενέσει χρῄζει τοῦ κ. τοῦ ἀπὸ τοῦ πυρός* Or.*hom.11.5 in Jer.*(p.83.15; M.13. 373D).

F. in spiritual life; of virtues purifying soul, [ref. Pr.1:7] *φόβος δέ, κ. ψυχῆς* Bas.*hom.*12.4(2.100E; M.31.393C); *μέγα κ. ἁμαρτημάτων ἡ εἰς τὸν πλησίον φιλοφροσύνη* Chrys.*ep.*117(3.659B); *τιμωρία ἐκ τοῦ μὴ φροντίζειν τῶν τῆς ψυχῆς κ., ἅπερ ἐστὶν ἀρετή* id.*hom.73.2 in Mt.* (7.709B); prayer, Nil.*epp.*2.24(M.79.89D); tears of repentance, Hyper. *mon.*115(M.79.1484D); martyrdom, Philost.*h.e.*4.4(M.65.520B); necessary for vision of God and myst. union *εἰ ποθεῖς ἰδεῖν...τὸν θεόν, κ. μεταλάμβανε θεοπρεπῶν* Clem.*prot.*1(p.10.9; M.8.65C); *πολλοὶ γὰρ καθαρσίων ἔτι...δεόμενοι...τῆς θείας ἀνόδου κατατολμῶσιν* Gr.Nyss. *v.Mos.*(M.44.376C); *τί γὰρ ἂν γένοιτο τούτου παραδοξότερον, ἢ τὸ αὐτὴν ποιῆσαι τὴν φύσιν τῶν ἰδίων παθημάτων κ., διὰ τῶν νομιζομένων ἐμπαθῶν ῥημάτων* [sc. of Cant.] *τὴν ἀπάθειαν νομοθετοῦσαν;* id.*hom. 1 in Cant.*(M.44.776C); of kiss of 'bridegroom' as purification of soul, *ib.*(780A).

G. in paganism *τῶν μυστηρίων τῶν παρ' Ἕλλησιν...τὰ κ.* Clem. *str.*5.11(p.373.24; M.9.108A); and Gnost., Or.*Cels.*6.35(p.104.22; M. 11.1349B).

H. neut. plur., as name of Purification festival *ἡ μὲν ἑορτὴ λέγεται καθαρσίων, ἣν οὐκ ἂν τις ἁμάρτοι, ἑορτῶν εἰπὼν ἑορτήν* Hesych.H.*serm.*6(M.93.1468B).

II. neut. plur. as subst.;

A. *prunings*, Or.*Jo.*6.28(14; p.137.33; M.14.249A).

B. *offscourings*, Synes.*regn.*20(p.47.10; M.66.1093C).

κάθαρσις, ἡ, *cleansing, purification*;

A. of men; **1.** by baptism *δεόμενος τῆς εἰλικρινεστάτης ταύτης κ. ...τυχεῖν* Dion.Al.ap.Eus.*h.e.*7.9.3(M.20.656A); *καθάρσεως τοῦτον εἶναι καιρὸν...ἀπορρύψασθαι τῆς ψυχῆς λόγων ἀπορρήτων δυνάμει σωτηρίῳ τε λουτρῷ πιστεύσας* Eus.*v.C.*4.61(p.142.26; M.20.1212C); *ἓν βάπτισμα, μία κ.* †Bas.*Is.*38(1.410A; M.30.193A); *ib.*39(410D; M. 193C); Gr.Naz.*or.*8.20(M.35.812C); *διττὴ καὶ ἡ κ., δι' ὕδατός τέ φημι καὶ πνεύματος, τοῦ μὲν θεωρητῶς τε καὶ σωματικῶς λαμβανομένου, τοῦ δὲ ἀσωμάτως καὶ ἀθεωρήτως συντρέχοντος* *ib.*40.8(M.36.368A); *ἴδιον δὲ τῆς θείας ἐνεργείας ἡ τῶν δεομένων ἐστὶ σωτηρία. αὕτη δὲ διὰ τῆς ἐν ὕδατι κ. ἐνεργὸς γίνεται* Gr.Nyss.*or.catech.*36(p.140.6; M.45.92D); Cyr. *glaph.Ex.*3(1.319D); *τῆς δὲ ψυχῆς ἡ κ. κατὰ τὸν ἀριθμὸν τῆς ἁγίας ἀποτελεῖται τριάδος* Thdt.*qu.19 in 4Reg.*(1.523); as *ἡ τοῦ ἁγίου πνεύματος κ.* id.*Mal.*3:2(2.1686); *τὴν ἁπάσης ὁμοῦ κακίας δι' ἐναρέτου καὶ θείας ζωῆς ἀποκάθαρσιν, τῇ δι' ὕδατος φυσικῇ κ. ... διαγγέλλουσα* Dion.Ar.*e.h.*2.3.1(M.3.397B); *ib.*5.1.3(504B); cf.*ib.*5.1.6(508B); *ἡ πλύσις τῶν ἱματίων...τὴν ἀπὸ νεκρῶν ἔργων κ. δηλοῖ, τὴν διὰ λουτροῦ ἀποτελουμένην εἰς τὸν μέλλοντα αἰῶνα* Proc.G.*Lev.*17:10(M.87.752C); **2.** by repentance *ἱκανὴ...ἀνθρώπῳ κ. μετάνοια ἀκριβής* Clem.*str.*4.22 (p.311.13; M.8.1352C); *διὰ τὴν τελείαν κ. καὶ πίστιν ἀποστερηθέντες τῶν τῆς σαρκὸς ἀτοπημάτων* Meth.*symp.*3.8(p.37.4; M.18.73D); *σοφία πρώτη, βίος...θεῷ κεκαθαρμένος...μόνην ἀπαιτοῦντι παρ' ἡμῶν θυσίαν, τὴν κ., ἣν δὲ καρδίαν συντετριμμένην...καὶ καινὴν ἐν Χριστῷ κτίσιν... τῇ γραφῇ καλεῖν φίλον* Gr.Naz.*or.*16.2(M.35.936B); **3.** ref. *γνῶσις*: *ἡ γνῶσις, ⟨ἢ⟩ τοῦ ἡγεμονικοῦ τῆς ψυχῆς κ. ἐστι* Clem.*str.*4.6(p.265.28; M.8.1249C); *ταχεῖα...εἰς κ. ἡ γνῶσις* *ib.*7.10(p.41.25; M.9.480C); *ἔνθα κ. ψυχῆς ἡ διὰ τῶν ἀρετῶν, ἐκεῖ καὶ ἔλλαμψις γνώσεως* Max.*ambig.* (M.91.1301D); **4.** through martyrdom, Clem.*str.*4.16(p.294.10; M.8. 1309C); and death which limits the duration of sin, Meth.*res.*1.42 (p.289.6; M.41.1112C); **5.** through ministration of priests, *Const.App.* 2.35.3; **6.** as stage of spiritual life *ἐν οὖν τῷ θεωρητικῷ βίῳ ἑαυτοῦ τις ἐπιμελεῖται...καὶ διὰ τῆς ἰδίας εἰλικρινοῦς κ. ἐποπτεύει τὸν θεόν* Clem. *str.*4.23(p.316.1; M.8.1361A); *ib.*7.10(p.42.1; M.9.481A); *τὴν τοῦ ἱεροῦ λαοῦ τάξιν, ὡς διὰ πάσης ἐληλυθυῖαν κ., καὶ τῆς ἱερᾶς...κοινωνίας, ὡς θεμιτόν, ἠξιωμένην* Dion.Ar.*e.h.*6.1.2(M.3.532C); *ἡ δὲ τῶν τελουμένων ἁπασῶν ὑψηλοτέρα τάξις ἡ τῶν μοναχῶν ἐστιν ἱερὰ διακόσμησις, πᾶσαν μὲν ἀποκεκαθαρμένην κ. ... θεωρεῖν...ἐγχειριζομένη* *ib.*6.1.3(532C); **7.** of souls after death; acc. Heraclitus, through fire, Clem.*str.*5.1(p.332. 1; M.9.21A) cit. s. *ἀνάστασις*; in Jewish and Christian teaching, ref. Is.4:4 *τὸν τρόπον τῆς κ. ἐπήγαγεν ὁ λόγος εἰπών· ἐν πνεύματι κρίσεως καὶ ἐν πνεύματι καύσεως* id.*paed.*3.9(p.264.13; M.8.620B); *Ἐννὼμ εὑρίσκομέν τι εἰς τὸν περὶ κολάσεων τόπον, μεταλαμβανομένων εἰς τὴν μετὰ βασάνου κ. τῶν τοιωνδὶ ψυχῶν* Or.*Cels.*6.25(p.96.3; M.11. 1332A); *ἐν δὲ τῷ πυρὶ καὶ τῇ φυλακῇ* [cf. Mt.5:25f.]*...εὐεργεσίαν ἐπὶ καθάρσει τῶν ἐν τῇ πλάνῃ κακῶν μετὰ σωτηρίαν λαμβάνοντες πόνων* id.*or.*29.15(p.390.13; M.11.544A); some souls having been purified by baptism and some needing purification by fire *ἐπειδὰν ἡ εἰς τὸ ἀρχαῖον ἀποκατάστασις...γένηται, ὁμόφωνος ἡ εὐχαριστία παρὰ πάσης ἔσται τῆς κτίσεως, καὶ τῶν ἐν τῇ κ. κεκολασμένων καὶ τῶν μηδὲ τὴν ἀρχὴν ἐπιδεηθέντων καθάρσεως* Gr.Nyss.*or.catech.*26(p.100.9; M.45. 69B); *ἐπεὶ οὖν ῥυπτική τίς ἐστι δύναμις ἐν τῷ πυρὶ καὶ τῷ ὕδατι, οἱ διὰ τοῦ ὕδατος τοῦ μυστικοῦ τὸν τῆς κακίας ῥύπον ἀποκλυσάμενοι τοῦ ἑτέρου τῶν κ. εἴδους οὐκ ἐπιδέονται· οἱ δὲ ταύτης ἀμύητοι τῆς κ. ἀναγκαίως τῷ πυρὶ καθαρίζονται* *ib.*35(p.139.6; 92C); **8.** exeg. Is.6:7, Dion.Ar.*c.h.*13.2(M.3.300B); *ὁ τὴν κ. τοῦ θεολόγου τελετουργῶν ἄγγελος...ὡς ἄν τις φαίη...ἐκδιδάσκων· ὅτι τῆς εἰς σὲ πρὸς ἐμοῦ τελετουργουμένης κ. ἀρχὴ μέν ἐστιν ἐξῃρημένη...ὁ καὶ τὰς πρώτας οὐσίας καὶ πρὸς τὸ εἶναι προσαγαγών, καὶ τῇ περὶ αὐτὸν ἱδρύσει συνέχων* *ib.* 13.4(305D); **9.** liturg., as first of three liturg. stages *αἱ μὲν ἅγιαι τελεταὶ κ. εἰσι καὶ φωτισμὸς καὶ τελείωσις· οἱ δὲ λειτουργοὶ* [i.e. deacons; so Max.*schol.e.h.*5.2.6(M.4.164D)] *καθαρτικὴ τάξις* Dion. Ar.*e.h.*6.3.5(M.3.536D); corresponding to a grade in celestial hierarchies *ἔστιν εἰπεῖν ἱερῶς ἐπὶ τῆς οὐρανίας ἱεραρχίας, ὅτι κ. ἐστι ταῖς ὑφειμέναις οὐσίαις ἡ παρὰ θεοῦ τῶν τέως ἀγνοουμένων ἔλλαμψις* *ib.* 6.3.6(537B); cf. *κ. τῶν οὐρανίων δυνάμεών ἐστιν ἡ ἐπὶ τελεωτέραν γνῶσιν ἔλλαμψις* Max.*schol.e.h.*6.3.6(M.4.173B); of priest washing fingers at celebration of eucharist, ref. Jo.13:10 *ὁ λελουμένος οὐ δεῖταί τινος ἑτέρας εἰ μὴ τῆς τῶν ἄκρων, εἴτουν ἐσχάτων ἑαυτοῦ νίψεως, δι' ἧς ἀκροτάτης κ., ἐν πανάγνῳ τοῦ θεοειδοῦς ἕξει...ἄσχετος ἔσται...ἡ δὲ τοῦ ἱεράρχου καὶ τῶν ἱερέων ἄχρι τῶν ἄκρων...ἀπόνιψις ἐπίπροσθεν γίγνεται τῶν ἁγιωτάτων συμβόλων, ὡς ἐπὶ Χριστοῦ τοῦ πάσας ἐφορῶντος ἡμῶν τὰς κρυφιωτάτας ἐννοίας, καὶ τῆς ἀκροτάτης κ. ἐν τοῖς αὐτοῦ...κρίσεσιν ὁριζομένης* Dion.Ar.*e.h.*3.3.10(440A,B); cf.Max. *schol.e.h.*3.3.10(145C); as primary aim of liturgy *ἡ...ἱερουργία πρώτην μὲν ἔχει θεοειδῆ δύναμιν τὴν ἱερὰν τῶν ἀτελέστων κ.* Dion.Ar. *e.h.*5.1.3(504A); **10.** at end of world *ἐκπυρωθήσεται...πρὸς κ. καὶ ἀνακαινισμὸν καταβασίῳ πᾶς ὁ κόσμος κατακλυζόμενος πυρί* Meth.*res.* 1.47(p.298.1; M.18.273B); cf. *Στωϊκοὶ...προσδέχονται δὲ ἐκπύρωσιν ἔσεσθαι καὶ κ. τοῦ κόσμου τούτου* Hipp.*haer.*1.21(p.26.4; M.16. 3049A).

B. in Dionysian theology as one of divine perfections *ἡ θεία μακαριότης...κ. ἱερὰ...ὑπὲρ κάθαρσιν* Dion.Ar.*c.h.*3.2(M.3.165C); *ὁ θεὸς καθαίρει πάντας τῷ πάσης κ. εἶναι αἰτίας* [vv.ll. *αἰτία, αἴτιος*] *ib.* 13.4(305C); *ib.*(308A); shared by angelic powers *καθαρτικαὶ δυνάμεις, οἱ πρῶτοι νόες ὀνομάζονται τῶν ὑφειμένων, ὡς δι' αὐτῶν ἐπὶ τὴν πάντων ὑπερούσιον ἀρχὴν ἀναγομένων, καὶ τῶν τελεταρχικῶν κ. ... ἐν μετουσίᾳ κατὰ τὸ αὐτοῖς θεμιτὸν γινομένων* *ib.*8.2(240C); *ib.*7.2(208A); *ἡ πρώτη τῶν οὐρανίων νοῶν ἱεραρχία...τῆς...κ. τοῦ ἀπλέτου φωτὸς... πληρουμένη, καθαίρεται* *ib.*7.3(209C); and by human believers *ἕκαστος οὐράνιός τε καὶ ἀνθρώπειος νοῦς...ἐν μετουσίᾳ γίνεται κατὰ τὸ αὐτῷ θεμιτὸν...τῆς ὑπεραγνοτάτης κ.* *ib.*10.3(273C); *κ. ἐστι τοῖς ὁπωσοῦν καθαροῖς ἡ τῆς θεαρχικῆς διαυγείας ἀγνότητος ὡς ἐφικτὸν μετουσία* *ib.* 13.4(305A); cf. *τί ἐστι κ., καὶ πῶς εἰς τὰ νοητὰ γίνεται παρὰ τοῦ θεοῦ ἡ κ. δηλαδὴ ἡ μετουσία. οὐ γὰρ οἷα ἐστὶ τῶν ἀνθρώπων ἡ κ., τοιαύτη ἐστὶ καὶ ἐπὶ τῶν ἀσωμάτων* Max.*schol.c.h.*13.4(M.4.100D).

καθαρτήριος, *purging, cleaning, purifying*, abs. *πῦρ κ., ὃ Χριστὸς ἦλθε βαλεῖν ἐπὶ τῆς γῆς* Gr.Naz.*or.*40.36(M.36.409D); *δαίμονές εἰσι κ., τέχνην ἔχοντες ἐπὶ ταῖς ψυχαῖς ἣν οἱ κναφεῖς ἐπὶ τοῖς ἱματίοις τοῖς πιναροῖς* Synes.*ep.*44(M.66.1368D); *ῥίψον πάντα βόρβορον κακίας ἀπὸ σοῦ, καὶ τότε ἐλθὼν ὑπόδεξαι τὸν κ. ἄνθρακα* Anast.S.*synax.*(M.89. 841C); *Χριστὸς...πάσχα τὸ κ.* Jo.D.*carm.anast.*40(p.219; M.96.841A); c. genit. *τὸ δημόσιον ξίφος...πόλεως κ.* Synes.*ep.*121(M.66.1501A); neut. as subst. *τοῖς τῆς ἀρετῆς κ.* *cat.Apoc.*4:4(p.241.30); *ἐκεῖνο μὲν* [sc. *βάπτισμα*] *τῶν προγεγονότων ἐν ἡμῖν κακῶν ἐστι κ.· τοῦτο δὲ* [sc. *τῶν δακρύων πηγή*] *τῶν μεταγεγονότων* Jo.Clim.*scal.*7(M.88.804B).

καθαρτικός, *purging, cleansing, purifying*, abs., Clem.*str.*5. 11(p.374.4; M.9.108B); *κ. τελετή* Synes.*insomn.*8(p.158.18; M.66. 1296A); Dion.Ar.*c.h.*13.4(M.3.305C) cit. s. *ἐμπυρίως*; *κ. τοίνυν ἐστὶν ἡ λειτουργικὴ διακόσμησις* id.*e.h.*5.1.6(M.3.508B); neut. as subst. *ὅτε τὰ κ. ποιεῖ ὁ...θεός* Or.*hom.6.2 in Jer.*(p.49.32; M.13.325C); *τὸ πρηστηρίως καὶ ὁλοκαύτως κ.* [of seraphim] Dion.Ar.*c.h.*7.1(M.3.205C); masc. as subst., *ib.*3.3(168A); c. genit. *τὸ πῦρ...κακοῦ κ.* Clem.*ecl.*25 (p.144.6; M.9.709C); '*πῦρ ἦλθον βαλεῖν ἐπὶ τὴν γῆν*', *δηλονότι δύναμιν τῶν...ἁγίων κ.* *ib.*26(p.144.23; 712A); ref. Jo.20:33 *τὸ...ἐμφύσημα κ. πως ἦν τῆς τῶν ἀποστόλων ψυχῆς* Eus.*e.th.*3.5(p.16.7; M.24.1008A).

καθαρτικῶς, *with purity*, Dion.Ar.*ep.*9.2(M.3.1108B).

***καθαρτισμός, ὁ,** *completeness* *οὐδὲν ἔλιπε τῷ θεῷ, οὕτως οὐδὲ τῷ κ. τῷ κατ' ἄνθρωπον, ἵνα τέλειος ἐν ἑκατέρᾳ φύσει τυγχάνει* Ambr.*fr.* (*SS* 1 p.360).

καθαρῶς, A. *purely, in purity*; **1.** ref. Christian life *ἡ κ. πολιτευσαμένη ψυχή* Clem.*str.*4.4(p.255.14; M.8.1228C); *ib.*7.11(p.45.14; M.9. 488A); *χαιρέτω κ. βιούντων ἡμῶν* *A.Jo.*107(p.205.6); *ib.*114(p.214.4); Chrys.*hom.10.4 in Heb.*(12.110A); **2.** ref. priesthood: Jewish *μόνοι ...οἱ κ. βιοῦντες ἱερεῖς ὄντως τοῦ θεοῦ* Clem.*str.*4.25(p.318.12; M.8. 1365C); Christian *μὴ κ. αὐτοὺς ἱερᾶσθαι διὰ τὴν ἐπιμιξίαν πρὸς τοὺς τὸ ὁμοούσιον θρησκεύοντας ἀποφαινόμενος* Philost.*h.e.*3.9(M.65.509B);

ἱεράρχην ὁ λέγων δηλοῖ...θεῖον ἄνδρα...ἐν ᾧ καὶ κ. ἡ κατ' αὐτὸν ἱεραρχία πᾶσα τελεῖται Dion.Ar.*e.h.*1.3(M.3.373C); **3.** ref. prayer and worship δεήσεται δὲ κ. ὑπὸ σοῦ προτιμώμενος ὡς ἄγγελος τοῦ θεοῦ Clem.*q.d.s.*41(p.187.21; M.9.648A); κ. ... διακονῆσαι ἐν τῇ λειτουργίᾳ Serap.*euch.*26.2; *Const.App.*8.46.10; **4.** ref. angelic life κράτιστον δὲ ἐν οὐρανῷ ἄγγελος,...καθαρώτερον τῆς αἰωνίου ζωῆς μεταλαγχάνων Clem.*str.*7.2(p.5.19; M.9.408B); angelic contemplation, Dion.Ar.*c.h.* 7.4(M.3.212A); **5.** ref. esoteric teaching ἱεροτελεστὰς...πείσεις ὁμολογῆσαι κατὰ θεσμὸν ἱεραρχικόν, καθαρῶν μὲν κ. id.*e.h.*1.5(M.3.377B).

B. *perfectly, completely* τὸ αὐτὸ δὲ ζῷον ἔσται κ., τῶν αὐτῶν ὄντων πάντων ἐξ ὧν ὡς μερῶν τὸ ζῷον Athenag.*res.*15(p.66.13; M.6.1004C); *ib.*16(p.67.14; 1005B); τὸ μὲν ἀγέννητον φῶς...κ. ἀπαθὲς καὶ ἀκήρατον Gr.Nyss.*Eun.*12(2 p.289.11; M.45.901B); exeg. Ps.8:5ff. οὔπω ἐκράτησεν ὁ βασιλεὺς κ. Chrys.*hom.*4.2 *in Heb.*(12.40D).

κάθαψις, ἡ, *consternation* ἐπάγουσαν μετὰ σφοδροτέρας τῆς ἀπορίας καὶ κ. ἡμῶν ὡς ἀλόγως λεγόντων αἵρεσιν Thdr.Stud.*epp.*1.48 (M.99.1072A).

καθέδρα, ἡ, A. thing sat upon; **1.** *seat* βίβλους...κατὰ τὴν ἀναγωγὴν παραδοῦναι, καθ' ἣν καὶ τοῖς Ἑβδομήκοντα ὁ Μωϋσῆς παρέδωκε τοῖς τὴν κ. αὐτοῦ παρειληφόσιν *Clem.ep.Petr.*1(M.2.26A); οὐκ ἐζήτησας... τίνος [sc. ἐστίν] ἡ τῆς προφητείας κ. *Hom.Clem.*3.18; of God τοῦτο τὸ ὄρος τὸ ὑψηλόν, οὗ ἡ κορυφὴ ὁμοία θρόνου, θεοῦ κ. ἐστίν, οὗ καθίζει... ὅταν καταβῇ ἐπισκέψασθαι τὴν γῆν ἐπ' ἀγαθῷ *Apoc.En.*25.3(p.56.9); fig. σὲ τῆς ἀφωρισμένης κ. κύκλῳ περιγράφειν τολμᾷ [sc. Arius] Const. ap.Gel.Cyz.*h.e.*3.19.27(M.85.1352B); exeg. Ps.1:1 ἢ νομίζειν ἡμᾶς χρὴ κ. λέγεσθαι τὴν ἑδραίαν καὶ μόνιμον ἐν τῇ κρίσει τῆς κακίας διατριβήν; Bas.*hom.in Ps.*1(1.95E; M.29.224C); of laity ἐν ταῖς δημοτικαῖς κ. Synes.*ep.*67(M.66.1432A); *couch* καθεζομένη...ἐπ' ἀμφικνεφάλου κ. ... ἀργυρόποδος *ib.*3(1325A); **2.** *chair*; **a.** in gen.; of teacher, ref. false prophets, Herm.*mand.*11.1; of judgement ἐκάθισαν αὐτὸν [sc. Jesus] ἐπὶ καθέδραν κρίσεως *Ev.Petr.*3(p.224); of torture τὴν σιδερᾶν κ., ἐφ' ἧς τηγανιζόμενα τὰ σώματα κνίσης αὐτοὺς ἐνεφόρει *Ep.Lugd.*ap.Eus.*h.e.*5.1.38(M.20.424A); *ib.*5.1.52(428B); *throne* δίφρος...ἔχων ὅλος ὡς πήχεις δύο ἥμισυ, ὡς αἱ παρ' ἡμῖν καλούμεναι κ. Cosm.Ind.*top.*2(M.88.101B); in sanctuary εὐχὴ τῆς ἄνω κ. *Lit.Bas.*(p.314.16); εὐχὴ τῆς κ. τοῦ θυσιαστηρίου *Lit.Chrys.*(p.314. 16); **b.** of presbyters, sts. fig. of their office πρεσβυτέρους τοὺς ἐπιθύσαντας ἔδοξε τῆς μὲν τιμῆς τῆς κατὰ τὴν κ. μετέχειν CAnc.(314)*can.* 1; καθέδρας μὲν μετέχειν [sc. πρεσβύτερον], τῶν δὲ λοιπῶν ἐνεργειῶν ἀπέχεσθαι Bas.*ep.*199.*can.*27(3.294A; M.32.724C); τὸν θεῖον Διόδωρον ...τῆς δευτέρας ἠξιωμένους κ. Thdt.*h.rel.*8(3.1180); **c.** of bishops, sts. fig., *see*; **i.** in gen. εἰς τὴν αὐτοῦ κ. καθεσθῆναί με ἐδυσώπησεν *Clem. ep.*19(M.2.56A); *ib.*2(36A); εἰς τὴν κ. αὐτοῦ ἕτερον ὑποκατασταθῆναι CSard.*can.*5; Ἀθανάσιος...τῆς...κ. ἐκπέπτωκε Constantius Imp.ap. Ath.*apol.Const.*31(M.25.636C); Bas.*ep.*188 *can.*1(3.270D; M.669C); τὴν κ. ταύτην δεξάμενοι, τὴν ἐπίμαχον καὶ ἐπίφθονον Gr.Naz.*or.*22.14 (M.35.1148A); κ. τιμία καὶ τιμίων ἀνδρῶν ἵδρυμα καὶ ἀνάπαυμα *ib.*33. 3(M.36.217B); αὐτῷ [sc. Bas.] περιῆν καὶ τὸ κράτος τῆς ἐκκλησίας, εἰ καὶ τῆς κ. εἶχε τὰ δεύτερα *ib.*43.33(541A); πρῶτος οὗτος [sc. S. James] εἴληφε τὴν κ. τῆς ἐπισκοπῆς Epiph.*ep.Arab.*ap.*haer.*78.7(p.457.21; M.42.709A); Synes.*ep.*67(M.66.1428C); Πρόκλος τοὺς οἴακας τῆς κ. ἐγχειρίζεται Evagr.*h.e.*1.8(p.16.31; M.86.2444B); **ii.** regarded as seat of Christ, *Clem.ep.*17(M.2.53A); ἵνα ἐπὶ τῆς Χριστοῦ κ. καθεσθεὶς τὴν αὐτοῦ ἐκκλησίαν εὐσεβῶς οἰκονόμῃ *Hom.Clem.*3.60; and of apostles, Bas.*ep.*197.1(3.288B; M.32.709C); **iii.** regarded as teacher's chair μὴ καταστήσῃς μηδένα τοιοῦτον ἐπὶ καθέδρᾳ διδασκόντων, ἵνα μὴ βεβηλώσῃ τὸ μαρτύριον τοῦ Χριστοῦ *A.Phil.*143(p.83.13); **iv.** of see of Rome as apostolic, Dam.Papa *ep.orient.*ap.Thdt.*h.e.*5.10.1(3.1034); *Cod. Afr.*proem.(H.1.861C); Horm.*ep.cler.*(p.55.16; M.*PL.*63.419C); *ib.* tit.(p.52.34; 415A); ὁμοίως καὶ ἀποστολικὴ κ. ὡς Κύριλλος πιστεύει Anast.S.*haer.*(p.262); and as that of S. Peter ὁ μακάριος Πέτρος, ὃς ἐν τῇ ἰδίᾳ κ. καὶ ζῇ καὶ προκάθηται, δίδωσι τοῖς ζητοῦσι τῆς πίστεως τὴν ἀλήθειαν Petr.Rav.*ep.*(p.46.13; M.*PL.*54.744A); **v.** as hieratic τοῦ δὲ λῦσαι τὴν αὐθεντίαν εἰς τὴν ἱερατικὴν κ. [sc. of Alexandria] ἀνέπεμψα Synes.*ep.*57(M.66.1425A); **vi.** of primatial see πρώτη ἐπίσκοποι πέραν θαλάσσης μὴ ἀποδημείτωσαν, εἰ μὴ μετὰ ψηφίσματος τῆς πρώτης κ. τοῦ ἰδίου ἑκάστης χώρας ἐπισκόπου *Cod.Afr.*23; τὸν τῆς πρώτης κ. ἐπίσκοπον μὴ λέγεσθαι ἔξαρχον τῶν ἱερέων ἢ ἄκρον ἱερέα ...ἀλλὰ μόνον ἐπίσκοπον τῆς πρώτης κ. *ib.*39; Ξάγκτιππος ἐπίσκοπος τῆς πρώτης κ. τῆς Νουμιδίας...Νικήτιος ἐπίσκοπος τῆς πρώτης κ. τῆς Μαυριτανίας Σιτιφένσης *ib.*85; **3.** *latrine*; plur., Ath.*ep.mort. Ar.*3 ap.Thdt.*h.e.*1.14.8(3.736; θάκας Opitz 2 p.179.26; M.25.688C); **4.** *saddle*, Chrysipp.*enc.in Thdr.*(pp.61.15,63.9).

B. *sitting*; **1.** *being seated* τῆς κ. τοῦ ὄνου Chrys.*hom.*66.2 *in Mt.* (7.655B); κ. καὶ στάσις ἀνθρώπινα ῥήματα, ἀλλὰ θεῖα νοήματα Sever. *sigill.*3(M.63.535); μετὰ τὸ γενέσθαι τὴν εἴσοδον τοῦ λυχνικοῦ καὶ τὴν πρώτην κ. *Euchol.*(p.291); Thphn.*chron.*p.69(M.108.224A); **2.** *session*; **a.** of a council, CNic.(787)*act.*3(H.4.129B); **b.** of righteous in heaven, Didym.(‡Bas.)*Eun.*4(1.295C; M.29.709A); **c.** of Christ at right hand of God, ref. Ps.109:1 ὥσπερ ῥητόν τινα χρόνον ὁρίζων αὐτῷ τῆς ἐν δεξιᾷ κ. Marcell.*fr.*104 ap.Eus.*Marcell.*2.4(p.53.31; M.24.813D); ἡ ἐκ δεξιῶν τοῦ πατρὸς ἀφωρισμένη τῷ υἱῷ κ., τί ποτε ἕτερον καὶ οὐχὶ τὸ ὁμότιμον τῆς ἀξίας ἀποσημαίνει; Bas.*Eun.*1.25(1.236B; M.29.568B); Chrys.*hom.in Mt.*26:39(3.17E); οὐδὲ γὰρ ὁρᾶται θεὸς ὁ πάντη ἀόρατος ἵνα καὶ ἡ ἐκ δεξιῶν κ. σωματικῶς θεωρεῖσθαι Vict.*Mc.*14:54(p.430. 26); Tim.III Al.*fr.*(p.317.13; M.86.269B); in anamnesis of liturgy μεμνημένοι...τῆς ἐκ δεξιῶν σου τοῦ θεοῦ καὶ πατρὸς κ. *Lit.Bas.*(p.329. 3); *Lit.Chrys.*(p.329.3); *Lit.Jac.*(p.204.5); **d.** of Trin. τὴν τριαδικὴν ὁμότιμον κ. αὐτῷ [sc. πνεύματι] καὶ τῷ πατρὶ *cat.Ac.*2:22(p.42.15); **e.** of God τί δὲ καὶ περὶ τῆς θείας στάσεως, ἤτοι κ., φαμέν; Dion.Ar. *d.n.*9.8(M.3.916B); **3.** *being stationed*; of troops, Synes.*ep.*130(M.66. 1512B); **4.** *sitting idle*, hence *truce*, Chrys.*comp.*3(1.119A).

***καθεδραιόω,** *make firm*, Ephr.2.61A.

καθέζ-ομαι, [fut. καθεσθήσομαι, Just.*1apol.*35.10(M.6.384C); Chrys. *hom.*3.2 *in 2Thess.*(11.525C); καθεδῶ v. 1 infra]; **1.** *sit down, take one's seat, sit*; of God as judge, Clem.*paed.*1.7(p.124.19; M.8. 320B); of a judge, Or.*hom.*14.17 *in Jer.*(p.124.3; M.13.428A); of presbyters τὸ ∼εσθαι ἐν πρεσβυτερίῳ *ib.*11.3(p.81.2; 369C); παρ' ἑκατέρου δὲ αὐτοῦ [sc. bishop's throne] ∼έσθω τὸ πρεσβυτέριον *Const.App.*2.57.4; of bishops, *ib.*2.11.2; 2.58.2; Ath.*fug.*24(p.84.16; M.25.676A); ὡς ἐν τάξει ἐπισκόπου ∼εται Evagr.*h.e.*2.18(p.72.3; M. 86.2556A); of a law court δεύτερον ἐπ' αὐτῷ καθεδεῖν δικαστήριον Synes.*provid.*3(p.121.11; M.66.1269C); **2.** *remain seated, be seated, sit*; **a.** as suppliant, Just.*dial.*90.5(M.6.692B); **b.** for one's portrait, Clem.*paed.*3.2(p.239.23; M.8.364A); **c.** of Christ seated at Father's right hand; **i.** in credal formularies ἔσται γὰρ ∼όμενος ἐν δεξιᾷ τοῦ πατρὸς οὐ μόνον ἐν τῷ αἰῶνι τούτῳ, ἀλλὰ καὶ ἐν τῷ μέλλοντι *Symb.Ant.* (341)4(p.251.10; M.26.725C) ∞ *Symb.Sirm.*1(p.254.27; M.26.736B); ∼εται ἐν δεξιᾷ τοῦ πατρός *Symb.CP*(360)(p.259.8; M.26.748B); ∼όμενον ἐν δεξιᾷ τοῦ πατρός *Symb.Nic.–CP*(p.80.11); ∼όμενον ἐν δεξιᾷ θεοῦ πατρός *Symb.App.*(p.30); **ii.** in liturg. formularies τὸ ὄνομα...ὀνομάζομεν τοῦ...∼ομένου ἐν δεξιᾷ τοῦ ἀγενήτου Serap.*euch.* 5.1; πιστεύω καὶ βαπτίζομαι...εἰς τὸν κύριον Ἰησοῦν τὸν Χριστὸν... καθεσθέντα ἐν δεξιᾷ τοῦ πατρός *Symb.*ap.*Const.App.*7.41.6; ἐκαθέσθη ἐκ δεξιῶν σοῦ τοῦ θεοῦ *Lit.*ap.*Const.App.*8.12.34; **iii.** theol. significance διὸ καὶ ∼εται μὲν αὐτὸς ἐν δεξιᾷ τοῦ πατρὸς ὡς λόγος· ἔνθα γάρ ἐστιν ὁ πατήρ, ἐκεῖ καὶ ὁ τούτου λόγος ἐστίν Ath.*decr.*11 (p.10.18; M.25.436B); αὐτὸς μὲν μετὰ τοῦ πατρὸς ∼εται, οἱ δὲ [sc. ἄγγελοι] παρεστήκασι λειτουργοῦντες id.*Ar.*1.62(M.26.141A); εἰς ποῖον ∼εται θρόνον; τὸ σῶμα τοίνυν ἐστιν ᾧ λέγει 'κάθου ἐκ δεξιῶν μου' ‡Ath.*serm.fid.*29(p.26; M.26.1284C); **3.** *be settled, established*, Jo.Mal. *chron.*8 p.199(M.97.313A); ∼ονται...ἐν τούτῳ τῷ ὄρει μοναχοί Jo.Mosch. *prat.*161(M.87.3028C); **4.** *have one's seat*, i.e. *see*, of a bishop ὅτε ἐν Ἀντιοχείᾳ ἐκαθέσθη [sc. Euzoïus] Ath.*syn.*31(p.260.6; M.26.749A); **5.** *be seated* upon; c. dat., Just.*dial.*88.6(M.6.688A).

***καθειργμός, ὁ,** *confinement*, Const.*or.s.c.*25(p.190.22; M.20. 1309B).

καθείργνυμι, 1. *shut in, confine, enclose* ψυχὴν...ἐν τῷ σώματι τῆς ταπεινώσεως καθειργμένην Or.*or.*2.3(p.301.17; M.11.420C); πῶς καθεῖρκται τῷ σώματι ἡ ψυχή Eus.*e.th.*1.12(p.71.20; M.24.848B); τῶν ἐν τῇ θανάτου φρουρᾷ καθειργμένων Gr.Nyss.*or.catech.*23(p.89.3; M. 45.61D); reflex. τῶν τὸν ἅπαντα χρόνον καθειρξάντων ἑαυτοὺς καὶ νηστείας δαπανηθέντων Chrys.*sac.*3.15(p.77.18; 1.393B); ptcpl. used abs. τοῖς καθειργμένοις παραπλησίως βιοτεύων Thdt.*h.rel.*20(3.1233); **2.** *confine in, enclose in* οἰκίσκῳ τινὶ καθειργμένος Gr.Nyss.*anim.et res.*(M.46.21C); of man before Inc. καθειργμένος τῷ σκότῳ id.*or. catech.*15(p.63.15; M.45.48B).

κάθειρξις, ἡ, *being shut up, confined*; in prison, Eus.*h.e.*3.24.8 (M.20.265B); Ast.Am.*hom.*5(M.40.232A); †Jo.D.*B.J.*5(M.96.892A); in death, Eus.*qu.Steph.*8.1(M.22.912C); of evil spirits, id.*Is.*13:2(M. 24.185B); of monks, Thdt.*h.rel.*20(3.1233).

καθεῖς, 1. *one by one*, Eus.*h.e.*10.4.8(M.20.849D); **2.** *each one individually, every one* κατάλογον πεποίηται...ἧς ὁ κ. αὐτῶν προηγεῖτο παροικίας *ib.*6.43.21(629A); Thdr.Mops.*Gal.*3:27–28(p.57.21; M.66. 905B); ‡Nil.*perist.*8.1(M.79.861B); written *divisim* κατὰ εἷς τῶν προφητῶν Clem.*exc.Thdot.*24(p.115.3; M.9.672A); Socr.*h.e.*6.13.5(M. 67.704A).

[*]**καθέκαστον, τό; καθεκάστην, τήν,** for καθ' ἕκαστον, καθ' ἑκάστην; **1.** neut., *individual, particular* ἐν μὲν τοῖς κ. τὴν φθοράν, ἐν δὲ τοῖς καθόλου τὴν φθαρσίαν ‡Just.*qu.Gr.*10(M.6.1477A); Chrys.*diab.* 2.3(2.263C); **2.** fem. [sc. ἡμέραν] *every day, daily*, *T.Abr.*A 9(p.86. 2); Barth.Edess.*Agar.*(M.104.1409A).

καθεκτός, *in the grip of* δεσμῷ τινι τοῦ κόσμου...γεγόνασι καθεκταί [sc. foolish virgins] Mac.Aeg.*elev*.4(M.40.892D).

***καθελκτικός**, **1.** ? *able to be drawn down*, i.e. *shut* κ. πύλαις Geo. Pis.*hex*.687(M.92.1488A); **2.** error for καθεκτικός *capable of holding* or *retaining*, Jo.D.*fr*.(M.95.228A) = Leont.B.*Nest.et Eut*.1(M.86. 1296D καθεκτ-).

καθέλκ-ω, **1.** *bring down, lower*, Nonn.*par.Jo*.4:23(M.43.777B); τὰς μετεώρους χεῖρας καθείλκυσε Jo.Eleem.*v.Tych*.(p.131); eyes in sleep, Philost.*h.e*.11.3(M.65.597B); met., *degrade* from office, *ib*.8.4 (560A); **2.** *drag down, cast down*, met. ὑπὸ τῆς λύπης ~όμενοι Or.*Jo*. 20.36(29; p.376.29; M.14.657D); ὁ τῷ βάθει τῆς ἁμαρτίας καθελκυσθείς id.*Ps*.70:1(p.89); τὸν λογισμὸν εἰς τὰ χείρω ~οντος τοῦ πονηροῦ Meth. *symp*.5.3(p.56.6; M.18.101A); οὐδενὸς ἐναντίου τὴν ψυχὴν πρὸς πάθος ~οντος Gr.Nyss.*or.dom*.1(p.6.31; M.44.1124A); ἡ τῆς φύσεως ἀσθένεια καθεῖλκεν [sc. ἡμᾶς] ἐπὶ τὸ πταίειν Thdr.Mops.*Gal*.1:3–5(p.8.21; M. 66.900B); **3.** *draw away*, Epiph.*haer*.42.12(p.167.16; M.41.792A); **4.** *compel* αἱ ἀντικείμεναι δυνάμεις τῶν ἐν ἡμῖν οἱονεὶ ~ονται καὶ νικῶνται ἀπὸ τῶν τοῦ θεοῦ ἐπῳδῶν Or.*hom.2.1 in Jos*.(p.418.29; M. 12.920C); Eus.*p.e*.3.16(126C; M.21.225A); Gr.Nyss.*Eun*.6(2 p.129.25; M.45.713A).

κάθεμα, τό, *necklace, collar*, †Bas.*Is*.126(1.467A; M.30.321D).

***καθεμάτιον, τό**, *necklace*, dim. of κάθεμα, *Pers*.(p.23.9).

καθεξῆς, **1.** *so on, so forth* οὐ πάντες εἰσὶν...ἑκατόνταρχοι οὐδὲ πεντηκόνταρχοι οὐδὲ τὸ κ. *1Clem*.37.3; **2.** *after, succeeding* καθὼς δηλώσω ἐν τῷ κ. *M.Polyc*.22.3.

κάθεξις, ἡ, *retention*, Const.ap.Eus.*v.C*.3.60(p.108.5; M.20.1132B).

[*]**καθερίζω**, = καθαρίζω, *A.Andr.et Mt*.10(p.77.2).

***καθερμηνεύω**, f.l. for καθαμαξεύω, Or.*hom.14.3 in Jer*.(M.13. 405D).

κάθεσις, ἡ, *degeneracy, decay*, Cyr.*glaph.Ex*.2(1.300D).

καθεστήριον, τό, *sitting-room*, *T.Job* 25(p.118.9).

καθετήρ, ὁ, = κάθεμα, Clem.*paed*.2.12(pp.231.1,233.31; M.8.545B, 552C).

κάθετος, **1.** *suborned*, Synes.*provid*.15(p.100.16; M.66.1249A); id. *ep*.44(M.66.1372D); **2.** κατὰ κάθετον, c. genit., *vertically below*, Or. *comm.in Gen*.ap.Eus.*p.e*.6.11(291A; M.12.72A); Eus.*d.e*.9.1(p.404.7; M.22.632C).

***καθέτως**, *vertically*; conj. for κατ' ἔτος cod., Philost.*h.e*.3.10(M. 65.493A).

καθεύδ-ω, **1.** *lie resting* ἐκάθευδεν [sc. Christ] ἐν τῷ πλοίῳ πειράζων ἡμᾶς· οὐκ ἦν γὰρ κοιμώμενος *A.Andr.et Mt*.8(p.75.2); **2.** *sleep*; **a.** exeg. 1Thess.5:6 ἔστι γὰρ ἐγρηγορότα ~ειν, μηδὲν πράττοντα ἀγαθόν Chrys.*hom.9.3 in 1Thess*.(11.489D); 'μὴ ~ωμεν'...τουτέστιν, οἱ τῇ δυσσεβείᾳ δουλεύοντες Thdt.*1Thess*.5:6(3.522); **b.** exeg. 1Thess. 5:10 'εἴτε ~ομεν' τὸν θάνατόν φησι τὸν σωματικόν Chrys.*hom.9.4 in 1Thess*.(11.491B); ~οντας δὲ τοὺς τετελευτηκότας [sc. καλεῖ] Thdt. *1Thess*.5:10(3.523); **c.** exeg. Eph.5:14 ζητήσεις, πῶς τῷ αὐτῷ λέγεται ὡς μὲν ζῶντι καὶ ~οντι 'ἔγειρε ὁ ~ων' ὡς δὲ τεθνηκότι τὸ 'ἀνάστα ἐκ τῶν νεκρῶν',...τὸ μὲν...λέγεται διὰ τὸ πνεῦμα, τὸ δὲ...διὰ τὴν ψυχήν Or.*comm.in Eph*.5:14(*JTS* 3 p.563); ~οντα καὶ νεκρόν, τὸν ἐν ἁμαρτίαις φησί. καὶ γὰρ δυσωδίας πνεῖ, ὡς ὁ νεκρός, καὶ ἀνενέργητός ἐστιν, ὡς ὁ ~ων Chrys.*hom.18.1 in Eph*.(11.128B); ~οντα λέγει τὸν ἐν ἁμαρτίαις κείμενον. καὶ γὰρ ὁ ἐν ἁμαρτίαις ζῶν νεκρὸς λέγεται εἶναι ‡Ath.*qu.script*.111(M.28.764A).

καθέψ-ω, **1.** *boil down*, Clem.*prot*.2(p.14.19; M.8.80A); **2.** *soften*, by hot baths ἀνθρωπογναφεῖα...τὰ σώματα...~οντα id.*paed*.3.9(p.263. 19; M.8.617B); **3.** *digest* πῶς οὐκ ἐν ἴσῳ τροφῆς δεδαπάνηται ~όμενος; [sc. Jonah] Cyr.*Jon*.11(3.375E).

***καθηγεμονιάω**, *bear rule* over κ. ... μοναστηρίων Thdr.Stud.*epp*. 2.143(M.99.1449B).

καθηγεμών, ὁ, **1.** *leader, guide* κ. [sc. Moses] τοῦ παντὸς ἔθνους Eus.*v.C*.1.12(p.13.17; M.20.925B); ὁ κ. ... ἁπάντων τοῦ θεοῦ λόγος id.*d.e*.4.7(p.161.13; M.22.269A); κ. τῆς ἐκκλησίας Gr.Naz.*or*.43.28 (M.36.533C); abs., of an army officer, Eus.*v.C*.4.51(p.138.19; 1201A); of a choir-master, Ath.*gent*.43(M.25.85B); of Christ ἕνα ἔχομεν κ. ... τὸν κύριον id.*tom*.8(M.26.805C); of a priest τὸν ἱερὸν κ. Dion.Ar.*e.h*. 3.3.14(M.3.445A); of a godfather κ. ... ἱερόν..., ἕξιν αὐτῷ [sc. baptized infant] τῶν θείων ἐμποιοῦντα *ib*.7.3.11(568C); of an archimandrite, Thdr.Stud.*or*.11.15(M.99.817B); **2.** *guide* to, *teacher* of θεοσεβείας κ. Clem.*paed*.1.1(p.90.4; M.8.249A); ὁ τῶν αἱρέσεων κ. διάβολος Ath.*ep.Aeg.Lib*.8(M.25.556B); τὸν θεοῦ λόγον κ. τῆς σπουδῆς ποιησάμενοι Gr.Nyss.*hom.9 in Cant*.(M.44.968A); πάσης ἱερᾶς ἐπιστήμης τε καὶ ἐνεργείας κ. [sc. θεόν] Dion.Ar.*c.h*.3.2(M.3.165A).

καθηγ-έομαι, **1.** *lead, guide*, c. genit. pers., Ath.*fug*.20(p.81.29; M. 25.669B); παρεκάλει [sc. Moses] αὐτὸν τὸν θεὸν ~εῖσθαι αὐτῶν Ath.*ep. Serap*.1.12(M.26.560C); Gr.Nyss.*v.Mos*.43(M.44.313C); ἡ γέρανος τριάκοντα ἡμέρας ~εῖται τῆς κοινῆς πτήσεως Nil.*epp*.3.241(M.79. 496A); pres. ptcpl. as subst., *leader, guide* τὸ πνεῦμα...~ούμενόν ἐστι τοῦ λαοῦ Ath.*ep.Serap*.1.12(561A); abs. δεόμεθα οἱ πεπλανημένοι...τοῦ ~ουμένου Clem.*paed*.1.9(p.139.3; M.8.349B); Hipp.*haer*.6.29(p.155. 21; M.16.3235B); τοῦ πρὸς τὴν ζωὴν ~ουμένου [i.e. Christ] Gr.Nyss.*or. catech*.37(p.141.3; M.45.93A); c. genit. rei τὸν ~ούμενον...ἀρίστου βίου Clem.*paed*.1.3(p.95.8; 260A); σώφρονος..., οὐκ ἐπιστημονικοῦ ~ήσασθαι βίου *ib*.1.1(p.90.21; 249B); Eun.*exp.fid*.3(p.259); c. genit. rei et pers. κατὰ μεταφόραν ἀπὸ τῶν ποιμένων τῶν ~ουμένων τοῖς προβάτοις ὁ ~ούμενος τῶν παίδων παιδαγωγὸς νοούμενος Clem.*paed*.1.7(p.121. 30; 313A); c. genit. rei et dat. pers., id.*str*.1.24(p.102.10; M.8.909C); Gr.Nyss.*v.Mos*.30(309B); **2.** *go before*, of things σκόπει τὰ ~ούμενα καὶ τὰ ἀκόλουθα, καὶ οὕτως ἅπτου τοῦ ἔργου ‡Nil.*Epict*.35(M.79.1300B); **3.** *initiate, begin*, c. genit. ~ήσατο δὲ τῆς μοναδικῆς γνώσεως Clem. *str*.3.2(p.197.26; M.8.1105A); Gr.Nyss.*or.catech*.5(p.21.3; M.45.20D); aor. ptcpl. as subst., *author, originator* οἱ ~ησάμενοι τῆς δόξης ταύτης Dion.R.ap.Ath.*decr*.26(p.22.27; M.25.464C); Gr.Nyss.*or.catech*. 35(p.131.4; 88A); **4.** *have authority over*, c. genit.; **a.** *preside over* ~ήσασθαί τε αὐτῶν πρῶτον ἐξ ἐθνῶν ἐπίσκοπον Eus.*h.e*.5.12.1(M.20. 457C); οἷός τις ὢν τῆς Χριστοῦ ~εῖτο ἐκκλησίας ἄνθρωπος id.*Marcell*. 2.1(p.31.27; M.24.776B); Jul.Papa *ep.Dian*.ap.Ath.*apol.sec*.35(p.113. 4; M.25.308A); Ath.*fug*.5(p.71.10; M.25.649B); **b.** *govern, rule* τῶν πώποτε τῆς 'Ρωμαίων ἀρχῆς ~ησαμένων Eus.*v.C*.1.3(p.9.4; M.20. 916B); ὧν πάντων ὁ βασιλικὸς ~εῖται λόγος id.*l.C*.3(p.202.2; M.20. 1332B); of superior of a monastery πάντων αὐτῶν ὡς πατὴρ ~εῖτο Ath.*v.Anton*.15(M.26.865C); ἀδελφὴν γηράσασαν ἐν παρθενίᾳ, ~ουμένην τε καὶ αὐτὴν ἄλλων παρθένων *ib*.54(921B); Bas.*ascet*.1.3(2.321A; M. 31.876B); πλειόνων ἀδελφῶν ~εῖσθαι Nil.*epp*.3.332(M.79.541B); pres. ptcpl. used abs. as subst., *superior* of a monastery; of men, Bas. *ascet*.1.5(2.322C; M.877D); Nil.*epp*.3.241 tit.(496A); *Mir.Geo*.6(p.76. 15); of women, Bas.*ascet*.2.2(326D; M.888B); Gr.Nyss.*v.Macr*.(p.388. 17; M.46.976C); CTrull.*can*.46; **5.** *teach*, c. genit. rei et dat. pers. τριὰς...ἰσότητος ~ησαμένη Eus.*l.C*.5(p.210.13; M.20.1348B); μηδ' ἐπισκόπους ~εῖσθαι γυναιξὶ θεοσεβῶν λόγων id.*v.C*.1.53(p.32.20; M.20. 968B); Gr.Nyss.*v.Mos*.(M.44.321A).

καθήγησις, ἡ, **1.** *guidance*; of God, ‡Caes.Naz.*dial*.126(M.38.1024); **2.** *position as superior of a monastery*, Thdr.Stud.*or*.11.26(M.99. 829A); id.*epp*.2.182(M.99.1564A).

καθηγητής, ὁ, *teacher*; of bishops, Const.*or.s.c*.1(p.154.5; M.20. 1233A); *Cod.Afr*.53; Socr.*h.e*.3.6.3(M.67.389A); exeg. Mt.23:10 εἷς κ. λεγόμενος ὁ Χριστὸς οὐκ ἐκβάλλει τὸν πατέρα τοῦ εἶναι κ. Chrys.*hom. 72.3 in Mt*.(7.704D); of Christ, *Mir.Geo*.1(p.5.12); in gen. κ. ... τῶν ἰδίων παίδων Eus.*d.e*.1.9(p.41.28; M.22.80C); id.*v.C*.4.51(p.138.14; M. 20.1201A); τὸν παράκλητον...τὸν κ. τῆς εὐσεβείας Eun.*exp.fid*.3(p.258); Chrys.*hom.2.1 in Rom*.(9.436E); Cyr.*Os*.70(3.106C); Max.*ambig*.(M. 91.1164B).

***καθηγουμένεια, ἡ**, *office of superior of a monastery*, Nil.*epp*.3.108 (M.79.433C).

καθηδύν-ω, *delight, gladden* ~όμενος [sc. ὁ νοῦς] ὑπὸ τοῦ τῆς εὐχῆς μάλιστα γλυκάσματος Diad.*perf*.68(p.84.8); act., *ib*.35(p.40. 14); Jo.Mon.*hymn.Chrys*.6(M.96.1381B).

καθηδυπαθέω, *squander in luxury and revelling* κ. τοῦ βίου Bas. *hom*.7.8(2.60C; M.31.301A); Cyr.*Ps*.48:8(M.69.1069A).

***καθηκεύω (καθηκετεύω)**, *yield* to, *comply* with; c. dat., Ath.*h. Ar*.70(p.221.19; M.25.776D); *ib*.44(p.208.36, v.l. καθηκετεύεις 748B); Mac.Mgn.*apocr*.3.29(p.122.2); c. acc., cf.Porphyry *adv.Christianos* 27 ap.eund.3.30(p.125.13) conj. καθικετεύων.

καθήκ-ω, **1.** *go down*; med., of raised hands, Cosm.Mel.*schol*.(M. 38.347) in Gr.Naz.*carm*.2.1.1.1; **2.** *come down to, reach to*, hence *connect, relate*; ptcpl. masc. as subst., *relative*, *A.Thom*.A 40(p.158.4); reflex., *join* oneself ~αμεν εἰς τόδε τὸ ἀσεβὲς σύστημα Thdr.Stud.*epp*. 1.13(M.99.953A); med., met., *grasp* οὐ ~όμενος τῆς ἐννοίας Olymp. *Job* 33:7(M.93.348D); **3.** *be meet, fitting*; ptcpl. neut. as subst., *seemly ordinance* τὸ ~ον τῆς βουλήσεως αὐτοῦ *1Clem*.41.3.

καθηλ-όω, **1.** *nail on, nail* ~ωμένον ὑπὲρ ἡμῶν ἐν σαρκί Ign. *Smyrn*.1.2; οἱ δὲ οὐ ~ωσαν μέν, προσέδησαν δὲ αὐτόν [sc. Polyc.] *M.Polyc*.14.1; Ath.*ep.Epict*.5(p.9.20; M.26.1060A); fig. ἐνόησα γὰρ ὑμᾶς...~ωμένους ἐν τῷ σταυρῷ τοῦ κυρίου Ign.*Smyrn*.1.1; **2.** *drive* a nail τοὺς τύπους τῶν ἥλων, οὓς ὑπέμεινεν αὐτὸς ὁ λόγος ὁρῶν ~ωμένους ἐν τῷ ἰδίῳ σώματι Ath.*ep.Epict*.6(p.10.8; M.26.1060B); **3.** *pierce with a nail*; **a.** lit., of beggars οἱ τὰς κεφαλὰς ~οῦντες Chrys.*hom.21.6 in 1Cor*.(10.188D); ἐκκλησίας...~ώσας τὰς θύρας ἄβατον τοῖς εἰς αὐτὴν ἀθροιζομένοις ἀπέφηνεν Thdt.*h.e*.3.12.1(3.925); **b.** met., exeg. Ps.118:120 δεῖ τὸν προσερχόμενον θεῷ...~ωμένον εἶναι τῷ φόβῳ τοῦ θεοῦ Bas.*ep*.22.3(3.101B; M.32.293A); id.*hom. in Ps*.33(1.149C; M.29.365B); οὕτω καὶ σὺ ~ωσον καὶ σύναψον, ὡσανεὶ ἥλῳ προσπεπερονημένῳ Chrys.*hom.54.1 in Jo.*(8.315B); Παῦλος...ὁ ~ωμένος τῷ φόβῳ τοῦ θεοῦ id.*hom.4.4 in 1Thess.*(11. 457A); τὰ μέλη παρακαλῶ τούτῳ ~ωθῆναι τῷ φόβῳ, ὥστε αὐτὰ νεκρὰ ἁμαρτίᾳ γενόμενα τῇ τῆς ψυχῆς ἀκολουθεῖν ποδηγίᾳ Thdt.*Ps.*118:120 (1.1468).

καθήλωσις, ἡ, *nailing*; plur., of a torture, Eus.*h.e.*4.15.47(M.20. 361A).

κάθ-ημαι, **1.** *be seated, sit*; **a.** in gen. ἐὰν προσεύχῃ ἢ ψάλλῃς ἢ ἀναγινώσκῃς, κατ' ἰδίαν ~ου Ath.*virg.*10(p.44.1; M.28.261D); τὸν ἐν αὐτῷ [sc. θρόνῳ] ~ήμενον ἐπίσκοπον id.*apol.sec.*17(p.100.9; M.25. 276C); ~ῆσθαί τε καὶ τὰ ἐπισκόπων πράττειν Epiph.*exp.fid.*13(p.513. 19; M.42.895B); when preaching, Chrys.*hom.8.8 in Eph.*(11.65A); **b.** of God ὁ ~ήμενος ἐπὶ τῶν χερουβὶμ Ath.*ep.fest.*43(p.298.2; M.26. 1441A); ὅ τε...ἑστάναι καὶ ὁ καθῆσθαι τὸ θεῖον λέγων οὐδὲν...περὶ τὸν νοῦν διαφέρονται· ὁ μὲν βεβηκέναι παγίως, ὁ δὲ καθιδρύσθαι ἀμεταθέτως τὸ θεῖον ἐν τῷ ἀγαθῷ δογματίζοντες Gr.Nyss.*Steph.*1(M.46. 720B); τί ἐστι, ~ηται ἐπὶ θρόνου [sc. ὁ θεός]; βασιλεύει, κρατεῖ Chrys. *exp.in Ps.*46:9(5.195D); θεὸς...λέγεται ~ῆσθαι διὰ τὸ ἑδραῖον· τὸ γὰρ ~ήμενον ἥδρασται Sever.*sigill.*3(M.63.536); Dion.Ar.*d.n.*9.1(M.3. 909B); **c.** of Christ ~ηται...ὁ ψυχικὸς Χριστὸς ἐν δεξιᾷ τοῦ δημιουργοῦ Clem.*exc.Thdot.*62(p.128.1; M.9.689A); ἐκ δεξιῶν...~ήμενος Ath.*Ar.* 1.61(M.26.140B); ἐπὶ τὸν αὐτὸν θρόνον τῷ πατρὶ ~ηται *ib.*(140A); οὔτε ~ηται ἐκ δεξιῶν ἀφ' ἑαυτοῦ, ἀλλ' ἀκούει λέγοντος τοῦ πατρός 'κάθου ἐκ δεξιῶν μου' *Symb.Sirm.*1 *anath.*18(p.255.33; M.26.740A); **2.** *be established, settle, live* εἰ...θέλει [sc. prophet] πρὸς ὑμᾶς ~ῆσθαι ...ἐργαζέσθω *Did.*12.3; *ib.*13.1; Jo.Mosch.*prat.*117(M.87.2981A); *ib.* 123(2985A); **3.** *sit upon, ride, ride in* τοῦ ~ημένου τὸ ὄχημα Chrys. *hom.11.2 in 1Tim.*(11.608F); οὐδὲ ἵππος...οὔτε ὁ ~ήμενος αὐτὸν ἄνθρωπος id.*hom.12.6 in Rom.*(9.540E, vv.ll. αὐτοῦ, ἐπ' αὐτὸν).

[*]**καθημέραν**, better written *divisim*, καθ' ἡμέραν *daily*, Hier. *vir.ill.*(tr.Sophr.Pal.)135(p.62.28; M.*PL.*23.718B); Thdr.Stud.*epp.*2. 66(M.99.1292A).

καθημερινός, *daily*, interpreting ἐπιούσιος (q.v.) in Lord's Prayer, Chrys.*hom.43.2 in Jo.*(8.257C); neut. as adv., *daily*, Hegem.*Arch.* 11(p.18.9; M.10.1445A).

καθημερόω, *mitigate*, Cyr.*hom.pasch.*18(5^2.240B).

***καθηνιοχέω**, *drive against*, fig. οὓς [sc. horses and chariot of Satan] δεῖ κ. τῷ ἅρματι τοῦ Χριστοῦ ‡Chrys.*circ.*(8.88B).

[*]**κάθησις**, ἡ, v. κάθισις.

καθησυχάζω, trans., *pacify, mollify*, Bas.*ep.*66.2(3.159D; M.32. 425B); pass., of winds, *be stilled*, Nil.*epp.*2.329(M.79.361B).

καθίδρυμα, τό, *statue*, Philost.*h.e.*7.8(M.65.545B).

καθίδρυσις, ἡ, **1.** *abode* ἐκεῖ...εἶναι χρὴ πιστεύειν κ. ἀμετάθετον... ἔνθα...ὁ νοῦς δι' ἀγάπης τὴν σφετέραν ἐρρίζωσε δύναμιν †Marc.Er. *temp.*7(M.65.1056C); **2.** *founding, establishment* ἡ τοῦ ἐν 'Ελευσῖνι τεμένους κ. Tat.*orat.*39(p.40.21; M.6.884A); of dedication of a church, Synes.*ep.*67(M.66.1420C); **3.** *sitting, session*, of Christ's heavenly session τὴν μὲν στάσιν καὶ τὴν κ. τὸ πάγιον τῆς φύσεως...ὑποφαίνειν Bas.ap.*cat.Ac.*7:56(p.129.5); οὔτε τὴν ἐπ' ἰσχίῳ κ. τοῦ ἀσχηματίστου παραληψόμεθα Gr.Nyss.*Steph.*1(M.46.720B); *enthronement* of bishop, Philost.*h.e.*9.10(M.65.576C).

καθιδρύ-ω, **1.** *set up, establish* ἀποστόλους δι' ὧν ~ται ἡ ἐκκλησία Hipp.*antichr.*61(p.41.17; M.10.780D); ~σθαι ἀμεταθέτως τὸ θεῖον ἐν τῷ ἀγαθῷ Gr.Nyss.*Steph.*1(M.46.720B); τῆς...τοῦ θεοῦ μνήμης τῇ καρδίᾳ ~μένης Nil.*epp.*3.261(M.79.516A); med. οἱ τὴν...ἐλπίδα...ἐπὶ τῶν θείων ~σάμενοι Const.ap.Eus.*v.C.*2.29(p.53.24; M.20.1008A); **2.** med., *settle* an agreement ἐκπέμπει...τοὺς περὶ συμβάσεως λόγους δυνατοὺς ~σασθαι πρεσβυτάς Thphyl.*exc.gent.*4(p.480.30; M.113. 940C); **3.** *consecrate* a bishop, Philost.*h.e.*9.8(M.65.576A).

***καθίδρως**, *sweating violently*, Bas.*hom.*13.7(2.120D; M.31.440C).

καθιερ-όω, *consecrate, dedicate, devote*; **1.** things τὴν αὐτοῦ πόλιν τῷ τῶν μαρτύρων ~ου θεῷ Eus.*v.C.*3.48(p.98.5; M.20.1108C); τὴν παρὰ πάντων πίστιν ἢ γοῦν τῆς πίστεως τὴν ὁμολογίαν ἑαυτῷ ~οῖ καὶ τῷ παναγίῳ πατρί Cyr.*apol.Thdt.*10(p.141.4; 6^1.235C); τὴν δὲ κυριακὴν ~οῦσι [sc. Ebionites] παραπλησίως ἡμῖν Thdt.*haer.*2.1(4.328); esp. churches, etc., Synes.*ep.*67(M.66.1420B); τὰ ἅπαξ ~ωθέντα μοναστήρια κατὰ γνώμην ἐπισκόπου μένειν εἰς τὸ διηνεκὲς μοναστήρια CChalc.*can.*24; ~ώθη ἡ ἐκκλησία τῶν ἁγίων ἀποστόλων *Chron.Pasch.* p.302(M.92.760B); **2.** persons πρεσβεύειν τοὺς τῷ θεῷ ~ωμένους Const. ap.Eus.*v.C.*3.12(p.83.5; M.20.1069A); ~ωθεῖσαν θεῷ παρθένον Hier. *vir.ill.*(tr.Sophr.Pal.)123(p.60.9; M.*PL.*23.712B); as a sacrificial victim αὐτὸν [sc. Isaac] ~ῶσαι ἐκελεύσθη Chrys.*scand.*13(3.496E); as a deity μηδένα θεὸν ὑπὸ βασιλέως ~οῦσθαι, πρὶν ὑπὸ τῆς συγκλήτου δοκιμασθῆναι Tert.ap.Eus.*h.e.*2.2.5(M.20.141A).

***καθιέρωμα**, τό, **1.** *shrine* δύο...κ. ἐπὶ δύο μυστικῶν ἄντρων [at Bethlehem] 'Ελένη...ἵδρυτο Eus.*v.C.*3.43(p.96.7; M.20.1104B); **2.** *consecrated, holy thing* ἱερεῦσι...καὶ ὑπουργοῦσι θείοις κ. [Lat. *sacramentis*] *Cod.Afr.*3.

καθιέρωσις, ἡ, *consecration, dedication* κορῶν καθιέρωσιν ἀπὸ πρεσβυτέρων μὴ γίνεσθαι *Cod.Afr.*6.

***καθιερωσύνη**, ἡ, prob. f.l. for foreg. τοὺς τρεῖς βαθμοὺς τούτους τοὺς συνδέσμῳ τινὶ τῆς ἁγνείας διὰ τῆς κ. συμπεπλεγμένους *Cod.Afr.*6 (v.l. καθιερώσεως).

***καθιερωτής**, ὁ, *initiator* in holy things τὴν μὲν...τῶν νοητῶν λογίων θέαν καὶ...διδασκαλίαν, πρεσβυτικῆς δεῖσθαι δυνάμεως· τὴν δὲ ...ἐπιστήμην καὶ ἐκμάθησιν τοῖς ὑφειμένοις κ. καὶ ἱερωμένοις ἁρμόζειν Dion.Ar.*d.n.*3.2(M.3.681C).

***καθίζησις**, ἡ, *sitting position, session*; of Son, ref. Ps.109:1, Heb. 1:13, Gr.Nyss.*Steph.*1(M.46.720C).

καθίζω, **1.** *sit*, of Christ ἐπιτρέπεται δὲ καθίσαι οὐχ ὡς μονογενής, κατὰ τοῦτο γὰρ συναΐδιος, ἀλλὰ ὡς πρωτότοκος καὶ κληρονόμος Or.*Ps.* 109:1(p.227); καθίσαντα ἐκ δεξιῶν τοῦ πατρός *Symb.Hier.*(M.33. 533A); κ. ἐν δεξιᾷ τοῦ πατρός ‡Ath.*interpr.*(p.66.20; M.26.1232B); κεκαθηκέναι [sic] τὸν σωτῆρα...ἐκ δεξιῶν τῆς μεγαλοσύνης Didym.*Ps.* 15:8(M.39.1232A); **2.** *settle*, of Christ πλανωμένης τῆς ἀνθρωπότητος ἐκάθισεν ὁ λόγος ἐπὶ ταύτην, καὶ ἄνθρωπος ἐπεφάνη Ath.*inc.*43.7(M.25. 173A); **3.** *remain, stay, live* ἐκάθισαν εἰς τὸ ὄρος *Ascens.Is.*A 2.9; *Apophth.Patr.*(M.65.401A); οὐ δύνασαι καθίσαι ὧδε Jo.Mosch.*prat.* 123(M.87.2985A); *ib.*124(2985C); met. ἐκάθισεν Βελιὰρ ἐν τῇ καρδίᾳ τοῦ Μανασσῆ *Ascens.Is.*A 3.11.

καθίημι, **A.** trans.; **1.** *send out*, hence, in gen. sense, *employ* ὁ διάβολος...καθεὶς ἀνθρώπους τινὰς λυμεῶνας Chrys.*hom.1.1 in 2Thess.* (11.510C); Synes.*ep.*44(M.66.1368A); **2.** *direct* the mind καθιέντας τὸν νοῦν ἐπ' αὐτὸ τὸ πνεῦμα τοῦ σωτῆρος Clem.*q.d.s.*5(p.163.30; M.9. 609D); Cyr.*ador.*3(1.115E); cf. ἔσπευδε τὸν λόγον καθεῖναι [i.e. *preach*] Chrys.*hom.43.2 in Ac.*(9.326E); **3.** *put in* ἐπὰν βράσῃ, καθιέντες τὰς χεῖρας οὐ καίονται Hipp.*haer.*4.3(p.58.14; M.16.3095A); **4.** reflex.; **a.** *bring* oneself *down, degrade* oneself, Const.*or.s.c.*25(p.191.16); **b.** met., *launch* oneself προήχθην εἰς τούτους ἐμαυτὸν καθεῖναι τοὺς λόγους Chrys.*hom.27.1 in 2Cor.*(10.627A); **c.** *apply* oneself ἐπὶ τὸ συγγράφειν ἑαυτοὺς καθήκαμεν Dion.Ar.*d.n.*3.3(M.3.684C).

B. intrans.; *come down, descend* ὁ...λόγος...κεκένωκεν ἑαυτόν, καθεὶς ἐθελοντὴς εἰς ὅπερ οὐκ ἦν Cyr.*glaph.Gen.*7(1.237E); esp. as if into arena, met. εἰς τὰς τῶν πέλας ζητήσεις καθιέναι Clem.*ecl.*36 (p.148.7; M.9.717A); ἐπὶ τήνδε καθεὶς τὴν πραγματείαν Eus.*p.e.*1.1 (4A; M.21.25D); εἰς γὰρ τὴν περὶ τῆς ἀναστάσεως ὑπόθεσιν καθεῖναι παρασκευάζομαι Chrys.*res.mort.*1(2.422A); id.*hom.5.6 in Rom.*(9. 470B); οὐκ εἶπε, μὴ κατακρίνῃς, ἀλλά, μηδὲ δέξῃ κατηγορίαν, μηδὲ ὅλως εἰς κρίσιν καθῇς id.*hom.15.3 in 1Tim.*(11.637F; καταθῇς Gaume).

***καθικετεία**, ἡ, *earnest supplication, entreaty*, Epiph.*haer.*59.13 (p.378.23, v.l. ἱκετείαν M.41.1037B).

καθικετεύ-ω, **1.** *entreat earnestly, beseech* τόν τε θεὸν ἵλεων αὐτοῖς γενέσθαι ~οντες Eus.*h.e.*8.1.9(M.20.801C); κ. ὡς... *ib.*10.4.72(880A); ἀνθρωποθυσίαις τοῖς πονηροῖς δαίμοσι ἐκαθικέτευον id.*p.e.*5.4(186B, v.l. ἐκαθήκευον; M.21.321C); πρὸς τὸν πατέρα ~ων λέγει, πάτερ, ἄφες αὐτοῖς Chrys.*hom.4.9 in Ac.princ.*(3.95A); κ. τὸν Θωμᾶν, ἵνα... ‡Chrys.*Thom.*3(12.804A); ~ω τὴν...γερουσίαν, βοηθήσατέ μοι Gel. Cyz.*h.e.*2.22.21(M.85.1293D); τοῦτο Χριστὸν ~σον Jo.D.*hom.*1.6(M. 96.556C); **2.** prob. f.l. for καθηκεύω: ~ων τοῖς τότε 'Ιουδαίοις Ath. *apol.Const.*33(M.25.640C, v.l. καθηκεύων); ἄνδρα βούλεσθαι γυναικὶ ~ειν Cyr.H.*procatech.*5.

***καθικέτης**, ὁ, Thdt.*h.rel.*26.18(3.1279; for οἰκέταις p.14.12).

καθικν-έομαι, **1.** *come down, descend*, Clem.*paed.*3.11(p.270.19; M.8.636A); of Christ κ. εἰς ἑκούσιον κένωσιν Cyr.*Pulch.*(p.45.25; 5^2.156E); ἐν ἀνθρωπότητι κ. διὰ τὴν τοῦ κόσμου σωτηρίαν id.*apol. Thdt.*4(p.125.23; 6^1.219D); **2.** *strike*; c. acc., Nil.*epp.*3.267(M.79. 517A); c. genit. τῇ μιᾷ πληγῇ τοῦ ἐλέγχου ἀμφοτέρων ὁμοῦ καθικέσθαι Bas.*Eun.*1.1(1.208C; M.29.501A); **3.** *reprove*, c. genit. οὔτε ~εῖται αὐτῶν σφοδρῶς, οὔτε ἀνεπιτιμήτους ἀφίησιν Chrys.*virg.*78(3.330C); σφοδρότερον αὐτοῦ ~εῖται, ἀπιστίαν ἐγκαλῶν id.*hom.27.1 in Jo.*(8. 154B).

καθιλαρεύ-ομαι, *rejoice greatly* over μὴ ~όμενος τῶν συμφορῶν [i.e. of others] Bas.*hom.*5.8(2.41D; M.31.257A).

καθιλαρύνω, *cheer, gladden*, †Cyr.*coll.VT*(6^4.37B; M.77.1229D).

καθιππεύ-ω, **1.** *ride through*, met. τὰ πάντα ~ων δικαιοσύνης ἥλιος ἐπ' ἴσης περιπολεῖ τὴν ἀνθρωπότητα Clem.*prot.*11(p.80.22; M.8. 232B); ὁ ἥλιος ~ων τοὺς κύκλους Meth.*symp.*8.15(p.103.12; M.18. 165D); ἀὴρ...μὴ ~όμενος ἡλίῳ *ib.*8.3(p.84.26; 144A); **2.** *ride upon*, c. genit., met. δεινοῖς μὲν ἡμῶν...καὶ λίαν εὐτροχωτάτοις ~εις λόγοις Cyr.*Jo.*4.1(4.333A).

καθίπταμαι, v. καταπέτομαι.

κάθισις ([*]κάθησ-), ἡ, *sitting, session* πνευματική ἐστιν ἡ κ. θεοῦ ἐπὶ πνευματικοῦ θρόνου καὶ ἡ Χριστοῦ ὁμοίως Or.*comm.in Mt.*16.4 (p.477.16; M.13.1377A); *Dial.Tim.et Aquil.*88 r°; δηλοῖ...ἡ κάθησις τὴν ἀνάπαυσιν Cyr.*ador.*2(3.90B); ἡ δὲ κ. ἡ ἐπ' αὐτοῦ τὴν οἱονεὶ βεβαιότητά τε καὶ ἐν ταυτότητι τῶν ἀγαθῶν ἵδρυσίν τε καὶ διαμονὴν ἔοικεν ὑποδηλοῦν id.*Is.*1.4(2.102C); τεκμηριοῖ...ἡ κάθησις τὸ ἀξίωμα τὸ δεσποτικόν id.*hom.pasch.*12(5^2.167C).

κάθισμα, τό, 1. *seat* of a chair, Cosm.Ind.*top.*2(M.88.101B); τὸ κ. τοῦ θρόνου †Polyb.*v.Epiph.*56(M.41.93C); **2.** imperial *box* in hippodrome at CP, Jo.Mal.*chron.*18 p.475(M.97.692A); *Chron.Pasch.*p.284 (M.92.708C); **3.** *session*; **a.** as name of church where BMV rested acc. tradition on way to Bethlehem with Joseph τὴν τοῦ κ. τῆς θεοτόκου ἐκκλησίαν Cyr.S.*v.Thds.*(p.236.20); ἐν τῇ τοῦ κ. ἐκκλησίᾳ id. *v.Sab.*14(p.97.6); Thdr.Pet.*v.Thds.*(p.14.9); τῷ λεγομένῳ παλαιῷ κ., τῷ ὄντι κατὰ τὴν λεωφόρον τὴν ἀπάγουσαν ἐπὶ τὴν ἁγίαν Βηθλεέμ [i.e. from Jerusalem] *ib.*(p.13.21); **b.** one of the twenty sections into which Psalter is divided for liturg. use, *ib.*(p.49.6); *Mir.Artem.*33 (p.50.27); **c.** short hymn sung after the preceding, *Euchol.*(p.30); ἀχρὶ τῆς Ἀναληψίμου ἑορτῆς προηγοῦνται τὰ ἀναστάσιμα στιχηρὰ καθισμάτων τῶν τε κατανυκτικῶν καὶ ἀποστολικῶν *Const.Stud.*5(M.99. 1708A); **4.** *settlement* of monks, *Apophth.Patr.*(M.65.364D); ἐν τρισὶ γενικωτάταις καταστάσεσι καθισμάτων ἅπασα ἡ μοναχικὴ πολιτεία περιέχεται Jo.Clim.*scal.*1(M.88.641B); hence *cell*, *V.Pach.Φ* 14(p.9. 26); **5.** *assiduity* in spiritual exercises ἀπὸ τοῦ νῦν φαίνεταί σου [sc. a novice] καὶ ἡ σπουδὴ καὶ ἡ ἁγνεία καὶ τὸ κ. Ephr.2.91A; hence *contemplation* συμβαίνει τινὰ εὑρεθῆναι ἀπὸ εὐχῆς, ἢ ἀπὸ καλοῦ κ. Dor.*doct.*7(M.88.1697A).

***καθισμάτιον, τό, 1.** *small cell* of a monk, Pach.*reg.*B 31(M.40. 952A); ἑκάστης οἰκίας τὰ κέλλια ἕως τῶν κ. *V.Pach.Φ* 144(p.91.1, v.l. καθισμάτων); **2.** ? *small seat* ἣν σύρων ἑαυτὸν [sc. a senile invalid] ἐπὶ τὸ κ. ἑαυτοῦ ἐν ὅλῃ τῇ συνάξει Ephr.2.115C.

καθιστάν-ω, = καθίστημι; **1.** *appoint*, *1Clem.*42.4; Epiph.*haer.* 75.4(p.336.8; M.42.508D); **2.** *bring* χορός σε παρθένων ~ει πρὸς οὐρανοὺς Meth.*symp.*11(p.136.22; M.18.213A).

καθιστ-άω, = καθίστημι; **1.** *appoint* τοὺς ἀρχιερεῖς ~ων Eus.*d.e.* 8.2(p.385.25; M.22.624B); CAnt.(341)*can.*22,23; Chrys.*hom.77.3 in Mt.*(7.746A); **2.** *render, make* ἀκύμονα ἑαυτοῖς ~ᾶν τὸν βίον καὶ πάνυ ῥᾴδιον Bas.*ep.*293(3.431E; M.32.1036A); Chrys.*hom.4.4 in Jo.*(8.32A); Cyr.*Os.*2(3.10B); **3.** *establish*, Chrys.*hom.5.2 in Eph.*(11.34E).

καθίστημι, 1. trans.; **a.** *appoint*, esp. clergy οἱ ἀπόστολοι... κατέστησαν τοὺς προειρημένους *1Clem.*44.2; Πολύκαρπος...ὑπὸ ἀποστόλων κατασταθεὶς...ἐπίσκοπος Iren.*haer.*3.34(M.7.852A)ap.Eus.*h.e.* 4.14.3; πόθεν...πρεσβύτερος Ἰσχύρας; τίνος καταστήσαντος; Ath. *apol.sec.*12(p.97.8; M.25.269A); ἀναγνώστης καθίσταται, ἐπιδιδόντος αὐτῷ βιβλίον τοῦ ἐπισκόπου. οὐδὲ γὰρ χειροθετεῖται *Const.App.epit.* 13; perf. in trans. sense, *bring about, cause* τοῦ γὰρ νοητοῦ ἄρτου βρῶσιν ἐργασία καθέστηκεν id.*Ps.*101:6(1.1317); **b.** med., *devote* ἡμεῖς...τὴν ζωὴν ἅπασαν εἰς τοῦτο κατεστησάμεθα Chrys.*hom.40.2 in 1Cor.*(10.381B); **2.** intrans.; **a.** *deposit a sediment* οἶνον...καταστάντα Proc.G.*Gen.*9:18–19(M.87.304D); **b.** *stand* or *become quiet* or *calm*, hence perf. ptcpl. act., *in a settled condition, in one's right mind* εἰ δὲ τοῦτο παραφρονούντων εἰπεῖν, οὐδὲ ἐκεῖνο καθεστηκότων Bas.*Eun.*2.5(1.241D; M.29.580C); τὴν μεθύουσαν καὶ παραπταίουσαν τῶν ἀνθρώπων φύσιν σωφρονοῦσαν καὶ καθεστηκυῖαν ἔδειξεν Thdt. *affect.*3(p.93.5; 4.784); neut. as subst., *T.Job* 36(p.126.6); εἰ ἐν τῷ καθεστηκότι ὑπάρχεις *ib.*37(p.127.4); Evagr.*h.e.*4.34(p.183.4; M.86. 2764D); **c.** *come into a certain state, become* καθίστατο τῆς ζωῆς τὸν θάνατον προαιρούμενος Thdt.*Jon.*4:8(2.1475, v.l. ἀπελέγετο).

καθιστήριον, τό, *seat*; met., Eus.*h.e.*10.4.66(M.20.876B).

***καθιστής, ὁ,** *sitter* on horseback, *rider*, Mac.Aeg.*hom.*23.2(M.34. 660D).

καθιστορέω, *observe*, hence **1.** *depict, paint* τὴν εἰκόνα τῆς θεομήτορος ἣν ὁ ἀπόστολος Λουκᾶς καθιστόρησεν Thdr.Lect.*h.e.*1.1(M. 86.165A); **2.** *narrate* τὸν δὲ νεκρόν, ὃν δὴ καὶ αὐτὸς καθιστόρησας, εὑρίσκω προκείμενον Sophr.H.*v.Anast.*(M.92.1728B).

καθοδηγ-έω, *guide, lead*; c. acc., Epiph.*haer.*8.6(p.192.23; M.41. 213C); Chrys.*hom.28.3 in Mt.*(7.337A); pass., *Orac.Sib.*1.384; *Tr. Phil.*1(p.161.11); intrans. ἀγαθὸν...ὁ...εἰς σωτηρίαν ~εῖ Clem.*paed.* 1.3(p.95.19; M.8.260B).

καθοδήγησις, ἡ, *guidance*, Clem.*paed.*3.12(p.284.3; M.8.665B).

καθοδηγός, ὁ, *guide*, *Orac.Sib.*1.385; ἐν σκότῳ βαθεῖ ἀλώμενοι τῷ βίῳ ἀπταίστου καὶ ἀκριβοῦς κ. δεόμεθα Clem.*paed.*1.3(p.95.14; M.8. 260A); θεὸς...κ. τῶν ἀποστόλων Epiph.*haer.*42.12(p.165.14; M.41. 788B).

κάθοδος, ἡ, *going down, descent*; **1.** in gen., to Egypt τὴν εἰς Αἴγυπτον κ. Mel.*pass.*87 p.14.25; Or.*Cels.*3.6(p.207.27; M.11.928B); Ath.*inc.*36.4(M.25.157D); to Judaea from Jerusalem, Or.*Jo.*10.3(2; p.173.24; M.14.312A); *attack, invasion* ἄχρι τῆς Περσῶν ἐπὶ τοὺς Ἀσσυρίους κ. Meth.*res.*3.9(p.403.13; M.18.324B); **2.** of Christ; **a.** at Inc. ἡ εἰς τὴν Μαρίαν αὐτοῦ κ. Iren.*haer.*3.22.2(M.7.956C); τὴν εἰς σάρκα κ. τοῦ κυρίου Clem.*str.*5.14(p.397.5; M.9.161A); Or.*fr.12 in Jo.* (p.494.17); θεοῦ κ. ἐπ' ἄνθρωπον Meth.*Porph.*1(p.504.22; M.18.400C); ἡ...πρὸς τὸ ταπεινὸν κ. Gr.Nyss.*or.catech.*24(p.91.15; M.45.64C); **b.** to death τὴν μέχρι θανάτου κ. αὐτοῦ Eus.*d.e.*6.7(p.257.21; M.22.424A); **c.** to Hades, Didym.*Trin.*3.21(M.39.905B) cit. s. ἀνόρμητος; Cyr. *Ps.*9:1(M.69.761B); τὴν ἐν τῷ ᾅδῃ κ. καὶ ἀνάβασιν αὐτοῦ ‡Bas.*h. myst.*49(p.391.5) v. ᾅδης; **d.** at second coming ὡς μέλλοντος κατὰ τὸν τῆς συντελείας καιρὸν...δευτέραν ποιεῖσθαι κ. ἐκ τοῦ οὐρανοῦ Eus. *e.th.*3.14(p.171.7; M.24.1028A); τῆς ἐξ οὐρανῶν αὐτοῦ κ. προδραμοῦντές τινες ψευδόχριστοι Cyr.*Lc.*21:5(M.72.896C); **3.** of H. Ghost; **a.** at Christ's baptism τοῦ πνεύματος τῇ κ. ἁγιάζεται Clem.*paed.*1.6(p.105. 17; M.8.280C); Hipp.*haer.*7.35(p.222.12; M.16.3343A); Or.*fr.49 in Jo.* (p.524.10); Ath.*Ar.*1.47(M.26.108C); Chrys.*hom.17.2 in Jo.*(8.98E); **b.** at Pentecost τὴν...τοῦ ἁγίου πνεύματος εἰς ἀνθρώπους κ. Eus. *v.C.*4.64(p.144.14; M.20.1220B); Cosm.Ind.*top.*5(M.88.261C); **c.** in response to epiclesis in liturgy, Petr.II Al.*encycl.*ap.Thdt.*h.e.*4.22.7 (M.33.1280A); **4.** of the soul; **a.** into body ὁ Πλάτων...κέκληκεν... ὕπνον...καὶ θάνατον τὴν εἰς σῶμα κ. τῆς ψυχῆς Clem.*str.*5.14(p.397. 1; M.9.160B); 'κ. ...' αὖθις 'στενὴν' τάχα οἱ τὴν μετενσωμάτωσιν εἰσάγοντες φήσουσιν Or.*Cels.*6.34(p.105.14; M.11.1352A); τὸ ἀπὸ τῶν ψαλμῶν [sc. Ps.125:5] δοκεῖ μοι δηλοῦν περὶ τῆς κ. τῶν εὐγενεστέρων ψυχῶν παραγινομένων εἰς τὸν βίον τοῦτον id.*Jo.*12.43(p.270.21; M.14. 477B); **b.** into Hades; of Odysseus, Just.*1apol.*18.5(M.6.356B); of sinners, Ath.*inc.*29.4(M.25.145C).

***καθοκνέω,** *hesitate*; c. infin., *Mir.Geo.*6(p.78.12).

καθολικός, A. *general, universal*; **1.** of God τῆς...ὑπερουσίου καὶ ...κ. ... πατρικῆς ὑποστάσεως Didym.*Trin.*2.4(M.39.484A); of providence τῇ κ. τοῦ θεοῦ προνοίᾳ Clem.*str.*6.16(p.508.18; M.9.380B); ἐλθεῖν ἐπὶ τὰς κ. εὐεργεσίας τοῦ θεοῦ, εἶτα μετὰ τὰς κ. εὐεργεσίας αὐτοῦ ἐπὶ τὰς ἰδικάς Or.*hom.3.1 in Jer.*(p.20.23; M.13.281D); ζητεῖται, εἰ τὰ κ. μόνον ποιήσας ὁ θεός, ἀφ' ἑαυτῆς τρέχειν τὴν φύσιν ἐποίησεν· ἢ κατὰ μέρος ἑκάστῳ τῶν τικτομένων παρίσταται Proc.G.*Ex.*4:11(M.87.536A); **2.** of Church (v. ἐκκλησία); **a.** as universal in scope τῆς ἀπὸ περάτων γῆς ἕως περάτων καθολικῆς τοῦ θεοῦ ἐκκλησίας Eus.*Marcell.*1.1 (p.8.23; M.24.728C); Adam.*dial.*1.8(p.16.14; M.11.1728C); ἔστιν οὖν ἡ ἁγία τοῦ θεοῦ κ. ἐκκλησία τὸ σύστημα τῶν ἀπ' αἰῶνος ἁγίων πατέρων, πατριαρχῶν, προφητῶν, ἀποστόλων, εὐαγγελιστῶν, μαρτύρων, οἷς προσετέθη πιστεύσαντα ὁμοθυμαδὸν πάντα τὰ ἔθνη Jo.V H.*icon.*11(M. 96.1357C); *Lit.Jac.*(p.186.13); **b.** implying orthodoxy ἡ κ. ἐκκλησία, ὀρθοῦ δόγματος προϊσταμένη Adam.*dial.*2.22(p.114.18; 1792A); τῶν Παυλιανισάντων, εἶτα προσφυγόντων τῇ κ. ἐκκλησίᾳ CNic.(325)*can.*19; Ath.*Ar.*1.4(M.26.20A); **c.** as extending throughout the world, teaching the fullness of Christian doctrine, disciplining all classes of mankind, curing all kinds of sin and possessing every virtue, Cyr.H.*catech.*18.23; **d.** of the whole Church opp. local churches νήσους δὲ τὰς κατὰ μέρος ἐκκλησίας. ἐξ ὧν ἡ μία καὶ κ. πανταχοῦ Proc. G.*Is.*49:14–26(M.87.2480D); **e.** of local churches τῆς ἐν Σμύρνῃ κ. ἐκκλησίας *M.Polyc.*16.2; τῇ κ. ἐκκλησίᾳ τῇ κατὰ Ναζιανζόν Gr.Naz. *test.*(M.37.389A); **f.** of Roman see τὴν κ. καθέδραν Eutych.*ep.Vigil.* (M.86.2404A); **g.** of Nicene council τὴν κ. σύνοδον Jul.Papa *ep.Dian.* ap.Ath.*apol.sec.*25(p.105.28; M.25.289B); Ath.*syn.*2(p.232.5; M.26. 684A); CArim.*decr.*ap.Ath.*syn.*11(p.238.34; 700C); **3.** of Christian faith as orthodox ἄνδρα τὸ γοῦν φρόνημα κ. ἔχοντα Malch.*ep.*ap.Eus. *h.e.*7.30.16(M.20.716B); as opp. schism τῆς κ. θρησκείας Const.ap.Eus. *h.e.*10.6.1(892A); τοῦτο δὲ κ. εἶναι οὐδεὶς ἀγνοεῖ, δύο πρόσωπα εἶναι, πατρὸς καὶ υἱοῦ *Symb.Sirm.*2(p.257.13; M.26.741C),; **4.** of Christians, in gen. ποίαν θρήσκειαν ἢ αἵρεσιν ἔχεις; ἀπεκρίνατο· τῶν κ. *M.Pion.* 19.4; as orthodox οἱ κ. Geo.Laod.*ep.dogm.*ap.Epiph.*haer.*73.21 (p.293.17; M.42.414C); τῶν κ. ἐπισκόπων Innoc.*ep.cler.*(M.52.538); **5.** of general epistles ἐν τῇ Βαρνάβα κ. ἐπιστολῇ Or.*Cels.*1.63 (p.115.20; M.11.777B); κ. ἐπιστολῶν τινὲς μὲν ἑπτά φασιν, οἱ δὲ τρεῖς μόνας χρῆναι δέχεσθαι, τὴν Ἰακώβου μίαν, μίαν δὲ Πέτρου, τήν τ' Ἰωάννου μίαν. τινὲς δὲ τὰς τρεῖς [i.e. 1–3 Jo. as well as Jac.], καὶ πρὸς αὐταῖς τὰς Πέτρου δέχονται, τὴν Ἰούδα δ' ἑβδόμην Amph. *Seleuc.*310(M.37.1597A); ἐν ταῖς κ. γράφει...ὁ μακάριος Ἰωάννης Pall. *v.Chrys.*20(p.131.11; M.47.73); αἱ κ. ἐπιστολαὶ οὖσαι ἑπτά...κ. δὲ ἐκλήθησαν, ἐπειδὴ οὐ πρὸς ἓν ἔθνος ἐγράφθησαν, ὡς αἱ τοῦ Παύλου, ἀλλὰ καθόλου πρὸς πάντα †Leont.B.*sect.*2.4(M.86.1204C); τὰς κ. αὐτῶν οἱ ἀπόστολοι τότε γράφουσιν, πρὸ τῆς διασπορᾶς αὐτῶν, εἰ καὶ Πέτρος μόνος ἀπὸ Ῥώμης γράφει *Chron.Pasch.*p.233(M.92.565B); **6.** of principal church of diocese, province, etc. ταῖς κ. προσερχέσθωσαν ἐκκλησίαις CTrull.*can.*59; ἐν ταῖς μεγάλαις καὶ κ. ἐκκλησίαις, ἤγουν ἐν τοῖς πατριαρχείοις καὶ ταῖς μητροπόλεσι καὶ ταῖς λοιπαῖς ‡Tim.CP *haer.suppl.*6(M.86.72C); Thphn.*chron.*p.314(M.108.761B); **7.** liturg., of general intercession τοῦ διακόνου τὴν κ. ὑπάγοντος πληρῶσαι εὐχήν Leont.N.*v.Jo.Eleem.*14(p.29.7); ὁ διάκονος ἄρχεται τῆς κ. *Lit.Jac.*(p.186.6); **8.** eschatol., of final consummation ἡ μὲν γὰρ προτέρα περὶ τῆς ἰδίας ἑκάστου συντελείας, ἥτις ἐγγὺς πάρεστιν. ἡ δὲ ἐν χερσί, περὶ τῆς κ. †Bas.*Is.*265(1.580E; M.30.584C); Max.*myst.*6(M. 91.685B); of general resurrection τὴν κ. ἀνάστασιν ἁπάντων ἀνθρώπων Thphl.Ant.*Autol.*1.13(M.6.1044B); Ammon.*Ac.*26:23(M.85.1597C); Eustrat.*stat.anim.*8(p.370); and judgement τὴν κ. ... πάντων...κρίσιν Just.*dial.*81.4(M.6.669A); Or.*Apoc.*30b(p.7.2); Olymp.*fr.Jer.*25:30 (M.93.680A); Max.*prol.Dion.*(M.4.16A); **9.** Gnost. (Valentinian) πρῶτος μὲν οὖν δημιουργὸς ὁ Σωτὴρ γίνεται κ. Clem.*exc.Thdot.*46 (p.121.17; M.9.681A); (Peratic) ὁ κ. ὄφις, φησίν, οὗτός ἐστιν ὁ σοφὸς τῆς Εὔας λόγος Hipp.*haer.*5.16(p.112.18; M.16.3174A); ref. demiurge οἱονεὶ μικρός τις βασιλεὺς ὑπὸ κ. βασιλέως τεταγμένος ἐπὶ μικρᾶς βασιλείας Heracleon ap.Or.*Jo.*13.60(59; p.291.23; M.14.513A); **10.** as official title ὁ κ.; **a.** of secular superintendents of finance, Const. ap.Eus.*v.C.*4.36(p.131.30; M.20.1185A); id.ap.Eus.*h.e.*10.6.1(M.20. 892A); Ath.*apol.Const.*10(M.25.608B); **b.** of archbishops κ. ἐπίσκοπος τῶν αὐτόθι κατασταθείς Cosm.Ind.*top.*2(M.88.73A); ὁ κ. Jo.Nic.*nativ.* (M.96.1448C); **c.** of superiors of several monasteries ἀναδέχεται τὴν φροντίδα...ὅλου τοῦ ὑπὸ τὴν μητρόπολιν μοναχικοῦ συστήματος, ὅθεν καὶ κ. ὠνομάζετο Eustrat.*v.Eutych.*18(M.86.2296A).

B. *canonical* τό γε μὴν τῶν ἐπικεκλημένων αὐτοῦ [sc. τοῦ Πέτρου] πράξεων καὶ τὸ κατ' αὐτὸν ὠνομασμένον εὐαγγέλιον τό τε λεγόμενον αὐτοῦ κήρυγμα καὶ τὴν καλουμένην ἀποκάλυψιν οὐδ' ὅλως ἐν καθολικοῖς ἴσμεν παραδεδομένα Eus.*h.e.*3.3.2(M.20.217A); ὁ [sc. Λουκᾶς] καὶ τὸ εὐαγγέλιον γράψας, καὶ τὰς πράξεις τὰς κ. Chrys.*hom.10.1 in 2Tim.* (11.720E).

*__καθολικότης__, ἡ, *comptrollership*, Eus.*h.e.*8.11.2(M.20.769A).

καθόλου, **1.** *in general, on the whole, LS*; **2.** *universal* τῷ κ. λόγῳ Clem.*str.*1.20(p.63.24; M.8.817A); τὴν κ. πρόνοιαν Dion.Al.ap.Eus. *h.e.*7.10.5(M.20.660A); πατὴρ ὁ...κ. νοῦς id.ap.Ath.*Dion.*23.4(p.64.2; M.25.516A); ἡ τῆς κ. ἐκκλησίας λαμπρότης Eus.*h.e.*4.7.13(320B); **3.** *altogether, as a whole* κ. ἡ...τριὰς καὶ τὴν δημιουργίαν καὶ τὴν ἐνανθρώπησιν καὶ τὴν ἀνάστασιν ἐργάζεται Cosm.Ind.*top.*5(M.88. 308C); **4.** *entirely, at all* κ. τὸ φῶς μὴ βλέπειν Papias *fr.*3.2; ἐπίσκοπος δὲ κ. γυναικὶ συνοικῶν καθαιρεῖται Phot.*nomoc.*8.14(M.104.689B).

*__καθομαλίζω__, *make level, flatten*, Bas.*ep.*45.1(3.134A; M.32.368A); fig., Thdr.Stud.*epp.*1.4(M.99.924A).

καθομηρίζω, *describe Homerically*, Gr.Naz.*or.*43.17(M.36.520A).

καθομιλ-έω, *be in daily intercourse* with, *be conversant* with υἱὸς ...τῷ τῶν ἀνθρώπων ~ῶν γένει Eus.*e.th.*1.13(p.73.32; M.24.852C); τοῖς ...θείοις οὐ παρέργως καθωμιληκότες id.*p.e.*10.9(487B; M.21.809D); εἰ τοῖς ἔξωθεν λόγοις ~οίημεν ἐν τῷ καιρῷ τῆς παιδεύσεως Gr.Nyss. *v.Mos.*(M.44.329C).

καθομολογ-έω, **1.** *confess, acknowledge* ~οῦσι τὸ ὁμοούσιον Socr. *h.e.*3.25.9(M.67.452B); τὸ πλήρωμα τῆς θεότητος κατοικεῖν ~οῦντες Thdt.*rect.conf.*17(M.6.1237C); ὅς...τὸν Ὄναγρον ταῦτα...δεδρακέναι καθωμολόγησεν id.*h.e.*2.10.1(3.852); Gel.Cyz.*h.e.*2.21.27(M.85.1289A); **2.** *devote, dedicate*, reflex. ἑαυτὰς εἰς τοῦτο ~ήσασαι Meth.*symp.*6.3 (p.66.10; M.18.116C); med. τῶν ἑαυτοὺς τῷ θεῷ ~ησαμένων Bas.*reg. fus.*14 tit.(2.355A; M.31.949C); παρθένων...~ησαμένων τὸν ἐν σεμνότητι βίον τῷ κυρίῳ id.*ep.*199 *can.*18(3.291B; M.32.717A); pass., *ib.*46.4 (138B; M.377A); Proc.G.*Dt.*33:7(M.87.980D); **3.** *promise, undertake* εἰρήνην ἄγειν καθωμολόγησεν Thphn.*chron.*p.214(M.108.548B).

καθοπλίζω, **1.** med., *arm oneself*, c. acc. of respect καθοπλισάμενος τὸν φόβον τοῦ κυρίου Herm.*mand.*12.2.4; **2.** pass., *be armed*, met. θώρακι...πνεύματος...καθωπλισμένος Tat.*orat.*16(p.18.5; M.6. 841A); Philost.*h.e.*12.11(M.65.620C); *be armed* καθωπλισμένον τὴν πανοπλίαν τοῦ θεοῦ Or.*sel.in Ex.*17:6(M.12.292A).

[*]**καθοπότερον**, *respectively*, better written *divisim*, *cat.Apoc.* 11:13(p.346.22).

καθορίζ-ω, **1.** *decree against, pronounce as punishment upon*; c. acc. et genit., Cyr.*ador.*6(1.179E); παντὸς ἑλομένου τοῦτο δρᾶν ποινὴν ~οντος τὴν ἐσχάτην *ib.*(187E); *call down upon* τὰ πάντων αἴσχιστα τῆς ἑαυτοῦ καθοριεῖ κεφαλῆς id.*hom.div.*9(5².110C); **2.** *declare, admit, allow* τῆς ἑαυτοῦ ζωῆς τὸ ἀτερπὲς ~οντα id.*Ps.*35:3(M. 69.916A); ~ει...τῶν ἱερουργῶν τὸ πλημμέλημα id.*Mal.*10(3.827C); id. *Juln.*7(6².222C); *condemn* ~ει δὲ τὸ ἀσύνηθες αὐτῆς [sc. τῆς λέξεως τῆς καθ' ὑπόστασιν] id.*apol.Thdt.*2(p.115.6; 6¹.209A); καθοριοῦμεν...τὸ εἰς ἄκρον ἀμαθὲς id.*inc.unigen.*(5¹.688A).

*__καθοριστικός__, *definitive*, Clem.*str.*7.8(p.37.21; M.9.472A).

*__καθορκόομαι__, *be bound by oath*, c. infin., *Schol.* in Bas.*ep.*188 *can.* 10(*Mon.*2 p.652).

καθορμίζω, *bring into harbour*, met. ἐγώ, φησίν, ὁ Χριστός, ἐγὼ ὁ... καθορμίσας τὸν ἄνθρωπον εἰς τὰ ὕψη τῶν οὐρανῶν Mel.*pass.*102 p.17. 17; ἕως ἂν ἀβλαβὲς καθορμίσῃ [sc. ὁ παιδαγωγός] τὸ παιδίον εἰς τὸν λιμένα τῶν οὐρανῶν Clem.*paed.*1.7(p.122.23; M.8.313C); τοῖς λιμέσι καθορμίσει [sc. σε] τῶν οὐρανῶν τὸ πνεῦμα τὸ ἅγιον id.*prot.*12(p.83.26; M.8.240A).

καθοσι-όω, **1.** *dedicate, devote* to ~ώσαντα...τῷ θεῷ τόπον Synes. *ep.*67(M.67.1420B); τὸ λογικὸν...ὅλον τοῖς θείοις νόμοις...~οῦν Thdt. *Ezech.*32:32(2.953); hence *destine* for ~ωθεὶς μετὰ θάνατον τάφῳ Nil.*perist.*12.12(M.79.964B); **2.** perf. ptcpl. pass., *dedicated, devoted* to τοὺς καθωσιωμένους τῷ Χριστῷ Clem.*str.*1.1(p.6.7; M.8.693A); τῷ σωτηρίῳ πίστει καθωσιωμένους Eus.*v.C.*2.44(p.59.28; M.20.1021A); μέγας ἀρχιερεὺς [sc. Christ]...τῇ τοῦ πατρὸς καθωσιωμένος τιμῇ id. *l.C.*1(p.198.25; M.20.1324B); καθωσιωμένος [sc. Ἀρτέμιος] τῇ τῶν Ῥωμαίων βασιλείᾳ ‡Jo.D.*Artem.*34(M.96.1284A); abs. ἡ θεία πρόνοια καθωσιωμένους ὑμᾶς διαφυλάττοι CSard.*ep.cath.*ap.Ath.*apol.sec.*47 (p.123.24; M.25.336C); CSard.*can.*17; καθωσιωμένῃ σπουδῇ Sabinus ap.Eus.*h.e.*9.1.3(M.20.800B); τῆς ἐμῆς κ. ψυχῆς Const.ap.Gel.Cyz. *h.e.*2.7.21(M.85.1236D); of imperial officials τῶν κ. δομεστικῶν CChalc.*act.*1(*ACO* 2.1.1 p.55.15; H.2.53C); ὁ κ. σηκρητάριος *ib.*(p.67. 34; 69E); τὸν κ. Εὐφρόνιον τὸν στρατηλατιανόν Thdt.*ep.*79(4.1135); *consecrated* ὄνομα ἔλαβε [sc. Χριστός] τὸ πάλαι κ. Clem.*prot.*1(p.7.16; M.8.61B); Ἰσαὰκ ὡς κ. ἱερεῖον id.*str.*2.5(p.123.13; M.8.952C).

καθοσίωσις, ἡ, **1.** *dedication*, hence *blessing* of gospel-book (liturg.), †Anast.S.*relat.*52(p.76); **2.** *devotion, fidelity* τῇ τῆς κ. εὐσεβείᾳ Const.*or.s.c.*2(p.155.27; M.20.1237A); εἰλικρινῆ τε κ. καὶ ἄχραντον πίστιν τῷ σωτῆρι id.ap.Ath.*decr.*42(p.45.34); τοῦ...βασίλεως τὴν εἰς τὸν...σωτῆρα κ. Eus.*v.C.*4.45(p.136.13; M.20.1196A); θρησκείας κ. CSard.*can.*11; ἣν [sc. πίστιν] καὶ ἡ Ῥωμαίων καὶ ἡ σῆς ἁγιότητος ἐκκλησία καὶ ἡ καθόλου κ. κατέχει Cael.*ep.Cyr.*(p.77.5; M.77.93B); πάσῃ τῇ κ. τὴν...πρεσβείαν ἐπλήρωσεν Leo Mag.*ep.*104(p.60.39; M. *PL.*54.998B); **3.** *sanctity*; **a.** as title of imperial officials τῆς ἐμῆς κ. Sabinus ap.Eus.*h.e.*9.1.5(M.20.800C); Flavius ap.Ath.*apol.sec.*85 (p.164.10; M.25.401B); τῆς σῆς κ. Constantius Imp.ap.Ath.*h.Ar.* 23(p.195.25; M.25.720C); **b.** as synonym for imperial power εἰς αὐτὴν δὲ τὴν κ. καὶ τοὺς τῆς ἡμετέρας θειότητος νόμους ἐξαμαρτάνων Marcian.Imp.*ep.Mac.*(p.131.28; H.2.665C); Isch.*libell.*(p.17.24; H.2. 325D); Sophr.Al.*libell.*(p.24.8; H.2.337B); **4.** (*crimen majestatis*) *high treason*, *Const.App.*5.14.11; Chrys.*hom.37.1 in Ac.*(9.280E); Socr. *h.e.*5.14.6(M.67.601A).

[*]**καθόσον**, *so far as*, better written *divisim*, Chrys.*hom.27.1 in Jo.*(8.153C).

[*]**καθοτιοῦν**, *inasmuch as*, better written *divisim*, Didym.(‡Bas.) *Eun.*4(1.287E; M.29.692B).

*__καθύβρισις__, ἡ, *contempt*, Thdr.Stud.*epp.*1.37(M.99.1040D).

*__καθυβριστέον__, *one must treat despitefully, insult*, Clem.*paed.*2.10 (p.208.13; M.8.497B); *ib.*(p.212.16; 505B).

καθυγραίνω, pass., *be well moistened*, i.e. *have one's thirst quenched*, Proc.G.*Jud.*4:17(M.87.1049B).

κάθυγρος, *very wet, moist*, met. χαύνης...καὶ κ. ἡδύτητος Diad. *perf.*33(p.38.8).

καθυλακτ-έω, *bark at*, c. genit., met., Bas.*hom.*10.3(2.86B; M.31. 360C); ὡς ἀγαθὸς σκύλαξ...τοῦ Φιλίππου καθυλάκτησεν [sc. eunuch] Gr.Nyss.*bapt.diff.*(M.46.421D); πικροῖς...ἡμῶν ~οῦσι λόγοις οἱ θεομάχοι Cyr.*Jo.*2.8(4.227B); c. acc. πάντας ~ῶν Nil.*epp.*2.50(M.79. 221C); pass., Max.*ambig.*(M.91.1204A).

καθυλομαν-έω, *run all to wood*; of an unpruned vine, Clem.*paed.* 1.8(p.129.11; M.8.329C); ‡Ath.*v.Syncl.*17(M.28.1496A); met., of souls ~ήσασαι τοῖς παραπτώμασιν Meth.*symp.*10.2(p.123.8; M.18.193C).

*__κάθυλος__, *well wooded*, *A.Xanthipp.*39(p.85.3).

*__καθυπάγομαι__, *be brought under subjection*, Eus.*v.C.*1.26(p.19.32; M.20.940D); καθυπαχθέντα [sc. ἄνθρωπον] σαρκικοῖς θελήμασιν Jo. Mon.*hymn.Blas.*8(M.96.1400B); ‡Jo.Jej.*can.*(p.433).

καθυπεμφαίνω, *suggest*, Them.*fr.*(H.3.1241B).

*__καθυπερκεῖμαι__, *be placed upon, superimposed*, Gr.Nyss.*ep.*25(M. 46.1100A).

καθυπηρετ-έω, **1.** *be of service* ὁ πλοῦτος...πρὸς δικαιοσύνην ~εῖ Clem.*q.d.s.*14(p.168.30; M.9.617C); **2.** *obey* τῷ σῷ ἔσομαι ~ῶν προστάγματι †Jo.D.*B.J.*16(M.96.1004A); *ib.*21(1045B).

καθυπισχνέομαι, *promise expressly*, Cyr.*Os.*23(3.45E); id.*Nah.*9 (3.485E); Jo.D.*hom.*12.19(M.96.808B).

καθυποβάλλω, **1.** *subject*, in phrase καθυποβαλεῖν ἀριθμῷ *count*, Marc.Diac.*v Porph.*64; **2.** *implicate* in τοῦ καθυποβαλεῖν αὐτὸν τῇ πλάνῃ Philost.*h.e.*7.13(M.65.552A); **3.** *assign* Ζαχαρίας...λαχμῷ μνηστῆρα αὐτῇ καθυπέβαλεν Rom.Mel.(*AS* 1 p.201); **4.** *add, append*, Gr.Mag.*dial.*(tr.Zach.)1.4(M.*PL.*77.178A).

καθυπογράφω, 1. *write down*, ref. debts, Isid.Pel.*epp*.2.127(M.78.569A); χρεώστην ὑμῖν ἐν τῷ παρόντι ἑαυτὸν καθυπογράψας Leont.B.*mesopent*.(M.86.1984A); Jo.Mosch.*prat*.194(M.87.3080A); 2. *subscribe* to document, Soz.*h.e*.6.14.1(M.67.705A); Jo.Ant.*ep.Ruf*.(p.40.12; M.83.1476C); Thdr.Lect.*h.e*.2.13(M.86.189B); 3. *confirm* αὐτὸς δὲ τὴν ἄφεσιν ὡς θεὸς κ. ‡Bas.*inc*.44(p.243.14).

***καθυποδέχομαι**, *submit to*, of BMV τὴν...ἄπειρον δύναμιν σοὶ ἐπισκιάσασαν καθυπεδέξω Jo.Mon.*hymn.Bas*.5(M.96.1373C).

***καθυποδηλόω**, *demonstrate*, Thdr.Stud.*cant*.8.5(p.352).

***καθυποζεύγνυμι**, *place beneath a yoke*; met., *subject absolutely*, of human nature τῷ θανάτῳ καθυπεζεύχθη Chrys.*coemet*.2(2.399C).

***καθυποκλίνω**, *bend* χαίροις, ὅτι τὸν αὐχένα σου καθυπέκλινας πατρί *Hymn*.(*SBBAW* 1892 p.328); med., *submit oneself* αὐτοῖς καθυπεκλίνοντο Chrys.*hom*.*24.2 in 2Cor*.(10.608C).

καθυποκρίν-ομαι, 1. trans.; a. *act* τὸ δρᾶμα...ὃ καθυπεκρίνατο Ast.Am.*hom*.3(M.40.208A); fig. ὁ δὲ Μωσέως χριστὸς ἐν δράματι τὸν τύπον...~άμενος Eus.*d.e*.4.16(p.194.29; M.22.324C); hence *represent* κίνησίν τε καὶ ἦχον καὶ σχήματα ~εται Gr.Nyss.*anim.et res*.(M.46.36B); b. *represent, bring forward, in counterfeit fashion* τὰς...ἀσωμάτους δυνάμεις οἱ φαῦλοι δαίμονες καθυπεκρίνοντο Eus.*p.e*.5.2(182A; M.21.316A); μυθικὰς...γενεαλογίας ~άμενος *ib*.13.14(692D; 1141C); 2. intrans., *dissemble*, Or.*adnot.in Ex*.20:4(M.17.16D); Petr.I Al.*ep.can*.5(M.18.473D); Eus.*d.e*.10.1(p.451.1; M.22.725B).

***καθυποκύπτω**, *bow down*, met. ἥττῃ κ. Jo.D.*hom*.11.1(M.96.764B); hence *incline* to an opinion, id.*trisag*.1(M.95.24C).

***καθυπομιμνήσκω**, *call to remembrance, mention*, *M.Ner.et Ach*.7(p.5.12).

καθυποπτεύω, 1. *suspect*, Gr.Nyss.*or.catech*.5(p.25.19; M.45.24B); id.*virg*.1(p.252.24; M.46.321A); 2. *consider* καθυπόπτευσον τὸν ἐν σαρκὶ φαινόμενον θεόν Cyr.H.*hom*.9(M.33.1141A).

***καθυποσημαίνομαι**, *subscribe* to; c. dat., *Ep*.ap.CChalc.*act*.4(*ACO* 2.1.2 p.119.35; H.2.429B); Evagr.*h.e*.3.16(p.114.27; M.86.2628A).

***καθυποσκελίζομαι**, *be tripped up*, Nil.*epp*.2.1(M.79.204A).

***καθυπόστασις**, ἡ, *individual person* γέγονεν ἡ κ. τῶν φύσεων ἕνωσις *Symb*.ap.*Euchol*.(p.253).

***καθυπόστατος**, *hypostatically united* καθυπόστατόν ἐστι τὸ ἐκ δύο μὲν πραγμάτων, ἐν ἑνὶ δὲ προσώπῳ *Doct.Patr*.33(p.262.23).

καθυποτάσσ-ω, 1. *subject to* θεὸς...πάντα γένη βαρβάρων τοῖς αὐτοῦ [sc. Const.] καθυπέταττε ποσίν Eus.*v.C*.1.46(p.29.17; M.20.961A); καθυποτάξας αὐτῷ [sc. Adam] τὴν κτίσιν *Lit*.ap.*Const.App*.8.12.20; αἱ δύο διαθῆκαι, αἱ τὴν γυναῖκα τότε καὶ νῦν καθυποτάξασαι τῷ ἀνδρί Epiph.*haer*.42.12(p.171.12; M.41.796D); τὸν ἀποστάτην ἄνθρωπον καθυποτάξας [sc. Christ] τῷ πλάσαντι Jo.D.*hom*.4.27(M.96.628B); fig. καθυποτάξαντες τὸν νοῦν τοῖς πάθεσι τοῖς ψυχικοῖς Clem.*str*.5.9(p.364.31; M.9.89A); ὅταν...ὅλην τὴν ψυχὴν ἑαυτοῦ καθυποτάξῃ κηδεμονίᾳ συγγενῶν Pall.*h.Laus*.6(p.22.22, v.l. καταπατήσῃ M.34.1018D); Jo.Mon.*hymn.Blas*.1(M.96.1401A); reflex. τῷ ἀλλοτρίῳ θελήματι ἑαυτὴν ...καθυποτάξαι *M.Ner.et Ach*.5(p.4.9); †Jo.D.*B.J*.12(M.96.969A); *ib*.14(985C); 2. *bring under subjection, subjugate*, Eus.*Ps*.149:8(M.24.72D); τὸ τῆς ψυχῆς ἄλογον μέρος ~ων ‡Proc.G.*Pr*.29:11(M.87.1516C); ὑπὸ τὸν...τοῦ κυρίου ζυγὸν τὸν ἑαυτῶν κ. τράχηλον Gr.Mag.*dial*.(tr.Zach.)2.8(M.*PL*.66.147A); τοὺς Βουλγάρους κ. ‡Jo.D.*ep.Thphl*.19(M.95.372A); 3. *subjoin, append* ἔκθεσιν κ. Epiph.*haer*.77.20(p.434.30; M.42.672B); *ib*.77.37(p.448.32; 696C); τὴν γενεαλογίαν ἐνταῦθα κ. *Chron.Pasch*.p.244(M.92.588A).

καθυπουργ-έω, 1. *render service* to, *serve*; c. dat., *T.Abr*.A 12(p.91.21); ‡Ath.*occurs*.2(M.28.976D); †Jo.D.*B.J*.18(M.96.1016C); abs., Jo.VI CP *ep*.(M.96.1428D); 2. *obey*, c. dat. πάσῃ προστάξει...~εῖν *M.Thdot.1* 27(p.78.15).

καθυστερίζω, *fall behind*, med. ἵνα κἂν τούτῳ μηδενὸς τῶν περιφανῶν καθυστερίζοιτο Jo.D.*f.o*.4.14(M.94.1157B).

καθυφαίν-ω, *interweave* χρυσῷ καὶ ἄνθεσι καθυφασμένας βαρβαρικὰς στολάς Eus.*v.C*.4.7(p.120.19; M.20.1156C); *ib*.1.31(p.22.8; 945B); Chrys.*hom*.*37.5 in Gen*.(4.381A); met. πολύχρωμον ζητημάτων κρόκην ~οντες Mac.Mgn.*apocr*.4.11(p.172.8).

***καθυφέλκομαι**, *draw, attract*, ‡Germ.CP *contempl*.(M.98.416D).

καθυφ-ίημι, 1. trans., *surrender, give up*, ref. Mt.26:41 οὐδὲν ~εὶς αὐτός, οὔτε μὴν εἰς ἰδίαν φύσιν τὸ ἀσθενῆσαι παθῶν συγκεχώρηκε τῇ σαρκί Cyr.*Nest*.5.3(p.98.32; 6¹.131B); 2. intrans.; a. *abate, slacken, cease* from, c. genit. ~εῖναι τοῦ τόνου Clem.*paed*.3.11(p.269.4; M.8.632A); τῶν...σημείων ~ίησιν [sc. Christ] Chrys.*hom*.*47.1 in Mt*.(7.493C); ~εῖναι τῆς κακίας id.*hom*.*4.4 in Phil*.(11.224C); Cyr.*Is*.3.4(2.484D); med. οὐδὲν προθυμίας ~ειμένη Meth.*symp*.6.1(p.64.7; M.18.113A); b. *desist, give way, condescend*, ref. Ac.26:2,3 ὁρᾷς Παῦλον ...πῶς ἐστι ~ιείς; Chrys.*hom*.*11.1 in Col*.(11.405A); οὐδὲ δημοσίᾳ ἐγκληθεὶς ~ῆκεν id.*hom*.*28.3 in 2Cor*.(10.637E); id.*hom*.*34.2 in Heb*.(12.315D); τὸ πραότητι ~εῖναι Isid.Pel.*epp*.4.205(M.78.1297C).

***καθυφικνέομαι**, καθυφίκοιτο perh. f.l. for καθυφήκατο, Cyr.*glaph.Gen*.5(1.159D).

καθωραΐζω, *beautify*, ‡Proc.G.*Pr*.8:27(M.87.1297A); pass., met., of soul, Meth.*creat*.1(p.494.10; M.18.333A); Gr.Agr.*Eccl*.1.2(M.98.756A).

***καθωρισμένως**, *in a binding way* κ. ὅρκον εἶναι τούτῳ τὸν βίον Clem.*str*.7.8(p.37.23; M.9.472A).

***κάθωρος**, *hourly* κ. στεναγμός Jo.Clim.*scal*.6(M.88.793B); v.l. for καθ' ὥραν Dan.Raith.*v.Jo.Clim*.(M.88.600B).

καθώσπερ, *just as*, ‡Jo.D.*Artem*.49(M.96.1297B).

καί, *and*; contrasted with δέ, ref. Ps.36:20 [οἱ ἁμαρτωλοὶ ἀπολοῦνται· οἱ δὲ ἐχθροὶ τοῦ κυρίου...ὡσεὶ καπνὸς ἐξέλιπον] ἡ τοῦ συνδέσμου ἐναλλαγὴ διαφορὰν προσώπων εἰργάσατο· καὶ ἄλλους μὲν ὑποβάλλει νοεῖν τοὺς ἁμαρτωλούς, ἄλλους δὲ ἐχθρούς. ... Ἀκύλας δέ, καὶ ὁ Σύμμαχος, ἀντὶ τοῦ 'δὲ' τὸν 'καὶ' σύνδεσμον τεθεικότες, τοὺς αὐτοὺς ἔδειξαν ἁμαρτωλοὺς καὶ...ἐχθρούς Thdt.ad loc.(1.837f.); in doxology, compared with σύν: εἰ...ἀντὶ τῆς 'καί,' τῇ 'σύν' ἐθελήσαιμεν χρήσασθαι, τί διάφορον πεποιηκότες ἐσόμεθα;...ὁ γὰρ εἰπὼν 'σὺν τῷ πατρὶ' τὸν υἱὸν εἶναι ὁμοῦ τήν τε τῶν ὑποστάσεων ἰδιότητα καὶ τὸ ἀχώριστον τῆς κοινωνίας ἔδειξεν...ὁ μὲν 'καὶ' σύνδεσμος τὸ κοινὸν τῆς ἐνεργείας παρίστησιν, ἡ δὲ 'σύν' πρόθεσις τὴν κοινωνίαν πως συνενδείκνυται Bas.*Spir*.59(3.50A; M.32.176C).

***Καϊάνισται**, οἱ, v. **Καϊνισταί*.

***Καϊανοί**, οἱ, v. **Καϊνισταί*.

καινίζ-ω, 1. *renew* Σολομὼν...ἀρχαῖον ἐκαίνισε θεσμὸν ἑορτῆς Nonn.*par.Jo*.10:22(M.43.836B); of spiritual renewal ~ων εἰς σωτηρίαν τὸν κατηχούμενον ἄνθρωπον Clem.*str*.7.9(p.39.6; M.9.473C); ref. 2Cor.5:17 κύριος παλαιὰ ~ων *ib*.3.12(p.233.22; M.8.1184A); 2. *make as something new*, ref. Creation οὗτός ἐσ[τιν ὁ] τὸν οὐρανὸν καὶ τὴν γῆν καιν[ίσας] Mel.*pass*.104 p.30.2.

καινισμός, ὁ, *renewal*, Max.*ep*.22(M.91.605B); *innovation* ὥστε τὴν πίστιν...μηδαμῶς συγχωρῆσαι κ. τινι διαφθείρεσθαι Leo Mag.*ep*.45(p.48.11; M.54.836B); νεώτερος κατὰ τῶν ἐκκλησιῶν κ. *Ep*.ap.CSyr.*act*.(*ACO* 3 p.93.32; H.2.1368A).

***Καϊνισταί**, οἱ, members of Gnost. sect stemming from Simonians, taking name from Cain, whom they honoured, Thdt.*haer*.1.1(4.289); forms *Καϊάνισται*, Clem.*str*.7.17(p.76.27; M.9.553A); Or.*Cels*.3.13(p.213.9; M.11.936C); *Καϊανοί*, Epiph.*haer*.38.1(p.62.16; M.41.653C); *Καϊνοί*, Thdt.*haer*.1.15(4.309).

***καινόδοξος**, *holding novel opinions*, Gr.Naz.*carm*.2.1.11.1760(M.37.1152A).

***καινοειδής**, *new in form*, Or.*Cels*.8.17(p.234.6; M.11.1540C).

***Καϊνοί**, οἱ, v. **Καϊνισταί*.

***καινοποίησις**, ἡ, *new creation*, ref. Inc. οὐ τῆς θεότητος μεταποίησιν...ἀλλὰ τῆς ἀνθρωπότητος κ. ‡Ath.*Apoll*.2.5(M.26.1140B).

καινοποιός, *making new*, *T.Neph*.1.12; τοῦ...κ. πνεύματος Gr.Naz.*or*.44.1(M.36.608B); ἀρετῆς...τῆς καινοποιοῦ Anast.Ant.*redit*.(p.255).

καινοπρεπής, *novel*; neut. as subst., *newness, novelty*, ref. Inc., Leont.B.*arg.Sev*.(M.86.1921B) cit. s. καινοτομέω.

καινός, *new*; 1. of the new covenant, v. διαθήκη; of the New Testament scriptures, v. διαθήκη; abs. ἡ κ., v. παλαιός; 2. ref. Pss. 32:3, 39:4, etc. ᾄδει...τῆς κ. ἁρμονίας τὸν ἀΐδιον νόμον, τὸν φερώνυμον τοῦ θεοῦ, τὸ ᾆσμα τὸ κ., τὸ Λευιτικόν Clem.*prot*.1(p.4.19; M.8.56A); ὅρα τὸ ᾆσμα τὸ κ. ὅσον ἴσχυσεν...τοῦτό τοι καὶ τὸ πᾶν ἐκόσμησεν ἐμμελῶς καὶ τῶν στοιχείων τὴν διαφωνίαν εἰς τάξιν ἐνέτεινε συμφωνίας, ἵνα δὴ ὅλος ὁ κόσμος αὐτῷ ἁρμονία γένηται *ib*.(p.5.30; 57B); of Christ, *ib*.(p.7.16; 61B); τὸ κ. ... ᾆσμα...τὴν κ. χάριν ἐξαγγέλλουσα τῆς ἐκκλησίας Meth.*symp*.6.5(p.69.23; M.18.121A); ἐπειδὴ τῶν παλαιῶν πραγμάτων κηρύττει μεταβολήν, καὶ κ. τινα πολιτείαν προαγορεύει, εἰκότως καὶ ᾆσμα κ. κελεύει προσενεγκεῖν τῷ θεῷ Thdt.*Ps*.97:1(1.1301); 3. exeg. Jer.31:22 ἡ οὖν ἐκ τοῦ σωτῆρος σωτηρία κτισθεῖσα κ., καθὼς λέγει Ἱερεμίας, ἔκτισεν ἡμῖν σωτηρίαν, καὶ ὡς Ἀκύλας φησίν, 'ἔκτισε κύριος κ. ἐν τῇ θηλείᾳ', τουτέστιν ἐν τῇ Μαρίᾳ. οὐδὲν γὰρ ἐκτίσθη καινὸν ἐν τῇ θηλείᾳ, εἰ μὴ τὸ ἐκ τῆς παρθένου Μαρίας τεχθὲν ἄνευ συνουσίας κυριακὸν σῶμα †Ath.*exp.fid*.3(M.25.205B); Thdt.*Jer*.31:22(2.548); cf.Chrys.*fr.in Jer*. ad loc.(M.64.980A); 4. exeg. 2Cor.5:17, Gal.6:15 (κ. κτίσις) Clem.*prot*.11(p.80.22; M.8.232B); Ath.*Ar*.1.16(M.26.45C); of resurrection, Meth.*symp*.9.1(p.114.9; M.18.177A); 5. of κ. ἄνθρωπος (ref. Eph.2:15, etc.) τὸν κ. ἄνθρωπον Ἰησοῦν Ign.*Eph*.20.1; κ. δὲ ἄνθρωπος θεοῦ πνεύματι ἁγίῳ μεταπεπλασμένος Clem.*prot*.11(p.79.19; M.8.229B); ἐκ τῆς...θεοτόκου...τὴν τοῦ Ἀδὰμ πλάσιν καὶ ποίησιν κ. ἀνεστήσατο ‡Ath.*Apoll*.1.13(M.26.1116B); μόνος...οὗτος ὡς ἀληθῶς κ. κυρίως ὀνομάζεται ἄνθρωπος Gr.Nyss.

*Eun.*3(2 p.19.11; M.45.584B); κ. τινα τὴν θεανδρικὴν ἐνέργειαν ἡμῖν πεπολιτευμένος Dion.Ar.*ep.*4(M.3.1072C); **6.** of gospel in gen. καί μου τὸ ᾆσμα τὸ σωτήριον μὴ κ. οὕτως ὑπολάβῃς ὡς σκεῦος ἢ ὡς οἰκίαν ...παλαιὰ δὲ ἡ πλάνη, κ. δὲ ἡ ἀλήθεια φαίνεται Clem.*prot.*1(p.7.4; M.8.61A); εἰπὲ τῷ διενεχθέντι πρὸς σέ,...ὅτι κ. τινα καὶ παρὰ τὴν ἀρχαίαν συνήθειαν, εἰσηγήσατο πολιτείαν τὸ εὐαγγέλιον, ὅτι·...τὴν πονηρὰν συνήθειαν καινότης μόνη παύειν πέφυκε. ... ὥστε...θαυμάζειν εἰκὸς ἦν, εἰ μεταβολῆς ἕνεκα πραγμάτων, δεῦρ' ἐπιφοιτήσας, μηδὲν κ. ἐπὶ τῶν νόμων παρεῖχε...οὐ γὰρ δεινὸν καινοτομεῖν εἰ τοῦ λυσιτελοῦντος ἡ μερὶς τῷ κ. προσείη Isid.Pel.*epp.*2.46(M.78.488A).

καινότης, ἡ, *newness*, esp. of Inc. and of spiritual renewal οἱ ἐν παλαιοῖς πράγμασιν ἀναστραφέντες εἰς κ. ἐλπίδος ἦλθον Ign.*Magn.*9.1; παρῴχηκε γὰρ τὰ ἀρχαῖα, καὶ μετακεχώρηκεν εἰς κ. τῶν πραγμάτων ἡ φύσις Cyr.*Soph.*40(3.618D); id.*Jo.*11.10(4.991B) cit. s. ἀνακτίζω; ἀνακαίνισις γὰρ γέγονε καινότητος ἐπανάληψις Gel.Cyz.*h.e.*2.24.10(M.85.1350D); ἀπέκδυσαι τὴν παλαιότητα καὶ ἔνδυσαι τὴν κ. ‡Meth.*Sym. et Ann.*7(M.18.365A); of the gospel, ref. accusation that it is a strange innovation, Isid.Pel.*epp.*2.46(M.78.488A) cit. s. καινός.

καινοτομ-έω, **1.** *innovate*; of heret. opinions, Clem.*str.*7.17(p.76.4; M.9.552A); Ath.*ep.encycl.*6(p.176.1; M.25.236B); Bas.*ep.*226.3(3.348C; M.32.848C) cit. s. καινοτομία; *inaugurate* a doctrine, Or.*dial.*12(p.146.14); *change, develop* meaning of a term, Leont.B.*arg.Sev.*(M.86.1921B,1924D); **2.** *make into something novel*, ref. Inc. τὰς φύσεις ἐκαινοτόμησεν τὸ καινοπρεπὲς τοῦ μυστηρίου Leont.B.*arg.Sev.*(M.86.1921B); παρθένος...~οῦσα τὴν φύσιν τῇ συνόδῳ τῶν ἀντικειμένων Max.*ambig.*(M.91.1052D); id.*ep.*19(M.91.592D); Anast.S.*hod.*2(M.89.72B) cit. s. καινοτομία; ἐν σοὶ [sc. BMV] καὶ νόμοι φύσεως ~ηθήσονται Jo.D.*fr.*(M.96.816B); **3.** abs., *make a new state of affairs*, Isid.Pel.*epp.*2.46(M.78.488B).

καινοτόμημα, τό, *new thing, innovation*, Epiph.*haer.*77.24(p.437.16; M.42.676C).

καινοτομία, ἡ, *innovation, new departure*, ref. Inc. κ. ἐστὶ τὸ κατὰ πάντα τρόπον παρηλλαγμένον τοῦ νόμου τῆς κοινῆς φύσεως, καὶ ἐν μηδενὶ τῇ τῶν ἀνθρώπων συνηθείᾳ ἐξομοιούμενον. τοῦτον δὲ τὸν ὅρον ἀναγκαῖον ἐπίστασθαι, διὰ τοὺς κακῶς νοοῦντας τὴν κ. ἐν τῷ Χριστῷ. εἰ γὰρ ἐκαινοτόμησε τὴν φύσιν ἀσπόρως γεννηθείς, ἀλλ' ὅμως μετὰ τὸν τόκον...πάντα ταῦτα [sc. physical growth] οὐ κατὰ κ. εἶχεν, ἀλλὰ καθ' ὁμοιότητα ἡμῶν χωρὶς ἁμαρτίας Anast.S.*hod.*2(M.89.72B,C); κ. δὲ κυρίως οὐ μόνον τὸ γεννηθῆναι χρονικῶς κατὰ σάρκα τὸν...λόγον, ἀλλὰ καὶ τὸ δοῦναι σάρκα τὴν ἡμετέραν φύσιν ἄνευ σπορᾶς Max.*ambig.*(M.91.1313C); id.*ep.*19(M.91.592D); Job.Mon.*inc.*(M.86.3320A); of believers, *newness* ζῶντες δὲ ἐν κ. κατὰ τὸ εὐαγγέλιον Ammon.*Jo.*19:18(M.85.1512C); in thinking or terminology, esp. in dogma ὀνόματα ἡμῖν ἀρκεῖ ἐκεῖνα ὁμολογεῖν, ἃ παρελάβομεν παρὰ τῆς ἁγίας γραφῆς, καὶ τὴν ἐπὶ τούτοις κ. ἀποφεύγειν Bas.*ep.*175(3.263A; M.32.653A); διαβάλλουσιν ἡμᾶς ὡς καινοτομοῦντας περὶ τοῦ πνεύματος τοῦ ἁγίου. ἐρωτήσατε οὖν τίς ἡ κ.; *ib.*226.3(348C; M.848C); καινοτομίαν κατὰ τῆς εὐαγγελικῆς πίστεως κινεῖσθαι μεμάθηκα Thdt.*ep.*146(4.1258); ref. Arians τὰς δὲ κ. ἀποστρέφεσθαι, καὶ διδάσκειν τοὺς λαοὺς μὴ προσέχειν πνεύμασι πλάνης Ath.*ep.Aeg.Lib.*21(M.25.588C); ref. Eunomius ἡ περὶ τὴν τάξιν [sc. of Trin.] κ. ... ὅλης τῆς πίστεώς ἐστιν ἄρνησις Bas.*ep.*52.4(146D; M.396C); of Aëtius, Gr.Nyss.*Eun.*1(p.33.3; M.45.260C); of Manicheanism, Eus.*h.e.*7.31.1(M.20.720D); of Apollinarius, Thdt.*eran.*3(4.257).

καινοτόμος, *innovating*, Chrys.*hom.*33.5 *in Mt.*(7.384D); in accusations of heresy νεωτεροποιοὺς ἡμᾶς καὶ κ. ... ἀποκαλοῦσιν Bas.*Spir.*13(3.10B; M.32.88A); Ἀπολλινάριον τὸν...κ. Nil.*epp.*2.49(M.79.221B).

καινουργέω, **1.** *make new*; of God renewing heaven and earth through Logos, Just.*dial.*113.5(M.6.737A); of man's renewal through H. Ghost, Cyr.*ador.*17(1.594B); ὁ δημιουργὸς καινουργῆσαι τὴν ἀμαυρωθεῖσαν εἰκόνα θελήσας, ὅλην τὴν φύσιν ἀναλαβών, πολλῷ τῶν προτέρων ἀμείνους ἐνετύπωσε χαρακτῆρας Thdt.*eran.*2(4.74); of Inc. as renewal of Adam, ‡Nil.*fr.ascens.*3(M.79.1500D); of inauguration of new life for those in Hades through Christ's descent, Bas.Sel.*or.*26.2(M.85.308A); of man's nature as renewed through dominical festivals, Jo.Nic.*nativ.*(M.96.1448D); **2.** *innovate, devise anew*, Eus.*h.e.*8.6.1(M.20.752B).

***καινούργημα**, τό, *innovation*, Geo.Pis.*Pers.*2.150(M.92.1221A), v. *κενούργημα.

καινουργία, ἡ, **1.** *renewal, recreation*; of man through Christ, Cyr.*Is.*5.2(2.771A); Jo.D.*carm.theoph.*32(p.210; M.96.828A); baptismal, Didym.*Trin.*2.14(M.39.700B); **2.** *innovation*; of a novel torture, Eus.*m.P.*2.3(p.909.23; νεουργίαν M.20.1468A).

***καινοφαής**, *new-shining*, *Orac.Sib.*8.476.

καινοφωνία, ἡ, *new term, untraditional expression*, of heresy μὴ ὃν παρέλαβε τρόπον δοξολογίας φυλάττων, ἀλλ' ἑαυτῷ κ., εἰς ἀρέσκειαν ἀνθρώπων, ἐπινοῶν Bas.*ep.*52.4(3.146C; M.32.396B); ἀντεισαχθῆναι δὲ τὴν παράλογον ταύτην κ., ἵνα νοῦς ἔνσαρκος ὁ μονογενής, καὶ μὴ σοφία κατονομάζηται Gr.Nyss.*Apoll.*36(M.45.1205B); Basilisc.*encycl.*(p.50.22); Eust.Mon.*ep.*(M.86.905A); τὸν ἀοίδιμον Ἰωάννην, τὸν πάσης κ. ἐξοριστήν Jo.D.*trisag.*26(M.95.57B), v. κενοφωνία.

***καινοφωνῶς**, *in novel terms, with new words*; of heretical doctrine, *Symb.CP*(681)(H.3.1397D).

καινόω, s.v.l., *make new*, Jo.Mosch.*prat.*200(M.87.3089A), perh. f.l. for κοινόω.

καίνωσις, ἡ, *innovation*; of Inc., Cyr.ap.*cat.Heb.*suppl.5:4(p.476.29).

καίριος, *important, crucial* οὐδὲ κ. τίς ἐστιν ἡ ἐν τούτοις [sc. gospels] δοκοῦσα διαφωνία Vict.*Mc.*6:7(p.323.20); of an important text τὸ κ. ὧδε ἐπιλεγόμενον Mac.Mgn.*apocr.*2.20(p.37.2); of principal doctrines, Gr.Naz.*ep.*7(M.37.33C); τὰ κ. τῆς τῶν πατέρων ἐκθέσεως Thdot.Anc.*exp.symb.*11(M.77.1329C); of principal customs handed down by tradition, Bas.*Spir.*66(3.54D; M.32.188A); in gen., Gr.Naz.*ep.*183(300B).

***καιροθέος**, *time-serving*, Gr.Naz.*carm.*2.1.10.24(M.37.1028A).

***καιρολουσία**, ἡ, *bathing-time*, *Const.App.*1.9.4.

καιρός, ὁ, *season, time*; **1.** *fit time, opportunity* κ. ... μετανοεῖν Ign.*Smyrn.*9.1; εἰσῆλθες εἰς ἀγῶνα, κάμε τὸν δρόμον. ἄλλον κ. τοιοῦτον οὐκ ἔχεις Cyr.H.*procatech.*6(M.33.345A); Chrys.*hom.*3.4 *in Eph.*(11.22B); ref. worship δοξάζουσα τὸν κύριον ἐν παντὶ κ. Herm.*mand.*5.2.3; τὸν κ. τοῦ πάσχα Or.*schol.in Cant.*6:10,11(M.17.280A); κ. τε ἑορτῶν ἐκκλησίαις ἐδόξαζον Eus.*v.C.*4.23(p.126.5; M.20.1172A); μὴ μόνον ἐν τῷ κ. τῶν κατηχουμένων, ἀλλὰ καὶ ἐν τῷ κ. τῶν πιστῶν Chrys.*hom.*2.8 *in 2Cor.*(10.440E); δίδοται ὁ κ. παρὰ τοῦ ἀρχιερέως τῷ πρώτῳ τῶν ἱερέων μέλλοντι ἄρχεσθαι τῆς θείας μυσταγωγίας. οὗτος δὲ ὁ κ. σχηματίζει τὸν περὶ τοῦ προφήτου [ref. Is.7:14] ἀναφωνηθέντα κ. τῆς προδρόμου γεννήσεως καὶ τοῦ Χριστοῦ...ἐπιδημίας ‡Sophr.H.*liturg.*11(M.87.3992A); **2.** of the present age and age to come μισήσωμεν τὴν πλάνην τοῦ νῦν κ., ἵνα εἰς τὸν μέλλοντα ἀγαπηθῶμεν *Barn.*4.1; τὸν κ. τοῦ ἀνόμου *ib.*15.5; κ. τῆς ἀναψύξεως Or.*schol.in Cant.*4:5(M.17.272C); κατὰ τὸν παρόντα κ. Meth.*res.*25(p.381.6; M.18.328C); Chrys.*hom.*43.4 *in Mt.*(7.464C); **3.** of ages of history οὐδὲ ...τῆς ἀδικίας κ. ... ἀλλὰ τὸν νῦν τῆς δικαιοσύνης *Diogn.*9.1; ἐν τῷ κ. τῷ Ἰουδαϊκῷ Chrys.*hom.*1.4 *in 1Thess.*(11.431A); κ. εὔθετον λέγει τῆς καινῆς διαθήκης τὴν πολιτείαν Thdt.*Ps.*31:6(1803); ἔσχατοι κ. Ign.*Eph.*11.1; λόγος...ἐν ἐσχάτοις κ. ἄνθρωπος...γεγονὼς Cyr.*expl.xii cap.*1(p.17.18; 6[1].148A); **4.** of time compared with eternity ἐπεὶ θεὸς ὁ κ. παρὰ τοῖς φαύλοις νομίζεται, δείκνυσιν ὡς κ. καὶ χρόνων αὐτὸς ποιητής Proc.G.*Gen.*9:4(M.87.292C); τὸ λοιπὸν δρόμου και[ρο]ῦ χρόνου αἰῶνος ἀνάπαυσιν ἐν σιγῇ *PRyl.*3.463; **5.** met., exeg. Ac.1:7 χρόνους δὲ καὶ κ. μή μοι νόει αἰσθητούς, ἀλλὰ διαστήματά τινα γνώσεως ὑπὸ τοῦ νοητοῦ ἡλίου γινόμενα Evagr.Pont.*ep.*7(M.32.260B).

καιροσκοπ-έω, *watch for opportunity*, Marc.Er.*opusc.*7.5(M.65.1077A); *ib.*10.10(1133C); *watch for opportunity of* τὸν αὐτοῦ ~οῦντι θάνατον Pall.*v.Chrys.*11(p.64.9; M.47.36).

***καιροσκόπος**, ὁ, *one who watches his opportunity* κ. δή τις πονηρὸς τὸν αἰῶνα τοῦτον περικέχηνεν Gr.Thaum.*Eccl.*3:11(M.10.996B).

καιροφυλακέω (καιροφυλακτέω), **1.** *observe the times* of stars, Dion.Al.ap.Eus.*p.e.*14.25(778A; M.21.1280B); **2.** *watch for the opportunity of* τὴν τοῦ πατρὸς τελευτὴν εἰς τὴν τῶν παίδων τιμωρίαν ἐκαιροφυλάκεις Isid.Pel.*epp.*5.86(M.78.1376C); *watch for, mark down*, of demons καιροφυλακτοῦντες ἡμᾶς †Chrys.*hom.prec.*1(2.783B).

***καισαρίκιος**, *belonging to a Caesar* τὰ κ. περικεφάλαια Thphn.*chron.*p.374(M.108.896B).

***καισαροειδής**, ὁ, *the seeming Caesar* περιέθηκαν δὲ αὐτῷ καὶ βασιλικὸν διάδημα, ὥστε μηδένα γινώσκειν, εἰ μὴ αὐτὸς οὗτος εἴη ὁ καῖσαρ...ὑπερνικήσας ὁ κ. τὸν τῶν Γόθθων βασιλέα Agath.*v.Gr.Ill.*20.

καίω, *burn*; perf. ptcpl. pass. κεκαυμένος, of Manicheans and encratite sects, ref. 1Tim.4:2 κεκαυτηριασμένους, μορφὴν εὐσεβοῦς καυτῆρος πρὸς ἀπάτην ἔχοντας, ἢ κεκαυμένους, οὓς ἡ δρόσος τοῦ ἁγίου πνεύματος οὐκ ἐπίανεν...οὓς ἡ φλόγωσις τῆς Χαλδαϊκῆς καμίνου κατέπρησεν Mac.Mgn.*apocr.*3.43(p.151.15).

κακεντρέχεια, ἡ, *activity in wickedness, perversity*, Bas.*hom.*12.6(2.103A; M.31.400A); of Devil, Or.*exc.in Ps.*1:1(M.17.152A); ref. one falling into heresy ἐξ ἀφελείας ἢ κ. Cyr.H.*catech.*7.7; ref. Nestorius, Anast.S.*hod.*20(M.89.277A).

***κακεντρεχῶς**, *wickedly, perversely*, Or.*exc.in Ps.*1:1(M.17.152A): Bas.*ep.*233.2(3.356D; M.32.865C).

***κακέσχατος**, ὁ, *utter villain*, Ephr.1.312E; Anast.Ap.*a.Max.*2.27 M.90.164C).

***κακευχία**, ἡ, *sad condition, distress*, Max.*ep.*3(M.91.412A).

κακηγκάκως** (κακιγκάκως**), *wretchedly*, †Jo.D.*B.J.*24(M.96.1088A); κακιγκάκως *M.Pers.*9.5(p.477.5); *M.Ariadn.*10(p.129.19).

***κακήκοια, ἡ**, *listening to slander*, Nil.*Eulog.*16(M.79.1113D).

κακία, ἡ, *evil*;

A. moral; **1.** def. and descriptions διπλοῦ...ὄντος τοῦ τῆς κ. εἴδους, τοῦ μὲν μετὰ ἀπάτης καὶ τοῦ λανθάνειν, τοῦ δὲ μετὰ βίας ἄγοντος Clem.*str.*2.6(p.127.1; M.8.961A); ἡ κ. κακὴν φύσιν ἔχει καὶ οὔποτ' ἂν καλοῦ τινος ὑποσταίη γεωργὸς γενέσθαι *ib.*1.1(p.13.11; 708B); ἡ κ. οὐκ ἄν τι ἐνάρετον ποιήσαι *ib.*6.17(p.513.30; M.9.392B); ὁ πλοῦτος οὐκ ὀρθῶς κυβερνώμενος ἀκρόπολίς ἐστι κακίας id.*paed.*2.3 (p.180.19; M.8.437B); ὄφις ἀλληγορεῖται ἡδονὴ...κ. γηΐνη id.*prot.*11 (p.78.28; M.8.228C); as negation of being ἐξειλήφασιν...τινες τῷ ἀνυπόστατον εἶναι τὴν κ. (οὔτε γὰρ ἦν ἀπ' ἀρχῆς οὔτε εἰς τὸν αἰῶνα ἔσται) ταῦτ' εἶναι τὰ 'μηδέν' Or.*Jo.*2.13(7; p.68.26; M.14.133D); δόγμα κάλλιστον περὶ τοῦ ἀόριστον εἶναι τὴν κ. id.*Cels.*4.63(p.334.8; M.11.1129C); dist. from τὸ κακόν, *ib.*4.66(p.336.29; 1133D); οὐ κατὰ τὸν τῆς οὐσίας λόγον ὑπάρχει κ., κατὰ δὲ τὸν τῆς προαιρέσεως τρόπον Meth.*arbitr.*13(p.180.6; M.18.264A); ὅτ' ἂν...ἐν διαστροφῇ τοῦ κατὰ φύσιν γένηται, τότε κ. τῆς ψυχῆς λέγεται Ath.*v.Anton.*20(M.26.873B); ἐν ὑποστάσει καὶ καθ' ἑαυτὴν εἶναι τὴν κ. censured as pagan error, id. *gent.*6(M.25.12D); πέφυκε πᾶσα κ. ἢ κατ' ἔλλειψιν, ἢ καθ' ὑπέρπτωσιν ἀρετῆς ἐνεργεῖσθαι Gr.Nyss.*v.Mos.*(M.44.420A); οὐ γὰρ ἔστιν ἄλλως κακίας γένεσιν ἐννοῆσαι, ἢ ἀρετῆς ἀπουσίαν id.*or.catech.*5(p.28.1; M.45.24D); ἡ κ. λογισμοὺς ἔχει πολλοὺς Mac.Aeg.*hom.*40.5(M.34.765B); οὔτε ἡ ἀρετὴ οὔτε ἡ κ. μένει ἀμετάπτωτος...κ. κακίαν ἐφέλκεται Nil. *epp.*2.124f.(M.79.253B); negative view discussed and elaborated, Dion.Ar.*d.n.*4.19(M.3.716Dff.); κ., οὐκ ὄν, ἀλλὰ τοῦ ὄντος, τουτέστι τοῦ νόμου τοῦ θεοῦ ἑκούσιος παρακοή Jo.D.*Man.*1.43(M.94.1545D); κ. ... ἡ τῆς τάξεως λύσις, εἴτουν ἀταξία *ib.*1.47(1548D); ἔστιν ἡ κ. ἡ τῶν φυσικῶν δυνάμεων παράχρησις *ib.*1.14(1517C); τὸ γὰρ τῆς κ. ὄνομα ὁμώνυμόν ἐστι. δύο γὰρ σημαίνει· ποτὲ μὲν γὰρ σημαίνει τὴν τῆς ἀρετῆς στέρησιν· ποτὲ δὲ τὴν τῆς χαρᾶς, τουτέστι τοῦ ἐπιθυμουμένου ...τοῦτο οὖν ἐστι κ., τὸ τῷ μὴ ὄντι ὡς ὄντι χρήσασθαι *ib.*1.60(1553A); **2.** origin; **a.** natural διὰ τὴν ἀπιστίαν τὴν ἀνθρωπίνην γένεσιν ἴσχει κ. Clem.*paed.*1.8(p.131.1; M.8.333B); ἡ δεισιδαιμονία...κ. ἀνοήτου γέγονε πηγή id.*prot.*3(p.34.1; M.8.129C); love of money and pleasure, id. *str.*7.12(p.54.8; M.9.504B); τὸ γὰρ ἑκάστου ἡγεμονικὸν αἴτιον τῆς ὑποστάσης ἐν αὐτῷ κ. Or.*Cels.*4.66(p.336.29; M.11.1133D); ἡμεῖς δὲ ἑαυτοῖς ἐκτίσαμεν τὴν κ. id.*hom.2.1 in Jer.*(p.16.24; M.13.277B); opinion attributed to Or. οὐ τὸ σῶμα τοῦτο παραίτιον κακίας ἐστίν, ἀλλ' αὐτὴ ἡ ψυχή Meth.*res.*1.29(p.261.7; M.41.1140A); discussed, *ib.*1.31(p.264.8; 1141A); through Adam's transgression, Mac.Aeg.*hom.*24.2(M.34.664A,B); worldly preoccupations, *ib.*40.7(768A); πολλὴ νομὴ τῆς κ. ἔνδον ἐστί *ib.*41.2(768D); ἐξ ἀρχῆς μὲν οὐκ ἦν ἡ κ. ... ἄνθρωποι δὲ ταύτην ὕστερον ἐπινοεῖν ἤρξαντο Ath.*gent.*2(M.25.5C); κ. ψυχῆς ἐστιν. αἰτία δὲ...οὐδεμία, ἀλλ' ἡ τῶν κρειττόνων ἀποστροφή *ib.*5(12B); αἱ κ. ἐκ τῆς αὐτῆς καρδίας ἐξερχόμεναι id.*ep.Aeg.Lib.*11(M.25.561B); consequence of this view ἐπειδὴ γὰρ ἔξω τῆς προαιρέσεως ἡ κ. εἶναι φύσιν οὐκ ἔχει, ὅταν πᾶσα προαίρεσις ἐν τῷ θεῷ γένηται, εἰς παντελῆ ἀφανισμὸν ἡ κ. μεταχωρήσειε [M. μὴ χωρήσει], τῷ μηδὲν αὐτῆς ὑπολειφθῆναι δοχεῖον Gr.Nyss.*anim.et res.*(M.46.101A); κ. being a wrong use of κινήματα indifferent in themselves such as θυμός and ἐπιθυμία, *ib.*(89A); κ. due to sin committed in previous existence (Origenist) Gr.Nyss.*ib.*(112C); theory criticized, *ib.*(113B–116A); ὅτι δὲ οὐδὲ κακίας αἴτιον τῇ ψυχῇ τὸ σῶμα, δῆλον ἐκ τοῦ δυνατὸν εἶναι ἄνευ σώματος παρυφίστασθαι κ., ὥσπερ ἐν δαίμοσι...πῶς δὲ γεννᾷ καὶ τρέφει τὴν φύσιν ἡ ὕλη κακὴ οὖσα;...εἰ δὲ φαῖεν, αὐτὴν μὲν οὐ ποιεῖν κ. ἐν ψυχαῖς, ἐφέλκεσθαι δὲ αὐτάς, πῶς ἔσται τοῦτο ἀληθές; πολλαὶ γὰρ αὐτῶν εἰς τὸ ἀγαθὸν βλέπουσι...ὥστε οὐκ ἐξ ὕλης ἐν ψυχαῖς τὸ κακόν, ἀλλ' ἐξ ἀτάκτου καὶ πλημμελοῦς κινήσεως Dion.Ar.*d.n.*4.27f.(M.3.728Dff.); **b.** preternatural; demons, Just.*2apol.*5.4(M.6.452C); Tat. *orat.*14(p.15.12; M.6.836B); ἀπό τινων πτερορρυησάντων καὶ κατακολουθησάντων τῷ πρώτῳ πτερορρυήσαντι ὑπέστη ἡ κ. Or.*Cels.*6.43 (p.114.17; M.11.1365B); Mac.Aeg.*hom.*24.3(664C); Devil called ὁ τῆς κ. πατήρ Ath.*v.Anton.*28(M.26.885A); ὁ τῆς κ. εὑρετής id.*ep.Aeg.Lib.*1(M.25.540B); Jo.D.*hom.*4.8(M.96.609B); **3.** opp.; **a.** ἀρετή, Just. *2apol.*7.6(M.6.456C); *ib.*9.1(460A); Athenag.*leg.*3.1(M.6.896C); Clem. *paed.*2.10(p.223.11; M.8.529A); and logos as identified with virtue, Or.*Jo.*32.7(p.444.2; M.14.769C); τὰ ἀπὸ κ. ἔργα ἐκτρέπεσθαι, τὴν δ' ἀρετὴν σέβειν id.*Cels.*5.39(p.43.16; M.11.1244B); Ath.*Dion.*20(p.61.26; M.25.509C); †Nil.*vit.*1(M.79.1140B); hence enemy of 'gnostic', Clem.*str.*7.11(p.47.13; M.9.492A); **b.** χάρις, esp. in Mac. Aeg. εἰσὶ γάρ τινες, ὅτι σύνεστιν αὐτοῖς ἡ χάρις...σύνεστι δὲ καὶ ἡ κ. ἔνδον *hom.*17.4(M.34.625D); *ib.*17.6(628B); οἱ κατεχόμενοι ἐν βάθει ὑπὸ... τῆς χάριτος...ἔτι εἰσὶ δοῦλοι...τῷ μέρει τῆς κ. *ib.*17.7(628C); struggle between κ. and χάρις in men, *ib.*26.10(680D); *ib.*26.22(689A,B); **4.** influence on men in guise of virtue ἡ γὰρ κ., πρόβλημα ἑαυτῆς τῶν πράξεων τὰ προσόντα τῇ ἀρετῇ καὶ ὄντως ὄντα καλὰ διὰ μιμήσεως ἀφθάρτων περιβαλλομένη...δουλαγωγεῖ τοὺς χαμαιπετεῖς τῶν ἀνθρώπων, τὰ προσόντα αὐτῇ φαῦλα τῇ ἀρετῇ περιθεῖσα Just.*2apol.*11.7(M.6.461C); ἢ γὰρ ἂν ἄπρακτος ἦν ἡ κ., μηδενὶ προσκεχρωσμένη καλῷ τῷ πρὸς ἐπιθυμίαν αὐτῆς ἐφελκομένῳ τὸν ἀπατώμενον Gr.Nyss.*hom.opif.*20(M.44.200A); πέφυκε γάρ πως ἡ κ. τῷ τοῦ καλοῦ προσχήματι ἐγκαλύπτεσθαι Jo.D.*hom.*4.9(M.96.609C); **5.** effects κ. ... τὴν ἀνθρώπων ἐπιβόσκεται φθοράν Clem.*prot.*1(p.6.34; M.8.60B); cf.id.*paed.*2.6 (p.189.10; M.8.456A); death and corruption, Ath.*inc.*5.3(M.25.105B); ἐκπίπτει τις ἀπὸ τοῦ πνεύματος διά τινα κ. id.*Ar.*3.25(M.26.376C); blinding of mind, id.*h.Ar.*71(p.222.8; M.25.777C); but κ. also regarded as temptation effecting chastisement, Mac.Aeg.*hom.*16.3 (M.34.616A); peace with Satan, *ib.*27.2(693D); excluding angels from heavenly ἁρμονία, Dion.Ar.*e.h.*6.3.6(M.3.537A); **6.** remedies; **a.** divine; providence bringing good out of evil, Clem.*str.*1.17(p.55.24; M.8.801A); κἂν συγχρήσηται τῇ κ. τῶν φαύλων εἰς τὴν διάταξιν τοῦ παντὸς ὁ θεός Or.*Cels.*4.70(p.339.26; M.11.1140A); through Christ's teaching, Clem.*paed.*3.8(p.261.25ff.; M.8.613C); through Inc., Mac. Aeg.*hom.*28.3(M.34.712C); through baptism, Dion.Ar.*e.h.*2.3.1(M.3.397B); through chastisements, Or.*Cels.*6.72(p.142.9; 1408B); symbolized by refining fire, Gr.Nyss.*anim.et res.*(M.46.100A); **b.** human; prayer and other good works, Clem.*paed.*3.12(p.289.17; M.8.676C); **7.** ref. God; **a.** κ. not in God, Just.*1apol.*8.2(M.6.337C); Or.*Cels.*5.23(p.24.18ff.; M.11.1216D); id.*hom.7.3 in Jer.*(p.54.19; M.13.333C); **b.** nor caused by God, Clem.*str.*1.17(p.54.16; M.8.800A); rel. to Logos discussed, Or.*Jo.*2.15(9; p.71.15ff.; M.14.140B); hated by God, Or.*fr.50 in Jo.*(p.524.21ff.); **c.** not in Christ, Or.*Cels.*4.15 (p.285.14; 1048A); **8.** Gnost.; related to matter τὴν ὑλικὴν πᾶσαν κ. δηλοῦσθαι διὰ τῶν ἓξ ἀνδρῶν (ref. Jo.4:17) Heracleon ap.Or.*Jo.*13.11(p.236.5; M.14.416C); ὁ δὲ κόσμος τὸ σύμπαν τῆς κ. ὄρος Heracleon *ib.*13.16(p.239.35; 421C); cf. Or.'s view of fall of souls into bodies διὰ κ. id.*princ.*1.8.4(p.103.8); **9.** Manichean; **a.** teaching οἱ δὲ ἀπὸ τῶν αἱρέσεων...ἀναπλάττονται δὲ ἑαυτοῖς παρὰ τὸν ἀληθινὸν τοῦ Χριστοῦ πατέρα θεὸν ἕτερον, καὶ τοῦτον ἀγένητον τοῦ κακοῦ ποιητὴν καὶ τῆς κ. ἀρχηγόν Ath.*gent.*6(M.25.13A); μίαν ἀρχὴν λέγεις τῶν ὄντων, ἢ δύο; δύο, μίαν μὲν ἀγαθήν, καὶ μίαν πονηράν...τὴν δὲ πονηρὰν... παντὸς πονηροῦ καὶ κ. ποιητικήν...ἡ δὲ ὕλη, ἤγουν ἡ κ., ἄζωος, ἀκίνητος Jo.D.*Man.*1.2(M.94.1508B,C); ἐκ γὰρ τῆς μοίρας τοῦ ἀγαθοῦ, ἐγένοντο αἱ ψυχαί, ἐκ δὲ τῆς οὐσίας τῆς κ., τὰ σώματα *ib.*(1508D); **b.** its consequences ὁ...βαρβαρικὴν ἀσέβειαν ἐπινοήσας, ἄναρχον κ. κατὰ τοῦ θεοῦ ἀνάρχου καὶ μόνου πλασάμενος, καὶ δευτέραν ἀρχὴν ταύτην μανικῶς ὁρισάμενος, οὐ μόνον ἐν ἴσῃ τάξει τίθησι κ. θεῷ, ὥσπερ τιμῆσαι ταύτην ὁ δῆθεν μισῶν προελόμενος, ἀλλὰ καὶ ἀνίατα πάντα τὰ ἐκ τῆς ἀνάρχου ῥέοντα κακὰ ἐπάναγκες φάσκων,...ὡς ἀδύνατον ἀνάρχου κ. ἐπισχεῖν τὴν φοράν Tit.Bost.*Man.*1.2(M.18.1072B); for soul τό τε δὴ σπουδαζόμενόν ἐστι τῷ ἀγαθῷ τὴν ψυχὴν ἐλευθερῶσαι τῆς κ.· καὶ ταύτην ἀντλῆσαι τρόπον τινὰ ἐκ τῆς ὕλης *ib.*1.13(1083C); **c.** refutation by *reductio ad absurdum* ἡ μὲν κ., φθορά. ὁ δὲ ἀγαθός, ζωή. οὐκοῦν ἡ μὲν κ. φθείρει τὸν ἀγαθόν, καὶ οὐχ ὑφίσταται· ὁ δὲ ἀγαθὸς ζωοῖ τὴν κ.· καὶ ὑποστήσεται μὲν ἡ κ., ἀπωλεῖται δὲ ὁ ἀγαθός Jo.D.*Man.*1.27(1532A); εἰ οὖν δημιουργεῖ ἡ κ., ἐκ μὴ ὄντων παράγει, καὶ οὐκέτι ἐκ τῆς ὕλης τὸ σῶμα. εἰ δὲ ἐκ τῆς ὕλης, τουτέστιν ἐκ τῆς οὐσίας τῆς κ., εἰ μὲν ἄναρχος ἡ κ., ἀθάνατος πάντως καὶ ἄτρεπτος...εἰ δὲ ἡ κ. ἄτρεπτος, καὶ τὸ ἐκ τῆς οὐσίας αὐτῆς σῶμα ἄφθαρτον ἔσται καὶ ἄτρεπτον *ib.*1.42(1545A); *ib.*1.63(1557B).

B. intellectual *error*, Or.*Cels.*6.53(p.125.5; M.11.1381A).

C. physical, *misfortune* ἐν τοῖς προφήταις ἡ κ. παιδεία λέγεται Max. *schol.d.n.*4.30(M.4.301B).

***κακιγκάκως**, v. *κακηγκάκως.

***κακίστως**, *very badly* ἵνα ταῖς καλλίσταις τῶν ἐντολῶν κακίστως χρησώμεθα Nil.*Eulog.*25(M.79.1128A).

***κακκαβοπυρφόρος**, *carrying cauldrons of fire*, Thphn.*chron.* p.294(M.108.720A); as subst., *fire-ship*, *ib.*p.352(845B).

***κακοαισχής**, *evil and shameful*, Gr.Naz.*carm.*1.1.2.14(M.37.402A).

***κακόβλαστος**, *bursting with evil*, Epiph.*haer.*31.1(p.383.17; M.41.473C).

***κακοβουλοσύνη, ἡ**, *evil design, wickedness*, *Orac.Sib.fr.*1.19.

***κακοβούλως**, *ill-advisedly, foolishly*, Epiph.*haer.*65.4(p.6.10; M.42.16D); Isid.Pel.*epp.*1.69(M.78.229C).

κακογάμιον, τό, *unlawful marriage*, Clem.*str.*2.23(p.191.9; μονογάμιον cod., M.8.1092A).

***κακόγηρος, ὁ**, *evil old man*, Ephr.1.312D; of Devil, Pall.*h.Laus.* 18(p.56.16; M.34.1065C); Jo.Mosch.*prat.*45(M.87.2900C).

***κακογνωμία, ἡ**, *corruption of the mind*, †Jo.Jej.*poenit.*(M.88.1905C).

κακογνώμων, *having corrupt judgement, Orac.Sib.*2.144; of heretics, Iren.*haer.*3.3.4(M.7.852B).

***κακογραφία, ἡ,** f.l. for *κακορραφία, contrivance of evil, mischievousness,* Eudoc.*Cypr.*2.123(M.85.849C; *κακορρ- Teub.*).

κακοδιδασκαλέω, *instruct in evil, 2Clem.*10.5.

***κακοδιδασκαλία, ἡ,** *false teaching,* of heresy φεύγετε τὸν μερισμὸν καὶ τὰς κ. Ign.*Philad.*2.1; τῶν δογμάτων τὴν κ. Hipp.*haer.* 9.8(p.241.5; M.16.3371A); Epiph.*haer.*40.1(p.80.31; M.41.677B); Pall. *h.Laus.*54(p.146.19; M.34.1227A).

***κακοδιδάσκαλος, ὁ,** *false teacher,* Epiph.*haer.*57.1(p.345.3, v.l. διδάσκαλος M.41.996C); *Clem.recogn.suppl.*2(M.1.1457D).

κακοδοξέω, *hold false beliefs,* Ath.*hom.in Mt.11*:27(M.25.220A); Bas.*reg.br.*20(1.422A; M.31.1097A).

κακοδοξία, ἡ, *false opinion, heresy* τὰ γὰρ τῆς πίστεως ὁμολογήματα, ταῖς τῶν αἱρέσεων οὐ συνδραμεῖται κ. Apoll.*fid.sec.pt.*24(p.175. 28; M.10.1113D); τῶν Ἀρειανῶν τὴν κ. Epiph.*haer.*65.6(p.8.25; M.42. 21A); τίς οὐκ ἐμπεσεῖται ῥαδίως εἰς κ. κρημνόν; Euther.*confut.*16(M. 28.1388C); ἵνα μὴ μέτοχοι τῆς κ. καὶ τῆς αὐτῶν γενώμεθα κατακρίσεως Jo.D.*f.o.*4.13(M.94.1153B); κ. ἤγουν πᾶσα αἵρεσις id.*virt.*(M.95.88B); ref. eccl. condemnation τῷ...ἐπισκόπῳ...κρίνοντι αὐτὸν ἐπὶ τῇ κ. Bas.*ep.*273.3(3.406A; M.32.977C); Leo Mag.*ep.*28.6(p.19.12; M.*PL.* 54.780A); Alex.Sal.*Barn.*34(448B).

κακόδοξος, 1. of persons, *holding false beliefs,* Ath.*hom.in Mt. 11*:27(M.25.213C); Gr.Naz.*or.*43.58(M.36.573B); id.*ep.*185(M.37. 304B); Didym.*Trin.*2.26(M.39.749B); ‡Jo.D.*ep.Thphl.*29(M.95.381D); **2.** of opinions, *unorthodox,* Epiph.*haer.*69.5(p.156.11; M.42.209B); Gel.Cyz.*h.e.*2.21.22(M.85.1288C); Thphn.*chron.*p.9(M.108.77B).

κακοδουλία (-εία), ἡ, *severe conditions of servitude, Const.App.* 4.6.4; *base servitude* ἠλευθέρωσεν ἡμᾶς ἐκ τῆς κακοδουλείας τῶν ἁμαρτιῶν Agath.*v.Gr.Ill.*36.

***κακοεκτέω,** *be indisposed,* Bars.*resp.*(M.88.1820B).

κακοεξία, ἡ, *evil disposition, evil state,* Nil.*epp.*2.57(M.79.225A); Dor.*doct.*12.3(M.88.1752C).

[*]κακοεργέω, = κακουργέω, *do evil,* Diad.*perf.*28(p.30.28).

κακοζήλως, *with misplaced zeal,* Hier.*ep.*57.11(M.*PL.*22.578).

***κακοήτωρ,** *of evil heart, Orac.Sib.*1.174.

κακοθέλεια (-ία), ἡ, *malevolence, ill will,* Eust.*engast.*26(p.57.11; M.18.668A); Leo Mag.*ep.*30.1(p.46.4; M.*PL.*54.788A); Isid.Pel.*epp.*1. 332(M.78.373C).

κακοθελής, *malevolent*; of Devil, Ath.*v.Anton.*28(M.26.885A); of heretics, Const.ap.eund.*apol.sec.*62(p.142.1; M.25.361A); Ath.*ep. Aeg.Lib.*8(M.25.556B); Ephr.3.213E.

***κακοθελῶς,** *with evil intent, from ill will,* Marc.Er.*opusc.*2.171 (M.65.957A); ref. heretics, Jo.Clim.*scal.*26(M.88.1060D); Anast.S. *hod.*21(M.89.284B).

***κακοιώνιστος,** *ill-omened,* Jo.Mal.*chron.*7 p.187(M.97.297B).

κακοκαρπία, ἡ, *production of evil fruit,* Jo.D.*Jacob.*1(M.94. 1436C).

***κακόκαρπος,** *bearing evil fruit,* Or.*Cant.*3(p.192.28; M.13.159D); Gr.Thaum.*pan.Or.*17(p.39.1; M.10.1101A).

***κακοκερδής,** *basely greedy of gain, Orac.Sib.*3.189; Gr.Naz. *carm.*2.2(epigr.)78.1(M.38.121A).

***κακολίμαστος,** *causing famine, Exorc.*2(p.333).

***κακολογίζομαι,** *have evil thoughts,* Diad.*perf.*28(p.32.1).

***κακομανία, ἡ,** *wicked madness,* Pall.*v.Chrys.*16(p.94.18; M.47. 53).

***κακόμαρτυς, ὁ,** *one who bears false witness,* Sophr.H.*carm.*12.65 (M.87.3793A).

***κακομαχία, ἡ,** *wicked quarrelsomeness,* Const.ap.Gel.Cyz.*h.e.* 3.18.2.

***κακόμαχλος,** *wickedly lustful,* Thdt.*qu.21 in Lev.*(1.198).

***κακόμαχος,** *wickedly contentious,* Isid.Pel.*epp.*1.114(M.78.260B).

***κακόμελος,** *discordant,* Melet.*nat.hom.*7(M.64.1181D).

[*]κακομηχαν-άομαι, *devise in wickedness* τὴν ἄλλην βλακείαν ~ώμεναι Clem.*paed.*3.2(p.238.18; M.8.560C).

κακομήχανος, *wickedly devised* κ. πρᾶξις Hipp.*ben.Jac.*13(p.28. 12).

***κακομυθία, ἡ,** *evil-speaking, falsehood,* Serap.*Man.*49(p.71; M. 18.1245A); Thdt.*haer.*tit.(4.280).

κακόνοια, ἡ, *perversity,* Chrys.*sac.*2.6(p.42.9; 1.378C); esp. of heresy, Ath.*ep.Aeg.Lib.*22(M.25.589A); Cyr.*Jo.*1 proem.(4.8E); Isid. Pel.*epp.*1.18(M.78.193A); Jo.VI CP *ep.*(M.96.1428D); of Judaism, *Const.App.*5.16.2.

κακοπάθεια, ἡ, *mortification*; in gen., Eus.*v.C.*3.5(p.79.16; M.20. 1060A); Ath.*virg.*19(p.54.22; M.28.276A); Marc.Diac.*v.Porph.*10; Mac.Aeg.*pat.*1(M.34.865C); Dor.*doct.*1.10(M.88.1629A); of its practice μήτε πρὸς τρυφήν, μήτε πρὸς κ. βλέπειν, ἀλλὰ φεύγειν ἐν ἑκατέρῳ τὴν ἀμετρίαν Bas.*ascet.*1.3(2.321C; M.31.876C); οὐ τὸ βλέπειν πρὸς τὴν τοῦ σώματος κ. ... ἀλλὰ πρὸς τὴν τῶν ψυχικῶν κινημάτων εὐκολίαν Nil.*epp.*3.268(M.79.517B); under obedience to superior, Bas.*ascet.*2.2(324E; M.884C).

***κακοπιστία, ἡ,** *wrong* or *erroneous belief*; of heresy, CSard.*ep. cath.*ap.Ath.*apol.sec.*42(p.119.13; M.25.324C); τῇ πέτρᾳ τῆς ἐκκλησίας προσρηγνύντες τὰ τῆς κ. αὐτῶν μηχανήματα Isid.Pel.*epp.*1. 311(M.78.364A); of Arians, Ath.*v.Anton.*68(M.26.940C); Marc.Diac. *v.Porph.*56; of Nestorius, Cyr.*expl.xii cap.*1(p.17.23; 6^{1}.148A) etc

***κακόπιστος,** *of wrong* or *erroneous belief*; of heretics, Epiph. *haer.*64.67(p.510.1); ‡Ath.*qu.Ant.*111(M.28.665B); ἀπίστοις, ἢ κ. Jo.Clim.*scal.*26(M.88.1060D); τῇ κ. ... δόξῃ Max.*schol.e.h.*6.3.6(M.4. 173A); Leont.N.*v.Sym.*30(M.93.1708B); Marc.Diac.*v.Porph.*8.

κακόπλαστος, *mis-shapen,* Chrys.*hom.15.3 in Heb.*(12.154C).

***κακοποδινός,** *bringing bad luck, ill-favoured,* Marc.Diac.*v.Porph.* 19; Leont.N.*v.Sym.*56(M.93.1740A).

κακοποι-έω, *injure* εἰ γὰρ μία φύσις τῶν θεῶν ὑπῆρχεν, οὐκ ὤφειλεν θεὸς θεὸν διώκειν οὔτε σφάζειν οὔτε ~εῖν Arist.*apol.*13.5.

κακοποιητικός, *prone to do evil,* Or.*fr.in Lam.*1:5(p.279.19; M.13. 616A); id.*Ps.*9:36(p.464); τὰ ἐν ἡμῖν καὶ ἐξ ἡμῶν φυόμενα ταῦτα ἡμέτερα τυγχάνουσι κ. ὄντα πονηρίας Meth.*Porph.*(p.507.18; M.18. 345B).

κακοπραγέω, *do evil,* Meth.*symp.*11(p.130.11; M.18.205B).

***κακοπράγημα, τό,** *evil action,* Meth.*symp.*6.3(p.67.5; M.18. 117A).

κακοπραγής, *given to doing evil* ἔθνη ἀνήμερα καὶ κακοπραγέστατα Thphyl.*exc.gent.*5(p.482.34; M.113.944A).

***κακοπραξία, ἡ,** *evil-doing, Clem.ep.*9(M.2.45A).

***κακόρεκτος,** v. **κακόρρεκτος.*

***κακορραφέω,** *contrive evil,* Synes.*ep.*148(M.66.1548A).

***κακορραφής,** *contriving evil,* †Apoll.*met.Ps.*14:4(M.33.1328C).

***κακορρέκτειρα, ἡ,** *destroyer* καρπῶν τε κ. χάλαζα *Orac.Sib.*3. 754.

κακορρέκτης, ὁ, *worker of evil* κ. δαίμων Eudoc.*Cypr.*2.374(M. 85.860C).

***κακόρρεκτος,** *working evil,* †Apoll.*met.Ps.*57:3(M.33.1392B); hence *noxious* κακόρ⟨ρ⟩εκτα...βλαστήματα Epiph.*haer.*31.1(p.383.5; κακόρεκτα M.41.473C).

***κακορρημονέω,** *speak ill, slander,* intrans., Nil.*epp.*3.333(M.79. 544A).

κακός, A. *wicked, evil*; **1.** in gen. κ. κολάσεις τοῦ διαβόλου Ign. *Rom.*5.3; Christians considered κ. by pagans διὰ τὸ ὄνομα Just. *1apol.*4.2(M.6.332B); κ. ζύμης ἔργα id.*dial.*14.2(M.6.504D); of lust and concupiscence ἐν ἡδονῇ κ. τὸ ἀποθανεῖν Ign.*Trall.*6.2; id.*Philad.*2. 2; Just.*1apol.*10.6(M.6.341B); of demons, *ib.*5.4(336C); *ib.*9.1(340A); ref. work on sabbath, id.*dial.*27.5(M.6.533C); of false doctrines ἐὰν πίστιν θεοῦ ἐν κ. διδασκαλίᾳ φθείρῃ Ign.*Eph.*16.2; *ib.*9.1; Judaizing opinions called κ. ζύμη id.*Magn.*10.2; **2.** masc. as subst. = *sinner,* Just.*dial.*5.3(M.6.488A); Clem.*str.*6.17(p.511.24; M.9.385C); opp. Christ ἀπέδοτο...τὸν ἄκακον ὑπὲρ τῶν κ. *Diogn.*9.2; more numerous than ἀγαθοί, Tat.*orat.*3(p.4.2; M.6.809B).

B. neut. as subst., *evil, sin*; **1.** in gen. μερισμοὺς φεύγετε ὡς ἀρχὴν κακῶν Ign.*Smyrn.*7.2; Herm.*mand.*5.2.4; ἐπιθυμίας τῶν κ. Just. *1apol.*16.3(M.6.352C); Clem.*str.*2.7(p.130.31; M.8.969A); Or.*or.*29.13 (p.388.9; M.11.540B); ultimate destruction foretold by prophets, id.*Cels.*8.72(p.289.12; M.11.1625A); opp. ἁγνεία, Polyc.*ep.*5.3; cannot be cause of good, Clem.*str.*4.5(p.258.11; M.8.1236A); **2.** a negative concept, cf. *certum...est malum esse bono carere,* Or.*princ.*2.9.2 (p.166.2; M.11.227A); Ath.*inc.*4.5(M.25.104C) cit. s. καλός; Adam. *dial.*3.2(p.116.25; M.11.1793B); στέρησις γὰρ ἀγαθοῦ ἐστι τὸ κ. Bas. *hom.*9.4(2.78A; M.31.341B); cf.id.*hex.*2.4(1.16D; M.29.37D); τὸ κ. οὐ τὸ εἶναι χαρακτηρίζει ἡ ἀνυπαρξία Max.*ambig.*(M.91.1332A); τὸ κ. στέρησίς ἐστι τοῦ εἶναι Jo.D.*Man.*1.13(M.94.1517A); **3.** origin; **a.** in free will, emphasized against dualists ἄνθρωπος...ὃς τῷ αὐτεξούσιος ὑπάρχειν τὸ κ. ἐπιγεννᾷ...ἐν γὰρ τῷ θέλειν καὶ νομίζειν τι κ. τὸ κ. ὀνομάζεται Hipp.*haer.*10.33(p.290.14ff.; M.16.3450B); ὁ ἄνθρωπος ἐντολὴν λαμβάνει παρὰ τοῦ θεοῦ, καὶ ἐντεῦθεν ἤδη τὸ κ. ἄρχεται... τοῦτο καὶ μόνον ἦν τὸ κ., ἡ παρακοή Meth.*arbitr.*17(p.189.14f.; M.18. 264B); τὰ κ. οὐδὲ κατὰ φύσιν, οὐδὲ κατ' οὐσίαν...ἀλλὰ τρόπῳ γίνονται τὰ κ. ἐκ τῆς αὐτεξουσιότητος Adam.*dial.*4.9(p.158.28ff.; M.11.1821A), ‡Just.*qu.Chr.*5(M.6.1412C); τὸ...κυρίως κ. ἡ ἁμαρτία...ἐκ τῆς ἡμετέρας προαιρέσεως ἤρτηται Bas.*hom.*9.5(2.76E; M.31.337D); dist. from evil of suffering, brought about by God as punishment of sin, *ib.*9.3(74B; M.332C); and not really evil, id.*hex.*2.5(1.17A; M. 29.40B); Diad.*perf.*3(p.6.16); καθέστηκε τὸ κ. ... ἐν τῇ πρὸς τὸ θεῖον θέλημα διαφορᾷ τοῦ κατὰ γνώμην ἡμετέρου θελήματος Max.*opusc.*(M. 91.56B); bad use being made of good things, Jo.D.*Man.*1.84(M. 94.1581C); **b.** in demons, Or.*mart.*45(p.41.27; M.11.624A); Plato's views discussed, id.*Cels.*4.62(p.333.19ff.; M.11.1129B); cf.*ib.*4.65 (p.336.12; 1133B); **4.** ref. God; **a.** in gen.; difficulties discussed, ref. Mt.6:13, Or.*or.*29.11(p.386.26; 537B); πάντων γὰρ τῶν ἐν ψυχῇ κ. δυνατώτερος ὢν ὁ λόγος id.*Cels.*8.72(p.289.6; M.11.1625A); κακὰ...ὁ θεὸς οὐ πεποίηκεν, ἀλλὰ τοῖς...αὐτοῦ ἔργοις ὀλίγα ὡς πρὸς τὴν τῶν ὅλων διάταξιν τυγχάνοντα ἐπηκολούθησεν *ib.*6.55(p.126.25; 1384C); ἐπειδὴ γὰρ θεοῦ ἔργον ὁ ἄνθρωπος, τοῦ δι' ἀγαθότητα τὸ ζῷον τοῦτο παραγαγόντος εἰς γένεσιν, οὐκ ἄν τις εὐλόγως...τοῦτον ἐν κακοῖς γεγενῆσθαι παρὰ τοῦ πεποιηκότος καθυποπτεύσειεν Gr.Nyss.*or.catech.* 5(p.25.18); **b.** in controversy with dualist heresies; **i.** orthodox affirmations ὁ δὲ κτίσας θεὸς κ. οὐκ ἐποίει οὐδὲ ποιεῖ Hipp.*haer.*10.33 (p.290.10; M.16.3450B); τὸ κ. οὐ παρὰ θεοῦ οὐδὲ ἐν θεῷ οὔτε ἐξ ἀρχῆς γέγονεν, οὔτε οὐσία τίς ἐστιν αὐτοῦ Ath.*gent.*7(M.25.16A); οὐδὲν κατ' οὐσίαν κ.· τῷ τὸ κ. ποιὸν εἶναι. οὐδὲν δὲ ποιὸν οὐσία. τὸ ἄρα κ. οὐκ οὐσία Didym.*Man.*2(M.39.1088C); Chrys.*hom.2.4 in Ac.*(9.20C); **ii.** heret. statements προσαγαγεῖν...αἰτίαν ὡς ἡμῶν φασκόντων ὑπὸ θεοῦ τὸ κ. ἐκτίσθαι Adam.*dial.*3.2(p.116.25; M.11.1793B); Manich. δύο ῥίζας φημί...τοῦ ἀγαθοῦ ἡ ποιότης...φῶς...τοῦ δὲ κ. ... σκότος *ib.* 3.4(p.118.27; 1796A); Manicheans οἱ τῶν ἁπλουστέρων καθηγεμόνες διδάσκουσιν...τὸ ἀγαθὸν καὶ τὸ κ. ἀπὸ τοῦ αὐτοῦ φέρεσθαι, καὶ μίαν ἀρχὴν εἰσηγούμενοι...σὺ δὲ...μὴ ἴσα τοῖς πολλοῖς τῶν ἀνθρώπων ἀλογίστως...ἀμφότερα...ἑνώσῃς Hegem.*Arch.*5(p.6.10; M.10.1433B); πόθεν λέγοντες...τὰ κ., εἰ μὴ ἔκ τινος ἀρχῆς καὶ ταῦτα τυγχάνει; Tit.Bost. *Man.*1.4(M.18.1073B); ἦν θεός, καὶ ὕλη...ἀγαθὸν καὶ κ. *ib.*1.5(1076A); **5.** *misfortune* φύγωμεν τὴν ἀσέβειαν, μὴ ἡμᾶς καταλάβῃ κακά *2Clem.* 10.1; Or.*Cels.*8.38(p.253.14; M.11.1573C); κ. δὲ αὐτὰ κέκληκεν, οὐχ ὡς φύσει κ., ἀλλ' ὡς οὕτως ὑπὸ τῶν ἀνθρώπων νομιζόμενα Thdt.*Is.*45:7 (p.180.13; 2.343).

κακοσιτεία, ἡ, for κακοσιτία, *bad feeding, lack of nourishment,* Cyr.*Is.*1.1(2.27B).

***κακόσκοπος,** *tiresome, difficult* ἀκολουθία εἰς παῖδας κ. *Euchol.* (p.753); *Exorc.*29 tit.(p.341).

***κακόσοφος,** *wise in evil,* Mac.Mgn.*apocr.*4.17(p.193.10).

***κακοσυμβουλία, ἡ,** *evil counsel,* Jo.Mosch.*prat.*45(M.87.2900D).

κακοσχολέω, *employ* one's *leisure ill,* Clem.*paed.*3.11(p.277.26; M.8.652B); in heretical quibblings κ. περὶ τὰς πεύσεις Leont.B.*Nest. et Eut.*1(M.86.1281A).

***κακοτελής,** *wholly evil,* Ephr.3.547A.

***κακοτερπής,** *taking pleasure in evil,* Eudoc.*Cypr.*1.52(M.85. 833D).

κακοτεχνέω, *distort,* ref. private interpretation of scripture or eccl. formularies, Hipp.*haer.*6.19(p.145.6; M.16.3222C); Bas.*Eun.* 1.9(1.221E; M.29.533A).

κακοτεχνία, ἡ, 1. *bad, debased art,* Clem.*prot.*4(p.35.25; M.8. 136A); of gladiatorial shows, Isid.Pel.*epp.*5.185(M.78.1437A); of luxury trades, Chrys.*hom.49.4 in Mt.*(7.509E); *false artifice*; of cosmetics, Clem.*paed.*2.10(p.219.24; M.8.521B); Isid.Pel.*epp.*1.461 (436B); **2.** plur., *evil arts*; of magical practices, Ign.*Polyc.*5.1; Cyr.H.*catech.*19.8; ref. Devil φεύγετε...τὰς κ. ... τοῦ ἄρχοντος Ign. *Philad.*6.2; Nil.*epp.*3.33(M.79.396A); *wicked schemes,* Ath.*fug.*10 (p.75.5; M.25.656C); sing., *wicked scheming,* Philost.*h.e.*7.4(M.65. 541B).

***κακότρεπτος,** *liable to be turned to evil,* of Adam οὔτε ἄτρεπτος ἦν, οὔτε μονομερῶς κακότρεπτος Marc.Er.*opusc.*4(M.65.1013C).

κακοτρόπως, 1. *maliciously, unfairly,* Ursac.*ep.Jul.*(p.138.13; M.25.353C); Cyr.*thes.*15(5[1].159D); **2.** *by dealing basely,* Tim.Ant. *caec.*6(M.28.1009D).

***κακούβιον, τό,** = καμψάκης, *cruse,* Epiph.*haer.*30.12(p.348.10; M.41.425C).

κακόυπνος, *of disturbed sleep* νύκτας κ. Pall.*v.Chrys.*20(p.139.7; M.47.77).

κακουχ-έω, 1. *maltreat, mortify,* of ascetics τὸ σῶμα ∼οῦσα ‡Ath. *v.Syncl.*17(M.28.1496A); pass., *practise mortification,* Nil.*Eulog.*33 (M.79.1137C); **2.** *suffer boredom* περὶ τὴν ἀνάγνωσιν τῶν θείων λογίων κ. Ephr.1.281D.

κακουχία, ἡ, *maltreatment*; ascet., *mortification* πρὸς τὴν τῶν δαιμόνων φυγὴν ἡ ἔνδεια καὶ ἡ νηστεία καὶ ἡ κ. ... ἐστι βοήθημα *Hom. Clem.*9.10; Bas.*reg.br.*90(2.447B; M.31.1145A); ‡Ath.*ep.Cast.*1.3(M. 28.853A); Nil.*epp.*3.195(M.79.473C).

κακοφροσύνη, ἡ, *folly, perversity,* Clem.*paed.*1.5(p.101.18; M.8. 272B); Meth.*symp.*3.10(p.38.19; M.18.76D); Ephr.1.84C; Isid.Pel. *epp.*1.352(M.78.384B); of heretics, Ath.*decr.*1(p.1.9; M.25.416A); ‡Gr.Nyss.*Ar.et Sab.*(M.45.1293B).

κακόχαρτος, *giving base delight,* Clem.*paed.*3.11(p.278.9; M.8. 653A); Gr.Naz.*carm.*1.2.9.20(M.37.669A).

κακύνω, *reproach, show to be bad,* Cyr.*Is.*3.5(2.513E).

κακωνυμία, ἡ, *bad name* τὴν Ἀρείου κ. Ath.*ep.Aeg.Lib.*5(M.25. 549A).

κάκωσις, ἡ, *ill-treatment,* esp. of divine *affliction* ἐν τῇ γῇ ταύτῃ τῆς κ. Or.*hom.7.3 in Jer.*(p.54.21; M.17.333C); τὰ δὲ παιδεύοντα, καὶ διὰ τῆς κ. εἰς ἐπιστροφὴν ἄγοντα Bas.*reg.br.*276(2.512A; M.31.1273D); ref. Am.3:6 κακίαν δὲ λέγει τὴν κ. Cyr.*Os.*87(3.118E); κ. δὲ τὴν νηστείαν Thdt.*qu.22 in Lev.*(1.203).

κακωτικός, *hurtful, distressing,* of mortification αἰνίττεται δὲ διὰ τοῦ σάκκου τὴν σκληρὰν καὶ κ. δίαιταν Diod.*Ps.*68:12(M.33.1604B); of divine affliction, Andr.Caes.*Apoc.*67(M.106.429A); ref. Gen.15:13 ὁ τέταρτος ἀριθμὸς ὑλικός τις καὶ σωματικὸς ὢν κ. ἐστιν Or.*fr.49 in Jo.* (p.546.25); πανταχοῦ τῆς γραφῆς κ. ἀριθμὸς ὁ τῶν μ' Proc.G.*Dt.*25:3 (M.87.940A).

καλαθίσκος, ὁ, *toy basket,* Chrys.*hom.4.6 in 1Cor.*(10.32E); id. *hom.4.4 in Col.*(11.356D).

κάλαθος, ὁ, *basket*; name of festival of Artemis, where carried in procession, Call.*v.Hyp.*(p.96).

καλαμάρι(ο)ν, τό, *pen-case, pen-holder,* Leont.N.*v.Jo.Eleem.*1 (p.7.17).

***καλαμητός, ὁ,** *gleaner,* SM ap.Thdt.*Is.*24:13(p.98.33).

καλάμιον, τό, 1. *corn stalk, Euchol.*(p.524); **2.** *token for corn-dole, Chron.Pasch.*p.263(M.92.461B).

καλαμίσκος, ὁ, 1. *branch of a candle-stick,* ref. Ex.25:30, Cosm. Ind.*top.*9(M.88.404C); **2.** a bone in the leg, Call.*v.Hyp.*(p.80).

***καλαμοειδῶς,** *like a reed,* Gr.Nyss.*hom.4 in Cant.*(M.44.841A).

κάλαμος, ὁ, *pipe,* of musical instrument ὀργάνῳ...ἔοικεν ἀπὸ χαλκῶν συγκειμένῳ καλάμων Thdt.*provid.*3(4.513).

καλαμόω, 1. med., *gather reeds,* Pall.*h.Laus.*23(p.76.17; M.34. 1089A); **2.** act., sens. dub., *Chron.Pasch.*p.393(M.92.1009A).

Καλάνδαι (-θαι), αἱ, (Lat. *Kalendae*) *Kalends*; observance as festival forbidden to Christians, CTrull.*can.*62; *Καλάνθαι M.Das.* 3.2.

***καλέσχατος,** *extremely good,* opp. κακέσχατος, Ephr.1.312E.

καλ-έω, *call*;

A. ref. divine calling; **1.** into being ἐκάλεσεν γὰρ ἡμᾶς οὐκ ὄντας καὶ ἠθέλησεν ἐκ μὴ ὄντος εἶναι ἡμᾶς *2Clem.*1.8; τὰ οὐκ ὄντα κ. διὰ τοῦ ἰδίου λόγου εἰς τὸ εἶναι Ath.*Ar.*2.22(M.26.192C); Thdt.*Is.*48:13(p.190. 36; 2.346); ὁ ∼έσας τὸ φῶς Gel.Cyz.*h.e.*2.17.11(M.85.1268C); **2.** to Christian faith and life δι' οὗ ἐκάλεσεν ἡμᾶς ἀπὸ σκότους εἰς φῶς, ἀπὸ ἀγνωσίας εἰς ἐπίγνωσιν δόξης ὀνόματος αὐτοῦ *1Clem.*59.2; Χριστὸς...κ. ἡμᾶς ἤδη ἀπολλυμένους *2Clem.*2.7; καθ' ἡμέραν ὡς ∼ούμενοι προκόπτωμεν Ath.*Ar.*3.59(M.26.428B); τὴν τοῦ ∼έσαντος θεραπείαν Thdt.*h.rel.*5(3.1162); εἰ...περὶ τῶν ἐθνῶν νοοῖτο, δηλοῖ [sc. Is.49:21] τὴν προτέραν αὐτῶν πρὶν κληθῆναι κατάστασιν Proc.G.*Is.* 49:21(M.87.2480C); Jo.D.*Eph.*4:1ff.(M.95.840B) cit. s. κλῆσις.

B. *summon* a council οἱ περὶ Εὐσέβιον δὲ πρὸς Ἰούλιον ἔγραψαν... ἠξίωσαν σύνοδον κ. Ath.*apol.sec.*20(p.102.2; M.25.280C).

C. *invoke* τὴν θείαν χάριν ἐπίκουρον κ. Thdt.*Cant.*4(2.134); angels ἀγγέλους γὰρ καλέσαι...οὐκ εὔλογον Or.*Cels.*5.5(p.4.29; M.11.1185C); a martyr ὀνόματι κληθεὶς...παρέστη Bas.*hom.*23.1(2.185C; M.31.589C).

D. *name* canonical books κ. οἱ ἅγιοι πατέρες, ποῖα βιβλία δεῖ δέχεσθαι †Leont.B.*sect.*3.2(M.86.1213C).

***καλιγάτος,** (Lat. *caligatus*) *wearing soldiers' boots,* hence *common, private* soldier στρατιώτας ἐνόπλους οὓς ὁ νόμος κ. καλεῖ Justn. *nov.*74.4(p.375.42); Ath.Scholast.*coll.*11.3(p.137).

***καλίγη, ἡ,** (Lat. *caliga*) *boot,* Ephr.1.42C; *-ίκη Const.Stud.*38(M. 99.1720B).

***καλιγραφίον, τό,** v.s. *καλλιγραφεῖον.

***καλιέργημα, τό,** *beautiful work,* ‡Jo.D.*ep.Thphl.*28(M.95.381A).

***καλίκη, ἡ,** v. *καλίγη.

***κάλληχος,** *sweet-sounding,* Thdr.Stud.*iamb.*10(M.99.1784B).

καλλίβοτρυς, *with beautiful clusters of grapes,* ref. BMV ἄμπελος ἡ κ. Chrysipp.*enc.in BMV* 1(p.337.7).

[*]καλλιγάριος, ὁ, (Lat. *caligarius*) *bootmaker,* Nil.*epp.*2.203 tit. (M.79.305D).

καλλίγονος, *having fair offspring*; of BMV, Leont.H.*Nest.*4.37 (M.86.1712A).

***καλλιγραφεῖον, *καλιγραφίον, τό,** *scriptorium, writing-room*; in Pachomian monastery, Pall.*h.Laus.*32(p.96.4); ἐσχόλαζεν εἰς τὰ καλιγραφία Jo.Mosch.*prat.*171(M.87.3037C).

καλλιγραφ-έω, *write beautifully*; of copyists writing in longhand, Gr.Nyss.*Eun.*1(1 p.204.23; M.45.452C); opp. shorthand writers ταχυγράφοι...αὐτῷ [sc. Origen] πλείους ἢ ἑπτὰ...παρῆσαν...βιβλιογράφοι τε οὐχ ἧττους ἅμα καὶ κόραις ἐπὶ τὸ κ. ἠσκημέναις Eus.*h.e.*6.23.2(M.20.576B); cf.Bas.*ep.*134(3.225E; M.32.572A); Gr.Mag.*dial.*(tr. Zach.)1.4(M.*PL*.77.171); met. βιβλίον σωφροσύνης ἑαυτὸν τῷ βίῳ ἐκαλλιγράφησα Ast.Soph.*hom.*5 *in Ps.*5(M.40.441C); δεῖ γὰρ τὰ... Χριστοῦ δόγματα...~εῖσθαι Anast.S.*hod.*proem.(M.89.36A).

καλλιγραφικός, *of beautiful writing*, ref. copyist's art κ. ἐπιστήμης ἔμπειρος Eus.*m.P.*11(p.939.29; καλλιγραφικῆς ἔμπειρος M.20.1452C).

καλλιγράφος, ὁ, *scribe, copyist* ὑπὸ τεχνιτῶν κ. καὶ...τὴν τέχνην ἐπισταμένων γραφῆναι Const.ap.Eus.*v.C.*4.36(p.131.26; M.20.1185A); Epiph.*haer.*67.3(p.136.17; M.42.177A); εἰ δὲ εὕροιμι κ. πέμψω σου τῇ ὁσιότητι...ἃ...συνέγραψα Thdt.*ep.*130(4.1219); *Apophth.Patr.*(M.65.293D); *artist*, cf. καλλιγράφων ἔργα καὶ πλαστῶν Philo ap.Eus.*p.e.*8.14(388C; M.21.657B).

καλλιελαία, ἡ, *cultivated olive*, ref. Rom.11:17 καθάπερ ἡ ἀγριέλαιος ἐγκεντρισθεῖσα τῷ...λόγῳ...κ. γίνεται Clem.*str.*6.15(p.491.15; M.9.341C); ὁ...ἀπόστολος οἶδεν ἐλαίᾳ παραβάλλειν τὴν παρὰ Ἰούδα διαδοχήν, καὶ ῥίζαν ἁγίαν...κ. αὐτὴν καλεῖ Eus.*Is.*17:5–6(M.24.209B); κοινωνοὶ ἐγίνεσθε τῆς κ. Ἰησοῦ Cyr.H.*catech.*20.3; Isid.Pel.*epp.*2.72(M.78.516C).

***καλλιέμπορος, ὁ, ἡ,** *fair trader*; met., of BMV χαίροις, κ. τοῦ παρθενικοῦ δηναρίου Thdot.Anc.*hom.BMV et Sym.*3(M.77.1393C).

***καλλιεξία, ἡ,** *fitness* for τοὺς...περὶ τὴν εὔθετον τῆς κ. σύνθεσιν ἐνδεομένους Eustrat.*v.Eutych.*101(M.86.2388C).

καλλιέπεια, ἡ, *eloquence, elegant style*, esp. of pagan writers ὑμεῖς μὲν τῇ κ. οὐκ ἐμποδίζετε τὴν τοῦ Χριστοῦ διδασκαλίαν Ath.*v.Anton.*78(M.26.952C); Cyr.*Ps.*11:5(M.69.797A); τὸ ψεῦδος τῇ κ. κοσμήσας, ἐν χρυσίδι τὸ δηλητήριον ἐκέρασεν Isid.Pel.*epp.*4.67(M.78.1125A); of heathen oracles, Eus.*v.C.*2.4(p.42.15; M.20.984A); of Eunomius' rhetoric, Gr.Nyss.*Eun.*1(1 p.158.8; M.45.400A).

καλλιεργία, ἡ, *work of beauty*; of the body, Dion.Al.ap.Eus.*p.e.*14.26(780B; M.21.1284A); of embellishment of a church, Const.ap. Eus.*v.C.*3.31(p.92.16; M.20.1092B); of acts of charity, Pamph.Mon. *Soter.*2(p.116.25).

καλλίεργος, ὁ, *good farmer*, met. τοῦ ἄνω κ. Rom.Mel.(*AS* 1 p.171).

καλλιερ-έω, *make acceptable sacrifice*, of Christ τὴν ἀπαρχὴν τοῦ τῶν ἀνθρώπων γένους ~ησάμενος Eus.*d.e.*10 proem.(p.445.17; M.22.717A); of martyrs ὑπὲρ τὸν Ἰσαὰκ ἐκαλλιερήθητε, τῇ ἑαυτῶν σφαγῇ τὴν θυσίαν τελέσαντες Const.Diac.*laud.*40(M.88.525A); of eucharist τὰ σεμνὰ τῆς Χριστοῦ τραπέζης θύματα, δι' ὧν ~οῦντες τὰς ἀναίμους καὶ λογικὰς...θυσίας...προσφέρειν θεῷ...δεδιδάγμεθα Eus.*d.e.*1.10(p.48.4; 92A); ἔνθα τὰ τῆς ἀναιμάκτου ~εῖται θυσίας Evagr.*h.e.*4.31(p.181.1; M.86.2760B).

καλλιέρημα, τό, *acceptable sacrifice*, to God μηδὲ ἀπωσθῆναι τὸ κ. Gr.Naz.*or.*18.11(M.35.997B); *ib.*43.71(M.36.592B); Chrys.*hom.*49.*1 in Gen.*(4.491C); κ. τῆς εἰς Χριστὸν...εὐσεβείας ‡Jo.D.*ep.Thphl.*3(M.95.348C).

***καλλιερητέον,** *one must make acceptable sacrifice*, Or.*Cels.*8.26(p.242.15; M.11.1556A).

***καλλιθέμειλος,** = καλλιθέμεθλος, *with beautiful foundations*, Paul.Sil.*ambo.*105(M.86.2256A).

καλλίκαρπος, *bearing fine fruit*; met., Rom.Mel.(*AS* 1 p.67).

καλλιλεξία, ἡ, *fairness of language, speciousness* τὰ μοχθηρὰ γὰρ αὐτοῦ δόγματα καλλιλεξίᾳ κεκόσμηται Or.*fr.*36 *in Jer.*(p.216.28); ref. 1Cor.4:19f. διδάσκων ὅτι οὐ...κ. ἀνύει πρὸς τὸ πείθειν, ἀλλὰ δυνάμεως θείας ἐπιχορηγία id.*Jo.*1.8(10; p.13.29; M.14.40A); Thdr.Mops.*1Cor.*1:17(p.173.15; M.66.877A); ὁ ἀμελῶν τῆς ἐργασίας τῶν κατὰ Χριστὸν ἀριστευμάτων, τῆς δὲ κ. ἀντιποιούμενος Nil.*epp.*3.52(M.79.416D); ἴσθι δὲ ἡμᾶς μὴ ἐσπουδακέναι περὶ τὴν φράσιν, ἐννοήσαντας ὡς εἰ σπουδάσαιμεν κ. χρήσασθαι, ἴσως μὲν καὶ ἀποπεσούμεθα τοῦ σκοποῦ Socr.*h.e.*6 proem.2(M.67.657A).

καλλίμαρτυς, ὁ, *excellent martyr*, Sophr.H.*aceph.Cyr.et Jo.*(M.87.3689D).

***καλλίμασθος,** *with beautiful breasts*, Jo.Mal.*chron.*5 p.101(M.97.189B).

καλλίνικος, *gloriously triumphant*; of emperors, Eus.*v.C.*1 proem.(p.7.3; M.20.912A); *Symb.Sirm.*3 proem.ap.Ath.*syn.*8(p.235.22; M.26.692B); of martyrs, Meth.*res.*1.56(p.316.8; M.41.1149D); Isid.Pel.*epp.*1.447(M.78.429A); Thdt.*Ps.*9:17(1.663).

***καλλιοτόκος,** v.l. for καλλιτόκος.

καλλιόω, *beautify*; pass., of the soul, Gr.Nyss.*hom.*9 *in Cant.*(M.44.953D).

καλλιπάρθενος, *of fair virginity*, *M.Pers.*8.2(pp.462.4,463.8); as subst. fem., *fair virgin*, Meth.*symp.*6.5(p.69.15; M.18.120C); Jo.D. *hom.*12.22(M.96.812B); of BMV, Cyr.*deip.BMV*(p.30.32; M.76.285C).

***καλλιπάτωρ, ὁ,** *glorious father*; of church fathers, *Hymn.*(*AS* 1 p.608).

***καλλίπενθος, ὁ,** *one blessed in his grief*, Jo.Clim.*scal.*7(M.88.808D).

καλλίπνους, *sweet-smelling, fragrant*; met., of virtue, Meth. *symp.*8.11(p.93.17; M.18.153D).

καλλίπολις, ἡ, *fair city*; of heavenly Jerusalem, Cyr.*ador.*13(1.473A).

***καλλιπονία, ἡ,** *work of excellence*, Nil.*Eulog.*4(M.79.1144C).

***καλλίπονος,** *toiling to produce beauty*, Paul.Sil.*Soph.*691(M.86.2145B).

***καλλιπρεπής,** *excellent*, Eus.*l.C.*3(p.200.20; M.20.1328B).

***καλλίσταχυς,** *growing fine corn*, *Orac.Sib.*11.118; *ib.*11.177; *ib.*11.241.

***καλλιτεχνέω,** *fashion beautifully*; of God creating world, Olymp.*Eccl.*5:8(M.93.544A).

καλλιτέχνης, *fashioning with fine artistry*; of God, Pall.*v.Chrys.*4(p.26.17; M.47.17); of Logos, Eus.*d.e.*4.5(p.157.34; M.22.264A); Gr. Naz.*carm.*1.2.10.110(M.37.688A).

καλλιτόκος, *having fair offspring*; of BMV, Cyr.*Arcad.*(p.66.32; καλλιοτόκος 5^2.49E).

***καλλίφαρος,** *having a fair bedspread* τοῦ κ. σκίμποδος *Hymn.*(*AS* 1 p.524).

καλλιφωνία, ἡ, 1. *euphony*, of style γραφαὶ δὲ αἱ θεῖαι...γυμναὶ... τῆς ἐκτὸς κ. Clem.*prot.*8(p.59.11; M.8.188A); Gr.Nyss.*Eun.*9(2 p.215.19; M.45.813C); **2.** *sweetness of sound*; met., of call of temptation, Meth.*symp.*8.1(p.81.15; M.18.140A).

καλλοποιός, *producing beauty*, of God τοῦ κ. καὶ ἀρχικοῦ κάλλους Dion.Ar.*c.h.*7.2(M.3.208C); id.*d.n.*4.7(M.3.701C).

κάλλος, τό, *beauty*;

A. of body οὐ γὰρ αὐτοποίητον ἐπὶ γῆς τὸ κ., ἀλλὰ...ὑπὸ χειρὸς καὶ γνώμης πεμπόμενον τοῦ θεοῦ Athenag.*leg.*34.1(M.6.968B); not desired by incarnate Christ οὐ τὸ κ. τῆς σαρκός, τὸ φανταστικόν, τὸ δὲ ἀληθινὸν καὶ τῆς ψυχῆς καὶ τοῦ σώματος ἐνεδείξατο κ. Clem.*paed.*3.1(p.237.22; M.8.557C); ὁ κύριος οὐ μάτην ἠθέλησεν εὐτελεῖ χρήσασθαι σώματος μορφῇ, ἵνα μή τις τὸ ὡραῖον ἐπαινῶν καὶ τὸ κ. θαυμάζων ἀφίστηται τῶν λεγομένων id.*str.*6.17(p.510.1; M.9.381C); cf.*ib.*3.17(p.244.1; M.8.1208A); Or.*Cels.*6.75–77(p.144.16ff.; M.11.1409ff.); not given to man to know his beauty, ‡Ath.*Apoll.*1.22(M.26.1132A).

B. spiritual; **1.** in gen. φιλοσοφίας...ἐστιν...κ. ἀληθινὸν παρὰ τὸ δεδολωμένον Clem.*str.*6.17(p.509.22; M.9.381B); περὶ τοῦ κάλλους τοῦ ἀληθινοῦ id.*paed.*3.1 tit.(p.235.19; M.8.556A); ἔστι κ. ἀνθρώπων ἀγαπή *ib.*3.1(p.237.11; 557B); τῶν ἠθῶν τὸ κ. *ib.*2.10(p.224.25; 532C); τὸ περὶ τὴν ἀρετὴν κ. id.*str.*2.21(p.182.18; M.8.1073A); τοῦ ἁγίου κάλλους *ib.*2.20(p.174.1; 1056B); θεῖον κ. Gr.Nyss.*virg.*12 tit.(p.297.10); **2.** of soul, opp. body κ. ... ἄριστον πρῶτον...τὸ ψυχικόν...ὅταν ἡ κεκοσμημένη ψυχὴ ἁγίῳ πνεύματι Clem.*paed.*3.11(p.272.2; M.8.640A); τὸ φυσικὸν τοῦ σώματος κ. ἔλαττον τοῦ ψυχικοῦ λογίζεται κύριος *ib.*3.2(p.243.10; 573A); ἐν μόνῃ...τῇ ψυχῇ καταφαίνεσθαι καὶ τὸ κ. καὶ τὸ αἶσχος...καλὸς...ἄνθρωπος, ὁ δίκαιος *ib.*2.12(p.230.5; 544B,C); τὸ κ. τῆς ψυχῆς 'νέως' γίνεται 'τοῦ ἁγίου πνεύματος' id.*str.*7.11(p.46.21; M.9.489B); ἐὰν εἰς κ. σώματος βλέψῃ τις...καὶ αὐτῷ ἡ σὰρξ εἶναι...δόξῃ καλή, σαρκικῶς ἰδὼν καὶ ἁμαρτητικῶς κρίνεται...ὁ δι' ἀγάπην τὴν ἁγνὴν προσβλέπων τὸ κ. οὐ τὴν σάρκα ἡγεῖται, ἀλλὰ τὴν ψυχὴν καλήν, τὸ σῶμα, οἶμαι, ὡς ἀδριάντα θαυμάσας, δι' οὗ κάλλους ἐπὶ τὸν τεχνίτην καὶ τὸ ὄντως καλὸν αὐτὸς αὐτὸν παραπέμπει *ib.*4.18(p.299.12; M.8.1324B); τὸ κ. τῆς νύμφης, ἧς ὁ 'νύμφιος' λόγος ὢν θεοῦ ἐρᾷ, ψυχῆς τυγχανούσης ἀνθούσης ὑπερουρανίῳ καὶ ὑπερκοσμίῳ κάλλει...τὸ γὰρ κυρίως κ. σὰρξ οὐ χωρεῖ Or.*or.*16.2(p.339.6; M.11.472B); κατὰ...τὴν συμμετρίαν καὶ ἁρμονίαν τῶν τῆς ψυχῆς θεωρημάτων, ἔνιοι τῶν σοφῶν νενοήκασι τὸ κ. ... ἵνα καὶ κ. ἐπιγένηται τῇ ψυχῇ...θείας...χάριτος χρῄζομεν...καλὴ μὲν οὖν πᾶσα ψυχὴ ἡ ἐν συμμετρίᾳ τῶν οἰκείων δυνάμεων θεωρουμένη· κ. δὲ ἀληθινόν, καὶ ἐρασμιώτατον, μόνῳ τῷ τὸν νοῦν κεκαθαρμένῳ θεωρητόν, τὸ περὶ τὴν θείαν...φύσιν Bas.*hom.in Ps.*29(1.128E,129A,B; M.29.317A,B); ἡ τῶν ἄλλων γυναικῶν κάλλει φιλοτιμουμένων...ἓν ἐπισταμένη κ., τὸ τῆς ψυχῆς, καὶ τὸ τὴν θείαν εἰκόνα...συντηρεῖν Gr.Naz.*or.*8.8(M.35.993B); marred by sin τὸ θεοειδὲς ἐκεῖνο τῆς ψυχῆς κ. τὸ κατὰ μίμησιν τοῦ πρωτοτύπου γενόμενον...οὐκέτι...τῆς οἰκείας αὐτῷ καὶ κατὰ φύσιν εἰκόνος τὴν χάριν διέσωζεν Gr.Nyss.*virg.*12(p.299.19; M.46.372B); restored by cleansing, *ib.* cit. s. κάλυμμα; cf.id.*hom.*4 *in Cant.*(M.44.832C,D) cit. s. καλός; ref. Ps.44:14 ὡς ἔνδον εὑρήσων τὸ κ. τὸ ἀληθινόν Clem.*paed.*3.2(p.238.23; 560C); κ. ἀπόθετον Gr.Naz.*or.*24.8(1180A); ὡς ἔνδον ὄντος τοῦ κάλλους τῆς νύμφης [sc. Χριστοῦ] Bas. *hom.in Ps.*44(1.168C; M.412A); **3.** revealed by Word ὁ...ἄνθρωπος ἐκεῖνος, ᾧ σύνοικος ὁ λόγος...κ. ἐστι τὸ ἀληθινόν, καὶ γὰρ ὁ θεός ἐστιν Clem.*paed*.3.1(p.236.24; M.8.556C); δεικνύντος ὡς ἀληθῶς τοῦ λόγου τὸ κ. τὸ ἀληθινόν *ib*.2.12(p.234.10; 553A); τὸν ἁπάντων ὑπὸ κάλλους ἀρρήτου ἐπακτικώτατον...λόγον Gr.Thaum.*pan.Or*.6(p.17.2; M.10.1072B); **4.** of God οἱ ἄγγελοι τοῦ θεοῦ τὸ κ. καταλελοιπότες διὰ κ. μαραινόμενον Clem.*paed*.3.2(p.244.24; M.8.576B); πᾶσα...ἡ κτίσις ἐνδεὴς ἐστι τοῦ κ. τοῦ θεοῦ Meth.*Porph*.3(p.506.11; M.18.401A); μορφὴν...ἔχει διὰ πρῶτον καὶ μόνον κ. καὶ πάντα μέλη, οὐ διὰ χρῆσιν *Hom.Clem*.17.7; of God as beauty and goodness τὸ ὑπὲρ πᾶν φῶς ἀγαθὸν...τοῦτο τἀγαθὸν ὑμνεῖται...καὶ ὡς καλόν, καὶ ὡς κ. ... καλὸν μὲν εἶναι λέγομεν τὸ κάλλους μετέχον, κ. δὲ τὴν μετοχὴν τῆς καλλοποιοῦ τῶν ὅλων καλῶν αἰτίας. τὸ δὲ ὑπερούσιον καλὸν κ. μὲν λέγεται, διὰ τὴν ἀπ' αὐτοῦ πᾶσι τοῖς οὖσι μεταδιδομένην οἰκείως ἑκάστῳ καλλονήν Dion. Ar.*d.n*.4.7(M.3.701C,D); τὸ θεοπρεπὲς κ., ὡς ἁπλοῦν, ὡς ἀγαθόν, ὡς τελεταρχικόν, ἀμιγὲς μέν ἐστι καθόλου πάσης ἀνομοιότητος, μεταδοτικὸν δὲ...καὶ τελειωτικὸν ἐν τελετῇ θειοτάτῃ id.*c.h*.3.1(M.3.164D); τοῦ καλλοποιοῦ καὶ ἀρχικοῦ κάλλους ὑπερουσίου *ib*.7.2(208C); πρὸς ἐκεῖνο τὸ νοητὸν καὶ εὐῶδες ἀφορῶν κ. ... ἑαυτὸ τυποῖ καὶ διαπλάττει πρὸς τὸ κάλλιστον μίμημα id.*e.h*.4.3.1(M.3.473B); imitated by Christian priest εἰς τὸ θεοειδέστατον ἀνηγμένος κ. *ib*.5.3.6(513B); by redeemed man, exeg. Cant.2:10 τὸ τῆς ἀνθρωπίνης φύσεως κάτοπτρον, οὐ πρότερον ἐγένετο καλόν, ἀλλ' ὅτε τῷ καλῷ ἐπλησίασε, καὶ τῇ εἰκόνι τοῦ θείου κ. ἐνεμορφώθη...βλέπει δὲ πρὸς τὸ ἀρχέτυπον κ. Gr.Nyss.*hom.5 in Cant*.(M. 44.868C,D); **5.** plur., *sights of beauty*, in contemplation τηλαυγέστερα κάλλη καὶ θειότερα...εὐπρεπέστερα καὶ ἑνοειδέστερα Dion.Ar.*e.h*.7.3. 11(M.3.568D,569A); *signs of* spiritual *beauty*, *ib*.3.3.11(441B).

κάλλυντρον ([*]**κάλυντρον**), τό, *palm-branch*, ref. use in Feast of Tabernacles τὰ κ., τὴν ἄσκησιν καὶ μελέτην τῶν γραφῶν Meth. *symp*.9.4(p.118.20; M.18.185B); κάλυντρα φοινίκων ἐδέχοντο...γράφοντος...τοῦ τύπου τὰς ἐν παραδείσῳ τρυφάς Cyr.*hom.pasch*.28(5^2.327E).

***καλλωπιστέος**, *fit to be adorned* ἡ ψυχὴ κ. τῷ τῆς καλοκἀγαθίας κοσμήματι Clem.*paed*.3.2(p.237.26; M.8.560A).

καλλωπιστής, ὁ, *one who paints* or *embellishes*, Agath.*v.Gr.Ill*.59.

***καλλώπιστος**, *adorned*, Ephr.3.472E.

***καλλωποιέομαι**, *adorn oneself*, Gr.Naz.*or*.7.20(M.35.781A).

καλόγηρος, *venerable*; of priests or ascetics, esp. in address, Pall.*h.Laus*.35(p.102.15; M.34.1113D); Dor.*doct*.7.6(M.88.1705B); Jo. Mosch.*prat*.1(M.87.2853B).

***καλογραῦς**, ἡ, *venerable lady*, ‡Caes.Naz.*dial*.140(M.38.1048).

***καλοδουλεία**, ἡ, *noble servitude* ἦλθεν γὰρ ἐξαγοράσαι ἡμᾶς ἐν τῷ ἰδίῳ αἵματι εἰς τὴν κ. τῆς θεότητος αὐτοῦ Agath.*v.Gr.Ill*.36.

καλοειδής, *of beautiful form*, *V.Zos*.3(p.97.27).

***καλοεργία**, ἡ, *good work*, Ephr.3.397B; of improvements made by a farmer; fig., of Christian life, Jo.Clim.*scal*.26(M.88.1025A).

***καλοήθεια**, ἡ, *goodness of disposition*, Gr.Mag.*dial*.(tr.Zach.)1.3 (M.*PL*.77.166A).

καλοθέλεια, ἡ, *goodwill*, Pall.*v.Chrys*.6(p.35.1; M.47.21); Gr. Mag.*dial*.(tr.Zach.)4.60(M.*PL*.77.427C).

καλοθελής, *well disposed*, *benevolent*, Ephr.3.213E; Leo Mag.*ep*. 106(p.58.8; καλοτελεῖ M.*PL*.54.1003A).

καλοθελῶς, *with good will*, Horm.*ep.Epiph*.(p.57.24; M.*PL*.63. 518C); *benevolently*, Leont.N.*v.Sym*.52(M.93.1736A).

καλοκἀγαθία, ἡ, *goodness*, *nobility of character* τὰ δὲ ἄλλα πάντα [sc. πίστις, ἀγάπη] εἰς κ. ἀκόλουθά ἐστιν Ign.*Eph*.14.1; ἡ ψυχὴ καλλωπιστέα τῷ τῆς καλοκἀγαθίας κοσμήματι Clem.*paed*.3.2(p.237.27; M.8.560A); ἴδωμεν εἰ μὴ Χριστιανοὶ μᾶλλον καὶ τούτων [sc. φιλοσόφων] βέλτιον πλήθη ἐπὶ καλοκἀγαθίαν προκαλοῦνται Or.*Cels*.3.51(p.247.2; M.11.988A); εἰ πάλαι εἶχεν ἡ τῶν ἀνθρώπων φύσις τὰ εἰς κ. σπέρματα Isid.Pel.*epp*.2.2(M.78.456B); opp. ἔχθρα, Clem.*str*.2.18(p.161.16,19; M.8.560A); *generosity*; of emperors, Ursac.*ep.Jul*.ap.Ath.*apol.sec*. 58(p.138.11; M.25.353B); Const.ap.Eus.*h.e*.10.5.10(M.20.884B); Eus. *v.C*.1.43(p.28.13; M.20.957C); as title of address, Ath.*apol.Const*.32 (M.25.637C); Bas.*ep*.112.1(3.204B; M.32.521B); Gr.Naz.*ep*.126(M.37. 221A).

***καλοκαίριον**, τό, *good season*, Thphn.*chron*.p.326(M.108.788B).

***καλοκῆρυξ**, ὁ, *noble proclaimer* Κύριλλος ὁ κ. τῆς ἁγίας θεοτόκου Jo.Not.*v.Eus*.1(M.86.301C).

***καλονοησία**, ἡ, *right-mindedness*, Dor.*doct*.9.3(M.88.1720C); *ib*. 17.3(1804C).

***καλοποδίνως**, *with good fortune*, *luckily*, Heracl.*ep*.(M.92.1025B).

***καλοποιΐα**, ἡ, *doing good*, *beneficence*; of God, Thphl.Ant.*Autol*. 1.3(M.6.1028C).

***καλοπραγμοσύνη**, ἡ, *good activity*, Pall.*h.Laus*.proem.(p.12.5; φιλοπραγμοσύναι M.34.1003).

***καλόρινος**, *with well-shaped nose*, *A.Barth*.2(p.131.19).

καλός, [superl. καλλίστατος, Procl.CP *hom*.2.3(M.65.840C)]; *beautiful*, *good*, *fair*;

A. of creatures; **1.** γεννήτωρ [sc. ὁ θεός] τῶν κ. Clem.*str*.7.3(p.12. 18; M.9.421A); πάντα...κ. καὶ καθαρὰ τὰ τοῦ θεοῦ ποιήματα Ath.*ep. Amun*.(M.26.1169A); οὐδὲ τοιαύτη παρ' αὐτῷ [sc. τῷ θεῷ] ἡ ἀποδοχὴ τῶν κ., οἵα παρ' ἡμῖν· ἀλλὰ κ. τὸ τῷ λόγῳ τῆς τέχνης ἐκτελεσθέν, καὶ πρὸς τὴν τοῦ τέλους εὐχρηστίαν συντεῖνον Bas.*hex*.3.10(1.32A; M.29. 76C); *ib*.4.6(38E; M.92B); παντὸς ζῴου κ. τυγχάνοντος ἅτε ὑπ' ἐμοῦ [sc. τοῦ θεοῦ] γενομένου *Const.App*.6.20.8; their proper use χρὴ δι' ὄψεως ἀπολαύοντας τῶν κ. δοξάζειν τὸν δημιουργόν Clem.*paed*.2.8 (p.200.9; M.8.480A); and avoidance τὰ πρόχειρα πάντα τοῦ κόσμου κ. οὐκ ἀγαπᾷ [sc. ὁ γνωστικός], ἵνα μὴ καταμείνῃ χαμαί id.*str*.7.11 (p.45.22; M.9.488B); *ib*.7.12(p.55.26; 508B); ἀπὸ τῶν νομιζομένων εἶναι ἐν κόσμῳ κ. ἀναχωροῦντα [sc. τὸν Ἰησοῦν] Or.*Jo*.28.23(18; p.419.31; M.14.732C); **2.** vocative, *dear*, *good* ὦ παῖ καλέ Dion.Ar.*e.h*.3.3.1(M. 3.428A); ὦ κ. Διονύσιε id.*ep*.7.3(M.3.1081C); κ. ἄνθρωπε Jo.Mosch. *prat*.207(M.87.3097C); **3.** c. prepp. εἰς τὰ καλά *well*, Dion.Ar.*ep*.9.6 (M.3.1113B); ἐν καλῷ *in a good position* or *place* δογματικῆς εὐτεχνίας ἐν κ. γεγονότες (i.e. well up, high up in the skill of doctrinal exposition) Cyr.*Is*.5.4(2.823C); *ib*.(847C); ἐπὶ καλοῖς *for good*, *favourably*, Ath.*apol.sec*.7(p.93.15; M.25.260D); **4.** c. ἵνα: οὐκ ἔστι κ. ἵνα ἀναγκασθῶσιν *Apophth.Patr*.(M.65.301A); κ. ἐστιν, ἵνα ἔχωμεν εὐλάβειαν Dor.*doct*.4.7(M.88.1665D).

B. spiritual; **1.** Trin. τριάδα...σοφὴν...καὶ κ. Dion.Ar.*d.n*.1.4 (M.3.592A); **2.** of God ὁ τοῦ μισθοῦ κ. ἀνταποδότης *Did*.4.7; ὁ κ. κύριος *Barn*.7.1; ἐσμὲν τοῦ κ. *A.Andr.fr*.1(p.38.13); Dion.Ar.*d.n*.1.6 (M.3.596B); **3.** of Christ ὁ σωτὴρ...κ. ... ὡς ἀγαπᾶσθαι μόνος πρὸς ἡμῶν τὸ κ. τὸ ἀληθινὸν ἐπιποθούντων Clem.*str*.2.5(p.123.18; M.8. 953A); ἀφ' οὗ...οὐδὲν ἄλλο μοι κ. εἶναι δοκεῖ...σὺ δὲ ἀληθῶς κ.· οὐ κ. δὲ μόνον, ἀλλ' αὐτῇ τῇ τοῦ κ. οὐσίᾳ ἀεὶ τοιοῦτος ὑπάρχων Gr.Nyss. *hom.4 in Cant*.(M.44.836A); of name of Christ τὸ κ. καὶ ὑπὲρ πᾶν ὄνομα τοῦ σωτῆρος Ath.*ep.Aeg.Lib*.3(M.25.544C); ταῦτα...φλυαροῦσι [sc. Arians]...προαιρέσει κατὰ τὸ αὐτεξούσιον καλός ἐστι [sc. ὁ λόγος] Ath.*Ar*.1.35(M.26.84B); Ar.*Thal.fr*.9 *ib*.1.5(21C); cf.Ath.*ep.Aeg. Lib*.12(564C) cit. s. τρεπτός; **4.** of fallen angels κ. ... γεγόνασι καὶ αὐτοί Ath.*v.Anton*.22(M.26.876A); **5.** of man, Clem.*paed*.2.12 (p.230.14; M.8.544C) cit. s. κάλλος; οὐκ...τὸν κ. τὸ σῶμα, ἀλλὰ τὸν κ. τὴν ψυχήν *ib*.3.2(p.243.9; 572C); ἀνδρὶ βουλομένῳ εἶναι καλῷ τὸ κάλλιστον ἐν ἀνθρώπῳ τὴν διανοίαν κοσμητέον *ib*.3.3(p.248.24; 584B); before Fall κ. γενόμενοι, ὕστερον παράβαται τῆς ἐντολῆς Ath.*Ar*.2.75 (M.26.305B); κ. μὲν ἤμην κατὰ τὴν φύσιν, ἀσθενὴς δὲ διὰ τὸ...νεκρωθῆναι τῷ παραπτώματι Bas.*hom.in Ps*.29(1.129A; M.29.317A); and after redemption, exeg. Cant.1:15 παιδεύει...ταύτην εἶναι τοῦ κάλλους τὴν ἐπανάληψιν, τὸ πλησίον γενέσθαι τῆς τοῦ καλοῦ πηγῆς, καὶ προσεγγίσαι πάλιν τῷ ἀληθινῷ κάλλει, οὗ ἀπεφοίτησε...πρότερον οὐκ ἦσθα καλή, διότι τοῦ ἀρχετύπου κάλλους ἀποξενωθεῖσα...πρὸς τὸ εἰδεχθὲς ἠλλοιώθης Gr.Nyss.*hom.4 in Cant*.(M.44.832C,D); ὁ δὲ ἅπαξ ἐν τῇ θείᾳ δόξῃ γενόμενος, ὅλος γίνεται κ., ἔξω τοῦ ἀντικειμένου μώμου γενόμενος *ib*.7(940B); *ib*.5(868C) cit. s. κάλλος; of soul, Clem.*str*.4.18(p.299.13; M.8.1325A) cit. s. κάλλος; γέγονε...καλὴ καὶ εὐθὴς Ath.*v.Anton*.20 (M.26.873A); of virtues ὁ φόβος αὐτοῦ [sc. τοῦ θεοῦ] κ. *1Clem*.21.8; ἡ πολυτέλεια κ. καὶ ἱλαρά Herm.*sim*.1.10; ἡ νηστεία...λίαν κ. ἐστι *ib*. 5.3.5; μετὰ κ. ἐλπίδος Constantius Imp.ap.Ath.*apol.Const*.30(M.25. 633D); ref. moral life ἡ ψυχὴ...δῆλος ἔστω ἐν τοῖς κ. ἔργοις *2Clem*. 12.4; τοῖς νῦν...παράδειγμα κ. ἐσόμενοι Constantius Imp.ap.Ath.*apol. Const*.30(633C); τινὸς οὐ κ. ἀγωγῆς *Const.App*.3.8.2; τῶν κ. ἕξεων τε καὶ ἐνεργειῶν Dion.Ar.*c.h*.7.4(M.3.212A); superl., id.*e.h*.4.3.1(M.3.473B) cit. s. κάλλος; ref. contemplation οὕτω κ. τὰ νοητὰ θεάματα *ib*.4.1 (472D); **6.** of law ὁ νόμος κ. καὶ ἅγιος *Const.App*.6.19.4; Thdt.*Rom*. 7:21(3.78); Thdr.Mops.*Rom*.7:19,20(p.131.35; M.66.816A); of divine teaching αἱ ἐντολαὶ κ. Herm.*mand*.12.3.4; τὰ λόγια τοῦ θεοῦ, ὡς κ. καὶ μέγαλα *2Clem*.13.3; τὰς τοῦ Χριστοῦ κ. ὑποθημοσύνας Just.*1apol*. 14.3(M.6.348C); *orthodox*, *correct* ἃ...ὁ κύριος διὰ τῶν ἀποστόλων τετύπωκε, ταῦτα κ. ... μένει Ath.*ep.Diac*.3(M.25.525D); ἀποδεξάμενοι ...ὡς κ. τὸ τῆς οὐσίας ὄνομα id.*syn*.37(p.264.7; M.26.760A); τὸ [Mc.13:32] κ. ἔχει τὸν νοῦν id.*ep.Serap*.2.9(M.26.621C); τὸ κ. δόγμα κηρύττειν Aen.*ep*.15(p.28).

C. neut. as subst., spiritual *beauty*, *goodness*; **1.** in gen. ἐργάσεσθε τὸ κ. *Barn*.21.2; μετακινηθῆναι ἀπὸ τοῦ κ. Or.*Jo*.20.27(22; p.363.13; M.14.636A); σκοπῶν...τὸ κ. ὁ ἅγιος Ath.*gent*.5(M.25.12C); μὴ... ἀφηνιάσωσι τοῦ κ. *Const.App*.4.11.1; Dion.Ar.*d.n*.8.9(M.3.897B); v. supra A.3; with soul ἐν τῇ ψυχῇ τὸ ὄντως κ. ὑπὸ τοῦ θείου λόγου ἀναζωπυρούμενον ἐκλάμπειν Clem.*prot*.11(p.82.25; M.8.236D); τὸ εὐγενὲς τῆς ἀληθείας, ἐν τῷ φύσει καλῷ κατὰ ψυχὴν ἐξεταζόμενον id.*paed*. 3.11(p.269.29; M.8.632C); τὸ ἀληθινῶς κ. τὸ ἐν τῇ ψυχῇ †Bas.*Is*.174(1. 505D; M.30.409B); as motive force ἡ δι' ἀγάπην εὐποιΐα ἢ δι' αὐτὸ τὸ κ. αἱρετή [sc. τῷ γνωστικῷ] Clem.*str*.4.22(p.308.16; M.8.1345B); *ib*. 7.7(p.37.16; M.9.469C); ἡ τὸ κ. δι' αὐτὸ τὸ κ. πράττουσα Isid.Pel.

ep.4.5(M.78.1053B); *ib*.4.135(1216D); cf. *ἐγγυμναζόμενοι...ἐν ταῖς ὑπὲρ τοῦ κ. περιστάσεσιν* Dion.Ar.*d.n*.8.8(896C); man's knowledge of it *τὸ κ. ... σοφίᾳ θεωρητὸν καὶ νοητόν...σωφροσύνῃ καὶ δικαιοσύνῃ διὰ πίστεως πρακτόν* Clem.*ecl*.37(p.148.13; M.9.717B); *ἔμφυτον...νόμον πρὸς τὸ κ. ἡμῶν ἐξεγείροντα τὸν λογισμόν* Meth.*res*.2.6(p.340.9; M.18.304C); *ὁ πονηρὸς...τὸ κ., ὅ τί ποτέ ἐστιν ἀγνοῶν* *Const.App*.6.6.8; *τῇ μὲν ψυχῇ αἱροῦμαι τὸ κ. ὑπὸ τοῦ νόμου παιδευόμενος...ἀκριβὴς ἐγκεῖται ἡμῖν ἥ τε τοῦ κ. καὶ τοῦ κακοῦ διάκρισις* Thdr.Mops.*Rom*.7:19,20(pp.131.27,132.4; M.66.816A,B); *τὴν ἀγνωσίαν τοῦ ὄντως κ.* Dion.Ar.*e.h*.2.2.5(M.3.396A); *τὸ κ. ἢ χεῖρον ἐφ' ἑαυτοῦ θεομιμήτως κρίναντες* *ib*.4.3.1(476A); Manich. *τὸ...φυτὸν ἐξ οὗ γνωρίζουσι τὸ κ. αὐτός ἐστιν ὁ Ἰησοῦς...ὁ δὲ λαμβάνων διακρίνει τὸ κ. καὶ τὸ πονηρόν* Hegem.*Arch*.11(p.18.4; M.10.1445A); real and apparent *εἴδωλον... τοῦ κ. τὴν φιλοκοσμίαν, οὐχὶ δὲ αὐτὸ ⟨τὸ⟩ κ. προστρεπομένους... δόξῃ, οὐκ ἐπιστήμῃ ὀνειροπολοῦντας τοῦ κ. τὴν φύσιν·...χρὴ...ἡμᾶς ἐπὶ τὸ ὄντως κ. καὶ κόσμιον σπεύδειν* Clem.*paed*.2.10(p.220.16; M.8.524A); *ἰδοῦσα* [sc. *ἡ ψυχή*] *καλὸν ἑαυτῇ εἶναι τὴν ἡδονήν, πλανηθεῖσα κατεχρήσατο τῷ τοῦ καλοῦ ὀνόματι, καὶ ἐνόμισεν εἶναι τὴν ἡδονὴν αὐτὸ τὸ ὄντως κ.* Ath.*gent*.4(M.25.9B); Mac.Aeg.*cust.cor*.3(M.34.824B); **2.** ref. God, Clem.*str*.4.18(p.299.17; M.8.1325A) cit. s. *κάλλος*; *εἴτε τὸ κ. ὑπάρχει ἐραστὸν αὐτῷ* [sc. *τῷ θεῷ*], *αὐτὸς ὢν τὸ μόνον κ., εἰς ἑαυτὸν βλέπει* Meth.*Porph*.3(p.506.15; M.18.401A); *ἀνελλιπὴς τυγχάνων ἐν τῷ κ.* Alex.Al.*ep.Alex*.7(p.23.20; M.18.557B); *μόνῃ τῇ διανοίᾳ τῇ καθ' ὑπερβολὴν κεκαθαρμένῃ τὸ κυρίως κ. ἐν τῇ θείᾳ φύσει γινώσκεται* †Bas.*Is*.175(1.506D; M.30.412C); *τὸ κ. ... ἐπὶ τῆς ὅλης θεότητος ὑμνεῖται* Dion.Ar.*d.n*.2.1(M.3.637B); as source of all, *ib*.4.7(701D) cit. s. *κάλλος*; *καὶ ἀρχὴ πάντων τὸ κ., ὡς ποιητικὸν αἴτιον...καὶ πέρας πάντων...ὡς τελικὸν αἴτιον (τοῦ κ. γὰρ ἕνεκα πάντα γίγνεται)* *ib*.(704A); *πρὸς τοῦ ὄντως κ. τὴν ὕπαρξιν ἐσχηκυῖα* [sc. *ὕλη*] id.*c.h*.2.4(M.3.144B); as object of participation *μηδὲ ἐν τῶν ὄντων εἶναι καθόλου τῆς τοῦ κ. μετουσίας ἐστερημένον* *ib*.2.3(141C); *διὰ...τῆς ἐνθέου καὶ ἱεραρχικῆς ἁρμονίας τοῦ ὄντως ὄντος κ. καὶ σοφοῦ καὶ ἀγαθοῦ μετέχειν* id.*e.h*.1.2(M.3.373A); but not source of evil *οὐ γὰρ ἐκ τοῦ κ. τὸ κακόν, οὐδὲ ἐν αὐτῷ ἐστιν, οὐδὲ δι' αὐτοῦ· ἐπεὶ οὐκέτι κ. ἂν εἴη μεμιγμένην ἔχον τὴν φύσιν, ἢ αἴτιον γινόμενον κακοῦ* Ath.*gent*.6(M.25.13A); **3.** without article *τὸ ἐν τῇ φύσει τῇ τῶν ἀνθρώπων εἶναι τὸ γνωριστικὸν καλοῦ καὶ αἰσχροῦ* Just.*2apol*.14.2(M.6.468B); *τοῦτον... ἐζήλωσεν ἐν καλῷ* Ath.*v.Anton*.3(M.26.844B); *οὐ καλῷ τὸ κακὸν ἰώμενοι, καλοῦ δὲ τὸ φαῦλον ἀντιλαμβάνοντες* Gr.Naz.*or*.8.13(M.35.804B); *οὐκ ἐγίνωσκε κ. καὶ πονηρὸν ὁ Ἀδάμ* ‡Ath.*Apoll*.1.15(M.26.1120B); *ib*.2.6(1141A); *περὶ...καλοῦ* Dion.Ar.*d.n*.4 tit.(M.3.693A); **4.** neut. plur.; **a.** in gen. *τὰ κ. ... ἐνώπιον αὐτοῦ ποιῶμεν* *1Clem*.21.1; *ἐν τῷ Μωυσέως νόμῳ τὰ φύσει κ. ... νενομοθέτηται πράττειν* Just.*dial*.45.3(M.6.572C); *φεύγειν τὰ αἰσχρὰ καὶ αἱρεῖσθαι τὰ κ.* id.*1apol*.43.3(M.6.393A); *χρὴ...ἀεὶ τῶν κ. ἐρᾶν* Meth.*symp*.1.1(p.9.7; M.18.40A); *ἃ ποιοῦμεν κ., μὴ δι' ἀνθρώπους, ἀλλὰ δι' αὐτὸν* [sc. *τὸν πατέρα*] *ποιῶμεν* Ath.*Ar*.3.19(M.26.361C); *ἀμετάπειστοι τῶν κ.* *Const.App*.5.8.2; *τὴν ...τῶν κ. καὶ τῶν οὐ τοιούτων γνῶσιν* Chrys.*hom.13.2 in Rom*.(9.560B); *πράττω...τἀναντία ὧν ἐπίσταμαί τε καὶ βούλομαι καλῶν* Thdr.Mops.*Rom*.7:19(p.131.30; M.66.816A); *ἐγὼ δὲ ὑμᾶς διαλάμπειν ἐν ἅπασι βούλομαι τοῖς κ.* Thdt.*Gal*.4:18(3.384); *τὰ κ. φιλῶ καὶ τἀναντία μισῶ* id.*Rom*.7:21(3.78); **b.** of spiritual benefits, *Const.App*.2.13.3; *τῶν οἰκείων ἀνέδειξε* [sc. *ὁ θεός*] *μετόχους καλῶν* Dion.Ar.*e.h*.3.3.11(M.3.441B); *τὰ κτηθέντα κ. βεβαίως...ἕξουσιν* *ib*.7.2(553D); *Ἰησοῦ... τῶν κ. διανέμοντος* id.*ep*.9.5(M.3.1113A); *προσεύχου πυκνῶς μετ' ἐλπίδος βεβαίας τῶν κ.* Jo.D.*spir.neq*.8(M.95.81C); liturg. *ἀναστάντες αἰτησώμεθα...τὰ κ. καὶ τὰ συμφέροντα* *Const.App*.8.36.3; superl. *αἰτεῖν τὰ κάλλιστα* Clem.*str*.7.12(p.52.18; M.9.501A); *οἱ πονεῖν ἕτοιμοι ἐπὶ τοῖς καλλίστοις* *ib*.7.16(p.66.1; 529A); **c.** *the true* opp. the false *οὐκ ὄντα...τὰ κακά, ὄντα δὲ τὰ κ., ἐπειδήπερ ἀπὸ τοῦ ὄντος θεοῦ γεγόνασι* Ath.*inc*.4.5(M.25.104C); *ὄντα δέ φημι τὰ κ., καθότι ἐκ τοῦ ὄντος θεοῦ τὰ παραδείγματα ἔχει* id.*gent*.4(M.25.9C); *ἀπὸ τοῦ ὄντος καλοῦ παρεκτρέπων ἐπὶ τὰ δοκήσει, ἀλλ' οὐκ ὄντως καλά. πᾶν γὰρ ὃ ἐὰν ποιῇ ἄνθρωπος κ., σπιλοῦν καὶ μιαίνειν ὁ πονηρὸς βούλεται* Mac.Aeg.*cust.cor*.3(M.34.824B); *οὐδὲ τῶν δοκούντων εἰκῇ κ. καὶ δικαίων, ἀλλὰ τῶν ὄντων ὄντως ἐρώσιν* Dion.Ar.*e.h*.4.3.2(M.3.476A).

D. *καλὸς καὶ ἀγαθός* (*καλὸς κἀγαθός*); **1.** of man, *perfect, excellent* in character and morals *μόνος ὁ σπουδαῖος κ. κἀγαθὸς ὄντως ἐστίν, καὶ μόνον τὸ κ. ἀγαθὸν δογματίζεται* Clem.*paed*.2.12(p.230.6; M.8.544B); *ἐκ προαιρέσεως κ. καὶ ἀγαθός* [sc. *ὁ γνωστικός*] id.*str*.7.12(p.53.22; M.9.504A); *τὸ θεῖον...ὅμοιον τοῖς κ. κἀγαθοῖς ἀνδράσι φαίνεται* *ib*.7.2(p.11.20; ...*μόνοις τοῖς κ.* 420A); of divine *ἔρως*, Dion.Ar.*d.n*.4.13(M.3.712A) cit. infra; **2.** neut. as subst., *beauty and goodness*; ref. God *ταὐτόν ἐστι τἀγαθῷ τὸ κ., ὅτι τοῦ κ. καὶ ἀγαθοῦ...πάντα ἐφίεται· καὶ οὐκ ἔστι τι τῶν ὄντων, ὃ μὴ μετέχει τοῦ κ. καὶ ἀγαθοῦ...τότε...καὶ αὐτὸ κ. καὶ ἀγαθόν, ὅταν ἐν θεῷ κατὰ τὴν πάντων ἀφαίρεσιν ὑπερουσίως ὑμνῆται. τοῦτο τὸ ἓν ἀγαθὸν καὶ κ. ἑνικῶς ἐστι πάντων τῶν πολλῶν κ. καὶ ἀγαθῶν αἴτιον* Dion.Ar.*d.n*.4.7(M.3.704A,B); responsible for all motion and rest, itself beyond motion and rest, *ib*.4.8,9,10(704D–705C); the principle of difference, unity, and being of all things *πᾶν ὂν ἐκ τοῦ κ. καὶ ἀγαθοῦ καὶ ἐν τῷ ἀγαθῷ καὶ κ. ἐστι, καὶ εἰς τὸ κ. καὶ ἀγαθὸν ἐπιστρέφεται...ἵνα συλλαβὼν εἴπω, πάντα τὰ ὄντα ἐκ τοῦ κ. καὶ ἀγαθοῦ· καὶ πάντα τὰ οὐκ ὄντα, ὑπερουσίως ἐν τῷ κ. καὶ ἀγαθῷ· καὶ ἔστι πάντων ἀρχή, καὶ πέρας ὑπεράρχιον, καὶ ὑπερτελές* *ib*.4.10(705D,708A); cf.*ib*.4.12(709D); the object of all desire, *ib*.(708A); itself being desire *ὁ πάντων αἴτιος, τῷ κ. καὶ ἀγαθῷ τῶν πάντων ἔρωτι δι' ὑπερβολὴν τῆς ἐρωτικῆς ἀγαθότητος ἔξω ἑαυτοῦ γίνεται...ὅλως τοῦ κ. καὶ ἀγαθοῦ ἐστι τὸ ἐραστόν, καὶ ὁ ἔρως, καὶ ἐν τῷ κ. καὶ ἀγαθῷ προΐδρυται, καὶ διὰ τὸ κ. καὶ ἀγαθόν ἐστι καὶ γίνεται* *ib*.4.13(712A,B); relationship towards demons, *ib*.4.18(716A); *ib*.4.23(725C).

***καλοστροφάω**, *turn over well*; of digging, Dor.*doct*.4(M.88.1756A).

***καλοτελής**, v. *καλοθελής*.

***καλοφροσύνη**, **ἡ**, *right-mindedness, good judgement*; iron. ref. heretics, Max.*opusc*.(M.91.97A).

κάλπις, **ἡ**, *pitcher*, plur. *κάλπεις*, Men.*exc.Rom*.8(p.194.9; M.113.888A).

καλύβη, **ἡ**, *cell* of a monk, Chrys.*stat*.1.2(2.3E); met., of heaven *ἐν θαυμασταῖς κ.* ‡Nil.*perist*.12.12(M.79.965A).

καλύβιον, **τό**, *small cell*; of a monk, ‡Pall.*h.mon*.2.5(p.25.17; M.34.1027B).

κάλυμμα, **τό**, *veil*; lit.; covering elements at eucharist, *Lit.Chrys*.(p.360.5,13,18; M.63.905); covering face of Moses, signifying lit. sense of Law opp. spiritual meaning, Cyr.*glaph.Dt*.(1.425B); met.; of literal meaning obscuring spiritual sense of scripture, Or.*Cels*.5.60(p.63.31; M.11.1276C); Ath.*Ar*.2.77(M.26.312A); *τὸ τοῦ γράμματος κ.* Thdt.*Cant*.4:7(2.96); of deception *ἵνα...μετὰ καλύμματος αὐτὴν* [sc. *βλασφημίαν*] *ἄλλοις σημαίνωσιν* Ath.*decr*.29(p.25.28; M.25.469C); *ὡς ἂν περιαιρεθέντος τοῦ γηΐνου κ.* [i.e. sin], *πάλιν τῆς ψυχῆς φανερωθῇ τὸ κάλλος* Gr.Nyss.*virg*.12(p.300.4; M.46.372C).

[*]**κάλυντρον**, **τό**, v. *κάλλυντρον*.

***καλυπτέον**, *one must conceal*, Or.*fr.in Mt*.13:20(p.130.10).

καλύπτρη, **ἡ**, **1.** *shroud*, Nonn.*par.Jo*.11:44(M.43.848A); **2.** *cupola*, Paul.Sil.*Soph*.529(M.86.2139B); **3.** *lid* of eye, Geo.Pis.*carm*.48.

καλύπτω, *cover, veil*; a virgin at dedication, *Cod.Afr*.126; met., *overshadow, be superior to*, Eus.*theoph.fr*.6(p.18*.8); Ath.*syn*.1(p.232.1; M.26.684A).

***καλωβατέω**, *walk on a tightrope*, Leont.H.*Nest*.1.23(M.86.1489C).

καλῶς, *well, rightly*; **1.** *for a good purpose*, opp. *ἄχρηστα*, *Diogn*.4.2; *kindly*, Pall.*h.Laus*.41(p.128.14; M.34.1233D); **2.** *κ. ποιῶ be right, do well*, Herm.*vis*.2.4.2; c. ptcpl. *κ. ἐποιήσατε ὑποδεξάμενοι you did well to receive*, Ign.*Smyrn*.10.1; **3.** c. genit. *κ. τῆς Θρᾴκης in a good position in Thrace*, Evagr.*h.e*.3.38(p.136.21; M.86.2677B); **4.** *κ. ἦλθον, be welcome* *κ. ἦλθες* Paul.Em.*hom*.1(p.10.23; M.77.1436C); *κ. ἦλθεν* Jo.Mosch.*prat*.93(M.87.2952C); *ib*.102(2960D).

***κάμακος**, **ὁ**, *pole*, Philost.*h.e*.11.3(M.65.597B).

καμάριον, **τό**, medic., *fornix* of the brain, Hipp.*haer*.4.51(p.76.12; M.16.3122B); *ib*.5.17(p.116.5; 3178C).

καμαρόω, *make a vault over*; of the vaulting of the sky, Dion.Al.ap.Eus.*p.e*.14.25(776D; M.21.1277B); at Creation; as work of Christ, Amph.*hom*.2.6(M.39.52D); ‡Epiph.*hom*.5(M.43.493D); Cosm.Ind.*top*.2(M.88.80D).

[*]**καμαρώδης**, = *καμαροειδής*, *vaulted*; of heavens, †Hipp.*theoph*.1(p.257.21; M.10.852B).

[*]**κάμασον**, **τό**, v. *καμίσιον*.

***καματηφόρος**, *bringing toil and trouble*, Hipp.*Graec*.1(M.10.797B).

κάματος, **ὁ**, *labour*, of spiritual discipline *οὐ μόνον δὲ περὶ τῆς εὐχῆς λέγομεν, ἀλλὰ καὶ περὶ παντὸς κ. ... ἢ παρθενίας, ἢ εὐχῆς, ἢ οἱουδήποτε κ. καὶ ἐργασίας ἀρετῆς ἕνεκεν ἐπιτελουμένου* Mac.Aeg.*cust.cor*.9(M.34.828B); Pall.*h.Laus*.19(M.34.1057D).

***καματουργία**, **ἡ**, *wearisome labour*, Epiph.*haer*.80.4(p.489.8; M.42.761C); *ib*.64.63(p.502.1, v.l. *κάματον* M.41.1177C).

***καματόω**, *give trouble to, inflict pain upon*, ‡Caes.Naz.*dial*.102(M.38.968).

***καμελαύκιον**, **τό**, **1.** kind of *cap*, esp. that worn by certain court officials, Ephr.2.14E; Thphn.*chron*.p.193(M.108.501B); **2.** *hood*, part of monastic habit, *Euchol*.(pp.379,380,381).

καμηλάριος, **ὁ**, *camel-driver*, Dor.*doct*.11.7(M.88.1741C); Jo.Mosch.*prat*.107(M.87.2968B); of certain monks in a Pachomian monastery, Pall.*h.Laus*.32(p.94.8; M.34.1100D).

***καμηλεύω**, *tend camels*, Thphn.*chron*.p.277(M.108.685A).

[*]καμῆλι, τό, dim. of *κάμηλος*, *little camel*, Barth.Edess.*Agar*.(M.104.1429C).

καμήλιον, τό, = foreg., Leont.N.*v.Sym*.45(M.93.1729B).

***καμηλοβάτης, ὁ**, *camel-rider*, Clem.*paed*.3.3(p.250.31; M.8.589B).

***καμηλόκεντρον, τό**, *camel-goad*, Sophr.H.*mir.Cyr.et Jo*.23(M.87.3489A).

***καμηλόνιον, τό**, *young camel*, ‡Barth.Edess.*Muham*.(M.104.1456B).

[*]κάμηλος, ὁ, as form of *κάμιλος*, *rope*, *cable*, exeg. Mt.19:24 *κ. οἱ μὲν τὸ σχοινίον τῆς μηχανῆς, οἱ δὲ τὸ ζῷον* Or.*fr.in Mt*.19:24(p.166); *κ. ἐνταῦθά φησιν, οὐ τὸ ζῷον..., ἀλλὰ τὸ παχὺ σχοινίον ἐν ᾧ δεσμεύουσι τὰς ἀγκύρας οἱ ναῦται* Cyr.*fr.Mt*.19:24(M.72.429D).

***καμηλοσφαγέω**, *sacrifice camels*, Isid.Pel.*epp*.4.57(M.78.1108C).

καμιναῖος, *of a furnace*, Gr.Naz.*or*.16.11(M.35.948C); Gr.Nyss.*hom.3 in Cant*.(M.44.812D); Chrys.*diab*.3.5(2.274A); of Gehenna *φυλάσσεται ἀπὸ τῆς κ. ἐκείνης ὀδύνης* Gr.Nyss.*v.Mos*.(M.44.349D).

καμίνιον, τό, *furnace*, Jo.Mal.*chron*.14 p.360(M.97.536A); Leont.N.*v.Sym*.54(M.93.1736D).

[*]καμίσι(ο)ν (κάμασον), τό, *garment*, perh. *shirt*, Pall.*h.Laus*.65(p.162.2; M.34.1252A); Jo.Mosch.*prat*.68(M.87.2917C); Thphn.*chron*.p.268(M.108.665A); *κάμασον ἕν* Gr.Naz.*test*.(M.37.393B); ref. military wear *ἕκαστος τῶν...πρὸς σαγὶν καὶ κάμισιν* *Chron.Pasch*.p.394(M.92.1012A).

καμμύω, *close the eyes*; as an ascetic practice, against worldly temptations, Cyr.H.*catech*.16.19; Pall.*h.Laus*.39(p.123.14; M.34.1195B); euphem., of the dead, Ephr.2.231D; met., of deliberate mental blindness, Ath.*Ar*.3.52(M.26.433B); Nil.*exerc*.25(M.79.753A); Thdt.*Is*.6:10(p.33.28; 2.212); *sleep*, *rest*, met., Gr.Nyss.*v.Mos*.(M.44.357B).

κάμν-ω, 1. *be sick in mind*, Mac.Mgn.*apocr*.3.5(p.59.7); **2.** *come to grief*, *be worn out*; of a garment, *ib*.2.20(p.38.14); **3.** *win by toil*, *earn*, *V.Dan*.9(p.256.21); **4.** c. prepp.: *κ. εἰς* *toil* or *labour* for *γυναικὶ ...~ούσῃ εἰς τὸ ὑδρεύσασθαι* Or.*Jo*.13.28(p.252.7; M.14.448A); *κ. εἰς δικαιοσύνην* Epiph.*haer*.80.4(p.489.10; M.42.761C); *κ. περί τινα* *labour* or *toil* on behalf of, Or.*Jo*.13.50(49; p.278.21; M.14.492A); *κ. ἄχρις* c. genit. *make a toilsome journey to*, CCP(381)*ep*.ap.Thdt.*h.e*.5.9.9(3.1031); **5.** med., c. *πρός* *grow weary of καμεῖται...πρὸς τὴν ἐν θεωρίᾳ ζωήν* Synes.*Dion* 6(p.249.11; M.66.1129A).

[*]κάμος, ὁ, = *κάβος*, *corn-measure*, Epiph.*mens*.24(M.43.281A).

***καμπάγιον, τό**, *soldier's boot*, Jo.Mal.*chron*.13 p.322(M.97.481C).

[*]Καμπάδοκες, οἱ, = *Καππάδοκες*, *Cappadocians*, Dam.*troph*.2.8(p.234.7).

καμπανίζω, *measure κ. τὸ ἔλαιον* ‡Jo.D.*Const*.14(M.95.329D).

***καμπανιστής, ὁ**, *user of false weights*, †Jo.Jej.*poenit*.(M.88.1924B).

καμπανός, ὁ, (Lat. *campana*) *weighing-machine*, Leont.N.*v.Jo.Eleem*.3(p.9.12).

κάμπη, ἡ, *caterpillar*; as a divine scourge, Thdr.Mops.*Joel*.1:4(M.66.213B) v. s. *βροῦχος*; Thdt.*Am*.1:2(2.1411); ref. Joel 2:25, interpreted to support Arian views *ὁ δὲ Χριστὸς πάλιν οὐκ ἔστιν ἀληθινὴ δύναμις τοῦ θεοῦ, ἀλλὰ μία τῶν λεγομένων δυνάμεών ἐστι καὶ αὐτός, ὧν μία καὶ ἡ ἀκρὶς καὶ ἡ κ.* Ar.Thal.*fr*.8 ap.Ath.*Ar*.1.5(M.26.21C); Ath.*ep.Aeg.Lib*.12(M.25.565B) cit. s. *βροῦχος*; divine, acc. Manichean doctrines of divinity of the soul and of metempsychosis, Chrys.*hom.2.5 in Ac*.(9.21C).

***καμπιδούκτωρ, ὁ**, (Lat. *campidoctor*) *trainer* or *driller of soldiers*, Chrys.*ep.Innoc*.1.3(p.13.28; 3.519C).

***κάμπος, ὁ**, (Lat. *campus*) *plain*, *Pet.Ar*.1 tit.(M.26.820A); *ib*.(820C); Cosm.Ind.*top*.11(M.88.444A); Gr.Mag.*dial*.(tr. Zach.)3.6(M.*PL*.77.227C).

***καμπτή, ἡ**, = *καμπτήρ*, *bend καθάπερ κ. τινα τὴν...διάνοιαν τῷ λόγῳ περιοδεύσας* Gr.Nyss.*Apoll*.24(M.45.1173A).

κάμπτρα, ἡ, *case*, *chest*, *Apophth.Patr*.(M.65.328A).

κάμπτω, *bend*; met., *move to pity*, *cause to relent*, Chrys.*hom.22.5 in Mt*.(7.282B); *ib.87.2*(819C); pass., Bas.*hom*.11.3(2.93B; M.31.376D).

καμπύλη, ἡ, *crooked dealing*, *crooked device*, plur., †Cyr.*hom.div*.14(5².411D).

***καμπυλοειδῶς**, *in a curve*, Thdt.*provid*.5(4.556).

[*]καμπυλόρινος, *crooked-nosed*, Jo.Mal.*chron*.12 p.314(M.97.472C).

[*]καμπυλώδης, *curved in shape*; of eyebrows, Melet.*nat.hom*.9(M.64.1188A).

καμψάκης, ὁ, *cruse*, Epiph.*mens*.21(M.43.272B); Gr.Naz.*carm*.1.2.3.85(M.37.639A); Gr.Nyss.*Placill*.(M.46.885D); met., ref. 3Reg.17:12 *ὁ κ. νοῦς τὴν...τῆς γνώσεως θεωρίαν πηγάυει* Max.*ambig*.(M.91.1125C).

***καμψαρικόν, τό**, *loin-cloth worn by a capsarius*, *V.Dan*.3(p.60.9).

καμψάριος, ὁ, (Lat. *capsarius*) *bathroom attendant*, Epiph.*haer*.55.2(p.313.2; M.41.956D).

***κανάλιον, τό**, *main road ἐν τῷ κ. τῆς Ἰταλίας* Ath.*apol.sec*.50(p.130.19; M.25.340B); *ἐν ταῖς παρόδοις, ἤτοι καναλίῳ* CSard.*can*.20.

***καναλίσκος, ὁ**, *conduit*, *server*, †Anast.S.*relat*.40(*OC* 2 p.85); met., of heresy, Anast.S.*hod*.4(M.89.97C).

[*]κανδῆλα, ἡ, *light*, *lamp*, Eus.Al.*serm*.6(M.86.352A); in pagan worship, Jo.Mal.*chron*.12 p.285(M.97.429B); *Chron.Pasch*.p.251(M.92.605A); in church, Epiph.*haer*.68.7(p.147.24; M.42.196B); Jo.Mosch.*prat*.105(M.87.2964B); Thdr.Stud.*poen*.1.71,72(M.99.1741C,D); symbolizing burning stars, ‡Sophr.H.*liturg*.3(M.87.3984C); or eternal light, *ib*.5(3985C); burning night and day *ἀκοιμήτου κανδήλας τῆς κρεμαμένης ἐπὶ τῇ κόγχῃ τοῦ θυσιαστηρίου* *Fr.hist*.2(M.85.1812B); placed before icon, Jo.Mosch.*prat*.185(3052C); Sophr.H.*mir.Cyr.et Jo*.36(M.87.3560C); containing oil for healing, *ib*.; *ib*.(3553B,C); *Euchol*.(p.346); cf. *τὸ ὕδωρ τῆς ἀσβέστου...κ. πίνουσα...ἠλευθερώθη ἀπὸ τοῦ δαίμονος* Cyr.S.*v.Euthym*.54(p.76.21).

***κανδηλάπτηρ, ὁ**, *lighter of church lamps*, *Euchol*.(p.439).

***κανδηλάριος, ὁ**, *one who tends lamps* in church, Thdr.Stud.*poen*.1.71ff.(M.99.1741C).

***κάνδιδα, τό**, *game* or *play exhibited by a candidate for office οὗτος ἔδωκεν τρίτον κάνδιδα ἐν τῇ Ῥώμῃ* *M.Eleuth*.1(p.149.8); *M.Bon*.1(p.284).

***κανδιδάτισσα, ἡ**, *wife of a κανδιδᾶτος*, Thdr.Stud.*epp*.2.195(M.99.1592C).

***κανδιδᾶτος, ὁ**, (Lat. *candidatus*) *military official* attached to court, Nil.*epp*.1.27(M.79.160B); Jo.Mal.*chron*.13 p.327(M.97.489A); Jo.Mosch.*prat*.185(M.87.3060A).

κάνεον (κανοῦν), τό, 1. *vessel*, *container*; for ink, Clem.*str*.6.4(p.449.8; *κανόνα* M.9.254B); Men.*exc.Rom*.8(p.194.16; M.113.888B); **2.** a dry measure, Epiph.*mens*.21(M.43.272B).

***κανθαροειδής**, *of the beetle kind*, Nil.*Magn*.16(M.79.989C).

κανθήλιον, τό, *pannier*, Jo.Mosch.*prat*.107(M.87.2968B).

***κανικλείων, ὁ**, *keeper of the royal inkstand*, †Gregent.*disp*.(M.86.781A).

κανίσκος, ὁ, *basket of reed* or *cane*, *Apoc.Bar*.12(p.92.32).

***καννίον, τό**, *cup*, Sophr.H.*mir.Cyr.et Jo*.44(M.87.3592C).

***καννοπλόκος, ὁ**, *basket-maker*, Ephr.2.176B.

***κανονάριον, τό**, *collection of rules*, Jo.Jej.*canonar*.1 tit.(p.101; *SS* 4 p.436).

***κανοναρχέω**, *exercise the office of κανονάρχης*, Thdr.Stud.*poen*.1.102(M.99.1748A).

***κανονάρχης, ὁ**, *precentor* of a monastic choir, who led singing and directed choir offices, mentioned as an important official in monastery, Nil.*epp*.3.241(M.79.496B); *ὁ κ. ἐξύπνιζέ με* Dor.*doct*.11.6(M.88.1741D); Cyr.S.*v.Sab*.43(p.134.1) al.; *ἐν μιᾷ νυκτὶ ἠγέρθην, ἐφ' ᾧ κροῦσαι τὸ ξύλον (ἤμην γὰρ κ.)* Jo.Mosch.*prat*.50(M.87.2905A); duties described, Thdr.Stud.*iamb*.10(M.99.1784B); id.*poen*.1.99 tit.(M.99.1745C); *Euchol*.(p.23); met., of S. Paul *ὁ μέγας κ. καὶ ὑπερβαίνων τοὺς λοιποὺς διδασκάλους τῆς ἐκκλησίας Παῦλος* Cosm.Ind.*top*.5(M.88.297D).

κανονίζ-ω, A. *regulate*, *control*; **1.** in gen., of Christian discipline *οἷς ὁ βίος ὡς πρὸς στάθμην τὸν θεὸν ~εται* Athenag.*leg*.31.2(M.6.961B); *τῇ κατὰ τὸ εὐαγγέλιον ἀκριβείᾳ ~ειν τὴν πολιτείαν* Bas.*hom.in Ps*.59(1.190D; M.29.464B); Isid.Pel.*epp*.2.89(M.78.533A); *ὁ τὸ σῶμα κανονίσας* Thal.*cent*.4.77(M.91.1465C); ref. prayer, Nil.*epp*.3.125(M.79.441B); **2.** *place under a rule*; **a.** ref. secular legislation, Gr.Nyss.*bapt.diff*.(M.46.416C); of Church *μὴ ἐν ἀκαταστασίᾳ εἶναι, ἀλλὰ διαμένειν ὥσπερ ὑπὸ τῶν ἀποστόλων ἐκανονίσθη* Jul.Papa *ep.Dian*.ap.Ath.*apol.sec*.34(p.112.13; M.25.305A); **b.** by eccl. legislation, *lay down by canon*; cf.CNic.(325)*ep*.(p.50.10; M.67.81B); *τὸ μηδὲ τροφῆς ὅλως ἅπτεσθαι...~εσθαι* Philost.*h.e*.10.12(M.65.592C); *αἱ κεκανονισμέναι σύνοδοι* CChalc.*can*.19; *τοῦτο...οἱ ἐπὶ τῆς Νικαέων ἅγιοι πατέρες συναγηγερμένοι ἐκανόνισαν* CChalc.*act*.4(*ACO* 2.1.2 p.111.37; H.2.417A); Leo Mag.*ep*.106.2(p.57.5; M.*PL*.54.1004B); *Βασίλειος ὁ μέγας περὶ πολλῶν ἐκανόνισεν* Jo.Scholast.*nomoc*.proem.(p.4.23); *Chron.Pasch*.p.223(M.92.544B); **c.** *discipline* by monastic rule *τοὺς τοῦ μοναστηρίου ὑμῶν ~ειν* Nil.*epp*.2.160(M.79.276C); pass. *τῶν ὑποτεταγμένων τοῖς δόγμασιν τῆς εὐσεβείας, ~ομένων τε ἅμα* *ib*.2.275(340A); *κανονισθῆναι παρ' αὐτοῦ* Jo.Clim.*scal*.4(M.88.724A); **3.** *measure*, *judge* of *οἱ δὲ μὴ ἐπιστάμενοι τὴν γνῶσιν οὐδὲ ~ειν δύνανται τὴν ἀλήθειαν* Clem.*str*.6.17(p.509.15; M.9.381B); *τὸν τῆς καθ' ἡμᾶς φύσεως οὐκ ἀναβαίνων νόμον, ~ει* [sc. Nicodemus] *τὰ θειότερα* Cyr.*Jo*.2.1(4.146D);

πατέρες, οἱ τοῦτο τὸ βιβλίον [sc. Cant.]...πνευματικὸν κανονίσαντες Thdt.*Cant.*proem.(2.3); **4.** c. ἐκ *judge* by ὁ ἀνθρώπινος νοῦς...ἐκ τῶν παρ' ἡμῖν ~εται *Disp.Phot.*(M.88.532A); *ib.*(541D); ἐκ τῆς ὑγιοῦς ζωῆς ...~εσθαι τὴν νόσον Sev.Ant.ap.Anast.S.*hod.*21(M.89.280C).

B. *include in the canon of scripture* τὰ ~όμενα...βιβλία Ath.*ep. fest.*39.2(M.26.1436B); ἔστι καὶ ἕτερα βιβλία...οὐ ~όμενα *ib.*39.11 (1437C); κεκανονισμένα...βιβλία ‡Ath.*synops.*1(M.28.284A); *ib.*2 (289B); οἱ κανονίσαντες τὰς ἐνδιαθήκους βίβλους Cosm.Ind.*top.*7(M.88. 372D); περὶ...τῶν κανονισθέντων βιβλίων Jo.Scholast.*nomoc.*50(p.30. 10); Tim.CP *haer.*(M.86.36A).

C. *watch, observe, scrutinize,* Leont.N.*v.Jo.Eleem.*1(p.5.12); id.*v. Sym.*32(M.93.1709B); CCP(681)*act.*12(H.3.1325B).

κανονικός, *canonical*; **1.** *pertaining to, according to ecclesiastical regulations, regular* ὁ παλαιὸς καὶ κ. νόμος CNic(325)*can.*13; πᾶσα... κ. τάξις Epiph.*haer.*70.10(p.242.25; M.42.356C); πραγμάτων κ. *ib.*73. 35(p.309.28; 468C); τὴν ἔννομόν τε καὶ κ. ἐπὶ τῶν πλημμεληκότων οἰκονομίαν Gr.Nyss.*ep.can.*(M.45.221B); τὰς κ. διατυπώσεις τῶν κοινοβίων ‡Ath.*ep.Cast.*1.1(M.28.849C); ἀκρόασιν κ. Cyr.*ep.*78(5^{2}.210B); πρᾶγμα ποιῶν κ. *ib.*11a(p.172.1; M.77.89A); κ. εὐταξίας *ib.*78(5^{2}.209D); αἰτίας κ. Jo.Mal.*chron.*18 p.483(M.97.700B); κ. δικαστήριον, κ. ἐπιτιμίοις Eustrat.*v.Eutych.*39(M.86.2320C,D); καθαιρέσει κ. CTrull.*can.* 3; τοῖς κ. τῶν πατέρων θεσμοῖς *ib.*84; κ. διατάξεων CNic.(787)*can.* 1; *ib.*5; κ. ζητήσεις *ib.*6; συνόδου...περὶ κ. καὶ εὐαγγελικῶν πραγμάτων *ib.*6; κ. ἀμφισβητήσεις Phot.*nomoc.*9.1(M.104.708C); esp. of letters of recommendation μηδὲ πρεσβυτέρους τοὺς ἐν ταῖς χώραις κ. ἐπιστολὰς διδόναι CAnt.(341)*can.*8; δειξάτωσαν ἢ κ. γράμματα παρ' ἐμοῦ πρὸς αὐτὸν [sc. Ἀπολινάριον] διαπεμπόμενα, ἢ παρ' ἐκείνου πρὸς ἐμέ Bas.*ep.*224.2(3.343B; M.32.836C); οὐ δεῖ ἱερατικὸν ἢ κληρικὸν ἄνευ κ. γραμμάτων ὁδεύειν CLaod.*can.*41; **2.** *containing canons* or *doctrinal formulations* τὰς κ. ἐπιστολὰς καὶ ἐκθέσεις τῶν ἁγίων πατέρων CChalc.*act.*1(*ACO* 2.1.1 p.195.38; H.2.273A); τὰς Κυρίλλου δύο κ. ἐπιστολάς *ib.*(p.196.2; 273B); Βασιλείου...κ. βιβλίου Justn.*Or.* (M.86.977B; ἀσκητικοῦ p.206.20); **3.** *regularly* or *properly appointed* τῶν κ. ψαλτῶν CLaod.*can.*15; = *orthodox* τοῖς κ. ἡμῶν ἐπισκόποις CCP(381)*can.*6; of Dion. Al., Bas.*ep.*188 *can.*1(3.268C; M.32.664C); cf. κ. πάντα ἄνθρωπον Χριστιανὸν κέκληκε ὁ ἅγιος *Schol.* in Bas.*ep.can.*2 (sic)(*Mon.*2 p.652); **4.** *pertaining to liturgical order,* of priestly functions forbidden to women κ. τι ἐργάζεσθαι ἐν ἐκκλησίᾳ Epiph. *haer.*79.3(p.477.28; M.42.744A); **5.** *within the canon of scripture* δεῖ ...λέγεσθαι ἐν τῇ ἐκκλησίᾳ...μόνα τὰ κ. [sc. βιβλία] τῆς καινῆς καὶ παλαιᾶς διαθήκης CLaod.*can.*59; ἐκτὸς τῶν κ. γραφῶν, μηδὲν ἐν τῇ ἐκκλησίᾳ ἀναγινώσκηται *Cod.Afr.*24(H.1.876E); **6.** masc. plur. as subst., *clergy,* Cyr.H.*procatech.*4; *ascetics,* ‡Bas.*const.*18 tit.(2.560D; M.31. 1381B); **7.** fem. as subst., *consecrated virgin* or *widow* τῶν κ. τὰς πορνείας εἰς γάμον μὴ καταλογίζεσθαι Bas.*ep.*188 *can.*6(3.272B; M.32. 673B); *ib.*173 tit.(260D; M.648B); ὑπηρέτει...αὐτῷ [sc. ascetic] κατὰ πίστιν κ. τις Mac.Aeg.*hom.*27.15(M.34.704D); οἱ μονάζοντες καὶ αἱ κ. Ammon.*Ac.*18:18(M.85.1569C); Chrys.*fem.reg.*tit.(1.248D); Cyr.*ep.* 28(p.50.30; 5^{2}.92A); CCP(518)*act.*(*ACO* 3 p.99.33; H.2.1377A); responsible for burials, Hypat.*fr.*(p.126.16); also adj. c. γυνή, ‡Ath. *qu.Ant.*97(M.28.657A); **8.** neut. as subst., *collection of canons,* CCP (381)†*cann.*tit.(p.164).

κανονικῶς, *canonically*; **1.** *according to ecclesiastical canon* or *regulations,* Ath.*ep.encycl.*2(p.171.14; M.25.228A) cit. s. κανών; δικαίως καὶ κ. Jul.Papa *ep.Dian.*ap.Ath.*apol.sec.*32(p.111.4; M.25. 301B); κ. καὶ ἐνθέσμως Bas.*ep.*92.3(3.186C; M.32.484A); *ib.*90.2(182C; M.475A); opp. τυραννικῶς, Gr.Naz.*or.*43.28(M.36.536A); ἐπίσκοπον...κ. ἐχειροτόνησαν CCP *ep.*ap.Thdt.*h.e.*5.9.16(3.1033); Eustrat.*v.Eutych.* 39(M.86.2320C); Εὐτυχῆ...καθαιρεθέντα κ. παρὰ τοῦ ἰδίου ἐπισκόπου Evagr.*h.e.*2.4(p.45.27; M.86.2504A); *ib.*2.8(p.57.15; 2524C); κανων- Ath.Scholast.*coll.*1.1(p.2); **2.** *in canonical writings* τὸν κ. ἐκτεθέντα νῦν παρὰ τοῦ κυρίου λόγον Ammon.*Jo.*3:8(M.85.1409B).

κανόνιον, τό, *diagram, table*; for finding Easter day, Max. *comput.*1(M.19.1217C).

κανονιστέον, *one must regulate, Chron.Pasch.*p.226(M.92.549A).

***κανονιστής, ὁ,** *one who draws up canons,* Jo.Jej.*serm.*1(M.88. 1932B).

***κανός, ὁ,** *chalice,* Eutych.*pasch.*6(M.86.2397D).

κανοῦν, τό, v. κάνεον.

κανών, ὁ, A. *rule* of faith; **1.** def. κ. δὲ ἐκκλησιαστικὸς ἡ συνῳδία καὶ ἡ συμφωνία νόμου τε καὶ προφητῶν τῇ κατὰ τὴν τοῦ κυρίου παρουσίαν παραδιδομένῃ διαθήκῃ Clem.*str.*6.15(p.495.5; M.9.349A); exeg. 2Cor.10:15 'κατὰ τὸν κ. ἡμῶν', τουτέστι κατὰ τὸ μέτρον ἡμῶν ὃ ἐπιστεύθημεν παρὰ θεοῦ *cat.2Cor.*10:15(p.418.22); **2.** in gen. κ. τῆς πίστεως Polycr.*fr.*ap.Eus.*h.e.*5.24.6(M.20.496A); Clem.*str.*4.15 (p.292.2; M.8.1305B); †Hipp.*Artem.*ap.Eus.*h.e.*5.28.13(516A); κ. τῆς ἀληθείας Clem.*str.*7.16(p.67.5; M.9.532A); Hipp.*haer.*10.5(p.265.17; M.16.3414B); κ. τῆς ἐκκλησίας Or.*Jo.*13.16(p.240.12; M.14.421D); abs. εἴ τι περὶ κανόνος λείπει, ὑπομνήσατε id.*dial.*10(p.144.1); Malch.*ep.* ap.Eus.*h.e.*7.30.6(M.20.712A); CAnt.(269)*act.*(H.1.196D); Ath.*Ar.*3. 28(M.26.385A); **3.** derived from scripture τοῖς πειθομένοις μὴ ἀνθρώπων εἶναι συγγράμματα τὰς ἱερὰς βίβλους, ἀλλ' ἐξ ἐπιπνοίας τοῦ ἁγίου πνεύματος...ἀναγεγράφθαι καὶ εἰς ἡμᾶς ἐληλυθέναι, τὰς φαινομένας ὁδοὺς ὑποδεικτέον, ἐχομένοις τοῦ κ. τῆς Ἰησοῦ Χριστοῦ κατὰ διαδοχὴν τῶν ἀποστόλων οὐρανίου ἐκκλησίας Or.*princ.*4.2.2(9; p.308. 15; M.11.360B); Bas.*Spir.*68(3.57C; M.32.193C); Gr.Nyss.*anim.et res.* (M.46.49C) cit. s. γραφή; exeg. Phil.3:16 κ. δὲ τὸ εὐαγγελικὸν ἐκάλεσε κήρυγμα Thdt.ad loc.(3.464); Dion.Ar.*d.n.*2.2(M.3.640A); **4.** transmitted by tradition, *1Clem.*7.2 cit. s. παράδοσις; Ath.*ep. encycl.*1(p.170.13; M.25.225A); Eun.*apol.*4(M.30.840B) cit. s. γνώμων; cf. παράδοσις; in baptism, Iren.*haer.*1.9.4(M.7.545B); embodied in Ath. ὁ τῆς ὀρθοδόξου πίστεως κ. ἀδιάστροφος Cyr.*hom.pasch.*8(5^{2}. 102E); **5.** opp. heresy τὴν Μαρκίωνος αἵρεσιν πολεμῶν τῷ τῆς ἀληθείας κ. Eus.*h.e.*4.23.4(M.20.385A); *ib.*6.2.14(525C); Gr.Nyss.*ep.*3(M. 46.1024C); Chrys.*hom.58.3 in Gen.*(4.566B); οἱ τῆς ὀρθῆς πίστεως τὸν εὐγενῆ κ. παρατρέχοντες Cyr.*Is.*4.2(2.612E); Socr.*h.e.*3.5.2(M.67.388B); κ. ὀρθοδοξίας Leont.H.*Nest.*2.14(M.86.1568C); **6.** abs. character κ. ... ἕως ἂν μηδὲν ἐνδέῃ τοῦ κανὼν εἶναι καὶ γνώμων, οὐδεμίαν προσθήκην εἰς ἀκρίβειαν ἐπιδέχεται Bas.*Eun.*1.5(1.213E; M.29.513C); **7.** ref. a private instruction on the true faith given by Christ to Polycarp, ‡Pion.*v.Polyc.*12.

B. *canon* of scripture, cf. τὸν ἐκκλησιαστικὸν φυλάττων κ., μόνα τέσσαρα εἰδέναι εὐαγγέλια μαρτύρεται Eus.*h.e.*6.25.3(M.20.581B); ref. Hermas μὴ ὂν ἐκ τοῦ κ. Ath.*decr.*18(p.15.20; M.25.448A); κ. ... τῶν θεοπνεύστων γραφῶν Amph.*Seleuc.*319(M.37.1598); κ. τῆς καινῆς διαθήκης Mac.Mgn.*apocr.*4.10(p.168.17); ref. apocryphal Acts used by Cathari παντάπασιν ἀλλότριοι τοῦ κ. τοῦ ἐκκλησιαστικοῦ Epiph. *haer.*61.1(p.381.3; M.41.1040D).

C. *rule of* eccl. *law*; **1.** in gen., body of laws and customs ἐπὶ τῶν ἄρτῳ καὶ ὕδατι κατὰ τὴν προσφορὰν μὴ κατὰ τὸν κ. τῆς ἐκκλησίας χρωμένων αἱρέσεων Clem.*str.*1.19(p.61.30; M.8.813A); τὸν κ. τῆς ἐκκλησιαστικῆς ἐπιστήμης...φυλαχθέντα Const.ap.Eus.*v.C.*3.61(p.109. 7; M.20.1133B); κατὰ τὸν τῆς ἐκκλησίας κ. ... οὕτω ῥυθμίσαι τὴν χειροτονίαν *ib.*3.62(p.110.26; 1137B); πολλὰ ἤτοι ὑπὸ ἀνάγκης ἢ ἄλλως ἐπειγομένων τῶν ἀνθρώπων παρὰ τὸν κ. τὸν ἐκκλησιαστικόν CNic. (325)*can.*2; CAnt.(341)*can.*9; τῷ ἐκκλησιαστικῷ κ. κατὰ τὸν παλαιὸν τύπον ὑποτάσσεσθαι Arsen.Hyps.*ep.*ap.Ath.*apol.sec.*69(p.147.14; M. 25.372B); Tim.CP *haer.*(M.86.56C) cit. s. θεοφάνια; *canon law* τάδε διατάσσομαι ὑμῖν τοῖς ἐπισκόποις...περὶ κανόνων *Const.App.*8.32.1; *ib.*4.48.1; ἐκτὸς...παντὸς...κ. ἐκκλησιαστικοῦ Chrys.*ep.Innoc.*1(3. 520C); τοῦτο δὲ ἔσεσθαι [ref. purity of priesthood] πιστεύομεν, εἴπερ ἡ τῶν ἱερῶν κ. παρατήρησις φυλάττοιτο, ἣν οἱ...παραδεδώκασιν ἀπόστολοι καὶ οἱ ἅγιοι πατέρες ἐφύλαξαν Justn.*nov.*6 proem.(p.36.18); with which bishops must be conversant, †Jo.D.*B.J.*33(M.96. 1177C); **2.** individual *regulation, canon* κατὰ δὲ τοὺς ἐκκλησιαστικοὺς κανόνας...πάντα κανονικῶς ἐξετασθῆναί τε καὶ πραχθῆναι Ath.*ep. encycl.*2(p.171.12; M.25.228A); ref. admission of heretics into Church οὐ γὰρ ἀντιδιδόναι αὐτοῖς ὑπεύθυνοι χάριν ἐσμέν, ἀλλὰ δουλεύειν ἀκριβείᾳ κανόνων Bas.*ep.*188 *can.*1(3.270D; M.32.669C); *ib.*54(148D; M.400B); ἀπόβλητον ἱερατικῆς χάριτος ὁ κ. ἀπεφήνατο Gr.Nyss.*ep.can.*5(M.45. 232C); ‡Gr.Nyss.*hom.6 in Jo.*(p.280.10,16); Cosm.Ind.*top.*5(M.88. 305A); παρὰ κανόνας πάντας Eustrat.*v.Eutych.*39(M.86.2320C); called θεῖοι, Cyr.*ep.*78(5^{2}.210D); Justn.*nov.*5.2(p.29.1,18); ἱεροί, *ib.*3(p.18. 21); ἅγιοι, *ib.*131.1(p.654.24f.); enforced by civil legislation, *ib.*131 proem.(p.654.20); θεσπίζομεν...τάξιν νόμων ἐπέχειν τοὺς ἁγίους ἐκκλησιαστικοὺς κ. τοὺς ὑπὸ τῶν ἁγίων τεσσάρων συνόδων ἐκτεθέντας ...τῶν γὰρ προειρημένων...συνόδων...τὰ δόγματα καθάπερ τὰς θείας γραφὰς δεχόμεθα καὶ τοὺς κ. ὡς νόμους φυλάττομεν *ib.*131.1(p.655); ref. deposition of bishops, Evagr.*h.e.*2.4(p.45.13; M.86.2501B); ref. penitential canons; to be applied with moderation, †Jo.Jej.*poenit.* (M.88.1904A); †Jo.Jej.*serm.*(M.88.1925C).

D. *canon* of behaviour, moral *standard*; **1.** in gen. φιλανθρωπία καὶ μεγαλοπρεπὴς θεοσέβεια γνωστικῆς ἐξομοιώσεως κ. Clem.*str.*7.3 (p.10.27; M.9.417A); *A.Jo.*57(p.179.29); δικαιοσύνη κ. ἐστιν ἀρετῶν Ath.*exp.Ps.*36:6(M.27.177B); πατριαρχῶν, ὧν οἱ βίοι ὑποδείγματα καὶ κ. προετέθησαν Bas.*ep.*261.1(3.401D; M.32.969A); Agath.*v.Gr.Ill.*155 (p.79); αὐτὸς [sc. φόβος κυρίου] ἀρετῆς...κ. ‡Proc.G.*Pr.*8:13(M.87. 1292D); [sc. Πέτρος] ὁ κ. τῶν ἀκολουθούντων σοι Rom.Mel.(*AS* 1 p.95); hence **2.** religious or monastic *rule* σὺ σεαυτῆς φρόντισον...καὶ πάλιν τὸν κ. σου ἑλκύσῃς Ath.*virg.*12(p.46.3; M.28.265A); οὐαὶ παρθένῳ τῇ μὴ οὔσῃ ὑπὸ κανόνα *ib.*14(p.48.20; 268C); τὴν ἀκρίβειαν τοῦ κ. φυλάσσει Bas.*reg.br.*156(2.467D; M.31.1184C); id.*reg.fus.*45.1(2.392A; M.31.

1032C); Gr.Naz.*ep*.6(M.37.29C); *τῶν...προσανεχόντων τῷ μονήρει κ.* Nil.*epp*.1.281(M.79.185A); Diad.*perf*.100(p.148.13); *τὸν κ. τοῦ μοναστηρίου* Jo.Mosch.*prat*.143(M.87.3005A); Niceph.Ur.*v.Sym*.249(M.86.3213C); also ref. office within monastery *ἕκαστος ἐν τῷ ἑαυτοῦ ἔργῳ φυλάσσει τὸν ἴδιον κ.* Bas.*reg.br*.147(2.464E; 1180A); **3.** of individual ascet. practices *ὑπὸ τὸν κ. τῆς παρθενίας* Bas.*ascet*.1.1(2.319B; M.31.872B); of fasting, *Apophth.Patr*.(M.65.244A); ‡Nil.*vit.cog*.(M.79.1436A); of *ἐγκράτεια*, ‡Ath.*ep.Cast*.2.1(M.28.873C); *ἄσκησις*, Isid.Pel.*epp*.1.74(M.78.233B); †Jo.D.*B.J*.40(M.96.1236D).

E. liturg. *order*; **1.** in gen., *1Clem*.41.1; *παρέδωκεν αὐτοῖς τὸν κ. τῆς ψαλμῳδίας καὶ τῆς ἱερᾶς λειτουργίας* *A.Thadd*.5(p.275.18); Eus.Al.*serm*.5(M.86.348D); **2.** eucharistic *κ. τῆς συνήθους συνάξεως* Ephr.2.96A; *τὸν κ. ἐπέτρεψεν γίνεσθαι κατὰ σάββατον καὶ κυριακήν* Cyr.S.*v.Sab*.18(p.102.7); **3.** of divine office *μέχρις ἐσχάτης προσευχῆς παράμενε τῷ κ.* Bas.*renunt*.8(2.209E; M.31.644C); *ib*.9(210B; M.644D); *μετὰ τὸν κ. τὸν νυκτερινόν* Jo.Mosch.*prat*.27(M.87.2873C); *ἐποίει ἐπάνω αὐτοῦ τὸν κ. καὶ ἔθαπτεν αὐτόν* *ib*.24(2869C); *τοῦ κ. ὥρας* Jo.Clim.*scal*.4(M.88.697D); **4.** *ὁ ἐπὶ τοῦ κ.* *choirmaster*, *ib*.22(952C).

F. liturg. *hymn*, divided into odes, Jo.D.*carm.dorm.BMV* tit.(M.96.1364A); *μετὰ...τροπαρίων καὶ κ.* Jo.Nic.*nativ*.(M.96.1449B); *Const.Stud*.1.104(M.99.1748A); *Mir.Geo*.5(p.55.4); Anast.*poenit*.1(p.281).

G. eccl. *rank, order*; **1.** of clergy *ὁ ἐν τῷ κ. ἐξεταζόμενος* CNic.(325)*can*.16; *τόν τε κ. τῆς ἐκκλησίας...ἐτίμα, καὶ πάντα κληρικὸν τῇ τιμῇ προηγεῖσθαι ἤθελεν ἑαυτοῦ* Ath.*v.Anton*.67(M.26.937C); *Const.App*.8.28.1; Epiph.*haer*.68.7(p.147.8; M.42.196A); CChalc.(451)*can*.2; **2.** of professed virgins and widows, *Chron.Pasch*.p.294(M.92.737B).

H. *logical sequence* *ὁ μὲν κ. συναγκάζει, ἄπορον δὲ τὸ λεχθέν* *Disp.Phot*.(M.88.548B).

I. *tax, revenue*, Marc.Diac.*v.Porph*.22; *ib*.41; Gr.Mag.*dial*.(tr. Zach.)4.30(M.*PL*.77.370).

***κανωνικῶς**, v. *κανονικῶς*.

***καπεπίλινον, τό**, perh. = *Καπετώλιον* *Capitol* of Rome, *Apoc.Dan*.B(p.40).

καπετώλιον, τό, (Lat. *capitolium*) *public meeting-place* *εἰς Ὀξύρυγχον πόλιν τινὰ τῆς Θηβαΐδος...ἔγεμον δὲ τῆς πόλεως οἱ ναοὶ καὶ τὰ κ. τῶν μοναχῶν* ‡Pall.*h.mon*.5.2(p.29.6; M.65.445D).

***Καπετωλίς**, *of the Capitol*, Paul.Sil.*Soph*.152(M.86.2125B).

καπηλεία, ἡ, **1.** *trade, transaction*; of a despicable type, Chrys.*hom.30.1 in Mt*.(7.347C); *ib.67.1*(661B); id.*hom.23.2 in Jo*.(8.134D); plur. *καπηλείας ἀνελευθέρους* id.*hom.20.3 in Mt*.(263A); *ib.61.3*(614B) cit. s. *καπηλεύω*; **2.** *petty bargaining* *μετὰ πολλῆς τῆς κ. ... ἀκριβολογούμεθα περὶ τῆς ἀντιδόσεως* id.*hom.5.7 in Rom*.(9.470E); **3.** *tricks of trade, trickery, fraudulence*, Meth.*symp*.5.4(p.57.23; M.18.104A); Gr.Nyss.ap.Proc.G.*Cant*.4:13f.(M.87.1665C); *οὐδὲν μετὰ κ. οὐδὲν μετὰ ὑποκρίσεως πεποιήκαμεν* Chrys.*hom.34.2 in Heb*.(12.314A); **4.** *tavern* *ἐπὶ μέθην καὶ κ. ... τρέχοντας* id.*pan.Pelag*.3(2.589B, v.l. *καπηλεῖα*).

καπηλεύ-ω, **1.** *retail dishonestly* or *in adulterated form, traffic (in)*, esp. of those who have no right to sell; **a.** exeg. 2Cor.2:17 *τοῦτο γάρ ἐστι ∼σαι, ὅταν τις νοθεύῃ τὸν οἶνον, ὅταν τις χρημάτων πωλῇ, ὅπερ δωρεὰν ἔδει δοῦναι* Chrys.*hom.5.3 in 2Cor*.(10.468D); *τὸν θεῖον ∼ουσι λόγον, μῦθον αὐτὸν ἐργαζόμενοι, καὶ τοὺς οἰκείους λογισμοὺς ἀναμιγνῦντες τῇ χάριτι, καθάπερ οἱ τοῦ οἴνου τὸ ἀκραιφνὲς τῷ ὕδατι κεραννῦντες* Thdt.*2Cor*.2:17(3.300); *οὐκ...∼ων καὶ νοθεύων τὴν δωρεὰν τοῦ θεοῦ...οὐ ∼ομεν τὸν λόγον ὡς καί τινες συμμεταβάλλοντες αὐτὸν τοῖς καιροῖς...αἰσχροῦ κέρδους χάριν* *cat.2Cor*.2:17(p.364.4,8); **b.** in gen. *∼οντας τὴν ἀλήθειαν* Clem.*paed*.2.11(p.279.31; M.8.657A); *τὴν ἁπλῆν τῶν θείων γραφῶν πίστιν ∼οντες* †Hipp.*Artem*.ap.Eus.*h.e*.5.28.15(M.20.516B); *μὴ ∼ειν τὴν χάριν μηδὲ πιπράσκειν τὰ ἐκ θεοῦ...δῶρα* Eus.*fr.Lc*.(M.24.544D); *ἔστωσαν...ὑμῖν ἀνάθεμα διὰ τὸ 'κεκαπηλευκέναι τὸν λόγον' τῆς ἀληθείας* CSard.*ep.cath*.ap.Ath.*apol.sec*.47(p.123.16; M.25.336B); *τὸ εὐαγγέλιον ∼σαντες* [sc. Manicheans] Serap.*Man*.37(p.54; M.18.1216D); *Μανιχαῖοι...καὶ Οὐαλεντῖνοι...∼οντες τὰς θείας γραφάς* Ath.*h.Ar*.66(p.219.27; M.25.772C); *μὴ ∼ωμεν τὴν φιλανθρωπίαν* Chrys.*hom.56.5 in Mt*.(7.573A); *νενοθευμένῃ γνώμῃ τὴν τιμὴν ∼ων* [sc. Cain] Bas.Sel.*or*.4.3(M.85.68D); pass., *ib*.6.2(89C); c. dupl. acc. *τὰς καπηλείας, ἃς αὐτοὺς ∼ουσιν* *the transactions they perform by means of them*, Chrys.*hom.61.3 in Mt*.(7.614B); **2.** *waste, fritter away* *τὰς ἡμέρας* Pall.*v.Chrys*.20(p.138.10; M.47.77); *χρόνον* *ib*.(p.139.15; M.47.78); **3.** med., *do trade, traffic* *ἐν τῷ ἱερῷ...τοὺς ∼ομένους* *cat.Mt*.21:23(p.172.2).

***καπηλοδυτέω**, *haunt taverns*, Cyr.H.*catech*.4.37.

κάπηλος, ὁ, **1.** *dishonest retailer, adulterator*; of wine, Gr.Nyss.*hom.9 in Cant*.(M.44.956A); **2.** met., *fraud, cheat*, opp. *διδάσκαλος*, Ath.*decr*.4(p.4.1; M.25.'429'(421)C); opp. *φιλόσοφος*, Thdt.*h.rel*.3(3.1145); **3.** c. genit., met., *dealer in* *κ. συμφορῶν ἀνθρωπίνων* Bas.*hom*.6.3(2.46C; M.31.268B).

***καπικλάριος, ὁ**, *turn-key, prison warder*, *M.Seb*.3(p.173.24); *ib*.7(p.177.10); Steph.Diac.*v.Steph*.(M.100.1161A).

***καπίλα, ἡ**, (Lat. *capillus*) *hair*, Call.*v.Hyp*.(p.58).

***κάπιτα, τά**, (Lat. *capita*) *poll-taxes* *ἀννονῶν καὶ κ.* Justn.*nov*.24.6(p.195.16); *ib*.appendix *Edict*.13.3(p.781.35).

***καπιτατίων, ἡ**, (Lat. *capitatio*) *poll-tax* *ἀννονῶν τε καὶ καπιτατιώνων* Justn.*nov*.8.2(p.67.31); *τὴν ἰδίαν καπιτατίονα* Phot.*nomoc*.1.34(M.104.557C).

***Καπιτώλιος**, (Lat. *Capitolinus*) *of the Capitol*, epithet of Zeus (Jupiter), Thphl.Ant.*Autol*.1.10(M.6.1040B).

καπνίζ-ω, **1.** pass., *be smoked to death, burned*; of sacrificed animals, Cyr.*Ag*.15(3.644D); of a criminal *ὑπὸ ἀχύρου ∼όμενον* †Gregent.*leg.Hom*.61(M.86.613C); **2.** met., *cause disturbance* *∼ων οἱονεὶ θρασύνων καὶ διεγείρων τὴν καρδίαν σου* Dor.*doct*.8.2(M.88.1709A); **3.** met., *befog* *ὁ σατανᾶς...∼ων ὥσπερ τὸν νοῦν διὰ...τὴν ἡδύτητα τῶν ἀλόγων ἡδονῶν* Diad.*perf*.76(p.96.2); in sense of *terrify* *προσεδόκησεν ταύτην ∼ειν...οὐκ ἔχεις με...καπνίσαι* Pall.*h.Laus*.46(p.135.8,13; M.34.1225C,D).

***καπνικός**, neut. as subst., *tribute levied on furnaces*, Thphn.*chron*.p.412(M.108.977B).

κάπνισμα, τό, *fume, fragrance, perfume*, Ephr.3.270B; Epiph.*haer*.69.72(p.220.22; M.42.320A).

***καπνοδόχος, ὁ**, *smoke-receiver*, a hole in the roof for smoke to pass through, Isid.Pel.*epp*.1.314(M.78.364D).

καπνός, ὁ, *smoke*; **1.** met., ?*faint image* *τῆς ἀθυμίας κ.* Chrys.*sac*.6.12(p.165.23; 1.432D); **2.** = *smoke-hole*, in phrase *λειτουργίαν...ὑπὲρ καπνοῦ* Jo.Mal.*chron*.10 p.246(M.97.376C).

***καπνοτόκειος**, *bringing forth smoke* *κ. σποδόν* †Apoll.*met.Ps*.147:5(M.33.1533C).

***καπνῳδία, ἡ**, *smokiness*, Nil.*epp*.1.188(M.79.153C).

κάρα, τό, *head*, genit. *καρός*, ‡Gr.Naz.*Chr.pat*.1207(M.38.233A).

κάρα, ἡ, = foreg., genit. *κάρης*: *τὴν κ. τοῦ δράκοντος* *T.Aser* 7.3; Epiph.*exp.fid*.11(p.511.20; M.42.801B); of Devil, Gr.Naz.*carm*.2.1.58.5(M.37.1402A).

***καραβιᾶς, ὁ**, *boatswain*, Jo.Mosch.*prat*.76(M.87.2929C).

καράβι(ο)ν, τό, *light boat*, *M.Areth*.(pp.54,56); *Chron.Pasch*.p.395(M.92.1012C); Thphn.*chron*.p.432(M.108.1020A).

κάραβος, ὁ, = foreg., *M.Areth*.(p.56); Jo.Mosch.*prat*.76(M.87.2929C); *Chron.Pasch*.p.395(M.92.1012C); *καστελλᾶτοι κ.* used in war, Const.Pogon.*sacr*.1(M.*PL*. 87.1154B).

καραδοκία, ἡ, *expectation*, Epiph.*haer*.66.4(p.22.14; M.42.36D); ref. Ps.38:8 *τὴν...ὑπόστασιν Ἀκύλας κ. ... εἴρηκεν* Thdt.*Ps*.38:8(1.853).

καρακάλλιον, τό, *hood*, Pall.*h.Laus*.46(p.135.5; M.34.1225C).

***κάραμις**, sens. dub., *σάνδαλον κάραμιν* *Didasc.Jac*.5.20(p.89.11).

***καρατόμημα, τό**, *beheading*, Chrysipp.*enc.in Jo.Bapt*.(p.42.21).

***καρατόμησις, ἡ**, = foreg., Jo.Mal.*chron*.18 p.473(M.97.688C).

***καρατομία, ἡ**, = foreg., Tat.*orat*.8(p.8.25; M.6.824A); Hipp.Th.*fr*.4.2(p.18.24).

***καρβούνη, ἡ**, (Lat. *carbo*) *coal*, *V.Amph*.3(M.39.20A).

κάρβων, ὁ, = foreg., Dor.*doct*.8.3(M.88.1709B); Hesych.S.*temp*.2.3(M.93.1512C).

***καρβωνίζ-ω**, *be charred* or *blackened* *αἱ ῥάβδοι ∼ουσαι ὡς ἀπὸ πυρός* †Anast.S.*relat*.38(*OC* 2 p.82).

[*]**καρβώνιον, τό**, *coal*, Thdr.Stud.*poen*.1.70(M.99.1741C).

καρδία, ἡ, **A.** *heart* (seat of affections and will); **1.** in gen. *οἱ δὲ τὸν κύριον ἔχοντες ἐπὶ τὰ χείλη, ἐπὶ τὴν κ. δὲ μὴ ἔχοντες* Herm.*sim*.9.21.1; *βιάζεσθαι χρὴ ἀεὶ εἰς πᾶν ἀγαθόν,...κἂν μὴ θελούσης τῆς κ. διὰ τὴν συνοῦσαν αὐτῇ ἁμαρτίαν* Mac.Aeg.*cust.cor*.13(M.34.836D); *δίψα καὶ ἀγρυπνία ἐξέθλιψαν καρδίαν· καρδίας δὲ θλιβήσης ἀπεπήδησαν ὕδατα* Jo.Clim.*scal*.6(M.88.796B); **2.** of Christ, ref. Ps.21:15 *ἐντρόμου τῆς κ. δῆλον ὅτι οὔσης καὶ τῶν ὀστῶν ὁμοίως καὶ ἐοικυίας τῆς κ. κηρῷ τηκομένῳ εἰς τὴν κοιλίαν, ὅπως εἰδῶμεν ὅτι ὁ πατὴρ τὸν ἑαυτοῦ υἱὸν καὶ ἐν τοιούτοις πάθεσιν ἀληθῶς γεγονέναι δι' ἡμᾶς βεβούληται, καὶ μὴ λέγωμεν ὅτι ἐκεῖνος, τοῦ θεοῦ υἱὸς ὤν, οὐκ ἀντιλαμβάνετο τῶν γινομένων καὶ συμβαινόντων αὐτῷ* Just.*dial*.103.8(M.6.720A); *τούτου δὲ καὶ ἡ κ. οὐδαμῶς ἐφοβεῖτο παρατασσομένης ἐπ' αὐτὸν ὅλης τῆς τοῦ σατανᾶ παρεμβολῆς. ἤλπιζε δὲ καὶ ἐπὶ θεῷ πεπληρωμένη ἱερῶν δογμάτων αὐτοῦ καρδία ἐπανισταμένου αὐτῷ πολέμου* Or.*mart*.29(p.25.17; M.11.597C); ref. dispersal of disciples at Passion *τάχα γίνεταί τινος ἡ κ. τηκομένη οἷα κηρὸς ἐν μέσῳ τῆς κοιλίας, ὅτ' ἂν ἴδῃ τοὺς ὠδινηθέντας καὶ γεννηθέντας ὑπ' αὐτοῦ συμφορὰν ὑπομένοντας. ἐπεὶ τοίνυν καὶ τὰ προειρημένα περὶ τοὺς μαθητὰς Ἰησοῦ γέγονεν, ἡ κ. αὐτοῦ διακειμένη πρὸς αὐτοὺς ἀγαπητικῶς πυρουμένη, κηροῦ πάθος ἀνεδέξατο ἐν* μέσῳ τῆς κοιλίας συμπαθούσης οἷς ἔτεκεν Didym.*Ps.*21:15(M.39.1281A); Cyr.*Ps.*21:15(M.69.837D); ἡ κ. μὲν γὰρ τῇ δειλίᾳ, ὡς ὁ κηρὸς τῷ πυρί, διελύθη Thdt.*Ps.*21:15(1.739); ref. Lc.12:39 ἐνετείλατο ἐν στρυφνότητι καρδίας Esaias *cap.spir.*13(M.40.1209B); **3.** met. and symbolically ὁ ὄντως θεός,...τοῦ ἄνω τε καὶ κάτω δὶς [καθ]υπαρχῶν κ. *Hom.Clem.*17.9; κ. [sc. θεοῦ] τὸ ἀπόκρυφον τῆς οὐσίας Ath.*exp.Ps.*32:11(M.27.165B); Gr.Nyss.*hom.1 in Cant.*(M.44.780B); ἔστω ὁ διάκονος τοῦ ἐπισκόπου...κ. καὶ ψυχή *Const.App.*2.44.4; ref. Christ ἐν τῷ σταυρῷ, φησί, τὸν ὑπὲρ ἀνθρώπων ἀναδεχόμενος θάνατον· ἀγρυπνεῖ δὲ ἡ κ., καθὸ ὡς θεὸς τὸν ᾅδην ἐσκύλευσεν Cyr.*fr.Cant.*5:2(M.69.1289B); 'κ. 'Ιερουσαλὴμ' τὸ κρεῖττον τοῦ λαοῦ τάγμα, καὶ τῆς ἐκκλησίας τὸ κυριώτατον, ὡς ἡ κ. τοῦ σώματος, δι' οὗ δηλοῦται τὸ λογικόν τε καὶ νοερώτερον τάγμα Proc.G.*Is.*40:1–8(M.87.2332A); ref. angels τὴν δ' αὖ κ., σύμβολον εἶναι τῆς θεοειδοῦς ζωῆς, τῆς τὴν οἰκείαν ζωτικὴν δύναμιν ἀγαθοειδῶς εἰς τὰ προνοούμενα διασπειρούσης Dion.Ar.*c.h.*15.3(M.3.332C); Max.*schol.c.h.*15.3(M.4.108B); **4.** esp. of moral intensity προτρέπεται οὖν ἡμᾶς πιστεύοντας ἐξ ὅλης τῆς κ. ἐπ' αὐτοῦ *1Clem.*34.4; οὐ δύναται [sc. Devil]...καταδυναστεύειν τῶν δούλων τοῦ θεοῦ τῶν ἐξ ὅλης κ. ἐλπιζόντων ἐπ' αὐτόν Herm.*mand.*12.5.2; ἐὰν μετανοήσητε ἐξ ὅλης κ. ὑμῶν πρὸς τὸν κύριον id.*vis.*4.2.5; Clem.*prot.*10(p.76.11; M.8.221C).

B. *mind*; **1.** as visible to God οἶδας...τῆς ἡμετέρας κ. τὰ νοήματα Ath.*exp.Ps.*8:11(M.27.80C); Proc.G.*Is.*1:20(M.87.1849C); **2.** as containing knowledge of natural law λόγιοι νόμοι...ἐν αὐταῖς ἐγγραφόμενοι ταῖς κ. Clem.*prot.*10(p.77.19; M.8.225A); Thdt.*Rom.*2:15(3.32); **3.** as illumined by God λέγει εἰς τὴν κ. Μωυσέως τὸ πνεῦμα, ἵνα ποιήσῃ τύπον σταυροῦ *Barn.*12.2; λαμψάτω οὖν ἐν τῷ ἀποκεκρυμμένῳ τοῦ ἀνθρώπου, ἐν τῇ κ., τὸ φῶς Clem.*prot.*11(p.81.22; M.8.236A); ὁ θεὸς...τοῖς δὲ θεωρητικοῖς καρδίᾳ θεωρητός, τουτέστι νῷ, κ. δὲ οὐ τῇ τυχούσῃ ἀλλὰ τῇ καθαρᾷ Or.*Cels.*6.69(p.139.11; M.11.1404A); ὁ κύριος 'Ιησοῦς...λαλησάτω ἐν ταῖς διανοίαις πάντων καὶ προοικονομησάτω εἰς πίστιν τὰς κ. Serap.*euch.*2.2; *Const.App.*6.30.8; *ib.*7.39.4; Thdt.*Rom.*10:10(3.113); κ. ἑαυτοῦ τὸν λαὸν...τῶν 'Ιουδαίων λέγει, διὰ τὰ λόγια αὐτοῦ ἐν ταῖς κ. αὐτῶν εἶναι Hesych.H.*Ps.tit.*21(M.27.724C); **4.** met., ref. God τὴν κ. τοῦ θεοῦ τὴν νοητικὴν αὐτοῦ καὶ προθετικὴν περὶ τῶν ὅλων δύναμιν ἐκληπτέον Or.*Jo.*1.38(42; p.49.31; M.14.100C); Trin. τινὲς ᾠήθησαν, ὡς ἐκ προσώπου τοῦ πατρὸς λέγεσθαι τὸν ψαλμὸν... περὶ τοῦ ἐν ἀρχῇ ὄντος πρὸς αὐτὸν λόγου, ὃν ἐκ τῆς οἱονεὶ κ.,...φησί, προήγαγε· καὶ ἀπὸ ἀγαθῆς κ. ἀγαθὸς λόγος προῆλθεν Eus.*Ps.*44:2(M.23.393B); ὁ ἐκ κ. τοῦ θεοῦ λόγος Ath.*Dion.*2(p.47.12; M.25.481B); id.*exp.Ps.*44:2(M.27.208B); κ. θεοῦ λεγομένης, οὐκ ἀνθρωπίνην νοοῦμεν αὐτήν ‡Ath.*Ar.*4.27(p.75.15; M.26.509B); τίς γὰρ ἀποστήσει καρδίας ἤτοι νοῦ λόγον, τὸν ἐν αὐτῷ τε καὶ ἐξ αὐτοῦ καὶ ἀεὶ σὺν αὐτῷ; ἀποστήσει δὲ οὕτως, ὡς ἔξω γενέσθαι παντελῶς αὐτοῦ;...οὐ γὰρ ἐνδέχεται νοῦν, ἤτοι κ., ἄλογον εἶναί ποτε· οὔτε μὴν λόγον, ὅς οὐκ ἔστιν ἐκ νοῦ καὶ εἰς νοῦν, ἤτοι καρδίαν καὶ ἐν κ. οὐκοῦν ὡς ἐν τάξει παραδείγματός τινος ἐπὶ θεοῦ δεξάμενοι κ. καὶ λόγον, τὸν τῆς ἑαυτῶν διανοίας ὑπερτείνωμεν ὀφθαλμὸν εἰς τὸ ἐπέκεινα τῶν αἰσθητῶν, καὶ θεοπρεπῆ τοῦ θεοῦ λόγου τὴν γέννησιν γενέσθαι πιστεύωμεν· ὃν ὡς λόγον ὁ πατὴρ ἐκ κ. ἐξηρεύξατο Cyr.*Ps.*44:1(M.69.1028A).

C. *soul*, i.e. the two foreg. together; **1.** as image of God ἁπλῆν αὐτὴν ἔπλασε καθ' ἑαυτὴν εἰκόνα σώζουσαν τὴν κ. ὁ δημιουργὸς τῶν ἀνθρώπων θεός· ὕστερον δὲ αὐτὴν τῇ πρὸς τὰ πάθη τῆς σαρκὸς ἐπιπλοκῇ ποικίλην ἐποιήσαμεν...ἡμεῖς τὴν κ. Bas.*hom.in Ps.*32(1.140B; M.29.344B); **2.** as source of moral acts ἡ κ., ἡ τῶν καλῶν ἔργων πηγή Or.*or.*22.3(p.348.15; M.11.485A); τῇ κ. μίασμα δέξασθαι Bas.*ascet.*1.1(2.319B; M.31.872B); id.*hom.in Ps.*1(1.94A; M.29.220B); **3.** as exposed to influence of good and evil spirits ὅταν οὖν οὗτος [sc. ὁ τῆς δικαιοσύνης ἄγγελος] ἐπὶ τὴν κ. σου ἀναβῇ, εὐθέως λαλεῖ μετὰ σοῦ περὶ δικαιοσύνης Herm.*mand.*6.2.3; ὅρα νῦν καὶ τοῦ ἀγγέλου τῆς πονηρίας τὰ ἔργα. ... ὅταν οὖν οὗτος ἐπὶ τὴν κ. σου ἀναβῇ, γνῶθι αὐτὸν ἀπὸ τῶν ἔργων αὐτοῦ *ib.*6.2.4; τὰ φερόμενα τοῦ πονηροῦ περὶ τὴν κ. φάσματα Meth.*symp.*8.4(p.85.11; M.18.144C); οἱ ὑπὸ τὴν τοῦ πνεύματος προσφυγόντες καὶ...τὴν τοῦ λόγου σκέπην οὐ δειλιάσουσιν οὐδὲ πτυρήσονται τὸν ταράσσοντα τὰς κ. *ib.*10.5(p.128.12; 201C); Mac.Aeg.*hom.*43.9(M.34.777B); **4.** as seat of divine presence and grace, *Barn.*6.15; δύναται...πασῶν τῶν ἐντολῶν τούτων κατακυριεῦσαι ὁ ἄνθρωπος ὁ ἔχων τὸν κύριον ἐν τῇ κ. αὐτοῦ Herm.*mand.*12.4.3; ‡*Diogn.*11.4; γίνεται δέ, ὅταν οἱ κτισθέντες ἄνθρωποι...λάβωσιν εἰς τὰς κ. ἑαυτῶν τὸ πνεῦμα τοῦ υἱοῦ αὐτοῦ Ath.*Ar.*2.59(M.26.273A); εἰς τὰς πλάκας τῆς κ. ἡ χάρις τοῦ θεοῦ ἐγγράφει τοὺς νόμους τοῦ πνεύματος...ἡ γὰρ κ. ...βασιλεύει ὅλου τοῦ σωματικοῦ ὀργάνου. καὶ ἐπὰν κατασχῇ τὰς νομὰς τῆς κ. ἡ χάρις, βασιλεύει ὅλων τῶν μελῶν, καὶ τῶν λογισμῶν· ἐκεῖ γάρ ἐστιν ὁ νοῦς, καὶ ὅλοι οἱ λογισμοὶ τῆς ψυχῆς καὶ ἡ προσδοκία αὐτῆς. διὸ καὶ διέρχεται ἡ χάρις εἰς ὅλα τὰ μέλη τοῦ σώματος Mac.Aeg.*hom.*15.20(M.34.589A); *ib.*15.38(597C); Chrys.*hom.*17.1 *in Mt.*(7.223A); ref. Christ ὁ κύριος ἦν ὁ λύχνος ὁ καιόμενος, διὰ τὸ πνεῦμα τῆς θεότητος τὸ μένον οὐσιωδῶς ἐν αὐτῷ, καὶ ἐκκαῖον αὐτοῦ τὴν κ. κατὰ τὸ ἀνθρώπινον Mac.Aeg.*hom.*43.2(772C).

καρδιακός, *of* or *belonging to the heart* κ. ἐνεργημάτων Marc.Er.*opusc.*1.26(M.65.909A); κ. ἀγνοίας καὶ λήθης *ib.*1.61(913A); ἐξομολόγησις κ. Hesych.S.*temp.*61(M.93.1500A).

καρδιογνώστης, ὁ, *one who knows the heart*; of God, Herm.*mand.*4.3.4; Or.*sel.in Ps.*9:38(M.12.108A); *Hom.Clem.*10.13; of Christ, *A.Thadd.*3(p.274.15); κ. ... οὐκ εἰσὶν οἱ δαίμονες Or.*exc.in Ps.*54:7(M.17.1469C); ref. Marcianists ἑαυτοὺς κ. φαντάζονται Tim.CP *haer.*(M.86.52B).

καρδιόπληκτος, *wounded in the heart,* Thphn.*chron.*p.401(M.108.956B).

***καρδιοπονέω,** *be exercised in heart,* Marc.Er.*opusc.*4(M.65.1017A); *ib.*(1021A).

καρδιότρωτος, *wounded in the heart,* ‡Ath.*v.Syncl.*85(M.28.1540A).

καρδιουλκία, ἡ, *drawing out the heart* of victim at sacrifice; plur., Clem.*prot.*2(p.13.5; M.8.76A).

καρδι-όω, 1. *ravish the heart, fascinate,* exeg. Cant.4:9 'ἐκαρδίωσας ἡμᾶς...' ὅπερ ἐστίν...τῷ ἐπεράστῳ σου βλέμματι τῆς συνέσεως ἀνεπτέρωσας ἡμῶν τὴν καρδίαν εἰς πόθον Meth.*symp.*7.2(p.73.1; M.18.128A); ταῦτά φησιν· τὴν μὲν ἔκπληξιν ἐπὶ πάντας φέρων Nil.ap. Proc.G.*Cant.*4:9(M.87.1657A,B); νῦν δέ μου ψυχὴν κεκαρδίωκας Jo. Clim.*scal.*30(M.88.1160B); **2.** *give heart to, make alive,* exeg. Cant.4:9 τοῦ δὲ 'ἐκαρδίωσας' τὸ σημαινόμενον τοιοῦτον...οἷον...τὸ 'ἐψύχωσας', ὥσει ἔλεγον πρὸς αὐτὴν ὅτι, καρδίαν ἡμῖν ἐνέθηκας Gr.Nyss.*hom.8 in Cant.*(M.44.948B); 'ἐκαρδίωσας', ὅπερ ἐστὶ ψυχήν τινα καὶ διάνοιαν πρὸς τὴν τοῦ φωτὸς κατανόησιν δι' ἑαυτῆς ἡμῖν ἐνεποίησας *ib.*(949C); cf. id.ap.Proc.G.*Cant.*4:9(1657A); pass., Gr.Nyss.*hom.8 in Cant.*(949A); ἡ λογικὴ ψυχή...ἐκ θεοῦ καρδίας ἡμῖν ~ωθεῖσα Anast.S.*serm.imag.*3(M.89.1164D).

***καρδίως,** *in the heart,* Max.*ambig.*(M.91.1117B).

καρηβαρής, *heavy of head, drowsy,* Synes.*provid.*4(p.71.17; M.66.1217D).

καρηβαρία, ἡ, *heaviness in the head*; *drunken stupor,* Gr.Nyss. *infant.*(M.46.185A); Chrys.*hom.44.5 in Mt.*(7.473E); *ib.69.3*(684C); met. μὴ ἐμπέσωμεν εἰς κ. id.*hom.8.4 in 1Cor.*(10.70E).

***καρήξανθος,** s.v.l., *yellow-haired* τὸν...κ. Μενέλαον Tat.*orat.*10(M.6.828C; κάρη ξανθόν p.11.19).

***καρκάλιον, τό,** *shroud, A.Jo.*71(p.185.24).

***Καρμήλιος,** *of Carmel* 'Ηλίου τὸ Κ. [sc. ὄρος] Niceph.Ur.*v.Sym.*69(M.86.3049D).

***καροία, ἡ,** *walnut* δένδρον κ. Socr.*h.e.*6.23.2(M.67.732A).

κάρος, ὁ, 1. *heavy sleep, torpor, unconsciousness,* ref. Lazarus ἵνα μηδεὶς ἔχῃ λέγειν, ὅτι...κ. ἦν...καὶ οὐ θάνατος Chrys.*hom.62.1 in Jo.*(8.369B); in fever πολλῷ τῷ κ. τῆς φλογὸς κατεχόμενος id.*ep.*14.2(3.596B); of Adam's sleep, id.*hom.15.2 in Gen.*(4.117C); **2.** *stupor, bewilderment* ὁ τῆς κακίας κ. Eus.*h.e.*1.2.21(κόρος M.20.64B); ref. apostles at Transfiguration ὕπνον ἐνταῦθα καλῶν τὸν πολὺν κ. τὸν ἀπὸ τῆς ὄψεως ἐκείνης αὐτοῖς ἐγγινόμενον Chrys.*hom.56.3 in Mt.*(7.569C); ref. S. Peter πόσῳ κ. κατείχετο...ἀπαγομένου τοῦ 'Ιησοῦ id. *hom.83.3 in Jo.*(8.493D).

καροῦχα, ἡ, (Lat. *carruca*) *carriage, M.Polyc.*8.2; Jo.Mal.*chron.*14(M.97.537B); *Chron.Pasch.*p.308(M.92.785A).

***καρουχαρεῖον, τό,** *carriage-house* τὸν...τῆς Ἀφροδίτης ναὸν ἐποίησε [sc. Theodosius] κ. Jo.Mal.*chron.*13 p.345(M.97.516B).

καρπεύ-ω, *gather, glean* ~ουσι στάχυν *Orac.Sib.*5.275; med. c. genit. ~εσθαι τῶν ὡραίων Meth.*symp.*proem.5(M.18.32A; ἀποκαρπεύεσθαι p.5.2); pass. ἀρετῆς ~ομένης παρὰ τῆς...θείας πολιτείας ‡Proc.G.*Pr.*11:30(M.87.1333B).

καρπέω, *yield as fruit,* met. τοὺς τῆς εὐσεβείας κεκάρπηκε τρόπους Cyr.*Is.*2.3(2.281D).

καρπισμός, ὁ, *legal transfer* of slaves, Clem.*str.*5.8(p.363.27; M.9.88A).

Καρπιστής, ὁ, *the Reaper,* name given to Horus in Valent. system, Val.Gn.ap.Epiph.*haer.*31.6(p.395.7; M.41.485B); Iren.*haer.*1.2.4(M.7.460A).

καρπογονία, ἡ, *productiveness, fruitfulness,* met. πίστις...τῶν ἀρετῶν ἡ ἀέναος κ. Max.*opusc.*(M.91.92A).

καρπογόνος, *fruitful, productive* εἰ δὲ μὴ κ. ἐστιν...ἡ θεία οὐσία, ἀλλ' ἔρημος...πῶς δημιουργικὴν ἐνέργειαν ἔχειν αὐτὸν λέγοντες οὐκ αἰσχύνονται; Ath.*Ar.*2.2(M.26.149C); neut. as subst., *fertility,* Cyr. *glaph.Gen.*1.2(1.14C); id.*ador.*13(1.464D).

***καρποδοσία, ἡ,** *fruitfulness,* Germ.CP *or.*1(M.98.229B).

καρποδότειρα, ἡ, *giver of fruit* γῆ κ. *Orac.Sib.*3.281.

***καρποδοτέω,** *yield fruit, Hymn.*(*AS* 1 p.546).

***καρποδότης**, ὁ, *yielder of fruit* or *crops*; of Nile, Gr.Naz.*or*.39.5 (M.36.340B); id.*carm*.2.2(poem.)7.268(M.37.1572A); met., of faithful in Egypt, id.*or*.34.2(241B).

***καρποζιζανηφόρος**, *bearing tares as fruit*; met., of heretics, Anast.S.*hex*.12(M.89.1073C).

***Καρποκράσιος**, ὁ, *follower of Carpocrates*, leader of a Gnost. sect, Epiph.*haer*.27 tit.(p.300.19; M.41.364B); tenets, *ib*.(pp.300–313; M.41.364B–377C); cf.Iren.*haer*.1.25.1–5(M.7.680A–686A).

καρπός, ὁ, **A.** *fruit, produce*; **1.** of handiwork, plur. *κ. τῶν χειρῶν* Clem.*paed*.2.12(p.233.26; M.8.552C); but cf. Thdt.*Ps*.127:2(1.1498); **2.** *seed, offspring*, of Jo. Bapt. *ἡ Ζαχαρίου σιωπή, ἀναμένουσα τὸν πρόδρομον τοῦ Χριστοῦ κ.* Clem.*prot*.2(p.10.7; M.8.65C); *φέρειν κ.* Thdt.*h.rel*.13(3.1213); Gnost. *τὸ σπέρμα...μορφωθὲν...υἱὸς νυμφίου γίνεται...ἀνδρωθεὶς ἄρρην γίνεται κ.* Clem.*exc.Thdot*.79(p.131.23; M.9.696A); Christol. *ὁ κύριος...ὁ τῆς παρθένου κ.* id.*paed*.1.6(p.115.6; M.8.300B); *κ. παντέλειος τοῦ πατρός* Ath.*gent*.46(M.25.93C); *ἐκ κ. τῆς κοιλίας αὐτοῦ* [sc. *τοῦ Δαβίδ*] *ἀναστῆσαι τὸν Χριστὸν τὸ κατὰ σάρκα* ‡Ath.*Apoll*.2.8(M.26.1145A); *οὐκ ἄρα ἓν τῶν ποιημάτων ἐστίν* [sc. *ὁ υἱός*], *ἀλλὰ κ. τῆς οὐσίας τοῦ πατρός* Cyr.*thes*.21(5^{1}.211D); = *spiritual offspring, disciple*, Geo.Pis.*carm*.24.1; **3.** spiritual *αὐτῷ* [sc. *τῷ Χριστῷ*] *δώσομεν...τίνα κ. ἄξιον;* 2*Clem*.1.3; *οὐδεὶς τῶν δικαίων ταχὺν κ. ἔλαβεν, ἀλλ' ἐκδέχεται αὐτόν ib*.20.2; *κ. ἄφθαρτος* opp. *κ. θανατηφόρος*, Ign.*Trall*.11.1,2; *τὸν κ. τῆς μακροθυμίας* Clem.*ecl*.45 (p.149.19; M.9.720A); *ὁ κ. τῆς εὐχῆς ταύτης* id.*paed*.3.12(p.285.17; M.8.668C); *κ., τὴν τῆς ψυχῆς εὐστάθειαν* id.*str*.4.23(p.314.20; M.8.1357C); *τὸν κ. τῆς ἑαυτῶν πίστεως* Jul.Papa *ep.Alex*.ap.Ath.*apol.sec*.52(p.133.20; M.25.344B); *τῆς ἀσκήσεως...κ. ἀγαθόν* Ath.*v.Anton*.66 (M.26.937B); *μετανοίας κ. Const.App*.2.39.6; *ib*.2.41.1; plur. *ποικίλοις κ. κεκοσμημένοι* ‡*Diogn*.12.1; *σωφροσύνης τοὺς κ.* Clem.*prot*.11(p.83.4; M.8.237B); *ἡ θεοσέβεια τοῦ γνωστικοῦ τοὺς κ. τῶν δι' αὐτοῦ πιστευσάντων ἀνθρώπων εἰς ἑαυτὴν ἀναδεχομένη* id.*str*.7.1(p.4.29; M.9.405B); *πρὸς ἐπίδειξιν καρπῶν δικαιοσύνης* †Bas.*Is*.153(1.487E; M.30.369C); *τοὺς κ. ὑμῶν...προσφέροντες* [sc. *τῷ ἐπισκόπῳ*] *Const.App*.2.34.5; *τῶν τῆς συκοφαντίας ἀπολαῦσαι κ.* Thdt.*ep*.103(3.1172).

B. *source* of fruit, met. *τῶν ἐλπιζόντων εἰς σὲ σωτηρίας, καὶ οὐκ αἰσχύνης ὑπάρχεις κ.* Thdt.*Ps*.68:7(1.1078).

***καρποτροφέω**, *suckle, nourish*, Thdr.Stud.*nativ.BMV* 4(M.96.685A).

***καρποφοράω**, v.l. for *καρποφορέω*.

καρποφορ-έω, **1.** *bear fruit*, met. *ἀναβαίνομεν* [i.e. from baptism] *~οῦντες ἐν τῇ καρδίᾳ Barn*.11.11; *ἐν τούτῳ* [sc. *παραδείσῳ*] *καὶ ὁ λόγος ἤνθησέν τε καὶ ἐκαρποφόρησεν σὰρξ γενόμενος* Clem.*str*.5.11 (p.375.2; M.9.109B); *καὶ πρὸς ἔκτασιν αὐτὴν* [sc. *τὴν πονηρίαν*] *ἐᾶσαι φῦναι καὶ ~εῖν* Meth.*res*.1.44(p.293.15; M.41.1116A) cit.ap.Leont.et Jo.*sacr*.2.3 (*καρποφορᾶν* M.86.2056B); **2.** *bear as fruit*, met. *~εῖ τὰς κατ' ἀρετὴν ἐνεργείας* Clem.*str*.7.12(p.50.26; M.9.497B); ref. Jo.12:24 *ὁ θάνατος τοῦ Ἰησοῦ τούτους πάντας ἐκαρποφόρησεν. εἰ δὲ ὁ θάνατος τοσούτους ἐκαρποφόρησε, πόσους ~ήσει ἡ ἀνάστασις;* Or.*hom*.10.3 *in Jer*.(p.73.20; M.13.361A); **3.** *offer*, of personal dedication *σαυτὸν ~ησον* Gr.Naz.*or*.40.25(M.36.393C); *πάντα τῇ εἰσόδῳ τοῦ Χριστοῦ ~ησον ib*.40.31(404B); *ἐκαρποφόρησαν ἑαυτοὺς οἱ ἅγιοι* Dor.*doct*.22.3 (M.88.1825A); of almsgiving *ἐλεημοσύνας ~ησας* Cyr.*Ps*.51:10(M.69.1105D); **4.** *make offerings, vow offerings*, ref. gifts to church, *Lit*.ap. *Const.App*.8.10.12; *οὐ δεῖ τοὺς ἐπισκόπους...ἀναγκάζειν τινὰς ~εῖν* Phot.*nomoc*.6.1(M.104.633B); to monks for their support *~εῖν μοναχοῖς* Nil.*epp*.1.129(M.79.137C); **5.** *vow as an offering* to church *ἐάν τις πρᾶγμα ~ήσῃ, γίνεται αὐτὸς ἔνοχος, οὐ μὴν τὸ πρᾶγμα* Phot.*nomoc*.2.1(569B); **6.** *derive fruit from ἵνα...ὁ ἄνθρωπος τὰς ἐντολὰς κυρίου...~ῇ* Eulog.*fr.Novat*.(M.104.349A).

***καρποφορητέον**, *one must bear fruit*; met., Or.*comm.in Mt*.15.3 (p.355.13; M.13.1260B).

καρποφορία, ἡ, **1.** *gathering of fruit*, Jo.Scholast.*coll.cap*.49 (p.388); **2.** met., *bringing forth fruit*, of spiritual fruit *τὴν...κατὰ θεὸν λογικὴν κ.* Eus.*d.e*.7.1(p.315.11; M.22.516B); *ὁ καταφυτεύσας τὸ ἑαυτοῦ ἡγεμονικὸν πάσῃ κ. πνευματικῇ* †Bas.*Is*.153(1.487E; M.30.369C); *τοσαύτην κ. ἀρετῶν V.Pach.Λ* 16(p.139.26); *εἰς κ. ἔργων ἀγαθῶν Lit.Jac*.(p.206.16); by repentance, Gr.Mag.*dial*.(tr.Zach.)4.44(M.*PL*.77.403C); **3.** *fruit brought forth, harvest*; met., of result of Christ's sacrifice *τῆς οἰκουμενικῆς κ.* Gr.Naz.*or*.4.67(M.35.588C); **4.** *offering*; in worship, Cyr.*Jo*.2(4.189E); Eus.Al.*serm*.4(M.86.341A); ref. gifts to church *ὑπὲρ σωτηρίας...τὴν μετρίαν ἡμῶν κ. δέχου, δέσποτα Inscr*.(*JHS* 11 p.236); *Mir.Geo*.11(p.109.13); *τίνας δεῖ λαμβάνειν, ἢ διδόναι κ.* Phot.*nomoc*.6.1(M.104.633C); plur., *offerings* to church, *Mir.Geo*.11(p.108.20); *ib*.(p.109.7); **5.** *making* or *vowing of offerings* to church *διαβαίνει...εἰς κληρονόμους ἡ τῆς κ. ἐνοχή* Phot.*nomoc*.2.1(M.104.569C); plur. *περὶ καρποφοριῶν ib*.6.6 tit.(632B).

καρποφόρος, *bearing offerings* to the church, *Mir.Geo*.11(p.109.27).

***καρποχειρίον**, τό, *palm of the hand*, Melet.*nat.hom*.2(M.64.1249C).

κάρπωσις, ἡ, **1.** *enjoyment*, Clem.*str*.2.18(p.159.8; M.8.1025B); **2.** *offering* of sacrifice, Mel.*fr*.9(p.312; M.5.1217B); Epiph.*haer*.79.9 (p.484.7; M.42.753C).

κάρταλ(λ)ος, ὁ, **1.** *basket*, Pall.*h.Laus*.36(p.107.13; M.34.1179D); Cyr.*Joel*.8(3.206B); Proc.G.*Gen*.4:2(M.87.236C); **2.** *bird-cage*, *T.Job* 27(p.120.2).

καρτερικός, **1.** *capable of endurance, steadfast κ. ἐν πόνῳ* Clem.*str*.7.9(p.40.5; M.9.477A); superl. *καρτερικωτάτης προθέσεως* Ath.*Ar*.3.57(M.26.444A); neut. as subst., *constancy, endurance*, Jo.D.*hom*.12 (M.96.797A); **2.** *requiring endurance, testing endurance τὸν κ. βίον* Eus.*d.e*.3.5(p.123.32; M.22.212A); *πόνους κ.* ‡Gr.Nyss.*or*.1 *in Gen*. 1:26(M.44.269D) ∾ ‡Bas.*struct.hom*.1(1.331C; M.30.25D).

***καρτερόαθλος**, *wrestling valiantly*; spiritually, *Hymn*.(*AS* 1 p.607).

***καρτεροκάρδιος**, *valiant-hearted*, Thdr.Stud.*cant*.16.2(p.371).

***καρτερόμητις**, *mighty in council*, Gr.Naz.*carm*.2.1.32.31(M.37.1303).

καρτεροψυχία, ἡ, *stoutheartedness*, Bas.*ep*.221(3.334D; M.32.817A).

καρυατίζω, *play childish game with nuts*, Max.*ambig*.(M.91.1413B).

***καρυδίζω**, = foreg., Leont.N.*v.Sym*.31(M.93.1708D).

καρύδιον, τό, *nut*, Leont.N.*v.Sym*.31(M.93.1708D).

καρύϊνος, *of walnut wood*, Or.*sel.in Gen*.30:37(M.12.125A); of Moses' rod, Gr.Nyss.*bapt.Chr*.(M.46.584A); Isid.Pel.*epp*.1.50(M.78.213A).

καρυκεία, ἡ, **1.** *concoction φαρμακῶν κ.* Cyr.*Jo*.6.1(4.607E); **2.** met., *richness τὴν κ. τοῦ βίου* Gr.Nyss.*infant*.(M.46.185B); Synes. *Dion* 10(p.263.17; M.66.1145A); Soz.*h.e*.3.16.2(M.67.1088A); *πνευματικῆς κ.* †Jo.D.*B.J*.38(M.96.1221A).

καρύκευμα, τό, *sauce, condiment*, Bas.*hex*.9.6(1.88E; M.29.208B); Chrys.*hom.52.5 in Ac*.(9.396D); Jo.VI H.*v.Jo.D*.7(M.94.440C); met. *εὐχῆς κ. κάλλιστον...δάκρυον* Bas.Sel.*v.Thecl*.2.28(M.85.613C).

***καρυκευτής**, ὁ, *fancy cook*, Clem.*paed*.3.4(p.251.23; M.8.592B).

***καρυκευτικός**, **1.** *rich, spiced*; of food and drink, Gr.Agr.*Eccl*. 2.12(M.98.836A); **2.** *ἡ καρυκευτική* [sc. *τέχνη*] *art of seasoning* or *cookery*, Chrys.*hom.49.4 in Mt*.(7.509C).

***καρύκευτος**, v. *ἀκαρύκευτος.

***καρυόκουφος**, *light as a nut*, Ant.Mon.*hom*.45(M.89.1573D).

καρυτίζω, = *καρυατίζω*, Nil.*exerc*.63(M.79.796C).

καρφολογ-έω, *pick bits out of ~είτω ἡμῶν τὸ ὄμμα* Bas.*ep*.204.4(3.304E; M.32.749A).

καρφολογία, ἡ, *collection of dry sticks*; for a fire, Leont.H.*Nest*. 1.19(M.86.1473A).

καρφόω, *nail ἐκάρφωσαν* [sc. *τὸν Ἰησοῦν*] *ἐν τῷ σταυρῷ A.Pil*.B 10 (p.305).

***κάσις**, ἡ, *whip*, †Cyr.*hom.div*.14(5^{2}.411C).

***κασιτήριος**, = *κασσιτέρινος*, *made of tin*, *Exorc*.(p.345).

***κάσος**, ὁ, *portion*, Phot.*nomoc*.11.1(M.104.840B).

***κασουδάριος**, ὁ, (? = Lat. *casularius*) *one who lives in a hut*, *Mir.Mich*.5(p.553.13).

[*]**κάσσαμον**, τό, = *κάσαμον*, a spice, Philost.*h.e*.3.6(M.65.488B).

***κασσίς**, ἡ, (Lat. *cassis*) *helmet*, Jo.Mal.*chron*.8 p.202(M.97.317A); Thphn.*chron*.p.266(M.108.660C).

***κάσταλδος**, ὁ, *governor of a town οἱ τὰ ἑσπέρια οἰκοῦντες μέρη, ῥῆγες ἔξαρχοί τε καὶ κ.* Thphn.*chron*.p.296(M.108.724A).

κασταναία, ἡ, *chestnut-tree*, ‡Ath.*def*.1(M.28.540B).

***καστελλᾶτος**, (Lat. *castellatus*) *fortified*, Const.Pogon.*sacr*.1 (M.*PL*.87.1154B).

***καστέλλι(ο)ν**, τό, (Lat. *castellum*) *stronghold, fort*, Jo.Mal.*chron*. 13 p.341(M.97.509A); of a monastery, Jo.Mosch.*prat*.167(M.87.3033C); *Chron.Pasch*.p.389(M.92.1020A); at CP *τὸ στρογγυλοῦν καστέλλιν ib*.p.382(980B).

***κάστελλος**, ὁ, = foreg., Epiph.*haer*.66.5(p.25.12; M.42.37C); *οἰκίαν κ. ἔχουσαν* Chrys.*ep*.14.3(3.397D); *V.Alex.Acoem*.33(p.683.12).

***καστελλόω**, *fortify*, Thphn.*chron*.p.250(M.108.625C).

καστόριον, τό, *beaver*, ‡Petr.I Al.*phys*.23.

***καστρησιανός** (*καστρισ-), ὁ, **1.** *military official*, *καστρισ-*, Jo. Mal.*chron*.18 p.430(M.97.633B); **2.** *court official*, responsible for the service of the imperial table, *CG–CI* 1 p.121.

***καστρομαχία**, ἡ, *siege warfare*, Thphn.*chron*.p.317(M.108.768B).

***κάστρον**, τό, (Lat. *castrum*) *stronghold*, Cyr.S.*v.Sab*.72(p.175.

18); *Chron.Pasch*.p.271(M.92.669A); †Hipp.Th.*fr*.7.1(p.33.1); applied to a city, Jo.Mosch.*prat*.112(M.87.2977B); to a monastery, Jo.Clim.*scal*.6(M.88.797A).

***καστροφύλαξ, ὁ,** *watchman* ὁ κ. τῆς πόλεως *Ep.Abg*.5(p.282.26).

***κάστυ, τό,** (Hebr. קֶסֶת) *ink-vessel* τίς ἦν ὁ ἑστὼς ἐπάνω τοῦ ὕδατος [ref. Dan. 12:6], εἰ μὴ αὐτὸς οὗτος...ὃς ἔμελλεν...ἐπὶ τῷ Ἰορδάνῃ...ὑπὸ τοῦ πατρὸς μαρτυρεῖσθαι...ὁ τὸ κ. τοῦ γραμμάτεως [ref. Ezech.9:2 (AQ, THDN): Hebr. קֶסֶת הַסֹּפֵר; LXX ζώνη σαπφείρου] περὶ τὴν ὀσφὺν φορῶν καὶ τὸ βαδδίν; Hipp.*Dan*.4.57.3 (M.10.668A).

καταβαίν-ω, *go down, descend*;

A. from heaven to earth; **1.** of angels ἀγγέλους φαμὲν...ἀναβαίνειν μὲν προσάγοντας τὰς τῶν ἀνθρώπων ἐντεύξεις...~ειν δ' αὖ ἐκεῖθεν φέροντας ἑκάστῳ κατ' ἀξίαν τῶν ἀπὸ θεοῦ τι αὐτοῖς διακονεῖν τοῖς εὐεργετουμένοις προστασσομένων Or.*Cels*.5.4(p.4.17; M.11.1185B); **2.** of God; denied of ingenerate deity, ref. OT theophanies μὴ ἡγεῖσθε αὐτὸν τὸν ἀγέννητον θεὸν κ. ἢ ἀναβεβηκέναι ποθέν Just.*dial*.127.1(M.6.772B); affirmed of Son in Inc. ὁ υἱὸς τοῦ θεοῦ...ἀπ' οὐρανοῦ κ. διὰ τὴν σωτηρίαν τῶν ἀνθρώπων Arist.*apol*.15.1; ὁ λόγος τοῦ θεοῦ ὁ μέχρι ἀνθρώπων καὶ τῶν ἐλαχίστων ~ων οὐδὲν ἄλλο ἐστὶν ἢ πνεῦμα σωματικόν [i.e. acc. Stoics]· κατὰ δὲ ἡμᾶς...οὐκ ἂν σῶμα εἴη ὁ θεὸς λόγος...ὁ φθάνων, ἵνα πάντα διὰ λόγου γίνηται Or.*Cels*.6.71(p.141.19; M.11.1405C); οὐ γὰρ ἂν ἄλλως ἡ ἐκκλησία...τοὺς πιστεύοντας...ἀναγεννῆσαι ...δύναιτο..., ἐὰν μὴ καὶ δι' αὐτοὺς ὁ Χριστὸς κενώσας ἑαυτὸν... ἀποθάνῃ καταβὰς ἐξ οὐρανῶν καὶ προσκολληθεὶς τῇ ἑαυτοῦ γυναικί, τῇ ἐκκλησίᾳ Meth.*symp*.3.8(p.36.2; M.18.73B); Ath.*inc*.35.8(M.25.157A); **3.** of soul (pagan) περὶ τῆς πιπτούσης ἀπὸ τῶν ἁψίδων τοῦ οὐρανοῦ ψυχῆς καὶ ~ούσης Or.*Cels*.1.20(p.71.25; M.11.696B).

B. to death, of Christ μέχρι θανάτου κ. ὑπὲρ ἀσεβῶν Or.*Jo*.6.57 (37; p.166.2; M.14.300B); ὡς ἄνθρωπος εἰς τὸν θάνατον κ. Ath.*inc*.50.3 (M.25.185B); to Hades; of Christ, Or.*Jo*.32.30(19; p.477.16; 824C); Ath.*hom.in Mt.11:27*(M.25.212C); cf. ὥσπερ οὖν μέλλων διδάσκεσθαι περὶ τῶν ἐπουρανίων ἀναβαίνω, οὕτως ἐὰν χρεία μοι ᾖ μανθάνειν περὶ τῶν καταχθονίων, κἂν προφήτης γένωμαι, ~ω, καὶ τάχα διὰ τοῦτο Σαμουήλ, ἡνίκα ἐδιδάχθη τὰ καταχθόνια, καταβέβηκε κάτω καὶ γέγονεν ἐν ᾅδου...τῶν γὰρ ἀκουόντων οἱ μὲν ἀναβαίνουσιν ἵνα διδαχθῶσιν, ἀναβαίνουσιν ⟨δὲ⟩ οὐ πάντως σωματικῶς· ⟨οἱ δὲ⟩ ~ουσι καὶ τὴν ψυχὴν ἔχουσιν ἄνω, ὑπὲρ τοῦ ἰδεῖν τὸν λόγον τὸν ἀνωτάτω περὶ τῶν κατωτάτω. αὐτὸς ὁ κύριός μου...Χριστὸς ἀναβέβηκε καὶ καταβέβηκεν Or.*hom.18.2 in Jer*.(p.152.28; M.13.465C); of believers into baptismal font, symbolizing death, *Barn*.11.11 cit. s. ἁμαρτία; εἰς τὸ ὕδωρ οὖν ~ουσι νεκροὶ καὶ ἀναβαίνουσι ζῶντες Herm.*sim*.9.16.4; νεκρὸς...καταβάς, ἀναβαίνεις ζωοποιηθεὶς...ὥσπερ γὰρ Ἰησοῦς... ἀπέθανεν...οὕτω καὶ σὺ καταβὰς εἰς τὸ ὕδωρ, καὶ τρόπον τινὰ ἐν τοῖς ὕδασι ἐνταφείς, ὥσπερ ἐκεῖνος ἐν τῇ πέτρᾳ Cyr.H.*catech*.3.12.

C. met., of moral decadence, esp. of idolatry ~οντας μετ' Αἰγυπτίων ἐπὶ τὰ πετεινὰ ἢ τετράποδα Or.*Cels*.6.4(p.74.2; M.11.1293B); Ath.*gent*.7(M.25.16C).

καταβαπτίζ-ω, 1. *sink, overwhelm*; **a.** lit., of Naaman dipping in Jordan, Didym.*Trin*.2.14(M.39.700C); **b.** met. τῶν πάνυ ὑπὸ τῆς κακίας καταβεβαπτισμένων Or.*Jo*.28.10(9; p.400.17; M.14.700B); ἐν πειρασμοῖς μὴ ~όμενοι Cyr.H.*catech*.23.17; τὸν νοῦν ὁ οἶνος ~ει †Bas.*Is*.156(1.489E; M.30.373D); τῷ τῶν παθῶν βυθῷ κατεβάπτισεν Arsen.*doct*.(M.66.1620C); τῷ μεγέθει τοῦ θαύματος τὸν λογισμὸν καταβαπτισθέντες Bas.Sel.*or*.33.2(M.85.364D); **2.** *baptize irregularly* or *in schism* οἱ ~οντες ἢ ἀναβαπτίζοντες Gr.Naz.*or*.33.17(M.36.236B); Ζωορᾶς... κατεβάπτισεν ἐν τῇ τοῦ πάσχα ἡμέρᾳ οὐκ ὀλίγους *Libell*.ap.CCP(536) *act*.1(*ACO* 3 p.139.2; H.2.1205E).

***καταβαπτιστήριον, τό,** *schismatical baptistery* καταβαπτιστήρια ᾠκοδόμησαν ἐξ ἐναντίας...τῆς ἁγίας κολυμβήθρας *Libell*.ap.CCP(536) *act*.5(*ACO* 3 p.43.36; H.2.1293A).

***καταβαπτιστής, ὁ,** *administrator of irregular* or *schismatic baptism*, Gr.Naz.*or*.40.44(M.36.421C).

καταβαρύνω, *oppress* κ. τὸ σῶμα ἐδέσμασι Call.*v.Hyp*.(p.49).

καταβασανίζω, in pass., *be put to the torture*, Petr.I Al.*ep.can*.11 (M.18.496B).

καταβασία, ἡ, an affliction of the eye τὴν κ. καὶ πάντα πόνον τοῦ ὀμματίου *Exorc*.14(p.337).

***καταβασιλεύω,** *rule over*, c. genit., *A.Xanthipp*.17(p.70.28).

καταβάσιος, *descending* κ. πᾶς ὁ κόσμος κατακλυζόμενος πυρί Meth.*res*.1.47(p.298.1; M.18.273B); *ib*.2.23(p.378.11); neut. as subst., *descent*, ref. Eleusinian mysteries τὸ κ. τὸ σκοτεινόν Ast.Am.*hom*.10 (M.40.324B); οἴκημα ὑπεράνω...καὶ κ. ἐκ τούτου λανθάνον ἐπὶ τοὺς μάρτυρας Soz.*h.e*.9.2.3(M.67.1597B).

κατάβασις, ἡ, A. *descent*; **1.** of Christ's descent into Hades, Or.*Jo*.6.35(18; p.144.8; M.14.260B); τὸ γὰρ βαπτίζεσθαι καὶ καταδύεσθαι, εἶτα ἀνανεύειν, τῆς εἰς ᾅδου κ. ἐστι σύμβολον καὶ τῆς ἐκεῖθεν ἀνόδου Chrys.*hom.40.1 in 1Cor*.(10.379C); ἡ ἀνάβασις δηλοῖ τὴν κ. Thdt.*Ps*.67:19(1.1065); Jo.D.*carm.assumpt.Chr*.79(p.228; M.96.845C) cit. s. ἀνυψόω; **2.** of Inc. τὸ μυστήριον τῆς τοῦ υἱοῦ τοῦ θεοῦ...κ. Or.*Jo*.6.5 (2; p.112.29; M.14.208B); Serap.*euch*.19(p.180.20); τῆς θείας φύσεως ἡ κ. τῆς ἀνθρωπίνης φύσεως ἐπραγματεύσατο τὴν ἀνάβασιν Thdt.*qu.19 in 4Reg*.(1.525); οὐ γὰρ ἦν σώματος ἡ κ. ἀλλὰ θείας ἐνεργείας βούλησις id.*rect.conf*.10(M.6.1224C); οὐ γὰρ τοπικὴ γέγονεν ἡ κ. ἀλλὰ θεϊκὴ πέπρακται συγκατάβασις Procl.CP *annunt*.5(M.85.448B); **3.** of the soul ἐπὶ τῆς νοητῆς κ. τῆς ψυχῆς Or.*Jo*.19.22(5; p.323.24; M.14.568A); τῇ ἀπὸ τῶν οὐρανῶν εἰς τὰ σώματα κ. καὶ παραπομπῇ τῶν ψυχῶν Meth.*symp*.2.5(p.21.5; M.18.53C); **4.** genealogical, Eus.*qu.Steph*.11(M.22.921C).

B. *fallen state*, Or.*Jo*.6.46(27; p.153.24; M.14.280D).

C. place beneath the altar for relics, *confession* ἡ κ. ἐκτίσθη, ἔνθα ...τιμᾶται [sc. ἡ κάρα τοῦ ἁγίου Ἰωάννου τοῦ προδρόμου] Thphn.*chron*.p.362(M.108.869A).

καταβάτης, ὁ, as adj., *steeply descending* τὸν κ. ᾅδην διαβάς ‡Gr.Naz.*Chr.pat*.1693(M.38.271A).

καταβατόν, τό, *sequel*, Anast.S.*hod*.12(M.89.201C).

***καταβδελύσσομαι,** *loathe*, Cyr.*ador*.1(1.41B).

καταβιβάζω, *lower, degrade*, Or.*Cels*.4.86(p.356.21; M.11.1160C); from eccl. orders, CChalc.*can*.29; in diptychs, *Fr.Hist*.4(M.85.1820A); κατεβιβάσθη τὸ ὄνομα Μηνᾶ πατριάρχου Κωνσταντινουπόλεως, καὶ προανεβιβάσθη τὸ ὄνομα Βιγιλίου προτασσομένου ἐν τοῖς διπτύχοις Thphn.*chron*.p.192(M.108.500A); *depose* διὰ τὸ καταβεβιβάσθαι τῶν ἀρχοντικῶν θρόνων τὸν λογισμόν Nil.*exerc*.69(M.79.801D).

***καταβλαβής,** *injurious*, Didym.*Trin*.2.8(M.39.608C).

***καταβλασφημέω,** *blaspheme against*, c. genit., Eus.*Ps*.62:9(M.23.616A).

***καταβλύζω,** *overwhelm*, Isid.Pel.*epp*.5.56(M.78.1361A).

καταβοή, ἡ, *outcry against*, Cyr.*Joel*.proem.(3.197A); id.*Am*.36 (3.291A, v.l. κατακοήν Aubert); id.*Nah*.21(3.506B); Isid.Pel.*epp*.2.21 (M.78.472A).

καταβόησις, ἡ, = foreg. ἡ τοῦ ἀσεβοῦς λαοῦ κ. φάσκοντος, αἶρε ἀπὸ τῆς γῆς τὸν τοιοῦτον Or.*Jo*.1.11(12; p.17.2; M.14.44D); ἀπειλῶν καὶ κ. ... ὑπομονήν Dion.Al.ap.Eus.*h.e*.7.11.18(M.20.669A); Isid.Pel.*epp*.1.154(M.78.285C).

***καταβοθρεύω,** *bury*, Cyr.*Zach*.22(3.681A; πεπτωκότων Aubert).

***καταβοθρόω,** = foreg., Tat.*orat*.34(p.35.27; M.6.876C).

καταβολή, ἡ, 1. *throwing down*, esp. of seed in propagation τὸ ἡγεμονικόν, ᾧ διαλογιζόμεθα, οὐ κατὰ τὴν τοῦ σπέρματος κ. γεννώμενον Clem.*str*.6.16(p.500.11; M.9.360B); Ἰησοῦν τὸν γεννηθέντα ἐκ τῆς παρθένου ἄνευ κ. σπέρματος ἀνδρός Or.*fr.27 in Jo*.(p.504.18); met., of mental propagation, Gr.Thaum.*pan.Or*.7(p.20.12; M.10.1076B); **2.** *beginning, foundation* μονὰς δὲ μήτηρ ἀριθμῶν...ἀρχὴ κ. τε καὶ στοιχεῖον Eus.*l.C*.6(p.209.30; M.20.1348A); esp. of Creation, *Barn*.5.5; Gr.Nyss.*hex*.(M.44.120A); Cosm.Ind.*top*.2(M.88.128C); interpreted as implying *descent* πῶς γὰρ δύναται ἔχειν τι ὁ κόσμος οὗτος ἄνω, οὗ ἡ κτίσις κ. ἐστιν; οὐ γὰρ ὡς ἔτυχεν ἀκουστέον τοῦ 'πρὸ κ. κόσμου' ἐπίτηδες διὰ τοιαύτην ἐπίνοιαν πλασάντων ὄνομα τῶν ἁγίων τὸ τῆς κ. καίτοι γε ἐδύναντο λέγειν 'πρὸ κτίσεως κόσμου' καὶ μὴ χρήσασθαι τῷ τῆς 'κ.' ὀνόματι. ὅλος οὖν ὁ κόσμος καὶ τὰ ἐν αὐτῷ ἐν κ. ἐστιν. ἔξω δὲ κ. κόσμου παντὸς γίνονται οἱ τοῦ Ἰησοῦ γνήσιοι μαθηταί Or.*Jo*.19.22(5; p.324.18ff.; M.14.568Df.); cf. *praetereundum esse non arbitror, quod scripturae sanctae conditionem mundi novo quodam et proprio nomine nuncuparunt, dicentes κ. mundi (quod latine satis improprie translatum constitutionem mundi dixerunt; κ. vero in graeco magis deicere significat, id est deorsum jacere)...per κ. a superioribus ad inferiora videtur indicari deductio*, id.*princ*.3.5.4 (pp.274ff.; M.11.328Bff.); καλῶς κ. εἶπεν, ὡς ἀπό τινος ὕψους καταβεβλημένον μεγάλου αὐτὸν δεικνύς Chrys.*hom.1.2 in Eph*.(11.4B); **3.** *sending forth, descent* εἰ μή τις εὐγένεια τύχοι ψυχῆς ἄνωθεν ἕλκουσα τὴν πρώτην κ. Synes.*Dion* 9(p.255.11; M.66.1136C); σημεῖον ἂν γένοιτο...ἡ χειρὸς ἐπίθεσις τῆς τοῦ παναγίου πνεύματος εἰς ἡμᾶς κ. Cyr.*ador*.11(1.404B).

***καταβολικός,** *casting down*; subst., *catabolici*, name given to persecuting demons, Tert.*de anima* 28(M.*PL*.2.698B).

καταβομβέω, *shout against* πιθανῶς καταβομβήσαντος ἡμῶν τοῦ λόγου καὶ ἀληθῶς δυναμένου ταράξαι καὶ κινῆσαι ἡμᾶς Or.*engast*.4 (p.285.30; καταπομπήσαντος M.12.1016D); ἐροῦμεν πρὸς τὸν τοσαῦτα ἡμῶν καταβομβήσαντα *ib*.(p.286.12; 1017B); τοσαύτην ἡμῖν ἐπὶ τοῦ βήματος καταβομβήσας δημηγορίαν ‡Jo.D.*Artem*.36(M.96.1284D).

καταβραβεύω, *give unjust judgement against, defraud*, Malch.*ep*.

ap.Eus.*h.e.*7.30.7(M.20.712B); Chrys.*hom.*7.*1 in Col.*(11.371E); Thdt. *Col.*2:18(3.489).

***καταβραχύνομαι**, *be short*, Philost.*h.e.*10.11(M.65.592B).

***καταβριθής**, *burdensome*, Cyr.*inc.unigen.*(5^1.678D).

καταβροντάω, *thunder down*; of psalmody, Gr.Naz.*or.*43.52(M. 36.561C); τῶν εὐαγγελικῶν κηρυγμάτων ἡ δύναμις κατεβρόντησε τὴν ὑπ' οὐρανόν Cyr.*Ps.*39:10(M.69.992A); Geo.Pis.*Pers.*1.178(M.92.1210A).

***καταβροχθισμός**, ὁ, *gulping down*, Clem.*paed.*2.2(p.175.16; M.8. 428A).

***καταβρυχάομαι**, *roar*, Cyr.*Ps.*9:30(M.69.784C); id.*Mich.*51(3. 442B); id.*Is.*3.4(2.497C).

κατάβρωμα, τό, *that which is devoured*; **1.** *prey*, †Jo.D.*B.J.*12(M. 96.973B); *ib.*(976B); of an excommunicated person κ. τοῦ διαβόλου Bas.*ep.*288 *can.*1(2.427A; M.32.1025A); **2.** *food*, Chrys.*hom.in Rom.* 5:3(3.148D).

κατάβρωσις, ἡ, *devouring*, Cyr.*Am.*66(3.323D); †Jo.D.*B.J.*23(M. 96.1068A).

κατάγαιος, variant of κατάγειος, neut. as subst. τὰ κ. opp. τὰ ἀνάγαια *ground floor (rooms)*, Pall.*h.Laus.*6 (v.l. for κατώγεα p.24. 10, M.34.1019B); met., of earth opp. firmament δύο οἴκους, τουτέστιν ἀνάγαιον καὶ κ. Cosm.Ind.*top.*2(p.59.8; ἀνώγεων καὶ κατώγεων M.88. 81C); *ib.*4(185B).

***καταγανόω**, *irradiate, make to shine*, Clem.*paed.*3.11(p.270.27; M.8.636A).

καταγγελεύς, ὁ, one who proclaims, *herald*, Clem.*str.*6.18(p.517. 31; M.9.400A); Οὐαλεντῖνος, τριάκοντα θεῶν κ. Cyr.H.*catech.*6.17.

καταγγελία, ἡ, *proclamation* of the gospel, Clem.*str.*6.18(p.518.11; M.9.400C); in OT types; exeg. Lev.16:5ff. οἱ...τράγοι δύο ὅμοιοι... τῶν δύο παρουσιῶν τοῦ Χριστοῦ κ. ἦσαν Just.*dial.*40.4(M.6.564A); τὰ ὑπὸ Μωυσέως διαταχθέντα...τύπους καὶ σύμβολα καὶ κ. τῶν τῷ Χριστῷ γίνεσθαι μελλόντων *ib.*42.4(565C).

καταγγέλλω, *proclaim*; pass., of spiritual truth, Just.*1apol.*42. 4(M.6.392C); id.*dial.*53.1(M.6.592C); Meth.*symp.*5.7(p.62.10; M.18. 109C); Ath.*syn.*6(p.243.29; M.26.689B); in a doxology, ‡Eust.*alloc.* (M.18.673D) cit. s. δοξολογέω; ref. Marcionite theory that Inc. had as object the proclamation of a more perfect God, Or.*princ.*4.2. 1(p.307.14; M.11.357C); of proclamation of gospel in OT; by prophets, Ign.*Philad.*5.2; in gen., Just.*dial.*85.1(M.6.676B); Or. *princ.*4.1.6(p.301.11; M.11.352B).

καταγγελτικός, *proclaiming* νόμοι...καινῆς δὲ καὶ ἀληθοῦς εὐσεβείας κ. Eus.*d.e.*3.6(p.138.12; M.22.233A); λόγοις βασιλείας οὐρανῶν καταγγελτικοῖς id.*pasch.*2(M.24.696B); τῇ κ. τοῦ θείου θελήματος δυνάμει ‡Proc.G.*Pr.*29:4(M.86.1513B).

καταγγίζ-ω, *put into a vessel*; met., of souls being embodied (Origenist) εἰ δὲ...ἡ ψυχὴ...προημάρτηκεν...ἔδει μὴ λέγειν τὸν... προφήτην 'καὶ πλάσσων πνεῦμα ἀνθρώπου ἐν αὐτῷ'· ἀλλὰ μᾶλλον, '~ων' Thphl.Al.*fr.ep.*ap.Justn.*Or.*(p.203.5; M.86.971A); Justn.*Or.* (p.191.21; 949D); Valent. παραδίδοσθαι ἀπὸ τοῦ ἄρχοντος τῷ ὑπηρέτῃ ...εἰς τὸ φέρειν τὰς ψυχὰς πάλιν καὶ εἰς σώματα κ. διάφορα Epiph. *haer.*27.5(p.307.8; M.41.369C); hence, *decant*, met. τὸν ἀλιτηρίως ἐκ τῶν σῶν ἀγγείων καταγγισθέντα τῶν ἐμῶν υἱῶν θάνατον ‡Pamph. Abyd.*ep.Petr.*(p.9.14; H.2.849C); *stuff* an animal, Cosm.Ind.*top.*11 (M.88.441C).

καταγελαστής, ὁ, *scorner*, Hipp.*haer.*4.15(p.50.1; M.16.3083B); Chrys.*hom.*5.4 *in 2Thess.*(Gaume; καταγελᾷ τῆς 11.543D).

§**κατάγελος**, ὁ, *laughing-stock*, *V.Zos.*21(p.108.6).

καταγεμίζω, *load*, fig. οἱ ὄνειροι...τῇ ψυχῇ προσεγγίζουσι πνευματικῆς αὐτὴν κ. θυμηδίας Diad.*perf.*37(p.42.14).

***καταγεραίρω**, *honour*, Gr.Nyss.*v.Ephr.*(M.46.833C); Cyr.*hom. pasch.*13.2(5^2.180D); δοξολογίαις τῶν ἁπάντων σωτῆρα κ. id.*Ps.*35:5(M. 69.916D); id.*dial.Trin.*1(5^1.415D); Andr.Cr.*Geo.*(p.xxvA).

καταγεύω, *give to taste*, Cyr.*Jo.*11(4.1016D).

καταγί(γ)νομαι, *abide, dwell*, of God οὐδὲ ἐν μέρει κ. Clem.*str.*2.2 (p.116.4; M.8.937A); πνεῦμα...τοῦ θεοῦ παρὰ πᾶσιν μὲν οὐκ ἔστι, παρὰ δέ τισι τοῖς δικαίως πολιτευομένοις κ. Tat.*orat.*13(p.15.2; M.6.836A); in a state (of punishment), Iren.*haer.*5.27.2(M.7.1196C); (of virginity), Meth.*symp.*7.1(p.71.23; M.18.125A).

***καταγκυλόω**, *bend*; perf. ptcpl. pass., of hair, *wavy*, Gr.Nyss. *hom.opif.*30(M.44.253A); neut. as subst., *crookedness* τὸ κ. τῆς τῶν σοφισμάτων πλοκῆς id.*Eun.*1(1 p.180.28; M.45.425A).

καταγλαΐζω, *glorify*, Jo.D.*hom.*8.4(M.96.705B); perf. ptcpl. pass., *glorified, resplendent*, Max.*ep.*13(M.90.532D); of man, Cyr.*ador.*1(1. 10A); τῷ τῆς ἀφθαρσίας τε καὶ ἀθανασίας κάλλει παρὰ θεοῦ κατηγλαϊσμένος ὁ ἄνθρωπος γέγονε Max.*ambig.*(M.91.1104A); of angelic intelligences, Dion.Ar.*d.n.*7.2(M.3.868B).

***καταγλαϊστικῶς**, *radiantly*, Steph.Diac.*v.Steph.*(M.100.1128C).

καταγλυκαίνω, *sweeten, fill with sweetness*, ref. Ex.15:22ff., Gr. Naz.*or.*36.4(M.36.269B); Cyr.*Am.*81(3.347B); met., Gr.Nyss.*hom.2 in Cant.*(M.44.800C); κ. ἡμῶν τὴν ἀκοήν id.*v.Macr.*(p.395.3; M.46. 981C); Chrys.*hom.12.2 in Rom.*(9.544C); Jo.Mon.*hymn.Bas.*9(M.96. 1376C).

καταγλύφω, *scratch, dig into*, Epiph.*haer.*78.4(p.455.3; M.42. 704D).

καταγλωττίζω, perf. ptcpl. pass.; **1.** *composed in elaborate language*, Gr.Naz.*or.*21.12(M.35.1093C); Thdt.*affect.*8(p.195.9; 4.898); **2.** of persons, *trained in rhetoric*, Cyr.*hom.pasch.*6(5^2.65A).

καταγλώττισμα, τό, *grandiloquent word*, Synes.*Dion* 11(p.263.17; M.66.1145A).

***καταγνωρίζω**, *recognize*, Cyr.*ador.*1(1.17E).

κατάγνωσις, ἡ, **1.** *condemnation, censure*, Bas.*jud.*5(1.217E; M.31. 664A); ref. confession of sins ἑαυτῶν κ. φέρουσιν *1Clem.*51.2; **2.** *reason of condemnation, charge* οὐ γὰρ τὸ μὴ θέλειν ἀποθανεῖν τὴν σάρκα, ἐστὶ κ. Chrys.*anom.*7.6(1.511B); **3.** *rejection* ἡ τοῦ τῶν ὅλων θεοῦ γνῶσις καὶ ἡ τῶν οἰκείων θεῶν κ. Eus.*p.e.*10.4(472D; M.21.785C); Ἰουδαίων κ. ἡ τῶν ἐθνῶν ἐπίγνωσις Bas.Sel.*or.*20.1(M.85.245D).

καταγογγύζω, *murmur against* μὴ κ. τῆς τῶν ἡμερῶν καθαρότητος Ast.Am.*hom.*14(M.40.377C); *ib.*13(365A).

***καταγογγυσμός**, ὁ, *murmuring against*, *Const.App.*2.32.1.

***καταγοήτευσις**, ἡ, *spell, charm*, Jo.D.*hom.*12.10(M.96.796B).

καταγοητεύω, **1.** *bewitch*; of magic, *Hom.Clem.*4.2; Cyr.*ador.*6(1. 190E); of snake-charming; fig., id.*Jo.*5(4.444E); of superstitious faith, id.*ador.*6(1.215A); **2.** *beguile, delude*; of the senses, Gr.Nyss. *hom.10 in Cant.*(M.44.993C); of rhetoric, Gr.Naz.*or.*16.1(M.35. 936B); of women, Isid.Pel.*epp.*4.71(M.78.1129B); ἡδονὴ κ. τὸν νοῦν Cyr.*ador.*1(1.10D); **3.** *soothe, hold spellbound*, Gr.Thaum.*pan.Or.*6 (p.16.13; M.10.1069D); of Christ τῶν Φαρισαίων κ. διάνοιαν Cyr.*Jo.* 6(4.640C).

[*]**κατάγομος**, τό, *burden, load*, *cat.Apoc.*14:20(p.400.26).

***καταγοριάρης**, ὁ, v. *κατηγοριάρης.

καταγραφή, ἡ, **1.** *diagram, map*, Clem.*str.*6.7(p.460.7; M.9.277C); Cosm.Ind.*top.*proem.1(M.88.53B); **2.** *description* (topographical), Eus.*onomast.*(p.2.8); **3.** *charge*, Euthal.Diac.*Ac.*(M.85.629A).

κατάγραφος, *painted*, Clem.*prot.*4(p.46.27; M.8.160A).

καταγράφω, **1.** *portray* ἐν τύποις...τὸ τοῦ...βαπτίσματος κ. μυστήριον Cyr.*ador.*15(1.540A); **2.** *assign, dedicate*, to God; of self-dedication, Ath.*inc.*37.5(M.25.161A); *V.Pach.A*(p.145.4); in gen., Cyr.*ador.*16(1.572D); **3.** *reckon, count as*, Cyr.*inc.unigen.*(5^1.679A).

κατάγχω, *strangle, suffocate*, Gr.Nyss.*or.dom.*5(p.108.23; M.44. 1188C); met., *press, urge*, Cyr.*ador.*1(1.38C); Arsen.*tent.*(M.66. 1624D); Areth.*Apoc.*49(M.106.708A); of curbing horses, Bas.*hom.*5.8 (2.42B; M.31.257C).

κατάγ-ω, **1.** *bring down*; **a.** from heaven to earth; pass., of God's condescension to creation, Dion.Ar.*d.n.*4.13(M.3.712B); (Platonist, etc.) of soul's descent into world as place of punishment, Clem.*str.* 3.3(p.201.16; M.8.1116B); **b.** of soul's descent in death to Hades, *T.Reub.*4.6; **c.** moral ἐπίγεια...ἔργα...κ. τὸν θησαυρίζοντα αὐτὰ ἐπὶ τῆς γῆς Or.*hom.*8.2 *in Jer.*(p.58.7; M.13.340A); **d.** *reduce*, Iren.*haer.* 1.15.6(M.7.625B); *ib.*1.15.4(624A); **e.** *subdue, cast down* ἡ...εἰδωλομανὴς πλάνη καταχθήσεται ‡Chrys.*pasch.*6(8.267D; παταχθήσεται p.141.5); **f.** *derive* succession πέμπτην ἀπὸ Πέτρου καὶ Παύλου ~ων διαδοχήν, τὴν ἐπισκοπὴν ἀπολαμβάνει Eus.*h.e.*4.1(M.20.303B); **2.** *bring in, introduce*, Athenag.*leg.*1.1(M.6.892A).

καταγωγή, ἡ, **1.** *place of hiding*, Eus.*h.e.*4.15.11(M.20.345D); **2.** *inn*, Athenag.*leg.*34.1(M.6.968B); *residence*, *ib.*16.1(920C); **3.** *halt, temporary suspense*; of life, Chrys.*hom.62.1 in Jo.*(8.369B).

***καταγωγία**, ἡ, *inn*, Gr.Nyss.*bapt.diff.*(M.46.421D).

καταγώγιον, τό, *shelter, stopping-place, inn, abode*, ‡Nil.*vit.cog.* (M.79.1452C); ref. Mt.8:20 οὐκ ἔχομεν κ. ὡρισμένον Chrys.*prod.Jud.* 1.4(2.382A); τὸ κ. τῶν ὀρφανῶν Evagr.*h.e.*2.11(p.63.7; M.86.2533C); τῶν πτωχῶν κ. Chrys.*Stag.*3.13(1.223D); of a monastic cell or house, ‡Pall.*h.mon.*24.1(p.84.20; M.34.1177B); Thdt.*h.rel.*3(3.1149); of a monastery guest house, ‡Pall.*h.mon.*19.2(p.78.19; 1177D); met. κ. ...τοῦ παραδείσου Meth.*symp.*proem.(p.6.14; M.18.36A); of death πάντων ὥσπερ ἐν ὁδῷ τῷ βίῳ τούτῳ πρὸς τὸ αὐτὸ κ. ἐπειγομένων... πάντας τὸ αὐτὸ ἀναμένει κατάλυμα Bas.*ep.*5.2(3.78C; M.32.241A); πρεσβύτην εἶναι καὶ ὅσον οὔπω τὸ πάντων ὑπελθεῖν κ. Evagr.*h.e.*3.11 (p.109.18; 2616B); of persons ἡ παρθένος οὖν αὐτὴ ἔστω ἁγία...ὡς... πνεύματος ἁγίου κ. *Const.App.*4.14.2; κ. ἔσται τῷ Χριστῷ...ἡ ψυχή Chrys.*stat.*2.6(2.29B); of martyrs Χριστοῦ κ. Const.Diac.*laud.*39(M. 88.524A); Εὐσέβιον...τὸ τῶν κακῶν κ. Thphn.*chron.*p.31(M.108. 136B); of Christ, in baptismal prayer κ. τῶν κεκμηκότων...κ. καὶ λιμὴν τῶν διιόντων ἀρχόντων χορῶν *A.Thom.*A 156(p.264.19).

καταδάκνω, *bite*; fig., of persecuting, Gr.Nyss.*Steph.*2(M.46.725A); met., of devouring the poor, Chrys.*hom.1.4 in Ps.48*:*17*(5.509E); pass., Just.*dial.*91.4(M.6.693B).

καταδαπανάω, 1. *consume*; met., Meth.*symp.*10.4(p.126.15; M.18.200A); of exhausting a topic, Chrys.*hom.19.4 in Jo.*(8.109D); **2.** *destroy, do away with,* Thdt.*Cant.*2:9(2.63).

καταδαρδάπτω, *devour,* Cyr.*ador.*14(1.509A).

***καταδάρπτω,** = foreg., Eudoc.*Cypr.*2.426(M.85.861C).

***καταδασύνομαι,** *be thickly wooded,* Cyr.*Os.*51(3.83A).

καταδεδίττομαι, *frighten, alarm,* Cyr.*Os.*158(3.190E); id.*Am.*81 (3.345A).

καταδεής, neut. as subst., *inferiority* οὐ χρή, φασί, πατρὶ καὶ υἱῷ συντετάχθαι τὸ ἅγιον πνεῦμα διὰ...τὸ τῆς ἀξίας κ. Bas.*Spir.*24(3.20E; M.32.112A); comp. *inferior* τὴν ἐν τοῖς κ. τῶν ὀνομάτων κοινωνίαν συγχωροῦντες τῷ πνεύματι, τῶν ὑπεραιρόντων κρίνειν ἀνάξιον Gr.Nyss. *Trin.*5(p.75.14; M.32.689B); in social status, Isid.Pel.*epp.*2.71(M.78.513C); of orders in Dionysian hierarchy, Dion.Ar.*d.n.*4.7,8(M.3.704B,D).

καταδεσμεύω, *bind up*; in healing, Eus.*Ps.*146:3(M.24.65C); of bondage to sin, Ath.*inc.*11.5(M.25.116C).

καταδεσμέω, *bind up*; in healing, Cyr.*Zach.*66(3.746B); *bind fast* τὰ σαυτοῦ κ. ἁμαρτήματα, οὐ τὰ τοῦ πλησίον Chrys.*hom.61.4 in Mt.*(7.616E); Mac.Aeg.*hom.*5.6(M.34.505C); in marriage, fig., Cyr.*ador.*5(1.153D); of Christ οὐδ' ἀνθρώπου ψυχῆς τρόπον τῷ σώματι κατεδεσμεῖτο Eus.*l.C.*14(p.242.8; M.20.1409B).

κατάδεσμος, ὁ, 1. *spell, charm*; in Jewish necromancy, Just.*dial.*85.3(M.6.676C); pagan, Eus.*l.C.*13(p.236.18; M.20.1397D); of love-philtres, Bas.*ep.*188 *can.*8(3.273C; M.32.677A); **2.** *bandage*, ref. Is.1:6 τῶν τραυμάτων τινά ἐστιν ἃ...δεῖται κ. ... ἄλλα δέ ἐστι τραύματα ἐφ' οἷς λέγεται 'οὔτε κ.' οὕτως ἔστι τινὰ ἁμαρτήματα Or.*hom.2.2 in Jer.*(p.18.25; M.13.280B).

καταδεύω, *soak*, typifying unction ἐλαίῳ τὴν σεμίδαλιν κ. Cyr.*ador.*10(1.364D).

καταδέχομαι, *receive, accept*; persons for ordination, CAnc.(314) *can.*10; as disciples, Nil.*exerc.*35(M.79.764B); teaching, *1Clem.*19.1; Gr.Nyss.*bapt.Chr.*(M.46.585A); Chrys.*hom.20.5 in Mt.*(7.267A); *admit, consent to*; of Christ's acceptance of suffering and death, Vict.*Mc.*14:1(p.417.19); Sev.Ant.ap.*cat.Mt.*27:27(p.235.16); *Lit.Jac.*(p.202.1).

καταδηϊόω, *ravage, pillage,* Eus.*Is.*2:20(M.24.105D); Cyr.*ador.*8(1.255C); id.*Nah.*12(3.490D).

***καταδηλόω,** *make plain, manifest,* Cyr.*inc.unigen.*(5^{1}.696A); *ib.*(710D); id.*schol.inc.*28(p.223.40).

***καταδημιουργία, ἡ,** *creative activity,* Zach.Mit.*opif.*(M.85.1053A).

***καταδήωσις, ἡ,** *devastation,* Cyr.*Joel.*4(3.200C).

***καταδιαβολή, ἡ,** *slander,* Cyr.*Ps.*36:14(M.69.933A).

***καταδιαδέχομαι,** *succeed as heir,* Ath.Scholast.*coll.*11.3(p.137).

καταδιαίρεσις, ἡ, *distribution,* ref. materialist idea of prior existence of substance to Persons in Trin. εἰ μὲν οὖν τὸ κοινὸν τῆς οὐσίας οὕτω νοήσας εἶπεν, ὡς ἐξ ὕλης προϋπαρχούσης...κ. εἰς τὰ ἀπ' αὐτῆς νοεῖν Bas.*Eun.*1.19(1.231B; M.29.556A).

καταδιαιρ-έω, *divide*; the unity of God in polytheism τάς τε τῶν αἰσθητηρίων δυνάμεις καταδιελὼν τῷ λόγῳ, παμπόλλους λέγοι εἶναι ἀνθρώπους τὸν ἕνα Eus.*l.C.*12(p.232.16; M.20.1392A); ὁ πατὴρ καὶ ὁ υἱὸς ἓν μέν εἰσι κατὰ φύσιν, δύο δὲ ἐν ἀριθμῷ, οὐχ ὡς ἑνός τινος εἰς δύο καταδιαιρεθέντος μέρη Cyr.*thes.*12(5^{1}.110A); the Person of Son εἴπερ ἦν τὸ μεσολαβοῦν μετὰ τὸ ἡνῶσθαι σαρκὶ τὸν λόγον, καὶ εἰς ἑτερότητα ~οῦν τὴν ὡς ἐν υἱῶν δυάδι, πῶς ἂν ἐκτίσθη τὰ πάντα διὰ Ἰησοῦ Χριστοῦ; id.*inc.unigen.*(5^{1}.709D); εἰς δύο υἱοὺς κ. τὸν ἕνα id.*apol. Thdt.*3(p.125.7; 6^{1}.219A).

***καταδιανθρώπησις, ἡ,** *formation of a man,* ‡Caes.Naz.*dial.*3(M.38.1080).

καταδίδωμι, *bestow,* Cyr.*ador.*7(1.234C).

καταδιΐστημι, *divide* κ. εἰς δύο τὸν ἕνα Χριστόν Cyr.*inc.unigen.*(5^{1}.679E); *ib.*(689A).

***καταδικάσιμος,** *damnable* τῆς κ. αἱρέσεως Cael.*ep.Jo.Ant.*(p.90.4; M.*PL.*50.500A).

***καταδικαστέον,** *one must condemn,* Clem.*q.d.s.*26(p.177.30; M.9.632D).

***καταδικαστικῶς,** *by way of condemnation* οὐ κ. ... ἀλλὰ πατρικῶς ἐπαίδευσεν Iren.*fr.*33(M.7.1245C).

καταδίκη, ἡ, *condemnation*; judicial, Chrys.*hom.in Mt.18:23*(3.13A); eccl., Philost.*h.e.*7.6(M.65.544A); divine ἑαυτὸν εἰς κ. ... τοῦ πυρὸς παρανάλωμα δέδωκεν Ath.*h.Ar.*70(p.221.20; M.25.776D); ὅπερ Ἀδὰμ ἀναμάρτητον καὶ ἀκαταδίκαστον εἰς φθορὰν καὶ κ. θανάτου κατενήνοχε ‡Ath.*Apoll.*1.7(M.26.1105A).

καταδίκος, ὁ, *condemned,* of Christ ὡς κ. ἐσταυρώθη Chrys.*hom.33.2 in Heb.*(12.304C); of martyrs μὴ ὡς κ. ἐπὶ κακοῖς ὁμολογουμένοις πάθωσι...ἀλλ' ὅτι Χριστιανοὶ πεφυκότες Basilides ap.Clem.*str.*4.12 (p.284.10; M.8.1292A); met., of slaves of avarice, Chrys.*hom.23.6 in 1Cor.*(10.209B,C); of sinners, *Hom.Clem.*12.30; Jo.D.*fr.Mt.*28:20 (M.96.1413B); of an excommunicate παρὰ θεῷ κ. *Const.App.*2.47.3; of penitents μετανοῶν ἐστι κ. ἀκαταίσχυντος Jo.Clim.*scal.*5(M.88.764B); οἱ...ἅγιοι κ. *ib.*(780D).

***καταδίψος,** *thirsting* for, met. κ. λόγου...ἐπιθυμοῦντες λόγου θεοῦ †Bas.*Is.*100(1.448E; M.30.281A).

***καταδονέω,** *shake, disturb,* Cyr.*Ps.*67:8(M.69.1148A); id.*hom.pasch.*30(5^{1}.346E); *ib.*26(307E).

καταδουλ-όω, *make into a servant* οἱ τὸ πνεῦμα ~ούμενοι Bas.*Spir.*52(3.44B; M.32.164B).

καταδράσσομαι, *take hold of, catch*; of fire, Cyr.*hom.pasch.*17(5^{2}.231B).

***καταδυναμόω,** *strengthen,* *Ascens.Is.*A 2.4(p.84).

καταδυναστεία, ἡ, *oppression, tyranny,* as a sin κ. τῶν ὑποδεεστέρων Bas.*hex.*7.3(1.65A; M.29.152D); τὴν...κατεστυγημένην θεῷ κ. Cyr.*Am.*48(3.302C); πᾶσι...ἀνθρώποις τὰ ἐκ τῆς τῶν τυράννων κ. ἐλεύθερα ἦν Eus.*h.e.*10.2.1(M.20.845B); of death, Eus.*theoph.fr.*3 (p.8*.5; M.24.615B); τῶν δαιμόνων κ. Or.*exc.in Ps.*80:2(M.17.149A); ref. Jo.8:32 ἐλευθερίαν, δηλονότι, ψυχῆς...ἐν τῷ ῥυσθῆναι ἀπὸ τῆς τῶν ἁμαρτημάτων κ. †Bas.*bapt.*1.1.2(2.625B; M.31.1516C); τοῦ ἀλλοτρίου κ. *Lit.*ap.*Const.App.*8.7.2; Thdr.Mops.*Eph.*4:8(M.66.920A); Mac.Aeg.*hom.*47.12(M.34.804C).

καταδυναστεύ-ω, 1. *oppress, tyrannize over*; pass., of Christians oppressed by Devil, Or.*hom.14.17 in Jer.*(p.124.4; M.13.428A); of heretics ~ουσι ψυχὰς χηρευούσας τοῦ ἀληθινοῦ νυμφίου †Bas.*Is.*232 (1.555C; M.31.525A); οὔτε ~ει ἡμῖν ὁ θάνατος ‡Chrys.*pasch.*2(8.255B); **2.** *govern, rule,* Thphn.*chron.*p.149(M.108.405A).

κατάδυσις, ἡ, A. *dipping, immersion*; **1.** threefold (baptismal), signifying; **a.** Christ's death and burial ἐν τῇ πρώτῃ ἀναδύσει τὴν πρώτην ἐμιμεῖσθε τοῦ Χριστοῦ ἐν τῇ γῇ ἡμέραν, καὶ τῇ κ. τὴν νύκτα... οὕτως ἐν τῇ κ., ὡς ἐν νυκτί, οὐδὲν ἑωρᾶτε Cyr.H.*catech.*20.4; *Const. App.*2.17.4; τὴν κ. τὸν τύπον τῶν τριῶν ἡμερῶν Bas.*ep.*236.5(3.363E; M.32.884A); τρεῖς κ. παραλαμβάνονται...τρίτον τοῦτο ποιήσαντες, τὴν τριήμερον ἑαυτοῖς τῆς ἀναστάσεως χάριν ἐξεικονίζομεν Gr.Nyss. *bapt.Chr.*(M.46.585A); τὸν...βαπτιζόμενον ἡ συμβολικὴ διδασκαλία μυσταγωγεῖ ταῖς ἐν τῷ ὕδατι τρισὶ κ. τὸν...τῆς τριημερονύκτου ταφῆς Ἰησοῦ...μιμεῖσθαι θάνατον Dion.Ar.*e.h.*2.3.7(M.3.404B); **b.** Trinity τρεῖς δὲ κ. γίνονται...ἵνα γνῶμεν, ὅτι δυνάμει πατρὸς καὶ υἱοῦ καὶ... πνεύματος τὰ πάντα πληροῦται Ammon.*Jo.*3:5(M.85.1409A); τρὶς μὲν αὐτὸν ὁ ἱεράρχης βαπτίζει, ταῖς τρισὶ τοῦ τελουμένου κ. καὶ ἀναδύσεσι τὴν τρισσὴν τῆς θείας μακαριότητος ἐβόησας ὑπόστασιν Dion.Ar.*e.h.*2.2.7(M.3.396D); **2.** single, as practised by Eunomians Εὐνομιανοὺς μέντοι...εἰς μίαν κ. βαπτιζομένους CCP(381)‡*can.*7; οἱ...Εὐνομιανοὶ μὲν διὰ τὸ μίαν κ. ποιεῖσθαι, λέγοντες μόνον εἰς τὸν θάνατον τοῦ κυρίου βαπτίζεσθαι Didym.*Trin.*2.15(M.39.720A); Philost.*h.e.*10.4(M.65.585B); Soz.*h.e.*6.26.2(M.67.1361Cf.); Tim.CP *haer.*(M.86.24B); Thphn. *chron.*p.53(M.108.188C); **3.** *ritual ablution* of Ebionites, Epiph.*haer.*30.2(p.334.19; M.41.408B) cit. s. βαπτισμός.

B. *descent* τὴν κ. τοῦ κυρίου...εἰς ᾅδην ‡Meth.*Sym.et Ann.*9(M.18.372B).

C. *lair*; met., of Devil, Chrys.*hom.8.6 in Rom.*(9.506D).

καταδυσωπέω, *entreat, implore,* Eus.*v.C.*3.13(p.83.23; M.20.1069C); id.*Marcell.*2.1(p.34.5; M.24.781A); Thdt.*h.e.*1.13.2(3.783).

καταδύω, *descend* into water; in baptism, Cyr.H.*catech.*20.4 cit. s. ἀναδύω; τὴν σωτήριον ταφὴν καὶ ἀνάστασιν...ὑποκρινόμεθα...ὡς ἡμεῖς ἐν τῷ ὕδατι, οὕτως ἐκεῖνος ἐν τῷ θανάτῳ κ. Gr.Nyss.*or.catech.*35 (p.135.16; M.45.89C); καθάπερ ἔν τινι τάφῳ, τῷ ὕδατι κ. ἡμῶν τὰς κεφαλάς, ὁ παλαιὸς ἄνθρωπος θάπτεται καὶ κ. Chrys.*hom.25.2 in Jo.*(8.146C); Cosm.Ind.*top.*7(M.88.352A); met. εἰς τὴν ἄβυσσον τῆς ταπεινώσεως τῶν μετανοούντων καταδύσαντας Jo.Clim.*scal.*5(M.88.777B).

καταζάω, *come back to life,* ‡Ath.*pass.*26(M.28.229B).

καταζεύγνυμι, *yoke*; fig., Clem.*prot.*12(p.85.20; M.8.244A); Cyr.*Ps.*32:12(M.69.877B).

***καταζωγραφέω,** *paint,* *Const.App.*1.8.24.

καταθαρρύνομαι, v. καταθρασύνομαι.

***καταθαυμάζω,** *wonder at,* Cyr.*Mich.*63(3.458E); id.*Ps.*4:2(M.69.733B); id.*hom.pasch.*17(5^{2}.231A).

καταθέλγω, *enchant,* Jo.D.*hom.*12.22(M.96.812C); esp. *beguile, delude*; of demons, Thdt.*Jer.*50:39(2.617); of music, Isid.Pel.*epp.*1.456(M.78.433B); of a woman, Thdt.*qu.28 in 2Reg.*(1.431); τῇ ὁμιλίᾳ κ. Chrysipp.*enc.in Thdr.*(p.70.6).

κατάθεμα, τό, = ἀνάθεμα, *curse* σωθήσονται ὑπ' αὐτοῦ τοῦ κ. *Did.* 16.5; *Clem.contest.*4(M.2.32B); ‡Just.*qu.et resp.*121(M.6.1372A); on heresy, CCP(536)*act.*5(p.88.19; H.2.1357E); Anast.Ap.*a.Max.*2.31(M. 90.168D).

καταθεματίζω, = ἀναθεματίζω, *put a curse upon, condemn*, Or. *hom.10.8 in Jer.*(p.78.1; M.13.365D); κ. τὸν σωτῆρα Eus.*d.e.*10.3 (p.460.18; ἀναθεματίζειν M.22.741A); esp. heresy, Iren.*haer.*1.13.3(M. 7.585A); *ib.*1.16.3(636A); ἐπὶ θεοῦ καὶ ἐκκλησίας, καὶ ⟨ὑπο⟩γράφω καὶ κ. Or.*dial.*6(p.134.11); ἀναθεματίζω καὶ κ. πάντας τοὺς Μανιχαίους *Clem.recogn.suppl.*3(M.1.1465D).

***καταθεματικός**, *accursed*, of astrol. prediction with play on μαθηματικός: τὴν μαθηματικὴν ταύτην, μᾶλλον δὲ κ., πρόγνωσιν Meth. *symp.*8.15(p.103.7; M.18.165C).

***καταθεματισμός**, ὁ, *cursing*, ‡Just.*qu.et resp.*121(M.6.1372A).

***καταθερίζω**, *harvest*; met., Sophr.H.*trop.*(M.87.4008C); Jo.D. *hom.*12.6(M.96.789D).

***καταθέρω**, *warm*, Cyr.*hom.pasch.*13(5^2.179A).

***καταθέσιον**, τό, *repository*, hence *sepulchre* κατὰ μίμησιν τοῦ ἐνταφιασμοῦ τοῦ Χριστοῦ...ὅπερ ἐστὶν ἀντίτυπον τοῦ ἁγίου μνήματος ἐκείνου τὸ θυσιαστήριον καὶ τὸ κ. ἐν ᾧ ἐτέθη τὸ ἅγιον καὶ πανάχραντον σῶμα, ἡ ἁγία τράπεζα ‡Bas.*h.myst.*50(p.391.13); containing relics τὰ κ. τῶν ἁγίων Pall.*h.Laus.*12(p.35n.; M.34.1034C); Sergia *Olymp.*2 (p.47.17).

κατάθεσις, ἡ, *deposition* of relics, Eus.*h.e.*3.31.1(M.20.280A); ἡ κ. τῶν τιμίων λειψάνων Ἀνδρέου, Λουκᾶ καὶ Τιμοθέου ἐν Κωνσταντινουπόλει Jo.Mal.*chron.*p.484(M.97.701B); *place of deposition* μίαν...τῆς καταπαύσεως...κ. *M.Seb.test.*1(p.116.21).

καταθήγ-ω, *incite, provoke* τὰ...ἀποπτώματα τοῦ τοιούτου [i.e. τῆς θυμιώδους διαθέσεως] ἐστὶν...αἱ...ἀμυντικαὶ διαθέσεις,...πολλοὺς εἰς φόνους καὶ αἵματα ~ουσαι Gr.Nyss.*ep.can.*(M.45.225B); τοῦ σατανᾶ τοὺς ἰδίους ὑπασπιστὰς ἐπ' αὐτοὺς ~οντος Cyr.*Ps.*36:28(M.69.944A); κ. [sc. Israel] ἐφ' ἑαυτοὺς τὸν...θεόν id.*Nah.*3(3.476E).

καταθήκη, ἡ, *putting down*; of money, *payment*, Cyr.*Jo.*2.5(4. 189A).

***καταθηρεύω**, *hunt down*, Cyr.*Nah.*25(3.504A).

καταθλάω, *crush*, *A.Pil.*B 11.2(p.311); Epiph.*haer.*29.9(p.333.1; M.41.405A); *ib.*48.15(p.241.17; 880A).

καταθοινάομαι, *feast upon*, met. κ. τὸν παρ' αὐτοῦ λόγον Cyr.*ador.* 14(1.500D); id.*Ps.*73:14(M.69.1188A); λύκος αἱρετικὸς κ. πρόβατον Bas.Sel.*or.*26.1(M.85.300A).

***καταθολ-όω**, *make turbid, darken*, met. κύλιξι...κ. τὸν νοῦν Cyr. *hom.pasch.*15(5^2.198E); id.*Ps.*37:11(M.69.964A); ἐστιν ἀμυδρὸς...ὁ νόμος...καὶ ~οῖ τὸν τῆς διανοίας ὀφθαλμόν id.*ador.*7(1.223D).

καταθρασύν-ομαι (**καταθαρρύνομαι**), **1.** *act boldly in the face of, face with confidence*, c. genit., temptation, Cyr.*Pulch.*(p.48.29; 5^2. 161D); ref. Mt.26:39 ἡ τοῦ κυρίου ψυχή, ὡς ἀληθῶς ἀνθρώπου γενομένου...αὖθις τῷ θείῳ νευρωθεῖσα θελήματι, τοῦ θανάτου καταθαρρύνεται Jo.D.*f.o.*3.18(M.94.1076A); **2.** *act defiantly* κ. κατὰ τοῦ ὄρους Σιὼν καὶ κατὰ τοῦ ἐν αὐτῷ τιμωμένου θεοῦ Eus.*Is.*10:2(M.24.156A); Cyr.*Ps.*9:4 (M.69.764B); of heresy defying truth, Ast.Am.*hom.*11(M.40.332C); **3.** *insult*; of blasphemy, Cyr.*ador.*1(1.35C); id.*Nah.*3(3.478A); exeg. Ac.2:36 χρὴ...τὸ 'ἐποίησε' μὴ εἰς τὴν οὐσίαν ἀναφέρειν τοῦ λόγου, μηδὲ τῆς ὑπάρξεως τοῦ υἱοῦ διὰ τὴν λέξιν ~εσθαι id.*thes.*21(5^1.214D).

***καταθράττω**, *destroy*, Sophr.H.*ep.syn.*(M.87.3197D).

καταθρέω, **1.** *perceive, observe*, Cyr.*ador.*4(1.137C); id.*Juln.*1(6^2. 7C); **2.** *see, contemplate*, id.*hom.div.*12(5^2.387E).

καταθρώσκω, **1.** *descend*, Cyr.*ador.*9(1.289B); **2.** *swoop down, strike*; of a hawk, Or.*sel.in Dt.*14:19(M.17.28A); **3.** met., *sink* Ἰουδαῖοι...κ. εἰς πολυθεΐαν Cyr.*Nah.*3(3.476D).

***καταθυμητικός**, *desired*, Gr.Nyss.*anim.et res.*(M.46.56A).

***καταθυμιάω**, *offer in sacrifice* κ. τῷ θεῷ τὴν οἰκείαν ζωήν Cyr. *ador.*15(1.520D); *ib.*12(440D).

καταθύμιος, *in the mind*; neut. as subst., *will, desire*, Eus.*d.e.*3.7 (p.146.20; M.22.245C); *that which is agreeable, pleasing* τὸ ζῆν διὰ τὴν τῶν κ. ἀπόλαυσιν αἱρετόν ἐστι τοῖς τοῦ βίου μετέχουσιν Gr.Nyss.*or. catech.*8(p.41.10; M.45.33A); esp. ref. free will ὁ θεὸς...προσέθηκε δύναμιν εὑρετικὴν τῶν κ. id.*hom.2 in Cant.*(M.44.796C); id.*or.catech.*5 (p.28.8; M.45.25A) cit. s. **αὐτεξουσιότης**.

***καταθυμίως**, *to one's liking, satisfaction*, Marc.Diac.*v.Porph.*62; Anast.S.*hod.*proem.(M.89.36A); Thphn.*chron.*p.10(M.108.80B); κ. ἔχω *hold in affection*, Jo.Mosch.*prat.*128(M.87.2993A); Max.*ep.*13(M. 91.512C).

καταθύω, *sacrifice*, met. τῆς φιλαργυρίας ἡ ἐπιθυμία...λέγει... κατάθυσόν μοι σαυτόν Chrys.*hom.65.3 in Jo.*(8.393A); id.*hom.17.4 in Rom.*(9.626B); in prayer to God ὅλον ἐμαυτόν σοι καταθῦσαι †Jo.D. *B.J.*25(M.96.1088C).

καταιβάσιος, *descending* τὸ κ. πῦρ Cyr.*Os.*130(3.163B, v.l. καταβαῖνον Aubert).

***καταιονέομαι**, *be bathed, drenched*, Clem.*paed.*3.9(p.263.29; M.8. 620A).

καταισχυμμός, ὁ, *ignominy, dishonour*, Clem.*str.*4.7(p.272.4; M.8. 1264B); *ib.*4.12(p.285.25; 1293B); Thdt.*Ezech.*32:23(2.950).

καταιωρέομαι, *hang down*, Nil.*serm.*8 (κατεώρηται M.79.1276D).

***κατακακχάζω**, *laugh at, mock*, ‡Jo.D.*Artem.*59(M.96.1305C).

κατακαλλύν-ω, *adorn*, med. διὰ πάσης ἀρετῆς τὴν τοῦ ἀνθρώπου ~εσθαι φύσιν Cyr.*Juln.*4(6^2.119D); ἔδει τοὺς τῆς ἐκκλησίας μυσταγωγοὺς ...τῇ τοῦ ἁγίου πνεύματος δόσει ~εσθαι id.*Joel.*35(3.226E); in language, id.*Juln.*4(6^2.114A).

***κατακαλλωπίζομαι**, *deck oneself*, Mac.Mgn.*apocr.*4.11(p.171.5).

κατακάλυμμα, τό, *veil*, met. κ. γὰρ ἔχει τὸ γράμμα καὶ κατακεκάλυπται...ἐν σκιαῖς Cyr.*ador.*10(1.338A).

***κατακάραν**, for κατωκάρα, *head downwards* Πέτρος...ὁ γενναίως τὸν σταυρὸν κ. παρακαλῶν ὑπομεῖναι Cosm.Ind.*top.*5(M.88.293B; κατωκάρα p.211.10).

κατακάρδιος, *in the heart*, Gr.Naz.*carm.*2.1.1.234(M.37.987A).

κατάκαρπος, *fruitful*; fig., Herm.*sim.*9.1.10; ref. Os.14:7, Chrys.*hom.24.3 in Jo.*(8.142C); Hesych.H.*fr.Ps.*51:7(M.93.1208A); Leont.N.*v.Jo.Eleem.*proem.(p.2.21); of BMV, Jo.D.*f.o.*4.14(M.94. 1160A).

***κατακαρυκεύω**, *season well*, Synes.*regn.*2(p.6.20; M.66.1056A).

κατακεν-όω, *expend (upon), exhaust (upon)* ἱκετεύει Δαβίδ...πᾶσαν τῶν οἰκτιρμῶν τὴν πηγὴν ~ῶσαι τῆς ἁμαρτίας τὸ ἕλκος Thdt. *Ps.*50:3(1.933); θυμὸν εἰς ἄλλον ~ῶσαι id.*qu.9 in 2Reg.*(1.408); ταμιεῖα...~ῶσαι εἰς τὸ ἀνοικοδομῆσαι...ναούς †Jo.D.*B.J.*25(M.96. 1089B).

***κατακεντάω**, **1.** *prick*, Epiph.*haer.*48.14(p.240.3; M.41.877C); *ib.* 48.15(p.241.11; 880A); *M.Artem.*49(p.170.20; M.96.1297A); **2.** *goad*, *Barn.*7.8.

κατακερματίζω, *chop up, divide* Valent. κ. αὐτὸν [sc. λόγον τοῦ θεοῦ] εἰς συλλαβὰς μὲν τέσσαρας, στοιχεῖα δὲ τριάκοντα Iren.*haer.*1. 15.6; Trin. διὰ τί οὖν τὰς τρεῖς ὑποστάσεις κ. εἰς διαφόρους φύσεις; Gr.Nyss.*bapt.Chr.*(M.46.585D); pass., ref. Christ's hypothetically single nature at death, Leont.H.*monoph.*33(M.86.1789B).

κατακερματισμός, ὁ, *dividing into parts*, Or.*comm.in Eph.*1:10 (p.241).

κατακέφαλα, *head downwards*, Chrys.*ep.*14.5(3.600E); Cosm.Ind. *top.*1(M.88.65C); Cosm.Mel.*schol.*102–114(M.38.551).

***κατακεχαρισμένως**, *acceptably* κ. μᾶλλον ἢ ἀληθῶς Or.*comm.in Eph.*1:9(p.240).

***κατακηδεύω**, *bury*, pass., Pall.*h.Laus.*20(M.34.1052D).

***κατακήλησις**, ἡ, *enchantment, charm*, Or.*Cels.*1.6(p.59.9; M.11. 665A).

***κατακιβδηλεύ-ω**, **1.** *adulterate* τῷ ἑαυτῶν κακῷ ~οντες τὰ περὶ τοῦ ἁγίου πνεύματος Didym.*Trin.*3.39(M.39.977D); **2.** *pronounce unsound*, Cyr.*apol.orient.*(p.35.6; 6^1.160B); id.*Nest.*1.1(p.16.19; 6^1. 6D).

κατακινέω, *exile*, ‡Max.*cap.al.*237(M.90.1460A).

κατακιρν-άω, *mix, fuse*; pass., of natural elements, Eus.*d.e.*4.15 (p.174.9; M.22.289D); Gr.Nyss.*diff.ess.*5(M.32.333C); of desire εἴτε γὰρ πρὸς τὸ καλόν, εἴτε πρὸς τὸ κακὸν ἡ τῆς ψυχῆς γένηται σχέσις, ~ᾶταί πως τῇ ψυχῇ τὸ ἀγαπώμενον id.*hom.8 in Eccl.*(M.44.733B); of Christ at Inc. ~ᾶται θεότης πρὸς τὸ ἀνθρώπινον id.*or.catech.*11(p.57. 6; M.45.44A); εἰ γὰρ...ὁ θεὸς...αἵματι καὶ σαρκὶ ~ᾶται id.*hom.15 in Cant.*(M.44.1097B); θεὸς τῇ ἀνθρωπίνῃ ~ᾶται φύσει, ἵνα συνεπαρθῇ τῷ ὕψει τοῦ θεοῦ τὸ ἀνθρώπινον id.*nativ.*(M.46.1137C).

κατακίρν-ημι, = κατακιρνάω, *mix, fuse*; pass., of eucharistic Christ τοῖς σώμασι τῶν πεπιστευκότων ~άμενος Gr.Nyss.*or.catech.* 37(p.152.4; M.45.97B).

κατάκλεισις, ἡ, *imprisonment*, Leont.H.*Nest.*1.19(M.86.1476A); ἐν τῷ ᾅδῃ...τῶν ψυχῶν κ. Max.*ep.*5(M.91.424A); ἐν τοῖς μοναστηρίοις ...κ. Thdr.Stud.*epp.*1.48(M.99.1076B).

κατάκλειστος, *imprisoned, prisoner*, *A.Andr.et Mt.*20(p.91.9); *A.Thom.*A 162(p.273.17); Socr.*h.e.*4.15.4(M.67.500B).

κατακλεί-ω, *enclose, confine* δεικνύειν...ὅτι μὴ μόνοι εἰς μονάδα τὸν θεὸν ~ομεν Athenag.*leg.*6.2(M.6.901B); Clem.*str.*7.7(p.27.25; M.9. 452A); of the name of Jesus μηκέτι [sc. κατὰ τὴν αὐτοῦ παρουσίαν] ...κατακεκλεισμένον ἐν ἀπορρήτοις Or.*schol.in Cant.*1(p.101.31; M. 17.253C); of soul in body (Origenist) τὴν ψυχὴν γὰρ τὴν ἀνθρωπείαν λέγει προϋπάρχειν, ἀγγέλους δὲ ταύτας εἶναι...εἰς τιμωρίαν εἰς τοῦτο τὸ σῶμα κατακεκλεισμένας Epiph.*haer.*64.4(p.411.4; M.41.1076D).

κατακληροδοτέω, *distribute, assign by lot*, Just.*dial.*132.3(M.6. 784A); Nil.*epp.*1.51(M.79.105A); Cyr.*Os.*24(3.47B).

κατακληρονομ-έω, **1.** *inherit, take possession of as inheritance* τὴν ἄνω ~οῦμεν πόλιν, τὴν ἐπουράνιον Ἱερουσαλήμ Cyr.*Mich.*70(3.469C); κατακυρίευσον τῆς καρδίας μου, δέσποτα, καὶ κ. αὐτήν Jo.D.*hom.*2.7 (M.96.588C); **2.** *leave an inheritance*, Hesych.H.*fr.Ps.*81:8(M.93.1260B).

κατάκλησις, ἡ, 1. *invocation*; of God, Or.*Cels.*4.34(p.304.10; M.11.1080B); **2.** *incantation*; in magic, *ib.*2.51(p.174.12; 877B); **3.** *enchantment* σωματικῆς κ. Jo.Clim.*scal.*5(M.88.764B).

κατάκλισις, ἡ, *prostration*; in prayer, Just.*dial.*90.5(M.6.692A).

κατακλυσμός, ὁ, the *flood*; **1.** in gen., as showing judgement and salvation σκόπει γοῦν ἐπὶ τοῦ κ., πόσος μὲν ἦν ὁ ἔλεος, πόσον δὲ τὸ δίκαιον Chrys.*exp.in Ps.*142:1(5.449B); **2.** as example of God's justice, being caused by sin οὐκ ἐν τῷ κ. γέγονε κατεφθαρμένη ἡ γῆ (τότε γὰρ ἀπελούσατο τὴν φθοράν), ἀλλ' ἐν τῇ ἀδικίᾳ Or.*sel.in Gen.*6:11(M.12.105A); Meth.*symp.*5.5(p.59.15; M.18.105C); ἥμαρτον οἱ γίγαντες, καὶ παρανομία πολλὴ τότε τῆς γῆς κατεχύθη, καὶ διὰ ταύτην κ. ἔμελλεν ἐπέρχεσθαι Cyr.H.*catech.*2.7; τότε φθορὰ τῆς γῆς...κ. πρὸς κάθαρσιν μόνον δεόμενος Bas.Sel.*or.*5.1(M.85.76C); Thdt.*qu.50 in Gen.*(1.63); Proc.G.*Gen.*6:8(M.87.272D); Cosm.Ind.*top.*2(M.88.93D); **3.** denial of other theories, e.g. that it was a recurrence of the cosmic cycle ἡμεῖς δὲ οὔτε τὸν κ. οὔτε τὴν ἐκπύρωσιν κύκλοις καὶ ἀστέρων περιόδοις ἀνατίθεμεν, ἀλλὰ τὴν τούτων αἰτίαν φαμὲν εἶναι κακίαν ἐπὶ πλεῖον χεομένην καὶ καθαιρομένην κ. ἢ ἐκπυρώσει Or.*Cels.* 4.12(p.282.15; M.11.1041B); or that it represents a change in the divine plan, *ib.*4.69(p.338.28; 1137B); **4.** comparison with pagan teaching ἡ δ' ἐν τῷ κ. διαφθορὰ τῶν ἀνθρώπων καθάρσιόν ἐστι τῆς γῆς, ὡς καὶ Ἑλλήνων οἱ...φιλοσοφήσαντες εἰρήκασιν *ib.*6.58(p.129.8; 1388C); **5.** as showing God's mercy; souls of those who perished not being destroyed, Clem.*str.*6.6(p.458.3; M.9.273C); Or.*Cels.*6.59(p.129.20; M.11.1388D); and being evangelized by Christ, ref. 1Pet.3:20, Clem.*str.*6.6(p.454.15; 268A); those destroyed having first been given time to repent, Cyr.H.*catech.*2.7; Bas.Sel.*or.*5.2(M.85.77B); mercy of God being symbolized by olive ἡ...ἐλαία διὰ τὸν καρπὸν τοῦ ἐλαίου τὴν εὐσπλαγχνίαν τοῦ θεοῦ μηνύει...μετὰ τὸν κ. Meth.*symp.* 10.2(p.124.13; M.18.196C); **6.** as type of baptism ὁ κ. ὁ τὴν ἀρχαίαν ἀδικίαν ἐκκαθάρας τοῦ κόσμου, προεφήτευεν οἱονεὶ πως ἐπικεκρυμμένως τὸν ἀπὸ τῆς θείας κολυμβήθρας τῶν ἁμαρτιῶν καθαρισμόν Didym.*Trin.* 2.14(M.39.696A); v. βάπτισμα; **7.** marking an epoch of history, exeg. Cant.6:7,8 βασιλίσσας...τὰς βασιλικὰς ἐκείνας τὰς πρὸ τοῦ κ. ψυχάς, εὐαρέστους τῷ θεῷ γεγενημένας, τουτέστι τὰς ἀμφὶ τὸν Ἄβελ καὶ τὸν Σὴθ καὶ τὸν Ἐνώχ, παλλακὰς δὲ τὰς μετὰ τὸν κ. τῶν προφητῶν Meth. *symp.*7.4(p.75.13; M.18.129C); ref. antediluvian souls who had direct knowledge of God, *ib.*7.5(p.76; 132A,C); τοῖς μετὰ τὸν κ. ἀπωτέρω λοιπὸν ἡ γνῶσις ἦν τοῦ θεοῦ *ib.*7.6(p.77.6; 132C); **8.** eschatological significance τὰ οὖν χ' ἔτη τοῦ Νῶε ἐφ' οὗ ὁ κ. ἐγένετο τὸν ἀριθμὸν...σημαίνουσι τοῦ ὀνόματος, εἰς ὃν συγκεφαλαιοῦται τῶν ς' ἐτῶν πᾶσα ἀποστασία καὶ ἀδικία καὶ πονηρία Iren.*haer.*5.29.2(M.7.1202C); μή ποτε πρὸς ἀντιδιαστολὴν μέλλοντος κ. γενέσθαι πυρὶ πρόσκειται ἐνταῦθα 'τοῦ ὕδατος' Or.*sel.in Gen.*7:6(M.12.105C); **9.** in rel. to Creation μεθ' ἑπτὰ δὲ τοῦ εἰσελθεῖν ἡμέρας ὁ κ. γίνεται...ἔστι δὲ ὁ ἑπτὰ ἀριθμὸς ὑπόμνημα τῆς τοῦ κόσμου γενέσεως Proc.G.*Gen.*9:3(M. 87.296B).

κατακοιμίζ-ω, 1. *lull to sleep*, met. κ. τὸν ἐρεθισμὸν τῆς...ἐπιθυμίας Clem.*paed.*2.2(p.168.30; M.8.413A); *ib.*2.5(p.187.3; 452A); ἔδειξε [sc. Christ] τοῦ πάθους τὰ γνωρίσματα...ἵνα πᾶσαν αὐτῶν ταραχὴν κατακοιμίσῃ Ammon.*Jo.*20:20(M.85.1517B); of putting out a light, fig. Ἰουδαῖοι...κατεκοίμισαν τῷ θανάτῳ μονονουχὶ τὸν ἀειφανῆ λύχνον κατασβεννύοντες [i.e. Jo. Bapt.] Cyr.*ador.*10(1.345C); **2.** *weaken, enfeeble* ⟨ὁ⟩ ἀναιρῶν τὸ ἰοβόλον ἢ ~ων Or.*Jo.*6.54(36; p.163.24; M. 14.296A).

κατακομίζ-ω, *bring down*, in view attributed to Cyril by opponents ἐξ οὐρανοῦ κατακομισθὲν καὶ οὐκ ἐκ τῆς...παρθένου λέγοντος τὸ...σῶμα Χριστοῦ Cyr.*ep.*39(p.17.26; 5².106D); met., *drag down*, ref. idolaters τὸ ὑπὲρ πᾶν ὄνομα ~οντες ἀμαθῶς εἰς ἀνθρωπίνης χειρὸς φιλοτέχνημα id.*ador.*6(1.174D); ~ουσι...τὸν...τοῦ θεοῦ λόγον τῆς ὑπερτάτης ὑπεροχῆς id.*Chr.un.*(5¹.715C).

κατάκομος, *luxuriant*; of woods, Isid.Pel.*epp.*2.66(M.78.509B); fig. ἔθος τῇ θείᾳ γραφῇ, τοῖς τῶν ὀρέων περιφανεστέροις ἔσθ' ὅτε τὴν τῶν Ἰουδαίων παρεικάζειν συναγωγὴν...πλείστοις...καὶ εὐκλεεστάτοις ἀνδράσιν...κ. Cyr.*Abac.*38(3.554A); met., of the mind τοῖς θείοις κ. ἀγαθοῖς Max.*ep.*20(M.91.600B); ἀνὴρ...συνέσει πολλῇ τὸν λογισμὸν κ. ἔχων †Jo.D.*B.J.*14(M.96.981C).

***κατακομπάζω,** *boast*; perf. ptcpl. pass., *vaunted*, Eust.*engast.*8 (p.25.29; M.18.625D).

***κατακομπέω,** *boast*, Eus.*p.e.*3.7(98A; M.21.180B).

κατακομψεύομαι, *speak plausibly, showily*, Bas.*hex.*1.10(1.10A; M.29.24B); Isid.Pel.*epp.*5.541(M.78.1632A); Zach.Mit.*opif.*(M.85. 1104C).

κατακονδυλίζ-ω, *strike with the fist*, met. ἔδωκε γὰρ ἡμῖν...ἄγγελον σατάν, ἱκανῶς ἡμᾶς ~οντα Bas.*ep.*248(3.384B; M.32.929A); κ. πένητας Nil.*epp.*3.5(M.79.368B); id.*praest.*5(M.79.1068A).

κατακόπτω, 1. *smite*; met., pass. κ. τὸ συνειδός Nil.*epp.*3.294(M. 79.529C); in mourning, Chrys.*hom.52.4 in Jo.*(8.373C); id.*hom.6.2 in 1Thess.*(11.468A); **2.** med., *waste* time, id.*hom.21.3 in Ac.*(9.174E).

***κατακορέννυμι,** *satiate, fill full with food*, met. κατεκόρεσας... τῶν ἄνωθεν ἀγαθῶν τὴν...γῆν Cyr.*Ps.*64:10(M.69.1129C).

κατάκορος, *satiated*, Max.*ambig.*(M.91.1373D).

***κατακοσμίζω,** *decorate*, *A.(Pass.)Andr.*10(p.24.18, v.l. for κοσμηθείς M.2.1236B); *M.Ner.et Ach.*5(p.4.12).

***κατακοῦμβαι, αἱ,** *the catacombs* κατέλαβεν αὐτοὺς ἐν τόπῳ λεγομένῳ κ. *A.Petr.et Paul.*87(p.221.2).

***κατακουστέον,** *one must understand*, Or.*sel.in Ps.*2:13(M.12. 1117B).

κατακράζ-ω, A. trans., *shout...(against)* φωνὰς ὑβριστικὰς ~οντες Jo.Mal.*chron.*p.468(M.97.681C); πολλὰ κατακράξας τῶν διαβαλλόντων αὐτόν Jo.Mosch.*prat.*108(M.87.2972C).

B. intrans.; **1.** *clamour* or *inveigh against*, c. genit., Cyr. *Ps.*62:10(M.69.1124A); *Chron.Pasch.*p.391(M.92.1004B); **2.** *cry down*, c. genit., *A.Barn.*8(p.295.2); **3.** *cry to*, c. genit., Ath.*v.Anton.*45 (M.26.913A); c. πρός and acc., Cyr.*ador.*15(1.528A).

***κατακραίνω,** pass., *be accomplished*, †Jo.D.*B.J.*28(M.96.1128B).

***κατακράτως,** s.v.l., adv. formed from prepositional phrase κατὰ κράτος written as one word, *mightily* κ. περιελάμφθησαν Andr. Cr.*or.*5(M.97.896C) prob. error for κατὰ κράτος.

κατακρημνάω, *cast headlong*, Isid.Pel.*epp.*1.280(M.78.348A).

κατάκριμα, τό, *judgement, condemnation*, Meth.*res.*2.2(p.332.4; M.41.1164D); Epiph.*haer.*61.7(p.387.21; M.41.1049A); Cyr.*Ps.*6:2(M. 69.744B).

κατάκρισις, ἡ, *condemnation*; in gen., *Hom.Clem.*11.33; of uncharitable judgements καταλαλιαὶ...κατακρίσεις Jo.D.*hom.*2.6(M.96. 585C); divine; *2Clem.*15.5; σατανᾶς...μηδέπω εἰδὼς αὐτοῦ τὴν κ. Iren.*haer.*5.26.2(M.7.1194C); Meth.*symp.*3.6(p.33.11; M.18.69B); τὴν προαπειληθεῖσαν τοῦ θανάτου κ. Ath.*inc.*4.4(M.25.104B); λυτρούμεθα τῆς...τῶν ἁμαρτιῶν κ. †Bas.*bapt.*1.1.3(2.626D; M.31.1520B); esp. ref. final judgement, Meth.*res.*1.44(p.293.8; M.41.1113D); Bas.*jud.*3(2. 215E; M.31.657C); Chrys.*hom.1.2 in Ac.princ.*(3.53A).

***κατακριτέον,** *one must judge*, Or.*Jo.*13.31(30; p.254.32; M.14. 452B).

κατάκριτος, *condemned*, in gen. ἐγὼ κ., ὑμεῖς ἠλεημένοι Ign.*Eph.* 12; id.*Trall.*3.3; ἐκεῖνοι ἀπόστολοι, ἐγὼ κ. id.*Rom.*4.3; *A.Jo.*10 (p.157.12); esp. ref. final judgement ἵνα μὴ ἀθανάτως ἁμαρτωλὸς ὢν ...αἰωνίως κ. γενηθῇ Meth.*symp.*9.2(p.116.14; M.18.181A); id.*res.*1.32 (p.269.13; M.18.268C); Gr.Nyss.*v.Mos.*(M.44.345D).

***κατακροαίνω,** *stamp*; of horses, Gr.Nyss.*infant.*(M.46.161A); Olymp.*Job* 39:21(M.93.416C).

κάτακρος, neut. as adv., *to the uttermost*, Amph.*Seleuc.*66(M.37. 1581A).

κατακροτέω, *strike* the ground in dancing, Bas.*hom.*14.1(2.123C; M.31.448A); *beat against, break on*, ‡Caes.Naz.*dial.*7(M.38.865); met., *come down on, attack with severity* ἐπὶ τοῦ παρόντος Thdt.*Ps.*57:4 (1.983).

κατακρούω, *strike* ὀρχήστραν τῷ ποδὶ κ. Chrys.*hom.1.1 in Jo.*(8. 2C); with comb in weaving, id.*hom.12.3 in Eph.*(11.94C).

***κατακρυαίνω,** *cool*, Eus.Al.*serm.*21.17(M.86.444B).

κατακρύπτω, *hide, conceal* τὴν ἀξίαν κατακρύψας τὴν ἄκραν ταπεινοφροσύνην εἵλετο [sc. Christ] Thdt.*Phil.*2:7(3.454); of burial, Gr.Nyss.*or.catech.*35(p.132.15; M.45.88C).

***κατάκρυψις, ἡ,** *lying hid*, of Christ τὴν κ. ἣν ἐν τῷ ᾅδῃ ἐκρύβη Anast.S.*hex.*12(M.88.1064A).

κατακτυπέω, 1. *resound throughout* ὁ εὐαγγελικὸς λόγος ὁ κατακτυπήσας τὴν ὑπ' οὐρανόν Cyr.*Ps.*76:19(M.69.1193B); πᾶσαν κ. τὴν κτίσιν ‡Caes.Naz.*dial.*20(M.38.876); **2.** *deafen, stun with noise*, Bas.*Spir.*75 (3.64D; M.32.209C); Soz.*h.e.*2.9.5(M.67.957A); **3.** *make resound* κ. τὸ τύμπανον Cyr.*Mich.*54(3.446C).

***κατακτύπημα, τό,** *thundering against*, Cyr.*Mich.*71(3.471A).

κατακυβιστάω, *turn somersault*; met., Cyr.*Jo.*3.6(4.326C).

***κατακυλιστικός,** *circular, wheel-shaped*, in interprn. of Γαλιλαία, Or.*comm.ser.141 in Mt.*(p.293.10; cf.M.13.1795B).

***κατακυλιστός,** = foreg. ἡ Γαλιλαία, ἡ κ. τῇ Ἑλλάδι γλώττῃ ἑρμηνεύεται, διὸ καὶ Γελγὲλ ὁ τροχὸς ὀνομάζεται Sev.Ant.*res.*2(p.856. 4; M.46.649D).

***κατακυμαίνω,** *rise against*; of the sea, Eus.*Is.*17:13(M.24.212B).

***κατακυμβαλίζω**, *deafen with cymbals*, ‡Just.*or.Gr.*3(M.6.236A).

κατακύπτω, *stoop*, met. πρὸς ταπεινοφροσύνην κ. Chrys.*hom.3.4 in 1Thess.*(11.446E).

***κατακυρίευσις**, ἡ, *domination*, Areth.*Apoc.*2:29(M.106.545B).

κατακυριεύω, *be lord over, dominate* κ. τῆς γῆς *Barn.*6.17; εἰ οὖν πάντων ὁ ἄνθρωπος κύριός ἐστι τῶν κτισμάτων...καὶ πάντων κ., οὐ δύναται καὶ τούτων τῶν ἐντολῶν κατακυριεῦσαι; Herm.*mand.*12.4.3; θηρίων κ. ... καὶ...παθῶν Clem.*str.*6.15(p.490.2; M.9.340B); Cyr.*Ps.* 9:9(M.69.765C); Jo.D.*hom.*2.7(M.96.588C); of evil, Mac.Aeg.*ep.*(M. 34.416C); Dor.*doct.*1.1(M.88.1620A); κ. μου τὸ πάθος τῆς ὀλιγωρίας Jo.Mosch.*prat.*164(M.87.3032A).

κατακωχή, ἡ, *indwelling, sojourn*; of divine presence in soul, Gr.Thaum.*pan.Or.*16(p.38.1; M.10.1100B); of Inc., Epiph.*haer.*69. 37(p.185.22; M.42.260C); διὰ τῆς κ. ἐν τῷ ᾅδῃ *ib.*69.66(p.214.11; 308C).

κατακώχιμος, (for κατοκώχιμος), met., *held, possessed* by an emotion, Synes.*Dion* 18(p.278.10; M.66.1161C).

καταλαλάζω, *exult over* Μαριὰμ...τὴν ἐκκλησίαν, ἣ τῆς τῶν ἐχθρῶν ἐπιβουλῆς καταλαλάξει Cyr.*Mich.*54(3.446E; ὑπερήρθη Aubert); id.*Os.*132(3.165E).

καταλαλ-έω, *speak against, slander*, *T.Isach.*4.3; μηδενὸς ~ει, μηδὲ ἡδέως ἄκουε ~οῦντος Herm.*mand.*2.2; *2Clem.*4.3; Or.*enarr.in Job* 19:3(M.17.69D); φύγωμεν τὸ ~εῖν Meth.*lepr.*6(p.457.14); Jo.Mosch. *prat.*191(M.87.3069D).

***καταλαλήτριος**, *slanderous*, *Ep.Chr.dom.*(p.26).

καταλαλιά, ἡ, *detraction, back-biting*, defined πονηρὰ ἡ κ., ἀκατάστατον δαιμόνιόν ἐστιν, μηδέποτε εἰρηνεῦον, ἀλλὰ πάντοτε ἐν διχοστασίαις κατοικοῦν Herm.*mand.*2.3; demonic, Or.*Jo.*20.36(29; p.376.5; M.14.657B) cit. s. δαιμόνιον; esp. among monastic vices κ. ἐστι, τὸ κατὰ ἀπόντος ἀδελφοῦ λαλεῖν, σκοπῷ τοῦ διαβάλλειν αὐτόν, εἰ καὶ ἀληθὲς ᾖ τὸ λεγόμενον Bas.ap.Jo.D.*parall.*(M.96.72D); συμφέρει σοι...τρώγειν κρέα, καὶ μὴ κατεσθίειν ἐν κ. σάρκας ἀδελφῶν Anon.*ib.* (73B); ἠρωτήθη πάλιν, τί ἐστι κ. καὶ ἀπεκρίθη, τὸ μὴ γνῶναι τὴν δόξαν τοῦ θεοῦ *Apophth.Patr.*(M.65.184A); τὸ οὖς...ἀποστρέψαι τοῦ μὴ ἀκούειν κ. Mac.Aeg.*hom.*4.3(M.34.473D).

κατάλαλος, ὁ, *scandal-monger*, Herm.*sim.*8.7.2; Bas.*renunt.*8(2. 209B; M.31.641C); Thal.*cent.*3.48(M.91.1452D).

καταλαμβάν-ω, **1.** *seize*; *gain possession of*; hence *receive to possess* or *hold* ὑποστάσεως ἀρχὴν οὐ κατέλαβον ἐν αὐτῷ Mac.Mgn. *apocr.*4.26(p.211.24); **2.** *occupy*; **a.** *repair* or *betake oneself to, go to live in* τὴν Ἰουδαίαν ἐδεδοίκει...κ. διὰ τὸν Ἀρχέλαον Chrys.*hom.9.4 in Mt.*(7.134D); id.*hom.40.1 in Ac.*(9.301D,302B); *Chron.Pasch.*p.8 (M.92.83D); freq. ref. eremitic life ὅπως...ποιεῖται τὴν ἡσυχίαν...τὴν ἐρημίαν ~ει Chrys.*hom.32.3 in Gen.*(4.320E); id.*hom.55.5 in Mt.*(7. 560E); τὰ ὄρη κ. καὶ μοναχοὺς γίνεσθαι *ib.*7.7(116B); id.*hom.25.6 in Rom.*(9.709D); Jo.Eub.*concept.BMV* 6(M.96.1469A); of Christ in womb of BMV οὗτος...ὁ τῶν ἐμῶν κόλπων μὴ χωρισθείς, καὶ τῆς Μαρίας τοὺς κόλπους καταλαβών Gr.Ant.*bapt.*2.5(M.88.1876B); **b.** of military occupation, Chrys.*hom.59.7 in Mt.*(7.604D); *ib.*37.6(423C); *Chron.Pasch.*p.392(M.92.1005B); met., Chrys.*hom.3.1 in Phil.*(11. 211D); **c.** *occupy, take* time ἡ...πάθησις μου...μιᾶς ἡμέρας διάστημα ~ει *A.(Pass.)Andr.*9(p.23.23; M.2.1236A); **3.** *arrive at, reach* a place κ. τὴν Ἔφεσον *A.Jo.*5(p.153.25); Epiph.*haer.*30.25(p.367.7; M.41.448C); Nil.*spir.mal.*2(M.79.1148A); of gospel reaching ends of earth, Chrys.*hom.75.2 in Mt.*(7.725B); id.*hom.2.1 in Rom.*(9.436E); abs., *arrive*, Eus.*v.C.*4.43(p.135.13; M.20.1193A); Philost.*h.e.*6.6(M. 65.537A); **4.** *come to, reach* a person κ. αὐτόν *A.Andr.fr.*14(p.44.3); κατείληφέ με ἡ εὐχή *A.Xanthipp.*30(p.79.21); *ib.*32(p.80.30); ὥρμησα ...κ. σου τὴν τιμιότητα...ἀλλ'...ἡ ἀρρωστία τοῦ σώματος διεκώλυσε Bas.*ep.*94(3.187B; M.32.485B); *rejoin* διασώζεσθαι τὴν ἀδελφὴν ἡμῶν ~ουσαν τὸν ἄνδρα Gr.Thaum.*pan.Or.*5(p.13.27; M.10.1068B); Gr. Nyss.*ep.*1(M.46.1008B); **5.** *follow closely* σπεύσατε κ. τὴν ἐμὴν ψυχὴν ἐπειγομένην πρὸς τὰ οὐράνια *A.(Pass.)Andr.*11(p.27.19; M.2.1240A); Chrys.*hom.31.1 in Mt.*(7.356E); **6.** *summon, call together* ἐγγύς ἐστιν τὸ πάσχα, κατάλαβε τοὺς ἀδελφοὺς κατὰ τὸν τύπον ὃν ἔχετε *V.Pach.Φ* 144(p.91.7).

καταλαμπρύν-ω, **1.** *make light*, Gr.Nyss.*hex.*(M.44.65C); **2.** *enlighten* ~οντος τὸ χρῆμα αὐτοῖς τοῦ ἁγίου πνεύματος Cyr.*Is.*1.1(2.1E); **3.** *make bright, glorify* ~έσθω θεός id.*Jo.*2.1(4.159B); τὸν...τῆς ἀσεβείας ἐραστὴν...~ουσιν οἱ πειρασμοί id.*Ps.*65:7(M.69.1137B); id.*Arcad.* (p.62.26; 5[2].43A); ὁ...τῆς...ἐκκλησίας θίασος νοητοῖς...~εται μυστηρίοις Amph.*hom.*1.1(M.39.36A); ‡Meth.*Sym.et Ann.*9(M.18.369A).

καταλάμπ-ω, *illuminate, enlighten* Χριστοῦ...τὴν θείαν αὐγὴν ~οντος ἐξ οὐρανοῦ Clem.*fr.*44(p.222.22); τὸ...~ειν τὰ ἡγεμονικὰ τῶν ἀνθρώπων Or.*Jo.*1.25(27; p.33.26; M.14.72D); Meth.*symp.*8.3(p.84. 24; M.18.144A); Eus.*l.C.*6(p.211.28; M.20.1349C); τὸ κήρυγμα... καταλάμψει τὴν οἰκουμένην Chrys.*hom.15.6 in Mt.*(7.195D); τῆς ἀποκαλύψεως ~ούσης αὐτοῦ τὴν ψυχὴν id.*comm.in Gal.*1:16(10.674C).

***καταλαξεύω**, *incise on stone*, Cosm.Ind.*top.*5(M.88.217A).

καταλγύνω, *give pain, hurt*, Cyr.*Nah.*3(3.477B); id.*Ps.*37:6(M.69. 957C).

καταλεαίνω ([*]**καταλειαίνω**), **1.** *smooth* ἡ...δεξιὰ...τὰ ἀνάντη καταλειαίνουσα Cyr.*Ps.*43:5(M.69.1048A); τὸν...τῆς πρὸς θεὸν ἐπιστροφῆς καταλειαίνει τρόπον id.*Os.*158(3.191B); **2.** medic., *rub*, Clem.*prot.*1(p.8.26; M.8.64B); **3.** *calm, placate*, Gr.Nyss.*Eun.*4(2 p.98.10; M.45.676B); Chrys.*hom.5.5 in Rom.*(9.468E).

***καταλεγμάτιον**, τό, *hymn* (Messalian), Epiph.*haer.*80.2(p.486.6; M.42.757B).

καταλέγω, **1.** *list in, count among* κατειλεγμένου τοῦ Πέτρου εἰς τὸν ἀριθμὸν τῶν δώδεκα Or.*Jo.*32.6(5; p.435.18; M.14.756C); τῶν κατειλεγμένων τῷ κλήρῳ Philost.*h.e.*2.5(p.17.11; M.65.468C); **2.** *indict, make a charge against*, Just.*dial.*17.1(M.6.513A); Or.*dial.*9(p.142); c. genit., Cyr.*Ps.*41:1(M.69.993A).

[*]**καταλειαίνω**, v. καταλεαίνω.

κατάλειμμα, τό, *remnant*, Cyr.*Os.*5(3.26C); id.*Nah.*9(3.486C).

***καταλειπτέος**, *to be given up, renounced*, Clem.*paed.*2.10(p.222. 11; M.8.525C).

καταλείπ-ω, **1.** *leave*, in gen. τοῦτο ἀπαρασήμαντον κ. Ath.*inc.* 35.6(M.25.156C); ὑπευθύνους...τοῦ θανάτου τοὺς ἀνθρώπους κ. id.*Ar.* 3.31(M.26.389B); c. infin. ἡμῖν δὲ κ. νοεῖν Or.*hom.16.6 in Jer.*(p.138. 19; M.13.448A); οὔτε διὰ παντὸς κατέλιπεν αὐτὴν [sc. τὴν ὕλην] οὕτω φέρεσθαι, ἀλλὰ δημιουργεῖν ἤρχετο Meth.*arbitr.*3.9(p.154.8; M.18. 248B); Nonn.*par.Jo.*11:48(M.43.848B); **2.** *leave* to ὄνομα τοῦ σωτῆρος ἡμῖν...κ. Ἀρειανοί Ath.*Ar.*1.3(M.26.17A); ὁ Συμεὼν τῷ κυρίῳ καταλέλειπται Proc.G.*Dt.*33:7(M.87.981A); ὁ τῶν μαθητῶν κορυφαῖος ...ἐπὶ τῇ θεαρχίᾳ τὴν ἐκλογὴν [sc. of Matthias]...καταλέλοιπεν Dion. Ar.*e.h.*5.3.5(M.3.512D); **3.** *relinquish, leave behind*; of soul leaving body at death, Just.*dial.*6.2(M.6.489B); ref. divine πνεῦμα and soul οὐκ ἔστιν ἀθάνατος...ἡ ψυχὴ καθ' ἑαυτήν·...γέγονε μὲν οὖν συνδίαιτον ἀρχῆθεν τὸ πνεῦμα τῇ ψυχῇ· τὸ δὲ πνεῦμα ταύτην ἕπεσθαι μὴ βουλομένην αὐτῷ καταλέλοιπεν Tat.*orat.*13(p.14.27; M.6.833C); ref. relation of Father to other Persons of Trin. τὸ οἰκεῖον ἅπαν φῶς οὐδέν τι τῶν ἑτέρων φώτων ἐν ἑαυτῷ συνεπισπώμενον ἢ τοῦ ἑαυτοῦ τοῖς ἑτέροις ~ον Dion.Ar.*d.n.*2.4(M.3.641B); ref. appearance of Logos at burning bush κ. τὰ ὑπὲρ οὐρανόν..., ἐν ὀλίγῳ γῆς μορίῳ πεφάνθαι Just.*dial.*60.2(612C); ref. Inc. κ. τὸν πατέρα καὶ τὴν μητέρα, τὴν ἄνω Ἱερουσαλήμ, καὶ ἔρχεται εἰς τὸν περίγειον τόπον Or.*hom.10.7 in Jer.*(p.77.12; M.13.365C); ὅταν εἴπω, ὅτι τὸν πατέρα κατέλιπε, μὴ τοιοῦτον νομίσῃς, οἷον ἐπ' ἀνθρώπων, τόπων μετάβασιν Chrys.*hom. 20.5 in Eph.*(11.172A); **4.** *abandon, forsake*; of God forsaking Israel, Just.*dial.*136.1(M.6.790C); Or.*princ.*3.1.12(p.215.4; M.11. 269C); not abandoning creation after Fall, Meth.*res.*1.44(p.292.2; M.41.1113C); *ib.*2.18(p.368.18; M.18.284A); of Christ forsaken, Ath. *h.Ar.*47(p.210.27; M.25.752B); of men forsaking God, Just.*dial.*8.3 (M.6.493B); Thdt.*Trin.*18(M.75.1189A); refusing to forsake Christ by apostasy in persecution, *M.Polyc.*17.2; abandoning truth and goodness, Herm.*sim.*8.9.1; Or.*princ.*3.1.17(p.226.12; M.11.284A); the scriptures, Ath.*Ar.*1.4(M.26.20A); of a bishop leaving his diocese, id.*apol.sec.*6(p.93.3; M.25.260B); id.*apol.Const.*25(M.25.628A); Gr.Naz.*ep.*87(M.37.161A); **5.** *give up, renounce*; evil, *2Clem.*10.1; Or.*princ.*3.6.2(p.282.22; M.11.335A); paganism, Just.*dial.*83.4(M.6. 673A); false teachers, Tat.*orat.*26(p.28.13; M.6.864A); lusts, Ath. *gent.*3(M.25.9A); κ. ἐκεῖνο τὸ σατανικόν, ἐλθὲ ἐπὶ τοῦτο τὸ πνευματικόν Chrys.*hom.in Is.*45:7(6.145E); the world in obedience to God δι' ὑπακοῆς ἐξῆλθεν [sc. Abraham] ἐκ τῆς γῆς αὐτοῦ...ὅπως γῆν ὀλίγην καὶ συγγένειαν ἀσθενῆ καὶ οἶκον μικρὸν καταλιπὼν κληρονομήσῃ τὰς ἐπαγγελίας τοῦ θεοῦ *1Clem.*10.2; *2Clem.*5.1; of Abraham compared with apostles in following the Word, Iren.*haer.*4.5.3(M.7.985B); οἱ ...ἀπόστολοι πάντα καταλιπόντες ἠκολούθησαν τῷ σωτῆρι Ath.*v.Anton.* 2(M.26.841B); ἡ παρθένος ἐγκρατευομένη ὀφείλει κ. τὰ γήϊνα πάντα, καὶ τῷ κυρίῳ μόνῳ κολληθῆναι id.*virg.*2(p.36.25; M.28.253C); Esaias *or.*13.1; Jo.Clim.*scal.*3(M.88.669C); esp. ref. prayer and contemplation ὁ νοῦς ὁ ἀνθρώπινος καταλιπὼν...τὸν θολερὸν...βίον, ἐπειδὰν καθαρὸς γενόμενος ἐν τῇ δυνάμει τοῦ πνεύματος, φωτοειδὴς γένηται Gr.Nyss.*virg.*11(p.295.7; M.46.365D); κ. ... πᾶν τὸ φαινόμενον, οὐ μόνον ὅσα καταλαμβάνει ἡ αἴσθησις, ἀλλὰ καὶ ὅσα ἡ διάνοια δοκεῖ βλέπειν id. *v.Mos.*(M.44.376D); ὁ προφήτης...εἰπὼν τὰ κτίσματα, καὶ τῇ ὄψει τῶν θεωμένων κ. τὸ κάλλος αὐτῶν καταμανθάνειν καὶ τὸ μέγεθος καὶ τὴν χρείαν Chrys.*exp.in Ps.*148:3–6(5.491A); Dion.Ar.*e.h.*3.3.2(M.3. 428C).

κατάλειψις, ἡ, *leaving behind*, Cyr.*Mal.*11(3.828B, v.l. κατάληξιν Aubert).

***καταλέκτια, τά,** *bed-clothes*, Ephr.3.48B; *Chron.Pasch.*p.395(M.92.1012C,1013A).

***καταλεπρόομαι,** *be leprous*, Cyr.*ador*.2(1.71B).

καταλεπτύν-ω, 1. *break up small* ἡ τοῦ σωτῆρος χάρις καταλέπτυνε τὸ ἐκείνου κέρας Cyr.*Zach.*11(3.666E); food in chewing, Bas.*hex*.9.5 (1.85C; M.29.200B); met. τοὺς ἀπὸ φυλῆς Λευί, οἳ βουσὶν ἐν ἴσῳ τὴν νοητὴν ἅλω ~οντες Cyr.*Abac.*60(3.576B); **2.** *refine, make subtle* ἐκ τύπου...τῶν σωματικῶν, εἰς ἀστειοτέρας ἡμᾶς ~ει βουλάς id.*ador*.12(1.413A).

***καταλευκαίνω,** *elucidate, make clear*; sense of scripture, Cyr. *Soph.*4(3.582A); id.*ador*.2(1.54E); id.*Ps*.7:15(M.69.756B).

***κατάλευσις, ἡ,** *stoning*, Chrys.*hom.88.2 in Jo.*(8.528C); Thdt. *eran*.2(4.98); id.*provid*.10(4.659).

καταλήγ-ω, *stop, desist* ἐν ἡμέρᾳ γὰρ ὀγδόῃ ~ει...τοῦ ἱεράσθαι Μωσῆς...χρόνος γὰρ δὴ τῆς ἱερωσύνης Χριστοῦ νοοῖτ' ἂν εἰκότως ὁ μετὰ τὸν νόμον, τοῦτ' ἔστιν ἡ ὀγδόη, καθ' ἣν ἡ ἀνάστασις Cyr.*ador*.11 (1.401A); of Sabbath rest τῆς ἐν κόσμῳ καταλήξαντες ζωῆς id.*Jo*.4.6 (4.424A); πνευματικῶς σαββατίζομεν, τῶν ἐν τῷδε κόσμῳ περισπασμῶν ~οντες id.*ador*.7(227C).

καταληΐζομαι, 1. *seize as plunder, prey upon*, met. κ. ... τὸν νοῦν Cyr.*Ps*.37:11(M.69.961D); τὴν ψυχὴν...ἡδονῶν κατεληΐζετο στῖφος id. *hom.pasch.*8(5^2.105D); **2.** *succeed in aim*, *ib*.14(194D).

κατάληξις, ἡ, *cessation* τὸν ἐν Χριστῷ νοούμενον σαββατισμὸν τουτέστιν...κ. τὴν ἐξ ἁμαρτίας Or.*exc.in Ps*.77:31(M.17.144D); cf. Cyr.*ador*.7(1.227C).

καταληπτικός, *apprehending* ἡ θεία φύσις πάσης ὑπέρκειται κ. διανοίας Gr.Nyss.*hom.3 in Cant.*(M.44.820D); πῶς ἂν εὑρεθείη, ὁ... πάσης κ. ἐφόδου ἐξώτερον ἀεὶ εὑρισκόμενον; *ib.12*(1028B); ὁ τῶν γινωσκομένων τι τὸν θεὸν εἶναι οἰόμενος, ὡς παρατραπεὶς ἀπὸ τοῦ ὄντος, πρὸς τὸ τῇ κ. φαντασίᾳ νομισθὲν εἶναι, καὶ ζωὴν οὐκ ἔχει id.*v.Mos.* (M.44.404B); πάσης αὐτοὺς τῆς περὶ θεοῦ κ. κατὰ τὸ τί ποτε εἶναι τὴν οὐσίαν ἐννοίας ἀπορραπίζων Max.*ambig*.(M.91.1224D).

καταληπτικῶς, *by direct apprehension*, Clem.*str*.1.19(p.61.1; M.8.812A); *ib*.6.16(p.502.11; M.9.364B); Pall.*v.Chrys*.5(p.31.7; M.47.19).

καταληπτός, *to be apprehended* by the mind, of God οὐκ ἔστιν ὀφθαλμοῖς...ὁρατὸν τὸ θεῖον...ἀλλὰ μόνῳ νῷ κ. Just.*dial*.3.7(M.6.481D); πῶς δὲ εἰ μὴ κ. ἐστιν ὁ πατὴρ τῷ υἱῷ...ἐπιδεικνύει; Cyr.*thes*.13 (5^1.137C); but denied οὐδὲ κ. τὸ θεῖον Clem.*str*.5.14(p.405.8; M.9.176A); as implied by Eunomians κ. αὐτὴν εἶναι...καὶ πεπερατωμένην Cyr.*resp*.(6^2.385E); or allowed paradoxically κ. ἐστι καὶ ἀκατάληπτος *Hom.Clem.*17.10; τὸ θεῖον...ἀκατάληπτον καὶ τοῦτο μόνον αὐτοῦ κ., ἡ ...ἀκαταληψία Jo.D.*f.o*.1.4(M.94.800B); cf. Gnost. τὸ μέγεθος τοῦ πατρὸς...οὐ κ. ἰδεῖν Iren.*haer*.1.2.1(M.7.453A); *ib*.1.2.5(464A).

***καταληστεύω,** *despoil*, Cyr.*Juln*.3(6^2.88E).

κατάληψις, ἡ, *apprehension* by the mind; of the divine, Tat. *orat*.11(p.12.12; M.6.829B); Or.*Jo*.13.24(p.248.17; M.14.440B); ἡ... τοῦ υἱοῦ...κ. γνῶσίς ἐστι περὶ τοῦ πατρός Ath.*Ar*.1.16(M.26.45A); Gr.Nyss.*or.catech*.1(p.13.2; M.45.16D); τὴν ὑψηλοτάτην τοῦ θείου μυστηρίου κ. Cyr.*hom.pasch*.5(5^2.57D); τύποι γάρ εἰσι...τὰ ἐμφανέστερα καὶ χειραγωγεῖ πρὸς κ. τῶν ὑπὲρ ἡμᾶς id.*Jo*.1.10(4.107B); ἡ τῶν θείων δογμάτων κ. Max.*opusc*.(M.91.12A); denied in full sense to human mind ὑψηλότερον τῆς ἀνθρωπίνης κ. Or.*exc.in Ps*.77:31(M.17.141B); τοῦ θεοῦ...οὐσίαν...ἐπέκεινα πάσης κ. Eus.*p.e*.7.12(320C; M.21.541B); Ath.*exp.Ps*.138:6(M.27.532D); κελεύεται...μηδὲ τινι τῶν ἐκ κ. γινωσκομένων ὁμοιοῦν τὴν τοῦ παντὸς ὑπερκειμένην φύσιν Gr.Nyss. *v.Mos*.47(M.44.317B); ἡ τῶν ἐσχάτων ἐν τοῖς ποιήμασιν ἀκριβὴς κ. τῆς καθ' ἡμᾶς λογικῆς ἐνεργείας ὑπερβαίνει τὴν δύναμιν Max.*ambig*.(M.91.1224D); denied to Son (Arian) οὐδὲν τῶν λεγομένων κατά τε κ. συνίει ἐξειπεῖν ὁ υἱός...τίς γοῦν λόγος συγχωρεῖ τὸν ἐκ πατρὸς ὄντα αὐτὸν τὸν γεννήσαντα γνῶναι ἐν κ.; Ar.*Thal.fr.*2 ap.Ath.*syn*.15(M.26.708B); Gnost. Χριστὸν διδάξαι αὐτοὺς συζυγίας φύσιν, ἀγεννήτου κατάληψιν γινώσκοντας, ἱκανοὺς εἶναι, ἀναγορεῦσαί τε ἐν αὐτοῖς τὴν τοῦ πατρὸς ἐπίγνωσιν, ὅτι...ἀκατάληπτος Iren.*haer*.1.2.5(M.7.461A).

***καταλίζω,** for παταγίζω, Epiph.*exp.fid*.11(M.42.801B; παταγιζόντων p.511.13; MS παταλιζόντων).

καταλιθάζω, *stone to death*, Epiph.*haer*.26.3(p.280.7; M.41.337A); met., Gr.Nyss.*Eun*.1(1 p.98.13; M.45.332B).

καταλιθοβολέω, = foreg., Heges.ap.Eus.*h.e*.2.23.17(M.20.201A); Dion.Al.*ib*.6.41.3(605B); Epiph.*haer*.66.82(p.123.19; M.42.157B).

καταλιπαίνω, *anoint*, Cyr.*Ps*.22:6(M.69.841D).

καταλλαγή, ἡ, *reconciliation* μέγιστον [v.l. -ος] τῷ θεῷ λόγῳ ὁ περὶ τῶν πρὸς ἀλλήλους καταλλαγῶν λόγος Isid.Pel.*epp*.4.111(M.78.1177A); with God ἐγὼ γὰρ ἥσθησθαί μοι δοκῶ, ὅτι...τῆς πρὸς τὸν θεὸν κ. οὐδὲν αἴτιον οὕτως ἄλλο γέγονε...ὡς ἁγνεία Meth.*symp*.4.2 (p.46.11; M.18.88B); ἡ κ. τοῦ θεοῦ πρὸς τὸν ἄνθρωπον ‡Ath.*Apoll.* 1.14(M.26.1117D); ἐσφάγη ὁ υἱὸς ἐπὶ καταλλαγὰς ἐλθὼν Chrys.*hom. 11.2 in 2Cor.*(10.516B); Thdt.*2Cor*.5:18(3.317); ‡Meth.*Sym.et Ann.* 8(M.18.368A); ref. H. Ghost τῆς κ. τοῦ θεοῦ δῶρόν ἐστι τὸ δοθῆναι τὸ πνεῦμα τὸ ἅγιον Chrys.*pent*.1.3(2.461C); ἡ δὲ χάρις καταλλαγῆς ἦν ἀπόδειξις id.*hom.51.2 in Jo.*(8.301A); of penitents with Church ὥστε σκηνικοῖς καὶ μίμοις...χάριν ἢ καταλλαγὴν μὴ ἀρνεῖσθαι *Cod. Afr.*45.

καταλλακτήριος, *reconciliatory*, Gr.Nyss.*ep*.16(M.46.1056B).

καταλλάκτης, ὁ, *reconciliator*, Chrys.*hom.16.2 in 1Cor.*(10.137A).

καταλλάσσω, *reconcile*, God to man εἰ γὰρ βούλει καταλλάξαι σου τὸν δεσπότην, ἔργα ἐπίδειξαι Chrys.*hom.82.4 in Jo.*(8.488B); οἱ... ἱερεῖς...αὐτὸν αὐτοῖς [sc. sinners] πολλάκις ὀργισθέντα κατήλλαξαν τὸν θεόν id.*sac*.3.6(p.58.2; 1.385A); penitents to Church μήτε δὲ καταλλάξαι τινὰ εἰς δημοσίαν λειτουργίαν πρεσβυτέρῳ ἐξεῖναι *Cod.Afr.* 6; ἑαυτὸν κ. τοῖς ἱεροῖς μυστηρίοις *ib*.7; κ. μετανοοῦντα *ib*.43; med., *be reconciled* ὁ υἱός, ἐν ᾧ ἡ κτίσις πρὸς τὸν θεὸν κατηλλάσσετο Ath. *Ar*.3.6(M.26.332C).

κατάλληλος, 1. *co-related*, of Trin. οὐσία μία, τρεῖς δὲ ὑποστάσεις ...κ. Or.*fr.572 in Mt.*(p.235.9; M.17.309D); **2.** *corresponding*; of the type and the thing signified, *Schol*.2 in Max.*qu.Thal*.53(M.90.505D); in gen. ἀναγκαῖον ἦν ἐγκραθῆναί τι τῇ ἀνθρωπίνῃ φύσει συγγενὲς πρὸς τὸ θεῖον, ὡς ἂν διὰ τοῦ κ. πρὸς τὸ οἰκεῖον τὴν ἔφεσιν ἔχοι Gr.Nyss.*or.catech*.5(p.23.5; M.45.21C); τὸ μὲν κ. τῇ νοητῇ φύσει χωρίον ἡ λεπτὴ...ἐστιν οὐσία *ib*.6(p.30.9; 25C); οἷς δὲ προσεπωρώθη τὰ πάθη...ἀνάγκη καὶ τούτους ἐν τῷ κ. [i.e. refining furnace] γενέσθαι *ib*. 35(p.138.16; 92B); *appropriate, due*, in natural or supernatural order οὐχ...παρεκαινοτόμησε...ἀλλὰ διὰ τῶν...κ. ἔδωκε τῷ καθ' ἑαυτὸν σώματι τὴν διαμονήν *ib*.37(p.148.7; 96C); βρῶσίς ἐστιν αὐτῷ... κ., ἡ τοῦ σωτηρίου...ἀποπλήρωσις id.*hom.in Cant.*proem.(M.44.760C); εἰς δύο καταστάσεις τὴν κτίσιν διελομένου θεοῦ καὶ κατάλληλον εὐτρεπικότος ἑκάστῃ...τὴν καταγωγήν Gennad.*fr.Gen*.1:6(M.85.1629C); νόμοις...κ. id.*fr.Heb*.1:1(p.421.1; M.85.1733A); πανταχοῦ μὲν οὖν τῆς γραφῆς κατάλληλα σπείρας τῆς γνώμης τὰ φάρμακα Bas.Sel.*or*.4.1(M.85.64A); of divine retribution, Clem.*paed*.3.12(p.291.16; M.8.681A); id.*prot*.10(p.66.31; M.8.204A); Ath.*exp.Ps*.17:26(M.27.1116B); Dion. Ar.*e.h*.3.3.11(M.3.442A); περιβαλόντες ἐσθῆτα...κ. *ib*.2.2.7(396D).

καταλλήλως, *appropriately*, of divine dispensation ἐν τῇ τῶν ἀλόγων φύσει...κ. ἕκαστον τῷ τῆς ζωῆς εἴδει κατασκεύασται Gr. Nyss.*or.catech*.5(p.23.7; M.45.21C); κ. ἑκάστῳ καιρῷ...ὁμιλήσας θεός Gennad.*fr.Heb*.1:1(p.420.23; M.85.1732D); of divine retribution κ. ἐκ τῆς ἑκάστου προαιρέσεως Gr.Nyss.*or.catech*.40(p.163.20; 105A); of priestly ministrations, Chrys.*sac*.2.4(p.35.9; 1.375B); *in conformity*; of a symbol, Iren.*haer*.5.29.2(M.7.1202A).

καταλογίζομαι, 1. *count among*, Cyr.*ador*.5(1.166B); **2.** *count, take as*, ref. sense of allegory εἰς τὸν διὰ τοῦ νόμου φωτισμὸν καταλογιεῖται τὸ πῦρ *ib*.7(1.223D); **3.** *enrol* προσῆλθον τῷ ἁγίῳ βαπτίσματι, καὶ λαβόντες τὴν ἐν Χριστῷ σφραγῖδα, κατελογίσθησαν μετὰ τῶν Χριστιανῶν †Gregent.*disp*.(M.86.780B).

κατάλογος, ὁ, *list* κ. τῶν προφητῶν Meth.*symp*.7.6(p.77.15; M.18.133A); of high priests, Eus.*d.e*.8.2(p.378.3; M.22.612C); τῶν θείων γραφῶν Chrys.*sac*.4.4(p.114.1; 1.409C); esp. of clergy πάντας τοὺς τοῦ ἱεροῦ κ. Const.ap.Ath.*apol.sec*.54(p.135.11; M.25.348B); *Can. App*.8; *Const.App*.3.15.5; εἰς τὸν κ. τῶν ἱερέων ἐτέτακτο Socr.*h.e*.1.36.5(M.67.173A); Ἄρειος τῷ κ. τῶν πρεσβυτέρων ἐντεταγμένος Thdt. *h.e*.1.2.9(3.726); κ. τῶν διδασκάλων καὶ ἱερέων Bas.Sel.*v.Thecl.* 2.27(M.85.613A); ἐν τῷ ἱερατικῷ καταλόγῳ Gr.Mag.*dial*.(tr.Zach.) 2.16(M.*PL*.66.163B); ἱερῶν παρθένων κ. ‡Jo.D.*ep.Thphl*.13(M.95.361B); in diptychs κέλευσον τοῦ κ. τῶν ἐπισκόπων ἐξαιρεθῆναι τὴν Ἰωάννου προσηγορίαν Cyr.*ep*.76(p.26.27; 5^2.206A).

κάταλσος, *wooded*, Gel.Cyz.*h.e*.3.10.10; Anast.S.*qu.et resp*.114(M.89.765D).

κατάλυμα, τό, 1. *dwelling*, met. ἐν τῷ ἀνωτέρῳ...κ. ἡ μεγάλη δόξα *T.Lev*.3.4; Bas.*ep*.5.2(3.78C; M.32.241A) cit. s. καταγώγιον; of BMV τῆς ἁγίας τριάδος τὸ κ. Procl.CP *or*.6.17(M.65.757B); ἡ ψυχὴ ...πορεύεται...αὐτῇ προητοίμασεν ἑαυτῇ κ. †Jo.D.*B.J*.8(M.96.924C); τὸ...κ. τῆς ἐννοίας [i.e. the mind] Areth.*Apoc*.49(M.106.708B); **2.** *inn*, Ephr.1.219B.

***καταλυπέω,** *grieve, distress* τὴν ἐπέκεινα καταλυποῦντες δόξαν Cyr.*ador*.6(1.181A); id.*Nest*.1.2(p.20.33; 6^1.13C); id.*Ps*.37:3(M.69.956A).

κατάλυσις, ἡ, *dissolution, abolition*; hence *breaking* fast, Jo. Clim.*scal*.14(M.88.864D); cf. κ. οἴνου καὶ ἐλαίου, κ. ἰχθύος N. Nilles *Kalendarium Manuale* (Innsbruck 1896, 1 pp.62,63,231).

καταλυτήριον, τό, 1. *lair, haunt*, Mac.Aeg.*hom*.28.2(M.34.712A); **2.** *termination, destruction*, Ephr.1.272E.

καταλύτης, ὁ, *destroyer* ὁ τοῦ γράμματος κ. Gr.Naz.*or*.45.21(M.36.652D); Epiph.*haer*.67.6(p.138.16; M.42.180D); τὸν θανάτου κ. θανάτῳ παραδίδωσιν Cyr.*Lc.*7:16(M.72.609D); *Νικηφόρου, τοῦ κ. τῶν Χριστιανῶν* Thphn.*chron.*p.422(M.108.1000A).

***καταλυττάω,** *rave, rage against*, Isid.Pel.*epp.*1.296(M.78.356A).

καταλύω, *break* a fast, Eus.*qu.Marin.*2.2(M.23.941C); *Apophth. Patr.*(M.65.96A); Dor.*doct.*15.2(M.88.1789B); Jo.Clim.*scal.*14(M.88. 864D).

καταλωβάω, *mutilate*; met., Cyr.*Os.*37(3.69A).

καταμαγγανεύω, 1. *call up by incantation*, Socr.*h.e.*3.2.5(M.67. 381A); **2.** *bewitch*, Bas.Sel.*v.Thecl.*1(M.85.508B).

καταμαίνομαι, *go raving mad*, ‡Ign.*Smyrn.*9; †Gregent.*disp.*(M. 86.640D); Anast.S.*hod.*4(M.89.96A).

καταμαλακίζω, *soften, make effeminate*, Chrys.*hom.10.5 in Mt.*(7. 145B); med., Jo.D.*hom.*12.10(M.96.796A); pass., *be* or *become soft, degenerate*, Clem.*str.*4.4(p.255.7; M.8.1228C); †Bas.*Is.*167(1.498D; M. 30.393C); Chrys.*hom.31.4 in Mt.*(362A); id.*hom.4.4 in Rom.*(9.459C).

καταμαλάσσω, *soften* τὸ τραχὺ τῆς γνώμης...κατεμάλαξε Chrys. *hom.11.1 in Mt.*(7.150C); the character, Bas.*renunt.*5(2.206D; M. 31.636C); Chrys.*Laz.*3.1(1.737E); Gr.Nyss.*virg.*6(p.279.27; M.46. 349D).

καταμαλθάσσω, *soften* καταμαλθάξαι [sc. τὰς καρδίας] δυνάμενος ὁ τῶν ὅλων θεός Cyr.*Is.*5.5(2.885A); *ib.*3.2(400A); *appease*, id.*Jo.*3.4 (4.297C).

***καταμαρτυρία, ἡ,** *evidence against*, *Const.App.*2.49.3.

***κατάμασθος,** *big-breasted*, Jo.Mal.*chron.*2 p.50(M.97.104C).

***καταμαστεύω,** *investigate*, Synes.*ep.*101(M.66.1472C).

καταμαστίζω, *scourge*, Philost.*h.e.*10.6(M.65.588B).

***καταμεγαλοφρονέω, 1.** *be high-souled*, Clem.*paed.*3.6(p.256.25; M.8.605A); id.*str.*4.5(p.257.20; M.8.1233B); **2.** *have a mind above, despise*, *ib.*3.7(p.223.9; 1161C); *ib.*3.16(p.243.7; 1205A).

καταμεθύ-ω, 1. *rave drunkenly against* κ. τῆς ἀληθείας Ath.*Ar.*2.25 (M.26.200B); **2.** *be intoxicated* τῶν οὐρανίων ἀγαθῶν ἀφθονίαις κ. Cyr. *ador.*7(1.221A); λύπῃ...~ουσαν ἔχειν τὴν διάνοιαν id.*Ps.*37:9(M.69. 961A); id.*hom.pasch.*17(5^2.232E); Jo.Eub.*innoc.*(M.96.1504D); ref. paganism πολυθείας δόξῃ κ. Didym.*Trin.*3.24(M.39.936C).

καταμειδιάω, *deride* κ. ... τοῦ θεοῦ Cyr.*Am.*12(3.262D); id.*ador.*1 (1.47C); κ. ... τοῦ διαβόλου Bas.Sel.*v.Thecl.*1(M.85.504A).

καταμελαίνω, *blacken*; *put into black* (i.e. mourning), Gr.Nyss. *virg.*3(p.263.9; M.46.332D); of countenance, *darken*, Cyr.*Nah.*23(3. 502A); met., the soul by sin, Gr.Nyss.*virg.*12(p.299.20; 372B); τοῦ θανάτου τὸ δεῖμα...κ. καρδίαν Cyr.*Joel.*42(3.241A).

***καταμελανόω,** *blacken*, Eus.*h.e.*9.11.2(M.20.837B).

***καταμελίζω,** *cut limb from limb*, Agath.*v.Gr.Ill.*83.

καταμερίζ-ω, *divide into parts* οὐ...~ειν χρὴ εἰς τρεῖς θεότητας τὴν ...θείαν μονάδα Ath.*decr.*26(p.23.10; M.25.465A); εἰς πολλοὺς καταμεμερίσθαι τὸ ὄνομα τῆς ἐνεργείας οὐ δύναται Gr.Nyss.*tres dii*(M.45. 128C); ἀπαγορεύει μὴ δεῖν ~ειν τὸν θεόν, μηδὲ τὸ μέν τι αὐτοῦ ἀγέννητον, τὸ δὲ γεννητὸν ὑποπτεύειν Bas.*Eun.*1.11(1.223E; M.29.537B); Christol. οὐ δίχα σαρκὸς ἀνθρωπίνης ὁ λόγος Χριστὸς γέγονεν, ἑαυτὸν καταμερίσας εἰς σαρκὸς ἐπίδειξιν...ἀλλὰ μένων ὃ ἦν ‡Ath.*Apoll.*2.23 θανάτου (M.26.1136B).

***καταμέσοθεν,** *in the middle*, Cosm.Ind.*top.*3(M.88.141C); *ib.*4 (184A).

κατάμεστος, *full* τοῦ εὐαγγελικοῦ κηρύγματος, ὃ καὶ δογμάτων ἐστὶν ἀληθινῶν κ. Cyr.*Is.*5.1(2.732C).

καταμηχανάομαι, *plot against*, *T.Job* 17(p.113.18).

καταμιαίν-ω, *pollute* κ. γῆν καὶ ἀέρα ταῖς δειναῖς αὐτῶν πράξεσιν Arist.*apol.*11.7; ref. Fall κατεμιάνθη...ὁ ἄνθρωπος Meth.*res.*1.38 (p.281.7; M.41.1105B); τὴν θεόθεν ἥκουσαν συνείδησιν ἀπιστίᾳ κ. Clem. *str.*2.6(p.129.1; M.8.965A); of sins ψυχὴν καὶ σῶμα ~ουσαι Cyr.*ador.*6 (1.196A).

καταμίγνυμι *mingle, join, unite* κατάμειξον αὐτοὺς εἰς τὴν σὴν ποίμνην *A.Thom.*A 25(p.140.9); *ib.*16(p.124.2); of the soul διὰ κακίας ...τῇ παχύτητι τῆς ὑλικῆς καταμιγνύμεναι φύσεως Or.*princ.*1.8.4(p.103. 16; M. om.); θεὸς...τῷ λύθρῳ τῆς ἀνθρωπίνης φύσεως καταμίγνυται Gr. Nyss.*or.catech.*14(p.62.13; M.45.45D); ὁ δὲ φανερωθεὶς θεὸς κατέμιξεν ἑαυτὸν τῇ ἐπικήρῳ φύσει, ἵνα τῇ τῆς θεότητος κοινωνίᾳ συναποθεωθῇ τὸ ἀνθρώπινον *ib.*37(p.151.12; 97B); *ib.*27(p.102.17; 72A).

***καταμικραμελέω,** *trouble about trifles*, ‡Ath.*renunt.*5(M.28. 1413D).

***καταμισθόομαι,** *bribe*, Cyr.*Nah.*28(3.506C); *ib.*31(508E); id.*Ps.* 40:12(M.69.1000B).

***καταμοιχάομαι,** *commit adultery*, Cyr.*Is.*5.3(2.798E).

καταμολύν-ω, *pollute, contaminate* μηδενὶ τρόπῳ τὸ τοῦ θεοῦ σκεῦος ἑαυτὸν τῇ ἐμπαθεῖ χρήσει ~ειν Bas.*ascet.*1.2(2.320A; M.31.873B); ὀφθαλμοῦ ῥομφαία...μηδενὶ τῶν ῥυπαρῶν θεαμάτων ~εσθαι Gr.Nyss. *hom.7 in Cant.*(M.44.904B); ψυχὴν...πάθεσι κ. Isid.Pel.*epp.*2.16(M. 78.469A); σκοτισμὸς δὲ κοσμικὸς...τὸν καθαρὸν...τῆς διανοίας αἰθέρα κ. Cyr.*ador.*1(1.37A); id.*Ps.*35:5(M.69.917A); *corrupt* truth, Gr.Nyss. *v.Mos.*(M.44.337B); of heresy, id.*Eun.*1(1 p.29.20; M.45.257B); τὴν εὐγένειαν τῆς ὀρθῆς κατεμόλυνεν πίστεως Jo.Mosch.*prat.*188(M.87. 3068A).

καταμόνας, v. μόνος.

***καταμυκάομαι,** *bray*, Chrys.*hom.76.3 in Jo.*(8.450A).

***καταμυρίζω,** *anoint*, *Const.App.*1.3.8; Cyr.*ador.*6(1.195D).

***καταμυσάττομαι,** *execrate, loathe*, Cyr.*ador.*2(1.69A); id.*Am.*72 (3.318D); id.*hom.pasch.*15(5^2.202C).

***καταμφιάζω,** *clothe*, met. τὸ γράμμα...κατημφίασταί πως τὴν ὡς ἐν σκιαῖς ἀσάφειαν Cyr.*ador.*10(1.388A); τῶν εὐαγγελικῶν θεσπισμάτων ...οὐδὲν ἐχόντων...τῇ τοῦ γράμματος ἀσαφείᾳ κατημφιασμένον, καθὰ καὶ ὁ νόμος ὁ διὰ Μωσέως id.*Ps.*32:4(M.69.872D).

καταμφιέννυμι, *cover*, Eus.*v.C.*1.31(p.21.32; M.20.945A); Cyr.*ador.* 13(1.458A); met. τῷ δὲ τοῦ θεοῦ φόβῳ κατημφιεσμένος Eus.*v.C.*1.44 (p.28.25; M.20.960A); ὁ μεγάλην κατημφιεσμένος ἀρετήν Cyr.*Jo.*1.7 (4.64A).

καταμωλωπίζω, *cover with weals* στιγματίαι τὴν συνείδησιν καὶ καταμεμωλωπισμένοι Gr.Nyss.*virg.*7(p.284.4; M.46.356A).

***καταμωμάομαι,** *reprehend, criticize*, Cyr.*Pulch.*(p.33.10; 5^2.138D); id.*Juln.*5(6^2.151A); *ib.*7(245A).

καταμωραίνω, *make foolish*, Gr.Nyss.*res.*1(M.46.605D).

κατανάγκη, ἡ, *charm*, Synes.*ep.*121(M.66.1500B).

καταναθεματίζω, *curse*, Just.*dial.*47.4(M.6.577C).

***καταναισχυντέω,** *bear oneself impudently towards*, †Bas.*Is.*296 (1.604A; M.30.637A); of monks, Bas.*hom.*14.1(2.123C; M.31.445C); κ. τῶν προεστώτων ‡Bas.*const.*31(2.578E; M.31.1421A).

καταναλίσκ-ω, 1. *consume* τὸ...χορτῶδες σῶμα τῆς ἀοιδίμου ταύτης [sc. BMV] τὸ ~ον πῦρ ἐδέξατο, καὶ χρυσὸς ὥσπερ ἀκίβδηλος ἀνάλωτον ἐχρημάτισε Jo.D.*hom.*2.7(M.96.733B); for exegesis of Dt.4:24, Heb.12:29 v. πῦρ; **2.** *destroy* men, Const.ap.Eus.*v.C.* 4.11(p.122.14; M.20.1160B); things, Thdt.*Zach.*10:11(2.1642); ‡Jo.D. *Artem.*5(M.96.1256D); **3.** *exhaust* ὁ ἐν τῷ ἀγῶνι καταναλωθεὶς Chrys. *hom.1.1 in Heb.*(12.6B).

***κατανάλωμα, τό,** *that which is consumed* by fire, i.e. *fuel*, *Const. App.*4.10.1.

κατανάλωσις, ἡ, 1. *consumption* of food, Clem.*str.*2.18(p.164.4; M.8.1036A); **2.** *expenditure* of money, id.*paed.*3.11(p.279.9; M.8. 656B).

***καταναλωτικός,** *consuming*, Or.*Jo.*13.23(p.247.10; M.14.437B); id.*sel.in Ps.*4:7(M.12.1164A).

καταναρκάω, 1. *lie heavy upon*; of tribulation, Gr.Naz.*or.*26.17 (M.35.1249B); **2.** *be slothful, reluctant*, Cyr.*glaph.Ex.*2(1.272D); *ib.*3 (342E); id.*Jo.*11.2(4.935C).

κατανδρίζ-ομαι, *fight manfully against, subdue* κ. χωρίων ἢ πόλεων Cyr.*Zach.*32(3.701B); κ. τῶν ἐχθρῶν τοῦ σταυροῦ τοῦ Χριστοῦ id.*ep.* 67(p.38.3; 5^2.194D); esp. ref. spiritual warfare, Or.*adnot.in Dt.*23:14 (M.17.32C) = Cyr.*glaph.Dt.*(1.423E); κ. παθῶν Cyr.*hom.pasch.*14(5^2. 187A); id.*Is.*5.5(2.868B); τὰς ἑαυτῶν ὀσφύας εὖ μάλα διεζωσμένοι ~εσθε τῶν παθῶν ψυχικῶν καὶ σωματικῶν id.*ep.*1.2(p.11.4; 5^2.2D); δυνάμεθα δὲ κ. καὶ ἐπιπλήττειν τοῖς τῆς σαρκὸς κινήμασι, θεοῦ συμπράττοντος id.*resp.*12(p.597.12; 6^2.379E); abs., CCP(681)*act.*9(H.3.1196E); of overcoming temptation, Cyr.*Chr.un.*(5^1.755C); and Satan, id. *ador.*1(1.35C).

κατανεανιεύομαι, 1. *prevail vigorously over* κ. παθῶν Cyr.*ador.*4(1. 107A); θανάτου κ. id.*glaph.Gen.*4(1.136A); id.*hom.pasch.*9(5^2.106A); **2.** *oppose rashly* κ. τῶν ἱερῶν γραμμάτων id.*Juln.*3(6^2.89E); Χριστοῦ ...δόξης κ. id.*hom.pasch.*24(5^2.289D).

κατανεκρ-όω, *deaden*, Cyr.*ador.*14(1.482E); ~ωθέντες πάθεσι Dion. Ar.*e.h.*3.3.12(M.3.444B); *mortify* οἱ ~ωθέντες ἐν ταῖς πολλαῖς βασάνοις Petr.I Al.*ep.can.*14(M.18.505A); τοὺς ~οῦντας τὸ κίνημα τῆς σαρκὸς Diod.*Ps.*93:19(M.33.1237B); ~ώσωμεν τὰ μέλη τὰ ἐπὶ τῆς γῆς Cyr. *Ps.*62:2(M.69.1121A); id.*hom.pasch.*20(5^2.262C).

***κατανεμέσησις, ἡ,** *indignant reproach*, Clem.*paed.*1.9(p.137.20; M.8.348A).

***κατανεόω,** *till, bring into cultivation* θείῳ ἀρότρῳ τοῦ σταυροῦ κ. τὴν γῆν ‡Sophr.H.*triod.*(M.87.3876C).

***κατανεύσιμος,** *indicated by a nod*, Cyr.*Juln.*4(6^2.136A).

κατάνευσις, ἡ, 1. *assent* μιᾶς ἐνεργείας καὶ βουλήσεως καὶ θελήσεως ἢ τῶν τριῶν θεαρχικῶν ὑποστάσεων κ. ‡Gr.Nyss.*hom.6 in Jo.*(p.227. 34); **2.** *inclination* of the head ἡ...κ. τῆς κεφαλῆς...ἀντὶ ὅρκου κρινέσθω [i.e. among monks] Bas.*ascet.*1.5(2.323B; M.31.881A); **3.** *casting down* of the eyes, Sophr.H.*v.Mar.Aeg.*15(M.87.3708D).

κατανεύ-ω, *incline towards* τοὺς ἀπὸ τῆς ἐκκλησίας πρὸς τὴν τῶν Ἐγκρατιτῶν αἵρεσιν ~σαντας Hier.*vir.ill.*(tr.Sophr.Pal.)31(p.26.

19; M.*PL*.23.680); *ib*.41(p.31.19; 692A); εἰς γῆν...κ. λογισμούς Max. *ambig*.(M.91.1148C).

***κατανθεμόω**, *deck with flowers*, Meth.*symp*.8.13(p.98.16; M.18.161A).

κατανο-έω, *contemplate* τῷ...νοητῷ κάλλει...εἰς ἔρωτα τὸν τὸ θεῖον κάλλος ~οῦντα οὐράνιον προκαλουμένῳ Or.*Jo*.1.9(11; p.14.30; M.14.40D); μία πρᾶξις ἔσται τῶν πρὸς θεὸν διὰ τὸν πρὸς αὐτὸν λόγον φθασάντων ἢ τοῦ ~εῖν τὸν θεόν *ib*.1.16(p.20.16; 49C); τὸ ὕψος καὶ μέγεθος τοῦ λόγου κ. id.*schol.in Cant*.7:8,9(M.17.284C); ref. Fall ὅθεν τῶν μὲν νοητῶν ἀπέστησαν ἑαυτῶν τὸν νοῦν, ἑαυτοὺς δὲ κ. ἤρξαντο Ath.*gent*.3(M.25.8C).

κατανόησις, ἡ, 1. *intellectual comprehension* ἐκεῖ πιστεύειν εἶναι τὸ θεῖον, ἐν ᾧ οὐκ ἐφικνεῖται ἡ κ. Gr.Nyss.*v.Mos*.46(M.44.317B); **2.** *contemplation*, of God or divine truth τὸ μακάριον τέλος, τὴν θεοῦ κ. Bas.*Spir*.18(3.16B; M.32.100C); ὁδηγεῖν τὸν νοῦν εἰς κ. τῶν τε κριμάτων καὶ δογμάτων τῆς εὐσεβείας †Bas.*bapt*.1.2.6(2.633E; M.31.1536B); τῆς πληρωθείσης οἰκονομίας ἡ κ. ‡Ath.*Apoll*.2.4(M.26.1137D); Gr.Nyss.*tres dii*(M.45.121B); Max.*schol.c.h*.5(M.4.61C); ref. Fall ἀποστάντες...τῆς πρὸς τὸν ἕνα καὶ ὄντα, θεὸν λέγω, κ. Ath.*gent*.3(M.25.9A).

***κατανουθετέω**, *advise, warn*, Synes.*ep*.140(M.66.1532B).

***κατανόχιον, τό,** *monk's cloak*, Jo.Mosch.*prat*.134(M.87.2997C).

καταντ-άω, 1. *come down to* τὴν ~ήσασαν ἐπὶ γῆς διὰ τῆς θεοφανείας τοῦ ἑνὸς τῆς ἁγίας τριάδος...δόξαν ‡Meth.*Sym.et Ann*.2(M.18.352C); **2.** *attain to*, *1Clem*.6.2; οἱ ~ῶντες ἐπὶ τὴν ἐκλογὴν τοῦ θεοῦ Or.*hom.4.3 in Jer*.(p.26.4; M.13.289A); εἰς τὴν ἑνότητα τοῦ κυρίου κ. Meth.*symp*.8.7(p.90.3; M.18.149B); ref. baptism εἰς θεὸν κ. *Hom.Clem*.11.24; ἄξιος γένηται καταντῆσαι εἰς τὴν εὐδοκίαν τοῦ θεοῦ †Bas.*bapt*.1.2.23(2.646A; M.31.1565A).

κατάντημα, τό, *end, goal*, Jo.D.*hom*.5(M.96.653C).

***κατάντικρυς, 1.** *exactly*, Epiph.*haer*.77.35(p.447.8; M.42.693A); **2.** = καταντικρύ, *immediately opposite*, Bas.Sel.*v.Thecl*.2.21(M.85.604D).

κατάντλημα, τό, *fomentation*, Bas.*hom.in Ps*.32(1.135A; M.29.332B).

***καταντλητέος**, *requiring a fomentation*, Cael.*ep.Nest*.(p.79.27; M.*PL*.50.476A).

***κατανυγμός, ὁ,** *compunction*, Or.*sel.in Ps*.4:5(M.12.1145A).

κατανυκτικός, 1. *piercing*; of bird-song, *A.Xanthipp*.6(p.61.33); **2.** *causing compunction, heart-searching*, †Bas.*Is*.147(1.482D; M.30.357C); ‡Chrys.*hom*.10(13.240F); ἀνάγνωσις τῶν θείων γραφῶν...μετὰ κ. λογίων τῶν θεοφόρων πατέρων Dor.*doct*.20(M.88.1812A); **3.** *of the night, nocturn*, ref. divisions of psalter for recitation in offices, *Lit.Chrys*.(p.378.21); ἄχρι τῆς ἀναληψίμου ἑορτῆς προηγοῦνται τὰ ἀναστάσιμα στιχηρὰ καθισμάτων τῶν τε κ. καὶ ἀποστολικῶν *Const.Stud*.5(M.99.1708A).

***κατανυκτικῶς**, *so as to cause compunction*, Thdt.*Trin*.2(M.75.1149B).

κατάνυξις, ἡ, *compunction* ἡ μὲν τοιαύτη κ. θεοῦ ἐστι δῶρον Bas.*reg.br*.16(2.420A; M.31.1092C); τοῦ χρόνου [sc. of penance] δὲ μέτρον, τὸ μέτρον τῆς κ. Gr.Naz.*ep*.163(M.37.272B); καιρὸς δακρύων καὶ κ. Chrys.*stat*.17.1(2.171B); ἔνθα φόβος ἐστίν, ἐκεῖ καὶ...δάκρυα...καὶ κ. *ib*.15.1(152D); Diad.*perf*.92(p.132.12); Marc.Er.*opusc*.1.15(M.65.908B); Jo.Mosch.*prat*.50(M.87.2905C); κ. κυρία ἐστίν, ἀμετεώριστος ὀδύνη ψυχῆς μηδεμίαν ἑαυτῇ παρηγορίαν παρέχουσα, μόνην δὲ τὴν ἑαυτῆς ἀνάλυσιν καθ' ὥραν φανταζομένη, καὶ τὴν τοῦ παρακαλοῦντος θεοῦ τοὺς ταπεινοὺς μοναχοὺς παράκλησιν...προσδεχομένη Jo.Clim.*scal*.7(M.88.808A); Ant.Mon.*hom*.107(M.89.1761A et passim).

κατανύσσ-ω, 1. *spur on, sting, goad*; met.; **a.** in gen., ref. conversion to Christianity κατανυχθέντες...ὑπὸ τοῦ ἁγίου πνεύματος *A.Barn*.13(p.297.3); οἱ δύο λαοὶ ~όμενοι ὑπὸ τοῦ ἐν αὐτοῖς ἐνεργοῦντος σατανᾶ Hipp.*Dan*.1.15.4(M.10.692B); τῷ θεῷ τῷ καὶ εἰς τοῦτο κατανύξαντι τὸν Κωνστάντιον Ath.*h.Ar*.22(p.194.17; M.25.717D); ref. Ps.29:13 ὥσπερ γὰρ ὁ ἐν εὐλαβείᾳ κατανενυγμένος οὐκ ἂν εὐκόλως μετασταίη· οὕτω καὶ ὁ ἐν πονηρίᾳ κατανυγεὶς πάλιν οὐκ ἂν ῥᾳδίως μεταβάλοιτο· κατανυγῆναι γὰρ οὐδὲν ἕτερόν ἐστιν ἢ τὸ ἐμπραγῆναί που καὶ προσηλῶσθαι Chrys.*hom.19.1 in Rom*.(9.643A); ἀνθρώπου τῷ τῆς ἁμαρτίας κέντρῳ κατανυγέντος Mac.Mgn.*apocr*.2.20(p.38.15); **b.** esp. of moving to repentance; Just.*dial*.91.3(M.6.693A); τῷ μέντοι 'κατανύγητε' ἰδίως πολλάκις ἐχρήσαντο· τάχα οὔτε παρὰ τοῖς φιλοκάλοις τῶν Ἑλλήνων κειμένῳ, οὔτε ἐν τῇ συνηθείᾳ τῶν ἐν Ἑλλάδι φωνῇ χρωμένων· καὶ ἀναγράφουσί γε τὴν λέξιν ταύτην ἐπὶ τῶν δακνομένων τῶν ἡμαρτημένων ἕνεκεν, ἢ ὧν δήποτε ἑτέρων Or.*sel. in Ps*.4:5(M.12.1144C); κατὰ διάνοιαν κατανυγέντες Ath.*inc*.51.6(M.25.188C); Gr.Naz.*ep*.163(M.37.272A); οὐ κατενύγησαν, τουτέστιν οὐ μετέγνωσαν ἐφ' οἷς κακῶς ἐβουλεύσαντο Didym.*Ps*.34:15(M.39.1332D); ref. means of procuring compunction τοῖς μὲν μεγάλοις ὑμῖν ἀρκεῖ πρὸς τὸ κατανυγῆναι, τὸ τῶν εὐεργεσιῶν ἀναμνησθῆναι τοῦ θεοῦ, τὸ μὴ μεμνῆσθαι τῶν οἰκείων κατορθωμάτων, τὸ μετὰ πολλῆς ἀκριβείας ἐξετάζειν εἴ πού τι καὶ μικρὸν ὑμῖν τύχοι πλημμεληθέν, τὸ πρὸς τοὺς μεγάλους ἄνδρας ὁρᾶν, καὶ σφόδρα εὐηρεστηκότας θεῷ· τὸ μετὰ ταῦτα ἅπαντα, ἐννοεῖν τὸ τοῦ μέλλοντος ἄδηλον, τὸ πρὸς τὴν κατάπτωσιν καὶ τὴν ἁμαρτίαν ὀξύρροπον Chrys.*compunct*.2(1.152C); id.*hom.41.4 in Mt*.(7.450B); κατανύξωμεν ἑαυτοὺς τῶν περὶ γεέννης ἀκούοντες λόγων *ib*.43.5(465C); ref. love of God οὐδὲν οὕτως ἡμᾶς κ. id.*hom.7.3 in Eph*.(11.49E); ptcpl. pass., of one habitually possessing compunction, *meek, sober*, Nil.*epp*.3.19(M.79.380A); κατανενυγμένον τῇ καρδίᾳ...τὸν πρᾶον τῇ καρδίᾳ Hesych.H.*Ps.tit*.108(M.27.1144A,B); **2.** *move deeply*, *A.Andr*.A 5(p.48.17); οἶδε γὰρ καὶ τράπεζα ἐφ' ἧς ὁ ἅγιος ἔφαγε...κατανύξαι τὸν ὑποδεξάμενον Chrys.*hom.30.4 in Rom*.(9.743B); Epiph.*mens*.15(M.43.261C).

***κατανώτιον, τό,** *cloak*, worn by monks, Ephr.1.326B.

καταξαίν-ω, *card* wool; *lacerate*; **1.** lit.; as form of torture, *M.Polyc*.2.2; Eus.*m.P*.4.11(M.20.1476D); CCP(381)*ep*.ap.Thdt.*h.e*.5.9.4(3.1028); as an expression of mourning κατακόπτεσθαι καὶ κ. παρειάς Chrys.*hom.6.2 in 1Thess*.(11.468B); **2.** met., Clem.*paed*.2.8(p.203.11; M.8.488A); κ. μαστίζων αὐτήν [sc. τὴν ψυχήν] Chrys.*hom.42.3 in Mt*.(7.455D); of Abraham offering Isaac τὴν φύσιν ἔχων...~ουσαν Thdt.*Heb*.11:18(3.618); *goad* ὁ διάβολος...λογισμοῖς κ. Chrys.*hom.8.5 in Col*.(11.386D).

καταξέω, 1. *polish smooth*; met., *soothe*, Clem.*paed*.3.6(p.256.26; M.8.605A); **2.** (= καταξαίνω) *tear, lacerate*; as form of torture, Chrys.*Jud*.3.3(1.609D); *M.Thdot*.2 2(p.86.11); Jo.D.*hom*.12.11(M.96.796D); met., Chrys.*ep*.3.13(3.567B).

καταξήρως, *in an ascetic way* τῷ λοιπῷ βίῳ κ. προσέχοντες [sc. Encratites], μᾶλλον Κυνικοὶ ἢ Χριστιανοί Hipp.*haer*.8.20(p.238.30; M.16.3367B).

***καταξινεῖ**, vox nihili καλῶς κ. πάντα *Dial.Tim.et Aquil*.83 r°; κατανύει conj. ed.; perh. iron. καταξαίνεις or καταπίνεις.

καταξιοπιστεύομαι, med., *demand implicit belief*, Ign.*Trall*.6.2.

καταξι-όω, 1. *esteem, deem worthy* of, usu. c. genit.; c. dat. τὸν δὲ φθόνον ἐκ τοῦ κρείττονι τιμῇ κατηξιῶσθαι τὸν ἄνθρωπον πρὸς τοῦ θεοῦ Meth.*arbitr*.18(p.194.5; M.18.265C); c. prep. ~ωθῆναι πρὸς φωτισμὸν τοῦ εὐαγγελίου Epiph.*haer*.51.6(p.256.17; M.41.900B); of punishment, Clem.*paed*.3.3(p.249.27; M.8.585B); act. and pass., *deserve*, *ib*.2.6(p.189.6; 456A); Chrys.*hom.2.1 in 1Tim*.(11.557A); in sense of *make worthy* τίς ἱκανός...εἰ μὴ οὓς ἂν καταξιώσῃ ὁ θεός; *1Clem*.50.2; αὐτοὺς εἰδωλολάτρας ὄντας κατηξίωσε γνῶναι Just.*dial*.130.4(M.6.780B); *Lit.Jac*.(p.46.18); freq. in pass. καταξιωθεὶς...ὀνόματος θεοπρεπεστάτου Ign.*Magn*.1.2; Just.*1apol*.65.1(M.6.428A); τὸ οἰκητήριον τοῦτο [sc. human body]...πνεύματος ἁγίου κατὰ τὸν...ἁγιασμὸν ~οῦται Clem.*str*.4.26(p.320.27; M.8.1373A); τῆς θείας δωρεᾶς καταξιωθέντες Mac.Aeg.*hom*.4.1(M.34.472D); *ib*.4.6(477A); ‡Ath.*dial.Trin*.1.1(M.28.1117B); **2.** *admit*; *appoint* τὸν μέλλοντα ~οῦσθαι τοῦ εἰς Συρίαν πορεύεσθαι Ign.*Polyc*.8.2; οὐ σοφίσμασι τὰ τῆς θρησκείας...γράφοντας, ἀλλ' ἐν ταπεινοφροσύνῃ καταξιωθέντας CIllyr.(374)*ep*.ap.Thdt.*h.e*.4.9.1(3.960); ref. penitents οὕτω τῆς προσφορᾶς ~οῦσθαι Bas.*ep*.217 *can*.77(3.329B; M.32.805A); δεῖ πρῶτον μαθητευθῆναι...καὶ τότε ~ωθῆναι τοῦ ἁγίου βαπτίσματος †Bas.*bapt*.1.1 tit.(2.624B; M.31.1513B); διὰ Πέτρου ἐπανακάμψας εὐαγγελίζεσθαι ~οῦται [sc. ὁ Μάρκος] Epiph.*haer*.51.6(p.256.10; M.41.900A); **3.** *deign, vouchsafe* 'ἀδελφοὺς'...καταξιώσαντος ἡμᾶς εἰπεῖν Clem.*str*.2.22(p.187.10; M.8.1084A); *ib*.4.6(p.263.13; 1248A); Epiph.*exp.fid*.14(p.514.26; M.42.809A); ref. Inc. σώματος οἰκητήριον κατηξίωσεν ἐκ παρθένου λαβεῖν Const.ap.Gel.Cyz.*h.e*.2.7.13(M.85.1236A); in genit. abs. as an expression parallel to D.V. θεοῦ ~οῦντος ἄσχιστον τὸ σῶμα τῆς ἐκκλησίας τηρήσομεν CCP(381)*ep*.ap.Thdt.*h.e*.5.9.18(3.1034).

καταξίωσις, ἡ, *esteem, repute*, Epiph.*haer*.69.69(p.218.5; M.42.313D).

καταπαιδεύω, *discipline*, Cyr.*Am*.41(3.296D, v.l. καταπαίοντες Aubert).

καταπαί-ω, *strike hard*, Cyr.*Ps*.9:33(M.69.785A); id.*Chr.un*.(5^1.766B); id.*ador*.8(1.278B); met., *outrage* αὐτὴν τὴν θεοῦ δόξαν...~οντες σκληραῖς...φωναῖς id.*Nah*.3(3.477E); pass., met., *be smitten*; by the conscience, id.*Ps*.37:1(M.69.952C); id.*Juln*.5(6^2.162A).

καταπαλαίω, 1. *overthrow in wrestling*, Clem.*str*.2.20(p.173.12; M.8.1053C); *ib*.8.9(p.98.17; M.9.596C); **2.** met., *overcome*; of temptation, or the Devil δύναται ὁ διάβολος ἀντιπαλαῖσαι, καταπαλαῖσαι δὲ οὐ δύναται Herm.*mand*.12.5.2; Iren.*fr*.14(M.7.1237B); Max.*ambig*.(M.91.1148A); in argument, Gr.Naz.*or*.21.33(M.35.1124A); Chrys.*sac*.4.7(p.120.19; 1.412B); Sophr.H.*v.Anast*.(M.92.1717D); **3.** *dispose of, disperse* διαθήκην ὕλης οὐ γράφει, ζῶν καὶ φρονῶν αὐτὴν κατεπάλαισεν (vv.ll. κατέπλασεν, κατέλειπεν) Pall.*v.Chrys.*20(p.138.14; M.47.77).

[*]**καταπανουργέομαι**, *deal craftily, treacherously with*, c. genit., Cyr.*Mich.*30(3.417D); pass., Iren.*fr.*14(M.7.1237B).

καταπατ-έω, *tread down, walk upon*, Arist.*apol.*4.3; Gel.Cyz.*h.e.* 2.7.18(M.85.1236C); met., *trample on* τῷ σημείῳ τοῦ σταυροῦ καὶ τῇ πίστει τῇ εἰς Χριστὸν ~εῖται Ath.*inc.*29.1(M.25.145B); κ. τοὺς νόμους ‡Jo.D.*Artem.*65(M.96.1312B); *despise*, Ath.*gent.*47(M.25.96A); ptcpl. pass. neut. plur., *things of no value*, Gr.Thaum.*pan.Or.*2(p.5.1; M.10.1056B); Chrys.*hom.20.2 in Heb.*(12.187D).

καταπάτημα, τό, 1. *thing trodden under foot, despised*, Eus.*Is.*1:8 (M.24.93B); Isid.Pel.*epp.*1.73(M.78.233A); †Gregent.*disp.*(M.86.653A); **2.** *trampling upon, scorn* ἀπώλεσεν αὐτὰ εἰς κ. *T.Jos.*19.8 (v.l. καταπάτησιν); οὐκ εἰς κ. τὸν οὕτω σεπτὸν ἐφίησι λόγον Cyr.*Jo.*3.6 (4.321B).

καταπάτησις, ἡ, *trampling upon*, *Pss.Sal.*2.20; *T.Sym.*6.6; *T.Zab.*3.3.

***καταπαύσιμος,** *of rest* ἄχρι τῆς ἑβδόμης καὶ κ. τῶν ἔργων ἡμέρας Gr.Naz.*or.*44.4(M.36.612A); Eustrat.*v.Eutych.*96(M.86.2381B).

κατάπαυσις, ἡ, 1. *place of rest, halting-place* οἶκον καταπαύσεως *A.Phil.*38(p.18.20); Cosm.Ind.*top.*5(M.88.217A); **2.** *rest*; of sabbath, Hipp.*haer.*8.14(p.233.21; M.16.3359C); Euthal.Diac.*epp.Paul.*(M.85.776A); after Creation ἀπὸ τῆς τοῦ κόσμου γενέσεως μέχρι κ. Meth.*creat.*12(p.499.27; M.18.344B); τρεῖς κ. κεκλημένας ἐν τῇ θείᾳ γραφῇ· καὶ πρώτην μὲν τὴν ἑβδόμην ἡμέραν, ἐν ᾗ τὴν κτίσιν πεπλήρωκεν ὁ θεός· δευτέραν δὲ τῆς ἐπαγγελίας τὴν γῆν· τρίτην δέ γε τὴν βασιλείαν τῶν οὐρανῶν Thdt.*Heb.*4:3(3.566); of heaven μεταστάντας ἐνθάδε πρὸς τὰς ἐκεῖθεν μονὰς καὶ κ. ‡Bas.*h.myst.*60(p.396.2); Thdr.Stud.*or.* 5.1(M.99.721A).

καταπαυστέον, *one must stop*, Clem.*str.*2.21(p.184.4; M.8.1076B); *ib.*5.14(p.420.14; M.9.204B).

***καταπεζεύω,** *walk upon*, Bas.*hom.*8.2(2.62E; M.31.305C).

καταπείθ-ω, med., *obey* ~εσθαι...τοὺς προεστηκότας Cyr.*Is.*2.1(2.189C).

καταπείρω, 1. *pierce through, transfix*, *A.Mt.*18(p.240.16); ὀστέοις τε καὶ νεύροις καταπεπαρμένον...τὸ σῶμα Eus.*p.e.*11.6(516D; v.l. for καταπεπαραμένον M.21.857A); **2.** *stick in* βέλη ἐν αὐτῷ...πηγνύμενα κατεπείρετο id.*v.C.*2.9(p.45.1; M.20.989A); cf.Soz.*h.e.*1.4.4(M.67.868C); **3.** met., pass., *be pierced, smitten* τὴν Βαλεντίνου φαντασίαν ἀφέντες, χείρονι κακῷ κατεπάρησαν Anast.Ap.*a.Max.*2.21(M.90.184C).

καταπέμπω, *send down*; **1.** of Father sending Son into world in Inc., Clem.*paed.*1.9(p.141.31; M.8.356A); Meth.*symp.*1.4(p.12.24; M.18.44D); **2.** of Father sending H. Ghost; at Pentecost, Chrys.*hom.4 in Ac.princ.*(3.89D); in gen., *Lit.Jac.*(p.160.16); in response to liturg. epiclesis καταξίωσον κ. τὸ πνεῦμα τὸ ἅγιόν σου ἐπὶ τὰ κτίσματα *Lit.Marc.*(*PDêr-Baliz.*p.24.26); κ. τὸ πνεῦμά σου τὸ ἅγιον ἐφ' ἡμᾶς καὶ ἐπὶ τὰ...δῶρα ταῦτα *Lit.Chrys.*(p.329.16); **3.** of God sending spiritual gifts and graces, Or.*Jo.*20.17(15; p.350.11; M.14.613A); Meth.*symp.*1.2(p.9.22; M.18.40C); *ib.*4.2(p.47.11; 89A); **4.** of soul (Origenist) εἴ τις λέγει...τὰς τῶν ἀνθρώπων ψυχὰς...τιμωρίας χάριν εἰς σώματα καταπεμφθείσας, ἀ. ἔ. Justn.*Or.*(p.213.16; M.86.989B); cf. Thphl.Al.*ib.*(p.202.35; 971A); ref. transmigration of souls ἐπὶ τιμωρίᾳ τὴν ψυχὴν τῶν προημαρτημένων ἐν τῷ ἀνθρωπίνῳ βίῳ εἰς σώματα [sc. of animals] κ. Nemes.*nat.hom.*2(M.40.588B).

καταπενθέω, *mourn*, intrans., Petr.I Al.*ep.can.*1(M.18.468B); Bas.*ep.*131.2(3.224A; M.32.568A).

***καταπερκάζω,** *turn purple*, Cyr.*Joel.*12(3.211A).

καταπερονάω, *rivet*, *A.Mt.*19(p.241.18).

καταπερπερεύομαι, *scorn*, c. genit., Cyr.*Jo.*2.6(4.222D).

***καταπετάζω,** *cover over*, Isid.Pel.*epp.*1.200(M.78.312A).

καταπέτασμα, τό, *curtain*; **1.** in gen. τὸ κ. τοῦ νυμφῶνος *A.Thom.* A 11(p.115.15); τὰ πρὸ θυρῶν συστέλλουσι κ. Bas.Sel.*or.*40.3(M.85.460B); **2.** met., *veil, covering* εἰς τὸ ἐσώτερον τοῦ γράμματος κ. παρεισδύνοντες εὑρήσομεν πάντως τὸ διὰ τούτων ἐσόμενον ‡Caes.Naz.*dial.*193(M.38.1176); **3.** *veil*; **a.** of Temple ὁ ἱερεὺς εἰσιὼν ἐντὸς τοῦ κ. τοῦ δευτέρου Clem.*exc.Thdot.*27(p.115.22; M.9.672C) v. d infra; ἐν μέσῳ...τὸ κ. διατείνας ἐν τύπῳ τοῦ στερεώματος, διχῇ διεῖλεν αὐτὴν [sc. τὴν σκηνήν] Thdt.*qu.60 in Ex.*(1.162, v.l. παραπέτασμα); τὸ δὲ κ. ἐξ ὑπερεχόντων δεσμῶν κατεώρηται, τὴν ἄνωθεν κατάπτησιν τῆς ὀθόνης ἐτυμολογοῦντος τοῦ ὀνόματος Nil.*serm.*8(M.79.1276D); πρόναον, εἰργόμενον δυσὶν ὑφάσμασι, τῷ μὲν ἔνδον, ὃ καλεῖται κ. Proc.G.*Ex.*27:1 (M.87.640); **b.** of a pagan temple, Clem.*paed.*3.2(p.238.10; M.8.560B); **c.** in church, of veil or curtain dividing sanctuary from nave, Synes.*ep.*67(M.66.1420D); τὸ κ. κείμενον ἐπάνω τοῦ ἁγίου θυσιαστηρίου Jo.Mosch.*prat.*150(M.87.3015C); *Ep.Chr.dom.*1(p.23); ὁ ἱερεύς...ὑψῶν τὸ κ. καὶ λέγων 'στῶμεν καλῶς' ‡Bas.*h.myst.*58(p.392.30); εὐχὴ τοῦ κ. *Lit.Jac.*(p.194.22); **d.** *firmament* (veil which divides heaven and earth), Chrys.*hom.1.3 in 2Cor.4:13*(3.263A); id.*hom.15.2 in Heb.*(12.152A); cf. τὴν σκηνὴν...ἣν καὶ διελὼν ὁ Μωϋσῆς διὰ τοῦ κ., τὴν μίαν εἰς δύο πεποίηκεν, καθάπερ καὶ ὁ θεὸς ἐξ ἀρχῆς τὸν χῶρον τὸν ἕνα τὸν ἀπὸ τῆς γῆς ἕως τοῦ οὐρανοῦ διὰ τοῦ στερεώματος διεῖλεν εἰς δύο χώρους Cosm.Ind.*top.*1(M.88.56D); Valent. ἐντὸς τοῦ κ. τοῦ δευτέρου, ἐν τῷ νοητῷ κόσμῳ, ὅ ἐστι δεύτερον ὁλοσχερὲς κ. τοῦ παντός Clem.*exc.Thdot.*27(p.115.31; M.9.672C); ὁ Τόπος...κ. ἔχει *ib.* 38(p.118.32; 677B); **e.** met., of the flesh τὸ τῆς σαρκὸς κ. περιβαλλόμενος [sc. ὁ Χριστός] Procl.CP *annunt.*3(M.85.433B); cf.Chrys.*hom.15.2 in Heb.*(12.152A); Cyr.*Chr.un.*(5^{1}.761C).

καταπέτομαι (late pres. καθίπταμαι), *settle, alight* ὁ ἀγρευτὴς τῶν ὀρνίθων ἐπὰν ἴδῃ ἀγέλην που καταπτᾶσαν Hipp.*haer.*4.46(p.68.27; M.16.3110D); καθίπτανται [sc. locusts]...βουνοῦ παντὸς Cyr.*Joel.*17(3.215D).

καταπεφρονημένως, *contemptuously*, Ephr.3.342E.

καταπημαίνω, *harm, do violence to*, Cyr.*apol.Thds.*10(6^{1}.232B; v.l. for παρασημ- p.137.29); id.*Juln.*6(6^{2}.197C); id.*ador.*7(1.251C).

καταπιαίν-ω, 1. *fatten, gorge*, Bas.*hom.in Ps.*29(1.130B; M.29.320C); Isid.Pel.*epp.*4.4(M.78.1052C); Cyr.*hom.pasch.*15(5^{2}.198E); **2.** *fatten, enrich*, ref. Os.6:4 ὁ Χριστὸς...ἐστιν ἡ ~ουσα δρόσος Cyr.*Os.*43(3.97B); met., Cyr.*ador.*17(1.590B); ref. spiritual refreshment or growth τοῦτο τὸ πόμα, φησὶν ἡ ἐκκλησία,...ἀγαλλιάματί με ~ει Ph.Carp.*Cant.*2(M.40.36C); τὸν ἐν αὐτῷ [sc. τῷ πνεύματι] ~εσθαι νοῦν Cyr.*Jo.*5.1(4.469C); θεὸς...διὰ φωνῆς ἁγίων ~ει πολλάκις id.*Os.*13(3.35B); τῇ τῶν ἀγαθῶν ἐλπίδι καταπιανοῦνται Cyr.*Ps.*41:5(M.69.1004B).

καταπιέζω, *repress, crush*, *M.Carp.*17(p.12.3); Bas.*reg.fus.*17(2.359E; M.31.961B); Thphyl.*exc.gent.*15(p.488.10; M.113.952A).

***καταπικραίνω,** *embitter*, Cyr.H.*catech.*19.8; Cyr.*Am.*16(3.267A).

κατάπικρος, *very bitter*, Cyr.H.*catech.*13.29; Chrys.*hom.3.5 in Jo.*(8.24B); id.*hom.4.1 in Phil.*(11.220B).

[*]**καταπι(μ)πράω,** = καταπίμπρημι, *burn to ashes*, Bas.*hex.*3.5 (1.29B; M.29.69A); Cyr.*ador.*10(1.351C); id.*Joel.*17(3.215D); -πιπράω, †Cyr.*coll.VT*(6^{4}.33E; M.77.1225A).

καταπίν-ω, 1. *swallow, devour*; of Devil devouring sinners, *Ep.Lugd.*ap.Eus.*h.e.*5.1.25(M.20.417B); ἵνα ἀποπνιχθεὶς ὁ θὴρ οὓς πρότερον ᾤετο καταπεπωκέναι, ζῶντας ἐξεμέσῃ *Ep.Lugd.ib.*5.2.6 (436B); of man swallowing Devil's 'fish-hook', Bas.*hom.*21.1(2.164B; M.31.541D); of death, ‡Dion.Al.*fr.Lc.22:42*(p.239.10); ἵνα ὥσπερ διὰ τὴν ἁμαρτίαν ἐνταῦθα κατέπιεν ὁ θάνατος ἰσχύσας, οὕτω καταποθήσεται δικαίως ἀσθενήσας ἐκεῖ διὰ τὴν χάριν Max.*ambig.*(M.91.1252B); in mythology Κρόνος...~ων τῶν παίδων τοὺς ἄρσενας Athenag.*leg.*20.2 (M.6.932A); ὁ Ζεὺς τὴν Μῆτιν ~ει Tat.*orat.*25(p.27.15; M.6.861A); *Hom.Clem.*4.16; *ib.*6.20; **2.** met., *overwhelm* μηδὲ καταποθῆναι τὴν ψυχὴν Bas.*ep.*5.2(3.78A; M.32.240B); ὑπὸ τοῦ πειρασμοῦ καταποθῆναι Jo.Mosch.*prat.*209(M.87.3101A); *overcome* τοῦτον [sc. τὸν πλησίον]...διὰ τῆς ἀγάπης...~ειν Dor.*ep.*8(M.88.1841C); **3.** *swallow up, absorb completely*, ref. origin of universe (Manich.) κρᾶσις...τῆς τε καταποθείσης δυνάμεως τοῦ ἀγαθοῦ καὶ τῆς ~ούσης ὕλης Tit.Bost.*Man.*1.12 (M.18.1085A); Christol.; of human nature as absorbed by divinity, Eus.*d.e.*4.14(p.173.13; M.22.170D) cit. s. ἄνθρωπος; Eutychian τὴν θεότητα μεμενηκέναι, καταποθῆναι δὲ ὑπὸ ταύτης τὴν ἀνθρωπότητα...ὡς ἡ θάλασσα μέλιτος προσλαβοῦσα σταγόνα Thdt.*eran.*2(4.114).

καταπιπράσκω, *T.Job* 25(p.118.17); Cyr.*ador.*14(1.491C); id.*Zach.* 82(3.767A).

[*]**καταπιπράω,** v. καταπιμπράω.

καταπίπτ-ω, *fall*, met.; **1.** of degradation through error, esp. idolatry οὐκ ἐπὶ τὰ πτωχὰ καὶ ἀσθενῆ στοιχεῖα ~ομεν Athenag.*leg.* 16.2(M.6.921A); ~οντες τὰς τῶν στοιχείων τροπὰς θεοποιοῦσιν *ib.*22.7(940C); οἱ καταπεπτωκότες ἀπὸ τῆς περὶ θεοῦ ὑγιοῦς ὑπολήψεως Or.*Cels.*4.26(p.295.2; M.11.1065A); *ib.*7.66(p.215.29; 1513C); κ. ἐπὶ γραφὰς καὶ εἰκόνας Eus.*h.e.*2.13.6(M.20.169A); ἐπὶ τὴν Ἑλληνικὴν καταπέσοιεν πολυθεΐαν id.*e.th.*2.20(p.129.20; M.24.953B); ἀπὸ τῆς πρὸς τὸν ἕνα θεὸν κατανοήσεως εἰς πολλὰ καὶ διάφορα καταπεπτώκασι Ath.*gent.*23(M.25.48A); abs., of apostasy in persecution περὶ τῶν ἐν τῷ διωγμῷ κατα[πεπτωκότων] κληρικῶν *CIG* 8957(c. 320); **2.** of fall of Devil and his angels ἄγγελοί τινες ἀκρατεῖς γενόμενοι...οὐρανόθεν δεῦρο καταπεπτώκασιν Clem.*str.*3.7(p.223.11; M.8.1161C); ὁ διάβολος ...ἐξ ἰδίας πονηρίας εἰς τοῦτο κατέπεσε Or.*princ.*1.8.3(p.100.5; M.96.505C); **3.** of fall of man κ. εἰς φθορὰν διὰ τὴν παράβασιν Meth.*res.*2.21 (p.375.2; M.18.285C); τῆς καταπεσούσης ἡμῶν οὐσίας Dion.Ar.*e.h.*3.3.12(M.3.441B); **4.** of fall of souls (Origenist) κακεῖθεν μέχρι τῆς φυσικῆς ταύτης καὶ ἀναισθήτου κ. ζωῆς Or.*princ.*1.8.4(p.103.6; M.46.112D); ἐπὶ τὴν γῆν κ. Gr.Nyss.*hom.opif.*28(M.44.233C); cf. εἴ τις λέγει...τὸ γένος τῶν δαιμόνων...συγκροτούμενον...ἐκ κρειττόνων ~όντων εἰς τοῦτο πνευμάτων...ἀ. ἔ. CCP(543)*anath.*6(Hahn p.228;

H.3.285A); εἴ τις λέγει, ὅτι ἡ ἀγωγὴ τῶν νοῶν ἡ αὐτὴ ἔσται τῇ προτέρᾳ, ὅτε οὔπω...καταπεπτώκεισαν, ὡς τὴν ἀρχὴν τὴν αὐτὴν εἶναι τῷ τέλει, καὶ τὸ τέλος τῆς ἀρχῆς μέτρον εἶναι· ἀ. ἔ. *ib.*15(p.229; 288A); ref. free will and soul's destiny hereafter διὰ τὰς προαιρέσεις τινὰς μὲν ἐκ χειρόνων εἰς κρείττονα προκόπτειν, ἑτέρους δὲ ἀπὸ κρειττόνων εἰς χείρονα ~ειν Or.*princ.*3.1.23(p.242.2; M.11.300B).

καταπιττόω, *remove hair by means of a pitch-plaster*, Clem.*paed.* 3.3(p.245.15; M.8.577B).

κατάπλασμα, τό, *plaster*; used as a cosmetic, Clem.*paed.*3.2 (p.239.19; M.8.561C).

κατάπλαστος, 1. lit., *plastered over*; **2.** met., *counterfeit, false* κ. ἔχοντα τὴν τῆς υἱότητος δόξαν Cyr.*Chr.un.*(5^1.766C); id.*ador.*14 (1.486A); κ. ἔχων τῆς Ἰουδαϊκῆς πολιτείας τὸ σχῆμα id.*glaph.Gen.*3 (1.104A).

καταπλατύνω, *spread abroad*, Areth.*Apoc.*63(M.106.757A).

καταπλέκω, *entangle*; c. genit., met., Epiph.*haer.*76.53(p.409.3; M.42.629B); Leont.N.*v.Sym.*6(M.93.1717C).

[*]**καταπληξία, ἡ,** = κατάπληξις, *astonishment*, Sophr.H.*v.Anast.* (M.92.1701B).

***καταπληρόω, 1.** *fill full,* Eus.*v.C.*3.26(p.90.10; M.20.1088A); **2.** *fulfil* πᾶσαν...τὴν γραφὴν...κ. Bas.*Eun.*2.7(1.243A; M.29.584C).

καταπλήσσω, *amaze, astound*; pass., *be impressed by* μὴ καταπλαγῆναι κάλλος σωμάτων καὶ μέγεθος Gr.Nyss.*v.Gr.Thaum.*(M.46. 933D); *admire* τὸν ἄνδρα καταπεπλήγμεθα Eus.*p.e.*14.1(717A; M.21. 1181C); Cyr.*hom.pasch.*17(5^2.233D); καταπλαγήσεται τὴν...τοῦ ἀνδρὸς φιλοσοφίαν Olymp.*Job* proem.(M.93.17B).

καταπλοκή, ἡ, *implication*, Leont.N.*v.Sym.*50(M.93.1732C).

***καταπλουτ-έω, 1.** *be rich,* Cyr.*ador.*15(1.533D); **2.** *possess in abundance,* id.*glaph.Gen.*3(1.75D); τὸ σῶμα Χριστοῦ φύσιν ἐν ἑαυτῷ τὴν θείαν ~οῦν id.*ador.*9(1.305D); κατεπλούτησε πᾶσαν σοφίαν Jo.D. *f.o.*3.22(M.94.1088B); c. genit. καταπλουτήσαντες ἀγαθῶν Cyr.*Ps.*31:7 (M.69.868B); pass., *abound,* id.*Juln.*6(6^2.201D).

***καταπνιγμός, ὁ,** *drowning, choking,* ‡Caes.Naz.*dial.*113(M.38. 996).

καταπνίγω, *suffocate*; met., pass., *be choked with* indignation, Chrys.*hom.67.1 in Mt.*(7.661D).

***καταποθούμενον,** αἷμα, οὐκ ἐπὶ γῆς ἐκχεόμενον καὶ κ. Thdt.*Ezech.* 24:8(2.877) prob. error for καταποθὲν μόνον.

***καταποιμαίνω,** met., *shepherd downwards* αὐτὸς...ἦν ὁ θάνατος, τουτέστιν ὁ θανάτου πρόξενος σατανᾶς καταποιμένων αὐτούς Cyr.*Ps.* 15:5(M.69.809C) prob. error for καταποιμαίνων.

***καταπολαύω,** *enjoy to the full, V.Chrys.*45(p.320.21); Germ.CP *or.*1(M.98.229B).

καταπολιτεύομαι, *gain power over,* Synes.*calv.*6(p.200.1; M.66. 1176D).

καταπομπεύω, *make a show of, Supplicatio* ap.Evagr.*h.e.*2.8(p.59. 2; M.86.2525C).

***καταπομπέω,** *guide*, v. καταβομβέω.

καταπομπή, ἡ, 1. *sending back*; of Jews to Jerusalem, Afric.ap. Eus.*d.e.*8.2(p.376.4; M.22.609C); **2.** *sending down*; of Elijah's fire, Chrys.*Stag.*3.11(1.219E); of soul τῇ ἀπὸ τῶν οὐρανῶν εἰς τὰ σώματα καταβάσει καὶ κ. τῶν ψυχῶν Meth.*symp.*2.5(M.18.53C; παραπομπῇ p.21.5).

καταπόνησις, ἡ, 1. *oppression, subjugation,* Chrys.*Laz.*6.1(1. 773B); met., ref. Mt.11:12 βίαν ἐκάλεσε τὴν τοῦ σώματος καταπόνησιν Bas.*renunt.*9(2.211A; M.31.645C); **2.** *affliction, trouble,* id.*ep.*66.1(3. 159B; M.32.424C).

καταποντίζ-ω, 1. = καταπίνω, *engulf, swallow up, A.Phil.*134 (p.65.10); κ. τοὺς ἀνθρώπους εἰς τὴν ἄβυσσον *ib.*137(p.69.18); Mac. Aeg.*hom.*11.12(M.34.553C); Thdt.*Ps.*105:17(1.1357, v.l. κατεπόθησαν); **2.** met., *overwhelm, engulf* μὴ βάρυνε αὐτὸ [sc. τὸ σῶμα] ἵνα μὴ καταποντίσῃς [i.e. through gluttony] Chrys.*hom.29.4 in Heb.*(12.277A); ~εσθαι ὑπὸ τῆς λύπης Nil.*epp.*2.146(M.79.268B); ~ων μὴ μόνον τὴν σαυτοῦ ψυχήν, ἀλλὰ καὶ ἄλλας πολλάς Isid.Pel.*epp.*2.65(M.78.509A); τὸν τῶν ἀνθρώπων ἐχθρὸν κ. ἐν τῷ...βαπτίσματι Chrysipp.*enc.in Jo.Bapt.* (p.40.10).

***καταπόντισις, ἡ,** *swallowing, engulfment* οἱ ἀνελθόντες...ἀπὸ... τῆς κ. τῆς ἀβύσσου *A.Phil.*141(p.76.6); met., of being plunged in slough of sin, Jo.Clim.*scal.*26(M.88.1016C).

καταποντισμός, ὁ, 1. *drowning,* Or.*schol.in Mt.*18:5(M.17.297C); id.*princ.*3.1.14(p.220.13; M.11.277A); Dion.Al.ap.Eus.*h.e.*7.21.6(M. 20.685A); Chrys.*hom.58.3 in Mt.*(7.588D); met., of submergence in evil, hence of moral and spiritual degradation ἠγάπα κακίαν... ἠγάπα πάντα ῥήματα καταποντισμοῦ Niceph.Ur.*v.Sym.*241(M.86. 3208A); **2.** *flood,* Eus.*d.e.*8.2(p.390.11; M.22.629C); Chrys.*hom. 7.2 in 2Tim.*(11.701C).

***καταποντιστέον,** *one must throw into the sea,* Clem.*q.d.s.*27(p.177. 29; M.9.632D).

καταποντόω, = καταποντίζω, met.; **1.** *cast, plunge into* εἰς τὸν πυθμένα τῆς κακίας κ. σαυτόν Isid.Pel.*epp.*5.445(M.78.1585B); **2.** *overwhelm* ἵνα μὴ...ταῖς τρικυμίαις καὶ ταῖς ἀπάταις τῆς ἡδονῆς περικλυσθεὶς καταποντωθῇ Meth.*symp.*3.6(p.33.6; M.18.69B); Jo. Mosch.*prat.*46(M.87.2901B).

***καταπόντωσις, ἡ,** *drowning in the sea,* Or.*comm.in Ex.*(M.12. 272D).

καταπορνεύω, met., *pander to* μὴ γεῦσιν καταπορνεύσωμεν Gr. Naz.*or.*38.5(M.36.316B).

κατάποσις, ἡ, met., *swallowing* ἐκ τῆς τοῦ...θανάτου παλαιᾶς κ. ἀνασπᾶν Dion.Ar.*e.h.*4.3.10(M.3.484B); theol., *absorption* Σαβελλίου τὴν ἀνάλυσιν καὶ τὴν σύγχυσιν καὶ τήν, ἵν' οὕτως εἴπω, κ., τὰ τρία εἰς ἓν συναιροῦντος Gr.Naz.*or.*33.16(M.36.233D); Σαβέλλιος...κατεξανίσταται αὐτῆς [sc. τῆς ἐκκλησίας] ἀνάχυσίν τινα καὶ κ. ἐπιτηδεύσας νομοθετῆσαι Germ.CP *syn.haer.*8(M.98.45B).

καταπότης, ὁ, *swallower*; of a dragon, *A.Thom.*A 108(p.220.8).

καταποφαίνομαι, *give judgement against,* ‡Ath.*hom.in Mt.21*:9 (M.28.1036C); Chrys.*fr.in Jer.*6:27(M.64.832A); Isid.Pel.*epp.*5.209 (M.78.1457A).

καταπραγματεύω, med., *make profit from,* c. genit., Gr.Naz.*or.* 43.34(M.36.544A); *ib.*43.36(545A).

***καταπρανῶς,** *headlong,* Germ.CP *or.*2(M.98.248D).

κατάπραξις, ἡ, *execution, performance,* Clem.*str.*1.1(p.5.23; M.8. 692C); *ib.*2.6(p.127.24; 961C); Leont.H.*Nest.*2.20(M.86.1581A).

καταπραΰνω, *assuage* grief, Gr.Nyss.*Pulch.*(M.46.864D).

***κατάπρησις, ἡ,** a *fanning wind,* ‡Bas.*Lac.*5(2.590E; M.31.1445D).

καταπρίζω, = καταπρίω, *tear in pieces, T.Sal.*11.7(p.41.5; M.122. 1333A); pass., met., *be cut up* by sorrow, ‡Amph.*poenit.*(p.91C).

καταπροδίδωμι, *abandon, fail to obtain,* Bas.*reg.fus.*9.1(2.351C; M. 31.941C); met., *abandon* ἡδοναῖς σάρκα κ. Bas.Sel.*v.Thecl.*1(M.85. 484C).

***καταπταίω,** *slip, err,* Eus.*fr.*11(M.22.1272C).

***κατάπτησις, ἡ,** *downward flight,* Nil.*serm.*8(M.79.1276D).

καταπτοέω, 1. *frighten,* Cyr.*ep.*50(p.96.13; 5^2.165D); Eus.Al.*serm.* 15(M.86.392A); Max.*ep.*13(M.91.532D); **2.** pass., *fear* ἐπεὶ τίνα τρόπον κατεπτοήθη θάνατον ἢ ζωή; Cyr.*Pulch.*(p.49.19; 5^2.162D).

***καταπτύστως,** *abominably,* Clem.*str.*3.11(p.231.9; M.8.1177B).

καταπτύω, *spit upon*; met., *reject* Ῥάχηλ...κατέπτυσεν συνουσίαν ἀνδρός *T.Isach.*2.1.

κατάπτωσις, ἡ, *fall*; **1.** fig., of death σκεῦος ἐμὸν...οὐ ῥαγώσει... σύντριμμα θανατοφθόρου κ. Germ.CP *or.*8(M.98.361C); **2.** of fall of Devil, Or.*princ.*3.1.12(p.216.7; M.11.272A); τὴν ἀπὸ τῶν κρειττόνων ἐπὶ τὰ χείρω κ. Eus.*d.e.*4.9(p.163.6; M.22.272C); **3.** of Adam's fall ἡ ἐκ τοῦ παραδείσου κ. Meth.*res.*1.55(p.314.18; M.41.1149A); **4.** of soul οὐδαμῶς...λέγοντες μετενσωμάτωσιν εἶναι ψυχῆς καὶ κ. αὐτῆς μέχρι τῶν ἀλόγων ζῴων Or.*Cels.*8.30(p.245.25; M.11.1561A); ἡ ἀπὸ τῶν οὐρανῶν κ. εἰς τὸν βίον Meth.*res.*1.54(p.313.2; M.41.1148A); ψυχῆς...κ. καὶ τὴν εἰς σῶμα κάθοδον Cyr.*Jo.*1.9(4.82C); cf.CCP(543) *anath.*7(Hahn p.228; H.3.285B); **5.** of moral lapse; into idolatry, †Bas.*Is.*83(1.436D; M.30.253C); in gen. ἡ πρὸς κακίαν κ. Gr.Nyss. *hom.opif.*28(M.44.233B); Anast.S.*Ps.*6(M.89.1124D).

καταπυκάζ-ω, *cover over,* Cyr.*ador.*9(1.296B); *ib.*13(457C); id.*Nah.* 4(3.479C); with idea of *protection* τὸν θεῖον ἐν ἑαυτῇ κατεπύκαζε [sc. ἡ κιβωτός] νόμον id.*ador.*5(158B); τὸν υἱόν...τὸν ἀποκρύπτοντα τοὺς ἁγίους καὶ οἷον ~οντα καθάπερ ἐν σκηνῇ id.*Ps.*30:22(M.69.865A).

καταπυρίζω, met., *become inflamed,* Eustrat.*v.Eutych.*53(M.86. 2336A).

***καταπυρσεύ-ω,** *illuminate*, met. ὁ πᾶσαν ταῖς τῆς αὐτοῦ θεολογίας ἀκτῖσι ~ων τὴν γῆν ‡Amph.*circ.*(p.16B); of BMV ὦ στήλη νεκρὰ καὶ στύλε ζωοποιέ...φῶς ἐνθέως ~ουσα Andr.Cr.*or.*14(M.97.1097B).

καταπωλέω, *sell,* Clem.*paed.*3.6(p.256.14; M.8.604C); Hipp.*Dan.* 4.19.5; Cyr.*ador.*14(1.516E); met. ἑαυτοὺς τῷ διαβόλῳ κ. id.*Jo.*4.6(4. 429B).

κατάρα, ἡ, *curse*; **1.** incurred through sin τὰ ἔτη τῆς ἀπωλείας ὑμῶν πληθυνθήσεται ἐν κ. αἰώνων *Apoc.En.*5.5(p.22.10); ὡς τοὺς μὲν εὐλογοῦντας ἡμᾶς εὐλογεῖσθαι ὑπὸ τοῦ θεοῦ, τοὺς δὲ καταρωμένους ὑπὸ κατάραν ἔσεσθαι Or.*Jo.*20.10(p.338.16; M.14.593A); ὑμεῖς οὖν μακάριοι, οἱ λυθέντες τῆς κ. ... Χριστὸς γάρ...τὸν νόμον κυρώσας ἐπλήρωσεν *Const.App.*6.22.1; **2.** *person* or *people accursed, T.Lev.*10. 4; οἴμοι...ὅτι κ. ἐγεννήθην ἐγὼ ἐνώπιον τῶν υἱῶν Ἰσραὴλ *Protev.*3 (p.7); **3.** ref. Gal.3:13, Eus.*d.e.*10.1(p.450.23; M.22.725A); εἰ γὰρ τὴν καθ' ἡμῶν γενομένην κ. ἦλθεν αὐτὸς βαστάσαι, πῶς ἂν ἄλλως ἐγένετο κ., εἰ μὴ τὸν ἐπὶ κατάρᾳ γενόμενον θάνατον ἐδέξατο; Ath.*inc.*25.2(M. 25.140A); οὐ τοῦτό φησιν, ὅτι ἡ οὐσία αὐτοῦ...εἰς κ. οὐσιώθη...ἀλλ' ὅτι τὴν καθ' ἡμῶν κ. δεξάμενος, οὐκ ἀφίησιν ἡμᾶς ἐπαράτους εἶναι λοιπόν Chrys.*hom.11.12 in Jo.*(8.64A).

***καταραΐζω**, *soothe* κ. τὴν λύπην Cyr.*Jo.*10.1(4.847D); *ib.*(841A); 'οὐδεὶς ἐπέβαλεν ἐπ' αὐτὸν τὰς χεῖρας'...μόνῃ...τῇ παρ' αὐτοῦ καταραϊσθέντες δυνάμει *ib.*5.2(478B, vv.ll. καταρασθέντες, καταρεσθέντες).

καταρ-άομαι, *curse*; **1.** in gen. ἁμαρτωλὸς...~ᾶται ζωὴν αὐτοῦ, τὴν ἡμέραν γενέσεως *Pss.Sal.*3.10; ἐν ὑμῖν καταράσονται πάντες οἱ ~ώμενοι *Apoc.En.*5.6(p.22.10); καθὼς ἐκατηράθητε παρὰ τῶν πενήτων Eus.Al.*serm.*21.5(M.86.429C); ἀνεχώρει εὐχαριστῶν αὐτῷ, καὶ ~ώμενος τῶν ἄλλων Dor.*doct.*5.3(M.88.1680B); **2.** of the curse invoked on Christians by Jews in synagogues, Just.*dial.*16.4(M.6.512A); *ib.*96.2(704A); *ib.*108.3(728A); cf.Epiph.*haer.*29.9(p.331.26; M.41.404D); **3.** of curse of God (implying condemnation) οὓς κατηράσατο κύριος ἐπὶ τοῦ κατακλυσμοῦ *T.Neph.*3.5; τοῖς κατηραμένοις ὑπὸ τοῦ θεοῦ *1Clem.*30.8; Just.*dial.*91.4(M.6.693B); θεὸς κατηραμένος *the God of the OT*, acc. Archontici καὶ λέγει τὸν ἄρχοντα τῶν ὀνομαζομένων ἀρχοντικῶν λέγεσθαι θεὸν κ. Or.*Cels.*6.27(p.97.10; M.11.1333A); *ib.*6.51(p.122.28; 1377C).

κατάρασις, ἡ, *cursing*, Ath.*exp.Ps.*27 arg.(M.27.149B); cf.Cyr.ad loc., cit. s. κατάρρησις.

καταργ-έω, 1. *bring to nought* αὐτοὶ νῦν ~ηθήσονται σὺν ταῖς πράξεσιν αὐτῶν *A.Thom.*A 77(p.192.11); ἡ γὰρ φαντασία τοῦ καλλωπισμοῦ ~εῖται, καὶ τὸ σῶμα γηράσκει *ib.*88(p.203.16); ἑαυτὸν ἐκένωσε [sc. ὁ Χριστός]...ἵνα τὴν ὑπερηφανίαν τοῦ ἐχθροῦ ~ήσῃ Anast.S.*hod.*13(M.89.237D); **2.** *render impotent* ~ηθέντων τῶν τυραννικῶν κολαστηρίων ὑπὸ τοῦ Χριστοῦ διὰ τῆς τῶν μακαρίων ὑπομονῆς *Ep.Lugd.* ap.Eus.*h.e.*5.1.27(M.20.417C); Serap.*euch.*10; Χριστὸς...~ήσῃ θανάτῳ τὸν θάνατον Cyr.H.*catech.*19.4; *defeat* τὸν διάβολον ~ήσας Clem.*paed.*2.8(p.203.9; M.8.488A); τὸν ἐπιδημήσαντα Χριστὸν Ἰησοῦν καὶ ~ήσαντα τὸν ἄρχοντα τοῦ αἰῶνος τούτου καὶ ~ήσαντα τὴν ἁμαρτίαν Or.*hom.*7.3 *in Jer.*(p.54.28; M.13.336A); met., *overcome* ἡ ἁγιωσύνη...~οῦσα τὴν πορνείαν *A.Thom.*A 85(p.201.15); ἵνα ~ήσωμεν τῆς σαρκὸς ἡμῶν τὰ πάθη Clem.*paed.*1.6(p.115.29; M.8.301A); ἡ ἐνθύμησις πάσας τὰς διαφορὰς τῶν πονηρῶν πνευμάτων ~εῖν δύναται Diad.*perf.*81(p.106.6); *counteract* εἴ τις...ἐκ τοῦ διαβόλου γεγέννηται καὶ μὴ κατήργησεν τὴν ἀπ' ἐκείνου γένεσιν ἐξ ἑαυτοῦ Or.*Jo.*20.22(20; p.354.5; M.14.620B); Tit.Bost.*Man.*1.30(M.18.1113A); **3.** *render unnecessary, do away with* οὐδέν ἐστιν ἄμεινον εἰρήνης, ἐν ᾗ πᾶς πόλεμος ~εῖται ἐπουρανίων καὶ ἐπιγείων Ign.*Eph.*13.2; πῶς λέγει κύριος ~ῶν αὐτόν [sc. τὸν ναόν]; *Barn.*16.2; †Just.*fr.res.*3(p.39; M.6.1577B); *supersede* ἡ περιτομὴ ...κατήργηται *Barn.*9.4; *A.Andr.et Mt.*14(p.81.10); τί τὸ ~ούμενον τῇ ἐπιφανείᾳ τῆς παρουσίας Χριστοῦ...ἢ πᾶν τὸ ἐπαγγελλόμενον εἶναι σοφία; Or.*Jo.*2.7(4; p.61.21; M.14.121A); exeg. 1Cor.13:8, id.*Cels.*1.13(p.65.27; M.11.680A); Chrys.*incomprehens.*1.2(1.446B); Thdt.*1Cor.*13:8(3.254); pass., *be idle* μὴ θαυμαζέτωσαν οὖν οἱ τῆς πίστεως ἐκτὸς εἰ τὴν ἀπὸ τοῦ νῦν ~ουμένην ἐν τοῖς ἔργοις τούτοις σάρκα καὶ ἐν τῷ μέλλοντι αἰῶνι ~ήσει †Just.*fr.res.*3(p.40; M.6.1577B); *put an end to*, *Barn.*15.5; ἰσχὺν ἔχει ~ῆσαι τὸν ἐπιγάστριον βίον Clem.*paed.*2.1(p.164.9; M.8.400C); *ib.*2.10(p.217.18; 517B); **4.** *set at nought*, †Just.*fr.res.*3(p.39; M.6.1577B); exeg. 1Cor.1:28 ἐὰν γάρ τις μετεσχηκὼς τοῦ εἶναι, ἐπιλαθόμενος τῆς μετοχῆς, ἑαυτῷ καταχαρίσηται τὴν τοῦ εἶναι αἰτίαν...τότε ~εῖται τὸ ὄν Or.*comm.in Eph.*1:1(p.235); **5.** *mishandle* κατήργησεν ὁ γέρων τὸ πρᾶγμα ἡμῶν *Apophth.Patr.*(M.65.137A); **6.** pass., *be set free from*; exeg. Rom.7:2, Or.*Jo.*13.8(p.232.17; M.14.409C); Thdt.*Rom.*7:6(3.70); **7.** *excommunicate* ~ήθητι ἀπὸ τῶν ἐλπιζόντων πρὸς κύριον· ἀπὸ ἐννοιῶν αὐτῶν...ἀπὸ ἀναστάσεως τῆς πρὸς θεὸν...ἀπὸ νηστειῶν...ἀπὸ εὐχαριστίας...ἀπὸ πάντων σε τούτων ἀνοσιώτατε...~ήσει σε Ἰησοῦς Χριστὸς *A.Jo.*84(p.192.24).

κατάργησις, ἡ, 1. *abolition*, Or.*comm.in Mt.*10.9(p.10.29; M.13.856D); ἵν' ὁ μὲν θάνατος λεγόμενος αὐτοῦ λύτρον ᾖ τῆς τῶν ἀνθρώπων ἁμαρτίας καὶ κ. τοῦ θανάτου Ath.*Ar.*1.45(M.26.105A); κ. τοῦ πονηροῦ Serap.*euch.*13.16; *Schol.*6 in Jo.Clim.*scal.*2(M.88.660D); **2.** met., *destruction*, ref. Rom.6:6 κ. τοῦ σώματος Max.*ep.*24(M.91.609A); **3.** *refutation* ἕως ἂν...τῶν ἐπεισάκτων δογμάτων τελείαν ποιήσωνται κανονικῶς τὴν κ. CLater.*act.*2(H.3.713D); *ib.*3(772C); ὅθεν εἰς παντελῆ τῶν τοιούτων κ., λέγω δὴ τῶν κατὰ καιροὺς τὰς ἀπατηλὰς ἐξερευνώντων ἐξερευνήσεις κατὰ τῆς πίστεως, καὶ συνοδικὸς ὁρίζεται κάλλιστα νόμος Max.*opusc.*(M.91.181A).

καταρδεύ-ω, 1. *water* τοῖς ληΐοις ἡ τοῦ ~εσθαι χρεία Cyr.*Am.*37(3.291E); **2.** *yield water*, met. τοῖς ἀρυσαμένοις κ. Or.*fr.54 in Jo.*(p.528.24); **3.** met.; **a.** *nourish* τῷ τῆς νηστείας ὕδατι ~έσθωσαν Bas.*hom.*2.2(2.11E; M.31.188B); **b.** *refresh* τῇ τοῦ ἁγίου πνεύματος ~όμενοι χάριτι Cyr.*glaph.Num.*(1.399A); id.*Jo.*10.2(4.875C); τοῖς θεορρύτοις τοῦ πνεύματος νάμασι τὴν οἰκείαν κατήρδευε διάνοιαν Jo.D.*hom.*4.27(M.96.629B).

κατάρδ-ω, 1. *water, irrigate*, Philost.*h.e.*3.11(p.42.32; M.65.500B); **2.** *feed* with liquid ἐλαίῳ ~όμενον...τὸ λυχνιαῖον Meth.*symp.*10.2(p.123.13; M.18.193D); **3.** met., *sprinkle, shower*, *ib.*8.3(p.84.23; 144A); αἱ νοηταὶ νεφέλαι, τουτέστιν οἱ...προφῆται...ζωοποιοῖς κηρύγμασι τῶν συνιέναι δυναμένων ~οντες νοῦν Cyr.*Nah.*4(3.480A); **4.** met., *refresh* παράκλησις ἡ πνευματικὴ...ὑετοῦ ~ουσα δίκην Cyr.*ador.*7(1.221B); *ib.*9(301E).

καταροῦν, for κατὰ ῥόον, *down stream*, Cyr.*ador.*13(1.467C).

***καταρραβδίζω**, *beat with a rod*, Thdr.Stud.*poen.*1(M.99.1745A).

καταρραθυμ-έω, *neglect* μὴ...~ῶμεν τῆς ἑαυτῶν σωτηρίας Chrys.*David* 3.9(4.782B); Nil.*epp.*3.33(M.79.389C); Cyr.*Nest.*1(p.15.13; 6^{1}.4E); τὸ τὴν ἀνάγνωσιν κατερρυθμῆσθαι...τραγῳδιῶν αἴτιον γέγονε Isid.Pel.*epp.*4.133(M.78.1216A; cod. κατερραθυμεῖσθαι).

καταρ(ρ)άκτης, ὁ, 1. *torrent*, ref. Flood ἀπὸ τοῦ οὐρανοῦ τῶν κ. ῥυέντων Thphl.Ant.*Autol.*3.19(M.6.1148A); *Apoc.Bar.rel.*5.24; **2.** *trap-door*; of floodgates of heaven (Gen.7:11), Ath.*Ar.*3.45(M.26.420B); Gr.Naz.*or.*28.28(p.66.3; M.36.65C); **3.** *stocks*, ref. Jer.20:2, Bas.*Spir.*54(3.46D; M.32.169A); Gr.Nyss.*castig.*(M.46.316C).

καταρ(ρ)άπτω, *plait* τὴν σπυρίδα κ. Pall.*h.Laus.*10(p.31.3; M.34.1028D); met., *set* or *fix in position* οἱ δὲ τὰ ἐκνεμηθέντα πρὸς καιρῶν ἐπίδειξιν καὶ ἐν φωστήρων τάξει κατερραμμένα θεοὺς ὠνόμαζον Cyr.*Os.*148(3.182A, v.l. κατεσταμένα Aubert, καθεσ- Migne).

καταρράσσω, 1. *throw down*, Chrys.*hom.19.8 in Mt.*(7.257B); Thdt.*haer.*1.1(4.287); **2.** met., *overthrow*; of Christ's victory over Devil in temptations, Chrys.*hom.78.4 in Mt.*(7.756A); **3.** met., perf. ptcpl. pass., *downcast* ἀλλ' ὁ μὲν κύριος...θέλει πάντας ἀνορθοῦσθαι τοὺς κατερραγμένους Ath.*Ar.*3.67(M.26.465C); Bas.*ep.*45.2(3.134D; M.32.368C); Ammon.*Ac.*18:23(M.85.1572B); **4.** intrans., *fall down*, Thdr.Mops.*Os.*7:6(M.66.165D).

***καταρραψῳδέω**, *rhapsodize* or *declaim against*, Cyr.*Jo.*1.9(4.78D); id.*hom.pasch.*6(5^{2}.66C).

καταρρ-έω, 1. *collapse, fall in ruins*; **a.** lit., ptcpl. pass., *ruined* τοίχους...~υέντας Bas.*hom.*7.4(2.55E; M.31.289C); **b.** met. ~εῖ ῥᾳδίως [sc. τὸ ψεῦδος] Chrys.*hom.29.1 in Jo.*(8.164B); *ib.29.2*(167A); **2.** met., *descend* καὶ ἐκ θεοῦ τὸ τῆς πατριᾶς ὄνομα καὶ εἰς ἡμᾶς ~εῖ Cyr.*Jo.*1.3(4.24E); **3.** *vomit forth* τὴν...γλῶσσαν σαπεῖσαν κατέρρευσε καὶ τοὺς ὀδόντας ἀπέβαλε Thphn.*chron.*p.40(M.108.156B).

κατάρρησις, ἡ, 1. *accusation, charge* πέπαυται καθ' ἡμῶν ἡ τῆς ἀνομίας κ. Cyr.*ador.*3(1.104D); *ib.*10(340E); id.*Jo.*12(4.1035C); **2.** *condemnation, denunciation* τῆς Ἰουδαίων ἀπονοίας κ. Cyr.*Ps.*27(M.69.853C); τὴν ἐκ νόμου κ. ὅπως ἂν ἔχοι δικαίαν ὁ σαρκικαῖς ἀρρωστίαις περιπεσὼν id.*ador.*15(1.536C); id.*Am.*19(3.269C); **3.** *criticism* τῆς μετὰ σαρκὸς οἰκονομίας...οὐ μετρίαν ποιοῦνται τὴν κ. Cyr.*expl.xii cap.*(p.16.2; 6^{1}.146A); id.*glaph.Gen.*6(1.193C); id.*apol.orient.*3(p.39.20; 6^{1}.165E); οὐ ψιλὴν κ. τῶν αὐτοῦ πεποιήμεθα λόγων, ἔλεγχον δὲ μᾶλλον σαφῆ τε καὶ ἀληθῆ id.*Nest.*4.2(p.78.36; -ρυσιν 6^{1}.100B); *ib.*(p.76.25; -ρυσις 96E); **4.** *calumny*, Cyr.*ador.*8(1.270D); Sophr.H.*mir.Cyr.et Jo.*51(M.87.3612B).

καταρρήσσω, = καταρράσσω, *fall*, *A.Mt.*4(p.220.12).

***καταρρητόρευσις, ἡ,** *rhetoric*, Leont.B.*mesopent.*(M.86.1981C).

καταρρητορεύω, 1. *overcome by rhetoric*, c. genit., Chrys.*hom.10.2 in Ac.*(9.82C); Nil.*epp.*2.204(M.79.308C); **2.** *declaim against*, c. genit., Bas.Sel.*v.Thecl.*1(M.85.496C); c. acc., Isid.Pel.*epp.*3.394(M.78.1033B); **3.** *declaim*, Mac.Mgn.*apocr.*2.17(p.28.1).

***καταρριγνύομαι**, = καταρρικνόομαι, Gr.Nyss.*anim.et res.*(M.46.137B, v.l. καταρρικνωθέντα).

***καταρρίζωμα, τό,** *root*, met., *foundation*, ‡Chrys.*pasch.*6.3(p.155.13; 8.269B).

καταρρικνόομαι, *be shrivelled*, *V.Max.*34(M.90.104C); v. *καταρριγνύομαι.

καταρρινέω (-ίζω), *file down*, hence met., perf. ptcpl. pass., *polished, accurate* ὦ...νοῦ κατερρινημένου καὶ συνιέντος ἰσχνῶς Cyr.*Juln.*9(6^{2}.295C); οἱονεὶ κατερρινισμέναις ἐννοίαις *ib.*1(19C).

καταρρίπτω, 1. *cast out*, *A.Phil.*1(p.1.14); παραβάντες τὴν κέλευσιν ἐκ τοῦ οὐρανοῦ κατερρίφησαν [sc. οἱ ἄγγελοι] Cosm.Ind.*top.*2(M.88.120A); *ib.*(120D); **2.** *make an incursion* Βουλγάρων...ἐπὶ τὸ Στενὸν καταρριψάντων Thphn.*chron.*p.320(M.108.776A); **3.** perf. ptcpl. pass., *mean, abject*, Cyr.*Is.*4.5(2.697B); *ib.*5.1(743A); id.*Juln.*8(6^{2}.252B).

***κατάρριψις, ἡ,** *overthrow*, Or.*Cels.*4.21(p.290.9; M.11.1053B).

***καταρρυθμέω**, s.v.l., *manipulate, fake* τὸ τὴν ἀνάγνωσιν κατερρυθμῆσθαι...τραγῳδιῶν αἴτιον γέγονε Isid.Pel.*epp.*4.133(M.78.1216A; cod. κατερραθυμεῖσθαι).

καταρ(ρ)υθμίζ-ω, 1. *arrange in order, regulate*, Cyr.*Juln.*5(6^{2}.153A); id.*ador.*6(1.173D); *ib.*7(1.226D); **2.** *manipulate, twist* εἰς τὸ τῆς οἰκονομίας πρόσχημα τὸ ἔκθεσμον αὐτοῖς ~ων καὶ ἀθέλητον Philost.*h.e.*6.3(M.65.536A); **3.** *attune* to ταῖς εἰς θεὸν ὑμνῳδίαις...~ειν τὴν γλῶτταν Cyr.*Ps.*33:14(M.69.889D); **4.** *make fit, train* for εἰς καινότητα

...ζωῆς...~ων τοὺς ἑαυτοῦ μαθητὰς Cyr.*Lc*.6:20(M.72.589A); id.*Juln.* 10(6².350B); πρὸς τὴν τοῦ θείου θεραπείαν τοὺς πειθομένους ~οντα Philost.*h.e.*2.5(M.65.469A).

***καταρρυπος**, *defiled, filthy*, Const.ap.Ath.*decr*.40(p.42.10; M.85. 1353B).

καταρρυπόω, *defile, sully*; met., Or.*fr.54 in Jo.*(p.528.29); Bas. *ep*.52.3(3.146B; M.32.396A); Chrys.*hom.32.3 in Jo.*(8.188C).

κατάρρυσις, ἡ, *dropping down*, Anast.S.*hod*.13(M.89.233B); v. *κατάρρησις*.

***καταρρωστέω**, met., *suffer* from, *be afflicted* with κατηρρώστησεν ἡ ἀνθρώπου φύσις τὴν ἁμαρτίαν Cyr.*ep*.17(p.39.9; 5².74C); id.*Soph*.30 (3.607D); id.*Juln*.2(6².66C).

καταρτάω, **1.** pass.; **a.** met., *hang over, threaten* κόλασις...τῆς τῶν φιλαμαρτημόνων καταρτηθήσεται κεφαλῆς Cyr.*Ps*.36:28(M.69.944C); id.*ador*.14(1.516A); **b.** *be properly furnished, equipped, Cod.Afr*.90; **2.** med., *make, render* τοὺς αἰχμαλώτους ἡμᾶς οἰκείους αὐτοῦ κατηρτήσατο Eus.*d.e*.4.17(p.199.18; M.22.332C).

***καταρτή**, ἡ, = κατάρτιον, *beam*; of wood, Jo.Mosch.*prat*.190 (M.87.3069C).

καταρτία, ἡ, *mast*, *Chron.Pasch*.p.394(M.92.1009B).

***καταρτίδιον**, τό, *small mast*, *M.Areth*.(p.56.1).

καταρτίζ-ω, **A.** *join together*; **1.** *fashion, frame*; **a.** lit. χρειῶδες... ἔργον οὐδὲν...συμβατικῶς ἀπεργάζεται, ἀλλὰ χειρουργούμενον, εἰς τὴν πρέπουσαν ὑπηρεσίαν ~εται Dion.Al.ap.Eus.*p.e*.14.24(773D; τίθεται M.21.1273A); ref. Creation διὰ ταύτην [sc. τὴν ἐκκλησίαν] ὁ κόσμος κατηρτίσθη Herm.*vis*.2.4.1; πιστεύομεν...εἰς...υἱὸν...δι' οὗ οἵ τε αἰῶνες κατηρτίσθησαν *Symb.Sirm*.3 ap.Ath.*syn*.8(p.235.27; M.26. 692C); Cyr.*Ps*.8:5(M.69.760B); of body of Christ (cf. Heb.10:5) τὸ καταρτισθὲν αὐτοῦ σῶμα Eus.*d.e*.1.10(p.47.29; M.22.89D); **b.** met. ζωὴν δέ φημι τὴν ~ομένην διὰ πλειόνων σπουδῆς, καὶ καρπῶν ἀξίων μετανοίας βεβαίας Nil.*epp*.3.43(M.79.412B); **2.** *restore, make up* ~ων εὐηκοΐαν αὐτοῖς Clem.*paed*.1.11(p.147.20; M.8.365B); καταρτίσαι τὰ ὑστερήματα...τουτέστι τὰ ἐλλείποντα πληρῶσαι Thdt.*1Thess*.3:10(3. 514); *restore, set right* ὑμεῖς οἱ πνευματικοὶ ~ετε τὸν τοιοῦτον· οὐκ εἶπε κολάζετε, οὐδὲ καταδικάζετε, ἀλλὰ διορθοῦσθε Chrys.*comm.in Gal*.6:1(10.723B); Thdt.*Gal*.6:1(3.392); **3.** *adapt, conform* τὸ νῖκος γάρ ἐστι τοῦ ἐργαζομένου, ὅταν καταρτίσῃ ἑαυτὸν ὅλον τῷ θεῷ Esaias *or*.23.5(p.146); Dor.*doct*.1.11(M.88.1632B); ὃς καὶ πνευματικῶς ζῆν κατηρτισμένος Areth.*Apoc*.1(M.106.504B); **4.** perf. ptcpl. pass., *established, settled* ἵνα ἐν μιᾷ ὑποταγῇ κατηρτισμένοι, ὑποτασσόμενοι τῷ ἐπισκόπῳ Ign.*Eph*.2.2; ἐνόησα γὰρ ὑμᾶς κατηρτισμένους ἐν ἀκινήτῳ πίστει id.*Smyrn*.1.1; ὡς ἄνθρωπος εἰς ἕνωσιν κατηρτισμένος id.*Philad*.8.1; **5.** *fasten upon* ὀθόνιον ἐφ' ἑαυτοῖς ~οντες ζυγόν Cyr. *Mich*.46(3.435B; καταστήσαντες Aubert).

B. *furnish, equip* τοὺς γενναιοτάτους ~ει εἰς πόλεμον Hipp.*Dan*. 4.9.2; *Clem.ep*.15(M.2.52A); *prepare, destine* for μάθετε...πρὸς ποίαν κόλασιν κατηρτίσθητε *Hom.Clem*.11.3; exeg. Rom.9:22 κατηρτισμένον εἰς ἀπώλειαν· τουτέστι, ἀπηρτισμένον, οἴκοθεν μέντοι καὶ παρ' ἑαυτοῦ Chrys.*hom.16.8 in Rom*.(9.616C).

C. *complete, finish, make perfect*; **1.** lit. ζητήσωμεν δὲ εἰ ἔστιν ναὸς θεοῦ. ἔστιν, ὅπου αὐτὸς λέγει ποιεῖν καὶ ~ειν *Barn*.16.6; Hipp.*haer*. 7.29(p.211.12; M.16.3326A); perf. ptcpl. pass., *finished product* τὸ ἔριον ἡ φύσις φέρει, τὸ δὲ κατηρτισμένον αἱ γυναῖκες ἐργάζονται ‡Chrys. *Chan*.4(8.187A); **2.** in moral and spiritual sense τί ἐστι, ~εσθε; τέλειοι γίνεσθε, ἀναπληροῦτε τὰ λείποντα Chrys.*hom.30.1 in 2Cor*. (10.649E); id.*hom.3.1 in 1Cor*.(10.15C).

D. *confirm, strengthen* οἰκοδομῶν καὶ ~ων αὐτοὺς ἐπὶ τὸ τοῦ θεοῦ μέγεθος *A.Jo*.111(p.210.6); Gr.Naz.*or*.8.3(M.35.792D); Bas.*reg.fus*.11 (2.354A; M.31.948B); as a work of H. Ghost κατηρτισμένοι τῷ πνεύματι Or.*Jo*.1.7(9; p.13.7; M.14.37B); *Lit.Jac*.(p.160.17).

κατάρτι(ο)ν, τό, *beam*; of wood, Jo.Mosch.*prat*.190(M.87.3069C); esp. *mast* of a ship, Gr.Mag.*dial*.(tr.Zach.)3.36(M.*PL*.77.303C); part of a loom, Clem.*str*.1.8(p.27.11; M.8.737A).

***κατάρτιος**, *ready, prepared*; neut. as subst., *preparedness*, Dor. *doct*.14.4(M.88.1781A).

κατάρτισμα, τό, *finished product*; of wool, ‡Chrys.*Chan*.4(8.187A).

καταρτισμός, ὁ, **1.** *restoration, reconciliation*; effected by Christ, *A.Phil*.49(p.21.31); τὸν τῆς ψυχῆς τε καὶ σώματος ἁγιασμὸν...τῷ τοῦ σωτῆρος κ. τελειούμενον Clem.*str*.4.26(p.320.28; M.8.1373A); **2.** *strengthening, perfecting* εἰς οἰκοδομὴν καὶ κ. τῶν ψυχῶν ἡμῶν Bas. *hex*.9.1(1.80E; M.29.189A); πρὸς κ. τῆς ἐκκλησίας Ammon.*Ac*.18:25 (M.85.1573A); CLater.*act*.5(H.3.888A); **3.** *correction, adjustment*, Chrys.*hom.2.1 in Tit*.(11.737D).

***καταρχάς**, = κατ' ἀρχάς, in phrase τὸ καταρχάς *in the beginning*, Gr.Nyss.*hom.2 in Cant*.(M.44.796B); id.*ep*.1(M.46.1008D; κατ' ἀρχάς p.10.11).

καταρχή, ἡ, *beginning*, *Orac.Sib*.3.155; Hipp.*haer*.9.16(p.254.24; M.16.3394A); *Chron.Pasch*.p.215(M.92.524C).

κατάρχ-ω, *rule, govern*; **1.** in gen. ἵνα...δυνηθείη...κατάρξαι... τῆς Μεσοποταμίας Epiph.*haer*.66.5(p.25.8; M.42.37C); δι' αὐτοῦ [sc. Χριστοῦ] τε καὶ σὺν αὐτῷ ~ει τῶν ὅλων ὁ θεός Tit.Bost.*fr.Lc*.10:2 (p.188.16); ἐν δικαιοσύνῃ κατάρξει...Χριστός Cyr.*Ps*.9:9(M.69.765C); **2.** of a ruling cause or principle, Athenag.*leg*.19.2(M.6.929A); **3.** *take the lead in* κάταρχε σοφίας καὶ ἀρετῆς Clem.*fr*.44(p.222.9); κ. τοῦ λόγου Meth.*res*.1.28(p.258.1); Chrys.*hom.1.1 in Rom*.(9.426C); **4.** *lead the way* Μάγοι μὲν ἀστέρος ~οντος ἠκολούθησαν Chrys.*hom.6.4 in Mt*. (7.91C).

***καταρωματίζω**, *spice*, Thphyl.*exc.gent*.15(p.488.25; M.113.952B).

***κατασαθρόω**, *corrupt, ruin*, †Cyr.*hom.div*.10(5².377B).

***κατασαλεύω**, pass., met., *be thrown backwards, reel*, Gr.Nyss. *v.Mos*.(M.44.376C).

***κατασάρκα**, τό, (or τὸ κατὰ σάρκα), the first of the linen cloths laid on the altar, *Euchol*.(p.181); *ib*.(p.498); *ib*.(p.659).

***κατασαρκ-όω**, **1.** *make fleshy, fatten*, Bas.*hom*.1.9(2.8A; M.31. 180A); *ib*.2.1(11A; M.185B); τῶν ἑκτηκόντων μὲν ἑαυτῶν τὸν νοῦν ἐν ἀτροφίᾳ τῶν...διδαγμάτων, ὑπερπιαινόντων δὲ καὶ ~ούντων τὸν ἔξω ἄνθρωπον †Bas.*Is*.32(1.406A; M.30.184B); **2.** pass.; **a.** perf., *be plump*, Bas.*hex*.5.2(1.41E; M.29.97C); **b.** met., *become carnal* ὁ ~ούμενος κατὰ τὸ γράμμα τοῦ νόμου ταῖς ἐναίμοις θυσίαις...ἄγνοιαν ἔχει *Schol*.24 in Max.*qu.Thal*.(M.90.777C).

***κατασαρόω**, *sweep down* or *away*, *Ep.Lugd*.ap.Eus.*h.e*.5.1.62(M. 20.432B).

κατάσβεσις, ἡ, met., *extinction*, Sophr.H.*v.Cyr.et Jo*.24(M.87. 3409C).

κατασείω, **1.** *shake*; met., *disturb, alarm* κ. αὐτῶν τὴν διάνοιαν Chrys.*hom.23.7 in Mt*.(7.294D); id.*hom.25.3 in Rom*.(9.705D); id. *hom.4.2 in 2Thess*.(11.531D); **2.** *cause an earthquake* κατασείσαντος δὲ τοῦ θεοῦ Synes.*ep*.67(M.66.1420A).

***κατασεμνύν-ω**, **1.** *glorify, honour*, †Dion.Al.*fr.Eccl*.1:3(p.211. 10); Φιλόστρατος...τὸν Ἀπολλωνίου βίον ἐξειλεγμέναις καλλιεπείαις ~ειν ἐπιχειρῶν Cyr.*Juln*.3(6².88A); id.*Am*.70(3.327E); **2.** med., *pride oneself on* ἑτέρῳ...~εσθαι κόσμῳ id.*Abac*.27(3.540D); id.*ador*.1(1. 45D); **3.** pass., met., *be adorned with* τῷ τῆς εὐπειθείας ~εσθαι κόσμῳ id.*Zach*.33(3.705C); id.*ep*.1.1(p.10.7,26; 5².1B,2C).

κατασημαίν-ω, **1.** *indicate* οἱ ἄγγελοι...τοῖς ποιμέσι ~οντες τὸν... θεὸν λόγον Cyr.*inc.unigen*.(5².681B); id.*Nah*.29(3.506D); Diad.*perf*. 91(p.132.1); **2.** *mean, signify* τὸ τῆς 'χρηστότητος' ὄνομα ἐνταῦθα ~ει πάντα τρόπον ἀρετῆς Or.*exc.in Ps*.36:3(M.17.120B); Nil.*epp*.2.282 (M.79.341A); Cyr.*ador*.1(1.4B); **3.** med., *observe, note*, Synes.*insomn*. 16(p.179.19; M.66.1312C).

κατασήπ-ω, met., *rot away* εἰς πολλὰς ~όμενον ἐπιθυμίας Clem. *paed*.2.2(p.172.22; M.8.421A); Meth.*lepr*.6.2(p.458.2); Chrys.*hom. 87.2 in Mt*.(7.820A); id.*hom.7.2 in Rom*.(9.485D) cit. s. δικαιοσύνη.

κατασθενέω, *grow weak*, Thphyl.*exc.gent*.9(p.486.17; M.113.948D).

***κατασιγαστέον**, *one must silence*, Clem.*paed*.2.6(p.189.12; M.8. 456A).

κατασιγάω, = κατασιγάζω, *put to silence*; pass., Meth.*symp*.3.10 (p.38.11; M.18.76C); met., *calm*, Thphn.*chron*.p.62(M.108.208A).

κατασιδηρόω, *bind with iron chains*; perf. ptcpl. pass., *Const. App*.2.22.10.

***κατασιελίζω**, *beslaver*, Gr.Nyss.*Eun*.12(1 p.387.5; M.45.1116C).

κατασίν-ομαι, *hurt, injure* ἀναπλέκοντες...τῇ ἀληθείᾳ τὸ ψεῦδος ~ονται τοὺς ἀκροωμένους Cyr.*ador*.6(1.185D); id.*Os*.17(3.39B); abs., id.*Jo*.3.4(4.298C).

κατασιωπάω, *silence*, *Hom.Clem*.1.11.

κατασκαίρω, *bound up and down, gambol*, Cyr.*Mich*.50(3.441C).

***κατάσκαλμος**, *rowing on the same bench*, met., Leont.N.*v.Sym*. 61(M.93.1744C).

κατασκάπτω, *destroy utterly*; met., Clem.*str*.3.4(p.208.22; M.8. 1133A); Or.*hom.1.9 in Jer*.(p.8.22; M.13.265C); Cyr.ap.*cat.Lc*.5:17 (p.45.4).

κατασκαφή, ἡ, *razing to the ground*; met., Or.*hom.1.9 in Jer*. (p.8.23; M.13.265C).

κατασκεδάζ-ω, = κατασκεδάννυμι, **1.** *scatter over* ὁ...πλεονέκτης ...ἐν σκότῳ ζῇ, καὶ σκότος πολὺ ~ει πάντων Chrys.*hom.18.4 in Eph*. (11.132B); **2.** *spread a report against* ἐπιβουλεύουσιν ἡμῖν ~οντες ὄχλον ἐγκλημάτων Athenag.*leg*.1.4(M.6.893B).

κατασκέλλομαι, in perf. ptcpl. act.; **1.** *hardened, frozen* τὸ κατεσκληκὸς ὑπὸ κρύους Clem.*paed*.3.9(p.263.10; M.8.617B); κλίσιν γονάτων κατεσκληκότων Gr.Naz.*or*.8.13(M.35.804C); ἄρτου οὐκ ὀδωδότος οὐδὲ κατεσκληκότος μετέλαβον Chrys.*ep*.120(3.661A); **2.** met.; **a.** *austere, ascetic* ἀπὸ τοῦ σεμνοτέρου καὶ κατεσκληκότος βίου ἦλθεν *εἰς τὴν ἡδονήν* †Dion.Al.*fr.Eccl.*2:1(p.214.2); *τὸ κατεσκληκός τε καὶ σύντονον τῆς ἀρετῆς* Gr.Nyss.*v.Mos.*(M.44.328B); Thdt.*Ps.*108:24(1.1388); **b.** *drawn, haggard τὸ κατεσκληκὸς τῆς ὄψεως Schol.*70 in Jo.Clim.*scal.*4(M.88.753C); **c.** *stubborn, obdurate,* Const.*or.s.c.*20(p.185.4; M.20.1297B); Cyr.*Nah.*3(3.477D); id.*glaph.Lev.*(1.358D).

κατασκέπτ-ομαι, = *κατασκοπέω,* **1.** *contemplate, examine μέχριπερ ἂν...δι' ἐπιστήμης κατασκέψηται τὸ ὄν* Meth.*symp.*8.11(p.94.10, v.l. *κατασκέπτηται* M.18.156A); *ψυχὴ λογικὴ ~ομένη τῷ νῷ τά τε ἤδη παρόντα καὶ πρός γε τούτοις τὰ συμβησόμενα* Cyr.*Pulch.*(p.58.29; 5[2].176B); *~εσθαι τὸ στερέωμα καὶ τὰ ἐν αὐτῷ* id.*Is.*4.5(2.707A); **2.** *regard μηδὲ ταπεινῶς ~ονται τὸν νοῦν τῶν ἐντολῶν* Meth.*symp.*4.5(p.50.25; M.18.93B).

κατασκευάζ-ω, **1.** *make, construct, prepare*; **a.** of God, in Creation *κόσμος...κατασκευή ἐστί τινος τεχνίτου· τὸ κατασκευασθὲν δὲ ἀρχὴν καὶ τέλος ἔχει* Arist.*apol.*4.2; *τοσαύτην ὕλην κατεσκεύασεν ὅσην ἠδύνατο διακοσμῆσαι* Or.*princ.*2.9.1(p.164.9; M.11.225D); *τὸ μηδέπω γεγενημένον ἐκ τοῦ μὴ ὄντος κατασκευάσαι* Meth.*res.*2.20(p.373.12; M.18.285A); ref. Gen.1:1,2 *τὸ...κατασκευάσαι καὶ τὸ ποιῆσαι οὐδὲν δοκεῖ διαφέρειν κατὰ τὴν ἔννοιαν* Gr.Nyss.*hex.*(M.44.65D); ref. Christ as second Adam *ὁ θεὸς...τὴν 'βοηθὸν' αὐτῷ ~ει, λέγω...τὰς ἡρμοσμένας αὐτῷ...ψυχάς* Meth.*symp.*3.8(p.36.19; M.18.73C); **b.** of Christ in Inc. *ἐν τῇ παρθένῳ ~ει ἑαυτῷ ναὸν τὸ σῶμα* Ath.*inc.*8.3(M.25.109C); **c.** of workmen, craftsmen *τὰ ἀνδροείκελα ~οντας ἀγάλματα* Meth.*symp.*2.7(p.24.17; 57C); Thdt.*Jer.*10:2(2.463); **d.** *make up* medicines, Arist.*apol.*10.5; Chrys.*hom.23.2 in Mt.*(7.285D); met. *τῇ νουθεσίᾳ χρὴ ἡδὺ ~ειν τὸ φάρμακον* id.*hom.10.2 in 1Thess.*(11.496E); **e.** met., *devise, produce τῇ ἀρνήσει τοῦ...Χριστοῦ τὸ καθ' ἑαυτῶν κατεσκεύασαν μῖσος* Thdt.*Ps.*80:16(1.1185); Gr.Ant.*bapt.*2.3(M.88.1873B); **2.** *furnish, supply, Diogn.*2.2; Or.*Cels.*1.5(p.58.26; M.11.664B); **3.** *bring it about that οὐ τὴν κτίσιν πάλιν προσκυνεῖσθαι παρασκευάσας, ἀλλὰ τὸν ποιητὴν...συνταχθῆναι τῇ κτίσει κατασκευάσας* Thdt.*h.e.*1.2.7(3.725); **4.** pass., *be conspired against Ζήνων...αἰτηθεὶς πρᾶγμα παρὰ...Βηρίνης, καὶ μὴ παρασχών, κατεσκευάσθη παρ' αὐτῆς Chron.Pasch.*p.325(M.92.832B); **5.** *discuss καὶ ταῦτα...αὐταρκῶς ἡμῖν κατασκευασθῶ περὶ τοῦ αὐτεξουσίου* Or.*princ.*3.1.24(p.244.3; M.11.301C); **6.** *establish, confirm καὶ ἀσκήσας κατασκευάσαι...~ων τὴν Χριστιανισμοῦ ἀληθότητα* Or.*Cels.*1.2(p.57.10; M.11.656A); **7.** in argument, *make out, affirm ~ων σαφῶς μὴ πάντας τοὺς ἀκούοντας τὸν λόγον κεχωρηκέναι τὸ μέγεθος τῆς γνώσεως* Clem.*str.*7.16(p.73.23; M.9.544B); Gr.Nyss.*fat.*(M.45.148B); Cyr.*Ps.*35:6(M.69.917C); **8.** *prove ἔκ τε τούτων ~ουσιν, ὡς νομίζουσιν, ἀδύνατον τὴν ἀνάστασιν* Athenag.*res.*4(p.52.24; M.6.981C); *κατασκευάσαι περὶ τῆς τῶν ἀλόγων ζῴων ψυχῆς ὡς θειοτέρας* Or.*Cels.*4.89(p.361.5; M.11.1165A); *οἴεται ἐντεῦθεν ~εσθαι τῇ οὐσίᾳ μὴ διεστηκέναι τοῦ υἱοῦ τὸν πατέρα* id.*Jo.*2.23(18; p.80.3; M.14.153C); *ὅρα ἐκ πόσων αὐτὸ ~ει* Chrys.*hom.2.1 in Philm.*(11.780D); *οὐ ~ει διὰ τί οὐ πολλῷ μᾶλλον* id.*hom.21.4 in 1Cor.*(10.185A); **9.** *construct an argument, solution,* etc., *Hom.Clem.*1.19; Chrys.*hom.3.3 in Heb.*(12.29B).

***κατασκεύασις,** ἡ, **1.** *making, manufacture,* Meth.*res.*1.29(M.41.1137D; *κατασκευάζονται* p.261.5); **2.** *apparatus,* Gr.Nyss.*Eun.*12(1 p.271.4; M.45.977A).

κατασκεύασμα, τό, **1.** *structure*; of the human body, ‡Bas.*struct.hom.*1.1(1.324E; M.30.12C); **2.** *arrangement, transaction,* CNic.(325) *can.*15; **3.** *argument, reasoning,* Cyr.*thes.*31(5[1].260E).

***κατασκευαστέον,** **1.** *one must maintain, contend κ. ὅτι οὐκ Αἰγύπτιοι ἦσαν οἱ ἐξεληλυθότες* Or.*Cels.*3.8(p.208.20; M.11.929B); **2.** *one must prove κ. ... ἀπὸ τῶν θείων γραφῶν τὰ εἰρημένα τοῦτον τὸν τρόπον* id.*or.*9.1(p.317.28; M.11.441D); id.*Cels.*3.22(p.218.31; 945A); *ib.*7.59(p.208.27; 1505A).

κατασκευαστής, ὁ, *creator, maker*; of God, Tat.*orat.*4(p.5.3; M.6.813A); *ὁ δὲ λόγος...θεὸς ἐν σαρκὶ...καὶ κ. ἐν τῷ κατασκευασθέντι ὑπ' αὐτοῦ* Ath.*Ar.*2.10(M.26.168C); Leont.H.*Nest.*1.19(M.86.1480C).

κατασκευαστικός, **1.** *creative αὐτὸν* [sc. *Χριστόν*]*...οὐρανοῦ δημιουργικόν, κόσμου κ.* Eus.*d.e.*4.4(p.155.4; M.22.257D); *τίς ἀπέδειξε λόγος ἐνεργείᾳ τινὶ κ. τὸν υἱὸν ὑποστῆναι;* Gr.Nyss.*Eun.*4(2 p.78.10; M.45.652C); **2.** *causing, productive of ταῦτα τοίνυν ἐστὶ φόβος καὶ ἐπιείκεια, ἀμφότερα εἰρήνης κ.* Adam.*dial.*1.15(p.32.14; M.11.1741A); Bas.*hex.*2.4(1.16A; M.29.37B); *αὐτὸν* [sc. *τὸν νόμον*] *ὄντα δείκνυσι τῆς ἁμαρτίας...κ.* Chrys.*hom.12.4 in Rom.*(9.548C); **3.** *tending to prove, establish οἴεται δὲ τοῦτο ὁ Κέλσος κατασκευαστικὸν εἶναι τοῦ μηδὲν τούτων ἔργον εἶναι θεοῦ* Or.*Cels.*4.57(p.330.19; M.11.1124B); *κ. λόγον τῆς ἀναστάσεως* ‡Just.*qu.Gr.*proem.15(M.6.1465C); Chrys.*hom.49.2 in Mt.*(7.505E); **4.** *of argument, reasoning οὐδὲ κ. δεῖ λόγων, ἀλλ' ἀρκεῖ καὶ ἀπαγορεῦσαι μόνον* Chrys.*comm.in Gal.*2:17(10.691D).

κατασκευαστικῶς, *by argument, by proof,* Chrys.*hom.3.3 in 1Cor.*(10.19C).

κατασκευαστός, *created, artificial* (Eunomian) *κ. ἐστι τοῦ υἱοῦ ἡ σημασία· γέννησιν δὲ τὴν κατασκευὴν ὀνομάζει* Gr.Nyss.*Eun.*4(2 p.96.12; M.45.673A).

κατασκευή, **A.** *preparation, construction, fabrication*; **1.** of Creation *ὁ...λόγος πρὸ τῆς τῶν ἀνθρώπων κ. ἀγγέλων δημιουργὸς γίνεται* Tat.*orat.*7(p.7.11; M.6.820B); *τοιαύτης...τῆς κ. τοῦ κόσμου γενομένης, παρ' αὐτοῖς* Hipp.*haer.*6.14(p.139.28; M.16.3214C); *εἶναί τινα οὐ τῇ ὑποστάσει ἐκ κ., ἀλλὰ ἐκ μεταβολῆς καὶ ἰδίας προαιρέσεως* Or.*Jo.*20.21(19; p.353.23; M.14.617D); Meth.*Porph.*1(p.505.3; M.18.400D); *τίς ἦν χρεία τῆς τοῦ ἡλίου κ.;* Gr.Nyss.*hex.*5(M.44.65C); Cyr.*Is.*3.2(2.432A); id.*Ps.*29:8(M.69.856C); employed by Eunomius to denote origin of Son, opp. *γέννησις,* Gr.Nyss.*Eun.*4(2 p.70.12,18; M.45.644A,B); *τῇ τῆς γεννήσεως λέξει τῆς κ. δηλουμένης ib.*(p.96.17; 673A); cf. B.2; **2.** *putting together, arrangement, compilation* of literary material *ἕκαστος οἰκείαις μεθόδοις τὴν...κ. πεποιημένος* Eus.*p.e.*10.9(487C; M.21.812A); *οὐκ ἀπέχρη τούτων ἕκαστος εἰς μιᾶς βίβλου ...κ.* Thdt.*xii proph.proem.*(2.1309); **3.** medical *treatment,* Chrys.*hom.2.1 in 1Tim.*(11.555D); **4.** moral *formation, training εἰς δικαιοσύνης κ.* Meth.*symp.*3.13(p.42.3; M.18.81B); Alex.Lyc.*Man.*1(p.3.2; M.18.412C); *ἡ ἐπερώτησις οὐκ ἐξ ἀγνοίας, ἀλλὰ πρὸς...τὴν οἰκείαν τῶν ἀκροατῶν κ.* Vict.*Mc.*4:34(p.312.4).

B. in concrete sense; **1.** *creation, construction, work* of artist or craftsman *κόσμος...κ. ἐστι τινὸς τεχνίτου* Arist.*apol.*4.2; **2.** *structure, formation, constitution κόσμου μὲν γὰρ ἡ κ. καλή, τὸ δὲ ἐν αὐτῷ πολίτευμα φαῦλον* Tat.*orat.*19(p.21.11; M.6.849A); *τὰς ὁρμὰς καὶ... φύσεις τῶν ζῴων καὶ τὰς κ. τῶν σωμάτων* Or.*princ.*4.1.7(p.303.12; M.11.353C); *ib.*3.1.5(p.200.5; 253B); Diod.*Gen.*3:8(M.33.1568C); *οὗτοι* [sc. *οἱ ἄνθρωποι*] *τῇ κ. συνεσπαρμένον ἔχουσι τὸ θεῖον* ‡Nil.*perist.*9.6(M.79.876C); esp. of the original nature of anything as created *ἀφωρίζετο...οὐ διὰ τὴν φύσιν ἔχουσάν τι ἐξαίρετον καὶ ὅσον ἐπὶ τῇ κ. ὑπὲρ τὰς τῶν μὴ τοιούτων φύσεις* Or.*comm.in Rom.*1:1(*JTS* 13 p.213); *εἰσάγειν τοὺς ἐκ κ. καὶ φύσεως σωζομένους ib.*(p.210); id.*Cels.*5.61(p.64.25f.; M.11.1277B); id.*princ.*3.1.18(p.229.11; 288A); *ib.*3.1.21(p.238.7; 297A); theol.: heret. of Son *αὐτοῦ τοῦ μονογενοῦς ἡ κ. κατὰ τὸν ἐκείνου λόγον τῆς ἐνεργείας ἐκείνης ἤρτηται* Gr.Nyss.*Eun.*1(1 p.94.19; M.45.328A); of H. Ghost *τοῦ μὲν πατρὸς ὡς τὴν αἰτίαν τῆς κ. ὑποβαλόντος, τοῦ δὲ μονογενοῦς ὡς αὐτουργήσαντος αὐτοῦ τὴν ὑπόστασιν ib.*(1 p.81.13; 312D); of Christ *τί...βούλεται καὶ τὸ ἑτεροίαν φάσκειν τὴν κ. τοῦ Ἰησοῦ Χριστοῦ τῆς ἡμετέρας;* Paul.Sam.*fr.*17(p.79.8)ap.Leont.B.*Nest.et Eut.*3 suppl.(M.86.1393A); cf. *μὴ τοῦτο ἔστι τὸ σκοπούμενον, πότερον ἑνώσει ἢ κ. φύσεως ἄφθαρτον γέγονεν* [sc. Christ's body] Leont.B.*Nest.et Eut.*2(1325C); of Christ's human soul *ἔζησεν τὸ σῶμα θεότητος ἁγιασμῷ καὶ οὐκ ἀνθρωπίνης ψυχῆς κατασκευῇ* Apoll.*corp.et div.*12(p.190.19; M.*PL*.8.875A); **3.** *occasion εἰς κ. ἐρωτήσεως τὸν παρὰ τοῦ Χριστοῦ λόγον λαμβάνει* [sc. Samaritan woman] Chrys.*hom.31.4 in Jo.*(8.180C).

C. of particular qualities of action; **1.** *art, craftsmanship,* Tat.*orat.*34(p.35.21; M.6.876B); *ἡ τέχνη δημιουργεῖ τὴν ὑποκειμένην ὕλην, εἰ δέξεται τὴν κ.* Meth.*symp.*2.5(p.22.10; M.18.56B); **2.** in bad sense, *plot κατασκευὰς τυρεύοντες ἐπισκόποις ἢ συγκληρικοῖς* CChalc.*can.*18.

D. *evidence, argument τὴν...διδασκαλίαν μετὰ κ. ποικίλης, πῇ μὲν τῆς ἀπὸ τῶν γραφῶν, πῇ δὲ καὶ ἀπὸ τοῦ εἰκότος λόγου* Or.*Cels.*3.16(p.214.25; M.11.940B); id.*Jo.*13.61(59; p.293.8; M.14.516B); *μετὰ πολλὰς ἀπορίας καὶ κ. καὶ ἀποδείξεις αὐτὴν* [sc. *τὴν λύσιν*] *τέθεικε* Chrys.*hom.16.10 in Rom.*(9.620A); *ib.*12.2(544C, v.l. *κατασκευάσματα*); opp. *ἀπόφασις: τοῦτο οὐκ ἔστι κ. ... ἀλλ' ἀπόφασις ib.*19.3(635A); *οὐδὲ κ. δεῖται, ἀλλ' ἀρκεῖται τῇ ἀποφάσει ib.*26.1(712D); id.*hom.12.2 in 1Tim.*(11.612B); id.*hom.32.1 in Jo.*(8.185C); cf. *χωρὶς πάσης κ. ...ἀποφαίνεται* Or.*Jo.*6.6.60(38; p.168.29; 304C); c. genit., *evidence* or *argument for, confirmation of μεγάλη κ. ἐστι τοῦ...Ἰησοῦν υἱὸν εἶναι θεοῦ* id.*Cels.*6.76(p.146.1; 1413B); *ἥρπασεν ὁ αἱρετικὸς πρὸς τὴν ἰδίαν κ. τῆς βλασφημίας* Bas.*hom.*23.4(2.188A; M.31.596D); Gr.Nyss.*or.catech.*34(p.126.9; M.45.85A); c. *πρός: πόσην ἔχει τὸ χωρίον τοῦτο κ. πρὸς τὴν τῶν μελλόντων ἐλπίδα* Chrys.*hom.9.3 in Rom.*(9.515D).

κατάσκεψις, ἡ, *careful investigation* or *examination ἀκριβῆ τὴν κ. ἔσεσθαι...τὴν ἐν ἁμαρτίαις κατειλημμένων* Cyr.*Is.*2.5(2.341B); id.*Ps.*38:5(M.69.973A).

κατασκέω, perf. pass.; **1.** *be trained, educated highly οὐδεὶς...τῶν πάνυ κατησκημένων τὸν νοῦν, καὶ περὶ τὴν...ῥέουσαν φύσιν ὀξυωπούντων* Bas.*hex.*3.5(1.26E; M.29.64B); **2.** ptcpl., *ascetic ὃν ἐκ παιδὸς... πρὸς τὴν ὀρθότητα καὶ τὸν κ. βίον τῷ τόνῳ χρώμενον* id.*ep.*291(3.429E; M.32.1032A).

κατασκηνάω, = *κατασκηνόω,* Synes.*calv.*7(p.204.1).

κατασκην-όω, **A.** *encamp*; hence *dwell*; **1.** of the divinity in the human body of Christ, Hipp.*fr.2 in Jo.*19:33–34(p.211.10) ap.Thdt.*eran*.3(4.233); τὸ σῶμα τοῦ Χριστοῦ...ἐν ᾧ...ἡ θεότης τοῦ μονογενοῦς κατεσκήνωσεν Eus.*d.e*.7.2(p.334.26; M.22.545C); **2.** of God; **a.** in the society of the elect: Jewish ἐν τῷ ~οῦν τὸ ὄνομά σου ἐν μέσῳ ἡμῶν *Pss.Sal*.7.5; Christian εὔχομαι...ἵνα εἰς πάντας κ. ὁ λόγος τοῦ θεοῦ *A.Thom*.A 88(p.203.7); κατασκηνώσει...ἁγίων ἐν μέσῳ Thdt.*Ezech*.43:7(2.1028); in heaven, Oecum.*Apoc*.7:15(p.101); **b.** in individuals, Synes.*calv*.7(M.66.1180C; p.204.1 κατεσκηνηκέναι); τοῦ...ἁγίου πνεύματος εἰς ἡμᾶς ~οῦντος Diad.*perf*.78(p.98.14); τὴν...χάριν εἰς τὸ βάθος τοῦ νοῦ κατεσκηνωκέναι *ib*.33(p.38.15); *ib*.79(p.100.11); **3.** of Christ with mankind in Inc. Ἰησοῦς ὁ κ. ἐν ἡμῖν Iren. *haer*.1.9.3(M.7.541B); κύριος...ὁ παραγενόμενος εἰς τὸν κόσμον, καὶ κατασκηνώσας ἐν ἀνθρώποις *Rit.Bapt*.(p.391); **4.** of various gifts and graces οἱ λόγοι μου ἐν σοὶ κ. Nil.*epp*.2.41(M.79.216B); παρθενίαν ἐν τῷ ἰδίῳ σώματι ~ῶσαι ἐκδεχόμενος Marc.Er.*opusc*.5.7(M.65.1040B).

B. trans.; **1.** *dwell in, inhabit* ψυχὴν...ἀνθρωπείαν...ἡγούμενοι εἶναι τὴν τὸ σῶμα Ἰησοῦ ~οῦσαν Eus.*d.e*.10.8(p.485.18; M.22.780C); of Christ in BMV, ‡Gr.Naz.*Chr.pat*.574(M.38.182A); **2.** *cause to indwell* ὑπὲρ τοῦ ἁγίου ὀνόματός σου, οὗ κατεσκήνωσας ἐν ταῖς καρδίαις ἡμῶν *Did*.10.2; *A.Thom*.A 149(p.258.19).

C. *dwell in peace, abide*, *1Clem*.58.1; τὸν ὀρθῶς παιδαγωγούμενον, ἐφ' ὃν ἡ εἰρήνη κατεσκήνωσεν Clem.*paed*.3.3(p.250.1; M.8.588A).

κατασκήνωσις, ἡ, *dwelling, abiding* θεὸς ἁγίων...οὗ ἀμετανάστευτος ἡ κ. *Const.App*.7.35.9; of God with men; **a.** in Inc. τὴν τοῦ Χριστοῦ γέννησιν καὶ τὴν τοῦ θεοῦ Ἰακὼβ κ. Eus.*d.e*.7.2(p.334.23; M.22.545C); Gr.Nyss.*Apoll*.51(M.45.1245C); of the Word in BMV, Marc.Er. *opusc*.5.9(M.65.1044B); **b.** in heaven ἀναμένειν τοῦ θεοῦ τὴν κ. Thdt. *Ezech*.43:7(2.1028); τὴν...κ. τοῦ θεοῦ, ἔφη τις τῶν ἁγίων, τὸ ἀδιάλειπτον αὐτοῦ μνήμην παραμένειν ταῖς τῶν ἁγίων ψυχαῖς Oecum.*Apoc*. 7:15(p.101).

κατασκιάζ-ω, **1.** *overshadow*; met., *obscure, veil, disguise*, Cyr. *Os*.65(3.98C); ἔθος...τοῖς...προφήταις...τοῦ κατ' αὐτὸν [sc. Χριστόν] μυστηρίου ποιεῖσθαι τὴν ἀφήγησιν, ἀσαφείαις ἔτι κατεσκιασμένην id.*Am*.75(3.335E); τὸ τῶν προσώπων κ. ἄνθος Thdt.*Is*.13:8(2.262; κατασβέσουσιν p.66.31); **2.** *cover*; **a.** med., oneself ᾧ [sc. ἁγνείας φύτῳ]...δεῖ ~εσθαι τὰς ὀσφύας Meth.*symp*.9.4(p.119.11; M.18.188A); **b.** *cover up, conceal* κρύπτοντας τὴν πονηρίαν, καὶ...κ. τὸ κακόν Cyr. *Ps*.9:28(M.69.784A).

***κατασκίασμα**, τό, *shadow, obscurity*; met., ref. old dispensation, Cyr.*ador*.12(1.450B); *ib*.6(215E); id.*glaph.Ex*.2(1.305C); of literal sense of Law, obscuring its typological meaning ἐτίθει...ὁ Μωσῆς χρησίμως...τὸ κάλυμμα. κ. γὰρ ὁ νόμος ἔχει τὸ παχὺ τοῦ γράμματος *ib*.3(341E); id.*ador*.7(223E).

***κατασκιασμός**, ὁ, *overshadowing* οὐκ ἀμαυρώσει τοῦτο [sc. the body of BMV] ζόφου κ. Germ.CP *or*.8(M.98.361C).

κατασκίδναμαι, pass. of κατασκεδάννυμι, *be diffused, spread abroad* over or among κ. τοῦ λαοῦ Cyr.*glaph.Ex*.3(1.322E).

***κατασκοπευτήριον**, τό, *watch-tower*; of the new Jerusalem, *M.Areth*.(p.36).

κατασκοπεύω, = κατασκοπέω 1, *1Clem*.12.2; *T.Sal*.10.6(p.38.14).

κατασκοπέω, **1.** *spy out, reconnoitre*; **2.** *watch, contemplate*, Clem. *paed*.1.5(p.103.2; M.8.276A).

κατασκόπησις, ἡ, *spying*, Jo.Disc.*v.Epiph*.32(M.41.63D).

κατάσκοπος, ὁ, **1.** *one sent on reconnaissance*; *spy*; fig., of apostles as typified by Joshua's spies τοῦ Χριστοῦ τοὺς ἀποστόλους ἐδέξατο...καὶ ἐπὶ τὸ δῶμα τούτους ἀνήγαγεν· οὐδεὶς γὰρ κ. Ἰησοῦ δύναται...μεῖναι κάτω Or.*hom.3.4 in Jos*.(p.305.28; M.87.1000B); of heretical bishops (a play upon ἐπίσκοπος) οἱ παρ' αὐτοῖς κ., οὐ γὰρ ἐπίσκοποι Ath.*h.Ar*.3(p.184.24; M.25.697C); *ib*.48(p.211.13; 753A); of other heretics or perh. iron., *inquisitor, busy-body*, Gr.Naz.*or*. 27.2(p.3.14; M.36.13B); **2.** *observer* τάχα...Σαμουὴλ...γέγονεν ἐν ᾅδου...ἵνα γένηται κ. καὶ θεωρητὴς τῶν μυστηρίων τῶν καταχθονίων Or.*hom.18.2 in Jer*.(p.152.31; M.13.465C); Bas.*hom*.13.1(2.114C; M. 31.425B); in an official capacity ἀπέστειλα Διονύσιον...ὃς...τῶν πραττομένων...τῆς εὐταξίας κ. παρέσται Const.ap.Eus.*v.C*.4.42(p.134. 30; M.20.1192B); **3.** *look-out man* λέγει σκοπόν...τὸν κ. ... ἐκεῖνος θεασάμενος ἐπιοῦσαν τὴν στρατείαν σημάνῃ τῇ σάλπιγγι Thdt.*Ezech*. 33:2ff.(2.954).

***κατασκοτέω**, s.v.l., = κατασκοτίζω, Cyr.*ador*.1(1.36A, perh. κατασκοτίζειν); cf.*ib*.(36E).

κατασκοτίζ-ω, *veil in darkness, obscure*, met. ἡ νὺξ ἐκείνη τῷ τῆς ἀπάτης γνόφῳ τὰ πάντα κ. Gr.Naz.*or*.35.2(M.36.260A); Cyr.*Nah*.20 (3.499B); σχολαίῳ...νῷ καὶ βεβηκότι μακρὰν τοῦ ~εσθαι κοσμικῶς... θύσομεν...τῷ θεῷ id.*ador*.1(1.36E).

κατασκυθρωπάζω, *look gloomy*; ref. persons fasting, Bas.*hom*.1.1 (2.2A; M.31.164A).

***κατασκύλλω**, **1.** *disarrange, make dishevelled*; a coiffure, Clem. *paed*.3.11(p.271.17; M.8.637A); **2.** *harass*, Chrys.(et Olymp.)*fr.Job* 16:8(M.64.617C).

κατασκώπτω, *mock, jeer at*, Cyr.*Ps*.9:24(M.69.780C); perf. ptcpl. pass., *despised*, id.*ador*.12(1.414A).

κατασμικρύν-ω, **1.** *lessen, detract from* ἐν προσποιήσει...τοῦ ὕψουν ...τὸν...πατέρα, τοῦ...υἱοῦ...τὴν δόξαν κ. Bas.*Eun*.1.26(1.237B; M.29. 569B); μήτε τῷ πατρὶ τὸ τῆς ἀρχῆς κ. ἀξίωμα Gr.Naz.*or*.20.6(M.35. 1072C); Nil.*epp*.2.323(M.79.357D); Christol. οὔτε τὴν θείαν αὐτοῦ κ. φύσιν τε καὶ δόξαν διὰ τὰ ἀνθρώπινα Cyr.*apol.Thdt*.4(p.125.25; 6¹. 219D); **2.** *belittle, disparage* πῶς κ. τοῖς βρεφικοῖς ἐπιχειρήμασι τὴν ἄφραστον τοῦ κυρίου μεγαλειότητα; Gr.Nyss.*Apoll*.28(M.45.1185B); διὰ τῆς τῶν δρωμένων ὑπεροχῆς εἰς ἐννοίας ἀναθρώσκειν τὰς ἐπ' αὐτῷ τοὺς ἀκροωμένους ἠθέλησε, ~ούσης αὐτὸν...τῆς ὁρωμένης σαρκός Cyr. *inc.unigen*.(5¹.702E); id.*Jo*.4.1(4.344E); **3.** pass., *fall short* of κ. τῆς τελειότητος Eulog.*fr.Novat*.ap.Phot.*cod*.280(M.104.344B).

***κατασμυρνόω**, *anoint with myrrh*, of athletes, met. οἱ μεγάλοι τῆς πίστεως πρόμαχοι...ἐν τοῖς ὑπὲρ εὐσεβείας ἀγῶσι κατεσμυρνώθησαν Gr.Nyss.*hom.14 in Cant*.(M.44.1068B).

κατασοβέω, **1.** *drive away*; c. genit., Cyr.*Os*.152(3.185D); usu. c. acc., id.*Jo*.3.4(4.269E); met. ταῖς μιαραῖς ἀντιπνοίαις τῶν ἔργων ἡμῶν τὴν φωτιστικὴν αὐτοῦ [sc. πνεύματος] φλόγα κ. *Schol.Clem.paed*.3.12 (p.339.25; M.9.794B); τὴν ἀρρωστίαν ἑνὶ κ. λόγῳ Cyr.*Jo*.3.4(4.278B); **2.** *frighten into, drive to* ἡ προαναφώνησις τοῦ θηρὸς κ. πρὸς φυγὴν Cyr. *Am*.27(3.277C); c. εἰς, id.*ador*.6(1.174C).

κατασοφίζομαι, **1.** persons, *outwit by sophisms* or *fallacies*; pass., in gen., *be tricked, let down*, Gr.Naz.*ep*.203(M.37.336B); **2.** things; **a.** *deal sophistically with, evade* οὐ χρὴ τὰ περὶ τοῦ...πνεύματος λόγια ...κ. Didym.*Trin*.2.3(M.39.480A); Marc.Er.*opusc*.1.36(M.65.909D); Cyr.*Jo*.3.5(4.301B); **b.** *explain away*; *misrepresent*, Eustrat.*stat. anim*.18(p.491); **c.** in good sense, *get the best out of*; *turn to good account* Ῥαχὴλ...ἀπορουμένη, τὸ τῆς ἀπαιδίας κ. χρῆμα Cyr.*glaph. Gen*.4(1.130D); κ. ... τὴν γραφὴν [sc. the inscription ἀγνώστῳ θεῷ] ὁ θεσπέσιος Παῦλος *ib*.(123C); **3.** *be made wise*; *understand, learn* κ. ὅτι τὰ δύο πνεύματα ταῦτα ἐδύναντο *T.Sal*.24.2(p.70.8); κ. ὅτι καὶ τὴν Εὐὰν μετὰ τοῦ Ἀδὰμ ἐγερεῖ ‡Tit.Bost.*palm*.2(M.18.1265C); εἶδον... καὶ ἔμαθον, καὶ κατεσοφίσθησαν σοφίαν *ib*.(1265B).

κατασοφιστεύω, = κατασοφίζομαι 1, Gr.Naz.*ep*.190(M.37.309A).

***κατάσοφος**, *very wise*, Jo.Not.*v.Eus*.3(M.86.309B).

κατασπάζ-ομαι, *embrace, kiss*; as an act of veneration, Sophr.H. *v.Anast*.(M.92.1713B,1720C); προσκυνοῦντες τὴν τοῦ δι' ἡμᾶς σαρκωθέντος μορφὴν...ὡς εἰκόνα τοῦ σαρκωθέντος θεοῦ κ. ... ὡσαύτως...καὶ τὸν τόπον τοῦ...σταυροῦ πίστει προσκυνῶν ~ου †Jo.D.*B.J*.19(M.96. 1032B,C); met., Bas.*hex*.4.6(1.38E; M.29.92B).

κατασπαταλάω, *live wantonly*, Gr.Naz.*or*.44.9(M.36.617A); Areth. *Apoc*.55(M.106.728D).

κατασπ-άω, **1.** *draw* or *pull down*; perf. ptcpl. pass., *stunted*, ‡Hipp.Th.*fr*.21(p.55.12); **2.** *draw down into oneself, absorb*, Hipp. *haer*.5.19(p.117.11; M.16.3179C); *ib*.10.11(p.271.3; 3423B); *ib*.10.16 (p.278.2; 3434B); **3.** ? *drag out* or *drive out*, Hipp.*Dan*.4.50.4; **4.** met.; **a.** *drag down, debase, degrade* τοῖς...τὴν τοῦ ἀγαθοῦ προσηγορίαν ~ῶσιν...ἀπὸ τῆς ἀρετῆς...ἐπὶ τὸν τυφλὸν πλοῦτον Or.*Cels*. 1.24(p.75.15; M.11.705B); Meth.*symp*.11(p.140.15; M.18.220B); *ib*.4. 2(p.47.17; 89A); *Hom.Clem*.13.18; *drag down to earth* τοὺς ἀνθρώπους κ. ... ἀπὸ τῆς περὶ θεοῦ ἐννοίας Or.*Cels*.4.32(p.302.16; M.11.1076D); *ib*.7.64(p.214.6; 1512B); *ib*.8.62(p.278.6; 1609B); τῆς εὐχῆς τὸ ὄμμα κ. Nil.*tract*.29(M.79.1132D); pass. κ. τὸ διὰ τῆς πίστεως ἀναγόμενον Clem. *str*.7.7(p.35.8; M.9.468A); Or.*Cels*.4.97(p.371.1; 1177A); *ib*.6.44(p.115. 27; 1368B); **b.** *bring down, abase* κ. τοῦ διαβόλου τὴν μανίαν Chrys. *hom.57.4 in Mt*.(7.581D); id.*hom.1.1 in Philm*.(11.774D); **c.** *subdue, repress* ὥστε...αἰρομένας κ. καὶ κωλύειν τὰς φήμας τὰς οὐκ ἀγαθάς Chrys.*sac*.6.9(p.158.12; 1.429B); *V.Dan*.(p.259.10); **d.** *draw along, bring* τὴν νηπιότητα...πρὸς τὴν τελειότητα κ. Mac.Aeg.*pat*.11(M.34. 873D).

κατασπείρω, **1.** *sow, plant*; met., *implant*, Marc.Er.*opusc*.3(M.65. 965D); Isid.Pel.*epp*.2.46(M.78.488D); ὁ κύριος...τῇ φύσει τῶν ἀνθρώπων τὰς τῆς ἀναστάσεως ἐλπίδας κ. Thdt.*provid*.10(4.672); **2.** *distribute* τοῦτο κερματίσας, ταῖς...Περσικαῖς κ. δυνάμεσιν Thphyl.*exc.gent*.8 (p.485.33; M.113.948B); **3.** *sprinkle with*, Chrys.*hom.2.3 in 1Tim*. (11.559C).

κατασπιλάζω, *break* or *burst suddenly upon* like a storm, ‡Chrys. *hom*.6(13.213E); ‡Nil.*perist*.11.3(M.79.905C); Cyr.*Is*.2.3(2.271A); id. *Juln*.6(6².185D).

***κατασπιλόω**, *stain, defile* ὁ σατανᾶς...αὐτοὺς...κ. ... τοῖς κακοῖς Cyr.*Jo*.3.6(4.325B); κ. μὲν τὴν σάρκα τὰ...πάθη, ψυχήν τε καὶ νοῦν id. *ador*.15(1.544B); *ib*.(535C); Andr.Cr.*can.mag*.2(M.97.1340C); pass.

κατεσπιλώθη τῷ ἁμαρτήματι †Bas.*Is*.44(1.414C; M.30.204A); Gr. Nyss.*v.Mos*.(M.44.376C); Nil.*epp*.3.195(M.79.473B).

***καταστοδόω**, *cover with ashes*, *Asen*.13(p.57.12); Thdt.ap.Proc. G.*Cant*.1:4(M.87.1553D).

κατασπορεύς, ὁ, *sower*, ‡Ath.*sem*.3(M.28.148A).

κατασπουδάζω, **1.** *be zealous, direct one's efforts against*, Gr.Naz. *or*.30.13(p.130.6; M.36.121B); **2.** *urge on, make to hurry*, *Apoc.En*. 14.8(p.38.12).

***κατασταθμάζω**, *appoint*, Or.*schol.in Mt*.24:45(M.17.301C).

***κατασταλάζω**, *let fall like rain* or *dew*; met., Germ.CP *or*.8(M. 98.368D).

καταστασιάζω, **1.** *make a disturbance* among κ. αὐτῶν Hipp. *haer*.9.12(p.247.13; M.16.3382B); **2.** of troops, *mutiny* against κ. τοῦ στρατηγοῦ Thphyl.*exc.Rom*.5(p.225.31; M.113.933B); **3.** pass., *be thrown into confusion*, Hipp.*haer*. l.c.

κατάστασις, ἡ, **A.** trans. senses; **1.** *establishment*; *appointment*, eccl.; in gen. τὴν...κ. τοῦ Ματθία...καὶ τὴν κ. τῶν ἑπτὰ διακόνων Euthal.Diac.*Ac*.(M.85.645B); περὶ καταστάσεως ἐπισκόπων καὶ πρεσβυτέρων, καὶ διακόνων *ib*.(781A); of consecration of bishops Εὐσέβιος τὴν κ. Ἀθανασίου μέμφεται, ἄνθρωπος τάχα μηδὲ κ. ὅλως ἐσχηκώς CAlex.*ep*.ap.Ath.*apol.sec*.6(p.92.29; M.25.260B); CAnt.(341)*can*.19; οὐδὲ ἠρνοῦντο τὸν Πιστὸν ὑπὸ Σεκούνδου ἐσχηκέναι τὴν κ. ... ἀδύνατον...τὴν κ. Σεκούνδου τοῦ Ἀρειανοῦ ἐν τῇ καθολικῇ ἐκκλησίᾳ ἰσχῦσαι Jul.Papa *ep.Dian*.ap.Ath.*apol.sec*.24(p.105.15,23; 289A); CSard.*can*. 10; ἐξ ἐμπορίας καὶ προστασίας αἱ κ. γίγνονται Ath.*ep.encycl*.2(p.171. 20; M.25.228A); Epiph.*haer*.68.7(p.147.15; M.42.196A); εἰ οἶσθα τὸν τρόπον τῆς κ. Πορφυρίου...ἢ τοὺς καταστήσαντας Pall.*v.Chrys*.16(p.93. 16; M.47.53); of election of a bishop ἡ...συμφωνία...ἐν τῇ σῇ κ. Ath.*ep.Drac*.1(M.25.524B); of a temporary appointment to a see, Gr.Naz.*ep*.139(M.37.236B); of ordination of priests χειροθεσία καταστάσεως πρεσβυτέρων Serap.*euch*.27 tit.; deacons διάκονοι...παρ' αὐτὴν τὴν κ. εἰ ἐμαρτύραντο καὶ ἔφασαν χρῆναι γαμῆσαι CAnc.(314) *can*.10; **2.** *control, direction* Ζεφυρῖνος συναράμενον αὐτὸν σχὼν πρὸς τὴν κ. τοῦ κλήρου Hipp.*haer*.9.12(p.248.12; M.16.3383B); *authority* οὐδὲ ἰσότυπον ἅπασιν εἶχε [sc. S. Peter] τὴν κ. Chrys.*hom.3.3 in Ac*. (9.26C); **3.** *settlement, establishment of order* οἱ...ἄρχοντες, οὓς ἔπεμψεν ὁ βασιλεὺς πρὸς κ. †Leont.B.*sect*.6.2(M.86.1236A); μεγάλην ἐποίησεν κ. ἐν Κωνσταντινουπόλει...πέμψας θείας σάκρας ὥστε τιμωρηθῆναι τοὺς ἀταξίας...ποιοῦντας *Chron.Pasch*.p.334(M.92.865B).

B. intrans. senses; **1.** *settled, orderly condition, peace* τῇ τοῦ κόσμου κ. Or.*or*.6(p.313.15; M.11.437A); τῇ παρούσῃ κ. τῆς ἐκκλησίας Gr.Naz.*ep*.168(M.37.277C); δὸς χεῖρα τῇ κοινῇ κ. *ib*.133(229A); of the individual, *tranquillity, composure* ὢ ἁγνεία...πλήρης εἰρήνης καὶ κ. Ephr.2.132E; ἐν πολλῇ κ. ἀνακρινόμενος τὸν στίχον *ib*.3.233C; οἱ προσερχόμενοι τῷ κυρίῳ ὀφείλουσι τὰς εὐχὰς ἐν ἡσυχίᾳ καὶ εἰρήνῃ καὶ κ. πολλῇ ποιεῖσθαι Mac.Aeg.*hom*.6.1(M.34.517C); Chrys.*Stag*.3.5(1. 211C); ἡ...προφήτης...μετὰ διανοίας νηφούσης καὶ σωφροσύνης καὶ κ. id.*hom.29.2 in 1Cor*.(10.259D; σωφρονούσης κ. Gaume); id.*hom. 16.3 in Eph*.(11.119E); ὀργὴ καταστάσεως ἀνασκευὴ †Nil.*vit*.3(M.79. 1144A); *sober senses, normal state*; *right mind* ὥσπερ οὐδὲ τὸν διάβολον...αὐτοψίᾳ, ἐν κ. ὤν, ἑωρακέναι, ἀλλ' ἐν ἐκστάσει Just.*dial*. 115.3(M.6.741B); of one exorcised, Gr.Nyss.*v.Gr.Thaum*.(M.46. 941D); **2.** in gen., *condition, state*; **a.** of Father ἐν ὁποίᾳ...ἦν...κ. ὁ θεός, μὴ ἔχων ἐν ἑαυτῷ τὸν οἰκεῖον λόγον; Eus.*e.th*.2.9(p.108.12; M.24. 916C); **b.** of Son ἐν τῇ κ. ὢν τῇ πρὸ τοῦ κενῶσαι ἑαυτόν Or.*Jo*.10.10 (8; p.180.9; M.14.321D); οὗτοι...δώσουσιν...τὸν υἱὸν τόπον ἐκ τόπου ἀμείψαντα...καὶ οὐχὶ κ. ἐκ κ., ὥσπερ ἡμεῖς ἐξειλήφαμεν *ib*.20.18(16; p.351.13; 614D); **c.** of Christ ὁ σωτὴρ...τὰ...ἄλλα ὑπέμεινεν ἔτι ὢν ἐν σαρκὶ καὶ φαινόμενος κατὰ τὴν ἀνθρωπίνην κ. Ant.Ptol.*Adam*. (p.652); **d.** of angelic beings ἐξ ἀγγελικῆς μὲν κ. καὶ ἀρχαγγελικῆς ψυχικὴν κ. γίνεσθαι, ἐκ δὲ ψυχικῆς δαιμονιώδη καὶ ἀνθρωπίνην Or. *princ*.2.8.3(p.160.8); Dor.*doct*.2.2(M.88.1644B); **e.** of mental or moral state of individuals οἶμαι νοεῖσθαι θεοῦ...βασιλείαν τὴν μακαρίαν τοῦ ἡγεμονικοῦ κ. Or.*or*.25(p.357.9; M.11.496C); τὴν προηγουμένην...τῆς ζωῆς κ. id.*Jo*.1.26(24; p.33.12; M.14.72B); ἵνα... ἀπιστίας λοιμώδει περιβάλλῃ κ. Cyr.H.*catech*.4.1; ἀτάραχον κ. τῆς ψυχῆς Bas.*hom.in Ps*.33(1.153E; M.29.376B); abs., *frame of mind*; *spiritual state* τὸ ὃ δεῖ, οἱ λόγοι εἰσὶ τῆς εὐχῆς, τὸ δὲ καθὸ δεῖ ἡ κ. τοῦ εὐχομένου Or.*or*.2(p.299.18; 417B); τὸ μὲν τῆς κ. εἰς τὴν ψυχὴν ἐγκαταθετέον, τὸ δὲ τοῦ σχήματος εἰς τὸ σῶμα *ib*.31(p.395.18; 549B); id.*Jo*.1. 36(29; p.376.24; 657D); οὐ πάντες γὰρ κ. ἴσοι ἐσμέν, οὔτε ταῖς αὐταῖς ἐννοίαις ἐλαυνόμεθα Marc.Er.*opusc*.4(M.65.1020D); καταστάσεως τῆς ἀπαθοῦς τε καὶ καθαρᾶς Nil.*epp*.1.107(M.79.129A); τρεῖς κ. εἰσὶν ἐν τῷ ἀνθρώπῳ· ἔστιν ὁ ἐνεργῶν τὸ πάθος, καὶ ἔστιν ὁ ἱστῶν αὐτό, καὶ ἔστιν ὁ ἐκριζῶν αὐτό Dor.*doct*.10.5(M.88.1729B); *character, behaviour*, Ephr. 3.405E; προσχὼν αὐτοῦ τῇ κ., τῷ ἀνεπιλήπτῳ τῆς παρρησίας Pall.*v. Chrys*.5(p.30.10; M.47.19) cf. 5; **f.** of men in rel. to God μένουσιν... ἐν τῇ πρὸ τῶν τέκνων τοῦ θεοῦ κ. τῶν πεπιστευκότων μόνον Or.*Jo*.20.33 (27; p.370.26; M.14.648C); δεύτερος Ἀδὰμ...ἀναδείξας...ἡμῖν τὴν μέλλουσαν κ. ... τὸν ὅμοιον...τρόπον καὶ δεύτερος ἄνθρωπος καλεῖται ὡς τὴν δευτέραν κ. ἐκφήνας Thdr.Mops.*symb*.(p.99.15,18; M.66.1020A, B); Oecum.*Apoc*.3:16(p.65); **3.** *appearance, look*, Pall.*v.Chrys*.4 (p.26.32; M.47.17); ἐκ τῆς τῶν ὀφθαλμῶν κ. γνωρίζουσι τοὺς σώφρονας ἄνδρας *ib*.5(p.31.1; M.47.19); **4.** *settled order, system*; of world as originally planned by God, Tit.Bost.*fr.Lc*.8:1(p.171); ‡Chrys. *hom.in Rom*.7:19(8.193A); †Jo.D.*B.J*.7(M.96.912C); of Christians θαυμάστην...τὴν κ. τῆς ἑαυτῶν [sc. Χριστιανῶν] πολιτείας *Diogn*.5.4; Or.*schol.in Cant*.6:3(M.17.276C); τήν τε τοῦ ἤθους κ. καὶ τοῦ βλέμματος τὸ εὔτακτον Cyr.S.*v.Abr*.(p.245.10); hence **a.** *political constitution, state, empire* πᾶσαν τὴν Ῥωμαϊκὴν κ. Jo.Mal.*chron*.16 p.400(M. 97.593A); **b.** eccl. *order*, Thdr.Mops.*1Tim*.1:3f.(p.70.22; M.66. 937A); ἐναντία...τῆς καθολικῆς κ. Justn.*conf*.(p.108.32; M.86.1033B); ἀγνοεῖς τῆς ἁγίας ἐκκλησίας τὴν κ. [ref. hour of eucharist] Jo.Mosch. *prat*.27(M.87.2873B); **5.** *way of life*, of those following a monastic rule ἀγγελικὴν κ. ἔχων ‡Pall.*h.mon*.4.1(p.28.8; M.34.1131D); πάντων ...οἰκοδομηθέντων εἴς τε τὴν αὐτοῦ κ. καὶ σεμνότητα καὶ πνευματικὴν σύνεσιν Cyr.S.*v.Jo.Hes*.(p.206.16); Jo.Mosch.*prat*.73(M.87.2925D); κρατοῦσι τοὺς ἄνδρας τῷ τε εἴδει καὶ τῇ κ. σεμνοτάτους, καὶ τὰ σήμαντρα τῆς ἐρημικῆς κ. ἐπὶ τῶν προσώπων φέροντας †Jo.D.*B.J*.22 (M.96.1061B); *religious rule* or *observance* ἔχων μετ' αὐτοῦ τὸν δευτερεύοντα τῆς τῶν κοινοβιακῶν κ. φροντίδων τὸν...Παῦλον Cyr.S. *v.Sab*.30(p.115.22); μαθὼν τὸ ψαλτήριον καὶ...τὴν μοναχικὴν κ. Jo. Mosch.*prat*.166(M.87.3033A); abs. ὡς ἔστιν ἡ κ. Leont.N.*v.Sym*.13 (M.93.1685C); **6.** *dispensation, order* ἕξομέν τι πλέον τῆς παρούσης κ. Or.*fr.10 in Jo*.(p.493.7); τὸ αὐτεξούσιον τῶν ἀνθρώπων...οὐ προσκαίρῳ θανάτῳ δικάζων, ἀλλ' ἐν ἑτέρᾳ κ. λογοθετῶν αὐτό *Const.App*. 6.22.1; τὴν ἐξ Ἀδὰμ ἕως Χριστοῦ κ. Arsen.*tent*.(M.66.1624B); ἄχρις ἂν ἡ παροῦσα μένῃ κ. Hadr.*introd*.97(M.98.1297C); μὴ χρονίζειν ἐν τῷ νῦν βίῳ τὴν τῆς νέας κ. Oecum.*Apoc*.11:2(p.127); ἁρπαγεὶς [sc. S. Paul] περιὼν ἐν τῇ νῦν κ. ἕως τρίτου οὐρανοῦ Cosm.Ind.*top*.5(M. 88.301C); ἡ τροπὴ ταύτης τῆς κ. *ib*.2(125B); τὴν μέλλουσαν δευτέραν κ. *ib*.1(57A) al.; τὰς δύο ταύτας μόνον κ. ἐποίησε, ταύτην πρῶτον ὁρίσας πολιτεύεσθαι, εἶθ' οὕτω τὴν μέλλουσαν *ib*.5(280C); Χριστὸς ὁ τῆς δευτέρας κ. ἀρχηγός *ib*.(297B).

***καταστεΐζομαι**, *make fun of*, c. genit., Mac.Mgn.*apocr*.3.15 (p.94.1).

καταστείχω, *come down, descend*, Nonn.*par.Jo*.4:51(M.43.784A).

καταστέλλω, **1.** *bring down* ἀπὸ τῆς πολλῆς δόξης καὶ ἀγωνίας κατασταλεὶς καὶ εἰς τὴν ἰδίαν ἕξιν τῆς ἀνθρωπίνης φύσεως ἐλθὼν Hipp. *Dan*.3.7.7; **2.** medic., *reduce, relieve* ὡς...ἰατρὸς...περιπλάσμασιν... πειρᾶται καταστεῖλαι τὸ οἴδημα Bas.*hom.in Ps*.32(1.135A; M.29.332B); fig. ταύτην...τὴν νόσον [i.e. heresy] καταστεῖλαι βουληθεὶς Const. ap.Eus.*v.C*.2.66(p.67.20; M.20.1037C); φλεγμαίνουσαν κ. τὴν ψυχὴν Chrys.*sac*.4.3(p.110.6; 1.408A); id.*Eutrop*.2.6(3.391A); **3.** *relieve, mitigate* ἵνα...συμφορὰν καταστείλῃς Gel.Cyz.*h.e*.3.12.7; **4.** pass., met., *be depressed*, Chrys.*Jud*.3.4(1.612A); **5.** *calm, restrain* persons ὁ Πέτρος...κ. τὸν ὄχλον εἶπεν *A.Petr.c.Sim*.7(p.90.11); Const.*or.s.c*. 15(p.175.16; M.20.1277B); Chrys.*hom.61.3 in Jo*.(8.366A); passions, Or.*Cels*.1.64(p.117.17; M.11.781A); Eus.*d.e*.3.7(p.146.9; M.22.245C); Tit.Bost.*Man*.2.13(M.18.1160A); in gen., *A.Phil*.52(p.22.34); ἀκηδίαν κ. ὑπομονή Nil.*inst*.(M.79.1236A); κ. τύφον Thdt.*Ps*.8:5(1.653); id.*Rom*.1:7(3.16); pass., *be restrained* or *subdued* οὐχ ὁρῶσιν, ὅσων πάθη καὶ ὅσων χύσις κακίας κ. Or.*Cels*.1.64(p.117.24; M.11.781A); συνεστραμμένῳ προσώπῳ κ. τε φωνῇ Eus.*v.C*.4.29(p.128.24; M.20. 1177B); Chrys.*hom.1.8 in Mt*.(7.18A); ὥστε...τόν τε Οὐρσῖνον παύσασθαι τῆς ἐπιχειρήσεως, καὶ κ. τοὺς βουληθέντας ἀκολουθῆσαι αὐτῷ Socr. *h.e*.4.29.6(M.67.544A); **6.** in bad sense; pass., *be repressed, cramped* τὸ...συνειδὸς αὐτὴν [sc. τὴν ψυχὴν] συστρέφον κατεστάλθαι ποιεῖ Chrys. *hom.9.4 in Heb*.(12.99A); **7.** perf. ptcpl. pass., *calm, sedate, moderate* of demeanour τῷ ἤθει κεκοσμημένος, τῷ σχήματι κ. Clem.*str*.7.11(p.45. 16; M.9.488A); Bas.*hom*.12.9(2.105A; M.31.404B); τὸν νηστεύοντα κ. εἶναι χρή, ἡσύχιον Chrys.*hom.8.6 in Gen*.(4.63C); ‡Nil.*perist*.12.10 (M.79.960B); neut. as subst., *calm, restraint, sobriety* τὴν γυναῖκα χρὴ ἔχειν μάλιστα εὐχομένην τὸ κ. Or.*or*.9(p.318.8; M.11.444A); **8.** *submit* κ. τῷ τοῦ θεοῦ θελήματι Didym.*Trin*.3.21(M.39.905A).

***καταστεμματίζω**, *crown*, Ephr.2.344A.

καταστενάζω, *bewail, deplore*; c. genit., Bas.*hom*.4.3(2.27E; M.31. 225A); Thdr.Stud.*epp*.2.157(M.99.1492D).

***καταστενόω**, *confine, shut in*; perf. pass., *be narrow*, Geo.Pis. *Pers*.2.341(M.92.1233A).

***καταστεπτέον**, *one must crown*, Clem.*paed*.2.8(p.202.6; M.8. 485A).

***καταστέρησις**, ἡ, *deprivation*, Or.*sel.in Ps*.29:6(M.12.1293C).

***κατάστερος**, **1.** *set with stars, starry*; of the peacock's tail, Gr. Naz.*or*.28.24(p.59.5; M.36.60B); Geo.Pis.*hex*.1272(M.92.1532A); met., of BMV χαῖρε οὐρανὲ...ἡ ταῖς τῶν ἀρετῶν λαμπηδόσι κατάστερος, ἐξ ἧς ὁ τῆς δικαιοσύνης ἥλιος ἀνέτειλεν Thdr.Stud.*nativ.BMV* 7(M.96. 692A); **2.** *marked with something starlike*; of one who had the imprint of the cross on his clothes, Gr.Naz.*or*.5.7(M.35.672B).

καταστερόω, perf. ptcpl. pass., *set with stars, starry*; of the heavens, Chrys.*incomprehens*.2.3(1.456D); id.*hom.6.5 in Gen*.(4. 45D).

καταστεφαν-όω, *crown*; pass., *be crowned with victory* over καταστεφανωθῆναι τοῦ ἀντιδίκου Bas.*hom*.9.9(2.81E; M.31.349C); τρόπαια ἱστῶσι, καὶ ~οῦνται τῶν ἐναντίων Nil.*epp*.4.4(M.79.552D); *ib*.2.172(288B).

καταστέφω, *crown*; perf. pass.; **1.** met., *be adorned*, with virtues, etc. ἀπεικάζεσθαι...λειμῶνι...τὴν ἐκκλησίαν, οὐ μόνον τοῖς τῆς ἁγνείας...κατεστεμμένην ἄνθεσιν, ἀλλὰ καὶ τοῖς τῆς τεκνογονίας καὶ τοῖς τῆς ἐγκρατείας Meth.*symp*.2.7(p.26.1; M.18.60B); Cyr.*Os*.4(3. 19D); id.*Lc*.9:1(M.72.640B); **2.** *be equipped* γυναιξὶν...κατόπτρῳ...τὴν ἀριστεράν, καὶ σείστρῳ τὴν δεξιὰν...κατεστεμμέναις Cyr.*ador*.9(1. 314A); *be invested* τοὺς ἐν ἱερωσύνῃ κατεστεμμένους *ib*.11(404D).

καταστηλόω, *plant like pillars*, Meth.*symp*.10.2(p.123.7; M.18. 193C).

καταστηρίζω, pass., *be set* στέφανος...κατεστήρικτο Eus.*v.C*.1.31 (p.22.1; M.20.945A); *be fixed*; of stars, Gr.Nyss.*hex*.67(M.44.116C).

***καταστιγής**, *spotted, speckled* τοὺς ποικίλους...καὶ κ. ὄρνεις Philost.*h.e*.3.11(M.65.500A).

καταστίζω, **1.** *mark, spot, speckle*, of leprosy τοὺς ἀλφούς, οἳ τὸ πρόσωπον αὐτοῦ κατεμάστιζόν τε καὶ κ. Philost.*h.e*.10.6(M.65.588B); τοῖς λέπρᾳ κατεστιγμένοις Isid.Pel.*epp*.1.24(M.78.197B); Cyr.*Am*.2(4. 251B); of scars (ref. Gal.6:17) ὑπὲρ ἧς [sc. τῆς τοῦ Χριστοῦ ὁμολογίας] πολλὰ παθὼν μικροῦ κατέστιγμαι τὸ σῶμα Thdr.Mops.*Gal*.6:17(p.110. 25); **2.** *punctuate* τὰ χαράγματα τέλεια ποίει, καὶ τοὺς τόπους ἀκολούθως κ. Bas.*ep*.333(3.452A; M.32.1076D); **3.** *spot, stain*; met., of sin, *A.Andr*.A 4(p.48.12); μηδέ σε κ. τὰ τοιαῦτα πάθη Gr.Nyss.*or.dom*.2 (p.44.15; M.44.1148C); *ib*.5(p.100.12; 1181D); Cyr.*ador*.14(1.482A); ἐμοὶ τῷ ἁμαρτωλῷ καὶ πᾶσι κηλῖσι κατεστιγμένῳ *Lit.Jac*.(p.160.15); of human nature assumed by Logos τὴν ἡμετέραν μορφὴν...ἀνέλαβε πολλοῖς ἁμαρτήμασι κατεστιγμένην Meth.*symp*.1.4(p.13.1; M.18.44D).

καταστίλβω, **1.** *glisten*; of gold, †Jo.D.*B.J*.16(M.96.1001A); **2.** perf. ptcpl. pass. neut. as subst., *brilliance*; of style, Gr.Nyss. *Eun*.1(1 p.158.17; M.45.400B).

καταστοιβάζω, perf. ptcpl. pass., *compressed*; of style, Gr.Nyss. *Eun*.1(1 p.158.1; M.45.400A).

καταστοιχει-όω, *reduce to elements* μηκέτι...ἀνέχεσθε τῶν μυθολογεῖν ἐπιχειρούντων, καὶ ~ουμένων τῆς γραφῆς, καὶ τὰ ἀπὸ τοῦ οἰκείου νοὸς ἐπεισφερόντων τοῖς θείοις διδάγμασιν Chrys.*hom.24.6 in Gen*.(4.226A).

καταστολή, ἡ, **1.** *dress* κ. ... αὐτῶν [sc. τῶν Ἐσσηνῶν] καὶ σχῆμα κόσμιον Hipp.*haer*.9.20(p.257.4; M.16.3398A); ἦν...ἡ κ. αὐτῶν εὐπρεπὴς *A.Phil*.60(p.25.12); Nil.*Magn*.53(M.79.1037B); met., *adornment* τοῦ ἔσωθεν ἀνθρώπου τῆς κ. Meth.*symp*.7.2(p.73.16; M.18. 128B); **2.** *putting down, subjugation*; *restraint* εἰς κ. τῶν τῆς ψυχῆς παθῶν Clem.*paed*.1.8(p.128.21; M.8.329A); id.*str*.6.9(p.469.27; M.9. 297A); προσευχὴ...ἐστι...τύφου κ. Gr.Nyss.*or.dom*.1(p.8.4; M.44. 1124A); Chrys.*hom.4.6 in Ac*.9:1(3.138D); **3.** *sobriety, moderation, reserve* εἰς κ. βίου Clem.*str*.7.10(p.41.14; M.9.480B); esp. with ἦθους, *ib*.6.11(p.476.27; 312A); Or.*Cels*.1.67(p.121.25; M.11.785C); †Nil.*vit*. 2(M.79.1142B); abs. τοὺς...τὸ πένθος...ἐπιδεικνυμένους τῇ πάσῃ κ. καὶ τῷ σχήματι καὶ τῇ τοῦ βίου ταπεινότητι CAnc.(314)*can*.3; ἐν τοῖς τῶν Ἑλλήνων μυστηρίοις αἱ ὀρχήσεις, ἐν δὲ τοῖς ἡμετέροις σιγὴ καὶ εὐκοσμία, αἰδὼς καὶ κ. Chrys.*hom.12.5 in Col*.(11.419C); Nil.ap.Proc.G.*Cant*. 4:3(M.87.1645D).

***καταστόρευσις**, ἡ, *quelling, removal* Χριστὸν εἰς ἐπιτίμησιν καὶ κ. τῆς κινδυνεύσεως διεγείροντες Thdr.Stud.*epp*.2.31(M.99.1204A).

καταστοχάζ-ομαι, **1.** *aim at* ὥσπερ...ὁ τοξότης πρὸς τὸν σκοπὸν ἀπευθύνει τὸ βέλος...οὕτως ὁ κριτὴς ὀφείλει τοῦ δικαίου κ. Bas.*hom*. 12.9(2.105D; M.31.405A); Dion.Ar.*d.n*.8.6(M.3.893B); id.*c.h*.15.8(M.3. 337B); **2.** *have regard for, be concerned with* παρακαλεῖ μὴ βαρὺ φορτίον...τὸ περὶ ἁγνείας τοῖς ἀδελφοῖς ἐπιτιθέναι, τῆς δὲ τῶν πολλῶν ~εσθαι ἀσθενείας Eus.*h.e*.4.23.7(M.20.388A); **3.** *guess, infer*; hence *assume* εἰς θεὸν οὐκ ἀσεβοῦμεν, μὴ τολμῶντες αὐτοῦ ~εσθαι χαλεπὴν ἀδυναμίαν, τοῦ ἀνθεστάναι κακίᾳ τῇ μὴ οὔσῃ Tit.Bost.*Man*.1.2(M.18. 1072A); Marc.Er.*opusc*.7.9(M.65.1085A); **4.** *anticipate* κ. τοῦ καιροῦ Proc.G.*ep*.62(M.87.2769A).

καταστοχασμός, ὁ, *conjecture*, Gr.Nyss.*anim.et res*.(M.46.84D).

καταστοχαστικός, *of conjecture* ref. Ex.28:3, πνεῦμα αἰσθήσεως... οὐδὲν ἀλλ' ἢ φρόνησίς ἐστι, δύναμις ψυχῆς...τῶν...μελλόντων κ. Clem. *str*.6.17(p.511.19; M.9.385B).

καταστράπτ-ω, **1.** *flash lightning*; pass., *be ablaze with lightning* καπνιζόμενον...τὸ ὄρος...καὶ κ. Gr.Naz.*or*.28.2(p.22.19; M.36.28B); **2.** *dazzle*; met., *illumine* τῆς ἁγνείας...τῷ φωτὶ ~ομένης...τοῦ λόγου Meth.*symp*.5.8(p.63.7; M.18.112B); ἡ τοῦ φωτὸς δύναμις...τὴν οἰκουμένην ἱερῷ λαμπτῆρι κ. Const.ap.Eus.*v.C*.2.67(p.67.29; M.20.1040A); Andr.Cr.*Agath*.66(M.97.1441B).

καταστρατεύ-ω, **1.** *lead in war* or *in an attack* κ. ὁ Ἀσσύριος τὴν ὑπὸ χεῖρα πληθὺν Cyr.*Os*.120(3.151A); ἐμπίδας κ. αὐτοῖς Thdt.*h.rel*.21(3. 1235); **2.** *make war upon, invade, attack* κ. ... τοῦ τυράννου Eus.*v.C*.1. 27(p.20.28; M.20.941C); Cyr.*Os*.119(3.150E); id.*Is*.2.1(2.187A); also med., Clem.*str*.6.18(p.518.14; M.9.400C); Cyr.*Ps*.41:8(M.69.1008B); met. σὺν Χριστῷ ~εσθαι τοῦ θανάτου Clem.*str*.4.13(p.288.19; M.8. 1300A); Or.*Jo*.6.2(1; p.107.30; M.14.200C); τῆς ἀρχαίας κ. πλάνης Cyr.*Is*.3.1(2.379A).

καταστρατηγέω, **1.** *overcome by generalship* or *stratagem*; met., *out-general, outwit*, ref. scheme of redemption δόλῳ...ὁ θάνατος κατεστρατηγήθη Clem.*exc.Thdot*.61(p.127.20; M.9.688D); of Christ παρέδωκεν ἑαυτὸν τῷ θανάτῳ...ἵνα μετὰ τοῦτο κ. καὶ καταργήσῃ τὸν θάνατον Or.*comm.in Rom*.6:8ff.(*JTS* 13 p.365); also c. genit., Synes. *provid*.1.15(p.99.6; M.66.1248B); **2.** *use strategy, campaign* ὁ...δαίμων ...ἑτέραις κατεστρατήγει μεθόδοις Eus.*h.e*.4.7.2(M.20.316B).

καταστρέφ-ω, **1.** *subvert* τοὺς δούλους τοῦ θεοῦ κ. Herm.*mand*.5. 2.1; **2.** *overthrow, destroy*, met. ἡ πλάνη...νενίκηται, τοῦ...Χριστοῦ καταστρέψαντος αὐτήν Meth.*symp*.10.5(p.127.12; M.18.200D); Ath. *inc*.1.2(M.25.97B); **3.** med., *subject to oneself, subdue, reduce* τοὺς Ἰουδαίους εἰς ἐσχάτην ἀμηχανίαν...κατεστρέψαντο Philost.*h.e*.7.9(M. 65.548A); **4.** *turn round*; met., *pervert* κ. αὐτοὺς ἀπὸ τῆς ἀληθείας Herm.*sim*.6.2.1; Hipp.*haer*.4.22(p.52.16; M.16.3087A); **5.** *bring to an end*, esp. τὸν βίον; also med. τὴν ζωὴν καταστρέψασθαι Philost.*h.e*. 3.22(M.65.509C); **6.** *cause to end in, bring at last to* οὐκ εἰς χλευασίαν μόνον ἀλλ' εἰς γέενναν κ. [sc. superstitions] τοὺς ἀπατωμένους Chrys. *hom.13.7 in 1Cor*.(10.107D); ἑτέρους κ. εἰς τὴν αὐτὴν ἡμῖν ἀπώλειαν id.*hom.2.5 in Col*.(11.340F; καταφέρειν Gaume); **7.** *apply to, be concerned with* ἡ θεία πρόνοια ⟨οὐ⟩ ~ει ἐπὶ μόνους τοὺς ἐν σαρκί Clem.*ecl*. 48(p.150.7; M.9.720B).

καταστρηνιάω, *behave wantonly in the face of* αἱ χῆραι μὴ σπαταλάτωσαν, ἵνα μὴ κ. τοῦ λόγου ‡Ign.*Ant*.11; κ. αὐτοῦ τῆς ἀγάπης Chrys. *hom.5.7 in Rom*.(9.471D); Nil.*Magn*.14(M.79.988B); cf. οἵτινες διαφόρους κ. μολύνουσιν τὰ ἑαυτῶν σώματα Ephr.1.207A.

καταστροφεύς, ὁ, *destroyer, subverter* οἱ...ἑαυτῶν τε καὶ τῶν πειθομένων αὐτοῖς κ. Iren.*haer*.3.12.5(M.7.898A).

καταστροφή, ἡ, **1.** *overturning, upsetting* τῆς ἁγίας τραπέζης κ. Ischyras *ep*.ap.Ath.*apol.sec*.64(p.143.22; M.25.364D); **2.** *ruin, destruction* Ἰωνᾶς Νινευΐταις κ. ἐκήρυξεν *1Clem*.7.7; τὴν κ. τοῦ ναοῦ Or. *Jo*.10.42(26; p.219.27; M.14.389A); Chrys.*hom.55.4 in Mt*.(7.560D); ref. persons δεινὴ κ. ἁμαρτωλοῦ *Pss.Sal*.13.7; of ruin caused by Arians μέχρι...τούτων ἡ κ. τῶν Ἀρειανῶν ἔφθασε Ath.ap.Thdt.*h.e*. 2.14.13(3.859); *undoing, subversion* τὴν αἰτίαν τῆς...κ. Ephr.2.150B; *Hom.Clem*.10.11; Thdr.Mops.*fr.Apoll*.3(p.320.14; M.66.1000D) cit. s. ἀντιστροφή; Cyr.*Ps*.118:67(M.69.1272B); λογομαχῶν ἐπὶ καταστροφῇ τῶν ἀκουόντων Dion.Ar.*ep*.8(M.3.1089B); of heresy, *pernicious teaching* ἀπέχου τῆς φωνῆς ταύτης, εἰς ἣν ἐντεῦθεν ἡ τῆς κ. ὑπόθεσις Gr. Nyss.*Eun*.1(1 p.175.17; M.45.420A); **3.** *turn of events* πρὸς τὴν ἀπάντων ἀθρόαν κ. Gr.Naz.*carm*.2.1.12.731(M.37.1219A).

καταστρώννυμι, **1.** *spread*; hence, *make one's bed* ἐὰν καταστρώσω εἰς τὰς ἀβύσσους, Hebr. וְאַצִּיעָה (Ps.138:8), *1Clem*.28.3 (LXX ἐὰν καταβῶ); met., *set forth, publish*, ‡Meth.*Sym.et Ann*.1(M.18. 348A); cf.Thdr.Balsamon *schol*.in CTrull.*can*.7,37(M.137.541B,641C); **2.** *strew, scatter over* τέρατα...ταῖς ἱστορίαις αὐτοῦ καταστρώννυσιν Philost.*h.e*.10.11(M.65.592C); **3.** *lay low, overthrow* γῆν Αἰγύπτου...κ. Hipp.*Dan*.4.49.4.

κατάστρωσις, ἡ, *strewing, scattering*, of quotations τῆς θείας κ. πεποίηται γραφῆς Eus.*h.e*.6.13.4(M.20.548B).

καταστυγέω, perf. ptcpl. pass., *abhorred, hateful*, Cyr.*fr.Mt*.(M. 72.472C); id.*apol.orient*.proem.(p.33.30; 6¹.158C); *ib*.10(p.55.30; 188A); id.*Lc*.17:7(M.72.836C).

***καταστυγητέον**, *one must loathe* or ***καταστυγητέος**, *detestable* κ. ... τὸ προσκεῖσθαι φιλεῖν ἀνοήτοις οἰωνοσκοπίαις Cyr.*ador*.6(1. 209C).

καταστυγνάζω, *look* or *be sad*, Cyr.*Os*.19(3.41D).

κατάστυγνος, *gloomy* μέλαινα κατὰ φύσιν ἡ γῆ καὶ κ. Mac.Mgn. *apocr*.3.42(p.145.17); ἡ τῆς ἀρετῆς ὁδὸς τοῖς μὲν ἀρχομένοις...τραχεῖα λίαν καὶ κ. φαίνεται Diad.*perf*.93(p.134.7).

καταστύφω, *astringe*; met., *bite, sting*, †Apoll.*met.Ps*.50 arg.(M.33.1381D); τὸν ἐν ἱερωσύνῃ βίον, ἐγκρατῆ τινα, καὶ κατεστυμμένον καὶ περιεσκληκότα τῇ φαινομένῃ ζωῇ· ἔνδοθεν δὲ τὸ ἐδώδιμον...περιέχοντα Gr.Nyss.*v.Mos*.(M.44.417C); *ib*.(428D); τῶν κατεστυμμένων ῥημάτων τὸ κέρδος Chrys.*hom.15.7 in Mt*.(7.195A).

κατασυκοφαντέω, *criticize captiously*; *calumniate*, Nil.*epp*.1.156 (M.79.148A).

***κατασυλάω**, *take, steal away*, Cyr.*ador*.6(1.185D).

κατασυλλογίζομαι, *rationalize* κ. πειρώμενος τὰ ἀσυλλόγιστα Thdr.Stud.*antirr*.1.11(M.99.341D).

***κατασυνήθειον, τό**, s.v.l., plur., *what is customary*, of the menses γυνή...ἐν τοῖς κ. ἤτοι καταμηνίοις εὑρέθῃ Anast.*liturg*.(*Mon*.2 p.278; perh. ἐν τοῖς κατὰ συνήθειαν).

***κατασυνίστημι**, *band together against*, Eus.*d.e*.8.2(p.390.12; M.22.629C).

κατασυρίζω, *hiss off the stage*; met., *reject* κ. τῆς Θεοφίλου μανίας Pall.*v.Chrys*.3(p.16.19; M.47.12).

κατασύρ-ω, **1**. *pull down*; hence *treat with violence, maltreat*, Thdt.*h.e*.5.17.1(3.1045); met., *drag down, debase, degrade* εἰς τοὔδαφος κ. τὴν εὐσέβειαν Clem.*prot*.4(p.44.11; M.8.153B); Eus.*Is*.9:7(M.24.153C); ἵνα μὴ...ἐπὶ μεῖζον κακὸν κ. σε Marc.Er.*opusc*.1.128(M.65.921B); τῆς πρὸς τὸν πατέρα θεὸν ὁμοουσιότητος...κ. τὸν υἱόν Cyr.*Ps*.90:3(M.69.1217C); pass. intrans., *fall back, lapse* διὰ τὸ μήπω χωρῆσαι τοῦ μυστηρίου τὸν λόγον ἐπὶ τὸν μητρῷον κολπὸν τοῖς λογισμοῖς κ. [sc. Nicodemus] Gr.Nyss.*or.catech*.39(p.159.1; M.45.101A); Cyr.*Am*.14 (3.265A); **2**. *carry off*; met., *seduce, carry away* Ἡρακλείδης...ἐπὶ τὰ Δημοκρίτου...∼εται εἴδωλα Clem.*prot*.5(p.51.9; M.8.172A); *Const.App*.2.6.17; οἱ...Ἕλληνες διὰ τῆς εὐγλωττίας ∼ουσι Cyr.H.*catech*.4.2; Gr.Nyss.*tres dii*(M.45.124B); κατεσύρη τῇ ἀπάτῃ τῆς ἡδονῆς Jo.Mosch.*prat*.108(M.87.2969C); Max.*ambig*.(M.91.1301C); *ib*.(1293A); **3**. *divert* the attention, Gr.Nyss.*Eun*.12(1 p.231.29; M.45.928C); ἵνα μή τις...κατασυρῇ πρὸς τὴν πρόχειρον ἔμφασιν τοῦ ὀνόματος *ib*.4(2 p.53.10; 624A); *distract* κ. τὸν νοῦν εἰς τὸ τῆς πολυνοίας πάθος Marc.Er.*opusc*.4(M.65.1016C); intrans., *digress* εἰς ἑτέραν...κ. ... σπουδήν Philost.*h.e*.8.13(M.65.565B); **4**. pass., *be reducible* to, *come* or *amount* to πρὸς τοῦτο [sc. doctrine of metempsychosis] τὸν λόγον ∼όμενον Gr.Nyss.*hom.opif*.28.3(M.44.232A).

κατασυστάδην, *standing together, face to face*, i.e. with both sides represented παρουσίᾳ αὐτοῦ κ. οὐδὲν ἐξετάσθη· ἀλλ' ἐκ μιᾶς μοίρας ᾐτιάσαντο CChalc.*act*.14(*ACO* 2.1.3 p.82.24; H.2.597A).

κατασφάζ-ω, *slaughter, murder*; properly, by the sword ἄλλοι μὲν ἐτόξευον, ἕτεροι δὲ κ. Jo.Mal.*chron*.18 p.476(M.97.692B); met., *destroy* τῇ πυρώσει τῶν τοῦ σώματος ἡδονῶν ἡ ψυχὴ ∼εται Marc.Er.*opusc*.5.7(M.65.1040D); τοὺς ἠδικηκότας θρηνοῦσιν...τὰ οἰκεῖα κατασφάξαντας μέλη Thdt.*ep*.119(4.1201).

κατασφαλίζω, **A**. act.; **1**. *fortify*, Men.*exc.Rom*.3(p.181.13; M.113.868A); **2**. *secure, imprison*, *A.Pil*.B 20.1(p.326); *shut up* διὰ τοῦτο ἐν ἀποκρύφῳ οἴκῳ κατησφαλισμένοι καθήμεθα, ἵνα μηδεὶς γνῷ εἰ μὴ μόνος ὁ θεός *Didasc.Jac*.1.55(p.779.26).

B. med.; **1**. *make* or *keep strong, safe* or *secure*, Meth.*symp*.5.8 (p.63.3; M.18.112B); αἱ κατησφαλισμέναι...καὶ σφραγισθεῖσαι ψυχαί *ib*.9.1(p.115.17; 180B); ἀρραγεῖ...ἑρκίῳ τὸ ἁπαλὸν τῆς σαρκὸς ἡ φύσις κ. Bas.*hex*.7.3(1.65C; M.29.153A); οἱ...σώφρονες...λογισμοὶ...κιβωτῷ...κ. Gr.Nyss.*v.Mos*.(M.44.329A); Ast.Am.*hom*.3(M.40.201D); pass., met., *be armed* τῷ θυρεῷ κατησφαλισμένος τῆς πίστεως Gr.Nyss.*Eun*.12(1 p.219.21; M.45.913A); **2**. *confirm*; **a**. *make certain, assure, guarantee*, Gr.Nyss.*v.Mos*.(M.44.353B); *ib*.29(309A); τὴν κληρονομίαν μοι κατησφαλίσατο Cyr.*Ps*.15:6(M.69.812B); **b**. *corroborate* μή τι διὰ τῶν ὑπολοίπων κατησφαλίσατο τὸν...λόγον Gr.Nyss.*Eun*.4(2 p.81.13; M.45.656B); *ib*.7(2 p.155.12; 744B); *ib*.8(2 p.178.5; 769D); **c**. *ratify* ἡ δὲ [sc. σύνοδος]...ὅμοιον...τὸν υἱὸν τῷ πατρὶ...ἀνακηρύξασα ὑπογραφαῖς ἰδίαις κ. Philost.*h.e*.4.10(M.65.524B); **3**. of persons, *bind*, e.g. by oath, Socr.*h.e*.5.21.13(M.67.624A); †Jo.D.*B.J*.2(M.96.877A).

***κατασφαλτόω**, *coat with pitch*, †Jo.D.*B.J*.6(M.96.904C).

***κατασφενδονάω** (*-έω or *-όω), **1**. *attack, smite down with a sling*, Cyr.*Is*.3.1(2.386C); **2**. met. τῶν τῆς ἀρρωστίας λειψάντων ἔτι ἡμᾶς κ. Isid.Pel.*epp*.3.154(M.78.845B); Cyr.*Is*.4.2(2.607C); id.*Jo*.1.7(4.54D); pass. ἐλεγχόμενοι τῆς θείας γραφῆς, καὶ τοῖς τῶν ἁγίων λόγοις ∼ούμενοι *ib*.1.3(4.25A).

κατασφηκόω, *fix, hold in place*, Paul.Sil.*Soph*.481(M.86.2138A).

κατασφίγγ-ω, **1**. *bind tightly*, Dion.Al.ap.Eus.*p.e*.14.25(775C; M.21.1276C); *gird* the loins, Clem.*paed*.2.10(p.224.20; M.8.532B); Eus.*Is*.21:3(M.24.240D); met. εἰκαῖον...λέγειν...ὅτι τύχη τε καὶ εἱμαρμένη, καὶ γένεσις...οὓς ἂν ἕλοιντο ∼ουσαι φαυλότητός τε καὶ ἀρετῆς ἀποτελοῦσιν ἐργάτας Cyr.*Is*.1.1(2.22E); δεσμὸς...ὁ νόμος ἦν...∼ων...ὥσπερ εἰς κόλασιν τοὺς ἠσθενηκότας *ib*.3.2(401E); *ib*.(402A); id.*ador*.1(1.47D); pass., freq. of persons *bound* by sin, Eus.*Ps*.145:7(M.24.64C); Gr.Naz.*or*.40.33(M.36.408A); Cyr.*Ps*.67:7(M.69.1145C); **2**. *constrict, hamper*, Cyr.*ador*.13(1.465C); **3**. *seize, grip* δριμυτέροις αὐτοὺς κ. λόγοις Cyr.*Jo*.4.4(4.394B); ὁ διάβολος...χερσὶ σφοδρῶς κ. νῦν τὸν νέον Ἰωσήφ Rom.Mel.(*AS* 1 p.76); **4**. *bind together, unite* τοῖς τῆς ἀγάπης δεσμοῖς εἰς ἑνότητα κ. Cyr.*Mich*.48(3.438A); ἀκρογωνιαῖον...εἶναί φησιν [sc. τὸν Χριστόν], ὡς διὰ πίστεως μιᾶς κ. πρὸς ἑνότητα τὴν πνευματικὴν τοὺς δύο λαούς id.*Is*.3.2(2.398A); theol. εἰς ἑνότητα...∼οντες [sc. Marcellus and Photinus] τόν τε ἐκ θεοῦ λόγον καὶ τὸν ἐκ τῆς ἁγίας παρθένου ναόν, κατοικῆσαί φασιν ἐν αὐτῷ τὸν λόγον...ψυχῆς...ἀναπληροῦν τὸν τόπον id.*inc.unigen*.(5^1.679D) = *Thds*.(p.45.20; 5^2.5B); **5**. *hold back, restrain*, Cyr.*Abac*.57(3.572C); Sophr.H.*v.Anast*.(M.92.1728B).

κατασφραγίζ-ω, **1**. *seal up, secure* κ. τὰς θύρας *A.Mt*.B 14(p.234.12); *T.Sal*.15.7(p.47.5; M.122.1337C); pass. (cf. English 'a sealed book') τὰς προφητικὰς ὁράσεις...πάλαι οὔσας ἀσαφεῖς καὶ κατεσφραγισμένας Eus.*d.e*.8.2(p.372.10; M.22.604D); **2**. act. and med., *confirm, testify to*, Hipp.*haer*.5.24(p.125.31; M.16.3191D); προφήτου...[Is.7:14] ∼οντος...τὴν προαναφώνησιν τοῦ...Γαβριὴλ Cyr.*inc.unigen*.(5^1.684C) = *Thds*.(p.49.20; 5^2.10C); cf. οὐ κατασφραγίσονται ὡς παιγνιώδές τι πασχόντων ἡμῶν; Thdr.Stud.*epp*.2.143(M.99.1452A); **3**. *seal* with seal of H. Ghost; **a**. in baptism τοῦ ἁγίου πνεύματος καὶ τοῦ σωτηρίου αὐτοῦ σημάντρου, ἐν ᾧ κατασφραγιζόμενοι ἀναστοιχειούμεθα εἰς εἰκόνα τὴν πρώτην Didym.*Trin*.2.15(M.39.717A); ἕκαστον τῶν προσιόντων αὐτῷ [sc. Χριστῷ] καθαρὸν ἀποφαίνει...διὰ τοῦ ἁγίου βαπτίσματος, καὶ κ. τῷ πνεύματι πρὸς ἁγιασμόν, καὶ ἐν τέκνοις καταγράφει θεοῦ Cyr.*Mich*.68(3.465B); κατεσφραγίσθημεν εἰς ὁμοιότητα τὴν πρὸς αὐτόν id.*Jo*.1.9(4.91B); **b**. at Creation, ref. Gen.2:7 κατεσφραγίζετο [sc. man] τῷ πνεύματι τῆς ζωῆς *ib*.(95A); **4**. *mark with sign of cross*; **a**. persons, in baptism (cf. 3.a) ὁ...ἐπίσκοπος...κ. αὐτὸν καὶ ἀλείψας ἐλαίῳ *A.Mt*.A 27(p.257.5); in gen. διϋπνισθεὶς καὶ κατασφραγίσας ἑαυτόν *ib*.B 11(p.228.8); τῇ δεξιᾷ χειρὶ ἐν ὀνόματι Χριστοῦ ∼ομεν τοὺς τῆς σφραγῖδος ταύτης δεομένους ‡Just.*qu.et resp*.118(M.6.1368C); Call.*v.Hyp*.(p.37); symbolism of liturg. use explained τὸ κατασφραγίσαι τὸν ἀρχιερέα τὸν λαὸν ὑποδεικνύει τὴν μέλλουσαν ⟨Χριστοῦ⟩ παρουσίαν ἐν τῷ ἑξακισχιλιοστῷ ⟨πεντηκοσιοστῷ⟩ ἔτει μέλλειν ἔσεσθαι διὰ τῆς ψηφῖδος τῶν δακτύλων ἐμφαινούσης ἑξακισχιλιοστὸν πεντακοσιοστόν ‡Bas.*h.myst*.45(p.389.13); **b**. things κ. τὴν κώμην τῷ σημείῳ τοῦ σταυροῦ τρίτον Ephr.2.7E; med. δεξάμενος τὸ φάρμακον καὶ κατασφραγισάμενος αὐτό *A.Jo*.9(p.156.32); **c**. med., oneself τὸ πρόσωπον τῷ σωτηρίῳ ∼όμενος σημείῳ Eus.*v.C*.3.2(p.78.6; M.20.1056C); περίφραττε σεαυτὸν τῷ τιμίῳ σταυρῷ ∼όμενος πάντα σου τὰ μέλη Ephr.3.221D; or for one's own use, v. b; abs., *sign oneself with sign of cross* μετὰ τὸ γεύσασθαι αὐτόν, κατεσφραγίσατο Ephr.2.9F; κατασφραγισάμενοι τῷ θεῷ διὰ τοῦ Χριστοῦ αὐτοῦ, κλίναντες εὐλογείσθωσαν παρὰ τοῦ ἐπισκόπου *Lit*.ap.*Const.App*.8.8.4; Pall.*h.Laus*.65(p.162.4); ‡Pall.*h.mon*.11.29(p.62.1; M.34.1155C); Jo.Not.*v.Eus*.3(M.86.309A); Eustrat.*v.Eutych*.94(M.86.2379C); Leont.N.*v.Sym*.43(M.93.1724B); ὕπαγε κατασφραγίσαι [prob. l. -άγισαι]· διαβολικὸν γάρ ἐστιν τὸ ἔργον τοῦτο *V.Dan*.(p.64.6).

***κατασφραγιστής, ὁ**, *one who seals*, ref. unholy wedlock ὁ...τῆς ἀθέσμου συμπλοκῆς συνάπτης καὶ κ. Thdr.Stud.*epp*.1.22(M.99.976C).

κατασχεδιάζω, **1**. *improvise*; pass., *happen*, Cyr.*glaph.Gen*.7(1.218B); **2**. *describe roughly, outline*, Eus.*p.e*.8.1(348D; M.21.585C).

***κατασχεία, ἡ**, *possession*, †Apoll.*met.Ps*.2:8(M.33.1316A; cf. p.11).

κατάσχεσις, ἡ, *possession* (cf.Gen.48:4; Num.13:3, etc.); **1**. *fact of possessing* κληροδοσία, καὶ γῆς τῆς ἁγίας κ. Gr.Naz.*or*.43.72(M.36.593C); Dion.Ar.*e.h*.3.3.4(M.3.429C); Max.*ambig*.(M.91.1164B); **2**. concrete, *that which is possessed* δότε αὐτὰ τοῖς τέκνοις ὑμῶν εἰς κ. αἰώνιον *T.Benj*.10.4; ἐθνῶν ὧν ἐπηγγείλατο ὁ θεὸς τῷ Ἀβραὰμ εἰς κ. δοῦναι Iren.*haer*.1.18.3(M.7.648A); ref. Christ opp. Joshua αἰώνιον ἡμῖν τὴν κ. δώσει Just.*dial*.113.4(M.6.736D); **3**. met., of the promised land τὰ...ὅρια τῆς κ. τῶν υἱῶν Ἰσραήλ Eus.*onomast*.(p.20.13); οὐδὲ ἐν τῇ κ. εὑρίσκεται πόλις οὕτω καλουμένη Proc.G.*Gen*.26:33(M.87.417A).

κατασχηματίζ-ω, **1**. *dress up, invest with* a certain form or appearance ἰσοθέους ἄνθρωποι κ. ἑαυτούς Clem.*prot*.4(p.42.19; M.8.149B); αὐτὸν κ. εἰς Ἥλιον *ib*.(p.42.14; 149A); τῶν...τὴν ἀκούσιον πρᾶξιν οἰκονομίας ῥήματι ∼όντων Philost.*h.e*.4.12(M.65.528A); pass., †Bas.*Is*.124(1.465D; M.30.320B); ref. docetism ἀντὶ τῆς ἀληθοῦς θεοφανείας δόκησίν τινα...δογματιζόντων ἐν σωματικῇ μορφῇ κατασχηματισμένην Gr.Nyss.*ep*.3(M.46.1020D); **2**. med., *simulate, pose* ἕκαστος κατασχηματισάμενος τοὺς ἀκεραίους φαντασιοσκοπεῖ ὡς βασιλεὺς Ath.*inc*.55.4(M.25.193C); †Bas.*hom.in Ps*.115(1.373A; M.30.108B); τὸ ὁμοούσιον πρεσβεύων...τὸ ἑτεροούσιον κατεσχηματίζετο Philost.*h.e*.5.5(M.

65.532A); pass., Bas.*hex*.5.2(1.41E; M.29.97D); **3.** pass.; **a.** *be conformed, take the form of* ὁ...ποικίλος καὶ ἔντεχνος [sc. λόγος]...μυρία ∼εται Bas.*hom*.12.7(2.103D; M.31.400C); **b.** gram., *be formed* or *derived* τὸ 'ἐπιούσιον' παρὰ τὸ ἐπιέναι κατεσχηματίσθαι Or.*or*.27(p.372.3; καὶ ἐσχηματίσθαι M.11.517A).

κατασχίζω, *split, tear*; pass. intrans., *split, branch* αἱρέσεις...κατασχίζονταί τινες, εἰς τὸ ἕτερά τε καὶ ἕτερα φρονεῖν Cyr.*Juln*.1(6^{2}.29A).

κατασχολέω (A), **1.** *busy, occupy* περὶ τούτου...τὴν διδασκαλίαν κατασχολήσωμεν Bas.Sel.*or*.14.1(M.85.184C); **2.** med., *be concerned* or *occupied*; of an affection, Gr.Nyss.*ep.can*.(M.45.224D); κ. ... ἡ φύσις τὰ πρῶτα περὶ τροφὴν καὶ πνεῦμα ‡Caes.Naz.*dial*.139(M.38.1045).

***κατασχολ-έω (B)**, **1.** *hinder, delay* τί μου τὰς πόδας ∼εῖς; Bas.Sel.*or*.19.1(M.85.240C); **2.** med., *have respite, cease* τὸν εὐεργέτην, ποθοῦντα πρὸς τὸ πλήττειν ∼εῖσθαι *ib*.27.2(316A).

κατασωρεύω, *heap* or *pile up, multiply, accumulate*, Cyr.*Ps*.34:20(M.69.893A); κ. ἑαυτοῖς...ἐλέου τινὸς ἐλπίδα id.*Juln*.3(6^{2}.94D); κ. εἰς νοῦν...τὴν τῆς εἰς Χριστὸν πίστεως γνῶσιν id.*Is*.4.4(2.689E); *gather together against* κ. τοῦ Χριστοῦ τοὺς ὑπὸ χεῖρα λαούς *ib*.3.3(461C).

κατασωτεύομαι, *squander on profligate living*, Or.*comm.in Mt*.15.37(p.459.26; M.13.1361A); Serap.*Man*.46(p.64; M.18.1233B).

κατατακτέον, *one must place, class* τὰ τοιαῦτα ἐν τοῖς τοιούτοις κ. Or.*Cels*.4.95(p.368.6; M.11.1173B).

κατάταξις, ἡ, **1.** *ordering, arranging, disposing*; of food, *digestion*, Clem.*paed*.2.9(p.205.1; M.8.492A); τὴν κ. τοῦ θεοῦ ᾗ κατατάσσει ἕκαστον εἴς τι τάγμα Or.*comm.in Eph*.1:22(p.401); **2.** *position, order* βουλεύεται οὐδὲν ἄξιοι τῆς ἐκ κ. ὑπεροχῆς Or.*Cels*.3.30(p.227.26; M.11.960A); κοινωνὸν τῆς τῶν ἐνθέων ἀποκληρώσεως καὶ ἱερᾶς κ. Dion.Ar.*e.h*.2.3.4(M.3.400D).

***καταταπεινόομαι**, *be utterly abased*, *A.Phil*.18(p.10.2); Proc.G.*Gen*.17:22ff.(M.87.361B).

καταταράσσω, *torment*, *T.Sal*.14.5(p.46.2; M.122.1336D).

κατατάσσ-ω, **1.** *arrange*; **2.** *refer* to a class, gen. c. εἰς; with ἐν: ἐν τοῖς...γνησίοις ∼εται Cyr.*ador*.9(1.287B); pass., *belong* to a class, Dion.Ar.*e.h*.7.2(M.3.556C); **3.** *refer* or *apply* a word to ἦν...ἐπὶ τῆς...θεοῦ δυνάμεως ∼ουσιν Eus.*p.e*.11.6(519D; M.21.861B); **4.** *appoint*, Dion.Ar.*e.h*.7.3.4(M.3.560A); pass., of the elect τὴν...ἐκκλησίαν...συνάγουσαν τοὺς ἤδη κατατεταγμένους Clem.*str*.7.17(p.76.15; M.9.552B); *condemn* οἱ ἐν ᾅδου καταταγέντες καὶ εἰς ἀπώλειαν ἑαυτοὺς ἐκδεδωκότες *ib*.6.6(p.454.9; 268A); εἰς ὑπερορισμὸν ⟨αὐτὸν⟩ κατέταξεν Epiph.*haer*.76.3(p.344.14; M.42.521C); **5.** eccl., *ordain* ἕκαστος...τῶν εἰς τὴν θείαν ἱερωσύνην κατατεταγμένων Cyr.*Jo*.2.1(4.138A); **6.** *translate* τὰς βίβλους εἰς Ἑλληνίδα κατέταξεν φωνήν Tat.*orat*.37(p.38.18; M.6.880C); **7.** *digest* κ. τὰς τροφάς Clem.*paed*.2.9(p.205.3; M.8.492A); εἰς πέψιν ∼ομένων...τῶν σιτίων *ib*.2.2(p.169.7; 413A); Meth.*res*.1.20(p.243.4; M.41.1088D); *ib*.1.22(p.244.18; 1089D).

***κατατάχος**, *quickly*, Thdt.*qu*.9 *in 2Reg*.2:14(1.408).

κατατέθηπα, perf. with pres. sense, *wonder, marvel at* κ. ... τὸ παράδοξον Cyr.*Juln*.6(6^{2}.216C); id.*Nest*.1.5(p.25.12; 6^{1}.19E); id.*ador*.5(1.146B); Jo.D.*haer.Nest*.20(M.95.197C).

κατατείν-ω, **A.** trans.; **1.** *stretch*; on the rack, *torture*; s.v.l., *ravage* ∼όμενος τὰ κάλλιστα τῆς χώρας...ἅπαντα Malchus *exc.Rom*.9(p.169.6; M.113.777C); **2.** *prolong, continue* μακρὸν...κ. λόγον Eus.*h.e*.4.18.3(M.20.373C); κ. δρόμον ἐπὶ τὸν λιμένα Synes.*ep*.61(M.66.1405A); *ib*.111(1493C).

B. intrans.; *strain*, in accusation, Malchus *exc.gent*.4(p.572.20; M.113.785D).

***κατατεκμαίρομαι**, *conjecture*, Cyr.*schol.inc*.8(p.220.25; 5^{1}.782C); id.*Juln*.2(6^{2}.52D).

***κατάτελμα, τό**, *mud* or *water* lying at bottom ἐν τοῖς κ. τῶν τάφων ἐνέπεσον [sc. οἱ ἐλέφαντες] Thphn.*chron*.p.33(M.108.140A).

κατατέμν-ω, **1.** *cut* τοῦτο...συνέσεώς ἐστι, καὶ κ. καὶ ἐπιδεσμεῖν τὸ ἕλκος Chrys.*hom*.27.2 *in 2Cor*.(10.628E); *slash* κακῶς ἀκούοντας, διαρρηγνυμένους, ∼οντας τὴν ἐσθῆτα id.*hom*.15.9 *in Mt*.(7.200A); **2.** *divide*, Eus.*v.C*.1.7(p.10.20; M.20.920A); Thdt.*1Cor*.13:11(3.254); in thought εἰς τρεῖς...κ. τὸν χρόνον ἡ...γραφή Proc.G.*Lev*.19:6(M.87.756C); *divide into* ἐκκλησία ἡ μία, ἣν εἰς πολλὰς κ. βιάζονται αἱρέσεις Clem.*str*.7.17(p.76.10; M.9.552A); **3.** *separate*, Philost.*h.e*.10.3(M.65.585A); ἰσχὺν...τοῖς τὰ αὐτοῦ σέβουσι διανέμοντος...καὶ οἷς ἂν...τὸ ∼εσθαί ποι πρὸς ἐκτόπους εἰκαιοβουλίας οὐκ ἀνεχομένοις Cyr.*Mich*.63(3.458B); **4.** *distinguish, differentiate* μυρίαις ἄλλαις ∼ονται διαφοραῖς νόμων, βίων, ἐθῶν Diod.*fat*.ap.Phot.*cod*.223(M.103.861C).

κατατέρπω, *delight*, ‡Meth.*palm*.1(M.18.384B).

***κατατερσαίνω**, *dry up, wither*, †Apoll.*met.Ps*.36:2(M.33.1360D).

κατατετραίνω, *perforate, make holes in*, met. τὰ διερρωγότα τοῦ ὕφους τοῦ σαρκικοῦ φιληδονίαις κατατετρημένα Clem.*paed*.2.2(p.172.20; M.8.421A).

***κατατεχνολογέω**, *subject to rules* or *canons*, Gr.Naz.*or*.31.20(p.170.8; M.36.156B).

***κατατηγανίζομαι**, *be tormented*, Jo.Jej.*poenit.cont.virg*.(M.88.1969A).

κατατήκω, **1.** *melt*; *dissolve*; *reduce* κ. τὴν [sc. γαστέρα] τοῦ πένητος ἐν ἐνδείᾳ Chrys.*hom*.*13.4 in 1Tim*.(11.623A); **2.** met., *reduce* to poverty τοῦτον...τῇ πενίᾳ κ. *ib*.*17.3*(651A); *take down, humiliate* κ. αὐτὰς καὶ ὀδυνᾷν id.*hom*.*28.6 in Heb*.(12.267A); *afflict* φροντίσιν ἑαυτοὺς κ. id.*hom*.*21.4 in Mt*.(7.273B); κ. ταῖς λύπαις Cyr.*Ps*.36:21(M.69.937C); *mortify* ὁ...κ. ἑαυτὸν οὐδὲ αἰσθήσεται τῆς στενοχωρίας Chrys.*hom*.*9.5 in 1Thess*.(11.493A); κ. ἑαυτῶν τὰ σώματα id.*hom*.*1.3 in 1Tim*.(11.555A); id.*hom*.*6.3 in Tit*.(11.769B); τὸ πιαίνειν τὴν σάρκα...τῆς ψυχῆς [sc. ἐστίν]· εἰ γὰρ βούλοιτο κ., αὐτὴ τὴν ἐξουσίαν...ἔχει id.*comm.in Gal*.5:3(10.717C); Marc.Er.*opusc*.5.11(M.65.1045D).

***κατάτηξις, ἡ**, *reducing by mortification* πολλὰ...τὰ κατ' ἀρετὴν ἐπιτηδεύματα ἐγκρατείας κ., ἀγρυπνίας νῆψις, δακρύων κένωσις Thdr.Stud.*or*.11.10(M.99.812C).

***κατατηρέω**, *spy upon*, *Didasc.Jac*.5.20(p.90.19).

κατατίθημι, **A.** act.; **1.** *put* or *lay down*; in writing, *record* Διαγορᾷ τὸν Ὀρφικὸν κατατιθέντι λόγον καὶ...δημεύοντι μυστήρια Athenag.*leg*.4.1(M.6.897A); cf. B.3; **2.** *lay down, ordain* ὁ θεὸς...οὕτως αὐτὸ κ. ἵνα ὦμεν ἀλλήλοις συνδεδεμένοι Chrys.*hom*.*33.3 in 1Cor*.(10.303B); **3.** id.*hom*.*15.3 in 1Tim*.(11.637F) v. s. καθίημι.

B. med.; **1.** *put off*; *lay down* office; *cease from* a war οὐ γὰρ νηποινὶ καταθέσθαι τοὺς ἡμαρτηκότας θέμις τὸν πόλεμον Thphyl.*exc.gent*.4(p.480.6; M.113.940A); intrans., *resign* πείσας καταθέσθαι τοὺς παρανόμως ἐπὶ τὸν θρόνον ἀναβεβηκότας Chrys.*hom*.*11.6 in Eph*.(11.89C); **2.** *bury*; hence *sow* seed, met. ἀποστολικὰ καταθησόμενοι σπέρματα Clem.*str*.1.1(p.9.8; M.8.700A); pass., *ib*.7.12(p.57.10; M.9.512A); **3.** *put down in writing, record* ἐν...εἰκόσι κατατέθειται συγγράμμασιν Eus.*h.e*.3.9.3(καταβέβληται M.20.241A); Areth.*Apoc*.66(M.106.764B); **4.** *lay up in the memory* εὐχαρίστως κατατίθεσθαι καὶ ἀντευεργετεῖν Const.*or.s.c*.23(p.189.21; M.20.1308A); **5.** *deposit money, pay* [sc. a ransom] αἰχμαλωτισθεὶς...διὰ τὸ μὴ δύνασθαι τὸν πατέρα πτωχὸν ὄντα καταθέσθαι ὑπὲρ αὐτοῦ Eus.*h.e*.1.6.3(M.20.88A); **6.** *lay down, affirm, declare* τὸ...'σμικρὸν ἐπὶ σμικρῷ' κατατίθεσθαι Bas.*leg.lib.gent*.8(2.184B; M.31.588B); κατάθου αὐτῷ, ὅτι ἡ φύσις πρόσωπον σημαίνει Anast.S.*hod*.10(M.89.161A); **7.** *engage in, undertake* κατὰ Πορφυρίου φησὶ...ὑπὲρ Χριστιανῶν ἀγῶνας καταθέσθαι Philost.*h.e*.10.10(M.65.592A); **8.** c. infin. (= συγκατατίθεμαι) *agree to*, with double augment ἐκατέθετο αὐτῷ δοῦναι ὡς ἠτήσατο Barth.Edess.*Agar*.(M.104.1416B).

κατατίλλ-ω, *pluck, tear* hair as a sign of grief, *Hom.Clem*.20.15; med., Bas.*hom*.4.6(2.30D; M.31.232B); abs., *tear one's hair* κλαίων καὶ ∼όμενος *A.Jo*.51(p.176.25).

***κατατινάσσω**, *shake*, *A.Thom*.A 31(p.147.20).

κατατολμ-άω, **1.** *face boldly*, Or.*Ps*.1:1(p.445) = Bas.*hom.in Ps*.1(1.93C; M.29.217C); κινδύνων καὶ θανάτων κ. Chrys.*hom*.*5.3 in Phil*.(11.232E); Nil.*exerc*.4(M.79.721D); **2.** *venture upon*, in the face of risk or difficulty ὅταν...πρὸς τὴν παροῦσαν ἀνάγκην [sc. ἀπίδῃ] κ. τοῦ δανείσματος Bas.*hom.in Ps*.14(1.108C; M.29.268B); εἰ...δυσκολωτέρα ἡ ἀπόδειξις, ἀλλ'...ἀναγκαῖον κ. τοῦ λόγου Chrys.*hom*.*37.2 in 1Cor*.(10.347A); γυμνοῖς...ποσὶ...λεπτῶν κλιμάκων κ. Thdt.*provid*.4(4.536); *venture upon, broach the subject of* οὐδέπω θαρρεῖ σαφῶς κ. τῶν βρωμάτων...οὐδὲ εἶπε, τὰ βρώματα, ἀλλ' [Mt.15:11] Chrys.*hom*.*51.3 in Mt*.(7.523E); *speak daringly of* ἐνταῦθα...αὐτοῦ [sc. Abraham] σφόδρα κ., καὶ δείκνυσι τὸν ἀκρόβυστον πολλῷ βελτίονα id.*hom*.*12.2 in Heb*.(12.123B); *venture into* a holy place αὐτοῦ ∼ᾷ τοῦ γνόφου Gr.Nyss.*v.Mos*.46(M.44.317A); τὸν ἀρχιερέα...τῶν ἀδύτων κ. Thdt.*qu*.*22 in Lev*.(1.199); *intrude into* τῆς ἱερωσύνης ἥρπασε τὴν ἀξίαν καὶ τῶν ἀδύτων...κ. [sc. Uzziah] id.*Is*.6:1(p.30.15; 2.206); *ib*.6:6(p.32.32; 2.210); *venture recklessly* or *rashly upon* οἱ ἐξ ἀρχῆς τὴν Ἑβραίων διάλεκτον εἰς τὴν Ἑλλάδα γλῶσσαν μεταβαλόντες, τινῶν ὀνομάτων τῆς ἑρμηνείας οὐ κ. Bas.*Eun*.2.7(1.243C; M.29.585A); τὸ κ. τῆς τῶν ἀγνοουμένων πείρας οὐκ ἔξω κινδύνου καθίσταται Gr.Nyss.*virg*.23(p.335.4; M.46.408A); τὰς γυναῖκας...οὐ προσήκει διδασκαλίας κ. Thdt.*1Cor*.11:3(3.233); **3.** *presume, dare* to κ. τις προσάπτειν τῷ κυρίῳ ἀδίκημα; *T.Job* 37(p.127.2); Gr.Naz.*ep*.176(M.37.288A); Chrys.*hom*.*6.5 in Phil*.(11.240E); **4.** *challenge, outdo* ὦ θερμότητος πνεύματος, κυνῶν ∼ώσης νυκτερινῶν δι' ἐπιθυμίαν εὐχῆς Gr.Naz.*or*.8.14(M.35.805B); **5.** *perpetrate* μιαιφονίας κ. Thdt.*Rom*.7:17(3.77).

κατατομή, ἡ, **1.** *cutting up*; *mutilation*, of members in martyrdom, Acac.Mel.*hom*.(p.92.3; M.77.1472B); derisively of circumcision, ref.

Phil.3:2 λαοὺς τοὺς ἀπὸ τῶν φυλῶν τῆς κ. [sc. ἡγούμεθα δηλοῦσθαι] Or.*sel.in Ps.*2:1(M.12.1101A); ὅταν...μὴ ᾖ νόμιμον τὸ γινόμενον, οὐδὲν ἄλλο ἢ σαρκὸς τομή ἐστι καὶ κ.· ἢ...ὅτι τὴν ἐκκλησίαν ἐπειρῶντο κατατέμνειν...καὶ ἡμεῖς δὲ κ. λέγομεν ἐπὶ τῶν εἰκῇ...τοῦτο ποιούντων Chrys.*hom.10.1 in Phil.*(11.276B); οἱ τῆς κ. Cosm.Ind.*top.*5(M.88.216C); **2.** *division* δίδοται...τὸ ἅγιον πνεῦμα, οὐ κατατομῇς μερισμοῖς, ἀλλὰ τῷ λόγῳ τῆς μετουσίας Didym.*Trin.*2.2(M.39.461A); ref. Arian heresy τὴν ἄτοπον...καὶ ἄλογον τοῦ λόγου κ. Gr.Naz.*or.*21.35(M.35.1125A); Christol. τίς οἴσει τὴν ἐν προσώποις τοῦ ἑνὸς κ.; Max.*opusc.*(M.91.225C).

***κατάτομος**, s.v.l., = τομός *cutting, incisive* τὸν λόγον ἐποίησε καὶ τομώτερον Chrys.*hom.67.3 in Mt.*(7.665C, v.l. κατατομώτερον).

***κατατρανόω**, *make plain, elucidate*, Cyr.*ador.*15(1.532B); ‡Jo.D.*Artem.*(M.96.1257B).

***κατατραχύνομαι**, ? *aggravate*, Petr.I Al.*ep.can.*9(M.18.484C).

κατατρέχω, *hasten after, pursue* ἀλλήλων κ. Chrys.*hom.33.3 in 1Cor.*(10.303B); id.*hom.10.5 in 2Tim.*(11.727C).

κατατριβή, ἡ, *waste of time*, Clem.*paed.*3.2(p.240.1; M.8.564A).

κατατρίβω, *wear out*; fig., *wear* by treading a path κατέτριψεν [sc. ὁ Χριστός] ἡμῖν ὁδὸν ἐν αὐτῷ τοῦ διαβῆναι ἐν ταῖς ζωοποιοῖς αὐτοῦ ἐντολαῖς πρὸς τὴν ἀλήθειαν Philox.*ep.*33(p.181).

***κατάτρυσμα**, τό, *sign of mourning* ἀμυχάς, κατατρύσματα Olymp.*fr.Jer.*16:6(M.93.664C).

κατατρυφ-άω, **1.** *delight in, enjoy* κ. τοῦ διηγήματος Gr.Naz.*or.*7.12(M.35.769B); Sev.Ant.ap.*cat.Lc.*18:12(p.134.9); †Jo.D.*B.J.*30(M.96.1148B); (*take*) *delight* κ. ἐν τοῖς ἀγαθοῖς *Apoc.Paul.*20(p.50); Eust.*engast.*14(p.39.21; M.18.644C); ‡Meth.*Sym.et Ann.*10(M.18.372B); abs., *frisk about*; of lambs, Cyr.*Mich.*50(3.441C); **2.** with God as object κατὰ πρόσωπον τῆς θείας ἐμφανείας κ. [sc. man before Fall] Gr.Nyss.*or.catech.*6(p.36.8; M.45.29B); ἵνα...τὴν πολυτροφίαν τοῦ πνεύματος...κατατρυφήσω Chrysipp.*enc.in Jo.Bapt.*(p.35.13); ref. Ps.36:4 κ. τοῦ κυρίου Bas.*reg.fus.*6(2.345A; M.31.928A); Chrys.*Thdr.*1.19(1.34C); Jo.Jej.*poenit.cont.virg.*(M.88.1952B); cf. τοῖς κατατρυφῶσι τῷ κυρίῳ Or.*Jo.*1.30(33; p.37.30; τοῦ κυρίου M.14.80B); **3.** myst. ἵνα...αὐτὸν...ἐν ἡμῖν οἰκοῦντα...ἔχοντες ~ῶμεν αὐτοῦ Marc.Er.*opusc.*9.4(M.65.1116D); μεθύουσα...ψυχὴ τῇ ἀγάπῃ τοῦ θεοῦ...θέλει κ. τῆς δόξης τοῦ κυρίου Diad.*perf.*8(p.10.9); τῆς ἀρρήτου δόξης κ. ἐν ταῖς... πρὸς αὐτὴν θεωρίαις Gr.Agr.*Eccl.*1.18(M.98.796D); τῶν διὰ θεωρίας ...θεῷ προσεδρευόντων καὶ τοῦ μακαρίου κάλλους ~ώντων Max.*ambig.*(M.91.1065D); Jo.D.*hom.*12.7(M.96.792B); θεωρία...τοῦ καινοῦ κόσμου ἐν τῷ πνεύματι τῆς ἀποκαλύψεως, ἐν ᾗ κ. πνευματικῶς ὁ νοῦς, ἐνέργειά ἐστι τῆς χάριτος Philox.*ep.*33(p.181); **4.** *behave wantonly, be insolent to*, c. genit., Gr.Naz.*or.*6.18(M.35.745A); Cyr.*Jo.*3.6(4.315E).

***κατατρύφησις**, ἡ, *delight* τῶν τοῦ θεοῦ λόγων τὴν ἐπιπόθησίν τε καὶ κ. Jo.D.*trisag.*1(M.95.21A).

κατατρύχ-ω, **1.** *afflict* ἵνα...μειζόνως ~ηται [sc. the rich man], ὁρᾷ, φησίν, τὸν Λάζαρον *cat.Lc.*16:22(p.125.10); **2.** med., *spend* time μακροὺς ἐν Βαβυλῶνι κατετρύχοντο χρόνους οἱ ἐξ Ἰσραὴλ Cyr.*glaph. Gen.*2.5(1.52B).

κατατυγχάνω, *have arrived, be present*, *Mir.Artem.*40(p.67.4).

***κατατυπόω**, **1.** *express* μυρίας...δυνάμεις...ὧν τὰς εἰκόνας ἐν τοῖς αἰσθητοῖς φασι κατατυπῶσαι Eus.*p.e.*11.23(546C; M.21.909B); **2.** *formulate* εἰρήνης πάκτα κ. Thphn.*chron.*p.154(M.108.416C).

κατατύπτω, *crush*, v. *κατατύφω.

κατατυραννέω, pass., *be subject to tyranny, be oppressed*, Or.*or.*25 (p.357.13,19; M.11.496C,497A); Eus.*h.e.*9.9.2(M.20.820C).

***κατατυρεύω**, *plot*, Thdt.*Ps.*69:3(1.1089).

***κατατυφλόω**, *strike stone blind, blind completely*, *A.Phil.*106 (p.40.26).

***κατατύφω**, pass. intrans., *smoulder*, met. ὁ...Φαραὼ...κατατυφεὶς τὴν ψυχὴν οὐκ ἐπιμένει τῇ τραχύτητι Serap.*Man.*27(p.43; κατατυφθεὶς M.18.1124B).

καταυγάζ-ω, **1.** *shine upon, illuminate*; fig., of divine light ὡς ἥλιον δικαιοσύνης...καὶ ὡς φῶς...νοητῶς κ. Dion.Ar.*c.h.*2.5(M.3.144D); met., of God τὰς...ἀσωμάτους δυνάμεις ὁ τοῦ θεοῦ κ. τέλειος λόγος Eus.*d.e.*4.6(p.158.16; M.22.214C); ἀπαύγασμα...ὧν [sc. ὁ υἱός] φωτὸς ἀϊδίου...τούτῳ...καὶ...τῷ ~ειν νοεῖται Dion.Al.ap.Ath.*Dion.*15(p.57.6; M.25.501C); τοὺς κεκαθαρμένους τὸ ὄμμα τῆς ψυχῆς κ. [sc. Christ] Bas.*Eun.*1.7(1.218D; M.29.525A); τὰ ἔθνη...τῷ τῆς θεογνωσίας κ. φωτί Cyr.*Ps.*58:6(M.69.1112C); διὰ τῆς ἐπιφοιτήσεως τοῦ... πνεύματος καταύγασον τοὺς ὀφθαλμοὺς τῆς διανοίας ἡμῶν *Lit.Marc.*(Brightman p.135.19); of truth ἡ [sc. ἀλήθεια] δὲ...κ. ... τοὺς ἐν σκότει κυλινδουμένους Clem.*prot.*1(p.4.10; M.8.53B); τῶν ἀποστολικῶν διδαγμάτων, μαργαριτῶν δίκην τὰς ψυχὰς ~όντων Meth.*creat.*1(p.494.3; M.18.333A); τὴν σύμπασαν οἰκουμένην ὁ σωτήριος κ. λόγος Eus.*h.e.*2.3.1(M.20.141B); of men inspired by God ὁ Δαβὶδ γέγονεν εἰς φῶς ἐθνῶν...τῇ μελῳδίᾳ ~ων τοὺς...πεπιστευκότας Χριστῷ Thdt.*qu.43 in 2Reg.*(1.447); of the Law αἱ...ἐντολαὶ κ. τὰ τῆς ψυχῆς ὄμματα Chrys.*Is.interp.*2(6.26B); pass., met. τῷ λαμπρῷ φωτὶ τῆς ἀληθείας ~όμενος τὴν ψυχήν Or.*Cels.*4.29(p.299.1; M.11.1072A); Ἀμβρόσιος...ὑπὸ φωτὸς καταυγασθεὶς τὴν διάνοιαν Eus.*h.e.*6.18.1(M.20.560B); φωτισμὸν καθ' ὃν ~όμεθα πρὸς θεογνωσίαν Thdr.Heracl.*Is.*53:11(M.18.1357D); τῷ προφητικῷ ~όμενος λύχνῳ Thdt.*Trin.*2(M.75.1149C); of conversion οἱ ἐκ πάσης φυλῆς...καταυγασθέντες Andr.Caes.*Apoc.*12(M.106.261C); **2.** intrans., *shine brightly* ὁ Ἰσραὴλ... στῦλον πυρὸς [sc. εἶχε] ~οντα Mac.Aeg.*hom.*15.3(M.34.577B); met. φαιδρῷ κάλλει κ. *A.Thom.*A 6(p.109.3); φωτὸς οὐρανίου βολαῖς...ταῖς ἐκκλησίαις τοῦ Χριστοῦ κατηύγαζεν Eus.*h.e.*10.1.8(M.20.945A); ἠμαυρώθη ἡ Ἰουδαϊκὴ συναγωγή, κ. δὲ τὸ εὐαγγέλιον Epiph.*haer.*50.2 (p.247.20; M.41.888A); τῆς...θείας ἑνότητος τὴν ὁμοίωσιν ἐν ἡμῖν ~εσθαι Jo.D.*Eph.*4:5f.(M.95.840D); **3.** *outshine* νύκτωρ χρησιμεύει τὸ κλέμμα [i.e. artificial light], ἡμέρας δὲ ~εται τὸ πῦρ Clem.*str.*5.5(p.345.8; M.9.52B); Or.*Jo.*2.17(11; p.74.15; M.14.144C); **4.** *show clearly, reveal* ἀστέρα...~οντά μοι τὸ τίς ἐστιν ὁ γέρων Jo.Mosch.*prat.*104(M.87.2961B); met. ἵνα ἐξ αὐτῶν τῶν ἔργων ὀφθῇ, τί μὲν οὗτός ἐστιν, οἱ δὲ τοῦ κυρίου λόγοι σαφῶς ἡμῖν καταυγάσωσιν Epiph.*haer.*76.5(p.345.24; M.42.524C); **5.** *give rise to, cause by shining, cast* a shadow φῶς...κ. τὴν σκιάν Clem.*str.*5.8(p.356.4; M.9.72C); **6.** med., *gaze at, see* φῶς...ὁ λόγος...δι' οὗ ~όμεθα τὸν θεόν Clem.*prot.*9(p.64.7; M.8.197A); act. intrans., *see* ~ειεν, ἔχων ὁμόφοιτον ἐν αὐτῷ ζωῆς ...φάος Nonn.*par.Jo.*8:12(M.43.813B).

***καταυθεντ-έω**, **1.** *lord it over* ἐπὶ τραπέζης μὴ ἀτακτείτω ἡ χείρ σου ἡ ἀριστερὰ μηδὲ ~είτω τῆς δεξιᾶς Bas.*renunt.*8(2.209E; M.31.644B); **2.** abs., *make an unlawful use of authority* φησί τινας τῶν...κληρικῶν κ. τοσοῦτον ὡς...καὶ ἐξῶσαι τῆς ἱερωσύνης αὐτόν Cyr.*ep.*77(p.66.32; 5².208E); **3.** in good sense, *control* καὶ ἔμεινε μετὰ τὸ πληρῶσαι αὐτόν, ὡς πατρίκιος ~ῶν τοῦ αὐτοῦ Θεοδοσίου Jo.Mal.*chron.*14 p.361 (M.97.537A).

***καταυλακίζω**, *plough into furrows*, met. τὰ δ' αἱμόφυρτα καὶ κατηυλακισμένα μέρη σά ‡Gr.Naz.*Chr.pat.*1470(M.38.253A).

καταυλ-έω, **1.** pass., *resound with flute playing*, Bas.*hom.*21.1(2.163E; M.31.541B); **2.** pass., *be piped down, depreciated* εἰ...κατηφῆ... τὰ τῶν ὁρωμένων ὑπάρχει πράγματα, καταψάλλεται καὶ τούτοις ὁ δημιουργός, ~ούμενος εὐλόγοις αἰτίαις Mac.Mgn.*apocr.*4.1(p.158.14).

καταυχένιος, *in* or *on the neck* ταῖς καταυχενίοις πληγαῖς Ath.*h.Ar.*12(p.189.11; M.25.708A); καταυχενίαις πληγαῖς *M.Tar.*1(p.453).

***καταφαιδρύν-ω**, **1.** *give light to, illuminate* τὴν νύκτα λαμπαδουχεῖ καὶ τοὺς ἀστέρας κ. ‡Jo.D.*Artem.*42(M.96.1289C); fig. ἡ νὺξ προέκοψε...τῷ δὲ φωτὶ τῆς ἡμέρας ἅπαν ~εται Gr.Naz.*or.*35.2(M.36.257C); Didym.*Trin.*1.28(M.39.409B); Jo.D.*hom.*8.4(M.96.705B); met., *enlighten* θείου...φωτὸς ἀναπιμπλάντος τὸν νοῦν, καὶ τῇ τοῦ ἁγίου πνεύματος χύσει ~οντος Cyr.*Mal.*44(3.867A); id.*Is.*4.1(2.565C); id.*Jo.*11.3(4.948A); *Lit.Marc.*(Brightman p.137.10); **2.** *make glorious, beautify, adorn* νεὼν...βασιλικῇ κατασκευῇ...κ. Eus.*v.C.*3.40(p.94.31; M.20.1100B); ‡Jo.D.*Artem.*42(M.96.1268D); met. λαμπρὰν αὐτῷ... τὴν ἑορτὴν κ. Eus.*v.C.*4.60(p.142.17; 1212B); τοῖς παρ' ἑαυτοῦ χαρίσμασι κ. Χριστός Cyr.*Lc.*9:1(M.72.640B); τοῖς εἰς εὐπάθειαν αὐχήμασι τὰς ἑαυτῶν κ. ψυχάς id.*Mal.*26(3.843E); *glorify, decorate*, met. στεφανοῖ, καὶ ταῖς ἀνωτάτω κ. τιμαῖς Cyr.*glaph.Gen.*5(1.168D); med., *be glorious* διὰ σοῦ [sc. τοῦ σταυροῦ]...ἑορταὶ ~ονται καὶ καταλάμπονται ‡Chrys.*cruc.venerand.*1(8.200B); ~εσθαι δεῖν τοῖς ἐξ ἀρετῶν αὐχήμασιν Cyr.*hom.pasch.*26.1(5².304D).

καταφαίν-ομαι, **1.** med., *declare, proclaim* μανίαν ἡμῶν ~ονται, δευτέραν χώραν μετὰ τὸν...θεὸν...ἀνθρώπῳ σταυρωθέντι διδόναι ἡμᾶς λέγοντες Just.*1apol.*13.4(M.6.348A); **2.** pass., *be clear, plain*; *be shown, revealed* ἄλλο τοῖς ἀνθρώποις νομιζόμενοι, καὶ ἄλλο τῷ κρυπτῷ γινωσκόμενοι καὶ ~όμενοι Marc.Er.*opusc.*5.2(M.65.1033B).

***καταφαίρετος**, *quite taken away, utterly abolished* ἵνα...ἐν τῷ μνήματι κ. ποιήσῃ τὴν φθοράν Epiph.*haer.*69.52(p.199.22; M.42.284B).

καταφάνεια, ἡ, *clear view*, Bas.*hex.*2.3(1.15A; M.29.36A); *ib.*2.7 (19B; M.45B); met. πάσῃ δυνάμει λογικῇ πρὸς τὴν τῆς ἀληθείας εὕρεσιν οἱόν τινα κ. δι' ἑαυτοῦ παρεχόμενον [sc. H. Ghost] id.*Spir.*22(3.19D; M.32.108C).

καταφαντάζω, *make apparent*, Bas.*ep.*210.3(3.314E; M.32.772B).

καταφαρμάσσω, *bewitch with drugs*; met., *beguile, relieve* λογισμοῖς τισι τὸ πάθος κ. Gr.Nyss.*Pulch.*(M.46.864D).

κατάφασις, ἡ, *affirmative proposition, affirmation* (ref. 1Cor.1:25; Ps.65:3) ταῖς ἀποφάσεσι τῶν ἡμετέρων ποιούμενος τὴν τῶν θείων κ. Max.*ambig.*(M.91.1409B); esp. ref. a theology of positive affirmations opp. negative theology, Dion.Ar.*c.h.*2.3(M.3.141A) cit. s. ἀπόφασις (A); δέον...μὴ οἴεσθαι τὰς ἀποφάσεις ἀντικειμένας εἶναι ταῖς κ.

id.*myst*.1.2(M.3.1000B); *ib*.3(1033C); δύο τῆς θεολογίας τρόπους...διὰ μόνης καὶ παντελοῦς ἀποφάσεως τὸ θεῖον ὡς ἀληθῶς καταφάσκοντα... καὶ τὸν ἑπόμενον τούτῳ καὶ σύνθετον, διὰ κ. ... ἐκ τῶν αἰτιατῶν ὑπογράφοντα Max.*ambig*.(M.91.1165B); *ib*.(1053B,1056C); Jo.D.*f.o*.1. 12(M.94.848B).

καταφάσκ-ω, *make a positive statement, affirm* τὰ ἐπὶ τῇ φιλανθρωπίᾳ τοῦ Ἰησοῦ ~όμενα δύναμιν ὑπεροχικῆς ἀποφάσεως ἔχοντα Dion. Ar.*ep*.4(M.3.1072B); id.*myst*.1.2(M.3.1000B); Max.*ambig*.(M.91. 1053C,1056D); *ib*.(1081B).

καταφατικός, *affirmative*; of theology making positive statements about God opp. theology of negation, *of affirmation* τῆς κ. θεολογίας Dion.Ar.*myst*.3(M.3.1032D); ‡Proc.G.*Pr*.23:5(M.87.1449D).

καταφατικῶς, *affirmatively, in the affirmative* ἡ οὐσία κτλ. ... κ. λέγεται...τὸ δὲ ἄναρχον...ἀποφατικῶς Thal.*cent*.4.83(M.91.1468A); Jo.D.*f.o*.1.12(M.94.845D) cit. s. ἀποφατικῶς (A); *ib*.(848B,C); *ib*.1.4 (800B) cit. s. δίκαιος.

***καταφέννης**, vox nihili, Petr.II Al.*encycl*.ap.Thdt.*h.e*.4.22.28(3. 997; κατὰ Φέννησον p.258.16).

καταφέρ-ω, **1.** *bring, carry down, Barn*.14.2; [sc. σῶμα] ὁ Ἀδὰμ ἐξ οὐρανοῦ ἐπὶ τὴν γῆν κατενήνοχε, Χριστὸς ἀπὸ γῆς εἰς οὐρανοὺς ἀνενήνοχε ‡Ath.*Apoll*.1.7(M.26.1105A); **2.** act. intrans., *descend* τὴν Ἑλένην ἀπὸ τῶν...οὐρανῶν κατενηνοχέναι λέγει τῷ κόσμῳ *Hom.Clem*. 2.25; **3.** pass. intrans., *sink* ᾠὸν...τὸ μὲν...κατὰ κορυφὴν αὐτοῦ Οὐρανὸς εἶναι ἐτελέσθη, τὸ δὲ κατενεχθὲν Γῆ Athenag.*leg*.18.3(M.6. 928B; conj. κάτω ἐνεχθέν p.21.1); ὑπὸ τῶν ἐλαφροτέρων τὸ βαρύτερον βαστάζεται, καὶ οὐ ~εται ἀλλ' ἕστηκεν ἀκίνητος ἡ γῆ Ath.*gent*.36(M. 25.72D); *descend* πυρὰν πολύφωτον...ἐκ τοῦ οὐρανίου χώρου μέχρις αὐτοῦ ~ομένην Dion.Ar.*ep*.8.6(M.3.1100A); into the arena, met. τῶν ψυχῶν...τῶν εἰς τὴν παγίδα τὸ σῶμα, ὡς εἰς ἀγώνισμα, κατενεχθεισῶν Meth.*res*.1.54(p.312.17; M.41.1148A); **4.** *cast down* ὁ σατανᾶς ...κατηνέχθη ἐκ τῶν οὐρανῶν Ath.*virg*.5(p.39.17; M.28.257A); **5.** *bring to ruin* μὴ φθονήσῃς τῷ κατορθοῦντι, ὁ φθονηθείς, καὶ φθονεῖσθαι πεισθείς, καὶ διὰ τοῦτο κατενεχθεὶς Gr.Naz.*or*.44.7(M.36.613D); οὔπω ~ομένους ὑπὸ τῆς τῶν οἰκείων ποδῶν ἀστασίας Dion.Ar.*ep*.8.6(M.3. 1100B); **6.** *destroy, kill* Ἄβελ ὑπὸ ἀδελφικῆς κατενεχθεὶς δεξιᾶς Chrys. *scand*.16(3.502C); id.*hom*.25.3 *in 2Cor*.(10.616B); id.*hom*.26.7 *in Mt*. (7.323C); **7.** *debase*; *depreciate* μὴ εἰς θηλείας κατέφερον τὴν θείαν προσηγορίαν Ath.*gent*.10(M.25.21C); *ib*.21(44A); κ. αὐτὴν [i.e. τὴν τριάδα] εἰς τὰ ἐξ οὐκ ὄντων id.*Ar*.1.18(M.26.49A); *ib*.3.2(325A); Didym.*Trin*.2.8(M.39.608A); Chrys.*hom*.14.2 *in 1Cor*.(10.119A); *disparage* προλήψεις μου κατέφερες *Hom.Clem*.19.24; *reduce* an amount καὶ τῶν μὲν Ἰσαμιτῶν τὰς ῥόγας ἀνήνεγκεν ἕως σ' νομισμάτων, τῶν δὲ Ἡρακιτῶν κατήνεγκεν ἕως λ' νομισμάτων Thphn.*chron*.p.289(M. 108.709B); **8.** *deal* one blows, *strike* κ. τὰς σάρκας σου πληγαῖς Ephr. 1.306B; pass. abs., *be stricken, afflicted* Ζήνωνα...δεινῶς ὑπὸ δαίμονος ~όμενον Call.*v.Hyp*.(p.60); **9.** *carry off, arrest* νυκτὸς οἱ Χριστιανοὶ κατεφέροντο Ath.*fug*.6(p.72.6; M.25.652A); id.*h.Ar*.59(p.216.15; M. 25.764C); *ib*.63(p.218.7; 768D); met., *lead away, seduce (into)* τὴν ἀφροσύνην κ. τούτους *ib*.78(p.227.4; 788C); Chrys.*hom*.5.4 *in Eph*. (11.37E); id.*hom*.9.3 *in 1Thess*.(11.490D); **10.** *bring a charge against, accuse* βλασφήμους...κ. ἡμῶν λόγους Clem.*str*.2.1(p.113.24; M.8. 932B); ἐκεῖνος ὁ ~όμενος ἀπολελύσθω...ὁ δὲ ~ων ἔνοχος ἔσται δίκης Marcus Aurelius ap.Eus.*h.e*.4.13.7(M.20.336B); ἵνα...δικαστὰς κατενέγκωσι τῷ βασιλεῖ Ath.*h.Ar*.31(p.200.12; M.25.728D); *ib*.53(p.213. 23; 757B).

καταφεύγ-ω, **1.** *flee for protection to*; *have recourse to, appeal* ὁ ἐκβαλλόμενος ἐχέτω ἐξουσίαν ἐπὶ τὸν ἐπίσκοπον τῆς μητροπόλεως τῆς αὐτῆς ἐπαρχίας ~εἰν CSard.*can*.14; **2.** *fall back* upon, *appeal* to ἐπὶ τὸν θεὸν...Ἰσραὴλ κατέφυγον Just.*dial*.110.2(M.6.729B); Or.*Jo*.13. 59(58; p.291.4; M.14.512C); ἀπέστησαν ἀπὸ τοῦ θεοῦ, οὕτως οὐ κ. πάλιν πρὸς αὐτόν; Ath.*gent*.34(M.25.68C); πρὸς τὸν θεὸν...κ. χρὴ τὸν ὄντως Χριστιανόν Cosm.Ind.*top*.2(M.88.133C); **3.** *escape, flee*, Didym. *Ps*.9:8(M.39.1204D).

***καταφευκτήριον, τό**, *refuge* τοῦ κ. ἡ πόλις Bas.*ep*.45.2(3.134D; M.32.368C); οὐκ ἔστι που κ. σώματος ἐν οἰκουμένοις Thdr.Stud.*epp*.2. 14(M.99.1160A).

καταφημίζω, *attribute, assign* to, Clem.*str*.1.21(p.69.18; M.8. 833A).

καταφθάν-ω, *arrive at, reach* καταφθάσας...τὴν...πόλιν οὐκ εἰσῆλθεν *Chron.Pasch*.p.299(M.92.752B); *ib*.p.274(680A); met. κἂν ἄχρι τῶν θυρίδων τῆς φύσεως τὰ τοῦ πανδήμου ἔρωτος ~ωσι βέλη Diad.*perf*. 57(p.64.9); δεῖ...εἰς ταύτην καταφθάσαι *ib*.74(p.92.17).

καταφθείρω, *corrupt*, morally and spiritually φιλότεκνος ὢν οὐκ ἐνουθέτεις σου τὸν οἶκον, ἀλλὰ ἀφῆκας αὐτὸν καταφθαρῆναι δεινῶς Herm.*vis*.1.3.1; ἡ λύπη...κ. τὸν ἄνθρωπον id.*mand*.10.1.2; *ib*.10.1.4; id.*sim*.6.2.4; *ib*.9.14.3 cit. s. ἀνανεόω.

καταφθορά, ἡ, **1.** *destruction, death, ruin* ὑπέμεινεν ὁ κύριος παραδοῦναι τὴν σάρκα εἰς κ. *Barn*.5.1; **2.** *corruption* opp. death ἀπόλλυνται ...εἰς θάνατον· τινὰ δὲ εἰς κ. ... οὗτοι...κατεφθαρμένοι εἰσὶν ἀπὸ τῆς ἀληθείας...ἡ κ. οὖν ἐλπίδα ἔχει ἀνανεώσεώς τινα ὁ δὲ θάνατος ἀπώλειαν ἔχει αἰώνιον Herm.*sim*.6.2.2,4; of the state of man unredeemed, ‡Meth.*Sym.et Ann*.8(M.18.368C).

***καταφιλικός**, *friendly* θίασον...καλεῖ τὴν κ. εὔοδον...πρὸς παράκλησιν τοῦ πενθοῦντος Chrys.*fr.in Jer*.16:5(M.64.912C).

***καταφλεγμαίν-ω**, *be inflamed* ~οντος τοῦ κακοῦ Cyr.*Nah*.40(3. 515B).

καταφλέγω, **1.** *burn up, consume*; of thirst, Gr.Nyss.*v.Mos*.35 (M.44.312B); of the fires of hell, Clem.*prot*.10(p.67.5; M.8.204A); Meth.*lepr*.10(p.464.14); Jo.D.*prec*.2(M.96.817B); of sin, Ephr.1.205F; of the action of baptism on sin λέβητα μὲν τὴν θείαν κολυμβήθραν τιμωροῦσαν καὶ κ. ... τὴν ἁμαρτίαν Thdt.*Ps*.59:10(1.1005); of truth on heresy τῆς ἐπταφώτου λυχνίας τῶν δογμάτων πυρσοὺς ἀνάπτων αἱρέσεις καταφλέγεις Geo.Pis.*carm*.11.2(p.17); of the glory of God εἰ πᾶσαν ὑπέδειξεν τὴν τῆς δόξης φανότητα [i.e. at Transfiguration], οὐκ ἂν κατεφλέχθησαν; Jo.D.*hom*.1.13(M.96.565C); **2.** *incite to anger, inflame, fire* με κατέδακνον, ὡς κ. μου τὴν διάνοιαν Thdt.*Ps*.56:5(1. 979).

***καταφλεκτικός**, *burning*, ref. Pentecost πυρὸς...οὐ κ. ἀλλὰ σωτηριώδους Cyr.H.*catech*.17.15.

***καταφληναφέω**, *utter nonsense*; of heretics, *V.Const*.34(p.564.19; *GCS* p.13.12).

καταφλογίζω, *set on fire*, Hipp.*Dan*.2.31.3.

καταφλυαρ-έω, *prate against, utter senseless abuse* of κ. ἡμῶν τῆς σιωπῆς Gr.Naz.*ep*.114(M.37.212B); μηδὲ τῆς τοῦ μονογενοῦς ~είτωσαν δόξης [sc. αἱρετικοί] Cyr.*Joel*.33(3.226A); Proc.G.*Is*.17:12(M.87. 2129C); ἄλλα τινὰ κατὰ τοῦ θείου Κυρίλλου κ. Justn.*typ.Thdr.Mops*. (M.86.1037A); *assert wildly* δύο υἱοὺς κατὰ Νεστόριον ὁμολογεῖν ἡμᾶς κ. *ib*.(1037B).

καταφοιτάω, **1.** *sink* morally κ. ... εἰς τὸ φρονεῖν ἑλέσθαι τὰ σαρκικά Cyr.*ador*.2(1.68E); **2.** *descend*; of God τὸ...ἐν ὄρει καταφοιτῆσαι τὸν θεόν *ib*.7(222E); *ib*.11(403E); esp. in Inc. ἐν τοῖς τῆς ἀνθρωπίνης πτωχείας κ.· μέτροις id.*Is*.4.5(2.691E); id.*expl.xii cap*.4(p.19.24; 6¹. 248C); οὐ γὰρ πρῶτον ἄνθρωπος ἐγεννήθη κοινός...εἶθ' οὕτως κ. ἐπ' αὐτὸν ὁ λόγος id.*ep*.4(p.27.13; 5².23E); κ. εἰς ὅπερ οὐκ ἦν id.*Thds*. (p.49.10; 5².10A) = *inc.unigen*.(5¹.684B); id.*ep*.50(p.93.23; 5².162B); id.*Nest*.3.1(p.56.40; 6¹.66E); of the second coming, id.*Lc*.9:26(M. 72.652B); of H. Ghost τὸ...πνεῦμα...ἐπὶ τοὺς ἱεροὺς μαθητὰς κ. Isid. Pel.*epp*.1.500(M.78.453C); Cyr.*Jo*.12.1(4.1099E); ref. soul of Christ οὐδὲ εἰς τὸν ᾅδην αὐτὴν καταπεφοιτηκέναι Leont.B.*Nest.et Eut*.2(M. 86.1341B); of divine grace in consecration of baptismal water καταφοιτῆσαι ἐν τοῖς ὕδασιν τούτοις τὴν καθαρτικὴν τῆς...τριάδος εὐεργεσίαν *Rit.Epiph*.(p.415).

***καταφοίτησις, ἡ**, *coming down, descent*, of Inc. τὴν κένωσιν, τὴν εἰς τὴν τοῦ δούλου μορφὴν κ. Cyr.*Nest*.3.4(p.69.40; 6¹.86C); id.*Zach*. 105(3.799B); id.*Juln*.4(6².139A); Gel.Cyz.*h.e*.2.24.9(M.85.1300C); of Christ's second coming, Jo.D.*hom*.9.6(M.96.732B).

καταφορά, ἡ, *bringing down*; **1.** *complete destruction* ἐπλήττοντο παρὰ θεοῦ ἀφορίαις ἔσθ' ὅτε, σωμάτων καταφοραῖς, πολέμων ἐμβολαῖς Cyr.*Is*.5.5(2.873D); κ. ἐστιν ἡ παντελὴς ἀπώλεια Anast.S.*hod*.2(M.89. 76B); **2.** (from pass.); **a.** menstrual *discharge*, Cyr.*ador*.15(1.552D); **b.** *inclination* τὴν ἐκ τοῦ ἔθους ἐπὶ τὴν συνουσίαν κ. Meth.*symp*.1.3 (p.11.22; M.18.44A).

[*]**καταφοράω**, v. καταφωράω.

***καταφορητικός**, *wasting, consumptive* ἡ...τὸν θώρακα καταφορητικῇ διαθέσει δουλεύουσα Sophr.H.*mir.Cyr.et Jo*.24(M.87.3489D); abs. τῆς κ. *ib*.(3492C).

καταφορικός, *vehement, denunciatory* κ. ποιεῖν τὸν λόγον Chrys. *hom*.83.1 *in Mt*.(7.792A); id.*hom*.2.4 *in Rom*.(9.441D); κ. ... τῇ γλώσσῃ χρησάμενος Socr.*h.e*.6.18.3(M.67.717A); comp., Chrys.*hom*. 3.3 *in 1Cor*.(10.19A); id.*hom*.1.1 *in 2Cor*.(10.418C); id.*hom*.54.2 *in Jo*.(8.317D).

καταφορικῶς, *by way of invective, in denunciation* κ. ἡμῖν ἐπελαύνων τὴν γλῶσσαν Gr.Nyss.*Eun*.6(2 p.134.17; M.45.717D); οὐδὲ ...κ., ἀλλ' ἐλεεινότερον μᾶλλον τὸν λόγον προσάγει Chrys.*hom*.81.2 *in Mt*.(7.775B); καθ' ἑαυτῶν κ. λέγειν Isid.Pel.*epp*.2.110(M.78.552B); *ib*. 2.135(577A); comp. ἐντρεπτικῶς αὐτὸ ποιεῖ· ὅταν δὲ πρὸς τοὺς αἰτίους, κ. Chrys.*hom*.14.1 *in 1Cor*.(10.118B); *ib*.4.2(25C); id.*hom*. 55.1 *in Ac*.(9.411D).

κατάφορος, **1.** *weighed down*; by grief, Cyr.*hom.pasch*.5.3(5². 48E); **2.** for κατάφωρος, *detected, found out*, Gr.Nyss.*Eun*.4(M.45. 653D; κατάφωρον 2 p.80.10); κ. εὑρίσκῃ...οὐκ ἐξ ὧν λέγεις...ἀλλ' ἐξ ὧν ἐργάζῃ Nil.*epp*.1.95(M.79.124B).

καταφορτίζω, *load heavily, burden, weigh down*; with weight of sin, †Bas.*Is*.30(1 403C; M.30.177C); with monastic discipline, Nil. *epp*.1.279(M.79.185A); τοὺς...νεοπαγεῖς οὔτε κ. δεῖ τῷ τοῦ κανόνος ζυγῷ Isid.Pel.*epp*.1.258(M.78.337B); *depress* δειλίαις αὐτῶν κ. τὸν νοῦν Cyr.*Nah*.22(3.500E).

***καταφορτόω**, ? *make a bundle of* μυρία ἀσεβείας πλήρη δόγματα καταφορτώσας εἰς μέσον κατέρριψε Germ.CP *syn.haer*.9(M.98.48A).

κατάφρακτα, τά, *coat of mail*, Mac.Aeg.*hom*.23.2(M.34.661A); Olymp.*Job* 39:21(M.93.416C); Thphn.*chron*.p.266(M.108.660B).

καταφράσσω, *protect*; Gr.Nyss.*ep*.19(M.46.1076B; error for καταφρυγεῖς p.63.8).

καταφρίσσω, in perf., *dread* κ. ... τὰ ἐφ' οἷς ἄν τις οὐδὲν ὑπομένει τὸ βλάβος Cyr.*ador*.6(1.196C); κ. ... τὸ...ἀνατλῆναι πόνους *ib*.5(170C); id.*Thds*.(p.46.22; 5^2.6D) = *inc.unigen*.(5^1.680E); id.*Nest*.1 proem. (p.14.10; 6^1.3B).

καταφρονέω, 1. *look down upon, despise*; s.v.l., c. dat. τῇ ἐπιεικείᾳ τοῦ διδασκάλου κ. ὡς οὐκ ἐλέγξαντος αὐτόν Chrys.ap.*cat. Mt*.26:21(p.220.31) for θαρρῶν id.*hom.81.2 in Mt*.(7.776C); **2.** *disregard, pay no attention*, abs. ὑβριζομένους μὲν ἀνέχεσθαι, ἀποστερουμένους δὲ κ. Ath.*inc*.52.5(M.25.189B); c. ἐπί: τὸ μὲν ὕψος ἐμιμεῖτο [sc. Shallum] τῆς κέδρου, τὸ δὲ ἄσηπτον αὐτῆς οὐκ ἐζήλωσεν, ἀλλ' ἐπὶ τῇ βασιλείᾳ κατεφρόνησε Thdt.*Jer*.22:15(2.511).

καταφροντίζ-ω, ? *adopt an attitude of, behave with...towards* μὴ πεσοῦσιν αὐτοῖς ἐπιμειδιᾶν...καὶ ~ειν αὐτοῖς ἀφιλοστοργίαν Cyr.*Juln*. '7'*fr*.(p.492; M.76.883A).

καταφρυάσσομαι, 1. *snort at* ὥσπερ πῶλος σκληρὸς καὶ δυσήνιος... τοῦ ἡνιόχου κ. Bas.*hom*.8.1(2.62C; M.31.305A); **2.** met., *be intransigent* ἐπὶ τῷ τὰ Μωυσέως ἡγεῖσθαι σεπτὰ κ. [sc. Pharisees] Cyr.*Jo*.5.1 4.461A, conj. edd.; κατωφρυαττόμενοι Aubert).

***Καταφρυγασταί, οἱ**, *Cataphrygians*, i.e. *Montanists*, Epiph. *anac*.48(M.41.845D; κατὰ Φρύγας p.211.7); Jo.D.*haer*.49(M.94.708A).

***Κατάφρυγες, οἱ**, = foreg., Cyr.H.*catech*.16.8(M.33.928A; κατὰ Φρύγας Reischl); cf. *Cataphrygas, Ophitas...et Manichaeos*, Hier. *comm.in Gal*.2(M.*PL*.26.356C).

καταφρύγ-ω (καταφρύσσω), 1. *burn up, burn to ashes* ὡς...τῶν ὀπτωμένων ἄρτων, οὓς εἰ μή τις μεταστρέφοι...ἀνάγκη καταφρύττεσθαι Cyr.*Os*.77(3.111C); of the final conflagration ὅτε...πάντα ~ήσεται Bas. *hex*.3.6(1.28C; M.29.68B); Proc.G.*Gen*.1:6(M.87.72B); **2.** *scorch*, esp. of sun's rays καταφρύσσει ὁ ἥλιος τὸν ἀέρα Bas.*hex*.6.8(1.57D; M.29.136B); †Bas.*parad*.3.4(1.349A; M.30.65B); τὴν ἔρημον...ἔνθα ...ἡ ἀκτὶς ἡ ἡλιακὴ καὶ λίθους αὐτοὺς ~ειν δύναται Chrys.*hom.9.6 in Phil*.(11.273C); **3.** *parch, consume* τοῦ ἡλίου...πᾶν τὸ ἐν σώματι ὑγρὸν τῇ φλογὶ καταφρύσσοντος Gr.Nyss.*ordin*.(M.46.552D); ‡Caes. Naz.*dial*.140(M.38.1053); of disease, Gr.Nyss.*v.Macr*.(p.398.19; M. 46.985A); τοῦ πυρετοῦ πᾶσαν τὴν δύναμιν αὐτῆς ~οντος *ib*.(p.390.17; 977C); of pleasures ὡς...ὁ καταξηραινόμενος ἐν τῇ φλογὶ πλούσιος ὑπὸ τῶν ἰδίων ἡδονῶν κατεφρύσσετο †Bas.*Is*.64(1.425D; M.30.229A).

καταφυγή, ἡ, 1. *place of refuge*, esp. of God σὺ ἡμῶν ἡ κ. *Lit. Marc*.(*PDêr-Baliz*.p.14); *Hom.Clem*.3.72; ἡ πρὸς θεὸν ἐξαρκεῖ κ. Ath.*h.Ar*.47(p.210.25; M.25.752B); of Church, ref. Mt.16:18 τοῦτο λιμὴν καὶ κ. Chrys.*hom.2.1 in Ac.princ*.(3.60E); of BMV χαίροις, βρότων ἡ πρὸς θεὸν κ. Mod.*dorm*.10(M.86.3304A); cf. *ave peccatorum refugium*, Ephr.3.576C; κ. σωτηρίας *safe retreat*, Thdr.Mops.*Rom*. 7:24(M.66.817A); **2.** *refuge* οἶκον καταφυγῆς (cf. Ps.30:2) Ath.*Ar*.1. 62(M.26.141Cff.); *ib*.2.14(176B); τὸν τῆς ἀληθείας λόγον...εἰς οἶκον κ. γενόμενον Marc.Er.*opusc*.3.1(M.65.965D); met., *way of escape* μία δὲ κ. τῆς πρὸς ταῦτα ἀπολογίας καταλείπεται Or.*Jo*.10.25(16; p.197.28; M.14.352B); **3.** *retreat to safety, flight for refuge* ἀπεκπέμπει ἀγγέλους παραδηλῶν ἄφιξιν...καὶ τὴν ἐς τὸν καίσαρα κ. Thphyl.*exc.gent*.5 (p.481.15; M.113.941A).

καταφύγιον, τό, *refuge* πολλοὶ...πιστεύοντες προσετίθεντο καὶ ἤρχοντο εἰς τὸ κ. τοῦ σωτῆρος *A.Thom*.A 27(p.143.13); of church of Resurrection at Jerusalem τὸ κ. ... πάντων τῶν ἀδικουμένων ἐκ παντὸς τοῦ κόσμου Cyr.S.*v.Sab*.57(p.153.26); of a monastery, Eustrat.*v.Eutych*.4(M.86.2280A); of BMV ἁπάντων Χριστιανῶν τὸ κ. Germ.CP *hymn.BMV*(M.98.453C).

καταφυσάω, 1. *breathe upon*, *Ev.Thom*.16.2(p.155); **2.** so as to exorcize; hence *reject* an opinion, Iren.*haer*.1.16.3(M.7.636A); *ib*.1. 13.4(585A).

***καταφύσημα, τό**, *blast*, met. κ. τοῦ πονηροῦ πνεύματος Meth. *symp*.11(p.139.13; M.18.217B); πειρασμῶν τὰ κ. Mac.Aeg.*hom*.44.7 (M.34.784B).

***καταφύτευμα, τό**, *plant*; met., ref. Jer.38:22 cit. as κύριος... ἔκτισεν εἰς κ. σωτηρίαν καινήν κτλ. ... ἡ δὲ κτισθεῖσα ἡμῖν εἰς κ. σωτηρία...Ἰησοῦς ἐστιν...ὃς ἑρμηνεύεται πῇ μὲν σωτηρία, πῇ δὲ σωτήρ †Ath.*exp.fid*.3(M.25.205A).

καταφύτευσις, ἡ, 1. *planting* κ. ἀμπελῶνος Clem.*str*.1.1(p.11.20; M.8.704C); τὰ περὶ τῆς οἰκοδομῆς καὶ τὰ περὶ τῆς κ. καὶ τῆς γεωργίας Or.*hom.18.5 in Jer*.(p.156.5; M.13.472B); **2.** met. τῶν ἀγαθῶν τὴν κ. opp. τῆς τῶν κακῶν ἐκκοπῆς Chrys.*hom.16.2 in Eph*.(11.117E).

καταφυτεύ-ω, *plant*; **1.** seedlings, trees, etc., Chrys.*hom.82.5 in Mt*.(7.789B); met. τῶν εἰς πίστιν καταπεφυτευμένων Clem.*str*.7.12 (p.53.9; M.9.501C); Chrys.*hom.33.4 in Mt*.(7.382E); τοῦ νοητοῦ καὶ μακαρίου σπέρματος, ὃ σπείρει...~ων ἐν τῷ βάθει τοῦ νοός Meth.*symp*. 3.8(p.35.17; M.18.73A); virtues, Chrys.*hom.18.5 in Mt*.(240D); id. *hom.4.4 in Col*.(11.357B); vices, id.*hom.9.2 in Jo*.(8.55E); Isid.Pel. *epp*.5.9(M.78.1329C); pass., of men in Christ τῆς ἀνημμένου καὶ ἀπίστου φύσεως καταπεφυτευμένης εἰς Χριστόν, τουτέστι τῶν εἰς Χριστὸν πιστευόντων Clem.*str*.6.15(p.492.8; M.9.344B); *ib*.6.1(p.423.13; 209B); **2.** ground, *Apoc.En*.10.18(p.34.1); ὄρει...συσκίῳ...ἐλαίαις καὶ συκαῖς καταπεφυτευμένῳ Clem.*str*.7.18(p.78.27; M.9.556C); καθαρὰν ἄρουραν κ. Chrys.*hom.75.4 in Mt*.(7.729B; εἰς καθαρὰν Gaume); met. ἡ γραφὴ ~θεῖσα τοῖς φανεροῖς τῶν ῥητῶν τῆς ἱστορίας καὶ τοῦ νόμου καὶ τῶν προφητῶν Or.*comm.in Mt*.10.5(p.5.15; M.13.845A).

καταφωνέω, *fill with sound*, Gr.Naz.*or*.28.24(p.58.17; M.36.60A); *ib*.44.11(620B).

καταφωράω ([*]-**φοράω**), *detect*, Eus.*h.e*.2.1.12(M.20.137C); *ib*.2. 14.4(169D); Cyr.*1Cor*.7:8(p.267.23; M.74.872C) cf. καταφορ-, *cat. 1Cor*.7:11(p.130.1); Cyr.*ador*.15(1.552B); καταφορ-, *ib*.14(1.484E) and id.*glaph.Num*.(1.397C); c. infin. κλέπτας γεγονέναι τοὺς Ἕλληνας... κατεφώρασεν Eus.*p.e*.10.2(463D; M.21.772C).

καταφωτίζ-ω, 1. *illuminate*, fig. τὴν ἡμέραν κυρίου τὴν μεγάλην, ἣν...ἀνατολὴ τοῦ τῆς δικαιοσύνης ἡλίου καταφωτίσει †Bas.*Is*.31(1. 404C; M.30.180B); met., *enlighten* τὴν διάνοιαν κ. Bas.*hex*.1.2(1.3C; M.29.8B); θάμνου...τὸ φέγγος...ᾧ ἡ ψυχὴ τοῦ προφήτου ~εται Gr. Nyss.*v.Mos*.(M.44.332C); οἱ τοῖς θείοις τὸν νοῦν καταφωτίσαντες λόγοις Max.*ambig*.(M.91.1405B); Gnost. κατεφώτισε πάντας...διὰ τῆς αὐτοῦ διδασκαλίας *A.Jo*.15(p.160.16); of Christ Χριστὸς...τῷ τηλαυγεῖ φωτὶ τῆς διδασκαλίας τὸν γνόφον κ. Gr.Nyss.*or.dom*.2(p.28.27; M.44. 1137B); τὸν...υἱόν...~οντα...τὸ ἐσκοτισμένον Cyr.*ador*.15(1.519D); id. *Zach*.23(3.683D); **2.** met., *render illustrious* Ἰωάννης δέ, ὁ μέγας διδάσκαλος, κατεφώτισεν...τὴν ἐκκλησίαν Κωνσταντινουπόλεως Thphn. *chron*.p.66(M.108.216B).

καταχαλάω, *let down*; pass., Pall.*h.Laus*.3(M.34.1012C; χαλασθῆναι p.19.12); pass. intrans., *hang* δέρρις εἰς τὴν θύραν...κατεκεχάλαστο Cosm.Ind.*top*.5(M.88.205C).

καταχαράσσ-ω, *score*; *mark*; *trace* τὸ σχῆμα [i.e. τῶν πόλεων] ~ουσιν Gr.Nyss.*fat*.(M.45.168A); τοὺς χαρακτῆρας τῶν γραμμάτων, σανίδι καταχαραγέντας εἰς βάθος...τοῖς δακτύλοις ἐφαπτόμενος Soz.*h.e*. 3.15.2(M.67.1084B conj. ed. καταχαραχθέντας).

καταχαρίζ-ομαι, *ascribe, attribute, credit with* τολμῶν τὰ τηλικαῦτα τῷ ἀνθρώπῳ καταχαρίσασθαι Or.*Jo*.1.26(24; p.33.6; M.14.72A); μὴ προπετῶς ἑαυτῷ ~όμενον τὸ νενοηκέναι ἐκ τοῦ ψιλὴν τὴν λέξιν ἐξειληφέναι *ib*.5.2(p.101.10; 188B); id.*comm.in Eph*.1:1(p.235); Max. *ambig*.(M.91.1208B).

***καταχειμάζω**, *vex with storms*; met., Cyr.*Is*.4.1(2.559B).

καταχείριος, *practised, habitual* οἷς δικαιοσύνη κ. ... ἐτύχθη †Apoll.*met.Ps*.105:3(M.33.1472C).

καταχειρόομαι, *subject to oneself, conquer*, Cyr.*ador*.4(1.138E); id.*hom.pasch*.13.2(5^2.180B).

***καταχειροποιέω**, Thphyl.*exc.gent*.3(M.113.940B; f.l. for καταχειροτόνεω p.480.11).

***καταχερσόομαι**, *be left* or *remain dry and barren*, Cyr.*Is*.1.3(2. 81B,84C).

καταχέω, 1. *pour down* upon or over; oil in anointing, Just.*dial*. 86.2(M.6.681A); in pre-baptismal unction for reception of H. Ghost οὐδέπω...ἦσαν δεξάμενοι τὸ ἐπισφράγισμα τῆς σφραγῖδος. λαβὼν δὲ ὁ ἀπόστολος τὸ ἔλαιον καὶ καταχέας ἐπὶ τῆς κεφαλῆς αὐτῶν καὶ...χρίσας αὐτούς *A.Thom*.A 27(p.142.11); *pour out* words, Clem.*str*.7.16(p.72. 30; M.9.541C); CAlex.*ep*.ap.Ath.*apol.sec*.3(p.90.9; M.25.253B); *heap charges* upon μυρία...ἡμῶν κ. Thdt.*ep*.87(4.1158); **2.** met., *suffuse* ἡ γνῶσις, φέγγος...καταχέουσα τῶν πραγμάτων Clem.*ecl*.32(p.147.5; M.9.716B); Or.*Jo*.1.11(12; p.16.24; M.14.44C); Thdt.*Rom*.12:21(3. 135).

καταχθέω, 1. pass., *be subject* κ. εἰς τὴν ἑαυτοῦ ἀρχὴν Afric.*chron*. (M.10.85A); **2.** perf. pass., *be oppressed* τοὺς ταῖς...πλεονεξίαις κατηχθημένους Cyr.*ador*.2(1.74A); id.*Is*.1.1(2.8C); id.*Nah*.12(3.489E) v. sq.

καταχθίζομαι, perf.; **1.** *be burdened* or *laden* with, Cyr.*hom. pasch*.17(5^2.224D); **2.** ptcpl., met., *oppressed*, id.*ador*.8(1.280B); id. *Is*.2.2(2.227B); id.*glaph.Gen*.4(1.127E); id.*Os*.12(3.33D); as *weighed down* by Law κατηχθισμένοι τῇ τῶν γραμματέων τε καὶ Φαρισαίων ἀπονοίᾳ...οὐ παρεδέχοντο τὴν πίστιν id.*Nah.*12(3.489E; κατηχθημένοι Aubert); id.*glaph.Gen.*7(1.217A); by cares, id.*Os.*19(3.41A).

καταχθονίζω, **1.** *bring to the earth, ground*, met. λογισμὸς... ῥυπαρὸς κ. αὐτήν [i.e. τὴν ψυχήν] Thal.*cent.*1.91(M.91.1436C); **2.** *lay low*; in health, Gr.Mag.*dial.*(tr.Zach.)4.31(M.*PL.*77.370C); in spirits, *ib.*4.35(378B).

καταχθόνιος, **1.** *below ground* πλήμμυρα τῶν κ. πνευμάτων Or. *mart.*48(p.44.10; M.11.632C); τῶν ἀερίων καὶ ἐπιγείων καὶ κ. πνευμάτων *T.Sal.*16.3(p.48.16; M.122.1340B); κ. ... τοὺς νεκροὺς τοὺς τεθαμμένους ἐν τῇ γῇ καλεῖ...[Phil.2:10] ἵνα εἴπῃ ἀγγέλων ὡς οὐρανίων, ἀνθρώπων ὡς ἐπιγείων, καὶ κ. ὡς ἐν τῇ γῇ τεθαμμένων Cosm.Ind.*top.*2(M.88.132A); cf. 2; neut. plur. as subst., one of the three divisions of the universe, *places under the earth, lower regions* (cf. Phil.2:10) χωρὶς αὐτοῦ ⟨οὐδὲν⟩ οὔτε τῶν οὐρανίων οὔτε τῶν ἐπιγείων οὔτε τῶν κ. συνέστηκεν Hipp.*haer.*5.16(p.113.23; M.16. 3175A); ὁ υἱὸς τοῦ θεοῦ ὁ λαβὼν τὴν πᾶσαν ἐξουσίαν τῶν ἐπουρανίων καὶ τῶν ἐπιγείων καὶ κ. id.*Dan.*4.52.4; σοφία περὶ τῶν οὐρανίων, πῶς διατέτακται τὰ οὐράνια· σοφία περὶ τῶν κ., ἐπεὶ σοφία θεοῦ ἐστι καὶ περὶ τῆς διατάξεως τῶν κ., ὁμοίως καὶ περὶ τῶν ἐπιγείων Or.*hom.18.2 in Jer.*(p.152.18; M.13.465B); θρόνος αὐτοῦ ὁ οὐρανὸς...ὑποπόδιον ἡ γῆ, ἀλλὰ φθάνει ἡ δύναμις καὶ μέχρι κ. Cyr.H.*catech.*6.8; δεσπόζεις τῶν ἐπουρανίων καὶ ἐπιγείων καὶ κ. *Lit.Jac.*(p.180.2); cf. *nemo...nec in caelo, nec in terra, nec subtus terram*, Iren.*haer.*4.20.2(M.7.1033A); of the infernal powers as ultimately to be eliminated φύσιν... ὑπεναντίως πρὸς τὸ καλὸν διακειμένην...ἥνπερ φασὶ καταχθονίοις ἐναριθμεῖν τὸν ἀπόστολον...σημαίνοντα, ὅτι τῆς κακίας ποτὲ...ἀφανισθείσης, οὐδὲν ἔξω τοῦ ἀγαθοῦ καταλειφθήσεται Gr.Nyss.*anim.et res.* (M.46.72B); **2.** *of the underworld*; **a.** as the abode of the departed οὐκέτι ἦν υἱὸς θεοῦ ἐπεὶ ἐν τῷ κ. γεγένηται τόπῳ; Or.*engast.*8(p.292.3; M.12.1025A); cf. c; neut. plur. as subst., of intermediate abode for souls of all departed, freq. equated with ᾅδης; esp. ref. 1Petr.3:19, cf. *dominum in ea quae sunt sub terra descendisse*, Iren.*haer.*4.27.2 (M.7.1058B); τὰ καλούμενα κ., ὧν εἰσι καὶ οἱ δαίμονες, ἤτοι πάντες, ἤ τινες...ὁ σωτὴρ...ὥσπερ πλέον ἔχων παρὰ ἀνθρώπους...οὕτως 'ἐν νεκροῖς' κατὰ τὸ μόνος ἐκεῖ εἶναι 'ἐλεύθερος'· οὐκ ἐγκαταλέλειπται ἡ ψυχὴ αὐτοῦ εἰς τὸν ᾅδην Or.*Jo.*1.31(p.39.10; M.14.81B); id.*Ps.*18:6 (p.474); ἕτερος ἀβύσσους τὴν τῶν κ. ἔφησε χώραν, κατὰ Παῦλον [Rom. 10:7] Eus.*Ps.*48:7(M.24.69B); κατῆλθεν εἰς τὰ κ. ἵνα κἀκεῖθεν λυτρώσηται τοὺς δικαίους Cyr.H.*catech.*4.11; ἀνέλθατε ἐξ ᾅδου οἱ δεδουλωμένοι ἐν τοῖς κ. τοῦ ᾅδου *Anaph.Pil.*B 8(p.447); in credal formulae εἰς τὰ κ. κατελθόντα *Symb.Sirm.*3 ap.Ath.*syn.*8(p.236.1; M.26.693A); *Symb.Nic.*(359)ap.Thdt.*h.e.*2.21.4(3.880); *Symb.CP* (360)ap.Ath.*syn.*30(p.259.5; M.26.748A); **b.** as place of destiny of wicked Σαμουὴλ ἐν τοῖς κ. ...; Σαμουὴλ ἐν ᾅδου...; ἵνα τί ἐν ᾅδου; Or. *engast.*3(p.285.12; M.12.1016C); Σαμουὴλ ἡνίκα ἐδιδάχθη τὰ κ., καταβέβηκε κάτω καὶ γέγονεν ἐν ᾅδου, οὐ δικαζόμενος ἵνα ἐν ᾅδου γένηται, ἀλλ' ἵνα γένηται...θεωρητὴς τῶν μυστηρίων τῶν κ. id.*hom.18.2 in Jer.* (p.152.29ff.; M.13.465C); οἳ [i.e. SS. Peter and Paul] καὶ ἐξ ἀέρος ἐπὶ γῆν κατήγαγον τὸν νομιζόμενον θεόν, μέλλοντα εἰς τὰ κ. κατάγεσθαι Cyr.H.*catech.*6.15; [1Cor.7:9] καὶ μὴ δυνάμενον φυλάξαι ἑαυτόν, ἐμπεσεῖν εἰς τὰ κ. τοῦ ᾅδου Eus.Al.*serm.*22.7(M.86.460D); τοῦ Ἀδὰμ γὰρ ἁμαρτήσαντος, πᾶσαι αἱ ψυχαὶ τῶν ἀνθρώπων μετὰ τὸ ἀποθανεῖν... ἐκρατοῦντο ὑπὸ τοῦ διαβόλου ἐν τοῖς κ. [i.e. before death of Christ] *Didasc.Jac.*1.28(p.762.28); cf.*ib.*4.4(p.65.28); **c.** as a state, not to be equated with 1 τούτων οὕτως ἐχόντων, οὐκέτ' ἂν τις ἡμᾶς ἀναγκάζοι τῷ τῶν κ. ὀνόματι τὸν ὑπόγειον ἐννοεῖν χῶρον Gr.Nyss.*anim.et res.*(M. 46.72C); ἐπουράνιον μὲν καλοῦντα τὸ ἀγγελικὸν καὶ ἀσώματον· ἐπίγειον δὲ τὸ συμπεπλεγμένον τῷ σώματι· κ. δὲ τὸ διακεκρυμμένον ἤδη τοῦ σώματος *ib.*(72A); **3.** *on the ground* τεθαύμακα τῶν τροχῶν τὰ κινήματα...τὰ...μέρη μετεωρούμενα αὖθις κ. γίνεται Thphyl.*exc.Rom.* 5(p.225.13; M.113.933A); **4.** met., *earthbound, of this world* opp. ἐπουράνιος: τὸν παλαιὸν καὶ κ. ἄνθρωπον Mac.Aeg.*hom.*2.4(M.34. 465D).

***καταχλεύαστος**, *ridiculous*, Epiph.*haer.*28.7(p.320.8; M.41. 388A).

καταχορδεύ-ω, *chop up*, cf. Eng. *make mincemeat of* τὰ τοῦ θεοῦ... ~ειν πλάσματα [i.e. human bodies] Dion.Al.ap.Eus.*h.e.*7.10.4(M.20. 660A).

καταχορεύω, **1.** *dance*, of the infant BMV κ. τοῖς ποσὶν αὐτῆς *Protev.*7.3(p.16); **2.** *dance in triumph over*; met., *exult over* κατακρατήσαντες τῆς 'Ιουδαίων χώρας οἱ Βαβυλώνιοι κ. τῶν ἑαλωκότων Cyr.*Is.*3.3(2.435B).

καταχραίνω, *defile*, in moral sense τὴν βασιλικὴν αὐλὴν κ. Isid. Pel.*epp.*1.118(M.78.261B); τῷ βορβόρῳ τῶν παθῶν κ. τὴν ἁγίαν... στολήν †Jo.D.*B.J.*30(M.96.1140D).

καταχράομαι, **1.** *make full use of*; *use* for a purpose, of God ὁ... λόγος, πάσῃ κ. σοφίας μηχανῇ Clem.*paed.*1.9(p.133.29; M.8.340B); ἑκάστου ἀριθμοῦ δύναμίν τινα ἔχοντος ἐν τοῖς οὖσιν, ᾗ κατεχρήσατο ὁ... δημιουργὸς εἰς τὴν σύστασιν Or.*sel.in Ps.*1(M.12.1084A); **2.** implying over-much use ἀρχῆς ἐπελάβου...ἐκκλησιαστικῆς;...ὡς ἀλλοτρίας τοίνυν φείδου, μὴ καταχρώμενος, μηδὲ ἀποχρώμενος εἰς τὰ μὴ προσήκοντα Chrys.*hom.10.3 in 1Cor.*(10.83E); οὐ γὰρ εἰ πορφύραν βασιλικὴν ἐνεχειρίσθης φυλάττειν, ἔδει καταχρήσασθαι τῇ στολῇ καὶ λυμήνασθαι *ib.*(84A); **3.** *mortify* κ. τῷ σώματί σου Nil.*paraen.*20(M.79.1252A).

καταχρειόω, **1.** *degrade*, Ephr.3.525B; **2.** pass., *be spoilt* οἶνος... ὀξώσας λοιπὸν κατηχρείωται †Gregent.*disp.*(M.86.672B).

***καταχρεμετίζω**, *neigh, whinny*, Cyr.*Abac.*57(3.572D); id.*Zach.*68 (3.747E).

κατάχρεος, also κατάχρεως, of persons, *in debt*; met., ref. Sap. 1:4 μὴ κατοικεῖν αὐτὸ [sc. τὸ πνεῦμα τὸ ἅγιον] ἐν σώματι κ. ἁμαρτίᾳ Or.*fr.85 in Jo.*(p.550.20); τὸ βάπτισμα ἄφεσιν ἔχει ἁμαρτημάτων καὶ ἀμεριμνίας πρόξενον γίνεται τοῖς κ. Bas.*hom.in Ps.*59(1.192B; M.29. 468A); Max.*cap.*1.73(M.90.1209A).

***καταχρηματικῶς**, v.l. for καταχρηστικῶς, Chrys.*hom.13.2 in Phil.*(11.300B).

κατάχρησις, ἡ, **1.** *full use*, Or.*princ.*3.1.24(22; p.243.13; M.11. 301C); **2.** use of a term in other than its proper connotation, *misuse, misapplication* of language δεησόμεθα...καὶ αὐτοῦ τοῦ λόγου... καὶ προσευξόμεθα δέ, ἐὰν δυνώμεθα κατακούειν τῆς περὶ προσευχῆς κυριολεξίας καὶ κ. id.*Cels.*5.4(p.4.28; M.11.1185B); εἰ δέ τι ἄλλο μετέχει ζωῆς, ἐν κ. τινὶ συνηθείας ἔμψυχον λέγομεν Gr.Nyss.*hom.opif.* 30.33(M.44.256B); Cyr.*Is.*4.3(2.618B); ἐκ κ. as adv., *catachrestically* πάντα...ἃ μὴ δι' ὅλων ἐστὶν ὅπερ λέγεται, ἐκ κ. ἔχει τὴν κλῆσιν Gr. Nyss.*hom.opif.*15.1(176D) = Melet.*nat.hom.*14(M.64.1208A); τοῖς... κατὰ μεταφοράν, ἐκ κ. λεγομένοις Gr.Nyss.*Eun.*3(2 p.41.3; M.45. 608D); id.*hom.7 in Cant.*(M.44.936A); opp. κυρίως, id.*hom.opif.*15.1 (176D); id.*or.catech.*16(p.67.6; M.45.49B).

***καταχρησμῳδέω**, *utter as an oracle, deliver oracularly*, Cyr.*ador.* 10(1.338E); *ib.*2(58C); id.*Nest.*3.2(p.61.10; 6^1.73C).

καταχρηστέον, *one must use*, Clem.*str.*7.15(p.65.12; M.9.528A).

καταχρηστικῶς, **1.** *inexactly, loosely*; of verbal expression; variant comp. καταχρηστικωτέρως λέγεται Or.*fr.in Pr.*1:1(M.17. 152B); **2.** *unnaturally*; of the practice of vice, †Jo.Jej.*serm.*(M.88. 1929A).

καταχρίω, *anoint*; *smear, coat*; met. οἷον μέλιτι κ. [sc. Devil] τοὺς τῆς φαυλότητος τρόπους Cyr.*Ps.*36:32(M.69.948A); of anointing with H. Ghost τῇ τοῦ πνεύματος δόσει κατακεχρισμένοι id.*ador.*9(1.299B); id.*Abac.*55(3.570C); οἱ μὲν...ἐχρίσθησαν εἰς βασιλέας...οἱ δὲ καὶ τὴν δι' αὐτοῦ τοῦ...Χριστοῦ λαβόντες λύτρωσιν, τουτέστιν ἡμεῖς καὶ τῷ ἁγίῳ πνεύματι κατακεχρισμένοι id.*Lc.*9:18(M.72.648C).

καταχρυσ-όω, *cover with gold, gild*; met., *make splendid*, of spiritual beauty τῇ τοῦ ἁγίου πνεύματος δόσει κατακαλλύνεσθαι...τῇ θείᾳ τε καὶ οὐρανίῳ ~οῦσθαι χάριτι Cyr.*Joel.*35(3.226E); pass., of God, *be glorified* τὸν...χορηγὸν ~οῦσθαι πρέπει δι' ὧν ἂν ἔχοιμεν παρ' αὐτοῦ id.*Os.*17(3.39C).

καταχρῴζω (καταχρώννυμι, καταχρωννύω), *colour* ὑπὸ πάσης χρωμάτων ἰδέας καταχρώννυται [sc. ὁ ἀήρ] Gr.Nyss.*hex.*25(M.44.88A); of artists, Andr.Cr.*or.*19(M.97.1213C); met., Bas.*mor.*18.4(3.571B; M.32.1345A); καλλιλεξίᾳ καταχρωννύντες τὸ ψεῦδος Thdr.Mops. *1Cor.*1:17f.(p.173.15; M.66.877A); Cyr.*Mich.*59(3.451B); s.v.l., *conceal*, id.*Os.*153(3.186B) v. s. καταχώννυμι.

κατάχυμα, τό, *abundance, superfluity*, Herm.*vis.*3.9.2.

***καταχωλεύω**, *limp, be lame*, Gr.Naz.*or.*4.122(M.35.661B).

καταχώννυμι (καταχωννύω), **1.** *cover with a heap, bury*, fig. τάλαντον, ὡς ἐν τάφῳ τῇ ἑαυτῶν καταχωννύσαντας ῥαθυμίᾳ Isid.Pel. *epp.*1.222(M.78.321D); **2.** met.; **a.** *bury, cover* τὰ αὐτῶν δόγματα τοῖς μύθοις κ. Clem.*str.*5.9(p.365.14; M.9.89B); Cyr.*Os.*153(3.186B; κατακεχρωσμένην Aubert); *bury in oblivion* so as to put an end to τῶν πονηρῶν λογισμῶν οἱ μὲν...βλαστάνουσιν ἂν δὲ...ἀποπνίγονται ταχέως καὶ καταχώννυνται Chrys.*hom.3.5 in Is.6:1*(6.119B); **b.** *clog, choke*, id.*hom.8.2 in Heb.*(12.85A); id.*hom.1.7 in Mt.*(7.15A); ἡ τῆς τρυφῆς ἀμετρία τὸ λογικὸν καταχώννυσιν Thdt.*1Tim.*5:6(3.663); **3.** *overwhelm, crush* κ. ... αὐτὸν [sc. Job] ταῖς...τῶν κακῶν φήμαις Bas.*hom.* 21.10(2.171B; M.31.557D); Chrys.*hom.63.2 in Mt.*(7.630B); Synes.*ep.* 57(M.66.1397C); βαρυτάτοις δανείσμασι τὴν ἐκκλησίαν *preces clericorum Antiochiae* ap.CCP (536)*act.*5(p.61.5; H.2.1320B); pass., *be overcome by sleep*, Chrys.*Eutrop.*2.11(3.395B).

καταχωρίζω, **1.** *enrol* in the army, Eus.*p.e.*8.4(352B; M.21.592B); **2.** *include* in a written record, cf.Aristeas *ib.*8.2(350D; M.589A).

καταχωρισμός, ὁ, *seclusion, solitude*; of the anchorite, Bas.*reg. fus.*7.1(2.345E; M.31.929A).

καταψάλλ-ω, **1.** *sing (psalms) against, oppose with a psalm*, Nil.

*Eulog.*2(M.79.1097A); abs. κ. αὐτοῦ [sc. δαίμονος] Ath.*v.Anton.*40(M. 26.901B); ἡνίκα ἂν βλέπητε καταγελῶντας τῆς ἡσυχίας ἡμῶν...∼ετε αὐτῶν, μὴ μέντοι μνησικακοῦντες Jo.Carp.*cap.*94(M.85.1856); **2.** *decry, detract* εἰ...λύπης αἴτια τὰ...πράγματα, ∼εται καὶ τούτοις ὁ δημιουργός Mac.Mgn.*apocr.*4.1(p.158.13).

καταψάω, *wipe away,* Chrys.*stat.*6.1(2.73C).

***καταψέγομαι,** *be censured,* Didym.*Trin.*1.30(M.39.417B); Cyr. *Nest.*5.2(p.97.32; 6¹.129D); id.*apol.orient.*9(p.52.12; 6¹.183A).

καταψεκάζ-ω, *wet* by continual dropping; pass., by rain, Nil.*epp.* 2.329(M.79.361B); met., *bedew, shed upon* ὅς [Mt.5:45] καὶ ∼ει τὴν δρόσον τῆς ἀληθείας Clem.*prot.*11(p.80.25; M.8.232C); σοφίᾳ κ. Meth.*symp.*4.3(p.49.8; M.18.92A).

καταψεύδομαι, **1.** *lie about, speak falsely of, accuse falsely;* c. κατά et genit., Athenag.*leg.*35.1(M.6.969A); κ. θεοῦ ὡς κωλύοντος ...τι ποιεῖν *Diogn.*4.3; c. acc. et infin., Tat.*orat.*3(p.4.6; M.6.812A); Ath.*decr.*22(p.18.27; M.25.456A); of things, *misrepresent* κ. τῶν θείων λογίων id.*Ar.*1.48(M.26.112B); id.*ep.Adelph.*8(M.26.1084A); κ. ... θεραπείας ἐξ αὐτῶν ἀποτελεσθείσας *Hom.Clem.*9.18; **2.** pass., *be false* ζύμην...τὴν ὡς ἐν φαυλότητι καὶ κατεψευσμένην Cyr.*ador.*17(1. 613D); id.*Abac.*1(3.518A).

***καταψηφηφορέω,** *vote against, condemn* one (*to*) κ. αὐτοῦ τὸν θάνατον Cyr.*Juln.*6(6².189E); id.*hom.pasch.*24.3(5².292A).

καταψηφίζομαι, A. = foreg.; hence **1.** *find guilty* of, *condemn* as, usu. τί τινος; c. genit. rei τίς...οὐ μανίας...καταψηφίσεται τῶν ὑπονοούντων; Ath.*Dion.*19(p.60.11; M.25.508A); **2.** met., *convict* or *accuse* of εἰ τὸ ποιεῖν ἐκ τοῦ μὴ ποιεῖν ἀλλοίωσιν τοῦ θεοῦ κ. Meth. *creat.*4(p.496.22; M.18.336C); Gr.Naz.*ep.*10(M.37.37A); Dion.Ar.*d.n.* 8.7(M.3.896A).

B. *decree* τῆς θείας...ψήφου τὸν εἰς τέλος τοῦ νεὼ ἀφανισμὸν καταψηφισαμένης Philost.*h.e.*7.14(M.65.553A); Thdt.*ep.*113(4.1191).

C. *reckon;* **1.** *reckon oneself among* κατεψηφισάμην βασιλεῦσιν *A.Thom.*A 100(p.212.18); **2.** c. εἰς, *reckon up to, put at* a figure τὸ πλῆθος τοῦ λαοῦ εἰς ἑξακοσίας χιλιάδας κατεψηφίσθη †Hipp.Th.*fr.*8 c. 2(p.36.19; M.117.1041D).

καταψιθυρίζω, *whisper against* κ. ... τοῦ θεοῦ καὶ Μωσέως Cyr. *ador.*5(1.159E).

καταψιλ-όω, 1. *strip bare,* τὰ πέδια...τῶν ἀκρίδων ὀδοῦσι ∼ούμενα Cyr.*Joel.*8(3.206E); pass. *be bald* ∼οῦσθαι τὴν κεφαλήν id.*Am.*75 (3.336B); fig., *smooth out* προστέταχε καὶ ∼οῦσθαι τὴν εἰσδρομήν id. *glaph.Gen.*7(1.225C); **2.** met., *smooth out* θεοῦ πᾶν αὐτοῖς ∼οῦντος τὸ ἄναντες id.*Os.*126(3.159A); id.*hom.pasch.*18.2(5².240E); *simplify* ἐν παχυτέραις ἀφηγήσεσιν...∼οῦν γὰρ ἔδει τῆς ἱστορίας τὸ ἄναντες εἶναι δοκοῦν id.*glaph.Gen.*4(1.115D).

καταψοφέω, *make* a place *resound* φιλήματι κ. τὰς ἐκκλησίας Clem. *paed.*3.11(p.281.6; M.8.660B).

κατάψυξις, ἡ, *cooling, becoming cold, chill,* met. νόσος ἐστὶν ἡ κ. τῆς ἀγάπης Chrys.*hom.27.3 in Rom.*(9.722D).

***καταψυχή, ἡ,** s.v.l., *frigidity, coldness* in human relationships μὴ ἔχειν κ. πρός τινα· ὁ γὰρ καταψυχῆς ἔχων ἡ ψυχὴ αὐτοῦ τῷ κυρίῳ οὐ προσδέδεκται ‡Ath.*syntag.*2(M.28.837C), κατὰ ψυχήν alternative version (M.28.1640B).

καταψύχ-ω, 1. *cool, chill,* lit. and met., *allow to cool;* pass. intrans., *be cold;* of land, Or.*Cels.*5.30(p.32.16; M.11.1227A); Cyr.*Zach.*12(3. 668A); pass., met., *grow cool, cool down* δράμε...ἐπὶ τὴν εὐχήν, καὶ κατεψυγεῖσάν σου τὴν διάνοιαν θέρμανον Chrys.*Anna* 4.5(4.737A); id. *hom.27.3 in Rom.*(9.722D); καταψυχθήσεσθαι...τὴν ἀγάπην Cyr.*Zach.* 12(668B); **2.** *cool, refresh,* met. δρόσου οὐρανίου...∼ούσης ἡμῶν τὸ ἡγεμονικόν Or.*mart.*33(p.28.20; M.11.604C); **3.** pass., *be dry* or *parched,* of land κατεψυγμένης ἀνομβρίᾳ τῆς γῆς Gr.Naz.*or.*21.7(M. 35.1089A).

κατεάσσ-ω, variant of κατάγνυμι *break;* met. of persons, *crush,* ref. Mt.12:28 συντετριμμένον...κάλαμον λογίζομαι εἶναι τὸν ἐν πάθει τινὶ ποιοῦντα ἐντολὴν θεοῦ· ὃν ∼ειν καὶ ἀποκόπτειν οὐ χρή Bas.*reg.br.* 291(2.517D; M.31.1285D); ‡Caes.Naz.*dial.*188(M.38.1165).

***κατεβδοματέω,** *divide into categories of seven, cat.Apoc.*8:2 (p.298.20).

***κατεγγελάω,** *mock, laugh at,* Eus.*h.e.*10.4.16(M.20.856; καταγελᾶν p.867.27); †Jo.D.*B.J.*37(M.96.1213C).

***κατεγγίζω,** *deposit, T.Job* 20(p.115.26; v.l. κατῴκιζον).

κατεγγυάω, *pledge, betroth,* met. τὴν νύμφην τὴν ἐκκλησίαν κατεγγυηθῆναι τῷ λόγῳ Meth.*symp.*7.6(M.18.133A); ὁ κατεγγυήσας ἑαυτὸν τῷ κυρίῳ *ib.*5.5(p.58.20; 105A).

***κατεγκαλ-έω,** *bring charges, accuse* ἤρξαντο...∼εῖν μοι Anast.S. *hod.*10(M.89.185D); οὐδεὶς κ. τὴν ἐπιμέλειαν Thdr.Stud.*epp.*2.162(M. 99.1509A); pass., Dion.Ar.*ep.*8.1(M.3.1088A); abs., *A.Barth.*8(p.147. 32).

***κατεγκεντρίζω,** *engraft,* met. κατεγκεντρισθεῖσα [sc. ἁπλότης] opp. φύσει ἐνυπάρχουσα, Jo.Clim.*scal.*24(M.88.984B).

***κατεγνωσμένως,** *reprehensibly* ἐπικινδύνως γινόμενα ἤτοι κ. †Bas. *bapt.*2.8.2(2.661D; M.31.1601A).

***κατεδαφέω,** = κατεδαφίζω, *bring down, raze to the ground* βώμους...μέχρις αὐτῶν κατηδάφουν τῶν θεμελίων †Jo.D.*B.J.*35(M.96. 1192B).

κατεδαφίζω, = foreg., *M.Artem.*(p.166.22); ‡Jo.D.*Artem.*59(M. 96.1305C).

κατεθίζω, *accustom;* perf. med., *be accustomed* or *wont,* Cyr.*Ps.* 48:2(M.69.1068D); *cat.Lc.*4:1(p.33.7).

κατεῖδον, of mental vision, *understand, discern the meaning of,* Iren.*haer.*5.13.2(M.7.1157B).

κατείδωλος, *full of idols; given to idolatry, A.Barn.*22(p.300.11); Cyr.*fr.Cant.*4:8(M.69.1288C); Thdt.*Os.*12:11(2.1370).

κάτειμι (*ibo*), **1.** *go* or *come down; step down* from a carriage, *M. Polyc.*8.3; into the arena, Tat.*orat.*23(p.25.26; M.6.857B); from bishop's throne μετὰ...τὴν...τοῦ...εὐαγγελίου ἀνάγνωσιν, ὅ τε ἀρχιερεὺς κ. τοῦ θρόνου Max.*myst.*14(M.91.692D); **2.** *descend* genealogically, Ath.Scholast.*coll.*1.1(p.9); Phot.*nomoc.*10.5(M.104.825B); **3.** from heaven, of H. Ghost ἐξ αὐτοῦ...εἰς αὐτὸν κατῄει, ἐκ τῆς θεότητος αὐτοῦ εἰς τὴν ἀνθρωπότητα αὐτοῦ [sc. Christ] Ath.*inc.et c.Ar.*9(M.26.997C); ref. Inc. εἰς αὐτὴν [sc. τὴν Μαρίαν] κατῄει Iren.*haer.*3.22.2(M.7.956C); Clem.*exc.Thdot.*18(p.112.19; M.9.665C); Eus.*d.e.*4.10(p.168.8; M.22. 280C); **4.** met., *stoop, condescend* εἰς τοσοῦτον κ., ὡς...καὶ...τῶν τοῦ θανάτου λῦσαι δεσμῶν *ib.*(p.167.18; 280A).

κατεῖπον, aor.; **1.** *denounce* as; *accuse* one *of* τούτων τίς ἂν κατείποι...ἀνδροφονίαν; Athenag.*leg.*35.1(M.6.969A); pass. κατερρήθη ...ὁ φιλόσοφος ὡς Ἕλλην Jo.Mal.*chron.*14 p.369(M.97.549C); **2.** *confess to* δι' αἰκισμῶν...ἐξαναγκάζουσι κατειπεῖν ταῦτα Just.*2apol.*12.4 (M.6.464B).

***κατειρηνεύ-ω, 1.** *bring into a state of peace, render peaceful,* Bas. *hom.*9.4(2.75C; M.31.336B); **2.** *give the greeting* εἰρήνη σοι: κ. μετά *exchange the greeting of peace* ὁ ἐξερχόμενος τοῦ μοναστηρίου... πρῶτον ἔρχεσθαι καὶ ∼ειν μετὰ τοῦ ἱερέως καὶ πατρὸς...καὶ οὕτως λοιπὸν ἀνεμποδίστως...προσέρχεσθαι τοῖς ἁγίοις μυστηρίοις κατὰ [Mt. 5:23] Call.*v.Hyp.*(p.87); *ib.*(p.88).

κατειρωνεύ-ομαι, abs., *dissimulate, conceal one's thoughts* οἱ μὲν... φόβῳ τὴν ἐκκλησίαν ὑπεδύοντο, τὸν καιρὸν ∼όμενοι Eus.*v.C.*3.66(p.113. 8; M.20.1144A); ∼όμενοι...καὶ τὴν ὑπόκρισιν ὑπεμφαίνοντες Cyr.*Ps.* 34:19(M.69.908C); Thphyl.*exc.Rom.*8(p.227.30; M.113.936D).

***κατεκκαθαρίζομαι,** *be thoroughly purified, Hom.Clem.*8.17.

***κατεκκλησιάζω,** *assemble,* Jo.Not.*v.Eus.*3(M.86.308D).

***κατεκνεύω,** *overhang, beetle over,* Cyr.*Abd.*3(3.357A).

***κατεκτυπέομαι,** perf. pass., *be moulded to the figure, cling;* of clothes, v.l. for ἐκτετυπωμένων, Chrys.*hom.*8.3 *in 1Tim.*(11.592E).

***κατεκχέω,** *pour out over,* irreg. aor. ptcpl. τὴν...κατεκχέασαν τῶν ποδῶν αὐτοῦ τὸ μύρον Vict.*Mc.*14:3(p.418.7).

***κατέλεος, τό,** *pity,* Mel.*pass.*p.16.36.

***κατέλευσις, ἡ,** *coming down, descent* τὸ...πνεῦμα...τὴν κ. πεποιημένον ἐπὶ τὴν τοῦ λόγου σάρκα Clem.*exc.Thdot.*16(p.112.6; M.9. 665A); of Inc. τῆς τοῦ Ἰησοῦ κ. Const.*or.s.c.*18(p.179.18; M.20. 1288A); *ib.*20(p.184.3; 1296A).

κατεμβλέπω, *look down at* or *upon;* of God from heaven, Cyr.*Am.* 79(3.343D; καταβλέψεται Aubert).

***κατεμπίμπλημι,** *fill,* Eus.*v.C.*4.72(M.20.1228A; κατεπίμπλα p.147. 24); Cyr.*Is.*3.2(2.402E).

***κατεμπίμπρημι,** *burn, destroy by fire,* Cyr.*Thds.*2(p.43.17; 5². 2C).

κατεμπορεύ-ομαι, *make profit out of, make a trade of,* Gr.Nyss. *v.Mos.*(M.44.429D); *trade on* ἐπίσταμαι τοὺς αὐτόθεν [sc. τεχνίτας] κρείττους εἶναι τῶν ἐνταῦθα ∼ομένων τῆς χρείας ἡμῶν id.*ep.*25(M.46. 1100A).

***κατέμπροσθεν,** *from the front* θυμιῶν τὴν ἁγίαν τράπεζαν κ. *Lit. Chrys.*(p.388.3).

***κατεμπυρίζω,** *burn up,* Cyr.*Am.*34(3.289A).

***κατεμφανίζω,** *reveal from above;* pass., of the Law, †Gregent. *disp.*(M.86.669C).

κατεμφορέομαι, med., *take one's fill of; stuff oneself with,* Gr.Agr. *Eccl.*2.12(M.98.836A); met. κ. τῆς θυμηδίας *ib.*3.5(852B).

***κατενάγω,** *lead up to,* in instruction εἰς τοῦτο [Os.6:6] κατενῆγεν Chrys.ap.*cat.Mt.*25:32(p.212.15), ἐνῆγε id.*hom.*79.1 *in Mt.*(7.758D).

κατέναντι, 1. prep.; **a.** *before, in front of,* of place βλέπω κ. μου καθέδραν Herm.*vis.*1.22; κ. τοῦ πατρὸς...σταθεῖσα *ib.*3.9.10; *A.Petr. et Sim.*3(p.82.12); cf.*T.Dan* 6.2; **b.** *in the face of* danger or hostility κ. τούτων ὁ Πέτρος ἀσθενοῦντας ἐθεράπευεν *A.Petr.et Paul.*33(p.193.

14) = *A.(Pass.)Petr.et Paul.*12(p.130.7); **c.** *over against, in contrast to* δύο ὁδοὺς...διὰ τοῦτο πάντα δύο δύο εἰσίν, ἓν κ. τοῦ ἑνός *T. Aser.*1.4; *ib.*5.1; **d.** *in the face of, against,* in hostility τὸν κονιορτὸν τῶν ποδῶν ἐξετινάξαμεν κ. τοῦ ἱεροῦ *A.Barn.*20(p.300.1); **2.** adj., *facing, opposite* ῥεόμενος [sc. ποταμός]...ἐπὶ τὴν κ. ἐκπεράσειε γῆν Philost.*h.e.*7.3 b(p.80.24).

***κατενδύω**, *clothe, invest* εἵμασίν...τινα...κ. Gr.Naz.*carm.*1.1.8.36 (M.37.449A).

κατένεξις (*-γξις), ἡ, **1.** *a throwing down* μετὰ τὴν κ. τῆς...συνοδικῆς τελείας εἰκόνος Agath.Diac.*epilog.*(H.3.1837A); **2.** *attack* τὴν...εἰς τὰς ἱερὰς εἰκόνας ὑπὸ τῶν κρατούντων κ. Thphn.*chron.*p.355(M.108.853B); **3.** (from pass.) κατένεγξις *downpour* of rain, Gr.Mag.*dial.*(tr.Zach.) 2.33(M.*PL.*66.193).

κατενεχυράζω, *pledge*, *Hom.Clem.*8.21.

κατεντρυφ-άω, *delight in* ἀνάπαυσιν οὐκ ἔχουσι...ὥσπερεὶ ∼ώντων πρὸς δόξαν...τοῦ θείου καὶ συντελουμένων Areth.*Apoc.*10(M.106.573C).

κατεντυγχάνω, *plead against, accuse,* opp. ὑπερεντυγχάνω, Didym. *Trin.*3.35(M.39.964A); Olymp.*Job* 7:21(M.93.104C); pass., Thdt.*ep.* 81(4.1140).

κατενώπιον, **1.** *before,* of persons, *in the presence of* διάκονοι ἄμεμπτοι κ. αὐτοῦ Polyc.*ep.*5.2; *A.(Pass.)Andr.*B 1(p.2.26; M.2. 1217A); of things, *in front of* κ. τοῦ ναοῦ στῆναι Just.*dial.*127.3(M. 6.773A); **2.** *in accordance with* ἐν τῷ διατάσσεσθαι αὐτὸν ταῦτα κ. τῆς τάξεως αὐτοῦ *A.(Pass.)Andr.*B 15(p.36.8; M.2.1248A).

***κατεξαίρετος**, for κατ' ἐξαίρετον; **1.** *exceptional, unique* τὴν... γνησίαν αὐτοῦ [sc. Christ] καὶ ἰδιότροπον καὶ φυσικὴν καὶ κ. υἱότητα Alex.Al.*ep.Alex.*8(M.18.560B; κατ' ἐξαίρετον p.24.25); cf.*ib.*3(p.21. 20; κατ' ἐξαίρετον 552C); τὴν κ. ὁμοιότητα τοῦ υἱοῦ πρὸς τὸν πατέρα Gr.Nyss.*Eun.*2(M.45.536C; κατ' ἐξαίρετον 2 p.357.28); *ib.*8(785B; κατ' ἐξαίρετον 2 p.190.21); neut. as subst. τὸ κ. τῆς ποιήσεως Proc.G. *Gen.*1:27(M.87.129D); **2.** neut. as adv., *specially* μὴ ἐν τούτοις [sc. instincts of anger and desire]...κ. ἡ ἀνθρωπίνη χαρακτηρίζεται φύσις Gr.Nyss.*anim.et res.*(M.46.53A, v.l. κατ' ἐξαίρετον); τις τῶν ἁγίων, οὗτινος κατ' ἐξαίρετον ἀπήρξατο καλοῦ Max.*ambig.*(for κ. M.91.1141C).

κατεξανάστασις, ἡ, *strife*, Chrys.*hom.10.1 in Eph.*(11.76B, v.l.).

κατεξανιστ-άω, = κατεξανίστημι; **1.** *raise up against* οἱ παρ' ἡμῶν κηρύγμασιν τὴν ἑαυτῶν σκαιότητα ∼ᾶν ἐθέλοντες Cyr.*Ps.*45:3(M.69. 1045D); **2.** *subdue, reduce* θηρίον, λιμοῦ ∼ῶντος αὐτὸ πρὸς τὸ δεῖν... βοῶν ἀγέλαις...ἐπιπηδᾶν id.*Is.*3.3(2.439C); **3.** med. intrans., *set oneself up, rebel against* ∼ᾶται [sc. ἡ σάρξ] τῆς ψυχῆς Chrys.*hom.13.6 in Rom.*(9.566A; κατεξανίσταται Gaume); ἵνα μή τις αὐτοῦ ∼ᾶται τῶν ἀπεγνωσμένων id.*hom.44.1 in 1Cor.*(Gaume; κατεξανιστῆται 10.406E).

κατεξανίστ-ημι, **1.** *raise up against* ∼άσης αὐτῶν τὸν πόλεμον τῆς Ῥωμαίων χειρός Cyr.*Is.*3.1(2.382B); id.*Nah.*29(3.506D); id.*ador.* 14(1.486C); id.*Ps.*33:21(M.69.893B); *raise up* as an enemy ὁ...θεὸς κατεξανέστησε τὸν Ναβουχοδονόσορ id.*Is.*3.2(2.421E); **2.** as med., *set oneself up against, despise* τὴν ἀποστολικὴν ∼ᾶσι ῥῆσιν, ὡς ἐπ' ἀνθρώπου κοινοῦ προενηνεγμένην id.*Chr.un.*(5[1].763B); **3.** intrans. 2nd aor. and med.; **a.** *rise up against, struggle against;* abs., *resist* φύσεως τυραννίς, ∼αμένη...καὶ ἐλευθεριάζειν βουλομένη Chrys.*hom. 23.2 in 1Cor.*(10.202B); ‡Nil.*perist.*2.3(M.79.820B); **b.** *set oneself up, vaunt oneself against, despise* ∼ασθαι τῶν πλημμεληκότων Chrys.*hom. 3.5 in Mt.*(7.41B); *ib.82.3*(785B,786D); τοὺς...ταῖς καινοτομίαις χαίροντας...καὶ τῶν συνηθῶν καὶ πάλαι γνωρίμων...ὡς μηδενὸς ἀξίων, ∼αμένους Max.*ambig.*(M.91.1209A); with κατά: κατεξαναστῆναι οὐκ ὀφείλεις κατὰ τοῦ πλησίον Chrys.*hom.10.1 in Eph.*(11.76B); abs. οὐ γὰρ ἐγὼ ∼αμαι· θεός ἐστιν ὁ ἐπιτάττων id.*hom.29.1 in Rom.*(9.730E); **c.** *face without fear, confront* πάντων ὡς παίδων ∼άμενον id.*hom.10.5 in Mt.*(7.145C); *ib.24.4*(305B).

***κατεξεστηκώς**, for καὶ ἐξεστηκώς: τίς...οὕτως παράφορος...καὶ ἐξεστηκὼς τὴν διάνοιαν; Gr.Nyss.*Eun.*1(1 p.159.14; κ. M.45.400D).

κατεξετάζ-ω, *examine carefully; question closely,* persons εἰ ταῦτα ...τις ἡμᾶς ∼οι Gr.Nyss.*Eun.*12(1 p.239.1; M.45.937A); matters τὰ νῦν ἡμῖν προκείμενα...κ. id.*anim.et res.*(M.46.52A); Cyr.*Ps.*5:2(M.69. 741B).

κατεξευμαρίζω, *make plain* or *easy*, Cyr.*Jo.*10.2(4.881E).

***κατεξωλεύομαι**, *be debauched*, Bas.Sel.*v.Thecl.*2.19(M.85.600B).

***κατεξουδεν-όομαι**, *be set at nought* καταπεφρόνηται καὶ ∼ωται... ἡ σοφία Gr.Agr.*Eccl.*9.1(M.98.1085C).

κατεξουσία, ἡ, *sovereignty, dominion,* Thphl.Ant.*Autol.*1.6(M.6. 1033C); sts. for κατ' ἐξουσίαν: ἡ κτίσις μεταλαμβάνεται τῶν χαρισμάτων, τὸ δὲ πνεῦμα κ. χαρίζεται Gr.Nyss.*fid.*(M.45.144A); [sc. εἰρήνην] ὡς αὐτοῦ τυγχάνουσαν...δίδωσιν κ. ἔφη γάρ [Jo.14:27] Didym.*Trin.* 1.26(M.39.384A); v. ἐξουσία.

κατεξουσιάζ-ω, *dominate, exercise authority over* ὕλη...τῆς ψυχῆς κ. ἠθέλησεν Tat.*orat.*15(p.17.3; M.6.840A); ποίμαινε τὸ ποίμνιον μὴ... ὡς ∼ων *Const.App.*2.20.11; Marc.Er.*opusc.*3.3(M.65.968D) etc.; of God τῷ πάντων ∼οντι θεῷ Cyr.*Nah.*4(3.479D); id.*Os.*82(3.115C); id. *Juln.*4(6[2].141B); of Christ φύσεως ἰδίας...καρπὸν τὸ...δύνασθαι ∼ειν τῶν τοῦ θανάτου δεσμῶν id.*Jo.*7(4.660C); *ib.*2.1(131D).

***κατεξουσιάστης**, ὁ, *ruler, potentate* τὸν σατανᾶν...τῆς καρδίας... κ. ποιεῖται Cyr.*Jo.*9(4.738E).

***κατεξουσιαστικός**, *sovereign,* Clem.*paed.*1.7(p.126.6; M.8.324A).

κατεπᾴδ-ω, *sing,* Gr.Naz.*or.*9.2(M.35.821B); τῷ Δαβὶδ...∼οντι τοῖς ὀρθότητος ἐρασταῖς Cyr.*Ps.*36 arg.(M.69.924B); αἱ λιταί, τοῖς... ἱεροῖς ∼όμεναι ὕμνοις Niceph.Ur.*v.Sym.*106(M.86.3085B).

κατεπαίρομαι, *behave arrogantly; crow over; disparage, Const. App.epit.*13; Gr.Naz.*or.*28.5(p.28.14; M.36.32C); Cyr.*Is.*2.2(2.236D); id.*Jo.*9(4.720A) cit. s. ἀνεθελήτως; of antichrist κ. εἰδώλων ἁπάντων Cyr.H.*catech.*15.15; c. dat. in Or.ap.*cat.Mt.*12:18ff.(p.92.4) for κ. τῆς ἀληθείας id. *fr.260 in Mt.*12:20(p.119).

***κατεπαΐσσω**, *swarm* καθάπερ μελίσσας...κατεπαΐξάσας ὄχλῳ πολλῷ Mac.Mgn.*apocr.*3.37(p.132.2).

***κατεπακούω**, *understand,* Mac.Mgn.*apocr.*3.13(p.85.2).

***κατεπανίστημι**, aor. 2 and pass. intrans.; **1.** *rise up against* κατεπανέστησάν μου πᾶς ὁ ὄχλος *V.Zos.*6(p.100.19, v.l. με; μοι Vassiliev, p.170); **2.** met., *be in opposition to, oppose* κατεπανέστησαν κατὰ τῆς πίστεως CSard.*ep.cath.*ap.Ath.*apol.sec.*42(p.119.9; M.25. 324B); πᾶσα κακία κατεπανισταμένη τῆς ἀρετῆς Max.*qu.Thal.*47(M. 90.425C); *resist, withstand* οὐ τῇ ἐμαυτοῦ δυνάμει τῶν ἀλγεινῶν κατεπανιστάμενος Bas.*hom.in Ps.*114(1.201C; M.29.488C).

***κατεπαρτικῶς**, *in* or *from superiority, arrogantly* μή με νομίσῃς... κ. σοι ἐνεχθῆναι· ἀλλὰ...ἀγαπητικῶς καὶ πεπονημένως Thdr.Stud.*epp.* 2.137(M.99.1440A).

***κατεπαφίημι**, *discharge upon;* hence *utter against,* Cyr.*Juln.*6 (6[2].185E).

***κατεπεγείρομαι**, *be aroused,* Marc.Er.*opusc.*2.78(M.65.941B).

κατεπείγ-ω, **1.** trans., *press hard, urge;* intrans., *be pressing* or *urgent* πρὸς τὴν...θεραπείαν ἡμᾶς...κ. *Hom.Clem.*4.1; *press for, demand urgently* τοῦ...μυστηρίου ἤδη λέγειν ∼οντος Just.*dial.*43.3 (M.6.568B); impers., *it is urgent, it is high time* [for one] *to* κ. με... πρὸς τὰ...εἰρημένα ἀποκρίνασθαι *ib.*68.9(636C); οὐ πάνυ κ. ... τροφῆς εὐπορίαν παρασχεῖν Or.*fr.53 in Jo.*(p.527.15); intrans., of persons, *be dangerously ill;* ptcpl., *urgent case* of illness ἀπὸ τῶν ∼όντων καὶ χείρονα πεπονθότων τὴν ἀρχὴν ποιεῖται τῆς θεραπείας id.*Jo.*32.6 (5; p.435.25; M.14.757A); **2.** neut. ptcpl.; **a.** *urgent matter;* hence *important matter, essential, point* ἡ...πίστις σύντομός ἐστιν...τῶν ∼όντων γνῶσις Clem.*str.*7.10(p.42.4; M.9.481A); τὸ κ. τοῦ ζητήματος id.*paed.*2.1(p.163.28; M.8.400B); πρὸς τὸ κ. ἴωμεν Chrys.*hom.36.1 in Jo.*(8.207C); **b.** *urgency* γράφειν μὲν ἀρξάμενος, διὰ δὲ τὸ κ. τῆς ἐξηγήσεως ὑπερθέμενος Tat.*orat.*35(p.37.10; M.6.877C); Thdr.Mops. *Nah.*1:1(M.66.401B); **3.** *hasten, expedite, Hom.Clem.*3.68.

κατεπεκτάδην, *at length* ἐποίησαν...λόγους κ., ἤγουν ἐκτεταμένους Jo.D.*dialect.*8(M.94.552D).

κατεπεμβαίν-ω, **1.** *trample on;* met. *attack* verbally, *insult* εἰ... πένητα προσιόντα...ἴδωμεν...∼ομεν Chrys.*ecl.*23(12.593C); τί ∼εις τῷ κειμένῳ; ‡Chrys.*publ.*1.1(8.117C); περιϋβρίζοντες τὸν Ἰησοῦν, ἀθύρῳ...γλώσσῃ ∼οντες Cyr.*Os.*35(3.65D); ἀλλήλοις ὡς πολεμίοις ∼οντες Thdt.*affect.*4(p.101.19; 4.793 some MSS only); c. genit. τηρήσει Χριστὸς τὰς καρδίας ἡμῶν, οὐκ ἐφιεὶς τῷ τῆς ἀνομίας εὑρετῇ ∼ειν αὐτῶν Cyr.*Is.*3.3(2.464A); θράσει ∼ετε μου ὡς ἀσεβοῦς Olymp. *Job* 21:27f.(M.93.292D); **2.** *embark upon,* met. ὁ...τολμῶν...ἐκτείνεσθαι πρὸς γνῶσιν θειοτέρων πραγμάτων, ἢ καὶ ἀΰλου ∼ων προσευχῆς Evagr.Pont.*or.*145(M.79.1197C).

***κατεπέρχομαι**, *seduce,* ‡Ath.*qu.Ant.*97(M.28.657A).

***κατεπιβαίνω**, *overcome* κατεπιβήσονται λοιπὸν τῆς τῶν δαιμόνων πονηρίας Nil.*Eulog.*15(M.79.1113A).

***κατεπιβαρέω**, *burden, put upon,* Ephr.1.84D.

***κατεπίδοσαν**, irreg. aor. from κατεπιδεῖν *look down and behold, see below* one κόσμος...τῶν καταχθονίων κατεπόθη...χάσμα τῆς γῆς ἐπειλημμένων βροντῶν ἤχῳ κ. *Anaph.Pil.*A 7(p.439).

κατεπιθύμιος, = sq., *A.Thom.*A 36(p.154.12).

κατεπίθυμος, *very desirous, eager,* Herm.*vis.*3.2.2; Hipp.*Dan.* 4.47.5.

κατεπίκειμαι, **1.** *be placed, lie,* Bas.*hex.*8.4(1.74E; M.29.176A); **2.** met., *attack, accuse* τῶν...ταπεινοτέρων μικράν τινα αἰτίαν εὕροντες, εὐθέως κατεπικείμεθα Marc.Er.*opusc.*3.3(M.65.968D).

***κατεπίκλησις**, ἡ, *additional name, title,* Or.*Cels.*4.34(p.304.25; M.11.1081A).

***κατεπιπλέκων**, vox nihili, Gr.Thaum.*pan.Or.*8(M.10.1077B; conj. κατ' ἐπιπλέκων p.22.8).

***κατεπισπεύδω**, *be in great haste,* Andr.Cr.*or.*8(M.97.976A).

κατεπιτηδεύ-ω, **1.** *labour, make a point of* μὴ ~οντας τὴν νουθεσίαν ‡Just.*ep.Zen.et Ser.*2(M.6.1185A); **2.** *strive* τὸ μὴ ~ειν πρωτείων ἀπολαύειν *ib.*3(1185B).

***κατεπιτρέχω**, *be eager, rush* for, Andr.Cr.*or.*8(M.97.973C).

***κατεπιτυγχάν-ω**, *attain* τινας αὐτῶν [i.e. those outside Church] καὶ ~οντας τῆς ἀληθείας Gr.Nyss.*Eun.*11(2 p.270.17; κατ' ἐπιτυγχάνοντας M.45.880B).

κατεπιφύ-ομαι *attack*, Cyr.*hom.div.*5(p.93.10; 5^2.359E); id.*Is.*3.1 (2.378A); ὅταν...~ωνται...αὐτῶν πειρασμοί *ib.*3.3(443A); abs. κατεπεφύοντο δεινῶς καὶ ἐζήτουν αὐτὸν ἀποκτεῖναι *ib.*1.5(136E); c. acc. κ. τινας id.*Ps.*37:14(M.69.965B).

κατεπιχειρέω, *make an attempt on*; **1.** *try* κ. τοῦ πράγματος Gr. Nyss.*virg.*23(p.335.1; M.46.408A); διασκεδάσαι κατεπεχείρησαν †Cyr. *hom.div.*10(5^2.378A); **2.** *attack* κ. τῆς ἀληθείας Gr.Nyss.*Eun.*3(2 p.42. 21; M.45.609C); id.*anim.et res.*(M.46.145B,152B); *assault* μοιχικῶς κ. τῆς ἀχράντου παστάδος id.*Melet.*(M.46.857D).

κατεργάζ-ομαι, **1.** *do, perform* τῆς δικαιοπραγίας ἧς κατειργάσαντο ...καὶ...ἔργων ὧν κατειργασάμεθα *1Clem.*32.3; τὸ θέλημα τοῦ νυμφίου ...κ. Ath.*virg.*2(p.37.29; M.28.253D); *perpetrate* τὰ δεινὰ κ. Athenag. *leg.*34.1(M.6.968B); **2.** abs., *work*; ptcpl., *active* πνεῦμα...ἐν τρισὶ ~όμενον...ἔργοις *T.Sal.*12.2(p.41.10; M.122.1333B); **3.** *subdue, consume, waste, wear* τὸ...πῦρ...κατεργασάμενον πᾶσαν ὕλην Iren.*haer.* 1.7.1(M.7.513A); Chrys.*hom.10.3 in Eph.*(11.78E); of Job τεταριχευμένῳ καὶ κατεργασθέντι id.*hom.28.4 in 1Cor.*(10.255Af.); id.*ep.*138 (3.681D); **4.** *work upon*; **a.** *work, knead* dough, Mac.Aeg.*hom.*24.4 (M.34.664D); **b.** *fashion* gems, Eus.*v.C.*3.49(p.98.20; M.20.1109B); **c.** pass., fig., of the soil of the mind, *be worked*, Gr.Thaum. *pan.Or.*7(p.20.10; M.10.1076A); **d.** met., *work upon, affect* κ. τι καὶ ποιῆσαι ἁπαλόν Chrys.*hom.50.3 in Ac.*(9.376E); the blood, *ib.42.4* (324B); οὕτω γὰρ αὐτὸν ὁ θεῖος κατειργάσατο πόθος...ὡς...προχέειν τὰ δάκρυα Thdt.*h.rel.*5(3.1165); **e.** *render, make* εὐήνιον...τὴν ἀρχὴν... τοῖς ἀρχομένοις κ. Eus.*v.C.*1.9(p.11.13; M.20.921A); *ib.*1.25(p.19.22; 940B); πνευματικὸν αὐτὸ [sc. τὸ σῶμα] κ. Chrys.*comm.in Gal.*5:22 (10.722B).

κατεργαστέον, *one must do* or *practise*, Nil.*epp.*1.142(M.79.141B).

κατεργαστικός, *of* or *for accomplishing* χεῖρα...νοοῦμεν τὴν τῶν θαυμάτων κ. αὐτοῦ δύναμιν Gr.Nyss.*hom.11 in Cant.*(M.44.1013A).

κάτεργον, τό, religious *service, office* οὐδενὶ πρέπον ἐν προσευχῇ πάρεργον, μᾶλλον δὲ κ. Jo.Clim.*scal.*19(M.88.937D).

***κατερεθίζω**, *provoke, incite*; to anger, *irritate*, Cyr.*Is.*3.4(2. 502C); κ. πρὸς ὀργὰς τοῦ νόμου τὸν ὁριστήν id.*Nah.*9(3.486B); κ. ἐφ' ἑαυτοῖς...τὸν...θεόν id.*Os.*95(3.126B); to evil, *ib.*119(150C); id.*Ps.* 36:1(M.69.924D); id.*ador.*4(1.108A); to good, *ib.*1(24E).

***κατερεικτός**, *crushed, ground* ὀσπρίων κ. Cyr.*glaph.Lev.*(1.345A).

κατερειπόω (κατεριπόω), *cast down, ruin*, Philost.*h.e.*4.11(M.65. 524C); ‡Nil.*perist.*12.7(M.79.953A); τὴν πάλαι Σαμαρείαν κατηριπωμένην *Chron.Pasch.*p.193(M.92.476B); Thphn.*chron.*p.42 (κατεριπώθη M.108.160C).

***κατερεύκεις**, vox nihili, †Apoll.*met.Ps.*77:38(M.33.1425D; κατερύκοις p.161).

κατερευνάω, *expose*, Sophr.H.*v.Anast.*(M.92.1709B).

[*]**κατεριπόω**, v. κατερειπόω.

κατερρήθη, v. κατεῖπον.

***κατερρινημένως**, *meticulously, accurately*, Cyr.*ador.*9(1.305D); id. *Mich.*5(3.394A).

[*]**κατερυθαίνω**, variant of κατερυθραίνω, *make red, flush*, Cyr. *Joel.*16(3.215A, v.l. -θραίνει Aubert).

κατερυθριάω, *blush deeply*, Cyr.*Thds.*(p.45.7; 5^2.4D); id.*Os.*131(3. 164A); id.*Am.*49(3.303D).

κατέρχ-ομαι, **1.** *go* or *come down*; c. acc. κ. τὸν ἔμβολον Jo.Mal. *chron.*18 p.490(M.97.709B); into waters of baptism κατελθόντος τοῦ Ἰησοῦ ἐπὶ τὸ ὕδωρ Just.*dial.*88.3(M.6.685B); ἵνα...καθαρὸς...κατέλθῃ [sc. ἐπὶ τὸ βάπτισμα] Clem.*exc.Thdot.*83(p.132.19; M.9.696D); Serap. *euch.*19.4; of Christ into Hades ὁ κύριος...εἰς ᾅδου κ. Clem.*str.*6.6 (p.454.31; M.9.268C); Meth.*res.*3.5(p.396.1; M.18.320B); Ath.*Ar.*3.23 (M.26.372A); ‡Ath.*Apoll.*1.18(M.26.1125B); in creeds ἀποθανόντα καὶ εἰς τὰ καταχθόνια κ. *Symb.Sirm.*3 ap.Ath.*syn.*8(p.236.1; M.26. 693A); *Symb.CP*(360)*ib.*30(p.259.5; 748A); **2.** morally, *decline, fall* εἰς τοῦτο τὸ τύφος κατεληλύθασιν Iren.*haer.*1.25.2(cf.M.7.681A); εἰς φθορὰν ~όμενον τὸ...τῶν ἀνθρώπων γένος Ath.*inc.*10.1(M.25.112D); εἰς πολυθεότητα κ. id.*ep.Aeg.Lib.*14(M.25.569B); **3.** theol., ref. Inc. πρόδρομος...σημαίνων...κατελεύσεσθαι τὸν σωτῆρα Hipp.*antichr.*45 (p.29.7; M.10.764B); κατῆλθεν...ὁ λόγος καὶ ἐσαρκώθη Meth.*res.*2. 24(p.380.12; M.18.329D); Ath.*inc.*18.5(M.25.128C); κατελθόντα καὶ σαρκωθέντα *Symb.Nic.*(325)(p.51; M.20.1540B); Eus.*e.th.*2.7(p.105.9; M.24.909C); Dion.Ar.*e.h.*4.3.10(M.3.484A); Gnost. (Valent.) τοῦτον διὰ Μαρίας διοδεύσαντα, καθάπερ ὕδωρ διὰ σωλῆνος ὁδεύει, καὶ εἰς τοῦτο ἐπὶ τοῦ βαπτίσματος κατελθεῖν ἐκεῖνον, τὸν...Σωτῆρα Iren.*haer.* 1.7.2(M.7.513A); (Marcosian) τὸ μὲν γὰρ βάπτισμα τοῦ φαινομένου Ἰησοῦ ἀφέσεως ἁμαρτιῶν, τὴν δὲ ἀπολύτρωσιν τοῦ ἐν αὐτῷ Χριστοῦ κατελθόντος εἰς τελείωσιν *ib.*1.21.2(657C); *ib.*1.14.5(604C); *ib.*1.15.2f. (620Af.); (Cerinthus) μετὰ τὸ βάπτισμα κατελθεῖν εἰς αὐτὸν τὸν... Χριστὸν ἐν εἴδει περιστερᾶς *ib.*1.26.1(cf.M.7.686B); (Theodotus) τοῦτο [sc. σαρκίον] στολισάμενος κατῆλθεν ὁ Σωτήρ Clem.*exc.Thdot.*1(p.105. 7; M.9.653A); *ib.*74(73; p.130.16; 693A); ὁ κατελθών *ib.*31(p.117.4; 673C); Manich. ἄνεμος, φῶς, ὕδωρ, πῦρ καὶ ὕλη...ταῦτα ἐνδυσάμενον ...κατελθεῖν κάτω καὶ πολεμῆσαι τῷ σκότει Hegem.*Arch.*7.3(p.10.8; M.10.1437B); *ib.*8.1(p.11.5; 1437C); **4.** error for παρερχόμενος, Dor. *doct.*10.5(M.88.1729B).

κατεσθί-ω, *eat up, devour*, fig. ἀντὶ...νύμφης θηρίον ἐγένετο, καὶ τὸν νυμφίον κατέφαγεν Thdt.*Jer.*12:8(2.476); met. τὰς ἀρετὰς αὗται καταφαγοῦσαι...χοιρώδη βίον...βιοτεύειν Meth.*creat.*1(p.494.14; M.18. 333B); ~είῃ for ~ει, Didym.*Ps.*13:3ff.(M.39.1221B); ~ωμεν ἑαυτούς, ἐὰν ῥῆμά ποτε φορτικὸν ἐκπηδήσῃ τῶν ὀδόντων Chrys.*hom.14.4 in Eph.*(11.109A); οὐχὶ κατεδηδόκασι τὸν σατανᾶν Cyr.*Lc.*9:1(M.72. 641A).

***κατεσκεμμένως**, *deliberately*, Cyr.*Juln.*5(6^2.174C).

***κατεσκευασμένως**, *speciously*, Cyr.*ep.*72(5^2.200E).

***κατεσκιασμένως**, *obscurely*, Cyr.*ador.*8(1.265C).

[*]**κατεσκληρός**, *hard, austere* ὁ καρτερικὸς καὶ κ. βίος τῶν δικαίων Oecum.*Apoc.*16:14(p.180.1).

***κατεσφαλμένως**, *erroneously*, Petr.I Al.*fr.*2(M.18.516A)ap.*Chron. Pasch.*p.3(M.92.73B).

***κατεσχηματισμένως**, *in affectation* or *pretence* μὴ ἐπιδεικτικῶς ἢ κ. ἐπιτελεῖν τὰς ἀρετάς Eustrat.*stat.anim.*18(p.489).

***κατεσωκλείω**, *shut up, imprison*, *Mir.Geo.hymn.*(p.152.14).

***κατευγλωττίζω**, *express well* or *fluently*, Chrys.*hom.in Mt.7:14* (3.27B); Jo.D.*hom.*12.21(M.96.809B).

κατευημερ-έω, *prosper, flourish at the expense of* ~οῦντος τῆς ἀληθείας τοῦ ψεύδους Gr.Nyss.*Trin.*1(p.72.3; M.32.685B); ἡ ἀδικία κ. ...τῆς δικαιοσύνης Gr.Agr.*Eccl.*8.2(M.98.1065B).

***κατευθύμιος**, *agreeable*, Gr.Nyss.*hom.opif.*6.1(M.44.140A).

κατευθυντήρ, ὁ, *one who straightens*; hence *corrector* διορθωτὴν ...καὶ κ. τῶν ἁμαρτιῶν Clem.*paed.*1.8(p.129.28; M.8.332B).

κατευθύν-ω, **1.** *straighten out* a difficulty, Gr.Mag.*dial.*(tr.Zach.) 3.24(M.*PL.*77.278D); **2.** *refer*, i.e. interpret as referring to πρὸς τὴν Χαλδαίαν Βαβυλῶνά τις ~ειν...τὸν λόγον Areth.*Apoc.*41(M.106.688C); **3.** *prosper, further* ~ομένην...τὴν δόξαν τοῦ σωτῆρος Cyr.*Ps.*8:10(M. 69.761A); Thdt.*Jer.*10:18(2.466); **4.** liturg. κατευθυνθήτω ref. Ps. 140:2, recited esp. in *Lit.Praesanct.*(p.346.13); *ib.*(*Euchol.*p.164); μετὰ τὸ 'κατευθυνθήτω', ἐν τῷ καιρῷ τοῦ εἰσάγεσθαι τὰ προηγιασμένα δῶρα *Chron.Pasch.*p.385(M.92.989B).

***κατευθυσμός, ὁ**, *right directing*, Clem.*paed.*1.7(p.122.9; M.8. 313B).

***κατευλαβέομαι**, *shrink from* μὴ κατευλαβηθῇς τοῦ βοᾶν πρὸς θεόν Ephr.3.460B.

κατευλογέω, *bless*, Bas.*hom.*5.2(2.35A; M.31.241B); Cyr.*glaph. Gen.*2(1.61E).

κατευμαρίζ-ω, *make easy* ~οντος...τὰ δεινὰ τοῦ Χριστοῦ Cyr. *Mich.*11(3.401C); id.*Jo.*4.1(4.345C); id.*Is.*2.3(2.267E).

κατευμεγεθ-έω, **1.** *be stronger, more powerful than, overcome* κ. τῶν ἀντικειμένων δυνάμεων Ath.*exp.Ps.*26:1(M.27.148D); Gr.Nyss. *mart.*2(M.46.780B); οὐ γὰρ ἂν φαίημεν τῆς θείας βουλῆς...~εῖν δύνασθαι ὄφεων δήγματα Germ.CP *vit.term.*15(M.98.117C); freq. in Cyr.: *Nah.*28(3.506B); *Jo.*11.2(4.945D); *Nest.*4.5(p.86.33; 6^1.112D); abs., *ib.*1.4(p.23.26; 17C); id.*Juln.*4(6^2.135E); **2.** *suppress* οὐ δύναμαι ...μὴ εἶναι ζῷον λογικόν, τῶν τῇ φύσει προσόντων ~ήσας πλεονεκτημάτων id.*Jo.*2.6(4.220D); **3.** *win, obtain* οὐ γάρ ἐστιν τῆς τοῦ ἐσταυρωμένου κυρίου μνήσεως κ., μὴ τῇ...τριάδι τὸ εἰσαγώγιμον εἰληχότα Areth.*Apoc.*67(M.106.769A); c. acc. τῆς ἀγγελιώτιδος τάξεως...τὴν ἐγγύτητα καὶ στάσιν ~ούσης *ib.*28(636D); τὸ θεὸν ὁρᾶν κ. *cat.Apoc.*7:9ff.(p.292.13); **4.** *accomplish* ἐξ αὐτῆς γὰρ προστάξεως τὰ θεῖα τὴν συντέλειαν κ. *ib.*16:19(p.422.12).

κατευνάζω, *lull, calm*; *appease* wrath of God, Cyr.*Os.*40(3.71E); id.*Zach.*6(3.661B); perf. pass., *be torpid, inactive*, id.*Jo.*4.5(4.410C).

***κατευναστήριον, τό**, *abode*, Nonn.*par.Jo.*11:19(M.43.841B).

κατευνήτειρα, ἡ, *she who soothes* χεῖρα τιθήνην ὀρφανικῶν, πάσης τε κ. ἀνάγκης Paul.Sil.*Soph.*994(M.86.2157A).

***κατευοδεύω**, = κατευοδόω, *bring prosperity, make prosper*, *Apoc. Bar.rel.*7.23(p.59).

κατευοδόω, *guide aright, make prosper*, Ast.Am.*phar.*(p.116.14); Chrys.*hom.48.4 in Gen.*(4.486E); *Lit.Marc.*(Brightman p.119.22);

pass. intrans., *prosper*, Or.*exp.in Pr.*4:2(M.17.172A); Eus.*Is.*53:11 (M.24.460D); Gr.Nyss.*or.dom.*4(p.78.4; M.44.1168C); c. infin. κατ-ευόδω⟨σον γ⟩ενέσθαι σου τὸ θέλημα Cyr.S.*v.Abr.*(p.247.21).

κατευόδωσις, ἡ, *good success*, Gr.Agr.*Eccl.*8.9(M.98.1081A).

κατευρύν-ω, 1. *stretch out* or *over* ἐπίσπαστρον...~εσθαι τῶν θυρῶν, κρύπτειν τὰ ἅγια Cyr.*ador.*10(1.336D); fig., *widen* ἀρετῆς κ. τρίβον id.*hom.pasch.*18(5^2.240C); id.*Os.*51(3.82E); *spread* a net ὁ σατανᾶς, ὁ τῆς ἑαυτοῦ δυστροπίας...λίνον ~ων id.*Nah.*41(3.516A); met., *open wide at, stretch* the mouth or tongue in blasphemy τῆς τοῦ σωτῆρος ἡμῶν ὑπεροχῆς...τὸ ἀκρατὲς καὶ βέβηλον κ. στόμα id. *Juln.*6(6^2.194E); κ. ἐπ' αὐτῷ [sc. τῷ οὐρανῷ] τὴν γλῶτταν id.*Soph.*4(3.582D); **2.** *extend, spread* power φιλεῖ [sc. ὁ Βαβυλώνιος]...τὴν ἑαυτοῦ ~ειν ἀρχήν id.*Abac.*7(3.523B); pass., id.*Juln.*6(6^2.212A); the race, *ib.*3 (77E); the new dispensation τοῖς τεθλιμμένοις κ. τῆς εὐαγγελικῆς πολιτείας τὸ ἐλεύθερον id.*Is.*3.2(2.398A); pass., *ib.*5.1(752E); id.*Os.*63 (3.97B); id.*1Cor.*15:17(p.302.12; M.74.900B); met. [Jo.11:42]...~ων τῇ ἀνθρώπου φύσει τὴν τοῦ πατρὸς ἀκοήν id.*Pulch.*(p.49.4; 5^2.162A); pass., *be brought to* the point of οὐκ ἀπήλλαγμαι...τοῦ ἐν μοχθηροῖς εἶναι πράγμασιν, ἀλλὰ...καὶ πρὸς εὐθυμίαν ~ομαι id.*Ps.*4:2(M.69.733D) cf. 4; **3.** *amplify, open up, explain* τὸν ὑγιᾶ τῆς πίστεως κ. λόγον id. *ep.*4(p.26.15; 5^2.22D); id.*apol.orient.*9(p.52.37; 6^1.184A); id.*ador.*14 (1.505E); **4.** med., *give oneself up* to ~ομένους αὐτοὺς ὁρῶν ἐν ἀπαθείᾳ id.*Abac.*15(3.529D); ἀνασκιρτᾶν ἡμᾶς ἀναγκαῖον ~ομένους εἰς θυμηδίας id.*hom.pasch.*24.1(5^2.287B); **5.** theol. ἥκιστα μὲν γὰρ τὴν τῆς θεότητος φύσιν συντελοῦμεν Ἰουδαϊκῶς, εἰς μόνον τὸν ἕνα θεὸν καὶ πατέρα, ~οντες δὲ ὥσπερ εἰς ἁγίαν τε καὶ ὁμοούσιον τριάδα Cyr.*ador.*6(1.175B) = Isid.Pel.*epp.*2.142(M.78.585A); μία...ἐστιν ὁμολογουμένως φύσις θεότητος...~εται δὲ νοητῶς εἰς ἁγίαν τριάδα Cyr.*Juln.*1(6^2.21A); **6.** Christol. καθὸ δὲ γέγονε σάρξ...εἰς θεωρίαν ἡμῶν διπλῆν ὁ ἐπ' αὐτῷ ~εται λόγος, θεῷ τε ὄντι καὶ γεγονότι ἀνθρώπῳ· ἀλλ' εἰ καὶ γέγονε διττός, ἀλλ' εἷς ἐστι Proc.G.*Gen.*17:23(M.87.360C).

κατευστοχ-έω, met., *assail successfully, score off* ὅταν...μορφὴ πορνικὴ...τοξεύῃ, νῶτα διδόναι καλόν...~εῖ γὰρ ὀφθαλμῶν ἡ πορνεία Gr.Nyss.int.opp.Chrys.*hom.suppl.*7(M.64.468A) for κατατοξεύει Gr. Nyss.*hom.in 1Cor.*6:18(M.46.492B).

***κατευστοχία, ἡ,** *shot in the centre of the target, bull's-eye*; fig., in argument, *Schol.Clem.paed.*(p.337.2; M.9.792D).

κατευτελίζ-ω, 1. of things, *make light of* τὸ...βαρὺ...ἀσέβημα... ~ουσιν Ephr.3.57C; **2.** of persons; *despise, disparage*, Bas.*hom.*3.5 (2.21C; M.31.209B); Andr.Sam.*fr.*ap.Cyr.*apol.orient.*10(p.53.35; 6^1.185C); perf. ptcpl. pass. ὡς ἄνθρωπος μέλλων ἀποθνήσκειν κατευτελισμένος Mac.Aeg.*hom.*26.26(M.34.692D); Nil.*epp.*2.145(M.79.268A); **3.** reflex., *humble, abase oneself* ὁ σεαυτὸν [sc. Christ] κατευτελίσας ἕως ἐμοῦ *A.Thom.*A 15(p.121.9); Nil.*epp.*2.51(M.79.221C).

***κατευτελισμός, ὁ,** *a making light of, frivolity*, Ephr.3.57C.

κατευφραίν-ω, *gladden, delight* τῇ συναφείᾳ κ. τὸν ἅγιον Sophr.H. *v.Anast.*(M.92.1716A); τῆς εὐποιΐας τὸν πλοῦτον...~οντα τῇ ἐλπίδι †Jo.D.*B.J.*33(M.96.1181B); ‡Jo.D.*Artem.*3(M.96.1256A); pass., Const.*or.s.c.*11(p.166.9; M. om.); with God as subject ἡ διὰ τοῦ ἁγίου βαπτίσματος χάρις...τῇ...ἐλπίδι ~ουσα καταπιαίνει Cyr.*Is.*2.5 (2.343B); *ib.*2.1(212C); id.*Joel.*35(3.227D); with God as object κ. τὸν δεσπότην διὰ τῆς ἐννόμου πολιτείας id.*Os.*132(3.166B); id.*Zach.*29(3.695D); id.*ador.*6(1.181A).

κατευωχέω, *feast, entertain*, Clem.*paed.*2.1(p.163.17; M.8.400A).

***κατέφοδος, ἡ,** *descent*; of H. Ghost on water of baptism, Didym.(‡Bas.)*Eun.*5(1.308B; M.29.740A).

κατεχθραίνω, *hate, detest*, Cyr.*ador.*14(1.507C).

κατέχ-ω, A. trans.; **1.** *hold fast*; *keep, hold down* a job πορισμὸν μὴ κ. Hipp.*haer.*4.21(p.52.8; M.16.3087A); med., *hold on* to καθάπερ ἐν ἁλύσει χρυσῇ...ἐν τοῦ ἑνὸς ~εται...οὕτω καὶ τὰ τῶν ἁγίων εὐαγγελίων θαύματα ‡Meth.*palm.*1(M.18.384A); mentally, *hold fast* to a truth ταῦτα...ἐν τῇ ἐμαυτοῦ ψυχῇ κ. ... ὡς ἐν τῇ διανοίᾳ δικαιοσύνην ἀεὶ φυλάττειν Const.ap.Ath.*apol.sec.*68(p.146.8; M.25.369B); τὴν τῆς καθολικῆς ἐκκλησίας διδασκαλίαν κ. CSard.*ep.Alex.ib.*37(p.115.24; 312B); κ. ... τὴν...πίστιν Ath.*ep.Aeg.Lib.*8(M.25.536A); a practice μακάριος ὁ ~ων σε [sc. ἐγκράτειαν] Ath.*virg.*24(p.59.20; M.28.281A); πῶς...αὐτῷ...προσέλθοιμεν...ἁγνείαν οὐ ~οντες σώματος; Sophr.H. *nativ.*(p.508.5); *keep* a commandment [sc. Adam] καὶ μιᾶς μὴ κατασχεῖν ἐντολῆς Chrys.*hom.59.2 in Mt.*(7.595B); **2.** *keep back, withhold*, a secret κατεῖχεν ἐν μυστηρίῳ καὶ διετήρει τὴν σοφὴν αὐτοῦ βουλὴν *Diogn.*8.10; *hold in* or *down, control* ὃν χεὶρ ἀνθρωπίνη οὐ κάτεσχεν αὐτὸς δὲ [sc. Logos] ~ει πάντα *V.Aberc.*16(p.14.9f.); *detain*; by force, *hold, keep* Χριστιανοὶ ~ονται μὲν ὡς ἐν φρουρᾷ τῷ κόσμῳ, αὐτοὶ δὲ συνέχουσι τὸν κόσμον *Diogn.*6.7; Hegem.*Arch.*7(p.10.15; M.10.1437B); *arrest*, Chrys.*hom.15.10 in Mt.*(7.202C); **3.** *possess, occupy*, of God in creation εἰ δὲ μήτε ἐν τῷ κόσμῳ ἐστὶν μήτε περὶ τὸν κόσμον (τὸ γὰρ περὶ αὐτὸν πᾶν ὑπὸ τούτου ~εται), ποῦ ἐστιν; Athenag.*leg.*8.3(M.6.905B); pass., met. ἡμέρας...προσομιλούντων τοῖς θείοις μυστηρίοις, καὶ νυκτὸς ὢν ἐν ἡμέρᾳ εἶδε...ἡ ψυχὴ ταῖς φαντασίαις ~ομένων Gr.Thaum.*pan.Or.*16(p.37.27; M.10.1100B); ἐγκράτεια...ὑπὸ ἀθανασίας ~ομένη Ath.*virg.*24(p.59.18; M.28.280D); pass., *be covered*; of soul in rel. to body, Meth.*res.*3.18(p.415.3; M.18.325B); *possess, hold in one's power, seize*, acc. Apollinarians ἡ ἁμαρτήσασα φύσις [sc. of Christ] ἐν θεῷ γέγονεν, ἁμαρτίαν μὴ ποιήσασα, ἀνάγκῃ...~εται ‡Ath.*Apoll.*2.9(M.26.1145C); of ideas and practices εἰδωλομανία... κ. τὴν οἰκουμένην Ath.*inc.*14.3(M.25.120D); pass. διδάγμασι ~όμενος Just.*1apol.*56.3(M.6.413B); of emotions φόβῳ τοῦ συνειδότος κατεσχέθησαν Ath.*apol.sec.*43(p.121.6; M.25.329B); *be overcome, borne down* by sleep, Jo.Thess.*dorm.BMV* 2.12(p.425.7); *be distressed, troubled* τοὺς οἰκείους...ὑπὲρ ἡμῶν ~ομένους Jo.Clim.*scal.*3(M.88.669C); of demons, *possess* ἰῶνται, καταργοῦντες...τοὺς ~οντας τοὺς ἀνθρώπους δαίμονας Just.*2apol.*6.6(M.6.456A); **4.** exeg. 2Thess.2:6 ~ει καὶ κωλύει τοῦ ἀνόμου τὴν παρουσίαν τὸ πνεῦμα τὸ ἅγιον Sever.*2Thess.*2:6 (p.334.20); τὸ ~ον...τουτέστι, τὸ κωλῦον· οἱ μὲν τοῦ πνεύματος τὴν χάριν φασίν, οἱ δὲ τὴν Ῥωμαϊκὴν ἀρχήν· οἷς ἔγωγε μάλιστα τίθεμαι Chrys.*hom.4.1 in 2Thess.*(11.529C); 'τὸ ~ον' ὡς ἂν τοῦ διαβόλου μὲν ἐθέλοντος καὶ ἤδη τοῦτο ποιῆσαι, τοῦ θεοῦ δὲ ~οντος αὐτόν...'~ον' ὁ ἀπόστολος ὀνομάζει, τοῦ θεοῦ [λέγων] τὸν ὅρον Thdr.Mops.*2Thess.*2:6 (p.54.15ff.; M.66.933Df.); τινὲς τὸ '~ον' τὴν Ῥωμαϊκὴν ἐνόησαν βασιλείαν· τινὲς δὲ τὴν χάριν τοῦ πνεύματος...οὐδέτερον τούτων...ἀλλὰ τὸ παρ' ἑτέρων εἰρημένον ἀληθὲς εἶναι ὑπολαμβάνω...ὁ τοῦ θεοῦ τοίνυν αὐτὸν ὅρος νῦν ἐπέχει φανῆναι. οἶμαι δὲ καὶ ἑτέραν ἔχειν διάνοιαν τὸ ῥητόν...πρότερον καταλυθήσεσθαι τῆς δεισιδαιμονίας τὸ κράτος, καὶ πανταχοῦ διαλάμψειν τὸ σωτήριον κήρυγμα, καὶ τότε φανήσεσθαι τὸν τῆς ἀληθείας ἀντίπαλον Thdt.*2Thess.*2:6(3.533f.); cf. τὴν κάκωσιν αὐτῶν [sc. τῶν πιστῶν] ὁ πονηρὸς ἐπιθυμεῖ, ἀλλὰ ~εται καὶ κωλύεται Photius.*2Thess.*2:6(Staab p.636.19); **5.** μηδὲ τοῖς κατόπιν εἴ τι πέπρακται σπουδαῖον ~ειν ‡Mac.Aeg.*ep.*(M.34.421A) = Gr.Nyss. *instit.*(προσέχειν p.65.10).

B. intrans.; **1.** *be current*; **a.** of *present* time τοῦ κατασχόντος καιροῦ τούτου Bas.*ep.*226.1(3.346B; M.32.844A); **b.** of *reports, rumours*; also ref. scripture, as scripture *has it*, scripture *has it* that ὁ παρὰ τούτοις [sc. τοῖς Ἑβραίοις] κ. λόγος Eus.*p.e.*7.8(306C; M.21.520B); τοῖς προφήταις αὐτοῖς ἐπιβουλεῦσαι αὐτοὺς κ. λόγος id.*d.e.*6 proem.(p.251.22; M.22.413B); **2.** *last, continue*, Jo.Mal.*chron.*7 p.190 (M.97.301A); **3.** *hold, believe* ~ειν...ὁμολογῶ ὡς ἡ...ἐκκλησία κ. Maur.*ep.*(M.*PL.*87.106A).

***κατεψευγμένως,** *under censure*, Cyr.*Is.*1.1(2.22B).

***κατεψευσμένως,** *slanderously, in calumny* κ. εἰρημένα Or.*Cels.*6.40(p.109.13; M.11.1357B).

***κατζίον, τό,** *brazier*, *Schol.Clem.paed.*3.5(p.337.31; M.9.793A) cit. s. ἄρουλα.

κατηγορ-έω, 1. *accuse*; **a.** persons, usu. c. genit.; c. acc. κ. τὸν Ἰησοῦν Or.*Cels.*3.1(p.204.3; M.11.921B); Ath.*decr.*18(p.15.12; M.25.'453'(445)D); c. acc. and infin. ἄνδρα...πεφονεῦσθαι ~οῦντες id.*apol. sec.*8(p.94.23; M.25.264B); Thdt.*ep.*90(4.1161); c. acc. of crime τοὺς αὐτοὺς ὠμότητα καὶ φιλανθρωπίαν ~εῖσθαι *ib.*111(4.1182); pass., of person accused Χριστιανοὶ...εἶναι ~ούμεθα Just.*1apol.*4.5(M.6.333A); Or.*Cels.*1.65(p.119.3; 784); Ἰσχύραν τὸν κατήγορον...Μακάριον τὸν ~ούμενον Ath.*apol.sec.*13(p.98.2; 272A); of those not numbered with the elect εἰς ἂν ἦν τῶν ~ουμένων Thdt.*Rom.*11:2(3.117); 'rarely c. dat., *cat.Mt.*12:22(p.92.31); cf.Chrys.*hom.41.1 in Mt.*(7.444D); *cat.Mt.*27:19(p.234.5); **b.** God ἠρέμα ~οῦντες τοῦ ἄρρεν καὶ θῆλυ εἰς γένεσιν ἀνθρώπων πεποιηκότος Iren.*haer.*1.28.1(M.7.690B); τῶν ~ούντων τοῦ θείου λόγου Or.*Cels.*6.66(p.136.29; 1400A); Thdt.*Dan.*3:37(2.1117); pass., Ath.*Ar.*3.42(M.26.412B); **c.** oneself, in penitence [sc. Job] ἑαυτοῦ κ. *1Clem.*17.4; εἰ...ἑαυτοῦ μεταμεληθεὶς ~ήσει CCP (381)†*can.*6(p.165); *confess* ἱκέτης ἐγένετο τῆς ἁμαρτάδος ~ῶν Thdt. *h.rel.*15(3.1220); in self-contradiction or self-exposure, Clem.*str.*2.20(p.174.23; M.8.1057A); **d.** things, *criticize adversely*; *frown upon, reject* κ. τῶν ὑγιῶν δογμάτων Or.*Cels.*7.49(p.200.4; 1492B); οὐδεὶς... ἐγκωμιάζων τινά, καὶ ~εῖ τῆς τούτου πολιτείας Ath.*gent.*17(M.25.36B); τῆς τοῦ σώματος κ. θεραπείας Thdt.*h.rel.*2(3.1121); ἰατρικὴν ~εῖσθαι διὰ τὰς ἐν αὐτῇ αἱρέσεις Or.*Cels.*5.61(p.64.14; 1277A); **2.** *predicate*; c. dat., *ascribe* ἀσθένειαν αὐτῇ [sc. τῇ ψυχῇ] ~οῦμεν Thdt.*ep.*144(4.1240).

κατηγόρημα, τό, gram., *mood* ἡ 'ὀργίζεσθε' φωνὴ σημαίνει τὸ προστακτικὸν κ. Or.*sel.in Ps.*4:5(M.12.1141D).

κατηγόρησις, ἡ, *accusation*, Epiph.*haer.*70.15(p.248.2; M.42.372C); ποία...πανήγυρις [sc. τῶν Ἰουδαίων] οὐ γέγονε κ.; Leont.B. *mesopent.*(M.86.1977B).

***κατηγορήτρια, ἡ,** fem. of κατήγορος, *accuser*; *betrayer*, Steph. Diac.*v.Steph.*(M.100.1184B).

κατηγορία, ἡ, = κατηγόρημα, *indication, evidence* τῆς προαιρέσεως...μεγίστη κ. Diod.*Gen.*17:14(M.33.1574A); Gr.Nyss.*Eun.*12 (1 p.268.15; M.45.973B).

κατηγοριάρης** (καταγ-**), ὁ, official at S. Sophia, CP ὁ καταγοριάρης φιλοκαλῶν τὴν ἐκκλησίαν· ἅπτει δὲ καὶ τὰς κανδήλας. φέρει δὲ καὶ λαμπρόν *Euchol.*(p.225); ὁ κατηγοριάρης, ἵνα ὑπομνίζῃ τὰς ἐπισήμους ἑορτὰς τοῦ λαοῦ ἵνα σχολάζουσι *ib.*(p.230).

κατηγορικός, *prone to accusation*; of constitution of city-state, Synes.*hom.*2(p.282.5; M.66.1564B); also against things, *raising objections, objecting* λόγος κ. τῆς ἑορτῆς τῶν Καλανδῶν Ast.Am.*hom.* 4 tit.(M.40.216A); cf.CTrull.*can.*62.

κατήγορος, ὁ, *accuser*; as adj. κ. χείλεα λύσας Nonn.*par.Jo.*5:45 (M.43.792C); cf. ποῖον ἔπος φθέγγεσθε, κ. ἀνδρὸς ὀλέθρου; *ib.*18:29 (896A); *ib.*(893C).

***κατηλίθιος,** s.v.l., *utterly foolish, senseless*, Or.*Jo.*19.19(4; M.14. 561D; κατ⟨ὰ πάντα⟩ ἠλίθιον p.320.30).

κάτηλυς, *descending*, Nonn.*par.Jo.*4:47(M.43.784A); *ib.*8:23 (816C).

κατημελημένως, *carelessly*, Cyr.*Os.*33(3.59E).

***κατῆνα (A), ἡ,** *vessel, ship* παμμεγέθεις ναῦς καὶ πολεμικὰς κατήνας Thphn.*chron.*p.331(M.108.797C); κ. σιτοφόρους *ib.*p.332 (800C).

***κατήνα (B), ἡ,** (Lat. *catena*) *chain*, Isid.Pel.*epp.*1.485(M.78.448A); Ath.ap.Thdt.*h.e.*2.8.12(3.835); cf.Ath.*apol.sec.*43(p.120.20; M.25. 328B); κ. εὕρομεν ταῖς θύραις ἐμβεβλημένην CCP(536)*act.*4(pp.175. 22,176.7; κατίναν H.2.1252E,1253B).

***κατηρεμ-έω,** *be quiet, be at rest*, Cyr.*Ag.*1(3.627B); ~ούσης ἁπάσης αἰσχρᾶς ἡδονῆς id.*fr.Rom.*5:18f.(p.186.27; M.74.789A); τοὺς ἤδη ~ήσαντας χάριτι τοῦ Χριστοῦ id.*ep.*67(p.39.7; 5².196A).

***κατηρτισμένως,** *correctly* ἀποκείρουσι...οὐ νομίμως καὶ κ. Thdr. Stud.*epp.*2.165(M.99.1525B).

***κατησχοιμένον,** ? for κατεσχημένον perf. ptcpl. pass. κατέχω: τὸ [sc. γένος] ζυγῷ δουλείας κατεσφιγμένον καὶ ταῖς τῶν πριαμένων ἐξουσίαις κ. Cyr.*ador.*8(1.263B).

κατήφεια, ἡ, **1.** *lowering* of eyes from grief or despondency, ‡Nil. *perist.*11.3(M.79.905D); **2.** *dejection, sorrow*; c. genit. τὴν τῆς ἀνομβρίας κ. Gr.Nyss.*laud.Bas.*17(p.36.20; M.46.805D); the work of demons, Ath.*v.Anton.*36(M.26.896B); Bas.*hex.*8.8(1.79C; M.29.185C); of state of sinners hereafter, ‡Nil.*perist.*8.1(M.79.861D); opp. state of blessed, Gr.Nyss.*or.catech.*35(p.138.4; M.45.92B); **3.** *sorrow* for sin προσδέχεται...ὁ κτίσας ἡμᾶς παρὰ τῶν σωθῆναι βουλομένων...κ. γινομένην ἐπὶ τοῖς ἐπταισμένοις Nil.*epp.*3.243(M.79.500C); Bas.Sel. *or.*12.3(M.85.165C); **4.** *gloom, obscurity* τὸν ἄρχοντα τῆς ἐξουσίας τοῦ σκότους...βορέαν τε καὶ σκληρὸν ὀνομάζει ὁ λόγος, τὸν τῆς κ. τοῦ χειμῶνος ἐργάτην Gr.Nyss.*hom.10 in Cant.*(M.44.984C); Gr.Ant. *bapt.*2.4(M.88.1873D) = ‡Chrys.*hom.*9(13.233E); τὴν τῶν δικαίων φαιδρότητα...καὶ τὴν τῶν ἁμαρτησάντων κ. Nil.*epp.*3.213(M.79.480C).

κατηφέω, *mourn* for sin, Chrys.*hom.9.5 in Heb.*(12.100B); Bas. Sel.*or.*18.2(M.85.232B).

κατηφής, **1.** *downcast, sorrowful* μηδὲν κ. ἢ λυπηρὸν παρὰ τῇ θείᾳ φύσει *cat.Lc.*12:37(p.103.8); cf.Cyr.*Lc.*12:37(M.72.745C); **2.** of things, *sad, depressing* τὸ κ. ἄκουσμα Hipp.*haer.*5.9(p.99.12; M.16.3155A); Gr.Mag.*dial.*(tr.Zach.)4.18(M.*PL.*77.351); *depressed, despondent*, Gr.quidam *ep.*(p.90.7); of life, *dreary*, superl., Const.ap.Eus.*v.C.*2. 30(p.54.14; M.20.1008C).

κατηχ-έω, **I.** pass., *ring, echo with*, with play on sense II.B ἤδη ὑμῶν τὰ ὦτα ὥσπερ ~εῖσθαι ποιήσατε ἐκείνην τὴν καλὴν ἠχήν Cyr.H. *procatech.*15(M.33.360A).

II. A. *teach, instruct*; **1.** esp. in Christian faith, ref. 1Cor.3:2 κατήχησα ὑμᾶς ἐν Χριστῷ...τροφῇ τῇ πνευματικῇ Clem.*paed.*1.6(p.111. 5; M.8.292C); cf. *gentes quidem primo catechizabat apostolus... discedere ab idolorum superstitione, et unum deum colere*, Iren.*haer.* 4.24.1(M.7.1049B); c. dupl. acc. ~ήσασα αὐτὴν τὸν λόγον τοῦ θεοῦ *A.Paul.et Thecl.*39(p.265.6); εὐαγγελίσασθαι αὐτοῖς καὶ κ. αὐτοὺς τὸν λόγον *Apoc.Bar.rel.*5.21(p.53); pass. c. acc. ~εῖσθαι τὰ τῆς εὐσεβείας δόγματα *Const.App.*3.5.3; *Lit.ap.Const.App.*8.6.12; other constructions κ. ... τὸν αὐτὸν ἀπὸ τῆς αἱρέσεως ἐκκλῖναι Epiph.*haer.*64.3 (p.405.16; M.41.1073A); τοῦ εὐαγγελίου, ἐν ᾧ κατηχήθησαν ‡Ath. *synops.*65(M.28.421A); cf. ὃν καὶ πολλὰ κατήχησε...εἰς τὴν πίστιν *A. Barn.*11(p.296.12); κ. τοὺς ἐμοὺς ⟨εἰς τὴν πίστιν τοῦ Χριστοῦ⟩ *Didasc. Jac.*5.17(p.88.1); abs. ἀπὸ τῶν εἰδώλων ἀποσπᾶν καὶ ~εῖν *2Clem.*17.1; μηδενὸς τῷ κατηχεῖν ἀνακειμένου Eus.*h.e.*6.3.1(M.20.528A); οἱ ~οῦντες πρῶτον ~ηθέντες ~ησάτωσαν· ὅτι περὶ ψυχῶν ἀνθρώπων τὸ ἔργον *Clem. ep.*13(v.l. ~είτωσαν M.2.48B); **2.** also under Law, Iren.*haer.*3.12.7 (M.7.900B); οἱ ἐκ νόμου ~ούμενοι Clem.*str.*6.15(p.494.14; M.9.348A); Ath.*exp.Ps.*35:7(M.27.176B); ἐκεῖνον [sc. Nebuchadnezzar] μετέβαλε καὶ κατήχησε καὶ εἰς πίστιν ἤγαγε Chrys.*hom.36.3 in 1Cor.*(10.337A); **3.** *evangelize*, cf. *Petrus...ad catechizandos eos missus est*, Iren.*haer.* 3.12.15(M.7.909A); πολλοὺς τῶν Γότθων ~ησεν Epiph.*haer.*70.14 (p.247.29; M.42.372B); τοὺς ἐν Φοινίκῃ ~οῦντας τοὺς Ἕλληνας Chrys. *ep.*51(3.621A); **4.** *catechize, instruct* catechumens τίς ὅτε ~οῦντο τοιαῦτα λελάληκεν αὐτοῖς; Ath.*Ar.*1.8(M.26.28B); Bas.*hom.*13.1(2.114C; M.31.425B); incl. instruction of the baptized κ. τούς...πεπιστευκότας Apollon.ap.Eus.*h.e.*5.18.5(M.20.477A); Ath.*h.Ar.*2(p.184.9; M. 25.697A); id.*ep.Marcell.*20(M.27.33B); Chrys.*hom.87.1 in Jo.*(8.519D).

B. as t.t.; **1.** *make, receive as a catechumen* Εὐνομιανούς... καὶ Μοντανιστὰς...καὶ Σαβελλιανούς...τὴν πρώτην ἡμέραν ποιοῦμεν αὐτοὺς Χριστιανούς, τὴν δὲ δευτέραν ~ουμένους, εἶτα τὴν τρίτην ἐξορκίζομεν αὐτούς...καὶ οὕτως ~οῦμεν αὐτούς, καὶ ποιοῦμεν αὐτοὺς χρονίζειν εἰς τὴν ἐκκλησίαν...καὶ τότε αὐτοὺς βαπτίζομεν CCP(381) ‡*can.*7 = CTrull.*can.*95; pass., *receive instruction, be under instruction* τοῖς...βουλομένοις ~εῖσθαι τὸν τῆς εὐσεβείας λόγον Ath.*ep. fest.*39.11(p.88; M.26.1438); ὁ μέλλων ~εῖσθαι τρία ἔτη ~είσθω *Const. App.*8.32.16; ref. catechumenate ἐν τῷ ~ουμένῳ βίῳ Bas.*ep.*199 *can.* 20(3.292D; M.32.721A); **2.** pass. ptcpl., *catechumen*; **a.** in gen., cf. *catechumenus dictus pro eo, quod adhuc doctrinam fidei audit, necdum tamen baptismum recepit. nam ~ούμενος Graece auditor interpretatur*, Isid.H.*etym.*7.14.7; νεανίσκοι ~ούμενοι *M.Perp.*2(p.63. 20); μηδέπω...τὸν Ἰησοῦν ἐνδυσάμενοι, ἀλλ' ἔτι καὶ ~ουμένοις ἐνάριθμοι Or.*adnot.in Dt.*27:19(M.17.33D); ἐπὶ ~ουμένων, καὶ...ἐπὶ Ἑλλήνων τραγῳδοῦντες τὰ μυστήρια Ath.*apol.sec.*11(p.96.8; M.25.268A); τὰ μυστήρια, ἃ νῦν ἡ ἐκκλησία διηγεῖταί σοι τῷ ἐκ ~ουμένων μεταβαλλομένῳ οὐκ ἔστιν ἔθος ἐθνικοῖς διηγεῖσθαι Cyr.H.*catech.*6.29; οὐ γὰρ ἦσαν ~ούμενοι τότε· ἀλλὰ περὶ πιστῶν καὶ ἀπίστων [sc. ὁ λόγος] Chrys. *hom.29.2 in 1Cor.*(10.261C); opp. πιστός, Or.*hom.14.4 in Jer.*(p.109. 3; M.13.408C); οἱ...μὴ εἰδότες τὴν τῶν λεγομένων τραχύτητα, ἀλλὰ μόνῃ τῇ ψιλῇ τῶν γραφῶν περιηχήσει προσέχοντες ~ούμενοι χρηματίζουσιν· οἱ δὲ τῆς τῶν φθόγγων διαστολῆς ἀκούοντες...οὗτοι οὐ ~ούμενοι, ἀλλὰ πιστοί id.*comm.in 1Cor.*14:18f.(*JTS* 10 p.38); cf. ἐν οἷς εἰσι ~ούμενοι καὶ Ἕλληνες, οἱ μηδέπω πιστεύσαντες id.ap.Ath.*ep.Serap.* 4.10(M.26.649C); Chrys.*hom.75.5 in Mt.*(7.730D); ‡Pall.*h.mon.*5.4 (p.29.15; M.65.448A); and νεοφωτιστός, Eus.*h.e.*6.4.3(M.20.532A); **b.** a comprehensive term ~ούμενος, ἐὰν εἰσερχόμενος εἰς κυριακὸν ἐν τῇ τῶν κ. τάξει στήκῃ, οὗτος δὲ [φανῇ] ἁμαρτάνων, ἐὰν μὲν γόνυ κλίνων, ἀκροάσθω μηκέτι ἁμαρτάνων· ἐὰν δὲ καὶ ἀκροώμενος ἔτι ἁμαρτάνῃ, ἐξωθείσθω CNeocaes.*can.*5; τοὺς κ. καὶ χειμαζομένους καὶ βαπτιζομένους καὶ τοὺς ἐν μετανοίᾳ *Const.App.*8.38.1; **c.** dist. from 'hearers' as well as from unbelievers μήτις τῶν ἀκροωμένων, μήτις τῶν ἀπίστων...εὔξασθε, οἱ κ. *Lit.*ap.*Const.App.*8.6.2; προέλθετε, οἱ κ. ἐν εἰρήνῃ...εὔξασθε, οἱ φωτιζόμενοι *ib.*8.6.14; *ib.*8.8.2; μή τις τῶν κ., μή τις τῶν ἀκροωμένων, μή τις τῶν ἀπίστων, μή τις τῶν ἑτεροδόξων *ib.*8.12.2; κ. ἔλεγου ἔξωθεν περιηχούμενος...οὐκ ἔτι περιηχῇ, ἀλλ' ἐνηχῇ Cyr.H. *procatech.*6; cf. *invocant* [sc. *exorcistae*]...*super catechumenos, vel super eos qui habent spiritum immundum, nomen...Jesu*, Isid.H. *etym.*7.12.31; ref. penance περὶ τῶν κ. καὶ παραπεσόντων...τριῶν ἐτῶν αὐτοὺς ἀκροωμένους μόνον, μετὰ ταῦτα εὔχεσθαι μετὰ τῶν κατηχουμένων CNic.(325)*can.*14; **d.** regulations and discipline: age for reception ἐὰν παιδίον κ., ὡς ἐτῶν ἑπτά...εὐκαιρήσῃ που προσφορᾶς γινομένης, καὶ ἀγνοῶν μεταλάβῃ...φωτισθῆναι ὀφείλει· παρὰ θεοῦ γὰρ κέκληται Tim.I Al.*resp.*1(M.33.1296B); three-year catechumenate, cf.Hipp.*trad.ap.*17.1; χρόνου δεῖ τῷ κ. CNic.(325)*can.*2; ref. penitents, *ib.*14; *Const.App.*8.32.16 cit. s. II.B.1; ref. reception of heretics, etc. ἐπὶ διετίαν θέλει τοὺς τοιούτους Σαμαρείτας ~εῖσθαι Tim.CP *haer.*5(M.86.72B); CCP(381)‡*can.*7 = CTrull.*can.*95 cit. s. II.B.1; cf. τεσσαράκοντα ἡμέρας οὐ σχολάζεις...διὰ τὴν σαυτοῦ ψυχήν; Cyr.H.*catech.*1.5; catechumens as objects of special prayer and blessing in liturgy, Serap.*euch.*3,4(titt.); *Lit.*ap.*Const.App.*8. 6.3,8.6.10; ὅταν γὰρ ὁ διάκονος λέγῃ, ὑπὲρ τῶν κ. ἐκτενῶς δεηθῶμεν, οὐδὲν ἄλλο ἢ τὸν δῆμον ἅπαντα τῶν πιστῶν διανίστησιν εἰς τὰς ὑπὲρ ἐκείνων εὐχάς· καίτοι γε ἀλλότριοι τέως εἰσὶν οἱ κ. οὐδέπω γὰρ τοῦ σώματός εἰσι τοῦ Χριστοῦ Chrys.*hom.2.5 in 2Cor.*(10.435B); after which they leave church εἰ γὰρ ἔνδον ἦσαν οἱ κ. οὔπω ἦν ὁ καιρὸς τῆς προσφορᾶς Jul.Papa *ep.Dian.*(p.108.17; M.25.296C); στρατιώτας ἐθνικούς...ἐξετάζοντας ἃ μηδὲ ~ουμένους ἔπρεπε θεωρεῖν Ath.*apol. sec.*72(p.152.5; M.25.380A); μετὰ τὰς ὁμιλίας τῶν ἐπισκόπων, καὶ τῶν κ. εὐχὴν ἐπιτελεῖσθαι, καὶ μετὰ τὸ ἐξελθεῖν τοὺς κ. CLaod.*can.*19; cf. *post lectiones atque tractatum, dimissis catechumenis*, Ambr.*ep.*20. 4(M.*PL.*16.995A); τινὲς...μὴ μόνον ἐν τῷ καιρῷ τῶν κ., ἀλλὰ καὶ ἐν τῷ καιρῷ τῶν πιστῶν ἑστάναι καὶ διαλέγεσθαι Chrys.*hom.2.8 in 2Cor.* (10.440E); τούς...κ. ἐνεργουμένους τε, καὶ τοὺς ἐν μετανοίᾳ ὄντας, ὁ τῆς ἁγίας ἱεραρχίας θεσμὸς ἐφίησι μὲν ἐπακοῦσαι τῆς ψαλμικῆς ἱερολογίας, καὶ τῆς ἐνθέου τῶν γραφῶν ἀναγνώσεως· εἰς δὲ τὰς ἑξῆς ἱερουργίας καὶ θεωρίας οὐ συγκαλεῖται τούτους Dion.Ar.*e.h.*3.3.6(M.3.432C); τοὺς κ. ἐξέρχεσθαι τοῦ ναοῦ καὶ στήκειν εἰς τὸν νάρθηκα †Jo.Jej.*poenit.*(M.88.1912D); Max.*myst.*14(M.91.692D); οἱ κ. ἐξέρχονται ὡς ἀμύητοι τοῦ θείου βαπτίσματος ‡Bas.*h.myst.*46(p.389.18); their place in church ἐὰν...κ. ... μὴ συνευχέσθω μετὰ τῶν πιστῶν Ath.*virg.*13(p.47.12; M.28.268A); κ. δὲ ἰδίᾳ εὐχέσθωσαν, ἢ ἔξωθεν τοῦ βήλου ‡Ath.*syntag.*8(M.28.845A); their reading matter, cf.Ath.*ep.fest.*39.11f.(p.88; M.26.1437C) cit. s. ἀναγινώσκω; ‡Ath.*synops.*2(M.28.289B); cf. τὰ δὲ λοιπὰ πάντα, ἐν δευτέρῳ κείσθω· καὶ ὅσα ἐν ἐκκλησίαις μὴ ἀναγινώσκεται, ταῦτα μηδὲ κατὰ σαυτὸν ἀναγίνωσκε Cyr.H.*catech.*4.36; their use of Lord's Prayer, Ephr.3.202A; content of instruction, *Const.App.*7.39.1ff.

κατηχήεις, *of* or *for catechumens* κ. λόγος...῎Εξιτε ἐκ νηοῖο θεοῦ βροτοὶ ἡμιτέλεστοι Eudoc.*Cypr.*1.277(M.85.841D).

κατήχησις, ἡ, 1. *instruction*; esp. in the faith λόγου δὲ γνῶσιν, τὴν κ. Gr.Naz.*carm.*1.2.34.234(M.37.962A); **a.** act of *teaching, instructing,* cf. *illis* [sc. Jews] *enim facilis catechizatio fuit,* Iren.*haer.*4.24.1(M.7.1049B); φυτεύει μὲν γὰρ διὰ τῆς κ. ὁ ἀπόστολος, ποτίζει δὲ βαπτίζων ὁ Ἀπολλῶς Gr.Nyss.*Eun.*2(2 p.383.25; καθηγήσεως M.45.565B); Cyr.*Ps.*43:4(M.69.1020B); **b.** matter of *instruction, teaching, doctrine* τὴν περὶ πατρὸς καὶ υἱοῦ κ. Ath.*ep.Serap.*4.11(M.26.652B); τῆς τῶν πατέρων κ. Nil.*epp.*4.1(M.79.549D); περιέχει ἡ...ἐπιστολὴ κ. εἰς Χριστόν Euthal.Diac.*epp.Paul.*(M.85.701A); **c.** esp. *elementary instruction* δίκην νηπίων γαλουχουμένων τὸν τῆς κ. ἐπιτρέπει δέχεσθαι λόγον ‡Ath.*serm.fid.*23(M.26.1276B); καὶ ἐν τῇ κ. διδαχθέντας ὑπομένειν τὰς θλίψεις ‡Ath.*synops.*66(M.28.421C); **d.** under Law ἐπὶ λόγῳ κατηχήσεως ἤρχετο πρός με, τοῦ μαθεῖν λόγον θεοῦ *T.Jos.*4.4; ἐντεθραμμένος τῇ νομικῇ κ. καὶ τῇ ἀκροάσει τῶν προφητικῶν λόγων Or.*or.*2(p.302.19; M.11.421C); Proc.G.*Is.*34:1ff.(M.87.2308C); **2.** as t.t. *instruction* of those preparing for baptism, *catechetical instruction*; **a.** in gen. ἡ...κ. εἰς πίστιν περιάγει, πίστις δὲ ἅμα βαπτίσματι ἁγίῳ παιδεύεται πνεύματι Clem.*paed.*1.6(p.108.9; M.8.285C); id.*ecl.*28(p.145.28; M.9.713B); γάλα μὲν ἡ κ. οἱονεὶ πρώτη ψυχῆς τροφὴ νοηθήσεται, βρῶμα δὲ ἡ ἐποπτικὴ θεωρία id.*str.*5.10(p.370.15; M.9.101A); τοῦ τῆς κ. προέστη διδασκαλείου Eus.*h.e.*6.3.3(M.20.528A); ταῦτα...μανθανέτω ἐν τῇ κ. ὁ προσιὼν *Const.App.*7.39.4; ἐν ἐκκλησίᾳ τὸν τῆς κ. ποιήσασθαι λόγον ‡Pion.*v.Polyc.*12; Chrys.*hom.17.2 in 1Tim.*(11.650C); καλῶς...ἔχειν δοκεῖ τὸ μηδὲ προχείρως αὐτοὺς [sc. Samaritans] εἰσδέχεσθαι τῷ...προστρέχοντας βαπτίσματι, ἀλλὰ μετά τινος παραφυλακῆς καὶ κ. ἐν ἀρκοῦντι χρόνῳ γινομένης Justn.*nov.*144.2(p.710.17); Jo.V H.*icon.*12(M.96.1357D); **b.** a single *instruction, lesson, lecture* ἐν τῇ πρώτῃ κ. Eus.*ep.Caes.*(p.43.5; M.20.1537A); ἐν ταῖς...κ. ... σοι εἴρηται Cyr.H.*catech.*19.9; id.*procatech.*9; δεῖ πρῶτον τὰς κ. γίνεσθαι καὶ...τότε...τὸ βάπτισμα Ammon.*Ac.*16:14(M.85.1556D); id.*1Petr.*3:19f.(M.85.1608D); **3.** *catechumenate* τοὺς ἐν κ. παίδευσον *Const.App.*8.15.5; τῆς κ. τὸ χρῖσμα Cyr.*Jo.*7(4.683E); **4.** monastic; **a.** *instruction, training* of a novice τὴν κ. ... εἰς τὸν μονήρη βίον Pall.*h.Laus.*35(p.103.19; M.34.1114B); **b.** monastic *discipline* κλαύσωμαι ...διὰ τὴν χαυνότητα τῆς κ. τῆς γινομένης ἐν ταῖς ἡμέραις ἡμῶν Ephr.1.40D.

***κατηχητής, ὁ,** *catechist* τιμᾶτε πρεσβυτέρους, κ., διακόνους χρησίμους *Hom.Clem.*3.71; Τιμόθεον τὸν πρεσβύτερον καὶ κ. Marc.Diac.*v.Porph.*100.

***κατηχητικός, 1.** *instructive, containing instruction* ὀρθοδοξίας κατηχητική [sc. ἐπιστολή] Eus.*h.e.*4.23.2(M.20.384B); γράφει πρὸς αὐτοὺς ταύτην τὴν ἐπιστολήν, ὥσπερ κ. ‡Ath.*synops.*63(M.28.420A); *ib.*65(421A); κ. εἰς τὸ...πάσχα ‡Chrys.*pasch.*1(8.250A); Cyr.*Is.*1.5(2.145E) ∞ Proc.G.*Is.*8:19ff.(M.87.1993A); **2.** *catechetical* κ. ... βιβλία Eus.*h.e.*4.24.1(M.20.389B); ῞Ελληνα...οὐκ ὀφείλει βαπτίζειν τις, ἐν ᾧ μὴ δύναται ἀκοῦσαι λόγον κ. καὶ καταδέξασθαι Ammon.*Ac.*16:32(M.85.1561B).

***κατηχουμένιον** [-ειον *Mir.Artem.*31(p.44.25)], **τό,** place in church allotted to catechumens ἀνέρχονται πρὸς αὐτὸν ἐν τῷ κ. τῆς ἐκκλησίας *V.Max.*25(M.90.161A); σωρεύσας τὸν λαὸν ἐν τοῖς κ. τῆς μεγάλης ἐκκλησίας Thphn.*chron.*p.348(M.108.837A).

***κατηχούμενον, τό,** = foreg. τὰ κ. εἰς τύπον τῶν μὴ κατερχομένων ἀγγέλων ‡Sophr.H.*liturg.*4(M.87.3985B); τῶν ἐν τοῖς σεβασμίοις ναοῖς κ. CTrull.*can.*97; ἐν τοῖς τῶν ἐκκλησιῶν ὑπερῴοις, ἃ πολὺς ἄνθρωπος κ. καλεῖν ἔγνω Leo VI Imp.*nov.*73(C. E. Zacharius v. Lingenthal *Jus Graeco-Romanum* 3 p.171, Leipzig 1856–65).

***κατιδιοποι-έομαι,** *make independent, distinct* τίς ὁ λέγων· ἡ ψυχή μου, ἡ σάρξ μου...καὶ ἓν ἕκαστον ~ούμενος ὡς ἕτερος αὐτῷ· τοῦτον νοεῖ [sc. Μονόϊμος] τέλειον Hipp.*haer.*10.17(p.279.12; M.16.3435B).

***κατίνα, ἡ,** v. *κατήνα (B).

κατισχν-όω, 1. *cause to waste away; reduce,* ref. fasting τήκει αὐτὸ [sc. τὸ σῶμα] καὶ λεπτύνει καὶ ~οῖ Chrys.*hom.12.2 in 1Tim.*(11.612B); Cyr.*Am.*13(3.263C); pass. ~οῦται καὶ ἀσθενεστέρα γίνεται Chrys.*hom.13.3 in 1Tim.*(621F); **2.** met., *refine* τὸ παχὺ τῶν τύπων ~ῶν [sc. ὁ Χριστός] εἰς ἀλήθειαν Cyr.*hom.pasch.*26.3(5^2.310D); id.*Juln.*9(6^2.301A); id.*glaph.Gen.*4(1.131D); **3.** *make precise* εἰ...τις ἕλοιτο ~οῦν ταῖς ἐρεύναις αὐτοὺς [sc. λόγους] καὶ ἀκριβῆ ποιεῖσθαι τῶν εἰρημένων τὴν βάσανον id.*Arcad.*(p.64.40; 5^2.47A); id.*Is.*1.4(2.115E).

κατισχύω, *have power, be able* ἣν αὐτὸς ῥύσασθαι τῆς φθορᾶς οὐ κ. Clem.*str.*4.13(p.288.23; M.8.1300A); *ib.*2.20(p.171.13; 1049C); Geo.Pis.*carm.*3.1(p.8).

***κατιχνεύω,** *investigate,* Tit.Bost.*Man.*3.12(M.18.1241C).

κατό, for κατὰ τό, *M.Thdot.1* 32(p.81.5).

κατοδυνάω, pass. intrans., *agonize, grieve intensely,* Or.*sel.in Ps.*4:7(M.12.1165C).

[*]**κατόδυνος,** v. κατώδυνος.

κατοδύρ-ομαι, 1. *bewail, lament* ἄρτι δέ σε, τλήμων Ἀσίη, ~ομαι οἰκτρῶς *Orac.Sib.*5.287; *ib.*7.114; Isid.Pel.*epp.*2.35(M.78.480A); **2.** *implore* ~εσθαι τῆς μάρτυρος Bas.Sel.*v.Thecl.*2.29(M.85.616A).

κατοικεσία, ἡ, [κατοικησία *T.Neph.*3.5] *habitation* πόλιν κατοικεσίας, τὴν ἐκκλησίαν Or.*Jo.*28.24(19; p.420.24; M.14.733A); Marc.Er.*opusc.*10.4(M.65.1121B); Jo.Disc.*v.Epiph.*19(M.41.45C).

κατοικέσια, τά, *anniversary festival of a colony,* Gr.Naz.*or.*40.1(M.36.360B).

κατοικ-έω, [imperf. ἐκατῴκουν, *Mir.Geo.*6(p.81.17)]; *inhabit; dwell,* **1.** in gen., of spirits in a man's soul ὅταν...ταῦτα τὰ πνεύματα πάντα ἐν ἑνὶ ἀγγείῳ ~ῇ, οὗ τὸ πνεῦμα τὸ ἅγιον ~εῖ, οὐ χωρεῖ τὸ ἄγγος ἐκεῖνο, ἀλλ' ὑπερπλεονάζει. τὸ τρυφερὸν οὖν πνεῦμα, μὴ ἔχον συνήθειαν μετὰ πονηροῦ πνεύματος ~εῖν...ἀποχωρεῖ ἀπὸ τοῦ ἀνθρώπου τοῦ τοιούτου καὶ ζητεῖ ~εῖν μετὰ πραότητος...εἶτα ὅταν ἀποστῇ ἀπὸ τοῦ ἀνθρώπου ἐκείνου οὗ ~εῖ, γίνεται ὁ ἄνθρωπος...πεπληρωμένος τοῖς πνεύμασι τοῖς πονηροῖς Herm.*mand.*5.2.5ff.; ἀμφότερα δὲ τὰ πνεύματα ἐπὶ τὸ αὐτὸ ~οῦντα, ἀσύμφορόν ἐστιν...τῷ ἀνθρώπῳ...ἐν ᾧ ~οῦσιν *ib.*5.1.4; cf.*Barn.*16.7ff.; τὰς ἐνεργείας...τοῖς δαιμονίοις...ἐπιτελεῖν φησι τοὺς ἁμαρτωλούς, οὐχὶ δὲ αὐτὰ τὰ πνεύματα ἐν τῇ τοῦ ἀπίστου ~εῖν ψυχῇ λέγει Clem.*str.*2.20(p.176.13; M.8.1060C); met., of things πάντες κατὰ ἀλήθειαν ζῆτε καὶ...ἐν ὑμῖν οὐδεμία αἵρεσις κ. Ign.*Eph.*6.2; ὁ...φόβος τοῦ θεοῦ κ. ἐν τῇ ἐπιθυμίᾳ τῇ ἀγαθῇ Herm.*mand.*12.2.4; ἡ ψυχὴ ἐν θνητῷ σκηνώματι κ. *Diogn.*6.8; τὴν ἁμαρτίαν τὴν κατοικήσασαν διὰ τῆς ἐπιθυμίας ἐν τῷ σώματι Meth.*res.*2.8(p.344.6; M.18.308A); **2.** ref. Inc. ὅτι αὐτὸς [sc. ὁ κύριος] ἐν σαρκὶ ἔμελλεν φανεροῦσθαι καὶ ἐν ἡμῖν ~εῖν *Barn.*6.14; κ. [sc. θεός]...ἐπὶ τῆς γῆς, σάρκα περιβαλλόμενος Clem.*fr.*36(p.218.31; M.9.769A); κατῴκησεν ἡ θεότης ἐν τῇ σαρκί Ath.*Ar.*3.31(M.26.389A); favoured by Diodorus as expressing essence of Inc. τὸν...θεὸν λόγον κατῳκηκέναι ἐν τῷ ἐκ σπέρματος Δαβίδ Diod.*synous.*(M.33.1560A); and Nestorius ἀλλὰ ναί, φησίν...ὁ ἐκ θεοῦ πατρὸς λόγος, ἐν μορφῇ τοῦ γεγεννηκότος ὑπάρχων...κατῴκησεν ἐν ἀνθρώπῳ...καὶ τοῦτό ἐστιν ἡ κένωσις Cyr.*ep.*1(p.16.20; 5^2.10B); rejected by Cyril, *ib.*(p.16.22; 10B); οὐδὲ ἐκεῖνο φαμὲν ὅτι κατῴκηκεν ὁ ἐκ θεοῦ λόγος ὡς ἐν ἀνθρώπῳ κοινῷ τῷ ἐκ τῆς ἁγίας παρθένου γεγεννημένῳ, ἵνα μὴ θεοφόρος ἄνθρωπος νοοῖτο Χριστός. εἰ γὰρ καὶ ἐσκήνωσεν ἐν ἡμῖν ὁ λόγος, εἴρηται δὲ καὶ ἐν Χριστῷ ~ῆσαι πᾶν τὸ πλήρωμα τῆς θεότητος σωματικῶς, ἀλλ' οὖν ἐννοοῦμεν ὅτι γενόμενος σάρξ, οὐχ ὥσπερ ἐν τοῖς ἁγίοις ~ῆσαι λέγεται, κατὰ τὸν ἴσον καὶ ἐν αὐτῷ τρόπον γενέσθαι διοριζόμεθα τὴν κατοίκησιν· ...ἀλλὰ...τοιαύτην ἐποιήσατο τὴν κατοίκησιν, ἣν ἂν ἔχειν λέγοιτο καὶ ἡ τοῦ ἀνθρώπου ψυχὴ πρὸς τὸ ἴδιον ἑαυτῆς σῶμα *ib.*17(p.36.6ff.; 5^2.70Df.); **3.** of divine indwelling in men; **a.** in gen. οὐ...μερισμός ἐστιν...θεὸς οὐ κ. Ign.*Philad.*8.1; ἐν τῷ κατοικητηρίῳ ἡμῶν ἀληθῶς ὁ θεὸς κ. ἐν ἡμῖν *Barn.*16.8; ὅπου ὁ κύριος κ., ἐκεῖ καὶ σύνεσις πολλή Herm.*mand.*10.1.6; ἐν ἡμῖν...διὰ τοῦ βαπτίσματος ἀπαρχὴ...θεότητος κ. Nil.*epp.*2.293(M.79.345B); in prophets, Epiph.*anc.*75(p.95.3; M.43.157C) cit. s. ἄνθρωπος; **b.** of image of God οὐ...τὴν εἰκόνα τοῦ θεοῦ ~οῦσαν ἔνδον εὑρήσει Clem.*paed.*3.2(p.238.24; M.8.561A); **c.** not to be equated with divinity in Christ ἐν ἡμῖν μὲν γὰρ ἀπαρχὴ καὶ ἀρραβὼν θεότητος κ., ἐν Χριστῷ δὲ πᾶν τὸ πλήρωμα τῆς θεότητος Ath.*inc.et c.Ar.*9(M.26.997B); cf. προσεύξονται ἐν αὐτῷ διὰ τὸ μείζονα ~εῖν ἐν αὐτῷ θεόν Eus.*d.e.*5.4(p.224.8; M.22.369B); **d.** of Father and Son (cf.Jo.14:23) προσεύχεται τῷ...μὴ...ἐγκαταλείποντι πατρὶ ἀλλ' ἐν αὐτῷ [sc. τῷ νῷ] ~οῦντι, συμπαρόντος αὐτῷ καὶ τοῦ μονογενοῦς Or.*or.*20(p.344.26; M.11.480C); of Son αὐτοῦ [sc. τοῦ κυρίου] ἐν ἡμῖν ~οῦντος Ign.*Eph.*15.3; ὅτι αὐτὸς [sc. ὁ κύριος] ἐν σαρκὶ ἔμελλεν φανεροῦσθαι καὶ ἐν ἡμῖν ~εῖν *Barn.*6.14; πιστεύομεν καὶ τὸν κύριον μεθ' ἡμῶν ~ήσειν Ath.*tom.*1(M.26.797A); **e.** of H. Ghost ἵνα τὸ πνεῦμα, ὃ ὁ θεὸς κατῴκισεν ἐν τῇ σαρκὶ ταύτῃ ἀληθὲς εὑρεθῇ...καὶ οὕτως δοξασθήσεται ὁ κύριος ὁ ἐν σοὶ ~ῶν Herm.*mand.*3.1; τὸ πνεῦμα τὸ ἅγιον τὸ ἐν σοὶ ~οῦν *ib.*10.2.5; *ib.*5.1.2; πᾶσα σὰρξ...ἄσπιλος, ἐν ᾗ τὸ πνεῦμα τὸ ἅγιον κατῴκησεν id.*sim.*5.6.7; *ib.*5.7.1; ~εῖν ἐν αὐτῷ [sc. human nature] βούλεται θεὸς διὰ τοῦ πρεσβεύοντος πνεύματος Tat.*orat.*15(p.16.23; M.6.837B); Meth.*symp.*11(p.138.12; M.18.216C); Ath.*inc.et c.Ar.*13(M.26.1005C); ὅπου γὰρ τὸ πνεῦμα τοῦ θεοῦ ~εῖ, ἐκεῖ ὁ θεὸς ~εῖ *ib.*14(1008B); Cyr.*thes.*34(5^{1}.349B) cit. s. ἀναγεννάω.

[*]**κατοικησία, ἡ,** v. κατοικεσία, ἡ.

κατοίκησις, ἡ, 1. *dwelling* in, *abiding*, ref. Inc. τὴν τοῦ πατρὸς ἐν αὐτῷ [sc. τῷ Χριστῷ] κ. Eus.*d.e.*5.4(p.224.30; M.22.372A); this terminology deprecated by later writers Ἰωάννης μὲν ἔργων ἦν δικαιοσύνη, Ἰησοῦς δὲ φύσει. οὐκοῦν ἄτοπόν ἐστιν τὸ λέγειν ἄνθρωπον τὸν Χριστὸν ἢ εὐδοκεῖσθαι παρὰ θεοῦ παρὰ πάντας ἀνθρώπους εἰς θεοῦ κ. ἄνευ τῆς ἀσκητικῆς καὶ ἐπιπόνου δικαιοσύνης ‡Dion.Al.*ep.Paul.Sam.*(p.4.11); οὐχ ὥσπερ ἐν τοῖς ἁγίοις κατοικῆσαι λέγεται, κατὰ τὸν ἴσον καὶ ἐν αὐτῷ τρόπον γενέσθαι διοριζόμεθα τὴν κ. ... ἀλλὰ...τοιαύτην ἐποιήσατο τὴν κ., ἣν ἂν ἔχειν λέγοιτο καὶ ἡ τοῦ ἀνθρώπου ψυχὴ πρὸς τὸ ἴδιον ἑαυτῆς σῶμα Cyr.*ep.*17(p.36.11f.; 5^{2}.70E); of Christ dwelling in men μετὰ ἀνθρώπων αὐτῷ κ. γίνεται ἐν τῇ κατὰ τοὺς δικαίους συνθέσει Clem.*fr.*36(p.218.32; M.9.769A); διὰ...τοῦ βαπτίσματος ἡ εἰς ψυχὰς...τοῦ κυρίου κ. †Bas.*hom.in Ps.*28(1.361E; M.30.81B); **2.** s.v.l., = οἴκησις, *government, administration* χειροτονήσαντές τε αὐτὸν ἐπίσκοπον...κατελείψαμεν αὐτὸν εἰς κ. τῶν ἐκεῖσε κατοικούντων ἀδελφῶν *A.Barn.*17(p.298.14; conj. διοίκησιν).

κατοικητήριον, τό, *dwelling, abode*; **1.** Gnost., ref. body as abode of demons καταλιμπάνω τὸ κ. τοῦτο τὸ σῶμά μου *A.Phil.*140(p.76.1); καταλιμπάνω τὸ κ. τοῦ δράκοντος τοῦ κολαφίζοντος πᾶσαν ψυχὴν ἁμαρτάνουσαν *ib.*(pp.75.25,76.12); (Valent.) ἔστι δὲ οὗτος ὁ ὑλικὸς ἄνθρωπος οἱονεὶ...πανδοχεῖον ἢ κ. ποτὲ μὲν ψυχῆς μόνης, ποτὲ δὲ ψυχῆς καὶ δαιμόνων Hipp.*haer.*6.34(p.163.14; M.16.3246C); **2.** of God ποιῆσαι τὴν οἰκίαν ἡμῶν τοῦ θεοῦ αὐτοῦ κ. *A.Phil.*51(p.22.15); Ἱερουσαλὴμ...ἐν ᾗ τὸ ἀληθὲς...κ. τοῦ θεοῦ Eus.*Ps.*134:18(M.24.33B); εἰς τὸ ἓν μέρος τῆς κτίσεως [sc. ἀνατολήν]...ποιοῦμεν τὴν προσκύνησιν, οὐχ ...ὡς εἰς κ. τοῦ θεοῦ τοῦτο ἀφωρισμένον, ἀλλ᾽ εἰς τόπον...τεταγμένον ‡Just.*qu.et resp.*118(M.6.1368D); in heart and mind of man ναὸς ἅγιος...τῷ κυρίῳ τὸ κ. ἡμῶν τῆς καρδίας *Barn.*6.15; πρὸ τοῦ ἡμᾶς πιστεῦσαι τῷ θεῷ ἦν ἡμῶν τὸ κ. τῆς καρδίας φθαρτὸν καὶ ἀσθενὲς *ib.*16.7; ἐν τῷ κ. ἡμῶν ἀληθῶς ὁ θεὸς κατοικεῖ ἐν ἡμῖν *ib.*16.8; μὴ εἶναι κοινόν τι τὸν νοῦν θεοῦ τε καὶ διαβόλου Diad.*perf.*82(p.110.6); ὁ ἑαυτὸν ἑτοιμάσας εἰς κ. τῆς...τριάδος Alex.Sal.*Barn.*proem.7(438E); σαυτὸν ὄντως Ἱερουσαλὴμ κατασκευάσας πόλιν θεοῦ ζῶντος εἰς κ. θείου πνεύματος Jo.Mon.*hymn.Chrys.*2(M.96.764C); of martyrs κ. πνεύματος Const.Diac.*laud.*(M.88.524A); of Church τὴν ἐκκλησίαν [sc. καλεῖ] ναὸν καὶ κ. Thdt.*Eph.*2:22(3.416); of Church triumphant ὑμεῖς ἐστε...ἡ ὕπαρξις τῆς ἄνω πόλεως, ἡ τερπνότης τοῦ κ.· οὗ ἡτοίμασεν ὁ θεὸς τοῖς ἀγαπῶσιν αὐτόν *A.Phil.*110(p.42.6,17).

κατοικία, ἡ, 1. *habitation, abode*, of God οὗ...ἀπρόσιτος ἡ κ. *Const.App.*7.35.9; in man πάσας...τὰς κ. ἑαυτοῦ ὁ θεός, ἃς πρὸς τοὺς ἀνθρώπους ἐποιήσατο, μερικῶς μὲν ἐν τοῖς προφήταις, ὁλοτελῶς δὲ... ἐν τῷ...Χριστῷ Cosm.Ind.*top.*5(M.88.233A); **2.** *community*, Dion.Ar.*ep.*8(M.3.1088A); ἐν τῇ ἐκκλησίᾳ τῶν πρωτοτόκων, ἔνθα εὐφραινομένων ἡ κ. Jo.D.*hom.*2.6(M.96.588A).

κατοικίζω, *cause to dwell, settle*, ref. Inc. τὸ πνεῦμα τὸ ἅγιον... κατῴκισεν ὁ θεὸς εἰς σάρκα ἣν ἐβούλετο Herm.*sim.*5.6.5; of H. Ghost in man τὸ πνεῦμα, ὃ ὁ θεὸς κατῴκισεν ἐν τῇ σαρκὶ ταύτῃ id.*mand.*3.1; πνεύματος ἁγίου ναοὶ καλούμεθα, ἐὰν κατοικίσωμεν τὸ αὐτοῦ πνεῦμα ἐν ἡμῖν Epiph.*haer.*69.27(p.177.25, v.l. κατοικήσωμεν M.42.248A).

κατοιμώζω, *bewail*, Cyr.*Is.*1.1(2.5B).

κατοίομαι, *be conceited*, Cyr.*Is.*1.4(2.94D) ∞ id.*Juln.fr.*11(M.76.1057C); id.*Soph.*23(3.604C).

***κατοιστρέομαι,** pass., *be maddened*; by desire, Cyr.*Juln.*5(6^{2}.177D).

κατοίχ-ομαι, 1. *have gone* οἱ ~όμενοι *the departed, dead*; sing. τὸ τοῦ κ. μνημόσυνον Gr.Nyss.*virg.*3(p.263.19; M.46.333A); Cyr.*ador.*14(1.481D); Thdt.*qu.2 in Ruth*(1.351); **2.** met., *fall* into sin κ. πρὸς ὀργήν Cyr.*ador.*5(1.153B).

***κατοκέλλω,** *run aground*, met. οὐδεὶς βίου ὡραϊσμὸς ἀπὸ τῶν ἐπουρανίων κατώκειλεν αὐτοῦ τὴν ψυχήν ‡Pion.*v.Polyc.*9.

κατοκλάζω, 1. *relax, enervate* φόβῳ τὸν λογισμὸν κατωκλάσατε Bas.Sel.*or.*40.2(M.85.456A); **2.** *fail* in a comparison, Paul.Sil.*Soph.*144(M.86.2125A).

***κατοκνῆ,** s.v.l., *sluggishly* τὸ...ἁλῶναι φυγάδα, καὶ κ. πονεῖν Cyr.*hom.pasch.*4.2(5^{2}.34B).

κατοκωχή, ἡ, *possession* (supernatural) τις αὐτὴν θεία κ. κατέλαβε Meth.*symp.*10.1(M.18.189D; ἀνακωχὴ p.121.15).

κατολιγωρ-έω, *neglect* persons; *be careless* about things πρὸς τὰ καλὰ κεκωφωμένοι. γλώττῃ μὲν...ἐπικροτοῦντες τὰ λεγόμενα, ἔργοις δὲ ~οῦντες αὐτῶν Eus.*v.C.*4.29(p.129.16; M.20.1180A); κ. τῶν παρηγγελμένων Diod.*Rom.*7:14(p.88.28)ap.*cat.Rom.*(p.100.25); κ. τῆς τοῦ θεοῦ θεραπείας Thdt.*Os.*9:4(2.1351); abs., *be negligent*, Isid.Pel.*epp.*5.261(M.78.1489A).

κατολισθαίνω, *slip; sink*, lit. and morally; c. πρός, Bas.*hom.in Ps.*1(1.96B; M.29.225A); Gr.Nyss.*or.dom.*5(p.106.2; M.44.1185C); of water, *fall*, ‡Caes.Naz.*dial.*92(M.38.956).

***κατολοθρεύω,** *destroy utterly*, Cyr.*Nah.*24(3.503B).

***κατομματόομαι,** pass., *be covered with eyes*; of the cherubim, Dion.Ar.*schol.d.n.*1.1(M.4.188C).

[*]**κατομοτικόν, τό,** *affirmation on oath*, Didym.*Ps.*109:4(M.39.1540D).

κατονειδίζω, *find fault with, blame* τοῖς τὰ Χριστοῦ φρονοῦσι...κ. Cyr.*Juln.*proem.(6^{2}.4A); τί τινι: κ. ... τὸ ἄναλκι id.*Os.*18(3.40C); id.*Ps.*14:3(M.69.805C); κ. ... τὸ μεθύειν αὐτοῖς id.*Is.*3.2(2.393E).

***κατονέομαι,** ? error for κατανεύομαι, *bow* the head as sign of dejection, *look downcast*, Jo.VI H.*v.Jo.D.*9(M.94.444C).

κατονομάζω, perf. pass., *be noted, famous* δύναμις αὐτοῦ [sc. Moses], ᾗ κατωνόμασται Diod.*Gen.*6:6(M.33.1571A).

κατονομασία, ἡ, *naming, denomination* θεοῦ κατονομασίας ἐν τῇ κατὰ τὸν θεὸν οὐσίας προσηγορίᾳ Epiph.*haer.*76.41(p.395.19; M.42.605C).

κατόπιν, 1. of place; **a.** *behind, after* εἰς τὸ κ. *backwards* ὁ τελειούμενος τοῖς ἔμπροσθεν ἐπεκτείνεται, οὕτως ὁ ἁμαρτάνων εἰς τὸ κ. ἀναποδίζει †Bas.*Is.*17(1.389B; M.30.144D); in moral sense ὁρῶντες... τὴν πολιτείαν κ. φερομένην ἐκ τῆς αὐτοῦ ἀπληστίας Thphn.*chron.* p.111(M.108.317B); **b.** met., *behind in, short of* κ. ἐρχόμενοι κόρου Cyr.*hom.pasch.*18.1(5^{2}.237C); id.*glaph.Gen.*4(1.123D); ἐστιν...τῆς εὐαγγελικῆς πολιτείας κ. ἡ νομικὴ id.*glaph.Ex.*2(1.287C); *as secondary* κ. πάντα τοῦ δικαίου τιθέμενος Isid.Pel.*epp.*1.165(M.78.292C); **2.** of time; **a.** *of yore* χρόνος οὖν οὐκ ἦν...ἐν ταῖς κ. ἡμέραις Bas.*Eun.*1.21(1.232D; M.29.560A); **b.** *previously* ὅπερ φησὶν ἐν τοῖς ἤδη κ. Cyr.*Jo.*5.1(4.470B); **3.** of contexts; **a.** *supra* ἐπιλαθόμενος αὐτὸς τῶν ἑαυτοῦ δογμάτων, ἃ ἐν τοῖς κ. λόγοις...ἐξετίθετο Bas.*Eun.*2.24(1.261B; M.29.628B); ἐν τοῖς κ. εἴρηται Gr.Nyss.*Eun.*11(2 p.260.15; M.45.868C); **b.** *infra* κατὰ τὸ μικρὸν κ. [sc. Apoc.20:8] ἐν ταύτῃ τῇ Ἀποκαλύψει φερόμενον *cat.Apoc.*16:12(p.417.18).

κατόπισθεν, ref. time, *behind one, past* ἐκλαθομένους τῶν κ. ἁμαρτιῶν Clem.*paed.*1.6(p.121.21; M.8.312C).

κατοπτάω, *roast, sear*, *M.Thdot.1* 34(p.82.34).

κατόπτευσις, ἡ, *seeing, sight* ἡ τῆς φύσεως αὐτοῦ [sc. of God] κ. ἐδηλοῦτο [sc. by the word πρόσωπον]...οὐ ταὐτὸν νοεῖται τῇ ὑποστάσει ὄν Leont.H.*Nest.*2.33(M.86.1592A).

***κατοπτευτής, ὁ,** *observer, investigator*, Epiph.*haer.*69.23(p.173.22; M.42.240B).

κατοπτεύ-ω, *observe, watch*; ptcpl., *onlooker*, Clem.*paed.*2.2(p.172.19; M.8.421A); pass., *be seen, appear*, *M.Polyc.*2.2 ap.Eus.*h.e.*4.15.4(M.20.344A); ὅπως...οἱ δαίμονες...~θῶσιν οὐκ ὄντες θεοί Meth.*Porph.*1(p.503.17; M.18.397D); met., *observe closely, examine*, Serap.*Man.*49(p.69; M.18.1241C); τὰς θείας...γραφὰς ~σωμεν Isid.Pel.*epp.*4.114(M.78.1185B); *ib.*2.143(588A); myst., *see, contemplate* God, Clem.*prot.*12(p.83.27; M.8.240A); ὁ ἱερεὺς...τὴν δόξαν τοῦ κυρίου ~ων ‡Bas.*h.myst.*59(p.393.20); med., ‡Pall.*h.mon.*1.26(p.11.16; καταγίνεσθαι M.34.1116D); spiritual things ἀτρανωτάτῳ λογισμῷ τὰ ἐκεῖ πράγματα ~οντες Meth.*res.*2.16(p.365.10; M.18.312B); προφήτης...ὢν ἄπταιστος, ἀπείρῳ ψυχῆς ὀφθαλμῷ πάντα κ. *Hom.Clem.*3.13; τῆς οἰκονομίας τὸ μέγεθος κ. Chrys.*comm.in Gal.*3:2(10.696C); the worship of heaven τῶν ἀοράτων δυνάμεων τὴν λειτουργίαν κατώπτευσε [sc. S. Paul] Cosm.Ind.*top.*5(M.88.301C).

κατοπτρίζ-ομαι, 1. *examine, inspect* κατοπτρισάμενος ἅπαντα τὰ κλήματα ‡Ath.*disp.*33(M.28.484A); abs., *look on, watch* κατοπτρισάμενοι ἅπαντες *ib.*36(485D); pass., ? *be admitted* or *allowed to watch* τῶν δυνάμεων...ἐμβατεύσας καὶ κατοπτρισθεὶς τὴν διακονίαν [ref. S. Paul rapt to third heaven] Cosm.Ind.*top.*5(M.88.301C); **2.** met.; **a.** *see mirrored* ἕκαστος...ὥσπερ εἰκόνι τινὶ ἐντυγχάνων τῇ μνήμῃ, τὸ τῶν πράξεων ~εται κάλλος, καὶ θεωρεῖ τὰς πράξεις τῇ τῆς μνήμης ἐγκειμένας εἰκόνι ‡Chrys.*Thecl.*(2.749A); **b.** *see, behold* simply ὅπως ἀΐδιον χαρὰν ἐνστερνίσωνται οἱ ~όμενοι τὸ ὡραιότατον ταύτης [sc. τῆς πρὸς θεὸν φιλίας] ἀξίωμα ‡Ath.*disp.*1(M.28.440B); τὰ ἐν αὐτῷ [sc. τῷ οὐρανῷ] κάλλη ~όμενος *M.Thdot.2* 4(p.87.28); τὸ διηνεκῶς τῷ θείῳ προσεδρεύειν ναῷ καὶ τὸ θεῖον...~εσθαι κάλλος Thdt.*Ps.*26:4f.(1.770); c. dat. ὥσπερ...οἱ τῷ ἡλίῳ ἀτενίσαι βουλόμενοι τὰς ὄψεις βλάπτονται, οὕτω καὶ οἱ ~εσθαι τῷ βίῳ ταύτης πειρώμενοι...σύγχυσιν ὑφίστανται τῇ διανοίᾳ ‡Ath.*v.Syncl.*2(M.28.1488B); **c.** ref. 2Cor.3:18, interpreted in Pauline context of Christians opp. Jews οἷς οὖν ἐπίκειται κάλυμμα, οὐκ ἂν εἴποιεν· πνεῦμα προσώπου ἡμῶν Χριστὸς κύριος, ἀλλ᾽ οἱ [2Cor.3:18] ὧν ἀεὶ πρὸ τῶν τῆς διανοίας ὀφθαλμῶν ἐστιν ὁ κύριος Or.*fr.116 in Lam.*4:20(p.276.16; M.13.657D); ἐὰν ἐπιστρέψῃ τις πρὸς τὸν κύριον...περιαιρεθεὶς τὸ κάλυμμα ἀνακεκαλυμμένῳ προσώπῳ τὴν ἐν τοῖς κεκρυμμένοις νοήμασι κατὰ τὰ γράμματα δόξαν τοῦ κυρίου ὡσπερεὶ ~εται καὶ μεταλαμβάνει τῆς...θείας δόξης id.*Cels*.5.60(p.64.1; M.11.1276D); Cyr.*Ps*.24:10(M.69.849A); id.*Jo*.3.6(4.317D); Const. Diac.*laud.mart*.13(M.88.496A); in other contexts τὴν ψυχὴν...ὡς πλησίον γενομένην ἀνακεκαλυμμένῳ προσώπῳ τὴν δόξαν τοῦ κυρίου ~εσθαι· πειθομένην τῷ λέγοντι [Cant.2:14 a] Or.*Cant*.3(p.231.26; M. 13.189D); δι' ἧς ἐδοξάσθη δόξης ἐν τοῖς ἐγνωκόσιν αὐτόν, περιεποίησεν δόξαν τοῖς ἐγνωκόσιν αὐτόν· οἱ γὰρ ἀνακεκαλυμμένῳ προσώπῳ τὴν δόξαν κυρίου ~όμενοι, τὴν αὐτὴν εἰκόνα μεταμορφοῦνται id.*Jo*.32.29 (18; p.474.28; M.14.820C); τοῖς ἔνδον ὀφθαλμοῖς τὴν δόξαν τοῦ κυρίου ~όμεθα ‡Ath.*v.Syncl*.99(M.28.1548D); τοῦτο...σημαίνει καὶ ἡ μετάληψις τῶν μυστηρίων τοῦ μεταλαβεῖν τοῦ δεδοξασμένου αὐτοῦ σώματος, ὥσπερ ἐν ἐσόπτρῳ ~όμενοι καὶ μεταλαμβάνοντες τῆς δόξης αὐτοῦ Cosm. Ind.*top*.5(M.88.308A); ἐν εὐτελείᾳ τὴν δόξαν κυρίου ~όμενοι Jo.D.*hom*. 4.24(M.96.621C); τὴν δόξαν κυρίου, καὶ τῆς θείας αὐτοῦ κιβωτοῦ ~όμεθα ‡Meth.*Sym.et Ann*.1(M.18.348A); v. 3 infra; **3.** *reflect*, Gr. Thaum.*pan.Or*.11(p.27.15; M.10.1084C) cit. s. ἀποθέωσις; ἱκανὴ...ἡ τῆς ψυχῆς καθαρότης ἐστὶ τὸν θεὸν δι' ἑαυτῆς ~εσθαι Ath.*gent*.2(M.25. 8B); ἡ ψυχὴ ~ομένη τὰ ἐπουράνια κατὰ τὴν τοῦ κυρίου δωρεάν Ephr. 1.330C; ref. 2Cor.3:18 οὕτω...ἡ ψυχὴ καθαιρομένη...δέχεται ἀκτῖνα ἀπὸ τῆς δόξης τοῦ πνεύματος, καὶ ταύτην ἀντιπέμπει. διὸ καί φησι '~όμενοι' τὴν αὐτὴν εἰκόνα μεταμορφούμεθα ἀπὸ δόξης τῆς τοῦ πνεύματος Chrys.*hom.7.5 in 2Cor*.(10.486E); ~όμεθα τὴν δόξαν κτλ.· τοῦτ' ἔστι καὶ ὁρῶμεν καὶ ἀπομασσόμεθα ὡς ἐν ἐσόπτρῳ ταῖς ψυχαῖς τὴν εἰκόνα τῆς δόξης τοῦ πνεύματος Sever.*2Cor*.3:18(p.286.25); ὥσπερ τὸ διαφανὲς ὕδωρ ἐκμάττεται τῶν εἰσορώντων τὰς ὄψεις...οὕτως ἡ καθαρὰ καρδία τῆς θείας δόξης οἷόν τι ἐκμαγεῖον καὶ κάτοπτρον γίνεται Thdt. *2Cor*.3:18(3.307); οὐ μόνον ὁρῶμεν εἰς δόξαν τοῦ θεοῦ, ἀλλὰ κἀκεῖθεν δεχόμεθά τινα τὴν ἀστραπήν, ὥσπερ ἄργυρος καθαρὸς πρὸς τὰς ἀκτῖνας κείμενος, καὶ αὐτὸς ἀκτῖνας ἐκπέμψειεν Jo.D.*2Cor*.3:18(M.95.724B).

κάτοπτρον, τό, *mirror*, met.; **1.** of brothers as mirrors of each other, Ath.*apol.Const*.10(M.25.608B); **2.** of Christ as mirror for soul ἀκολουθεῖν...τῷ σωτῆρι...καὶ τελειότητα τὴν ἐκείνου μετερχόμενον καὶ πρὸς ἐκεῖνον ὥσπερ κ. κοσμοῦντα...τὴν ψυχήν Clem.*q.d.s*.21 (p.174.9; M.9.628A); **3.** of soul as mirror of Word ὅτε πάντα τὸν ἐπιχυθέντα ῥύπον τῆς ἁμαρτίας ἀφ' ἑαυτῆς [sc. ψυχῆς] ἀποτίθεται, καὶ μόνον τὸ κατ' εἰκόνα καθαρὸν φυλάττει, εἰκότως, διαλαμπρυνθέντος τούτου, ὡς ἐν κ. θεωρεῖ τὴν εἰκόνα τοῦ πατρὸς τὸν λόγον, καὶ ἐν αὐτῷ τὸν πατέρα Ath.*gent*.34(M.25.68D); ὅτι...διὰ πάντων γένοιτο τέλειος, πρὸς αὐτὸν μὲν τὸν θεὸν λόγον, ὡς πρὸς ἡλίου κύκλον ἀτενῶς ἐνιδεῖν φύσιν οὐκ ἔχει· ἐν ἑαυτῷ δὲ καθάπερ ἐν κ. βλέπει τὸν ἥλιον. αἱ γὰρ τῆς ἀληθινῆς ἐκείνης...ἀρετῆς ἀκτῖνες τῷ κεκαθαρμένῳ βίῳ...ἐκλάμπουσαι, ...τῷ ἡμετέρῳ κ. ἐνζωγραφοῦσαι τὸν ἥλιον Gr.Nyss.*hom.3 in Cant*.(M. 44.824C); cf.*ib*.7(920C); ref. virginity, †Bas.Anc.*virg*.2(M.30.672C); **4.** ref. 2Cor.3:18 τὰς γνωστικὰς ψυχὰς...οὐκ ἐν κατόπτροις ἢ διὰ κατόπτρων ἔτι τὴν θεωρίαν ἀσπαζομένας τὴν θείαν Clem.*str*.7.3(p.10. 11; M.9.416C); **5.** of scripture τοῦτο τὸ κ. οὐ δείκνυσι τὴν ἀμορφίαν μόνον, ἀλλὰ καὶ μετατίθησιν...εἰς κάλλος ἀμήχανον Isid.Pel.*epp*.2.135 (M.78.577C).

κατορθ-όω, A. trans.; **1.** *set upright, establish* ~ώσει αὐτοῦ τὴν βασιλείαν Just.*dial*.68.5(M.6.633C); τὸν ἀρχισυνάγωγον μέλλοντα διαπιστεῖν...~οῖ Chrys.*hom.31.1 in Mt*.(7.358B); Max.*opusc*.(M.91. 29D); of God ὁ...ἅπαντα ~ῶν Thdt.*Ps*.71:5(1.1104); pass. ἐν τῷ... δίκαια βουλεύεσθαι αὐτὸν ~οῦται ἡ δόξα αὐτοῦ ἐν τοῖς οὐρανοῖς Herm. *vis*.1.1.8; ὁ βίος...καὶ τῆς ἀγωγῆς ὁ τρόπος...ἐννοίαις τῶν πάλαι θεοφιλῶν ἀνδρῶν κατωρθοῦτο Eus.*h.e*.1.4.4(M.20.77B); Thdt.*Ps*.71:1(1. 1101); **2.** *keep straight, set right*; **a.** *correct, emend* a text ~ώσῃς αὐτὸ πρὸς τὸ ἀντίγραφον Iren.*fr*.1(M.7.1225A); **b.** morally, *amend* τὸν βίον ἡμῖν διώρθου...καὶ διὰ πάντων τὴν ζωὴν ~ῶν τὴν ἡμετέραν Chrys. *hom.66.1 in Mt*.(7.655C); id.*hom.83.5 in Jo*.(8.497E); οἱ ἀπόστολοι τὴν οἰκουμένην κατώρθωσαν id.*exp.in Ps*.110:9(5.275D); ref. work of Christ πάντα τὰ τῶν ἀνθρώπων διὰ τῆς ἑαυτοῦ δυνάμεως ~ώσας Ath. *inc*.10.1(M.25.113A); ὕστερον...γέγονεν ὁ λόγος σάρξ...ἵν' ἐν αὐτῷ τὰ ὅλα ~ωθῇ id.*hom.in Mt.11*:27(M.25.212C); ἵνα...παραδῷ τὴν ἀνθρωπίνην βασιλείαν κατωρθωμένην τῷ πατρὶ id.*inc.et c.Ar*.20(M.25. 1021A); Gr.Naz.*or*.44.8(M.36.616C); ὁ...ἅπαντα ~ῶν Thdt.*Ps*.71:5(1. 1104); med. ἵνα ~ώσωνται τὰς ὁδοὺς αὐτῶν ἐν δικαιοσύνῃ Herm.*vis*. 2.2.6; pass. intrans., *be correct* ~ωθείσης...ἢ παρασφαλείσης τῆς τοῦ αἱρουμένου...κρίσεως Max.*opusc*.(M.91.29A); ptcpl., *perfect* τῶν εἰς δόξαν τοῦ θεοῦ...~ουμένων †Bas.*bapt*.1.2.9(2.635B; M.31.1540B); τοῖς ἤδη κατωρθωμένοις Cyr.*Jo*.3.4(4.294A); **3.** *accomplish successfully* in moral sphere; **a.** *perform, do* good works τὴν ἔννομον ἀρχὴν εἰς τυραννίδα μεταβαλών, μοιχοὺς καὶ ἀνδροφόνους ἀνευθύνους ἐᾷς καὶ ἀποδέχῃ ὡς μεγάλα ~οῦντας *M.Thdot*.3(p.134.22); τί μοι κεκατώρθωται μέγα; ‡Nil.*vit.cog*.(M.79.1465B); pass. ptcpl. neut., *exploit* ἀλλά τινα κατ' ἐξαίρετον ~ούμενα ποιοῦσιν γενέσθαι υἱὸν θεοῦ τὸν ~ώσαντα Or. *Jo*.20.17(15; p.349.23; M.14.612B); κατορθωμένων for ~ουμένων or κατωρθωμένων Thdt.*qu.1 in Jud*.(1.321); *good deed* τῆς ἐπὶ τοῖς ~ωθεῖσι τιμῆς Athenag.*res*.21(p.73.28; M.6.1016A); εἰς ζῆλον αὐτοὺς τῇ διηγήσει τῶν ἑτέροις ~ουμένων ἄγων Chrys.*hom.43.1 in 1Cor*.(10. 400C); ἕπεται ἡ ὄχλησις τοῦ πάθους τοῖς ~ουμένοις Diad.*perf*.99(p.146. 22); *ib*.proem.(p.5.7); ἀναλόγως τοῖς κατωρθωμένοις ἡ μονή Cyr.*Jo*. 4.6(4.428B); **b.** *perform, carry out* precepts ~οῦντα τὰς ἐντολάς Mac. Aeg.*perf*.11(M.34.849B); τοὺς δὲ μαθητὰς οὐκ αὐτοὺς μόνους ταῦτα ~οῦν, ἀλλὰ καὶ ἑτέρους διορθοῦν ἐκέλευσε Chrys.*hom.23.3 in Mt*.(7. 288D); Cyr.*Ps*.33:11(M.69.889A); med. κατωρθώσαντο τὰς ἐντολάς Herm.*vis*.3.5.3; pass. ~οῦται τὸ...προστεταγμένον Or.*Jo*.2.24(19; p.81.21; M.14.157A); τὸ...οὐράνιον ἐπάγγελμα ~οῦται...παρὰ μόνοις ...τοῖς Χριστιανοῖς Ath.*apol.Const*.33(M.25.640B); †Bas.*bapt*.1.2.16(2. 641C; M.31.1553C); ref. a monastic rule ὁ ζυγὸς...~ούμενος Bas.*reg. fus*.11(2.353D; M.31.948A); *ib*.proem.2(2.328D; M.893A); **c.** *attain to, achieve* virtues τὸ ἀναμάρτητον πάντοτε ~ῶν Clem.*str*.7.9(p.40.6; M.9.477A); Ammonas *ep*.1(p.433.3); οἱ ὁσιότητα ~ώσαντες Diod. *Ps*.51:11(M.33.1590B); Chrys.*hom.78.4 in Jo*.(8.464C); Nil.*epp*.3.35 (M.79.404B); ὑπὸ τῆς φύσεως βοηθούμενος ~οῖ δίχα πόνων τὴν σωφροσύνην Thdt.*1Cor*.3:8(3.181); id.*Heb*.12:14(3.627); pass. τὰ τῆς δικαιοσύνης κατωρθῶσθαι μεμαρτύρηται Eus.*d.e*.1.6(p.24.33; M.22. 52B); *ib*.(p.23.15; 49A); εὐκολώτερον...διὰ τῆς πενίας ἡ ἀρετὴ ~οῦται Chrys.*hom.10.4 in Phil*.(11.280E); τοῦτο δὲ διὰ τῆς ἄνωθεν βοηθείας ...τοῦ ἁγίου πνεύματος μόνης ~οῦσθαι δυνατόν Marc.Er.*opusc*.5.7(M. 65.1040B); **d.** *achieve, realize* a state of mind or way of life τὸ φρόνημα εὐάρεστον τῷ θεῷ ~ώσαντες †Bas.*bapt*.1.1.1(2.624E; M.31. 1516A); τὴν ὑψηλὴν φιλοσοφίαν, ἔργῳ μᾶλλον ἢ λόγῳ ~ουμένην Gr. Nyss.*or.catech*.18(p.76.2; M.45.36A); τοῖς εὐαγγελικὴν ~οῦσι ζωήν Cyr. *Ps*.33:20(M.69.892D); Thdt.*qu.24 in 2Reg*.10:16ff.(1.423); **e.** *bring to perfection* ἵνα κατὰ τὸν ἀρχηγὸν τῆς σωτηρίας ἡμῶν κατορθωθῇ τοῖς ἑπομένοις ἡ μίμησις Gr.Nyss.*or.catech*.35(p.131.5; 88A); *ib*.(p.136.11; 89D); οὕτω τὰς τέχνας κατωρθώσαμεν, οὐκ ἀθρόον παρὰ τῶν διδασκάλων πάντα μανθάνοντες Chrys.*hom.31.1 in Jo*.(8.174D); *ib*.*79.2*(8.467D); Nil.*Magn*.58(M.79.1045B).

B. intrans., *do well*; **1.** in moral sense, *live a good life*, **a.** in gen. ἀεὶ...~οῖ [sc. ὁ γνωστικός] ἐν πᾶσι πάντως Clem.*str*.7.9(p.40.9; M.9. 477A); *ib*.4.16(p.293.21; M.8.1309A); ἐὰν ἀφέξω τὸ πορευτικὸν διεστραμμένας ὁδοὺς πορεύεσθαι, ἀνατέθεικα καὶ τοὺς πόδας...εἰς τὸ κατορθῶσαι πληρώσασά τι τῶν ἐντολῶν Meth.*symp*.5.4(p.58.4; M.18.104B); δυνατὰς εἶναι τὰς ἐντολὰς εἰς τὸ ~οῦν Ath.*v.Anton*.93(M.26.973C); οὐ γὰρ ὁ νηστεύων ἀπὸ βρωμάτων μόνον ἐκεῖνος κατώρθωσεν, ἀλλ' ὁ ἀπεχόμενος ἀπὸ παντὸς πονηροῦ πράγματος id.*virg*.7(p.41.24; M.28.260C); Bas. *reg.fus*.10.1(2.352C; M.31.944D); Chrys.*hom.11.1 in Heb*.(12.203C); Thdr.Mops.*Gal*.3:18(p.45.26; M.66.904B); opp. ἁμαρτάνω: κατὰ μὲν τὴν προαίρεσιν ἕκαστον ~οῦν ἢ ἁμαρτάνειν Just.*2apol*.7.3(M.6.456B); Athenag.*res*.14(p.65.11; M.6.1001C); οἱ μὲν γὰρ ἁμαρτάνοντες ποιοῦσι τὰ ἔργα τοῦ...διαβόλου, οἱ δὲ ~οῦντες...τὰ...τοῦ πατρὸς αὐτῶν θεοῦ Or. *Jo*.20.14(13; p.345.3; M.14.604C); Gr.Naz.*or*.7.22(M.35.785A); Chrys. *hom.33.3 in Jo*.(8.194B); opp. σφάλλομαι, Just.*1apol*.43.4(M.6.393A); opp. πλημμελέω, Meth.*symp*.6.3(p.67.3; M.18.117A); opp. ἀναπέπτωκα, Chrys.*hom.10.3 in 2Cor*.(10.509C); **b.** perf. ptcpl. *just, righteous* ἕπεσθαι ἑτέροις δοκιμασθεῖσιν ἤδη καὶ κατωρθωκόσιν Clem. *str*.1.1(p.5.22; M.8.692B); *ib*.7.11(p.45.18; M.9.488B); οὐ μὴν ἤδη κατωρθωκότας, ἀλλ' ἔτι ἁμαρτάνοντας Or.*Jo*.20.26(21; p.362.23; M.14. 633C); Chrys.*hom.27.1 in Rom*.(9.719D); id.*hom.35.5 in Mt*.(7.405B); opp. παραπεπτωκώς, Or.*princ*.3.1.19(18; p.233.12; M.11.292B); also pres. εἰ γὰρ τοῖς ~οῦσιν ἀναγκαῖον ἡ θλῖψις, πολλῷ μᾶλλον τοῖς ἁμαρτάνουσιν Chrys.*hom.13.5 in Mt*.(7.174D); *ib*.*64.5*(642Aff.); Cyr. *Ps*.43:19(M.69.1024D); **c.** neut. ptcpl., moral *triumph* (cf. A.3.a) τὰ ~οῦντα Or.*Jo*.20.27(22; p.363.15; M.14.636B); **d.** med. ὅσοι ἂν... κατορθώσωνται, ζήσονται τῷ θεῷ Herm.*sim*.8.11.4(omit. ed. C.Bonner p.115); ἐφ' ἡμῖν [sc. κεῖται] τὸ κατορθώσασθαι καὶ ἁμαρτῆσαι Meth. *res*.1.57(p.319.8; M.41.1153A); πρὸς πάσας τὰς ἐντολὰς ~ούμενοι Marc. Er.*opusc*.4(M.65.992C); *ib*.7.6(1080A); **2.** *be accomplished, proficient* καθ' ἕκαστον παιδείας μέρος ~οῦντες Athenag.*leg*.6.2(M.6.901B); Cyr. *apol.Thdt*.3(p.120.21; 6^1.214B).

κατόρθωμα, τό, A. in pass. senses; **1.** *success*, of Church in world συμπνέων τε αὐτοῖς καὶ συνεργῶν ἐπιστώσατο τὸ κ. Eus.*theoph*.8 (p.22*.21; M.24.632B); **2.** *triumph, achievement, work* in moral or spiritual sphere πίστεως...ἡ μετάνοια κ. Clem.*str*.2.6(p.127.15; M.8. 961B); οὐ γὰρ ἐμόν ἐστι τοῦτο κ. ... ἀλλὰ τοῦ σωτῆρός ἐστι ἡ θεραπεία Ath.*v.Anton*.58(M.26.928A); id.*virg*.7(p.41.17; M.28.260B); Gr.Nyss. *v.Mos*.(M.44.337C); οὐδὲ ἀνθρωπίνης ἐστὶ φύσεως κ. τὰ προκείμενα δῶρα, ἀλλ' ἡ τοῦ πνεύματος χάρις Chrys.*pent*.1.4(2.463C); καιρὸς...ὁ πρέπων τοῖς οὕτω λαμπροῖς...κ., ὁ μετὰ τὸ ἅγιον βάπτισμα Cyr.*Pulch*.

(p.46.14; 5².158A); id.*Jo.*2.3(4.166B); of martyrs διαπρέψας τοῖς ἐν θεοσεβείᾳ κ. Eus.*h.e.*8.11.2(M.20.769A); μόνα καὶ ταῦτα τῶν ὑμετέρων ἱδρώτων τὰ κ. Gr.Naz.*or.*35.1(M.36.257B); Cyr.*Juln.*6(6².203E); of saints ἐπὶ πᾶσι τοῖς τῆς εὐσεβείας κατορθώμασι μεμαρτύρηται [sc. Job] Eus.*p.e.*7.8(311A; M.21.525C); Jov.*ep.*(M.26.813A); of Church in NT, Thdt.*Ps.*64:8(1.1033); δυνατὸν [sc. David] ἐν τοῖς τῆς ἀρετῆς ...κ. *ib.*88:21(1237); id.*Rom.*16:13(3.159); of Cyril τὰ ὑπὲρ τῆς ὀρθῆς πίστεως κ. Dalmat.*ep.Eph.*2(M.85.1800B); *feat* of asceticism, Thdt. *h.rel.*3(3.1148); of work of Christ σύμβολόν ἐστι [sc. crown of thorns] δεσποτικοῦ κ. βαστάσαντος αὐτοῦ τῇ κεφαλῇ...πάντα ἡμῶν τὰ πονηρά, δι' ὧν ἐκεντούμεθα Clem.*paed.*2.8(p.203.5; M.8.485C); οὗ...λέγεται τὰ πάθη...τούτου καὶ τὸ κ. καὶ ἡ χάρις Ath.*Ar.*3.32(M.26.392B); ἡμεῖς μετέχοντες τοῦ κ. πίστει σωζόμεθα Apoll.*tom.syn.*(p.263.9; M.86.1952B); τὸ κ. τοῦ Χριστοῦ...καὶ γὰρ ἐνίκησε τὸν θάνατον Chrys.*hom.* *31.3 in Mt.*(7.361A); id.*hom.8.2 in Heb.*(12.84B); οὐκ ὀπτάνεται [sc. risen Christ] Πιλάτῳ ἵνα μὴ τὸ κ. λύσωσιν οἱ τὰ καλὰ μεμαθηκότες λύειν Mac.Mgn.*apocr.*2.19(p.33.4); Cyr.*hom.pasch.*1.2(5².5B); plur., Eus.*l.C.*17(p.254.12; M.20.1429B); Ath.*inc.*54.4(M.25.192C); id.*Ar.*3.41(M.26.409C); Chrys.*pan.Ign.*4(2.599B); Thdr.Mops.*Gal.*3:23(p.52.28; M.66.905A); Cyr.*hom.pasch.*2.1(5².16E); τῆς οἰκονομίας τὰ κ. Thdt.*Is.*11:10(p.62.2; 2.254); ‡Cyr.*Trin.*28(6³.34D; M.77.1173B); of works of God οὕτω θείου πράγματος ὄντος τοῦ τὴν οἰκουμένην πᾶσαν τῆς αὐτοῦ γνώσεως πεπληρῶσθαι, ἀνάγκη τὸν ἀρχηγὸν...τοῦ τοιούτου κ. εἶναι θεὸν καὶ θεοῦ λόγον Ath.*gent.*1(M.25.5B); of sanctification through baptism, Gr.Nyss.*or.catech.*36(p.140.1; M.45.92D); Chrys. *pan.Pelag.Ant.*1(2.587D); id.*hom.25.3 in Mt.*(7.310D); κ. τῆς βουλῆς τοῦ θεοῦ Cyr.*Ps.*91:5(M.69.1225D); ὑπηρετοῦμαι μεγάλῳ θαύματι καὶ κ. [i.e. Inc.] Antip.Bost.*annunt.*18(M.85.1789B); **3.** more generally; *good deed* ἴδιον ἡγούμενοι [sc. polytheists] κ. τὴν πρὸς τὰ κρείττονα, ὡς αὐτοὶ νομίζουσι, μίμησιν Ath.*gent.*25(M.25.49C); μὴ γὰρ κ. σου τοῦτό ἐστι [sc. wearing large phylacteries, etc.]...ἐλεημοσύνῃ καὶ νηστείᾳ, καίτοι ἐπιπόνοις καὶ κ. οὖσιν ἡμετέροις, φιλοτιμεῖσθαι οὐ δεῖ Chrys.*hom.72.2 in Mt.*(7.703cf.); τὸ...θύραν ἐπιθεῖναι τῇ γλώττῃ... κ. ἐστι Cyr.*Ps.*33:14(M.69.889D); ironically καλά γε αὐτῶν τὰ ἐν ταῖς ἑορταῖς τὰ κ. Chrys.*hom.49.1 in Jo.*(8.288B); τὸ πανάγιον πνεῦμα... λέγοντες...Μοντανοῦ διακονοῦντος δεδόσθαι...μοιχοῦ δὲ φανερῶς ἑαλωκότος καὶ τῷ κ. τούτῳ θεοφάνειαν λέγοντες πεπιστεῦσθαι Isid.Pel. *epp.*1.243(M.78.332B); τοιαῦτα μὲν οὖν τὰ Μακεδονίου ὑπὲρ τοῦ Χριστιανισμοῦ κ., φόνοι καὶ μάχαι Socr.*h.e.*2.38.31(M.67.329B); plur., *good works* διὰ τοῦ λόγου...πάντα τὰ κ. κατωρθῶσθαι τοῖς μακαρίοις νοεῖν ἀναγκαῖον Or.*Jo.*2.13(7; p.68.24; M.14.133D); ἀνδρὸς ἴδιος ἔπαινος...ἐκ τῶν ὑπαρχόντων αὐτῷ κ. μαρτυρούμενος Bas.*hom.*23.2(2.185E; M.31.592A); Chrys.*serm.4.1 in Gen.*(4.658E); ἀρετῶν τινων καὶ κ. μέτοχοι ἐτύγχανον Marc.Er.*opusc.*5.4(M.65.1036A); Cyr.*resp.*(6².378E); ref. Origen's theory of salvation ἐκ προτέρων τινῶν κ. γενόμενον νῦν σκεῦος τιμῆς Or.*princ.*3.1.23(21; p.240.11; M.11.300A); useless without Christian faith οὐ γὰρ ὀνήσει ὑμᾶς τὰ πρότερα κ. ἐὰν ἀποπλανηθῆτε τῆς πίστεως *Const.App.*7.31.6; cf. ὀκνηρίαν...πρὸς τὴν πίστιν τὰ ταύτης [sc. the soul] κ. ἔχουσιν Ph.Carp.*Cant.*239(M.40.149A); not a subject for pride, Chrys.*hom.in Mt.7:14*(3.31B); ἵνα τῇ τοῦ κριτοῦ συγγενείᾳ θαρρήσωμεν, οἱ ἐξ οἰκείων κ. παρρησίαν οὐκ ἔχοντες Thdot.Anc.*exp.symb.*21(M.77.1344D); ταπείνωσίς ἐστι, τὸ ἐπιγράφειν τῷ θεῷ τὰ κ. Dor.*doct.*2.6(M.88.1645C); *ib.*6.2(1688A); Max.*ambig.*(M.91.1161C); opp. ἁμαρτήματα, Clem.*paed.*1.11(p.147.20; M.8.365B); Or.*Jo.*13.43(p.269.25; M.14.476C); Jo.D.*fr.Mt.*28:10 (M.96.1413B); opp. πταίσματα, Const.*or.s.c.*6(p.159.24; M.20.1245C); Diad.*perf.*28(p.30.14); opp. πλημμελήματα, *Const.App.*5.7.23; **4.** *perfection, virtue* ὡς τὸ κ. κατὰ τὸν ὄρθον γίνεται λόγον, οὕτως ἔμπαλιν τὸ ἁμάρτημα παρὰ τὸν λόγον Clem.*paed.*1.13 tit.(p.150.19; M.8.372A); ὥσπερ οὖν τὸ μὲν ἁπλῶς σώζειν τῶν μέσων ἐστίν, τὸ δὲ ὀρθῶς καὶ δεόντως κ., οὕτως καὶ πᾶσα πρᾶξις γνωστικοῦ μὲν κ., τοῦ δὲ ἁπλῶς πιστοῦ μέση πρᾶξις λέγοιτ' ἂν id.*str.*6.14(p.487.25f.; M.9.336A); of Christ οὐ προαιρετικόν, ἀλλὰ οὐσιωδές τὸ κ. Leont.H.*Nest.*1.19(M.86.1473A); a *virtue, good quality* οὐδὲ τῆς αὐτῆς φύσεως κ. τὸ συντακτικὸν καὶ διδασκαλικὸν εἶδος Clem.*ecl.*27(p.144.29; M.9.712B); τοῖς...τῆς ἀγέλης παραβάλλεται κ. Thdt.*Cant.*4:2(2.91); id.*Rom.*7:15(3.76); of the 'counsels' τὸ 'οὐ μοιχεύσεις' ἐὰν τηρήσω...ὃ ὤφειλον ποιῆσαι πεποίηκα. ἐὰν δὲ παρθένος μείνω, οὐ κελευσθεὶς...οὐκέτι λέγω ἐπὶ τῷ τῆς παρθενίας κ. 'δοῦλοι ἀχρεῖοί ἐσμεν' Or.*comm.in 1Cor.*7:25(*JTS* 9 p.509); οὐκ...ἐν μόνῃ τῇ τοῦ σώματος φυλακῇ τὸ κ. τῆς παρθενίας περισώζοντες Bas.*ascet.*1.2(2.319E; M.31.873A); τῶν εὐαγγελικῶν κ. Mac.Aeg.*pat.*11(M.34.873C); τὸ τῆς εὐπειθείας κ. Gr.Nyss.*v.Mos.*2 (M.44.300B); τὸ τῆς ἀκτημοσύνης κ. Nil.*Magn.*2(M.79.969D); of other individual virtues μέγιστόν ἐστι κ. ἀμνησικακία Or.*or.*9(p.319.9; M.11.444D); κ. ἡ ἀκακία ‡Chrys.*hom.in Ps.100*(5.639B); τρία...εἶχε κ., φιλόξενος ἦν, καὶ εὐμετάδοτος, καὶ ἐλεήμων *M.Bon.*1(p.326); τὸ τῆς φιλοξενίας κ. *cat.Lc.*10:38(p.89.30); cf.Cyr.*Lc.*10:38(M.72.684C); τὸ κ. τῆς ἁγνείας ‡Nil.*vit.cog.*(M.79.1445B); τοῦ...κ. τῆς ταπεινώσεως Isid.Pel.*epp.*1.286(M.78.352A); ἐν...τοῖς παλαιοῖς σπάνιον τὸ τῆς παρθενίας κ. Andr.Caes.*Apoc.*39(M.106.341B); **5.** *credit, merit* εἰ τὸν Ἰακὼβ ἄγεις ἐν μείζονι τιμῇ καὶ θαυμασίῳ κ., ἐπεὶ παρέσχεν ὑμῖν ὕδωρ Or.*fr.54 in Jo.*(p.528.19); οὐ τοῦ φυλάξαντος κ., ἀλλὰ τοῦ...θεοῦ, τὸ μηδὲν πεπονθέναι ἀπὸ πολεμίων τήνδε τὴν πόλιν id.*princ.*3.1.19(p.231.10; M.11.289B); μεῖζον ἔσται σοι τοῦ σφάλματος τὸ κ. Dion.Al.ap. Eus.*h.e.*6.45(M.20.633C); Chrys.*hom.56.1 in Gen.*(4.540C); ἐν τῇ μελλούσῃ ἡμέρᾳ ἀμέμπτους...φανῆναι, ὄγκον ἐπαγομένους κατορθωμάτων Thdr.Mops.*Phil.*1:10(p.204.24; M.66.921C); *cat.2Cor.*6:8(p.390.25); **6.** *end, object* ὁ συνημμένος...ἐκείνῳ [sc. Χριστῷ] πρὸς τὸ αὐτὸ κ. βλέπων, τὸ κατὰ τὴν ζωὴν λέγω πέρας Gr.Nyss.*or.catech.*35(p.133.3; M.45.88D); τῶν τεχνῶν...ἐν ἑκάστῃ ἀπολαβοῦσα ἔχει κ.· οἷον ἡ γεωργία, τὸ τρέφειν Chrys.*hom.52.3 in Mt.*(7.534B); id.*hom.in Mt.* *26:39*(3.18A).

B. in act. sense; **1.** *right ordering* or *exercise* τὸ τῆς θεοσεβείας κ. δι' ἔργων τὸ καθῆκον ἐκτελεῖ Clem.*paed.*1.13(p.151.18; M.8.373B); ἡ ...πονηρία ἐκ φύσεως ἀλλ' οὐχ εἱμαρμένης, ἥ τε ἀρετὴ ἤθους καὶ τρόπων ἐστὶ κατορθώματα Const.*or.s.c.*6(p.159.21; M.20.1245C); Eus. *p.e.*6.6(247B; M.21.420D); μνήματα...ἁγίων οὐ...στῆλαι καὶ γράμματα, ἀλλ' ἔργων κατορθώματα καὶ πίστεως ζῆλος Chrys.*pan.Eust.Ant.*(2.605B); τῆς οἰκονομίας τὰ κ. καὶ τὴν ἀρχὴν Thdt.*Is.*11:10(p.62.2; 2.254); freq. κ. προαιρέσεως: οὐκέτ' οὖν προαιρέσεως κ. ἡ πίστις εἰ φύσεως πλεονέκτημα Clem.*str.*2.3(p.118.22; M.8.941B); ἵνα...μὴ ἀναγκασμένον εἴη τὸ ἀγαθὸν καὶ ἀκούσιον ἀλλὰ κ. προαιρέσεως Gr.Nyss. *hom.2 in Cant.*(M.44.796D); Chrys.*hom.67.1 in Gen.*(4.636E); Antip. Bost.*annunt.*18(M.85.1788B); and κ. βουλήματος: εἰ γὰρ ἀνάγκη ἐστὶ ταπεινῶσθαι καὶ ἄκοντα, οὐκέτι τῆς φρονήσεώς ἐστι τὸ κ. οὐδὲ τοῦ βουλήματος Chrys.*hom.6.2 in Phil.*(11.236E); cf. αὐτοῦ ποιῆσαι τὸ κ. καὶ τῆς αὐτῆς προαιρέσεως id.*hom.22.1 in Eph.*(11.166C); ἐστὶν δὲ ταῦτα συντυχίας οὐ γνώμης κ. Thdr.Mops.*1Tim.*3:2(p.104.22; M.66.941A); **2.** *perfection, consummation* ποῦ δὲ ἔτι γραφῆς καὶ μαθήσεως κ. τῇ ψυχῇ...τῇ καθαρᾷ γενομένῃ, ὅπου καὶ ἀξιοῦται...θεὸν ὁρᾶν; Clem. *exc.Thdot.*27(p.116.7; M.9.673A); οὐ κακῶς γε ἐκεῖνο τῇ ἐξουσίᾳ παρακεῖται οὔ γε ἡ ἀποχὴ τελείας ἀρετῆς κ. Tit.Bost.*Man.*2.34(M.18.1200B); *ib.*2.2(1133C); *establishment* εἰρήνης τὸ κ. Thds.Imp.*ep.Jo.* *Ant.*(p.3.6; M.77.1460A).

κατόρθωσις, ἡ, **1.** *right ordering, setting right*; **a.** in Church οὐδεμία δὲ τηλικαύτη δύναται πρὸς αὐτῶν [sc. workers of schisms] κ. γενέσθαι, ἡλίκη τοῦ σχίσματος ἐστὶ ἡ βλάβη Iren.*haer.*4.33.7(M.7.1076B); ἄλλως...οὐ δυνατὸν τὰ μεγάλα τῶν σκεμμάτων ἢ διὰ συνόδων κατορθώσεως τυγχάνειν Eus.*v.C.*1.51(p.31.28; κατορθώσασθαι M.20.965B); πρώτην ὑπάρχειν καὶ μόνην καὶ ἀληθῆ κ. εὐσεβείας τὴν διὰ τῆς τοῦ Χριστοῦ διδασκαλίας παραδοθεῖσαν ἡμῖν id.*h.e.*1.4.15(M.20.80C); **b.** in moral sense τὴν ἀκολουθοῦσαν τῇ κ. τῶν πράξεων θεωρίαν Or.*Jo.*2.36 (29; p.95.11; M.14.180B); τῶν ἠθῶν κ. Eus.*p.e.*11.4(511D; M.21.849B); γενέσθω σοι ἡ ἱστορία βίου κ. Chrys.*exp.in Ps.*3(5.1B); **2.** *recovery* of health ἐάν ἐστιν ἀσθενέστερος, πολλοῦ πάνυ χρεία καὶ κόπου καὶ χρόνου πρὶν ἢ γένηται αὐτοῦ ἡ κ. Dor.*doct.*11.1(M.88.1736A); **3.** *achievement, work* οὐκ ἄρα ἡ τοῦ νόμου κ. ἐστιν, ἀλλ' ἡ τοῦ θεοῦ ὑπόσχεσις ἡ τὴν κοινωνίαν ἡμῶν τῆς εὐλογίας χαριζομένη Thdr.Mops.*Gal.*3:18 (p.45.30; M.66.904C); Ammon.*Ac.*26:29(M.85.1597D); of precepts, *performance, fulfilment* πρὸς κ. πασῶν τῶν ἐντολῶν συνεργοῦσαν τὴν προσευχήν Marc.Er.*opusc.*7.4(M.65.1077A); *ib.*5.7(1037D); *consummation*, ref. work of Christ ἡ διὰ τῶν παθημάτων κ., ἥτις...τῷ τὸν σταυρὸν δεξαμένῳ γεγένηται Hesych.H.*fr.Ps.*98:9(M.93.1269C); *establishment* of virtue, Marc.Er.*opusc.*5.2(M.65.1032A); Cyr.*Jo.*3.4 (4.293E); Thdt.*Rom.*8:30(3.93); **4.** abs., *practice of virtue, good life* ὁ...νόμος Μωϋσέως οὐκ ἄδικος, ἀλλὰ σκληρὸς...διὸ ἀδύνατος εἰς κ. ἀνθρώποις ἐφάνη Ammon.*Ac.*13:39(M.85.1541C).

κατορθωτέον, *one must practise rightly*, ‡Nil.*vit.cog.*(M.79.1460C).

κατορθωτικός, *conducive to right performance* or *to right living* τῇ κ. τῶν πρακτέων...ἀσκήσει Clem.*str.*7.7(p.33.27; M.9.464B); τῆς ἐπηβόλου καὶ κ. πίστεως *ib.*6.9(p.470.7; 297B).

κατορρωδέω, intrans., *be dismayed, frightened* οὐ κατορρωδήσας ὁ Ὅσιος...ἔγραψε...τοιαῦτα Ath.*h.Ar.*43(p.207.17; M.25.744C); Men. *exc.Rom.*3(p.185.18; M.113.873B).

κατορύσσ-ω, **1.** *bury*; also med. τίς ἐὰν ἀνοίξῃ τὴν ληνὸν τούτων... εἴτε τέκνα ἔχει κατορύξαιτο αὐτά *CG–CI* 1.15; met. οἱ ἐν σκότει...ἂν εἶεν οἱ ἐν τῇ εἰδωλολατρείᾳ κατορυγμένον ἔχοντες τὸ ἡγεμονικόν Clem. *str.*6.6(p.453.27; M.9.265A); Eus.*p.e.*2.5(69D; M.21.133D); Bas.*leg.* *lib.gent.*7(2.182C; M.31.584B); ἐν τοῖς νοεροῖς ταμείοις τὴν πλεονεξίαν χρυσοῦ δίκην κατορύξαντες Marc.Er.*opusc.*3.5(M.65.973A); **2.** reflex., *bury oneself, sink into the ground*, for shame τοῦτο...ἄξιον ἐπαίνου; καὶ οὐ ∼εις σαυτόν; Chrys.*hom.7.5 in Phil.*(11.253B); id.*hom.12.5* in *1Cor.*(10.103B); κ. ἑαυτὸν βούλεται id.*hom.*40.4 *in Mt.*(7.443D); also med. φιλοτιμοῦνται ἐφ' οἷς ~εσθαι ἔδει *ib.*70.4(692C); **3.** *make away with, destroy* αὐτὸν...κ. ὡς λυμεῶνα id.*hom.4.1 in 2Thess.*(11.529D); **4.** *mine*, Jo.Mal.*chron.*18 p.470(M.97.684C); τὰ ἀφανῆ τῶν θεμελίων κ. Thphn.*chron.*p.43(M.108.164B); **5.** *suppress, conceal* τὴν νεκρέγερσιν κ. δόλῳ ‡Gr.Naz.*Chr.pat.*2376(M.38.322A).

***κατορφανεύω**, *deprive* μὴ κατορφανεύσῃς ἡμᾶς τῆς ἱκεσίας σου [sc. BMV] *Hymn.*(*AS* 1 p.536).

κατορχ-έομαι, **1.** *dance in triumph over; exult over; disdain*; c. acc., Bas.Sel.*or.*18.1(M.85.229A); **2.** *please* or *win by dancing* κ. τῶν θεατῶν παντοίοις...λυγίσμασι Gr.Naz.*or.*21.12(M.35.1093C); **3.** pass., *be escorted with dances* (ref. funeral of Juln. Imp.) καταυλούμενός τε καὶ ~ούμενος *ib.*5.18(688A).

***κατότεχνος**, Eus.Al.*serm.*4(M.86.340A), error for κακότεχνος.

***κατούδιον, τό**, dimin. of κάττος (Lat. *catus*), *young cat* ἐὰν φορεῖς γοῦνα ὑπὸ δέρματος κατουδίου Barth.Edess.*Agar.*(M.104.1405A).

κατουράνιος, *heavenly*; τὰ κ. opp. τὰ χαμαὶ...καὶ περίγεια Ath. *apol.Const.*30(M.25.633C).

***κατοφρυάομαι**, variant of κατοφρυόομαι, Gr.Naz.*or.*43.64(M.36.580D).

κατοφρυ-όομαι, *be supercilious towards, despise* δι' ὧν αὐτοῦ ἐδόκει ~οῦσθαι *A.Andr.fr.*18(p.45.18); abs., *be supercilious*, freq. in perf., Bas.*hom.*3.1(2.17B; M.31.200C); Cyr.*Is.*3.2(2.417A); ἐπὶ τῇ τοῦ νόμου γνώσει κατωφρυωμένοι id.*Jo.*1.10(4.108C); *ib.*6.1(618E).

***κάτοφρυς**, *low-browed* or *with heavy eyebrows*; of Paris, Jo.Mal. *chron.*5 p.106(M.97.196A).

κατοχή, ἡ, **1.** *detention*; **a.** in prison, ‡Ath.*serm.fid.*35(p.29; M.26.1288D); **b.** esp. in the grip of death or Hades κάτω ἦν...ἡ κ. τῶν ψυχῶν Or.*fr.84 in Lc.*23:46(p.274); τὸν Ἀδὰμ...ὑπὸ κατάραν καὶ κ. θανάτου ‡Ath.*serm.fid.*13(p.9; 1269C); οὔτε...θάνατος ὑπερισχύσας ὑπηγάγετο ἑαυτῷ τὴν ἀνθρωπίνην τοῦ λόγου ψυχὴν εἰς δεσμῶν κ. ‡Ath. *Apoll.*1.14(M.26.1117C); *ib.*2.17(1161C); τὴν ἐν ᾅδῃ κ. ἡμῶν γενομένην διὰ θανάτου ‡Caes.Naz.*dial.*182(M.38.1156); **2.** *grasp* ὤμων ἀχθοφορίαι, καὶ κ. δακτύλων Dion.Al.ap.Eus.*p.e.*14.26(779D; M.21.1281D); **3.** *possession, occupation*, of a see ἐπιψηφίσαι τὴν κ. τοῦ θρόνου Philost.*h.e.*2.11(M.65.473B); **4.** met., *possession, grasp* Παῦλος ...ἐν κ. τοῦ θείου γεγονὼς ἔρωτος Dion.Ar.*d.n.*4.13(M.3.712A); of a sudden *wave* of emotion αἰφνίδιός τις κ. τῆς εὐσεβείας γίνεται ἐν τῇ καρδίᾳ μου ‡Ath.*disp.*1(M.28.440A).

κατόχιον, τό, *bolt*, Jo.Disc.*v.Epiph.*13(M.41.37D); τὸ κ. τοῦ θυριδίου Cyr.S.*v.Jo.Hes.*(p.215.27); met. κ. ἐπὶ τῷ στόματι Eulog. *palm.*10(M.86.2929C).

κάτοχος, **A.** act. senses; **1.** *holding fast, retentive* κ. ἀρετῆς [sc. ὁ μαθητής] Cyr.*Jo.*2.1(4.131C); **2.** masc. as subst., *anchor* ῥίψαντες τοὺς κ. ἔμενον Pall.*v.Chrys.*14(p.89.2; M.47.50).

B. pass. senses; **1.** *overcome* by, *subject* to passions, sins κ. ἐπιθυμίας Meth.*symp.*2.2(p.17.3; M.18.49B); τῇ δυσσεβείᾳ κ. Cyr.*Os.*73(3.109C); τῷ πλημμελήματι κ. id.*Mich.*28(3.414D); **2.** *possessed, gripped*, ref. states of the soul ἁρπάζεται παρ' αὐτῆς [sc. εὐχῆς] ὁ ἔσω ἄνθρωπος, καὶ κ. ἀπείρῳ βάθει τοῦ αἰῶνος ἐκείνου γίνεται Mac. Aeg.*carit.*8(M.34.916A); ἡδονῇ κ. γίνονται θαυμασίᾳ *ib.*6(913B); **3.** *possessed, inspired*, by H. Ghost τὸν κ. τῷ θείῳ πνεύματι Or.*Cels.* 7.3(p.155.26; M.11.1426A); Eus.*v.C.*3.26(p.90.14; M.20.1088B); id. *d.e.*4.15(p.176.32; M.22.293D); c. ὑπό: τοσοῦτον...ἦν τὸ διάφορον τῶν ὑπὸ τοῦ θείου πνεύματος κ. καὶ τῶν ὑπὸ δαιμονικῆς ἐνεργείας μαντεύεσθαι προσποιουμένων *ib.*5 proem.(p.207.37; 345A).

κατοχυρόω, *fortify*, Jo.Mon.*hymn.Bas.*3(M.96.1372C); of persons τούτους ἱεροῖς λόγοις...κ. *V.Chrys.*43(p.320.11).

κάττα, ἡ, *cat* ὁ δὲ ἔφη αἴλουρον εἶναι, ἣν κ. ἡ συνήθεια λέγει Evagr. *h.e.*6.23(p.239.13; M.86.2880B); ‡Caes.Naz.*dial.*110(M.38.985).

κάττυμα, τό, plur., *patchings*; met., of concoctions from other doctors' medicines, Sophr.H.*mir.Cyr.et Jo.*30(M.87.3516B).

καττύω, *stitch, sew up*; hence *devise, plot* ἐκάττυσαν ἐπιστολὴν ἐπιδοθῆναι *Ep.Aeg.*(p.157.27; M.25.389A); *ib.*(p.157.13; 388C); τὸν ἐμὸν κ. θάνατον Ath.*exp.Ps.*30:16(M.27.160A); Thdt.*qu.48 in 1Reg.*(1.385B); abs., Alex.Thess.*ep.Ath.*(p.160.27; M.25.393C); κ., ἀπόντων ἡμῶν, ὡς βούλονται Ath.*apol.sec.*72(p.151.19; M.25.377B).

κάτω, **A.** of place; **1.** in gen., *below*; τὰ κ. *the depths, the bottom* ἀπὸ τῶν κ. ἐπὶ τὰ ἄνω ὁρμὴν ἔχων Hipp.*haer.*5.7(p.85.22; M.16.3136A); ὥσπερ τῶν ἀναβαθμῶν ὁ μέν ἐστιν πρῶτος ἐπὶ τὰ κ. Or.*Jo.* 19.6(p.305.20; cf.M.14.536C); **2.** *in the nether regions, in the world below* Χριστὸς ἦν καὶ κ. ὢν...ἐν τῷ κ. τόπῳ ὢν Or.*engast.*8(p.292.6; M.12.1025A); τὰς κ. δυνάμεις Meth.*Porph.*1(p.504.14; M.18.400B); *A.Phil.*138(p.70.11); *ib.*139(p.72.9); τὰς κ. ποινάς Synes.*ep.*44(M.66.1369D); comp. ὁ σταυρὸς ὁ...διορίσας τὰ ἀπὸ γενέσεως καὶ κατωτέρω *A.Jo.*99(p.200.18); superl. εἰς τὰ κατώτερα μέρη τῆς γῆς ὁ καταβὰς... διὰ τοὺς ἐν τοῖς κ. τῆς γῆς Or.*Jo.*19.20(5; p.322.10; M.14.565A); ἡ πλάνη...πολλοὺς...κατέρριψε τοῖς κ. μέρεσι παραδοῦσα Const.ap.Eus. *v.C.*4.10(p.121.30; M.20.1160A); **3.** *in this world, on earth, here below* opp. in heaven κἂν μὴ τὴν φωνήν τις ἐξικνεῖσθαι πρὸς τὸν θεὸν λέγῃ κ. περὶ τὸν ἀέρα κυλινδουμένην Clem.*str.*7.7(p.29.5; M.9.453A); τὴν κ. νομιζομένην Ἰουδαίαν Or.*Cels.*7.28(p.179.20; M.11.1461A); *ib.*2.5(p.132.15; 804A); τὸν ἀέρα τὸν ὧδε κ. πλανᾶται Ath.*inc.*25.5(M.25.140B); id.*inc.et c.Ar.*9(M.26.997C) cit. s. ἄνωθεν; ‡Ath.*nativ.Chr.*4(M.28.965B) cit. s. γέννησις; πᾶν ἀτιμάζω τερπνὸν κ. μένον, εἰς τοῦτό μοι πᾶν ἐκενώθη τὸ φίλτρον μετὰ θεόν Gr.Naz.*or.*6.5(M.35.728B); παρὰ τῷ κ. καίσαρι Thdr.Stud.*epp.*1.44(M.99.1069A); οἱ κ. *men on earth* τῷ Χριστῷ...μεθ' ἡμῶν τῶν τοπικῶς κ. ἐπὶ γῆς τυγχάνοντι Or.*Cels.*5.12(p.13.9; cf.M.11.1197D); ὁ σωτὴρ ὢν μὲν ἐν τῷ πατρὶ...οὐκ οἶδε φθέγγεσθαι τοῖς κ. id.*hom.1.8 in Jer.*(p.8.7; M.13.265A); id.*Jo.*28.4(p.392.31; M.14.685B).

B. implying value, *beneath*; **1.** often best translated by adj., *inferior, lower*; **a.** in the order of being ὥστε διὰ τὸ αἰσθητὸν φῶς ἐκείνων [i.e. the sun, etc.] νομίσαι ἑαυτοὺς κ. που εἶναι Or.*Cels.*5.10(p.11.8; M.11.1196B); τὰ...γενητὰ κ. που τῆς τριάδος ἐστὶ...δουλεύοντα Ath. *Ar.*1.58(M.26.133B); id.*ep.Serap.*1.30(M.26.600A); τῆς κ. φύσεως [i.e. of man opp. God] Gr.Nyss.*tres dii* (M.45.120C); implying motion, *downwards* πρὸς τὴν ὕλην νεύει κ. Tat.*orat.*13(p.14.22; M.6.833B); comp., of *lower* forms of life, Ath.*gent.*19(M.25.40A); superl., of *lowest* part of the soul, Or.*Jo.*32.2(p.427.13; M.14.744A); **b.** morally, of one fallen or laid *low* in sin τίς...ἔτι μέριμνα τῷ διαβόλῳ παλαίειν τοῖς ἀεὶ κ. κειμένοις; Marc.Er.*opusc.*7.7(M.65.1081A); **c.** socially, οἱ κ. *the lower classes of society* πολλοὶ μὲν τῶν ἐν δυναστείαις καὶ ὕψεσιν...πολλοὶ δὲ τῶν κ. καὶ ἀριθμῷ μόνῳ γνωριζομένων Gr.Naz.*or.*4.65(M.35.588A); οὐκ ὀλίγην...τοῦ λαοῦ μοῖραν...ὅση τε τῶν κ., καὶ ὅση τῶν ἐπ' ἀξίαις *ib.*43.8(M.36.536A); **2.** *in the sphere of the literal* or *physical*; of persons, *immersed in the world* or *in things of sense*; **a.** in gen. δικαιωθήσεται...πᾶς ζῶν...οὐκ ἐνώπιον τοῦ θεοῦ· ὅτι δὲ τοῖς κ. συγκρίνεται καὶ ὑπὸ τοῦ σκότους κεκρατημένοις Or.*Jo.*2.17(11; p.74.17; M.14.144D); ref. Lc.6:20 μὴ κ. εἰσὶν οἱ τοῦ Ἰησοῦ μαθηταί *ib.*28.4(p.392.27; 685B); ὁ ὑπὸ τοῦ λόγου προσαχθεὶς ἐπὶ τὸ σέβειν τὸν...θεὸν καὶ διὰ τὰ πάτρια κ. που μένων παρὰ τοῖς ἀγάλμασι καὶ τοῖς ἀνθρωπίνοις ἱδρύμασι id.*Cels.*5.35(p.39.9; M.11.1236B); τοῖς μὲν ἔτι κ. τυγχάνουσι καὶ μηδέπω ἐπὶ τὸ ἀναβαίνειν παρεσκευασμένοις ὁ λόγος οὐκ ἔχει εἶδος οὐδὲ κάλλος *ib.*6.77(p.147.6; 1416A); ἀμφὶ τὰς σωμάτων γενέσεις καὶ τὸν κ. θνητὸν βίον καταπεσόντες, ἀνθρώπους θνητοὺς ἐξεθείασαν Eus.*l.C.*13(p.236.4; M.20.1397C); τὰς ἐλπίδας ἔχοντες...κ. που κειμένας Ath.*h.Ar.*58(p.215.29; M.25.764A); id.*inc.*14.7(M.25.121B); κἂν... μικρά τις ὁμοίωσις [i.e. of earthly things to God] εὑρεθῇ, φεύγει τὸ πλεῖον, ἀφέν με κ. μετὰ τοῦ ὑποδείγματος Gr.Naz.*or.*31.31(p.186.15; M.36.169A) ∞ Didym.*Trin.*2.5(M.39.505A); τὰ κ. *earthly things, things of sense* ὁ τὰ κ. ἀπὸ τοῦ ἐν οὐρανοῖς...κατοικοῦντος κυρίου αἰτῶν Or.*or.*21(p.345.14; M.11.481A); πότερόν ποτε ταὐτόν ἐστιν τὸ 'ἐκ τῆς γῆς εἶναι' τῷ 'ἐκ τῶν κ. εἶναι'...ἄλλη μέντοι γε ἡ ἐπίνοια ἡ ἐκ τῶν κ. καὶ τῆς γῆς. κ. γὰρ ὥσπερ τόπῳ τινὶ νοεῖται οὕτως καὶ δόγμασιν καὶ διανοίᾳ· καὶ πᾶς γε ὁ τούτοις δόγμασιν καὶ διανοίᾳ χρώμενος, ἅτινά ἐστιν ἐκ τῶν κ., ἐκ τῶν κ. ἐστίν...τὸν μὲν ἐκ τῶν κ. πάντως εἶναι ἐκ τοῦ κόσμου τούτου, τὸν δὲ ἐκ τοῦ κόσμου τούτου μὴ πάντως εἶναι ἐκ τῶν κ. ... ἔξεστιν μέντοι γε τὸν ἐκ τῶν κ. καὶ ἐκ τοῦ κόσμου τούτου καὶ ἐκ τῆς γῆς μεταβαλεῖν καὶ γενέσθαι ἐκ τῶν ἄνω...ὁ σωτὴρ...ἦλθεν τοὺς κ. καὶ πολιτογραφηθέντας ἐν τοῖς κ. μεταστῆσαι ἐπὶ τὰ ἄνω id.*Jo.* 19.20(5; p.321.4,20ff.,30; p.322.2,8; M.14.564A,Cff.); λαμβάνων [sc. ὁ λόγος] ἑαυτῷ σῶμα...ἐκ τῶν κ.—λέγω δὴ διὰ τῶν τοῦ σώματος ἔργων Ath.*inc.*14.8(M.25.121B); τοσοῦτον τῷ πηλῷ συνεσχέθη, ὡς μὴ...ὑπὲρ τὰ κ. γενέσθαι, γεγονὼς ἄνωθεν, καὶ πρὸς τὰ ἄνω καλούμενος Gr. Naz.*or.*21.2(M.35.1084C); comp. κ. ... ἐν ὑποδεεστέροις Or.*Jo.*10.9(7; p.179.2; 320C); δυνατὸν...μεταβῆναι ἀπὸ τοῦ σήμερον εἶναι ἐν τοῖς κ., ὥστε γενέσθαι τοῦ θεοῦ σῶμα τὸ ἀνωτέρω id.*hom.11.5 in Jer.*(p.83.25; M.13.376A); superl., *ib.18.2*(p.153.12; 468A) cit. s. ἄνω; **b.** ref. Inc., Ath.*inc.*16.3(M.25.124C) cit. s. ἄνω; γενόμενος ἄνθρωπος ὁ κ. θεὸς Gr.Naz.*or.*29.19(p.103.2; M.36.100A) cit. ap. Max.*ambig.*(M.91.1040B) and paraphrased thus κενωθεὶς ὁ λόγος, καὶ ὑπὸ τὴν φυσικὴν ...γενόμενος αἴσθησιν, θεὸς ὁρατὸς καὶ κ. θεὸς προσηγορεύθη *ib.* (1040C); τὴν κ. συγγένειαν i.e. of Christ with men acc. the flesh, Thdt.*eran.*1(4.39); comp. οἱ μὲν πάντες εἰσὶν ἀναβαθμοὶ ὁ σωτήρ· ὁ δὲ ...πρῶτος κ. τὸ ἀνθρώπινον αὐτοῦ Or.*Jo.*19.6(p.305.22; M.14.536C).

C. of time; **1.** *afterwards, later*; comp., Or.*princ.*4.3.7(p.333.22; M.11.387A); ὁ ἔτι κ. Ἰωσίας περὶ ἔτη γεγονὼς ἑπτὰ τῆς ἀρχῆς ἀντελάβετο Ath.*inc.*36.1(M.25.157B); Jo.D.*haer.*3(M.94.681A); **2.** as prep., *after, later than* κ. ... τῆς Μωϋσέως ἡλικίας οἱ παρ' Ἕλλησι σοφοὶ γεγόνασι Clem.*str.*1.14(p.38.10; M.8.760A).

κατῶβλεψ, ὁ, *down-looker*; an African beast resembling a bull,

Geo.Pis.*hex*.947(M.92.1507A); cf.Aelian *NA* 7.5(*Teub*.p.171.30); Pliny *nat.hist*.8.21(32; *Teub*.p.104.8).

κατώγεως, **1.** *below ground*; of cellars τῶν κ. οἴκων *A.Thom*.A 22 (p.135.10); **2.** neut. as subst. τὰ κ. opp. τὰ ἀνώγεα *ground floor* [*rooms*], Pall.*h.Laus*.6(p.24.10; κατάγαια M.34.1019B); met., of earth opp. firmament, v. καταγαῖος.

κατώδυνος ([*]**κατόδυνος**), **1.** of persons, *in anguish, afflicted*, *A. Xanthipp*.1(p.58.10); Gr.Nyss.*res*.3(M.46.657C); Chrys.*hom.44.3 in Gen*.(4.450E); of Christ, ref. Jo.12:27 νῦν ἡ ψυχή μου τετάρακται καὶ κ. ἐστι ‡Ath.*Apoll*.1.16(M.26.1124A); *grieving, mourning* μοναχός ἐστιν κ. ψυχὴ ἐν διηνεκεῖ μνήμῃ θανάτου...γρηγοροῦσα Jo.Clim.*scal*.1 (M.88.633C); κατόδ- Gr.Mag.*dial*.(tr.Zach.)3.33(M.*PL*.77.298C); **2.** of things, *grievous*, Isid.Pel.*epp*.1.196(M.78.309A); τὸν τραχὺν καὶ ἐμμέριμνον, καὶ κατόδυνον βίον Jo.D.*hom*.2.3(M.96.581A).

*__κατωδύνως__, *sorrowfully, in affliction*, Jo.Clim.*scal*.7(M.88.804D).

κάτωθεν, *from below*; **1.** *upside down* ὁ Πέτρος κ. ἀνεσκολοπίσθη Chrys.*hom.5.2 in 2Tim*.(11.687C); **2.** *from the nether regions* φωναὶ ...ἀνερχόμεναι κ. *A.Phil*.133(p.64.13); κ. ... ἀπὸ τοῦ χάσματος ὄφεις ἀνέρπειν Dion.Ar.*ep*.8(M.3.1100B); **3.** *on earth, here below*, opp. heaven, denoting origin in the world of sense and matter, Tat.*orat*. 13(p.14.25; M.6.833B) cit. s. ἄνω; τὸν μηδαμῶς ἀπὸ τῶν παλαιοτέρων καὶ κ. ζυμούντων ἄζυμον...ἄρτον Or.*Jo*.10.18(13; p.189.19; κατωτέρω M.14.357C); ὁ γὰρ γεννηθεὶς ἄνωθεν ἐκ πατρὸς λόγος...ὁ αὐτὸς ἐν χρόνῳ γεννᾶται κ. ἐκ παρθένου...ἵνα οἱ κ. πρότερον γεννηθέντες ἄνωθεν γεννηθῶσιν ἐκ δευτέρου Ath.*inc.et c.Ar*.8(M.26.996A); from anything lower than Godhead, *from created world* παρὰ τῷ πατρὶ μὴ φθάσαντα πρῶτον κ. ἀναβαίνοντα ἐπὶ τὴν τοῦ υἱοῦ θεότητα Or.*Jo*.1.27(29; p.35.5; 76A); λέγει [sc. Paul of Samosata] Ἰησοῦν Χριστὸν κ. Malch.*ep*.ap.Eus.*h.e*.7.30.11(M.20.713B); τῶν...λεγομένων θεῶν...τῶν κ. Ath.*gent*.11(M.25.25A); Gr.Nyss.*or.catech*.39 (p.159.3; M.45.101B) cit. s. ἄνωθεν.

κατωθ-έω, *compel, force*, Cyr.*Os*.4(3.19D); ἢ πῶς κατωθήσειε πρός γε τὸ δεῖν id.*Juln*.6(6^2.211D); pass. ὁ πτωχὸς...πρὸς πᾶν εἶδος φαυλότητος ~ούμενος id.*Ps*.9:23(M.69.780B).

*__κατωθίζω__, *push down*, *Ev.Thom*.B 8.1(p.161).

*__κατωκλινῶς__, [*while bending*] *downwards*; of animals on all fours opp. man who walks upright, Anast.S.*hod*.2(M.89.68B).

κατωμαδόν, *on the shoulders*, met. τὰς ἁπάντων φροντίδας κ. ἀράμενος φέρω Synes.*ep*.66(M.66.1409C).

κατωρύ-ομαι, **1.** *howl*; of dogs, Chrys.*hom.68.4 in Mt*.(7.675B); **2.** *roar against*, met. εἴ...τις οἴοιτο...ὡς ἐν τάξει λεόντων ~εσθαι τοῦ Χριστοῦ τοὺς γραμματεῖς Cyr.*Zach*.76(3.757C).

*__κατωρύχιος__, *underground*; of rivers, Philost.*h.e*.3.9(M.65.492B).

κατώτατος, κατώτερος, (superl. and comp. adjs. from κάτω); comp., *lower*; superl., *lowest*; **1.** of the nether regions, comp. ἡ ὑπερηφανία αὐτὸν [sc. Satan] κατέβαλεν εἰς τὰ κ. μέρη τῆς ἀβύσσου Ath.*virg*.5(p.39.19; M.28.257A); τὸ σκότος τὸ κ. *Hom.Clem*.20.9; superl. εἰς τὰ κ. τῆς γῆς Or.*hom.5.17 in Jer*.(p.46.23; M.13.321B); Hegem.*Arch*.8(p.11.13; M.10.1440A); v. 2.a; **2.** exeg. Eph.4:9; **a.** εἰς τὰ κ. μέρη τῆς γῆς, εἰς ᾅδου Or.*Jo*.19.21(5; p.323.10; M.14.565D); ὑψῶσθαι λέγεται αὐτὸς ἀπὸ τῶν κ. μερῶν τῆς γῆς, ἐπεὶ καὶ αὐτοῦ λέγεται ὁ θάνατος εἶναι Ath.*Ar*.1.45(M.26.104C); τὰ κ. μέρη τῆς γῆς τὸν θάνατόν φησιν ἀπὸ τῆς τῶν ἀνθρώπων ὑπονοίας Chrys.*hom.11.2 in Eph*.(11.82C); Thdt.*Eph*.4:9(3.423); καταβὰς οὐ μόνον γῆν, ἀλλὰ καὶ ὑπὸ γῆν Jo.D.*Eph*.4:9(M.95.841B); **b.** *non sub terra dicit. nam illa quae sub terra sunt, jam ultra terram esse non poterunt...ipsam terram nominat in comparatione caeli*, Thdr.Mops.*Eph*.4:9(p.167.13); **3.** *lower, inferior* in kind or degree; **a.** ref. Trisagion as illustrating divine being in three Persons οὐδαμοῦ τις...ἀπήγγειλεν ἡμῖν...τὸν πρῶτον ἁγιασμὸν κυριολογοῦντα, τὸν δὲ δεύτερον ὑποτάσσοντα, καὶ τὸν τρίτον κ. τιθέντα Ath.*hom.in Mt.11*:27(M.25.220A); **b.** in spiritual or intellectual sphere <εἰ μὲν τὰ κ.> διδάσκομαι, καταβαίνω τῷ λόγῳ, ἵνα ἴδω τὰ κ.· εἰ δὲ τὰ ἀνώτερα μανθάνω, ἀναβαίνω τῷ λόγῳ ἐπὶ τὰ ἀνώτερα Or.*hom.18.2 in Jer*.(p.152.8; M.13.465A); ἔδει μὲν αὐτὰς ἀνωτέρας εἶναι τῶν βιωτικῶν· ἐπειδὴ δὲ κ. γεγόνασι κἂν ἐν αὐτοῖς στηκέτωσαν Chrys.*hom.15.1 in 1Tim*.(11.635E); superl., Or.*hom. 18.2 in Jer*.(p.153.16; M.13.468A); **c.** socially οἱ κ. *the lower classes* ταῦτα ἐννοῶμεν διαπαντὸς, τοὺς κ., τοὺς ἐν μείζοσι συμφοραῖς Chrys. *hom.11.4 in 1Thess*.(11.507C); **4.** temporal, *later* πολὺ τῆς Μωσέως ἡλικίας κ. Tat.*orat*.36(p.38.11; M.6.880B); κ. Κύρου Eus.*p.e*.10.14 (504D; M.21.840C); *ib*.10.9(484C; M.805C).

*__κατωτικός__, **1.** *low, pertaining to things below*; Gnost., of evil principle from which created world is derived ἡ κ. ῥίζα, ἀφ' ἧς ἡ τῶν γινομένων προῆλθεν φύσις *A.Jo*.98(p.200.15); ὁ δὲ περὶ τὸν σταυρὸν μονοειδὴς ὄχλος ἡ κ. φύσις ὑπάρχει *ib*.100(p.201.1); ref. mystical significance of number four ὁ τέταρτος ἀριθμὸς ὑλικός τις καὶ σωματικὸς ὢν κ. ἐστιν Or.*fr.79 in Jo*.(p.546.25); **2.** of the *lower* countries relative to Constantinople τῶν κ. μερῶν Thphn.*chron*. p.360(M.108.865A).

κατωφερής, *with a downward tendency*; morally, *inclined* κ. εἰς συνουσίαν Clem.*str*.7.6(p.25.19; M.9.448A); πρὸς τὸ...πάθος...κ. Gr. Nyss.*v.Mos*.(M.44.413C); abs., *likely to deprave* καρδίαν καθελκομένην ὑπὸ τῆς κακίας οὔσης κ. Or.*sel.in Ex*.7:13f.(M.12.284A); *prone to vice* κ. ... καὶ ἀκρατής Chrys.*hom.28.6 in Heb*.(12.267B); Isid.Pel.*epp*.2. 53(M.78.497A); cf. τοῦτο τὸ ἡμισφαίριον κ. θηλυκόν τε καὶ κακοποιόν Hipp.*haer*.4.43(p.66.13; M.16.3107A); *ib*.4.44(p.67.9; 3107C).

κατώφορος, *steep, sloping*; neut. as subst., *slope* κατέβησαν τὸ κ. τῆς Ἱεριχὼ Leont.N.*v.Sym*.5(M.93.1676A).

κατωχριάω, *turn pale*, Cyr.*Is*.2.5(2.337B); id.*ador*.11(1.381B); med., †Jo.D.*B.J*.6(M.96.901B).

καυκάλιον, τό, v. βαυκάλιον.

καυκίον ([*]**καυχίον**), **τό**, *vessel, cup*, *V.Eudoc*.2(p.875); Ephr.2. 3A; Jo.Mosch.*prat*.196(M.87.3081A); for holding bread, *V.Euprax*.26 (p.732F); Cyr.S.*v.Jo.Hes*.19(p.216.2); met., of sun's orb δίσκος... καυχίον τοῦ ἡλίου ‡Ath.*qu.al*.4(M.28.776B).

*__καυκοδιάκονος, ὁ__, *cup-bearer* τὸν ἀπὸ καυκοδιακόνων σοφιστὴν γεγονότα τῆς ἰατρικῆς ἐπιστήμης Thphn.*chron*.p.320(M.108.773C).

καῦκος, ὁ, *cup*, Thphn.*chron*.p.248(M.108.624B).

*__καυλακαῦ__, קַו לָקָו Is.28:10 (i.e. prob. *Q* (in answer) to *Q*, ref. teaching of alphabet to children), taken as sacred name and applied to σωτήρ by Basilides, cf. *quemadmodum et mundus nomen esse, in quo dicunt descendisse et ascendisse salvatorem, esse Caulacau*, Iren.*haer*.1.24.5(M.7.678B); τὸν...σωτῆρα καὶ κύριον καυλακαύαν ὀνομάζουσι Thdt.*haer*.1.4(4.292); by Ophites οὗτοί εἰσιν οἱ τρεῖς ὑπέρογκοι λόγοι *K*., Σαυλασαῦ, Ζεησάρ, *K*. τοῦ ἄνω, τοῦ Ἀδάμαντος Hipp.*haer*. 5.8(p.89.20; M.16.3139C); and by Nicolaitans ἄλλοι δὲ τὸν κ. ὡσαύτως δοξάζουσιν, ἄρχοντά τινα τοῦτον οὕτως καλοῦντες Epiph.*haer*.25.3 (p.270.16; M.41.324C); κ. ... ἐν τῷ Ἠσαΐᾳ γέγραπται, λέξις τις οὖσα ἐν τῇ δωδεκάτῃ ὁράσει...κ. κ. ἐλπὶς ἐπ' ἐλπίδι *ib*.25.4(p.271.19ff.; 325B).

καυλός, ὁ, *stem* of a candlestick, Cyr.*Jo*.4.4(4.390C).

*__καυλοτομ-έω__, *mutilate* τοὺς ἐν παιδεραστίαις εὑρισκομένους ~εῖσθαι Jo.Mal.*chron*.18 p.436(M.97.644B).

*__καυματινός__, of climate, *torrid, hot*, Epiph.*haer*.66.84(p.126.16; M.42.164A); *Chron.Pasch*.p.28(M.92.124A).

*__καυσοκόπος, ὁ__, *worm, insect*; harmful to crops, *Euchol*.(p.555).

*__καυσοπολίτης, ὁ__, *incendiary*, as nickname ὅτε οἱ πράσινοι... ἔκαυσαν τὴν μέσην...τοὺς Χριστιανοὺς ὡς πρασίνους ὑβρίζων καὶ κ. ἀπεκάλουν καὶ Μανιχαίους *Didasc.Jac*.1.53(p.777.1).

*__καυσόχειρ__, *having a burnt hand* ἐκάη ὁ...δάκτυλος...καὶ ἔκτοτε... Ὀρέντιος ὁ κ. ἐπέγραφεν †Anast.S.*relat*.18(*OC* 2 p.71.3).

καυσόω, pass.; **1.** *bear the heat of the day*, ref. Mt.20:12, ‡Nil. *perist*.12.2(M.79.940D); **2.** *become feverish*, Gr.Naz.*carm*.1.2.10.483 (M.37.715A).

καυστήρ, ὁ, v. καυτήρ.

καυστήριον, τό, v. καυτήριον.

καυστικός, **1.** *burning, inflammatory* τὴν καυτικὴν δύναμιν [i.e. of fire] Mac.Mgn.*apocr*.4.14(p.183.13, cod. καυστικήν); met. λόγον ζῶντος θεοῦ...καυστικώτερον παντὸς πυρός Or.*Jo*.6.58(37; p.166.27; M. 14.300D); δὸς...κἀμοὶ...διαβάντι τὸ πῦρ ἀναλγητί, καὶ τῶν ῥευμάτων εἰς τὴν κ. μεταβληθέντων φύσιν ὑπεξαλύξαντι τὰς ὁρμάς Meth.*res*.1.56 (p.317.9; M.41.1152B); τὸν καυστικώτατον τῆς πρὸς τὴν θείαν συνουσίαν...ἐφέσεως ἔρωτα Max.*ambig*.(M.91.1364D); **2.** = καυστός, *inflammable*, Meth.*res*.2.23(p.377.17; M.18.288A); Epiph.*haer*.29.5 (p.327.3; M.41.400A); Chrys.*hom.16.8 in Mt*.(7.215A).

καύστρα, ἡ, *burning*, †Anast.S.*relat*.38(*OC* 2 p.82.12).

καύσωμα, τό, *scorching, burning heat*, ref. Pr.25:13 κ. διαλύει, μεγάλα τὸν σῖτον βλάπτοντα, ὡς πρὸ ὥρας πεσεῖν πολλάκις ἀφανισθέντα ὑπὸ τῆς καύσεως ‡Hipp.*fr.49 in Pr*.(p.174.19).

καύσων, ὁ, *fever, flame*, met. ἐν σκιρτήματι νεοτησίῳ καὶ τῷ κ. τῆς ἡλικίας Clem.*q.d.s*.8(p.165.6; M.9.612D); ὅταν ὁ κ. τοῦ παρόντος βίου παύσηται, καὶ καιρὸς τῆς ἀναψύξεως ἐπιστῇ Or.*schol.in Cant*.4:5(M. 17.272C); ὁ...πειρασμὸς τὸν φλογώδη καύσωνα...ἐπιβαλών, ἁπαλὴν ἔτι ...τὴν πρώτην βλάστην κατέβαλε Gr.Nyss.*hom.2 in Cant*.(M.44. 793B); ref. state of demons δαίμονες...τῷ πυρὶ χωνευόμενοι, ὅπερ ἐκ τῆς ὀπτασίας τοῦ σωτῆρος ἔλαμψεν...ἐπιβάθραν τῶν χοίρων τὴν ἀγέλην ἐζήτησαν, ἵνα δι' αὐτῶν εἰσελθόντες τὸν κ. λύσωσι Mac.Mgn.*apocr*.3.11 (p.77.7).

*__καυσωνίζομαι__, *suffer from fever*, ‡Just.*ep.Zen.et Ser*.12(M.6. 1197C).

[*]**καυτεριάζω**, v. καυτηριάζω.

καυτήρ (καυστήρ), ὁ, **1.** *cauterizing apparatus, branding iron* καυστ- Or.*Cels*.4.72(p.342.14; M.11.1144A); ὡς...ὁ κ. μετὰ τοῦ πυρὸς νοεῖται, καὶ ἄλλο μέντοι ἡ ὑποκειμένη ὕλη καὶ ἄλλο τὸ πῦρ Bas.*Spir*. 38(3.32C; M.32.137A); as instrument of torture, Eus.*v.C*.1.58(p.35.6; M.20.972D); **2.** *cautery, branding*, Or.*sel.in Ps*.4:6 ap.*philoc*.26.6 (p.238.21; καυστ- M.12.1160A); *Const.App*.6.21.2; καυστ- ‡Just.*ep. Zen.et Ser*.5(M.6.1189A); Thdt.*1Tim*.4:2(3.659); ref. practice of Carpocratians σφραγῖδα...ἐν κ. ἢ δι' ἐπιτηδεύσεως ξυρίου...ἐπιτιθέασιν οὗτοι ἀπὸ Καρποκρᾶ ἐπὶ τὸν δεξιὸν λοβὸν τοῦ ὠτός Epiph.*haer*.27.5 (p.308.3; M.41.372A); v. καυτήριον, καυτηριάζω; **3.** *mark made by branding* ὡς πρόβατα ἄλογα τῷ κ., κἂν πλανηθῇ ῥᾳδίαν ἔχει τὴν... εὕρεσιν Or.*sel.in Jos*.5:2(M.12.821B); καθάπερ τις κ. σώματι, ταῖς ἀμφοτέρων ὑπολήψεσιν ἐγκαίεται Chrys.*fem.reg*.6(1.259D); Pall.*h. Laus*.32(p.90.2; καυστῆρας M.34.1100A); met. ὀνοματοποιίαις χρήσασθαι, ἵν', ὥσπερ διὰ κ. τινῶν...τὸ ἰδίωμα ἑκάστου γένους ἐπιγινώσκηται Bas.*hex*.8.3(1.72E; M.29.169C); ζητήσωμεν...τὸν κ. τοῦ κυρίου καὶ τὴν σφραγῖδα ἐν ἑαυτοῖς ἔχειν Mac.Aeg.*hom*.12.13(M.34. 564D); ὥστε αὐτοῖς ἐνθεῖναι καυτῆρα ἀνίατον τῆς ἥττης...τὸ ὄνομα τὸ ἑαυτοῦ τοῖς τῆς πόλεως ἐπέθηκε λειψάνοις Chrys.*Jud*.5.11(1. 645D).

καυτηριάζ-ω (καυτεριάζω), **1.** *brand*; ref. Carpocratian practice ~ουσι τοὺς...μαθητὰς ἐν τοῖς ὀπίσω μέρεσι τοῦ λοβοῦ τοῦ δεξιοῦ ὠτός Iren.*haer*.1.25.6 ap.Hipp.*haer*.7.32(M.16.3339B); met. ἐκ τῆς νέας σοφίας κεκαυτηριασμένα τὰ ῥήματα Bas.*Spir*.16(3.13D; M.32.96A); esp. exeg. 1Tim.4:2 πολλὰς ἐξηπατήκασι γυναῖκας, αἵτινες κεκαυτηριασμέναι τὴν συνείδησιν, αἱ μὲν...ἐξομολογοῦνται, αἱ δὲ...ἔνιαι μὲν ἀπέστησαν, ἔνιαι δὲ ἐπαμφοτερίζουσι Iren.*haer*.1.13.7(M.7.592A); κατὰ βάθους τῆς ψυχῆς συνέχειν τὰ ἁμαρτήματα, τὴν συνείδησιν ~ομένους †Bas.*hom.in Ps*.37(1.366A; M.30.92B); Chrys.*hom.12.1 in 1Tim*.(11.610C); διὰ τοὺς κεκαυτηριασμένους τὴν συνείδησιν, ὡς διὰ συντόμου ἀπολογητέον περὶ τῶν ἀποστόλων Ammon.*Ac*.15:39(M.85. 1552D); κέκληκε, τὴν ἐσχάτην αὐτῶν ἀναλγησίαν διδάσκων· ὁ γὰρ τοῦ καυτῆρος τόπος νεκρωθεὶς τὴν προτέραν αἴσθησιν ἀποβάλλει Thdt. *1Tim*.4:2(3.659); κεκαυτεριασμένην τὴν ἰδίαν συνείδησιν ἔχοντες Jo. D.*haer*.103(M.94.777A); **2.** *cauterize*, medic. ὑπὸ ἰατρῶν τοῖς θεραπείας ἕνεκεν τεμνομένοις ἢ ~ομένοις Or.*Cels*.6.56(p.127.5; M.11. 1384D); id.*hom.12.5 in Jer*.(p.92.20; M.13.385C); Mac.Aeg.*hom*.6.1 (M.34.517C); met. κ. αὐτὸ καὶ τὴν σηπεδόνα ἔκκοψον, στιβώσας νηστείαις *Const.App*.2.41.6; **3.** *brand, burn*; as a punishment, *M.Tar*.5(p.460); **4.** *burn* glass, Leont.N.*v.Sym*.54(M.93.1736D).

καυτήριον (καυστήριον), τό, *mark of burning, brand* τὰ κ. καὶ τοὺς μώλωπας καὶ τὰ τραύματα ἔχοντες *Ep.Lugd*.ap.Eus.*h.e*.5.2.2(M.20. 433B); εἶπεν ὁ Κέλσος ἀκοῆς καυστήριά τινας ὀνομάζεσθαι παρὰ Χριστιανοῖς Or.*Cels*.5.64(p.67.16; M.11.1285A).

καυτικός, v. καυστικός.

καυχ-άομαι (-έομαι), *boast, glory*; **1.** c. prep., *boast* of ἐν ἀρετῇ... ἐν σημείοις κ. Ath.*v.Anton*.38(M.26.900A); Marc.Er.*opusc*.2.209(M. 65.964A); κ. ἐν νόμῳ Dion.Ar.*ep*.8.2(M.3.1092A); κ. ... ἐπὶ εὐγενείᾳ Or.*hom.11.4 in Jer*.(p.81.25; M.13.372B); ἐπὶ τῷ δαίμονας ἐκβάλλειν κ. Ath.*v.Anton*.38(897B); εἰσί τινες...εἰς οὓς ~ώμεθα πλείω πάντων Dam.*troph*.2.8(p.234.7); **2.** *glory, exult* οὐ...δίκαιον τὸν νυμφίον... παθεῖν καὶ σταυρωθῆναι, καὶ τὴν νύμφην, δι' ἣν ὁ νυμφίος παρεγένετο, καὶ ~ουμένην εἶναι καὶ ῥέμβεσθαι Mac.Aeg.*hom*.27.2(M.34.693C); in God, *Pss.Sal*.17.1; Ath.*apol.fug*.18(p.81.8; M.25.668C); ὁ νοῦς, ὅτε ἐπάνω τοῦ τῆς σαρκὸς ~ᾶται φρονήματος δύναται γεύεσθαι τῆς παρακλήσεως...τοῦ...πνεύματος Diad.*perf*.30(p.34.8).

καύχημα, τό, **1.** *boast* τὸ κ. ἡμῶν...ἔστω ἐν αὐτῷ [sc. τῷ κυρίῳ] *1Clem*.34.5; ἄκουε οἷα καυχᾶται κ. [2Cor.11:23ff.] Or.*hom.11.4 in Jer*.(p.82.13; M.13.373A); Diad.*perf*.17(p.22.9); **2.** *vainglorious speech* τῷ ἀποτετάχθαι παντὶ κ. Or.*hom.17.5 in Jer*.(p.149.10; M.13. 461A); κενὸν ὑμῶν ἄρα τὸ κ. Ath.*Ar*.2.82(M.26.321A); Diad.*perf*.13 (p.16.7); **3.** *occasion of boasting* or *pride*, of Macrina τὸ κοινὸν κ. τῆς γενεᾶς Gr.Nyss.*v.Macr*.(p.395.18; M.46.981D); σταυρὸς...τὸ τοῦ Παύλου κ. Chrys.*hom.in Mt.26:39*(3.19B); Cyr.*Ps*.35:5(M.69.916D); *glory* μὴ ἀκλεῶς ἀποθνήσκειν, ἀλλ' ἔχειν...τοῦ μαρτυρίου τὸ κ. Ath. *apol.fug*.17(p.80.12; M.25.665C); ἔχεις κ. τοῦ βαπτίσματος, αὐτὸν τὸν υἱὸν τοῦ θεοῦ Cyr.H.*catech*.3.9; of Christ ἡ...πρᾳότης κ. αὐτοῦ *A. Thom*.A 86(p.202.12).

***καυχηματικῶς**, *boastfully*, Didym.*Trin*.3.31(M.39.952C).

***καυχημον-έω**, *boast, vaunt* ἡ ἀγάπη...οὐ ~εῖ Ephr.2.112C (1Cor. 13:4 περπερεύεται).

καύχησις, ἡ, **1.** *boasting* ἔστιν τινά, ἐν οἷς καυχώμεθα...οὐκ οὖσιν καυχήσεως ἀξίοις...ἀλλοτρία ἐστὶν ἡ κ. καυχήσεως ἁγίων...μανθάνομεν ...καυχήσεων εἶναι διαφοράς· ὡς τινὰς μὲν κ. εἶναι αἰσχύνης ἀξίας Or. *hom.11.4 in Jer*.(p.81.25,30; p.82.16; M.13.372Bff.); **2.** *vaingloryíng* πολλὰ φρονῶ ἐν θεῷ, ἀλλ' ἐμαυτὸν μετρῶ, ἵνα μὴ ἐν κ. ἀπόλωμαι Ign. *Trall*.2.1; καυχήσεως καὶ ὑψηλοφροσύνης καὶ ὑπερηφανίας Herm. *mand*.8.3; ἀσφάλισαι λόγον ἀπὸ κ. Marc.Er.*opusc*.2.176(M.65.957B); **3.** *glorying, exultation*, Or.*mart*.41(p.39.1; M.11.617A); δώῃς αὐτῷ στέφανον καυχήσεως ἐν ἡμέρᾳ ἀποκαλύψεως ἐπισκοπῆς σου *Const.App*. 3.13.1; ὁ Παῦλος μυρία ὑπομείνας δεινὰ...ἐκαυχᾶτο...ἡ δὲ κ. ἡδονῆς ἐστιν ἐπίτασις Chrys.*stat*.18.3(2.186C); **4.** *pretext for boasting* τῶν τειχέων [i.e. of Jericho]...πεπτωκότων αὐτομάτως ἄνευ ἀνθρωπίνης κ. *Chron.Pasch*.p.77(M.92.229A).

[*]**καυχίον, τό**, v. καυκίον.

καχεκτ-έω, *be ill-disposed, disaffected*, Chrys.*hom.24.5 in Eph*. (11.186B); ~ούσας ψυχάς ‡Proc.G.*Pr*.27:23–24(M.87.1500C).

***καχέσπερος**, *of a bad evening*, Jo.D.*carm.theoph*.37(p.210; M.96. 828A).

***καχημερία**, ἡ, *evil day, black day* μοναχὸς γαστρίμαργος τὴν νηστείαν κ. ἀποκαλεῖ Ephr.1.108B.

καχλάζ-ω, *crackle* πῦρ...~ον Mac.Aeg.*hom*.16.13(M.34.624A).

καψάκης, ὁ, *flask*, Gr.Naz.*carm*.1.2.6.49(M.37.647).

[*]**κεάτας**, ὁ, = καιάδας, *pit* or *underground cavern* at Sparta; used as prison, *Schol.Clem.prot*.(p.314.8; M.9.786D).

[*]**κεγχρεμίς**, ἡ, = κεγχραμίς, *millet-seed*, hence of any *fine grain*, Cyr.*ador*.12(1.446A).

κεγχριδίας, *made of κέγχρος*: ἄρτος ὁ κ. Thdt.*h.rel*.2(3.1120).

κεγχρίς, ἡ, = κέγχρος, *millet*, hence anything in small grains; of gold dust, Mac.Aeg.*hom*.15.52(M.34.612B); κ. σύκου Chrys.*hom. 17.2 in 1Cor*.(10.148C, v.l. κέγχρος).

κεγχρῖτις, ἡ, a kind of serpent, Epiph.*haer*.66.88(pp.131.19,132.1; M.42.172A).

κεγχροειδής, *like grains of millet* κ. ἐπαναστήματος Philost.*h.e*.3.11 (p.41.20; M.65.497B).

κέγχρος, ὁ, ἡ, *millet*, hence *grain*; met., of specks on a precious stone, Epiph.*gemm*.11(M.43.501A); ὀφθαλμόν, τὴν μικρὰν ἐκείνην κ. ‡Chrys.*fid*.(1.828E).

[*]**κεδραία**, ἡ, = κεδρία, *oil of Syrian cedar*, *Mir.Cosm.et Dam*.11 (p.122).

[*]**κεδρέα**, ἡ, = foreg., Anast.S.*hod*.2(M.89.68A).

κέδρος, ἡ, *cedar-tree*; **1.** etym. κ. ... *quasi καιομένης δρυὸς ὑγρόν, id est arboris humor ardentis*, Isid.H.*etym*.17.7.33; **2.** allegorical interprn. ἡ κ. ποτὲ μὲν ὡς μόνιμον, καὶ σήψεως βέλτιον...παρὰ τῆς γραφῆς ἐπαινεῖται· ποτὲ δὲ ὡς ἄκαρπον...διαβάλλεται, ὡς καὶ εἰκόνα πληροῦν τοῦ ἀσεβοῦς Bas.*hom.in Ps*.28(1.119C; M.29.293B); αἱ κ. λαμβάνονται μέν ποτε καὶ εἰς εἰκόνα ψυχῶν μεγάλων, καὶ ἀξιόλογον ἐχουσῶν δίαρμα, ἐκ τοῦ διανεστηκέναι τῷ φρονήματι...ἤδη δὲ καὶ τὰ σκληρὰ...ἤθη, τὰ ἐπαιρόμενα κατὰ τῆς γνώσεως τοῦ θεοῦ, κέδρους ἔγνωμεν λεγόμενα...καὶ οἱ ἐπαιρόμενοι ἐπὶ τῇ ψευδωνύμῳ γνώσει...κ. λέγονται †Bas.*Is*.228(1.552Af.; M.30.517Af.); on account of the combination of its magnificence with the uselessness of its fruit signifying the proud and wicked, Bas.*hom.in Ps*.28(1.119Cf.; M.29.293C); †Bas.*Is*.228(1.552B; M.30.517B) cit. supra; ὁ δὲ ἄνευ ἐργασίας τινὸς ἀγαθῆς, ἢ διὰ πλοῦτον, ἢ δι' εὐγένειαν...μετεωριζόμενος, κ. ἐστίν, ἀκάρπῳ ζωῇ καὶ ἀνονήτῳ ἐπαγαλλόμενος *ib*.90(442C; M.265D); ἁπαλὰ δὲ τῆς κ., τούς...τρυφῇ προσέχοντας...κ. ... τοὺς ἐπὶ πλούτῳ βριθομένους, καὶ ἐν ἀξιώμασι λαμπρυνομένους Thdt.*Cant*.proem.(2.7); signifying pagan temples ἐπειδή...ὑψηλὰ ἦν...τὰ τῶν εἰδώλων τεμένη, καρπὸν οὐδένα τοῖς σεβομένοις ὀρέγοντα, ταῖς τοῦ Λιβάνου κ. ἀπείκασε ταῦτα, αἳ ὑψηλαὶ μέν εἰσιν, ἐδώδιμον δὲ καρπὸν οὐ πεφύκασι φέρειν id.*Ps*.28:5(1.782); because of its many virtues likened to the just, †Bas.*Is*.228(552A; M.517A) cit. supra; ὁ δὲ δίκαιος τῆς μὲν κ. τὸ δασύ, καὶ θερμόν, καὶ θρέψιμον, τοῦ δὲ φοίνικος μιμήσεται τὸ ὑψίκομόν τε καὶ κάρπιμον· διαρκεῖ δὲ ἀμφότερα καὶ ἐπὶ πλεῖστον διαμένοντα χρόνον, χρόνου δὲ καὶ εἰς αὔξησιν δεῖται Thdt.*Ps*.91:13(1.1268); cf. *sicut cedrus non putrescit, ita nec majorum gloria ulla vetustate corrumpitur*, Ambr.*serm.4.20 in Ps.118*(M.*PL*.14.1247C); to sovereigns, Thdt.*Ps*.79:11(1175); to ministers of Church, cf. *cedros dei esse eos qui ecclesiam contegunt*, Or.*Cant*.3(p.177.14; M.13.149A); to prophets, Ph.Carp.*Cant*.33(M.40.57C); as not liable to decay it is referred to humanity of Christ κέδρον δὲ καλεῖ τὴν ἀνθρωπείαν, ὡς σηπεδόνα τῆς ἁμαρτίας οὐ δεξαμένην· ἄσηπτος γὰρ ἐν ξύλοις ἡ κ. Thdt.*Cant*.5:16(2.120); κ. δὲ αὐτὸν προσηγόρευσε κατὰ τὸ ἀνθρώπινον ...ἔχει δὲ καὶ ἄσηπτον ἡ κ., ὥσπερ καὶ ὁ δεσπότης, καὶ κατὰ τὸ ἀνθρώπειον τὸ ἀναμάρτητον ἔσχηκε id.*Ezech*.17:22(2.807).

κεῖμαι, *lie*; **1.** *lie outstretched*, of eucharistic gifts οὐρανίων δυνάμεων ἅπαν τὸ βῆμα καὶ ὁ περὶ τὸ θυσιαστήριον πληροῦται τόπος, εἰς τιμὴν τοῦ κειμένου Chrys.*sac*.6.4(p.147.19; 1.424C); ὅταν ὁ κύριος ἡμῶν...κεῖται ἐσφαγμένος id.*hom.14.1 in Heb*.(12.141A); **2.** *be situated, lie, be* in a place; **a.** of persons, *be* in an attitude or position ἐπὶ γόνυ...οἱ ἱεροὶ κελεύουσι κεῖσθαι νόμοι, ὥστε καὶ διὰ τοῦ σχήματος ὁμολογῆσαι τὴν δεσποτείαν Chrys.*catech.*3.4(p.171.30); εὑρίσκει αὐτὸν ἐπὶ γόνατα κείμενον· ἣν γὰρ μετάνοιαν ποιῶν...καὶ οὕτως ἀπέδωκεν τὴν ψυχήν. ἔμεινεν οὖν τὸ σῶμα αὐτοῦ ἔτι κείμενον εἰς μετάνοιαν *V.Dan.*11(p.390.17); **b.** met., of God, *have one's place, be* τὸ περὶ τοῦ πνεύματος, ὡς...τῷ θεῷ καὶ τῷ υἱῷ κειμένου †Apoll.*ep.Bas.*2(M.32.1108B); εἰ...ἄνω παντὸς κεῖσθαι πάθους τὴν θείαν τοῦ πατρὸς ἐροῦσι φύσιν, ἔξω δηλονότι καὶ τῆς ἐπὶ τοῦτο κατηγορίας κείσεται Cyr.*Jo.*1.3(4.26E); of persons οὐ διϊστάντες εἰς ἄνθρωπον ἰδικῶς τε καὶ ἀνὰ μέρος κείμενον τὴν ἐπ' αὐτῷ [i.e. Christ] θεωρίαν, καὶ εἰς θεὸν λόγον id.*expl.xii cap.*2(p.18.7; 6^1.148D); of abstracts ἐν τῇ αἱρέσει τῆς γνώμης κεῖται τῆς τελειότητος ἡ κατόρθωσις Thdt.*Eph.*2:15(3.414); of events, *take place, happen* ⟨ἐ⟩κεῖτο δὴ μετὰ ταῦτα ἐπὶ γῆς σκυβάλων ἐκβλητότερον Eus.*l.C.*16(p.253.25; M.20.1428B); *go* according to plan ταῦτα κατὰ λόγον ἔκειτο αὐτῷ id.*v.C.*1.25(p.19.25; M.20.940C); **3.** *be laid down, ordained, established*; **a.** of persons, *be appointed, set* over ἄγγελος...κείμενος ἐπὶ τῆς τιμωρίας Herm.*sim.*6.3.2; **b.** esp. of laws, *be in force* παιδαγωγὸς...ὁ νόμος ἦν, ἔκειτο δὲ καὶ μέχρι καιροῦ διορθώσεως, ἣν δὲ οὗτος ὁ τῆς τοῦ σωτῆρος...ἐπιδημίας Cyr.*Is.*4.2(2.607B); **c.** of an allegory or metaphor, with εἰς or ἐπί, *be applied* to, *used of, refer* to αὕτη...ἡ παραβολὴ εἰς τοὺς δούλους τοῦ θεοῦ κεῖται Herm.*sim.*2.4; Dion.Ar.*d.n.*2.11(M.3.652A); ὁ ...καταποντισμὸς ἐπὶ κολάσεως κεῖται Olymp.*Eccl.*10:12f.(M.93.601A); of the subject of the metaphor, *be denoted* or *represented* διατί...ὁ υἱὸς τοῦ θεοῦ εἰς δούλου τρόπον κεῖται ἐν τῇ παραβολῇ; Herm.*sim.*5.5.5; *ib.*6.1; **4.** *be available* τούτοις...μετάνοια κεῖται, ἐὰν ταχὺ μετανοήσωσιν *ib.*9.19.2; *ib.*9.19.3; **5.** of words and phrases, *be found, occur*; τὸ κείμενον the *text*, κατὰ τὸ κ. au pied de la lettre, *according to the superficial meaning, literally*, Meth.*symp.*3.1(p.27.16; M.18.61B).

[*]**κειμηλιαρχεῖον, τό,** *repository, treasury*; of a church, Cyr.S.*v.Cyriac.*(p.227.7); Jo.Mosch.*prat.*195(M.87.3080D); †Gr.II Papa *ep.Leon.*2(H.4.16D).

κειμηλιάρχης, ὁ, *treasurer*; of a church, Cyr.S.*v.Cyriac.*(p.226.27); Jo.Mosch.*prat.*48(M.87.2904A); *ib.*195(3080D); κιμιλιάρχης *MAMA* 3.349 (Corycus).

κειμήλιον, τό, anything stored up as valuable, *treasure, heirloom*; **1.** of treasures of a church, partic. sacred vessels, Eus.*v.C.*3.43(p.95.28; M.20.1104A); Pall.*v.Chrys.*16(p.95.1; M.47.54), Cyr.*ep.*78(5^2.211A); πρεσβύτερος καὶ φύλαξ τῶν ἱερῶν κ. Eustrat.*v.Eutych.*8(M.86.2284B); cf. τὰ κ., ἤγουν τὰ ἱερά Theodorus Balsamon *schol.* in CNic.(787)*can.*12(M.137.932A); cf. τὰ σεπτὰ κ. ἐπὶ μόνῃ ἀναρρύσει αἰχμαλώτων ἐκποιείσθωσαν id.*constitutionum ecclesiasticarum collectio* 2.2(M.138.1313B); prob. of *relics* ἤνοιξεν τὰ ἁρμάρια τῶν κ. Cyr.S.*v.Euthym.*48(p.69.14); met. ὥσπερ ἴδια κ. τὰ μαθήματα σφραγίζων ἐν ἡμῖν Ath.*ep.Aeg.Lib.*1(M.25.540A); *inheritance* οὐ...νεώτερον τὸ ἐφεύρημα [i.e. νηστεία]· πατέρων ἐστὶ τὸ κ. Bas.*hom.*1.3(2.3A; M.31.165C); ref. Rom.9:3 οὐ γὰρ θάνατον, φησίν, ἀλλὰ κ. καὶ ἀνάθημα ηὔχετο εἶναι τοῦ Χριστοῦ Chrys.*hom.16.3 in Rom.*(9.606E); of Jo. Bapt. ὁ πρόδρομος...τὸ κρυπτόμενον ἐν τῇ ἐρήμῳ κ. Jo.D.*hom.*1.3(M.96.549B); of BMV χαίροις, Μαρία, τὸ κ. τῆς οἰκουμένης †Cyr.*hom.div.*11(5^2.380D); **2.** *precious vessel*: idea of vessel as well as treasure is present in following instances where τὸ κ. is not only precious in itself but also because of its contents; **a.** of Christ's body δῶρον...ὄφρα φυλάξῃ σώματος ἡμετέρου κ. Nonn.*par.Jo.*12:7 (ἡμετέρων κτερέων M.43.852A); **b.** of BMV τριάδος νύμφη ὑπάρχει ἡ ...Μαρία, τὸ πανάρρητον τῆς οἰκονομίας κ. ‡Epiph.*hom.*5(M.43.489A); ὦ παρθένε, φρικτὸν τῆς ἐκκλησίας κ. *ib.*(497A); τὸ ἀμόλυντον τῆς παρθενίας κ. Procl.CP *or.laud.BMV* 1(p.103.12; M.65.681A); κ. τῆς ἐπουρανίου βασιλείας Mod.*dorm.*10(M.86.3304B); χαίροις, ὦ θεοῦ θεοφόρον κ. ‡Jo.D.*hom.*5(M.96.649C); **c.** of other holy persons παρθένους φύλαττε, ὡς Χριστοῦ κειμήλια ‡Ign.*Her.*5; δι' οὗ [i.e. Chrys.] ὁ σωτὴρ ὡς διὰ κρατῆρος ἢ κ. ἐλογοπότει τοῖς ἐρασταῖς τοῦ λόγου τὰ πρόσφορα τῆς σωτηρίας Pall.*v.Chrys.*20(p.147.4; M.47.82).

***κειμηλιοφύλαξ, ὁ,** *keeper of sacred vessels* and other valuables of the church, *sacristan*, CBeryt.*act.*(*ACO* 2.1.3 p.24.15; H.2.517C).

κεῖρα ([*]**κήρα**), **ἡ,** *age* ἐκ ποίας κ. κρίνονται παρὰ θεοῦ τὰ ἁμαρτήματα,...οἱ μὲν ἀπὸ δεκαετοῦς κ., οἱ δὲ καὶ μείζονος Tim.I Al.*resp.*(M.33.1308B); νεότης ἡ ἄθεος κ. ‡Chrys.*pat.*1(9.808A); μετὰ τὸ εἰς κ. λογισμοῦ δεκτικὴν παραγενέσθαι *Cod.Afr.*57; *ib.*62; οὐδὲ ταῦτα [sc. νήπια] διὰ τὴν κ. περὶ τῆς παραδοθείσης αὐτοῖς μυσταγωγίας ἀποκρίνασθαι ἐπιτηδείως ἔχουσι CTrull.*can.*84; κήρα Gr.Mag.*dial.*(tr.Zach.)3.18(M.*PL.*77.267A); *ib.*4.47(407C).

κειρία, ἡ, plur., *grave-clothes*, Bas.*hom.*4.5(2.29B; M.31.228C); ‡Nil.*fr.pasch.*1(M.79.1493A); allegorical significance διὰ τὸ μηδέπω ἀπολελύσθαι τῶν τῆς ἁμαρτίας δεσμῶν...δεδεμένος [sc. ὁ Λάζαρος] τοὺς πόδας καὶ τὰς χεῖρας δεσμοῖς νεκρῶν κειρίαις Or.*Jo.*28.7(6; p.398.12; M.14.696C); ὁ γὰρ ἁμαρτίας ἐλεύθερος ἐν νεκροῖς λελόγισται· καὶ κειρίαις περίκειται ὁ Λαζάρου λύσας τὰ σπάργανα ἵνα τὸν νεκρωθέντα τῇ ἁμαρτίᾳ ἄνθρωπον, καὶ ταῖς ταύτης περισφιγέντα σειραῖς, λύσῃ τῶν δεσμῶν Jo.D.*hom.*4.22(M.96.620C).

κείρ-ω, [aor. act. ἔκορσεν v. 2 infra]; **1.** *crop, cut off* the hair; ref. tonsure: of nuns πᾶσαί εἰσι κεκαρμέναι, ἔχουσαι κουκούλια Pall.*h.Laus.*34(p.98.8; M.34.1106B); of monks μηδεὶς τὴν κεφαλὴν ~ηται χωρὶς τοῦ πατρός Pach.*reg.*B(p.19.11; M.40.952B); ἐκάρη καὶ τὸ μοναχικὸν σχῆμα ἠμφιέσατο Anast.S.*qu.et resp.*16(M.89.476D); clerical τῷ τοῦ κλήρου ~έσθωσαν σχήματι CTrull.*can.*21; its origin τίνος χάριν περὶ τρίχα ~όμεθα; ὁ ἐν τῇ κεφαλῇ τοῦ ἱερέως περικείμενος διπλοῦς ⟨στέφανος ἐκ τῆς τῶν τριχῶν σημειώσεως⟩ εἰκονίζει τὴν τοῦ...Πέτρου κάραν ‡Bas.*h.myst.*13(p.260.25); τίνος χάριν ~ονται [sc. οἱ μοναχοί] τὴν κόμην; τὸ δὲ ~εσθαι τὴν κάραν ὁλοτελῶς κατὰ τὴν μίμησιν τοῦ... ἀποστόλου Ἰακώβου καὶ...τῶν λοιπῶν *ib.*22(p.262.26); **2.** met., *cut off, cut short*, ref. Adam νεκροφόρος (θανάτῳ γὰρ ἁμαρτάδα Χριστὸς ἔκορσεν) Gr.Naz.*carm.*1.1.8.116(M.37.455A).

***κεκαλυμμένως,** *in veiled terms, obscurely* τὰ νομικὰ καὶ τὰ προφητικὰ ἀκριβῶς...νενοημένα Μωσεῖ καὶ τοῖς προφήταις καὶ...κ. καὶ ἐσκεπασμένως ἀναγεγραμμένα Or.*Jo.*13.48(46; p.275.22; M.14.485C); τὰ [sc. λόγια] τῶν ἐκ περιτομῆς ἕνεκα κ. ἀποδεδόσθαι, διὰ τὰ θεσπιζόμενα κατ' αὐτῶν σκυθρωπά Eus.*d.e.*6 proem.(p.251.19; M.22.413A); κ. ... ἠγόρευσεν Jo.Eleem.*v.Tych.*(p.119).

***κεκιβδηλευμένως,** *dishonestly, falsely*, Cyr.*Ps.*90:9(M.69.1220C).

***κεκινδυνευμένως,** *dangerously, hazardously*, ‡Just.*ep.Zen.et Ser.*8(M.6.1192B).

κεκλασμένως, *mincingly, effeminately* κ. βαδίζοντας Cyr.*hom.div.*19(M.77.1108B).

***κεκλείσκονται,** v. κλείω.

κεκολασμένως, *in a qualified manner* κ. μεθοδεύει Chrys.*hom.19.1 in 2Cor.*(10.571B).

κεκριμένως, 1. *judiciously, with discretion* ἐλεῶν κ. τοῖς ἀξίοις ἐπιμετρεῖ τοὺς οἰκτιρμούς Bas.*hom.in Ps.*114(1.201E; M.29.489A); σοφῶς ἁπάντων συλλέγων τὸ χρήσιμον, φεύγων δ' ἑκάστου τὴν βλάβην κ. Amph.*Seleuc.*40(M.37.1580A); τὰ ἔθνη καλῶν...ὁ θεός, καὶ ταῦτα λέγειν...ἐν τῇ ἐκκλησίᾳ διδάσκων, κ. τε τὸ Χριστοῦ καταγγέλλειν μυστήριον Proc.G.*Is.*41:1ff.(M.87.2345C); **2.** *advisedly, after consideration* τήν τε περὶ τὰ Ἑβραίων λόγια σπουδὴν κ. ἡμῖν καὶ εὐλόγως γεγενημένην παραστήσαντες Eus.*d.e.*1.1(p.7.8; M.22.21C); ὁ ἀπόστολος...ἡμᾶς παιδεύει κ. νεκροὺς μὲν εἶναι τῇ ἁμαρτίᾳ, ζῶντας δὲ τῷ θεῷ ἐν Χριστῷ Ἰησοῦ †Bas.*bapt.*1.2.16(2.641A; M.31.1553A); ἔστιν... δόξα ἡ μέν τις φυσική...ἡ δέ τις ἔξωθεν ἢ ἐκ προαιρέσεως κ. τοῖς ἀξίοις προσαγομένη Bas.*Spir.*46(3.39B; M.32.152C); διασκεδάσαι τοὺς λόγους αὐτῶν, καίτοι γεγονότας ἐν κρίσει, τοῦτ' ἔστιν, οὐκ ἀτημελῶς, κ. δὲ μᾶλλον Cyr.*Is.*3.3(2.445D).

κεκρυμμένως, 1. *secretly, covertly* ἕως...κ. κλέψωσιν οἱ οἰκεῖοι τὰ τῶν ἰδίων σώματα Ath.*apol.Const.*27(M.25.629C); ὁ δόλους συμπλέκων καὶ κ. κακοποιῶν ὄφις ἐστί Marc.Er.*opusc.*1.122(M.65.920D); opp. φανερῶς: φανερῶς εἰπεῖν ἃ κ. φρονοῦσιν Ath.*decr.*15(p.13.12; M.25.'449'(441)B); ἔδει...ἐκδικεῖν φανερῶς τὰ Ἀρείου, ἵνα μὴ κ. ἀλλὰ φανερῶς Χριστομάχοι δεικνύωνται id.*ep.Aeg.Lib.*10(M.25.560B); Mac.Aeg.*pat.*9(M.34.872D); opp. λάθρα, *in a deliberately hidden manner, in secret* but without stealth κἂν γὰρ αὐτοὶ κ. πράττουσι [sc. monks and hermits], κἂν λανθάνειν ἐθέλωσιν· ἀλλ' ὁ κύριος αὐτοὺς ὡς λύχνους δείκνυσι Ath.*v.Anton.*93(M.26.973C); μὴ λάθρα ἁπλῶς, ἀλλὰ κ. τὰς εὐχὰς ποιοῦ Chrys.*hom.8.1 in 1Tim.*(11.589D); *ib.15.3*(638A); **2.** of scripture, Or.*Cels.*6.18(p.89.14; M.11.1317C) cit. s. σεραφίμ; (ref. Pr.8:22) τὰ...ἐν παροιμίαις λεγόμενα οὐκ ἐκ φανεροῦ λέγεται ἀλλὰ κ. ἀπαγγέλλεται Ath.*Ar.*2.44(M.26.241A); *allegorically, mystically* opp. literally ἀρκεῖ...τὰ κ. ὡς ἐν ἱστορίας τρόπῳ εἰρημένα κατὰ τὸν τῆς ἱστορίας παραστῆσαι τρόπον, ἵν' οἱ δυνάμενοι ἑαυτοῖς ἐπεξεργάσωνται τὰ κατὰ τὸν τόπον Or.*Cels.*5.29(p.31.13; M.11.1225C); ὁ Ἰουδαῖος οὐκ ἀκούει κ. τοῦ νόμου· διὰ τοῦτο φανερῶς περιτέμνεται...ὁ δὲ ἀκούων τῆς περιτομῆς κ. ἐν κρύπτῳ περιτμηθήσεται· ὁ ἀκούων τῶν περὶ τοῦ πάσχα νενομοθετημένων κ. ἐσθίει ἀπὸ τοῦ προβάτου Χριστοῦ id.*hom.12.13 in Jer.*(p.99.24; M.13.396Bf.); Bas.*hom.in Ps.*44(1.158C; M.29.388A).

***κεκωλυμένως,** *under restriction*, Chrys.*hom.55.2 in Ac.*(9.414C).

***κεκωνωμένον,** error in Gr.Nyss.*instit.*(M.34.428A, conj. κεκοινωμένον p.72.14).

κελάδημα, τό, *singing, song*, Paul.Sil.*Soph.*333(M.86.2132B).

***κελαδισμός, ὁ,** *singing, note*; of a bird, *A.Xanthipp.*6(p.61.27).

κελαρύζω, med.; **1.** *babble, murmur*; of running water, *Orac.Sib.*1.229; *ib.*3.440; **2.** *gush*, *ib.*3.453.

***κελαρυσμός, ὁ,** *gurgling*, Clem.*paed.*2.2(p.175.13; M.8.428A); ‡Nil.*narr.*5(M.79.645B).

κέλευσις, ἡ, 1. *command*; divine, Just.*dial*.42.3(M.6.565B); *A.Jo.* 73(p.186.12); ἔκ τε τῆς τοῦ θεοῦ κ. καὶ τοῦ τῆς σῆς εὐσεβείας προστάγματος CArim.*ep.Const*.1(p.237.3; M.26.696B); κελεύσει τοῦ παντοκράτορος αἱ σφραγῖδες διεφυλάχθησαν σῶαι...ἡ οὖν παρθενία τῆς... Μαρίας κελεύσει ἀλλ' οὐδὲ κυήσει διεφυλάχθη *Dial.Tim.et Aquil*.96 r°; abs. παραβάντες τὴν κ. ἐκ τοῦ οὐρανοῦ κατερρίφησαν Cosm.Ind.*top*.2 (M.88.120A); as nature of divine Word ὁ δὲ Παῦλος ὁ Σαμοσατεὺς οὐκ ἔλεγε τὸν αὐθυπόστατον λόγον γεγενῆσθαι ἐν τῷ Χριστῷ, ἀλλὰ λόγον ἔλεγε τὴν κ. καὶ τὸ πρόσταγμα †Leont.B.*sect*.3.3(M.86.1216A); **2.** imperial *dispatch* or *rescript*, *A.Petr.et Paul*.3(p.179.12); **μετὰ τὴν ἡμετέραν κ.** Const.ap.Eus.*v.C*.3.53(p.100.25; M.20.1116A); ἀντέγραψεν ἡμῖν...ὅτι...ἡνίκα δέξηται δευτέραν ἡμῶν κ. ... πρὸς ἡμᾶς αὐτὸς ἔρχεται Heracl.*ep*.(M.92.1024D); also of the *order* of a senior official κ. τοῦ ἡγεμόνος *M.Niceph*.8(p.287).

κελευστής, ὁ, *house-steward*, '*major domo*', Gr.Naz.*carm*.2.1.12. 612(M.37.1210A).

***κελευστικῶς,** *commandingly*, *authoritatively*, ‡Ath.*serm.fid*.24 (p.20; M.26.1277B).

κελεύ-ω, 1. *urge*, *exhort*, *bid* πάτερ, ~εις λάβω αὐτό; *Apophth. Patr*.(M.65.112C); πόσον ~εις ἵνα ἀπέχῃ διάστημα τὰ...κέλλια; *ib*. (85D); *Chron.Pasch*.p.317(M.92.808B); **2.** imper., *if you please, please* ~σον, εἰσέλθε εἰς τὸ ἱερατεῖον ‡Amph.*v.Bas*.13(p.203C); *ib*.(p.204B); ~σον, πάτερ, εἰς τὸν κανόνα...λέγει, πάτερ, ~σον, ἵνα μεταλάβῃς Jo. Mosch.*prat*.127(M.87.2988D,2989B); *ib*.93(2952B); Thdr.Stud.*epp*.1. 37(M.99.1041A); liturg., spoken by one minister to the other as a sign that one is ready to proceed λέγει ὁ ἱερεύς· ~ετε *Lit.Marc.* (Brightman, p.138.27); cf. εἶτα λέγει ὁ διάκονος πρὸς τὸν ἱερέα, ~σον, δέσποτα *Lit.Chrys*.(p.370.22).

κελεφία, ἡ, kind of *leprosy*, Epiph.*haer*.55.9(p.337.14; M.41.988D).

κελεφός, ὁ, *leper* πεφονευκυῖα ψυχὴ [i.e. in Manich. doctrine] εἰς κελεφῶν σώματα μεταφέρεται Hegem.*Arch*.10(p.15.9; M.10.1441C); *Apophth.Patr*.(M.65.116C).

κελητίζω, *ride*; intrans., Jo.VI H.*v.Jo.D*.7(M.94.440B).

κελήτιον, τό, *fast sailing yacht* κ. δισκάλμου Synes.*ep*.4(M.66. 1337C).

κέλλα ([*]**κέλλη**), **ἡ,** (Lat. *cella*); **1.** *cell* of a monk, Bas.*renunt*.5 (2.206C; M.31.636C); Evagr.Pont.*cap.pract*.A.19(M.40.1225C); Nil. *epp*.2.29(M.79.212B); esp. of anchorites and those who have joined them from the coenobium, Pall.*v.Chrys*.7(p.39.17; M.47.24); Cyr.S. *v.Euthym*.17(p.27.19,21); Jo.Mosch.*prat*.211(M.87.3104A); κέλλη *ib*. 19(2868A); **2.** *store-chamber*, *PLond*.1914.12 (? anno 335).

***κελλαράριος, ὁ,** *cellarer*; in a monastery, Gr.Mag.*dial*.(tr.Zach.) 2.28(M.*PL*.66.185B).

κελλαρικά, τά, *stores*, *provisions*, Pall.*h.Laus*.13(p.37.2; M.34. 1035C); *Chron.Pasch*.p.292(M.92.729A).

κελλάριον, τό, *store-room*; of a monastery, Bas.*reg.br*.156 tit.(2. 467C; M.31.1184C); Cyr.S.*v.Euthym*.17(p.27.14); Eustrat.*v.Eutych*. 62(M.86.2344D).

κελλάριος, ὁ, *cellarer*; in a monastery, Bas.*reg.br*.147 tit.(2.464D; M.31.1180A); ‡Bas.*poen.mon*.51(2.530A; M.31.1313A).

κελλαρίτης, ὁ, = foreg., Dor.*doct*.11.8(M.88.1744D); *ib*.4.10 (1672C); *Apophth.Patr*.(M.65.149A); †Anast.S.*relat*.7(*OC* 2 p.64.23; M.88.608C).

[*]**κέλλη, ἡ,** v. κέλλα.

κελλίον, τό, 1. *chamber*, *room*, *A.Jo*.5(p.153.27); Jul.Papa *ep. Dian*.ap.Ath.*apol.sec*.28(p.108.12; M.25.296B); νοσοῦντα [sc. Ἰσχύραν] καὶ κατακείμενον ἐν κ. Ath.*apol.sec*.63(p.143.3; 364A); of the cenacle οἱ μαθηταὶ...ἦσαν εἰς κ. κρυπτόμενοι id.*fr.Cant*.2(M.27. 1353B,D); ἔχε οἴκημα...εἰπέ, τοῦτο τὸ κ. τοῦ Χριστοῦ· ἡ οἰκία αὕτη αὐτῷ ἀφώρισται Chrys.*hom.45.4 in Ac*.(9.343C); **2.** monastic *cell*, esp. of anchorites, Ammonas *fr*.2(p.486.4); τῆς ἐν τῷ κ. ἡσυχίας Evagr.Pont.*rer.mon*.5(M.40.1257A); Nil.*epp*.2.130(M.79.256A); plur., of cells in a laura τὰ κ. ἐκ διαστήματος ἔχουσιν...μόνον δὲ ἐν σαββάτῳ καὶ κυριακῇ ἐν ταῖς ἐκκλησίαις συνάγονται, καὶ ἀλλήλους ἀπολαμβάνουσιν ‡Pall.*h.mon*.23.3(p.84.4; M.34.1177A); **3.** *group of cells* forming a laura; name of monastery in Nitria ἦν τις γέρων...εἰς τὰ κ. *Apophth.Patr*.(*PO*.11 p.404.3; M.65.120B); πρεσβυτέρῳ ὄντι τῶν λεγομένων κ. Pall.*h.Laus*.18(p.47.23; M.34.1050A); ἕτερός ἐστι τόπος...ὄνομα κελλία. ἐν τούτῳ δὲ σποράδην ἐστὶ μοναχικὰ οἰκήματα πολλά, καθὸ καὶ τοιαύτης ἔλαχε προσηγορίας Soz.*h.e*.6.31.2(M.67. 1388B); **4.** met. μιγάδων λογισμῶν...τραχυνόντων πῶς [τὸ] διανοίας τε καὶ νοῦ διειδέστατον κ. ‡Eust.*Laz*.24(p.47.1).

***κελλιώτης, ὁ,** *monk* who has left the coenobitic life for greater solitude in a laura δεῖ εἶναι τὸν κ. μοναχὸν διακριτικὸν καὶ σπουδαῖον ...διδακτικὸν οὐ διδασκαλίας χρῄζοντα Cyr.*v.Sab*.28(p.113.10); καὶ ποιήσαντα ἐκεῖσε χρόνον ἱκανὸν καὶ παιδευθέντα...ἐδέξατο αὐτὸν κ. εἰς τὴν λαύραν *ib*.47(p.138.9); Dor.*doct*.16 tit.(M.88.1793C); Thdr.Stud. *epp*.1.11(M.99.948A).

***κελλιωτικός,** *eremitic*, *pertaining to monastic life* or *life in a laura* opp. coenobitic κληρικὸς γινόμενος ἢ ἐν κ. μονῇ καταταττόμενος Phot.*nomoc*.1.24(M.104.1008C); cf. τὰ κ. μοναστήρια opp. τὰ κοινοβιακά, Theodorus Balsamon *schol*.in CNic.(787)*can*.19(M.137. 981C).

κέλλ-ω, 1. *lead*, of God's guidance πνεύματι ~ων ἀσεβοῦντας ἐθνῶν ἄρχοντας ‡Rom.Mel.(*AS* 1 p.232); **2.** med., v.l. for κεκλόμενος †Apoll.*Ps*.105:9(M.33.1472D, conj. *Teub*.); *ib*.106:25(1477C, conj. *Teub*.).

κελτίς, *Celtic*, *Orac.Sib*.7.103; *ib*.12.133.

[*]**κέμφος** ([*]**κέφφος**), **ὁ,** = κέπφος; **1.** cf.Pr.7:22, *sea-bird*, perh. *stormy petrel*, Hipp.*fr.13 in Pr*.(p.161.23; M.10.620B); Or.*exp.in Pr*. 7:22(M.17.181D,184A); **2.** met., *feather-brained fellow* ὀργίλου καὶ κέφφου *Mir.Cosm.et Dam*.6(p.110).

[*]**κεμφόω,** v. κεπφόω.

κένανδρος, *empty of men*, Cyr.*Is*.1.7(2.180E); id.*Os*.39(3.70C); id. *Am*.44(3.298A).

***κενεαυχήν,** for κενεαυχής, *vainglorious*, †Apoll.*Ps*.3:8(M.33. 1316C; conj. *Teub*.).

***κενεήγορος,** *talking vanity*; of the oracle of Ammon, Gr.Naz. *carm*.2.2(poem.)7.258(M.37.1571A).

***κενεήφατος,** ? *fabulous*, *Orac.Sib*.3.372.

κενεμβατ-έω, 1. *step on emptiness*; met., *tread a void* λόγον ὁμολογοῦντες ἀρνοῦνται αὐτὸν εἶναι υἱόν, καὶ κατ' ἐπίνοιαν υἱὸν λέγεσθαι τὸν λόγον βούλονται, ἐξ ἴσου ~οῦντες ‡Ath.*Ar*.4.8(p.53.3; κενοβ- M.26.480A); σου δὲ μὴ ~είτω ὁ νοῦς, εἰς αἰῶνας ὑπερβαίνειν πρεσβυτέρους τοῦ υἱοῦ, τοὺς οὔτε ὄντας, οὔτε γενομένους †Bas.*Chr. generat*.1(2.596B; M.31.1460A); οὐδενὶ τῷ μεταξὺ διαστήματι τῆς διανοίας ἀπὸ τοῦ υἱοῦ πρὸς τὸν πατέρα ~ούσης Gr.Nyss.*Eun*.2(2 p.335. 24; M.45.512A); **2.** *step into a hole*; met., *tumble into a pitfall*, Bas. *hom*.16.2(2.135D; M.31.476A); πρὸς ψιλὸν τὸ ὄνομα τοῦ υἱοῦ καὶ τοῦ μονογενοῦς ἐπιδραμόντας, ~ῆσαι τῷ βόθρῳ Gr.Nyss.*Eun*.4(2 p.89.20; M.45.665B); **3.** *make a vain attempt*, *fail* οὐκ ἀπέκαμεν ἡ διάνοια τῶν τοιούτων ~οῦσα Chrys.*hom.7.3 in 1Thess*.(11.476A); ~ούσης τῆς φορᾶς τῶν ὀμμάτων πρὸς τὴν ἀμυδρὰν τῆς ῥοπῆς θεωρίαν Geo.Pis.*hex*. 96(M.92.1439A); **4.** *tread on air*, *soar aloft*; met. διὸ καὶ ἀετὸς μετωνόμασται [sc. S. John], ὡς τὰ ὕψη...~ήσας, κακεῖθεν τὰ ἀπόρρητα μυηθεὶς ‡Ath.*qu.script*.46(M.28.729B).

***κενοβατέω,** v. foreg.

***κενοβουλία, ἡ,** *vain counsel*, Cyr.*Abac*.31(3.546C).

κενοδοξ-έω, 1. *imagine vainly* εἰ ~εῖς ἵνα ὀμόσω τὴν Καίσαρος τύχην *M.Polyc*.10.1; μετὰ τοῦ καὶ εἰς χάριν τοῦ τότε βασιλέως ~ῆσαι Epiph.*haer*.20.1(p.224.14; M.41.269C); **2.** *be vainglorious*; **a.** *vaunt oneself*, *call attention to oneself*, of demons τῇ σφῶν ἀβελτερίᾳ πρὸς τὸ ~εῖν τραπέντες...λῃσταὶ θεότητος γενέσθαι προεθυμήθησαν Tat. *orat*.12(p.13.22; M.6.832C); of men ἴσμεν...πολλοὺς καὶ τῶν ἐπὶ φιλοσοφίᾳ μεγαλοφρονούντων ~οῦντας, ἢ χρηματισμοῦ χάριν περιβεβλημένους τὸν τρίβωνα *Hom.Clem*.4.9; Chrys.*hom.22.1 in 2Cor*. (10.589A); πρὸς...τοὺς ὁμοτίμους...φθονοῦσι καὶ ~οῦσι id.*hom.61.2 in Mt*.(7.613B); τῶν φιλοχρημάτων καὶ τῶν ~ούντων *ib*.65.4(650A); ὁ ~ῶν ἐν ταπεινῷ σχήματι Marc.Er.*opusc*.1.35(M.65.909C); whether by deeds πρὸς τὸ...κ. ταῦτα πράττοντες Or.*Cels*.8.74(p.291.19; M.11. 1629A); or by words, ref. Mt.16:13 οὐ ~ῶν ἀλλὰ τὴν ἀλήθειαν αὐτοῖς δεῖξαι βουλόμενος Cyr.H.*catech*.11.3; ~ῶν...ἕκαστος καὶ βουλόμενος ἑαυτῷ συνάγειν ἄθροισμα Epiph.*haer*.35.2(p.41.11; M.41.629A); Chrys. *hom.27.3 in Mt*.(7.329C); ~οῦντες λέγουσι *ib*.74.1(716A); in respect of graces or good works εἰ αὐτὴ [sc. ἀγάπη] ἦν...οὐκ ἂν ἐκενοδόξησαν ἐπὶ τοῖς χαρίσμασι id.*hom.44.1 in 1Cor*.(10.408C); τὸ μὲν ἐπὶ τοῖς ἄλλοις...~εῖν, θαυμαστὸν οὐδέν· τὸ δὲ ἐπὶ νηστείᾳ καὶ εὐχῇ, τοῦτό ἐστι τὸ ξένον id.*hom.71.2 in Mt*.(697D); *ib.19.1*(244D); νηστεύων ~εῖ Marc.Er.*opusc*.1.181(M.65.957D); **b.** less overtly, *covet praise and attention* οὐ ~ῶν χαίρεις ἐπὶ τοῖς ἑτέρου καλοῖς Chrys.*hom.11.4 in Col*.(11.410D); or perh. with explanatory phrases *pride oneself on* [*one's virtues*] πολλοὶ διὰ τὸ μὴ ~εῖν ~οῦσιν id.*hom.2.3 in Philm*.(11. 783A); Nil.*epp*.3.231(M.79.492A); ἐπὶ τῇ ἰδιωτείᾳ κ. Marc.Er.*opusc*. 1.81(M.65.916A); τὸ...νήπιον...ἐὰν τιμηθῇ οὐ ~εῖ Dor.*doct*.1.13(M.88. 1633D); πρόδρομον...τῆς...ἀπαθείας τὸ πένθος γέγονε...ὁ τοῦ πένθους ἔσωθεν...λογισμός...φησι· μὴ ~ήσῃς, ἐπεὶ ἀναχωρῶ σου Jo.Clim. *scal*.7(M.88.813B); **3.** c. infin., *be too proud to*, *scorn to*, Meth.*lepr*.12 (p.466.11).

κενοδοξία, ἡ, 1. *idle*, *senseless opinion*, Clem.*paed*.2.1(p.155.3; M. 8.380B); *vain doctrine* φθειρόμενοι ταῖς κ. τῶν ἐθνῶν Herm.*sim*.8.9.3; ἡ τῶν Ἐγκρατιτῶν κ. Hipp.*haer*.8.7(p.225.20; M.16.3347B); of Arian heresy διὰ τῆς σιωπῆς ὡμολόγουν τὴν ἐπὶ τῇ κ. αὐτῶν αἰσχύνην Ath.

*decr.*3(p.3.6, v.l. κακοδοξίᾳ M.25.'428'(420)C); αὐτὸς [sc. Ἄρειος] τῷ βίῳ ἐφεύρατό τινα μεγάλην μυθώδη κ. Epiph.*haer.*75.1(p.333.16; M. 42.504B); **2.** *vainglory*, desire for and delight in praise or reputation, described κ. ἐστὶ κατὰ μὲν τὸ εἶδος φύσεως ἐναλλαγή, καὶ ἠθῶν διαστροφή, καὶ παρατήρησις μέμψεως· κατὰ δὲ τὴν ποιότητα, καμάτων σκορπιστήριον...ὑπερηφανίας πρόδρομος...λεπτὸς μὲν ὑπάρχων, παντὶ δὲ καμάτῳ καὶ καρπῷ ἐπιβουλεύων Jo.Clim.*scal.*22(M.88.949Af.); in gen. ὃν ἐπίσκοπον ἔγνων οὐκ ἀφ' ἑαυτοῦ οὐδὲ δι' ἀνθρώπων κεκτῆσθαι τὴν διακονίαν...οὐδὲ κατὰ κενοδοξίαν, ἀλλ' ἐν ἀγάπῃ θεοῦ Ign. *Philad.*1.1; πρὸς πάντας τοὺς εἰσερχομένους...μοναχούς, τοῦτο...εἶχε τὸ παράγγελμα,...φεύγειν...κ. Ath.*v.Anton.*55(M.26.921B); ἀνὴρ οὕτως τὸν τῆς κ. ἀποδυσάμενος χιτῶνα ὡς καὶ παράφορον τοῖς οὐκ εἰδόσι δόξαι αὐτὸν εἶναι Evagr.*h.e.*4.34(p.182.27; M.86.2764C); plur., Philox. *ep.*36(p.184); Jo.D.*hom.*2.6(M.96.585D) cit. infra; in lists of sins κ. τε καὶ ἀφιλοξενίαν *1Clem.*35.5; ...ἀπάτη, κ., ἀλαζονεία Herm.*mand.* 8.5; ὑπερηφανίᾳ, κ., ἀνθρωπαρεσκείᾳ Marc.Er.*opusc.*5.4(M.65.1036B); καὶ ἡ τοῦ διαβόλου πομπή, ὑπερηφανίαι, κενοδοξίαι, οἴησις, ἔπαρσις κτλ. Jo.D.*hom.*2.6(585D); freq. associated with ὑπερηφανία (v. supra) and φιλαργυρία, †Bas.*Is.*276(1.590B; M.30.605B); Chrys.*hom.13.4 in 2Cor.*(10.536E); *Ascens.Is.*A 3.28 cit. infra i; φιλαργυρία...καὶ κ., ἀσπλαγχνίας καὶ ὑποκρίσεως [sc. εἰσὶν αἴτια] Marc.Er.*opusc.*2.80 (941B); Jo.Mosch.*prat.*110(M.87.2973B); but not identified with either, Gr.Nyss.*hom.13 in Cant.*(M.44.1061A); τὴν μητέρα τῆς ὑπερηφανείας τὴν καλουμένην κ. ‡Pall.*proem.*(p.5.7; M.34.995); †Nil. *vit.*4(M.79.1144C); Marc.Er.*opusc.*8.2(1104D); *ib.*4(1000B); τινὲς... ἰδιαιρέτῳ τάξει καὶ λόγῳ τὴν κ. παρὰ τὴν ὑπερηφανίαν φιλοῦσιν ὁρίζειν...τοσαύτην δὲ μόνον πρὸς ἀλλήλας τὴν διαφορὰν κέκτηνται, ὅσην ἔχει τῇ φύσει ὁ παῖς παρὰ τὸν ἄνδρα, καὶ ὁ σῖτος παρὰ τὸν ἄρτον· ἀρχὴν μὲν γὰρ τὸ πρότερον, τέλος δὲ τὸ δεύτερον Jo.Clim.*scal.*22(M.88. 948Df.); associated with ἡδονή etc., Marc.Er.*opusc.*1.102f.,107(917Cf.) citt. infra c, d; ὕλη...νοός, κ. καὶ ἡδονή *ib.*2.106(945B); *ib.*8.5 (1108Df.); τοῦ...ἀνθρώπου διὰ φιληδονίαν καὶ κ. ἡδέως προσομιλήσαντος *ib.*2.211(964C); ὑπὸ φιληδονίας καὶ κ. σκοτισθεῖσα ἡ ψυχή *ib.*4 (1020D); partic.; **a.** as having no place in Christ or in perfected Christian life, Tat.*orat.*32(p.33.1; M.6.872A); μηδὲν κατ' ἐρίθειαν καὶ κ. ποιεῖν, ἀλλὰ διὰ τὸν θεόν, καὶ πρὸς τὴν ἑαυτοῦ ἀρέσκειαν Bas.*ascet. disc.*2(2.213B; M.31.652B); βλέπω πρὸς τὰ τῶν ἀγαθῶν ὑποδείγματα τὰ ἐν τῷ νυμφίῳ δεικνύμενα. ἐκεῖ...τὸ μακρόθυμον, τὸ πάσης κ. τε καὶ ἀπάτης βιωτικῆς ἀνεπίμικτον Gr.Nyss.*hom.4 in Cant.*(M.44.852A); καθαρὸς δὲ ἂν τις γένοιτο, οὐχὶ εἰ πορνείας ἀπαλλαγείη μόνον, ἀλλὰ καὶ πλεονεξίας καὶ...κ. Chrys.*hom.13.3 in 2Cor.*(10.534E); avoided by bridling tongue, Nil.*epp.*3.232(M.79.492C); cf.Dion.Ar.*e.h.*4.3.1(M.3. 473B); **b.** as in fact entering not infrequently into motive of good works: not so with the 'gnostic', Clem.*str.*7.13(p.58.17; M.9.513B); οἱ ποιοῦντες πρὸς τὸ δοξασθῆναι ὑπὸ τῶν ἀνθρώπων...δίκαιον μέν τι πεποιήκασιν, οὐ μὴν ἀπὸ ἕξεως δικαιοσύνης ἀλλ' ἀπὸ κ. Or.*Jo.*28.13 (12; p.405.8; M.14.708B); τοὺς κατὰ πρόφασιν κενοδοξίας...ἐπὶ τοῦτο [sc. virginity] παρεληλυθότας Meth.*symp.*3.14(p.44.3; M.18.84C); ἐκ πόνων ἐλέησον, καὶ μὴ θέλε ἀδικεῖν, προφασιζόμενος ἐξ ἀδικίας τῷ θεῷ προσάγειν τὸν ἔλεον. κ. τὰ τοιαῦτα, καὶ πρὸς τοὺς ἐξ ἀνθρώπων ἐπαίνους †Bas.*miser.*(2 p.1069A; M.31.1709B); Chrys.*hom.71.2 in Mt.*(7.697D); *ib.71.3*(698A); ὁρᾶτε...εἰ μὴ πρὸς κενοδοξίαν τὰς ἡμετέρας ἀρετὰς θηράσητε, ἵνα δὴ ὡς ἐπιδεικτιῶντες τοῖς ἀνθρώποις φάνησθε τὰ ἡμῶν ἔργα μιμούμενοι ‡Pall.*h.mon.*1.24(p.11.3; M.34. 1116C); κ. πάθος ἐστὶν ἄλογον καὶ παντὶ ἔργῳ ἀρετῆς εὐκόλως συμπλέκεται...κ. ... ταῖς ἀρεταῖς παραφύεται Nil.*spir.mal.*15(M.79.1160cf.); οὔτε...ὑπὸ τῆς κ. αὐτὸν [sc. τὸν νοῦν] ὑποσυρῆναι διαφορηθέντα διὰ τῆς πολλῆς χαρᾶς καὶ τῆς πολυλογίας [i.e. in prayer] παραχωρήσωμεν Diad.*perf.*68(p.84.3); ἡ...τῆς κ. κακία...ἐν παντὶ ἐπιτηδεύματι παρυφίσταται, ἔν τε σχήματι...καὶ ἐν φωνῇ...καὶ ἐν εὐχῇ, καὶ ἐν ἀναγνώσει, καὶ ἐν ἡσυχίᾳ καὶ ἐν μακροθυμίᾳ Ant.Mon.*hom.*43(M.89.1568A); entering into conquest of other vices ἐχθραίνει πολλάκις κ. τῇ γαστριμαργίᾳ...ἡ μὲν καταλύειν βιάζεται, ἡ δὲ τὴν ἑαυτοῦ ἀρετὴν θριαμβεύειν ὑποτίθεται Jo.Clim.*scal.*14(M.88.864D); into conquest of itself, Nil.*epp.*3.233(M.79.492D); Chrys.*hom.1.2 in 1Tim.*(11.551B); **c.** as root of many other sins, *Apoc.Paul.*24(p.53); ὡς εἶναι τὴν κ. οὐ μόνον καθαιρέτιν τῶν καλῶν πράξεων, ἀλλὰ καὶ τῶν πονηρῶν ὁδηγόν ‡Bas.*const.*10.2(2.557A; M.31.1373B); Chrys.*hom.74.3 in Jo.* (8.437E); Nil.*exerc.*40(M.79.768D); ἡ αἰτία πάσης κακίας, κ. καὶ ἡδονή Marc.Er.*opusc.*1.102(M.65.917C) ∾ Ant.Mon.*hom.*43(M.89.1565D); ἡ κ. ἀναιρουμένη μέν, οἴησιν ἐμποιεῖ· μένουσα δέ, ἀλαζονείαν *Schol.*22 in Jo.Clim.*scal.*22(M.88.964C); and of heresy πᾶσαν...αἵρεσιν...ἢ κενοδοξίας ἢ ἐπάρσεως φρόνημα εἰργάσατο Epiph.*haer.*75.1(p.333.4; M. 42.504A); **d.** as enemy of virtue μέγα τοῖς ἀνθρώποις ἡ κ. πρὸς ἀρετὴν ἐμπόδιον Gr.Naz.*or.*2.51(M.35.461A); Chrys.*hom.13.4 in 2Cor.* (10.536C); οὕτω μισῆσαι δεῖ φιλαργυρίαν καὶ κ. καὶ ἡδονήν, ὡς μητέρας τῶν κακῶν, καὶ μητρυιὰς τῶν ἀρετῶν Marc.Er.*opusc.*1.107 (917D); κ., καὶ φιλαργυρία, καὶ ἡδονὴ ἄσπιλον εὐποιΐαν διαμεῖναι οὐκ ἀφιᾶσιν *ib.*2.129(949A); τῆς ἀρετῆς κωλυτικαί εἰσι κακίαι δύο, κ., καὶ ἡδονή *ib.*8.5(1108D); ἡ κ. ἀπόλλυ⟨σι⟩ πάντα τὸν κόπον τοῦ μοναχοῦ Esaias *or.*1.2(p.3); νηστεία...προσευχὴ...καὶ ξενοδοχία, φύσει καλὰ ἔργα εἰσίν, ἀλλ' ὅταν διὰ κενοδοξίαν γίνωνται, οὐκ ἔστι καλά *Schol.*14 in Jo.Clim.*scal.*22(M.88.961B); robbing man of its reward φύγωμεν οὖν κ., τὸν γλυκὺν σκυλευτὴν τοῦ πνευματικοῦ πλούτου...τὸν σῆτα τῶν ἀρετῶν, τὸν μεθ' ἡδονῆς τὰ ἡμέτερα καλὰ ληϊζόμενον ‡Bas.*const.*10.2 (2.556D; M.31.1373A); κ. ἀπόλλυσι μισθοὺς ἀρετῶν Nil.*spir.mal.*15(M. 79.1160D) = Ant.Mon.*hom.*43(M.89.1568B); jeopardizing his salvation, ‡Bas.*const.*10.1(556A; M.1372B); μήτηρ...γεέννης κ., καὶ τὸ πῦρ ἀνάπτει...καὶ τὸν σκώληκα τὸν ἰοβόλον Chrys.*hom.17.3 in Rom.* (9.625E); id.*hom.13.4 in 2Cor.*(10.536E); **e.** opp. pursuit of holiness, as a road of pleasure, ‡Bas.*const.*10.2(2.556D; M.31.1373A); Marc. Er.*opusc.*1.42(M.65.912A) = Ant.Mon.*hom.*43(M.89.1565D); **f.** its occasions ὅταν προσβάλλωσί σοι λογισμοὶ...δίκην φλεγμονῆς ἐξοιδοῦντες εἰς κ., ἢ ἐκ τύχης ἁπλῶς, ἢ καὶ ἀπὸ προτερημάτων καὶ κατορθωμάτων τινῶν...σύνες, ὅπως ἐκτίσθης ‡Bas.*struct.hom.*2.10(1.343E; M. 30.53B); **g.** as caused by refusal to love glory given by God, Jo.D. *Man.*1.14(M.94.1520A); **h.** as subject of Christ's third temptation τίνες...εἰσὶν οἱ τρεῖς; ἡ γαστριμαργία, ἡ φιλαργυρία, ἡ κ., ἄλλους... πειρασμοὺς οὐκ ἔχει *cat.Lc.*4:13(p.35.18); **i.** to become prevalent before parousia καὶ ἔσονται καταλαλιαὶ πολλαὶ καὶ κ. πολλὴ ἐν τῷ ἐγγίζειν τὸν κύριον...καὶ οὐκ ἔσονται...προφῆται πολλοὶ...διὰ τὸ πνεῦμα τῆς πλάνης...καὶ τῆς κ. καὶ τῆς φιλαργυρίας *Ascens.Is.*A 3.26, 28(p.94); **3.** *empty praise* ἵνα τῆς μὲν [sc. τιμῆς i.e. of a bishop] παρὰ θεοῦ δοθείσης καταφρονῇ, τὴν δὲ τῶν ἀνθρώπων κ. ἀγαπήσῃ Ath.*apol. sec.*25(p.106.7; M.25.289C).

κενόδοξος, **1.** of a bird, *vain*, Hipp.*antichr.*55(p.36.18; M.10. 773B); **2.** *vainglorious*; **a.** implying ostentation or boastfulness κ. ... ἐστιν ὁ ψιλῆς ἕνεκεν τῆς ἐν κόσμῳ δόξης, τῆς παρὰ τῶν ὁρώντων ἢ ἀκουόντων, ποιῶν τι ἢ λέγων Bas.*reg.br.*52(2.432D; M.31.1117B); in gen. μηδὲ φιλάργυρος μηδὲ κ.· ἐκ γὰρ τούτων...κλοπαὶ γεννῶνται *Did.* 3.5; *Const.App.*7.6.6 cit. s. ἀλαζονεία; ὁ...τῆς τοῦ κόσμου σοφίας λόγος...πλάσμα ὢν κ. ἀνθρώπων Diad.*perf.*11(p.12.24); **b.** inwardly, *honour-loving*, coveting and relishing praise or reputation (as implying undeserved reputation, opp. φιλόδοξος) κ. δὲ [sc. κλητέον], τὸν ἐφ' οἷς μὴ πράττει δοξάζεσθαι βουλόμενον· φιλόδοξον δέ, τὸν ἐφ' οἷς πράττει ἐναβρυνόμενον Isid.Pel.*epp.*3.381(M.78.1025C); ὁ...κενὸς ὢν πράξεων ἀγαθῶν, δόξαν δὲ ζητῶν μὴ προσήκουσαν, κ. ἐστιν, ἐφ' οἷς μὴ πράττῃ σεμνυνόμενος, καὶ ἀλλοτρίῳ προσώπῳ ἐναβρυνόμενος. οὐ γὰρ τὴν δόξαν κενὴν μόνον χρὴ νομίζειν (εἰ γὰρ τοῦτο δοθείη καὶ ὁ φιλόδοξος κ. εἰκότως ἂν κληθείη), ἀλλ' εἰ κυριολεκτοῖτο τοὔνομα, ὁ κενὸς ὢν ἔργων χρηστῶν, ἀντιποιούμενος δὲ δόξης, κ. ἂν δικαίως καλοῖτο *ib.*5.411(1572Af.); in gen. ἡ...γλῶττα πολλοὺς τῶν κ. εἰς ὄλεθρον ἤγαγεν Nil.*epp.*3.232(M.79.492C); ὑψηλόφρων καὶ κ. ἀλλήλοις ἡδέως συναλλάσσουσιν· ὁ μὲν γὰρ δουλικῶς ὑποπίπτοντα ἐπαινεῖ τὸν κ., ὁ δὲ συνεχῶς ἐπαινοῦντα μεγαλύνει τὸν ὑψηλόφρονα Marc.Er.*opusc.*2. 151(M.65.953B); κ. ἐστιν εἰδωλολάτρης πιστός, θεὸν μὲν τῷ δοκεῖν σεβόμενος, ἀνθρώποις δὲ...ἀρέσκειν βουλόμενος. κ. ἐστι πᾶς φιλενδείκτης Jo.Clim.*scal.*22(M.88.949C).

***κενοδόξως**, **1.** *vaingloriously*, *ostentatiously*, *for self-aggrandisement* ἐπιδεικτικῶς καὶ κ. προκαλεῖσθαι Bas.*reg.br.*66(2.438E; M.31. 1129B); σκοπεῖτε πῶς ἐποικοδομεῖτε, εἰ κ., εἰ πρὸς ἀνθρώπους ἀποσπῶντες τοὺς μαθητάς Chrys.*hom.8.4 in 1Cor.*(10.70A); **2.** *high-handedly*, *arrogantly* τῷ...κ. ἀποσκορακίζοντι τὰς θειοτάτας ἑρμηνείας Tat.*orat.*12(p.13.12; M.6.832B).

***κενοθρησκεία**, ἡ, *vain*, *empty religion*, *cat.Jac.*1:26(p.9.6).

***κενοκάματος**, *labouring in vain*, Ephr.2.123D.

***κενόκρανος**, *empty-headed*, *Orac.Sib.*3.430.

***κενολατρεία**, ἡ, *worship of vain things* βλάβην εἰδωλολατρείας καὶ κενολατρείας Epiph.*ep.Arab.*ap.*haer.*78.23(p.473.25; M.42.736D).

***κενολεκτέω**, *talk nonsense*, Serap.*Man.*40(p.58; M.18.1221C); Epiph.*haer.*76.48(p.404.20; M.42.621B).

***κενολεξία**, ἡ, *vain*, *nonsensical talk*, Epiph.*haer.*56.3(p.342.24, v.l. κενολογία M.41.993C).

κενολογ-έω, *babble about* τρεῖς...~οῦντες θεότητας Sophr.H.*ep. syn.*(M.87.3156C).

κενολογία, ἡ, *idle speech*, *nonsense*, Eust.*engast.*25(p.56.29; M.18. 665D); of heretics, Ath.*Ar.*2.33(M.26.217A); Didym.*Trin.*1.15(M.39. 321B); cf. κενολεξία.

κενολόγος, *talking nonsensically*, Eust.*engast.*25(p.56.26; M.18. 665D); κ. τισὶ νεκρομάντεσι Cyr.*Is.*1.5(2.146A); v. κενοφωνέω.

κενοπαθ-έω, **1.** *have false* or *misleading impressions* μὴ ~οῦντες, ἀλλὰ τρανῶς καταλαμβάνειν φάσκοντες Or.*or.*23.3(p.351.8; M.11.

488D); Serap.*Man*.36(p.53; M.18.1213C); **2.** *have useless ideas*, i.e. ideas impossible of realization through lack of material πρόνοιά τις πρεσβυτέρα θεοῦ...τὴν ὕλην...ὑποβεβληκυῖα...προνοουμένη τοῦ τὴν τέχνην τὴν ἐνυπάρχουσαν αὐτῷ μὴ κενοπαθῆσαι Or.*comm.in Gen*.ap. Eus.*p.e*.7.20(335C; M.12.49A).

κενός, 1. *empty, vain, void*; of pagan sacrifice, *V.Glyc*.1(p.12*C); of baptism by Arians παντελῶς κ. καὶ ἀλυσιτελὲς τὸ παρ' αὐτῶν διδόμενόν ἐστι Ath.*Ar*.2.42(M.26.237A); in blessing of water for baptism ὅπως τὸ μυστήριον τὸ νῦν ἐπιτελούμενον μὴ κ. εὑρεθῇ ἐν τοῖς ἀναγεννωμένοις Serap.*euch*.19.2; of persons ἀποπλανῶσι κ. ἀνθρώπους Polyc.*ep*.6.3; τοῦ πνεύματος τοῦ ἐπιγείου καὶ κ. καὶ δύναμιν μὴ ἔχοντος Herm.*mand*.11.11; τοῖς διψύχοις καὶ κ. *ib*.11.13; ψυχὴ μὴ κ. ἀλλὰ μυελοῦ γέμουσα πνευματικοῦ Clem.*exc.Thdot*.53(p.124.27; M.9.685A); in adverbial phrases: *in vain, fruitlessly* ὁ...λόγος οὐ κατὰ κενοῦ χωρήσας Tat.*orat*.5(p.5.24; M.6.816A); ἐπὶ κενῷ *for a trifling cause, without good reason*, Thphl.Ant.*Autol*.2.10(M.6.1065A); **2.** *destitute, bereft* οὐδὲν...αὐτοῦ [sc. τοῦ θεοῦ λόγου] κενὸν ὑπολέλειπται τῆς κτίσεως μέρος Ath.*inc*.8.1(M.25.109A); usu. of persons; of Pneumatomachoi γινόμενοι...ἐρημοὶ καὶ κ. τοῦ πνεύματος Ath.*ep. Serap*.1.32(M.26.605B); c. prep. ἐκεῖνος κ. ἀπὸ τοῦ πνεύματος τοῦ δικαίου Herm.*mand*.5.2.7; *ib*.11.4; αὐτὸν...κ. ἐκ τῆς ταπεινώσεως Philox. *ep*.38(p.185); ref. Ex.23:15 οὐκ ὀφθήσῃ ἐνώπιόν μου κ.: ἀλλ' εἴ τι καλόν, μετὰ σεαυτοῦ φέρων. νῦν δὲ ὄφθητι καινός [i.e. redeemed] Gr.Naz.*or*.44.8(M.36.616C); εἰ μὲν χρήματα ἔχοιμεν, μετὰ τῆς τῶν πενήτων θεραπείας προσεύχεσθαι τῷ θεῷ· εἰ δὲ τὸν ἀκτήμονα προαιρούμεθα βίον, μὴ κ. ἔχειν τῶν ἀγαθῶν τὴν ψυχήν, ἀλλ' ἔχουσαν τὸν πλοῦτον τῆς ἀρετῆς Thdt.*qu.53 in Ex*.23:15(1.158); **3.** *lacking, devoid of*; **a.** theol. οὐ γὰρ ὡς ἐκεῖνοι νομίζουσιν ἀντεμβιβαζόμενοι εἰς ἀλλήλους εἰσίν...[Jo.14:10] ὥσπερ ἐν ἀγγείοις κ. ἐξ ἀλλήλων πληρούμενοι· ὥστε τὸν μὲν υἱὸν πληροῦν τὸ κ. τοῦ πατρός, τὸν δὲ πατέρα πληροῦν τὸ κ. τοῦ υἱοῦ Ath.*Ar*.3.1(M.26.324B); ἐκ πολλῆς...ἀσυνεσίας...λέγειν, ὅτι γενόμενος ἄνθρωπος ὁ...λόγος...κενοὺς ἀφῆκε τῆς ἑαυτοῦ θεότητος τοὺς οὐρανούς Cyr.*resp*.3(p.581.22; 6².388E); **b.** Christol. εἰ μὲν [sc. ἐπεδήμει ὁ λόγος] ἵνα λάβῃ ταῦτα [i.e. sanctification and resurrection] ἅπερ λέγει εἰληφέναι· κ. ἦν τούτων πρὸ τούτου Ath.*Ar*.3.39(M.26.408A); ὁ γεννηθεὶς ἐκ Μαρίας οὐ κ. ἐγεννήθη...ἀλλὰ μετὰ τοῦ ναοῦ ...οὔτε δὲ τὸν ναὸν καλῶ Ἰησοῦν χωρὶς τοῦ λόγου, οὔτε τὸν λόγον χωρὶς τοῦ ναοῦ Ἰησοῦν ‡Ath.*dial.Trin*.4.5(M.28.1260A); **c.** ref. eucharistic presence ἡ...μετάδοσις...μεταποιοῦσα...τοὺς ἀξίως μεταλαμβάνοντας ...ὥστε καὶ αὐτοὺς δύνασθαι εἶναι...θεούς, διὰ τὸν αὐτοὺς ὅλως πληρώσαντα ὅλον θεὸν καὶ μηδὲν αὐτῶν τῆς αὐτοῦ παρουσίας κενὸν καταλείψαντα ‡Bas.*h.myst*.62(p.397.23).

***κενοσπουδαστής, ὁ,** *place-hunter* μηδένα...διὰ τοὺς κ. ἐκ τῆς ἐκκλησίας εἰς τὴν ἐπισκοπὴν προχειρίζεσθαι Socr.*h.e*.7.29.1(M.67.804A).

κενοσπουδία, ἡ, *eager pursuit of frivolities*, esp. *worldly ambition, place-hunting* οὐ παιδιαὶ αἱ φιλοδοξίαι...ἀλλ' οὐδὲ αἱ κ. καὶ αἱ ἀλόγιστοι φιλοτιμίαι Clem.*paed*.3.11(p.279.8; M.8.656B); κ. τῆς...ἐν τῷ παρόντι βίῳ ἐξουσίας *cat.Apoc*.19:9(p.465.19).

κενοσπούδως, *with wasted zeal*, ref. idolatry ἃ περὶ τὴν ὕλην κ. δαπανᾶτε Clem.*prot*.10(p.73.2; M.8.216B).

κενότης, ἡ, 1. *empty space*, not in Trin. οὔτε διαστήματός τινος ἀνυποστάτου κ., ἥτις κεχηνέναι ποιεῖ τῆς θείας οὐσίας τὴν πρὸς ἑαυτὴν ἁρμονίαν, τῇ παρενθήκῃ τοῦ κενοῦ τὸ συνεχὲς διαστέλλουσα Gr. Nyss.*diff.ess*.4(M.32.332B); **2.** ref. Phil.2:7, *emptying, humiliation* of Christ ἀπὸ τῆς παρ' ἡμῖν κ., ἣν 'ἐκένωσεν ἑαυτόν', ἐπὶ τὸ ἴδιον 'πλήρωμα' παλινδρομοῦντα· ἔνθα καὶ ἡμεῖς...πληρωθέντες πάσης κ. ἀπαλλαγησόμεθα Or.*or*.23(p.350.23ff.; M.11.488Bf.).

***κενοτομ-έω,** *make empty innovations*, pun on καινοτομέω: νέαν ~οῦντες ἐτεκτονήσαντο πίστιν Jo.V H.*icon*.2(M.96.1349C); *ib*.3 (1352B).

***κενούργημα, τό,** prob. for καινούργημα, Ath.Scholast.*coll*.9.6 (p.102).

***κενουργός, ὁ,** for καινουργός, *restorer* Χριστέ...κενουργὲ τῆς ἡμετέρας φύσεως *Lit.Jac*.(*NBP* 10² p.107).

***κενοφρόνημα, τό,** *vain thought*, Epiph.*haer*.66.14(p.36.12; M.42.49A).

κενόφρων, *empty-minded, silly*, Clem.*prot*.4(p.44.10; M.8.153B).

κενοφων-έω, *speak foolishly*, of heretics ὡς ὁ Ἄρειος ~ῶν ἐδογμάτισεν Epiph.*haer*.62.3(p.392.5; M.41.1053B); *ib*.76.37(conj., p.387.31, for κενολόγους φωνοῦντας cod., M.42.592D); Cyr.*Is*.5.4(2.825C); pres. ptcpl. pass., *foolishly spoken* τὰ ὑπ' αὐτῶν ~ούμενα Epiph.*haer*.31.33(p.435.15; M.41.537D); ὁ τούτου ~ούμενος μυθώδης λόγος *ib*.42.16 (p.185.31; 816D); Cyr.*Jo*.1.4(4.32B).

***κενοφώνημα, τό,** *vain, foolish statement* or *talk*, ref. heresy, Epiph.*ep.Arab*.ap.*haer*.78.23(p.473.10; M.42.736B); id.*haer*.80.9(p.494.24; 769D); *ib*.42.15(p.184.20; M.41.813D).

κενοφωνία, ἡ, *vain, foolish talking*, of heretics τοῖς τῆς κ. λόγοις Apollon.ap.Eus.*h.e*.5.18.5(M.20.477A); ἡ κατὰ συζυγίαν πνευματικοῦ δῆθεν Πληρώματος κ. Epiph.*haer*.31.3(p.386.16; M.41.477B) al.; Cyr. *ep*.17(p.36.1, v.l. καινοφωνία 5².70C).

***κενόφωνος, 1.** *idly, carelessly spoken* κ. ... μηδὲν τὴν ἀνυπόστατον τῶν ἀτόμων φύσιν διὰ τῶν τοιούτων φωνῶν ἐνδεικνύμενος [sc. Ἐπίκουρος] Gr.Nyss.*hex*.17(M.44.80C); Epiph.*haer*.66.83(p.125.2; M.42.160B); **2.** masc. as subst., *trifler, talker of nonsense*, Thdr.Stud.*epp*.1.33(M.99.1020C).

κεν-όω, I. in gen.; **A.** *empty* a vessel, opp. πληρόω; **1.** οὔτε ὅθεν ἔρχονται [sc. οἱ ποταμοί] ~οῦνται, οὔτε ὅπου ἀπέρχονται πληροῦσιν *Hom.Clem*.3.35(v.l. ~οῦται); met. ὅταν...ἔλθῃ εἰς συναγωγὴν πλήρη ἀνδρῶν δικαίων...~οῦται...ἐκεῖνος, καὶ τὸ πνεῦμα τὸ ἐπίγειον...φεύγει ἀπ' αὐτοῦ Herm.*mand*.11.14; πολλοὶ ἐκενώθησαν ὑψοῦντες ἑαυτούς id. *sim*.9.22.3; *humble, deflate* καὶ κ. τὸ φύσημα τῆς διανοίας Chrys.*hom. 1.3 in Rom*.(9.434A); perh., Herm.*sim*.9.22.3 cit. supra; **2.** *purge, rid*, cf. *Ialdabaoth voluisse excogitare evacuare hominem per feminam, et...eduxisse feminam, quam illa Prunicos suscipiens invisibiliter evacuavit a virtute*, Iren.*haer*.1.30.7(M.7.698B); τῶν προτέρων διανοημάτων κ. ἑαυτούς Clem.*str*.6.16(p.509.17; M.9.381B); ~οῖ τῆς ὕλης τὴν ψυχὴν ἡ νηστεία id.*ecl*.14(p.140.28; M.9.705A); Or.*Jo*.6.54(36; p.163.24; M.14.296A); **3.** *deprive, rob, strip*, Clem.*paed*.2.10(p.214.9; M.8.509B); Or.*Jo*.13.2(p.227.16; M.14.401A); ὡς βασιλεὺς πληρούμενος τῆς βασιλείας καθ' ἕκαστον τῶν αὐξόντων τὴν βασιλείαν, ~ούμενον δὲ ταύτης ἐν τοῖς ἀφισταμένοις id.*comm.in Eph*.1:23(p.402); ~ωθέντες μὲν τοῦ ἐμφυσήματος τοῦ θεοῦ, πληρωθέντες δὲ ἐπιθυμίας ὑλικῆς Meth. *res*.2.6(p.339.15; M.18.304B); Ath.*inc*.4.5(M.25.104Bf.); ~ῶσαι τὸν Ἰαλδαβαὼθ ἀπὸ τῆς δυνάμεως Epiph.*haer*.37.4(p.55.16; cf.M.41.648A); **4.** *nullify, destroy* τὰ περιττὰ καὶ ~οῦντα τὸ εὐαγγέλιον Gr. Naz.*or*.29.21(p.106.14; M.36.101C); ~ῶσαι τὴν ἑαυτοῦ δύναμιν Epiph. *haer*.37.4(p.56.1; M.41.648A); Chrys.*comm.in Gal*.4:11(10.706A); τὴν σὴν ἐλπίδα ~ώσαντες Cyr.*Nah*.38(3.513C); id.*Is*.1.2(2.61A).

B. *empty, pour out* the contents of a vessel; **1.** *shed* blood or tears, *A.Thom*.B 45(p.39.4); Gr.Naz.*carm*.2.1.27.7(M.37.1286A); *ib*. 2.2(epitaph.)129.13(M.38.80A); ‡Bas.*h.myst*.31ᵇ(p.264.30); met. αἷμα ~οῖ ὁ καθειργμένος, ὁ...στενοχωρούμενος...ὁ πεινῶν, ὁ διψῶν Thdr. Stud.*epp*.2.21(M.99.1181B); **2.** verbally, *set out, declare*, cf. Eng. *pour out* ἐπὶ Κορινθίους ὁλόκληρον τὴν αἰτίαν ~οῖ λέγων Chrys.*hom. 24.2 in 1Cor*.(10.608B); id.*hom.31.4 in Ac*.(9.247C); ἤκουσα...ἕως ὅτε πᾶσαν ἑαυτῶν τὴν φρόνησιν ~ώσητε Olymp.*Job* 32:10(M.93.344B); **3.** exeg. Cant.1:3 v. μύρον, ἐκκενόω; **4.** *spend, expend, exhaust* ὁ τὸ πολὺ τοῦ βίου ~ώσας ἀμέμπτως Gr.Naz.*or*.16.3(M.35.937B); Chrys.*Laz*.5.4(1.768A); *spend*, etc., on or for Χριστῷ σῶμα, βίον, δάκρυα, πάντ' ἐκένωσα φέρουσα Gr.Naz.*carm*.2.2(epitaph.)91.3 (M.38.57A); εἰς τοῦτό μοι πᾶν ἐκενώθη τὸ φίλτρον id.*or*.6.5(M.35.728B); ἐβουλόμεθα...καὶ τὰς ψυχὰς εἰς ὑμᾶς ~ῶσαι Chrys.*hom.2.3 in 1Thess*.(11.437A); πᾶσα εἰς τὴν σάρκα ἡ σπουδὴ ~οῦται id.*hom.30.6 in Mt*.(7.356B); τὸν τοῖς δεομένοις τὰ ὄντα ~οῦντα *ib*.78.1(751A); ‡Proc. G.*Pr*.10:2(M.87.1309C); *spend, expend* against εἰς δέ με πάντας σῆς γλυκερῆς παλάμης πικροὺς ἐκένωσας ὀϊστούς Gr.Naz.*carm*.2.1.19.30 (M.37.1273A); εἰς τὸν ἀέρα κ. τὴν δύναμιν Chrys.*hom.22.3 in Rom*.(9.683C); πάντα τὸν θυμὸν...~ούτω κατὰ τῆς τοῦ διαβόλου κεφαλῆς id. *hom.22.5 in Eph*.(11.173D); id.*hom.84.3 in Jo*.(8.502A); *squander* πολλὰς ἐκένωσεν οὐσίας id.*hom.67.3 in Mt*.(7.665E); **5.** *get rid of, shed* χρήματα ~ῶσαι οὐ δύνασαι πάντα;...ἀλλὰ μὴ ἁρπάζειν ἐκέλευσε Chrys.*hom.9.2 in 1Cor*.(10.75D); καὶ χωρὶς τῆς ἐλεημοσύνης τὸ τὰ χρήματα ~οῦν πολὺ ἔχει τὸ κέρδος id.*hom.6.3 in Tit*.(11.768D); id. *hom.23.2 in Heb*.(12.213D); τὸ ~ωθῆναι τὰς ποιητικὰς τῶν παθῶν μορφὰς εὔκολον γίνεται Nil.*exerc*.48(M.79.780A); *expel, banish* πρότερον ~ώσας αὐτῶν τὴν ἀπιστίαν Chrys.*hom.12.1 in Heb*.(12.121A); ἵνα τὴν ~ωθεῖσαν εἰς γῆν διαφθορᾶς ἀνθρωπότητα, πάλιν ἐκ γῆς ἀναστήσῃ Sophr.H.*or*.2.42(M.87.3273C).

II. theol., *void, discard*, rejected as explanation of Son's generation by Father ὁ θεὸς...τοῦτον τὸν λόγον ἐγέννησε προφορικὸν ...οὐ ~ωθεὶς αὐτὸς τοῦ λόγου, ἀλλὰ λόγον γεννήσας, καὶ τῷ λόγῳ αὐτοῦ διαπαντὸς ὁμιλῶν Thphl.Ant.*Autol*.2.22(M.6.1088B); οὐ τοίνυν ὡς ἕτερον ἐν ἑτέρῳ...ἦν ὁ υἱὸς ἀγέννητος ἐν τῷ πατρί, μέρος ὢν αὐτοῦ ὃ μεταβληθὲν ὕστερον καὶ ~ωθὲν ἐκτὸς αὐτοῦ γέγονεν Eus.*d.e*.5.1(p.212.14; M.22.352D).

III. Christol., v. κένωσις; *empty*, ref. Christ's body ἔκειτο ἐν μνημείῳ, οὐχὶ ~ωθὲν τῆς θεότητος Hipp.*pasch.fr*.3(p.268.29; M.10.701B).

[*]κενσίτωρ, ὁ, v. κηνσίτωρ.

***κένταρχος, ὁ,** *centurion*, Thphn.*chron*.p.241(M.108.608A).

***κενταυρόμορφος,** *formed like a centaur*, of two different incomplete natures in one person, characterizing monophysite belief ὅπως ἐφεῖται τοῖς ὁδηγοῖς τῆς πλάνης κενταυρόμορφον δογματίζειν εἰκόνα ἢ μηδέν ἐστιν ἐντελὲς πρὸς τὰς φύσεις ἐξ ὧν συνῆλθεν· ἐνδεεῖς γὰρ αἱ δύο Geo.Pis.*Sev*.43(M.92.1625A).

κεντάω, = sq., *stab, pierce*; met., in conscience, irreg. form of pres. indic. med. and pass. κεντᾶσαι...καὶ τῶν φλεγομένων...ἀλγεῖς, ἀκούων τοῦ Χριστοῦ *M.Thdot*.3(p.137.23).

κεντ-έω, 1. *wound, stab*; pass., by demons, Ath.*v.Anton*.9(M.26.857B); met. ~ῶν [sc. θάνατος] τὴν...ψυχὴν Or.*Cels*.5.19(p.21.10; M.11.1209B); ~οῦσι...με...οἱ πόνοι Gr.Naz.*carm*.1.2.8.190(M.37.662A); of false friends λάθρᾳ ~οῦσι Chrys.*hom.58.5 in Mt*.(7.591C); κεντηθήσονται οἱ ~οῦντές σε νῦν Nil.*epp*.2.138(M.79.257B); *prick*, of the conscience ὑπὸ τῆς συνειδήσεως ~ούμενος Or.*sel.in Ps*.51:3(M.12.1457B); Meth.*fr.10 in Job*(p.513.10); †Jo.Jej.*serm*.(M.88.1968D); **2.** *plait, weave* ἐκέντουν...κανίσκια Jo.Mosch.*prat*.160(M.87.3028B); **3.** *work in mosaic, IGC As.Min*.93 (Clazomenae).

κέντημα, τό, 1. *hole* pierced in stocks used for torture βαλόντες αὐτῷ σίδηρα εἰς τέσσαρα κεντήματα, αὐτὸν διατείνατε *M.Tar*.2(p.455); **2.** *point, dot*, Epiph.*mens*.8(M.43.248C); **3.** *stitch* in basket-making, Pall.*h.Laus*.10(p.31.4; M.34.1033A).

κεντηνάριον, τό, (Lat. *centenarium*), a sum of money, Zos. *alloquia* 5(M.78.1689B); Leont.N.*v.Jo.Eleem*.11(p.21.16); identified with δηνάριον, Jo.Mosch.*prat*.195(M.87.3077D).

κεντηνάριος, ὁ, (Lat. *centenarius*), a fiscal official, *Ep.Mareot*.2 (p.155.35; M.25.385A).

κέντησις, ἡ, 1. *piercing* οὔτε ἡ κ. ἀληθὴς κ. [i.e. of Christ, if not true man] Anast.S.*hod*.13(M.89.221A); **2.** *mosaic, MAMA* 1.170.16 (Phrygia, saec. iv); Gr.Naz.*or*.33.7(M.36.224B); *IGC As.Min*.90 (Smyrna, ? saec. iv).

κεντητήρι(ο)ν, τό, *awl, needle, Apophth.Patr*.(M.65.152C); met. ὁ ἐχθρὸς...ὁρῶν ἑαυτὸν...τοῖς τῆς...εὐχῆς κ. ... τιτρωσκόμενον Nil.*epp*.1.30(M.79.97B).

κεντητός, 1. *of mosaic* or *embroidery, Inscr.*(*Hesp*.7 p.262); **2.** neut. as subst.; **a.** prob. *basket work*, Ephr.2.176B; **b.** *embroidery* χλανίδα...ἔχουσαν ταβλὶν χρυσοῦν ἐν ᾧ ἐκ κεντητοῦ ἐνεκεχάρακτο ἡ εἰκὼν τοῦ βασιλέως Ἰουστίνου Thphn.*chron*.p.144(M.108.393A); **c.** *tattooing* Τούρκων ἐν τοῖς μετώποις τὸν τύπον τοῦ σταυροῦ διὰ μέλανος κ. ἐχόντων *ib*.p.224(569C); *ib*.p.396(941C).

***κεντινάριος,** (Lat. *centenarius*), sens. dub., perh. *costing a* centenarium auri πύργον κ. *CIG* 8664 (Nicaea, saec. viii); cf. Nicetas Choniates *de Andronico Comneno* 2.11(M.139.708A).

***κεντιονάριος, ὁ,** sens. dub., perh. f.l. for ⟨κεστιονάριος⟩ (Lat. *quaestionarius*) δηλώσας τοῖς κ. ἵνα δεθῇ τὰς χεῖρας *A.*(*Pass.*)*Andr*. 10(p.23.18).

***κεντονάριον, τό,** *garment made of patches, Apophth.Patr*.(M.65.296B); cf. κεντώνιον.

***κεντόνη, ἡ,** v. κεντώνη.

κεντουρίων, ὁ, v. κεντυρίων.

κέντριον, τό, 1. *axis* τὸ κοσμαγωγὸν...κ. Geo.Pis.*hex*.151(M.92.1444A); **2.** error for κέντρον *sting*, Epiph.*haer*.44.7(M.41.832B; κέντρον p.198.20).

***κεντροβρίθομαι,** *be weighed down to the centre* [sc. of the earth], *be loaded to the ground*; met., Germ.CP *or*.1(M.98.228B).

κέντρον, τό, 1. any sharp point; of the *nails* which fixed Christ to the Cross, Nonn.*par.Jo*.19:6(M.43.897C); of ? *studs* in headwear of Pachomius' monks προσέταττε...τιάραις ἐρίναις τὰς κεφαλὰς σκέπεσθαι· κατασημαίνεσθαι δὲ ταύτας τὰς τιάρας κέντροις πορφυροῖς προσέταξε Soz.*h.e*.3.14.13(M.67.1072B); **2.** *stinging* or *sharp-pointed plant* (cf. κεντρόω), *A.Thom*.B 14(p.31.9); **3.** *stationary point* of a pair of compasses, Dor.*doct*.6.9(M.88.1696B); plur. = *compasses* οὐ μέτρων, οὐ κ., οὐ γωνιῶν δεομένη Thdt.*provid*.5(4.547).

κεντροφόρος, *sting-bearing, armed with a sting*, Germ.CP *or*.2(M.98.256A).

κεντρόω, *furnish with a sting* or *prick*; pass., of rushes, Cyr.*Joel*.44(3.244C); met., of Assyrians and Persians likened to bees, id.*Is*.1.5(2.126D).

κεντρώδης, *prickly*, Epiph.*haer*.37.1(p.62.23; M.41.655D); met., *piercing* τὴν κ. καὶ ἰοβόλον πηγήν *ib*.66.88(p.131.20; M.42.173A).

κέντρων, ὁ, *cento* τοῦ λόγου τὸν κ. Gr.Nyss.*Eun*.12(1 p.252.4; M.45.953A).

κεντυρίων (κεντουρίων), ὁ, (Lat. *centurio*) *centurion, M.Polyc*.18.1; *Ev.Petr*.8(p.282.3); *A.Paul*.6(*PHamb*.p.11.4; *LB* p.116.5); κεντουρίων Steph.Diac.*v.Steph*.(M.100.1156C).

***κεντώνη (*κεντόνη), ἡ,** *patched cloak*; met., Nil.*exerc*.65(M.79.797D); κεντόνη *V.Dan*.2(p.52.25); cf. sq.

***κεντώνιον, τό, 1.** *rag covering, much-patched garment* κ. πολυετὲς τὸ ἔνδυμα Nil.*Alb*.(M.79.708B); δύναταί τις ἀρκεσθῆναι ἑνὶ κ. Dor. *doct*.3.3(M.88.1657A); οὐκ ἐκτήσατο δύο χιτῶνας, ἀλλ' ἐν στιβαδίῳ... ἐκάθευδεν ἐπὶ ψιαθίου καὶ κ. Cyr.S.*v.Sab*.44(p.135.4); ἀπωσάμενοι ὡς προσαίτην τινὰ...κ. ῥυπαρὰ καὶ πολύραφα φοροῦντα αὐτὸν θεασάμενοι *ib*.51(p.142.8); **2.** met., *sorry garment* τῆς κακοηθείας ἀμφιέννυται κ. Nil.*epp*.3.137(M.79.448B).

κέντωρ, ὁ, *goader, driver*; as adj., *piercing*, Nonn.*par.Jo*.19:37 (M.43.905B); met. κ. μύθῳ *ib*.8:49(821A).

κένωμα, τό, 1. the result of κένωσις; **a.** *empty space* μὴ οἷόν τὸν θεὸν κ. τι ἔχειν ἐν ἑαυτῷ ᾧ ὑποδέδεκται τὸν περιεχόμενον ‡Gr.Nyss. *Ar.et Sab*.12(M.45.1297C); **b.** *state of emptiness* αὐτὸς γὰρ κενὸς ὢν κενὰ καὶ ἀποκρίνεται κενοῖς· ὃ γὰρ ἐὰν ἐπερωτηθῇ, πρὸς τὸ κ. τοῦ ἀνθρώπου ἀποκρίνεται Herm.*mand*.11.3; Clem.*paed*.2.10(p.211.3; M.8.504A); Christol. τὸ ἐπιδημῆσαν τῷ βίῳ ἐκένωσεν ἑαυτό, ἵνα τῷ κ. αὐτοῦ πληρωθῇ ὁ κόσμος. εἰ δὲ ἐκένωσεν ⟨ἑαυτὸ⟩ ἐκεῖνο τὸ ἐπιδημῆσαν τῷ βίῳ, αὐτὸ ἐκεῖνο τὸ κ. σοφία ἦν [1Cor.1:25] Or.*hom.8.8 in Jer*.(p.61.33ff.; M.13.345A); **2.** *void*, ref. Gen.1:2[AQ] 'κ. καὶ οὐδέν'. ἀόρατος δὲ λέγεται, οὐχ ὅτι οὐκ ἐφαίνετο, ἀλλ'...ἀκόσμητος Sever. *creat*.2.3(M.56.441); interpreted of state of potentiality opp. actuality τὴν...αὐτὴν διάνοιαν [sc. ὅτι ἐνεργείᾳ μὲν οὔπω ἦν· ἐν μόνῃ δὲ τῇ δυνάμει τὸ εἶναι εἶχε] ἐνδείκνυται ἡμῖν καὶ τὸ 'κ. καὶ οὐθέν'· τὴν γὰρ χωρητικὴν τῶν ποιοτήτων δύναμιν τῇ τοῦ κ. φωνῇ παρεδήλωσεν Gr.Nyss.*hex*.17(M.44.80Bf.); **3.** (Gnost.) antithesis of πλήρωμα, *state of privation and unreality* ἀφορισθεῖσαν τοῦ ἄνω πληρώματος...ἐν σκιᾶς καὶ σκηνώματος [l. κενώματος] τόποις Iren.*haer*.1.4.1(M.7.480A); *ib*.1.4.2(484A); Clem.*exc.Thdot*.31(p.117.11; M.9.676A); Thdt.*haer*.1.7 (4.298).

κένωσις, ἡ, A. in gen. contexts; **1.** *emptiness* ὡς Μάγδαλ' εἶπε Μαρία...τὴν κ. μηνύσασα τοῦ τάφου ‡Gr.Naz.*Chr.pat*.2420(M.38.325A); **2.** *making void, nullification* ἐπὶ δικαιοσύνῃ τὸ φυσᾶσθαι κ. δικαιοσύνης ἐστί Chrys.*poen*.1.2(2.282D); κένωσιν ἡ θεία γραφή φησιν τὸ μηδέν Thdr.Mops.*Phil*.2:7(p.216.15; M.66.924B); of the Cross (ref. 1Cor.1:17) κ. τοῦ σταυροῦ, τὸ τοῦ λόγου κομψὸν ἀναδείκνυται Gr.Naz.*or*.29.21(p.107.2; M.36.104A); πείσαντες οὐκ ἐν πόνοις εὐσεβείας καὶ προσευχῆς, ἀλλ' ἐν πειθοῖ ἀνθρωπίνης σοφίας, καὶ λόγοις φιλοσοφεῖν· ἣν καὶ ὁ ἀπόστολος...κ. τοῦ σταυροῦ ὀνομάζει Marc.Er.*opusc*.7.8(M.65.1084B); *privation, deprivation* ὀλιγοσιτία καὶ κ. Chrys.*hom.63.3 in Mt*.(7.631D); μὴ παύσησθε οὖν εὖ ποιοῦντες ἐνδεέσιν, ἵνα τῇ κ. τὸ πλήσμιον ἀμείωτον ἔχητε Max.*ep*.3(M.91.412A); **3.** *evacuation*; *shedding* of tears; as an act of virtue, Thdr.Stud.*or*.11.10(M.99.812C); cf. κενόω; met., *expulsion* κ. νοημάτων ἐμπαθῶν Hesych.S. *temp*.2.20(M.93.1517C); δόσις ἐστὶν ἴασις παθῶν τῶν ἐντός, καὶ κ. ῥύπου ἀοράτου Jo.Clim.*past*.2(M.88.1169A).

B. Christol. κ. and κενόω (ref. Phil.2:7): denoting abasement in Inc.; **1.** in gen.; **a.** with ταπείνωσις, συγκατάβασις, καθίεμαι: τὴν... οἰκονομίαν τῆς ἑαυτοῦ κ. τε καὶ ταπεινώσεως Eus.*d.e*.10.8(p.489.15; M.22.785C); τὸ γενέσθαι ἀρχιερέα οὐχὶ φύσεώς ἐστιν ἀλλὰ χάριτος καὶ συγκαταβάσεως καὶ κ. Chrys.*hom.7.2 in Heb*.(12.76A); αὐτὸν...φαμὲν τὸν...λόγον ὅτε δι' ἡμᾶς κεκενῶσθαι λέγεται...τότε καὶ ἐν τοῖς τῆς ἀνθρωπότητος μέτροις ἑαυτὸν καθεῖναι Cyr.*Nest*.3 proem.(p.54.27; 6^1.63C); καθεὶς ἑαυτὸν. εἰς κ. ὁ πάντα πληρῶν id.*hom.pasch*.27(5^2.324C); id.*Is*.4.5(2.691E); οἰκονομίαν θεοῦ, καὶ διὰ κενώσεως συγκατάβασιν λέγομεν Thdot.Anc.*exp.symb*.2(M.77.1317A); **b.** abs. σάρκωσις κένωσις Apoll.*fr*.124(p.237.30)ap.Thdt.*eran*.1(4.70); ὢ Χριστοῦ κ., καὶ δούλου μορφή, καὶ παθήματα Gr.Naz.*or*.8.14(M.35.805C); καθιγμένον εἰς κ. καὶ τὸ τῆς ἀνθρωπότητος ὑποδύντα μέτρον Cyr.*Juln*.8(6^2.257B); ὁ...ἄνωθεν...γεγεννημένος υἱὸς...κεκένωκεν ἑαυτόν, καὶ λαγόνων ἐξεδόθη τῶν παρθενικῶν τὸ κατὰ σάρκα, οὐκ ἐξ ἀνθρωπίνης καταβολῆς λαβούσης [? l. λαβὼν] τὴν γένεσιν, ἀλλ' ἐκ δυνάμεώς τε καὶ ἐνεργείας τοῦ ἁγίου πνεύματος id.*Is*.1.4(2.122C); id.*Pulch*.(p.54.37; 5^2.170D) cit. s. 7; τὴν κ. τοῦ μονογενοῦς τὴν εἰς τὴν θεοτόκον παρθένον Hesych.H. *fr.Ps*.71:6(M.93.1236D); περὶ τῆς...σαρκώσεως, ταὐτὸν δὲ εἰπεῖν ὑπερτάτης κ. Sophr.H.*ep.syn*.(M.87.3160B); Max.*ep*.11(M.91.457B); **2.** as a voluntary act, Or.*hom.1.7 in Jer*.(p.6.25; M.13.264Af.) cit. s. προκόπτω; cf. *quoniam evacuaverat se formam servi accipiens, id quod amiserat resumebat*, id.*hom.20 in Lc*.(M.13.1853B); εἰ καὶ καθῆκας... ἑαυτὸν διὰ τὴν ἡμετέραν σωτηρίαν εἰς ἑκούσιον κ. Ath.*exp.Ps*.56:6(M.27.260C); Χριστὸς...ἐθελούσιον ὑπὲρ ἡμῶν ὑπομείνας κ. Cyr.*hom.pasch*.10.1(5^2.128C); id.*ep*.1(p.18.10; 5^2.12D); id.*dial.Trin*.5(5^1.572A); Vict.*Mc*.1:37(p.280.14); Ammon.*Jo*.1:6(M.85.1396B) cit. s. αὐτοδέσποτος; ‡Gr.Nyss.*hom.5.71 in Jo*.(p.196.12); Max.*ambig*.(M.91.1316D); for man's salvation [Phil.2:6f.] ὁ φιλοικτίρμων θεός, σῶσαι τὸν ἄνθρωπον γλιχόμενος...αὐτὸς...ὁ λόγος λαλεῖ...ὁ λόγος ὁ τοῦ θεοῦ ἄνθρωπος γενόμενος, ἵνα δὴ καὶ σὺ παρὰ ἀνθρώπου μάθῃς, πῇ ποτε ἄρα ἄνθρωπος γένηται θεός Clem.*prot*.1(p.9.6; M.8.64C); διὰ φιλανθρωπίαν ἑαυτὸν ἐκένωσεν ἵνα χωρηθῆναι ὑπ' ἀνθρώπων δυνηθῇ Or.*Cels*.4.15(p.284.30; M.11.1045B); Gr.Naz.*carm*.1.2.8.107(M.37.656A); Cyr.

*hom.pasch.*13.4(5^{2}.184A); κεκένωκεν ἑαυτόν, ἵνα τὴν ἀνθρώπου φύσιν ἐπίμεστον ἀποφήνῃ τῶν ἄνωθεν ἀγαθῶν *ib.*22.3(275E); ὁ...λόγος, καθιεὶς ἑαυτὸν εἰς κ., κέχρισται παρὰ τοῦ πατρός, καὶ γέγονε καθ' ἡμᾶς. καὶ ὁ τῆς κ. σκοπὸς εἰς τὸ διασῶσαι τοὺς ἐπὶ τῆς γῆς id.*glaph.Gen.*5 (1.166D); Max.*opusc.*(M.91.57B); τῆς **αὐτοῦ** [sc. τοῦ Ἀδάμ] ἀνακλήσεως καὶ ἀνασώσεως ἕνεκεν, τὸ τῆς κ. ἅπαν ἐπράχθη μυστήριον Germ. CP *or.*2(M.98.256B); **3.** the subject of the action; **a.** not a man ἡ δὲ κ. οὐκ ἄνθρωπον, ἀλλὰ υἱὸν ἀνθρώπου τὸν κενώσαντα ἑαυτὸν ἀπέφηνε κατὰ τὴν περιβολήν, οὐ κατὰ μεταβολήν Apoll.*fr.*124(p.237.30f.)ap. Thdt.*eran.*1(4.70); Eun. charges Bas. with teaching that it is εἰ... μὴ περὶ τοῦ ἐν ἀρχῇ ὄντος λόγου...ὁ μακάριος διαλέγεται Πέτρος, ἀλλὰ περὶ τοῦ βλεπομένου καὶ κενώσαντος ἑαυτόν, καθώς φησι Βασίλειος... [Phil.2:7] οὐ γάρ ἐστιν ἀνθρώπων οὐδεὶς ὃς τοῦτον οἰκειώσεται τὸν λόγον Eun.ap.Gr.Nyss.*Eun.*5(2 p.107.29ff.; M.45.688A); ἄνθρωπον εἰς ἄνθρωπον κεκενῶσθαι λέγειν Gr.Nyss.*Eun.*5(2 p.110.30; 689C); οὐκ ἔστι τοῦτο κ., τὸ φύσεως ὄντα ἀνθρωπίνης καὶ ἄνθρωπον ψιλόν, νίψαι τοὺς ὁμοδούλους Chrys.*hom.*7.2 *in Phil.*(11.247B); τίς ὁ κενώσας ἑαυτόν...; εἰσκομίζει γάρ...ἡμῖν...ὁ παρ' αὐτῶν [sc. Nestorians] λόγος ἐκ τῆς καθ' ἡμᾶς ταπεινότητος ὑψούμενον ἄνθρωπον καὶ ἐκ τῆς καθ' ἡμᾶς κ. εἰς τὸ πλῆρες τῆς θεότητος ἀναβαίνοντα...πῶς οὖν ἄρα κεκενῶσθαί φασι τὸν μονογενῆ...οὐκ ἔχει νοεῖν, εἰ μὴ κεκενῶσθαί φασιν αὐτόν, ὅτι τῇ ἰδίᾳ δόξῃ τετίμηκεν ἄνθρωπον...τῆς τοίνυν...γραφῆς κ. ὀνομαζούσης, καὶ δούλου μορφὴν καὶ μέντοι καὶ ἀνθρωπότητα καὶ τὸν ταῦτα ἐθελουσίως ὑπομείναντα λεγούσης εἶναι τὸν ἐκ θεοῦ πατρὸς λόγον Cyr. *ep.*50(p.93.11ff.; 5^{2}.161Dff.); οἴεσθαι δεῖν ὅτι κενοῦται τὸ πλῆρες καὶ ἐν δούλου μορφῇ γένοιτ' ἄν, οὐ τὸ τῇ φύσει δοῦλον, ἀλλὰ τὸ τῶν τῆς δουλείας ἐπέκεινα μέτρων id.*Pulch.*(p.35.34; 5^{2}.142B); **b.** but the pre-existent Son, Clem.*paed.*3.1(p.237.5; M.8.557A); (Valent.) ὁ Ἰησοῦς τὸ φῶς ἡμῶν...ἑαυτὸν κενώσας, τουτέστιν ἐκτὸς τοῦ Ὅρου γενόμενος κατὰ Θεόδοτον id.*exc.Thdot.*35(p.118.10; M.9.676C); Meth.*symp.*3.8 (p.36.1; M.18.73B) cit. s. ἐκκλησία; [Phil.2:5ff.] συνορᾷς ὅτι πρὸ τοῦ κενῶσαι ἑαυτὸν...ἦν καὶ προῆν...οὐκ ἄρα λόγος ψιλὸς καὶ ἀνυπόστατος ἔσται ἀλλ' υἱὸς...ὃς...ἑαυτὸν ἐκένωσεν Eus.*e.th.*1.20(pp.90.35,91.27; M.24.884A,C); περὶ τῆς θεότητος...τοῦ υἱοῦ ὁ ἀπόστολος διδάσκει λέγων [Phil.2:6f.] id.*Marcell.*1.4(p.25.22; M.24.765A); [Phil.2:5ff.] οὐ γὰρ ἐξ ἐλαττόνων βελτίων γέγονεν· ἀλλὰ μᾶλλον θεὸς ὑπάρχων τὴν δούλου μορφὴν ἔλαβε, καὶ ἐν τῷ λαβεῖν, οὐκ ἐβελτιώθη, ἀλλ' ἐταπείνωσεν ἑαυτόν Ath.*Ar.*1.40(M.26.93C); εἰ μὴ νοῦς ἔνσαρκος γέγονεν ὁ λόγος, ἀλλὰ σοφία ἦν τῷ νῷ, οὐ κατέβη ὁ κύριος οὐδὲ ἐκένωσεν ἑαυτόν Apoll. *fr.*71(p.221.15)ap.Gr.Nyss.*Apoll.*37(M.45.1208A); εἰ θεὸς ἐν ἀνθρώπῳ κατῴκησεν, οὐκ ἐκενώθη. ἐκενώθη δὲ ὁ ἐν μορφῇ θεοῦ μορφὴν δούλου λαβών· οὐκ ἄρα ἐν ἀνθρώπῳ κατῴκησεν. θεὸς ἐν ἀνθρώπῳ κατοικῶν οὐκ ἔστιν ἄνθρωπος· πνεῦμα δὲ σαρκὶ ἡνωμένον ἄνθρωπός ἐστιν· ἄνθρωπος Χριστός, ὡς εἴρηται, ὁμωνύμως· πνεῦμα ἄρα θεῖόν ἐστιν ἡνωμένον σαρκί id.*anac.*15f.(p.243.29; M.28.1273A); ἡ κενωθεῖσα θεότης ...ἡ προσληφθεῖσα σάρξ Gr.Naz.*or.*2.23(M.35.432B); σκεψώμεθα...τί τὸ ἀνακαινούμενον καὶ τί τὸ κενούμενον. κενοῦται μὲν γὰρ ἡ θεότης, ἵνα χωρητὴ τῇ ἀνθρωπίνῃ φύσει γένηται Gr.Nyss.*Eun.*5(2 p.124.25; M.45.705D); id.*Apoll.*14(M.45.1149A); Cyr.*glaph.Num.*(1.402C); εἰς τοσαύτην ἑαυτὸν καθῆκεν ὁ ἀκένωτος κ. ἵνα τὴν κενωθεῖσαν εἰς γῆν διαφθορᾶς ἀνθρωπότητα...ἀναστήσῃ Sophr.H.*or.*2.42(M.87.3273C); Jo.D.*f.o.*1.2(M.94.793B); acc. Origen, *quidam autem volunt de ipsa anima dictum videri, cum primum de Maria corpus adsumit, etiam illud, quod apostolus dicit* [Phil.2:6f.], Or.*princ.*4.5(p.356.2; M.11. 406C); **4.** divinity suffering no change πευσόμεθα πῶς λέγει μεταβολήν. εἰ μὲν γὰρ τῆς οὐσίας, οὐ δίδοται...εἰ δ' ὅτι πάσχει τι ὑπὸ τοῦ σώματος...τί ἄτοπον ἀπαντᾷ τῷ λόγῳ, ἀπὸ πολλῆς φιλανθρωπίας καταβιβάζοντι σωτῆρα τῷ γένει τῶν ἀνθρώπων;...ἑκουσίως εἰς τὰς ἀνθρωπίνας κῆρας ὑπὲρ τοῦ γένους ἡμῶν καταβᾶσα [sc. soul of Jesus]. ταῦτα δ' ἐπιστάμενος ὁ θεῖος λόγος...[Phil.2:5ff.] Or.*Cels.* 4.18(p.288.14; M.11.1052A); cf. *quamvis enim vilem servi gesserit formam, plenitudo tamen in eo divinitatis habitabat*, id.*hom.*2.3 *in Lev.*(M.12.416C); ὑπέστη κ. ... ἐθελούσιον...περινοήσωμεν δὲ μᾶλλον ἐκεῖνο σοφῶς, ὅτι καὶ ἐν σαρκὶ γεγονότα τὸν ἴδιον υἱόν, οὐκ ἔξω τίθησιν ὁ πατὴρ τῶν ἐνόντων αὐτῷ φυσικῶν ἀξιωμάτων Cyr.*hom.pasch.*17.2 (5^{2}.226Af.); οὐ γὰρ ἐκ μόνων ἡμῖν τῶν τῆς κ. τρόπων γνώριμος ὁ υἱός, ἀλλὰ καὶ ἐξ ὧν ἐστι θεός id.*ador.*9(1.307A); Dion.Ar.*d.n.*2.10(M.3. 649A); Hypat.*fr.*(p.126); because divine by nature ὁ τῆς φιλανθρωπίας λόγος κενοῦται, ἀκένωτος τὴν φύσιν τυγχάνων Attic.*fr.*ap.Cyr. *apol.orient.*4(p.45.10; 6^{1}.173C); ζωὴ κατὰ φύσιν ὑπάρχων ὁ...λόγος, καθίκετο μὲν οὖν εἰς ἑκούσιον κ., γέγονε δὲ καθ' ἡμᾶς...οὐ τροπὴν ὑπομείνας τὴν ἀπό γε τῆς ἰδίας φύσεως εἰς σάρκα τὴν ἀπὸ γῆς· ἐρήρεισται γὰρ ἡ θεοῦ φύσις ἐν ἰδίοις ἀγαθοῖς Cyr.*hom.pasch.*18.4(5^{2}. 243B); τοῦ πιστοῦ κυρίου φύσει...υἱός ἐστι καὶ εἰ πέφηνεν οἰκονομικῶς ἐν εἴδει τῷ καθ' ἡμᾶς καὶ τὸ τῆς κ. ὑπέδυ μέτρον id.*Is.*4.4(2.667C); κεκενῶσθαι δὲ λέγεται ὡς πρὸ τῆς κ. τὸ πλῆρες ἔχων ἐν ἰδίᾳ φύσει, καθὸ νοεῖται θεός· οὐ γὰρ ἐκ τοῦ κενὸς εἶναί τις εἰς τὸ πλῆρες ἀνέβη· ἐταπείνωσε δὲ μᾶλλον ἑαυτὸν ἐξ ὑψωμάτων θεϊκῶν id.*ep.*55(p.55.5f.; 5^{2}.182Bf.); ἄτρεπτος κατὰ φύσιν ὡς θεός, μεμενηκὼς ὅπερ ἦν ἀεὶ... κεχρημάτικεν καὶ υἱὸς ἀνθρώπου...καθῆκε γὰρ ἑαυτὸν εἰς κ. id.*Arcad.* (p.63.29; 5^{2}.44E); **5.** the object of κ. not οὐσία but δόξα or ἀξία or εἶναι ἐν ἰσότητι τοῦ πατρός: οὐδ' ἄρα τοπικῶς ταῦτα ἐκδεκτέον· ἀλλ' ὁ λόγος τοῦ θεοῦ, ἡμῖν συγκαταβαίνων καὶ ὡς πρὸς τὴν ἰδίαν ἀξίαν, ὅτε παρὰ ἀνθρώποις ἐστὶ ταπεινούμενος, μεταβαίνειν λέγεται...πρὸς τὸν πατέρα, ὅπως καὶ ἡμεῖς ἐκεῖθι τέλειον αὐτὸν θεασώμεθα, ἀπὸ τῆς παρ' ἡμῖν κενότητος, ἣν ἐκένωσεν ἑαυτόν, ἐπὶ τὸ ἴδιον πλήρωμα παλινδρομοῦντα Or.*or.*23(p.350.23; M.11.488B); ὁ αὐτὸς θεὸς καὶ ἄνθρωπος, Ἰησοῦς Χριστός...πεπίστευται θεὸς μὲν κενώσας ἑαυτὸν ἀπὸ τοῦ εἶναι ἴσα θεῷ, ἄνθρωπος δὲ κτλ. Hymen.*ep.*8(p.329.6); κενωθεὶς...καὶ τὴν μορφὴν τοῦ δούλου προσλαβὼν εἰς τὴν ἑαυτοῦ τελειότητα πάλιν ἀνεπληρώθη καὶ τὴν ἀξίαν. αὐτὸς γὰρ ἐν ἑαυτῷ σμικρυνθείς, καὶ ἐν τοῖς ἑαυτοῦ μέρεσιν ἀναλυθείς, ἐκ τῆς ἑαυτοῦ σμικρότητος καὶ τῶν ἑαυτοῦ μερῶν εἰς τὴν συμπλήρωσιν πάλιν τὴν ἑαυτοῦ καὶ τὸ μέγεθος κατέστη, οὐδέποτε τοῦ τέλειος εἶναι μειωθείς Meth.*symp.*8.11(p.95.17; M.18.157A); κενοῦται δι' ἡμᾶς...κ. δὲ λέγω τὴν τῆς δόξης οἷον ὕφεσίν τε καὶ ἐλάττωσιν, διὰ τοῦτο χωρητὸς γίνεται Gr.Naz.*or.*37.3(M.36. 285B); ὁ πλήρης κενοῦται· κενοῦται γὰρ τῆς ἑαυτοῦ δόξης ἐπὶ μικρόν, ἵν' ἐγὼ τῆς ἐκείνου μεταλάβω πληρώσεως *ib.*45.9(636A); id.*carm.*1.1. 9.39(M.37.459A) = *ib.*1.2.1.144(533A); ἡ τοῦ ἐκένωσεν λέξις σαφῶς παρίστησι τὸ μὴ ἀεὶ τοῦτο εἶναι, ὅπερ ἡμῖν ὤφθη, ἀλλ' εἶναι μὲν ἐν τῷ πληρώματι τῆς θεότητος ἴσα θεῷ, ἀπρόσιτον...καὶ μάλιστά γε τῇ βραχύτητι τῆς ἀνθρωπίνης οὐδενείας ἀχώρη[σ]τον· χωρητὸν δὲ ...τότε γενόμενον, ὅτε ἐκένωσε...τὴν ἄφραστον αὐτοῦ τῆς θεότητος δόξαν Gr.Nyss.*Apoll.*20(M.45.1164Bf.); Chrys.*hom.*8.2 *in Eph.*(11. 54B); τὸ οὖν ἑαυτὸν ἐκένωσεν, ἀντὶ τοῦ οὐκ ἔδειξεν ἑαυτόν,...τὴν ἀξίαν ἐκείνην ἀπέκρυψεν Thdr.Mops.*Phil.*2:7(p.217.12; M.66.924B); τὸ πλήρωμα τοῦ δι' ἡμᾶς ἑαυτὸν κενώσαντος...τῆς δόξης τὸ ὕψος τοῦ καθέντος ἑαυτὸν δι' ἡμᾶς εἰς ταπείνωσιν Cyr.*Heb.*1:1(p.365.2); ἔχων...τὸ εἶναι κατὰ φύσιν ἐν ἰσότητι τοῦ πατρός, κεκένωκεν ἑαυτόν, καὶ μορφὴν δούλου λαβὼν...τεταπείνωκεν ἑαυτὸν εἰς κ. id.*Arcad.* (p.106.26; 5^{2}.108D); it is a σχῆμα: ὑποβιβάζει δέ πως [sc. τὸν λόγον] ἡ κ. εἰς τὸ καθ' ἡμᾶς...τῆς ἑκουσίου κ. ὁ τρόπος...τὸ τῆς ταπεινώσεως περικείμενος σχῆμα, διὰ τὸ ἀνθρώπινον ἐν ἐλάττοσί πως ἢ ἐν οἷς ἐστιν ὁ πατὴρ φαίνεσθαι ποιεῖ τὸν...θεὸν μονογενῆ id.*Jo.*11.9(4.970B,D); perh. in some such sense is to be understood *in forma enim dei manens formam servi assumpsit, non demutatus sed se ipsum exinaniens et intra se latens et intra suam ipse vacuefactus potestatem*, Hil.Pict. *Trin.*11.48(M.*PL.*10.432A); but in Hilary *natura* is the object, cf. *haurienda fuit natura caelestis, ut exinaniens se ex dei forma in formam servi hominisque decideret*, id.*Ps.*68:2f.(M.*PL.*9.472B); but the divinity is not thereby destroyed, cf.*ib.*68:27ff.(486A); it is even present, cf. *cumque accipere formam servi nisi per evacuationem suam non poterit qui manebat in dei forma, non conveniente sibi formae utriusque concursu...evacuatio formae non est abolitio naturae: quia qui se evacuat, non caret sese; et qui accipit* [sc. *formam servi*] *manet* [sc. *in forma dei*] id.*Trin.*9.14(292Bff.); cf.*ib.*11. 48 cit. supra; (these passages have also been interpreted as implying a reduction in scale) *per ipsam sui exinanitionem studet nobis deitatis plenitudinem demonstrare. verbi causa, si facta esset aliqua statua talis, quae magnitudine sui universum orbem terrae teneret et pro sui immensitate considerari a nullo posset, fieret autem alia statua...per omnia similis...hanc videntes, illam se vidisse confiderent...tali quadam similitudine exinaniens se filius de aequalitate patris et viam nobis cognitionis ejus ostendens, figura expressa substantiae ejus efficitur*, Or.*princ.*1.2.8(p.38.26; M.11.137A); cf.Meth. *symp.*8.11 cit. supra; σμικρὸν μὲν γὰρ ὁμολογουμένως αὐτῷ τὸ γενέσθαι καθ' ἡμᾶς· καλεῖται γὰρ κένωσις Cyr.*hom.pasch.*15(5^{2}.206C); **6.** an assumption rather than a change or essential addition or loss, Apoll.*fr.*124(p.237.30f.)ap.Thdt.*eran.*1(4.70) cit. s. 3.a; ἄκτιστος θεὸς κτιστῇ περιβολῇ φανερούμενος, κενώσας μὲν ἑαυτὸν κατὰ τὴν μόρφωσιν ⟨δούλου⟩, ἀκένωτος δὲ καὶ ἀναλλοίωτος καὶ ἀνελάττωτος κατὰ τὴν θείαν οὐσίαν Apoll.*corp.et div.*6(p.188.1; M.*PL.*8.874A); Gr.Naz.*or.*29.18f.(p.101.15ff.; M.36.97B) cit. s. σύνθετος; ἵνα γὰρ μή, ἀκούσας ὅτι ἐκένωσεν ἑαυτόν, μεταβολὴν νομίσῃς καὶ μετάπτωσιν καὶ ἀφανισμόν τινα, μένων, φησίν, ὃ ἦν ἔλαβεν ὃ οὐκ ἦν καὶ σὰρξ γενόμενος ἔμεινε θεὸς λόγος ὤν Chrys.*hom.*7.2 *in Phil.*(11.247F); cf. *'semetipsum exinanivit', non mutando divinitatem suam, sed nostram mutabilitatem assumendo*, Aug.*Trin.*7.3.5(M.*PL.*42.938); ποία τίς ἐστιν ἡ κ.; τὸ ἐν προσλήψει γενέσθαι σαρκὸς...ἡ πρὸς ἡμᾶς ὁμοίωσις τοῦ μὴ καθ' ἡμᾶς κατ' ἰδίαν φύσιν Cyr.*Chr.un.*(5^{1}.742B); ἥτις γέννησις χρονικὴ τῆς θείας αὐτοῦ καὶ ἀϊδίου γεννήσεως οὔτε τι ἀπεμείωσεν οὔτε μήν τι ταύτῃ προσέθηκεν, ἀλλ' ὅλην ἑαυτὴν εἰς τὸ σῶσαι τὸν ἄνθρωπον

...ἐκένωσεν Leo Mag.*ep.*28.2(p.11.29; M.*PL.*54.760A); οὐ φαντασίᾳ ταῦτα γινόμενος...ἀλλ' ἀληθείᾳ καὶ πράγματι ὅλον ἑαυτὸν κενώσας πατρικῷ καὶ οἰκείῳ θελήματι, καὶ ὅλον προσλαβὼν τὸ ἡμέτερον φύραμα Sophr.H.*ep.syn.*(M.87.3161A); θεοῦ...δι' ἀγαθότητα πρὸς ἀνθρώπους ὑπῆρχεν· αὐθαίρετος κ. τὸ μυστήριον, ἀλλ' οὐ θεότητος ἔκπτωσις, ἡ διὰ σαρκὸς ἑκούσιος συγκατάβασις· μεμένηκε γὰρ ὅπερ ἦν, καὶ γενόμενος ὅπερ οὐκ ἦν Max.*ep.*19(M.91.592D); μήτε τι πεπονθὼς εἰς τὴν ἰδίαν οὐσίαν πρὸς τῆς...κ., μήτε τι τῆς ἀνθρωπίνης διὰ τὴν...πρόσληψιν ἀμείψας id.*ambig.*(M.91.1048C); **7.** true κ. demands union of natures εἰ μὲν οὖν τὸν ἐκ τῆς ἁγίας παρθένου γεγεννημένον...ὑπομεῖναί φασι τὴν κ., πῶς ἐκενώθη δεδοξασμένος;...εἰ δὲ ἐπ' αὐτοῦ λέγοιεν πεπράχθαι τὴν κ. τοῦ μονογενοῦς, κεκένωταί τι παθών· ᾧ γὰρ τὸ παθεῖν συμβέβηκε, πρέποι ἂν μᾶλλον καὶ τὸ τῆς κ. χρῆμα Cyr.*Heb.*2:9(p.390.25ff.); κἂν εἰ λέγοιτο λαβεῖν παρὰ τοῦ πατρὸς δόξαν...ἀναθετέον μὲν τὸ λαβεῖν τοῖς τῆς κ. μέτροις...κεκενῶσθαι μὲν λέγεται διὰ τὸ ἀνθρώπινον, ὑψοῦται δὲ πάλιν...ἀνθρωπίνως, καίτοι κατὰ φύσιν ὕψιστος ὢν ἀεί. γέγονε γὰρ ἄνθρωπος, καὶ τοῦτο...ἐστὶ τὸ τῆς ὑφέσεως μέτρον καὶ ἡ λεγομένη κ. id. *Pulch.*(p.54.21,33ff.; 5^2.170A,cf.); τίνα κεκένωται τρόπον;...οἱ μὲν οὖν εἰς δύο τέμνοντες τὸν...Χριστὸν...τὸν ἐκ τῆς ἁγίας παρθένου φασὶν ὑπομεῖναι τὴν κ. ... προαποδεικνύντων ὅτι καὶ ἐν μορφῇ καὶ ἰσότητι... ἦν τοῦ πατρός, ἵνα καὶ τὸν τῆς κ. ὑπομείνῃ τρόπον, εἰς ὅπερ οὐκ ἦν καθιγμένος id.*ep.*1(p.16.8ff.; 5^2.9Df.); οὐ...ταὐτὸν ὡς ἐν ποιότητι φυσικῇ θεότης τε καὶ ἀνθρωπότης. ἐπεὶ πῶς κεκένωται θεὸς ὢν ὁ λόγος, καθεὶς ἑαυτὸν ἐν μείοσιν, τουτέστιν ἐν τοῖς καθ' ἡμᾶς; *ib.*40(p.26.27; 5^2.116C); εἰκῇ...τὸ τῆς ἐνανθρωπείας λαλεῖται μυστήριον καὶ κεκένωκε μὲν ἑαυτὸν κατ' οὐδένα τρόπον [i.e. acc. teaching of Nestorius] id. *Nest.*1.6(p.26.23; 6^1.21E); κ. δὲ τῷ θεῷ λόγῳ παθεῖν οὐκ εἰδότι τὴν τροπήν, τὸ δρᾶσαί τι καὶ εἰπεῖν τῶν ἀνθρωπίνων διὰ τὴν πρὸς σάρκα σύνοδον οἰκονομικήν id.*apol.Thdt.*4(p.125.20; 6^1.219C); ποῖος ἂν γένοιτο πτωχείας αὐτῷ καὶ κ. τρόπος; ὡς ἕν γε δὴ μόνῳ τῷ ἐθελῆσαι τυχὸν τιμήσας τινὰ τῶν καθ' ἡμᾶς ἄνθρωπον;...θεὸς ὢν φύσει...δουλοπρεπὲς ὑπέδυ μέτρον τουτέστι τὸ ἀνθρώπινον *ib.*10(p.138.29; 6^1.233C); εἰ μὴ τὰ ἀνθρώπινα πέπονθε, ποῦ ἐκενώθη;...πάθος γὰρ περιῆψε θεῷ, οὐ φύσις παθητή, ἀλλὰ πρὸς τὸ παθητὸν ἕνωσις Thdot.Anc.*hom.*3.5(M.77.1389B); τίς ἐκένωσεν ἑαυτὸν...εἰ μὴ ὁ τούτου κοινωνήσας τοῖς ἀνθρώποις θεὸς ἑκουσίως, οὐ τὴν φύσιν ἀναγκασθείς; [Phil.2:5ff.]...τί τῆς κ. τὸ εἶδος;...εἰ μὲν γὰρ μὴ συγκαταβὰς ἀνθρώπῳ θεὸς ἀνέλαβεν ἄνθρωπον, μορφὴν ἔλαβε δούλου μόνον, καὶ ἑαυτὸν οὐκ ἐκένωσεν id. *exp.symb.*19(M.77.1341Af.); ὁ...θεὸς λόγος κατὰ φύσιν ἑνωθεὶς τῇ ἰδίᾳ σαρκὶ...πάντα τὰ τοῦ ἀνθρώπου ἴδια ᾠκειώσατο...ἐν τούτῳ γάρ ἐστιν αὐτοῦ καὶ ἡ κ. Pamph.H.*panopl.*4.1(p.611); τὰ μὲν δουλικὰ δεσποτικῶς ἐνεργῶν...τὴν ἀπαθῆ...ἐν τοῖς σαρκικοῖς ἐπεδείκνυτο δύναμιν...τὰ δεσποτικὰ δὲ πράττων δουλικῶς...τὴν ἄφατον ἐνεδείκνυτο κ. Max. *ambig.*(M.91.1044C); so that full humanity may be predicated of the Word τὰς μὲν τοῦ...πάθους ταπεινώσεώς τε καὶ κ. καὶ τῆς καλουμένης αὐτοῦ πτωχείας...φωνὰς...παρατίθενται ἐπὶ παραγραφῇ τῆς ἀνωτάτω καὶ ἀρχῆθεν αὐτοῦ θεότητος Alex.Al.*ep.Alex.*9(p.25.18; M.18.561B); συμπλάττεται...πανταχοῦ τοῖς τῆς ἀνθρωπότητος μέτροις, καὶ τὸ τῇ κ. πρέπον οὐκ αἰσχύνεται διὰ τὴν οἰκονομίαν Ath.*exp.Ps.*15:8(M.27.105A); ἀνθρωπίνως...διὰ τὴν κ. πρὸς τὸν ἑαυτοῦ πατέρα ποιεῖται τὸν λόγον *ib.*40:11(200A); ὁ...καθεὶς ἑαυτὸν δι' ἡμᾶς εἰς ἑκούσιον κ., διὰ ποίαν αἰτίαν παραιτοῖτ' ἂν τοὺς τῇ κ. πρέποντας λόγους; ἑνὶ τοιγαροῦν προσώπῳ τὰς...πάσας ἀναθετέον φωνάς· ὑποστάσει μιᾷ, τῇ τοῦ λόγου σεσαρκωμένῃ Cyr.*ep.*17(p.38.20f.; 5^2.73D); id.*Arcad.*(p.104.29; 5^2.106A); δι' ἡμᾶς κεκενῶσθαι λέγεται...ἐπείπερ γέγονε καθ' ἡμᾶς, προσκεκύνηκε μεθ' ἡμῶν ὡς ἄνθρωπος, καίτοι προσκυνούσης αὐτὸν τῆς ἄνω πληθύος id.*Nest.*3 proem.(p.54.27ff.; 6^1.63C); including human weakness and subjection τὴν Χριστοῦ κ. τὴν ὑπὲρ ἡμῶν, καὶ τὰ τοῦ ἀπαθοῦς πάθη Gr.Naz.*or.*17.12(M.35.980A); εἰ...τεταπείνωκεν ἑαυτόν, καὶ καθῆκεν ἑκὼν εἰς κ., δεῖ δὴ πάντως καὶ τὸ τῆς κ. ὁρᾶσθαι μέτρον, καὶ δι' αὐτῶν τῶν πραγμάτων νοεῖσθαι τὸ ταπεινόν Cyr.*Is.*3.5(2.538E); id. *ep.*55(p.54.19; 5^2.181B); καίτοι κατὰ φύσιν ἰδίαν ἐλεύθερος ὢν...πλὴν ὡς ἰδίαν ἔχων τὴν τοῦ δούλου μορφὴν διὰ τὸ τῆς κ. μέτρον τοῖς τῶν τελῶν πράκτορσιν ὑπόφορος ἦν id.*apol.Thdt.*6(p.129.10; 6^1.223C); Oecum.*Apoc.*3:12(p.62); and ignorance ἀνθρωπότητος δὲ μέτροις πρέποι ἂν εἰκότως καὶ τὸ ἀγνοεῖν τὰ ἐσόμενα...ὥσπερ δὲ αὐτὸς ὢν ἡ πάντων ζωὴ...τροφὴν ἐδέχετο σωματικήν, οὐκ ἀτιμάζων τὸ τῆς κ. μέτρον,...οὕτω καὶ πάντα εἰδὼς τὴν τῇ ἀνθρωπότητι πρέπουσαν ἄγνοιαν οὐκ ἐρυθριᾷ προσνέμων ἑαυτῷ Cyr.*resp.*4(6^2.382D); cf. εἰ...οὐ γέγονεν ἄνθρωπος ὁ λόγος, ἔστω τοῦ λόγου καθ' ὑμᾶς τὸ λαβεῖν, καὶ τὸ χρῄζειν δόξης, καὶ τὸ ἀγνοεῖν· εἰ δὲ γέγονεν ἄνθρωπος· γέγονε γάρ· ἀνθρώπου δέ ἐστι τὸ λαβεῖν, καὶ τὸ χρῄζειν, καὶ τὸ ἀγνοεῖν Ath.*Ar.*3.39(M.26.405C); v. γνῶσις.

κενωτικός, *cathartic, purgative,* ref. drugs κ. ἐνεργείας Anast.S. *hod.*2(M.89.65D).

κεπφόω ([*]**κεμφόω**), *deceive, gull* ἐπαγγελίᾳ ἐλπίδος κεπφώσας τοὺς ὑπὸ σοῦ ἠπατημένους Epiph.*haer.*36.4(p.48.1; M.41.637A); usu. pass., Iren.*haer.*1.13.3(M.7.584A); τοὺς πειθομένους τῇ πονηρίᾳ κεμφουμένους...δι' ἀκολασίαν Or.*exp.in Pr.*7:22(M.17.184A); Cyr.*hom. div.*4(p.103.21; 5^2.357A).

***κέπφωσις**, ἡ, *instability,* Mac.Aeg.*pat.*1(M.34.868A).

κεραία, ἡ, any *projection* like a horn; **1.** of arms of Cross, Gr. Nyss.*Eun.*5(2 p.115.15; M.45.696B); esp. transverse beam, *ib.* (p.115.19; 696C); also called ἡ μέση as dividing upright beam τὴν μέσην κ. μιᾷ προσηγορίᾳ διαλαμβάνει, πᾶν τὸ διὰ μέσου τῶν ἐπουρανίων καὶ ὑποχθονίων ὀνομάσας ἐπίγειον id.*or.catech.*32(p.121.6); exeg. Mt. 5:18 ἡ δὲ ἐγκαρσίως ἀγομένη διὰ πλαγίου, κ. ὀνομάζεται...τὸ...ξύλον... οὐ...τὴν ὀθόνην ἐξαπλοῦσι, κ. λέγουσιν, ἐκ τοῦ σχήματος ὀνομάζοντες. διὸ...ἡ θεία τοῦ εὐαγγελίου φωνή...οἷον δι' αἰνίγματος...τοῦ κατὰ τὸν σταυρὸν σχήματος ὑποδείκνυσι id.*res.*1(M.46.625A); and Abac.3:4 τοῦτ' ἔστι τοὺς ἥλους τοῦ σταυροῦ ἢ τὰς κ. αὐτοῦ Mac.Mgn.*apocr.*3.8 (p.66.13); **2.** of the small projection occurring in strokes of certain Hebrew letters such as differentiates ב from כ πρέπει...τὰ ἅγια γράμματα πιστεύειν μηδεμίαν κ. ἔχειν κενὴν σοφίας θεοῦ Or.*fr.hom.21 in Jer.*(p.195.23); ἑκάστη κ. τῶν θείων λογίων ἰδίαν δύναμιν καὶ θεωρίαν κέκτηται ‡Tit.Bost.*palm.*4(M.18.1269B); Chrys.*hom.36.1 in Jo.*(8.206D); τοῦτο [i.e. a decree]...τῇ χειρὶ πειραθεὶς βεβαιῶσαι οὐδεμίαν στοιχείου κ. ἐξέτεινεν Thdt.*h.e.*4.19.15(3.983); ref. confusion between Abimelech and Ahimelech (LXX 1Reg.21:1; Ps.33:1) παρὰ...τὴν ὁμοιότητα τοῦ στοιχείου τοῦ βὴθ...καὶ τοῦ χὰφ διαφόρως ἐξεδόθη τοὔνομα· σχεδὸν γὰρ ἓν καὶ ταὐτόν ἐστι τὰ δύο στοιχεῖα, βραχυτάτης κ. μόνης ἐναλλαττούσης Eus.*Ps.*33:1(M.23.292C); Proc. G.*1Reg.*21:1(M.87.1108C); exeg. Mt.5:18 διὰ τοῦ ἰῶτα καὶ τῆς κ. ἡ δικαιοσύνη κέκραγεν αὐτοῦ...[Mt.5:18] τουτέστιν οὔτε ἡ τοῖς εὐθέσι κατάλληλος ἐπαγγελία οὔτε ἡ τοῖς πλαγιάζουσιν ἠπειλημένη κόλασις Clem.*fr.*58(p.227.1ff.; M.9.765D); as if in apposition to ἰῶτα: τοῦ τελείου ἀνθρώπου κατανοεῖ [sc. Monoïmus]...μεγίστην εἰκόνα ἰῶτα, ἕν, τὴν μίαν κ. Hipp.*haer.*8.12(p.232.22; M.16.3358C); τῇ ἁπλῇ καὶ ἀσυνθέτῳ τοῦ ἰῶτα κ. μιᾷ...τῆς μιᾶς κ. τοῦ ἰῶτα *ib.*8.13(p.233.3,6; 3359A); μία κ. οὐ παρ' Ἕλλησι μόνον ἐστὶ τὸ ἰῶτα, ἀλλὰ καὶ παρ' Ἑβραίοις τὸ...ἰώθ. δύναται δὲ τὸ ἰῶτα ἓν ἢ μία κ. συμβολικῶς λέγεσθαι ὁ Ἰησοῦς, ἐπείπερ ἡ ἀρχὴ τοῦ ὀνόματος αὐτοῦ οὐ παρ' Ἕλλησι μόνον, ἀλλὰ καὶ παρ' Ἑβραίοις ἀπὸ τοῦ ἰὼθ γράφεται· καὶ ἔστιν οὕτως τὸ ἰῶτα ἓν ἢ μία κ. ὁ Ἰησοῦς, ὁ λόγος τοῦ θεοῦ ἐν τῷ νόμῳ Or.*fr.75 in Lc.* 16:17(p.270); **3.** *written communication, letter, message* κεραίαν ἐποιήσατο πρὸς ἡμᾶς Serg.*ep.*3 ap.CCP(681)*act.*12(H.3.1317C); Thdr. Stud.*epp.*2.121(M.99.1397B); //γράμμα, Thphyl.*exc.gent.*5(p.481.29; M.113.941B); //λόγος, *ib.*3(p.480.21; 940C).

κεραίν-ω, *confuse, disturb* φιλονεικεῖν βουλόμενοι ~ονται πρὸς τὰ ῥηθέντα ‡Caes.Naz.*dial.*168(M.38.1132).

κεραϊστής, ὁ, *plunderer,* Orac.Sib.2.261.

***κεραιώδης**, *principal,* Or.*fr.4 in Lc.*(M.17.333B; κεφαλαιωδέστερα p.234).

κεράμβηλον, τό, *scarecrow,* Olymp.*fr.Ep.Jer.*69(M.93.777D).

κεραμεύς, ὁ, *potter* (ref. Jer.18:6, Rom.9:21) καθὼς...οἶδεν ὁ κ. τὸ σκεῦος πόσον χωρεῖ, καὶ πρὸς αὐτὸ φέρει τὸν πηλόν, οὕτω καὶ ὁ κύριος πρὸς ὁμοίωσιν τοῦ πνεύματος ποιεῖ τὸ σῶμα *T.Neph.*2.2; *ib.*2.4; ὁ κ. θεὸς τῶν σωμάτων ἡμῶν, ὁ δημιουργὸς τῆς κατασκευῆς ἡμῶν Or.*hom. 18.4 in Jer.*(p.154.30; M.13.469B); cf.id.*princ.*3.1.21(p.235f.; M.11. 293C); τέκτων...καὶ κ. τὴν...πρὸ αὐτῶν ὕλην...ἐργάζεται...αὐτὸς δὲ ὁ... θεὸς τὸν...γενόμενον ἤδη παρ' αὐτοῦ χοῦν...λαβὼν πλάττει τὸν ἄνθρωπον· καὶ αὐτὴν μέντοι τὴν γῆν...εἰς τὸ εἶναι πεποίηκε διὰ τοῦ ἰδίου λόγου Ath.*Ar.*1.24(M.26.61A); ὁ κ. τοῦ κόσμου Rom.Mel.(*SBBAW* 1901 p.743); in illustration showing necessity for repentance while still in this world ὁ κ., ἐὰν ποιῇ σκεῦος καὶ ἐν ταῖς χερσὶν αὐτοῦ διαστραφῇ...πάλιν αὐτὸ ἀναπλάσσει, ἐὰν δὲ προφθάσῃ εἰς τὴν κάμινον τοῦ πυρὸς αὐτὸ βαλεῖν, οὐκέτι βοηθήσει αὐτῷ *2Clem.*8.2.

***κεραμευτής**, ὁ, = foreg., Cyr.*Juln.*4(6^2.120C).

***κεραμευτικῶς**, *like a pot* ὅσον ἐσμὲν ἐν τῷ βίῳ τούτῳ, μορφούμεθα, ἵν' οὕτως ὀνομάσω διὰ τὸ πήλινον ἡμῶν σκεῦος, κ. Or.*hom.18.1 in Jer.* (p.151.9; M.13.464B).

[*]**κεραμία**, ἡ, = κεραμεία, *the potter's craft,* figuratively attributed to God in scripture (cf. Jer.18:6, Rom.9:21), Dion.Ar.*ep.*9(M. 3.1105A).

κεραμίδιον, τό, *tile, Ep.Abg.*5(p.282.24ff.).

κεράμιος, neut. plur. as subst.; **1.** *pots, crockery,* Chrys.*hom.7.4 in Col.*(11.377D); **2.** ? variant of κεράμεα *tiling,* hence *roof* μέγας κτύπος ἐν τοῖς κ. τῆς...ἐκκλησίας γέγονεν Gr.Mag.*dial.*(tr.Zach.)3.30 (M.*PL.*77.287C).

κεραμοποιός, ὁ, *potter,* Thphn.*chron.*p.371(M.108.888B).

κέραμος, ὁ, *jar,* hence *jarful* μ' κάδους ἢ κεράμους [sc. τοῦ ὕδατος] ‡Ath.*poenit.can.*5(p.457).

κεράμωσις, ἡ, *tiled roofing*, met. ἦν ἰδέσθαι [sc. at Crucifixion] τὸν οὐρανὸν...τὸν τῆς κτίσεως ὄροφον, τὴν τῆς πανδήμου οἰκίας κ. ‡Chrys. *ador*.2(11.825C).

κεράννυμι, 1. *mix*; **a.** wine ποτήριον κεκερασμένον Or.*hom.12.2 in Jer*.(p.88.6; M.13.380C); met. οὐκ ἐντραπήσεται [sc. Satan]...καὶ σοὶ κεράσαι τὸ πρῶτον αἴτιον τῶν κακῶν Bas.*renunt*.6(2.207E; M.31. 640A); **b.** any liquids τὸ ὕδωρ...κραθήσεσθαι τῷ αἵματι Thdt.*Is*.15:8 (p.76.16; 2.275); **c.** eucharistic ὡσαύτως καὶ τὸ ποτήριον κεράσας, ἔδωκε τοῖς μαθηταῖς Thdt.*Ps*.109:4(1.1396); ‡Bas.*h.myst*.63(p.397. 28); in preparation for eucharist προθέντων ἄρτον νεόπτητον, καὶ οἶνον ἐν ξυλοποτηρίῳ κερασάντων Leont.H.*monoph*.(M.86.1900B); liturg., *Lit*.ap.*Const.App*.8.12.37; cf.Hipp.*trad.ap*.23.1; *Lit.Jac*. (p.202.13); **2.** *mingle, blend* notes in harmony, Ath.*gent*.38(M.25. 77A); light, Eudoc.*Cypr*.2.202(M.85.853A); κραθεῖσα [sc. ἡ ἡμέτερα γνώμη] ταῖς ἀρεταῖς, καὶ ἑαυτῇ ταύτας κεράσασα Max.*ambig*.(M.91. 1136B); moral qualities ἀσεβείας, ἥν, μετὰ...ἀφροσύνης ἑαυτοῖς κεράσαντες Ath.*Ar*.2.25(M.26.200B); **3.** *compound* elements, *Hom. Clem*.6.25; *ib*.19.9; τοῦ πονηροῦ ἡ...οὐσία...ὑπὸ τοῦ θεοῦ προεβλήθη, ἔξω δὲ αὐτῆς...ἐκράθη πρὸς τὴν κρᾶσιν ἡ κακοῖς χαιροῦσα προαίρεσις *ib*.20.8; τὰ ἐναντία τῇ φύσει συνημμένα...πῦρ ψυχρῷ, καὶ ξηρὸν ὑγρῷ κεκραμένον Ath.*gent*.36(M.25.72B); **4.** of close physical contact, pass., *be joined* (ref. Lc.24:39) αὐτοῦ ἥψαντο, καὶ ἐπίστευσαν κραθέντες τῇ σαρκὶ αὐτοῦ καὶ τῷ αἵματι Ign.*Smyrn*.3.2; met. (s.v.l.), Clem.*exc.Thdot*.32(p.117.19, v.l. ἐκρατήθη M.9.676A); *join, add, unite* πόθος...κατὰ προκοπὴν πίστεως ἅμα ζητήσει κραθεὶς συνίσταται id.*str*.7.11(p.44.5; M.9.485A); πίστιν ἐλπίδι κεράσας *ib*.7.13(p.59.6; 516A); **5.** *temper, mitigate* ὡς κερασθῆναι τὴν τιμωρίαν Chrys.*ep*.3.14 (3.570A); Thdt.*provid*.1(4.482); *ib*.5(4.562); ἡ σελήνη...τῆς νυκτὸς τὸ ζοφῶδες κεράννυσι id.*affect*.3(p.70.11; 4.761); **6.** Christol.; ref. union of two natures; **a.** in gen. σχηματισάμενος αὐτὸν [sc. man] ὁ κύριος, θεότητι ἐκέρασεν Meth.*Porph*.1(p.50.4; M.18.400D); id.*symp*.3.4(p.30. 22; M.18.68A) cit. s. ἄνθρωπος; Gr.Naz.*carm*.2.1.46.15(M.37.1379A) cit. s. σάρξ; εἷς...ὁ Χριστὸς ἔκ τε ἀνθρωπότητος καὶ θεοῦ λόγου κεκερασμένος, οὐκ ἐκ τοῦ τετράφθαι πρὸς ὅπερ οὐκ ἦν, ἀλλ' ἐκ τοῦ προσλαβεῖν τὸν ἐκ παρθένου ναόν Cyr.*thes*.20(5[1].197A) cf. 6.c infra; opp. συγχύω: ὁ αὐτὸς θεός, ὁ αὐτὸς ἄνθρωπος, ὁ μὴ σύγχυσιν ἀπεργασάμενος, ἀλλὰ τὰ δύο κεράσας εἰς ἕν Epiph.*anc*.80(p.100.26; M.43.168C); πῶς τὰ τοσοῦτον κατὰ τὴν φύσιν παρηλλαγμένα...ἀλλήλοις τε συνέβη, καὶ κραθέντα οὐ συγκέχυται; ἀλλὰ καὶ ἔστιν ἕν, καὶ γνωρίζεται δύο Leont.B.*Nest. et Eut*.1(M.86.1300A); Andr.Cr.*Agath*.96(M.97.1441D); **b.** used as parallel to συγκεράννυμι: τῶν συγκιρναμένων αἱ ποιότητες κεράννυνται καὶ οὐκ ἀπόλλυνται Apoll.*fr*.127(p.238.14)ap.Thdt.*eran*.2(4.170); ὁ κεκραμένος ἐκ σώματος καὶ θεότητος *ib*.11(p.207.26)ap.Leont.B.*Apoll*. (M.86.1961D); **c.** rejected as savouring of Apollinarianism οὐ κραθείς, ἀλλ' ἐν ἑκατέραις ταῖς οὐσίαις εἷς καὶ ὁ αὐτὸς φανείς Ambr.*fr*.ap. Thdt.*eran*.2(4.140) and *Doct.Patr*.7(p.50.19); Cyr.*hom.div*.21.1(p.539. 21,26; M.77.1113A).

κέρας, τό, 1. *horn*, a symbol esp. of power and glory εἴωθε...ἡ γραφὴ κ. τῆς βασιλείας ὀνομάζειν Eus.*Is*.5:1(M.24.116C); cf. ad loc. τουτέστιν, ἐν στερρᾷ καὶ τροφίμῃ †Bas.*Is*.140(1.477E; M.30.348B); ref. 1Reg.2:1 τί ποτ' οὖν λέγει κ.; τὴν δύναμιν, τὴν δόξαν, τὴν περιφάνειαν, ἀπὸ μεταφορᾶς τῶν ἀλόγων ζῴων αὐτὸ τιθείς Chrys.*Anna* 4.3 (4.733D); λαμβάνεται...τὸ κ. παρὰ τῇ θείᾳ γραφῇ εἰς ἰσχὺν καὶ εἰς δύναμιν, καὶ εἰς δόξαν τὴν βασιλικήν Cyr.*Is*.1.3(2.78E); id.*Zach*.10(3. 664C); κ. ἡ θεία γραφὴ ποτὲ μὲν καλεῖ τὴν εὐσέβειαν, ποτὲ δὲ τὴν δύναμιν, ποτὲ δὲ τὴν βασιλείαν Thdt.*Ezech*.29:21(2.927); ref. Apoc. 5:6 καὶ τὰ κ. τὸ φρουρητικὸν καὶ ἀκράτητον Dion.Ar.*c.h*.15.8(M.3. 337A); κ. τὴν δύναμιν σημαίνει καὶ τὴν δόξαν Areth.*Apoc*.12(M.106. 580D); whether of God τὸ κ. ὑπὸ τῆς γραφῆς ἀντὶ τῆς δόξης πολλαχοῦ παρειλημμένον ἐστὶν εὑρεῖν...ἢ...ἀντὶ δυνάμεως πολλάκις παραλαμβάνεται Bas.*hom.in Ps*.28(1.120D; M.29.297A); Thdt.*Abac*.3:4(2. 1551); of Christ τὸ...κ. ἰσχυρόν τι δηλοῖ καὶ μόνιμον id.*Ps*.131:17(1. 1511); of the just, Bas.*hom.in Ps*.28(120D; M.297A) cit. supra; Thdt.*Ps*.111:9(1.1406); *ib*.148:14(1581); or of the wicked ὅμοιον...τὸ [Ps.74:11]. λέγει δὲ νῦν τοὺς ἄρχοντας, ἐν οἷς ἡ τοῦ ἔθνους ἰσχὺς καθάπερ ἐν τοῖς κερασφόροις τῶν ζῴων, καὶ διότι τοῦ σώματος ἐξέχει καθὰ τῶν ὑπηκόων οἱ ἄρχοντες...δηλοῖ δὲ καὶ τὴν ὑπεροψίαν τοῦ ἡγεμονικοῦ τὸ κ. Or.*fr.45 in Lam*.2:3(p.255.12ff.; M.13.632D); exeg. Ps.74:11 τὰ κ. τῶν ἁμαρτωλῶν, ἐπειδὴ ἐκ διαφόρων συλλεγέντες τῶν ἐθνῶν...κ. δὲ δικαίου τὸ εὐσεβὲς ἐκάλεσε φρόνημα Thdt.*Ps*.74:11(1. 1139); πάντα ὡς ἐπὶ προβάτων εἴρηκεν, ὤμους καὶ κ., καὶ πλευράς· διὰ πάντων δὲ τῶν ἐν δυνάμει τὴν ἄδικον δυναστείαν διήλεγξεν id.*Ezech*. 34:22(2.970); in gen. καὶ τοῦ τετάρτου βοὸς ἀνέβησαν τὰ κ. μέχρι τοῦ οὐρανοῦ καὶ ἐγένοντο ὡς τεῖχος τῶν ποιμνῶν *T.Jos*.19.6; τέσσαρα κ. οὐ...ἀνθρώπους λέγει, ἀλλ' ἐπειδὴ εἰς τέσσαρα πέρατα μεμερίσθαι τὴν οἰκουμένην φαμέν Thdr.Mops.*Zach*.1:18(M.66.516B); τὰ κερασφόρα ζῷα ὅπλον τὸ κ. παρὰ τῆς φύσεως ἔλαβον· ἡμεῖς δὲ κ. σωτηρίας, καὶ νικηφόρον ὅπλον, τὸ σὸν ἔχομεν ὄνομα Thdt.*Ps*.43:6(1.880); οὐχ οἷόν τε ἡμᾶς μὴ ἀλγεῖν, ὁρῶντας τῶν Ἰουδαίων τὸ κ. εἰς ὕψος αἰρόμενον, καὶ τοὺς Χριστιανοὺς ἐν ὀδυρμοῖς id.*ep*.79(4.1136); **2.** anything resembling a horn; **a.** of projections of the Cross, Just.*dial*.91.2(M.6.693A); of the transverse beam ὑψηλὸν δόρυ...κ. εἶχεν ἐγκάρσιον Eus.*v.C*.1.31 (p.21.32; M.20.945A); *ib*.(p.22.6; 945B); hence **b.** of Cross itself τὸ 'κατεχόμενος' τῶν κ. ὁ Σύρος καὶ ὁ Ἑβραῖος 'κρεμάμενός' φησιν, ὡς σαφέστερον τυποῦν τὸν σταυρόν †Mel.*fr*.12(p.313; M.5.1220); τὸ ξύλον ...τὸ κ. τὸ ποθούμενον *Orac.Sib*.8.245; τὸ κ. τοῦ σταυροῦ ὅπλον κατὰ παθῶν καὶ δαιμόνων Thdt.*Ps*.91:11(1.1267); *ib*.88:18(1236); **c.** plur., *extremities of the earth*, so, of four quarters of the wind κ. τῶν ἀνέμων *A.Andr.et Mt*.4(p.69.8); **3.** plur., acc. Theodoret, ad loc. (2.901), *objects of ebony* in Ezech.27:15(SM), but this appears to be a confusion: SM's ἐβένους must translate הבנים, not קרנות, i.e. sense 1.

κερασβόλος, of hard seed commonly believed to have struck the horn of the ox in ploughing which subsequently will not soften (cf. Theophrastus *De Causis Plantarum* 4.12.13); hence, of human seed, *unproductive, wasted*, Clem.*paed*.2.10(p.212.17; M.8.505B).

κέρασμα, τό, 1. *mixture, potion*, met. τὸ τρισφάρμακον κ. [i.e. κενοδοξία, ὑπερηφανία, φθόνος] τῶν παθῶν †Nil.*vit*.4(M.79.1144C); **2.** *drink poured out* πορφύρεον τὸ κ. ἐποίει φαίνεσθαι Hipp.*haer*.6.39 (p.171.2; M.16.3258A); *ib*.6.40(p.172.7; 3259A); Thdr.Mops.*Ps*.74:8 (M.66.696C); eucharistic πίστις...δὲ προῆγεν...καὶ τοῦτον [sc. Χριστόν] ἐπέδωκε φίλοις ἐσθίειν διὰ παντός, οἶνον χρηστὸν ἔχουσα κ. διδοῦσα μετ' ἄρτου Aberc.*epitaph*.16.

***κεράσσω**, *butt with the horns*, Gr.Naz.*or*.4.94(M.35.628A).

κεραστής, ὁ, *one who mixes*; of a servant who prepares drinks, Gr.Naz.*carm*.1.2.8.147(M.37.659A); met., of God as creator, *ib*.1.1. 4.14(416A).

κερασφορέω, *have horns*, Cyr.*hom.pasch*.5(5[2].51C).

[*]**κεραταία, ἡ, 1.** = κερατέα; **2.** = κεραία, *yard-arm*, *M.Areth*. (p.56, v.l. κερατάρια).

κερατέα (κεραταία), ἡ, *carob-tree*, Thdr.Lect.*h.e*.2.2(M.86.1884B); Cyr.S.*v.Sab*.35(p.120.26); -αία Alex.Sal.*Barn*.40(p.450E).

κερατίζ-ω, 1. *butt with the horns*, Ath.*v.Anton*.9(M.26.857A); †Bas. Anc.*virg*.64(M.30.800B); Gr.Nyss.*res*.5(M.46.685C); met., *repulse* ἀοράτους καὶ ἀντικειμένας δυνάμεις ὠθούμενος καὶ ~ων Eus.*d.e*.6.15 (p.271.31; M.22.448A); τὸ ὑπὸ τοῦ...Δαβὶδ εἰρημένον· 'ἐν σοὶ τοὺς ἐχθροὺς ἡμῶν κερατιοῦμεν' Thdt.*Abac*.3:4(2.1551); **2.** *gore, toss*, *M.Perp*.20(p.91.22); met., *wound deeply*, ref. Dt.33:17 κερατισθέντες ..., τουτέστι κατανυγέντες Just.*dial*.91.3(M.6.693A).

κεράτινος, *made of horn*, fem. (sc. σάλπιγξ) *horn, trumpet*, *Const. App*.2.6.10; ‡Chrys.*ador*.2(11.825C).

κεράτιον, τό, *carat*, a small coin ἐγὼ καταλύω ἐκ τοῦ ἐργοχείρου μου δύο κ. καθ' ἡμέραν *Apophth.Patr*.(M.65.368C); ἐν κ. ... τὰ κδ' κ., ὅ ἐστιν νόμισμα Jo.Mosch.*prat*.184(M.87.3057B); τοὺς αἰχμαλώτους...Χαγάνος τῷ βασιλεῖ ἐδίδου λύτρον...κατὰ ψυχῆς νόμισμα αἰτήσας...τοῦ δὲ μηδὲ τέσσαρα κ. λαβεῖν τοὺς αἰχμαλώτους ἀπολογησαμένου...Χαγάνος πάντας ἀπέκτεινεν *Chron.Pasch*.p.379(M.92.972A).

κερατιστής, ὁ, *one that has horns*; as adj., *horned*; of cattle, Just.*dial*.103.1(M.6.716B); Or.*sel.in Gen*.9:4–5(M.12.108B); †Bas. Anc.*virg*.63(M.30.797C,D).

***κέρατον, τό,** *horn*, Gr.Mag.*dial*.(tr.Zach.)2.30(M.*PL*.66.187A).

κερατοποιέω, *make* hard *like horn*, Chrys.*stat*.2.8(2.32B).

κερατόω, = κερατίζω, *gore*, met. τὴν...ἀντικειμένην θεῷ πᾶσαν ἐκεράτωσε [sc. Christ] δύναμιν Diod.*Ps*.88:25(M.33.1621D).

κεραυνίτης, ὁ, kind of precious stone, perh. *bloodstone*, Clem. *paed*.2.12(p.227.25; M.8.540B).

κεραυνοβολ-έω, *strike with a thunderbolt* ἵνα μὴ...τοὺς ἁμαρτάνοντας...~ῶσιν ‡Chrys.*Petr.et El*.1(2.732C); pass., Epiph.*haer*.80.2 (p.486.10; M.42.760A).

***κεραυνοβόλησις, ἡ,** *hurling of thunderbolts*, *A.Mt*.14(p.233.6).

κεραυνοβόλος, *hurling the thunder*, title of Roman twelfth legion, attributed to miracle of thunderstorm by Claud., Eus.*h.e*. 5.5.4(M.20.441C); cf. Lat. title of legion, *fulminata* (κεραυνόβολος).

***κεραψία, ἡ,** v. *κηραφία.

κεράω, metr. gr. for κεράννυμι: ἐκέρων ἐξ ὕδατος οἶνον Gr.Naz. *carm*.1.1.23.3(M. 37.494A).

κερβικάριον ([*]**κερβηκάριον**), **τό,** (Lat. *cervicarium*) *pillow, cushion*, Herm.*vis*.3.1.4; *Apophth.Patr*.(M.65.356A); κερβηκάριον Dor.*doct*.3.3(M.88.1656D).

***κερβούκολος, ὁ,** (cf. Lat. *cervulus*) plur., pagan New Year games, forbidden to Christians παιγνίοις δαιμόνων κ ὶ κερβουκόλοις Nil.*epp*.3.252(M.79.506B).

κερδαίν-ω, *gain* κερδήσας εἰς θεὸν μὴ ἁμαρτάνειν *Hom.Clem.*2.40; τοῦτο...∼οντες, ὅτι ἡμᾶς πλεῖον πιστεύειν τῇ γραφῇ παρασκευάζουσι Marc.Er.*opusc.*7.8(M.65.1084A); with personal object κ. τὸν ἀκροατήν Or.*schol.in Cant.*4:3(M.17.269D); Gr.Naz.*or.*2.51(M.35.461A); ἵνα κερδήσῃ αὐτοὺς μὴ ἐναντία δοξάζειν Didym.*Job* 13:16(M.39.1149C).

***κερδαντήρ, ὁ,** *one out for gain, Orac.Sib.*7.136.

κερδέμπορος, *trafficking in gain*, Chrys.ap.Jo.D.*parall.*(M.95.1512A).

***κερδόμισθον, τό,** *reward, recompense*, Thdr.Stud.*or.*11.12(M.99.813D).

κέρδος, τό, moral and spiritual *benefit, advantage* συμφερόντως... τοῦτο ποιεῖ καὶ ἐπὶ κέρδει τῶν πειραζομένων Chrys.*paralyt.*2(3.34E); τὸν...μὴ ὑπακούοντα...τὸ κ. ὃ ἀπέβαλεν ἐκεῖνος, σὺ περιποίησαι σεαυτῷ Marc.Er.*opusc.*2.200(M.65.961B); ref. God ἀμέτρῳ...φιλανθρωπίᾳ χρώμενος, οἰκεῖον ἡγεῖται κ. τὴν τῶν ἀνθρώπων ζωήν Thdt.*Ps.*97:1(1.1301); of death (cf. Phil.1:21) βίου τὸ κ., ἐκβιοῦν καθ' ἡμέραν Gr.Naz.*carm.*1.2.30.2(M.37.909A); Χριστὸς ἦν τὸ ζῆν ἀμφοτέροις, καὶ ὁμοίως ἑκατέρῳ κ. ὁ θάνατος Gr.Nyss.*laud.Bas.*12(M.46.801A); *merits* τέθεικε δὲ αὐτὸ...ὑπερβολικῶς δεῖξαι βουλόμενος τῆς ἀγάπης τὸ κ. Thdt.*1Cor.*13:1(3.251); plur., of rewards ἵν' αὐτὸς μὲν τῆς ἀγαθῆς ἀπολαύσῃ παραψυχῆς, ἀντιδῷ δὲ αὐτοῖς τὰ ἐπουράνια καὶ μόνιμα κ. id.*ep.*52(4.1110).

***Κερδωνιανοί, οἱ,** followers of a dualistic heresy initiated by Cerdon *K.* οἱ ἀπὸ Κέρδωνος ⟨τοῦ⟩ ἀπὸ Ἡρακλέωνος διαδεξαμένου τὴν μετοχὴν τῆς πλάνης, προσθέντος δὲ τῇ ἀπάτῃ Epiph.*anac.*41(p.2.20; M.41.580C); Κολοβασίων, Κ., καὶ τῶν ἄλλων id.*ep.Arab.*ap.*haer.*78.3 (p.453.22; M.42.701D); described, *ib.*41(p.90ff.; M.41.692f.) cf.Iren.*haer.*1.27.1(M.7.687Bf.).

κερδῷος, *foxy*, i.e. *wily*, Gr.Naz.*carm.*2.1.17.32(M.37.1264A).

[*]**κερείη, ἡ,** = κειρία, Nonn.*par.Jo.*11:44(M.43.848A bis).

***κέριον (*κέρειον), τό,** ? = καίριον, *main point* αὐτὸ τῆς ὀρθῆς πίστεως τὸ κ. Didym.*Trin.*1.19(M.39.364A); οἱ εὐαγγελισταὶ ἐν πᾶσι μὲν τοῖς ἀναγκαίοις ὁμοφώνησαν...καὶ ἁπλῶς εἰς πάντα τὰ κέρεια Dam.*troph.*3.10(p.258.12).

***κερκέσιον (*κερκήσιον), τό,** *circus*, at Rome, *Chron.Pasch.*p.110 (M.92.292B); κερκή- *ib.*p.319(812B).

κερκίδιον, τό, *shuttle*, Jo.Mosch.*prat.*60(M.87.2913B).

κέρκιος, ὁ, (Lat. *circius*) a violent wind blowing (to the Romans) from west-north-west, Jo.D.*f.o.*2.8(M.96.900D).

κερκίς, ἡ, 1. *shuttle*, met. κ. ... ὁ λόγος, οἱ δὲ ἐργαζόμενοι πατριάρχαι τε καὶ προφῆται οἱ τὸν...ποδήρη...χιτῶνα ὑφαίνοντες Χριστοῦ, δι' ὧν ὁ λόγος διϊκνούμενος κερκίδος δίκην ἐξυφαίνει...ταῦθ' ἅπερ βούλεται ὁ πατήρ Hipp.*antichr.*4(p.7.6ff.; M.10.732Bf.); **2.** *backbone*; of a fish, id.*haer.*5.9(p.102.1; M.16.3158C); *ib.*5.17(p.115.21; 3178B).

***κερκώπειος**, *befitting a* κέρκωψ, *cunning* τὰ ἀμφότερα μέρη...κ. λόγοις πρὸς ἑαυτοῦ φιλίαν κατασκευάζων [sc. Κάλλιστος] Hipp.*haer.*9.11(p.245.18; M.16.3378C); Synes.*provid.*15(p.97.20; M.66.1245C).

κερματίζ-ω, 1. *cut into pieces*; met., *dissect*, by severing νοῦς from ψυχή of Christ, ref. Apollinarians, Gr.Nyss.*Apoll.*30(M.45.1189D); **2.** med., *collect coppers*, ref. Montanists τοὺς λεγομένους...προφήτας καὶ μάρτυρας μὴ μόνον παρὰ πλουσίων, ἀλλὰ καὶ παρὰ πτωχῶν καὶ ὀρφανῶν καὶ χηρῶν ∼ομένους Apollon.ap.Eus.*h.e.*5.18.7(M.20.477C).

κερματιστής, ὁ, *money-changer*, Or.*Jo.*10.3(2; p.173.3; M.14.309C); ‡Caes.Naz.*dial.*109(M.38.984).

***κερμοδότης, ὁ,** *money-changer*, as adj. κ. χορόν Nonn.*par.Jo.* 2:14(M.43.764A).

κερνοφορέω, *carry the* κέρνος (sacrificial dish) *in the dance*, in formulae of Phrygian mysteries, Clem.*prot.*2(p.13.12; M.8.76B).

***κερνόω**, variant of κιρνάω, *mix* wine and water; *serve* or *pour* it *out*, *Mir.Geo.*5(p.59.2).

***κερόχρυσος**, *with gilded horns, golden-horned, Orac.Sib.*5.355.

***κευθμωνοχαρής**, *delighting in the nether world*, Synes.*hymn.*4.46 (p.28; M.66.1604).

***κεφαλαιογράφιον, τό,** *epitome*, Justn.*ep.Thdr.Mops.*(p.60.28; M.86.1073C).

κεφάλαιος, A. ? *having a head, headed* εἰ...μήτε ξύλον ἐπάγῃ κατὰ τῆς γῆς, μήτε τις ἧλος ὠξύνθη κ. Mac.Mgn.*apocr.*3.8(p.66.11); or perh. as B.

B. *principal, chief* ἀνῆλθον πρὸς αὐτὸν κ. τε τῶν κληρικῶν καὶ οἱ μεγιστᾶνες τῆς πόλεως Jo.Not.*v.Eus.*1(M.86.300D); neut. as subst., etym. κ. ... λέγεται...ἀπὸ τοῦ καὶ τὴν κεφαλὴν ἡμῶν ἅπαντα ἔχειν ἐν αὐτῇ καὶ τὰ ὅλα ἡμῶν τῆς ζωῆς αἰσθητήρια ὡς ἐν κ. Or.*comm.in Eph.* 1:10(p.241).

C. as subst., *head*; hence **1.** *poll-tax* τούτων ἕκαστος προσθήκῃ κεφαλαίων δέκα Const.ap.Gel.Cyz.*h.e.*3.19.39 (κεφαλῶν M.85.1353D); **2.** of persons, *author, source* αὐτὸ τὸ κ. τῆς ἁπάντων ἡμῶν σωτηρίας, τὸν υἱόν Eus.*e.th.*1.7(p.65.26; M.24.836C); τὸ...κ. τῆς τῶν γενητῶν ἁπάντων...συστάσεώς τε καὶ σωτηρίας αὐτὸς ἦν *ib.*3.2(p.142.5; 976D); of Father ἀπ' αὐτοῦ...τοῦ κ. τῶν χαρισμάτων Gr.Nyss.*tres dii*(M.45.125D); **3.** *chief* or *main point, culmination*; **a.** of faith or salvation εἴ τις δοκῶν πιστεύειν εἰς τὸν Ἰησοῦν μὴ πιστεύοι ὅτι εἷς ἐστιν ὁ θεὸς ὁ νόμου καὶ εὐαγγελίου...οὗτος ἂν μεγίστῳ λείποι τῆς πίστεως κ. Or.*Jo.*32.16(9; p.452.2; M.14.784A); τὸ τέλος τῆς [sc. τοῦ Χριστοῦ] ἐν σώματι διαγωγῆς...τὸ κ. τῆς πίστεως ἡμῶν ἐστι τοῦτο Ath.*inc.*19.4 (M.25.129C); [Mt.6:9] τὸ κ. ... τῆς πίστεως ἡμῶν εἰς τοῦτο συντείνειν ἠθέλησεν id.*decr.*31(p.27.22; M.25.473C) = id.*Ar.*1.34(M.26.81C); τὸ ...κ. πάσης τῆς πίστεως...ἵνα τριὰς ἀεὶ φυλάττηται, καθὼς...[Mt. 28:19] *Symb.Sirm.*2 ap.Ath.*syn.*28(p.257.22; M.26.744A); κ. ... τῆς σωτηρίας ἡμῶν ἡ τοῦ λόγου σάρκωσις Apoll.*fid.sec.pt.*11(p.170.28; M.10.1109A); Didym.(‡Bas.)*Eun.*5(1.304D; M.29.729D); τὸ τῆς σωτηρίας κ., τοῦ κυρίου καὶ σωτῆρος ἡμῶν ἡ κατὰ σάρκα γέννησις Thdt.*Jer.* 31:15(2.545); **b.** of providence ἀνάστασις, τῆς τοῦ κυρίου προνοίας τὸ κ. ‡Nil.*fr.pasch.*2(M.79.1493D); **c.** of sacraments τὸ...τέλος ἁπάσης καὶ τὸ κ. ἡ τῶν θεαρχικῶν μυστηρίων τῷ τελουμένῳ μετάδοσις Dion.Ar.*e.h.*3.1(M.3.425A); *ib.*6.3.5(536C); **4.** abstract, *supremacy* ἡ...ἐπὶ τῆς κεφαλῆς ἶρις τὸ κ. ὑπογράφει τῆς ἀγγελιώτιδος τάξεως Areth.*Apoc.*28(M.106.636C); **5.** of money, *capital* opp. interest, met. μὴ ἀπαιτήσῃς με...τῆς ψυχῆς τὸ κ. καὶ τῆς σαρκὸς τὸν τόκον ‡Chrys.*meretr.*1.2(8.52D); ὁ θεὸς τοῖς μὲν ἁμαρτωλοῖς καὶ τὸ κ. παραχωρεῖ μετανοοῦσιν *Apophth.Patr.*(M.65.165C).

D. as subst., *topic, subject*; **1.** *matter* τοῦ...γεγονότος κ. Gr.Mag.*dial.*(tr.Zach.)2.22(M.*PL.*66.175C); **2.** *point* in an accusation ἐάν τις ἐπὶ πολλοῖς ἐγκλήμασιν κληρικοῦ κατηγορήσας μὴ ἀποδείξῃ τὸ προτεθὲν πρῶτον κ. Phot.*nomoc.*9.3(p.543; M.104.1101A); ὑπὲρ τῶν κ. [= Lat. *causa*] *on behalf of* συνηγόρων ἀντίληψις ὑπὲρ τῶν κ. τῆς ἐκκλησίας *Cod.Afr.*97 tit.; **3.** *proposition, article* τὰ κ. ὑπὸ σοῦ συντεθεῖσθαι Epiph.*haer.*76.16(p.362.19; M.42.549A); *ib.*76.18 tit. (p.363.5; 549B); Justn.*conf.anath.*12(p.94.16; M.86.1017D); id.*ep.Thdr.Mops.*(p.47.31ff.; M.86.1045A); of a *summa* of theology, Dion.Ar.*d.n.*3.2(M.3.681A); **4.** *section* of a written work; **a.** *chapter* or larger section, Hipp.*haer.*9.10(p.244.2; M.16.3375C); οἱ δὲ λοιποὶ [sc. τῶν προφητῶν] οὐχ ἑαυτοῖς συνέγραφον, ἀλλὰ γραμματεῖς ἦσαν ἐν τῷ ἱερῷ, οἳ ἔγραφον...ὡς ἐπὶ ἡμερολογίου λόγον...εἰ ἐκήρυξεν περὶ ἑτέρου πράγματος...πάλιν ἔγραφον...ὡς ἀρχὴν κεφαλαίου ποιούμενοι...ὅθεν ἐστὶν εὑρεῖν ἐν ταῖς αὐτῶν βίβλοις κ. ἁρμόζον εἰς τὴν αἰχμαλωσίαν Βαβυλῶνος κτλ. Cosm.Ind.*top.*5(M.88.276B); Didym.*Trin.*3.36(M.39.965C); *ib.*3.16(868C); Thdt.*Rom.*5:21(3.60); ἐνταῦθα τὸ πρῶτον κ. πεπλήρωκεν ὁ ἀπόστολος id.*1Cor.*6:20(3.199); **b.** a single division of a chapter, Max.*schol.e.h.*3.2(M.4.137A); **c.** a sentence or two, *passage*, esp. of scripture, Clem.*str.*1.21(p.91.18; M.8.889A); Or.*hom.12.7 in Jer.*(p.93.17; M.13.388B); Eus.*d.e.*5.30(p.249.4; M.22.409D); **d.** *division* of text, *short paragraph*, ref. gospels so arranged by Ammonius Alexandrinus, Eus.*ep.Carp.*(M.22.1276C); *ib.*(1277B); of the four gospels, 1162 in number, Epiph.*anc.*50(p.60.3; M.43.105A) ∞ ‡Caes.Naz.*dial.*39(M.38.905); 40 of Acts ἀναγνώσεις εἰσὶν ις', κεφάλαια μ' Euthal.Diac.*Ac.*(M.85.636B); ἐγχειροῦμεν...τῇ δὲ τῶν κ. ἐκθέσει *ib.*(652B); id.*epp.Paul.*(M.85.716A) cit. s. ἀνακεφαλαίωσις; Apocalypse divided into 72 by Andrew of Caesarea, Areth.*Apoc.*proem.(M.106.493A); **5.** of persons, *generation* εἴκοσι δύο κ. ἀπὸ Ἀδὰμ ἄχρι τοῦ Ἰακώβ Epiph.*mens.*22(M.43.277B).

κεφαλαι-όω, *sum up*; hence pass., *amount to*; *be multiplied* πέντε ...δωδεκάκις ∼ούμενος τὸ πλήρωμα ποιεῖ τῶν ἑξήκοντα Gr.Nyss.*hom.6 in Cant.*(M.44.904A).

κεφαλαιώδης ([*]**κεφαλεώδης**), **1.** *principal* τὸ μυστήριον τῆς θείας ἐνανθρωπήσεως τὸ κεφαλεωδέστερον Leont.H.*Nest.*1.12(M.86.1449A); **2.** *punishable by death* or *by loss of civil rights, capital* ἔκλεψε κ. κλέμματα †Jo.Jej.*poenit.*(M.88.1909C).

κεφαλαιωτής, ὁ, *chieftain, leader*; of heads of seventy-two nations descended from Noah's sons, Epiph.*haer.*2(p.175.17; M.41.184A); *ib.*39.8(p.77.31; 673B).

***κεφαλαιωτός**, = foreg. ἔχοντες συνεργὸν...τὸν τοῦδε τοῦ δράματος κ. διάβολον Geo.Al.*v.Chrys.*28(p.194.43).

κεφαλαλγέω, *suffer from headache*; med., Thphn.*chron.*p.199(M.108.513B).

***κεφαλάλγημα, τό,** *headache*, *cat.Ps.*72:5(2 p.485).

κεφαλαλγία, ἡ, *headache*, Isid.Pel.*epp.*2.240(M.78.680C); rejected as explanation of S. Paul's 'thorn in the flesh', Chrys.*hom.26.2 in 2Cor.*(10.620Df.).

***κεφαλεύ-ω**, *be at the head of, rule* ∼σαι ἀδελφότητα *Apophth.Patr.al.*(M.34.236B) ∞ ∼σαι ἀδελφότητος *Schol.*5 in Jo.Clim.*scal.*23(M.88 972D).

[*]**κεφαλεώδης**, v. *κεφαλαιώδης*.

κεφαλή, ἡ, *head*;

I. of men or animals;

A. with preps. *κατὰ κεφαλῆς* and *ἐπὶ κεφαλῆς*; **1.** *upside down, head downwards, on one's head εἰμι κρεμάμενος κατὰ κ. A.Phil.*140 (p.74.16); *ἐπὶ κ. ἐκρέμασάν με ib.*132(p.62.8,20); ref. rebaptism by Eunomians, Epiph.*haer.*76.54(p.414.8; M.42.637C) cit. s. *ἀναβαπτίζω*; id.*anac.*76(p.232.9; M.42.337C); *κατὰ κ. περιπατούντων* Chrys.*hom. 5.4 in Jo.*(8.41C); **2.** *head to the ground*, i.e. grovelling on all fours opp. man's normal upright position *τὸν...τύπον φέρω τοῦ πρώτου ἀνθρώπου κατὰ κ. ἐνεχθέντος ἐπὶ τῆς γῆς A.Phil.*140(p.74.5); *ἐπὶ κ. ib.*(p.74.25); *κατὰ κεφαλήν A.Petr.et Sim.*9(p.94.6, v.l. *κατὰ κεφαλῆς*).

B. its significance *κ., τὸ τῶν αἰσθήσεων ἐργαστήριον* Gr.Naz.*or.*40. 39(M.36.413C); *οἱ...τὸν ἐγκέφαλον ἀφιεροῦντες τῷ λογισμῷ. ὥσπερ ἀκρόπολίν τινα τοῦ παντὸς σώματος τὴν κ. δεδομῆσθαι...λέγουσιν* Gr. Nyss.*hom.opif.*12.1(M.44.156D); *οὐ τῷ τόπῳ τοσοῦτον ὑπερέχει τοῦ λοιποῦ σώματος ὅσον τῇ προνοίᾳ, καθάπερ τις κυβερνήτης, ἅπαν αὐτὸ εὐθύνουσα, ἐν γὰρ τῇ κ. καὶ οἱ τοῦ σώματος καὶ οἱ τῆς ψυχῆς ὀφθαλμοί* Chrys.*hom.5.5 in 2Thess.*(11.545D); *τὴν κ. ... ὥσπερ ἀκρόπολίν τινα τῆς τοῦ σώματος πόλεως ἐν ὕψει καθημένην, καὶ οἱόν τινα πλοῦτον...ἐν ἰσχυροτάτῳ φρουρίῳ φυλάττουσαν τὸν ἐγκέφαλον* Thdt.*provid.*3(4. 524).

C. *life*; **1.** in phrase *εἰς κίνδυνον* (or *κινδύνῳ*) *τῆς κ. at the risk of, in peril of one's life*, Const.ap.Ath.*apol.sec.*87(p.166.16; M.25.405B); Marc.Diac.*v.Porph.*27; **2.** of capital punishment *τούτῳ θάνατος ἔσται ζημία. παραχρῆμα γὰρ ἁλοὺς ἐπὶ τούτῳ κεφαλῆς ὑποστήσεται τιμωρίαν* Const.ap.Gel.Cyz.*h.e.*2.36.2 cf. *κεφαλικὴν* Socr.*h.e.*1.9.31(M.67.89A); *ὥστε, εἰ εὑρεθείημεν, κεφαλῆς ὑποστῆναι τιμωρίαν* Ath.*apol.fug.*3 (p.70.9; M.25.648C); of punishment in gen., as literal translation of ܦܪܥܝܢ ܒܪܫܢ *τιμωρίαν ἀποτίσομεν τῆς ἑαυτῶν κ. A.Thom.*A 66 (p.184.10); *ib.*101(p.214.12); cf.*ib.*76(p.191.1) prob. due to misreading of ܪܫܢܐ (F. C. Burkitt, *JTS* 1 pp.283ff.).

II. met.;

A. of things; **1.** main *dish*; *plateful, helping* of food, Pach. *reg.*B 35(p.173.18; M.40.948B); **2.** ? a child's toy *καθάπερ τρόχους καὶ ἀστραγάλους καὶ κ. καὶ σφαίρας, οὕτω ταῦτα...ἡγεῖται εἶναι εὐκαταφρόνητα* Chrys.*hom.47.4 in Mt.*(7.492E); **3.** *main thoroughfare ἦν... ἡ ὁδὸς κ. μία Ep.*ap.CEph.(431)(*ACO* 1.1.2 p.66.6; H.1.1588B).

B. of persons; **1.** *head* of the house, Herm.*sim.*7.3; **2.** *chief, headman*, Thphn.*chron.*p.343(M.108.828A); **3.** religious *superior μηδεὶς χωρὶς τῆς κ. καλέσῃ τοὺς ἀδελφοὺς εἰς τὴν σύναξιν* Pach.*reg.*A 11 (p.172.15); *μηδεὶς ἑαυτῷ κτήσηται μηδέν, χωρὶς τῶν διδομένων παρὰ τῆς κ. ib.*B 81(p.178.10; M.40.952A); **4.** of bishops *κεφαλαὶ...ἐκκλησιῶν* Ath.*apol.sec.*89(p.167.16; M.25.409A); *τοῦ...ἐπισκόπου τῆς Ῥωμαίων πόλεως κ. ὑπάρχοντος πασῶν τῶν ἐκκλησιῶν* CChalc.*act.*1 (*ACO* 2.1.1 p.65.19; H.2.68A); *κατὰ τὴν ὑμετέραν ἀποστολικὴν προεδρίαν...κεφαλὴν τῆς κατὰ Χριστὸν ἱερωσύνης κανονικῶς ὑμᾶς λογιζόμενοι* Jo.VI CP *ep.*(M.96.1417A); **5.** *κ. εἶναι* c. genit., *take precedence* of *ὅταν εἰσέλθῃς οἰκῆσαι μετὰ ἀδελφοῦ ὡς πάροικος...μὴ θελήσῃς αὐτοῦ κ. εἶναι* Esaias *or.*3(p.10; cf.M.40.1110B).

C. of Christ; **1.** as head of creation *γίνεται κ. τῶν ὅλων μετὰ τὸν πατέρα* Clem.*exc.Thdot.*43(p.120.12; M.9.680B); *Symb.Sirm.*1 *anath.* 26 ap.Ath.*syn.*27(M.26.740B), Cyr.*Arcad.*(p.76.20ff.; 5^2.63E) citt. s. 4; Oecum.*Eph.*1:22(p.448.10ff.); and of the new creation, v. 4 infra; **2.** as head of Church *τῆς κ. τοῦ ὅλου τῶν σωζομένων σώματος, Χριστοῦ Ἰησοῦ* Or.*Jo.*1.13(14; p.18.11; M.14.45D); *τότε...αὐτὸς ὑποταγήσεται ἀνθ' ἡμῶν τῷ πατρί, ὡς κ. ὑπὲρ τῶν ἰδίων μελῶν* Ath.*inc. et c.Ar.*20(M.26.1020C); [1Cor.12:27] *κρατούσης δηλονότι καὶ συναπτούσης ἕκαστον τῷ ἄλλῳ πρὸς ὁμόνοιαν τῆς μιᾶς καὶ μόνης ἀληθῶς κ. ἥτις ἐστὶν ὁ Χριστός* Bas.*jud.*3(2.216B; M.31.660A); *εἷς Χριστός, μία κ. τῆς ἐκκλησίας* Gr.Naz.*or.*37.8(M.36.292B); *ib.*40.39(413C); *υἱὸν καὶ εἰκόνα τοῦ θεοῦ, καὶ οὕτω πρωτότοκον καὶ κ. τοῦ σώματος τῆς ἐκκλησίας* Didym.*Trin.*3.4(M.39.829C); *ἐνδυόμεθα τὸν Χριστὸν... μέλη γιγνόμεθα τῆς μακαρίας ἐκείνης κ.* Chrys.*sac.*3.5(p.56.1; 1.384A); Thdt.*Ps.*108:30(1.1390); *Χριστὸν ἐνταῦθα τὸ κοινὸν σῶμα τῆς ἐκκλησίας ἐκάλεσεν, ἐπειδὴ κ. τοῦδε τοῦ σώματός ἐστιν ὁ δεσπότης Χριστός* id.*1Cor.*12:12(3.246); id.*Eph.*1:23(3.409); Cosm.Ind.*top.*5(M.88. 304A); *ἡ...τῆς ἐκκλησίας κ. κατὰ τὴν ἐπίνοιαν τῆς ἀνθρωπότητός ἐστιν ὁ Χριστός* Max.*qu.Thal.*63(M.90.672B); relationship of body and head, v. *σῶμα*; **3.** exeg. 1Cor.11:3, *Symb.Sirm.*1 *anath.*26 ap. Ath.*syn.*27(M.26.740B); *ἄνδρα δὲ τὸν πιστὸν...ὀνομάζεσθαι (οὐ γὰρ δὴ καὶ τῶν ἀπίστων ἂν εἴη κ. ὁ Χριστός), πάντως ὁ τῆς σωζούσης πίστεως ἀποτμηθεὶς ἀκέφαλος ἂν εἴη...τῆς ἀληθινῆς κ. μεριζόμενος* Gr.Nyss.*Eun.*12(1 p.218.3ff.; M.45.912Aff.); *εἰ ἀνδρὸς κ. ὁ Χριστός, Χριστοῦ δὲ κ. ὁ θεός, ἄνθρωπος δὲ τῷ θεῷ Χριστῷ οὐχ ὁμοούσιος (οὐ γὰρ θεός), Χριστὸς δὲ θεῷ ὁμοούσιος (θεὸς γάρ), οὐκ ἄρα ὡς ἀνδρὸς κ. Χριστός, οὕτω θεὸς Χριστοῦ* Didym.*Eun.*4(1.291C; M.29. 700B); *εἰ...σῶμά ἐσμεν τοῦ Χριστοῦ καὶ μέλη ἐκ μέρους, καὶ ταύτῃ ἐκεῖνος ἡμῶν κ., τῶν οὐκ ὄντων ἐν τῷ σώματι...οὐκ ἂν εἴη κ.· ὥστε ὅταν εἴπῃ 'παντὸς' τοῦ πιστοῦ δεῖ προσυπακούειν...εἰ κ. γυναικὸς ὁ ἀνήρ, ὁμοούσιος δὲ ἡ κ. τῷ σώματι, κ. δὲ τοῦ Χριστοῦ ὁ θεός, ὁμοούσιος ὁ υἱὸς τῷ πατρί* Chrys.*hom.26.2 in 1Cor.*(10.229Aff.); *κ. ... ὧδε κατὰ τὸ ἀρχοντικὸν εἴρηται, οὐ κατὰ τὸ ποιητικόν...τῷ Χριστῷ ὑποτεταγμένοι τῷ...πατρὶ ὑποτετάγμεθα, ὅτι καὶ τοῦ Χριστοῦ κ. ὁ θεός* Sever.*1Cor.*11:3(p.260.20ff.); *κ. δὲ ἡμῶν ἐστιν, οὐ κατὰ τὴν θεότητα ἀλλὰ κατὰ ἀνθρωπότητα...τῷ δὲ σώματι ὁμόφυλον εἶναι προσήκει τὴν κ. κατὰ τὴν ἀνθρωπότητα τοίνυν ἡμῶν κ. οὐκοῦν καὶ κατὰ ταύτην αὐτοῦ κ. ὁ θεός...κ. δὲ αὐτοῦ ὡς πατὴρ καὶ αἴτιος ὀνομάζεται* Thdt.*1Cor.*11:3 (3.233); Oecum.*1Cor.*11:3(p.440.9); cf. *κ. μὲν ἡμῶν τῶν πιστῶν ἐστιν ὁ Χριστός, ὡς συσσώμων...αὐτῷ γεγεννημένων...δι' αὐτὸν γὰρ ἅπαντες ἓν σῶμα χρηματίσαντες κ. ἔχομεν αὐτόν. 'κ. δὲ τοῦ Χριστοῦ' ὁ... πατήρ, ὡς γεννήτωρ καὶ προβολεὺς καὶ ὁμοούσιος αὐτοῦ. κ. δὲ γυναικὸς ὁ ἀνήρ, ὅτι καὶ αὐτὸς γεννήτωρ αὐτῆς καὶ προβολεὺς καὶ ὁμοούσιος ὑπάρχει αὐτῇ* Phot.*1Cor.*11:3(p.567.1ff.); **4.** exeg. 1Cor.11:3 (cont.), as equivalent of *ἀρχή*: *κ. γάρ, ὅ ἐστιν ἀρχὴ πάντων, ὁ υἱός. 'κ. δὲ' ὅ ἐστιν ἀρχὴ 'τοῦ Χριστοῦ ὁ θεός', οὕτω γὰρ εἰς μίαν ἄναρχον τῶν ὅλων ἀρχὴν δι' υἱοῦ...τὰ πάντα ἀνάγομεν Symb.Sirm.*1 *anath.*26 ap. Ath.*syn.*27(M.26.740B); *ἀρχὴν τῷ ἀνθρώπῳ τιθεὶς* [i.e. S. Luke in his genealogy] *τὸν ποιήσαντα θεόν. οὕτως εἶναί φαμεν παντὸς ἀνδρὸς κ. τὸν Χριστόν· πεποίηται γὰρ δι' αὐτοῦ...θεϊκῶς. κ. δὲ γυναικὸς ὁ ἀνήρ, ὅτι ἐκ τῆς σαρκὸς αὐτοῦ ἐλήφθη...κ. δὲ ὁμοίως Χριστοῦ ὁ θεός, ὅτι ἐξ αὐτοῦ κατὰ φύσιν* Cyr.*Arcad.*(p.76.20ff.; 5^2.63E); esp. of the new creation *παθητοὶ μὲν γὰρ ὄντες κεφαλὴν ἡγούμεθα τὸν Ἀδὰμ ἐξ οὗπερ τὸ εἶναι εἰλήφαμεν, ἀπαθεῖς δὲ γενόμενοι κ. ἡγούμεθα τὸν Χριστὸν ἐξ οὗπερ ἀπαθεῖς εἶναι ἐσχήκαμεν. ὁμοίως δέ...καὶ ἀπὸ τῆς γυναικὸς ἐπὶ τὸν ἄνδρα, ἐπειδὴ ἀπ' ἐκείνου τὸ εἶναι εἴληφεν* Thdr.Mops. *1Cor.*11:3(p.187.12ff.; M.66.888C); *αὐτὸς μὲν ἡμῶν ἀρχή, τουτέστι κ., καθὸ πέφηνεν ἄνθρωπος, ἔχει γε μὴν κ. αὐτὸς ὡς φύσει θεὸς τὸν... πατέρα...ὅτι δὲ ἡ κ. σημαίνει τὴν ἀρχήν, ἐμπεδοῖ πρὸς ἀλήθειαν τῶν ἐνδοιαζόντων τὸν νοῦν τὸ κ. λέγεσθαι τὸν ἄνδρα τῆς γυναικός...εἰς οὖν ἄρα Χριστὸς...ὁ κεφαλὴν μὲν ἔχων ὡς θεὸς κατὰ φύσιν τὸν πατέρα, γεγονὼς δὲ ἡμῶν κ. διά τοι τὸ κατὰ σάρκα συγγενές* Cyr.*Pulch.*(p.28. 17ff.; 5^2.131D); *ὥσπερ κ. ἐστιν ὁ Ἀδὰμ πάντων τῶν ἀνθρώπων ἐν τούτῳ τῷ κόσμῳ, ὡς αἴτιος αὐτῶν ὧν καὶ πατὴρ οὕτω καὶ ὁ δεσπότης Χριστὸς κατὰ σάρκα τῆς ἐκκλησίας κ. καὶ πατὴρ τοῦ μέλλοντος αἰῶνος* Cosm.Ind.*top.*5(M.88.224Af.).

κεφαλικός, *capital*; of sentences and punishments, Eus.*h.e.*5.21.4 (M.20.488B); Ath.*h.Ar.*19(p.192.23; M.25.716A); Socr.*h.e.*7.22.11(M. 67.785C).

κεφαλίς, ἡ, **1.** *roll* forming [part of] a book, *book* in scroll form *τόμον καινόν, μέγαν, ἢ 'τεῦχος' ἢ 'διφθέρωμα', ἢ 'κ.' κατὰ τοὺς λοιπούς* Eus.*Is.*8:1(M.24.140D); *κεφαλίδα...καλεῖ τὰ εἱλητὰ βιβλία* Thdt.*Ezech.*3:1(2.699); *τὴν κ. εἴλημα εἰρήκασιν Ἀκύλας καὶ Σύμμαχος. οὕτω δὲ τὰς θείας γραφὰς μέχρι καὶ τήμερον Ἰουδαῖοι κατασκευάζειν εἰώθασι* id.*Ps.*39:8(1.860); *κ. τουτέστι τόμον Apophth. Patr.*(M.65.168B); of OT scriptures *πᾶσαν τὴν θεόπνευστον γραφήν, τὴν ἐπαγγέλλουσαν περὶ αὐτοῦ. πάντα δέ φησι μίαν κ. βιβλίου* Or.*Ps.* 39:8(p.36); id.*Jo.*5.6(4; p.103.20; M.14.192C); ref. Jer.43:4 *Ἱερεμίας ...προστάσσεται παρὰ κυρίου κ. βιβλίου λαβεῖν καὶ γράψαι Chron. Pasch.*p.123(M.92.317C); **2.** *headship, authority* over *καὶ τοσοῦτον ὅσον τῶν ἁπάντων εἰ ὑπερέχων τῇ κ. τῆς ἱερωσύνης* Thdr.Stud.*epp.*2.9 (M.99.1140C).

***κεφαλιτιόνα**, ἡ, *capitation tax*, Justn.*cod.*10.16.1(p.401).

***κεφαλιτιῶν**, ἡ, = foreg., Thphn.*chron.*p.407(M.108.969B).

κεφαλοδέσμιον, τό, *headband*; worn by women, *Protev.*2(p.5); Ath.*virg.*11(p.45.2; M.28.264B).

κεφαλόδεσμον, τό, = foreg., Chrys.*subintr.*9(1.242A); id.*Is.interp.* 3(6.44E).

***κεφαλοκλισία**, ἡ, *bowing of the head εὐχὴ τῆς κ. Lit.Bas.*(M.31. 1645C).

***κέφαλον**, τό, *ἐπὶ κέφαλα head downwards*, *Narr.Jo.Bapt.*(p.3).

κεφαλοτομέω, *behead*, Just.*dial.*110.4(M.6.729C).

[*]**κέφφος**, ὁ, = *κέπφος*, v. [*]*κέμφος*.

κεχαρισμένως, *gratuitously*, Eus.*d.e.*3.5(p.128.24; M.22.217C); Cyr. *Jo.*9(4.772A).

***κεχηνός**, τό, *aimlessness, ennui κ. καὶ ῥᾴθυμον τῆς διανοίας* Chrys.*hom.15.1 in 1Tim.*(11.635A).

***κεχρεωστημένως**, *deservedly, duly*, Cyr.*Jo.*6.1(4.595A).

κεχυμένως, *unrestrainedly κ. ἐγέλασαν* ‡Nil.*vit.cog.*(M.79.1448A); Ant.Mon.*hom.*18(M.89.1484C).

κεχωρισμένως, *separately, apart*; **1.** ref. place of women in church καθεζέσθωσαν...αἱ γυναῖκες κ. *Const.App.*2.57.4; **2.** Trin.; **a.** not applicable to Persons of Trin. in respect of deity ἐνέργεια... μία ἐστὶ...παρὰ...τῆς τριάδος κατορθουμένη, οὐ μὴν κατὰ τὸν ἀριθμὸν τῶν...προσώπων...ἢ τοῦ πατρὸς εἶναι μόνου, ἢ τοῦ μονογενοῦς ἰδιαζόντως, ἢ διὰ τοῦ ἁγίου πνεύματος κ. Gr.Nyss.*tres dii*(M.45.129A); οἱ ἀπονέμοντες [i.e. Eunomians] ὄνομα κ., τῷ μὲν πατρὶ τὸ 'θεός', τῷ δὲ υἱῷ τὸ 'κύριος' Didym.*Trin.*1.33(M.39.432C); Cyr.*thes.*6(5^1.49D) cit. s. διαστατῶς; **b.** but to Son as second Person *in distinction* (ref. Jo.8:42 and 14:10) ἐν πατρὶ καὶ ἐκ τοῦ πατρός, ἀδιαστάτως τε ἅμα καὶ κ. id.*Jo.*3.5(4.306E); **3.** Christol. οὐκ ἄν τις εἴποι μετὰ τὴν ἕνωσιν, τὸν μὲν κ. υἱὸν τὸν θεῖον λόγον, τὸν δὲ υἱὸν τὸν ἄνθρωπον· ἀλλ' ἕνα καὶ τὸν αὐτὸν ἑκάτερα νοήσει Thdt.*rect.conf.*12(M.6.1229C); cf. μετὰ τὴν ἀνάληψιν οὐ δύναται καλεῖσθαι κεχωρισμένος υἱός, ἵνα μὴ δύο υἱοὺς δογματίσωμεν Nest.*fr.*C 10(p.275.4)ap.Cyr.*Nest.*2.8(p.44.10; κ. 6^1.47E); in spite of this disavowal it was claimed as logical outcome of Nestorius' teaching, Cyr.*ib.*(p.44.35; 48E); οἱ δὲ Νεστοριανοὶ δύο υἱοὺς εἰσάγειν βουλόμενοι κ. λέγουσιν τὸν θεὸν λόγον καὶ κ. τὸν Χριστὸν ψιλὸν ἄνθρωπον Justn.*ep.Thdr.Mops.*(p.59.18f.; M.86.1071A); τοὺς ὑπὲρ φύσιν τρόπους καὶ τοὺς κατὰ φύσιν λόγους...ἔχων ἀλλήλοις συνημμένους...μηδετέρῳ τὸ παράπαν ὧν ὑπόστασις ᾖ θατέρου κ. ἐνεργῶν, δι' ἑκατέρου δὲ μᾶλλον πιστούμενος θάτερον...θεϊκῶς μὲν...τὸ πάσχειν ἔχων, ἑκούσιον γὰρ...ἀνθρωπικῶς δὲ τὸ θαυματουργεῖν, διὰ σαρκὸς γάρ Max.*ambig.*(M.91.1056A).

κηδεία, ἡ, *care for the dead, funeral*; not a cause of defilement as supposed, Chrys.*hom.36.1 in Jo.*(8.207B); of *burial* of Christ ἀνέστη μετὰ τὴν κ. ὁ Ἰησοῦς Clem.*paed.*1.5(p.104.4; M.8.277B); ἐλθὼν Ἰωσὴφ ὁ ἀπὸ Ἀριμαθίας, μαθητὴς ὢν...τῶν ἑβδομήκοντα ἴσως... νομίσαντες ἐσβέσθαι τὴν ὀργὴν τῷ σταυρῷ...τῆς κ. ἐπεμελοῦντο Chrys.*hom.85.3 in Jo.*(508C); μετὰ τὸν σταυρὸν δὲ πολλὴν τὴν ἐπιμέλειαν τῆς τοῦ δεσποτικοῦ σώματος φαίνεται κηδείας ποιούμενος id.ap.*cat.Jo.*3:1 (p.202.27); cf.id.*hom.24.1 in Jo.*(138C).

[*]**κηδεμον-έω,** *care for*, ref. Job 29:16 πατέρα...ἑαυτόν, οὐ τῷ γεννῆσαι πάντας, ἀλλὰ τῷ ~εῖν, ὠνόμασεν Cyr.H.*catech.*7.9; of God's care and protection, *ib.*7.10.

κηδεμονία, ἡ, 1. *care, solicitude*, c. πρός: κοινὴν πρὸς ἅπαντας ἐνδεικνύμενος πατρικὴν κ. Eus.*v.C.*4.1(p.118.6; M.20.1149B); also c. εἰς: κατὰ κ. τὴν εἰς ἡμᾶς Clem.*str.*7.3(p.10.20; M.9.417A); Chrys.*hom.9.2 in Jo.*(8.54C); c. περί: τὴν περὶ τὸν λαὸν κ. Thdr.Mops.*Os.*proem.(M.66.125A); c. possessive adj. in pass. sense κ. τῇ σῇ *care for you*, Synes.*ep.*44(M.66.1372B); **2.** *concern, preoccupation* ἕως...νήπιός ἐστιν ἕκαστος ἡμῶν...οὐδεμίαν τοῦ μέλλοντος κ. ποιεῖται Bas.*hom.in Ps.*1(1.95C; M.29.224A); **3.** ?*guardianship* ἐπίσκοπος ἢ μοναχὸς μὴ καλείσθω πρὸς κηδεμονίαν Ath.Scholast.*coll.*1.2(p.6); **4.** of divine *care, providence* ἀπαξιωθέντων τῆς θείας κ. Meth.*symp.*10.4(p.125.3; M.18.197C); πᾶσα πρόνοια καὶ κ., καὶ τοῦ παντὸς ἐπιστασία Gr.Nyss.*tres dii*(M.45.129D); δίκην προβάτων αὐτοὺς ὑπὸ τὴν ἐμὴν ἀφώρισα κ. Thdt.*Ezech.*36:37(2.993); plur. πατὴρ ἡμῶν ὁ θεὸς...ὀνομάζεται...εἰς τὸ εἶναι ἡμᾶς...παραγαγών, καὶ ταῖς κ. προσοικειούμενος Bas.*Eun.*2.23(1.259C; M.29.624B).

κηδεμών, ὁ, *protector, guardian*, as a civil appointment ἄρχουσι ...πόλεων μέν, ἄρχοντες· κωμῶν δέ, κ.· στρατηγοὶ στρατείας Thdt.*provid.*7(4.601); ref. divine care ὁ θεὸς...ὡς πάντων κ. *Hom.Clem.*2.9; of the Word ὁ ζῶν...λόγος...φύλαξ πάντων πραγμάτων, τῆς ἡμετέρας σωτηρίας κ. Const.ap.Gel.Cyz.*h.e.*2.7.29(M.85.1237D); ὁ σωτὴρ πάντων...πάντων κ. καὶ ἰατρός, λόγος, ὁ ἄγρυπνος φύλαξ πάντων ἀνθρώπων Gr.Thaum.*pan.Or.*17(p.38.18; M.10.1101A); of H. Ghost τὸν παράκλητον...ἁπάντων κ. Eun.*exp.fid.*3(p.259); of angels ἀγγέλους...τοὺς κ. τῶν λαῶν Ath.*ep.Serap.*1.14(M.26.565C); of a guardian angel πρὸς τῷ κοινῷ πάντων ἀνθρώπων κυβερνήτῃ καὶ τοῦτον, ὅστις ποτ' ἐστὶν ἰδίᾳ παιδαγωγὸς ἡμῶν...ὃς τά τε ἄλλα πάντῃ πάντα ἀγαθὸς ὢν τροφεὺς καὶ κ. ἐμός Gr.Thaum.*pan.Or.*4(p.10.5; M.10.1061C); of celebrant of eucharist τὸ συλλεγόμενον παρὰ τῷ προεστῶτι ἀποτίθεται, καὶ αὐτὸς ἐπικουρεῖ ὀρφανοῖς τε καὶ χήραις...καὶ πᾶσι τοῖς ἐν χρείᾳ οὖσι κ. γίνεται Just.*1apol.*67.6(M.6.429C).

κηδεστής, ὁ, *task-master, overseer*, Cyr.*Is.*4.1(2.543A).

κηδέστρια, ἡ, *mother-in-law*, Const.ap.Eus.*v.C.*3.52(p.99.23; M.20.1112B); Chrys.*hom.12.7 in Col.*(11.423A); Thdt.*Mich.*7:5f.(2.1511).

κήδευμα, τό, *funeral, burial*, Chrys.*hom.4.5 in Heb.*(12.47B).

κήδ-ομαι, *be concerned about*, of Christ οὐ τῆς ἐκείνων δόξης ἐφιέμενος...ἀλλ' αὐτῶν ~όμενος Chrys.*hom.47.2 in Jo.*(8.278D); *care for*; of God, Clem.*ecl.*21(p.142.23; M.9.708B); Ath.*gent.*35(M.25.69A); CHier.(350)*ep.*(p.137.3; M.25.352B); of H. Ghost τὸ πνεῦμα τὸ ἅγιον σφόδρα ἡμῶν ~εται Chrys.*hom.15.1 in Rom.*(9.594B).

§**κηλητικός,** *of a rupture* βουβῶνος κ. *Mir.Artem.*24(p.34.20).

κηλιδ-όω, *stain, defile*, morally οἱ νόθῳ ψυχῇ καὶ κεκηλιδωμένῃ τὰ ῥήματα [sc. ἀπὸ γραφῆς] φέροντες κλέπτουσι Or.*fr.21 in Jer.*(p.208.3; M.13.573C); οὔτε ἡδονὴ...οὐ φιλοχρηματία, οὐκ ἄλλο τι τῶν τὴν ψυχὴν ...~ούντων Gr.Nyss.*hom.15 in Cant.*(M.44.1096A); Isid.Pel.*epp.*1.349(M.78.381C).

κηλίς, ἡ, *stain*, moral κ. ... κακίας Meth.*res.*1.38(p.281.8; M.41.1105B); τὰς τῶν ἁμαρτημάτων...κ. Thdt.*Eph.*1:7(3.403); abs. ἁμαρτήσασα ψυχὴ...παύεται τῆς κ. καὶ παύεται τῆς ἁμαρτίας Or.*hom.2.2 in Jer.*(p.18.3; M.13.280A); ἀπονιψάμενοι ἐν τῷ βαπτίσματι τὰς κ. Chrys.*hom.10.5 in Mt.*(7.146A); οἱ...μολυσμῶν ἀνάπλεοι καὶ ἀνίερων κ. Dion.Ar.*e.h.*7.1.2(M.3.553D).

***κηλόγραφος,** *writing on the subject of hernia* οἱ κ. χειρουργοί *Mir.Artem.*28(p.41.17).

***κηλοποιός,** *causing hernia*, *Mir.Artem.*17(p.18.17).

***κηλοτομέω,** *operate for hernia*, *Mir.Artem.*24(p.35.2); pass., *undergo an operation for hernia*, *ib.*44(p.73.1).

κήλων, ὁ, *stallion*; fig. of a licentious person Τιμόθεον...κ. Thphn.*chron.*p.133(M.108.365B); cf. Τιμόθεον...ὃν ἐκάλουν...κόλωνα [prob. error for κήλωνα] Thdr.Lect.*h.e.*2.28(M.86.200A).

κημ-όω, *muzzle* βόες μὴ ~ούμενοι Isid.Pel.*epp.*1.394(M.78.404B).

***κήμωτρον, τό,** met., *restraint* κήμωτρα τῶν ἀλογίστων παθῶν Nil.*epp.*1.169(M.79.149C); †Nil.*vit.*4(M.79.1144C).

***κηνσιτορία, ἡ,** (cf. Lat. *censura*), *office of censor, censorship*, Isid.Pel.*epp.*1.275(M.78.345A).

κηνσίτωρ ([*]**κενσίτωρ**), **ὁ,** (Lat. *censitor*) *censor, magistrate*, Bas.*ep.*83 tit.(3.176A; M.32.461A); *ib.*284 tit.(424E; M.1020B); *ib.*312 tit. (443D; M.1060C); κενσίτωρ *MAMA* 3.358.

κῆνσος, ὁ, (Lat. *census*) *poll-tax* τὸν κ. κατὰ κεφαλὴν ἐπιτρόπων... εἰσπραττομένων Eus.*fr.Lc.*9:7(M.24.548A); πρεσβυτέρους καὶ διακόνους ὁ παλαιὸς κ. ἀτελεῖς ἀφῆκεν Bas.*ep.*104(3.198E; M.32.509C); *ib.*312(3.443D; M.1060C); νομικοὶ πυνθανόμενοι περὶ τελειότητος καὶ Ἡρωδιανοὶ περὶ κήνσου Gr.Naz.*or.*37.5(M.36.288B).

***κηνσουάλιος, ὁ,** (Lat. *censualis*) *one responsible for drawing up the censor's lists*, Justn.*nov.*17.8(p.122.32); v. κλησουάλιος.

***κηνσοφύλαξ, ὁ,** *keeper of the census*, Nil.*epp.*2.146 tit.(M.79.268B); Ath.Scholast.*coll.*20.1(p.171).

***κήνσωρ, ὁ,** (Lat. *censor*) *censor, magistrate*, Ath.*apol.sec.*65 (p.144.6f.,19; M.25.365Aff.); *Chron.Pasch.*p.286(M.92.713B).

***κηπάριον, τό,** *little garden*, *M.Ner.et Ach.*17(p.16.23).

***κηπευτικός,** *concerned with gardens* τῆς κ. ἐπιμελείας Clem.*str.*7.15(p.65.6; M.9.528A).

κῆπος, ὁ, *garden*; met., of Church, Gr.Nyss.*hom.10 in Cant.*(M.44.985A); Cyr.*Is.*5.4(2.823A); of BMV χαῖρε, ὁ κ. ὁ τοῦ πατρός Chrysipp.*enc.in BMV* 1(p.337.3); χαῖρε κ. κεκλεισμένος Thdr.Stud.*nativ.BMV* 7(M.96.692C).

κηποτάφιον, τό, *tomb in a garden*, Pall.*h.Laus.*18(p.49.9; M.34.1051D).

***κηποῦριν, τό,** *garden*, of Eden οὐ κ. ἦν ὁ παράδεισος, μικρὸν ἔχων μέτρον Sever.*creat.*5.5(M.56.478).

κηπωρός, ὁ, *gardener*, Synes.*ep.*132(M.66.1517B); Thphn.*chron.*p.46(M.108.169A).

[*]**κήρα, ἡ,** v. κεῖρα.

κηραψία (***κεραψία**), **ἡ,** *lighted candle, light*, Thdr.Stud.*poen.*1.102(M.99.1748A); κερ- *Chron.Pasch.*p.383(M.92.981C).

κηρέλαιον, τό, *cerate, mixture of wax and oil* τὰς ὑπήνας κηρελαίῳ ἀλείφων Thphn.*chron.*p.376(M.108.900B).

***κήρη, ἡ,** v. κηρός.

κηρία, ἡ, = κειρία, *girth* αἱ κ. τῶν πώλων ἀπεσπάθησαν *M.Eleuth.*8(p.157.11).

***Κηρινθιανοί, οἱ,** *followers of Cerinthus*, Epiph.*haer.*28.1(p.313.7; M.41.377C); *Κ.* ... Ἰουδαῖοί τινες περιτομὴν αὐχοῦντες, τὸν δὲ κόσμον ὑπὸ ἀγγέλων γεγενῆσθαι, Ἰησοῦν δὲ κατὰ προκοπὴν Χριστὸν καλεῖσθαι λέγοντες id.*anac.*28(p.236.6; M.41.284B); only used part of first gospel, id.*haer.*28.5(p.317.10f.; 384A); acc. Epiph. taught that Christ was not yet raised from the dead, *ib.*28.6(p.318.1ff.; 384B) but cf. Iren.*haer.*1.26.1(M.7.686A,B).

κηρίολος, ὁ, *wax taper* or *candle* ἀπαντῶσι τοῖς λαοῖς...μετὰ κηριόλων ψάλλοντες *Ep.*ap.CEph.(431)(*ACO* 1.1.2 p.66.8, v.l. κηρῶν H.1.1588B); v. κηρίων.

κηρίον, τό, 1. *honeycomb*; met., title of anthologies, Clem.*str.*6.1(p.423.2; M.9.209A); **2.** *beehive* καθάπερ μέλιτται κ. βομβοῦσαι, οὕτω τὴν ἀγορὰν περιίπταντο καθ' ἑκάστην ἡμέραν οἱ οἰκοῦντες Chrys.*stat.*2.1(2.21A); **3.** *wax candle*; burnt at feasts, *Mir.Artem.*18(p.21.25).

κηριτρεφής, *causing destruction* or *death*, Synes.*hymn.*3.66(p.9; M.66.1594); ‡Synes.*hymn.*10.9(p.64; M.66.1615).

κηρίων, ὁ, *wax taper* or *candle* τοὺς κ. τῆς ἐκκλησίας τοῖς εἰδώλοις ἀνῆπτον Ath.*ep.encycl*.4(p.173.7, v.l. κηριόλους M.25.229C).

κηρογραφ-έω, *paint with wax and fix by burning in*; of encaustic painting, Eust.*engast*.27(p.59.27; M.18.669D); ἄνθρωπος...εἰκών ἐστι τοῦ υἱοῦ, τοῦ καὶ ἐξ ἀνομοίων ~εῖσθαι χρωμάτων εἰκόνας id.*fr.in Pr.* 8:22(M.18.677D).

κηροειδής, *soft like wax, impressionable*, Gr.Nyss.*hom.opif*.30.7 (M.44.241D).

***κηρομάστιχος**, ἡ, *wax mixed with mastic*, *Euchol*.(pp.490f.).

***κηροπλαστεῖον**, τό, *tool for working in wax*, Epiph.*haer*.23.3 (p.251.18f.; M.41.301B).

κηροπλαστ-έω, **1.** *mould as in wax*, of God ὁ ἀριστοτέχνης...τὸν ἄνθρωπον...κ. ἐξ ὑγρῶν...σπερμάτων ἐν μήτρᾳ Meth.*symp*.2.6(p.23.7; M.18.56D); **2.** *make wax cells* ὁρμῇ...ἐν τῇ μελίσσῃ ἐπὶ τὸ ~εῖν Or. *princ*.3.1.2(p.197.7; M.11.252A); fig. τῷ λειμῶνι τῶν θεοπνεύστων ἐφιπτάμενον λόγων, ἀφ' ἑκάστου τι πρὸς τὴν κτῆσιν τῆς σοφίας ἀπανθιζόμενον, ~εῖν ἑαυτῷ τὸ κηρίον Gr.Nyss.*hom.9 in Cant*.(M.44.960A).

***κηροπράτης**, ὁ, *seller of wax*, Thdr.Stud.*ep*.22 tit.(p.20).

κηρός, ὁ, **1.** *bees-wax*, ref. Lc.22:44 (cf. Ps.21:15) ἐντρόμου τῆς καρδίας...ἐοικυίας...κ. τηκομένῳ εἰς τὴν κοιλίαν Just.*dial*.103.8(M.6.720A); in simile of monophysite Christology εἰς φύσιν μίαν...γένοιτο ἕνωσις, οἷον γίνεται ἐπὶ τῆς κλαύρας χίας, καὶ τοῦ μαλθακοῦ κ. εἰς μαστιχήματος σύστασιν Leont.H.*monoph*.(M.86.1816A); as used for candles, etc., Eus.*v.C*.4.22(p.125.27; M.20.1169A); Gr.Nyss.*ep*.6 (κήρης M.46.1036A); **2.** *lighted taper, lighted candle*, freq. plur., *lights*; **a.** ref. Christian ceremonies: at funerals ὥστε μὴ φαίνεσθαι τὸ ὄρος ἐκ τοῦ πλήθους καὶ τοῦ καπνοῦ τῶν θυμιαμάτων καὶ τῶν κ. καὶ λαμπάδων τῶν καιομένων Anton.Hag.*v.Sym.Styl*.29(p.68.13); ἐποίησε πᾶσαν τὴν πόλιν μετὰ κηρῶν ἐλθεῖν Jo.Mosch.*prat*.88(M.87.2945C); in public processions ὑπερέβαλλον [sc. τοὺς ἀπὸ τῆς Ἀρείου αἱρέσεως] τῷ πλήθει καὶ τῇ προόδῳ. καὶ γὰρ δὴ καὶ σταυρῶν ἀργυρᾶ σημεῖα ὑπὸ κηροῖς ἡμμένοις προηγοῦντο αὐτῶν Soz.*h.e*.8.8.4(M.67.1537A); v. κηρίολος; as measuring duration of devotions φῶτα ποιήσας καὶ κηρὸν ἑκατέρᾳ χειρὶ κατέχων, οἷς συνεμέτρει τὸν ἐπινίκιον· οὐ γὰρ πρότερον ἡ γλῶττα τῶν ὕμνων πέπαυτο, ἕως τοῖς κ. καυθεῖσι τὸ φῶς ἔσβεστο Niceph.Ur.*v.Sym*.48(M.86.3032A); symbolism οἱ κ. τύπος εἰσὶ τοῦ αἰωνίου φωτός ‡Sophr.H.*liturg*.5(M.87.3985C); **b.** ref. non-religious occasions τινὸς...ὑφάψαντος κηροὺς ἐν τῷ θεάτρῳ Jo.Mal.*chron*.18 p.467(M.97.681B); τὴν...στήλην διριγευομένην ὑπὸ τῶν στρατευμάτων μετὰ χλανιδίων καὶ καμπαγίων, πάντων κατεχόντων κ. λευκούς *ib*.13 p.322(M.97.481C); *Chron.Pasch*.p.327(844B); Leont.N.*v.Jo.Eleem*. 36(p.72.10).

***κηρουλ(λ)άριος**, ὁ, *seller of wax lights*, *Mir.Artem*.21(p.27.1); -λλάριος Thphn.*chron*.p.412(M.108.980A).

***κηρούλλιον**, τό, *wax taper*, *Mir.Artem*.24(p.34.5).

***κηρουργία**, ἡ, *work of wax*, *cell* of bees, Ephr.2.354D.

κηρόχυτος, **1.** *encaustic*; of paintings, Eus.*v.C*.1.3(p.8.20; M.20.913B); *ib*.3.3(p.78.16; 1057A); ‡Chrys.*leg*.6(6.413E); Taras.*ep*.1(M.98.1429B); **2.** *moulded from wax* πινακίδιον κ. ‡Chrys.*nat.Jo.Bapt*. (10.817B).

κήρυγμα, τό, **A.** *preaching*; **1.** *proclamation* τοῦτο τῆς δικαιοσύνης τὸ κ., ὑπακούουσιν εὐαγγέλιον, παρακούσασιν κριτήριον Clem.*prot*.11 (p.82.2; M.8.236B); ἵνα...ἀκούοντες ἄνθρωποι...ἀποστρέφωσι τὰς ἀκοὰς αὐτῶν ἀπὸ τοῦ τῆς ἀληθείας κ. Hipp.*haer*.7.32(p.220.1; M.16.3339B); ἐφυλάττετο...τῇ ἑαυτοῦ παρουσίᾳ ἡ χάρις τοῦ κ. τῆς περὶ αὐτοῦ θεολογίας, ἣν καθ' ὅλης τῆς οἰκουμένης ὥσπερ τι πάλαι κρύφιον... μυστήριον παραλαβοῦσα σεμνύνεται Eus.*e.th*.1.20(p.96.7; M.24.892C); **2.** abs., *preaching, proclamation of the gospel* οἱ μὲν προφῆται ἐν προφητείᾳ τέλειοι, οἱ δίκαιοι δὲ ἐν δικαιοσύνῃ καὶ οἱ μάρτυρες ἐν ὁμολογίᾳ, ἄλλοι δὲ ἐν κ. Clem.*str*.4.31(p.307.20; M.8.1344C); οὐ τὴν ἐπέκτασιν τοῦ κ. τὴν κατὰ τὸν τόπον λέγων...ἀλλὰ τὴν γνῶσιν *ib*. 6.18(p.516.30; M.9.397B); *A.(Pass.)Petr.et Paul*.10(p.128.8); [Rom. 8:2a] ὃ δή ἐστι τὸ εὐαγγέλιον...διὰ τοῦ κ. πρὸς ὑπακοὴν τεθεὶς καὶ ἄφεσιν ἁμαρτημάτων Meth.*res*.2.2(p.345.4; M.18.308B); ref. Am.4:13, in connexion with Pentecost τῆς...βροντῆς...τὸ εὐαγγελικὸν κ. δηλούσης Eus.*e.th*.3.2(p.141.5; M.24.976A); προϊόντος τοῦ σωτηρίου κ. id.*h.e*.2.1.13(M.20.137C); μὴ γινώσκοντες θεὸν διὰ τοῦ κ. πιστεύσαντες *Const.App*.5.16.5; **a.** by Christ, Clem.*str*.6.6(p.454.30; M.9.268B); τοὺς λ' ἢ...δώδεκα τὸ κ. δηλοῦν ἱστοροῦσιν, ὅτι τριακοστῷ μὲν ἐκήρυξεν ὁ κύριος ἔτει, ιβ' δὲ ἦσαν οἱ ἀπόστολοι *ib*.6.11(p.475.14; 308C); τὸ πιστεῦσαι τῷ τοῦ Ἰησοῦ κ. Or.*Jo*.28.10(9; p.400.16; M.14.700B); τὰ...εὐαγγέλια ἄρξασθαι τὸν κύριόν φασι τοῦ σωτηρίου κ. ἐπὶ Ἄννα ἀρχιερέως, σταυρωθῆναι δὲ ἐπὶ Καϊάφα *Chron.Pasch*.p.222(M.92.541A); τὸ ιδ' ἔτος...Τιβερίου Καίσαρος...ἐν ᾧ ἡ παρουσία ἡ ἐπὶ τὸ βάπτισμα καὶ ἡ ἀρχὴ τοῦ σωτηρίου κ. τοῦ...Χριστοῦ *ib*.p.164(404B); ἀπὸ μὲν πεντεκαιδεκάτου ἔτους...Τιβερίου Καίσαρος καὶ τοῦ σωτηρίου κ. ἀρχῆς *ib*.p.247(596A); **b.** pre-eminently by apostles, *A.Petr.et Paul*.59(p.204.11); *A.Phil*.9(p.5.14); *Symb.Caes*.ap.Eus.*ep.Caes*.3 (p.43.17; M.20.1537C); κύριε...ὁ διὰ Χριστοῦ κ. γνώσεως δοὺς ἡμῖν εἰς ἐπίγνωσιν τῆς σῆς δόξης *Lit*.ap.*Const.App*.8.11.2; *Const.App*.3.6.2 cit. s. γύνη; τὰς ὕβρεις...ἐδέξαντο [i.e. apostles] ὑπὲρ τοῦ πληρῶσαι τὸ κ. κατὰ τὴν ἐντολὴν τοῦ κυρίου †Bas.*bapt*.2.13.1(2.673B; M.31.1628A); Euthal.Diac.*Ac*.proem.(M.85.636A); ἡ τοῦ θεοῦ...δύναμις...τὸ κ. αὔξουσα Chrys.*stat*.1.6(2.8E); *ib*.1.7(10C); **c.** and their successors, Ath.*ep.Drac*.5(M.25.529A); ὥστε εἰς ὅ τι μὲν ἀπεστάλη τις, μὴ πληρώσας τὸ κ. ἔργῳ καὶ λόγῳ, ἔνοχός ἐστι τοῦ αἵματος τῶν μὴ ἀκουσάντων †Bas.*bapt*.2.12.2(2.672C; M.31.1625A); Chrys.*hom.80.1 in Jo*.(8.473C); assisted by those vowed to chastity ἵνα...συνεργὴ σωσι βοηθοῦντες τῷ κ. πρὸς τὴν τῶν λοιπῶν σωτηρίαν Meth.*symp*.3.8 (p.37.9; M.18.76A); **3.** the matter preached: *proclamation, message, teaching, doctrine*; **a.** in gen.; ref. Plato ἐπιμελεῖσθαι σώματος δεῖν ψυχῆς ἕνεκα ἁρμονίας, δι' οὗ βιοῦν τέ ἐστι καὶ ὀρθῶς βιοῦν καταγγέλλοντα τῆς ἀληθείας τὸ κ. Clem.*str*.4.4(p.256.23; M.8.1232A); ref. patriarchs πρῶτον...τὸ κ. μετὰ τὴν παράβασιν πέμπεται τὸ διὰ Νῶε Meth.*symp*.10.3(p.125.10; M.18.197A); and prophets τοῖς τῶν προφητῶν κ. τοῖς αὐτὸν εὐαγγελισαμένοις...εἰς πάντας Just.*dial*.136.3(M 6.789D); Gr.Naz.*carm*.1.2.34.231ff.(M.37.962A); τοῦ ἀψεύδους αὐτῶν κ. πληρουμένου Jo.Eub.*concept.BMV* 4(M.96.1465B); ref. Jo. Bapt., Chrys.*hom.40.1 in Jo*.(8.237E); of any message from God, *Apoc. Bar.rel*.7.15(p.58); **b.** also of what is opposed to the truth: pagan teaching, Hipp.*haer*.5.7(p.85.11; M.16.3135A); ζῶσαν ἠπείλουν κατακαύσειν, εἰ μὴ συνεκφωνήσειεν αὐτοῖς τὰ τῆς ἀσεβείας κ. Dion.Al. ap.Eus.*h.e*.6.41.7(M.20.608A); heresies, ref. Arians τῆς ἀσεβείας ἑαυτῶν τὸ κ. Alex.Al.*ep.Alex*.1(p.20.10; M.18.549A); ref. Eunomius τὸ ἄθεον τοῦτο παρὰ τοῦ διαβόλου προκαταβέβληται κ. Gr.Nyss.*Eun.* 11(2 p.273.11; M.45.884A); ὥστε τοὺς ἀλογωτέρους, ταὐτὸν εἶναι τῇ ἀληθινῇ πίστει τὸ τούτων κ. ... νομίζοντας κτλ. *ib*.4(2 p.89.18; 665B); τὸ κ. [sc. τῶν ἀποστόλων]...τοῖς ἀντιθέοις κ. ... κατωχύρωσας, *Βασίλειε* Jo.Mon.*hymn.Bas*.3(M.96.1372C); **4.** content of apostolic preaching, the *gospel*; **a.** as preached by Christ // λόγος, δίδαγμα, μάθημα: (exeg. Jo.12:48) τὸ κ. ... φησὶ κρίνειν τὸν μὴ φυλάξαντα τὴν ἐντολήν ‡Ath.*Ar*.4.17(p.62.24; M.26.492D); φαίνεταί πως αὐτοὺς... διδαγμάτων ἐξέλκων τῶν Μωσαϊκῶν...προσκεῖσθαι κελεύων...τῷ λόγῳ τῷ παρ' αὐτοῦ, ὅπερ ἐστὶν...τὸ εὐαγγελικόν...κ. ἐλάλει γὰρ καὶ πάλιν πρὸς ἡμᾶς διὰ τῶν...προφητῶν, ἀλλ' ἦσαν οἱ μεσιτεύοντες...λόγος κυρίως αὐτοῦ τὸ εὐαγγελικὸν νοηθήσεται κ. ... διά τοι τοῦτο λόγος αὐτοῦ κυρίως ὀνομασθήσεται μάθημα τὸ εὐαγγελικόν Cyr.*Jo*.5.5(4.534Af.); *ib*.(534D); ἄλλοις τὰ καθ' ἑαυτὸν ἐπιτάττει κηρύττειν, φωναῖς ἀλλοτρίαις καταπιστεύσας τὸ κ. Bas.Sel.*or*.25.3(M.85.293D); καλέσας [sc. ὁ Χριστὸς] τοὺς μαθητὰς πιστεύσαντας καὶ δεξαμένους τὸ κ. τῆς εὐσεβείας *Chron.Pasch*.p.210(M.92.513D); to souls in prison ἵνα...αἱ [sc. ἐν ᾅδου] ψυχαὶ ἀκούσασαι τοῦ κ. ... τὴν μετάνοιαν ἐνδείξωνται Clem.*str*.6.6(p.456.13; M.9.272A); **b.** by Church, Herm.*sim*.8.3.2; ἀπόστολοι καὶ διδάσκαλοι τοῦ κ. τοῦ υἱοῦ τοῦ θεοῦ *ib*.9.15.4; εἷς ἐξ αὐτῶν [sc. δώδεκα μαθητῶν] τὰς καθ' ἡμᾶς περιῆλθε χώρας, τὸ δόγμα κηρύττων τῆς ἀληθείας. ὅθεν οἱ εἰσέτι διακονοῦντες τῇ δικαιοσύνῃ τοῦ κ. αὐτῶν καλοῦνται Χριστιανοί Arist.*apol*.15(p.110.28); *A.Andr.* A 7(p.50.8); *A.Phil*.116(p.47.3); οἱ τοῦ προφητικοῦ πνεύματος ὑπηρέται καὶ οἱ τοῦ εὐαγγελικοῦ κ. διάκονοι Or.*Jo*.6.1(p.106.14; M.14.197B); προκείσθω...τῶν αἱρετικῶν τὰ δόγματα, καὶ τῆς ὑμετέρας φρονήσεως ἡ γνώμη, καὶ τῆς ἡμετέρας πίστεως ὁ λόγος, καὶ τοῦ εὐαγγελίου τὸ ὅρος, καὶ τῶν ἀποστόλων τὸ κ., καὶ τῶν προφητῶν ἡ μαρτυρία, καὶ τῆς πληρωθείσης οἰκονομίας ἡ κατανόησις ‡Ath.*Apoll.* 2.4(M.26.1137C); Gr.Nyss.*or.catech*.13(p.61.1; M.45.45B); id.*ep*.3(M.46.1024C); id.*Eun*.1(1 p.96.6; M.45.329A); μετὰ μείζονος τῆς προθυμίας τὸ τῆς ἀληθείας κατήγγελλον κ. Chrys.*stat*.1.11(2.17E); Thdt. *1Cor*.proem.(3.163); *ib*.16:15f.(284); ὥστε πάντας...διὰ τῆς τοῦ κ. διδασκαλίας ἀποφῆναι τελείους id.*Col*.1:28f.(3.483); ἦλθον τὸν σπόρον τοῦ θείου κ. τῇ σῇ καταβαλεῖν καρδίᾳ...ἰδοὺ...τὴν διακονίαν μου πεποίηκα, τὴν αὐτοῦ καταγγείλας σοι γνῶσιν καὶ τὸ τῶν προφητῶν καὶ ἀποστόλων γνωρίσας κ. †Jo.D.*B.J*.18(M.96.1020C); heret. (Naassene) τὰ τῶν δώδεκα μαθητῶν κ. οὔτε πάντες ἀκηκόασιν οὔτε, ἐὰν ἀκούσωσι, παραδέξασθαι δύνανται Hipp.*haer*.5.8(p.91.14; M.16.3143A); denoting Christian religion opp. paganism and heresy ἔδωκεν αὐτοῖς τὴν σφραγῖδα τοῦ κ. Herm.*sim*.9.16.5; ὡς κατὰ καιρὸν ἥκει τὸ κ. νῦν, οὕτως κατὰ καιρὸν ἐδόθη νόμος μὲν καὶ προφῆται βαρβάροις, φιλοσοφία δὲ Ἕλλησι, τὰς ἀκοὰς ἐθίζουσα πρὸς τὸ κ. Clem.*str*.6.6 (p.453.16ff.; 265A); Or.*Jo*.5.8(p.105.14; M.14.196B) cit. s. ἀντιπαραβάλλω; σχεδὸν παντὸς τοῦ κόσμου ἐγνωκότος τὸ κ. Χριστιανῶν μᾶλλον ἢ τὰ τοῖς φιλοσόφοις ἀρέσκοντα id.*Cels*.1.7(p.60.1; M.11.668A); Geo. Laod.*ep.dogm*.ap.Epiph.*haer*.73.6(p.275.19; M.42.413A); πολλοί... τῶν παραδεξαμένων τὸν ἐλευθερωτὴν...τῆς τυραννίδος λόγον, καὶ προστιθέμενοι τῷ κ. ... [others] τὸ λυσιτελεῖν αὐτοῖς μᾶλλον ἀνηκόοις μεῖναι τοῦ τῆς ἐλευθερίας κ. Gr.Nyss.*v.Mos.*(M.44.341Cf.); οὔπω πάντων περιγέγονε τὸ κ. Chrys.*hom.4.2 in Heb.*(12.40D); opp. Judaism, Procl.CP *or.*17.4(M.65.813B); plur. ἔργα θεοῦ εἶναί φαμεν τὴν εὐσεβῆ πολιτείαν...ἣ διὰ τῶν εὐαγγελικῶν κ. γέγονεν ἡμῖν ἐμφανής Cyr.*Ps.*44:2(M.69.1028C); denoting Christian dispensation τύπος... ὁ διαδεξάμενος ἦν Μωσῆν Ἰησοῦς τοῦ διαδεξαμένου τὴν διὰ τοῦ νόμου οἰκονομίαν τῷ εὐαγγελικῷ κ. Ἰησοῦ τοῦ Χριστοῦ Or.*Jo.*6.44(26; p.153.18; M.14.277A); τῶν χρόνων τοῦ εὐαγγελικοῦ κ. *ib.*13.44(p.271.4; 477C); ἐν τοῖς ἔτεσι τοῖς πρὸ τοῦ κ., καὶ τοῖς ἐν τῷ κ. τὸ νομικὸν καὶ σκιῶδες πάσχα ἐπετέλεσεν ‡Petr.I Al.*fr.*(M.18.517C)ap.*Chron.Pasch.* p.5(M.92.77A); Chrys.*hom.72.4 in Jo.*(8.427E); **c.** of written gospels ὁ εὐαγγελιστὴς Ἰωάννης...ὑπερεφώνησε τὰ προλαβόντα κ. τῇ μεγαλοφυΐᾳ τῆς γνώσεως Bas.*Eun.*2.15(1.250C; M.29.601B); διὰ τῆς τρίτης ἐπαναλήψεως [sc. of the word λόγος in Jo.1:1] τελειῶν τὸν σκοπὸν τοῦ κ. Gr.Nyss.*Eun.*4(2 p.55.5; M.45.625A); *ib.*(2 p.54.7; 624C); **5.** *the apostolic tradition, the faith* τοῦτο τὸ κ. παρειληφυῖα, καὶ ταύτην τὴν πίστιν...ἡ ἐκκλησία...ἐπιμελῶς φυλάσσει...καὶ συμφώνως ταῦτα κηρύσσει, καὶ διδάσκει, καὶ παραδίδωσιν Iren.*haer.*1.10.2(M.7.552A); ὁ διάκονος...καὶ τὸ κ. καὶ τὸ βάπτισμα Clem.*str.*2.8(p.133.8; M.8.973B); *ib.*4.4(p.254.15; 1228A); Or.*princ.*3.1.1(p.195.4; M.11.249A); *ib.* proem.10(p.16.1; cf.120C); τὸν ὑγιῆ κανόνα τοῦ σωτηρίου κ. Eus.*h.e.*3.32.7(M.20.284C); τὴν ἀπλανῆ παράδοσιν τοῦ ἀποστολικοῦ κ. *ib.*4.8.2 (321B); οὓς [i.e. heretics] ἐκτραπεῖσα ἡ ἐκκλησία τοῦ θεοῦ τῷ τῆς ἀληθείας εὐαγγελικῷ κ. σεμνύνεται id.*e.th.*1.3(p.64.3; M.24.832D); πῶς δ' ἂν εἴημεν ἔτι τῶν μακαρισμῶν ἄξιοι...οἱ μόνοις τοῖς κατὰ λογισμὸν ἐναργέσι πειθόμενοι;...οὐκ ἐπειδὴ τοῖς ἐκ τῶν λογισμῶν φαινομένοις ἀκολουθοῦντες, τῷ κ. τοῦ πνεύματος ἀπειθοῦσι; Bas.*Eun.*2.24(1.261A; M.29.628A); ματαία μὲν ἡ πίστις ἀποδειχθήσεται, κενὸν δὲ τὸ κ., περιττὸν δὲ τὸ βάπτισμα Gr.Nyss.*Eun.*10(2 p.231.13; M.45.832D); τινὰ παραχαράττοντα τὰ ἐν τῷ ἐκκλησιαστικῷ κ. καὶ θεσμῷ τῆς ἐκκλησίας Epiph.*haer.*70.1(p.233.15; M.42.340B); ὀνόματα λέγειν τῶν τελευτησάντων...πιστεύειν...ὅτι οἱ ἀπελθόντες...ζῶσι παρὰ τῷ δεσπότῃ; καὶ ὅπως ἂν τὸ σεμνότατον κ. διηγήσοιτο, ὡς ἐλπίς ἐστιν ὑπὲρ ἀδελφῶν εὐχομένοις...ὠφελεῖ δὲ καὶ ὑπὲρ αὐτῶν γινομένη εὐχή *ib.*75.7(p.338.31; 513B); Marc.Er.*opusc.*4(M.65.988B); συνίστησι...δι' αὐτοῦ τοῦ σχήματος, καὶ τῆς τοῦ κόσμου κατασκευῆς καὶ αὐτῆς τῆς φύσεως τῶν πραγμάτων, τὴν θείαν γραφὴν ἀληθεστάτην οὖσαν καὶ τῶν Χριστιανῶν τὸ κ. Cosm.Ind.*top.*proem.1(M.88.53C); ἑτέρας γὰρ ἐγὼ δόξης καθέστηκα, καὶ οὐ τοῦ τῆς ἐκκλησίας κ. Sophr.H.*mir.Cyr.et Jo.*36 (M.87.3553B); incl. discipline, Clem.*prot.*10(p.72.14; M.8.213B); ref. practice of baptism [Mt.28:19] καὶ τοῦτό ἐστιν εἰς πᾶσαν τὴν... ἐκκλησίαν τὸ κ. Ath.*ep.Serap.*1.28(M.26.596C); θόρυβος ἐκινεῖτο ἐν τῷ ἐκκλησιαστικῷ κ. περὶ τοῦ τῆς ἑορτῆς...ζητήματος Epiph.*haer.*70.9 (p.242.14; M.42.356A); τὸ κ. ... τὰ πάντα εἶχε, τὸ εὐαγγέλιον...τὴν ζωήν, τὴν εὐσέβειαν, τὴν πίστιν, πάντα ὁμοῦ Chrys.*hom.1.1 in Tit.* (11.732A); χρὴ...ἡμᾶς τῷ ἀποστολικῷ κ. πιστεύειν [i.e. on subject of baptism], καὶ ἐμμένειν ταῖς ἑαυτῶν ὁμολογίαις...εἰ οὖν τὸ κ. ἀληθὲς ἔχομεν, τελέσωμεν πάσας τὰς ἐντολάς Marc.Er.*opusc.*4(M.65.985Bf.); διπλοῦν...ἐν ἐκκλησίαις τὸ...κ.· ἓν μὲν...εἰς ὀρθότητα τὴν δογματικὴν ἀποφέρει τοὺς πεπιστευκότας...ἕτερον δὲ πρὸς ἠθικὴν ἐπανόρθωσιν ξεναγεῖ Cyr.*ador.*5(1.166Bf.); in Basil opp. δόγμα, q.v.; of Nicene definition of faith κατὰ τὴν Νικαίαν...τὸ μέγα...κ. Bas.*ep.*52.1(3.145A; M.32.392C); and of public prayers of Church μέμνησαι...τῶν κ. τῶν ἐκκλησιαστικῶν...ὅτι καὶ ὑπὲρ τῶν ἐν ἀποδημίαις ἀδελφῶν δεόμεθα *ib.*155(244C; M.612C); cf. ἐν κ.· τουτέστι, φανερῶς, μετὰ παρρησίας Chrys.*hom.1.1 in Tit.*(11.732A); **6.** of an individual item of the faith, *doctrine, dogma* τὸ περὶ κρίσεως κ. Or.*Cels.*6.55(p.126.12; M.11.1384B); τὸ σεμνότατον κ. τῆς ἐκκλησίας τοῦ θεοῦ, τὴν μοναρχίαν Dion.R.ap.Ath.*decr.*26(p.22.2; M.25.461D); *ib.*(p.23.15; 465A); συλλογίζεσθαι περὶ τοῦ κ. τοῦ θείου σταυροῦ Ath.*v.Anton.*74(M.26.945B); τὸ διπλοῦν κ. τῆς αὐτοῦ [sc. Christ] ἐπιδημίας ‡Ath.*Apoll.*1.10 (M.26.1112A); τοῖς ἁπλούστερον δεχομένοις τὸ περὶ τὸν σταυρὸν καὶ τὴν ἀνάστασιν κ. Gr.Nyss.*Eun.*12(2 p.288.19; M.45.901A); plur., *the faith*, Meth.*creat.*1(p.493.12f.; M.18.332B); Ἰουδαῖοι καὶ Ἕλληνες, οἱ τοῖς Χριστοῦ κ. ἀντιπίπτοντες *cat.Heb.*suppl.(p.376.7); **7.** as title of work Πέτρου κ., freq. cit.: Clem.*str.*1.29(p.112.3; M.8.929A) al.; and Heracleon πολὺ δέ ἐστιν νῦν παρατίθεσθαι τοῦ Ἡρακλέωνος τὰ ῥητά, ἀπὸ τοῦ ἐπιγεγραμμένου 'Πέτρου κ.' παραλαμβανόμενα, καὶ ἵστασθαι πρὸς αὐτὰ ἐξετάζοντας καὶ περὶ τοῦ βιβλίου, πότερόν ποτε γνήσιόν ἐστιν ἢ νόθον ἢ μικτόν Or.*Jo.*13.17(p.241.13; M.14.424C); τὸ...λεγόμενον αὐτοῦ Κ. καὶ τὴν καλουμένην Ἀποκάλυψιν οὐδ' ὅλως ἐν καθολικοῖς ἴσμεν παραδεδομένα, ὅτι μήτε ἀρχαίων μήτε μὴν καθ' ἡμᾶς τις ἐκκλησιαστικὸς συγγραφεὺς ταῖς ἐξ αὐτῶν συνεχρήσατο μαρτυρίαις Eus.*h.e.*3.3.2(M.20.217A); τὰ...συγγράμματα, τουτέστι...τρίτον Κ. ... ὡς ἀπόκρυφα ὄντα ἀποδοκιμάζεται Hier.*vir.ill.*(tr.Sophr.Pal.)1(p.3.2; M.*PL.*23.610A) cit. Jo.D.*parall.*(M.95.1157B); *ib.*(1461D); **8.** ref. Easter, of Resurrection as cardinal doctrine of κ.: κανονίζοντες τὴν...ἀνάστασιν ἐν τῇ ἁγίᾳ κυριακῇ, ἑορτάζομεν τὸ ἐκκλησιαστικὸν κ. η' ἡμέρας, ὥς φησιν ὁ ἅγιος Ἰωάννης [i.e. Jo.20:26a] *Chron.Pasch.* p.223(M.92.544C).

B. *acclamation* καθάπερ ἐκ σταδίου τοῦ βίου...νικηφόρος...μετὰ...κ. ἀγγελικῶν ἐπανέρχεται Clem.*q.d.s.*3(p.162.8; M.9.608C).

C. *declaration, avowal* κ. ἦν κατὰ τῆς ἀσεβείας αὐτῶν ἡ τούτων ἀποδημία Ath.*h.Ar.*34(p.202.20; M.25.733A).

D. *call, invitation* of Wisdom (Pr.9:4) μετὰ ὑψηλοῦ κ. αὐτὴ τῶν δεομένων αὐτῆς...ἐφιεμένην (v.l. ἐφιεμένη) Dion.Ar.*ep.*9.3(M.3.1109B).

κηρυκεία, ἡ, v. [*]κηρυκία.

***κηρυκή**, ἡ, *proclamation*, *M.Con.*1.2.

[*]**κηρυκία (-εία)**, ἡ, *preaching* προφητῶν ἀνάγνωσις καὶ εὐαγγελίου κ. καὶ θυσίας ἀναφορά *Const.App.*2.59.4; τῆς κηρυκείας τοῦ Ἰωνᾶ ‡Chrys.*circ.*(8.89E).

***κηρυκικός**, *of heralding*, Clem.*str.*1.1(p.5.1; M.8.692A).

κῆρυξ, ὁ, **A.** *herald*; **1.** of sun, moon, and stars ἔστω καὶ κ. αὐτοῦ [sc. τοῦ θεοῦ] εἶναι καὶ ἀληθῶς οὐρανίους ἀγγέλους, πῶς οὖν οὐχὶ καὶ οὕτως τὸν κηρυσσόμενον ὑπ' αὐτῶν θεὸν καὶ τὸν ἀγγελλόμενον μᾶλλον προσκυνητέον ἢ τοὺς κ. καὶ τοὺς ἀγγέλους αὐτοῦ; Or.*Cels.*5.12(p.14.5ff.; M.11.1200C); met., *witness* κ. ὑμεῖς γίνεσθε τῆς οἰκείας ἀχαριστίας Thdt.*Os.*12:11(2.1370); **2.** of those who preach gospel: Jo. Bapt. κ. αὐτοῦ τῆς παρουσίας Just.*dial.*88.2(M.6.685B); *ib.*49.3(584B); apostles μεθ' ὃν [sc. τὸν πρόδρομον] οἱ κ. τῆς ἐπιφανείας τὴν δύναμιν... μηνύουσιν Clem.*str.*6.18(p.517.35; M.9.400B); τούτων ἔχοντες τὴν πληροφορίαν, ὧν κ. ἐπαγγελλόμεθα εἶναι *Const.App.*5.7.17; ἐδόθη... τοῦτο [sc. gift of tongues] τοῖς κ. διὰ τὰς διαφόρους τῶν ἀνθρώπων φωνάς Thdt.*1Cor.*14:2(3.256); id.*2Cor.*12:16ff.(3.352); S. Paul κ. γενόμενος ἔν τε τῇ ἀνατολῇ καὶ ἐν τῇ δύσει *1Clem.*5.6; ἐθνῶν κ. Clem.*fr.*22(p.202.4; M.9.749B); Ath.*apol.Const.*1(p.279.4; M.25.596A); Thdt.*affect.*12(p.299.22; 3.1013); apostles, evangelists, and other authors of scripture ὁ Ἰωάννης ὁ κ. τοῦ λόγου Clem.*prot.*1(p.10.4; M.8.65C); *A.Mt.*17(p.238.3); ὁ...τῆς ἐκκλησίας κ. πρὸς τῷ προτέρῳ καὶ τὸ δεύτερον μὴ ἀγνοεῖν διδάσκει...[1Cor.8:6] Eus.*e.th.*1.20(p.90.6; M.24.881B); οἱ...ἅγιοι...τῆς ἀληθείας κ. ἀλλήλοις...συμφωνοῦσι...εἰ γὰρ καὶ διαφόροις χρόνοις γεγόνασιν, ἀλλ' εἰς ταὐτὸν ἀλλήλοις ὁρμῶσιν ἑνὸς ὄντες τοῦ θεοῦ προφῆται. καὶ τὸν αὐτὸν συμφώνως εὐαγγελιζόμενοι λόγον Ath.*decr.*4(p.4.7; M.25.'429'(421)D); assumed by Tatian as author of an apology, Tat.*orat.*17(p.18.22; M.6.841C); of bishops τῆς ἀληθείας κήρυκες Ath.*apol.fug.*4(p.71.4; M.25.649B); *Const.App.* 2.17.6; of Ath., Eustrat.*stat.anim.*14(p.430); of clergy in gen. ἐὰν μὲν ὦσιν κ. τῆς εὐσεβείας, προσδεχέσθωσαν *Can.App.*33; of any who bear witness to Christ, Chrys.*hom.52.1 in Jo.*(8.304C); of the man born blind, *ib.58.3*(341D); ὁ...ἐγγίσας τῷ κυρίῳ ἀκολουθεῖ αὐτῷ, καὶ κ. γίνεται τῶν τελειοτέρων δογμάτων Marc.Er.*opusc.*1.13(M.65.908A); **3.** of pagans ψευδοθέων κ. Ath.*gent.*15(M.25.32C); of heretics and schismatics (Arians) τῆς δυσσεβοῦς φρονήσεως κ. ἑαυτοὺς ἀνήγγειλαν CArim.*ep.Const.*1 ap.Ath.*syn.*10(p.237.33; M.26.697B); ὁ τούτου [sc. τοῦ διαβόλου as inspirer of Meletian schism] κ. ἀντίχριστος Ath.*h.Ar.*78(p.227.13; M.25.788D); **4.** *precentor*, Gr.Nyss.*v.Macr.*(M.46.993D).

B. *trumpet-shell*; as instrument of torture, *M.Polyc.*2.4; Eus.*h.e.* 4.15.4(M.20.344A).

κήρυξις, ἡ, *announcement* περὶ τοῦ μέλλοντος λυτροῦσθαι τὸν Ἰσραὴλ κ. *T.Lev.*2.10; *preaching*, Clem.*str.*7.9(p.39.11; M.9.473C); κ. τοῦ εὐαγγελίου Or.*Cels.*1.62(p.114.23; M.11.776C); κ. Θαδδαίου *Ep. Chr.suppl.*ap.Eus.*h.e.*1.13.21(M.20.129A).

κηρύσσ-ω, **1.** *announce, proclaim*; c. ὅτι, Just.*dial.*107.2(M.6.724C); Or.*hom.4.2 in Jer.*(p.24.6; M.13.288A); c. acc. and infin., Meth.*res.*1.49(p.303.7; M.18.277C); Ath.*h.Ar.*42(p.206.32; M.25.744A); liturg. ὁ διάκονος ἐφ' ὑψηλοῦ τινος ἀνελθὼν ~έτω *Lit.*ap.*Const. App.*8.6.2; in writing τοῖς Ἡροδώρου βιβλίοις...γῆν ἄνω κ. Tat.*orat.* 27(p.29.12; M.6.865B); Ματθαῖος...τὴν κατὰ ἄνθρωπον αὐτοῦ γέννησιν κ. Iren.*haer.*3.11.8(M.7.887B); abs. τοῦ υἱοῦ τοῦ θεοῦ...ἑνὸς καὶ τοῦ αὐτοῦ ὄντος, ὡς...οἱ προφῆται κ. *ib.*3.17.4(931B); of things *proclaim*, i.e. be a sign of, show ὁ...ναὸς τὸν ἐνοικοῦντα κ. θεόν Cyr.*dial.Trin.*24 (M.75.1181C); of thieves τῷ πειρᾶσθαι λανθάνειν τὸ δέος ~ουσιν Thdt.*provid.*7(4.592); id.*Ps.*148:7(1.1579); **2.** abs., *preach (the gospel)* κατὰ χώρας...καὶ πόλεις ~οντες *1Clem.*42.4; ὁ Παῦλος...ἀπεστάλη ~ειν Clem.*exc.Thdot.*23(p.114.23; M.9.669C); τοῖς τοιούτοις ἐκήρυξεν ὁ σωτήρ Or.*princ.*3.1.17(p.228.6; M.11.285B).

κήρωμα, τό, (Lat. *ceroma*) *wrestling-ring*, met. τὸ σπήλαιον τοῦτο ...κ. ἐστι· δός, λάβε Jo.Mosch.*prat.*181(M.87.3053B).

***κηρωματίτης**, ὁ, *apothecary, medical practitioner*, Cyr.S.*v.Sab.*45 (p.136.10).

κήρωσις, ἡ, *covering with wax, waxing*, as simile of Inc. ἵνα... ὡς χαρακτὴρ...ἐντυπώσῃ ἐν ἑαυτῷ τὴν σάρκωσιν, ὡς κ. ταύτην φέρων, ἢ χρύσωσιν ‡Ath.*annunt*.6(M.28.924D).

κητώεις, perh. *monstrous, vast* κόσμου κητώεντος ὁρῶν εὔπηκτα θέμεθλα tr. *aspice convexo nutantem pondere mundum*, Vergil *ecl*.4. 50 ap.Const.*or.s.c*.20(p.186.10; M.20.1300A).

***κητῷος**, *of a sea-monster*, Gr.Nyss.*res*.1(M.46.604B).

κιβδηλεύω, **1.** *forbid* τὴν αἵματος βρῶσιν κεκιβδήλευκεν ὁ νόμος Cyr.*ador*.10(1.356A); id.*Juln*.9(6².316D); **2.** perf. ptcpl. pass.; **a.** *spurious*, of *Susannah* τοῦ μέρους τοῦ βιβλίου κ. ὄντος Or.*ep*.1.2(M. 11.49A); **b.** *debased*; of money, Gr.Nyss.*or.catech*.35(p.138.16; M.45. 92B); **c.** *perverted* κ. ἐννοιῶν Cyr.*ador*.7(1.237C); **d.** *forbidden* τὰ θεοῦ νόμῳ κ. *ib*.6(193D).

κίβδηλος, *adulterated*; hence **1.** *spurious*; of a book, Afric.*ep.Or*.1 (p.78.7; M.11.44A); **2.** *forbidden*, Thdt.*qu.27 in Lev*.(1.206).

***κιβδηλόω**, = κιβδηλεύω, *adulterate*, Leont.H.*Nest*.4.32(M.86. 1697C).

κιβώριον ([*]**κιβούριον**), **τό**, **κιβώριος**, **ὁ**, **1.** *cup* ἴσως ὡς κ. μικρά [i.e. in temple of Diana] Chrys.*hom.42.1 in Ac*.(9.318B); **2.** *cupola, dome* τὸ...μέσον αὐτοῦ [sc. τοῦ εἰδωλείου] ἦν ἀναφυσητὸν κ. Marc. Diac.*v.Porph*.75; **3.** *baldachino, canopy*; **a.** over altar ἠμφίεσεν ἅπαν τὸ ἱερατεῖον μετὰ τοῦ κ. ‡Amph.*v.Bas*.9(184C); συνέτριψε τὸ κιβούριον σὺν τῇ ἁγίᾳ τραπέζῃ Jo.Mal.*chron*.18 p.490(M.97.708B); Thdr.Stud.*iamb*.42 tit.(M.99.1793D); etym. and symbolism τὸ κιβούριόν ἐστι ἀντὶ τοῦ τόπου ἔνθα ἐσταυρώθη ὁ Χριστός· ἐγγὺς γὰρ ἦν ὁ τόπος καὶ ὑπόβαθρος ὅπου ἐτάφη...ἔστι δὲ καὶ κατὰ τὴν κιβωτὸν τῆς διαθήκης κυρίου ἐν ᾗ λέγεται ἅγια ἁγίων...ἐν ᾗ προσέταξεν ὁ θεὸς γενέσθαι δύο χερουβὶμ...τὸ γὰρ κιβ ἐστὶ κιβωτός, τὸ δὲ οὔριν...φῶς κυρίου ‡Bas.*h.myst*.4(p.258.18); ὁ κιβώριός ἐστιν εἰς τύπον τῆς κιβωτοῦ τοῦ Νῶε· τὸ μὲν κιβ κιβωτός, τὸ δὲ ὥριον τουτέστι διάταξις αὐτοῦ ‡Sophr.H.*liturg*.2(M.87.3984B); **b.** covering seats of royalty, Call.*v.Hyp*.(p.56).

κιβώτιον, **τό**, *box*, of *poor-box* in churches τὸ κ. δὲ τοῦτο ἐκείνου τοῦ κ. πολλῷ βέλτιον...οὐ γὰρ ἱμάτια, ἀλλ' ἐλεημοσύνην ἔχει συγκεκλεισμένην Chrys.*hom.32.6 in Mt*.(7.373D); τέως δὲ παρὰ σαυτῷ τίθει...καὶ ποίησόν σου τὴν οἰκίαν ἐκκλησίαν, τὸ κ. γαζοφυλάκιον id. *hom.43.1 in 1Cor*.(10.401B); *ib*.43.4(405Df.).

κιβωτός, ἡ, *box, chest, coffer*; hence

A. *ark*; **1.** of Noah; **a.** as type of Church ἡ κ. ... σώσασα τοὺς ἐν αὐτῇ εἰσφρήσαντας, εἰκὼν τῆς σεπτῆς ἐτύγχανεν ἐκκλησίας Didym. *Trin*.2.14(M.39.696A); Νῶε κατεσκεύασε τὴν κ. ... χαρακτηρίζων τὴν ...ἐκκλησίαν, ἔχουσαν διόροφα καὶ τριόροφα, ἐπίκλησιν πατρὸς καὶ υἱοῦ καὶ ἁγίου πνεύματος ‡Ath.*proph*.1(M.28.1064A); Chrys.*Laz*.6.7(1. 783A,B); Cyr.*glaph.Gen*.2(1.36C); ref. Callistus' attitude to Church discipline τὴν κ. τοῦ Νῶε εἰς ὁμοίωμα ἐκκλησίας ἔφη γεγονέναι, ἐν ᾗ καὶ κύνες καὶ λύκοι καὶ κόρακες καὶ πάντα τὰ καθαρὰ καὶ ἀκάθαρτα, οὕτω φάσκων δεῖν εἶναι ἐν ἐκκλησίᾳ ὁμοίως Hipp.*haer*.9.12(p.250.5; M.16.3386C); **b.** as type of BMV κ. ἁγία, δι' ἧς τοῦ τῆς ἁμαρτίας κατακλυσμοῦ διεσώθημεν Ephr.3.529D; Jo.Thess.*dorm.BMV* 1.12 (p.397.28); Jo.Eub.*concept.BMV* 4(M.96.1464B); Thdr.Stud.*nativ. BMV* 7(M.96.689B); **c.** instanced as etym. of κιβώριον, q.v.; **2.** of covenant; **a.** as type of Christ's humanity ὥσπερ γὰρ ἡ κ. κεχρυσωμένη ἔσωθεν καὶ ἔξωθεν χρυσίῳ καθαρῷ ἦν, οὕτω καὶ τὸ τοῦ Χριστοῦ σῶμα...ἔσωθεν μὲν τῷ λόγῳ κοσμούμενον, ἔξωθεν δὲ τῷ πνεύματι φρουρούμενον Iren.*fr*.8(M.7.1233A); κ. τοῦ ἁγιάσματος τὴν ἁγίαν αὐτοῦ σάρκα φησίν Ath.*exp.Ps*.131:8(M.27.521B); προανετυποῦτο... ὡς ἔν γε τῇ κ. Χριστός. κατεσκεύαστο γὰρ ἐκ ξύλων ἀσήπτων ἐκείνη, καὶ τὸν θεῖον ἐν ἑαυτῇ κατεπύκαζε νόμον, ὅς ἐστι λόγος θεοῦ Cyr.*ador*.5 (1.158B); *ib*.9(293Bff.); ‡Meth.*Sym.et Ann*.1(M.18.349A); **b.** as type of BMV αὕτη ἡ κεχρυσωμένη ἔσωθεν καὶ ἔξωθεν κ., σώματι καὶ πνεύματι ἡγιασμένη Procl.CP *or*.6.17(M.65.753B); Chrysipp.*enc.in BMV* 2(p.338.2); Germ.CP *hymn.BMV*(M.98.453C); ‡Jo.D.*hom*.5(M.96. 648C); ref. Ps.131:8, Mod.*dorm*.4(M.86.3289A); Andr.Cr.*or*.4(M.97. 869B); ‡Ath.*occurs*.16(M.28.993C).

B. *cube* (math.) ἑβδόμῃ καὶ εἰκάδι τοῦ μηνὸς...ἐν ἀριθμῷ τῇ κ. ἀπὸ τοῦ τρία Proc.G.*Gen*.7:11(M.87.284B).

κιγκλίζω, *surround*, Jo.Mosch.*prat*.150(M.87.3016B).

κιγκλίς, ἡ, **1.** *latticed partition* in law courts, Chrys.*incomprehens*. 4.4(1.477C); id.*Laz*.2.2(1.729E); Isid.Pel.*epp*.3.360(M.78.1016A); in race-course, Gr.Naz.*ep*.10(M.37.37B); **2.** *chancel screen* in a church, Gr.Naz.*carm*.2.1.13.1361(M.37.1122A); Thdt.*h.e*.5.18.20(3.1050); id. *qu.84 in Gen*.(1.94); **3.** ? *grill* or *railing*, Bas.Sel.*v.Thecl*.2.2(M.85. 568D); Niceph.Ur.*v.Sym*.154(M.86.3129B).

***κιγκραμίς**, ἡ, *pruning* of a tree, Or.*comm.in 1Cor*.15:35(*JTS* 10 p.40).

κιθάρα, ἡ, *lyre*, as image of harmony and concord τὸ...πρεσβυτέριον...συνήρμοσται τῷ ἐπισκόπῳ, ὡς χορδαὶ κιθάρᾳ Ign.*Eph*.4.1; συνευρύθμισται...ταῖς ἐντολαῖς ὡς χορδαῖς κ. id.*Philad*.1.2; of soul as giving praise to God, Clem.*str*.6.11(p.476.6; M.9.309B); in metaphor of inspiration, id.*paed*.2.4(p.182.23; M.8.441B), ‡Just.*coh.Gr*.8 (M.6.257A) citt. s. πλῆκτρον; as image of world, Gr.Naz.*or*.28.6(p.29. 11ff.; M.36.32Df.); met., of S. Barnabas ἡ κ. τοῦ πνεύματος Alex.Sal. *Barn*.5(437C).

κίθαρις, ἡ, **1.** *diadem* forming part of Jewish high priest's head-*dress*, cf.Ex.28:4, Or.*sel.in Ps*.34:2(M.12.1309D); Chrys.*sac*.3.4(p.51. 11; 1.382C); Thdt.*Ezech*.21:26(2.847); **2.** *part of a woman's head-dress*, *Asen*.10(p.52.5); *ib*.13(p.57.9).

***Κιλικάρχης**, ὁ, *chief priest of imperial cult in Cilicia*, *M.Tar*.10 (p.472).

κιλίκιον, **τό**, **1.** a liquid measure, Jo.Mosch.*prat*.184(M.87.3057C); **2.** *coarse cloth*, Gr.Mag.*dial*.(tr.Zach.)3.31(M.*PL*.77.291A).

***κιλικίσιον**, **τό**, = foreg. 1, Pall.*h.Laus*.17(p.47.4; M.34.1049B); *ib*. 27(p.83.1; 1092B).

[*]**κίλικος**, *made of coarse cloth* (strictly, of Cilician goat's hair), *Const.Stud*.38(M.99.1720B).

κιμβικία, ἡ, *stinginess*, Pall.*h.Laus*.proem.(p.10.11; M.34.1002).

[*]**κιμιλιάρχης**, ὁ, v. κειμηλιάρχης.

Κιμμέριος, *Cimmerian*, i.e. *dwelling in darkness*; met., Clem.*prot*. 9(p.65.27; M.8.200B).

κινάρα, ἡ, *rod*, *A.Petr.et Paul*.79(p.212.12); *A.*(*Pass.*)*Petr.et Paul*.58(p.168.8).

***κινδύνευσις**, ἡ, *danger*, Thdr.Stud.*epp*.2.31(M.99.1204A).

***κινδυνευτέον**, *one must run risks*, Isid.Pel.*epp*.2.164(M.78.617B).

κινδυνεύ-ω, **1.** *run a risk, be in danger* (*of*) κατεχόμενος κ. Hegem. *Arch*.7(p.10.15; M.10.1437B); ἵνα μὴ ∼σῃ πάλιν εἰς τὸ μὴ εἶναι [sc. creation] Ath.*gent*.41(M.25.84A); abs., sc. of death ἐπαγγειλάμενος τῷ πατρὶ περὶ τῆς ζωῆς τοῦ ∼οντος διὰ τοῦ [Jo.4:50] Or.*Jo*.13.59(58; p.290.10; M.14.509D); Ῥουβεὶμ...ἐπειδὴ...τὸ παιδάριον οὐ τεθέαται, κεκινδυνευκέναι νομίσας, περιρρήγνυσι...τὸ ἱμάτιον Cyr.*glaph.Gen*.6(1. 183E); **2.** *be liable* κανόνι πειθόμενος, ὃς ∼ειν παρακελεύεται τὸν καλούμενον εἰς σύνοδον, καὶ παραγίνεσθαι μὴ βουλόμενον Thdt.*ep*.81(4. 1140); ∼ων εἰς τὰ δημόσια μετὰ τῆς οἰκείας τάξεως Ath.Scholast.*coll*. 4.1(p.49); theol., of self-imposed liability in Inc., *subject oneself* υἱὸν...σαρκὶ ∼σαντα Cyr.*thes*.32(5¹.319C); **3.** *venture, dare* οὐ τινὰ μέν, τινὰ δὲ οὔ, ἀλλὰ ∼ω λέγειν πάντας Cyr.*Ps*.36:8(M.69.928C); **4.** with neg., *be safe*, i.e. in no danger of error (cf. Eng. 'it is safe to say') τὰ γεγραμμένα λέγω. καὶ σὺ λέγε, καὶ οὐ ∼εις ‡Ath.*dial.Trin*.3.4(M. 28.1209A); *ib*.3.6(1212C).

κίνδυνος, ὁ, **1.** *danger*, not to be courted by Christians, Gr.Naz. *or*.7.14(M.35.772B); Chrys.*hom.26.3 in Heb*.(12.240C); id.*hom.in Mt. 26:39*(3.23D); for εἰς κ. τῆς κεφαλῆς and similar phrases, v. κεφαλή; of threat to logical position, Clem.*str*.7.16(p.69.4; M.9.536A); ὁ λόγος ἀναβὰς εἰς κ. ἐμπέσῃ Meth.*res*.1.49(p.303.16; M.18.280A); spiritual ὅσῳ πλείονος κατηξιώθημεν γνώσεως, τοσούτῳ μᾶλλον ὑποκείμεθα κινδύνῳ *1Clem*.41.4; *Const.App*.3.9.1; **2.** *liability, cost* οὐχ ἁπλῶς ἀκινδύνως ἐχαρίσατο, φησίν, ἀλλὰ μετὰ τοῦ κ. τοῦ υἱοῦ Chrys. *hom.17.1 in Eph*.(11.121E).

κιν-έω, *move*, **I.** trans.;

A. *set in motion*; **1.** *move*; in phrases, *leave no* stone *unturned*, Gr.Thaum.*pan.Or*.6(p.15.7; M.10.1069A); ὁ πάντα κάλων ∼ῶν εἰς τὴν αὐτοῦ κατασκευήν ‡Ign.*Phil*.4; πάντα δεῖ λίθον κ. ... ὥστε τὸ ἀληθὲς ἐξευρεῖν Thdt.*eran*.2(4.125); **2.** *remove*, met. κ. τοὺς δοκοῦντας ἐπισκόπους CAlex.*ep*.ap.Ath.*apol.sec*.8(p.94.13; M.25.264A); θάνατον ἀπὸ σώματος κ. Chrys.*hom.57.3 in Mt*.(7.580B); *overthrow* Law, *ib*. *16.1*(203E); **3.** *raise* or *discuss* a subject μηδὲ ἐπιτρέψαι τι σεαυτῷ ἐν τῇ συνόδῳ κ. περὶ τῶν καθ' ἡμᾶς πραγμάτων Alex.Thess.*ep.Dion*. (p.160.16; M.25.393B); πολλοὺς κ. λογισμούς, καὶ πανταχόθεν ἐπιχειρεῖ λῦσαι τὴν ἀπορίαν Chrys.*hom.16.4 in Rom*.(9.609C); ἕτερον ἐκίνει τόπον ἀγωνιστικώτατον id.*comm.in Gal*.5:4(10.697E); εἰς καιρὸν τὸν περὶ τῶν θείων μυστηρίων ἐκίνησας λόγον Thdt.*eran*.2(4.125); id. *Rom*.3(3.40); pass. τοῦ κεκινημένου ζητήματος Eus.*h.e*.5.24.18(M.20. 508B); *be introduced* περὶ...τοῦ νῦν ∼ηθέντος...δόγματος Dion.Al.*ib*. 7.6(M.20.645B); ptcpl. pass. neut. as subst., *subject under discussion* διασαφούσας σοι τὸ κ. Isid.Pel.*epp*.1.449(M.78.429B); *Pers*. (p.39.6); **4.** *hold* converse, *speak* λόγους τινὰς πνευματικοὺς πρὸς ἀλλήλους ∼ήσωμεν Chrys.*hom.in 1Cor.10:1*(3.229D); **5.** pass., of a council, *be held*, Ath.*syn*.6(p.234.14; M.26.689A); **6.** *move, impel*, ref. deliberative action ἱκανός ἐστι κ. ψυχὴν ἀκροατοῦ μάλιστα ἡμαρτηκότος, τοιούτους εὔχεται λόγους λέγειν, οἵτινες...κ. ἐπὶ πένθος Or.*hom.20.6 in Jer*.(p.186.6ff.; M.13.513B); κ. πρὸς τὸ πιστεῦσαι id. *Jo*.28.10(9; p.400.15; M.14.700B); usu. pass., *be moved, activated*, of man and his faculties λογικῶς κ. ἡ ψυχὴ ἡ προμηνεύουσα τὰ μέλλοντα ἢ θεραπεύουσα τὰ ἐνεστηκότα Athenag.*leg*.27.2(M.6.953A); θέλησίς ἐστι...νοῦς περί τι αὐθαιρέτως κ. αὐτεξουσιότης ἐστὶ νοῦς κατὰ φύσιν κ. ἡ νοερὰ τῆς ψυχῆς κίνησις αὐτοκρατής Clem.*fr*.40(p.220.16f.; M.9.752B); ὡς...ἀπὸ θεοῦ ἔχομεν τὸ εἶναι ζῷα καὶ τὸ εἶναι ἄνθρωποι, οὕτω καὶ τὸ καθόλου θέλειν...καὶ τὸ καθόλου κ. ... ἡμεῖς δὲ τῷ θέλειν ἢ ἐπὶ τοῖς καλλίστοις ἢ ἐπὶ τοῖς ἐναντίοις χρώμεθα, ὁμοίως καὶ τῷ ἐνεργεῖν Or.*princ*.3.1.20(19; p.234.17; M.11.293A); διαφόρως περὶ τούτου [i.e. nature of God] κ. *ib*.4.2.1(8; p.307.15; 357C); πᾶς νοῦς αὐτοκράτωρ ἐστὶ ἰδικῷ θελήματι κατὰ φύσιν ~ούμενος Apoll.*fr*.150(p.247.24)ap.*Doct.Patr*.41(p.307.6); of Arian Christ οὐκ ἔχει τὴν προαίρεσιν ἐλευθέραν εἰς τὸ κ. καὶ ῥέπειν εἰς ἑκάτερα; Ath.*Ar*.1.35(M.26.84B); of God τὸ πνεῦμα τὸ ἅγιον τὸ ~ῆσαν τοὺς ἀνθρώπους Or.*engast*.4(p.286.8; M.12.1017A); ὁ...Ἀντώνιος, ὥσπερ θεόθεν ~ούμενος ἠγάπησε τὸν τόπον Ath.*v.Anton*.50(M.26.916A); πάντες οἱ συνελθόντες [i.e. in synods] τοὺς μὲν [sc. Ursacius, Valens, etc.]...ὡς ἀφ' ἑνὸς πνεύματος ~ούμενοι, ἀνεθεμάτισαν id.*ep.Epict*.1(p.1.10; M.26.1052A); Jo.Mosch.*prat*.176(M.87.3045A); ref. inspiration of scripture, Dion.Ar.*e.h*.3.3.5(M.3.432B) cit. s. διαθήκη; esp. to prophecy χάριν μὴ λυπῶν ἐπιγνώσῃ, ἃ λόγος ὁμιλεῖ δι' ὧν βούλεται, ὅτε θέλει. ὅσα γὰρ θελήματι τοῦ κελεύοντος λόγου ἐκινήθημεν ἐξειπεῖν μετὰ πόνου...γινόμεθα ὑμῖν κοινωνοί ‡*Diogn*.11.7f.; ἀπὸ τοῦ ~οῦντος αὐτοὺς θείου λόγου Just.*1apol*.36.1(M.6.385A); τῷ παρὰ τοῦ θεοῦ πνεύματι ὡς ὄργανα κεκινηκότι τὰ τῶν προφητῶν στόματα Athenag.*leg*.7.2(M.6.904C); ὁ...Δαβὶδ...τὴν πρόρρησιν ἐκινεῖτο Proc.G.*Num*.24:8(M.87.868A); v. ἔκστασις, πλῆκτρον; of demons, Chrys.*diab*.1.5(2.256B), id.*Stag*.2.1(1.180A) citt. s. δαίμων; in Messalian teaching, Tim.CP *haer*.(M.86.48B) cit. s. δαίμων; **7.** theol.; **a.** of God as prime mover ἰδὼν...τὸν κόσμον...συνῆκα τὸν κ. καὶ διακρατοῦντα εἶναι θεόν· πᾶν γὰρ τὸ ~οῦν ἰσχυρότερον τοῦ ~ουμένου...~εῖται δὲ ὁ οὐρανὸς κατὰ ἀνάγκην. ... ὁρῶμεν...αὐτὸν [sc. τὸν ἥλιον] ~ούμενον κατὰ ἀνάγκην. ... ὁρῶμεν...αὐτὸν [sc. τὸν ἄνθρωπον] κ. κατὰ ἀνάγκην Arist.*apol*.1.2,4.2,6.1,7.1; πανταχόθεν...ἀκούει [sc. ὁ θεός], νοεῖ, κ. *Hom.Clem*.17.7; τί τὸ ταῦτα κ.;...ἆρ' οὐχ ὁ τεχνίτης τούτων; Jo.D.*f.o*.1.3(M.94.797A); himself unmoved οὔτε ~ούμενος ὁ τόπῳ τε ἀχώρητος Just.*dial*.127.2(M.6.772B); σὲ τὴν κατὰ τὸν τόπον ~εῖσθαι, δέσποτα, κίνησιν οἴεται [sc. Arius] Const.ap.Gel.Cyz.*h.e*.3.19.27(M.85.1352B); οὐδέ γε παθητικῶς κ. ... ὑφίστη αὐτόν [sc. τὸν υἱόν] Eus.*e.th*.1.12(p.72.16; M.24.849A); πῶς τὸ αὐτὸ καὶ ~εῖ καὶ ~εῖται; Gr.Naz.*or*.20.11(M.35.1077C); *ib*.28.8(p.34.1ff.; M.36.36A); τὸ...ἄπειρον κατ' οὐδένα τρόπον ἢ λόγον ἐπιδέχεται κίνησιν, οὐκ ἔχον ὅπου καὶ περὶ ὃ ~ηθήσεται. τροπὴ γὰρ τοῦ κατὰ φύσιν ἀπείρου ~εῖσθαι μὴ πεφυκότος ἡ κίνησις ‡Hipp.*Ber.Hel*.2(p.321.21f.; M.10.832A); τριὰς...πανταχοῦ παροῦσα μὴ ~ουμένη Geo.Pis.*Pers*.1.8(M.92.1199A); πᾶν γὰρ ~ούμενον ὑφ' ἑτέρου ~εῖται...καὶ τοῦτο εἰς ἄπειρον, ἕως ἂν καταντήσωμεν εἴς τι ἀκίνητον. τὸ γὰρ πρῶτον ~οῦν, ἀκίνητον, ὅπερ ἐστὶ τὸ θεῖον Jo.D.*f.o*.1.4(M.94.797Cf.); **b.** pass., of God εἰ...διὰ τὴν προσοῦσαν ἀγαθότητα τῷ θεῷ ὅλην μὲν κεκινῆσθαι λέγοι τὴν τοῦ πατρὸς δύναμιν εἰς τὴν γέννησιν τοῦ υἱοῦ, ὅλην δὲ πάλιν τὴν τοῦ μονογενοῦς εἰς τὴν ὑπόστασιν τοῦ ἁγίου πνεύματος Bas.*Eun*.2.32(1.269C; M.29.648B); μονὰς ἀπ' ἀρχῆς, εἰς δυάδα ~ηθεῖσα, μέχρι τριάδος ἔστη Gr.Naz.*or*.29.2(p.75.8; M.36.76B); ποτὲ μὲν ἔρωτα καὶ ἀγάπην αὐτόν [sc. θεόν] φασι, ποτὲ δὲ ἐραστὸν καὶ ἀγαπητόν...τῷ μὲν ~εῖται, τῷ δὲ ~εῖ Dion.Ar.*d.n*.4.14(M.3.712C); τί δὲ...~ούμενόν φασι τὸν ἀκίνητον;...~εῖσθαι...αὐτὸν...οἰητέον, οὐ κατὰ φοράν, ἢ ἀλλοίωσιν...ἢ τοπικὴν κίνησιν...ἀλλὰ τὸ εἰς οὐσίαν ἄγειν τὸν θεὸν καὶ συνέχειν τὰ πάντα...καὶ τὸ παρεῖναι πᾶσι τῇ πάντων ἀσχέτῳ περιοχῇ, καὶ ταῖς ἐπὶ τὰ ὄντα πάντα προνοητικαῖς προόδοις καὶ ἐνεργείαις. ἀλλὰ καὶ κινήσεις θεοῦ τοῦ ἀκινήτου, θεοπρεπῶς τῷ λόγῳ συγχωρητέον ὑμνῆσαι *ib*.9.9(916C); in comment on Gr.Naz.*or*.29.2 cit. supra τὸ θεῖον ἀκίνητον...λέγεται ~εῖσθαι, τῷ ~εῖν προνοητικῶς ἕκαστον τῶν ὄντων καθ' ὃν ~εῖσθαι πέφυκε λόγον Max.*ambig*.(M.91.1260B); ~εῖσθαι...ἡ θεότης λέγεται ὡς αἰτία τῆς καθ' ὃν ὑπάρχει τρόπον ἐξετάσεως...λέγεται δὲ ~εῖσθαι πάλιν καὶ διὰ τὴν κατὰ μέρος φανέρωσιν...κατὰ τὴν...γραφήν, ἀπὸ τοῦ πατέρα ὁμολογεῖν ἀρχομένου, καὶ εἰς τὸ υἱὸν συνομολογεῖν πατρὶ προβαίνοντος, καὶ πατρὶ καὶ υἱῷ συμπαραδέχεσθαι τὸ πνεῦμα τὸ ἅγιον *ib*.(1260Df.); **8.** Christol. v. θέλημα, θέλησις, κίνησις.

B. *disturb*; **1.** *bestir* ἐκίνησαν ἑαυτοὺς καὶ συνήγαγον ἅπαντας *Pers*.(p.38.9); *vent* one's anger πλὴν τοῦ θυμοῦ ὃν ἐκίνει κατὰ τῶν ἐχθρῶν τῆς πίστεως Marc.Diac.*v.Porph*.8; **2.** *disturb, distress* μηδὲ...~ήσῃς σαυτόν, μηδὲ κάμῃς Chrys.*hom*.84.4 *in Mt*.(7.802D); freq. pass., Meth.*symp*.9.5(p.121.2; M.18.192A); Chrys.*hom*.3.4 *in Ac*.(9.29C); **3.** *adduce in objection*, ‡Gr.Nyss.*Ar.et Sab*.13(M.45.1300A).

II. intrans.; **A.** κ. ἀπό *leave*; **1.** ref. Gen.11:2, *move camp from* ἐκίνησαν ἀπὸ ἀνατολῶν Or.*hom*.12.3 *in Jer*.(p.90.7; M.13.384A); Ath.*ep.fest*.43(p.297.20; M.26.1440C) ∞ Cosm.Ind.*top*.3(M.88.136C); **2.** usu. pass.; **a.** *leave* δοῦλος...ἀκολουθῶν τῷ κυρίῳ αὐτοῦ, καὶ μὴ κ. ἀπ' αὐτοῦ Ammonas *opusc*.2.7(p.464.1); **b.** met., *depart from, desert* ὡς...μὴ κ. ἀπὸ τοῦ γράμματος, μηδὲν θειότερον μάθωμεν Or.*princ*.4.2.9(p.321.10; M.11.373B); **c.** οἱ ~ούμενοι ? *the winds* ὁ ἡνιοχεύων τὴν τῶν κ. πνοήν Rom.Mel.(*AS* 1 p.125).

B. *take action* μηδὲν ἔτι περὶ τοῦ ποτηρίου ~ήσας Ath.*apol.sec*.17(p.99.33; M.25.276B); *take legal action, go to law*, Ath.Scholast.*coll*.2.2(p.33); *bring an action* against ἐπίσκοπος κ. ἐπισκόπῳ Phot.*nomoc*.9.8(M.104.1104A).

κίνησις, ἡ, **A.** *motion*; **1.** in gen., of different kinds τῆς...κ. οὐ μόνον κατὰ τὴν τοπικὴν μετάστασιν νοουμένης, ἀλλὰ καὶ ἐν τροπῇ...θεωρουμένης Gr.Nyss.*hom.opif*.1.4(M.44.129C); **a.** local motion specified as one of divine gifts to man at Creation, *Lit*.ap.*Const.App*.8.12.17; **b.** of mental impulses, emotions; also of rational mental processes ἀπὸ τῆς φυσικῆς...ἡμῶν κ. καὶ τῆς συνηθείας ἐστὶ τούτῳ ἐπιστῆναι Didym.*Trin*.2.19(M.39.736A); of voluntary acts ψυχῆς νοερᾶς αὐτεξούσιος κ. Ath.*fr*.(M.26.1292D); ἡ δ' οἱ θέλω κ., ἐξουσιότης Gr.Naz.*carm*.1.1.34.37(M.37.948A); Max.*opusc*.(M.91.153A) cit. s. θέλημα; *ib*.(280A); **2.** Trin., voluntary *activity*; one in Trin., Gr.Nyss.*Maced*.13(M.45.1317B), id.*tres dii*(M.45.128A) citt. s. θέλημα; *ib*.(129B) cit. s. βούλημα; θεὸν τὰ τρία μετ' ἀλλήλων νοούμενα, τῷ ταὐτῷ τῆς κ. καὶ τῆς φύσεως Just.Imp.*edict*.ap.Evagr.*h.e*.5.4(p.198.28; M.86.2796C); τὸ ταὐτὸν τῆς οὐσίας καὶ...τοῦ θελήματος, καὶ τὴν τῆς γνώμης σύμπνοιαν...καὶ τὸ ἓν ἔξαλμα τῆς κ. ‡Cyr.*Trin*.10(6^3.15C; M.77.1141D); ref. Jo.5:19 οὐχ ὡς δι' ὀργάνου ἢ δούλου, ἀλλ' ὡς δι' οὐσιώδους καὶ ἐνυποστάτου αὐτοῦ λόγου...διὰ τὸ μίαν ἐν πατρὶ καὶ υἱῷ θεωρεῖσθαι κ. *ib*.23(29A; M.1164D); **3.** Christol.; **a.** Apollinarian, cf. ἓν ζῷον ἐκ κινουμένου καὶ κινητικοῦ συνίστατο καὶ οὐ δύο ἢ ἐκ δύο τελείων καὶ αὐτοκινήτων Apoll.*fr*.107(p.232.16)ap.Justn.*monoph*.(M.86.1124A); v. θέλημα; **b.** monothelite ἐπειδὴ...εἷς ὁ ἐνεργῶν, καὶ μία αὐτοῦ ἐστιν ἡ ἐνέργεια, καὶ ἡ κ. ἡ ἐνεργητική Sev.Ant.*fr*.(H.3.893B); μία γὰρ ἡ ἐνέργεια, τουτέστιν ἡ κ. ἡ ἐνεργητική *ib*.; ὕπνον καὶ κάματον...καὶ τὴν ἐν τούτοις κ. καὶ ἠρεμίαν τῇ...τοῦ λόγου ἐνεργείᾳ προσάπτομεν κἀντεῦθεν μίαν τοῦ αὐτοῦ...ἐνέργειαν προσάπτομεν Thdr.Pharan.*fr*.(H.3.765D); cf. τὴν ὡς ἑνὸς μίαν θέλησιν...πῇ μὲν ἀνθρωπίνως κινεῖσθαι πῇ δὲ θεοπρεπῶς Them.*fr*.(H.3.1240D); **c.** orthodox εἷς οὖν ἐκ δύο φύσεων ὁ Χριστός...δύο τε φυσικὰς καὶ γενικάς, καὶ τῶν ἐξ ὧν ἦν συστατικὰς κ., ἤγουν ἐνεργείας ἔχων, ὧν ἀποτελέσματα τὰ κατὰ μέρος ἦν ἐνεργήματα Max.*opusc*.(M.91.36C); cf. ἔδει...τὸ τῆς σαρκὸς θέλημα κινηθῆναι, ὑποταγῆναι δὲ τῷ θελήματι τῷ θεϊκῷ *Symb.CP*(681)(H.3.1400D).

B. *initiative, incentive* ἡ ψυχὴ ἀποστᾶσα τῆς πρὸς τὰ καλὰ θεωρίας, καὶ τῆς ἐν αὐτοῖς κ. ... κινεῖται τὰ ἐναντία Ath.*gent*.4(M.25.9D); ἢ ἐξ οἰκείας κ. ὁ ἄρχων ἢ ὁ ἔκδικος τοῦτο πράττεται Ath.Scholast.*coll*.5.5(p.76).

C. *disturbance* λῃστῶν κ. Ath.*v.Anton*.36(M.25.896B).

D. *action, proceedings* τὴν κ. διηγήσασθαι τῆς ἐξανυσθείσης πρεσβείας *Cod.Afr*.90(Lat. *cursum*).

E. *sentence, punishment* τί...ἄλλο τέλος τῆς...ἐξετάσεως ἢ θάνατος ἐκ βασιλικῆς κ. ἐπαγόμενος; CAlex.*ep*.ap.Ath.*apol.sec*.3(p.90.15; M.25.253C); Cyr.*Jo*.4.3(4.373A); ἰσομεγέθη...ὥσπερ αἰτιάμασιν ἀποτορνεύων τὴν κ. id.*ador*.8(1.258D); Ath.Scholast.*coll*.1.17(p.24).

κινητής, ὁ, *one who overthrows* κ. τῶν ἀντιτεταγμένων Gr.Nyss.*v.Mos*.(M.44.372D).

κινητικός, *setting in motion, causing to move*; c. genit., Clem.*paed*.2.8(p.203.32; M.8.488C); ὡς...θεὸς τῆς ἰδίας ἦν κινητικὸς ἀνθρωπότητος Max.*ambig*.(M.91.1056A).

κινητός, *movable*; of property, Ath.*v.Anton*.2(M.26.843A); Gr.Naz.*test*.(M.37.389B).

***κινίζ-ω**, s.v.l., ? *excite* καιρὸς θρηνεῖν καὶ δακρύειν, οὐχὶ δὲ τὸ ~ειν καὶ μετεωρίζεσθαι ‡Chrys.*hom.jej*.5(9.801A).

[*]**κίνν-υμαι**, metr. gr. for κίνυμαι, ? *stamp* θεοῦ λόγος...σφρηγὶς ~υμένη πατρώϊος Gr.Naz.*carm*.1.1.1.31(M.37.400A).

[*]**κιννύρα**, ἡ, (Hebr. כִּנּוֹר) variant of κινύρα, Jewish stringed instrument, ‡Chrys.*ador*.2(11.825F).

[*]**κιννυρίζ-ω**, *play a stringed instrument*; met., *make music* ἔστιν τις ~ων ἐν ἐμοί *A.Xanthipp*.14(p.68.5).

***κιννυρικός**, *of a stringed instrument*, ‡Caes.Naz.*dial*.103(M.38.969).

***κινυρίστρια**, ἡ, *female player on the* κιννύρα (or κινύρα), *Pers*.(p.13.4; M.10.101B).

***κιονάκιον**, τό, *column*; supporting mensa of an altar, Thphn.*chron*.p.318(M.108.769B).

κιόνιον, τό, **1.** *leg*; of a table, *Fr.hist*.4(M.85.1821B); of a chair, Cosm.Ind.*top*.1(M.88.101B); **2.** *pillar* κιόνια ἤτοι τὰ στήθεα τὰ διαχωρίζοντα τὸ βῆμα ἀπὸ τοῦ λοιποῦ ναοῦ, εἰσὶν ἃ δηλοῦσι ‡Germ.CP *contempl*.(M.98.389D).

***κιονίτης, ἡ,** *one who dwells on a pillar, stylite,* Evagr.*h.e.*2.10 tit.(p.35.1; M.86.2532A); Thphn.*chron.*p.285(κίων M.108.700C); *ib.*p.361 (865C); Thdr.Stud.*epp.*1.15 tit.(M.99.957A).

κιονοειδής, *like a column* κιονοειδὲς φωνῆς ὄργανον Melet.*nat.hom.* 10(M.64.1196B).

κιρν-άω, = κίρνημι and κεράννυμι; **1.** abs., *mix wine in a cup, mix a drink,* Jo.Mosch.*prat.*94(M.87.2952D); **2.** gen., *mix, blend* τὸ ἀγαθὸν καὶ τὸ κακὸν ἀπὸ τοῦ αὐτοῦ φέρεσθαι...οὐ διαιροῦντες...τὸ ἀγαθὸν ἀπὸ τοῦ κακοῦ...ἀλλὰ ~ῶντες καὶ ἐγκαταμιγνύντες θάτερον θατέρῳ Hegem.*Arch.*5(p.6.14; M.10.1433C); **3.** myst., *unite* ἡ θεία χάρις τῇ ἀνθρωπίνῃ ~ωμένη προθυμίᾳ, σώζει τὸν ἄνθρωπον Isid.Pel. *epp.*4.51(M.78.1101A); **4.** *temper, mitigate* δεῖ...μετρίως ~ᾶν [sc. austerities] ἵνα τῇ πάντῃ ἀκρασίᾳ μὴ τὸ σπουδάζον παθαίνοιτο Ephr.3. 404A; ἡ φρόνησις τῇ ἁπλότητι ~ωμένη Isid.Pel.*epp.*2.175(M.78. 625C); τῶν ὁμιλούντων αὐτῷ τὸν τόνον ἐκίρνα Soz.*h.e.*1.13.6(M.67. 897B); **5.** Christol., pass., *be joined, united,* ref. mutual interaction of divine and human natures οὐδὲν αὐτὸς ἀπὸ τῆς κοινωνίας τῆς περὶ τὸ σῶμα καὶ τὴν ψυχὴν ἀλλοιούμενος...γίνεται σὺν αὐτοῖς ἓν...καὶ ~ᾶται καὶ μένει...ἀμετάβλητος, οὐ συμπάσχων, ἀλλὰ συμπράττων μόνον Nemes.*nat.hom.*3(M.40.601B); Thdr.Raith.*praep.*(p.194.15; M.91. 1496A) cit. s. κίρνημι.

κίρν-ημι, = κιρνάω and κεράννυμι; **1.** *mix* wine, fig. οἶνος ὃν ἡ σοφία ~ησιν Or.*hom.12.1 in Jer.*(p.86.26; M.13.377D); met. ~αταί σοι ὁ θυμὸς καὶ ἡ κόλασις *ib.12.2*(p.88.27; κιρνᾶται 381A); **2.** *mingle,* of two streams ἕνα...ἀποτελοῦσι ποταμὸν...τό τε ῥεῦμα καὶ τὴν προσηγορίαν ~άμενοι Philost.*h.e.*7.4(M.65.628A); **3.** *compound* (ref. Is. 19:14) τὸ πνεῦμα τῆς πλανήσεως ~άμενον ἀπὸ τοῦ θεοῦ Or.*hom.20.3 in Jer.*(p.182.17; M.13.507B); **4.** pass., of intimate contact, *be joined, be united;* **a.** myst., in eucharist οἱ μὴ παρέχοντες ἐπιτήδειον τὸ σῶμα πρὸς τὴν ἀνάκρασιν τοῦ σώματος αὐτοῦ [sc. τοῦ Χριστοῦ], ὅπερ ἡμῖν ἔδωκεν, ἵνα πρὸς αὐτὸ ~άμενοι, πρὸς τὸ πνεῦμα τὸ ἅγιον ἀνακιρνώμεθα ‡Chrys.*pasch.*2(8.256B); **b.** Christol. [1Cor.15:47f.] νομιστέον λέγεσθαι...οὐ κατὰ τὸ φαινόμενον τοῦ θεοῦ, ἀλλὰ κατὰ τὸ νοούμενον, ~αμένων ὥσπερ τῶν φύσεων, οὕτω δὴ καὶ τῶν κλήσεων, καὶ περιχωρουσῶν εἰς ἀλλήλας τῷ λόγῳ τῆς συμφυΐας Gr.Naz.*ep.*101(M.37. 181C); ~αμένων...τῶν...φύσεων καὶ περιχωρουσῶν εἰς ἀλλήλας τῷ λόγῳ τῆς συμφυΐας..., κιρνῶνται καὶ περιχωροῦσιν εἰς ἀλλήλας ὡσαύτως καὶ αἱ κλήσεις Thdr.Raith.*praep.*(p.194.13; M.91.1496A).

***κίσηρος (*κίσσηρος),** *of pumice* λίθου κ. Max.*qu.dub.*(M.90. 837A); as subst., *pumice-stone* κισσήρων ἐπιπολαζόντων Thphn. *chron.*p.339(M.108.816C).

κισσάω, *conceive,* ref. Gen.30:38f., Gr.Nyss.*Apoll.*1(M.45.1125B); Cyr.*glaph.Gen.*5(1.147E); fig. ὁ παμμίαρος τὴν κακίαν ἐκίσσησεν Thphn.*chron.*p.347(M.108.833C).

***κίσσηρος,** v. *κίσηρος.

κίσσησις, ἡ, *pregnancy,* ref. Gen.30:38f., Didym.*Trin.*1.15(M.39. 329B); *conception,* fig. ἡ κ. τῆς φαντασιολογίας Epiph.*haer.*25.4(p.271. 25; M.41.325B).

κισσόφυλλον, τό, *ivy-leaf,* Steph.Diac.*v.Steph.*(M.100.1120C); Melet.*nat.hom.*10(M.64.1196C).

***κιστέρνα, ἡ,** (Lat. *cisterna*) *cistern,* Jo.Mal.*chron.*16 p.399(M.97. 592A); *ib.*18 p.477(692C); *Chron.Pasch.*p.312(M.92.796A).

***κιτατόρι[ο]ν, τό,** (Lat. *citatorium*) *proclamation,* Thphn.*chron.* p.322(M.108.780A).

κιχλισμός, ὁ, *giggling, tittering,* Clem.*paed.*2.5(p.186.3; M.8. 448C) cit. s. γέλως.

κιχρ-άω, A. act.; **1.** *lend* ~ῶν...ὡς τὴν ἔκτισιν...προσμένων Thdt. *Ps.*111:5(1.1405); ref. divine gifts ~ῶντος ἡμῖν τὸ τῆς ἰδίας φύσεως ἀμετάπτωτον τοῦ μονογενοῦς Cyr.*Jo.*5.2(4.473B); within Trin., acc. Eunomians ~ῶντος...τοῦ πατρὸς τῷ υἱῷ τὴν [sc. δόξαν] ἑαυτοῦ id. *thes.*6(5¹.49B); met. κ. ὁρμάς id.*Jo.*6(4.568B); γλῶτταν αὐτῇ κ. καὶ κάλαμον [i.e. information both oral and in writing] Sophr.H.*mir. Cyr.et Jo.*34(M.87.3536C); *give, devote* οὐ δεῖ κ. ἑαυτὸν εἰς τὴν περὶ τῶν βιωτικῶν φροντίδα Bas.*moral.*28(2.303A; M.31.840C); τῷ ἔργῳ κ. τὰς χεῖρας Nil.*Magn.*29(M.79.1005B); κ. ἡμῖν σεαυτήν Thdr.Stud. *epp.*2.214(M.99.1644B); χεῖρα κ. τῷ παρατατομένῳ δεσπότῃ [i.e. God] Bas.Sel.*or.*15.2(M.85.196A); **2.** *proclaim* as an oracle (cf. χράω) ἐξ ὧν ἐσπούδαζε τὸ Ἑλληνικὸν ~ᾶν τὰ δαιμόνια...ἐκ τούτων ...τὸ ἀσθενὲς αὐτῶν διελέγχειν...συνηλαύνοντο Philost.*h.e.*7.12(M.65. 549C).

B. med., *borrow* ὁ...διάβολος...~ᾶται τὰς λέξεις τῶν γραφῶν Ath. *Ar.*1.8(M.26.25C); Pall.*h.Laus.*63(p.159.10; M.34.1235C); Thdt.*affect.* 4(p.117.1; 4.811); Jo.Mosch.*prat.*200(M.87.3088D).

κίων, ὁ, *pillar;* as home of pillar-ascetics, Thdt.*h.rel.*26(3.1270); Evagr.*h.e.*1.13(p.21.2; M.86.2453B); Jo.Mosch.*prat.*129(M.87.2993B).

***κλάβαξ, ἡ,** *drain, Didasc.Jac.*5.20(p.90.18).

***κλαβίον, τό,** *bracelet,* Jo.Mal.*chron.*18 p.457(M.97.669B, conj. for κλανίον); Thphn.*chron.*p.207(M.108.532A).

κλαγγή, ἡ, *crowing,* Epiph.*exp.fid.*22(p.524.4; M.42.928D); *squeak* of weasel, Gr.Mag.*dial.*(tr.Zach.)3.4(M.*PL.*77.226A).

***κλαγγόφωνος,** *crowing,* ‡Caes.Naz.*dial.*140(M.38.1072).

***κλάγγω, 1.** *howl;* of a sinner at death, Eus.Al.*serm.*4(M.86. 336A); **2.** *crow,* Nonn.*par.Jo.*13:38(M.43.865C).

κλαδαρός, *lascivious,* Clem.*paed.*3.9(p.274.25; M.8.645A); neut. sing. as adv. κ. περιβλέπουσαι *ib.*(p.274.1; 644A).

κλαδεών, ὁ, *branch,* Gr.Naz.*carm.*1.2.2.280(M.37.600A).

κλαδηφόρος, *bearing branches,* ref. Entry into Jerusalem, ‡Sophr.H.*triod.*(M.87.3900C).

κλάδος, τό, *branch;* met., *offspring,* Thdt.*ep.*18(4.1081); Geo.Pis. *carm.*4.116; theol., of Son in rel. to Father, Didym.*Trin.*1.30(M.39. 417A) cit. s. ῥίζα.

[*]κλαδοφορέω, = κλαδηφορέω, *bear branches,* ref. Entry into Jerusalem, ‡Sophr.H.*triod.*(M.87.3897C).

[*]κλάνω, v. κλάω.

κλάσις, ἡ, 1. *breaking,* in gen. ποτηρίου κ. Ischyras *ep.*(p.143.22; M.25.364D); Ath.*apol.sec.*85(p.163.14; M.25.400B); of eucharistic breaking of bread κλίσις γονάτων καὶ κ. ἄρτου καὶ λόγος θεοῦ *A.Paul.et Thecl.*5(p.238.10); μετὰ τὴν εὐχὴν ἡ κ. καὶ ἐν τῇ κ. εὐχή Serap.*euch.*14 tit.; ἡ κ. ... τοῦ ἄρτου...τὴν σφαγὴν δηλοῖ Eutych. *pasch.*3(M.86.2396A); of the broken bread μετὰ τὸ διαδοῦναι τὴν κ. Serap.*euch.*15 tit.; **2.** *heart-break* ἐμοὶ...ταῦτ᾽ ἦν κ. μέν, ἀλλ᾽ ὅμως ἐκαρτέρουν Gr.Naz.*carm.*2.1.11.1796(M.37.1155A); **3.** *modulation* of voice, *ib.*1.2.8.100(656A); **4.** plur., *looseness* of morals, *ib.*1.2.6.32 (645A).

κλάσμα, τό, 1. *fragment* συλλέξατε...κλάσματα...τραπέζης Nonn. *par.Jo.*6:12(M.43.796A); eucharistic, *broken bread* περὶ δὲ τοῦ κ.· εὐχαριστοῦμέν σοι, πάτερ ἡμῶν *Did.*9.3; ὥσπερ ἦν τοῦτο ⟨τὸ⟩ κ. διεσκορπισμένον ἐπάνω τῶν ὀρέων καὶ συναχθὲν ἐγένετο ἓν *ib.*9.4; cf. ἐπέδωκεν αὐτῷ...ποτήριον καὶ κ. ἄρτου ‡Ath.*Melch.*(M.28.529C); **2.** *breach, rupture,* Gr.Nyss.*Apoll.*26(M.45.1180A); **3.** *breaking* into a house κλάσμα αὐτῷ πεποίηκεν *Mir.Artem.*18(p.20.10).

***κλασματίζ-ω,** *break in pieces* τὰ πεζικὰ...~οντες Thphn.*chron.* p.332(M.108.801B).

***κλασσικός, ὁ,** (Lat. *classicus*) *naval official* to whom dues were paid by ships passing through Hellespont, *IGC As.Min.*4.24 (Abydus, saec. v–vi).

[*]κλαυθμηρίζω, = κλαυθμυρίζω, intrans., *weep,* ‡Nil.*narr.*5(M. 79.645A).

***κλαυθμυρικῶς,** *with tears, sadly,* Thdr.Stud.*epp.*2.50(M.99. 1260D).

***κλαυθμύρισμα, τό,** *wailing* of infants; fig., ‡Chrys.*nat.Jo. Bapt.*(10.814A).

κλαυθμών, ὁ, *weeping,* ref. Ps.83:6, Chrys.*hom.3.3 in Col.*(11. 347A).

***κλαῦρος,** sens. dub., epithet applied to gum, Leont.H.*monoph.* (M.86.1816A) cit. s. κηρός.

κλαυσείω, *whimper,* Synes.*regn.*14(p.30.14; M.66.1077B).

***κλαυσίδειπνος,** *lamenting the loss of a dinner,* Bas.*ep.*115(3. 208B; M.32.532A).

κλαύσιμος, *pitiable;* of an excommunicated person, *Cod.Afr.*138 (Lat. *dolendus*).

κλάω, *break* ποτήριον...κεκλᾶσθαι Ath.*apol.sec.*8(p.94.18; M.25. 264A); κεκλασμένων...τῶν αὐχένων id.*virg.*14(p.48.21; M.28.268C); esp. of breaking bread, *A.Paul.*p.4.4; as technical eucharistic term, v. ἄρτος, σῶμα, εὐχαριστία; in form κλάνω, *Lit.Marc.*(p.138.19).

κλειδάρχης, ὁ, *keeper of the keys;* of S. Peter, Mac.Mgn.*apocr.*3.27 (p.117.4).

κλειδοποιός, ὁ, *locksmith,* Nil.*epp.*2.217 tit.(M.79.313A); Anast.S. *hod.*10(M.89.188D).

κλειδοῦχος, ὁ, *holder of the keys* of kingdom of heaven; of S. Michael, *Apoc.Bar.*11(p.92.7); of S. Peter κ. τῶν οὐρανῶν Didym. *Trin.*2.18(M.39.728A); κ. τῆς τῶν οὐρανῶν βασιλείας Anast.S.*Ps.*6(M. 89.1128C); Jo.D.*hom.*1.6(M.96.556C).

***κλειδοφυλακέω,** *keep locked,* met. τὰς διανοίας Serap.*Man.*54 (p.78; M.40.924B).

κλειδοφύλαξ, ὁ, *keeper of the keys, Orac.Sib.*8.122; Serap.*Man.*54 (p.78; M.40.924A).

κλείδωμα, τό, *fastening, bolt* of a door, *V.Aberc.*4(p.5.3).

κλείδωσις, ἡ, *fastening,* Sophr.H.*mir.Cyr.et Jo.*35(M.87.3545A).

κλειθρία, ἡ, *keyhole, chink,* Const.Diac.*laud.*13(M.88.493D).

***κλειθρίδιον, τό,** *narrow opening* prob. covered by a grating, Evagr.*h.e.*1.14(p.24.13; M.86.2461A); *ib.*2.3(p.41.8; 2496A).

κλείς, ἡ, *key*; met., ref. Mt.16:19 ἄρα...τῷ *Πέτρῳ μόνῳ δίδονται ὑπὸ Χριστοῦ αἱ κ. τῆς τῶν οὐρανῶν βασιλείας, καὶ οὐδεὶς ἕτερος τῶν μακαρίων αὐτὰς λήψεται*; Or.*comm.in Mt*.12.11(p.87.2; M.13.1001A); *Πέτρος...ἃς ἐπιστεύθη παρὰ Χριστοῦ κ. τῶν οὐρανῶν βαστάζων* Cosm. Ind.*top*.5(M.88.296D); ἀντὶ γὰρ κ. τὴν γλῶτταν ἐκέκτητο [sc. ὁ Πέτρος] ἀνοίγουσαν τὸν οὐρανὸν καὶ κλείουσαν ‡Caes.Naz.*dial*.194(M. 38.1180); defined as γνῶσις, *Hom.Clem*.3.18; as baptism τὸ φώτισμα, κ. οὐρανῶν βασιλείας Gr.Naz.*or*.40.3(M.36.361B); deposited in Roman see, Thdr.Stud.*epp*.2.63(M.99.1281A).

κλεῖσις, ἡ, *shutting*; of church doors after Gospel, Max.*myst*.13 (M.91.692B); *ib*.15(693C).

κλεισούρα, ἡ, *fortified place on a mountain pass*, Thphn.*chron*. p.258(M.108.644C); *ib*.p.325(785C).

***κλεισουράρχης, ὁ,** *military official in charge of a* κλεισούρα, Thphn.*chron*.p.307(M.108.749A).

***κλεισουροφύλαξ, ὁ,** *guard of a* κλεισούρα, Thphn.*chron*.p.291 (M.108.713A).

***κλειστάς, ἡ,** sens. dub., ? *door*, *A.Thom*.A 7(p.110.3; perh. παστάς).

§**κλειτός,** *shut*, Gr.Naz.*carm*.2.2(poem.)6.76(M.37.1548A).

κλείω, *shut*, irreg. perf. pass. αἱ θύραι κεκλείσκονται Thdr.Stud. *praesanct*.(M.99.1689A).

***κλέον,** for πλέον, Geo.Pis.*hex*.1667(M.92.1564A, conj. *Teub*.).

κλέπτης, ὁ, *thief*; **1.** met., *plagiarist* κλέπτας τῆς βαρβάρου φιλοσοφίας Ἕλληνας Clem.*str*.2.1(p.113.3; M.8.929D); Eus.*p.e*.10.2 (463D; M.21.772C); *ib*.11.1(507D; M.844B); **2.** as adj., superl. Ἰούδαν...κλεπτίστατον Cyr.*Os*.35(3.66A).

κλεπτικός, *thieving*; met., *plagiaristic*, Clem.*str*.1.8(p.26.3; M.8. 736B); *ib*.6.2(p.424.20; M.9.212C).

κλέπτω, 1. *steal*, met.; **a.** *take away, destroy* ὕπνον Serap.*ep.mon*.5 (M.40.932A); ‡Bas.*Lac*.5(2.591B; M.31.1448B); ἀλήθειαν Thdt.*h.rel*.1 (3.1113); τὸ δίκαιον id.*ep*.2(4.1061); pass. τῆς ἐλευθερίας ἐκλάπη τὸ νόμισμα Mac.Mgn.*apocr*.2.21(p.43.26); **b.** *plagiarize*; of poets, Eus. *p.e*.10.2(462B; M.21.769B); of false prophets, Thdt.*Jer*.23:30–32(2. 519); **c.** *catch* the eye, Oecum.*Apoc*.13:14(p.157); **2.** *steal from, rob* τοὺς δημοσίους ναοὺς κ. Phot.*nomoc*.2.2(M.104.581B).

***κλεσίη, ἡ,** v. *κλισίη.

***κλεψία, ἡ,** *theft*, *Apoc.Bar*.13(p.93.17); ‡Chrys.*poenit*.2.1(9. 782B); Jo.D.*disp*.(M.96.1336C).

***κλεψιγαμέω,** *ravish*, abs., Bas.*ep*.217 *can*.69(3.327D; M.32.800C).

***κλεψιγαμία, ἡ,** *illicit love*, Epiph.*haer*.59.6(p.371.10; M.41.1028B).

κλεψίγαμος, *seeking illicit love, adulterous*, *Orac.Sib*.2.258; Meth. *symp*.2.4(p.19.11; M.18.52C); Cyr.*Ps*.50:1(M.69.1085B); masc. as subst., Tim.Ant.*descr.BMV* 6(M.28.952C).

***κλεψιλογέω,** *steal arguments, plagiarize*, Hipp.*haer*.9.31(p.264. 22; M.16.3411B); of Marcionites borrowing dualistic principle from Empedocles, *ib*.7.31(p.217.20; 3335C).

***κλεψίλογος,** *stealing arguments, plagiaristic*, Hipp.*haer*.4.51 (p.76.32; M.16.3122D); of Marcion, *ib*.7.29(p.210.14; 3323B).

κλεψιμαῖος, 1. *stolen* σμάραγδοι κ. Pall.*h.Laus*.6(p.23.13; M.34. 1018D); *V.Pach.A* 23(p.150.14,15); **2.** in adv. phrases ἀπὸ κλεψιμαίων *by stealth*, Meth.*symp*.2.5(p.22.7; M.18.56B); κ. τρόπῳ Gr.Mag. *dial*.(tr.Zach.)1.3(M.*PL*.77.166A).

κλεψίνοος, *deceitful*, ‡Ign.*Phil*.4; Nonn.*par.Jo*.7:12(M.43.805C).

***κλεψίσοφος,** *sophistical* κ. δόγμασι Meth.*symp*.2.3(p.18.17; M.18. 52B).

***κλεψιφάγος,** *eating in secret*, Thdr.Stud.*epp*.2.156(M.99.1489B).

κλεψίφρων, *misleading the mind* κ. βουλῇ Gr.Naz.*carm*.1.1.9.13 (M.37.457A).

***κλεψόγονος, ὁ,** *one who steals children*; of Devil, Thdot.Anc. *hom.BMV et Sym*.12(M.77.1408B).

***κλεψοσύνη, ἡ,** *thieving*, Leont.N.*v.Jo.Eleem*.38(p.77.10).

κλεψύδριον, τό, *extract, snippet* χρησείδια καὶ κλεψύδρια πατρικά Anast.S.*hod*.3(M.89.92A); *ib*.12(201A).

κληδονίζομαι, *observe omens, practise divination*, Cyr.H.*catech*. 12.6; †Bas.*Is*.77(1.433C; M.30.248A); Chrys.*hom.5.3 in Tit*.(11.760A).

κληδονισμός, ὁ, *observation of signs* or *omens*, Cyr.H.*catech*.19. 8; †Bas.*Is*.77(1.433B; M.30.248A); Chrys.*hom.6.4 in Eph*.(11.44C); κληδωνισμοί Cyr.*Is*.4.3(M.70.984A, conj. for κλυδωνισμοί 2.621D).

κληδοῦχος, *holding the keys*, of S. Peter κληδοῦχος ἐπουρανίων πυλεώνων Paul.Sil.*Soph*.788(M.86.2149B).

***κλῆθος, τό,** prob. error for πλῆθος, *M.Bon*.10(p.329).

[*]**κληιδοφόρος,** *bearing keys*, Synes.*hymn*.3.634(p.24, v.l. κληιδηφόροι; M.66.1602).

κλῆμα, τό, *vine-switch, cane* carried by Roman centurion, Eus. *h.e*.7.15.2(M.20.676C).

***κληματηδόν,** *like a spreading vine*, ref. veins and arteries coursing through the body, Melet.*nat.hom*.synops.(M.64.1129D; vv.ll. κλημακηδόν, κληματοειδῶς).

***κληματίδιον, τό,** *small vine-twig*, Leont.N.*v.Sym*.58(M.93.1741A); Jo.Eleem.*v.Tych*.10(p.121); *ib*.19(p.127).

***Κλημέντια, τά,** *the Clementine writings*, ‡Ath.*synops*.76(M.28. 432B).

κληρικός, ὁ, *one who receives a lot* or *portion*, hence *one who holds official position in Church, member of clerical order, cleric*; **1.** in all ranks, opp. laity τοὺς τῆς καθολικῆς ἐκκλησίας κ. καὶ λαούς Ath.*apol. sec*.33(p.111.23; M.25.304A); id.*syn*.9(p.236.24; M.26.696A); Serap. *euch*.15 tit.; *M.Niceph*.3(p.284); including bishops, presbyters, and deacons, Epiph.*haer*.68.3(p.143.17; M.42.189A); τοῦ τάγματος τῶν κ. πρεσβύτεροι δύο, διάκονοι δὲ πέντε Pall.*v.Chrys*.4(p.25.4; M.47.16); νεωστὶ γεγαμηκότες τινὲς...χειροτονοῦνται κ. ἤγουν πρεσβύτεροι Cyr. *ep*.79(5^2.211E); ἐποίησεν αὐτὸν κ. καὶ ἔπεμψεν αὐτὸν ἐπίσκοπον εἰς Σμύρναν *Chron.Pasch*.p.318(M.92.809B); **2.** in lower ranks λειτουργοὶ καὶ κ. πάντες Ath.*apol.sec*.7(p.93.31; M.25.261B); τοὺς περὶ ἐμὲ κ. ὅσους παρῃτησάμην Gr.Naz.*ep*.67(M.37.132B); ἐπίσκοποι κατ᾽ ἐπισκόπων καὶ κ. κατὰ κληρικῶν Cyr.H.*catech*.15.7; ἔχειν τιμὴν τοὺς διακόνους ὑπὸ τῶν ὑπηρετῶν καὶ πάντων τῶν κ. CLaod.*can*.20; τοὺς τῶν ἐπισκόπων κ. Thdt.*h.e*.2.9.9(3.851); κ. δέ τις τοῦ αὐτοῦ πρεσβυτέρου *M.Ner.et Ach*.17(p.16.20); dist. from ἱερατικοί, CLaod.*can*.27; **3.** dist. from monks, Ath.*v.Anton*.67(M.26.937C); Pach.*reg*.B(M.40.949A); Dam.Papa *ep.orient*.ap.Thdt.*h.e*.5.10.3(3.1035); ministering in monasteries, Cyr.*ep*.79(5^2.211E); *Apophth.Patr*.(M.65.104B); CChalc. *can*.8; **4.** appointed to a particular place κ. κατὰ τὴν...Ἀλεξανδρέων ...ἐκκλησίαν *Supplicatio* ap.Evagr.*h.e*.2.8(p.57.1; M.86.2524B); τῶν ἐν ἑκάστῃ [sc. ἐκκλησίᾳ] κ. Pall.*v.Chrys*.2(p.9.29; M.47.9); ἵνα καταστήσῃ κατὰ πόλεις κληρικούς Euthal.Diac.*epp.Paul*.(M.85.785C); με ...ἐποίησαν κ. εἰς τὴν κώμην *Apophth.Patr*.(M.65.257C); forbidden to move to another church without bishop's permission, *Can.App*. 15; CChalc.*can*.20; not to minister, nor be received in another city without letter from bishop, *Can.App*.12; CChalc.*can*.13; **5.** privileges: exemption from curial *munera*, Const.ap.Eus.*h.e*.10.7.2(M. 20.893B) cit. s. ἀλειτούργητος; Constantius Imp.ap.Ath.*apol.sec*.54 (p.135.10; M.25.348B); *ib*.56(p.136.16ff.; 349C–352A); outside sphere of secular courts, CSard.*ep.Alex*.ap.Ath.*apol.sec*.39(p.117.28; M.25. 316B); supported from church funds administered by bishops, *Can. App*.4; *ib*.59; *Const.App*.2.34.3; *ib*.3.15.5; **6.** duties incl. care of widows, Ath.*h.Ar*.61(p.217.20; M.25.768A); investigation of eccl. offences, Jul.Papa *ep.Dian*.ap.Ath.*apol.sec*.31(p.110.15; M.25.300D); administration of sacraments, Tim.I Al.*resp*.(M.33.1304B,C); Cyr. *ep*.79(5^2.211E); **7.** prohibition against man becoming cleric if he had been married to two sisters, or to a niece, *Can.App*.19; if self-mutilated, *ib*.22; if possessed, *ib*.79; cleric deposed by bishop, *Const.App*.8.28.1, for major offences, such as fornication, cf.Pall. *h.Laus*.141(p.166.3; M.34.1242A) and debt, cf.Gel.Cyz.*h.e*.2.32.17(M. 85.1333), but not excommunicated, cf.*Can.App*.25; sundry prohibitions laid upon clerics, *Can.App*.12,20,23.

κληροδοσία, ἡ, 1. *distribution of land*, esp. the promised land, Clem.*str*.1.21(p.87.5; M.8.876C); τὴν ἀληθῆ κ. ἀπὸ Ἰησοῦ μεριζομένην τοῖς υἱοῖς Ἰσραήλ Or.*hom.20.1 in Jos*.(p.415.23; M.12.917C); *Chron. Pasch*.p.209(M.92.512B); τῶν τοῦ...λαοῦ κ. διανεμήσεις καὶ κατασχέσεις Dion.Ar.*e.h*.3.3.4(M.3.429C); met. Χριστὸς...τοῖς ἰδίοις ἱερουργοῖς οὐχὶ...μόνον τὴν Ἰουδαίαν ἀλλὰ...ἅπασαν τὴν γῆν. καὶ δευτέρα μετὰ τὴν πρώτην κ. γέγονε Cyr.*Is*.5.5(2.865D); **2.** *assignment of a portion* διαφόρου κ. ἀποκειμένης ἐν τῇ γῇ τῆς κληρονομίας †Bas.*Is*.138(1.476A; M.30.344A); τὴν...κ. εἰς ἣν ἔπεσέ μοι τὰ τῆς κ. σχοινία Cyr.*Ps*.15:6 (M.69.812B); met., of Anomoeans' assignment of status to Persons of Trin. ἡ καινὴ τούτων κ. Bas.*Spir*.7(1.6D; M.32.80A); **3.** *inheritance* τοῦ Βενιαμὶν κ. ἐστὶν Ἱερουσαλήμ Or.*hom.19.12 in Jer*.(p.168.22; M. 13.488C); Κωνσταντῖνος...πρὸς τὴν τοῦ...ἀδελφοῦ κ. ἐπανελθών ‡Jo. D.*Artem*.9(p.30.10; M.96.1260C); τὰς δύο κ. *ib*.10(p.30.27; 1261A); of the Christian inheritance τὴν κ. τὴν οὐρανίαν Or.*exp.in Pr*.13:22(M. 17.192D); ὁ Χριστὸς τὴν ἀληθῆ κ. διδούς id.*hom.18.1 in Jos*.(p.406. 23; M.87.1028A); κ. τῆς μελλούσης *ib*.23.4(p.444.27; M.87.1037B).

κληροδοτ-έω, 1. *endow with an allotted portion* or *inheritance*, *T.Isach*.5.7; pass. οἱ ὑπὸ τῷ Μωσῇ ~ούμενοι πρῶτοι εἰλήφασι τὴν ἐπαγγελίαν· οἱ δὲ ὑπὸ τῷ Ἰησοῦ ~ούμενοι ὕστερον Or.*comm.in 1Cor*. 4:8(*JTS* 9 p.359); id.*Jo*.6.42(25; p.151.21; M.14.273B); met., *forecast the inheritance* in heaven of those who postpone baptism, Gr.Nyss. *bapt.diff*.(M.46.428B); **2.** *give as an inheritance*, *T.Isach*.5.7; Ἰησοῦν ...τὸν ~ήσαντα ὃ ἀνείληφεν ἀνθρώπινον Or.*Jo*.6.42(25; p.151.29; M. 14.273C); **3.** *distribute in portions, allot*; the promised land, Proc.G.*Is*.44:10(M.87.2412C); Cyr.*Is*.3.2(2.422C); pass. ἡ χώρα τοῖς Ἰσραηλίταις ἐκληροδοτεῖτο Thdr.Heracl.*Is*.44:9(M.18.1337D); ‡Hipp.Th.*fr*.14(p.44.21).

***κληροδότης**, ὁ, *dispenser, divider* κ. θεός Or.*exc.in Ps*.36:9(M.17.125C); of Anomoeans *διαιρεῖται…τῆς θεότητος καὶ κ.* Chrys.*pan.Phoc*.3(2.708D); *Χριστὸς…κ. τῶν ἀξίων τῆς χάριτος* Max.*ambig*.(M.91.1120C); *ὁ…τῶν θείων μονῶν κ.* Thdr.Stud.*epp*.2.16(M.99.1165B).

κληρονομ-έω, *inherit, obtain as one's inheritance* or *lot*, of Christ *∼οῦντος διαθήκην κυρίου* *Barn*.14.5; esp. of people of God inheriting divinely promised blessings *Ἀβραὰμ…ὅπως…∼ήσῃ τὰς ἐπαγγελίας τοῦ θεοῦ* *1Clem*.10.2; *οἱ…ὑπομένοντες…δόξαν καὶ τιμὴν ἐκληρονόμησαν* *ib*.45.8; *Barn*.13.1; Just.*dial*.119.5(M.6.753A) cit. s. *κληρονομία*; *οἱ τὸν Χριστὸν διώξαντες…οὐ ∼ήσουσιν ἐν τῷ ὄρει τῷ ἁγίῳ οὐδέν· τὰ δὲ ἔθνη τὰ πιστεύσαντα εἰς αὐτόν…∼ήσουσι τὴν ἁγίαν τοῦ θεοῦ κληρονομίαν* *ib*.26.1(532A); *∼ήσουσι τὸν θεόν* *A.Paul.et Thecl*.5(p.239.1); *πάντων ⟨τῶν⟩ ∼ουμένων οὐρανῶν ὄντων ἄνω* Or.*Jo*.19.22(p.323.22; M.14.568A); *ὁ θεὸς…νικήσας τὸν θάνατον ἀπέδωκε* [sc. *τὴν σάρκα*] *τῇ ἀφθαρσίᾳ, ἵνα μὴ ∼ήσῃ ἡ φθορὰ τὴν ἀφθαρσίαν* Meth.*res*.2.18(p.369.2; M.18.313A); *∼εῖσθαι μὲν τὸ ἀποθνῆσκον, ∼εῖν δὲ τὸ ζῶν* *ib*.(p.370.12; 313B); *οὐ ∼εῖσθαι βασιλείαν θεοῦ…ὑπὸ τοῦ σώματος, ἀλλὰ τὸ σῶμα ὑπὸ τῆς ζωῆς…νῦν δὲ τὸ τεθνηκὸς ἡ ζωὴ ∼εῖ* *ib*.(p.371.3; 313B); *βασιλείαν κ.* Ath.*v.Anton*.17(M.26.869A); *ἐν ἐκείνῳ* [sc. future life] *∼οῦσι τὴν γῆν τῶν ζώντων οἱ ἄξιοι* Thdt.*Is*.60:21(p.239.24; 2.382); *∼ήσας βασιλείαν ἀτελεύτητον* †Gregent.*disp*.(M.86.784A).

κληρονόμημα, τό, *inheritance*, Clem.*str*.7.12(p.55.29; M.9.508B); Epiph.*haer*.76.1(p.341.12; M.42.516D).

κληρονομία, ἡ, *inheritance, heritage*; **1.** abs. *ὁ δεσπότης συντέτμηκεν τοὺς καιροὺς…ἵνα ταχύνῃ ὁ ἠγαπημένος αὐτοῦ καὶ ἐπὶ τὴν κ. ἥξῃ* *Barn*.4.3; *Μωϋσῆς θεράπων ὢν ἔλαβεν, αὐτὸς δὲ ὁ κύριος ἡμῖν ἔδωκεν εἰς λαὸν κληρονομίας δι' ἡμᾶς ὑπομείνας* *ib*.14.4; *σὺν τῷ Ἀβραὰμ τὴν ἁγίαν κληρονομήσομεν γῆν, εἰς τὸν ἀπέραντον αἰῶνα τὴν κ. ληψόμενοι* Just.*dial*.119.5(M.6.753A); *καλή γε καὶ ἐράσμιος ἡ κ., οὐ χρύσιον, οὐκ ἄργυρος…ἀλλ' ἐκεῖνος ὁ θησαυρὸς τῆς σωτηρίας* Clem.*prot*.10(p.68.21; M.8.205C); *ἡ κ. οὐκ ἔξωθέν ἐστι τοῦ κληρονομοῦντος ἀλλ' ἐν τῷ νῷ καὶ τῇ ψυχῇ αὐτοῦ* Or.*comm.in Eph*.1:14(p.243); *κ. δὲ ἀληθής, ἡ αἰώνιος ζωή* Thdt.*Ps*.60:6(1.1010); *κληρονομίαν…ἐν τῷ αἰῶνι τούτῳ ἡ ἐκκλησία οὐ κέκτηται, πλὴν μόνον τὸν θεόν* Hesych.*fr.Ps*.15:2(M.93.1185B); **2.** inherited by saints *οἱ πρὸ Μωυσέως γενόμενοι δίκαιοι…σώζονται ἐν τῇ τῶν μακαρίων κ. ἢ οὔ;* Just.*dial*.67.7(M.6.632A); *ζητήσεις εἰ ἔστι αὐτὸς ὁ θεὸς τῶν ἁγίων κ.* Or.*comm.in Eph*.1:18–20(p.399); *τῶν…προφητῶν τὸν κύριον κληρονομίαν λεγόντων τῶν ἁγίων, ὁ Παῦλος τὸ ἅγιον πνεῦμα κληρονομίαν εἶναι εἶπεν* Ath.*inc.et c.Ar*.15(M.26.1009B); *ὁ κύριος…κ. γίγνεται τῆς ψυχῆς* [sc. in contemplation], *καὶ ἡ ψυχὴ κ. γίγνεται τοῦ κυρίου* Mac.Aeg.*hom*.47.4(M.34.796A); **3.** specified as heavenly *οὐκ ἀποκέκοπται τέλεον αὐτοῖς* [sc. the rich] *ἡ κ. τῆς βασιλείας τῶν οὐρανῶν* Clem.*q.d.s*.3(p.161.15; M.9.605D); id.*prot*.1(p.9.21; M.8.65A); Or.*Jo*.19.22(5; p.325.22; M.14.568A); **4.** of Israel and gentiles as inheritance of God or Christ *τίς οὖν ἡ κ. τοῦ Χριστοῦ; οὐχὶ τὰ ἔθνη;* Just.*dial*.122.6(M.6.760C); *εἰ καὶ μὴ σαββατίζουσι* [sc. Jews], *μηδὲ περιτέμνονται μηδὲ τὰς ἑορτὰς φυλάσσουσι, πάντως κληρονομήσουσι τὴν ἁγίαν τοῦ θεοῦ κ.* *ib*.26.1(532A); *εὐλογοῦντος…τοῦ θεοῦ καὶ Ἰσραὴλ τοῦτον τὸν λαὸν καλοῦντος καὶ κληρονομίαν αὐτοῦ βοῶντος εἶναι, πῶς οὐ μετανοεῖτε ἐπί τε τῷ ἑαυτοὺς ἀπατᾶν, ὡς μόνοι Ἰσραὴλ ὄντες, καὶ ἐπὶ τῷ καταρᾶσθαι τὸν εὐλογημένον τοῦ θεοῦ λαόν;* *ib*.123.6(764A); *εἰς τὸ γενέσθαι τὰ ἔθνη κ. τοῦ θεοῦ* Or.*Jo*.13.50(49; p.278.26; M.14.492A); *ἐκλεκτὸς δὲ λαὸς κ. θεοῦ προσαγορευόμενος, πάλαι μὲν ὁ Ἰουδαϊκός, μετὰ δὲ ταῦτα ὁ ἐκ τῶν ἐθνῶν ἐκλεγείς, καὶ τῆς πίστεως τὰς ἀκτῖνας δεχόμενος* Thdt.*Ps*.32:12(1.810).

***κληρονομίζω**, *inherit*, Cyr.*ador*.4(1.119A).

κληρονόμος, ὁ, *heir*; **1.** of Son in rel. to Father, Herm.*sim*.5.2.6; *πάντων ὢν κ.* Ath.*Ar*.3.36(M.26.401A); *υἱὸν…καὶ ἴδιον κ.* *ib*.2.30(212A); *κ. … τοῦ πατρὸς καὶ πάντ' ἔχοντα ὅσα καὶ ὁ πατήρ* Eus.*e.th*.1.20(p.97.26; M.24.896A); *πάντων…τῶν ἐνόντων τῷ πατρὶ φυσικῶς ἰδιωμάτων κ. ὁ υἱός* Cyr.*Jo*.1.2(4.36E); *οὐδενὶ ἐξῆν αὐτὴν* [sc. *τὴν διαθήκην*] *ἀποσφραγίσαι εἰ μὴ μόνῳ τῷ κ. ὅς ἐστι Χριστός· οὗτος γὰρ θανάτῳ βεβαιωθείσης τῆς διαθήκης ἀναφανεὶς κ. περιεῖλε τὰς σφραγῖδας* Proc.G.*Gen*.17:8(M.87.356C); **2.** of Christians *κ. τῆς διαθήκης κυρίου* *Barn*.6.19; *ζωῆς ἀνωλέθρου…κ.* Arist.*apol*.17(*TS* p.112.8); *κ. τῆς αὐτοῦ* [sc. *Ἰησοῦ*] *βασιλείας* *Const.App*.5.16.6; *μονονουχὶ κ. τῆς ὑπ' οὐρανὸν ἔσονται…οἱ τῶν ἁγίων ἐκκλησιῶν ἡγούμενοι* Cyr.*Is*.5.5(2.865C); *ὁ νοῦς…τὰς θείας ἐπαγγελίας προσμένει ὧν μετὰ τοῦ συνεργήσαντος σώματος γίνεται κ.* Thdt.*Ps*.26:14(1.773); in baptism *κ. … τῶν πρὸς ἀφθαρσίαν γεννησάντων σε γόνεων* *Hom.Clem*.11.24; **3.** of Abraham *κ. τοῦ κόσμου* *Lit*.ap.*Const.App*.8.12.23; **4.** of the sinner *τοῦ οὐαὶ κ.* *Const.App*.1.3.6; 1.10.1.

κλῆρος, ὁ, **1.** *lot, inheritance*; **a.** in gen.; of martyrdom, Ign.*Trall*.12.3; *M.Polyc*.6.2; *Ep.Lugd*.ap.Eus.*h.e*.5.1.10(M.20.428A); of death *ἀνθρωπίνῳ κ.* Const.ap.Ath.*apol.sec*.87(p.166.23; M.25.405C); Gr.Nyss.*Eun*.1(1 p.23.11; M.45.252A); of judgement, Ath.*Ar*.2.76(M.26.308B); **b.** of inheritance of Christ *τούτῳ…κ. ἐξαίρετον…ἀγγέλους καὶ ἀρχαγγέλους…καὶ…θεοφιλεῖς ψυχὰς ἀφωρίσατο* Eus.*d.e*.4.6(p.160.20; M.22.268A); *ἴδιον…κ. τοὺς ἐπὶ τῆς γῆς* Cyr.*Heb*.1:1(p.366.3); consisting of gentiles offered by him to God, Jo.D.*carm.theog*.63(p.207; M.96.821B); **2.** *office, appointment*, esp. in Church *γυμνούσθω τοῦ κ.* Ath.Scholast.*coll*.1.2(p.10); *διδόναι κλήρους ordain*, *Lit*.ap.*Const.App*.8.5.7; hence of an order in Church: episcopate, ‡Procl.CP *tract*.(M.65.849B); presbyterate *πρεσβυτερίου κ.* Corn.ap.Eus.*h.e*.6.43.17(M.20.624B); Gr.Nyss.*Eun*.1(1 p.53.12; M.45.281C); *πρεσβυτίδες*, *cat.Tit*.2:3(p.94.14); **3.** *clergy* in gen., Clem.*q.d.s*.42(p.188.6; M.9.648B); Or.*exp.in Pr*.26:17(M.17.240B); id.*hom.11.3 in Jer*.(p.80.17; M.13.369C); CAnc.(314)*can*.3; *Const.App*.6.17.3; Chrys.*sac*.3.15(p.78.22; 1.393D); Thdr.Mops.*1Tim*.3:2(p.101.20; M.66.940A); dist. from bishops, *Lit*.ap.*Const.App*.8.11.9; Pall.*v.Chrys*.1(p.8.1; M.47.8); *ib*.13(p.79.12; M.47.45); Evagr.*h.e*.2.8(p.56.27; M.86.2524B); to whom they are subject, *Const.App*.2.44.1; dist. from monks *οὐδένα ἂν εὕροις…οὐ βιωτικὸν ἄνδρα, οὐ μοναχόν, οὐ τοῦ κλήρου ἐλεύθερον τῆς ἁμαρτίας* Chrys.*compunct*.1.7(1.130E); Jo.D.*haer*.100(M.94.761B); belonging to partic. church *ἔστι κ. κατὰ πᾶσαν…τοῦ θεοῦ παροικίαν* Bas.*ep*.204.4(3.305B; M.32.749B); *τοῦ κλήρου τῆς ἐκκλησίας τῆς Ἐφεσίων* Pall.*v.Chrys*.13(p.88.14; M.47.50); *ὁ ἐν Κωνσταντινουπόλει κ.* Philost.*h.e*.9.7(M.65.573B).

κληρουχία, ἡ, **1.** *apportionment of land* *τὰς…τῶν δώδεκα φυλῶν…κληρου⟨χία⟩ς* Eus.*onomast*.(p.2.9); **2.** sens. dub., Nil.*epp*.2.183(M.79.296B).

κληρ-όω, med. and pass.; **1.** *inherit, receive as one's portion*, of Christ *ὁ τὴν ἐνδεικτικὴν καὶ παιδευτικὴν ἡγεμονίαν κεκληρωμένος λόγος* Clem.*paed*.1.11(p.149.19; M.8.369A); *οὐκ ἀπὸ τοῦ γεννῆσθαι αἰτία⟨ν⟩ πάθους ∼ωθήσεται ὁ υἱός* Epiph.*haer*.76.44(p.398.27; M.42.612A); of bishops *τὴν ἐπισκοπὴν κ.* Eus.*h.e*.3.36.2(M.20.288B); *τοῦ δεσμεῖν ἐκληρώσω τὴν ἐξουσίαν…καὶ τοῦ λύειν* *Const.App*.2.18.3; *τῆς ἐν Κωνσταντίνου πόλει ἐκκλησίας τὸν θρόνον ἐκληρώθη* Socr.*h.e*.7.41.3(M.67.832A); in gen. *ἐλευθερίαν ἐκληρώσαντο* Meth.*arbitr*.16(p.186.11); *τὸν διδασκαλικὸν κεκληρῶσθαι θρόνον* id.*lepr*.12(p.466.10); *παρὰ τοῦ πατρὸς…τοῦ διαβόλου τὴν Χριστομάχον ἐκληρώσαντο* [sc. Arians] *μανίαν* Ath.*Dion*.3(p.48.6; M.25.484B); *ἀντὶ ἀναπαύσεως αἰωνίαν κόλασιν ∼ωσάμενοι* [sc. idolators] *Const.App*.6.10.11; *τὰ…ὑπὸ αἰτίαν πεπτωκότα καὶ αἰτίαν κεκληρωμένα* Epiph.*haer*.76.44(p.398.16; 609D); *τὴν τοῦ ἀέρος…κεκληρωμένος* [sc. Devil] *διοίκησιν* Bas.Sel.*or*.32.1(M.85.269C); *τάφον…∼ώσασθαι* Evagr.*h.e*.3.32(p.131.9; M.86.2665C); **2.** pass., *be appointed, be destined* *οὐδὲ ἁπλῶς ἐκληρώθημεν* Chrys.*hom.2.1 in Eph*.(11.9E); *οἱ μὲν τῶν κατὰ γῆν ἔφοροι θυσιαστηρίων ἐκληρώθησαν* Areth.*Apoc*.44(M.106.696A); c. prep. *οὐδὲ…ἱερεὺς ἔσται, μὴ πρὸς τῶν ἱεραρχικῶν τελειώσεων εἰς τοῦτο κεκληρωμένος* Dion.Ar.*e.h*.5.1.5(M.3.505C); *εἰς τὴν ἀποστολὴν κ.* Eus.*h.e*.2.1.1(M.20.133B); *εἰς ἣν ἐκληρώθη ὑπὸ τοῦ θεοῦ ἐκκλησίαν* CAnt.(341)*can*.21; c. infin. *κεκλήρωται ἡ ψυχὴ συνεζεῦχθαι τῷ…σώματι* Or.*Jo*.6.52(p.161.17; M.14.292B); *ἵνα ∼ωθῶ ἄξιος γενέσθαι* *A.Thom*.A 24(p.139.13); *τὰ…ἄλλα τῶν ζῴων…ἕρπειν ∼ωθέντα νόμῳ τῆς φύσεως* Bas.Sel.*or*.1.3(M.85.36A); **3.** pass., *be assigned, be allotted* *τῶν αὐτῷ* [sc. *Χριστῷ*] *κεκληρωμένων ψυχῶν* Eus.*h.e*.10.4.61(M.20.873A); *τούτῳ* [sc. *Χριστῷ*] *κἂν…τῇ φύσει κεκληρωμένον ᾖ τὸ ἅπαξ ἀποθανεῖν* Chrys.*hom.15.4 in Rom*.(9.599A); *κἂν ∼ωθῇς, ὦ γύναι, συνοίκῳ τούτῳ* id.*hom.26.7 in 1Cor*.(10.238A); **4.** *appoint* *θεὸς…ὁ ∼ωσάμενος* Chrys.*hom.2.1 in Eph*.(11.9E).

***κλήρωμα**, τό, s.v.l., *that which is allotted, destiny*, Ammon.*Ac*.13:46(M.85.1541D) but prob. f.l. for *πλήρωμα*; cf. *κληρώματι* Justn.*conf*.tit.ap.*Chron.Pasch*.p.345(M.92.901A) for *πληρώματι* *ib*.(p.72.5; M.86.993C).

κλήρωσις, ἡ, **1.** (Lat. *clericatus*) *the clerical order* *τάξιν κληρώσεως* *Cod.Afr*.57; *πρὸς κ. καταδέχεσθαι* *ib*.90; **2.** *designation, naming* *οἱ ὅροι καὶ αἱ κ.* Jo.D.*trisag*.2(M.95.25A).

κλῆσις, ἡ, **A.** *calling*, from God; **1.** in gen., of Abraham *ὁ Χριστὸς…διὰ τῆς ὁμοίας κ. ἐκάλεσεν αὐτὸν…καὶ ἡμᾶς* Just.*dial*.119.5(M.6.752D); of apostles, Or.*fr.21 in Jo*.(p.502.6); Euthal.Diac.*Ac*.proem.(M.85.636A); *ἐν τῷ καιρῷ τῆς κ. ἐτυφλώθη* [sc. S. Paul] Chrys.*laud.Paul*.4(2.491A); of Jews, Thdt.*Jer*.2:2(2.410); *κοσμικὴ…ἡ τοῦ προτέρου λαοῦ κ. καὶ τῇ ἑξάδι σύστοιχος τῇ κοσμογόνῳ* Apoll.ap.Proc.G.*Cant*.(M.87.1721B); **2.** partic. of Christian vocation; **a.** in gen. *μία κ. ἐν Χριστῷ* *1Clem*.46.6; *Barn*.16.9; *τὴν κ. ἐκείνην μεγάλην καὶ σεμνήν* Herm.*mand*.4.3.6; *τῆς κ. τῆς καινῆς καὶ αἰωνίου διαθήκης, τοῦτ' ἔστι τοῦ Χριστοῦ* Just.*dial*.118.3(M.6.749C); *τοῦτο…περιεμένομεν, τὴν κ.* Or.*hom.5.2 in Jer*.(p.32.8; M.13.297C); *ἡ κ. ἄνωθεν* Ath.

*ep.fest.*43(p.297.11; M.26.1440B); τὸ βραβεῖον τῆς ἄνω κ. id.*ep.Drac.* 8(M.25.532C); †Bas.*bapt.*1.2.6(2.633D; M.31.1536B); ὑπηκούσατε τῇ κ. *Const.App.*5.15.3; τὴν κ. πλουτήσαντες Cyr.*Is.*5.5(2.865B); ref. new birth εἰς κ. καὶ σωτηρίαν νεογνοὶ γεγόναμεν Clem.*paed.*1.7(p.125.14; M.8.321B); its fairness and universality ὁ θεῖος λόγος...πάντας συλλήβδην καλῶν δικαίαν τὴν κ. πεποίηται id.*str.*2.6(p.127.6; M.8.961B); εἰ...ὁμότιμος ἐπὶ πάντας ἡ κ. οὔτε ἀξίας, οὔτε ἡλικίας, οὔτε τὰς κατὰ τὰ ἔθνη διαφορὰς διακρίνουσα Gr.Nyss.*or.catech.*30(p.112.2; M.45.76D); τὸ...δόγμα τῆς προαιρέσεως ὁμολογεῖται, διὰ τοῦτο καὶ ἡ κ. Tit.Bost. *fr.Lc.*6:43(p.163.12); illustrated in Christ's parables, Clem.*exc.Thdot.* 9(p.109.9; M.9.660B); Or.*Jo.*13.34(p.259.27; M.14.460A); due to God's will ἡ κ. ἡμῶν ὥς ποτε αὐτῇ μὴ οὖσα, νῦν δὲ ἐπιγενομένη προηγουμένην ἔχει τὴν βούλησιν καὶ...κατὰ τὴν εὐδοκίαν τοῦ θελήματος γέγονε Ath.*Ar.*3.61(M.26.452A); ἀπὸ ἀγάπης...θεοῦ ἡ κ. Apoll.*Rom.*1:5(p.57. 11, not.); τῆς τοῦ δεσπότου Χριστοῦ κ. δι' οἶκτον φιλανθρωπίας γεγόναμεν ἄξιοι *Chron.Pasch.*p.223(M.92.544B); its demands, exeg. Eph.2:3 ἐπὶ ἁγίᾳ ζωῇ...κέκλησθε, καὶ ἀπαιτεῖ κ. τὸ πνευματικόν Jo. D.*Eph.*4:1–3(M.95.840B); **b.** to martyrdom διὰ τὴν πρὸς τὸν θεὸν ἀγάπην ἑκόντες πείθονται τῇ κ. Clem.*str.*7.11(p.48.10; M.9.493A); *ib.* (p.46.2; 488C); **c.** of gentiles Ἰησοῦς...ἐξαπέστειλε...τὸν λόγον τῆς κ. ... πρὸς τὰ ἔθνη πάντα Just.*dial.*83.4(M.6.673A); following upon Jews' disbelief συνεχρήσατο [sc. ὁ Ἰησοῦς] τῇ ἀπιστίᾳ τῶν Ἰουδαίων πρὸς τὴν κ. τῶν ἐθνῶν Or.*Cels.*2.78(p.200.12; M.11.917B); ἐχρῆν...τὸ Ἰουδαίων ἔθνος ἀνάστατον γεγονέναι καὶ ἐπ' ἄλλους τὴν τοῦ θεοῦ εἰς μακαριότητα κ. μεταβεβηκέναι *ib.*4.22(p.292.11; 1060A); initiated by Christ's death, Ath.*inc.*25.3(M.25.140A); first proclaimed by S. Philip, *Chron.Pasch.*p.229(M.92.556B); **d.** *those called by God, the elect* ὁ κύριος θέλει τὴν κ. τὴν γενομένην διὰ τοῦ υἱοῦ αὐτοῦ σῴζεσθαι Herm.*sim.*8.11.1; τῇ ἐξ ἐθνῶν κ. Clem.*str.*2.6(p.128.20; M.8.964C); cf. τοὺς τῆς κ. ἀνθρώπους id.*exc.Thdot.*9(p.109.4; M.9.660A); οὔτε τῇ κ. τῶν ἐθνῶν ἥρμοζε κατὰ τὸν Μωϋσέως...πολιτεύεσθαι νόμον Or.*Cels.* 7.26(p.177.2; 1457B); τὸ οἰκετικὸν γένος τῆς κ. Eus.*p.e.*1.1(3A; M.21. 25A); **e.** Valent., Clem.*exc.Thdot.*21(p.113.21; 668B) cit. s. ἐκλογή; εὐαγγελιζομένη τῇ κ. τὴν Χριστοῦ παρουσίαν Heracleon ap.Or.*Jo.*13. 31(30; p.255.17; M.14.452D); cf. πάντων τῶν τῆς κ. Iren.*haer.*1.14. 4(M.7.604A).

B. *name, appellation*; **1.** Trin. οὐδὲ τρεῖς θεοί...κἂν ἐφαρμόζει ἡ τοιαύτη κ. τῇ ἁγίᾳ τριάδι Gr.Nyss.*tres dii*(M.45.129C); ἑκάστη...τῶν κ. τούτων...κανὼν ἀληθείας καὶ νόμος εὐσεβείας...Χριστὸς παραμένειν ἀποφηνάμενος...τῇ τοῦ πατρός τε καὶ τοῦ υἱοῦ καὶ τοῦ ἁγίου πνεύματος κ. id.*Eun.*2(2 p.298.17ff.; M.45.469A); ἡ τοῦ πατρὸς κ. οὐκ οὐσίας ἐστὶ παραστατική· ἀλλὰ τὴν πρὸς τὸν υἱὸν σχέσιν ἀποσημαίνει *ib.* (2 p.302.23; 473B); διὰ τῶν κ. τούτων οὐ φύσεων διαφορὰν διδασκόμεθα ἀλλὰ μόνας τὰς τῶν ὑποστάσεων γνωριστικὰς ἰδιότητας Eulog.*fr.dogm.*(M.86.2948D); **2.** Christol. κιρναμένων ὥσπερ τῶν φύσεων οὕτω...καὶ τῶν κ. Gr.Naz.*ep.*101(M.37.181C); τὴν κ. ἑνικήν Leont.B.*cap.Sev.*15(M.86.1905B); **3.** of Christians τῷ ἁγίῳ πνεύματι κατακεχρισμένοι τὴν τοῦ Χριστοῦ κ. ἐσχήκαμεν Cyr.*Lc.*9:18(M. 72.648C).

C. *invocation*, magical ψυχῶν ἀνθρωπίνων κλήσεις Just.*1apol.*18.3 (M.6.356A); δαιμόνων κλήσεις Chrys.*hom.24.4 in Rom.*(9.699D).

D. *inheritance* τὴν ἐξ ἀδιαθέτου κ. Ath.Scholast.*coll.*3.3(p.46); plur., *ib.*9.10(p.104).

***κλῄσκ-ω**, *shut up, confine* ~εται εἰς φυλακήν *A.Andr.*B 1(p.58. 22).

***κλησουάλιος**, perh. error for κησουάλιος, Nil.*epp.*1.156 tit.(M. 79.148A).

***κλητορεύω**, *invite, summon* πρὸς ἀριστόδειπνον κ. Thphn.*chron.* p.313(M.108.761A).

κλητός, *called*, by God to salvation τῇ ἐκκλησίᾳ...κλητοῖς ἡγιασμένοις *1Clem.*proem.; ἵνα μήποτε ἐπαναπαυόμενοι ὡς κλητοὶ ἐπικαθυπνώσωμεν ταῖς ἁμαρτίαις *Barn.*4.13; ὁ παιδαγωγὸς ἐκκαλεῖται ...τοὺς κ. ἐπὶ τὰ βελτίω Clem.*paed.*1.8(p.133.19; M.8.340A); *Const. App.*2.56.3; exeg. Rom.8:28 ἡ πρόθεσις γνησία οὖσα κ. σε ποιεῖ Cyr. H.*procatech.*1; Gnost. τρεῖς ἐκκλησίαι...ὀνόματα δὲ αὐταῖς ἐκλεκτή, κ., αἰχμάλωτος Hipp.*haer.*5.6(p.78.21; M.16.3126B); cf. τὸ ἐκλεκτὸν καὶ τὸ κ. Clem.*exc.Thdot.*58(p.126.12; M.9.688A); τῶν κ. [οὖν] τὰ ἀγγελικά *ib.*39(p.119.10; κλήρων M.9.677B).

κλήτωρ, ὁ, 1. *one who sends* or *summons*, Sophr.H.*mir.Cyr.et Jo.*60(M.87.3636C); **2.** *host*, of Christ τὸν κ. τῆς ἐπουρανίου ἑορτῆς *M.Ariadn.*2(p.123.23).

[*]**κλίβανον, τό,** = κρίβανον, *breastplate*, Mac.Aeg.*hom.*17.7(M.34. 628D).

κλίμα, τό, *region*, hence *district* in a city, Socr.*h.e.*2.38.19(M.67. 328A); *Cod.Afr.*93(H.1.917E).

κλιμακηδόν, *like a ladder* or *stairs* τῶν...στίχων κειμένων κ. Bas. *ep.*334(3.452B; M.32.1077A); ὁ...φιλόσοφος...ὁδὸν...παρεσκευάσατο καὶ κ. ἄνεισιν Synes.*Dion* 8(p.255.4; M.66.1136B).

κλιμακόεις, *gradual*; of a psalm, †Apoll.*met.Ps.*119 tit.(M.33. 1505C).

κλιμακτήρ, ὁ, 1. *rung of a ladder*, met. τὰ τῶν πειρασμῶν πάθη κ. κικλήσκουσί τινες Eust.*fr.*(p.71; M.18.696B); **2.** *dangerous crisis*, Nil.*epp.*2.258(M.79.332D); κ. θανατηφόρῳ Pall.*v.Chrys.*20(p.146.24; M.47.82).

κλῖμαξ, ἡ, *ladder*; met., *way of ascent* to heaven, by astronomy ὥσπερ διὰ κ. τινος οὐρανομήκους Gr.Thaum.*pan.Or.*8(p.22.23; M.10. 1077C); spiritual κ. ... εἰς ὕψος ἀνάγουσα...εἰκὼν σημείου πάθους Χριστοῦ ἕλκουσα τοὺς πιστοὺς εἰς ἀνάβασιν οὐρανῶν Hipp.*antichr.* 59(p.40.5; M.10.780A); of Cross, Eust.*fr.*13(p.70; M.18.696B); of virtues τῆς πνευματικῆς τῶν ἀρετῶν κ. Gr.Nyss.*v.Ephr.*(M.46.828D); Nil.*epp.*4.42(M.79.569C); of created universe κλίμακος...δίκην θεὸς ἁρμόσας τὴν κτίσιν δι' αὐτῆς πρὸς ἑαυτὸν...ἀνάβασιν ἐτεχνήσατο Bas. Sel.*or.*1.1(M.85.29A); exeg. Mt.18:3 αὐτὴ...τῶν οὐρανίων κ. *ib.*28.2 (321B); of BMV κ. ἐστηριγμένη ἀπὸ γῆς εἰς οὐρανόν Thdr.Stud.*or.*5. 4(M.99.725B); ref. gradations in Trin. τὸ...ἐκ μεγάλου καὶ μείζονος καὶ μεγίστου συνιστᾶν τὴν τριάδα...κ. ἐστὶ θεότητος οὐκ εἰς οὐρανὸν ἄγουσα, ἀλλ' ἐξ οὐρανοῦ κατάγουσα Gr.Naz.*ep.*101(M.37.192B).

κλιματάρχης, ὁ, as adj., *ruling celestial regions*, astrol. κ. ἀστέρα ἢ ζώδιον Proc.G.*Gen.*1:5(M.87.93C).

[*]**κλιματήρ, ὁ,** for κλιμακτήρ, Nil.*epp.*2.151(M.79.269D).

***κλινάς, ἡ,** *couch*, Eus.*v.C.*3.15(p.84.9; M.20.1073A).

***κλινηφόρος**, *carrying one's bed*, ‡Chrys.*publ.*1.1(8.116D).

***κλινοκοιτέω**, *sleep on a bed*, opp. χαμοκοιτέω, Ephr.3.152E = id. 1.42D.

κλίν-ω, A. *bend, incline*; **1.** liturg.; **a.** head, in prayer, *Const. App.*8.39.4; κ. τὰς κεφαλὰς...τεκμήριον τοῦ τὰς εὐχὰς ἀκουσθῆναι Chrys.*hom.2.8 in 2Cor.*(10.440D); neck, at anaphora, Anast.S. *synax.*(M.89.836D); for bishop's blessing, *Lit.*ap.*Const.App.*8.6.10; fig. τοὺς κεκλικότας σοι αὐχένα ψυχῆς καὶ σώματος *ib.*8.9.8; **b.** of prostration and genuflexion ἄμφω τὼ πόδε ~ας [sc. bishop at consecration, priest at ordination] ἐπίπροσθεν τοῦ θυσιαστηρίου Dion. Ar.*e.h.*5.2(M.3.509Af.); *ib.*5.3.8(516B); λειτουργικὴ διακόσμησις, τὸν ἕνα [sc. πόδα] κ. *ib.*5.3.7(516A); ὁ...τελούμενος [sc. monk] ἕστηκεν οὐκ ἄμφω τὼ πόδε ~ων, οὐχ ἕνα τοῖν ποδοῖν *ib.*6.2(533B,C); v. γόνυ; **2.** met. τὴν καρδίαν...εἰς εὐμένειαν κ. Ath.*apol.Const.*12(M.25.609B); οὗς *V.Mac.*A(p.154); Dam.*troph.*4.4(p.267.2).

B. intrans.; **1.** *kneel, bow*, at baptism ~αντες εὐλογείσθωσαν παρὰ τοῦ ἐπισκόπου *Lit.*ap.*Const.App.*8.8.4; to idols, Ath.*ep.Aeg.Lib.*21 (M.25.588A); **2.** *turn, incline*, ‡Petr.I Al.*phys.*20(p.51.15); c. infin., Thphl.Ant.*Autol.*2.32(M.6.1105A); met. τὴν...αἵρεσιν ~ουσαν ἐπὶ τὰ κρείττονα ἢ ἐπὶ τὰ χείρονα Or.*princ.*3.1.21(p.244.2; M.11.301C); of God οὐ...ἔκλινεν εἰς τὸ ἀπολέσαι ἀλλ' εἰς τὸ σῶσαι Chrys.*hom.9.4 in 1Thess.*(11.490E, v.l. ἐκάλεσεν); *falter, waver* τὴν ψυχὴν ~ουσαν Ath. *v.Anton.*19(M.26.872B).

C. pass., *sink* to death ἐπικρατήσαντος τοῦ θανάτου ~εται τὸ σῶμα εἰς φθοράν Meth.*res.*2.18(p.368.11; M.18.312C); *ib.*(p.368.16; 284A); of Christ κέκλιται...ὁ κύριος Clem.*prot.*11(p.79.5; M.8.228C).

κλισιάς, ἡ, *entrance, gate*, Meth.*symp.*7.1(p.70.15; M.18.121B).

***κλισίη (*κλεσίη), ἡ,** *assembly, congregation* δήμων κλισίη †Apoll. *met.Ps.*61:9(κλεσίη M.33.1397A); κλισίη πολυηχέϊ *ib.*39:10(1368C); plur. κλισίαις *ib.*39:11(κλισίης 1368C).

κλίσις, ἡ, *bending* or *bowing* in prayer κ. γονάτων *A.Paul.et Thecl.* 5(p.238.10); at one's consecration, Gr.Naz.*carm.*2.1.12.506(M.37. 1202A).

κλισμός, ὁ, *chair of office*, Eudoc.*Cypr.*1.308(M.85.844B).

κλίτος, τό, *side* of a person, ‡Sophr.H.*v.Mar.Aeg.*10(M.87.3705A).

***κλιτός**, *mutable*, Gr.Naz.*carm.*1.1.9.86(M.37.463A).

***κλοβομαχ-έω**, *fight in a coop* περδίκων...καθ' ἑαυτοὺς ~ούντων Jo.Clim.*scal.*8(M.88.832A).

κλοιός, ὁ, *fetter*, Serap.*ep.mon.*7(M.40.933A); Chrys.*hom.3.3 in Eph.*(11.21B); plur. κλοιά, Jo.Clim.*scal.*15(M.88.881C); *collar* worn by ascetics, plur., Chrys.*hom.13.3 in Eph.*(11.99E).

***κλοιοφορέω**, *wear a prisoner's collar*, Pall.*v.Chrys.*17(p.103.18; M.47.58); Thdt.*Ezech.*1:4(2.682).

***κλοιοφόρος**, *wearing an ornamental collar* κ. παῖδας χρυσοζώνους ‡Pall.*h.mon.*30.2(p.92.14; M.34.1050C).

κλον-έω, *shake violently* ~ῆσαι [sc. Σαμψών] τοὺς...κίονας Thdt. *qu.22 in Jud.*(1.340); pass. τὴν γῆν ~ουμένην [sc. at general resurrection] Chrys.*hom.8.1 in 1Thess.*(11.479B); met. in pass., *be upset*, Thdt.*1Thess.*3:1–3(3.512).

***κλονίζω**, *disturb, agitate*, Ant.Mon.*hom.*18(M.89.1484B).

***κλονισμός, ὁ,** *spray of leaves*, ‡Caes.Naz.*dial.*85(M.38.949).

***κλονοτομέω**, *cut off the branches of*, *Phys.*B 2(p.154.2), cf. κλωνοκοπάω.

κλοπεύς, ὁ, *plunderer*, ref. Mc.7:11 τῶν ἱερῶν ἀναθημάτων κ. Cyr. *ador.*16(1.573E).

κλοπή, ἡ, 1. *theft* αὐτὰ κλοπὴν ἠθέλησε ποιῆσαι Gr.Mag.*dial.*(tr. Zach.)3.26(M.*PL.*77.279C); met. κ. τῆς ἀληθείας Clem.*str.*6.2(p.424. 9; M.9.212B); Ath.*ep.Aeg.Lib.*11(M.25.561B); **2.** *plagiarism* τὴν ἐκ τῆς βαρβάρου φιλοσοφίας Ἑλληνικὴν κ. Clem.*str.*5.14(p.384.16; M.9. 129B); τῆς ἐν λόγοις κ. Eus.*p.e.*10.1(461C; M.21.768C); Thdt.*affect.*5 (p.144.22; 4.342).

κλοπιμαῖος, *done by stealth, clandestine* κ. ... μοιχείας Ath.*gent.*11 (M.25.25A); γάμων κ. †Bas.*Is.*301(1.608A; M.30.647A).

κλοπιμαίως, *stealthily* λαθραίως καὶ κ. Eus.*l.C.*5(p.245.25; M.20. 1416B).

κλοποφορέω, *get by stealth*, Steph.Diac.*v.Steph.*(M.100.1161A).

κλουβός, ὁ, 1. *coop*, Philost.*h.e.*10.11(M.65.992B); **2.** *monk's cell* or *cave*, Steph.Diac.*v.Steph.*(M.100.1101C).

κλυδωνίζω, pass.; **1.** *become rough*; of the sea, Mac.Aeg.*hom.*43.4 (M.34.773D); **2.** *be buffeted, tossed* on the sea; met., Dion.Al.*fr.* (p.255.8)ap.Leont.et Jo.*sacr.*2(M.86.2081C); Constantius Imp.ap. Ath.*apol.sec.*51(p.132.12; M.25.341A); ref. Eph.4:14, Gr.Nyss.*hom. 9 in Cant.*(M.44.956D).

κλυδωνισμός, ὁ, *surging of waves*; met., *confusion*, Epiph.*haer.* 69.27(p.177.13; M.42.245C); error for κληδονισμός, Cyr.*Is.*4.3(2.621D).

κλυτόπαις, *famous for one's child*; of BMV, Leont.H.*Nest.*4.37 (M.86.1712A).

***κλυτόφρων**, *famous for wisdom*; of S. John, Sophr.H.*carm.*11.77 (M.87.3789A).

κλύω, = κλύζω, *rinse out* χύτρας κλύε Thdr.Stud.*iamb.*14(M.99. 1785B).

κλώζω, *caw*, Clem.*prot.*10(p.74.34; M.8.220B).

κλώθω, perf. ptcpl. pass., *fated*, ‡Chrys.*provid.*5(2.770A).

***κλωνοκοπάω**, *knock off the branches of*, ‡Epiph.*phys.*3(M.43. 520C), cf. κλονοτομέω.

κλῶσμα, τό, *thread, cord*; in Jewish clothing, Or.*comm.ser.11 in Mt.*(p.22.8); ref. Num.15:38, Thdt.*qu.31 in Num.*(1.240).

κλωσμός, ὁ, *hooting*; a sound of disapproval in theatre, etc., Pall.*v.Chrys.*10(p.61.23; M.47.35); *ib.*20(p.146.6; M.47.81).

***κλῶταξ, ὁ**, ? *support for a lathe-chisel* ἀνάγκη αὐτὸν [sc. τὸν οὐρανόν] ὑπὸ κλωτάκων ὡς ὁ τόρνος...βαστάζεσθαι Cosm.Ind.*top.*1(M. 88.64D); *ib.*4(189C).

κναφεύω, *cleanse, purify like a fuller*, of Petr. Full. οἷόν τι ἀφιλοκάλητον ὕφασμα κναφεῦσαι τὸν τρισάγιον Jo.D.*trisag.*5(M.95.33A).

κναφικός, *of a fuller*, Hier.*vir.ill.*(tr.Sophr.Pal.)2(p.4.19; M.*PL.* 23.612B); Sophr.H.*v.Anast.*(M.92.1720B).

***κνεφώδης**, *clouded*; comp., of pearls, Or.*comm.in Mt.*10.7(p.9.4; M.13.852B).

[*]**κνήδιος**, v. κνίδιος.

κνήθ-ω, 1. *irritate, afflict* φρικτὴ...τῶν ποδῶν ὑποψία...~ει με Geo. Pis.*carm.*1.25; **2.** met., *tickle* κ. καὶ γαργαλίζοντες Clem.*str.*1.3(p.15. 4; M.8.712C).

κνημόω, *bind up*, met. κ. τοὺς πόδας εὐαγγελικοῖς μαθήμασι Ant. Mon.*hom.*111(M.89.1776A).

[*]**κνηπία, ἡ**, v. κνιπεία.

[*]**κνηπός**, v. κνιπός.

κνῆσις, ἡ, *tickling*, met. τῆς ἀκοῆς ἡ κ. Thdt.*2Tim.*4:3(3.692); hence *stimulus* διὰ κνήσεις δαιμόνων Agath.*v.Gr.Ill.*24(p.15); prob. error for κνῖσα, *ib.*35(p.21).

κνηστιάω, *lust*, Clem.*paed.*2.10(p.210.19; M.8.501C); id.*str.*5.8 (p.361.9; M.9.81A).

κνίδιος ([*]**κνήδιος**), *of* or *from Cnidus*; of wine, κνηδ-, Sophr.H. *mir.Cyr.et Jo.*60(M.87.3636C); hence neut. as subst., name of a measure of wine, *ib.*; *Apophth.Patr.*(M.65.693B); fem. as subst., name of a dry measure, *PLond.*1918.13,14 (saec. iv).

κνιπεία (κνιπία, κνηπία), ἡ, 1. *miserliness*, Dor.*doct.*14.5(M.88. 1784A); in form κνηπία, tr. Lat. *avaritia*, Gr.Mag.*dial.*(tr.Zach.)1.9 (M.*PL.*77.195B); *ib.*4.38(391C); **2.** v. σκνιπία.

κνιπεύομαι, *be miserly*, †Max.*loc.comm.*21(M.91.852B).

κνιπός (κνηπός), 1. *niggardly, miserly*, Jo.Mal.*chron.*18 p.454(M. 97.665A); κνηπ-, tr. Lat. *avarus*, Gr.Mag.*dial.*(tr.Zach.)3.14(M.*PL.* 77.246C); **2.** *highly-priced*, *Mir.Geo.*10(p.107.5).

***κνιπῶς** *in a niggardly fashion* φειδωλῶς καὶ κ. *cat.2Cor.*9:6 (p.408.31).

κνισμός, ὁ, *tickling, irritation*, Nil.*Magn.*65(M.79.1057A).

κνισοδιώκτης, ὁ, *pursuer of roast meat*, Pall.*v.Chrys.*12(p.74.15; M.47.42).

κνώδαλον, τό, 1. *wild beast, animal*, Eus.*d.e.*8.5(p.401.9; M.22. 648C); Cyr.*Jon.*11(3.375C); **2.** *infant, child* μήτηρ διδάσκει...τῷ ἑαυτῆς κ. τὸ πατὴρ ὄνομα Diad.*perf.*61(p.70.5).

***κογγιάριον, τό**, (Lat. *congiarium*); **1.** *a liquid measure*, Epiph. *mens.*21(M.43.272C); **2.** *gift divided among the people, dole* Νοῦμμας Πομπήλιος κογγιάριον ἔδωκεν ἐν Ῥώμῃ ἀσσάρια ξύλινα καὶ ὀστράκινα *Chron.Pasch.*p.117(M.92.305B).

***κογνατικός**, *pertaining to a kinsman*; τὰ κ. *the rights of kinsmen*, Ath.Scholast.*coll.*3.4(p.49).

***κογνᾶτος, ὁ**, (Lat. *cognatus*) *kinsman, blood-relation*, Ath. Scholast.*coll.*9.10(p.104).

***κογνιτίων, ἡ**, (Lat. *cognitio*) *judicial inquiry* τῶν θείων κ. CCP (449)*act.*1(*ACO* 2.1.1 p.149.20,30; H.2.173D).

κογχάριον, τό, *little apse* ἐκτυποῖ προσευχῆς κ. Steph.Diac.*v. Steph.*(M.100.1101B).

κόγχη, ἡ, *apse* of a church, Eus.*v.C.*3.32 tit.(p.73.27; M.20. 1049C); τῆς ἱερᾶς κ. Evagr.*h.e.*4.31(p.180.33; M.86.2760B); *Fr.hist.*2 (M.85.1812C) cit. s. κανδῆλα; derivation of name κ. εἴτ' ἀπὸ κόγχου εἰναλίου καλέουσι...εἴτ' ἀπὸ τέχνης Paul.Sil.*Soph.*359(M.86.2133B); ἡ κ. ἐστὶν κατὰ τὸν ἐν Βηθλεὲμ σπήλαιον ὅπου ἐγεννήθη ὁ Χριστὸς καὶ κατὰ τὸ σπήλαιον ὅπου ἐτάφη ‡Bas.*h.myst.*2(p.258.4); ‡Sophr.H. *liturg.*2(M.87.3984A); Jo.Jej.*liturg.*(p.441); of other buildings κ. τῆς βασιλικῆς Jo.Mal.*chron.*12 p.287(M.97.433A); βασιλικὴν ἔχουσαν κ. *Chron.Pasch.*p.284(M.92.709A).

[*]**κογχλιάριον, τό**, = κοχλιάριον, *spoon*, †Anast.S.*relat.*42(*OC* 3 p.62).

***κογχλοειδῶς**, v. *κοχλοειδῶς.

κόγχος, ὁ, *oyster*; fig., of BMV, Jo.D.*fr.*(M.96.816B).

***κογχοστάτης, ὁ**, *shell-shaped dish* or *container* κ. σιδηροῦν *A. Xanthipp.*21(p.73.25); cf. *conchae ferreae quibus depletur oleum*, Columella *de re rustica* 12.52.8.

κογχύλη, ἡ, 1. *murex, shellfish from which purple dye is obtained*, Jo.Mal.*chron.*2 p.32(M.97.101A); *Chron.Pasch.*p.43(M.92.161C,D); Jo.D.*imag.*1(M.94.1264B); **2.** *purple dye*, Jo.Mal.*chron.*2 p.32(101A).

***κογχυλουργής**, *produced by the murex* κ. πορφύραν Geo.Pis. *carm.*48.1.

κογχωτός, *shell-shaped, concave*; of teeth, Melet.*nat.hom.*10(M. 64.1193C).

***κοδίμεντον, τό**, kind of herb; used as a condiment, Gr.Mag. *dial.*(tr.Zach.)3.1(M.*PL.*77.219A); †Anast.S.*relat.*13(*OC* 2 p.67).

κοδράντης, ὁ, (Lat. *quadrans*) *quarter of an as*, Hipp.*haer.*6.25 (p.152.6; M.16.3231B); Epiph.*mens.*24(M.43.285A).

***κόδρι(ο)ν, τό**, (Lat. *quadrum*) *square box* containing money, Cyr.S.*v.Euthym.*48(p.69.19); id.*v.Thds.*109(p.238.9).

κόθορνος, *variable* τὸν ἀσταθῆ καὶ κ. βίον Evagr.*h.e.*6.17(p.234.9; M.86.2869C).

***κοθωκίδης**, sens. dub. (cf. Aristophanes *Thesmophoriazusae* 620) ἢ γὰρ ἂν πλείω λέγοντας εὗρες, καὶ οὐκ ἂν ἡμῖν τὸ κοθωκίδην ἔφης, τὸ τῶν αὐλῶν πάθος τοῖς σοφισταῖς ἐπισκώπτοντα Proc.G.*ep.*136(77; M. 87.2780B).

***κόθωνος, ὁ**, (Hebr. כְּתֹנֶת) *vestment* worn by Jewish priests, *Hymn.*(*AS* 1 p.543).

κοιαίστωρ, ὁ, v. [*]κυαίστωρ.

***κοιαιστώριον, τό**, v. *κυαιστώριον.

κοιλαίν-ω, 1. *hollow*, ref. reception of eucharistic bread by communicant κοιλάνας τὴν παλάμην, δέχου τὸ σῶμα τοῦ Χριστοῦ Cyr.H.*catech.*23.21; Chrys.*ecl.*47(12.771C); **2.** med., fig., *be tormented in mind* ὁ περὶ πάντα...τὰ καλὰ καὶ θεοφιλῆ πράγματα καὶ διανοήματα ~όμενος ὄφις ‡Jo.D.*fid.dorm.*2(M.95.248B).

κοίλανσις, ἡ, *hollow* ἡ κ. τῆς λέπρας Max.*qu.dub.*78(M.90.852B).

***κοιλιόδουλος**, *enslaved to the belly*, Ant.Mon.*hom.*4(M.89.1444C); Jo.Clim.*scal.*14(M.88.864D); ‡Jo.D.*conf.*7(M.95.292B).

***κοιλιολάτρης, ὁ**, *belly-worshipper*, Pall.*v.Chrys.*12(p.77.29; M. 47.44).

***κοιλιομανία, ἡ**, *madness of gluttony*, Nil.*epp.*4.58(M.79.576D); Jo.Carp.*cap.*76(M.85.1854); Jo.Clim.*scal.*26(M.88.1028C).

***κοιλιοπονέω (-πονάω)**, *struggle in childbirth*, Leont.N.*v.Sym.*39 (M.93.1717C); *Exorc.*21(p.339); κοιλιοπονᾷ *ib.*(p.340).

***κοιλιοφορέω**, *bear in the womb, be pregnant*, ‡Epiph.*hom.*5(M.43. 496D).

***κοιλιοφορῶς**, *by bearing in the womb* ἡ τὴν ἀστραπὴν ἔνδον κ. βαστάσασα [sc. BMV] ‡Epiph.*hom.*5(M.43.492D).

κοιμ-άομαι, [imper. κοιμοῦ *Apophth.Patr.*(M.65.172C)]; *lie down*; *fall asleep*, met. κοιμᾶται ἡ νύξ *1Clem.*24.3; esp. *fall asleep in death*, *die*; **1.** in gen. ὁ ~ώμενος...ὁ ἀπηλλαγμένος τοῦ βίου Or.*engast.*9 (p.293.17; M.12.1028A); τις τῶν κεκοιμωμένων φαινόμενος Meth.*res.*

3.7(p.414.8; M.18.325A); ὡς ἐν θανάτῳ ~ωμένου Ath.*gent*.33(M.25.65C); **2.** of Christ τοῦ ~ηθέντος καὶ ἀναστάντος *Const.App*.6.30.8; within the believer ἀδύνατον...τοῦ πνεύματος τοῦ ἁγίου μετασχεῖν τινα...ἐὰν μὴ πρότερον καὶ ἐπὶ τούτου συγκατελθὼν ὁ λόγος ἐκστῇ ~ηθείς Meth.*symp*.3.8(p.36.13; M.18.73C); **3.** of those who died before Inc. οἱ πρὸ τῆς παρουσίας...~ώμενοι Or.*engast*.9(p.294.16; M.12.1028C); τῆς...χάριτος τῆς προφητικῆς αἱ ψυχαὶ τῶν ~ωμένων ἐδέοντο *ib*.(p.293.15; 1025D); ‡Ath.*serm.fid*.38(p.31; M.26.1289C); *Const.App*.2.22.18; *ib*.6.30.5; **4.** of the redeemed; **a.** in gen., *1Clem*.44.2; Ign.*Rom*.4.2; ἐν δικαιοσύνῃ ἐκοιμήθησαν καὶ ἐν μεγάλῃ ἁγνείᾳ Herm.*sim*.9.16.7; τοῖς ἐν Χριστῷ κεκοιμημένοις Eus.*Marcell*.1.1(p.2.2; M.24.712B); τοῦτον...μακαρίως...ἀναπεπαυμένον πάλαι τε κεκοιμημένον *ib*.1.4(p.18.7; 752A); ἐν τῇ ἐκκλησίᾳ κεκοίμηται καλῶς Ath.*Dion*.3(p.48.10; M.25.484B); ἐκοιμήθησαν ἐν Χριστῷ id.*syn*.43(p.268.22; M.26.768D); πῶς...οἱ πιστοὶ διὰ τοῦ Ἰησοῦ ~ῶνται; δηλονότι τὸν Χριστὸν ἔχοντες ἐν ἑαυτοῖς Chrys.*hom.7.1 in 1Thess*.(11.473E); μὴ πενθεῖν τοὺς κεκοιμημένους id.*hom.79.5 in Mt*.(7.764E); id.*coemet*.1(2.398A) cit. s. κοιμητήριον; περὶ τῶν ἐν πίστει κεκοιμημένων ‡Jo.D.*fid.dorm*.tit.(M.95.247); **b.** ref. resurrection ἀναβίωσις τῶν κεκοιμημένων *Const.App*.7.32.3; οἱ...θεῷ πεπιστευκότες ἐὰν καὶ ~ηθῶσιν οὐκ εἰσὶν νεκροί *ib*.6.30.4; ὁ θεὸς...ἀναστήσει ἡμᾶς σὺν πᾶσι τοῖς ἀπ' αἰῶνος ~ηθεῖσιν *ib*.5.7.1; **c.** death not a cause for sorrow ψάλλοντες ὑπὲρ τῶν κεκοιμημένων μαρτύρων καὶ...τῶν ἀδελφῶν...τῶν ἐν κυρίῳ κεκοιμημένων καὶ...ἐν ταῖς ἐξόδοις τῶν κεκοιμημένων ψάλλοντες προπέμπετε αὐτούς *Const.App*.6.30.2; οἱ τοῦ ~ηθέντος οἰκεῖοι αὐτὸν...μακαρίζουσι πρὸς τὸ νικηφόρον εὐκταίως ἀφικόμενον τέλος Dion.Ar.*e.h*.7.1.3(M.3.556B); **d.** rites of burial described, Dion.Ar.*e.h*.7(M.3.552Cff.); esp. prayer ὁ...ἱεράρχης εὐχὴν ἱερὰν ἐπὶ τῷ κεκοιμημένῳ ποιεῖται...ἡ μὲν...εὐχὴ τῆς θεαρχικῆς ἀγαθότητος δεῖται πάντα μὲν ἀφεῖναι τὰ ἡμαρτημένα τῷ κεκοιμημένῳ, κατατάξαι δὲ αὐτὸν ἐν φωτὶ καὶ χώρᾳ ζώντων *ib*.7.3.4(560A); τοῖς ἀνιέροις οὐκ ἐπεύχεται ταῦτα κεκοιμημένοις *ib*.7.3.7(564A); v. εὐχή; kiss αὐτός τ' ὁ ἱεράρχης ἀσπάζεται τὸν κεκοιμημένον καὶ μετ' αὐτὸν οἱ παρόντες ἅπαντες *ib*.7.2(556D); cf. ὑμεῖς...ἀπαρατηρήτως ἁπτόμενοι τῶν κεκοιμημένων μὴ νομίσητε μιαίνεσθαι *Const.App*.6.30.7; anointing ἐπιχέει τῷ κεκοιμημένῳ τὸ ἔλαιον ὁ ἱεράρχης Dion.Ar.*e.h*.7.2(556D); τὸ ἐπιχεόμενον ἔλαιον ἐμφαίνει κατὰ τοὺς ἱεροὺς ἀγῶνας ἀθλήσαντα καὶ τελειωθέντα τὸν κεκοιμημένον *ib*.7.3.8(565A); **e.** commemoration of dead in liturgy, Serap.*euch*.13.17 cit. s. ἀνάμνησις; ἐπιτελείσθω δὲ τρίτα τῶν κεκοιμημένων ἐν ψαλμοῖς καὶ ἀναγνώσμασιν καὶ προσευχαῖς διὰ τὸν διὰ τριῶν ἡμερῶν ἐγερθέντα, καὶ ἔνατα εἰς ὑπόμνησιν τῶν περιόντων καὶ τῶν κεκοιμημένων *Const.App*.8.42.1,2; οὐδὲ μάτην ὁ παρεστὼς τῷ θυσιαστηρίῳ τῶν φρικτῶν μυστηρίων τελουμένων βοᾷ· πάντων τῶν ἐν Χριστῷ κεκοιμημένων καὶ τῶν τὰς μνείας ὑπὲρ αὐτῶν ἐπιτελούντων Chrys.*hom.41.4 in 1Cor*.(10.393A); τὸ πρᾶγμα πάντως ἐπωφελὲς καὶ θεάρεστον τὸ μνήμην...ποιεῖν ἐπὶ τῆς...μυσταγωγίας, τῶν ἐν ὀρθῇ τῇ πίστει καὶ κεκοιμημένων Gr.Nyss.ap.‡Jo.D.*fid.dorm*.7(M.95.253A).

κοίμησις, ἡ, *a falling asleep in death*; **1.** in gen. μέχρι τῆς κ. αὐτῶν Herm.*sim*.9.15.6; Or.*engast*.5(p.287.25; M.12.1020A); Epiph.*haer*.79.5(p.480.4; M.42.748B); ἡ τῶν ἱερῶν ἐστι κ. ἐν εὐφροσύνῃ καὶ ἀσαλεύτοις ἐλπίσιν Dion.Ar.*e.h*.7.1.1(M.3.553B); plur. τὰς κ. τῶν ἱερῶν *ib*.7.1.3(556A); in prayers for the dead δεόμεθά σου περὶ τῆς κ. καὶ ἀναπαύσεως τοῦ δούλου σου τοῦδε Serap.*euch*.30.2; ὑπὲρ τῆς κ. τοῦδε...δεηθῶμεν *Const.App*.8.41.2; **2.** as peculiarly Christian conception of death τῆς γραφῆς...τὸν θάνατον...κ. ἀποκαλούσης Eus.*d.e*.8.1(p.364.12; M.22.592B); id.*Ps*.149:5(M.24.72B); ὅταν...μετὰ τὸ ἀποθανεῖν ζήσῃ...οὐ θάνατος τοῦτό ἐστιν ἀλλὰ κ. Chrys.*hom.17.2 in Heb*.(12.166B); ἐπειδὰν δ' ἦλθεν ὁ Χριστὸς...οὐκέτι θάνατος καλεῖται λοιπὸν ὁ θάνατος ἀλλὰ ὕπνος καὶ κ. id.*coemet*.1(2.398B); **3.** of dormition of BMV περὶ τῆς πανεντίμου κ. αὐτῆς οὐ πέφηναν...διὸ κατὰ τὴν ἡμέραν τῆς θεομητρικῆς κ. πλεῖστοι κεχήνασι ὅσοι φιλομαθεῖς...τι ἀπόρρητον μαθεῖν γλιχόμενοι περὶ αὐτῆς Mod.*dorm*.1(M.86.3280B); ὦ παμμακαρία κ. τῆς...θεοτόκου *ib*.7(3293Aff.); πανηγυρίζομεν...τὴν ζωηφόρον αὐτῆς κ. Jo.Eub.*concept.BMV* 22(M.96.1497B); λόγος εἰς τὴν κ. τῆς ἁγίας θεοτόκου *Dorm.BMV* tit.(p.95); the festival μέχρι τῆς κ. τῆς θεοτόκου ‡Anast.Ant.*serm*.4(M.89.1397B).

κοιμητήριον, τό, *resting-place for the dead*; **1.** *cemetery*; **a.** in gen. ἀπὸ τῶν κ., προπέμψαντες τοὺς μάρτυρας, ἠρχόμεθα ἐπὶ τὰς συναγωγάς Or.*hom.4.3 in Jer*.(p.25.20; M.13.288D); ἐν ἐρήμῳ τόπῳ πλησίον τοῦ κ. Ath.*apol.Const*.27(M.25.629C); ἡ Πέτρου καὶ Παύλου εἰς δεῦρο κρατήσασα ἔτι τῶν αὐτόθι κ. πρόσρησις Eus.*h.e*.2.25.5(M.20.208C); τὴν θήκην...ἐν τῷ καλουμένῳ κ. κατέθεσαν ‡Jo.D.*Artem*.(p.92.14; M.96.1301D); διὰ ταῦτα...ὁ τόπος κ. ὠνόμασται, ἵνα μάθῃς ὅτι οἱ τετελευτηκότες καὶ ἐνταῦθα κείμενοι οὐ τεθνήκασι ἀλλὰ κοιμῶνται Chrys.*coemet*.1(2.398A); ἐτάφη ἐν τῷ κ. τῆς μεγάλης ἐκκλησίας †Gregent.*disp*.(M.86.784A); ἐκέλευσεν...εἰς τὸ κ. αὐτὸν ταφῆναι ἔνθα ἐπίσκοπος ἔκειτο Jo.Mosch.*prat*.40(M.87.2892C); **b.** used for worship τῇ...ἑβδομάδι μετὰ τὴν ἁγίαν πεντηκοστὴν ὁ λαὸς νηστεύσας ἐξῆλθε περὶ τὸ κ. εὔξασθαι Ath.*fug*.6(p.72.9; M.25.652B); in cult of martyrs τὴν...δεκτὴν εὐχαριστίαν προσφέρετε ἔντε ταῖς ἐκκλησίαις...καὶ ἐν τοῖς κ. *Const.App*.6.30.2; cf.CLaod.*can*.9 cit. s. μαρτύριον; **c.** Christians denied access in times of persecution, Dion.Al.ap.Eus.*h.e*.7.11.10(M.20.665B); Eus.*h.e*.9.2.1(804A); right restored, *ib*.7.13.1(676A); **2.** *tomb, family grave* κατεσκεύασα τὸ κυμητή[ρ]ιον ἐμαυτῷ καὶ τῇ γυναικί μου *JHS* 4 p.407 (Phrygia); κοιμητήριον *ib*.p.429; κ]οιμητήρι[ο]ν ἐν Χριστῷ Ἰησοῦ...ου καὶ Εὐτυ[χίδ]ος καὶ Ἐλπι[δίου *BCH* 1 p.406 (Attica); κυμιτίριον *ib*.p.405 (Attica); κ[ατεσκεύασε ἑ]αυτῷ κοιμητή[ριον τοῦτο] μνήμης χάρ[ιν *MAMA* 1.205 (Phrygia).

***κοιμήτωρ, ὁ,** *one who induces sleep*, Gr.Naz.*carm*.1.2.8.144(M.37.659A).

κοιμισμός, ὁ, *putting to sleep*, Epiph.*anc*.83(p.103.16; M.43.172C).

***κοινοβιακός (-βιαϊκός),** *cenobitic, belonging to a community* of religious κ. κανόνων ‡Ath.*ep.Cast*.1(M.28.857D); *Apophth.Patr*.(M.65.245C); Cyr.S.*v.Sab*.2(p.88.1); κ. βίος id.*v.Jo.Hes*.6(p.206.9); †Jo.D.*B.J*.12(M.96.969A); Thdr.Stud.*epp*.2.164(M.99.1520C); κοινοβιαϊκὴν ζωήν id.*or*.11.11(M.99.813A); μία ἐκκλησία κ. id.*epp*.2.53(M.1264D); ὁ κ. *one who belongs to a community* τὰ τῶν κ. κατορθώματα ‡Bas.*const*.18.4(2.562D, v.l. κοινωνικῶν; M.31.1385B).

***κοινοβιακῶς,** *in accordance with a common life*, opp. ἰδιοβούλως, Thdr.Stud.*epp*.2.133(M.99.1428D).

***κοινοβιαρχέω,** *rule over a religious community*, Cyr.S.*v.Sab*.27(p.111.27); id.*v.Thds*.(p.237.15).

κοινοβιάρχης, ὁ, *head of a religious community*, *Apophth.Patr*.(M.65.224D); τὸν ἀββᾶν...τὸν γεγονότα τῆς ἐρήμου...μέγαν κ. καὶ τῶν κοινοβίων ἀρχιμανδρίτην Cyr.S.*v.Euthym*.8(p.16.15); Jo.Mosch.*prat*.97(M.87.2956A); *ib*.146(3009B); *ib*.147(3012A).

κοινόβιον, τό, *community* of religious, *monastery*; **1.** in gen. τοὺς ἐν κ. μοναχούς Gr.Naz.*carm*.1.2.5 tit.(M.37.642A); τοὺς ἐν κ. ἀσκοῦντας ‡Bas.*const*.1 tit.(2.533A; M.31.1321); τοὺς ἐν κ. κανονικοὺς *ib*.18 tit.(560D; M.1381B); ἄπελθε εἰ...θέλεις μοναχὸς γενέσθαι εἰς κ. πλειόνων ἀδελφῶν Pall.*h.Laus*.28(p.70.17; M.34.1081A); τοῖς ἐν κ. ... τὸν σκοπὸν τῆς ἐγκρατείας κατορθοῦσι Diad.*perf*.53(p.58.13); *Apophth.Patr*.(M.65.81D); τὸ κ. ... τοῦ ἀββᾶ Σάβα Jo.Mosch.*prat*.52(M.87.2908A); τὸ κ. τοῦ βαπτίσματος *ib*.3(2856B); building of κ. described, Cyr.S.*v.Euthym*.43(p.64.14ff.); possessions of κ., *Apophth.Patr*.(M.65.152B); **2.** contrasted with λαύρα, Cyr.S.*v.Jo.Hes*.6(p.206.5) cit. s. λαύρα; οὔτε εἰς τὴν λαύραν εἰς κέλλιον ἠφίει αὐτοὺς οἰκῆσαι, ἀλλὰ μικρὸν κ. κατὰ τὸ ἀρκτῷον μέρος τῆς λαύρας συστησάμενος καὶ ἄνδρας εἰς αὐτὸ ἐστυμμένους καὶ νηφαλέους καταστήσας ἐκεῖσε τοὺς ἀποτασσομένους μένειν ἐκέλευσεν, ἕως οὗ τό τε ψαλτήριον μάθωσι καὶ τὸν τῆς ψαλμῳδίας κανόνα καὶ τὴν μοναχικὴν παιδευθῶσιν ἀκρίβειαν id.*v.Sab*.28(p.113.6); id.*v.Euthym*.39(p.58.29) cit. s. λαύρα; cf.*ib*.9(p.16.25ff.); **3.** of women's convent τὰς...γυναῖκας βουλομένας...τῇ ἁγίᾳ...κοινωνίᾳ τῆς καθολικῆς ἐκκλησίας προσελθεῖν, ἔχειν τὰ ἴδια κ. ἀπαρεγχείρητα Max.*ep*.12(M.91.464D).

[*]**κοινοβιώτης, ὁ,** *member of a community*, Nil.*epp*.1.307 tit.(M.79.193B).

κοινοβουλία, ἡ, *common purpose, common will* τὴν πρὸς τὸν θεὸν καὶ πατέρα κ. [i.e. of Christ] Cyr.*Jo*.7(4.661C).

***κοινογαμία, ἡ,** **1.** *communal marriage* advocated by Platonists, ‡Epiph.*epit.haer*.6(p.346.15); and Secundian Gnostics, *ib*.32(p.363.6); **2.** *public union* of Crates, Gr.Naz.*or*.25.7(M.35.1208B); v. κυνογαμία.

***κοινοδέσποτος,** *common to several masters*; opp. μονοδέσποτος, Leont.H.*Nest*.2.13(M.86.1561C).

***κοινοεργ-έω,** *work upon together* τὴν...τροφὴν...ἡ γαστὴρ καὶ τὸ ἧπαρ ~οῦσιν Melet.*nat.hom*.21(M.64.1225B).

κοινοεργής, *working in common*, Melet.*nat.hom*.21(M.64.1228A).

κοινολογέω, *converse*, ‡Ath.*disp*.3(M.28.441B).

κοινολογία, ἡ, *conversation*, Or.*Jo*.13.28(p.252.29; M.14.448C); Cyr.*Am*.22(3.272D).

***κοινόμυια, ἡ,** v. κυνόμυια.

κοινοποι-έω, **1.** *make common*; **a.** one's own with another, *impart*, of God τὰ ἴδια μυστήρια διὰ τῶν προφητῶν ~ήσαντα Hipp.*ben.Jac*.1(p.14.2); Gr.Naz.*ep*.165(M.37.277C); Cyr.*Ps*.43:19(M.69.1024D); θεῷ...τὰ τῆς ἰδίας φύσεως ἀγαθὰ ~εῖν εἰωθότι τῷ ἰδίῳ σώματι id.*inc.unigen*.(5[1].711A); ἡ τιμὴ καὶ ἡ προσκύνησις ~οῦνται μέχρι καὶ τοῦ τυχόντος ἀνθρώπου Thdr.Stud.*epp*.2.151(M.99.1472C); acc. Eunomians εἰ γάρ τις ~εῖν πρὸς ἕτερον ἢ μεταδιδόναι τινὶ τῆς οὐσίας ταύτης ἐθελήσειεν, ἤτοι κατὰ διάστασιν καὶ μερισμόν, ἢ κατὰ σύγκρισιν τοῦτο κατασκευάσειεν ἂν Eun.*apol*.9(M.30.844B); ~ηθήσεται τὸ τῆς οὐσίας ἀξίωμα *ib*.(844C); med. ~εῖται [sc. ἡ γυνή] πρὸς τοῖς ἄλλοις τὸ

...ἀγαθόν Cyr.*Jo*.2.5(4.194B); **b.** with oneself, *share in, assume*, of Christ τὰς ἡμετέρας ~εῖ εἰς ἑαυτὸν ἁμαρτίας Eus.*d.e*.10.1(p.449.30; M.22.724B); med. ~οῦμαι...τὴν σὴν εὐπραγίαν Gr.Naz.*ep*.88(M.37.161C); Cosm.Ind.*top*.5(M.88.304D); **2.** *regard as common, attribute to another* or *others* ἐκοινοποίησεν ὁ Κέλσος...φάσκων αὐτὰ καὶ παρ' Ἕλλησιν εἰρῆσθαι Or.*Cels*.7.59(p.208.9; M.11.1504C); *ib*.6.1(p.70.4; 1289A); τὴν ἰδίαν ἀσθένειαν ~εῖς Gr.Nyss.*Eun*.9(2 p.209.8; M.45.805D); πῶς...οὐδαμοῦ τοῦ πατρὸς ἑαυτὸν ἀπόστολον εἶναί φησιν, ἀλλὰ τοῦ Χριστοῦ; πάντα ~εῖ Chrys.*hom.1.1 in 1Tim*.(11.549F); πῶς εἰς αὐτὸν οὐκ ἀσεβήσομεν τὸν πατέρα...τὸ μόνου τοῦ μονογενοῦς ἐξαίρετον ἀγαθὸν ~οῦντες πρὸς ἄλλοις; Cyr.*Jo*.1.10(4.107A); *ib*.2.2(162C); *regard alike* or *equally* as truth δημοσίας...βίβλους εἴτε τὰς Ἰουδαϊκὰς ...γραφὰς εἴτε τὰς τῶν φιλοσόφων ~εῖ [sc. Valentinus] τὴν ἀλήθειαν Clem.*str*.6.6(p.458.18; M.9.276A); **3.** *apply equally* to another case ἅπερ...λέγει...δύναται ~εῖσθαι εἰς τὴν Μωϋσέως κατηγορίαν Or.*Cels*.2.53(p.176.6; M.11.880C); *ib*.2.55(p.179.6; 885A); τὸ...τοῦ ἁγίου καὶ τοῦ ἀφθάρτου...οὐδαμοῦ ~ούμενον πρὸς τὰ μὴ δέοντα Gr.Nyss.*Trin*.5(p.77.3; M.32.692B); of Arians τὸ τοῦ υἱοῦ ~οῦντες ὄνομα πρὸς τοὺς δούλους Apoll.*fid.sec.pt*.1(p.167.6; M.10.1105A); **4.** *regard, treat as like*; **a.** Christol. τὰς δὲ εὐαγγελικὰς καὶ ἀποστολικὰς περὶ τοῦ κυρίου φωνὰς ἴσμεν τοὺς θεολόγους ἄνδρας τὰς μὲν ~οῦντας ὡς ἐφ' ἑνὸς προσώπου, τὰς δὲ διαιροῦντας ὡς ἐπὶ δύο φύσεων Jo.Ant.*ep.Cyr*.2(p.9.6; M.77.173A); τοὺς...λέγοντας ὅτι οὐ χρὴ ~εῖν τὴν σάρκα τῇ θεότητι τοῦ μονογενοῦς οὐδὲ τὴν θεότητα τῇ σαρκὶ ἐν ταῖς θαυματουργίαις...τῆς ἀληθείας διημαρτηκέναι φαμέν Cyr.*resp*.5(p.585.24; 6^{2}.390A); μετὰ τὴν καθ' ὑπόστασιν ἕνωσιν ~εῖ τὰ τῆς σαρκὸς καὶ τῆς θεότητος κατὰ τῆς ἐνεργείας, οὐ κατὰ μεταβολὴν τῶν ἐξ ὧν ὁ Χριστός Ammon.*Jo*.3:13(M.85.1409C); ~εῖ τὸ πᾶν, οὐκ εἰδὼς χωρισμὸν μετὰ τὴν ἕνωσιν *ib*.3:16(1412A); **b.** in derogatory sense, *treat as comparable, confuse*, act. Ἐλιφὰζ...~εῖ αὐτὸν [sc. τὸν Ἰώβ] τοῖς πᾶσιν ἀνθρώποις Didym.*Job* 15:7(M.39.1152A); *Const.App*.2.61.2; Cosm.Ind.*top*.5(M.88.256C) cf. *Chron.Pasch*.p.90(M.92.252B); Christ's miracles ~εῖ [sc. Celsus] αὐτὰ πρὸς τὰ ἔργα τῶν γοήτων Or.*Cels*.1.68(p.122.5; M.11.788A); *ib*.2.16(p.145.25; 832A); and resurrection appearances ~εῖν πρὸς ἕτερα φαντάσματα καὶ ἄλλους φαντασθέντας τὰ κατὰ τὸν Ἰησοῦν *ib*.2.62(p.184.25; 893D); in Eunomian teaching on Christ ἔφη ~εῖν τὸν μονογενῆ πρὸς τὴν κτίσιν Bas.*Eun*.2.24(1.261B; M.29.628B); μηδεὶς... τὸν υἱὸν ἀκούων ποίημα δυσχεραινέτω, ὡς ~ουμένης τῆς οὐσίας ὑπὸ τῆς τῶν ὀνομάτων κοινωνίας *ib*.2.24(261C; M.628C); ἡ τῶν ὀνομάτων κοινωνία οὐ ~ήσει καὶ τὰς οὐσίας *ib*.; πῶς ~οῦσιν ἢ πρὸς τὴν αἰσθητὴν κτίσιν τὸν τῆς κτίσεως κύριον, ἢ πρὸς τὴν τῶν ἀγγέλων φύσιν τὸν ὑπ' αὐτῶν προσκυνούμενον; Gr.Nyss.*Eun*.4(2 p.61.16; M.45.632D); πρὸς τὰ μικρότατα τῆς κτίσεως μόρια ~εῖται παρ' αὐτῶν τοῦ μονογενοῦς ἡ οὐσία *ib*.(p.97.4; 673C); οὐκέτ' ἂν εἴη μονογενής, ὁ τισὶ τῆς γεννήσεως ἰδιώμασι πρὸς τὰ λοιπὰ τῶν γεννηθέντων ~ούμενος *ib*.8(2 p.190.26; 785B); *ib*.6(2 p.132.11; 716C); οὐ ~οῦμεν...τοῦ μονογενοῦς τὴν οὐσίαν πρὸς τὰ ἐκ μὴ ὄντων γενόμενα Eun.*apol*.15(M.30.849C); such teaching condemned εἴ τις...~ῶν αὐτὸν [sc. τὸν υἱόν] πρὸς τὰ λοιπὰ ποιήματα ...ἀ. ἔ. CAnc.(358)*anath*.ap.Epiph.*haer*.73.11(p.284.1; M.42.424D); εἴ τις...~ῶν τὴν τοῦ πατρὸς καὶ τοῦ υἱοῦ ἔννοιαν ἐπὶ τῶν λοιπῶν ποιημάτων...ἀ. ἔ. *ib*.(p.280.25; 421A); cf. ὁ υἱὸς 'κύριος ἔκτισέ με' εἰπών, ἵνα ⟨μὴ⟩ ~ουμένην αὐτοῦ πρὸς τὰ λοιπὰ κτίσματα ὑποπτεύσωμεν τὴν φύσιν, ἐπήνεγκεν ἀναγκαίως 'πρὸ δὲ πάντων βουνῶν γεννᾷ με' Geo.Laod.*ep.dogm*.ap.Epiph.*haer*.73.20(p.293.8; 440C); in teaching of Pneumatomachoi οὐ ~εῖται τοῖς πᾶσιν μοναδικὸν ὂν τὸ ἅγιον πνεῦμα ‡Ath.*Maced.dial*.1.8(M.28.1300C); **5.** *make like* or *equal*, med. οὐ... ἡ κοινότης τῶν λέξεων ~εῖται τὰς φύσεις *ib*.(1300D).

***κοινοπρεπής**, *befitting alike* the divine and human nature of Christ, Anast.S.*hod*.1(M.89.48A).

***κοινοπρεπῶς**, *in a manner consonant with both* the divine and human θεανδρικήν...ἐνέργειαν νοοῦμεν τὴν κ. πως ὑπὸ Χριστοῦ πραττομένην Anast.S.*hod*.1(M.89.45D); comp., for καινοπρεπέστερον, Ath.Scholast.*coll*.2.8(p.40).

κοινός, *common*; **1.** *shared in common*; **a.** of abstracts τοῦ κ. ὀνόματος καὶ ἐλπίδος Ign.*Eph*.1.2; τὸ ἐπικατηγορούμενον ὄνομα κ. ἐστι Just.*1apol*.7.3(M.6.337A); κ. πίστις Clem.*str*.4.16(p.293.2; M.8.1308B); κ. ἀρετῶν *ib*.4.21(p.307.21; 1344C); κ. βίος *ib*.7.7(p.37.18; M.9.469C); τὴν κ. πάντων ἀνάστασιν Ath.*inc*.10.5(M.25.113C); κ. διαίτης *Const.App*.2.40.1; cf. κ. τραπέζας Thdt.*1Cor*.11:20(3.237); ἡ...τοῦ ἑνὸς καὶ ταὐτοῦ καὶ ἄρτου καὶ ποτηρίου κ. ... μετάδοσις Dion.Ar.*e.h*.3.3.1(M.3.428B); κ. ... τὰς ἀγγελικὰς ὀνομασίας id.*c.h*.5(M.3.196C); κ. τινα...τῶν ἁγίων...κοινωνίαν id.*ep*.9.5(M.3.1112D); neut. as subst., *the common element* τὸ κ. τῆς ἐλπίδος *1Clem*.51.1; τὸ κ. τῆς πίστεως Clem.*str*.7.16(p.69.8; M.9.536A); τὸ τῆς γενέσεως κ. id.*exc.Thdot*.27(p.116.14; M.9.673B); plur. τὰ κ. τῆς πρός σε φιλίας Meth.*arbitr*.4(p.156.1; M.18.248D); **b.** of persons: Christ ὁ λόγος ὁ κ. ἀμφοῖν θεοῦ μὲν υἱός, σωτὴρ δὲ ἀνθρώπων Clem.*paed*.3.1(p.237.1; M.8.557A); τῷ κ. πάντων ἀνθρώπων κυβερνήτῃ Gr.Thaum.*pan.Or*.4(p.10.2; M.10.1061C); τὸν κ. πάντων σωτῆρα *ib*.(p.9.25; 1061C); Ath.*inc*.15.2(M.25.121C); ὁ κ. πάντων κύριος *ib*.49.1(184B); spiritual parents τῆς... κ. ... πάντων ἡμῶν μητρός [i.e. Church] Const.ap.Gel.Cyz.*h.e*.2.7.39(M.85.1241B); τοῦ...κ. ἡμῶν πατρὸς Ἀκακίου Jo.Ant.*ep.Nest*.(p.94.21; M.77.1453A); τῶν κ. ἡμῖν πατέρων Thdt.*h.e*.1.11.7(3.775); Dion.Ar.*d.n*.2.11(M.3.649D); κ. τις...πατὴρ...ὁ ἱερεύς Chrys.*hom.6.1 in 1Tim*.(11.578D); **c.** Christol. τὸ...σῶμα ὡς καὶ αὐτὸ κοινὴν ἔχον τοῖς πᾶσι τὴν οὐσίαν Ath.*inc*.20.4(M.25.132A); ἐκ δύο μὲν τῆς τε θείας καὶ τῆς κ. ἀνθρωπείας ἄμφω προϋπαρχουσῶν τῆς ἑνώσεως Χριστοῦ φαμεν· ἐν δύο δέ, τῆς τε ὑπὲρ τὸν κ. λόγον καὶ ἰδικὸν οὔσης κ. θεότητος καὶ τῆς ἰδικῆς μόνον αὐτοῦ ἀνθρωπότητος Leont.H.*monoph*.58(M.86.1801B); v. ἰδικός; **d.** Trin. θεότης τὸ 'εἶναι' κ. ταῖς ὑποστάσεσι σημαίνει ‡Ath.*dial.Trin*.1.16(M.28.1141C); οὐκ εἶπον· τὰ ἴδια τοῦ πατρὸς καὶ τοῦ υἱοῦ καὶ τοῦ πνεύματός εἰσι κ.· ἀλλά, τὰ ἴδια τῆς οὐσίας τοῦ θεοῦ, τοῦ πατρὸς καὶ τοῦ υἱοῦ καὶ τοῦ ἁγίου πνεύματός εἰσι κ. *ib*.25(1153D); *ib*.22(1149B,C); τῷ μὲν τῶν ἰδιοτήτων δηλοῦντες τὸν ἀριθμόν· τῷ δὲ τὸ κ. τῆς δεσποτείας μηνύοντες Thdt.*affect*.2(p.53.17; 4.744); ἡνωμένον μέν ἐστι τῇ ἐναρχικῇ τριάδι καὶ κοινὸν ἡ ὑπερούσιος ὕπαρξις κτλ. Dion.Ar.*d.n*.2.4(M.3.641A); τὰς κ. καὶ ἡνωμένας τῆς ὅλης θεότητος διακρίσεις *ib*.2.11(652A); *ib*.2.5(644A); ὁ Φιλόπονος ἔλεγεν ὅτι εἰσὶ τρεῖς μερικαὶ οὐσίαι ἐπὶ τῆς ἁγίας τριάδος, καὶ ἔστι μία κ. †Leont.B.*sect*.5.6(M.86.1233B); αἱ τρεῖς [sc. ὑποστάσεις] ἔχουσι μίαν φύσιν καὶ οὐσίαν κ. τῆς θεότητος Jo.D.*fid.Nest*.7(p.562); acc. Valentinus κοινὸν τῆς τριάδος τὸ πάθος ‡Ath.*Apoll*.2.3(M.26.1136C), cf.*ib*.2.2(1133C); acc. monophysites μὴ εἶναι...τούτων ἕκαστον καθ' ἑαυτὸν θεὸν φύσει, ἀλλ' ἔχειν κ. θεόν, ἤγουν θεότητα ἐνύπαρκτον...καλοῦσι δὲ...τὸ...κ. αὐτῶν θεόν, οὐσίαν καὶ φύσιν Tim.CP *haer*.(M.86.60A,B); acc. Nest. εἰ τὸ 'εἷς τῆς τριάδος' λεγόμενον κ. τῆς θεότητος καὶ τῆς ἀνθρωπότητος Χριστοῦ ἐστιν ἢ...ἐστι κ. τῷ πατρὶ καὶ τῷ πνεύματι, ἢ καθ' ἕτερον καὶ ἑτερόν πως ἐξ ἀμφοῖν ἀποτελουμένου λόγου ἑνός Leont.H.*Nest*.7.4(M.86.1768A); **e.** οὐδὲν κ. ἔχω πρός τινα *have nothing in common with* ἡμῶν ...μηδὲν ἐχόντων κ. πρὸς τὴν πατρικὴν θεότητα Eus.*e.th*.3.20(p.181.7; M.24.1044D); οὐδὲν κ. τῷ λόγῳ πρὸς τοὺς αἰῶνας Ath.*decr*.18(p.15.18; M.25.456A); of H. Ghost μηδὲν κ. μηδὲ ἴδιον ἔχειν τι τῇ φύσει καὶ τῇ οὐσίᾳ πρὸς τὰ κτίσματα id.*ep.Serap*.1.27(M.26.593C); τί...κ. πόλεμος πρὸς ἐπισκόπους; id.*h.Ar*.11(p.189.1; M.25.705C); Chrys.*oppugn*.2(1.68B); id.*hom.20.1 in Rom*.(9.657B); **f.** in prepositional phrases ἀπὸ κοινοῦ, κατὰ κοινοῦ *with like* or *common application* in interprn. of a phrase, ref. Jo.8:51 ζητῶ μήποτε τὸ 'εἰς τὸν αἰῶνα', ἀπὸ κ. ληπτέον, ὥστ' ἂν εἶναι τοιοῦτον τὸ ὅλον· ἐάν τις τὸν ἐμὸν λόγον τηρήσῃ εἰς τὸν αἰῶνα...Or.*Jo*.20.39(31; p.382.11; M.14.668B); *ib*.13.8(p.232.14; 409B); id.*comm.in 1Cor*.3:3(*JTS* 9 p.241); cf.Hier.*comm.in Mt*.5:22(M.*PL*.26.37A); κατὰ κ. κεῖται τὸ 'κατὰ τὰς γραφάς' Chrys.*hom.38.3 in 1Cor*.(10.354A); Ammon.*Ac*.19:23(M.85.1580B); Andr.Caes.*Apoc*.4(M.106.236A); ἀπὸ κ. *commonly, generally*, Or.*comm.in Gen*.ap.*philoc*.14.1(p.68.5; M.12.88B om.); κατὰ κοινοῦ *universally*, Dion.Ar.*c.h*.5 tit.(M.3.196A); *ib*.6 tit.(284B); κατὰ τὸ κοινότερον *in general*, Or.*Jo*.2.30(24; p.87.24; M.14.168A); **g.** τὸ κ. *the* Christian *community* εἰς τὸ κ. εἰσελθεῖν Or.*Cels*.3.51(p.247.7; M.11.988A); id.*hom.12.5 in Jer*.(p.92.4; M.13.385B); τὸ κ. τῆς ἐκκλησίας Chrys.*stat*.3.5(2.42B); cf. ἀπὸ κ. τοῦ τῶν πιστῶν συναθροίσματος *Const.App*.3.18.1; with preps. ἀπὸ τοῦ κοινοῦ *from common* or *Church funds*, Ign.*Polyc*.4.3; ἐπὶ τοῦ κ. τῆς ἐκκλησίας *publicly* in Church, Eus.*h.e*.6.19.16(M.20.569B); *ib*.6.37.1(597B); **2.** *ordinary*; **a.** of Christ as man: denied οὐκ ἔστιν ὁ Χριστὸς ἄνθρωπος. ἐξ ἀνθρώπων κατὰ τὸ κ. τῶν ἀνθρώπων γεννηθείς Just.*dial*.54.2(M.6.596A); οὐκ ἴσασι τὴν αἰτίαν τοῦ μὴ γῆμαι τὸν κύριον;...οὐδὲ ἄνθρωπος ἦν κ. Clem.*str*.3.6(p.218.28; M.8.1152C); ἵνα μή τις αὐτὸν κ. ἄνθρωπον ἐκ τοῦ πάθους ὑπολάβῃ Ath.*inc*.34.3(M.25.156A); id.*Ar*.3.32(M.26.392C); εἰ δὲ ἄνθρωπος ἦν κ. ὁ Ἐμμανουήλ, πῶς ἂν ὠφέλησε τὴν ἀνθρώπου φύσιν ὁ ἀνθρώπου θάνατος; Cyr.*Arcad*.7(p.64.10; 5^{2}.45E); *ib*.(p.108.22; 111E); id.*Pulch*.(p.43.24; 5^{2}.153E); οὐ ...ἔδει κ. ἄνθρωπον τὴν ὑπὲρ τῆς τοῦ κόσμου ζωῆς θυσίαν προσενεγκεῖν id.*Heb*.3:1(p.467.25; M.74.972A); **b.** in argument about Christ 'on the level of an ordinary man' τοῖς ἀπειθοῦσι ταῖς προφητικαῖς γραφαῖς ἰδίως ἀπαντήσομεν, ὡς περὶ ἀνδρὸς κ., καὶ τοῖς λοιποῖς παραπλησίου τέως τὴν ἐξέτασιν ποιούμενοι· ἵνα, ὁπόταν πάντων τῶν ἐξ αἰῶνος βοηθέντων ἐν ἀνθρώποις πολὺ κρείττων...ἀναφανῇ, τοτηνικάδε καὶ τὰ περὶ τῆς θειοτέρας αὐτοῦ φύσεως...διαλάβωμεν Eus.*d.e*.3.2(p.108.16; M.22.185D); cf. ταῦτα...ὡς περὶ κοινοῦ τὴν φύσιν ἀνθρώπου *ib*.3.3(p.113.27; 193D); *ib*.8.1(p.353.31; 593C); asserted by Christ's enemies μὴ εἶναι αὐτὸν Χριστόν, ἀλλ'...ὡς κ. ἄνθρωπον ἐν ᾅδου μένειν Just.*dial*.99.3(M.6.709A); τὰς ἐπανισταμένας αὐτῷ δυνάμεις, ἃς εἰκὸς ...κ. ἄνθρωπον καὶ τοῖς πολλοῖς ὅμοιον αὐτὸν ὑπειληφέναι Eus.*d.e*.8.1(p.363.17; M.22.589C); in teaching of Paul. Sam. περὶ τοῦ Χριστοῦ

...ὡς κοινοῦ τὴν φύσιν ἀνθρώπου γενομένου id.*h.e.*7.27.2(M.20.705B); Ath.*Ar*.3.51(M.26.429B); **c.** of ordinary, opp. consecrated, bread and wine οὐ γὰρ ὡς κ. ἄρτον οὐδὲ κ. πόμα ταῦτα λαμβάνομεν Just. *1apol*.66.2(M.6.428C); Iren.*haer*.4.18.5(M.7.1028B) cit. s. εὐχαριστία; cf.Cyr.H.*catech*.23.15; **3.** *profane, unclean* opp. holy or consecrated οὐ διὰ τὸ εἶναι αὐτὰ κ. ἢ ἀκάθαρτα οὐκ ἐσθίομεν Just.*dial*. 20.3(M.6.520A); ref. Mt.15:18, Clem.*paed*.2.6(p.187.11; M.8.452B); *Const.App*.6.12.6; βέβηλον δέ ἐστι τὸ μὴ ἅγιον, τούτεστι τὸ κ. Thdt. *Is*.56:2(p.220.33; 2.365); οἱ δὲ Ἀρειανοί...ἐν οἴκῳ κ. συνήγοντο Thphn. *chron*.p.40(M.108.156A); **4.** *mutually dependent* ἀμφότερα [sc. σὰρξ καὶ πνεῦμα]...κ. ἐστι καὶ ἄτερ ἀλλήλων μιανθῆναι οὐ δύναται Herm. *sim*.5.7.4; *sharing in common*; of one living a common life, Thdr. Stud.*or*.11.11(M.99.813B).

***κοινοτέρως**, *quite generally, in the ordinary sense*, Eus.*d.e*.4.16 (p.187.24; M.22.313A).

κοινότης, ἡ, 1. *a sharing in common, community*; **a.** in gen., of the sharing in revealed truth by Jews and gentiles, Clem.*str*.6.6(p.458. 11; M.9.276A); *mutual* or *shared interest*, *ib*.7.11(p.49.11; 496A); ἰσότητι καὶ κοινότητι μερίσας *ib*.3.2(p.198.25; M.8.1108B); ὁ κοινότητα πρὸς ἀνθρώπους...οὐκ ἔχει *which has no reference to men*, *Hom. Clem*.11.28; of a monastic *community*, Thdr.Stud.*or*.11.11(M.99. 813B); **b.** Trin. αὐτῶν τὴν κ. καὶ ἑνότητα ‡Ath.*dial.Trin*.3.13(M.28. 1221D); ἐν τῇ τῆς οὐσίας κ. ἀσύμβατά φαμεν εἶναι καὶ ἀκοινώνητα τὰ ἐπιθεωρούμενα τῇ τριάδι γνωρίσματα Gr.Nyss.*diff.ess*.4(M.32.332A); οὔτε τῆς κατὰ τὴν οὐσίαν κ. τὸ ἰδιάζον τῶν γνωρισμάτων ἀναχεούσης *ib*.(333A); οὐδεμίας ἐν τούτοις ἀντιστροφῆς, ἢ ὅλως κ. ἐπεισαγομένης Dion.Ar.*d.n*.2.3(M.3.640C); **c.** with preps. εἰς κ., κατὰ κοινότητα *communally*, Clem.*str*.3.2(p.198.31; M.8.1108C); *ib*.(p.198.16; 1108A); **2.** *common* or *universal quality*, denied of God οὐ πιστεύσαιμι... αὐτοὺς...φάναι τὸν θεὸν...ὥσπερ κ. τινα λόγῳ...θεωρητήν Bas.*Spir*.41 (3.35D; M.32.144C); **3.** *common* or *crude usage* of a word, Dion.Al. *ep.can*.1(p.97.12; M.10.1276A); Procl.CP *hom*.2.1(M.65.837D).

κοινόω, *make public* property, *appropriate for the state*, Thphn. *chron*.p.414(M.108.981C).

κοινων-έω, A. c. dat., *take part, be involved, participate* in; **1.** in gen. ἀνόμοις καὶ ἀθέοις τελεταῖς κ. Just.*dial*.35.6(M.6.552B); κ. ... ταῖς πραγματείαις Tat.*orat*.22(p.25.5; M.6.857A); ταῖς παρ' ὑμῶν εὐεργεσίαις κεκοινώνηκε Athenag.*leg*.2.1(M.6.893C); Or.*Jo*.2.24(19; p.81.17; M.14.157A); τὴν τῷ λόγῳ ~οῦσαν ψυχήν id.*Cant*.3(p.230. 28; M.13.189D); μηδὲν ~οῦσαν [sc. τὴν παρθενίαν] ταῖς σαρκὸς ἀκαθαρσίαις Meth.*symp*.5.6(p.61.7; M.18.108D); κ. τῷ μυστηρίῳ τῷ ἁγίῳ CLaod.*can*.7; δόξῃ κ. Chrys.*hom.87.1 in Mt*.(7.819A); of angels ~οῦσι ταῖς θεουργικαῖς [sc. τοῦ Ἰησοῦ] καὶ φιλανθρώποις ἀρεταῖς Dion.Ar.*c.h*.7.2(M.3.208C); **2.** Christol. κ. τῇ ἀνθρωπίνῃ φύσει Or.*Cels*.3.28(p.226.8; M.11.956C); ὁ λόγος...τῇ ἀνθρωπίνῃ γενέσει ~ήσας Ath.*v.Anton*.74(M.26.945C); αὐτὸν κεκοινωνηκέναι τῇ ἡμετέρᾳ σαρκί ‡Ath.*Ar*.4.22(p.68.23; M.26.500D); τὸ τῷ ἀκτίστῳ ~ῆσαν ἢ ἑνωθέν ‡Ath.*Apoll*.1.4(M.26.1100A); ἀναλλοιώτως ἡμῖν καὶ ἀσυγχύτως κεκοινώνηκε Dion.Ar.*d.n*.2.10(M.3.649A); ὁ μεσίτης ὀφείλει ἀμφοτέροις ~εῖν ὧν ἐστι μεσίτης *cat.1Tim*.2:2(p.17.30); in teaching of Marcion and Manicheans θεὸν...ἀνεπιδέκτως ἔχοντα ~ῆσαι φύσει ἀνθρωπίνῃ ‡Ath.*Apoll*.2.3(1136C); ref. Christ's human experiences τούτοις...ὁ πατὴρ καὶ τὸ πνεῦμα κατ' οὐδένα κεκοινώνηκε λόγον Dion.Ar.*d.n*.2.6(644C); acc. Nest. εἰ...καθ' ἕτερον ~εῖ ὁ λόγος καὶ καθ' ἕτερον ἡ σὰρξ τῷ πατρὶ καὶ πνεύματι, πῶς οὐ δύο τὰς φύσεις τῆς...τριάδος εἰσάγετε; Leont.H.*Nest*.7.4(M.86.1768A); c. acc. cogn. δευτέραν ~εῖ κοινωνίαν...τῆς προτέρας παραδοξοτέραν Gr.Naz.*or*.38.13 (M.36.325C).

B. c. genit.; **1.** *receive a share of, partake* of ἁλῶν Chrys.*hom.32.7 in Mt*.(7.375C); *ib.31.1*(357B); τραπέζης id.*hom.47.5 in Jo*.(8.281D); id.*hom.48.6 in Mt*.(7.501D); τραπέζης σὺν αὐτῷ Thdt.*Jer*.41:1(2. 574); more gen. τῆς βασιλείας τῆς πατρῴας ~ήσει τῷ γνησίῳ Clem. *prot*.9(p.62.24; M.8.193B); abstracts, id.*str*.2.9(p.135.8; M.8.977A); *ib*.2.18(p.157.18; 1024A); the image of God, Ath.*inc*.13.6(M.25. 120B); divine nature in Christ, id.*v.Anton*.74(M.26.945C); πῶς κεκοινώνηκεν [sc. Christ] αἵματος καὶ σαρκός; Cyr.ap.*cat.Heb*.suppl. 2:15(p.407.34); *share* τῶν πόνων [sc. of Christ] Chrys.*hom.55.3 in Jo*.(8.325C); **2.** *receive, partake* of body and blood of Christ sacramentally τοῦ σώματος Χριστοῦ Cyr.H.*catech*.23.22; τὸ ποτήριον οὗ κ. Gr.Naz.*or*.40.31(M.36.404A); τῆς εὐχαριστίας *A.Mt*.8(p.226.5); *A. Thom*.A 49(p.166.4); τραπέζης πνευματικῆς Chrys.*hom.32.7 in Mt*. (7.375C); τοῦ αὐτοῦ ἄρτου id.*hom.72.1 in Jo*.(8.423E); δεῖ τοὺς μοναχοὺς καθ' ἑκάστην ἡμέραν τῶν μυστηρίων...~εῖν ‡Pall.*h.mon*.8.56 (p.48.12; M.34.1148A); ref. fasting before communion οὐ πρότερον τῆς τροφῆς μετελάμβανον πρὶν ἢ τῆς εὐχαριστίας...~ήσωσι *ib*.8.53 (p.47.3; M.34.1147B).

C. c. dat. pers. *associate, have fellowship* with one (in); **1.** in gen. οὐ μιᾷ ψυχῇ ~ῶν [sc. reason], ἀλλὰ πλείοσι Or.*schol.in Cant*. 6:7(M.17.277C); μηδὲ μέχρι λόγου ~εῖν τινι τῶν παραχαρασσόντων τὴν ἀλήθειαν Iren.*haer*.3.3.4(M.7.854A); *Const.App*.2.14.3; ἡ τῶν ἀρχαγγέλων τάξις...ταῖς...ἁγιωτάταις ἀρχαῖς κ., καὶ τοῖς ἁγίοις ἀγγέλοις Dion.Ar.*c.h*.9.2(M.3.257C); id.*e.h*.5.1.2(M.3.501D); **2.** sacramentally with Christ ἐλθὲ [sc. Ἰησοῦ] καὶ ~ησον ἡμῖν *A.Thom*.A 49 (p.166.5); *ib*.50(p.166.9,15); τῷ κυρίῳ ~εῖν διὰ τοῦ...αὐτοῦ σώματος καὶ αἵματος Thdt.*1Cor*.10:21(3.229); cf. πῶς...καὶ τῷ κυρίῳ κ. ... καὶ πάλιν τοῖς δαίμοσι διὰ τῆς εἰδωλοθύτου τροφῆς; *ib*.; and in him with each other κοινωνία [sc. λέγεται] διὰ τὸ ~εῖν ἡμᾶς δι' αὐτῆς τῷ Χριστῷ...~εῖν δὲ καὶ ἑνοῦσθαι καὶ ἀλλήλοις δι' αὐτῆς Jo.D.*fr. Mt*.26:27(M.96.1409D); **3.** *associate* in Christian fellowship with, *hold communion* with ὧν οὐδενὶ ~οῦμεν οἱ γνωρίζοντες αὐτοὺς ἀθέους Just.*dial*.35.5(M.6.552A); ἐκοινώνησαν ἑαυτοῖς Iren.*ep.Vict*. ap.Eus.*h.e*.5.24.17(M.20.508A); προσευχῶν αὐτοῖς καὶ ἑστιάσεων ἐκοινώνησαν Dion.Al.*ib*.6.42.5(613C); ~ήσουσι τῷ λαῷ τῶν προσευχῶν CNic.(325)*can*.11; τῶν αὐτῷ [sc. Ἀθανασίῳ] κεκοινωνηκότων Constantius Imp.ap.Ath.*apol.sec*.54(p.135.8; M.25.348B); τοὺς... ~οῦντας τοῖς ἐκβάλλουσι τὸ ὁμοούσιον...οὐδενὶ τῶν τοιούτων ~οῦμεν Apoll.*fid.sec.pt*.34(p.180.21; M.10.1117C); οὔτε...ἐν τοῖς μετάλλοις ἀλλήλοις ἐκοινώνουν Epiph.*haer*.68.3(p.143.27; M.42.189B); οὐ βούλονται [sc. οἱ καθαροί] τοῖς διγάμοις ~εῖν *ib*.59.3(p.366.10; M.41.1021B); καὶ εὐχῶν καὶ ὕμνων...καὶ τῶν ἄλλων...πλὴν τῆς μυστικῆς ἐκοινώνουν [i.e. Arians with orthodox] θυσίας Philost.*h.e*.3.14(M.65.501B); cf. κ. τῇ ἀσεβείᾳ τῶν αἱρετικῶν Ἀρειανῶν Ath.*ep.encycl*.5(p.174.14; M. 25.233A); **4.** *administer communion*, Eus.*d.e*.3.2(p.109.1; M.22. 188B); μόνοις ἔξον...τοῖς ἱερατικοῖς...κ. CLaod.*can*.19; *communicate*; (c. genit. rei) *communicate* one (with) ~ήσας τοῖς ἀδελφοῖς...τῆς τοῦ κυρίου εὐχαριστίας *A.Jo*.86(p.193.14); ᾧ [sc. ἐπισκόπῳ]...ἐκοινωνήσαμεν λαϊκῷ Corn.ap.Eus.*h.e*.6.43.10(M.20.620B); Ἰησοῦς...ἐν ὑπερῴῳ τοῦ μυστηρίου ~εῖ τοῖς τὰ ὑψηλότερα τελουμένοις Gr.Naz. *or*.41.12(M.36.445B); Χριστὸς αἵματός μοι καὶ σαρκὸς ~ήσας Cyr.H. *catech*.19.4; Dion.Ar.*e.h*.1.5(M.3.377B); **5.** *agree* κ. ἡμῶν τοῖς δόγμασι Tat.*orat*.19(p.21.8; M.6.849A); **6.** abs., *give alms*, Clem.*q.d.s*.30 (p.180.32; M.9.637B); *ib*.13(p.168.21; 617B).

D. c. acc., *admit to communion* λέγουσιν ὅτι τινὰς ἐκοινώνησα μετὰ τὸ φαγεῖν αὐτούς Chrys.*ep*.125(3.668D); Thphn.*chron*.p.48(M.108. 177A); pass., †Hipp.*Artem*.ap.Eus.*h.e*.5.28.12(M.20.513D).

E. abs., Trin., *be associated, united*, Bas.*Spir*.60(3.50D; M.32. 177C) cit. s. σύν; παρηλλάχθαι [sc. in teaching of Aëtius] τὴν τοῦ γεννηθέντος οὐσίαν πρὸς τὴν τοῦ γειναμένου καὶ κατὰ μηδὲν ~εῖν Philost.*h.e*.4.12(M.65.525C).

F. abs., *communicate, receive communion*, *V.Dan*.(p.52.18); εἰσέρχεται πρὸς ἡμᾶς ὁ Χριστός, ἡνίκα ἂν ~ῶμεν Chrys.*hom.30.2 in 2Cor*.(10.650E); Cyr.S.*v.Sab*.76(p.183.1); πάντων...βαρύτερον ἁμάρτημα τὸ ἀναξίως ~εῖν †Jo.Jej.*serm*.(M.88.1929B); Jo.Mosch.*prat*.100 (M.87.2960A); ὁ μὴ ~ῶν ἐν ταῖς ἐκκλησίαις, ἐν αἷς οἱ ἐντόπιοι συνέρχονται ἐπίσκοποι, αἱρετικός ἐστιν Ath.Scholast.*coll*.3.1(p.44); how frequently τὸ ~εῖν καθ' ἑκάστην ἡμέραν...καλόν Bas.*ep*.93(3.186D; M.32.484B); καλὸν...τὸ ~εῖν συνεχῶς Anast.S.*qu.et resp*.7 tit.(M.89. 385C); on Sundays and special days, Bas.*ep*.93(3.186D; M.484B); *Apophth.Patr*.(M.65.252C); exclusion from communion ἐπίσκοπος ὃν οὐδὲ ὡς λαϊκὸν ~εῖν ἐχρῆν Ath.*h.Ar*.28(p.198.2; M.25.725A); μηδεὶς ~είτω τῶν μὴ μαθητῶν Chrys.*hom.82.6 in Mt*.(7.790A); οὐκ ἔξον αὐτοὺς [i.e. Nestorians] ~ῆσαι Cyr.S.*v.Sab*.38(p.128.6); ἕως θανάτου τὸ ἐπιτίμιον ἔχει...μὴ ~εῖν †Jo.Jej.*poenit*.(M.88.1904C); διερευνᾶν...εἰ φαγὼν ἢ πιὼν ἐκοινώνησε *ib*.(1896A); ~ήσας μετέλαβεν τροφῆς Jo.Mosch.*prat*.100(M.87.2960A).

κοινωνητέον, *one must have communion* or *fellowship with*; c. dat., Clem.*paed*.2.8(p.202.4; M.8.484B).

κοινωνία, ἡ, A. *communion*; **1.** *association, connexion*, Just. *1apol*.55.2(M.6.412B); of abstracts θάνατος...ἡ ἐν σώματι κ. τῆς ψυχῆς, ἁμαρτητικῆς οὔσης Clem.*str*.4.3(p.253.17; M.8.1224C); τῆς πίστεως ἡ κ. ἡ πνευματικὴ πρὸς τὸν...ἄνθρωπον id.*paed*.1.6(p.120.28; M.8.312A); πρὸς τὸ χεῖρον κ. Gr.Thaum.*pan.Or*.6(p.18.14; M.10. 1072A); τὰς τῆς ἀλαμποῦς κακίας...κ. Dion.Ar.*e.h*.2.3.5(M.3.401B); theol. (Eunomian) ἀγέννητος ὢν...ἐκφύγοι τε ἂν πᾶσαν σύγκρισιν καὶ κ. τὴν πρὸς τὸ γεννητόν Eun.*apol*.8(M.30.844B); Christol. τὸ...θνητὸν αὐτοῦ σῶμα, καὶ τὴν ἀνθρωπίνην ἐν αὐτῷ ψυχὴν τῇ πρὸς ἐκείνου οὐ μόνον κ. ἀλλὰ καὶ ἑνώσει...τὰ μέγιστά φαμεν προσειληφέναι καὶ τῆς ἐκείνου θειότητος κεκοινωνηκότα εἰς θεὸν μεταβεβληκέναι Or.*Cels*.3.41 (p.237.8; M.11.975A); in adv. phrase κατὰ κοινωνίαν *by association*, Clem.*str*.1.26(p.104.26; 916B); **2.** *combination, mingling*, Athenag. *leg*.33.2(M.6.968A); Clem.*paed*.1.6(p.120.15; M.8.309B); id.*str*.1.21 (p.88.12; M.8.880A); οὐκ ἐκ κ. τῆς πρὸς ἕτερον τὴν τῶν ὄντων δημιουργίαν συστησάμενον Eun.*apol.*26(M.30.864A); *sexual intercourse* πρός τινα Or.*Jo.*13.30(29; p.254.20; M.14.452A); τὸ...τῆς μοιχείας ὄνομα κοινωνίας...ἀνδρὸς καὶ γυναικός. ... ἐὰν κοινωνῇ τις τῇ γυναικὶ... παιδοποιίας ἕνεκα...ἀγαθή τις ἡ κ. γίνεται. εἰ δέ τις καταλιπὼν τὴν νομίμην κ. ἐνυβρίζοι γάμοις ἀλλοτρίοις...πράττει κακόν·...ἡ κ. χωρὶς τοῦ τρόπου τῆς χρήσεως ἐξεταζομένη, κακὸν οὐκ ἔστι Meth.*arbitr.*15 (p.183.9)ap.Adam.*dial.*4.10(M.11.1824C); Bas.*ep.*160.2(3.249C; M.32. 624B); *ib.*199 *can.*48(297B; M.732B); ref. illicit intercourse with heretics, CLaod.*can.*10; ref. virgin birth οἱ λέγοντες ἀδύνατον εἶναι χωρὶς κ. τῆς πρὸς ἄνδρα γυναῖκα τεκεῖν Procl.CP *annunt.*4(M.85. 437A); plur., *acts of intercourse, Hom.Clem.*5.12; ref. Carpocratians μελετήσαντες ἐν τοιαύτῃ 'ἀγάπῃ' τὴν κ. Clem.*str.*3.2(p.200.12; M.8. 1112A); ref. Adamites τὴν σαρκικὴν καὶ συνουσιαστικὴν κ. ἱεροφαντοῦσι *ib.*3.4(p.208.24; 1133A); *ib.*(p.209.29; 1136A); Thdt.*haer.*1.6(4. 296); τὰς ἀσυμφυεῖς ἀνδρογύνους κ. Clem.*paed.*2.10(p.210.23; M.8. 501C); fig., of Logos engendering children by Church in baptism, Meth.*symp.*3.8(p.35.21; M.18.73B); **3.** *relationship* ἡ ἁμαρτία...οὐ δύναται κ. ἔχειν μετὰ τῆς ἀφθαρσίας Clem.*str.*3.17(p.244.18; M.8. 1208B); τὸ βάπτισμα ὃ παρὰ τοῖς αἱρετικοῖς βεβάπτιστο μὴ...ἔχειν τινὰ πρὸς τοῦτο κ. Dion.Al.ap.Eus.*h.e.*7.9.2(M.20.656A); οἱ τῆς φύσεως νόμοι οὐχὶ διάστασιν ἀπ' ἀλλήλων υἱῷ πρὸς πατέρα, ἀλλ' ἀναγκαίαν καὶ ἄρρηκτον τὴν κ. ποιοῦσιν Bas.*Eun.*2.30(1.267B; M.29.644A); of heavenly powers κατὰ μὲν τὸ ἀξίωμα ἡ διαφορά, κατὰ δὲ τὴν φύσιν ἡ κ. *ib.*3.2(1.273C; M.657C); **4.** *communion, fellowship*; **a.** of heavenly powers with the divine αἱ ἅγιαι δυνάμεις ἐκ τῆς πρὸς τὸ φύσει ἅγιον κ. Bas.*Eun.*3.3(1.274B; M.29.660B); ὁ μέντοι ἁγιασμὸς ἔξωθεν ὢν τῆς οὐσίας τὴν τελείωσιν αὐτοῖς ἐπάγει διὰ τῆς κ. τοῦ πνεύματος id.*Spir.* 38(3.32D; M.32.137A); πρὸς θεὸν κ. Dion.Ar.*c.h.*9.2(M.3.260B); τὰς πρὸς τὴν θεαρχικὴν ἐμφέρειαν κ. *ib.*4.2(180A); **b.** of man with God κ. θεοῦ, ζωὴ καὶ φῶς Iren.*haer.*5.27.1(M.7.1196B); Or.*Cels.*3.28(p.226.17; M.11.956D); κ. θεοῦ πρὸς ἄνθρωπον Gr.Naz.*or.*41.12(M.36.445B); τὴν πρὸς θεὸν κ. Dion.Ar.*e.h.*3.1.9(M.3.425A); τὴν ἐκ θεοῦ κ. id.*c.h.*5(M.3. 196D); as natural ἦν δέ τις ἔμφυτος ἀρχαία πρὸς οὐρανὸν ἀνθρώποις κ. Clem.*prot.*2(p.19.1; M.8.93B); mediated by Christian teaching, id. *str.*7.9(p.38.31; M.9.473B); through Christian life πρὸς τὸ θειότερον κ. Or.*Cels.*3.28(p.226.15; M.11.956D); ref. Phil.3:10, Thdt.*Rom.*8:17(3. 87); ref. 1Petr.4:13, Euthal.Diac.*epp.cath.*(M.85.681A); **c.** among heavenly powers τὴν μίαν ἁπάντων ἐναρμόνιον καὶ συνδετικὴν κ. Dion.Ar.*c.h.*12.2(M.3.292C); *ib.*13.2(300B); **d.** among saints, †Bas. *bapt.*1.2.17(2.642B; M.31.1556B); Dion.Ar.*ep.*9.5(M.3.1112D); **e.** of sacramental fellowship τῆς κ. εἴρχθησαν Anon.ap.Eus.*h.e.*5.16.10(M. 20.468C); CAnc.(314)*can.*16; Ath.*ep.mort.Ar.*2(p.179.10; M.25.688A); τῆς κ....ἀπεστερήθη *ib.*3(p.179.27; 688C); ἐκύρωσαν...εἰς ἡμᾶς τήν τε κ. καὶ ἀγάπην id.*apol.sec.*36(p.115.6; M.25.309C); ἀποβάλλειν τινὰ τῆς κ. Jul.Papa *ep.Dian.*ap.Ath.*apol.sec.*32(p.111.3; 301B); ὑπὸ ἐπισκόπου ἀπὸ κ. ἐγένετο Tim.CP *haer.*(M.86.29C); esp. κ. ἐκκλησιαστική Ursac.*ep.Ath.*(p.138.27; M.25.356A); Bas.*ep.*69.2(3.163A; M.32.432C); Gr.Nyss.*ep.*5(M.46.1029C); κ. τῆς καθολικῆς ἐκκλησίας *ib.*(1029B); ἐν τῇ ἐκκλησίᾳ καὶ ἐν τῇ κ. Epiph.*haer.*68.2(p.142.14; M.42.188A); περὶ καθολικῆς κ. τῶν πιστευσάντων Euthal.Diac.*Ac.*(M.85.653B); with named individuals and groups ἀντιποιούμεθα τῆς κ. τοῦ... Ἀθανασίου Ursac.*ep.Jul.*(p.138.10; M.25.353B); CSard.*ep.Alex.*ap. Ath.*apol.sec.*37(p.116.4; 312D); τὴν πρὸς τοὺς Ἀρειομανίτας κ. CAlex. *ep.*ap.Ath.*apol.sec.*7(p.93.20; 261A); τῇ τοῦ Ἀρείου κ. Epiph.*haer.* 69.10(p.160.18; M.42.217C); with Eunomians, Philost.*h.e.*10.1(M.65. 584B); cf. ἀπέχεται κοινωνίας ἁπάντων αἱρέσεων Epiph.*exp.fid.*24.3 (p.525.7; M.42.829D); ref. canonical letters εἰ...ἐλέγχουσί μου τὴν κ., δειξάτωσαν ἢ κανονικὰ γράμματα παρ' ἐμοῦ πρὸς αὐτὸν διαπεμπόμενα, ἢ παρ' ἐκείνου πρὸς ἐμέ Bas.*ep.*224.2(3.343B; M.32.836C); ἀνταπέστειλεν ...ὁ πάπας ἀμφοτέροις τοῖς μέρεσι τὰ ἴσα τῆς κ. Pall.*v.Chrys.*3(p.16.8; M.47.12); *ib.*6(p.35.12; M.47.22); plur., *claims to fellowship* τὰς τῶν ἐντυγχανόντων κ. καὶ τὰς ἐγγράφως γινομένας Bas.*ep.*129.3(3.221E; M. 32.561A).

B. *act of sharing*; **1.** *community* of life ἀγάπη...κ. βίου Clem.*str.*2.9 (p.134.20; M.8.976B); abs., of coenobitic life παραδόσεις εἰς σύστασιν τῆς κ. *V.Pach.Φ* 89(p.60.12); **2.** *participation* in; **a.** of table-fellowship ἅλῶν κ. *Hom.Clem.*14.8; Chrys.*hom.70.1 in Jo.*(8.414A); τραπέζης κ. *Chron.Pasch.*p.291(M.92.729A); **b.** in gen. κ. ἀφθαρσίας Clem.*str.*4.6(p.260.11; M.8.1240B); ἐκ τῆς κατὰ τὸν βίον κ. (*consistent with remaining alive*) *ib.*6.9(p.471.16; M.9.300B); ref. Pr.8:22, Jo. 1:1 κατὰ μὲν τὴν σύστασιν τῆς περὶ τῶν ὅλων θεωρίας καὶ νοημάτων τῆς σοφίας νοουμένης, κατὰ δὲ τὴν πρὸς τὰ λογικὰ κ. τῶν τε τεθεωρημένων τοῦ λόγου λαμβανομένου Or.*Jo.*1.19(22; p.23.23; M.14.56B); with the body in human nature, Meth.*res.*1.33(p.270.9; M.41. 1097A); τὴν τοῦ γιγνομένου κ. Ath.*gent.*39(M.25.77C); κ. τῆς δόσεως ἐν ἡμῖν id.*ep.Serap.*1(M.26.600C); of human beings in one nature, Chrys.*hom.37.3 in Jo.*(8.214D); ἡ τῶν πανιερῶν θεὰ καὶ κ. Dion.Ar. *e.h.*3.3.7(M.3.433C); τῆς θείων ἐποψίας καὶ κ. *ib.*3.2(425C); in prayer κ. εὐχῆς Bas.*ep.*224.2(3.343B; M.32.837A); *ib.*217 *can.*82(330B; M. 808A); **3.** *community* of essence; **a.** denied of God in rel. to creatures, Eus.*e.th.*1.9(p.67.10; M.24.840A); ‡Just.*qu.Chr.*5(M.6.1457B); Dion. Ar.*d.n.*2.5(M.3.644B); **b.** of Father and Son, Athenag.*leg.*12.2(M.6. 913B); ἡ 'πατὴρ' προσηγορία δηλοῖ τὴν κ. Dion.Al.ap.Ath.*Dion.*17 (p.58.21; M.25.505A); cf. πῶς...οὐ τολμηρὸν τῆς κατὰ τὴν δοξολογίαν κ. ἀποστερεῖν τὸν υἱόν; Bas.*Spir.*15(3.13A; M.32.93B); τῆς ἀϊδίου κ. ... τὸ ἀχώριστον τῆς κ. *ib.*59(50B; M.177A); ἀπωθεῖται [sc. by Eunomians] ὡς πορρωτάτω τὸν μονογενῆ τῆς τοῦ πατρὸς κ. id.*Eun.*2.30(1. 267B; M.29.641B); ref. deity of H. Ghost τὸ...πνεῦμα διὰ τὴν ἐκ φύσεως κ. τέτακται τῷ θεῷ id.*Spir.*30(25C; M.121A); μάθοις πρὸς πατέρα καὶ υἱὸν τοῦ πνεύματος κ. ἐκ τῶν δημιουργημάτων τῶν ἐξ ἀρχῆς *ib.*38(31C; M.136A); ref. Mt.28:19 οὐκ ἀπαξιῶν τὴν πρὸς αὐτὸ [sc. τὸ πνεῦμα] κ. *ib.*24(20E; M.112A); of Trin. τινὰ συνεχῆ καὶ ἀδιάσπαστον κ. ἐν αὐτοῖς Gr.Nyss.*diff.ess.*4(M.32.332A); ἄρρητος καὶ ἀκατανόητος ἐν τούτοις ἡ κ. καὶ ἡ διάκρισις *ib.*(332D); cf. (ref. baptism) ἐπειδὴ περὶ τοῦ πατρὸς οὐδεὶς ἀμφιβάλλει, τὸ δὲ ἀμφίβολον ἦν περὶ τοῦ υἱοῦ καὶ τοῦ πνεύματος..., παρείληπται ἐν τῇ μυσταγωγίᾳ ἵνα ἐν τῇ κ. τῆς χορηγίας τῶν...ἀγαθῶν, καὶ τὴν κ. τῆς ἀξίας καταμανθάνωμεν Chrys.*hom.78.3 in Jo.*(8.462A); **4.** Christol.; participation in, taking of human nature by Logos, *union* τῷ ἀνθρωπίνῳ σώματι προσθήκη μεγάλη γέγονεν, ἐκ τῆς τοῦ λόγου πρὸς αὐτὸ κ. τε καὶ ἑνώσεως Ath.*ep.Epict.*9(p.15.9; M.26.1065B); τῆς ἀνθρωπίνης ἀσθενείας διὰ τῆς πρὸς τὸ ἀκήρατον κ. τὸ κρεῖττον ἀλλοιωθείσης Gr. Nyss.*Eun.*6(2 p.131.17; M.45.716A); ἡ οὐσία τοῦ λόγου...κ. ἠσπάσατο πρὸς τὴν...τῆς ἀνθρωπότητος φύσιν Procl.CP *annunt.*5(M.85.445B); ἐνεργεῖ...ἑκατέρα μορφὴ μετὰ τῆς θατέρου κ. ὅπερ ἴδιον ἔσχηκεν Leo Mag.*ep.*28.4(p.14.27; M.*PL.*54.768B); ἐποιήσατο κ. αὐτὴν τὴν φύσιν οὐσιωδῶς ἑαυτῷ καθ' ὑπόστασιν ἑνώσας Max.*ambig.*(M.91.1289C); **5.** *union* of faithful with Christ τίς γάρ, ἄκτιστον ἀκούων τὸ τοῦ κυρίου σῶμα, ἑαυτὸν δὲ ποιηθέντα...εἰδώς, οὐκ ἐννοηθήσεται...ἑαυτὸν μὴ ἔχειν πρὸς τὸν Χριστὸν κ.; ‡Ath.*Apoll.*1.4(M.26.1100B); τὴν πρὸς αὐτὸν [sc. τὸν λόγον] ἡμῶν ἑνοποιὸν κ. Dion.Ar.*e.h.*3.3.12(M.3.444A); perfected in life to come πάντα...ἡμῖν ἐκ τῆς αὐτοῦ κ. ὑπάρξει Eus. *Marcell.*2.1(p.34.18; M.24.781B); id.*e.th.*3.18(p.179.35; M.24.1041C); sacramentally ἐν ἀθανασίᾳ γενέσθαι τὸ ἡμέτερον σῶμα...διὰ τῆς πρὸς τὸ ἀθάνατον κ. ἐν μετουσίᾳ τῆς ἀφθαρσίας Gr.Nyss.*or.catech.*37(p.144. 7; M.45.93C); and with H. Ghost τὴν κ. τοῦ ἁγίου πνεύματος ἔχοντος Ἰωάννου [i.e. Baptist] Or.*Jo.*6.22(13; p.132.18; M.14.240C); λέγεται πνευματικόν [sc. resurrection body], οὐ τὸ λεπτομερὲς καὶ ἀερῶδες... ἀλλὰ...τὸ χωροῦν πᾶσαν τοῦ ἁγίου πνεύματος τὴν ἐνέργειαν καὶ κ. Meth.*res.*3.16(p.413.9; M.118.888A); Gr.Thaum.*pan.Or.*15(p.34.13; M.10.1093D); exeg. Ps.44:8 ἐχρίσθη...ἡ σὰρξ τοῦ κυρίου τῇ τοῦ ἁγίου πνεύματος εἰς αὐτὴν ἐπιδημίᾳ...ὑπὲρ πάντας ἀνθρώπους τοὺς μετέχοντας τοῦ Χριστοῦ. διότι ἐκείνοις μὲν μερική τις ἐδίδοτο πνεύματος κ. Bas. *hom.in Ps.*44(1.165E; M.29.405A); γινόμεθα...θείας κοινωνοὶ φύσεως τῇ κ. τοῦ ἁγίου πνεύματος ‡Ath.*dial.Trin.*1.7(M.28.1125D); τὴν κ. τοῦ ἁγίου πνεύματος οἷον τὴν μετοχὴν αὐτοῦ καὶ μετάληψιν *cat.2Cor.*13:13 (p.444.12).

C. eucharistic; **1.** *partaking* in, *receiving* of body and blood of Christ in Communion ἀποκαταστήσονται εἰς τὴν κ. τοῦ σώματος τοῦ Χριστοῦ Bas.*ep.*217 *can.*82(3.330B; M.32.808A); κ. τῶν ἁγιασμάτων *ib.can.*61(327A; M.800A); Gr.Nyss.*ep.can.*(M.45.225C); κ. τοῦ σώματος τοῦ Χριστοῦ Mac.Aeg.*carit.*29(M.34.932C); τῶν φρικτῶν μυστηρίων κ. Chrys.*prod.Jud.*1.1(2.76A); τῆς τῶν τελεστικῶν μυστηρίων ...κ. Dion.Ar.*e.h.*2.3.8(M.3.404D); κ. τοῦ δεσποτικοῦ σώματος καὶ αἵματος Hesych.H.*fr.Ps.*49:23(M.93.1197D); hence **2.** *Communion* καταξίωσον ἡμᾶς τῆς κ. καὶ ταύτης Serap.*euch.*14.1; δεκτοὺς γενέσθαι εἰς τὴν κ. Bas.*ep.*217 *can.*81(3.329D; M.32.805C); τῷ τόπῳ τῆς κ. *ib.* 188 *can.*4(272A; M.673B); ἀποδοῦναί τινι κοινωνίαν Gr.Nyss.*ep.can.* (M.45.229B); καιρὸν...προσόδου καὶ κ. Chrys.*hom.28.1 in 1Cor.*(10. 250D); τῇ θείᾳ προσελθὼν κ. Nil.*epp.*3.41(M.79.408A); μυστικῆς... μεταλαχεῖν κ. Thdt.*ep.*111(4.1182); ἐνιαίως ἀνηγορεύεται κ. τε καὶ σύναξις Dion.Ar.*e.h.*3.1(3.424C); παῖδας...μετόχους γίγνεσθαι...τῶν ἱερωτάτων τῆς θεαρχικῆς κ. συμβόλων *ib.*7.3.11(565D); παρατηρεῖ... ἰδεῖν τί ποιεῖ ὁ ἀδελφὸς εἰς τὴν κ. Dor.*doct.*9.2(M.88.1717C); μεταλαβεῖν τῆς ἁγίας κ. *ib.*(1717D); τῆς ζωοποιοῦ κ. ἀλλήλοις μετέδοσαν Evagr. *h.e.*1.13(p.21.7; M.86.2453B); τὴν ἀποχὴν...τῆς ἀχράντου κ. †Jo.Jej. *poenit.*(M.88.1905B); κ. κέκληται ἡ τῶν θείων μυστηρίων μετάληψις διὰ τὸ τὴν πρὸς Χριστὸν ἡμῖν χαρίζεσθαι ἕνωσιν καὶ κοινωνοὺς ἡμᾶς τῆς αὐτοῦ ποιεῖν βασιλείας ‡Bas.*h.myst.*63(p.397.24); partic. of the consecrated bread τὴν κ. λαμβάνειν τῇ ἰδίᾳ χειρὶ Bas.*ep.*93(3.187A; M.32.485A); πάντες...οἱ κατὰ τὰς ἐρήμους μονάζοντες...κ. οἴκοι κατέχοντες ἀφ' ἑαυτῶν μεταλαμβάνουσιν. ἐν Ἀλεξανδρείᾳ δὲ καὶ ἐν Αἰγύπτῳ ἕκαστος καὶ τῶν ἐν λαῷ τελούντων...ἔχει κ. ἐν τῷ οἴκῳ αὐτοῦ *ib.*; Thdt.*Ps.*105:48(1.1365); *Apophth.Patr.*(M.65.433A); πάσας τὰς ἡμέρας τῶν νηστειῶν διετέλει ἄσιτος, τῇ κατὰ σάββατον καὶ κυριακὴν ἀρκούμενος κ. Cyr.S.*v.Sab.*24(p.109.1); Jo.Mosch.*prat.*29 (M.87.2877A); ἐάσαντα κατὰ λήθην τὰς ἁγίας κ. ἐν τῷ ἀρμαρίῳ *ib.*79 (2936D).

D. *communication, distribution, imparting* αἱ κ. τῶν λόγων Just. *2apol.*3.4(M.6.449A); ἡ κ. τοῦ λόγου Clem.*str.*1.1(p.5.30; M.8.692C); of secrets, Chrys.*hom.77.1 in Jo.*(8.452B); of charitable giving, Clem.*str.*3.4(p.208.13; 1132B); τὴν πρὸς τοὺς πτωχοὺς κ. Ath.*ep.fest.* 45(p.298.19; M.26.1441C); Bas.*ep.*223.2(3.337C; M.32.824B); κ. καλεῖ τὴν ἐλεημοσύνην *cat.2Cor.*8:3(p.400.31); ref. God's bounty ἰσότης καὶ κ. τοῦ θεοῦ ἡ αὐτὴ πρὸς πάντας Clem.*paed.*1.6(p.108.11; M.8. 285C); φιλίας ἐπιστατικῆς κ. *ib.*1.7(p.123.22; 317B); cf. δικαιοσύνην τοῦ θεοῦ κ. τινὰ...μετ' ἰσότητος Epiph.Gn.ap.eund.*str.*3.2(p.198.1; 1105A).

κοινωνικός **1.** *sharing*; **a.** *possessing a share* κ. τῶν πλημμεληθέντων *Const.App.*2.15.2; **b.** *giving a share, generous* ἀγάπη κ. Clem. *str.*2.18(p.159.18; M.8.1028A); κοινωνικὸν ἡ σοφία καὶ φιλάνθρωπον *ib.* 1.1(p.3.15; 688A); κ. τῶν ἐπιτηδείων *ib.*(p.6.6; 693A); †Bas.*Is.*106(1. 452D; M.30.289B); ‡Pall.*proem.*(p.3.10; M.34.995); neut. as subst., *generosity*, Eus.*d.e.*3.2(p.109.1; M.22.188B); **2.** *social*; **a.** neut. as subst., *community, reciprocity*, Or.*Cels.*1.64(p.118.2; M.11.781A); τοῦ κ. ἕνεκεν *for the good of society*, *ib.*7.59(p.209.9; 1505B); †Bas.*Is.*310 (1.613B; M.30.660A); **b.** *living in a society* opp. μοναστικός, Bas.*reg. fus.*3.1(2.340B; M.31.917A); Gr.Naz.*or.*43.62(M.36.577B); **c.** *shared, common* βίος κ., of married life, Clem.*paed.*1.4(p.96.9; M.8.260C); Bas.*reg.fus.*7.2(2.346E; M.31.932A); opp. μοναδικός, Thdt.*Ps.*24:13 (1.760); Thdr.Stud.*epp.*1.42(M.99.1061D); **3.** *being in fellowship* or *communion*; **a.** in gen., abs. ἔχε κοινωνικούς Gr.Naz.*ep.*102(M.37. 196A); opp. φιλόνεικος, Gr.Ant.*bapt.*2.10(M.88.1884A); κ. αὐτῶν Bas. *ep.*113(3.206C; M.32.528A); τῶν Μελιτίου κοινωνικῶν Thdt.*h.e.*1.30.1 (3.818); κ. τῆς ἐκκλησίας Sophr.H.*mir.Cyr.et Jo.*40(M.87.3576A); κ. ...τῶν πνευμάτων τῆς πονηρίας Jo.D.*haer.*80(M.94.729A); **b.** of those in eccl. fellowship, Or.*hom.5.14 in Jer.*(p.44.1; M.13.317A); Bas. *ep.*120(3.211D; M.537C); κ. ἐπισκόπους CCP(381)*ep.*ap.Thdt.*h.e.*5.9.9 (3.1030); Thphn.*chron.*p.76(M.108.237B); **4.** *commending* or *exhorting to eccl. fellowship* κ. γράμματα Malch.*ep.*ap.Eus.*h.e.*7.30.17(M.20. 717A); Photinus et al.*ep.*ap.Epiph.*haer.*72.11(p.265.22; M.42.397B); Cyr.*ep.*48(p.31.32; 5^2.156B); ἐπιστολαὶ κ. Gr.Naz.*ep.*101(M.37.177A); μηδένα ἄνευ κοινωνικοῦ δεχέσθω τὸν ξένον *Nomoc.*454; **5.** neut. as subst., *communion hymn*, *Chron.Pasch.*p.390(M.92.1001C); *Lit.Bas.* (p.341.26); cf.*Lit.Chrys.*(p.393.17); **6.** fem. as subst., *consort*, Mac. Aeg.*hom.*7.1(M.34.524C).

κοινωνικῶς, *as befits a communicant*, *Const.App.*2.58.2(v.l. κοινωνικός).

***κοινωνίς**, ἡ, *fellowship, partnership* τῇ κοινωνίδι *cat.Phil.*1:3 (p.232.32) [Phil.1:3 κοινωνίᾳ].

κοινωνός, ὁ, ἡ, **1.** *participant, one who shares*, of Christians χάριτος κ. Just.*dial.*58.1(M.6.608A); οἱ κ. τῶν παθημάτων...κ. ἔσονται τῆς παρακλήσεως Or.*mart.*42(p.39.14; M.11.617C); κ. τῆς θείας φύσεως Ath.*Ar.*3.40(M.26.409A); in sacraments, Dion.Ar.*e.h.*3.13(M.3.444C); *ib.*5.1.6(505D); *Lit.Jac.*(p.226.9); of Jews τῆς τοῦ...Ἀβραὰμ εὐλογίας ...κ. Eus.*d.e.*2.3(p.66.4; M.22.120D); **2.** *partner*, of Son ὁ πατὴρ... προσελάβετο κ. Ath.*hom.in Mt.11*:27(M.25.209B); of Christians at eucharist κ. θεοῦ Dion.Ar.*e.h.*3.3.13(M.3.444D); *fellow-communicant*, Bas.*ep.*218(3.331C; M.32.809C); **3.** title in Montanist hierarchy, cf. *cenonas* Hier.*ep.*41.3(M.*PL.*22.476A, v.l. *cenonos*).

κοίνωσις, ἡ, *profanation, defilement*; of sin, Or.*comm.in Mt.*11.15 (p.58.16; M.13.952B); Epiph.*haer.*46.5(p.209.18; M.41.845A); κ. μοναστηρίων Thphn.*chron.*p.378(M.108.905A).

***κοινώτης**, ὁ, *one who defiles*, Jo.Carp.*cap.*55(M.85.1848).

κοινωφελής, **1.** *benefiting all in common, for the general benefit* κ. ... αἱ τοῦ θεοῦ δωρεαί Clem.*str.*2.19(p.166.7; M.8.1040B); of a style of writing, *popular*, Or.*Cels.*6.1(p.70.14; M.11.1289B); of Son τοῖς πᾶσιν κ. καὶ σωτήριος Eus.*e.th.*3.2(p.143.1; M.24.977C); διδασκαλία κ. Epiph.*mens.*9(M.43.252B); comp. κ. ἰατρόν Or.*Cels.*7.59(p.209.13; 1505C); id.*comm.in 1Cor.*14:5(*JTS* 10 p.36); **2.** τὸ κ. *benefit of all, public interest*, opp. τὸ ἑαυτοῦ, *1Clem.*48.6; εἰς τὸ κ. Chrys.*hom.15.3 in Jo.*(8.88C); τὸ χρήσιμον καὶ τὸ κ. Isid.Pel.*epp.*3.185(M.78.873D); τὸ κ. τῆς διδαχῆς *the general profit of the teaching*, Ammon.*Jo.*6:29 (M.85.1433D); plur., *matters of general benefit*, Eus.*l.C.*18(p.259.10; M.20.1440D); Ammon.*Jo.*4:29(1425B); Cyr.ap.*cat.Mt.*14:23(p.118.9); comp., Gr.Nyss.*ep.can.*(M.45.233D).

***κοινωφελῶς**, *for the general good* or *benefit* τὸ κ. ζῆν Chrys.*laud. Paul.*3.1(2.487A); id.*hom.78.3 in Mt.*(7.755A, v.l. κοινωφελές).

κοιτάριον, τό, *cubicle*, Thdr.Stud.*poen.*1.48(M.99.1740A); *ib.*2.24 (1752C).

κοίτη, ἡ, myst., *union, intercourse*; of soul with God, Max.*myst.* (M.91.680D).

κοιτών, ὁ, *bed-chamber*; ὁ περὶ τὸν κοιτῶνα *chamberlain*, Bas.*ep.* 79(3.173A; M.32.453C); πραιπόσιτον τοῦ εὐσεβεστάτου κ. Pall.*h.Laus.* epilog.(p.169.8; M.34.1259A); οἱ ἐν τῷ κ. *servants of the bed-chamber*, Philost.*h.e.*10.6(M.65.585C); Socr.*h.e.*2.2.5(M.67.188A); ‡Jo.D.*Artem.* 18(p.157.12; M.96.1268C).

***κοιτωνάριον**, τό, *small bed* in a monk's cell, Ephr.3.256E; *Apophth.Patr.*(M.65.109B).

κοκκάριον, τό, *pellet*; of hail, Herm.*mand.*11.20.

κοκκηρός, *scarlet*, Epiph.*haer.*76.54(p.413.13; M.42.636D); *Chron. Pasch.*p.286(M.92.716A).

κοκκινοβαφής, *dyed scarlet* ἱμάτια κ. ‡Pion.*v.Polyc.*21 (v.l. κογχυλιοβαφῆ).

κοκκίον, τό, *dice*; plur., Jo.Mal.*chron.*5 p.103(M.97.192B).

***κοκκυάω**, s.v.l., *rave, talk foolishly*, Anast.S.*haer.*(p.267).

κόλαβρος, ὁ, *young pig*, Olymp.*Job* 5:4(M.93.81B).

κολάζ-ω, **1.** *punish, chastise*; of divine punishment; **a.** in gen., Clem.*ecl.*39(p.148.22; M.9.717B); ὁ θεὸς τοὺς πονηροὺς ἐκόλασεν ὕδατι καὶ πυρί *Const.App.*7.39.3; κολάσας τοὺς Αἰγυπτίους *ib.*7.39.24; **b.** purpose and operation ὁ λόγος...προμηνύει πάντως τινὰς καὶ ἀγγέλους καὶ ἀνθρώπους κολασθήσεσθαι μέλλοντας Just.*dial.*141.2(M. 6.797C); θεὸς...~ει...πρὸς τὸ χρήσιμον καὶ κοινῇ καὶ ἰδίᾳ τοῖς ~ομένοις Clem.*str.*7.16(p.72.21; M.9.541B); ἐπὶ ταῖς ἑκουσίαις [sc. ἁμαρτίαις] ~όμεθα *ib.*4.34(p.316.18; M.8.1364A); οἱ παῖδες ἁμαρτήσαντες οὐκ αὐτοὶ μόνοι κολασθήσονται, ἀλλὰ καὶ ὑπὲρ αὐτῶν οἱ γονεῖς...κριθήσονται *Const.App.*4.11.5; τοῖς διὰ τῶν ἔργων ~εσθαι μέλλουσι Chrys.*hom. 42.5 in Jo.*(8.253E); of punishment hereafter as corporeal ~εσθαι ἐν αἰσθήσει καὶ μετὰ θάνατον οὔσας τὰς τῶν ἀδίκων ψυχάς Just.*1apol.*20.4 (M.6.357C); κἂν τοῖς αὐτοῖς σώμασι μετὰ τῶν ψυχῶν γινομένων καὶ αἰωνίαν κόλασιν κολασθησομένων *ib.*8.4(337C); τίς χρεία τοῖς ~ομένοις ὀδόντων; [i.e. for gnashing] Meth.*res.*1.24(p.248.11; M.41.1093B); θάνατος παρὰ θεοῦ ἐπελεύσεταί σοι αἰώνιος ἐν αἰσθήσει πικρῶς ~ομένῳ *Const.App.*1.3.3; as eternal, Just.*dial.*5.3(M.6.488B); *Hom.Clem.*15. 11; and by fire, Just.*2apol.*9.1(M.6.460A); *Hom.Clem.*3.6; *ib.*8.23; Ath.*ep.Serap.*4.18(M.26.665B); in Hades, *Hom.Clem.*2.13; Meth.*res.* 3.17(p.414.13; M.18.325A); **2.** *torture, harm* ποικίλων βασάνων ἰδέαις ~όμενοι *M.Polyc.*2.4; Clem.*str.*4.12(p.284.6; M.8.1289A); the soul, Ath.*v.Anton.*42(M.26.905B); κ. τὴν ψυχὴν ἐπιθυμίαις Chrys.*hom.14.5 in 1Cor.*(10.123C); **3.** *discipline* κ. ἑαυτόν *Hom.Clem.*11.15; of monks, Chrys.*sac.*6.5(p.150.14; 1.425D); **4.** *temper* a statement, Bas.*Spir.* 70(3.59D; M.32.200A); Chrys.*hom.12.2 in Heb.*(12.123D); Thdt.*haer.* 5.24(4.461); κ. τὴν λιτήν Cyr.*Is.*5.6(2.890B); τὸ ἄγαν ψυχρὸν ~ομεν τῷ θερμῷ Thdt.*Rom.*7:17(3.77).

[*]**κολακάσσιον**, τό, = κολοκάσιον, *root of plant* Nelumbium speciosum, tr. Vergil *ecl.*4.20 ap.Const.*or.s.c.*20(p.183.7; M.20.1293B).

κολακευτής, ὁ, *flatterer*, *M.Seb.*3(p.173.13); Jo.Clim.*scal.*22(M.88. 949D).

κολακεύ-ω, **1.** *flatter*; τὰς θύρας κ. *pay court*; **2.** *adulate, worship* τὰ στοιχεῖα κ. *Hom.Clem.*10.9; *ib.*11.21; **3.** *treat gently, coax, mollify* τὰ φαινόμενα εἰς πρόσωπον κ. Ign.*Polyc.*2.2; τὰ θηρία κ. id.*Rom.*4.2; *Hom.Clem.*13.16; τὴν γαστέρα κ. Cyr.H.*catech.*19.6; c. infin., *coax, persuade*, Ign.*Rom.*5.2; Nil.*Eulog.*2(M.79.1097A); **4.** *beguile, seduce* ~ούσῃ ἁμαρτίᾳ *Hom.Clem.*20.4; c. prep. ἐπὶ τῇ ὕβρει τινὰ κ. *ib.*12. 15; **5.** c. dat., *gratify, satisfy* ταῖς τοῦ βίου χρείαις κ. Bas.Sel.*or.*14. 1(M.85.182B).

***κολακός**, *soft* κ. στρωμνῇ Ephr.3.35D.

κολαπτός, *carved*, Jo.D.*imag.*1.20(M.94.1252A).

κόλασις, ἡ, **1.** *punishment* κ. τῆς πονηρίας Herm.*sim.*9.18.1; κολάσεις βλασφημιῶν Clem.*ecl.*38.2(p.148.20; M.9.717B); of divine punishment; **a.** its operation σωτήριοι καὶ παιδευτικαὶ αἱ κ. τοῦ θεοῦ εἰς ἐπιστροφὴν ἄγουσαι καὶ τὴν μετάνοιαν τοῦ ἁμαρτωλοῦ...αἱρούμεναι id.*str.*6.6(p.455.4; M.9.268C); εὑρήσεις τὸν θεὸν ἐπιμετροῦντα κολάσεις μετὰ φειδοῦς Or.*hom.7.1 in Jer.*(p.52.1; M.13.329B); οἱ ἐπὶ τῶν κ. τεταγμένοι *ib.19.14*(p.170.25; 492A); **b.** of punishment hereafter τὰς μελλούσας κ. *ib.7.1*(p.52.7; 329C); ἡ κατ' ἀξίαν κ. ἐν τῷ τῆς κρίσεως καιρῷ ἀποδίδοται τῇ ψυχῇ μετὰ τὴν τοῦ σώματος ἀνάλυσιν *Hom.Clem.*3.28; τὰ...μέλλοντα ἑκάτερα ἀθάνατα...τά τε κολάσεως τά τε τῆς βασιλείας Chrys.*hom.44.2 in Jo.*(8.260E); **c.** corporeal οἱ τῆς κ. ἄξιοι ἀπελεύσονται εἰς αὐτὴν [sc. ζωήν]...ἰδίας ἔχοντες ψυχάς, καὶ ἴδια σώματα Iren.*haer.*2.33.5(M.7.834A); cf.*A.Thom.*A 55ff.(p.171. 16ff.); by fire τὸ τῆς μελλούσης κρίσεως καὶ αἰωνίου κ. τοῖς ἀσεβέσι τηρούμενον πῦρ *M.Polyc.*11.2; v. πῦρ; **d.** persons affected ἀμετανόητος τηρεῖται εἰς αἰώνιον κ. *T.Gad* 7.5; ὁ δεσπότης...τοὺς ἑτεροκλινεῖς ὑπάρχοντας εἰς κ. καὶ αἰκισμὸν τίθησιν *1Clem.*11.1; κ. ἀφόρητος [sc. τοὺς μεθύοντας] ἀναμένει Chrys.*stat.*1.5(2.7E); **e.** its place τὴν αἰώνιον ἐν γεέννῃ κ. *Ep.Lugd.*ap.Eus.*h.e.*5.1.26(M.20.417B); κ. τὰς ἐν τῷ ᾅδῃ καὶ τὰς βασάνους τὰς αἰωνίους Ath.*virg.*17(p.52.18; M.28.272D); **f.** eternal οὐδὲν ἡμᾶς ῥύσεται ἐκ τῆς αἰωνίου κ. ἐὰν παρακούσωμεν τῶν ἐντολῶν αὐτοῦ *2Clem.*6.7; Or.*Cels.*3.78(p.269.20; M.11.1021C); εἰ...τῆς αἰωνίου κ. ἔσται ποτὲ τέλος, ἕξει πάντως καὶ ἡ αἰώνιος ζωή Bas.*reg.br.*267(2.507B; M.31.1265A); τῆς ἀιδίου κ. ἐντὸς κατέστη *Const. App.*5.6.7; ἀνάγκη κολάζεσθαι κ. τέλος οὐκ ἔχουσαν, πέρας οὐκ ἐπισταμένην Chrys.*hom.42.5 in Jo.*(8.253E); αἰώνιος...ζωὴ καὶ αἰώνιος κ. τὸ ἀτελεύτητον τοῦ μέλλοντος αἰῶνος δηλοῖ Jo.D.*f.o.*2.1(M.94.364B); eternity of punishment doubted εἰς...τὰ ὑπερέκεινα [sc. κολάσεως] οὐ χρήσιμον ἀναβαίνειν διὰ τοὺς μόγις φόβῳ τῆς αἰωνίου κ. κἂν συστέλλοντας Or.*Cels.*6.26(p.96.16; M.11.1332B); συγκρίνωμεν καθ' ἑαυτούς, τί λυσιτελεῖ τῇ μονογάμῳ...οἴεσθαι...αἰωνίῳ κ. παραδίδοσθαι τὴν δίγαμον ἵνα μείνῃ μονόγαμος, ἢ γνῶναι τὸ ἀληθὲς καὶ διγαμῆσαι id.*hom. 20.4 in Jer.*(p.182.25; M.13.508C); cf.id.*comm.in Rom.*6:23(*JTS* 13 p.368); cf.id.*princ.*1.6(p.78.8ff.; M.11.165Aff.); εἰ δ' εἰς αἰώνιόν τι διάστημα ἡ ἄσχετος ἐκείνη ὀδύνη παραταθείη, τίς ἐκ τῆς ὕστερον ἐλπίδος ὑπολέλειπται παραμυθία, ᾧ πρὸς ὅλον αἰῶνα συνδιαμετρεῖται ἡ κ.; Gr.Nyss.*anim.et res.*(M.46.101B); λέγουσι [sc. οἱ Ὠριγενισταί]...ὅτι τὸ τοῦ αἰῶνος ὄνομα ἐπὶ ὡρισμένου χρόνου λαμβάνεται, καὶ ὅταν εἴπῃ ἡ γραφὴ ὅτι αἰωνία ἐστὶν ἡ κ., οὐ λέγει εἰ μὴ ἐπὶ ὡρισμένου χρόνου †Leont.B.*sect.*10.6(M.86.1265D); τῶν...τὴν ἀποκατάστασιν τῆς κ. τερατολογούντων Anast.S.*haer.*(p.264); **g.** in paganism τὰς...μετὰ θάνατον κ. ... ἀπὸ τῆς βαρβάρου φιλοσοφίας ἡ Ἑλληνικὴ φιλοσοφία ὑφείλετο Clem.*str.*5.14(p.385.24; M.9.132B); in Greek mysteries, Cels. ap.Or.*Cels.*8.48(p.262.28; M.11.1588B); acc. Plato, Hipp.*haer.*1.19 (p.22.1; M.16.3044B); **2.** *torture*, ref. martyrdom κακαὶ κ. τοῦ διαβόλου Ign.*Rom.*5.3; οἱ εἰς τὰ θηρία κατακριθέντες ὑπέμειναν δεινὰς κ. *M.Polyc.*2.4; *Ep.Lugd.*ap.Eus.*h.e.*5.1.38(M.20.424A); **3.** κεφαλικὴ κ. *capital punishment, execution*, Eus.*h.e.*5.21.4(M.20.488B).

***κολασταῖος**, *punishable* τὰ ψεκτὰ καὶ κ. Didym.ap.Leont.et Jo. *sacr.*2.11(M.86.2065B).

κολαστέος, *to be condemned* τέχνας κ. CSard.*can.*2.

κολαστήριος, *punitive, used for torture*; **1.** in gen. τόποι κ. *A. Thom.*A 57(p.174.11); πῦρ κ. Gr.Naz.*or.*40.36(M.36.412A); ξύλον κ. Eus.*h.e.*6.39.5(M.20.601A); **2.** neut. as subst.; **a.** *punishment, torture* of the sinner μεῖζόν τι ζητῶ κ. τῆς γεέννης τοῦ πυρός Or.*hom.19. 15 in Jer.*(p.175.12; M.13.497C); τῶν ὑπὸ γῆς κ. Const.ap.Eus.*v.C.*2. 27(p.52.28; M.20.1005A); γεέννης διάφορα κ. Bas.*reg.br.*267(2.507C; M.31.1265B); ἀπαλλαγησόμεθα...τῶν κατὰ τὸν μέλλοντα αἰῶνα κ. Chrys.*hom.10.4 in Rom.*(9.519B); ref. persecution τυραννικῶν κ. *Ep.Lugd.*ap.Eus.*h.e.*5.1.27(M.20.417C); Gr.Nyss.*ep.can.*(M.45.225A); †Bas.*hom.in Ps.*115(1.374C; M.30.109C); **b.** *place of punishment* σκυθρωπὸν κ. Gr.Nyss.*ep.*1(M.46.1004C); in pagan philosophy κατάγουσι...τὴν ψυχὴν...καθάπερ εἰς κ. τὸν κόσμον Clem.*str.*3.3(p.201.17; M.8.1116B); of future punishment acc. Plato εἰς τὴν παίδευσιν σωφρονίζοντα παρεισάγων κ. *ib.*5.14(p.386.13; M.9.133B).

κολαστικός, **1.** *punitive*; c. genit. κρίσιν...κ. τῶν ἁμαρτανόντων Max.*ambig.*(M.91.1133D); κρίσις...κακίας κ. *ib.*(1400B); ἡ κ. [sc. τέχνη] *chastisement*, Clem.*str.*1.26(p.104.28; M.8.916B); *ib.*7.3(p.13.15; M.9.421C); **2.** *given to punishment* νομοθέτης κ. Chrys.*hom.32.1 in Heb.*(12.295A); of God, id.*hom.14.2 in 1Cor.*(10.120A); c. genit. τῆς ἀδιαφορίας κολαστικός Max.*ambig.*(M.91.1161C).

***κολαστικῶς**, *so as to punish*, opp. ἰατρικῶς, Thdt.*Ps.*6:2(1.641).

κολαφίζ-ω, *slap, strike*, Mac.Aeg.*hom.*27.6(M.34.697A); pass., *Orac.Sib.*8.292; Thphn.*chron.*p.416(M.108.988A); met. πειρασμοῖς τὴν ψυχὴν ~οντες Jo.Carp.*cap.*19(M.85.1841).

***κολάφισμα, τό**, *slap, blow*, Isid.Pel.*epp.*1.54(M.78.217A); Philox. *ep.*38(p.185); ‡Jo.D.*Artem.*38(M.96.1285D).

***κολαφισμός, ὁ**, *beating* κ. τῆς κεφαλῆς Chrys.*hom.13.4 in 1Cor.* (10.114C); κολαφισμοῖς βαλλόμενος Pall.*h.Laus.*47(p.141.14; M.34. 1202D).

κόλαφος, ὁ, *slap, blow* ἡ...μετὰ τῶν δακτύλων γινομένη πληγή...κ. λέγεται Melet.*nat.hom.*27(M.64.1253A); met., *affliction*, Call.*v.Hyp.* (p.64).

κολεόπτερος, *sheath-winged*; of beetles, Bas.*hex.*8.3(1.72E; M.29. 169C).

κολίανδρον, τό, = κορίανδρον, *coriander*, *T.Sal.*18.20(M.122. 1344C).

***κολικευμός, ὁ**, *colic*, Sophr.H.*mir.Cyr.et Jo.*1(M.87.3428A).

***κόλλαθον, τό**, a liquid measure, Epiph.*mens.*21(M.43.272B); *ib.* 24(292B).

κολλ-άω, **1.** *fasten, join* ~ᾷ περὶ τὴν ὀσφὺν...τὸ περίζωμα Or.*hom. 11.6 in Jer.*(p.84.1; M.13.376A); spiritually ἀγάπη ~ᾷ ἡμᾶς τῷ θεῷ *1Clem.*49.5; *ib.*56.2; οἱ μαθηταὶ...τοὺς ἔτι μακρὰν...~ῶντες τῷ Χριστῷ Cyr.*glaph.Gen.*3(1.89B); **2.** pass., *cleave* to, *devote oneself* to, *1Clem.*46.1; κ. τοῖς μετ' εὐσεβείας εἰρηνεύουσιν *ib.*15.1; ~ηθέντος αὐτῇ [sc. τῇ σαρκί] τοῦ πνεύματος τοῦ ἁγίου *2Clem.*14.5; οὐ κ. ... ἀνθρώποις τοιούτοις *Barn.*16.3; τοῖς τοιούτοις πνεύμασιν οὐ ~ῶνται Herm. *mand.*11.4; κ. τῷ κυρίῳ *ib.*10.1.6; ref. Mt.19:5 οὕτως...πᾶς ἀνὴρ ἢ γυνὴ ~ώμενος τῷ κυρίῳ ἓν πνεῦμα Ath.*virg.*2(p.36.22; M.28.253B); εἰς ἑνότητά τινα ἐν πνεύματι κεκολλήμεθα τῷ πατρί Cyr.*glaph.Gen.*2 (1.49E); τῇ εὐχῇ ~ηθῶμεν Nil.*epp.*1.10(M.79.85D); ref. Arian Trin. doctrine μὴ δίδους...ἐκ τῆς μονάδος εἶναι τὸν λόγον, ἀλλ' ἁπλῶς κεκολλῆσθαι τῷ πατρὶ λόγον, δυάδα οὐσίας εἰσάγει ‡Ath.*Ar.*4.3(p.47.9; M. 26.472B); c. prep. οὐ ~ηθήσεται ἡ ψυχή σου μετὰ ὑψηλῶν *Did.*3.9; οὐ κ. μετὰ τῶν πορευομένων ἐν ὁδῷ θανάτου *Barn.*19.2; **3.** pass., *fasten upon, attack* ἡ ὀξυχολία ὅταν ~ηθῇ τῷ ἀνθρώπῳ Herm.*mand.* 10.2.3; κ. τοῖς πλουσίοις Chrys.*Eutrop.*2.3(3.389A); Cyr.*Ps.*9:28(M. 69.784A).

***κόλλεον, τό**, *cock's comb*, Clem.*paed.*3.3(p.247.8; M.8.581A); *Schol.Clem.paed.*(p.336.14; M.9.792C).

[*]**κόλλη, ἡ**, = κόλλα, *solder* κόλλην ἐκ μολύβδου καὶ κασσιτέρου κεραννυμένην Thdt.*eran.*2(4.101).

κολλήγας, ὁ, (Lat. *collega*) *colleague*, Const.ap.Eus.*h.e.*10.5.18ff. (M.20.888Af.).

κολλήγιον, τό, (Lat. *collegium*) *band, company*; of robber bands, Pall.*h.Laus.*19(p.59.15; M.34.1066A); *Apophth.Patr.*(M.65. 377C); CEph.(431)*ep.*(*ACO* 1.1.3 p.7.22; H.1.1508B).

κόλλυβα, τά, *boiled wheat*; food of a monk, Pall.*v.Chrys.*20(p.127. 4; M.47.71).

***κολλυβίζω**, *exchange money*, Or.*comm.in Mt.*16.21(p.549.11; M. 13.1448A).

κολλυριδιανοί** (κολλουριδιανοί**), **οἱ**, *Collyridians*, a Mariolatrous sect οἱ εἰς ὄνομα...Μαρίας...κολλυρίδα τινὰ προσφέροντες Epiph. *anac.*79(p.415.14, v.l. -ουρ-; M.42.640B) = Jo.D.*haer.*79(M.94.728A); described, Epiph.*haer.*79 tit.(p.475.26; M.42.740B).

κολλυρίς, ἡ, *small loaf*; offered to BMV by Collyridians, Epiph. *anac.*79(p.415.15; M.42.640C) = Jo.D.*haer.*79(M.94.728A); Epiph. *haer.*78.23(p.473.11; M.42.736B); ref. 1Par.16:3, Thdt.*qu.1 in 1Par.* (1.562).

κολόβιον, τό, *short-sleeved garment*, *A.Barth.*(p.131.22); identified with dalmatic, -βίων, Epiph.*haer.*14.1(p.209.15; M.41.245A); Jo.D.*haer.*15(M.94.688A); esp. worn by monks, ‡Ath.*ep.Cast.*1.6(M. 28.856D); λεβιτὼν ὅνπερ τινὲς κ. προσαγορεύουσι ‡Pall.*h.mon.*(p.34. 11; M.34.1138A); Max.*qu.dub.*67(M.90.840B).

***κολοβοδάκτυλος**, *stump-fingered*; of S. Mark, Hipp.*haer.*7.30 (p.215.16; M.16.3334A).

κολοβόκερκος, *with docked tail*; of sacrificial victim, Chrys.*hom. 21.2 in Rom.*(9.657E).

κολοβόρριν, ὁ, *one with a mutilated nose*, †Cyr.*coll.VT*(6^4.27C; M.77.1216B).

***κολοβόρρινος**, *with mutilated nose*, Cyr.*Mal.*1(3.817D).

κολοβότης, ἡ, *shortness* of stature, Anast.S.*hod.*2(M.89.64C).

***κολοβόχειρ**, *with hands cut off*, Jo.Thess.*dorm.BMV* 13(p.428. 39); Jo.D.*hom.*9(M.96.740C).

κολόβωσις, ἡ, *vitiation, imperfection*, of human nature according to Apollinarius συμβαινούσης τῷ λόγῳ τῆς θεότητος τῆς κατὰ τὴν φύσιν ἡμῶν κολοβώσεως Gr.Nyss.*Apoll.*50(M.45.1245B); denied of resurrection body οὐ σωματικὴν...κ. id.*anim.et res.*(M.46. 160B).

***κολοκύνθιον (κολοκύντιον), τό**, *gourd*, Cyr.S.*v.Sab.*48(p.138.11); *gourd-shaped container* κολοκύντιον οἴνου *Apophth.Patr.*(M.65.184B); Cyr.S.*v.Sab.*46(p.137.9); κ. ὄξους *ib.*(p.136.27).

***κολουστέος**, *fit to be checked* or *stopped*, Clem.*paed.*3.11(p.274.16; M.8.644C).

κόλπος, ὁ, **A.** *bosom*; **1.** met. φήμη...Μωϋσέα...μέσοις αὐτοῖς τυραννικοῖς οἴκοις τε καὶ κόλποις τραφῆναι Eus.*v.C.*1.12(p.13.10; M.20. 925A); ἡ τοῦ φωτὸς δύναμις καὶ ὁ τῆς ἱερᾶς θρησκείας νόμος...οἷον ἔκ τινων τῆς ἀνατολῆς κ. ἐκδοθεὶς Const.ap.Eus.*v.C.*2.67(p.67.28; 1040A); **2.** exeg. Ps.73:11 κ. θεοῦ ὁ τῶν ἀγαθῶν θησαυρός· τέθεικε δὲ αὐτὸ ἐκ μεταφορᾶς τῶν πεπληρωμένον ἐχόντων τὸν κ., καὶ αἰτουμένων μέν, δοῦναι δὲ μὴ βουλομένων ἀλλ' ἐπιστρεφόντων εἰς τοὐπίσω τὴν χεῖρα Thdt.*Ps.*73:11(1.1128); **3.** exeg. Lc.16:22 of future state of blessed δοκεῖ τὴν ἀγαθὴν τῆς ψυχῆς κατάστασιν, ἐν ᾗ τὸν τῆς ὑπομονῆς ἀθλητὴν ἀναπαύει ὁ λόγος, κόλπον τοῦ Ἀβραὰμ ὀνομάσαι Gr.Nyss. *anim.et res.*(M.46.84B); δεηθῶμεν ὅπως ὁ...θεὸς προσδεξάμενος αὐτοῦ τὴν ψυχὴν...κατατάξῃ εἰς χώραν εὐσεβῶν ἀνειμένων εἰς κόλπους Ἀβραὰμ καὶ Ἰσαὰκ καὶ Ἰακώβ *Const.App.*8.41.2; *ib.*8.41.5; Chrys. *hom.40.2 in Gen.*(4.407A); Dion.Ar.*e.h.*7.3.4(M.3.560B); v. βασιλεία;

4. Trin., ref. Jo.1:18 (ὁ ὢν εἰς τὸν κ. τοῦ πατρός): various interpretations προϋπάρχων ἦν [sc. ὁ υἱός] οὐκ ἐν τῇ διανοίᾳ τοῦ πατρός, ὡς ἐδόκει Μαρκέλλῳ, ἀλλ' ἐν τοῖς κ. αὐτοῦ· ὥσπερ δὴ ἡμῖν ἐπήγγελται ὁ σωτὴρ εἰς κόλπους Ἀβραὰμ καὶ Ἰσαὰκ καὶ Ἰακὼβ διαναπαύσασθαι, οὕτως καὶ ὁ υἱὸς 'εἰς τὸν κ.' ἦν 'τοῦ πατρός' Eus.*e.th.*1.20(p.83.28ff.; M.24.869C); οὐ γὰρ ἀμφότερα, ὅ τε λόγος καὶ ὁ υἱός, ἐν τοῖς κ., ἀλλ' ἕνα εἶναι δεῖ καὶ τοῦτον τὸν υἱόν, ὅς ἐστι μονογενής ‡Ath.*Ar.*4.16(p.60.22; M.26.489B); κ. μὲν γὰρ πατρικὸς υἱῷ καθέδρα πρέπουσα Bas.*Spir.*15(3.12B; M.32.92B); ὁ μὲν...ἁπλῶς ὁρῶν, οὐ πάντως ἀκριβῆ τοῦ φαινομένου τὴν γνῶσιν ἔχει· ὁ δὲ τοῖς κ. ἐνδιατρίβων, οὐδὲν ἀγνοήσειέ ποτε (cf. Jo.6:46) Chrys.*hom.15.2 in Jo.*(8.86D); ἐν κ. φαμὲν...ἀντὶ τοῦ ἐν ἀγαπήσει, καθὰ καὶ αὐτός πού φησιν, 'ὁ πατὴρ ἀγαπᾷ τὸν υἱόν' Cyr.*Jo.*1.10(4.106D); demonstrating relationship to Father τὸ ἐν κ. σημαίνει...τὴν γνησίαν ἐκ τοῦ πατρὸς τοῦ υἱοῦ γέννησιν Ath.*decr.*21(p.18.20; M.25.453C); οὐ...τὸν ἑτερούσιον ἐν τοῖς κ. ἂν ἔσχεν ὁ πατήρ· ἀλλ' οὐδὲ ἂν αὐτὸς ἐτόλμησε, δοῦλος ὢν καὶ τῶν πολλῶν εἷς, ἐν τῷ κ. στρέφεσθαι τοῦ δεσπότου· τοῦτο γὰρ υἱοῦ γνησίου μόνον Chrys.*hom.15.2 in Jo.*(8.87A); τὸν κ. ἀκούων, μὴ κ. εἶναι νόμιζε, μηδὲ τόπον, ἀλλ' ἀπὸ τῆς τοῦ κ. προσηγορίας τὴν πρὸς τὸν γεγεννηκότα ἐγγύτητα καὶ τὴν παρρησίαν ἐκλάμβανε id.*incomprehens.*4.4(1.476C); ἐν 'κ.' εἶναί φησι 'τοῦ πατρός', ἵνα φαίνηται πάλιν τῆς πρὸς τὴν κτίσιν ὁμοφυΐας ἔξω κείμενος, καὶ ἰδιάζουσαν ἔχων ἐκ πατρὸς καὶ ἐν πατρὶ τὴν ὕπαρξιν Cyr.*Jo.*1.10(4.105B); 'ἐν τοῖς κ.'...ἵνα νοῆται καὶ υἱὸς ἐξ αὐτοῦ καὶ ἐν αὐτῷ φυσικῶς, ἀντὶ τῆς οὐσίας τὸν κ. τοῦ πατρὸς εἰπών *ib.*(107B); this state eternal ἀνάρχως καὶ ἀϊδίως ἐν τῷ κ. τοῦ πατρός ἐστιν ὁ υἱός Chrys.*hom.15.2 in Jo.*(8.87B); cf. πρὸ γὰρ...τῆς διὰ Δαυὶδ προφητείας, ἐν κ. τοῦ πατρὸς ἦν ὁ λόγος ‡Ath.*serm.fid.*28(p.25; M.26.1284A); *ib.*30(p.27; 1285A); eternity denied by Arians ὕστερον ἐν κ. τοῦ πατρὸς γέγονε ‡Ath.*Ar.*4.23(p.69.26; M.26.501C); ref. Inc. κατελθὼν [sc. ὁ λόγος] ἐκ τῶν κ. τοῦ πατρός †Ath.*exp.fid.*1(M.25.201B); οὐδέποτε δὲ ἐκενώθη ὁ κ. τοῦ πατρὸς τῆς τοῦ υἱοῦ θεότητος, φησὶ γάρ [Pr.8:30] *ib.*2(204B); Manich. τὸν μονογενῆ τὸν ἐκ τῶν κ. τοῦ πατρὸς καταβάντα Χριστόν *Ep.*ap.Hegem.*Arch.*5(p.7.9; M.10.1436A); τὸν υἱὸν ἀπέστειλεν ὁ ἀγαθὸς πατὴρ ἐκ τῶν κ. εἰς τὴν καρδίαν τῆς γῆς Hegem.*ib.*8(p.11.12; 1437C).

B. *hollow, recess, chasm* πνευμάτων ἐναπολαμβανομένων τοῖς κ. τῆς γῆς Philost.*h.e.*12.10(M.65.620A); met. τοῦ νοὸς τὸν κ. ἁπλώσας Gr. Mag.*dial.*(tr.Zach.)4.7(M.*PL.*77.231B); φόβος ἐνέσκηψε τοῖς τῆς διανοίας κ. Bas.*ep.*45.1(3.133A; M.32.365A); Chrys.*hom.43.1 in Gen.*(4.435A).

κόλπωμα, τό, *deep abyss,* Philost.*h.e.*3.9(M.65.492C).

κολυμβ-άω, *swim, Barn.*10.5; Pall.*h.Laus.*19(p.59.9; M.34.1066A); met., Clem.*paed.*2.2(p.170.18; M.8.416B); of those born under sign Virgo ὀφθαλμοῖς...~ῶσιν Hipp.*haer.*5.20(p.51.22; M.16.3086C).

κολυμβήθρα, ἡ, A. *pool, cistern* ἡ κ. τοῦ κναφέως near Jerusalem, Eus.*onomast.*(p.102.16); exeg. Jo.5:2: Or.*fr.61 in Jo.*(p.533.3) cit. s. προβατικός; cf.Ammon.*Jo.*5:2(M.85.1428D); Chrys.*paralyt.*1(3.32B); as type of baptism, id.*hom.36.1 in Jo.*(8.207B); *ib.26.2*(151B); id. *hom.5.4 in Col.*(11.364D); of cistern seen by Perpetua in vision, signifying baptismal purification, *M.Perp.*7(p.73.21); *ib.*8(p.75.8); ref. Is.22:9 ὕδωρ δὲ ἦν παλαιᾶς κ. ... ὁ τῆς παλαιᾶς...γραφῆς λόγος Eus.*Is.*22:9(M.24.248C); Proc.G.*Is.*22:1–14(M.87.2176C–2177A).

B. *font;* **1.** in gen., Chrys.*ep.Innoc.*1.3(p.13.7; 3.519A); Pall.*v. Chrys.*9(p.57.26; M.47.33); ‡Ath.*qu.script.*92(M.28.753C) cit. s. ἀναδύω; τὴν κ. τοῦ βαπτιστηρίου πληρωθῆναι Socr.*h.e.*7.17.12f.(M.67.773A); but equated with βαπτιστήριον, Thdr.Lect.*h.e.*1.8(M.86.169B); Thdt.*eran.*1(4.37); Bas.Sel.*pasch.*1.5(M.28.1080D) cit. s. ἀναγέννησις; Eustrat.*v.Eutych.*8(M.86.2284A); **2.** equivalent to βάπτισμα: δύναμιν τοῦ μυστηρίου τῆς κ. Ephr.2.378F; οἱ πολέμιοι μετὰ τὴν ἁγίαν κ. εὐκαταγώνιστοι ἐγένοντο Thdt.*Ps.*73:15(1.1131); δευτέρας κ. κατάδυσιν †Jo.D.*B.J.*11(M.96.952A); ref. ceremonies of actual baptism, as distinct from subsidiary rites, ‡Just.*qu.et resp.*137(M.6.1389C) cit. s. ἔλαιον; of entry into monastic life as δευτέρα κ., Steph.Diac. *v.Steph.*(M.100.1089B); **3.** as source of removal of sin τὴν θείαν κ. τιμωροῦσαν μὲν καὶ καταφλέγουσαν καὶ ἐξαναφίζουσαν τὴν ἁμαρτίαν Thdt.*Ps.*59:10(1.1005); and liberation from Devil, id.*Mich.*7:20(2.1516); of regeneration ἄνθρωπος...θεὸς δι' ὕδατος καὶ πνεύματος ἁγίου μετὰ τὴν τῆς κ. ἀναγέννησιν γίνεται †Hipp.*theoph.*8(p.262.11; M.10.860A); Didym.*Trin.*2.13(M.39.692A); ἡμεῖς γεννώμεθα διὰ τῶν τοῦ θεοῦ ῥημάτων. ἐν γὰρ τῇ κ. τῶν ὑδάτων ῥήματά ἐστι θεοῦ τὰ γεννῶντα ἡμᾶς καὶ διαπλάττοντα Chrys.*hom.16.4 in Rom.*(9.608E); id.*comm. in Gal.*4:22(10.711C) cit. s. ἀναγεννάω; exeg. Mt.21:15 τίνα τὰ θεολογοῦντα νήπια;...τίνες αἱ τούτων μητέρες; αἱ τοῦ βαπτίσματος κ. αἱ τοὺς πιστοὺς ἀναγεννῶσαι ‡Epiph.*hom.*6(M.43.504D); μεθ' ἡμῶν ὁ θεός, καὶ ἡ κ. τίκτουσα οὐ κάμνει Procl.CP *or.*5.4(M.65.721A); μία γάρ ἐστι περιστερά μου...μία ἐστὶ τῇ μητρὶ αὐτῆς· μητέρα δὲ ἔχει τὴν ἱερὰν κ., τὴν ἄνω Ἱερουσαλήμ Thdt.*Cant.*6:7(2.129); Oecum.*Gal.*6:15(p.448.3); διὰ βαπτίσματος δευτέρα ἀναγέννησις ἐν ὕδατι τῆς κ. διὰ τοῦ πνεύματος ἐγγινομένη †Jo.D.*B.J.*11(M.96.956C); of illumination διὰ... τὸν τῆς δικαιοσύνης ἥλιον Χριστὸν οὐρανὸς ἡ ἐκκλησία γεγένηται... ἀστέρας νεοφωτίστους ἐκ κ. ἀναφέρουσα ‡Epiph.*hom.*3(465C); of sonship towards God through action of H. Ghost λαμβάνει αὐτὸν ἡ τοῦ πνεύματος χάρις εἰς τὴν κ., καὶ τὸν ἡταιρηκότα υἱὸν θεοῦ κατασκευάζει Chrys.ap.*cat.Heb.*8:11(p.596.9); οἱ τῆς τοῦ πνεύματος κ. υἱοί Bas.Sel. *or.*27.2(M.85.313A); cf. ἐκγόνων τῆς τιμίας κ. †Gregent.*disp.*(M.86.744C); hence of Pentecostal 'wind' καθάπερ κ. γέγονεν ὕδατος Chrys. *hom.4.2 in Ac.*(9.34D); **4.** types of baptismal κ.; **a.** in OT; Red Sea as type of font in which burial and resurrection are effected, Chrys.*hom.7.2 in Col.*(11.374B); τύπον ἔχει τῆς κ. ἡ θάλαττα· ἡ δὲ νεφέλη, τοῦ πνεύματος Thdt.*qu.27 in Ex.*(1.144); id.*Mich.*7:20(2.1516); id.*1Cor.*10:2(3.225); ‡Anast.S.*Jud.disp.*3(M.89.1268A); exeg. Is.7:3 τινὲς δὲ καὶ τοῦ...βαπτίσματος τὴν κ. ἀπεφήσαντο τύπον Proc. G.*Is.*7:1–9(M.87.1956D); exeg. Is.41:18, Hesych.H.*fr.Ps.*106:35(M.93.1305C); **b.** in NT, Christ's baptism ἐν ποταμῷ τὸ τῆς κ. μυστήριον ἐσκιογράφησε Procl.CP *or.*2.2(M.65.693C); **c.** in church ornament ἡ γαστὴρ τοῦ θυμιατηρίου δηλοῖ τὴν κ. τοῦ ἁγίου βαπτίσματος ‡Bas.*h. myst.*42(p.388.5).

κόλυμβος, ὁ, 1. *diver, Orac.Sib.*5.335; **2.** as adj., *swimming,* ‡Pall. *h.mon.*(p.91.21; M.34.1026C); *Chron.Pasch.*p.396(M.92.1013C,D).

§**κόλων,** v. κήλων.

κολωνία, ἡ, (Lat. *colonia*) Roman *colony,* Serap.Ant.ap.Eus.*h.e.* 5.19.3(M.20.481B); Phot.Tyr.*libell.*(p.14.11; H.2.504B).

κομ-άω, 1. *flourish;* fig., Chrys.*hom.2.5 in Jo.*(8.15B); met. τῆς εὐσεβείας τὸν λόγον πανταχοῦ κατασπειρόμενον καὶ ~ῶντα id.*hom.1.2 in Mt.*(7.4C); *ib.19.1*(244E); πονηροὺς ἀνθρώπους...~ῶντας πανταχόθεν id.*hom.28.3 in 1Cor.*(10.254B); **2.** c. dat. rei *abound in* ταῖς ἀρεταῖς κ. Bas.*renunt.*2(2.204D; M.31.632B); Chrys.*hom.13.4 in Mt.*(7.174A).

***κόμβενδος,** v. *κόμβεντος.

***κομβέντιον, τό,** (Lat. *conventio*) *assembly,* Jo.Mal.*chron.*7 p.183 (M.97.293A).

***κόμβεντος,** (Lat. *conventus*) *convoked, convened* γενομένου σιλεντίου κομβέντου Jo.Mal.*chron.*18 p.438(M.97.648A); *ib.*18 p.494 (713C); as subst. κόμβεντος, ὁ *assembly, council, ib.*5 p.102(189C); κόμβενδος *Chron.Pasch.*p.323(M.92.825B); κομβέντον Thphn.*chron.* p.145(M.108.397A).

***κομβίνευμα, τό,** *yoking together of horses for racing* μὴ τερπέτω σε τὰ προϊππικὰ κ. ‡Chrys.*circ.*(8.88E).

***κομβινεύω,** (cf. Lat. *combino*) *race with yoked horses,* ‡Chrys. *circ.*(8.88E).

κόμβος, ὁ, *knot* or *joint in a stalk,* Cyr.H.*catech.*9.10; Gr.Nyss.*res.* 3(M.46.669B).

κομβόω, A. *bind* or *weave together,* met. ὁ θεὸς...ὁ κομβώσας τὸ σῶμα ‡Chrys.*BMV* 3(8.241A).

B. *deceive, trick;* **1.** c. acc. pers., Jo.Mal.*chron.*16 p.395(M.97.585A); Thphn.*chron.*p.128(M.108.353B); **2.** abs., *say deceitfully* οὐκοῦν μεριστὸς [sc. ὁ Χριστός] ὡς ἐκόμβουν οἱ πάλαι Andr.Cr.*Agath.* (M.97.1441B); **3.** c. acc. rei, *gain fraudulently* ἐκόμβωσε πολλὰ χρήματα Jo.Mal.*chron.*16 p.395(M.97.585A).

***κόμβυλος, ὁ,** *vessel, jar,* v.l. for βόμβυλος, Thdt.*provid.*4(4.539).

[*]**κομβώνω,** = κομβόω, *deceive, trick,* Thphn.*chron.*p.128(M.108.353B).

***κομενταρήσιος (-αρίσιος, -άριος), ὁ,** (Lat. *commentariensis*) *public official in charge of state documents;* of one who keeps prison records, *M.Tar.*6(p.462); *M.Pion.*21.1; in gen. -άριος Ath.*apol.sec.* 8(p.94.12; M.25.264A); -αρίσιος Jo.Mal.*chron.*18 p.492(M.97.712B); -αρίσιος ‡Jo.D.*Artem.*2(M.96.1253B).

***κομενταρίον, τό,** (Lat. *commentarium*) *magistrate's court,* Ath. *apol.Const.*29(M.25.632C).

***κομερκιάριος, *κομέρκιον,** v. *κομμερκιάριος, *κομμέρκιον.

***κομετᾶτος,** v. *κομιτᾶτον.

κόμης, ὁ, (Lat. *comes*), title of the occupant of certain state offices κομήτων δὲ οἱ μὲν πρώτου τάγματος...οἱ δὲ δευτέρου, οἱ δὲ τρίτου Eus.*v.C.*4.1(p.118.12; M.20.1152A); πῶς δὲ σύνοδον ὀνομάζειν τολμῶσιν, ἧς κόμης προυκάθητο; Ath.*apol.sec.*8(p.94.11; M.25.261D); ὁ...βασιλεὺς...κόμητα...αὐτὸν κατέστησε Epiph.*haer.*30.11(p.347.9; M.41.424D); κ. *consistorian*ῶν Justn.*nov.*13.3(p.102.9) etc.; with office defined τῶν οἰκείων κ. Gr.Naz.*ep.*151(M.37.257A); κ. ... πριβάτων Thdt.*h.e.*3.12.2(3.925); κ. τῶν σακρῶν *Ep.*ap.CEph.*act.*(*ACO* 1.1.3 p.32.8; H.1.1556B); κ. τοῦ ὀψαρίου *Chron.Pasch.*p.391(M.92.1004B); κ. τῶν λαργιτιώνων Thphn.*chron.*p.158(M.108.428B); κ. τῶν βασιλικῶν σταύλων *ib.*p.208(533B) etc.; of a province κ. Ἀντιοχείας Pall.*v.*

*Chrys.*5(p.30.2; M.47.19); κ. ἀνατολῆς *Chron.Pasch.*p.321(M.92.820B); κ. τοῦ Ὀψικίου Thphn.*chron.*p.321(776C) etc.; military, Gr.Nyss.*ep.* 19(M.46.1077A); κ. ἐξκουβιτώρων *Chron.Pasch.*p.331(857B); κόμητες σχολῶν Thphn.*chron.*p.118(333C); κ. Φοιδεράτων *ib.*p.134(368C); εὗρε βάνδον τῶν Περσῶν, καὶ φονεύσας αὐτοῦ τὸν κ. *ib.*p.265(657C) etc.

*__κομητατήσιος__, (Lat. *comitatensis*) *of the court* ὁ τῶν κ. λαργιτιόνων κόμης Petr.II Al.*encycl.*ap.Thdt.*h.e.*4.22.10(M.33.1280C).

*__κομητᾶτον__, v. *κομιτᾶτον.

*__κομητιανός__ (*__κομιτιανός__), *of a* κόμης: οἱ ἐκ τῆς κ. τάξεως πράκτορες Thdt.*ep.*42(4.1101); κομιτιανός, CChalc.*act.*11(*ACO* 2.1.3 p.49. 19; κομητ- H.2.553B).

*__κομητικός__, = foreg., CChalc.*act.*10(H.2.508B; κομιτιανὴν *ACO* 2. 1.3 p.17.4).

*__κομῆτις__, *covered with hair*, Synes.*calv.*8(M.66.1181C).

*__κομήτισσα__, ἡ, *wife of a* κόμης, Nil.*epp.*2.213 tit.(M.79.312B); id. 2.218 tit.(313B).

__κομίατος__, ὁ, (Lat. *commeatus*) *leave of absence*; met., of an extension of life on earth to a sick person αἴτησαί μοι κ. Or.*hom.17.6 in Jer.*(p.150.11; ἀνοχήν M.13.461D); Pall.*h.Laus.*38(p.120.3; M.34. 1194A).

__κομίζ-ω__, **1.** *bring*, met. δειλίας σοφίσματα εἰς μέσον κ. Clem.*str.*4.4 (p.256.9; M.8.1229B); *ib.*7.11(p.43.31; M.9.485A); **2.** med., *obtain, acquire*; met. τὴν περὶ αὐτοῦ [sc. τοῦ θεοῦ] κομίσασθαι γνῶσιν *ib.* 7.10(p.40.29; 477C); τῷ ἀγαπᾶν τὸν πατέρα εἰς οἰκείαν ἰσχὺν καὶ δύναμιν ἀφθαρσίαν ~ομένους id.*q.d.s.*27(p.178.15; M.9.633B); of reward or punishment μισθὸν κ. *2Clem.*11.5; Ign.*Polyc.*6.2; οὐ ~όμενοι τὰ ἐπίχειρα τῶν ἁμαρτημάτων Clem.*ecl.*11(p.139.21; M.9. 704A); **3.** *admit, allow* αὐλητρίδας ἐκόμιζε Synes.*Dion* 1(M.66. 1113A; ἐνόμιζεν p.234.17); **4.** *offer, provide, devise* ἀπολογίαν...κ. Or. *Jo.*10.27(17; p.200.7; M.14.356B); ἀπόδειξιν...κ. Eus.*p.e.*4.3(137A; M. 21.241A); **5.** *produce* ῥάβδος ἡ Ἀαρὼν βλαστὸν κομίσασα ἀρχιερέα αὐτὸν ἀπέδειξε Just.*dial.*86.4(M.6.681B); **6.** pass., *be sent*, of Christ ἐπ' ἀγαθὸν αὐτῷ [sc. τῷ Χριστῷ] ~ομένῳ Eus.*d.e.*10.8(p.483.34; M.22. 777B); **7.** f.l. prob. for κοσμείσθωσαν, Thdt.*1Tim.*3:8(3.656).

*__κομιτᾶτον__, τό, (Lat. *comitatus*) *court, retinue*, esp. imperial, Ath.*ep.encycl.*2(p.170.28; M.25.225B); Epiph.*haer.*30.11(p.347.2; κομητᾶτον M.41.424C); Pall.*v.Chrys.*8(p.49.14; M.47.29); κομετᾶτος Jo.Mal.*chron.*13 p.319(M.97.477B).

*__κομιτιανός__, v. *κομητιανός, *κομητικός.

*__κομίτισσα__, ἡ, *wife of a* κόμης, Thdr.Stud.*epp.*2.157(M.99. 1493A).

__κόμμα__, τό, *piece cut off*; hence **1.** *sect* τὸ κ. τὸ Ἰουδαϊκόν Bas.*hom.* 23.4(2.187D; M.31.596B); **2.** *section*; of Bible, Chrys.*hom.1.3 in Mt.* (7.8A); **3.** παρὰ κόμμα *immoderately*, Leont.N.*v.Sym.*7(M.93.1732D).

*__κομμαμοφόριον__, τό, ? *cloak* ἔλαβον κ. καὶ ἐσκέπασα τοὺς ὤμους αὐτοῦ Ephr.3.360D.

[*]__κομματικός__, = κομμωτικός, *for embellishment* ἑταίρας εἰδεχθοῦς κομματικῷ κόσμῳ τὸ φυσικὸν ἐπικαλυπτούσης εἶδος ‡Nil.*narr.*6(M.79. 673A).

__κομμάτιον__, τό, *fragment* κομμάτια κομμάτια *in little pieces*, *Didasc.Jac.*5.17(p.88.6).

*__κομμενταρία__, ἡ, *office of a* κομενταρήσιος, *Mir.Geo.*5(p.56 not.).

*__κομ(μ)ερκιάριος__, ὁ, (Lat. *commerciarius*) *tax-collector*, Jo.Mal. *chron.*16 p.396(M.97.588A); Jo.Mosch.*prat.*186 (κομερκιάριος M.87. 3061D); *Chron.Pasch.*p.394(M.92.1009C).

*__κομ(μ)έρκιον__ (*__κωμέρκιον__) τό, (Lat. *commercium*), *tax, tribute*, Jo.Mosch.*prat.*186 (κομέρκιον M.87.3064A); Thphn.*chron.*p.396 (κωμέρκιον M.108.945A); *ib.*p.401 (κωμέρκιον 956C).

*__κόμμιδας__, ? τό, *gum*, Leont.H.*Nest.*2.13(M.86.1561B).

*__κομμονιτώριον__, τό, (Lat. *commonitorium*) *letter of instruction*, *Cod.Afr.*93; CChalc.*act.*1(*ACO* 2.1.1 p.96.32; H.2.105D); Evagr.*h.e.* 2.18(p.71.23; κομμονητόριον M.86.2553C).

*__κομμουλᾶτον__, τό, (Lat. *cumulatus*) *overplus* γαβὶς λέγεται τὸ ὑπερέχον τοῦ χείλους τοῦ μεδίμνου, ὃ καλεῖται κ. Or.*enarr.in Job* 28:18 (M.17.89D).

*__κομμωτίζομαι__, *beautify oneself*, Synes.*calv.*20(p.225.19; M.66. 1200D).

__κομμώτρια__, ἡ, *beautifier, embellisher*, met. τῆς...εὐμορφίας ἡ νηστεία κομμώτρια Ast.Am.*hom.*14(M.40.385A).

*__κομπαγωγία__, ἡ, *boasting*, Isid.Pel.*epp.*1.374(M.78.393D).

__κομπάζ-ω__, **1.** *boast, brag*; c. acc., *utter boastfully*, Eus.*Hierocl.*2 (512D; M.22.800B); Isid.Pel.*epp.*1.96(M.78.248C); ‡Nil.*perist.*9.9(M. 79.881C); **2.** c. dat., *make a great show with* οἱ Αἰγυπτίων ναοί... κάλλει λίθων ~οντες Pall.*v.Chrys.*4(p.27.21; M.47.18).

__κομπαστικός__, *braggart* λόγῳ κ. Epiph.*haer.*76.37(p.389.26; M.42. 596B).

__κομπαστικῶς__, *boastfully*, Nil.*epp.*2.245(M.79.328A).

*__κομπεία__ (*__κομπία__), ἡ, *boasting* κομπίας Eus.*p.e.*15.1(M.21.1293B; conj. κομψείας 788D); Epiph.*haer.*76.15(p.361.6; κομπία M.42.545D).

__κομπέω__, **1.** *ring* a coin, Pall.*v.Chrys.*4(p.26.14; M.47.17); ‡Caes. Naz.*dial.*140(M.38.1060); **2.** pass., *be full of pride*, ‡Pion.*v.Polyc.*9.

__κομπηρός__, *pretentious, boastful*, Cyr.*Ps.*16:1(M.69.813C).

*__κομπία__, ἡ, v. *κομπεία.

*__κομπλατίων__, ἡ, (Lat. *completio*) *legal ratification*, Jo.Mosch. *prat.*193(M.87.3073B).

*__κομπολογέω__, *debate grandiloquently*, Just.*dial.*113.2(M.6.736C).

__κομπολογία__, ἡ, *grandiloquence*, Hyper.*mon.*122(M.79.1485A); Men.*exc.Rom.*3(p.177.3; M.113.860D).

*__κομπολόγος__, *using empty* or *boastful words*, v. κομπολόγως.

*__κομπολόγως__, *with empty* or *boastful words*, Hipp.*haer.*10.31 (p.288.4; κομπολόγῳ M.16.3446C).

*__κομποποιέω__, *boast, brag*, Epiph.*haer.*66.54(p.91.6; M.42.109D); Call.*v.Hyp.*(p.53).

*__κομπορ(ρ)ήμων__, ὁ, *braggart*, *Mir.Artem.*24(p.34.19); κομπορήμων Geo.Pis.*hex.*1253(M.92.1531A).

*__κομπορύαξ__, ὁ, *braggart*, Nil.*epp.*2.215(M.79.312D).

__κόμπος__, ὁ, **1.** *boasting*, hence *pomp, ostentation* Ἰησοῦς οὐκ ἦλθεν ἐν κ. ἀλαζονείας οὐδὲ ὑπερηφανίας *1Clem.*16.2; ref. a well dressed person in church μετὰ κόμπου καθίσει Chrys.*hom.3.3 in 2Thess.*(11. 527A); **2.** *empty statement*, of threats of punishment after death μή τις εἴπῃ...ὅτι κ. καὶ φόβητρά ἐστι τὰ λεγόμενα Just.*2apol.*9.1(M.6. 460A); **3.** *magnificence, flamboyance* ποίῳ κ. λόγου Παῦλος ἔλεγε Chrys.*hom.3.4 in 2Thess.*(11.528B).

__κομπός__, *pompous, ostentatious*; of language, *V.Pelag.Ant.*6(p.7. 12); Marc.Diac.*v.Porph.*3; *ib.*74.

*__κομποστολ-έω__, *array smartly*, met. ἁβροῖς ἀναλώμασι ~οῦντες ἀπολογίας Nil.*exerc.*55(M.79.788A).

*__κομπωδεία__, ἡ, *boastfulness*, Nest.*hom.tent.*2(p.347; M.61.685).

*__κομπῳδία__, ἡ, *boastful language*, Nil.*epp.*2.49(M.79.220C).

*__κομφέκτωρ__, ὁ, (Lat. *confector*) *one appointed to give the death-stroke* to a victim in the amphitheatre, *M.Polyc.*16.1.

__κομψία__, ἡ, *boastfulness*, Didym.*Trin.*2.18(M.39.385C; conj. κομψεία).

*__κομψοέπεια__, ἡ, *fine language*, Cyr.*Juln.*3(6².76A); ‡Meth.*Sym.et Ann.*10(M.18.373B).

*__κομψοεπής__, *elegantly phrased* or *expressed*, Cyr.*Nah.*28(3.506A).

*__κομψολογέω__, *speak finely* or *elegantly*, Dam.*troph.*suppl.(p.284.9).

*__κομψολογία__, ἡ, *fine speaking*, Ath.*Ar.*3.59(M.26.448A); Cyr. *Juln.*3(6².76A); Men.*exc.Rom.*3(p.174.10; M.113.856C).

*__κομψοφανής__, *specious*, Isid.Pel.*epp.*5.149(M.78.1413B).

*__κονδάπτω__, *stumble*, Jo.Mal.*chron.*12 p.309(M.97.465B).

*__κονδαρής__, *short of stature*; of persons, opp. πλήρης, *V.Mac.*A (p.149).

*__κονδισάμος__, ὁ, ? *tool-grinder*, *MAMA* 3.724.

*__κονδῖτος__, **1.** *spiced, seasoned*, ‡Ath.*dial.Trin.*1.27(M.28.1157B); *Apophth.Patr.*(M.65.376C); **2.** neut. as subst., *condiment*, Mac.Aeg. *hom.*16.9(M.34.620C).

*__κονδοειδής__, *short of stature*, Jo.Mal.*chron.*5 p.100(M.97.188C).

*__κονδοήλικος__, *short of stature*, *A.Barth.*2(p.131.21).

*__κονδόθριξ__, *short-haired*, Jo.Mal.*chron.*4 p.88(M.97.172C); *ib.*10 p.232(357B).

*__κονδοκούρευτος__, *with cropped head*, †Anast.S.*relat.*7(*OC* 2 p.64. 21) = Dan.Raith.*v.Jo.Clim.*(M.88.608C).

__κονδός__, ὁ, *short garment* ἀμανίκωτον κ. Thphn.*chron.*p.372 (κοντός M.108.389B).

*__κονδοτζάγγιον__, τό, *short-legged boot*; worn by monks, *Const. Stud.*38(M.99.1720B).

*__κονδυλέω__, *stumble* ἐκονδύλησεν ὁ ἵππος *Chron.Pasch.*p.270(M.92. 665A) or perh. for ἐκονδύλισεν (κονδυλίζω).

__κονδυλισμός__, ὁ, *striking with the fist*; *maltreatment*, Chrys.*poenit.* 4.3(2.305E).

__κόνδυλος__, ὁ, *fist*; *blow with the fist*, met. γυνὴ πονηρὰ ἁμαρτιῶν ἐστι κ. Chrys.*exp.Ps.*3:1(5.3B).

*__κονδωμῆνος__, ὁ, (Lat. *condominus*) *householder*, *MAMA* 3.486.

*__κονδῶμος__, ὁ, (Lat. *condomus*) *household*, *MAMA* 3.486.

__κονιάω__, **1.** *whitewash* οἰκήματι...ἄρτι κεκονιαμένῳ Philost.*h.e.*8.8 (M.65.561B); met., of painting face with cosmetics, Chrys.*hom.30.5 in Mt.*(7.354D); *ib.*(355B); **2.** *reduce to dust*, Steph.Diac.*v.Steph.*(M. 100.1137C); **3.** med., *be sprinkled with dust* (like wrestlers), hence met., *prepare to wrestle* or *struggle*; of philosophers, Eus.*p.e.*14.2 (718B; κονίομαι M.21.1184C).

*__κονιορτάω__, *dust*, Thdr.Stud.*poen.*1.48(M.99.1740A).

κονιορτός, ὁ, *dust raised* or *stirred up, cloud of dust*; met., Tat. *orat.*30(p.30.22; M.6.868B); πολλοὶ καὶ μετὰ τὸ λουτρὸν [i.e. baptism] κονιορτοῦ τῶν ἁμαρτημάτων πληροῦνται Or.*Jo.*32.2(p.427.14; M.14. 744A); πολὺν ἤγειρεν αὐτῷ κ. λογισμῶν ἐν τῇ διανοίᾳ Ath.*v.Anton.*5 (M.26.848A).

κονιορτ-όω, pass., *turn to dust* Μωϋσῆς...ἐν ἀγνώστῳ τάφῳ ~ωθείς Tim.Ant.*cruc.*(M.86.260A).

κονιορτώδης, *blown about like dust, unstable*, Gr.Nyss.*Eun.*4(2 p.79.27; M.45.653C); id.*hom.opif.*27.6(M.44.228C).

κονίπους, ὁ, 1. *one who has dusty feet*, Firm.*ep.*44(M.77.1512C); **2.** a kind of sandal, Clem.*paed.*2.11(p.227.10; M.8.540A).

κόνις, ἡ, *dust* σε κόνιν ἄψυχον ὄντα θεοειδεῖ κάλλει κατακοσμήσας [sc. ὁ θεός] Gr.Nyss.*Eun.*11(2 p.253.1; M.45.860B); ἡ πίστις...τῆς κ. τῶν σωμάτων τὴν ἀθανασίαν παρασκευάζει φαντάζεσθαι Thdt.*Heb.* 11:1(3.613); id.*Rom.*12:2(3.130); of a saint; used for healing, Niceph.Ur.*v.Sym.*225(M.86.3193B); *ib.*236(3204A).

***κονρήκτωρ, ὁ,** (Lat. *corrector*) *governor*, *M.Eupl.*1; κονρήκτορος Σικελίας Const.ap.Eus.*h.e.*10.5.23(κορρήκτορος M.20.889C); κορρίκτωρ Isid.Pel.*epp.*1.116 tit.(M.78.260C); κορρήκτωρ *ib.*2.25(473B).

***κονσιλάριος, ὁ,** (Lat. *consiliarius*) *councillor*, Anast.Ap.*a.Max.* 2.32(M.90.169B).

***κονσιστοριανός,** *belonging to the consistory*, Proc.G.*ep.*24(M.87. 2740B).

***κονσιστόριον (*κονσιστώριον), τό,** (Lat. *consistorium*) *consistory* τοῦ θείου κ. CChalc.*act.*1(*ACO* 2.1.1 p.67.34; -ωρίου H.2.72A,D); *ib.*14 (*ACO* 2.1.3 p.64.39; H.2.572D) cit. s. βοηθός; Proc.G.*ep.*24(M.87. 2740B); τοῦ κωνστιτουρίου Marc.Diac.*v.Porph.*51, vv.ll. κωνστητουρίου, κωνσισταρίου; *meeting-place of the consistory*, -ώριον, Cyr.S. *v.Sab.*51(p.142.15, vv.ll. -στόριον, κοσσιστόριον).

***κονσουλάριος, ὁ,** (Lat. *consularis*) *provincial governor*, Chrys. *ep.*61 tit.(3.626E); *ib.*139 tit.(682A); Pulch.*ep.Strat.*tit.(p.29.5; H.2. 48A).

***κονσουλτατίων, ὁ,** (Lat. *consultatio*) *consultation*, Ath.Scholast. *coll.*6.9(p.91).

κοντάκιον, τό, *contakion*; **1.** name of volume containing *Lit.Bas.*, *Lit.Chrys.*, and *Lit.Praesanct.*, read by priest after his ordination ἵσταται μετὰ τῶν πρεσβυτέρων ἀναγινώσκων τὸ κ. *Euchol.*(p.243); **2.** name of a type of liturgical hymn in honour of a saint or holyday, Rom.Mel. tit.(*SBBAW* 1898² p.114; *SBBAW* 1899² p.658); ‡Serg.*acath.*tit.(p.140; M.92.1335A); *Max.offic.*2 tit.(M.90.216C); Andr.Cr.*can.mag.*6(M.97.1361A).

[*]**κόνταξ, ὁ,** = κόνδαξ, gambling game played with an unpointed dart, Phot.*nomoc.*13.29(M.104.964A).

***κονταρέα, ἡ,** *spear-wound*, Thphn.*chron.*p.266(M.108.660B).

***κοντεύω,** *spear, put on a spear* or *pole* τὴν κεφαλὴν Ὁλοφέρνου κοντευθεῖσαν Jo.Mal.*chron.*6 p.160(M.97.261C); *ib.*10 p.245(376A).

***κοντοπνευστί,** *with short breaths*, Steph.Diac.*v.Steph.*(M.100. 1104B).

***κοντούμαξ, ὁ,** (Lat. *contumax*) *one who repeatedly defies a judicial summons*, Ath.Scholast.*coll.*7.4(p.90).

[*]**κονωπίων, ὁ,** = κωνώπιον, *couch with mosquito-curtains*, Jo. Mosch.*prat.*161(M.87.3028D).

***κόξα, ἡ,** (Lat. *coxa*) *hip-bone*, *Mir.Artem.*19(p.24.4).

κοπάδι(ο)ν, τό, *piece of food*, Pall.*h.Laus.*103(M.34.1210B; κόπεον p.132.12); *Apophth.Patr.*(M.65.200A).

κοπανίζω, 1. *break up* clods of earth, Dor.*doct.*12.4(M.88.1756A); **2.** *treat, prepare* hemp used for spinning, Ephr.2.329B.

***κοπενδάριον, τό,** *staff, walking-stick*, Dor.*doct.*1.14(M.88.1636B).

***κόπεον, τό,** v. κοπάδιον.

κοπή, ἡ, 1. *curtailing, denying* ὀδεύων...τὴν ὁδὸν τῆς κ. τοῦ θελήματος Dor.*doct.*1.14(M.88.1636B); **2.** *cutting down, slaughter*, Thphn.*chron.*p.400(M.108.953A); **3.** *hilt* of a sword, *Asen.*23(p.74. 16).

κοπιάτης, ὁ, 1. *industrious person*; of those born under Taurus, Libra, and Sagittarius, Hipp.*haer.*4.16(p.50.13; M.16.3083C); *ib.*4.21, 23(p.52.8,23; 3087A,B); **2.** *undertaker, grave-digger*; as minor church official, Epiph.*exp.fid.*21.11(p.522.24; M.42.825A).

κοπιάω, *strive, toil*; *make haste* κοπίασον εἰς τὴν...πόλιν †Anast.S. *relat.*54(*OC* 3 p.81.2).

***κοπιδερμία, ἡ,** *lacerating of the skin*, as sign of slavery μὴ ποιεῖν τινα ἔγγραφον κοπιδερμίας Jo.Mal.*chron.*16 p.401(M.97.593B).

κοπίδερμος, ὁ, *one who lacerates the skin*, as sign of slavery μήτε ...αὐτὸ τὸ ὄνομα τοῦ κ. ὀνομάζεσθαι Jo.Mal.*chron.*16 p.401(M.97. 593B).

***κοπολογία, ἡ,** for κομπολογία, *fine speech* σοφία μοναχοῦ μὴ ἐν κ. γινέσθω ἀλλ' ἐν εὐσταθίᾳ καὶ πρᾳότητι Ephr.2.362A.

κοπόω, 1. *weary, harass* ἐκόπωσεν ὑμᾶς...ὁ διάβολος Bas.Sel.*or.* 29.1(M.85.325C); **2.** med., *work hard*, Bas.*ascet.*1.5(2.322E; M.31. 880B).

***κοπριοσύλλεκτος,** *picked from a rubbish heap*, Cosm.Mel.*schol.* proem.(M.38.344).

κοπροθέσιον, τό, *cess-pit, midden*, Thphn.*chron.*p.370(M.108. 888A).

***κοπρομόχθος,** *toiling in dung*; of beetles, Geo.Pis.*hex.*1079(M.92. 1516A).

κόπρον, τό, *filth*; plur., Herm.*sim.*9.10.3.

***κοπροπηλόφυρτος,** *covered with dung and mud*, Jo.VI H.*v.Jo.D.* 30(M.94.472A).

κοπροποιός, *producing excrement*, Gr.Nyss.*hom.6 in Eccl.*(M.44. 709B).

***κοπρόρυκτος,** *burrowing in dung*, Agath.*v.Gr.Ill.*109.

***κοπρώνης, ὁ,** *dung-dealer, scavenger*, Chrys.*hom.38.6 in 1Cor.* (10.360B); id.*hom.10.2 in Eph.*(11.77E).

***κόπται, οἱ,** *those who sunder* or *divide*, name given to Mohammedans as dividers of Trin., Jo.D.*haer.*101(M.94.768D).

κοπτικός, *cleaving asunder*, Synes.*hymn.*3.368(p.16; M.66.1599).

κόπτ-ω, 1. *smite*; met., *attack viciously, harm*, Eus.*e.th.*2.25(p.136. 18; M.24.965C); δι' ὅλης τῆς...προφητείας...~όμενα τὰ...ξόανα *ib.*2.22 (p.132.24; 960B); ἑαυτοὺς ~ουσι οἱ Ἀρειανοί Ath.*hom.in Mt.11:27* (M.25.217B); Chrys.*hom.11.6 in Eph.*(11.89C); τὴν ψυχὴν ~ειν id. *hom.2.4 in 2Thess.*(11.521D); **2.** *cut off*, met. ὁδὸν κ. *obstruct the road*, Jo.Mal.*chron.*5 p.98(M.97.185B); from Church, *excommunicate*; pass., †Jo.Jej.*poenit.*(M.88.1904C); **3.** *cut one's way forward, make progress* κόψον ἐκ πάντων ἐν τῇ ἀγάπῃ Philox.*ep.*24(p.174); **4.** med. ~εσθαί τινα *mourn for one*, Ath.*gent.*10(M.25.24A); Philost.*h.e.*9.17 (M.65.581C); **5.** pass., *be worried* or *worn out* ὑπὲρ τούτων...~ονται Chrys.*hom.85.4 in Mt.*(7.429D); id.*hom.15.2 in 1Tim.*(11.636E); by effort μὴ εἰκῇ ~ώμεθα *let us not strive in vain*, id.*hom.4.2 in Phil.* (11.214C).

κόπωσις, ἡ, *toiling*, hence *weariness*, ‡Ath. *Apoll.*1.1(M.26.1093A); Max.*ambig.*(M.91.1370C,D); *ib.*(1372A).

***κορακιστί,** *like the ravens, nonsensically* κ. φθέγγεσθε Chrys.*hom.* *4.4 in Ac.*(9.39D).

***κορακόφωνος,** *croaking like a raven*, Tat.*orat.*15(p.16.10; M.6. 837A).

κόραξ, ὁ, an instrument of torture κ. σιδηροῦς *A.Phil.*125(p.55. 1); *ib.*140(p.173.10).

***κορασηνός,** (prob. Arabic قرشي), *belonging to the tribe Koreish*, Thphn.*chron.*p.278(M.108.688C).

***κόρδα, ἡ,** (χορδή; Lat. *chorda*) *rope*, Thphn.*chron.*p.312(M.108. 757A).

[*]**κορείη, ἡ,** = κορεία, *maidenhood*, Gr.Naz.*carm.*1.2.2.711(M.37. 573A); ref. BMV, Nonn.*par.Jo.*2:2(M.43.760C); ‡Gr.Naz.*Chr.pat.* 2398(M.38.324A).

κόρη, ἡ, *maiden*; of BMV, *Pers.*(p.9.2); Jo.Eub.*concept.BMV* 18 (M.96.1489B); in invocation, Jo.Mon.*hymn.Petr.*(M.96.1389A); id. *hymn.Blas.*(M.96.1408B).

***κοριάλιος,** v. *κουριάλιος.

κορικός, *girlish, of a girl*, Nil.*epp.*2.68(M.79.232A); id.*exerc.*47(M. 79.777A); Bas.Sel.*v.Thecl.*1(M.85.517C).

κορμίον, τό, *small log*, *M.Areth.*(pp.50,51).

κορμός, ὁ, *block*; of an anvil, *Mir.Artem.*26(p.38.1).

κορνικουλάριος, ὁ, (Lat. *cornicularius*) *secretary, assistant*; to a civil official, *M.Tar.*3(p.456); *ib.*6(p.461).

***κορνοῦτος,** (Lat. *cornutus*) *horned*, title of a legion κόμης τῶν λεγομένων κ. Philost.*h.e.*7.7(M.65.544C); τάγματος κορνούτων *Chron. Pasch.*p.297(M.92.744C).

κοροκόσμιον, τό, *girl's ornament*, Tat.*orat.*8(p.9.7; M.6.824B); Clem.*prot.*4(p.45.22; M.8.157A); id.*paed.*2.12(p.230.2; M.8.544B).

κοροπλαθικός, *modelling*; ἡ κ. [sc. τέχνη], *art of modelling*, Athenag.*leg.*17.2 (κοροπλαστική M.6.924A).

***κορρεκτόριος,** *pertaining to a* corrector (*governor*) ἀρχήν, μήτε ὑπατικήν μήτε ἡγεμονικήν, ἃς δὴ κονσουλαρίας καὶ κ. καλοῦσιν Justn. *nov.*8.1(p.67.10).

***κορρήκτωρ (*κορρίκτωρ), ὁ,** v. *κονρήκτωρ.

κόρση, ἡ, *top of an arch*, Paul.Sil.*Soph.*278(M.86.2130B); *ib.*560 (2141B).

***κορτάλινος, ὁ,** (Lat. *cohortalinus*) *member of the imperial guards*, Marcian.Imp.*const.Eut.*(p.123.30; H.2.677D).

§**κόρτη, ἡ,** (Lat. *cohors*) *cohort*, Thdr.Stud.*epp.*2.38(M.99.1232A); Thphn.*chron.*p.390 (κόρτις M.108.929B); *ib.*p.395(940C).

***κορτίνη, ἡ,** *curtain*, Cyr.S.*v.Sab*.80(p.186.5); Cosm.Ind.*top*.5 (M.88.204A).

κορυβαντιάω, *be filled with Corybantic frenzy, be possessed*, Thdt. *eran*.2(4.97); hence *be filled with religious enthusiasm*, Pall.*v.Chrys*. 20(p.138.2; M.47.77).

κορυφαῖος, 1. *chief*, freq. of S. Peter τῆς ἐκκλησίας ὁ κ. κῆρυξ Cyr.H.*catech*.11.3; τῷ κ. Πέτρῳ Mac.Aeg.*pat*.3(M.34.868C); ὁ κ. τῶν μαθητῶν Chrys.*hom.1.1 in Rom*.(9.429E); ὁ κ. τῶν ἀποστόλων ‡Tit. Bost.*palm*.4(M.18.1269C); superl. ὁ κ. τῶν ἀποστόλων Epiph.*anc*. 9.4(p.16.17; M.43.32C); of SS. Peter and Paul τοὺς ἁγίους καὶ κ. ἀποστόλους *A.(Pass.)Petr.et Paul*.63(p.172.10); of SS. Peter, James, and John κ. τῶν μαθητῶν Chrys.*comm.in Gal*.1:1(10.659B); cf.Thdt. *Gal*.1:10(3.363); of the twelve apostles τῶν πνευματικῶν κορυφαίους καὶ διδασκάλους id.*eran*.2(4.76); **2.** neut. as subst., *the most important point* or *matter*, Clem.*paed*.1.13(p.151.1; M.8.372B); Mac.Mgn. *apocr*.2.21(p.42.5); Const.ap.Gel.Cyz.*h.e*.2.7.1(M.85.1232C); plur., *chief positions* τὰ κ. τῆς...γερουσίας Evagr.*h.e*.2.18(p.67.25; M.86. 2548B); **3.** masc. as subst., *bishop*, Bas.*ep*.94(3.188B; M.32.488B).

***κορυφαιοτάτης, ἡ,** *excellency, supremacy*; as title of address to pope, Thdr.Stud.*epp*.1.33(M.99.1020C).

κορυφή, ἡ, *head, summit*; hence **1.** *source* of a river, Cosm.Ind. *top*.2(M.88.100D); met., *original principle* δύο...ἀρχαὶ...μιᾶς ἐξημμέναι κ. Dion.Ar.*d.n*.4.28(M.3.729A); **2.** *highness*, as title of emperor τῇ...εὐαγεστάτῃ ὑμῶν κ. Soz.*h.e*.proem.21(M.67.852B); τὴν καλλίνικον κ. Thdt.*ep*.119(3.1202); τῇ θείᾳ κ. CChalc.*act*.4(*ACO* 2.1.2 p.92.30; H.2.384D).

***κορυφιακός,** *exalted, supreme*; of Roman see, Thdr.Stud.*epp*. 2.63(M.99.1281A).

κορυφ-όω, 1. act., *bring to a head*; met., *pile up* ἐκορύφωσε τὴν ἑαυτοῦ ἁμαρτίαν ‡Bas.*Lac*.3(2.590B; M.31.1445A); **2.** pass.; **a.** *be increased* or *enlarged*, Trin. ταῦτα τρία ὄντα...οὐ ~ούμενα, οὐ συναγόμενα ‡Caes.Naz.*dial*.3(M.38.861); with pride, Chrys.*Eutrop*.2.6(3. 391D); τὴν πόαις...ἀρίσταις ~ουμένην πιότητα Sophr.H.*ep.syn*.(M.87. 3197C); τῇ ἀγάπῃ κορυφωθέντες *filled with love*, Ephr.1.274C; **b.** *rise up*; in attack, Gr.Nyss.*hom.5 in Cant*.(M.44.864A); in exaltation, *soar* ~ούμεθα πρὸς τὰ ὕψη ‡Ath.*v.Syncl*.44(M.28.1513B); with evil ambition, Nil.*epp*.3.99(M.79.432B).

κορύφωσις, ἡ, *swelling*; met., *exaltation* in pride κ. τῆς ψυχῆς ‡Caes.Naz.*dial*.121(M.38.1009).

κορωνίς, ἡ, *completion*; met., *height, extremity, crown*, Isid.Pel. *epp*.2.201(M.78.645B); ἡ κ. τῆς εὐλογίας Chrys.*hom.53.3 in Gen*.(4. 518C); τὴν κ. τῆς ἀνδρίας Socr.*h.e*.3.15.7(M.67.417C); ἡ κ. τῆς τοῦ θεοῦ λόγου σαρκώσεως ἐπιτίθεται Jo.D.*hom*.4.2(M.96.604A).

κοσκινίζω, *sift*; met., Thdr.Stud.*epp*.2.37(M.99.1228D).

κοσμαγοί, οἱ, *guides of the universe*, supernatural beings in 'Chaldean' belief, Synes.*hymn*.3.271(M.66.1597).

***κοσμαγωγός,** *supporting the world* τὸ κ. ... κέντριον Geo.Pis. *hex*.151(M.92.1444A); met., of CP τῇ κ. ... ὁλκάδι id.*bell.Avar*.211 (M.92.1277A).

κοσμ-έω, 1. *order, set in order* τὰ οὐράνια στοιχεῖα...~ήσας [sc. God] Just.*2apol*.5.2(M.6.452B); τὴν ἀρχὴν δι' αὐτοῦ [sc. τοῦ Χριστοῦ] πάντα ἔκτισε καὶ ἐκόσμησε *ib*.6.3(453A); τῷ λέγειν ἡμᾶς, ὑπὸ θεοῦ πάντα κεκοσμῆσθαι...Πλατῶνος δόξομεν λέγειν δόγμα id.*1apol*.20. 4(M.6.357C); τὸ πᾶν ἐκόσμησεν ἐμμελῶς Clem.*prot*.1(p.5.33; M.8. 57C); τοῦ πάντα ~ήσαντος λόγου Or.*Cels*.4.84(p.355.7; M.11.1157C); met. ~οῦντα καὶ ῥυθμίζοντα τὴν ψυχήν Clem.*q.d.s*.21.7(p.174.9; M.9. 628A); κατὰ τοὺς νόμους ἡ ψυχὴ κεκοσμημένη Ath.*gent*.47(M.25. 96B); of God's power ~οῦσα τὴν ἀταξίαν καὶ ἀκοσμίαν Dion.Ar.*d.n*. 8.9(M.3.897B); by baptism τὸ ἄκοσμον ~εῖται id.*e.h*.2.3.8(M.3. 404C); Gnost. ὅτε...ἐφωτίσθη ὁ ἄνθρωπος, τότε εἰς τὸν κόσμον ἦλθεν, τουτέστιν ἑαυτὸν ἐκόσμησεν Clem.*exc.Thdot*.41(p.119.28; M.9.677D); **2.** *adorn, embellish* τὸν ἄνδρα καθάπερ τοὺς λέοντας γενείοις ~ήσας [sc. God] id.*paed*.3.3(p.247.6; M.8.580C); τὸ φαινόμενον στερέωμα ἄστροις ἐκόσμησεν *Hom.Clem*.3.33; met. ἐν ἔργοις ἀγαθοῖς...ἐκοσμήθησαν οἱ δίκαιοι *1Clem*.33.7; κεκοσμημένοι ἐν ταῖς ἐντολαῖς Ἰησοῦ Ign. *Eph*.9.2; ἀνθρώπου...νοῦς...ἁγίῳ πνεύματι κεκοσμημένος Just.*dial*.4.1 (M.6.484A); κεκοσμημένη ψυχὴ ἁγίῳ πνεύματι Clem.*paed*.3.11(p.272. 4; 640C); ἁγίῳ ~εῖσθαι λόγῳ, τῷ λόγῳ τοῦ θεοῦ *ib*.2.12(p.228.5; 540C); ὁ κεκοσμημένος τῷ λόγῳ τοῦ θεοῦ καὶ τοῖς ἔργοις αὐτοῦ Or.*Cels*.8.10 (p.228.12; M.11.1532B); ἐν ταύτῃ τῇ ἀρετῇ ~ησόν σου τὸ σῶμα Ath. *virg*.6(p.40.5; M.28.257C); ~εῖσθαι τῇ φιλίᾳ Chrys.*hom.1.1 in 2Tim*. (11.659E); τοῖς θεοειδέσιν ἐκόσμησε τὸ ἀνείδεον κάλλεσι Dion.Ar.*e.h*. 3.3.11(M.3.441B); τῶν τῆς ψυχῆς ἐκοσμεῖτο καλῶν *V.Const*.36(p.566. 23).

κοσμητέον, *one must set in order, compose* τὴν διάνοιαν κ. Clem. *paed*.3.3(p.248.25; M.8.584B).

κοσμητής ([*]κοσμίτης), ὁ, 1. *sweeper, cleaner*; in a monastery κοσμίτης *Apophth.Patr*.(M.65.381A,B); Thdr.Stud.*poen*.1.98 tit.(M. 99.1745C); **2.** *entablature*, ‡Bas.*h.myst*.7(p.259.20); ‡Sophr.H.*liturg*.4 (M.87.3984D).

κοσμητικός, *skilled in ordering*, of H. Ghost κ. τῶν ὄντων τὸ πνεῦμα Diod.*Gen*.1:26(M.33.1563D).

κοσμήτρια, ἡ, *woman who adorns, tire-woman*, Epiph.*haer*.76.43 (p.397.32; M.42.609B).

κόσμητρον, τό, *broom*, Meth.*symp*.9.4(p.118.11; M.18.185A).

κοσμήτωρ, ὁ, ἡ, 1. = κοσμητής, *sweeper, cleaner*; in a monastery, Pall.*h.Laus*.18(p.55.21; M.34.1060B); **2.** fem., perh. f.l. for ⟨κοσμομήτωρ⟩ *world-mother*; of Eve, ‡Jo.D.*hom*.5(M.96.649B).

κοσμίδιον, τό, *adornment*, Leont.N.*v.Jo.Eleem*.7(p.14.5).

***κοσμίζω,** *adorn*, Nil.*epp*.4.1(M.79.544B).

κοσμικός, 1. *belonging to the world as a whole, universal* αἶσχος κ. Clem.*prot*.2(p.25.22; M.8.112A); τὴν ἐσομένην διὰ Χριστοῦ πάντων κ. ἀνάστασιν ‡Just.*qu.et resp*.45(M.6.1292A); of the sanctuary, ref. Heb.9:1 κ. λέγει, ἐπειδὴ πᾶσιν ἠφίετο ἐπιβαίνειν...ἐπεὶ οὖν καὶ Ἕλλησι βατὸν ἦν κ. αὐτὸ καλεῖ Chrys.*hom.15.1 in Heb*.(12.149B); **2.** *belonging to the world of sense*; **a.** ref. Inc. οὐκ ὢν κ. ὡς κ. εἰς ἀνθρώπους ἦλθεν Clem.*str*.6.15(p.495.26; M.9.349B); **b.** of man πάντα τὸν κ. *anyone in the world, everybody*, *ib*.2.18(p.160.8; M.8.1028B); **c.** *physical, material* κ. βασάνων *M.Polyc*.2.3; ἀναστροφῆς οὔσης κ. Or.*Jo*.13.31(30; p.255.30; M.14.453A); κ. ὕλης Gr.Naz.*or*.43.33(M.36. 541A); Proc.G.*Num*.31:49(M.87.885A); of a visible symbol of a spiritual reality μυστήριον κ. ἐκκλησίας *Did*.11.11; **d.** with additional meaning of *decorative, ornamental* λαμπάδας...κεκοσμημένας... κ. κόσμῳ Meth.*symp*.6.4(p.69.12; M.18.120B); Chrys.*hom.5.3 in 1Tim*. (11.577E) cit. s. παραπέτασμα; **e.** *normal* κ. μίξει γάμου Epiph.*haer*. 26.11(p.290.9; M.41.349B); **f.** of an historical event *taking place in this world*, Apoll.ap.Proc.G.*Cant*.(M.87.1721B) cit. s. κλῆσις; **3.** *belonging to the world, worldly, secular*, opp. spiritual; **a.** in gen. of persons πᾶς ὁ τὴν γνώμην κ. ‡Just.*ep.Zen.et Ser*.6(M.6.1189D); 'ὡς Ἠσαῦ βέβηλος'· τουτέστι...κ. Chrys.*hom.31.1 in Heb*.(12.286A); Max.*carit*.2.53(M.90.1001B); of life, Gr.Naz.*carm*.1.2.8.3(M.37.649A); Chrys.*hom.5.3 in 1Thess*.(11.462E); Socr.*h.e*.4.23.7(M.67.509D); ref. Heb.13:12 τὸ ...ἔξω τῆς πύλης ἔξω τοῦ κόσμου νοεῖν ἔοικε· ζωῆς γὰρ ἡμᾶς ἐξίστησι κοσμικῆς τὸ ἐθέλειν ἕπεσθαι Χριστῷ Cyr.*Heb*.13:12 (p.418.20; M.74.1000C); Αἴγυπτος...νοηθήσεταί πως...εἰς ἕξιν τὴν κ. id.*Jo*.3.6(4.313C); **b.** of natural affections ὀρέξεων...κ. Meth.*symp*. 11.2(p.138.28; M.18.217A); τέρψεις...κ. Cyr.*ador*.10(1.361A); πάντα ὅσα ἂν τῷ παρόντι κόσμῳ συγκαταλύηται, κ. ἐστιν ἐπιθυμία Chrys.*hom. 5.1 in Tit*.(11.758A); **c.** of mental states κ. σοφίας Athenag.*leg*.24. 5(M.6.948B); Clem.*paed*.3.2(p.241.15; M.8.569A); Mac.Aeg.*hom*.18.15 (M.34.633C); κ. ἐννοίας καὶ σαρκικάς Chrys.*hom.53.1 in Jo*.(8.310D); φροντίδος κ. Cyr.*Abac*.1(3.532C); **d.** of reputation τὴν κ. μου δόξαν *T.Jos*.17.8; τῶν ἀπὸ κ. ἀξιωμάτων μεγάλων Or.*hom.12.8 in Jer*.(p.94. 18; M.13.389A); Gr.Nyss.*ep*.17(M.46.1064A); **e.** of powers βασιλείας σωματικὰς καὶ κ. Or.*hom.1.16 in Jer*.(p.16.2; M.13.276C); Eus.*h.e*.7. 30.19(M.20.720A); ἀρχὴν κ. Ath.*h.Ar*.14(p.189.32; M.25.708C); *Const. App*.2.45.2; κ. δικαστήρια *ib*.2.52.1; **f.** opp. Christian τῶν ἔξωθεν εἶναι δοκούντων καὶ κ. λόγων †Just.*fr.res*.(p.41; M.6.1580C); τῆς...παιδείας ...κ. Eus.*m.P*.4.3(p.912.9; M.20.1473A); *Hom.Clem*.1.10; **g.** opp. μοναχικός: κ. εἰμι ἀνήρ Chrys.*Jud*.8.4(1.678D); κ. ... τάξει †Jo.Jej. *poenit*.(M.88.1909B); ἀδελφὸν...κ. Jo.Mosch.*prat*.65(M.87.2916C); cf. infra 4.a; **h.** of secular affairs κ. ... πραγμάτων Chrys.*sac*.6.3(p.145. 13; 1.423C); CChalc.*can*.3; opp. θεῖα πράγματα, Leo Mag.*ep*.104.3 (p.59.37; M.*PL*.996A); cf. infra 4.c; **4.** *in the world*, as subst.; **a.** masc., of Christians living in the world, opp. religious οἱ κατοικοῦντες ἐν τῇ ἐκκλησίᾳ κοσμικοί Mac.Aeg.*hom*.15.15(M.34.585A); *ib*.17.8(629A); ‡Pall.*h.mon*.22(p.83.1; M.34.1172C); Leont.B.*Nest. et Eut*.3(M.86.1361C); **b.** fem., opp. virgins, Ath.*virg*.11(p.45.21; M. 28.264D); Chrys.*hom.4.5 in Heb*.(12.46D); opp. κανονικαί, Nil.*epp*.2. 46(M.79.217C); **c.** neut. τὸ κ. ἅπαν ζημίαν [sc. ἔχει] ἐσχάτην Chrys. *hom.75.5 in Jo*.(8.445B); plur., *the things of the world*, opp. πνευματικά, *2Clem*.5.6; Clem.*paed*.1.5(p.99.1; M.8.268A); Or.*fr.in Mt*.5:21 (p.164; M.17.300C).

κοσμικῶς, *in a worldly fashion*, Or.*hom.28.23 in Jo*.(18; p.420. 3; M.14.732C); Chrys.*hom.15.1 in Phil*.(11.310A); Cyr.*ador*.1(1.36E); opp. μοναχικῶς, †Jo.Jej.*poenit*.(M.88.1913A).

κόσμιον, τό, 1. *ornament*, Clem.*paed*.3.7(p.258.22; M.8.608C); Chrys.*hom.12.7 in Col*.(11.422E); Socr.*h.e*.1.12.5(M.67.105A); **2.** *ornamentation*, ‡Sophr.H.*liturg*.4(M.87.3984D).

κοσμιότης, ἡ, *propriety, decorum*, as form of address τῇ κ. ὑμῶν Gr.Naz.*ep*.238(M.37.381A); Bas.*ep*.180(3.265B; M.32.657B); Firm.*ep*. 25(M.77.1500B).

[*]**κοσμίτης**, ὁ, v. κοσμητής.

***κοσμιώδης**, *decorous* διαπόνησις κοσμιωδεστέρα Clem.*paed*.3.10 (p.266.3; M.8.624B).

***κοσμόβιος**, ὁ, *one who dwells in this world*, Gr.Naz.*carm*.1.2.29. 326(M.37.908A).

κοσμογονία (**κοσμογένεια**), ἡ, **1.** *creation of world* κ. ἐν ἓξ περαιοῦται ἡμέραις Clem.*str*.6.16(p.502.15, v.l. κοσμογένεια M.9.364C); Gr.Nyss.*Eun*.1(1 p.118.25; M.45.353B); **2.** *account of creation, creation-story* ὁ τῆς κοσμογενείας λόγος id.*hom.12 in Cant*.(M.44. 1020C); ὁ τῆς κ. λόγος id.*or.catech*.5(p.24.3; M.45.21D); Cyr.*Juln*.1 (6².21C); confined to creation of sensible world, Bas.*Spir*.38(3.31D; M.32.136A; vv.ll. κοσμογένειαν, κοσμοποιΐαν); cf.Clem.*str*.5.14(p.388. 5; M.9.137B); ref. Moses as author Μωσῆς...θεὸν τῶν ὅλων αἴτιον ὑποστησάμενος, κ. ... ὑπογράψας Eus.*p.e*.11.4(512B; M.21.849C); as inspired, Or.*Cels*.1.44(p.94.23; M.11.741C); Bas.*Eun*.1.21(1.232D; M. 29.560A); Gr.Nyss.*hex*.proem.(M.44.61A).

***κοσμογόνος**, **1.** *world-creating* κ. νοῦς Gr.Naz.*carm*.1.1.4.68(M. 37.421A); of Christ, Sophr.H.*carm*.2.59(M.87.3741A); **2.** *of the Creation* τῇ ἑξάδι...τῇ κ. Apoll.ap.Proc.G.*Cant*.6:7,8(M.87.1721B).

κοσμογραφία, ἡ, *description of the world*, Clem.*str*.6.4(p.449.10; M.9.253B).

κοσμογράφος, ὁ, *describer of the world*; of Moses, Didym.*Trin*.2. 14(M.39.693A); Cosm.Ind.*top*.1(M.88.76A); *Chron.Pasch*.p.66(M.92. 228A).

***κοσμοδόχος**, *world-receiving* ἐν τῷ κ. κήτει τοῦ ᾅδου κεῖται εἰς τύπον Ἰωνᾶς Χριστοῦ ‡Epiph.*hom*.2(M.43.453A).

***κοσμοθέτης**, ὁ, *founder of the world*; of Christ, Gr.Naz.*carm*. 1.1.1.34(M.37.401A).

***κοσμοκίνητος**, *moving the universe*, Geo.Pis.*hex*.230(M.92.1451A).

***κοσμοκρατορέω**, *rule the world*, Areth.*Apoc*.20:7(M.106.756A).

***κοσμοκρατορικός**, *world-ruling*, Eus.*l.C*.6(p.211.9; M.20.1349A); Mac.Mgn.*apocr*.2.19(p.34.13).

***κοσμοκρατορικῶς**, *with worldly power* τῶν κ. κρατούντων δαιμόνων καὶ ἀνθρώπων Thdr.Stud.*epp*.1.36(M.99.1033D).

κοσμοκράτωρ, ὁ, **A.** *ruler of the world, world-ruler*; **1.** human; of Const., Eus.*v.C*.3.46(p.97.1; M.20.1105C); of other earthly rulers, id. *Is*.2:13–17(M.24.105B); Mac.Mgn.*apocr*.4.30(p.221.33); **2.** pagan Ζεὺς ...μαγείας δυνάμει κ. ἀναφανεὶς *Hom.Clem*.6.21; **3.** of evil spiritual powers as rulers; **a.** of this world (cf. Jo.14:30) ὁ μυστικῶς ὀνομαζόμενος Βαβυλῶνος βασιλεὺς ὁ κ. τοῦ κόσμου τούτου ἐστὶν †Bas.*Is*.279 (1.592C; M.30.609C); συνέτριψε [sc. Christ] τὸν σατανᾶν καὶ τοὺς κ. τοῦ κόσμου τούτου Cyr.*Is*.4.5(2.705E); τοῖς ἐχθροῖς· δῆλον δὲ ὅτι τοῖς κ. τοῦ αἰῶνος τούτου id.*Mich*.69(3.466C); id.*Zach*.14(3.669D); **b.** of (this) darkness (cf. Eph.6:12), plur. θάνατος...τῷ ἄρχοντι τοῦ κόσμου τούτου, καὶ τοῖς κ. τοῦ σκότους, καὶ τοῖς πνευματικοῖς τῆς πονηρίας, καὶ πάσῃ τῇ ἐχθρᾷ τῆς θείας φύσεως δυνάμει συντέτακται Bas.*Eun*. 2.27(1.264B; M.29.636A); τοὺς...καταδυναστευθέντας ὑπὸ τῶν κ. τοῦ σκότους τούτου τῆς τυραννίδος ἀπήλλαξεν [sc. Christ] Proc.G.*Is*.41:1–7 (M.87.2348C); sing., †Bas.*Is*.309(1.612E; M.30.657B); ref. Lc.16:22 ταφὴ...ἐστι τὸ μὴ δυνηθῆναι διαβῆναι καὶ παρελθεῖν τὸν κ. τοῦ σκότους καὶ τὰς ὑπ' αὐτὸν ἀποστατικὰς δυνάμεις τε καὶ τάξεις Eustrat.*stat. anim*.27(p.538); exeg. Eph.6:12 ἄρα οὖν μὴ καὶ ἐνταῦθα [i.e. Eph. 3:9–10] λέγει ὅτι οἱ δαίμονες τότε ἔγνωσαν; οὐδαμῶς. ... αὗται δὲ αἱ ἀρχαὶ καὶ ἐξουσίαι ὑπὸ τὸν οὐρανόν. διὰ τοῦτο καὶ κοσμοκράτορας αὐτοὺς καλεῖ, δεικνὺς ὅτι ἄβατος αὐτοῖς ἐστιν ὁ οὐρανὸς καὶ τὴν τυραννίδα πᾶσαν ἐν τῷ παρόντι κόσμῳ ἐπιδείκνυνται μόνον Chrys.*incomprehens*.4.2(1. 474B); ποίου σκότους;...τῆς πονηρίας...κοσμοκράτορας δὲ αὐτούς φησιν, οὐχ ὡς τοῦ κόσμου κρατοῦντας, ἀλλ' οἶδε τὸν κόσμον τοῦτον καλεῖν ἡ γραφὴ τὰς πονηρὰς πράξεις. ... κόσμον ἐνταῦθα τοὺς πονηροὺς ἀνθρώπους φησίν· οἱ δὲ δαίμονες μᾶλλον τούτων κρατοῦσι id.*hom.22.3 in Eph*. (11.169E); ἀρχάς τε καὶ ἐξουσίας καὶ τοὺς κ. τοῦ σκότους τούτου, τουτέστι τὰ βδελυρὰ τῶν δαιμονίων στίφη Cyr.*Zach*.58(3.737B); κ. δὲ αὐτοὺς ὠνόμασεν, οὐχ ὡς παρὰ τοῦ θεοῦ τήνδε τὴν ἀρχὴν δεξαμένους, ἀλλ' ὡς τῶν ῥαθυμίᾳ συζώντων γνώμῃ τὴν δουλείαν ἀσπασαμένων Thdt.*Eph*. 6:12(3.438); astrol. πνεύματα ἑπτὰ...εἶπον· ἡμεῖς ἐσμεν στοιχεῖα κοσμοκράτορες τοῦ σκότους *T.Sal*.8.2(M.122.1328B); **c.** of wickedness οἱ τοῦ σκότους ἄρχοντες, οἱ κ. τῆς πονηρίας *Apophth.Patr*.(M.65. 200B); **d.** unqualified, sing. ὃν [sc. Χριστὸν] ἐφοβήθη...τοῦ κ. ἅπασα ἡ δύναμις *A.Jo*.23(p.163.28); τῶν ἀσωμάτων δυνάμεων, τῶν ἀρχῶν, τῶν ἐξουσιῶν, τοῦ κ. Chrys.*hom.6.3 in 1Thess*.(11.470D); τὸν πλάνον φύγωμεν κόσμον καὶ κ. Max.*ep*.1(M.91.389C); *ib*.43(637C); κατῆλθεν [sc. Χριστὸς] ἐν τῷ ᾅδῃ καὶ ἐξήγαγεν οὓς κατεῖχε δεσμίους ὁ δεινὸς κ. †Jo.D.*B.J*.31(M.96.1161A); *ib*.18(1020C); *ib*.24(1085C); plur. κύριε... ἔνδυσόν με τὴν ἔνδοξόν σου στολὴν...ἕως ἂν παρέλθω πάντας τοὺς κ. καὶ τὸν πονηρὸν δράκοντα *A.Phil*.144(p.86.7); listed with ἀρχαί and ἐξουσίαι (cf. Eph.6:12), Eus.*e.th*.2.20(p.128.9; M.24.952B); Proc.G. *Is*.5:24–30(M.87.1929A); Gnost. (Valent.) ἐκ τῆς λύπης τὰ πνευματικὰ τῆς πονηρίας διδάσκουσι γεγονέναι· ὅθεν ⟨καὶ⟩ τὸν διάβολον τὴν γένεσιν ἐσχηκέναι, ὃν καὶ Κ. καλοῦσι. ... λέγουσι τὸν Κ. κτίσμα τοῦ Δημιουργοῦ· καὶ τὸν μὲν Κ. γινώσκειν τὰ ὑπὲρ αὐτόν, ὅτι πνεῦμά ἐστι τῆς πονηρίας, τὸν δὲ Δημιουργὸν ἀγνοεῖν, ἅτε ψυχικὸν ὑπάρχοντα· οἰκεῖν δὲ τὸν Δημιουργὸν...εἰς τὸν ἐπουράνιον τόπον...τὸν ⟨δὲ⟩ Κ. ἐν τῷ καθ' ἡμᾶς κόσμῳ Iren.*haer*.1.5.4(M.7.497Af.).

B. as adj., *ruling the world* τὸν κ. διάβολον Nil.*epp*.4.11(M.79. 556A); τῷ κ. ἐχθρῷ Jo.Mon.*hymn.Nic.Myr*.9(M.96.1389C).

***κοσμοκτόνος**, ὁ, *slayer of the world*, Geo.Pis.*hex*.1835(M.92. 1575A).

***κοσμολάλητος**, *spoken of by the world, world-famous*, *Hymn*. (*AS* 1 p.571).

***κοσμολατρεία**, ἡ, *worship of, attachment to the world* γονικὴν ἐβδελύξω κ. *Hymn*.(*AS* 1 p.615).

***κοσμόλεθρος**, *world-destroying*; of Chosroes, Geo.Pis.*hex*.353(M. 92.1461A); cf.Thphn.*chron*.p.258(M.108.644B).

***κοσμολέτης**, ὁ, as adj., *world-destroying*, Gr.Naz.*carm*.1.2.14.88 (M.37.762A).

***κοσμομανής**, *raging the world over* ἔσσεται ὑστατίῳ καιρῷ...κ. πόλεμος *Orac.Sib*.5.362; *ib*.5.462.

***κοσμοπάτωρ**, ὁ, *world's ancestor*; of Adam, ‡Jo.D.*hom*.5(M.96. 649B).

***κοσμοπλάνης**, ὁ, *world-deceiver*; of antichrist, *Did*.16.4.

***κοσμοπλάνος**, ὁ, = foreg., *Const.App*.7.32.2; as. adj. τὸν κ. διάβολον *ib*.7.32.4.

κοσμοπόθητος** (κοσμωπ-**), *desired* or *beloved by the world*; of BMV, κοσμω-, Ephr.3.530E; of Chrys., Thdr.Stud.*cant*.11.5(p.359); of emperor, id.*epp*.2.86(M.99.1332B).

κοσμοποιΐα, ἡ, *creation of world*; **1.** as described by Moses Μωϋσῆς...τὴν κ. ἐξηγούμενος Or.*fr.1 in Jo*.(p.484.9); Eus.*e.th*.2.14 (p.117.11; M.24.932B); μηδεμίαν αὐτὸν μνήμην ποιήσασθαι ἀγγέλων κτίσεως ἐν τῷ τῆς κ. λόγῳ *ib*.2.20(p.127.30; 952A); Gr.Nyss.*Eun*. 12(1 p.279.4; M.45.985C); Proc.G.*Gen*.2:4(M.87.149D); **2.** of the Creation story εὑρήσεις...τὸν λόγον τὸν λέγοντα ἐν τῇ κ. 'γεννηθήτω φῶς' †Hipp.*Laz*.(p.226.35; M.62.778); Or.*fr.95 in Jo*.(p.558.14); ἀναπλάσαι θεὸν ἕτερον καὶ κ. ἄλλην παρὰ τὴν ὑπὸ τοῦ πνεύματος ἀναγεγραμμένην id.*hom.16.19 in Jer*.(p.140.28; M.13.449C); Eus.*e.th*.3.3(p.150. 4; M.24.989B); Diod.*Ps*.89:1(M.33.1624D); Mac.Aeg.*ep*.(M.34.412B); Isid.Pel.*epp*.3.95(M.78.801C); of book of Genesis γέγραπται...ἐν τῷ τῆς κ. βιβλίῳ Cyr.*ep*.41(p.47.30; 5².131A); **3.** in gen. τοῦτο τὸ παιδίον γηγενὴς οὐκ ἔστι...τάχα τοῦτο πρὸ τῆς κ. ἐστὶν γεγεννημένον *Ev. Thom*.A 7.2(p.147); Clem.*prot*.4(p.48.17; M.8.164A); Or.*comm.in Gen*. ap.Eus.*p.e*.6.11(p.287C; M.12.64B); *ib*.ap.*philoc*.23.20(p.209.20; M. 12.84B); καταπαύσαντος ἀπὸ τῶν ἔργων τῆς κ. τοῦ θεοῦ Meth.*symp*.9.1 (p.114.11; M.18.177B); Eus.*e.th*.2.14(p.117.11; M.24.932B); †Bas.*Is*. 280(1.592E; M.30.612B); ἀπ' ἀρχῆς...κατὰ τὴν κ. πρὸς τὸν υἱὸν καὶ τὸ πνεῦμα διαλεγόμενος δῆλός ἐστιν ὁ θεὸς Didym.(‡Bas.)*Eun*.5(1.315B; M.29.756B); Nemes.*nat.hom*.1(M.40.516A); *Dial.Tim.et Aquil*.79 v°; Cosm.Ind.*top*.3(M.88.141B); μετὰ τὴν πρώτην ἑβδομάδα τῆς κ. οὐχ εὑρίσκομεν οἱονδήποτε πρᾶγμα πλάσαντα τὸν θεὸν ἢ πλάττοντα Jo.D. *disp*.(M.96.1345C).

κοσμοποιός, *world-creating*; **1.** (Gnost.) of angels; in Simonian system, Iren.*haer*.1.23.3 ap.Hipp.*haer*.6.19(M.16.3223C) cit. s. ἄγγελος; in system of Saturninus, *ib*.1.24.2 ap.Hipp.*haer*.7.28(3323A) cit. *ib*.; cf.Epiph.*haer*.23.2(p.251.3; M.41.301A); Carpocratian τὸν ὑπεράνω τῶν κ. ἀγγέλων θεὸν Iren.*haer*.1.25.4 ap.Hipp.*haer*.7.32 (3339B); ref. soul of Jesus ὅπως τὰ ὁραθέντα αὐτῇ ἀναμνημονεύουσα καὶ ἐνδυναμωθεῖσα φύγῃ τοὺς κ. ἀγγέλους Epiph.*haer*.27.2(p.302.1; M.41.365A); αἱ τοιαῦται...[sc. ψυχαί]...καταφρονήσασαι τῶν κ. ἀγγέλων...ὑπερβαίνουσι τὴν τῶν αὐτῶν μυθοποιῶν (οὐ γὰρ ἂν εἴποιμι κοσμοποιῶν) ἐξουσίαν *ib*.27.3(p.303.22; 368A); as subst. masc., Iren. *haer*.1.24.2 ap.Hipp.*haer*.7.28(3323A); ὑπ' ἐκείνου [sc. ἀγενήτου θεοῦ] αὐτῇ [sc. soul of Jesus] καταπεμφθῆναι δύναμιν, ὅπως τοὺς κ. ἐκφυγεῖν δι' αὐτῆς δυνηθῇ *ib*.1.25.1 *ib*.7.32(3338A); of Devil ἄγγελον ἐξυπηρετούμενον τῷ κριτῇ τῷ κ. εἰς τὸ φέρειν τὰς ψυχὰς πάλιν...εἶναι δὲ τὸν ἀντίδικον τοῦτον...ἄγγελον ἕνα τῶν κ. ... ὄνομα ἔχοντα διάβολον Epiph. *haer*.27.5(p.307.7; 369C); cf.*ib*.(p.307.16; 372A); of ἄρχοντες: τὴν... ὁμοίως ἐκείνῃ τῇ τοῦ Χριστοῦ ψυχῇ δυναμένην καταφρονῆσαι τῶν κ. ἀρχόντων ὁμοίως λαμβάνειν δύναμιν πρὸς τὸ πρᾶξαι τὰ ὅμοια Iren. *haer*.1.25.1 ap.Hipp.*haer*.7.32(3338B); *ib*.(3339A); **2.** of demiurge opp. supreme God (Archontic) ἐξουσίας καὶ ἀρχὰς τοῦ κ. θεοῦ Epiph. *haer*.40.7(p.88.4; M.41.688C); as subst., (Cerinthian) *ib*.28.6(p.318. 22; 384B); (Cerdonian) ἐληλυθέναι...τὸν Χριστὸν...ἐκ τοῦ ἀγνώστου πατρός, εἰς ἀθέτησιν τῆς τοῦ κ. καὶ δημιουργοῦ ἀρχῆς *ib*.41.1(p.92.2; 692D); (Valent.) φησίν, ὅτι ὁ διάβολος ἐγέννησεν ἄλλους, οἵτινες κατεσκεύασαν τὸν κόσμον· καὶ ὅτι ὁ Χριστὸς κατῆλθεν, ἐπὶ τὸ ἀποστῆσαι τοὺς ἀνθρώπους τοῦ κ. Cyr.H.*catech*.6.18; in gen. φιμούσθω πᾶσα αἵρεσις διαφόρους ποιητὰς καὶ κ. εἰσάγουσα *ib*.11.21; πολλοὶ τῶν ἀπὸ αἱρέσεων διαιροῦσι τὴν θεότητα λέγοντες ἄλλον εἶναι θεὸν τὸν κ. καὶ ἄλλον τὸν πατέρα τοῦ Χριστοῦ Didym.*Ac*.4:24(M.39.1664A); Max. *schol.d.n*.5.2(M.4.312A); **3.** of God πᾶς ὁ κόσμος γενητὸς ὤν, τῷ ἀγενήτῳ κ. θεῷ ἐνυφέστηκεν Leont.H.*Nest*.2.23(M.86.1585A); as subst., Eus.*h.e*.1.2.4(M.20.56A); id.*l.C*.6(p.208.24; M.20.1345A); of Logos, *ib*.12(p.235.12; 1396C); μία...ἡ καθόλου κ. δύναμις καὶ εἷς ὁ τῶν ὅλων δημιουργὸς λόγος id.*d.e*.(p.155.10; M.22.260A).

κοσμοπολίτης, ὁ, *citizen of the world*, of man τέλος τῆς δημιουργίας τὸ λογικὸν ζῷον τὸν κ. *Const.App*.7.34.6.

***κοσμορύστης, ὁ,** *deliverer of the world*, of Heraclius τὸν κ. τὸν διώκτην Περσίδος Geo.Pis.*hex*.1846(M.92.1575A); id.*Sev*.452(M.92.1656A); of Heracles compared with Heraclius, id.*Heracl*.1.70(M.92.1304A).

κόσμος, ὁ, A. *order* πάντα τὸν κ. τοῦ οὐρανοῦ Or.*Jo*.2.3(p.56.18; M.14.112C); οὐδὲ ἐν ὕλῃ τὸ κακὸν...καὶ αὐτὴ τοῦ κ. ... καὶ εἴδους ἔχει μετουσίαν Dion.Ar.*d.n*.4.28(M.3.729A); βασιλεία [sc. ἐστίν] ἡ παντὸς ὅρου καὶ κ. καὶ θεσμοῦ καὶ τάξεως διανέμησις *ib*.12.2(969B).

B. *ornament, decoration* τὰ δέσμα κ. εὐπρεπῆ περικεῖσθαι αὐτοῖς *Ep.Lugd*.ap.Eus.*h.e*.5.1.35(M.20.421A); connexion of meanings *ornament* and *world* pointed out, Or.*princ*.2.3.6(p.121.5; M.11.194B); in gen. κ. ... ἁρμόδιος γυναικὶ ἡ πρὸς τὸν ἄνδρα ὑπακοὴ Eus.ap.*cat. 1Petr*.3:1(p.59.16); *adornment*, with play on meaning *world* φῶς... ὃ φωτίζει πάντα ἄνθρωπον ἐρχόμενον εἰς τὸν κόσμον, τὸν τοῦ διαφόρου σπέρματος· ὅτε γὰρ ἐφωτίσθη ὁ ἄνθρωπος, τότε εἰς τὸν κ. ἦλθεν, τουτέστιν ἑαυτὸν ἐκόσμησεν, χωρίσας αὐτοῦ τὰ ἐπισκοτοῦντα...πάθη Clem.*exc.Thdot*.41(p.119.28; M.9.677D); in gen. διὰ τὰς τρίχας κολάζεσθαι καὶ τὸν κ. τὰς γυναῖκας id.*ecl*.39(p.148.22; M.9.717C); πάλιν...ἀπολήψεται τὸν ἑαυτῆς κ. ἡ ἐκκλησία Ath.*v.Anton*.82(M.26.960B); χρώματα πρὸς κόσμον ταῖς γυναιξὶν ἐπιτετηδευμένα τοῦ προσώπου †Bas.*Is*.126(1.467B; M.30.324A); ref. resurrection body κ. ἄλλος καὶ ἄλλα ἐνδύματα Mac.Aeg.*elev*.2(M.34.892B); plur., Just. *2apol*.11.5(M.6.461C); Thdt.*Cant*.4:9(2.99); Dion.Ar.*myst*.3(M.3.1033B); id.*ep*.9.1(M.3.1105A); of Church as κ. τοῦ κόσμου with play on meaning *world*, Or.*Jo*.6.59(38; p.167.22; M.14.301C); of man as κ. τοῦ κ. (i.e. of world), Meth.*res*.1.35(p.275.10; M.41.1100D); *Const. App*.7.34.6.

C. *world, universe*; including earth and heaven ἐν ὅλῳ τῷ κ., οὐ μόνον τῷ περιγείῳ τόπῳ, ἀλλὰ καὶ παντὶ τῷ συστήματι τῷ ἐξ οὐρανοῦ καὶ γῆς Or.*Jo*.1.15(p.19.20; M.14.49A); **1.** as created; **a.** as created order κ. καλεῖται [esp. ref. heaven, not to be regarded as a deity]· κ. δὲ κατασκευή ἐστί τινος τεχνίτου Arist.*apol*.4.2; ὑπὸ...τοῦ δημιουργοῦ ἡ ὕλη εἰς οἷον ἠθέλησε κόσμον ἠνέχθη σχῆμα *Hom.Clem*.19.17; **b.** created by God τὸν πατέρα καὶ κτίστην τοῦ σύμπαντος κ. *1Clem*.19.2; Just.*dial*.41.1(M.6.564B); on man's account, id.*2apol*.4.2(M.6.452A); ὁ μὲν κ. σφαιρικὸς ἀποτελεσθείς, ὁ δὲ τοῦ κ. ποιητὴς ἀνωτέρω τῶν γεγονότων, ἐπέχων αὐτὸν τῇ προνοίᾳ Athenag.*leg*.8.2(M.6.905A); οὐδὲν ἄτοπον τὸν ἐξ ἀνομοίων συνεστηκότα κ. ὑπὸ ἑνὸς γεγονέναι τεχνίτου Or.*Cels*.4.54(p.327.24; M.11.1120A); μήπω τοῦ κ. γεγονότος οὐδὲν ἕτερον ἦν πλὴν θεοῦ μόνου Marcell.*fr*.93 ap.Eus.*Marcell*.2.2(p.40.7; M.24.792A); γενητὸν εἶναι τὸν κ. Eus.*e.th*.2.14(p.117.15; M.24.932C); **c.** created through Logos τοῦτον [sc. Logos] ἴσμεν τοῦ κ. τὴν ἀρχήν Tat.*orat*.5(p.5.25; M.6.816A); ὁ κ. ... διὰ...τοῦ φωτὸς γέγονε τοῦ κρείττονος, δηλαδὴ τοῦ πατρὸς διὰ τοῦ υἱοῦ τὸ πᾶν συνισταμένου Eus.*e.th*.1.20(p.82.5; M.24.868B); *ib*.(p.81.12; 865C); (Arian) ἐδεῖτο...ὁ θεὸς ὑπουργοῦ εἰς τὴν τοῦ ἀνθρώπου καὶ τοῦ κ. κατασκευὴν Gel.Cyz.*h.e*.2.16.2(M.85.1260C); **d.** world as expressing its creator ὁ σύμπας οὗτος κ., τὸ μέγα τοῦ θεοῦ στοιχεῖον..., ᾧ καὶ δηλοῦται θεὸς σιωπῇ κηρυττόμενος Gr.Naz.*or*.6.14(M.35.740C); **2.** nature of world: material, Tat.*orat*.12(p.12.22; M.6.829C); cf.*ib*.6(p.7.1; 820A); composite, yet a unity, Ath.*Ar*.2.28(M.26.205C); perceptible, opp. heavenly powers, Eus.*e.th*.3.2(p.143.29; M.24.980B); (Epicurean) composed of atoms, Dion.Al.ap.Eus.*p.e*.14.23(773A; M.21.1272B); temporal and corruptible, Tat.*orat*.13(p.14.14; 833A); Ἀριστοτέλης... λέγει...ἄλυτον εἶναι τὸν κ., ἐγὼ δὲ λυόμενον *ib*.25(p.27.6; 861A); Thdr. Mops.*Gal*.1:3(p.6.13; M.66.900A); question of world's temporality in rel. to metempsychosis οὐκ ἔσται τάχα ὅτε ψυχὴ οὐ μετενσωματωθήσεται· ἀεὶ γὰρ διὰ τὰ πρότερα ἁμαρτήματα ἐπιδημήσει τῷ σώματι καὶ οὕτω οὐχ ἕξει χώραν ἡ τοῦ κ. φθορά Or.*comm.in Mt*.13.1(p.174.5; M.13.1088B); **3.** Origenist plurality of worlds ὑποτίθεται δὲ [sc. Or.] διαφόρους κ. συστῆναί τε καὶ συνίστασθαι, τοῦτο μὲν παρελθόντας, τοῦτο δὲ μέλλοντας Justn.*Or*.(p.190.23; M.86.949A); **4.** world in rel. to God and man; controlled by God, Just.*dial*.29.3(M.6.537B); Christ as lord of world, *Barn*.5.5; defiled by sin, Const.ap.Gel.Cyz.*h.e*.2.7.31(M.85.1240A); restored by Christ ζητῶ...εἰ ταὐτόν ἐστι τὸ φῶς τοῦ κ. τῷ φωτὶ τῶν ἀνθρώπων, καὶ ἡγοῦμαι πλείονα δύναμιν παρίστασθαι τοῦ φωτὸς ὅτε φῶς τοῦ κ. προσαγορεύεται ἤπερ φῶς τῶν ἀνθρώπων, ὁ γὰρ κ. οὐ μόνον ἄνθρωποι...κ. ἐστιν ἡ ἐλευθερουμένη κτίσις...ἀπὸ τῆς δουλείας τῆς φθορᾶς Or.*Jo*.1.26(24; p.31.34; M.14.69A,B); preserved on account of Church ἐπιμένει ὁ θεὸς τὴν σύγχυσιν καὶ κατάλυσιν τοῦ παντὸς κ. μὴ ποιῆσαι...διὰ τὸ σπέρμα τῶν Χριστιανῶν Just.*2apol*.7.1(M.6.456A); diversity of world as part of its fallen character ποικιλωτάτου κ. τυγχάνοντος καὶ τοσαῦτα διάφορα λογικὰ περιέχοντος...τί ἄλλο χρὴ λέγειν αἴτιον γεγονέναι τοῦ ὑποστῆναι αὐτόν...ἢ τὸ ποικίλον τῆς ἀποπτώσεως τῶν οὐχ ὁμοίως τῆς ἑνάδος ἀπορρεόντων; Or.*princ*.2.1.2(p.107.2; M.11.182B); **5.** of 'sensible' and 'intelligible' worlds ὁ κύριος...ἔμελλεν...τὸν σύντροφον τοῦ κ. ἄνθρωπον ἐπὶ τὰ νοητὰ καὶ κύρια διὰ τῆς γνώσεως ἀνάγειν ἐκ κόσμου εἰς κόσμον Clem.*str*.6.15(p.495.27; M.9.349B,C); ἐστίν τις καὶ ἕτερος παρὰ τὸν...αἰσθητὸν κ. ... ἐν ᾧ ἐστιν τὰ μὴ βλεπόμενα· καὶ ὅλον τοῦτο κ. ἀόρατος, κ. οὐ βλεπόμενος, καὶ νοητὸς κ., οὗ τῇ θέᾳ καὶ τῷ κάλλει ἐνόψονται οἱ καθαροὶ τῇ καρδίᾳ Or.*Jo*.19.22(5; p.323.32ff.; M.14.568B); ὁ νοῦς...τοῦ νοητοῦ κ. ἐστὶ φῶς *ib*.1.25(24; p.31.1; 68B); ὁ θεὸς... ἐδημιούργησε...δύο κ., τὸν μὲν ἄνω τοῖς λειτουργικοῖς πνεύμασι καὶ τὴν πολιτείαν ἔχειν ἐκεῖ διετάξατο· τὸν δὲ κάτω τοῖς ἀνθρώποις ὑπὸ τὸν ἀέρα τοῦτον Mac.Aeg.*hom*.45.5(M.34.789B); Chrys.*hom.81.3 in Jo*.(8.481D); invisible world identified with 'world to come', Cosm.Ind.*top*.2(M.88.92A); **6.** of 'this world', opp. 'next world' or 'eternal life' ἀπηλλάγη τοῦ κ. καὶ εἰς τὸν ἅγιον τόπον ἀνελήφθη *1Clem*.5.7; *2Clem*.5.5; *ib*.19.3; ὁ δίκαιος καὶ ἐν τούτῳ τῷ κ. περιπατεῖ καὶ τὸν ἅγιον αἰῶνα ἐκδέχεται *Barn*.10.11; Or.*hom.14.17 in Jer*.(p.124.1; M.13.428A); id.*Jo*.19.22(5; p.324.18; M.14.569A); τοῦ νῦν κ. ὡς θήλεια [sc. Eve] ὁμοίως ἄρχουσα...ὁ δὲ ἕτερος [sc. Adam] ὡς υἱὸς ἀνθρώπου...τῷ μέλλοντι αἰῶνι προφητεύει *Hom.Clem*.3.22; opp. heaven, Or.*Jo*.19.20(5; p.322.3; 564D); **7.** in spiritual sense, of 'the world'; **a.** ref. worldly things and interests; of life acc. the flesh, Polyc.*ep*.5.3; ἡ ἄσκησις τῆς κατὰ τὸ εὐαγγέλιον τοῦ Χριστοῦ εὐαρεστήσεως ἐν τῇ ἀναχωρήσει τῶν μεριμνῶν τοῦ κ. ... ἡμῖν κατορθοῦται Bas.*reg.fus*.5(2.341E; M.31.920C); κόσμον...λέγει πᾶσαν τὴν ὑλικὴν ζωήν, τὴν μητέρα τῆς φθορᾶς, ἧς ὁ μετασχεῖν ἐθέλων ἐχθρὸς γίνεται τοῦ θεοῦ *cat.Jac*.4:4(p.26.14); κ. λέγει ἡ γραφὴ τὰ ὑλικὰ πράγματα· καὶ κοσμικοί εἰσι οἱ τούτοις τὸν νοῦν ἐνασχολοῦντες Max. *carit*.2.53(M.90.1001B); ξενωθῶμεν τοῦ κ., τὸν νοῦν εἰς οὐρανοὺς μεταθέντες ‡Serg.*acath*.169(p.144; M.92.1341D); cf.Or.*Jo*.19.20(5; p.322.3; M.14.564D); ref. worldly wisdom, Eus.*v.C*.3.60(p.106.24; M.20.1128B); **b.** opp. monastic life μηδὲ εἰς τὸν κ. βλέποντες, νομίζωμεν μεγάλοις τισὶν ἀποτετάχθαι Ath.*v.Anton*.17(M.26.868C); Bas.*reg.fus*.5(2.342B; M.31.921A); ἀναχωρήσας τοῦ κ. ... καὶ ἐν τῇ ἐρήμῳ διατελέσας ‡Pall.*h.mon*.8.3(p.33.11; M.34.1137C); ἄνδρες βροτοί, φύγωμεν ἐκ κ. πλάνου· Χριστὸς καλεῖ, δράμωμεν Thdr.Stud.*iamb*.3(M.99.1780D); **c.** of world as sphere of evil and opposed to God, *T.Isach*.4.6; καλὸν τὸ δῦναι ἀπὸ κόσμου πρὸς θεόν Ign.*Rom*.2.2; μισεῖ... Χριστιανοὺς ὁ κ. μηδὲν ἀδικούμενος, ὅτι ταῖς ἡδοναῖς ἀντιτάσσονται *Diogn*.6.5; ἀμήχανον...συνυπάρχειν τὴν πρὸς τὸν κ. ἀγάπην τῇ πρὸς τὸν θεὸν ἀγάπῃ, ὡς ἀμήχανον συνυπάρχειν ἀλλήλοις φῶς καὶ σκότος Or.*Jo*.19.21(5; p.323.3; M.14.565C); ὁ...θάνατός ἐστιν ὁ κ., ἡ δὲ ζωή ἐστιν ἡ δικαιοσύνη. μακρὰν οὖν ὁ κ. ἀπὸ τῆς δικαιοσύνης, καθ' ὅσον ὁ θάνατος ἀπὸ τῆς ζωῆς· ἐὰν οὖν πορεύῃ ἐν τῷ κ., ἐν τῷ θανάτῳ πορεύῃ καὶ ἐκτὸς τοῦ θεοῦ γίνῃ Ath.*virg*.18(p.53.19; M.28.273B); μεταθῶμεν τὴν ψυχὴν πρὸς οὐρανὸν καὶ νενίκηται ὁ κ. ἅπας Chrys.*hom.79.3 in Jo*.(8.468E); Eulog.*fr.Novat*.(M.104.348C); cf.*cat.Jac*.4:4(p.26.14); κ. λέγεται διττῶς· καὶ ἡ σύστασις ἡ δημιουργικὴ καὶ τῶν ἀνθρώπων τὸ σύστημα τὸ πονηρόν Sever.*Eph*.2:2(p.307.27); τρία...ὑπάρχουσι τὰ τὸν ἄνθρωπον ἄγοντα...θεὸς καὶ φύσις καὶ κ. Max.*ep*.9(M.91.445C); εἰ ...φύσις ἐστὶν ἡ ἄγουσα τὸν ἄνθρωπον,...φύσει τὸν ἄνθρωπον διαδείκνυσι, μέσον θεοῦ καὶ κ. τυγχάνουσα...εἰ δὲ κ. ἐστὶν ὁ φέρων, κτῆνος ἐργάζεται...ἐμπάθειαν αὐτῷ δι' ἀπάτης δημιουργῶν *ib*.(445D); αἱ... ἀκρότητες, θεὸν δέ φημι καὶ κ., ἀλλήλων καὶ τῆς μεσότητος, λέγω δὲ τὴν φύσιν, ἀπάγειν τὸν ἄνθρωπον εἰώθασιν *ib*.; ἡ...μεσότης...οὔτε πρὸς τὸν θεὸν αὐτὸν ἀναδραμεῖν συγχωροῦσα καὶ πρὸς τὸν κ. ἀφιέναι καταπεσεῖν αἰδουμένη *ib*.(448A); σκοπὸς...τῷ δοτῆρι τῶν ἐντολῶν κ. καὶ φύσεως ἐλευθερῶσαι τὸν ἄνθρωπον *ib*.(448C); εἰ πνεύματι θεοῦ ἄγεσθαι ποθεῖς...κ. καὶ φύσιν σαυτοῦ περίελε *ib*.(448B); θέωσιν... ὑπὲρ φύσιν...δωρούμενος καὶ τῶν δύο...ἀποτέμνει, κ. λέγω καὶ φύσεως *ib*.(445C); **d.** in sense of *mankind* considered as alienated from God, Dion.Al.ap.Eus.*h.e*.7.25.21(M.20.701B); Const.ap.Gel.Cyz.*h.e*.2.7.35(M.85.1240D); τὸ πλέον τοῦ κ. ὑπὸ τὰς τοῦ διαβόλου χεῖρας ἑαυτοὺς ἔδωκαν Chrys.*hom.8.4 in 2Tim*.(11.712E); γράφει...ὁ Ἰωάννης [1 Jo. 3:13]· φανερόν ἐστι...κόσμον μισοῦντα τοὺς ἁγίους, τοὺς πονηροὺς ἀνθρώπους σημαίνων *cat.1Jo*.5:19(p.144.18); **8.** ref. correspondence bet. spiritual and material worlds; from elements answering to four cardinal virtues, Max.*ambig*.(M.91.1245A); detailed analysis of this parallelism, *ib*.(1245B,C); **9.** of the earth, opp. heaven, *1Clem*. 59.2; *αἱ τῶν γιγάντων ψυχαὶ οἱ περὶ τὸν κ. εἰσὶ πλανώμενοι δαίμονες* Athenag.*leg*.25.1(M.6.948C); *ὁ Ἰωάννης ἀπεστάλη...εἰς τὸν κ.* (*κ. λαμβανομένου τοῦ περιγείου τόπου, ἔνθα εἰσὶν οἱ ἄνθρωποι*) Or.*Jo*.2.29(24; p.85.33; M.14.164C); *οὐ τὸ ἐξ οὐρανοῦ καὶ γῆς σύστημά ἐστι...ὁ κ., ἀλλ' ὁ περίγειος μόνος τόπος, καὶ οὗτος οὐ καθ' ὅλην νοούμενος τὴν γῆν, ἀλλ' ὁ κατὰ τὴν ἡμετέραν οἰκουμένην* id.*comm.in Mt*.13.20 (p.235.5; M.13.1149A); Cyr.H.*catech*.19.3; as scene of life, *1Clem*. 38.3; Arist.*apol*.1.1; **10.** *world* in sense of *sphere*; of the 'Roman world' *ἐν τῷ τῶν Ῥωμαίων κ.* Dam.Papa *ep.Illyr*.ap.Thdt.*h.e*.2.22.5 (3.882); Gel.Cyz.*h.e*.1 proem.1(M.85.1192D); ref. Hades *πρὸς τὸν κ. τῶν ἐκεῖ ἐγκεκλεισμένων* Eus.Al.*serm*.12(M.86.381D); plur., *realms ὠκεανὸς ἀπέραντος ἀνθρώποις καὶ οἱ μετ' αὐτὸν κόσμοι* *1Clem*.20.8; Hegem.*Arch*.10(p.17.18; M.10.1444C); **11.** in sense of *mankind, inhabitants of the world* *τὸ αἷμα τοῦ Χριστοῦ...διὰ τὴν ἡμετέραν σωτηρίαν ἐκχυθὲν παντὶ τῷ κ. μετανοίας χάριν ὑπήνεγκεν* *1Clem*.7.4; *Barn*.4.12; '*καὶ ὁ κ. αὐτὸν οὐκ ἔγνω*', *οἱ ἐν τῷ περιγείῳ τόπῳ ἄνθρωποι, τάχα δὲ καὶ αἱ οἰκεῖαι τῷ χωρίῳ τούτῳ δυνάμεις* Or.*comm.in Mt*.13.20 (p.235.18; M.13.1149A); cf.*cat.Jac*.3:5(p.21.13); Ath.*ep.Serap*.4.19 (M.26.665D); Mac.Mgn.*apocr*.2.7(p.6.10); *σῶσαι θέλων τὸν κ. ὁ τῶν ὅλων κοσμήτωρ* ‡Serg.*acath*.217(p.145; M.92.1344D); as sphere of Church's life and influence *ὅπερ ἐστὶν ἐν σώματι ψυχή, τοῦτ' εἰσὶν ἐν κ. Χριστιανοί· ἔσπαρται κατὰ πάντων τῶν τοῦ σώματος μελῶν ἡ ψυχὴ καὶ Χριστιανοὶ κατὰ τὰς τοῦ κ. πόλεις* *Diogn*.6.1–2; *Χριστιανοὶ γινώσκονται μὲν ὄντες ἐν τῷ κ., ἀόρατος δὲ αὐτῶν ἡ θεοσέβεια μένει* *ib*. 6.4; *Χριστιανοὶ κατέχονται μὲν ὡς ἐν φρουρᾷ τῷ κ., αὐτοὶ δὲ συνέχουσι τὸν κ.* *ib*.6.7; **12.** of Logos as *κόσμος* because world is created in him and *λόγοι* of all things are in him *ζητήσεις...εἰ δύναται ὁ πρωτότοκος πάσης κτίσεως εἶναι κ., καὶ μάλιστα καθ' ὃ σοφία ἐστὶν ἡ πολυποίκιλος· τῷ γὰρ εἶναι πάντας...τοὺς λόγους...ἐν αὐτῷ, εἴη ἂν καὶ αὐτὸς κ., τοσούτῳ ποικιλώτερος τοῦ αἰσθητοῦ κ. καὶ διαφέρων, ὅσῳ διαφέρει γυμνὸς πάσης ὕλης τοῦ ὅλου κ. λόγος τοῦ ἐνύλου κ., οὐκ ἀπὸ τῆς ὕλης ἀλλὰ ἀπὸ συμμετοχῆς τοῦ λόγου καὶ τῆς σοφίας τῶν κοσμούντων τὴν ὕλην κεκοσμημένων* Or.*Jo*.19.22(5; p.324.5ff.; M.14.568B,C); *ὅρα εἰ δύναται ὁ λέγων· 'οὐκ εἰμὶ ἐγὼ ἐκ τοῦ κ. τούτου' ἡ ψυχὴ εἶναι τοῦ Ἰησοῦ ἐμπολιτευομένη τῷ ὅλῳ κ. ἐκείνῳ καὶ πάντα αὐτὸν ἐμπεριερχομένη καὶ χειραγωγοῦσα ἐπ' αὐτὸν τοὺς μαθητευομένους. οὐδὲν ἔχει ἐκεῖνος ὁ κ. κάτω, ὡς οὐδὲ οὗτος...ἄνω* *ib*.(p.324.13; 568C); cf. ref. Inc. *ὁ δυνάμενος ἀπὸ τῆς κατὰ τὴν οἰκονομίαν γνώσεως, ἀφ' ἧς ὁ τῆς σαρκὸς τοῦ λόγου κ. γέγονε παρὰ τῷ πατρί, εἰς τὴν τῆς πρὸ τοῦ τὸν κ. τῆς τοῦ λόγου σαρκώσεως εἶναι παρὰ τῷ πατρὶ δόξης ἔννοιαν ἀναχθῆναι* Max.*ambig*.(M.91.1385B); **13.** of man as microcosm *ἡ σοφία...τὸν ἄνθρωπον οὕτως ἐδείματο...ὥστε κ. εἶναι μικρὸν τὸν ἄνθρωπον ἔχοντα ἐν ἑαυτῷ πάντα τὰ μέρη τοῦ ὅλου, μέγαν δὲ τὸν κ. ἄνθρωπον* Meth. *res*.2.10(p.350.11); *ὁ μικρὸς οὗτος κ. ... ὁ ἄνθρωπος* Gr.Naz.*or*.28.22 (p.56.15; M.36.57A); *ὁ τεχνίτης...λόγος...ζῷον ἐν ἐξ...ἀοράτου...καὶ ὁρατῆς φύσεως δημιουργεῖ τὸν ἄνθρωπον· καὶ παρὰ μὲν τῆς ὕλης λαβὼν τὸ σῶμα...παρ' ἑαυτοῦ δὲ πνοὴν ἐνθείς...οἷόν τινα κ. δεύτερον ἐν μικρῷ μέγαν ἐπὶ τῆς γῆς ἵστησιν* *ib*.38.11(324A); *οὔτε πρότερον ἡνίκα τὸν κ. ... παρήγαγεν* [sc. *ὁ λόγος*], *οὔτε ὕστερον ὅτε τὸν μέγαν ἐν μικρῷ κόσμον τὸν ἄνθρωπον ἑαυτῷ περιέπηξεν, περιεγράφη* Leont.B. *Nest.et Eut*.1(M.86.1284C); *ὁ...λόγος...ἀνακτίζει τὸν μικρὸν κ., τὸν σύνδεσμον πάσης τῆς κτίσεως, τουτέστιν τὸν ἄνθρωπον* Cosm.Ind.*top*.5 (M.88.320A); **14.** Gnost.; of sphere outside Pleroma, separated from it by *ὁ Σταυρός*, Clem.*exc.Thdot*.42(p.120.2; M.9.680A); cf. *ἐν τῷ κ. οὐκ εἶχεν ἄνδρα ἡ Σαμαρεῖτις· ἦν γὰρ αὐτῆς ὁ ἀνὴρ ἐν τῷ αἰῶνι* Heracleon ap.Or.*Jo*.13.11(p.236.1; M.14.416C); acc. Heracleon, *ib*.2. 14(8; p.70.5; 137A); *ib*.13.38(p.263.22; 465B); *ὁ...κ. τὸ σύμπαν τῆς κακίας ὄρος, ἔρημον οἰκητήριον θηρίων, ᾧ προσεκύνουν πάντες οἱ πρὸ νόμου καὶ οἱ ἐθνικοί* *ib*.13.16(p.239.34; 421C); exeg. Jo.1:27 *εἰ...καὶ ...νενόηται...πᾶς ὁ κ. ὑπόδημα εἶναι τοῦ Ἰησοῦ τῷ Ἡρακλέωνι, ἀλλ' οὐκ οἶμαι δεῖν συγκατατίθεσθαι* Or.*Jo*.6.39(23; p.148.23; 268C); *ὁ... Ἡρακλέων κ. τὸ ὑπόδημα ἐνδεξάμενος...οἴεται τὸν δημιουργὸν τοῦ κ. ἐλάττονα ὄντα τοῦ Χριστοῦ τοῦτο ὁμολογεῖν διὰ τούτων τῶν λέξεων* *ib*.(p.148.14; 268B); for Gnost. doctrine of creation of world by angels, v. *ἄγγελος*; Manich. *ὁ...κ. οὐδ' αὐτός ἐστι τοῦ θεοῦ, ἀλλ' ἢ ἀπὸ μέρους τῆς ὕλης ἐπλάσθη* Hegem.*Arch*.11(p.18.6; M.10. 1445A); created by *ζῶν πνεῦμα* *ib*.8(p.11.4; 1437C); *ib*.12(p.20.7; 1448A); *τὸ...σῶμα τοῦτο κ. καλεῖται πρὸς τὸν μέγαν κ.* *ib*.9(p.14.13; 1441B); of paradise *περὶ τοῦ παραδείσου ὃς καλεῖται κ.* *ib*.11(p.18.1; 1445A).

***κοσμοσέβαστος**, *venerated by the world*, of BMV *κ. τοῦ θεοῦ κιβωτός* ‡Jo.D.*hom*.5(M.96.648C).

***κοσμόσωστος**, *saving the world* *τῶν ἁγίων καὶ κ. ἀποστόλων* Jo. Jej.*canonar*.2(p.438); *τῆς τῶν ἀποστόλων κ. διδασκαλίας* ‡Jo.D.*ep. Thphl*.12(M.95.360C).

***κοσμοσώτειρα**, ἡ, *saviour of the world*, of BMV *σῶσόν με, κόρη κ.* Jo.Mon.*hymn.Blas*.9(M.96.1408B).

***κοσμοσωτήριος**, *world-saving*; of Cross, ‡Ath.*qu.al*.20(M.28. 793B); of Passion, ‡Gr.Naz.*Chr.pat*.proem.4(M.38.133A).

***κοσμοτέχνης**, ὁ, *framer of the world*; of God, Synes.*hymn*.3.424 (p.19; M.66.1599).

***κοσμοτεχνῖτις**, ἡ, *framer of the world*; of Wisdom, Synes.*hymn*. 2.30(p.44; M.66.1592).

***κοσμοτόκος**, *who gave birth to the world*; of Wisdom, Sophr.H. *carm*.1.123(M.87.3737D).

***κοσμότροπος**, *worldly*, *Hymn*.(*AS* 1 p.628).

***κοσμουργία**, ἡ, *making of the universe, creation of the world*, Dion.Ar.*ep*.9.2(M.3.1108B); Geo.Pis.*hex*.tit.(M.92.1426A).

κοσμοφθόρος, *world-destroying*; of lion killed by Heracles, Geo. Pis.*Heracl*.1.77(M.92.1305A).

***κοσμοφόρησις**, ἡ, *wearing of secular attire*, Thdr.Stud.*epp*.2.52 (M.99.1264B).

κοσμοφόρος, *world-carrying*; of Noah's ark, Cosm.Ind.*top*.2(M. 88.92C); *ib*.5(p.164.30; M. om.).

***κοσμόφρων**, *worldly-minded*, Ant.Mon.*hom*.5(M.89.1445C).

***κοσμοφύλαξ**, *guarding the universe* *κ. ἄγγελοι* Gr.Thaum.*Eccl*. 12:3(M.10.1016C).

***κοσμοφυσάω**, *be puffed up with worldly pride*, ‡Chrys.*hom.in Ps*.76:4(10.745A).

***κοσμοχώρητος**, *bounding the world*; of the sea, ‡Jo.D.*hom*.5(M. 96.852D).

***κοσμωπόθητος**, v. **κοσμοπόθητος*.

***κοσμωφελής**, *of benefit to the world*, Germ.CP *or*.1(M.98.232C).

***κοσσίζω**, *box on the ears, strike*, Pall.*h.Laus*.35(p.103.14; M.34. 1114B); Jo.Mosch.*prat*.105(M.87.2964D); Leont.N.*v.Sym*.5(M.93. 1703D).

κόσσος, ὁ, *box on the ear, blow*, Pall.*h.Laus*.23(p.76.19; M.34. 1089A); Leont.N.*v.Sym*.7(M.93.1728A); id.*v.Jo.Eleem*.36(p.73.14).

κόσ(σ)υμβος, ὁ, *netted head-dress*, Cyr.*Is*.1.3(2.69D); *ib*.(71D); Thdt.*Is*.3:18(p.21.2; *κόσσυμβος* 2.194).

κοσυμβωτός, *fringed*; of dress of Jewish priests, Cosm.Ind.*top*.5 (M.88.212D).

***κότζιον**, τό, *ankle-bone*, Melet.*nat.hom*.29(M.64.1265B).

κοττίζω, *play dice*, Jo.Mal.*chron*.13 p.345(M.97.516B).

κοττιστής, ὁ, *dice-player*, Jo.Mal.*chron*.18 p.451(M.97.661C).

κόττος, ὁ, *dicing*, Jo.Mal.*chron*.18 p.451(M.97.661C).

***κουβαλέω**, *carry away, carry off*, *Apophth.Patr*.(M.65.196A); *V. Dan*.9(p.257.23).

***κουβάρι(ο)ν**, τό, *ball*, Call.*v.Hyp*.(p.19); *οὐ δύνανται ἁπλῶσαι τοὺς ἑαυτῶν πόδας, ἀλλὰ κοιμῶνται ὡς κουβάριν* Leont.N.*v.Jo.Eleem*. 21(p.38.22).

κουβικουλαρία, ἡ, (Lat. *cubicularia*) *lady of the bed-chamber*; court title, *V.Aberc*.65(p.46.8); Jo.Mal.*chron*.5 p.95(M.97.181A); Thphn.*chron*.p.396(M.108.945A; *κουβικουλαρέα* de Boor).

***κουβικουλάριος**, ὁ, (Lat. *cubicularius*) *chamberlain*, a palace official, a eunuch; office held by Eutropius, Marc.Diac.*v.Porph*. 26; and Narses, Jo.Mal.*chron*.18 p.469(M.97.684B); Thphn.*chron*. p.109(M.108.313C).

***κουβουκλεῖον**, τό, (Lat. *cubiculum*) *bed-chamber*; in a palace, Mac.Aeg.*hom*.15.33(M.34.597C); Marc.Diac.*v.Porph*.45; Jo.Mal. *chron*.4 p.85(M.97.169A).

***κουβουκλείσιος** (**-κλείων**), ὁ, (Lat. *cubicularius*) *chamberlain*; a patriarchal official, CNic.(787)*act*.4(H.4.168C); *-κλείων* *ib*.5(312C).

***κουκίον**, τό, *bean*, *Const.Stud*.30(M.99.1716C).

***κουκούλλιον** (**κουκούλιον**), τό, (Lat. *cucullus*) *cowl, hood*; **1.** worn by children, not adults, Dor.*doct*.1.13(M.88.1633D) cit. s. 4 infra; **2.** of virgins *κεφαλοδέσμιον ἐρεοῦν, περισφίγγον τὴν κεφαλὴν καὶ κ.* Ath.*virg*.11(p.45.3; M.28.264B); in a convent *πᾶσαί εἰσι κεκαρμέναι, ἔχουσαι κουκούλλια* Pall.*h.Laus*.34(p.98.8; M.34.1106B); **3.** of monks; as part of monastic habit, *V.Pach.Φ* 41(p.26.1); *μηδεὶς ἑαυτῷ κτήσηται μηδὲν...παρεκτὸς τοῦ ἐνδύματος· ἅπερ εἰσὶν... σανδάλια, κ. δύο* Pach.*reg*.A,B(p.17.14; M.40.952A); *Apophth.Patr*. (M.65.180B); *ἐνδύσας αὐτὸν λευιτῶνα καὶ κ. αὐτοῦ τῇ κεφαλῇ περιθείς* ‡Pall.*h.mon*.11.7(p.56.2; M.65.449D); *γίνεταί τις τοῦ ῥαφιδίου δοῦλος ἢ τοῦ κ. ἢ τοῦ μανδυλίου* Zos.*alloquia* 5(M.78.1689B); *V.Dan*.7(p.67. 21); *μὴ μόνον ἐπὶ τοῦ στήθους κ. βραχὺ περικείμενος* Niceph.Ur.*v. Sym*.80(M.86.3061A); ‡Jo.D.*ep.Thphl*.28(M.95.380D); worn in church *ἀπιόντες...εἰς τὴν κοινωνίαν...μετὰ κ. μόνου εἰσιέτωσαν* Pall. *h.Laus*.32(p.89.13; M.34.1099D); in refectory *ἐσθίοντες...τὰς κεφαλὰς* καλυπτέτωσαν τοῖς κ., ἵνα μὴ ἀδελφὸς ἀδελφὸν μασώμενον ἴδῃ *ib.*(p.92.1; 1100B); in monastic profession ὁ ἀδελφὸς ἡμῶν ὁ δεῖνα ἐνδύεται τὸ κ. τῆς ἀκακίας εἰς περικεφαλαίαν ἐλπίδος *Euchol.*(p.411); in confession εἰ δὲ ἀββᾶς, ἐπάνω τῆς κεφαλῆς αὐτοῦ τὸ ἑαυτοῦ κ. βαλεῖν †Jo.Jej.*poenit.*(M.88.1892D); **4.** symbolic meaning τὸ...κ. σύμβολόν ἐστι τῆς χάριτος τοῦ...θεοῦ, σκεπαζούσης...τὸ ἡγεμονικὸν καὶ περιθαλπούσης τὴν ἐν Χριστῷ νηπιότητα διὰ τοὺς ῥαπίζειν ἀεὶ καὶ τιτρώσκειν ἐπιχειροῦντας Evagr.Pont.*cap.pract.*A proem.(M.40.1220C); κουκούλια ...αὐτοῖς ἐτύπωσεν ἄμαλλα ὡς παιδίοις, ἐν οἷς καὶ καυτῆρα τύπον σταυροῦ διὰ πορφυρίου ἐκέλευσεν ἐντίθεσθαι Pall.*h.Laus.*32(p.90.1; M.34.1099D); τὸ δὲ ἐπὶ τῆς κεφαλῆς σκέπασμα, ὃ κ. καλοῦσιν, ὥστε ἐπίσης ἀκεραίως καὶ καθαρῶς βιοῦν τοῖς γάλακτι τρεφομένοις παισίν, οἷς αἱ τοιαῦται τιάραι ἐπίκεινται, τὸ ἡγεμονικὸν σκέπουσαί τε καὶ περιθάλπουσαι Soz.*h.e.*3.14.7(M.67.1069C); λαμβάνομεν δὲ κ.· τοῦτο δέ ἐστι σύμβολον τῆς ταπεινώσεως· τὰ νήπια γὰρ τὰ μικρὰ τὰ ἄκακα φοροῦσι κουκούλια. ἄνθρωπος δὲ τέλειος κ. οὐ φορεῖ. ἡμεῖς οὖν διὰ τοῦτο φοροῦμεν, ἵνα νηπιάζωμεν τῇ κακίᾳ Dor.*doct.*1.13(M.88.1633C,D); τὸ δὲ κ. δηλοῖ τὴν φρουροῦσαν καὶ σκέπουσαν τὸν νοῦν ἡμῶν χάριν τοῦ θεοῦ· ὁ γὰρ ἀποκειράμενος τὰ τοῦ κόσμου νοήματα, τὴν περικεφαλαίαν δέχεται τοῦ σωτηρίου Max.*qu.dub.*67(M.90.841B); τὰ κ. κατὰ τὸν λέγοντα ἀπόστολον ὅτι ἐσταύρωταί μοι ὁ κόσμος κἀγὼ τῷ κόσμῳ ⟨δι' ὃ καὶ πορφυροῖς καὶ λευκοῖς λωρίοις καὶ σταυρίοις κεκόσμηται διὰ τὸ ῥυὲν ἐκ τῆς πλευρᾶς τοῦ κυρίου αἷμα καὶ ὕδωρ ὁμοῦ⟩ ‡Bas.*h.myst.*24(p.263.6).

κουκούμι(ο)ν, τό, *vessel, pitcher*, Cyr.S.*v.Thds.*(p.237.12).

κούκουμος, ὁ, (Lat. *cucuma*) = foreg., Thdr.Stud.*poen.*1.41(M.99.1737D).

***κούκουρον**, τό, *bag* κ. γέμον νομισμάτων Thphn.*chron.*p.306 (v.l. κουρκουρόν M.108.744B).

***κουλλίκιον**, τό, *unleavened bread*; so called by children, ‡Jo.D.*azym.*1(M.95.389C).

***κουνδοῦρος**, ὁ, *courier-horse*, *V.Aberc.*51(p.37.13, v.l. βερέδοις).

κουνίον, τό, *dormitory*, ‡Bas.*poen.mon.*15(2.527E; M.31.1308C).

***κούντουρον**, τό, ? *reckoning, estimated period* of time κράτει τὰ αὐτὰ κούντουρα τῶν χιλιοντάδων καὶ ἑκατοντάδων τῶν ἀπὸ κτίσεως κόσμου †Andr.Cr.*cycl.*(M.19.1329B).

***κουπανίζω**, *bruise, pulverize*, ‡Ath.*synops.*15(M.28.317D).

***κουπισμός**, ὁ, *beating*, Thdr.Stud.*epp.*1.48(M.99.1076B).

κουρά, ἡ, *cropping of hair, tonsure,* of monks μοναχὸν οὐχ ἡ κ. καὶ ἡ περιβολὴ συνίστησιν, ἀλλ' οὐράνιος πόθος καὶ ἡ ἔνθεος πολιτεία Ephr.1.276F; of priests μηδέ τινα...συγχωρεῖν ἐπ' ἄμβωνος...τοὺς...λόγους ἀποφωνεῖν, εἰ μή τι ἂν ἱερατικῇ κ. χρήσηται ὁ τοιοῦτος CTrull.*can.*33; cf.CNic.(787)*can.*14; ἡ ἐν τῇ κεφαλῇ τοῦ ἱερέως στρογγύλη κ. δηλοῖ τὸν ἀκάνθινον στέφανον ‡Sophr.H.*liturg.*6(M.87.3985D).

κουρατορεύω, *serve as curator of*, Pamph.Mon.*Soter.*2(p.116.4).

κουρατορία, ἡ, *crown possessions*, consisting of buildings and estates, often obtained by confiscation, Thphn.*chron.*p.412 (v.l. κουρατωρία M.108.977B).

κουράτωρ, ὁ, (Lat. *curator*); **1.** *protector*; of Christ, Jo.Mosch.*prat.*201(M.87.3089B); of BMV, Leont.N.*v.Jo.Eleem.*34(p.67.1); **2.** legal *guardian*, Thphn.*chron.*p.69(M.108.221A,B); **3.** *executor* ἐποίησεν τὸν ἄνβωνα...διὰ Κυριακοῦ τοῦ κ. *IGC* 1.94; ἀνηνέχθη ἡ διαθήκη τῷ βασιλεῖ διὰ τοῦ κ. Jo.Mal.*chron.*18 p.439(M.97.648C); **4.** *curator, administrative official* τὸν κ. τῆς πόλεως *M.Ner.et Ach.*19(p.19.6); Nil.*epp.*2.179 tit.(M.79.292C); *ib.*2.222(316B); κ. τῶν βασιλικῶν οἴκων, *curator domus divinae* (part of emperor's private property, comprising palaces in CP usually having provincial estates attached, which had been acquired by inheritance or confiscation), Thphn.*chron.*p.220(M.108.561A); having under him lesser curators of different properties which retained names of their old owners, Eustrat.*v.Eutych.*76(M.86.2361B); κ. τοῦ δεσποτικοῦ οἴκου τῶν Πλακιδίας Jo.Mal.*chron.*18 p.490(M.97.709A); cf.*IGC As.Min.*240; κ. τῶν Μαρίνης Thphn.*chron.*p.200(M.108.517A).

***κουράω**, *cut down, kill*, Thphn.*chron.*p.377(M.108.904B).

κουρεύ-ω, **1.** *cut the hair of, tonsure,* of monks ἐκούρευσα αὐτὸν... ἐνδύσας αὐτὸν τὸ μοναχικὸν σχῆμα Jo.Mosch.*prat.*78(M.87.2936C); *ib.*(2981C); †Anast.*relat.*34(*OC* 2 p.80.8ff.; M.88.608B); cf.*ib.*6(p.63.28); ἀγαγὼν τὸ ψαλίδιον καὶ...τεθεικὼς ἐπὶ τοῦ...θυσιαστηρίου ἐκούρευσεν αὐτούς Leont.N.*v.Sym.*12(M.93.1684D); εἶτα ~ει αὐτὸν σταυροειδῶς *Euchol.*(p.386); novices, *ib.*(p.379); *ib.*(p.380); of compulsory tonsure of politically dangerous persons ἐδήμευσεν αὐτὸν καὶ ~σας ἐποίησε παπᾶν τῆς μεγάλης ἐκκλησίας Κωνσταντινουπόλεως Jo.Mal.*chron.*14 p.361(M.97.537A); δείρας καὶ ~σας αὐτὸν καὶ σιδηρώσας, ἐξώρισεν Thphn.*chron.*p.319(M.108.772B); **2.** pass., *receive the tonsure, be professed*, Leont.N.*v.Sym.*12(M.93.1685A); **3.** med., *wear hair short*, Epiph.*exp.fid.*10(p.10.8; M.42.800A).

κουριάλιος** (κοριάλιος**), ὁ, (Lat. *curialis*) *courtier*, Gr.Mag.*dial.*(tr.Zach.)4.32(M.*PL*.77.371B); κορι-, *ib.*2.11(M.*PL*.66.155A).

κουρικός, *for cutting the hair*; of scissors, Clem.*paed.*3.11(p.270.31; M.8.636B).

***κουρικός**, ὁ, (cf. Lat. *curriculum*) *carriage* γυναῖκες κουρικόν τινα κοσμοῦσαι ἤτοι δίφρον Epiph.*haer.*79.1(p.476.16; M.42.741A).

***κουρίσκος**, ὁ, *barber*, Thphn.*chron.*p.39(M.108.153C).

***κουριῶσος**, ὁ, (Lat. *curiosus*) *official informer to the emperor*, *Ep.Alex.*ap.Ath.*apol.sec.*73(p.152.24; M.25.380C); *Ep.Mareot.*2 *ib.*76(p.155.34; 385A); Chrys.*ep.Innoc.*1.2(p.11.4; 3.517D).

***κουρκουρόν**, τό, v. *κούκουρον.

[*]**κούρκωμον**, τό, *snaffle* χαλινὸν...ὁλόχρυσον, διὰ μαργαριτῶν ὂν τὸ κ. αὐτοῦ Jo.Mal.*chron.*16 p.395(M.97.585A).

***κουροπαλάτης**, ὁ, *comes curiae*; originally title of one of several officials under the *castrensis*, concerned with administration of imperial palace; by Justin's reign, of a high official holding patrician rank, *Chron.Pasch.*p.332(M.92.861B); as dignity and unique title, conferred by Justinian on his nephew and heir, Evagr.*h.e.*5.1(p.195.9; M.86.2788D); thenceforward until 10th century bestowed only occasionally and only on members of imperial family, *Chron.Pasch.*p.379(M.92.969C); Thphn.*chron.*p.245(M.108.617A); *ib.*p.331(797B); *ib.*p.416(988C).

κουρόσυνος, *of hair-cutting*, Gr.Naz.*or.*40.1(M.36.360B).

κουρσεύω, *make predatory expeditions*, Thphn.*chron.*p.264(M.108.657A); *ib.*p.321(777A).

***κοῦρσον**, τό, *predatory band*, Thphn.*chron.*p.391(M.108.932B); *ib.*396(945A).

[*]**κοῦρσορ**, ὁ, v. κούρσωρ.

***κοῦρσος**, ὁ, (Lat. *cursus*) *predatory expedition*, Thphn.*chron.*p.271(M.108.669C).

κούρσωρ ([*]**κοῦρσορ**), ὁ, (Lat. *cursor*) *courier*, *Ep.Tib.*(p.78.4); τοὺς δρομεῖς, κούρσωρας καλουμένους Ῥωμαϊστί ‡Chrys.*hom.3.2 in Job*(6.588E); κοῦρσορ ‡Caes.Naz.*dial.*107(M.38.976).

[*]**κούρταλον**, τό, = κρόταλον, *clapper*; used in dances, *Contrad.*2(p.8).

[*]**κουσούλλιον**, τό, v. [*]κουσσούλιον.

***κουσπισμός**, ὁ, *putting in the stocks*, Thdr.Stud.*epp.*1.48(M.99.1076B).

***κοῦσπος**, ὁ, *wooden fetter* or movable *stocks* for the feet, Jo.Mal.*chron.*2 p.50(M.97.124B).

[*]**κουσσούλιον** ([*]**κουσσούλλιον**), τό, = κουσούλιον, monastic cloak, *Apophth.Patr.*(M.65.225B); Jo.Mosch.*prat.*151(M.87.3018A); -λλ-, *ib.*68(2920A).

κουστωδία, ἡ, (Lat. *custodia*); **1.** *guard*; at Christ's tomb, Chrys.*hom.89.1 in Mt.*(7.832B); ‡Hesych.H.*m.Long.*3(M.93.1548A); Alex.Sal.*cruc.*(M.87.4036C); **2.** *guard-house, prison*, *V.Eudoc.*13(p.884); Pall.*h.Laus.*38(p.118.4; M.34.1193A); **3.** *vigilance, attention*, Chrysipp.*enc.in Jo.Bapt.*(p.44.6).

***κουτζαίνομαι**, *become lame*, *Nomoc.*31.

***κουτζός**, *lame*, *Nomoc.*94; *Mir.Geo.*5(p.63.3).

[*]**κούτζουλον**, τό, = [*]κουσσούλιον, Geo.Al.*v.Chrys.*42(p.217.22).

***κούτουλος**, ? *with bowed head*, Barth.Edess.*Agar.*(M.104.1428B).

κουφίζ-ω, **1.** *reduce in weight, make light* ἐπὶ πελάγους ~εται [sc. Christ]...ἀλλὰ Πέτρον ~ει βαπτιζόμενον Gr.Naz.*or.*29.20(p.104.15f.; M.36.100C); **2.** *relieve* from burden of sin, Or.*comm.in Ex.*(M.12.272C); *Clem.ep.*15(M.2.52B); **3.** *remit*, ref. excommunication κουφισθήτω αὐτῷ καὶ ἕτερος χρόνος Thdr.Stud.*epp.*2.67(M.99.1293C); **4.** *elevate*, liturg. ~ων ὁ ἱεράρχης τὸν ἅγιον ἄρτον, ἐδείκνυ τὴν εὐλογίαν λέγων· 'τὰ ἅγια τοῖς ἁγίοις' Max.*schol.e.h.*3.3(M.4.148B).

κουφισμός, ὁ, **1.** *lightening, mitigation* ἄνεσιν ἕξειν καὶ κ. τῆς ἐκεῖ τιμωρίας Dion.Al.*fr.*(p.60.5); of impiety, Const.ap.Eus.*v.C.*2.28(p.53.3; M.20.1005B); of sin, id.ap.Gel.Cyz.*h.e.*3.19.3(M.85.1345A); Pall.*h.Laus.*6(p.23.9; M.34.1018D); of spiritual evils, Jo.Mon.*hymn.Geo.*7(M.96.1397D); of mental disquietude, Dor.*doct.*1.17(M.88.1640D); of sufferings and disasters, Thdr.Mops.*Joel.*1:4f.(M.66.213C); **2.** *remission* of taxation, Thdt.*ep.*43(4.1103); **3.** *elevation*, liturg. τὸν κ. τῆς μιᾶς εὐλογίας τοῦ θείου ἄρτου...ὃν ὑψοῖ ὁ ἱερεὺς λέγων· 'τὰ ἅγια τοῖς ἁγίοις' Max.*schol.e.h.*3.2(M.4.137A).

***κουφόγλωσσος**, *light-tongued, flippant in speech*, Or.*sel.in Ezech.*3:5(M.13.773C).

***κουφογνώμων**, *light-minded, shallow*, Pall.*h.Laus.*proem.(p.9.8; εὐεξαπατήτων M.34.1001).

***κουφοδοξία**, ἡ, *vainglory, futile opinion*, Pall.*h.Laus.*proem.(p.12.27; M.34.1004); Nil.*epp.*2.49(M.79.220C).

κοῦφος, **1.** *light, vain*; c. genit., *empty, void* πίστεως τοῦ μυστηρίου κ. ὢν Εὐτυχὴς...καὶ ἀμέτοχος Leo Mag.*ep.*28(p.17.13; M.*PL*.54.774B);

2. *lightened*; **a.** *unhampered, unfettered*; of Lazarus unbound, Nonn.*par.Jo.*11:44(M.43.848A); **b.** *relieved of burden*, hence *fine, subtle, immaterial* ἐάν...τις ἐπὶ κύριον καταφύγῃ, ἀποτρέχει τὸ πονηρὸν πνεῦμα ἀπ' αὐτοῦ, καὶ γίνεται ἡ διάνοια κ. *T.Sym.*3.5; κενοῖ τῆς ὕλης τὴν ψυχὴν ἡ νηστεία καὶ καθαρὰν καὶ κ. σὺν τῷ σώματι παρίστησι τοῖς θείοις λόγοις Clem.*ecl.*14(p.140.29; M.9.705A); αἱ δὲ [sc. ψυχαί]...κ. εἰς τὸν ὑπερκόσμιον τόπον ὑπερκύψασαι τοῦ βίου Meth. *symp.*8.2(p.82.12; M.18.140C); Gr.Nyss.*anim.et res.*(M.46.88A); εἰ... κ. καὶ ἀπέριττος τύχῃ [sc. ἡ ψυχή]...εὔκολος αὐτῇ ἡ πρὸς τὸν ἐπισπώμενον [sc. θεόν] προσχώρησις γίνεται *ib.*(97B); Chrys.*hom.8.4 in 1Thess.*(11.484E); of spiritual body τὸ...οὐράνιον σῶμα λεπτόν τε καὶ κ. καὶ ἀεικίνητον Gr.Nyss.*infant.*(M.46.173B); τίς γὰρ ἂν γένοιτο τοῦ...κ. πρὸς τὸ βαρύ τε καὶ ἐμβριθὲς κοινωνία; *ib.*; of spiritual realm ἡ... νοητὴ [sc. κτίσις]...τοῖς κ. τε καὶ αἰθεριώδεσι τόποις ἐνδιατρίβουσα id. *or.dom.*4(p.74.17; M.44.1165C); hence **c.** *spiritual, not devoted* to material things, Chrys.*hom.24.3 in Eph.*(11.184A); **3.** as subst.; **a.** κουφότατον, τό, *fineness, subtlety* βαρὺ πᾶν τοῦ γράμματος φορτίον ἐστὶν τὸ ἀνώφορον καὶ κ. τοῦ πνεύματος χωρεῖν μὴ δυναμένου Or.*Jo.*10.29(18; p.202.19; M.14.360A); **b.** κοῦφον, τό, *jar*, *Apophth.Patr.*(M.65.257C).

***κουφοσιτία, ἡ,** *living on light food*, Pall.*v.Chrys.*12(p.69.27; M.47.39).

***κουφοσύνθετος,** *lightly built, insecure*, Geo.Pis.*van.*21(M.92.1583A).

***κοφινίς, ἡ,** *basket*, Thdt.*h.e.*3.20.3(3.937).

***κοχλαδόν,** *in bubbles*, ‡Chrys.*virt.spei*(9.860D).

κοχλάζω, = καχλάζω, *boil, bubble, quiver*, *A.Mt.*3(p.220.1); *Apoc. Paul.*31(p.57); *M.Bon.*9(p.329); Jo.Mal.*chron.*17 p.419(M.97.620B).

κόχλασμα, τό, *hissing, bubbling*; of boiling liquids, Ephr.3.250B.

κοχλίας, ὁ, *spirally twisted object*; hence **1.** *screw, rack*; as instrument of torture, *M.Pers.*1.16(p.434.4); *ib.*1.17(p.435.7); *M.Niceph.*4(p.285); **2.** *spiral staircase*, Cyr.S.*v.Sab.*18(p.102.24); *Chron.Pasch.* p.313(M.92.796D); esp. of that bet. palace and emperor's seat in circus, Jo.Mal.*chron.*13 p.320(M.97.480A); Thphn.*chron.*p.107(M.108.309C).

κοχλιοειδής ([*]**κοχλιώδης**), *spiral*; of the winding staircase leading to the middle chamber of Solomon's temple -ιώδης Thdt. *qu.24 in 3Reg.*(1.469); Proc.G.*3Reg.*6:24(M.87.1156D); Jo.Mal.*chron.* 2 p.32(M.97.101A, cod. -ιώδης).

***κοχλογένητος,** *born from a shell*, Evagr.*h.e.*1.11(p.20.6; M.86.2452C).

***κοχλοειδῶς,** *in the form of a spiral*, Gr.Nyss.*ep.*25(p.77.17, v.l. κογχλοειδῶς M.46.1096B).

κόχλος, ὁ, *shell-fish*; used for purple dye, Nonn.*par.Jo.*19:5(M.43.897C); *oyster*; believed to have no natural progeny but to produce pearls from dew fallen from heaven, hence of BMV τὴν ἄσπορον κ., τὴν τὸν οὐράνιον...μαργαρίτην τίκτουσαν Χριστόν Jo.Eub. *concept.BMV* 4(M.96.1465A).

***κοψίχη, ἡ,** *scrap*; thrown to dogs, Cosm.Mel.*schol.*119(M.38.562) in Gr.Naz.*carm.*1.2.10.313.

***κραβαταρία (-ρέα), ἡ,** *litter, bier* -ρέαν Jo.Mal.*chron.*16 p.397(M.97.588B); *ib.*18 p.436(644B).

κράβατος, ὁ, v. κράββατος.

***κραβαττοπυρία, ἡ,** *gridiron*; as instrument of torture, *M.Ign. Rom.*9.

***κραββατίζω,** ? *fling down* ἐστύλισαν ἐκραββάτισαν καὶ ἐπτέρνισαν Thal.CP *Thds.*3(p.8.30, v.l. ἐκρεβάτισαν M.91.1476A).

[*]**κραββάτιον, τό,** *bed, mattress*, CChalc.*act.*11(*ACO* 2.1.3 p.46.22; H.2.549A).

κράβ(β)ατος, ὁ, 1. *bed, mattress*, *A.Thom.*A 53(p.169.13); avoided as a vulgar word, ref. Mc.2:10, Jo.5:8 σκίμποδα ἀντὶ τοῦ κ., μεταβαλὼν τὸ ὄνομα, εἶπε Soz.*h.e.*1.11.9(M.67.889A); κράβατος Jo.Mal. *chron.*18 p.482(M.97.697C); met. μὴ πάλιν ἐπὶ κραββάτου ῥιφῇς ἁμαρτήσας Gr.Naz.*or.*40.33(M.36.405C); **2.** *bier*, Jo.Mal.*chron.*18 p.489(M.97.708B); Germ.CP *or.*8(M.98.369A); **3.** *gridiron*; an instrument of torture, *M.Eleuth.*4(p.152).

***κραββατοφόριος, ὁ,** *bier*, *V.Eudoc.*11(p.882).

κράζ-ω, 1. *cry aloud*, in mystery rites, Hipp.*haer.*4.28(p.54.15; M.16.3090C); *ib.*(p.55.14; 3091A); *ib.*5.8(p.96.17; 3150C); *ib.*(p.92.4; 3143B); to God in prayer, *Pss.Sal.*5.3; οἱ μαθηταὶ...εὐχαῖς σχολάζοντες πρὸς κύριον κεκράγασιν Or.*schol.in Cant.*5:11(M.17.276A); Meth.*symp.*1.1(p.8.21; M.18.37C); *ib.*11(p.134.22; 212A); *ib.*(p.135.20; 212B); inwardly ἔστιν...ὁμιλία πρὸς τὸν θεὸν ἡ εὐχή· κἂν...μηδὲ τὰ χείλη ἀνοίγοντες μετὰ σιγῆς προσλαλῶμεν, ἔνδοθεν κεκράγαμεν· πᾶσαν γὰρ τὴν ἐνδιάθετον ὁμιλίαν ὁ θεὸς...ἐπαΐει Clem.*str.*7.7(p.30.17; M.9.456B); of angel's salutation to BMV ~ω σοι· χαῖρε, νύμφη ἀνύμφευτε ‡Serg.*acath.*6(p.140; M.92.1335A); ἄγγελος πρωτοστάτης...ἵστατο ~ων πρὸς αὐτήν *ib.*11(p.140; 1337A); **2.** *proclaim aloud, preach* ὁ... ἀπόστολος κεκραγὼς καὶ γράφων περιτομὴν τὴν χειροποίητον οὐδὲν ὠφελεῖν Clem.*str.*7.9(p.39.17; M.9.476A); κέκραγε μυστικῶς ταῦτα λέγων ὁ προφήτης Or.*hom.16.1 in Jer.*(p.133.20; M.13.440C); τὸ πνεῦμα τὸ ἅγιον τοιαῦτα μελῳδεῖ...κεκραγός Meth.*symp.*1.3(p.12.7; M.18.44B); Marcell.*fr.*89 ap.Eus.*Marcell.*1.4(p.29.23; M.24.772B); Thdt. *affect.*7(p.189.22; 4.892); met. Ἰησοῦς...αὐτὸς μὲν...σιωπᾷ..., ἀπολογεῖται δὲ ἐν τῷ βίῳ τῶν...ἑαυτοῦ μαθητῶν, κεκραγότι τὰ διαφέροντα καὶ πάσης ψευδομαρτυρίας ὄντι κρείττονι Or.*Cels.*proem.2(p.52.22; M.11.645A); *Hom.Clem.*3.14; ἡ...περὶ τῆς θεοσεβείας...γνῶσις...καθ' ἡμέραν τοῖς ἔργοις κέκραγε Ath.*gent.*1(M.25.4A); **3.** *acclaim*, *Chron. Pasch.*p.318(M.92.809A); *ib.*p.330(853B); *ib.*p.339(885A); **4.** *call upon, summon* ὁ θάνατος...φοβούμενος οὐκ ἐτόλμα προσεγγίσαι αὐτῷ [sc. Christ]· διὰ τοῦτο ἔκλινεν ὁ Χριστὸς τὴν κεφαλήν, ~ων αὐτόν ‡Ath.*qu. script.*41(M.28.725A); **5.** *crow*; of a cock, Nonn.*par.Jo.*18:27(M.43.893C).

***κραιπαλικός,** *intoxicated*, *Vaticin.*1(p.49).

κρᾶμα, τό, 1. *mixture*; of liquids, Clem.*paed.*2.3(p.177.24ff.; M.8.432B); esp. of wine and water, *ib.*1.6(p.118.6; 305B); Nemes.*nat. hom.*3(M.40.593A); met. τὸ κ. τοῦ νόμου τοῦ παλαιοῦ καὶ τοῦ λόγου τοῦ νέου Clem.*paed.*2.2(p.174.3; 424B); of influx of H. Ghost upon man's inward vision οὐρανόθεν ἐπεισρέοντος ἡμῖν τοῦ ἁγίου πνεύματος· κ. τοῦτο αὐγῆς ἀϊδίου *ib.*1.6(p.106.26; 284A); eucharistic, Just. *1apol.*65.3(M.6.428A) cit. s. προΐστημι; Clem.*paed.*2.2(p.168.4; 412A) cit. s. κρᾶσις; ἐν...τῇ τῶν μυστηρίων παραδόσει σῶμα τὸν ἄρτον ἐκάλεσε καὶ αἷμα τὸ κ. Thdt.*eran.*1(4.26); ὁ τὰ μυστικὰ αὐτοῦ κ. ἀδεῶς...δεχόμενος ‡Caes.Naz.*dial.*140(M.38.1065); **2.** *union* of soul and body, hence of human nature τὸ θεῖον κ. τὸν ἄνθρωπον Clem.*paed.*2.2(p.168.8; M.8.412A); οὐ τῷ κρείττονι τὸ χεῖρον ὑποζεύγνυμεν, τὸν χοῦν λέγω τῷ πνεύματι, ὡς ἂν οἱ τῷ κ. δικαίως δικάζοντες; Gr.Naz.*or.*27.7(p.12.7; M.36.20C); *ib.*28.3(p.26.11; 29B); τῶν ἐκ τοῦ αὐτοῦ πηλοῦ καὶ κράματος *ib.*38.5(316C); *ib.*45.7(632A).

***κράνη, ἡ,** *skull*, ‡Caes.Naz.*dial.*140(M.38.1057).

κρανίον, τό, *skull*; **1.** *Golgotha, Calvary*, as burial-place of Adam πόθεν...ἡ ἐπωνυμία τοῦ κ., ἀλλ' ἐπειδὴ τοῦ πρωτοπλάστου ἀνθρώπου ἐκεῖ τὸ κ. ηὕρηται καὶ ἐκεῖ τὸ λείψανον ἐναπέκειτο, τούτου ἕνεκα κ. τόπος ἐπεκέκλητο Epiph.*haer.*46.5(p.209.10ff.; M.41.845A); Nil.*epp.*1.2(M.79.84A); κρανίου τόπον, ὃν Ἑβραίων οἱ διδάσκαλοί φασι τοῦ Ἀδὰμ εἶναι τάφον ‡Ath.*pass.*12(M.28.208A); ‡Bas.Sel.*or.*38.3(M.85.409A); Thphn.*chron.*p.21(M.108.112B); *ib.*p.74(233A); **2.** *the church on Calvary*, Marc.Diac.*v.Porph.*7; Cyr.S.*v.Sab.*56(p.149.3); *ib.*(p.152.10); Ant.Mon.*ep.Eust.*(M.89.1428A).

***κρασί(ο)ν, τό,** *cup, draught* of liquid, *A.Thom.*A 120(p.230.15); Jo.Mosch.*prat.*113(M.87.2977C).

κρᾶσις, ἡ, *blending, blend*, def. κ. ἐστιν οὐσιῶν ἀλλήλαις ἑτεροίων συνδρομὴ καὶ τῶν περὶ αὐτὰς ποιοτήτων ἀντεμβολή Jo.D.*dialect.*65(M.94.664B); **1.** process of *blending, composition*; **a.** in gen.; of alloys, Clem.*str.*1.16(p.49.1; M.8.785A); of the human body, Melet. *nat.hom.*synops.(M.64.1088B); freq. of wine with water ἡ κ....τοῦ οἴνου καὶ τοῦ ὕδατος ἀμφότερα συνδιαφθείρει Nemes.*nat.hom.*3(M.40.593A); Dion.Ar.*ep.*9.6(M.3.1113C); in eucharist κίρναται ὁ μὲν οἶνος τῷ ὕδατι, τῷ δὲ ἀνθρώπῳ τὸ πνεῦμα, καὶ τὸ μὲν εἰς πίστιν εὐωχεῖ, τὸ κρᾶμα, τὸ δὲ εἰς ἀφθαρσίαν ὁδηγεῖ, τὸ πνεῦμα, ἡ δὲ ἀμφοῖν αὖθις κ., ποτοῦ τε καὶ λόγου, εὐχαριστία κέκληται Clem.*paed.*2.2(p.168.5; M.8.412A); **b.** mental, *synthesis* τὴν...κ. τῶν ὄντων ἤτοι σύνθεσιν τῆς ἡμετέρας γνώμης εἶναι σύμβολον Max.*ambig.*(M.91.1136A); **c.** Gnost. ἔστιν Ἰησοῦς καὶ ἡ Ἐκκλησία καὶ ἡ Σοφία δι' ὅλων κρᾶσις τῶν σωμάτων δυνατὴ κατὰ τοὺς Οὐαλεντινιανούς Clem.*exc.Thdot.*17(p.112.8; M.9.665B); λέγουσιν οἱ Σηθιανοὶ τὸν περὶ κράσεως καὶ μίξεως λόγον συνεστάναι Hipp.*haer.*5.21(p.123.7; M.16.3187C); freq. in Clementine cosmological speculations τὰ...στοιχεῖα θεὸς εἶναι οὐ δύναται τὰ ὑπὸ ἄλλου γενόμενα, οὐχ ἡ μίξις, οὐχ ἡ κ., οὐχ ἡ γένεσις *Hom. Clem.*6.24; ἢ τῇ κ. συμβέβηκεν αὐτοῦ ἡ προαίρεσις ἢ ἄνευ κ. καὶ θεοῦ βουλῆς συνέβη γενέσθαι ἐξ οὐκ ὄντων *ib.*19.9; **d.** ref. Creation ἐξ αὐτοῦ, καὶ δι' αὐτοῦ, καὶ οὐσία, καὶ ζωὴ πᾶσα...καὶ αἱ τῶν ὄντων ἀναλογίαι, καὶ ἁρμονίαι, καὶ κράσεις Dion.Ar.*d.n.*4.10(M.3.705C); *ib.*5.7(821B); *ib.*8.5(892D); **2.** composition in particular proportions τῶν...συγκραμάτων οὐχ ὡσαύτως ἀεὶ διαμενόντων τὰ σπέρματα ἄλλοτε ἄλλην ἔχοντα κ. ἀποκρίνονται, οἷς πρὸς τὴν τοῦ καιροῦ κ. καὶ αἱ γνῶμαι ἕπονται εἴτε ἀγαθαί, εἴτε κακαί *Hom.Clem.*20.5; τὰς ὥρας τῶν ἰδίων ἐξήγαγε [sc. human sin] φύσεων καὶ τῶν καιρῶν τὰς ἰδέας εἰς ἀλλοκότους κ. διήμειψεν Bas.*hom.*8.2(2.63D; M.31.308C); freq. of the atmosphere τὴν τῶν ἀέρων καὶ πρὸς τὸ χρήσιμον ζῴοις καὶ μάλιστα ἀνθρώποις κ. Or.*Cels.*8.52(p.267.22; M.11.1593C); *Const. App.*7.34.7; Chrys.*sac.*4.3(p.110.2; 1.408A); hence *temperament*, constitution ἐλλέβορος...ὀρτύγων ἐστὶ τροφή, ἰδιότητι κράσεως τὴν βλάβην ἀποφευγόντων Bas.*hex*.5.4(1.43C; M.29.101D); ἵνα πρὸς τὴν αὐτοῦ ἕκαστος κ. ἐπιτηδείῳ χρήσηται φαρμάκῳ *Hom.Clem*.17.12; *ib.* 19.12; ὁ πονηρὸς σκότῳ χαίρειν κατὰ τὴν κ. γεγονὼς *ib*.20.9; τὴν εὔτακτον τῶν ἐν ἡμῖν στοιχείων κ. Cyr.*hom.pasch*.7(5^{2}.82B); τρία ὑπάρχουσι πράγματα, δι' ὧν λαμβάνεις λογισμούς· ἡ αἴσθησις καὶ ἡ μνήμη, καὶ ἡ κ. τοῦ σώματος Thal.*cent*.1.46(M.91.1432C); *ib*.3.32 (1452A); Jo.D.*f.o*.1.8(M.94.828B); **3.** product of composition, *mixture, compound, combination* in creation generally σύνθετος...ὁ κόσμος καὶ ἐκ διαφόρων οὐσιῶν τε καὶ κ. τὴν σύστασιν ἔχει Meth. *arbitr*.12(p.176.1); Ath.*gent*.37(M.25.73B); of colour, Eus.*v.C*.4.7 (p.120.14; M.20.1156B); between classes of people κ. τις...λευιτικῶν καὶ Ἰσραηλιτικῶν ταγμάτων Proc.G.*Jos*.21:27ff.(M.87.1040B); esp. of mixture of wine and water τὴν γοῦν ἕνωσιν τῶν θείων νοημάτων καὶ τῶν ἐπιγείων λόγων κ. οὐκ ἀπεικότως ἐκάλεσε Isid.Pel.*epp*.2.3(M. 78.460A); of a *drink* whether mixed or not τὸ δὲ κεράσματος οὐ κεκραμένου λέγει...ἐπειδὴ κρᾶσιν πολλάκις καλοῦμεν τὸ μέτρον ὃ πρὸς πόσιν ἀρκεῖ Thdr.Mops.*Ps*.74:8(M.66.696C); of union of soul and body δύο τινὰ συναγόντων τῇ φύσει ἐναντία εἰς κ. μίαν Or.*Jo*.13.50(49; p.277.24; M.14.489A); ἡ ψυχῆς πρὸς σῶμα κ. Apoll.*fr*.134(p.239.27)ap. Thdt.*eran*.2(4.172); **4.** Christol.; **a.** *union* of natures πολλῷ...μᾶλλον ἐπὶ τῆς τοῦ ἀσωμάτου πρὸς σῶμα κ. μένει τὸ τῆς φύσεως τῶν ἑνωθέντων Apoll. *fr*.147(p.246.24)ap.Leont.B.*Apoll*.(M.86.1965B); ἓν ἐκ δύο τῶν ἐναντίων, σαρκὸς καὶ πνεύματος...ὢν τῆς καινῆς μίξεως· ὢ τῆς παραδόξου κ. Gr.Naz.*or*.38.13(M.36.325C); τὴν πρὸς ἡμᾶς τοῦ θεοῦ λόγου κ. id.*carm*.2.1.11.612(M.37.1071A); γίνεται σὺν αὐτοῖς [sc. soul and body] ἕν, μένων ἐν ᾧπερ ἦν καὶ πρὸ τῆς ἑνώσεως· καινότερος οὗτος ὁ τρόπος τῆς κ. ἢ ἑνώσεως Nemes.*nat.hom*.3(M.40.601B); *ib.* (605A); orthodox usage explained τὸ μὲν γὰρ τῆς κ. ὄνομα τεθείκασί τινες καὶ τῶν ἁγίων πατέρων...μὴ ἄρα τις ἀνάχυσις συμβῆναι νομισθῇ καθάπερ ἐν τάξει τῶν ἀλλήλοις συγκεκραμένων ὑγρῶν...κατακέχρηνται δὲ τῇ λέξει, τὴν εἰς ἄκρον ἕνωσιν τῶν ἀλλήλοις συμβεβηκότων καταδηλοῦν σπουδάζοντες Cyr.*Nest*.1.3(p.22.7; 6^{1}.15C); usage reappearing in later writers περὶ δὲ τῶν κατὰ σύνθεσιν ἤγουν συμπλοκὴν ἢ κ. ἢ ἕνωσιν ἢ ὅπως ποτὲ φίλον καλεῖν τὰς...σχέσεις λεκτέον Leont.B.*Nest. et Eut*.1(M.86.1304A); ἐφ' ἑαυτόν, ἐν ᾧ ὥς τινι κρατῆρι κατὰ τὸ τῆς οἰκονομίας μυστήριον, ἡ παράδοξος κ. τῆς θείας φύσεως καὶ τῆς ἀνθρωπίνης ἀσυγχύτως καθ' ὑπόστασιν γέγονε ‡Proc.G.*Pr*.9:3(M.87. 1301D); ταῦτα...ἐκ τῆς πρὸς τὸ ἀνθρώπινον κ. ἐπιλέγεται τῷ λόγῳ Jo.D.*f.o*.4.18(M.94.1184B); **b.** *fusion*, implying *confusion* (in this sense freq. coupled with σύγχυσις and suspect to such writers as Thdr. Mops., Nest., and Thdt.) περιττὸν μὲν τὸ τῆς κ. καὶ ἀπρεπὲς καὶ ἀφαρμόζον, ἑκάστης τῶν φύσεων ἀδιαλύτως ἐφ' ἑαυτῆς μεινάσης, πρόδηλον δὲ ὡς τὸ τῆς ἑνώσεως ἐφαρμόζον Thdr.Mops.*fr.inc*.8(p.299. 1; M.66.981A); Nest.*fr*.C 10(p.273.8)ap.Cyr.*apol.orient*.4(p.42.27; 6^{1}. 170B) cit. s. διαιρέω; *ib*.C 4(p.229.7,16)ap.Cyr.*Nest*.5.4(6^{1}.132C,D); συνάφειαν κηρύττομεν καὶ οὐ σύγχυσιν, ἕνωσιν, οὐ κ. Jo.Ant.*hom*.(p.84. 20); τοὺς δὲ λέγοντας ὅτι κ. ἢ σύγχυσις ἢ φυρμὸς ἐγένετο τοῦ θεοῦ λόγου πρὸς τὴν σάρκα, καταξιωσάτω ἡ σὴ ὁσιότης ἐπιστομίζειν Cyr.*ep*.39 (p.19.2; 5^{2}.107E); ἡ καθ' ὑπόστασιν ἕνωσις, ἣν ἀντὶ κ. ἡμῖν, ὡς οἶμαι, προβάλλεται Thdt.ap.Cyr.*apol.Thdt*.2(p.115.2; 6^{1}.208E); ἐπιφημίζει πάλιν ἡμῖν τῆς Ἀπολιναρίου κακοδοξίας τὸν μῶμον, καὶ οὐκ αἰσχύνεται λέγων ὅτι λέξεσιν ἑτέραις τὸ τῆς κ. ἤτοι συγχύσεως ἐπικρύπτει χρῆμα Cyr.*apol.Thdt*.11(p.143.19; 237E); οἱ ἐπ' ἀναιρέσει τῶν δύο φύσεων, οἱ τὰ τῆς κ. καὶ συγχύσεως, καὶ τῆς ἀπὸ σώματος εἰς θεότητα μεταβολῆς ...πραγματευόμενοι Thdt.*rect.conf*.15(M.6.1233B); συνουσίωσιν λέγει [sc. Πολέμιος] γεγενῆσθαι καὶ κρᾶσιν τῆς θεότητος καὶ τοῦ σώματος id.*haer*.4.9(4.363); οἱ δὲ σύγχυσιν καὶ κ. εἰσάγοντες καὶ μίαν εἶναι φύσιν τῆς σαρκὸς καὶ τῆς θεότητος ἀνοήτως ἀναπλάττοντες *Symb.Chalc.* (p.324.21; H.2.453D).

κραταίβολος, *wielded with violence*, ‡Gr.Naz.*Chr.pat*.667(M.38. 189A).

κραταιός, **1.** *strong, mighty*; of God, *Pss.Sal*.2.33; *ib*.4.28; of his power, Herm.*vis*.1.3.4; esp. of his hand, *T.Jos*.1.5; *1Clem*.28.2; denoting Son ὁ υἱός, ἡ...κ. χεὶρ τοῦ πατρὸς Meth.*creat*.9(p.498.29; M. 18.341A); Serap.*euch*.25.1; superl. in phrase κατὰ τὸ κ. *most decisively* κατὰ τὸ κ. καταπολεμηθείς Philost.*h.e*.3.26(M.65.513B); **2.** *powerful* either in position or influence, Thphyl.*exc.Rom*.5(p.224. 14; M.113.932B).

κραταιότης, ἡ, **1.** *power, might*; **a.** of God 'ὄρη' ὀνομάζων τοὺς μεγαλοφρονοῦντας...ἀγνοοῦντας...τὴν τοῦ θεοῦ κ. Bas.*hom.in Ps*.45 (1.172D; M.29.421A); Gr.Nyss.*hom.5 in Cant*.(M.44.861B); **b.** of men ἡ κ. τῶν ἀρχῶν Isid.Pel.*epp*.1.290(M.78.352D); **c.** of mountains διαφέρει κραταιότητι τῆς λοιπῆς γῆς τὰ ὄρη Nil.ap.Proc.G.*Cant*.2:9(M. 87.1597A); **2.** *firmness, constancy* γενναιότητος καὶ κ. Thdr.Stud.*epp*. 1.51(M.99.1097B).

κραται-όω, **A.** *strengthen*; **1.** act., *increase* ἐκραταίωσας ἐφ' ἡμᾶς τὸ ἔλεός σου ‡Meth.*Sym.et Ann*.8(M.18.368C); **2.** pass.; **a.** *grow strong* ἐκραταιοῦτο ἡ παῖς [sc. BMV] *Protev*.6.1(p.12); **b.** *be strengthened*, fig. οἱ δὲ...στῦλοι τοῦ κυρίου, ~ωθέντες ὑπ' αὐτοῦ...γεγόνασιν...μάρτυρες Dion.Al.ap.Eus.*h.e*.6.41.14(M.20.609A); in temporal power μονάρχου δυναστείας μιμήματι ~ούμενος Eus.*l.C*.3(p.201.21; M.20.1329B); ~ουμένης...τῷ Νέρωνι τῆς ἀρχῆς id.*h.e*.2.25.1(M.20.208A); substituted for ἰσχύω in citation of 3Reg.2:2, Thdt.*qu.3 in 3Reg*.(1.456); εἰσπνεόμενος ἀπὸ τοῦ πονηροῦ νόμος...ὑπὸ τοῦ ἐν σαρκὶ...~οῦται νόμου Meth.*res*.2.7(p.342.7; M.41.1173B); in spirit δυναμούμενος...καὶ ~ούμενος ἀνήρει πᾶν 'τὸ φρόνημα τῆς σαρκός' Or.*Cels*.7.22(p.174.1; M.11.1452D); οὐδὲν εἰς τὸ καθελεῖν αὐτήν [sc. τὴν ἐκκλησίαν], ὡς ἂν ὑπὸ τοῦ θεοῦ ~ουμένην, ἰσχύσουσι Eus.*d.e*.1.1(p.5.11; M.22.20A); τῇ τοῦ θεοῦ ~ούμενοι δυνάμει Chrys.*hom.13.2 in Mt*.(7.169B); of the knowledge of God, *be mighty, overwhelming*, ref. Ps.138:6 κεκραταιῶσθαί τε πλέον ἢ κατὰ τὴν ἑαυτοῦ δύναμιν καὶ περίδραξιν Gr.Naz.*or*. 28.21(p.54.6; M.36.53C).

B. *solidify* τὸν Ἀδὰμ...τηκτὸν ὄντα...καὶ μηδέπω φθάσαντα δίκην ὀστράκου τῇ ἀφθαρσίᾳ ~ωθῆναι...ὁ θεός, ἐν τῇ παρθενικῇ ~ώσας... μήτρᾳ...ἄθραυστον ἐξήγαγεν Meth.*symp*.3.5(p.31.16ff.; M.18.68B).

C. *confirm*; **1.** act. τὸ τῆς ὀρθοδοξίας ἐκραταίωσαν σύμβολον *Chron. Pasch*.p.304(M.92.769A); **2.** pass., *be confirmed in* a belief δοξάζων τὸν κύριον ἐκραταιώθη καὶ εἶπεν, ὅτι...τὸ χθὲς ἀπέθανεν ἡ σάρξ μου *T.Neph*.1.4.

D. *restrain, hold in check*, exeg. Ps.73:14 σὺ...ἐδωρήσω πορείαν, τὴν ῥοώδη φύσιν στεγανὴν ἐργασάμενος...ἣν ἐφ' ἡμῶν ἐκραταίωσας θάλασσαν, ἐπ' ἐκείνων διέλυσας Thdt.ad loc.(1.1129).

***κραταιπαγής**, *massive*, Paul.Sil.*Soph*.619(M.86.2143A).

κραταίρινος, *hard-shelled*, Paul.Sil.*ambo*.118(M.86.2256B).

κραταίωμα, τό, *support, stay* ἔστι...τοῦτο...τὸ σχῆμα [sc. the cross] νίκης κ. Meth.*Porph*.1(p.504.21; M.18.400C); ἰσχὺν καὶ κ. καὶ καταφυγὴν...θεὸν...καλῶν Gr.Nyss.*Eun*.1(1 p.121.14; M.45.356D); in 1Reg.2:35 Theodoret reads καὶ ἐπιβλέψει κ. ὃν and comments κ. ... ὃν τοῦ ὄντος λέγει θεοῦ...τούτου κ. κέκληκε τὴν ἱερωσύνην, τὴν κατὰ τὴν τάξιν Μελχισεδέκ Thdt.*qu.7 in 1Reg*.(1.360) where Theodotion reads κ. Μαών; ἡ βασιλεία ἱερωσύνης ἰσχὺς καὶ κ. Taras.*ep*.5(M.98. 1469B).

κραταιῶς, *strongly, firmly*, *Pss.Sal*.8.16; ὁ...ἄρχων κ., φίλος ἐστὶ θεοῦ Isid.Pel.*epp*.1.290(M.78.352D).

κρατ-έω, **A.** *rule*; **1.** *rule* (*over*) ~εῖν...φαμεν τὸν σωτῆρα...πάντων μὲν τῶν ὑποτεταγμένων αὐτῷ...ἀλλ' οὐχὶ καὶ τοῦ ~οῦντος αὐτὸν πατρὸς Or.*Cels*.8.15(p.233.14; M.11.1540A); as bishop, Pall.*v.Chrys*. 4(p.25.22; M.47.16); **2.** *be strong, powerful* ἡ μὲν πρώτη...ἡ ~οῦσα τὰς χεῖρας, Πίστις καλεῖται Herm.*vis*.3.8.3; *A.Jo*.77(p.189.16).

B. *conquer*; **1.** *gain victory* (*in*) τάγματα...ὡσανεὶ κεκρατηκότα τῆς μάχης Eus.*v.C*.2.6(p.43.25; M.20.985B); ref. Passion εἰπὲ τί δύναται ~ῆσαι, ὅτι ἔπαθε Eus.Em.*fr.dogm*.1(M.86.540B); **2.** *surpass* (*in*) πάντων ~εῖτε Athenag.*leg*.6.2(M.6.901B); παντὸς...~ῶν ἀρετῇ Gr.Naz.*or*.43.10(M.36.505C); Philost.*h.e*.8.14(M.65.565C); c. acc. τὴν ...δορκάδα διὰ τοῦ δρόμου ἐκράτουν *T.Jud*.2.3; **3.** *achieve, accomplish* ὃς ἂν...δουλεύσῃ ταύταις [sc. πίστει, ἐγκρατείᾳ κτλ.] καὶ ἰσχύσῃ ~ῆσαι τῶν ἔργων αὐτῶν Herm.*vis*.3.8.8; ἐκράτει...γνώμης Eus.*v.C*.2.2(p.41. 11; M.20.980C); *do* penance εἰ δὲ λέγοι μετανενοηκέναι καὶ ἐπιτίμια ~εῖν Thdr.Stud.*epp*.2.42(M.99.1241C); **4.** *prevail* τὰ ἀρχαῖα ἔθη ~είτω CNic.(325)*can*.6; ~είτω ἡ τῶν πλειόνων ψῆφος *ib.*; ἐκ τῆς κεκρατηκυίας ἐν ταῖς ἐκκλησίαις...συνηθείας Eus.*qu.Marin*.2.2(M.22. 941D); ἐκράτει...παρὰ τοῖς πᾶσι μία γνώμη id.*v.C*.3.21(p.88.21; M.20. 1084A); αὐτῶν...ἡ συκοφαντία καὶ αἱ διαβολαὶ κεκρατήκασιν CAlex. *ep*.ap.Ath.*apol.sec*.11(p.96.20; M.25.268B); abs. impers. ἐκράτει *the custom was*, *Chron.Pasch*.p.332(M.92.861A); *prevail* over τὰ... γράμματα μετὰ πάσης δυνάμεως...εἰρημένα καὶ τοῦτο τῆς ἀπὸ τῶν ἐθνῶν ἐκλογῆς κεκρατηκότα Or.*princ*.4.1.6(p.301.13; M.11.352B); pass. πολυθεΐᾳ κεκρατημένη Thdt.*Ps*.53:5(1.955); *hold good* [Mt. 6:24] καὶ μᾶλλον ὁ περὶ τῆς ⟨πρὸς⟩ τὸν θεὸν δουλείας μόνον...~ήσει λόγος Or.*Cels*.8.8(p.226.31; M.11.1529B); Bas.*hom*.21.5(2.167C; M.31. 549B); ~ήσει πάντως καὶ ἐναντίον Cyr.*thes*.32(5^{1}.298E); of legislation, *remain in force* ὁ...νόμῳ κυρωθὲν ~ῆσάν τε Eus.*v.C*.4.2(p.118.24; M. 20.1152B); Heracl.*nov*.25(p.47); pass., *be generally accepted*, Barth. Edess.*Agar*.(M.104.1385C); ptcpl., *established truth* πλέκων [sc. Eun.] συνδέσμους καὶ διαλύων ~ούμενα Gr.Naz.*or*.28.11(p.39.5; M.36.40A); **5.** *extend, reach* εἶδον τεῖχος νεφέλης ~οῦν ἀπὸ τῶν ὑδάτων ἕως τοῦ οὐρανοῦ *V.Zos*.2(p.97.20); in time, *persist, last* ἀλλ' οὐκ ἐν Χριστῷ τοὺς τύπους ἔδει ~οῦντας ὁρᾶσθαι Cyr.*Ps*.34:28(M.69.911D); τοῦ... πολέμου ἐπὶ πέντε ἔτη ~ήσαντος Thdr.Lect.*h.e*.2.9(M.86.188A); ἡ βασιλεία...~ήσασα ἔτη ϡζ' Jo.Mal.*chron*.4 p.72(M.97.152B); ~εῖ ἕως τῆς πεντηκοστῆς τὸ ὕδωρ Jo.Mosch.*prat*.215(M.87.3108A); **6.** *master*, *control* ὅπως ἀνάρχως λέγοιτο ~εῖν τοῦ τεχνάσματος ὁ τεχνίτης Meth.*creat*.7(p.498.5; M.18.340A); οὐ...τοῦ κλέπτου τὸ ἀδίκημα...ᾧ γε οὐδὲ βουλομένῳ δυνατὸν ἦν ~εῖν τῆς χειρός Bas.*hex*.6.7(1.57A; M.29.133B); oneself τοὺς ἐν κλήρῳ πρεσβυτέρους ἢ διακόνους ὄντας καὶ ἀπερχομένους κρεῶν ἔδοξεν ἐφάπτεσθαι, καὶ οὕτως, εἰ βούλοιντο ~εῖν ἑαυτῶν CAnc.*can*.14; pass. ~οῦνται...ὑπ' ἀλλήλων αἱ δυνάμεις αὐτῶν [sc. the virtues] Herm.*vis*.3.8.7; ψυχαὶ...ὅποσαι...παραληφθεῖσαι καὶ ~ηθεῖσαι περιπολοῦσιν...μετὰ Χριστοῦ τὸν οὐρανόν Meth.*symp*.4.2 (p.47.16; M.18.89A); *be subject* εἰ οὐκ ἔστι δημιουργὸς ἄνευ δημιουργημάτων...οὐδὲ παγκράτωρ ἄνευ τῶν ~ουμένων id.*creat*.2(p.494.19; M.18.333B); to Christ τοσοῦτον ὑπὸ τοῦ λόγου ~ούμενοι, ὡς φόβῳ τῶν ...αἰωνίων κολάσεων...θανάτου καταφρονεῖν Or.*Cels*.3.78(p.269.19; M.11.1021C); of Christ ἐκρατήθη τῇ σαρκί Gel.Cyz.*h.e*.2.19.25(M.85.1280D); **7.** *keep, restrain* oneself from ~ήσας ἑαυτὸν τῆς προσφορᾶς, πρὸ τοῦ τὸ πάθος τῆς ἁμαρτίας [i.e. leprosy] σκιρρῶσαι Meth.*lepr*.6(p.458.25); pass., *abstain from* τοῦ συναγελάζεσθαι ~ηθείς *ib*.7(p.460.8); intrans., *practise abstinence* ~εῖν...τοὺς μὲν κοσμικοὺς τὸ κρέας, τοὺς δὲ μοναχοὺς τὸν τυρόν †Jo.Jej.*poenit*.(M.88.1913C); ~είτωσαν. τὸ μηδόλως ἁμαρτῆσαι εἰς γυναῖκα †Jo.Jej.*serm*.(M.88.1932A).

C. *lay hold of*; **1.** *seize*; **a.** c. genit. ~ήσας τῶν κεράτων *T.Jud*.2.7; met. τὰ πανταχοῦ...στρατόπεδα...μιᾶς ἐκράτει γνώμης Eus.*v.C*.4.68 (p.146.3; M.20.1224B); *ib*.1.36(p.24.10; 952A); **b.** c. acc. ~ήσας τὸν ἀσκόν *T.Sal*.22.10(p.66.16; M.122.1352D); met. ἐκράτησεν αὐτὸν πόνος *Apophth.Patr*.(M.65.93B); **2.** *detain*, Eus.*h.e*.7.32.21(M.20.732A); ἐκράτησεν ἡμᾶς φαγεῖν *Apophth.Patr*.(M.65.145A); ἐκρατήθη τὸ ~ούμενον [i.e. body of Christ] Eus.Em.*fr.dogm*.1(M.86.540A); **3.** *hold fast*; **a.** *retain* sins, Nonn.*par.Jo*.20:23(M.43.912C); *cherish* in the mind ἐν τῇ ψυχῇ σου μὴ ~ήσῃς δόλον *T.Gad* 6.3; a grudge, Chrys.*hom.14.2 in Eph*.(11.105B); Dor.*doct*.8.5(M.88.1712D); *keep* a secret, *Didasc.Jac*.3.2(p.52.29); **b.** met., *hold fast, persevere in* belief or practice συνήσετε τὸ θέλημα τοῦ θεοῦ ~εῖν, καὶ ἀπορρίπτειν τὸ θέλημα τοῦ Βελίαρ *T.Neph*.3.1; ~ούντων τὴν...συνήθειαν εἰς τὸ μετέπειτα πεποιηκότων Iren.*ep.Vict*.ap.Eus.*h.e*.5.24.13(M.20.504A); ~εῖν τὴν ἐν Νικαίᾳ πίστιν Gel.Cyz.*h.e*.3.12.12; Jo.Mal.*chron*.7 p.180(M.97.288B); οὐ κλίνομεν γόνυ μέχρι τῆς κυριακῆς τῆς πεντηκοστῆς, διά τε τὰς ἑπτὰ ἡμέρας μετὰ τὸ ἅγιον πάσχα ἑπταπλωμένως ~εῖν ‡Sophr.H.*liturg*.5(M.87.3985C); τὴν ὁδὸν τῆς ἀληθείας· ἥνπερ...ἡ καθολικὴ...ἐκκλησία ~εῖ ‡Jo.D.*Const*.1(M.95.309A); abs., *persist* τοῦ...βασιλέως ...λιπαροῦντος καὶ ~οῦντος Gel.Cyz.*h.e*.3.9.12; **4.** *hold in the hand* τὸν ἄρτον ~ήσας λέγει σφραγίζων *Lit.Jac*.(p.202.3); pass., *be held, handled* as something palpable ἔδει δὲ τὸν εἰς κόσμον ἀφικνούμενον [sc. Christ]...ὀφθῆναι, ~ηθῆναι Clem.*exc.Thdot*.59(p.126.23; M.9.688B); **5.** *hold* so as to lead φαίνεται αὐτοῖς ὁ ἅγιος ἐφ' ἵππου λευκοῦ καθεζόμενος καὶ δύο νεανίσκοι...ἐκράτουν αὐτὸν ἔνθεν καὶ ἔνθεν *Mir.Geo*.5(p.57.3); **6.** *maintain, uphold, support*, Herm.*sim*.9.8.5; in being τεθεμελίωται...ὁ πύργος τῷ ῥήματι τοῦ παντοκράτορος...~εῖται δὲ ὑπὸ τῆς...δυνάμεως τοῦ δεσπότου id.*vis*.3.3.5; ὁ κόσμος διὰ τεσσάρων στοιχείων ~εῖται *ib*.3.13.3; Clem.*str*.7.2(p.8.26f.; M.9.413Af.); Gr.Naz.*carm*.2.1.11.688(M.37.1076A); τὴν καινὴν ἐκράτησαν αἵρεσιν Thdt.*ep*.142(4.1236); *Chron.Pasch*.p.261(M.92.636C); cf.Eus.*h.e*.4.29.4(M.20.400C); **7.** *endure, put up with* ὅταν μὴ ~ῇ ἄνθρωπος τὸ ἑαυτὸν μέμφεσθαι Dor.*doct*.1.8(M.88.1628A); **8.** (cf. *LS* IV.4) *hold, possess* ~εῖν...πρόσρημα Const.ap.Eus.*v.C*.2.38(p.57.19; M.20.1016B); τὸ ἐπισκοπεῖον κ. Cyr.S.*v.Sab*.75(p.180.5); id.*v.Euthym*.3(p.10.7).

κράτημα, τό, 1. *grasp, laying hold of*; met., by the willing subject, ‡Ath.*def*.2(M.28.540D) = Anast.S.*hod*.2(M.89.61D) cit. s. θέλημα; **2.** *support, assistance* τὰ κ. [sc. of grace] Rom.Mel.(*AS* 1 p.76); **3.** *strength* (of character), *resolution*, *ib*.(p.113).

κρατήρ, ὁ, *bowl for mixing wine and water*; hence *chalice* ἡ σοφία συγκαλεῖ ἐπὶ τὸν ἑαυτῆς κ. λέγουσα [Pr.9:5] Or.*hom.12.1 in Jer*.(p.86.24; M.13.377C); eucharistic ἢ περὶ τὰς ἱερὰς τραπέζας ἐξυβρίσασιν ἢ περὶ τοὺς μυστικοὺς κ. μανεῖσιν Gr.Naz.*or*.5.2(M.35.665B); in representation κίονας ἐστεφάνουν...κ. μεγίστοις Eus.*v.C*.3.38(p.94.20; M.20.1100A); liturg., *Lit.Jac*.(p.228.24,29; p.230.10); ‡Bas.*h.myst*.53(p.391.22); ‡Sophr.H.*liturg*.5(M.87.3985C); symbolism ὁ...κ., περιφερὴς ἦν καὶ ἀναπεπταμένος, σύμβολον ἔστω τῆς...προνοίας Dion.Ar.*ep*.9.3(M.3.1109B); Gr.Nyss.*ep*.11(M.46.1044B; βρωτῆρες p.40.4).

κράτησις, ἡ, A. *dominion*; **1.** civil *power*, Eus.*v.C*.4.50(p.138.1; M.20.1200C); met. τὴν τοῦ θανάτου κ. Ath.*inc*.8.2(M.25.109B); ‡Ath.*Apoll*.1.17(M.26.1124C); **2.** *accession* of emperor τοῦ τεθνεῶτος ἀναβίωσιν τὴν τοῦ παιδὸς κ. ἐδόξαζον Eus.*v.C*.1.22(p.18.30; M.20.937C); Κόμμοδος ἐπὶ τῆς αὐτοῦ κ. παύει τὸν διωγμὸν τῆς ἐκκλησίας *Chron.Pasch*.p.262(M.92.641A).

B. *possession*; **1.** in gen., Or.*schol.in Cant*.3:1ff.(M.17.269B); **2.** *taking possession, occupation* (ref. Jos.11:23) νοεῖ...τοῦ κυρίου Ἰησοῦ...κράτησιν τῆς γῆς Or.*hom.16.3 in Jos*.(p.396.28; M.87.1024C); **3.** *holding, taking hold* τὸ...ἀποτέλεσμα τοῦ...σώματος, ἡ ἁφὴ καὶ ἡ κ. Jo.D.*f.o*.3.15(M.94.1049A); *hold, grasp* προστάσσω ταῖς πονηραῖς δυνάμεσιν...ἀφεῖναι τῆς κ. *Const.App*.6.9.4; **4.** *detention, arrest* τὸν ἀσπασμὸν τοῦ Ἰούδα, τὴν κ. τῶν Ἰουδαίων ‡Jo.D.*Const*.3 (M.95.316A); **5.** *abstinence* from ἢ βρώσεως, ἢ πόσεως, ἢ κοινωνίας τὸ σύνολον κ. †Jo.Jej.*poenit*.(M.88.1908C); **6.** that which holds, *tradition* περὶ πίστεως ὀρθοδόξου καὶ κ. τῆς ἐκκλησίας ‡Jo.D.*Const*.1(M.95.309A).

κρατητέον, *one must master, control* γαστρὸς...κ. Clem.*str*.2.20 (p.171.6; M.8.1049B).

κρατητικός, 1. *of power, relating to power*, ref. Pr.8:22 'ἀρχήν'... οὐ χρονικὴν λέγει ἀλλὰ τὴν κ. ‡Gr.Nyss.*Ar.et Sab*.5(M.45.1288B); **2.** *capable of holding, retentive*, of hyssop πυκνόν ἐστι καὶ κ. Chrys.*hom.16.2 in Heb*.(12.159B).

κρατητός, *capable of being held, detained*, ref. death of Christ ὁ ἀθάνατος θανών, ὁ ἀκράτητος κ. γενόμενος Epiph.*haer*.66.78(p.119.19; M.42.152C).

***κρατίκλη, ἡ,** (Lat. *craticula*) *gridiron*; as instrument of torture, Chrys.*hom.3.5 in 1Thess*.(11.447C, v.l. κραββάτου).

κράτος, τό, A. *might*; **1.** *strength*; κατὰ κράτος or ἀνὰ κ. *with all one's might*, hence *thoroughly, completely*, Clem.*str*.7.11(p.46.27; M.9.489B); Philost.*h.e*.4.12(M.65.525C); *ib*.9.17(581B); Thdt.*qu.14 in Jos*.10:13 (1.312); **2.** *power* of God ἐλπιοῦμεν ἐπὶ θεόν...ὅτι τὸ κ. τοῦ θεοῦ ἡμῶν εἰς τὸν αἰῶνα μετ' ἐλέου *Pss.Sal*.17.3; σύ, δέσποτα, ἔδωκας τὴν ἐξουσίαν τῆς βασιλείας αὐτοῖς διὰ τοῦ μεγαλοπρεποῦς καὶ ἀνεκδιηγήτου κ. σου *1Clem*.61.1; ἐμήνυσεν [sc. second commandment]...μὴ δεῖν ...ἐπιφέρειν τὸ μεγαλεῖον κ. τοῦ θεοῦ Clem.*str*.6.16(p.501.15; M.9.364A); ὁ θεὸς ὁ πάντων ἔχων τὸ κ. Ath.*inc*.11.1(M.25.113D); σοῦ τὸ κ. ἀνήγγειλαν οἱ οὐρανοὶ καὶ γῆ *Const.App*.7.35.2; of Son ὡς υἱὸς ἔχει τὸ πατρικὸν κ. Ath.*Ar*.2.50(M.26.253B); esp. in forms of doxology, v. διά, δόξα, ἐν, σύν; **3.** ref. power of Devil, Dion.Ar.*e.h*.3.3.11(M.3.441B); plur., Meth.*Porph*.1(p.503.3; M.18.397C) cit. s. δαίμων; so of death (Heb.2:14), Ath.*inc*.24.3(M.25.137C); Dion.Ar.*e.h*.2.3.6(404A); **4.** of spiritual power, exeg. Lc.1:3 πᾶς 'θεόφιλος' 'κράτιστός' ἐστιν ἔχων τὸ κ. καὶ τὴν δύναμιν τὴν ἀπὸ τοῦ θεοῦ Or.*hom.1 in Lc*.(p.12.3; M.17.313A).

B. imperial *majesty*; **1.** *sovereign power*, Mel.*fr*.1.3(p.308; M.5.1212A) cit. s. διάδοχος; κ. ἐδέξατο παρὰ θεοῦ ἡ τῶν Ῥωμαίων βασιλεία Cosm.Ind.*top*.2(M.88.113A); the *crown*, fig. φιλονεικῶν τὸ τῆς ἀσεβείας κ. ἀναδήσασθαι Gr.Naz.*or*.43.5(M.36.500B); the *Crown*, i.e. the emperor ἐπ' ἀνδρὶ...λαχόντι ἐν τοῖς αὐτόθι παρὰ τοῦ κ. χαρτουλαρεύειν Thdr.Stud.*epp*.2.190(M.99.1580A); **2.** as form of address: to emperor ταῦτα...ἀνήγαγον τῷ κ. σου *A.Petr.et Paul*.42(p.197.14); δεόμεθά σου τοῦ κ., καὶ τοῦ βασιλείου σου, καὶ τῆς εὐσεβείας σου *Pet.Ar*.1(M.26.820A); Cyr.H.*ep.Const*.5(M.33.1172A); to empress συντάξασθαι τῷ ὑμετέρῳ κ. Marc.Diac.*v.Porph*.52; Thdt.*ep*.43(4.1102); of emperor in first person προσέταξε τὸ ἡμέτερον κ. Valent.Imp.*ep.episc*.ap.Thdt.*h.e*.4.8.2(3.956); in third person εἰ...βούλεται αὐτῶν [sc. emperor and empress] τὸ κ. Thdt.*ep*.138(4.1231); *ib*.140(1235); βασιλέα τιμῶμεν, καὶ ὑπὲρ τοῦ κ. αὐτοῦ εὐχόμεθα *M.Apollon*.6(p.30.27); **3.** in address to officer of the crown, *A.Thom*.B 31(p.35.12).

***κρατοτύραννος, ὁ,** *powerful tyrant*, ‡Epiph.*hom*.2(M.43.453D).

κρατύν-ω, A. *strengthen*; **1.** *strengthen* in κ. πρὸς εὐσέβειαν Eun.*exp.fid*.3(p.259); pass., *derive force*, ref. 1Cor.6:10 εἰ...πληροῦνται... ταῦτα καὶ κ. διὰ τοῦ σώματος Meth.*res*.1.60(p.324.14; M.41.1157B); of arguments, Athenag.*res*.18(p.69.23; M.6.1009A); **2.** *support*; **a.** with arguments ἔλαττον...τὸ 'τὸ ψεῦδος ἐλέγχειν' τοῦ 'τὴν ἀλήθειαν ~ειν' *ib*.11(p.60.10; 993C); διδάσκαλος εἶναι λέγων, οὐκ ᾔδει τὸ διδασκόμενον ὑπ' αὐτοῦ ~ειν Rhod.ap.Eus.*h.e*.5.13.7(M.20.461B); ἰσχυρῶς κ. τὴν ἔνστασιν τῆς παρθενίας Meth.*symp*.3.13(p.43.9; M.18.84B); γράμματα...τὸ μὲν ὁμοούσιον διασύροντα ~οντα δὲ τὸ ἑτεροούσιον Philost.*h.e*.2.1(M.65.465B); *hold* an opinion τούτου...τὸ δόγμα ἐκράτυνε Μαρκίων Hipp.*haer*.7.37(p.223.16; M.16.3346A); Thdt.*haer*.5(4.397); **b.** *confirm, corroborate* ᾧ μαθητεύσας...ἐκράτυνε τὸ δόγμα Hipp.*haer*.9.7(p.240.20; M.16.3370C); ταῦτα οὕτως ὡς γέγραπται παραλαμβάνεσθαι ~οντος τοῦ Χριστοῦ τὴν γραφήν Meth.*res*.1.39(p.282.16; M.18.268B); ἀληθὴς...ὁ λόγος, καὶ...τὸν θεὸν ἀγένητον εἶναι κ. Dion.Al.ap.Eus.*p.e*.7.19(334C; M.21.564C); ~ειν διὰ τούτων τὴν ἑαυτοῦ δόξαν ἡγεῖται Eus.*e.th*.2.24(p.135.9; M.24.964C); pass. ἐκεῖνα φρονεῖν ...ἅπερ ἐν τῇ κατὰ Νίκαιαν συνόδῳ δι' ὑμῶν ὡρίσθη καὶ ἐκρατύνθη Const.ap.Gel.Cyz.*h.e*.3.15.2; Thdr.Stud.*epp*.2.72(M.99.1304A); **c.** *establish, set up* ἐβούλοντο ἂν...οἱ νομοθέται...~αι τοὺς φανέντας νόμους εἶναι καλοὺς...παρὰ παντὶ τῷ τῶν ἀνθρώπων γένει Or.*princ*.4.1.1(p.293.17; M.11.344B); ἑνὸς ἀνθρώπου παράβασις ἐκράτυνε τοῦ θανάτου τὴν δυναστείαν Thdt.*Rom.*5:17(3.58); **d.** *maintain, insist* οὐδὲ ἡμεῖς ἄθεοι, ὑφ' οὗ λόγῳ δεδημιούργηται...τὰ πάντα, τοῦτον...~οντες θεόν Athenag.*leg.*6.3(M.6.901C); ὅταν...~ωμεν τὸν διακοσμήσαντα τὸ πᾶν τοῦτο, τοῦτον εἶναι τὸν θεόν *ib.*7.1(904B); c. ὅτι, Just.*dial.*20.3(M.6.520A); *A.Jo.*65(p.183.4); τοῦτο μόνον κ. ἐν ἑαυτῷ ὅτι συμβολικῶς πάντα ὁ κύριος ἐπραγματεύσατο *ib.*102(p.202.7); *assert* one's will οὐκέτι τὸ αὐτοῦ κ., τὸ δὲ τοῦ πατρὸς ἵστησι βούλημα ‡Dion.Al.*fr.in Lc.*22:42(p.235.15).

B. *be strong enough, have the power* to τίς βασιλεὺς νόμους...ἀπὸ περάτων γῆς...ἀναγινώσκεσθαι ἐκράτυνεν; Eus.*h.e.*10.4.17(M.20.856B); *be strong enough for, endure bravely* τὴν προλαβοῦσαν ἐκράτυναν ζωήν Athenag.*res.*12(p.62.20; M.6.997B).

C. *become master of*; *master* mentally τῶν προκειμένων ἐπιβατεύειν καὶ κ. αὐτὰ πειρώμενοι Dion.Al.ap.Eus.*h.e.*7.24.8(M.20.696B).

***κραυγάρης**, *noisy*, Ephr.1.99A.

κραύγασος, *clamorous, noisy*, *Const.App.*3.5.1.

κραυγή, ἡ, 1. *crying, proclaiming* ἡ παρθενία Μαρίας καὶ ὁ τοκετὸς αὐτῆς, ὁμοίως καὶ ὁ θάνατος τοῦ κυρίου· τρία μυστήρια κραυγῆς, ἅτινα ἐν ἡσυχίᾳ θεοῦ ἐπράχθη Ign.*Eph.*19.1; Athenag.*leg.*11.1(M.6.912A); **2.** *cry* of lamentation, *Hom.Clem.*14.9; of loud, clamorous speech, Clem.*fr.*44(p.222.3); inward οὐ φωνὴν...καὶ βοὴν τὴν κ. νοητέον, ἀλλὰ τὴν τῆς ψυχῆς προθυμίαν Thdt.*Ps.*3:4f.(1.627); **3.** of animals and birds, *crowing*, *Const.App.*5.19.3; *braying*, Gr.Mag.*dial.*(tr.Zach.)3.4(M.*PL.*77.226A); *croaking*, Geo.Pis.*carm.*1.67.

***κραυγητικός**, *loud*, Anast.S.*qu.et resp.*125(M.89.776A).

***κραυγικῶς**, *vociferously*, Thphn.*chron.*p.316(M.108.765B).

κρεανομέω ([*]κρεων-), **1.** *divide the flesh of* a sacrifice, Isid.Pel.*epp.*1.72(M.78.232C); **2.** *tear in pieces*, κρεων-, Epiph.*anc.*85(p.105.10; M.43.176A); Cyr.*Zach.*84(3.770C).

***κρεβατίζω**, v. *κραββατίζω.

[*]**κρεηβορέω**, v. κρεοβορέω.

κρεισσ-όω, *make better, give superiority to*, ref. Christ; **1.** in Nestorian doctrine ~οῖ [sc. ἡ χάρις] τοῦτον κατὰ τὴν φύσιν αὐτοῦ, ᾧ κεχάρισται Leont.H.*Nest.*3.7(M.86.1624B); τί πεποίηκεν αὐτὸν εἶναι τῇ φύσει ἐγγενομένη καὶ ~ώσασα αὐτὸν κατ' οὐσίαν; *ib.*; cf.*ib.*(1624C); **2.** ref. monophysite doctrine εἰ μία φύσις...Χριστοῦ μετὰ τὴν ἕνωσιν ...ἆρά γε...~ωθῆναί πως ταύτην μετὰ τὴν...ἀνάστασιν id.*monoph.*9(M.86.1773C); εἶναι...τι...ἐν...τῇ ἀναστάσει τοῦ δεσπότου ~ούμενον καὶ ἕτερον μὴ ~ούμενον *ib.*(1773D); εἰ...εἶναί τι...τὸ ~ούμενον κατὰ φύσιν καὶ ἕτερον...~οῦν κατὰ φύσιν...φατέ, αὐτόθεν...τὰς δύο φύσεις συνομολογεῖτε *ib.*; **3.** orthodox ἐκρειττώθη τι τῶν τοῦ κυρίου φυσικὴν κρείττωσιν λαβὸν μετὰ τὴν...ἀνάστασιν *ib.*44(1796B).

κρείσσων, *mightier, stronger*; **1.** οἱ κ. *the higher powers*; **a.** of angels μηδὲ τὰς οὐσίας τῶν κ. συνεξισοῦσθαι ταῖς καθ' ὑπόβασιν διαφερούσαις Athenag.*res.*16(p.67.15; M.6.1005B); **b.** of God θεία τις ὑπάρχει οἰκονομία καὶ δύναμις κρειττόνων ἡ συνέχουσα τὰ ὅλα, ἣν καὶ θεὸν δικαίως ἂν εἴποιμεν Meth.*arbitr.*2(p.149.19; M.18.244C); **2.** τὸ κρεῖττον; **a.** *the Almighty*, *Hom.Clem.*5.5; Meth.*arbitr.*15(p.185.3); ἐντολήν τινα φυλάττει [sc. ὁ ἥλιος] κρείττονος *ib.*2(p.149.9; M.18.244B); ὀρθῶς καὶ σωφρόνως περὶ τοῦ κ. δοξάζουσιν Const.ap.Eus.*v.C.*2.24(p.51.6; M.20.1001B); βουλήσει τοῦ κ. id.ap.Ath.*apol.sec.*54(p.135.5; M.25.348B); Eus.*v.C.*1.16(p.16.6; M.20.932B); ἠξιώθημεν τῇ χάριτι τοῦ κ. †Ath.*fr.Mt.*6:22(M.27.1376C); Gr.Naz.*ep.*85(M.37.157C); Didym.*Trin.*2.11(M.39.660C); Nil.*epp.*3.11(M.79.373A); Proc.G.*Gen.*4:23f.(M.87.261B); partic. of Father ὁ κόσμος...διὰ τοῦδε τοῦ φωτὸς γέγονεν, τοῦ κ., δηλαδὴ τοῦ πατρός Eus.*e.th.*1.20(p.82.5; M.24.868B); **b.** *higher state*, *A.Jo.*84(p.192.18); ἐσμὲν τοῦ κ. διὰ τοῦτο ἀπὸ τοῦ χείρονος φεύγομεν *A.Andr.fr.*(p.38.11); ταχεῖα...εἰς κάθαρσιν ἡ γνῶσις καὶ ἐπιτήδειος εἰς τὴν ἐπὶ τὸ κ. εὐπρόσδεκτον μεταβολήν Clem.*str.*7.10(p.41.26; M.9.480C); Meth.*symp.*10.2(M.18.196B); **3.** τὰ κρείττονα; **a.** *higher things*; in moral or religious sense, *A.Jo.*52(p.177.15); Or.*hom.1.8 in Jer.*(p.7.16; M.13.264D); πευσόμεθα πῶς ἡ ἀπολλυμένη φύσις θέλει τὰ κ. id.*princ.*3.1.18(p.230.5; M.11.288A); Meth.*symp.*8.4(p.85.8; M.18.144B); Eus.*e.th.*3.3(p.152.12; M.24.993B); id.*d.e.*1.9(p.40.29; M.29.77D); πάντα...τὰ κρείττω τῇ τοῦ προδρόμου συντρέχει γεννήσει ‡Thdt.*nativ.Jo.Bapt.*(5.96); **b.** of the better or the good ὃς [sc. θεός]...ἐστιν ἀγαθὸς καὶ τῶν κ. ποιητής, τῶν δὲ φαύλων αὐτῷ πρόσεστιν οὐδέν Meth.*arbitr.*3(p.152.12; M.18.245C); **c.** of higher orders of being, angels τοῦ τῶν κ. τάγματος Eus.*e.th.*2.20(p.128.13; M.24.952B); not applicable to status of Father in rel. to Son διὰ τοῦτο...αὐτὸς ὁ υἱὸς οὐκ εἴρηκεν· ὁ πατήρ μου κρείττων μού ἐστιν, ἵνα μὴ ξένον τις τῆς ἐκείνου φύσεως αὐτὸν ὑπολάβοι Ath.*Ar.*1.58(M.26.133B).

***κρείσσωσις, ἡ,** *superiority* τοῦ κυρίου φυσικὴν κρείττωσιν...μετὰ τὴν...ἀνάστασιν Leont.H.*monoph.*44(M.86.1796B); id.*Nest.*3.7(M.86.1624C).

κρεμασμός, ὁ, *suspension of judgement, indecision*, Or.*hom.20.5 in Jos.*(p.424.23; M.87.1032B).

κρεμαστάριον, τό, *chandelier*, Thdr.Stud.*poen.*1.74(M.99.1741D).

κρεοβορέω ([*]κρεηβ-), *eat flesh*, Bardesanes ap.Eus.*p.e.*6.10(274B; M.21.465A); Andr.Cr.*or.*19(M.97.1220C) ∾ κρεηβ- ‡Caes.Naz.*dial.*145(M.38.1096).

κρεοδοσία, ἡ, *meat-offering*, Proc.G.*Num.*11:4(M.87.821A).

κρεοδοτέω, *give meat*, *Const.App.*6.3; *ib.*6.20.6.

κρεοκοπέω, *cut into pieces*; met., *distribute*, Pall.*v.Chrys.*18(p.119.25; M.47.67).

[*]**κρεονομία** ([*]**κρεωνομία**), **ἡ,** *distribution of meat*, Clem.*prot.*2(p.11.16; κρεων- M.8.72A); κρεωνομίαν μυῶν Epiph.*anc.*106(p.129.9; κληρονομίαν μείων M.43.209B).

[*]**κρεοπωλεῖον, τό,** *butcher's shop*, Ast.Am.*hom.*14(M.40.373B).

***κρεοφόρος,** *bearing flesh*, ‡Chrys.*Marth.*(10.755B).

κρεΰλλιον, τό, *flesh*, Synes.*ep.*131(M.66.1517B).

***κρεωβορία, ἡ,** *eating of flesh*, Gr.Nyss.*v.Mos.*(M.44.321D); Isid.Pel.*epp.*1.69(M.78.229A); ‡Caes.Naz.*dial.*110(M.38.985).

[*]**κρεωνομέω,** v. κρεανομέω.

[*]**κρεωνομία, ἡ,** v. [*]κρεονομία.

***κρημνηστής, ὁ,** as adj., *that hurls one headlong*, Gr.Naz.*carm.*1.2.25.531(M.37.850A); Thdr.Stud.*epp.*1.49(M.99.1088C).

***κρήμνισμα, τό,** *fall from a precipice*, Gr.Naz.*carm.*1.2.10.718(M.37.732A); *ib.*2.1.65.5(1407A).

κρημνοβάτης, ὁ, *rope-dancer*, Gr.Naz.*carm.*2.1.17.8(M.37.1267A).

κρημνός, ὁ, 1. *precipice*, in sneering allusion of Celsus to Cross εἰ ἔτυχεν ἐκεῖνος [sc. Christ] ἀπὸ κ. ἐρριμμένος...ἦν ἂν ὑπὲρ τοὺς οὐρανοὺς κ. ζωῆς ap.Or.*Cels.*6.34(p.103.23; M.11.1348C); met. ἐπὶ...τοὺς κ. τῆς ἀπωλείας ὑπὸ τῆς ἀνοίας φερόμενοι Clem.*prot.*10(p.66.25; M.8.201B); τί...κατὰ κρημνῶν ὠθεῖς, περὶ ὧν μὴ μεμάθηκας ὁριζόμενος ἐγγράφως Eus.*Marcell.*2.4(p.56.15; M.24.820A); αὐτὸν ὠθῶν ἐπὶ τὸν προφανῆ τῆς αὐτῆς δυσσεβείας κ. id.*e.th.*1.15(p.75.17; M.24.856B); ἐναντίοι...ἀλλήλοις οὗτοι κ.· μέση δὲ ἡ τῶν εὐαγγελικῶν δογμάτων ὁδός [ref. Nestorianism and monophysitism] Thdt.*ep.*109(4.1178); **2.** *gulf, abyss*, met. εἰς ὅσον ἀφροσύνης πεπτώκασι κ. Ath.*Ar.*3.67(M.26.465C).

***κρημνόω,** *throw down from a height, precipitate* ἀνῃρέθη κρημνωθείς ‡Epiph.*v.proph.Mich.*(p.26; MS κρημνῷ M.43.415B).

κρήνη, ἡ, 1. *fountain*; in atrium of church for cleansing of worshippers before entering church itself, Eus.*h.e.*10.4.40(M.20.865A); κρήνας εἶναι ἐν ταῖς αὐλαῖς τῶν εὐκτηρίων οἴκων νενόμισται, ἵνα... πρότερον ἀπονιψάμενοι τὰς χεῖρας, οὕτως αὐτὰς εἰς εὐχὴν ἀνατείνωσιν Chrys.*hom.3.11 in 2Cor.*4:13(3.289D); **2.** *source, fount* of any liquid for πηγήν Mc.5:29 τῆς αἱμόρρου τῶν αἱμάτων τὴν κ. ἐξήρανεν Jo.D.*hom.*1.6(M.96.553B).

[*]**κρηνιαῖος,** = κρηναῖος, *from a spring*, Thdt.*h.rel.*11(3.1200).

***κρηπιδοπώλης, ὁ,** *shoemaker*, Synes.*ep.*52(M.66.1380C).

κρηπίδωμα ([*]-δημα), **τό,** *foundation, base* -δημα Ast.Am.*hom.*8(M.40.268D); Eustrat.*v.Eutych.*14(M.86.2289B); *ib.*98(2384D).

***κρηπίζομαι,** *be furnished with a foundation*, *Orac.Sib.*8.147(conj. for κριπισθέν).

κρηπίς, ἡ, 1. *shoe, slipper*, of elegant shoes κ. Ἀττικὰς καὶ τὰς Σικυωνίας Clem.*paed.*2.11(p.226.25; M.8.537A); *Const.App.*1.3.9; **2.** *foundation* κ. ... πρὸς τὴν τελείωσιν ἡ εὐλάβεια Bas.*hex.*1.5(1.6C; M.29.16A); προκαταθείσης...ἐν ἡμῖν κρηπῖδος...δίκην τῆς...πίστεως Cyr.*Jo.*4.4(4.393B); met., of faith κ. ἀληθείας Clem.*str.*2.6(p.129.30; M.8.968A); of knowledge of God as κ. ζωῆς, id.*q.d.s.*7(p.164.18; M.9.612B); εὐσέβεια...κ. ἀσφαλής Synes.*regn.*9(p.20.17; M.66.1069A); Στέφανος...κ. τῆς καλῆς ὁμολογίας Ast.Am.*hom.*12(M.40.340B); of S. Peter's confession as foundation of Church, Isid.Pel.*epp.*1.235(M.78.328C); Cyr.*Mich.*(3.464B); Trin., of Father παιδὸς κ. Synes.*hymn.*5.60(p.38; M.66.1609); of Son as basis and source of creation, Eus.*e.th.*1.8(p.66.27; M.24.837C); **3.** *platform*, Eus.*v.C.*4.71(p.147.4; M.20.1225B); Synes.*ep.*67(M.66.1412B).

***κριανός,** *born under Aries*, Bas.*hex.*6.6(1.55D; M.29.132A).

***κριέλαφος, ὁ,** *ram-stag*, invented word without corresponding object, Leont.H.*Nest.*3.5(M.86.1616A).

κριθόμαντις, ὁ, *one who divines by barley*, Clem.*prot.*2(p.11.4; M.8.69A); Chrys.ap.*cat.Jer.*(1.15E).

κρίκιον, τό, *link* in a chain, ‡Chrys.*palm.*1.1(8.231A).

κρίμα, τό, 1. *judgement*, divine κρίματος, τοῦ διαστεῖλαι ἀνὰ μέσον δικαίου καὶ ἁμαρτωλοῦ *Pss.Sal.*2.37; in relation to divine righteousness and acts of righteousness τὸ δὲ κ. τὴν δικαιοπραγίαν, ἤτοι τὴν δικαιοσύνην. ... κ. γὰρ ὁ νόμος ὠνόμασται παρά γε τῇ...γραφῇ Cyr.*Os.*139(3.172D); κ. μὲν λέγει [sc. ἡ γραφή] τοὺς λόγους διαστείλαντας τῶν οὐ πρακτέων τὰ πρακτέα...δικαιώματα δὲ λέγει τῶν κ. τὴν ὀρθότητα

‡Just.*qu.et resp.*92(M.6.1333A); ref. Apoc.17:1 *κ. τὴν διαγωγὴν καὶ τὴν διοίκησιν καλεῖ* Areth.*Apoc.*17:1(M.106.716C); **2.** *decision, decree*; **a.** of God's providential decrees *τὰ κ. σου ἐπὶ πᾶσαν τὴν γῆν μετ' ἐλέου Pss.Sal.*18.3; Meth.*fr.22 in Job*(p.517.18); Didym.*Ps.*17:22 (M.39.1252B); Diad.*perf.*82(p.110.20); Andr.Caes.*Apoc.*23(M.106. 292C); **b.** eccl. *τούτους* [sc. eunuchs of Constantius] *νῦν τῶν ἐκκλησιαστικῶν κ. κυρίους ἐλογίσαντο* Ath.*h.Ar.*38(p.204.31; M.25.737C); **3.** *sentence of condemnation, condemnation ἀπολίπωμεν φαύλων ἔργων ...ἐπιθυμίας...ἵνα σκεπασθῶμεν ἀπὸ τῶν μελλόντων κ. 1Clem.*28.1; *τὸ...βάπτισμα τοῖς μὲν...κακοῖς βαπτιζομένοις εἰς πῦρ καὶ εἰς κ. γίνεται* Or.*hom.26 in Lc.*(p.165.13); *τὸ ψωμίον...ἐκείνοις μὲν εἰς σωτηρίαν, τῷ δὲ Ἰούδᾳ εἰς κ.* id.*Jo.*32.24(16; p.468.12; M.14.809B); *ἵνα καὶ τὸ καθ' ἡμῶν κ. τοῦ θανάτου...παραδοθῇ τῷ υἱῷ* Ath.*hom.in Mt.*11:27(M.25. 213A); ref. condemnation of heretics at Last Judgement, Cyr.*Jo.* 12.1(4.111E); **4.** *responsibility κ. βαστάζεις ὅλων τῶν ἀδελφῶν ὡς ἡγουμένη* Jo.Mosch.*prat.*128(M.87.2992C); *ib.*95(2953B).

***κρινόχροος,** *lily-white*, ‡Chrys.*Joseph*(6.604C).

κρίν-ω, I. *judge*;

A. of divine judgement; **1.** in gen., men and angels by divine law, Just.*dial.*141.1(M.6.797C); by reference to man's disposition, Clem.*str.*3.5(p.217.20; M.8.1149B); men's works to be judged by purifying fire, Gr.Naz.*carm.*2.1.1.524(M.37.1009A); **2.** by Son *αὐτῷ δέδοται τὸ κρῖναι πάντας ἁπλῶς* Just.*dial.*46.1(M.6.573A); cf.*Diogn.* 7.5,6; *ὁ τὴν ἐξουσίαν...λαβὼν παρὰ τοῦ πατρὸς κ. ζῶντας καὶ νεκρούς A.Andr.*A 12(p.53.15); *ἡμεῖς δὲ στήκομεν ~όμενοι παρ' αὐτῷ, ὡς ποιήματα* Ath.*decr.*11(p.10.19; M.25.436B); *Χριστὸς γάρ ἐστιν ὁ ~ων. οὐδὲ γὰρ ὁ πατὴρ ~ει οὐδένα, ἀλλὰ τὴν κρίσιν πᾶσαν δέδωκε τῷ υἱῷ, οὐκ ἀπαλλοτριῶν ἑαυτὸν τῆς ἐξουσίας, ἀλλὰ διὰ τοῦ υἱοῦ ~ων. νεύματι τοίνυν πατρὸς ~ει ὁ υἱός* Cyr.H.*catech.*15.25; *δικαιοσύνῃ ~ει ὡς νομοθέτης Const.App.*5.7.23; *σὺν τῷ υἱῷ ὁ πατὴρ μέλλει κ. τοὺς ἀπιστοῦντας τῷ ἀπεσταλμένῳ ἐξ αὐτοῦ* Ammon.*Jo.*8:16(M.85.1448D); in virtue of his divinity, Cyr.*Jo.*2.7(4.224C); *ὁ πατὴρ οὐδένα ~ει, τὴν δὲ κρίσιν πᾶσαν δέδωκε τῷ υἱῷ· ἔκρινε γάρ, ὁ πατὴρ δηλονότι, καὶ ὁ υἱός, ὡς θεός, καὶ τὸ πνεῦμα τὸ ἅγιον· αὐτὸς δὲ ὁ υἱὸς ὡς ἄνθρωπος σωματικῶς καταβήσεται καὶ καθιεῖται ἐπὶ θρόνου δόξης· σώματος γὰρ περιγραπτοῦ ἡ κατάβασις καὶ ἡ καθέδρα· καὶ ~εῖ πᾶσαν τὴν οἰκουμένην* Jo.D.*f.o.*1.13(M.94.853C); ref. Mt.24:36 *ὁ μὲν πατὴρ οἶδε τὴν ἡμέραν, [ἅμα] οἶδεν αὐτὴν καὶ εἰργάσατο καὶ πέπραχε καὶ ἔκρινεν, ὡς ἔφη ἐν τῷ κατὰ Ἰωάννην εὐαγγελίῳ ὅτι ὁ πατὴρ οὐδένα ~ει, ἀλλὰ τὴν πᾶσαν κρίσιν δέδωκε τῷ υἱῷ· ἐν γὰρ τῷ δεδωκέναι κέκρικεν· κρίνας τοίνυν ἔγνω· γνοὺς οἶδε πότε ἔρχεται* Epiph.*haer.*69.45(p.192.32; M.42.272D); cf.‡Caes.Naz.*dial.*21(M.38.880); **3.** by Trin. *τρία πρόσωπα...πάντα ~οντα* Dam.Papa *anath.*ap.Thdt.*h.e.*5.11.11(3.1039); **4.** ref. present and future judgement, exeg. Jo.3:18 *πῶς ὁ μὴ πιστεύων ἤδη κέκριται, εἰ μηδέπω πάρεστι τῆς κρίσεως ὁ καιρός;...καθάπερ γὰρ ὁ φονεύων, καὶ μὴ τῇ ψήφῳ τοῦ ~οντος καταδικασθῇ, τῇ τοῦ πράγματος καταδεδίκασται φύσει, οὕτω καὶ ὁ ἄπιστος* Chrys.*hom.28.1 in Jo.*(8.159D); Cyr.*Jo.*2.1(4.154E); cf.Didym.*Ps.*1:5(M.39.1160B); **5.** ref. resurrection *μὴ λεγέτω τις ὑμῶν, ὅτι αὕτη ἡ σὰρξ οὐ ~εται οὐδὲ ἀνίσταται 2Clem.*9.1; *κ. οὖν ζῶντας μὲν τοὺς τότε ζῶντας, νεκροὺς δὲ τοὺς ἀνισταμένους ἐκ τῶν νεκρῶν* ‡Just.*qu.et resp.*109(M.6.1357B); *ἀναστήσονται μέν* [sc. the wicked], *οὐ κριθήσονται δέ, τυγχάνοντες αὐτοκατάκριτοι* Didym.*Ps.*1:5(M.39.1160B); **6.** by saints; apostles judging Israel, ‡Chrys.*advent.*5(8.148C); cf.Thdt.*Rom.*6:2(3.194); martyrs judging demons, Andr.Caes.*Apoc.*61(M.106.412A); **7.** successively, by Abel as son of Man (Adam), twelve tribes, and God *υἱὸς Ἀδὰμ τοῦ πρωτοπλάστου, ὁ ἐπιλεγόμενος Ἄβελ,...καὶ κάθηται ὧδε κρῖναι πᾶσαν τὴν κτίσιν...διότι εἶπεν ὁ θεός· ἐγὼ οὐ ~ω ὑμᾶς, ἀλλὰ πᾶς ἄνθρωπος ἐξ ἀνθρώπων κριθήσεται. τούτου χάριν αὐτῷ δέδωκεν κρίσιν, κρῖναι τὸν κόσμον μέχρι τῆς μεγάλης καὶ ἐνδόξου παρουσίας· καὶ τότε...γίνεται τέλεια κρίσις καὶ ἀνταπόδοσις...πᾶς γὰρ ἄνθρωπος ἐκ τοῦ πρωτοπλάστου γεγέννηται, καὶ διὰ τούτου ἐνταῦθα πρῶτον ἐκ τοῦ υἱοῦ αὐτοῦ ~ονται· καὶ ἐν τῇ δευτέρᾳ παρουσίᾳ κριθήσονται ὑπὸ τῶν δώδεκα φυλῶν τοῦ Ἰσραήλ* [vv.ll. *ὑπὸ τῶν ιβ ἀποστόλων; ὑπὸ τῶν ἀποστόλων κριθήσονται αἱ δώδεκα φυλαὶ τοῦ Ἰσραήλ*] *...τὸ δὲ τρίτον ὑπὸ τοῦ δεσπότου θεοῦ τῶν ἁπάντων κριθήσονται T.Abr.* A 13(p.92.7).

B. of human judgement; **1.** causes of fallibility *δύο εἰσὶν ἀρχαὶ πάσης ἁμαρτίας, ἄγνοια καὶ ἀσθένεια...τούτων δὲ δι' ἣν μὲν οὐ καλῶς ~ουσι, δι' ἣν δὲ οὐκ ἰσχύουσι τοῖς ὀρθῶς κριθεῖσιν ⟨ἀκολουθεῖν⟩* Clem. *str.*7.16(p.71.27; M.9.540C); *ib.*(p.69.30; 536C); Bas.*moral.*3 tit.(2. 274C; M.31.781A); *οὐδὲ γὰρ δεῖ...~ειν ἑτέρους, ὅταν τις τῶν αὐτῶν ὑπεύθυνος ᾖ* Chrys.*hom.23.2 in Mt.*(7.286E); Anast.S.*qu.et resp.*70 (M.89.696B); Jo.D.*Rom.*2:1–2(M.95.452C); **2.** in rel. to divine, exeg. Mt.7:1, Jo.7:24, Bas.*reg.br.*161(2.470A; M.31.1189B); ref. 1Cor.4:5, Isid.Pel.*epp.*4.94(M.78.1156C); Anast.S.*qu.et resp.*70(M.89.696B); delegated by God *ὁ γάρ τοι τὸ ~ειν πεπιστευμένος, καθιεῖταί που πάντως ἐν τάξει θεοῦ, ᾧ δὴ τὸ ~ειν καὶ μόνῳ οἰκεῖον* Cyr.*Am.*15(3. 266B); to S. Peter and all who imitate his confession *ὥστε τὰς κρίσεις μένειν βεβαίας τούτου, ὡς ~οντος ἐν αὐτῷ τοῦ θεοῦ, ἵνα ἐν αὐτῷ τῷ ~ειν μὴ κατισχύσωσιν αὐτοῦ πύλαι ᾅδου. τοῦ μὲν οὖν ἀδίκως ~οντος...πύλαι ᾅδου κατισχύουσιν* Or.*comm.in Mt.*12.14(p.98.10; M. 13.1013A); **3.** clergy not to be judged by laity, Gr.Naz.*or.*19.10(M. 35.1053C); bishop not to be judged by laity, *Const.App.*2.36.9; ref. formal legal processes *μηδένα τῶν δικαστῶν, οἷς περὶ μόνων τῶν δημοσίων μέλειν προσήκει, μήτε ~ειν κληρικούς* CSard.*ep.Alex.*ap. Ath.*apol.sec.*39(p.117.28; M.25.321D); **4.** Christians not to seek judgement from secular tribunals *οἱ πράγματα ἔχοντες ἀδελφοὶ ἐπὶ τῶν ἐξουσιῶν κοσμικῶν μὴ κρινέσθωσαν, ἀλλ' ὑπὸ τῶν τῆς ἐκκλησίας πρεσβυτέρων συμβιβαζέσθωσαν Clem.ep.*10(M.2.45A); *Hom.Clem.* 3.67.

II. *condemn*;

A. ref. judgement by God and his ministers; **1.** divine condemnation of sinners through example of saints, *1Clem.*17.5; cf.*ib.*11.1; Chrys.*diab.*3.3(2.270C); Jo.D.*1Cor.*6:2(M.95.613A); **2.** of condemnation to eternal punishment as already pronounced *εἰς τέλος εἰσὶν ἀσεβεῖς καὶ κεκριμένοι ἤδη τῷ θανάτῳ Barn.*10.5; Herm.*mand.*12.3.6; **3.** of apostles judging the twelve tribes *οἱ δώδεκα ἀπόστολοι ~οῦσι τὰς δώδεκα φυλὰς τοῦ Ἰσραήλ, τουτέστι κατακρινοῦσι. κατακρινοῦσι δέ, ὡς ἐξ αὐτῶν ὄντες, τῷ κυρίῳ πιστεύοντες, καὶ μυρία θανάτων εἴδη ὑπομεμενηκότες, καὶ τὴν εἰς αὐτὸν οὐκ ἀρνησάμενοι πίστιν* Thdt.*Rom.* 6:2(3.194); cf. I.A.6 supra; cf.Areth.*Apoc.*61(M.106.749D); **4.** of condemnation of Devil *αὕτη τῆς ἐνανθρωπήσεως ἡ αἰτία τὸ κ. τὴν καθ' ἡμῶν πλεονεξίαν τοῦ σατανᾶ* Ath.*exp.Ps.*71:2(M.27.324B); *κέκριται, οὐ μόνον ὅτι οὗτος οὐκ ἐπίστευσεν, ἀλλὰ καὶ ἐπείρασε τὸν κύριον, καὶ εἰς τὸν Ἰούδαν εἰσῆλθεν, ἵνα παραδῷ αὐτὸν εἰς θάνατον* Ammon. *Jo.*3:18(M.85.1412B).

B. ref. human judgement; ref. plea that Christians should not be condemned for name of Christian *~εσθαι ἐφ' ὅτῳ ἂν καὶ εὐθύνῃ τις* Athenag.*leg.*2.3(M.6.896A); cf.Just.*1apol.*7.4(M.6.337A); Mel.*fr.*2 (p.307; M.5.1209).

III. *correct κ. καὶ σῶσαι πάντας τοὺς ἐπικαλουμένους τὸν κύριον T.Jud.*24.6; Meth.*fr.1 in Job*(p.511.3); *Const.App.*4.11.5.

IV. *decide, decree ὁ πατὴρ θανατωθήσεσθαι αὐτὸν ἐκεκρίκει ὃν ἐγεγεννήκει* Just.*dial.*102.2(M.6.713B); *ὅταν κ. ὁ θεὸς παθεῖν τι ἡμᾶς...* Meth.*fr.22 in Job* 22(p.517.21); cf.id.*res.*2.23(p.379.4); Ath.*exp.Ps.* 71:2(M.27.324B).

κριοκέφαλος, *with the head of a ram*, Ath.*gent.*9(M.25.20B).

***κριοκρούω,** *batter with a battering-ram*, †Cyr.*hom.div.*14(5^2. 416A).

κριός, ὁ, A. *ram*; allegorical senses based on **1.** OT sacrifices; **a.** in gen., cf. *iracundiam quasi arietem iugulet*, Or.*hom.9.4 in Ex.* (p.241.21; M.12.366D); *ib.13.*5(p.277.3; 393A); of any means of overcoming sin, id.*hom.4.5 in Lev.*(p.322.14ff.; M.12.439B); of works of righteousness, Hesych.H.*Ps.tit.*65(M.27.908C); **b.** as type of Christ *ἦν γὰρ ὁ κύριος ὁ ἀμνὸς ὡς ὁ κ., ὃν εἶδεν Ἀβραὰμ κατεχόμενον ἐν φυτῷ σαβέκ* Mel.*fr.*11(p.312; M.5.1216B); cf.Or.*hom.3.8 in Lev.*(p.313.23; M.12.433A); *caro, cujus hic aries forma est*, id.*hom.8.9 in Gen.*(p.84. 26; M.12.209A); *κ. ... εἰς ὁλοκαύτωσιν, γέγονε γὰρ εἰς ὀσμὴν εὐωδίας ὁ κύριος ἡμῶν Ἰησοῦς Χριστός, τῷ θεῷ καὶ πατρί* Cyr.*glaph.Lev.*(1. 372E); **2.** characteristic features: to lead, cf. *arietes duces sunt gregum. qui sunt ergo duces gregis Christi, nisi apostoli?* Or.*hom. 27.11 in Num.*(p.271.10; M.12.792C); *κριοὺς μὲν τοὺς ἄρχοντας τῶν ἐκκλησιῶν* Eus.*Ps.*65:15(M.23.668A); Bas.*hom.in Ps.*28(1.114D; M. 29.284A); *κρινῶ κ. πρὸς κ. ... τοῦτ' ἔστιν ἐπίσκοπον πρὸς ἐπίσκοπον Const.App.*2.19.1; perfection as compared with sheep and lambs *οὐ γὰρ εἶπεν ἀμνός, νέος, ὡς ὁ Ἰσαάκ, ἀλλὰ κ., ὡς ὁ κύριος, τέλειος* Mel.*fr.*12(p.313); Christ thus called ram of God, Heracleon ap.Or. *Jo.*6.60(38; p.169.2; M.11.304C); *πρόβατα καὶ κριούς, ἄνδρας βρίθοντας καλοῖς* Proc.G.*Is.*60:1–22(M.87.2625B); power of attack *κριοὺς ὀνομάζει προβάτων καὶ τοὺς ἁγίους ἀποστόλους, ὡς προκύψαντας καὶ τοὺς ἐχθροὺς κερατίζειν ἰσχύοντας* Ath.*exp.Ps.*64:14(M.27.285D); lack of reason; ref. Church of gentiles *τούτους υἱοὺς κριῶν διὰ τὸ ἄλογον ἀποκαλεῖ* Eus.*Ps.*28:1(M.23.253B); cf.Ath.*exp.Ps.*28:1(M.27.152B); Thdt.*Ps.*28:1(1.781).

B. *battering-ram*; met., cf. *urbes mendacii veritatis ariete subvertit*, Or.*hom.18.3 in Jos.*(p.409.3; M.12.915A).

κριόω, perf. ptcpl. pass., *belonging to rams οἵ καὶ ὑπομένουσιν οἰκεῖν ἐν τοῖς κεκριωμένοις ἐθέλοντες, ὃ δηλοῖ τὸ Ἐλὼμ* Or.*hom.24.1 in Jos.*(p.448.26; M.87.1037D); *τὸ ὅριον τῆς Μωαβίτιδος Γαλλὶμ ὠνόμασται. ὅμως ἑρμηνεύεται κεκριωμένον, ἐπώνυμον τῷ ἡγεμονικῷ ζῴῳ καὶ ἀρχικῷ* †Bas.*Is.*299(1.606C; M.30.644A).

κρίσις, ἡ, *judgement*;
A. of Last Judgement; **1.** in gen. ἡμέρα κρίσεως κυρίου *Pss. Sal.*15.13; Ath.*v.Anton.*19(M.26.872B); **2.** described, *T.Lev.*3.2,3; *2Clem.*16.3, etc.; **3.** teaching; in scripture gen., Bas.*hom. in Ps.*48 (1.179B; M.29.436D); †Bas.*Is.*119(1.462A; M.30.312A); ref. Ezech. 33:3 μάχαιρα μὲν ἔστιν ἡ κ. *Const.App.*2.6.11; in Christ's preaching ἵνα...μηδενὶ τῶν ἐν τῷ βίῳ τῶν ἀνθρώπων ἀπολογίας καταλίπῃ τόπον ὡς οὐκ ἐγνωκότι περὶ τῆς ἐσομένης κ. Or.*Cels.*1.56(p.107.7; M.11. 764A); **4.** ref. judge; **a.** Son, Just.*1apol.*53.2(M.6.405C); id.*dial.*58. 1(M.6.608A); Or.*Jo.*1.35(p.45.2; M.14.92C); πάρεστι τοίνυν ἐν τῇ κ. τότε ὁ θεὸς ὁ πάντων πατήρ, συγκαθεζομένου Ἰησοῦ Χριστοῦ, καὶ συμπαρόντος ἁγίου πνεύματος Cyr.H.*catech.*15.24; ὁ πατὴρ...τὴν κ. πᾶσαν δέδωκε τῷ υἱῷ αὐτὸς κρίνων οὐδένα, οὐ τῷ μὴ δύνασθαι ἢ σῶσαι τὸν ἀπολόμενον ἢ κρῖναι τὸν ἁμαρτήσαντα διὰ τοῦ υἱοῦ ταῦτα ποιῶν, ἀλλὰ τῷ διὰ τῆς ἰδίας δυνάμεως, δι' ἧς τὰ πάντα ἐργάζεται, καὶ ταῦτα ποιεῖν· δύναμις δὲ τοῦ πατρός ἐστιν ὁ υἱός Gr.Nyss.*Eun.*6(2 p.139.9; M.45.724C); ref. Jo.5:22 δεδόσθαι γεμὴν τὴν κ. ἑαυτῷ φησι παρὰ τοῦ πατρός, οὐχ ὡς ἔξω τῆς ἐπὶ τούτῳ κείμενος ἐξουσίας, ἀλλ' ὡς ἄνθρωπος οἰκονομικῶς Cyr.*Jo.*2.7(4.224C); **b.** angels ὁ ἄγγελος τῆς κ. *T.Abr.*A 13(p.93.12); φοβοῦμαι τοὺς ἀγγέλους τοὺς ἐπὶ τῆς κ., ὅτι ἀνελεήμονές εἰσι †Cyr.*hom.div.*14(5^2.400A); **5.** time of final judgement; **a.** at resurrection and parousia Ἰωάννης...ἐν ἀποκαλύψει γενομένῃ αὐτῷ χίλια ἔτη ποιήσειν ἐν Ἰερουσαλὴμ τοὺς τῷ ἡμετέρῳ Χριστῷ πιστεύσαντας προεφήτευσε, καὶ μετὰ ταῦτα τὴν καθολικὴν... ἀνάστασιν γενήσεσθαι καὶ κ. Just.*dial.*81.4(M.6.669A); Cyr.*Is.*2.5(2. 340A); τῆς ἐν τῇ δευτέρᾳ παρουσίᾳ τοῦ Χριστοῦ...γενησομένης κ. Gr. Agr.*Eccl.*3.19(M.98.881B); **b.** ref. Mt.24:36 ἔστι δὲ ἓν τῶν πάντων, ὧν ἐν τῷ υἱῷ ἐργάζεται...ὁ πατήρ, τὸ γινώσκειν τὴν ἡμέραν καὶ ὥραν τῆς κ.·...ὁ γοῦν μὴ γινώσκων τὴν ἡμέραν τῆς κ., ὁ ἐκ τῆς Μαρίας γεννηθείς ἐστιν Ἰησοῦς· οὐδὲν γὰρ ἀγνοεῖ ὁ ἐκ καρδίας πατρὸς θεὸς λόγος ‡Ath. *serm.fid.*33(p.29; M.26.1288B); διὰ σὲ καὶ τὴν ὥραν καὶ τὴν ἡμέραν τῆς κ. ἀγνοεῖ· καίτοι οὐδὲν λανθάνει τὴν ὄντως σοφίαν...ἀλλὰ τοῦτο οἰκονομεῖ διὰ τὴν σὴν ἀσθένειαν, ἵνα μήτε τῷ στενῷ τῆς προθεσμίας οἱ ἁμαρτήσαντες τῇ ἀθυμίᾳ καταπέσωσιν, ὡς οὐχ ὑπολελειμμένου καιροῦ μετανοίας· μηδ' αὖ πάλιν οἱ πολεμοῦντες μακρὰν τῇ ἀντικειμένῃ δυνάμει, διὰ τὸ μῆκος τοῦ χρόνου λειποτακτήσωσιν Evagr.Pont.*ep.*6(M.32. 256A); Didym.(‡Bas.)*Eun.*4(1.290A; M.29.696C); **6.** as instantaneous ὁ τῆς προσδοκωμένης κ. καιρὸς οὐ δεῖται χρόνων. ἀλλ' ὡς ἡ ἀνάστασις γίνεσθαι λέγεται ἐν ἀτόμῳ...οὕτως οἶμαι καὶ ἡ κ. Or.*fr.79 in Lc.* (p.272.18); id.*comm.in Mt.*14.9(p.298.10; M.13.1205C); **7.** accusation being by conscience τίς δ' ἡ κ.; οἰκεῖον ἔνδον τοῦ συνειδότος βάρος, ἢ κουφότης, νόμου τε πρὸς βίον σταθμή Gr.Naz.*carm.*1.2.34.254(M.37. 964A); Nil.*epp.*3.284(M.79.524D); cf.†Bas.*Is.*43(1.413C; M.30.201A); **8.** criterion ἐν ἡμέρᾳ κρίσεως ταῖς τῶν πεπλανημένων εὐποιΐαις αἱ τῶν ἀλήθειαν ἐγνωκότων ἰσάζονται πράξεις *Hom.Clem.*11.33; Israel, but not other peoples, being judged on observance of Law, †Bas. *Is.*120(1.462B; M.30.312B); **9.** mindfulness of judgement a preservative agst. sin, *Barn.*19.10; *Clem.ep.*10(M.2.45B); Ath.*v.Anton.* 81(M.26.956C); ὁ δὲ περὶ τῆς μελλούσης πεπεικὼς ἑαυτὸν κ., καὶ τὸ φοβερὸν δικαστήριον ἐκεῖνο πρὸ τῶν ὀφθαλμῶν ἔχων...παντὶ τρόπῳ πειράσεται σωφροσύνης μὲν καὶ...τῆς ἄλλης ἀρετῆς Chrys.*res.mort.*1 (2.422C); Diad.*perf.*81(p.106.13); **10.** unorthodox views; judgement denied, Polyc.*ep.*7.1; by followers of Simon Magus, *Const.App.* 6.10.1; its force attenuated μή τις νομίσῃ ὡς ἐν ἐκστάσει εἶναι τὴν κ. ἐκείνην. πολλοὺς γὰρ οἶδα λέγοντας, ὅτι ὥσπερ ἐν ὕπνῳ τις ὑπάρχων κολάζεται, οὕτως ἔσται καὶ ἡ κ. ἐκείνη Eus.Al.*serm.*20(M.61.775); acc. Marcellus, marking end of Christ's kingdom δι' ἡμᾶς τὴν ἀνθρωπίνην ἀνείληφεν σάρκα. εἰ δὲ δι' ἡμᾶς ἀνειληφὼς φαίνεται, πάντα δὲ τὰ καθ' ἡμᾶς τῇ αὐτοῦ προνοίᾳ καὶ ἐνεργείᾳ ἐν τῷ καιρῷ τῆς κ. τέλους τεύξεται, οὐκέτι οὐδὲ ταύτης τῆς ἐν μέρει βασιλείας ἔσται χρεία Marcell.*fr.*106 ap.Eus.*Marcell.*2.4(p.55.7; M.24.817A); cf.*Symb.Ant.*(345)ap.Ath. *syn.*26(p.252.40; M.26.732A); **11.** in arguments against unorthodox, ref.; **a.** pre-existence of soul ἡ κ. πῶς δὲ ἐπιφέρεσθαι, ὡς μέλλουσα, προσδοκᾶσθαι ἔτι δύναται, καθ' ἣν ὁ θεὸς ἑκάστῳ κατὰ τὰ ἔργα... ἀποδίδωσι, καὶ οὐχ ὡς ἤδη παροῦσα νομισθήσεται, εἴ γε τὸ γεννηθῆναι μὲν καὶ εἰς σῶμα ἐλθεῖν τὴν ψυχὴν κριθῆναί ἐστιν ἤδη...; Meth.*res.*1.57 (p.319.10; M.41.1153A); **b.** God as author of evil, Or.*Cels.*6.55(p.126. 12; M.11.1384B); εἰ τῶν ἁμαρτητικῶν λογισμῶν δημιουργὸς ὁ θεός,... ἄδικος ἔσται πάλιν ἡ κ. καταδικάζουσα τὸν ἁμαρτήσαντα ‡Ath.*Apoll.* 2.6(M.26.1140C); **c.** fatalism εἰ γὰρ ἀνάστασίς ἐστι καὶ κ., οὐκ ἔστιν εἱμαρμένη Chrys.*hom.45.4 in Jo.*(8.267D); **d.** Arianism, Ath.*Ar.*2.6 (M.26.157B) cit. s. κρίτης; **12.** as represented by eighth day ἑβδόμη ἡμέρα λέγεται ὁ αἰὼν οὗτος πληροῦσθαι, καὶ μετὰ τοῦτο ἐφίστασθαι τὴν ἡμέραν τῆς κ., τὴν ὀγδόην ‡Bas.*struct.hom.*2.8(1.342C; M.30.49D); **13.** of judgement of angels ἐὰν μὴ πιστεύσωσιν εἰς τὸ αἷμα τοῦ Χριστοῦ, κἀκείνοις κ. ἐστίν Ign.*Smyrn.*6.1.

B. of God's continual and recurring judgements καλὴ ἡ κ. τοῦ θεοῦ, παίδευσις οὖσα Clem.*ecl.*40(p.148.27; M.9.717C); μὴ περιεργάζου τοῦ δεσπότου τὴν κ. Bas.*hom.*21.12(2.172E; M.31.680C); ἀγαπᾷ ἐλεημοσύνην καὶ κ.... ἵνα μήτε ὁ ἔλεος χαυνώσῃ ἡμᾶς, μήτε μόνη ἡ κ. ἀπόγνωσιν ἐνεργάσηται Nil.*epp.*1.36(M.79.100A).

C. of human judgement τοῦ γνωστικοῦ δὲ καὶ ἡ βούλησις καὶ ἡ κ. καὶ ἡ ἄσκησις ἡ αὐτή Clem.*str.*2.16(p.153.23; M.8.1016B); id.*paed.*1.12 (p.151.21; M.8.376A); conditions of its exercise ἀπεχόμενοι πάσης... κ. ἀδίκου Polyc.*ep.*6.1; cf.*Did.*5.2; detachment from world necessary for moral judgement, Diad.*perf.*18(p.22.18).

D. *differentiation, discrimination* ἐλεημοσύνας δεῖ ποιεῖν...μετὰ κ. καὶ τοῖς ἀξίοις Clem.*fr.*53(p.225.25; M.9.744A); μόνος δὲ ὁ θεὸς οἶδεν ἀξίως καὶ ἐπαινέσθαι τὸν ἐπαινετὸν καὶ τοῦ ψεκτοῦ τὴν κ. ἀξίως ποιῆσαι, ἐπειδὴ βλέπει ἐν τῷ κρυπτῷ Or.*hom.2 in Lc.*(p.17.10); ref. Christ πρὸ μὲν τοῦ πάθους ἀπαξαπλῶς φανέντος τοῖς πλείοσι...μετὰ δὲ τὸ πάθος...μετά τινος κ. ἑκάστῳ id.*Cels.*2.66(p.188.19; M.11.900D); Bas.*fid.*2(2.225B; M.31.680C); Gr.Naz.*or.*43.68(M.36.588A).

E. *condemnation*, *T.Abr.*A 14(p.93.24); οὐκ ἐκφεύξεσθε τὴν ἐσομένην τοῦ θεοῦ κ., ἐὰν ἐπιμένητε τῇ ἀδικίᾳ Just.*1apol.*68.2(M.6. 432A); id.*dial.*138.3(M.6.793C); ref. pre-existence of souls πέμψονται δὲ ἀπὸ θεοῦ πρὸς τιμωρίαν, ὅπως ἐνταῦθα πρώτην κ. ὑποδέξονται Or. *princ.*1.8.1(p.97.3).

F. *decree*; **1.** divine, Or.*Cels.*2.66(p.188.16; M.11.900C); κ. τινὶ θείᾳ λαβόντες [sc. demons] ἐξουσίαν *ib.*8.31(p.247.7; 1564A); Ath. *apol.Const.*7(M.25.604D); id.*fug.*15(p.79.10; M.25.664C); **2.** eccl., ref. restoration of lapsed to communion at request of confessors τὴν κ. αὐτῶν...φυλάξωμεν...ἢ τὴν κ. αὐτῶν ἄδικον ποιησώμεθα; Dion.Al.ap. Eus.*h.e.*6.42.6(M.20.616A); Dion.Al.*ib.*6.42.5(613B); ref. heresy κρίσει τῆς ἀποστολικῆς καθέδρας Dam.Papa *ep.orient.*ap.Thdt.*h.e.*5.10.5(3. 1036); conciliar, Ath.*Ar.*1.7(M.26.25B); τὸν ψήφῳ καὶ κ. τοῦ κλήρου παντὸς εἰς πρεσβυτέριον ἐπιδοθέντα [sc. ordinand] *Const.App.*8. 16.4.

G. variations of meaning in exegesis; ref. Mt.7:1 κ. δὲ ὀνομάζει τὴν τραχυτέραν κατάκρισιν Ast.Am.*hom.*13(M.40.360D); Jo.5:24 τὸ δέ, εἰς κ. οὐκ ἔρχεται, τοῦτό ἐστιν, οὐ κολάζεται Chrys.*hom.39.2 in Jo.* (8.229A); ὁ Παῦλος...οἶδε...κ. τὴν δικαιοσύνην λέγειν id.*hom.40.2 in Mt.*(7.440A); Is.26:7, Cyr.*Is.*3.1(2.360E); id.*Ps.*36:28(M.69.945A); Jo.12:31 τῷ μὲν κόσμῳ κ. ἔσται, τουτέστιν, ἐκδίκησις id.*Jo.*8(4. 707B); Ps.36:28, *justice*, Hesych.H.*Ps.tit.*36(M.27.789D).

κριτήριον, τό, **1.** *standard of judgement, criterion*, ref. Pr.1:3 τὸ κ. τὸ ἐν ἡμῖν ὑγιὲς καὶ ἀπλανὲς ἔχειν δεῖν μηνύει Clem.*str.*2.2(p.116.17; M.8.937B); κυριώτερον...τῆς ἐπιστήμης ἡ πίστις καὶ ἔστιν αὐτῆς κ. *ib.* 2.4(p.120.27; 948A); cf.*ib.*7.16(p.67.23; M.9.532C); **2.** *judgement, discrimination* ἀμεταπτώτῳ κ. τῇ πίστει ἐπαναπαυώμεθα *ib.*2.4(p.119.6; M.8.944A); at Last Judgement κ. τῶν τοῦ θεοῦ προβάτων Eus.*e.th.*3. 17(p.177.8; M.24.1040A); **3.** *testing*; of martyr's torments κ. πολλά *A.Petr.et Paul.*84(p.219.8); κ.... πίστεως Const.ap.Gel.Cyz.*h.e.*3.19. 19(M.85.1349B); torture, Gr.Mag.*dial.*(tr.Zach.)2.31(M.*PL.*66.189B); **4.** *judgement-seat, tribunal*; **a.** of God ὁ θάνατος...ἀπάγει αὐτὰς εἰς τὸν τόπον τοῦ κ. *T.Abr.*B 9(p.114.7); τὸ κ. τὸ ἀδέκαστον Chrys.*hom.* 1.6. *in Ps.48*:17(5.514B); Max.*ep.*1(M.91.384A); the thought of it as a preservative against sin, Bas.*ep.*174(3.262B; M.32.652A); Chrys.*Laz.*5.1(1.763C); Diad.*perf.*17(p.20.26); **b.** ref. eccl. court, *Const.App.*2.49.1; **c.** ref. secular tribunal μὴ ἐρχέσθω ἐπὶ κ. ἐθνικόν *ib.*2.45.1; **d.** met., of conscience τὸ μικρὸν ἔνδον καὶ σαφὲς κ. Gr. Naz.*carm.*1.2.28.300(M.37.300).

κριτής, ὁ, *judge*; **1.** of God, in gen. ἐξᾶραι ὁ θεὸς τοὺς ποιοῦντας... πᾶσαν ἀδικίαν, ὅτι κ. μέγας...ὁ θεὸς ἡμῶν *Pss.Sal.*4.28; Ath.*ep.Aeg. Lib.*19(M.25.581B); **2.** of Christ; **a.** in gen. μόνος κ., ὅτι ἀναμάρτητος μόνος Clem.*paed.*1.2(p.91.28; M.8.252C); πάσης γὰρ φύσεως καὶ παντὸς νόμου, καὶ θέσμου, καὶ τάξεως, ὁ τοῦ θεοῦ λόγος ἐστὶ ποιητής, καὶ τῶν ἐν φύσει καὶ νόμῳ καὶ θέσμῳ καὶ τάξει κ.·...εἴτε οὖν ἐν νόμῳ τις κρίνεται, ὡς ἐν Χριστῷ κριθήσεται· εἴτε χωρὶς νόμου, πάλιν ἐν αὐτῷ πάντως κριθήσεται Max.*qu.Thal.*19(M.90.308C); **b.** as Messiah, Just. *dial.*36.1(M.6.583A); *ib.*49.2(584A); *ib.*132.1(784A); **c.** at Last Judgement, Clem.*paed.*3.12(p.291.3; M.8.680B); ὁ τοὺς ἀπειθήσαντας τῷ εὐαγγελίῳ βαπτίσων ὡς κ. τῷ πυρὶ τῆς γεέννης Or.*hom.26 in Lc.*(p.165. 7); ref. Arian notion of Son as a creature ποῦ λοιπὸν ἡ κρίσις, κρινομένου τοῦ κ.; Ath.*Ar.*2.6(M.26.157B); ref. Mt.25:13 εἰπέ ποτε καὶ τό, οὐδὲ ὁ υἱός,...ἵνα δείξῃ, ὅτι, ὡς ἄνθρωπος, οὐκ οἶδεν·...εἰ μέντοι λόγος ἐστί, καὶ αὐτὸς ἐστιν ὁ...κ., οἶδε πότε...ἔρχεται *ib.*3.46 (420C); †Bas.*Is.*117(1.460A; M.30.308A); *Const.App.*5.20.4; *ib.*5.20. 12; ἐπειδὴ τῆς ἀρρήτου οὐσίας ἐκείνης ἐστὶν υἱός, διὰ τοῦτό ἐστι κ. Chrys.*hom.39.3 in Jo.*(8.230A); κ., ὡς δημιουργὸς καὶ δεσπότης τῆς κτίσεως Andr.Caes.*Apoc.*9(M.106.252C); **3.** of Abel and Enoch at the judgement τίς ἐστιν οὗτος ὁ κ., καὶ τίς ἐστιν ὁ ἄλλος, ὁ ἐλέγχων τὰς ἁμαρτίας; καὶ λέγει Μιχαὴλ...θεωρεῖς τὸν κ.; οὗτός ἐστιν ὁ Ἄβελ, ...καὶ ἤνεγκεν αὐτὸν ὧδε ὁ θεὸς κρινεῖν· καὶ ὁ ἀποδεικνύμενος οὗτός ἐστιν...Ἐνώχ *T.Abr.*B 11(p.115.14); **4.** of eccl. judges νομίζοντες ἡμᾶς ἐκφοβεῖν, ἠξίωσαν σύνοδον καλέσαι, καὶ αὐτὸν Ἰούλιον, εἰ βούλοιτο, κ. γενέσθαι Ath.*apol.sec.*20(p.102.2; M.25.280C); γίνεσθε δίκαιοι κ. [i.e. bishops], εἰρηνοποιοί *Const.App.*2.53.1; **5.** ref. human judges in gen. πενήτων ἄνομοι κ. *Barn.*20.2; *Did.*5.2; ἄνω γὰρ δεῖ τῆς ἁμαρτανούσης ψυχῆς εἶναι τὸν ταύτης κ. Cyr.*Lc.*6:37(M.72.690B); κρίτην ἀδικίας ἐν τῷ εὐαγγελίῳ παραβολικῶς ὑπάρχειν καὶ λέγεσθαι, τὸν ἡμέτερον λογισμόν, ἀρχῆθεν ἐκ παραβάσεως ἄδικον πεποιημένον τὴν κρίσιν Max.*qu.Theop.*(M.90.1396B).

κροαίνω, **1.** *stamp*; of a horse, Gr.Naz.*or.*43.24(M.36.529B); *ib.*44.11(620B); **2.** met., *spurn*, Clem.*paed.*1.5(p.99.1; M.8.268A).

[*]**κροβύλος**, ὁ, = κρωβύλος, *roll* or *knot of hair on the crown of the head*, Nil.*Magn.*30(M.79.1005C).

[*]**κροκοδείλινος**, *of the crocodile*, ref. a sophistical fallacy κ. σωρίτου Clem.*str.*5.1(p.333.21; M.9.25B).

κροσσός, ὁ, *tassel*; met.; **1.** on garment of Church in Ps.44:14 οἱ κ., οἱ ἐκλεκτοί Clem.*paed.*2.10(p.223.25; M.8.529B); ὁ λόγος πλείων ἐστὶ τοῦ ἔργου, οἱονεὶ κ. τίς ἐστιν ἀπὸ τοῦ πρὸς τὴν πρᾶξιν ὑφάσματος περισσεύων Bas.*hom.in Ps.*44(1.168E; M.29.412C); κ. δὲ [sc. σημαίνει] τὰς πολυειδεῖς ἀρετάς Ath.*exp.Ps.*44:14(M.27.212D); Chrys.*exp.in Ps.*44:14(5.180B); Cyr.*Ps.*44:14(M.69.1044C); κ. ἀπείκασε χρυσοῖς τὴν τῶν χαρισμάτων διαίρεσιν Thdt.*Ps.*44:14(1.895); **2.** on high priest's breastplate signifying good deeds of saints, Cyr.*ador.*11(1.384B).

κροσ(σ)ωτός, *tasselled*, hence neut. plur. as subst., *fringes*; **1.** on garment of Church in Ps.44:14 τὰ κ. τὰ χρυσᾶ, τὴν ἐκ μέρους γνῶσιν Eus.*Ps.*44:14(M.23.404A); Bas.*hom.in Ps.*44(1.168C; M.29.412A); representing doctrines of Christianity, Didym.*Ps.*44:14(M.39.1369C); Cyr.*ador.*11(1.384B); **2.** ref. BMV ὡς κ. χρυσοῖς, τὴν τῶν ἀρετῶν περιβεβλημένην εὐπρέπειαν ‡Jo.D.*hom.*6.9(M.96.673D); **3.** ref. soul called to union with God κ. χρυσοῖς περιβεβλημένην Chrys.*hom.*69.2 *in Mt.*(7.682D); **4.** on high priest's breastplate, Cosm.Ind.*top.*5(M.88.213B; κροσω- p.151.12).

***κροταλιστής**, ὁ, *rattler, castanet-player*, in proverb about wealth put to bad use τὰ Ταντάλιστῶν φάγονται κροταλισταί Nil.*epp.*2.153(M.79.272D).

***κροταφιαῖος**, *on the temples*, Synes.*ep.*122(M.66.1501C).

κροταφίζω, *strike on the temples*; **1.** lit., Const.Ind.*top.*11(M.88.441C); Hipp.Th.*fr.*2(p.2.9; M.117.1036D); **2.** met. ὁ διάβολος, διὰ Χριστοῦ...κροταφισθείς Anast.S.*hod.*4(M.89.97A).

***κροτιστής**, ὁ, *rattler, castanet-player*, †Gregent.*leg.Hom.*36(M.86.661B).

κροῦμα (κροῦσμα), τό, **1.** *blow, knock* εἴ τις κληρικὸς...ἀπὸ τοῦ ἑνὸς κ. ἀποκτείνῃ, καθαιρείσθω *Can.App.*66; Mac.Mgn.*apocr.*3.24(p.109.3); met. τοὺς σώφρονας περιτίθησι λόγους...ὡς μὴ δύνασθαι ἐξικνεῖσθαι εἰς θραῦσιν τῆς ψυχῆς τὸ κ. τῆς πορνείας Clem.*paed.*2.6(p.187.16; M.8.452B); **2.** *musical note, melody*; met., of Psalms, Thdt.*Pss.proem.*(1.607); as prophecies of Christ νῦν ἀληθῶς γέγονε τὰ κ. πράγματα Bas.Sel.*ascens.*1(M.28.1093B); **3.** in monasteries, a *striking* on wood or metal as a signal for divine office, etc., Cyr.S.*v.Sab.*43(p.133.18); τὸ κ. δέδωκε καὶ κατάδηλον ἐκ τούτου ποιεῖ τὴν τοῦ πατρὸς κοίμησιν Steph.Diac.*v.Steph.*(M.100.1096A).

***κρουσματέω**, *give the signal*; for rising, Thdr.Stud.*iamb.*20(M.99.1788B).

κρουσμός, ὁ, *striking, smiting*, Nil.*epp.*3.243(M.79.500C).

κρού-ω, **1.** *strike* στήθη ∼εται θρήνοις Clem.*paed.*3.2(p.244.14; M.8.576A); met. τῷ συνειδότι τῆς δυσγενείας κ. Afric.ap.Eus.*h.e.*1.7.13(M.20.96B); Gr.Naz.*carm.*2.1.34.132(M.37.1316A); **2.** *strike, play on* stringed instrument τὸ στόμα οἱονεὶ πλήκτρῳ κ. τῷ πνεύματι Clem.*paed.*2.4(p.182.23; M.8.441B); id.*str.*6.11(p.476.6; M.9.309B); παρακαλέσωμεν αὐτὸν...εἰς τὴν ἡμετέραν κροῦσαι καρδίαν Chrys.*hom.*8.7 *in Rom.*(9.507E); **3.** *knock, sound gong* as signal for divine office in monasteries κ. εἰς τὴν σύναξιν Ephr.2.101B; *V.Pach.Φ* 61(p.41.35); Cyr.S.*v.Sab.*43(p.134.1); Leont.Abb.*v.Gr.Agr.*55(M.98.645A); κ. τὰ γʹ...ἐπὶ τοῦ κάνονος *Const.Stud.*36(M.99.1717C); **4.** *knock on* door τῷ ἐξυπνιστικῷ σφυρίῳ τὰς πάντων κ. κέλλας συνάγων αὐτοὺς εἰς τοὺς εὐκτηρίους οἴκους Pall.*h.Laus.*43(p.130.14; M.34.1210C); met. ζητεῖν τὴν διάνοιαν τῶν γραφῶν καὶ...κ. αὐτῶν τὰ κεκλεισμένα Or.*Cels.*6.7(p.77.19; M.11.1300B); Const.ap.Gel.Cyz.*h.e.*2.7.39(M.85.1242A); ἐρχόμενον [sc. Christ] πρὸς ἕκαστον μὴ βιάζεσθαι, ἀλλὰ μᾶλλον κ. τε καὶ λέγειν· ἄνοιξόν μοι Ath.*h.Ar.*33(p.201.18; M.25.732A); **5.** met. phrases σταθμὸν μὴ κ. ἑτερόζυγον, ἀλλ' ἴσον ἕλκειν *tilt the scale, hold balance unfairly*, *Orac.Sib.*2.67; ἔγνωμεν πρύμναν κρούσασθαι τὸ τοῦ λόγου *turn about, change tactics*, Gr.Naz.*ep.*87(M.37.161A); id.*or.*43.17(M.36.520A).

***κρυμόω**, *freeze*; pass., Gr.Naz.*carm.*2.1.88.138(M.37.1440A); Olymp.*Job* 37:9–10(M.93.388B).

***κρυπτάζω**, **1.** *hide, conceal*, Epiph.*haer.*76.3(p.344.10; M.42.521B); med., *hide oneself*, Eus.*h.e.*9.10.4(M.20.744B); τῶν ἐκκλησιῶν ποιμένας...κ. *ib.*8.3.1(744B); id.*p.e.*12.9(582C; M.21.968A); **2.** *dissemble*; med., Epiph.*anc.*81(p.101.25; M.43.169B); id.*haer.*37.2(p.52.14; M.41.644B).

κρυπτή, ἡ, *vault*, *M.Ner.et Ach.*18(p.17.28); *T.Job* 46(p.134.2).

κρυπτήρ, ὁ, *vault, treasure-chamber* τὰ νεχοθὰ [Hebr. נְכֹת], ὃ ἑρμηνεύεται κ. *Dial.Tim.et Aquil.*97 v°(p.78).

κρυπτήριος, fem. as subst., *hiding-place*, Const.ap.Ath.*apol.sec.*62(p.142.3; M.25.361A); Gr.Nyss.*beat.*5(M.44.1261C); †Nil.*vit.*4(M.79.1144D).

κρυπτός, *hidden*; **1.** in gen., of spiritual sense of scripture ὁ δὲ σταυρὸς εἰ μέν τινα καὶ ἕτερον περιέχει λόγον βαθύτερον, εἰδεῖεν ἂν οἱ τῶν κ. ἐπιίστορες Gr.Nyss.*or.catech.*32(p.117.11; κρυπτομένων M.45.80C); of Devil ἄνεμός τις κ. Mac.Aeg.*hom.*5.3(M.34.497A); **2.** ref. God τὰ κ. τοῦ θεοῦ Ign.*Philad.*9.1; as dwelling in soul ἔνδον κ. ἐνοικεῖ ὁ πατὴρ καὶ ὁ τούτου παῖς Clem.*q.d.s.*33(p.182.15; M.9.640B); **3.** of Christ, Christol. τῆς μὲν φωνῆς ἢ τῆς πράξεως ἀνθρωπικῶς διεξαγομένης, τοῦ δὲ κατὰ τὸ κ. νοουμένου τὸ θεῖον ἐμφαίνοντος Gr.Nyss.*or.catech.*32(p.118.6; M.45.80C); ref. Jo.7:10 τί δήποτε δὲ ἐν παρρησίᾳ διαλεγόμενος ἀεί, ὡς ἐν κ. νῦν τοῦτο ποιεῖ;...οὕτω γὰρ ἐχρῆν ...παιδεύων ἡμᾶς τὰ πράγματα οἰκονομεῖν Chrys.*hom.*49.1 *in Jo.*(8.288A); **4.** of secrets of heart οὐδὲν λανθάνει τὸν κύριον, ἀλλὰ καὶ τὰ κ. ἡμῶν ἐγγὺς αὐτῷ ἐστιν Ign.*Eph.*15.3; cf.id.*Philad.*7.1; Ἰησοῦς, οὐ ψιλὸς ἄνθρωπος ὤν, ἀλλὰ θεὸς γενόμενος ἄνθρωπος, πάντα οἶδεν, τὸ κ. καταλαμβάνων τοῦ νοῦ Or.*fr.*33 *in Jo.*(p.509.1); id.*Jo.*32.28(18; p.473.18; M.14.817C); ὁ θεὸς...ὁ τῶν κ. γνώστης id.*princ.*3.1.17(p.226.1; M.11.284A); ref. Christ ὁ νεκροὺς ζωοποιῶν...πολλῷ μᾶλλον τὰ κ. πάντων ἐπιγινώσκει Ath.*Ar.*3.38(M.26.405A); id.*v.Anton.*55(M.26.924A); ref. secretly held heresy τὰ κ. τοῦ σκότους Bas.*ep.*125.1(3.215A; M.32.545C); **5.** ref. inner life, exeg. Rom.2:29 τῶν ἐν κ. Ἰουδαίων ἐστί τι ἔθνος, τῆς ψυχῆς τὴν εὐγένειαν ταύτην κατά τινας λόγους ἀπορρήτους κεκτημένης Or.*princ.*4.3.6(p.332.15; M.11.388A); cf.Jo.14:27 λαβεῖν τὴν ἐν κ. εἰρήνην ἀπὸ τοῦ αἰεὶ τοῖς ἀξίοις διδόντος αὐτήν id.*Jo.*6.1(p.106.15; M.14.197B); Bas.*hom.*1 *in Ps.*14(1.353D; M.29.253C); Gr.Mag.*dial.*(tr. Zach.)3.26(M.*PL*.77.282C); **6.** in teaching of Simon Magus εἶναι [τὴν] τοῦ πυρὸς διπλῆν τινα τὴν φύσιν, καὶ τῆς διπλῆς ταύτης καλεῖ τὸ μέν τι κ., τὸ δέ τι φανερόν Hipp.*haer.*6.9(p.136.25; M.16.3210B).

κρύπτ-ω, **1.** *hide*; **a.** in gen. ἵνα ἀνομία μὲν πολλῶν ἐν δικαίῳ ἑνὶ κρυβῇ *Diogn.*9.5; τῆς δαιμονικῆς πλάνης...∼ούσης τὴν περὶ τοῦ ἀληθινοῦ θεοῦ γνῶσιν Ath.*inc.*13.1(M.25.117C); ref. Arianism νομίζει δὲ δύνασθαι ∼ειν ἑαυτὴν ἐν τῷ λέγειν id.*Ar.*2.19(M.26.185C); ref. *disciplina arcani* ἁμαρτάνει τῷ θεῷ ὁ ἀξιωθεὶς λογίων ἀπορρητοτέρων, καὶ ∼εσθαι ἀπὸ τῶν πολλῶν ἀξίων, καὶ μὴ ∼ων αὐτὰ ἀφ' ὧν δεῖ id.*exp.Ps.*118:11(M.27.481C); exeg. Mt.5:14 ὥσπερ γὰρ ἐκείνην κρυβῆναι ἀμήχανον, οὕτω τὸ κήρυγμα ἀδύνατον σιγηθῆναι καὶ λαθεῖν Chrys.*hom.*15.6 *in Mt.*(7.195C); εἰ βούλει ἀνθρώπους ἰδεῖν σου τὰ κατορθώματα, κρύψον αὐτὰ νῦν, ἵνα μετὰ πλείονος τιμῆς τότε αὐτὰ πάντες θεάσωνται, τοῦ θεοῦ φανερὰ ποιοῦντος *ib.*19.2(246C); Thdt.*Ps.*118:11(1.1441); **b.** of Christ ∼ομένου σαρκί Ath.*Ar.*3.34(M.26.396B); ref. Mt.24:36 ἀμφότερα δὴ οὖν καὶ τὸ καθόλου τέλος, καὶ τὸ ἑκάστου πέρας ἔκρυψεν ἀφ' ἡμῶν ὁ λόγος...ἵνα...καθ' ἡμέραν ὡς καλούμενοι προκόπτωμεν, τοῖς ἔμπροσθεν ἐπεκτεινόμενοι, τῶν δὲ ὄπισθεν ἐπιλανθανόμενοι *ib.*3.49(428B); ref. Jo.16:15, Mt.24:36 εἰ δὲ οἶδεν τὴν ἡμέραν, ∼ειν δὲ βουλόμενος ἀγνοεῖν λέγει, ὅρα εἰς ποίαν βλασφημίαν χωρεῖ τὸ συναγόμενον Thdt.ap.Cyr.*apol.Thdt.*4(p.121.23; 6[1].215C); of the divine nature φύσιν...τὴν κεκρυμμένην id.*affect.*6(p.175.18; 4.876); **c.** of spiritual sense of scripture ἡ...θεία φύσις...συγκατέβη τῇ ἰδιωτείᾳ τοῦ πλήθους τῶν ἀκροωμένων, ἵνα ταῖς συνήθεσιν αὐτοῖς χρησαμένη λέξεσι προκαλέσηται ἐπὶ ἀκρόασιν τὸ τῶν ἰδιωτῶν πλῆθος, δυνάμενον ἐξ εὐχεροῦς μετὰ τὴν ἅπαξ γενομένην εἰσαγωγὴν φιλοτιμήσασθαι πρὸς τὸ καὶ βαθύτερα τῶν κεκρυμμένων νοημάτων ἐν ταῖς γραφαῖς καταλαβεῖν Or.*Cels.*7.60(p.210.24; M.11.1508B); id.*princ.*4.2.18(p.320.4; M.11.373A); μὴ κατὰ τὸ πρόχειρον ταῦτα γεγράφθαι, ἀλλὰ κατὰ κεκρυμμένον id.*Apoc.*25(p.32.5); ref. OT τί δὴ ἄρα κἂν τούτῳ τὸ κεκρυμμένον; Cyr.*ador.*3(1.82A); id.*glaph.Dt.*(1.425C); Thdt.*Is.*8:6(p.42.34; 2.224); **d.** exeg. Col.3:3 συνετάφητε γὰρ ἐν τῷ βαπτίσματι τῷ Χριστῷ, ἐδέξασθε δὲ τὴν ἐλπίδα τῆς ἀναστάσεως. τοῦτο γὰρ λέγει, ἡ ζωὴ ὑμῶν κέκρυπται σὺν τῷ Χριστῷ ἐν τῷ θεῷ Thdt.ad loc.(3.492); **e.** met., of Christ τοῦ Δαυιτικοῦ γένους τὸ ἄμαχον διὰ τὸ ἐν αὐτῷ ∼όμενον σπέρμα id.*Is.*9:7(p.50.32; 2.237); **2.** *conceal, keep silent about*, ref. Lc.2:40, Is.11:1,2 τοῦ Χριστοῦ...φύσιν...τὴν ἀόρατον ὑπὸ τοῦ εὐαγγελιστοῦ καὶ τοῦ προφήτου ∼ομένην Thdt.*pental.*(5.121); **3.** *hide from* ἦλθε τοὺς πολλοὺς ~ων Chrys.*exp.in Ps.*49:3(5.225B); Cyr.*thes.*22(5^{1}.219C); **4.** *make invisible, throw into the shade*, ref. Christ's second coming ὡς καὶ τὴν σελήνην καὶ τὸν ἥλιον καὶ ἅπαν ~εσθαι φῶς ὑπὸ τῆς αὐγῆς ἐκείνης καταλαμπόμενον Chrys.*hom.14.10 in Rom.*(9.591C); id.*hom.3.6 in Col.*(11.388C); Thdt.*2Cor.*3:10(3.304).

***κρυπτῶς**, *in a hidden manner, secretly*, Clem.*str.*1.13(p.10.6; M.8.701B); Mac.Aeg.*hom.*5.11(M.34.516E); ‡Ath.*qu.Ant.*80(M.28.648C).

κρυσταλλίζω, *be clear as crystal*, ‡Jo.D.*hom.*5(M.96.657D).

κρυσταλλόομαι, *be frozen*, *A.Phil.*24(p.13.5); Philost.*h.e.*10.6(M.65.588A).

κρυφιμαῖος, *secret*, ref. baptism μυστήριον κ. *A.Thom.*A 121 (p.230.23); τῇ Μαρίᾳ...οὐχ ἁπλῶς προσετέθη, ἀλλὰ δύναμίν τινα κ. ἐκ τῆς αὐτοῦ οὐσίας ἔδωκεν [sc. Christ] αὐτῇ [sc. Mary of Bethany] Mac.Aeg.*hom.*12.16(M.34.568B).

***κρυφιογνωμέω**, *form secret plans*, Steph.Diac.*v.Steph.*(M.100.1125C).

***κρυφιογνώμως**, *with secret purpose*, Steph.Diac.*v.Steph.*(M.100.1177B); *ib.*(1180B).

***κρυφιογνώστης, ὁ,** *one who knows secret things*; of God, ‡Chrys.*hom.*3.3 *in Gen.*(6.546E).

***κρυφιόγνωστος**, *secretly known* μυσταγωγῷ κρυφιογνώστου σοφίας Παύλῳ Max.*ambig.*(M.91.1409A).

***κρυφιοειδῶς**, *in a hidden manner, mysteriously*, Dion.Ar.*c.h.*9.2 (M.3.260A).

***κρυφιόμυστος**, *of hidden mystery* σὺ τὴν κ. αἴνεσιν τῷ πρυτάνει τῶν ὅλων ἀναπέμπεις Chrysipp.*enc.in Jo.Bapt.*(p.34.22); θεολογίας κατὰ τὸν ὑπέρφατον ἐγκεκάλυπται τῆς κ. σιγῆς γνόφον Dion.Ar.*myst.*1(M.3.997B); τῇ κ. καὶ πολυφωνοτάτῳ σιγῇ Max.*opusc.*(M.91.229A); τῆς...πάντων ἐπέκεινα κ. ... ἀπειρίας id.*ambig.*(M.91.1165D).

***κρυφιομύστως**, *in a hidden mystery*, ‡Epiph.*hom.*2(M.43.453B); Χριστιανῶν βάπτισμα...κ. ὁ θεὸς διὰ τοῦ προφήτου ᾐνίξατο †Gregent.*disp.*(M.86.728B); θεὸς...τὴν ὑπὲρ πάντων ἐν σοὶ [sc. BMV] κ. ἱερουργήσων λατρείαν Andr.Cr.*or.*4(M.97.877D).

***κρυφιοπνευστί**, f.l. for *κρυφιοπευστεί, *by secret inquiry*, Steph. Diac.*v.Steph.*(M.100.1161A, v.l. κρυφιοπνεύστως).

κρύφιος, *hidden, obscure*; **1.** of God, ref. Jo.5:19,20 δεικνύντος ἄρα τοῦ πατρὸς τὰ ἑαυτοῦ κ. θεωρῶν ὁ υἱὸς δι' ἔργων ὑφίστη τὰ τῆς πατρικῆς βουλῆς ἔργα Eus.*e.th.*3.3(p.155.30; M.24.1000B); τοῦ κ. θεοῦ Dion.Ar.*e.h.*1.1(M.3.372A); *ib.*4.3.1(473B); αἱ τοῦ θεοῦ κρύφιαι καὶ ὑπὲρ νοῦν εὐώδεις εὐπρέπειαι *ib.*; id.*d.n.*1.3(M.3.589B); **2.** of Christ's divine nature τὸ γὰρ...κ. Ἰησοῦ...τῇ καθ' ἡμᾶς ἐνανθρωπήσει πρὸς τὸ...ὁρατὸν...προελήλυθε id.*e.h.*3.3.12(444A); **3.** of divine mysteries; **a.** in gen., of teaching about divinity of Christ ἡ... ἐκκλησία, ὥσπερ τι πάλαι κ. ... μυστήριον παραλαβοῦσα σεμνύνεται Eus.*e.th.*1.20(p.96.9; M.24.892C); κ. περὶ τοῦ λόγου μυστήριον *ib.*2.18(p.122.15; 941B); ἡ κ. καὶ ἱερατικὴ παράδοσις Dion.Ar.*c.h.*2.3(M.3.140D); id.*e.h.*2.3.7(M.3.404C); ὁπόταν οἱ τῆς ἀπορρήτου σοφίας πατέρες, διὰ δή τινῶν κ. ... αἰνιγμάτων ἐκφαίνωσι τὴν θείαν καὶ μυστικὴν καὶ ἄβατον τοῖς βεβήλοις ἀλήθειαν id.*ep.*9(M.3.1104B); ref. Ps.9:1 κρύφια τοίνυν τοῦ υἱοῦ, τὰ κρυφίως πεπραγμένα τῷ σωτῆρι·...ἀπέκρυψε γὰρ αὐτὰ καὶ τοὺς ἄρχοντας τοῦ κόσμου τούτου Cyr.*Ps.*9:1(M.69.761B); **b.** as revealed by God, *Barn.*6.10; δύναται δὲ καὶ ὁ λόγος ὁ υἱὸς εἶναι παρὰ τὸ ἀπαγγέλλειν τὰ κ. τοῦ πατρὸς ἐκείνου Or.*Jo.*1.38(42; p.49.4; M.14.100A); **c.** as transmitted through angels μυστηρίων ὑπερκοσμίων κρυφίους ὁράσεις...ἀναφαίνοντες Dion.Ar.*c.h.*4.2(M.3.180A); ref. first order κρυφιωτέρᾳ...τῆς θεαρχίας φωτοδοσίᾳ καθαίρεται ...κρυφιωτέρᾳ μέν, ὡς ἐνοτοτέρᾳ, καὶ μᾶλλον ἁπλωτικῇ καὶ ἑνοποιῷ *ib.*10.1(272D); ἐλλάμπει δὲ τοῖς καθ' ἕκαστον δευτέροις διὰ τῶν πρώτων, καί, εἰ δεῖ συντόμως εἰπεῖν, πρώτως ἐκ τοῦ κ. τὸ ἐμφανὲς ἄγεται διὰ τῶν πρώτων δυνάμεων *ib.*13.4(305B); **d.** symbolized τὴν μὲν... μορφὴν ἐμφαίνειν οἰητέον...τῶν ἵππων τὸ εὐπειθὲς...λευκῶν μὲν ὄντων τὸ λαμπρόν...κυανῶν δὲ ὄντων, τὸ κ. *ib.*15.8(337A); **4.** of secret thoughts τότε [sc. in day of judgement] φανήσεται τὰ κ. καὶ φανερὰ ἔργα τῶν ἀνθρώπων *2Clem.*16.3; θεὸν τὸν τὰ κ. εἰδότα Ign.*Magn.*3.2; Or.*princ.*3.1.13(p.218.3; M.11.273A); τὰ κ. τοῦ ἀνδρὸς συνορῶν [sc. Christ] Eus.*Marcell.*2.4(p.58.26; M.24.824B); Dion.Ar.*e.h.*3.3.10 (M.3.440B); **5.** in system of Simonians πάντων τῶν ὄντων αἰσθητῶν τε καὶ νοητῶν, ὧν ἐκεῖνος κρυφίων καὶ φανερῶν προσαγορεύει Hipp.*haer.*6.9(p.137.5; M.16.3210C).

κρυφιότης, ἡ, *hiddenness, mystery* θεὸν...ἐν τῷ...υἱῷ...τὸ τῆς πατρικῆς κ. γνώρισμα προάγοντα Thdot.Anc.*hom.BMV et Sym.*12 (M.77.1408D); τῆς θεαρχικῆς κ. Dion.Ar.*c.h.*4.2(M.3.180A); *ib.*15.9 (340B); τὴν ὑπερούσιον κ. θεὸν ἢ ζωὴν ἢ οὐσίαν ἢ φῶς ἢ λόγον ὀνομάσαιμεν id.*d.n.*2.6(M.3.645A); *ib.*9.5(913B); τῇ κ. τῶν ἀπορρήτων id.*c.h.*2.3 (141A); τῇ κατὰ νοῦν κ. τὰ ἅγια περιστείλας *ib.*2.5(145C); ἡ τῆς θεαρχικῆς ἀγνότητος μετουσία...εἰς...τοὺς ἱεροὺς νόας ὑπερουσίῳ κ. τελετουργουμένη *ib.*13.4(305B); πρὸς τὸ ἓν τῆς αὐτοῦ [sc. πατρός] κ. κατ' ἔκστασιν πάντων συναχθήσεται Max.*myst.*23(M.91.701B); ἔστω ταῦτα...τῇ θείᾳ μυστικῶς κ. τιμώμενά τε καὶ συντηρούμενα Andr.Cr.*or.*12(M.97.1053C).

κρυφιώδης, *hidden, mysterious*, ref. spiritual sense of scripture τὴν ἀγλαΐαν τοσοῦτον ὑπερλάμπουσαν τοῦ φαινομένου, ὅσον τὸ νοούμενον τοῦ φαινομένου κρυφιωδέστερόν τε καὶ διαρκέστερον Andr.Cr.*or.*7(M.97.940B).

***κρυφιωδῶς**, *in hidden, mysterious fashion*, ref. spiritual sense of scripture κρυφιωδέστερον...καὶ μυστικώτερον, πρόσωπον μὲν τοῦ θεοῦ καὶ πατρὸς ὁ υἱός, φῶς δὲ τὸ ἐξ αὐτοῦ πεμπόμενον πνεῦμα εἰς ἡμᾶς Cyr.*Ps.*4:7(M.69.740B); τὴν δευτέραν [sc. order of angels] τῆς πρώτης μὲν ἱεραρχίας ἐμφανέστερον, τῆς δὲ μετ' αὐτὴν κρυφιωδέστερον Dion.Ar.*c.h.*9.2(M.3.260A).

κρυφίως, *secretly, in hidden fashion*, ref. Jo.1:5 κ. ... δηλοῖ ὡς... φαίνει ἀιδίως ὡς ἀχώριστον ἀπαύγασμα τοῦ θεοῦ Didym.*Trin.*1.15 (M.39.301B); ἡ θεαρχικὴ δύναμις...ὡς κ. ἐπὶ πάντας διεῖσα τὰς προνοητικὰς αὐτῆς ἐνεργείας Dion.Ar.*c.h.*13.3(M.3.301A).

***κρυφογαμία, ἡ,** *secret marriage*, *Nomoc.*326.

***κρυφοπομπαῖος**, *discharged secretly* κ. βέλη Agath.*v.Gr.Ill.*60.

***κρυψοτάλαντος**, *hiding one's talent*, ‡Ath.*v.Syncl.*21(M.28.1500A).

***κρυψώνυμος**, *anonymous*, Leont.H.*monoph.*(M.86.1852A).

κτέαρ, τό, *possession*; met., of the Cross ὄλβιος, ὃς πάντων κτεάνων ὠνήσατο Χριστόν, καὶ κ. οἷον ἔχει σταυρόν Gr.Naz.*carm.*1.2.17.6(M.37.782A); the Church σῶμα μέγα Χριστοῖο...θεοῦ κ. ἔνθα καὶ ἔνθα σείεται *ib.*2.1.13.29(1229A).

κτενοειδής, *like a comb*, *Schol.Clem.paed.*3.3(p.336.14; M.9.792C).

κτῆμα, τό, *possession*; **1.** in gen., dist. from χρῆμα, Clem.*q.d.s.*14 (p.168.24; M.9.617C); ref. Logos ὁ πρὸς μηδένα ἔχων κοινὸν κ. ἢ χρῆμα, ἀλλὰ πάντων κύριος ‡Ath.*serm.fid.*28(p.25; M.26.1284A); **2.** of persons, often with implicit notion of *slave* τὸν Ἰούδαν...τοῦ Ἰησοῦ ...κ. Or.*Jo.*32.14(9; p.449.6; M.14.777C); ἐὰν τὰ ἀγαθά τις πράσσειν ἔληται, τοῦ...βασιλέως γίνεται κ. *Hom.Clem.*20.3; ref. Pr.8:22 τὸ... μέγα κ. τοῦ θεοῦ ὁ μονογενὴς υἱός, καθ' ὃ μὲν ἐξ αὐτοῦ γεγένηται...καθ' ὃ δὲ τοῖς πᾶσιν κοινωφελὴς καὶ σωτήριος...κ. τοῦ πατρός Eus.*e.th.*3.2 (p.142.35; M.24.977C); **3.** of spiritual gifts, Clem.*paed.*3.11(p.279.18; M.8.656C); id.*q.d.s.*34(p.182.20; M.9.640B); τὰ ἐν τοῖς προφήταις πνεύματα...δεδωρημένα αὐτοῖς ὑπὸ θεοῦ...κ. Or.*Jo.*6.11(p.120.18; M.14.220B); Meth.*symp.*4.6(p.52.9; M.18.96B); κοινὸν...κ. τῆς καθόλου ἐκκλησίας ἡ ἐν ἐκείνῳ χάρις Gr.Nyss.*ep.*17(M.46.1065C); of spiritual sacrifice τὸ κάλλιστον τῶν κ. ... σφᾶς αὐτοὺς ἐπιτρέπειν τῷ θεῷ Clem.*prot.*12(p.86.7; M.8.244B); **4.** *estate, property, farm*, Thdt.*ep.*42(4.1101); Jo.Mal.*chron.*2 p.47(M.97.120C); Jo.Mosch.*prat.*27(M.87.2873B).

***κτηματίσκιον, τό,** *small farm*, Gr.Mag.*dial.*(tr.Zach.)3.21(M.*PL.*77.272C).

***κτήνειος**, **1.** *of cattle*, Or.*Cels.*4.54(p.327.15; M.11.1117C); **2.** *of animals* or *beasts* ἆρα...ὁ πρῶτος ἄνθρωπος...κτηνείαν τινὰ ψυχὴν εἶχε; Gr.Nyss.*Apoll.*10(M.45.1144B).

***κτηνικός**, *belonging to a beast*, Anast.S.*hod.*2(M.89.72D).

κτηνίτης, ὁ, *cattle-driver*, *Apophth.Patr.*(M.65.148B); Thdr.Stud.*catech.parv.*125(M.99.673C); id.*poen.*1.91 tit.(M.99.1745A).

***κτηνοβασία (κτηνοβατία), ἡ,** *bestiality*, †Jo.Jej.*poenit.*(M.88.1893D); †Jo.Jej.*serm.*1(M.88.1921D); Jo.D.*virt.*(M.95.88C).

***κτηνογενής**, *produced by a beast*, Anast.S.*hex.*12(M.89.1053A).

***κτηνόθυτος**, *of a sacrificed beast*, ‡Epiph.*hom.*2(M.43.441C).

***κτηνομέτωπος**, *with the brow of a beast*, Geo.Pis.*carm.vit.*22.

***κτηνόμορφος**, *having the shape of a beast*; met., Geo.Pis.*Heracl.*2.51(M.92.1321A); τὰς κ. τῶν παθῶν παρεμφάσεις id.*van.*68(M.92.1586A).

***κτηνόομαι**, *become brutish*, Cyr.*Juln.*9(6^{2}.321C); Max.*cap.theol.*2.67(M.90.1156A).

***κτηνοπρεπής**, *befitting a beast*, ref. man's unredeemed state εὗρον ἀποκτηνωθέντα τὸν ἄνθρωπον·...ἐν φάτνῃ ὡς ἐν τάξει τροφῆς τέθειται, ἵνα τὸν κ. μεταμείψαντες βίον, εἰς τὴν ἀνθρώπῳ πρέπουσαν ἀνακομισθῶμεν σύνεσιν Cyr.*Lc.*2:7(M.72.488D); ref. Israel, id.*Os.*33 (3.61B); ref. gentiles, id.*Juln.*8(6^{2}.278D).

***κτηνοπρεπῶς**, *in a manner befitting a beast*, i.e. irrationally, Cyr.*Juln.*4(6^{2}.140C); *cat.Lc.*14:23(p.114.32); Areth.*Apoc.*15(M.106.592A).

***κτηνοσφαγία, ἡ,** *slaughter of cattle*, ‡Caes.Naz.*dial.*153(M.38.1108).

***κτηνοφθορία, ἡ,** *bestiality*, †Gregent.*leg.Hom.*2(M.86.584A).

***κτηνοφθόρος**, *committing bestiality*, *T.Lev.*17.11.

***κτηνόφρων**, *brute-minded* κ. ἄνθρωποι Agath.*v.Gr.Ill.*151.

***κτηνωδεία**, ἡ, v. **κτηνωδία*.

κτηνώδης, *like a beast* τὴν θηριώδη φύσιν καὶ τὴν κ. *A.Phil.*99(p.38.35); κ. γαστέρα *T.Job* 39(p.128.21); as irrational, sensual ὁ δὲ κ. βίος ἄριστος, ἀρετὴ δὲ ἀνόητος Athenag.*res.*19(p.72.8; M.6.1012D); τὸ πολυσκελὲς καὶ κ. καὶ ὁρμητικὸν πάθος, τὴν ἐπιθυμίαν Clem.*str.*5.8(p.362.4; M.9.84A); κ. φύσιν Gr.Nyss.*hom.opif.*28(M.44.232C); βοσκήματα...τοὺς ἀνθρώπους...οὓς ἡ κ. καὶ ἄλογος...ὁρμὴ ἐκλάθεσθαι τῆς ἀνθρωπίνης ἀνέπεισε φύσεως id.*v.Mos.*(M.44.424C); id.*virg.*5(p.277.21; M.46.348C); expressing man's dependence on God, exeg. Ps. 72:22 σοῦ δὲ ἄγοντος, ἐρρῶσθαι φράσας ἐκείνῳ τῷ λογικῷ, τοῦ κτήνους μιμοῦμαι τὸ εὐπειθές, καὶ τοῖς ἄλλοις ὢν λογικός, κ. γίνομαι παρὰ σοί Thdt.*provid.*5(4.555); of a life opposed to grace οἱ προσελθόντες... τῷ λόγῳ κτηνώδεις Or.*sel.in Lev.*5:2(M.12.400B); τίς οὕτω κ. ὥστε ἀκούων θεὸν λόγον...πρὸς τὰ σώματος πάθη τοῖς λογισμοῖς καταπίπτειν; Bas.*Eun.*2.5(1.241E; M.29.581B); with ἄλογος, Gr.Nyss.*hom. 1 in Cant.*(M.44.765A); οὐδὲν οὕτω κ. καὶ ἀλόγου ψυχῆς δεῖγμα...ὡς τῶν θείων ὑπερορᾶν λογίων Chrys.*hom.1.1 in Ac.*9:1(3.98C); of fallen man οἱ πρότερον μὲν κ. ὑπὸ δὲ τῆς εἰς αὐτὸν πίστεως φωτισθέντες Diod.*Gen.*49:11(M.33.1580A); of men without respect for the law οἱ δὲ κ. ...ἐν τοῖς ὑψηλοῖς τόποις προσέφερον τὰς θυσίας Thdt.*Is.*36:5ff.(p.143.17; 2.318); stupid σύμβολον...τῶν...ἀνοήτων καὶ κ. τὸ πρόβατον Or.*Jo.*10.24(16; p.196.31; M.14.349C); Gr.Nyss.*Eun.*1(1 p.89.10; M.45.321A); of the unbaptized παντελῶς κ. ἢ θηριώδεις, ὡς ἂν ἀνοίας ἢ πονηρίας ἔχωσιν Gr.Naz.*or.*40.23(M.36.389A); σοφίζεται ὁ Ὠριγένης ...πολὺ δὲ κτηνωδέστερον τὸ τοιοῦτον Epiph.*anc.*62(p.74.15; M.43.128C); of heretics, Epiph.*haer.*42.11(p.139.20; M.41.749A); *ib.*66.45(p.83.5; M.42.97C).

***κτηνωδία** (-εία), ἡ, **1.** *brutishness* μεταίρει [sc. Satan] τὴν φύσιν εἰς παρὰ φύσιν τῶν παθῶν κτηνωδίαν Geo.Pis.*hex.*766(M.92.1493A); id.*van.*70(M.92.1586A); ἄλλος τρόπος τῆς τῶν ἀνθρώπων αὐξήσεως προεγνωσμένος θεῷ, εἰ...πρὸς κτηνωδίαν ἑαυτὸν [sc. Adam]...μὴ κατέβαλε Max.*ambig.*(M.91.1309A); **2.** *animal form, animal-like appearance*, -δεία, Dion.Ar.*c.h.*2.1(M.3.137A).

κτηνωδῶς, *like cattle*; comp., Or.*Jo.*13.6(p.231.13; M.14.408C).

[*]**κτησίδιον**, τό, = κτησείδιον, *property*, ‡Nil.*Epict.*24(M.79.1293C).

κτῆσις, ἡ, **1.** *acquisition* τὴν τοῦ τέλους κ. Clem.*str.*7.11(p.47.3; M.9.489C); of virtues, Thdt.*Is.*38:17(p.152.6; 2.325); τὸ σῶμα...προξενεῖ...τῇ ψυχῇ τῆς ἁμαρτίας τὴν ἐπιζήμιον κ. id.*eran.*3(4.179); **2.** *possession*, in gen. ὁ λόγος τῆς κ. ἀφίστασθαι οὐ κελεύει, ἀλλ' ἀπροσπαθῶς διοικεῖν τὴν κ. Clem.*ecl.*47(p.150.3; κτίσεως M.9.720B); of spiritual possessions, *Const.App.*7.45.3; Mac.Aeg.*hom.*9.10(M.34.538B); of persons βεβαιῶν [sc. Christ] ἑαυτῷ κ. τῶν ἀπὸ ταύτης τῆς γῆς πιστευόντων εἰς τὸν πατέρα δι' αὐτοῦ Or.*Jo.*13.57(56; p.288.8; M.14.508B); Gr.Nyss.*ep.*17(M.46.1060D); ref. Pr.8:22 τὴν μὲν κτίσιν...τὴν ἐκ τοῦ μὴ ὄντος εἰς τὸ εἶναι πάροδον σημαίνειν· τὴν δὲ κ. τοῦ προϋπάρχοντος ἰδιάζουσαν οἰκειότητα πρὸς τὸν κτώμενον Eus.*e.th.*3.2(p.143.16; M.24.980A); **3.** *property, estate*, *Cod.Afr.*58.

κτήτωρ, ὁ, *possessor, owner*; **1.** in gen., *landowner* οἱ ταῖς εὐτελεστάταις χρώμενοι τροφαῖς ἰσχυρότεροί εἰσι...ὡς οἰκέται δεσποτῶν καὶ γεωργοὶ κτητόρων Clem.*paed.*2.1(p.157.5; M.8.385B); κ. παρ' οἷς ἡ ἐκείνων [sc. Donatists] εὑρεθῇ συναγωγὴ *Cod.Afr.*93; Jo.Mosch.*prat.*196(M.87.3081D); Gr.Mag.*dial.*(tr.Zach.)3.26(M.*PL.*77.282B); *householder*, Leont.N.*v.Jo.Eleem.*13(p.26.9); *Chron.Pasch.*p.322(M.92.824A); of men of substance in gen. ψηφίζεσθαι...παρὰ τῆς ἑκάστης μητροπόλεως κληρικῶν καὶ κ. καὶ λαμπροτάτων ἀνδρῶν καὶ... ἐπισκόπων CChalc.*act.*17(*ACO* 2.1.3 p.98.39; H.2.641E); Geo.Al.*v.Chrys.*4(p.161.39); of the worldly man μοναχὸς φιλοκτήμων... κοσμικὸς κ.· μοναχὸς δὲ πένης, οὐράνιος πολίτης Ephr.3.151B; met., of humility as possessor of the soul, Jo.Clim.*scal.*25(M.88.996A); **2.** Christol. ὁ θεότητος κ. ἐξ ἀνθρώπων ληφθεὶς Nest.ap.Cyr.*Nest.*3.1(p.57.9; 6¹.64B); **3.** *founder* of church or monastery δεόμεθα ὑπὲρ ἀναπαύσεως τῶν ψυχῶν τῶν...κ. τῆς...μονῆς *Euchol.*(p.150); *Nomoc.*12; **4.** *patron*; of martyr over whose grave church had been built, Chrysipp.*enc.in Thdr.*(p.57.17).

κτίζ-ω, **I.** *create*;

A. in rel. to other terms; dist. from γεννάω, Ath.*Ar.*2.59(M.26.272B); but τὸ γεννᾶν καὶ τὸ κ. τὸ αὐτό ἐστιν ‡Chrys.*Jud.*(1.825B); v. ποιέω.

B. of God as creator; **1.** in gen., Clem.*str.*6.10(p.471.30; M.9.301A); Or.*hom.*2.1 *in Jer.*(p.17.22; M.13.277D); Ath.*exp.Ps.*103:24(M.27.410D); ὁ κύριος ἡμῶν οὔτε θεοὺς εἶναι ἐφθέγξατο παρὰ τὸν κτίσαντα τὰ πάντα *Hom.Clem.*16.15; **2.** Trin. ~ουσά ἐστι...ἡ τριάς Ath.*Ar.*1.18(M.26.49A); id.*ep.Serap.*1.28(M.26.596A) cit. s. δημιουργέω; εἰ μὴ γὰρ ὑπὸ τῆς τριάδος ἐκτίσθημεν, πῶς ἐκ τριάδος ἀναγεννώμεθα βαπτιζόμενοι; Proc.G.*Gen.*2:7(M.87.156D); ref. rel. of Father and Son; of Creation by Father through Son, Just.*2apol.*6.1(M.6.453A); κτίστης ἐστὶν ὁ θεός, διὰ υἱοῦ δὲ τὰ ποιήματα κ. Ath.*Ar.*1.17(M.26.48A); *Const.App.*7.36.1; Cyr.*thes.*7(5¹.59E); otherwise expressed τὸ ~ειν μόνου τοῦ θεοῦ ἐστιν, καὶ τοῦ ἰδίου αὐτοῦ λόγου Ath.*Ar.*2.27(M.26.204A); ὁ λόγος τοῦ πατρός, ἐν ᾧ καὶ δι' οὗ τὰ πάντα κ. *ib.*1.16(45B); of Son as creator τὰ πάντα γοῦν ἔκτισεν ὁ τοῦ θεοῦ λόγος †Ath.*exp.fid.*4(M.25.205C); Jo.D.*disp.*(M.96.1345A); of H. Ghost τὸ πνεῦμα τὸ ἅγιον..., τὸ κτίσαν πᾶσαν τὴν κτίσιν Herm.*sim.*5.6.5; ὁ γὰρ πατὴρ διὰ τοῦ λόγου ἐν τῷ πνεύματι κ. τὰ πάντα Ath.*ep.Serap.*3.5(M.26.632B); δέδεικται ὅτι κ. τὸ πνεῦμα. ηὑρέθη γὰρ ἡ ἁγία Μαρία ἐν γαστρὶ ἔχουσα ἐκ πνεύματος τοῦ ἁγίου. ... τὸ οὖν 'ἐκ πνεύματος ἁγίου' τί ἄλλο ἠγῇ πλὴν τοῦ κτίσαι; ‡Ath.*dial.Trin.*3.25(M.28.1241D); **3.** reasons for Creation ἔκτισας τὰ πάντα ἕνεκεν τοῦ ὀνόματός σου *Did.*10.3; περὶ τὸν θεὸν δείκνυται δύναμις μὲν καὶ ἀγαθότης ἐν τῷ τὰ μηδέπω ὄντα ἑκουσίως ~ειν Iren.*haer.*4.38.3(M.7.1107B); **4.** creation *ex nihilo* ὁ θεὸς...κτίσας ἐκ τοῦ μὴ ὄντος τὰ ὄντα Herm.*vis.*1.1.6; Ath.*decr.*11(p.9.35; M.25.433C); Eun.*apol.*18(M.30.852D); **5.** angels in rel. to Creation, v. ἄγγελος; **6.** heret. (Valent.) διὰ τῆς τοῦ Σωτῆρος ἐπιφανείας ἡ Σοφία ⟨ἀπαθὴς⟩ γίνεται καὶ τὰ ἔξω ~εται Clem.*exc.Thdot.*45(p.121.11; M.9.680C); ὁ δημιουργὸς...οὐσιωδῶς ~ων πνευματικὰ τῆς πονηρίας *ib.*48(p.122.13; 681B); θανάτου δὲ γένεσιν ἔργον εἶναι τοῦ κτίσαντος id.*str.*4.13(p.287.18; M.8.1297A); (Manich.) τὸ ζῶν πνεῦμα ἔκτισε τὸν κόσμον Hegem.*Arch.*8(p.11.4; M.10.1437C); (Apelles) ὁ αὐτὸς ἅγιος ἄνωθεν θεὸς...ἐποίησεν ἕνα ἄλλον θεόν· ὁ δὲ γενόμενος ἄλλος θεὸς ἔκτισε τὰ πάντα Epiph.*haer.*44.1(p.191.3; M.41.821C); **7.** for theory of Son as created, v. δημιουργέω, εἰμί, λόγος, ποίησις; **8.** ptcpl. as subst.; ref. creatures below man τῶν ὑπὸ θεοῦ κτισθέντων εἰς χρῆσιν ἀνθρώπων *Diogn.*4.2; Valentinian οἱ μὲν δίκαιοι διὰ τῶν ἐκτισμένων τὴν ὁδὸν ποιούμενοι παρὰ τῷ τόπῳ κατείχοντο..., οἱ δὲ ἕτεροι ἐν τῷ τοῦ σκότου ἐκτισμένῳ ἐν τοῖς ἀριστεροῖς, ἔχοντες συναίσθησιν τοῦ πυρὸς Clem.*exc.Thdot.*36(p.118.25; M.9.677A).

C. of spiritual re-creation; **1.** in Christ τὸν ἐν Χριστῷ κτισθέντα καὶ ἀνακαινισθέντα νοῦν Ath.*ep.Serap.*1.9(M.26.553C); cf.id.*Ar.*2.46(M.26.244C); οὕτω κ. Χριστός, ἀναμορφῶν δι' ἁγιασμοῦ πρὸς ἑαυτὸν τοὺς πιστεύοντας Cyr.*Is.*5.2(2.771A); ὁ ~ων ἡμᾶς ἐστι θεὸς ἐν Χριστῷ Jo.D.*Eph.*2:10(M.95.832A); **2.** on conversion to Christianity λαβόντες τὴν ἄφεσιν τῶν ἁμαρτιῶν καὶ ἐλπίσαντες ἐπὶ τὸ ὄνομα ἐγενόμεθα καινοί, πάλιν ἐξ ἀρχῆς ~όμενοι *Barn.*16.8; Didym.*Ps.*88:12(M.39.1489C); **3.** through baptism, Evagr.Pont.*ep.*11(M.32.264C); τὸ 'κτισθέντες' ἐνταῦθα ἐπὶ τῆς ἀναγεννήσεως τέθεικεν Thdt.*Eph.*2:10(3.412); cf.‡Ath.*dial.Trin.*3.26(M.28.1244D); **4.** through repentance; ref. Is.45:7 κ. δὲ [sc. God] κακά· τουτέστι, μετακοσμεῖ αὐτὰ καὶ εἰς βελτίωσιν ἄγει Bas.*hom.*9.4(2.75C; M.31.336C); **5.** at resurrection of dead, cf.Ps.103:30 ἀποστελεῖ τὸ πνεῦμα τὸ ἅγιον, καὶ κ. ἡμᾶς Evagr.Pont.*ep.*11(M.32.264C).

II. *establish*; ref. chosen people ὁ θεὸς...τὸν λαὸν ἔκτισε Herm.*sim.*5.6.2; κτίσας τὴν ἁγίαν ἐκκλησίαν αὐτοῦ id.*vis.*1.3.4; *ib.*2.4.1; ref. growth in virtue ἑαυτὸν κ. ... ὁ γνωστικός Clem.*str.*7.3(p.10.22; M.9.417A); ref. Apoc.4:11, etc. τὰ λογικὰ δὲ μετὰ τὸ οὐσιωθῆναι καὶ εἶναι δέχονται τὸ κτισθῆναι·...~εται γάρ τις ἐπὶ ἔργοις ἀγαθοῖς, πρὸ τούτο ὢν θεοῦ ποίημα, εἰς καρδίαν καθαράν Or.*Apoc.*26(p.32.2); cf.id.*hom.1.10 in Jer.*(p.9.9; M.13.268A); ἔκτισεν ὁ θεὸς τοὺς εἰς αὐτὸν πεπιστευκότας Bas.*hom.in Ps.*32(1.138B; M.29.340A).

III. *produce* ἡμεῖς δὲ ἑαυτοῖς ἐκτίσαμεν τὴν κακίαν καὶ τὰς ἁμαρτίας Or.*hom.*2.1 *in Jer.*(p.16.24; M.13.277B).

κτίσις, ἡ, **I.** *creation*;

A. of act of Creation; **1.** lit., in gen. *Pss.Sal.*8.7; *Barn.*15.3; Or.*hom.1.10 in Jer.*(p.8.30; M.13.265D); τῆς ἐξ οὐκ ὄντων κ. Eus.*e.th.*1.9(p.67.9; M.24.840A); as work of Trin., Bas.*Spir.*38(3.31D; M.32.136A) cit. s. πνεῦμα; ref. Christ οὐδὲν ἐν τοῖς διὰ τῆς κ. οὖσι χωρὶς αὐτοῦ γεγενῆσθαι Gr.Nyss.*Eun.*3(2 p.6.6; M. om.); Gnost. βλασφημοῦσι...τὸ μυστήριον τῆς κ., τὴν γένεσιν διαβάλλοντες Clem.*str.*3.17(p.243.11; M.8.1205A); as synonym for Genesis τῆς κ. τὸ βιβλίον Thdt.*Jer.*49:28(2.608); *Didasc.Jac.*1.23(p.760.15); **2.** spiritual; of re-creation by grace κατὰ τὴν κ. τὴν ἐξειλεγμένην Clem.*str.*7.12(p.54.28; M.9.505A); ἡ μὲν γένεσις τὴν τῶν λογικῶν οὐσίωσιν δηλοῖ· ἡ δὲ κ. τὴν ἀπὸ τοῦ κρείττονος ἐπὶ τὸ χεῖρον μεταβολήν· εἴ τις γὰρ ἐν Χριστῷ καινὴ κ., ἀνακαινίζεται Or.*sel.in Ps.*32:9(M.12.1305B); ‡Ath.*comm.essent.*24(M.28.56A); κτίσιν καλεῖ τὴν οὐσίωσιν τῆς ἀρετῆς Chrys.*hom.13.2 in Eph.*(11.98B); ref. regeneration in Christ κ. τὸ πρᾶγμά ἐστι, καὶ τῆς ἑτέρας τιμιωτέρα· ἐξ ἐκείνης μὲν γὰρ τὸ ζῆν, ἐκ δὲ ταύτης τὸ καλῶς ζῆν ἡμῖν περιγέγονεν Chrys.*hom.4.3 in Eph.*(11.28E); id.*hom.20.3 in 1Cor.*(10.172C); ref. baptism καινὴν γὰρ κ. ταύτην καλεῖ τὴν καθ' ὑμᾶς πολιτείαν id.*comm.in Gal.*6:15(10.729A); Thdt.*Dan.*9:24(2.1244); **3.** of resurrection of dead, ref.

Ps.103:30, Rom.8:11, ‡Ath.*comm.essent*.24(M.28.56A); **4.** three creations described *τρεῖς κ. εὑρήκαμεν ὀνομαζομένας ἐν τῇ γραφῇ· μίαν μὲν καὶ πρώτην, τὴν ἀπὸ τοῦ μὴ ὄντος εἰς τὸ εἶναι παραγωγήν· δευτέραν δέ, τὴν ἀπὸ τοῦ χείρονος εἰς τὸ κρεῖττον ἀλλοίωσιν· τρίτην δέ, τὴν ἐξανάστασιν τῶν νεκρῶν. ἐν ταύταις εὑρήσεις συνεργὸν πατρὶ καὶ υἱῷ τὸ ἅγιον πνεῦμα* Evagr.Pont.*ep*.11(M.32.264B); *ἡ πρώτη κ.* Ath.*Ar*.2.65(M.26.285B); *Hom.Clem*.13.15; Gr.Nyss.*Eun*.3(2 p.12.11; M.45.576C); Sever.*creat*.5.2(M.56.473); *ἡ δευτέρα κ.* Bas.*hom.in Ps*.32(1.138A; M.29.340A); ref. baptism *διπλῆν γὰρ τῆς φύσεως ἡμῶν τὴν κ. ἐγνώκαμεν, τήν τε πρώτην καθ' ἣν ἐπλάσθημεν καὶ τὴν δευτέραν καθ' ἣν ἀνεπλάσθημεν. ἀλλ' οὐκ ἂν ἦν τῆς δευτέρας ἡμῶν κ. χρεία, εἰ μὴ τὴν πρώτην διὰ τῆς παρακοῆς ἠχρειώσαμεν* Gr.Nyss.*Eun*.4(2 p.65.4; 636D); Gnost. *πρώτη γάρ, φησίν, κ. ἡ κατὰ τὸν Ἀδὰμ ἐν πόνοις. ...δευτέρα δὲ κ. ἐστὶν ἡ κατὰ Χριστόν, δι' ἧς ἀναγεννώμεθα* Hipp.*haer*.4.47(p.71.22ff.; M.16.3144Df.).

B. of universe; **1.** of whole of creation; **a.** in gen., *T.Lev*.4.1; *ἁρμονίαν κτίσεως καλλίστην* Clem.*str*.4.6(p.266.19; M.8.1252B); Or.*Jo*.1.26(24; p.32.5; M.14.69B); Gr.Nyss.*bapt.Chr*.(M.46.600A); created from nothing, id.*Eun*.5(2 p.120.8; M.45.701A) cit. s. *εἰμί*; as raising mind to God, Chrys.*Anna* 1.3(4.703C); id.*hom.3.2 in Rom*.(10.449E); **b.** ref. its author *πᾶσα ἡ κ. διὰ τοῦ υἱοῦ βαστάζεται* Herm.*sim*.9.14.5; *οὐκ ἔστι διελεῖν τὴν κ., ὥστε εἰπεῖν τοῦτο μὲν τοῦ πατρός, τοῦτο δὲ τοῦ υἱοῦ* Ath.*decr*.7(p.7.8; M.25.428C); *ἀχώριστος γὰρ ἀεὶ ἡ... τριάς, ὅ τε πατὴρ καὶ ὁ υἱὸς καὶ τὸ ἅγιον πνεῦμα, δημιουργήσασα ἅμα πᾶσαν τὴν κ. τήν τε νοητὴν καὶ αἰσθητήν* Gel.Cyz.*h.e*.2.21.8(M.85.1285A); **c.** in Gnost. teaching; (Marcosian) *αὐτὴν τὴν κ. κατ' εἰκόνα τῶν ἀοράτων ὑπὸ τοῦ δημιουργοῦ, ὡς ἀγνοοῦντος αὐτοῦ, κατασκευάσθαι διὰ τῆς μητρὸς λέγουσι* Iren.*haer*.1.17.1(M.7.637A); (Valentinian) *τῆς κ. τῆς καθ' ἡμᾶς* Hipp.*haer*.6.36(p.166.14; M.16.3250D); *τῆς κ. τῆς πονηρᾶς* *ib*.4.49(p.73.27; 3118B); (Naassene) *τῆς κ. κάτωθεν* *ib*.5.7(p.82.7; 3131A); **2.** of mankind *ἡ κ. τῶν ἀνθρώπων* *Did*.16.5; *τῆς κ.* Ath.*gent*.1(M.25.5A); Diad.*perf*.80(p.102.12); Thdt.*Heb*.2:17(3.561); **3.** of lower creation; **a.** as subject to man, Herm.*mand*.12.4.2; Or.*sel.in Ps*.73:18(M.12.1532C); *Hom.Clem*.16.19; *Lit*.ap.*Const.App*.8.12.20; but *τῷ ἁμαρτωλῷ πᾶσα ἡ κ. πολεμεῖ* Or.*hom.4.1 in Jos*.(p.308.22; M.87.1005C); **b.** as raising mind to God, Cyr.*Abac*.26(3.539E); Thdt.*Rom*.1:20(3.24); **c.** as witnessing to Christ at Crucifixion, Ath.*Dion*.4(p.48.18; M.25.484C); Cyr.*Am*.75(3.338A); **d.** ref. its proper use *τῇ κ. χρώμενοι, μετ' εὐχαριστίας* Clem.*str*.3.14(p.240.10; M.8.1196B); *ὅταν...ἀγαπήσῃ τὴν κ. διὰ τὸν πάντων θεόν τε καὶ ποιητήν* *ib*.3.10(p.227.18; 1172A); **e.** to be ultimately renewed, cf. Rom.8:20 *τί ἐστι 'τῇ ματαιότητι ἡ κ. ὑπετάγη'; φθαρτὴ γέγονε. τίνος ἕνεκεν καὶ διὰ τί; διὰ σὲ τὸν ἄνθρωπον. ἐπειδὴ γὰρ σῶμα ἔλαβες θνητὸν καὶ παθητόν, καὶ ἡ γῆ κατάραν ἐδέξατο καὶ ἀκάνθας ἤνεγκε καὶ τριβόλους. ... ἐλευθερωθήσεται γάρ, φησίν, ἀπὸ τῆς δουλείας τῆς φθορᾶς· τουτέστιν, οὐκέτι ἔσται φθαρτή, ἀλλὰ ἀκολουθήσει τῇ τοῦ σώματος εὐμορφίᾳ τοῦ σοῦ* Chrys.*hom.14.5 in Rom*.(9.582B); *ib*.(583A); id.*comm.in Gal*.6:15(10.729B); Cyr.*Rom*.8:19(p.216.11ff.; M.74.821Bff.); id.*Zach*.105(3.801A); Thdt.*Gal*.6:15(3.395); id.*Eph*.1:10(3.405); Andr.Caes.*Apoc*.22(M.106.421A).

C. of Church as new spiritual creation *ἀποστελεῖς τὸ πνεῦμά σου, τὸ διὰ τοῦ ἁγίου βαπτίσματος ἐπιφοιτῶν, καὶ κτισθήσονται εἰς καινὴν κ., εἰς νέον λαόν* Eus.*Ps*.103:30(M.23.1288B); Ath.*Ar*.2.65(M.26.285B); Thdt.*2Cor*.5:17(3.317).

II. *creature*;

A. in gen.; plur., Herm.*vis*.1.1.3; *A.Jo*.104(p.202.26); *Hom.Clem*.16.14; *ἡ μὲν κ., εἰκὼν καὶ χαρακτὴρ τῆς δημιουργικῆς βουλήσεως αὐτοῦ* [sc. God] Ath.*Ar*.2.2(M.26.149B).

B. characteristics; ref. defects such as death and disease *τὰ τοιαῦτα κτίσεως ἀνάγκην εἶναι* Clem.*str*.7.11(p.44.29; M.9.485C); Cyr.*Jo*.9.1(4.100B); not to be adored, Bas.*hom.in Ps*.28(1.116B; M.29.285C); Thdt.*Rom*.1:25(3.26).

C. ref. Christ *τοὺς διὰ τῶν Ἀρείου δογμάτων εἰδωλοποιοῦντας τὴν κ.* Gr.Nyss.*ep*.3(M.46.1017B); *ὡς οὐδεμία παραλλαγὴ οὐσίας...τῷ μονογενεῖ υἱῷ πρὸς τὸν θεὸν πατέρα, διαφορὰ δὲ πᾶσα, εἴ γε θέμις τοῦτο φάναι, πρὸς τὴν κ.* Didym.*Trin*.2.2(M.39.464C); v. *πρωτότοκος*.

D. of H. Ghost, ref. Pneumatomachoi *οὐ τριάς ἐστιν, ἀλλὰ δυάς, καὶ λοιπὸν ἡ κ. ...;* Ath.*ep.Serap*.1.2(M.26.533B); *τὸ πνεῦμα ἄρα οὐ κ.* Didym.(‡Bas.)*Eun*.5(1.302E; M.29.725C).

III. *production* *κ. τοῦ εἶναι ἐν αὐτοῖς πᾶν ἔργον ἀνθρώπου* *T.Reub*.2.3.

IV. *activity* *κ. δὲ συνωνύμως καὶ ἐνέργεια λέγεται ἔργον ἡμέτερον οὖσα* Clem.*str*.4.14(p.290.24; M.8.1304A).

κτίσμα, τό, A. *creature*; **1.** in gen. def. *τὰ φύσει τὴν οὐσίαν ἔχοντα κτιστὴν κτίσματα λέγεται* Ath.*Ar*.2.46(M.26.244B); *ταὐτὸν γάρ ἐστιν κ. καὶ ποίημα, καὶ ἔργον* *ib*.2.70(297A); opp. *γέννημα*, v.s.v.; of virtues and vices, Herm.*mand*.8.1; (Valent.) *τὸν δὲ κοσμοκράτορα κ. τοῦ δημιουργοῦ* Iren.*haer*.1.5.4(M.7.497B); ref. Devil *οὐδενὸς κτιστοῦ ὄντος παρὲξ τοῦ θεοῦ ἡμῶν, θεοῦ ἐστι κ.* Or.*Jo*.2.13(7; p.69.20; M.14.136C); *τοῖς λογικοῖς κ.* Cyr.*thes*.4(5^{1}.24E); **2.** characteristics; **a.** formed from nothing *ἐξ οὐκ ὄντων ἐστὶ τὰ κ., καὶ ἀρχὴν ἔχει τοῦ εἶναι* Ath.*ep.Serap*.3.2(M.26.628B); Chrys.*hom.4.3 in Heb*.(12.43C); **b.** in time *πρὸ πάντων τῶν κ.* Just.*dial*.61.1(M.6.613C); *ib*.129.4(777B); *κ. ... ἤρξατο ...χρονικῶς* Gr.Naz.*or*.42.17(M.36.477C); **c.** reflection of God, Bas.*hom.in Ps*.33(1.145E; M.29.357A); *ἐκ γὰρ καλλονῆς τῶν κ. ἀναλόγως ὁ γενεσιουργὸς αὐτῶν θεωρεῖται τῇ δημιουργίᾳ* Proc.G.*Gen*.11:17(M.87.324C); **d.** not to be adored, Or.*mart*.7(p.9.1; M.11.573A); *ἵνα ἐκ τῶν δημιουργημάτων τὸν τεχνίτην τοῦ παντὸς καταμαθόντες προσκυνήσωσι τὸν ἐργασάμενον, καὶ μὴ ἐναπομείνωσι τοῖς κ.* Chrys.*hom.2.2 in Gen*.(4.10B); **3.** created by God alone *οὐ τὰ ἴδια κ. συνάγει ὁ διάβολος,...ἀλλ' ἐπὰν φωνήσῃ, συνάγει τὰ ἄλλου κ. καὶ ποιεῖ αὐτὰ ἴδια* Or.*hom.17.2 in Jer*.(p.144.10; M.13.456A); by Logos, id.*Jo*.2.13(7; p.68.22; M.14.133D); id.*fr.1 in Jo*.(p.484.18); **4.** of divine Persons; **a.** Son, v. *γέννημα, εἰμί, εἷς, ἔμμονος, πατήρ, ποίημα, υἱός*; of difference between creatureliness and sonship, Ath.*ep.Serap*.2.7(M.26.620A); **b.** H. Ghost, v. *πνεῦμα*; **c.** relationship of Father to creatures implied by Arianism *εἰ ὅμοιον τὸ γενητὸν τῷ ἀγενήτῳ θέλουσιν,...οὐ μακρὰν εἰσιν εἰπεῖν, ὅτι καὶ τὸ ἀγένητον καὶ κτισμάτων ἐστὶν εἰκών* Ath.*Ar*.1.31(M.26.76C); *ib*.2.43(240A); *ποία δὲ ὑμῶν τόλμα...ὅτι τὸν πατέρα καὶ τὸν τούτου λόγον εἰς τὰ κ. κατάγετε, καὶ πάλιν τὸ κ. συνεξισοῦτε τῷ θεῷ; τοῦτο γὰρ ποιεῖτε φανταζόμενοι περὶ τοῦ πνεύματος ὡς κ., καὶ συντάσσοντες αὐτὸ εἰς τριάδα. τί δὲ καὶ τὸ μανιῶδες ὑμῶν,...ὅτι μὴ...πάντα τὰ κ., ἀλλ' εἷς ἐκ τούτων συναριθμεῖται τῷ θεῷ καὶ τῷ λόγῳ αὐτοῦ;* id.*ep.Serap*.1.29(M.26.597A); **5.** of lower creation *ὁ ἄνθρωπος κύριός ἐστι τῶν κ. τοῦ θεοῦ* Herm.*mand*.12.4.3; id.*vis*.3.9.2; ref. pagan ideas of the elements as divine *εἴ τις τῶν λόγων ἀποδεκτός ἐστι, δύναιτ' ἂν καὶ τῶν λοιπῶν κ. ἓν ἕκαστον ὁμοίως ἀποφαίνεσθαι θεόν* *Diogn*.8.3.

B. *building*, Const.ap.Eus.*v.C*.3.31(p.92.15; M.20.1092B); Nonn.*par.Jo*.2:20(M.43.764C); Jo.Mosch.*prat*.37(M.87.2888A).

***κτισματολατρεία, ἡ,** *creature-worship*; of paganism, Didym.*Trin*.2.18(M.39.728A); of Arianism, *ib*.3.2(792C); Eunomianism, ‡Chrys.*hom.in Lc*.8:5(10.830D); ‡Chrys.*haer*.(9.830B); of teaching of monophysite *incorrupticolae*, Leont.B.*Nest.et Eut*.3(M.86.1372D); of image-worship, CNic.(787)*refut*.(H.4.332C); Steph.Diac.*v.Steph*.(M.100.1121C).

***κτισματολάτρης, ὁ,** *creature-worshipper*; of pagans, Didym.*Trin*.1.15(M.39.308A); Thdr.Stud.*antirr*.1.16(M.99.348A); of Arius, ‡Eust.*alloc*.(M.18.676A); applied to orthodox by Julianists who believed Christ's body to be *οὐ μόνον ἄφθαρτον ἐξ αὐτῆς τῆς... συλλήψεως, ἀλλὰ καὶ ἄκτιστον* Tim.CP *haer*.(M.86.58B).

κτίστης, ὁ, A. *builder*, Ath.*decr*.29(p.26.13; M.25.472A).

B. *creator*; **1.** rel. to other notions *ὁ...οὐδὲν ἡγούμενος διαφέρειν, ἢ πατέρα ὁμολογεῖν ἢ κ.,...ποῦ τετάξεται παρ' ἡμῶν;* Bas.*Eun*.2.22(1.258A; M.29.620C); v. *ποιητής*; **2.** of God *τὸν...κ. τῶν ὅλων* Eus.*l.C*.10(p.222.18; M.20.1373A); *Hom.Clem*.16.20; *ὁ...κ.* Cyr.H.*catech*.2.1; Jo.Mon.*hymn.Bas*.6(M.96.1373D); **3.** of Trin. *τὸν θεὸν κ. ... τῶν ἁπάντων...[ἐν υἱῷ μονογενεῖ καὶ πνεύματι ἁγίῳ]* Arist.*apol*.15.3; *οὐκ ἔστιν ὡς τὰ γενητὰ ὁ θεός, ἀλλὰ καὶ τούτων κ. διὰ τοῦ υἱοῦ* Ath.*Ar*.1.33(M.26.80B); *Const.App*.7.35.10; *τοῦ ἑνὸς...κ., πατρὸς καὶ υἱοῦ καὶ ἁγίου πνεύματος* Epiph.*haer*.69.17(p.167.7; M.42.228D); **4.** of Father; **a.** in gen., *1Clem*.19.2; Just.*2apol*.6.2(M.6.453A); Clem.*str*.6.16(p.507.3; M.9.377A); *Const.App*.7.35.1; **b.** in credal formulae *θεὸν πατέρα...κ. οὐρανοῦ καὶ γῆς* *Symb.App*.(p.32); *θεὸν πατέρα...τὸν τῶν ὅλων κ.* *Symb.Ant*.(341)3(p.250.9; M.26.724C); *θεόν, πατέρα...κ. ... τῶν πάντων* *Symb.Ant*.(341)4(p.251.1; M.26.725B); *Symb.Ant*.(345)(p.251.22; M.26.725B); *Symb.Sirm*.1(p.254.17; M.26.736A); *Symb.Sirm*.3(p.235.24; M.26.692B); *τὸν πατέρα τοῦ Χριστοῦ, κ. ... τῶν ἁπάντων* *Symb*.ap.*Const.App*.7.41.4; **5.** of Son *τὸν τῶν πάντων κ. ... λόγον τοῦ θεοῦ* Iren.*haer*.1.15.5(M.7.625A); Clem.*exc.Thdot*.19(p.113.9; M.9.668A); Ath.*ep.Adelph*.8(M.26.1084B); Gr.Nyss.*fid*.(M.45.137B); Didym.(‡Bas.)*Eun*.5(1.314A; M.29.753A); **6.** Gnost. *οἱ τὸν κ. ἄλλον εἶναι παρὰ τὸν πρῶτον θεὸν δογματίζοντες* Clem.*str*.4.13(p.289.28; M.8.1301A).

C. *one who supports* or *establishes*, of emperors *σωτῆρες καὶ κ. τῆς οἰκουμένης* *M.Ariadn*.(p.125.10); of God *κ. τοιᾶσδε χάριτος* Clem.*str*.2.18(p.157.20; M.8.1024A).

***κτιστικός,** *creative*, Didym.(‡Bas.)*Eun*.4(1.291D; M.29.700B).

***κτιστικῶς,** *by way of creation*, opp. *γεννητικῶς*, Epiph.*haer*.76.40(p.394.28; M.42.604D).

***κτιστολάτρης, ὁ,** = *κτισματολάτρης*, Didym.*Trin*.1.32(M.39.429C).

κτιστός, *created*; **1.** ref. characteristics of created things τὸ κ. opp. ἀΐδιον, Ath.*decr.*28(p.25.9; M.25.469B); ἡ δὲ τῶν...κ. φύσις ἐστὶ τρεπτή id.*ep.Serap.*1.26(M.26.592A); ἡ γὰρ κ. φύσις ἅπασα πῶς καὶ ἰδεῖν δυνήσεται τὸν ἄκτιστον; Chrys.*hom.15.1 in Jo.*(8.85D); created nature corruptible, Thdt.*Heb.*2:9(3.557); opp. ἄκτιστος, v.s.v.; **2.** created things dist. from God οὐ γάρ ἐστι κατὰ τὴν κ. φύσιν ὁ θεός, ὥστε τὸ εἶναι αὐτόν, καὶ τὸ ἔχειν, νοηθῇ ἐν συνθέσει ‡Just.*qu.et resp.*144(M.6.1396D); θεὸς οὐ κ. Procl.CP *Arm.*12(p.193.7; M.65.868C); **3.** of Christ; **a.** orthodox; **i.** divine nature not created κ. οὐσία οὐ δύναται ἂν...εἰπεῖν 'πάντα, ὅσα ἔχει ὁ πατήρ, ἐμά ἐστιν' Ath.*ep.Serap.*2.5(M.26.616B); cf.id.*ep.Afr.*7(M.26.1041C); ὅμοιος γὰρ ὢν κατὰ τὴν οὐσίαν τοῦ πατρός, οὐκ ἂν εἴη κ. id.*ep.Aeg.Lib.*17(M.25.577B); ἐκφεύγειν τοιγαροῦν τὸ ἔγκλημα τὸ περὶ τῆς δόξης τῶν κ. θεῶν τοὺς πιστεύοντας τῷ υἱῷ Didym.*Trin.*1.7(M.39.269A); **ii.** human nature created τῷ πατρὶ ὁμοούσιος, οὐχ ἡ σάρξ, οὐδέ γε ἡ ψυχή· κ. γὰρ αὗται· ἀλλ' ἡ θεότης Thdt.*eran.*3(4.229); id.*Trin.*27(M.75.1172C); ‡Proc.G.*Pr.*8:22(M.87.1296B); Leont.H.*Nest.*1.39(M.86.1560C); ἐκ ἀκτίστου θεότητος, καὶ κ. ἀνθρωπότητος Anast.S.*hod.*18(M.89.268B); **b.** heret. teaching stated and refuted, 'Origenism' σαφές ἐστιν ὅτι κτιστὸν ὁρίζεται. ... πᾶν γὰρ τὸ κ. οὐ προσκυνητόν, ὡς ἔφην. εἰ δὲ ὅλως προσκυνητόν, πολλῶν ἄλλων ὑπαρχόντων κ. οὐδὲν ἂν διοίσει τὸ καὶ ἡμᾶς μετὰ τοῦ ἑνὸς κ. τὰ ὅλα προσκυνεῖν Epiph.*haer.*64.8(pp.417.14,418.7; M.41.1084A,B); Arianism τοὺς δὲ...φάσκοντας εἶναι...κ. ... τὸν υἱὸν τοῦ θεοῦ τοὺς τοιούτους ἀναθεματίζει ἡ...ἐκκλησία *Symb.Nic.*(325)(p.52.4; M.20.1540C); Eus.Nic.*ep.Paulin.*(p.16.9; M.82.913C); τὸ ἄρα 'ἔκτισε' καὶ τὸ 'ἔπλασε' καὶ τὸ 'κατέστησε'...οὐδὲ τὴν οὐσίαν αὐτοῦ κ. δείκνυσιν, ἀλλὰ τὴν εἰς ἡμᾶς αὐτοῦ κατ' εὐεργεσίαν γενομένην ἀνανέωσιν Ath.*Ar.*2.53(M.26.260A); *ib.*2.56(265A); εἰ ἡ κτίσις οὐ γινώσκει τὸν πατέρα, εἰ μὴ ἃ ἀποκαλύψῃ ὁ υἱός, ὁ δὲ υἱὸς γινώσκει, οὐδενὸς ἀποκαλύπτοντος αὐτῷ· οὐκ ἔστιν κ., ἀλλὰ γεννητός Didym.*Trin.*3.2(M.39.792B); Apollinarianism διὰ τί οὐ λογίζεσθε, ὅτι καὶ ποιηθὲν τὸ σῶμα τοῦ κυρίου οὐ κτιστὴν ἀποφέρεται τὴν προσκύνησιν; ‡Ath.*Apoll.*1.6(M.26.1101C); Eunomianism τί οὖν ποιοῦσιν οἱ λέγοντες, ὅτι κ. ἐστι; προσκυνοῦσι τὸν κ. αὐτόν, ἢ οὐχί; εἰ μὲν γὰρ οὐ προσκυνοῦσιν, Ἰουδαΐζουσιν,...εἰ δὲ προσκυνοῦσιν, εἰδωλολατροῦσι Gr.Nyss.*fid.*(M.45.137A); Thdt.*Is.*26:12(p.105.28; 2.296); cf. against monophysites οὐ γὰρ οἷόν τε τὴν αὐτὴν καὶ μίαν ἐνέργειαν, ἢ θέλησιν, ἢ φύσιν...ὑπάρχειν...ἄκτιστον, καὶ κ. Max.*opusc.*(M.91.117A); **4.** of H. Ghost; **a.** orthodox position; τοὺς δὲ φάσκοντας εἶναι ἢ τρεπτὸν τὸν υἱὸν τοῦ θεοῦ ἢ τὸ ἅγιον πνεῦμα τούτους ἀναθεματίζομεν ‡Ath.*theopasch.*(p.212.33); Bas.*ep.*140.2(3.233E; M.32.589A); Gr.Naz.*or.*40.42(M.36.420A); ἀεὶ γὰρ τὸ πνεῦμα σὺν πατρὶ καὶ υἱῷ,...οὐ κ. Epiph.*haer.*62.4(p.392.20; M.41.1053D); arguments from scripture ἀσεβὲς οὖν ἐστι κ. ἢ ποιητὸν λέγειν τὸ πνεῦμα τοῦ θεοῦ· ὁπότε πᾶσα γραφὴ ...μετὰ πατρὸς καὶ υἱοῦ αὐτὸ συναριθμεῖ Ath.*inc.et c.Ar.*9(M.26.997A); τὸ δὲ 'πάντα δι' αὐτοῦ ἐγένετο' οὐδαμῶς ἡμῖν κ. εἶναι τὸ πνεῦμα τὸ ἅγιον παρίστησιν Bas.*Eun.*3.7(1.278C; M.29.669C); from his sanctifying function εἰ δὲ τῇ τοῦ πνεύματος μετουσίᾳ γινόμεθα κοινωνοὶ θείας φύσεως, μαίνοιτ' ἄν τις λέγων τὸ πνεῦμα τῆς κ. φύσεως Ath.*ep.Serap.*1.24(M.26.585C); Didym.(‡Bas.)*Eun.*5(1.296E; M.29.712C); **b.** called κ. by Macedonians, Gr.Nyss.*fid.*(M.45.141B); Thdt.*h.e.*2.6.2(3.831); *Chron.Pasch.*p.304(M.92.772A); **5.** ref. Gnost. conception of world as γεννητός, not κ., Epiph.*haer.*32.2(p.441.5; M.41.545C) cit. s. γεννητός.

[*]**κυαίστωρ (κοιαίστωρ, [*]κυέστωρ)**, ὁ, (Lat. *quaestor sacri palatii*) chairman of imperial consistory and minister of justice, Pall.*v.Chrys.*3(p.19.19; M.47.14); κοιαίσ-, Justn.*nov.*24.4(p.193.40); κοιαίσ-, Jo.Mal.*chron.*18 p.479(M.97.696B); κυέσ-, *Chron.Pasch.*p.293(M.92.732B).

***κυαιστώριον (*κοιαι-)**, τό, **1.** *office of* quaestor sacri palatii, Evagr.*h.e.*6.24(p.240.34; M.86.2884B); **2.** *residence of quaestor*, κοιαι-, Thphn.*chron.*p.394(M.108.937C).

***κυανάντυξ**, *blue-vaulted*, Synes.*hymn.*9.45(p.55; M.66.1613).

κυάνεος, *blue*; of political and circus faction usu. called Βένετοι, Evagr.*h.e.*4.32(p.181.19; M.86.2761B).

***κυανοβόστρυχος**, *with dark locks, curls*, Meth.*symp.*11(p.136.5; M.18.212D).

[*]**κυανόχρωος**, *of dark blue colour*, *Orac.Sib.*13.160.

κυβεία, ἡ, *trickery*; ref. wiles of heretics, cf.Eph.4:14, Hipp.*haer.*9.13(p.251.11; M.16.3387B); Or.*Jo.*32.5(p.434.1; M.14.753B); μηδὲ τῇ τῶν ἀνθρώπων κ. ἑαυτοὺς ἀν⟨α⟩τιθέντες Epiph.*anc.*74(p.93.10; M.43.156A); id.*haer.*22.1(p.246.7; M.41.296C); *ib.*24.3(p.260.9; 312C); Jo.D.*haer.*80(M.94.733D); ass. magic, Hipp.*haer.*6.39(p.170.12; 3258A); μαγικῆς κ. ἐμπειρότατον Eus.*h.e.*4.11.4(M.20.329A); σωματικὰ πάθη ...κ. Ephr.3.426F.

κυβερν-άω, **1.** *steer, direct the course of* a boat; fig. of man ναῦς ...μόναις ἁγίων εὐχαῖς ~ωμένη Clem.*q.d.s.*34(p.182.29; M.9.640C); αἱ δὲ [sc. ψυχαί] ~ἂν ἀπαλλαγήσασαι τὰ σφέτερα σκάφη Meth.*symp.*4.2(p.47.3; M.18.88C); hence **2.** *manage, direct* πλοῦτος οὐκ ὀρθῶς ~ώμενος Clem.*paed.*2.3(p.180.18; M.8.437B); of Christ ἐκ θελήματος πατρὸς ~ῶντα τὴν πάντων σωτηρίαν id.*str.*7.2(p.8.15; M.9.413A); **3.** *govern*, in gen. Μωυσῆς...νόμος ἔμψυχος τῷ χρηστῷ λόγῳ ~ώμενος *ib.*1.26(p.104.24; M.8.916B); αἱ τῶν ἀποστησάντων βουλαὶ...~ῶνται... ὑπὸ τῆς καθόλου προνοίας *ib.*1.17(p.55.21; 801A); ὡς ὑπὸ τοῦ λόγου ~ώμενος Ath.*v.Anton.*14(M.26.865A); of God τὸ πᾶν ἀπταίστως θείας βουλῆς ~ᾶσθαι προστασίᾳ Meth.*res.*2.10(p.350.6); ~ῶν τὰ πάντα Ath.*gent.*36(M.25.72B); τριὰς...ἐν πᾶσιν οὖσα...~ῶσα Didym.(‡Bas.)*Eun.*5(1.317C; M.29.760D); πῶς ὑπὸ πολλῶν ~ηθήσεται ὁ κόσμος καὶ οὐ διαλυθήσεται; Jo.D.*f.o.*1.5(M.94.802B).

κυβέρνησις, ἡ, *steering, direction*; of a boat, fig. ἵνα χειμαζομένην [sc. ἀνθρωπότητα] περισώσῃ διὰ τῆς κ. Ath.*inc.*43.7(M.25.173B); hence *government*, divine ἡ κτίσις καὶ ἡ ταύτης...κ. Jo.D.*f.o.*1.1(M.94.789B); ref. H. Ghost's direction of men, Chrys.*hom.3.3 in 2Cor.*(10.445B); of spiritual government exercised by men, cf.Or.*hom.11.4 in Num.*(p.85.15; M.12.649D); exeg. 1Cor.12:28 πεπονθυίας τῆς ψυχῆς δεῖ τινος οἰκονομίας...αὗταί εἰσιν αἱ ἀντιλήψεις καὶ κ. Cyr.*ep.*58(p.21.7; M.77.321C); κ. αἱ διοικήσεις αἱ ἐκκλησιαστικαί *cat.1Cor.*12:28(p.243.16).

κυβερνήτης, ὁ, *pilot, guide, governor*; **1.** in gen. δεῖ πάντως σε τὸν σοβαρὸν καὶ δυνατὸν καὶ πλούσιον ἐπιστήσασθαι ἑαυτῷ τινα ἄνθρωπον θεοῦ καθάπερ...κ. Clem.*q.d.s.*41(p.187.10; M.9.645C); ὁ λογισμὸς καὶ τὸ ἡγεμονικὸν...τῆς ψυχῆς κ. αὐτῆς εἴρηται id.*str.*2.11(p.141.6; M.8.988B); id.*paed.*2.2(p.173.17; M.8.424A); Meth.*symp.*11(p.139.2ff.; M.18.217A); of bishop ὡς ἂν κ. νηὸς μεγάλης...κέλευε ποιεῖσθαι τὰς συνόδους, παραγγέλλων τοῖς διακόνοις ὡσανεὶ ναύταις τοὺς τόπους ἐκτάσσειν τοῖς ἀδελφοῖς καθάπερ ἐπιβάταις *Const.App.*2.57.2; *ib.*2.57.9; ref. pagan deification of elements ὅμοιον εἰ καὶ ναῦν τις, ἐν ᾗ ἔπλευσεν, ἀντὶ τοῦ κ. ἄγοι Athenag.*leg.*22.7(M.6.941A); **2.** of Christ τὸν σωτῆρα τῶν ψυχῶν ἡμῶν καὶ κ. τῶν σωμάτων ἡμῶν *M.Polyc.*19.2; βλέποιεν πρὸς τὸν κύριον ἀτενεῖ τῷ βλέμματι, καθάπερ εἰς ἀγαθοῦ κ. νεῦμα δεδορκότες, τί βούλεται Clem.*q.d.s.*26(p.177.7; M.9.632A); id.*paed.*1.7(p.122.12; M.8.313B); σοφὸς κ. τὸν κλῆρον παρὰ τοῦ πατρὸς ὑποδεδεγμένος, ἐπιβὰς τοῦ σύμπαντος κόσμου ἄνω τε πρὸς τὸν αὐτοῦ πατέρα βλέπων, ἄγει καὶ φέρει πηδαλιουχῶν τὸ πᾶν, οὐδὲ τὸ σμικρότατον τῶν δεομένων τῆς ἐξ αὐτοῦ χορηγίας παρορῶν οὐδ' ὑπερφρονῶν τῶν βραχυτάτων Eus.*e.th.*1.13(p.73.16; M.24.852A); Serap.*euch.*7.1; Gr.Naz.*or.*4.78(M.35.604B); ἄνευ γὰρ τοῦ ἐπουρανίου κ. Χριστοῦ, ἀδύνατόν τινι παρελθεῖν τὴν πονηρὰν θάλασσαν τῶν δυνάμεων τοῦ σκότους, καὶ τῶν πικρῶν πειρασμῶν τὰ καταφυσήματα Mac.Aeg.*hom.*44.7(M.34.784B); **3.** Manich., of apostles (with astrol. reference) ὁ Ἰησοῦς ὁ ἐν τῷ μικρῷ πλοίῳ, καὶ ἡ μήτηρ τῆς ζωῆς, καὶ οἱ δώδεκα κ. Hegem.*Arch.*13(p.21.11; M.10.1448C).

***κύβευμα, τό**, *laughing-stock, reproach*, Gr.Naz.*carm.*2.1.12.334(M.37.1190A); *ib.*2.1.12.660(1214A).

κυβευτικός, *deceptive, false*, Or.*Cels.*3.39(p.235.23; M.11.972A); Epiph.*haer.*34.21(p.38.15; M.41.625B); *ib.*42.2(p.205.7; 840C).

***κυβευτικῶς**, *deceitfully, falsely*, Or.*comm.in Eph.*4:15(p.415); comp., id.*Cels.*3.36(p.232.22; M.11.965C).

κυβεύω, **1.** *deceive*, Hipp.*haer.*6.41(p.172.17; M.16.3259B); **2.** *debase* gold, Jo.Mosch.*prat.*200(M.87.3088D).

***κυβιστεύω**, *hurl* oneself, of fish ἑαυτοὺς ἐκυβίστευον ἐπὶ τὸ πλοῖον ‡Chrys.*hom.*13(13.254D).

κυβιστής, ὁ, **1.** *juggler*, of Eunomians κ. λόγων Gr.Naz.*or.*27.1(p.2.7; M.36.13A); **2.** prob. = κυβευτής, *gambler* ὁ κ. ... καὶ πάροινος ἱερεὺς...καθαιρείσθω Sophr.H.*conf.*(M.87.3368C).

κυβιστητήρ, ὁ, as adj., *tumbling*, Nonn.*par.Jo.*2:15(M.43.764A).

κυδιάνειρα, ἡ, as fem. adj., *famous for men*; of Rome, *Orac.Sib.*14.171.

***κυδοιμοτόκος**, *causing an uproar*, Gr.Naz.*carm.*1.1.28.2(M.37.506A).

***κυεστόριος, ὁ**, *ex-quaestor*; *man of quaestorian rank*, *Chron.Pasch.*p.322(M.92.821B); *ib.*(824B).

[*]**κυέστωρ, ὁ**, v. [*]κυαίστωρ.

κύημα, τό, *that which is conceived* in the mind or spirit; of virtue, Gr.Nyss.*v.Mos.*(M.44.328C); of true and false beliefs, Cyr.*ador.*8(1.261B,262C); Thdt.*Trin.*proem.(M.75.1148A).

κύησις, ἡ, *conception* διτταὶ...γίνονται κ. ἀνθρώποις, ἡ μὲν ἐκ σώματος ἡμετέρου, ἡ δὲ ἐκ τοῦ θείου πνεύματος Didym.*Trin.*2.12(M.39.669A).

***κυητικός**, *for conception* κ. ὄργανα Clem.*paed.*2.10(p.213.6; M.8.508A).

***κυϊνκεννάλια, τά,** *quinquennalia*; celebration of emperor's fifth anniversary, *Chron.Pasch.*p.308(M.92.784A); *ib.*p.309(788A).

***κυϊντανός,** Lat. *quintanus*, Phot.*nomoc.*13.29(M.104.964A).

κύκησις, ἡ, *confusion*; of mind, Sophr.H.*or.*2.24(M.87.3244B *κύνησις* misprint).

κυκλάζω, *surround*, *M.Eleuth.*9(p.158.8).

***κυκλάριος,** *wandering τις τῶν κ. ψευδηρεμιτῶν* ‡Jo.D.*ep.Thphl.* 17(M.95.368B).

κυκλάς, 1. *revolving*; of time, Nonn.*par.Jo.*2:4(M.43.760D); *ib.* 11:9(840C); **2.** *long-continued, chronic*; of disease, *ib.*7:23(808C); **3.** of the head, *all round λινέῳ πεπύκαστο* [sc. Lazarus] *καλύμματι κυκλάδα κόρσην ib.*11:44(848A); *νίψον...καὶ χεῖρας ἐμὰς καὶ κ. κόρσην ib.*13:9(861A).

κύκλευμα, τό, *wandering, vagrancy*, ‡Jo.D.*ep.Thphl.*18(M.95. 369A).

§**κυκλευτής, ὁ,** *vagrant monk*, Ephr.1.94F; Nil.*Eulog.*26(M.79. 1128B); id.*spir.mal.*13(M.79.1160A).

κυκλεύω, 1. *walk round, wander about*, Herm.*sim.*9.9.6; Ath.*gent.* 23(M.25.48B); Pall.*h.Laus.*46(p.134.15; M.34.1225B); **2.** *form a circle*, *A.Jo.*94(p.197.18); **3.** *revolve*; of the firmament in Manichean system, Hegem.*Arch.*8(p.11.8; *κυκλῆσαι* M.10.1437C); **4.** met., *encompass* with the mind, Didym.*Trin.*1.15(M.39.312A).

***κυκλίσκομαι,** for *κικλήσκομαι*, *T.Sal.*8.7(*καλοῦμαι* M.122.1328C).

***κυκλοδράκων, ὁ,** *coiled serpent*, Epiph.*haer.*79.7(p.482.14; M.42. 752A).

***κυκλόπους, ὁ,** *circular snow-shoe*, Thphn.*chron.*p.329(M.108. 793C).

κύκλος, ὁ, 1. *circle, sphere*, of heaven *ὁ...κόσμος σφαιρικὸς ἀποτελεσθείς, οὐρανοῦ κύκλοις ἀποκέκλειται* Athenag.*leg.*8.2(M.6. 905A); Or.*Cels.*5.44(p.47.27; M.11.1249B); Ath.*gent.*35(M.25.72A); of a *ball, cake* of food, Aen.*ep.*14; of circle as symbol of perfection: of Trin., Dion.Ar.*d.n.*2.5(M.3.644A); of God's love and goodness, *ib.*4.14(712D) cit. s. *ἀποκαθίστημι*; *ib.*5.6(821A); of Son as source and unity of powers of intellect, Clem.*str.*4.25(p.318.1; M.8.1365B); ref. symbolism of winding staircase leading to middle chamber of Solomon's temple, Or.*Jo.*10.41(25; p.218.4; M.14.385C) cit. s. *ἑλικοειδής*; of virtue *ἀρετῆς ἐν κ. καλῷ* Cyr.*ador.*7(1.218A); of the number ten, Anat.Laod.*decad.*(p.39); symbolizing Leviathan (in Ophite cosmology), Or.*Cels.*6.24(p.95.3; M.11.1329A); **2.** met., *sphere*; of work, authority, etc. *περιγράψαι τῷ 'Ισαύρων* [sc. *ἐπισκόπῳ*] *τὸν ἴδιον κ.* Bas.*ep.*190.1(3.282E; M.32.1700A); *scope βραχυπορησάντων ἡμῶν τῆς παραγγελίας τοῦ θεοῦ τὸν κ.* Meth.*res.*2.6(p.339.17; M.41. 1172C); **3.** *roundabout way of speaking, riddle*, Thdt.*qu.28 in 2Reg.* (1.432); **4.** *cycle, revolution*; **a.** period of time; of fifteen years, Evagr.*h.e.*3.33(p.131.24; M.86.2668A); of a year, *Libell.*ap.CCP 536 (*ACO* 3 p.106.18; H.2.1388D); of a day, Bas.*ep.*45.1(3.133D; M.32. 366C); *ib.*193(285E; M.705B); **b.** *revolution, change κ. τῶν ἀνθρωπίνων πραγμάτων* Gr.Naz.*or.*17.4(M.35.969B); †Jo.D.*B.J.*36(M.96.1204C); **c.** *course* of medical treatment, Synes.*calv.*12(p.212.15; M.66.1188D); **d.** *turn κάμὲ πρὸς τὸ λέγειν ὁ κ. ἀνίστησιν* Thdt.*serm.Chrys.*(5.103); **5.** in adverbial phrases; of circular movements and positions; of order of heavenly powers around God, Ath.*Ar.*2.49(M.26.252A); Dion.Ar.*c.h.*7.4(M.3.209D); of movement of soul in contemplation *ψυχῆς κίνησίς ἐστι κυκλικὴ μὲν ἡ εἰς ἑαυτὴν εἴσοδος ἀπὸ τῶν ἔξω... ὥσπερ ἔν τινι κ. τὸ ἀπλανὲς αὐτῇ δωρουμένη* id.*d.n.*4.9(M.3.705A,B); *ψυχαὶ τὸ λογικὸν ἔχουσι διεξοδικῶς μὲν καὶ κύκλῳ περὶ τὴν τῶν ὄντων ἀλήθειαν περιπορευόμεναι ib.*7.2(868B); of one of the divine movements (together with *τὸ εὐθύ* and *τὸ ἑλικοειδές*) *τὸ δὲ κατὰ κύκλον τὸ ταὐτόν, καὶ τὸ τὰ μέσα καὶ ἄκρα περιέχοντα καὶ περιεχόμενα συνέχειν, καὶ τὴν εἰς αὐτὸν ἀπ' αὐτοῦ προεληλυθότων ἐπιστροφήν ib.*9.9 (916D).

***κυκλοφερής,** *circular*, Cyr.*Juln.*9(6².300A); Agath.*v.Gr.Ill.*113 (p.57).

κυκλοφορέω, *revolve*, Gr.Nyss.*Eun.*12(1 p.237.14; M.45.936A); pass., *ib.*9(2 p.205.27; 801C).

***κυκλοφόρητος,** *set in a circle*, Paul.Sil.*Soph.*870(M.86.2152A).

κύλινδρος, ὁ, *circuit, pacing round and round*; of animals in a cage, Bas.*hex.*9.6(1.87C; M.29.205B).

***κυλιοπονέω,** *be in labour*, Leont.N.*v.Sym.*39(M.93.1717C).

κυλίστρα, ἡ, *urn* from which lots were drawn in horse-racing, CTrull.*can.*71.

***κυλλάω,** *chastise, subdue*, Nil.*paraen.*59(M.79.1253C).

***κυλλότης, ἡ,** *mutilation, deformity*, Or.*comm.in Mt.*11.18(p.65. 34; M.13.965C).

κυλλόω, *maim, mutilate*, Mac.Aeg.*hom.*15.8(M.34.581A); Leont. N.*v.Sym.*41(M.93.1721A); aor. *ἐκύλλωνα*, *Didasc.Jac.*53(p.777.1).

κυματίζω, *be agitated*, met. *κ. τὴν ψυχήν* Gr.Mag.*dial.*(tr.Zach.) 4.7(M.*PL.*77.331B).

κυμάτιον, τό, *cymatium*; *waved moulding* carved at the extremity of a piece of architecture or masonry, Thdt.*Ezech.*40:26(2.1022); Cosm.Ind.*top.*1(M.88.92B); *ib.*5(209C).

κυματόω, pass., *be tossed about, be agitated*, ‡Nil.*fr.pasch.*2(M. 79.1496C); met., Gr.Nyss.*v.Mos.*(M.44.328D); Chrys.*hom.37.3 in Jo.* (8.215C).

κυνηγέσιον, τό, *wild-beast fight* in circus, *M.Polyc.*12.2; Bas.Sel. *v.Thecl.*1(M.85.529B); Diod.*fat.*ap.Phot.*cod.*223(M.103.869A).

***κυνηγέτρια, ἡ,** *huntress*; of Artemis, Epiph.*anc.*103(p.123.25; M.43.201B).

κυνηγικός, *of* or *for hunting οἱ τῆς καλουμένης κυνηγικῆς* [? sc. *χώρας*] *μοναχοί* Evagr.*h.e.*3.32(p.130.31; M.86.2665B).

κυνήγιον, τό, = *κυνηγέσιον*, Cyr.H.*catech.*19.6; Epiph.*exp.fid.* 24(p.525.11; M.42.832A); Thdr.Lect.*h.e.*2.53(M.86.209B); *Κυνῆγιν*, name of a circus, *Chron.Pasch.*p.265(M.92.649C).

***κύνησις,** v. *κύκησις*.

κυνικός, *dog-like, brutish*; of the sinner, Chrys.*hom.9 in 1Cor.* (10.78D); of devils, *A.Petr.et Paul.*48(p.199.20).

κυνίσκος, ὁ, a sea-fish of the cartilaginous kind, Bas.*hex.*7.2(1. 64B; M.29.152A).

κυνογαμία, ἡ, *dog-marriage*; of Crates and Hipparchia, Tat.*orat.* 3(p.4.9, codd. *κοινογ-*; M.6.812A, v.l. *κοινογ-*); Clem.*str.*4.19(p.302. 11; M.8.1332A for *γυνογ-*); Thdt.*affect.*12(p.312.9; 4.1026, v.l. *κοινογ-*).

***κυνογλωσσέω,** *howl like a dog*, Tim.Ant.*descr.BMV* 4(M.28. 949A).

κυνόδηκτος, *bitten by a dog*, Hipp.*haer.*9.14(p.253.4; M.16.3390C); *ib.*9.15(p.254.1; 3391B).

κυνοδρομέω, *run* or *chase with dogs*, Clem.*str.*1.2(p.14.11; M.8. 709C).

***κυνοκομέω,** *take care of dogs*, Chrys.*fr.Job* 30:1(M.64.533A); Synes.*calv.*4(p.197.4; M.66.1173C).

***κυνοκτονία, ἡ,** *slaughter of dogs*, Eus.*h.e.*9.8.10(M.20.817B).

κυνόμυια, ἡ, *swarm of flies*, cf. *κυνόμυια non, ut Latini interpretati sunt, 'musca canina' dicitur per υ Graecam litteram; sed juxta Hebraicam intelligentiam per δίφθογγον debet scribi οι, ut sit κοινόμυια, id est 'omne muscarum genus'*, Hier.*ep.*106.86(*CSEL* 55 p.289.12; M.*PL.*22.867).

κυνοπόταμος, ὁ, *beaver*, ‡Caes.Naz.*dial.*102(M.38.969A).

***κυνοτροφικός,** *of dog-keeping κ. τέχνη* Clem.*str.*1.7(p.24.27; M.8. 732C).

κυνοφθαλμίζομαι, *gaze impudently*, Synes.*provid.*2.8(p.130.7; M. 66.1280A).

***Κυντίλιος, ὁ,** *Quintilis, the month July*, *Chron.Pasch.*p.187(M. 92.461A).

κυοφόρημα, τό, *offspring*, ‡Jo.D.*Artem.*33(M.96.1281B).

***κυοφορικός,** *pertaining to pregnancy*, Epiph.*haer.*78.12(p.463.9; M.42.717B).

κυπαρίσσιον, τό, *cypress*, Dor.*doct.*11.3(M.88.1737A).

***κυπάσσιον, τό,** a *short frock*, *Orac.Sib.*5.187.

κυπελλοφόρος, ὁ, *cup-bearer*, Gr.Naz.*carm.*1.2.15.26(M.37.767A).

Κυπριανίζω, *behave as a Cypriot*; met., *act as a turncoat*, Thdr. Stud.*epp.*2.63(M.99.1281C).

κυπρίζω, *bloom*, Gr.Naz.*ep.*57(M.37.112B); Gr.Nyss.*v.Ephr.*(M. 46.841C); Ph.Carp.*Cant.*29(M.40.56B).

***Κυπριώτης, ὁ,** *Cypriot*, †Polyb.*v.Epiph.*58(M.41.97B); Cyr.S.*v. Euthym.*40(p.60.7).

***κῦρ,** v. **κύρις*.

***κυρεβοειδής,** sens. dub., qualifying one of the three parts of the brain, Jo.D.*ep.*(M.95.244C).

κυρεία, ἡ, *dominion, power*; of the Godhead, Dion.Ar.*d.n.*2.1(M. 3.637B); *ib.*8.1(889C); *cat.Apoc.*4:6(p.244.6); of Christ, Clem.*str.*4.7 (p.267.9; M.8.1253B); Eus.*d.e.*5.6(p.230.4; M.22.380B); of believers, Or.*adnot.in Num.*24:7(M.17.21C); of spiritual light, Dion.Ar.*d.n.*4. 6(701B).

κυρία, ἡ, *mistress, lady*; in gen., as title of address, Herm.*vis.* 1.1.5; *κ. ἀδελφή M.Perp.*4(p.67.3); *δεῦρο, κ.* Pall.*h.Laus.*8(p.27.7; M.34.1025A); of BMV *κ. καὶ δέσποινα* ‡Ath.*annunt.*15(M.28.940C); *κ. ... πάντων τῶν ποιημάτων* Jo.D. *f.o.*4.14(M.94.1157B); of Sunday *κ. τῶν ἡμερῶν M.Apollon.*47(p.35.6); Eus.Al.*serm.*16.1(M.86.416B; p.414 om.); cf.Bas.*hom.*13.3(2.116B; M.31.429B).

κυριακός, *belonging to the Lord*; **1.** in OT *ὁ κ. ἔλεγχος* [i.e. Pr. 1:24] Clem.*paed.*1.9(p.140.13; M.8.352C); *ἡ κ. φωνή* [sc. Dt.4:12] id. *str.*6.3(p.448.15; M.9.252C); *Const.App.*2.9.2; **2.** of what pertains to

Christ τῇ κεφαλῇ τῇ κ. Clem.*str*.5.6(p.352.9; M.9.64C); Isid.Pel.*epp*.1.491(M.78.449C); Jo.D.*fr.Mt*.27:37(M.96.1412B); ἐν τῷ κ. σώματι Ath.*inc*.8.4(M.25.109D); Chrys.*hom.13.8 in Rom*.(9.571A); Pamph.H.*panopl*.3.3(p.609); κ. σάρκα Didym.(‡Bas.)*Eun*.5(1.314E; M.29.753C); ψυχὴν κ. ‡Ath.*dial.Trin*.4.10(M.28.1265A); κ. αἷμα *ib.*; eucharistic μεταλαμβανέτω ἑκάστη τάξις καθ' ἑαυτὴν τοῦ κ. σώματος *Const.App*.2.57.14; of Christ's passion, Clem.*paed*.1.10(p.146.14; M.8.364A); Mac.Mgn.*apocr*.3.9(p.70.17); Isid.Pel.*epp*.1.253(M.78.336B); Cross, Ath.*inc*.30.1(M.25.147A); Nil.*epp*.3.278(M.79.521C); burial, ‡Ath.*dial.Trin*.4.10(M.28.1265A); of Christ's sayings and teaching λόγος κ. Clem.*str*.1.5(p.19.7; M.8.721A); *ib*.3.12(p.235.2; 1185B); *Const.App*.2.39.3; παραβολὰς κ. Iren.*haer*.1.8.1(M.7.521A); ἐντολαὶ κ. Clem.*paed*.1.13(p.151.27; M.8.376A); *Const.App*.8.45.2; ‡Gr.Nyss.*hom.7 in Jo*.(p.254.14); κ. διδασκαλία Clem.*paed*.2.8(p.194.9; 465B); κ. ὀνομασία τῆς τριάδος Epiph.*inc*.3(p.231.4; M.41.277C); for λογίων κ. ἐξήγησις (title of work of Papias) v. λόγιον; of Christ's power and authority, Clem.*paed*.2.3(p.178.22; 433B); id.*str*.7.10(p.42.16; M.9.481B); ἀξίωμα id.*paed*.1.7(p.124.17; 320B); ὄνομα Ath.*syn*.20(p.247.13; M.26.717A); **3.** Christol. κ. ἄνθρωπος the *Christ-man*, term applied to Christ's humanity, v. ἄνθρωπος; κ. ἕνωσις the *union* of natures *in the Lord*, Leont.H.*Nest*.2.12(M.86.1551D), v. ἕνωσις; **4.** of things emanating from Christ, *the Lord's*; **a.** of benefits given by Christ κ. μεταλαβεῖν ἀφθαρσίας Clem.*paed*.2.2(p.168.2; M.8.409B); τῇ κ. τῇ φωτεινῇ ἀγωγῇ id.*str*.3.7(p.223.3; M.8.1161B); ἡ κ. ἄσκησις ἀπάγει τὴν ψυχὴν *ib*.4.6(p.260.7; 1240A); δύναμιν λαβοῦσα κ. ἡ ψυχὴ *ib*.6.14(p.488.27; M.9.337A); κ. κληρονομίας ἀνάπαυσιν ἀπολαβεῖν *ib*.6.16(p.503.25; 369A); ἐπὶ τὴν κ. ... ἐπείγεται μονὴν *ib*.7.10(p.42.14; 481B); τοῖς κ. ὅπλοις id.*exc.Thdot*.85(p.132.28; M.9.897A); γάλακτι τῇ κ. τροφῇ id.*paed*.1.6(p.116.29; M.8.304A); τῆς κ. υἱοθεσίας κληρονόμοις id.*str*.6.8(p.466.5; M.9.289B); **b.** of things appointed by Christ, bearing Christ's authority or belonging to Christ, in Church's life and worship κ. γραφῶν Dion.Cor.ap.Eus.*h.e*.4.23.12(M.20.389A); Clem.*str*.6.11(p.477.34; M.9.313A); Meth.*res*.1.62(p.327.15; M.41.1160D); διαθηκῶν κ. Clem.*str*.6.17(p.515.9; 393C); λαοῦ κ. *ib*.7.16(p.72.18; 541B); τὸ κ. δεῖπνον...ὀφείλει κοινὸν εἶναι. τὰ γὰρ τοῦ δεσπότου οὐχὶ τοῦδε μὲν ἔστι τοῦ οἰκέτου, τοῦδε δὲ οὐκ ἔστιν...τὸ οὖν κ. τοῦτό φησι τὸ κοινόν Chrys.*hom.27.3 in 1Cor*.(10.244B), v. δεῖπνον; ποτήριον κ. *Ep.Mareot*.2(p.156.4; M.25.385B); **c.** of Church as 'Lord's house' or 'household', Clem.*str*.3.18(p.246.19; M.8.1212B); τῆς πίστεως τὸ κ. οἰκητήριον Const.ap.Gel.Cyz.*h.e*.2.7.1(M.85.1232C); *ib*.2.7.5(1233A); *ib*.2.7.6(1233B); cf.CAnc.(314)*can*.15; of a church building κ. τόπος *M.Ariadn*.18(p.133); Ath.*apol.Const*.17(M.25.616C); κ. οἶκος ‡Pion.*v.Polyc*.31; *CIG* 8652 (Syria saec. vi–vii); neut. as subst. τὰ κ. ὅπως κατασκευάζοιεν συγχωρεῖται Maximinus Daia ap.Eus.*h.e*.9.10.10(M.20.833C); Eus.*l.C*.17(p.255.3; M.20.1432B); Ath.*v.Anton*.1(M.26.841A); κἂν ἐπιδημῇς...μὴ ἁπλῶς ἐξέταζε ποῦ τὸ κ. ἐστι (καὶ γὰρ αἱ...αἱρέσεις κ. τὰ ἑαυτῶν σπήλαια καλεῖν ἐπιχειροῦσι)...ἀλλὰ ποῦ ἡ καθολικὴ ἐκκλησία Cyr.H.*catech*.18.26; ψάλλοντες ἐν τοῖς κ. *Const.App*.2.59.1; οὐ δεῖ ἐν τοῖς κ. ἢ ἐν ταῖς ἐκκλησίαις τὰς λεγομένας ἀγάπας ποιεῖν CLaod.*can*.28; CTrull.*can*.74; **d.** ἡ κ. ἡμέρα or ἡ κ., *the Lord's day, Sunday*; **i.** as regular day of worship, *Did*.14.1 cit. s. ἄρτος; Dion.Cor.ap.Eus.*h.e*.4.23.11(M.20.388C); Μελίτωνος...ὁ περὶ κυριακῆς λόγος Eus.*ib*.4.26.2(392A); Clem.*str*.7.12(p.54.18; M.9.504C); Eus.*v.C*.4.18(p.124.6; M.20.1165A); συνάξεις...ἐπιτελούμεναι ταχθεῖσαί εἰσιν ἀπὸ τῶν ἀποστόλων...κυριακῇ Epiph.*exp.fid*.22(p.522.27; M.42.825B); εὐχὴ πρώτη τῆς κ. Serap.*euch*.1 tit.; εἰρηνεῦσαι εἰς τὴν κυριακὴν τοὺς διαφερομένους πρὸς ἀλλήλους *Const.App*.2.47.1; ἐν...τῇ τοῦ κυρίου ἀναστασίμῳ τῇ κ. ἀπαντᾶτε *ib*.2.59.3; καὶ ἐν παρασκευῇ καὶ ἐν σαββάτῳ καὶ ἐν κυριακῇ ἡ αὐτὴ θυσία ἐπιτελεῖται Chrys.*hom.5.3 in 1Tim*.(11.577E); as day of respite from discipline ἐν τῇ κ. ἑστῶτας...ἔδοξε...τὰς εὐχὰς ἀποδιδόναι CNic.(325)*can*.20; τὸ σάββατον...καὶ τὴν κ. ἑορτάζετε *Const.App*.7.23.3; μὴ συντυγχάνειν τινὶ ἐκτὸς σαββάτου καὶ κυριακῆς Nil.*epp*.4.1(M.79.544C); v. νηστεύω, νηστεία; some activities forbidden on Sunday οὐδὲ ἐν ταῖς κ. ἡμέραις τῶν εὐφροσύνων ἐπιτρέπομεν ἄσεμνόν τι φθέγγεσθαι *Const.App*.5.10.1; δεῖ...τὴν κ. προτιμῶντες...σχολάζειν ὡς Χριστιανοί CLaod.*can*.29; πάντα τεχνίτην τῇ ἁγίᾳ κ. μιᾶς τριχὸς ἔργον...ἅψασθαι οὐ προστάττομεν †Gregent.*leg.Hom*.63(M.86.616B); τὰς κ. ἀπράκτους ἐκέλευσε γενέσθαι...ἵνα μήτε αὐλὸς ἢ κιθάρα ἢ ἄλλο τι μουσικὸν λέγειν ἐν κ. ἀλλὰ πάντα ἀργεῖν *Chron.Pasch*.p.322(M.92.825A,B); μὴ χρῆναι ἐν κυριακῇ θεώρια γίνεσθαι ἢ γόνυ κλίνειν Phot.*nomoc*.7.4 tit.(M.104.1076A), v. γόνυ; **ii.** as day of Christ's Resurrection, *Ev.Petr*.9(p.292.1); ἡ [sc. ἡμέρα] τῆς...ἀναστάσεως αὐτοῦ...ἥντινα ὡς ἀληθῶς κυρίαν οὖσαν καὶ κ. κρείττονα εἶναί φασιν...μυρίων...ἡμερῶν Eus.*d.e*.4.16(p.187.23; M.22.313A); ταῖς κ. ἡμέραις τὰ τῆς ἀναστάσεως ἐπετέλουν id.*h.e*.3.27.5(M.20.273C); ἡ πρώτη κ. ... τὸ σωτήριον...μεθόριον τῆς ταφῆς καὶ τῆς ἀναστάσεως Gr.Naz.*or*.44.5(M.36.612C); αὐτοῦ...ἀναστάντος ἐπιφωσκούσης κ. *Const.App*.5.19.6; τῇ κ. πρωῒ θανάτῳ παραδοθήσῃ *A.Pil*.B 12.1(p.315); τὴν διὰ τοῦ Χριστοῦ ἡμῖν δοθεῖσαν...ἀνάστασιν...τελεσθεῖσαν κατὰ τὴν κ. Nil.*epp*.3.132(M.79.444D); ὁ κύριος...τρεῖς ἡμέρας καὶ...νύκτας ὑπὸ γῆς διέτριψεν, τὴν μὲν παρασκευὴν τὸ δὲ σάββατον...τὴν δὲ κ. Thdt.ap.*cat.Mt*.16:4(p.129.15); Cosm.Ind.*top*.2(M.88.128A); as eighth day ἡ ὀγδόη...κ. κατωνόμασται, ὡς εἰς τέλος τὸν τοῦ νόμου καιρὸν κατακλείουσα, ἀρχὴν δὲ ἡμῖν κυριακῶν εἰσφέρουσα χρόνων Cyr.*hom.pasch*.6(5^2.72C); cf.Olymp.*Eccl*.11:2(M.93.605C) cit. s. ὄγδοος; **iii.** as day of Creation ἡ πρώτη κτίσις τὴν ἀρχὴν ἀπὸ κυριακῆς λαμβάνει Gr.Naz.*or*.44.5(M.36.612C); ἐν τῇ α' ἡμέρᾳ, τουτέστιν τῇ κυριακῇ...ἡ ἀρχὴ τῆς κτίσεως ἐγένετο, ἀφ' ἑσπέρας ἀρξάμενος ὁ θεὸς κτίζειν τὰ περιεκτικὰ τοῦ παντὸς κόσμου Cosm.Ind.*top*.2(p.90.3; M.88.125D); **iv.** of Easter αἱ κ. τοῦ πάσχα Hipp.*can.pasch*.tit.(M.10.879); αὐτὴν τὴν κ. τῆς ἁγίας ἑορτῆς Ath.*ep.encycl*.5(p.174.4; M.25.232C); ἐν τῷ πάσχα καὶ ταῖς κ. id.*apol.Const*.27(M.25.629C); τῆς πρώτης κ. *Const.App*.5.20.2 τῇ μεγάλῃ κ. †Jo.Jej.*poenit*.(M.88.1913A); its date ἐκ τριῶν...συνέστηκεν ὁ τοῦ πάσχα σύνδεσμος, ἔκ τε τοῦ ἡλιακοῦ δρόμου διὰ τὴν κ. καὶ τὸν μῆνα κτλ. Epiph.*haer*.70.11(p.243.25; M.42.360A); ἀδύνατον ἢ ἡμᾶς ἢ ὑμᾶς ἢ ἕτερον ὀντινοῦν αὐτῆς ἐπιλαβέσθαι τῆς κ. ἡμέρας Chrys.*Jud*.3(1.615C); v. πάσχα; **v.** of Sunday after Easter εἰς τὴν καινὴν κ. Gr.Naz.*or*.44 tit.(M.36.608A); τὴν καλουμένην νέαν κ. Evagr.*h.e*.1.3(p.8.31; M.86.2428B); Max.*ambig*.(M.91.1389A); τῆς δευτεροπρώτης κ. Eustrat.*v.Eutych*.96(M.86.2381B); τῆς καινῆς κ. CTrull. *can*.66; **vi.** of Pentecost, *Chron.Pasch*.p.223(M.92.544B); v. πεντηκοστή; **vii.** of fifth Sunday after Easter τῇ κ. τῆς ἐπισωζομένης Chrys.*stat*.19 tit.(2.188D); **viii.** Annunciation and other events assigned to Sunday κυριακῆς εὐηγγελίσθη ἡ...Μαρία ὑπὸ τοῦ...Γαβριήλ, καὶ κυριακῆς ἐτέχθη...ὁ σωτήρ, καὶ κυριακῆς...ἐξῆλθον μετὰ βαΐων...καὶ κυριακῆς ἀνέστη καὶ κυριακῆς ἔχει ἐλθεῖν κρῖναι...καὶ κυριακῆς ἐλθεῖν πρὸς δόξαν...τῆς ἀναλύσεως τῆς...παρθένου τῆς τεκούσης αὐτόν *Dorm.BMV*(p.107); **ix.** of Last Day ὅτε τὰ ὀστᾶ ταῦτα ἐν τῇ μεγάλῃ κ. ἐγερθήσεται Or.*Jo*.10.35(20; p.209.30; M.14.572A); **x.** name given to ὀγδοάς, Clem.*exc.Thdot*.63(p.128.9; M.9.689B).

***κυριακῶς**, *in the manner of Lord* τὴν φύσιν αὐτὴν ὑπὸ τοῦ θεοῦ κ., ὡς εἰπεῖν, ποιηθεὶς ἐν τῷ κτίζεσθαι κύριός ἐστι πάντων Leont.H.*Nest*.5.14(M.86.1736D).

***κυριαρχέω**, *control* πλοίου τῆς σαρκὸς κ. ‡Proc.G.*Pr*.1:5(M.87.1224D).

***κυριαρχία**, ἡ, *power, dominion* κυριότητος καὶ κ. Dion.Ar.*c.h*.8.1(M.3.237C); Areth.*Apoc*.54(M.106.724B).

***κυριαρχικός**, *all-controlling, absolute*, Dion.Ar.*c.h*.8.1(M.3.237C).

***κυρίευμα**, τό, *dominion, control*, ‡Gr.Nyss.*or.1 in Gen.1:26*(M.44.272A).

***κυρίευσις**, ἡ, *control*, Anast.S.*hod*.2(M.89.77D).

κυριευτικός, *possessing lordship, superior* ὅτε δοῦλος κατὰ τὸ σῶμα ὀνομάζεται [sc. Christ], μή τις ἀρνήσηται τὴν κ. φύσιν Apoll.*corp.et div*.4(p.186.18; M.*PL*.8.873C); τὴν...ἰατρικὴν ὕλαις χρωμένην...κ. τῶν ὑλῶν Didym.(‡Bas.)*Eun*.5(1.308C; M.29.740A).

κυριεύ-ω, **1.** *hold sway, rule* τῷ υἱῷ τὸ ~ειν ἴδιον Apoll.*fid.sec.pt*.(p.173.10; M.10.1112B); τὸ ~ον Dion.Ar.*d.n*.12.2(M.3.969C); τυραννικῶς κ. Max.*ambig*.(M.91.1044C); met. τῆς ὁρμῆς τῆς ~ούσης Clem.*str*.3.11(p.228.21; M.8.1173A); **2.** *control, be master of* ἐντολῆς κ. Herm.*mand*.5.2.8; κ. τῆς ψυχῆς Just.*dial*.105.3(M.6.721A); ζωὴ ἧς μόνος [sc. ὁ Χριστός] ~ει Clem.*exc.Thdot*.77(p.131.10; M.9.693C); τὰ πνευματικὰ...ἐκυρίευσεν ἡμῶν id.*ecl*.20(p.142.12; M.9.708A); ~εσθαι ὑπὸ τοῦ κακοῦ Meth.*res*.1.5(p.226.18); ref. Christ's body μηκέτι ὑπὸ θανάτου...~όμενον Epiph.*inc*.2(p.230.7; M.41.276D); ἡ ~ουσα πάντων φυσικῶς οὐσία...ἡ θεία Leont.H.*Nest*.5.14(M.86.1736D); ~όμενον ὑπὸ λύπης †Jo.Jej.*serm*.(M.88.1921C).

***Κυριλλιανός**, *following Cyril* σύνοδος Κ. †Leont.B.*sect*.9(M.86.1257D).

***κυριόδουλος**, *being both Lord and servant*; denied of any Person of Trin., Jo.D.*haer*.epilog.(M.94.780A).

***κυριοέργος**, ὁ, *the Lord's workman*, Leont.et Jo.*sacr*.2(M.86.2023B).

***κυριοκτονέω**, *slay the Lord*, Cyr.*Os*.6(3.26B); id.*Nah*.25(3.504A).

***κυριοκτονία**, ἡ, *slaying of the Lord*, Const.ap.Eus.*v.C*.3.18(p.85.22; M.20.1076B); Didym.*Ps*.9:7(M.39.1192B); Cyr.*Ps*.7:14(M.69.753D).

κυριοκτόνος, *slaying the Lord*, ref. Jews, Eus.*v.C*.4.27(p.127.28; M.20.1176B); κ. μιαιφονία *ib*.3.33(p.93.11; 1093B); 'Ιουδαῖοι κ. Ath.*ep.encycl*.3(p.172.17; M.25.229A); Cyr.*Juln*.8(6^2.288D); κ. συναγωγή

‡Caes.Naz.*dial*.4.183(M.38.1160); neut. as subst. τὸ κ. τῶν Ἰουδαίων Cyr.H.*catech*.10.12; of followers of Paul. Sam. as δεύτεροι κ. Epiph.*haer*.65.2(p.5.3; M.42.13D); also of Arians, *ib*.69.13(p.163.18; 224A).

κυριολεκτ-έω, **1.** *use words in their proper* or *literal sense*, opp. καταχρῶμαι, Isid.Pel.*epp*.4.58(M.78.1112A); Leont.B.*Nest.et Eut*.1 (M.86.1289B); Eulog.*fr.dogm*.(M.86.2956D); pass., Or.*comm.in Gen.* ap.*philoc*.14.2(p.69.2; M.12.89A); **2.** *designate by the correct name*, Or.*Cels*.1.25(p.76.3; M.11.705C); ἐπὶ μόνου τοῦ λόγου ∼εῖσθαι αὐτόν [sc. Χριστόν] φησιν [sc. ὁ Μάρκελλος] ὡς οὐδὲν ὄντα ἕτερον ἢ λόγον Eus.*e.th*.2.10(p.110.32; M.24.920C); **3.** *call Lord, describe as Lord*, pass., of Christ τοῦτο...ἀπὸ τοῦ ∼εῖσθαι...καὶ γὰρ...ἡ θεία γραφὴ...κύριον ἀποκαλεῖ Eus.*d.e*.5.4(p.234.19; M.22.388A); of H. Ghost ὡς σὺν πατρὶ καὶ υἱῷ ∼εῖται Epiph.*haer*.74.1(p.314.2; M. 42.473D).

***κυριόλεκτος**, **1.** *properly* or *accurately expressed* τὸ τῶν ὑψηλῶν νοημάτων ∼ον ‡Gr.Nyss.*occurs*.(M.46.1173C); **2.** *chosen by the Lord* κ. σταυρόν ‡Chrys.*ador*.2(11.824B).

***κυριολέκτως**, *by a proper* or *distinct use of words*, Olymp.*Eccl.* 4:17(M.93.537C).

κυριολογ-έω, **1.** *use words in their proper* or *literal sense*; οὐδὲν... ὄνομα ἐπὶ θεοῦ ∼εῖσθαι δυνατόν ‡Just.*coh.Gr*.21(M.6.272A); **2.** *express clearly* or *accurately*, Clem.*str*.5.4(p.339.16; M.9.40B); κατὰ τὸ ∼ούμενον εἶδος *ib*.(p.339.19; 40B); **3.** *call Lord, describe as Lord*; of Father and Son, Just.*dial*.56.14(M.6.601B); of Christ τὸν σωτῆρα ...μυρία πλήθη...∼εῖ Eus.*d.e*.3.2(p.101.11; M.22.176B); ὁ Θωμᾶς... τὸν Χριστὸν οὐχ ὡς ἄνθρωπον ἐκυριολόγει Ast.Soph.*hom.1 in Ps.5* (M.40.401C); τὸ πνεῦμα τοῦ θεοῦ ∼εῖν μὴ βουλόμενοι Didym.(‡Bas.) *Eun*.5(1.314B; M.29.753A); of angels in Gen.19 προσεκύνησεν [sc. ὁ Λώτ] αὐτοὺς καὶ ∼εῖ ‡Ath.*dial.Trin*.3.12(M.28.1220C); pass., of Christ τοῦ πρὸς ἡμῶν μετὰ τὸν πατέρα ∼ουμένου θεοῦ λόγου Eus. *d.e*.1.5(p.22.28; M.22.48C); ‡Jo.D.*hom*.5(M.96.652C); of H. Ghost μαρτυρίαι...τοῦ ∼εῖσθαι τὸ πνεῦμα Bas.*Spir*.52(3.43D; M.32.164A); οὐ θεολογεῖται τὸ πνεῦμα, ὅμως ∼εῖται ‡Ath.*Maced.dial*.1.3(M.28. 1293A).

κυριολογία, ἡ, *title of Lord*, of Christ τὴν κ. οὐκ ἀρνουμένου τὴν περὶ ἑαυτοῦ ‡Ath.*Sabell*.4(M.28.105A); Cyr.*deip.BMV* 21(p.28.27; M.76.281B).

***κυριολογικός**, *expressing clearly* or *accurately*, opp. συμβολικός, Clem.*str*.5.4(p.339.15; M.9.40B).

***κυριολογικῶς**, *by a literal use of words*, opp. τροπολογικῶς, Jo.D.*disp*.(M.96.1344B = 94.1588B); *ib*.(M.96.1344D).

***κυριοπρασία**, ἡ, *selling of the Lord*, ‡Chrys.*transfig*.(Savile 7 p.340.6).

κύριος, ὁ, *lord, master*;

A. in gen.; **1.** with power to dispose of things and persons πάντων ὁ ἄνθρωπος κ. ἐστι τῶν κτισμάτων τοῦ θεοῦ Herm.*mand*.12.4. 3; πονηρὰ...ἡ βουλὴ αὕτη, ἵνα δοῦλος κύριον ἴδιον ἀρνήσηται id.*sim*.9. 28.4; ὑποταγήσῃ κυρίοις ὡς τύπῳ θεοῦ *Barn*.19.7; μισθὸν ἐλπίζειν ἀπὸ τοῦ κ. τῶν χωρῶν καὶ χορηγοῦ τῶν σπερμάτων Or.*Jo*.13.47(46; p.273. 22; M.14.481D); φύσει...αὐτὸς κ. ἦν καὶ ἡμεῖς δοῦλοι Chrys.*hom.71.1 in Jo*.(8.418B); of a husband ἡ σώφρων γυνὴ...κ. τὸν ἄνδρα γνωρίζει *Hom.Clem*.13.18; of angels ἁγίους δὲ καὶ βασιλεῖς καὶ κ. καλεῖ τὰ λόγια τὰς ἐν ἑκάστοις ἀρχικωτέρας διακοσμήσεις Dion.Ar.*d.n*.12.4 (M.3.972B); **2.** as title of respect, *lord, sir*, given to various dignitaries; also, mere form of polite address: to an angel, Herm.*vis*. 3.10.9; *Pers*.(p.17.14; M.10.105D); to emperors, *M.Eupl*.1.1; Ath. *syn*.55(p.278.12; M.26.792B); an apostle, *A.Andr.et Mt*.21(p.93.13); *M.Ner.et Ach*.12(p.11.15); an eparch, Hipp.*haer*.9.12(p.247.21; M. 16.3382C); bishops, Cyr.*ep*.39(p.15.23; 5^2.104C); *ib*.(p.16.7; 5^2.105A); abbots, Cyr.S.*v.Sab*.50(p.141.9); relatives, Gr.Naz.*ep*.7(M.37.33A); *ib*.14(45C); *M.Seb.test*.1(p.116.25); husband, Pall.*h.Laus*.8(p.27.16; M.34.1025B); **3.** as divine title applied to pagan emperors; but refused by Christians, *M.Polyc*.8.2; cf.Hipp.*haer*.9.26(p.260.16; M. 16.3403B); to false gods, *ib*.6.20(p.148.6; 3226A).

B. of God; **1.** in LXX representing both אֲדֹנָי and יהוה οὐκ ἀγνοητέον δὲ περὶ τοῦ ἐκφωνουμένου παρὰ μὲν Ἕλλησι τῇ 'κ.' προσηγορίᾳ, παρὰ δὲ Ἑβραίοις τῇ 'Ἀδωναΐ'. δέκα γὰρ ὀνόμασι παρ' Ἑβραίοις ὀνομάζεται ὁ θεός, ὧν ἐστιν ἓν τὸ 'Ἀδωναΐ', καὶ ἑρμηνεύεται 'κ.'. καὶ ἔστιν ὅπου λέγεται τὸ 'Ἀδωναΐ' παρ' Ἑβραίοις καὶ παρ' Ἕλλησι 'κύριος', τῆς λέξεως τῆς γεγραμμένης ἐν τῇ γραφῇ τοῦτο ἀπαγγελλούσης. ἔστι δὲ ὅτε τὸ ''Ἰαή' κεῖται, ἐκφωνεῖται δὲ τῇ 'κ.' προσηγορίᾳ παρ' Ἕλλησι, ἀλλ' οὐ παρ' Ἑβραίοις...ἔστι δέ τι τετραγράμματον ἀνεκφώνητον παρ' αὐτοῖς...καὶ λέγεται μὲν τῇ 'Ἀδωναΐ' προσηγορίᾳ, οὐχὶ τούτου γεγραμμένου ἐν τῷ τετραγραμμάτῳ· παρὰ δὲ Ἕλλησι τῇ 'κ.' ἐκφωνεῖται Or.*sel.in Ps*.2:1–2(M.12.1104A,B); τὸ γὰρ ἀλληλούϊα, ὡς καὶ ἤδη ἡρμηνεύκαμεν, αἰνεῖτε τὸν κ. ἐπὶ τῇ Ἑλλάδι φωνῇ. σημαίνει γὰρ τὸ ἀλληλοὺ αἰνεῖτε, τὸ δὲ ἰὰ κύριον, ἢ τὸν ὄντα Thdt.*Ps*.110(1. 1399); hence **2. a.** normal appellation of God without distn. of Persons, *1Clem*.60.1; καρδίαν ἔχετε πρὸς τὸν κ. Herm.*mand*.10.1.6; ὁ ἔχων τὸν κ. ἐν τῇ καρδίᾳ αὐτοῦ *ib*.12.4.3; τῶν τριῶν λαῶν...διαφόροις...παιδευομένων διαθήκαις τοῦ ἑνὸς κ. Clem.*str*.6.5(p.452.28; M.9.261B); πάντες...κατὰ διάνοιαν...προσευχέσθωσαν λέγοντες· κ. ἐλέησον *Lit*.ap.*Const.App*.8.6.4; in adjurations κατὰ τοῦ κ. Herm. *vis*.3.2.3; echo of κ. as personal name of God in OT δέσποτα, κ. ὁ θεός μου *Lit.Jac*.(p.160.10); **b.** perh. referring more to Father, in OT terms, or as exercising supreme dominion ἐκεῖνο μηνύων, ὡς δυνάμει μὲν ὁ κ. καὶ θεὸς πάντων ἂν εἴη καὶ τῷ ὄντι παντοκράτωρ, κατὰ δὲ τὴν γνῶσιν οὐ πάντων θεός· οὔτε γὰρ ὅ ἐστιν οὔθ' ὅπως κ. καὶ πατὴρ καὶ ποιητής, οὐδὲ τὴν ἄλλην ἴσασιν οἰκονομίαν τῆς ἀληθείας Clem.*str*. 5.14(p.417.18f.; M.9.197B); τὸν κ. τῶν πνευμάτων ποθῶ, τὸν κ. τοῦ πυρός, τὸν κόσμου δημιουργόν, τὸν ἡλίου φωταγωγόν id.*prot*.6(p.51. 24; M.8.172C); as κ. τῶν δυνάμεων v. δύναμις; **c.** prob. referring more to Son in his claim on mankind through redemption βαστάσαι ...τὸν ζυγὸν τοῦ κ. *Did*.6.2; ἐν πνεύματι προφήτης ἐστὶν...ἐὰν ἔχῃ τοὺς τρόπους κυρίου *ib*.11.8; κατὰ κυριακὴν δὲ κυρίου *ib*.14.3; ἐν γὰρ τῇ μακροθυμίᾳ ὁ κ. κατοικεῖ, ἐν δὲ τῇ ὀξυχολίᾳ ὁ διάβολος Herm.*mand*. 5.1.3; ἦν ὡς ἀληθῶς διὰ μὲν Μωσέως παιδαγωγὸς ὁ κ. τοῦ λαοῦ τοῦ παλαιοῦ, δι' αὐτοῦ δὲ τοῦ νέου καθηγεμὼν λαοῦ Clem.*paed*.1.7(p.124. 14; M.8.320B); ὁ γνωστικός, ἰδίαν σωτηρίαν ἡγούμενος τὴν τῶν πέλας ὠφέλειαν, ἄγαλμα ἔμψυχον εἰκότως ἂν τοῦ κ. λέγοιτο id.*str*.7.9(p.39.9; M.9.473C); ὁ καθ' ἡμᾶς ἱεράρχης ἄγγελος κυρίου παντοκράτορος ὑπὸ τῶν λογίων ὠνόμασται Dion.Ar.*c.h*.12.1(M.3.292C); id.*e.h*.7.3.7(M.3.561C); **3.** of Father ὁ παντεπόπτης θεὸς...καὶ κ. πάσης σαρκός, ὁ ἐκλεξάμενος τὸν κ. Ἰησοῦν Χριστόν *1Clem*.64; τὸ θέλημα τοῦ πατρὸς ἡμῶν θεοῦ... τὸ θέλημα κυρίου *2Clem*.14.1; κ. ὁ θεὸς ὁ παντοκράτωρ, ὁ τοῦ...παιδός σου Ἰησοῦ Χριστοῦ πατήρ *M.Polyc*.14.1; οὗτός ἐστιν ὁ τοῦ υἱοῦ πατήρ, ὁ δημιουργὸς τῶν συμπάντων, ὁ παντοκράτωρ κ. Clem.*str*.4.13 (p.288.27; M.8.1300B); ἄρχειν...τῶν ὅλων ὑπὸ κ., τοῦ αὐτοῦ πατρός, κατατεταγμένος Eus.*e.th*.3.2(p.140.12; M.24.973C); ἡμεῖς...ἕνα μόνον θεὸν καταγγέλλομεν, νόμου καὶ προφητῶν κ., τὸν ὄντων δημιουργόν, τοῦ Χριστοῦ πατέρα *Const.App*.6.11.1; **4.** of Son τιμήσεις...ὡς κ. ὅθεν γὰρ ἡ κυριότης λαλεῖται, ἐκεῖ κ. ἐστιν *Did*.4.1; τὸν...ἐπίσκοπον...ὡς αὐτὸν τὸν κ. δεῖ προσβλέπειν Ign.*Eph*.6.1; ὁ λόγος δὲ τοῦ θεοῦ ἐστιν ὁ υἱὸς αὐτοῦ...καὶ ἄγγελος δὲ καλεῖται καὶ ἀπόστολος· αὐτὸς γὰρ ἀπαγγέλλει...καὶ ἀποστέλλεται...ὡς καὶ αὐτὸς ὁ κ. εἶπεν· ὁ ἐμοῦ ἀκούων ἀκούει τοῦ ἀποστείλαντός με Just.*1apol*.63.5(M.6.424B); cf. ὁ κ., ἀπόστολος ὢν τοῦ παντοκράτορος, ἀπεστάλη πρὸς τοὺς Ἑβραίους Clem.*fr*.22(p.201.26; M.9.749B); id.*str*.7.14(p.61.2; M.9.520A); ὁ κ., ἀλήθεια καὶ σοφία καὶ δύναμις θεοῦ *ib*.2.11(p.141.21; M.8.989A); ὁ κ. πνεῦμα καὶ λόγος id.*paed*.1.6(p.116.2; M.8.301B); ὁ νόμος κυρίου τοῦ θεοῦ μου *M.Eupl*.1.3; in professions of faith ἡ...ἐκκλησία...παραλαβοῦσα τὴν...πίστιν...εἰς ἕνα Χριστὸν Ἰησοῦν...καὶ τὴν...εἰς τοὺς οὐρανοὺς ἀνάληψιν τοῦ ἠγαπημένου Χριστοῦ Ἰησοῦ τοῦ κ. ἡμῶν καὶ τὴν ἐκ τῶν οὐρανῶν ἐν τῇ δόξῃ τοῦ πατρὸς παρουσίαν αὐτοῦ...ἵνα Χριστῷ Ἰησοῦ τῷ κ. ἡμῶν καὶ θεῷ καὶ σωτῆρι καὶ βασιλεῖ...πᾶν γόνυ κάμψῃ Iren.*haer*.1.10.1(M.7.549A,B); χρὴ...πιστεύειν ὅτι κ. Ἰησοῦς Χριστός, καὶ πάσῃ τῇ περὶ αὐτοῦ κατὰ τὴν θεότητα καὶ τὴν ἀνθρωπότητα ἀληθείᾳ Or.*Jo*.32.16(9; p.451.28; M.14.784A); cf.*Symb.Nic*.(325)(p.51. 6; M.20.1540B); *Symb.Nic.–CP*(p.80.4; H.2.288B); ἕνα καὶ τὸν αὐτὸν ὁμολογεῖν υἱὸν τὸν κ. ἡμῶν Ἰησοῦν Χριστόν...ἐκδιδάσκομεν...ἕνα καὶ τὸν αὐτὸν Χριστὸν υἱὸν κ. μονογενῆ...ἕνα καὶ τὸν αὐτὸν υἱὸν μονογενῆ θεὸν λόγον κ. Ἰησοῦν Χριστόν *Symb.Chalc*.(p.129.23,30; p.130.1; H. 2.456Bf.); in Trin. controversy οὐκ ἐκβάλλει τῆς κυριότητος τὸν πατέρα, τὸ λέγεσθαι ὅτι εἷς κ. Ἰησοῦς Χριστός Chrys.*incomprehens*. 5.1(1.482A); κ. in OT interpreted of Son νοητέον...ὅτι οὗτός ἐστιν ὁ κ. ὁ κτίσας τὴν λογιστικὴν σοφίαν εἰς ἀρχὴν ὁδῶν αὐτοῦ...ὁ κατασκευάσας τὴν γῆν εἰς τὸν αἰῶνα χρόνον [ref. Pr.8:22f.] Gel.Cyz.*h.e*.2. 17.12(M.85.1268C); **5.** of Father and Son as one God; ref. Gen. 19:24 ὁ Μωσῆς ἄμφω δυοῖν μνημονεύων κυρίων, πατρὸς δηλαδὴ καὶ υἱοῦ, ὧδέ πῃ...ἱστορεῖ, λέγων· καὶ ἔβρεξε κ. παρὰ κυρίου Eus.*p.e*.7.12 (322C; M.21.544D); εἴ τις τὸ [Gen.19:24] μὴ ἐπὶ τοῦ πατρὸς καὶ τοῦ υἱοῦ ἐκλαμβάνοι...ἀ. ἔ., ἔβρεξε γὰρ κ. ὁ υἱὸς παρὰ κυρίου τοῦ πατρός... εἴ τις ἀκούων κ. τὸν πατέρα καὶ τὸν υἱὸν κ. ... δύο λέγοι θεούς, ἀ. ἔ. ... υἱόν...ὑποτεταγμένον τῷ πατρί...οὔτε ἔβρεξεν ἀφ' ἑαυτοῦ, ἀλλὰ παρὰ κ. αὐθεντοῦντος δηλαδὴ τοῦ πατρός *Symb.Sirm*.1 *anath*.17f.(p.255. 26ff.; M.26.737C); Chrys.*hom.3.2 in 2Tim*.(11.674D,E); ref. Dt.6:4 τὸ γὰρ 'κ. ὁ θεός σου κ. εἷς ἐστι', καὶ τὸ τῆς οὐσίας διδάσκει μοναδικόν, καὶ παραδηλοῖ τῶν προσώπων τὸν ἀριθμόν Thdt.*qu.2 in Dt*.(1. 263); in gen. ὑπὲρ τοῦ...ὑμᾶς...δοξάζειν ἡμῶν τὸν κ. ἐν Χριστῷ Ἰησοῦ τῷ κ. ἡμῶν CHier.(350)*ep*.(p.137.15,16; M.25.352C); **6.** of H. Ghost τίς ὁ κατευθύνων κ. εἰς τὴν τοῦ θεοῦ ἀγάπην καὶ εἰς τὴν ὑπὲρ τῶν θλίψεων τοῦ Χριστοῦ ὑπομονήν; ἀποκρινάσθωσαν ἡμῖν οἱ τὸ πνεῦμα καταδουλούμενοι Bas.*Spir*.52(3.44B; M.32.164B); καὶ τὸ πνεῦμα κ. Didym.(‡Bas.)*Eun*.5(1.310C; M.29.744C); καὶ κ. τὸ πνεῦμά ἐστι Dion.Ar.*d.n*.2.1(M.3.637B); credal πιστεύομεν...εἰς τὸ πνεῦμα τὸ ἅγιον τὸ κ. *Symb*.ap.Epiph.*anc*.118(p.147.12; M.43.232D); *Symb. Nic.–CP*(p.80.12; H.2.288B); cf. κ. καὶ ἡγεμονικὸν...πνεῦμα Clem. *str*.6.17(p.512.4; M.9.388B); **7.** of all three Persons, ref. Gen.19:12–24 ποτὲ οὖν τὸ 'ἡμεῖς' λέγει διὰ τὰς ὑποστάσεις, ποτὲ δὲ τὸ 'ἐγὼ' διὰ τὴν φύσιν...Ἀβραὰμ τὰς τρεῖς ὑποστάσεις ἐγνωκώς, κύριον λέγει· καὶ Λὼτ τὰς δύο ἐγνωκώς, ὁμοίως κύριον λέγει ‡Ath.*dial.Trin*.3.14(M.28.1224D); ἑνὸς ὄντος κ. τοῦ υἱοῦ, κ. ὁ πατὴρ τῷ τῆς εἰκόνος ὀνόματι καλούμενος...οὕτω καὶ τὸ πνεῦμα κ., ἀπὸ τοῦ κ. τὴν ἐπωνυμίαν ἔχον, ἀφ' οὗ καὶ μεταδίδοται Didym.(‡Bas.)*Eun*.5(1.310C; M.747C); **8.** θεός and κ. coupled; **a.** as in OT φοβοῦμεν κ. τὸν θεόν Clem.*str*.1.26(p.107.27; M.8.921A); ὁ δι' ἀγάπην τὴν πρὸς τὸν θεὸν παθὼν διὰ τὴν ἰδίαν σωτηρίαν, ὅ τε αὖ διὰ τὴν ἰδίαν ἀποθνῄσκων σωτηρίαν διὰ τὴν ἀγάπην ὑπομένει τοῦ κ. *ib*.4.6(p.267.21; 1256A); *ib*.4.22(p.309.10; 1348B); with passage from one Person to another in common concept of lordship εἰ οὖν δεόμεθα τοῦ κ. ἵνα ἡμῖν ἀφῇ, ὀφείλομεν καὶ ἡμεῖς ἀφιέναι· ἀπέναντι γὰρ τῶν τοῦ κ. καὶ θεοῦ ἐσμεν ὀφθαλμῶν, καὶ πάντας δεῖ παραστῆναι τῷ βήματι τοῦ Χριστοῦ Polyc.*ep*.6.2; **b.** in Trin. controversy, vindicated for both Father and Son διδάσκων ἕνα μὲν εἰδέναι θεὸν ἀγέννητον, τὸν πατέρα· ἕνα δὲ γεννητὸν κ., τὸν υἱόν· θεὸν μέν, ὅταν καθ' ἑαυτὸν λέγηται, προσαγορευόμενον· κ. δέ, ὅταν μετὰ πατρὸς ὀνομάζεται· τὸ μὲν διὰ τὴν φύσιν, τὸ δὲ διὰ τὴν μοναρχίαν Gr.Naz.*or*.25.15 (M.35.1220B); τὸ...πατὴρ καὶ υἱὸς ⟨ὄνομά ἐστιν⟩ ἴδιον ἑκάστης ὑποστάσεως, τὸ δὲ θεὸς καὶ κ., κοινόν Chrys.*incomprehens*.5.2(1.482D); exeg. Ps.141:2 φωνῇ μου πρὸς κύριον ἐκέκραξα· φωνῇ μου πρὸς τὸν θεὸν ἐδεήθην· οὐκοῦν καὶ κ. καὶ θεὸν αὐτὸν ὀνομάζει...οὐκοῦν θεὸς ὁ υἱός, καὶ κ. ὁ πατήρ...ἕν ἐστι τὸ κ. καὶ τὸ θεός id.*pan.Phoc*.3(2.708D–709A); exeg. 1Cor.8:6 δείξας...ἰσοδυναμοῦσαν τῇ θεὸς προσηγορίᾳ τὴν κ. ... ἐνταῦθα...τὸν μὲν θεὸν προσηγόρευσε, τὸν δὲ κ. ... τὴν κύριος ἰσοδυναμοῦσαν τῇ θεὸς ἐπιδείξας...ὁ τοίνυν ὄντως θεός, πάντως καὶ κ.· καὶ ὁ ὄντως κ. πάντως καὶ θεός Thdt.*1Cor*.8:6(3.215); **c.** dist.: θεός = Father; κ. = Son; ref. 1Cor.8:6 ἐπειδὴ...τὰ πάντα δι' αὐτοῦ ἐγένετο, εἰκότως ἡμῖν τοῖς τοῦτ' ἐπιστ[αμ]ένοις κ. εἶναι τῶν ὅλων μετὰ τὸν ἐπὶ πάντων θεὸν πεπίστευται Eus.*e.th*.1.20(p.90.12; M.24.881B).

κυριότης, ἡ, *lordship, dominion*; **1.** in gen., of man's control in exercise of free will ἡ...ἐξουσία, κ. ἔννομος τῶν ἐφ' ἡμῖν πρακτῶν, ἡ κ. ἀκώλυτος τῆς τῶν ἐφ' ἡμῖν χρήσεως Max.*opusc*.(M.91.17C); of God's lordship, opp. man's servitude τὴν διαφορὰν τοῦ κτιστοῦ πρὸς τὸ ἄκτιστον· ὧν ἡ παραλλαγὴ κυριότητι καὶ δουλείᾳ χαρακτηρίζεται Gr.Nyss.*Eun*.5(2 p.120.22; M.45.701B); revealed in incarnate Christ, Ath.*Ar*.2.16(M.26.181B); cf. 4 infra; κ. οὐχ ἡ τῶν χειρόνων ὑπεροχὴ μόνον, ἀλλὰ καὶ πᾶσα τῶν καλῶν τε καὶ ἀγαθῶν ἡ παντελὴς παγκτησία Dion.Ar.*d.n*.12.2(M.3.969B); Christol. καθ' ὑπόστασιν ἐν Χριστῷ τὸ ἀνθρώπινον τῇ τῆς ἀληθοῦς κ. στεφανοῦται τιμῇ Cyr.*Heb*.2:9(p.391); **2.** of Trin. πατὴρ καὶ υἱὸς καὶ ἅγιον πνεῦμα, ἡ μία κ. †Ath.*serm.fid*. 32(p.28; M.26.1288A); λέγομεν...καὶ μίαν κ. ... τὴν τριάδα Apoll. *fid.sec.pt*.26(p.176.14; M.10.1116B); εἷς...θεὸς...καθ' ὃ θεότης μιᾶς κυριότητος *ib*.16(p.172.23; 1112A); τρισὶν δοξολογίαις μίαν κ. ὁμολογοῦσαι Procl.CP *hom*.1.5(M.65.837C); Sophr.H.*ep.syn*.(M.87.3153A,B); Jo.D.*trisag*.(M.95.25B); exeg. Eph.4:5 τὰς...τρεῖς κ. εἰς μίαν κ. συναγαγών ‡Ath.*comm.essent*.6(M.28.33C); ref. address to Persons in prayer εἰπὲ...υἱῷ καὶ πνεύματι...ἐναντίον σου, οὐκ, ἐναντίον ὑμῶν, ἵνα μὴ διέλῃς τὴν κ. ‡Ath.*dial.Trin*.3.13(M.28.1224A); ref. indwelling of God in saints ἐν οἷς οἰκεῖ ἡ...μία κ. πατρὸς καὶ υἱοῦ καὶ ἁγίου πνεύματος Didym.(‡Bas.)*Eun*.5(1.317E; M.29.761B); Arian τὸ δυσσέβημα...εἰς ἑτερογονεῖς τρεῖς κ. τὴν μίαν διϊστῶν κ. Sophr.H.*ep.syn*.(3153B); **3.** of Father, in rel. to Son πάντων... κύριος τυγχάνει οὗτος, ὅτι...τῇ τοῦ πατρὸς κ. ἥνωται Ath.*Ar*.3.64(M.26.460A); ἔφησεν ὑποταχθήσεσθαι τῷ υἱῷ διὰ τοῦ πατρὸς τὰ πάντα, ἵνα μὴ τῆς ἁπάντων κ. ἔξω γεγονὼς ὁ πατὴρ ὑποπτεύηται...ἵνα τῆς πάντων κ. τὸ πᾶν ἔχοι κράτος ὁ πατήρ Cyr.*thes*.29(5[1].255D,E); **4.** of Son ὅθεν...ἡ κ. λαλεῖται, ἐκεῖ κύριός ἐστιν *Did*.4.1; ὁ υἱός...εἰς ἐξουσίαν...κεῖται καὶ κ. Herm.*sim*.5.6.1; τῇ κ. τοῦ ἄρχοντος Or.*Jo*. 32.10(7; p.442.20; M.14.768B); ‡Hipp.*consumm*.43(p.307.10; M.10.945C); Areth.*Apoc*.1:5(M.106.508A); in rel. to Father, Acac.Caes. *fr.Marcell*.ap.Epiph.*haer*.72.8(p.262.30; M.42.393A); Didym.*Trin*.1. 26(M.39.384A); ἔσται οὐ τελείως ἐλεύθερος, εἴπερ ἐστὶν ἐλάττων ἐν κ. Cyr.*Jo*.1.3(4.23B); Eunomian οὐσίαν ὀνομάζει [sc. Eunomius] τὴν κ. Gr.Nyss.*Eun*.7(2 p.151.12; M.45.740A); ἡ κ. οὐχὶ οὐσίας ὄνομα, ἀλλ' ἐξουσίας *ib*.6(2 p.149.3; 736A); ref. Inc. ὁ νῦν κύριος...οὐκ ἀρχὴν ἔχει τοῦ γενέσθαι...κύριος ἀλλὰ τοῦ τὴν κ. ἑαυτοῦ δεικνύειν Ath.*Ar*.2.12 (M.26.173A); οὐ τὴν οὐσίαν τοῦ υἱοῦ πεποιῆσθαι ἔλεγεν [ref. Ac.2:36] ...ἀλλὰ τὴν εἰς ἡμᾶς αὐτοῦ κ. γενομένην ὅτε γέγονε ἄνθρωπος *ib*.2.13 (173B); cf.Gr.Nyss. supra; ἦν...ἐν Χριστῷ...ἐν οἰκετικῇ μορφῇ κ. Cyr. *Chr.un*.(5[1].753C); κυριότητος ἀληθοῦς ἡ τοῦ θεοῦ λόγου μεμέστωται φύσις *ib*.(753B); αὐτὸς ἀξίᾳ τινὶ καὶ κωδικέλλοις ἔλαβε τὴν κ. ποιηθεὶς κύριος Leont.H.*Nest*.5.14(M.86.1736D); οὐκ ἀφῄρηται τὴν κατὰ πάντων κ. τῷ γενέσθαι ἄνθρωπος Andr.Caes.*Apoc*.54(M.106.384C); demonstrated by forgiveness of sins τῇ τῶν ἁμαρτιῶν ἀφέσει τὴν κ. αὐτοὺς ἐννοῆσαι ποιῶν Cyr.*deip.BMV* 21(p.29.3; M.76.1281B); exeg. Mt.11:27 'πάντα' λέγοντες τὴν κ. τῆς κτίσεως Ath.*hom.in Mt.11:27* (M.25.209A); in rel. to work of H. Ghost τὸ πνεῦμα τὴν τοῦ υἱοῦ κ. διαπέμπον εἰς τὴν ἁγιαζομένην κτίσιν Apoll.*fid.sec.pt*.25(p.180.28; M.10.1117D); **5.** of H. Ghost τῇ δουλείᾳ τοῦ γράμματος τὴν τοῦ πνεύματος ἀντιδιαιρῶν κυριότητα Gr.Nyss.*Eun*.7(2 p.155.7; M.45.744A); ἀλλαχοῦ [i.e. Ac.13:2]...αὐτοῦ τὴν κ. ἔστιν ἰδεῖν Chrys.*hom.7.5 in 2Cor*.(10.487A); τὸ ἐνεργεῖν...καθὼς βούλεται, δείκνυσιν αὐτοῦ...τὴν κ. *ib*.(487B); v. πνεῦμα; **6.** plur., *dominions* (cf. Col.1:16), an angelic order ἐν τῇ διατάξει τῶν ὅλων εἶναί τινας τοὺς καλουμένους θρόνους καὶ ἄλλους κ. καὶ...ἐξουσίας Or.*Cels*.4.29(p.298.17; M.11.1069C); id.*or*. 17.2(p.339.21; M.11.472D); many in number, Ath.*ep.Serap*.1.27(M. 26.593B); their superiority, *ib*.2.4(613B); ἄγγελοι...καὶ κ. ... τοῦ λόγου μετέχοντες βλέπουσι διαπαντὸς τὸ πρόσωπον τοῦ πατρός id.*Ar*. 3.51(M.26.432A); devoted to service of God, *ib*.2.27(204B); Cyr.H. *procatech*.15; creatures of God, ‡Chrys.*hom*.8(13.221E); hence inferior to Christ, Cyr.*inc.unigen*.(5[1].697D); Arian εἰ γὰρ διὰ ταῦτα ἕν εἰσιν ὁ υἱὸς καὶ ὁ πατήρ [i.e. through unity of will, etc.]...ὅρα καὶ τοὺς ἀγγέλους...καὶ θρόνους καὶ κ. ... εἶναι καὶ αὐτούς, ὡς τὸν υἱόν, υἱούς Ath.*Ar*.3.10(M.26.341B); Marcellan τὸν πρωτότοκον πάσης κτίσεως διὰ τὴν σάρκα κεκλῆσθαι λέγει [sc. Marcellus], ἐπιμένει δὲ... ἐν τῇ σαρκὶ φάσκων τὰ ἐν τοῖς οὐρανοῖς καὶ τὰ ἐπὶ τῆς γῆς ἐκτίσθαι... οὐδὲ διατρέπεται θρόνους καὶ κ. ... διὰ τῆς σαρκὸς τοῦ σωτῆρος λέγων τῆς ἐν Χριστῷ κτίσεως ἠξιῶσθαι Eus.*e.th*.3.7(p.165.11; M.24.1016C); in Marcosian initiation formula τὸ ὄνομα τὸ ἀποκεκρυμμένον ἀπὸ πάσης θεότητος καὶ κ. ... ὃ ἐνεδύσατο Ἰησοῦς Iren.*haer*.1.21.3(M.7.664A); in Valent. application of Col.1:16 ὅπως ἐν αὐτῷ [sc. τῷ σωτῆρι] τὰ πάντα κτισθῇ...θρόνοι, θεότητες, κ. *ib*.1.4.5(488A); **7.** as style of address ἡ σὴ κ. *Mir.Geo*.6(p.71.16).

***κυριοτόκος,** *bearing the Lord, who is mother of the Lord* ἡ κ. Μαρία καὶ ἀειπάρθενος, Ath.*fr.Lc*.(M.27.1393C); preferred to θεοτόκος by Nestorius, as more scriptural term Χριστοτόκον, κ., ἀνθρωποτόκον, ἐμάθομεν ἀπὸ τῆς γραφῆς λέγειν, θεοτόκον δὲ οὐδαμῶς ἐδιδάχθημεν λέγειν Nest.ap.Cyr.*dial.Nest*.(M.76.249A); accepted by orthodox in conjunction with θεοτόκος: εἰ οὖν κύριος ὁ τεχθείς, πῶς οὐ κ. ἡ παρθένος; ἐγὼ δὲ λέγω καὶ Χριστοτόκον καὶ κ. καὶ σωτηριοτόκον καὶ θεοτόκον ‡Ath.*nativ.Chr*.4(M.28.965C); Thdr.Stud.*antirr*. 2.7(M.99.356C); and independently ἁγία κ. παρθένος †Jo.D.*creat*.4 (p.123); *ib*.6(p.142); Thdr.Stud.*or*.5.1(M.99.720D).

***κυριοφόρος,** *bearing the Lord* κ. φάτνην Isid.Pel.*epp*.1.378(M.78. 396C).

***κύρις (*κῦρις), ὁ,** form of κύριος used as title of respect; *Lord, Sir* (voc. κύρι, acc. κύριν, genit. κυροῦ), Ephr.2.155A, 394C; CChalc. (451)*act*.1(*ACO* 2.1.1 p.142.29); *Didasc.Jac*.1.14(p.751.14); Jo.Mal. *chron*.12 p.293(M.97.444B); Cyr.S.*v.Sab*.64(p.165.20); Thphn.*chron*. p.312(M.108.757C, v.l. κύριον); in form κῦρ, Leont.H.*monoph*.tit.(M. 86.1769).

***κυριώδης,** *important, authoritative*; comp., Isid.Pel.*epp*.3.249 (M.78.929B).

***κυριώνυμος,** *properly* or *aptly named*; of BMV, Thdr.Stud. *nativ.BMV* 5(M.96.685C).

***κυρτοβατέω,** *walk with bent back*; of the aged, ‡Chrys.*Zach*. (2.792A); Isid.Pel.*epp*.5.231(M.78.1473A); ‡Caes.Naz.*dial*.100(M.38. 965).

***κυρτοκάπηλος, ὁ,** ? *dealer in fishing tackle*, *CIG* 9180.

***κυρωτέον,** *one must acknowledge* τὴν Πέτρου κ. ἐπιστολήν Eus. *h.e*.3.25.2(M.20.268D).

***κυρωτικός,** *confirmatory*, Clem.*str*.8.5(p.89.11, cod. κυριωτική M. 9.580B).

***κυτάζομαι,** ? *lurk*, Ephr.2.348D.

§**κυφοειδής,** *hump-shaped, curved*; of cheek-bones, Melet.*nat. hom*.5(M.64.1181A); τὸ κ., of the ankle-bone, *ib*.29(1265B).

κυφότης, ἡ, *rotundity*; of the head, Melet.*nat.hom*.1(M.64.1148D).

***κώδηξ, ὁ,** (Lat. *codex*) *codex, volume of writings*, Tim.Ant.*descr. BMV* 2(M.28.945B); Evagr.*h.e*.1.12(p.20.21; M.86.2452D); Jo.Mosch. *prat*.38(M.87.2889A).

***κωδικίλλιον, τό,** *writing*; of emperor confirming privilege, *diploma* (= κωδίκελλος 2), Jo.Mal.*chron*.15 p.384(M.97.569B).

***κωδίκελλος, ὁ,** (Lat. *codicillus*) **1.** *writing-tablet* κ. γραφῶν... Χριστιανῶν *M.Agap*.(p.98.2); **2.** *writing* of emperor confirming privilege, *diploma*, Mac.Aeg.*hom*.39.1(M.34.761C); Max.*ambig*.(M. 91.1284B); **3.** *testamentary order, codicil*, Gr.Naz.*test*.(M.37.393C); **4.** theol., *testament*; ref. Cant.5:14 κ. ... ἐπουρανίου βασιλείας Ph. Carp.*Cant*.154(M.40.109D) ∞ Proc.G.*Ex*.24:11(M.87.633A); Leont.H. *Nest*.5.14(M.86.1736D) cit. s. κυριότης.

*__κωδίκιον, τό,__ dim. of κώδηξ, *codex, collection of writings*, *Chron. Pasch*.p.330(M.92.856B κωδίκου); CCP(681)*act*.10(H.3.1204D).

*__κωδωνισμός, ὁ,__ *proclamation by bell-ringing*, Thdr.Stud.*or*.11 (M.99.841A).

κώλυμα, τό, *interdict*, Jo.Mal.*chron*.13 p.347(M.97.517C).

κωλυτικός, *forbidden* κ. δένδρου *A.(Pass.)Andr*.5(p.12.21; M.2. 1225B).

*__κωλυτικῶς,__ *so as to hinder*, Or.*Jo*.6.22(13; p.132.6; M.14.240B).

κωλύω, 1. *prevent*, c. ὥστε: οὐ κωλύων ὥστε [v.l. οὔτε] χεῖρας νίπτειν οὐδὲ [v.l. οὔτε] στόμα Chrys.*hom.51.4 in Mt*.(7.526B); **2.** *check, prune* plants, Chrys.*hom.15.4 in 2Cor*.(10.548D); **3.** τὸ κεκωλυμένον *forbidden thing* εἰς ὄρεξιν καταπεσεῖν τῶν κ. Meth.*res*. 2.2(p.331.5; M.41.1164B); Chrys.*hom.15.2 in Mt*.(7.187C); *ib.51.5* (526C).

*__κωλῶθις,__ = κολλυρίς, *loaf*; in children's language at Amasea, of eucharistic bread before consecration, Eustrat.*v.Eutych*.52(M. 86.2333C).

κωμασία, ἡ, *procession of images of gods* in Egypt, Clem.*str*.5.7 (p.354.29; M.9.69B).

κωμαστήριον, τό, 1. *sacred object*; property of Egyptian priests, Synes.*calv*.10(p.208.5; M.66.1184D); **2.** *council of priests* in Egypt, id.*provid*.6(p.74.18; M.66.1221B).

κωμαστής, ὁ, in Egypt, *one who carries sacred images in procession*, Synes.*provid*.6(p.75.3; M.66.1221C).

κωμαστικός, *belonging to the* κωμασταί: κ. ψῆφος Synes.*provid*.6 (p.75.6; M.66.1221C).

*__κωμέρκιον, τό,__ v. *κομμέρκιον.

κωμοδρομέω, *wander from village to village*, Jo.Mal.*chron*.18 p.453 (M.97.664D).

*__κωμοδρόμος, ὁ,__ *one who wanders from village to village*, Thphn. *chron*.p.189(M.108.489D).

κωμύδριον, τό, *small village, hamlet*, Gr.Naz.*carm*.2.1.11.442(M. 37.1059A); Mac.Mgn.*apocr*.2.14(p.23.9); Pall.*v.Chrys*.7(p.38.21; M. 47.23).

κωμῳδία, ἡ, 1. *derision, mockery* ὑπέπεσαν τῇ ἀποστολικῇ ἀρᾷ καὶ κωμῳδίᾳ Nil.*epp*.2.140(M.79.261C); Thdt.*Dan*.5:23(2.1169); Chrys. *hom.85.1 in Mt*.(7.803E); **2.** *object of derision*, Chrys.*hom.14.10 in Rom*.(9.572D); id.*hom.7.7 in 1Cor*.(10.61C).

*__κωμῴδιον, τό,__ *mockery, baiting*, Serap.*ep.mon*.7(M.40.933A).

κωνάριον, τό, *pineal gland* in the brain, Hipp.*haer*.4.51(p.76.16; M.16.3122B); *ib*.5.17(p.116.5; 3178C).

κῶνος, ὁ, *cone*; met., *the heart*, Geo.Pis.*carm.vit*.41.

*__κωνστιτούριον,__ v. *κονσιστόριον.

*__κώφευσις, ἡ,__ *dumbness*, Isid.Pel.*epp*.1.131(M.78.269B); ‡Caes. Naz.*dial*.1(M.38.856).

κωφεύω, *be deaf* or *dumb*, Meth.*fr.4 in Job*(p.521.10); Isid.Pel. *epp*.1.54(M.78.217A); Procl.CP *or*.2.3(M.65.693D).

κώφησις, ἡ, *deformity, deficiency*, Sophr.H.*mir.Cyr.et Jo*.10(M.87. 3448B).

Λ

*__λάαρος,__ ‡Bas.Sel.*or*.38(M.85.416A), perh. for ἱλαρός or γαυρός.

*__λάβαρον, τό__ (other forms v. infra), perh. = λαβ(υ)ρᾶτον *standard* adopted by Const. as result of vision before battle of Milvian Bridge (described, Eus.*v.C*.1.31(p.21.31ff.; M.20.945A)); ἔκφρασις σταυροειδοῦς σημείου, ὅπερ νῦν οἱ Ῥωμαῖοι λ. καλοῦσιν *ib*.tit.(p.5.4; 908A); apparent attempt to derive word from *laborare* ἄγει τὸν στρατὸν...καμάτων [? *laborum*] λυτήριον ὅν τε καὶ κατὰ Ῥωμαίους ὀνομαζόμενον Gr.Naz.*or*.4.66(M.35.588B); σημεῖον τὸ βασιλικὸν...τὸ λεγόμενον...λάβουρον Chrys.*hom.3.1 in 1Tim*.(11.562D some MSS only); σταυροῦ σύμβολον...τὸ παρὰ Ῥωμαίοις καλούμενον λάβωρον Soz.*h.e*.1.4.1(M.67.868A); of Cross as standard of Christ's empire ἐπίσημον λ. Gr.II Papa *ep.Germ*.(M.98.149A); of standard of pagan emperor (λαύορον), Ephr.2.344A.

λαβή, ἡ, *handle, grip*; met.; **1.** *means of obtaining* παρέχοιμι...λ. σωτηρίους ‡Just.*ep.Zen.et Ser*.1(M.6.1184A); **2.** mental *grasp* τῶν λογισμῶν τὴν λ. Gr.Nyss.*hom.6 in Cant*.(M.46.892D); *ib.12*(1028B); **3.** *handle, hold*, metaphor from wrestling παράσχῃ λαβὴν τοῖς κεφαλαίοις καταχρῆσθαι τούτοις τοὺς πρεσβεύοντας προφάσει τεκνογονίας σωμάτων παρατριβάς Meth.*symp*.3.11(p.39.3; M.18.77A); δώσει τοῖς αἱρετικοῖς καθ' ἡμῶν λαβήν Bas.*ep*.188 *can*.6(3.272B; M.32.673B); Gr.Nyss.*hom.in 1Cor.6:18*(M.46.496A); Chrys.*hom.40.1 in Mt*.(7. 437C); id.*hom.2 in Rom.16:3*(3.187B); id.*hom.1.2 in Heb*.(12.15E); Thdt.*Ps*.9:1(1.656); λαβὰς εἰς κατάλυσιν...κηρύγματος τοῖς ἀντιπάλοις παρείχετο Gennad.*fr.Rom*.9:19–23(p.392.14; M.85.1709A).

λαβίς, ἡ, I. *pair of tongs*; exeg. Is.6:6–7:

A. interpreted as typifying **1.** spiritual apprehension of divine gifts and teaching, †Bas.*Is*.183(1.514A; M.30.429B) = Proc.G.*Is*. 6:6–13(M.87.1941A); πίστιν...καὶ γνῶσιν καθάπερ τινὶ λ. δεχώμεθα διὰ νομικῶν...καὶ προφητικῶν παιδευμάτων Cyr.*Is*.1.4(2.108C); **2.** ἡ διὰ τοῦ δεσποτικοῦ σώματος...τῶν ἁμαρτημάτων ἀπαλλαγή Thdt.*Is*.6:6 (p.32.34; 2.210); **3.** BMV νοεράν σε λ. τὸν ἀληθινὸν ἄνθρακα φέρουσαν Χριστόν Jo.Mon.*hymn.Blas*.3(M.96.1402C); her hands when presenting Christ to Symeon, ‡Meth.*Sym.et Ann*.7(M.18.364B).

B. its purpose; **1.** to signify altar's sanctity, †Bas.*Is*.183(1.513D; M.30.428C); ἐλέγχει...τὴν...Ὀζίου παρανομίαν τὸ γεγονός Thdt.*Is*.6:6 (p.32.27; 2.210); Proc.G.*Is*.6:6–13(M.87.1941A); **2.** to convey Christ, who is the ἄνθραξ, Cyr.*Is*.1.4(2.107C); ‡Germ.CP *contempl*.(M.98. 393C); cf.Proc.G.*Is*.6:6–13(M.87.1940B); **3.** to denote divine condescension, Chrys.*Is.interp*.6(6.69C); **4.** to contrast Isaiah's call with Jeremiah's ἐπειδὴ οὗτος ἁγιάσθη ἐκ μήτρας οὐ λ. αὐτῷ πέμπεται Or.*hom.1.14 in Jer*.(p.12.7; M.13.272A); cf.Proc.G.*Is*.6:1–5(M.87. 1937D).

C. in Trin. simile ὡς γὰρ οὐδὲν διαφέρει τὸ τῇ λ. ἐκ τοῦ θυσιαστηρίου τὸν ἄνθρακα, μὴ αὐτῇ χειρὶ λαμβάνεσθαι, εἰ καὶ διὰ ταύτης ἡ χαλκευτικὴ εἴη, τὸ ἐπελαύνειν τὸν σίδηρον (ἔσται γὰρ καὶ ἡ λ. καὶ ὁ διὰ ταύτης ἐλαυνόμενος σίδηρος τοῦ γένους τῶν ποιημάτων) οὕτως οὐδὲν διοίσει τῶν ποιημάτων ὁ δι' οὗ τὰ πάντα, εἰ μὴ ἔστιν υἱός CAnc.(358)*ep.syn*. ap.Epiph.*haer*.73.4(p.274.2; M.42.409C).

II. *communion-spoon*, *Mir.Geo*.6(p.69.14); ἡ λαβὶς [sc. αἰνίττεται] κατὰ τὸν προφήτην Ἡσαΐαν λέγοντα [Is.6:6]...σημαίνει δὲ καὶ τὴν παρθένον, βαστάζουσαν καὶ αὐτὴν τὸν οὐράνιον ἄρτον ‡Sophr.H.*liturg*. 5(M.87.3985B); cf.*Euchol*.(p.130).

*__λαβνεῖον, τό,__ a kind of *caustic salve*, Sophr.H.*mir.Cyr.et Jo*.47 (M.87.3600B).

λαβραγόρης, ὁ, *impetuous talker*, †Apoll.*met.Ps*.139:12 (v.l. λαυραγόρην M.33.1524C).

*__λαβρᾶτον, τό,__ *laurel-wreathed standard* bearing emperor's portrait εἰσῆλθεν τὰ λ. αὐτοῦ ἐν Κωνσταντινουπόλει *Chron.Pasch*.p.323 (M.92.828A); λαβράτοις προσκυνοῦσιν οἱ ἄνθρωποι Jo.D.*imag*.3.41 (M.94.1359A).

*__λάβρες, αἱ,__ *tongs*, Cosm.Ind.*top*.5(λαβίδες M.88.209B).

*__λαβυρίνθιος,__ *complicated, tortuous* λ. ... μύθους Sophr.H.*carm*. 10.41(M.87.3781B).

*__λαγγᾶς, ὁ,__ a measure of length, ? about 6 miles, Jo.Mosch. *prat*.157(M.87.3025D).

*__λαγκίδιον, τό,__ *small lance*, Jo.Mal.*chron*.18 p.458(M.97.669C); Thphn.*chron*.p.207(M.108.532B).

*__λαγκούριον, τό,__ a precious stone, identified with λιγύριον (cf. Ex.28:19) and tentatively with ὑάκινθος, Epiph.*gemm*.7(M.43. 297D).

λαγνεία, ἡ, 1. *lust, lechery*, def. as ὕβρις...ἐπειδὰν ἐκτραπῇ κατὰ τοῦτο τῆς ἀταξίας τὸ μέρος τὸ κατὰ τὴν ἀφροδίτην, λ. κέκληται, τὸ λαϊκὸν καὶ δημῶδες καὶ ἄναγνον, τὸ περὶ τὰς ὀχείας καταφερές, ἐμφαίνοντος τοῦ ὀνόματος Clem.*paed*.2.10(p.213.16; M.8.508B); τὸ δὲ περὶ τὴν φωνὴν σωφρονεῖν ἀσκεῖν ἐστι λαγνείας καρτερεῖν *ib*.2.6(p.188. 23; 453C); *ib*.2.10(p.209.32; 501A); Isid.Pel.*epp*.1.135(M.78.272B); Thdt.*Am*.4:3(2.1425); **2.** plur., *lustful acts*, Clem.*paed*.3.11(p.272. 32; M.8.556B); τὸν...λ. καὶ γαστριμαργίαις ὑποπεπτωκότα Bas.*hom. in Ps*.29(1.129C; M.29.317C); ἡδονῶν ἐξοιστρουσῶν ἐπὶ λαγνείας id. *hom*.14.4(2.125C; M.31.452A); Nil.*epp*.1.140(M.79.141A).

*__λαγνικός,__ error in Clem.*paed*.2.10(M.8.508B, cod.; conj. λαϊκόν p.213.16).

*__λάγνιος,__ *lecherous*, Bas.*hex*.8.3(1.73D; M.29.172C).

*__λαγούριον, τό,__ = λαγκούριον, Epiph.*gemm*.7(M.43.300A).

*__λάγχηρος,__ *fleecy*, Cosm.Ind.*top*.5(M.88.216C).

λαγών, ἡ, usu. plur.; **1.** *belly*, Cyr.*Jon*.18(3.380D); **2.** *bowels* of the earth, Bas.*hom*.5.2(2.35A; M.31.241B); Chrys.*hom.3.3 in 2Thess*.(11. 526E); Thdt.*Ps*.77:19–20(1.1153); of *depths* of sea, Nonn.*par.Jo*. 21:10(M.43.817A); of *well* of water, *ib*.4:15(776C); **3.** *womb*, *Orac. Sib*.8.457; Pall.*h.Laus*.57(p.150.8; M.34.1250B); Cyr.*Os*.158(3.191A); ἐκ λ. παρθενικῶν id.*Mich*.47(3.437A); Mod.*dorm*.2(M.86.3285A); *ib*.5 (3292A); **4.** *hollow, cranny*, ‡Meth.*Sym.et Ann*.9(M.18.369B).

λαγωός, ὁ, *hare*, ref. Lev.11:5 *οὐ μὴ γένῃ παιδοφθόρος, οὐδὲ ὁμοιωθήσῃ τοῖς τοιούτοις, ὅτι ὁ λ. κατ' ἐνιαυτὸν πλεονεκτεῖ τὴν ἀφόδευσιν Barn.*10.6, cf.Clem.*paed*.2.10(p.208.22; M.8.497C).

***λαζάριον, τό,** *lazar-house, hospital*, Cyr.S.*v.Euthym*.8(p.15.23); *ib*.(p.16.7); *ib*.48(p.70.5).

***λαζούριος,** *azure* λ. χρῶμα Areth.*Apoc*.21:19f.(M.106.773A).

λαθικηδής, *banishing care ἄλλος...νόον λαθικηδέα τέρπει so as to forget care*, Paul.Sil.*Soph*.894(M.86.2153A).

***λαθρογαμία, ἡ,** *secret marriage*, CLaod.*can*.1; †Jo.Jej.*poenit*.(M.88.1896A).

[*]**λαθρόδακνος,** *biting secretly*, hence *backbiting*, Nil.*epp*.1.309 (M.79.196A).

λαθροδάκτης, ὁ, as adj., *biting stealthily* λ. *κύων* Pall.*v.Chrys*.6 (p.36.6; M.47.22).

λαθροδήκτης, ὁ, *one who takes a surreptitious bite*, fig. of dissident Christians *κύνες λυσσῶντες*, λ. Ign.*Eph*.7.1; of the malicious, Chrys.*hom.15.4 in Eph*.(11.115A).

***λαθροδιδασκαλέω,** *teach in secret*, Iren.*haer*.3.4.2(M.7.857A).

***λαθροκακουργέω,** *do evil secretly*, Thdr.Raith.*praep*.(p.194.2; M.91.1493D).

***λαθροκακοῦργος,** *secret evil-doer*, Marc.Er.*opusc*.1.121(M.65.920D).

***λαθροπορέω,** *devise* plots *secretly*, Steph.Diac.*v.Steph*.(M.100.1125C).

***λαθροφαγία, ἡ,** *secret gluttony*, Bas.*renunt*.8(2.209A; M.31.641B); Ephr.3.426E = Jo.D.*virt*.(M.95.88C); *Schol*. in Jo.Clim.*scal*.4.41(M.88.744A).

λαθροφάγος, *secretly gluttonous*, Bas.*renunt*.6(2.208B; M.31.640B).

***λαθροφθορέω,** *corrupt secretly*, Meth.*symp*.3.14(p.44.21; M.18.85B).

***λαθροφονευτής, ὁ,** *murderer in secret*, ‡Chrys.*poenit*.1(9.778A).

***λαθροφόνος,** *slaying in secret*, ‡Chrys.*hom*.2(13.207D, v.l. *-φόρους*).

***λαιβίον, τό,** a sound expressing derision, Anast.Ap.*a.Max*.1.3(M.90.113C).

λαϊκός, A. *common, profane*, Clem.*paed*.2.10(p.213.16; M.8.508B) cit. s. *λαγνεία*.

B. *lay*; freq. as subst., *layman*; **1.** in Judaism, in comparison of OT with Church order *τῷ γὰρ ἀρχιερεῖ ἴδιαι λειτουργίαι δεδομέναι εἰσὶν καὶ τοῖς ἱερεῦσιν ἴδιος ὁ τόπος προστέτακται, καὶ λευΐταις ἴδιαι διακονίαι ἐπίκεινται...ὁ λ. ἄνθρωπος τοῖς λ. προστάγμασιν δέδεται 1Clem.*40.5; *τὸ...κάλυμμα κώλυμα λ. ἀπιστίας* Clem.*str*.5.6(p.347.19; M.9.57A); *Ἀβραὰμ ὁ πρόγονος τῶν λευϊτῶν, τῶν...ἱερέων, ἐπὶ τοῦ Μελχισεδέκ, ὃς ἦν τύπος τῆς καθ' ἡμᾶς ἱερωσύνης, λαϊκοῦ τάξιν ἐπεῖχε* Chrys.*Jud*.7.5(1.669D); ‡Just.*qu.et resp*.97(M.6.1340C); **2.** Christian; **a.** as order in Church *οἱ μὲν ἐν τῷ λ. ὄντες τάγματι* Bas.*ep*.188 *can*.3(3.271B; M.32.672B); cf. *ἦν τις πρεσβύτερος...καὶ ἦν ἄλλος...τῇ τάξει λαϊκός M.Niceph.*1; *τί οὖν πρὸς ἐμὲ τὸν λ., εἰ... ἀρχιερωσύνην ἐνεδύσατο; τί πρὸς ἐμὲ τὸν ἐν λ. τάξει κατηλεγμένον;... διὰ πάντας ἀνθρώπους γέγονεν ἄνθρωπος· εἰ δὲ βούλει αὐτὸν καὶ λαϊκοῦ τάξιν ὑπερχόμενον ἰδεῖν διὰ σέ,...σκόπησον. ... ὅρα...'Ιωάννην ἐν τάξει ἱερέως βαπτίζοντα, καὶ τὸν Χριστὸν ἐν λ. τάγματι βαπτιζόμενον* Sever.*appar*.7(M.65.20C); *ἰδιώτην καλεῖ τὸν ἐν τῷ λ. τάγματι τεταγμένον· ἐπειδὴ καὶ τοὺς ἔξω τῆς στρατιᾶς ὄντας ἰδιώτας καλεῖν εἰώθασι* Thdt.*1Cor*.14:16(3.259); Eus.Al.*serm*.1(M.86.316A); **b.** functions and place in Church, in gen. *ὡς γάρ σοι ἀσεβές ἐστι, τὰς βιωτικὰς φροντίδας ἀναδέξασθαι, καταλείψαντα ποιεῖν ὃ ἐκελεύσθης, οὕτως ἑκάστῳ λ. ἁμαρτία ἐστίν, ἐὰν μὴ ἀλλήλοις καὶ ἐν ταῖς βιωτικαῖς χρείαις παρίστανται Clem.ep.*5; *ὑμεῖς, οἱ λ., ἡ ἐκλεκτὴ ἐκκλησία τοῦ θεοῦ· καὶ γὰρ ὁ λαὸς πρότερον θεοῦ λαὸς ὠνομάζετο, καὶ ὑμεῖς οὖν ἐστε ἁγία τοῦ θεοῦ ἱερὰ ἐκκλησία Const.App.*2.26.1; *ποιμένα τὸν ἀγαθὸν ὁ λ. τιμάτω, ἀγαπάτω, φοβείσθω ὡς πατέρα, ὡς κύριον, ὡς δεσπότην ib.*2.20.1; *πᾶς λ. ἄνευ τοῦ ἱερέως ἐπιτελῶν τι ματαιοπονεῖ ib.*2.27.3; *οὔτε λαϊκοῖς ἐπιτρέπομεν ποιεῖν τι τῶν ἱερατικῶν ἔργων, οἷον θυσίαν ἢ βάπτισμα ἢ χειροθεσίαν ἢ εὐλογίαν μικρὰν ἢ μεγάλην ib.*3.10.1; *ὅ τε γὰρ ἐπίσκοπος καὶ οἱ πρεσβύτεροί τινών εἰσιν ἱερεῖς, καὶ οἱ λ. τινών εἰσιν λ.· καὶ τὸ μὲν εἶναι Χριστιανὸν ἐφ' ἡμῖν, τὸ δὲ...ἐπίσκοπον ἢ ἄλλο τι οὐκ ἐφ' ἡμῖν, ἀλλ' ἐπὶ τῷ...θεῷ ib.*8.1.21; functions may include teaching, cf.Hipp.*trad.ap*.19.1; *ὁ διδάσκων εἰ καὶ λ. ᾖ, ἔμπειρος δὲ τοῦ λόγου...διδασκέτω Const.App.*8.32.17; this discouraged, cf.Gr.Naz.*or*.32.12ff.(M.37.189ff.); *ὁ λ., τὴν ἀκοὴν εὐτρέπισον καὶ πρὸς τὴν...γραφῶν ἀκρόασιν ἕτοιμος γενοῦ* Eus.Al.*serm*.8(M.86.361D); forbidden *οὐ χρὴ δημοσίᾳ λ. λόγον κινεῖν ἢ διδάσκειν, ἀξίωμα ἑαυτῷ διδασκαλικὸν...περιποιούμενον, ἀλλ' εἴκειν τῇ παραδοθείσῃ παρὰ τοῦ κυρίου τάξει καὶ τὸ οὖς τοῖς τὴν χάριν τοῦ διδασκαλικοῦ λαβοῦσι λόγου διανοίγειν* CTrull.*can*.64; baptizing; gen. forbidden, Bas.*ep*.188 *can*.1(3.270B; M.32.669A); *Const.App*.3.10.1 but v. *βάπτισμα*; preaching; allowed in time of Or. in many districts but described by Demetrius as unheard of in cases where bishops are present, Alex.H.*fr*.ap.Eus.*h.e*.6.19.18(M.10.205A); place assigned to laity in church, *Const.App*.2.57.4; who are not to usurp priests' place in sanctuary, cf.Thdt.*h.e*.5.18.21(3.1050); *μὴ ἐξέστω τινὶ τῶν ἁπάντων ἐν λαϊκοῖς τελοῦντι ἔνδον ἱεροῦ εἰσιέναι θυσιαστηρίου, μηδαμῶς ἐπὶ τοῦτο τῆς βασιλικῆς εἰργομένης ἐξουσίας...ἥνικα ἂν βουληθείη προσάξαι δῶρα τῷ πλάσαντι* CTrull.*can*.69; not to bless at *agape*, cf.Hipp.*trad.ap*.26.12; to make response of 'Amen' in liturgy, Chrys.*hom.35.3 in 1Cor*.(10.325E); ass. with bishop in reconciliation of penitents, †Hipp.*Artem*.ap.Eus.*h.e*.5.28.12(M.20.513C); and clergy in approval of candidates for priesthood, Corn.*ib*.6.43.17(624B); **c.** reconciliation as layman of penitent bishop (one of Novatian's consecrators) *ᾧ καὶ ἐκοινωνήσαμεν λαϊκῷ ib*.6.43.10(620B); deposition to lay status, CSard.*can*.19; Bas.*ep*.54(3.149A; M.32.401B); *ib*.188 *can*.3(271B; M.672B); Pall.*h.Laus*.18(p.54.19; M.34.1059B); **d.** of layman opp. monk, CChalc.*can.2*; *εἴασε τὸ σχῆμα μοναχικόν, καὶ γέγονε λ.* Jo.Mosch.*prat*.118(M.87.2981C); CTrull.*can*.81; CNic.(787) *can*.22.

λαῖλαψ, ἡ, ὁ, *tempest* λ. *ἐστι συστροφὴ ἀνέμου Doct.Patr*.33(p.263.3); met., of storms of passion, Clem.*paed*.3.1(p.236.19; M.8.556C); Nonn.*par.Jo*.7:7(M.43.805B); masc. λ. ... *γενομένου μεγάλου* Thphn.*chron*.p.242(M.108.609C).

λαιμαργέω, 1. *devour greedily*, Cyr.H.*catech*.6.31; ‡Just.*ep.Zen. et Ser*.13(M.6.1200A); **2.** *be greedy*, Gr.Nyss.*infant*.(M.46.185C).

***λαιμαργικός,** *greedy*; neut. as subst., *greed*, Steph.Diac.*v.Steph*.(M.100.1173D).

λαιμάω, *eat greedily*, Melet.*nat.hom*.10(M.64.1197A).

***λαΐτης, ὁ,** *one of the crowd, one of the people ἄνδρα...ἐν τοσούτῳ ἀξιώματι ὄντα, λ. ... εἶναι οὐχ ὑπολαμβάνω* Gr.Mag.*dial*.(tr.Zach.)3.1(M.*PL*.77.219C).

λακάω, *burst asunder* (cf. Ac.1:18) *ὁ δὲ δράκων...ἐλάκησε A.Thom*. A 33(p.150.18); ref. death of Arius likened to that of Judas *ἐλάκησε μέσος* Ath.*ep.mort.Ar*.(p.179.27; M.25.688C, v.l. *ἐλάκισε*); *ἐλάκησε καθάπερ καὶ 'Ιούδας* Epiph.*haer*.68.6(p.147.1; *ἐλάκισε* M.42.193D); *εὑρέθη λακήσας ib*.69.10(p.160.22; 217C).

λακίζ-ω, 1. *break*, Ephr.2.83F; *ὥσπερ δράκοντος κεφαλὴν ξύλῳ τῆς πίστεως ἐπὶ γῆς λακίσαντες* Epiph.*haer*.27.8(p.313.4; *λακήσαντες* M.41.377C); *νηὸς...λακισθείσης ib*.56.1(p.340.7; M.41.992A); of a corpse *~όμενον καὶ θρυπτόμενον ib*.64.69(p.514.20; 1192C); **2.** in gen., *destroy φλογὶ ~όμενον* Men.*exc.Rom*.8(p.193.5; M.113.885A); **3.** v.l. *ἐλάκισε* for *ἐλάκησε*, v. *λακάω*.

***λακκ-άω,** *? stagnate*; met., *be forgotten ἄφες τὸν λογισμόν σου ~ᾶν Apophth.Patr*.(M.65.364A).

λάκκος, ὁ, *cistern, pit* (*for water*);

A. lit.; **1.** in gen., in illustration of Arian doctrine of Son as a creature *οὐκ ἔτι πηγὴν...δείκνυσιν, ἀλλά τινα λ. ὥσπερ ἔξωθεν ὕδωρ λαβόντα, κεχρημένον τῷ ὀνόματι τῆς πηγῆς* Ath.*decr*.15(p.13.16; M.25.441C); **2.** of Jeremiah's pit, Or.*hom.1.13 in Jer*.(p.11.14; M.13.269C); Cyr.*Am*.49(3.303E); Esaias *or*.8.2(p.53); **3.** of Daniel's den, *1Clem*.45.6; Clem.*str*.1.21(p.77.17; M.8.825B); Or.*or*.13(p.326.27; M.11.456A); *τοὺς λέοντας νηστεύειν ἐδίδαξεν, εἰσελθὼν εἰς τὸν λ.* Bas.*hom*.1.7(2.6A; M.31.173B); *ib*.8.5(68C; M.320A); Chrys.*hom.in Rom. 12:20*(3.159E).

B. met.; **1.** ref. 2Reg.23:15 *ᾔδει...ὡς ἀπειθήσουσιν 'Ιουδαῖοι Χριστῷ τῷ...ζωογονοῦντι...ὕδατι Βηθλεὲμ...ἀνατέλλοντι καὶ ἐκ λ. παρθενικοῦ...φαίνοντι* Sophr.H.*nativ*.(p.514.4); *λ. γὰρ καὶ πύλη μυστικῶς ἡ...παρθένος διώρισται ib*.(p.514.15); **2.** ref. Jer.2:13 *οὓς δὲ ὑμεῖς ὠρύξατε λ. ἑαυτοῖς συντετριμμένοι εἰσί* Just.*dial*.14.1(M.6.504C); cf.Or.*exc.in Ps*.27:1(M.17.116D); **3.** ref. 2Par.26:9–10 *λάκκους λαοτομεῖ ὁ κύριος ἐν τῇ ἐρήμῳ· λέγω δὲ τῷ κόσμῳ καὶ τῇ φύσει τῶν ἀνθρώπων...λ. καλεῖ...τὰς δεκτικάς...καρδίας* †Cyr.*coll.VT*(6^4.59A,B; M.77.1261C,D); **4.** in gen., of evil *ἐκ τοῦ λ. τῶν κακῶν A.Phil*.112 (p.44.12); *λ. ταλαιπωρίας, τουτέστιν ἐκ βάθους ἁμαρτιῶν* Cyr.*Ps*.39:1 (M.69.980B); of death, Thdt.*Ps*.27:1(1.775).

***λακταία, ἡ,** *heel*, Gr.Mag.*dial*.(tr.Zach.)3.37(M.*PL*.77.311B).

***λακτία, ἡ,** *kick*, *M.Ner.et Ach*.3(p.3.7).

***λακωνάριος,** (cf. Lat. *lacunar*) *panelled καμάραν...λ.* Const.ap. Eus.*v.C*.3.32(p.92.27; M.20.1092C); as subst., *panelled ceiling περὶ τῶν...κιόνων...καὶ περὶ τῶν λ. ib*.(p.93.6; 1093A).

λαλ-έω, A. *speak*; **1.** in gen. *ὃς* [sc. *ἐπίσκοπος*] *σιγῶν πλείονα δύναται τῶν μάταια ~ούντων* Ign.*Philad*.1.1; *ἐὰν δὲ...περὶ...Χριστοῦ μὴ ~ῶσιν, οὗτοι ἐμοὶ στῆλαί εἰσιν...νεκρῶν ib*.6.1; of apostles *ἄνδρες ...ἰδιῶται, ~εῖν μὴ δυνάμενοι* Just.*1apol*.39.3(M.6.388B); Athenag.*leg*.

31.3(M.6.961C); Clem.*str*.7.14(p.62.14; M.9.521A); πῶς παραστήσεις μέγα καὶ ἔνδοξον εἶναι τὸ 'οὐκ ἐπίσταμαι ~εῖν' λεγόμενον ὑπὸ τοῦ σωτῆρος; τὸ ~εῖν ἀνθρώπινόν ἐστι· τὸ ~εῖν διαλέκτῳ χρήσασθαί ἐστιν. ...ἐάν...εἰδῇς αὐτὸν λόγον ἐν ἀρχῇ πρὸς τὸν θεόν, ὄψει ὅτι οὐκ ἐπίσταται ~εῖν ἀνθρωπίνου ὄντος τοῦ ~εῖν, ἀλλ' ⟨οὐκ ἐπίσταται⟩, ἐπεί ἐστι μεῖζον ὃ ἐπίσταται τοῦ ~εῖν Or.*hom.1.8 in Jer.*(p.7.21; M.13.264D); πᾶσα ἡ λογικὴ κτίσις ποτὲ ἀφ' ἑαυτῆς ~εῖ, ποτὲ τὰ τοῦ θεοῦ Didym. (‡Bas.)*Eun*.5(1.319A; M.29.765A)∞‡Ath.*dial.Trin*.1.23(M.28.1152C); Epiph.*haer*.69.41(p.189.15; M.42.265C); τὸν ὑπ' αὐτοῦ ~ούμενον τῆς διδασκαλίας λόγον Max.*ambig*.(M.91.1365D); Νεστόριος...~ῶν κατὰ τοῦ θεοῦ ἀδικίαν Dam.*troph*.suppl.(p.278.10); **2.** of God, *1Clem*.8.1; Χριστὸς...τὸ ἀψευδὲς στόμα, ἐν ᾧ ὁ πατὴρ ἀληθῶς ἐλάλησεν Ign.*Rom*. 8.2.; δέκα λόγοις, ἐν οἷς ἐλάλησεν...πρὸς Μωϋσῆν *Barn*.15.1; *ib*.16.5; Just.*1apol*.63.1(M.6.424A); Meth.*res*.1.56(p.316.22; M.41.1152A); λ. λέγεται θεὸς οἷς ἀποκαλύπτει τὸ βούλημα. καὶ Παῦλος γὰρ οὐ δι' αἰσθήσεως ἤκουε παρὰ τοῦ ἐν αὐτῷ ~οῦντος Χριστοῦ Proc.G.*Ex*.32:11 (M.87.669B); Manich. τὸν δὲ λαλήσαντα μετὰ Μωυσέως καὶ τῶν Ἰουδαίων καὶ τῶν ἱερέων τὸν ἄρχοντα...εἶναι τοῦ σκότους Hegem. *Arch*.12(p.20.13; M.10.1448B); **3.** of Christ ὁ λόγος φανείς, παρρησίᾳ ~ῶν ‡*Diogn*.11.2; τὸν σταυρωθέντα...λ. ... ἐν στύλῳ νεφέλης Just.*dial*. 38.1(M.6.557A); ὥσπερ διὰ τοῦ σώματος ὁ σωτὴρ ἐλάλει...οὕτως καὶ πρότερον μὲν διὰ τῶν προφητῶν, νῦν δὲ διὰ τῶν ἀποστόλων καὶ τῶν διδασκάλων Clem.*ecl*.23(p.143.4; M.9.708D); **4.** of H. Ghost in OT scriptures, Just.*dial*.52.1(M.6.589B); Clem.*prot*.9(p.62.9; M.8.192D); Didym.(‡Bas.)*Eun*.5(1.319A; M.29.765A); esp. in prophecy, *Barn*. 10.2; ὁ νοῦς τοῦ προφητικοῦ καὶ τοῦ διδασκαλικοῦ πνεύματος ἐπικεκρυμμένως ~ούμενος Clem.*str*.1.9(p.30.4; M.8.741B); Cyr.H.*catech*.16.4; *Symb*.ap.Epiph.*anc*.118(p.147.13; M.43.232D); *Symb.ib*.119(p.148.26; 236A); *Symb.Nic.–CP*(p.80.14; H.2.288B); speaking the things of God, as being divine, ‡Ath.*dial.Trin*.1.23(M.28.1152C); πάντα γὰρ ὅσα ~εῖ τὸ πνεῦμα καὶ ὁ υἱός, τοῦ θεοῦ εἰσι λόγια Didym.(‡Bas.)*Eun*.5 (319A; M.765A); *Lit.Jac*.(p.204.26); of Montanist inspiration, Anon. ap.Eus.*h.e*.5.16.17(M.20.472A); **5.** of prophets διὰ πνεύματος...περὶ μετανοίας ἐλάλησαν *1Clem*.8.1; οὐ πᾶς δὲ ὁ ~ῶν ἐν πνεύματι προφήτης ἐστίν, ἀλλ' ἐὰν ἔχῃ τοὺς τρόπους κυρίου ‡*Did*.11.8; δίκαιοι...θείῳ πνεύματι λαλήσαντες Just.*dial*.7.1(M.6.492A); **6.** of preachers and teachers in gen., Ign.*Trall*.9.1; *Barn*.10.11; *Diogn*.10.7; Tat.*orat*. 33(p.34.23; M.6.873C); οὐδὲ τὰ περὶ τῶν μυστηρίων ἐπὶ κατηχουμένων λευκῶς ~οῦμεν Cyr.H.*catech*.6.29.

B. *speak of, have on one's lips* μὴ ~εῖτε Ἰησοῦν Χριστόν, κόσμον δὲ ἐπιθυμεῖτε Ign.*Rom*.7.1; ἄτοπόν ἐστιν, Ἰησοῦν Χριστὸν λ. καὶ Ἰουδαΐζειν id.*Magn*.10.3; τούτων ~ουμένων *Barn*.11.11.

C. *address* λ. ἔχω τὸν στρατόν Thphn.*chron*.p.271(M.108.672A); c. ἵνα, *approach* ἐὰν λαλήσῃς τὸν στρατόν, ἵνα δέξωνταί με *ib*.

λαλητός, **1.** *endowed with speech*, Iren.*fr*.14(M.7.1237A); **2.** *argumentative* ἑρμηνεύονται δὲ Ἀμορραῖοι μὲν λ. παραπικραίνοντες. ... οἱ δεινοὶ γὰρ πρὸς ἀπάτην σοφιστικὴν καταπικραίνοντές εἰσι λ. Eus.*Ps*. 135:19(M.24.36A).

*__λαλίς,__ ἡ, *tongue*, †Apoll.*met.Ps*.21:16(M.33.1340C; *Teub*. om.).

λαμβάν-ω, **1.** *take, receive*, in allegory of Sarah taking the meal ~ει ἡ τοῦ θεοῦ σοφία Σάρρα, ἡγεμόνισσα ἢ ἄρχουσα, ~ει σῶμα, ψυχὴν καὶ πνεῦμα καὶ ἐγκρύπτει τῷ πυρί...τὴν εἰς πατέρα καὶ υἱὸν καὶ πνεῦμα ὁμολογίαν ‡Chrys.*hom*.7(13.218B); ref. Inc. in gen. σώματος οἰκητήριον ἐκ παρθένου λαβεῖν Gel.Cyz.*h.e*.2.7.13(M.85.1236A); ~ει σῶμα ἐκ γυναικός *ib*.2.24.12(1301A); Thdr.Mops.*fr.inc*.(p.319.26; M.66.1000B); τὸν ὑπὸ τοῦ μονογενοῦς εἰλημμένον ἄνθρωπον *ib*.(p.320.35; 1001A); εἰ μὴ σάρκα λαβὼν ἐγένετο σάρξ, τραπεὶς ἐγένετο σάρξ Thdt.*eran*.1(4. 12); τῆς ληφθείσης φύσεως id.*Ps*.40:12(1.869); abs., *receive*, theol., of H. Ghost πεμπόμενος ὑπ' αὐτοῦ [sc. Son] καὶ παρ' αὐτοῦ ~ων Eun. *exp.fid*.3(p.259); Epiph.*haer*.69.56(p.204.7; M.42.292A); ἀπὸ πατρὸς ἐκπορευόμενον καὶ τοῦ υἱοῦ ~ον *ib*.62.3(p.392.1; M.41.1053B); *ib*.69. 34(p.182.32; M.42.256B); ~ειν εὐχήν *receive* someone's *prayers, have benefit of* someone's *intercession* βαλόντα μετάνοιαν καὶ λαβόντα εὐχήν ‡Sophr.H.*v.Mar.Aeg*.4(M.87.3701A); *ib*.6(3704A); **2.** abs., *receive money*, *Did*.1.5; Herm.*mand*.2.5; *T.Job* 11(p.110.15); in an accusation ἀπὸ χειροτονιῶν ~ει CBeryt.*act*.(*ACO* 2.1.3 p.24.22; H.2.517C); **3.** *marry* [sc. a wife] ἄλλοι...ἔλαβον συναρπαχθέντες ὑπὸ τοῦ σατανᾶ Nil.*epp*.2.140(M.79.261C); **4.** ~ειν εἰς πρόσωπον *be a respecter of persons*, *Sent.App*.(p.77).

*__λαμπαδάριος,__ ὁ, eccl. official responsible for arranging and cleaning lamps in church, *Euchol*.(pp.225,230).

*__λαμπάδη,__ ἡ, *lamp*, Eus.Al.*serm*.21.7(M.86.432D).

*__λαμπαδηκόμος,__ *with shining head*, Synes.*calv*.11(p.210.20, conj. for λαμπηδοκόμος M.66.1188A).

λαμπαδηφορέω, *be a torch-bearer*, Pall.*h.Laus*.25(p.80.7; M.34. 1090D).

λαμπαδηφόρος, ὁ, ἡ, *torch-bearer* ἀδύτων γέγονα λ. φώτων Meth. *symp*.6.5(p.69.22; M.18.120C); Pall.*h.Laus*.25(p.80.7; M.34.1090D).

λαμπαδουχ-έω, *illuminate* λαμβάνει ἡ τοῦ θεοῦ σοφία...σῶμα... καὶ ἐγκρύπτει τῷ πυρί, τουτέστι τῇ ἀσβέστῳ θεότητι ~οῦσα ‡Chrys. *hom*.7(13.218B); τῷ πνεύματι ~ούμενος Jo.D.*carm.dorm.BMV* 139 (p.232; M.96.1365D); ‡Jo.D.*Artem*.42(p.162.26; M.96.1289C).

λαμπαδουχία, ἡ, *illumination*, ‡Chrys.*pasch*.6.2(p.135.9; 8.267A); ‡Chrys.*ascens*.1(3.777E); τὰς πασῶν τῶν ἀρετῶν λ. Nil.*epp*.3.184(M. 79.469D).

λαμπαδοῦχος, *illuminating, giving light* λ. ἀστέρα *M.Tar*.9 (p.475); ἀσθενεία...πίστεως λαμπαδοῦχε †Hipp.*Laz*.(p.217.2; M.62. 776); †Cyr.*hom.div*.11(5².381A).

*__λαμπαδοφανῶς,__ *with shining light* ἀκτὶς...καταβαινομένη λ. ‡Ath. *qu.al*.4(M.28.776B).

*__λαμπαδοφεγγέω,__ *glow with light, shine brilliantly*, †Sophr.H. *orat*.(M.87.4004B); σήμερον λαμπαδοφεγγεῖ πᾶσα ἡ κτίσις ἀρδεύεται *Rit.Epiph*.p.426(conj. λαμπαδοφεγγής).

λαμπάς, ἡ, **1.** *light* in eccl. ceremonies, illuminating church at Easter vigil, Eus.*v.C*.4.22(p.125.28; M.20.1169A); κηρῶν καὶ λ. Anton.Hag.*v.Sym.Styl*.29(p.68.13); cf. προπορευομένων αὐτῶν λ. ποιοῦσι τὴν μικρὰν εἴσοδον *Lit.Chrys*.(p.367.30); *ib*.(p.372.23); met. ἡ πεντάφωτος...λ. ἡ σάρξ ἐστιν [ref. Mt.25:1–12] Meth.*symp*.6.3(p.67. 12; M.18.117B); τὰς τῆς πίστεως λ. Cyr.H.*catech*.1.1; **2.** *flame*, Eus. *Hierocl*.18(523C; M.22.824C); Chrys.*hom.21.2 in Rom*.(9.658B); id. *hom.5.5 in 1Cor*.(10.40E); id.*hom.10.2 in Eph*.(11.77C).

*__Λαμπετιανοί,__ οἱ, members of Euchite sect, otherwise called Messalians, Tim.CP *haer*.(M.86.48A); Max.*schol.d.n*.6.2(M.4.169D); Jo.D.*haer*.98(M.94.760B).

*__λαμπηδογλωσσ-έω,__ *speak with tongues of light* ἀστέρες ~οῦσιν Germ.CP *or*.4(M.98.356C).

*__λαμπηδοκόμος,__ v. *λαμπαδηκόμος.

λαμπηδών, ἡ, *brilliance of light*; **1.** of physical light in gen.; lamps in pagan rites, Const.ap.Eus.*v.C*.4.10(p.121.28; M.20.1157C); heavenly bodies, lightning, etc., id.*l.C*.1(p.197.28; M.20.1321B); *ib*. 6(p.207.31; 1344B); Ath.*gent*.29(M.25.57B); of light of eyes, Cyr.H. *catech*.12.30; Gr.Nyss.*v.Mos*.(M.44.325C); Chrys.*hom.63.4 in Mt*.(7. 632E); **2.** of principle of light opp. darkness in Gnost. (Sethian) system τὸ...σκότος...βιάζεται κατέχειν εἰς ἑαυτὸν τὴν λ. καὶ τὸν σπινθῆρα Hipp.*haer*.5.19(p.117.16; M.16.3179C); ἀντιποιεῖται τὸ σκότος τῆς λ. *ib*.(p.117.20; 3179D); λέγουσι...θεὸν...⟨ὃν⟩ ἐκ τῶν ὑδάτων καὶ...φωτὸς λαμπηδόνος γεγονέναι *ib*.10.11(p.272.2; 3426A); **3.** of supernatural light in visions and theophanies, Herm.*sim*.9.2.2; at martyrdom λ. ἐκ τοῦ οὐρανοῦ ἐξελθοῦσα κατηύγασεν αὐτόν *A.(Pass.) Andr*.14(p.33.12; M.2.1245A); ref. burning bush τοῦ φωτὸς τὴν λ. Gr.Nyss.*v.Mos*.(M.44.401B); ref. S. Paul's vision, Ammon.*Ac*.22:15 (M.85.1585C); **4.** fig. φιλοσοφία τῇ ἐκ τῆς θρυαλλίδος ἔοικεν λ. Clem.*str*. 5.5(p.345.4; M.8.52B); of Christ at parousia ὑπὲρ ἅπασαν...λ. φωτός Cyr.H.*catech*.4.15; Gr.Nyss.*or.catech*.26(p.99.8; M.45.69A); of Son's generation ἐκ...τοῦ ἡλιακοῦ κύκλου ἡ τοῦ φωτὸς λ. ἀπαυγάζεται id. *Eun*.8(2 p.108.13; M.45.773B); Mac.Mgn.*apocr*.4.15(p.186.5); **5.** met., of divine illumination, Ephr.3.406A; Isid.Pel.*epp*.1.32(M.78.201C); τοῦ Χριστοῦ φῶς...μεταδιδὸν ἡμῖν τῆς αὐτοῦ λ. †Jo.D.*B.J*.15(M.96. 996A); of sevenfold gifts of H. Ghost, Gr.Nyss.*v.Mos*.(M.44.384C); of scriptures, id.*hom.10 in Cant*.(M.44.980B); Chrys.*hom.1.1 in Rom*. (9.426B); of Christian doctrine, Mac.Mgn.*apocr*.4.30(p.226.19); ‡Chrys.*hom*.8(13.222A); of virtues and good works, Gr.Nyss.*v.Mos*. (389A); id.*hom.3 in Cant*.(808D); Mac.Mgn.*apocr*.4.13(p.178.8); Thdt.*2Cor*.8:23(3.332); †Jo.D.*B.J*.12(964B); **6.** *glory, distinction* ἴσην ἐπὶ πάντων ἐκέκτητο λ. Thdt.*Dan*.6:2(2.1177).

λαμπήνη (-πίνη), ἡ, **1.** *covered chariot*, Thdt.*qu.12 in Jud*.(1.331); λαμπίνη...εἶδος ἁρμαμάξης, ὥσπερ καὶ ἀπήνη. ... Ἀκύλας οὐκ εἶπε 'λ.' ἀλλὰ 'στρογγυλώσει' [ref. 1Reg.26:7] id.*qu.60 in 1Reg*.(1.396); exeg. Is.66:20 λ. ... σημαίνειν ἐοίκασι τὰ τῆς ἀναστάσεως σώματα...λ. διὰ τὴν ἐκλάμπουσαν αὐτοῖς δόξαν Eus.ad loc.(M.24.524A); Ἡσαΐας τὴν τῆς ἐκκλησίας κατάστασιν προφητεύων...λέγει...παῖδας ἐν λαμπήναις κομιζομένους...τὸν ἐν ἀρετῇ διαγράφει βίον...τῆς νηπιώδους ἡλικίας ὑποδεικνύων τὸ...ἄκακον Gr.Nyss.*hom.2 in Cant*.(M.44.793C); Thdt.*Ps*.41:5(1.872); **2.** *candle* διὰ...λαμπηνῶν πρὸς τοὺς νυκτερινοὺς διεγείρεις καμάτους Bas.*ep*.232(3.355C; M.32.864B).

*__λαμπούθιον,__ τό, *mould*, Dor.*doct*.7.1(M.88.1700C).

λαμπροειδής, *shining brightly, glorious*; of flesh of Christ, ‡Ath. *qu.al*.19(M.28.792A).

*__λαμπρόκλωστος,__ *brightly-spun* λ. νήματα πλέκειν Geo.Pis.*hex*. 1279(M.92.1532A).

*__λαμπροπυρσόμορφος,__ *of purple splendour*, ‡Gr.Naz.*Chr.pat*. 2055(M.38.299A).

λαμπρότης ἡ, **1.** *brightness*; of stars, Or.*Cels*.6.73(p.143.14; M.11.1409A); id.*princ*.3.1.19(p.232.15; M.11.292A); Const.ap.Gel.Cyz.*h.e*.2.7.3(M.85.1232D); of Christ's garments at Transfiguration, Or.*Cels*.6.68(p.138.21; 1401C); of God τὸν ἥλιον ἀμαυροῖ τῇ ἑαυτοῦ λαμπρότητι Meth.*fr.Job* 2(p.511.14); λ. θεοῦ καὶ ἰδεῖν καὶ παθεῖν Gr.Naz.*or*.38.11(M.36.324A); ref. angels ὑπέστησαν λαμπρότητες δεύτεραι, λειτουργοὶ τῆς πρώτης λ. *ib*.38.9(320C); of brightness of divine light, Const.ap.Gel.Cyz.*h.e*.2.7.7(1233B); *ib*.2.7.30(1240A); of soul μετὰ τὴν ἀνάστασιν...ἥξει...δεχομένη...τὴν λ. στολῆς σχήματι περιβεβλημένη τοῦ λόγου Meth.*symp*.8.5(p.87.14; M.18.145C); of new Jerusalem, Iren.*haer*.5.36.1(M.7.1222B); met., ref. scriptures τῇ κεκρυμμένῃ λ. τῶν δογμάτων Or.*princ*.4.1.7(p.304.2; 356A); of spiritual illumination ἡ γνῶσις, φέγγος καὶ λ. καταχέουσα τῶν πραγμάτων Clem.*ecl*.32(p.147.5; M.9.716B); θαυμαστήν τινα κόσμου λαμπρότητα σωτήριος προσήγαγε λογισμός Const.ap.Gel.Cyz.*h.e*.2.7.5(1233A); **2.** *beauty* of lily, Gr.Nyss.*hom.4 in Cant*.(M.44.840C); **3.** *whiteness* of milk, Mac.Mgn.*apocr*.3.23(p.104.1); **4.** *clarity*, Thdt.*1Cor*.1:20(3.170); **5.** *joy*, *1Clem*.35.2; μεταλαμβάνοντος τραπέζης μυστικῆς...μετὰ...λ.,...παρρησίας Chrys.*hom.1.3 in Eph*.(11.6D); **6.** *glory* τὰς τιμὰς [sc. in future life]...τὴν λ. Cyr.*Os*.9(3.30D); worldly *distinction, eminence* λ. κοσμική id.*Am*.33(3.286E); as honorific style of address, Ath.*apol.sec*.78(p.158.29; M.25.392B); Nil.*epp*.2.302(M.79.349B); Thdt.*ep*.76(4.1124).

λαμπροφανής, *appearing brightly*, Gel.Cyz.*h.e*.1.10.2(M.85.1212B).

λαμπροφεγγής, *shining brightly*, Germ.CP *or*.3.1(M.98.292C).

***λαμπροφορ-έω**, **1.** *wear bright robes, festal attire* χοροὺς...δικαίων ~οῦντας ‡Pall.*h.Laus*.46(M.34.1130D); Thdot.Anc.*hom.BMV et Sym*.1(M.77.1392A); οἱ μετ' ἐμοῦ ἐν τῇ παλιγγενεσίᾳ λαμπροφορήσουσι Andr.Caes.*Apoc*.7(M.106.244D); **2.** *be more resplendent* ὑπερέχει καὶ ~εῖ ἡ τῶν ἀγγέλων οὐσία τῆς οὐσίας τῶν ψυχῶν ἀνθρώπων ‡Ath.*qu.Ant*.27(M.28.613C).

***λαμπροφορία**, ἡ, *splendid attire*, Gr.Naz.*or*.25.2(M.35.1200A); ref. white garments of neophytes, *ib*.45.2(M.36.624C); τὸν πρὸς τὴν ἄνω λ. καλούμενον ἄνθρωπον CTrull.*can*.102; †Jo.D.*B.J*.29(M.96.1136B).

***λαμπροφόρος**, *brilliantly arrayed* τοῦ γὰρ νυμφίου Χριστοῦ βαπτιζομένου ἔδει τὸν οὐράνιον θάλαμον τὰς λ. ἀνοῖξαι πύλας †Hipp.*theoph*.6(p.261.2; M.10.857B); ἔβλεπέ τινα λ. ἐξερχόμενον ἐκ τοῦ ἱερατείου Dor.*doct*.11.6(M.88.1741A); esp. of Easter, *Poen.App*.1.1 cit. s. διακαινήσιμος; τῆς λ. ἡμέρας τῆς ἐγέρσεως Jo.D.*carm.pasch*.92(p.220; M.96.841D); and Low Sunday τῇ...κυριακῇ τῆς λ. [sc. ἡμέρας] *Const.Stud*.3(M.99.1705B).

***λάμπρυνσις**, ἡ, *making bright*, Didym.*Ps*.17:19(M.39.1249C).

λαμπρύν-ω, **1.** *brighten*, Ath.*gent*.27(M.25.53C); met. βεβαπτισμένας...ψυχὰς...λελαμπρυσμένας πίστει Ph.Carp.*Cant*.93(M.40.89B); ὁ Ἰσραὴλ τῇ εἰς Χριστὸν πίστει λελαμπρυμένος Cyr.*Os*.30(3.54E); *ib*.38(69D); *make bright and clean*, Bas.*hom*.1.6(2.5D; M.31.173A); ~ων ...τὴν ὑμετέραν διάθεσιν Chrys.*hom.17.1 in 2Cor*.(10.558D); **2.** *adorn*, pass. ἡ σώφρων γυνὴ...λευκὴ...τυγχάνει...ὅταν τὰς φρένας ᾖ λελαμπρυμένη *Hom.Clem*.13.16; οἵῳ χρὴ τὸν ἱερέα κόσμῳ ~εσθαι Gr.Nyss.*v.Mos*.(M.44.320A); **3.** *make distinguished* μητέρα...ἐλάμπρυνεν ἀρετῆς κατορθώμασι Thdt.*Rom*.16:13(3.159); in bad sense ~ης τῇ φιλοτιμίᾳ τὰς ἐπιδόσεις Gr.Nyss.*or.dom*.4(p.86.30; M.44.1173C); pass., *be distinguished*, Eus.*h.e*.3.5.1(M.20.221B); id.*v.C*.2.20(p.49.19; M.20.997C).

λαμπτήρ, ὁ, **1.** *lantern*, Nonn.*par.Jo*.18:3(M.43.889A); **2.** *lamp* in church, Paul.Sil.*Soph*.488(M.86.2138A); *ib*.893(2153A); **3.** *shining light*, met. Γρηγόριον...οἷον...λ. ... ἐν τῇ ἐκκλησίᾳ...διαλάμψαντα Bas.*Spir*.74(3.62C; M.32.205B); λ. τῆς εὐσεβείας Thdt.*Tit*.1:15(3.702).

***λάμπυρος**, ὁ, *fire-fly*, Geo.Pis.*hex*.1037(M.92.1511A).

λάμπ-ω, [λάψη for λαμ-, *CG-CI* 1.16 (Corinth, saec. iv)]; **1.** *shine*, of Christ φῶς ~ειν μέλλων Just.*dial*.113.5(M.6.737A); **2.** *be resplendent, shine forth*, of persons ἐν τῇ πρώτῃ παρουσίᾳ...τοσοῦτον ἔλαμψεν *ib*.121.3(757B); Eus.*theoph.fr*.5(p.17*.7; M.24.623C); Chrys.*stat*.5.3(2.63B); ‡Nil.*perist*.10.2(M.79.888D); of power of God, Or.*princ*.4.1.7(p.304.4; M.11.356A); of spiritual sense of Law revealed at Christ's coming, *ib*.4.1.6(p.301.14; M.11.352B); ὁ ~ων *shining one*, name given by Egyptians to planet Saturn, Jo.Mal.*chron*.2 p.25(M.97.92A).

***λαμυρῶς**, *wantonly*, Synes.*Dion* 1(p.235.7; M.66.1116A).

λάμψις, ἡ, *shining, brilliance*; of divine light, Ath.*decr*.17(p.15.5; M.25.445C).

***λανάτος**, ὁ, *woollen garment*, Dor.*doct*.4.3(M.88.1657A).

λανθάν-ω, **1.** *escape notice of* οὐδὲν λέληθεν αὐτὸν [sc. τὸν θεόν] τῶν ἐννοιῶν ἡμῶν *1Clem*.21.3; Ign.*Eph*.15.3; ἔλαθεν τὸν ἄρχοντα τοῦ αἰῶνος τούτου ἡ παρθενία Μαρίας καὶ ὁ τοκετὸς αὐτῆς, ὁμοίως καὶ ὁ θάνατος τοῦ κυρίου *ib*.19.1; θεὸν ἀδύνατον εἶναι ~εῖν Just.*1apol*.12.1(M.6.344A); **2.** ptcpl. in adv. phrases, *secretly, imperceptibly* ἐν τῷ λεληθότι †Gregent.*leg.Hom*.42(M.86.604C); Jo.Mal.*chron*.3 p.62(M.97.140B); εἰς τὸ λεληθὸς Eus.*l.C*.15(p.245.30; M.20.1416B); κατὰ τὸ λανθάνον Bas.*reg.fus*.6.1(2.344B; M.31.925B); κατὰ τὸ λεληθὸς id.*jud*.3(2.215B; M.31.656D); Pall.*h.Laus*.67(p.163.22; M.34.1235A).

λαξεία, ἡ, *sculpture*, ‡Caes.Naz.*dial*.140(M.38.1049).

λαξευτήριον, τό, *mason's chisel*, Eus.*h.e*.10.4.33(M.20.861C).

λαξευτής, ὁ, *mason*, ‡Jo.D.*Artem*.60(M.96.1308C).

λαξευτός, *hewn out of rock*; in gen., Thdt.*qu.32 in Lev*.(1.210); ‡Caes.Naz.*dial*.114(M.38.997); ref. Christ's tomb μνημείῳ λ. *A.Pil*.A 11(p.250); Or.*Cels*.1.69(p.191.4; M.11.904C); πέτραν λ. Germ.CP *or*.2(M.98.261A).

λαξεύω, **1.** *hew out* of rock, Eus.*theoph.fr*.3(p.14*.11; M.24.620A); Pall.*h.Laus*.48(p.142.11; M.34.1211B); **2.** *hollow out* ἐν πέτρᾳ λελαξευμένῃ καλύπτεται Jo.D.*hom*.4.30(M.96.632C); **3.** *carve* out of stone εἴδωλα ἐλαξεύσατε Thdr.Heracl.*Is*.2:18(M.18.1312A); πλάκας...ἃς ἐλάξευσε Μωυσῆς Hier.H.*cruc*.(M.40.865D); *cat.2Cor*.3:3(p.365.14); **4.** *cut away* ἀπάτην ἐκ τῶν ψυχῶν...λαξεύσαντες Ephr.3.463D.

***λαοβόρος**, *devouring people*, of Cerberus λ. κύων Synes.*hymn*.9.21(p.54; M.66.1613).

***λαοηγησία**, ἡ, *leadership of the people* (Israel), Just.*dial*.49.6(M.6.584D).

[*]**λαοξικός**, *of stone work*, Gr.Nyss.*ep*.25(M.46.1100A).

λαοξόος, ὁ, *sculptor*, Gr.Naz.*carm*.1.1.4.17(M.37.417A); Gr.Nyss.*ep*.25(M.46.1100A).

***λαοπλανής**, *deceiving the people*, Jo.D.*hom*.12.14(M.96.800A).

λαοπλάνος, *deceiving the people*, esp. of demons, pagan gods, and pagan or heret. ideas; ref. Montanist prophesying λ. πνεῦμα Anon.ap.Eus.*h.e*.5.16.8(M.20.468A); λ. δαιμόνιον Eus.*h.e*.7.17.1(680A); of pagan gods λ. δαιμόνων id.*p.e*.10.4(472C; M.21.785B); id.*l.C*.2(p.199.35; M.20.1328A); of pagan rites λαοπλάνου φάσματα κακίας *ib*.8(p.217.17; 1362A); λ. αἵρεσις [i.e. Arianism] Bas.*ep*.91(3.183C; M.32.476D); ref. Thphl. Al. καθάπερ λ. τις δαίμων Pall.*v.Chrys*.8(p.44.24; M.47.27); of demon impersonating Samuel, Thdt.*qu.63 in 1Reg*.(1.398); Anast.S.*qu.et resp*.39(M.89.581A); masc. as subst., Just.*dial*.69.7(M.6.640A); CCP(681)*act*.15(H.3.1377C); †Jo.D.*B.J*.23(M.96.1065D); λεωπ- *ib*.26(1104A, v.l. λαοπ-).

λαός, ὁ, *people*; **1.** in gen., of a number or crowd of people ἦλθον οἱ...βασιλεῖς...καὶ λ. πολὺς μετ' αὐτῶν *T.Jud*.3.1; ἐπανῆλθεν...Ἡσαῦ...ἐν λ. βαρεῖ καὶ ἰσχυρῷ *ib*.9.2; of a person's household retinue ὑμεῖς...ὁ ἐμὸς λ., ἐπιμελεῖσθε τὸν οἶκον *A.Thom*.B 18(p.32.9); ἐβάπτισεν αὐτὴν σὺν παντὶ τῷ λ. αὐτῆς *ib*.28(p.34.18); ὁ ἐν γυναιξὶ λ. Gr.Nyss.*hex*.4(M.44.65A); Leont.H.*monoph*.(M.86.1877C); συνελθόντων δὲ ἀπείρων λ. †Jo.D.*B.J*.26(M.96.1105B); **2.** *nation, people*; in gen., *Pss.Sal*.5.13; σὺ κριτὴς δίκαιος ἐπὶ πάντας τοὺς λ. τῆς γῆς *ib*.9.4; *ib*.17.48; πάντες οἱ λ. δοξάσουσι τὸν κύριον *T.Jud*.25.5; Just.*1apol*.36.2(M.6.385A); οἱ οὐ προσδοκήσαντες αὐτὸν λ. τῶν ἐθνῶν προσκυνήσουσιν αὐτὸν *ib*.49.1(400C); διὰ τοῦ λουτροῦ...ὃ ὑπὲρ τῆς ἀνομίας τῶν λ. τοῦ θεοῦ γέγονεν...ἐπιστεύσαμεν id.*dial*.14.1(M.6.504C); of heathen collectively, Clem.*paed*.3.8(p.261.20; M.8.613B); of Jews, gentiles, and Christians as three λαοί, id.*str*.6.5(p.452.26; M.9.261B); **3.** partic. of Israel as people of God, *1Clem*.55.6; *Barn*.8.1; περιτέτμηται ὁ λ. εἰς σφραγῖδα *ib*.9.6; Just.*1apol*.60.2(M.6.417A); id.*dial*.22.1(M.6.521A); πρεσβυτέρων τοῦ λ. *ib*.78.1(657A); παιδαγωγὸς ὁ κύριος τοῦ λ. τοῦ παλαιοῦ Clem.*paed*.1.7(p.124.14; M.8.320B); τῷ πρεσβυτέρῳ λ. πρεσβυτέρα διαθήκη...καὶ νόμος ἐπαιδαγώγει τὸν λ. *ib*.(p.124.30; 321A); *ib*.3.2(p.243.21; 573A); λ. εἰς περιποίησιν κληθέντες ὑπὸ θεοῦ εἶναι ὁ Ἑβραίων λ. Or.*Cels*.5.10(p.10.10; M.11.1193C); ὁ πρὸ ἡμῶν λ. καὶ μερὶς ὢν τοῦ θεοῦ id.*comm.in Mt*.17.6(p.591.14; M.13.1488A); προσέταξεν ὁ θεὸς τῷ πρώτῳ λ. Meth.*arbitr*.18(p.194.11); *Hom.Clem*.18.18; προφητῶν τινος τῷ προτέρῳ λ. διακονησαμένου Eus.*Marcell*.1.1(p.3.12; M.24.716B); id.*e.th*.2.22(p.132.32; M.24.960B); Cyr.H.*catech*.19.2; *Const.App*.2.1.4; ἡ θεολογία...ἄρχοντα τοῦ Ἰουδαίων λ. τὸν Μιχαὴλ ὀνομάζουσα Dion.Ar.*c.h*.9.2(M.3.260B); *ib*.9.4(261D); **4.** of Church τοὺς πλανωμένους τοῦ λ. σου ἐπίστρεψον *1Clem*.59.4; *2Clem*.2.3; *Barn*.3.6; αὐτὸς ἑαυτῷ τὸν λ. τὸν καινὸν ἑτοιμάζων *ib*.5.7; ἴδωμεν δέ, εἰ οὗτος ὁ λ. κληρονομεῖ ἢ ὁ πρῶτος *ib*.13.1; Herm.*sim*.5.5.2; λ. ὁ εἰς αὐτὸν πιστεύειν προεγνωσμένος Just.*dial*.70.5(M.6.641A); τοῦ νέου καθηγεμὼν λ. Clem.*paed*.1.7(p.124.14; M.8.320B); ἐκ τοῦ λ. τοῦ κυριακοῦ id.*str*.7.16(p.72.18; M.9.541B); λ. δ' εἶδον ἐκεῖ [i.e. at Rome] λαμπρὰν σφραγῖδαν ἔχοντα Aberc.*epitaph*.9; ἵνα γεννήσῃ τὸν λ. ἡ νοητὴ Σιὼν τὸν ἄρσενα...εἰς τὴν ἑνότητα τοῦ κυρίου καταντήσαντα Meth.*symp*.8.7(p.90.1; M.18.149B); Cyr.H.*catech*.4.24(ed.); **5.** *congregation* πᾶς ὁ παρὼν λ. ἐπευφημεῖ λέγων, ἀμήν... εὐχαριστήσαντος δὲ τοῦ προεστῶτος, καὶ ἐπευφημήσαντος παντὸς τοῦ λ. Just.1apol.65.3(M.6.428B); cf.Hipp.*trad.ap*.16.1; Corn.ap.Eus. *h.e*.6.43.10(M.20.621A); πάντας τοὺς εἰσιόντας εἰς τὴν ἐκκλησίαν...μὴ κοινωνοῦντας δὲ εὐχῆς ἅμα τῷ λ. ... ἀποβλήτους γίνεσθαι τῆς ἐκκλησίας CAnt.(341)*can*.2; Serap.*euch*.4.1; Bas.*ep*.190.1(3.282C; M.32.697A); of Montanist congregations, Epiph.*haer*.49.2(p.243.6; M.41.881A); ποιμαίνοντα [sc. bishop] τὸν λ. σου *Lit.Jac*.(p.208.6); **6.** *laity*; **a.** in Israel, Thdt.*qu.34 in Dt*.(1.282); ἱερεῖς παρανομίᾳ συζήσαντες τιμωρίᾳ παραδοθήσονται, τινὲς δὲ εἰς τὸν τοῦ λαοῦ τελοῦντες κατάλογον, εἰς τὸ ἐκείνων μεταβήσονται τάγμα id.*Is*.24:2(p.97.37; 2.290); **b.** Christian τὴν εὐχαριστίαν τινὲς διανείμαντες...αὐτὸν δὴ ἕκαστον τοῦ λ. λαβεῖν τὴν μοῖραν ἐπιτρέπουσιν Clem.*str*.1.1(p.5.19; M.8.692B); Eus.*v.C*.3.24 (p.89.9; M.20.1085A); *ib*.4.71(p.147.3; 1225B); Ath.*ep.encycl*.2(p.170.24; M.25.225B); *ib*.5(p.174.1; 232C); id.*apol.sec*.63(p.142.28; M.25.364A); ἐν Ἀλεξανδρείᾳ δὲ καὶ ἐν Αἰγύπτῳ ἕκαστος καὶ τῶν ἐν λ. τελούντων...ἔχει κοινωνίαν ἐν τῷ οἴκῳ αὐτοῦ, καὶ ὅτε βούλεται, μεταλαμβάνει δι' ἑαυτοῦ Bas.*ep*.93(3.187A; M.32.485A); *ib*.188 *can*.1(269A; M.665A); τὸ γάρ, 'δεηθῶμεν', οὐ τοῖς ἱερεῦσι λέγεται μόνον, ἀλλὰ καὶ τοῖς εἰς τὸν λ. συντελοῦσιν Chrys.*hom.2.5 in 2Cor*.(10.435D); Pall. *v.Chrys*.16(p.97.16; M.47.55); *ib*.18(p.116.22; M.47.65); Thdt.*h.e*.2.24.13(3.890); ὑπὲρ εὐχῆς ...παντὸς τοῦ κλήρου καὶ τοῦ λ. *IGC As.Min*.144 (Cos, saec. v–vi); Dion.Ar.*e.h*.3.3.4(M.3.429C); ἱερεῖς ἀποχειροτονεῖ τοὺς ἠξιωμένους ἀγαθότητι φέρειν τὰ ἀγνοήματα τοῦ λ. id.*ep*.8.4(M.3.1096A); *Lit.Jac*.(p.208.10).

λαοσσόος, *saving the people*, Nonn.*par.Jo*.1:6(M.43.749B); *ib*. 7:31(809B); *ib*.12:54(849A).

λαοτομέω, *hew out*, †Cyr.*coll.VT*(6⁴.59A; M.77.1261C) cit. s. λάκκος.

***λαοτόρος, ὁ**, *designer in stone*, Paul.Sil.*ambo*.263(M.86.2261B); id. *Soph*.648(M.86.2144A); *ib*.605(2142B).

λαοτύπος, ὁ, *stone-mason*, Paul.Sil.*ambo*.155(M.86.2257B); *ib*.265 (2261B).

λαργιτίων, ἡ, (Lat. *largitio*) *imperial treasury*, Jo.Mal.*chron*.16 p.398(M.97.589A); cf. λαργιτίωνες, τουτέστιν ὅπου αἱ δημόσιαι εἴσοδοι εἰς δημοσίας ἀναλίσκονται χρείας *Schol*.ad loc.(590D); usu. in title of count of the sacred largesses ὁ...λαργιτιόνων κόμης Petr.II Al.*encycl*.ap.Thdt.*h.e*.4.22.10(3.990); Nil.*epp*.2.304 tit.(M.79.349B); κόμης τῶν θείων λαργιτιώνων Cyr.*ep*.28(p.252.20; 5².92A); Jo.Mal. *chron*.16 p.400(593A); *Chron.Pasch*.p.308(M.92.785B); Thphn.*chron*. p.158(M.108.428B).

***λάρδιον, τό**, *ham*, Leont.N.*v.Sym*.48(M.93.1729B).

***λαρνακίδιον, τό**, *little box*, Steph.Diac.*v.Steph*.(M.100.1180C).

λάρναξ, ἡ, 1. *ark*; of Noah, *Hom.Clem*.8.17; Eus.*onomast*.(p.4.6); Const.*or.s.c*.11(p.168.27; M.20.1256A); Epiph.*haer*.1.6(p.173.8; M.41.180B); *ib*.1.7(p.173.12; 180B); *ib*.26.1(p.276.15; 333A); **2.** *coffin* or *sarcophagus*, Eus.*v.C*.4.60(p.145.8; M.20.1212A); Chrys.*hom.27.4 in Mt*.(7.331C); id.*hom.24.3 in Ac*.(9.197B); id.*hom.7.2 in Col*.(11.374B); Jo.Ant.*ep.senat.CP*(p.128.11; M.83.1445C); Thdt.*h.e*.3.10.3 (3.923); ‡Jo.D.*Artem*.20(M.96.1270C).

λαρυγγίζ-ω, 1. *make a guttural sound* ~ειν μίμησίς ἐστι φωνῆς, ὅτ' ἄν τις...ἐπιβήσει τῇ φωνῇ καὶ στενοῖ αὐτήν, ὥστε δοκεῖν ἐν τῷ λαρυγγιᾶν παρακατέχεσθαι Cosm.Mel.*schol*.(M.38.630); **2.** *declaim loudly* σὺ τί καυχᾶσαι ~ων ἁπλῶς, καὶ οὐ πράττων; Isid.Pel.*epp*.1.88 (M.78.244B); Gennad.*fr.Gen*.1:1(M.85.1624C); **3.** *shout*, Cyr.*Jo*.5.1 (4.469E).

λαρύγγιον, τό, dim. of λάρυγξ, *throat*, *Apophth.Patr*.(M.65.365A).

***λαρύγγισμα, τό**, *mouthing* πομφόλυγας διὰ κενῶν λ. ἐξερευγομένη Germ.CP *vit.term*.1(M.98.89B); Jo.D.*hom*.12.1(M.96.784A); ‡Meth. *Sym.et Ann*.10(M.18.373B).

***λασιόομαι**, *be hairy*, Leont.H.*Nest*.4.36(M.86.1704D).

[*]**λασιοτριχής**, *with hairy skin*, Cyr.*glaph.Gen*.3(1.102A).

***λατέρκουλον, τό**, (Lat. *laterculum*) *instructions issued to praetor on assuming office*, Justn.*nov*.24.6(p.194.33).

***Λατινίδης, ὁ**, a *Latin*, *Orac.Sib*.5.1; *ib*.12.1.

Λατινίς, ἡ, 1. as subst., *Latium* Λατινίδος ἔκγονε 'Ρώμη (codd. 'Ρώμης) *Orac.Sib*.3.356; *ib*.8.75; **2.** as adj., *Latin* Λ. ἀρχῆς *Roman empire*, Thphyl.*exc.gent*.6(p.484.25; M.113.945B).

λατόμος, ὁ, 1. *stone-mason*, Herm.*sim*.9.9.2; Thdt.*qu.23 in 3Reg*. (1.467); *M.Artem*.(p.172.7); ‡Jo.D.*Artem*.60(M.96.1308B); **2.** *engraver*, met. τῶν σῶν καρδιῶν λατόμος, ὥστε ἐν ταύταις τὰ θεῖα λόγια ἐγκεχαράχθαι Gr.Nyss.*v.Mos*.(M.44.428C).

λατρεία, ἡ, *service*;

A. secular, ref. Lev.23:3 πᾶν ἔργον λατρευτὸν...λ. ἐνταῦθα τὴν δουλείαν καλεῖ Isid.Pel.*epp*.1.71(M.78.232A).

B. of service of God in gen. διὰ τῆς ἐμῆς πρὸς θεὸν λ. τὰ πανταχοῦ εἰρηνεύεται Const.ap.Ath.*apol.sec*.86(p.165.21; M.25.404B); id.ap. Eus.*v.C*.4.9(p.121.15; M.20.1157B); CAnc.(358)*ep.syn*.ap.Epiph. *haer*.73.2(p.269.14; M.42.405A).

C. esp. *worship*; **1.** of Jewish cultus ποῦ ἡ λ., ὁ ναός, αἱ θυσίαι; Or.*hom.4.2 in Jer*.(p.24.30; M.13.288C); as σωματικὴ λ., Heracleon ap.eund.*Jo*.13.17(p.241.23; M.14.428A); as συμβολικὴ λ., Eus.*h.e*.1.3.4(M.20.69B); πρόσκαιρος γὰρ ἡ λ., καὶ πρὸς ὀλίγον ἀνθήσασα †Bas.*Is*. 21(1.393D; M.30.153C); τὴν τοπικὴν λ. ἑτέρως μετεποίησεν *Const. App*.6.23.5; παλαιᾶς λ. καὶ πολιτείας Chrys.*hom.4.4 in Ac.princ*.(3.87D); id.*hom.51.3 in Jo*.(8.302C); τῆς ἐν νόμῳ λ. ἡ δύναμις οὐκ ἀπόχρη πρὸς κάθαρσιν Cyr.*ador*.9(1.312C); **2.** pagan, *Diogn*.3.2; Arist.*apol*.2.1; ματαίαν λ. *Hom.Clem*.9.7; [sc. ἀποτάσσομαί σοι, σατανᾶ,] καὶ πάσῃ τῇ λ. σου. λ. δέ ἐστι διαβόλου, ἡ ἐν εἰδωλείοις εὐχή Cyr.H.*catech*.19.8; δαιμόνων λ. Gr.Nyss.*Eun*.8(2 p.177.22; M.45.769C); λ. τῶν πονηρῶν πνευμάτων *Const.App*.2.28.8; Oecum.*Apoc*. 13:8(p.153); **3.** of Christian worship in gen.: as heavenly, opp. typical worship of Law, Or.*hom.4.2 in Jer*.(p.24.30; M.13.288C); Chrys.*hom.80.2 in Jo*.(8.475A); τῆς ἐν πνεύματι λ. ἱερουργοί id.ap.*cat. Heb*.2:1(p.141.28); Esaias *or*.1(p.5); identified with προσκύνησις, ref. worship to be paid to H. Ghost, Gr.Nyss.*Maced*.14(M.45.1317C); *ib*. 23(1329C); Cyr.*ador*.9(1.309B); esp. of eucharistic worship, Apoll. *fid.sec.pt*.9(p.170.17; M.10.1108D); Epiph.*haer*.75.3(p.334.30; M.42.505C); id.*exp.fid*.22(p.524.1; M.42.828C); μυστικῆς λ. *Lit*.ap.*Const. App*.8.15.11; *Lit.Marc*.(*PStrasb*.12 r°); *Lit.Jac*.(p.194.10); **4.** of daily morning and evening prayer, Chrys.*hom.6.1 in 1Tim*.(11.579A); **5.** of preaching as priestly sacrifice, part of apostolic λειτουργία and ἱερουργία which is more than ἁπλῶς λ., id.*hom.29.1 in Rom*. (9.731A); **6.** *cult, mode of worship* εἰς τὴν Ἀρείου μετεβαπτίσατο λ. Thdr.Lect.*fr*.(M.86.224B); ἡ...τῆς πλάνης λ. ταῖς ἐκκλησίαις ἐπεισέφρησε ‡Just.*qu.et resp*.100(M.6.1344D); **7.** *service, act of worship* τὰς ὑπὲρ βασιλέως διηνεκεῖς ἐξετέλουν λ. Eus.*v.C*.1.17(p.16.28; M.20.933A); οὐκ ἦν ὥρα ἡμερινὴ οὐδὲ νυκτερινή, ἐν ᾗ τὰς λ. οὐκ ἐπετέλουν [sc. Oxyrhynchus monks] τῷ θεῷ ‡Pall.*h.mon*.5.4(p.29.13; M.65.448A); **8.** λογικὴ λ. (exeg. Rom.12:1), interpreted of Christian service to God as ἀναίμακτος θυσία opp. pagan animal sacrifices, Athenag.*leg*.13.2(M.6.916C); πνεῦμά εἰσιν οἵτινες κατὰ ἀλήθειαν καὶ οὐ κατὰ πλάνην προσκυνοῦσιν Heracleon ap.Or.*Jo*.13.25(p.249.4; M.14.441A); τί δέ ἐστι λογικὴ λ.; ἡ πνευματικὴ διακονία, ἡ πολιτεία ἡ κατὰ Χριστόν. ... ἐὰν καθ' ἑκάστην ἡμέραν προσφέρῃς αὐτῷ θύματα, καὶ ἱερεὺς τοῦ οἰκείου σώματος γίνῃ καὶ τῆς κατὰ ψυχὴν ἀρετῆς· οἷον, ὅταν σωφροσύνην προσενέγκῃς...ταῦτα γὰρ ποιῶν, ἀναφέρεις λογικὴν λ., τουτέστιν, οὐδὲν ἔχουσαν σωματικόν, οὐδὲν παχύ, οὐδὲν αἰσθητόν Chrys.*hom.20.2 in Rom*.(9.658C); τί δέ ἐστιν ἡ λογικὴ λ.; τὰ διὰ ψυχῆς, τὰ διὰ πνεύματος...ὅσα μὴ δεῖται σώματος, ὅσα μὴ δεῖται ὀργάνων, μὴ τόπων·...οἷον ἐπιείκεια, σωφροσύνη id.*hom.11.3 in Heb*. (12.115A); cf.Thdt.*Rom*.12:1(3.129); of eucharistic oblation, *Lit.Jac*. (p.194.10); **9.** in iconoclastic controversy, λ. as being directed to God dist. from προσκύνησις of saints, sacred objects, etc., Jo.D. *imag*.1.14(M.94.1244A) cit. s. προσκύνησις; Taras.*ep*.1(M.98.1433C); CNic.(787)*act*.6(H.4.441C); τιμητικὴν προσκύνησιν ἀπονέμειν, οὐ μὴν τὴν κατὰ πίστιν ἡμῶν ἀληθινὴν λ., ἣ πρέπει μόνῃ θείᾳ φύσει *Symb. Nic*.(787)(H.4.456A); λ. being offered only to Trin., Thdr.Stud.*epp*. 2.151(M.99.1472B); **10.** dist. from δουλεία, cf. λατρεία *vero secundum consuetudinem...aut semper, aut tam frequenter ut pene semper, ea dicitur servitus quae pertinet ad colendum deum*, Aug. *de civitate dei* 10.1.2(M.*PL*.41.278); *at illo cultu, quae graece* λατρεία *dicitur, latine uno verbo dici non potest, cum sit quaedam proprie divinitati debita servitus, nec colimus, nec colendum docemus, nisi unum deum*, id. *c.Faustum* 20.21(M.*PL*.42.385).

λατρεύς, ὁ, *worshipper*; plur., *A.Thom*.A 131(p.239.4, v.l. λάτραι); Bas.*ep*.45(3.134A; M.32.368A).

***λατρευτέον**, *one must worship* λ. θεῷ τῷ κατὰ φύσιν μόνῳ Cyr. *ador*.1(1.40A); ref. orthodox distn. of λατρεία from προσκύνησις in iconoclastic controversy τῇ Χριστοῦ εἰκόνι οὐ λ. Thdr.Stud.*epp*.2.161(M.99.1504A); προσκυνητέον...τῇ εἰκόνι...οὐ λ. *ib*.2.212(1640D).

***λατρευτέος**, v. λατρευτός.

***λατρευτής, ὁ**, *worshipper*; of God, Just.*dial*.64.1(M.6.621C); of Baal, Isid.Pel.*epp*.1.69(M.78.229A); ref. S. Joseph οὐκ ἔτι...ὡς ἀνήρ, ἀλλ' ὡς λ. ... ἐξυπηρετεῖτο...τῇ λεγομένῃ γυναικὶ...Μαρίᾳ Nil.*epp*.1.271(M.79.181C).

λατρευτικός, *of the nature of worship* or *adoration* ἐπ' αὐτοῦ δὴ Χριστοῦ λ. ἡ προσκύνησις...ἐπὶ δὲ τῆς εἰκόνος, ἡ αὐτὴ μέν, σχετικὴ δὲ ὅμως ἤγουν ὁμωνυμική Thdr.Stud.*epp*.2.85(M.99.1329A).

***λατρευτικῶς**, *by way of worship* (as offered to God alone), †Gr. II Papa *ep.Leon*.1(H.4.5C) cit. s. προσκύνησις; *Euchol*.(p.255) cit. s. σχετικῶς.

λατρευτός, 1. *to be worshipped* οὐδὲ λ. ἡ κτίσις Epiph.*anc*.70(p.87.

14; M.43.145C) = id.*haer*.74.7(p.323.14; v.l. λατρευτέα M.42.488C); Jo.V H.*icon*.3(M.96.1352B); Thdr.Stud.*epp*.2.151(M.99.1472B) cit. s. λατρεύω; **2.** *servile* (Lev.23:3), Isid.Pel.*epp*.1.71(M.78.232A); Jo.D. *hom*.4.29(M.96.632A).

***λατρευτῶς**, = λατρευτικῶς: λ. ... προσακτέον τὴν προσκύνησιν τῷ ...Χριστῷ Thdr.Stud.*epp*.2.212(M.99.1640A).

λατρεύ-ω, **1.** *serve, be a slave* γῇ...οὐδ' εἰσέτι ~ουσα *Orac.Sib*.2.31; **2.** *serve* God, *worship*; **a.** pagan ἔθνη...χειρῶν ἔργοις ~οντα Just. *1apol*.53.6(M.6.408A); δαίμονες...δικαστὰς ἔχοντες...~οντας id. *2apol*.1.2(M.6.444A); αὐτοῖς [sc. demons] καὶ τοῖς ~ουσιν αὐτοῖς ἐσομένης ἐν πυρὶ αἰωνίῳ κολάσεως *ib*.8.4(457B); Or.*hom.5.3 in Jer*. (p.34.6; M.13.300B); in anti-Arian argument πῶς δὲ προσκυνῶν τὸν Χριστὸν ὁ...ἀπόστολος, τοὺς τῇ κτίσει ~οντας παρὰ τὸν κτίσαντα, εἰδωλολατρεῖν διορίζεται; ἢ γὰρ οὐκ ἂν προσεκύνησεν εἰ κτιστὸς ἦν, ἢ οὐκ ἂν τοῖς εἰδωλολάτραις συνέταξε τοὺς τῇ κτίσει ~οντας· ἵνα μὴ καὶ αὐτὸς εἰδωλολατρεῖν δόξῃ, προσάγων τῷ κτιστῷ τὴν προσκύνησιν Gr. Nyss.*Eun*.2(2 p.339.13; M.45.516A); ἔθνη...τρέχει ἐπὶ τὰ εἴδωλα τοῦ λ. αὐτοῖς *Const.App*.2.60.2; Cyr.*ador*.9(1.313E); of worship of mammon in place of God, *Const.App*.3.7.4; **b.** OT and Christian; **i.** in gen. τῶν ἐν καθαρᾷ συνειδήσει ~όντων τῷ...ὀνόματι αὐτοῦ *1Clem*.45.7; ᾧ πᾶσα πνοὴ ~ει Polyc.*ep*.2.1; of serving God in Christian life, Serap.*euch*.20.2; διὰ τῆς ἁπλῆς...ὁμολογίας ~οντες τῷ κυρίῳ Bas.*ep*.172(3.260D; M.32.648B); *ib*.235.3(360C; M.876A); in anti-Arian argument εἰ μὴ ἀΐδιος θεὸς ὁ υἱός, ἐξ ἀνάγκης πρόσφατος· εἰ μὴ ἀληθινός, ψευδής· εἰ μὴ φύσει, θέσει. ἀσεβῶν δὲ προσφάτοις καὶ ψευδέσι καὶ μὴ φύσει ~ειν...ἀσεβεῖς οἱ οὕτω Χριστῷ ~οντες Didym. (‡Bas.)*Eun*.4(1.287A; M.29.689C); εἰ δὲ προσκυνοῦντες αὐτῷ, καὶ τῷ πατρὶ...προσκυνοῦμεν, καὶ αὐτῷ μόνῳ ~ομεν· μία ἄρα θεότης πατρὸς καὶ υἱοῦ ‡Ath.*dial.Trin*.3.7(M.28.1213A); τοῖς τριάδι ~ουσι Jo.D. *hom*.1.1(M.96.545A); **ii.** in iconoclastic controversy dist. by orthodox from προσκυνέω (formerly synonymous), cf.†Gr.II Papa *ep. Leon*.1(H.4.5C); ἵνα μὴ ὡς θεὸς ~ομένη προσκυνῆται ἡ κτίσις Jo.D. *imag*.1.15(M.94.1244C); προσεκύνησεν...Δανιὴλ ἀγγέλῳ θεοῦ, ἀλλ' οὐκ ἐλάτρευσε. ἕτερον γάρ ἐστι λατρείας προσκύνησις *ib*.1.8(1240B); *ib*.3. 33–41(1352A–1357C) cit. s. προσκυνέω; προσκυνοῦμεν ἁγίοις, ἀλλ' οὐ ~ομεν αὐτοῖς Thdr.Stud.*ep.imag*.(M.99.504B); but former usage also continues προσκυνήσωμεν καὶ λατρεύσωμεν μόνῳ τῷ κτίστῃ Jo.D. *imag*.3.41(1357A); cf. ~εται ὁ Χριστὸς ἐν τῇ αὐτοῦ εἰκόνι· ὥστε καὶ ἡ εἰκὼν λατρευτή Thdr.Stud.*epp*.2.151(M.99.1472B).

***λάτρης, ὁ,** *worshipper*; in gen., Ath.*Ar*.3.32(M.26.392B); Jo.D. *haer*.epilog.(M.94.780C); Christol. κἂν εἰ γέγονεν ἄνθρωπος λ. ἔχει τὸν οὐρανόν Cyr.*Nest*.4.6(6¹.117B; λάτριν p.89.42); μὴ γὰρ ὅτι ἱερεὺς λέγεται, λ. καὶ λειτουργὸς μόνον...νοείσθω Leont.H.*Nest*.5(M.86. 1729A).

λάτρις, ὁ, *servant*, of Gabriel λ. ... θεοῦ Sophr.H.*or*.2.26(M.87. 3249B).

***λαύορον, τό,** v. *λάβαρον.

λαύρα, ἡ, **1.** *alley, lane* in a city, Ath.*h.Ar*.58(p.216.8; M.25. 764C); ἀμφόδων ἤτοι λ. ἐπιχωρίως καλουμένων ὑπὸ τῶν τὴν Ἀλεξανδρέων κατοικούντων πόλιν Epiph.*haer*.69.1(p.152.25; λαβρῶν M.42. 204A); **2.** *monastery*, collection of individual cells of monks gathered together under one leader; described φροντιστήρια καὶ τὰς καλουμένας λ.· ἐν οἷς ἡ μὲν δίαιτα διάφορος, ἡ δέ γε πολιτεία εἰς ἕνα τελευτᾷ θεοφιλῆ σκοπόν. οἱ μὲν γὰρ ἀγεληδὸν ζῶντες οὐδενὶ τῶν εἰς γῆν βριθόντων κρατοῦνται...ὡς καὶ τὴν πάντων ἐσθῆτα ἑνὸς εἶναι δοκεῖν καὶ τὴν ἑνὸς ἁπάντων. καὶ κοινὴ τράπεζα παρατίθεται...κοινὰς δὲ τὰς πρὸς θεὸν λιτὰς διημερεύουσί τε καὶ διανυκτερεύουσιν Evagr. *h.e*.1.21(p.29.24; M.86.2477A); in gen. ἔμεινεν εἰς τὸν Καλαμῶνα...καὶ ἄλλος γέρων ἠσθένει εἰς τὴν ἄλλην λ. *Apophth.Patr*.32(M.65.401D); ἀπέκρυψεν ἑαυτὸν ἐν κελλίῳ ἔξω τῆς λ. ἡσυχάζοντι *ib*.(432B); διάκονον ...τῆς λ. τοῦ ἀββᾶ Γερασίμου Zos.*alloquia* 13(M.78.1697A); λαβὼν τινὰς τῆς λ. ἐπιτηδείους...κτίζει εὐκτήριον καὶ κελλία κύκλῳ· καὶ καταστήσας τινὰς τῆς Μεγίστης λ. ἐκεῖσε...λ. τὸν τόπον συνεστήσατο Ἑπτάστομον ταύτην ἐπονομάσας Cyr.S.*v.Sab*.39(p.130.22); εὐδόκησεν ὁ θεὸς κοινόβιον ταύτην γενέσθαι τὴν λ. id.*v.Euthym*.39(p.58.29); συνέβη κτίζεσθαι τὸ κατὰ βορρᾶν ἔξω τῆς λ. κοινόβιον πρὸς τὸ ἐκεῖσε τοὺς ἀποτασσομένους τῷ βίῳ τὴν μοναχικὴν πρότερον εἰς αὐτὸ παιδεύεσθαι ἀκρίβειαν, εἶθ' οὕτως εἰς τὴν λ. οἰκεῖν τὸν κοινοβιακὸν κανόνα ἀκριβῶς διδαχθέντας, τοῦ...Σάβα...λέγοντος ὅτι ὥσπερ ἄνθος προηγεῖται καρποφορίας, οὕτως ὁ κοινοβιακὸς βίος τοῦ ἀναχωρητικοῦ προηγεῖται id.*v.Jo.Hes*.6 (p.206.4); ἐν τῇ λ. τοῦ ἐν ἁγίοις πατρὸς ἡμῶν Σάβα Jo.Mosch.*prat*.3 (M.87.2853C); *ib*.4(2856B); τὴν λ. τῶν Πυργίων τοῦ Ἰορδάνου *ib*.5 (2856C); τὸν πρεσβύτερον τῆς λ. τοῦ ἀββᾶ Γερασίμου *ib*.12(2861A); Jo. Clim.*past*.14(M.88.1200D); τῶν ἁγίων πατέρων τῆς καθ' ἡμᾶς λ. Ant. Mon.*ep.Eust*.(M.89.1421C).

***λαυραγόρης,** v. λαβραγόρης.

***λαυρᾶτον, τό,** *laurel-wreathed portrait of emperor* θείων λ. ἐπ' εὐτυχίᾳ οἰκουμενικῇ εἰσερχομένων καὶ ἐν τῇ...Ἀλεξανδρείᾳ Sophr.Al. *libell*.(p.24.8; H.2.337B); †Gr.II Papa *ep.Leon*.1(H.4.12A); Thphn. *chron*.p.247(M.108.620A); in anti-iconoclastic argument βασιλέων λαυράτοις...ἀπαντῶσι λαοὶ μετὰ κηρῶν καὶ θυμιαμάτων οὐ τὴν... σανίδα τιμῶντες ἀλλὰ τὸν βασιλέα Thds.Am.*libell*.(H.4.45B).

***λαυρήτης, ὁ,** (prob. for λαυρίτης) *dweller in a λαύρα*, Jo.Mosch. *prat*.4(M.87.2856B).

***λαυρίζω,** *burn furiously*, Thphn.*chron*.p.331(M.108.800A).

λαῦρος, = λάβρος, *violent*, Or.*exp.in Pr*.28:3(M.17.241D); Ast. Am.*hom*.8(M.40.269A); Nil.*epp*.4.14(M.79.556D).

***λαύρως,** *violently*, Amph.*Seleuc*.120(M.37.1585A).

λάφυξις, ἡ, *gluttony*, Gr.Naz.*carm*.1.2.34.89(M.37.952A).

λαφυραγωγέω, *carry off as booty*, Philost.*h.e*.7.10(M.65.549A); met. ὁ διάβολος ἡμᾶς...λαφυραγωγήσας Nil.*epp*.2.238(M.79.321C); Manich. τὴν οὐσίαν τῆς ψυχῆς...ὑπὸ...τοῦ πονηροῦ λαφυραγωγηθεῖσαν Serap.*Man*.51(p.72; M.18.1248D).

λαφυραγωγία, ἡ, **1.** *plundering*, Pall.*v.Chrys*.3(p.18.27; M.47.13); Socr.*h.e*.6.6.13(M.67.677B); **2.** *booty*, Epiph.*haer*.55.9(p.335.15; M. 41.988A); Cyr.*ador*.5(1.144A).

λαφυραγωγός, ὁ, *plunderer*, Men.*exc.Rom*.3(p.185.16; M.113. 873B).

***λαφυρία, ἡ,** *booty*, ‡Caes.Naz.*dial*.188(M.38.1165).

λάφυρον, τό, *piece of booty, spoil*; **1.** lit., Gr.Nyss.*virg*.13(p.307. 27; M.46.380C); id.*Eun*.10(2 p.233.29; M.45.836B); Chrys.*pan.Bab*. 2.21(2.572E); Isid.Pel.*epp*.2.92(M.78.537A); **2.** met., ref. Christ's spoiling of Devil τὰ λ. κρέμαται ἄνω...ἐπὶ τοῦ σταυροῦ Chrys.*coemet*. 3(2.402B); of S. Paul as spoil taken from Devil, id.*hom.19.3 in Ac*. (9.156D); of penitent thief as spoil with which Christ entered paradise, Sever.ap.*cat.Lc*.23:43(p.170.26); of soul (in Manich. doctrine) as spoil taken from God, Serap.*Man*.51(p.72; M.18.1248D).

***λαχάνη, ἡ,** *dish of vegetables*, Dor.*doct*.7.6(M.88.1705A).

λαχανηφόρος, *producing herbs*, Gr.Naz.*ep*.26(M.37.61B).

λαχανοειδής, *like vegetables*, ‡Ath.*pat*.(M.26.1300C).

***λαχνιστήριον, τό,** *casting of lots, sortilegium* (by opening Bible), permitted, when preceded by prayer, as opp. recourse to diviners, Anast.S.*qu.et resp*.108(M.89.761A).

***λαχνός, ὁ,** *lot*, Ath.Scholast.*coll*.18.4(p.165).

λαψάνη, ἡ, *charlock*, Pall.*h.Laus*.32(p.95.9; M.34.1105B).

***λαψάνιον, τό,** = foreg., *V.Pach.A* 15(p.139.5).

***λεανώμενος,** prob. f.l. for λεαινόμενος, Didym.*Ps*.17:43(M.39. 1261D).

λέβης, ὁ, *cauldron, basin*; as instrument of torture, *M.Con*.5.5 (p.66.10); *M.Thdot.1* 22(p.75.9).

λεβητάριον, τό, *small metal basin* κομίζεται ὕδωρ θερμότατον εἰς μικρὸν λ. καὶ κιρνῶσιν ἐξ αὐτοῦ τὰ προκείμενα τῇ θείᾳ τραπέζῃ ‡Germ. CP *contempl*.(M.98.449B).

***λεβητονάριον, τό,** a garment, Pach.*reg*.A,B(p.17.11, v.l. λεβιτωνάρια; λευιτωνάρια M.40.952A).

***λεβιτών, ὁ,** v. *λευιτών.

***λεγατάριος, *λεγατεύω, *λεγάτον,** v. *ληγ-.

λεγεών (λεγιών), ὁ, (Lat. *legio*); **1.** *legion*, Or.*hom.13.1 in Jer*. (p.102.11; M.13.400B); Eus.*h.e*.5.5.1(M.20.441A); of legions of angels λ. ὄντων ἀγγέλων τῶν τεταγμένων ἐπὶ τῷ βοηθεῖν τῇ τῶν ἀνθρώπων φύσει Or.*hom.13.1 in Jer*.(p.102.11; 400B); Gr.Nyss.*hom.14 in Cant*. (M.44.1080D); of demons, Clem.*ecl*.46(p.149.24; M.9.720B); *T.Sal*.11. 3(p.40.4; M.122.1332D); Gr.Nyss.*hom.5 in Cant*.(881A); **2.** *band of soldiers* ἐπῆλθεν...τῇ ἐκκλησίᾳ ὁ δοὺξ...μετὰ πολλῶν λ. στρατιωτῶν Ath.*h.Ar*.81(p.229.17; M.25.793C).

***λεθέκ, τό,** (Hebr. לֶתֶךְ), a Hebrew measure, Epiph.*mens*.21 (M.43.272B); ref. Os.3:2 λ. δέ, ὡς ἐν τῷ Ὠσηὲ...εἴρηται, ὅτι ἐμισθωσάμην ἐμαυτῷ λ. κριθῶν· ἐν ἀντιγράφοις δέ, γόμορ κριθῶν, τὸ αὐτό εἰσι· δέκα γὰρ καὶ πέντε μόδιοι σημαίνονται οὗτοι. λ. δὲ κατὰ τὴν τῶν Ἑβραίων φωνὴν κέκληται, ὅ ἐστιν ἔπαρμα...τὸ δὲ αὐτὸ καὶ τὸ γόμορ καλεῖται...δεκαπέντε καὶ αὐτὸ ὂν μοδίων *ib*.(272C).

***λείανσις, ἡ,** *smoothing, making smooth*, Clem.*paed*.3.3(p.247.27; M.8.581B).

λειμών, ὁ, *meadow*; met., of spiritual purification ἣν τόποι καθαροὶ καὶ λ. ἐδέξαντο Clem.*ecl*.34(p.147.14; M.9.716C); of future life ἀγγέλους...εἰς τοὺς...παραπέμπειν λ. αὐτάς Meth.*symp*.8.2(p.83. 14; M.18.141A); of spiritual enlightenment εἰς τὸν...λ. τοῦδε τοῦ παραδείσου χειραγωγήσω Cyr.H.*catech*.19.1; of Church ἀπεικάζεσθαι ...λ. λόγος ἔχει προφητικὸς τὴν ἐκκλησίαν Meth.*symp*.2.7(p.25.22; 60B); id.*arbitr*.1.1(p.147.10; M.18.241B); of monasteries, Thdt.*h.rel*. 4(3.1160); of anthologies, Clem.*str*.6.1(p.423.1; M.9.209A); sources of historical information, Eus.*h.e.*1.1.4(M.20.52A); collection of virtuous lives, Jo.Mosch.*prat.*proem.(M.87.2852B); of scripture τῷ λ. τῶν γραφῶν ποιμαινόμενοι Philox.*ep.*26(p.176); of a festival, Germ.CP *or.*3(M.98.292C).

λειμωνάριον, τό, dim. of foreg., title of work of Jo. Mosch. attributed to Sophr. H., Jo.D.*imag.*1(M.94.1280A); *ib.*3(1336B) but cf. Jo.Mosch.*prat.*proem.(M.87.2852B).

λειότης, ἡ, *smoothness*, met. βίβλων...ἐν αἷς...πολλαὶ δὲ ἡδοναὶ καὶ λ., πολλαὶ δὲ τραχύτητες Gr.Naz.*ep.*165(M.37.273C); τῇ τῆς ζωῆς λ. (opp. τραχύτης of μέριμναι) Jo.D.*hom.*2.3(M.96.580D).

λειουργέω, *make smoothe*, Clem.*paed.*3.3(p.245.19; M.8.577B).

[*]**λειποθυμέω,** v. λιπ-.

***λειποτακτίτης, ὁ,** *deserter*, Jo.Carp.*cap.*84(M.85.1854).

[*]**λειποψυχία, ἡ,** *faintheartedness, depression*, Chrys.*pan.Macc.* 2.2(2.630C).

λειτουργ-έω, 1. *perform public service*, Synes.*regn.*13(p.38.12; M.66.1085A); **2.** *minister*; met., *be a slave to* κύβοις καὶ πόρναις, οἱ δὲ ἑτέραις τοιαύταις ~οῦσι δαπάναις Chrys.*hom.*87.4 *in Jo.*(8.524E); ὄψει καὶ...γεύσει ~εῖν ‡Nil.*narr.*3(M.79.616A); ‡Nil.*perist.*9.7(M.79.877A); Bas.Sel.*or.*36.2(M.85.385B); **3.** *serve* God; **a.** of angels, *T.Lev.* 3.5; τῷ θελήματι αὐτοῦ ~οῦσιν παρεστῶτες *1Clem.*34.5; Serap.*euch.* 10.1; θρόνους καὶ κυριότητας ~οῦντας Cyr.H.*procatech.*15; ἄγγελοι πάντες...λειτουργίαν ἐκπληροῦσι χρειώδη τοῖς οὐρανοῖς καὶ τοῖς διὰ τὸν ἄνθρωπον· οἱ δὲ ~εῖν εἰληφότες τὸ παρέπεσθαι τοῖς ἀνθρώποις φύλακες ἀεὶ μὲν αὔξονται, μειοῦνται δὲ οὐδέποτε ‡Just.*qu.et resp.*30(M.6.1277C); ὥσπερ ~οῦσιν ἄγγελοι τοῦ θεοῦ, οὕτως ἐν τῷ ἁγίῳ βήματι ἵστανται καὶ οἱ ἔνυλοι ἱερεῖς...λατρεύοντες τῷ κυρίῳ ‡Sophr.H.*liturg.*3 (M.87.3984C); **b.** of OT saints τοὺς τελείως ~ήσαντας τῇ μεγαλοπρεπεῖ δόξῃ αὐτοῦ...Ἐνώχ,...Νῶε *1Clem.*9.2; **c.** of OT ministry ἱερεῖς καὶ λευῖται...οἱ ~οῦντες τῷ θυσιαστηρίῳ τοῦ θεοῦ *ib.*32.2; *Const.App.*2.25.4,7; Diad.*perf.*13(p.20.4); contrasted with office of Son ref. Heb. 10:11 τὸ ἑστάναι τοῦ ~εῖν ἐστι σημεῖον· οὐκοῦν τὸ καθῆσθαι τοῦ ~εῖσθαι Chrys.*hom.*18.1 *in Heb.*(12.175A); **d.** Christian; **i.** of service to God in gen., Herm.*mand.*5.1.3; id.*sim.*7.6; *ib.*9.27.3; *M.Sab.*7.6; *Const.App.*2.63.1; ἐλπίζομεν...λ. αὐτῷ μετ' ἀγγέλων *cat.Heb.*7:19 (p.210.17); σῶμα...δύναται...καλῶς ὑπὸ τῆς ψυχῆς κυβερνούμενον τῷ θεῷ λ. Thdt.*Rom.*6:13(3.65); **ii.** of Church's official ministry, as ministering to flock of Christ, *1Clem.*44.3; χειροτονήσατε οὖν ἑαυτοῖς ἐπισκόπους καὶ διακόνους...ὑμῖν γὰρ ~οῦσι...τὴν λειτουργίαν τῶν προφητῶν καὶ διδασκάλων *Did.*15.1; τὴν ἐπισκοπὴν λελειτουργηκότα Eus.*h.e.*5.22(M.20.489A); ἁγίασον...διακόνους, ἵνα...δυνηθῶσιν...~εῖν καὶ παραστῆναι τῷ ἁγίῳ σώματι καὶ τῷ ἁγίῳ αἵματι Serap.*euch.*11.1; ἐπίσκοπον...καλῶς σοι ~ήσαντα *Const.App.*3.13.1; ἐπίσκοπον...~οῦντα νυκτὸς καὶ ἡμέρας *Lit.*ap.*Const.App.*8.5.6; καταξίωσον αὐτὸν... ~ήσαντα τὴν...διακονίαν...μείζονος ἀξιωθῆναι βαθμοῦ *Const.App.*8.18.3; CChalc.*can.*10; of preaching ministry, exeg. Ac.13:2 τί ἐστι, ~ούντων; κηρυττόντων Chrys.*hom.*27.1 *in Ac.*(9.216A); esp. of eucharistic ministry ~ήσας θυσιαστηρίῳ Eus.*Marcell.*2.1(p.33.19; M.24.780B); abs., *perform liturgy, celebrate*, Jul.Papa *ep.Dian.*ap. Ath.*apol.sec.*28(p.108.15; M.25.296C); CSard.*can.*12; εἴ τις διακρίνοιτο παρὰ πρεσβυτέρου γεγαμηκότος, ὡς μὴ χρῆναι ~ήσαντος αὐτοῦ προσφορᾶς μεταλαμβάνειν, ἀνάθεμα ἔστω CGangr.*can.*4; Bas.*ep.*199 *can.* 27(3.294B; M.32.724C); Pall.*h.Laus.*18(p.54.12; M.34.1059A); *Lit.Jac.*(p.178.27); *Lit.Bas.*(p.317.15); of office of higher clergy opp. deacons, Chrys.*hom.*20.2 *in 2Cor.*(10.579D); **4.** of deacon, *serve* or *assist* bishop, *Const.App.*2.26.2.

***λειτουργητέον,** *one must minister* τῷ βίῳ λ. τὰ πρέποντα Cels.ap. Or.*Cels.*8.55(p.272.2; M.11.1600B).

λειτουργία, ἡ, A. *public service*, Eus.*h.e.*8.9.7(M.20.761A); of curial *munera* ἐπισκόπους...εἰς λ. δημοσίας παραδίδοσθαι Jul.Papa *ep.Dian.*ap.Ath.*apol.sec.*33(p.111.22; M.25.304A); τοὺς...ἐν κλήρῳ κατειλεγμένους εἰς τὴν τῶν βουλευτῶν ἀνέστρεφε [sc. Julian] λ. Philost.*h.e.*7.4(M.65.541C).

B. *service*, in gen. of men to each other τῇ πρὸς τὸν πλησίον λ. *Ep.Lugd.*ap.Eus.*h.e.*5.1.9(M.20.412A); of charitable work in gen., Chrys.*hom.*62.5 *in Jo.*(8.375A); Μάρθας...τῆς περὶ τὴν σωματικὴν λ. περισπωμένης Nil.*praest.*16(M.79.1080B); of Elijah's ravens ἐνίκησαν ...τὴν φύσιν τῇ περί σε λ. Bas.Sel.*or.*11.1(M.85.152B); ref. paradise πάντα εἶχεν δεδομένα τῷ ἀνθρώπῳ εἰς λ. ‡Ath.*diab.*5(p.6.35); of service to man performed by times and seasons, Chrys.*stat.*8.1(2.91C); of servitude to evil desires, Ephr.1.210C; and worldly interests, Chrys.*hom.*80.3 *in Jo.*(476B); in argument agst. dualistic heretics πῶς οὖν πρὸς τὴν σύστασιν τοῦ πονηροῦ βίου τοσαύτην εἰσάγουσι λ. οὗτοι οἱ καθ' ὑμᾶς θεοί [i.e. heavenly bodies]; id.*comm. in Gal.*1:4(10.664D).

C. *service* to God; **1.** in gen. ἔχει...ὁ γάμος ἰδίας λ. καὶ διακονίας τῷ κυρίῳ Clem.*str.*3.12(p.231.29; M.8.1180A); πληροῖ...τὴν προσταχθεῖσαν αὐτῷ θεόθεν λ. Const.*or.s.c.*23(p.189.13; M.20.1305C); Bas. Sel.*or.*12.2(M.85.161C); **2.** *worship*; **a.** in gen., Clem.*str.*7.10(p.41.21; M.9.480B); ἐσθήμασιν...τῇ λ. πρεπωδεστέροις Cyr.*Is.*3.4(2.482E); θείαν ἐπιτελέσαντες λ. *Lit.Jac.*(p.168.13); πᾶσαν τὴν ἐν τῷ ναῷ σου πληρώσαντες θείαν λ. *ib.*(p.240.22); of Arian worship of Son δουλοπρεπὴς...λ. Thdt.*Trin.*(M.75.1165C); **b.** *system of worship, cult*, ‡Hipp.*consumm.*34(p.303.7; M.10.937A); οὐδὲ γάρ, καθάπερ τὴν παλαιὰν λατρείαν...περιέγραψεν, οὕτω καὶ τὴν καινὴν λ. ἑνὶ περιορίζει χωρίῳ Thdt.*Is.*49:9(p.196.14; 2.350); id.*Dan.*12:11(2.1301); ἐκκλησιαστικῆς λ. ... τὴν τάξιν id.*1Tim.*proem.(3.638); ἔχει δὲ ἡ... νῆσος καὶ ἐκκλησίαν...καὶ πρεσβύτερον...καὶ πᾶσαν τὴν ἐκκλησιαστικὴν λ. Cosm.Ind.*top.*11(M.88.445C); **c.** *service, rite*; **i.** Jewish, Chrys. *hom.*16.2 *in Heb.*(12.159D); Thdt.*qu.*7 *in Ex.*(1.123); Cosm.Ind.*top.* 5(M.88.209D); **ii.** Christian; of a fast, Herm.*sim.*5.3.8; of baptism ἵνα...τὴν τοῦ θείου βαπτίσματος ἐπιτελῇ λειτουργίαν Thdt.*h.e.*2.27.2 (3.894); of offices τὴν αὐτὴν λ. τῶν εὐχῶν πάντοτε καὶ ἐν ταῖς ἐννάταις καὶ ἐν ταῖς ἑσπέραις ὀφείλειν γίνεσθαι CLaod.*can.*18; ποιῶ μικράν μου λ. *Apophth.Patr.*(M.65.389A); ἑσπερινὰς ἢ...ἑωθινὰς λ. Jo.Ant.*relat. imp.*1(p.124.35; M.83.1441A); especially of eucharistic *liturgy* ψυχῆς σκῆνος...μυστικῆς λ. ἀξιούμενον Eus.*v.C.*4.71(p.147.14; M.20.1225C); λογικῶν θυσιῶν ἱεροπρεπεῖς λ. id.*l.C.*16(p.253.10; M.20.1428A); ‡Pion. *v.Polyc.*20; εἰώθασιν ἐν ταῖς ἐκκλησίαις, μετὰ τὴν μυστικὴν λ., ἑστιᾶσθαι κοινῇ πλούσιοί τε καὶ πένητες Thdt.*1Cor.*11:16(3.235); id.*h.rel.* 16(3.1172); τὴν τῆς μυστικῆς λ. ἔκθεσιν ‡Procl.CP *tract.*(M.65.849B); *ib.*(852A); for the dead, ‡Jo.D.*fid.dorm.*12(M.95.256C); **3.** *ministry*, of Christ in his humanity περὶ τῆς ἀνθρωπίνης αὐτοῦ λ. ἔλεγεν, 'οὐδὲ ὁ υἱός' Ath.*Ar.*3.44(M.26.416B); of angels, ref. Mal.3:1 of Jo. Bapt. ἄγγελος ὄνομα λειτουργίας μᾶλλόν ἐστιν, ἤπερ οὐσίας σημαντικόν Cyr.*Jo.*1.7(4.61E); in gen., ‡Just.*qu.et resp.*30(M.6.1277C); Thdt.*haer.*5.7(4.403); Cosm.Ind.*top.*5(M.88.301C); for ministry of angels in gen. v. ἄγγελος, λειτουργικός; of public ministry of sacrifice, worship, sacraments, etc.: Jewish ἀρχιερέων...ἐνιαύσιον λ. ἐκτετελεκότων Eus.*h.e.*1.10.6(M.20.112B); id.*d.e.*8.2(p.381.25; M.22.624B); of Levites' office as λ. τῆς σκηνῆς *Const.App.*2.25.4; Μωσῆς...διεῖλε τίνα μὲν χρὴ ὑπὸ τῶν ἀρχιερέων ἐπιτελεῖσθαι, τίνα δὲ ὑπὸ τῶν ἱερέων, τίνα δὲ ὑπὸ τῶν λευιτῶν, ἑκάστῳ τὴν οἰκείαν καὶ ἀνήκουσαν τῇ λ. θρησκείαν ἀπονείμας *ib.*8.46.3; Christian; of episcopal office, *1Clem.*44.2, Iren.*haer.*3.3.3(M.7.849A) citt. s. ἀπόστολος; Eus.*h.e.*3.13(248B); CAnc.(314)*can.*17; Chrys.*sac.*1.7(p.12.6; 1.366A); *ib.*2.4(p.37.12; 376B); Pall.*v.Chrys.*20(p.132.7; M.47.73); Eustrat.*v.Eutych.*22(M.86.2300A); of ministerial office in gen. χειροτονήσατε οὖν ἑαυτοῖς ἐπισκόπους καὶ διακόνους ἀξίους τοῦ κυρίου ...ὑμῖν γὰρ λειτουργοῦσι καὶ αὐτοὶ τὴν λ. τῶν προφητῶν καὶ διδασκάλων *Did.*15.1; ἐκλεξάμενος ἐπισκόπους καὶ πρεσβυτέρους καὶ διακόνους εἰς λ. τῆς καθολικῆς σου ἐκκλησίας Serap.*euch.*26.1; ἐπεσχέθη τῆς λ. Bas.*ep.*188 *can.*1(3.269A; M.32.665A); καὶ γὰρ ἀκούσαντες τοῦ προφήτου λέγοντος· ὑμεῖς ἱερεῖς θεοῦ κληθήσεσθε· οὔτε πάντες τῆς τοιᾶσδε ἱερωσύνης ἢ λ. τὴν ἐξουσίαν ἁρπάζομεν †Bas.*bapt.*2.8.3(2.662B; M.31.1601C); of preaching ministry, Chrys.*hom.*29.1 *in Rom.* (9.731A); of diaconate, Pall.*v.Chrys.*8(p.45.3; M.47.27); id.*h.Laus.* 18(p.54.11; M.34.1059A); τὴν τοῦ κλήρου λ. Thdr.Mops.*1Tim.*3:2 (p.101.20; M.66.940A); τὸ φοβερὸν τῆς θείας λ. Nil.*epp.*2.294(M.79.348A); Εὐδόξιος...εἰς διακονίαν Εὐνόμιον προχειρίζεται· ὁ δὲ...τὴν λ. οὐ δέχεται Philost.*h.e.*4.5(M.65.520B); of ministry of eucharist, *Lit. Jac.*(p.190.27) al.

λειτουργικός, 1. *servile, belonging to a servant* οὐ λ. ἡ δόξα Χριστοῦ, ἀλλὰ θεϊκὴ καὶ ποιητική Euthal.Diac.*epp.Paul.*(M.85.777A); **2.** *belonging to divine service, liturgical* λ. ... σκεύη Or.*fr.*49 *in Lam.*2:7(p.257.2; M.13.633D); Gr.Naz.*or.*33.3(M.36.217B); in ordination prayer of subdeacon δὸς αὐτῷ πνεῦμα ἅγιον πρὸς τὸ ἐπαξίως ἐφάπτεσθαι τῶν λ. σου σκευῶν *Const.App.epit.*12.2; λ. ... τράπεζα Bas.Sel.*v.Thecl.*1(M.85.560A); *ib.*2.12(588B); στολὰς...λ. Ἀαρών Cosm.Ind.*top.*3(M.88.172D); λ. καὶ ἀναιμάκτου θυσίας...ἱερουργίαν *Lit.Jac.*(p.180.1); **3.** *ministering*; of angels as λ. πνεύματα Or. *schol.in Cant.*3:1(M.17.269B); λ. πνεύματα πρὸς διακονίαν ἀποστελλόμενα Bas.*Eun.*3.2(1.273E; M.29.660A); λ. πνεύματα, δι' ὧν οἱ ἄνθρωποι σῴζονται Gr.Nyss.*hom.*1 *in Cant.*(M.44.772D); λ. δυνάμεσιν Didym. *Trin.*2.1(M.39.448A); ref. ordination παρόντος...τοῦ ἁγίου πνεύματος καὶ πάντων τῶν ἁγίων καὶ λ. πνευμάτων *Const.App.*8.4.5; Ἰσραὴλ οὐχ ὑπὸ λ. δυνάμεσι κείμενον, ὥσπερ τὰ ἄλλα ἔθνη Proc.G.*Dt.*33:26 (M.87.989C); Oecum.*Apoc.*4:3(p.69); *ib.*9:13(p.115); ‡Caes.Naz.*dial.* 104(M.38.972); dist. as λ. from H. Ghost, Bas.*Eun.*2.21(1.257C; M.29.620A); *ib.*3.2(273E; M.660A); hence denial that H. Ghost is λ., id. *ep.*125.3(3.216E; M.32.549C); id.*Spir.*25(3.21D; M.32.112C); πνεῦμα... ἀναπνευσθὲν ἀνάρχως, καὶ οὐ γενόμενον ὡς ἓν τῶν λ. πνευμάτων

Didym.*Trin.*2.2(460B); Son as οὐκ...λ., ἀλλὰ συνεργός dist. from λ. πνεύματα Sever.ap.*cat.Heb.*1:14(p.139.31); Creation being διὰ τοῦ ὁμογενοῦς υἱοῦ...οὐχ ὡς δι' ὀργάνου λ., ἀλλὰ φυσικῆς καὶ ἐνυποστάτου δυνάμεως ‡Cyr.*Trin.*8(6^3.12E; M.77.1137D); **4.** *of* or *pertaining to the diaconate* καθαρτικὴ τοίνυν ἐστὶν ἡ λ. διακόσμησις, ἐπὶ τὰς φανὰς τῶν ἱερέων ἱερουργίας ἀνάγουσα τοὺς κεκαθαρμένους Dion.Ar.*e.h.*5.1.6(M.3.508B).

***λειτουργικῶς**, *so as to minister* παρεστάναι τῷ θρόνῳ λ. προσετάχθημεν ‡Bas.*inc.*17(p.237.8); Max.*ep.*4(M.91.415C).

λειτουργός, ὁ, *servant*; **1.** in gen. λ. καὶ διάκονος Chrys.*hom.29.3 in Jo.*(8.168C); λ. τῆς βασιλείας τὸν βασιλέα Synes.*regn.*14(p.42.12; M.66.1089A); Anast.S.*qu.et resp.*60(M.89.641C); met. τοῖς τῆς ἀληθείας λ. Cyr.*Jo.*1.6(4.62C); Christol., ref. Gen.1:26 ποιήσωμεν γὰρ εἶπεν, ἵνα τὴν συνέργειαν εἴπῃ, οὐχί, ποιήσατε, ἵνα μὴ σὺ πάλιν ὑπουργὸν καὶ λ. εἴπῃς ‡Ath.*dial.Trin.*3.16(M.28.1228C); μὴ τοίνυν αὐτὸν ἱερέα ἀκούσας, ἀεὶ ἱερᾶσθαι νόμιζε· ἅπαξ γὰρ ἱεράσατο, καὶ λοιπὸν ἐκάθισεν. ἵνα γὰρ μὴ νομίσῃς ἄνω ἑστάναι αὐτόν, καὶ λ. εἶναι, δείκνυσιν ὅτι οἰκονομίας τὸ πρᾶγμά ἐστιν. ὥσπερ γὰρ δοῦλος ἐγένετο, οὕτω καὶ ἱερεὺς καὶ λ.· ἀλλ' ὥσπερ δοῦλος γενόμενος, οὐκ ἔμεινε δοῦλος· οὕτω καὶ λ. γενόμενος, οὐκ ἔμεινε λ.· οὐ γὰρ λειτουργοῦ τὸ καθῆσθαι, ἀλλὰ τὸ ἑστάναι Chrys.*hom.13.3 in Heb.*(12.134C); **2.** of servants of God; in gen., *1Clem.*8.1; *Protev.*23.1(p.45); Eus.*Marcell.*1.1(p.1.16; M.24.712A); esp. of eccl. ministry; **a.** OT priesthood, *T.Lev.*2.10; *Asen.* 2.2; *1Clem.*41.2; **b.** Christian clergy in gen., Eus.*v.C.*1.51(p.31.17; M.20.965A); *ib.*3.9(p.81.6; 1064A); Ath.*ep.encycl.*4(p.173.11; M.25.232A); Gr.Naz.*ep.*208(M.37.345B); καθιστάναι ἐκκλησίας καὶ λειτουργοὺς ἐν αὐταῖς *A.Barn.*22(p.300.14); of deacons, Bas.*ep.*93(3.186E; M.32.484B); Dion.Ar.*e.h.*2.2.7(M.3.396C); *ib.*3.2(425B,C); *ib.*5.1.6 (508A); Max.*schol.e.h.*3.2(M.4.136C) cit. s. ὑποδιάκονος; **3.** of angels as ministers, Athenag.*leg.*10.3(M.6.909B); Clem.*str.*6.17(p.513.5; M.9.389A); τοὺς λ. τῶν ἀναφερομένων εὐχῶν ἀγγέλους id.*exc.Thdot.*27 (p.116.1; M.9.673A); of inferior orders of angels, Meth.*res.*1.49 (p.302.12; M.18.277B); †Bas.*hom.in Ps.*37(1.368E; M.30.97B); ἀγαθαὶ δυνάμεις, λ. τῶν ἁγίων †Bas.*parad.*12(1.351D; M.30.72B); τῶν κατ' οὐρανὸν λ. μυριάδες Gr.Nyss.*Eun.*4(2 p.98.26; M.45.676C); as God's λ. in Creation, not as co-equal συνεργοί, Sever.*creat.*4.6(M.56.464).

λειψανδρία, ἡ, *under-population*, Cyr.*Is.*4.4(2.678E).

λείψανον, τό, *remnant, remainder*; **1.** in gen. τά τε τῶν θηρίων, τά τε τοῦ πυρὸς λ. [i.e. *remains left over from*] *Ep.Lugd.*ap.Eus.*h.e.*5.1.59 (M.20.432A); Ath.*gent.*24(M.25.48C); Manich. τὸ ζῶν πνεῦμα ἔκτισε τοὺς φωστῆρας, ἅ ἐστι τῆς ψυχῆς λείψανα Hegem.*Arch.*8(p.11.8; M.10.1437C); λ. διχονοίας CSard.*can.*18; Νῶε λ. τοῦ κόσμου γεγονότα Epiph.*anc.*112(p.136.9; M.43.220B); of remains of pagan temples χρήσιμα τὰ λ., ἵνα μάθωμεν τίνων ἀπηλλάγμεθα ‡Ath.*diab.*7(p.8.24); ref. vegetarianism of Marcionites ἵνα μὴ φάγωσι σῶμά τι λ. ψυχῆς ὑπὸ τοῦ δημιουργοῦ κεκολασμένης Hipp.*haer.*7.30(p.216.9; M.16.3334B); **2.** of eucharistic remains, Cyr.*ep.Calos.*(p.605.23; 6^2.365B); Leont.H.*monoph.*(M.86.1892A); θείων λ. ‡Germ.CP *contempl.*(M.98.452B); **3.** *dead body, corpse* (freq. in plur.); **a.** in gen., Tat. *orat.*17(p.19.19; M.6.844C); Hipp.*Dan.*4.51.1; Ath.*Ar.*2.16(M.26.180A); ἐκ τῆς θήκης τοῦ τιμίου σου λ. βρύον ἔλαιον Thdr.Pet.*v.Thds.* (p.92.12); ἐκ τοῦ τιμίου αὐτοῦ λ. μύρων ἰαματικὴν εὐωδίαν πᾶσιν ἀναβλύσαι Leont.N.*v.Jo.Eleem.*46(p.102.2); **b.** (plur.), esp. of relics of martyrs and other saints, cf.*M.Polyc.*17.1 s.v. σαρκίον; τοὺς ἀπὸ θεῶν ἐπὶ τοὺς νεκροὺς καὶ τὰ λ. μετατετραμμένους Juln.Imp.*ep.*114(p.178.22); ἔψαλλα...ἔμπροσθεν τῶν λ. ὑμῶν τῶν ἁγίων Ephr.3.254B; ἐὰν δὲ δυνηθῶμεν περινοῆσαι λ. μαρτύρων, εὐχόμεθα καὶ αὐτοὶ συμβαλέσθαι ὑμῶν τῇ σπουδῇ Bas.*ep.*49(3.142C; M.32.385C); καλῶς δὲ ποιήσεις, ἐὰν καὶ λείψανα μαρτύρων τῇ πατρίδι ἐκπέμψῃς *ib.*155(245A; M.613B); *ib.*197.2(288E; M.712C); οὐκ ἔτι προσάξουσι πῦρ μαρτύρων μνήμασιν... οὐκ ἔτι πυρὶ καταναλώσουσιν ἁγίων λείψανα Gr.Naz.*or.*5.29(M.35.701B); τῶν ἁγίων λ. *ib.*24.17(1189C); τῶν ἐμῶν πατέρων τὰ σώματα τοῖς τῶν στρατιωτῶν παρεθέμην λ. Gr.Nyss.*mart.*2(M.46.784B); ἐδόκουν γὰρ λ. μαρτύρων διὰ χειρὸς φέρειν, εἶναι δὲ ἀπ' αὐτῶν αὐγὴν...ὥστε μοι τὰς ὄψεις...ἀμβλύνεσθαι id.*v.Macr.*(p.387.12; M.46.976A); τῶν παρὰ θεῷ ζώντων οὐδὲ τὰ λ. ἄτιμα *Const.App.*6.30.5; ἡ πόλις ἡμῖν τοῖς λ. τῶν ἁγίων τειχίζεται Chrys.*coemet.*1(2.397C); id.*pan.Bab.*2.11(2.555D); τὰ λ. τῶν ἁγίων εἴασεν ἡμῖν ὁ θεὸς βουλόμενος ἡμᾶς πρὸς τὸν αὐτὸν ἐκείνοις χειραγωγῆσαι ζῆλον id.*pan.Ign.*5(2.601A); προσπέσωμεν αὐτῶν τοῖς λ.· συμπλακῶμεν αὐτῶν ταῖς θήκαις, δύνανται γὰρ καὶ θῆκαι μαρτύρων πολλὴν ἔχειν δύναμιν id.*pan.Bern.*7(2.645C); id.*ep.*126(3.672D); παρείπετο [sc. Eudoxia] τοῖς λ., συνεχῶς ἐφαπτομένη... οὕτω δὴ καὶ ἡ τοῦ πνεύματος χάρις ἡ τοῖς ὀστέοις παρακαθημένη...εἰς ἑτέρους πρόεισι...καὶ ἀπὸ ψυχῆς εἰς σώματα, καὶ ἀπὸ σωμάτων εἰς ἱμά-τια. ... τῶν γὰρ λ. φερομένων, ἐμπρησμοὶ δαιμόνων, ὀλολυγαὶ... πανταχόθεν ἤροντο, τῆς ἀκτῖνος τῶν ὀστῶν ἐκπηδώσης id.*hom.div.* 2.1(12.331E); πολλαχοῦ μερισθέντα τὰ λ., ὁλόκληρον πανταχοῦ τῷ τρισμακαρίῳ σώζει τὴν εὐφημίαν Ast.Am.*hom.*9(M.40.309A); λαβὼν τὸν νεανίσκον εἰσῆλθεν εἰς τὸ μαρτύριον ἑαυτοῦ...ἐν ᾧ λ. κατακεῖται Ἰωάννου τοῦ βαπτιστοῦ. καὶ ἐπευξάμενος αὐτῷ...ὑγιῆ ἀπέδωκε τὸν νεανίσκον τῇ αὐτοῦ μητρί Pall.*h.Laus.*44(p.131.25; M.34.1210A); θυσιαστήρια ὡσανεὶ εἰς μνήμην μαρτύρων καθιστάμενα ἐν οἷς οὐδὲ ἓν σῶμα ἢ λ. (Lat. *reliquiae*) μαρτύρων ἀποκείμενα δείκνυνται...καταστρέφωνται *Cod.Afr.*83; βραχύτατον λ. τὴν ἴσην ἔχει δύναμιν τῷ μηδαμῇ μηδαμῶς διανεμηθέντι μάρτυρι· ἡ γὰρ ἐπανθοῦσα χάρις διανέμει τὰ δῶρα Thdt.*affect.*8(p.199.13; 4.902); id.*eran.*3(4.207); id. *h.rel.*3(3.1148); ἀλαβαστροθῆκαι ἀργυραῖ...ἐν αἷς τὰ ἱερὰ λ. ἔκειντο Soz.*h.e.*9.2.16(M.67.1601B); εἰσῆλθον [sc. under Constantius] ἐν Κωνσταντινουπόλει τὰ λ. τῶν ἁγίων ἀποστόλων Τιμοθέου...Ἀνδρέα... καὶ Λουκᾶ Thdr.Lect.*h.e.*2.61(M.86.212C); ἱδρύσας ἐν τούτῳ τοῦ... μάρτυρος Γεωργίου τὸ τίμιον λ. *CIG* 8627 (Syria, 516); σηκὸς εὐαγὴς καὶ τέμενος ἅγιον τῷ Ἰγνατίῳ τὸ πάλαι Τυχαῖον γέγονε, τῶν ἱερῶν αὐτοῦ λ. μετὰ πομπῆς ἱερᾶς ἀνὰ τὴν πόλιν ἐπ' ὀχήματος ἐνεχθέντων καὶ κατὰ τὸ τέμενος τεθέντων Evagr.*h.e.*1.16(p.26.5; M.86.2465B); Φιλιππικοῦ δεηθέντος παραφυλακῆς ἕνεκα τῶν ἑῴων ἐκστρατευμάτων τίμια λ. οἱ ἐκπεμφθῆναι *ib.*1.13(p.23.16; 2457B); θυσιαστήριον ἐν ἀγρῷ ἢ ἐν ἀμπελῶσι γενόμενον ἐν ᾧ λ. οὐκ ἐναπόκειται μαρτύρων καταστρεφέσθω Sophr.H.*conf.*(M.87.3369A); ὅσοι οὖν σεπτοὶ ναοὶ καθιερώθησαν ἐκτὸς ἁγίων λ. μαρτύρων, ὁρίζομεν ἐν αὐτοῖς κατάθεσιν γενέσθαι λειψάνων, μετὰ καὶ τῆς συνήθους εὐχῆς. καὶ εἴ ἀπὸ τοῦ παρόντος τις εὑρεθῇ ἐπίσκοπος χωρὶς ἁγίων λ. καθιερῶν ναόν, καθαιρείσθω, ὡς παραβεβηκὼς τὰς ἐκκλησιαστικὰς παραδόσεις CNic.(787)*can.*7.

λεῖψις, ἡ, **1.** *want, shortage*, *Chron.Pasch.*p.321(M.92.820A); **2.** = ἔκλειψις, *eclipse*, Hipp.*haer.*4.10(p.43.3; M.16.3074B).

[*]**λειψοφωτ-έω**, = λειψιφωτέω, *be on the wane*, met. Σευῆρος ὑποβάλλων τὸν Χριστόν, ποτὲ μὲν αὐτὸν ~οῦντα, ποτὲ δὲ πάλιν πληροσέληνον ὄντα φανταζόμενος, καὶ νῦν μὲν διφυῆ, νῦν δὲ μονοφυῆ γινόμενον Anast.S.*hod.*7(M.89.116A).

λεκανομαντεία, ἡ, *divination from dishes*, Hipp.*haer.*4.35(p.61.10; M.16.3099B).

***λεκτίκη, ἡ,** (= Lat. *lectica*) *litter*, Cyr.S.*v.Sab.*76(p.182.11).

λεκτίκιον, τό, dim. of foreg., Chrys.*ep.*14.3(3.598B); Pall.*h.Laus.* 55(p.149.10; M.34.1244C); Jo.Mal.*chron.*14 p.366(M.97.548A).

***λεκτίνιον, τό,** = foreg., *V.Chrys.*110(p.358.9,16).

***λεκτίον, τό,** = foreg., Thdr.Trim.*v.Chrys.*4(M.47.lvi).

***λέκτριος**, *on a bed, bedridden*, Gr.Naz.*carm.*2.1.19.94(M.37.1278A); *ib.*2.1.50.71(1390A).

***λεκτροκλόπος, ὁ,** *adulterer*, *Orac.Sib.*1.178; *ib.*3.38.

λεληθότως, **1.** *secretly*, Eus.*h.e.*7.32.11(M.20.725C); Cyr.*Ps.*65:17 (M.69.1140A); id.*Os.*48(3.79A); ὁ Νικόδημος...ὁ λ. εἶναι πιστὸς βουλόμενος Ammon.*Jo.*3:1(M.85.1408B); of something connived at γίνεται...κριτήρια λ. κατὰ τὸν νόμον Or.*ep.*1.14(M.11.84A); **2.** *furtively, by insinuation*, Clem.*str.*7.18(p.79.6; M.9.557A); Κέλσος λ. βουλόμενος διαβάλλειν τὴν...κοσμοποιΐαν Or.*Cels.*1.19(p.70.19; M.11.693B).

***λεμίν, τό,** dim. of λαιμός *throat*; hence *portrait bust*, Jo.Mal. *chron.*10 p.265(M.97.401B).

λέντιον, τό, (= Lat. *linteum*) *linen cloth*; **1.** in gen., Herm. *vis.*3.1.4; *A.Jo.*6(p.155.1); *towel*, Nonn.*par.Jo.*13:4 (λίντιον M.43.860C); Geo.Pis.*hex.*1762(M.92.1570A); towel of Jo.13:4 symbolized by maniple, ‡Sophr.H.*liturg.*8(M.87.3988B); **2.** *apron*, *Apoc.Bar.*3 (p.68.7); *A.Phil.*6(p.4.7); *A.Petr.et Andr.*4(p.119.5); *ib.*13(p.123.11); worn by monks, cf.*PLond.*1922.6; ‡Pall.*h.mon.*11.7(p.56.3; M.65.449D); *Apophth.Patr.*(M.65.237A); ζῶσαι...τὴν ὀσφύν σου λ. ὑπακοῆς Jo.Clim.*scal.*4(M.88.700B); **3.** as headgear λ. μικρὸν ἐπὶ τὴν κεφαλὴν αὐτοῦ ‡Pall.*h.mon.*8.5(p.34.11; M.34.1138A).

λεξείδιον (-ίδιον), τό, **1.** *little word* τό, τίς, δὴ τοῦτο πλειστάκις ἀναφωνεῖς τὸ λ. Cyr.*inc.unigen.*(5^1.701E); **2.** *term, expression* τὸ τοῦ ἀγενήτου λ. οὐ πρὸς τὸν υἱὸν ἔχει τὴν σημασίαν Ath.*Ar.*1.33(M.26.80A); πάντα γὰρ ταῦτα τὰ λ. [i.e. υἱὸς ἀνθρώπου, κατεστάθη, νυμφίος, κτλ.] τῆς ἀνθρώπων συστάσεως ἴδια τυγχάνει ὄντα *ib.*2.11(169A); **3.** *phrase, sentence*, ref. Gen. 49:10 οὐ περὶ τοῦ λ. συζητῆσαι ὑμῖν ἔρχομαι Just.*dial.*120.5(M.6.756A); οὐχ ἑνός μοι λεξειδίου χρεία ἐστὶν Or.*hom.8.9 in Jer.*(p.62.33; λεξειδίου M.13.345D); **4.** esp. with connotation of *vain, empty*, or *meretricious word* or *expression* σωθῆναι γὰρ...καὶ συνάρασθαι τοῖς σώζεσθαι γλιχομένοις βέλτιστόν ἐστιν, οὐχὶ συνθεῖναι τὰ λ. καθάπερ τὰ κόσμια Clem.*str.*1.10(p.31.21; M.8.745A); Or.*Cels.*2.28(p.156.21; M.11.848B); *ib.*6.34(p.104.5; 1349A); οὐ λ. ἀλλὰ πράγματα *ib.*8.6(p.225.14; 1528A); οὐκ ἐν φωναῖς καὶ λεξειδίοις ζητῶ τὸ διδόναι κυρίῳ...δόξαν, ἀλλ' ἐν πράξεσιν id.*hom.12.11 in Jer.* (p.97.14; λεξειδίοις M.13.393A); λ. μόνον θηρᾶν Ath.*Dion.*4(p.49.6; M.25.485B); μελετᾶτε κενὰ λ. κατὰ τοῦ κυρίου id.*Ar.*1.11(M.26.33C);

ἐν εὐκαταφρονήτοις λ. πολὺ τὸ ἀγωγὸν καὶ πρὸς σωτηρίαν ὁλκὸν ἔχει τοῦ εὐαγγελίου τὸ κήρυγμα Bas.*hom.in Ps.*44(1.162D; M.29.397A); Socr.*h.e.*4.7.5(M.67.472C); **5.** *extract, passage* of book, Gr.Nyss.*Eun.* 1(1 p.24.11; M.45.252C); Anast.S.*hod.*3(M.89.92A); **6.** *tract, treatise,* Epiph.*haer.*33.9(p.459.12; M.41.569D).

***λεξίθηρ, ὁ,** *word-hunter, text-hunter,* Epiph.*haer.*69.61(p.209.15; M.42.300B); *ib.*69.76(p.224.26; 325C); *ib.*77.33(p.445.26; 689D); τοὺς λ. καὶ τοὺς κομπορύακας καὶ πάντας τοὺς φιλενδείκτας Nil.*epp.*2.215 (M.79.312D).

***λεξίθηρας, ὁ,** *investigator of words, pursuer of stylistic effect,* Isid.Pel.*epp.*5.245(M.78.1480C); *ib.*5.258(1488A).

λεξιθηρ-έω, 1. *investigate, hunt for words,* Socr.*h.e.*6.22.21(M.67. 729C); μὴ τὴν ἄκαιρον γλῶσσαν ~ει Nil.*Eulog.*25(M.79.1125C); Cyr. *Jo.*4.6(4.178C); **2.** *search for texts* ~οῦντες τὰ καλῶς...εἰρημένα ἀπὸ ἑκάστης γραφῆς Epiph.*haer.*69.50(p.196.20; M.42.277D); esp. of collecting texts in support of false doctrine ~οῦντες τοιαῦτα, ἔνθα ἐμφαίνεται...ὠμότης τοῦ δημιουργοῦ Or.*princ.*3.1.16(p.224.11; M.11. 281B); τὰ καλῶς διεσταλμένα κακῶς ~ῶν προφέρει Adam.*dial.*2.16 (p.90.12; M.11.1785A); Didym.*Trin.*2.13(M.39.688C); τοῖς ~οῦσι τὰ εἰς ἑαυτῶν καταστροφήν Epiph.*haer.*30.25(p.366.24; M.41.448B); ~οῦντες ἐκεῖνα μόνα ἅτινα κατὰ τὸν νοῦν αὐτῶν μεταχειρίζονται *ib.*45. 4(p.201.17, v.l. ~ῶντες 836A).

***λεξιθηρία, ἡ,** *investigation of words, pursuit of stylistic effect,* Clem.*paed.*1.6(p.117.11; M.8.303B).

***λεξίθηρος,** *given to pursuing words* or *stylistic effect, Const.App.* 3.5.1.

λεξικός, *wordy* λ. τῦφον Socr.*h.e.*4.7.11(M.67.473B).

λέξις, ἡ, 1. *language, speech* Δωριέων μὲν γὰρ οὐχ ἡ αὐτὴ λ. τοῖς ἀπὸ τῆς Ἀττικῆς Tat.*orat.*1(p.2.3; M.6.805A); ἡ πρώτη Ἰουδαίων λ., ᾗ οἱ προφῆται χρησάμενοι καταλελοίπασιν ἡμῖν βιβλία Or.*Cels.*7.59 (p.208.22; M.11.1505A); **2.** *diction, style* λ. Ἀττικὴ καὶ φιλοσόφων σωρεία Tat.*orat.*27(p.29.13; M.6.865B); μοι πεισθῆναι ταύταις [sc. ταῖς γραφαῖς] συνέβη διά τε τῶν λ. τὸ ἄτυφον καὶ τῶν εἰπόντων τὸ ἀνεπιτήδευτον *ib.*29(p.30.8; 868A); Dion.Al.ap.Eus.*h.e.*7.25.25(M.20. 704A); τοὺς σκώπτοντας τοὺς εὐλαβεῖς ἐπὶ τῇ ἀμαθείᾳ τῶν λ. Nil.*epp.*2. 215(M.79.312D); **3.** *phraseology*; of religion, Tat.*orat.*26(p.27.17; M. 6.861B); of doctrine μήπω ἀναφανεισῶν τῶν αἱρέσεων ἁπλούστερον ἐκέχρηντο ταῖς λ. †Leont.B.*sect.*10(M.86.1264C); **4.** *phrase, expression* ἡ 'ἐνεφυσίωσε' λ. Clem.*str.*7.16(p.74.10; M.9.545A); id.*ecl.*56(p.153.2; M.9.724C); in baptismal renunciation ἐν δευτέρᾳ λ. μανθάνεις λέγειν· καὶ πᾶσι τοῖς ἔργοις σου Cyr.H.*catech.*19.5; Chrys.*hom.*55.2 *in Jo.* (8.324B); δέχεται γὰρ οὕτω τὴν λ. ἡ...γραφή Cyr.*Ps.*24:21(M.69. 849D); οὐ γὰρ ἡ κοινότης τῶν λ. κοινοποιεῖται τὰς φύσεις ‡Ath. *Maced.dial.*1.8(M.28.1300D); **5.** *words* collectively, *language* διὰ λέξεως ἣν τὸ πνεῦμα...ἐφθέγξατο Just.*dial.*74.2(M.6.649A); χρησάμενοι λ. εὐαγγελικῇ Or.*hom.*12.10 *in Jer.*(p.96.8; M.13.392A); ἡ προκειμένη τῆς εὐαγγελικῆς λ. διήγησις id.*Jo.*32.27(17; p.472.23; M.14. 816D); **6.** *text, passage* τὰς τῆς προφητείας λ. Just.*1apol.*35.10(M.6. 384C); id.*dial.*34.1(M.6.548A); *ib.*70.5(641B); Clem.*paed.*1.7(p.125. 22; M.8.321C); εἰ μὴ ἔχοι νοῦν τινα κεκρυμμένον...ἡ προκειμένη λ. Or.*Jo.*5.1(p.100.10; M.14.188A); Eus.*p.e.*11.9(524B; M.21.869A); Ath. *tom.*8(M.26.805A); **7.** *extract* from book, Or.*Cels.*proem.6(p.55.11; M.11.649C); Eus.*h.e.*5.16.20(M.20.472B); **8.** *text,* dist. from *content* or *sense,* Clem.*str.*7.1(p.3.20; M.9.404B); Or.*Jo.*5.2(p.101.10; M.14. 188B); διϊόντων...ἐκ τῆς προχείρου λ. ἐπὶ τὸν ἐξ αὐτῆς νοῦν Eus. *Marcell.*1.3(p.17.4; M.24.749A); id.*e.th.*2.10(p.110.31; M.24.920C); **9.** hence *letter, literal meaning* opp. allegorical, typological, or 'spiritual' sense οὐ περὶ τὴν λ., ἀλλὰ περὶ τὰ σημαινόμενα ἀναστρεπτέον Clem.*str.*6.17(p.510.3; M.9.381C); *ib.*7.16(p.68.13; 533B); οἱ τῆς λ. δοῦλοι Or.*Jo.*10.18(13; p.188.16; M.14.336D); id.*princ.*4.3.2(p.326.6; M.11.380B); Eus.*p.e.*2 proem.(44B; M.21.92C); κατὰ λέξιν ἑρμηνεία Diod.*proem.Pss.*(p.82.24); **10.** phrases αὐταῖς λ. or κατὰ λέξιν, *word for word,* hence κατὰ λ., *in so many words,* Clem.*str.*1.7(p.25.27; M.8.736A); Eus.*v.C.*3.51(p.99.18; M.20.1112B); Socr.*h.e.*4.7.12(M.67. 473B); κατὰ [τὴν] λ. *literally,* Or.*hom.*3.2 *in Jer.*(p.21.20; M.13. 284B); id.*or.*13.4(p.328.12; M.11.457A); ταῦτα δοκεῖ...κατὰ λ. πεπληρῶσθαι Thdr.Mops.*exp.in Ps.*7:17(M.66.652C); ἐπὶ λέξεως *literally,* Eust.*engast.*21(p.50.5; M.18.657B); πρὸς λέξιν, *in plain language,* Clem.*str.*2.4(p.122.4; M.8.949B); Eus.*p.e.*10.7(477A; M.21.793B); id. *d.e.*7.1(p.319.35; M.22.521D).

***λεοντιαῖος,** *like a lion,* ‡Epiph.*hom.*1(M.43.433A); Steph.Diac. *v.Steph.*(M.100.1173D); Areth.*Apoc.*28(M.106.637C).

***λεόντιος,** *of a lion,* Clem.*fr.*32(p.217.28).

***λεοντόβρωτος,** *eaten by a lion,* Ephr.3.447E.

***λεοντόγνωμος,** *lion-minded,* punning epithet of Leo III, Jo.VI H.*v.Jo.D.*2(M.94.432C).

λεοντοειδής, *of leonine appearance*; of Michael acc. Ophite diagram, Or.*Cels.*6.30(p.100.8; M.11.1340A); of angels, Dion.Ar.*c.h.*15 tit.(M.3.325D); cf.*ib.*15.18(336D).

***λεοντοειδῶς,** *like a lion* λ. βρύξας ὁ ἀνήμερος θήρ [sc. Leo III] ‡Jo.D.*ep.Thphl.*12(M.95.360B).

***λεοντοπίθηκος, ὁ,** *lion-ape,* Philost.*h.e.*3.11(M.65.495C).

***λεοντώνυμος,** *bearing the name of lion*; of Leo III, ‡Jo.D.*ep. Thphl.*12(M.95.359B); Jo.VI H.*v.Jo.D.*2(M.94.432C).

λεόπαρδος, ὁ, *leopard, A.Phil.*96(p.37.28); Jo.Clim.*scal.*7(M.88. 812D); met. θηριομαχῶ...ἐνδεδεμένος δέκα λ., ὅ ἐστιν στρατιωτικὸν τάγμα Ign.*Rom.*5.1.

λεπράω, *become a leper,* Iren.*haer.*4.20.12(M.7.1043A); Meth.*lepr.* 12(p.446.3).

λεπριάω, = foreg., ‡Ath.*dial.Trin.*1.23(M.28.1152B).

λεπρ-όω, *make leprous* ἐλέπρωσε...τὴν χεῖρα Thdt.*qu.10 in Ex.*(1. 124); pass., Or.*adnot.in Num.*12:1(M.17.21A); Eus.*Is.*6:1(M.24. 121A); Chrys.*hom.3.4 in Col.*(11.349A); Nil.*epp.*2.166(M.79.279B); met. τὴν ταῖς ἁμαρτίαις...λεπρωθεῖσαν ψυχήν *ib.*1.104(128C); ἅμα τις λοιδορήσῃ τὸν πλησίον, εὐθέως ~οῦται τὴν καρδίαν *ib.*2.166(279B); λελεπρῶσθαι...τὴν τῶν Ἰουδαίων συναγωγήν Cyr.*glaph.Lev.*(1.361D).

λέπρωσις, ἡ, *turning leprous,* Thdt.*qu.10 in Ex.*(1.124).

***λεπτανικός,** *thin,* Jo.Mal.*chron.*10 p.232(M.97.357B) perh. for λεπτακινός *LS.*

λεπτεπίλεπτος, *thin-upon-thin,* neut. as subst.; *minutest subdivision,* as astrological term of subdivisions of sphere of fixed stars ἑκάστου γὰρ δωδεκατημορίου...εἰς τριάκοντα μοίρας διαιρουμένου...ἑκάστης δὲ μοίρας εἰς ἑξήκοντα λεπτά, καὶ τούτων ἑκάστου πάλιν εἰς ἑξήκοντα τὰ λεγόμενα λ. Proc.G.*Gen.*1:15(M.87.92D).

***λεπτηγορέω,** *mention in detail,* ‡Caes.Naz.*dial.*28(M.38.888).

λεπτίζομαι, *be turned into scales, become scaly,* Sophr.H.*mir.Cyr. et Jo.*8(M.87.3441C).

***λεπτοβόης,** *of feeble voice*; of Law, Cyr.*Jo.*3.2(4.258D).

***Λεπτογένεσις, ἡ,** *Little Genesis* (i.e. *Book of Jubilees*), Epiph. *haer.*39.6(M.41.672B; λεπτῇ γενέσει p.76.16).

λεπτόγεως (-γαιος, -γειος), *with poor soil,* Chrys.*sac.*2.4(p.35.16; 1.375C); *ib.*5.8(p.137.13; -γειον 1.419E, v.l. -γαιον); id.*hom.26.8 in 1Cor.* (λυπρόγεως 10.239A).

λεπτόγραφος, *neatly written,* Pall.*h.Laus.*proem.(p.14.17; M.34. 1009).

***λεπτοδάκτυλος,** *delicately-fingered,* Geo.Pis.*hex.*1166(M.92. 1524A).

***λεπτοεπέω,** *speak precisely,* Cyr.*ador.*15(1.546E); id.*dial.Trin.*5 (5^1.567A).

***λεπτόκλονος,** *with slender branches,* ‡Eust.*hex.*(M.18.740C); *Phys.*A 36(p.116.7).

λεπτολάχανον, τό, *chopped-up vegetable* in monastic diet, Pall.*h. Laus.*2(p.17.7; M.34.1011B); *ib.*32(p.95.10; 1105B); ὁ εἰς τὴν ἔρημον περιπατῶν ἄρτον οὐκ ἐσθίει, ἀλλὰ βοτάνας· σὺ δὲ διὰ τὴν ἀσθένειάν σου φάγε λ. *Apophth.Patr.*(M.65.152C).

λεπτολογ-έω, *specify precisely,* Epiph.*anc.*35(p.45.24; M.43. 81B); *ib.*54(p.63.21; 112C); ἡ οὖν ἀκρίβεια ~εῖ καὶ συλλογίζεται Ammon.*Ac.*26:5(M.85.1596C).

***λεπτολόγημα, τό,** *subtlety,* Epiph.*anc.*9(p.16.26; M.43.33A); id. *haer.*72.10(p.265.3; M.42.396D).

λεπτολογία, ἡ, 1. *precise reckoning,* Afric.*chron.*18.2(M.10.89D); *ib.*18.3(92A); **2.** *precise language,* Gr.Nyss.*hom.in 1Cor.6:18*(M.46. 492D); Epiph.*haer.*51.15(p.268.13; M.41.916C); *ib.*69.62(p.211.2; M. 42.301C); **3.** *hair-splitting,* Bas.*Spir.*4(3.4D; M.32.73C); Epiph.*haer.* 31.8(p.398.12; M.41.488D).

***λεπτολόγως,** *with precise definition,* Epiph.*haer.*19.4(p.222.7; M.41.268A).

λεπτομέρεια (-ία), ἡ, 1. *minute division,* Gr.Nyss.*Eun.*2(2 p.322. 1; M.45.496B); **2.** *detailed knowledge,* Evagr.*h.e.*2.4(p.44.12; M.86. 2500C); Leont.N.*v.Sym.*63(M.93.1745C); Jo.D.*spir.neq.*(M.95.96C).

λεπτομερής, A. *composed of fine particles, subtle*; **1.** in gen., Clem. *paed.*1.6(p.113.19; M.8.297A); *ib.*2.8(p.203.32; 488C); λεπτομερεστέροις τῶν στοιχείων Eus.*p.e.*7.10(314B; M.21.532C); Gr.Nyss.*hom.6 in Cant.*(M.44.896B); **2.** of bodies, Meth.*Porph.*2(p.506.2); ὁ δὲ ἀπὸ τοῦ χοῦ πλασθείς, τὸ λ. σῶμα καὶ ἄξιον τῆς ἐν παραδείσῳ διαγωγῆς Proc. G.*Gen.*3:21(M.87.221A); ref. bodies assumed by souls after supramundane fall λ. ἢ καὶ παχύτερα σώματα ἀμφιάσασθαι Justn.*ep.CP* (M.86.991A); of resurrection bodies ὁμοιότης...ἐν λ. μεταπεπλασμένη σώματι Meth.*res.*3.6(p.398.3; M.18.521C); *ib.*3.16(p.413.6) cit. s. ἀνάστασις; of Christ's risen body τὸ παχυμερὲς λ. καὶ τὸ θνητὸν ἀθάνατον Epiph.*anc.*91(p.112.11; M.43.184C); id.*inc.*3(p.230.12; M. 41.277A); *ib.*(p.231.1; 277B); id.*haer.*77.29(p.441.28; M.42.684B); **3.** of

God, Or.*Jo*.13.21(p.244.21; M.14.432C) cit. s. *αἰθερώδης*; *ἔστι...ὁ αἰθὴρ ἀὴρ λεπτομερέστατος...ἀέρα λέγων* [sc. Porphyry] *εἶναι αὐτὸν λεπτομερέστατον* Eus.*p.e.*3.11(108B; M.21.196B); *ὁ δὴ νοῦς...Διὸς ἐλήλεκται σῶμα τυγχάνων εἰ καὶ τὸ πάντων λεπτομερέστατον ib.*(108C; M.196B); **4.** of the soul *τὸ λεπτομερέστερον, ἡ ψυχή* Clem.*str.*6.6 (p.458.6; M.9.273C); *πνεῦμα λ. ὅ ἐστι ψυχή* Ammon.*Ac.*17:30(M.85.1568A); *σῶμά ἐστιν ἡ ψυχή...εἰ καὶ λεπτομερέστατον* Nemes.*nat.hom.* 2(M.40.540A).

B. *subtle, refined*, of ideas, etc. λ. *τί λέγει Δανιήλ* Hipp.*antichr.* 19(p.14.21; *λεπτομερέστερον* M.10.741D); *τὸ λ. τῆς προνοίας* Or.*fr. 54 in Lc.*(p.261.12; M.17.357A); Gr.Nyss.*Eun.*1(1 p.111.24; M.45.345C); λ. *διηγήσεως* Didym.ap.*cat.Ac.*18:28(p.312.11); Cyr.*Jo.*1.9(4.98C).

λεπτομερῶς, **1.** *in a rarefied manner, subtly*, Hipp.*haer.*7.21(p.196.19; M.16.3303A); Epiph.*haer.*76.12(p.374.18; M.42.569A); λ. ... *ἐκρέει τὸ πνεῦμα* Thdt.*provid.*3(4.518); **2.** *carefully, subtly*; of exegesis, etc., Hipp.*Dan.*4.13.1; id.*ben.Jac.*17(p.33.22); id.*haer.*5.13(p.107.7; M.16.3166A); Gr.Nyss.*Eun.*1(1 p.111.10; M.45.345D); Epiph.*haer.*51.7 (p.257.3; M.41.900C); Chrys.*hom.in Ps.115:1–3*(p.351.27); Pall. *v.Chrys.*13(p.82.21; M.47.47); Cyr.*Os.*32(3.57E); **3.** *craftily* λ. *ἀπατῶσα* Leo Mag.*ep.*44(p.26.13; M.*PL.*54.830B).

***λεπτομυθέω**, *explain precisely, go into details*, Cyr.*Jo.*3.3(4.267E); *ib.*12(1064B); id.*Rom.*8:3(p.211.24; M.74.817B).

***λεπτόνους**, *of subtle mind*, Cyr.*glaph.Gen.*2(1.57B).

***λεπτόομαι**, *suffer from consumption*, ‡Ath.*synops.*77(M.28.433C).

λεπτοποι-έω, *grind up small*, †Bas.*Is.*178(1.509D; M.30.420B); Gr. Nyss.*hom.6 in Cant.*(M.44.896B); met. *τοῖς ~οῦσιν ἐν τοῖς ὀδοῦσι τὸν λογισμόν ib.14*(1061D).

λεπτοποίησις, **ἡ**, *making small, reduction to small particles*, †Bas. *Is.*25(1.398E; M.30.165D).

***λεπτοποιητικός**, *making small, grinding up*, Gr.Nyss.*hom.7 in Cant.*(M.44.924C).

λεπτόπους, *with small feet*, Gr.Naz.*carm.*1.2.28.240,245(M.37.874A).

λεπτοπυρέτιον, **τό**, *slight fever*, Dor.*doct.*11.7(M.88.1741D).

***λεπτόρινος**, *with a small nose*, Jo.Mal.*chron.*5 p.103(M.97.192A).

λεπτός, **1.** *thin, slight*; in phrases: *ἐπὶ λεπτοῦ subtly*, Gr.Mag. *dial.*(tr.Zach.)4.3(M.*PL.*77.322C); *κατὰ λεπτόν in detail*, *V.Dan.*2 (p.56.15); **2.** *τὸ λ.*; **a.** *small coin, half-farthing*, ref. Mc.12:42 *χήραν λ. βάλλουσαν δύο τάχα τῷ γνωστικῷ τόπῳ ἢ τῷ πρακτικῷ* Or.*Jo.*19.8 (2; p.307.32; M.14.541A); cf. *duo minuta...libenter suscipiuntur, in quo amplius aliquid quam quod Moyses praeceperat de suscipienda pecunia demonstratur, ille enim ab his, qui habebant accipiebat; hic autem accipit etiam ab his qui non habent*, Hegem.*Arch.*47(p.70.6; M.10.1497B); Cyr.*Lc.*21:1(M.72.896A); Leont.N.*v.Jo.Eleem.* proem.(p.3.4); **b.** *minute*, subdivision of degree, *Chron.Pasch.*p.14 (M.92.93A); **c.** *minute* of time, *ib.*p.221(537B); **d.** *morsel, fragment*, Jo.Mosch.*prat.*42(M.87.2896B).

λεπτόσωμος, *of tenuous substance*; of air, Geo.Pis.*hex.*202(M.92.1449A).

λεπτότης, **ἡ**, **1.** *lightness*, Mac.Mgn.*apocr.*4.17(p.192.19); **2.** *immateriality*; of the soul, Clem.*str.*6.6(p.458.8; M.9.273C) cit. s. *ἁπλότης*; *ὁ τοιοῦτος ἐν λ. ... ἤδη κοινωνεῖ τῷ θεῷ* Mac.Aeg.*pat.*8(M.34.872B); of Christ's resurrection body *εἰς λ. πνεύματος κοσμηθέν* Epiph.*anc.*91(p.112.7; M.43.184C); of Christ's divinity, Mac.Aeg. *hom.*16.5(M.34.617A); **3.** *subtlety*, Or.*Jo.*2.7(4; p.62.1; M.14.121B); id.*comm.in Rom.*1:2(*JTS* 13 p.211.54; cf.M.14.842B); Mac.Mgn. *apocr.*2.17(p.29.14); *ib.*4.11(p.172.7); Mac.Aeg.*pat.*18(M.34.880C).

λεπτουργέω, *work out carefully* or *in detail*, Clem.*str.*7.18(p.78.8; M.9.556B); Bas.*Eun.*1.5(1.214E; M.29.516C); Nil.*epp.*3.10(M.79.372C).

λεπτουργία, **ἡ**, **1.** *skilful craftsmanship*; of Creation, Geo.Pis. *hex.*1270(M.92.1532A); *τὴν συντομουργὸν τοῦ θεοῦ λ. ib.*1505(1550A); **2.** *subtlety*, Gr.Nyss.*virg.*22(p.331.17; M.46.404B); Thdt.*Is.*19:9(p.84.22; 2.282).

***λεπτοχαράκτηρος**, *with fine features*, Jo.Mal.*chron.*5 p.103(M.97.192A); *ib.*10 p.243(372C); *Chron.Pasch.*p.312(M.92.793D).

λέπυρον, **τό**, *outer covering, shell, rind ἀλήθειαν...φιλοσοφίας, δόγμασι...ἐγκεκαλυμμένην...καθάπερ τῷ λ. τὸ ἐδώδιμον τοῦ καρύου* Clem.*str.*1.1(p.13.3; M.8.708A); *σιωπώμενα δόγματα ὡς κόκκους ῥόας ὑπὸ τὸ λ. αὐτῆς* Or.*schol.in Cant.*4:3(M.17.272A).

λέσχη, **ἡ**, *sect τῆς λ. ταύτης* [sc. Novatianists] *πρεσβύτερος* Tim. CP *haer.*(M.86.37B).

λεσχηνεύω, *talk idly*, *cat.1Cor.*12:6(p.230.17).

***Λευιαθάν**, **τό**, *Leviathan*, in Ophite diagram *κύκλου, ὃς ἐλέγετο εἶναι ἡ τῶν ὅλων ψυχὴ καὶ ὠνομάζετο Λ.* Or.*Cels.*6.25(p.95.5; M.11.1329A); *ἀντὶ δὲ τοῦ 'δράκων' Λ. ἦν ἐν τῷ 'Εβραϊκῷ* [ref. Ps.103:26] *ib.* (p.95.11; 1329A); *τὸ...διάγραμμα...Λ. ἔλεγεν εἶναι τὴν διὰ τῶν ὅλων πεφοιτηκυῖαν ψυχήν ib.*(p.95.12; 1329A).

λευίτης, **ὁ**, *Levite*; **1.** in comparison of OT hierarchy with gen. ordering of Christian church *τῷ γὰρ ἀρχιερεῖ ἴδιαι λειτουργίαι δεδομέναι εἰσίν...καὶ λευίταις ἴδιαι διακονίαι ἐπίκεινται 1Clem.*40.5; hence **2.** equated with Christian *deacon*, λ. coming to be synonymous with *διάκονος*: *οἱ λ. ὑμῶν οἱ νῦν διάκονοι Const.App.*2.26.3; *δεῖ γὰρ τοὺς τῇ ἐκκλησίᾳ προσεδρεύοντας ἐκ τῆς ἐκκλησίας διατρέφεσθαι, ἅτε ἱερεῖς, λευίτας, προέδρους, λειτουργοὺς θεοῦ, καθὼς ἐν βίβλῳ τῶν Ἀριθμῶν γέγραπται περὶ τῶν ἱερέων ib.*2.25.14; *ib.*4.8.1; cf.*ib.*8.46.5ff.; ‡Pion.*v.Polyc.*23; *1Apoc.Jo.*24(p.90); Pall.*v.Chrys.*17(p.107.2; M.47.60); *Cod.Afr.*3; *εἴτε λ. ἐστίν, εἴτε πρεσβύτερος, εἴτε ἐπίσκοπος* Synes.*ep.*58(M.66.1401D); cf.Thdt.*qu.1 in 2Par.*(1.596); exeg. Jer.33:18 *μαρτυρεῖ τοῖς λεγομένοις τὰ πράγματα. ἅπασα γὰρ γῆ καὶ θάλαττα πλήρεις ἀρχιερέων, καὶ τῶν λευιτικὴν λειτουργίαν πληρούντων διακόνων* id.ad loc.(2.558); Proc.G.*2Par.*29:34(M.87.1217A); Ant. Mon.*hom.*123(M.89.1817Dff.); **3.** name of group among Gnostics *οἱ δὲ Λ. παρ' αὐτοῖς καλούμενοι οὐ μίσγονται γυναιξίν, ἀλλὰ ἀλλήλοις μίσγονται* Epiph.*haer.*26.13(p.292.9; M.41.352C).

λευιτικός, **1.** *of Levi ἡ λ.* [sc. *φυλή*] Or.*princ.*4.3.6(p.332.1; M.11.385C); **2.** *Levitical*; of Law, institutions, etc., Clem.*prot.*1(p.4.20; M.8.56A); Gr.Nyss.*Eun.*12(1 p.283.14; M.45.992A); Cyr.*hom.pasch.*4 (5^2.40C); of work of deacons as λ. *λειτουργία*, Thdt.*Jer.*33:18(2.558); **3.** neut. as subst., title of book of OT, Clem.*str.*1.21(p.75.24; M.8.848A); Or.*mart.*30(p.27.11; M.11.601B); Cyr.*glaph.Lev.*tit.(1.343); **4.** masc. plur. as subst., name of Gnostic group *Λ. καὶ Βορβορῖται καὶ οἱ λοιποί* Epiph.*haer.*25.2(p.268.21; M.41.321C); v. *λευίτης*.

***λευιτών** (**λεβιτών*), **ὁ**, a monastic garment, ‡Pall.*h.mon.*(p.56.1; *λεβιτῶνα* M.65.449C); *λεβιτών ib.*(p.34.11; M.34.1138A).

***λευιτωνάριον**, **τό**, v. **λεβητονάριον*.

***λευκάζω**, *be white*, †Max.*hymn.*1(M.91.1421C).

λευκαντής, **ὁ**, *one who makes white, fuller*, *CG–CI* 31 (Corinth, saec. iv–v).

***λευκαντίζω**, *λελευκαντισμένη* prob. f.l. for *λελευκανθισμένη*, Jo. D.*hom.*8.11(M.96.716D); cf.*ib.*10.4(757D).

λευκάς, **1.** *white* λ. *χαίτην* Nonn.*par.Jo.*3:4(M.43.765C); *ib.*8:21 (816B); **2.** *clear* λ. *φωνῇ ib.*16:25(881C).

λευκάς, **ἡ**, *leaf* of palm-tree *οἱ φοίνικες...ἐκβάλλουσι λ. Apophth. Patr.*(M.65.208A).

λευκασμός, **ὁ**, *making white λίβανος γὰρ λ. ἑρμηνεύεται, ὅπερ ἐστὶν ὁ κύριος ὁ λευκαίνων πάντας* Hesych.H.*Ps.tit.*103(M.27.1093D).

***λευκόδερμος**, *with a white surface*; of pearls, Geo.Pis.*hex.*1630 (*λευκόδεσμος* M.92.1561A).

***λευκοειδής**, *of white appearance*, ‡Jo.D.*hom.*5(M.96.657D).

***λευκοπόρφυρος**, *pale purple*, Soz.*h.e.*9.2.13(M.67.1601A).

***λευκόπυρσος**, *gleaming white*; of moon, Geo.Pis.*hex.*143(M.92.1443A).

λευκός, *white*; of baptismal robe, *Chron.Pasch.*p.276(M.92.685A); fig. *διὰ παντὸς ἔστω σου τὰ ἱμάτια λ., ὅτι εὐδόκησε κύριος τὰ ποιήματά σου...ἐνδυσάμενον τὰ πνευματικῶς λ., χρὴ λευχειμονεῖν διαπαντός* Cyr.H.*catech.*22.8; v. *βάπτισμα, φωτεινός*; met., *Hom.Clem.*13.16 cit. s. *λαμπρύνω*; of the 'white' faction in circus, representing air and associated with 'green' faction representing earth, while 'blue' and 'red' symbolize water and fire, *Chron.Pasch.*p.112(M.92.296A); *λευκή, ἡ white line*, starting-point for chariot races in hippodrome, ‡Chrys.*circ.*(8.88A).

λευκόστολος, *in white robes*, *Pers.*(p.23.9).

***λευκοσχήμων**, *white*, *Hymn.*(*AS* 1 p.601).

***λευκοφανής**, *shining white*; of angels, ‡Epiph.*v.proph.Eliae* 2 (p.32; M.43.396B).

λευκοφορ-έω, *wear white robes*, ref. pagan festival *πάντων ~ούντων μόνος ἐνδυσάμενος μέλανα A.Jo.*38(p.170.2); ref. angelic appearances, ‡Pall.*h.mon.*8.18(p.38.11; M.34.1139C); of Moses and Elijah at Transfiguration, Socr.*h.e.*6.22.7(M.67.728C); opp. *Αἰθίοπες*, Jo.Mosch.*prat.* 66(M.87.2917A).

λευκοχίτων, *dressed in a white robe*, ‡Gr.Naz.*Chr.pat.*2123 (M.38.304A); met., of day of Resurrection, ‡Chrys.*serm.pasch.* (p.108).

λευκόω, *make white*; pass., of a tablet to be used for painting, Athenag.*leg.*17.2(M.6.924A); of a leper, Clem.*paed.*3.11(p.267.16; M.8.628B).

λευχειμον-έω, *wear white*; **1.** of men, ref. Essenes *πάντες δὲ ἀεὶ ~οῦσι* Hipp.*haer.*9.19(p.256.25; M.16.3395B); *λευχειμονήσας τὸν λίβανον ἐπιθῶ* Or.*comm.in 1Cor.*5:9–11(*JTS* 9 p.366); ref. Mt.22:11

τὸ ~οῦν πάντων Cyr.H.*procatech*.3; ref. neophytes τὴν...γῆν... ~οῦσαν Pall.*v.Chrys*.9(p.58.13; M.47.34); **2.** of angels and spiritual beings appearing in visions ~οῦντες ἄγγελοι *A.Thom.*A 6(p.109.8 not., one MS); ἀναστάσεως δι' ἣν καὶ ~οῦντες ἐφαίνοντο Ammon. *Jo*.20:11(M.85.1516D); Thdt.*h.rel*.21(3.1246); Cosm.Ind.*top*.2(M.88. 121D); Thdr.Lect.*fr*.(M.86.224A); Jo.Mosch.*prat*.105(M.87.2964A); ~οῦσαν ἁγίων ὁμήγυριν Sophr.H.*mir.Cyr.et Jo*.11(M.87.3453B); Leont.N.*v.Sym*.22(M.93.1697D); Niceph.Ur.*v.Sym*.13(M.86.2997C); ref. angels at Ascension, ‡Epiph.*hom*.5(M.43.485B); Anton.Hag. *v.Sym.Styl*.10(p.32.9); **3.** met. χρὴ ~εῖν διαπαντός Cyr.H.*catech*.22.8; ~οῦντες τοῖς καθαροῖς νοήμασι Gr.Nyss.*hom.1 in Cant*.(M.44.765A); Geo.Pis.*res*.1(M.92.1373A); Jo.D.*carm.theoph*.111(p.212; M.96.832A); ~ῶ τῷ λόγῳ id.*hom*.3.2(M.96.592A).

***λευχείμων**, *dressed in white*; in gen., of Montanist prophetesses εἰσέρχονται λαμπαδηφοροῦσαι ἑπτά τινες παρθένοι, λ. δῆθεν ἐρχόμεναι, ἵνα προφητεύσωσι τῷ λαῷ Epiph.*haer*.49.2(p.243.4; M.41.381A); of a bride, Gr.Nyss.*virg*.3(p.263.8; M.46.332D); στιχάριον λ. ὡς ἀγγέλου ‡Sophr.H.*liturg*.8(M.87.3988C); of angels, at Resurrection, Eus. Em.*fr.Jo*.20:7(M.86.552D); in visions, Niceph.Ur.*v.Sym*.13(M.86. 2997C); Jo.Mosch.*prat*.38(M.87.2889A); ref. resurrection of saints πάντας λ. καὶ ὡσπερεὶ λαμπροτάταις στολαῖς τοῖς τῆς ἀναστάσεως ἀφθαρτοῖς σώμασιν ἐξαστράπτοντας Eus.*e.th*.3.16(p.175.12; M.24. 1033C).

λεχώ, ἡ, *woman in child-bed*; *woman in puerperal condition* τοῖς πολλοῖς...δοκεῖ ἡ Μαριὰμ λ. εἶναι διὰ τὴν τοῦ παιδίου γέννησιν, οὐκ οὖσα λ. (καὶ γὰρ μετὰ τὸ τεκεῖν αὐτὴν μαιωθεῖσάν φασί τινες παρθένον εὑρεθῆναι) Clem.*str*.7.16(p.66.21; M.9.529B).

[*]**λεωπλάνος**, v. λαοπλάνος.

λεωφόρος, **1.** adj., *carrying people*; hence, of a road, *main*, *frequented* οὐδεμία δὲ ὁδός, οὐ λ., οὐ στενωπός Dion.Al.ap.Eus.*h.e.* 6.41.8(M.20.608A); Nil.*Magn*.19(M.79.993C); ‡Nil.*perist*.10.5(M.79. 896A); met., Clem.*str*.7.15(p.65.3; M.9.528A); **2.** λ. [sc. ὁδός], ἡ, *main road*, *highway*, Hipp.*fr.5 in Pr*.(p.158.14); Eus.*d.e*.3.4(p.114.15; M.22.196C); Bas.Sel.*or*.5.2(M.85.84A); fig., ‡Bas.*const*.2.3(2.542D; M.31.1344C); Thdt.*eran*.1(4.6); met., of monastic discipline θείας λ. Nil.*epp*.3.108(M.79.433D); of pleasure, Isid.Pel.*epp*.5.485(M.78. 1609A); of parenthood λ. τῆς φύσεως Bas.Sel.*or*.4.2(M.85.68A); of way of truth, Gel.Cyz.*h.e*.1 proem.23(M.85.1197B); of doctrinal orthodoxy βασιλικῆς λ.,...τῆς ἀποστολικῆς πίστεως *ib*.2.20.4(1281C); Evagr.*h.e*.4.39(p.190.1; M.86.2781A).

***ληγατάριος** (*λεγατάριος), ὁ, (Lat. *legatarius*), *legatee*, Justn. *nov*.1.1(p.2.37) al.; Ath.Scholast.*coll*.3.3(p.46); λεγατάριον *ib*.5.2 (p.71).

***ληγατεύ-ω** (*λεγατεύω), **1.** *bequeath*, pass. λιτιγιόσου πράγματος λεγατευθέντος Ath.Scholast.*coll*.5.2(p.71); Phot.*nomoc*.2.1(M.104. 565B); **2.** *make* someone *a legatee* ~σας πολλούς Marc.Diac.*v.Porph.* 103; **3.** abs., *make bequests* διάταξις ἐπιτρέπει Σαμαρίτας...~ειν Ath.Scholast.*coll*.3.2(p.45); **4.** *pay a dole* ἐκέλευσεν τοῖς ἐπάρχοις ληγατεῦσαι αὐτοῖς ἀπὸ δημοσίων Παλαιστίνης Marc.Diac.*v.Porph.* 54.

***ληγατίων**, ἡ, (Lat. *legatio*) *dole*, *payment from public funds*, Marc.Diac.*v.Porph*.54.

***ληγάτον** (*λεγάτον), τό, (Lat. *legatum*) *legacy* βούλομαι...δοθῆναι αὐτῷ λεγάτον λόγῳ χρυσᾶ νομίσματα πέντε Gr.Naz.*test*.(M.37.392C); Epiph.*exp.fid*.7(p.503.6; M.42.785A); μεγάλοις λεγάτοις Ath.Presb. *libell*.(p.20.26; H.2.332B); Jo.Scholast.*coll.cap*.24(p.395); Ath. Scholast.*coll*.2.3(p.35).

***ληγάτος**, ὁ, (Lat. *legatus*), *deputy*; **1.** official acting as lieutenant of a higher authority, esp. *provincial governor*, *M.Das.* 5.3; Nil.*epp*.2.246 tit.(M.79.328B); *IGC As.Min*.124.4 (Hypaepa); **2.** papal representative at councils, CEph.(431)*act*.2(*ACO* 1.1.3 p.53. 23; H.1.1465C); *ib*.3(p.62.12; 1480B).

λήγω, **1.** *cease*; hence, of the moon, *wane*, *Apoc.Bar*.9(p.91.4); **2.** *finally turn into*, *end up in* ἀὴρ...εἰς πῦρ ἔληξε *Hom.Clem*.20.6; πάντων...εἰς εὐφροσύνην ληξάντων Anat.CP *ep*.2(p.54.7; M.*PL*.54. 982C).

[***ληδιόνοστος**, ὁ, v. ληίς.

ληθαῖος, *forgetful*, Nonn.*par.Jo*.14:24(M.43.872A).

ληθαργ-έω, *forget* πάσας τὰς ἁμαρτίας ἃς ἐποίησα ἐν τῷ κόσμῳ ἐληθάργησα· ἐνταῦθα δὲ οὐκ ἐληθάργησαν *T.Abr*.B 10(p.115.10); ἐληθάργησε τὴν ἡτοιμασμένην κόλασιν ‡Chrys.*ascet.facet*.(1.808E); Procl.CP *or*.5.3(M.65.720B); Jo.Mal.*chron*.6 p.155(M.97.256B); ἡ ψυχὴ...εἰσπίπτει ἐν ἄλλῳ σώματι...καὶ ~εῖ ποίαν δορὰν ἀφῆκε Cosm. Mel.*schol*.(M.38.465) in Gr.Naz.*carm*.1.1.8.28–29.

ληθαργικός, **1.** *causing to forget* ὕπνος λ. †Hipp.*Laz*.(p.218.7); Socr.*h.e*.7.7.1(M.67.749B); **2.** *forgetting*, *forgetful*, v. λήθαργος.

λήθαργος, *forgetting*, *forgetful* τὸ γῆρας ἔχει...τὸ λ. Chrys.*hom. 4.1 in Tit*.(11.750B, v.l. ληθαργικόν).

***ληθοποιός**, *causing forgetfulness*, Eust.ap.Leont.et Jo.*sacr*.2.1 (M.86.2040A).

ληθώ, ἡ, = λήθη, *forgetfulness* ἡ Λητὼ...λ. τις καλείσθω...ὅτι λήθη ξυνομαρτεῖ ταῖς ὑπὸ σελήνην γενομέναις ψυχαῖς Eus.*p.e*.3.13 (119A; M.21.213C).

ληΐζ-ω, *ravage*, met. θάνατος διαφθείρων ἡμῶν τὰ ~οντα τὴν φύσιν Meth.*res*.1.45(p.295.10; M.41.1116C).

ληίς, ἡ, *people* δωρήσαο ληΐδι νόστον †Apoll.*met.Ps*.84:2 (v.l. ληδιόνοστον M.33.1437C).

ληΐστωρ, ὁ, *robber*; as adj., *of a robber*, Nonn.*par.Jo*.10:1(M.43. 832B); *ib*.10:8(833A); *ib*.18:20(893A).

λημματίας, ὁ, *one who is high-spirited*; hence *one who is audacious*, Cyr.*Abac*.20(3.534D).

λημ-άω, *have sore eyes*, met. ~ῶντας τῷ ῥύπῳ τῶν ἁμαρτιῶν Thdt. *rect.conf*.17(M.6.1240A).

λήμ(μ)η, ἡ, *discharge in the eye*, met. τῆς ἀπιστίας λ. Thdt.*2Cor.* 3:18(3.307); νηστείας ἡ σάλπιγξ...τῶν ἔνδον ὀφθαλμῶν περιαιροῦσα τὰς λ. Bas.Sel.*or*.1.1(M.85.28B); τῇ λήμμῃ τῆς βασκανίας τὸ ὀξυκερδὲς ἀφῃρημένοι τοῦ ὄμματος Jo.D.*hom*.1.7(M.96.557B).

λῆμμα, τό, *something taken*; **1.** *gain*, Herm.*sim*.9.19.3; ὅλους τοῦ λ. Chrys.*hom.81.3 in Mt*.(7.776D); Thdr.Mops.*Ac*.2:11–15(M.66. 489C); εὐτελεστάτων λ. Cyr.*Am*.15(3.266C); Proc.G.*Is*.4:22–25(M. 87.1908B); **2.** *something picked*; **a.** lit., *vegetable* λαχάνων ἢ λ. Thdt. *1Cor*.4:13(3.189); **b.** met., *something selected* τὸ λ. τῆς χάριτος Cyr. *ador*.3(1.90B); λ. κατ' ἐκλογὴν χάριτος id.*Is*.5.6(2.895D); **3.** *something assumed* in argument, Clem.*str*.8.3(p.83.8; M.9.565B); *ib*.(p.84.15; 568C); Bas.*Eun*.2.10(1.246A; M.29.592A); Chrys.*hom.39.4 in 1Cor.* (10.369A); id.*hom.30.1 in Mt*.(7.437C); **4.** of prophetic oracles in OT (Eng. versions *burden*), *subject*, *theme* (in Abac.1:1 = מַשָּׂא *uplifting* of eyes, hence *vision*), interprn. ῥῆσις καὶ λόγος καὶ λ. ταὐτόν ἐστι Chrys.*fr.in Jer*.1:1(M.64.745D); τινὲς δὲ...τοῦ...πνεύματος δι' αὐτῶν ἐνεργοῦντος ἐφθέγγοντο...τοῦτο ἐκάλουν λ. Thdt.*qu.31 in 4Reg*.(1.531B); ἐκάλουν...λ. τὴν προφητείαν id.*Jer*.23:34(2.520); id. *Nah*.1:1(2.1519); Olymp.*Jer*.23:33(M.93.677A); τὸ λ. ἴσον εἶναι τὸ δόμα παρὰ θεοῦ Proc.G.*Is*.1:1(M.87.1825A); ἀντὶ τοῦ, ἡ ὅρασις, λ. Σύμμαχός φησιν *ib*.30:6–17(2261B); **5.** = λῆμα, *spirit*, *courage*, Meth. *symp*.8.12(p.97.2; M.18.157C); ἥκιστα τοῦδε λ. ἔφυ τυραννικόν (cf. Euripides *Medea* 348) ‡Gr.Naz.*Chr.pat*.251(M.38.157A).

λημμάτιον, τό, **1.** *paltry gain*, Cyr.*Soph*.31(3.608A); id.*Juln*.10 (6^2.358A); Sophr.H.*mir.Cyr.et Jo*.(M.87.3605B); **2.** *premise* of argument, Zach.Mit.*opif*.(M.85.1081B).

[*]**λήμμη**, ἡ, v. λήμη.

λημνίσκος (*λιμν-), ὁ, a critical mark [÷] used by Or. to show that same sense was rendered in two different ways, λιμν-, Epiph. *mens*.8(M.43.248C); described, λιμν-, *ib*.(248B); Cyr.*Pss*.proem.(M. 69.717B); cf.Isid.H.*etym*.1.21.5.

ληναΐζω, *compose* drama *for the Lenaea*, Clem.*prot*.1(p.4.4; M.8. 53B).

***ληνιαῖος**, *of the wine-press* σαβιθά· τοῦτο...ἑρμηνεύεται λ. ἄντλημα Epiph.*mens*.24(M.43.284C, v.l. λιμνιαῖον).

ληνοβατ-έω, *tread out in the wine-press* ἐφ' ἑνὸς θυσιαστηρίου τοὺς τῶν ἀνθρώπων καρποὺς ~οῦσιν οἱ ἱερεῖς Thdt.*Ps*.8:1(1.650); ληνὸς...ἡ ἐκκλησία, διὰ τὸν θεὸν τὸν ἐν αὐτῇ ~οῦντα τὸ μυστήριον Hesych.H.*fr.Ps*.55:1(M.93.1221C); Jo.D.*hom*.2.4(M.96.729B).

ληνοβάτης, ὁ, *one who treads the wine-press* βλέπω τὸν σταυρὸν... καὶ τὰ ἱμάτια τοῦ κυρίου ὡς τὰ τοῦ λ. κεχρωσμένα τῷ αἵματι Ast.Am. *hom*.5(M.40.225C).

ληνός, ἡ, **1.** *wine-press*; **a.** exeg. Ps.8:1 λ. εἰσὶ φύσεις λογικαί, τοὺς ἐκ τῆς πνευματικῆς ἀμπέλου καρποὺς ὑποδεξάμεναι Or.*sel.in Ps*.8:1 (M.12.1184A); ἐν γὰρ τῇ λ. τῆς ψυχῆς (λ. δέ ἐστιν ἡ συνείδησις) ὁ ἐκ τῶν ἔργων βότρυς τὸν οἶνον ἡμῖν εἰς τὸν ἐφεξῆς ἀποθήσεται βίον Gr.Nyss. *Pss.titt*.B 5(M.44.505C); οὐ μία...ἡ λ., πολλαὶ γὰρ αἱ πρακτικαὶ ἀρεταὶ καὶ τοῦ καρποῦ ἑκάστης οἰκεία τις ἔσται λ. Didym.*Ps*.8:1(M.39. 1184D); φασὶ δέ τινες καὶ εἰς τὸν κοινὸν εἰρῆσθαι ἄνθρωπον ἐν τῇ τῶν σκηνοπηγίων ἑορτῇ...τὸν ψαλμὸν...καθ' ὃ ἡ τῶν καρπῶν συγκομιδὴ γίνεται· καὶ διὰ τοῦτο ἐπιγέγραπται παρὰ τῶν λ. Thdr.Mops.*Ps*.8:1 (p.42.21; M.66.653A); ὑπὲρ τῶν λ. ... ὑπὲρ τῶν ἐχόντων ἐν ἑαυτοῖς τὸν οἶνον...τουτέστι τὸν κύριον Hesych.H.*Ps.tit*.8(M.27.674B); interpreted of churches ὑπὲρ δὲ τῶν λ. διὰ τὰς ἐν πάσῃ τῇ γῇ συστάσας ἐκκλησίας...τὸ δὲ πλῆθος νυνὶ τῶν λ. τὰ πολλὰ μηνύει θυσιαστήρια ταῖς κατὰ μέρος ἐκκλησίαις συνδιαιρούμενα Eus.*Ps*.8:1(M.23.125D); αὗται δὲ ἂν εἶεν αἱ ἐκκλησίαι, αἱ τοὺς τῶν κατορθούντων ἐν θεοσεβείᾳ δεχόμεναι καρπούς...μετὰ δὲ τὴν τῶν ἐθνῶν κλῆσιν πολλαὶ λ. Ath.*exp. Ps*.8:1(M.27.80D); λ. ... τὰς ἐκκλησίας...εἰς ἃς...συγκομίζουσιν οἱ μυσταγωγοὶ τοὺς ἐκ...᾿Ιουδαίων καὶ ἐκ τῶν ἐθνῶν πιστεύοντας...καὶ... ἐξ ἀμπελῶνος δεσποτικῆς καρποὺς συνεγείρουσιν Cyr.*Ps.*8:1(M.69.757A); λ. δὲ τὰς ἐκκλησίας προσαγορεύει ἐπειδὴ καὶ τὸν κύριον ἄμπελον ...ταύτην δὲ τρυγῶντες οἱ πεπιστευκότες τὸν μυστικὸν κατασκευάζουσιν οἶνον Thdt.*Ps.*8:1(1.650); λ. τὰς ἐκκλησίας ἐν αἷς ἐκχεῖται ὁ οἶνος ἤτοι τὸ...αἷμα τοῦ κυρίου ‡Ath.*qu.script.*77(M.28.744B); **b.** exeg. Is.63:2–3; of inheritance of gentiles in place of Jews, Just.*dial.*26.4(M.6.532A–C); μόνῳ γὰρ αὐτῷ τὴν κρίσιν δέδωκεν ὁ πατήρ, τὴν δὲ ἁμαρτημάτων ἔκπραξιν λ. εἴωθε καλεῖν...τῶν ἀγαθῶν καρπῶν...τρυγωμένων λ. θεοφιλεῖς...γίνονται Eus.*Is.*63:2–3(M.24.501C); cf.Proc.G.*Is.*63:2–3(M.87.2668A); λ. δὲ ὀνομάζει τὴν πολεμίων κατάλυσιν Thdt.*Is.*63:2f.(p.245.33; 2.388); λ. γὰρ ἡ Γὲθ ἑρμηνεύεται· λ. δὲ καὶ ἡ ἐκκλησία, διὰ τὸν θεὸν τὸν ἐν αὐτῇ ληνοβατοῦντα τὸ μυστήριον Hesych.H.*fr.Ps.*55:1(M.93.1221C); **c.** exeg. Mt.21:33–43 λ. ὁ τόπος τῶν σπονδῶν [sc. in Temple] Or.*comm.in Mt.*17.6(p.591.19; M.13.1488B); **d.** exeg. Mt.26:26–28, Jo.15:1, cf. *ego sum vitis vera, et est sanguis uvae illius, quae missa in torcular passionis protulit potum*, id.*comm.ser.85 in Mt.*(p.196.27; M.13.1734B); **2.** *basin* of fountain, *Asen.*(p.42.9); Thdt.*provid.*3(4.519); for sacrificial blood, *A.Andr.et Mt.*22(p.96.8); **3.** *cistern*, Just.*dial.*86.2(M.6.680C); Cyr.*glaph.Ex.*1(1.256D); **4.** *sarcophagus*, in form λανός *IG* 14.150; ἐὰν ἀνοίξῃ τὴν λ. *CG–CI* 1.15; *ib.*1.30 (Corinth, saec. v–vi).

***λῃξίπονος**, *relieving pain*, Sophr.H.*mir.Cyr.et Jo.*16(M.87.3473A).

λῆξις, ἡ, (A), 1. *obtaining of a portion* or *lot* ἀγαθῶν...λ. Chrys.*hom.in Rom.5:3*(3.143A); Cyr.*thes.*32(5[1].323B); **2.** *lot, portion* τὴν... παππῴαν λ. τῷ μείζονι...διένειμε Eus.*v.C.*4.51(p.138.9; M.20.1201A); Chrys.*stat.*18.4(2.187C); id.*hom.18.3 in Mt.*(7.237D); of heavenly reward τῆς ἐκεῖ λ. ... ἐκβαλεῖν *ib.13.4*(173D); Thdt.*affect.*8(p.207.16; 4.911); Oecum.*Apoc.*14:13(p.165); Dion.Ar.*ep.*9.1(M.3.1105A); μῆτερ ...θεοῦ...προκληθεῖσα εἰς λ. μακαριότητος Mod.*dorm.*10(M.86.3301C); **3.** *side taken* τῆς ἐναντίας προκατάρχοντες λ. Eus.*v.C.*2.10(p.45.8; M.20.989C); **4.** *appointed place, allotted sphere* ὄμματα...τῆς ἰδίας λ. ἀποπεσόντα Eus.*h.e.*9.10.15(M.20.836D); γῆν καὶ...ὑποχθόνιον λ. Gr.Nyss.*Eun.*5(2 p.103.18; M.45.681C); αἰσθητῆς κτίσεως...μεθ᾿ ἣν ἡ νοητὴ...διαδέχεται λ. *ib.*12(1 p.293.16; 1004A); ἡ...νοητὴ [sc. φύσις]... τὴν ἄνω λ. ἐπιπορεύεται id.*or.dom.*4(p.74.16; M.44.1165B); id.*or.catech.*6(p.30.11; M.45.25D); τὰς ἐν οὐρανῷ λ. ὅπου τὸ φῶς Dion.Ar.*c.h.*15.4(M.3.333A); id.*e.h.*1.4(M.3.376B); of bosoms of patriarchs as θειόταται λ., *ib.*7.3.6(560B); cf.*cat.Lc.*16:29(p.127.22); Max.*schol.c.h.*6(M.4.64C); of future life, in gen. δοῦλον...ὃν...προσελάβου εἰς ἑτέραν λ. *Const.App.*8.41.5; Dion.Ar.*e.h.*7.1.2(M.3.553C); heaven, Ath.*exp.Ps.*14:1(M.27.100A); τὴν ψυχὴν ἐπὶ τὴν...πρέπουσαν αὐτῇ λ. ἀνέπεμψε Bas.*hom.*5.2(2.34E; M.31.241A); Gr.Nyss.*hom.2 in Cant.*(M.44.804C); Chrys.*hom.47.3 in Jo.*(8.280B); Dion.Ar.*e.h.*2.1(M.3.392A); τὴν...θεοειδῆ λ. *ib.*3.3.9(437B); ἀθάνατον...λ. *ib.*7.1.2(553D); θείαις...λ. *ib.*7.2.1(557A); μακαριωτάτων λ. *ib.*7.2.2(557B); λ. ... ἀμοιβαίαν *ib.*7.3.6(560D); id.*d.n.*1.5(M.3.592B); id.*ep.*8.5(M.3.1097A); Evagr.*h.e.*4.26(p.173.8; M.86.2745A); Max.*cap.*4.29(M.90.1316B); as compared with present life τὴν κρείττονα λ. Eus.*v.C.*3.46(p.96.33; M.20.1105C); μείζονα λ. Chrys.*hom.42.3 in 1Cor.*(10.396D); τυχὼν ἀμείνονος λ. Synes.*ep.*27(M.66.1357A); Bas.Sel.*v.Thecl.*2 proem.(M.85.565C); Evagr.*h.e.*4.1(p.153.5; 2704A); contrasted with hell, †Just.*fr.*118(p.52; M.6.1596C); of hell πρέπουσα λ. τοῖς τῇ δυναστείᾳ ...ἐπὶ κακῷ χρησαμένοις ‡Nil.*perist.*9.7(M.79.880A); hence **5.** phrase τῆς ὁσίας, θείας, etc., λήξεως used to describe the departed, Marcian.Imp.*ep.Leo.*3(p.55.29; M.*PL.*54.974B); Θεοδόσιον τὸν τῆς εὐσεβοῦς λ. Justn.*conf.*(p.108.24; M.86.1033A); *Chron.Pasch.*p.377(M.92.964B); **6.** *state, condition* οὐρανὸς...πρὸς τὴν ἀμείνω λ. ... μεταστήσεται Chrys.*hom.14.5 in Rom.*(9.582B); τὰ ὀνόματα ταῦτα [sc. of ministry] τῆς ἄνω λ. ὑπάρχει, ἐπεὶ οὐδὲν πρεσβύτερον θεοῦ, οὐδὲν ἐπισκοπώτερον Pall.*v.Chrys.*9(p.55.8; M.47.32); Nil.*epp.*3.318(M.79.537B); Max.*cap.*5.51(M.90.1369C); ref. state of Adam in paradise, Eus.*p.e.*7.10(317B; M.21.536C); of demons, *ib.*4.5(142A; M.248B); of angels λ. τὴν ἀγγελικήν Chrys.*hom.68.5 in Mt.*(7.677B); id.*hom.1.1 in Jo.*(8.2B); Thdt.*haer.*5.8(4.407); Proc.G.*Gen.*18:1(M.87.365B).

λῆξις, ἡ, (B) 1. *rest* τὸν τῶν ἀγγέλων...βίον...μεθέξοντας ἀπαθείας καὶ λ. Bas.Sel.*v.Thecl.*1(M.85.485A); βασιλείας καὶ λ. *ib.*(485B); Max.*ambig.*(M.91.1089A); **2.** *limit*; **a.** geographical ἑῴας τε καὶ δύσεως...λ. Max.*ep.*44(M.91.648A); Jo.D.*hom.*9.3(M.96.746C); τὰς τέσσαρας λ. τῆς οἰκουμένης Areth.*Apoc.*63(M.106.753D); **b.** εἰς, πρός, λῆξιν *to the limit*; **i.** without vb. or genit. τοῖς εἰς λ. κακοῖς Cyr.*ador.*7(1.235E); id.*glaph.Gen.*6(1.180D); id.*Is.*1.1(2.8D); πραότητος... τῆς εἰς λ. *ib.*5.4(820D); id.*Chr.un.*(5[1].757E); id.*ep.*41(p.40.12; 5[2].121C); id.*hom.pasch.*24(5[2].290B); **ii.** c. vb. τῶν εἰς λ. ἡκόντων ἐπαίνων id.*ador.*6(1.202B); τοῦ πρὸς λ. ἰόντος...κακοῦ *ib.*(206B); id.*glaph.Gen.*1(1.7A); γενέσθαι εἰς λ. τὴν ἀνωτάτω id.*ador.*9(1.312D); εἰς λ. ... ἀρετῆς ἀναβαίνειν id.*Is.*1.3(2.65A); *ib.*4.1(556D); id.*Nah.*13(3.491A); διὰ τὸ εἰς λ. ἰέναι τὴν ἀνωτάτω id.*dial.Trin.*5(5[1].566C); **c.** perh. as prepositional phrase λῆξιν *as far as* κεκόσμηται γῆ ἀέρος καὶ ὕδατος λ. Proc.G.*Gen.*1:20(M.87.100B).

ληπτός, 1. *capable of being apprehended* οὐ...τὴν θεότητα τοῦ μονογενοῦς ὀφθαλμοῖς ἀνθρώπων λ. ἔσεσθαι †Thdt.*Nest.*(4.1051); in number, i.e. *few* ἀριθμῷ...ληπτούς Eus.*p.e.*10.1(461A; M.21.768B); id.*d.e.*1.9(p.41.19; M.22.80B); *ib.*2.3(p.84.3; M.149C); **2.** *to be grasped, desirable* ληπτὸν ἡγεῖται Clem.*str.*1.17(p.54.23; M.8.800A); **3.** *receiving bribes* δικαστῶν λ. καὶ δωροδοκουμένων Jo.D.*parall.*index(M.95.1052).

***ληπτῶς**, *by being taken*, of creation of Eve οὔτε γεννητῶς οὔτε... ἀναιτίως, ἀλλὰ λ. ἤτοι ἐκπορευτῶς ‡Anast.S.*serm.imag.*(M.89.1145A).

ληραίνω, *be foolish*, Tat.*orat.*33(p.34.5; M.6.873B).

[*]**ληρία, ἡ**, v. λῃρωδία.

***ληρολόγημα, τό**, *nonsensical utterance*; of heret. doctrine, Epiph.*haer.*66.47(p.85.7; M.42.101A); *ib.*79.4(p.479.26; 745D).

***ληρολογία, ἡ**, *nonsensical talk*; of heret. teaching, Epiph.*haer.*26.13(p.294.1; M.41.354C); *ib.*31.4(p.389.8; 479C); *ib.*32.2(p.440.27; 546C).

***ληρολόγος**, *talking nonsense*, of Gnostics λ. σοφισταί Iren.*haer.*1.11.5(M.7.569A); of Simon Magus as ὁ λ., Epiph.*haer.*21.6(p.245.5; M.41.293C); of dreaming, *ib.*32.7(p.447.10; 553C).

***ληροπαραπαίω**, *speak nonsensically, rave*, Leont.H.*Nest.*1.48(M.86.1509B).

***ληρόσοφος**, *wise in nonsense*; as subst. masc., †Chrys.*pan.Bab.*2.18(2.566E).

***ληροφρονέω**, *think foolishly*, Pall.*v.Chrys.*20(p.139.18; M.47.78).

λῃρωδέω, *say* or *speak foolishly*; trans., Philost.*fr.*(M.65.637B); Cosm.Ind.*top.*1(M.88.61C); intrans., *Dial.Christ.et Jud.*17(p.82.18).

λῃρώδημα, τό, *nonsensical utterance*, Anast.S.*hod.*8(M.89.132B).

λῃρωδία, ἡ, *nonsense, foolish talking*, Gr.Naz.*carm.*2.1.14.3(M.37.1245A); esp. of heresy and paganism, Epiph.*haer.*21.6(p.245.1; M.41.293C); *ib.*31.1(p.383.21; 473D); *ib.*36.6(p.49.20; 640B) al.; Chrys.*hom.67.1 in Mt.*(7.662D); id.*hom.10.5 in Rom.*(9.526D); id.*hom.12.2 in Eph.*(11.92E, v.l. ληρίας); Cyr.*Nah.*29(3.506A); plur., *absurdities* λῃρωδίας πλάττει Chrys.*hom.24.3 in Jo.*(8.141B); †Thdt.*Nest.*(4.1048C); Jo.D.*haer.*101(M.94.769B).

***λῃρώδως**, *foolishly*, Sophr.H.*ep.syn.*(M.87.3184A).

***λησμονέω, 1.** *forget*; c. genit., Nil.*epp.*2.175(M.79.289B); pass., Leont.N.*v.Sym.*33(M.93.1712A); **2.** *neglect* to do something ἐλησμόνησα δοῦναι αὐτῷ τὸν ποτόν Marc.Diac.*v.Porph.*24; **3.** *leave inadvertently* λησμονήσας αὐτὴν ἐν τῷ κελλίῳ ‡Ath.*imag.Beryt.*A 2(M.28.797C).

***λησμονή, ἡ**, *forgetfulness*, Epiph.*haer.*51.18(M.41.924A, v.l. ἐπιλησμονήν p.275.14).

***λῃσταρχέω**, *proceed to plunder*, Jo.Mal.*chron.*14 p.363(M.97.541A).

λῄσταρχος, ὁ, 1. *brigand chief*, Clem.*q.d.s.*42(p.189.7; M.9.648D); Cels.ap.Or.*Cels.*2.12(p.140.19; M.11.816D); Chrys.*hom.8.4 in 2Tim.*(11.712D); id.*coemet.*(2.399C); *Chron.Pasch.*p.327(M.92.840B); in gen., *brigand, robber*, Chrys.*hom.24.2 in Heb.*(12.222A); id.*pan.Macc.*(2.623A); Nil.*epp.*2.32(M.79.212D); **2.** as adj., *of a robber* λ. ... βίον Gr.Naz.*carm.*1.2.28.170(M.37.869A).

λῃστεία, ἡ, *robbery*, met. τὴν τοῦ χειμῶνος λ. Thdt.*provid.*8(4.615).

λῃστεύ-ω, 1. *plunder, rob*, met. ~ων γάμον ἀλλότριον Meth.*arbitr.*3.4(p.151.13; M.18.245B); Thdt.*1Thess.*4:6(3.516); τοῦ...Ποιμένος ~σαντες ὄνομα id.*Jer.*3:3(2.423); id.*h.rel.*3(3.1141); id.*affect.*9(p.229.15; 4.935); ref. Lc.23:43 ~ει τὴν βασιλείαν Chrys.*cruc.*2.3(2.415D); τῇ ~ομένῃ λέγει ὡς κληρονόμῳ...ὦ ἐκκλησία...σήμερον ἀποθνήσκω καὶ εἰς νομὰς εἰσέρχῃ τῆς κληρονομίας Ast.Am.*hom.*15(M.40.392C); οὐ μόνον γλώσσῃ ~εται κύριος πρὸς τὸ σῶσαι, καθάπερ ἐπὶ τοῦ λῃστοῦ ...ἀλλὰ καὶ λογισμῷ Jo.Carp.*cap.*56(M.85.1848); **2.** pass., *be infested with robbers*, †Jo.D.*creat.*6(p.135); ref. demons as brigands ἡ ὁδὸς... ~εται κατὰ τὸν ἀέρα, δαίμονές μοι ἀπαντῶσι ‡Chrys.*Abr.*3(2.748A).

λῃστήριον, τό, 1. *den of robbers*, ref. public bakehouses οἱ μάγκιπες...λ. τοὺς οἴκους πεποίηνται Socr.*h.e.*5.18.3(M.67.612A); **2.** *band of robbers*; of Arian party, Const.ap.Ath.*apol.sec.*61(p.141.18; M.25.359C); id.ap.Gel.Cyz.*h.e.*3.19(M.85.1345A).

λῃστής, ὁ, *robber*; **1.** in gen.; met., of adultery ἀλλοτριόγαμον λ. Thdt.*Ps.*50:9(1.939); id.*ep.*145(4.1257); of evil thoughts, Meth.*res.*2.4(p.337.17; M.41.1169C); of demons, Tat.*orat.*12(p.13.22; M.6.832C); *ib.*18(p.20.17; 848A); Clem.*exc.Thdot.*53(p.124.18; M.9.684C); of Satan, ‡Chrys.*annunt.*3(2.797C); antichrist, Thdt.*haer.*5.23(4.454);

2. exeg. Mt.21:13, Jo.2:17, etc.; **a.** cf. *τῶν μηδενὶ χάριτι διδόντων, ἀλλ' ἐμπορίαν καὶ κέρδος τὴν τῶν ξένων εἰς τὸ ἱερὸν εἴσοδον νομιζόντων...κέρδους ἕνεκεν τὰς...θυσίας χωρηγούντων* Heracleon ap.Or.*Jo.* 10.33(19; p.207.4; M.14.365C); representing sinners within spiritual temple of Church, Or.*comm.in Mt.*16.21(p.546.7ff.; M.13.1444Cff.); corrupt bishops, *ib.*16.22(p.549.22; 1448B); and laity, *ib.*(p.551.19; 1449C); id.*Jo.*10.23(16; p.195.15; M.14.348B); human souls *πεπληρωμένοις λ. λογισμῶν* id.*comm.in Mt.*16.23(p.555.30; 1453C); cf. *οὐκ ἐκβάλλει τοὺς ἀγοράζοντας...ἀλλὰ τοὺς ἀποδιδομένους τὰ...χρήσιμα καὶ λαμβάνοντας...τὰ νενομισμένα εἶναι τίμια* id.*hom.38 in Lc.*(pp.224f.; M.13.1897Df.); devils, id.*Jo.*10.25(18; p.203.9; 360C); **b.** purpose of their expulsion; to defend Law, Iren.*haer.*4.2.6(M.7.978C); demonstrate sanctity of Temple, Eus.*d.e.*7.2(p.388.26; M.22.628C); abrogate legal sacrifices, Or.*Jo.*10.24(16; p.196.5; M.14.349A); Thdr. Mops.*fr.in Jo.*2:19(p.320.8; M.66.740D); Ammon.*Jo.*2:15(M.85.1405D); and legal system as whole, Cyr.*Lc.*19:45(M.72.880D); id.*fr.Mt.*21:23(M.72.433C); symbolizing rejection of Jews, cf.Cyr.*Jo.*2.1(4.140B); rebuking irreverence of Jewish observance of feasts, Or.*fr.32 in Jo.*(p.507.10); **3.** exeg. Lc.10:30–36; *λῃσταί* represent devils; Samaritan is Christ, Clem.*q.d.s.*28(p.179.4; M.9.633D); Or.*hom.34 in Lc.*(p.201.22; M.13.1886C); Cyr.*Lc.*10:30(M.72.681A); or sins in which soul becomes involved, Or.*Cant.*proem.(p.70.18; M.13.69D); **4.** exeg. Jo.10:1ff.; λ. represent antichrist and false Messiahs, Theudas and Judas, Thdr.Heracl.ap.*cat.Jo.*10:5(p.296.26); Chrys.*hom.59.3 in Jo.*(8.348D); Thdr.Mops.*fr.in Jo.*10:7–9(p.350.23); Cyr.*Jo.*6.1(4.641E); *λ. ἀποκαλεῖ...τὸν ἐκ βίας...τὴν οὐ δοθεῖσαν αὐτῷ τιμὴν δύνασθαι λαβεῖν οἰόμενον ib.*(4.637Dff.); Scribes and Pharisees, Thdr.Heracl.ap.*cat.Jo.*10:5(p.296.33ff.); Cyr.*Jo.*6.1(4.640C,D); *λῃσταὶ χρηματίζοντες οὐκ ἠδύναντο ἀκολουθῆσαί τινι, δοκοῦντες τὴν ἀρχὴν ἐγχειρίζεσθαι τοῦ λαοῦ* Thdr.Mops.*fr.in Jo.*10:12f.(p.351.23ff.; M.66.760A); cf.*ib.*10:4(p.348.20; 757B); Law and Prophets acc. Valentinians, Hipp.*haer.*6.35(p.164.7; M.16.3247A); heretics, Iren.*haer.*3.4.1(M.7.855A); false exegetes, Or.*fr.21 in Jer.*(p.208.6); Devil as instigator of false prophets, Clem.*str.*1.17(p.54.26; M.8.800B); Cyr.*Jo.*6.1(4.641B); philosophers, as stealing their teaching from Hebrew prophets, Clem.*str.*1.17(p.56.1; 801B); pagan seers, *ib.*1.21(p.84.2; 869B); pagan gods, Or.*Cels.*7.70(p.219.10; M.11.1520A); **5.** ref. Barabbas *μέχρι σήμερον οἱ Ἰουδαῖοι Ἰησοῦν...οὐκ ἔχουσιν...ἔχουσι...Βαραββᾶν τὸν λ. ... διὰ τοῦτο ἄρχει τῶν...Ἰουδαίων Βαραββᾶς ὁ λ.* Or.*fr.80 in Lc.*23:18(p.272); **6.** exeg. Mt.26:55; Christ's saying demonstrates his peaceful character, Or.*comm.ser.103 in Mt.*(p.223.26; M.13.1753C); his voluntary submission, Isid. Pel.ap.*cat.Mt.*26:55(p.227.9); **7.** ref. *λῃσταί* at Crucifixion; **a.** as fulfilling Is.53:12, Or.*comm.ser.131 in Mt.*(p.267.23; M.13.1779B); cf. *ἄκοντες...τὴν προφητείαν πληροῦντες* Chrys.*hom.85.1 in Jo.*(8.504B); *ἄλλος λ. ἦν ἐσταυρωμένος, ἵνα πληρωθῇ ἐκεῖνο* id.*cruc.*1.2(2.405E); Ammon.*Jo.*19:18(M.85.1512B); **b.** *ἔγραψε τοῦτο* [Jo.19:19] *ἵνα μὴ νομισθῇ καὶ αὐτὸς εἶναι λ. ib.*19:19(1512C); **c.** compared with revilers of Christians, Or.*comm.ser.131 in Mt.*(p.267.23; 1779B); ref. Celsus' vilification of Christ as λ.: *ὁμοιόν τι λῃσταῖς ἔχουσιν* [sc. Christians] *...αἰκίαν...ἀναδεχόμενοι* id.*Cels.*2.44(p.167.5; M.11.865C); **d.** penitent λ. (v. *παράδεισος*); **i.** as example of justification by faith alone, cf.Or.*comm.in Rom.*3.9(M.14.952D); his 'baptism', Thdr.Stud.*or.*4.6(M.99.716D) cit. s. *πλευρά*; **ii.** his penitence demonstrating Christ's power, Chrys.*cruc.*1.2(2.404E); id.*hom.85.1 in Jo.*(504C); **iii.** his virtues *εἶδες παρρησίαν λῃστοῦ...εἶδες φιλοσοφίαν ἐντιμωρίᾳ*; id.*cruc.*1.3(406C); *εἶδες σύνεσιν καὶ διδασκαλίαν*; *ib.*(406E); *τί...ὁ λ. ἐπεδείξατο*;*...εἴπω τὴν ἀνδρείαν αὐτοῦ*; *ib.*1.2(405C); Cyr.*Lc.*23:38(M.72.937C); **iv.** contrasted with S. Peter at the denial, *ib.*; and with Judas *ὁ λ. μετὰ τοῦ Χριστοῦ καὶ ὁ μαθητὴς Ἰούδας μετὰ τοῦ διαβόλου* ‡Chrys.*latr.*1(8.248B); **v.** *λ. ... λῃστεύει τὴν βασιλείαν* Chrys.*cruc.*2.3(2.415D); **vi.** representing those who by mortification of passions are crucified with Christ, cf.Or.*comm.inRom.*5.9(1045A); ‡Ammon.*Mt.*27:44(M.85.1389B); **vii.** reasons for his repentance: Christ's prayer (Lc.23:34), *cat.Lc.*23:33(p.167.16); darkness and wonders, Or.*comm.ser.133 in Mt.*(p.271.6; M.13.1781C); **viii.** first to enter paradise since Adam, cf.Or.*hom.9.5 in Lev.*(p.425.10; M.12.514A); Chrys.*cruc.*1.2(2.404D); **ix.** entered with Christ at ninth hour, the time of Adam's expulsion, Cosm.Ind.*top.*1(M.88.124C); as sign of Christ's triumph, ‡Chrys.*latr.2*(8.249D); and as spoil taken from Devil, *cat.Lc.*23:43(p.170.29); **x.** question whether he entered *paradisus deliciarum* (Ezech.28:13), cf.Or.*hom.13.2 in Ezech.*(p.447.25; M.13.763A); **xi.** his entry into paradise in rel. to Christ's descent into Hades *γέγονε σημεῖον εὐεργετουμένῳ λ. εἰς παράδεισον εἰσελθεῖν... μετὰ τοῦτο καταβαίνων εἰς ᾅδου* Or.*comm.in Mt.*12.3(p.73.1; M.13.980C); id.*fr.81 in Lc.*23:43(p.273); id.*Jo.*32.32(19; p.480.1; M.14.828C); cf. *σήμερον...ἐπὶ ὅλον παρατείνει τὸν ἑστηκότα αἰῶνα* Tit.Bost. *fr.Lc.*23:43(p.245); *ἐν τῷ σταυρῷ ἦν διὰ τὴν σάρκα, καὶ ἐν τῷ οὐρανῷ διὰ τὴν θεότητα, καὶ...ἐν τῷ ᾅδῃ ὑπῆρχεν, καὶ τὸν λ. εἰς τὸν παράδεισον εἰσήγαγε cat.Lc.*23:43(p.168.6); **xii.** apparent disagreement between Lc.23:43 and Heb.11:13 *τινὲς λέγουσιν ὡς ὁ ἀπόστολος οὐκ...τὸν λ. συνηρίθμησεν...ὡς τῶν ἐπηγγελμένων ἤδη τυχόντα...ἕτεροι...μηδέ πως τὸν λ. τετυχέναι* (the promises being referred to God's kingdom on earth) Sev.Ant.ap.*cat.Lc.*23:43(p.168.15); **xiii.** promise to repentant λ. extended to all Christians, cf.Or.*hom.15.5 in Gen.*(p.134.12; M.12.245B); **e.** *λῃσταί* as types of repentant and unrepentant sinners, ‡Ammon.*Mt.*27:44(M.85.1389A,B); of *ὁ τῆς σαρκὸς νόμος* and *ὁ τοῦ πνεύματος νόμος ib.*; of Jew and gentile, Cyr.*fr.Mt.*27:38(M.72.464D); id.*Lc.*23:38(M.72.937C); of law-breaking Jews and idolatrous gentiles who must be crucified with Christ, id.*Jo.*12(4.1059B); Ammon.*Jo.*19:18(M.85.1512C); of goats in Day of Atonement ritual, one belonging to God, the other being scapegoat, cf.Or.*hom.9.5 in Lev.*(p.425.1; M.12.513C); **f.** apparent disagreement bet. evangelists on whether or not both λ. reviled Christ; explanation that at first both did so, but one afterwards repented, Or.*comm.ser.133 in Mt.*(p.271.4; M.13.1781C); *cat.Lc.*23:33(p.167.11); Vict.*Mc.*15:29(p.438.29).

λῃστοδιώκτης, ὁ, *pursuer of brigands, police officer*, Jo.Mal. *chron.*15 p.383(M.97.568B); *Chron.Pasch.*p.327(M.92.841A).

***λῃστοδόχος,** *harbouring robbers*, Socr.*h.e.*5.18.8(M.67.612B).

***λῃστοτροφέω,** *maintain robbers*, Tat.*orat.*23(p.25.28; M.6.857B).

***λῃστοτρόφος,** *maintaining robbers*, of worldly life as λ. *ὁδός* Nil.*praest.*19(M.79.1084A).

***λῃστουργία, ἡ,** plur., *depredations of robbers*, Mac.Aeg.*hom.*16.11(M.34.621A).

λῃστρικός, *of robbers, predatory, with intent to plunder*, met. *λ. συγκεκρότηται λόγος* Gr.Nyss.*Eun.*2(1 p.216.11; M.45.909A); *μετὰ... λ. ἡσυχίας* Pall.*v.Chrys.*6(p.34.15; M.47.21); *σπήλαια λ.* (of Messalian monasteries) Thdt.*h.e.*4.11.3(3.965); Vict.*Mc.*11:15(p.393.27); Jo.D. *imag.*2.12(M.94.1297A); of CEph.(449), cf.Leo Mag.*ep.*95(p.51.4; M.*PL.*54.943B); Justn.*typ.Thdr.Mops.*(M.86.1039B); Cyr.S.*v.Euthym.*27(p.41.6); Thphn.*chron.*p.86(M.108.261A).

λῃστρικῶς, *like robbers* or *bandits*, Or.*Cels.*5.40(p.44.12; M.11.1245A); Evagr.*h.e.*1.1(p.6.21; M.86.2421B); CTrull.*can.*1; comp., Eus.*d.e.*8 proem.(p.350.8; M.22.569B).

λῆψις, ἡ, 1. *taking up σκευῶν...λ.* Clem.*paed.*2.3(p.177.25; M.8.432B); **2.** *taking* money *τῷ τρόπῳ τῆς λ.* Meth.*arbitr.*15(p.184.10); **3.** *reception*; of answer to prayer, Clem.*str.*7.7(p.32.19; M.9.460B); Gel.Cyz.*h.e.*3.9(p.184.25 where prob. l. *λείψει*); **4.** *assumption*, Clem. *str.*8.6(p.90.19; M.9.581B); **5.** ecstatic *rapture*, Thdt.*Nah.*1:1(2.1519).

***ληψοδοσία, ἡ,** *exchange of benefit*, Epiph.*haer.*27.3(p.304.12; M.41.368B).

λιβάδιον, τό, *marshy place, damp meadow*, Thphn.*chron.*p.325(M.108.785B).

λίβανος, ὁ, 1. *incense φοῖνιξ...σηκὸν ἑαυτῷ ποιεῖ ἐκ λ. καὶ σμύρνης 1Clem.*25.2; ref. prophetess of Apollo *διὰ λιβάνων ἔκφρων γίνεται* Tat.*orat.*19(p.21.20; M.6.849B); ref. martyrs' refusal to offer incense, Ath.*ep.Aeg.Lib.*21(M.25.588A); ref. gift of Magi *λ. ... ὅτι θεὸς ἦν ὁ τεχθείς· τοῦτον...ἐξ ἔθους προσεκόμιζον τοῖς...θεοῖς* Thdot.Anc. *hom.*1.5(p.83.29; M.77.1356B); **2.** *Lebanon*, exeg. Jer.23:23 *οὐκ ἐκλείψουσιν...τὰ ὕδατα τοῦ Ἰησοῦ, ἢ χιὼν ἀπὸ τοῦ Λ., τὰ ὕδατα τὰ πατρικά·...λ. ... τὸ θυμίαμα...ἐστι...καὶ προσφέρεται ἐπὶ τὸ θυσιαστήριον λ. ... ἴσως ἴσῳ, καὶ ὁμώνυμον τὸ ὄρος τούτῳ τῷ λ., καί ἐστι χιὼν ἀπὸ τοῦ Λ. κατερχομένη, ὃν τρόπον τὸ ὕδωρ τοῦ ἁγίου πνεύματος* Or.*hom.18.9 in Jer.*(p.164.1; M.13.481D); ref. Jos.10:11–12 *Λ. δὲ...τὴν Ἱερουσαλὴμ αἰνίττεται* Eus.*d.e.*2.3(p.80.31; M.22.144D); ref. Is.10:33–34 *Λ. ... Ἱερουσαλὴμ ἀλληγορικῶς σύνηθές ἐστι ἀποκαλεῖν ib.*6.21(p.290.12; 477A); ref. Ps.71:16 *λιβάνου...ἐπινοουμένης τῆς Ἱερουσαλὴμ...διὰ τὸ...θυσιαστήριον...ὁ τοῦ Χριστοῦ καρπὸς ἡ ἐξ ἐθνῶν ἐκκλησία ὑπὲρ τὸν λ. ἀρθήσεσθαι θεσπίζεται ib.*7.3(p.342.9; 557C); ref. Zach.11:1 *Λ. ... τὸ ἱερὸν ὀνομάζει ἐπεὶ...δι' ἑτέρων... ἀποδέδεικται Λ. ... ὁ νεὼς ἐπικεκλημένος ib.*8.4(p.397.23; 641C).

***λιβελλήσιος, ὁ,** (Lat. *libellensis*) *clerk* in law-court, Justn.*nov.*20.9(p.144.15).

***λιβελλικῶς,** *by means of* libelli, CSyr.*act.*(*ACO* 3 p.99.30n.; H.2.1376E).

λίβελλος, ὁ, (Lat. *libellus*); **1.** *small book, document*, esp. of statements of orthodoxy, CCP(381)‡*can.*7; Gennad.*fr.*5(p.83.14); CTrull.*can.*95; Thphn.*chron.*p.275(M.108.681B); explanatory statements or apologies, Ursac.*ep.Jul.*(p.138.17; M.25.353C); Epiph. *haer.*68.9(p.149.21; M.42.197C); *ib.*72.1(p.256.6; 384B); *ib.*72.4(p.259.14; 388C); Eust.Mon.*ep.*(M.86.936B); ‡Jo.D.*ep.Thphl.*21(M.95.

372D); of polemical statements ποιῆσαι λ. κατὰ τῶν Ὠριγενιαστῶν Cyr.S.*v.Sab.*85(p.191.28); *ib.*90(p.198.16); Evagr.*h.e.*4.38(p.188.26; M.86.2777A); lists of heresies anathematized, Justn.*Or.*(p.208.8; M. 86.979D); **2.** *accusation* δανειστὴς...λιβέλλους καθ' ὑμῶν γράψας ἄρχοντι παρέστησεν Serap.*ep.mon.*7(M.40.933B); λ. διδόναι καθ' ἡμῶν Chrys.*ep.Innoc.*1.1(p.9.29; 3.517A); λ. ἐπιδιδόναι κατά Pall.*v.Chrys.*8 (p.45.2; M.47.27); Gel.Cyz.*h.e.*2.8.1(M.85.1244A); Evagr.*h.e.*1.9(p.17. 4; M.86.2445A); **3.** *petition*, Bas.*ep.*117(3.209D; M.32.533C); ἐντευκτικοὺς λ. ἐπέδωκεν Pall.*v.Chrys.*1(p.7.24; M.47.8); *Chron.Pasch.*p.310 (M.92.792A); of prayers τοὺς πρὸς τὸν θεὸν λ. Nil.*epp.*3.266(M.79. 517A).

Λιβυκός, *like Libya*, comp. εἰς τραχυτέρους καὶ Λιβυκωτέρους τόπους Dion.Al.ap.Eus.*h.e.*7.11.14(M.20.668A).

λιγαίνω, *sing in praise of*, Gr.Naz.*carm.*1.1.29.6(M.37.507A).

***λίγνη, ἡ**, *smoke*, Gr.Nyss.*anim.et res.*(M.46.141B, v.l. λιγνῦν).

λιγνυώδης, *like smoke*; of the breath, Nemes.*nat.hom.*23(M.40. 693B, vv.ll. ληγγνῶδες, λιγνῶδες); *ib.*24(700); Thdt.*provid.*3(4.514); *ib.*(528); Melet.*nat.hom.*synops.(M.64.1109A).

λιγύθροος, v. *λιγυρόθροος.

***λιγυπτερόφωνος**, *with wings sounding shrill*, *Orac.Sib.fr.*3.10 (conj. for λιγυροπτ-).

λιγύριον, τό, a precious stone (Ex.28:19) identified with λαγκούριον, and tentatively with ὑάκινθος, Epiph.*gemm.*7(M.43.297D).

***λιγύρισμα, τό**, *song*, Anast.S.*hex.*12(M.89.1076C).

***λιγυρόθροος**, *clear-sounding*, *Orac.Sib.fr.*3.9, v.l. λιγύθροος.

***λιγυρόκτυπος**, v. λυροκτύπος.

λιγυρός, *fresh*; of wind, met. πνεῦμα...πάσαις ἡμῖν λ. οὖρον πνεῦσαν γνώσεως Meth.*symp.*7.1(p.71.5; M.18.121A).

λιγυρῶς, *clearly*; of sound, Cyr.*Jo.*4.5(4.402E).

***λιγυφωνία, ἡ**, *clarity, sweetness of voice*, *Schol.Clem.paed.*(p.331. 2; M.9.790A).

λιγύφωνος, *sweet-* or *clear-voiced*, *MAMA* 1.496 (Laodicea Combusta, saec. iv).

λιθάριον, τό, *gem*, Jo.Mosch.*prat.*185(M.87.3061A).

***λίθασμα, τό**, *stoning*, Gr.Naz.*carm.*2.1.40.21(M.37.1338A).

λιθασμός, ὁ, = foreg., Gr.Naz.*carm.*1.2.25.234(M.37.830A); id. *ep.*95(M.37.170A); Isid.Pel.*epp.*1.54(M.78.218A).

λιθαστής, ὁ, *stoner*, Gr.Naz.*carm.*1.2.25.236(M.37.830A); Gr.Nyss. *res.*5(M.46.685D).

λιθία (λιθέα), ἡ, *jewellery*, Epiph.*mens.*10(M.43.255B); λιθέα Thphn.*chron.*p.191 (θέα M.108.497C).

λίθινος, *made of stone, stony*; met., *obstinate, stubborn*, Chrys. *hom.7.4 in Mt.*(7.109B); *ib.41.4*(451A); id.*sac.*6.7(p.154.3; 1.427B); cf. ψυχὴν...χρυσῆν...εἰληφώς, λ. ... καὶ μολυβδίνην ἀπέδειξας Nil.*epp.* 3.10(M.79.372C); exeg. Ezech.11:19, as fulfilled in Inc., *Barn.*6.14; τὸ ἐμποδίζον ὑπεξῃρηκέναι, τὴν λ. καρδίαν Or.*princ.*3.1.7(p.205.6; M. 11.260B); εἰ...ὅτε βούλεται ὁ θεὸς ἐξαίρει τὰς λ. καρδίας...οὐκ ἔστι τὴν κακίαν ἀποθέσθαι ἐφ' ἡμῖν *ib.*3.1.15(p.221.6; 280A).

λιθόβλητος, *of thrown stones* λ. νιφετοῖο Nonn.*par.Jo.*8:59(M.43. 824A).

λιθοβολέω, *stone*; ref. legendary stoning of Jeremiah, *Apoc.Bar. rel.*9.21; Hipp.*Dan.*1.12.4(M.10.689B); *Apoc.Paul.*49; of Zacharias, Hipp.Th.*fr.*1.2(p.2.9; M.117.1036C); of Achan after crossing of Jordan, compared with convert's destruction of evil as result of baptism, Gr.Nyss.*bapt.diff.*(M.46.421A).

λιθοβολία, ἡ, *stoning*; of S. Stephen, Hipp.Th.*fr.*1.3(p.3.14; M. 117.1037A); of Zacharias (identified with father of Jo. Bapt.), *ib.*1.2 (p.2.8; 1036C); cf.*ib.*3.2(p.16.5; 1029B).

***λιθοβολίστρα, ἡ**, *sling*, Anast.S.*hod.*9(M.89.144C).

***λιθογλυφής**, *hollowed out of rock*, Nonn.*par.Jo.*20:8(M.43. 909A).

***λιθογλυφικός**, *of stone-carving*; [sc. τέχνη] as subst. fem., *sculpture*, Niceph.Ur.*v.Sym.*110(M.86.3089C).

λιθογλύφος, ὁ, 1. *sculptor*, Didym.(‡Bas.)*Eun.*5(1.301E; M.29. 724B); **2.** *gem-cutter*, Gr.Nyss.*hom.14 in Cant.*(M.44.1072C).

***λιθόδρομος**, *of hurtling stones*, Geo.Pis.*hex.*553(M.92.1478A).

λιθοκάρδιος, *stony-hearted, stubborn*, Or.*hom.4.6 in Jer.*(p.29.12; M.13.293B); ὑπὸ λ. καὶ ἀπεριτμήτων Evagr.Pont.*ep.*7(M.32.260C); ‡Just.*qu.Gr.*14(M.6.1465B); †Jo.D.*B.J.*31(M.96.1161B).

***λιθολαμπής**, *brilliant with gems*, ‡Jo.D.*hom.*5(M.96.657C).

λιθολευστέω, *stone*, Thdt.*eran.*2(4.94); met. οὐ λιθολευστήσεται ταῖς τοῦ μώμου βολαῖς Germ.CP *or.*2(M.98.248C).

λιθολογέω, *make into a heap of stones*; pass., ref. Mich.3:12 (AQ), interpreted as *build with unworked stones*, Eus.*d.e.*8.3(p.393.23; M. 22.636C).

λιθολογία, ἡ, *heap of stones*, Eus.*d.e.*8.3(p.393.19; M.22.636B).

***λιθολόγιος**, *built of unworked stones*, Ath.*exp.Ps.*78:1(M.27. 357C).

***λιθομανής**, *mad on stones* for building; of Thphl. Al., Isid.Pel. *epp.*1.152(M.78.286A); on precious stones, Thphn.*chron.*p.382(M. 108.916A).

***λιθομανία, ἡ**, *mania for building*, Pall.*v.Chrys.*6(p.35.19; M.47. 22).

***λιθόξεστος**, *carved out of stone*, *Orac.Sib.*4.7.

λιθόξοος, ὁ, *carver in stone*, in gen. σταυρῷ ἐνηλώθη καὶ ἦν τέκτων...εἰ ἔτυχεν ἀπὸ κρημνοῦ ἐρριμμένος [sc. Christ] ἢ...σκυτοτόμος ἢ λ. Cels.ap.Or.*Cels.*6.34(p.103.24; M.11.1348D); Bas.*hom.*7.4(2. 55E; M.31.289C); esp. *sculptor*; of makers of idols, *Orac.Sib.*3.13; *Diogn.*2.3; Thphl.Ant.*Autol.*2.2(M.6.1048B); Clem.*prot.*4(p.41.26; M.8.148B); of sculptor in relief, opp. ἀνδριαντοποιός, *ib.*(p.45.26; 157A); Gr.Nyss.*Thdr.*(M.46.737D); Isid.Pel.*epp.*2.115(M.78.556C).

***λιθοπλάξ**, *made of stone slabs*, *Apoc.En.*14.10.

λίθος, ὁ, *stone*;

A. lit.; of stones used in making fire συμβαίνει περὶ τοὺς πυροβόλους λ. ... ἵνα δύο λ. προσκρουσάντων πῦρ γενηθῇ Or.*hom.8.4 in Jer.* (p.60.3; M.13.341C); τὸν ἄρρην λ. εἰ σπείσεις τῇ θηλείᾳ, πυρκαιὰ γίνεται †Bas.*contub.*5(M.30.820C); εἰσὶν γὰρ λ. πυροβόλοι, ἄρσεν καὶ θῆλυ. ἐν ὅσῳ μακρὰν εἰσὶν ἀπ' ἀλλήλων, οὐδαμοῦ πῦρ καίει· ἐὰν δὲ πλησιάσῃς τὸν ἄρρενα τῇ θηλείᾳ, ἀνάπτεται καὶ ἐμπυρίζει πολλά ‡Petr.I Al.*phys.*4; of heathen idolatry as worshipping of stones, *2Clem.*1.6; Clem. *prot.*10(p.73.1; M.8.216B); Tit.Bost.*fr.Lc.*19:40(p.233); of altar as constructed of stone, Gr.Nyss.*bapt.Chr.*(M.46.581C).

B. met.; **1.** of Christians as spiritual stones λίθοι ναοῦ πατρός, ἡτοιμασμένοι εἰς οἰκοδομὴν θεοῦ πατρός Ign.*Eph.*9.1; Herm.*sim.* 9.3.3ff.; Or.*comm.in Mt.*16.21(p.546.8; M.13.1444C); **2.** of Christ, exeg. Is.28:16, Ps.117:22, Dan.2:34; cf.Rom.9:33, 1Petr.2:6 ἐπὶ λίθον οὖν ἡμῶν ἡ ἐλπίς; μὴ γένοιτο· ἀλλ' ἐπεὶ ἐν ἰσχύϊ τέθεικεν τὴν σάρκα αὐτοῦ ὁ κύριος *Barn.*6.3; ref. Jos.5:2–3 λ. καὶ πέτρα ἐν παραβολαῖς ὁ Χριστὸς διὰ τῶν προφητῶν ἐκηρύσσετο Just.*dial.*113.6(M.6. 737B); τί δεῖ λοιπὸν περιμένειν, ἀλλ' ἢ Χριστὸν ἀπ' οὐρανῶν ἐρχόμενον, ὡς λ. ἀπὸ ὄρους τεμνόμενον, ἵνα τὰς τοῦ κόσμου βασιλείας μεταστήσῃ, ἀναστήσῃ δὲ τὴν ἐπουράνιον τῶν ἁγίων βασίλειαν; Hipp.*Dan.*2.13.2 (p.68.14); οὐ γὰρ πᾶς λ. εἰς γωνίαν ἐπιτήδειος, ἀλλ' ὁ δοκιμώτατος. ... ὁ ἀποδοκιμασθεὶς παρὰ τῶν Ἰουδαίων...οὗτος ἐφάνη θαυμαστός, ὥστε μὴ μόνον οἰκοδομὴν ὑφῆναι, ἀλλὰ συνδῆσαι δύο τοίχους, τοὺς ἐξ Ἰουδαίων καὶ Ἑλλήνων πιστεύσαντας Or.*Ps.*117:22(p.243); πολυτελῆ δὲ ὄντα τὸν λ. τοῦτον...θήσειν εἰς τὰ θεμέλια τῆς ἐκκλησίας ἐπαγγέλλεται...εἴη δ' ἂν τὸ ἀνθρώπινον τοῦ σωτῆρος ἡμῶν οὕτως ὠνομασμένον σῶμα· ἐπεὶ καὶ κατὰ τὸν Δανιήλ, λ. τμηθεὶς ἄνευ χειρῶν ἑωρᾶτο· λ. μὲν τοῦ ἀνθρωπίνου νοουμένου σώματος· ὄρους δὲ τῆς κατὰ τὸν σωτῆρα θεότητος Eus.*Is.*28:16(M.24.292B); τοῦ μὲν ὄρους τὴν προΰπαρξιν τῆς θεότητος αὐτοῦ σημαίνοντος, τοῦ δὲ λ. τὴν ἀνθρωπότητα id.*e.th.*1.20 (p.94.26; M.24.889B); οὕτω δέ τις περὶ τοῦ κυρίου διανοούμενος, οὐ προσκόψει τῷ λ. τοῦ προσκόμματος Ath.*decr.*17(p.15.4; M.25.'453' (445)C); σοὶ αὐτῷ τῷ γεγονότι δι' ἡμᾶς λ. ἀπηγορευμένῳ ἀπεδοκίμασαν μὲν οἱ οἰκοδομοῦντες· μετὰ δὲ τὴν τῶν ἐθνῶν μεταβολὴν ἑτέρας γωνίας κεφαλὴ γέγονας id.*exp.Ps.*117:22(M.27.480A); φεῦγε εἰς τὸ ὄρος πρὸς...Χριστόν, τὸν τμηθέντα λ. ἄνευ χειρῶν, καὶ τὴν οἰκουμένην πληρώσαντα Cyr.H.*catech.*19.8; τὸ γὰρ 'λ. πολυτελῆ κτλ.' ... οὐδὲν ἕτερόν ἐστιν ἢ ἔπαινος παρὰ πατρὸς εἰς υἱὸν γινόμενος Thdr.Heracl.*Is.* 28:16(M.18.1317D); εἷς Χριστός· ἀλλ' εἰς πτῶσιν κεῖται καὶ ἀνάστασιν ...τοῖς μὲν ἔστι πέτρα προσκόμματος...τοῖς δὲ λ. ἀκρογωνιαῖος...ὅσοι συνδεσμοῦνται τῷ λόγῳ Gr.Naz.*or.*17.7(M.35.973B); ref. Gen.29:9 ὁ δὲ Ἰακὼβ μόνος ἀποκυλίει τὸν λ. ... τίς γὰρ ὁ ἐπικείμενος λ. ἢ αὐτὸς ὁ Χριστός; περὶ οὗ φησιν Ἡσαίας...καὶ Δανιὴλ ὁμοίως· ἐτμήθη λ. ἄνευ χειρός· τουτέστιν· ἐγεννήθη Χριστὸς ἄνευ ἀνδρός. ... ἐπέκειτο τοίνυν τῷ φρέατι ὁ λ. ὁ νοητὸς Χριστός, κρύπτων ἐν βάθει καὶ μυστηρίῳ τὸ τῆς παλιγγενεσίας λουτρόν. ... οὐδεὶς δὲ τὸν λ. ἀπεκύλισεν, εἰ μὴ Ἰσραήλ, ὅς ἐστι νοῦς ὁρῶν θεόν Gr.Nyss.*bapt.Chr.*(M.46.589A); λ. ὀρεινόν...ὅνπερ οὐ χεῖρες ἐλατόμησαν ἀλλ' ἡ χάρις ἐφεῦρεν *Pers.*(p.32. 2); *ib.*(p.32.10ff.); ἀληθῶς...λ. ὁ...υἱός, ὅπως ἂν τὴν κατὰ θεὸν οἰκοδομὴν συνδέων, καὶ τὰς δύο γωνίας τῆς τε παλαιᾶς οἰκοδομῆς τῆς ἐκ περιτομῆς, καὶ τῆς νέας τῆς ἐξ ἐθνῶν, ὑπὸ μίαν συνάπτων γωνίαν Didym.*Ps.*117:22(M.39.1561D); cf.†Didym.*1Petr.*2:7–8(M.39. 1762C); ὁ δὲ λ. ἀπὸ ὄρους ἔπεσε...τὸ ἑκούσιον δείκνυσι, καὶ ὡς οὐκ ἀναγκασθείς. ... καὶ ἐτμήθη ἄνευ χειρῶν· τὴν κατὰ σάρκα γέννησιν αἰνίττεται. ... καὶ ἐγένετο ὁ λ. εἰς ὄρος μέγα· τὰ ἀποστολικὰ ῥήματα τὴν οἰκουμένην ἐπλήρωσεν ἅπασαν. ποτὲ μὲν οὖν ὄρος ὁ λ., ποτὲ δὲ ἀκρογωνιαῖος, ποτὲ δὲ θεμέλιος, ἵνα μάθῃς ὅτι τὰ πάντα πληροῖ Chrys.*Dan.*2:34(6.214E); λ. ... τὸν κύριον...ἀποκαλεῖ, καὶ τῇ τῆς θεότητος δόξῃ...διαπρέποντα Cyr.*Is.*3.2(2.397E); γέγονεν ἡμῖν κρηπὶς καὶ ἀσφάλεια, καὶ ἀκλόνητος ὑποβάθρα, καὶ θεμέλιος ἀρραγής·

ὠνόμασται δὲ διὰ τοῦτο λ. id.*ador*.3(1.102D); ὅταν τοίνυν ἀναβῶμεν εἰς Βαιθήλ, τουτέστιν, εἰς οἶκον θεοῦ, ἐκεῖ τὸν λ. ἐπιγνωσόμεθα, λ. τὸν ἐκλεκτόν, τὸν εἰς κεφαλὴν γεγονότα γωνίας, τουτέστι Χριστόν. ὀψόμεθα δὲ χριόμενον παρὰ τοῦ πατρὸς εἰς εὐφροσύνην id.*glaph.Gen*.5 (1.177C); ὁ δὲ...Χριστὸς τοὺς δύο τοίχους, τοὺς ἀπ' ἀλλήλων ἑστῶτας ἐκ διαμέτρου, τοὺς ἐξ Ἰουδαίων...καὶ τοὺς ἐξ ἐθνῶν πεπιστευκότας... εἰς ἓν...συνέζευξε...γωνίαν τινὰ μιμησάμενος. ... τοῦτον μέντοι τὸν λ. οἰκοδόμοι πάλαι ὄντες, φαρισαῖοί τε καὶ σαδδουκαῖοι...ἀπεδοκίμασαν Thdt.*Ps*.117:22(1.1432–3); ἀνοίας ἐσχάτης εἶναι νομίζω, τὸ ταύτην τῷ Ἑζεκίᾳ προσαρμόζειν τὴν προφητείαν. ... ὁ προφητικὸς ἐπαινεῖ λόγος τοὺς εἰς τὸν λ. τοῦτον πιστεύοντας. ἀκρογωνιαῖος δὲ λ. ὁ...Χριστός, ὁ ποιήσας τὰ ἀμφότερα ἕν...αὐτὸς δὲ καὶ θεμέλιος κέκληται id.*Is*.28:16(2.301); ὄρος μὲν ἡ Δαβιτικὴ φυλή, λ. δὲ ὁ Χριστὸς κατὰ τὸ ἀνθρώπινον, οὐ κατὰ τὸν νόμον τῆς φύσεως τμηθείς id.*Dan*.2:34(2.1093); ‡Ammon.*Mt*.21:42(M.85.1385A); ὁ λ. ὁ ἀκρογωνιαῖος καὶ ἀχειρότμητος ἐν πέτρᾳ λελαξευμένῃ καλύπτεται Jo.D.*hom*.4.30(M.96.632C).

C. λ. χαλάζης *hailstone*, Thdt.*Is*.13:13(p.67.29; 2.263).

D. medic., *anchylosed joint* λ. ... τῶν ποδῶν Geo.Pis.*hex*.1584(M.92.1558A).

***λιθοσσόος**, *stone-throwing*, Nonn.*par.Jo*.8:59(M.43.824A).

λιθόστρωτος, *paved*, of 'Pavement' at Jerusalem λ. παρὰ χώρῳ Nonn.*par.Jo*.19:13(M.43.900C); as subst., Hesych.H.ap.*cat.Jo*.19:17(p.390.15); at Alexandria; as subst., Dion.Al.ap.Eus.*h.e*.6.41.4(M.20.605B).

λιθοτομία, ἡ, *art of stone-cutting*, Clem.*str*.1.16(p.49.7; M.8.788A).

λιθοτόμος, *stone-cutter*, in simile of Christ's birth ἐγεννήθη...ἄνευ ἀνδρός...λίθον πέτρας ἀποτμηθῆναι ἄνευ λ. Gr.Nyss.*bapt.Chr*.(M.46.589A).

λιθουργέω, *fashion in stone* ἄτοπον...λ. ... τὸν θεόν Dion.Al.ap.Eus.*p.e*.7.19(334B; M.21.564B).

λιθουργία, ἡ, 1. *work in quarries* ἐπισκόπους...εἰς λ. παραδεδώκασι Ath.*h.Ar*.72(M.25.780B; λειτουργίαν p.223.6); **2.** *fashioning of hailstones* τίς τὰς ἀφορμὰς...ταύτης ἀπηκρίβωσε τῆς λ.; Geo.Pis.*hex*.544 (M.92.1477A).

λιθόω, *turn to stone*; lit., Clem.*prot*.10(p.74.25; M.8.220B); Geo.Pis.*hex*.551(M.92.1478A); met., perf. ptcpl. pass., *stubborn* τῶν εἰς ἀλήθειαν λελιθωμένων Clem.*prot*.1(p.5.15; 57A); τοῖς μὴ τὸν νοῦν λελιθωμένοις Eus.*v.C*.4.67(p.145.29; M.20.1224A); id.*l.C*.17(p.256.2; M.20.1433A); μὴ ἔστω λελιθωμένη ἡ καρδία Chrys.*hom.9.3 in 2Tim*.(11.718E).

***λίκμησις, ἡ,** *winnowing*, Gr.Naz.*or*.21.22(M.35.1108A).

λικμητήριον, τό, *winnowing fan*, met. ἁμαρτιῶν λ. ‡Caes.Naz.*dial*.135(M.38.1040).

***λικμητηρίς, ἡ,** *winnowing fan*, Mac.Mgn.*apocr*.4.11(p.171.26).

λικμητός, ὁ, *winnowing*, Gr.Nyss.*hom.in Cant*.proem.(M.44.761D); Nil.*exerc*.19(M.79.745A).

λικμήτωρ, ὁ, *winnower*, Gr.Nyss.*hom.in Cant*.proem.(M.44.764A); met., of Devil, Jo.Clim.*scal*.22(M.88.953B).

λικμίζ-ω, *winnow*, met. τὰ ἀπειθῆ...ἔθνη ~εται Thphyl.*exc.gent*. (p.482.15; M.113.941D).

***λικμών, ὁ,** *winnower*, Chrys.*hom.32.3 in Mt*.(Gaume; λικμῶντος 7.368A).

λικνίζω, *winnow*; met., *test, tempt*, *Apophth.Patr*.(M.65.149A).

λικνοειδής, *concave* λ. ... καὶ μεσόκοιλος Bas.*hex*.9.1(1.80D; M.29.188C); ἢ κυλινδρός ἐστιν ἢ λ. Isid.Pel.*epp*.2.273(M.78.704A).

λιμαγχονέω, *make hungry, starve*, ref. Dt.8:3 ἐλιμαγχόνησέν σε ἐν τῇ ἐρήμῳ Clem.*str*.1.27(p.107.4; M.8.920B); Or.*comm.in Ex*.(M.12.277A); Proc.G.*Is*.8:18–20(M.87.1996B); fig. λιμαγχονῆσαι τῶν θείων λόγων ‡Ath.*v.Syncl*.110(M.28.1553D).

λιμαγχονία, ἡ, *abstinence* ἄρτου λ. ‡Ath.*v.Syncl*.17(M.28.1496A).

λιμβός, 1. *greedy*, Ephr.1.13E; **2.** *appetising*, Leont.N.*v.Sym*.55 (M.93.1737B).

***λιμενάριον, τό,** *little harbour*, Jo.Mal.*chron*.14 p.372(M.97.556A); *Chron.Pasch*.p.324(M.92.809A).

***λιμενίσκιον, τό,** = foreg., Synes.*ep*.4(M.66.1337C).

λιμήν, ὁ, *harbour*; met., of divine peace, Ign.*Smyrn*.11.3; id.*Polyc*.2.3; ὥσπερ ἐν λ. ... τῷ θείῳ φωτὶ τοῦ σωτῆρος Clem.*fr*.44(p.222.16); τὸν τῆς ἀναπαύσεως...λ. *Clem.ep.Petr*.13(M.2.49A); ὁδηγήσει σε ἐπὶ λιμένα θελήματος αὐτοῦ Jo.D.*hom*.2.7(M.96.588B); τὸν...σωτηρίας λ. Thst.*v.Nic.Heg*.10(p.xxivB); of a place of refuge, Leont.N.*v.Jo.Eleem*.7(p.13.14); of absence of persecution ἐκκλησίαν...εἰς...λ. κατῆγεν Soz.*h.e*.proem.17(M.67.852A); of persons τὸν πάνδοκον λ. ... τὸν...πατριάρχην Leont.N.*v.Jo.Eleem*.30(p.62.21); λ. θεογνωσίας ἐγένετο *V.Alex.Acoem*.22(p.673.17).

***λιμιτάνεος**, (Lat. *limitaneus*) *of the frontiers*; as adj. and subst., of troops guarding frontiers οὐδεμίαν μετιέναι [sc. monks] στρατείαν ...εἰ μὴ...κορταλίνων ἢ τῶν λ. Marcian.Imp.*const.Eut*.(p.123.30; H.2.677D); στρατιωτῶν τε καὶ λ. καὶ φοιδεράτων Justn.*nov*.103.3(p.499.9); Jo.Mal.*chron*.18 p.426(M.97.628B); στρατιώτας λ. *ib*.12 p.308(464D).

λίμιτον, τό, (cf. Lat. *limes*) *frontier* εἰς τὸ λ. Jo.Mal.*chron*.5 p.39 (M.97.237A); εἰς τὰ λ. *ib*.12 p.308(464C); ἐν τῷ λ. *ib*.5 p.43(241B); διὰ τοῦ ἐξωτέρου λ. *ib*.18 p.445(656A); ἐπὶ τὸ λ. *Chron.Pasch*.p.43(M.92.160D); *border-country* ἐν ταῖς κατὰ τὸ βαρβαρικὸν λεγόμενον λ. ἐρήμοις Leont.H.*monoph*.(M.86.1900A); τὰς πανερήμους τῶν λεγομένων λ. περινοστῶν Evagr.*h.e*.6.22(p.238.24; M.86.2877B).

λιμνάζ-ω, *be soaked*, Epiph.*mens*.8(M.43.248C); Chrys.*hom.13.2 in Phil*.(11.299E); ‡Nil.*narr*.5(M.79.645B); met. ~οντα λογικῶν ὑδάτων χωρία Proc.G.*Is*.42:16(M.87.2377A).

***λιμνηδόν**, *like a lake*, Ph.Carp.*Cant*.7:4(M.40.125B).

***λιμνιαῖος**, v. *ληνιαῖος.

***λιμνίσκος**, v. ληνίσκος.

***λιμνόδρομος**, *lake-faring* λ. πλοίοις ‡Chrys.*hom*.13(13.252B).

***λιμνόω**, *make watery*, Nil.*Magn*.19(M.79.993C).

λιμώδης, v. λοιμ-.

λιμώσσ-ω, 1. *suffer hunger*, *A.Thom*.A 145(p.252.10); Hipp.*ben.Jac*.(p.13.27); Cels.ap.Or.*Cels*.4.47(p.319.31; M.11.1104C); *Hom.Clem*.13.20; Gr.Naz.*or*.34.2(M.36.241C); Chrys.*hom.5.5 in Mt*.(7.82A); medic., *be on starvation diet*, Thdt.*affect*.1(p.5.13; 4.694); met., of hunger for spiritual food, Eus.*Is*.65:11–12(M.24.512B); Ath.*ep.Drac*.2(M.25.525B); Procl.CP *or*.3.30(M.65.713C); Antip.Bost.*annunt*.24(M.85.1792A); **2.** *make hungry*, †Gregent.*leg.Hom*.53(M.86.609A); met., ref. Ps.58:7 τροφῆς ἐπουρανίου τὰς ψυχὰς ~ουσι κατὰ τὴν γραφήν Eus.*Is*.5:13(M.24.120A); Germ.CP *or*.2(M.98.249C).

***λινηφικός, 1.** masc. as subst., *linen-maker*, †Gregent.*leg.Hom*.63 (M.86.616B, v.l. λινυφικόν); **2.** neut. as subst., *linen-making*, Ephr.2.176C.

***λινοειδής**, *made of linen*, Ammon.*Ac*.19:12(M.85.1576A).

λίνον, τό, 1. *fishing net*, *Ev.Petr*.12(p.338); met. τὸ τοῦ εὐαγγελικοῦ κηρύγματος...λ. Cyr.*Is*.5.4(2.845D); id.*Lc*.5:2(M.72.553A); **2.** *snare*; met., in gen., †Apoll.*met.Ps*.34:7(M.33.1357B); Isid.Pel.*epp*.2.289(M.78.720A); Cyr.*Os*.6(3.26C); *ib*.51(83B); of snares of sin, id.*Is*.4.4(2.681E); of Devil, *ib*.4.3(620A); id.*Jo*.11.12(4.1012C); of wrath of God λίνα φθισίμβροτα πέμψει †Apoll.*met.Ps*.10:6(1325A); τὸ λ. τῆς θείας ὀργῆς Cyr.*Ps*.34:8(M.69.900B).

***λινόπληγος**, *caught in a snare*; of the damned, †Cyr.*hom.div*.14 (5^{2}.411E).

λινοπλήξ, *afraid of the snare* λ. τινος ζῴου Chrys.*Jud*.8.1(1.674A); id.*hom.25.1 in 1Cor*.(10.221C).

λινοπλόκος, *weaving nets*, Nonn.*par.Jo*.21:3(M.43.913C).

λινοῦφιον, τό, *linen-factory*, Const.ap.Eus.*v.C*.2.34(p.55.25; M.20.1012A); λινύφιον Soz.*h.e*.1.8.3(M.67.877A).

***λινόχρυσος**, *made of linen interwoven with gold thread*, Jo.Mal.*chron*.18 p.457(M.97.669B).

[*]λίντιον, τό, v. λέντιον.

***λινυφαρία, ἡ,** *female linen-worker*, Jo.Disc.*v.Epiph*.1(M.41.24B).

[*]λινυφής, ὁ, = λινοϋφής, *linen-weaver*, Ephr.2.176C.

[*]λινυφικός, = λινοϋφικός, v. *λινη-.

[*]λινύφιον, τό, v. λινοῦφιον.

λίξ, word used in magic; explained Ἀνδροκύδης...ὁ Πυθαγορικὸς τὰ Ἐφέσια...γράμματα...συμβόλων ἔχειν φησὶ τάξιν...λ. ... ἐστιν ἡ γῆ κατὰ ἀρχαίαν ἐπωνυμίαν καὶ τετρὰξ ὁ ἐνιαυτός Clem.*str*.5.8(p.356.4; M.9.72C); λὶξ τετράξ as name of a demon, *T.Sal*.7.4–8(pp.29.7–31.3).

λιπαίνω, 1. *make smooth* or *sleek*, esp. with oil, Clem.*paed*.2.8 (p.197.25; M.8.473B) etc.; met., of feeding a flame αὐγὴν τῆς ἀρετῆς ἐλαίῳ λ. Meth.*symp*.10.2(p.124.16; M.18.196C); **2.** *pamper, make fat* or *prosperous*, *Hom.Clem*.13.18; Chrys.*hom.44.5 in Mt*.(7.474B); id.*hom.13.2 in Phil*.(11.298C); **3.** *adorn, elaborate*; of literary composition, Chrys.*hom.8.3 in 1Cor*.(10.69C); *ib*.*29.3*(262B); Pall.*v.Chrys*.1 (p.4.29; M.47.6); *use ornamental diction*, Chrys.*hom.17.1 in 2Cor*.(10.559E); Nil.*epp*.2.163(M.79.277C); **4.** *enervate*, Pall.*v.Chrys*.4(p.24.28; M.47.16).

***λιπαλγής**, *free from sorrow*, Paul.Sil.*Soph*.891(M.86.2153A).

λιπαρῶς, *thoroughly, earnestly*, Clem.*ecl*.27(p.145.13; M.9.742C); Gr.Thaum.*pan.Or*.5(p.12.18; M.10.1065B); λ. ἱκετεύσαντος Eus.*h.e*.5.21.4(M.20.488B); Chrys.*hom.30.3 in Rom*.(9.743A).

λιπασμός, ὁ, *fatness*, Chrys.*hom.12.1 in Eph*.(11.90E); Thdr.Mops.*Ps*.16:10(M.66.660C); met., of fatness of soul through spiritual nourishment, Proc.G.*Is*.58:1(M.87.2593B).

***λιπαυγέω**, *be bereft of light*, Bas.Sel.*v.Thecl*.1(M.85.537D); *ib*.2.20 (604A).

λιπάω, *be fat*, Gr.Naz.*ep*.2(M.37.24A).

***λιποβλέφαρος**, *eyeless*, Nonn.*par.Jo*.9:1(M.43.824B).

***λιπόγεως**, *deficient in soil*, Mac.Aeg.*hom*.26.4(M.34.676D).

λιποθυμέω (λειπο-), *faint*, *Ev.Thom*.A 14.2(p.153); λειποθυμοῦντας ἀναψυχοῦσι Gr.Naz.*ep*.4(M.37.28A); *be faint-hearted, despondent* λιποθυμήσας ἐν τῷ πράγματι Pall.*h.Laus*.51(p.144.19; M.34.1212D).

***λιποκτέανος**, *needy*, Paul.Sil.*Soph*.993(M.86.2157A).

***λιπόμαστος**, *weaned*, Gr.Naz.*carm*.2.1.50.33(M.37.1387A).

λιπόσκιος, *deprived of shadow*, Nonn.*par.Jo*.1:44(M.43.757B); ἐχάραξε λιπόσκιον ὄρθρος ὁμίχλην *ib*.6:22(797A); νύκτα λ. ἔσχισεν ἠώς *ib*.12:12(852C); ref. blind man ὕδασι...λ. φάεα νίπτων *ib*.9:7(825A).

λιπόтακτος, ὁ, *deserter*, Gr.Nyss.*v.Gr.Thaum*.(M.46.945D).

***λιπόχριστος**, *deserting Christ*, Gr.Naz.*carm*.1.2.2.133(M.37.589A); Pamph.Mon.*Soter*.3(p.118.16).

λιρόφθαλμος, *lewd-eyed*, Melet.*nat.hom*.2(M.64.1176B).

***λίσγον, τό**, *spade*, ‡Caes.Naz.*dial*.102(M.38.968).

λιτανεία, ἡ, 1. *supplication, petition* οὔτε ἀργύρια ἔπειθεν οὔτε λ. ἐδυσώπει *Ep.Lugd*.ap.Eus.*h.e*.5.1.61(M.20.432B); **2.** *congregational supplication* or *prayer*; ref. praying for a miracle τῆς ἐκκλησίας πάσης αἰτησαμένης μετὰ νηστείας καὶ λ. πολλῆς ἐπέστρεψεν τὸ πνεῦμα τοῦ τετελευτηκότος Iren.*haer*.2.31.2(M.7.825A); for remission of sins πρεσβεύων ὑπὲρ σοῦ πρὸς θεὸν καὶ λ. συνήθεσι μαγεύων τὸν πατέρα Clem.*q.d.s*.41(p.187.19; M.9.648A); for healing τῷ τῶν μαρτύρων εὐκτηρίῳ ἐνδιατρίψας οἴκῳ ἱκετηρίους εὐχάς τε καὶ λ. ἀνέπεμπε τῷ θεῷ Eus.*v.C*.4.61(p.142.25; M.20.1212C); for public welfare σύν γε ταῖς χερσὶν εὐχαῖς τε καὶ λ. πᾶν, ὅσον ἤνυσται ὑπὲρ συμφέροντος κατορθοῦσθαι Const.*or.s.c*.26(p.192.15; M.20.1316A); *ib*.(p.192.28; 1316B); developed in form οὐκ ἦν...ταῦτα ἐπὶ τοῦ μεγάλου Γρηγορίου...ἀλλ' οὐδὲ αἱ λ. ἃς ὑμεῖς νῦν ἐπιτηδεύετε Bas.*ep*.207.4(3.311D; M.32.764B); as expression of penitence καιρὸς δακρύων...στεναγμῶν προσπτώσεως...λ. συντεταμένης, ἱκετηρίας πολλῆς Chrys.*virg*.32(1.291B); τὴν σπουδὴν τὴν περὶ τὰς λ. id.*a.exil*.1.3(3.416E); ποιήσαντες νηστείας καὶ λ. *Pers*.(p.4.4); ταῖς νυκτεριναῖς λ. παρεκάλει τοὺς δήμους Pall.*v.Chrys*.5(p.32.24; M.47.20); **3.** *liturgical prayer* said by deacon, consisting of a number of rogations, *litany* κυριακοῦ πληρώσαντος τὴν τοῦ λυχνικοῦ λ. καὶ εἰπόντος 'ἐλέησον ἡμᾶς ὁ θεὸς κατὰ τὸ μέγα ἔλεός σου, δεόμεθά σου, κύριε, ἐπάκουσον καὶ ἐλέησον' Eustrat.*v.Eutych*.96(M.86.2381C); **4.** *religious procession* accompanied by prayers, with crosses borne by the people ὑπάγωμεν τὸν σταυρὸν βαστάζοντες...λιτανείαν, κἀκεῖ εἰσβῶμεν CTyr.(518)*act*.(p.87.14; H.2.1357A); held on extraordinary occasions (e.g. earthquakes) or as memorial of such events ἡ ἀνάμνησις κατ' ἔτος ἐπιτελεῖται...τῆς λ. ὑπὲρ τῆς τοῦ θεοῦ μακροθυμίας ἐν τῷ Τρικόγχῳ *Chron.Pasch*.p.317(M.92.805C); *ib*.p.319(812A); in drought, Jo.Mal.*chron*.18 p.492(M.97.712B).

λιτανεύ-ω, 1. *appeal to*; in preaching, *Orac.Sib*.1.149; **2.** *supplicate* God in prayer; **a.** privately ἐλιτάνευσεν τὸν δεσπότην λέγουσα, ὁ θεὸς...ἐπάκουσον τῆς δεήσεώς μου *Protev*.2.4(p.6); **b.** publicly θεὸν ...πάντες ~σατε *Orac.Sib*.1.159; Ign.*Rom*.4.2; οἱ μὲν...ἐπ' ὄψιν κείμενοι ἐλιτάνευον· οἱ δὲ τὰ γόνατα κλίνοντες ἔκλαιον *A.Jo*.42(p.172.3); οὐχ ἡ φωνὴ προεφέρετο, ἡ γνώμη δὲ παρεφέρετο· ἀλλὰ συντεταμένως ἑκάτερα τὸν θεὸν ἐλιτάνευε Chrys.*hom.suppl*.2(M.64.428C); esp. for remission of sins, Bas.*ep*.207(3.312A; M.32.764B); of eucharistic prayer ἐν τοῖς μυστηρίοις...κοινὰς ποιούμεθα τὰς εὐχὰς ~οντες ὑπὲρ νοσούντων καὶ τῶν καρπῶν τῆς οἰκουμένης καὶ γῆς καὶ θαλάττης Chrys.*hom*.78.3 *in Jo*.(8.464D); of prayer in time of earthquake, id.*Laz*.6.1(1.773A); τῷ λαῷ ἔφη ~οντας ᾆσαι καὶ στήσασθαι τὴν ἀπειλήν... καὶ ὁ σεισμὸς...πέπαυτο Niceph.Ur.*v.Sym*.109(M.86.3089A); of incessant prayer, Nil.*epp*.4.25(M.79.561B); **3.** *pray in procession, utter litany* ~οντες ἐξ οἴκου κυρίου ἐξέρχεσθαι †Gregent.*disp*.38(M.86.601C); in time of earthquake σεισμῶν πολλάκις γενομένων...παρακαλέσαντος τοῦ βασιλέως...ἐξελθεῖν καὶ ~σαι μηδέποτε πεισθῆναι ἐξελθεῖν CEph.(431)*ep*.(*ACO* 1.1.2 p.65.29; H.1.1588A); cross being carried in procession τὸ τοῦ σταυροῦ σημεῖον, ὃ ἀντὶ διδασκάλου ἐπ' ὤμων φέροντες ἐπὶ τῆς ἀσπόρου ἐλιτάνευον Pall.*v.Chrys*.16(p.97.6; M.47.55); patriarch and emperor participating, Thdr.Lect.*h.e*.1.6(M.86.169A); *Chron.Pasch*.p.318(M.92.812A); procession outside town during earthquake ἔφυγον ἔξω τῆς πόλεως πάντες ~οντες ἡμέρας καὶ νυκτός *ib*.p.317(805D); of processions from palace to church ὁ Αἴλουρος...ἐκ τοῦ οἴκου τοῦ Βασιλίσκου ~ων εἰς τὴν ἐκκλησίαν ἤρχετο, αὐτοῦ ἐκείνου ἐπὶ ὄνου ὀχουμένου Thdr.Lect.*h.e*.1.30(180B); hymn τρισάγιον being sung at these processions ἀπεκάλυψε...Πρόκλῳ τὸ τρισάγιον εἰς παῦσιν ὀργῆς ~οντας αὐτοὺς φωνεῖν ‡Asclep.*ep*.(p.11.21; H.2.853A); γέγονε σεισμός...ὥστε πᾶσαν τὴν πόλιν συναχθῆναι εἰς τὸν φόρον Κωνσταντίνου καὶ ~ειν καὶ λέγειν· ἅγιος ὁ θεός *Chron.Pasch*.p.341(M.92.889B); ὁ πᾶς δῆμος τῶν ~όντων ἐξεβόησεν *ib*.; cf. ~ειν τὸ τρισάγιον καὶ λέγειν ἅγιος ὁ θεός...καὶ οὕτως ~σάντων ἔστησαν οἱ σεισμοί· οὕτως οὖν καὶ σὺ ~ε ‡Quint.*ep*.(p.17.26ff.; M.85.1740D); ~οντος τοῦ λαοῦ διὰ τὴν θεήλατον ἀπειλήν Jo.D.*f.o*.3.10(M.94.1021A); **4.** of prayer to BMV τοῦ θήλεος τούτου τὸ πρόσωπον ~ουσιν πλούσιοι τοῦ λαοῦ ‡Jo.D.*hom*.6.9(M.96.673D); **5.** of intercession of saints ὅταν ~ωσι [sc. οἱ ἅγιοι] τότε ἐμοὶ ἔννοια ἐπέστη καὶ ἐχάρη τῇ αὐτῶν πραότητι Ephr.1.176E; Sophr.H.*carm*.12.108(M.87.3796A).

λιτή, ἡ, 1. *supplication*; **a.** of pagan prayers ὁπόταν ἐποχὴ ὑετοῦ γένηται, πρὸς οὐρανὸν...ἀφορῶντες εὐχὰς καὶ λ. ἀπονέμετε *Hom.Clem*.11.13; **b.** of Christ's prayer at Crucifixion τὰς πρὸς θεὸν καὶ πατέρα λ. ὑπὲρ αὐτῶν ἐποιεῖτο Cyr.*Lc*.6:27(M.72.596A); **c.** of Church's prayers εἰρήνην αἰτοῦμεν...ἐν ταῖς ἐκκλησίαις...ἐν ταῖς εὐχαῖς, ἐν ταῖς λ. Chrys.*hom*.3.3 *in Col*.(11.347D); **2.** *prayer uttered in procession, litany* (v. λιτανεία); emperor participating, Thdr.Lect.*h.e*.1.6(M.86.169A); Thphn.*chron*.p.94(M.108.280A); with candles and incense μετὰ ψαλμῳδιῶν καὶ κηρῶν καὶ θυμιαμάτων ἐν τῷ ἁγίῳ οἴκῳ καταντήσαντες τὴν λ. ... πληρώσωμεν CTyr.(518)*act*.(p.90.12; H.2.1361B); γέγονε σεισμὸς μέγας ὡς ἐξ ἀνάγκης...λ. γενέσθαι εἰς τὸν Κάμπον καὶ ψαλθῆναι τὸ τρισάγιον *Chron.Pasch*.p.384(M.92.984B); as expiation in time of plague, Eustrat.*v.Eutych*.84(M.86.2369C); at reception of a bishop or in his honour ἐξῆλθεν ὁ ἡγούμενος...μετὰ τῶν ἀδελφῶν... καὶ ἐδέξαντο τὸν...Γρηγόριον...μετὰ λ. ψάλλοντες τὸ 'ἅγιος ὁ θεός' Leont.Abb.*v.Gr.Agr*.48(M.98.632A); ἐρχομένου αὐτοῦ μετὰ τῆς λ. ... μετὰ τοῦ κλήρου αὐτοῦ Jo.Mosch.*prat*.210(M.87.3101B); at dedication of a church γέγονε τὰ...ἐγκαίνια τῆς μεγάλης ἐκκλησίας καὶ ἐξῆλθεν ἡ λ. ... καθημένου...τοῦ πατριάρχου ἐν τῷ βασιλικῷ ὀχήματι καὶ τοῦ βασιλέως συλλιτανεύοντος τῷ λαῷ Thphn.*chron*.p.184(480A); ἐξῆλθεν ...ὁ πατριάρχης μετὰ τῆς λ. ... φορῶν τὸ ἀποστολικὸν σχῆμα...πάντων ψαλλόντων τὸ 'ἄρατε πύλας' *ib*.p.202(520B); in drought, *ib*.p.201(517A).

***λιτήσιος**, *prayerful, in prayer*, Nonn.*par.Jo*.4:23(M.43.777B).

***λιτιγάτωρ, ὁ**, (Lat. *litigator*) *litigant*, Ath.Scholast.*coll*.4.15(p.58); *ib*.5.3(p.72).

***λιτιγιόσος**, (Lat. *litigiosus*) *as being subject of litigation* τοῦτο θεσπίζομεν λ. ... πρᾶγμα κινητὸν ἢ ἀκίνητον ἢ αὐτοκίνητον οὗτινος περὶ τῆς δεσποτείας ζήτησις...κινεῖται Justn.*nov*.112.1(p.524.1); cf.Ath. Scholast.*coll*.5.2(p.71).

λιτός, 1. *plain, frugal*, *Orac.Sib*.7.89; *in plain clothes* opp. episcopal garb, Thphn.*chron*.p.121(M.108.337C); **2.** *ordinary, common*; in gen., of a private soldier στρατιώτης...λ. Thphn.*chron*.p.89(M.108.268B); eucharistic, of elements before epiclesis of Trin. (v. ἐπίκλησις) compared with food offered to idols before invocation of demons which profanes it, Cyr.H.*catech*.19.7; cf.Jo.D.*f.o*.4.13(M.94.1149B) cit. s. ἄνθραξ; of incarnate Christ at baptism by John παραγίνεται λ., μόνος, γύμνος,...ὡς ἄνθρωπος λ. καὶ ὑπόχρεως ἁμαρτιῶν †Hipp.*theoph*.4(p.259.11; M.10.856A).

***λιτοφαγία, ἡ**, *plain fare*, *Schol*.22 in Jo.Clim.*scal*.14(M.88.877C); Thal.*cent*.4.31(M.91.1461B).

λιτρισμός, ὁ, *measurement by λίτραι*, Epiph.*mens*.24(M.43.285A).

***λιτροβουλής, ὁ**, *dirty glutton*, Thdr.Lect.*h.e*.2.28(M.86.200A, conj. -βούλβην); Thphn.*chron*.p.133(M.108.365B).

λιτῶς, *plainly*; ref. diet, Bas.*hom*.1.4(2.4A; M.31.169A); ref. dress, opp. ceremonially, Thphn.*chron*.p.148(M.108.401B); opp. in priestly vestments, *ib*.p.121(337C, v.l. λιτός).

λιχανός, ὁ, *licking*; as subst., *tip of tongue*, Synes.*ep*.158(M.66.1560B).

***λιχνίζω**, *make gluttonous*; pass., *Apophth.Patr*.(M.65.149A).

λιχνώδης, *gluttonous, luxurious* οὐ...πάντων τὰ κοινόβια διὰ τὸ λ. Jo.Clim.*scal*.1(M.88.641D).

***λόβωσις, ἡ**, ? for λώβωσις (cf. λωβόω) or perh. for λώβησις, *incapacitation*, Sophr.H.*v.Cyr.et Jo*.24(M.87.3409C).

λογάριν (λογάρην), τό, 1. *sum of money*, Leont.N.*v.Sym*.44(M.93.1725A); *ib*.52(1733C); id.*v.Jo.Eleem*.37(p.76.8); -ρην Jo.Mosch.*prat*.155(M.87.3024C); **2.** *piece of money*, Leont.N.*v.Jo.Eleem*.1(p.5.4); *ib*.44(p.89.25); -ρην Jo.Mosch.*prat*.184(M.87.3056D).

λογάς, ὁ, 1. sing. and plur., *picked man (men), leading person(s)*; in gen., Or.*Cels*.2.78(p.200.28; M.11.917C); Gr.Nyss.*usur*.(M.46.433B); Thphn.*chron*.p.78(M.108.241A); esp. of authors, Mac.Mgn.*apocr*.3.37(p.132.1); partic. of pagan writers (as iron. term of contempt) σοφοὶ καὶ λ., ποιηταὶ δὲ μάλιστα Cyr.*ador*.6(1.178D); λ., ποιηταί τε καὶ συγγραφεῖς *ib*.17(596A); id.*glaph.Gen*.1(1.15C); ἱερομύστας...καὶ ποιητὰς καὶ λ. id.*Is*.3.1(2.352D); of philosophers and rhetoricians, *ib*.5.2(773E); **2.** λ. λίθοι *unhewn stones*, ref. Christ's tomb οὐκ ἐκ λ. λίθων οἰκοδομηθέντι Or.*Cels*.2.69(p.191.15; M.11.904D).

λογεῖον, τό, v. λόγιον.

***λογίδριον, τό**, = λογύδριον λογίδιον; **1.** *contemptible little* *pamphlet*, Jo.D.*hom*.12.23(M.96.813B); of heret. books, Sophr.H. *ep.syn*.(M.87.3189B); *ib*.(3196B); ‡Jo.D.*ep.Thphl*.20(M.95.372B); **2.** *contemptible utterance*, †Jo.D.*B.J*.28(M.96.1124C); Thst.*v.Nic. Heg*.29(p.xxviiiE).

λογικεύ-ομαι, **1.** *endow with reason*· ἑαυτὸν ὅλοις τοῖς οὖσι καταμειγνὺς ἵνα ~ηται τὰ λογικὰ καὶ φρόνησιν ἔχῃ τὰ φρονήσεως δεκτικά Cyr.*Jo*.1.5(4.58E); **2.** *argue*, Meth.*res*.1.27(p.256.2; M.41.1133B); *ib*. 1.62(p.326.22; 1160B).

λογικός, **A.** *rational, endowed with reason*; **1.** of man πλησίον δὲ ἀνθρώπου οὐδὲν ἄλλο ἐστὶν ἢ τὸ ὁμοιοπαθὲς καὶ λ. ζῷον, ὁ ἄνθρωπος Just.*dial*.93.3(M.6.697C); δυνάμενον αἱρεῖσθαι τἀληθῆ...τὸ γένος τὸ ἀνθρώπινον πεποίηκεν, ὥστ' ἀναπολόγητον εἶναι τοῖς πᾶσιν ἀνθρώποις παρὰ τῷ θεῷ· λ. γὰρ καὶ θεωρητικοὶ γεγένηνται id.*1apol*.28.3(M.6. 372C); ἔστι γὰρ ἄνθρωπος οὐ...ζῷον λ., νοῦ καὶ ἐπιστήμης δεκτικόν· δειχθήσεται γὰρ...τὰ ἄλογα νοῦ καὶ ἐπιστήμης δεκτικά. μόνος δὲ ἄνθρωπος εἰκὼν καὶ ὁμοίωσις τοῦ θεοῦ Tat.*orat*.15(p.16.11; M.6. 837A); Iren.*haer*.5.3.2(M.7.1130A); θνητὸν λ. ὁ ἄνθρωπος Or.*Jo*.1.31 (34; p.38.24; M.14.81A); through partaking of Logos ὁ δὲ σωτὴρ ἐλλάμπων τοῖς λ. καὶ ἡγεμονικοῖς, ἵνα αὐτῶν ὁ νοῦς τὰ ἴδια ὁρατὰ βλέπῃ, τοῦ νοητοῦ κόσμου ἐστὶ φῶς· λέγω δὲ τῶν λ. ψυχῶν τῶν ἐν τῷ αἰσθητικῷ κόσμῳ *ib*.1.25(24; p.30.33; 68B); ἐὰν γὰρ νοήσωμεν τὸν ἐν ἀρχῇ λόγον, τάχα δυνησόμεθα μόνον τὸν τούτου...μετέχοντα λ. εἰπεῖν· ὥστε καὶ ἀποφήνασθαι ἄν, ὅτι μόνος ὁ ἅγιος λ. *ib*.2.16(p.73.13; 144A); ἐὰν δέ τις ᾖ λογικώτερος καὶ διὰ τοῦτο καὶ νοητὸς ἄνθρωπος, τὸν νοητὸν ἄρτον ἐσθίει *ib*.13.33(p.258.31; 457B); id.*or*.6.1(p.312.5; M.11.436A); τὴν λογικωτάτην εἰκόνα καὶ ἔμψυχον τὸν ἄνθρωπον...ἑαυτοῦ τεκταινόμενος Meth.*symp*.2.6(p.23.5; M.18.56D); ἐπαινῶν μὲν φιλοσοφίαν καὶ τοὺς φιλοσοφίας ἐραστάς...τούτους μόνους ζῆν ὄντως τὸν λογικοῖς προσήκοντα βίον λέγων, τοὺς ὀρθῶς βιοῦν ἐπιτηδεύοντας Gr.Thaum. *pan.Or*.6(p.15.10; M.10.1069A); *Hom.Clem*.10.17; κατὰ τὴν ἑαυτοῦ εἰκόνα ἐποίησεν αὐτούς, μεταδοὺς αὐτοῖς καὶ τῆς τοῦ ἰδίου λ. δυνάμεως, ἵνα ὥσπερ σκιάς τινας ἔχοντες τοῦ λόγου καὶ γενόμενοι λ. διαμένειν ἐν μακαριότητι δυνηθῶσι Ath.*inc*.3.3(M.25.101B); ὁ δὲ λ. καὶ κατ' εἰκόνα γενόμενος ἄνθρωπος ἠφανίζετο *ib*.6.1(105C); *ib*.8.2(109A); μέρος μὲν ὄντα [sc. man] τοῦ παντός, ὅμως δὲ πολίτην ἐπιστήσας λ. τὸν ἄνθρωπον ὁ θεός, τὰ μὲν ἄλλα ὅσα μήτε πρὸς ἀρετὴν μήτε πρὸς κακίαν ὁρᾷ, ἑαυτῷ τετήρηκεν οἰκονομεῖν Tit.Bost.*Man*.2.2(M.18.1133C); λόγος υἱὸς λογικῶν ποιητής Cyr.H.*catech*.4.8; Σινᾶ...ὁ μόνοις ἀνείθη... τοῖς λ. εἰς ἐπίβασιν Gr.Nyss.*v.Mos*.45(M.44.316A); οὔτε γὰρ τὸ λ., οὔτε τὸ διανοητικόν, οὔτε τὸ ἐπιστήμης δεκτικόν, οὔτε ἄλλο τι τοιοῦτον, ὃ τῆς ἀνθρωπίνης ἴδιον οὐσίας ἐστί, τῷ λόγῳ τῆς ἀρετῆς ἠναντίωται id.*or.catech*.15(p.66.9; M.45.49A); ταῦτα [sc. sinful πάθη] οὐκ ἔστι τοῦ λ., ἀλλ' εἰς μωρίαν τὸ λ. παρατρέποντος id.*castig*.(M.46.309B); τέλος τῆς δημιουργίας τὸ λ. ζῷον, τὸν κοσμοπολίτην, τῇ σῇ σοφίᾳ διαταξάμενος κατεσκεύασας *Const.App*.7.34.6; οὐδὲ γὰρ ἄνθρωπος ἀλόγου βελτίων τῷ μὴ εἶναι ἄψυχος...ἀλλὰ τῷ εἶναι λ. Didym. (‡Bas.)*Eun*.4(1.285E; M.29.688A); φιλοσόφων...τοῦτον ποιησαμένων ...ὅρον...ζῷον λ. θνητόν Chrys.*stat*.11.2(2.117A); how dist. from ἄλογοι: διακρίνειν τὸ καλὸν ἀπὸ τοῦ κακοῦ δύνα⟨ν⟩ται [sc. οἱ λ.] Thdr. Mops.*Rom*.11:15(p.156.16; M.66.853C); οὐδὲ γὰρ ἀδίδακτον ἔχειν ἡμᾶς τῆς ἀρετῆς ἐνεδέχετο τὴν ἕξιν λ. γεγονότας τὴν φύσιν *ib*.(p.156.23; 853D); λ. ... αἱ ἄνω δυνάμεις...ὁμοίως δὲ λ. ἐπὶ γῆς ὁ ἄνθρωπος... βραχὺ δὲ ὑποβέβηκε τὴν τῶν ἀγγέλων ἀξίαν διὰ τὴν πρὸς τὸ γεῶδες σῶμα συνάφειαν Cyr.*Ps*.8:6(M.69.760B); μόνος γὰρ αὐτὸς παρὰ πάντα τὰ ἐπὶ γῆς ζῷα λ. ἐστι...ἐπιτηδειότητα πρὸς πᾶσαν ἀρετὴν ἔχων, λαχὼν δὲ καὶ τὸ ἄρχειν ἁπάντων...οὐκοῦν κατὰ τὸ εἶναι ζῷον λ. ... ἐν εἰκόνι θεοῦ πεποιῆσθαι λέγεται id.*ep.Calos*.(p.605.9,12; 6^2.364E); Thdt. *provid*.4(4.543); id.*qu.8 in Jud*.(1.328); ὁ θεὸς...νόμῳ φυσικῷ τὸ λ. ἐτίμησε ζῷον Procl.CP *Arm*.5(p.189.19; M.65.860C); v. εἰκών, ἄνθρωπος; **2.** partic. of man's rational soul γυμνὴ δὲ ἡ ψυχὴ...μεταβαίνει εἰς τὰ πνευματικά, λ. τῷ ὄντι καὶ ἀρχιερατικὴ γενομένη, ὡς ἂν ἐμψυχουμένη ὡς εἰπεῖν ὑπὸ τοῦ λόγου προσεχῶς ἤδη Clem.*exc.Thdot*.27(p.116. 3; M.9.673A); id.*fr*.38(p.219.29; M.9.769C) cit. s. αἰσθητικός; θεὸς γὰρ οἰκονομεῖ τὰς ψυχὰς οὐχ ὡς πρὸς τὴν...πεντηκονταετίαν τῆς...ζωῆς, ἀλλ' ὡς πρὸς τὸν ἀπέραντον αἰῶνα· ἄφθαρτον γὰρ φύσιν πεποίηκε τὴν νοερὰν...καὶ οὐκ ἀποκλείεται ὥσπερ ἐπὶ τῆς ἐνταῦθα ζωῆς ἡ λ. ψυχὴ τῆς θεραπείας Or.*princ*.3.1.13(p.218.13; M.11.273A); ἐτεκτήνατο κατ' εἰκόνα τῆς εἰκόνος ἑαυτοῦ τὴν ψυχήν. δίο καὶ λ. καὶ ἀθάνατός ἐστι Meth.*symp*.6.1(p.64.18; M.18.113B); λ. τῆς ψυχῆς δύναμις Eus.*p.e*.6.6 (249A; M.21.424A); θεοῦ λόγος, ὁ τῆς ἐν ἀνθρώποις λ. καὶ νοερᾶς πατὴρ οὐσίας id.*l.C*.4(p.202.32; M.20.1333A); id.*e.th*.2.13(p.114.12; M.24. 925D); Cyr.*dogm*.2(6^2.368C); Thdt.*qu.20 in Gen*.(1.28) cit. s. εἰκών; id.*eran*.1(4.13); **3.** of the rational soul of Christ incarnate μεγαλειότερα μὲν οὖν πάσης ἀνθρωπείου διδασκαλίας φαίνεται τὰ ἡμέτερα διὰ τοῦ τὸ λ. τὸ ὅλον τὸν φανέντα δι' ἡμᾶς Χριστὸν γεγονέναι, καὶ σῶμα καὶ λόγον καὶ ψυχήν Just.*2apol*.10.1(M.6.460B); λαβὼν δὲ καὶ ψυχὴν τὴν ἀνθρωπείαν, λ. δὲ λέγω Hipp.*Noët*.17(p.261.25; M.10.825D; prob. anti-Apollinarian interpolation, v. p.114); Or.*Cels*.4.18(p.288.4; M.11.1049D) cit. s. ψυχή; ἄνθρωπος γέγονε χωρὶς ἁμαρτίας, κατὰ πρόσληψιν πάσης τῆς ἀνθρωπείας φύσεως, τουτέστι ψυχῆς λ. καὶ νοερᾶς καὶ σαρκὸς ἀνθρωπίνης Photinus et al.*ep*.ap.Epiph.*haer*.72.12(p.266. 19; M.42.400A); γέγονεν ἄνθρωπος...οὐκ ἄψυχον...σῶμα λαβών, ἐψυχωμένον δὲ μᾶλλον ψυχῇ καὶ λ. ... καὶ ὥσπερ οἰκειοῦται πάντα τὰ τοῦ ἰδίου σώματος, οὕτω καὶ τὰ τῆς ψυχῆς Cyr.*Pulch*.(p.58.34; 5^2. 176C); σάρκα ἐψυχωμένην ψυχῇ λ. ἑνώσας ὁ λόγος ἑαυτῷ καθ' ὑπόστασιν id.*ep*.4(p.26.27; 5^2.23B); ἐκ ψυχῆς λ. καὶ σώματος *Symb. Chalc*.(p.129.26; H.2.456C); Thdt.*eran*.1(4.13); Vict.*Mc*.7:31(p.339. 2); ἐκ δύο μὲν φύσεων ἀεὶ διαβεβαιούμενοι τὸν Χριστόν, οὐδέποτε δὲ αὐτὸν ἐκ τριῶν φύσεων καλέσαντες· καίπερ καὶ ψυχὴν λ. τῇ σαρκὶ... παρέχουσιν Leont.B.*Nest.et Eut*.1(M.86.1296B); CCP(543)*anath*.9; Justn.*conf*.(p.74.27; M.86.997B) cit. s. ὑπόστασις; **4.** ref. theory of pre-existence of souls, CCP(543)*anath*.4; *ib*.14; **5.** of angelic powers, Or.*Jo*.1.31(34; p.38.26ff.; M.14.81A); λ. ... αἱ ἄνω δυνάμεις, μακράν τε καὶ ἀτελεύτητον τρίβουσαι ζωήν Cyr.*Ps*.8:6(M.69.760B); id.*Is*.2.4 (2.282D); τὴν κτίσιν τὴν ἄνω τε καὶ λ. *ib*.3.4(485D); *ib*.4.2(592E); ταῖς ἄνω δυνάμεσι λ., αἷς ἐπαναπαύεται θεός id.*dogm*.(6^2.371C); CCP(543) *anath*.4; Proc.G.*Is*.49:1–13(M.87.2476A); **6.** of rational creatures in gen. ὁ δὲ σωτὴρ ἐλλάμπων τοῖς λ. ... τοῦ νοητοῦ κόσμου ἐστὶ φῶς· λέγω δὲ τῶν λ. ψυχῶν τῶν ἐν τῷ αἰσθητικῷ κόσμῳ, καὶ εἴ τι παρὰ ταῦτα συμπληροῖ τὸν κόσμον Or.*Jo*.1.25(24; p.30.33; M.14.68B); ὁ μὲν... πατὴρ...φθάνει εἰς ἕκαστον τῶν ὄντων...ἐλαττόνως δὲ...ὁ υἱὸς φθάνων ἐπὶ μόνα τὰ λ. id.*princ*.1.3.5(p.56.3; M.11.150B); ποικιλωτάτου κόσμου τυγχάνοντος καὶ τοσαῦτα διάφορα λ. περιέχοντος *ib*.2.1.1(p.107.2; 187B); ᾧ πάντα πείθονται τὰ λ. Meth.*symp*.3.6(p.32.11; M.18.68D); μακρὸν ἂν εἴη μεταξὺ πατρὸς ἀγεννήτου, καὶ τῶν κτισθέντων ὑπ' αὐτοῦ ἐξ οὐκ ὄντων, λ. τε καὶ ἀλόγων Alex.Al.*ep.Alex*.11(p.26.26; M.18. 564C); Didym.(‡Bas.)*Eun*.5(1.319A; M.29.765A); ‡Ath.*dial.Trin*.1. 8(M.28.1129B); ref. heret. ascetics κρεῶν ἀπέχεσθαι οὐχ ὡς ἀλόγων ζῴων, ἀλλ' ὡς λ. ἐχόντων ψυχήν *Const.App*.6.10.2; εἴ τις λέγει, πάντων τῶν λ. τὴν παραγωγὴν νόας ἀσωμάτους...γεγονέναι...ὡς ἑνάδα πάντων τούτων γενέσθαι CCP(543)*anath*.2; **7.** theol., ref. Gen.1:26 πρός τινα καὶ ἀριθμῷ ὄντα ἕτερον, λ. ὑπάρχοντα, ὡμιληκέναι αὐτόν Just. *dial*.62.2(M.6.617B); Tat.*orat*.5(p.5.20; M.6.813C); *ib*.7(p.7.7; 820B), Athenag.*leg*.10.2(M.6.909A) citt. s. λόγος; ἐν αὐτῷ εἶναι τῷ πατρὶ ὡς βουλὴν καὶ λόγον βουλευτικὸν καὶ λ. Leont.H.*Nest*.2.17(M.86.1576B).

B. *pertaining to the reason, comprehensible by reason, logical, intellectual* ἀποδείξεως λ. Or.*princ*.4.1.1(p.293.13; M.11.344A); λ. ἐπιστήμαις Eus.*h.e*.7.32.28(M.20.733A); λογικωτέραν διδασκαλίαν id. *v.C*.3.51(p.99.15; M.20.1112B); χρεωστεῖς δὲ ἡμῖν...καὶ τὰ πνευματικά, ἀρχιερεὺς ἀρχιερεῦσι, καὶ τὰ λ., ὡς λόγιος φιλολόγοις Gr.Naz. *ep*.167(M.37.277B).

C. *spiritual* (= νοερός, νοητός, πνευματικός); **1.** of persons ἐὰν δέ τις ᾖ λογικώτερος καὶ διὰ τοῦτο καὶ νοητὸς ἄνθρωπος, τὸν νοητὸν ἄρτον ἐσθίει Or.*Jo*.13.33(p.258.31; M.14.457B); of angelic host λ. στρατιᾶς Eus.*h.e*.1.2.3(M.20.53C); πάσης νοερᾶς καὶ λ. οὐσίας id.*e.th*. 1.8(p.66.34; M.24.837D); †Ath.*exp.fid*.3(M.25.204C); **2.** *spiritual* opp. material, esp. of spiritual reality denoted by a material image or metaphor; **a.** in gen. λ. γὰρ αἱ τοῦ λόγου πύλαι, πίστεως ἀνοιγνύμεναι κλειδί Clem.*prot*.1(p.10.14; M.8.68A); Eus.*h.e*.1.1.3(M.20.52A); ψυχῆς ἄρτος θρεπτικός τις λόγος, καὶ ποτὸν ὡσαύτως λ. id.*Is*.3:1–2(M.24. 108C); λ. γεωργίαν Thdt.*Is*.5:6(p.24.31; 2.199); λ. ἁλιέων Procl.CP *or*.19.1(M.65.824A); of BMV ἡ θεοφερὴς λ. ὁλκάς Mod.*dorm*.4(M.86. 3288C); of Church or Christ's disciples as a spiritual flock, Eus. *h.e*.8.13.3(M.20.773C); λ. προβάτων id.*m.P*.12(p.946.23; M.20.1512B); *Const.App*.2.19.2; Cyr.*Is*.1.3(2.63D); Eus.Al.*serm*.5(M.86.348B); of Christ τὸ πρόβατον τὸ λ. Epiph.*anc*.19(p.27.25; M.43.52B); ‡Chrys. *pasch*.4(8.260A); of Israel, Cyr.*Soph*.42(3.620E); **b.** esp. of spiritual worship opp. material offerings; **i.** λ. θυσία of prayer and worship in gen., Eus.*d.e*.1.6(p.30.33; M.22.61A); of eucharist, v. θυσία; **ii.** λ. λατρεία v. λατρεία.

λογικῶς, *rationally, in accordance with reason*; *spiritually* opp. corporeally ἄρτον λαβὼν...εὐχαρίστησε...ἵνα φάγωμεν λ. Clem.*str*.1. 10(p.30.21; M.8.744A).

λόγιον, τό, **A.** *utterance, saying*; **1.** plur., of teaching or discourse in gen. ὁρῶ...τὰ λ. σου ὡς λ. Παύλου *A.Xanthipp*.28(p.78.25); τὰ τῆς θεογνωσίας προσλαλεῖν λ. †Jo.D.*B.J*.30(M.96.1144B); **2.** of God's creative words οὔτε γὰρ προσφορᾷ δημιουργεῖ ῥημάτων θεός, κἂν ἀνθρωπινωτέρως ὀνομάζηται λ. θεοῦ προφορικὰ ῥήματα Didym. (‡Bas.)*Eun*.5(1.303E; M.29.728C); of ten commandments, *Const. App*.2.36.1; *ib*.7.36.4; Eustrat.*v.Eutych*.26(M.86.2304D); Proc.G. *Jos*.3:2(M.87.1004C); **3.** esp. of oracular or inspired utterances; **a.** pagan χρηστήρια...χρησμοὺς ἀνεδίδου καὶ λ. Philost.*h.e*.7.12(M.65.

549B); Bas.Sel.*v.Thecl.*2(M.85.564C); *τὰ τῆς μαντείας λ.* ‡Just.*qu.et resp.*81(M.6.1324A); **b.** of utterances of OT prophets, prophecies *Ματθαῖος μὲν οὖν Ἑβραΐδι διαλέκτῳ τὰ λ. συνετάξατο, ἡρμήνευσεν δ' αὐτά, ὡς ἦν δυνατὸς ἕκαστος* Papias *fr.*2.15 (if λ. here denotes OT prophetic proof-texts; to be included under d infra, if λ. here denotes *sayings* of Christ); cf. *τοῦ δὲ Παπία συγγράμματα πέντε τὸν ἀριθμὸν φέρεται, ἃ καὶ ἐπιγέγραπται λ. κυριακῶν ἐξηγήσεως* Eus. *h.e.*3.39.1(M.20.296A) (where λ. may similarly denote either *prophecies* relating to the Lord or *sayings* of the Lord); *Ἰεσσαὶ προπάτωρ μὲν κατὰ τὸ λ. γεγένηται* Just.*1apol.*32.14(M.6.380C); id. *dial.*18.1(M.6.516A); *τὰ προφητικὰ λ.* Eus.*e.th.*2.25(p.136.8; M.24.965B); *τῶν περὶ αὐτῶν λ. ... πληρωθησομένων ib.*3.16(p.174.29; 1033B); id.*d.e.*1 proem.(p.2.19; M.22.16B); Evagr.Pont.*ep.*2(M.32 248C); Cyr.*Mich.*4(3.392E); **c.** plur., of OT scriptures in gen. *ἐπίστασθε τὰς ἱερὰς γραφάς,...καὶ ἐγκεκύφατε εἰς τὰ λ. τοῦ θεοῦ 1Clem.*53.1; *ἀνδράσιν...ἐλλογιμωτάτοις καὶ ἐγκεκυφόσιν εἰς τὰ λ. τῆς παιδείας τοῦ θεοῦ ib.*62.3; *Ἰουδαίους...οἱ τὰ μὲν λ. τοῦ θεοῦ ἀνὰ στόμα ἔχουσιν* Clem. *str.*7.18(p.77.14; M.9.556A); Or.*hom.10.1 in Jer.*(p.71.5; M.13.357B); Eus.*p.e.*11 proem.(507D; M.21.844B); Mac.Mgn.*apocr.*4.16(p.189.27); **d.** of sayings of Christ, cf.Papias *fr.*2.15 (v. 3.b supra); *ὃς ἂν μεθοδεύῃ τὰ λ. τοῦ κυρίου πρὸς τὰς ἰδίας ἐπιθυμίας καὶ λέγῃ μήτε ἀνάστασιν μήτε κρίσιν, οὗτος πρωτότοκός ἐστι τοῦ σατανᾶ* Polyc.*ep.*7.1; cf.Eus.*h.e.*3.39.1(M.20.296A) (v. 3.b supra); *ὁ δεχόμενος* [sc. Thomas] *αὐτοῦ τὰ ἀπόκρυφα λ. A.Thom.*A 39(p.156.15); Bas.*ep.*296 (3.434B; M.32.1040B); *τὰ τοῦ Χριστοῦ λ. ... διηνεκῶς μελέτα Const. App.*1.4.1; Thdt.*eran.*1(4.27); Leont.B.*mesopent.*(M.86.1977B); *Chron.Pasch.*p.289(M.92.724A); **e.** of the gospels *ὅτε...ἀπένιψεν τοὺς πόδας, καθὰ τὰ θεόπνευστα διδάσκει λ. ib.*p.218(532C); *ib.*p.221(540A); **f.** of Bible as a whole *μεμελετηκότι τὰ καθαρὰ τῶν λ.* Gr.Thaum.*pan. Or.*15(p.34.1; M.10.1093C); Eus.*v.C.*3.1(p.77.1; M.20.1053B); *διαπαντὸς τοῖς θείοις λ. προσηλῶσθαι* Ath.*exp.Ps.*1:2(M.27.61A); *δὸς ἡμῖν...ἐκζητεῖν τὰ...σου λ.* Serap.*euch.*12.3; *ib.*27.1; Bas.*Eun.*1.6(1.217B; M.29.521C); Chrys.*hom.84.3 in Jo.*(8.503A); *ἐξησκήθη τοῖς λόγοις πρὸς διακονίαν τῶν θείων λ.* Pall.*v.Chrys.*5(p.28.5; M.47.18); *οἱ μὲν τὰ θεῖα λ. ἀναγινώσκοντες, οἱ δὲ βαπτίζοντες ib.*9(p.56.21; M.47.33); *θεοῦ τὰ λ. παρ' ᾧ ψεῦδος οὐδὲν ἢ ἄλογον* Proc.G.*Gen.*proem.(M.87.24A); as utterance of H. Ghost *εἴ τις ἑτεροδιδασκαλεῖ, καὶ... παρωθούμενος τὰ τοῦ πνεύματος λ., τὴν οἰκείαν διδασκαλίαν κυριωτέραν ποιεῖται τῶν εὐαγγελικῶν διδαγμάτων* Bas.*ep.*261.3(3.403B; M.32.972C); Nil.*epp.*3.278(M.79.521C); Cyr.*thes.*proem.(5¹.2B); *ib.*10 (82B); **g.** of a passage or text of scripture, *T.Benj.*9.1; *τοιοῦτον ἐγκεῖται λ. ἐν τοῖς ἱεροῖς γράμμασι* Gr.Thaum.*pan.Or.*15(p.34.17; 1096A); *εἰκὼν ὑπάρχων τοῦ θεοῦ, ὡς τὸ λ. δείκνυσιν* Ath.*Ar.*1.46(M.26.108A); *τὸ ἀποστολικὸν λ.* Gr.Nyss.*anim.et res.*(M.46.13A); *Const. App.*2.16.3; Nil.*epp.*1.225(M.79.165A); Diad.*perf.*64(p.76.10); *τὸ ψαλμικὸν...λ.* Jo.Eub.*concept.BMV* 8(M.96.1472A); **h.** sing., of scripture as a whole *τῇ φύσει μὲν σαφέστατον...πᾶν τὸ θεῖον λ. ὄν* Gr.Thaum.*pan.Or.*15(p.33.22; M.10.1093B); *λέγεται δὲ λ. καὶ ἡ θεόπνευστος γραφή* Ath.*exp.Ps.*118:81(M.27.493D); **i.** of inspiration of H. Ghost in gen. *ὁρῶ ὅτι καὶ ἐν τοῖς λ. τοῦ πνεύματος οὐ παντὶ ἐξὴν ἐπιβάλλειν τῇ ἐξετάσει τῶν εἰρημένων, ἀλλὰ τῷ ἔχοντι τὸ πνεῦμα τῆς διακρίσεως* Bas.*ep.*204.5(3.305D; M.32.752A); **j.** of gospel in gen. as *λόγια τοῦ θεοῦ 2Clem.*13.3; *A.Paul.et Thecl.*42(p.268.3); sing. *οὐδὲν ἄλλο ποιεῖ ζῆν λογικὴν ψυχὴν τὴν ἑαυτῆς ζωὴν ὡς τὸ λ. τοῦ θεοῦ· καθ' ὃ γὰρ αὔξει τὸ λ. τοῦ θεοῦ,...παραλαμβανόμενον εἰς τὴν τοῦ ἀνθρώπου ψυχήν, κατὰ τοῦτο αὔξεται καὶ τὰ τῆς ζωῆς* Ath. *exp.Ps.*118:50(M.27.488D); *Const.App.*6.30.5; ‡Proc.G.*Pr.*3:1(M.87.1241B); Cosm.Ind.*top.*2(M.88.128C); **4.** of Logos *ἐξέλιπον οἱ ὀφθαλμοί μου εἰς τὸ λ. σου εἰς τὸν κύριον ἡμῶν Ἰησοῦν Χριστόν* Ath. *exp.Ps.*118:82(M.27.496A); cf. *ἐγὼ ἕνα μόνον λόγον τοῦ θεοῦ ἐν ὑποστάσει ὁμολογῶ ἄκτιστον ὄντα...τὴν δὲ ἅπασαν γραφήν μου, οὐ λέγω λόγια, ἀλλὰ ῥήματα θεοῦ* Jo.D.*disp.*(M.96.1344A).

B. *oracular breast-plate* of high priest (also *λογεῖον*) *τὸ λόγιον... οὐ τὸ αὐτὸ μηνύει. ἀλλ' ὅταν μὲν ἡ πρώτη ὀξύνηται συλλαβή, χρησμὸν δηλοῖ, ὅταν δ' ἡ δευτέρα, τὸ ἐπὶ τοῦ στήθους τοῦ ἀρχιερέως ἐπιτεθῆναι θεσπισθέν, οἷον λόγου ἱερόν, ἢ οἶκον, ἢ τέμενος* Isid.Pel.*epp.*3.10(M.78.733B); *τὸ λόγιον τῆς συνέσεως T.Lev.*8.2; *λογεῖον* Iren.*haer.*1.18.4 (M.7.648B); *τοῦ λ. (τὸν λόγον δὲ τοῦτο αἰνίσσεται)* Clem.*str.*5.6(p.352.2; M.9.64B); *λογεῖον* Ath.*Ar.*2.7(M.26.161B); *Μωυσῆς λ. ἐπιτίθησι* Nil.*exerc.*56(M.79.788D); *τὸ...λ. τὴν λογικὴν συγκαλύπτον καρδίαν* Thdt.*qu.60 in Ex.*(1.167); *διὰ τοῦ λ. τῆς κρίσεως* id.*qu.47 in Num.*(1.253); cf. *τὸ λογεῖον τῆς κρίσεως* Cosm.Ind.*top.*5(M.88.213A); met., of BMV *τὸ...χρυσοΰφαντον λ.* ‡Jo.D.*hom.*5(M.96.649C).

λογιότης, ἡ, 1. *rationality, reasonableness,* Ath.*gent.*32(M.25.65A, conj. for *λογικότητος*); Mac.Mgn.*apocr.*3.43(p.149.27); *λ. δέ φησιν ἐπὶ τοῦ θεοῦ, οὐχ ὅτι λογικὸν θέλει δηλῶσαι τὸν θεόν, ὡς μετέχοντα λόγου...ἀλλ' ὅτι αὐτολογιότης ἐστίν, ὅλος λόγος ὤν* Max.*schol.c.h.*2.3 (M.4.40C); *καὶ ἐπὶ ἀγγέλων λ. λέγει ib.*2.4(44A); in honorific address *τῇ λ. σου συνεσόμεθα* Bas.*ep.*1(3.70C; M.32.221B); Isid.Pel.*epp.*5.125(M.78.1396D); **2.** *argumentation, logic-chopping,* Leont.H.*Nest.*2.8(M.86.1553B); *ib.*4.9(1668A).

λογισμός, ὁ, 1. *argument*; in gen., in rel. to faith *λογισμοὶ γὰρ θνητῶν δειλοί...τί ἐστι δειλοί; ὁ δειλὸς κἂν ἐπ' ἀσφαλοῦς βαίνῃ χωρίου, οὐδέπω θαρρεῖ...οὕτω καὶ τὸ λογισμοῖς ἀποδειχθέν, κἂν ἀληθὲς ᾖ, οὐδέπω πληροφορίαν τῇ ψυχῇ παρέχει καὶ πίστιν ἱκανήν* Chrys.*anom.*11.1(1.542B); *ὁρᾶτε πῶς, ὅταν τοῖς οἰκείοις λ. ἐπιτρέψῃ τις τὰ πνευματικά, καὶ καταγέλαστα φθέγγεται...ὅταν...μὴ δέχηται τὴν τῆς πίστεως συγκατάθεσιν* id.*hom.24.3 in Jo.*(8.141B); *τῶν λ. τὴν ἀσθένειαν ἀφέντες τὴν κάτω, πρὸς τὸ ὕψος τῆς πίστεως ἀναβαίνωμεν ib.25.1*(144A); *τοῦτο ἐκείνου ἀπορώτερον, ἐὰν λογισμοῖς ἐξετάζῃς, καὶ μὴ τῇ πίστει παραχωρῇς* id.*hom.26.1 in 2Cor.*(10.619B); *ὥσπερ γὰρ οἱ λ. διαιροῦσι καὶ σαλεύουσιν, οὕτως ἡ πίστις στερεοῖ καὶ παγῆναι ποιεῖ* id.*hom 5.3 in Col.*(11.361E); *μηδὲ...περιεργάζου, μηδὲ λογισμοὺς ἀπαίτει· πίστεως δεῖται τὰ ἡμέτερα* id.*hom.19.1 in Heb.*(12.182A); *τὸ τῆς πίστεως γενναίας...δεῖται ψυχῆς, καὶ...τὴν ἀσθένειαν τῶν λ. τῶν ἀνθρωπίνων παρερχομένης ib.22.1*(201C); **2.** *thought, imagining;* **a.** def. *λ. ἐστι κίνησις ψυχῆς περί τι Doct.Patr.*33(p.262.25); *λ. ἐστι τὸ πρῶτον ἐν τῷ νοΐ ἀνελθὸν νόημα ib.*(p.263.9); **b.** in gen. *λέληθεν αὐτὸν οὐδὲν οὔτε λ. οὔτε ἐννοιῶν* Polyc.*ep.*4.3; *γενέσθαι τὸν υἱὸν λ. καὶ βουλήσεως τάχιον* Hipp.*haer.*8.12(p.232.11; M.16.3358B); *ὁ λ. ἔχων ἀπαθεῖς* id.*fr.7 in Pr.*4:25(p.159.2; M.10.617B); *γήϊνον καὶ φιλοσώματον λ.* Or.*mart.*37(p.35.9; M.11.612D); *δεῖ ὑπὲρ τοῦ μὴ ἐπιθολοῦσθαι τὸν νοῦν ὑπὸ ἑτέρων λ. πάντων ἐπιλελῆσθαι τῶν ἔξω τῆς εὐχῆς* id.*or.*9.1 (p.318.2; M.11.444A); *πάντα πράττειν ὡς ἐν ὀφθαλμοῖς θεοῦ, ἐπὶ θεατοῦ, ἐνορῶντος ἡμῶν καὶ τοῖς λ.* id.*Cels.*7.51(p.202.15; M.11.1496B); *ὁ θεὸς...βλέπει...οὐ μόνον τὰς πράξεις, ἀλλὰ καὶ τοὺς λ.* id. *hom.2 in Lc.*(p.17.13); *τῷ λ. ἀνατυπούμενος ἐν ἑαυτῷ τὸ κάλλος αὐτοῦ* [sc. God] *τῆς τέχνης* Meth.*arbitr.*22(p.205.13); *θεοφιλεῖ λ. Hom. Clem.*16.14; *σωτήριος...λ.* Const.ap.Gel.Cyz.*h.e.*2.7.5(M.85.1233A); *φησὶ γὰρ ἡ γραφή* [not in LXX]· *καὶ παρελογίσατο Ἀμὼν λ. παραβάσεως κακόν Const.App.*2.23.3; *πρὸς τὸ ἀτάραχον τῶν μιαρῶν λ. τὴν ...φυλάξαι ψυχήν* Chrys.*sac.*6.3(p.144.14; 1.423A); *μὴ πάντων ἐστὶν ὑμνεῖν τὸν θεόν, ἀλλὰ μόνον τῶν μετ' εὐθύτητος λ. τοῦτο ποιουμένων* Thdr.Mops.*Ps.*32:1(p.143.8; M.66.668C); *ἐὰν λ. εἰσέλθῃ σοι, καὶ διακρῖναι τοῦτον οὐ δύνασαι, Χριστὸν...δυσώπησον, ἵνα εἰ μὲν ἐκ δαιμόνων ἐστί, φεύξηται* Jo.Jej.*doct.*1(p.229); **c.** partic. of evil thoughts or desires *οἱ λ. ... ἐν ἡμῖν ἔξωθεν ἐπισυνίστανται, καθαπερεὶ κύνες λυσσῶντες* Meth.*res.*2.4(p.337.15; M.41.1169C); Ephr.1.321D; *ὀκτώ εἰσιν οἱ λ. ... γαστριμαργία, πορνεία, φιλαργυρία, θυμός, λύπη ἄκαιρος, ἀκηδία, κενοδοξία, ὑπερηφανία ib.*2.428B; Chrys.*stat.*1.1(2.1B); *τοὺς βασιλέων κρατοῦντας λ.* id.*hom.47.4 in Mt.*(7.492D); *ὅταν ἡμῶν κατατρέχωσι λ. καὶ θλίψεις* Cyr.*Ps.*31:7(M.69.868A); *τοῦ ἁγίου βαπτίσματος λύτρωσιν, δι' ἧς καὶ μόνης τοὺς ἐκ τῆς ἁμαρτίας ἀποτριβόμεθα λ.* id.*Is.*5.6(2.903A); *ἀσκήσει, ὑπομονῇ, καθαιρέσει τῶν λ. καὶ τοῖς λοιποῖς* ‡Philox.*ep.*24(p.175); *ψυχὴν...τοῖς λογισμοῖς ἔχρανα* Anast.*poenit.*3 (p.282); *ὀκτὼ...οἱ λ. οἱ πολεμοῦντες τὸν μοναχόν* Jo.D.*spir.neq.*1(M.95.80A); **3.** *notion, principle of interpretation παρὰ τὸν ὀρθόδοξον βιάζεσθαι...λ. τὰς γραφάς* Meth.*symp.*3.10(p.38.13; M.18.76C); **4.** *attitude, disposition,* Or.*or.*8.2(p.317.18; M.11.441C); id.*fr.61 in Jo.*5:2(p.533.17); *χαυνῶσαι τὸν λ. φαντασίαις ἐκτόποις* Meth.*symp.*4.5(p.51.23; M.18.96A); *ἕνα καὶ τὸν αὐτὸν ἔχετε λ.* Const.ap.Eus.*v.C.*2.25(p.51.22; M.20.1004A); *ἂν μὲν γὰρ ὀρθῷ λ. τὸ πρᾶγμα διαθῆται* Chrys.*sac.*3.15(p.82.5; 1.395A); Hier.*vir.ill.*(tr.Sophr.Pal.)95(p.52.17; M.*PL*.23.698A); **5.** *reason, mind, T.Gad* 6.2; *ἄνθρωπος...αἴσθησιν... ἔχει καὶ λ. Diogn.*2.9; *ἐπεὶ μὴ ἐκ λ. ἀνδρίζεται* Clem.*str.*7.10(p.43.20; M.9.484B); Or.*or.*29.18(p.392.10; M.11.545A); *οὐ λ. εἶναι ἐν μύρμηξι* id. *Cels.*4.83(p.354.7; M.11.1157A); *πολλοὶ δὲ...πνεῦμα ἡγεμονικὸν ἐκάλεσαν τὸν αὐτοκράτορα λ.* id.*Ps.*50:14(p.52); *ἐλθὲ ὁ πρεσβύτερος τῶν πέντε μελῶν, νοὸς ἐννοίας φρονήσεως ἐνθυμήσεως λ. A.Thom.*A 27(p.143.1); *φύλαξον...τὴν ψυχὴν...καὶ τὴν σάρκα καὶ τὸν λ.* Meth.*symp.*5.2(p.54.9; M.18.97C); *τοὺς ἔχοντας λ. ἐνουθέτει Hom.Clem.*11.33; *ἡ τοῦ ὑγιοῦς λ. ... κατάληψις* Const.ap.Eus.*v.C.*2.48(p.61.28; M.20.1025B); ref. '*ποιήσωμεν ἄνθρωπον*' in Marcellus' interpretation *ὑποτίθεσθαι τὸν θεὸν τῇ ἑαυτοῦ ἐνθυμήσει καὶ τῷ ἰδίῳ λ. προσδιαλεγόμενον...λέγειν* Eus.*e.th.*1.17(p.78.17; M.24.860C); Thdt.*Ps.*50:14(1.941); *δεσπότης τῶν παθῶν...ὁ...φρόνιμος λ.* Ant.Mon.*hom.*79(M.89.1672B); partic. of conscience *τοῦ λ. τὰς ἀκίδας ἀμβλῦναι θελήσας* Thdt.*h.rel.*13(3.1207); **6.** λ. as fifth aeon in Simonian system, Hipp.*haer.*4.51(p.75.33; M.16.3122A); *ῥίζας καλεῖ νοῦν καὶ ἐπίνοιαν, φωνὴν καὶ ὄνομα, λ. καὶ ἐνθύμησιν ib.*6.12(p.138.13; 3211B); *ὁ δὲ λ. καὶ ἡ ἐνθύμησις ἀὴρ καὶ ὕδωρ ib.*6.13(p.139.9; 3214A); **7.** *confession,* i.e. *account, reckoning, of sins γυναικῶν μὴ δέχεσθαι λογισμούς Nomoc.*41; *γίνεται γὰρ διὰ τὸ* ῥαββὶ καὶ πατέρες καλεῖσθαι, ἀλλοτρίους ἀναδέχεσθαι λ. ‡Jo.D.*conf*.9 (M.95.293C).

λογιστεία, ἡ, *exchange, treasury*, Or.*ep*.1.13(M.11.81A).

***λογιστευτής, ὁ,** *one who calls to account, auditor*, met. θεὸν λ. τούτων *Const.App*.2.25.2.

λογιστεύω, 1. *calculate*, *Hom.Clem*.3.36; **2.** *hold office of* λογιστής: λ. τὰ κατὰ πόλιν *be curator of city*, Eus.*h.e*.9.2(M.20.804A); abs., *OGIS* 722 (Egypt, 374); **3.** *call to account* οὐ λογιστεύσεις σου τὸν ἐπίσκοπον *Const.App*.2.35.4; *ib*.2.25.13; **4.** in gen., *scrutinize, examine*, Attic.*ep.Call*.ap.Socr.*h.e*.7.25.8(M.67.793C); Thdt.*Ps*.35:3 (1.829); id.*1Cor*.11:31(3.239).

λογιστήριον, τό, *law-court*, Synes.*ep*.154(M.66.1553C).

***λογιστικῶς,** *in thought* opp. deed εἰσὶ πάθη λ. μορφούμενα καὶ... ἕτερα πρακτικῶς ἐγκείμενα Marc.Er.*opusc*.1.179(M.65.928A); ref. Manicheans μολυμένους λ. τε καὶ πρακτικῶς Anast.S.*hod*.14(M.89.252C).

λογογράφημα, τό, *prose work*, *Schol.Clem.paed*.2.2(p.327.17).

λογογραφικός, *like a book* εἰς λ. μῆκος Gr.Nyss.*fat*.(M.45.148B).

λογογράφος, ὁ, 1. *historian*, Ath.*h.Ar*.38(p.204.33; M.25.737C); Thdt.*h.e*.1.1.1(3.723); *V.Thdr.fr*.(p.177.30); **2.** as term of abuse, *long-winded, prosy, writer*, Gr.Nyss.*Apoll*.3(M.45.1128C); *ib*.11 (1144C); id.*Eun*.1(1 p.136.5; M.45.373D); **3.** *registrar* Γεώργιον τὸν πρεσβύτερον καὶ λ. τῆς ἐκκλησίας αὐτῶν Anast.S.*hod*.10(M.89.188D).

λογοθεσία, ἡ, *audit, scrutiny, calling to account* ἀρχὴν...μυρίαις λ. ὑποκειμένην [ref. episcopate] Isid.Pel.*epp*.5.6(M.78.1329A).

λογοθέσιον, τό, 1. *examination of accounts, audit, calling to account* πρὸ τοῦ λ. ποιῆσαι τὴν συγχώρησιν Chrys.*hom.in Mt.18*:*23*(3.10B); id.*hom.61.3 in Mt*.(7.615B); Jo.Clim.*scal*.4(M.88.721B); met., of self-examination, Ast.Am.*hom*.2(M.40.181B); ἐν ἑσπέρᾳ λ. ἀπαιτεῖ τὴν ψυχήν Chrys.*exp.in Ps*.4:8(5.19B); Hesych.S.*temp*.65(M.93.1501C); of final judgement, Or.*fr.79 in Lc*.(p.272); Chrys.*hom.19.6 in Rom*.(9.639D); λ. καὶ παγκόσμιον δικαστήριον ‡Chrys.*ascens*.1(3.777E); τοῦ μέλλοντος...λ. Isid.Pel.*epp*.1.187(M.78.303B); Bas.Sel.*or*.27(M.85.316B); λογωθ- Ath.Scholast.*coll*.4.4(p.54); ref. devils τῶν ἐχθρῶν...τῶν λογοθέσιον ἡμῖν ἐν τῷ ἀέρι κινούντων †Jo.D.*B.J*.13(M.96.981A); **2.** *office of accountant* as bureau in imperial administration λογοθέτου τοῦ στρατιωτικοῦ λ. CNic.(787)proem.(H.4.33B); γραφεὺς ...εἰς τὸ λεγόμενον λ. Thst.*v.Nic.Heg*.11(p.xxivB).

λογοθετ-έω, 1. *count up*, Chrys.*ascens*.10(3.767A); **2.** *settle accounts with*, ‡Chrys.*hom*.13(13.255C); **3.** *scrutinize, call to account*, Chrys.*exp.in Ps*.3(5.3D); Isid.Pel.*epp*.2.127(M.78.569C); Philost.*h.e*.6.4(M.65.536B); ~εῖς τοῦ θεοῦ τὸν διάκονον; Antip.Bost.*Jo.Bapt*.7(M.85.1769B); of disputations about doctrine, ‡Chrys.*hom*.9(13.236D) = Gr.Ant.*bapt*.2.9(M.88.1880D); οὐ ~οῦσι τὴν τῆς ἁγίας τριάδος ταυτότητα *ib*.(13.233C = M.1873B); of divine judgement πᾶσα γὰρ ἡ τοῦ βίου ψῆφος τηνικαῦτα ~εῖται Const.*or.s.c*.23.3(p.189.27; M.20.1308A); Nil.*epp*.3.318(M.79.537A); Jo.Clim.*scal*.4(M.88.705B); Ant.Mon.*hom*.122(M.89.1813B); of testing of soul by demons at final judgement, *Pers.capt*.(M.86.3261C); Anast.S.*defunct*.(M.89.1200C) cit. s. λογοθέτης.

λογοθέτης, ὁ, 1. *auditor, one who calls to account*, Chrys.*hom.9.2 in 1Tim*.(11.597C); fig., of aerial powers who seize upon departed souls τελωνάρχαι καὶ λ. ... τοῦ ἀέρος †Cyr.*hom.div*.14(5².405B); τῷ ἀέρι ἐν ᾧ οἱ δεινοὶ τελῶναι καὶ λ. ... λογοθετοῦντες Anast.S.*defunct*.(M.89.1200C); **2.** *logothete* = ancient *rationalis*; lit., *accountant*; imperial official, originally a subordinate of the financial bureaux but by seventh cent. of high rank ὁ ἐνδοξότατος πατρίκιος καὶ λ. *Chron.Pasch*.p.394(M.92.1009D); four chief logothetes: **a.** ὁ λ. τοῦ δρόμου *Logothete of the Course, Postmaster General*, often called simply ὁ λ., head of administrative bureaux and foreign minister, Thphn.*chron*.p.362(M.108.868C); *ib*.p.368(884A); **b.** *financial minister* γενικὸς λ. *ib*.p.305(M.108.741C); **c.** *treasurer of the army* τοῦ ἐνδοξοτάτου ἀπὸ ὑπάτων πατρικίου καὶ στρατιωτικοῦ λ. CCP(681)*act*.1(H.3.1056C); λ. τοῦ στρατιωτικοῦ λογοθεσίου CNic.(787)proem.(H.4.33B); **d.** ὁ λ. τοῦ πραιτωρίου lesser official under City Prefect, concerned with administration and police, cf.Const.Porphyrogenitus *de ceremoniis* 1.1(A. Vogt, Paris 1935, p.9.18; M.112.149); **3.** eccl. official, *financial officer* of patriarch of Alexandria, Leont.N.*v.Jo. Eleem*.11(p.21.11).

***λογοθωπεία, ἡ,** *persuasive talk*, ‡Eust.*alloc*.(M.18.676B).

λογολεσχέω, *prate*, Anast.S.*synax*.(M.89.829C).

λογολέσχης, ὁ, *arguer, prater*; of heretics, Gr.Naz.*or*.31.13(p.161.7; M.36.148B); Niceph.Ur.*v.Sym*.169(M.86.3141D).

***λογολεσχία, ἡ,** *idle talk, prating*, Olymp.*Job* 2:12f.(M.93.49A); Pamph.Mon.*Soter*.3(p.118.24); ‡Meth.*Sym.et Ann*.10(M.18.373B).

λογομαχ-έω, 1. *contend with words, indulge in empty argument* ~εῖν ἐπ' οὐδὲν χρήσιμον Ath.*tom*.8(M.26.805B); ~οῦντας καὶ ἐν ῥήμασι κενοῖς ἔχοντες τὴν ἐλπίδα †Bas.*hom.in Ps*.115(1.372B; M.30.105B); ~ῶν ἐπὶ καταστροφῇ τῶν ἀκουόντων Dion.Ar.*ep*.8.1(M.3.1089B); **2.** *contend against the Logos* ~εῖν μελετήσαντες καὶ...πνευματομαχοῦντες Ath.*ep.Serap*.4.1(M.26.637B).

λογομαχία, ἡ, *battle of words, empty argument*, Bas.*fid*.5(2.228E; M.31.689A); esp. of pagan arguments, Eus.*p.e*.14.9(740D; M.21.1217C); σοφιστικαῖς λ. Ath.*v.Anton*.78(M.26.952B); †Bas.*Is*.75(1.432D; M.30.245A); οὐ δύναται κατορθῶσαι φιλοσοφίαν [i.e. contemplation] ὁ λογομαχίαις προασχολούμενος Isid.Pel.*epp*.1.220(M.78.321A); περὶ ἡλίου λ. Thdt.*affect*.1(p.27.25; 4.718); and heret. disputations, Ath.*syn*.54(p.277.18; M.26.789B); id.*ep.Aeg.Lib*.10(M.25.560B); τὴν τῶν αἱρετικῶν λ. Apoll.*ep.Dion*.13(p.262.3; M.*PL*.8.935B).

***λογομάχος, ὁ, 1.** *contender about words, quibbler*, Gr.Naz.*or*.31.11(p.158.14; M.36.145A); **2.** *contender against the Logos* [i.e. one holding Arian view], ‡Meth.*palm*.5(M.18.393B).

***λογοπείθεια, ἡ,** *belief in gossip*, ‡Ath.*doct.Ant*.120(M.28.676A).

***λογοπλάστης, ὁ,** *fabricator of words*, Leont.H.*Nest*.2.19(M.86.1580A).

***λογοποτέω,** *give to drink of the Word*; eucharistic, Pall.*v.Chrys*.20(p.147.4; M.47.82).

λογοπραγ-έω, *make a bargain for*, ref. Judas δῶρον ἀξιόθεον ~εῖ Cosm.Mel.*hymn*.5(10.54, p.190; M.98.476B).

***λογοπράτης, ὁ,** *seller of the Logos*; of Judas, ‡Gr.Naz.*Chr.pat*.266(M.38.158A).

λόγος, ὁ, *word*;

I. in gen.;

A. *spoken expression*; **1.** *word* εἰς λόγους ἐλθεῖν *hold converse* or *discussion* with, Just.*dial*.112.4(M.6.736A); Athenag.*leg*.28.1(M.6.953B); ref. reception in audience ἐς λόγους πρὸς τὸν αὐτοκράτορα ἧκεν Thphyl.*exc.gent*.9(p.486.25; M.113.949A); **2.** *statement, sentence* οὐδεὶς δὲ ἁπλοῦς καὶ πρῶτος λ. ὀνομάζεται συλλογισμός..., ἀλλ' ἔστι τοὐλάχιστον ἐκ τριῶν τοιούτων σύνθετον Clem.*str*.8.3(p.83.13; M.9.565B); partic. *answer* πολλάκις...ἠρώτησα, καὶ οὐδείς μοι λ. ἀπέδωκεν Just.*dial*.94.4(M.6.701A); *question* οὐδέποτε ἐρωτηθεὶς λ. γραφικὸν ἢ ἄλλον τινὰ πραγματικὸν πάραυτα ἀπεκρίνατο Pall.*h.Laus*.10(p.32.1; M.34.1033B); *proverb*, Const.ap.Eus.*v.C*.4.42(p.134.10; M.20.1192A); ὥστε...καὶ τυφλούς, τοῦτο δὴ τὸ τοῦ λ., μὴ ἀμφιβάλλειν...τὴν... ἑρμηνείαν Didym.*Trin*.3.3(M.39.812B); **3.** *command*, of divine authority in gen. ἐν λ. τῆς μεγαλωσύνης αὐτοῦ συνεστήσατο τὰ πάντα, καὶ ἐν λ. δύναται αὐτὰ καταστρέψαι *1Clem*.27.4; τοῖς παραβαίνουσιν τὸν λ. τοῦ θεοῦ *M.Agap*.5.2; contained in scripture τοῖ[ς] ...συμφορᾷ παραπεσοῦσιν βοηθ[εῖ]ν π[α]ρ[α]γγέλλεται ἡμῖν ὁ θεῖος λ. πᾶσι, μάλιστα τοῖς ἀδελφοῖς ἡμῶν *PLond*.1915.4 (saec. iv); Eus.*Marcell*.2.2(p.36.10; M.24.785A); ref. Inc. and eucharistic consecration, Just.*1apol*.66.2(M.6.428C) cit. s. αἷμα; ὁ ἄρτος...ἁγιάζεται διὰ λ. θεοῦ καὶ ἐντεύξεως...πρὸς τὸ σῶμα διὰ τοῦ λ. μεταποιούμενος Gr.Nyss.*or.catech*.37(p.151.1,3; M.45.97A); of decalogue ἐν τοῖς δέκα λ. *Barn*.15.1; Clem.*str*.6.16(p.501.14; M.9.364A); **4.** *promise* δῶμεν... λ. ὥστε ἔχειν μετ' ἀλλήλων ἀγάπην Ephr.1.221A; λ. ... δέδωκα τῷ Χριστῷ τοῦ μὴ γεύσασθαι ἄρτου *V.Dan*.9(p.256.30); δός μοι οὖν λ. ὅτι ὧδε κατοικεῖς·...ὁ δὲ...συνέθετο μετὰ λόγου παραμένειν Jo.Mosch.*prat*.1(M.87.2853B); λαβόντας λ. ὅτι οὐκ ἀποκεφαλίζονται *Chron.Pasch*.p.326(M.92.836B); ἀνήνεγκεν αὐτοὺς ὑπὸ λόγον *ib*.p.313(796B); hence *pledge, security* ἀπεδέξατο αὐτούς, μὴ φονεύσας αὐτούς, ἀλλὰ δοὺς λόγον αὐτοῖς, ἵνα ἐκβάλωσι τὸν στρατὸν ἐκ τῆς ἐρήμου χώρας Jo.Mal.*chron*.13 p.332(M.97.496A); *oath* σωματικοῦ λ. CCP(381)*act*.13(H.4.1352A); **5.** *story, conversation, discourse* τοὺς τῶν πρεσβυτέρων ἀνέκρινον λ. Papias *fr*.2.4; Just.*1apol*.14.5(M.6.349A); Chrys.*hom.58.5 in Jo*.(8.344A); συντακτήριον λ. Thphn.*chron*.p.59(M.108.200B); **6.** *report, tale* οὐ γάρ εἰσιν ὧν ψευδεῖς οἱ λ. Athenag.*leg*.30.3(M.6.960C); Eus.*p.e*.1.6(17B; M.21.48B); **7.** *treatise*, dist. from sermon, cf. εἰ καὶ 'λόγοι' ἔχει τὴν ἐπιγραφὴν τὸ βιβλίον...ἀλλὰ μᾶλλον ἐοίκασιν ὁμιλίαις...ὅτι ἐν πολλοῖς πολλάκις ὡς παρόντας ὁρῶν τοὺς ἀκροατάς Phot.*cod*.172–174(M.103.501C); **8.** *sermon, homily*, Gr.Naz.*or*.1 tit.(M.35.396A); Amph.*hom*.1 tit.(M.39.36A); Bas.Sel.*or*.2.1(M.85.37B); **9.** *passage* of scripture, *1Clem*.13.3; Just.*dial*.56.4(M.6.597B); *ib*.58.4 (608B); ὁ προφητικὸς λ. ... σημαίνει *ib*.56.6(597D); ὅσα περιέχει τῆς κοσμογονίας ὁ λ. Gr.Nyss.*hex*.7(M.44.68D); τοῦ δὲ λ. βαθύνοντος, τὸν νοῦν ἀναπτυκτέον Didym.*Trin*.1.7(M.39.276A); plur., of collection of texts, Just.*dial*.56.8(M.6.600B); *ib*.85.8(680A); of scriptures in gen., Clem.*str*.7.16(p.73.5; M.9.544A); sing., of scripture as a whole, id.*ecl*.47(p.150.3; M.9.720B); τὸν πατέρα μὲν δημιουργὸν εἶναι παρὰ τῆς γραφῆς ἐδιδάχθημεν· ὡσαύτως καὶ διὰ τοῦ υἱοῦ τὰ πάντα γεγενῆσθαι ἐμάθομεν, οὐδὲν δὲ τοιοῦτο περὶ τοῦ πνεύματος ἡμᾶς ὁ λ. ἐδίδαξεν Gr.Nyss.*Maced*.11(M.45.1313D); **10.** *form of words, manner of speaking*, opp. literal sense χθὲς καὶ πρῴην γεγόνασιν, ὡς λόγῳ εἰπεῖν Athenag. *leg.*17.1(M.6.921C); Meth.*arbitr.*2(p.148.8; M.18.244A); **11.** *mere talk* opp. truth or fact εἰ δὲ λ. τοῦτό ἐστι καὶ ἀναπλασμός Gr.Naz.*ep.*101 (M.37.177A); but contrast opposition of λ. to mere φωνή: ἐὰν γὰρ σιωπήσητε ἀπ' ἐμοῦ, ἐγὼ λ. θεοῦ· ἐὰν δὲ ἐρασθῆτε τῆς σαρκός μου, πάλιν ἔσομαι φωνή Ign.*Rom.*2.1; **12.** substance of what is said, *teaching, opinion, knowledge,* esp. of doctrine; **a.** of philos. schools ἕκαστος τῶν φιλοσοφεῖν νομιζόντων,...ἀπὸ τοῦ πατρὸς τοῦ λ. τὸ ὄνομα ἧς φιλοσοφεῖ φιλοσοφίας ἡγεῖται φέρειν Just.*dial.*35.6(M.6.552B); opp. θεοῦ παραγγέλματα Tat.*orat.*32(p.33.2; M.6.872A); τὸν Ὀρφικὸν ...λ. Athenag.*leg.*4.1(M.6.897A); στωϊκὸν λ. Or.*Cels.*1.10(p.63.7; M. 11.676A); **b.** of Christian gospel or 'the Faith' ὁ λ. ... τῆς πίστεως *Barn.*16.9; οἱ τὸν λ. ἀκούσαντες καὶ θέλοντες βαπτισθῆναι Herm.*vis.* 3.7.3; id.*sim.*9.25.2; τὸν ἐξ ἀρχῆς ἡμῖν παραδοθέντα λ. Polyc.*ep.*7.2; πειθαρχεῖν τῷ λ. τῆς δικαιοσύνης *ib.*9.1; τὸν τοῦ Χριστιανισμοῦ μαθεῖν λ. *M.Polyc.*10.1; γενόμενος...καινὸς ἄνθρωπος ὡς ἂν καὶ λόγου καινοῦ ...ἀκροατὴς ἐσόμενος *Diogn.*2.1; τὸν λ. τῆς κλήσεως καὶ τῆς μετανοίας πρὸς τὰ ἔθνη Just.*dial.*83.4(M.6.673A); Or.*Jo.*5.8(p.105.11; M. 14.196A); λ. τῆς ἀληθείας *V.Aberc.*7(p.7.7); abs. μετὰ τὸ τῷ λ. πεισθῆναι ἐκείνων μὲν ἀπέστημεν Just.*1apol.*14.1(M.6.348B); οὐδεὶς γὰρ Χριστιανὸς πονηρός, εἰ μὴ ὑποκρίνεται τὸν λ. Athenag.*leg.*2.3(M.6. 896A); ἀπολογεῖσθαι ὑπὲρ τοῦ λ. *ib.*2.4(896B); ἀπὸ Ἑλληνικῶν τις δογμάτων...ἐλθὼν ἐπὶ τὸν λ. Or.*Cels.*1.2(p.57.9; M.11.656A); δυσφημίαν τοῦ λ., ὡς ἄρα...οἱ ἀπὸ τοῦ λ. τὰ τοῦ σκότου πράττειν βουλόμενοι *ib.*6.27(p.97.24; 1333B); ref. bishops τοῖς τοῦ λ. προεστῶσιν Eus.*h.e.*7. 13(M.20.673C); ἀνίστησι δὲ [sc. Ath.] πεπτωκότα τὸν λ. Gr.Naz.*or.*21. 31(M.35.1120A); plur., Didym.*Trin.*3.1(M.39.777C); **13.** hence, plur., *learning, education,* Eus.*h.e.*7.32.6(M.20.724A); λόγων μητρόπολιν Gr.Naz.*or.*43.13(M.36.512A); Thdt.*h.e.*3.21.6(3.938D); **14.** *speech, language,* in gen. οὐκ ἔσται ὁ λ. σου ψευδής, οὐ κενός, ἀλλὰ μεμεστωμένος πράξει *Did.*2.5; διὰ λόγου κοπιῶν...καὶ μελετῶν εἰς τὸ σῶσαι ψυχὴν τῷ λ. *Barn.*19.10; Tat.*orat.*1(p.2.1; M.6.805A); πᾶς λ. ὅ γε ἀληθῶς λ. σημαντική τίς ἐστι τῶν κατ' ἔννοιαν κινημάτων φωνή Gr. Nyss.*Eun.*12(1 p.376.5; M.45.1101D); πάντα ὑπερβαῖνον λ. καὶ πᾶσαν ἐκφεῦγον διάνοιαν Chrys.*exp.in Ps.*41:2(5.135D); Thdt.*Ezech.*12:25 (2.756D).

B. *immanent rationality*; **1.** *reason, understanding* ὁ γὰρ θεὸς τοὺς ἀνθρώπους ἠγάπησε,...οἷς λ. ἔδωκεν, οἷς νοῦν *Diogn.*10.2; ὁ λ. ... οὗ βασιλικώτατον καὶ δικαιότατον ἄρχοντα μετὰ τὸν γεννήσαντα θεὸν οὐδένα οἴδαμεν ὄντα Just.*1apol.*12.7(M.6.344B); τὸ λογικὸν τὸ ὅλον τὸν...Χριστὸν γεγονέναι, καὶ σῶμα καὶ λ. καὶ ψυχήν id.*2apol.*10.1(M. 6.460B); Or.*Jo.*1.37(42; p.47.24; M.14.97A); Gr.Nyss.*castig.*(M.46. 308A), cf. II.D infra; ἔδειξεν...ἑαυτὸν ὑπὲρ λόγον ἐνανθρωπήσαντα Procl.CP *Arm.*7(p.190.30; M.65.864A); esp. of practical reason opp. speculative (νοῦς), Just.*1apol.*2.1(M.6.329A); *ib.*68.1(432A); τῶν κατὰ τὸν ἔμφυτον νόμον καὶ λ. ἐνεργούντων Athenag.*res.*24(p.77.31; M.6. 1021A); Clem.*str.*5.3(p.336.26; M.9.33B); ἐν ἡμῖν γὰρ αὐτοῖς τρία μέτρα, τρία κριτήρια, μηνύεται, αἴσθησις μὲν αἰσθητῶν, λεγομένων δὲ καὶ ὀνομάτων καὶ ῥημάτων ὁ λ., νοητῶν δὲ νοῦς *ib.*2.11(p.139.16; M.8. 985B); Cyr.H.*catech.*19.5; λόγῳ κράτει τῆς ἁμαρτίας Bas.*hom.*13.5(2. 118E; M.31.436B); τὸ μὲν θεωρητικὸν ἐκάλει νοῦν, τὸ δὲ πρακτικὸν λ., ὡς πρώτας δηλαδὴ δυνάμεις τῆς ψυχῆς, καὶ πάλιν τὸν νοῦν σοφίαν, τὸν δὲ λ. φρόνησιν, ὡς πρώτας ἐνεργείας Max.*myst.*5(M.91.499D); **2.** *ground, reason, motive,* Just.*1apol.*53.2(M.6.405C); δικαίῳ τινὶ λ. *Hom.Clem.*2.38; Bas.*hom.*6.7(2.50A; M.31.276C); *ib.*5.5(38B; M.249A); id.*Eun.*1.12(1.224E; M.29.540B); ποῖος γὰρ νοῦς ἱκανὸς ἐξετάσαι τῆς σῆς προνοίας τοὺς λ.; Thdt.*Ps.*91:6(1.1265D); c. infin. τίς γὰρ τοῖς μὲν πιστεύειν λ., τοῖς δὲ ἀπιστεῖν; Athenag.*leg.*30.3(M.6.960C); λόγος ἔχει *have point, be reasonable* τοὺς δὲ μηδὲν ἀνεξέταστον ἔσεσθαι... πεπεισμένους, οὐδεὶς λ. ἔχει οὐδὲ τῶν βραχυτάτων τι ἁμαρτεῖν *ib.*36.2 (969C); **3.** *explanation* δότε μοι λ., ὅτου χάριν...ἔστησε Just.*dial.*94.3 (M.6.700B); Athenag.*leg.*22.1(M.6.936C); Eus.*v.C.*1.32(p.22.27; M.20. 948B); **4.** *definition, description* ἔστι γὰρ συνώνυμα ὧν τό τε ὄνομα ἀμφοῖν κοινόν, τὸ ζῷον, καὶ ὁ λ. ὁ αὐτός, τουτέστιν ὁ ὅρος, οὐσία ἔμψυχος Clem.*str.*8.8(p.95.8; M.9.592A); ἄλλος οὖν ὁ τοῦ τί ἐστι, καὶ ἄλλος ὁ τοῦ πῶς ἐστι λ. Gr.Nyss.*tres dii*(M.45.133C); hence, *category, class* ὡς ἐν μύθου λ. Eus.*h.e.*9.9.4(M.20.821A); οὐκοῦν ἐν ὀργάνου λ. θεία δύναμις Alex.Lyc.*Man.*23(p.34.11; M.18.444B); **5.** *principle*; **a.** *ground,* of cosmic order αὐτὸς γάρ ἐστιν ὁ πάντων τῶν ὄντων λ., οὐδὲν οὖν οἷός τε παρὰ λόγον, οὐδὲ παρ' ἑαυτὸν ἐργάσασθαι Cels.ap. Or.*Cels.*5.14(p.15.24; M.11.1201C); of sinful life of fallen man λ. ὁ πονηρός [i.e. Devil] Mac.Aeg.*hom.*11.5(M.34.548B); **b.** formative and regulative *law* of being, *essential disposition* οἱ περὶ ἑκάστου λ., ὄντες ὡς ἐν ὅλῳ μέρη ἢ ὡς ἐν γένει εἴδη τοῦ ἐν ἀρχῇ λ. πρὸς τὸν θεὸν θεοῦ λόγον οὐδαμῶς παρελεύσονται. θέλομεν γὰρ ἀκούειν τοῦ εἰπόντος, ...οἱ δὲ λ. μου οὐ μὴ παρέλθωσιν Or.*Cels.*5.22(p.23.25; 1216B); λ. τις ἐγκεῖται τῷ σώματι ἀφ' οὗ μὴ φθειρομένου ἐγείρεται τὸ σῶμα ἐν ἀφθαρσίᾳ *ib.*5.23(p.24.5; 1216C); καὶ δίχα τοῦ...σώματος, ἀεὶ καὶ διὰ παντὸς ἥκων δι' ὅλης τῆς τῶν στοιχείων...ὕλης, οἷά τις θεοῦ λ. ὢν δημιουργός, τῆς ἐξ αὐτοῦ σοφίας ἐν αὐτῇ τοὺς λ. ἀποσφραγίζεται Eus. *d.e.*4.13(p.171.6; M.22.285A); τοὺς τῶν ἁπάντων δημιουργικούς τε καὶ ποιητικοὺς λ. *ib.*5.5(p.228.13; 377A); νεφέλη ἀγγελικὸν ἐχούσῃ τὸν λ. τῆς οὐσίας Mac.Mgn.*apocr.*4.12(p.176.9); ὁ υἱὸς οἶδε μὲν ἐξ ὧν ἐστι τὸν ἑαυτοῦ γεννήτορα, τηρεῖ δὲ τὸν λ. αὐτοῦ, τουτέστιν ὅλον ἔχει σῳζόμενον ἐν ἑαυτῷ τῆς οὐσίας αὐτοῦ τὸν ὅρον· δηλοῖ γὰρ ὁ λ. τὸν ὅρον Cyr.*Jo.*6(4.582E); οὐ...τῇ ἀντιδόσει τῶν ἰδιωμάτων ἀναιροῦμεν τὸν ἴδιον λ. τῆς θατέρου ἐν ταὐτῷ ἰδιότητος Leont.B.*Nest.et Eut.*1(M. 86.1289C); τί γὰρ ἂν εἴη μία φύσις θεότητος ἢ ὁ κοινὸς τῆς θείας φύσεως λ. ...; καὶ ἰδικώτερον πάλιν τὸ τῆς φύσεως γινώσκομεν ὄνομα, τὸν κοινὸν λ. τῆς φύσεως ἐφ' ἑκάστου τῶν ἀτόμων, ἤγουν τῶν ὑποστάσεων ἑκάστης ἴδιον γενόμενον θεωροῦντες καὶ οὐδενὶ λοιπὸν ἑτέρῳ τῶν ὑπὸ τὸ κοινὸν εἶδος ἐφαρμόζειν δυνάμενον Jo.Philop.*arb.*(pp.276. 29,277.7; M.94.748C); **c.** *principle* or *rule* embodying the result of λογισμός: ἀρχὴν τῆς οἰκίας καὶ τῆς νεὼς ἐχόντων τοὺς ἐν τῷ τεχνίτῃ τύπους καὶ λ. Or.*Jo.*1.19(22; p.24.5; M.14.56D); **6.** for λ. σπερματικός, v. σπερματικός.

C. *reckoning*; **1.** *computation,* Or.*Jo.*6.40(24; p.149.20; M.14. 269B); ἀληθεῖ λ. μακάριον οἶδ' ἐμαυτόν Const.ap.Eus.*v.C.*4.63(p.143. 28; M.20.1217A); Max.*schol.d.n.*5.5(M.4.320A); **2.** *account* ἵνα...λ. ἀποδῶ ὑπὲρ ὑμῶν...τῷ κυρίῳ Herm.*vis.*3.9.10; hence, with idea of penalty ἐγὼ Χριστῷ λ. δώσω ὑπὲρ σοῦ· ἂν δέῃ, τὸν σὸν θάνατον ἑκὼν ὑπομενῶ Clem.*q.d.s.*42(p.190.5; M.9.649B); plur. ἀποτίσειν...τῷ κρίτῃ τῶν ἰδίων πλημμελημάτων τοὺς λ. Cyr.*ador.*7(1.233B); **3.** financial *account*; hence *credit account, credit* τὰ εἰς λ. τῶν πενήτων...βαλλόμενα Or.*Cels.*2.11(p.139.15; M.14.816A); εἰσὶ πρὸς λ. ἑκατὸν λίτραι χρυσίου Mac.Aeg.*cust.cor.*12(M.34.832D); *ib.*(833C); **4.** εἰς λόγον *on account of, for the sake of* εἰς λ. τιμῆς Ign.*Philad.*11.2; ἐπηκολούθησάν μοι εἰς λ. θεοῦ id.*Smyrn.*10.1; πόλις...ἠράσθη...εἰς λ. ἐπισκόπου Pall. *h.Laus.*11(p.33.1; M.34.1033D); *in regard to, in respect of* οὐδὲν χείρους εἰς ἀρετῆς λ. Athenag.*leg.*31.1(M.6.961B); **5.** λόγῳ c. genit., *for, on behalf of* λαμβάνετε...καὶ λ. τῶν γυναικῶν ὑμῶν Leont.N.*v.Sym.*55 (M.93.1737B).

D. *matter, fact* ἐκ τῆς τῶν πρακτικῶν λ. γνώσεως Hipp.*haer.*4.2 (p.33.14; M.16.3059B); οὐκ ἦν...βασιλεῖ φορητὸς ὁ λ. Eus.*v.C.*4.5(p.119. 19; M.20.1153B); Cyr.*Jo.*6.1(4.654B).

E. *regard, esteem, Diogn.*4.1; ὁρᾷς ὅσον ὑπὲρ τούτων πεποίηται λ. ἡ...γραφή Chrys.*hom.*3.4 *in Ac.*(9.28D); οἷς ἂν εἶεν ἐν λ. Cyr.*hom. pasch.*24.1(5^2.286C).

F. *concern, interest* τίς ἡμῖν κοινὸς πρὸς τούτους λ.; Bas.*ep.*217 *can.* 84(3.330C; M.32.808C); θυγατέρες τῶν ἱερέων, αἷς οὐδεὶς πρὸς τὴν ἱερωσύνην λ. Chrys.*sac.*6.11(p.160.25; 1.430C).

G. *relation,* Hipp.*haer.*4.10(p.42.25; M.16.3074A); Or.*or.*17.1(p.338. 10; M.11.469D); Eus.*l.C.*6(p.210.21; M.20.1348C).

H. *manner, arrangement* τούτῳ τῷ λ. καὶ οἱ ἀπὸ τῆς Στοᾶς...φασίν Athenag.*leg.*19.2(M.6.929A); *Hom.Clem.*3.16(M.2.121A); ἑορτὴν...μιᾷ τάξει καὶ φανερῷ λ. παρὰ πᾶσιν...φυλάττεσθαι Const.ap.Eus.*v.C.*3.18 (p.85.7; M.20.1073D); τριάδος λόγῳ τριττὴν γονὴν παίδων...κτησάμενος Eus.*v.C.*4.40(p.133.9; M.20.1188D); Mac.Mgn.*apocr.*3.14(p.93.3).

I. *condition, limitation* οὐδεὶς οὖν τὸν Ἰησοῦν μετὰ τὴν ἀνάστασιν λ. περιέκλεισεν, οὐ τόπος οὐ χρόνος οὐ ποσὸν οὐ ποιόν Mac.Mgn.*apocr.*3. 14(p.93.8); Chrys.*hom.64.1 in Mt.*(7.635A); Cyr.*Jo.*9(4.736E).

J. *status* στοιχειώσεως μὲν ἔχειν λ. τὴν πίστιν, προκοπῆς δὲ τὴν ἐλπίδα Or.*comm.in Rom.*4:18(*JTS* 13 p.361).

K. *function* ἑτέρους τὸν τῶν χειρῶν καὶ ἄλλους τὸν τῶν ποδῶν ἐπέχοντας λ. Bas.*hom.in Ps.*33(1.154A; M.29.376C); τῆς λειτουργίας τὸν λ. πληρώσασα Mac.Mgn.*apocr.*4.12(p.174.18); Thdt.*Ezech.*27:8 (2.899); of a proxy Παύλῳ...ποιουμένῳ τὸν λ. καὶ ὑπὲρ τοῦ...Ἀκακίου CEph.Orient.*ep.*(*ACO* 1.1.3 p.37.2; H.1.1561B); *ib.*(p.37.5; 1561C).

II. theol., of second Person of Trinity;

A. associations and significance of term; **1.** with emphasis on idea of revelation εἷς θεός ἐστιν, ὁ φανερώσας ἑαυτὸν διὰ Ἰησοῦ Χριστοῦ τοῦ υἱοῦ αὐτοῦ, ὅς ἐστιν αὐτοῦ λ. ἀπὸ σιγῆς προελθών Ign. *Magn.*8.2; τὴν δύναμιν τὴν παρὰ τοῦ πατρὸς...φανεῖσαν τῷ Μωυσεῖ...λ. καλοῦσιν, ἐπειδὴ καὶ τὰς παρὰ τοῦ πατρὸς ὁμιλίας φέρει τοῖς ἀνθρώποις Just.*dial.*128.2(M.6.776A); cf. *hic pater domini nostri Jesu Christi, per verbum suum, qui est filius ejus, per eum revelatur et manifestatur omnibus quibus revelatur,* Iren.*haer.*2.30.9(M.7.823A); *per ipsam conditionem revelat verbum conditorem deum...sed per legem et prophetas similiter verbum et semetipsum et patrem praedicabat...et per ipsum verbum visibilem...factum, pater ostendebatur, ib.*4.6.6 (989B); κατὰ τὴν μὲν σύστασιν τῆς περὶ τῶν ὅλων θεωρίας καὶ νοημάτων τῆς σοφίας νοουμένης, κατὰ δὲ τὴν πρὸς τὰ λογικὰ κοινωνίαν τῶν τεθεωρημένων τοῦ λ. λαμβανομένου Or.*Jo.*1.19(22; p.23.24; M.14.56B); cf. *verbum dei eam* [sc. *sapientiam*] *esse intelligendum est per hoc, quod ipsa ceteris omnibus, id est universae creaturae, mysteriorum et arcanorum rationem…aperiat; et per hoc verbum dicitur, quia sit tamquam arcanorum mentis interpres,* id.*princ.*1.2.3(p.30.11; M.11.132A); τοῦτον καὶ ἀνάπαυσιν καλοῦμεν καὶ ἄμπελον καὶ χάριν καὶ λ. τοῦ πατρός *V.Aberc.*16(p.14.18); πῶς οὖν εἰκόνα τοῦ ἀοράτου θεοῦ τὸν τοῦ θεοῦ λ. Ἀστέριος εἶναι γέγραφεν; αἱ γὰρ εἰκόνες τούτων ὧν εἰσιν εἰκόνες καὶ ἀπόντων δεικτικαί εἰσιν. … εἰ δὲ τοῦ θεοῦ ἀοράτου ὄντος ἀόρατον εἶναι καὶ τὸν λ. συμβαίνει, πῶς εἰκὼν τοῦ ἀοράτου θεοῦ καθ' ἑαυτὸν ὁ λ. εἶναι δύναται, καὶ αὐτὸς ἀόρατος ὤν; Marcell.*fr.*93 ap.Eus.*Marcell.*2.3(p.48.34; M.24.805B); λ. καὶ παραινέτης Gr.Naz.*or.*30.14 (p.131.10; M.36.124A); ἄγγελός τε καὶ λ. … κατὰ τὴν αὐτὴν ἔννοιαν λέγεται, ὁ τὴν πατρικὴν ἀγαθότητα δι' ἑαυτοῦ γνωρίζων. … καὶ ὁ λ. ὡσαύτως ἐκκαλύπτει τὸ ἐγκείμενον νόημα Gr.Nyss.*Eun.*11(2 p.264.19; M.45.872D); **2.** on idea of reason τὸν Χριστὸν πρωτότοκον τοῦ θεοῦ εἶναι ἐδιδάχθημεν…λ. ὄντα οὗ πᾶν γένος ἀνθρώπων μετέσχε· καὶ οἱ μετὰ λόγου βιώσαντες κτλ. Just.*1apol.*46.2(M.6.397B); λ. γὰρ ὁ ἐπουράνιος, πνεῦμα γεγονὼς ἀπὸ τοῦ πατρός, καὶ λ. ἐκ τῆς λογικῆς δυνάμεως,…εἰκόνα τῆς ἀθανασίας τὸν ἄνθρωπον ἐποίησεν Tat.*orat.*7 (p.7.6f.; M.6.820A); θεόν φαμεν, καὶ υἱὸν τὸν λ. αὐτοῦ, καὶ πνεῦμα ἅγιον, ἑνούμενα μὲν κατὰ δύναμιν, τὸν πατέρα, τὸν υἱόν, τὸ πνεῦμα, ὅτι νοῦς λ. σοφία ὁ υἱὸς τοῦ πατρός, καὶ ἀπόρροια, ὡς φῶς ἀπὸ πυρός, τὸ πνεῦμα Athenag.*leg.*24.1(M.6.945B); Thphl.Ant.*Autol.*2.10(M.6.1065A); *ib.*2.15(1077B); cf. *ante omnia enim deus erat solus…ceterum ne tunc quidem solus; habebat enim secum quam habebat in semetipso, rationem suam scilicet…quae ratio sensus ipsius est, hanc Graeci λ. dicunt, quo vocabulo etiam sermonem appellamus, ideoque jam in usu est nostrorum…sermonem dicere in primordio apud deum fuisse, cum magis rationem competat…quia ipse quoque sermo ratione consistens priorem eam ut substantiam suam ostendat,* Tert.*adv. Praxeam* 5(M.*PL.*2.160A); Clem.*prot.*10(p.71.25; M.8.212C) cit. s. εἰκών; οὗτος οὖν μόνος…θεὸς λόγον πρῶτον ἐννοηθεὶς ἀπογεννᾷ, οὐ λ. ὡς φωνήν, ἀλλ' ἐνδιάθετον τοῦ παντὸς λογισμόν Hipp.*haer.*10.33(p.289.3; M.16.3447B); ὁ γὰρ ἐν ἑκάστῳ λ. τῶν λογικῶν τοῦτον τὸν λ. ἔχει πρὸς τὸν ἐν ἀρχῇ λ. πρὸς τὸν θεὸν ὄντα λ. θεόν, ὃν ὁ θεὸς λ. πρὸς τὸν θεόν· ὡς γὰρ αὐτόθεος…ὁ πατὴρ πρὸς εἰκόνα…οὕτως ὁ αὐτόλογος πρὸς τὸν ἐν ἑκάστῳ λ. Or.*Jo.*2.3(p.55.15; M.14.109C); cf. *deus pater omnibus praestat ut sint, participatio vero Christi secundum id, quod verbum (vel ratio) est, facit ea esse rationabilia. … cum ergo primo ut sint habeant ex deo patre, secundo ut rationabilia sint habeant ex verbo, tertio ut sancta sint habeant ex spiritu sancto,* id.*princ.*1.3.8(p.61.1; M.11.154B); acc. followers of Paul. Sam. λ. γὰρ οἷον τὸν ἐν καρδίᾳ εἶναι…καὶ σοφίαν οἵαν ἐν ψυχῇ ἀνθρώπου ἕκαστος ἔχει τὴν ἐκ θεοῦ φρόνησιν ἐκ θεοῦ κεκτημένος Epiph.*haer.*65.3(p.5.15; M.42.16A); **3.** on idea of will or fiat δύναμις θεοῦ ὁ λ. αὐτοῦ ἦν Just.*1apol.*14.5(M.6.349A); οὐχὶ καὶ τὸ λέγειν ἔργον ἐστὶ καὶ τὸ ποιεῖν ἐκ τοῦ λ. γίνεται;… καὶ οὐδὲν χωρὶς αὐτοῦ ἐγένετο, φησί, τοῦ λ. τοῦ θεοῦ. ἢ οὐχὶ καὶ ὁ κύριος λόγῳ πάντα ἔπρασσεν; Clem.*str.*1.9(p.30.13; M.8.741C); *ib.*5.14 (p.392.6; M.9.149A); Hipp.*Noët.*10(p.251.22; M.10.817B) cit. s. B.3 infra; αἴτιον τοῖς γινομένοις λ. ἦν, ἐν αὐτῷ φέρων τὸ θέλειν τοῦ γεγεννηκότος id.*haer.*10.33(p.289.6; M.16.3447B); οὐ χρῄζει τοίνυν λόγῳ μαθεῖν τοῦ πατρὸς τὸ θέλημα, αὐτὸς ὢν τοῦ πατρὸς ὁ λ. κατὰ τὴν ὑψηλοτέραν σημασίαν τοῦ λ. Gr.Nyss.*Eun.*12(1 p.276.9; M.45.984A); for identification of God's λ. and θέλημα v. θέλημα; **4.** with various connotations λ. δέ, ὅτι οὕτως ἔχει πρὸς τὸν πατέρα, ὡς πρὸς νοῦν λ.· οὐ μόνον διὰ τὸ ἀπαθὲς τῆς γεννήσεως, ἀλλὰ καὶ τὸ συναφές, καὶ τὸ ἐξαγγελτικόν. τάχα δ' ἂν εἴποι τις, ὅτι καὶ ὡς ὅρος πρὸς τὸ ὁριζόμενον, ἐπειδὴ καὶ τοῦτο λέγεται λ. … καὶ σύντομος ἀπόδειξις…τῆς τοῦ πατρὸς φύσεως, ὁ υἱός…εἰ δὲ καὶ διὰ τὸ ἐνυπάρχειν τοῖς οὖσι λέγοι τις, οὐχ ἁμαρτήσεται τοῦ λ.· τί γάρ ἐστιν ὃ μὴ λόγῳ συνέστηκεν; Gr.Naz.*or.*30.20(p.139.3ff.; M.36.129A); λ. ἐστὶν ὁ οὐσιωδῶς τῷ πατρὶ ἀεὶ συμπαρών. λ. ἐστὶν ἐνδιάθετος ὁ ἐν καρδίᾳ λαλούμενος. λ. ἐστὶν ἄγγελος νοήματος *Doct.Patr.*33(p.263.5f.).

B. ref. unity of Godhead; **1.** in gen. θεὸς ἦν ἐν ἀρχῇ· τὴν δὲ ἀρχὴν λόγου δύναμιν παρειλήφαμεν…τὰ πάντα σὺν αὐτῷ…αὐτὸς [καὶ ὁ λ. ὃς ἦν ἐν αὐτῷ] ὑπέστησεν. θελήματι δὲ τῆς ἁπλότητος αὐτοῦ προπηδᾷ λόγος·…ὥσπερ γὰρ ἀπὸ μιᾶς δᾳδὸς ἀνάπτεται μὲν πυρὰ πολλά,… οὕτω καὶ ὁ λ. προελθὼν ἐκ τῆς τοῦ πατρὸς δυνάμεως οὐκ ἄλογον πεποίηκε τὸν γεγεννηκότα Tat.*orat.*5(p.5.16ff.; M.6.813C); λόγος… πνεῦμα γεγονὼς ἀπὸ τοῦ πνεύματος, καὶ λ. ἐκ λογικῆς δυνάμεως *ib.*7 (p.7.6; 820A); ἐστὶν ὁ υἱὸς τοῦ θεοῦ λ. τοῦ πατρὸς ἐν ἰδέᾳ καὶ ἐνεργείᾳ· …ἑνὸς ὄντος τοῦ πατρὸς καὶ τοῦ υἱοῦ. ὄντος δὲ τοῦ υἱοῦ ἐν πατρὶ καὶ πατρὸς ἐν υἱῷ, ἑνότητι καὶ δυνάμει πνεύματος, νοῦς καὶ λ. τοῦ πατρὸς ὁ υἱὸς τοῦ θεοῦ Athenag.*leg.*10.1(M.6.908B); *ib.*24.1(945A,B); οὐδὲν ἄρα μισεῖται ὑπὸ τοῦ θεοῦ. ἀλλ' οὐδὲ ὑπὸ τοῦ λ.· ἓν γὰρ ἄμφω, ὁ θεός, ὅτι εἶπεν, ἐν ἀρχῇ ὁ λ. ἦν ἐν τῷ θεῷ, καὶ θεὸς ἦν ὁ λ. Clem.*paed.*1.8 (p.127.5; M.8.325B); πνεῦμα γάρ, φησίν [sc. Callistus], ὁ θεὸς οὐχ ἕτερόν ἐστι παρὰ τὸν λ. ἢ ὁ λ. παρὰ τὸν θεόν. ἓν οὖν τοῦτο πρόσωπον, ὀνόματι μὲν μεριζόμενον, οὐσίᾳ δὲ οὔ. τοῦτον τὸν λ. ἕνα εἶναι θεὸν ὀνομάζει καὶ σεσαρκῶσθαι λέγει Hipp.*haer.*10.27(p.283.17; M.16.3442A); οὐ γὰρ ἐκτός ἐστι τοῦ λ. τὸ πνεῦμα, ἀλλά, ἐν τῷ λ. ὄν, ἐν τῷ θεῷ δι' αὐτοῦ ἐστιν…αὐτὸς γὰρ ὁ πατὴρ διὰ τοῦ λ. ἐν τῷ πνεύματι ἐνεργεῖ Ath.*ep.Serap.*3.5(M.26.633A); **2.** distn. bet. λ. ἐνδιάθετος (*immanent reason*) and λ. προφορικός (*uttered word*) used to illustrate unity of Father and Logos and distn. between them (from standpoint of finite observer) through act of Creation and redemption in which Logos is the expression of infinite Father; **a.** used with approval, cf.Ign.*Magn.*8.2; Just.*dial.*61.1(M.6.616A); ἔστιν ὁ υἱὸς τοῦ θεοῦ λ. τοῦ πατρὸς ἐν ἰδέᾳ καὶ ἐνεργείᾳ…πρῶτον γέννημα εἶναι τῷ πατρί, οὐχ ὡς γενόμενον (ἐξ ἀρχῆς γὰρ ὁ θεὸς νοῦς ἀΐδιος ὤν, εἶχεν αὐτὸς ἐν ἑαυτῷ τὸν λ., ἀϊδίως λογικὸς ὤν) Athenag.*leg.*10.2 (M.6.908Bff.); ἔχων οὖν ὁ θεὸς τὸν ἑαυτοῦ λ. ἐνδιάθετον ἐν τοῖς ἰδίοις σπλάγχνοις, ἐγέννησεν αὐτὸν μετὰ τῆς ἑαυτοῦ σοφίας ἐξερευξάμενος πρὸ τῶν ὅλων Thphl.Ant.*Autol.*2.10(M.6.1064C); οὐχ ὡς οἱ ποιηταὶ… λέγουσιν υἱοὺς θεῶν ἐκ συνουσίας γεννωμένους, ἀλλὰ ὡς ἀλήθεια διηγεῖται τὸν λ., τὸν ὄντα διαπαντὸς ἐνδιάθετον ἐν καρδίᾳ θεοῦ. πρὸ γάρ τι γίνεσθαι, τοῦτον εἶχε σύμβουλον, ἑαυτοῦ νοῦν καὶ φρόνησιν ὄντα· ὁπότε δὲ ἠθέλησεν ὁ θεὸς ποιῆσαι ὅσα ἐβουλεύσατο, τοῦτον τὸν λ. ἐγέννησε προφορικόν…οὐ κενωθεὶς αὐτὸς τοῦ λ., ἀλλὰ λ. γεννήσας, καὶ τῷ λ. αὐτοῦ διαπαντὸς ὁμιλῶν *ib.*2.22(1088A); Hipp.*haer.*10.33(p.289.3; M.16.3447B) cit. s. A.2 supra; cf. τὸ δὲ πᾶν πατήρ, ἐξ οὗ δύναμις λόγος id.*Noët.*11(p.253.11; M.10.817C); ἕτερός ἐστιν ὁ υἱὸς παρὰ τὸν ἐνδιάθετον, ἤτοι ἐν κινήσει νοηματικῇ λ., οὐ μετέχων καὶ ἀναπιμπλάμενος καλεῖται λ. ὁ προφορικὸς καὶ τῆς τοῦ πατρὸς οὐσίας ἐκφαντικός, τουτέστιν ὁ υἱός Eun.ap.Cyr.*Jo.*1.4(4.31A); used as illustration (from human reason and speech) of orthodox doctrine, †Gr. Thaum.*ep.Philagr.*(M.46.1105B); Cyr.*thes.*4(5[1].31D,E); *ib.*6(47E); **b.** condemned: in its use by Valentinians, cf. *hi qui generationem prolativi hominum verbi transferunt in dei aeternum verbum, et prolationis initium donantes…quemadmodum et suo verbo,* Iren. *haer.*2.13.8(M.7.747B); *ib.*2.28.5(808B); ὁ γὰρ τοῦ πατρὸς τῶν ὅλων λ. οὐχ οὗτός ἐστιν ὁ προφορικός, σοφία δὲ καὶ χρηστότης φανερωτάτη τοῦ θεοῦ δύναμίς τε αὖ παγκρατής Clem.*str.*5.1(p.329.21; M.9.16B); cf.Or. *Jo.*1.24(23; p.29.21; M.14.65A); μὴ γὰρ οὖν τις ὑπολάβοι τῷ παρὰ ἀνθρώποις ἐκ συλλαβῶν συνεστῶτι…ἐνάρθρῳ καὶ προφορικῷ λ. τὸν τοῦ θεοῦ παρόμοιον τυγχάνειν…ἀλλ' οὐ καὶ ὁ τοῦ θεοῦ τοιοῦτος, ἔχων δὲ καθ' ἑαυτὸν οἰκείαν ὑπόστασιν…διὸ καὶ σοφίαν αὐτὴν καὶ θεοῦ λ. οἱ θεῖοι χρησμοὶ προσαγορεύουσιν Eus.*d.e.*5.5(p.228.17; M.22.377A); διὰ τούτων ἐναργῶς καὶ ἐνδιάθετον λ. ᾧ διαλογίζεταί τις καὶ προφορικὸν ᾧ διαλέγεται προσῆψεν [sc. Marcellus] τῷ θεῷ, τοιοῦτόν τινα οἷον τὸν καθ' ἡμᾶς καὶ τὸν ἐν τῷ θεῷ εἶναι λ. ὑποθέμενος id.*e.th.*2.15(p.119.26; M.24.936C); μηδὲ ποτὲ μὲν ἐνδιάθετον ὡς ἐπ' ἀνθρώπῳ λόγον, ποτὲ δὲ σημαντικὸν ὥς ἐν ἡμῖν προφορικὸν καὶ ἐν τῷ θεῷ ὑποτίθεσθαι. ταῦτα γὰρ Σαβελλίου ἢ Ἰουδαίων τινὸς…ἀνεκτὸν ἦν μᾶλλον ἢ Χριστιανοῦ λέγοντος ἀκούειν *ib.*1.17(p.78.16; 860D); cf. Marcell. cit. s.v. ἔνδον; βδελυσσόμεθα δὲ…τοὺς λ. μὲν μόνον αὐτὸν ψιλὸν τοῦ θεοῦ καὶ ἀνύπαρκτον ἐπιπλάστως καλοῦντας, ἐν ἑτέρῳ τὸ εἶναι ἔχοντα, νῦν μὲν ὡς τὸν προφορικὸν λεγόμενον ὑπό τινων, νῦν δὲ ὡς τὸν ἐνδιάθετον, Χριστὸν δὲ αὐτὸν καὶ υἱὸν…μὴ εἶναι πρὸ αἰώνων θέλοντας *Symb.Ant.*(345)5(p.252.34; M.26.729D); *ib.*6(p.253.4; 732A) cit. s. ἁπλῶς; εἴ τις ἐνδιάθετον ἢ προφορικὸν λ. λέγοι τὸν υἱὸν τοῦ θεοῦ, ἀνάθεμα ἔστω *Symb.Sirm.*1 *anath.*8; λ. δὲ οὐ προφορικόν, οὐκ ἐνδιάθετον, οὐκ ἀπόρροιαν τοῦ τελείου, οὐ τμῆσιν τῆς ἀπαθοῦς φύσεως, οὔτε προβολήν, ἀλλ' υἱὸν αὐτοτελῆ †Ath.*exp.fid.*1(M.25.201A); Ath.*Ar.*2.35(M.26.221B); λ. οὐ προφορικὸς εἰς ἀέρα διαχεόμενος, οὔτε λόγοις ἀνυποστάτοις ἐξομοιούμενος Cyr.H.*catech.*4.8; προφορικὸν οὖν φῂς τὸν υἱὸν λ.;…μὴ γένοιτο. τὸν γὰρ λ. ἐγώ φημι ἐνούσιον, καὶ οὐ ῥῆμα διαλυόμενον, οὔτε μὴν προεληλυθότα ἐκ τοῦ θεοῦ καὶ πάλιν…ἀναλυθέντα κατὰ Σαβέλλιον ‡Ath.*disp.*25(M.28.469A); cf.Bas.*hex.*3.2(1.23Aff.; M.29.56A,B); cf. id.*hom.*24.1(2.190A,B; M.31.601A,B); ἵνα δὲ μὴ δοκῶμεν τὸν υἱὸν εἶναί ποτε ὅτε ἀφανὴς ἦν τῷ πατρὶ κρυπτόμενος, καὶ ἵνα μὴ προφορικὸν λ. καὶ ἐνδιάθετον ὑπολαμβάνωμεν ‡Gr.Nyss.*Ar.et Sab.*10(M.45.1296B); Σαβελλίου δὲ τὴν μανίαν ἀνούστατον εἶναι τὸν θεὸν λ., ὡς τὸν προφορικὸν καὶ ἀναλυόμενον Didym.*Trin.*3.23(M.39.924C); id.(‡Bas.)*Eun.*5(1.297C; M.29.713B); Παύλου τοῦ Σαμοσατέως…οὗτος ἀνύπαρκτον τὸν Χριστὸν…διαβεβαιοῦται, λ. προφορικὸν αὐτὸν σχηματίσας Epiph. *anac.*65(*GCS* 3 p.1.6; M.42.9A); Chrys.*hom.3.3 in Jo.*(8.20B); cf. Cyr.*Thds.*6(p.45.15; 5[2].5A); ἐπειδὰν τὸν προφορικὸν λ. ὑπόδειγμα τοῦ ἐνυποστάτου θεοῦ λ. φέρω, μὴ νομίσῃς με προφορικὸν λέγειν τὸν θεὸν λ. Thdot.Anc.*hom.*2.5(p.76.25; M.77.1376B); Jo.D.*f.o.*1.7(M.94.808A); opp. ἐνυπόστατος, v.s.v.; **c.** distinction of 'economic' from eternal (ἐνδιάθετος) Logos λέγεται μὲν καὶ ὁ υἱὸς λ., ὁμωνύμως τῷ πατρικῷ λ., ἀλλ' οὐχ οὗτός ἐστιν ὁ σὰρξ γενόμενος. οὐδὲ μὴν ὁ πατρῷος λ., ἀλλὰ δύναμίς τις τοῦ θεοῦ, οἷον ἀπόρροια τοῦ λ. αὐτοῦ νοῦς γενόμενος τὰς τῶν ἀνθρώπων καρδίας διαπεφοίτηκε Clem.*fr*.23 (p.202.19)ap.Phot.*cod*.109(M.103.384B); cf. ἕτερος γινόμενος τοῦ ἐν καρδίᾳ λ. ὁ διὰ γλώσσης νοῦς προπηδῶν Dion.Al.ap.Ath.*Dion*.23 (p.63.8; M.25.513B); **3.** subordinationist tendency in Logos speculation ὅτε ἠθέλησεν, καθὼς ἠθέλησεν, ἐγέννα τὸν λ. αὐτοῦ...πάντα γὰρ τὰ γενόμενα διὰ λ. καὶ σοφίας τεχνάζεται λόγῳ μὲν κτίζων, σοφίᾳ δὲ κοσμῶν ...ὃν λ. ἔχων ἐν ἑαυτῷ ἀόρατόν τε ὄντα τῷ κτιζομένῳ κόσμῳ ὁρατὸν ποιεῖ· πρότερον φωνὴν φθεγγόμενος καὶ φῶς ἐκ φωτὸς γεννῶν προῆκεν τῇ κτίσει κύριον τὸν ἴδιον νοῦν...καὶ οὕτως αὐτῷ παρίστατο ἕτερος, ἕτερον δὲ λέγων οὐ δύο θεοὺς λέγω, ἀλλ' ὡς φῶς ἐκ φωτός Hipp.*Noët*.10 (p.251.19; M.10.817B); σωτῆρι, ὡς μετ' αὐτὸν δευτέρῳ καὶ θεῷ λ. Or. *Jo*.6.39(23; p.149.3; M.14.268D); ἀλλ' ὅμως τῶν τοσούτων...ὑπερέχων οὐσίᾳ καὶ πρεσβείᾳ καὶ δυνάμει καὶ θειότητι (ἔμψυχος γάρ ἐστι λ.), καὶ σοφίᾳ, οὐ συγκρίνεται κατ' οὐδὲν τῷ πατρί. εἰκὼν γάρ ἐστιν τῆς ἀγαθότητος αὐτοῦ καὶ ἀπαύγασμα οὐ τοῦ θεοῦ ἀλλὰ τῆς δόξης αὐτοῦ *ib*.13.25(p.249.28; 444A); cf.id.*princ*.1.3.5(p.56.3; M.11.150B); μετὰ τὴν ἄναρχον καὶ ἀγένητον τοῦ θεοῦ...οὐσίαν...δευτέραν οὐσίαν καὶ θείαν δύναμιν...ἐκ τοῦ πρώτου αἰτίου γεγενημένην, εἰσάγουσι [sc. Hebrew scriptures], λ. καὶ σοφίαν...προσαγορεύοντες Eus.*p.e*.7.12 (320C; M.21.541B); οὐ γὰρ δὴ γενητῶν πρῶτος ὁ ἐπὶ πάντων θεός... μόνου τοῦ θείου λ. πάντων τῶν γενητῶν πρώτου χρηματίζοντος id.*d.e*. 5.6(p.229.21; M.22.380A); εἰ καὶ δύο κυρίους...ὁμολογοῦμεν, ἀλλ' οὐ καὶ ταῖς ὁμοίαις ἐπ' ἀμφοτέροις χρώμεθα θεολογίαις· εὐσεβῶς δὲ τῇ τάξει χρώμενοι, τὸν μὲν ἀνωτάτω πατέρα καὶ θεὸν καὶ κύριον καὶ τοῦ δευτέρου κύριον καὶ θεὸν εἶναι πεπαιδεύμεθα, τὸν δὲ τοῦ θεοῦ λ. τὸν δεύτερον κύριον, τῶν μὲν ὑπ' αὐτὸν δεσπότην, οὐκέτι δὲ ὁμοίως καὶ τοῦ μείζονος· οὐ γὰρ τοῦ πατρὸς κύριος οὐδὲ τοῦ πατρὸς θεὸς ὁ θεὸς λ., ἀλλ' ἐκείνου μὲν εἰκὼν καὶ λ. καὶ σοφία..., τῶν δὲ μετ' αὐτὸν δεσπότης καὶ κύριος καὶ θεός· ὁ δέ γε πατὴρ καὶ τοῦ υἱοῦ πατὴρ καὶ κύριος καὶ θεός. ὅθεν εἰκότως ἀνατρέχουσιν εἰς μίαν ἀρχήν, καὶ εἰς ἕνα θεὸν συνίσταται ἡμῖν τὰ τῆς εὐσεβοῦς θεολογίας *ib*.5.8(p.230.23; 381A); διελεῖν γὰρ τὸν λ. τοῦ θεοῦ τολμήσας [sc. Eus.] καὶ ἕτερον θεὸν τὸν λ. ὀνομάσαι, οὐσίᾳ τε καὶ δυνάμει διεστῶτα τοῦ πατρός...τοῦ μὲν **Εὐσεβίου Οὐλεντίνῳ** τε καὶ Ἑρμῇ ὁμοίως εἰρηκότος Marcell.*frr*.72,75 ap.Eus.*Marcell*.1.4(p.26.14,25; M.24.765C,768A); in Arianism (with impersonal conception of Logos), Ar.*Thal.fr*.16 ap.Ath.*Dion*.23 (p.62.28; M.25.513A) cit. s. ξένος; ἦν γάρ...μόνος ὁ θεός, καὶ οὐκ ἦν ὁ λ. ... εἶτα θελήσας ἡμᾶς δημιουργῆσαι, τότε πεποίηκεν τοῦτον, καί... ὠνόμασεν αὐτὸν λ. ... καὶ λ. ἕτερον εἶναι...παρὰ τὸν υἱὸν ἐν τῷ θεῷ καὶ τούτου μετέχοντα τὸν υἱὸν ὠνομάσθαι πάλιν κατὰ χάριν λ. καὶ υἱὸν αὐτόν *ib*.4f.ap.Ath.*Ar*.1.5(M.26.21A); οὐκ ἔστιν ὁ ἀληθινὸς καὶ μόνος αὐτὸς τοῦ πατρὸς λ., ἀλλ' ὀνόματι μόνον λέγεται λ. *ib*.7 ap.Ath. *Ar*.1.9(29B); acc. followers of Ar. πῶς δύναται ὁ υἱὸς λ. εἶναι, ἢ ὁ λ. εἰκὼν τοῦ θεοῦ; ὁ γὰρ ἀνθρώπων λ. ἐκ συλλαβῶν συγκείμενος, μόνον ἐσήμανε τὸ βούλημα τοῦ λαλήσαντος, καὶ εὐθὺς πέπαυται Ath.*Ar*.2.34 (220C); ἄλλον μὲν εἶναι τὸν ἴδιον καὶ φύσει λ. τοῦ πατρός...τὸν δὲ ἀληθῶς υἱὸν κατ' ἐπίνοιαν μόνον λέγεσθαι λ., ὡς ἄμπελον, καὶ ὁδόν, καὶ θύραν Ar.*Thal.fr*.16 ap.Ath.*Ar*.2.37(225A); cf.Eun.ap.Cyr.*Jo*.1. 4(4.31A) cit. s. B.2.a supra; **4.** refutation of theories that Logos is only immanent in nature, or is an impersonal attribute of God, Ath.*gent*.40(M.25.81A) cit. s. σπερματικός; subordinationism attacked οὐ γάρ ἐστι δεύτερος θεὸς ὁ υἱός, ἀλλὰ λ. τοῦ ἑνὸς καὶ μόνου θεοῦ id.*inc.et c.Ar*.19(M.26.1017A); **5.** Gnost.; **a.** pagan antecedents Ἑρμῆν μὲν λ. τὸν ἑρμηνευτικὸν καὶ πάντων διδάσκαλον Just.*1apol*.21.2 (M.6.360A); εἰ δὲ καὶ ἰδίως...γεγενῆσθαι αὐτὸν ἐκ θεοῦ λέγομεν λ. θεοῦ...κοινὸν τοῦτο ἔστω ὑμῖν τοῖς τὸν Ἑρμῆν λ. τὸν παρὰ θεοῦ ἀγγελτικὸν λέγουσιν *ib*.22.2(361B); cf. *apud vestros quoque sapientes Logon, id est sermonem atque rationem, constat artificem videri universitatis*, Tert.*apol*.21(M.*PL*.1.398A); Ἑρμῇ, ὃν δὴ λ. εἶναί φασι Clem.*str*.6.15(p.498.19; M.9.356B); as rational cosmic principle controlling fate of men, in poems of Aratus as allegorized by Gnostics, Hipp.*haer*.4.48(p.70.16ff.; M.16.3114ff.); identified with Dog-star, *ib*.(p.72.27; 3115C); οὗτοι [sc. Brahmins] τὸν θεὸν φῶς εἶναι λέγουσιν...ἀλλ' ἔστιν αὐτοῖς ὁ θεὸς λ., οὐχ ὁ ἔναρθρος, ἀλλ' ὁ τῆς γνώσεως...τοῦτο δὲ τὸ φῶς, ὅ φασι λ. τὸν θεὸν *ib*.1.24(p.28.7; 3052B); **b.** Gnost. theories; *Λ*. as fifth aeon in Valent. system, produced with *Ζωή* from *Μονογενής* as πατέρα πάντων τῶν μετ' αὐτὸν ἐσομένων, καὶ ἀρχήν, καὶ μόρφωσιν παντὸς τοῦ πληρώματος Iren.*haer*.1.1.1(M.7. 448A); identified with Simonian aeon *Λογισμός*, Hipp.*haer*.6.20 (p.148.20; 3226C); not incarnate οὐχ ὁ *Λ*. σὰρξ ἐγένετο, ὅς γε οὐδὲ ἦλθέ ποτε ἐκτὸς πληρώματος, ἀλλὰ ὁ...μεταγενέστερος τοῦ *Λ*., *Σωτήρ* Iren.*haer*.1.9.2(M.7.541A); πάντα δι' αὐτοῦ ἐγένετο...πᾶσι γὰρ τοῖς μετ' αὐτὸν αἰῶσι μορφῆς καὶ γενέσεως αἴτιος ὁ *Λ*. ἐγένετο *ib*.1.8.5 (533B); giving special revelation to Valentinus, Hipp.*haer*.6.42 (p.173.24; M.16.3262A); in system of Colorbasus as product of *Ἄνθρωπος* and *Ἐκκλησία* instead of vice versa as in Valentinus' system, Iren.*haer*.1.12.3(M.7.576A); in Marcosian system, mode of revelation emitted as spoken word by Father, *ib*.1.14.1(596A); all aeons known as λόγοι by Marcosians, *ib*.1.14.2(597B); λέγουσι δὲ καὶ τοὺς αἰῶνας ὁμωνύμως τῷ λ. λόγους Clem.*exc.Thdot*.25(p.115.11; M.9. 672B); represented at birth of Jesus by Gabriel, Iren.*haer*.1.15.3 (M.7.620B); cf.Clem.*exc.Thdot*.25(p.115.10; M.9.672B); Logos being associated with rest of ogdoad in possessing Jesus, Iren.*haer*.1.15.3 (621B); τῷ δὲ λ. τῷ ἐν τῇ ἀρχῇ, τοῦτ' ἔστιν ἐν τῷ *Μονογενεῖ*, ἐν τῷ *Νῷ* καὶ τῇ *Ἀληθείᾳ*, μηνύει τὸν *Χριστόν*, τὸν *Λ*., καὶ τὴν *Ζωήν* Clem.*exc. Thdot*.6(p.107.17; 657A); as second aeon in Basilidean system, Iren. *haer*.1.24.3(M.7.675B); (Peratic) καθέζεται οὖν μέσος τῆς ὕλης καὶ τοῦ πατρὸς ὁ υἱός, ὁ λ., ὁ ὄφις ἀεὶ κινούμενος πρὸς ἀκίνητον τὸν πατέρα καὶ κινουμένην τὴν ὕλην Hipp.*haer*.5.17(p.114.18; M.16. 3175B); **6.** in credal formulations εἷς θεός, πατὴρ λ. ζῶντος...εἷς κύριος...λ. ἐνεργός Gr.Thaum.*symb*.(p.3.2ff.; M.10.984f.); εἰς ἕνα κύριον Ἰησοῦν Χριστὸν τὸν τοῦ θεοῦ λ. *Symb.Caes*.(p.43.10; M.20. 1537B); τὸν ἐξ αὐτοῦ πρὸ πάντων τῶν αἰώνων γεγεννημένον, θεὸν λ. Ar.*ep.Const*.(p.64.7; M.67.1012A); εἰς ἕνα μονογενῆ λ., σοφίαν, υἱόν †Ath.*exp.fid*.1(M.25.200A); θεὸν ἐκ θεοῦ...λ. ζῶντα *Symb.Ant*.(341)2 (p.249.15; M.26.721C); εἷς...υἱὸν θεοῦ καὶ γέννημα μονογενὲς καὶ ἀΐδιον λ., ζῶντα καὶ ὑφεστῶτα καὶ ἐνεργόν, ἀεὶ συνόντα τῷ πατρί Apoll.*fid.sec.pt*.34(p.180.5; M.10.1117B); **7.** in doxologies δόξα σοι πάτερ...δόξα σοι λόγε...δόξα σοι χάρις...δόξα σοι τὸ πνεῦμα *A.Jo*.94 (p.197.19); *ib*.96(p.199.2); *A.Thom*.A 80(p.196.10).

C. ref. Inc.; **1.** λ. applied without qualification to Christ incarnate τὰ διὰ λόγου δειχθέντα φανερῶς μαθηταῖς, οἷς ἐφανέρωσεν ὁ λ. φανείς ‡*Diogn*.11.2; λόγου ἡ Βηθλεὲμ πατρίς *Orac.Sib*.8.479; cf. *verbum ei, qui a nativitate caecus fuerat, formavit visionem*, Iren. *haer*.5.15.3(M.7.1166A); τὴν ἀνάστασιν τοῦ λ. Or.*Cels*.5.56(p.60.3; M. 11.1272A); τοῦ σωτηρίου λ. παρ' ἡμῖν φάντος· ἐγώ εἰμι ἡ ἄμπελος Eus. *p.e*.11.18(538B; M.21.896A); Cyr.*Is*.1.4(2.122D); in eucharistic context τρώγειν καὶ πίνειν τὸν λ. τοῦ θεοῦ Iren.*haer*.4.38.1(M.7.1106A); τὴν σάρκα τοῦ λ. Or.*hom.12.13 in Jer*.(p.99.30; M.13.396C); id.*Cels*. 8.22(p.239.21; M.11.1552A); τὸ αὐτοῦ τοῦ λ. σῶμα ζωοποιόν ἐστιν Cyr.*Nest*.4.5(p.85.27; 6.110E); **2.** of divine person of Christ in relation to humanity ὥσπερ γὰρ ἦν ἄνθρωπος ἵνα πειρασθῇ, οὕτω καὶ λ. ἵνα δοξασθῇ· ἡσυχάζοντος μὲν τοῦ λ. ἐν τῷ πειράζεσθαι...καὶ ἀποθνήσκειν, συγγινομένου δὲ τῷ ἀνθρώπῳ ἐν τῷ νικᾶν καὶ...ἀνίστασθαι Iren.*haer*.3.19.3(M.7.941A); θεὸς ἐν ἀνθρώπου σχήματι ἄχραντος...λ. θεός, ὁ ἐν τῷ πατρί,...σὺν καὶ τῷ σχήματι θεός Clem.*paed*.1.2(p.91. 24; M.8.252C); ἦν αὐτὸς ὁ λ., ἐκ πνεύματος ἁγίου καὶ παρθένου ἕνα τέλειον υἱὸν θεοῦ ἀπεργασάμενος Hipp.*Noët*.4(p.241.26ff.; M.10. 809A); τὸν λ., ὃν υἱὸν προσηγόρευε διὰ τὸ μέλλειν ἄνθρωπον γενέσθαι... οὔτε γὰρ ἄσαρκος καὶ καθ' ἑαυτὸν ὁ λ. τέλειος ἦν υἱός, καίτοι τέλειος ⟨λ.⟩ ὢν μονογενής, οὔθ' ἡ σὰρξ καθ' ἑαυτὴν δίχα τοῦ λ. ὑποστᾶναι ἠδύνατο *ib*.15(p.259.16; 824B); εἰ καὶ σῶμα θνητὸν καὶ ψυχὴν ἀνθρωπίνην ἀναλαβὼν ὁ ἀθάνατος θεὸς λ., ὁ λ. τῇ οὐσίᾳ μένων λ. οὐδὲν μὲν πάσχει ὧν πάσχει τὸ σῶμα ἢ ἡ ψυχή Or.*Cels*.4.15(p.285.15; M.11. 1048A); ὁ ἐν τῷ Ἰησοῦ ἐπιδημήσας λ., καὶ πρότερον δὲ θεοφορήσας *ib*.8.54(p.270.24; 1597C); λ. υἱὸν τοῦ θεοῦ...θεὸν καὶ ἄνθρωπον id.*dial*.2 (p.122.11); in teaching of Paul. Sam. ὁ ἄνθρωπος Ἰησοῦς χρίεται, ὁ λ. οὐ χρίεται...ὁ λ. μὲν γὰρ ἄνωθεν, Ἰησοῦς δὲ Χριστὸς ἄνθρωπος ἐντεῦθεν. Μαρία τὸν λ. οὐκ ἔτεκεν, οὐδὲ γὰρ ἦν πρὸ αἰώνων. Μαρία τὸν λ. ὑπεδέξατο καὶ οὐκ ἔστι πρεσβυτέρα τοῦ λ.· ἀλλὰ ἄνθρωπον ἡμῖν ἴσον ἔτεκεν. ... λέγει ἄλλον εἶναι τὸν Ἰησοῦν Χριστὸν καὶ ἄλλον τὸν λ. ... τὸν θεὸν λ. ἐν αὐτῷ εἶναι, ὅπερ ἐν ἡμῖν ὁ ἔσω ἄνθρωπος Paul.Sam. *fr*.B 4(p.331.2ff.)ap.Leont.B.*Nest.et Eut*.3 suppl.(M.86.1392B); acc. followers of Paul. Sam. τὸν μὲν υἱὸν εἶναι τὸν Χριστόν, τὸν δὲ λ. ἄλλον εἶναι ‡Ath.*Ar*.4.30(p.79.3; M.26.513D); τὸν παθόντα Ἰησοῦν κύριον ἐποίησε, καὶ οὐ τὴν σοφίαν οὐδὲ τὸν λ. τὸν ἀνέκαθεν ἔχοντα τῆς δεσποτείας τὸ κράτος Eust.*fr.in Pr*.8:22(M.18.681A); ἐν σώματι λ. ἦν θεοῦ Ath.*Dion*.8(p.51.25; M.25.492B); λ. γινόμενον ἐν σαρκί id.*Ar*.2. 15(M.26.177B); ποῖος ᾅδης ἠρεύξατο ὁμοούσιον εἰπεῖν τὸ ἐκ Μαρίας σῶμα τῇ τοῦ λ. θεότητι; ἢ ὅτι ὁ λ. εἰς σάρκα καὶ ὀστέα...μεταβέβληται id.*ep.Epict*.2(p.4.11f.; M.26.1052C); Ἰουδαῖοι...οὐ λ. γινόμενον ἐν σαρκί, ἀλλὰ ψιλὸν αὐτὸν ἄνθρωπον γίνεσθαι, ὡς πάντες γεγόνασιν οἱ βασιλεῖς ὑπολαμβάνουσιν id.*Ar*.2.15(M.26.177B); ὥσπερ γὰρ οἱ ἄνθρωποι λαμβάνοντες τὸ πνεῦμα τοῦ θεοῦ, γίνονται τέκνα δι' αὐτοῦ· οὕτως ὁ λ. τοῦ θεοῦ, ὅτε καὶ αὐτὸς ἐνεδύσατο τῶν ἀνθρώπων τὴν σάρκα, τότε λέγεται καὶ κτίζεσθαι καὶ πεποιῆσθαι. εἰ μὲν οὖν ἡμεῖς κατὰ φύσιν υἱοί, δῆλον ὅτι κἀκεῖνος κατὰ φύσιν κτίσμα καὶ ποίημα· εἰ δὲ ἡμεῖς θέσει καὶ κατὰ χάριν γινόμεθα υἱοί, δῆλον ὅτι καὶ ὁ λ. διὰ τὴν εἰς ἡμᾶς χάριν γενόμενος ἄνθρωπος εἴρηκε, κύριος ἔκτισέ με *ib*.2.61(277A); εἰμὶ μὲν [sc. ἡ σάρξ] ἐκ τῆς γῆς κατὰ φύσιν θνητή, ἀλλ' ὕστερον τοῦ λ. γέγονα σάρξ, καὶ αὐτὸς ἐβάστασέ μου τὰ πάθη, καίτοι ἀπαθὴς ὤν· ἐγὼ δὲ γέγονα τούτων ἐλευθέρα, οὐκ ἀφιεμένη δουλεύειν ἔτι τούτοις διὰ τὸν ἐλευθερώσαντά με κύριον ἀπὸ τούτων·...ὅρα μὴ ἐγκαλέσῃς, ὅτι ὁ τοῦ θεοῦ λ. τὴν ἐμὴν τῆς δουλείας ἔλαβε μορφήν· ὡς γὰρ ὁ κύριος ἐνδυσάμενος τὸ σῶμα, γέγονεν ἄνθρωπος, οὕτως ἡμεῖς οἱ ἄνθρωποι παρὰ τοῦ λ. θεοποιούμεθα προσληφθέντες διὰ τῆς σαρκὸς αὐτοῦ *ib*.3.34(397A); οὔτε τὸ παθεῖν τὸν μονογενῆ ἐν σαρκὶ πάθος περιποιεῖται τῇ αὐτοῦ θεότητι, καίτοι γε ἐξ ἀληθινῆς ὁμολογίας πιστευόμενον...ὅτι πέπονθεν ὁ ἀπαθὴς θεὸς ὢν λ. Epiph.*haer*.76.39(p.393.3; M.42.601A); Apoll.*fid.inc*.6(p.198.26; M. *PL*.8.877C) cit. s. ἐνέργεια; τὸν...θεὸν λ. λέγων κατῳκηκέναι ἐν τῷ ἐκ σπέρματος Δαβὶδ Diod.*synous*.1(M.33.1560A); εἴ τις βούλοιτο καταχρηστικῶς καὶ τὸν...λ. υἱὸν Δαβὶδ ὀνομάζειν, διὰ τὸν ἐκ Δαβὶδ τοῦ...λ. ναόν, ὀνομαζέτω· καὶ τὸν ἐκ σπέρματος Δαβὶδ υἱὸν τοῦ θεοῦ χάριτι καὶ οὐ φύσει προσαγορευέτω *ib*.(1560B); *ib*.(1560C) cit. s. χάρις; μὴ τῆς Μαρίας υἱὸς ὁ θεὸς λ. ὑποπτευέσθω *ib*.; εἶχεν δὲ καὶ ῥοπὴν οὐ τὴν τυχοῦσαν πρὸς τὰ κρείττω τῇ πρὸς τὸν θεὸν λ. ἑνώσει, ἧς ἠξίωτο κατὰ πρόγνωσιν τοῦ θεοῦ λόγον ἄνωθεν αὐτὸν ἑνώσαντος ἑαυτῷ. ... ἔσχεν μὲν πολλὴν πρὸς τὸ κακὸν τὴν ἀπέχθειαν...τὴν τοῦ θεοῦ λ. συνέργειαν δεχόμενος...οὐδεμίαν ἔχων κεχωρισμένην καὶ ἀποτετμημένην ἐνέργειαν τοῦ θεοῦ λ., ἔχων δὲ ἅπαντα ἐν ἑαυτῷ διαπραττόμενον τὸν θεὸν λ. διὰ τὴν πρὸς ἑαυτὸν ἕνωσιν Thdr.Mops.*fr.inc*.7(p.296.32; M.66.977B); *ib*.8 (p.299.20; 981B) cit. s. ἀπρόσωπος; τὸν θεὸν λ. φησὶν διὰ παθημάτων τετελειωκέναι τὸν ἀναληφθέντα ἄνθρωπον *ib*.12(p.304.8; 985C); ὁ μὲν θεὸς λ. κατὰ τὴν φυσικὴν γέννησιν υἱὸς εἶναι λέγεται, ὁ δὲ ἄνθρωπος... διὰ τὴν πρὸς ἐκεῖνον συνάφειαν *ib*.(p.306.16; 988B); τὸν ναὸν καὶ τὸν ἐν τῷ ναῷ θεὸν λ. id.*fr.Apoll*.(p.313.4; M.66.997B); οὐχ ὁ θεὸς λ. ἐκ γυναικὸς γεγέννηται *ib*.(p.314.3); εἷς υἱὸς κατ' οὐσίαν, ὁ θεὸς λ., ὁ μονογενὴς υἱὸς...ᾧπερ οὗτος συνημμένος τε καὶ μετέχων θεότητος κοινωνεῖ τῆς υἱοῦ προσηγορίας id.*symb*.(p.98.28; M.66.1017C); εὐδοκίας, καθ' ἣν ἡνώθη τῷ θεῷ λ. ὁ...ἄνθρωπος id.*ep.Domn*.7(p.339.14; M.66.1003D); ref. Phil.2:5–8 ἐπειδὴ γὰρ ἔμελλε τοῦ θανάτου μεμνῆσθαι, ἵνα μὴ τὸν θεὸν λ. ἐντεῦθέν τις παθητὸν ὑπολάβῃ, τίθησι τό, Χριστός, ὡς τῆς ἀπαθοῦς καὶ παθητῆς οὐσίας...προσηγορίαν σημαντικήν. ... τὴν μὲν τῶν φύσεων ἐπῄνουν διαίρεσιν κατὰ...τὸ τὸν θεὸν λ. δευτέρας ἐκ γυναικὸς μὴ φάσκειν δεδεῆσθαι γεννήσεως Nest.*ep.Cyr*.2 (p.30.20; M.77.52C); οὐ σὰρξ ὁ τοῦ θεοῦ λ., ἀλλ' ἄνθρωπον ἀνειληφώς id.*fr*.B 5(p.217.20)ap.Cyr.*Thds*.6(p.46.3; 5².5E); οὐκ ἄλλος ἦν ὁ θεὸς λ. καὶ ἄλλος ὁ ἐν ᾧ γέγονεν ἄνθρωπος. ἓν γὰρ ἦν ἀμφοτέρων τὸ πρόσωπον ἀξίᾳ καὶ τιμῇ id.*fr*.B 9(p.224.11)ap.CLater.*act*.5(H.3.896C); τί οὖν ἀνθερμηνεύεις τῷ Παύλῳ, τὸν ἀπαθῆ θεὸν λ. ... παθητὸν ἀρχιερέα ποιῶν; id.*hom.in Heb.3*: *1*(p.236.13; M.64.484D); ἀνθρωπότητα τῆς τοῦ θεοῦ λ. θεότητος ὄργανον id.*fr*.C 8(p.247.6)ap.Leont.B.*Nest.et Eut*.3(M.86.1392C); θεὸς τοῦ Χριστοῦ ὁ ἐκ τοῦ θεοῦ λ. id.*fr*.C 15 (p.291.8); for phrase μία φύσις τοῦ θεοῦ λ. σεσαρκωμένη [Apoll.*ep. Jov*.1(p.250.7; M.28.28A)] in rel. to Nestorian controversy and as expounded by Cyr., v. φύσις; for Cyrilline doctrine of Logos incarnate also v. ἕνωσις; **3.** doctrine that Logos occupied place of human soul in Christ, v. ψυχή, νοῦς.

D. as source of man's rationality and of his communion with God οὐδὲν δὲ θαυμαστόν, εἰ τοὺς οὐ κατὰ σπερματικοῦ λόγου μέρος, ἀλλὰ κατὰ τὴν τοῦ παντὸς λ., ὅ ἐστι Χριστοῦ, γνῶσιν...πολὺ μᾶλλον μισεῖσθαι οἱ δαίμονες ἐλεγχόμενοι ἐνεργοῦσιν Just.*2apol*.8.3(M.6.457B); ὅσα οὖν παρὰ πᾶσι καλῶς εἴρηται, ἡμῶν τῶν Χριστιανῶν ἐστι· τὸν γὰρ ἀπὸ ἀγεννήτου...θεοῦ λ. μετὰ τὸν θεὸν προσκυνοῦμεν *ib*.13.4(465C); v. σπερματικός; κήδεται...τοῦ ἀνθρώπου ὁ θεός. τοῦτο δὲ ἐνδείκνυται ἔργῳ παιδαγωγῶν αὐτὸν λόγῳ, ὅς ἐστι τῆς τοῦ θεοῦ φιλανθρωπίας συναγωνιστὴς γνήσιος Clem.*paed*.1.8(p.127.21; M.8.328A); ὁ δὲ ἄνθρωπος ἐκεῖνος, ᾧ σύνοικος ὁ λ.,...μορφὴν ἔχει τὴν τοῦ λ. ... θεὸς δὲ ἐκεῖνος ὁ ἄνθρωπος γίνεται, ὅτι βούλεται ὁ θεός *ib*.3.1(p.236.22; 556C); λ.,...πᾶν ἄλογον ἡμῶν περιαιρῶν καὶ κατὰ ἀλήθειαν λογικοὺς κατασκευάζων...εἰς δόξαν θεοῦ ἐπιτελοῦντας διὰ τὸν λ. καὶ τὰ...τελειότερα τοῦ βίου ἔργα. ... δῆλον ὅτι...λογικοὶ γινόμεθα, τὰ ἐν ἡμῖν ἄλογα... ἀφανίζοντος αὐτοῦ, καθ' ὃ λ. ἐστί. ... ἐπίστησον δὲ εἰ μετέχουσί πως αὐτοῦ πάντες ἄνθρωποι, καθ' ὃ λ. ἐστί Or.*Jo*.1.37(42; p.47.21; M.14.96D); *ib*.2.15(9; p.72.2; 140D); Gr.Nyss.*castig*.(M.46.308B); Didym. *Trin*.3.1(M.39.780A).

***λογοσκόπος, ὁ,** *one who spies on words* ἐργοσκόπους καὶ λ. Pall. *v.Chrys*.6(p.35.25; M.47.22).

***λογοσοφία, ἡ,** *wordy wisdom, wisdom in words alone*, Max.*ambig*. (M.91.1124A).

***λογοσυνακτέω,** s.v.l., *count the wealth of*, *Pers*.(p.38.4).

***λογοχαρής,** *delighting in verbiage*, Evagr.Pont.*or*.148(M.79.1199A).

λογόω, *endow with reason*, i.e. give a share in divine Logos ὁ λόγος τοῦ θεοῦ ὁ λογώσας καὶ διδάξας ὡς φίλον ἐστὶ τῷ θεῷ *M.Apollon*. 35(p.33.30); ζωοποιούμεθα...λογωθείσης τῆς σαρκός Ath.*Ar*.3.33(M.26.396A).

λογύδριον, τό, = λογίδριον, *foolish tale*, ‡Jo.D.*Artem*.47(p.164.14; M.96.1296A); ‡Ath.*Lat*.2(M.28.828A).

λογχεύ-ω, *pierce with a spear*, *A.Thom*.A 164(p.278.14); ref. Christ, *A.Pil*.B 11.2(p.311); CChalc.*act*.4(*ACO* 2.1.2 p.120.21; H.2.429E); ‡Sophr.H.*triod*.(M.87.3957B); liturg., of cutting eucharistic bread with λόγχη: ∼ων...αὐτὴν σταυροειδῶς *Lit.Chrys*.(*Euchol*.p.85); αὐτὸς μόνος ὁ...ἄρτος...ὡς ἀμνὸς θύεται, τὰ δ' ἄλλα τῶν...δώρων οὐ ∼ονται σταυροειδῶς, ἀλλὰ...μερίζονται ‡Germ.CP *contempl*.(M.98.449A).

λόγχη, ἡ, *spear*, *lance*, ref. Crucifixion, *A.Jo*.97(p.199.15); *Const.App*.5.20.1; ὡς ἀμνὸς σφαττόμενος τῇ λ. τὴν πλευρὰν αὐτοῦ ‡Bas.*h.myst*.48(p.390.13); brought to CP in 644 ἠνέχθη ἡ τιμία λ. ἀπὸ τῶν ἁγίων τόπων...καὶ...προσεκυνήθη *Chron.Pasch*.p.385(M.92.988C); hence, liturg., of instrument used to cut eucharistic bread, ‡Bas.*h.myst*.31(p.264.20) cit. s. σταυροειδῶς; λαμβάνει ὁ ἱερεὺς ἐν ἀριστερᾷ χειρὶ τὴν προσφοράν, ἐν...δεξιᾷ τὴν ἁγίαν λ. ... πήγνυσι τὴν λ. ἐν δεξιῷ μέρει τῆς σφραγίδος *Lit.Chrys*.(p.356.28); ‡Germ.CP *contempl*.(M.98.449A); interpreted ref. Is.53:7, ‡Bas.*h.myst*.29(p.264.7); as symbolizing spear of Crucifixion, *ib*.31 a(p.264.12); ‡Germ. CP *contempl*.(397B); Thdr.Stud.*icon*.1(M.99.489B); also Christ's birth, ‡Sophr.H.*liturg*.10(M.87.3989C); ‡Germ.CP *contempl*.(397D); λ. being heated and dipped into chalice if hot water unobtainable, *Nomoc*.90; and used in blessing the sick with sign of cross, *Euchol*. (p.709).

***λογχιάζω,** *pierce with spears*, *A.Thom*.A 164(p.278.4); *ib*.166 (p.280.2).

***λογχίας, ἡ,** *spear*, *Chron.Pasch*.p.323(M.92.828A, v.l. λοχίας).

***λογχοβολέω,** *strike with a spear, hurl a spear at*, ‡Chrys.*remiss*. (9.846D).

[*]**λογχοδρέπανος,** *in the form of a long-handled knife* Περσεὺς ...λ. ξίφει ἀπέτεμεν αὐτῆς τὴν κάραν Jo.Mal.*chron*.2 p.35(M.97.105B).

λογχοειδής, *in the form of the spear* (i.e. instrument of Passion) ἡ σταυροειδὴς εἰκὼν...καὶ ἡ λ. ... καὶ ἡ σπογγοειδὴς Thdr.Stud.*epp*.2.36 (M.99.1220B).

[*]**λογωθέσιον, τό,** v. λογοθέσιον.

***λόγωσις, ἡ,** *endowing with Logos* θέωσιν τῆς σαρκὸς καὶ λ. καὶ ὑπερύψωσιν ‡Cyr.*Trin*.24(6³.29D; M.77.1165B) = Jo.D.*f.o*.4.18(M.94.1184B).

λοετρόν, τό, v. λουτρόν.

λοιδορητικός, *abusive* λόγῳ παράκειται...τῷ ἐγκωμιαστικῷ τὸ λ. Clem.*paed*.1.8(p.128.26; M.8.329A).

λοιδόρως, *with abuse*, Gr.Naz.*carm*.2.1.11.1192(M.37.1110A).

λοίμη, ἡ, *pestilence*, met. φέρει λύμην Chrys.*hom.87.3 in Mt*.(7.821E, cj. λοίμην); cf.*ib.89.4*(837D).

λοιμικός, *pestilential*, met. τοῦ συνεδρίου τοῦ λ. Chrys.*hom.59.1 in Jo*.(8.344D); Isid.Pel.*epp*.3.47(M.78.764B); λ. τρόποις...διαφθείρειν *ib*.1.484(445C).

λοιμοποιός, *pestiferous*, Isid.Pel.*epp*.1.55(M.78.218C).

λοιμότης, ἡ, *pestilent conduct* ἀλαζονία, ἢ καλεῖται λ. Ant.Mon. *hom*.130(M.89.1841D).

λοιμοφόρος, *pestiferous*, met. λ. γυναικός Marc.Diac.*v.Porph*.86.

λοιμώδης, *pestilential*, met. λοιμώδεις διδασκαλίας †Just.*fr.res*. (p.49; λιμώδεις M.6.1589D); λ. ... καταστάσει Cyr.H.*catech*.4.1; Isid. Pel.*epp*.5.290(M.78.1505B); Diad.*perf*.58(p.64.23).

λοιπάζ-ω, *leave*; pass., *be left over* μῆνες...ἐξ ἔτι ∼όμενοι Cosm. Ind.*top*.5(M.88.197A); *be found wanting* ∼όμεθα τοῦ χρέους ἡμῶν Jo. Clim.*scal*.4(M.88.721B); med., *owe* σῖτον...τῷ δημοσίῳ ∼εσθαι Isid. Pel.*epp*.1.299(M.78.356D); ∼όμενον καὶ χρεωστοῦντα χρυσίου λίτρας ἑκατόν Jo.Clim.*scal*.4(721B).

λοιπάς, ἡ, 1. *remainder*, *Apophth.Patr*.(M.65.132C); **2.** plur., *arrears of payment, debt* ὁ βασιλεὺς λ. χρημάτων ἀφίησιν, ὁ δὲ ἱερεὺς λ. ἁμαρτημάτων Chrys.*hom.4.5 in Is.6*: *1*(6.127D).

λοῖσθος, 1. *last*, Cyr.*glaph.Gen*.2(1.43B); **2.** *extreme*; of extremities of body, id.*ador*.11(1.397D); πρὸς...τὸ λ. τῶν κακῶν *ib*.(400C); *ib*.15 (531B).

***λοξίν,** *crookedly, astray*, Nil.*epp*.2.217(M.79.313A).

λοξόβαμος, *walking sideways*, Gr.Naz.*carm*.1.2.1.714(M.37.575A).

λοξοβάτης, ὁ, as adj. = foreg., *Orac.Sib*.13.169, v.l. τοξο-.

***λοξόδρομος,** *moving crookedly*, Geo.Pis.*hex*.62(M.92.1432A).

***λοξοειδῶς,** *crookedly, obliquely*, Geo.Pis.*hex*.793(M.92.1495A).

***λοξοεργέω,** *act crookedly*, Thdr.Stud.*epp*.1.5(M.99.925A).

λοξοκίνητος, *moving crookedly*; of serpents; fig., of Severus and Acephali, Geo.Pis.*Sev*.320(M.92.1645B); *ib*.71(1628A).

***λοξονοέω**, *have crooked, perverse opinions*, Thdr.Stud.*epp*.2.21 (M.99.1181D).

***λοξοτενής**, *stretching across, transverse*, Paul.Sil.*Soph*.632(M.86. 2143B); id.*ambo*.74(M.86.2255A).

***λοξώδης**, *crooked, misdirected*, *Max.invect*.(M.90.204A).

***λοπόδεικτος**, ? *portrayed on bark*, hence *on thin tablets*; of diagrams (prob. Gnost.) τῶν λ. ὁρίων, καὶ μεθορίων Nil.*epp*.1.296(M. 79.192A).

***λορδόπους**, *with twisted legs*, Sophr.H.*mir.Cyr.et Jo*.55(M.87. 3625A).

***λοσώριος**, v. *λουσόριος.

***λουδάριος, ὁ**, s.v.l., ? *gladiator* ἐκέλευσεν μαχαιροφόνους τῶν λ. εἰσελθεῖν καὶ ἀποσφάττειν αὐτούς *M.Tar*.11(p.474), perh. for δουλάριον.

***λουδεμπιστής, ὁ**, *trainer, supervisor of athletes in the games*, *Const.App*.8.32.9.

***λοῦδος, ὁ**, (Lat. *ludus*) *game, show* εἴ τις...κατεκρίθη...εἰς λ. *Const.App*.5.1.1.

***λούπαξ, ὁ**, *rapacious person*, Cosm.Mel.*schol*.(M.38.548) in Gr. Naz.*carm*.2.2(epigr.)57.

***λούπ(π)εος, ὁ**, v. *λουππαῖος.

***λούπινον, τό**, *lupin-seed* μόδιον τοῦ λ. Thphn.*chron*.p.352(M.108. 845B).

***λουππαῖος, ὁ**, *licentious person*, Jo.D.*parall*.index(M.95.1057); λουππέων *ib*.tit.(M.96.101B); λουπέων Leont.et Jo.*sacr*.titt.(M.86. 2025B).

λοῦσις, ἡ, *bathing, washing*; of mixed bathing in public baths, forbidden, *Const.App*.1.9.1; excessively frequent bathing forbidden μὴ περισσοτέραν δὲ λ. ποιείσθω...ἀλλ' εἰ δυνατὸν μηδὲ καθ' ἡμέραν *ib*.1.9.3; of ablutions prescribed by Mosaic Law, typifying baptism, Proc.G.*Lev*.17:3(M.87.752C).

***λοῦσμα, τό**, *washing*, of baptism ἔσται αὐτῷ [sc. penitent] ἀντὶ τοῦ λ. ἡ χειροθεσία *Const.App*.2.41.2; μετὰ τὸ νυμφικὸν λ., μετὰ τὸ πνευματικὸν χρῖσμα Ast.Am.*hom*.19(M.40.441C); (Marcosian) λούσματα καὶ ἀπολυτρώσεις Hipp.*haer*.6.42(p.173.13; M.16.3259D).

λουσόριος** (λοσώριος**), (Lat. *lusorius*); **1.** *for pleasure* λ. πλοίῳ Epiph.*anc*.106(p.130.3; M.43.209C); **2.** *for the games* ἀχθῆναι λοσώριον *M.Eleuth*.10(p.159.7).

λούστης, ὁ, *bath attendant*, Gr.Naz.*carm*.1.2.8.147(M.37.659A).

λουτέον, *one must bathe*, Clem.*paed*.3.9(p.263.21; M.8.617C).

λουτήρ, ὁ, *laver*;

A. ref. Ex.30:18, 4Reg.8:8, etc., as interpreted; **1.** by Jews πρὸ τῆς ἐξωτέρας ναοῦ Σολομῶντος λουτῆρες ἄφετοι ἐχρημάτιζον πάντοτε. νόμος δὲ ἔκειτο, ἵνα ὁ ἁμαρτάνων ἐπί τινι πράγματι, καὶ βουληθεὶς μεταμεληθῆναι...ἀπολουόμενος [MSS ἀπολυόμενος]...ἐπιτελεῖ τὰς λατρείας †Gregent.*disp*.(M.86.725C); **2.** by Christians as symbol; **a.** of baptism καὶ σύμβολον ἔκειτο τοῦ βαπτίσματος, λ. ἔνδον ἀποκείμενος τῆς σκηνῆς Cyr.H.*catech*.3.5; Cyr.*ador*.9(1.311D); **b.** of ministers of baptism λουτῆρας δέ τις ἀκούων, νοήσει πάντως τοὺς διὰ τοῦ μυστικοῦ ὕδατος τὸν μολυσμὸν ἀποκλύζοντας τῶν ἁμαρτιῶν. λ. ἦν ὁ Ἰωάννης...λ. ἦν ὁ Πέτρος...λ. τοῦ Κανδάκου ὁ Φίλιππος Gr.Nyss.*v. Mos*.(M.44.385B).

B. of laver at church door, *stoup*, for washing of hands before entry to worship ὥσπερ οἱ λ. ὕδατος πεπληρωμένοι εἰσὶ πρὸ τῶν θυρῶν τῆς ἐκκλησίας, ἵνα νίψῃ τὰς χεῖρας, οὕτως οἱ πένητες καθέζονται, ἵνα πλύνῃς τὰς χεῖρας τῆς ψυχῆς Chrys.*poenit*.3.2(2.296E); cf.Synes. *ep*.121(M.66.1501A).

C. *baptistery* ἐλθόντες ἐν τῷ λ. τῆς...ἐκκλησίας ἄλλος τις ἄλλο ἔκραζε *CNic*.(787)proem.(H.4.25E); ἐξερχόμεθα πάντες ἐν τῷ λ. *Euchol*.(p.366).

D. equivalent to λουτρόν; **1.** of baptism τῷ λ. τῆς παλιγγενεσίας †Gregent.*disp*.(M.86.741C); **2.** hence of a church λ. ὑπάρχει ὁ θεῖος ναός, ἀπορρίπτων τὰ ἁμαρτήματα Jo.D.*hom*.11.14(M.96.777B); **3.** of penitence λ. ἀγαθὸς τῇ ψυχῇ τὸ τῆς προσευχῆς δάκρυον Nil.*sent*.58 (M.79.1245B).

λουτήριον, τό, = λουτήρ; **1.** *laver*, for Jewish ritual ablutions τό, λούσασθε...περὶ τῶν νομικῶν λ. λελάληται †Gregent.*disp*.(M.86. 728A); **2.** *baptistery* εἰσάγεις αὐτὸν ἐν τῷ λ. τοῦ βαπτίσματος ‡Jo.D. *Const*.10(M.95.325D).

λουτρόν (**λοετρόν**), **τό**, **I.** in gen.;

A. *washing* σώματα...λ. τε καὶ περιστολαῖς κατακοσμοῦντες Dion. Al.ap.Eus.*h.e*.7.22.9(M.20.689B); *Hom.Clem*.11.28.

B. *bath*, Eus.*onomast*.(p.22.26); id.*v.C*.4.59(p.141.22; M.20.1209B); *ib*.4.61(p.142.23; 1212B); Gr.Nyss.*hom.3 in Eccl*.(M.44.657B); Pall. *v.Chrys*.9(p.56.20; M.47.33); reasons for taking bath παραληπτέον δὲ τὸ λ. ταῖς μὲν γυναιξὶ καθαριότητος ἕνεκεν καὶ ὑγιείας, ὑγιείας δὲ μόνης ἀνδράσι Clem.*paed*.3.9(p.263.8; M.8.617A).

II. religious;

A. of Jewish ritual washings, *Const.App*.2.35.1; Chrys.*hom.70.2 in Jo*.(8.416C); †Gregent.*disp*.(M.86.725C).

B. of Christ's baptism τελειοῦται δὲ τῷ λ. μόνῳ καὶ τοῦ πνεύματος τῇ καθόδῳ ἁγιάζεται; οὕτως ἔχει. τὸ δὲ αὐτὸ συμβαίνει τοῦτο καὶ περὶ ἡμᾶς Clem.*paed*.1.6(p.105.17; M.8.280C); τὸ λ. ἦν κάθαρσις ὑδάτων ἐμῶν Gr.Naz.*carm*.1.2.34.200(M.37.960A); v. βάπτισμα.

C. of Christian baptism; **1.** equivalent to βάπτισμα, rite of *baptism*, in title of treatise by Melito, Eus.*h.e*.4.26.2(M.20.392A); ἔλαβον τὸ λ. *A.Paul.et Thecl*.40(p.266.8); δόξα ὁ τὸ λ. τοῦ βαπτίσματος ἐνδυόμενος *A.Thom*.A 132(p.239.17); λοετρόν Gr.Naz.*carm*.2.1.1.325 (M.37.994A); τὰ δ' ἄλλα μυστήρια περὶ λουτροῦ καὶ τῶν ἔνδοθεν μυστηρίων Epiph.*exp.fid*.22(p.524.6; M.42.828D); Chrys.*hom.11.2 in Rom*.(9.532B); id.*hom.2.3 in Eph*.(11.12B); id.*hom.4.1 in 1Tim*. (11.568B); λοετρόν Nonn.*par.Jo*.1:26(M.43.753C); Proc.G.*Lev*.16:10 (M.87.752C); ἀχράαντα λοετρά Paul.Sil.*Soph*.564(M.86.2141A); Gnost. λουτροῖς χρεισαμένη Χριστοῦ μύρον ἄφθιτον, ἅγνον *CIG* 4.9595a; **2.** of water-baptism opp. baptism of blood (v. βάπτισμα) πλευρᾶς δὲ ῥεῦσαν αἷμα καὶ ὕδωρ ἅμα, τὸ δισσὸν ἦν βάπτισμα, λ. καὶ πάθους Gr.Naz. *carm*.1.2.34.217(M.37.961A); and opp. blood of Christ (in eucharist), Proc.G.*Dt*.32:43(M.87.976B); **3.** in connexion with particular parts of baptismal rite; **a.** Trinitarian formula ἐπ' ὀνόματος γὰρ τοῦ πατρὸς...καὶ τοῦ σωτῆρος ἡμῶν Ἰησοῦ Χριστοῦ καὶ πνεύματος ἁγίου τὸ ἐν ὕδατι...λουτρὸν ποιοῦνται Just.*1apol*.61.3(M.6.420C); τὸ διὰ τοῦ ὕδατος λ. ... καθ' αὐτὸ τῷ ἐμπαρέχοντι ἑαυτὸν τῇ θειότητι τῆς δυνάμεως τῶν τῆς προσκυνητῆς τριάδος ἐπικλήσεών ἐστιν ἡ χαρισμάτων θείων ἀρχὴ καὶ πηγή Or.*Jo*.6.33(17; p.142.27; M.14.257A); ἀρνήσονται ...τὸ ἅγιον λ., ὅτι εἰς πατέρα καὶ εἰς υἱόν, καὶ οὐκ εἰς κτίστην καὶ κτίσμα δίδοται Ath.*syn*.36(p.263.11; M.26.757A); Epiph.*exp.fid*.18 (p.520.1; M.42.820A); Chrys.*hom.4.2 in 2Thess*.(11.532C); **b.** confession of faith καθὼς παρελάβομεν...ἐν τῇ πρώτῃ κατηχήσει, καὶ ὅτε τὸ λ. ἐλαμβάνομεν...τὴν ἡμετέραν πίστιν...προσαναφέρομεν Eus. *ep.Caes*.2(p.43.6; M.20.1537A); δι' ὧν συντασσόμεθα τῷ Χριστῷ; τῆς ὁμολογίας ἐκείνης τῆς πρὸ τοῦ λ.; τῆς μετὰ τὸ λ.; Chrys.*hom.1.3 in Eph*.(11.6E); v. βάπτισμα; **c.** chrismation, λ. being baptism which preceded this (v. βαπτίζω) καθαρίσας αὐτοὺς τῷ σῷ λ. καὶ ἀλείψας αὐτοὺς τῷ σῷ ἐλαίῳ *A.Thom*.A 25(p.140.10); ἐπίκλησις ὀνόματος καινοῦ, καὶ χρῖσις ἐλαίου (here prob. ref. pre-baptismal unction) καὶ λ. ὕδατος *A.Xanthipp*.2(p.59.6); Serap.*euch*.22.2; **d.** post-baptismal fasting μέγα [? μετὰ] λουτρόν, οὐ τρυφῇ καὶ μέθῃ καὶ τραπέζῃ πληθούσῃ, ἀλλὰ νηστείᾳ προσέχειν δεῖ Chrys.ap.*cat.Lc*.4:3(p.34.19); **4.** effects; **a.** cleansing; **i.** in gen., *A.Thom*.A 25(p.140.10); λ. σύμβολον τυγχάνον καθαρσίου ψυχῆς Or.*Jo*.6.33(17; p.142.27; M.14. 257A); λουσάμενοι τῷ μυστικῷ τούτῳ λ., καθαροὶ τὰς προαιρέσεις γενοίμεθα Gr.Nyss.*or.catech*.40(p.160.12; M.45.101D); Epiph.*exp.fid*. 18(p.520.1; M.42.820A); τί δέ ἐστιν ὁ ἁγιασμός; τὸ λ., ὁ καθαρισμός Chrys.*hom.1.1 in 1Cor*.(10.4B); **ii.** as conferring remission of sins, Just.*1apol*.66.1(M.6.428B); λ. ... δι' οὗ τὰς ἁμαρτίας ἀπορρυπτόμεθα Clem.*paed*.1.6(p.105.24; M.8.281A); Chrys.*hom.3.2 in Philm*.(11. 788D); and cleansing from stain of original sin ἐκβάλλεσθαι...πιστεύομεν ἐκ τῶν ταμιείων τοῦ νοῦ διὰ τοῦ λ. ... τὸν πολύμορφον ὄφιν...τὸ λ. ...τὸν...ἐκ τῆς ἁμαρτίας σπίλον περιαίρει ἐξ ἡμῶν Diad.*perf*.78(p.98. 23); **iii.** through which the 'old man' is put off, Ph.Carp.*Cant*.171(M. 40.116B); **b.** regeneration τὸ...εἰς ἀναγέννησιν λ. Just.*1apol*.66.1(M.6. 428B); τῆς ἀναγεννήσεως τοῦ θείου λ. μετόχους γενέσθαι *A.Thom*.A 16 (one MS only; p.124.10–12n.); οἱ γεγεννημένοι διὰ τοῦ λ. Meth.*symp*. 3.8(p.36.6; M.18.73B); Gr.Nyss.*or.catech*.35(p.137.9; M.45.92A); esp. in phrase λ. παλιγγενεσίας (Tit.3:5), v. παλιγγενεσία; which is compared with generation of living creatures from water on fifth day of Creation, Thphl.Ant.*Autol*.2.16(M.6.1077C); **c.** illumination καλεῖται δὲ τοῦτο τὸ λ. φωτισμός Just.*1apol*.61.12(M.6.421B); δύο τάγματα...τὸ μὲν εἰσέτι στοιχειούμενον, τὸ δ' ἤδη διὰ τοῦ λ. πεφωτισμένον Eus.*d.e*.2.3(p.77.27; M.22.140B); hence also διὰ τοῦ λ. ... τῆς ...γνώσεως τοῦ θεοῦ Just.*dial*.14.1(M.6.504C); v. βάπτισμα; **d.** union with Christ in death and resurrection, Chrys.*hom.8.3 in Col*.(11. 384C); id.*hom.5.1 in 2Tim*.(11.686A); v. βάπτισμα; **e.** resurrection and immortality τὸ λ. λάβω τῆς ἀφθαρσίας, *A.Thom*.A 120(p.229. 24n.); Gr.Nyss.*or.catech*.35(p.137.9; M.45.92A); τὸ τῆς ζωῆς λ. *Const. App*.2.7.2; λ. τῆς ἀφθαρσίας Diad.*perf*.78(p.98.23); **f.** adoptive sonship, *cat.2Cor*.6:18(p.393.15); v. παλιγγενεσία; **g.** character of king, priest, and prophet, Chrys.*hom.3.7 in 2Cor*.(10.454A); **h.** reception of H. Ghost μὴ ὡς ὕδατι λιτῷ πρόσεχε τῷ λ. ἀλλὰ τῇ μετὰ τοῦ ὕδατος δεδομένῃ πνευματικῇ χάριτι Cyr.H.*catech*.3.3; καταξιωθήσονται τῆς πνεύματος ἁγίου ἐν τῷ λ. τῆς δωρεᾶς, καὶ ἀφέσεως ἁμαρτιῶν διὰ τῆς χάριτος τῆς ὑπ' αὐτοῦ δοθείσης Epiph.*haer*.51.20(p.278.19; M.41. 925B); Chrys.*hom.24.2 in Jo*.(8.140C); ‡Germ.CP *contempl*.(M.98.

385D); contrast αἱ τοῦ λόγου ἐντολαί...τοῦ ἁγίου πνεύματος δύναμις, αἷς μετὰ τὸ λουτρὸν...χρίονται οἱ πιστεύοντες Hipp.*Dan*.1.16.3(M.10.693A); **i.** as a seal σφράγισόν με καθάπερ Παῦλος σφραγίζει διὰ λουτροῦ παλιγγενεσίας *A.Xanthipp*.28(p.78.34); τὸ λ. ἐστι δευτέρου βίου σφραγίς Gr.Naz.*carm*.1.2.34.237(M.37.962A); contrast *A.Thom.*(*consumm.*)(p.291.7) where τὸ λ. appears to be dist. from τὴν ἐν Χριστῷ σφραγῖδα (consignation); **j.** as replacing circumcision, Epiph.*exp.fid*.24(p.525.5; M.42.829C); **k.** ref. angels assuming guardianship of men from time of their rebirth διὰ λουτροῦ παλιγγενεσίας Or.*comm.in Mt*.13.27(p.254.8; M.13.1165B); **5.** qualifications and preparation for λ.; **a.** repentance, Just.*1apol*.61.10(M.6.421B); id.*dial*.14.1(M.6.504C); with faith and love, Hipp.*Dan*.1.16.5(M.10.692D); **b.** period of catechetical preparation prescribed, CNic.(325)*can*.2; but catechumens baptized in emergency by Cerinthians without full preparation (on authority of 1Cor.15:29), Epiph.*haer*.28.6(p.318.26; M.41.385A); this practice deprecated, Chrys.*hom.1.7 in Ac*.(9.12C); **6.** ref. ministry of women at λ., v. βάπτισμα; **a.** administration of λ. allowed to women by Marcion, Epiph.*anac*.42(p.3.13; M.42.861B) = Jo.D.*haer*.42(M.94.704A); **b.** their office restricted to attendance on women at baptism, Epiph.*haer*.79.3(p.478.18; M.42.744D); **7.** ref. post-baptismal sin v. βάπτισμα; **a.** in gen. οἱ μὲν οὖν πολλοὶ καὶ μετὰ τὸ λουτρὸν κονιορτοῦ τῶν ἁμαρτημάτων πληροῦνται Or.*Jo*.32.2(p.427.14; M.14.744A); cf. ἁμαρτάνω; ἡ ἁμαρτία ...μετὰ τὸ λουτρὸν καὶ τὴν ψυχὴν φθεῖραι δύναται Chrys.*hom.24.6 in Eph*.(11.186C); **b.** regarded by Novatian as unforgivable μετὰ δὲ τὸ λ. μηκέτι δύνασθαί τινα ἐλεεῖσθαι παραπεπτωκότα Epiph.*haer*.59.1(p.364.4; M.41.1017B); hence Νοουατιανῷ...εὐλόγως ἀπεχθανόμεθα ...τὸ λ. ἀθετοῦντι Dion.Al.ap.Eus.*h.e*.7.8(M.20.652B); **c.** regarded by orthodox as forgivable, Ath.*ep.Serap*.4.13(M.26.653C) cit. s. μετάνοια; Chrys.*hom.20.1 in Heb*.(12.186D); contrast ἐπόρνευσέ τις μετὰ τὸ λ. τοῦ θείου βαπτίσματος. ἐνταῦθα οὐδὲ παραμυθία λοιπὸν τῷ ἁμαρτήματι λείπεται id.*hom.76.5 in Mt*.(7.730C); **d.** but baptism, in any case, not repeatable λ. οὐκ ἔστι δεύτερον id.*hom.11.2 in Rom*.(9.532B); id.*hom.2.3 in Eph*.(11.12B); v. βάπτισμα; παρ' αὐτῷ [sc. Marcion]...δίδοται ἕως τριῶν λ. καὶ ἐπέκεινα Epiph.*haer*.42.3(p.98.10; M.41.700A); **8.** ref. rebaptism of heretics, advocated by Cyprian διὰ λουτροῦ πρότερον τῆς πλάνης ἀποκαθηραμένους προσίεσθαι δεῖν ἡγεῖτο Eus.*h.e*.7.3(M.20.641A); v. βάπτισμα; **9.** ref. heret. rites of baptism: Naassene, Hipp.*haer*.5.7(p.83.6; M.16.3131C); Marcosian, *ib*.6.42(p.173.17; 3259D); Manichean, Cyr.H.*catech*.6.33; **10.** ref. imitation of Christian baptism by demons (i.e. similarity to it of pagan rites), Just.*1apol*.62.1(M.6.421B); cf. οὐκ ἀπεικότως ἄρα καὶ τῶν μυστηρίων τῶν παρ' Ἕλλησιν ἄρχει μὲν τὰ καθάρσια, καθάπερ καὶ τοῖς βαρβάροις τὸ λ. Clem.*str*.5.11(p.373.24; M.9.108A); **11.** ref. repudiation of baptism by Archontici, Epiph.*haer*.40.2(p.82.27; M.41.680C); Thdt.*haer*.1.11(4.303).

D. of martyr's baptism of blood (v. βάπτισμα) λουσάμενος ἐν τῷ ἰδίῳ αἵματι τὸ τῆς παλιγγενεσίας λ. Gr.Nyss.*mart*.3(M.46.781C).

E. of 'baptism of tears', Gr.Nyss.*hom.3 in Eccl*.(M.44.657B); cf. δάκρυον.

λούω, [impf. med. ἐλεώμην as if from λεάω, Dor.*doct*.10.2(M.88.1725A)]; **A.** *bathe*; in gen.; med., bathing avoided by Manicheans εἴ τις λούεται, εἰς τὸ ὕδωρ τὴν ἑαυτοῦ ψυχὴν πήσσει Hegem.*Arch*.10(p.16.10; M.10.1444A); prohibited on sabbath by Jews, Or.*hom.12.13 in Jer*.(p.100.8; M.13.396D); abstained from as spiritual discipline ἄνδρα ἀπὸ πεντήκοντα ἐτῶν ὀρθόδοξον ὄντα, μηδέποτε μηδὲ λουσάμενον CBeryt.(449)*act*.(p.29.15; H.2.524E); to be practised in moderation, Clem.*paed*.3.9(p.263.28; M.8.620A); mixed bathing in public baths discouraged, *ib*.3.5(p.254.15; 600B); *Const.App*.1.6.13; Epiph.*haer*.30.7(p.342.25; M.41.417A); Nil.*epp*.2.211(M.79.312A); forbidden under penalty of deposition for clerics and excommunication for laity, CTrull.*can*.77.

B. *baptize*; **1.** of Christ's baptism by John, Cels.ap.Or.*Cels*.1.41(p.91.32; M.11.736C); Or.*Jo*.6.48(29; p.157.24; M.14.285A); **2.** of Christian baptism; act., of baptizer; med., of person getting himself baptized; **a.** in gen. ἡμεῖς μετὰ τὸ οὕτως λοῦσαι τὸν πεπεισμένον ...ἐπὶ τοὺς...ἀδελφοὺς ἄγομεν Just.*1apol*.65.1(M.6.428A); τοῦ τὸν λουσόμενον ἄγοντος ἐπὶ τὸ λουτρόν *ib*.61.10(421B); Or.*Jo*.32.7(6; p.436.21; M.14.757C); λουσάμενόν τινα τὸ τῆς ζωῆς λουτρόν *Const.App*.2.7.2; τὸν ἐθνικὸν λούσας εἰσδέχῃ *ib*.2.41.2; **b.** partic. as a cleansing from sin εὐχαριστία, ἧς οὐδενὶ ἄλλῳ μετασχεῖν ἐξόν ἐστιν ἢ τῷ πιστεύοντι... καὶ λουσαμένῳ τὸ ὑπὲρ ἀφέσεως ἁμαρτιῶν...λουτρόν Just.*1apol*.66.1(M.6.428B); λουόμενος εἰς ἄφεσιν ἁμαρτιῶν Clem.*str*.2.13(p.144.15; M.8.996C); **c.** as cleansing of soul and body together, hence as sign of resurrection of body, †Just.*fr.res*.(p.46; M.6.1585C); **d.** of Thecla's self-baptism εἶπεν, νῦν καιρὸς λούσασθαί με. καὶ ἔβαλεν ἑαυτὴν λέγουσα ἐν τῷ ὀνόματι Ἰησοῦ Χριστοῦ ὑστέρᾳ ἡμέρᾳ βαπτίζομαι *A.Paul.et Thecl*.34(p.260.6); cf. ἔλαβον τὸ λουτρόν, Παῦλε· ὁ γὰρ σοὶ συνεργήσας εἰς τὸ εὐαγγέλιον κἀμοὶ συνήργησεν εἰς τὸ λούσασθαι *ib*.40(p.266.10); **e.** of heret. baptism (Naassene) ἡ γὰρ ἐπαγγελία τοῦ λουτροῦ οὐκ ἄλλη τίς ἐστι κατ' αὐτούς, ἢ τὸ εἰσαγαγεῖν εἰς τὴν ἀμάραντον ἡδονὴν τὸν λουόμενον κατ' αὐτοὺς ζῶντι ὕδατι Hipp.*haer*.7.13(p.83.7; M.16.3131C); **3.** of baptism by fire (Lc.3:16), interpreted as punishment of post-baptismal sin, Or.*hom.2.3 in Jer*.(p.19.13; M.13.281A).

C. of spiritual cleansing without direct allusion to baptism λούειν δὲ δεῖ μάλιστα μὲν τὴν ψυχὴν καθαρσίῳ λόγῳ Clem.*paed*.3.9(p.263.31; M.8.620A); ἐν ποταμοῖς οὐδεὶς ἀγαθὸς εἰ μὴ ὁ Ἰορδάνης, καὶ λέπρας ἀναλλάξαι δυνάμενος τὸν μετὰ πίστεως τὴν ψυχὴν λουόμενον εἰς Ἰησοῦν Or.*Jo*.6.47(27; p.156.24; M.14.281C); (Gnost.) in Christ's hymn to Father ἐφ' ᾧ...εὐχαριστοῦμεν λέγω...λούσασθαι θέλω καὶ λούειν θέλω *A.Jo*.95(p.198.2).

§**λόφωσις, ἡ,** for λώφησις, *cessation*, Jo.D.*hom*.10.5(M.96.761C).

λοχαγός, ὁ, *centurion*, Eus.*v.C*.4.51(p.138.19; M.20.1201A); Thdt.*h.e*.5.24.7(3.1064).

λοχάω, *lie in wait*; esp. of Devil and evil spirits, Meth.*symp*.8.4(p.85.20; M.18.144C); *ib*.8.10(p.92.7; 153A); Nil.*epp*.3.72(M.79.121C).

λοχεία, ἡ, *childbirth*; **1.** lit., of BMV Χριστοῖο διαγγέλλουσι λ. Paul.Sil.*ambo*.32(M.86.2253B); τῆς ὑπερφυοῦς σου λ. ‡Meth.*Sym.et Ann*.5(M.18.357C); term not inconsistent with miraculous birth, cf.*ib*.4(356B); but used with hesitation, Gr.Nyss.*hom.13 in Cant*.(M.44.1052D); *ib*.(1053A); τούτου...μόνου χωρὶς λ. ἡ γέννησις...οὐ γάρ ἐστιν ἐπὶ τῆς ἀφθόρου τε καὶ ἀπειρογάμου κυρίως τὸ ὄνομα τῆς λ. εἰπεῖν *ib*.; cf.*ib*.(1053C); cf.Procl.CP *or*.3.3(M.65.705D); hence plur., of Christmas observance condemned by CTrull. ἀλόχευτον τὸν... τόκον ὁμολογοῦντες...ἐπειδή τινες μετὰ τὴν ἡμέραν τῆς...γεννήσεως δείκνυνται σεμίδαλιν ἕψοντες...προφάσει τιμῆς...λοχείων...παρθενομήτορος, ὁρίζομεν μηδὲν τοιοῦτον...τελεῖσθαι *can*.79; **2.** met., of regeneration θαυμαστῆς καὶ παραδόξου λ. Chrys.*hom.25.2 in Jo*.(8.145E); ‡Chrys.*hom.in Mt.20:1*(8.105D); Nonn.*par.Jo*.3:3(M.43.765B).

λόχευμα, τό, plur., *travail, childbirth*; fig., ref. Passion ἐκκλησίαν ...παιδίον...ἐκύησεν ὁ κύριος ὠδῖνι σαρκικῇ· ὢ τῶν ἁγίων λ. Clem.*paed*.1.6(p.115.20; M.8.301A); ref. baptism as new birth καινῶν λ. Chrys.*hom.3.6 in Ac.princ*.(3.80D); παράδοξον τῶν λ. νόμον id.*hom.15.3 in Rom*.(9.579A); Isid.Pel.*epp*.4.24(M.78.1076A).

*λόχευσις, ἡ, *bringing to birth*, Sophr.H.*or*.2.29(M.87.3523A).

λοχεύτρια, ἡ, *mother*, of BMV τὴν τοῦ...θεοῦ...κατὰ σάρκα λ. Jo.D.*hom*.8.6(M.96.708D); ref. Gen.2:21 πλευρὰν...τοῦ βίου λ. Geo.Pis.*hex*.1026(M.92.1513A).

λοχεύω, pass., *be born*, Meth.*symp*.2.6(p.23.9; M.18.57A).

*λοχηφόρος, *of child-bearing* λ. δίφρου *delivery stool*, Marc.Diac.*v.Porph*.44.

λόχιος, *of* or *connected with childbirth*, Nonn.*par.Jo*.7:22(M.43.808C); *ib*.9:25(829A).

λόχος, ὁ, **1.** *detachment of troops, century*, Eus.*h.e*.9.9.3(M.20.820D); *V.Const*.16(p.555.2); **2.** *ambuscade*; of Devil, Bas.*hom*.21.1(2.164B; M.31.541C).

*λοχοῦς, ἡ, = λοχός *LS*, *woman in childbirth* παρθένον λ. ‡Epiph.*v.proph.Jer*.A 7(M.43.400B; λοχόν p.21).

λύγισμα, τό, *contortion* λ. ... ὀρχηστικά CNic.(787)*refut*.(H.4.352D); met., of sophistical arguments, Gr.Naz.*or*.21.12(M.35.1093C); id.*carm*.2.1.11.268(M.37.1048A); of the twists and turns of complicated musical tunes, *ib*.1.2.33.66(933A); id.*or*.5.35(M.35.709B); of the waving of branches τοῖς λ. θρῆνον τὰ δένδρα ἐποίουν ἠχοῦντα, ποῦ εἶ ὁ Ἀδάμ; *Hymn*.(*KlT* p.14).

λυγμός, ὁ, *hiccough*, Clem.*paed*.2.2(p.170.27; M.8.417A); *catching of breath* in weeping, Gr.Nyss.*v.Macr*.(p.413.14; M.46.997D).

*λυγοδοπλέκω, *weave of willow twigs*, ‡Chrys.*transfig*.3(Savile 7 p.340.30).

*λυγρώδης, *dismal*, Hipp.*fr.21 in Pr*.(p.164.11; M.10.621B).

Λυδός, *Lydian*; Λυδὴ λίθος (= Λυδία λίθος, *LS*); siliceous stone used to assay gold, Clem.*str*.1.9(p.29.19; M.8.741A).

λύθρον, τό, (**λύθρος, ὁ**), **1.** *gore, defilement from blood* λύθρους καὶ αἵματα Eus.*p.e*.4.10(148D; M.21.257C); id.*l.C*.2(p.200.3; M.20.1328A); of sacrifices, id.*v.C*.3.27(p.90.29; M.20.1088C); βωμοὺς λύθροις αἱμάτων μιαινομένους *ib*.3.48(p.98.9; 1108C); περὶ τὰ εἴδωλα καὶ τὸν ἐπιβώμιον λ. Gr.Nyss.*Eun*.7(2 p.164.14, v.l. τὸ ἐ. λ. M.45.753C); of blood shed in murder, ref. martyrs ἐν πολλῷ τῷ λ. ... θαυμάζουσι τοὺς νικηφόρους Clem.*str*.2.20(p.173.15; M.8.1056A); λ. φοινίῳ κόνιν δεύων Meth.*symp*.11(p.135.19; M.18.212B); ὁμογνίῳ λ. ...ἐξεμίανεν Philost.*h.e*.5.4(M.65.532A); ref. edicts of persecution διατάγματα λύθρων μιαιφόνοις...ἀκωκαῖς Const.ap.Eus.*v.C.*2.51(p.62.29; M.20.1028C); *ib.*2.52(p.63.7; 1029A); **2.** *defilement,* ref. Inc. τῷ λ. τῆς ἀνθρωπίνης φύσεως καταμίγνυται Gr.Nyss.*or.catech.*14(p.62.13; M.45.40D); **3.** *blood* (= αἷμα) λύθροις λουσαμένους ἰδίοισι Paul.Sil.*ambo*.42(M.86.2253B).

λυκάβας, ὁ, *month,* tr. Vergil *ecl.*4.61 ap.Const.*or.s.c.*21(p.187.7; M.20.1301A); *year,* Nonn.*par.Jo.*11:49(M.43.848C); *ib.*18:13(892A); Paul.Sil.*Soph.*935(M.86.2154B).

λύκαινα, ἡ, *she-wolf* of Rome, rationalized as *shepherdess* λ. καλοῦσιν...τὰς χωρικὰς τὰς βοσκούσας τὰ πρόβατα *Chron.Pasch.*p.114 (M.92.297C).

λυκίσκος, ὁ, *skylight,* Marc.Diac.*v.Porph.*98 (v.l. οἰκίσκου).

***λυκόθηρ, ὁ,** *hunter of wolves,* ‡Meth.*palm.*6(M.18.393C).

***λυκουργός,** perh. f.l. for λυρουργός, *playing on the lyre* Σμύρνα ἐὸν κλαίουσα λ. [perh. ref. Homer] *Orac.Sib.*5.306.

[*]**λυκτικός,** v. λυτικός.

λῦμα, τό, *offscourings*; hence **1.** *cleansing* (in fullers' trade, of *cleansing of cloth*), fig. ἔστω ὁ...χιτὼν τῆς ψυχῆς...νήματι, μᾶλλον δὲ λύματι ἀμνησικακίας ἐξυφασμένος Jo.Clim.*scal.*28(M.88.1129C); **2.** *removal* of a curse περὶ δέματος καὶ λ. †Jo.Jej.*serm.*(M.88.1924A).

***λύμανσις, ἡ,** *destructiveness,* Sophr.H.*or.*4(M.87.3305D).

λυμαντήριος, *destroying* λ. τῆς ψυχῆς πάθη Meth.*symp.*3.5(p.56.15; M.18.101B).

λυμαντής, ὁ, *destroyer, A.Andr.*A 9(p.51.15).

λυμαντικός, *destructive*; in gen., Clem.*str.*7.6(p.25.19; M.9.447A); λ. ζῷα *Hom.Clem.*8.17; ὃν [sc. sinner] ὥσπερ τινὰ...λ. ῥίζαν ὁ τῶν ψυχῶν γεωργὸς ἐκτίλλει ‡Chrys.*hom.in Ps.51*(5.601A); ἥλιον...λ. ὀφθαλμῶν Chrys.*hom.8.2 in Jo.*(8.50B); of evil thoughts λ. βλαστήματα Eus.*l.C.*5(p.203.34; M.20.1336A); of false doctrine λ. τῆς ἀληθοῦς ἐννοίας, τὸ λέγειν Eun.*apol.*8(M.30.844A); Epiph.*haer.*36.6(p.50.5; M.41.640D); *ib.*57.2(p.346.19; 997C); of devils λ. ἐξουσίαις Clem.*str.*2.15(p.149.14; M.8.1008A); μοχθηρῶν καὶ λ. δαιμονίων Eus.*d.e.*5.2 (p.217.28; M.22.360A); δαίμονας λ. ἀνθρώπων id.*Lc.*12:11(M.24.556A).

λυμεών, ὁ, *destroyer,* of Devil and evil spirits δαίμονας...λ. ὄντας Clem.*prot.*3(p.33.4; M.8.128B); ὁ λ. τῆς ζωῆς ἡμῶν διάβολος Bas.*hom.*11.4(2.94A; M.31.378D); ἐξαπατᾶσθαι ὑπὸ τοῦ λ. Nil.*epp.*1.81(M.79.120A); ὁ κοινὸς τῆς ἀνθρωπότητος λ. Gr.Ant.*bapt.*2.10(M.88.1881A); of heretics, e.g. Paul. Sam. λ. τῆς Χριστοῦ ποίμνης Eus.*h.e.*7.27.2(M.20.705B); Arius ὦ λ. καὶ ὀλέθριε Const.ap.Gel.Cyz.*h.e.*3.19.30(M.85.1352C); Arians, id.ap.Thdt.*h.e.*1.20.10(3.800); Simon Magus, *Const. App.*6.9.3; of false teachers in gen., Chrys.*hom.73.1 in Mt.*(7.708A); of a corrupt bishop, id.*sac.*3.16(p.85.11; 1.396D).

***λυμήτης, ὁ,** = foreg., *Orac.Sib.*3.470.

λυπέω, A. *grieve*; **1.** ref. worldly grief ἐὰν ζημιωθῆτε ἑκουσίως ἢ ἀκουσίως μὴ λυπεῖσθε *T.Dan* 4.6; ἐπισυμβάντος δέ τινος μὴ ἀγανακτεῖν, μηδὲ λυπεῖσθαι Clem.*ecl.*47(p.150.4; M.9.720B); Bas.*reg.br.*192 (2.480C; M.31.1212A) cit. s. λύπη; κατὰ κόσμον...ἐὰν λυπηθῇς διὰ χρήματα, διὰ δόξαν, διὰ τὸν ἀπελθόντα, πάντα ἐκεῖνα κατὰ κόσμον. διὸ καὶ θάνατον ποιεῖ [sc. λύπη]. ὁ γὰρ διὰ δόξαν λυπούμενος φθονεῖ, καὶ ἀναγκάζεται πολλάκις ἀπολέσθαι· οἷαν καὶ ὁ Κάϊν ἐλυπήθη λύπην Chrys.*hom.15.1 in 2Cor.*(10.543E); as sinful, Herm.*mand.*10.3.3 cit. s. λύπη; τὸ ἀκαίρως λυπεῖσθαι, ἐκ τοῦ φθονεροῦ δαίμονός ἐστιν. ... ὁ λυπούμενος συνεχῶς, καὶ προσποιούμενος ἀπάθειαν, ὅμοιός ἐστιν νοσοῦντι, καὶ ὑγείαν ὑποκρινομένῳ...ὁ ἀγαπῶν τὸν κόσμον, λυπηθήσεται πολλά Ant.Mon.*hom.*25(M.89.1509A,D); **2.** ref. godly sorrow, for one's own sins, Herm.*mand.*10.2.3; Or.*hom.20.9 in Jer.*(p.191.20; M.13.521B); Bas.*reg.br.*192(2.480C; M.31.1212A); ὁ λυπούμενος ἐφ' ἁμαρτίαις, οὗτος μόνος ἀνύει τι πλέον ἀπὸ τῆς λύπης Chrys.*hom.15.1 in 2Cor.*(10.544A); οὐδεὶς γὰρ ἑαυτοῦ καταγνώσεται, ἐὰν λυπηθῇ ἐφ' ἁμαρτίᾳ *ib.15.2*(544D); for sins of others, *T.Lev.*2.4; ὑπὲρ τούτων χρὴ λυπεῖσθαι...οὕτως ἐλυπεῖτο Παῦλος ὑπὲρ τῶν ἁμαρτανόντων Chrys.*hom.15.6 in Phil.*(11.319B); **3.** of sins grieving H. Ghost, Herm.*mand.*10.2.4; v. λύπη; of grief caused to Christ by association in prayer of righteous with impenitent excommunicated offenders, *Const.App.*3.8.3.

B. *injure* τῶν λυπησάντων τὴν βασιλείαν Or.*hom.12.3 in Jer.*(p.90.20; M.13.384B); id.*comm.in Gen.*ap.Eus.*p.e.*6.11(293D; M.12.77B); Chrys.*poenit.*4.5(2.308C).

C. *hinder,* Cyr.*Ag.*9(3.637A).

D. *be vexed, angry* εἰς Ἀθανάσιον...ἐλυποῦντο Ath.*apol.sec.*6(p.92.4; M.25.257B); ἐλυπήθη πρὸς αὐτούς Jo.Mal.*chron.*2 p.43(M.97.116A); Max.*carit.*1.53(M.90.972A).

λύπη, ἡ, 1. *grief*; **a.** worldly ἀπὸ γὰρ λ. ἐγείρεται καὶ θυμὸς μετὰ ψεύδους *T.Dan* 4.6; οὐκ ἐπερρίψατε ἑαυτῶν τὰς μερίμνας ἐπὶ τὸν κύριον ...ἀλλὰ...ἐπαλαιώθητε ταῖς λ. ὑμῶν Herm.*vis.*3.11.3; ἡ [sc. λ.] τοῦ κόσμου, ὅταν τι ἀνθρώπινον καὶ τοῦ κόσμου ἄξιον ᾖ τὸ λυποῦν Bas.*reg. br.*192(2.480C; M.31.1212A); τὴν κατὰ κόσμον λ. ... ταύτην τὴν ἐπὶ βλάβῃ τῶν λυπουμένων Chrys.*hom.15.1 in 2Cor.*(10.543E); κόσμου δὲ λ., τὴν ἐπὶ ζημίᾳ χρημάτων, τὴν ἐπὶ θανάτῳ παίδων ἢ γυναικῶν, ἧς ἡ ἀμετρία τὸν θάνατον οἶδεν ἐπάγειν Thdt.*2Cor.*7:10(3.324); hence, as a sin διατί...οὐκ ἀναβαίνει ἐπὶ τὸ θυσιαστήριον ἡ ἔντευξις τοῦ λυπουμένου; ὅτι...ἡ λ. ἐγκάθηται εἰς τὴν καρδίαν αὐτοῦ· μεμιγμένη οὖν ἡ λ. μετὰ τῆς ἐντεύξεως οὐκ ἀφίησι τὴν ἔντευξιν ἀναβῆναι καθαρὰν ἐπὶ τὸ θυσιαστήριον. ὥσπερ γὰρ ὄξος οἴνῳ μεμιγμένον ἐπὶ τὸ αὐτὸ τὴν αὐτὴν ἡδονὴν οὐκ ἔχει, οὕτω καὶ ἡ λ. μεμιγμένη μετὰ τοῦ ἁγίου πνεύματος τὴν αὐτὴν ἔντευξιν οὐκ ἔχει. καθάρισον οὖν σεαυτὸν ἀπὸ τῆς λ. τῆς πονηρᾶς ταύτης...καὶ πάντες ζήσονται τῷ θεῷ ὅσοι ἂν ἀποβάλωσιν ἀφ' ἑαυτῶν τὴν λ. καὶ ἐνδύσωνται πᾶσαν ἱλαρότητα Herm.*mand.*10.3.3–4; personified, id.*sim.*9.15.3; μηδενὸς ἄλλου γενώμεθα, μὴ πνεύματος ὀργῆς, μὴ πνεύματος λύπης Or.*hom.5.2 in Jer.*(p.32.24; M.13.300A); Meth.*res.*1.30(p.263.11; M.41.1140D); ὅταν τὸ πονηρὸν πνεῦμα τῆς λ. περιδράξηται τῆς ψυχῆς, ὅλην τὴν εὐτονίαν αὐτῆς καὶ καρτερίαν παραλύει, καὶ σκοτίζει...ἀλλ' ἡμῖν εὐθὺς κατὰ τῆς λ. ἀγωνιστέον, διὰ τῆς προσευχῆς, καὶ τῆς εἰς θεὸν ἐλπίδος, καὶ τῆς ἀναγνώσεως τῶν...γραφῶν, καὶ τῆς μετὰ εὐλαβῶν ἀνθρώπων ἀναστροφῆς. ... τὴν οὐ κατὰ θεὸν λ., φαύλης ὀρέξεως ἀποτυχία συνίστησιν...λ., σκώληξ καρδίας, εἰς ἑαυτὴν ἕλκουσα ...τὸν νοῦν...ἡ λ. γὰρ ἐμπόδιον παντὸς κατορθώματος. οὐκ ἰσχύει λ., μὴ παρόντων παθῶν, λ. γὰρ παθῶν ἔλεγχος ἀψευδής. ὁ κρατῶν οὖν παθῶν, ἐκράτησε λύπης †Nil.*vit.*(M.79.1453D–1456B) ∞ ‡Ath.*ep.Cast.*2.5(M.28.896Cff.); τοῦ ἀλάστορος τοῦ τῆς λ. δαίμονος. ὅταν γὰρ τὸ... τοῦτο πνεῦμα περιδράξηται τῆς ψυχῆς, καὶ ὅλην αὐτὴν σκοτίσῃ, οὐκ εὐχὰς ἐκτελεῖν μετὰ προθυμίας συγχωρεῖ, οὔτε ἱερῶν ἀναγνωσμάτων τῇ ὠφελείᾳ ἐγκαρτερεῖν. ... λ. οὖν ἐστιν κατήφεια μὲν ψυχῆς...σκώληξ καρδίας, κατεσθίων τὴν τεκοῦσαν μητέρα Ant.Mon.*hom.*25(M.89.1509A–C); cf.Max.*loc.comm.*28(M.91.877A); **b.** godly; of grief for sins, Herm.*vis.*5.4; αὕτη οὖν ἡ λ. δοκεῖ σωτηρίαν ἔχειν, ὅτι τὸ πονηρὸν πράξας μετενόησεν id.*mand.*10.2.4; Bas.*reg.br.*192(2.480C; M.31.1212A); εἰς ἁμαρτίας μόνον ἡ λ. χρήσιμον Chrys.*hom.15.1 in 2Cor.*(10.544A); λυπηθῶμεν τοίνυν λύπην χαρᾶς μητέρα, καὶ μὴ ἡσθῶμεν χαρὰν λύπην τίκτουσαν id.*hom.15.6 in Phil.*(11.320A); τὴν...κατὰ θεὸν λ., καὶ μᾶλλον ἀσκητέον, τὴν ἐφ' οἷς ἁμαρτάνομεν, καὶ ῥαθυμοῦμεν, καὶ τὸν θεὸν παροργίζομεν. αὕτη...διεγείρει πρὸς ἐργασίαν ἀρετῶν, καὶ σπουδαίους ἀποτελεῖ †Nil.*vit.*(M.79.1456A); χαίρω, οὐ γυμνὴν τὴν λ., ἀλλὰ τῆς λ. θεωρῶν τὸν καρπόν· ἡ λ. γὰρ ἐκείνη βεβλάστηκε τὴν ἐπαινουμένην μετάνοιαν Thdt.*2Cor.*7:9(3.324) Ant.Mon.*hom.*25(M.89.1512D); ἀπαύστως εὔχομαι...συντηρηθῆναι τῷ εὐλογημένῳ μου δεσπότῃ ταύτην τὴν σωτήριον λ., τὴν ὄντως, τῶν μὲν παθῶν ἀπότομον δέσποιναν, τῶν ἀρετῶν δὲ μητέρα σεμνήν...σπέρμα γὰρ θεῖον ὑπάρχει σαφῶς ἡ κατὰ θεὸν λ.· καρπὸν ὥριμον τὴν τῶν αἰωνίων ἀγαθῶν εὐφροσύνην παρέχουσα Max.*ep.*4(M.91.413B,D); for sins of others, *T.Jud.*23.1; Chrys.*hom.15.6 in Phil.*(11.319C); in def. of ἔλεος, v.s.v.; **c.** ref. sin as causing grief to H. Ghost (Eph.4:30), Herm.*mand.*3.4; cf.*ib.*10.2.1; cf.Chrys.*hom.15.4 in Eph.*(11.115C); Ant.Mon.*hom.*25(M.89.1512C); **2.** *grievance* μὴ ἀναμένοντες τῇ λ. τῇ κατ' ἀλλήλων ἐπιδῦναι τὸν ἥλιον Thdt.*Ezech.*25:15–17(2.889); id.*Gal.*4:15(3.384); **3.** *damage, loss, Can.App.*82.

***λυπητήριος,** *causing sorrow,* Chrys.*hom.1.1 in 2Cor.4:13*(3.260C).

***λυπικός,** *painful,* Jo.D.*hom.*2.5(M.96.688A).

λύρα, ἡ, *lyre,* in metaphors of divine inspiration Ἐφραὶμ ἡ τοῦ πνεύματος λ. Thdt.*ep.*145(4.1252); id.*serm.Chrys.*(5.99); χρῆσον ἡμῖν, ὦ πάτερ Ἰωάννη, τὴν λ. τὴν σήν *ib.*(5.103); ἡ ἐκκλησιαστικὴ λ. τὸ ἀρχαῖον πλῆκτρον [i.e. Chrys.] ἐπιγινώσκει *ib.*(5.102); ref. prophets; metaphor pressed by Montanus to imply passivity and unconsciousness, Mont.*fr.*ap.Epiph.*haer.*48.4(p.224.22; M.41.861A), orthodox use of simile, ‡Just.*coh.Gr.*8(M.6.257A) citt. s. πλῆκτρον.

***λύρισμα, τό,** *tune on the lyre,* Gr.Naz.*carm.*2.1.39.44(M.37.1352A).

***λυροκτυπέω,** *strike the lyre,* Cyr.*Ps.*32:2(M.69.872A).

λυροκτύπος, *striking the lyre* λ. Δαβίδ Nonn.*par.Jo.*8:42(M.43.812B); *accompanied by the lyre* λ. αἶνον ἀείσω †Apoll.*met.Ps.*107:4 (v.l. λιγυρόκτυπον M.33.1479C).

***λυρουργός,** v. *λυκουργός.

λυσίγαμος, *dissolving marriage,* Gr.Naz.*carm.*1.2.29.186(M.37.898A).

λυσίκομος, *with unbound hair,* Mel.*pass.*29 p.5.12.

***λυσίνομος,** *lawbreaking,* Nonn.*par.Jo.*9:28(M.43.829B).

λυσιπόνιον, τό, *means of release from suffering, A.Andr.*A 13 (p.54.10); Ephr.1.138B.

λυσίπονος, *releasing from suffering*; in gen., Nonn.*par.Jo.*5:10 (M.43.785C); *ib.*7:31(809B); of serpent in wilderness, *ib.*3:14(768D); of Cross, Jo.D.*hom.*3.1(M.96.589A); eucharistic τὸ λ. ... πόμα Epiph.*exp.fid.*14(p.515.21; M.42.809D).

λύσις, ἡ, 1. *release, loosing*, from sin ἡ λ. τοῦ φθόνου διὰ φόβου θεοῦ γίνεται *T.Sym.*3.4; as essential constituent of gospel, Chrys.*hom.* *1.2 in Mt.*(7.4B); ὁ γὰρ θάνατος αὐτοῦ [sc. Χριστοῦ], τῆς ἁμαρτίας λ. id.*hom.39.2 in 1Cor.*(10.365A); id.*hom.1.2 in Philm.*(11.777C); Nonn.*par.Jo.*20:23(M.43.912B); as result of penitence, Jo.Jej. *poenit.cont.virg.*(M.88.1964A); **2.** *dissolution*; of world, *Hom.Clem.* 1.1; in death τοὺς δερματίνους χιτῶνας διὰ τοῦτο κατεσκεύασεν,... ὅπως διὰ τῆς λ. τοῦ σώματος πᾶν τὸ ἐν αὐτῷ γεννηθὲν κακὸν ἀποθάνῃ Meth.*res.*1.38(p.282.1; M.18.293B); *Hom.Clem.*1.5; ἦν...πάλαι... φοβερὸς...ὁ...θάνατος, καὶ λ. ἐνομίζετο τῆς ὅλης ἀνθρώπου φύσεως...ἡ τούτου δυναστεία Eus.*theoph.*3(p.12*.2; M.24.617A); of destruction of death through work of Christ, *ib.*(p.8*.5; 613B); Chrys.*hom.11.6 in Mt.*(7.157B); of dissolution of Mosaic Law by Christ's coming, id.*hom.78.3 in Jo.*(8.462D); **3.** *breaking* of laws, etc. ἐν τῇ λ. τῆς μιᾶς καὶ τὰς λοιπὰς ἐξ ἀνάγκης συγκαταλύεσθαι Bas.*reg.fus.*proem.2 (2.328D; M.31.893A); ref. Mt.12:5 ἐκεῖ μὲν γὰρ...ἡ περίστασις τὴν λ. ἐποίησεν [sc. of Sabbath law]· ἐνταῦθα δὲ καὶ χωρὶς περιστάσεως ἡ λ. Chrys.*hom.39.2 in Mt.*(7.433C); δακνομένους ἐπὶ τῇ τοῦ σαββάτου λ. id.*hom.37.2 in Jo.*(8.213D); **4.** *dissolution* of marriage, ref. Montanus (perh. alluding to desertion of husbands by Priscilla and Maximilla) οὗτός ἐστιν ὁ διδάξας λύσεις γάμων Apollon.ap.Eus.*h.e.* 5.18.2(M.20.476B); ἐγένετο μεταξὺ αὐτῶν [sc. Theodosius II and Eudocia] λ. καὶ ἀπομερισμός *Chron.Pasch.*p.316(M.92.804B); **5.** *reconciliation*; of a church polluted by heret. use, *Euchol.*(p.494); **6.** *solution*; hence *remedy* for difficulty or trouble, Chrys.*stat.*3.2 (2.38B); *CG–CI* 1.5 (Corinth saec. iv–v).

λυσιφάρμακον, τό, *remedy against spells* λυσιφάρμακον τοῦ ὑπ' αὐτῶν [sc. Arians] ἀπατηθέντος λαοῦ Alex.Al.*ep.Alex.*14(p.29.19; M. 18.569D).

λυσίφρων, *distracted*, Mel.*pass.*29 p.5.13.

λύσσα, ἡ, 1. *rage, madness, frenzy*; caused by demons, Nonn. *par.Jo.*8:52(M.43.821B); of persecutors, Thdt.*h.e.*1.7.5(3.755); *ib.* 3.18.2(935); **2.** of raging passions, *T.Sal.*5.8(p.23.4, one MS); λ. ἔρωτος *Hom.Clem.*2.2; ὁ ὄφις...ἐπὶ τὴν ἀκόλαστον λ. ... κατασύρεται Gr.Nyss.*or.dom.*4.4(p.84.25; M.44.1173A); of gluttony, Isid.Pel. *epp.*1.192(M.78.305C); of avarice, Nonn.*par.Jo.*13:2(M.43.860B); **3.** *rabies*; hence, met., *folly*, esp. of senseless refusal to believe, ref. paganism [sc. Ἕλληνες] κακῶν...μαθημάτων γέμοντες...τοῖς συναμιλλωμένοις, ὥσπερ λ., τοῖς πλησίον μεταδιδόασιν ὧν πεπόνθασιν αὐτοί *Hom.Clem.*4.19; τούτῳ [sc. baptismal water] ὁ μήπω προσελθεῖν θέλων ἔτι τὸ τῆς λ. φέρει πνεῦμα, οὗ ἕνεκα ἐπὶ τῇ αὐτοῦ σωτηρίᾳ ὕδατι ζῶντι προσελθεῖν οὐ θέλει *ib.*11.26; ref. Judaism, Nonn.*par.Jo.* 2:23(M.43.765A) al.; ref. heresy ταύτης τῆς λ. ἤρξατο...Ἄρειος Gr. Naz.*or.*21.3(M.35.1096A); τὴν πονηρὰν Μανιχαίων...λ. Chrys.*hom.* *58.3 in Mt.*(7.587E); Thdt.*h.e.*1.11.7(3.775); Philost.*h.e.*3.15(M.65. 508A); *ib.*9.1(568A); ref. spiritual folly of neglect of God and religion, Isid.Pel.*epp.*2.188(M.78.637C); Nonn.*par.Jo.*5:29(M.43.789B).

λυσσ-άω, *be mad, frenzied, suffer from rabies*; fig., of heretics and false teachers εἰσίν...κύνες ~ῶντες Ign.*Eph.*7.1; met., of Arians ἔσχατα ~ῶντας Ath.*ep.encycl.*5(p.173.26; M.25.232B); οἱ τὰ Ἀρείου ~ῶντες Chrys.*sac.*4.4(p.114.16; 1.409D); κατὰ τῶν ἀποστολικῶν ἐλύσσα δογμάτων Thdt.*h.e.*2.25.2(3.891).

λυσσητήρ, ὁ, as adj.; *frenzied, raging in madness* μανέντες δίκην λ. κυνῶν Epiph.*ep.Arab.*ap.*haer.*78.3(p.454.8; M.42.704A); δαίμων λ. καὶ ἄγριος Bas.Sel.*v.Thecl.*2.18(M.85.597B).

λυσσόδηκτος, *bitten by a mad dog*, Or.*comm.in Ex.*10:27(M.12. 277A); *ib.*(272A); met. πόνους...λ. Geo.Pis.*hex.*1545(M.92.1554A).

***λυσσοφόρος,** *carrying rabies* λ. κύων Ephr.2.242E.

λυσσώδης, = foreg. λ. γαστριμαργίαν Clem.*fr.*44(p.222.28); Bas. *ep.*2.6(3.74E; M.32.232C); λ. ἀκολασία id.*hom.*13.7(2.120D; M.31. 440C); λ. ὑπονοίας *Hom.Clem.*10.21; ref. Caiaphas ἔφ λ. γάμβρῳ Nonn.*par.Jo.*18:24(M.43.893B).

λυτέον, *one must solve*, Or.*Jo.*2.22(16; p.78.16; M.14.152B).

λυτήρ, ὁ, *redeemer, rescuer* of ὅλης λ. γενέθλης Nonn.*par.Jo.*17:21 (M.43.888A); from λ. τῆς πλάνης ‡Caes.Naz.*dial.*107(M.38.973).

λυτήριος, 1. *delivering, releasing* from λ. ... οἱ τοῦ θεοῦ...οἰκτιρμοὶ θανάτου καὶ ἁμαρτημάτων Meth.*symp.*10.2(p.123.13; M.18.193D); of Cross λ. τῶν ἐκ τῆς παρακοῆς κατασκευασθέντων ἡμῖν δεσμῶν id. *Porph.*3(p.506.22; M.18.401B); **2.** *being the deliverer* of με...ἀνδρομέου βιότοιο λυτήριον Nonn.*par.Jo.*17:23(M.43.888B); **3.** neut. as subst., *that which delivers, remedy* ἐν ἁμαρτίας λ., τὸ ἐκχυθὲν ὑπὲρ τῆς σωτηρίας τοῦ κόσμου αἷμα †Bas.*Is.*26(1.400B; M.30.169B); Synes. *ep.*94(M.66.1464B); ὕδωρ δὲ τὸ λ. τῶν ἁμαρτημάτων...τὸ παν(άγιον) βάπτισμα Thdt.*Is.*32:20(p.131.7; 2.311); **4.** *destructive* αὕτη γὰρ λ. γέγονε τῆς...εὐπραγίας Thphyl.*exc.Rom.*8(p.227.29; M.113.936D).

λυτικός, *destructive* φῶς λ. ... σκοτίας καὶ ἀγνοίας Or.*fr.3 in Jo.* (p.486.29); πνεῦμα ἅγιον λ. καὶ συγχωρητικὸν...ἁμαρτίας Eus.*qu. Marin.suppl.*2.9(M.22.1013B); of baptism as λ. παθῶν Gr.Naz.*or.*40. 2(M.36.360C); λυκτικός (? f.l.) in Cyr.*ador.*2(1.79E); of orthodoxy as λ. ... Ἰουδαϊσμοῦ, καὶ Ἑλληνισμοῦ, ὕστερον...καὶ τῶν αἱρέσεων ‡Just. *qu.et resp.*1(M.6.1252B).

λύτρον, τό, A. *ransom*; **1.** def. λ. ἐστὶ δόμα τι τοῖς πολεμίοις διδόμενον πρὸς τῶν ἡττωθέντων, ἢ πρὸς τοῦ τῶν ἡττωθέντων προνοουμένου ἐπὶ σωτηρίᾳ καὶ ἀφέσει τῶν αἰχμαλωτισθέντων Or.*sel.in Ps.*33:23(M. 12.1309B); **2.** of ransom or redemption for sins; **a.** of OT sacrifices as vicariously offered in place of lives of the offerers, Eus.*d.e.*1.10 (p.44.12; M.22.84D); **b.** of Christ's death as a ransom (cf. Mc.10:45; v. λύτρωσις, ἀπολύτρωσις) ἐλεῶν αὐτὸς τὰς ἡμετέρας ἁμαρτίας ἀνεδέξατο, αὐτὸς τὸν ἴδιον υἱὸν ἀπέδοτο λ. ὑπὲρ ἡμῶν, τὸν ἅγιον ὑπὲρ ἀνόμων...τὸν ἄφθαρτον ὑπὲρ τῶν φθαρτῶν *Diogn.*9.2; cf.Iren.*haer.* 5.1.1(M.7.1121B); Clem.*paed.*1.9(p.140.1; M.8.352B); τίνι δὲ ἔδωκε τὴν ψυχὴν αὐτοῦ λ. ἀντὶ πολλῶν; οὐ γὰρ δὴ τῷ θεῷ· μήτι οὖν τῷ πονηρῷ; οὗτος γὰρ ἐκράτει ἡμῶν, ἕως δοθῇ τὸ ὑπὲρ ἡμῶν αὐτῷ λ. ἡ τοῦ Ἰησοῦ ψυχή, ἀπατηθέντι...ὡς δυναμένῳ αὐτῆς κυριεῦσαι καὶ οὐχ ὁρῶντι ὅτι οὐ φέρει τὴν ἐπὶ τῷ κατέχειν αὐτὴν βάσανον. ... οὐκοῦν ἠγοράσθημεν μὲν τῷ τιμίῳ τοῦ Ἰησοῦ αἵματι, δέδοται δὲ λ. ὑπὲρ ἡμῶν ἡ ψυχὴ τοῦ υἱοῦ τοῦ θεοῦ, καὶ οὔτε τὸ πνεῦμα αὐτοῦ (πρότερον γὰρ αὐτὸ παρέθετο τῷ πατρί) [Lc.23:46]...οὔτε τὸ σῶμα (οὐδὲν γὰρ εὕρομέν πω τοιοῦτον περὶ αὐτοῦ γεγραμμένον). καὶ ἐπεὶ δέδοται ἡ ψυχὴ αὐτοῦ λ. ἀντὶ πολλῶν, οὐκ ἔμενε δὲ παρ' ἐκείνῳ ᾧ ἐδέδοτο λ. ἀντὶ πολλῶν·...πυθώμεθα γὰρ...εἰ ἡ θειότης τῆς εἰκόνος τοῦ θεοῦ..., εἰ ἐκεῖνος ἐν ᾧ ἔκτισται τὰ πάντα...λ. ἐδόθη ἀντὶ πολλῶν· καὶ τίνι ἐδόθη ἐκείνη λ. πολεμίῳ κατέχοντι ἡμᾶς αἰχμαλώτους ἕως λάβῃ τὸ λ., καὶ εἰ ἐχώρει τὸ τηλικοῦτον...ἐκεῖνος λ. ἀντὶ τῶν αἰχμαλώτων λαβεῖν. καὶ οὐ ταῦτά φημι ὡς καταφρονῶν τῆς ψυχῆς Ἰησοῦ...ἀλλὰ βουλόμενος ταύτην μὲν κατὰ τὸ ἐνδεχόμενον λ. δεδόσθαι ὑπὸ τοῦ ὅλου σωτῆρος, τὴν δὲ... θεότητα ἐκείνην μηδ' ἂν δεδυνῆσθαι λ. δοθῆναι. πλὴν...οὐ λύω τὸν Ἰησοῦν ἀπὸ τοῦ Χριστοῦ Or.*comm.in Mt.*16.8(p.498.20ff.; M.13. 1397Aff); cf. πόθεν ἀπολύεις [ref. Lc.2:29]; ἐκ τοῦ βιωτικοῦ σκάμματος· λύτρα γὰρ καὶ δεσμωτήριον ὁ βίος id.*hom.15 in Lc.*(p.105.9 where perh. punctuate λύτρα γάρ, καὶ...[i.e. Christ is ransom]); εὕρηται τὸ μέγα καὶ τίμιον λ. Ἰουδαίων ὁμοῦ καὶ Ἑλλήνων, τὸ... πάντων ἀνθρώπων ἀντίψυχον...ὁ ἀμνὸς τοῦ θεοῦ...οὗ διὰ τῆς ἐνθέου καὶ μυστικῆς διδασκαλίας πάντες ἡμεῖς...τὴν ἄφεσιν τῶν προτέρων ἁμαρτημάτων εὑράμεθα Eus.*d.e.*1.10(p.46.6; M.22.88B); λ. ἑαυτὸν ἐπιδοὺς καὶ ἀντίψυχον τῶν μελλόντων δι' αὐτοῦ σωθήσεσθαι id.*theoph.* 4(p.24*.5; M.24.633B); ἀπέθανε διὰ τὸ ὑπὲρ πάντων λ. Ath.*inc.*21.7 (M.25.133C); ὅτε δὲ ἠθέλησεν ὁ πατὴρ ὑπὲρ πάντων λύτρα δοθῆναι... τότε δὴ ὁ λόγος...ἔλαβε τὴν ἀπὸ τῆς γῆς σάρκα...ἵνα ἔχων τὸ προσφερόμενον...ἑαυτὸν προσενέγκῃ τῷ πατρί, καὶ τῷ ἰδίῳ αἵματι πάντας ἡμᾶς ἀπὸ τῶν ἁμαρτιῶν καθαρίσῃ id.*Ar.*2.7(M.26.161B); οὐχ οἷόν τε ἦν ἕτερον ἀνθ' ἑτέρου ἀντιδοῦναι λ.· ἀλλὰ σῶμα ἀντὶ σώματος, καὶ ψυχὴν ἀντὶ ψυχῆς δέδωκε, καὶ τελείαν ὕπαρξιν ὑπὲρ ὅλου ἀνθρώπου· τοῦτ' ἔστι τὸ ἀντάλλαγμα τοῦ Χριστοῦ ‡Ath.*Apoll.*1.17(M.26.1125A); ψυχὴ ἡ ἁμαρτάνουσα, αὕτη καὶ ἀποθανεῖται· ὑπὲρ ἧς τὴν ἰδίαν ψυχὴν τέθεικεν ὁ Χριστὸς λ. ἀντιδιδοὺς *ib.*1.19(1125D); Gr.Naz.*or.*30.20(p.141.9; M.36. 132A) cit. s. ἀπολύτρωσις; ἔδει...τὸν δίκαιον τρόπον ἐπινοηθῆναι τῆς ἀνακλήσεως. οὗτος δέ ἐστί τις τὸ ἐπὶ τῷ κρατοῦντι ποιήσασθαι πᾶν ὅπερ ἂν ἐθέλοι λ. ἀντὶ τοῦ κατεχομένου λαβεῖν Gr.Nyss.*or.catech.*22 (p.85.19; M.45.61A); αὐτὸν αἱρεῖται λ. τῶν ἐν τῇ τοῦ θανάτου φρουρᾷ καθειργμένων γενέσθαι *ib.*23(p.89.2; 61D); προσκομίζειν ὁ νόμος... διετάξατο λ. τῆς οἰκείας ἕκαστον κεφαλῆς, τὸ ἥμισυ τοῦ διδράχμου. ἐν δὲ ἑνὶ στατῆρι τὸ δίδραχμον ἦν. ἀλλὰ καὶ ἐν τούτῳ πάλιν...ἐσκιαγραφεῖτο Χριστός, ὁ ὑπὲρ πάντων, ὡς παρὰ πάντων, λ. ἑαυτὸν προσαγαγὼν τῷ...πατρί, καὶ νοούμενος μέν, ὡς ἐν μιᾷ δραχμῇ, πλὴν τῆς ἑτέρας οὐ κεχωρισμένως, διὰ τὸ ὡς ἐν νομίσματι τῷ ἑνὶ...τὰς δύο κεῖσθαι δραχμάς Cyr.*Jo.*3.5(4.307A); πίστιν γὰρ μόνην εἰσενεγκόντες, τῶν ἁμαρτημάτων τὴν ἄφεσιν ἐδεξάμεθα, ἐπειδὴ οἷόν τι λ. ὑπὲρ ἡμῶν ὁ ...Χριστὸς τὸ οἰκεῖον προσενήνοχε σῶμα Thdt.*Rom.*3:24(3.43); οὕτως γὰρ ἠγάπησεν ἡμᾶς ὁ...πατήρ, ὥστε τὸν υἱὸν αὐτοῦ τὸν μονογενῆ ἔδωκε λ. ὑπὲρ ἡμῶν Jo.D.*hom.*2.2(M.96.580A); **c.** of baptism μέγα τὸ ...βάπτισμα· αἰχμαλώτοις λ. Cyr.H.*procatech.*16; **d.** ref. almsgiving, of possessions as λ. ψυχῆς, Bas.*hom.*7.7(2.59C; M.31.297C); τὸ λ. ψυχῆς αὐτῶν γενέσθαι ὀφείλοντα χρήματα τῇ εἰς τοὺς ἐνδεεῖς εὐποιΐᾳ, κατακρίσεως αἰτία...πεποίηνται ‡Nil.*perist.*5.3(M.79.853C).

B. *deliverance, redemption* (without thought of ransom) ἐπὶ σοὶ ...φανερώσει κύριος τὸ λ. αὐτοῦ τοῖς υἱοῖς Ἰσραὴλ *Protev.*7.2(p.15).

***λυτροχαρής,** *rejoicing in ransom*, *Orac.Sib.*8.493.

λυτρ-όω, 1. *release, deliver*, in gen. ἀποστῆναι αὐτοὺς ἀπὸ κυρίου τοῦ ~ωσαμένου αὐτοὺς *Pss.Sal.*9.1; ἠρξάμην...ἐρωτᾶν τὸν κύριον ἵνα με ~ώσηται ἐξ αὐτοῦ [sc. τοῦ θηρίου] Herm.*vis.*4.1.7; χάριν ἔχε τῷ θεῷ τῷ...σε ἐκ...θανάτου ~ωσαμένῳ *A.Jo.*12(p.159.2); εὐλογητὸς κύριος ὁ θεός, ὃς ἐλυτρώσατο τὸν Ἰσραὴλ ἀπὸ τοῦ μὴ ἐκχέειν αὐτοὺς αἷμα ἀθῷον *A.Pil.*A 15.3(p.268); ἣν [sc. Ἑλένην] ~ωσάμενος...περιῆγε [sc. Simon Magus] Hipp.*haer.*6.19(p.146.5; M.16.3223A); of Israel λελύτρωνται διὰ Μωυσέως Or.*fr.51 in Lc.*11:24(p.257); λ. αὐτοὺς ἐκ τῆς τοῦ διαβόλου πλάνης *A.Thom.*B 46(p.39.3); ἔθνους ἀπὸ τῆς τῶν Αἰγυπτίων κακουχίας μέλλοντος ~οῦσθαι *Hom.Clem.*2.33; ἀπέστειλε τοὺς ἀποστόλους...ὅπως ~ώσῃ τὸν λαὸν αὐτοῦ ἐκ τῆς πλάνης τοῦ διαβόλου *A.Barth.*5(p.139.25); Δαυὶδ...τοῦ θανάτου ~οῦται *Const.App.*2.22.2; τοὺς πατέρας ἡμῶν...ἐλυτρώσω ἐκ χειρὸς Φαραὼ *ib.*7.36.3; ὅπως ...~ώσηται αὐτοὺς ἀπὸ τῆς παγίδος τοῦ διαβόλου *Lit.*ap.*Const.App.* 8.9.2; λ. αὐτὸ [sc. ποίμνιον] πάσης ἀγνοίας *ib.*8.11.3; πολλοὺς δὲ μεγιστᾶνας...προσφεύγειν τοῖς...μοναχοῖς καὶ ~οῦσθαι μὲν κινδύνων θανατηφόρων Nil.*epp.*1.1(M.79.81A); λ. ἡμᾶς ἀπὸ αἰσχύνης παραπτωμάτων *Lit.Jac.*(p.182.9); **2.** partic., *redeem, ransom*, *T.Lev.*2.10; πολλοὺς ἐν ἡμῖν παραδεδωκότας ἑαυτοὺς εἰς δεσμά, ὅπως ἑτέρους ~ώσονται *1Clem.*55.2; λ. τοὺς δεσμίους ἡμῶν *ib.*59.4; ἐξ ἀναγκῶν ~οῦσθαι τοὺς δούλους τοῦ θεοῦ Herm.*mand.*8.10; ἐξανδραποδισθέντες ὑπὸ...Σαρακηνῶν· ὧν οἱ μὲν μόλις ἐπὶ πολλοῖς χρήμασιν ἐλυτρώθησαν Dion.Al.ap.Eus.*h.e.*6.42.4(M.20.613B); Gel.Cyz.*h.e.*2.24.26(M.85.1304C); **3.** esp. of Christ as both rescuing and ransoming sinners αὐτὸς ~ώσεται πᾶσαν αἰχμαλωσίαν υἱῶν ἀνθρώπων *T.Zeb.*9.8; Ign.*Philad.*11.1; καρδίας...παραδεδομένας τῇ...ἀνομίᾳ ~ωσάμενος ἐκ τοῦ σκότους *Barn.*14.5; δοξάσεις τόν σε ~ωσάμενον ἐκ θανάτου *ib.*19.2; τὸ αἷμα αὐτοῦ, ᾧ ~ούμεθα Clem.*paed.*1.6(p.119.23; M.8.308C); διττὸν δὲ τὸ αἷμα τοῦ κυρίου· τὸ μέν ἐστιν αὐτοῦ σαρκικόν, ᾧ τῆς φθορᾶς λελυτρώμεθα, τὸ δὲ πνευματικόν, τοῦτ' ἔστιν ᾧ κεχρίσμεθα *ib.*2.2(p.167.29; 409B); id.*exc.Thdot.*78(p.131.18; M.9.696A); ὁ μέλλων λυτρώσασθαι τὴν Ἱερουσαλήμ, τοῦτ' ἔστι τὴν τῶν ἐν θεοσεβείᾳ διαπρεπόντων... πόλιν Or.*hom.17 in Lc.*(p.119.15); παρέστη τῷ πατρὶ ὁ σωτὴρ... καὶ ἐδεήθη περὶ τῆς ἡμετέρας αἰχμαλωσίας, ἵνα ~ωθῶμεν...ἀπὸ τοῦ ἐχθροῦ id.*hom.14.11 in Jer.*(p.116.1; M.13.417A); ὁ ~ωσάμενός με ἀπὸ τῆς πτώσεως καὶ εἰς τὸ κρεῖττόν με παραγαγών *A.Thom.* A 15(p.121.6); ὁ ἀγαθὸς ποιμὴν ὁ ἑαυτὸν ἐκδοὺς ὑπὲρ τῶν...προβάτων καὶ τὸν λύκον νικήσας καὶ ~ωσάμενος τοὺς ἰδίους ἄρνας *ib.*39(p.157.15); κυρίου, ὃς τῆς Αἰγυπτιακῆς εἰδωλολατρίας πάντας ἡμᾶς τοὺς ἐξ ἐθνῶν ἐλυτρώσατο Eus.*d.e.*4.17(p.198.16; M.22.329C); ὁ ~ούμενος τὰς πάντων ἁμαρτίας Ath.*inc.*40.2(M.25.165A); αὐτὸς μὲν οὐδὲν ἐβλάπτετο ἀναφέρων τὰς ἁμαρτίας ἡμῶν ἐπὶ τὸ ξύλον...ἡμεῖς δὲ...ἀπὸ μὲν τῶν ἰδίων παθῶν ἐλυτρούμεθα, τῆς δὲ τοῦ λόγου δικαιοσύνης ἐπληρούμεθα id.*Ar.*3.31(M.26.389C); ὁ τῷ ἰδίῳ αἵματι πᾶσαν ~ωσάμενος τὴν γῆν id.*exp.Ps.*99:3(M.27.424B); ὁ ~ωσάμενος τὸ πλάσμα τὸ ὑπὸ σοῦ δημιουργηθὲν διὰ τῆς ἐπιδημίας τοῦ...λόγου Serap.*euch.*19.1; σαρκωθεὶς ἐν τῇ...παρθένῳ ἐλυτρώσατο ἡμᾶς ἐκ τοῦ θανάτου Gr.Nyss.*Eun.*2(2 p.303.16; M.45.473D); ὑπὸ Χριστοῦ ἐλυτρώθημεν, καὶ τῷ χρυσίῳ δουλεύομεν Chrys.*hom.76.3 in Jo.*(8.449D); ὁ θεὸς ἐκινήθη...συμβαλεῖν τῷ ἀντικειμένῳ, ἵνα σε ~ώσηται ἐκ τοῦ θανάτου Mac.Aeg.*hom.*15.46 (M.34.608C); τῷ αἵματι τοῦ υἱοῦ αὐτοῦ ἐλυτρώσατό σε ἀπὸ θανάτου τῆς ἁμαρτίας Hesych.H.*Ps.tit.*102(M.27.1085C); τὴν πάντων κατὰ ψυχὴν αἰχμαλωσίαν, ἣν μέλλει ~οῦσθαι ὁ ἀνερχόμενος ἐπὶ τοῦ σταυροῦ ‡Bas.Sel.*or.*38.2(M.85.405A); of redemption at parousia ὅτε ἐλθὼν ~ώσεται ἡμᾶς, ἕκαστον κατὰ τὰ ἔργα αὐτοῦ *2Clem.*17.4; of redemption of Jesus by aeon Christ at his baptism (Valent.), Clem.*exc. Thdot.*22(p.114.13; M.9.669B); **4.** *redeem, recover* one's property from despoilers, *Pss.Sal.*8.12; **5.** *deliver* from illness, *cure*, *M.Ner.et Ach.* 19(p.19.6); of a demoniac ἐν αὐτῇ τῇ ὥρᾳ ἐλυτρώθη ὁ ἄνθρωπος *A.Barth.*3(p.133.14); **6.** *free* from condemnation, *excuse* ἐκ τοῦ διαμαρτύρασθαι οὐ ~οῦται τῆς κατακρίσεως *Schol.* in Jo.Clim.*past.*6(M.88.1181A).

λύτρωσις, ἡ, 1. *deliverance, release*; **a.** in gen. κλίνας γόνυ πρὸς κύριον...αἰτῶν λ. ἐξ αὐτῆς *T.Jos.*8.1; λ. καὶ ἐλευθερίαν τῶν...κακῶν οὐδετέρως εὑράμενοι Eus.*p.e.*2.1(51D; M.21.104B); **b.** of deliverance of Israel from Egypt, *T.Lev.*2.10; τὰ ἐπὶ τῆς προτέρας λ. ... θαυμάσια Ath.*exp.Ps.*77:13(M.27.353A); Thdr.Heracl.*Is.*48:17(M.18.1348D); **2.** *redemption* effected by Christ, sometimes in sense 1, sometimes also with idea of *ransoming* (metaphor of release of prisoners) διὰ τοῦ αἵματος τοῦ κυρίου λ. ἔσται πᾶσιν τοῖς πιστεύουσιν καὶ ἐλπίζουσιν ἐπὶ τὸν θεόν *1Clem.*12.7; ὁ γεγευμένος ἀληθείας καὶ κατηξιωμένος τῆς μεγάλης λ. Clem.*q.d.s.*34(p.182.24; M.9.640C); ὁ Χριστὸς οὐκ αἰχμαλωτισθεὶς ἦν ἐν τῷ τόπῳ τῶν αἰχμαλώτων, ἀλλὰ λυτρώσεως αὐτῶν χάριν Or.*hom.1.5 in Ezech.*(p.329.29; M.13.769B); οἱ...τὸν Χριστὸν ἐπεγνωκότες...καὶ τὴν διδασκαλίαν αὐτοῦ παραδεδεγμένοι...τὴν τῶν πολεμίων λ. εὑράμενοι Eus.*d.e.*2.3(p.87.3; M.22.153D); ὥσπερ δι' αὐτοῦ γεγόναμεν, οὕτω καὶ ἐν αὐτῷ τῶν πάντων λ. ἀπὸ τῶν ἁμαρτιῶν γένηται Ath.*Ar.*1.49(M.26.113C); τὸ μὲν γὰρ ἐλέσθαι σῶσαι τῆς ἀγαθότητός ἐστι μαρτυρία· τὸ δὲ συναλλαγματικὴν ποιήσασθαι τὴν τοῦ κρατουμένου λ. τὸ δίκαιον δείκνυσι Gr.Nyss.*or. catech.*23(p.90.12; M.45.64A); δοὺς ἀντάλλαγμα τῆς λ. τῶν ψυχῶν ἡμῶν τὸ τίμιον αὐτοῦ αἷμα id.*Eun.*2(2 p.303.18; M.45.476A); ref. Apollinarian Christology ταῦτα γὰρ ἅπαντα τὰ τῆς ἡμετέρας λ. μυστήρια ματαιοῦται, εἴ γε ὁ...υἱὸς τὴν ἀληθῆ τοῦ ἀληθοῦς ἀνθρώπου καὶ τὴν ὅλην φύσιν ἀνειληφὼς οὐ πιστεύεται Leo Mag.*ep.*35(p.41.10; M.*PL.*54.806B); σαφεστάτη...τῆς λ. ἀπόδειξις, τὸ ἐν μεθέξει γενέσθαι πνεύματος ἁγίου Proc.G.*Is.*59:19–21(M.87.2616B); **3.** esp. associated with baptism μετὰ τὴν σφραγῖδα καὶ τὴν λ. Clem.*q.d.s.*39(p.185.12; M.9.644C); τῆς καθ' ὅλου γενησομένης τῶν ἁμαρτημάτων λ. τὴν διὰ τοῦ ἁγίου βαπτίσματος προφήτειαν Ath.*exp.Ps.*50 proem.(M.27.237B); τὴν διὰ τοῦ ἁγίου βαπτίσματος λ. Cyr.*Is.*5.6(2.903A); **4.** of redemption obtained through almsgiving ἐὰν ἔχῃς διὰ τῶν χειρῶν σου, δώσεις λ. ἁμαρτιῶν σου *Did.*4.6; *Const.App.*7.12.2; by works διὰ τῶν χειρῶν σου ἐργάσῃ εἰς λ. ἁμαρτιῶν σου *Barn.*19.10; **5.** Gnost.; of redemption obtained by 'spiritual' baptism connected with chrismation (opp. baptism in water), corresponding to descent on Jesus of aeon Christ at Jordan ἄλλοι δὲ πάλιν τὴν λ. ἐπιλέγουσιν οὕτως· τὸ ὄνομα...ὃ ἐνεδύσατο Ἰησοῦς...Χριστοῦ ζῶντος διὰ πνεύματος ἁγίου, εἰς λ. ἀγγελικήν Iren.*haer.*1.21.3(M.7.664A); ἐν τῇ χειροθεσίᾳ λέγουσιν ἐπὶ τέλους 'εἰς λ. ἀγγελικήν', τουτέστιν ἣν καὶ ἄγγελοι ἔχουσιν ἵν' ᾖ ⟨ὁ⟩ βεβαπτισμένος ὁ τὴν λ. κομισάμενος τῷ αὐτῷ ὀνόματι, ᾧ καὶ ὁ ἄγγελος αὐτοῦ προβεβάπτισται. ἐβαπτίσαντο δὲ ἐν ἀρχῇ οἱ ἄγγελοι ἐν λ. τοῦ ὀνόματος τοῦ ἐπὶ τὸν Ἰησοῦν ἐν τῇ περιστερᾷ κατελθόντος καὶ λυτρωσαμένου αὐτόν. ἐδέησεν δὲ λυτρώσεως καὶ τῷ Ἰησοῦ Clem.*exc. Thdot.*22(p.114.9; M.9.669A); ref. Ascodruti πνευματικὴν...δεῖ καὶ τὴν λ. ὑπάρχειν· διὰ τοῦτο...οὐδὲ ἐπιτελεῖται παρ' αὐτοῖς τοῦ βαπτίσματος τὸ μυστήριον. λ. γὰρ καλοῦσι τὴν τῶν ὅλων ἐπίγνωσιν Thdt.*haer.*1.10(4.302); **6.** exeg. Jud.1:15 τί ἐστι, δός μοι λ. ὕδατος, καὶ λ. μετεώρων, καὶ λ. ταπεινῶν; οἱ περὶ τὸν Σύμμαχον ἀρδείαν ὕδατος... ᾔτησε τοίνυν ἀρδείαν ὕδατος Thdt.*qu.3 in Jud.*(1.322) i.e. confusion of גְּאֻלָּה with גֻּלָּה.

***λυτρωτήριος,** *redemptive*, *Chron.Pasch.*p.9(M.92.85B).

λυτρωτής, ὁ, *deliverer, redeemer*; **1.** of Messiah προφῆται...λ. καὶ βασιλέα Ἰουδαίων ἥξειν αὐτὸν οὐχὶ δὲ τῶν ἀλλοφύλων...κατήγγειλαν Eus.*p.e.*1.2(5D; M.21.29B); **2.** of Christ as deliverer βοηθὸν γὰρ ἐκεῖνον καὶ λ. καλοῦμεν, οὗ καὶ τὴν τοῦ ὀνόματος ἰσχὺν καὶ τὰ δαιμόνια τρέμει Just.*dial.*30.3(M.6.540B); ὁ τοῦ καθαιμάξαντος ἑαυτὸν ἀνθρώπου λ. *A.Jo.*77(p.189.21); τὸν σωτῆρα καὶ λ. πάλαι μὲν ἐξ Αἰγύπτου, νῦν δὲ δαιμόνων λατρείας Or.*fr.101 in Lam.*4:6(p.271.18; M.13.652D); compared with Moses as deliverer from Egypt, id.*fr.51 in Lc.*11:24(p.257); abs. τὸν λ. id.*schol.in Lc.*1:36(M.17.320C); λ. τῶν αἰχμαλώτων *A.Thom.*A 10(p.114.8); ὁ λ. καὶ βοηθός *ib.*60(p.177.11); *ib.*167(p.281.6); λ. ... τῶν ψυχῶν *A.Andr.*A 16(p.56.23); Eus.*h.e.*10.1.1(M.20.841B); id.*Ps.*130 proem.(M.24.25A); λ. καὶ σωτῆρος ἁπάντων id.*qu.Steph.*10.1(M.22.920A); τὸν ἀναβησόμενον εἰς τοὺς οὐρανοὺς...λ. Cyr.H.*catech.*2.12; ref. reason for Inc. ἐπεζήτει τὸν λ. ὁ αἰχμάλωτος Gr.Nyss.*or.catech.*15(p.63.15; M.45.48B); ἀρχιερέως καὶ λ. τῶν ψυχῶν *Const.App.*5.6.10; τοῦ σωτῆρος καὶ λ. τῶν ἐλπιζόντων ἐπ' αὐτόν *ib.* 5.16.5; as ὁ ἀληθινὸς λ. typified by Moses, Mac.Aeg.*hom.*11.6(M.34.548D); οὐδὲν βλάψει ἁμαρτία τοὺς ἐν ἐλπίδι καὶ πίστει τὸν λ. ἐκδεχομένους, ὃς παραγενόμενος μεταβάλλει τοὺς λογισμοὺς τῆς ψυχῆς *ib.*31.2 (729B); τὸν λ. ἐπιζητεῖν καὶ τῆς ἀφέσεως ἐπιθυμεῖν Chrys.*hom.10.2 in Mt.*(7.141B); Cyr.*Is.*1.1(2.29B); *ib.*1.5(146A); id.*Os.*72(3.107C); σωτῆρα καὶ λ. καὶ εὐεργέτην *Lit.Jac.*(p.180.16); τὸν λ. τοῦ κόσμου Jo.D.*carm.assumpt.Chr.*(M.96.845D); in baptism λ. δέ, ὡς διὰ τῆς παλιγγενεσίας τοῦ...βαπτίσματος, τῆς μὲν προτέρας ἐλευθεροῦντα φθορᾶς, καὶ τῆς τῶν δαιμόνων δουλείας λυτρούμενον Thdt.*Ps.*18:15(1.724); as deliverer of souls in Hades ὁ τῶν νεκρῶν εὐαγγελιστὴς καὶ τῶν ψυχῶν λ. Hipp.*Cant.Mos.*1(p.83.6; M.10.609D); *cat.Mt.*11:3(p.84.20); **3.** of Ὅρος in Valent. system συλλυτρωτήν [for σταυρὸν καὶ λ.] Iren.*haer.*1.2.4(M.7.460A); **4.** of Const. as greeted on entry into Rome λ. ... σωτῆρά τε καὶ εὐεργέτην Eus.*v.C.*1.39(p.26.10; M.20.953C).

***λύττια, ἡ,** *madness, frenzy*; of lust, Isid.Pel.*epp.*3.11(M.78.736C).

λυχναῖος, = λυχνιαῖος, Jo.Mosch.*prat.*51(M.87.2908A).

λυχναψία, ἡ, *lighting of lamps*; **1.** in worship; pagan, *T.Sal.*9.7 (p.37.in.); of Messalians μετὰ πολλῆς λ. ... συναθροιζόμενοι Epiph.*haer.*80.2(p.486.6; M.42.757B); **2.** partic. = λυχνικόν *evening office*, Socr.*h.e.*5.22.54(M.67.640A); ἐν Καισαρείᾳ τῆς Καππαδοκίας καὶ ἐν Κύπρῳ ἐν ἡμέρᾳ σαββάτου καὶ κυριακῆς ἀεὶ...μετὰ τὴν λ. οἱ πρεσβύτεροι καὶ ἐπίσκοποι τὰς γραφὰς ἑρμηνεύουσιν *ib.*5.22.55(640A); **3.** as gen. sign of rejoicing, Cyr.*ep.*28(p.118.8; 5^2.87D); *Chron.Pasch.*p.309 (M.92.788A).

λυχνεύς, λ. λίθος *shining stone*, name given to *Parian marble*, Clem.*prot.*4(p.36.4; M.8.136B).

λυχνία, ἡ, *candlestick, lampstand*; **1.** in gen., ref. pagan accusations of immoral behaviour at Christian meetings λυχνίας...· ἀνατροπὴν καὶ τὰς ἀνέδην μίξεις καὶ ἀνθρωπείων σαρκῶν βορὰς Just. *1apol.*26.7(M.6.369A); **2.** in Temple, in objector's allusion to OT ritual εἰ λύχνοις καὶ λυχνίαις τέρπεται, καὶ τίς τοὺς φωστῆρας ἔταξεν ἐν οὐρανῷ; *Hom.Clem.*2.44; εἰς δὲ τὴν πρώτην σκηνὴν διαγράφει ἐν μὲν τῷ νότῳ τὴν λ., ἑπτὰ λύχνους ἔχουσαν...τύπον ὑπάρχουσαν τῶν φωστήρων Cosm.Ind.*top.*2(M.88.92B); *ib.*5(209B); ref. Zach.4:2 as type of Christ's humanity, Sever.*Abr.*1(M.56.554) cit. s. ἑπτάφωτος; **3.** *sanctuary lamp* in church, Ath.*ep.encycl.*4(p.173.6; M.25.229C); τῷ καιρῷ τῷ δέοντι πλὴν νέων χίδρων ἢ σταφυλῆς μὴ ἐξὸν ἔστω προσάγεσθαί τι πρὸς τὸ θυσιαστήριον, καὶ ἔλαιον εἰς τὴν λ. καὶ θυμίαμα τῷ καιρῷ τῆς...ἀναφορᾶς *Can.App.*3; its oil used for unction of sick, Chrys.*hom.32.6 in Mt.*(7.373C); cf.*Typicon Sabae* (Venice, 1615, p.15); **4.** met., of bishop's chair ἅπτει λύχνον ὁ θεὸς ἱερέα, καὶ τίθησιν ἐπὶ λυχνίας τῆς ἑαυτοῦ φωτοφόρου καθέδρας Isid.Pel.*epp.*1.32(M.78.201C); τῆς ἑπταφώτου λ. τῶν δογμάτων πυρσοὺς ἀνάπτων αἱρέσεις καταφλέγεις Geo.Pis.*carm.*11.1; of BMV, Procl.CP *or.*6.17 (M.65.753B); Thdr.Stud.*nativ.BMV* 7(M.96.696C); of the Church, ref. Zach.4:2f. λ. ... ἐστιν ὁλόχρυσος, ἡ τοῦ θεοῦ...ἐκκλησία...ἀκίβδηλος...καὶ τοῦ ἀληθινοῦ φωτὸς δεκτική Max.*qu.Thal.*63(M.90.665B); **5.** = λύχνος, Jo.Thess.*dorm.BMV* 2.13(p.428.1).

λυχνιαῖος, *of a lamp*, Meth.*symp.*10.2(p.123.13; M.18.193D); Bas. *hex.*3.7(1.29A; M.29.69A); fig., of grace quenched by worldly preoccupations καθάπερ τις ἐπὶ τοῦ λ. ... φωτὸς ὕδωρ κατασκεδάσας... ἔσβεσε τὸ φῶς Chrys.*hom.11.1 in 1Thess.*(11.502C); of Law opp. Christ's teaching ἡλίου...φανέντος οὐκ ἔτι δυνατὸν τὸ λ. ἐνεργεῖν φῶς id.*hom.59.1 in Gen.*(4.569D); μηκέτι προσεδρεύειν τῷ λ. φωτὶ τοῦ νόμου, ἀλλὰ τῷ ἀληθινῷ τὰς ψυχὰς καταυγάζειν Thdt.*Is.*2:5(p.14.27; 2.186); ἐθνικοί...μηδὲ...ἔχοντες τὸ λ. φῶς *ib.*9:2(232); of present life as λ. φῶς opp. heaven as ἥλιος, Chrys.*hom.56.3 in Jo.*(8.330C); εἰ... ἥλιος ἀπὸ λ. φωτὸς οὐκ ἂν λάβοι προσθήκην...ἐγὼ [sc. Christ] τῆς ἀνθρωπίνης ἀφέξω δεηθῆναι δόξης *ib.41.1*(243D).

***λυχνικός**, *at lamp-lighting, evening*; **1.** of prayers and hymns in gen. προσευχαὶ ἑωθιναί, λ. τε ἅμα ψαλμοὶ καὶ προσευχαί Epiph.*exp.fid.* 23(p.524.10; M.42.829A); Chrys.*hom.18.5 in Ac.*(9.150D); *V.Marth.* (404E); **2.** partic. of hymn φῶς ἱλαρόν, called also ἐπιλύχνιος εὐχαριστία, Bas.*Spir.*73(3.62B; M.32.205A); said to have been composed by martyr Athenogenes (saec. ii–iii), *ib.*; during singing of which unction with blessed oil took place, *Euchol.*(p.511); **3.** of evening service, vespers ἐν ἀρχῇ πάσης ἑωθινῆς τε καὶ λ. τελετῆς πρῶτον τῆς παλαιᾶς ψάλλονται οἱ ψαλμοί ‡Sophr.H.*liturg.*12(M.87.3992C); ‡Germ.CP *contempl.*(M.98.401D); neut. (sing. and plur.) as subst., *office of lamp-lighting, vespers* (Lat. *lucernarium*) or more exactly the first part of the office, taking place after sunset when lamps are lit to give light and for symbolic reasons; office beginning with Ps.103, cf. ἑσπέρας γενομένης συναθροίσεις τὴν ἐκκλησίαν... καὶ μετὰ τὸ ῥηθῆναι τὸν ἐπιλύχνιον ψαλμὸν *Const.App.*8.35.2; office consisting in Pachomian monasteries of six prayers each accompanied by a psalm, *V.Pach.*5(Nau, *PO* 4 p.428) but cf. ἐν τῷ λ. δώδεκα [sc. εὐχάς] Pall.*h.Laus.*32(p.92.5; M.34.1100B); cf.Ammon. Aeg.*ep.*22(p.110.31); one of seven daily offices, ‡Chrys.*hom.3 in Ps. 118*(5.716E); held in church, CTyr.(518)*act.*(p.89.1; H.2.1360A); preceded in monasteries by meal and followed by retirement to individual cells, ‡Bas.*poen.mon.*41(2.529C; M.31.1312B); Dor.*doct.*10. 2(M.88.1725B); Cyr.S.*v.Sab.*60(p.161.10); reckoned as first service of eccl. day (beginning at sunset), hence kneeling, forbidden on Sundays, begins at λ. on Sunday evening, CTrull.*can.*90; at beginning of service during introductory psalm (Ps.103) priest reads secretly seven special prayers, whether or not the vespers constitute first part of liturgy of presanctified, Thdr.Stud.*praesanct.* (M.99.1688C); *Lit.Praesanct.*(p.345.11); *Euchol.*(p.2); *ib.*(p.28); litany said during service, Eustrat.*v.Eutych.*94(M.86.2380B); when connected with liturgy of presanctified a prayer for catechumens also being said, *Lit.Praesanct.*(p.346.20); before dedication of new church this service was held in neighbouring church where relics destined for new church were deposited, *Euchol.*(p.661); acc. some texts baptism took place μετὰ τὸ γενέσθαι τὴν εἴσοδον τοῦ λ. *ib.*(p.291).

λυχνίτης, λ. λίθος *red lychnite*, *T.Sal.*C 11.9(p.84.10).

λυχνοκαΐα, ἡ, *lighting of lamps* as act of worship, Christians being accused of so honouring image of Constantine, Philost.*h.e.* 2.17(M.65.480A).

λύχνος, ὁ, *lamp, light*;

A. lit; **1.** etym. λ. λέγεται παρὰ τὸ λύειν τὸ νύχος, τουτέστι τὸ σκότος *Doct.Patr.*33(p.262.27); **2.** used in worship as mark of devotion; **a.** pagan, *Hom.Clem.*10.24; λατρεία δέ ἐστι διαβόλου...τὸ ἅπτειν λύχνους, ἢ θυμιᾶν παρὰ πηγὰς ἢ ποταμοὺς Cyr.H.*catech.*19.8; *Can.App.*71 cit. infra; used in magic *T.Sal.*6.10(p.28.1); **b.** Jewish; in OT cultus, *Hom.Clem.*2.44 cit. s. λυχνία; seven lamps signifying days of week, Cosm.Ind.*top.*1(M.88.92A) v. λυχνία; in synagogue worship εἴ τις Χριστιανὸς ἔλαιον ἀπενέγκοι εἰς ἱερὸν ἐθνῶν ἢ εἰς συναγωγὴν Ἰουδαίων ἢ ἐν ταῖς ἑορταῖς αὐτῶν λύχνους ἅψῃ, ἀφοριζέσθω *Can.App.*71; **c.** Christian, at baptism ἐκέλευσε προσενεγκεῖν αὐτοὺς ἔλαιον, ἵνα διὰ τοῦ ἐλαίου δέξονται τὴν σφραγῖδα. ἤνεγκαν οὖν τὸ ἔλαιον, καὶ λ. ἀνῆψαν πολλούς· νὺξ γὰρ ἦν. καὶ...ὁ ἀπόστολος ἐσφράγισεν αὐτοὺς *A.Thom.*A 26(p.142.6); *ib.*27(p.143.6); cf.Gr. Naz.*or.*40.46(M.36.425A); cf.*ib.*45.2(624C); before portrait, *A.Jo.*27 (p.165.26).

B. met.; of Christ, *Hymn*.ap.*A.Jo.*95(p.198.11); ὁ λ. ὁ τὸ ἀληθινὸν ὑποδεξάμενος φῶς· καλεῖ δὲ οὕτω τὴν τοῦ δούλου μορφὴν Thdt.*Ps.* 117:29(1.709); of Jo. Bapt. (opp. Christ as ἥλιος or φῶς), Or.*fr.17 in Jo.*(p.496.23); Thdt.*Ps.*118:105(1.1464); Nonn.*par.Jo.*5:35(M. 43.789C); τὸ βρέφος...προσεκύνησε τῷ δεσπότῃ...ὁ λ. τῷ φωτὶ τῷ ἀκοιμήτῳ Chrysipp.*enc.in Jo.Bapt.*(p.33.2); of Magi οἱ τῆς ἀνατολῆς λ. Rom.Mel.(*BZ* 24 p.6; *AS* 1 p.6); of Law (opp. Christ as sun of righteousness), Thdt.*Ps.*118:105(1464); ref. Mt.25:1ff. οἱ λ. ὑμῶν μὴ σβεσθήτωσαν *Did.*16.1; τοὺς λ. ἅψαντες τῶν καρδιῶν, γρηγορήσωμεν ἐντόνως Jo.Thess.*dorm.BMV* 2.4(p.410.26); λ. ἐντολή, νόμος δὲ φῶς CNic.(787)*can.*6.

λύω, **A.** *loose, release*; **1.** *let slip, utter* τὸν λόγον λ. Mac.Mgn. *apocr.*3.27(p.116.20); **2.** abs., *set sail* λ. ἐκ Βενδιδείου Synes.*ep.*4(M. 66.1328B); **3.** *deliver* λύσατέ με ἀπὸ τῆς κρίσεως *T.Jos.*15.6.

B. *dissolve*; **1.** in death εἰ δὲ λυθείην, ποιμένος οἶδε τύχοιεν ἀρείονος Gr.Naz.*carm.*2.1.19.101(M.37.1279A); Epiph.*anc.*100(p.121.14; M.43. 197C); **2.** *relax* μηδὲ λύε τὸν τῆς ψυχῆς τόνον ἐν εὐωχίᾳ Clem.*fr.*44 (p.222.23); pass., of calm sea, Gr.Naz.*or.*28.27(p.63.10; M.36.64C); **3.** *put an end to*; **a.** in gen.; c. acc., also c. genit. θορύβου λ. Anast. *mort.*19(p.246); **b.** partic., *break* a fast οὐ δεῖ ἐν τεσσαρακοστῇ τῇ ὑστέρᾳ ἑβδομάδι τὴν πέμπτην λύειν, καὶ ὅλην τὴν τεσσαρακοστὴν ἀτιμάζειν CLaod.*can.*50 = CTrull.*can.*92; Ephr.3.452C; μὴ χάριν παρουσίας φίλου λύσῃς τὴν νηστείαν Eus.Al.*serm.*1(M.86.324A); Eutych.*pasch.*3(M.86.2396B); καλόν ἐστι...ἐὰν παραβάλῃ ἡμῖν τις λύειν ἐκ τοῦ οἴνου; ἀπεκρίθη...οὔ. λέγομεν...καὶ πῶς οἱ ἀρχαῖοι ἔλυον πατέρες; ἀπεκρίθη...οἱ πατέρες...ἴσχυον καὶ λῦσαι καὶ πάλιν δῆσαι· ἡ δὲ ἡμετέρα γενεὰ...οὐκ ἔστιν ἱκανὴ λῦσαι καὶ δῆσαι· ἀλλ' ἐὰν λύσωμεν, οὐκ ἔτι κρατοῦμεν τὴν ἄσκησιν ἡμῶν Jo.Mosch.*prat.*162(M.87.3029C); **c.** *break* law, *LS*; sabbath, Chrys.*hom.49.2 in Jo.*(8.290C); *ib.49.3* (292B); Nonn.*par.Jo.*5:18(M.43.788B); **d.** *violate* a boundary ὅριον οὐκ ἔλυσα *T.Isach.*7.5; **e.** *end* travail; *be delivered*, of child τὰς ὠδῖνας ἔλυσεν Chrys.*hom.8.1 in Mt.*(7.118B); τὰς αὐτὰς λῦσαι ὠδῖνας *be born of same mother*; **i.** lit., id.*hom.16.5 in Rom.*(9.610E); id *hom. 34.4 in 1Cor.*(10.315B); **ii.** met., of spiritual brotherhood of those born by one baptism as children of God τὰς αὐτὰς πάντες ἐλύσαμεν ὠδῖνας id.*hom.32.7 in Mt.*(7.375A); id.*hom.8.8 in Rom.*(509E); **4.** *forgive, absolve* sins αὐτῷ [sc. Clement] μεταδίδωμι τὴν ἐξουσίαν τοῦ δεσμεύειν καὶ λύειν...δήσει γὰρ ὃ δεῖ δεθῆναι, καὶ λύσει ὃ δεῖ λυθῆναι, ὡς τὸν τῆς ἐκκλησίας εἰδὼς κανόνα *Clem.ep.*2(M.2.36B) or perh. here in sense of *allow* opp. forbid; *ib.*6(41A); σὺ δὸς ἐξουσίαν τῷ προκαθεζομένῳ λύειν ἃ δεῖ λύειν καὶ δεσμεῖν ἃ δεῖ δεσμεῖν *Hom.Clem.*3.27; ἐβαπτίσθη μὲν ὡς ἄνθρωπος, ἀλλ' ἁμαρτίας ἔλυσεν ὡς θεός Gr.Naz.*or.* 29.20(p.104.7; M.36.100C); γνώριζε, ὦ ἐπίσκοπε, τὸ ἀξίωμά σου, ὅτι ὡς τοῦ δεσμεῖν ἐκληρώσω τὴν ἐξουσίαν, οὕτως καὶ τοῦ λύειν *Const. App.*2.18.3; of bishop λύων τοὺς ἡμαρτηκότας *ib.*2.20.10; *ib.*2.34.4; ἃ...θεοῦ μόνου ἐστὶν ἴδια, τό τε ἁμαρτήματα λῦσαι, καὶ τὸ ἀπερίτρεπτον τὴν ἐκκλησίαν ποιῆσαι...ἐπαγγέλλεται δώσειν Chrys.*hom.54.2 in Mt.* (7.548C); ref. Levitical priesthood ἐν χειρὶ γὰρ ἱερωσύνης ἐλύετο καὶ ἐδεσμεύετο τὰ ἁμαρτήματα Epiph.*anc.*97(p.118.10; M.43.193A); εὐχὴ ἐπὶ τοῦ ἐν δεσμῷ ὄντος ὑπὸ ἱερέως καὶ λυομένου †Jo.Jej.*poenit.*(M.88. 1917B); **5.** *absolve* from penalty ἐλύθη ἐκ τοῦ ἀφορισμοῦ Jo.Mosch. *prat.*192(M.87.3072C); εὐχὴ λύουσα αὐτὸν ἐκ τοῦ ἀφορισμοῦ *Euchol.* (p.531); **6.** *remit* sentence or penalty, Athenag.*res.*19(p.72.26; M.6. 1013A); Marcell.*fr.*52 ap.Eus.*Marcell.*2.2(p.41.25; M.24.793B).

λωβ-άω, **1.** *damage*; act., *Orac.Sib.*11.71; τὴν πίστιν ~ήσουσι, μᾶλλον δὲ ἑαυτούς Epiph.*haer.*69.25(p.174.32; M.42.211B); ref. Marcion and gospel of S. Luke ἐλώβησε καὶ...παρέκοψε πολλὰ τῶν μελῶν *ib.*42.13(p.181.21; M.41.813A); med., Meth.*lepr.*6(p.458.2); Thdt. *provid.*1(4.492); of moral damage τὴν ἀγάπην...~ήσασθαι Meth. *symp.*11(p.130.10; M.18.205B); Thdt.*provid.*9(635); id.*ep.*146(4. 1267); τοῖς οὐδέπω...ἐσχηκόσι...ἐλωβᾶτο τὸ...γινόμενον id.*1Cor.* 7:39(3.213); abs. τί ~ᾶται; *what harm does it do?* id.*eran.*2(4.84); **2.** perf. ptcpl. pass.; **a.** *damaged* ἄγαλμα...λ. Meth.*res.*1.43(p.289.15;

M.18.272A); **b.** of persons, *maimed, mutilated,* Epiph.*haer*.75.1 (p.333.25; M.42.504C); τοῖς τὰ σώματα λ. Chrys.*hom.66.3 in Mt*.(7. 658B); ὁ πρεσβύτερος καὶ ἀφηγούμενος τοῦ πτωχείου τῶν λ. Pall.*h. Laus*.6(p.23.9; M.34.1018D); Cyr.*Lc*.14:12(M.72.788B); partic. of lepers, *Apophth.Patr*.(M.65.252C); Thdt.*h.e*.5.19.2(3.1051); Aen. *dial*.(M.85.921A); **c.** met., of those *harmed* by sin, Meth.*res*.1.42 (p.289.2; M.41.1112B).

λώβη, ἡ, *damage*; **1.** in gen. ἀδικία...λ. ἐργάζεται Thdt.*Ps*. 118:122(1.1469); **2.** *maiming, damage to body,* Athenag.*res*.21(p.75. 3; M.6.1016D); *Can.App*.77; Chrys.*hom.33.6 in Mt*.(7.386B); *ib.69. 2*(682B); **3.** esp. of leprosy, Isid.Pel.*epp*.1.28(M.78.200C); Leont.H. *Nest*.1.6(M.86.1424A); **4.** of effect of false doctrine, Thdt.*h.e*.4.1.6(3. 946); *ib*.5.6.3(1023); Gel.Cyz.*h.e*.3.16.29.

***λώβημα, τό,** *flaw,* Meth.*res*.1.43(p.290.15; M.18.272B).

λώβησις, ἡ, *damage, mutilation,* physical λ. ... λοβοῦ ὠτίου †Bas. *bapt*.1.2.1(2.630A; M.31.1528A); πῶς ἐνδέχεται...ἐν βασιλείᾳ οὐρανῶν ἐν σώματι λ. γίνεσθαι; Epiph.*haer*.58.2(p.359.19; M.41.1013A); partic. of leprosy, *ib*.55.9(p.337.14; 988D); met., *ib*.59.9(p.374.13; 1032B); τῶν λ. τῶν...παρατραπόντων λόγων Max.*ambig*.(M.91.1400B).

λωβητήρ, ὁ, as adj., *damaging,* Nonn.*par.Jo*.8:22(M.43.816C); *ib*. 8:48(821A).

λωβήτωρ, ὁ, as adj., = foreg., Nonn.*par.Jo*.8:23(M.43.816C).

λωβός, *maimed, T.Sal*.12.2(p.41n. conj. for βωβά); *Nomoc*.94; Thphn.*chron*.p.61(M.108.205C); of a leper, ‡Amph.*v.Bas*.(p.201A).

***λωβόω,** *damage physically, maim*; of leprosy, cf. λωβάω, †Gregent.*leg.Hom*.61(M.86.613D).

λωδίκιον, τό, *cloak,* Epiph.*haer*.68.3(p.143.4; M.42.188B).

λῶμα, τό, 1. *necklace,* Clem.*paed*.3.3(p.246.31; M.8.263C); **2.** *fringe* of high priest's robes, †Bas.*Is*.18(1.466E; M.30.321C); ‡Chrys.*leg*.(6.411B); **3.** *thread* μὴ στρέφε οὕτως τὸ λ. [i.e. in weaving] *V.Pach.Σ* 79(p.256.23); Thdr.Stud.*poen*.1.110(M.99.1748C).

λωποδυσία, ἡ, *waylaying and robbery,* Clem.*q.d.s*.42(p.188.21; M.9.648C).

λωποδύτης, ὁ, *robber, highwayman,* of Satan λ. τῆς ἀρετῆς Thdt. *h.rel*.3(3.1141); of devils ψυχῶν λ. id.*Ps*.118:11(1.1441).

***λωρίζω,** *beat with thongs,* Leont.N.*v.Sym*.46(M.93.1725D).

***λωρικάτος,** (Lat. *loricatus*) *in armour, wearing a cuirass,* Thphn. *chron*.p.157(M.108.425B, v.l. λουρ-).

λωρίκιον, τό, *cuirass,* Thphn.*chron*.p.266(M.108.661A; v.l. λουρ-); *ib*.p.324(784B).

λωρί(ο)ν, τό, *strip of leather, thong*; as shoe-lace, Chrys.ap.Phot. *cod*.274(M.104.237C) cit. s. σφαιρωτήρ; Gr.Mag.*dial*.(tr.Zach.)3.20 (M.*PL*.77.270D); of reins, Jo.Mal.*chron*.4 p.89(M.97.173A); of laces on vestments τὰ εἰς τὰ μανίκια λ. δεικνύουσι τὰ δεσμὰ τῶν χειρῶν αὐτοῦ ‡Sophr.H.*liturg*.7(M.87.3988B); τὰ λ. τοῦ στιχαρίου εἰσὶ τὰ ἐν τῇ χειρὶ ἐμφαίνοντα τὸν δεσμὸν τοῦ Χριστοῦ...τὰ λ. εἰς τὰ πλαγιά εἰσι τὸ αἷμα τὸ...ἐκ τῆς πλευρᾶς ‡Germ.CP *contempl*.(M.98.393C); ‡Bas. *h.myst*.17(p.262.3); *ib*.18(p.262.6); on monk's hood signifying blood and water, *ib*.24(p.263.7) cit. s. κουκούλλιον; *Euchol*.(p.438); of strip of skin, Gr.Mag.*dial*.(tr.Zach.)3.13(M.*PL*.77.242B,C).

***λωρόπους (λουρ-),** *with twisted legs* Μηνᾶν...τὴν λουρόποδα Sophr.H.*mir.Cyr.et Jo*.7(M.87.3436B); ταυρίνου λ. *ib*.43 tit.(3588A); *ib*.(3588C).

λωροτομ-έω, *cut strips,* of skin, pass. κελεύει...~εῖσθαί σε ἀπὸ τοῦ σώματός σου...λώρους ἑπτά *M.Bas.Presb*.15(p.17*A).

λῶταξ, ὁ, *pimp, Const.App*.8.32.11; Chrys.*hom.13.3 in Eph*.(11. 99C, conj. for λωβούς, λω...τούς).

λωτάριον, τό, *lotus,* Cosm.Ind.*top*.2(M.88.117B).

λωτός, ὁ, ? = λῶταξ, Chrys.*hom.10.5 in Col*.(11.403D, v.l. λωβοῦ; εἴλωτος Gaume).

M

***μαβλησία, ἡ,** *procuration, pandering,* †Jo.Jej.*serm*.(M.88.1924A).

***μαγαρίζω,** *become a Mohammedan* εἰ δὲ τυχὸν ἁρπαχθῇ ὑπὸ ἔθνους, καὶ μαγαρισθῇ, εὐλόγησον αὐτῷ *Nomoc*.48; Thphn.*chron*. p.334(M.108.805C).

***μαγαρικόν, τό,** *earthen vessel, Mir.Artem*.32(p.45.23).

***μαγαρισμός, ὁ, 1.** *Mohammedanism* ἦλθεν ὁ Μουχαμὲθ κηρύττων τὸν μ. Jo.D.*disp*.8(M.94.1596C); **2.** *pollution,* †Jo.Jej.*serm*.(M.88. 1924A).

[*]**μαγγανάρις, ὁ,** = μαγγανάριος, *mechanical engineer,* Thphn. *chron*.p.218(M.108.557A, v.l. μαγγανάρην).

μαγγανεία (-νία metr. gr., Eudoc.*Cypr*.2.310(M.85.857B)), **ἡ, A.** *trickery*; **1.** of magical arts οἱ δι' ἐπῳδῶν καὶ μ. μεμαθηκότες καλεῖν καὶ ἐπάγεσθαι δαίμονας Or.*Cels*.7.69(p.218.25; M.11.1517C); πνεύματα...προσδεθέντα ὥσπερ...μαγγανείαις τισὶν...οἰκοδομαῖς καὶ τόποις *ib*.7.5(p.157.2; 1428A); οὐδὲ γὰρ τὴν ἄλογον λογικὴν ἐποίησε [sc. ὁ Πυθαγόρας] φύσιν...ἀλλὰ μαγγανείαις τοὺς ἀνοήτους ἠπάτα Chrys.*hom.2.2 in Jo*.(8.10A); φάσματα μαγγανείαις γενόμενα Isid.Pel. *epp*.1.397(M.78.405A); heathen explanation of power or protection given by God Αἰγυπτίων διαβαλλόντων [sc. Μωϋσέα] ὡς γόητα καὶ μαγγανείᾳ τὰς δυνάμεις πεποιηκέναι δοκοῦντα Or.*Cels*.1.45(p.95.12; 744B); τὰ ὑπὸ Ἰησοῦ γενόμενα παράδοξα οὐ μαγγανείᾳ...ἀλλὰ θειότητι *ib*.8.9(p.227.24; 1532A); Bas.Sel.*v.Thecl*.1(M.85.540A); in good sense ὦ μεγάλη τῆς ἀληθοῦς μ. ⟨δύναμις⟩ *A.Phil*.23(p.12.20); **2.** of wiles of Devil or of demons, tempting men, Mac.Aeg.*libert.ment*.7(M. 34.940B); Chrys.*hom.2.6 in Rom*.(9.444E); Bas.Sel.*v.Thecl*.1(M.85. 503D); of their tricks in the physical realm, ref. Mc.16:18 πάσας τὰς μ. τοῦ διαβόλου καὶ τῶν τούτου ὑπηρετῶν *A.Jo*.10(p.157.27); δαίμονες ἐφαντασιοκόπουν τοὺς ἀνθρώπους, προκαταλαμβάνοντες πηγὰς ἢ ποταμοὺς...καὶ οὕτως ταῖς μ. ἐξέπληττον τοὺς ἄφρονας Ath.*inc*.37.2 (M.25.180C); **3.** in gen.; of meretricious arts, *T.Reub*.3.4; Chrys. *hom.67.3 in Mt*.(7.666A); of heret. and misleading opinions πολλή σου τῆς ἰατροσοφιστικῆς κακοπίστου γνώμης μ. Epiph.*haer*.64.67 (p.510.1); τὰ ὑπὸ...Ἀετίου εἰρημένα ἐν διαλεκτικῇ τινι τέχνῃ καὶ συλλογιστικῇ ὑπονοίᾳ ἀνθρωπίνης μ. *ib*.76.54(p.410.34; M.42.632D); **4.** met., *spell, fascination* τὰς μ. τὰς ἐν ταῖς ἱπποδρομίαις Chrys. *hom.12.5 in 1Cor*.(10.104A); of wealth, *ib.23.5*(208C).

B. = μάγγανον, *engine of war,* Sever.ap.*cat.Ac*.2:7(p.27.3).

μαγγάνευμα, τό, plur., *luxurious dishes,* Gr.Naz.*or*.14.17(M.35. 880A); id.*carm*.1.2.8.23(M.37.658A).

μαγγανευτήριον, τό, plur., *magical arts,* Thdt.*serm.Chrys*.(5.102).

μαγγανευτής, ὁ, *sorcerer,* Eus.*d.e*.3.6(p.131.30; M.22.224A).

μαγγανεύτρια, ἡ, *sorceress,* Chrys.*dimiss.Chan*.5(3.436D).

μαγγανεύω, 1. *use magical arts*; met., *play tricks*; of verbal subtlety, Dor.*doct*.9.3(M.88.1721A); perf. ptcpl. pass., *faked* τὸ ἀγαπᾶν...οὐδὲν σοφιστικὸν οὐδὲ μεμαγγανευμένον [sc. ἔχον] ‡Hipp. *fr.39 in Pr*.(p.173.1); **2.** *lure, beguile*; of sexual attraction, †Bas. Anc.*virg*.5(M.30.680B); *ib*.18(708B).

***μαγγανικός, 1.** *magical,* Epiph.*haer*.24.2(p.258.9; M.41.309C); **2.** neut. as subst. = μάγγανον, *engine of war, Chron.Pasch*.p.290 (M.92.724B); *ib*.p.393(1009A); Thphn.*chron*.p.317(M.108.768B).

***μαγγανοδαίμων,** *juggler with demons,* Leont.B.*mesopent*.(M.86. 1980B).

μάγγανον, τό, 1. *engine of war, catapult* αἰφνίδιον ἐπίσκοπος ὥσπερ ἐκ μ. τινὸς εἰς τὸ μέσον ῥιφεὶς ἀναφαίνεται Corn.ap.Eus.*h.e*.6. 43.7(M.20.617C); Epiph.*haer*.66.82(p.124.13; M.42.160A); Thphn. *chron*.p.32(M.108.137B); fig. ὁ...διάβολος ἔχων μάγγανα...κατέχει τὰς νομὰς τῆς ψυχῆς Mac.Aeg.*hom*.27.19(M.34.708A); met., *device* of Devil or of demons, Nil.*Eulog*.28(M.79.1129D); Dor.*doct*.8.5(M.88. 1713D); **2.** machine for hoisting or lowering weights, *windlass* or *crane,* Eus.*h.e*.8.9.1(M.20.760A); Gr.Mag.*dial*.(tr.Zach.)4.6(M.*PL*.77. 330B); used to lower dead body of S. Symeon Stylites, Anton.Hag. *v.Sym.Styl*.29(p.68.8).

[*]**μάγγιψ, ὁ,** v. μάγκιψ.

μαγεία (-γία), **ἡ, 1.** *wisdom of the Magi* Περσῶν οἱ Μάγοι (οἳ μαγείᾳ καὶ τοῦ σωτῆρος προεμήνυσαν τὴν γένεσιν) Clem.*str*.1.15(p.45.23; cod. μέν γε M.8.77B); **2.** *magic* Μάγους ἀφ' ὧν ἡ παρώνυμος...μ. καὶ τοῖς λοιποῖς ἔθνεσιν ἐπὶ διαφθορᾷ...τῶν χρωμένων αὐτῇ ἐπιδεδήμηκε Or. *Cels*.6.80(p.151.24; M.11.1420B); ἡ καλουμένη μ. οὐ...πρᾶγμά ἐστιν ἀσύστατον πάντῃ ἀλλ', ὡς οἱ περὶ ταῦτα δεινοὶ ἀποδεικνύουσι, συνεστὸς μὲν λόγους δ' ἔχον σφόδρα ὀλίγοις γινωσκομένους·...δύναται ταῦτα τὰ ὀνόματα [sc. τὸ Σαβαὼθ καὶ τὸ Ἀδωναΐ] λεγόμενα μετά τινος τοῦ συνυφοῦς αὐτοῖς εἱρμοῦ *ib*.1.24(p.74.22; 704A); οὐ μόνον [sc. τοὺς Ἰουδαίους] χρῆσθαι...ἐν τῷ κατεπᾴδειν δαίμονας τῷ ὁ θεὸς Ἀβραὰμ...ἀλλὰ γὰρ σχεδὸν καὶ πάντας τοὺς τὰ τῶν ἐπῳδῶν καὶ μαγειῶν πραγματευομένους *ib*.4.33(p.304.1; 1080A); ὑποστάτην εἶναι μαγείας καὶ γοητείαν, ἐνεργουμένην ὑπὸ πονηρῶν δαιμόνων...ἀνθρώποις γόησιν ὑπακουόντων *ib*.2.51 (p.174.12; 877B); enumerated among τὰ ἀπολλύντα τὴν ψυχήν *Barn*. 20.1, cf.*Did*.5.1; contrasted with power of God, *Hom.Clem*.2.27; with persuasion ὁ μὲν τῇ τῆς μ. βίᾳ ἐπαναγκάσας·...ὁ δὲ λόγῳ πείσας *ib*.5.7; overthrown at Inc. ἀστὴρ ἐν οὐρανῷ ἔλαμψεν...ὅθεν ἐλύετο πᾶσα μ. καὶ πᾶς δεσμός Ign.*Eph*.19.3; rendered ineffectual by sign of cross ἔνθα τὸ σημεῖον τοῦ σταυροῦ γίνεται, ἀσθενεῖ μὲν μ., οὐκ ἐνεργεῖ δὲ φαρμακεία Ath.*v.Anton*.78(M.26.952C); by prayer and piety, Or.*Cels*.6.41(p.110.12; 1360A); anti-Christian explanation of miracles of Christ and apostles ἃς [sc. παράδοξας] Ἰησοῦς ἐποίησεν διαβάλλειν...βουλόμενος, ὡς ἀπὸ μ. καὶ οὐ θείᾳ δυνάμει γεγενημένας *ib.*

1.38(p.89.29; 733A); *A.Pil.*B 1(p.288); *πάντας ἀπατῶσιν ἐν τῇ μ. ἐκείνου τοῦ Ἰησοῦ A.Phil.*15(p.9.3); *A.Mt.*(p.246.6); Christian explanation of pagan myths *οἱ ὑπ' αὐτῶν ᾀδόμενοι θεοὶ κακοί τινες γεγόνασι μάγοι, οἵτινες ἄνθρωποι ὄντες μοχθηροί, μαγείᾳ μεταμορφούμενοι...βίους διέφθειρον Hom.Clem.*6.20; associated with Marcosian Gnostics, Iren.*haer.*1.13.1(M.7.580A); *τίνα τὰ Μάρκῳ καὶ Κολαρβάσῳ νομισθέντα; καὶ ὅτι τινὲς αὐτῶν μαγείαις καὶ ἀριθμοῖς Πυθαγορείοις ἔσχον* Hipp.*haer.*6.5(p.134.6; M.16.3206B); *ib.*9.4(p.240.6; 3370A); plur., *sorceries, spells, Did.*5.1; Cyr.H.*catech.*19.8; *μαγίαι Const. App.*7.18.1 (v.l. *μαγεῖαι*), cf.*Did.*5.1; Chrys.*hom.21.6 in 2Cor.*(10.586D).

μαγειρεῖον, τό, *place where food is cooked*; ? *fireplace* or *oven οὐκ ἐκτήσατο...χαλκίον ἢ μ. ἢ χαλάδριον* Cyr.S.*v.Sab.*44(p.135.2).

μαγεύ-ω, 1. *conjure up* spirits, *T.Sal.*15.5(M.122.1337B); **2.** perf. ptcpl. pass., *poisoned τὸ ποτήριον...μεμαγευμένον* Jo.Mosch.*prat.*94 (M.87.2953A); **3.** met., *charm, captivate πρεσβεύων ὑπὲρ σοῦ πρὸς θεὸν καὶ λιτανείαις συνήθεσι ~ων τὸν πατέρα* Clem.*q.d.s.*41(p.187.19; M.9.648A).

μαγικός, *magical δαίμονες...ἀγωνίζονται ἔχειν ὑμᾶς δούλους...διὰ μ. στροφῶν* Just.*1apol.*14.1(M.6.348B); *μ. τελεταῖς Hom.Clem.*9.7; a charge *of sorcery, A.Petr.c.Sim.*3(p.84.9); Hipp.*haer.*9.14(p.253.2; M.16.3390C).

***μάγιος,** *magical*; of a philtre, *Nomoc.*217.

***μαγιστόριον, τό,** *office of a μάγιστρος, M.Cyriac.*1(M.10.553A).

***μαγιστριανός, ὁ,** an official on the staff of *magister officiorum νεανίσκῳ τινὶ μ.* Pall.*h.Laus.*65(p.161.21; M.34.1251D); Nest.*ep.Thds.*(p.14.4; H.1.1437D); *Κωνσταντῖνος ὁ καθωσιωμένος μ. καὶ σηκρητάριος τοῦ θείου κονσιστωρίου* CChalc.*act.*1(*ACO* 2.1.1 p.92.3; H.2.100A).

***μαγίστριον, τό,** = *μαγιστόριον,* Thphn.*chron.*p.117(M.108.332B).

***μάγιστρος, ὁ,** (Lat. *magister*); **1.** *master of the imperial household Παλλάδιος ὁ γενόμενος τοῦ παλατίου μ.* Ath.*apol.Const.*22(M.25.624A); *ib.*3(600B); Thdt.*h.e.*5.18.6(3.1047); *μ. τῶν θείων ὀφφικίων* CCP(449)*act.*(*ACO* 2.1.1 p.177.3; H.2.209D); *τὴν τοῦ μ. ἀρχὴν...ὃν ἡγεμόνα τῶν ἐν τῇ αὐλῇ τάξεων οἱ πρόσθεν ἐκάλουν* Evagr.*h.e.* 3.2(p.125.28; M.86.2056B); as honorary title, Philost.*h.e.*11.2(M.65.593C); Jo.Mal.*chron.*14 p.356(M.97.529C); **2.** as military title; **a.** under Republic *ἐπὶ τῶν προκειμένων ὑπάτων γέγονε μ. Βούβουλκος Chron.Pasch.*p.171(M.92.424A); **b.** under Empire *ὁ...δοὺξ τῆς Αἰγύπτου,...ὁ δὲ μ. ... ἐκεῖ, καὶ...ὁ τοῦ παλατίου μ.* Ath.*apol.Const.*10(M.25.608B); *IGC As.Min.*100² (Ephesus, saec. vi); **3.** *president* of collegium (Lat. *magister augustalis*) *αὐγουστάλιος καὶ ἀπὸ μαγίστρων MAMA* 1.216.

***μαγιστρότης, ἡ,** *office* or *position of μάγιστρος,* Eus.*h.e.*8.11.2(M.20.769A).

[*]**μαγκίπιον** ([*]**-ιπεῖον,** [*]**-ήπιον,** [*]**-ηπεῖον**), **τό,** *flour-mill* or *bakery -ηπεῖον* Socr.*h.e.*5.18 tit.(M.67.609B); *-ιπεῖον* Cyr.S.*v.Euthym.*15(p.24.19, v.l. *-ηπίον*); *Chron.Pasch.*p.341(M.92.889A, v.l. *-ηπίον*); Thphn.*chron.*p.63 (vv.ll. *-κήπιον, -κηπεῖον, -κιπεῖον* M.108.209B).

μάγκιψ ([*]**μάγκηψ,** [*]**μάγγιψ**), **ὁ,** (Lat. *manceps*) *baker,* Socr.*h.e.*5.18.3(M.67.609C); *μάγγιψ* Eus.Al.*serm.*21.17(M.86.444C); Cyr.S.*v.Sab.*5(p.89.21, v.l. *μάγκηψ*).

[*]**μαγνίτης,** *magnetic ὁ μ. λίθος* ‡Pall.*gent.Ind.*(p.4).

***μαγοδείκτης, ὁ,** *juggler, impostor*; met., *V.Alex.Acoem.*40 (p.689.8).

μάγος, ὁ, 1. *Magian,* a Persian priest *κατὰ τῶν τῆς εὐσεβείας τροφίμων...ζάλη...ὑπὸ τῶν μ. ... ῥιπιζομένη* Thdt.*h.e.*5.39.5(3.1082); Socr.*h.e.*7.8.5ff.(M.67.752B); **2.** plur., *Magi* of Nativity, various accounts of their origins: Arabian (ref. Is.8:4), Just.*dial.*78.5(M.6.660A); *Dial.Ath.et Zacch.*33(p.23); confused with Chaldeans by Celsus, Or.*Cels.*1.58(p.109.23; M.11.768B); descendants of Balaam (ref. Num.24:17) *τοὺς ἀπ' αὐτοῦ τὸ γένος κατάγοντας M., ἐπιτηροῦντας κατὰ τὴν πρόρρησιν τοῦ προπάτορος τὴν τοῦ καινοῦ ἀστέρος ἀνατολήν* Gr.Nyss.*nativ.*(M.46.1133D); ancestors of Persian royal line, Cosm.Ind.*top.*2(M.88.113D); **3.** *magician, sorcerer,* esp. associated with Egypt *μάγοι δαίμοσιν ὁμιλοῦντες καὶ τούτους...καλοῦντες* Or.*Cels.* 1.60(p.116.23; M.11.769B); *ib.*8.59(p.275.30; 1605C); *εἰς Αἴγυπτον πορεύσομαι...καὶ μ. ζητήσας καὶ εὑρὼν χρήμασι πολλοῖς πείσω, ὅπως ψυχῆς ἀναπομπήν, τὴν λεγομένην νεκρομαντείαν ποιήσῃ Hom.Clem.* 1.5; *ἀνάγκην ἔχουσιν οἱ δαίμονες τοῖς μ. ὑπείκειν περὶ ὧν κελεύονται·... ἀδύνατόν ἐστι τοὺς δαίμονας μὴ ὑπουργεῖν τοῖς αὐτῶν ἡγουμένοις ἀγγέλοις...αὐτοὶ οἱ ἄγγελοι...ἀπὸ μάγων ὁρκιζόμενοι, ὑπείκουσιν ib.*5.5; of pagan gods, *ib.*6.20 cit. s. *μαγεία*; charge against Christ and apostles *μάγον εἶναι αὐτὸν ἐτόλμων λέγειν* Just.*dial.*69.7(M.6.640A); *οὐκ οἶδ' ὅπως ἂν μ. ἠγωνίσατο διδάξαι λόγον...ὡς θεοῦ κρίνοντος ἕκαστον ἐπὶ πᾶσι τοῖς πεπραγμένοις* Or.*Cels.*1.38(p.89.28; 733B); *A.Thom.*A 20(p.131.2); *Hom.Clem.*4.2.

***μαγουδαῖος, ὁ,** plur., *Jewish magicians,* ‡Jo.D.*ep.Thphl.*11(M.95.360A).

μάγουλον, τό, plur., *cheeks,* Melet.*nat.hom.*5(M.64.1181A).

μαγουσαῖος, ὁ, *mage,* member of a Persian sect widespread in eastern provinces, holding esoteric doctrines, practising vegetarianism, worshipping heavenly bodies, and accused of incestuous marriages, Eus.*p.e.*6.10(275D; M.21.468B); *ib.*(278D; M.473C); Bas.*ep.*258.4(3.394D; M.32.952C); *μυστηρίων πολλῶν...ἀρχηγοὶ παρὰ Πέρσαις μαγουσαῖοι* Epiph.*exp.fid.*12(p.512.18; M.42.804C); Leont.B.*Nest.et Eut.*3.37(M.86.1376C); *μή μοι πρόσεχε ὡς μαγουσαίῳ· δοῦλος γάρ εἰμι τοῦ ἐσταυρωμένου* Jo.Disc.*v.Epiph.*16(M.41.41C).

***μάγωζος, ὁ,** *secret cabinet* or *casket,* ref. AQ Ezech.27:24 [Hebr. בִּגְנְזֵי perh. misread] *τὸ δὲ 'ἐν μαγώζοις' ἀπὸ τοῦ Ἑβραίου ἐξελλήνιζει· σημαίνει δὲ ἐν ἀποκρύφοις σκεύεσιν* Thdt.*Ezech.*27:24(2.904).

μᾶζα, ἡ, 1. *barley-cake*; met., *sop,* ref. Pr.25:22, Chrys.*hom.* *50.4 in Ac.*(9.378C); **2.** *lump οὐδὲ γὰρ τό, ἐκ γῆς γεγενῆσθαι, ποιεῖ χοϊκὸν ἁπλῶς, ἐπεὶ καὶ ὁ κύριος ἀπὸ τῆς μ. καὶ τοῦ φυράματος τούτου ἦν, ἀλλὰ τὸ γήϊνα πράττειν* Chrys.*hom.42.1 in 1Cor.*(10.395D); met., of treasures of scripture *μ. χρυσίου* id.*hom.31.1 in Rom.*(9.745A).

***μαζάριον, τό,** ? *basket* or *trencher* for barley-bread, Jo.Mosch.*prat.*160(M.87.3028B).

μαζί(ο)ν, τό, dim., of *μᾶζα, lump, Apophth.Patr.*(M.65.88A).

μαζός, ὁ, *breast,* met. *πηγαὶ πρὸς ἀπόλαυσιν καὶ ὑγείαν δημιουργηθεῖσαι...παρέχονται τοὺς πρὸς ζωῆς ἀνθρώποις μ. 1Clem.*20.10.

***μαζουρώθ, ὁ,** (Hebr. מַזָּרוֹת) *signs of the zodiac ὁ μ., ὁ λεγόμενος ἐξάστερος* Eus.Al.*serm.*22.1(M.86.453B); *μ. τὰ συστήματα λέγει τῶν ἀστέρων, ὃ...ζῴδια καλοῦνται...ἄλλοι δέ φασι, μ. ... σημαίνειν τὸν ἀστρῷον κύνα* Olymp.*Job* 38:32(M.93.408D).

μάθημα, A. *something learnt, learning, knowledge*; **1.** plur., *studies οἱ...ἀπαρχόμενοι εἰς σωτηρίαν τῶν μ.* Meth.*symp.*3.8(p.37.10; M.18.76A); **2.** *astrology ὅτι δέ ἐστι...εἱμαρμένη...ἐναργὴς ἀπόδειξις καὶ ἡ τῶν μ. θεωρία* Clem.*exc.Thdot.*75(p.130.24; M.9.693B); id.*str.* 6.16(p.504.19; M.9.693B); **3.** in bad sense, *magic arts,* Hipp.*haer.*4.34 (p.60.13; M.16.3098C); Or.*Cels.*3.46(p.243.7; M.11.981A); *Const.App.* 7.6.2.

B. *teaching, doctrine*; **1.** in gen., Just.*1apol.*3.4(M.6.332A); id. *2apol.*2.9(M.6.445A); Or.*Cels.*3.75(p.267.9; M.11.1020A); ref. Rom. 14:2 *πάντα κατ' ἀναλογίαν μετενεκτέον ἐστὶ καὶ ἐπὶ τὰς διαφορὰς τῶν νομιζομένων τροφίμων μ.* id.*or.*27.9(p.369.18; M.11.513A); ref. Mt.7:6 *μαργαρίτας...τὰ μυστικώτερα τῆς θεοσδότου θρησκείας...μ.* Meth.*creat.*1(p.493.4; M.18.332A); id.*symp.*1.1(p.8.17; M.18.37C); **2.** of Christ, Or.*Cels.*3.29(p.227.1; M.11.957B); *τοῦτο...τοῦ Ἰησοῦ μ. ... καταφρονεῖσθαι μὲν τὸ ὑπὸ τῶν πολλῶν περιεπόμενον ζῆν· σπουδάζεσθαι δὲ τὸ παραπλήσιον τῷ ζῆν τοῦ θεοῦ ζῆν ib.*2.45(p.168.9; 868C); ref. Jo.6:48 *ὁ ἄρτος τρέφει...ὁ δὲ οἶνος ἥδει. ... οὕτως τὰ μὲν ἠθικὰ μ., ζωὴν περιποιοῦντα τῷ μανθάνοντι καὶ πράττοντι, ἄρτος ἐστὶ τῆς ζωῆς...τὰ δὲ εὐφραίνοντα...ἀπόρρητα καὶ μυστικὰ θεωρήματα* id.*Jo.*1.30(33; p.37.27; M.14.80A); ref. Jo.15.1ff. *ἄμπελος...κλημάτων δίκην ἐκ τῶν μ. τοὺς βότρυς ἱλαρῶς ἀπαιωροῦσα τῶν χαρισμάτων...ὁ κύριος ἡμῶν ἐστιν Ἰησοῦς* Meth.*symp.*5.5(p.59.4; M.18.105B); *ib.*1.4(p.12.18; 44C); **3.** of apostles, Or.*Cels.*3.57(p.252.22; M.11.996C); *μ. παρὰ Ματθαίου εἰληφὼς βίβλον τῆς τοῦ θεοῦ φωνῆς καὶ θαυμάτων καὶ διδαγμάτων σύγγραμμα A.Barn.*15(p.297.23); *ib.*24(p.301.13); of a precept of S. Paul, Eus.*h.e.*10.8.10(M.20.897A); = NT *ἀναγνωστέον δὲ οὐ μόνον τὰ τῶν ἱερῶν ἀποστόλων μ., ἀλλὰ καὶ τὰ τῶν θείων προφητῶν θεσπίσματα* Thdt.*affect.*2(p.66.7; 4.757); hence **4.** *θεῖα μ. scripture,* Or.*Cels.*3.22(p.219.2; M.11.945B); *ἄσκησιν τῶν θείων μ., οἷς ἐκκαθαίρεται...ψυχή* Meth.*symp.*9.4(p.118.8; M.18.185A); Philost.*h.e.*3.27(M.65.543C); = the gospel (ref. Mt.13:20) *τὸ ἐν χαρᾷ δοκεῖν παρειληφέναι τὰ ἅγια μ.* Or.*mart.*49(p.45.13; M.11.633A); of passages from scripture used in exorcism *ἀπελαύνειν* [sc. *δαίμονας*] *εὐχαῖς καὶ τοῖς ἀπὸ τῶν ἱερῶν γραμμάτων μ.* id.*Cels.*7.67(p.216.26; 1514B); **5.** *creed τῶν θυρῶν κλεισθεισῶν καὶ τοῦ ἁγίου μ. κατὰ τὸ σύνηθες λεχθέντος* CCP(536)*act.*5(*ACO* 3 p.76.20; H.2.1340E); *ἐκτίθενται ὅρον ἤτοι μ. πίστεως, ὅπερ λέγομεν* †Leont.B.*sect.*4(M.86.1220D); *τοῖς εὐαγγελικοῖς παραγγέλμασι καὶ τῷ ἁγίῳ συμβόλῳ ἤτοι μ. τῶν ἁγίων πατέρων* Just.Imp.*edict.*(p.198.11; M.86.2796A); *ὅτι καὶ τότε πίστεώς τι σύμβολον προελέγετο· ἢ μᾶλλον ὅπερ τότε παρελάμβανον μ. καὶ συμμάθημα τῆς πίστεως* Max.*schol.e.h.*3.2(M.4.136D).

μαθηματικός, *fond of learning, learned,* of an inventor *πανοῦργος καὶ μ. Chron.Pasch.*p.44(M.92.164C).

μαθηματικῶς, *with readiness to learn* τοὺς πλουσίους μ. ἀκουστέον ...μὴ σκαιῶς μηδὲ ἀγροίκως Clem.*q.d.s.*18(p.171.4; M.9.621C).

***μαθησία, ἡ, 1.** *knowledge*, Isid.Pel.ap.*cat.Ac.*13:10(p.216.10); Alex.Sal.*Barn.*1(p.438B); **2.** *education* παραδόσεως καὶ μ. Leont.N. *v.Jo.Eleem.*1(p.5.19, v.l. μαθήσεως).

μάθησις, ἡ, 1. *act of learning, acquisition of knowledge* εὐλογηθείη τὰ σώματα τοῦ λαοῦ εἰς σωφροσύνην...εὐλογηθείησαν αἱ ψυχαὶ αὐτῶν εἰς μ. Serap.*euch.*6.2; **2.** *knowledge, learning* ἀρχὴν εἶναι μαθήσεως τῇ μὲν φύσει Χριστὸν καθ' ὃ σοφία καὶ δύναμις θεοῦ, πρὸς ἡμᾶς δὲ ⟨τὸ⟩ 'ὁ λόγος σὰρξ ἐγένετο' Or.*Jo.*1.18(20; p.23.3; M.14.53D); ref. Lc.2:32 τῷ Ἰσραὴλ ἀκόλουθος ἡ μ. [i.e. not revelation but knowledge based on the prophets] id.*hom.15 in Lc.*(p.106.9); of scripture τὰ εἰς τὴν ἱερὰν μ. Philost.*h.e.*8.11(M.65.564C); **3.** *instruction* ὁ θεὸς...διὰ Χριστοῦ διδασκάλους τοὺς μαθητὰς ἐπιστήσας πρὸς μάθησιν τῆς εὐσεβείας *Lit.* ap.*Const.App.*8.6.11; *means of learning, lesson* ἡ τοῦ υἱοῦ καὶ τοῦ πατρὸς ἑνότης...ὑπογραμμὸς καὶ μ. ἐστι, καθ' ἣν δύνανται μανθάνειν... πῶς καὶ αὐτοὶ ὀφείλουσιν ἓν πρὸς ἀλλήλους γίνεσθαι τῷ φρονήματι Ath. *Ar.*3.21(M.26.368A).

μαθητεία (-ία), ἡ, *training, discipleship* παραλαβόντες τὰ ἔθνη εἰς μ. Eus.*Ps.*149:9(M.24.73A); -ία, Bas.Sel.*or.*31.3(M.85.349A); ref. Mt.11:25 κἂν ἐν τοῖς χρόνοις τῆς μ. ὦσιν νήπιοι *Hom.Clem.*18.16; τὰ κωλυτικὰ τῆς μ. †Bas.*bapt.*1.2.26(2.648A; M.31.1569B); of distributing the loaves and fishes ἡ λειτουργία κατὰ τὸ οἰκεῖον τῆς μ. Vict. *Mc.*8:15(p.341.20); *making disciples* ἡ τῶν δώδεκα μ. [sc. by Christ] *Ascens.Is.*A 3.13(p.92); Mac.Mgn.*apocr.*3.37(p.133.4); ref. Mt.28:19 τὴν τῶν ἐθνῶν μ. Thdt.*rect.conf.*6(M.6.1213D); *becoming disciples* ζηλωτὰς...μυρίους, καταλιπόντας τοὺς πατρῴους νόμους... τῆς τηρησέως τῶν Μωσέως νόμων καὶ τῆς μ. τῶν Ἰησοῦ Χριστοῦ λόγων Or.*princ.*4.1.1(p.294.9; M.11.344C); ὅθεν πρὸ τῆς μ. τοῦ Ἰησοῦ περιεποίουν ἑαυτοῖς τὰς τροφάς id.*Cels.*1.62(p.113.22; M.11. 773C).

μαθητεύ-ω, A. intrans., *be a pupil, disciple* χωρήσωμεν τὸ φῶς καὶ ~σωμεν τῷ κυρίῳ Clem.*prot.*11(p.80.6; M.8.232A); φασὶ τὸν Βαλαὰμ ἔχειν φοιτητὰς...~σαντας αὐτῷ τῇ μαγικῇ Or.*adnot.in Num.*24:17(M. 17.21C); pres. ptcpl. as subst., *disciple*, id.*Cels.*2.9(p.136.25; M.11. 809C); id.*or.*13.5(p.329.20; M.11.460A); met. φιλοσοφίαν...προπαιδεύουσαν εἰς τὴν διὰ Χριστοῦ τελείωσιν, ἣν μὴ ἐπαισχύνηται γνώσει βαρβάρῳ ~ουσα [φιλοσοφία] προκόπτειν εἰς ἀλήθειαν Clem.*str.* 6.17(p.510.24; M.9.384C); *attach oneself* to a sect τοῖς βουλομένοις τῇ αἱρέσει μ. Hipp.*haer.*9.23(p.258.9; M.16.3399B).

B. trans.; **1.** *instruct, teach* ἵνα κἀκεῖνα βέβαια ᾖ, ἃ ~οντες ἐντέλλεσθε Ign.*Rom.*3.1; οἱ γὰρ ἐξ ἀνθρώπων εἰς ἀγγέλους μεταστάντες χίλια ἔτη ~ονται ὑπὸ τῶν ἀγγέλων, εἰς τελειότητα ἀποκαθιστάμενοι Clem.*ecl.*57(p.154.9; M.9.725C); πάλαι ἠκούσαμεν τῶν Ἰησοῦ λόγων καὶ ἤδη πολλῷ χρόνῳ τῷ εὐαγγελίῳ μεμαθητεύμεθα Or.*mart.*48(p.43. 20; M.11.632A); τινες τῶν ἐνσωματουμένων ψυχῶν πρὶν εἰς γένεσιν ἐλθεῖν μεμαθητευμέναι παρὰ τῷ πατρί id.*Jo.*20.7(p.335.14; M.14. 588C); τινὲς οἱ μὴ δι' ἀνθρώπων πρότερον μαθητευθέντες θεῷ, ἀρχῆθεν δεδύνηνται...χωρῆσαι τὰς ἐμφάσεις τοῦ πνεύματος †Bas.*Is.*198(1. 526E; M.30.460A); ref. Jo.16:14, of H. Ghost 'learning' from Christ, Or.*Jo.*2.18(12; p.75.23; 145D); **2.** *make disciples* μ. πάντα τὰ ἔθνη... εἰς τὴν ἀνάστασιν τοῦ ἀγαπητοῦ *Ascens.Is.*A 3.18(p.93); ἄνδρες οἱ κληθέντες ὑπὸ τοῦ λόγου τοῦ θεοῦ καὶ...μ. ὑπὸ τῆς αὐτοῦ σοφίας *A.Andr.*A 1(p.46.6); *A.Petr.c.Sim.*12(p.100.21); μετὰ τελωνῶν ἐσθίει καὶ παρὰ τελώναις καὶ ~ει τελώνας Gr.Naz.*or.*38.14(M.36.328C); οἱ δὲ δώδεκα ἦσαν σὺν αὐτῷ οὐκ εὐαγγελιζόμενοι ἀλλὰ μ. καὶ παιδαγωγούμενοι πρὸς τὸ εὐαγγέλιον *cat.Lc.*8:1(p.63.25); **3.** pass., *become a disciple* καθ' ἡμέραν τινὰς ~ομένους εἰς τὸ ὄνομα τοῦ Χριστοῦ Just. *dial.*32.2(M.6.560B); id.*1apol.*15.6(M.6.349B); †Bas.*bapt.*1.1.2(2.525E; M.31.1517B); ref. Ps.104:16 τῶν ἁγίων ἕκαστος...στρουθίων δίκην δεχόμενος τοὺς ὑπ' αὐτῷ μ. βουλομένους Cyr.*Abac.*30(3.545B); **4.** pres. ptcpl. as subst., of one under instruction; **a.** *learner* ἐπὶ τῶν ἀποστόλων...τοὺς πρότερον μανθάνοντας διδασκάλους καθιστῶντες ἑτέρων τινῶν μ. Chrys.*hom.9.2 in Col.*(11.392A); id.*hom.9.1 in 1Tim.* (11.594E); **b.** *apprentice* τῶν τεχνῶν ἡ ὑπόστασις ἐκ τῶν διδασκόντων ὅλη τοῖς μ. ἐγγινομένη Bas.*Eun.*2.16(1.252A; M.29.605A); **c.** *disciple*; of followers of Jo. Bapt., dist. from those whom he merely baptized, Or.*or.*2.4(p.303.2; M.11.421D); of the multitude who followed Christ, dist. from μαθηταί, id.*Jo.*13.34(p.259.21; M.14.460A); of disciples of Christian teachers Χριστοῦ ἐπιτάξαντος τοὺς τὸ εὐαγγέλιον κηρύττοντας ἐκ τῶν μ. ζῆν Chrys.*hom.21.1 in 1Cor.*(10. 179C); ref. Jo.1:9, cf.Mt.5:14 οὐδέν τινων διακονουμένων ἀποστόλων καὶ προφητῶν δέονται...αὐτῷ τῷ πρωτογεννήτῳ ~όμενοι φωτί Or.*Jo.* 1.25(p.31.25; M.14.69A); met., in bad sense τῷ δουλεύοντι τῇ ἁμαρτίᾳ καὶ τῷ ~ομένῳ τοῖς ψεύδεσιν *ib.*32.11(7; p.444.13; 769D); **5.** perf. ptcpl. pass., of fully trained disciple qualified to teach others τὸ ...τῷ ἀναστάντι ἐκ νεκρῶν μεμαθητευμένοις λεγόμενον καὶ ἀποστελλομένοις ~εῦσαι πάντα τὰ ἔθνη *ib.*10.9(7; p.179.14; 321A); *ib.*10.29 (18; p.202.23; 360A).

μαθητής, ὁ, 1. *learner, pupil* τοῦτο γὰρ μαθητοῦ, τὸ μὴ περιεργάζεσθαι τὰ τοῦ διδασκάλου, ἀλλ' ἀκούειν καὶ πείθεσθαι, καὶ τὸν προσήκοντα καιρὸν ἀναμένειν τῆς λύσεως Chrys.*hom.46.2 in Jo.*(8.272A); ἐπὶ μὲν τῆς γῆς τὸ πᾶν τοῦ γεωργοῦ γίνεται· ...ἐπὶ δὲ ταύτης τῆς γῆς τῆς πνευματικῆς...οὐ τῶν διδασκάλων ἐστὶ τὸ πᾶν, ἀλλ' εἰ μὴ τὸ πλέον, τὸ γοῦν ἥμισυ καὶ τῶν μ. id.*hom.3.3 in 2Thess.*(11.526B); in Church καθάπερ γὰρ ἐπὶ τῶν στρατοπέδων οὐ πάντες εἰς ἓν εἶδος στρατεύονται, ἀλλ' ἐν διαφόροις τάγμασιν· οὕτω καὶ ἐν τῇ ἐκκλησίᾳ, ὁ μὲν εἰς διδασκάλου τάξιν, ὁ δὲ εἰς μ., ὁ δὲ εἰς ἰδιώτου id.*hom.5.1 in 1Tim.*(11. 575C); ὀφείλοντες εἶναι διδάσκαλοι διὰ τὸν χρόνον, οὐδὲ μαθητῶν τάξιν ἐπέχετε id.*hom.11.1 in Heb.*(12.92B); ἐν τῷ τῶν μ. καταλόγῳ ταχθεὶς Thdt.*1Tim.*3:6(3.655); **2.** *disciple*; **a.** Christ's: the twelve, opp. the many, ref. Jo.6:66 τῶν γνησίων Ἰησοῦ μ. Or.*hom 17.4 in Jer.* (p.148.13; M.13.460B); cf. πεπιστευκότων μὲν αὐτῷ καὶ μαθητευθέντων πως, οὐ μὴν ἤδη ἀληθῶς χρηματισάντων μ. τοῦ Ἰησοῦ id.*Jo.*20.13 (p.343.10; M.14.601A); οὐχὶ δὲ οἱ πολλοὶ τῶν πεπιστευκότων εἰς αὐτὸν μένουσιν ἐν τῷ λόγῳ αὐτοῦ, οὐδὲ οἱ πολλοὶ ἀληθῶς αὐτοῦ μ. γίνονται *ib.* 19.11(3; p.310.26; 545C); S. John εἰ καὶ ἀνακείμενος οὖν πρότερον μὲν ἦν ἐν τῷ κόλπῳ τοῦ Ἰησοῦ, ὕστερον δὲ ἀνέπεσεν ἐπὶ τὸ στῆθος τοῦ Ἰησοῦ, διὰ τοῦ δευτέρου...χαρακτηρίζεται...ὁ τοῦ Ἰησοῦ γνήσιος μ. *ib.*32.21(13; p.463.34; 801D); the seventy, *A.Phil.*108(p.41.14); *Const.App.*2.55.2; Joseph of Arimathaea μ. ὤν· οὐ τῶν δώδεκα, ἀλλὰ τῶν ἑβδομήκοντα ἴσως Chrys.*hom.85.3 in Jo.*(8.508C); the five hundred, ref. 1Cor.15:6, Or.*fr.85 in Lc.*24:15(p.274); the evangelists ταῦτα ἀναγραφῆς ἀξιωθέντα ὑπὸ τῶν ἁγίων μ. αὐτοῦ id.*Jo.*20. 36(29; p.375.22; M.14.657A); certain Christians in sub-apostolic age Ἀριστίων καὶ ὁ πρεσβύτερος Ἰωάννης, τοῦ κυρίου μ. Papias *fr.*2; plur., = apostles παρὰ τῶν τοῦ Χριστοῦ μ. ... ἐκηρύχθη [sc. τὰ ἀποστολικὰ κηρύγματα] Meth.*creat.*1(p.493.17; M.18.332B); cf. ἀνεληλυθὼς ἀπὸ τῆς θαλάσσης ὑποπεσὼν τοῖς δικτύοις τῶν μ. Ἰησοῦ Or.*hom. 16.1 in Jer.*(p.132.24; M.13.140A); but dist. from apostles οὐκ ἀπῆλθε πρὸς τοὺς ἀποστόλους, ἀλλὰ τοῖς μ. ἐπειρᾶτο κολλᾶσθαι, ἅτε οὐ διδάσκαλος ὢν ἀλλὰ μ. Chrys.*hom.21.1 in Ac.*(9.168E); μ. δὲ καλεῖ καὶ τοὺς μὴ τελοῦντας εἰς τὸν χορὸν τῶν δώδεκα· διότι μ. πάντες ἐκαλοῦντο τότε διὰ τὴν πολλὴν ἀρετήν· ἦν γὰρ ἡ εἰκὼν τῶν μ. δήλη *ib.21.3*(9.172B); one who attains full discipleship by martyrdom ἐλπίζοντα τῇ προσευχῇ ὑμῶν ἐπιτυχεῖν ἐν Ῥώμῃ θηριομαχῆσαι, ἵνα διὰ τοῦ ἐπιτυχεῖν δυνηθῶ μ. εἶναι Ign.*Eph.*1.2; νῦν ἄρχομαι μ. εἶναι id. *Rom.*5.3; μήπω...ἐφαψάμενος...τῆς τελείας τοῦ μ. τάξεως *M.Ign.Ant.* 1; ἐκοσμήθησαν τῷ μάρτυρες εἶναι Χριστοῦ πολλοὶ τῶν γνησίων Χριστοῦ μ. Or.*Jo.*2.34(p.92.14; M.14.176A); Christians in general μ. ποιμένος ἁγνοῦ Aberc.*epitaph.*3; ἄμπελός ἐστιν ἀληθινὴ...ἐπεὶ βότρυς ἔχει τὴν ἀλήθειαν καὶ κλήματα τοὺς μ., μιμητὰς αὐτοῦ καὶ αὐτοὺς καρποφοροῦντας τὴν ἀλήθειαν Or.*Jo.*1.30(33; p.37.21; M.14.80A); οὐκ εἰρήνην ἐπὶ τὴν γῆν βαλεῖν ἀλλ' ἐπὶ τὴν ψυχὴν τῶν μ. ἑαυτοῦ id.*mart.* 37(p.34.23); ἡμεῖς [sc. S. Andrew and his followers] μ. ἔσμεν τοῦ κυρίου *A.Andr.et Mt.*6(p.71.12); ὁ εὐχόμενος ἐκείνου μ. εἶναι ζηλούτω τοὺς αὐτοῦ ἀγῶνας, μιμείσθω τὴν ὑπομονὴν *Const.App.*5.6.10; μ. Χριστοῦ πάντες ὑπάρχοντες οἱ πιστοί *ib.*5.7.24; ποίου βιοθανοῦς πᾶς ὁ κόσμος μαθητῶν ἐπληρώθη; *M.Pion.*13.4(p.52.21); the prophets in spiritual sense οὗ [sc. Χριστοῦ] οἱ προφῆται μ. ὄντες τῷ πνεύματι ὡς διδάσκαλον αὐτὸν προσεδόκων Ign.*Magn.*9.2; **b.** μ. of H. Ghost; Hermas, Or.*princ.*4.2.4(11; p.314.4; M.11.365B); **c.** of holy men: of the apostles ἀποστόλων γενόμενος μ. γίνομαι διδάσκαλος ἐθνῶν *Diogn.* 11.1; Ἰγνάτιος ὁ τοῦ ἀποστόλου Ἰωάννου μ. *M.Ign.Ant.*1; Ἀνδρέας μετὰ τῶν αὐτοῦ μ. *A.Andr.et Mt.*6(p.72.11); of Jo. Bapt. ὁ κύριος εὗρε τοὺς περὶ Πέτρον καὶ Ἰωάννην...ὄντας τὸ πρότερον Ἰωάννου τοῦ βαπτιστοῦ μ. Or.*fr.3 in Lc.*(p.233); of Elijah and Elisha, *Const.App.* 8.1.15; of a bishop ὁ ἐπίσκοπος...ἀνεπίληπτος ἀδικίας ὢν ποιμήν, τοὺς ἰδίους αὐτοῦ μ. ἀναγκάσει...μιμητὰς ἀξίους γενηθῆναι *ib.*2.6.5; of monks, Ephr.3.360E; Cosm.Ind.*top.*2(M.88.73A); of martyrs ὧν πάντων ταῖς πρεσβείαις γένοιτο ἡμᾶς συγκοινωνοὺς τε καὶ μ. γενέσθαι *Chron.Pasch.*p.258(M.92.629A); **d.** of Church οἱ τῆς καθολικῆς τοῦ Χριστοῦ ἐκκλησίας μ. *ib.*p.226(M.92.549A).

μαθητία, ἡ, v. μαθητεία.

μαθητι-άω, 1. *become a disciple* οὗτοί με ~ᾶν ἑαυτοῖς ἀξιοῦσι Synes.*ep.*154(M.66.1553C); **2.** *learn* ὀρέξεις τὰς ἐπί γε τὸ μαθητιᾶν Cyr.*glaph.Gen.*7(1.241B); **3.** pres. ptcpl. as subst., *disciple* ὁ συνετὸς ...σὺν τοῖς μ. Or.*exp.in Pr.*15:31(M.17.193C); Μάρθας...ἐν ταῖς μ. λελογισμένης *cat.Lc.*7:36(p.60.28).

μαθητικός, *belonging to a disciple*, ref. Mary of Bethany μ. σχολήν Clem.*q.d.s.*10(p.166.17; M.9.613D).

μαίευμα, τό, *thing delivered* by a midwife; met., of *Benedictus* *τοῦτο τῆς μυστηριώδους* [sc. *Ζαχαρίου*] *σιωπῆς ἀγαθὸν ὡς εἰκὸς μ.* ‡Thdt.*nativ.Jo.Bapt.*(5.94).

μαιεύ-ομαι, *bring to birth*; met., of catechumens *τῶν ἱερῶν ἡ πάνσοφος ἐπιστήμη...αὐτοὺς τῇ τῶν...ζωοποιῶν λογίων εἰσαγωγικῇ τροφῇ ~εται* Dion.Ar.*e.h.*3.3.6(M.3.433A); *αἱ τῶν λογίων ᾠδαὶ καὶ ἀναγνώσεις τοὺς μὲν ἀτελέστους ~ονται ib.*4.3(476D); pass. *εἰσαγωγικὴν* [sc. *τάξιν*], *τῶν ἔτι ~ομένων* Thdr.Stud.*epp.*2.165(M.99.1524C).

μαίευσις, ἡ, *bringing to birth,* met. *τῆς τῶν κατηχουμένων ἐν θεοειδεῖ τῶν ἱεραρχικῶν τάξει μ. καὶ ζωῆς* Dion.Ar.*e.h.*3.3.6(M.3.433B); *ib.*6.1.1(532A).

μαιεύτρια, ἡ, *one who brings to birth,* of BMV *ὦ χαρᾶς τῆς ὑπερτάτης μ.* Sophr.H.*or.*3.18(M.87.3237B).

μαιμάσσ-ω, 1. *quiver with eagerness,* ref. Jer.4:19 *τοῦτο γὰρ τὸ μαιμάσσειν οἷον προθυμία τις θυμῷ σύγκρατος* Gr.Naz.*or.*17.1(M.35.965A); Nil.*Magn.*19(M.79.993C); Olymp.*Job* 38:8(M.93.400C); *τὴν φοβερὰν...τοῦ ᾅδου γαστέρα, τὴν ~ουσαν ὑποδέξασθαι τοὺς τὰ παρόντα τερπνὰ τῶν μελλόντων ἀγαθῶν προκρίνοντας* †Jo.D.*B.J.*12(M.96.977A); **2.** trans., *make to tremble δεινὴν φλόγα, ἢ σφόδρα μ. με καὶ στροβεῖ κέαρ* ‡Gr.Naz.*Chr.pat.*28(M.38.139A); *τὰ αἰσθητήριά μου ~ει με, ἡνίκα ἀκούσω ἀπευκτὴν ἀκοὴν ἐπί τινι* Thdr.Stud.*epp.*2.131(M.99.1424C).

μαινάς, ἡ, 1. as subst., *mad woman*; fig., of wine, Bas.*hom.*2.4(2.12E; M.31.189C); of anger, Dan.Raith.*v.Jo.Clim.*(M.88.600B); **2.** as adj., *frenzied ὁ θυμὸς...μέθης ἔργον ἀποφαίνει τὸν νοῦν, μαινάδα τὴν φρένα ποιῶν* Isid.Pel.*epp.*1.479(M.78.444B).

[*]**μαινόλας,** = *μαινόλης, frenzied,* Or.*Cels.*3.23(p.219.21; M.11.945C).

μαίν-ομαι, 1. *be mad οὔτε νοσῶν ἢ μεμηνὼς οὐδεὶς θεῷ φίλος* Cels. ap.Or.*Cels.*4.18(p.287.10; M.11.1049B); met.; **a.** with anger, hostility *θαυμαστὸν οὐδὲν τοὺς οὕτω κατὰ τῆς τοῦ μονογενοῦς μανέντας θεότητος ἀδεῶς τοὺς ἄλλους παραβῆναι νόμους* Thdt.*h.e.*1.19.2(3.797); **b.** with greed or ambition *πρὸς δόξαν μ.* Or.*hom.8.8 in Lev.*(p.406.23; M.87.736A); *μ. ἐπὶ πλούτῳ* Ephr.2.185C; *περὶ τὰ χρήματα μ.* Chrys.*hom.7.2 in 2Tim.*(11.702B); **2.** *burn* with enthusiasm or devotion, ref. 1Cor.13:5 *ἡ ἀγάπη...περὶ* [sc. *τὸν ἀδελφόν*] *σωφρόνως μ.* Clem.*q.d.s.*38 (p.184.23; M.9.644A); Ephr.2.114F; *Μωϋσῆς...ἐξεκαίετο καὶ ἐμεμήνει καὶ ὑπὲρ αὐτῶν* [sc. Israelites] *πάσχειν ἕτοιμος ἦν* Chrys.*hom.7.4 in Eph.*(11.51C); *εἴ τις μ. καὶ περικαίεται τοῦ δεσπότου ib.8.1*(53A); **3.** *be deluded,* ref. 2Cor.4:7 *~ονται* [sc. death and Devil] *περὶ τὸ σαρκίον, οὗ καταφρονοῦσιν ὡς ἀσθενοῦς, τῶν ἔνδον ὄντες τυφλοὶ κτημάτων* Clem. *q.d.s.*34(p.182.19; M.9.640B); ref. pagan world *τὴν οἰκουμένην ἔτι μεμηνυῖαν ὁρῶν* [sc. *Κωνσταντῖνος*] Thdt.*h.e.*5.21.1(3.1055); of Herod and Pilate, Oecum.*1Cor.*2:8(p.432.8).

μαινομένη, ἡ, *salt fish,* Leont.N.*v.Jo.Eleem.*20(p.37.18).

μαι-όομαι, 1. *bring to birth*; of God at Nativity, ref. Ps.21:10 *σὺ αὐτὸς ὁ θεός μου καὶ πατήρ μου ὥσπερ ~ούμενος τὴν ἐμοὶ κατεσκευασμένην ἐξ ἁγίου πνεύματος σάρκα ἐξέσπασας* Eus.*d.e.*10.8(p.481.10; M.22.773B); **2.** *suckle,* Synes.*provid.*8(p.78.9; M.66.1225A); **3.** pass., *be born,* Nonn.*par.Jo.*9:34(M.43.829C).

***Μαϊουμᾶς, ὁ,** *May-day,* Thphn.*chron.*p.380(M.108.912A).

μαίωσις, ἡ, *giving birth,* ref. Ps.109:3 *τῆς πατρικῆς μαιώσεως φυσικὴν ἐνδείκνυται υἱότητα* Alex.Al.*ep.Alex.*8(p.25.1; *μαιεύσεως* M.18.560B).

μάκαρ, *blessed, happy*; **1.** of God *ἀθανάτου πατρὸς...μ. Hymn.*(*AGC* p.40); *σοί, μ. ὑψιμέδον CIG* 4.8608 (inscr. of Jov., c. 363); of heavenly Bridegroom, in invocation, Meth.*symp.*11(p.132.9,19; M.18.208D,209A); **2.** of men, as sharing in God's beatitude partic. after death: of a martyr named Macar *τὴν προσηγορίαν...ἀληθὴς M.* Dion.Al.ap.Eus.*h.e.*6.41.17(M.20.609B); plur., the *blessed dead τὰ μακάρων ἀγαθά* Clem.*str.*4.22(p.312.27; M.8.1356A); *μετενεχθεὶς εἰς τὴν μακάρων πόλιν, τοὺς οὐρανούς* Meth.*symp.*6.2(p.65.12; M.18.116A).

μακαρία, ἡ, *happiness, bliss*; name of Gnostic aeon, last of ten aeons produced by Logos and Zoe, Iren.*haer.*1.1.2(M.7.449A).

μακαρίζ-ω, 1. *pronounce happy* or *blessed* (act of God so making blessed in fact), *bless*; **a.** of God *μακάρισον κοινῇ πάντας* Serap.*euch.*18.2; *ὑπὸ θεοῦ μεμακαρισμένοι καὶ ὑπὸ ὁσίων ἀνδρῶν τετιμημένοι Const.App.*5.8.2; in respect of a particular gift *ἵνα...ἐπὶ σοὶ* [sc. *ὦ γύναι*] *μακαρισθῇ ὁ ἀνήρ ib.*1.8.2; in life to come, *ib.*4.3.3; **b.** of Christ *οἱ...~όμενοι πανταχοῦ οἱ ἐλεήμονές εἰσιν, οἱ ταπεινοὶ κτλ.* Chrys.*virg.*36(1.295D); esp. in beatitudes *τοὺς ἐθελήσαντας...πτωχοὺς γενέσθαι, τούτους μ.* Clem.*str.*4.6(p.260.1; M.8.1240A); Or.*Cels.*6.16 (p.87.11,14; M.11.1315A); *ὁ ~όμενος...κλαυθμός* id.*hom.20.6 in Jer.* (p.185.27,29; M.13.513A); *τοῦ ~ομένου ἐπὶ τῷ πεινῆν καὶ διψῆν τὴν δικαιοσύνην* id.*Jo.*13.4(p.229.13; M.14.404C); Gr.Nyss.*ordin.*(M.46.552C); *ὑπάρχει...τῷ...~ομένῳ τὸ εὐφραίνεσθαι τοῖς προκειμένοις εἰς ἀπόλαυσιν αὐτῷ* id.*beat.*1(M.44.1197A); S. Peter (ref. Mt.16:17) *ὁμοίως αὐτῷ ~όμενοι* Or.*comm.in Mt.*12.10(p.84.33; M.13.997A); id.*engast.*7(p.291.12; M.12.1024C); Dion.Al.ap.Eus.*h.e.*7.25.10(M.20.700A); *Clem.ep.*1(M.2.33A); *Hom.Clem.*17.18; Eus.*Marcell.*1.2(p.10.33; M.24.736A); id.*e.th.*1.16(p.75.26; M.24.856C); Didym.*Trin.*1.30 (M.39.417B); (ref. Jo.20:29) *πῶς...οὐ μακαριώτεροι οἱ ὀφθαλμοὶ οἱ ὑπὸ τοῦ Ἰησοῦ ~όμενοι ἐπὶ τοῖς τεθεωρημένοις τῶν μὴ φθασάντων ἐπὶ τὴν τῶν τοιούτων θέαν*; Or.*Jo.*10.43(27; p.222.6; M.14.393A); *ἐνταῦθα...οὐ τοὺς μαθητὰς μ. μόνους ἀλλὰ καὶ τοὺς μετ' ἐκείνους πιστεύοντας* Chrys.*hom.87.1 in Jo.*(8.520B); **c.** in scripture (ref. Apoc.22:27) *μ. ὁ προφήτης τοὺς...φυλάσσοντας αὐτήν* [sc. *τὴν προφητείαν*] Dion.Al.ap.Eus.*h.e.*7.25.6(M.20.697C); Gr.Nyss.*Pss.titt.* A 1(M.44.433D); *ἐνταῦθα...τὸ ἐπιγνῶναι τὸ ἀγαθὸν ~εται ib.*12(552C); (ref. Ps.143:15) *τὸν εὐσεβείᾳ κομῶντα...ἐγὼ μ., φησί* Chrys.*stat.*1.9 (2.14B); Thdt.*Ps.*118:2,3(1.1438); **2.** of angels, *call happy* or *blessed,* med. *μακάριοι ἐκεῖνοι ἐφ' οἷς οἱ ἄγγελοι οὐκ ἐροῦσι τὸ 'οἴμοι', ἀλλὰ ~ονται* Or.*hom.15.4 in Jer.*(p.128.21; M.13.433B); **3.** of persons, *call happy, deem happy* or *blessed*; **a.** angels *εὐφημοῦμεν αὐτοὺς* [sc. *τοὺς ἀγγέλους*] *καὶ μ.* Or.*Cels.*8.57(p.274.15; M.11.1604B); prophets, id.*hom.15.1 in Jer.*(p.125.11; M.13.428D); Church, Meth.*symp.*7.7 (p.78.5; M.18.133B); martyrs and confessors *τοὺς ὑπομένοντας ὑπὲρ δικαιοσύνης μακαρίσεις Diogn.*10.8; *~ετε ἑαυτούς* Herm.*sim.*9.28.6; *οἱ μὲν γὰρ ἄκοντες πάσχοντες...καταθρηνοῦνται· οἱ δ' ἑκουσίως ἀθλοῦντες ~ονται* Isid.Pel.*epp.*2.166(M.78.620B); other holy persons *οὐδένα χρὴ μ., ἀλλ' ἢ τὸν κατὰ θεὸν ζῶντα μόνον* Chrys.*stat.*18.3(2.185D); individuals, e.g. David, id.*David* 2.3(4.763B); the apostle John *μὴ μέχρι τούτου στῶμεν...τοῦ μακαρίζειν τὸν ἀπόστολον, ἀλλ' ὥστε καὶ τῶν ~ομένων γενέσθαι,...μιμώμεθα τὸν εὐαγγελιστήν* id.*hom.33.3 in Jo.*(8.193C); pre-eminently BMV *ἐν παντὶ τῷ κόσμῳ μ. καὶ εὐφημεῖται* Nil.*epp.*2.180(M.79.293A); *ἄξιόν ἐστιν ὡς ἀληθῶς ~ειν σέ Lit.Chrys.*(M.63.917); applicable esp. to those who have finished their course on earth *ὁ ἐν τῷ βίῳ τυγχάνων, οὔπω μακαριστός ...ὁ δὲ...ἀναντιρρήτῳ τέλει τὴν ζωὴν κατακλείσας, οὗτος ἤδη ἀσφαλῶς μ.* Bas.*hom.in Ps.*1(1.93A; M.29.217A); *οὐ χρὴ μ. πρὸ τελευτῆς ἄνθρωπον* Gr.Naz.*or.*16.3(M.35.937A); Chrys.*Laz.*7.3(1.794E); ways of life and thought *~ει μου ἡ ψυχὴ τὴν εἰς θεὸν αὐτοῦ γνώμην* Ign.*Philad.*1.2; Chrys.*hom.80.3 in Jo.*(8.476D); **b.** in error *δοξάζοντες καὶ ~οντες τοὺς ἐν ταῖς πλατείαις ἀσεβεῖν αὐτοῖς νενομισμένους* Or.*or.*19(p.343.5; M.11.477B); *τοὺς χαίροντας ἐπ' αὐτῷ* [sc. Montanus] *~οντος τοῦ* [sc. *νόθου*] *πνεύματος* Anon.ap.Eus.*h.e.*5.16.9(M.20.468B); *ἀμαθεῖς ἄνθρωποι...μ. ... τὰ μηδενὸς ἄξια* Bas.*hom.in Ps.*1 (1.92C; M.29.216C); Chrys.*exp.in Ps.*143:15(5.466B,C); Dion.Ar.*e.h.*4.3.1(M.3.476A); **4.** *felicitate, congratulate, 1Clem.*1.2; *ὑμᾶς ~ω τοὺς ἐνκεκραμένους οὕτως* [i.e. to their bishop] Ign.*Eph.*5.1; *παρὰ τῶν κολάκων μακαρισθῆναι* Bas.*hom.in Ps.*48(1.187B; M.29.456B); *αὐτὸν ...μ. πρὸς τὸ νικηφόρον...ἀφικνούμενον τέλος* Dion.Ar.*e.h.*7.1.3(M.3.556B); oneself, intrans. *~ων ἐπήγαγεν* †Dion.Al.*fr.Eccl.*2:12(p.218.16; M.10.1584A).

***μακαριοποιός,** *producing happiness, making for happiness ἀπαθῆ καὶ μ. φόβον...δηλοῦσθαι ἐκ τοῦ 'ἐν φόβῳ Χριστοῦ'* Or.*comm.in Eph.*5:21(p.566).

μακάριος, *happy, blessed* [superl. *μακαριέστατος* Epiph.*haer.*67.4 (p.137.8; M.42.177C)];

A. properly a divine epithet *μ. ... τῷ ὄντι τὸ αὐτόκαλον* Bas.*hom. in Ps.*1(1.92B; M.29.216B); Gr.Nyss.*Pss.titt.*A 1(M.44.433C) cit. s. B infra; cf. *ἔστι...τὸ κυρίως καὶ πρώτως μακαριστὸν τὸ ἀληθινῶς ἀγαθὸν* Bas.*hom.in Ps.*1 l.c.; Thdt.*Ps.*1:1(1.610); **1.** of God *τῆς μ. φύσεως τοῦ θεοῦ* Meth.*symp.*2.6(p.23.16; M.18.57A); Bas.*ep.*243(3.375C; M.32.909A); Thdr.Mops.*1Tim.*1:11(p.77.18f.; M.66.937B) cit. s. B infra; *μ. αὐτὸν ἐκάλεσεν ἐπὶ συστάσει τῆς μελλούσης προσέσεσθαι ἡμῖν ἀτρεπτότητος ib.*6:15(p.184.17; M.66.944C); Thdt.*1Tim.*6:15(3.672); Dion.Ar.*d.n.*8.6(M.3.893C); Zach.Mit.*opif.*(M.85.1096C); *συναΐδιον τῇ μ. φύσει ib.*(1097A); Jo.D.*f.o.*1.1(M.94.789A); of Son *ἑαυτὸν...ἐταπείνωσεν, οὐδὲν δ' ἧττον μ. ἦν* Or.*Cels.*4.15(p.285.5; M.11.1045B); incarnate *ἐμακαρίσθη* [sc. *ὁ Πέτρος*] *ὑπὸ τοῦ μόνου μ. δεσπότου* Didym.*Trin.*1.30(M.39.417B); *ἡ σάρξ...ἡ ἄχραντος καὶ μ.* Meth.*symp.*7.8(p.79.11; M.18.136B); comp. of Christ in relation to the just *Χριστὸς...*[sc. *οὐσίας*] *θειοτέρας καὶ ἐνδοξοτέρας καὶ μακαριωτέρας* Or.*dial.*3(p.126); of Trin. *τὴν ἁγίαν καὶ μ. τριάδα* Eus.*p.e.*11.20 (541B; M.21.901B); id.*Marcell.*1.1(p.3.24; M.24.716C); Didym.(‡Bas.) *Eun.*5(1.297B; M.29.713A); **2.** of what pertains to God: image of God in man *τὰς τὴν μ. χαρακτῆρων ἐμφάσεις...τὴν μ. ... μορφὴν* Gr.Nyss.*beat.*1(M.44.1197C); as presented to mystical contemplation *ὀψόμεθα θεωρίαν, τὸ μ. ἀποστίλβουσαν ἐμφανῶς τῶν ἀρχετύπων κάλλος* Dion.Ar.*e.h.*3.3.2(M.3.428C); *ib.*4.3.2(476B); *τῆς ὑπὲρ νοῦν* ἑνώσεως ἐν ταῖς τῶν ὑπερφανῶν ἀκτίνων ἀγνώστοις καὶ μ. ἐπιβολαῖς id.*d.n.*1.4(M.3.592C).

B. of other things in God μ. ἐστιν, ὃ κυρίως λέγεται. καὶ πρώτως, ἡ τοῦ παντὸς ἐπέκεινα φύσις· τὸ δὲ ἐν ἀνθρώποις μ., τῇ μεθέξει τοῦ ὄντως ὄντος Gr.Nyss.*Pss.titt.*A 1(M.44.433C); τὸ ἀληθῶς ἀγαθὸν... μόνον ἐστὶ...μ. ... τῇ φύσει, οὐ πᾶν τὸ μετέχον μ. γίνεται *ib.*; μ. αὐτὸν ἐνταῦθα καλεῖ, ὡς ἂν αὐτοῦ μὲν τὸ μ. ἔχοντος ἐν τῇ φύσει...ἡμῖν δὲ χάριτι τοῦτο περιποιοῦντος Thdr.Mops.*1Tim.*1:11(p.77.18f.; M.66.937B); opp. τὸ ἄθλιον, Gr.Nyss.*beat.*1(M.44.1197A); **1.** of good angels τὰ σπουδαῖα καὶ μ. ... οἱ ἀγαθοὶ δαίμονες εἴτε ὡς ἡμῖν ἔθος ὀνομάζειν, οἱ τοῦ θεοῦ ἄγγελοι Or.*Cels.*4.24(p.293.26; M.11.1061B); οὐ πάντες ἄγγελοι ἄγγελοι λέγονται εἶναι τοῦ θεοῦ ἀλλὰ μόνοι οἱ μ. *ib.*8.25(p.241.31; 1553C); id.*or.*31(p.400.3; M.11.556B); Dion.Ar.*c.h.*1.2(M.3.121B); *ib.*13.4(304C); **2.** of man in Christ ἡ [sc. πύλη] ἐν Χριστῷ, ἐν ᾗ μ. πάντες *1Clem.*48.4; διὰ τοῦ λόγου...πάντα τὰ κατορθώματα κατορθῶσθαι τοῖς μ. νοεῖν ἀναγκαῖον Or.*Jo.*2.13(7; p.68.24; M.14.133D); cf. εἰ δ' οἰκεῖοι τοῦ σωτῆρος ἦσαν καὶ τῆς μ. φύσεως, πῶς ἐζήτουν αὐτὸν ἀποκτεῖναι; *ib.*20.8(p.336.11; 589B); of women because of BMV, Procl.CP *or.*5.3(M.65.720B); of all Christians μ. ... ἡμεῖς οἱ περιτμηθέντες...τὴν δευτέραν περιτομὴν Just.*dial.*114.4(M.6.740B); τὸ...ἐν ταῖς καρδίαις τῶν μ. κρᾶζον...πνεῦμα Or.*or.*2(p.301.10; M.11.420C); ὑμεῖς...μ. ... ἔθνος ἅγιον *Const.App.*5.15.1; 6.22.1; esp. of the holy τῇ δικαίᾳ ψυχῇ, ὅταν μ. μὲν αὐτὴ τυγχάνῃ...μ. δὲ διαπραττομένη ἔργα Clem.*str.*7.5(p.21.32; M.9.440A); θείας τινὸς γενικῆς αἰσθήσεως ἣν μόνος ὁ μ. εὑρίσκει Or.*Cels.*1.48(p.98.10; M.11.749A); *ib.*6.5(p.75.18; 1297A); μ. ... ὁ βαπτιζόμενος ἐν ἁγίῳ πνεύματι καὶ μὴ δεόμενος βαπτίσματος τοῦ ἀπὸ πυρός id.*hom.2.3 in Jer.*(p.19.14; M.13.281A); ‡Nil.*perist.*10 tit.(M.79.885A); of different classes of persons: blessed in observance of Christian practices οἱ...τοῖς προτεταγμένοις καιροῖς ποιοῦντες τὰς προσφορὰς αὐτῶν εὐπρόσδεκτοί τε καὶ μ. *1Clem.*40.4; μ. πᾶς ὁ εὑρεθεὶς ἐν τούτοις [sc. ἐλεημοσύνῃ, μετανοίᾳ, νηστείᾳ, προσευχῇ] πλήρης *2Clem.*16.4; open to all alike οὐ γὰρ εἶπεν ὁ δεῖνα καὶ ὁ δεῖνα, ἀλλ' ὁ ταῦτα ποιοῦντες μ. πάντες Chrys.*hom.15.2 in Mt.*(7.187B); in embracing the gospel, Or.*Jo.*1.9(11; p.15.3; M.14.41A); in knowledge and practice of divine will, *ib.*32.13(8; p.446.13; 773B); and of the good, Gr.Nyss.*Pss.titt.*B 12(M.44.552C); in intimacy with God Ἰησοῦν ἐν ἑαυτῷ ἔχοντος καὶ ἀπαξαπλῶς μ. Or.*or.*32.13(8; p.446.19; 773C); μ. ὁ γευσάμενος τῆς ἀγάπης αὐτοῦ Ephr.1.49A; ᾧτινι...ἐξεγένετο...θεῷ συγγενέσθαι...μ. οὗτος Gr.Naz.*or.*21.2(M.35.1084C); πάντων...οὗτος μακαριώτατος, τὸν θεὸν ἔχων φίλον Chrys.*kal.*4(1.702C); id.*stat.*1.9(2.14B); id.*exp.in Ps.*143:15(5.466D); and with BMV σοι θνησκούσῃ συναποθνήσκειν μ. Jo.D.*hom.*9.9(M.96.736A); associated with ἀρετή: ἡ ἀρετὴ ἡ γνωστικὴ...μ. ... τὸν ἄνθρωπον κατασκευάζουσα Clem.*ecl.*37(p.148.9; M.9.717A); ἡ αὐτὴ ἀρετή ἐστι τῶν μ. πάντων, ὥστε καὶ ἡ αὐτὴ ἀρετὴ ἀνθρώπου καὶ θεοῦ Or.*Cels.*4.29(p.298.27; M.11.1069D); μ. εἶναι...τοὺς κατ' ἀρετὴν βιώσαντας ἢ τὰς κατ' ἀρετὴν πράξεις ποιήσαντας *ib.*6.55(p.126.13; 1384B); cf. μ. γίνεται ἐν τῇ ζωῇ αὐτοῦ, ὅτι πάντων τῶν πονηρῶν ἔργων ἀφέξεται Herm.*vis.*3.8.4; id.*mand.*8.9; ἡ τῆς ἀρετῆς κτῆσις πρὸς τὸ μ. γενέσθαι τὸν κατ' αὐτὴν ζῶντα βλέπει Gr.Nyss.*Pss.titt.*A 1(M.44.433B); τὸ...μ. ὄνομα τῆς κατ' ἀρετὴν τελειώσεως ὑπάρχει καρπός Thdt.*Ps.*1:1(1.610); **3.** as title of the saints; **a.** of Bible; OT: Judith, *1Clem.*55.4; prophets, Hipp.*Dan.*3.2.3; Hannah, *Const.App.*5.20.15; Job, *ib.*6.5.5; Abraham, Didym.(‡Bas.)*Eun.*5(1.313E; M.29.752C); Joseph, Chrys.*hom.71.3 in Jo.*(8.420E); οἱ τρεῖς μ. παῖδες Thdt.*qu.7 in Gen.*(1.12); τῶν μ. πατριαρχῶν καὶ τῶν λοιπῶν ἁγίων ἁπάντων Dion.Ar.*e.h.*7.3.5(M.3.560B); NT: of BMV, Or.*hom.7 in Lc.*(p.46.5; M.17.320D); ἡ Μαρία καθ' ἑκάστην ἡμέραν ἀκούει παρὰ πάντων μακαρία Sever.*creat.*6.10(M.56.497); ἐκ τῆς μ. παρθένου Nest.*fr.*C 10(p.274.13)ap.Cyr.*Nest.*2.2(p.36.29; 6¹.36C); Jo.D.*hom.*9.9(M.96.736A); and Elisabeth, Or.*hom.8 in Lc.*(p.55.7; 321A); S. Andrew, *A.Andr.fr.*12(p.43.14); S. Philip, *A.Phil.*26(p.14.17); S. Stephen, both as NT character and as protomartyr, *Const.App.*6.30.10; οἱ μ. ἀπόστολοι Iren.*haer.*3.3.3(M.7.849A); of biblical writers: Moses, *1Clem.*43.1; as a prophet, Just.*dial.*112.3(M.6.733C); David, *ib.*32.3(544B); Ath.*apol.sec.*2(p.88.23; M.25.249D); τῶν μ. προφητῶν Just.*dial.*48.4(581A); Or.*Cels.*1.48(p.98.19; M.11.749B); S. Paul, *1Clem.*47.1; Polyc.*ep.*3.2; S. Peter, Clem.*fr.*36(p.219.3; M.9.769A); S. John, *A.Jo.*26(p.165.14); Hipp.*Noët.*14(p.255.26; M.10.821A); author of Apoc., Dion.Al.ap.Eus.*h.e.*7.25.13(M.20.700C); S. Luke, Or.*hom.1 in Lc.*(p.10.9); τῶν μ. εὐαγγελιστῶν Hipp.*haer.*5.23(p.125.4; M.16.3191A); **b.** post-biblical times, esp. of martyrs, *M.Polyc.*1.1; *ib.*19.1; Polyc.*ep.*9.1; Iren.*ep.Flor.*ap.Eus.*h.e.*5.20.6f.(M.20.483f.); Dion.Al.*ib.*7.11.24(672B); *A.Xanthipp.*14(p.67.10); Ath.*syn.*4(p.233.27; M.26.688B); *Const.App.*5.1.1; *M.Das.*2; *M.Ner.et Ach.*8(p.7.17); of one who ministers to martyrs μ. ἔσται καὶ φίλος τοῦ Χριστοῦ *Const.App.*5.1.3; and shares their lot, *ib.*5.2.3; of Christian writers ἤδη τοῦ μ. πρεσβυτέρου Εἰρηναίου...τὰ δόγματα αὐτῶν διελέγξαντος Hipp.*haer.*6.55(p.189.11; M.16.3291B); πολλοὶ τῶν μ. ἡμῶν διδασκάλων...λόγοι· οἷς ἐάν τις ἐντύχοι, εἴσεται μέν πως τὴν τῶν γραφῶν ἑρμηνείαν Ath.*gent.*1(M.25.4A); and other saints (but v. 4 infra) ὁ μακαριώτατος ἐπίσκοπος Ἀθανάσιος Bas.*ep.*214.2(3.321C; M.32.785C); *ib.*258.3(3.394B; M.952A); τὸν μακαριώτατον Διονύσιον [i.e. of Milan] *ib.*197.2(3.288B; M.712A); and what appertains to them τοὺς...φύλακας τοῦ μ. σώματος...τῇ μ. ψυχῇ *ib.*(288D,289A; M.712B,C); τοῦ μ. Κυρίλλου *Doct.Patr.*2.35(p.21.9); **c.** abs., *saint*, of martyrs ἕκαστος τῶν μ. Or.*mart.*31(p.27.20; M.11.601C); ἤνεγκεν ὁ μ. ἀλγηδόνας Eus.*m.P.*4.12(p.916.12; M.20.1477A); ἔρριψαν ἐκεῖ τὸν μ. Alex.Sal.*Barn.*2.29(p.445B); and others (ref. Ps.142:2) ὡς πρὸς τὸν θεὸν καὶ τὴν ἐν αὐτῷ δικαιοσύνην οὐδεὶς δικαιωθήσεται τῶν πάνυ μ. Or.*Jo.*2.17(11; p.74.13; M.14.144C); τὴν τῶν δικαίων καὶ μ. πανήγυριν id.*Cels.*6.61(p.131.23; M.11.1392B); **4. a.** eccl. title, of bishops of Roman see τὸν μ. Οὐΐκτορα, ὄντα ἐπίσκοπον τῆς ἐκκλησίας Hipp.*haer.*9.12(p.247.29; M.16.3382D); ὁ μ. ὑμῶν ἐπίσκοπος Σωτήρ Dion.Al.ap.Eus.*h.e.*4.23.10(M.20.388B); μακαριωτάτῳ πάπᾳ Ἰουλίῳ Ath.*apol.sec.*58(p.138.3; M.25.353B) etc.; cf. τὸν ἐπίσκοπον τοῦ μ. θρόνου *Cod.Afr.*proem.(H.1.865D); and others Ἀθανασίῳ μ. πάπᾳ ...μακαριώτατε πάπα Arsen.Hyps.*ep.*(pp.147.11,148.8; M.25.372B, 373A); οἱ μ. συλλειτουργοὶ ἡμῶν Ath.*apol.sec.*89(p.167.11; M.25.408B); Bas.*ep.*225(3.345B; M.32.841A); superl., Capr.*ep.Eph.*tit.(p.52.16; M.*PL.*53.844B); and other clergy διὰ Κλήμεντος τοῦ μ. πρεσβυτέρου Alex.H.ap.Eus.*h.e.*6.11.6(M.20.544B); **b.** mode of address ὦ μακαρία Meth.*symp.*proem.(p.6.13; M.18.36A); to the reader, Ath.*gent.*1(M.25.4A); Dion.Ar.*d.n.*1.1(M.3.585B).

C. of states and activities having God as their object; **1.** of angels ἡ...τῶν Σεραφὶμ τάξις...τοῖς μακαριωτάτοις αὐτοῦ [sc. Ἰησοῦ] θεάμασιν...ἐπιβάλλουσα Dion.Ar.*e.h.*4.3.5(M.3.480B); αἱ...τῶν ἀγγελικῶν νοῶν δυνάμεις τὰς ἁπλᾶς καὶ μ. ἔχουσι νοήσεις id.*d.n.*7.2(M.3.868B); τῆς πρὸς αὐτὸ [sc. τὸ ἕν] μακαριωτάτης ἑνώσεως *ib.*1.5(593C); **2.** of men καὶ οἶμαι νοεῖσθαι θεοῦ μὲν βασιλείαν τὴν μ. τοῦ ἡγεμονικοῦ κατάστασιν Or.*or.*25(p.357.9; M.11.496C); δεῖ...ἐπιλελῆσθαι τῶν ἔξω τῆς εὐχῆς κατὰ τὸν καιρόν, ἐν ᾧ τις εὔχεται (τοιοῦτον δὲ εἶναι πῶς οὐκ ἐστὶ μακαριώτατον;) *ib.*9(p.318.4; 444A); ὑπόθεσίς ἐστι τῆς μ. ζωῆς, ἡ τῶν παθῶν νέκρωσις Isid.Pel.*epp.*3.227(M.78.909B); τῶν θεουργιῶν γνώσεως...δι' ἧς...μακαριωτάτη κοινωνία τελεσιουργεῖται Dion.Ar.*e.h.*5.1.3(M.3.504C); ἐν μ. καὶ νοητοῖς θεάμασιν *ib.*3.2(428A); id.*d.n.*2.9(M.3.648B).

D. of all that brings salvation to man: death of Christ μακαριωτάτῃ ἐξόδῳ Or.*Jo.*10.18(13; p.189.31; M.14.340A); Church τῇ μ. Ἀντιοχέων ἐκκλησίᾳ Alex.H.ap.Eus.*h.e.*6.11.5(M.20.544B); the faith τὴν ἀληθῆ τῆς μ. σῴζοντες διδασκαλίας παράδοσιν Clem.*str.*1.1(p.9.4; M.8.700A); and means by which it is imparted ἀρκεῖ...ἡ μ. γλῶττα [i.e. of S. Paul] φήσασα 'καθὼς γέγραπται' Thdt.*2Cor.*2:9(3.177); new life τοῦ νοητοῦ καὶ μ. σπέρματος Meth.*symp.*3.8(p.35.16; M.18.73A).

E. in connexion with life to come; **1.** of the departed μ. οἱ προοδοιπορήσαντες πρεσβύτεροι *1Clem.*44.5; ἔθετο νόμους, καθ' οὓς οἱ βιοῦντες μ. ἔσονται Or.*Cels.*4.32(p.302.19; M.11.1077A); id.*princ.*3.1.8(p.208.5; M.11.261C); αἱ...μ. ψυχαὶ πατριαρχῶν καὶ προφητῶν καὶ ἀποστόλων Eus.*e.th.*2.9(p.109.33; M.24.917D); Gr.Naz.*or.*7.17(M.35.776B); abs. σῴζονται ἐν τῇ τῶν μ. κληρονομίᾳ Just.*dial.*67.7(M.6.632A); εἰς ἀπεράντους αἰῶνας ἡ τῶν μ. ἐστὶν ἀνάπαυσις Or.*fr.58 in Lc.*12:19(p.261); id.*hom.12.3 in Jer.*(p.90.16; M.13.384B); τοὺς ἐξεληλυθότας μ. opp. τοῦ ὄντος ἐν τῷ σώματι, id.*or.*31(p.399.10; M.11.556A); of individuals who have died in the faith: clergy, Serap.Ant.ap.Eus.*h.e.*5.19.2(M.20.481A); Bas.*ep.*81(3.174B; M.32.457A); *ib.*263.3(3.406A; M.977C); *ib.*(3.406C; M.980A); *ib.*95(3.189C; M.489C); and laity, Gr.Naz.*test.*(M.37.392A); *CIG* 4.9117 (Nubia); *IGC As.Min.*255 (saec. vi); of deceased emperors, Juln.Imp.*ep.*60(p.67.2); with μνήμη: ὁ θεοφιλέστατος καὶ μ. μνήμης βασιλεὺς Κωνσταντῖνος Ath.*apol.sec.*70(p.148.10; M.25.373A); ὑπὲρ ἀναπαύσεως κοιμήσεως κὲ μακαρήας μνήμης τοῦ δούλου...τοῦ θ(εο)ῦ *MAMA* 1.260; τῆς εὐλαβοῦς καὶ μ. μνήμης Τιμοθέου διακ[όνου] *Inscr.*, *ib.*1 p.xxv; **2.** of state of faithful departed; **a.** μακάριος αὐτὸν ἀναμένει χρόνος *2Clem.*19.4; ἡ μέλλουσα μ. ζωή Or.*Cels.*3.81(p.271.17; M.11.1025B); ταῖς ...ὑπερκοσμίοις καὶ μ. λήξεσιν Dion.Ar.*e.h.*1.4(M.3.376B); *ib.*7.1.1(553B); *ib.*7.1.2(553C); id.*ep.*8.5(M.3.1097A); ἀνάπαυλαν...τῶν πολλῶν πόνων, καὶ ζωὴν ἀπήμονα...καὶ μ. ἀγαθῶν ἄφθονον χορηγίαν *ib.*9.5(1113A); **b.** ref. general resurrection τὴν ἐλπιζομένην μ. καὶ τελείαν ἀνάστασιν Or.*Jo.*10.35(20; p.210.10; M.14.372C); ὥστε καὶ ἀγγέλους καὶ πᾶσαν τὴν κτίσιν ἀνακαινίζεσθαι εἰς κρείττονα καὶ μ. κατάστασιν Cosm.Ind.*top.*2(M.88.128B); **c.** with τέλος: ἵν'...εἰς τέλος ἀγάγῃ τῶν ἐξουσιαζομένων μ. Or.*or*.26(p.361.19; M.11.501C); τὸ καθ' ἡμᾶς παρὰ θεῷ ἐν Χριστῷ...τέλος μ. τοῖς ἀμέμπτως καὶ καθαρῶς βιώσασι id. *Cels*.3.81(p.271.23; M.11.1025C); ἐν τέλει εὑρίσκεται μακαριωτάτῳ id. *Jo*.19.21(p.322.20; M.14.565B); Eus.*e.th*.3.17(p.176.19; M.24.1036D); and τελείωσις: αἰτῆσαι τὴν ἐν Χριστῷ μ. τελείωσιν Dion.Ar.*e.h*.7.2 (M.3.556D); *ib*.7.3.3(560A); *ib*.7.3.5(560C) cit. s. μακαριστός; **3.** neut. as subst., *beatitude*, summum bonum ἐξ ἀμφοτέρων [sc. faith and works]...πιστεύωμεν ἢ τὸ ἀνέγκλητον ἔξειν ἢ κατὰ τὸ μ., ἢ ἐναντίον τούτοις Or.*dial*.9(p.142); τὸ μ. οὐκ εἶναι ἐνταῦθα, ἀλλ' ἐν τῷ...μέλλοντι αἰῶνι id.*Cels*.2.42(p.165.30; M.11.864B); τὸ πάντων μακαριώτατον, εἴτε ἀΐδιός ἐστι ζωή, ἢ παράμονος ὑγίεια, ἢ τέλειος νοῦς κτλ.*Hom.Clem*.2.5; also in paradise before Fall ἐν ἀρχῇ...τὴν πρώτην ἐν μακαρίοις ζωήν Eus.*h.e*.1.2.18(M.20.61C); **4.** of heavenly Jerusalem, Meth.*symp*.4.5 (p.51.18; M.18.96A).

F. of material objects in allegories μακαριωτέρων λίθων [sc. of Temple] Or.*Jo*.10.40(24; p.218.8; M.14.385C); cf. *felix hoc genus* [sc. *lapidum*], Herm.*sim*.9.30.3; κοσμήσαντες...τὴν σκηνὴν κλάδοις ἁγνείας, τῷ θεοποιῷ καὶ μ. φυτῷ Meth.*symp*.9.4(p.119.10; M.18. 188A).

G. Gnost. ἡ πρώτη καὶ μ. κατ' αὐτοὺς ἀσχημάτιστος οὐσία Hipp. *haer*.5.7(p.83.1; M.16.3131C); ἡ τῶν ὑπερκοσμίων...μ. φύσις *ib*.(p.82. 2; 3131A); τῆς μ. φύσεως τοῦ λόγου *ib*.(p.86.18; 3135C); μία...ἡ μ. φύσις τοῦ μ. ἀνθρώπου τοῦ ἄνω *ib*.5.8(p.89.11; 3139B); υἱόν, οὐ ψυχικόν, οὐ σωματικόν, ἀλλὰ μ. αἰῶνα αἰώνων *ib*.(p.97.19; 3151C); τὴν μ. υἱότητα *ib*.7.27(p.207.27; 3319C).

μακαριότης, ἡ, *beatitude, bliss, happiness*;

A. properly only of Godhead ἔστι γὰρ αὐτῷ ἀρετὴ καὶ μ. καὶ θειότης Or.*Cels*.6.62(p.132.26; M.11.1393A); *ib*.3.47(p.243.25; 981B); ἐχθρὸς...τῇ μ. σου id.*hom.14.15 in Jer*.(p.121.23; M.13.424C); μ. ἐστὶν ἡ ἀκήρατος ἐκείνη ζωή, τὸ ἄρρητον...ἀγαθόν, τὸ ἀνέκφραστον κάλλος Gr.Nyss.*beat*.1(M.44.1197A); *ib*.(1197B); ἡ ἀφθορία, ἡ μ.,... πᾶν τίμιον ὄνομα οὕτως λέγεται ἐπὶ τοῦ ἁγίου πνεύματος, ὡς καὶ ἐπὶ τοῦ πατρὸς καὶ ἐπὶ τοῦ υἱοῦ id.*fid*.(M.45.144A); Gel.Cyz.*h.e*.2.15.8(M.85. 1260B); ἡ θεία μ. Dion.Ar.*c.h*.3.2(M.3.165C); id.*e.h*.2.2.7(M.3.396D); *ib*.1.3(373D); hence of risen and glorified Christ ἐκεῖνος ἐν τῷ θανάτῳ καταδυείς, πάλιν ἐπὶ τὴν ἰδίαν ἀναλύειν μ. Gr.Nyss.*or.catech*.35 (p.135.16; M.45.89C); γυμνὸν ἀναστήσας τὸ σῶμα, δόξης...καὶ μ. ἐμπεπλησμένον Chrys.*delic*.6(3.343B); ἵνα...συνυψώσῃ τὴν ἑνωθεῖσαν αὐτῷ ἀνθρωπότητα...τῆς...ἀϊδίου τιμῆς καὶ μ. ἀπαρχομένην Leont.H. *Nest*.5.1(M.86.1724C).

B. *summum bonum* of angels, state in which angels were created by God ἐκπεσὼν [sc. Satan] τῆς μ. Or.*Cels*.6.44(p.115.14; M.11. 1368A); lesser angels, id.*princ*.1.8.1(p.97.5,16); *ib*.4.2.7(p.319.11; M. 11.372B); in which unfallen angels remain, Meth.*res*.1.49(p.302.8; M.18.277A).

C. *summum bonum* of man, counterpart of eternal life μ. ... ὅταν εἴπω, τὴν κορυφὴν λέγω τῶν ἀγαθῶν ἁπάντων Chrys.*hom.8.2 in Rom*.(9.499B); **1.** its source; divine beatitude in which man participates through Christ, Or.*Jo*.1.27(29; p.35.7; M.14.76A); id.*Cels*.7.44 (p.196.8; M.11.1485B); *ib*.8.6(p.225.13; 1528A); **2.** in what it consists; **a.** knowledge of God (Jo.17:3), Clem.*fr*.44(p.223.18); τὴν ἀπὸ τοῦ γινώσκεσθαι ἡμῖν αὐτὸν ἐγγινομένην ταῖς ψυχαῖς ἡμῶν μ. Or.*Cels*. 4.6(p.279.1; M.11.1036D); μηδὲ ἄλλο τι...τὴν βασιλείαν τῶν οὐρανῶν νομίσητε ἢ τὴν τῶν ὄντων ἀληθῆ κατανόησιν, ἣν καὶ μ. ὀνομάζουσιν αἱ... γραφαί Evagr.Pont.*ep*.12(M.32.265C); εἰ τὸ γνῶναι μ. πηλίκον τὸ γινωσκόμενον; Gr.Naz.*or*.23.11(M.35.1164B); μ. ... περίληψις πάντων τῶν κατὰ τὸ ἀγαθὸν νοουμένων Gr.Nyss.*beat*.1(M.44.1196D); **b.** likeness to God ὅρος ἐστὶ τῆς ἀνθρωπίνης μ. ἡ πρὸς τὸ θεῖον ὁμοίωσις Gr.Nyss.*Pss.titt*.A 1(M.44.433C); **c.** adoption εἰς τὴν τῆς υἱοθεσίας εἰσποιηθήσεσθαι ἀξίαν, ἥτις ἐστὶν ὁ ἀκρότατος τῆς μ. ὅρος Isid.Pel. *epp*.4.169(M.78.1261C); **d.** in rel. to εὐδαιμονία: opposed τοὺς... κακοδαίμονας ἐπὶ εὐδαιμονίαν [sc. προτρέπομεν] ἤ, ὅπερ κυριώτερόν ἐστιν εἰπεῖν, ἐπὶ μ. Or.*Cels*.3.59(p.254.11; M.11.1000A); equated, Max.*ambig*.(M.91.1173A); also with εὐζωΐα, Gr.Naz.*carm*.1.2.34.257 (M.37.964A); **e.** associated with ἀπάθεια: ἡ...ἀποτελουμένη μορφὴ [i.e. in Cant.], μ. ἐστὶ καὶ ἀπάθεια, καὶ ἡ πρὸς τὸ θεῖον συνάφεια Gr. Nyss.*hom.1 in Cant*.(M.44.776B); v. infra 3.a; **3.** its recipients; **a.** man as originally created in image of God, Gr.Nyss.*mort*.(M. 46.521D); τῇ μ. τῆς ἀθανασίας ἐρειδομένη [sc. ἡ ἀνθρωπίνη φύσις] id. *hom.opif*.4(M.44.136D); of Eden τῶν φωτεινῶν...τῆς μ. τόπων id.*or. dom*.5(p.102.15; M.44.1184C); τίς ἐξοικισθέντα με τοῦ παραδείσου... ἐπὶ τὴν πρώτην ἕλκει μ.; *ib*.1(p.10.37; 1125C); ἀπόκληρος τῆς πατρίδος ἐγώ, καὶ τῆς...μ. ὑπερόριος Germ.CP *or*.1(M.98.229B); lost by Fall (ref. Gen.3:22) διὰ τὸν ἕνα ἐκπεσόντα τῆς μ. Or.*Jo*.32.18(11; p.457.3; M.14.792B); τῆς κατὰ τὸ ἀπαθὲς νοουμένης μ. ἐκπεσόντες Gr.Nyss.*or. catech*.8(p.42.9; M.45.33B); **b.** man redeemed by Christ ἐν ἑκάστῳ ...τῶν τελείων, ἐχόντων τὸ ἄθροισμα τῶν συμπληρούντων τὴν μ. ... ἐστὶν ἡ...ἐκκλησία Or.*comm.in Mt*.12.10(p.86.9; M.13.997B); ἐν μ. ἀρξαμένων καὶ μεινάντων τῶν ἁγίων id.*Jo*.1.20(22; p.25.13; M.14. 57C); possession of the baptized ἔχοντες τὴν μ. τοῦ φωτὸς μὴ ζητήσητε τὸ σκότος *A.Phil*.140(p.75.13); ἤδη μακαριότητος ὀσμὴ πρὸς ὑμᾶς, ὦ φωτιζόμενοι Cyr.H.*procatech*.1; οὐκ ἔστιν ἡ βασιλεία τοῦ θεοῦ βρῶσις καὶ πόσις, ἀλλὰ δικαιοσύνη καὶ ἀπάθεια, καὶ μ. Gr.Nyss. *hom.5 in Eccl*.(M.44.696B); begun here, continued hereafter λαμβάνει Γονέθλαν τὴν κάτω...καὶ Γονέθλαν τὴν ἄνω· ἡ γὰρ κατὰ θεὸν μ. ἐπαγγελίαν ἔχει ζωῆς, καὶ τῆς παρούσης, καὶ τῆς μελλούσης Proc.G. *Jos*.15:19(M.87.1032C); **c.** fully realized in life of heaven, Clem.*fr*. 44(p.223.18); Or.*Jo*.1.9(11; p.14.25; M.14.40D); id.*hom.17.6 in Jer*. (p.150.15; M.13.461D); ἵνα...συνῶσιν αὐτῷ καὶ ἀπολαύωσι μ. Meth. *res*.1.37(p.278.15; M.41.1104B); Eus.*e.th*.3.16(p.174.28; M.24.1033A); *ib*.3.17(p.178.9; 1040B); ἐπειδή...τις ἀξιωθῇ τῆς μακαρίας ἐκείνης σκηνῆς, εἰς ἀπεράντους αἰῶνας ἕξει τὴν μ. Ath.*exp.Ps*.14(M.27.100B); Gr.Naz.*or*.7.21(M.35.781C); *ib*.33.17(M.36.237A); τῆς παρούσης ζωῆς ...ὁ καρπός, τουτέστι μ. ἀτελεύτητος ‡Just.*qu.et resp*.123(M.6.1373A); γνώσεως φυσικῆς, ἣν διαδέχεται θεολογία καὶ ἐσχάτη μ. Pall.*h.Laus*.40 (p.126.5; M.34.1204C) = Evagr.*cap.pract*.A proem.(M.40.1221C); preeminently by saints and martyrs, Or.*Jo* 1.17(p.21.13; M.14.52B); id.*mart*.31(p.27.16; M.11.601C); Max.*opusc*.(M.91.33A) cit. s. ἐκθεωτικός; οὐχ...ἡμεῖς ἐσμεν ἄξιοι μνημονεύειν τῆς ἐκείνων [sc. τῶν ἁγίων] μ. *Lit.Jac*.(p.218.13); in Manicheism ἡ παρ' αὐτοῖς ἐλπιζομένη σωτηρία καὶ μ. Tit.Bost.*Man*.1.29(M.18.1112A); associated with ἀνάπαυσις, Or.*mart*.47(p.43.12; M.11.632A); id.*hom.15.1 in Jer*. (p.125.16; M.13.429A); Ἰησοῦ Χριστὲ...ἀνάπαυσόν με ἐν τῇ μ. σου *A.Phil*.144(p.87.2); **4.** in rel. to man's free will; **a.** not man's by nature πᾶν ὁτιποτοῦν λογικὸν μὴ οὐσιωδῶς ἔχειν ὡς ἀχώριστον συμβεβηκὸς τὴν μ. Or.*Jo*.2.18(12; p.75.9; M.14.145C); but by gift and calling of God, id.*princ*.3.1.12(p.217.2; M.11.272B); id.*Cels*.4.22 (p.292.11; M.11.1060A); τὴν ἐκλογὴν τοῦ θεοῦ καὶ τὴν μ. id.*hom.4.3 in Jer*.(p.26.5; M.13.289A); **b.** but which man may win by grace of God or reject at will, Or.*Cels*.3.69(p.262.9; M.11.1012B); id.*comm.in Gen*.ap.Eus.*p.e*.6.11(281D; M.12.52A); εἰ καὶ ἄξιοι διὰ τὰ δεύτερα αὐτῶν ἔργα μακαριότητος εἶεν, ἐπεὶ ἄνθρωποί εἰσι...πρῶτον δεῖ ἀπολαβεῖν αὐτοὺς τὰς ἁμαρτίας αὐτῶν id.*hom.16.5 in Jer*.(p.137.19; M.13.445A); πᾶσα μ. ... ἐκ τοῦ ἐφ' ἡμῖν ἤρτηται †Bas.*Is*.45(1.415D; M.30.205B); Gr.Naz.*or*.40.6(M.36.365B); ἄθλιοι...οἱ τῆς μ. ἐκείνης ἑαυτοὺς ἐκβάλλοντες Chrys.*hom.39.5 in Jo*.(8.234D); under old dispensation gained by obedience to Law and prophets, Epiph.*haer*. 42.11(p.143.18; M.41.753D); now by knowledge and practice of spiritual truth, Bas.*hom.in Ps*.14(1.354C; M.29.256C); and Christian virtues, Nil.*epp*.1.177(M.79.152B); Max.*ambig*.(M.91.1173A).

D. in more general sense, *happiness, blessedness* αἴτιον προκοπῆς καὶ μ. Or.*hom.14.3 in Jer*.(p.108.14; M.13.408A).

E. as title: of bishops, CEph.(431)*act*.2(*ACO* 1.1.3 p.54.28; H.1. 1465E); *Cod.Afr*.proem.(H.1.865E) (Lat. *beatitudo*); Justn.*Or*.(p.207. 30; M.86.979C) etc.; of pope, Pulch.*ep.Leon*.(p.9.18; M.*PL*.54. 906B); Eutych.*ep.Vigil*.(M.86.2404A); Jo.VI CP *ep*.(M.96.1421A); of abbots, Jo.Mosch.*prat*.127(M.87.2989C); Leont.N.*v.Sym*.17(M.93. 1692A).

F. Valent., one of dodecad of aeons emanating from Ἄνθρωπος and Ἐκκλησία: Ἐκκλησιαστικὸς καὶ Μ. Iren.*haer*.1.1.2(M.7.449B); Hipp.*haer*.6.30(p.157.22; M.16.3239A); one of thirty aeons, coupled with Θελητός, Epiph.*haer*.31.2(p.386.4,11; M.41.477A).

μακαρισμός, ὁ, 1. *promise of blessedness* τῶν τοὺς μ. φερόντων ἔργων καὶ λόγων Or.*Jo*.32.1(p.425.16; M.14.740C); ἀνθολογούμενοι τὸν μ. τοῦ πάθους ἑαυτῶν [of those about to be martyred] *M.Perp*.17 (p.87.13); or *pronouncement of blessedness* (two senses not always distinguishable) ἄλλο εἶδος αὐτοῦ παιδαγωγίας, ὁ μ. Clem.*paed*.1.10 (p.144.5; M.8.360A); ὃς μὲν [sc. ὁ δεδωκὼς] ἔχει τὸν τῆς εὐποιΐας μισθόν, σὺ δὲ τὸν τῆς εὐσυνειδήτου οἰκονομίας μ. *Const.App*.3.4.2; dist. from ἔπαινος: ἔστι δὲ...ἕτερον ἑκάτερον, μ. καὶ ἔπαινος. μακαρίζεται μὲν γάρ τις ἐπὶ τοῖς ἔξωθεν· ἐπαινεῖται δὲ ἐπὶ τοῖς ἔνδοθεν Synes.*regn*.4(p.10.3; M.66.1060A); by Christ (see also 2) τὰ δὲ ἐφόδια τῆς κυριακῆς ὁδοῦ οἱ μ. τοῦ κυρίου Clem.*ecl*.12(p.140.1; M.9.704B); τὸν ὑποδεέστερον λαβεῖν μ. [Jo.20:29] Or.*Jo*.10.43(27; p.222.5; M.14.393A); opp. κόλασις, Chrys. *hom.54.4 in Jo*.(8.320E); of partic. pronouncements: to S. Peter, Or.*comm.in Mt*.12.10(p.84.33; M.13.997A); to Mary of Bethany, ‡Eust.*Laz*.(p.47.1); in scripture (ref. Ps.31:1f., cit. Rom.4:7f.) οὗτος ὁ μ. ἐγένετο ἐπὶ τοὺς ἐκλελεγμένους ὑπὸ τοῦ θεοῦ *1Clem*.50.7 = Clem.*str*.2.15(p.148.8; M.8.1004A) cf.Rom.4:9; (ref. Ps.128:1) τὸν ⟨τοῖς⟩ ἐν τῷ εὐαγγελίῳ ἐμφερῆ μ. *ib*.2.13(p.144.27; 997A); σπουδάζωμεν ἐπὶ τοὺς μ. τῶν προφητῶν Or.*hom.15.2 in Jer*.(p.126.23; M.13. 429C); Gr.Nyss.*Pss.titt*.B 12(M.44.552C); ἐπὶ τὸν ἀληθῆ θησαυρὸν τὸν μ. ἐκτείνει Chrys.*exp.in Ps.*143:15(5.466B); id.*hom.33.3 in Jo.*(8.193C); for women equally with men (ref. Ps.1:1) ἆρα μὴ τοῦ μ. τὰς γυναῖκας ἀπέκλεισε; μὴ γένοιτο. μία γὰρ ἀρετὴ ἀνδρὸς καὶ γυναικός Bas.*hom.in Ps.*1(1.92D; M.29.216D); μηδεὶς...ἄνδρα μόνον ὁρῶν ἐνταῦθα μακαριζόμενον ἐστερῆσθαι νομίσῃ τοῦδε τοῦ μ. τῶν γυναικῶν τὸ γένος... συμπεριλαμβάνει γὰρ τοῖς ἀνδράσι καὶ τὰς γυναῖκας ὁ λόγος Thdt. *Ps.*1:1(1.611); **2.** *beatitudes* of sermon on mount; plur., Or.*or.*18 (p.340.31; M.11.473D); id.*Jo.*10.19(14; p.190.7; M.14.340B); Eus.*d.e.*3.1(p.94.24; M.22.165B); †Bas.*bapt.*1.2.2(2.630B; M.31.1528B); Gr.Nyss. *ordin.*(M.46.552C); Cosm.Ind.*top.*5(M.88.288D); sing. ὅπου τὸν μ. διαγγέλλει [sc. ὁ κύριος] Gr.Nyss.*ep.*2(M.46.1009C); οὐκ εἰσάγει ἐν τάξει παραινέσεως τὰ λεγόμενα...ἀλλ' ἐν τάξει μ. Chrys.*hom.15.2 in Mt.*(7.187A); of a single beatitude, Gr.Nyss.*beat.*1(M.44.1196D); Chrys.*hom.77.3 in Jo.*(8.454E); a beatitude common to all ἐπὶ πάντων τὸν μ. ἔθηκεν ἵνα μηδὲν αἰσθητὸν ἀναμένῃς id.*hom.15.5 in Mt.* (7.191A); οὐδὲν...ταπεινοφροσύνης ἴσον. διὰ τοῦτο τῶν μ. ἐντεῦθεν ἤρξατο ὁ Χριστός id.*hom.33.3 in Jo.*(8.194A); τριπλῆς τριάδος εἰκών, ἡ τῶν μ. ἀρίθμησις *Apophth.Patr.*(M.65.165B); ἐν τῇ νέᾳ [sc. διαθήκῃ] οἱ μ. καὶ αὐτοὶ δέκα· ὁμοίως καὶ τὸ 'πάτερ ἡμῶν' δέκα λόγοι εἰσίν Jo.Eub.*concept.BMV* 22(M.96.1497C); of other beatitudes περὶ μ. καὶ ταλανισμῶν Ephr.2.334B tit.; **3.** *beatification, making blessed* or *happy* πάνυ ὀλίγοι χύσεως μ. ἐπιτεύξονται ἐξαιρέτου Or.*mart.*14(p.14.6; M.11.581B); τοῖς ἀξίοις μ. κλαίουσι λεγέσθω [Jer.38:16] id.*fr.55 in Jer.*(p.225.23); Dion.Al.ap.Eus.*p.e.*14.27(783A; M.21.1288B); τυχεῖν τοῦ παρ' αὐτοῦ μ. ἐν ἐλέει καὶ ζωῇ τῇ ἀπεράντῳ ‡Eust.*Laz.*(p.51.1); ἡ ...γραφὴ...τὴν μέθοδον τῆς τοῦ μ. κτίσεως τεχνολογοῦσα Gr.Nyss.*Pss. titt.*A 1(M.44.433D); ὥσπερ...μισθοῦ πλέον ἡ δικαιοσύνη, οὕτω δικαιοσύνης πλέον ὁ μ. Chrys.*hom.8.2 in Rom.*(9.499C); id.*exp.in Ps.* 143:15(5.466C); ἔπαθλον...τῆς...τῶν θείων μαθημάτων στοργῆς ἐστιν ὁ μ. Euthal.Diac.*Ac.*(M.85.633A); **4.** *estimate of beatitude, opinion as to beatitude* ἀμφοτέρων δὲ τελευτησάντων, διάφοροι μ. τούτων ἐγένοντο, ὡς ἀμφοτέρων τελειωθέντων Pall.*h.Laus.*14(p.38.11; M.34.1036B); **5.** *virtue* associated with a beatitude σὺν τοῖς ἄλλοις μ. καθαρὸς τῇ καρδίᾳ *V.Pach.Φ* 18(p.11.21).

μακαριστέον, *one must deem happy* or *blessed* τοὺς...ἀρετῆς ἆθλον τὴν ἱερωσύνην ἐσχηκότας ἐγκωμιαστέον καὶ μ. Isid.Pel.*epp.*5.379(M.78.1553C).

μακαριστός, 1. *to be deemed happy* or *blessed*; **a.** properly only of God ἔστι...τὸ κυρίως καὶ πρώτως μ. τὸ ἀληθινῶς ἀγαθόν. τοῦτο δέ ἐστιν ὁ θεός Bas.*hom.in Ps.*1(1.92B; M.29.216B); Gr.Nyss.*beat.*1(M.44.1197A); **b.** in secondary degree of man ἐπεὶ δὲ ὁ πλάσας τὸν ἄνθρωπον, κατ' εἰκόνα θεοῦ ἐποίησεν αὐτόν· δευτέρως ἂν εἴη μ. τὸ κατὰ μετουσίαν τῆς ὄντως μακαριότητος ἐν τῷ ὀνόματι τούτῳ γινόμενον *ib.* (1197B); of 'gnostic' ἐν πολλῷ τῷ βίῳ μ. οὐ διὰ τὸ μακρὸν ζῆν Clem. *ecl.*31(p.146.16; M.9.713C); μόνον κρίνομεν μ. τὸν ἐνάρετον Gr.Nyss. *v.Gr.Thaum.*(M.46.897B); in friendship τίς μακαριστότερος τοῦ ὑπὸ τοσούτων φίλων δορυφορουμένου; Isid.Pel.*epp.*5.172(M.78.1428B); of life of evangelical poverty, Clem.*q.d.s.*17(p.170.32; M.9.621B); **c.** strictly applicable only to the departed, Bas.*hom.in Ps.*1(1.93A; M.29.217A); **2.** *happy* οἱ κακοδαίμονες...μ. ἡγοῦνται βίον τὴν ἀκοσμίαν τὴν περὶ τὰ συμπόσια Clem.*paed.*2.2(p.171.21; M.8.420A); **3.** *blessed* ἡ μ. πίστις Const.ap.Eus.*v.C.*2.28(p.53.13; M.20.1005C); of life of grace μακαριστότατον δι' αἰῶνος καὶ ἀεὶ θάλλοντα πρὸς ἀθανασίαν βίον Meth.*res.*2.2(p.331.15; cf. M.18.297C); θεοφιλῆ βίον... ⟨καὶ⟩ μ. Eus.*d.e.*3.2(p.97.34; M.22.169C); τί...θεοφιλίας μακαριστότερον; id.*p.e.*1.1(2C; M.21.24C); Gr.Nyss.*Placill.*(M.46.881C); Dion. Ar.*e.h.*3.3.9(M.3.437B); of what appertains to the next world κολποὶ δέ εἰσιν...τῶν μακαρίων πατριαρχῶν καὶ τῶν λοιπῶν ἁγίων ἁπάντων αἱ θειόταται καὶ μ. λήξεις...ὑποδεχόμεναι πάντας εἰς τὴν...μακαριωτάτην τελείωσιν *ib.*7.3.5(560B); of a holy place τὸν ἐν τοῖς Ἱεροσολύμοις τῆς σωτηρίου ἀναστάσεως μακαριστότατον τόπον Eus.*v.C.*3.25(p.89.10; M.20.1085A).

***μακαρίστρια, ἡ,** *one who speaks well of, eulogist* ἀκηδία ἐστὶ... κοσμικῶν μ., θεοῦ διαβλήτωρ Jo.Clim.*scal.*13(M.88.860A).

μακαριστῶς, *happily*, †Bas.*Is.*42(1.412D; M.30.200A).

μακαρίτης, ὁ, *one blessed*; also adjectivally, *of happy memory*, usu. of one lately dead; bishops Διονύσιον...καὶ Φιρμιλιανὸν...τοὺς μ. Malch.*ep.*ap.Eus.*h.e.*7.30.3(M.20.709C); ὑπὸ τοῦ μ. Ἀλεξάνδρου τοῦ πρὸ ἐμοῦ ἐπισκόπου Ath.*ep.encycl.*7(p.177.6; M.25.237C); *Pers.capt.* (M.86.3236A); so of Chrys., Synes.*ep.*66(M.66.1408D); of Const., Epiph.*haer.*30.4(p.338.15; M.41.409D); id.*mens.*20(M.43.269D); of biblical characters and writers (= 'Saint') ὁ μ. Δαβίδ Cosm.Ind. *top.*5(M.88.256C); ὁ μ. Παῦλος *ib.*(253B).

μακαρῖτις, ἡ, fem. of foreg., of BMV τῆς ἁγίας ταύτης καὶ μ. ἀειπαρθένου Epiph.*ep.Arab.*ap.*haer.*78.23(p.472.33; M.42.736A); of soul of one dead, Synes.*ep.*44(M.66.1369B).

μακαρίως, *in a state of blessedness* εἰρηνευόντων καὶ μ. διαγόντων Or.*Cels.*6.44(p.115.14; M.11.1368A); τῷ ζῶντι μ. id.*fr.95 in Jo.* (p.558.26); μ. μὲν βεβιωκότα, μ. δ' ἀναπεπαυμένον Eus.*Marcell.*1.4 (p.18.6; M.24.752A).

***Μακεδονιανοί, οἱ,** *followers of Macedonius*, Didym.*Trin.*2.6(M.39.545B); Πνευματομάχοι οἱ καὶ Μ. ... οἱ τὸ ἅγιον τοῦ θεοῦ πνεῦμα βλασφημοῦντες Epiph.*rescr.*4(p.159.3; M.41.164A); ἀναθεματίζομεν τοὺς Μ. οἵτινες ἐκ τῆς Ἀρείου ῥίζης καταγόμενοι Dam.Papa *anath.* ap.Thdt.*h.e.*5.11.21(3.1037); Socr.*h.e.*1.8.24(M.67.65B).

§Μακεδονικός, *of Macedonius M.* αἱρέσεως Cyr.*ep.*45(5^2.135D; Μακεδονιανῆς p.151.17).

μακελλεῖον, τό, *butcher's stall*, Mac.Mgn.*apocr.*3.42(p.147.19, v.l. μακέλλιον).

***μακελλεύω,** *keep a butcher's stall*, Mac.Mgn.*apocr.*3.42(p.145.4).

***μακελλικός,** *of* or *belonging to a butcher*, ‡Ath.*qu.Ant.*94(M.28.656B); Jo.Clim.*scal.*22(M.88.952B).

μάκελλον, τό, *butcher's shop*, ref. Absalom's death ὡς ἔριφος ἐν μ. ὁ λέων ἐκρέματο Ast.Soph.*Ps.*7(M.40.473B); ὥσπερ κύων ἐν μ. τῇ συνηθείᾳ οὐκ ἀφίσταται, ἂν δὲ κλεισθῇ τὸ μ. ... οὐκέτι ἐγγίζει· οὕτω σὺ ἐὰν ἐπιμείνῃς, ἀκηδιάσας ὁ δαίμων ἔχει σε ἀποστῆναι Pall.*h.Laus.*19 (p.60.17; M.34.1066D); ref. 1Cor.10:25 καθάπερ ἐν μ. τῇ ἐκκλησίᾳ καὶ οἱ ἔπαινοι γίνονται τῶν κατορθούντων καὶ οἱ ψόγοι τῶν ἀμελούντων id. *v.Chrys.*18(p.118.25; M.47.66).

μακραίων, *long-lasting*; of that which is eternal, Dion.Al.ap.Eus. *p.e.*14.25(775A; M.21.1276B); προσδοκῶμεν...τὸν μ. βίον Cyr.*glaph. Gen.*3(1.106B); ἄρτος...ὁ ἐξ οὐρανοῦ ἀποτρέφων ἡμᾶς εἰς μ. ζωήν id. *Jo.*3.6(4.323B).

***μακρακόντιον, τό,** *long spear*, Geo.Pis.*hex.*1087(M.92.1518A).

μακράν, *far* οἱ κλάδοι αὐτῶν εἰς μ. ἔσονται *T.Sym.*6.2; τὸν οἶκον... κάτω μέχρι μ. τῆς εἰσόδου Meth.*symp.*2.4(p.19.15, v.l. μέχρις ἄκρων M.18.52C); πολλοὺς τῶν μ. ἐπισκόπων Malch.*ep.*ap.Eus.*h.e.*7.30.3(M.20.709C); οὐδὲν γὰρ τόπῳ μ. τοῦ θεοῦ Ath.*Ar.*3.22(M.26.369B); met. ὁ...ἔχων ἀγάπην μ. ἐστιν πάσης ἁμαρτίας Polyc.*ep.*3.3; *Barn.*20.2; γινώσκει ὁ υἱὸς τὸν πατέρα...καὶ ἑαυτὸν γινώσκων, ὅπερ καὶ αὐτὸ οὐ μ. ἀποδεῖ τοῦ προτέρου Or.*Jo.*32.28(18; p.473.16; M.14.817B); μ. τῆς θείας φύσεως φθόνος Jo.D.*f.o.*1.1(M.94.792A).

[*]**μακρήμερος,** = μακροήμερος, Or.*Ps.*22:6(p.481).

[*]**μακροβιοτία, ἡ,** *longevity*, Clem.*paed.*2.2(p.169.28; M.8.416A).

***μακροβιόω,** *live long*, Ephr.2.167A.

μακροβίωσις, ἡ, *longevity*, Thdr.Heracl.*Is.*65:20(M.18.1373B); Bas.*hom.*3.3(2.18D; M.31.204B); of future life, ref. Ps.22:6, Gr. Nyss.*hom.12 in Cant.*(M.44.1032C).

***μακρόγηρος,** *aged*, Geo.Pis.*hex.*1113(M.92.1520A).

μακροδάκτυλος, *long-fingered*; of figure of Christ in a picture, ‡Jo.D.*ep.Thphl.*3(M.95.349C).

***μακροδαπής,** neut. as subst., *great extent*; of a diocese, *Cod.Afr.* 17 tit.; τὸ μ., τῆς ἀποστολῆς [i.e. of S. Thomas] μέχρις Ἰνδῶν... ἐκτελεσθείσης Areth.*Apoc.*21:19f.(M.106.773D).

***μακροείκελος,** *elongated*, Epiph.*haer.*51.35(p.311.6; M.41.953C).

μακροημέρευσις, ἡ, *length of days*, in this life εἴπωμεν...ὑπὲρ σωτηρίας...τε καὶ μ. τοῦ ἁγίου πατρὸς ἡμῶν καὶ ἀρχιεπισκόπου Πέτρου, παντὸς τοῦ κλήρου καὶ τοῦ...λαοῦ *Lit.Praesanct.*(p.499.29); in future life, Ath.*exp.Ps.*20 proem.(M.27.128D); τότε κληρονομήσομεν γενεὰς γενεῶν μ. δηλονότι καταργηθέντος θανάτου Cyr.*Is.*5.4(2.823E); ζωὴν...αἰώνιον, οὐ μ. ἧς πάντες μέλλουσιν ἀπολαύειν μετὰ τὴν ἀνάστασιν καλοί τε καὶ κακοί· ἀλλὰ καὶ τὸ ἐν εὐθυμίᾳ διάγειν id.*Jo.*7(4.666A).

***μακροημερεύω,** *live long*, *Lit.*ap.*Const.App.*8.10.7; *Lit.Bas.*(p.336.6); cf.*Lit.Chrys.*(p.389.21).

***μακροημερία, ἡ, 1.** *lapse of time* before second advent, Hipp. *Dan.*4.16.2; **2.** *length of days, long life*, ref. Ex.20:12, Isid.Pel.*epp.* 4.204(M.78.1293A); Proc.G.*Num.*20:24(M.87.856C).

μακροήμερος, *long-lived*, fig. τοῖς τετελειωμένοις καὶ πνευματικῶς μ. γενομένοις...δόξα...αἱ κοσμοῦσαι αὐτοὺς νοηταὶ πολιαί Or.*Jo.*20.10 (p.340.1; M.14.596C).

μακρόθεν, *long since* μ. καὶ προφητικῶς ἀνακόπτοντος...τοῦ νόμου Clem.*str.*2.18(p.163.4; M.8.1033A).

μακροθυμ-έω, 1. *be patient, slow to anger* μ. ... μετ' ἀλλήλων ἐν πραότητι, ὡς ὁ θεὸς μεθ' ὑμῶν Ign.*Polyc.*6.2; *Diogn.*9.2; Iren.*haer.* 1.10.3(M.7.556A); θεὸς μ. ... βλασφημούμενος [i.e. by heretics] Hipp. *haer.*proem.(p.2.7; M.16.3020A); ref. Jer.15:15 ἐμακροθύμησας ἀεὶ ἐπὶ τὸν λαὸν ἐπὶ τοῖς ἁμαρτήμασιν, ἐπὶ δὲ τοῖς κατ' ἐμοῦ τετολμημένοις μὴ μ. Or.*hom.14.13 in Jer.*(p.118.11; M.13.420B); μή τις ἐννοείτω...ὡς εἰς τέλος...διαμένει θεὸς...εἰ καὶ τέως μακροθυμῇ·...οὐκ ἔστι τινὰ τῶν ἀσεβῶν τὴν θείαν διαδρᾶναι δίκην Meth.*fr.Job* 6(p.512.10); πολλάκις εἰς αὐτοὺς ~ήσας οὐκέτι λοιπὸν ἀνέξομαι Thdt.*Am.*1:9 (2.1414); **2.** *be slow* to help ἀφῆκεν αὐτοὺς εἰς χαλεπωτέρους χειμῶνας πραγμάτων ἐμπεσεῖν, καὶ ἐμακροθύμησε Chrys.*hom.28.1 in Mt.*(7.334A); **3.** *be patient, enduring* in temptation or trial, *T.Jos.*2.7; ὡς μακροθύμου θεοῦ υἱοὶ καὶ μακροθύμου Χριστοῦ ἀδελφοὶ μ. ἐν πᾶσι τοῖς συμβαίνουσι Or.*mart.*43(p.40.15; M.11.620B); in prayer οὔτε προλαμβάνειν...τὴν τοῦ θεοῦ βουλήν· ἀλλὰ μ. καὶ δέεσθαι Hipp.*Dan.*4.5.4(M.10.681D); **4.** c. infin., *wait patiently* to τὴν κατὰ φύσιν γεωργίαν μ. ὕστερον πολλῷ χρόνῳ λαβεῖν Or.*princ.*3.1.14(p.220.6; M.11.276B); πάντες οἱ τῷ πονήματι ἡμῶν συμποιοῦντες καὶ σπουδάσματι ἐντυγχάνειν μ. Epiph.*exp.fid.*20(p.521.7; M.42.821A); **5.** trans., *bear with patiently* παρακουόμενον μ. καὶ ἀνέχεσθαι Ant.Mon.*hom.*111(M.89.1776D).

μακροθυμία, ἡ, **1.** *long-suffering, patience, endurance* ἐν δέκα πειρασμοῖς...ἐμακροθύμησα, ὅτι μέγα φάρμακόν ἐστιν ἡ μ. *T.Jos.*2.7; ἐμὲ γὰρ ἔδει ὑφ' ὑμῶν ὑπαλειφθῆναι πίστει,...μ. Ign.*Eph.*3.1; *Barn.*2.2; ὀλιγοψύχοις...δίδωσι...μ., τοῦτ' ἔστι καρτερίαν καὶ ὑπομονήν Cyr.*Is.*5.3(2.809A); **2.** *forbearance*; **a.** of men ἡ μ. γλυκυτάτη ἐστὶν...καὶ εὔχρηστός ἐστι τῷ κυρίῳ...ἡ δὲ ὀξυχολία πικρὰ καὶ ἄχρηστός ἐστιν. ἐὰν οὖν μιγῇ ἡ ὀξυχολία τῇ μ., μιαίνεται ἡ μ. καὶ οὐκ εὔχρηστός τῷ θεῷ ἡ ἔντευξις Herm.*mand.*5.1.6; ἡ ἰσότης καὶ ἡ μ. καὶ ἡ φιλανθρωπία τοῖς δεσπόταις εὐάρμοστος Clem.*paed.*3.11(p.277.5; M.8.649C); ἄλλον μὲν εἶναι μικροψυχίας καιρὸν...τὸν τῆς ἀδείας, ἄλλον δὲ μ., τὸν τῆς ἀνάγκης Gr.Naz.*or.*43.31(M.36.540A); **b.** of God, Ign.*Eph.*11.1; κρατεῖ καὶ τῶν ἀθετούντων αὐτὸν αἱρετικῶν...καὶ τοῦ διαβόλου, ἀλλ' ἀνέχεται διὰ μακροθυμίαν Cyr.H.*catech.*8.4; μ. πρὸς ἀλλήλους, ὑπομονὴν πρὸς τοὺς ἔξω· μακροθυμεῖ γάρ τις πρὸς ἐκείνους οὓς δυνατὸν καὶ ἀμύνασθαι, ὑπομένει δὲ οὓς οὐ δύναται ἀμύνασθαι...ἐπὶ μὲν θεοῦ οὐδέποτε ὑπομονὴ λέγεται, μ. δὲ πολλαχοῦ Chrys.*hom.2.2 in Col.*(11.334F); **c.** of Christ Ἰούδας...οὐκ ἀπεβλήθη ὑπὸ τοῦ κυρίου διὰ μακροθυμίαν *Const.App.*5.14.2; πραότητι καὶ μ. πείθων τοὺς ἀνθρώπους αἱρεῖσθαι τὴν ἀρετήν Jo.D.*f.o.*4.4(M.94.1109B).

μακρόθυμος, *long-suffering,* ὁ μ. = ὁ θεός, *Barn.*3.6; τὸ μ. αὐτοῦ [sc. θεοῦ] βούλημα *1Clem.*19.3; epithet of God, Gr.Nyss.*Eun.*1(1 p.154.10; M.45.396A); ref. 1Cor.13:4 μ. διὰ τοῦτο λέγεται, ἐπειδὴ μακράν τινα καὶ μεγάλην ἔχει ψυχήν· τὸ γὰρ μακρὸν καὶ μέγα λέγεται Chrys.*hom.33.1 in 1Cor.*(10.299D); *patient* under rebuke, Or.*Jo.*32.5(p.434.16; M.14.753D).

μακρολογία, ἡ, *length of speech, wordiness,* Bas.*hom.in Ps.*18(1.123A; M.29.304A).

***μακρομεγέθης,** *very large,* Or.*comm.in Mt.*10.7(p.9.5; M.13.852B).

μακροπερίοδος, *using long periods,* Didym.*Trin.*3.1(M.39.781B).

μακρόπορος, *travelling far,* †Apoll.*met.Ps.*103:18(M.33.1468A).

***μακρόπους,** *long-footed*; of an insect, *long-legged, Euchol.*(p.555).

μακροπρόσωπος, *long-faced* Ἰώσηπος...ἱστορεῖ ὁραθῆναι τὸν κύριον...μακροπρόσωπον Andr.Cr.*imag.*(M.97.1304C).

***μακρόρινος,** *long-nosed,* Jo.Mal.*chron.*11 p.281(M.97.425B).

μακρός, *long,* ἐκ μ. *long before,* Eus.*v.C.*4.60(p.142.11; M.20.1212A); ἐν μ. *at length,* †Bas.Anc.*virg.*1(M.30.669A).

μακρόσκιος, *with long shadow,* comp., Or.*or.*17.1(p.338.12; M.11.469D).

***μακρόστιχος,** *with long lines,* hence *lengthy*; of creed of Antioch (345), Socr.*h.e.*2.19 tit.(M.67.224B); γραφὴν ἣν μ. ἔκθεσιν ὀνομάζουσιν Soz.*h.e.*3.11.1(M.67.1060B).

μακροτέρω, *farther off, more distant*; ref. kinship, Chrys.*hom.70.2 in Mt.*(7.689D).

***μακροτζάγγιον, τό,** *high boot, Const.Stud.*38(M.99.1720B).

μακρότης, ἡ, *forbearance,* cf. μακροθυμία, *Apoc.En.*13.6.

***μακροχαράκτηρος,** *long-faced,* Jo.Mal.*chron.*5 p.106(M.97.196B).

μακροχρονίζω, *live long,* Eus.Al.*serm.*21.11(M.86.437B).

μακροχρόνιος, *aged,* Socr.*h.e.*2.38.11(M.67.325B); Cosm.Ind.*top.*5(M.88.260B).

***μάκροψις,** *long-faced,* Jo.Mal.*chron.*4 p.88(M.97.172C); *ib.*5 p.104(192C).

μακρύν-ω, **1.** *prolong* ἕξιν μακρυνθεῖσαν μακρᾷ συνηθείᾳ Nil.*Magn.*41(M.79.1020A); **2.** *remove to a distance, separate* ἑαυτοὺς ~όντων ἀπὸ τοῦ θεοῦ...διὰ τῆς περὶ θεοῦ ἀπιστίας Or.*Cels.*5.53(p.57.13; M.11.1264C); ref. Ps.72:27 ἀπ' οὐδενὸς ὁ θεὸς μ. ἑαυτόν id.*hom.18.9 in Jer.*(p.163.22; M.13.481C); τοῦ δὲ υἱοῦ συγκαθημένου τῷ πατρί, ἐνθυμεῖσθε τοῦτον ~ειν ἀπ' αὐτοῦ Ath.*Ar.*1.18(M.26.49A); οὔτε τὸν λόγον προσκυνῆσαι θέλοντες, ~ομεν αὐτὸν ἀπὸ τῆς σαρκός id.*ep.Adelph.*3(M.26.1076A); ἕκαστος ἁμαρτάνων ~εται...ἀπὸ θεοῦ, οὐ τόπῳ ἀλλὰ τρόπῳ Nil.*epp.*2.186(M.79.297A); οἱ τῆς ἐκκλησίας καὶ τῆς κοινωνίας ἑαυτοὺς μ. †Cyr.*hom.div.*14(5^2.414E).

μακρυσμός, ὁ, *separation,* ‡Proc.G.*Pr.*13:2(M.87.1348B); ‡Sophr.H.*triod.*(M.87.3848D).

μακτήριον, τό, *towel,* conj. for ἀλητήριον, Nonn.*par.Jo.*13:4 (ἀλκτήριον M.43.860C).

μάκτρα, ἡ, *coffin, sarcophagus, A.Petr.c.Sim.*11(p.100.3).

μάλα, *very, exceedingly,* with superl. εὖ μ. ῥᾷστα Gel.Cyz.*h.e.*2.13.4(M.85.1253A); comp. μᾶλλον *more, rather*; with verbs, *the more, indeed, in truth* οὐδὲν φαινόμενον καλόν. ὁ γὰρ...Χριστός, ἐν πατρὶ ὤν, μ. φαίνεται Ign.*Rom.*3.3; μ. ὁ θεὸς θέλει σε βασιλεῦσαι *Chron.Pasch.*p.339(M.92.884B); with superl. adj., *much, in the fullest sense* μ. αὐτῶν χείριστος εἶ Chrys.*hom.18.3 in Eph.*(11.130F); with ὅσον, *so much* as οὐχὶ πρὸς πίστωσιν μ. ὅσον πρὸς ἔλεγχον *V.Const.*35(p.565.19); with negative, not *so much* οὐ καθ' ἕνα μ., ἀγεληδὸν δέ Cyr.*Is.*5.4(2.844A); superl. μάλιστα *above all, especially* ὅπερ μ. πάντων δάκνειν ἡμᾶς εἴωθεν ἢ αἱ συμφοραί Chrys.*hom.8.3 in Phil.*(11.261C); with comp. adj., *ib.15.5*(318E); id.*hom.88.2 in Mt.*(7.827A).

***μαλαγή, ἡ,** *softening,* ‡Caes.Naz.*dial.*140(M.38.1052).

μάλαγμα, τό, *emollient*; met., of persons μ. [sc. τὸ θῆλυ] ἡδονῆς...τῷ ἄρρενι †Bas.Anc.*virg.*4(M.30.676C); iron. of Job's wife, Chrys.*a.exil.*2.2(3.422E).

μαλακίζομαι, **1.** *be softened, show weakness* or *cowardice* εἰδὼς φέρειν μαλακίαν, οὐ μὴν μεμαλακισμένος SM.ap.Proc.G.*Is.*53:3(M.87.2520D); *be made weak, bear infirmity,* ref. Is.53:5 παραδοθεὶς ὑπὸ τοῦ πατρὸς καὶ μαλακισθεὶς καὶ τὰς ἀνομίας ἡμῶν ἀνειληφώς Eus.*d.e.*10.8(p.477.21; M.22.768B); **2.** *be ill, T.Reub.*1.8; *T.Gad* 1.4.

§**μαλάκιον, τό,** small *basket* made of palm-leaves, used by monks to contain food, Ephr.2.176A; Pall.*h.Laus.*32(p.96.4; M.34.1105B); *Apophth.Patr.*(M.65.300D); Cyr.S.*v.Sab.*10(p.94.12).

***μαλακίσκιον, τό,** *little basket,* hence *present,* Thdr.Stud.*epp.*2.215(M.99.1653D).

***μαλακισμός, ὁ,** *softness, moral weakness* τὸν ὡς ἐν φαυλότητι μ. Cyr.*ador.*1(1.17C); *ib.*12(440A); ἔστι...πρωτοτόκος τε καὶ ἄρσην [sc. ὁ Χριστός], ὅτι μὴ οἶδε μ. εἰς ἁμαρτίαν· μαλακισμοῦ δὲ τύπος τὸ θῆλυ id.*glaph.Ex.*2(1.278B).

***μαλακοφορέω,** *wear fine raiment,* Thdr.Stud.*epp.*1.11(M.99.945A).

***μαλακοψυχία, ἡ,** *faint-heartedness, cat.Rom.*7:18(p.112.22).

μαλακόψυχος, *faint-hearted,* Chrys.*hom.90.3 in Mt.*(7.843C).

μαλακόω, *soften,* ‡Caes.Naz.*dial.*8(M.38.865).

μαλακώδης, *effeminate,* Chrys.*hom.49.5 in Mt.*(7.511A).

***μαλθακόσαρκος,** *soft-fleshed,* Melet.*nat.hom.*7(M.64.1184D).

***μαλθακτός,** *softened,* Leont.H.*monoph.*(M.86.1816A).

***μαλθάκων, ὁ,** *effeminate person,* Cyr.*Os.*46(3.77E).

***μαλλί(ο)ν, τό,** *flock of wool,* Cyr.S.*v.Euthym.*50(p.73.14); plur., of fleecy lining of a cloak, Jo.Mosch.*prat.*126(M.87.2988B).

μαλλωτάριον, τό, *sheepskin rug, Const.Stud.*38(M.99.1720B).

[*]**μαλός, ὁ,** = μαλλός, *fleece,* Max.*qu.dub.*79(M.90.853A).

***μαλωᾶ, τοῦ** (genit.), **1.** ? *wild fruit, wild berries* ἐκ τῶν εὑρισκομένων βοτανῶν καὶ τοῦ μαλωᾶ διαιτώμενος Cyr.S.*v.Euthym.*11(p.22.6); **2.** *fruit tree* or *shrub* καθεζομένων ἡμῶν καὶ μαλωὰν καθαριζόντων *ib.*56(p.77.14).

[*]**μάμμα, ἡ,** = μάμμη, *grandmother,* Jo.Mosch.*prat.*128(M.87.2992B).

[*]**μαμπάριος, ὁ,** v. μαππάριος.

μαμωνᾶς, ὁ, (Aramaic מָמוֹן) *wealth* τὸν μάγον Σίμωνα ἐθέλειν τὸ δικαιότατον διὰ τοῦ μ. τῆς ἀδικίας Or.*Jo.*6.33(17; p.143.7; M.14.257A); Gr.Nyss.*ep.*25(M.46.1100B); *Const.App.*3.7.3; τοῦ μ. ἡ τυραννίς Chrys.*hom.76.3 in Jo.*(8.449D).

***μαναά, τό,** *gift, offering,* ref. Dan.2:46, Chrys.*Thdr.*1.5(1.6A).

***μανδᾶτον, τό,** (Lat. *mandatum*) *command,* usu. from emperor, Eus.Dor.*ep.imp.*(p.67.13; M.86.2549D); imperial *message,* implying command, Jo.Mal.*chron.*14 p.352(M.97.525A); ἀπέπλευσαν κατὰ τα ἴδια μανδᾶτα πρῶτον *ib.*5 p.108(200A).

***μανδάτωρ, ὁ,** (Lat. *mandatorius*) *one to whom a charge or commission is given,* †Gregent.*leg.Hom.*45(M.86.605B); of imperial officials, Anast.Ap.*a.Max.*1.1(M.90.109C); CNic.(787)*act.*2(H.4.76E); Thphn.*chron.*p.155(M.108.420Aff.).

***μανδίον, τό,** v. μανδύας.

***μανδόβαρα, τό,** (Hebr. מִדְבָּר) *desert, Apoc.En.*28(p.58.16).

μάνδρα, ἡ, **A.** *fold, sheepfold*; fig. and met.; **1.** of a family, Gr.Naz.*or.*8.11(M.35.801B); **2.** of Church οὐ μόνον νηῒ ἀλλὰ καὶ μ. ὡμοίωται ἡ ἐκκλησία *Const.App.*2.57.12; ὑπὸ τὸν αὐτὸν τῆς ἐκκλησίας σηκόν, ὑπὸ τὴν αὐτὴν μ. μεθ' ὁμονοίας ἑστῶτας Chrys.*hom.8.7 in Rom.*(9.508B); εἰ τῆς βδελυκτῆς Μανιχαίου...τυγχάνεις μερίδος, οὐδείς σοι τῆς ἡμετέρας συστήσεται μ. Isid.Pel.*epp.*1.52(M.78.216A); πᾶς...πιστὸς ἐν τῇ μ. τῶν προβάτων μενέτω, τῷ σημείῳ τῷ τοῦ Χριστοῦ σφραγιζόμενος Proc.G.*Jos.*2:20(M.87.1001C); Max.*opusc.*(M.91.92D); **3.** of Temple μίαν ἔσχον [sc. οἱ Ἰουδαῖοι] μ., τὸν ἐν Ἱεροσολύμοις ναόν, ἡμεῖς δὲ ἀριθμῶν κρείττους κατὰ πᾶσαν τὴν οἰκουμένην ἐκκλησίας Thdt.*Ezech.*34:14(2.968); **4.** of heret. sects, Proc.G.*Dt.*16:5(M.87.913A); **5.** of a monastery Αὐδιανοὶ...τὰς ἑαυτῶν μονάς, ἤτοι μ. ἔχουσιν Epiph.*haer.*70.1(p.233.1; M.42.340A); ἐν μοναστηρίοις...μ. καλουμέναις *ib.*80.6(p.491.20; 765C); ἐν τῇ πνευματικῇ σου μ. Nil.*epp.*3.241(M.79.496B); *ib.*2.62(228D); Thdr.Stud.*epp.*1.14(M.99.957A); **6.** of heaven ἐπιστρέφου ψυχήν μου εἰς τὴν μ. παραδείσου Ephr.1.299A; ποιμὴν...τὸ πλανώμενον ἐπιστρέφων...καὶ πρὸς τὴν ἐκεῖθεν μ. συνάγων λόγοις ποιμαντικῆς ἐπιστήμης Gr.Naz.*or.*30.21(p.143.5; M.36.132C); ποιμένες...πρὸς τὴν ἄνω μ. φωναῖς σύριγγος πνευματικῆς ἀνάγειν...εἰδότες Max.*ambig.*(M.91.1064A); **7.** ref. Mt.25:41 ἄδηλον γὰρ εἰ μὴ τρίβος ἐρίφων ἐστὶ τὸ φαινόμενον, οἷς σὺ ἀκολουθοῦσα...ἐπειδὰν παρήλθες τὸν βίον...κατολίσθῃς ἐν τῇ τοῦ θανάτου μ. Gr.Nyss.*hom.2 in Cant.*(M.44.805B); **8.** of conscience μ. καὶ σηκὸς ἐν ᾧ φυλάξομεν τοὺς λογισμοὺς ἀσινεῖς Chrys.*hom.17.4 in Ac.*(9.142A).

B. lion's *den*, Thdr.Mops.*Am.*3:4(M.66.261A); id.*Os.*5:14(M.66.160A).

μανδραγόρας, ὁ, *mandrake*, ref. Gen.30:14 μ. ... ἦσαν...μῆλα εὔοσμα *T.Isach.*1.3.

***μανδραρχαΐζω,** *rule a monastery*, Thdr.Stud.*iamb.*80(M.99.1800D).

***μανδρεῖον, τό,** *monastery*, Evagr.*h.e.*6.23(p.240.1; M.86.2881A).

***μανδρεύω,** *fold* sheep, ‡Chrys.*hom.in Ps.139:1*(5.721C).

§μανδρίτης, ὁ, *monk*, CTyr.(518)*act.*(*ACO* 3 p.88.18; H.2.1357D); *ib.*(p.89.11; 1360C).

μανδύας, ὁ (*μανδίον, *μανδύον, τό), *outer garment, cloak* τί ἐστι μ.; εἶδός ἐστιν ἐφεστρίδος...παρὰ πολλῶν μαντίον ὀνομαζόμενον Thdt.*qu.44 in 1Reg.*(1.383); τοὺς μανδύας ἢ τὰ καλούμενα Ἀρκαδίκια, τὰ μαντία Proc.G.*2Reg.*8:4(M.87.1133A); royal *mantle*, Jo.Mal.*chron.*2 p.33(M.97.101C); esp. monk's *cloak* ὁ ἄνευ τοῦ μανδύου αὐτοῦ ἢ τοῦ κουκουλλίου ἐργαζόμενος...ἐπιτιμάσθω Thdr.Stud.*poen.*2.4(M.99.1749A); τὸ δὲ μανδίον ἐμφαῖνον διὰ τῆς ἀπολελυμένης ἁπλώσεως τὴν πτερωτικὴν τῆς τῶν ἀγγέλων μιμήσεως ‡Germ.CP *contempl.*(M.98.396B); ἀκολουθία τοῦ μικροῦ σχήματος ἤτοι τοῦ μανδίου *Euchol.*(p.382); cf.*ib.*(p.393 not.); εὐχὴ ἐπὶ τοῦ μέλλοντος λαμβάνειν μανδύον *ib.*(p.390); worn by candidate at ordination of sub-deacon, *ib.*(p.203); of a lector, *ib.*(p.194); as monk's shroud, *ib.*(p.438); v. μαντίον.

***μανδύλιον, τό,** *mantle*, *A.Pil.*B 1.2(p.288); of a monk, Zos.*alloquia* 5(M.78.1689B); *Nomoc.*500; *Euchol.*(p.208).

***μανδύον, τό,** v. μανδύας.

[*]**μανδυώδης,** *cloaklike*, *Schol.Clem.paed.*(p.333.24; M.9.791A).

***μανέω,** *predict the future, divine*, Isid.H.*etym.*4.7.8.

***μάνζηρος (*μάντζηρος, *μαύζηρος), ὁ,** (Hebr. מַמְזֵר) *bastard*; as term of abuse applied to Jo. D. by emperor, with play on his name Μανσούρ, Thphn.*chron.*p.350(M.106.841B); to a Jew μάντζηρος Leont.N.*v.Sym.*54(M.93.1736D); μαύζηρος †Gregent.*disp.*(M.86.669A).

§μάνη, ἡ, = μήνη, *moon*, Synes.*hymn.*3.31(p.8; M.66.1593).

§Μάνης, ὁ, *Manes* (*Mani*), originator of Manichean heresy, name often declined as if it were μανείς, aor. ptcpl. pass. of μαίνομαι, as a play on the word, Tit.Bost.*Man.*1.7(M.18.1077B); Philox.*ep.*35(p.183); Jo.D.*Man.*1.67(M.94.1564A).

μανθάνω, *teach* μ. ἑτέρους κακίας †Jo.Jej.*serm.*(M.88.1924C).

μανία, ἡ, 1. *madness*; met., of heresy, Hipp.*haer.*1 proem.(p.1.19; M.16.3017B); τὴν τῶν Σαβελλιανῶν μ. Ath.*Dion.*26(p.65.21; M.25.517C); Gr.Naz.*or.*21.13(M.35.1096A); of paganism τὴν πολύθεον μ. *Const.App.*5.15.3; in good sense, ref. Ex.32:32 ὄντως μ., ὄντως ἔρως μέγας Chrys.*hom.7.4 in Eph.*(11.51B); **2.** *rage*, of Devil ἡ μ. αὐτοῦ ἠρεμησάτω *A.Jo.*114(p.214.10).

μανιάκι(ο)ν, τό, *necklace, torque*, Ephr.1.107A; *Apophth.Patr.*(M.65.104A); Eus.Al.*serm.*21.17(M.86.444B); Jo.Mal.*chron.*18 p.457(M.97.669B).

***μανιαστής, ὁ,** *madman*, Hesych.H.*Ps.tit.*27(M.27.748C).

***μανίζω,** *think like a madman*; met., *cherish the illusion*, c. ὅτι, *M.Ariadn.*13(p.130.5).

***μανιητόκος,** *maddening*, Gr.Naz.*carm.*2.2(poem.)7.262(M.37.1571A).

μανίκια, τά, (cf. Lat. *manicae*) *cuffs*, ‡Sophr.H.*liturg.*7(M.87.3988B) cit. s. λωρίον; *Euchol.*(p.292).

μανικός, 1. *mad*; met., of heretics, Hipp.*haer.*7.29(p.210.5; M.16.3323A); Const.ap.Gel.Cyz.*h.e.*3.19.42(M.85.1355); *extravagant*, in good sense, of S. Paul ἐρώμενος...μ. ... καὶ ἀκαρτέρητος περὶ φιλίαν Chrys.*hom.3.2 in 1Thess.*(11.443D); **2.** *furious, violent-tempered* μὴ γίνου...ζηλωτὴς μηδὲ μ. μηδὲ θρασύς *Const.App.*7.5.5; Chrys.*Jud.*1.8(1.600B).

μανικῶς, 1. *madly*; met., of heresy μανικώτερον εἰς αὐτὴν τὴν θεότητα κατατετόλμηκε Ath.*ep.Aeg.Lib.*17(M.25.580A); **2.** *frenziedly* μ. ἐνθυσιώντων...παρὰ βωμοῖς *Hom.Clem.*3.13.

***Μανιχαΐζω,** *become a Manichean*, Didym.*Trin.*2.6(M.39.548B); Mac.Ant.*symb.*(H.3.1173D); Thdr.Stud.*epp.*2.162(M.99.1516A).

***Μανιχαϊκός,** *Manichean* οἱ τοῖς Μ. δόγμασι δι' ἀπάτης παρασυρέντες...πονηρὸν εἶναι τὸν τῆς ἀνθρωπίνης φύσεως κτίστην ἀποδεικνύοντες Gr.Nyss.*or.catech.*7(p.37.15; M.45.29D); τὰ διάφορα ὀνόματα τοῦ διαβόλου ἐνεργείας αὐτοῦ διαφόρους, οὐκ οὐσίας, δηλοῖ... ὅπερ ἀνατρεπτικόν ἐστι τοῦ Μ. δόγματος Didym.*Job* 3:8(M.39.1129D); μένει...ἡ θεία οὐσία ἀμέριστος...παραβιασθεῖσα ὑπὸ τῆς Μ. ὑποθέσεως...εἰς μερισμόν *Disp.Phot.*(M.88.537A).

***Μανιχαϊκῶς,** *in Manichean fashion, as the Manicheans do* ἢ ἂν τὸν θεὸν ταῦτα πεποιηκέναι φαῖεν...ἢ μὴ πεποιηκέναι...ἐξ ἀνάγκης ἄλλην ἀρχὴν Μ. τὴν ταῦτα ποιοῦσαν εἰσάγοντες Max.*ambig.*(M.91.1332A); ἤρνησαν...Μ. τὴν φύσιν...οἰόμενοι ὅτιπερ ἐὰν ὁμολογήσωσιν ἐπ' αὐτοῦ σαρκὸς φύσιν, ἀκάθαρτόν τι καὶ...ἀνάξιον θεοῦ πρᾶγμα ὁμολογοῦσι Anast.S.*hod.*14(M.89.253B); λέγουσι Μ. δύο μόνα εἶναι θελήματα, τὸ ἓν τὸ θεῖον, τὸ ἀγαθόν· τὸ δὲ ἕτερον τὸ διαβολικόν, τὸ πονηρόν Jo.D.*volunt.*32(M.95.169A).

***Μανιχαῖος, ὁ,** *follower of Manes, Manichee* ὁ πατὴρ...ἀπέστειλεν ...δύναμιν...λεγομένην ζῶν πνεῦμα, καὶ...δέδωκεν [sc. τῷ πρώτῳ ἀνθρώπῳ] δεξιὰν καὶ ἀνήνεγκεν ἐκ τοῦ σκότους...διὰ τοῦτο Μ. ἐὰν συναντήσωσιν ἀλλήλοις, δεξιὰς διδόασιν ἑαυτοῖς σημείου χάριν, ὡς ἀπὸ σκότους σωθέντες Hegem.*Arch.*7(p.11.1; M.10.1437B); ἐκεῖνοι [sc. Μ.] μόνον ἄχρις ὀνόματος ἀγαθὸν θεὸν ὀνομάζουσι, καὶ ἔργον αὐτοῦ οὔτε βλεπόμενον οὔτε ἀόρατον δεικνύειν δύνανται Ath.*ep.Aeg.Lib.*16(M.25.573A); Μ. ... ἥλιον σέβοντες καὶ σελήνην, ἄστροις τε καὶ δυνάμεσι καὶ δαίμοσι εὐχόμενοι, ἀρχὰς δύο εἰσάγοντες, πονηράν τε καὶ ἀγαθὴν ἀεὶ οὔσας· Χριστὸν δὲ δοκήσει πεφηνέναι καὶ δοκήσει πεπονθέναι· παλαιὰν διαθήκην βλασφημοῦντες καὶ τὸν ἐν αὐτῇ λαλήσαντα θεόν, κόσμον δὲ οὐ τὸν πάντα ἀλλὰ μέρος ἐκ θεοῦ γεγενῆσθαι ὁριζόμενοι Epiph.*anac.*66(p.1.10; M.42.9A); ἀπὸ ψυχῶν τῶν Μ. γεμίζεται ἡ σελήνη...οὐδεὶς μετὰ τὴν πεντεκαιδεκάτην τῆς σελήνης Μ. [sc. τελευτᾷ] id.*haer.*66.23(p.51.13; M.42.69A); τὴν κτίσιν ὑβρίζοντες καὶ τὰ κτίσματα τοῦ θεοῦ διαβάλλοντες...τοιοῦτοι...Μ. παῖδες ἐξεφοίτησαν Mac.Mgn.*apocr.*3.43(p.151.21); ὑδροπότησε Πυθαγόρας καὶ Διογένης καὶ Πλάτων ἐν οἷς καὶ οἱ Μ. Pall.*h.Laus.*proem.(p.12.26; M.34.1004); δύο θεοὺς λέγουσιν [sc. οἱ Μ.], ἕνα ἀγαθὸν καὶ ἕνα κακὸν...καὶ [sc. ἀνατιθέασι] τὴν ὕλην τῷ κακῷ θεῷ, τὸ δὲ εἶδος τῷ ἀγαθῷ θεῷ...οὐχ ὁμολογοῦσιν ἀληθῆ γενέσθαι τὴν ἐνανθρώπησιν τοῦ Χριστοῦ, ἀλλὰ κατὰ φαντασίαν, καὶ ἐν τοῖς πάθεσιν ὅτι ἄλλον ἄνθρωπον ὑπέβαλεν ἀντ' αὐτοῦ καὶ αὐτὸς ἔφυγεν †Leont.B.*sect.*3.2(M.86.1213A–C).

***Μανιχαϊσμός, ὁ,** *Manicheism*, Gr.Nyss.*ep.can.*(M.45.225C); id.*Eun.*1(1 p.164.11; M.45.405C); Thdr.Stud.*epp.*2.162(M.99.1513C).

μάννα, τό, *manna* ἐξουδενοῦντες τὸ μ. ... καὶ ἔλεγον, μα ἄν, οὐδέν, ὃ ἑρμηνεύεται, τί ἐστι τοῦτο; *Dial.Tim.et Aquil.*99 r°; ref. Ex.16:20 ὅτι...οὐ τῆς τοῦ μ. φύσεως ἦν τὸ πάθος, μαρτυρεῖ τὸ σάββατον ἐν ᾧ ἀλώβητον διετηρήθη τὸ τῇ παρασκευῇ συλλεγέν Thdt.*qu.31 in Ex.*(1.145); ref. Ps.77:25 ἄρτον ἀγγέλων τὸ μ. προσηγόρευσεν ὁ προφήτης ὡς ἀγγέλων τῇ τούτου δωρεᾷ διακεκονηκότων...οὕτως ἄρτος οὐρανοῦ προσηγορεύθη ἐπειδὴ ἄνωθεν κατηνέχθη, οὐκ ἐξ αὐτοῦ τοῦ οὐρανοῦ, ἀλλ' ἐκ τοῦ ἀέρος *ib.*29(144); contrasted with loaves and fishes, Gr.Nyss.*or.catech.*23(p.88.7; M.45.61C); as type of bread of life τὸ μ. εἰ καὶ ἀπὸ τοῦ θεοῦ διδόμενος, ἄρτος ἦν προκοπῆς, ἄρτος τοῖς ἔτι παιδαγωγουμένοις χορηγούμενος, ἄρτος τοῖς ὑπὸ ἐπιτρόπους καὶ οἰκονόμους ἁρμονιώτατος Or.*Jo.*6.45(26; p.154.31; M.14.280A); ἔλεγεν... αὐτὸς εἶναι ὁ τῆς ζωῆς ἄρτος πολλῷ κρείττων τοῦ μ. *ib.*8.35(28; p.374.4; 653C); Bas.*Spir.*31(3.26A; M.32.121C); ref. Ex.16:33 τότε γὰρ κενὸν γίνεται τῆς ψυχῆς τὸ ἀγγεῖον τῆς οὐρανίας τροφῆς, ἐὰν ἁμαρτία...τὴν ἐπιρροὴν τοῦ μ. κωλύσῃ Gr.Nyss.*laud.Bas.*(M.46.812B); Ammon.*Jo.*6:32(M.85.1436A); ὁ τὸ μ. τὸ νοητὸν ἀποθησαυρίζων ἐν ἑαυτῷ Cyr.*Jo.*3.6(4.319C); τὸ μ. τὸ ἐκπορευόμενον ἐκ τοῦ στόματος, ῥῆμα ἦν... ἐξ οὗ διδασκόμεθα οὐκ ἐπ' ἄρτῳ μόνῳ ζῆν τὸν ἄνθρωπον Proc.G.*Dt.*8:3(M.87.900A); ref. Ex.16:20,24, type of corruptible bodies and Christ's incorruptible body, Germ.CP *or.*2(M.98.264A–C).

***μαννάδιν, τό,** *basket*, *Apophth.Patr.*(M.65.112A).

***μανναδοτέω,** v. *μαννοδοτέω.

***μανναδόχος (*μαννοδόχος),** *receiving manna*; of BMV, Ephr.3.529E; μαννοδ-, Jo.Mon.*hymn.Nic.Myr.*3(M.96.1384D).

[*]**μάννη, ἡ, 1.** = μάννα, ἡ, *frankincense*, Hipp.*haer.*4.31(p.58.3; M.16.3094A); **2.** = μάννα, τό, *Orac.Sib.*7.49.

***μαννοδοσία, ἡ,** *giving of manna*, Mel.*pass.*88 p.14.31.

***μαννοδοτέω (*μανναδοτέω),** *give manna*; of God, Mel.*pass.*85 p.14.9; *Const.App.*6.20.6; of Moses, *ib.*6.3.1; fig., of BMV χαῖρε, στάμνε...ἀφ' ἧς μανναδοτεῖται ἅπας ὁ κόσμος Thdr.Stud.*nativ. BMV* 7(M.96.689B).

***μαννοδότης**, ὁ, *giver of manna*, *Orac.Sib.*2.347.

***μαννοδόχος**, v. *μανναδόχος.

***μαννούθιον**, τό, *faggot*; plur., Cyr.S.*v.Sab.*8(p.92.8); *ib.*40(p.130.30, v.l. μανουθίων).

§**μαννοφόρος**, *holding manna*, Leont.N.*serm.*3(M.93.608A); ‡Jo.D.*hom.*6.6(M.96.672A).

***μανουάλιον**, τό, *candlestick* carried in processions, *V.Olymp.*1.1(p.417.28); *Euchol.*(pp.4,162); *Rit.Epiph.*(p.430).

***μανούβριον**, τό, (Lat. *manubrium*) *handle, haft*, Gr.Mag.*dial.*(tr.Zach.)2.6(M.*PL.*66.143D).

***μανσιονάριος**, ὁ, (Lat. *mansionarius*) = παραμονάριος, *keeper of a church*, Gr.Mag.*dial.*(tr.Zach.)3.25(M.*PL.*77.279A).

***μάντζηρος**, ὁ, v. *μάνζηρος.

μαντί(ο)ν, τό, *cloak, mantle*, Thdt.*qu.44 in 1Reg.*(1.383); Proc.G.*2Reg.*8:4(M.87.1133A); δίχα διαδήματος εἰσῆλθεν ἐν ἐκκλησίᾳ μετὰ πορφυροῦ μ. κλαίων Jo.Mal.*chron.*17 p.421(M.97.621C); an anchorite's dress στιχάριον τρίχινον καὶ ἀπὸ σειρᾶς μ. Jo.Mosch.*prat.*87(M.87.2945A); monastic dress generally, Leont.Abb.*v.Gr.Agr.*81(M.98.693A); κουκούλλια...ἐμφαίνοντα διὰ τῆς τοῦ μ. ἀπολελυμένης ἁπλώσεως τὴν πτερωτικὴν τῆς τῶν ἀγγέλων μιμήσεως ‡Bas.*h.myst.*24(p.263.9); Cyr.S.*v.Euthym.*50(p.73.20).

μαντιπόλος, ὁ, *soothsayer*, Eudoc.*Cypr.*2.63(M.85.848B).

[*]**μαντιχόρα**, ὁ, = μαντιχόρας, fabulous man-eating beast, Eus.*Hierocl.*22(525D; M.22.829A).

***μαντώδης**, *prophetic*, Nonn.*par.Jo.*4:25(M.43.777C).

***μάππα**, ἡ, (Lat. *mappa*) *napkin*; of handkerchief or flag used as starting signal in hippodrome, hence *races, games* ἐν τῷ ὑπατεύειν αὐτὸν μετὰ τὴν πρώτην αὐτοῦ μ. ἐσφάγη Jo.Mal.*chron.*17 p.412(M.97.609B).

μαππάριος, ὁ, ([*]**μαμπάριος**), official who gave the signal for beginning the races, *starter*, μαμπ-, ‡Chrys.*circ.*(8.89B); *Chron.Pasch.*p.383(M.92.981B).

***μαραγγιάω**, *die away, go slowly out*; of fire, Leont.H.*Nest.*1.19(M.86.1473A).

***Μαρὰν ἀθά** (**Μαραναθά**), (Aramaic מרנא תא or perh. מרן אתא) *our Lord, come* (or *has come*) (cf. 1Cor.16:22); in eucharistic prayer μ. ἀ.· ἀμήν *Did.*10.6; *Const.App.*7.26.5; interpreted ref. 1Cor.16:22 as a curse ἀνάθεμα ἤτω Μαραναθάν *CIG* 9303 (Salamis).

μαραντικός, *wasting* νόσῳ μ. *Ep.Her.*(p.68.28).

μαρασμός, ὁ, *wasting* πυρετὸς...μ. ... ἐπήγαγεν Bas.*ep.*138.1(3.229C; M.32.580A); τὸν ἐκ τοῦ χρόνου μ. id.*hom.*13.5(2.118D; M.31.436B); met., *decay* γνώσεως ἀληθοῦς μ. Or.*fr.54 in Lam.*(p.258.19; M.13.636D); *withering*, Cyr.*Ps.*36:2(M.69.925A); id.*Joel.*6(3.203E); fig. ἵνα κλαιόντων ἡμῶν περὶ τῶν ἁμαρτιῶν ἡμῶν, ἀναθάλλῃ ἡμῶν ἡ ψυχὴ τοῦ μ. τῶν ἁμαρτιῶν Ephr.1.227B.

μαργαίνω, *rage, be mad*, of gluttony μ. ἐστὶ τὸ μαίνεσθαι, γαστρὸς μὲν μανία περὶ τὸ ποσὸν καταγίνεται· λαιμοῦ, περὶ τὸ ποιόν ‡Nil.*vit.cog.*(M.79.1437C).

***μαργάρεος**, ὁ, = μαργαρίτης, Gr.Naz.*carm.*2.1.38.34(M.37.1328A).

μαργαρίτης, ὁ, *pearl*, fig. and met.; **1.** of Christ, *A.Jo.*109(p.207.14); ἔξον ἁγίῳ κοσμεῖσθαι λίθῳ, τῷ λόγῳ τοῦ θεοῦ, ὃν μ. ἡ γραφὴ κέκληκέν που, τὸν διαυγῆ καὶ καθαρὸν Ἰησοῦν Clem.*paed.*2.12(p.228.5; M.8.540C); ref. Mt.13:46, Or.*comm.in Mt.*10.8(p.9.23; M.13.856A); ἐξετάζων τοῦ νοητοῦ μ. τὴν φύσιν Ephr.2.271D; ἐπίβλεψον τῷ μ. καὶ βλέπεις τὰς δύο φύσεις συνέχοντα· φαιδρότατός ἐστι διὰ τὴν θεότητα, λευκὸς διὰ τὴν πρόληψιν Ephr.Ant.*fr.*(M.86.2109A) = Ephr.2.269B; ἐὰν μή τις γεννηθῇ ὑπὸ τοῦ βασιλικοῦ καὶ θεϊκοῦ πνεύματος...τὸν ἐπουράνιον...μ., τὴν εἰκόνα τοῦ φωτὸς...ἥτις ἐστὶν ὁ κύριος, οὐ δύναται φορέσαι Mac.Aeg.*hom.*25.1(M.34.660D); μ. κέκληται [sc. ὁ κύριος] ἐπειδὴ τῷ βυθῷ τῆς θεότητος ἥνωται καὶ μόνοις τοῖς ἁλιεῦσι καὶ τοῖς αὐτοῦ ὑποφήταις ἐγνώρισται Isid.Pel.*epp.*1.182(M.78.301B); ref. BMV πήραν ἧς ὁ μ. τοῦ ἡλίου λαμπρότερος Hesych.H.*serm.*5(M.93.1461A); Chrysipp.*enc.in BMV* 1(p.337.5); of name of Christ, Diad.*perf.*59(p.66.20); of eucharistic body of Christ ὥραν ἐν ᾗ τὸν ἀτίμητον μ. τοῦ Χριστοῦ σώματος ὑποδεξόμεθα ἐν ταῖς χερσὶν ἡμῶν ‡Epiph.*hom.*3(M.43.473A); Anast.S.ap.Jo.D.*imag.*3 suppl.(M.94.1416C); esp. of a particle of the bread μετὰ πολλοῦ φόβου τὸ σῶμα τοῦ Χριστοῦ ὑπόδεξαι, ἵνα μή τις μ. ἐκπέσῃ ἐκ τῆς χειρός σου Chrys.*ecl.*47(12.771C); διὰ τὸ μὴ κολλᾶσθαι τοὺς μ. ἐν τῷ δισκοκαλύμματι ‡Sophr.H.*liturg.*5(M.87.3985C); ὁ ἱερεύς...ἀποπλύνει τὸ ἅγιον ποτήριον...καὶ ὁρᾷ μὴ μείνῃ τὸ λεγόμενον μ. *Euchol.*(p.68); **2.** ref. Mt.7:6; **a.** of Christian teaching μαργαρίτας...τὰ μυστικώτερα τῆς θεοσδότου θρησκείας μαθήματα Meth.*creat.*1(p.493.3; M.18.332A); πάλιν γίνεται ὁ μ. τὸ εὐαγγέλιον· ὅτι ἐν εὐτελεῖ γράμματι τοσαύτην ἐμπεριέχει δύναμιν μυστηρίων Ephr.2.274C; Chrys.*hom.1.3 in Jo.*(8.4D); Isid.Pel.*epp.*4.181(M.78.1273A); of teaching of prophets, Thdt.*Dan.*proem.(2.1053); of Christ's teaching, ‡Germ.CP *contempl.*(M.98.385A); **b.** of Christian fellowship ὥσπερ γὰρ τὸ τοῖς χοίροις ῥίπτειν τὸν μ. ἀπείρηται, οὕτω τὸ ἀποστερεῖν τοῦ τιμίου μ. τὸν ἤδη ἄνθρωπον διὰ τῆς καθαρότητος ...γενόμενον, τῶν ἀτόπων ἐστίν Gr.Nyss.*ep.can.*(M.45.229D); **3.** of soul ὁ φόρτος τῶν ἄνω [sc. ἐστίν]...λίθοι ἐξ Ἰνδῶν οἱ χαλκεδόνιοι, καὶ μ. ἐκ Κοσάνων *A.Thom.*A 108(p.220.1); **4.** in gen. τὰ δεσμὰ περιφέρω, τοὺς πνευματικοὺς μ. Ign.*Eph.*11.2; τιμίους μ. περίκειται [sc. ἡ σώφρων γυνή], τοὺς σωφρονίζοντας λόγους *Hom.Clem.*13.16; ἄγγελοι ...ἐγένοντο λίθος τίμιος καὶ μ. περίβλεπτος *ib.*8.2.

***μαργαριτοειδής**, *pearl-like*, ‡Epiph.*hom.*5(M.43.500D).

***μαργαριτοφόρος**, *pearl-bearing*, Or.*comm.in Mt.*10.7(p.9.6; M.13.852B).

μάργαρος, ὁ, = μαργαρίτης, *T.Sal.*C 10.45; Gr.Naz.*ep.*12(M.37.44C); Chrys.*hom.4.10 in Mt.*(7.66B); Sophr.H.*v.Anast.*(M.92.1685B).

***μαργαρώδης**, *pearl-like*, met. θείων καὶ μ. λόγων ‡Proc.G.*Pr.*23:9(M.87.1452C); ref. 1Cor.3:12, Max.*cap.theol.*2.12(M.90.1129C); Thdr.Stud.*icon.*7(M.99.497C); neut. as subst., *effulgence* τὸ διαυγὲς ἤτοι τὸ μ. τῶν ὑμετέρων λόγων Martin.*ep.*4(M.*PL.*87.148D).

***μαργόνιον**, τό, *wallet*, Jo.Mosch.*prat.*125(M.87.2988B).

***μάρης**, ὁ, a Pontic liquid measure; larger than Macedonian μάρις (*LS*), Epiph.*mens.*24(M.43.292A).

***Μαρία**, ἡ, *Mary*; of BMV; **1.** name explained τῇ ἁγίᾳ παρθένῳ λίαν πρέπον ὄνομα. Μ. γὰρ ἐκέκλητο· ὅπερ δὲ φωτισμὸς ἑρμηνεύεται. τί γὰρ τοῦ φωτὸς τῆς παρθενίας λαμπρότερον; ‡Gr.Thaum.*annunt.*2(M.10.1164D); αὕτη γὰρ οὐρανὸς καὶ ναὸς καὶ θρόνος εὑρίσκεται. ἡ γὰρ Μ. ἑρμηνεύεται κυρία, ἀλλὰ καὶ ἐλπίς. κύριον γὰρ ἔτεκε, τὴν ἐλπίδα τοῦ παντὸς κόσμου Χριστόν. ἑρμηνεύεται πάλιν τὸ Μ., σμύρνα θαλάσσης· σμύρναν δὲ ἐρεῖ, ὃ καὶ φημί, περὶ ἀθανασίας, ὅτι ἤμελλε τὸν ἀθάνατον μαργαρίτην τίκτειν ἐν τῇ θαλάσσῃ, τουτέστιν ἐν τῷ κόσμῳ... πάλιν...ἑρμηνεύεται...φωτιζομένη, ἥτις ἐφωτίσθη παρὰ τοῦ υἱοῦ τοῦ θεοῦ, καὶ ἐφώτισε τοὺς πιστεύσαντας...τῇ τριάδι ‡Epiph.*hom.*5(M.43.488Dff.); τοῦτο γὰρ [sc. κυρία] τῆς Μ. σημαίνει τὸ ὄνομα Jo.D.*f.o.*4.14(M.94.1157B); as an acrostic *ΜΑΡΙΑΜ*· Μόνη· Αὕτη· Ῥύσεται· Ἰοῦ· Ἅπαντας· Μισοκάλου ‡Hipp.Th.*fr.*17(p.49.21); **2.** as source of Christ's human nature, v. μήτηρ; καὶ ἐκ Μ. καὶ ἐκ θεοῦ Ign.*Eph.*7.2; οὐδὲ δύο υἱούς, ἄλλον μὲν υἱὸν θεοῦ ἀληθινόν...ἄλλον δὲ ἐκ Μ. ἄνθρωπον Apoll.*ep.Jov.*1(p.251.4; M.28.28A); Ath.*ep.Epict.*4(p.8.8; M.26.1057A); hence emphasis on her humanity ὁ δὲ Γαβριὴλ ἀποστέλλεται ...πρὸς παρθένον μεμνηστευμένην ἀνδρί, ἵν' ἐκ τοῦ μνηστῆρος δείξῃ τὴν Μ. ἀληθῶς ἄνθρωπον οὖσαν *ib.*5(p.9.3; 1057C); Gr.Nyss.*Eun.*5(2 p.118.28; M.45.700B); Epiph.*haer.*77.18(p.432.21; M.42.668B); **3.** as contrasted with Eve, Just.*dial.*100.5(M.6.712A) cit. s. παρθένος; κατὰ μὲν τὸ αἰσθητὸν ἀπ' ἐκείνης τῆς Εὔας πᾶσα τῶν ἀνθρώπων ἡ γέννησις ἐπὶ γῆς γεγένηται· ὧδε δὲ ἀληθῶς ἀπὸ Μ. αὐτὴ ἡ ζωὴ τῷ κόσμῳ γεγέννηται, ἵνα ζῶντα γεννήσῃ καὶ γένηται ἡ Μ. μήτηρ ζώντων Epiph.*haer.*78.18(p.468.27; M.42.728C); ἡ μὲν γὰρ Εὔα πρόφασις γεγένηται θανάτου τοῖς ἀνθρώποις·...ἡ δὲ Μ. πρόφασις ζωῆς *ib.*(p.469.9; 729A); Chrys.*pasch.*2(3.752C) cit. s. παρθένος; οὐ διὰ τῆς Μ. τὴν πεσοῦσαν Εὔαν ἀνέστησας; ‡Chrys.*praecurs.*1.1(2.806B); Nil.*epp.*1.266(M.79.180D); cf.Iren.*haer.*3.22.4(M.7.959Aff.); cf.*ib.*5.19.1(1175B); **4.** her relation to Christians οὗ [sc. S. John's gospel] τὸν νοῦν οὐδεὶς δύναται λαβεῖν μὴ ἀναπεσὼν ἐπὶ τὸ στῆθος Ἰησοῦ, μηδὲ λαβὼν ἀπὸ Ἰησοῦ τὴν Μ. γενομένην καὶ αὐτοῦ μητέρα Or.*Jo.*1.4(6; p.8.17; M.14.32A); τὴν παρθένον Μ. ἱκετεύουσα βοηθῆσαι παρθένῳ κινδυνευούσῃ Gr.Naz.*or.*24.11(M.35.1181A); ἔχομεν...τὴν...θεοτόκον Μ. πρεσβεύουσαν ὑπὲρ ἡμῶν Chrys.*leg.*7(6.415D); ἡ Μ. ἐν τιμῇ, ὁ κύριος προσκυνείσθω Epiph.*haer.*79.9(p.484.10; M.42.753D); μακαριζομένην τὴν ἁγίαν Μ. ἐν παντὶ ἔθνει Nil.*epp.*2.180(M.79.293A); worship offered by Collyridians, Epiph.*haer.*79.1(p.476.18; M.42.741A).

***Μαρκιανισταί**, οἱ, *followers of Marcianus*, members of a Euchite sect Μ. καὶ Μεσσαλιανοὶ καὶ εὐτυχῖται [perh. for εὐχῖται]. ... ἐκλήθησαν δὲ Μ. ὡς ἀπὸ Μαρκιανοῦ τοῦ τραπεζίτου τοῦ ἐν χρόνοις γενομένου Ἰουστινιανοῦ Tim.CP *haer.*(M.86.45C); τόν ποτε τῆς Μαρκιανιστῶν ἐκκλησίας ἐπίσκοπον †Andr.Cr.*or.*18.7(p.425.20; M.97.1201B).

***Μαρκιανοί**, οἱ, = sq., Just.*dial.*35.6(M.6.552B).

Μαρκιωνιστής** (Μαρκιον-**), ὁ, *follower of Marcion*, Anon.ap.Eus.*h.e.*5.16.21(M.20.472C); Hipp.*haer.*7.31(p.216.17; M.16.3334C); *OGIS* 608.1 (Syria, 318–319); Cyr.H.*catech.*18.26; Epiph.*haer.*42.1(p.93.22; M.41.696A); Μαρκιον-, Thdt.*h.e.*5.31 tit. (vv.ll. Μαρκιων-, Μαρκιαν- 3.1070).

μαρμαράριος, ὁ, *marble-mason*, *MAMA* 3.21 (Seleucia).

μαρμάρι(ο)ς, ὁ, = foreg., *Euchol.*(p.664); μαρμάρις *MAMA* 3.25 (Seleucia).

μάρμαρον, τό, *marble*, Hipp.*haer.*4.34(p.60.28; M.16.3099A); plur., *blocks of marble* μ. κόπτειν εἰς τὴν οἰκοδομὴν τοῦ ναοῦ *T.Sal.*

10.10 (μαρμαροκοπεῖν M.122.1332C); Chrys.*hom.21.1 in Mt.*(7.270B); Thdt.*qu.28 in 3Reg.*(1.476); *marble pavement*, Marc.Diac.*v.Porph.* 76; Jo.Mosch.*prat.*185(M.87.3060C).

μάρμαρος, *of marble*, Nonn.*par.Jo.*12:3(M.43.849C).

μαρμαρυγή, ἡ, *radiance, gleam*; **1.** lit., ref. Transfiguration τὸ πρόσωπον αὐτοῦ...φωτὸς μαρμαρυγὰς ἐκλάμψαι Eus.*e.th.*3.10(p.166. 6; M.24.1017C); **2.** fig. and met.; **a.** of Christ's divinity τῷ μὴ δυναμένῳ αὐτοῦ τὰς μ. καὶ τὴν λαμπρότητα τῆς θειότητος βλέπειν οἱονεὶ σὰρξ γίνεται Or.*Cels.*4.15(p.285.19; M.11.1048A); υἱοὶ θεοῦ κατὰ μετοχὴν τῆς τοῦ μονογενοῦς αὐτοῦ κοινωνίας ἀποτελεσθέντες μετουσίᾳ τῶν τῆς θεότητος αὐτοῦ μ. Eus.*e.th.*3.18(p.179.36; M.24. 1041C); **b.** of illumination of human soul by divine light καὶ τῶν ἐκεῖθεν μ. ἀναπλησθεὶς ὁ προφήτης Bas.*hom.in Ps.*7(1.102B; M.29. 396C); θείαν τινὰ καὶ νοητὴν ἐντιθέντος μ. τοῖς τῆς καρδίας αὐτῶν ὀφθαλμοῖς τοῦ ἁγίου πνεύματος Cyr.*Jo.*9.1(4.814C); Dion.Ar.*e.h.*3.3.10 (M.3.440B); ἵνα τηλαυγῶς τὰς φωτοειδεῖς μ. τοῦ θείου λόγου δεξώμεθα Jo.D.*hom.*4.1(M.96.601C); **c.** in Trin. simile μ. τινα ἡλιακὴν τοίχῳ προσαστράπτουσαν καὶ περιτρέμουσαν ἐξ ὑδάτων κινήσεως, ἣν ἡ ἀκτὶς ὑπολαβοῦσα διὰ τοῦ ἐν μέσῳ ἀέρος, εἶτα σχεθεῖσα τῷ ἀντιτύπῳ, παλμὸς ἐγένετο Gr.Naz.*or.*31.32(p.188.8; M.36.169C); **d.** of truth, Clem.*str.* 6.15(p.499.10; M.9.357B); Gr.Nyss.*v.Mos.*(M.44.332C); τὸ κρίνον... τὴν τῆς σωφροσύνης μ. ὑπαινίσσεται id.*hom.4 in Cant.*(M.44.840C); of virtue, Thdt.*Dan.*9:23(2.1238); **e.** of martyrs μ. καὶ λαμπηδόνες ἐκ τῶν σωμάτων ἐξαλλόμεναι τούτων αὐτὰς ἀποτυφλοῦσι τοῦ διαβόλου τὰς ὄψεις Chrys.*pan.Macc.*1.1(2.623A).

μαρμαρυγώδης, *sparkling*; neut. as subst., Clem.*paed.*3.11(p.272. 14; M.8.640B).

μαρμαρύσσω, of stars, *twinkle*, fig. ἐν λαμπρῷ τῆς ἀληθείας φωτὶ μ. Gr.Naz.*or.*35.2(M.36.257C).

μαρμαρώδης, s.v.l., *like marble*; met., *hard*; of demons, ‡Ath. *v.Syncl.*81(M.28.1536B, conj. βαρβαρώδης).

μαρμάρωσις, ἡ, *marble pavement*, Marc.Diac.*v.Porph.*76; *marble facing*, CQuerc.(M.103.108A).

***μαρτύραθλος**, *of a victorious martyr* μ. ... τέλος Thdr.Stud. *iamb.*119(M.99.1809C).

μαρτυρ-έω, **I.** *bear witness, testify*;

A. in gen. ὁ ταπεινοφρῶν μὴ ἑαυτῷ ~είτω, ἀλλ' ἐάτω ὑφ' ἑτέρου ἑαυτὸν ~εῖσθαι *1Clem.*38.2; Herm.*sim.*5.2.6; ἐπὶ πλείσταις ~ουμένης ἀνδραγαθίαις τῆς ὑπ' αὐτὸν ἐκκλησίας Eus.*h.e.*4.23.5(M.20.385A); ταῦτα ὡς ἐπὶ θεοῦ ~οῦμεν Ath.*apol.sec.*75(p.154.36; M.25.384C).

B. of divine witness; **1.** God's witness αὐτὸς [sc. θεός] δέ μοι μ. *Barn.*15.4; Just.*dial.*116.3(M.6.745A); Clem.*paed.*3.1(p.237.20; M.8. 557B); *ib.*1.8(p.131.23; 336A); **2.** in scripture, Clem.*paed.*3.1(p.237.3; M.8.557A); μ. αἱ θεῖαι γραφαί Or.*Jo.*1.8(10; p.13.24; M.14.37D); *ib.*5.6 (p.103.17; 192C); introducing a citation ~ήσει μοι εἷς τῶν δώδεκα προφητῶν φήσας Clem.*str.*3.16(p.242.22; M.8.1201A); Or.*Jo.*1.5(7; p.10.14; 33B); **3.** in baptism κύριος ἐν τῷ φωτισμῷ ὑμῶν, τῇ τοῦ ἐπισκόπου χειροθεσίᾳ ~ῶν *Const.App.*2.32.3.

C. of human witness; **1.** to God, in gen. Ἀπόλλων, ~ῶν τῇ δόξῃ τοῦ θεοῦ Clem.*str.*5.14(p.415.18; M.9.193A); ref. OT prophets εἰσὶ Χριστοῦ μάρτυρες τῷ ~εῖν περὶ αὐτοῦ κοσμούμενοι καὶ οὐ πάντως ἐκείνῳ τι διὰ τοῦ ~εῖν περὶ τοῦ υἱοῦ θεοῦ καταχαριζόμενοι Or.*Jo.*2.34 (28; p.92.20f.; M.14.176A); of Christians ὁ θεὸς τῆς ἐλπίδος οὗτός ἐστιν ᾧ ~οῦμεν Clem.*str.*4.7(p.271.11; M.8.1261B); μ. τῇ ἀληθείᾳ μόνος ὁ γνωστικὸς καὶ ἔργῳ καὶ λόγῳ *ib.*7.9(p.40.8; M.9.477A); τοῖς ~οῦσι τῷ Χριστιανισμῷ μέχρι θανάτου Or.*Cels.*1.8(p.60.16; M.11.669A); **2.** through Christian life πλείονας ὑπήνεγκεν [sc. ὁ Πέτρος] πόνους καὶ οὕτω ~ήσας ἐπορεύθη εἰς τὸν...τόπον τῆς δόξης *1Clem.*5.4; *ib.*5.7; γνώσεως ἀληθοῦς...~ουμένης ὑπὸ τῆς ζωῆς ‡*Diogn.*12.6; ὃς ἐὰν πτωχὸς ᾖ διὰ δικαιοσύνην ~εῖ δικαιοσύνην ἀγαθὸν εἶναι ἣν ἠγάπησεν, κἂν πεινῇ κἂν διψῇ διὰ δικαιοσύνην, ~εῖ δικαιοσύνην τὸ ἄριστον τυγχάνειν. ὁμοίως δὲ καὶ ὁ κλαίων...διὰ δικαιοσύνην ~εῖ τῷ βελτίστῳ νόμῳ εἶναι καλῷ Clem.*str.*4.6(p.259.16ff.; M.8.1237B); ὁ γνωστικὸς... ~ήσει νύκτωρ, ~ήσει μεθ' ἡμέραν· ἐν λόγῳ, ἐν βίῳ, ἐν τρόπῳ ~ήσει *ib.* 2.20(p.170.10f.; 1048C,D); ὅσοι δὲ τὰς ἐντολὰς τοῦ σωτῆρος ἐπιτελοῦσιν, καθ' ἑκάστην πρᾶξιν ~οῦσι...ὀνομάζοντες τὸν κύριον καὶ δι' ἔργου ~οῦντες ᾧ πείθονται *ib.*4.7(p.267.27f.; 1256A); **3.** other kinds of witness, ref. human spirit τὴν σάρκα σου ταύτην φύλασσε καθαράν... ἵνα τὸ πνεῦμα τὸ κατοικοῦν ἐν αὐτῇ ~ήσῃ αὐτῇ Herm.*sim.*5.7.1; of soldiers crowning Christ with thorns ὃν...παρεπίκραναν ἐπιδείξασθαι τὸν κύριον, τούτῳ αὐτῷ ὑφουμένῳ μεμαρτυρήκασι, τὸ διάδημα τῆς δικαιοσύνης...περιάψαντες Clem.*paed.*2.8(p.202.29; M.8.485C); Abel's blood ὅτι δὲ τὸ αἷμα ὁ λόγος ἐστίν, μ. τοῦ Ἄβελ...τὸ αἷμα *ib.*1.6(p.118. 18; 305C); ἀγαθῷ συνειδότι...~ούμενος Cyr.*Ps.*25:1(M.69.852A).

D. pass. ptcpl., *approved, of attested merit* λέγομεν δὲ Ἠλίαν καὶ Ἐλισαιέ...πρὸς τούτοις καὶ τοὺς μεμαρτυρημένους. ἐμαρτυρήθη μεγάλως Ἀβραάμ *1Clem.*17.1,2; τί δὲ εἴπωμεν ἐπὶ τῷ μεμαρτυρημένῳ Δαυείδ; *ib.*18.1; *ib.*19.1; τοὺς...μεμαρτυρημένους...ὑπὸ πάντων *ib.*44. 3; Παύλου...μεμαρτυρημένου Ign.*Eph.*12.2; id.*Philad.*5.2; Cosm.Ind. *top.*3(M.88.164A); of ministers of Church διάκονοι...μεμαρτυρημένοι παρὰ τοῦ πλήθους *Ordo Eccl.App.*20(p.234.18); bishops εἰ...ἐν παροικίᾳ μικρᾷ ὑπαρχούσῃ που προβεβηκὼς τῷ χρόνῳ μὴ εὑρίσκηται μεμαρτυρημένος καὶ σοφὸς εἰς ἐπισκοπὴν κατασταθῆναι, νέος δὲ ᾖ ἐκεῖ, μεμαρτυρημένος ὑπὸ τῶν συνόντων αὐτῷ ὡς ἄξιος ἐπισκοπῆς...εἰ ὑπὸ πάντων οὕτως ~εῖται, καθιστάσθω ἐν εἰρήνῃ *Const.App.*2.1.3; of widows, *ib.*3.3.1; of canonical scripture λέγει...Σολομῶν ἐν τῷ Ἐκκλησιάστῃ, γραφὴ δέ ἐστιν αὕτη ~ουμένη, οὐ παραγραφομένη Sever. ap.Cosm.Ind.*top.*10(424D).

II. *be martyred, suffer martyrdom*;

A. in gen. ἐγράψαμεν ὑμῖν...τὰ κατὰ τοὺς ~ήσαντας *M.Polyc.*1.1; *ib.*19.1; *ib.*21.1; Iren.*haer.*3.3.4(M.7.852A); *ib.*3.3.3(851A); Clem.*str.* 4.4(p.254.27; M.8.1228B); Heges.ap.Eus.*h.e.*2.23.18(M.20.201B); ὑπομνήματα μεμαρτυρηκότων Eus.*h.e.*4.15.48(361B); Cyr.*Zach.*68(3. 748D).

B. desire for martyrdom εἰ ~ῶ, ἐβουλόμην καὶ τέκνα καταλιπεῖν μετὰ ἀγρῶν καὶ οἰκιῶν, ἵνα καὶ παρὰ τῷ θεῷ...ἁγιωτέρων τέκνων χρηματίσω πατήρ Or.*mart.*14(p.14.22; M.11.581C); πόθον μὲν εἶχε ~ῆσαι· παραδοῦναι δὲ μὴ θέλων ἑαυτόν, ὑπηρέτει τοῖς ὁμολογηταῖς... ἐν ταῖς φυλακαῖς Ath.*v.Anton.*46(M.26.909C).

C. for Christ and the faith, Eus.*h.e.*5.21.4(M.20.488B); Chrys. *hom.66.1 in Gen.*(4.629D); id.*hom.11.4 in Eph.*(11.86D); Proc.G. *Gen.*1:15(M.87.97D); *Chron.Pasch.*p.252(M.92.608B).

D. necessary conditions: assistance of H. Ghost τῇ δυνάμει τοῦ ἁγίου πνεύματος οἱ μάρτυρες ~οῦσι...ἀδύνατον γὰρ ~ῆσαι περὶ τοῦ Χριστοῦ ἐὰν μή τις διὰ πνεύματος ἁγίου ~ήσῃ Cyr.H.*catech.*16.21; charity, Chrys.*hom.27.3 in Rom.*(9.723A).

E. in teaching of Basilides πῶς δὲ ἔτι μισθὸς ὁ ἐνδοξότατος ἐν οὐρανῷ ἀπόκειται τῷ ~ήσαντι διὰ τὸ ~ῆσαι; Clem.*str.*4.12(p.285.14; M.8.1293A); his teaching on refusal of martyrdom following from his contention that Simon of Cyrene died in place of Christ διδάσκει...μὴ δεῖν μ. ὁ γὰρ ~ῶν ἄμισθος εὑρεθήσεται, μὴ ~ῶν ὑπὲρ τοῦ πεποιηκότος τὸν ἄνθρωπον· ~εῖ γὰρ ὑπὲρ τοῦ ἐσταυρωμένου Σίμωνος...δεῖ τοίνυν ἀρνεῖσθαι καὶ μὴ προαλῶς ἀποθνήσκειν Epiph. *haer.*24.4(p.261.13ff.; M.41.313A).

III. pass., *be testified to by martyrs* τοῦ ~ουμένου σωτῆρος ἡμῶν, ...τὴν θείαν δύναμιν ἐπιπαροῦσαν ἐναργῶς τε αὐτὴν τοῖς μάρτυσιν ἐπιδεικνῦσαν ἱστορήσαμεν Eus.*h.e.*8.7.2(M.20.756B); τὴν εἰς τὸν ~ούμενον θεὸν ἀνεκήρυττεν ὁμολογίαν id.*m.P.*4(p.917.16).

μαρτυρία, ἡ, **A.** *testimony, witness*; **1.** which God bears to Son τὰ ὑπ' αὐτοῦ [sc. Christ] γενόμενα παράδοξα...τὴν ἀπὸ θεοῦ εἶχε μ. Or. *Cels.*8.9(p.227.26; M.11.1532A); ref. Mt.3:17, Gr.Ant.*bapt.*2.1(M.88. 1872C); ref. testimonies concerning his birth, Clem.*str.*6.15(p.493. 10; M.9.345A); **2.** which God bears to Christians θεοῦ μ. δούλοις πρέπουσα Just.*dial.*123.4(M.6.761B); μέχρις ἂν...οἱ ἄνθρωποι...τῆς τοῦ τελείου θεοῦ γνώσεως τελειοτέραν διὰ τῶν ἀγώνων ἐν ἡμέρᾳ κρίσεως τὴν μ. λάβωσιν Tat.*orat.*12(p.13.27; M.6.832C); **3.** of scripture, *proof text* μετὰ μαρτυρίας τῶν γραφῶν Just.*dial.*67.3(M.6.629B); *ib.*79.2 (661C); μετὰ μ. προφητικῆς Clem.*paed.*1.9(p.134.12; M.8.340C); id. *str.*1.5(p.19.21; M.8.724A); μ. τῶν ἐν τοῖς νομικοῖς καὶ προφητικοῖς λόγοις κειμένων Or.*Jo.*1.3(5; p.6.20; M.14.28B); τὰς διὰ τῶν προφητῶν περὶ Χριστοῦ μ. *ib.*2.34(28; p.91.13; 173A); διὰ μυρίων μ. πιστώσασθαι Eus.*h.e.*1.2.10(M.20.57C); αἱ...παρὰ τοῦ κυρίου παρενεχθεῖσαι μ. [sc. at Temptation] Chrys.*hom.13.3 in Mt.*(7.171C); *ib.27.2*(327D); coupled with patristic testimony, Eustrat.*v.Eutych.*30(M.86.2309A); *reference* ἐν τῇ βίβλῳ τῶν Πράξεων τῶν ἀποστόλων...κεφάλαια μ', μαρτυρίαι λ' Euthal.Diac.*Ac.*(M.85.636B et passim); **4.** of Christians ἡ τῶν εἰς τέλος ὑπομεινάντων μ. Clem.*paed.*1.5(p.103.16; M.8.276B); id. *str.*4.7(p.268.4; M.8.1256B); Or.*mart.*30(p.27.4; M.11.601A); γραμματεῖς καὶ φαρισαῖοι πρὸς ἀλλήλους ἔλεγον, κακῶς ἐποιήσαμεν τοιαύτην μ. παρασχόντες τῷ Ἰησοῦ [sc. by persecuting Christians] Heges.ap. Eus.*h.e.*2.23.14(M.20.201A); μετὰ τὴν ἐν τοῖς ἡγεμονικοῖς δικαστηρίοις λαμπρὰν...μ. Eus.*h.e.*6.39.3(600B); *ib.*7.15.2(676C); with play on double meaning of word μ. ἣν ὁμώνυμος, οἶμαι, τῷ παρὰ τὸ μαρτυρεῖν καὶ ἀποθνήσκειν ὑπὲρ θεοσεβείας σημαινομένῳ Or.*Jo.*32.18(11; p.456. 26; M.14.792A).

B. *martyrdom*; **1.** def. ἡ πρὸς θεὸν ὁμολογία μ. ἐστί Clem.*str.*4.4 (p.255.13; M.8.1228C); **2.** in gen., *Ep.Lugd.*ap.Eus.*h.e.*5.1.11(M.20. 413A); Iren.*haer.*1.28.1(M.7.690C); Hipp.*haer.*9.11(p.246.13; M.16. 3379B); Eus.*h.e.*3.2.1(M.20.216B); **3.** conditions of true martyrdom; charity οὐ τὴν ἁπλῆν ἐμφαίνων μ., ἀλλὰ τὴν γνωστικήν, ὡς κατὰ τὸν κανόνα τοῦ εὐαγγελίου πολιτευσάμενος διὰ τῆς πρὸς τὸν κύριον ἀγάπης Clem.*str.*4.4(p.255.20; M.8.1229A); *ib.*4.7(p.269.10; 1257B); νόμος δὲ *μαρτυρίας, μήτε ἐθελοντὰς πρὸς τὸν ἀγῶνα χωρεῖν, φειδοῖ τῶν διωκόντων καὶ τῶν ἀσθενεστέρων, μήτε παρόντας ἀναδύεσθαι· τὸ μὲν γὰρ θράσους, τὸ δὲ ἀνανδρίας ἐστίν* Gr.Naz.*or*.43.6(M.36.500D); martyrdom also for unity of Church *ἦν οὐκ ἀδοξοτέρα τῆς ἕνεκεν τοῦ μὴ εἰδωλολατρῆσαι γινομένης ἡ ἕνεκεν τοῦ μὴ σχίσαι μ.* Dion.Al.ap.Eus.*h.e.*6.45 (M.20.633B); **4.** its joy and efficacy *τὴν μὲν δύναμιν τῆς μ. ἔργῳ ἐπεδείκνυντο, πολλὴν παρρησίαν ἄγοντες τὰ ἔθνη Ep.Lugd.*ap.Eus.*h.e.* 5.2.4(M.20.436A); *ἡ χαρὰ τῆς μ. ib.*5.1.34(421A); **5.** Gnost. *τινὲς δὲ τῶν αἱρετικῶν...μ. λέγοντες ἀληθῆ εἶναι τὴν τοῦ ὄντως ὄντος γνῶσιν θεοῦ, ὅπερ καὶ ἡμεῖς ὁμολογοῦμεν, φονέα δὲ εἶναι αὐτὸν ἑαυτοῦ καὶ αὐθέντην τὸν διὰ θανάτου ὁμολογήσαντα* Clem.*str*.4.4(p.256.6; M.8.1229B).

***μαρτυριανοί, οἱ,** *Martyrians*, members of a pagan ascetical sect (= *Μασσαλιανοί* 1) *M. ἑαυτοὺς ἐπωνόμασαν, δῆθεν διὰ τοὺς ὑπὲρ τῶν εἰδώλων μαρτυρήσαντας* [i.e. who were slain by imperial authorities] Epiph.*haer*.80.2(p.486.20; M.42.760B); Jo.D.*haer*.80(M.94.729A).

***μαρτυρικός, 1.** *of a martyr ἀγὼν μ. A.Paul.et Thecl.*43(p.269. 6n.); ‡Just.*qu.Gr*.15(M.6.1488C); *στέφανος* Philost.*h.e.*7.8(M.65.545C); voice, Chrys.*pan.Juln*.3(2.675D); death, Philost.*h.e.*2.12(476C); in wider sense, of a tragic accident *μ. θανάτῳ τέθνηκεν ὁ ἄνθρωπος ἐκεῖνος* Eus.Al.*serm*.6(M.86.352A); martyr's blood, Jo.Mon.*hymn. Bas*.10(M.96.1377A); relics *ἐκ μ. λειψάνων μύρον εὐῶδες ἀναβλύζειν* Jo.D.*f.o*.4.15(M.94.1165A); *αἱ μ. βίβλοι διηγοῦνται περὶ τῶν παθημάτων τῶν μαρτύρων* Taras.*ep*.4(M.98.1453C); **2.** neut. plur. as subst.; **a.** *martyrs' lives ἀναγίνωσκε δὲ τὴν νέαν διαθήκην, μαρτυρικὰ δέ, καὶ τοὺς βίους τῶν πατέρων* Nil.*epp*.4.1(M.79.545A); **b.** *hymns in honour of martyrs, Const.Stud.*6(M.99.1708A).

***μαρτυρικῶς,** *as befits martyrs, like martyrs*, †Jo.D.*B.J.*proem. (M.96.860B); Thdr.Stud.*epp*.2.14(M.99.1157D); *ib*.2.55(1268C).

μαρτύριον, τό, I. *testimony, evidence, proof*;

A. in OT *ἡ σκηνὴ τοῦ μ.* Just.*dial*.36.2(M.6.553B); *ib*.36.6(556A); Or.*Jo*.28.1(p.389.14; M.14.681A); without *σκηνή*: *θυσιαστήριον ἔνδον ἐν τοῖς ἁγίοις τῶν ἁγίων ἀνακείμενον κατὰ πρόσωπον τοῦ μ.* Meth. *symp*.5.8(p.63.1; M.18.112B).

B. in gen. *εἰς μ. τῶν φυλῶν...εἰς μ. Ἀβραάμ, Ἰσαάκ, Ἰακώβ Barn.* 8.3,4; ref. circumcision *τὴν μείωσιν τῆς σαρκὸς μ. ἐκλογῆς ἀλαζονεύεσθαι...πῶς οὐ χλεύης ἄξιον; Diogn.*4.4; Just.*dial*.88.1(M.6.685A); Or.*Jo*.2.14(8; p.70.3; M.14.137A).

C. from scripture, for truths of the faith *τίνι γὰρ ἂν λόγῳ ἀνθρώπῳ σταυρωθέντι ἐπειθόμεθα, ὅτι πρωτότοκος τῷ...θεῷ ἐστι... εἰ μὴ μ. πρὶν ἢ ἐλθεῖν αὐτὸν ἄνθρωπον γενόμενον κεκηρυγμένα περὶ αὐτοῦ εὕρομεν;* Just.*1apol*.53.2(M.6.405C); id.*dial*.61.1(M.6.613C); *τὰ τῆς πίστεως ἐκ τῆς παρ' ἡμῖν ἱστορίας ἀναλεγόμενος παρατίθεμαι μ.* Clem.*str*.2.4(p.119.18; M.8.944B); *ib*.6.15(p.493.30; M.9.345C); Or. *Jo*.5.6(p.103.9; M.14.192B); *περὶ...τοῦ κυρίου ἡμῶν Ἰησοῦ Χριστοῦ, καὶ περὶ τῆς πρὸς τὸν πατέρα ἑνότητος αὐτοῦ γέγραπται καὶ δείκνυται τὰ μ.* Ath.*Ar*.2.39(M.26.229B).

D. from pagan writings *περὶ...πίστεως ἱκανὰ μ. τῶν παρ' Ἕλλησι γραφῶν παρατεθείμεθα* Clem.*str*.5.2(p.335.1; M.9.29A).

E. ref. Passion *ὃς ἂν μὴ ὁμολογῇ τὸ μ. τοῦ σταυροῦ, 'ἐκ τοῦ διαβόλου ἐστίν'* Polyc.*ep*.7.1; exeg. 1Tim.2:6 *μ. δὲ τὸ πάθος ἐκάλεσε, πρῶτον μὲν διὰ τὸ ἄδικον τῆς σφαγῆς· ἔπειτα δὲ καὶ διὰ τὸ πάντας ἔχειν μάρτυρας τοὺς προφήτας* Thdt.*1Tim*.2:6(3.648); *Χριστὸς...ἀπέθανεν ὑπὲρ Ἑλλήνων...τὸ δὲ αὐτοῦ μέρος ἐγένετο. 'μ.' τὸ πάθος φησίν. ... ἦλθε γὰρ μαρτυρήσων, φησί, τῇ ἀληθείᾳ τοῦ πατρός* Chrys.*hom.7.1 in 1Tim.*(11.586D).

II. *martyrdom*;

A. of Christ's Passion, exeg. Mt.14:36 *'παρένεγκε τὸ ποτήριον τοῦτο ἀπ' ἐμοῦ.' ὅρα τοίνυν εἰ δύνασαι, παντὸς μ. τοῦ καθ' ὁποιανοῦν πρόφασιν ἐξόδου ἀποτελουμένου ποτηρίου καλουμένου, φάσκειν ὅτι οὐ τὸ γένος τοῦ μ. παρῃτεῖτο ὁ λέγων· 'παρελθέτω ἀπ' ἐμοῦ τὸ ποτήριον τοῦτο' (ἔφασκε γὰρ ἂν· παρελθέτω ἀπ' ἐμοῦ τὸ ποτήριον) ἀλλὰ τάχα τὸ εἶδος τόδε. καὶ πρόσχες εἰ δυνατὸν ἐνορῶντα τὸν σωτῆρα τοῖς εἴδεσιν... τῶν ποτηρίων...τόδε τὸ εἶδος τῆς ἐξόδου παραιτεῖσθαι τοῦ μ. ἄλλο δὲ τάχα βαρύτερον αἰτεῖν λεληθότως* Or.*mart*.29(p.26.1ff.; M.11.600A); cf.*ib*.28(p.24.23; 597A); *τὸ τοῦ σωτῆρος μ.* Diod.*Ps*.87:11(M.33. 1618C); *ἀθλητὴς μ. γεγένημαι. ἐπὶ τοῦ σταυροῦ...ἐπάλαισα* Procl.CP *or*.17.7(M.65.817B).

B. of martyrdom of Christians in strict sense, as death for the faith; **1.** scriptural basis *περὶ δὲ τοῦ μ. διαρρήδην ὁ κύριος εἴρηκεν* Clem.*str*.4.9(p.279.27; M.8.1280D); *οὐκ ἐν τοῖς πρὸς τοὺς πολλοὺς λόγοις τὰ περὶ μ. προφητεύεται ὑπὸ τοῦ σωτῆρος ἀλλ' ἐν τοῖς πρὸς τοὺς ἀποστόλους* Or.*mart*.34(p.29.5; M.11.605A); *ταῦτα δὲ παρὰ τῷ Ματθαίῳ ἐπὶ μαρτύριον προτρεπόμενα οὐ πρὸς ἄλλους ἢ τοὺς δώδεκα εἴρηται· ὧν ἀκούειν καὶ ἡμᾶς δεήσει ἐν τῷ ἀκούειν ἐσομένους ἀδελφοὺς τῶν ἀκουσάντων ἀποστόλων καὶ ἀποστόλοις συγκαταριθμησομένους ib.* (p.30.10; 605D); **2.** as foundation of Church *οἱ...ἀπόστολοι εἰς πῆξιν...τῶν ἐκκλησιῶν εἰς πεῖραν καὶ μ. τελειότητος ἤχθησαν* Clem.*str.* 7.12(p.53.17; M.9.501C); *θῶμεν αὐτὴν* [sc. *ψυχήν*]...*ὑπὲρ τῶν ἐν τῷ μ. ἡμῶν οἰκοδομηθησομένων* Or.*mart*.41(p.38.28; M.11.617A); **3.** conditions of true martyrdom *μακάρια...τὰ μ. πάντα τὰ κατὰ τὸ θέλημα τοῦ θεοῦ γεγονότα· δεῖ γὰρ εὐλαβεστέρους ἡμᾶς ὑπάρχοντας τῷ θεῷ τὴν κατὰ πάντων ἐξουσίαν ἀνατιθέναι M.Polyc.*2.1; *ib*.1.1; *εἴ που μ. δι' αἵματος χωροῦντος ἐπικαταλάβοι χρεία, βούλεται* [sc. *ὁ νόμος*] Clem. *str*.2.18(p.155.26; M.8.1020C); *διδάσκει ἡμᾶς ὁ κύριος, ὡς οὐκ ἄνευ προνοίας ἔρχεταί τις ἐπὶ τὸν τοῦ μ. ἀγῶνα* Or.*mart*.34(p.30.17; M.11. 608A); false martyrdom rejected *ψέγομεν δὲ καὶ ἡμεῖς τοὺς ἐπιπηδήσαντας τῷ θανάτῳ...οὐ γὰρ τὸν χαρακτῆρα σῴζουσι τοῦ μ. τοῦ πιστοῦ, τὸν ὄντως θεὸν μὴ γνωρίσαντες, θανάτῳ δὲ ἑαυτοὺς ἐπιδιδόασι κενῷ* Clem.*str*.4.4(p.256.16; M.8.1229C); ref. Montanists *ἐπειδὰν οἱ ἐπὶ τὸ τῆς κατ' ἀλήθειαν πίστεως μ. κληθέντες ἀπὸ τῆς ἐκκλησίας τύχωσι μετά τινων τῶν ἀπὸ τῆς τῶν Φρυγῶν αἱρέσεως λεγομένων μαρτύρων* Anon.ap.Eus.*h.e.*5.16.22(M.20.472C); **4.** excellence of martyrdom; **a.** gen. affirmations *τελείωσιν τὸ μ. καλοῦμεν οὐχ ὅτι τέλος τοῦ βίου ὁ ἄνθρωπος ἔλαβεν ὡς οἱ λοιποί, ἀλλ' ὅτι τέλειον ἔργον ἀγάπης ἐνεδείξατο* Clem.*str*.4.4(p.255.1; M.8.1228B); *οἱ βασάνους καὶ πόνους ὑπομείναντες τῶν μὴ ἐν τούτοις ἐξητασμένων λαμπροτέραν ἐπεδείξαντο τὴν ἐν τῷ μ. ἀρετὴν* Or.*mart*.15(p.15.7; M.11.584A); ref. Ps. 115:4 *'ποτήριον δὲ σωτηρίου' ἔθος ὀνομάζεσθαι τὸ μ. ib*.28(p.24.19; 596D); *λόγον γὰρ ἔχει τὸ ἰδίως τὸν ἐν μ. θάνατον ὕψωσιν καλεῖσθαι, ὡς δῆλον ἐκ τοῦ* [Jo.12:32] *ib*.50(p.47.1; 636A); *τότε ἦσαν πιστοί, ὅτε τὰ μ. τὰ γενναῖα ἐγίνοντο* id.*hom.4.3 in Jer.*(p.25.19; M.13.288D); Meth.*fr.mart.* 1(p.520.2; M.18.345C) cit. s. *ἁρπαγμός*; **b.** does not give claim to highest honours, exeg. Mt.10:38ff., Chrys.*anom*.8.6(1.522A); being inferior to charity *ἀγάπης οὐδὲν οὔτε μεῖζον οὔτε ἴσον ἐστίν, οὐδὲ αὐτὸ τὸ μ., ὃ πάντων ἐστὶ κεφάλαιον τῶν ἀγαθῶν...ἀγάπη μὲν γὰρ καὶ χωρὶς μ. ποιεῖ μαθητὰς τοῦ Χριστοῦ, μ. δὲ χωρὶς ἀγάπης οὐκ ἂν ἰσχύσειε τοῦτο ἐργάσασθαι...μ. χωρὶς ἀγάπης οὐ μόνον μαθητὰς οὐ ποιεῖ, ἀλλ' οὐδὲ ὠφελεῖ τι τὸν ὑπομένοντα* id.*pan.Rom*.1.1(2.612C); *ὁ μὴ φιλῶν τὸν ἀδελφὸν...κἂν ἐν μ. διαλάμψῃ, οὐδὲν ἀνύει πλέον* id.*hom. 7.6 in Rom.*(9.491A); **c.** receives a crown *εἰς πᾶν εἶδος διῃρεῖτο τὰ μ. τῆς ἐξόδου αὐτῶν. ἐκ διαφόρων γὰρ χρωμάτων...πλέξαντες στέφανον Ep.Lugd.*ap.Eus.*h.e.*5.1.36(M.20.421B); Chrys.*hom.15.2 in Rom.*(9. 596D); *ib.30.4*(742D); *M.Niceph*.7(p.287); **5.** effects; **a.** cleansing from sin, Clem.*str*.4.9(p.281.26; M.8.1284C) cit. s. *ἀποκάθαρσις*; ref. Sap.3:1ff. *ἡ θεία σοφία...κάθαρσιν ἔνδοξον τὸ μ. διδάσκουσα ib*.4.16 (p.294.10; 1309C); being a baptism *τὸ μ. γὰρ οἶδε βάπτισμα καλεῖν ὁ σωτὴρ* [sc. Mc.10:38] Cyr.H.*catech*.3.10; *μὴ θαυμάσητε, εἰ βάπτισμα τὸ μ. ἐκάλεσα· καὶ γὰρ καὶ ἐνταῦθα τὸ πνεῦμα μετὰ πολλῆς ἐφίπταται τῆς δαψιλείας, καὶ ἁμαρτημάτων ἀναίρεσις καὶ ψυχῆς γίνεται καθαρμὸς θαυμαστός τις καὶ παράδοξος· καὶ ὥσπερ οἱ βαπτιζόμενοι τοῖς ὕδασιν, οὕτως οἱ μαρτυροῦντες τῷ ἰδίῳ λούονται αἵματι* Chrys.*pan.Lucn*.2(2. 526A); but *οὐδὲν οὕτω παροξύνει τὸν θεόν, ὡς τὸ ἐκκλησίαν διαιρεθῆναι ...ἀνὴρ δέ τις ἅγιος...οὐδὲ μ. αἷμα ταύτην ἔφησε δύνασθαι τὴν ἁμαρτίαν ἐξαλείφειν* id.*hom.11.4 in Eph.*(11.86D); **b.** other effects *εἰ θέλομεν ἡμῶν σῶσαι τὴν ψυχήν, ἵνα αὐτὴν ἀπολάβωμεν κρείττονα ψυχῆς, καὶ μ. ἀπολέσωμεν αὐτὴν* Or.*mart*.12(p.12.25; M.11.580B); receiving 'a hundredfold', *ib*.14(p.14.21; 581C); procuring *παρρησία* with God, *ib*.28(p.24.7; 596C); *τόπον διὰ τῆς εἰς τὸ μ. προθυμίας δότε τῷ τοῦ πατρὸς ὑμῶν πνεύματι λαλοῦντι τοῖς διὰ θεοσέβειαν παραδοθεῖσιν ib*.39 (p.36.11; 613C); *ὁ εἰς μ. ἑλκόμενος, οὕτω νικᾷ, δεσμούμενος, καὶ μαστιγούμενος* Chrys.*hom.84.4 in Mt.*(7.802C); **6.** literary tradition: as title of martyrs' legends, *A.Andr.*A tit.(p.46.1); *A.Phil.*tit.(p.41. 19); Sophr.H.*v.Anast*.tit.ap.CNic.(787)*act*.4(H.4.173D); accounts in pagan literature *ἡ τῆς ἡμετέρας πίστεως διέλαμπεν διδασκαλία, ὡς καὶ τοὺς ἄποθεν τοῦ καθ' ἡμᾶς λόγου συγγραφεῖς μὴ ἀποκνῆσαι ταῖς αὐτῶν ἱστορίαις τόν τε διωγμὸν καὶ τὰ ἐν αὐτῷ μ. παραδοῦναι* Eus.*h.e.* 3.18.4(M.20.252B); description by martyr of persecutions *ἥτις* [sc. S. Perpetua] *πᾶσαν τὴν τάξιν τοῦ μ. ἐντεῦθεν διηγήσατο, ὡς καὶ τῷ νοΐ αὐτῆς καὶ τῇ χειρὶ συγγράψασα κατέλιπεν οὕτως εἰποῦσα M.Perp.*2 (p.63.26); *Παπίας καὶ ἄλλοι πολλοί, ὧν καὶ ἔγγραφα φέρονται τὰ μ. Chron.Pasch.*p.258(M.92.628C); **7.** liturg., celebration of anniversary of martyrdom *ἔνθα ὡς δυνατὸν ἡμῖν συναγομένοις ἐν ἀγαλλιάσει καὶ χαρᾷ παρέξει ὁ κύριος ἐπιτελεῖν τὴν τοῦ μ. αὐτοῦ ἡμέραν γενέθλιον, εἴς τε τὴν τῶν προηθληκότων μνήμην καὶ τῶν μελλόντων ἄσκησιν M.Polyc.*18.3; Euthal.Diac.*epp.Paul.*(M.85.701A); **8.** refutation of Basilides, who held that martyrdom was a punishment for sins committed in an earlier life *εἰ δὲ τὸ μ. ἀνταπόδοσις διὰ κολάσεως, καὶ ἡ πίστις καὶ ἡ διδασκαλία, δι' ἃς τὸ μ.· σύνεργοι ἄρα αὗται κολάσεως, ἧς τίς ἂν ἄλλη μείζων ἀπέμφασις γένοιτο;* Clem.*str*.4.12(p.285. 27f.; M.8.1293B); *ib*.(p.284.6; 1289A); **9.** refusal of martyrdom, ref. Is.14:9f. *οὐδὲν δὲ ἄτοπον ἰδεῖν ἐκ τῶν τῷ Ἡσαΐᾳ γεγραμμένων τὰ λεχθησόμενα ὑπὸ τῶν ἐν ᾅδου τοῖς νενικημένοις καὶ ἀπὸ τοῦ οὐρανίου μ.*

καταπεπτωκόσιν Or.*mart*.18(p.17.12; M.11.588A); ἄλλων δὲ τοῦ μ. ἐκπεσόντων, καὶ τὴν ἀθεμιτουργίαν τῆς τῶν εἰδώλων θρησκείας πραξάντων Epiph.*haer*.68.2(p.141.22; M.42.185B).

C. in wider sense; **1.** in gen., of endurance of sufferings of life φέρε τοίνυν τὰ συμπίπτοντα πάντα γενναίως· τοῦτο γάρ σοι μ. ἐστιν. οὐ γὰρ τὸν κελευόμενον θῦσαι, τὸ μὴ θῦσαι, ἀλλὰ καταξανθῆναι μᾶλλον, ἢ τοῦτο ποιῆσαι, ποιεῖ μ. μόνον· ἀλλὰ καὶ τὸ τῆς ὀδύνης εἰς βλασφημίαν ἐξαγούσης, ἑλέσθαι ἐγκαρτερῆσαι τῷ πόνῳ, καὶ μηδὲν ἀπηχὲς εἰπεῖν, μάρτυρα ἐργάζεται Chrys.*exp.in Ps*.127:1(5.362B); ref. Pr.3:12, Heb.12:6 πόσοι ποσάκις ἐπεθύμησαν μ. στέφανον λαβεῖν; τοῦτο ἀπηρτισμένος ἐστὶ μ. στέφανος. οὐ γὰρ τὸ κελευσθῆναι, εἶτα ἑλέσθαι μᾶλλον ἀποθανεῖν ἢ θῦσαι, ποιεῖ μάρτυρα μόνον, ἀλλὰ καὶ τὸ ὁτιοῦν φυλάττοντα μόνον δυνάμενον θάνατον ἐπισπάσασθαι, μ. ἐστι σαφές id. *Jud*.8.7(1.685E); τί πάθω, φησίν, ὅτι μ. καιρὸς οὐ πάρεστι νῦν; τί φής; οὐ πάρεστι μ. καιρός; οὐδέποτε...οὗτος ἄπεστιν,...οὐδὲ γὰρ τὸ ἐπὶ ξύλου κρέμασθαι μόνον, τοῦτο ποιεῖ μάρτυρα· ἐπεὶ εἰ τοῦτο ἦν, ἐκτὸς τῶν στεφάνων τούτων ὁ Ἰὼβ ἦν id.*hom.1.4 in 2Cor*.(10.424C); δεῖ οὖν εὐχαριστοῦντας ὑπομένειν τὴν βουλὴν τοῦ θεοῦ· τό τε γὰρ ἡμῖν εἰς λόγον δευτέρου μ. τό τε συνεχὲς τῶν νόσων καὶ ἡ πρὸς τοὺς δαιμονιώδεις λογισμοὺς μάχη λογισθήσεται Diad.*perf*.94(p.138.14); τὸ μ. τῆς συνειδήσεως *ib*.(p.138.26); **2.** various examples; **a.** giving one's life nursing in epidemics, Dion.Al.ap.Eus.*h.e*.7.22.8(M.20.689A); and in other ways risking one's life for one's neighbour, Chrys.*hom.9.3 in Phil*.(11.268B); **b.** defending faith against heretics οὐ γὰρ μόνον τὸ μὴ θῦσαι λίβανον δείκνυσι μάρτυρας· ἀλλὰ καὶ τὸ μὴ ἀρνήσασθαι τὴν πίστιν, ποιεῖ τὸ μ. τῆς συνειδήσεως λαμπρόν Ath.*ep.Aeg.Lib*.21(M.25.588A); τὰ γὰρ τοιαῦτα παθήματα [sc. those inflicted by heretics] μέρος ἐστὶ μ. CSard.*ep.Alex*.ap.Ath.*apol.sec*.38(p.117.16; M.25.316A); **c.** illness, loss of property, etc., Chrys.*hom.3.5 in 1Thess*.(11.447E,F); id.*hom.1.5 in 2Cor*.(10.425A); **3.** ascetical life as martyrdom ἐὰν μηδεὶς διώκῃ σε τύραννος Ἕλλην, ἀλλ' ὅμως γίνου ἕτοιμος εἰς μ. ... πάρεστι διωγμὸς διὰ παντὸς τοῦ βίου· πάρεστιν θυμός, πάρεστιν ἐπιθυμία αἰσχρά...ἀγωνίζου τοίνυν, καὶ ἀνδρίζου κατ' αὐτῶν Nil.*epp*.3.71(M.79.421B); τοὺς νηπιάζοντας παιδαγωγοῦντες, καὶ τὸν καλοῦντα περιμένοντες λόγον· ὃς ἐν τοῖς νομίμως τοὺς ὑπὲρ εὐσεβείας ὑπερμαχομένοις ἀγῶνας ἀοράτως παραγινόμενος, τὸν τῆς μαρτυρίας διέξεισι δρόμον· ὡς μόνος αἴσθησιν καὶ φύσιν νικῆσαι δυνάμενος· ἐπειδὴ σαφῶς αἰσθήσεως νίκη καὶ φύσεώς ἐστι τὸ μ., δι' οὗ πέφυκε νοῦ τε καὶ λόγου γίγνεσθαι κατὰ τῶν παθῶν ἐπανάστασις Max.*ep*.14(M.91.544B); cf. τὸ γυμνάσιον τῆς εὐσεβείας μ. ἐστι ‡Chrys.*hom.in Ps.95:1*(5.635C); τοὺς θεοφόρους ἀσκητάς, τοὺς τὸ χρονιώτερον καὶ ἐπιπονώτερον μ. τῆς συνειδήσεως διαθλήσαντας Jo.D.*f.o*.4.15(M.94.1168B).

III. *martyr's sanctuary*, hence gen. *chapel* or *church*;

A. in gen., coupled with ἐκκλησία etc. πόλιν...εὐκτηρίοις...ἐφαίδρυνεν μ. τε μεγίστοις Eus.*v.C*.3.48(p.98.2; M.20.1108C); *ib*.4.61(p.143.2; 1213A); Didym.*Trin*.2.16(M.39.721A); Chrys.*hom.11.4 in 1Thess*.(11.507D); Jo.Ant.*relat.imp*.1(p.124.36; M.83.1441A); ἐν ἐκκλησίᾳ πόλεως...ἢ μ., ἢ μοναστηρίῳ CChalc.*can*.6; οἱ κληρικοὶ τῶν...μοναστηρίων καὶ μ. *ib*.8.

B. *martyr's shrine* δώσω ὑμῖν τὸ παλάτιόν μου εἰς μ. τοῦ Ματθαίου *A.Mt*.27(p.256.9); οἱ κατηχούμενοι ἐπὶ τοῖς μ. κατηχοῦντο Or.*hom.4.3 in Jer*.(p.25.22; M.13.289A); in Rome ἀπελθὼν εἰς τὸ μ. Πέτρου Ath.*h.Ar*.37(p.204.3; M.25.736D); οὐδὲ τὰς ἐν τοῖς μ. γινομένας ἀγορασίας οἰκείας ἡμῖν ὁ λόγος δείκνυσιν. οὐ γὰρ ἄλλου τινὸς ἕνεκεν ἐν τοῖς μ., ἢ ἐν τοῖς περὶ αὐτὰ τόποις φαίνεσθαι ἐπιβάλλει Χριστιανοῖς, ἢ προσευχῆς ἕνεκεν, καὶ τοῦ εἰς ὑπόμνησιν ἐλθόντας τῆς τῶν ἁγίων ὑπὲρ εὐσεβείας μέχρι θανάτου ἐνστάσεως, πρὸς τὸν ζῆλον τὸν ὅμοιον προτραπῆναι Bas.*reg.fus*.40(2.386A,B; M.31.1020B); directions for building such, Gr.Nyss.*ep*.25(M.46.1093Cff.); τῆς γὰρ μελλούσης κρίσεως ἴχνη...τὰ μ. τῶν ἁγίων παρέχεται, δαιμόνων μαστιζομένων, ἀνθρώπων κολαζομένων καὶ ἐλευθερουμένων Chrys.*hom.26.5 in 2Cor*.(10.626C); desecrated by Juln. Imp., id.*pan.Bab*.1.3(2.534E); ἐν τῷ μ., ἔνθα τὸ σῶμα τῆς μάρτυρος Εὐφημίας ἀπόκειται Socr.*h.e*.6.6.12(M.67.677A); τὸ λείψανον τῆς ἁγίας Ἀναστασίας...κατετέθη ἐν τῷ μ. αὐτῆς Thdr.Lect.*h.e*.2.65(M.86.216B); ἤνεγκε τὸ λείψανον τοῦ ἁγίου Συμεώνος ἐν Ἀντιοχείᾳ...καὶ ἐκτίσθη αὐτοῦ μ. μέγα *Chron.Pasch*.p.321(M.92.820B); apptly. inhabited, prob. by guardians of relics Σάμος...μᾶλλον τῶν τὸ μ. οἰκούντων ἐνδιέτριβε τῷ ναῷ Bas.Sel.*v.Thecl*.2.30(M.85.617A); legislation concerning those of heretics περὶ τοῦ μὴ συγχωρεῖν εἰς τὰ κοιμητήρια ἢ εἰς τὰ λεγόμενα μ. πάντων τῶν αἱρετικῶν ἀπιέναι τοὺς τῆς ἐκκλησίας εὐχῆς ἢ θεραπείας ἕνεκα CLaod.*can*.9; met., of a hermit's cell ἔσται γὰρ τὸ σπήλαιόν σου μ. τῆς ἐρήμου *V.Zos*.18(p.107.3).

C. sanctuaries in Jerusalem called μ.; **1.** Holy Sepulchre τὸ σεμνὸν καὶ πανάγιον τῆς σωτηρίου ἀναστάσεως μ. Eus.*v.C*.3.28(p.91.1; M.20.1088D); κατ' αὐτὸ τὸ σωτήριον μ. ἡ νέα κατεσκευάζετο Ἱερουσαλὴμ *ib*.3.33(p.93.9; 1093A); id.*l.C*.11(p.225.11; M.20.1377C); *ib*.18(p.259.29; 1440B); **2.** Church of Holy Sepulchre τάς τε περὶ τὸ μ. μεγαλουργίας διεξιόντες τῷ λόγῳ id.*v.C*.4.45(p.136.13; 1196A); τῷ...θεῷ ἀμφὶ τὸ μνῆμα τὸ σωτήριον εἰρήνης ἀνάθημα τὸ μ. βασιλέως ἀφιεροῦντος *ib*.4.47(p.137.13; 1197C); id.*l.C*.9(p.221.16; 1369C); *ib*.11(p.224.11; 1376B, v. not. ad loc.); ἐπὶ ἀφιερώσει τοῦ σωτηρίου μ. CHier.(335)*ep*.ap.Ath.*syn*.21(p.247.27; M.26.717C); Marc.Diac.*v.Porph*.5; **3.** Church of Resurrection τὸν νεὼν σωτηρίου ἀναστάσεως ἐναργὲς ἀνίστη μ. βασιλεύς Eus.*v.C*.3.40(p.94.30; 1100B).

***μαρτυρογραφή, ἡ,** = sq., Eustrat.*stat.anim*.20(p.501).

μαρτυρογράφιον, τό, *record of martyrdom* σχεδὸν πάντα τὰ μ. ἀνεπίγραφά εἰσιν Thdr.Stud.*epp*.2.42(M.99.1244D).

***μαρτυρολόγιον, τό,** *life of a martyr*, CTrull.*can*.63.

μάρτυς, ὁ, ἡ, I. *witness*;

A. ref. God μ. δέ μοι ἐν ᾧ δέδεμαι, ὅτι ἀπὸ σαρκὸς ἀνθρωπίνης οὐκ ἔγνων Ign.*Philad*.7.2; as witness to Christians θεὸν...μ. ἔχοντες τῶν τε λογισμῶν καὶ τῶν πράξεων Just.*2apol*.12.4(M.6.464B); θεὸς μ. τοῦ ἡμετέρου συνειδότος Or.*Cels*.1.46(p.96.16; M.11.745B); id.*Jo*.2.34(28; p.93.5; M.14.176C); *Const.App*.8.1.5; Proc.G.*Dt*.19:15(M.87.920D); as witness to Christ βαπτιζομένῳ τῷ κυρίῳ ἀπ' οὐρανῶν ἐπήχησε φωνὴ μ. ἠγαπημένου Clem.*paed*.1.6(p.105.5; M.8.280B); ἦν γὰρ ἐμπρεπὲς τὸν ἁπάντων μείζονα τῶν ἄλλων μετὰ τὸν πατέρα μόνῳ τῷ ἑαυτοῦ μείζονι πατρὶ χρήσασθαι μ. καὶ δὴ καὶ τῆς ἁγνείας οὐκ εἰς ἀνθρωπίνην ἀνοίσω κἀγὼ δόξαν τοὺς ἐπαίνους, ἀλλ' εἰς αὐτόν, ᾧ μέλομεν...γεωργὸν αὐτῆς...καὶ ἐραστὴν τῆς ὥρας ὄντα καὶ ἀξιόχρεω μ. Meth.*symp*.7.1(p.71.17ff.; M.18.124B–125A); ref. H. Ghost τοῦ πνεύματος ἡ συμπαράληψις ὡς μάρτυρος *Const.App*.3.17.2; *Lit*.ap.*Const.App*.8.5.3.

B. ref. scriptures; **1.** in gen., Clem.*paed*.1.5(p.98.17; M.8.265B); λαβὼν μ. δύο ἀπὸ καινῆς καὶ παλαιᾶς διαθήκης, λαβὼν μ. τρεῖς ἀπὸ εὐαγγελίου, ἀπὸ προφήτου, ἀπὸ ἀποστόλου Or.*hom.1.7 in Jer*.(p.6.13f.; M.13.264A); of prophets in gen. ἀξιόπιστοι μ. τῆς ἀληθείας Just.*dial*.7.2(M.6.492B); Athenag.*leg*.7.2(M.6.904C); τῶν ἑτεροδόξων τινὲς πιστεύειν φάσκοντες εἰς τὸν Χριστόν...οὐ προσιέμενοι τὴν ἐπιδημίαν αὐτοῦ ὑπὸ τῶν προφητῶν προκατηγγέλθαι, ἀνατρέπειν πειρῶνται τὰς διὰ τῶν προφητῶν περὶ Χριστοῦ μαρτυρίας, φάσκοντες μὴ δεῖσθαι μαρτύρων τὸν υἱὸν τοῦ θεοῦ...εἰ Μωσῆς πεπίστευται διὰ τὸν λόγον καὶ τὰς δυνάμεις, οὐ δεηθεὶς μαρτύρων πρὸ αὐτοῦ τινων αὐτὸν καταγγειλάντων,...πῶς οὐχὶ μᾶλλον Μωυσέως καὶ τῶν προφητῶν διαφέρων δύναται χωρὶς προφητῶν μαρτυρούντων τὰ περὶ αὐτοῦ ἀνῦσαι ὃ βούλεται; Or.*Jo*.2.34(28; p.91.13; M.14.173A); ref. OT saints in gen. [cf.Mt.13:17] τοιαῦτα νῦν ὁρᾶν...ἠξιώθημεν, οἷα τῶν πρὸ ἡμῶν πολλοὶ...θεοῦ μ. ἐπεθύμησαν ἐπὶ γῆς ἰδεῖν Eus.*h.e*.10.1.4(M.20.844A); **2.** of individuals, Isaiah, Clem.*paed*.1.5(p.99.14; M.8.268B); Jeremiah, Meth.*symp*.3.5(p.31.10; M.18.68B); David, *Const.App*.2.41.4; Jo. Bapt. μ. ... Ἰησοῦ ἐστιν ὁ Ἰωάννης Or.*Jo*.2.37(30; p.96.9; M.14.181B); S. Paul (ref. Eph.4:17ff.) τοιοῦτον μ. ἐλέγχοντος τὴν τῶν ἀνθρώπων ἄνοιαν Clem.*prot*.9(p.63.13; M.8.196A); id.*str*.5.1.(p.327.3; M.9.12A); Meth.*symp*.2.7(p.25.9; M.18.60A); S. John (but may also mean *martyr* here) Ἰωάννης...μ. καὶ διδάσκαλος Polycr.ap.Eus.*h.e*.5.24.3(M.20.493C); ref. relatives of Christ προηγοῦνται πάσης ἐκκλησίας ὡς μ. καὶ ἀπὸ γένους τοῦ κυρίου Heges.*ib*.3.32.6(284B); S. Barnabas (ref. *Barn.*) οὔ μοι δεῖ πλειόνων λόγων παραθεμένῳ μ. τὸν ἀποστολικὸν Βαρνάβαν Clem.*str*.2.20(p.176.6; M.8.1060B); 'authors' of *Const.App.* referring to themselves ἡμεῖς...μ. τῆς παρουσίας αὐτοῦ σὺν Ἰακώβῳ τῷ τοῦ κυρίου ἀδελφῷ καὶ ἑτέροις ἑβδομήκοντα δύο μαθηταῖς *Const.App*.2.55.2; ref. Transfiguration Μωσῆς...καὶ Ἠλίας...συνῆσαν ἐν τῇ μεταμορφώσει τοῦ κυρίου ἐν τῷ ὄρει μάρτυρες αὐτοῦ τῆς ἐνανθρωπήσεως καὶ τῶν παθημάτων *ib*.6.19.4.

C. ref. Christians, ref. 'Νατάλιος ὁμολογητής': Χριστὸς οὐκ ἐβούλετο ἔξω ἐκκλησίας γενόμενον ἀπολέσθαι μάρτυρα τῶν ἰδίων παθῶν †Hipp.*Artem*.ap.Eus.*h.e*.5.28.11(M.20.513C); ἐπίσκοποι...φθόγγοι τοῦ θεοῦ καὶ μ. τοῦ θελήματος αὐτοῦ *Const.App*.2.25.7; with play on double meaning of *witness* and *martyr* τὸ δὲ σωμάτιον μ. ἦν τῶν συμβεβηκότων, ὅλον τραῦμα καὶ μώλωψ *Ep.Lugd*.ap.Eus.*h.e*.5.1.23(417A); οἱ μακάριοι μ. ἑκόντες ἠγέρθησαν· ᾐσχύνοντο γὰρ ὀλίγους μ. ἔχειν ἐπὶ τῷ μακαρίῳ θανάτῳ αὐτῶν *M.Perp*.21(p.93.23f.); μάρτυρας δέχου τοὺς μ., τοὺς καθάπερ προοίμιον ἀθανασίας τὸν θάνατον ἀσπασαμένους Isid.Pel.*epp*.4.52(M.78.1104A).

D. ref. abstracts ἐχρῆν μὲν ὑμᾶς, ὦ ἄνθρωποι, αὐτοῦ πέρι ἐννοουμένους τοῦ ἀγαθοῦ ἔμφυτον ἐπάγεσθαι πίστιν, μάρτυρα ἀξιόχρεων αὐτόθεν οἴκοθεν Clem.*prot*.10(p.70.6; M.8.209A).

E. Gnost., of the 'seven witnesses' of baptismal formula of Elchezaites ἁγνευσάτω καὶ ἐπιμαρτυρησάσθω αὐτῷ τοὺς ἑπτὰ μ. γεγραμμένους ἐν τῇ βίβλῳ ταύτῃ, τὸν οὐρανὸν καὶ τὸ ὕδωρ καὶ τὰ πνεύματα τὰ ἅγια καὶ τοὺς ἀγγέλους τῆς προσευχῆς καὶ τὸ ἔλαιον καὶ τὸ ἅλας καὶ τὴν γῆν Hipp.*haer*.9.15(p.253.17; M.16.3391A); Epiph.*haer*.19.1(p.218.12; M.41.261B).

F. of witnesses of baptism ἤρεσε περὶ τῶν νηπίων, ὁσάκις μὴ εὑρίσκονται βέβαιοι μ., οἱ ταῦτα ἀναμφιβόλως βαπτισθέντα εἶναι λέγοντες *Cod.Afr*.72.

II. *martyr*;

A. def. and descriptions, cf. *martyres testantur et contemnunt mortem, non secundum infirmitatem carnis, sed secundum quod promptus est spiritus*, Iren.*haer*.5.9.2(M.7.1145A); ὁ μ. ἡδονὴν τὴν δι' ἐλπίδος διὰ τῆς παρούσης ἀλγηδόνος αἱρεῖται Clem.*str*.4.5(p.258.8; M.8.1233D); εἰ δὲ καὶ πολιτεύσαιτο ὀρθῶς...μ. τε ἐπὶ τοῖσδε ὀρθότατα ὁμολογήσας δι' ἀγάπην γένοιτο...οὐδ' οὕτως φθάσει τέλειος ἐν σαρκὶ κληθείς, ἐπεὶ τὴν προσηγορίαν ταύτην προείληφεν ἡ συμπεραίωσις τοῦ βίου, φθάσαντος ἤδη τοῦ γνωστικοῦ μ. τὸ τέλειον ἔργον ἐνδείξασθαι καὶ παραστῆσαι κυρίως δι' ἀγάπης γνωστικῆς εὐχαριστηθέντος αἵματος παραπεμπομένου τὸ πνεῦμα *ib*.4.21(p.305.32–306.3; 1341A); οἱ μ., τὰ πρόσωπα μὲν τοῦ σώματος πρὸς τοὺς δικαστὰς ἐξ ἀνάγκης ἔχοντες, τῇ δὲ δυνάμει λοιπὸν ὄντες ἐν παραδείσῳ Cyr.H.*catech*.16.20; ὁ γὰρ διὰ τὸ ὄνομα κυρίου τοῦ θεοῦ καταδικαζόμενος, οὗτος μ. ἅγιος *Const.App*.5.1.2; ὁ γὰρ ἐν μαρτυρίῳ ἐξελθὼν ἀψευδῶς ὑπὲρ τῆς ἀληθείας, οὗτος ἀληθινὸς μ. *ib*.5.9.2.

B. in relation to God; **1.** to Father καὶ ἐν ἀνθρώποις εὑρεθήσονται πολλοὶ ὅμοιοι τῷ πατρί, πλεῖστοι μὲν μ. γενόμενοι Ath.*Ar*.3.10(M.26.341C); **2.** to Christ ἐκείνῃ τῇ ὥρᾳ βασανιζόμενοι τῆς σαρκὸς ἀπεδήμουν οἱ...μ. τοῦ Χριστοῦ, μᾶλλον δέ, ὅτι παρεστὼς ὁ κύριος ὡμίλει αὐτοῖς *M.Polyc*.2.2; Χριστέ...γένωμαι κἀγὼ μ. ἀληθὴς τῆς σῆς θεότητος *A. Andr*.A 16(p.57.2); οὗτος οὖν ⟨οὐ⟩ φόβῳ τὸ ἀρνεῖσθαι Χριστὸν διὰ τὴν ἐντολὴν ἐκκλινεῖ, ἵνα δὴ φόβῳ μ. γένηται· οὐ μὴν οὐδὲ ἐλπίδι δωρεῶν ἡτοιμασμένων πιπράσκων τὴν πίστιν, ἀγάπῃ δὲ πρὸς τὸν κύριον ἀσμενέστατα τοῦδε τοῦ βίου ἀπολυθήσεται Clem.*str*.4.4(p.254.20; M.8.1228A); γενέσθαι μ. ἐν Χριστῷ Or.*mart*.14(p.14.18; M.11.581C); οἱ μ. ὁμολογοῦσι τὸν υἱὸν τοῦ θεοῦ *ib*.35(p.32.11; 609A); *ib*.42(p.39.23; 617C); ἐὰν ἴδῃς μοι τοὺς πανταχοῦ μ. δικαζομένους ⟨καὶ⟩ καθ' ἑκάστην ἐκκλησίαν παρισταμένους τοῖς δικασταῖς, ὄψει τίνα τρόπον Ἰησοῦς Χριστὸς ἐν ἑκάστῳ τῶν μ. δικάζεται id.*hom.14.7 in Jer*.(p.112.15,17; M.13.412C,D); hence called Χριστοφόροι μ. Phil.Thm.*ep*.ap.Eus.*h.e*.8.10.3(M.20.764B); πάντες μ. τῷ εὐαγγελικῷ γράμματι προσέχοντες τὸν νοῦν, ἐν ᾧ προτρέπων τοὺς ἱεροὺς ἀθλητὰς...ὁ κύριος λέγει· [Mt.10:32] ὑπὲρ ταύτης τῆς ὁμολογίας ἤνεγκαν ἀτρέπτοις τοῖς λογισμοῖς σίδηρον τεθηγμένον, καὶ πυρκαϊὰς ἐπέβησαν Ast.Am.*hom*.10(M.40.317A); ζῇ καὶ ἐνεργεῖ ταῖς τῶν μ. ψυχαῖς ὁ Χριστός Chrys.*pan.Dros*.2(2.691B); τούς τε κυρίου μ. ἐκ παντὸς τάγματος ἐκλελεγμένους, ὡς στρατιώτας Χριστοῦ, καὶ τὸ αὐτοῦ πεπωκότας ποτήριον, τότε ζωοποιοῦν αὐτοῦ θανάτου βαπτισθέντας βάπτισμα ὡς κοινωνοὺς τῶν παθημάτων αὐτοῦ καὶ τῆς δόξης Jo.D.*f.o*.4.15(M.94.1168B); also called αὐτοῦ τῆς βασιλείας μ. Dion.Al.ap.Eus.*h.e*.6.41.14(609A); **3.** to H. Ghost ὁρᾷς πῶς τὸ πνεῦμα τοῦ πατρὸς μελετᾶν τοὺς μ. ⟨δι⟩δά⟨σκει⟩ Hipp.*Dan*.2.21.1; οἱ μακάριοι μ. ἐν τοῖς κατὰ καιροὺς διωγμοῖς...διωκόμενοι μὲν ἔφευγον,...εὑρισκόμενοι δὲ ἐμαρτύρουν. εἰ δὲ καί τινες ἐξ αὐτῶν αὐτοῖς προσήρχοντο τοῖς διώκουσι, καὶ τοῦτο οὐχ ἁπλῶς ἔπραττον· ἐμαρτύρουν γὰρ εὐθὺς καὶ πᾶσιν ἐγίνετο φανερόν, ὅτι παρὰ τοῦ πνεύματος ἦν...ἡ τοσαύτη πρόσοδος Ath.*fug*.22(p.83.19; M.25.673A); τῇ δυνάμει τοῦ ἁγίου πνεύματος οἱ μ. μαρτυροῦσι...ἀδύνατον γὰρ μαρτυρῆσαι περὶ τοῦ Χριστοῦ, ἐὰν μή τις διὰ πνεύματος ἁγίου μαρτυρήσῃ Cyr.H.*catech*.16.21; πνεῦμα τοῦ θεοῦ...τὸ...μάρτυρας ἀντιστῆναι τυραννικῇ ὠμότητι ἐνισχύσαν Didym.*Trin*.2.1(M.39.452B); ref. Lc.24:49 καὶ λήψεσθε δύναμιν ἐπελθόντος τοῦ ἁγίου πνεύματος· δύναμιν ἥν τινα οὐχ οἷόν τέ ἐστι μάρτυρας γενέσθαι μὴ δεξαμένους ‡Chrys.*ascens.Ac*.4(3.762B); number of martyrs claimed as criterion of Montanists' possession of H. Ghost, Eus.*h.e*.5.16.20(M.20.472B).

C. martyr's power; **1.** martyrs as true conquerors δύο παρατάξεις, ἡ μὲν τῶν μ., ἡ δὲ τῶν τυράννων· ἀλλ' οἱ μὲν τύραννοι εἰσι καθωπλισμένοι, οἱ δὲ μ. γυμνῷ τῷ σώματι μάχονται, καὶ ἡ νίκη τῶν γυμνῶν οὐ τῶν καθωπλισμένων γίνεται Chrys.*pan.mart*.3.1(2.712C); τοὺς μ. γυμνοὺς ἄγοντες, καὶ τὰς χεῖρας ὀπίσω δήσαντες καὶ πάντοθεν παίοντες οὕτως ἡττῶντο· οἱ δὲ τὰ τραύματα δεχόμενοι, τὸ κατὰ τοῦ διαβόλου τρόπαιον ἔστησαν. καὶ καθάπερ ἀδάμας πληττόμενος αὐτὸς μὲν οὐκ ἐνδίδωσιν...οὕτω δὴ καὶ αἱ ψυχαὶ τῶν ἁγίων, τοσούτων ἐπαγομένων βασάνων, αὐταὶ μὲν οὐδὲν ἔπασχον δεινόν, τῶν δὲ παιόντων τὴν δύναμιν καταλύουσαι, αἰσχρῶς...ἡττηθέντας ἐκ τῶν ἀγώνων ἐξέπεμπον μετὰ πολλὰς...πληγάς *ib*.(713A); δι' ἣν αἰτίαν νομίζεις τοὺς μ. τῷ τεθνάναι ἡττᾶσθαι, καὶ μὴ διὰ τοῦτο μᾶλλον ἀνακηρύττεις; τέλος γάρ ἐστι τῆς μάχης ταύτης οὐ τὸ σῶμα...ἀλλὰ τὸ μὴ διαφθεῖραι τὸ τῆς ἀρετῆς κλέος Isid.Pel.*epp*.5.5(M.78.1328C); **2.** breaking powers of evil τῇ πείρᾳ μαθόντες οἱ δαίμονες ἑαυτοὺς ἡττωμένους καὶ κρατουμένους ὑπὸ τῶν μ. Or.*Cels*.8.44(p.258.31; M.11.1581C); κατάλυσιν οὖν νομιστέον γίνεσθαι δυνάμεων κακοποιῶν διὰ τοῦ θανάτου τῶν ἁγίων μ., οἷον τῆς ὑπομονῆς αὐτῶν καὶ τῆς ὁμολογίας τῆς μέχρι θανάτου καὶ τῆς εἰς χρ εὐσεβὲς προθυμίας ἀμβλυνούσης τὸ ὀξὺ τῆς ἐκείνων κατὰ τοῦ πάσχοντος ἐπιβουλῆς, ὥστε ἀμβλυνομένης καὶ ἀτονησάσης τῆς δυνάμεως αὐτῶν καὶ ἑτέρους πλείονας τῶν νενικημένων ἀνίεσθαι ἐλευθερουμένους τοῦ βάρους, οὗ αἱ πονηραὶ δυνάμεις ἐπικείμεναι ἐφόρτιζον καὶ ἔβλαπτον...τῷ θανάτῳ τῶν εὐσεβεστάτων μ. γίνεσθαι, πολλῶν ἀφάτῳ τινὶ δυνάμει ὠφελουμένων ἀπὸ τοῦ θανάτου αὐτῶν id.*Jo*.6.54(36; p.163.14ff.; M.14.293D–296B); **3.** a certain redemptive power therefore attributed to them τάχα δὲ καὶ ὥσπερ 'τιμίῳ αἵματι' τῷ τοῦ Ἰησοῦ ἠγοράσθημεν... οὕτως τῷ 'τιμίῳ αἵματι' τῶν μ. ἀγορασθήσονταί τινες id.*mart*.50(p.46.27; M.11.636A); which is sacrificial, id.*Jo*.6.54(36; p.162.15; M.14.293A) cit. s. αἷμα; and priestly, cf. *hostia autem cum immolatur, ad hoc immolatur, ut eorum, pro quibus jugulatur, peccata purgentur. de martyribus autem scribit Johannes apostolus in Apocalypsi quia 'animae eorum, qui jugulati sunt propter nomen domini Jesu, adsistant altari'; qui autem 'adsistit altari', ostenditur fungi sacerdotis officio; sacerdotis autem officium est pro populi supplicare peccatis. unde ego vereor, ne forte, ex quo martyres non fiunt et hostiae sanctorum non offeruntur pro peccatis nostris, peccatorum nostrorum remissio non fiat...quia hostiae martyrum non offeruntur pro nobis, idcirco manent in nobis peccata nostra*, id.*hom.10.2 in Num*.(pp.72.25–73.9; M.12.638B,C); martyrs as mediators κοινωνίαν ἔχητε μετὰ τῶν ἁγίων μ., καὶ δι' αὐτῶν μετὰ τοῦ κυρίου ἡμῶν Ἰησοῦ Χριστοῦ *M.Perp*.1(p.63.16); **4.** efficacy of their intercession μάρτυρες τοῖς μὴ μάρτυσιν ἐχαρίζοντο *Ep.Lugd* ap.Eus.*h.e*.5.1.45(M.20.425B); ἀφέντες καὶ πόνους χειρῶν ἡμῶν καὶ ἐλπίδας, καὶ πολλὰ τοῖς ἁγίοις ἀπολογησάμενοι μ. Gr.Naz.*ep*.203(M.37.336B); μήτηρ ἀραμένη τὸν ἄρρωστον παῖδα...πρὸς ἕνα τῶν μ. ἐλθοῦσα, δι' ἐκείνου τῷ δεσπότῃ προσάγει τὴν αἴτησιν Ast.Am.*hom*.10(M.40.317D); τίς εἰς πλοῦν ἐπειγόμενος, οὐ πρότερον τῆς νεὼς λύει τὰ πείσματα, πρὶν ἂν τὸν τῆς θαλάσσης δεσπότην διὰ τῶν μ. ἐπικαλέσηται; πτωχῶν δὲ φυλαί... κοινὴν ἑστίαν κέκτηνται τὴν τῶν μ. ἀνάπαυσιν· ᾄδονται δὲ πανταχοῦ γῆς καὶ θαλάττης οἱ μ. *ib*.(320A); prayer to martyrs defended ἐπειδὴ γὰρ οὐκ ἀρκεῖ ἡ ἡμετέρα εὐχὴ δυσωπῆσαι θεὸν ἐν καιρῷ ἀνάγκης...διὰ τοῦτο τοῖς ἀγαπωμένοις παρὰ τοῦ δεσπότου ὁμοδούλοις προσφεύγομεν, ἵνα ἐκεῖνοι ἐν τοῖς ἰδίοις κατορθώμασι τὰ ἡμέτερα θεραπεύσωσι πλημμελήματα. ποῖον οὖν ἔγκλημα, ὅτι τιμῶντες μ. καὶ αὐτοὶ σπουδάζομεν ἀρέσκειν θεῷ; *ib*.(324A); ὅταν ἴδῃς τὸν θεόν σε κολάζοντα,...καταφύγῃς...πρὸς τοὺς φίλους αὐτοῦ, τοὺς μ., τοὺς ἁγίους, καὶ εὐηρεστηκότας αὐτῷ, καὶ πολλὴν ἔχοντας παρρησίαν Chrys.*Jud*.8.6(1.683B); **5.** procuring moral improvement ἔχομεν τοίνυν τοὺς μ., οὐ διδασκάλους μόνον ἀγαθῆς πολιτείας, ἀλλὰ καὶ κατηγόρους τῆς ἁμαρτίας. πῶς δ' ἂν γένοιτο μ. κατήγορος, ἄκουσον· εἰ ἐκεῖνος ἐνίκησε φλόγα πυρὸς τῇ καρτερίᾳ, σὺ πῶς πορνείαν οὐ δαμάζεις τῇ σωφροσύνῃ; εἰ ὁ μ. οὐκ ἐλέησε πλοῦτον ὃν ἠφίει...διὰ τί σὺ ὀλίγου οὐ καταφρονεῖς ἀργυρίου ὑπὲρ δικαιοσύνης;...εἰ ὁ μ. τὸ σῶμα διὰ θεὸν ἐξεδύσατο, πῶς αὐτὸς ἑνὸς οὐ καταφρονεῖς χιτωνίσκου εἰς σκέπην γυμνοῦ;...ἢ τοίνυν ὡς διδασκάλους τοὺς ἁγίους αἰδεσθῶμεν, ἢ ὡς κατηγόρους φοβηθῶμεν Ast.Am.*hom*.10(M.40.316B,C); τοῦ φωτὸς τῶν μ. εἰς τὰς ὑμετέρας καταλάμποντος διανοίας, ἅπαντα κατορύττεται τὰ νοσήματα, καὶ ἡ λαμπρὰ τῆς φιλοσοφίας ἀνάπτεται φλόξ Chrys.*mart*.2(2.668C); id.*pan.Phoc*.1(2.704C).

D. martyr's eternal reward εὐλογῶ σε, ὅτι ἠξίωσάς με τῆς ἡμέρας καὶ ὥρας ταύτης, τοῦ λαβεῖν μέρος ἐν ἀριθμῷ τῶν μ. ἐν τῷ ποτηρίῳ τοῦ Χριστοῦ σου 'εἰς ἀνάστασιν ζωῆς' αἰωνίου ψυχῆς τε καὶ σώματος ἐν ἀφθαρσίᾳ πνεύματος ἁγίου *M.Polyc*.14.2; οἱ θεῖοι μ. ... οἱ νῦν τοῦ Χριστοῦ πάρεδροι καὶ τῆς βασιλείας αὐτοῦ κοινωνοὶ καὶ μέτοχοι τῆς κρίσεως αὐτοῦ καὶ συνδικάζοντες αὐτῷ Dion.Al.ap.Eus.*h.e*.6.42.5(M.20.613B); *ib*.7.22.4(688B); ref. 1Cor.2:9 οὐδεὶς δὲ ἀνθρώπων οὕτως αὐτὸν [sc. θεόν] ἠγάπησεν ὡς οἱ μ. οὐ μὴν ἐπειδὴ καὶ λόγον καὶ διάνοιαν ὑπερβαίνει τῶν ἀποκειμένων ἀγαθῶν τὸ μέγεθος, διὰ τοῦτο σιγήσομεν, ἀλλ' ὡς οἷόν τε καὶ εἰπεῖν ἡμῖν καὶ ὑμῖν ἀκοῦσαι, πειρασόμεθα ὑμῖν ἀμυδρῶς ἐνδείξασθαι τὴν ἐκεῖ διαδεξομένην αὐτοὺς μακαριότητα...τὰ μὲν γὰρ δεινὰ ταῦτα καὶ ἀφόρητα ἐν βραχείᾳ καιροῦ ῥοπῇ πάσχουσιν οἱ μ.· μετὰ δὲ τὴν ἐντεῦθεν ἀπαλλαγὴν εἰς οὐρανοὺς ἀναβαίνουσιν, ἀγγέλων αὐτοῖς προηγουμένων, καὶ ἀρχαγγέλων δορυφορούντων· οὐ γὰρ αἰσχύνονται τοὺς συνδούλους Chrys.*pan.mart*.3.2(2.714C,D); counted with prophets and apostles, Hipp.*antichr*.59(p.40.8; M.10.780A); id.*Dan*.4.14.3; Or.*hom.10.2 in Num*.(p.71.15; M.12.638A); Ath.*Ar*.3.10(M.26.341C); Evagr.*h.e*.1 proem.(M.86.2420A); only martyrs saved without baptism, Cyr.H.*catech*.3.10.

E. martyr's place in Church; **1.** in gen., place of honour, *M. Polyc*.19.1; ἥτις [sc. Church]...ἐν διωγμοῖς...τοὺς ἁγίους μ. τοῖς τῆς ὑπομονῆς...ἔστεψε στεφάνοις Cyr.H.*catech*.18.27; μέλη ἡμῶν εἰσιν οἱ μ. εἴτε δὲ πάσχει ἓν μέλος, συμπάσχει πάντα τὰ μέλη· εἴτε δοξάζεται ἓν μέλος, συγχαίρει πάντα τὰ μέλη. ἡ κεφαλὴ στεφανοῦται, καὶ τὸ λοιπὸν σῶμα ἀγάλλεται...πόδες ἐσμὲν ἡμεῖς, οἱ μ. κεφαλή Chrys.*pan. Rom.*1.1(2.611A,B); marriage honourable if only because without it there would be no saints and martyrs, Meth.*symp.*2.2(p.17.13; M.18.49C); special veneration of women martyrs, Chrys.*pan.Dros.*3(2.692C); **2.** as proving truth of Christianity, Ath.*inc.*28.4(M.25.144D); ὅταν οὖν πρὸς Ἕλληνας ἡμῖν ἀγῶνες κινῶνται καὶ μάχαι περὶ δογμάτων...μετὰ τῶν ἄλλων καὶ τοῦτο προβαλλώμεθα πρὸς ἐκείνους, τῶν μ. φημὶ τὸν θάνατον, λέγοντες, τίς τούτους ἔπεισε τῆς παρούσης καταφρονῆσαι ζωῆς; Chrys.*pan.Dros.*2(2.690D); **3.** reasons for veneration περὶ δὲ τῶν μ. λέγομεν ὑμῖν, ὅπως πάσῃ τιμῇ ὦσιν παρ' ὑμῖν...οὗτοι γάρ εἰσιν καὶ ὑπὸ θεοῦ μεμακαρισμένοι καὶ ὑπὸ ὁσίων ἀνδρῶν τετιμημένοι *Const.App.*5.8.1; τοὺς ἁγίους μ. ὅταν μακαρίζωμεν, ἀπὸ τῶν τραυμάτων πρότερον μακαρίζομεν, καὶ τότε ἀπὸ τῶν βραβείων· ἀπὸ τῶν πληγῶν, καὶ τότε ἀπὸ τῶν ἀποκειμένων στεφάνων Chrys.*Anna* 5.2(4.742E); ἀνθρώπου...ἁπλῶς οὐκ ἂν γένοιτο κατορθώματα μετὰ τελευτήν· μάρτυρος δὲ γένοιτ' ἂν πολλὰ καὶ μεγάλα, οὐχ ἵνα ἐκεῖνος λαμπρότερος γένηται...ἀλλ' ἵνα σὺ μάθῃς...ὅτι θάνατος μαρτύρων οὐκ ἔστι θάνατος, ἀλλὰ ζωῆς βελτίονος ἀρχή...μὴ γὰρ δὴ τοῦτο ἴδῃς, ὅτι γυμνὸν τοῦ μ. τὸ σῶμα πρόκειται τῆς ψυχικῆς ἐνεργείας ἔρημον· ἀλλ' ἐκεῖνο σκόπει, ὅτι τῆς ψυχῆς αὐτῆς ἑτέρα παρακάθηται μείζων αὐτῷ δύναμις, ἡ τοῦ ἁγίου πνεύματος χάρις...δι' ὧν θαυματοποιεῖ id.*pan.Bab.*1(2.531D); μαρτύρων γὰρ θάνατος πιστῶν ἐστι παράκλησις, ἐκκλησιῶν παρρησία, Χριστιανισμοῦ σύστασις, θανάτου κατάλυσις, ἀναστάσεως ἀπόδειξις, δαιμόνων γέλως, διαβόλου κατηγορία, φιλοσοφίας διδασκαλία,...καὶ πάντων τῶν ἀγαθῶν ῥίζα id.*pan.Dros.*2(2.690B); id.*Jud.et gent.*15(1.578D); τὰ καθ' ἑκάστην ἡμέραν ὑπὸ τῶν μ. γινόμενα θαύματα †Chrys.*pan.Bab.*2(2.555D); **4.** their sanctity in proportion to their sacrifice ἐὰν δέ τις μακαρίζων πλουσίους μ. ... 'ἑκατονταπλασίονα' γεννήσοντας τέκνα καὶ ἑκατονταπλασίονας ἀγροὺς καὶ οἰκίας ληψομένους ζητῇ...παρὰ τοὺς ἐν βίῳ πένητας μ. Or.*mart.*15(p.15.2,4; M.11.581D); ὑπὲρ γὰρ πάντας μ. ἐγώ φημι εἶναι τοὺς τότε [sc. in times of antichrist] μ.· οἱ μὲν γὰρ πρὸ τούτου, μόνοις ἀνθρώποις ἐπάλαισαν, οἱ δὲ ἐπὶ τοῦ ἀντιχρίστου, αὐτῷ σατανᾷ...πολεμήσουσιν Cyr.H.*catech.*15.17; **5.** public veneration; **a.** dist. from worship of God τοῦτον [sc. Χριστόν] μὲν γὰρ υἱὸν ὄντα τοῦ θεοῦ προσκυνοῦμεν, τοὺς δὲ μ. ὡς μαθητὰς καὶ μιμητὰς τοῦ κυρίου ἀγαπῶμεν ἀξίως ἕνεκα εὐνοίας ἀνυπερβλήτου τῆς εἰς τὸν ἴδιον βασιλέα καὶ διδάσκαλον *M.Polyc.*17.3; ἡμεῖς μ. οὐ προσκυνοῦμεν, ἀλλὰ τιμῶμεν, ὡς γνησίους προσκυνητὰς θεοῦ· οὐ σέβομεν ἀνθρώπους, θαυμάζομεν δὲ τοὺς ἐν καιρῷ πειρασμῶν καλῶς σεβασθέντας θεῷ Ast.Am.*hom.*10(M.40.321D); **b.** keeping of their feasts νεύματι βασιλέως καὶ μαρτύρων ἡμέρας ἐτίμων καιρούς τε ἑορτῶν ἐκκλησίαις ἐδόξαζον Eus.*v.C.*4.23(p.126.4; M.20.1172A); τὴν ἡμέραν Στεφάνου τοῦ πρωτομάρτυρος ἀργείτωσαν καὶ τῶν λοιπῶν ἁγίων μ. τῶν προτιμησάντων Χριστὸν τῆς ἑαυτῶν ζωῆς *Const.App.*8.33.9; εἰ μὴ γὰρ ἐδίωξεν Χριστιανοὺς ὁ διάβολος,...οὐκ ἂν εἴχομεν μ.· μ. δὲ μὴ ὄντων, σκυθρωπὸς ἡμῶν ὁ βίος καὶ ἀνέορτος Ast.Am.*hom.*10(M.40.316A); πολλὰς ἡμέρας τῆς τῶν μ. ἀπελαύσαμεν πανηγύρεως, καὶ ἄκαιρον ἦν ἐν τάφοις μαρτύρων διατρίβοντας, τῶν τοῖς μ. πρεπόντων ἐγκωμίων ἀμοίρους ἀπελθεῖν Chrys.*Anna* 1.1(4.701A,B); μνήμην μ. ἐπιτελοῦμεν, καὶ οὐδεὶς ἀπήντησεν...οἱ μ. τὸ ἴδιον αἷμα ἐξέχεαν ὑπὲρ τῆς ἀληθείας, σὺ δὲ οὐδὲ βραχείας ὁδοῦ καταφρονεῖς;...μνήμη μαρτύρων, καὶ σὺ ἀθυμεῖς καὶ ἀναπέπτωκας; δέον ἐστί σε παραγενέσθαι, καὶ ἰδεῖν τὸν διάβολον ἡττώμενον, καὶ μ. νικῶντα ‡Chrys.*Petr.et El.*1(2.730A,B); **c.** liturg., ref. Feast of Martyrs παρακαλοῦμεν νῦν ἐπιφανῆσαί σε ἡμῶν τῇ πόλει, ἐπὶ τῷ σεμνοτέραν γενέσθαι τὴν πανήγυριν, ἣν δι' ἔτους ἄγειν ἐπὶ τοῖς μ. ἔθος ἐστὶν ἡμῶν τῇ ἐκκλησίᾳ Bas.*ep.*176(3.263B; M.32.653B); date of its celebration ἐξ οὗ τὴν ἱερὰν πανήγυριν τῆς πεντηκοστῆς ἐπετελέσαμεν, οὔπω παρῆλθεν ἡμερῶν ἑπτὰ ἀριθμός, καὶ πάλιν κατέλαβεν ἡμᾶς μαρτύρων χορός Chrys.*pan.mart.*3.1(2.711A); feasts of individual martyrs not permitted in Lent, CLaod.*can.*51; mentioned individually in liturgy, *Lit.*ap.*Const.App.*8.13.6 cit. s. ἄθλησις; τί οἴει τὸ ὑπὲρ μαρτύρων προσφέρεσθαι, τὸ κληθῆναι ἐν ἐκείνῃ τῇ ὥρᾳ; κἂν μ. ὦσι, κἂν ὑπὲρ μ., μεγάλη τιμὴ τὸ ὀνομασθῆναι τοῦ δεσπότου παρόντος, τοῦ θανάτου ἐπιτελουμένου ἐκείνου, τῆς φρικτῆς θυσίας Chrys.*hom.21.4 in Ac.*(9.176B); in preface ψυχαὶ μαρτύρων καὶ ἀποστόλων *Lit.Jac.*(p.198.27); in commemoration of living, *ib.*(p.212.17); **d.** as patrons of cities προνοοῦσιν οἱ πολιοῦχοι μ. τῆς ταλαίνης [sc. Πηλουσίου] Isid.Pel.*epp.*1.226(M.78.324B); **6.** veneration by imitation of their virtues ἐτίμησας τὴν μ. τῇ παρουσίᾳ [sc. at celebration]; τίμησον αὐτὴν καὶ τῇ διορθώσει τῶν οἰκείων μελῶν Chrys.*pan.Pelag.Ant.*4(2.589D); αἱ τῶν μ. ἑορταὶ οὐκ ἐν τῇ περιόδῳ τῶν ἡμερῶν μόνον, ἀλλὰ καὶ τῇ γνώμῃ τῶν ἐπιτελούντων κρίνονται. ... ἐμιμήσω μάρτυρα; ἐζήλωσας αὐτοῦ τὴν ἀρετήν; κατ' ἴχνος αὐτοῦ τῆς φιλοσοφίας ἔδραμες; καὶ οὐκ οὔσης ἡμέρας μάρτυρος, ἑορτὴν μ. ἐπετέλεσας. τιμὴ γὰρ μάρτυρος, μίμησις μ. id.*pan.mart.*2(2.667C); *ib.*(668A,B); ἐτίμησας τοὺς μ. τῇ παρουσίᾳ...τίμησον αὐτοὺς καὶ τῇ κοσμίῳ ἀναχωρήσει *ib.*(668E); id.*pan.Juln.*4(2.677C); ‡Chrys.*mart.*4(3.818E); καλὸν μὲν τὸ τιμᾶν τοὺς μ. τῆς εὐσεβείας τοῖς ἀναθήμασιν...κρεῖττον δὲ τὸ θεραπεύειν αὐτοὺς οἷς ἐποίησαν κατορθώμασιν Isid.Pel.*epp.*1.189(M.78.304C).

F. true and false martyrs, cf. *ecclesia omni in loco ob eam quam habet erga deum dilectionem, multitudinem martyrum in omni tempore praemittit ad patrem; reliquis autem omnibus non tantum non habentibus hanc rem ostendere apud se, nec quidem necessarium esse dicentibus tale martyrium; esse enim martyrium verum sententiam eorum: nisi si unus, aut duo aliquando, per omne tempus ex quo dominus apparuit in terris, cum martyribus nostris, quasi et ipse misericordiam consecutus, opprobrium simul bajulavit nominis, et cum eis ductus est, velut adjectio quaedam donata eis. opprobrium enim eorum, qui persecutionem patiuntur propter justitiam, et omnes poenas sustinent, et mortificantur propter eam quae est erga deum dilectionem, et confessionem filii ejus, sola ecclesia pure sustinet*, Iren.*haer.*4.33.9(M.7.1078A,B); ref. Montanists ὅταν τοίνυν ἐν πᾶσι τοῖς εἰρημένοις ἐλεγχθέντες ἀπορήσωσιν, ἐπὶ τοὺς μ. καταφεύγειν πείρωνται, λέγοντες πολλοὺς ἔχειν μ., καὶ τοῦτ' εἶναι τεκμήριον τῆς δυνάμεως τοῦ...προφητικοῦ πνεύματος...καὶ γὰρ τῶν αἱρέσεών τινες πλείστους ὅσους ἔχουσι μ. ... οὐδὲ ἀλήθειαν ἔχειν αὐτοὺς ὁμολογήσομεν. καὶ πρῶτοί γε...Μαρκιωνισταὶ...πλείστους ὅσους ἔχειν Χριστοῦ μ. λέγουσιν, ἀλλὰ τόν γε Χριστὸν αὐτὸν κατ' ἀλήθειαν οὐχ ὁμολογοῦσιν Anon.ap.Eus.*h.e.*5.16.20f.(M.20.472B,C); Θεμίσων...ὁ μὴ βαστάσας τὸ τῆς ὁμολογίας τὸ σημεῖον, ἀλλὰ πλήθει χρημάτων ἀποθέμενος τὰ δεσμά,...ὡς μ. καυχώμενος Apollon.ap.Eus.*h.e.*5.18.5(M.20.477A); *ib.*5.18.6(477B).

G. exeg.: Gen.4:10 τὸ γάρ· 'φωνὴ αἵματος...' νομίσωμεν λέγεσθαι καὶ περὶ ἑκάστου τῶν μ., ὧν ἡ φωνὴ τοῦ αἵματος βοᾷ πρὸς τὸν θεόν Or.*mart.*50(p.46.23; M.11.636A); Ps.115:4 σωτηρίου ποτήριον ὁ τῶν μ. ἐστὶ θάνατος *ib.*29(p.26.14; 600B); Ps.78:11 ὑπομιμνήσκου τοῦ εὐξαμένου ἐν πνεύματι περὶ τέκνων μαρτύρων διὰ τὴν πρὸς θεὸν ἀγάπην αὐτῶν καταλελειμμένων καὶ φήσαντος· 'περιποίησαι τοὺς υἱοὺς τῶν τεθανατωμένων' *ib.*38(p.35.27; 613B); Is.43:10 'γένεσθέ μοι μ., κἀγὼ μάρτυς...'. πᾶς δὲ ὁ μαρτυρῶν τῇ ἀληθείᾳ, εἴτε λόγοις εἴτε ἔργοις... μ. εὐλόγως ἂν χρηματίζοι. ἀλλ' ἤδη κυρίως ⟨ὡς⟩ τὸ τῆς ἀδελφότητος ἔθος ἐκπλαγέντες διάθεσιν τῶν ἕως θανάτου ἀγωνισαμένων ὑπὲρ ἀληθείας ...κυρίως μόνους μ. ὠνόμασαν τοὺς τῇ ἐκχύσει τοῦ ἑαυτῶν αἵματος μαρτυρήσαντας τῷ τῆς θεοσεβείας μυστηρίῳ, τοῦ σωτῆρος πάντα τὸν μαρτυροῦντα τοῖς περὶ αὐτοῦ καταγγελλομένοις μ. ὀνομάζοντος id.*Jo.*2.34(28; p.93.8ff.; M.14.176C,D); Ps.65:10 δοκιμασθέντες διαρκῶς οἱ μ. ἐν ταῖς κατὰ τοὺς πειρασμοὺς τῶν βασάνων προσβολαῖς Meth.*res.*1.56(p.315.7; M.41.1149A); Ps.123:2–7 οἱ μ. εἰσιν οἱ ψάλλοντες. δύο δὲ τῶν καλλινίκων οἱ χοροὶ μαρτύρων. εἷς μὲν τῆς διαθήκης τῆς καινῆς, θάτερος δὲ τῆς παλαιᾶς *ib.*(p.316.8f.; M.41.1149Cf.).

H. Constantine's legislation concerning their property τῶν...μ. τῶν ἐν ὁμολογίᾳ τὴν τελευτὴν ἀποθεμένων τοῦ βίου τὰς οὐσίας ἐκέλευε τοὺς τῷ γένει προσήκοντας ἀπολαμβάνειν, εἰ δὲ μὴ τούτων τις εἴη, τὰς ἐκκλησίας ὑποδέχεσθαι τοὺς κλήρους Eus.*v.C.*2.21(p.49.31; M.20.1000A).

I. refutation of Basilides' theory (v. μαρτύριον) εἰ...τις αὐτῶν λέγοι κολάζεσθαι μὲν τὸν μ. διὰ τὰς πρὸ τῆσδε τῆς ἐνσωματώσεως ἁμαρτίας, τὸν καρπὸν δὲ τῆς κατὰ τόνδε τὸν βίον πολιτείας αὖθις ἀπολήψεσθαι, οὕτω γὰρ διατετάχθαι τὴν διοίκησιν, πευσόμεθα αὐτοῦ, εἰ ἐκ προνοίας γίνεται ἡ ἀνταπόδοσις· εἰ μὲν γὰρ μὴ εἴη τῆς θείας διοικήσεως, οἴχεται ἡ οἰκονομία τῶν καθαρσίων καὶ πέπτωκεν ἡ ὑπόθεσις αὐτοῖς, εἰ δὲ ἐκ προνοίας τὰ καθάρσια, ἐκ προνοίας καὶ αἱ κολάσεις. ἡ πρόνοια δὲ εἰ καὶ ἀπὸ τοῦ Ἄρχοντος, ὥς φασιν, κινεῖσθαι ἄρχεται, ἀλλ' ἐγκατεσπάρη ταῖς οὐσίαις καὶ τῇ τῶν οὐσιῶν γενέσει πρὸς τοῦ θεοῦ τῶν ὅλων. ὧν οὕτως ἐχόντων ἀνάγκη ὁμολογεῖν αὐτοὺς ἢ τὴν κόλασιν μὴ εἶναι ἄδικον (καὶ δικαιοπραγοῦσιν οἱ καταδικάζοντες...τοὺς μ.) ἢ ἐκ θελήματος ἐνεργεῖσθαι τοῦ θεοῦ καὶ τοὺς διωγμοὺς Clem.*str.*4.12(pp.286.31–287.5; M.8.1296A,B).

J. veneration of martyr's relics; **1.** their power τοσοῦτο δ' ἐστὶν τῆς ἀθλήσεως σέβας, ὡς καὶ κόνιν βραχεῖαν, ἤ τι λείψανον ὀστῶν παλαιῶν, ἢ τριχῶν μικρὸν μέρος...ἀρκεῖν εἰς ὅλου τιμήν ποτε. καὶ κλῆσιν ἔγνων, ἔστιν ὧν ἀλείψανον, τόποις δοθεῖσαν ἀνθ' ὅλου τοῦ μ., ἰσχύν τ' ἴσην λαβοῦσαν, ὢ τοῦ θαύματος Gr.Naz.*carm.*1.2.10.750(M.37.734); τῶν ἁγίων μ. τὰ σώματα...φυλακτικὰ ὄντα ἀπὸ τῆς τῶν δαιμόνων ἐπιβουλῆς, καὶ ἰαματικὰ νοσημάτων τῶν κατὰ τὴν ἰατρικὴν τέχνην ἀνιάτων ‡Just.*qu.et resp.*28(M.6.1276C); τὰ εὐσεβῆ σώματα...φυλάσσομεν, φρουροῦμεν δὲ αὐτοῖς ὡς ἡμετέροις πλεονεκτήμασιν, καὶ τοῖς μ. ἡ ἐκκλησία τετείχισται ὡς πόλις ὁπλίταις γενναίοις...πρεσβευτὰς αὐτοὺς τῶν εὐχῶν καὶ αἰτημάτων, διὰ τὸ ὑπερβάλλον τῆς παρρησίας, ποιοῦμεν. ἐντεῦθεν πενίαι λύονται, καὶ ἰατρεύονται νόσοι, καὶ ἀρχόντων ἀπειλαὶ κοιμίζονται· πασῶν δὲ τῶν ταραχῶν καὶ χειμώνων τοῦ βίου λιμένες εἰσὶν εὔδιοι, οἱ ἱεροὶ τῶν μ. σηκοί Ast.Am.*hom*.10(M.40.317B,C); esp. over demons, Chrys.*pan.Macc*.1.1(2.623A); λαβὼν γάρ τινα δαιμονῶντα...εἰσάγαγε πρὸς τὸν ἅγιον τάφον ἐκεῖνον, ἔνθα τοῦ μ. τὰ λείψανα, καὶ ὄψει πάντως ἀποπηδῶντα id.*pan.Juln*.2(2.674D); σκηνὴ γάρ ἐστι στρατιωτικὴ τῶν μ. ὁ τάφος· κἂν ἀνοίξῃς τοὺς τῆς πίστεως ὀφθαλμούς, ὄψει τὸν θώρακα τῆς δικαιοσύνης ἐνταῦθα κείμενον...τὴν μάχαιραν τοῦ πνεύματος, αὐτὴν τοῦ διαβόλου τὴν κεφαλὴν ἀπερριμμένην χαμαί. ὅταν γὰρ ἴδῃς δαιμονῶντα ἄνθρωπον παρὰ τὸν τάφον τοῦ μ. κείμενον ὕπτιον...οὐδὲν ἕτερον ἀλλ' ἢ τὴν κεφαλὴν τοῦ πονηροῦ τετμημένην ὁρᾷς id.*pan.Barl*.4(2.686A,B); id.*stat*.8.2(2.93B); δύνανται γὰρ καὶ θῆκαι μαρτύρων πολλὴν ἔχειν δύναμιν, ὥσπερ οὖν καὶ τὰ ὀστᾶ τῶν μ. πολλὴν ἔχει τὴν ἰσχύν id.*pan.Barn*.7(2.645C); **2.** its causes εἴδετε πῶς δυνατωτέρα καὶ σιγώντων ἡ φωνὴ τῶν μ.; διὰ τοῦτο ἀφῆκεν ἡμῖν τὰ σώματα αὐτῶν ὁ θεός· διὰ τοῦτο πάλαι νικήσαντες, οὐδέπω καὶ νῦν ἀνέστησαν, ἀλλὰ τοὺς μὲν ἄθλους ὑπέμειναν πρὸ τοσούτου χρόνου, τῆς δὲ ἀναστάσεως οὐδέπω ἐπέτυχον, οὐδέπω διὰ σὲ καὶ τὴν ὠφέλειαν τὴν σήν, ἵνα καὶ σὺ ἐκεῖνον τὸν ἀθλητὴν ἐννοῶν πρὸς τὸν αὐτὸν δρόμον διεγερθῇς...καίτοι γε ἄφωνος ὁ μ. κεῖται ἐν πολλῇ τῇ σιγῇ. τί ποτ' οὖν ἐστι τὸ κεντοῦν τὸ συνειδός, καὶ ποιοῦν ὥσπερ ἐκ πηγῆς ἀναβλύζειν τοὺς τῶν δακρύων κρουνούς; αὐτὴ τοῦ μ. ἡ φαντασία, καὶ τῶν κατορθωθέντων πάντων ἡ μνήμη id.*pan.mart*.1.2(2.652E–653B); power as proof of truth of the faith, id.*pan.Dros*.2(2.691C,D); ἀπέδωκεν ἡμῖν τὴν ἁγίαν ταύτην κιβωτὸν τὸ σῶμα τοῦ μ.· ταύτην κατέχομεν μέχρι τῆς παρούσης ἡμέρας μυρίων οὖσαν ἀγαθῶν θησαυρόν. καὶ γὰρ ἐμερίσατο ὁ θεὸς πρὸς ἡμᾶς τοὺς μ., τὰς ψυχὰς λαβὼν αὐτός, τὰ σώματά πως ἡμῖν ἔδωκεν, ἵνα ἔχωμεν ὑπόμνησιν ἀρετῆς διηνεκῶς τὰ ἅγια τούτων ὀστέα id.*pan.Juln*.4(2.676E); **3.** relics honoured τοὺς τόπους αὐτούς, οἳ τοῖς σώμασι τῶν μ. τετίμηνται καὶ τῆς ἀναχωρήσεως τῆς ἐνδόξου ὑπομνήματα καθεστᾶσιν, τίς ἂν ἀμφιβάλοι μὴ οὐχὶ ταῖς ἐκκλησίαις προσήκειν, ἢ οὐχὶ καὶ προστάξειεν ἄν; Const.ap.Eus.*v.C*.2.40(p.58.15; M.20.1017A); εἰς δόξαν τοῦ ὀνόματος τοῦ Χριστοῦ οἶκον ἠγείρατε...ἐὰν δὲ δυνηθῶμεν περινοῆσαι λείψανα μαρτύρων, εὐχόμεθα καὶ αὐτοὶ συμβαλέσθαι ὑμῶν τῇ σπουδῇ Bas.*ep*.49(3.142C; M.32.385C); τιμῆσαι τοὺς μ. σπεύδοντες...εἰ γὰρ καὶ πρὸ τούτου ἔδει πρὸς τοὺς...τῆς εὐσεβείας ἀθλητὰς τρέχειν, ὅτε ὑπὸ τὸ ἔδαφος ἔκειντο· πολλῷ μᾶλλον νῦν τοῦτο ποιεῖν χρή, ὅτε καθ' ἑαυτοὺς οἱ μαργαρῖται, ὅτε ἀπηλλάγη τῶν λύκων τὰ πρόβατα...αὐτοῖς...οὐδεμία βλάβη ἦν, οὐδὲ πρὸ τούτου· ὁ δὲ λαὸς ἡμῖν οὐ τὴν τυχοῦσαν ζημίαν ὑπέμεινεν ἀπὸ τῶν τόπων, τρέχων μὲν πρὸς τὰ λείψανα τῶν μ., μετὰ δὲ ἀμφιβολίας...ποιούμενος τὰς εὐχὰς διὰ τὸ ἀγνοεῖσθαι τὰς θήκας τῶν ἁγίων...ἐβάδιζε μὲν ὁ λαὸς πρὸς τὰς καθαρὰς τῶν μ. πηγάς· αἰσθανόμενος δὲ δυσωδίας αἱρετικῆς ἐγγύθεν ἀνιούσης, ἀνεχαιτίζετο πάλιν. ὅπερ οὖν συνειδὼς ὁ σοφὸς οὗτος ποιμὴν [i.e. Flavian]...οὐκ ἠνέσχετο μέχρι πολλοῦ ταύτην τὴν ζημίαν περιϊδεῖν οὗτος...ζηλωτὴς τῶν μ. ἀλλὰ τί ποιεῖ;...τὰ μὲν θολερὰ...ῥεύματα κατέχωσε...τὰς δὲ καθαρὰς τῶν μ. πηγὰς ἐν καθαρῷ χωρίῳ κατέστησε...ἐπεδείξατο καὶ περὶ τοὺς μ. τὴν τιμήν, καὶ περὶ τὸν λαὸν τὴν κηδεμονίαν...περὶ δὲ τοὺς μ. τιμήν, ἀπαλλάξας αὐτοὺς τοῦ πονηροῦ γειτονήματος Chrys.*ascens*.1(2.447A–448B); Philost.*h.e*.7.12(M.65.549B); εἴσω δὲ τοῦ θόλου πρὸς τὰ ἑῷα εὐπρεπής ἐστι σηκός, ἔνθα τὰ...τῆς μ. ἀπόκειται λείψανα ἔν τινι σορῷ τῶν ἐπιμήκων...ἐξ ἀργύρου εὖ μάλα σοφῶς ἠσκημένῃ Evagr.*h.e*.2.3(p.40.25ff.; M.86.2493B); **4.** eccl. legislation εἴ τις αἰτιῷτο, ὑπερηφάνῳ διαθέσει κεχρημένος καὶ βδελυττόμενος τὰς συνάξεις τῶν μ. ἢ τὰς ἐν αὐτοῖς γινομένας λειτουργίας καὶ τὰς μνήμας αὐτῶν CGangr.*can*.20; faithful forbidden to venerate relics of heretics, CLaod.*can*.34; ref. non-authentic sanctuaries ἤρεσεν, ἵνα πανταχοῦ ἀνὰ τοὺς ἀγροὺς...θυσιαστήρια, ὡσανεὶ εἰς μνήμην μ. καθιστάμενα, ἐν οἷς οὐδὲ ἓν σῶμα ἢ λείψανον μ. ... δείκνυνται, ἀπὸ τῶν ἐντοπίων ἐπισκόπων, εἰ ἔστι δυνατόν, καταστρέφωνται...καὶ παντελῶς μηδὲ μνήμη μ. ἐπιτελεσθῇ, εἰ μή που ἢ σῶμα ἤ τινα λείψανα ὦσιν, ἢ ἀρχαιότητι παραδιδῶνται *Cod.Afr*.83.

III. *confessor*;

A. of those who survived tortures; designation at first rejected from humility, *Ep.Lugd*.ap.Eus.*h.e*.5.2.2,3(M.20.433A,B); but soon gen. applied, Hipp.*haer*.9.12(p.247.27; M.16.3382C); Αὐρήλιος Κυρίνιος μ. ἐρρῶσθαι ὑμᾶς εὔχομαι in signature appended to a letter (but sometimes interpreted as *witness*), Serap.Ant.ap.Eus.*h.e*.5.19.3(M.20.481B); ζῶντες μ., ἔμπνοοι στῆλαι Gr.Naz.*or*.43.5(M.36.500C); Philost.*h.e*.3.12(M.65.501A); Γολιανδοὺχ μ. ζῶσα παρ' ἡμῖν ἦν, ἡ διὰ πολλῶν μὲν πόνων τὸ μαρτύριον διενέγκασα Evagr.*h.e*.6.20(p.235.5; M.86.2872D).

B. hence of any true Christian εἰ τοίνυν ἡ πρὸς θεὸν ὁμολογία μαρτυρία ἐστί, πᾶσα ἡ καθαρῶς πολιτευσαμένη ψυχὴ μετ' ἐπιγνώσεως τοῦ θεοῦ, ἡ ταῖς ἐντολαῖς ὑπακηκυῖα, μ. ἐστὶ καὶ βίῳ καὶ λόγῳ, ὅπως ποτὲ τοῦ σώματος ἀπαλλάττεται, οἷον αἷμα τὴν πίστιν ἀνὰ τὸν βίον ἅπαντα, πρὸς δὲ καὶ τὴν ἔξοδον προχέουσα Clem.*str*.4.4(p.255.15; M.8.1228C); *ib*.4.14(p.290.27; 1304A); *ib*.4.21(p.305.21; 1340B); ἀνελάμβανεν δὲ ἐνθέου καὶ προφητικοῦ βίου τρόπον καὶ θεοῦ μ. ἀληθῆ αὑτὸς ἑαυτὸν καὶ πρὸ τῆς ὑστάτης τελευτῆς τοῦ βίου παρίστη Eus.*m.P*.11(p.934.30; M.10.1540B); cf. *non dubito et in hoc conventu esse aliquos ipsi* [sc. *deo*] *soli cognitos, qui jam apud eum martyres sint testimonio conscientiae, parati, si quis exposcat, effundere sanguinem suum pro nomine domini*, Or.*hom*.10.2 *in Num*.(p.72.22; M.12.639A); Meth.*symp*.8.17(p.112.10; M.18.176A); *Const.App*.5.2.3; τοὺς διωκομένους δὲ διὰ τὴν πίστιν...προσλαμβάνεσθε...ὡς μ. *ib*.5.3.1; ref. Bas. προστίθεται τοῖς ἱερεῦσιν ὁ ἀρχιερεύς...ὁ μ. τοῖς μ. καὶ νῦν, ὁ μέν ἐστιν ἐν οὐρανοῖς, κἀκεῖ τὰς ὑπὲρ ἡμῶν, ὡς οἶμαι, προσφέρων θυσίας, καὶ τοῦ λαοῦ προσευχόμενος [? l. προευχ-] Gr.Naz.*or*.43.80(M.36.601C); ἓν γάρ ἐστιν τῶν ἀμηχάνων, ἢ μαρτυρῆσαι γενναίως, ἢ κηρῦξαι σπουδαίως...ἐὰν μὴ πνεύματος ἁγίου δύναμις νευρώσῃ τὸν τόνον τοῦ μ.· ἄλλως γὰρ οὐ δύνανται μ. εἶναι. μ. δὲ λέγω νῦν, οὐ μόνον τὸν διὰ παθῶν τελειούμενον, ἀλλὰ καὶ τὸν τῷ λόγῳ μαρτυροῦντα τῆς χάριτος. πᾶς γὰρ κῆρυξ ἀληθείας, μ. ἐστὶ τοῦ θεοῦ ‡Chrys.*ascens.Ac*.4(3.762A).

C. of ascetics, ref. Symeon Stylites ὁ πανάγιος καὶ ἀέριος μ. Evagr.*h.e*.1.13(p.22.20; M.86.2456C); οὐ μόνον οἱ διὰ τὴν εἰς Χριστὸν πίστιν δεξάμενοι τὸν θάνατον, μ. εἰσιν, ἀλλὰ καὶ διὰ τὴν τῶν ἐντολῶν αὐτοῦ τήρησιν ἀποθνήσκοντες *Schol*.13 in Jo.Clim.*scal*.4(M.88.733C).

[*]**μαρυκάζω**, v. μηρυκάζω.

***Μαρωνίζω**, *play the Maronite heretic*, Jo.D.*trisag*.5(M.95.33B, v.l. παροινήσομεν).

***μαρώνιον, τό**, *wine-cask*, *M.Thdot*.1 33(p.82.6).

[*]**μάσαι**, = μάσσαι, aor. infin., *seek*, *inquire*; *Musae...appellatae* ἀπὸ τοῦ μ. *id est a quaerendo, quod per eas...vis carminum et vocis modulatio quaereretur*, Isid.H.*etym*.3.15.1.

μασάομαι, *chew*, Pall.*h.Laus*.32(p.92.1; M.34.1100B) cit. s. κουκούλλιον; in punishment of blasphemers and false witnesses γυναῖκες καὶ ἄνδρες μασώμενοι αὐτῶν τὰ χείλη...ἄλλοι...τὰς γλώσσας αὐτῶν μ. *Apoc.Petr*.28f.; fig., of Satan τὸν πτωχὸν τῇ ἀρετῇ καὶ ἀσύνετον... εἰς τὸ σπήλαιον τῆς κακίας λαβὼν μασᾶται, καθάπερ λέων Cyr.*Ps*.9:30(M.69.784B); τοῦτο [sc. Christ's body] μ. τοῖς ὀδοῦσιν τῆς διαφθορᾶς θέλων, οὐκ ἴσχυσε [sc. ὁ θάνατος] Gr.Ant.*mul.ung*.5(M.88.1853A); met., *chew* one's words, *mumble*, Mac.Mgn.*apocr*.2.17(p.30.10).

***μασητικός**, **1.** *able to masticate*, met. ἡ ψυχὴ μ. ... τῶν ἰδίων τροφῶν Or.*fr.in Mt*.13:42(p.136); **2.** *of mastication* δύναμιν μ., met., Meth.*res*.1.24(p.248.19; M.41.1093C).

μασθός, ὁ, v. μαστός.

***μάσσα, ἡ**, (Lat. *massa*) a named *plot of ground*, *A.Petr.et Paul*.80(p.214.8).

***Μασσαλιανοί, οἱ**, (Syriac ܡܨܠܝܢܐ); **1.** a pagan sect ἦσαν δὲ πρὸ χρόνου τινός, ὡς ἀπὸ τῶν καιρῶν Κωνσταντίου...εὐφημῖται εἴτ' οὖν Μ. καλούμενοι...ἀλλ' ἐκεῖνοι μὲν ἐξ Ἑλλήνων ὡρμῶντο, οὔτε Ἰουδαϊσμῷ προσανέχοντες οὔτε Χριστιανοὶ ὑπάρχοντες οὔτε ἀπὸ Σαμαρειτῶν, ἀλλὰ μόνον Ἕλληνες ὄντες...καὶ θεοὺς μὲν λέγοντες, μηδενὶ δὲ ⟨τούτων⟩ προσκυνοῦντες, ἑνὶ δὲ μόνον δῆθεν τὸ σέβας νέμοντες καὶ καλοῦντες Παντοκράτορα Epiph.*haer*.80.1(p.485.7; M.42.756B); assemblies for worship, *ib*.80.2(p.486.1ff.; 757B); said to worship Satan; hence known as σατανιανοί, *ib*.80.3(p.486.29; 760C); also called μαρτυριανοί from their veneration of members of the sect slain by Lupicianus [perh. Lucillianus, governor of Mesopotamia], *ib*.80.2(p.486.20; 760B); perh. identical with ὑψιστάριοι, cf.Gr.Naz.*or*.18.5(M.35.989D–992A); **2.** (also *Μεσσαλιανοί, *Μεσσαλῖται) an heret. sect also called εὐχῖται (q.v.), Epiph.*haer*.80.3(p.487.7ff.; M.42.760C); Μεσσαλιανοί: condemned by synods at Side under Amphilochius and at CP under Flavian, Thdt.*h.e*.4.10(3.964–966); id.*haer*.4.11(4.367–368); cf.Phot.*cod*.52(M.103.88B); Μεσσαλῖται: Cyr.*ep*.82(p.20.14; M.77.376A); also called Μαρκιανισταί (q.v.), Tim.CP *haer*.(M.86.45C); apptly. confused with 1 supra, Jo.D. *haer*.80(M.94.728A).

***μάσσινος**, sens. dub.; epithet of a rope, Jo.Mal.*chron*.7 p.186(M.97.296D).

μαστεύω, *seek*, *search after* ἡμῖν αὐτὸς ὁ Χριστὸς ἡ τροφὴ τοῖς νηπίοις...ἐντεῦθεν τὸ ζητῆσαι μ. καλεῖται, ὅτι τοῖς ζητοῦσιν νηπίοις τὸν λόγον αἱ πατρικαὶ τῆς φιλανθρωπίας θηλαὶ χορηγοῦσι τὸ γάλα Clem.*paed*.1.6(p.117.21; M.8.304C).

***μαστιγόπληκτος**, *scourged*, *lashed*, Jo.Mal.*chron*.5 p.123(M.97.217B).

μαστιγ-όω, *whip*; fig., ref. Ex.14:21 τὴν Ἐρυθρὰν θάλασσαν... νότῳ βιαίῳ μ. Philost.*h.e*.12.10(M.65.620B); met., *be a scourge*, Ign.*Trall*.4.1; of a plague of locusts, *Apoc.Dan*.C(p.116); *afflict* ὅλην τὴν ἡμέραν τοῦ βίου τούτου ὁ δίκαιος ~οῦται ἐν λύπαις...ἐν ὀνειδισμοῖς Nil.*epp*.1.37(M.79.100C).

μαστίζω, = foreg., fig., ref. Eccl.2:22 *οἷόν τισι κέντροις, ταῖς... ἐπιθυμίαις τὴν καρδίαν μ.* †Dion.Al.*fr.Eccl.*2:22(p.223.7; M.10.1585C); *διὰ πυρετῶν καὶ νόσων...τὸ δοῦλον σῶμα τὴν δέσποιναν ψυχὴν μ. ἁμαρτήσασαν* Chrys.*exp.in Ps.*3:1(5.4C); of conscience, Zach.H.*ep.*(M.86.3233B); *οὐ δύνασαι ἀκούειν τοῦ φοβεροῦ ὀνόματος* [sc. *Χριστοῦ*] *καὶ διὰ τοῦτο μαστίζῃ τὴν διάνοιαν* *M.Thdot.*3(p.37.7); met., *afflict* *πλεῖον τῆς νηστείας ἢ καθ' ὑπακοὴν μετάληψις μ. τοὺς δαίμονας* Nil.*epp.*1.307(M.79.193C); Isid.Pel.*epp.*1.39(M.78.208A); Bas.Sel.*or.*26.2(M.85.308B); Nonn.*par.Jo.*11:20(M.43.841C).

μαστικτήρ, ὁ, *scourger*, *Orac.Sib.*2.344.

μάστιξ, ἡ, *scourge, rod*; met., of chastening *μ. παιδείας σου* *Pss. Sal.*7.8; *μακάριος ἀνὴρ οὗ ὁ κύριος ἐμνήσθη ἐν ἐλέγχῳ, καὶ ἐκυκλώθη ἀπὸ ὁδοῦ πονηρᾶς ἐν μ.* *ib.*10.1.

***μαστίχημα, τό**, *plaster*, Leont.H.*monoph.*(M.86.1816A,B).

μαστός (μασθός), ὁ, *breast*; fig., ref. 1Cor.3:2 *ἡ τοῦ γάλακτος ζωοτρόφος οὐσία, φιλοστόργοις πηγάζουσα μ.* Clem.*paed.*1.6(p.111.7; M.8.292C); ref. 1Petr.2:2 *μακάριοι...ὅσοι τοῦτον θηλάζουσι τὸν μ.* *ib.*(p.116.10; 301B); *τῶν τοῦ νυμφίου μ. δηλούντων τὰ ὑψώματα* Or.*Cant.*7:8(M.13.213B); cf. *τῶν...μασθῶν δηλούντων τὰ πυκνώματα* id.*schol. in Cant.*7:8(M.17.284C); *τοὺς τοῦ νυμφίου μ. ... προτιμῶσα...οἴνου τοῦ ἐν νόμῳ τε καὶ προφήταις* Apoll.ap.Proc.G.*Cant.*1:2(M.87.1549A).

***μαστοφαγής, ὁ**, a bird of prey *ὠκύπτερον μ.* Clem.*paed.*3.11(p.278.10; M.8.653A).

[*]μαστροπέω, *flatter, pander*, Thdr.Stud.*epp.*1.31(M.99.1012A).

***μαστροπότης, ἡ**, *pandering*, Leont.B.*mesopent.*(M.86.1980C).

[*]μαστυγίας, ὁ, for *μαστιγίας*, *one that deserves a whipping*, Jo. Mon.*hymn.Geo.*8(M.96.1400B).

μαστώδης, *rounded*, Herm.*sim.*9.1.4.

μασχάλη, ἡ, *armhole* *στιχάριον...τύπος...τῆς σαρκὸς τοῦ Χριστοῦ... ἔχει...μασχάλας διὰ τὴν ἐκ λόγχης κεντηθεῖσαν πλευράν* ‡Sophr.H.*liturg.*7(M.87.3988B); cf.‡Germ.CP *contempl.*(M.98.393C).

***ματαιεργία, ἡ**, *vain labour*, Epiph.*haer.*30.7(p.343.4; M.41.417A).

***ματαιοκόπος, ὁ**, *fruitless toiler*, Ant.Mon.*hom.*13(M.89.1469A).

***ματαιοκοσμία, ἡ**, *worldly triviality*, Thdr.Stud.*iamb.*28(M.99.1792A).

ματαιολογία, ἡ, *idle talk*; of pagan and heret. teaching, Ath.*inc.*3.1(M.25.101A); id.*ep.Epict.*1(p.3.1; M.26.1049A); of casting horoscopes, Thdt.*qu.15 in Gen.*(1.18).

ματαιοπονέω, *labour in vain upon* *τόμοι οὓς ἐματαιοπόνησεν εἰς τὴν πρὸς Ῥωμαίους τοῦ ἀποστόλου ἐπιστολήν* Socr.*h.e.*4.7.7(M.67.473A).

ματαιοπονία, ἡ, *labour in vain*; of resistance to God's will, *1Clem.*9.1; of pursuit of wealth, Clem.*str.*4.7(p.271.24; M.8.1264A); of heresy, Hipp.*haer.*6.43(p.176.12; M.16.3266B); Hegem.*Arch.*5(p.7.9; M.10.1436A); of pursuit of secular learning, Chrys.*sac.*2.7(p.45.9; 1.379D); *ὁ ὀργῆς καθαρεύων...οὐκ ἀναλώσει τὸν βίον εἰς μ. καὶ ὀδύνας* id.*hom.61.5 in Mt.*(7.618A).

***ματαιοσκόπος**, *studying vanity* *μετεωρολόγων ἢ μ. ἀνθρώπων* Meth.*symp.*8.17(p.111.10; M.18.173C).

***ματαιοσπουδέω**, *be devoted to trifles*, Philost.*h.e.*11.1(M.65.593B).

***ματαιοσπουδία, ἡ**, *exertion in vain, devotion to trifles*, Olymp. *Eccl.*5:6(M.93.541C).

***ματαιοσυκοφαντία, ἡ**, for *μάταιος συκοφαντία*, Epiph.*haer.*51.4(M.41.892C; *divisim* p.251.17).

***ματαιοσυμβουλία, ἡ**, *false counsel*, ‡Chrys.*Marth.*(10.753B).

ματαιοσύνη, ἡ, = sq., Ant.Mon.*hom.*18(M.89.1485A).

ματαιότης, ἡ, **1.** *vanity, purposelessness* *πάσης μ. νοημάτων καὶ λέξεων* Or.*Cels.*5.46(p.50.15; M.11.1253B); ref. Rom.8:20 *ἐλευθερωθήσονται* [sc. *ἄγγελοι καὶ ἀρχαὶ καὶ ἐξουσίαι*] *ἀπὸ τῆς μ. τοῦ κόσμου παρὰ τὴν ἀποκάλυψιν τῆς δόξης τῶν υἱῶν τοῦ θεοῦ* Clem.*q.d.s.*29(p.179.16; M.9.636A); *ἡ κτίσις...μηκέτι τῇ μ. δουλεύουσα ἀλλὰ τῇ δικαιοσύνῃ* Meth.*res.*1.47(p.299.6; M.18.276A); *ἡ κτίσις...συνωδίνει τῇ καθ' ἡμᾶς μ.* Gr.Nyss.*Eun.*4(2 p.63.28; M.45.636B); *μ. λέγει τὸν ῥευστὸν τοῦτον καὶ φθαρτὸν βίον ἡμῶν* Gennad.*fr.Rom.*8:20(p.330.17; M.85.1696C); of idolatry, Eus.*v.C.*3.57(p.104.15; M.20.1124B); of heresy, *ib.*3.64(p.111.20; 1140B); of a fallacious argument *ἐπὶ τοῦ θεοῦ...μετακομίζειν τὴν μ.* Bas.*Eun.*2.2(1.246D; M.29.592C); of rhetoric or secular education in gen. *πλάσματος οἷα ἐν τοῖς διδασκαλείοις τῆς μ. ... τοῖς μειρακίοις προβάλλεται* *ib.*2.1(1.238D; M.537B); of astronomy, id. *hex.*1.3(1.4C; M.29.9C); of pomps of Devil *διαβόλου ἐστὶ...ἱπποδρομίαι, κυνηγεσία καὶ πᾶσα τοιαύτη μ.* Cyr.H.*catech.*19.6; **2.** *folly*; of men, *Const.App.*8.46.4; of Devil *ὑμᾶς ἀποστάντας αὐτοῦ τῆς μ. ἄλλοτε ἄλλως πειράζει* *ib.*6.5.5.

***ματαιοφιλοτιμέομαι**, *be ostentatious*, ‡Chrys.*hom.in Mt.6*:*1*(8.92A).

ματαιοφρονέω, *have vain thoughts*, Epiph.*haer.*30.34(p.380.27, v.l. *ματαίως φρονεῖς* M.41.469D); Marc.Er.*opusc.*7.10(M.65.1084C).

ματαιοφροσύνη, ἡ, **1.** *vanity of thought*; of heresy, Epiph.*haer.*30.30(p.375.11; M.41.457B); *ib.*37.3(p.53.16; 645A); **2.** *vaingloriousness*, *Orac.Sib.*8.80.

ματαιόφρων, *empty-minded, foolish*, Clem.*prot.*2(p.16.22; M.8.88A); †Bas.*Is.*237(1.560A; M.30.536B); *οἱ...τῆς νόθου σοφίας μ. ἐρασταί* Bas.Sel.*or.*21.1(M.85.256B); of heretics, Dion.Al.ap.Ath. *decr.*26(p.22.12; M.25.464A); Sophr.H.*ep.syn.*(M.87.3165A); ‡Gr. Nyss.*hom.6 in Jo.*(p.218.15); of ideas *μ. λογισμῷ* *Dorm.BMV* 29(p.104); as subst., *fool, foolish person*, ref. Lc.12:20, Gr.Nyss.*bapt. diff.*(M.46.425A); Epiph.*haer.*30.32(p.377.18; M.41.464A).

μαται-όω, **1.** *frustrate, bring to naught*, †Dion.Al.*fr.Eccl.*2:1(p.214.5; M.10.1580B); *μεματαίωται τοῖς Ἀρειανοῖς ἡ περὶ τοῦ 'γενόμενος' πρόφασις* Ath.*Ar.*1.56(M.26.129B); ref. 1Cor.15:17 *μεματαιώμεθα... καὶ ἐσμὲν οὐδὲν ἧττον καὶ νῦν ἐν τοῖς πάλαι καὶ πρὸ τῆς ἐπιδημίας* Cyr. *Nest.*3.3(p.66.7; 6¹.81A); *ὁ νηστεύων καὶ μὴ μεταδιδοὺς πεινῶντι τὸν ἄρτον αὐτοῦ, ~οῖ τὴν νηστείαν αὐτοῦ* Eus.Al.*serm.*1(M.86.316A); *τὴν κρίσιν* [sc. *τοῦ θεοῦ*] *~οῦσαν τὰς σπουδὰς τῶν οἰομένων ἀνύειν τι δύνασθαι σπουδῇ τῆς οἰκείας δυνάμεως* ‡Nil.*perist.*5.2(M.79.852C); *do away with*, †Bas.*Is.*29(1.402B; M.30.176A); **2.** *make foolish* *ῥαθυμίας τῆς ~ούσης...τὸν νοῦν* Marc.Er.*opusc.*5.3(M.65.1032C).

***ματαίωμα, τό**, *vanity* *τῶν μ. τοῦ αἰῶνος τούτου* Herm.*mand.*9.4.

***ματαίωσις, ἡ**, *vanity*, Ath.*exp.Ps.*23:4(M.27.141B).

ματίζω, *seek, inquire*; pass., AQ ap.Proc.G.*Is.*33:20(M.87.2301D).

ματί(ο)ν ([*]μάττιν), τό, an Egyptian measure of capacity, *Apophth.Patr.*(M.65.381C); *μάττιν* Jo.Mosch.*prat.*161(M.87.3029A).

***ματλαῖον, τό**, (Lat. *matula*) *pot* or *vessel*, hence a liquid measure, *Euchol.*(p.508).

***ματρίκιον, τό**, **1.** (Lat. *matricula*) *roll, register*, of a diocese *τὸ μ. καὶ ἀρχέτυπον* *Cod.Afr.*86; of a monastery, kept by taxiarch, Thdr.Stud.*poen.*1.106(M.99.1748B); **2.** = *μάτριξ* q.v. *ἐὰν ἐν τοῖς μ. ἤγουν ἐν ταῖς καθέδραις* *Cod.Afr.*123.

μάτριξ, ἡ, (Lat. *matrix*) *mother* or *cathedral church*, *Cod.Afr.*33; *ib.*119.

***ματρῶνα, ἡ**, (Lat. *matrona*) *matron* *τῶν εὐγενῶν γυναικῶν τὰς περιφανεστέρας, καὶ ἃς ὁ λόγος μ. οἶδε καλεῖν* *Clem.epit.*A 144(M.2.576C); *A.Petr.c.Sim.*1(p.78.5); *ib.*5(p.86.3); of Perpetua *μ. Χριστοῦ* *M.Perp.*18(p.87.24).

***ματτιάριος, ὁ**, *javelin-carrier*, Jo.Mal.*chron.*13 p.330(M.97.492C).

[*]μάττιν, τό, v. *μάτιον*.

***μαύζηρος, ὁ**, v. ***μάνζηρος**.

μαῦρος, *dark*, Or.*schol.in Cant.*6:10(M.17.280A); *A.Petr.et Paul.*16(p.186.5); *δαίμονα...ὡς Αἰθίοπα μ.* *A.Barth.*7(p.146.23); *τὸ δὲ μ. τὰ ἐνδύματα* [sc. *μοναχικά*] *εἶναι σημαίνει ὅτι χρὴ ἡμᾶς ἀφανεῖς εἶναι τῷ κόσμῳ ὡς τὸ πολίτευμα ἔχοντας ἐν οὐρανῷ* Max.*qu.dub.*67(M.90.841C); neut. plur. as subst., name of symptoms of plague, *Mir. Artem.*34(p.52.13).

***μαυρότριχος**, *dark-haired*, *A.Barth.*2(p.131.18).

μαυρόω, *darken, obscure*, met. *ὁ θεὸς...ἅγιος εἶ ὅ[ν] ἡ φύσις οὐκ ἐμαύρωσεν* *Pap.Chr.*(p.431).

μαφόριον, τό, *veil* covering head and shoulders; **1.** worn in public by women *εἰ μὲν οὐ ποιεῖς τὰ νεωτερικὰ σχήματα,...τὸ μ. ἄκροσσον, ὡσαύτως τῆς αὐτῆς χρόας* Ath.*virg.*11(p.44.24; M.28.264B); ref. Cant.5:7 *θέριστρον λέγει τὸ λεγόμενον μ.* Ph.Carp.*Cant.*140(M.40.105C); *γυναῖκα εὐδαιμονεστάτην...καταλείψασαν τὸ ἑαυτῆς μ., μεταμφιασαμένην τὸ σχῆμα τὸ τῶν δουλίδων* Pall.*v.Chrys.*10(p.59.16; M.47.34); id.*h.Laus.*59(p.153.18; *ὠμοφόριον* M.34.1236B); *σεμνὰς γυναῖκας ...ἐκ τῶν οἰκιῶν αὐτῶν σύροντες...ἀσχήμως δημοσίᾳ ἄνευ μ. καὶ ὑποδημάτων* *Fr.hist.*2(M.85.1813A); **2.** worn by monks *ἕνα χιτῶνα φορῶν* [sc. *πτωχός*] *κατὰ τὴν εὐαγγελικὴν παράδοσιν, καὶ μικρὸν μ.* Pall.*h.Laus.*(M.34.1220A); *αἰτησάντων* [sc. *πτωχῶν*] *αὐτὸν ἔδωκε...τὸ ἱμάτιον ὃ ἐφόρει, καὶ εἰσῆλθεν εἰς τὸ κελλίον περιζωσάμενος τὸ μ.* *Apophth.Patr.*(M.65.192B); *ἀποδύεται...τὰ ἱμάτια αὐτοῦ...καὶ ζώννυται τὸ μ. αὐτοῦ καὶ βάλλει ἑαυτὸν εἰς τὸν ποταμόν* Dor.*doct.*1.15(M.88.1637B); *κύριε Ἰησοῦ...οἵανπέρ μοι ἰσχὺν δέδωκας τῷ σῷ ἁμαρτωλῷ οἰκέτῃ, πάρασχε καὶ ταύτῃ μου βακτηρίᾳ σὺν τῷ μ.* ‡Sophr.H.*v.m.Cyr. et Jo.*13(M.87.3688A); cf. *angusto palliolo...colla pariter atque humeros tegunt, quae mafortes tam nostro quam ipsorum nuncupantur eloquio*, Cassianus *coen.instit.*1.7(M.*PL.*49.72A); **3.** in paraphrase of Mt. 5:40 *τῷ αἴροντι αὐτοῦ τὸ ἱμάτιον προσδιδόναι καὶ τὸ μ.* *Hom.Clem.*15.5.

μάχαιρα, ἡ, *sword*, ref. Lc.22:38 *ἴσως δὲ πνευματικὴν χρὴ νοῆσαι τὴν μ.* Tit.Bost.*fr.Lc.*22:38(p.243); *ὁ σωτὴρ...διαγελᾷ τὸ...εἰρημένον, ὅτι 'ἰδοὺ ὧδέ εἰσι μ. δύο', καί φησιν· 'ἱκανόν ἐστι.' ναί, φησίν, ἀρκέσουσι δύο ξίφη πρὸς ἀντίστασιν τοῦ πολέμου τοῦ μέλλοντος ἥξειν κατ' αὐτῶν, πρὸς ὃν οὐδὲν ἂν ὠφέλησαν οὐδὲ πολλαὶ ξιφῶν χιλιάδες*; Cyr.*Lc.*22:38(M.72.917D); *ἡ ἑρμηνεία τῶν δύο μ. αὕτη ἐστίν, τὸ πρακτικὸν καὶ τὸ θεωρητικόν* Jo.Mosch.*prat.*40(M.87.2893D).

***μαχαιροφόνος**, ὁ, *gladiator*, *M.Tar.*11(p.474; perh. f.l. for *μαχαιροφόρος*).

***μαχῆτις**, ἡ, fem. of *μαχητής*, *warrior*; met., of Church, Anast.S. *hex.*12(M.89.1076A).

μάχιμος, *quarrelsome ἀντέχου τοίνυν, φησὶ κατὰ λέξιν ὁ Ἰσίδωρος ἐν τοῖς Ἠθικοῖς μαχίμης γυναικός* [cf. Pr.21:19 *γυναικὸς μαχίμου*] Clem.*str.*3.1(p.196.2; M.8.1101A); Chrys.*hom.17.5 in Mt.*(7.229B); *ὁ οἶνος...ποιεῖ...τοὺς μὲν φιλικούς, τοὺς δὲ μ.* Isid.Pel.*epp.*2.109(M.78. 549C); neut. as subst., *Const.App.*1.10.1.

***μαχλάω**, in pres. ptcpl. only, = *μάχλος*, *lewd*, *wanton*; of persons, Clem.*paed.*2.10(p.223.16; M.8.529B); Cyr.*glaph.Gen.*6(1. 202B); id.*Os.*3(3.12C); of *ὄργια*, Clem.*prot.*2(p.12.12; M.8.73A); of *ἡδοναί*, *ib.*(p.23.24; 105B); Meth.*creat.*1(p.494.13; M.18.333B); id.*res.* 2.18(p.368.7; M.18.312C).

***μαχοσύμβουλος**, *counselling strife*, *Const.App.*3.6.4; Jo.Carp. *cap.*88(M.85.1855A); Ant.Mon.*hom.*27(M.89.1528B).

[*]**μεγακληείς**, *glorious*; of God's arm, †Apoll.*met.Ps.*76:16(M.33. 1421C).

***μεγαλαυχενία**, ἡ, *boastfulness*, *Orac.Sib.*8.76.

***μεγαλαύχησις**, ἡ, *boastfulness*, Meth.*Porph.*1.4(p.503.18; M.18. 397D).

μεγαλεῖος, **A.** *magnificent, splendid*; of things pertaining to God, *mighty*, Clem.*str.*6.16(p.501.15; M.9.364A); Gr.Nyss.*or.catech.*2(p.14. 18; M.45.17B); of Christian truth, *sublime μεγαλειότερα...πάσης ἀνθρωπείου διδασκαλίας...τὰ ἡμέτερα* Just.*2apol.*10.1(M.6.460B); *Ἰωάννης...ὁ τὰ μεγαλειότατα καὶ θειότατα τῶν τοῦ σωτῆρος λόγων... ὑπομνηματισάμενος* ‡Dion.Al.*fr.in Lc.22:42*(p.237.12; M.10.1592A).

B. neut. as subst.; **1.** sing., *majesty, greatness, sublimity*; esp. of God, Gr.Nyss.*hom.6 in Cant.*(M.44.892A); of Son, Bas.*Spir.*16(3.13B; M.32.93C); *τὸ μ. ἐξαγγέλλοντες τῷ ἀρνίῳ* Areth.*Apoc.*14:17ff.(M.106. 700C); of angels, Chrys.*fr.Job* 4:18(M.64.588A); *τὸ μ. τῆς ἐπαγγελίας 1Clem.*26.1; plur., *mighty works*; of God, Herm.*sim.*9.18.2; *τὴν τῶν μ. τοῦ θεοῦ κατάληψιν* Cyr.*Ps.*33:4(M.69.885B); of Christ, *A.Paul.et Thecl.*1(p.236.3); **2.** as complimentary address *οὐκ ἂν πρὸς τὸ μ. τὸ σὸν αὐτὸν ἤγομεν A.Pil.*B 3.1(p.293); **3.** *book containing the gospels μὴ κτησάμενός τί ποτε τοῦ αἰῶνος τούτου, πλὴν στιχαρίου τριχίνου, καὶ σαγίου καὶ μ.* Jo.Mosch.*prat.*51(M.87.2908A); *ἐκράτει δὲ καὶ μ. ἔχον ἀργυροῦν σταυρόν ib.*87(2945A); *ἀνῆλθεν ὁ βασιλεὺς ἐν τῷ ἱππικῷ βαστάζων τὸ ἅγιον μ.* Jo.Mal.*chron.*18 p.475(M.97.689C); hence *gospel παρεγγυήσας αὐτοῖς τὸ μ. καὶ τὴν λοιπὴν ἀκολουθίαν ἐν ταῖς συνάξεσιν Ἀρμενιστὶ καθ' ἑαυτοὺς λέγειν* Cyr.S.*v.Sab.*32(p.117.22); *τὸ μ. τὸ κατὰ Ματθαῖον ἀπὸ τοῦ Ἀβραὰμ ἄρχεται ἕως Ἰωσὴφ Didasc. Jac.*1.54(p.778.2); *ib.*(p.779.16); *ὁ τοῦ μ. μὴ ὑπακούων παραστηκέτω τῇ τραπέζῃ* Thdr.Stud.*poen.*1.8(M.99.1733D).

μεγαλειότης, ἡ, **1.** *greatness, majesty, magnificence*; **a.** of God, Ign.*Rom.*proem.; *Diogn.*10.5; Clem.*str.*6.3(p.448.9; M.9.252B); of his providence, *1Clem.*24.5; **b.** of Christ *ἀποστόλων διηγουμένων τὴν μ. ⟨τοῦ⟩ υἱοῦ τοῦ θεοῦ* Or.*Jo.*2.34(28; p.92.18; M.14.176A); *A.Thom.* A 143(p.250.5); *τοῖς δὲ μαθηταῖς τὴν θεότητα καὶ τὴν μ. δεικνὺς ἑαυτοῦ* Ath.*Ar.*1.50(M.26.116B); *ἐκπληττομένη* [sc. BMV] *ταῖς τοῦ υἱοῦ καὶ θεοῦ παρεμφαινομέναις μ.* Procl.CP *annunt.*5(M.85.448A); *μὴ καταφλέξῃς ἡμᾶς τῷ...πυρὶ τῆς μ. σου Lit.Jac.*(*NBP* 10² p.107); ref. parousia, Max.*ep.*4(M.91.416C); **c.** of BMV, ‡Meth.*Sym.et Ann.*10 (M.18.373C); **d.** of future life, Chrys.*hom.68.4 in Mt.*(7.676D, v.l. *μακαριότης*); **e.** of moral or spiritual *greatness* of men *καταφρονήσας ...τῶν ὑπαρχόντων...διὰ τῆς σῆς μ.* Clem.*str.*4.6(p.261.4; M.8.1241A); Or.*hom.6.3 in Jer.*(p.51.10; M.13.329A); of evangelists *τῆς ἐν τῷ δύνασθαι θεωρεῖν μ.* Cyr.*Jo.*1(4.7A); **f.** of size or importance; of stars, Mac.Aeg.*hom.*36.1(M.34.749A); of a city, *ib.*42.1(769C); **2.** as style of address, *majesty οἱ προσενεχθέντες τῇ μ. σου M.Tar.*1 (p.452); Heracl.*ep.*(M.92.993C).

μεγαλέμπορος, ὁ, *wholesale merchant*; hence fig., ref. Mt.13:45, *rich* or *successful merchant μ. ... τῶν μικρῶν καὶ...φθαρησομένων ὠνησάμενος τὰ μεγάλα μὴ λυόμενα* Gr.Naz.*or.*6.5(M.35.728B).

***μεγαλεμπόρως**, *like a rich* or *successful trader*, Thdr.Stud.*epp.* 2.191(M.99.1581C).

μεγαλεπίβολος, *of great enterprise*, ‡Ath.*polit.*1(M.28.1396A).

***μεγαλευχερῶς**, *very readily*, Sev.Ant.*res.*(M.46.633D; *μᾶλλον εὐχερῶς* p.812.10).

μεγαληγορέω, **1.** *speak boldly*, Chrys.*hom.2.2 in Phil.*(11.204F); *speak loftily, nobly τοῖς μ. μὲν ἐν τῷ φανερῷ καὶ τὰ θεῖα σεμνύνουσι, κρύβδην δὲ τἀναντία πράττουσιν* Isid.Pel.*epp.*4.154(M.78.1240A); **2.** *extol highly οὐ μὲν τὸ τῆς ἀληθείας φρόνημα δεῖ σιωπᾶν, ἀλλὰ...μ.* Ath.*Ar.*2.31(M.26.212A).

***μεγάληχος**, *high-sounding*, Amph.*hom.*1.3(M.39.40B).

μεγαλίζω, *magnify, exalt*, †Apoll.*met.Ps.*33:4(M.33.1356B).

***μεγαλοβοάω**, *shout aloud*, Niceph.Ur.*v.Sym.*220(M.86.3189A).

***μεγαλοβούλως**, *with high counsel*, Thdr.Stud.*epp.*2.206(M.99. 1625C).

***μεγαλογράφος**, ὁ, *writer on great subjects*; of Psalmist, Didym. *Trin.*1.27(M.39.396B); v. *μελογράφος*.

***μεγαλοδαίμων**, ὁ, *great deity*; of Serapis, Clem.*prot.*4(p.37.5; M.8.137B); *οὐδ' αὐτὸς ὁ Πύθιος...οὐδ' ἕτερος τῶν μ.* Eus.*l.C.*9(p.218. 17; M.20.1364B); *great demon*, of Devil *εἴτε δαιμόνων εἴτε καὶ χειρόνων ἄλλων πνευμάτων...ἔτι τε καὶ τοῦ πάντων ἐν τούτοις ἄρχοντος δεινοῦ τινος μ.* id.*d.e.*4.9(p.162.16; M.22.272A).

μεγαλόδοξος, **1.** *very glorious*; of BMV, ‡Jo.D.*hom.*5(M.96.649A); **2.** *high-minded*; neut. as subst., Meth.*symp.*11.3(p.138.2; M.18.216A).

μεγαλοδύναμος, *very powerful ἡ ἔνδοξος καὶ μ. τοῦ κριτοῦ ἐπιφάνεια* ‡Bas.*struct.hom.*2.9(1.343A; M.30.52C); of Christ, †Gregent. *disp.*(M.88.708C).

[*]**μεγαλοδωρεά** (-ία), ἡ, **1.** *munificence, generosity*; **a.** of God, ref. Pr.19:17 *ὅταν πτωχῷ παρέχειν μέλλῃς...δάνεισμα...διὰ τὴν μ. τοῦ δεσπότου* Bas.*hom.in Ps.*14(1.112E; M.29.277C); ref. Ex.33:18 *τὸ... πληρῶσαι τὴν ἐπιθυμίαν αὐτῷ ἡ τοῦ θεοῦ μ. κατένευσε* Gr.Nyss.*v.Mos.* (M.44.404A); *οὐ κωλύει τὴν μ. ἡ δύναμις* id.*or.dom.*5(p.98.1; M.44. 1181A); *τῆς θείας εὐσπλαγχνίας καὶ συγκαταβάσεως καὶ μ.* Nil.*epp.*1.40 (M.79.101B); Isid.Pel.*epp.*3.195(M.78.880D); ref. Tit.3:5 *εἰς αἴσθησιν τῆς μεγαλοδωρίας* Cyr.*Is.*2.1(2.212A); id.*Am.*57(3.312B); id.*Jo.*4.3(4. 671D); **b.** of Christ *ὑπὲρ τὴν αἴτησιν ἐπιδαψιλούμενος τῇ μ. τῶν χαρισμάτων* Gr.Nyss.*engast.*(p.63.9; M.45.108A); *αὕτη ἡ τιμὴ* [sc. baptism] *τῆς τοῦ τιμήσαντός ἐστιν ἀξία μ.* Chrys.*catech.*2.3(p.157.27); **2.** *large* or *generous gift μιᾶς...καὶ τῆς ἴσης πάντας...μεγαλοδωρεᾶς ἠξίωσε τὴν πρὸς αὐτὸν γνῶσιν...δωρούμενος* Eus.*p.e.*1.1(3B; M.21.25A); *τῶν μ. καὶ τῆς ἐν τῷ βαπτίσματι ἀναγεννήσεως τὸ πρὸς τὸν θεὸν πατέρα ἐπίκοινον τοῦ ἁγίου πνεύματος* Didym.*Trin.*2.6(M.39.524C).

μεγαλόδωρος, *munificent, bountiful*; of God, Meth.*res.*2.23(p.379. 1; M.18.283B); *πρόκειται ἀνάπαυσις αἰωνία...κατὰ χάριν τοῦ μ. θεοῦ* Bas.*hom.in Ps.*114(1.202E; M.29.492A); id.*hom.*13.3(2.116A; M.31. 429A); *αὐτῷ ὁ μ. τὸ τῶν ἰαμάτων ἐδωρήσατο χάρισμα* Thdt.*h.rel.*16(3. 1222); of Christ *μ. οὖν ὁ τὸ μέγιστον ὑπὲρ ἡμῶν, τὴν ψυχὴν αὐτοῦ, ἐπιδιδούς* Clem.*paed.*1.9(p.140.2; M.8.352B); Cosm.Ind.*top.*5(M.88. 313D); of God's gifts, Chrys.*hom.23.3 in Heb.*(12.214B); neut. as subst., *munificence*, Men.*exc.Rom.*5(p.190.24; M.113.881B).

***μεγαλοζῶος**, *giant, huge*; of Goliath's limbs, Cosm.Mel.*schol.* (M.38.475); Gr.Naz.*carm.*2.2(poem.)2.3.

***μεγαλοήλιξ**, *tall*, Thdr.Stud.*epp.*2.188(M.99.1573D).

***μεγαλοθύμων**, *valiant*, Eus.Al.*serm.*13(M.86.517A).

***μεγαλόκλονος**, *loud-sounding*, Clem.*prot.*11(p.82.3; M.8.236B).

***μεγαλόμαρτυς**, ὁ, *great martyr*, Nect.*Thdr.*11(M.39.1829C); Chrys.*pan.Dros.*tit.(2.688A); *οἱ τρεῖς παῖδες οἱ ὄντως...μ.* Marc.Er. *opusc.*3.12(M.65.984B); *χρήσασθαι...τῇ ἱερᾷ εἰκόνι τοῦ μ. Δημητρίου* Thdr.Stud.*epp.*1.17(M.99.961B).

***μεγαλομέγεθος**, *vast*; of the sea, ‡Jo.D.*hom.*5(M.96.652D).

μεγαλόνοια, ἡ, **1.** *magnanimity, greatness of spirit θεὸς ὁ κτίστης τοιᾶσδε χάριτος· ἤδη δὲ ὁ μεταδοτικὸς καὶ τόκους ἀξιολόγους λαμβάνει, τὰ τιμιώτατα τῶν ἐν ἀνθρώποις, ἡμερότητα, χρηστότητα, μ., εὐφημίαν* Clem.*str.*2.18(p.157.22; M.8.1024A); ref. Mt.3:7, of courage of Jo. Bapt., Chrys.*hom.11.1 in Mt.*(7.149D); of S. Paul's love for Christ, id.*hom.15.5 in Rom.*(9.601A); ref. Lev.26:8 *αἱ πέντε αἰσθήσεις τῇ μ. καὶ θεόθεν χορηγουμένῃ ἰσχύϊ...περιχαρακωθεῖσαι, ἑκατοντάδα τῶν πολεμίων ἐλαύνουσιν* Nil.*epp.*3.181(M.79.469B); **2.** *elevation of thought* of S. Paul, Chrys.*hom.16.4 in Rom.*(9.608C); *loftiness of mind, largeness of intellect ὁ μὴ πιστεύσας τῇ ἐκδοχῇ τοῦ γράμματος, διὰ μεγαλόνοιαν πιστεύει τῇ πνευματικῇ τοῦ νόμου διηγήσει* Or.*Jo.*32.21(13; p.462.31; M.14.801A); †Bas.*Is.*26(1.299C; M.30.168C); *ib.*89(441E; M. 265A); *φιλοσοφεῖν...χαλεπώτατον καὶ οὐ...ἄλλων ἢ τῶν ὑπὸ τῆς θείας προκεκλημένων μ.* Gr.Naz.*or.*7.9(M.35.765B); *τὴν μ. καὶ τὴν πνευματικὴν διάνοιαν* Chrys.*hom.8.2 in Rom.*(498E); **3.** as honorific title *βασιλικῆς μ. μεγαλουργήματα* Eus.*l.C.*9(p.220.15; M.20.1368B); Gr. Naz.*ep.*129(M.37.224B); Isid.Pel.*epp.*3.195(M.78.880B).

***μεγαλοπιστία**, ἡ, *greatness of faith*, Thdr.Stud.*epp.*2.94(M.99. 1345B).

μεγαλοποιέω, **1.** *do great things*, Or.*Cels.*1.33(p.85.7; M.11.724B); **2.** *enlarge*, Chrys.*hom.72.2 in Mt.*(7.703C).

μεγαλοπρέπεια, ἡ, **1.** *exalted position*, ref. Rom.8:17 *τὴν Ἰουδαίων μικροπρέπειαν...καὶ τὴν Χριστιανῶν μ.* Isid.Pel.*epp.*5.197(M.78. 1452A); **2.** esp. *majesty* of God *θαυμαστὸς ἐν ἰσχύϊ καὶ μ. 1Clem.*60.1; *τὸν ἐν δεξιᾷ τῆς μ. αὐτοῦ...θρόνον* Eus.*e.th.*1.11(p.70.8; M.24.845A); *εἴπερ καθαρεύῃ πάσης μορφῆς ἐν εἴδει θεωρουμένης ἡ τῆς πατρικῆς δόξης μ.* Gr.Nyss.*Apoll.*57(M.45.1264D); *τὸν χορὸν τῶν ἀστέρων ἐν οὐρανῷ καταγράψας εἰς αἶνον τῆς σῆς μ. Lit.*ap.*Const.App.*8.12.9;

theol. τὸ αὐτὸν ὑποταγήσεσθαι τῷ πατρὶ...σημαίνοι ἂν...τὴν δόξαν... τήν τε μ. τήν τε...ὑπακοὴν ἣν καὶ αὐτὸς ἀποδώσει τῷ...πατρί Eus. *e.th.*5.15(p.172.21; M.24.1029A); ascribed to God in doxology, *Pap. Chr.*(p.430); *Lit.*ap.*Const.App.*8.15.9; Pall.*v.Chrys.*20(p.147.24; M. 47.82); Jo.Eub.*innoc.*5(M.96.1508B); **3.** as honorific title, Thdt. *haer.*proem.(4.280); id.*ep.*15(4.1076); Firm.*ep.*12(M.77.1489C).

μεγαλορ(ρ)ημονέω, *boast*, *1Clem.*17.5; Malch.*ep.*ap.Eus.*h.e.*7.30. 9(M.20.713A); ἀνταποκρινόμενοι καὶ μεγαλορη⟨μο⟩νοῦντες *T.Job* 41 (p.130.9); Gr.Nyss.*Eun.*1(1 p.23.30; M.45.252B).

μεγαλορ(ρ)ημοσύνη, ἡ, *boasting*, Ign.*Eph.*10.2; Ephr.3.366D.

μεγαλορρήμων, 1. *boastful*, Eus.*qu.Steph.*8.2(M.22.913B); ref. Is. 13:13 τῇ μ. ταύτῃ καρδίᾳ τῆς γῆς Gr.Nyss.*res.*1(M.46.608C); **2.** *long-winded*, Men.*exc.Rom.*3(p.172.5; M.113.853B).

μεγαλόσαρκος, *great of flesh*, hence *carnal*, Or.*Jo.*6.19(11; p.128. 18, v.l. φιλόσαρκος M.14.233B).

[*]**μεγαλόσθενος**, = μεγαλοσθενής, *of great strength*, *Orac.Sib.*5. 196; of cities, *ib.*5.63; *ib.*14.208.

[*]**μεγαλοσύνη, ἡ,** v. μεγαλωσύνη.

μεγαλόσχημος, of monks and nuns, *wearing the great habit*, i.e. *of the higher order*, opp. μικρόσχημος, †Jo.Jej.*poenit.*(M.88.1893B); Thdr.Stud.*poen.*2.47(M.99.1753D); *Nomoc.*147; cf.*Euchol.*(p.581n.).

μεγαλόσωμος, *large-bodied*, Eus.*p.e.*2.1(48D; M.21.100B).

***μεγαλοτόκος, ἡ,** *mother of majesty*; of BMV, Ant.Ptol.*fr.*ap. Cyr.*Arcad.*(p.66.32; 5².49E).

[*]**μεγαλούργημα, τό,** = μεγαλοέργημα, **1.** *great achievement*; of buildings, Eus.*l.C.*11(p.226.2; M.20.1380B); **2.** *mighty work, miracle*; performed by God, Nect.*Thdr.*4(M.39.1825A); τῶν ἐν Αἰγύπτῳ μ. Cyr.*Is.*4.5(2.711C); id.*Jo.*4.2(4.360A); *Rit.Epiph.*(p.416); by Christ, Or.*Ps.*77:4(p.113) = Ath.*exp.Ps.*77:4(M.27.352A); Cyr.*Arcad.*(p.93. 22; 5².89C); by apostles, Alex.Sal.*Barn.*16(p.441A).

μεγαλουργία, ἡ, 1. *mighty work, miracle*, of God τῆς προνοίας [sc. τοῦ κυρίου] τὰς μ. καταλέξας Eus.*Ps.*134:15(M.24.32C); Cyr.*Os.*5(3. 24C); id.*Ps.*95:2(M.69.1244B); ἐπαινέτης [sc. ὁ κόσμος] σιγῶν τὰς μ. Melet.*nat.hom.*31(M.64.1301A); of Son, ref. Inc., Eus.*d.e.*4.10 (p.169. 1; M.22.281A) cit. s. ἀνακιρνάω; ἀναθετέον...τῷ θειοτάτῳ πατρὶ τὰς τοῦ υἱοῦ μ. Eust.*fr.in Pr.8:22*(M.18.681C); of Christ's earthly ministry, Cyr.*Lc.*4:31(M.72.545B); **2.** *mighty working, miracle-working*; of God, Gr.Naz.*or.*38.11(M.36.321C); τὴν τοῦ ποιητοῦ μ. Thdt.*qu.7 in Gen.*(1.11); ἡ ἐξ ἐθνῶν ἐκκλησία τῶν ἔργων σου τὴν μ. κηρύξει id.*Ps.*144:4(1.1560); of Christ, ‡Pion.*v.Polyc.*5; Cyr.*Lc.*5:2 (M.72.553B); of H. Ghost τῇ τῶν τεράτων μ. τοὺς ἀπίστους εἰς θεογνωσίαν ἐφελκόμενον Thdt.*h.rel.*proem.(3.1106); of a saint, Sophr.H.*mir.Cyr.et Jo.*14(M.87.3468B).

μεγαλουργός, *performing great deeds*; of God, Eus.*h.e.*10.4.9(M. 20.852B); of emperor, id.*l.C.*11(p.226.17; M.20.1380C).

μεγαλουργῶς, *magnificently*, Thphyl.*exc.gent.*6(p.483.24; M.113. 944D).

μεγαλοῦχος, *overweening*, Clem.*str.*3.6(M.8.1152B; μεγάλαυχοι p.218.23).

μεγαλοφυής, *of noble nature*; neut. as subst., *nobility* τὸ μ. τῆς ἀρετῆς Eus.*d.e.*2.3(p.80.1; M.22.144A); τὸ μ. τῆς ψυχῆς †Bas.*hom. in Ps.*115(1.375B; M.30.112D); Chrys.*hom.20.4 in Rom.*(9.662B); ref. Christ τὸ μ. τῆς θεότητος Tim.III Al.*fr.*(p.316.15; M.86.268A).

μεγαλοφυΐα, ἡ, *noble nature, nobility*; **1.** of persons τὸ πνεῦμα τὸ ἅγιον ἐν τῇ τοῦ Στεφάνου μ. γενόμενον Gr.Nyss.*Steph.*1(M.46.705C); of God φαίνεται οὐ δι' ὑπερβολὴν καὶ μ. εἰς ἀγριότητα θεὸς ἀποκλίνων· ἀλλὰ μᾶλλον...εἰς ἡμερότητα Cyr.*thes.*13(5¹.136D); **2.** of abstracts μ. τῆς γνώσεως Bas.*Eun.*2.15(1.250C; M.29.601B); ῥημάτων μ. Gr.Nyss. *or.dom.*2(p.32.6; M.44.1140B); θείων δογμάτων μ. id.*Eun.*1(1 p.187.3; M.45.432C); **3.** as honorific title, Thdt.*ep.*23(4.1087); *M.Ner.et Ach.* 11(p.10.27).

μεγαλοφυῶς, 1. *as befits a noble nature, nobly, generously*, Clem. *str.*1.4(p.17.24; M.8.717B); Gel.Cyz.*h.e.*2.33.8(M.85.1337D); Max. *ambig.*(M.91.1172A); iron. οὕτως μ. τὴν γέννησιν ἡμῖν τοῦ μονογενοῦς θεολογεῖ Bas.*Eun.*2.14(1.249A; M.29.597C); comp., of sayings of Jesus τοὺς μ. εἰρημένους λόγους Or.*Jo.*19.18(4; p.318.9; M.14.557D); Gr.Nyss.*hom.10 in Cant.*(M.44.985A); **2.** *exaggeratedly*, comp., Isid. Pel.*epp.*2.191(M.78.640C).

μεγαλοφωνία, ἡ, 1. *loud utterance*, fig. and met. Ἰωάννης τῇ μ. τοῦ πνεύματος ἐμβοᾷ σοι Bas.*Eun.*2.27(1.263D; M.29.633B); Gr.Nyss.*hom. 1 in Cant.*(M.44.785D); μετὰ τῆς μ. τῶν πράξεων...θυσίας αἰνέσεως ἀναφέρειν...τῷ θεῷ Sev.Ant.ap.*cat.Ac.*16:28(p.274.3); **2.** *lofty utterance*, Or.*Cels.*3.58(p.253.17; M.11.997B); μείζονι ἢ κατὰ ἄνθρωπον μ. τὸν σωτῆρα...θεολογῶν Eus.*d.e.*7.1(p.297.15; M.22.488B); τὴν...τῶν ἁγίων μ. Didym.*Trin.*3.21(M.39.901C); Ἰωάννης ὁ υἱὸς ὄντως βροντῆς, τῇ οἰκείᾳ μ. CAnc.(358)*ep.syn.*ap.Epiph.*haer.*73.7(p.278.5; M.42.417A).

μεγαλόφωνος, 1. *loud-voiced*; fig., of words, Or.*Cels.*6.77(p.147. 23; M.11.1416C); **2.** *lofty in utterance, grandiloquent* μ. προφητείας Didym.*2Reg.*22:14(M.39.1117C); Socr.*h.e.*4.27.4(M.67.536B).

μεγαλοφώνως, 1. *loudly*, fig. and met. τίς κωφὸς ἀλλ' ἢ ὁ μὴ ἀκούων οὕτω μ. ἐμβοῶντος τοῦ πνεύματος; Bas.*hex.*3.4(1.26C; M.29. 64A); Synes.*ep.*128(M.66.1508D); Sev.Ant.ap.*cat.Ac.*10:2(p.171.17); comp. μυρίων ἐπιστολῶν μακρῷ μεγαλοφωνότερον ὁ νεανίσκος ἂν διηγήσαιτο Synes.*ep.*85(1453D); Nil.*epp.*1.191(M.79.189A); **2.** *in noble language* ὁ περὶ τῶν μεγάλων δογμάτων ἀπαγγέλλων ὡς δεῖ μ. Or.*fr. 10 in Jo.*(p.492.1); ‡Hipp.*consumm.*4(p.290.23; M.10.908B).

***μεγαλόφωτος**, *of great light*; of BMV, ‡Jo.D.*hom.*5(M.96.653C).

μεγαλοψυχ-έω, 1. *be exalted* πάντες ~οῦμεν, σοῦ ἡδρασμένου Thdr. Stud.*epp.*1.2(M.99.912C); **2.** *be generous*, Chrys.*hom.19.4 in 2Cor.* (10.576C).

μεγάλως, *greatly*, comp. μειζόνως, ref. Father εἰ ἀληθινὸς θεὸς καὶ φῶς...καὶ κύριος ὁ υἱός, ταῦτα δὲ καὶ ὁ πατὴρ ὤν, οὐχ ὁμοίως ἐστίν, ἀλλὰ μ.· οὐχ οὐσίας ὑπεροχῇ ἀλλὰ ποιότητος ὑπερβολῇ Didym.(‡Bas.) *Eun.*4(1.282A; M.29.677C); superl. μεγίστως, *Pers.*(p.25.15).

μεγαλωσύνη (μεγαλοσύνη), ἡ, *majesty, greatness*; **1.** in gen., Val. Gn.ap.Clem.*str.*4.13(p.287.23; M.8.1297B); ἐκ τῶν κτισμάτων ἢ τῆς μεγαλοσύνης αὐτῶν φανερόν ἐστιν ὅτι ὁ θεὸς παντοδύναμος Or.*exp.in Pr.*18:10(M.17.204C); ἑρμηνεία ἐστὶ τοῦ...ὡσαννά, μεγαλοσύνη ὑπερκειμένη ‡Just.*qu.et resp.*50(M.6.1296A); **2.** of God; **a.** = his power ἐν λόγῳ τῆς μ. αὐτοῦ συνεστήσατο τὰ πάντα *1Clem.*27.4; εὐλογῶν τῷ κυρίῳ τῆς μεγαλοσύνης *Apoc.En.*12.3; μὴ ἔχειν ὅρον τὴν θείαν μ. Gr. Nyss.*Eun.*3(2 p.35.3; M.45.601B); ὁ κόσμος...ὥσπερ τι βιβλίον...τὴν... ἀόρατον τοῦ θεοῦ μ. δι' ἑαυτοῦ διαγγέλλον σοι τῷ νοῦν ἔχοντι ‡Bas. *struct.hom.*2.1(1.338D; M.30.41C); διὰ τοῦ μονογενοῦς...τὴν λύτρωσιν ἡμῶν ποιησάμενος, ἀνάξιον κρίνας τῆς σῆς μεγαλοσύνης καὶ χρηστότητος, οἰκέτῃ τὴν τῶν σῶν οἰκετῶν καταπιστεῦσαι σωτηρίαν ‡Meth.*Sym. et Ann.*8(M.18.368A); **b.** = his person ὁ οὐρανὸς καὶ ἡ γῆ...ἀπὸ προσώπου τῆς μ. αὐτοῦ σαλεύονται *T.Lev.*3.9; πεποιθότες ἐπὶ τὸ ὁσιώτατον τῆς μ. αὐτοῦ ὄνομα *1Clem.*58.1; εἰσελθεῖν εἰς τὸν κόσμον... ἀδύνατον, μὴ χειραγωγηθέντα τῷ θελήματι τῆς μεγαλοσύνης Meth. *symp.*2.3(p.18.3; M.18.52A); εὐχαριστῶ τῇ μ. σου *A.Pil.*B 8.1(p.330); **c.** being ascribed to him by Son, ref. 1Cor.15:28 αὐτῷ τὴν μ. ἅτε δὴ πάντων τῶν ἀγαθῶν αἰτίῳ προσοίσων Eus.*e.th.*3.15(p.174.5; M.24. 1032C); by men in doxology, *1Clem.*20.12; *Pap.Chr.*(p.430); Pall. *v.Chrys.*20(p.147.24; M.47.82); shared with men αὐτὸς [sc. Messiah] δώσει τὴν μ. κυρίου τοῖς υἱοῖς αὐτοῦ...εἰς τὸν αἰῶνα *T.Lev.*18.8; **3.** of Son and H. Ghost ἡ τοῦ ἁγίου πνεύματος μ. ἀδιάλυτος, ἀπέραντος, ...ἀεί ἐστιν Didym.*Trin.*2.6(M.39.509A); ref. Ps.144:3 οὔτε τῆς μ. τοῦ υἱοῦ ἐστι πέρας, οὔτε τῆς μ. τοῦ πνεύματος ‡Ath.*dial.Trin.*1.25 (M.28.1156A); καθὸ ἔστι καὶ νοεῖται θεὸς...δόξαν ἔχων ἀπόρρητον...μ. ἀνείκαστον *cat.2Cor.*8:9(p.402.22).

μεγαλωφελής, *very serviceable, of great benefit*; of Christ, Clem. *paed.*1.9(p.140.3; M.8.352B); τὸ ὅπλον τῆς μ. καὶ σωτηρίου εὐχῆς τῆς ἐν Χριστῷ Nil.*epp.*3.36(M.79.404D).

§**μεγαρίζ-ω**, *go to the* μέγαρα (v. *LS* s.v. μέγαρον IV) τὰς ὗς τὰς Εὐβουλέως τὰς συγκαταποθείσας τοῖν θεαῖν, δι' ἣν αἰτίαν ἐν τοῖς θεσμοφορίοις ~οντες χοίρους ἐμβάλλουσιν Clem.*prot.*2(p.14.4; M.8.77B; conj. μεγάροις ζῶντας); αἱ ~ουσαι γυναῖκες καὶ θεσμοφορι⟨ά⟩ζουσαι ἄλληλαι πρὸς ἀλλήλας διαφέρονται Epiph.*exp. fid.*10(p.510.11; M.42.800A).

μέγας, *great, mighty*;

A. neut. plur. as subst., *mighty works*, ref. Exodus, Just.*1apol.* 62.4(M.6.424A); prepositional phrase as adv. τοῦ παναγίου πνεύματος ἐπὶ μέγα χυθέντος ἐπ' αὐτούς Max.*schol.d.n.*1.3(M.4.193B); *long*, of Ps.118, Pall.*h.Laus.*26(p.81.20; M.34.1091D); τοῦ μ. κανόνος Andr.Cr. *can.mag.*tit.(p.147; M.97.1329C); μ. τῷ βίῳ *old*, Cyr.S.*v.Cyriac.*6 (p.225.27); without τῷ βίῳ: θέλεις, ὦ μ., λαμβάνω σε εἰς τὴν οἰκίαν; Pall.*h.Laus.*21(p.64.22; M.34.1073C).

B. comp.; **1.** μεγαλώτερος *elder*, *A.Barth.*8(p.147.27); **2.** μειζότερος; **a.** of a *senior* monk θέλων γενέσθαι μοναχὸς...ἐβουλήθη μεῖναι εἰς κελλίον μετὰ μειζοτέρου Ephr.1.301A; ἀπεκρίθη...ὁ ἀδελφός· ἐγὼ δοῦλός εἰμι, καὶ ὅ με κελεύουσιν οἱ μ. μου, τοῦτο ποιῶ id.1.309C; μὴ μετελθεῖν [sc. τοὺς νεοκατηχητούς] ἀπὸ μ. πρὸς ἕτερον id.1.318B; id.2.85E; δεῖ δὲ τοὺς μ. τύπους εἶναι τοῖς μικροτέροις πρὸς πᾶσαν ἀρετήν id.2.87F; but *superior* of a monastery, opp. ὁ δεύτερος, Pall.*h.Laus.*32(p.90. 8; M.34.1100A); **b.** *headman* of a village acting under jurisdiction of an abbot, *IGC As.Min.*47 [Adramyttium]; **3.** μειζονότερος, *mightier*, Ephr.3.316E; **4.** μείζων; **a.** in gen., masc. as subst., *Grand Chamberlain* πρεσβύτης τις εὐνοῦχος, τροφεὺς Σαβώρου, καὶ μ. τῆς βασιλέως οἰκίας Socr.*h.e.*2.9.6(M.67.957A); *ib.*2.24.6(997C); μ. ... τῶν βασιλέως εὐνούχων *ib.*8.7.1(1533A); μ. τῆς βασιλικῆς αὐλῆς *ib.*5.5.8 (1220A); **b.** theol.; **i.** of Father in rel. to Son, ref. Ps.44:7 ἔχρισέν σε, ὦ θεέ, ὁ ἀνωτάτω καὶ μείζων αὐτὸς ὁ καί σου θεός Eus.*d.e.*4.15

(p.183.3; M.22.305A); θεὸς εἶναι λέγεται ἠγαπηκὼς δικαιοσύνην καὶ μεμισηκὼς ἀδικίαν καὶ τούτου χάριν ὑφ' ἑτέρου μ. θεοῦ καὶ πατρὸς αὐτοῦ κεχαρισμένος ib.4.16(p.193.15; 321C); ref. Ps.90:9 μονονουχὶ λέγων ὅτι σὺ αὐτός, ὦ κύριε, ὃς ἐμοῦ τοῦ προφητεύοντος ἐλπὶς ὢν τυγχάνεις, μείζονα σαυτοῦ τὸν θεὸν ὕψιστον εἰδώς, ἐκεῖνον αὐτὸν 'ἔθου καταφυγήν σου' ib.9.7(p.421.2; 677D); ref. Jo.14:28 οὐδέ τις ἀρνεῖταί ποτε τὸν πατέρα τοῦ υἱοῦ μ., οὐ δι' ἄλλην ὑπόστασιν, οὐ δι' ἄλλην διαφοράν, ἀλλ' ὅτι αὐτὸ τὸ ὄνομα τοῦ πατρὸς μ. ἐστι τοῦ υἱοῦ CSard. ep.cath.ap.Thdt.h.e.2.8.45(3.846); οὐδενὶ δὲ ἀμφίβολόν ἐστι μ. εἶναι τὸν πατέρα, οὐδὲ γὰρ διστάσειεν ἄν τις τὸν πατέρα τιμῇ καὶ ἀξίᾳ καὶ θειότητι καὶ αὐτῷ τῷ ὀνόματι τῷ πατρικῷ μ. εἶναι, διαμαρτυρουμένου αὐτοῦ τοῦ υἱοῦ ὁ ἐμὲ πέμψας πατὴρ μ. μού ἐστι Symb.Sirm. 2(p.257.11; M.26.741C); ὁ υἱὸς οὐκ εἴρηκεν ὁ πατήρ μου κρείττων μοῦ ἐστιν, ἵνα μὴ ξένον τις τῆς ἐκείνου φύσεως αὐτὸν ὑπολάβοι· ἀλλὰ 'μ.' εἶπεν, οὐ μεγέθει τινὶ οὐδὲ χρόνῳ ἀλλὰ διὰ τὴν ἐξ αὐτοῦ τοῦ πατρὸς γέννησιν· πλὴν ὅτι καὶ ἐν τῷ εἰπεῖν 'μ. ἐστιν' ἔδειξε πάλιν τὴν τῆς οὐσίας ἰδιότητα Ath.Ar.1.58(M.26.133C); ἐπειδὴ γὰρ ἀπὸ τοῦ πατρὸς ἡ ἀρχὴ τοῦ υἱοῦ, κατὰ τοῦτο μ. ὁ πατήρ, ὡς αἴτιος καὶ ἀρχή Bas.Eun.1.25(1.236C; M.29.568B); μεγέθει μὲν ὁ πατὴρ τοῦ υἱοῦ οὐκ ἂν λεχθείη μ.· ἀσώματος γάρ·...οὔτε ὡς αἴτιος· ἐπεὶ ὁμοίως καὶ αὐτοῦ καὶ ἡμῶν μ. εἴπερ γὰρ αὐτοῦ καὶ ἡμῶν αἴτιος·...τιμὴν τοίνυν μᾶλλον τὸ ῥηθὲν υἱοῦ πρὸς πατέρα...δείκνυσιν, ἔπειτα τὸ μ. οὐ πάντως καὶ ἑτεροούσιον...μ. γὰρ ἄνθρωπος ἀλόγου οὐ κυρίως λέγεται...ἀλλ' ἄνθρωπος ἀνθρώπου καὶ ἄλογος ἀλόγου· ὁμοούσιος οὖν ὁ πατὴρ τῷ υἱῷ, κἂν μ. λέγηται Didym.(‡Bas.)Eun.4(1.289 B–D; M.29.693C–696A); οὐ τοῦ υἱοῦ μ. ἐστὶν ἀσυγκρίτῳ ὑπεροχῇ, ἀλλ' ὡς πατὴρ υἱοῦ...οὐκ ἄρα ἄλλῳ τινὶ μείζονα ἑαυτοῦ τὸν πατέρα λέγει, ἀλλ' ὡς υἱὸς μορφὴν δούλου λαβὼν καὶ τιμῶν τὸν ἑαυτοῦ πατέρα ‡Ath.Maced.dial.1.19(M.28. 1325B,C); ὅτε οὖν ἀκούσομεν ἀρχὴν καὶ μείζονα τοῦ υἱοῦ τὸν πατέρα, τῷ αἰτίῳ νοήσομεν ‡Cyr.Trin.8(6^{3}.12D; M.77.1137C); acc. Ar., though only Father was greater than Son, other beings could be his equals ἴσον μὲν τοῦ υἱοῦ γεννᾶν δυνατός ἐστιν ὁ κρείττων, διαφορώτερον δὲ ἢ κρείττονα ἢ μ. οὐχί Ar.Thal.fr.2 ap.Ath.syn.15(p.243.10; M.26.708B); **ii.** of Son; no greater than H. Ghost τὸ γὰρ ἐκ μεγάλου καὶ μ. καὶ μεγίστου συνιστᾶν τὴν τριάδα, ὥσπερ ἐξ αὐγῆς καὶ ἀκτῖνος καὶ ἡλίου, τοῦ πνεύματος καὶ τοῦ υἱοῦ καὶ τοῦ πατρὸς...κλίμαξ ἐστὶ θεότητος, οὐκ εἰς οὐρανὸν ἄγουσα, ἀλλ' ἐξ οὐρανοῦ κατάγουσα Gr.Naz.ep.101(M. 37.192B); αὐτοῦ [sc. Ἀπολιναρίου]...ἐστιν εὕρεμα, τὸ μέγα, μεῖζον, μέγιστον· ὡς μεγάλου μὲν ὄντος τοῦ πνεύματος, τοῦ δε υἱοῦ μείζονος, μεγίστου δὲ τοῦ πατρός Thdt.haer.4.8(4.362); exeg. Mt.11:11 τινὲς τὸ μέρος τοῦτο περὶ τοῦ δεσπότου ἐνόησαν, μικρότερον μὲν κατὰ τὴν τοῦ δούλου μορφήν, καθ' ἣν ἥσσων προφητῶν καὶ ἱερέων ὑπωπτεύετο τυγχάνειν, μ. δὲ κατὰ τὴν θεότητα Didym.Trin.3.18(M.39.885C).

C. superl. μέγιστος; as description of high-ranking Montanist clergy, CLaod.can.8.

***μεγαφρονέω**, **1.** abs. *exult, be self-confident*, Thdt.Abd.12(2. 1454); id.Mich.1:10(2.1482); **2.** *make one's boast, put one's confidence* in τῇ βασιλικῇ δυνάμει μ. id.Zach.12:7(2.1653); id.1Cor.1:1(3.165); Anast.S.qu.et resp.28(M.89.556B).

***μεγέθης**, *big* μ. ζῷον Phys.B 2(p.153.2); τὰ μ. δένδρα ib.(p.154.1).

μέγεθος, τό, 1. of God, *majesty* ἀποπίπτοντες τοῦ μ. τοῦ θεοῦ... τὰς τῶν στοιχείων τροπὰς θεοποιοῦσιν Athenag.leg.22.7(M.6.940B); A.Phil.96(p.37.31); ὁ πατήρ μου ὁ Χριστός, ὁ πατὴρ τοῦ μ. ib.132 (p.62.14); (Gnost.) μόνος ὁ Νοῦς...ἐτέρπετο θεωρῶν τὸν πατέρα καὶ τὸ μ. τὸ ἀμέτρητον αὐτοῦ κατανοῶν Iren.haer.1.2.1(M.7.452B); met., *stature* ἔπαθε γὰρ σαρκὶ τῷ σταυρῷ προσπαγεὶς ὁ λόγος, ἵνα ἁπλώσῃ... τὸν ἄνθρωπον, πρὸς τὸ ἄνω τε καὶ θεῖον μ. τῷ ξύλῳ ἐξισώσας τῆς ζωῆς αὐτόν Meth.Porph.3(p.506.25; M.18.401B); ἦλθε θεὸς ἐπὶ γῆς ὁ υἱός, σαρκὶ κρύψας...τὸ τῆς αὐτοῦ θεότητος μ. Gel.Cyz.h.e.2.19.26(M.85. 1281A); **2.** moral and spiritual *greatness* or *force* μεγέθους ἐστὶν ὁ Χριστιανισμός, ὅταν μισῆται ὑπὸ κόσμου Ign.Rom.3.3; τό τε μ. αὐτοῦ τῆς μαρτυρίας M.Polyc.17.1; **3.** of weather, *severity*, Philost.h.e.8.8 (M.65.561C); **4.** as title τὸ μ. σου Bas.ep.225(3.345A; M.32.840C); Thdt.ep.34(4.1095); μὰ τὸ σὸν μ. M.Tar.6(p.462); **5.** Gnost.; **a.** name of Valent. aeon, Val.Gn.ap.Epiph.haer.31.5(p.391.2; M.41.481B); cf. Ἰησοῦς...παρὰ τοῖς Αἰῶσι τοῦ Πληρώματος πολυμερὲς τυγχάνον...γινωσκόμενον ὑπ' ἐκείνων...ὧν τὰ μ. παρ' αὐτῶν [v.l. αὐτῷ] ἐστι διαπαντός Iren.haer.1.14.4(M.7.604A); **b.** = ἄγγελος: ὁ δὲ τόπος τοῦ μ. ἐν ἡμῖν ἐστι ib.1.13.3(581B); ὦ πάρεδρε θεοῦ καὶ μυστικῆς πρὸ αἰῶνος Σιγῆς, ἣν τὰ μ. διαπαντὸς βλέποντα τὸ πρόσωπον τοῦ πατρός, ὁδηγῷ σοι...χρώμεθα [l. χρώμενα] ib.1.13.6(589A).

***μεγιστᾶνος, ὁ,** = μεγιστάν, *grandee*, †Gregent.leg.Hom.22(M.86. 592C); Thphn.chron.p.245(M.108.616C).

***μεγιστόφωνος**, *of very loud voice*, Geo.Pis.hex.1111(M.92.1519A).

***μεδεκώθ**, a liquid measure μ. λέγει τοὺς κυάθους ἡ γραφή Epiph. mens.24(M.43.284B).

μεδιμναῖος, *holding a* μέδιμνος (a measure of corn), proverb οὐ μ. ἀγγεῖον χωρήσει διμέδιμνον Jo.D.Man.1.25(M.96.1529C); quoted by heretics, ref. two natures of Christ, id.f.o.3.6(M.96.1005C).

μέδων, ὁ, *lord*; of Christ, Jo.D.carm.pent.117(p.217; M.96.837C).

μεθαρμόζ-ω, A. act.; **1.** *adapt* ἀπὸ τῆς...γνωστικῆς αἱρέσεως τὰς ἀρχὰς εἰς ἴδιον χαρακτῆρα διδασκαλείου μ. Οὐαλεντῖνος Iren.haer.1.11. 1(M.7.560A); βούλονται κατὰ πάντα ~ειν τὸ παράδειγμα τοῦ ἀνθρώπου ἐπὶ τοῦ Χριστοῦ †Leont.B.sect.7.6(M.86.1245C); in bad sense, *pervert* τὸν προφήτην...εἰπόντα· Ἰσραὴλ δέ με οὐκ ἔγνω...τὴν τοῦ ἀοράτου βυθοῦ ἀγνωσίαν εἰρηκέναι ~ουσι Iren.haer.1.19.1(652A); **2.** *translate*, Clem.fr.51(p.255.11).

B. med., *adapt* ὁ κύριος...θυρὰν ἑαυτὸν λέγων καὶ ὁδόν...ἄλλοτε ἄλλως ἑαυτὸν ὀνομάζει, ταῖς ἐπινοίαις διαφερούσαις ἀλλήλων τὰς προσηγορίας ~όμενος Bas.Eun.1.7(1.218C; M.29.525A); id.ep.226.3 (3.348B; M.32.848B); abs., *make a change*, Synes.ep.133(M.66.1520A); in music, *change the mode*, fig. ἡ πρὸς τοὺς ἁμαρτάνοντας ἐπίπληξις ἔχει σκοπὸν τὴν σωτηρίαν, ~ομένου μουσικῶς τοῦ λόγου κατὰ τοὺς οἰκείους ἑκάστων τρόπους Clem.paed.1.8(p.129.15; M.8.329D).

C. pass., *be transformed*, Bas.hom.in Ps.114(1.203D; M.29.493B); Chrys.hom.31.5 in Mt.(7.363B); *be translated*, of BMV ταύτην ἐξαρπασθῆναι τοῦ τάφου, καὶ πρὸς τὸν υἱὸν τὴν μητέρα μεθαρμοσθῆναι Jo.D.hom.9.14(M.96.741A).

[*]**μεθαύριον**, v. μεταύριον.

***μέθειρξις, ἡ,** *captivity, incarceration*, Thdr.Stud.epp.2.67(M.99. 1293B).

***μεθέκτης, ὁ,** *partaker* τῆς ἀληθείας μ. Clem.str.1.12(p.35.20, conj. μεθεκτικοί; cod. μεθεκτοί M.8.753A).

μεθεκτικός, *capable of participating*, Max.ambig.(M.91.1329A); neut. as subst. πνεῦμα δὲ τὸ πνευματικὸν σῶμα προσεῖπεν ἐκ τοῦ μ. τὸ μέτοχον καλέσας Gennad.fr.Rom.8:9(p.377.3; M.85.1692B).

μεθεκτός, 1. *shared, communicated*, of Father ἀκοινώνητος, φασί, καὶ οὐ μ. ἡμῖν ὁ πατὴρ δι' ἑαυτοῦ διὰ τὴν ὑπερβολήν Cyr.thes.13(5^{1}. 136B); of indwelling Christ ὡς οὖν αὐτὸς [i.e. the Christian] ἐν τῷ μετεχομένῳ, οὕτω καὶ ὁ μ. ἐν τῷ μετέχοντι Diod.Ps.70:6(M.33.1609B); αὐτὸν εἶναι...τὴν ζωήν, οὕτω τε δύνασθαι ζωογονεῖν τοῖς ἐν οἷς ἂν γένοιτο μ. Cyr.thes.32(5^{1}.322C); οὐκοῦν εἰ μ. ἐν τοῖς γενητοῖς ἐστιν ὁ ζωογονῶν αὐτὰ λόγος, οὐκ ἐν τοῖς μετέχουσιν ἔσται καὶ αὐτός, ἀλλ' ἕτερος...παρ' ἐκεῖνα id.Jo.1.6(4.50E); of H. Ghost μὴ ἁγιαζόμενον παρ' ἑτέρου, μηδὲ μετέχον ἁγιασμοῦ, ἀλλ' αὐτὸ μ. ὄν, ἐν ᾧ καὶ τὰ κτίσματα πάντα ἁγιάζεται Ath.ep.Serap.1.23(M.26.584B); ref. attributes of H. Ghost οὐδὲ εὐσεβές, ὥσπερ ἐπὶ τῶν ἀνθρώπων, οὕτω καὶ ἐπὶ τοῦ πνεύματος, μ. λέγειν αὐτοῦ τὴν θεότητα τετιμῆσθαι, καὶ οὐχὶ φύσει αὐτῷ συνυπάρχειν Bas.Eun.1.5(1.276D; M.29.665C); and of Son, ref. Jo.1:16 οὐ μ. ... ἔχει τὴν δωρεάν, ἀλλ'...αὐτορίζα ἐστὶ πάντων τῶν καλῶν Chrys.hom.14.1 in Jo.(8.78B); **2.** act., *participating, partaking*, Clem.str.1.12(M.8.753A; μεθέκτης p.35.20); Didym.(‡Bas.) Eun.5(1.297A; M.29.713A); Mac.Mgn.apocr.3.23(p.103.18).

***μεθεκτῶς**, *by participation* ἡ κτίσις...μ. ἔχει [sc. ἀλήθειαν καὶ ἀγαθότητα καὶ ἁγιωσύνην] Didym.Trin.3.2(M.39.601C); οἱ μακάριοι μαθηταὶ...τῆς ἄνωθεν ὑπεροχῆς τὴν λαμπρότητα μ. ἐκπεπλουτηκότες Cyr.ador.9(1.294A); κατὰ φύσιν ὑπάρχων [sc. ὁ υἱός] τὸ φῶς, μ. γε μὴν ἐν τοῖς ἁγίοις καὶ παρ' αὐτοῦ id.Zach.23(3.683D); τοῦ θεοῦ ἑαυτῷ ὁμοίους ἡμᾶς ποιήσαντος (τῷ ἔχειν τῆς αὐτοῦ ἀγαθότητος μ. ἀκριβῆ γνωρίσματα) Max.ambig.(M.91.1097C); ref. God ἔνεστι μόνῃ τῇ πασῶν ἐπέκεινα φύσει τὸ εἶναί τε καὶ ζῆν, οὐ μ. παρ' ἑτέρου λαχούσῃ ταῦτα Cyr.Is.4.5(2.713D); ref. Son εἰ οὕτως ἔχει τὴν ζωὴν ὁ υἱὸς ἐν ἑαυτῷ ...οὐσιωδῶς ἄρα καὶ οὐ μ. id.thes.32(5^{1}.323A); cf.id.Jo.11.10(4.992A); πάντα καὶ περὶ τὴν ὑπόστασιν τοῦ υἱοῦ θεωρεῖται [sc. ἀθανασία... δικαιοσύνη...κυριότης], ὁμοίως τῷ πατρί, καὶ οὐ μ. ‡Ath.dial.Trin.1. 18(M.28.1145A).

μεθέλκω, 1. met.; **a.** *draw over* to oneself, *appropriate*, Philost. h.e.11.3(M.65.596C); πρὸς ἑαυτοὺς τὴν τιμὴν καὶ τὰς θυσίας μ. †Jo.D. B.J.32(M.96.1169A); **b.** *draw aside, divert*, Synes.ep.105(M.66.1484C); **2.** *relax* a bowstring, Geo.Pis.hex.455(M.92.1471A).

μέθεξις, ἡ, *participation*, in Christ τὸ ἐν μ. γενέσθαι τῇ πνευματικῇ τοῦ...Χριστοῦ Cyr.hom.pasch.19(5^{2}.249E); in the Spirit ἡτοίμασε... ὁ θεὸς...ἁμαρτιῶν ἀπόθεσιν, πνεύματος ἁγίου μ. id.Lc.14:16(M.72. 789B); id.1Cor.15:35(p.307.27; M.74.904B); οὔπω...τῆς τελείας τοῦ πνεύματος μ. τετυχήκασιν Jo.D.hom.1.19(M.96.573C); in sacraments μ. τῶν ἁγιασμάτων Gr.Thaum.ep.can.11(M.10.1048B); ἡ τῶν μυστηρίων μετάδοσις...ὁμοίους τῷ...ἀγαθῷ κατὰ χάριν καὶ μ. ἀποφαίνουσα τοὺς ἀξίως μεταλαμβάνοντας ‡Bas.h.myst.62(p.397.20); in gifts of God ἧς [sc. τῆς σοφίας] ἡ μ. Clem.str.6.16(p.502.10; M.9.364B); τῆς ἐπηγγελμένης ἐλπίδος τὴν μ. Cyr.Lc.9:27(M.72.653D); freq. κατὰ μέθεξιν, ἐν μ., μεθέξει *by participation, derivatively* ἔστι γὰρ αὐτοσοφία καὶ δικαιοσύνη· ἡμεῖς δὲ κατὰ μ. σοφοί τε καὶ δίκαιοι Or.schol.

*in Cant.*1:1(M.17.253B); of Son ᾗ μὲν...ὑπάρχων αὐτὸς ὁ τῆς δόξης κύριος, ᾗ δὲ γέγονεν ὁ κατὰ μ. θεοῦ δοξαζόμενος ἄνθρωπος *cat.Heb.*1:7 (p.322.21); τὸ γὰρ ὅλως κατ' ἀλήθειαν φῶς οὐκ ἂν γένοιτο μ. τῇ πρὸς ἕτερόν τινα φῶς Cyr.*Jo.*1.8(4.66D); ἐν μ. καὶ κατὰ χάριν ἀπονέμουσι [sc. Nestorians] τῷ Χριστῷ τὸ τῆς υἱότητος ὄνομα id.*hom.pasch.*20 (5^2.259E); εἰ δέ τῳ δοκεῖ...διισχυρίζεσθαι ὅτι κατὰ μ. ἐν τῷ υἱῷ τὸ πνεῦμά ἐστιν, ἢ καὶ τότε γέγονεν ἐν αὐτῷ, πρότερον οὐκ ἐνυπάρχον, ὅτε καὶ ἐβαπτίσθη id.*Jo.*2.1(4.124D); ref. Inc. οὗτος κύριος ὁ μηδενὸς ἑτέρου ἐν μ. γενόμενος πλὴν τοῦ φυράματος Ἀδάμ ‡Meth.*Sym.et Ann.* 14(M.18.380B).

***μεθεόρτιος,** = sq., *of mid-Pentecost* προεόρτιος καὶ μ. [i.e. as falling between Easter and Ascension–Pentecost] Leont.N.*serm.* 2(M.93.1584B).

μεθέορτος, *after the feast* εἰς τὴν κοίμησιν τῆς παναγίας θεοτόκου ἤγουν εἰς τὸ λυχνικὸν τὸ μ. *Const.Stud.*13(M.99.1708D); met., of Resurrection as new creation ἡ καινὴ κτίσις, καὶ μ. ἑορτή Gr.Naz.*or.* 44.4(M.36.612B).

***μεθερμηνευτής, ὁ,** *interpreter,* Eus.*v.C.*4.32(p.129.33; M.20.1181A).

μεθερμηνεύ-ω, 1. *translate*; of Theodotion and Aquila, ref. exegesis of Is.7:14 τῶν νῦν ~ειν τολμώντων τὴν γραφὴν Iren.*haer.* 3.21.1(M.7.946A); Eus.*p.e.*10.5(474B; M.21.788C); **2.** *interpret,* Hipp. *haer.*6.19(p.145.7; M.16.3222C); οὐ προσήκει καθ' ὁμοιότητα τῶν λοιπῶν ὀνομάτων καὶ τὴν τοῦ υἱοῦ προσηγορίαν ~εσθαι Gr.Nyss.*Eun.*3(2 p.45. 31; M.45.613C).

μεθετέον, *one must give up,* Clem.*paed.*3.3(p.246.3; M.8.577C).

μέθη, ἡ, A. *drunkenness* μ. ... ἐστιν ἀκράτου χρῆσις σφοδροτέρα Clem.*paed.*2.2(p.172.8; M.8.420B); condemned, *ib.*(p.173.23; 424B); Eus.*h.e.*1.2.21(M.20.64B); Chrys.*hom.29.1 in Gen.*(4.282A); met. ἡ μ. τῆς ὕλης Mac.Aeg.*hom.*24.5(M.34.665B); μ. ἀγνοίας *ib.*31.5(732B); μέθη γὰρ δεινή, φιλοδοξία, καὶ φιλαρχία †Bas.*Is.*178(1.509A; M.30.417C).

B. met., *inebriation, spiritual intoxication*; **1.** non-mystical (in modern technical sense); **a.** with a sacramental connotation, also nected with conception of Christ as true vine προσθετέον...πῶς ἐστιν ὁ υἱὸς 'ἀληθινὴ ἄμπελος'· τοῦτο δὲ δῆλον ἔσται τοῖς συνιεῖσιν ἀξίως χάριτος προφητικῆς τὸ 'οἶνος εὐφραίνει καρδίαν ἀνθρώπου'. εἰ γὰρ ἡ καρδία τὸ διανοητικόν ἐστι, τὸ δὲ εὐφραῖνον αὐτὸ ὁ ποτιμώτατός ἐστι λόγος, ἐξιστῶν ἀπὸ τῶν ἀνθρωπικῶν καὶ ἐνθουσιᾶν ποιῶν καὶ μεθύειν μέθην οὐκ ἀλόγιστον ἀλλὰ θείαν Or.*Jo.*1.30(33; p.37.18; M.14. 80A); cf. *potus iste quem deus verbum sanguinem suum fatetur, verbum est potans et inebrians praeclare corda bibentium,* id.*comm. ser.85 in Mt.*(p.196.24; M.13.1734B); τὴν κρατύνουσαν, ἀλλ' οὐ διαλύουσαν μ. Eus.*Ps.*22:5(M.23.220A) = Thdt.*Ps.*22:5(1.749); ἐσθίειν τὸν ζῶντα ἄρτον καὶ τὰς ζωοποιοὺς αὐτοῦ σάρκας, πίνειν τε τὸ σωτήριον αὐτοῦ αἷμα. τούτοις τρεφόμενος καὶ πιαινόμενος, τῆς ἐνθέου μ. ἀπολαύων Eus.*Ps.*36:2ff.(M.23.325C); αὕτη ἡ καλὴ μ.· κάρωσόν σου τὴν ψυχὴν τῷ πνεύματι, ἵνα μὴ καρώσῃς τῇ μ. ... ἔστιν ἡμῖν ποτήριον μέθης καλόν, ἐστὶ ποτήριον μέθης σωφροσύνην ποιοῦν, οὐ παράλυσιν. ποῖον δὲ τοῦτο; τὸ ποτήριον τὸ πνευματικόν, τὸ ποτήριον τὸ ἄχραντον τοῦ αἵματος τοῦ δεσποτικοῦ. ἐκεῖνο οὐ ποιεῖ μέθην, ἐκεῖνο οὐ ποιεῖ παράλυσιν...καινὸς τρόπος μέθης, ἰσχὺν ἐντίθησιν, ἐγκρατῆ ποιεῖ καὶ δυνατόν· ἀπὸ γὰρ τῆς πέτρας ἔρρευσε τῆς πνευματικῆς· οὐκ ἔστι παρατροπὴ λογισμῶν, ἀλλὰ προσθήκη λογισμῶν πνευματικῶν Chrys. *res.Chr.*2(2.440C–E); οὐ μόνον πιεῖν, ἀλλὰ καὶ μεθυσθῆναι...ἔστι γὰρ μ. σωφροσύνην, ἀλλ' οὐ παραφροσύνην ἐργαζομένη Thdt.*Cant.*5:1 (2.108); **b.** without sacramental connotation τὴν τῶν ἀρετῶν μ. εἰσοικίσαι ταῖς οἰκείαις ψυχαῖς· μέθην σωφροσύνης μητέρα, μ. ἀγνοίας διδάσκαλον, μ. ἄγρυπνον τηροῦσαν τὸ βλέμμα τοῦ νοῦ· μ. ἀληθείας φῶς ἐναποτιθεμένην ταῖς ἀεὶ πληρουμέναις ψυχαῖς· μ. οὐ παραφόρους ἐργαζομένην...ἀλλὰ μᾶλλον τὰ μέλη κρατύνουσαν...μ. ἧς ὁ τῶν ἀποστόλων ἐνεπλήσθη χορὸς Bas.Sel.*or.*37.1(M.85.389A,B); **2.** without marked sacramental connexion, as a mystic state; **a.** in gen. ἡ λαμπὰς πάντοτε καιομένη...πλέον ἐν μέθῃ ἐξάπτεται τῆς ἀγάπης τοῦ θεοῦ Mac.Aeg.*hom.*8.2(M.34.529A); τὴν μ. ἐκβάλλων τὴν ἐπιβλαβῆ, τὴν πνευματικὴν ἀντεισήγαγε Thdt.*Eph.*5:18(3.432); id.*carit.*(3. 1301) cit. s. ἔρως; **b.** as a mystic state preceding ecstasy ὡς γὰρ ἐφ' ἡμῶν κατὰ τὸ χεῖρον ἡ μ. καὶ ἀσύμμετρος ἀποπλήρωσίς ἐστι, καὶ νοῦ καὶ φρενῶν ἔκστασις· οὕτω κατὰ τὸ κρεῖττον ἐπὶ θεοῦ τὴν μ. οὐκ ἄλλο τι χρὴ διανοεῖσθαι παρὰ τὴν ὑπερπλήρη κατ' αἰτίαν προοῦσαν ἐν αὐτῷ πάντων τῶν ἀγαθῶν ἀμετρίαν, ἀλλὰ καὶ τὴν ἐπακολουθοῦσαν τῇ μ. τοῦ φρονεῖν ἔκστασιν, τὴν ὑπεροχὴν τοῦ θεοῦ τὴν ὑπὲρ νόησιν οἰητέον Dion. Ar.*ep.*9.5(M.3.1112C); cf.Gr.Nyss.*hom.10 in Cant.*(M.44.989C) cit. s. ἔκστασις; of pentecostal inebriation ἡ ἔκχυσις καὶ ἡ μ. τοῦ πνεύματος Mac.Aeg.*hom.*50.4(M.34.817D); **c.** called νηφάλιος: οἶκος μὲν θεοῦ ἐστιν ἡ ἐκκλησία αὐτοῦ· πιότης δὲ τοῦ οἴκου τὰ θεόπνευστα ἀναγνώσματα· μ. δὲ σώφρων καὶ νηφάλιος ἡ ἀπὸ τῶν ἀναγνωσμάτων ὠφέλεια Eus.*Ps.*35:9f.(M.23.321B); of apostles at Pentecost μεθύουσι μ. νηφάλιον Cyr.H.*catech.*17.19; of mystic state of those inebriated by divine wisdom οὕτω μοι νόησον καὶ τὴν κυπρίζουσαν ἄμπελον, ἧς ὁ μὲν οἶνος, ὁ τὴν καρδίαν εὐφραίνων, πληρώσει ποτὲ τὸν τῆς σοφίας κρατῆρα· καὶ προκείσεται τοῖς συμπόταις ἐκ τοῦ ὑψηλοῦ κηρύγματος κατ' ἐξουσίαν ἀρύσασθαι εἰς ἀγαθήν τε καὶ νηφάλιον μ. ἐκείνην λέγω τὴν μ., δι' ἧς τοῖς ἀνθρώποις ἐκ τῶν ὑλικῶν πρὸς τὸ θειότερον ἡ ἔκστασις γίνεται Gr.Nyss.*hom.5 in Cant.*(M.44.873B); πρὶν γὰρ τὴν σωματικὴν τροφὴν προσενέγκασθαι,...γίνεται αὐτῷ [sc. S. Peter] ἡ θεία τε καὶ νηφάλιος μ., δι' ἧς ἐξίσταται αὐτὸς ἑαυτοῦ *ib.10*(992A); sacramental and mystical ὁ τοῦ ποτηρίου ἄκρατος, ὁ τὴν νηφάλιον μ. ἐργαζόμενος *ib.12*(1032B); προσθεὶς αὐτῷ οἶνον τὸν τὴν καρδίαν εὐφραίνοντα, τὴν νήφουσαν ἐκείνην μ. ἐμποιεῖ τῇ ψυχῇ, στήσας τοὺς λογισμοὺς ἀπὸ τῶν προσκαίρων πρὸς τὸ ἀΐδιον id.*ascens.*(M.46.692B).

***μεθηλικιόομαι,** *advance in years,* ref. Lc.2:52, ‡Ath.*serm.fid.* 18(p.12; M.26.1272C); ‡Bas.*struct.hom.*1.17(1.331A; M.30.25B); ‡Nil. *perist.*12.6(M.79.949A).

***μεθηλικίωσις, ἡ,** *advance in age,* Bas.*hom.in Ps.*114(1.203D; M.29. 493B) = Nil.*epp.*2.76(M.79.233C); ‡Bas.*struct.hom.*1.17(1.331A; M.30. 25B); of Christ, Mod.*dorm.*12(M.86.3308C); Sophr.H.*ep.syn.*(M.87. 3173A).

***μεθῆλιξ,** *belonging to a later age,* Ast.Am.*hom.*1(M.40.173C).

***μεθημέραν,** *by day,* Nil.*paraen.*31(M.79.1252C); Thdr.Stud.*epp.* 2.103(M.99.1360B).

μεθίδρυσις, ἡ, *change of position,* met. μετὰ τὴν ἄφιξιν τοῦ θεάνδρου, διὰ τοῦ εὐαγγελικοῦ κηρύγματος ἡ πρὸς θεοσέβειαν γέγονε μ. ‡Caes.Naz.*dial.*111(M.38.989).

μεθίημι, med., *neglect, abandon*; c. acc., Cyr.*ador.*1(1.25A).

μεθιστάν-ω, = μεθίστημι, *remove, transfer* ὁ θεὸς...~ει τοὺς οὐρανοὺς καὶ τὰ ὄρη Herm.*vis.*1.3.4.

μεθιστ-άω, = foreg.; **1.** *place* in a different position εἰς ἀνάγκην αὐτὸν...~ᾶν τοῦ...ποιῆσαι Chrys.*hom.45.1 in Jo.*(8.262B); **2.** *change* people from one state to another ~ῶν...τοὺς αὐτῷ προσανέχοντας ἐκ μὲν ἀκολασίας ἐπὶ σώφρονα βίον Eus.*d.e.*4.10(p.167.12; M.22. 277D); ἠρέμα αὐτοὺς τῶν πραγμάτων μεθιστῶντες, τῶν ὀνομάτων οὐ μεθίστων Chrys.*comm.in Gal.*1:6(10.667B).

μεθίστημι, A. trans.; **1.** *remove, transfer* νοσοκομήσαντες καὶ ῥώσαντες ἑτέρους, ἐτελεύτησαν αὐτοί, τὸν ἐκείνων θάνατον εἰς ἑαυτοὺς μεταστησάμενοι Dion.Al.ap.Eus.*h.e.*7.22.7(M.20.689A); τὴν κιβωτὸν... ὁ Δαβὶδ εἰς Σιὼν...μετεστήσατο Diod.*Ps.*88:5(M.33.1619D); **2.** *change* people from one state to another ἀναστὰς ὁ κύριος εὐηγγελίσατο τοὺς δικαίους τοὺς ἐν τῇ ἀναπαύσει καὶ μετέστησεν αὐτοὺς καὶ μετέθηκεν Clem.*exc.Thdot.*18(p.112.24; M.9.665C); ref. change of opinion εἰς ἕτερόν σε μεταστῆσαι δόγμα *Hom.Clem.*1.22; οὐδαμῶς αὐτὸν ἴσχυσε τῆς εὐσεβείας μεταστῆσαι Philost.*h.e.*7.7(M.65.544C); **3.** *translate* a bishop, *ib.*4.4(520A); *ib.*2.10(472C).

B. intrans. and pass.; **1.** *be moved* διὰ τῆς εὐχῆς μεταστήσεσθαι τὸν ἥλιον ἐπὶ τὰ ἐαρινὰ σημεῖα Or.*or.*5.3(p.309.20; M.11.432B); **2.** *be changed* εἰ τὸ ἀγέννητον στέρησις, ἡ δὲ στέρησις ἕξεως ἀποβολή ἐστιν ...πῶς οἷόν τε ἕξει μεθισταμένῃ ἢ ἀπολλυμένῃ κατονομάζεσθαι τὴν οὐσίαν τοῦ θεοῦ, τῇ τοῦ ἀγεννήτου φύσεως προσηγορίᾳ; Aët.*synt.*24 (p.357.13; M.42.541B); **3.** of persons, *be changed* or *translated* οἱ γὰρ ἐξ ἀνθρώπων εἰς ἀγγέλους μεταστάντες χίλια ἔτη μαθητεύονται ὑπὸ τῶν ἀγγέλων Clem.*ecl.*57(p.154.9; M.9.725C); of Isaiah ὁ βασιλεὺς...ἔγνω ὅτι οὐκ ἀπέθανεν ἀλλ' ἀνελήφθη ἤγουν μετέστη *Ascens.Is.*B 2.2(p.142); of a bishop, Philost.*h.e.*9.14(M.65.580A); **4.** *depart* this life ἐν ταῖς μνείαις...πρεσβεύειν ὑπὲρ τῶν μεταστάντων *Const.App.*8.44.1; τὸν βίον μεταστῆναι τοῦτον Chrys.*hom.20.8 in Eph.*(11.155E, v.l. μετελθεῖν).

μεθοδεία (μεθοδία), ἡ, 1. *craft, wiliness*; plur., *cunning devices, wiles*; of Devil, Ath.*ep.Adelph.*1(M.26.1072A); Bas.*fid.*2(2.225C; M. 31.680C); Chrys.*hom.2.5 in Col.*(11.340B); of heretics, Iren.*haer* 1.9. 1(M.7.537B); Gr.Naz.*or.*26.3(M.35.1232A); in good sense, *devices* to outwit Devil, ‡Pall.*h.mon.*1.55(p.21.11; M.34.1129A); ‡Nil.*perist.*12. 3(M.79.944A); **2.** = μέθοδος, *system, set of rules* τῆς περὶ πρᾶξιν καὶ ἀρετὴν πολυτρόπου μ. Max.*ambig.*(M.91.1356A); **3.** ? *moving about, disturbance* ἐν τῷ πάθει τῷ κυριακῷ...τὰ μνήματα πρὸς μεθοδείαν σωμάτων ἐτρόμαζον Isid.Pel.*epp.*1.253(M.78.336B); **4.** *action for recovery of debt,* Ath.Scholast.*coll.*15.3(p.154).

***μεθοδευτικῶς,** *wilily,* ref. sophistical arguments, Leont.N.*v. Sym.*47(M.93.1728C).

μεθοδεύ-ω, 1. *treat, deal with*; **a.** persons or situations διὰ...τῶν πρεσβυτέρων ἑαυτοῦ καὶ διὰ γραμμάτων μεθώδευσε τοὺς περὶ Εὐσέβιον CSard.*ep.Alex.*ap.Ath.*apol.sec.*37(p.116.3; M.25.312C); γράμμασι τῆς σῆς χρηστότητος ~θέντες...οὐκ ἠδυνήθημεν λόγον ἀποδοῦναι Ursac.*ep. Jul.*(p.138.5; M.25.353B); τὸ μάλιστα λυποῦν αὐτοὺς...μεθώδευσε Chrys.*hom.79.3 in Mt.*(7.761B, v.l. ἐμεθόδευσε); ἀρετὴ διδασκάλου, τὸ ποικίλοις δύνασθαι ~ειν τρόποις τῶν ἀκρωμένων τὸν νοῦν Cyr.*Jo.*2.1

(4.148B); σαφῶς τὰ κατὰ τὸν προφήτην ἐμεθώδευεν Bas.Sel.or.11.2(M.85.152C); perh. with idea of implicating τῶν ἐπισκόπων τοὺς μὲν διὰ γραμμάτων ~ουσι, πλάττοντες κατ' αὐτῶν προφάσεις Ath.h.mon.32(p.200.25; M.25.729B); **b.** c. εἰς, *treat...so as to obtain* τὸ ἀπὸ ἡλίου φῶς...μ. ἡ τέχνη εἰς πῦρ Clem.str.6.17(p.508.27; M.9.380C); **c.** *treat* medically; fig., of God ὅρα φιλανθρωπίαν δεσπότου, πῶς...καθάπερ ἰατρὸς ἄριστος μ. αὐτῶν τὴν νόσον Chrys.hom.25.3 in Gen.(4.234A); id.hom.in Mt.18:23(3.10C); **2.** *manipulate*; **a.** *bamboozle* persons διὰ τῆς...φαντασίας μ. τοὺς ἀπειροτέρους Iren.haer.1.8.1(M.7.521B); **b.** *express, put* in words διὰ τὴν τῶν ἀκουόντων ἀσθένειαν οὕτω μ. τὸν λόγον Chrys.hom.30.2 in Jo.(8.171D); τοῦτον μὲν τὸν τρόπον οὐ ~ει τὰ εἰρημένα, ἑτέρως δέ, πληκτικώτερον μέν, ἀνεπαχθέστερον δὲ id. hom.13.1 in 1Cor.(10.109C); id.hom.11.1 in 2Cor.(10.513A); Thdt. Rom.6:1(3.61); in field of action, *go about, contrive* οὐ δύνασαι νηστεῦσαι;...ἔνεστί σοι μισθὸν λαβεῖν, ἂν ἑτέρως τὸ πρᾶγμα μ., τὸν ἐν τούτοις κάμνοντα θεραπεύων Chrys.hom.1.2 in Phil.(11.197B); **c.** *twist* words ὃς ἂν μ. τὰ λόγια τοῦ κυρίου πρὸς τὰς ἰδίας ἐπιθυμίας...πρωτότοκός ἐστι τοῦ σατανᾶ Polyc.ep.7.1; λέξιν εἰς τὸν ἑαυτῶν νοῦν ~οντες Epiph.anac.40(p.2.19; M.41.580B); id.haer.30.22(p.362.25; M.41.441C); οὐδὲ γὰρ μέρος τι τῆς πίστεως τῆς ἡμετέρας μὴ ὂν σαφὲς ~εται, ἀλλ'...ὅπερ ὁ ἡμέτερος δεσπότης ἐν τῇ ἰδίᾳ ἐκκλησίᾳ οὐδαμῶς ἀγνοεῖσθαι ἠθέλησεν Leo Mag.ep.30(p.46.26; M.PL.54.788C); **3. a.** *make a way for, contrive* τὴν ἀντιλογίαν ἐξηγήσεως σχήματι μ. †Apoll.ep.Bas.2(M.32.1108A); Epiph.haer.21.5(p.244.26; M.41.293B); ἐπειδὴ ἀπὸ λόγων οὐχ οὕτως ἔπειθεν, ἀπὸ τῆς τῶν πραγμάτων πείρας αὐτὸ μ. Chrys.hom.66.2 in Jo.(8.397C); c. acc. and infin., *arrange for* τοὺς...ἐπισκόπους μεθώδευσα τοὺς μὴ συναθροισθέντας μετ' αὐτῶν ἀναμεῖναι τὴν τῆς ὑμετέρας ἁγιωσύνης παρουσίαν CEph.Orient.act. (ACO 1.1.5 p.120.24, v.l. ἐμεθόδευσα H.1.1452B); **b.** abs., *use craft*, of demons εἰ τὸ δυνατὸν ὑπῆρχεν αὐτοῖς, οὐκ ἂν...φαντασίας ἐποίουν οὐδὲ μετασχηματιζόμενοι ἐμεθόδευον Ath.v.Anton.28(M.26.883C); of a heretic ποικίλως ~ων ἣν ἐπενόησε συνεργείᾳ τοῦ διαβόλου πλάνην ἰσχύειν ἐπιχειρεῖ Tit.Bost.Man.3 proem.(M.18.1208B); τί ἐστι μεθοδεία; ~εῦσαί ἐστι τὸ ἀπατῆσαι, καὶ διὰ συντόμου ἑλεῖν, ὅπερ καὶ ἐπὶ τῶν τεχνῶν γίνεται καὶ ἐν λόγοις, καὶ ἐν ἔργοις...οἷόν τι λέγω... εἰδωλολατρείαν οὐ λέγει, ἀλλ' ἑτέρως αὐτὸ κατασκευάζει ~ων, τοῦτ' ἔστι, πιθανὸν κατασκευάζων τὸν λόγον Chrys.hom.22.3 in Eph.(11.168F); **4.** *exact* a debt μύρια τάλαντα ἐμεθόδευεν Chrys.hom.27.7 in Gen.(4.265E); pass., of debtor, *be compelled to pay* ὅταν καὶ τὸν ὑπὲρ τούτων [sc. τῶν καταβληθέντων] τόκον ~ωνται...ὁ ~θεὶς εἰς ἐσχάτην πενίαν ἀθρόον καταφέρεται ib.42.2(413B,C).

μέθοδος, ἡ, **1.** *pursuit, aim* ἡ καπηλεία τὴν μ. ἐναλλάξασα ἐπισκοπῆς ἔργον ἐπλήρου ἐν εὐτελεῖ προσχήματι M.Thdot.13(p.62.31); **2.** *way, means* ἐπὶ τοῦ κατακλυσμοῦ...οὐκ ἦν μ. σωθῆναί τινα... παρελθόντα τῆς κιβωτοῦ ib.7(p.65.26); hence *means of livelihood* τῆς καπηλείας τὴν μ. ἐνεπορεύετο ib.1(p.61.22); **3.** *stratagem, device* ἐπαναπαλαίσαντας μήτε ἐκ μ. τινὸς ἀλλ' ἐξ ἀληθείας CAnc.(314)can.1; μ. γοήτων ἀπειρημέναις Eus.p.e.5.9(197C; M.21.341A); δαίμονες...πρὸς θάνατον τὰς ψυχὰς μεθόδοις ἀπάτης ἀγκιστρευσάμενοι Meth.Porph.1 (p.503.16; M.18.397D); of Inc., by which God outwitted Satan νομίσαι ἀπάτην τινὰ τοιαύτην μ. ἐπινενοῆσθαι ὑπὲρ ἡμῶν τῷ θεῷ Gr. Nyss.or.catech.26(p.96.13; M.45.68A); οὐκ ἐκ μεταμελείας ὁ θεὸς ἐπὶ ταύτην ἐλήλυθε τῆς σωτηρίας τὴν μ. Thdt.Rom.proem.(3.11); **4.** (cf. μεθοδεύω 4) *debt* ἀπαιτοῦνται...μετὰ τοῦ τόκου τὴν μ. Chrys.hom.41.2 in Gen.(4.412E).

***μεθοράω**, *observe*, Bas.Sel.or.20.1(M.85.218A).

***μεθορία**, ἡ, *banishment*, Philost.h.e.2.18(M.65.480A).

μεθορίζω, *deport, banish*, Philost.h.e.5.2(M.65.529B); med., *go beyond the boundaries* of a monastery, Mac.Aeg.pat.25(M.34.885C); fig., *carry away* τὰς νοητὰς πτέρυγας...αἳ πρὸς τὸ οὐράνιον αὐτὰς [sc. ψυχάς] μ. φρόνημα id.elev.2(M.34.892B).

μεθόριος, *on the borders*; **1.** met., of men or of human nature ὁ σπουδαῖος ὀλιγοδεής, ἀθανάτου καὶ θνητῆς φύσεως μ. Clem.str.2.18 (p.155.18; M.8.1020B); ὁ ἄνθρωπος...μεθόριος τοῦ τῆς ζωῆς ξύλου καὶ τοῦ γνωστοῦ καλοῦ τε καὶ πονηροῦ τεθεὶς Meth.symp.3.7(p.34.10; μεθόριον M.18.72A); μεθόριος τῆς ἀφθαρσίας...καὶ τῆς φθορᾶς ἡ σάρξ id.res.2.18(p.368.13; μεθόριον M.18.312C); οἷς μ. πρὸς ἀρετήν τε καὶ κακίαν ἡ φύσις Gr.Nyss.Eun.3(2 p.41.6; M.45.608D); ἡ ἀνθρωπίνη ψυχὴ δύο φύσεων οὖσα μ., ὧν ἡ μὲν ἀσώματός ἐστι καὶ νοερὰ καὶ ἀκήρατος· ἡ δὲ ἑτέρα σωματικὴ καὶ ὑλώδης καὶ ἄλογος id.hom.11 in Cant.(M.44.1009A); **2.** as fem. subst., *the frontier*, Philost.h.e.2.7(M.65.472A); ib.3.18(509A); τῶν μ. τοὺς κατεψηφισμένους ἀνεῖναι... προστάξαι ib.4.10(524A); **3.** neut. as subst. μεθόριον ἑκατέρου, οὐδὲν ἕτερον ὂν Serap.Man.9(p.33; μεθόδιον M.40.908B); ἐν μεθορίοις ἐστὶ νοητῆς καὶ αἰσθητῆς οὐσίας [sc. ὁ ἄνθρωπος] Nemes.nat.hom.1(M.40.508A); τῶν...ἐν μ. γάμου καὶ ἀγαμίας ἑστώτων Thdt.1Cor.7:28(3.209); of Christ ἦν γὰρ κατὰ τὴν ἀνάστασιν αὐτοῦ ὡσπερεὶ ἐν μ. τινὶ τῆς παχύτητος τῆς πρὸ τοῦ πάθους σώματος καὶ τοῦ γυμνὴν τοιούτου σώματος φαίνεσθαι ψυχήν Or.Cels.2.62(p.184.12; M.11.893B); τὸ μυστήριον...τῆς ἐκ νεκρῶν ἀναστάσεως, τὸ διαλυθῆναι μὲν τῷ θανάτῳ τοῦ σώματος τὴν ψυχὴν...εἰς ἄλληλα δὲ πάλιν ἐπαναγαγεῖν διὰ τῆς ἀναστάσεως, ὡς ἂν αὐτὸς γένοιτο μ. ἀμφοτέρων θανάτου τε καὶ ζωῆς Gr.Nyss.or.catech.16(p.72.12; M.45.52D); μεθόριον γὰρ ὥσπερ τι θεότητός τε τῆς ἀνωτάτω καὶ ἀνθρωπότητός ἐστιν ὁ Χριστός Cyr.Jo.6.1 (4.653D); acc. Arians ἐπειδὴ μὴ ἐχώρει ἡ ἀνθρωπίνη φύσις δι' ἑαυτῆς προσελθεῖν τῷ θεῷ, μεθόριον γίνεται τῆς κτιστῆς καὶ τῆς ἀκτίστου φύσεως ὁ υἱὸς προσάγων τὴν οἰκουμένην Sever.sigill.2(M.63.535); as astrological term, *degree* in zodiacal sign (in Gnostic diagrams), Nil. epp.1.296(M.79.192A) cit. s. λοπόδεικτος.

***μεθορισμός**, ὁ, *going beyond the boundaries* of a monastery, Mac.Aeg.pat.1(M.34.865C).

μεθορμάω, [aor. ἐμεθώρμησαν], *remove from one anchorage to another*, Jo.Mal.chron.5 p.116(M.97.209A).

***μεθύπαρξις**, ἡ, *subsequent coming into existence* οὐκ ἔστιν παρὰ τῷ θεῷ μ. γεννήματος, ἐπειδὴ οὐδὲ προΰπαρξις γεννήσεως ‡Just.qu.et resp.16(M.6.1264B); οὔτε προΰπαρξιν οὔτε μ. ψυχῆς ἢ σώματος Max. ambig.(M.91.1325D); ‡Caes.Naz.dial.140(M.38.1049).

μεθυπάρχ-ω, *exist after, come into being after* κατὰ τὴν ἡμετέραν φύσιν...γέννημα...~ει τοῦ γεννήσαντος ‡Just.qu.et resp.16(M.6.1264B); Leont.H.Nest.4.3(M.86.1657B); ψυχὴν καὶ σῶμα...ἀλλήλων... ~ειν ἀμήχανον Max.ambig.(M.91.1100D); id.ep.12(M.91.489A).

***μεθυπέρβατος**, *transposed, in inverted order*; of words or phrases, Thdt.Ps.44:6(1.890); ib.61:4(1.1013); ib.89:4(1.1250).

μεθυπερβατῶς, *by changing the order of words*, Leont.H.Nest.3.8 (M.86.1625D).

***μεθυπλανής**, *staggering*, Gr.Naz.carm.2.1.1.490(M.37.1006A).

μεθύσκω, **1.** *intoxicate, make drunk*, met. ἐμέθυσσεν ὅλον δόμον ἔνθεος ὀδμή Nonn.par.Jo.12:3(M.43.849C); pass. τοῦ μεμεθυσμένου τῇ οἰήσει...τῶν δαιμόνων Philox.ep.36(p.184); spiritually ὥσπερ ἐμεθύσθη...Δαβίδ, ὅτι ἐκβὰς αὐτὸς ἑαυτοῦ καὶ ἐκστάσει γενόμενος, εἶδε τὸ ἀθέατον κάλλος Gr.Nyss.hom.10 in Cant.(M.44.989D); ὁ δεδεμένος πνεύματι ἁγίῳ καὶ μεμεθυσμένος εἰς τὰ ἐπουράνια Mac.Aeg. hom.15.36(M.34.600C); ib.15.40(604A); **2.** perf. ptcpl. pass., *insolent* μεμεθυσμένων ῥημάτων Men.exc.gent.21(p.462.27; M.113.825B).

μέθυσμα, τό, *drunkenness*, †Bas.Is.178(1.509A; M.31.417C) cit. s. μεθύω.

***μεθυστέον**, *one ought to be drunk*, Clem.prot.10(p.70.8; M.8.209A).

μεθυστικός, *intoxicating*, Clem.paed.2.4(p.181.16; M.8.440B) ∞ Isid.Pel.epp.1.456(M.78.433A).

μεθύ-ω, **1.** trans. = μεθύσκω, met. δεινὸν μέθυσμα φθόνος...οἷς μεθυσθεῖσα ἡ ψυχή, ἐπιλανθάνεται τῆς σοφίας †Bas.Is.178(1.509A; M. 30.417C); αἱ πέρα μέτρου συμφοραὶ...~ουσαι τοὺς πεπονθότας Cyr.Is. 4.5(2.720E); **2.** intrans., **a.** *be intoxicated, be drunk*; met., ref. Abraham's devotion in offering Isaac ~ων τῷ πόθῳ Chrys.hom.14.6 in 1Tim.(11.633A); Thdt.h.rel.2(3.1121); with grief, Cyr.hom.pasch. 5.3(5^2.48E); **b.** of things, *be steeped, immersed* in a liquid; met., of promised land, *be flooded* with good things, id.Am.57(3.312C).

μειαγωγέω, *measure short* ὕδωρ...πρὸς κλεψύδραν...ὅ τις ἂν καὶ ὑπηρέτης μ. δημόσιος Synes.Dion 11(p.267.5; M.66.1149A); id.ep. 148(M.66.1548C).

μείδημα, τό, *smile*, Orac.Sib.1.182.

μειλίχιος, **1.** *gentle*; neut. as subst., *softness* τὸ στερρὸν...τῷ πράῳ συγκεκραμένον, καὶ τὸ ἐν τῷ μ. μὴ συμπεπτωκός Gr.Naz.ep.10 (M.37.40A); **2.** *penitent*, Nonn.par.Jo.19:32(M.43.905A).

***μειλιχόμυθος**, *smooth-spoken*, Gr.Naz.carm.1.2.29.121(M.37. 893A).

μεῖξις, ἡ, v. μῖξις.

μειονεκτ-έω, **1.** *deprive, stint*, Clem.str.7.12(p.55.16; M.9.508A); **2.** pass., *be diminished, be inferior*; of men opp. angels τὸ... ~ούμενον φύσει τε καὶ δόξῃ Cyr.Am.46(3.300A); of Christ, ref. Phil. 2:7 οὐδὲ γὰρ ~εῖσθαί πως, ἢ εἰς τὸ τοῦ χεῖρον ἔχοντος μέτρον καταφέρεσθαι Didym.Trin.3.4(M.39.837A); εἰ δὲ νοοῖτο γεγονὼς ἐν τῇ δούλου μορφῇ ὁ υἱός...οὐδὲ ὅλως ὑπομένει τὸ βλάβος εἰς τὸ εἶναι καὶ ὁμοούσιος αὐτῷ καὶ ἰσοκλεὴς καὶ κατ' οὐδὲν ὅλως ~ούμενος Cyr.Jo.7(4.670B); ref. Heb.2:9 ἔδοξε [sc. ὁ λόγος] δέ πως...αὐτῶν ~εῖσθαι τῶν ἁγίων ἀγγέλων, καὶ τῆς ἐκείνων εὐκλείας ἰέναι κατόπιν id.Abac.39(3.554C).

***μειονέκτημα**, τό, **1.** *smaller quantity of property*, opp. πλεονέκτημα, Tit.Bost.Man.2.8(M.18.1148D); **2.** *deficiency, diminution*, Cyr.Jo.2.1(4.158B); οὐκ ἐκμετρουμένης δὲ τῆς ἀξίας τοῦ πατρός, ποία δεῖξις ἐν υἱῷ τοῦ μ.; ib.1.3(26A); ib.2.6(215E).

μείουρος, *with docked tail*, Synes.ep.148(M.66.1548D).

μειόω, **1.** *lessen, diminish*, ref. Phil.2:7 τὴν τοῦ θεοῦ μορφὴν ἡ τοῦ δούλου μόρφωσις οὐκ ἐμείωσεν Leo Mag.*ep.*28.3(p.14.2; M.*PL.* 54.766A); ‡Cyr.H.*occurs.*10(M.33.1197B); **2.** pass., *become smaller, decrease* ἄλλοι...ἐκ τῆς οὐσίας [sc. φασί] τοῦ πατρὸς γεγεννῆσθαι τὸν υἱόν, οἱονεὶ μειουμένου καὶ λείποντος τῇ οὐσίᾳ ᾗ πρότερον εἶχεν τοῦ θεοῦ Or.*Jo.*20.18(16; p.351.6; M.14.613C); ὡς γὰρ μένων ὁ ἥλιος ὁ αὐτὸς οὐ μειοῦται ταῖς ἐκχεομέναις ὑπ' αὐτοῦ αὐγαῖς, οὕτως οὐδὲ ἡ οὐσία τοῦ πατρὸς ἀλλοίωσιν ὑπέμεινεν, εἰκόνα ἑαυτῆς ἔχουσα τὸν υἱόν Thgn. *hypot.fr.*2(p.76; M.10.240A); Eus.*e.th.*2.9(p.108.33; M.24.917A); of Trin. as consequence of Arian view μηδὲ ἑαυτῇ ὁμοία τυγχάνουσα, ἀλλ' ἐκ προσθήκης χρόνων πληρουμένη...οὐκ ἀμφίβολον...ὅτι καὶ δυνατὸν αὐτὴν μειοῦσθαι Ath.*Ar.*1.17(M.26.48C).

μειράκιον, τό, *lad, stripling*; also *girl* μικρὰ μ. i.e. aged 11, 13 and 15, ‡Sophr.H.*v.m.Cyr.et Jo.*8(M.87.3681C).

***μειράκιος,** *belonging to a girl,* Jo.D.*hom.*12.20(M.96.809B).

***μειρακοειδής,** *of childhood,* ‡Caes.Naz.*dial.*140(M.38.1073).

μείρομαι, *receive a share*; aor. ptcpl. μορήσας *sharing,* Cosm.Mel. *schol.*(M.38.475) in Gr.Naz.*carm.*2.2(poem.)2.3; perf. ptcpl. fem. as subst., v. εἱμαρμένη.

μείων, *lesser, less* ἐν μείω, ἐν μείοσιν *on a lower level, in an inferior position,* of angels τοῖς ἀπείρως...ἐν μείω τὴν εἰκόνα καὶ ὁμοίωσιν ἔχουσιν...τῆς...ἀρρήτου τριάδος Didym.*Trin.*2.7(M.39.565B); of Christ σύνθρονόν τε αὐτοῦ [sc. θεοῦ] καὶ συγκατάρχοντα τῶν ὅλων, ὡς ἐν ὑφέσει τε ὄντα καὶ ἐν μείοσιν διά τοι τὴν πρὸς ἡμᾶς ὁμοίωσιν Cyr.*Ps.* 40:11(M.69.997B).

μείωσις, ἡ, *diminution,* denied of Father, ref. generation of Son οὐδὲ γὰρ σῶμα ἦν [sc. ὁ πατήρ], ὡς ἀπόρροιαν ἢ μ. ... ἐπ' αὐτῷ λογίσασθαι Eus.*e.th.*1.12(p.72.18; M.24.849A); id.*d.e.*4.15(p.181.22; M.22.501C); πάθει γεννῶμεν καὶ γεννώμεθα, τῆς ἡμετέρας φύσεως... τομὴν ὑποδεχομένης...τε καὶ μ. καὶ τὰ ἄλλα πάντα...ἐν θεῷ δὲ οὐδὲν τούτων ἐν τῷ τὸν υἱὸν γεγεννηκέναι ἐνυπῆρξεν Epiph.*haer.*76.31(p.380. 24; M.42.580B); οὐκ...ἐν χρόνῳ τὸ τέλειον ἔσχεν ἡ τοῦ πατρὸς οὐσία, ἀεὶ ὡσαύτως ἔχουσα, καὶ οὔτε προσθήκης τινὸς δεομένη οὔτε μ. ὑποστῆναι δυναμένη Cyr.*thes.*6(5^1.42D); denied of Son τὸ 'μείζων' καὶ τὸ 'πέμψας' τῷ πρὸς τὸν πατέρα ὁμοουσίῳ μ. οὐ ποιεῖ Didym.*Trin.*3.18 (M.39.885C); ref. Inc. and Passion εἴ τις τὸν μονογενῆ...ἐσταυρωμένον ἀκούων τὴν θεότητα αὐτοῦ φθορὰν...ἢ μ. ἢ ἀναίρεσιν ὑπομεμενηκέναι λέγοι, ἀ. ἔ. *Symb.Sirm.*1 *anath.*13; μηδαμῇ μηδαμῶς πεπονθὼς μ. τῆς ὑπερουσίου καὶ θείας μεγαλειότητος, τὴν ἀνθρωπίνην οὐσίαν... ἀνέλαβεν ὁλικῶς ‡Gr.Nyss.*hom.3 in Jo.*(p.137.28); τοὺς κατ' ἔννοιαν μειώσεως ἢ φύρσεως τῶν συνελθόντων διαβάλλοντας αὐτὸν λέγειν τὴν μίαν φύσιν Leont.H.*monoph.*(M.86.1813B).

***μελάγγυιος,** *black-limbed,* Paul.Sil.*Soph.*987(M.86.2156B).

***μελάγκορος,** *with black pupils,* Jo.Mal.*chron.*5 p.103(M.97.192B).

***μελαγκρήδεμνος,** *black-capped,* Nonn.*par.Jo.*6:17(M.43.796C); Paul.Sil.*Soph.*905(M.86.2153B).

μελαγκρήπις, *with black shoes,* Paul.Sil.*Soph.*261(M.86.2130A).

***μελάγριον, τό,** a herb found in the desert, Cyr.S.*v.Euthym.* 38(p.56.30); *ib.*(p.57.7); περιῄει τὴν ἔρημον συλλογῆς ἕνεκεν τῶν αὐτομάτως φυομένων μ. ἐξ ὧν οἱ κατὰ τὴν ἔρημον τρέφονται ἀναχωρηταί id.*v.Jo.Hes.*11(p.209.19); id.*v.Cyriac.*8(p.227.9, v.l. μελάγριαι) one MS reads μελιάγριον throughout.

μελαγχολία, ἡ, 1. *melancholy,* Bas.*leg.lib.gent.*8(p.61; M.31. 589A); **2.** *anger,* Nil.*epp.*2.190(M.79.300B); *ib.*2.233(364B); **3.** *folly* τὰ ἀναγκαίως συμβαίνοντα περιστατικὰ τῷ τῶν ἀνθρώπων γένει εἴ τις οἴοιτο διὰ τὸ εὔχεσθαι μὴ πείσεσθαι, πᾶσαν ⟨ἂν⟩ ὑπερβάλλοι μ. Or.*or.*5. 3(p.309.23; M.11.432B).

μέλαθρον (μέλεθρον), τό, 1. *beam*; **2.** *house, palace* τῶν βασιλικῶν μελέθρων *Pers.*(p.11.8, v.l. μελάθρων M.10.100A); **3.** ref. 3Reg.6:5 (Hebr. יָצִיעַ), *projecting lower story,* hence *side-chamber* μέλαθρα δὲ καλεῖ, τοὺς ἐν κύκλῳ τοῦ ναοῦ δεδομημένους οἰκίσκους Thdt.*qu. 23 in 3Reg.*(1.468); **4.** ref. 3Reg.7:9 (Hebr. כֹּתֶרֶת), *capital* μ. δὲ κέκληκε τὸ νῦν παρά τινων ἐπίστυλον προσαγορευόμενον *ib.24*(471).

μελαίν-ω, *blacken,* fig. τὴν [sc. νύμφην] τῷ κακῷ μελανθεῖσαν Gr. Nyss.*hom.4 in Cant.*(M.44.832B); Αἰθίοπας...εἶναι νοητούς φησιν, τούς...οἱονεὶ ~ομένους τὸν νοῦν Cyr.*Ps.*71:9(M.69.1181C); Hesych.S. *temp.*2.93(M.93.1541C).

μελαμβαφής, *dark-dyed,* †Apoll.*met.Ps.*104:29(M.33.1469D); Geo. Pis.*senar.*(M.92.1733B).

***μελαμπέδιλος,** *with black sandal,* Geo.Pis.*Pers.*3.118(M.92. 1242A).

***μέλαμψος,** *dark*; of red meat opp. white, Cosm.Ind.*top.*11(M.88. 445B).

***μελάμψωμα, τό,** *murkiness,* Ant.Mon.*hom.*87(M.89.1701D).

μέλαν, τό, *black bile, malus appellatus a nigro felle, quod Graeci μέλαν dicunt,* Isid.H.*etym.*10.176.

***μελανδόχος,** *in* or *from an inkpot,* Geo.Pis.*hex.*447(M.92.1470A).

***μελανεία, ἡ,** prob. f.l. for μαγγανεία, Thdr.Lect.*h.e.*1.8(M.86. 169B); cf.Thphn.*chron.*p.94(M.108.280A).

μελανειμον-έω ([*]**μελανημ-**), *be clad in black* ἐρημίτας οἵτινες ~οῦντες CTrull.*can.*42; fig., of one uttering a funeral oration μ. τῷ λόγῳ Gr.Nyss.*Melet.*(M.46.853A); ref. Crucifixion ἐμελανημόνησεν ὁ οὐρανός Ephr.3.474B; ἡ κτίσις πᾶσα ἐμελανειμόνει Cosm.Ind.*top.*2 (M.88.124C).

***μελανεμβαφής,** *dyed black,* met. μ. σκότος ‡Jo.D.*ep.Thphl.*6(M. 95.352D).

[*]**μελανημονέω,** v. μελανειμονέω.

[*]**μελάνι, τό,** *ink, Exorc.*(p.343).

μελανία, ἡ, 1. *blackness*; met., of sin οἱ Αἰθίοπες, οἱ ἐθνῶν τῇ πίστει προστρέχοντες καὶ...τῷ μυστικῷ ὕδατι τὴν μ. ἀποκλυσάμενοι Gr.Nyss.*hom.7 in Cant.*(M.44.909C); **2.** ? snake-*venom* ἀπὸ τῆς τοῦ ὄφεως πληγῆς μελανίᾳ...εὗρεν αὐτὸν τεθνηκότα καὶ τὴν μ. νεμομένην καὶ ἀψαμένης [l. ἀψαμένην] τῆς καρδίας αὐτοῦ *A.Jo.*86(p.193.17).

μελανός, *black,* comp., Or.*hom.11.6 in Jer.*(p.84.22; M.13.376C); Cyr.S.*v.Euthym.*50(p.73.20); neut. plur. as subst., *mourning* Ἀκάκιος δὲ μελανειμονήσας τὸν θρόνον καὶ τὸ θυσιαστήριον μελανοῖς ἠμφίασεν Thphn.*chron.*p.104 (μελανῷ M.108.304B).

μελανότης, ἡ, *darkness*; of complexion, Anast.S.*hod.*2(M.89.64C); met. δόγματα μελανότητος Or.*hom.19.14 in Jer.*(p.170.23; M.13.492A).

***μελανοφανής,** *black in appearance,* Agath.*v.Gr.Ill.*130(p.66).

***μελανωπός,** *black-faced*; of devils, Eudoc.*Cypr.*1.140(M.85.837B).

***μελάνωσις, ἡ,** = μέλανσις, *becoming black* ἡ ἄνω Ἰερουσαλὴμ... ὅπου οὐκ ἔνι ἁμαρτία καὶ μ. Ephr.3.27C; φυλάττουσαν αὐτὰς [sc. τὰς ψυχάς] ἀνωτέρας τῆς ἐκ τοῦ φλογμοῦ τῶν παθῶν μ. ‡Proc.G.*Pr.*8:12 (M.87.1292B).

μέλας, *black*; as subst., *the Evil One, Barn.*4.9; *ib.*20.1.

[*]**μελαχίτων,** = μελαγχίτων, *black-robed*; of Devil, Geo.Pis.*res.* 43(M.92.1377B).

[*]**μέλεθρον, τό,** v. μέλαθρον.

***μελεία, ἡ,** *care,* Oecum.*Apoc.*7:17(p.102).

μελειστί, *limb by limb,* ref. Christ ἐθυμιᾶτο...μ. ... ὅλος ὡς ὑπὲρ ἑκάστου καὶ ὑπὲρ πάντων Cyr.*ador.*11(1.402D).

μελετ-άω, 1. *attend to, study, meditate upon* τὸν νόμον καὶ τὰ προστάγματα τοῦ θεοῦ λέγειν καὶ μ. ἐβούλοντο Just.*dial.*86.6(M.6. 681C); Iren.*haer.*1.6.4(M.7.509A); Chrys.*hom.5.2 in Mt.*(7.74A); αἰτήσας γὰρ νοῦν ἔνθεον...πῶς ἂν γένοιτο...ἐκ τοῦ διαπαντὸς αὐτὸν [sc. θεόν] ~ᾶν id.*hom.2.7 in 2Cor.*(10.438A); μὴ κατοκνῶμεν...προσεύχεσθαι καὶ ψάλλειν, καὶ μ. διδασκαλίαν τοῦ ἁγίου...πνεύματος Nil.*epp.* 3.195(M.79.529C); c. ἐν: ~ῶν καὶ σπουδάζων ἐν ταῖς κυριακαῖς βίβλοις *Const.App.*2.5.4; ~ήσαντες ἐν τοῖς ῥήμασι Chrys.*hom.35.1 in Mt.*(7. 398C); *devise* a plot, Thphn.*chron.*p.201(M.108.517B); **2.** *take thought, take pains* τῶν ματαίων προφάσεων αὐτῶν [sc. Ἀρειανῶν] ἃς τῆς ἀσεβοῦς ἑαυτῶν χάριν αἱρέσεως ἀναπλάττειν ἐν αὐτοῖς μεμελετήκασιν Ath.*decr.*32(p.28.24; M.25.476C); οἱ γὰρ 'κατὰ τοῦ κυρίου καὶ κατὰ τοῦ Χριστοῦ αὐτοῦ' ~ᾶν ἐπιχειρήσαντες id.*Dion.*1(p.46.13; M.25.480A); **3.** *practise* τῆς ψυχῆς ἑαυτὴν ὥσπερ ἐν κατόπτρῳ ὁρᾶν ~ώσης Gr. Thaum.*pan.Or.*11(p.27.13; M.10.1084C); Bas.*hom.*7.1(2.52C; M.31. 281B); τὰ τοῦ Χριστοῦ λόγια ἀναμιμνησκόμενος διηνεκῶς μελέτα *Const. App.*1.4.1; [sc. ἡμῶν] ~ώντων αὐτοῦ [sc. θεοῦ] καταφρονεῖν καὶ ὑπερορᾶν Chrys.*Thdr.*1.4(1.5C); hence perf. ptcpl. act., *accustomed* τὴν σάρκα τὴν ἤδη μεμελετηκυῖαν καὶ εἰθισμένην βαστάζειν τὴν ζωήν Iren.*haer.*5.3.3(M.7.1132A); Gr.Thaum.*pan.Or.*2(p.5.24; M.10.1057A); **4.** *con over* τὰ παιδία...τὰ μαθήματα...δι' ὅλης μ. τῆς ἡμέρας Chrys. *hom.5.1 in Mt.*(7.72B); id.*subintr.*1(1.228B); hence perf. ptcpl. pass., *learnt* τὰς κυριακὰς ἡμέρας...μεμελετημένην εὐχὴν...ἀναπέμπειν θεῷ Eus.*v.C.*4.19(p.124.25; M.20.1168A); **5.** *repeat* τοιαῦτα [i.e. pagan myths] ~ῶντες πῶς ἡμᾶς διαγελᾶτε; Tat.*orat.*21(p.23.11; M.6.853A); Iren.*haer.*1.9.4(M.7.544B); Didym.*Trin.*3.36(M.39.965B); Chrys.*hom. 2.9 in 2Cor.4:13*(3.277E); Bas.Sel.*or.*33.2(M.85.365A); of doves cooing ὀδυρόμενοι γὰρ καὶ θρηνοῦντες περιστεραῖς ~ώσαις ἀπεικασθήσονται Thdt.*Ezech.*7:16(2.727); **6.** *train oneself* μ. εἰς τὸ σῶσαι ψυχὴν τῷ λόγῳ *Barn.*19.10; ~ήσαντος [sc. τοῦ γνωστικοῦ] ἀεὶ τῶν παθῶν κρατεῖν Clem.*str.*7.11(p.48.20; M.9.493A); μ. εἰς πίστιν διὰ πολλῆς τῆς δεήσεως id.*ecl.*27(p.145.14; M.9.712D); **7.** pass., of disaster, *threaten,* Chrys.*Laz.*5.4(1.768E).

***μελετ-έω,** *attend to* ~οῦντες τὸν νόμον *A.Pil.*A 16.4(p.278).

μελέτη, ἡ, 1. *care, attention* οὐ γὰρ ⟨ἐν⟩ μ. λόγων ἀλλ' ἐπιδείξει καὶ διδασκαλίᾳ ἔργων τὰ ἡμέτερα Athenag.*leg.*33.2(M.6.965A); Bas.*ep.* 237(3.365D; M.32.385C); **2.** *practice, exercise* ὁ λόγος...τραφεὶς τῇ μ. καὶ βεβαιωθεὶς τοῖς δόγμασι πρὸς τὸ καλόν Or.*princ.*3.1.4(p.199.9; M. 11.253A); μελέταις τῆς ἀρετῆς...μελέταις ἐπιπόνοις καὶ ἀσκήσεσι καθαιρόμενος ὁ νοῦς Meth.*symp.*9.4(p.118.12; M.18.185B); ἐκ μ.

πολλῆς καὶ ἀσκήσεως ἡ βία καὶ ἡ ἀγριότης τῶν παθῶν ἀσθενεῖς Didym. *fr.*2(M.39.1109B); **3.** *trial, rehearsal* τὸ ὑπνοῦν ἀπὸ τοῦ ἐγρηγορέναι καὶ τὸ ἀνίστασθαι ἀπὸ τοῦ καθεύδειν...θανάτου καὶ ἀναστάσεως μ. Meth.*res.*1.53(p.309.8; M.41.1128C); Gr.Nyss.*virg.*3(p.262.14; M.46.332C); id.*Eun.*1(1 p.71.8; M.45.300D); τί γὰρ εὐτελέστερον, εἰπέ, βάτος ἢ μήτρα παρθενικὴ καθαρὰ τῆς ἁμαρτίας παθῶν; οὐκ οἶδας ὅτι τὰ ἀρχαῖα μελέτη...τῶν νῦν γενομένων ἐστί Thdot.Anc.*hom.*2.2(p.74.26; M.77.1372A); **4.** *usage, habit,* Clem.*str.*2.13(p.144.19; M.8.996C); ἀδιαφορίας μ. Bas.*ep.*190(3.282B; M.32.697A); Ἰουδαίους...καὶ τὴν πονηρὰν αὐτῶν μ. καὶ τὴν φθόνων γεμοῦσαν ψυχήν Chrys.*hom.*5.5 *in 1Cor.*(10.40D); Cyr.*Am.*31(3.281A); **5.** *study, meditation* μ. ἐστὶν ἔργον εὐφροσύνης *Barn.*10.11; λάβε σπέρματα...ἀπὸ τοῦ νόμου...ἀπὸ τῶν προφητῶν, ἀπὸ τῶν εὐαγγελικῶν γραφῶν, ⟨ἀπὸ τῶν⟩ ἀποστολικῶν λόγων, καὶ...σπεῖρον τὴν ψυχὴν διὰ...τῆς μ. Or.*hom.*5.13 *in Jer.*(p.42.30; M.13.313C); Bas.*ep.*207.3(3.311B; M.32.764A); ἐν τῇ μ. τῶν λογίων τοῦ κυρίου διάγειν *ib.*296(434B; M.1040B); Nil.*epp.*1.262(M.79.180B) cit. s. μελιτώδης; μ. δὲ λέγει οὐ τὴν ἐν λόγοις [sc. θεοῦ] μόνον, ἀλλὰ καὶ τὴν ἐν ἔργοις Thdt.*Ps.*118:117(1.1467); as 'sabbath' occupation σαββατιζέτω πνευματικῶς μελέτῃ νόμων χαίρων ‡Ign.*Magn.*9; σαββατισμὸν μελέτης νόμων, οὐ χειρῶν ἀργίαν *Const.App.*2.36.2; κύριε παντοκράτορ...σάββατον ὥρισας...ὅτι ἐν αὐτῷ κατέπαυσας ἀπὸ τῶν ἔργων εἰς μ. τῶν σῶν νόμων *ib.*7.36.1; as monastic duty, Ephr.1.306C; καθήμενος ἐν τῷ κελλίῳ σου, τῶν τριῶν τούτων φρόντισον συνεχῶς· τοῦ ἐργοχείρου, τῆς μ. καὶ τῆς εὐχῆς Esaias *cap.spir.*6(M.40.1208A); purposes of meditation μεγίστη δὲ ὁδὸς πρὸς τὴν τοῦ καθήκοντος εὕρεσιν, καὶ ἡ μ. τῶν θεοπνεύστων γραφῶν Bas.*ep.*2.3(3.72E; M.32.228B); ἡ μ. ἐν φόβῳ φυλάττει τὴν ψυχὴν ἀπὸ τῶν παθῶν Ammonas *opusc.*4(p.476.14); ἡ μ. τῶν λογίων τοῦ ἁγίου πνεύματος τὴν τῶν φαύλων λογισμῶν ὕλην ἐξαφανίζει Nil.*epp.*3.278(M.79.521C); meditation on evil things περὶ ἀπαθείας προϊέμενος λόγους, ἡ τῶν αἰσχρῶν παθῶν μ. ἐν ἐμοὶ ὑπάρχει ἡμέρας καὶ νυκτός Ephr.1.19A; cf. τὸ μέντοι τῆς μ. ἄμεμπτον οὐκ ἄλλοθεν ἢ ἐκ σοῦ ὑπῆρκται, καθαρίσαντός με ἀπὸ τῶν κρυφίων μου Didym.*Ps.*18:15(M.39.1272B); **6.** *subject of meditation* νύκτωρ καὶ μεθ' ἡμέραν τὰς σὰς ἐντολὰς μελέτην ποιήσομαι Thdt.*Ps.*34:29(1.827); hence *subject of thought, plan* ἀπ' ἀρχῆς ἡ μ. τοῦ πάθους [sc. Χριστοῦ], ἐν τέλει δὲ τὸ πάθος ‡Chrys.*pasch.*5(8.263B); *design, plot,* Philost.*h.e.*11.8(M.65.604B); Thphn.*chron.*p.201(M.108.517B).

μελέτησις, ἡ, *study,* Cyr.*ador.*2(1.58C).

μελετητικός, 1. *causing meditation,* Clem.*paed.*2.7(p.193.26; M.8.465A); **2.** of doves repeating the same sound, *cooing,* simile of persons ἐν αὐτοῖς [sc. ἀποστόλοις καὶ εὐαγγελισταῖς] ἀποστοματίζοντες καὶ ταῖς αὐτῶν κεχρημένοι φωναῖς καὶ ἀκραίφνεσι μυσταγωγίαις, ἵν' ὦμεν...ὡς περιστεραὶ μ. Cyr.*Ps.*47:13(M.69.1065B); Nil.*exerc.*20(M.78.745D); neut. as subst., *lament,* Thdt.*Ezech.*16:55(2.792).

***μεληγορέω,** *sing,* Gr.Thaum.*pan.Or.*4(p.9.18; M.10.1061B).

μεληδόν, *limb from limb,* ‡Jo.D.*Artem.*69(p.101.29; M.96.1317B); ‡Jo.D.*hom.*5(M.96.652B); fig. μ. τεμαχίζει τὸν νόμον Mac.Mgn.*apocr.*3.34(p.129.5).

***μέλησις, ἡ,** *care, anxiety,* ‡Gr.Naz.*Chr.pat.*2286(M.38.316A); Thphyl.*exc.gent.*8(M.113.948B; μελλήσεως p.485.25); στενάζειν [sc. τὴν κτίσιν] ἐπὶ τῇ μ. τῆς ἐντεῦθεν ἀποδημίας Chrys.*hom.*14.6 *in Rom.*(Gaume; μελλήσει 9.583C).

μελησμός, ὁ, *care,* Cyr.*Jo.*4.2(4.357E).

μέλι, τό, *honey,* exeg. Is.7:15 ὅτι μὲν γὰρ ἐν σαρκὶ γέγονε κατ' ἀλήθειαν, πειρᾶται πληροφορεῖν, τροφὴν αὐτῷ γεγενῆσθαι λέγων τὴν νηπίοις πρέπουσαν, βούτυρόν τε καὶ μ. Cyr.*Is.*1.5(2.122E); exeg. Is.7:22 τῆς τῶν ἀνθρώπων ἐρημίας μέγιστόν ἐστι τεκμήριον...τὸ μ. ... εἰώθασι γὰρ τοῖς ἐρήμοις ἐμφιλοχωρεῖν αἱ μέλιτται Chrys.*Is.interp.*7(6.87C); ref. austerities of Jo. Bapt. μ. ὀρείου ὑπὸ μελισσῶν ἀγρίων...πικρότατον...καὶ πάσῃ γεύσει πολέμιον Isid.Pel.*epp.*1.132(M.78.269C); cf. ἀκρίς; fig. τῷ λόγῳ παιδεύων τοὺς ἡλκωμένους τὴν καρδίαν, καθάπερ μ. σωτηρίῳ, γλυκεῖ τε ὄντι καὶ δηκτικῷ Clem.*ecl.*31(p.146.19; M.9.713D); ψιλὸν τὸ γράμμα τῆς θεοπνεύστου γραφῆς κηρίον ἂν λέγοιτο· ὁ δέ γε ἐν τῷ γράμματι τεθησαυρισμένος νοῦς, μ. τροπικῶς ῥηθήσεται Nil.*epp.*1.264(M.79.180C); πλήρη...τὰ τῶν γραφῶν κηρία τοῦ μ. Bas.Sel.*or.*37.1(M.85.389A); τὰ [sc. γράμματα] παρὰ τῶν τοῦ σοῦ μ. γεγευμένων συμφώνως λεγόμενα Thdt.*ep.*143(4.1237).

***μελίδριον, τό,** *short psalm,* †Apoll.*met.Ps.*56 tit.(M.33.1389C).

μελιειδής, prob. f.l. for μελιηδής, *honey-sweet*; superl., Jo.D.*hom.*9.1(M.96.724A).

μελίζ-ω, *dismember,* Just.*dial.*120.6(M.6.756B); liturg., *break* eucharistic bread τὸν δεσπότην ~όμενον καὶ διαδιδόμενον καὶ μὴ δαπανώμενον Eus.Al.*serm.*16.2(M.86.416C); Jo.Mosch.*prat.*196(M.87.3081B); *Lit.Jac.*(p.63.27); ‡Sophr.H.*liturg.*9(M.87.3989B) cit. s. μερίς; *Lit.Chrys.*(p.393.23).

μελικηρίς, ἡ, *honeycomb,* †Apoll.*met.Ps.*18:11(M.33.1336C); *ib.*118:103(1500D); *Apophth.Patr.*(M.65.105B).

***μελιπηκτής, ὁ,** *confectioner,* ‡Nil.*perist.*11.16(M.79.928A).

μελίρρυτος, *flowing with honey*; lit., ref. manna αἰθέρος ἄρτον...μ. Nonn.*par.Jo.*6:32(M.43.800A); fig. οἱ τὰ μ. πηγάζοντες νάματα, οἱ τῆς θεοῦ φρονήσεως πνευματικοὶ ῥήτορες †Cyr.*hom.div.*11(5^{2}.379D); met., of religious teaching, *M.Ner.et Ach.*8(p.7.16); Nonn.*par.Jo.*6:68(M.43.804B); †Gregent.*disp.*(M.86.673B); of voices of children crying Hosanna, ‡Meth.*palm.*5(M.18.392C).

μέλισμα, τό, 1. *song*; of a psalm of David, ‡Hipp.*fr.17 in Pss.*(p.145.19); **2.** *melody,* Max.*myst.*24(M.91.708A).

μέλισσα, ἡ, *bee* μ. τινὲς τοὺς προφήτας κικλήσκουσι, μελισσουργεῖον δ' αὐτῶν τὴν θείαν εἶναι γραφήν Nil.*epp.*1.262(M.79.180B).

μελισσήεις, *of bees,* Paul.Sil.*ambo*.88(M.86.2255B).

μελίσσιον, τό, *honeycomb,* Gr.Mag.*dial.*(tr.Zach.)3.26(M.*PL.*77.282C).

μελισσουργεῖον, τό, *hive,* Nil.*epp.*1.262(M.79.180B) cit. s. μέλισσα.

μελισσουργικός, *of bee-keeping* ἡ βουκολικὴ...καὶ μ. τέχναι Clem.*str.*1.7(p.24.27; M.8.732C).

***μελισταγέω,** *drop honey* γλῶσσα μελισταγέουσα *Orac.Sib.*5.240 (μὲν σταγέουσα, μὲν στυγέουσα codd.).

μελισταγής, *sweet as dropped honey,* lit. νᾶμα μελισταγές ἀπὸ πέτρης *Orac.Sib.*5.282; μ. ... ἄρτου θεσπεσίοιο Nonn.*par.Jo.*19:29(M.43.904C); met. ἡδίστης καὶ μ. διδασκαλίας *A.Xanthipp.*8(p.63.18); τὴν Πλάτωνος γλῶσσαν μ. Gr.Naz.*carm.*1.2.10.43(M.37.684A); τὸ ἐν τῷ βάθει τοῦ γράμματος κείμενον μ. νόημα Chrys.*hom.in Ps.115:1–3*(p.351.21); μ. δάκρυον Nil.*epp.*2.96(M.79.244C); καὶ τὴν ὁμιλίαν καὶ τὴν φωνὴν μελισταγής Isid.Pel.*epp.*3.245(M.78.924B).

μελίστακτος, = foreg., met. τοῖς τοῦ θεοῦ...μ. κολαστηρίοις Jo.Carp.*cap.*suppl.(M.85.1858); of Barnabas τῆς ἀθανασίας ὁ μ. βότρυς Alex.Sal.*Barn.*5(p.437C).

§**μελιστής, ὁ,** *master of the mint,* Thphn.*chron.*p.201(M.108.517B).

μελιτόω, *sweeten*; met., Gr.Nyss.*ep.*18(M.46.1068B).

***μελιττοκόμος, ὁ,** *beekeeper,* Cyr.*Nah.*25(3.503D); Thdt.*Is.*5:26(2.205).

[*]**μελιττούτα, ἡ,** = μελιτούττα, *honey-cake,* Cyr.*Os.*33(3.59B).

μελιτώδης, *like honey,* met. βρῶσιν...μ. τὴν ἀνάγνωσιν καὶ τὴν μελέτην τῶν λογίων τοῦ πνεύματος Nil.*epp.*1.262(M.79.180B).

***μελίφθεγκτος,** *honey-tongued,* *Orac.Sib.*4.2.

μελλάκιον, τό, *lad,* Pall.*h.Laus.*18(M.34.1042C; μειράκιον p.42.10).

μελλησμός, ὁ, 1. *delay, procrastination* ὅπερ ἂν εὔξῃ, διαπεραίνειν ἐπείγου...χρῆμα γὰρ ἐν τούτοις ὁ μ. οὐκ ἀζήμιον Cyr.*ador.*16(1.576C); ref. Lc.10:4 χρὴ...μηδὲ χαρίζεσθαι φιλίαις τὸν ἀνωφελῆ μ. id.*fr.4Reg.*5:26(M.69.693C); ref. Creation τὴν [sc. δύναμιν ποιητικήν] ἐξ οὐκ ὄντων γυμνῷ τῷ βουλήματι χωρὶς μ. ἅμα τῷ θελῆσαι αὐτουργοῦσαν ὃ βούλεται ποιεῖν Meth.*creat.*9(p.498.26, v.l. μελησμοῦ; μελισμοῦ M.18.341A); Cyr.*Juln.*1(6^{2}.22A); **2.** *postponement* of an event, id.*glaph.Gen.*6(1.194C).

***μελληστής, ὁ,** *procrastinator,* Cyr.*Nest.*1.3(6.13C; μελλητής p.20.33).

μελλητικός, 1. *inclined to delay, dilatory* τὸ δὲ σεμνὸν καὶ τὸ σχολαῖον ἐκλεκτέον, οὐ τὸ βάδισμα τὸ μ. Clem.*paed.*3.11(p.276.21; M.8.649B); neut. as subst., *readiness to wait* τὸ δι' ὑπομονὴν καὶ τὸ μ. τῆς μακροθυμίας Epiph.*haer.*42.8(p.104.11; M.41.708A); **2.** *future* ἐλλιπὲς τὸ φρόνημα, ὅτι μ. τινα ἐν θεῷ...λογίζεται *ib.*69.76(p.224.20; M.42.325C); οὐδέν τι μ. τυγχάνει αὐτῷ [sc. θεῷ], ἀλλ' ἅμα πάντα ἐν αὐτῷ ἐστι τέλεια *ib.*69.70(p.218.17; 316A).

***μελλητικῶς, 1.** *with hesitation,* ref. God's creative acts οὐκ ἀπὸ βουλήματος μόνον...ὡς ἂν εἴποι τις, μ. ἢ κατὰ μετάμελον Epiph.*haer.*76.35(p.385.8; M.42.583C); ἐλεύθερός ἐστιν ὁ θεὸς πάσης αἰτίας...οὐ μ. οὐδὲ μεταμεμελημένως τὸν υἱὸν μετὰ χρόνους ἔχων *ib.*76.48(p.402.9; 617B); **2.** *proleptically,* ref. Lc.13:28 περὶ μὲν τοῦ 'ἐκβαλλομένους' μ. ἀπεφήνατο *ib.*42.11(p.141.22; M.41.752B); *in the future tense,* Eus.*Is.*9:14(M.24.156C).

***μελλοβασιλεύς, ὁ,** *future king,* Thphn.*chron.*p.366(M.108.877B).

***μελλοπατρίκιος, ὁ,** *one who is to be a patrician,* Anast.Ap.*a.Max.*2.2(M.90.140A).

***μελλοφανής,** *to be manifested, appear in the future* τὸν υἱὸν τὸν θεοῦ λόγον τὸν ἀπαθῆ, παθητὸν μ. Jo.Mal.*chron.*4 p.85(M.97.168B).

***μελλοφωτιστής, ὁ,** *candidate for baptism,* *Ep.*ap.CSyr.*act.*(*ACO* 3 p.95.39; H.2.1369E).

***μελογραφέω, 1.** *write songs,* Isid.Pel.*epp.*4.182(M.78.1273C); **2.** prob. error for μελογράφω q.v., ‡Caes.Naz.*dial.*139(M.38.1044).

μελογράφος, ὁ, *song-writer,* ‡Just.*monarch.*1(M.6.313C); *psalmist,* Eust.*engast.*7(p.25.5; M.18.625B); Eus.*Ps.*135:4(M.24.33B); Thdt.*Ps.*135:6(1.1521, v.l. μεγαλογράφος); οὐ πάντες οἱ μ. ᾖδον οὐδὲ πάντες οἱ ᾄδοντες ἐμελογράφουν Isid.Pel.*epp.*4.182(M.78.1273C).

***μελογράφω**, *ascribe members to* τοὺς μ. τὸ θεῖον καὶ ἀνθρωπόμορφον λέγοντας ‡Caes.Naz.*dial*.169(M.38.1132); μελογραφεῖς (sic) τὸ θεῖον *ib*.139(1044).

μελοποιία, ἡ, *forming of limbs*, Iren.*haer*.5.3.2(M.7.1130B).

μέλος, τό, *limb*; **1.** in gen. ἔξαρθρον μ. Or.*hom.14.18 in Jer*.(p.124.22; M.13.428C); τῶν πάντων μ. τὴν συζυγίαν ἰσχυροτάτοις νεύροις συνέδησεν Const.ap.Gel.Cyz.*h.e*.2.7.17(M.85.1236B); **2.** any *member* or *part* of body 'τὰ δὲ ἐλάχιστα μ. τοῦ σώματος ἡμῶν ἀναγκαῖα' καὶ εὔχρηστά εἰσιν ὅλῳ τῷ σώματι *1Clem*.37.5; πολλῶν ἀριθμουμένων μ. τὰ σύμπαντα ἓν καλεῖται καὶ ἔστι σῶμα Just.*dial*.42.3(M.6.565B); τοῖς μ. τοῖς ὑμετέροις ἐνεφώλευον αἱ ἀντικείμεναι δυνάμεις Cyr.H.*catech*.20.2; οὐχὶ θάνατος ἀλλὰ ῥῆξίς ἐστι μελῶν...ἀπελύθη ὁ Συμεών, ἠλευθερώθη ἐκ τῶν δεσμῶν τοῦ σώματος Gr.Nyss.*Melet*.(M.46.861B); ἔχει θέλημα ἡ ψυχὴ τοῦ ἀποστρέψαι καὶ κωλῦσαι τὰ μ. τοῦ σώματος ἀπὸ κακίστων θεαμάτων καὶ ἀκοῆς πονηρᾶς καὶ αἰσχρᾶς καὶ λόγων ἀπρεπῶν, καὶ ἐπιτηδευμάτων κοσμικῶν καὶ πονηρῶν Mac.Aeg.*hom*.4.3(M.34.473D); ἡ γραφὴ πολλαχοῦ στόμα μαχαίρας ὠνόμασε· καὶ οὐδεὶς οὕτω μέμηνεν ὥστε λέγειν μ. ἔχειν τὴν μάχαιραν, ὃ καλεῖται στόμα ‡Ath.*dial.Trin*.1.20(M.28.1148B); of members ascribed to God μορφὴν γὰρ ἔχει, διὰ πρῶτον καὶ μόνον κάλλος, καὶ πάντα μ. οὐ διὰ χρῆσιν *Hom.Clem*.17.7; but only fig. ἄτοπον...τὰ θεοῦ λεγόμενα μ. μὴ τὸν αὐτὸν ἀκούεσθαι τρόπον [i.e. τροπικῶς] Or.*fr.31 in Lam*.(p.250.8; M.13.625B); ἐπὶ θεοῦ ὅταν λέγωνται μ. ἢ μέρη, ἀνθρωποπαθῶς μὲν λέγονται, θεοπρεπῶς δὲ νοοῦνται ‡Ath.*dial.Trin*.1.6(M.28.1125C); denied of angels ἄγγελος ἁπλοῦς ἐστι, καὶ ψυχὴ καὶ τὸ φῶς· οὐ γὰρ ἐκ μερῶν ἢ μ. σύγκειται *ib*.1.4(1121C); of Christ, ref. eucharist οἱ τοίνυν ἐσθίοντες τοῦ νυμφίου τὰ μ. καὶ πίνοντες αὐτοῦ τὸ αἷμα, τῆς γαμικῆς αὐτοῦ τυγχάνουσι κοινωνίας Thdt.*Cant*.3:11(2.89); **3.** *part* or *faculty* of soul, Or.*hom.6.2 in Jer*.(p.49.15; M.13.325B); τῶν πέντε μ., νοῦ ἐννοίας φρονήσεως ἐνθυμήσεως λογισμοῦ *A.Thom*.A 27(p.142.19); ὥσπερ τὰ μ. τοῦ σώματος πολλὰ ὄντα εἷς ἄνθρωπος λέγεται, οὕτω καὶ μ. ψυχῆς εἰσι πολλά, νοῦς, συνείδησις, θέλημα, λογισμοὶ κατηγοροῦντες καὶ ἀπολογούμενοι, ἀλλὰ ταῦτα πάντα εἰς ἕνα λογισμόν εἰσιν ἀποδεδεμένα, καὶ μέλη ἐστὶ ψυχῆς· μία δέ ἐστι ψυχή, ὁ ἔσω ἄνθρωπος Mac.Aeg.*hom*.7.8(M.34.528B); τοῦ διανοητικοῦ καὶ διακριτικοῦ μ. τῆς ψυχῆς ...ἐπιμελεῖσθαι ὀφείλουσιν...ὡς ὀφθαλμῷ τῆς διακρίσεως μέλει χρώμενοι *ib*.4.1(472D); τὰ μ. τῶν λογισμῶν [sc. τῆς ψυχῆς] *ib*.4.4(473D); of soul and body τὴν ψυχὴν καὶ ὅλην τὴν ὑπόστασιν αὐτῆς ἐνέδυσε τὴν ἁμαρτίαν ὁ ἄρχων ὁ πονηρός, καὶ...οὐκ ἀφῆκεν οὔτε ἓν μ. αὐτῆς ἐλεύθερον ἀπ' αὐτοῦ, οὐ λογισμούς, οὐ νοῦν, οὐ σῶμα, ἀλλ' ἐνέδυσεν αὐτὴν πορφυρίδα τοῦ σκότους *ib*.2.1(464B); **4.** *member*; met., of persons, ref. Mt.18:3 οὐ περὶ μ. ταῦτα λέγων· ἄπαγε· ἀλλὰ περὶ φίλων, περὶ τῶν προσηκόντων, οὓς ἐν τάξει μ. ἔχομεν ἀναγκαίων Chrys.*hom.59.4 in Mt*.(7.598D); esp. of members of Church as Christ's body ἵνα τί διέλκομεν καὶ διασπῶμεν τὰ μ. τοῦ Χριστοῦ...καὶ εἰς τοσαύτην ἀπόνοιαν ἐρχόμεθα, ὥστε ἐπιλαθέσθαι ἡμᾶς, ὅτι μ. ἐσμὲν ἀλλήλων; *1Clem*.46.7; ἐν τῷ πάθει αὐτοῦ προσκαλεῖται ὑμᾶς ὄντας μ. αὐτοῦ Ign.*Trall*.11.2; πῶς δεκτικὴν μὴ εἶναι λέγουσι τὴν σάρκα τῆς δωρεᾶς τοῦ θεοῦ, ἥτις ἐστὶ ζωὴ αἰώνιος, τὴν ἀπὸ τοῦ σώματος καὶ αἵματος τοῦ κυρίου τρεφομένην, καὶ μ. αὐτοῦ ὑπάρχουσαν; Iren.*haer*.5.2.3(M.7.1126A); τοῦ...σοῦ βασιλέως γῆ τε ἅπασα καὶ ὅσα ἐκφύεται· ὡς μ. δὲ αὐτοῦ ⟨τὰ σώματα⟩ τῶν αὐτοῦ θεραπόντων ὑπερβαλλόντως περιέπει καθάπερ ἱερὰ καὶ ναοὺς αὐτοῦ Clem.*fr*.44(p.223.3); τὰ πολλὰ μ. ἕν ἐστι σῶμα, ὅπερ ἐστὶν ἡ ἐκκλησία Ath.*inc.et c.Ar*.5(M.26.992B); Bas.*ep*.243.1(3.372D; M.32.904A); Gr.Naz.*or*.6.1(M.35.721A); Gr.Nyss.*hom.7 in Cant*.(M.44.917C); τὸ βλεπόμενον, ὃ διὰ τῶν καθ' ἕκαστον μ. τῶν συμπληρούντων τὴν ἐκκλησίαν, σωματοποιεῖ ὁ ἀπόστολος *ib.14*(1080B); Chrys.*serm.9.2 in Gen*.(4.691A); τὰ ἀπερρηγμένα τῆς ἐκκλησίας μ. συνάπτειν id.*sac*.2.4(p.35.13; 1.375B); ἡμεῖς ὡς μ. σώματι συναρμολογηθῶμεν αὐτῷ Dion.Ar.*e.h*.3.3.12(M.3.444B); **5.** plur., *bodies, persons* δαίμονες...τοῖς τινων ἐπιφοιτῶντες μ. Tat.*orat*.18(p.20.19; M.6.848A); **6.** *corpse*, Jo.Mosch.*prat*.21(M.87.2868C).

***μελοτομέομαι**, *be cut limb from limb*, Thdr.Stud.*epp*.2.11(M.99.1148A).

μελουργέω (A), *compose music*, Jo.D.*hom*.10.3(M.96.757B); Jo.VI H.*v.Jo.D*.27(M.94.460B).

§**μελουργέω (B)**, *make sweet*, Geo.Pis.*hex*.906(M.92.1504).

***μελούργημα, τό**, *musical composition*, Jo.VI H.*v.Jo.D*.31(M.94.472D).

***μελουργία (A), ἡ**, *musical composition, song*, Jo.VI H.*v.Jo.D*.31(M.94.473A).

***μελουργία (B), ἡ**, *making of honey*, fig. ἀΰλον ἐν σοὶ τῶν φρενῶν μ. Geo.Pis.*Pers*.1.85(M.92.1204A).

μελουργός, *tuneful*, Jo.Mon.*hymn.Chrys*.6(M.96.1381B).

***Μελχισεδεκιανοί, οἱ**, members of sect, holding Melchizedek to be or represent a divine power τὸν Μελχισεδὲκ τὸν ἐν ταῖς γραφαῖς λεγόμενον...μειζότερον τοῦ Χριστοῦ...φάσκουσι Epiph.*haer*.55.1(p.324.1; M.41.972A); φάσκει [sc. Hieracas] ὡς...ἐν τῇ τῶν Μ. αἱρέσει δεδήλωται, περὶ τοῦ ἁγίου πνεύματος ὅτι αὐτός ἐστιν ὁ Μελχισεδέκ *ib*.67.3(p.135.12; M.42.476B); Thdt.*haer*.2.6(4.332).

***Μελχισεδεκῖται, οἱ**, = foreg. Μ. εἰσιν οἱ νῦν προσαγορευόμενοι Ἀθίγγανοι Tim.CP *haer*.(M.86.33B, v.l. Μελχισεδεκιανοί).

μελω, 1. perf. ptcpl. act., *setting* one's *thoughts on* ἐκ δὲ κακῶν σώζοιντο μεμηλότες ἐλπίδι θείῃ †Apoll.*met.Ps*.36:40(M.33.1364B); also in pass. sense, *dear* χῶρον...μεμηλότα θέσπιδι βουλῇ Nonn.*par Jo*.4:20(M.43.777A); **2.** perf. ptcpl. pass. μεμελημένος, *cared for*, hence *dear*, *ib*.1:18(252C); also in act. sense, *giving thought to*, †Apoll.*met.Ps*.36:7(1361A).

μελῳδέω, *sing* ἐν τῇ Σοφίᾳ...τὸ πνεῦμα τὸ ἅγιον τοιαῦτα μ. Meth.*symp*.1.3(p.12.7; M.18.44B); fig., of book of Psalms, Ath.*ep.Marcell*.2(M.27.12C); *play* a tune, fig. ὅτε...ἐδέξατο [sc. ὁ ἄνθρωπος]...τὴν ἁρμονίαν, τουτέστι τὴν δικαιοσύνην, γέγονεν εὐάρμοστον ὄργανον...ὅπως ὁ κύριος...εὐήχως τὴν ἀνάστασιν μ. τῇ σαρκί Meth.*symp*.3.7(p.34.25; 72C).

μελῴδημα, τό, *song*, Isid.Pel.*epp*.1.414(M.78.412D); Jo.VI H.*v.Jo.D*.31(M.94.473A).

μελῳδία, ἡ, 1. *chant, choral song*, of Psalms τῆς πνευματικῆς ἐν ψυχῇ ἁρμονίας τὴν ἐκ τῶν λόγων μ. σύμβολον εἶναι θέλων ὁ κύριος Ath.*ep.Marcell*.28(M.27.40C); Thdt.*h.e*.2.24.9(3.889) cit. s. ἀντίφωνος; of prophetic writings, id.*haer*.5.28(4.476); **2.** *tune* opp. words Ἄρειον...ᾄσματά τε ναυτικὰ καὶ...ὁδοιπορικὰ γράψαι, καὶ...εἰς μελῳδίας ἐντεῖναι ἃς ἐνόμιζεν ἁρμόζειν, διὰ τῆς ἐν ταῖς μ. ἡδονῆς ἐκκλέπτων ...τοὺς ἀμαθεστέρους Philost.*h.e*.2.2(M.65.465C).

***μελῳδίζω**, *make melody*, Ephr.1.161C.

μελῳδικός, *fit to be sung, melodious*, as subst. μ. καὶ ᾀσμάτων Jo.Clim.*scal*.15(M.88.893A).

***μελῳδικῶς**, *melodiously*, Nect.*Thdr*.1(M.39.1821A); ‡Chrys.*ascet.facet*.(1.812C).

μελῳδός, ὁ, *singer*; of psalmist, Didym.*Trin*.2.11(M.39.652A); θεῖος μ. Cyr.*ador*.15(1.522D); id.*Os*.61(3.94D); id.*Jo*.6 proem.(4.579E); Oecum.*Apoc*.1:13(p.41).

***μελωπή, ἡ**, prob. f.l. for μηλωτή, Niceph.Ur.*v.Sym*.25(M.86.3099A).

***μεμαρτυρημένως**, *with abundant testimony*, Cosm.Ind.*top*.10(M.88.416B).

μεμβράνα, ἡ, (Lat. *membrana*) *parchment* μ. τὰ εἰλητὰ κέκληκεν· οὕτω γὰρ Ῥωμαῖοι καλοῦσι τὰ δέρματα Thdt.*2Tim*.4:13(3.695); ἐν βίβλῳ ἀρχαιοτάτῃ ἐγγεγραμμένα ἐν μεμβράναις ἅπαντα ἀπαραλείπτως ἐχούσαις Gel.Cyz.*h.e*.1 proem.2(M.85.1193A); σκυτάλης ἢ μ.· ἡλίῳ μὲν διαφυσσομένων, μηδὲ τὴν ἀφὴν ἄψοφον ἔχειν, νοτιζομένων δέ, μηδὲ τὴν διαρραγὴν σημαίνειν ἢ συστολήν ‡Caes.Naz.*dial*.8(M.38.865); ἐὰν ὁ πρωτοκαλλιγράφος...μὴ περιστέλλῃ καλῶς τὰς μ. Thdr.Stud.*poen*.1.60(M.99.1740D).

μεμελημένως, *carefully*, Meth.*symp*.3.2(p.28.16; M.18.61C); *ib*.8.1(p.80.15; 157A); id.*res*.2.5(M.41.1172B, μεμελετημένως p.338.19).

μεμερισμένως, 1. *separately* οὐκ ἰδίᾳ δὲ καὶ μ. τοῦτο...ἐνεργεῖ, ἀλλὰ συνεργάζεται ὁ πατὴρ τῷ υἱῷ Cyr.ap.*cat.Jo*.6:44(p.252.1); ὅπου γὰρ φύσεως ἡ εἰσάπαν ταυτότης...ἐκεῖ τῆς ἀξίας...ἡ δόξα, οὐ μ. ἐνί τι τῶν ὄντων ἀνατιθεῖσα τυχὸν...ἀλλ' ἴσην μίαν τε καὶ τὴν αὐτὴν τὴν εἰς ἅπαν ὁτιοῦν ἐκτείνουσα δόξαν id.*Jo*.11.8(4.968C); **2.** *partially* ὑποτυπῶν διὰ τῶν ὁλοκαυμάτων τὴν...ἀνάθεσιν οὐ μ. ἀλλ' εἰσάπαν καὶ ὁλοτελῶς id.*ador*.17(1.618C); id.*inc.unigen*.(5¹.704A); **3.** *as a share* τοῖς μὲν τὴν ἀρετήν, τοῖς δὲ τὸν πλοῦτον μ. περιγίνεσθαι Isid.Pel.*epp*.5.186(M.78.1441B).

μεμηνότως, *madly*, ‡Caes.Naz.*dial*.3(M.38.861).

μεμηχανημένως, *by stratagem*, Chrys.*fr.Job* 1:19(M.64.532B).

***μεμοράδιος, ὁ**, = sq., Epiph.*haer*.71.1(p.250.26; M.42.376C).

***μεμοριάλιος, ὁ**, (Lat. *memoralius*) *notary, recorder*, Nil.*epp*.1.86(M.79.120D); *ib*.1.264(180C).

μεμόρι(ο)ν, τό, *martyr-sanctuary*, CChalc.*act*.4(*ACO* 2.1.2 p.115.9; H.2.421C); *ib*.(p.115.3; 421B).

***μεμορίτης, ὁ**, *custodian of a martyr-sanctuary*, CChalc.*act*.4(*ACO* 2.1.2 p.114.34; H.2.421B); *ib*.(p.115.2; 421B).

***μεμοροφύλαξ, ὁ**, = foreg., CChalc.*act*.4(*ACO* 2.1.2 p.114.32; H.2.421B).

[*]**μεμπταῖος**, = μεμπτέος, *to be blamed*, *cat.Mt*.11:27(p.88.6).

***μεμπτικός**, *censorious*, ‡Just.*ep.Zen.et Ser*.1(M.6.1184A).

***μέμυξ, ὁ**, f.l. for βέμβιξ, *buzzing insect*, Epiph.*haer*.41.3(M.41.693B; βέμβικος p.93.12).

μέμφομαι, *complain*, c. ὅτι, Meth.*arbitr*.4(p.155.6; M.18.248C); μ. τῷ δεῖν *complain of the necessity of*, Eus.*Marcell*.1.4(p.20.26; M.24.757A); c. dat. rei, Sophr.H.*v.Anast*.(M.92.1684B).

***μέναυλος, ὁ,** (cf. Lat. *venabulum*) *hunting spear*, Thphn.*chron.* p.187(M.108.484D).

***μενεφώθ,** v. *ἐφώθ.

μενοινή, ἡ, *design, purpose*, Nonn.*par.Jo.*2:1(M.43.761C); *ib.*3:26 (772A); *ib.*6:6(793B).

μερίζ-ω, 1. *divide, separate*; **a.** Persons of Trin. *οὔτε τρεῖς ὑποστάσεις μεμερισμένας καθ' ἑαυτὰς...ἔστι λογίσασθαι, ἵνα μὴ πολυθεΐαν...φρονήσωμεν* †Ath.*exp.fid.*2(M.25.204A); ref. Dion. Al. and others *διαιροῦντας...τὴν μοναρχίαν εἰς τρεῖς δυνάμεις τινὰς καὶ μεμερισμένας ὑποστάσεις καὶ θεότητας τρεῖς* Dion.R.ap.Ath.*decr.*26(p.22.3; M.25.461D); *ὁ μὲν* [sc. *Σαβέλλιος*] *προσώπων συγχέων ὑπόστασιν, ὁ δ'* [sc. *Ἄρειος*] *αὖ ~ων δυσσεβῶς τὴν οὐσίαν* Amph.*Seleuc.*207(M.37. 1590A); *οὐ ξένος ὁ υἱός, οὐδὲ ἀλλότριον τὸ πνεῦμα τοῦ θεοῦ καὶ υἱοῦ, οὐ τόποις μεμερισμένα* Didym.(‡Bas.)*Eun.*5(1.314B; M.29.753A); **b.** Father, ref. generation of Son *θεὸν...οὐ τὴν οὐσίαν καθ' ἥν ἐστιν εἷς, χωριζόμενον ἢ ~όμενον εἰς πλείους...οὐκ ἐν τῷ γεννᾶν τὴν ἰδίαν οὐσίαν* [sc. *~οντα*] Eun.*exp.fid.*1(p.254); *ὀνομάζεται...λόγος, ὡς ἀχρόνως καὶ ἀπαθῶς προελθών, καὶ μὴ μερίσας τὸν φύσαντα* Thdt. *affect.*2(p.63.22; 4.755); **c.** Father and Son *οὐ γὰρ ἐξίσταταί ποτε τῆς αὐτοῦ περιωπῆς ὁ υἱός...οὐ ~όμενος, οὐκ ἀποτεμνόμενος...εἰδὼς πάντα, δυνάμει τὰς δυνάμεις ἐρευνῶν* Clem.*str.*7.2(p.5.26; M.9.408C); in teaching of Dion. Al. acc. Dion. R. *διαιρεῖ καὶ μακρύνει καὶ ~ει τὸν υἱὸν ἀπὸ τοῦ πατρός* Ath.*Dion.*16(p.58.13; M.25.504C); *μὴ μερίσῃς τὰ ἀμέριστα, μὴ σχίζε τὰ ἄσχιστα* Didym.(‡Bas.)*Eun.*5(1.317C; M.29. 760D); *ἡ...οἰκονομία...δι' ἣν ὁ θεὸς ἐμερίσθη ἀμέριστος ὢν* *Disp.Phot.* 1(M.88.537A); cf. *οὐ κατὰ ἀποτομήν, ὡς ἀπομεριζομένης τῆς τοῦ πατρὸς οὐσίας τὰ ἄλλα πάντα ~όμενα καὶ τεμνόμενα οὐ τὰ αὐτά ἐστιν ἃ καὶ πρὶν τμηθῆναι* Just.*dial.*128.4(M.6.776B); *γέγονεν δὲ κατὰ μερισμόν, οὐ κατὰ ἀποκοπήν· τὸ γὰρ ἀποτμηθὲν τοῦ πρώτου κεχώρισται, τὸ δὲ μερισθὲν οἰκονομίας τὴν διαίρεσιν προσλαβὸν οὐκ ἐνδεᾶ τὸν ὅθεν εἴληπται πεποίηκεν* Tat.*orat.*5(p.5.24; M.6.816A); **d.** H. Ghost as united with Father and Son *μὴ ~όμενον* Didym.*Trin.*2.1(M.39.449B); **e.** Christol., ref. Eph.4:10 *οὐδέποτε τοῦ μείναντος ὁ καταβὰς ~εται* Clem.*exc. Thdot.*7(p.108.5; M.9.657C); *μὴ ~ωμεν τὰ ἀμέριστα μήτε τὴν θεότητα διαιροῦντες τοῦ σώματος ὡς δι' εὐφημίαν, ὅταν τὸ σῶμα πεπλασμένον ἐκ κοιλίας λέγηται· μήτε τὸ σῶμα ~οντες τῆς θεότητος ὡς δι' ὁμολογίαν τῆς παρουσίας, ὅταν ἡ θεότης ἄκτιστος δοξάζηται* Apoll.*ep.Dion.*10 (p.260.21; M.*PL.*8.935A); *ἵνα μὴ δύο νοῶμεν υἱούς, ~οντες τὸν ἀμέριστον* Cyr.*apol.Thdt.*3(p.118.26; 6^1.212C); id.*ep.*40(p.24.26; 5^2.114B); *Symb.Chalc.*(p.129.33; H.2.456D) cit. s. διαιρέω; *αἱρετικοὺς ἡμᾶς ἀποκαλοῦντες καὶ εἰς δύο ~ειν υἱοὺς συκοφαντοῦντες τὸν ἕνα κύριον* Thdt. *ep.*82(4.1142); **f.** Christ in eucharist *ὑπὲρ...ἀναριθμήτων λαῶν τὴν ἀναίμακτον θυσίαν προσέφερεν ἀεὶ τῷ θεῷ ἀμερίστως ~ομένην* Eustrat. *v.Eutych.*3(M.86.2277B); *ὁ κύριος ὁ μελιζόμενος καὶ μὴ ~όμενος καὶ τοῖς πιστοῖς μεταδιδόμενος* *Lit.Jac.*(p.63.27); cf. 2.b infra; **g.** of God and man *εἴ τις δὲ διϲταγμῷ εἴσι ἢ παραρρύει, μερισθῇ κατὰ τοῦ θεοῦ καὶ τῆς ἁγίας αὐτοῦ ἐκκλησίας* Ephr.2.243C; *ἀποφοιτᾶν ἔσθ' ὅτε* [sc. *ὁ θεός*] *λέγεται τῶν ἡμαρτηκότων, οὐ ταῖς κατὰ τόπον διαστάσεσι ~όμενος* Cyr.*Zach.*39(3.714E); **2.** *share*; **a.** med., *take a share in* *τὰ μὲν τῶν ἀδελφῶν ἁμαρτήματα μερίσασθαι εὐχόμενος* Clem.*str.*7.12(p.57. 7; M.9.509C); *ἵνα μὴ τὰ ὅπλα μερίσωνται τὴν τῶν κατορθωμάτων νίκην* Proc.G.*1Reg.*17:46(M.87.1101C); *give a share* *θεοῦ ~ομένου πρὸς ἐκείνους* [sc. *τοὺς τῆς ὕλης*] *τὴν δημιουργίαν* Tit.Bost.*Man.*1.30(M.18. 1112C); *~εται αὐτῷ τοὺς κατὰ βαρβάρων ἀγῶνας* Socr.*h.e.*5.2.3(M.67. 568B); **b.** pass., *be shared*, of Christ's body in eucharist *τὸ ἐν ἐκεῖνο σῶμα τοῦ Χριστοῦ πᾶσαν ζωοποιεῖ τὴν τῶν ἀνθρώπων φύσιν, ἐν ὅσοις ἡ πίστις ἐστί, πρὸς πάντας ~όμενον καὶ αὐτὸ οὐ μειούμενον* Gr.Nyss. *or.catech.*37(p.147.5; M.45.96B); **3.** pass.; met.; **a.** of the mind, *be distracted*, Or.*Apoc.*5(p.22); Bas.*reg.fus.*8.3(2.350B; M.31.940A); *χαρᾷ τε ~όμενος καὶ λύπῃ* Nil.*Eulog.*4(M.79.1100B); *ἀπαλλαττόμενος ὁ νοῦς τῶν ἔξωθεν περισπώντων καὶ μηκέτι τῇδε κἀκεῖσε ~όμενος ἀλλ' εἰς ἑαυτὸν νεύων* Thdt.*Ezech.*3:22(2.707); *οἱ ἀμετάστρεπτοι πρός σε ἀτενίζοντες διὰ τὸ μὴ ~εσθαι δεσμῷ σώματος, αἱ ἄϋλοι...ἀγγελικαὶ τάξεις* id.*Cant.*8:13(2.163); **b.** *have, receive in scattered portions* *τῆς καμίνου τὰ λείψανα ὁ κόσμος ἐμερίσθη* Gr.Nyss.*mart.*2(M.46.784B).

μερικός, 1. *partial*; **a.** opp. complete *φθάνειν...ἀπὸ τοῦ ἀπαυγάσματος τούτου τῆς ὅλης δόξης μ. ἀπαυγάσματα ἐπὶ τὴν λοιπὴν λογικὴν κτίσιν* Or.*Jo.*32.28(18; p.474.10; M.14.820A); *πρόσωπον γὰρ κυρίου ἐστὶ θεωρία πνευματικὴ πάντων τῶν ἐπὶ γῆς γεγονότων. φῶς δὲ προσώπου ἐστὶν ἡ μ. γνῶσις τούτων αὐτῶν* id.*Ps.*4:7(p.454) = Cyr.*Ps.* 4:7(M.69.740B); *οὐκ ἄρα ἡ γνῶσις καταργεῖται, ἀλλὰ τὸ μ. εἶναι γνῶσις* Chrys.*hom.34.1 in 1Cor.*(10.311A); *πάσχα ἡμεῖς ἑορτάζομεν, οὐ μ. ἀποφυγὴν θανάτου...ἀλλὰ τελείαν μὲν ἐκ θανάτου λύτρωσιν* ‡Chrys.*pasch.*4(8.259D); *μ. οὔτι που δικαίωσις ἐν Χριστῷ, τελεία δὲ μᾶλλον τοῦ κατασπιλοῦν εἰωθότος ἀπόνιψις* Cyr.*ador.*15(1.535B); *ταύτης ...φύσεως Χριστοῦ...τὸν θεὸν λόγον τί φατε εἶναι, μέρος ἢ ὅλον; εἰ μὲν γὰρ μέρος, καὶ μέρους φύσεως πατέρα λέγετε τὸν πατέρα· μ. γὰρ ὄντος τοῦ λόγου κατὰ τὴν φυσικὴν υἱότητα, καὶ τοῦ πατρὸς ἔσται κατὰ τὴν φυσικὴν πατρότητα μ. ἡ πατρότης* Leont.H.*monoph.*19(M.86.1780D); superl. *μεθ' ὑπερβολῆς δεικνὺς μερικωτάτην τὴν παροῦσαν γνῶσιν* Chrys.*hom.34.2 in 1Cor.*(10.311C); **b.** opp. impartial *ἀπόβλητός ἐστιν ἀπὸ συνοδίας ἥ τε ἀπρεπὴς μάχη καὶ ἡ μ. διάθεσις* Bas.*ascet.*2.2 (2.325B; M.31.885A); cf. 5 infra; **c.** neut. sing. as adv., *in part, partly* *τὸ παιδίον...μερικὸν τῆς τεκούσης χαρακτῆρα ἔχον* *Pers.*(p.17.20; M.10. 108A); **2.** *of a part, partial* *εἰ κεχωρισμέναι ἀπ' ἀλλήλων εἰσὶν αἱ δύο ἀρχαί, ἀνάγκη ἐν μέρει εἶναι λέγειν τὸν θεόν· μ. δὲ τὸν θεὸν καὶ πέρας ἔχοντα οὐκ ἄν τις εὖ φρονῶν ὑπολάβοι* Adam.*dial.*2.1(p.62.11; M.11. 1764A); *περιτομὴ...ἦν μ. ... ἡ δὲ ἀληθὴς περιτομὴ καθ' ὅλης ἐστὶ σαρκός* ‡Chrys.*pasch.*3(8.257E); *οὐκ ἐκ τοῦ συντεθῆναι...εὐλόγως τῆς θείας τελειότητος μερικὴν ἀτέλειαν κατηγορήσετε·...μέρος ὁ λόγος, οὐ μετὰ μ. ἀτελείας λέγεται. καὶ συντιθέμενος...οὔτε ἔλαττον...τὴν ἑαυτοῦ ἄκτιστον οὐσιώδη τελειότητα ἐπιδείκνυται* Leont.H.*Nest.*1.10(M.86. 1444C,D); **3.** *particular* opp. general *τό, ἀποδιδοὺς ἁμαρτίας πατέρων ἐπὶ τέκνα, οὐ γενικῆς ἐστι νομοθεσίας, ἀλλὰ μ. τοῖς ἐπελθοῦσιν ἐκ τῆς Αἰγύπτου ῥηθείσης* Diod.*Ex.*20:5(M.33.1583C); Cyr.*Is.*4.3(2.632E); Proc.G.*Is.*43:14(M.87.2392C); *κοινὸν μὲν...καὶ καθολικὸν...ἤγουν γενικὸν...ἡ οὐσία καὶ ἡ φύσις...ἴδιον δὲ καὶ μ. ἡ ὑπόστασις καὶ τὸ πρόσωπον* Max.*ep.*15(M.91.545A); neut. as subst. *ἀπὸ τοῦ μ. πρὸς τὸ καθόλου* Proc.G.*Is.*46:1(2437C); **4.** belonging to *particular* persons and places, hence *private, localized* *οὔτε μ. οὔτε καθολικὸς κόσμῳ... πόλεμος* Anon.ap.Eus.*h.e.*5.16.19(M.20.472B); *πνευμάτων κινήσεως, ἢ μ. ἢ καθόλου* Bas.*hex.*6.4(1.53B; M.29.125A); Gr.Nyss.*fat.*(M.45. 169A); denied of God and his works, Clem.*str.*6.8(p.463.33; M.9. 285B); *ὁ θεὸς οὐκ ἔστι μ. θεὸς ἀλλὰ πάντων πατήρ* Chrys.*hom.8.4 in Rom.*(9.503C); *οὐκ ᾔδεσαν οἱ Σαμαρεῖται ὃ προσεκύνουν ὅτι τοπικὸν καὶ μ. θεὸν ἐνόμιζον εἶναι* id.*hom.33.1 in Jo.*(8.190C); Thdt.*qu.63 in 3Reg.*(1.507); as subst., of people who conceive of a localized God *πᾶσιν ἐγγὺς εἶναι λέγει τοῖς πανταχοῦ τῆς οἰκουμένης οὖσι...καθαιρεῖ τοὺς μ.* Chrys.*hom.38.8 in Ac.*(9.290C); **5.** *particular, special, individual* *ἐν τῇ κοινῇ ταύτῃ συσκηνίᾳ μερικὰς φιλίας καὶ ἑταιρείας ὁ τῆς ἀγάπης θεσμὸς οὐ συγχωρεῖ* Bas.*ascet.*1.5(2.322C; M.31.880A); *ἡ νοερὰ τῆς ψυχῆς φύσις...οὐ διακόπτεται οὐδὲ πρὸς τὸν ἀριθμὸν τῶν στοιχείων εἰς μ. τμήματα κατακερματίζεται* Gr.Nyss.*anim.et res.*(M. 46.48B); Cyr.*Is.*2.1(2.194B); comp., Bas.*Spir.*41(3.35C; M.32.144B).

μερικῶς, 1. *partly, in part* *εἰ...μέρος αὐτοῦ καὶ ὁμοουσίους ἡμᾶς τῷ θεῷ...εἴη ἂν οὕτως...μ. ἁμαρτάνων ὁ θεός* Clem.*str.*2.16(p.152.13; M.8. 1013A); opp. *ὁλοκλήρως*, Chrys.*hom.10.1 in 2Cor.*(10.506D); Cyr. *Abac.*55(3.570E); *γράφων* [sc. *ὁ Εὐσέβιος*]...*εἰς τὸν βίον Κωνσταντίνου, τῶν κατ' Ἄρειον μ. μνήμην πεποίηται* Socr.*h.e.*1.1.2(M.67.33A); **2.** *particularly* opp. generally *τὸ μὲν ἐπὶ τοῦ Σαμψὼν μ. γεγένηται, τὸ δὲ καθ' ὅλον πληρωθήσεται ἐπὶ τὸν ἀντίχριστον* Hipp.*antichr.*15 (p.12.2; M.10.757C); *of a part, particularly* *ὥσπερ ἀκούοντες τοῦ Παύλου τὸν Χριστὸν παθητὸν οὐ μ. ἠκούσαμεν οὔτε τὴν θεότητα παθητὴν ἐνομίσαμεν, οὕτω καὶ τὸ κτιστὸν καὶ δοῦλον οὔτε μ. λέγεται οὔτε τὴν θεότητα ποιεῖ κτιστὴν οὔτε δούλην* Apoll.*ep.Dion.*9(p.260.6; M.*PL.*8.934B); *ἀπὸ μὲν τῆς θεότητος, μόνον τὸ ἄκτιστον καὶ ἀπαθὲς φάσκοντες εἶναι αὐτοῦ, ἀπὸ δὲ τοῦ σώματος, τὸ κτιστὸν καὶ παθητόν, οὔτε μ. ἀκούειν οὔτε λέγειν τάδε ἐπὶ Χριστοῦ εἰρήκατε, ἀλλ' ἐκ τοῦ ὅλου Χριστοῦ* Leont.H.*monoph.*(M.86.1873A); *in detail, point by point* *τῆς ...ἐκκλησίας τὰ δόγματα, ἅπερ μ. ὑμῖν καὶ διὰ βραχέων ἐκτέθειμαι* Sophr.H.*ep.syn.*(M.87.3196B); *in particular cases* *οἱ μ. τὰς ἐντολὰς ἐργασάμενοι* Marc.Er.*opusc.*4(M.65.1005B); **3.** *with partiality*, acc. Marcion *προσωποληπτῆν* [sc. *θεόν*]...*μὴ τὸ ἀγαθὸν ἴσως πᾶσιν ἀλλὰ μ. ποιοῦντα* Epiph.*haer.*42.11(p.138.13; M.41.748A).

μεριμνάω, *care for, be anxious about*; c. genit., Or.*hom.17.2 in Jer.*(p.145.1; M.13.456C); perf. ptcpl. med., *careful*, Chrys.*hom.47.2 in Mt.*(7.489D); id.*hom.7.1 in Col.*(11.371C); id.*hom.20.4 in Rom.* (9.716E).

μεριμνητής, ὁ, 1. *one who cares for, is anxious about*, *A.Xanthipp.* 24(p.75.15); Jo.Jej.*poenit.cont.virg.*(M.88.1937B); abs., ref. Mt.6:19 *τοὺς φιλοκτήμονας...τοὺς ἁπλῶς μ. καὶ φροντιστὰς...τοὺς φιλοσωμάτους* Clem.*str.*4.6(p.263.1; M.8.1245A); **2.** *student* of astronomy, Hipp.*haer.*4.12(p.44.25; M.16.3075B).

μεριμνητικός, *careful* *τῇ τῶν θείων μεριμνητικῇ ψυχῇ* Nest.*ep.Cyr.* 2(p.32.9; M.77.56C).

μερίς, ἡ, A. *portion*; **1.** of eucharistic bread *ὁ ἱερεὺς ἐπιδίδωσι τὴν μ. καὶ κατέχει αὐτὴν ὁ ὑποδεχόμενος* Bas.*ep.*93(3.187B; M.32.485A); *τῆς τοῦ ἁγιάσματος μ. ἀξιωθήσεται* Gr.Nyss.*ep.can.*(M.45.225C); *προσκομίζεται ἡ προσφορὰ διὰ τὸ κοινωνεῖν τὸν λαὸν ἕκαστον μ.· εἰ δὲ πληθύνει ὁ ὄχλος, χρὴ μελίζειν τὰς μ.* ‡Sophr.H.*liturg.*9(M.87.3989B); *μ. ἅγια Χριστοῦ πληρὴς χάριτος καὶ ἀληθείας πατρὸς καὶ ἁγίου πνεύματος* *Lit.Jac.*(p.62.29); **2.** met.; **a.** *lot, fate*, Or.*hom.14.12 in Jer.*

(14; p.119.11; M.13.421A); *Const.App.*5.4.1; Thdt.*Ps.*27:1(1.774); **b.** of men as God's *portion* ἁγίου οὖν μ. ὑπάρχοντες ποιήσωμεν τὰ τοῦ ἁγιασμοῦ πάντα *1Clem.*30.1; οἱ...σωζόμενοι...διὰ τούτου [sc. τοῦ κυρίου] σώζονται, καὶ ἐν τῇ τούτου μ. εἰσί Just.*dial.*64.3(M.6.624A); τῷ αὐτοῦ υἱῷ...τοὺς Ἑβραίους ἔδωκε [sc. ὁ πατήρ] μερίδα *Hom.Clem.*18.4; μ. γίνεταί τις θεοῦ, τῆς ἐκλογῆς αὐτὸν ἄξιον ἐργαζόμενος, καὶ μετὰ Δαβὶδ διὰ τοῦτο βοῶν, μ. μου ὁ κύριος Proc.G.*Dt.*32:9(M.87.960B).

B. *division, class* τοὺς ταύτην ὁμολογοῦντας τὴν πίστιν ἐγκατέτασσον τῇ μ. τῶν κοινωνικῶν Bas.*ep.*204.6(3.307A; M.32.753C); *party* τοὺς τῆς μ. τοῦ...Μελετίου, τοῦ ἐπισκόπου *ib.*214.2(321B; M.785B); τῆς τῶν εὐσεβῶν μ. Thdt.*Jer.*proem.(2.404); heretical *sect* οὗτοι...τῆς Ἀρείου μ. ὄντες Ath.*syn.*1(p.231.15; M.26.684A); Bas.*ep.*226.2(3.346D; M.844C).

***μερισία**, ἡ, *allotment of portions,* Anast.S.*qu.et resp.*28(M.89.557B,C).

***μέρισις**, ἡ, *division, Dial.Tim.et Aquil.*87 r°; *Chron.Pasch.*p.26 (M.92.117).

μερισμός, ὁ, **1.** *dividing, division*; **a.** theol., τὴν λέξιν τοῦ ὁμοουσίου ἀκούοντες, μὴ...μ. καὶ διαιρέσεις τῆς θεότητος λογιζώμεθα Ath.*decr.*24(p.20.3; M.25.457B); μιᾶς ἀμερίστως...τὰ τρία πρόσωπα πληρούσης θεότητος...θεότης γὰρ μ. οὐχ ὑφίσταται Sophr.H.*ep.syn.*(M.87.3157C); ref. generation of Son ἀπόρροια τῆς τοῦ πατρὸς οὐσίας, οὐ μερισμὸν ὑπομεινάσης τῆς τοῦ πατρὸς οὐσίας Thgn.*hypot.fr.*2(p.76; M.10.240A); οὐδ' ἄρα πάθος καὶ μ. τῆς οὐσίας τοῦ θεοῦ σημαίνομεν, λέγοντες υἱὸν καὶ γέννημα Ath.*Ar.*1.16(M.26.45B); εἴτε γὰρ διαιροῖτο καὶ μερίζοιτο [sc. ὁ πατήρ] οὐκ ἔτι ἀγέννητος εἴη...οὔτ' ἄφθαρτος· τοῦ μ. τὸ τῆς ἀφθαρσίας ἀξίωμα λυμαινομένου Eun.*apol.*9(M.30.844C); in adoptionist view τῷ θεῷ συναφθεὶς ὁ σωτὴρ οὐδέποτε δέχεται μ. εἰς τοὺς αἰῶνας ‡Paul.Sam.*fr.*5(p.339.29); **b.** *schism* οὗ...μ. ἐστιν καὶ ὀργή, θεὸς οὐ κατοικεῖ Ign.*Philad.*8.1; **c.** *separation,* Or.*Jo.*13.62(60; p.295.15; M.14.520B); **2.** *assignment* of functions τὸν ἥλιον...μερισμοὺς ἔχοντα μετὰ τῶν λοιπῶν ἀστέρων Arist.*apol.*6.1; **3.** *sharing, participation* γέγονεν [sc. ὁ κόσμος] κατὰ μ. οὐ κατὰ ἀποκοπήν Tat.*orat.*5(p.5.24; M.6.516A).

μεριστής, ὁ, **1.** *divider* οἱ τῆς συζυγίας [i.e. τοῦ γάμου] μ. Clem.*str.*3.6(p.217.22; M.8.1149C); of Eun. μ. τῶν ἀδιαιρέτων καὶ γεωμέτρης τῆς ἡμετέρας εἰς Χριστὸν σωτηρίας Epiph.*haer.*76.8(p.348.23; M.42.529A); name of a Jewish sect, Just.*dial.*80.4(M.6.665B); cf. *meristae appellati eo quod separent scripturas, non credentes omnibus prophetis, dicentes aliis et aliis spiritibus illos prophetasse,* Isid.H.*etym.*8.4.8; **2.** *partaker* τίνα κοινωνὸν τῶν λυπηρῶν...μ. τῆς εὐφροσύνης; Bas.*ep.*29(3.109C; M.32.312B); οὐ κοινωνὸν ἔχων τῆς θεότητος, οὐ μ. τῆς δόξης...εἷς...καὶ μόνος θεός Eun.*exp.fid.*1(p.254); μ. τῶν ἐμῶν πόνων Chrys.*hom.*1.2 *in Phil.*(11.196A); **3.** ? *parting* of the hair, *Const.App.*1.3.9.

μεριστικός, *fit for dividing, able to divide,* Iren.*haer.*1.3.5(M.7.476A); Epiph.*haer.*76.31(p.380.1; M.42.581D).

μεριστός, **1.** *divided* ἡ τριὰς μεθ' ὧν ἡ πανεπίσκοπος τοῦ θεοῦ δύναμις ἀμερῶς μ. Clem.*str.*3.10(p.227.13; M.8.1169C); εἰ τὴν ὕλην ἐν τῷ θεῷ εἶναί τις λέξει...ὥσπερ ἐν ἀέρι ζῴων ὑπάρχει γένη...μ. ἀνάγκη τὸν θεὸν εἰπεῖν Meth.*arbitr.*6(p.161.3; M.18.252B); neut. as subst. ἡ θεία ἔλλαμψις...τὰ μ. πρὸς τὴν ἑαυτῆς ἁπλότητα συνάγουσα Jo.D.*f.o.*1.14(M.94.860C); **2.** *divisible,* ref. God οὔτε...συντιθέμενος ὡς σῶμα ἢ μ. τις φύσις συντεθήσεται, ἵνα ὡς μέρος ἢ ὅλον, μ. συγκείμενος λογισθήσεται Leont.H.*Nest.*1.1(M.86.1412A); οἴονται...μ. εἶναι τὴν τῆς θεότητος οὐσίαν, καὶ τὸ μέρος αὐτῆς ἐν πατρὶ θεωρεῖσθαι, τὸ δὲ ἐν υἱῷ, τὸ δὲ ἐν ἁγίῳ πνεύματι Eulog.*fr.dogm.*(M.86.2944D).

μεριστῶς, *dividedly, as a result of division, in separate portions* θεότης...ἐν τοῖς προσώποις πληρωτικῶς καὶ ἐντελῶς, οὐ μ. ἤγουν ἐκ μέρους πληροῦσα, ἀλλὰ...μία μένουσα Sophr.H.*ep.syn.*(M.87.3157C).

μεριτεία, ἡ, *apportionment,* Epiph.*haer.*23.1(p.248.5; M.41.297C).

μεροπηΐς, *human,* †Apoll.*met.Ps.*20:11(M.33.1337C).

μέρος, τό, **A.** *share, portion* τὸν...εὔσπλαγχνον πατέρα ἡμῶν, ὃς ἐκλογῆς μέρος ἡμᾶς ἐποίησεν ἑαυτῷ *1Clem.*29.1; ἠξίωσάς με...τοῦ λαβεῖν μ. ἐν ἀριθμῷ τῶν μαρτύρων *M.Polyc.*14.2; Manich. τὸν θεὸν μὴ ἔχειν μ. μετ' αὐτοῦ τοῦ κόσμου μηδὲ χαίρειν ἐπ' αὐτῷ Hegem.*Arch.*12(p.20.8; M.10.1448A).

B. *turn*; κατὰ μέρος *one by one, point by point,* Apoll.*fid.sec.pt.*tit.(p.167; M.10.1104); hence *bit by bit, gradually,* Nemes.*nat.hom.*1(M.40.512A); Chrys.*stat.*3.7(2.48B); Nil.*Magn.*38(M.79.1016B); ἀνὰ μ. *separately* ὅταν ὁμολογοῦσιν ἕνα υἱόν...πεπαύσονται διαιροῦντες...εἰς δύο, ὡς ἕνα μὲν ἰδικῶς καὶ ἀνὰ μ. υἱὸν νοεῖσθαι τὸν...λόγον, ἕτερον δὲ πάλιν ἰδικῶς καὶ ἀνὰ μ. υἱὸν τὸν...ἀναληφθέντα ἄνθρωπον Cyr.*resp.*5(p.586.20; 6^{2}.390D).

C. *part* one takes, *function* τὰ τῶν ἐπάρχων [codd. ἐπαρχιῶν] μ. Eus.*v.C.*3.31(p.92.17; M.20.1092B); τὰ τῆς ἀγάπης ἀποπληρῶσαι μ. *Hom.Clem.*4.1; *ib.*12.6; in periphrasis τὸ θεολογικὸν ἡμῶν...μ. Athenag.*leg.*10.3(M.6.909B); τὸ τῆς θεοσεβείας...μ. *Hom.Clem.*2.25.

D. *part,* opp. whole; **1.** Trin. αἱρετικῶς πυνθάνεσθαι...πῶς δύναται ἐκ τῆς οὐσίας εἶναι τοῦ πατρὸς καὶ μὴ μ. εἶναι Ath.*Ar.*2.32(M.26.217A); εἴ τις τὸν ἀγέννητον ἢ μ. αὐτοῦ ἐκ Μαρίας λέγειν γεγεννῆσθαι τολμῷ, ἀ. ἔ. *Symb.Sirm.*1 *anath.*4; εἴ τις τὸ πνεῦμα τὸ ἅγιον μ. λέγοι τοῦ πατρὸς ἢ τοῦ υἱοῦ, ἀ. ἔ. *ib.*22; μὴ αὐτὸς ὁ πατὴρ ἢ μ. πατρὸς...οὐ τὸ πρωτότυπον ἀλλ' εἰκών †Apoll.*ep.Bas.*1(M.32.1104D); Eun.*apol.*8(M.30.844A); θεὸς γάρ, οὐ μέρος, ὁ υἱός, ἀλλὰ τέλειος ὥσπερ ὁ πατήρ Gel.Cyz.*h.e.*2.12.3(M.85.1249C); οἴονται γὰρ ἴσως μεριστὴν εἶναι τὴν τῆς θεότητος οὐσίαν, καὶ τὸ μ. αὐτῆς ἐν πατρὶ θεωρεῖσθαι, τὸ δὲ ἐν υἱῷ, τὸ δὲ ἐν ἁγίῳ πνεύματι, ὡς ἐκείνης ὑποστάσεως ἐκ μ., ἀλλ' οὐκ ἐν πᾶσι τοῖς τῆς θεότητος ἰδιώμασι γνωριζομένης Eulog.*fr.dogm.*(M.86.2944D); **2.** Christol., in view ascribed to Apoll. τὸν ἄνωθεν ἥκοντα τὸν νοῦν μὴ ἔχειν, ἀλλὰ τὴν θεότητα τοῦ μονογενοῦς τὴν τοῦ νοῦ φύσιν ἀναπληρώσασαν, μέρος γενέσθαι τοῦ ἀνθρωπείου συγκράματος τὸ τριτημόριον Gr.Naz.*ep.*202(M.37.333A); οὐ γὰρ μ. αὐτῆς [sc. ἀνθρωπότητος] προσείληφεν, ὡς Ἀπολινάριός φησι, σάρκα δίχα λογικῆς ψυχῆς, ἀλλὰ πᾶσαν τὴν οὐσίαν, ὅ ἐστι σὰρξ ἐμψυχωμένη Eulog.*fr.dogm.*(M.86.2945B); λέγειν ἐτόλμησας μ. θεοῦ τὴν σάρκα τὴν ἐκ σπέρματος Δαβίδ...τὴν οὐ φαντασίᾳ σάρκα ἀλλ' ἀληθείᾳ, καὶ μετὰ τὴν ἀνάστασιν φανεῖσαν. τοῦ δὲ ἀμεροῦς θεοῦ πῶς οἷόν τέ ἐστιν μ. νοῆσαι, καὶ ταῦτα σάρκα; ‡Ath.*dial.Trin.*5.29(M.28.1284D); πᾶς ἄνθρωπος μ. κόσμου, καὶ οὐδὲν μ. κόσμου αἴρει τὴν ἁμαρτίαν τοῦ κόσμου *ib.*5.2(1265D); πολλάκις τὸ ὅλον ἐκ μ. καὶ τὰ μ. τῇ τοῦ ὅλου κλήσει προσαγορεύομεν, υἱὸν ἀνθρώπου τὸν λόγον ὀνομάζοντες, καὶ κύριον τῆς δόξης ἐσταυρῶσθαι ὁμολογοῦντες Leont.B.*Nest.et Eut.*1(M.86.1289C); Leont.H.*Nest.*1.10(M.86.1444C,D); ταύτης τῆς καθ' ἡμᾶς φύσεως Χριστοῦ...τὸν θεὸν λόγον τί φατε εἶναι, μ. ἢ ὅλον; εἰ μὲν γὰρ μ. καὶ μέρους φύσεως πατέρα λέγετε τὸν πατέρα id.*monoph.*19(M.86.1780D); εἰ ὥσπερ τὴν ψυχὴν καὶ τὸ σῶμα μέρη ὅλου τοῦ ἀνθρώπου ὡς φυσικοῦ εἴδους φαμέν, οὕτω καὶ τὸν λόγον καὶ τὴν σάρκα μ. Χριστοῦ οὐχ ὡς συνθέτου τινὸς μόνον, ἀλλ' ὡς φυσικοῦ εἴδους λέγομεν, εἰπὲ τί τὸ ὅλον τοῦτο εἶδος; *ib.*48(1797A); μέρη δὲ Χριστοῦ ἡ θεότης αὐτοῦ καὶ ἡ ἀνθρωπότης ἐστίν, ἐξ ὧν καὶ ἐν αἷς ὑφέστηκε Max.*ep.*13(M.91.525A); **3.** in gen. οὐχ ὡς μ. θεοῦ ἐν ἑκάστῳ ἡμῶν τὸ πνεῦμα Clem.*str.*5.13(p.384.11; M.9.129A); ref. eucharist ὅλον οὖν ἅπας τὸ ἅγιον σῶμα καὶ τὸ τίμιον αἷμα τοῦ κυρίου δέχεται, κἂν εἰ μ. τούτων δέξηται. μερίζεται γὰρ ἀμερίστως ἐν ἅπασι Eutych.*pasch.*2(M.86.2393C); of angels ἄγγελος ἁπλοῦς ἐστι...οὐ γὰρ ἐκ μερῶν ἢ μελῶν σύγκειται ‡Ath.*dial.Trin.*1.4(M.28.1121B); of the human spirit σπεύδοντι δή μοι πρὸς ὑμᾶς καὶ τῷ πλείονι μ. σὺν ὑμῖν ὄντι Const.ap.Eus.*v.C.*2.72(p.71.14; M.20.1048B); Manich. ὡς ἂν προβάλῃ [sc. ὁ θεός] μέρη τινὰ ἐκ τῆς οἰκείας οὐσίας, καὶ ῥίψῃ τῇ ἐναντίᾳ ἀρχῇ *Disp.Phot.*1(M.88.536D); **4.** *class* or *party,* of followers of Christ τὸ περὶ αὐτὸν μ. *Pers.*(p.9.17); of the sexes μία γὰρ προθυμία ἐν ἑκατέροις τοῖς μ. Pamph.Mon.*Soter.*1(p.113.5); *party* in a lawsuit, Men.*exc.Rom.*3(p.182.3; M.113.868C); **5.** *passage* of scripture, Didym.*Trin.*3.18(M.39.385C); **6.** *premiss* in a syllogism, Chrys.*hom.*39.3 *in Jo.*(8.230C); **7.** prepositional phrases; **a.** ἀπὸ μ. c. genit., *a part of* ταῦτα ἀπὸ μ. ὧν ἤμεσαν ἐκ τῆς ἑαυτῶν αἱρετικῆς καρδίας οἱ περὶ Ἄρειον, ἐστί Ath.*syn.*17(p.244.21; M.26.712A); *ib.*15(p.242.7; 705C); **b.** ἐπὶ μέρους *in particular,* Athenag.*leg.*24.3(M.6.948A); ἀδύνατον εἶναι λέγειν πάντα τὰ ἐπὶ μ. γινώσκειν τὸν θεόν Clem.*str.*6.17(p.512.13; M.9.388B); *in part* εἴ πως τῶν τελείων διαμαρτάνων, τῶν ἐπὶ μ. γοῦν τεύξηται ἡμῖν ὁ λόγος Gr.Thaum.*pan.Or.*3(p.7.10; M.10.1057D); **c.** περὶ μέρους *in particular* τὸν περὶ προνοίας τῶν τε καθόλου καὶ τῶν περὶ μ. λόγον Eus.*v.C.*4.29(p.128.33; M.20.1177C); **d.** ἐκ μ. *in particular,* Athenag.*leg.*24.5(M.6.948B); **e.** ἐν μ. *partly* τὸ πνεῦμα...ἀεὶ πᾶσιν ἐπιπνέον ὁμοίως καὶ οὐκ ἐν μ. Didym.*Trin.*2.1(M.39.449B); *in the case of* ὁ γνωστικὸς...ἀληθεύει, πλὴν εἰ μή ποτε ἐν θεραπείας μ., καθάπερ ἰατρὸς πρὸς νοσοῦντας Clem.*str.*7.9(p.39.15; M.9.476A); *in the class of* οἱ λέγοντες [sc. υἱόν] ὡς ἐν χάριτος μ. λαβεῖν παρὰ τοῦ πνεύματος τὴν εἰς οὐρανοὺς ἀνάληψιν Cyr.*expl.xii cap.*9(p.23.26; 6^{1}.155A); **8.** in local sense; **a.** *region,* Const.ap.Eus.*v.C.*4.11(p.122.18; M.20.1161A); *Const.App.*2.57.18; τὸ μ. Γαλιλαίας Chrys.*hom.*9.4 *in Mt.*(7.135C); **b.** *side* ἐκείνων ἐστὶν τὰ δεξιὰ μ. τοῦ ἁγιάσματος, καὶ ὃς ἐὰν πάθῃ διὰ τὸ ὄνομα· τῶν δὲ λοιπῶν τὰ ἀριστερὰ μ. ἐστίν Herm.*vis.*3.2.1; *Ev.Petr.*9(p.86.11); *Const.App.*5.14.15; **c.** *face* of a coin, Eus.*v.C.*4.73(p.148.1; 1228B).

***μερρά**, ἡ, (Hebr. מָרָה), *bitterness,* Gr.Nyss.*v.Mos.*(M.44.373A).

μεσάζ-ω, **A.** intrans.; **1.** *be in the middle, midway*; of a period of time, Cyr.*hom.div.*17(M.77.1097B); of a point of time, c. genit. ἕως ἐπιφωσκούσης πεντεκαιδεκάτης, ~ούσης τῶν δύο δρόμων νυκτός τε καὶ ἡμέρας Epiph.*haer.*70.12(p.245.26; M.42.365A); of a person ἀρχομένῳ καὶ ~οντι καὶ τελευτῶντι τῆς βασιλείας Eus.*v.C.*1.4(p.9.8; M.20.916B); **2.** *take a central position,* Jo.Mal.*chron.*7 p.185(M.97.296A);

fig. πολιτείας θεοφιλοῦς κατορθουμένης, μακαριότητος δὲ ~ούσης, φίλοι τοῦ δημιουργοῦ καθιστάμενοι Gr.Ant.*bapt*.2.10(M.88.1881B); ἐκβαλῶ τοῦ συνεδρίου τήν τε ἐπιθυμίαν καὶ τὸν θυμόν, ~ειν δὲ τὴν φρόνησιν καὶ τὴν δικαιοσύνην ποιήσω †Jo.D.*B.J*.2(M.96.869B); **3.** *reach the middle*, Chrys.*poenit*.6.1(2.317C); ‡Chrys.*ascens.Ac*.16 (3.775B); **4.** *be a middleman, agent* Ἰωσὴφ ἐμέσασε πράγματος ἐν Αἰγύπτῳ Ephr.1.109B; πᾶς ἐπίσκοπος προῖκα χειροτονείσθω, τοῦ διδοῦντος ἢ λαμβάνοντος ἢ ~οντος τῆς ἱερωσύνης ἐκπίπτοντος Ath. Scholast.*coll*.1.2(p.5); μ. τῇ μοιχείᾳ τῆς πορνείας Jo.Mal.*chron*.4 p.85 (M.97.169A); μ. τῷ γαμῷ *ib*.14 p.356(529C); **5.** *interfere*, abs., *Apophth.Patr*.(M.65.309A).

B. trans.; **1.** *place in the middle*, Evagr.Pont.*or*.112(M.79.1192C); διεῖλεν ὁ θεὸς τὸν ἕνα χῶρον ἀπὸ τῆς γῆς ἕως τοῦ ἀνωτέρου οὐρανοῦ, μεσάσας τὸν δεύτερον οὐρανόν Cosm.Ind.*top*.3(M.88.177B); pass., *occupy a central position*, Sophr.H.*mir.Cyr.et Jo*.70(M.87.3669B); **2.** *divide in two* τὸ καταπέτασμα...ὃ καὶ ~ει τὴν σκηνὴν εἰς δύο σκηνάς Cosm.Ind.*top*.1(M.88.92A); **3.** *interfere, intervene in*, *Apophth.Patr*. (M.65.89D); ἡ ἀγαθοθέλεια ~ει τὴν ἐξουσίαν· ἧττον γὰρ τολμᾷς ἤπερ δύνῃ *Cod.Afr*.55; ὡς βραβευτὴς...μ. τὴν μάχην Geo.Pis.*hex*.527(M. 92.1476A); **4.** *be in the middle of* a task, Ephr.1.218D; **5.** of an agent, *transact* business, *convey* a message ἐὰν προχειρισθῆς ~ειν τι id.1.109B; Jo.D.*parall*.1.28 tit.(M.95.1228D); **6.** *celebrate* Easter *in the middle* διαφόρως παρά τισιν ἐφυλάττετο [sc. τὸ πάσχα]· οἱ μὲν γὰρ προελάμβανον, οἱ δὲ ἐμέσαζον, οἱ δὲ μετέπειτα ἐπετέλουν Epiph.*haer*. 69.11(p.161.3; M.42.220A).

***μεσαιόλιον, τό,** for μαυσωλεῖον, *mausoleum*, Afric.*chron*.17.3(M. 10.85D).

***μεσαπώλειον, τό,** *mule*, fig. *hybrid* οὐκέτι οὐδὲ Ἰουδαῖοι καθαροὶ γίνεσθε, οὐδὲ Χριστιανοὶ εἰς πλήρης, ἀλλὰ μεσαπώλεια Dam.*troph*. 2.8(p.233.14).

μεσαραϊκός, *intestinal*, Melet.*nat.hom*.18(M.64.1220C).

***μέσασμα, τό,** *middle*, Thdr.Stud.*catech.parv*.tit.135(M.99.25D).

***μεσασμός, ὁ,** *central place* οἱ φαρισαῖοι...τὰς προεδρίας, τοὺς μ. ἐπιζητοῦντες Chrys.*hom.62.4 in Mt*.(7.625C); ταῦτα ὁ μεσίτης θεοῦ καὶ ἀνθρώπων γενέσθαι πεποίηκεν, ὁ τὴν ἡμῶν σωτηρίαν ἐν μέσῳ τῆς γῆς τῇ σωτηρίῳ αὐτοῦ τοῦ σταυροῦ προσηλώσει κατεργασάμενος, καὶ τῷ μ. τῆς θείας ταύτης νηστείας χρηστὰς ἡμῖν ἐλπίδας ὑπέφηνε τῆς ἀναστάσεως Sophr.H.*or*.5(M.87.3312D); ‡Sophr.H.*triod*.(M.87.3872B).

***μεσατώριον, τό,** v. *μιτατώριον.

μεσαύλιον, τό, *forecourt* of church, Eus.*v.C*.3.39 tit.(p.74.6; M.20. 1100A); Jo.Mosch.*prat*.105(M.87.2964C).

***μεσαχαρακτήρ, ὁ,** *middle stroke of a letter*, *Ev.Thom*.A 6(p.146).

μεσέμβολος, *interposed, inserted*, ref Mt.27:45 μ. ἦν ἄρα τὸ σκότος [sc. ἐν ἡμέρᾳ μέσῃ] Cyr.H.*catech*.13.24.

[*]**μεσέμβριον, τό,** = μεσήμβριον, cf. μεσημβρία *midday*, *Mir. Artem*.3(p.4.7).

***μεσέμβρος,** = μεσημβρινός, *Pers.capt*.(M.86.3245B).

μεσεύ-ω, *stand midway, act as go-between* θεοῦ λόγος...~ων ἀμηγέπη καὶ συνάγων πρὸς τὸν ἀγέννητον τὴν γεννητὴν οὐσίαν Eus.*l.C*. 12(p.231.14; M.20.1389A).

***μεσηλικιότης, ἡ,** *middle age*, Thdr.Stud.*epp*.2.112(M.99.1373D).

μεσημβρία, ἡ, *midday*, met. ἐν μ. τοῦ βίου φιλοσοφεῖν Synes.*ep*. 154(M.66.1553C).

μεσημβρινός, *belonging to noon* or *noontide* οἱ μὲν ἄλλοι δαίμονες ἀνατέλλοντι ἢ δύνοντι τῷ ἡλίῳ ἐοίκασιν, ἑνός τινος μέρους τῆς ψυχῆς ἐφαπτόμενοι· ὁ δὲ μ. ὅλην περιλαμβάνειν εἴωθε τὴν ψυχὴν καὶ ἐναποπνίγειν τὸν νοῦν Evagr.Pont.*cap.pract*.A 25(M.40.1228C); τὸ πνεῦμα τῆς ἀκηδίας...μ. καλεῖται ‡Nil.*vit.cog*.(M.79.1456D); *Euchol*.(p.583); v. ἀκηδία; μεσημβρινόν *at midday*; fig., ref. Mt.20:5 ὅτε ἐμέσασαν οἱ χρόνοι ἀπ' ἀρχῆς κτίσεως καὶ ἕως συντελείας, τότε μ. ἀπεστάλη Μωϋσῆς καὶ Ἀαρών Cyr.*hom.div*.17(M.77.1097B).

[*]**μεσήτης, ὁ,** v. μεσίτης.

***μεσήτρια, ἡ,** *mediatrix*; of BMV, Ephr.3.525F.

[*]**μεσίαυλον, τό,** = μέσαυλον; **1.** *central space* in a church before sanctuary, Jo.Mal.*chron*.18 p.435(M.97.644A); *Mir.Artem*.34(p.51. 26); **2.** *connecting passage*, Cyr.S.*v.Sab*.32(p.117.12).

μεσιτεία, ἡ, 1. *mediation*; **a.** between God and man; **i.** of Christ τὰ ἐν μέρει τοῖς κατὰ μέρος ἀξίοις διὰ τῆς τοῦ δευτέρου [sc. τοῦ λόγου] διακονίας τε καὶ μ. κατὰ τὸ ἑκάστῳ ἐφικτὸν ἐμπαρέχειν [sc. τὸν πατέρα] Eus.*p.e*.7.15(326A; M.21.549D); id.*Marcell*.1.1(p.7.11; M.24.725A); συνανεκράθη θεῷ τὸ ἀνθρώπινον, τοῦ κατὰ Χριστὸν ἀνθρώπου τὴν μ. ἐργασαμένου Gr.Nyss.*Eun*.2(2 p.355.8; M.45.533A); αὐτὸς καὶ νῦν μεσιτείᾳ τοῦ Χριστοῦ σου δι' ἡμῶν ἐπίχεε τὴν δύναμιν τοῦ ἡγεμονικοῦ σου πνεύματος *Lit*.ap.*Const.App*.8.5.5; θεὸς...ὑμᾶς...καταξιώσει τε τῆς αἰωνίου ζωῆς...διὰ τῆς μ. τοῦ...Ἰησοῦ Χριστοῦ *Const.App*.8.48. 3; ref. Ex.20:19 τὸ χρῆμα τὴν διὰ Χριστοῦ μ. προανετύπου Cyr. *Jon*.1(3.365D); †Diad.*Ar*.7(M.65.1161B); between man and God ὅπως ὁ ἀγαθὸς θεὸς προσδέξηται αὐτὸ [sc. τὸ δῶρον] διὰ τῆς μ. τοῦ Χριστοῦ αὐτοῦ εἰς τὸ ἐπουράνιον αὐτοῦ θυσιαστήριον *Lit*.ap.*Const. App*.8.13.3; εὐπρόσδεκτοι ἡμῶν αἱ δεήσεις...τῇ τοῦ κυρίου γεγόνασι μ. καὶ καταλλαγῇ Oecum.*Apoc*.20:1(p.214); between man and man, *A.Andr.fr*.2(p.38.25); **ii.** of angels ἄγγελον ἄνωθεν πεμφθέντα πρὸς τὸ χαμόθεν τοὺς ἀνθρώπους...ἀναγαγεῖν εἰς οὐρανοὺς τῇ οἰκείᾳ μ. θεομιμήτως Andr.Caes.*Apoc*.40(M.106.344C); **iii.** of BMV ἡ δεξιὰ τοῦ ὑψίστου ἡ ἀπὸ σοῦ σαρκωθεῖσα πολλὰς ποιεῖ τὰς δυνάμεις διὰ τῆς σῆς μ. Jo.VI H.*v.Jo.D*.18(M.94.457B); **iv.** of saints τούτους ἐπικαλοῦμαι τοῦ ...διὰ τῆς μ. αὐτῶν ἵλεών μοι γενέσθαι τὸν...θεόν †Bas.*ep*.360(3.462E; M.32.1100B); τῇ μ. τῶν ἁγίων καὶ βοηθείᾳ τῶν ὑμετέρων εὐχῶν Max. *ambig*.(M.91.1033C); ref. intercessory prayer ἐπίσχες τὴν ὀργὴν κυρίου τῇ μ. Gr.Naz.*or*.16.20(M.35.961C); **v.** of a sponsor at baptism ἀξιοῦντός τε διὰ τῆς ἱερᾶς αὐτοῦ μ. θεοῦ καὶ τῶν θείων τυχεῖν Dion.Ar.*e.h*.2. 2.5(M.3.396A); **vi.** fig., of virginity as reconciling God and man, Gr. Nyss.*virg*.2(p.255.12; M.46.324C); **b.** between men and men παραγγέλλω τε ἐν ὀνόματι καὶ μ. θεοῦ *CIG* 9546 (Rome, saec. ii); τὰ δεόμενα τῆς ἡμετέρας μ. πρὸς τὴν διόρθωσιν Bas.*ep*.278(3.422D; M.32.1016A); **2.** *communication* between communities of monks and nuns διὰ τῆς [sc. τῶν πρεσβυτέρων] μ. ἡ τοῦ λόγου χρεία πληρούσθω id.*reg.fus*.32(2. 376E; M.31.997D); **3.** *means* οὐκ εἶπεν ὅτι ὁ θεὸς λόγος προέκοπτεν ...ἀλλὰ προέκοπτεν κατὰ τὴν μ. τῆς οἰκονομίας Tim.Ant.*Sym*.(M. 86.248B); Max.*myst*.(M.91.661C); Hadr.Papa *ep.Const*.(M.*PL*.96. 1218C); **4.** *intermediate position* ὁ ἀὴρ τῇ ἑαυτοῦ μ. διαλλακτὴς γίνεται τῆς μαχομένης φύσεως ὕδατος καὶ πυρός Bas.*hex*.4.5(1.38B; M.29. 89D); Gr.Nyss.*hex*.19(M.44.81A); of Son τῆς τοῦ υἱοῦ μ. [sc. between Father and H. Ghost] καὶ αὐτῷ τὸ μονογενὲς φυλαττούσης καὶ τὸ πνεῦμα τῆς φυσικῆς πρὸς τὸν πατέρα σχέσεως μὴ ἀπειργούσης Gr. Nyss.*tres dii*(M.45.133C); **5.** = μεσῖτις, *mediatrix*, of BMV ἀκαταίσχυντον πρέσβιν καὶ μ. εὐμενῆ Jo.Mon.*hymn.Bas*.10(M.96.1377B).

μεσιτεύ-ω, 1. *mediate*; **a.** *act as arbiter* or *mediator*, Eus.*v.C*.3. 23(p.88.33; M.20.1084C); τῷ ~οντι τῇ δίκῃ Chrys.*hom.16.3 in 1Cor*. (10.138E); Pall.*h.Laus*.29(p.84.14; M.34.1097D); bet. Father and Son (a *reductio ad absurdum*) οὐκοῦν περιττὸν ἤδη φανεῖται τὸ δι' ἑτέρου μανθάνειν οἴεσθαι τὸν υἱὸν τοῦ πατρὸς θέλησιν, ἀργήσει δὲ πάντως ἡ χρεία τοῦ μάτην ~οντος λόγου κατὰ τὴν ἐκείνων ἀπαιδευσίαν Cyr.*Jo*.1.4 (4.42C); of Christ mediating between God and man ἄνθρωπος φίλος τῷ θεῷ, ~οντος τοῦ λόγου Clem.*prot*.12(p.86.10; M.8.244C); προφήτης ὅμοιον Μωσεῖ τι ἔχων, τὸ ~σαι θεοῦ καὶ ἀνθρώπων Or.*Jo*.6.15(8; p.125.3; M.14.228C); ἵν' αὐτὸς ἡμᾶς...πρὸς ἑαυτὸν ἐπαναγάγῃ διὰ τοῦ υἱοῦ ~σαντος Gr.Naz.*or*.45.22(M.36.653B); acc. Eunomius μηδενὸς δὲ ὄντος τοῦ ~οντος ἄμεσον καὶ συναφῆ τὴν κοινωνίαν εἶναι οὐ καταδέχεται Gr.Nyss.*Eun*.9(2 p.208.20; M.45.805C); εἰ ὑπάρχοι γενητὸς δεῖται πάλιν τοῦ ~οντος Cyr.*thes*.15(5[1].151B); διὰ τοῦτο μεσίτην αὐτὸν εἴρηκεν θεοῦ καὶ ἀνθρώπων, ὡς ἐξ ἀμφοτέρων τῶν οὐσιῶν ἕνα ὄντα· τὸ γάρ τινων ~ον ἀμφοτέρων ἔχεται πάντως id.*deip.BMV* 2(p.24.14; M. 76.269B); of BMV, Ephr.3.532A; of priesthood τὴν ἱερωσύνην ~ουσαν θεῷ καὶ ἀνθρώποις *Supplicatio* ap.Evagr.*h.e*.2.8(p.58.29; M.86. 2525B); **b.** trans., *mediate for* or *in respect of*, of BMV εἰς οὐρανοὺς εἰσαχθεῖσα, ἐξοστρακίζει τοὺς δαίμονας, ~ουσα τὰ πρὸς κύριον Thdr. Stud.*or*.5.2(M.99.721C); οὐ δὲ πάντες οἱ τὸν βασιλέα γνωρίζοντες καὶ τοὺς ἄλλους εἰς αὐτὸν δύνανται ~ειν ‡Jo.D.*conf*.10(M.95.293C); pass., *be reconciled* τοῦ λόγου...συνευχομένου πρὸς τὸν πατέρα τῷ ὑπ' αὐτοῦ ~ομένῳ Or.*or*.10.2(p.320.19; M.11.445D); φυσικῶς τῶν ~ομένων ἐπιθιγγάνοντος [sc. Χριστοῦ]...τήν τε ~ομένην ἀνθρωπότητά φημι καὶ πατέρα θεόν Cyr.*Jo*.3.3(4.266C); of Jews and gentiles οἱ μὲν δι' οἰκέτου ἐμεσιτεύοντο, οἱ δέ, δι' αὐτοῦ τοῦ κατὰ φύσιν υἱοῦ id.*Juln*.3 (6[2].109C); Max.*ep*.12(M.91.468C); **c.** *interpose* between disputants; fig. πανταχοῦ τῆς δικαιοσύνης ἐν τοῖς ἀμφισβητουμένοις ~ούσης Gr. Nyss.*or.dom*.1(p.6.23; M.44.1121D); **2.** *act as go-between* or *agent* τῷ πατρὶ καὶ ἀγγέλοις ~ειν [sc. ὁ υἱός] Eus.*Marcell*.1.1(p.8.8; M.24.728A); Ἀαρὼν...ἐμεσίτευε τῇ ὀπτασίᾳ τοῦ θεοῦ καὶ ταῖς τῶν ἀνθρώπων θυσίαις Ath.*Ar*.2.7(M.26.161B); ὁ θεὸς...τὸν Ἰσραὴλ...ἐξ οἴκου δουλείας ἐξήγαγεν ~οντος τοῦ Μωυσέως Cyr.*Os*.144(3.178A); of a prophet κἂν εἰ ~οιμι τυχὸν ὡς ἄνθρωπος, ἀλλ' αὐτὸς ὑμῖν ὁ τῶν ὅλων διαμαρτύρεται θεός id.*Mich*.4(3.392E); βασιλεύειν οὖν τεταγμένοι παρὰ θεοῦ σύνδεσμοί τε τῆς τῶν ὑπηκόων εὐσεβείας τε καὶ εὐπραγίας τυγχάνοντες...τῇ τε προνοίᾳ καὶ ἀνθρώποις ~οντες Thds.Imp.*ep.Cyr*.2(p.115.6; H.1.1344C); εἴ τις ἐπίσκοπος ἐπὶ χρήμασι χειροτονίαν ποιήσαιτο...εἰ δέ τις καὶ ~ων φανείη τοῖς οὕτως αἰσχροῖς καὶ ἀθεμίστοις λήμμασιν...ἀναθεματιζέσθω CChalc.*can*.2; ὁ πατὴρ...ὁμολογῶν εἰληφέναι ὅπερ ἔλαβε ~σας ὁ πτωχός [sc. between God and the almsgiver] ‡Nil.*perist*.9.5(M.79. 872C); ref. Heb.1:1 οὐδεὶς γὰρ ἡμῖν, ὡς τοῖς παλαιοῖς, ἐμεσίτευσεν Proc.G.*Is*.54:13(M.87.2544B); †Gregent.*leg.Hom*.16(M.86.588D); fig. οὐκ ἔστι διδαχὴ ~ουσα μεταξὺ τῶν αἰσθητικῶν καὶ τῶν αἰσθητῶν

Philox.*ep*.22(p.173); hence pass. *ὁ σὸς λόγος καὶ ἐκ τοῦ νοῦ ἀναφαίνεται καὶ οὐ ∼εται πάθει* Gr.Nyss.*Eun*.4(2 p.54.12; M.45.624D); *ib*. 12(1 p.275.16; 981C); **3.** *assist, promote* a cause or process, c. genit. or dat., ref. Gal.3:19 *∼ων τῇ τῶν ἀνθρώπων σωτηρίᾳ, πρὶν ἢ τὴν σάρκα ἀναλαβεῖν* Eus.*e.th*.2.21(p.130.22; M.24.956B); Bas.*ep*.156.2(3. 245D; M.32.616A); *τῆς πνευματικῆς ∼ούσης ἀγάπης* CCP(381)*ep*.ap. Thdt.*h.e*.5.9.17(3.1033); *θεώσεως...ἧς οἱ μάρτυρες ∼ουσι* Gr.Naz.*or*. 11.5(M.35.837C); Didym.*Trin*.2.14(M.39.696B); Thdr.Mops.*fr.inc*.15 (p.311.5; M.66.992C); *οὔτε γὰρ τῇ ἑνώσει τροπή τις ἢ φυρμὸς ἐμεσίτευσεν* Sophr.H.*ep.syn*.(M.87.3164B); *Ἰησοῦν Χριστὸν...ἐνεργοῦντα τὰ θεῖα ∼ούσης τῆς ἀνθρωπότητος τῆς ἑνωθείσης αὐτῷ τῷ θεῷ λόγῳ καθ' ὑπόστασιν* Honor.*ep.Serg*.1(H.3.1320B); c. acc. and infin. *∼ουσι καὶ ἑτέρους φίλους θεῷ γενέσθαι* Chrys.*fr.in Pr*.15:28(M.64.705D); **4.** *mingle with, supervene upon οὐκέτι μαχομένοις τισὶ συμπλεκόμενοί τε καὶ ∼οντες* Gr.Nyss.*v.Mos*.(M.44.332B); *ἐν ᾗ κάλλους ἐπιθυμία ∼ει τῷ πόθῳ* id.*hom.1 in Cant*.(M.44.772B); Chrys.*Anna* 3.2(4.724C); Thdr.Mops.*Philm*.2(p.269.17; M.66.949C); *τοῦ σαρκωθέντος θεοῦ... μητέρα μονογενῆ καὶ μονότροπον σύλληψιν δεξαμένην...οὔτε σπορᾶς γενομενῆς οὔτε φθορᾶς ∼σάσης* Isid.Pel.*epp*.1.54(M.78.216C); **5.** *be between, intervene*, as a link or a barrier *τὸ πνεῦμα, φωτὸς τύπον ἐπέχον, ἐμεσίτευεν τοῦ ὕδατος καὶ τοῦ οὐρανοῦ* Thphl.Ant.*Autol*.2.13 (M.6.1073A); ‡Nil.*perist*.9.4(M.79.869A); *αὐτῷ νεφέλη* [i.e. at Transfiguration] *πρὸς ἀνθρώπους λαλοῦντι ἐμεσίτευσεν* Bas.Sel.*or*.40.1(M. 85.453B); *occupy an intermediate position*; of marriage in respect of prayer-life on one hand and child-bearing on the other, Clem. *str*.3.12(p.233.3; M.8.1181B); theol. *ὧν* [sc. *ἀγεννήτου πατρὸς καὶ κτισθέντων*] *∼ουσα φύσις μονογενής, δι' ἧς τὰ ὅλα ἐξ οὐκ ὄντων ἐποίησεν ὁ πατήρ* Alex.Al.*ep.Alex*.11(p.26.27; M.18.564C); *τὸ φῶς αὐτὸς* [sc. *ὁ λόγος*] *ἦν...∼όν τε καὶ διεῖργον τῆς τῶν γενητῶν οὐσίας τὴν ἄναρχον καὶ ἀγένητον ἰδέαν* Eus.*l.C*.1(p.198.28; M.20.1324B); *εἰ δὲ οὐκ ἀεὶ... συνῆν ὁ υἱός...ἀνάγκη χρόνον καὶ αἰῶνα πατρὶ καὶ υἱῷ ∼ειν* Thdt.*Trin*. 6(M.75.1152C); *ἐπὶ...τῆς τοῦ υἱοῦ γεννήσεως ἀσεβὲς λέγειν χρόνον ∼ειν* Jo.D.*f.o*.1.8(M.94.812B) = ‡Cyr.*Trin*.7(6^3.9D; M.77.1133A); *ἡνωμένον πατρὶ κατὰ πνεῦμα, ἡμῖν δὲ κατὰ σάρκα, καὶ οὕτω ∼σαντα θεῷ καὶ ἀνθρώποις* Ath.*inc.et c.Ar*.22(M.26.1024B); *ὁ ἀχώρητος χωρεῖται διὰ μέσης ψυχῆς νοερᾶς ∼ούσης θεότητι καὶ σαρκὸς παχύτητι* Gr.Naz. *or*.38.13(M.36.325C); *ἑκατέροις ∼ει, πρὸς τὸν πατέρα αὐτοῦ, θεὸς ὢν φύσει...πρὸς δὲ τοὺς ἀνθρώπους, ἄνθρωπος φυσικός* Epiph.*anc*.44(p.55. 4; M.43.97A); of BMV *χαῖρε κεχαριτωμένη, ∼ουσα θεῷ καὶ ἀνθρώποις, ἵνα τὸ μεσότοιχον ἀναιρεθῇ* Procl.CP *annunt*.5(M.85.444A); *σὺ ∼σασα καὶ κλίμαξ γεγονυῖα τῆς πρὸς ἡμᾶς τοῦ θεοῦ καταβάσεως, τοῦ τὸ ἀσθενὲς ἡμῶν ἀναλαβόντος φύραμα* Jo.D.*hom*.8.8(M.96.713A).

μεσίτης, ὁ, 1. *mediator*; **a.** between God and man; **i.** of Christ, Iren.*haer*.3.18.7(M.7.937B) cit. s. *γνωρίζω*; *μ. ὁ λόγος ὁ κοινὸς ἀμφοῖν, θεοῦ μὲν υἱός, σωτὴρ δὲ ἀνθρώπων, καὶ τοῦ μὲν διάκονος, ἡμῶν δὲ παιδαγωγός* Clem.*paed*.3.1(p.236.28; M.8.557A); Hipp.*Bal*.(p.82.7f.; M.10.605B) cit. s. *ἀρραβών*; *διὰ μεσίτου καὶ ἀρχιερέως καὶ παρακλήτου* Or.*Jo*.2.34(28; p.93.1; M.14.176B); *ἀληθινὸς θεός ἐστιν ὁ υἱός, καὶ πρὸ τοῦ γενέσθαι αὐτὸν ἄνθρωπον, καὶ μετὰ τὸ γενέσθαι μ. θεοῦ καὶ ἀνθρώπων ἄνθρωπον Ἰησοῦν Χριστόν* Ath.*inc.et c.Ar*.22(M.26.1024B); *μέγα τῇ Χριστοτόκῳ τὸ τεκεῖν ἀνθρωπότητα, τῆς τοῦ θεοῦ λόγου θεότητος ὄργανον· ἀρκοῦν αὐτῇ πρὸς τιμὴν ὑπεραίρουσαν τὸ γεννῆσαι μεσίτην τῇ τοῦ θεοῦ συνημμένον ἀξίᾳ* Nest.ap.Leont.B.*Nest.et Eut*.3(M.86. 1392C); *ἑνώσει γὰρ πάντως ὁ υἱὸς ὡς μ. ἐν τῇ ἑαυτοῦ σαρκὶ...ἐμὲ... τῷ πατρί* †Diad.*Ar*.7(M.65.1161B); *μεσήτης θεοῦ καὶ ἀνθρώπων Χριστέ* *Lit.Jac*.(*NBP* 10^2 p.107); **ii.** of an angel *τῷ ἀγγέλῳ τῷ παραιτουμένῳ ὑμᾶς·...οὗτός ἐστι μ. θεοῦ καὶ ἀνθρώπων* *T.Dan* 6.2; **iii.** of BMV *πρόστατιν καὶ μ. πρὸς τὸν ἐκ σοῦ τεχθέντα θεόν* Ephr.3.532D; **iv.** of saints: departed *δι' ἐκείνου* [sc. *μάρτυρος*] *τῷ δεσπότῃ προσάγει τὴν αἴτησιν, τοιαύταις κεχρημένη πρὸς τὸν μ. φωναῖς* Ast.Am.*hom*. 10(M.40.317D); Niceph.Ur.*v.Sym*.145(M.86.3121C); living *διὰ μεσίτου τὸν θεὸν τοῦ οἰκείου θεράποντος ἐπεκαλοῦντο* *ib*.74(3056B); **v.** of clergy *ἐπίσκοποι...οἱ μ. θεοῦ καὶ τῶν πιστῶν* *Const.App*.2.25.7; *δώσεις τῷ ἱερεῖ τὰ ὀφειλόμενα...ὡς μεσίτῃ θεοῦ καὶ...τῶν δεομένων καθάρσεως καὶ παραιτήσεως* *ib*.2.35.3; *εἰ ἀληθῶς βούλει θεῷ δωροφορεῖν, τὸν μ. τῶν δώρων μὴ ἀτίμαζε, οὗ ταῖς χερσὶ διακόνοις κεχρῆσθαι θεὸς φιλανθρώπως ἠξίωσεν* Isid.Pel.*epp*.1.349(M.78.381B); †Gregent.*disp*.(M. 86.784B); *Supplicatio* ap.Evagr.*h.e*.2.8(p.59.5; M.86.2525C); *τοῦ δὲ ἀγγέλου τούτου τύπον ἐπέχει ἕκαστος ἱεράρχης, ὡς μ. θεοῦ καὶ ἀνθρώπων· καὶ τῶν μὲν τὰς κλήσεις ἀνάγων· τῶν δὲ τὸν ἱλασμὸν κατάγων· τοὺς δὲ τῶν ἁμαρτανόντων ἐπιστρέφων* Andr.Caes.*Apoc*.21(M.106.288D); **vi.** of Moses as mediator of Law, Hipp.*Dan*.4.40.5(M.10.660B); **vii.** fig. *εὐχὴ φωτισμὸς ψυχῆς...θεοῦ καὶ ἀνθρώπων μεσίτης* ‡Chrys. *hom.suppl*.6(M.64.464A); **b.** *umpire* of a disputation *ὁ τῶν λόγων μ.* *Hom.Clem*.16.5; **c.** *witness* of an oath, of God *τὸν θεὸν μεσίτην εἰσάγων* Chrys.*David* 3.9(4.782D); **2.** *agent, intermediary ζητήσαις ...εἰ...οἱ ἄγγελοι αὐτοὶ ὄψονται τὰ παρὰ τῷ πατρί, οὐκέτι διὰ μεσίτου καὶ ὑπηρέτου βλέποντες αὐτόν* Or.*Jo*.20.7(p.334.24; M.14.588A); Ath. *ep.Adelph*.5(M.26.1077C); *τί δέ ἐστιν, 'ἐμὲ οὐκ ἐρωτήσετε'; οὐ δεήσεσθε μεσίτου, ἀλλ' ἀρκεῖ τὸ ὄνομα μόνον εἰπόντας πάντα λαβεῖν* Chrys.*hom.79.1 in Jo*.(8.466D); *channel* of the water of life, *ib.46.4* (273E); *προμνήστωρ ὑμῶν ἐγενόμην καὶ τοῦ γάμου μ. δι' ἐμοῦ ἐδέξασθε τοῦ νυμφίου τὰ δῶρα* Thdt.*2Cor*.11:2(3.341); **3.** *one who comes between, occupies an intermediate position*; **a.** of Jo. Bapt. *τὸν πρὸ τοῦ μεσίτου μεσίτην, μεσίτην παλαιᾶς διαθήκης καὶ νέας* Gr.Naz.*or*.21.3 (M.35.1085B); *ὁ βαπτιστὴς...ὁ τῆς ἀρχαίας ὁμοῦ καὶ τῆς νέας διαθήκης μ.* Bas.Sel.*or*.18.2(M.85.229C); **b.** of Son *μήτε αὐτὸν εἶναι τὸν ἐπὶ πάντων θεόν...μήτε τῶν ἀγγέλων ἕνα, τούτων δὲ μέσον καὶ μ.* Eus. *Marcell*.1.1(p.8.7; M.24.728A); *εἰ ἵνα τὰ γενητὰ γένηται, μεσίτου γέγονε χρεία, γενητὸς δὲ καθ' ὑμᾶς* [sc. Arians] *ἐστιν ὁ υἱός, ἔδει καὶ πρὸ αὐτοῦ μέσον τινὰ εἶναι ἵνα κτισθῇ· τοῦ δὲ μ. πάλιν καὶ αὐτοῦ κτίσματος τυγχάνοντος, ἄραρεν ὅτι κἀκεῖνος ἐδέετο μ. ἑτέρου πρὸς τὴν ἰδίαν σύστασιν* Ath.*decr*.8(p.7.24; M.25.'437'(429)A); *εὑρήσει* [sc. *τις*] *πολὺν ὄχλον ἐπιρρεόντων μεσιτῶν καὶ οὕτως ἀδύνατον ὑποστῆναι τὴν κτίσιν ἀεὶ τοῦ μ. δεομένην* id.*Ar*.2.26(M.26.201C); *τὸν ἀμφοῖν ἀναμέσον, θεοῦ τε φημὶ καὶ κτίσεως, ταύτῃ γάρ τοι καὶ μεσίτην αὐτὸν κεκλῆσθαί φησιν* Cyr.*dial.Trin*.1(5^1.410D); **c.** hence *locum tenens* of a see *μηδενὶ ἐξεῖναι μεσίτῃ τὴν καθέδραν κατέχειν ᾗτινι μεσίτης δέδοται* *Cod.Afr*.74(Lat.*intercessor*); **d.** *boundary διομολογεῖται Ῥωμαίοις καὶ Ἀβάροις ὁ Ἴστρος μ.* Thphyl.*exc.Rom*.6(p.226.29; M.113.936A).

***μεσῖτις, ἡ,** fem. of foreg.; **1.** *mediatrix*, of BMV *ἡ νόμου μ. καὶ χάριτος* Andr.Cr.*or*.4(M.97.865A); *θεοτόκος, ἡ τῆς ἡμῶν ἀναπλάσεως καὶ σωτηρίας μ.* Niceph.Ur.*v.Sym*.145(M.86.3121B); **2.** *mean* between two extremes, ‡Max.*cap.al*.223(M.90.1453C).

***μεσιτολογέω,** *speak as a mediator*; of BMV, ‡Jo.D.*hom*.5(M.96. 660A).

μεσοδάκτυλον, τό, *space between two fingers* or *toes*, *M.Tar*.9 (p.470).

***μεσοδίκτυος,** *in the midst of a net*, Bas.Sel.*or*.8.2(M.85.121A).

***μεσόδμητος,** *built in μ. ... μολύβδῳ* Paul.Sil.*Soph*.479(M.86. 2138A).

μεσόθεν, *from the middle*; *ἐν μ.* *in the midst ἐν μ. τῆς ἁγίας συνόδου* Leont.Abb.*v.Gr.Agr*.73(M.98.677B).

***μεσόκληρος,** ? for *μεσόσκληρος*, *hard in the middle*, Geo.Pis.*hex*. 1224(M.92.1528A).

μεσολαβ-έω, A. trans.; **1.** in wrestling, *grip round the waist*; fig., Nil.*Magn*.60(M.79.1049B); **2.** *intercept*, Socr.*h.e*.7.20.9(M.67.780C); hence *divide in two οἱ δὲ ∼οῦσι τὸν χρόνον, δὶς τῆς ἑβδομάδος παρατιθέμενοι τράπεζαν* ‡Nil.*narr*.3(M.79.617A); **3.** met., *interrupt, impede*, Chrys.*pan.Barl*.5(2.696C); *∼ουμένη δὲ λογισμοῖς προσευχή* Nil.*Magn*.28(1004C); **4.** *separate οὐδὲν γὰρ ὅλως τὸ ∼οῦν πατέρα καὶ τὸν υἱόν, ὅσον εἰς οὐσίας ταυτότητά φαμεν* Cyr.*Jo*.6(4.571E); *διαστήματος οὐδενὸς ὄντος μεταξὺ τοῦ ∼οῦντος τὸ εἶναι τοῦ πατρὸς καὶ τὴν γέννησιν τοῦ υἱοῦ* id.*thes*.7(5^1.58E); *νόμος δὲ παρεισῆλθε τὴν ἀρχαίαν καὶ τὴν ὑστάτην μίαν οὖσαν ∼ήσας πολιτείαν* Nil.ap.Proc.G.*Cant*.2:14(M. 87.1609B); **5.** *place in the middle ∼ήσας καταπέτασμα μεσόθεν* (v.l. *ἔσωθεν*) *ποιεῖ αὐτὴν* [sc. *τὴν σκηνήν*] *χώρους δύο* Cosm.Ind.*top*.3(M.88. 160D); pass., *be in the middle ∼ούμενον δὲ τὸ Ἰουδαίων ἔθνος, ποτὲ μὲν ὑπὸ Σύρων ἐπολεμεῖτο, ποτὲ δὲ ὑπὸ Πτολεμαίων* Eus.*Is*.19:23(M. 24.236A); ref. virtue as the mean, Gr.Nyss.*v.Mos*.(M.44.420B); of a group *τὰ ἔθνη καὶ τὰς μεταξὺ τῶν ἐθνῶν ∼ουμένας τοῦ θεοῦ ἐκκλησίας* Eus.*Is*.49:1(428D); *be flanked γραμμὴ μία, ∼ουμένη ὑπὸ κεντημάτων δύο εἴτουν στιγμῶν* Epiph.*mens*.8(M.43.248C).

B. intrans.; *intervene*, Isid.Pel.*epp*.2.189(M.78.640A); *τὸ στερέωμα ...μερίζον τὰ ὕδατα ἄνωθεν καὶ κάτωθεν μεσολαβοῦν* Cosm.Ind.*top*.3 (M.88.141C); hence **a.** *form a barrier ἐσχήκαμεν...εἰρήνην τὴν πρὸς τὸν πατέρα...τὴν ∼οῦσάν τε καὶ διϊστῶσαν ἡμᾶς τῶν τρόπων ἀκαθαρσίαν ἀπονιψάμενοι* Cyr.*glaph.Gen*.2(1.61D); id.*Is*.5.2(2.779B); pres. ptcpl. as subst., *gulf, barrier εἰ δὲ ἀκατάληπτόν τι τὸ ∼οῦν εὑρίσκεται, τί τὰ τῆς ἡμετέρας φύσεως ἡττήματα κανόνα καὶ σταθμὸν ὁρίζουσι τῷ θεῷ;* id.*Jo*.11.11(4.996E); *ἔστι πολὺ τὸ ∼οῦν καὶ ἀσυγκρίτοις διαφοραῖς τῆς τοῦ σωτῆρος ἡμῶν εὐκλείας καὶ ὑπεροχῆς ἀποτειχίζον τὰ καθ' ἡμᾶς* id.*ep*.1(p.14.29; 5^2.7D); *λέλυται γὰρ τὸ ∼οῦν ἐν Χριστῷ, καὶ οἱ πάλαι διεστηκότες...συνειςδυόμεθα δι' αὐτοῦ τε καὶ ἐν αὐτῷ τῷ θεῷ* id.*ador*.3(1.99C); **b.** *act as mediator* or *agent τεθαυματούργηκε γὰρ ἐν Αἰγύπτῳ ∼οῦντος μὲν τοῦ Μωσέως* id.*Is*.5.5(2.881B); *οἰκειότητα...τὴν διὰ νόμου...διακονοῦντος Μωσέως καὶ ∼ούντων ἀγγέλων* id.*Os*.28(3.51E); *ἐβασιλεύετο...ὁ Ἰσραὴλ ἐν ἀρχαῖς ὑπὸ θεοῦ, ∼ούντων ἁγίων* id.*Mich*.46(3.434E); id.*glaph.Gen*.6(1.206E); *αὐτὸς ἡμῖν δι' ἑαυτοῦ λελάληκεν ὁ υἱός· οὐ ∼οῦντος ἔτι προφήτου καὶ φωνῆς ἁγίων* id.*Heb*.1:1(p.364.15); of things, *be the means of obtaining τὰ τῶν χαρισμάτων ἐξαίρετα ∼οῦσι πόνοι* id.*glaph.Ex*.3(1.311E).

***μεσονήστιμος,** *in the middle of the fast* (mid-Lent), Germ.CP *or.* 1 tit.(M.98.221B).

***μεσονυκτέω,** pres. ptcpl. prob. f.l. for *μέσων νυκτῶν* Chrys.*hom.* 83.1 *in Jo.*(8.489C).

***μεσονυκτικός,** = *μεσονύκτιος, of* or *at midnight μ. εὐχάς* Leont. Abb.*v.Gr.Agr.*54(M.98.644C); of evil spirits, *Euchol.*(p.583).

***μεσοπελαγίζω,** *be in the middle of the sea, T.Job* 18(p.114.23).

***μεσοπέλαγος, τό,** *mid-ocean,* Jo.Mosch.*prat.*174(M.87.3041D).

***μεσοπεντηκοστή, ἡ,** *Mid-Pentecost, the fourth week in Eastertide,* feast kept from fourth day after third Sunday after Easter until fourth day of following week; ref. Jo.7:14, Amph.*mesopent.* tit.(M.39.120); Leont.B.*mesopent.*tit.(M.86.1976B); Leont.N.*serm.*2 (M.93.1584B); *Catech.Stud.*10(M.99.1700D).

***μεσοπετής,** *flying in the middle*; hence of angels, *of intermediate rank,* Dion.Ar.*c.h.*7.3(M.3.209B); Max.*schol.c.h.*7.3(M.4.72C).

μέσος, 1. *middle, in the middle*; **a.** of space, plur. *μέσοις αὐτοῖς τυραννικοῖς οἴκοις...τραφῆναι* Eus.*v.C.*1.12(p.13.9; M.20.925A); *ἐν μέσοις...τοῖς πολεμίοις* Chrys.*hom.*31.2 *in Rom.*(9.747C); **b.** of time, of noonday prayer *τὴν μ. τῶν τριῶν εὐχὴν τὴν...παρὰ τοῦ Δαυὶδ λεγομένην* Or.*or.*12(p.325.10; M.11.453A); of Lord's Prayer in liturgy, *Lit.Bas.*(p.338.2); **2.** *intermediate between,* c. genit.; of Christ *μ. ἑστὼς θεοῦ τοῦ ἀγενήτου καὶ τῶν μετ' αὐτὸν γενητῶν* Eus. *d.e.*4.10(p.167.34; M.22.280B); acc. Arians *θέλων ὁ θεὸς τὴν γενητὴν κτίσαι φύσιν...ποιεῖ καὶ κτίζει πρώτως μόνος μόνον ἕνα, καὶ καλεῖ τοῦτον υἱὸν καὶ λόγον, ἵνα, τούτου μ. γενομένου, οὕτω λοιπὸν καὶ τὰ πάντα δι' αὐτοῦ γενέσθαι δυνηθῇ* Ath.*Ar.*2.24(M.26.200A); of angels *οὔτε θεοὺς οὔτε δαίμονας ἀποκαλεῖν ἄξιοί, μέσας δὲ οὔσας θεοῦ καὶ δαιμόνων ...μέση προσηγορία ἀγγέλους θεοῦ καὶ πνεύματα λειτουργικά* Eus.*p.e.* 4.5(142A; M.21.248C); of Jo. Bapt. *ὁ μ. τῆς παλαιᾶς καὶ καινῆς διαθήκης* Cosm.Ind.*top.*5(M.88.277A); of Gnostic demiurge, Ptol. *ep.*ap.Epiph.*haer.*33.7(p.456.20; M.41.565D); as subst., *mediator, go-between μ. τῆς πρὸς ἀλλήλους ὑμῶν ἀμφισβητήσεως οἷον εἰρήνης πρύτανιν ἐμαυτὸν...προσάγω* Const.ap.Eus.*v.C.*2.68(p.68.10; M.20. 1041A); Evagr.*h.e.*1.20(p.28.25; M.86.2473A); *sequester dicitur qui certantibus medius intervenit, qui apud Graecos ὁ μέσος dicitur, apud quem pignora deponi solent,* Isid.H.*etym.*10.260; neut. as subst., *intermediate state θεότητος καὶ κτίσεως μηδὲν εἶναι τὸ μ.* Thdt.*rect. conf.*7(M.6.1220A); *intervening* as a barrier *ἀλλοτρίους...ὅσον μέσα ἔθνη καὶ ὄρη καὶ ποταμοὺς διείργειν ἡμᾶς* Gr.Thaum.*pan.Or.*4(p.10. 18; M.10.1064A); neut. as subst., *difference, gap δείκνυσι...τὴν πρὸς τὸν πατέρα συγγένειαν, καὶ ὅτι οὐδὲν τὸ μ.* Apoll.ap.*cat.Jo.*12:46(p.333. 31); *ἐπ' αὐτοῦ καὶ τοῦ πατρὸς...πολλὴ ἡ ἰσότης διὰ τὴν τῆς φύσεως συγγένειαν· οὕτως...ἐφ' ἡμῶν καὶ αὐτοῦ...πολὺ τὸ μ. καὶ ἄπειρον ἑκατέρας τῆς φύσεως* Chrys.*hom.*72.1 *in Jo.*(8.483C); *οὐ...τι μ. τῆς θεότητος* [i.e. between Father and Son] *ib.*4.3(30D); *ὅσον τὸ μ. τοῦ τε μαρτυρουμένου καὶ τοῦ μαρτυροῦντος* *ib.*6(43D); id.*hom.*11.3 *in Heb.*(12.114D); *τὸ μ. φύσεως σαρκὸς καὶ θεότητος* Thdt.*eran.*1(4.12); an *interval* of time, Philost.*h.e.*12.4(M.65.612A); **3.** *middling, moderate*; **a.** *in a middle class,* spiritually *οἱ τέλειοι δίκαιοι καὶ οἱ μ. καὶ οἱ ἀσεβεῖς. ... ἕκαστος τῶν πιστῶν ὀρθὴν καὶ ἀνυπόκριτον πίστιν καὶ βίον καλὸν ἔχων μετὰ παρρησίας εἰσέρχεται εἰς τὴν βασιλείαν. ... οἱ δὲ ἕνα μὲν ἔχοντες, ἕνα δὲ μὴ ἔχοντες, μέσοι τινές εἰσιν, ἔξωθεν μένειν τοῦ νυμφῶνος κατακρινόμενοι, τουτέστι τοῦ στερεώματος* Cosm.Ind. *top.*5(M.88.284A); of infants *μέσα...μήτε στεφάνους ληψόμενα μήτε τιμωρίας ὑπομένοντα* *ib.*7(377C); **b.** morally *indifferent,* Clem.*str.* 6.14(p.487.25; M.9.333B); hence *ordinary εἰς τὴν μ. καὶ κοινότερον καλουμένην ζωὴν σπῶντος τοῦ περὶ ἡμᾶς πνεύματος. ... τὸ πνεῦμα κατὰ τὴν γραφὴν λέγεται ζωοποιεῖν, φανερὸν ὅτι ζωοποίησιν οὐ τὴν μ. ἀλλὰ τὴν θειοτέραν* Or.*Jo.*13.23(p.247.12; M.14.437B); *τοῦ κοινοτέρου θανάτου...νῦν τοῦ μ. ὀνομαζομένου* id.*comm.in Rom.*6:8–10(*JTS* 13 p.364); *κατὰ τὸν μ. θάνατον πάντες ἄνθρωποι ἀποθνήσκομεν* id.*dial.* 25(p.168.15); **c.** *indeterminate οὐ τοῦτο τέθεικεν, ἀλλ' ἀφῆκεν αὐτὸ μέσον, ἵνα πλήξῃ μειζόνως* Chrys.*hom.*15.1 *in 1Cor.*(10.126A); **4.** with prepositions; **a.** *ἐν μέσῳ in the midst ἐν μ. θεάτρου A.Paul.et Thecl.* 20(p.249.7); *ἐν μ. βαρβάρων τραφείς* Chrys.*hom.*24.4 *in Rom.*(9.716E); met., *in public life τὰς ἀγορὰς καὶ τὸ ἐν μ. στρέφεσθαι* id.*hom.*6.4 *in 1Cor.*(10.49A); *available, convenient τοῖς...ἐν μ. καὶ προχείροις* Clem. *str.*7.16(p.69.6; M.9.536A); *ψυχὴ...εἶχε τὴν κτίσιν ἀντὶ βιβλίου προκειμένην ἐν μ.* Chrys.*hom.*7.4 *in 1Cor.*(10.56C); **b.** *εἰς μέσον to the centre, forward τὸν ἄξιον εἰς μ. παράγειν* id.*hom.*5.1 *in 1Tim.*(11. 574B); *ἄρτους ἀγαγεῖν τοὺς οὐκ ὄντας εἰς μ.* Vict.*Mc.*8:14(p.343.14); Thdt.*1Cor.*4:5(3.187); met., *to the forefront* of the discourse *σταυρὸν εἰς μ. φέρων cat.Gal.*1:1(p.6.34); Chrys.*hom.*3.2 *in Jo.*(8. 18C); *in the middle,* Herm.*sim.*9.2.1; *ib.*9.6.1; **c.** *διὰ μέσου by means of εἰς ἓν συνήγαγε τά τε νοητὰ καὶ τὰ ὁρατὰ διὰ μ. τῆς τῶν ἀνθρώπων γενέσεως* Nemes.*nat.hom.*1(M.40.512B); *ὁ πατὴρ διὰ μ. Χριστοῦ ὡς μεσίτου καταλλάσσων ἑαυτῷ τὸν κόσμον cat.2Cor.*5:19(p.386.9); *ib.* 13:10(p.443.5); *τὸ διὰ μέσου the difference ἕτερον μέν τι εἶναι τὴν ὕλην ἄλλο δὲ τὸν θεὸν καὶ τὸ διὰ μ. πολύ* Athenag.*leg.*4.1(M.6.897B); **d.** *ἀνὰ μέσον* c. genit., judge *between,* Thphyl.*exc.Rom.*6(p.226.23; M.113.936A); **5.** neut.; **a.** as adv., *in the midst, Pers.*(p.27.7); *τούτων* [sc. Sabellius and Arius] *οὕτως ἀλλήλοις μαχομένων, ἡ ἐκκλησία μ. χορεύουσα* †Leont.B.*sect.*1(M.86.1200A); **b.** as prep. **i.** c. genit., *in the midst of, Pers.*(pp.22.12,26.6); *παράδεισοι μ. τῆς πόλεως* Jo.Mosch.*prat.*207(M.87.3097C); *μ. ἡμέρας at midday,* Clem.*str.* 7.12(p.57.15; M.9.512A); *between,* Chrys.*comm.in Gal.*1:2(10.660C); **ii.** c. acc., *during διεσώθη μ. νυχθήμερα τρία* Barth.Edess.*Agar.*(M. 104.1433C); **6.** superl.; **a.** *μεσαίτατος*: of tabernacle *μ. οὐρανοῦ...καὶ γῆς* Clem.*str.*5.6(p.347.17; M.9.57A); *ἔστησεν* [sc. *ὁ θεὸς τὴν γῆν*] *'ἐπ' οὐδενί'...ἰσχύϊ θεοῦ κατὰ τὸ μ. κεῖται* Or.*hom.*8.1 *in Jer.*(p.55.20; M.13.336B); **b.** *μεσώτατος*: *ἐξεπέτασεν ἐν σταυρῷ τὰς χεῖρας, ἵνα περιλάβῃ τῆς οἰκουμένης τὰ πέρατα· τῆς γὰρ γῆς τὸ μ. ὁ Γολγοθᾶς οὗτός ἐστιν* Cyr.H.*catech.*13.28; ref. Ps.73:13 *τὸν Γολγοθᾶν τόπον μ. καὶ οἱονεὶ κέντρον τῆς ὑπουρανόν* Didym.*Trin.*1.15(M.39.324B).

***μεσόστιχον, τό,** *middle verse τὰ τροπάρια δὲ τῶν καθισμάτων διπλοῦνται, λεγομένου μ. Const.Stud.*13(M.99.1709A).

μεσότης, ἡ, 1. *central position, middle πάντων οὐσιοποιὸς ἀρχὴ καὶ μ. καὶ τελευτή* Dion.Ar.*d.n.*5.8(M.3.824A); **2.** *interval,* of space *τῶν μὲν ὀκτὼ αἱ μ. γίνονται ἑπτά, τῶν δὲ ἑπτὰ φαίνονται εἶναι τὰ διαστήματα ἕξ* Clem.*str.*6.16(p.503.28; M.9.369A); of time, Epiph.*haer.*51.19 (p.276.12; M.41.924B); **3.** *difference πολλὴ δὲ διαφορὰ καὶ μ. τυγχάνει, τοῦ τε λόγου τοῦ θεοῦ καὶ τοῦ λόγου τοῦ κόσμου* Mac.Aeg.*hom.*46.1(M. 34.792C); *gulf, barrier τὸ δὲ 'ἐσχίσθη τὸ καταπέτασμα ἀπὸ ἄνωθεν ἕως κάτω εἰς δύο' τύπος ἡμῶν ἐστιν ὅτι ἐὰν ἐλευθερωθῇ ὁ νοῦς, ἡ μ. ἣν ἔχει μεταξὺ αὐτοῦ καὶ τοῦ θεοῦ ἀπέρχεται* Esaias *or.*13.3(p.77); **4.** *mean, intermediate state,* Or.*Apoc.*23(p.31); of Christ acc. Marcion *εἰ γὰρ μ. ἐστίν, ἀπήλλακται...πάσης τῆς τοῦ κακοῦ φύσεως· κακὸς δ' ἐστὶν...ὁ δημιουργὸς καὶ τούτου τὰ ποιήματα. διὰ τοῦτο ἀγέννητος κατῆλθεν ὁ Ἰησοῦς...ἵνα ᾖ πάσης ἀπηλλαγμένος κακίας. ἀπήλλακται... τῆς τοῦ ἀγαθοῦ φύσεως ἵνα ᾖ μ.* Hipp.*haer.*7.31(p.217.11; *μέσος* bis M.16.3335B); acc. Apoll. *μεσότητες γίνονται ἰδιοτήτων διαφόρων εἰς ἓν συνελθουσῶν ὡς ἐν ἡμιόνῳ ἰδιότης ὄνου καὶ ἵππου...οὐδεμία δὲ μ. ἑκατέρας ἔχει τὰς ἀκρότητας ἐξ ὁλοκλήρου ἀλλὰ μερικῶς ἐπιμεμιγμένας· μ. δὲ θεοῦ καὶ ἀνθρώπων ἐν Χριστῷ· οὐκ ἄρα οὔτε ἄνθρωπος ὅλος οὔτε θεός, ἀλλὰ...μίξις* Apoll.*fr.*113(p.234)ap.Justn.*monoph.* (M.86.1140C); of orthodoxy, between Sabellianism and Arianism, Gr.Naz.*or.*20.6(M.35.1072B); of semi-Arianism, *ib.*21.22(1108A); cf. Bas.*ep.*128(3.219C; M.32.556C); of human life *μεσότητα εἶχεν ἡ πλάσις θνητότητος δυναμένης ἀθανατίζεσθαι· ὡς καὶ νῦν ἐφ' ἡμῶν μ. τοῦ σπειρομένου μὲν ἐν φθορᾷ ἐγειρομένου δὲ ἐν ἀφθαρσίᾳ* Proc.G. *Gen.*3:18(M.87.216D); of Christian life in this world *τὸν ἀνακαινισμὸν τῆς μ. τοῦ ἐλευθερωθῆναι τῆς δουλείας τῆς φθορᾶς ἐν τῇ ἐλευθερίᾳ τῶν τέκνων τοῦ θεοῦ* Philox.*ep.*42(p.187); **5.** *moderate amount ὁ μὲν φόβος τῶν ἔτι καθαριζομένων ἐστὶ μετὰ μεσότητος ἀγάπης* Diad.*perf.*16(p.20.2); *ib.*92(p.132.7); **6.** (Gnost.) *intermediate state* between Pleroma and seven heavens *τὴν μητέρα...ἔχειν τὸν τῆς μ. τόπον καὶ εἶναι ὑπεράνω μὲν τοῦ Δημιουργοῦ ὑποκάτω δὲ ἢ ἔξω τοῦ Πληρώματος μέχρι συντελείας* Iren.*haer.*1.5.3(M.7.496B); *ib.*1.7. 1(512Bf.); *τὸν δὲ ἐκ Καφαρναοὺμ υἱὸν αὐτοῦ* [sc. *βασιλικοῦ*]...*τὸν ἐν τῷ ὑποβεβηκότι μέρει τῆς μ. τῷ πρὸς θάλασσαν, τουτέστιν τῷ συνημμένῳ τῇ ὕλῃ* Heracleon ap.Or.*Jo.*13.60(59; p.291.25; M.14.513A); *ἡ Ὀγδοὰς...ἀνέδειξε πεντάδα προυνίκων ἀθηλύντων...οὗτοι τῆς μ. ὠνομάσθησαν υἱοί* Val.Gn.ap.Epiph.*haer.*31.6(p.395.8; M.41.485B); *δημιουργὸς...ἕτερος ὢν παρὰ τὰς τούτων* [sc. God and Devil] *οὐσίας μέσος τε τούτων καθεστώς, ἐνδίκως καὶ τὸ τῆς μ. ὄνομα ἀποφέροιτο ἄν* Ptol.*ep.*ap.Epiph.*haer.*33.7(p.456.21; M.41.565D); *ἀπὸ μιᾶς ἀρχῆς... ἀγαθῆς, συνέστησαν καὶ αὗται αἱ φύσεις, ἥ τε τῆς φθορᾶς καὶ ⟨ἡ⟩ τῆς μ.* *ib.*(p.457.11; 568B); ref. psychic soul *τὸ μὲν χοϊκὸν εἰς φθορὰν χωρεῖν· καὶ τὸ ψυχικόν, ἐὰν τὰ βελτίονα ἕληται, ἐν τῷ τῆς μ. τόπῳ ἀναπαύ⟨σ⟩εσθαι· ἐὰν δὲ τὰ χείρω, χωρήσειν καὶ αὐτὸ πρὸς τὰ ὅμοια· τὰ δὲ πνευματικὰ...τελειότητος ἀξιωθέντα, νύμφας ἀποδοθήσεσθαι τοῖς τοῦ Σωτῆρος Ἀγγέλοις...τῶν ψυχῶν αὐτῶν ἐν μ. κατ' ἀνάγκην μετὰ τοῦ Δημιουργοῦ ἀναπαυσαμένων εἰς τὸ παντελές* Iren.*haer.*1.7.5(520A); *ἀναγκαίαν ἡμῖν τὴν ἐγκράτειαν καὶ ἀγαθὴν πρᾶξιν, ἵνα δι' αὐτῆς ἔλθωμεν εἰς τὸν τῆς μ. τόπον* *ib.*1.6.4(512A); Clem.*str.*4.13(p.288.2; M.8.1297B); *τινὲς αἱρετικοὶ λέγουσι περὶ τῆς μ. ἣν καὶ ψυχικὴν φύσιν καλοῦσιν, ὅτι αὐτὴ ἡ μ. ὧδε ἔχει μετάπτωσιν, ὅπερ καλεῖται ἔγερσις. ... ἡμεῖς οὕτω δοξάζομεν, ὅτι ἑκάστη ψυχὴ ἐν μ. ἐστι, καὶ ὅπου θέλει ῥέπει, ἢ εἰς ἀρετὴν ἢ εἰς κακίαν· καὶ τοῦτο ἐπὶ πάσης ἀνθρώπων ψυχῆς λέγομεν, ὅπερ αὐτοὶ ἐπὶ μόνης λέγουσιν εἶναι τῆς μ.* Didym.ap.*cat.Ac.* 24:14(p.378.13).

μεσότοιχος, ὁ (μεσότοιχον, τό), 1. *party-wall τὴν ἐκκλησίαν...*

ἔχουσάν τινα μ., μή ποτε σκοτισθῶσιν αἱ προσευχαὶ τῶν νεοφωτίστων ἐν τῇ ὁράσει τῶν ὀφθαλμῶν *A.Phil.*142(p.81.24); met., ref. Eph.2:14 ἡ ἔχθρα [sc. τῶν ἐν κόσμῳ ἀνθρώπων] τὸ μ. ἣν τοῦ φραγμοῦ κωλῦον τοῦ ἑνοῦσθαι τὴν ἀνθρώπων φύσιν τῇ μακαριότητι τῶν κρειττόνων Or. *comm.in Eph.*2:14(p.406); τινὲς μέν φασιν ὅτι ὁ νόμος μ. ... ἐμοὶ δὲ οὐ τοῦτο δοκεῖ· ἀλλὰ τὴν ἔχθραν ἐν τῇ σαρκὶ μ. λέγει...ἣν καὶ πρὸς Ἰουδαίους εἶχε καὶ πρὸς Ἕλληνας...μ. οὐκέτι αὐτοὺς ἐν ἀσφαλείᾳ καθιστῶν, ἀλλὰ χωρίζον αὐτοὺς ἀπὸ τοῦ θεοῦ Chrys.*hom.5.2 in Eph.*(11.34C); τί τὸ μ.; τὸ πρὸς τοὺς Ἕλληνας ἄμικτον· κεκώλυτο γὰρ Ἕλλησιν ἐπιμίγνυσθαι Ἰουδαίους, ἵνα μὴ...εἰς τὴν εἰδωλολατρείαν καταπέσωσιν Sever.*Eph.*2:14(p.309.1); μ. ... ὅπερ ὁ Ἀδὰμ ᾠκοδόμησε τῇ παρακοῇ, ἐργάτην τῆς ἔχθρας τὸν φυγόντα δράκοντα μισθωσάμενος Leont.B.*mesopent.*1(M.86.1977A); καθάπερ μ. κατασπάσας τὴν ἐκ τῆς ἁμαρτίας μνησικακίαν Chrys.*hom.26.2 in 1Cor.*(10.230D); **2.** in gen. *barrier, obstacle* οὐκ ἔστιν ἡσυχάσαι τὸν νοῦν ἄνευ σώματος, οὔτε λῦσαι τὸ τούτων μ. ἄνευ ἡσυχίας καὶ προσευχῆς Marc.Er.*opusc.*2.29 (M.65.936A); ἢ γὰρ ἐξ ἀρχῆς ἐμίγνυτο τῷ φωτὶ τὸ σκότος...ἢ ἕτερόν τι μ. ἣν ἀπ' ἀρχῆς τὸ ταῦτα χωρίζον Jo.D.*Man.*1.22(M.94.1525D); ἐκλείπει ὁ ἥλιος τοῦ σώματος τῆς σελήνης ὥσπερ μ. γενομένου καὶ ἀποσκιάζοντος id.*fr.Mt.*27:45(M.96.1412C); met., *distinction* τὸ τῆς ἁμαρτίας μ. ... ἡ μία φυλὴ εἰς τὴν γυναῖκα ἐπόρνευσεν, αἱ δὲ ἕνδεκα φυλαὶ εἰς τὰ εἴδωλα Chrys.*exp.in Ps.*3(5.3C).

***μεσοτρόπως,** *indifferently*, Marc.Er.*opusc.*1.89(M.65.916C).

μεσόχορος, ὁ, *chorus-leader*; fig., of Arians, Eust.*fr.*61(M.18. 692B); of demon inspiring them, Anast.S.*hod.*4(M.89.96D).

***μεσοχρονία, ἡ,** *middle period*, Iren.*haer.*4.36.7(M.7.1097B).

***Μεσσαλιανοί, *Μεσσαλῖται,** v. **Μασσαλιανοί*.

μεσσοπαγής, *fixed up to the centre, firmly fixed* βουλᾶς πατρικᾶς... ἃ πατρὸς λοχίους ἔφηνε καρπούς, καὶ φήνασα φάνη μ. νοῦς Synes.*hymn.* 6.9(p.40; M.66.1609).

μεσσοφανής, *appearing in the midst*, Nonn.*par.Jo.*6:3(M.43. 793A).

μεστός, *full*; neut. as subst., *fullness, capacity* οὐ μ. αὐτῆς τῆς πόλεως ἔχεσθαι τῆς τοῦ αὐτοκράτορος μεγαλονοίας Thphyl.*exc.gent.*6 (μεοστὸν αὐτῆς M.113.944D; μετὸν αὐτοῖς p.483.28).

μεστόω, *fill full*; met., *fulfil, accomplish* ὁ λόγος σου...οὐ κενὸς ἀλλὰ μεμεστωμένος πράξει *Did.*2.5.

μετά, A. in gen.; **1.** c. acc.; **a.** *below*, in space οἱ τὰ μ. σελήνην ἀπρονόητα λέγοντες Tat.*orat.*2(p.3.5; M.6.808B); Thdt.*affect.*6(p.151. 11; 4.848); Χριστὲ βασιλεῦ τῶν οὐρανῶν καὶ τῶν μ. οὐρανὸν <καὶ> ὑπὲρ οὐρανὸν Bas.Sel.*v.Thecl.*1(M.85.528B); **b.** *after*, in time μ. ἔτη δύο τῆς τελευτῆς Ἰωσὴφ *T.Reub.*1.2, etc.; **c.** *in accordance with* μ. νόμον Chrys.*hom.32.2 in Ac.*(9.250B); cf. μ. συγχώρησιν Vict.*Mc.*6:7(p.323. 11); μ. γνώμην τῶν γερόντων Dor.*doct.*11.7(M.88.1741C); μ. θεόν *ib.*6. 7(1693C); **d.** *towards* τὸ φίλτρον μ. θεόν Gr.Naz.*or.*6.5(M.35.728B); **e.** *with a view to* μ. προσαύξησιν πιστοῖς Euthal.Diac.*epp.Paul.*(M. 85.704A); **f.** μ. χεῖρας; v. χείρ; **g.** *with* (i.e. carrying) μ. λίβανον... ἦλθεν ἐπὶ τὸ θυσιαστήριον *Apoc.Mos.*33(p.18); **h.** *with* (of instrument), Geo.Pis.*carm.vit.*3; (by the agency of) θαύματα ἃ ὁ κύριος ἐποίησεν μ. τὸν ἅγιον Γεώργιον *Mir.Geo.*15(p.144.2); **2.** c. genit.; **a.** *with*, mostly superseded by σύν but implying closer association, *in common with, in the same way as* μ. θεοῦ καὶ σὺν θεῷ ἀκλινεῖς καὶ ἀπαθεῖς τὴν ψυχήν Athenag.*leg.*31.3(M.6.961C); ὡς θεὸς καὶ υἱός, μ. πατρὸς καὶ σὺν πατρὶ τὴν δόξαν ἔχει Bas.*Spir.*17(3. 15A; M.32.97B); **b.** *after* παρὰ πολὺ μ. τοῦ μέτρου τῆς ἀξίας τῶν πραγμάτων ἀπολειφθήσεται Alex.Sal.*Barn.*proem.(436F).

B. theol., c. acc. *after*, c. genit. *with*; **1.** in doxology, c. genit. in early orthodox use, Ath.*inc.*57.3(M.25.197A) cit. s. σύν; μ. οὗ τῷ πατρὶ ἅμα τῷ ἁγίῳ πνεύματι ἡ δόξα καὶ τὸ κράτος id.*ep.Serap.*4.23 (M.26.676C); δι' οὗ καὶ μ. οὗ ἡ δόξα τῷ πατρὶ...σὺν τῷ ἁγίῳ πνεύματι Gr.Naz.*or.*9.6(M.35.825C); Epiph.*ep.Arab.*ap.*haer.*78.24(p.475.2; M. 42.737D); Chrys.*hom.1.4 in Jo.*(8.7A); Cyr.*glaph.Gen.*1(1.25B); Thdt. *h.rel.*30(3.1295); Max.*opusc.*(M.91.132D); Jo.D.*hom.*8.14(M.96.721B); usage defended μοι...τὴν δοξολογίαν ἀποπληροῦντι...νῦν μὲν μ. τοῦ υἱοῦ σὺν τῷ πνεύματι τῷ ἁγίῳ, νῦν δὲ διὰ τοῦ υἱοῦ ἐν τῷ ἁγίῳ πνεύματι ἐπέσκηψάν τινες Bas.*Spir.*3(3.3D; M.32.72C); ὅταν μὲν γὰρ τὸ μεγαλεῖον τῆς φύσεως τοῦ μονογενοῦς...θεωρῶμεν, 'μ. πατρὸς' εἶναι αὐτῷ τὴν δόξαν μαρτυροῦμεν, ὅταν δὲ τὴν εἰς ἡμᾶς χορηγίαν τῶν ἀγαθῶν ἐννοήσωμεν...'δι' αὐτοῦ' καὶ 'ἐν αὐτῷ' ἐνεργεῖσθαι ἡμῖν τὴν χάριν ταύτην ὁμολογοῦμεν. ὥστε ἡ μὲν ἰδία τῶν δοξολογούντων ἐστὶν ἡ 'μ. οὗ', ἡ δὲ 'δι' οὗ' τῶν εὐχαριστούντων ἐξαίρετος...ἡ δόξα κοινὴ πατρὶ καὶ υἱῷ· διὸ 'μ. τοῦ υἱοῦ' τὴν δοξολογίαν προσάγομεν τῷ πατρί *ib.*16(13Bff.; M.93C–96A); τὸ 'δι' αὐτοῦ' τὴν χρῆσιν ἁρμοδιωτάτην καὶ εὔσημον ἀποδίδωσιν, ὅταν ὡς θύρα καὶ ὡς ὁδὸς λέγηται. ὡς μέντοι θεὸς καὶ υἱὸς 'μ. πατρὸς' καὶ 'σὺν πατρὶ' τὴν δόξαν ἔχει *ib.*17(3.15A; M. 97B); ὅταν μὲν τὴν οἰκείαν ἀξίαν τοῦ πνεύματος ἐννοῶμεν, 'μ.' πατρὸς αὐτὸ καὶ υἱοῦ θεωροῦμεν, ὅταν δὲ τὴν εἰς τοὺς μετόχους ἐνεργουμένην χάριν ἐνθυμηθῶμεν, 'ἐν' ἡμῖν εἶναι τὸ πνεῦμα λέγομεν *ib.*63(3.53B; M. 184C); **2.** c. acc., used by Arians of relationship of Persons of Trin. but replaced by μ. c. genit. by orthodox τοῦ υἱοῦ ὑποτεταγμένου τῷ πατρί, ἐκτὸς δὲ αὐτοῦ πάντων μ. αὐτὸν βασιλεύοντος *Symb.Ant.* (345)9(p.254.3; M.26.733C); οὐ μ. πατρός, φασίν, υἱός, ἀλλὰ μ. τὸν πατέρα· διόπερ ἀκόλουθον δι' αὐτοῦ τὴν δόξαν προσάγειν τῷ πατρί, ἀλλ' οὐχὶ μ. αὐτοῦ. τὸ μὲν γὰρ μ. αὐτοῦ τὴν ἰσοτιμίαν δηλοῖ, τὸ δὲ δι' οὗ, τὴν ὑπουργίαν παρίστησιν Bas.*Spir.*13(3.10C; M.32.88B); τὸ μ. τὸν πατέρα πῶς τὸν υἱὸν λέγουσιν; ὡς χρόνῳ νεώτερον ἢ ὡς τάξει ἢ ὡς ἀξίᾳ; *ib.*14(10D; M.88C); τὸν υἱὸν...ἐκ τοῦ θεοῦ...καὶ οὐ μ. τὸν θεὸν οὐδὲ ἐκτὸς τοῦ θεοῦ ἀλλὰ μ. τοῦ θεοῦ καὶ ἐν τῷ θεῷ καὶ σὺν τῷ θεῷ ‡Ath.*dial.Trin.*2.1(M.28.1160A); cf.Gr.Naz.*or.*29.3(p.76.19; M.36. 77A); **3.** Christol., ref. Ac.17:31, of the two natures after the Resurrection οὐ...θεὸν μ. ἀνδρός, ἀλλὰ θεὸν ἐν ἀνδρί Euther.*confut.*17 (M.28.1393C).

μεταβαίν-ω, *pass over* from one place to another μεταβήσεται τὸ πνεῦμα τοῦ θεοῦ ἐπὶ τὰ ἔθνη *T.Benj.*9.4, v.l. καταβήσεται; met., *pass* from one state to another, of Persons of Trin. acc. Sabellian teaching φεύγοι ἂν ἅπερ ἐστίν, εἰς ἄλληλα μεταχωροῦντα καὶ ~οντα Gr.Naz. *or.*20.6(M.35.1072B); of conversion from paganism to Judaism, *Pers.*(p.38.13).

μεταβάλλ-ω, I. act. and pass.;

A. trans.; **1.** *turn, turn round* or *about*; hence **a.** *transfer, distribute* τὰ ἀπὸ ἑκάστου...ἐμπορίων δεχομένη, καὶ τοῖς ἐνδοτέρω ~ουσα, καὶ τὰ ἴδια ἅμα ἑκάστῳ ἐμπορίῳ ἐκπέμπουσα Cosm.Ind.*top.*11 (M.88.448A,B); passage in writing, *plagiarize* τὴν ἀρχὴν τοῦ λόγου ἐκ τῆς...Δευκαλιωνείας μετέβαλεν Clem.*str.*6.2(p.443.10; M.9.244A); **b.** *transcribe*, Andr.Cr.*Agath.*tit.(p.508; M.97.1437C); **c.** *substitute* ἀντὶ τῶν διδασκάλων καὶ τῶν μαθητῶν τοὺς γονέας καὶ τὰ τέκνα ~ων Chrys.*hom.27.2 in 2Cor.*(10.629B); **2.** *change, alter*; **a.** the appearance, *transform* πολλὰ τῶν ἀερίων τὰς μορφὰς ~οντα Bas.*hex.*8. 8(1.78E; M.29.184D); or condition τὴν κτίσιν ἐκ τῆς δουλείας εἰς τὴν ἐλευθερίαν μεταβληθήσεσθαι Eus.*Marcell.*2.4(p.54.22; M.24.816B); Thdt.*Is.*58:12(p.229.10; 2.374); **b.** qualities, character, etc. καὶ ὁ ἄρτος καὶ τὸ ἔλαιον...οὐ τὰ αὐτὰ ὄντα κατὰ τὸ φαινόμενον οἷα ἐλήφθη· ἀλλὰ δυνάμει εἰς δύναμιν πνευματικὴν μεταβέβληται Clem.*exc.Thdot.*82 (p.132.12; M.9.696C); *ib.*46(p.121.14; M.9.681A); ὁ...ὑπὸ τῶν ἔξωθεν ὑπεισιόντων καὶ προσπιπτόντων ἀεὶ ~εται, πῶς ἂν ποτε ἐν ἕξει καὶ διαθέσει...γένοιτ' ἄν; id.*str.*6.9(p.470.18; M.9.297C); εἰς εὐχρηστίαν ~ουσι ...τοῦ χυμοῦ τὴν δυσχέρειαν Bas.*hex.*5.7(1.46E; M.29.109D); γεωργία... τὰς τῶν φυτῶν ποιότητας ~ει *ib.*(1.47A; M.109D); εἰ δὲ κατὰ μεταβολήν, δῆλον, ὅτι ἐκ τοῦ ἐναντίου εἰς τὸ ἐναντίον ~εται...ἐκ τοῦ ψυχροῦ εἰς τὸ θερμὸν ~όμενον ‡Just.*qu.Chr.*5(M.6.1460C); **c.** substance Ἡρακλέα προσκυνοῦσιν...ὡς ἐξ ἀνθρώπου εἰς θεὸν μεταβληθέντα Or.*hom.5.3 in Jer.*(p.33.23; M.13.300C); ὁ ἄνθρωπος...οὔποτε μεταβληθήσεται οὔτε εἰς τὴν τῶν ἀγγέλων οὔτε εἰς τὴν τῶν ἑτέρων μορφήν Meth.*res.*1.49(p.303. 3; M.18.277C); hence, *transmute* τὸν χαλκὸν εἰς χρυσὸν μεταβαλὼν Aen. *dial.*(M.85.984B); *ib.*(992A); **d.** ref. eucharistic elements, cf.Clem. *exc.Thdot.*82(p.132.12; M.9.696C) cit. s. b supra; οὗ ἂν ἐφάψηται τὸ ἅγιον πνεῦμα, τοῦτο ἡγίασται καὶ μεταβέβληται Cyr.H.*catech.*23.7; διὰ τῆς γενομένης εὐχαριστίας εἰς σάρκα καὶ αἷμα ~εσθαι Thdr.Mops. *Mt.*26:26(M.66.713B); οὐ γὰρ ἀλλοιοῦται Χριστός, οὐδὲ τὸ ἅγιον αὐτοῦ σῶμα μεταβληθήσεται, ἀλλ' ἡ τῆς εὐλογίας δύναμις, καὶ ἡ ζωοποιὸς χάρις διηνεκής ἐστιν ἐν αὐτῷ Cyr.*ep.Calos.*(p.606.1; 6².365B); Thdt. *eran.*1(4.26) cit. s. αἷμα; *ib.*3(4.269) cit. s. ἀντίτυπος; ποίησον τὸν μὲν ἄρτον τοῦτον...σῶμα τοῦ Χριστοῦ σου μεταβαλὼν τῷ πνεύματί σου τῷ ἁγίῳ *Lit.Chrys.*(p.330.5); in Eutychian argument τὰ σύμβολα τοῦ δεσποτικοῦ σώματός τε καὶ αἵματος...μετὰ...τὴν ἐπίκλησιν ~εται, καὶ ἕτερα γίνεται Thdt.*eran.*2(4.126); **3.** morally, *turn, change, convert* λόγου παιδευτικοῦ...παραλαμβάνοντος...καὶ ~οντος· ὥστε...γεγονέναι ...τὴν ἐπὶ τὸ κρεῖττον μεταβολὴν Or.*princ.*3.1.5(p.200.7; M.11.253C); λῃστὴν ἐν σταυρῷ μεταβαλεῖν καὶ εἰς παράδεισον εἰσαγαγεῖν Chrys. *hom.85.1 in Jo.*(8.504C); ἕνδεκα ἄνδρας...πᾶσαν τὴν οἰκουμένην μεταβαλεῖν Thdt.*Jer.*1:8(2.407); v. ἀλλοιόω; pass. τῶν...τὴν γνώμην μεταβληθέντων Philost.*h.e.*4.12(M.65.528A).

B. intrans.; **1.** *undergo change, change*; **a.** in appearance ~ειν... φάναι τὸ θεῖον καὶ σχηματίζεσθαι εἰς ἀνδρὸς εἶδος καὶ μορφήν, οὐκ εὐαγές Eus.*d.e.*5.9(p.232.3; M.22.384A); *ib.*5.11(p.234.14; 388A); id. *h.e.*1.2.8(M.20.57A); **b.** of a stream, *change current*, Anat.Laod. *decad.*(p.36); **c.** in substance (Stoic) ἐκπύρωσιν ἔσεσθαι πάντων εἰς πῦρ ~όντων Or.*Cels.*8.72(p.288.23; M.11.1624C); Ἀσκληπιὸν προσκυνοῦσιν ὡς ἐξ ἀνθρώπων δι' ἀρετὴν εἰς θεὸν μεταβεβληκότα id.*hom.5.6 in Jer.*(p.33.24; M.13.300C); τὸ μεταβεβληκὸς εἰς οἶνον ὕδωρ id.*Jo.* 13.39(p.264.13; M.14.468A); τὴν ὑδάτων...οὐσίαν...εἰς οἶνον μεταβαλοῦσαν Ath.*inc.*18.6(M.25.128D); ὁποῖα καὶ περὶ τοῦ Ἰνδικοῦ σκώληκος ἱστορεῖται...ὃς εἰς κάμπην...μεταβαλών, εἶτα...βομβυλιὸς γίνεται Bas.*hex*.8.8(1.78E; M.29.184D); **2.** morally; **a.** *change*, direction of change being expressed ~ει πᾶν τὸ ἐνάρετον εἰς ἀμείνους οἰκήσεις, τῆς μεταβολῆς αἰτίαν τὴν αἵρεσιν τῆς γνώσεως ἔχον, ἣν αὐτοκρατορικὴν ἐκέκτητο ἡ ψυχή Clem.*str*.7.2(p.9.31; M.9.416B); οὐδὲ τὸ ἀγαθὸν εἰς κακόν *ib*.7.12(p.51.2; 497B); δυνατὸν...~ειν ἐξ ἑτέρου ἔθνους εἰς ἕτερον κρεῖττον ἢ χεῖρον Or.*fr.25 in Jer*.25:14ff.(p.210.17); Eus. *l.C*.10(p.222.12; M.20.1372C); **b.** partic. of change wrought by repentance, *be converted* τὸν Ἰησοῦν...σωτῆρα...πάντων τῶν ~όντων ἀπὸ τῆς χύσεως τῆς κακίας γεγενημένον Or.*Cels*.5.55(p.59.3; M.11.1269A); αἱ...ἐκκλησίαι τῶν μεταβαλόντων ἀπὸ...κακῶν *ib*.1.67(p.121.22; 785C); ἄνθρωποι...μετάνοιαν ἐπιδέχονται καὶ ἐξ ἀπιστίας εἰς πίστιν ~ουσιν id.*Jo*.13.59(58; p.291.2; M.14.512B); Eus.*d.e*.9.1(p.405.8; M.22.653B); εἰ...νῦν μεταβάλοις καὶ θεραπεύσοις τὴν ἁμαρτίαν Gr. Naz.*ep*.217(M.37.353C); **c.** and by gift of supernatural life θεὸς ὑπὲρ τὴν ἀνθρωπίνην φύσιν ἀναβιβάζων τὸν ἄνθρωπον, καὶ ποιῶν αὐτὸν ~ειν ἐπὶ φύσιν κρείττονα καὶ θειοτέραν Or.*Cels*.5.23(p.24.27; M.11.1217A); εὐθέως σου ~ει ἡ ψυχὴ καὶ μεταμορφοῦται καὶ γίνεται κρεῖττόν τι καὶ θειότερον id.*hom.16.1 in Jer*.(p.133.2; M.13.440A); **d.** pass. intrans., ? *be mollified, change one's purpose* οὐκ ἐν τῇ τοῦ θυμοῦ ὀξύτητι φθεγξάμενος μετεβλήθη Diod.*Gen*.27:41(M.33.1576C).

II. med.;

A. *turn* oneself; met. (cf. parallel usage in C infra) *turn* to ὑπέρθεσθε οὖν τὴν κακὴν ζύμην...καὶ μεταβάλεσθε εἰς νέαν ζύμην Ign. *Magn*.10.2; *be moved* to μήτε ~εσθε μήτε εἰς τέρψιν μήτε εἰς ἀηδίαν *T.Dan* 4.3; *turn away* from τοὺς...μηδαμῶς τῆς προθέσεως ~ομένους Iren.*ep.Flor*.ap.Eus.*h.e*.5.21.4(M.20.489A); μεταβαλομένην τοῦ μίσους *Hom.Clem*.20.20.

B. *change* what is one's own; **1.** one's form; of demons, *T.Sal*. 15.3(p.46.22; M.122.1337B); Jo.D.*f.o*.2.4(M.94.877A); **2.** one's way of life ~εσθε τὸν τρόπον ἀπὸ τῶν χειρόνων ἐπὶ τὰ κρείττονα *Hom. Clem*.1.7; abs., of apostasy, Dion.Al.ap.Eus.*h.e*.7.11.4(M.20.664B); **3.** abs. ? *change one's mood* χρηστὸν ὄναρ εἶδε καὶ ~εται Proc.G.*ep*.16 (M.87.2733A).

C. morally, esp. of change wrought by repentance, *be converted* ἀπὸ τῆς ἁμαρτίας...~εσθαι Clem.*str*.1.19(p.59.11; M.8.808B); Or.*Jo*. 2.11(6; p.66.13; M.14.129C); τῆς πατρικῆς δεισιδαιμονίας μεταβεβλῆσθαι Eus.*d.e*.1.2(p.10.8; M.22.28A); *ib*.4.15(p.181.9; 301B); abs. κἂν μὴ πιστεύσῃ κόλασιν...ἐπηρτῆσθαι τῷ πλημμελοῦντι...οὐδ' οὕτως μεταβαλεῖται Clem.*str*.2.5(p.127.18; M.8.961C); *Hom.Clem*.18.2; Chrys.*stat*.5.5(2.67C); id.*hom.28.2 in Jo*.(8.160C); *ib.34.3*(199B).

III. theol., *change*;

A. of motion as involving change (cf. I.A.1, II.A) οὐκ...ἦν ὁ υἱὸς ἀγένητος ἐν τῷ πατρί, μέρος ὢν αὐτοῦ ὁ μεταβληθὲν ὕστερον καὶ κενωθὲν ἐκτὸς αὐτοῦ γέγονε...προβεβλημένον Eus.*d.e*.5.1(p.212.13; M.22.352D).

B. idea of change (cf. I.A.2, B, II.B) in Godhead directly combated σοφία...οὔποτε ~ουσα Clem.*paed*.1.5(p.102.9; M.8.273B); Meth. *creat*.4 passim(p.496; M.18.336f.); *ib*.2(p.494.25; 333C) cit. s. ἀλλοιόω; partic. ref. Inc. μένων...αὐτὸς ἄυλος, οἷος καὶ πρὸ τούτου παρὰ τῷ πατρὶ ἦν, οὔτι μεταβαλὼν τὴν οὐσίαν, οὐδ' ἀφανισθείσης τῆς αὐτοῦ φύσεως Eus.*l.C*.14(p.243.6; M.20.1412A); *ib*.(p.242.9; 1409B); ἐνανθρώπησεν, οὐκ ἐκ τῆς ἰδίας φύσεως αὐτὸς ἑαυτῷ σῶμα μεταβαλών Cyr.*ep*. 50(p.91.21; 5².159D); οὐ μεταβαλὼν θεότητα, ἀλλὰ προσλαβὼν...τὴν ἀνθρωπότητα Thdot.Anc.*exp.symb*.(M.77.1316C); ὁ θεὸς γέγονεν ἱερεύς, οὐ τὴν φύσιν μεταβαλών Procl.CP *or.laud.BMV* 3(p.104.15; M.65.684B); τὸν...λόγον...μηδὲν μεταβαλόντα τῆς θείας οὐσίας διὰ τὴν πρὸς σάρκα κοινωνίαν *Euchol*.(p.255); pass. εἴ τις...τὸν λόγον εἰς σάρκα μεταβεβλῆσθαι νομίζοι ἢ τροπὴν ὑπομεμενηκότα ἀνειληφέναι τὴν σάρκα λέγοι, ἀ. ἔ. *Symb.Sirm*.1 *anath*.12; οὐ γὰρ εἰς ἄνθρωπον μετέπεσεν ὁ θεὸς λόγος, οὐδὲ οὐσία μετεβλήθη Chrys.*hom.7.3 in Phil*.(11.248B); οὐ γὰρ φαμὲν ὅτι ἡ τοῦ λόγου φύσις μεταποιηθεῖσα γέγονε σάρξ, ἀλλ' οὐδὲ ὅτι εἰς ὅλον ἄνθρωπον μετεβλήθη τὸν ἐκ ψυχῆς καὶ σώματος Cyr.*ep*.4(p.26.26; 5².23B); id.*Arcad*.(p.64.3; 5².45C); Jo.D.*f.o*.4.18 (M.94.1184C) cit. s. σύνθετος.

C. used in restricted sense in attempt to express effect on human nature of union with the divine τὸ δὲ θνητὸν αὐτοῦ σῶμα καὶ τὴν ἀνθρωπίνην ἐν αὐτῷ ψυχὴν τῇ πρὸς ἐκεῖνον οὐ μόνον κοινωνίᾳ ἀλλὰ καὶ ἑνώσει καὶ ἀνακράσει...τῆς ἐκείνου θειότητος κεκοινωνηκότα εἰς θεὸν μεταβεβληκέναι Or.*Cels*.3.41(p.237.10; M.11.973A); τί θαυμαστὸν τὴν ποιότητα τοῦ θνητοῦ κατὰ τὸ τοῦ Ἰησοῦ σῶμα...μεταβαλεῖν εἰς...θείαν ποιότητα; *ib*.(p.237.17; 973B); ὁ δὲ εἴς τι ~όμενος ἐκεῖνο γίνεται ὃ μὴ πρότερον ἦν; ὥσπερ οὖν ὁ μὴ γνοὺς ἁμαρτίαν ἁμαρτία γίνεται, ἵνα ἄρῃ τὴν ἁμαρτίαν τοῦ κόσμου, οὕτως πάλιν ἡ δεξαμένη τὸν κύριον σὰρξ Χριστὸς καὶ κύριος γίνεται, ὃ μὴ ἦν τῇ φύσει, εἰς τοῦτο μεταποιουμένη διὰ τῆς ἀνακράσεως Gr.Nyss.*Eun*.6(2 p.144.8; M.45.729B).

***μεταβαπτίζω**, *baptize anew into another faith* εἰς τὴν Ἀρείου μετεβαπτίσατο λατρείαν Thdr.Lect.*fr*.(M.86.224B)ap.Jo.D.*imag*.3(M.94.1389C).

μεταβάπτ-ω, *dip successively* χαλκεύς τις μετακοσμῶν σίδηρον καὶ ἐκ πυρὸς εἰς ὕδωρ ~ων Hipp.*haer*.7.29(p.213.23; M.16.3330B).

***μεταβασία, ἡ**, *removal, migration*, Thdr.Stud.*epp*.2.107(M.99.1365D).

μετάβασις, ἡ, 1. *change of place*, ref. Abraham λιμὸς καὶ μ. καὶ γυναικὸς ἁρπαγή Chrys.*hom.53.4 in Mt*.(7.643B); τὰ μὲν σκιρτῶντα ταῖς μ. τὰ δὲ δεσμῷ φύσεως προσηλωμένα τῇ γῇ Bas.Sel.*or*.1.3(M.85.33B); denied of Persons of Trin. ὁ θεὸς...πανταχοῦ ἐπιφαινόμενος ...καὶ οὐχὶ κατὰ μετάβασιν ὃν τρόπον οἱ ἄγγελοι κατερχόμενοι ἐξ οὐρανοῦ ἐπὶ τὴν γῆν Mac.Aeg.*hom*.16.5(M.34.616D); ref. Ps.103:29, of H. Ghost ἀποστολὴν δὲ καλεῖ τὴν πρὸς τὸ ἔργον αὐτοῦ συγκατάβασιν, οὐ τὴν ἐκ τόπου εἰς τόπον μ. Didym.(‡Bas.)*Eun*.5(1.297E; M.29.716A); ref. Eph.4:9 ταῦτα ἀκούων, μὴ μ. νόμιζε Chrys.*hom.11.2 in Eph*.(11.82B); ref. Jo.13:1, either of Christ's death or ascension, Jo.Philop.*pasch*.(p.220.36); of death ἐπὶ τὸ κρεῖττον μ. Eus.*v.C*.4.60(p.142.20; M.20.1212B); Gr.Nyss.*v.Ephr*.(M.46.848D); Chrys.*hom.70.1 in Jo*.(8.413C); *translation* of bishops, *Cod.Afr*.48; **2.** *movement* τὴν [sc. κιθάρας] μ. Thdt.*Ps*.97:5(1.1303); **3.** *transfer* ἀπειθήσαντος γὰρ τοῦ Ἰσραὴλ...μ. ἐπὶ τὴν γῆν τοῦ ὑετοῦ γέγονεν Diod.*Ps*. 71:6(M.33.1611C); λῆμμα καλεῖ...τὴν ἀπὸ τῶν ἀνθρωπίνων μ. ἐπὶ τὴν θείαν ἀποκάλυψιν Thdt.*Abac*.1:1(2.1538); of an accusation, Const.ap. Ath.*apol.sec*.68(p.146.20; M.25.369C); *transmission* of speech, Tat. *orat*.5(p.6.5; M.6.817A).

μεταβάτης, ὁ, *one who moves from one place to another*; met., *apostate*, ref. Ex.12:45 πάροικον...ὅτῳ πιστεύειν ἑδραίως οὐκ ἔστι, ὑπονοστοῦντα δὲ ὥσπερ καὶ εἰς ἰδίαν ἀποστρέφοντα πόλιν ἢ χώραν, τὴν ἀπιστίαν, ὃν ἡμᾶς ἔθος μ. ἀποκαλεῖν Cyr.*hom.pasch*.9(5².123E); of *translated* bishops, CCP(536)*act*.5(*ACO* 3 p.88.25; H.2.1357E).

μεταβατικός, *transitional*; gram., of conjunctions, *cat.Apoc*.2:24 (p.215.30) cit. s. ἀπολύτως.

μεταβατικῶς, *from one place to another* οὐδὲ γὰρ ὁ υἱὸς ἐν τόπῳ οὐδ' αὖ ὁ πατήρ, ἵνα καὶ τὸ ἅγιον πνεῦμα μ. κινούμενον ἐκ τοῦ πατρὸς εἰς τὸν υἱὸν μεταβαίνῃ Or.*fr.20 in Jo*.1:31(p.501.20); οὐ πέμπεται...τὸ πνεῦμα...μ. ἐπειδὴ οὐδὲ ὁ πατὴρ οὔ τῆς ὑποστάσεως πνεῦμά ἐστιν, πέρασι περιγέγραπται Didym.*Trin*.3.38(M.39.977C); *by transition* τίνα τρόπον ἐν σαρκὶ ἡ θεότης; ὡς τὸ πῦρ ἐν σιδήρῳ· οὐ μ. ἀλλὰ μεταδοτικῶς †Bas.*Chr.generat*.2(2.596E; M.31.1460C).

μεταβιβαστέος, *to be transferred*, Or.*Cels*.7.60(p.209.16; M.11.1505C).

μεταβιόω, [aor. infin. μεταβιῶσαι]; *change one's manner of life*, Nil.*Eulog*.14(M.79.1112A).

***μεταβίωσις, ἡ**, *decease*, Sophr.H.*v.Cyr.et Jo*.24(M.87.3409A).

***μετάβλησις, ἡ**, *change*, Sophr.H.*ep.syn*.(M.87.3148C).

***μεταβλήσκω**, = μεταβάλλω, *Rit.Epiph*.(p.418) cit. s. ἐπιφάνεια.

μεταβλητός, *subject to change*, v. τρεπτός with which it is often linked, partic. of what pertains to creation, Hipp.*haer*.4.49(p.74.1; M.16.3118B); ἡ μ. γένεσις *ib*.5.7(p.84.8; 3134B); *ib*.6.17(p.143.15; 3219B); Or.*or*.27(p.368.18; M.11.512C); ass. ῥευστός, Athenag.*leg*.22.2(M.6.937A); Hipp.*haer*.1.23(p.27.19; 3049D); denied of God ὁ θεὸς ἔσται μ. οὐσίᾳ...ὅπερ ἄτοπον ‡Just.*qu.Chr*.2(M.6.1416D).

μεταβοθρεύω, *transplant*, Cyr.*ador*.9(1.301E); id.*Is*.2.3(2.280D).

μεταβολή, ἡ, *change*; (from med.) *change* undergone;

A. in gen.; **1.** physical and chemical *change*; to be found throughout universe, Gr.Thaum.*pan.Or*.8(p.22.10; M.10.1077B); *Hom.Clem*.20.6; ‡Just.*qu.Chr*.5(M.6.1460C) cit. s. ἀλλοίωσις; Aen. *dial*.(M.85.984B); part of divine order in nature, Clem.*fr*.42(p.221.2)ap.Anast.S.*qu.et resp*.96(M.89.744A); **2.** *change* of qualities or characteristics ἡ...αὐτὴ ψυχὴ κατὰ μεταβολὰς ἄλλας καὶ ἄλλας ποιότητας...ἀναδεχομένη Clem.*ecl*.46(p.149.25; M.9.720B); πᾶν πνεῦμα...ἐπιδέχεται ὅσον ἐπὶ τῇ ἑαυτοῦ φύσει τὴν εἰς τὸ παχύτερον μ. Or.*Jo*.13.21 (p.245.19; M.14.436A); τὰς τρεῖς ἡμῶν τῆς ἡλικίας...μ., τὴν μειρακιώδη καὶ τὴν πρόσηβον καὶ τὴν πρεσβυτικήν Meth.*symp*.5.2(p.55.5; M.18.100B); ref. Trin. controversy τὸ ἦν καὶ τὸ ἔσται καὶ τὸ γεγονέναι ...τῆς ἐν χρόνῳ μ. ὄντα δηλωτικά Eus.*e.th*.2.9(p.108.30; M.24.917A); ἀμήχανον...ᾧ θάτερον συνυπάρχει, ἐκ μ. ἄν ποτε πρὸς τὸ ἀντικείμενον μεταβῆναι, ὥστε...ἐξ ἀγεννήτου γεννητὸν γενέσθαι Bas.*Eun*.2.28 (1.264D; M.29.636C); Anomoean argument εἰ...γέννημα λέγεται οὐκ ἀμετάβλητος ἡ οὐσία αὐτοῦ [sc. τοῦ θεοῦ], τῆς μ. ἐργασαμένης τὴν τοῦ υἱοῦ ἰδιοποίησιν ‡Ath.*dial.Trin*.2.15(M.28.1180D); **3.** in degree ἀσθένεια...τί ἕτερόν ἐστιν ἢ τῆς καθ' ἕξιν δυνάμεως ἀλλοίωσις καὶ μ. Leont.B.*Nest.et Eut*.2(M.86.1344C); **4.** of substance, *transformation*, *renewal* of world after conflagration (Stoic), Just.*1apol*.20.2(M.6.357C); id.*2apol*.7.3(M.6.456B); ref. deification ἥρωας ἐκ μ. συστάντας ἀγαθῆς ἀνθρωπίνης ψυχῆς Or.*Cels*.3.37(p.234.7; M.11.968C); of men into angels, id.*Jo*.10.30(18; p.203.21; M.14.361A); of water into wine, *ib*.13.62(60; p.294.18; 517B); 5. of state ἡ δύναμις...τῆς μ. τοῦ βαπτισθέντος οὐ περὶ τὸ σῶμα...ἀλλὰ περὶ ψυχήν Clem.*exc.Thdot*.77 (p.131.10; M.9.693C); of change involved by death τῆς εἰς τὴν ἀφθαρσίαν μ. Meth.*symp*.4.2(p.46.10; M.18.88B); id.*res*.3.4(p.393.9); and by end of world τὴν εἰς τὸ κρεῖττον...ἀπὸ ταύτης τῆς καταστάσεως τοῦ κόσμου μ. *ib*.1.48(p.300.10; M.18.276B); Thdt.*Gal*.6:15 (3.396); 6. of mind, cf. C.3; εὔκολος πρὸς μεταβολὴν ἡ διάνοια Bas. *ep*.293(3.431E; M.32.1036A); *ib*.226.3(3.348B; M.848B); Thdr.Mops. *Gal*.1:6(pp.9.18,10.23; M.66.901B); συναπαχθῆναι μὲν τῇ κατὰ Νίκαιαν συνόδῳ, ἀνενεχθῆναι δὲ τῆς μ. Philost.*h.e*.2.15(M.65.477A); *ib*.5.1(528C); of mood τὴν ἀπὸ τοῦ φόβου...εἰς τὴν χαρὰν...μ. Meth.*symp*.10.2(p.124.11; M.18.196C); contrasted with course of generation whereby like begets like, Bas.*hex*.2.4(1.16C; M.29.37C).

B. in rel. to eucharistic elements τροφήν, ἐξ ἧς αἷμα καὶ σάρκες κατὰ μ. τρέφονται ἡμῶν Just.*1apol*.66.2(M.6.429A); ref. consecration τῇ ἐκ χάριτος γενεννημένῃ μ. ... οὐ τὴν φύσιν μεταβαλὼν ἀλλὰ τὴν χάριν τῇ φύσει προστεθεικώς Thdt.*eran*.1(4.26).

C. moral; **1.** with direction of change expressed τῆς ἐπὶ τὸ χεῖρον καὶ κρεῖττον...μ. Or.*Jo*.2.20(14; p.77.21; M.14.149C); id.*schol.in Cant*.7:6f.(M.17.284A); Bas.*ep*.223.5(3.340B; M.32.829B); Thdt.*Is*. 2:8f.(p.15.17; 2.187); **2.** abs., *amendment*, Just.*2apol*.2.5(M.6.444B); *degradation, debasement* οὐ τῇ ὑποστάσει...ἀλλὰ ἐκ μ. καὶ ἰδίας προαιρέσεως τοιοῦτον γεγεννημένον Or.*Jo*.20.21(p.353.24; M.14.617D); **3.** Christian *conversion, repentance, renewal* μ. σωτήριος ἡ ἐξ ἐθνῶν εἰς πίστιν Clem.*str*.7.10(p.42.8; M.9.481A); μ. ... καὶ μετάθεσιν...τῆς γεώδους ζωῆς ἐπὶ τὴν οὐράνιον Eus.*v.C*.3.46(p.97.8; M.20.1105D); μ. ἐκ τῆς Ἑλληνίδος θρησκείας εἰς τὸν Χριστιανισμόν Philost.*h.e*.1.6(M. 65.464B); abs. ὡς ἐκ νεκρῶν ἀναστάντες, ἐὰν ἀξιόλογον ἐνδείξωνται μ. Or.*Cels*.3.51(p.248.2; M.11.988C); ἐκ μ. γίνεσθαί τινα υἱὸν θεοῦ id.*Jo*. 20.33(27; p.371.22; M.14.649B); ἐπεὶ τοίνυν τοσαύτη γέγονε μ. ... εὐχαριστήσωμεν τῷ ἀγαπήσαντι πᾶσαν μ. ‡Ath.*diab*.7(p.8.4); effect of Inc. ἐπὶ ἀνακαινισμῷ καὶ μ. τῆς φύσεως ἡμῶν τὴν σωτήριον...γέννησιν Gr.Nyss.*or.catech*.40(p.159.15; M.45.101C); τῆς...ἀνθρωπείας φύσεως τὴν σωτηρίαν, καὶ...τὴν παράδοξον τῶν πραγμάτων μ. Thdt.*Ps*.67:1 (1.1054); and redemption θεοῦ μὴ συγχωροῦντος ἄγαν ἀθυμεῖν, ὡς ἕξοντας τῶν παρόντων μεταβολήν, ἁπάντων ἀνθρώπων δι' αἵματος λυτρουμένων Χριστοῦ Proc.G.*Is*.43:10(M.87.2385B); and in course of Christian life ἐν τῇ ὁδῷ τῶν ἀρετῶν ἐστὶ πτώματα...ἐστὶ καὶ μ. Esaias *or*.24 p.150(cf.M.40.1174B); δείκνυσί σοι ἡ...γραφὴ καὶ δικαίους πολλάκις σφαλέντας, καὶ ἁμαρτωλοὺς πολλὴν μ. ἐπιδειξαμένους Chrys. *hom.29.1 in Gen*.(4.279B).

D. theol.; **1.** not applicable to divine essence, Eus.*e.th*.1.12(p.72.18; M.24.849A) cit. s. ἔκτασις; τὸ...ὡσαύτως ἔχον ἀεὶ...τὸ πρὸς πᾶσαν μ. τήν τε πρὸς τὸ κρεῖττον καὶ τὴν πρὸς τὸ χεῖρον ἐπίσης ἀκίνητον Gr. Nyss.*v.Mos*.(M.44.333B); id.*or.catech*.6(p.34.2; M.45.28C) cit. s. τροπή; therefore not relevant to Inc. as regards either divine nature κατάβασιν θεοῦ πρὸς τὰ ἀνθρώπινα...οὐ μεταβολῆς...οὔτε τροπῆς Or.*Cels*.4.14(p.284.14; M.11.1044D); υἱὸν ἀνθρώπου τὸν κενώσαντα ἑαυτὸν...κατὰ τὴν περιβολήν, οὐ κατὰ μ. Apoll.*fr*.124(p.237.32) ap.Thdt.*eran*.1(4.70); ὁ λόγος σὰρξ ἐγένετο, οὐ...κατὰ τοὺς...λέγοντας μ. ... αὐτὸν πεπονθέναι Paulin.T.*symb*.(p.435.6; M.42.672C); οὐκ ἄρα ἕξει τὴν μ. τὴν εἰς λόγον ὁ πατήρ, ἀλλ' ἔσται πατὴρ ἀεί Cyr.*Jo*.1.4(4.36D); σάρκα γεγονότα...ἄνευ μ. καὶ μειώσεως Sophr.H.*or*.2.36(M.87.3265A); or human nature οὔτε...τῆς σαρκὸς εἰς τὴν τῆς θεότητος φύσιν γενέσθαι φαμὲν μεταβολήν Cyr.*Nest*.1.3(p.22.3; 6^{1}.15B); **2.** referred to God's dealings with mankind, exeg. Ps.76:11 μεταβολῆς ...ταῦτα σημεῖα καὶ ἀλλοιώσεως τῆς πάλαι τοῦ θεοῦ περὶ τὸν λαὸν κηδεμονίας Eus.*Ps*.76:11(M.23.893C); ἐγώ φησι πρόξενος ἐγενόμην ἐμαυτῷ τῆς τοιαύτης μ. Thdt.*Ps*.76:11(1.1145).

μετάβολος, *changed, transferred*; neut. as subst., *copy*, Jo.Clim. *past*.1(M.88.1165C).

μεταγγίζ-ω, *pour from one vessel into another*, fut. ptcpl. μεταγγιῶν Cyr.*Ag*.17(3.647C; conj. μετ' ἀγγείων); met., of metempsychosis, Clem.*str*.3.3(p.201.20; M.8.1116B); (Manichean), Hegem. *Arch*.10(p.15.6; M.10.1441C); (Stoic), Jo.D.*haer*.7(M.94.684B); ref. Elchezaites Χριστὸν ἕνα οὐχ ὁμολογοῦσιν, ἀλλ' εἶναι τὸν μὲν ἄνω ἕνα, αὐτὸν δὲ ~όμενον ἐν σώμασι, πολλοῖς πολλάκις καὶ νῦν δὲ ἐν τῷ Ἰησοῦ ὁμοίως ⟨π⟩οτὲ μὲν ἐκ τοῦ θεοῦ γεγενῆσθαι, ποτὲ δὲ πνεῦμα γεγονέναι... καὶ τοῦτον δὲ μετέπειτα ἀεὶ ἐν σώμασι ~εσθαι καὶ ἐν πολλοῖς κατὰ καιροὺς δείκνυσθαι Hipp.*haer*.10.29(p.284.11; M.16.3442C).

*Μεταγγισμονῖται, οἱ, an heretical sect, cf. *Metangismonitae ideo tale nomen acceperunt, quia ἄγγος Graece vas dicitur, adserunt enim sic esse in patre filium, tanquam vas minus intra vas majus*, Isid.H.*etym*.8.5.47.

μεταγγισμός, **ὁ**, *transference, transmigration*, (Marcionite), Epiph. *haer*.42.4(p.100.8; M.41.701A); (Manichean), *ib*.66.55(p.91.12; M.42. 112A); Jo.D.*haer*.5(M.94.684A).

μεταγενής, *born after*; comp., *later, of later times* οὗτος μὲν [sc. ἄνθρωπος] μ. κτισθεὶς...ἐν τῇ τῆς κτίσεως παρόδῳ, ὁ δὲ [sc. κόσμος] μ. τοῦ ἀνθρώπου ἐν τῇ τοῦ θεοῦ ἐνθυμήσει Gel.Cyz.*h.e*.2.17.22(M.85. 1269B); ref. generation of Son εἰ τῷ υἱῷ ὁ πατὴρ ἀπήγγειλεν, εὑρεθήσεται ἀγνοῶν ὁ υἱὸς καὶ τῶν ἔργων μ. Or.*sel.in Ps*.44:2(M.12.1428D); ἀδιανόητον γάρ...τὸν αἴτιον γενόμενόν τινος αὐτὸν μ. λέγειν τῆς ἐκείνου γενέσεως Alex.Al.*ep.Alex*.6(p.23.19; M.18.557A); ὁ τοίνυν μ. τὸν υἱὸν λέγων τοῦ πατρὸς...αὐτὸ τὸ χαρακτηρίζον τὴν ἀκήρατον οὐσίαν...ἀναιρεῖ Isid.Pel.*epp*.3.63(M.78.772D); ἀεὶ συνυπάρχει τῷ πατρὶ ὁ υἱός, οὐ μ. χρόνοις, οὐκ ἐλάσσων δυνάμει Gel.Cyz.*h.e*.2.15.3(M. 85.1257C); πατὴρ ὁ παντοκράτωρ...καὶ αἴτιος τοῦ υἱοῦ αὐτοῦ...ὡς ἀκτῖνος ἥλιος...αἰτία μέν, οὐ προγενεστέρα δέ. ὁμοίως καὶ τὰ ἐξ αὐτῶν αἴτια μέν, οὐ μ. δέ ‡Caes.Naz.*dial*.2(M.38.857); of H. Ghost ἔσται κατ' αὐτοὺς ἑαυτοῦ τι πρεσβύτερον καὶ ἑαυτοῦ τι πάλιν μ. Gr.Nyss. *Maced*.17(M.45.1324A); (Gnost.) ἡ τοῦ Πρώτου Χριστοῦ σὺν τῷ Πνεύματι τῷ ἁγίῳ ἐκ μετανοίας ὑπὸ τοῦ Πατρὸς αὐτῶν μ. τῶν Αἰώνων γένεσις Iren.*haer*.1.3.1(M.7.468A); οὐχ ὁ λόγος σὰρξ ἐγένετο, ὅς γε οὐδὲ ἦλθέ ποτε ἐκτὸς πληρώματος, ἀλλὰ ὁ τῆς οἰκονομίας μ. τοῦ Λόγου, Σωτήρ *ib*.1.9.2(541A); neut. as subst., *posteriority* τοὺς...τὸ μ. τῷ λόγῳ κατασκευάζοντας Gr.Nyss.*Eun*.8(2 p.181.9; M.45.773C); neut. plur. as subst., *later passage* in a book, ‡Ath.*disp*.43(M.28.497A).

μεταγεννάω, *beget later* οὐδὲ συγγεγεννημένος ἢ προγεγεννημένος ἢ μεταγεγεννημένος υἱὸς ἕτερος τοῦ θεοῦ τῷ μονογενεῖ υἱῷ Gel.Cyz.*h.e*. 2.19.9(M.85.1277B).

μεταγί(γ)νομαι, *become something else, undergo change* εἰ μὲν ἕπεται τῷ θεῷ τὸ γενέσθαι τὸν Πλάτωνα ἄνθρωπον, ἀνάγκη, μεταγομένου τοῦ Πλάτωνος...μεταγενέσθαι καὶ τὸν θεὸν τοῦ εἶναι ὅ ἐστιν ‡Just.*qu.Gr*.15.21(M.6.1484D); μεταγενόμενα τὰ τῆς φύσεως καὶ οὐσίας καὶ ὑποστάσεως καὶ προσώπου ὀνόματα ἐπὶ τῆς οἰκονομίας Leont.H. *monoph*.testimonia(M.86.1852A).

μεταγι(γ)νώσκ-ω, *change one's mind, repent* ἀπαλλαγὴν τοῦ θανάτου τοῖς ~ουσιν ἀπὸ τῶν φαύλων Just.*dial*.100.6(M.6.711A); εἰ ἐφ' οἷς ἥμαρτεν...μετέγνω, ὅπερ ἐστὶ μετὰ ταῦτα ἔγνω· βραδεῖα γὰρ γνῶσις μετάνοια, γνῶσις δὲ ἡ πρώτη ἀναμαρτησία Clem.*str*.2.6(p.127.13; M.8. 961B); τοῦτ' ἔστι μεταγνῶναι, τὸ καταγνῶναι τῶν παρῳχημένων καὶ αἰτήσασθαι τούτων ἀμνηστίαν παρὰ πατρὸς id.*q.d.s*.40(p.186.8; M.9. 645A); ref. 2Cor.7:10 τῷ ἄξια τοιαύτης λύπης ποιήσαντι καὶ ~οντι ἐπ' αὐτοῖς Or.*Jo*.28.4(p.393.10; μέγα γινώσκοντι M.14.685C); Meth.*res*.1. 30(p.265.20; M.41.1141C); *Const.App*.2.7.2; οἱ ἐν ἁμαρτίαις γινόμενοι καὶ μὴ μεταγνόντες...οὐκ εἰσακουσθήσονται προσευχόμενοι *ib*.4.6.9; only effective in this life οὐδὲν ἡμῖν ὄφελος ἔσται τότε ~ουσι Chrys. *hom.19.3 in Gen*.(4.167A); of the rich fool τὸ φορτίον τῶν ἁμαρτημάτων ἐπὶ τῶν οἰκείων ὤμων ἐπιφερόμενος, καὶ ἄπρακτα λοιπὸν ~ων *ib*. *48.1*(482A); denied of God εἰ...ἐκ μεταμέλου φαίη...[sc. τὸν Χριστὸν ἀποστέλλειν] τὸν θεὸν ὁ ἀντιλέγων, ἀσθενὴς αὐτῷ ὁ λόγος ~οντα τὸν θεὸν εἰσάγων Meth.*res*.1.39(p.284.2; M.41.1108B); οὔτε ὡς φαῦλον τεκτηνάμενος ὁ θεὸς τὸν ἄνθρωπον...μεταγνοὺς ὥσπερ φαυλότατοι τῶν δημιουργῶν *ib*.1.49(p.303.19; M.18.280B).

μετάγνωσις, **ἡ**, **1.** *change of mind*, of apostasy μ. τῶν ὀρθῶς βεβουλευμένων Cyr.*thes*.12(5^{1}.123C); **2.** *repentance*, *Lit*.ap.*Const.App*. 8.9.9; Diod.*Gen*.6:6(M.33.1570C) cit. s. μεταμέλεια; Cyr.*Nah*.3(3. 477D); plur., *acts of repentance* λιταῖς τε καὶ μ. ἐκμειλίσσεσθαι θεόν id.*Os*.94(3.125B); id.*Jon*.24(3.385E).

*μεταγράμματον, τό, *charge sheet*, fig. ὅπως ἐξαλείψῃς τὸ μ. τῶν ἐμῶν ἁμαρτιῶν Ephr.3.486A.

μεταγραφή, **ἡ**, **1.** *transcribing*, fig. Χριστὸς...ἐνεφάνισε τὴν μυστικὴν δύναμιν τῆς διαθήκης, καὶ παντὶ βουλομένῳ δέδωκεν αὐτὴν εἰς μ. Proc.G.*Gen*.17:8(M.87.356D); **2.** *transcription, copy*, Epiph. *exp.fid*.25(p.526.8; M.42.832C); **3.** *altered copy* μὴ συγγραφὴν...τὰ τούτων συντάγματα ἀλλὰ μ. μᾶλλον, τὰ ἐκείνου εἰς τὰ οἰκεῖα μεταβαλλόντων Leont.B.*Nest.et Eut*.3(M.86.1392D).

μεταγράφ-ω, **1.** *copy*; med., *M.Polyc*.22.2; Herm.*vis*.2.1.3; ὁρκίζω σε τὸν μεταγραψόμενον τὸ βιβλίον...ἵνα ἀντιβάλῃς ὃ μετεγράψω καὶ κατορθώσῃς αὐτὸ πρὸς τὸ ἀντίγραφον τοῦτο, ὅθεν μετεγράψω, ἐπιμελῶς Iren.*fr*.1(M.7.1225A); †Hipp.*Artem*.ap.Eus.*h.e*.5.28.18(M. 20.517A); **2.** *alter* a judicial sentence, fig. λύει θεὸς τὴν ἀπόφασιν καὶ μ. τὸν κίνδυνον Bas.Sel.*or*.12.3(M.85.165C); **3.** in portrait painting, *copy* εἰκὼν ὑπὸ τῆς τῶν κατὰ καιροὺς ~όντων ἀμελείας κατὰ μικρὸν ἐλαττουμένη Nil.*exerc*.6(M.79.724D); fig. εἰκόνα πάσης ἀρετῆς τὸν... βίον...μ. id.*epp*.3.332(M.79.541C); *reproduce with a difference, alter*, Gr.Nyss.*ep*.19(M.46.1072B); met. ἡγοῦνται καθάπερ ὄφις τῆς κεφαλῆς ἀπεκδύσασθαι τὸ γῆρας ~οντες ἑαυτοὺς καὶ νεοποιοῦντες Clem.*paed*. 3.3(p.246.4; M.8.577C).

***μεταγυμνάζω**, *make a change and practise, practise instead*, Cyr. H.*hom*.10(M.33.1144B).

μετάγ-ω, 1. *bring from one place to another*; *displace* from office ἐνίους ὑμεῖς μετηγάγετε...ἐκ τῆς...λειτουργίας *1Clem*.44.6; *translate* a bishop, Philost.*h.e*.9.8(M.65.574A); met., *bring* people from one state to another μέγιστον...ἀγαθόν, ὅταν τινὰ ἐκ τοῦ κακῶς πράττειν εἰς ἀρετήν τε καὶ εὐπραγίαν μ. δύνηταί τις Clem.*str*.1.27(p.107.12; M.8. 920B); *ib*.6.15(p.491.27; M.9.344A); τὸ 'μετατίθεσθε' προστεθεικώς, οὐ '~εσθε'· ὡς ἐπὶ ἀψύχων φησὶν μετατίθεσθε Thdr.Mops.*Gal*.1:6 (p.9.20; M.66.901B); pass., *be changed* for the worse μ. ἡ διάνοια ὑπὸ ἡδονῆς Clem.*paed*.3.2(p.244.21; M.8.576A); of metempsychosis ~ομένου τοῦ Πλάτωνος ἐκ τοῦ εἶναι αὐτὸν ἄνθρωπον εἰς τὸ γενέσθαι αὐτὸν μύρμηκα ‡Just.*qu.Gr*.15.21(M.6.1484D); *change* things εἰς ἐρήμους...τόπους καταφεύγων...τὴν ἀνάγκην εἰς προαίρεσιν μετῆγεν Hier.*v.Paul*.A 5(p.8.14); **2.** of thought or discourse; **a.** *lead* to a different point συνέσεως δόσιν, ἐκ τῶν αἰσθητῶν εἰς τὰ νοητά...~ούσης ἡμᾶς Clem.*str*.6.11(p.474.25; M.9.308B); πάλιν ἐπὶ τὴν θάλασσαν τὸν λόγον μ. Meth.*fr.Job* 21(p.517.4); οὐχ ἵσταταί πω λόγος τῷ Μάνεντι, ἀλλ' ὧδε κἀκεῖσε ~όμενος ὑφ' ἑαυτοῦ διελέγχεται Tit.Bost.*Man*.1.30 (M.18.1112C); ἐπὶ τὰς προφητικὰς...βίβλους τὴν εὐσεβῆ φροντίδα μ. Leo Mag.*ep*.28.2(p.12.14; M.*PL*.54.762A); **b.** *transfer* to a different context τὴν ὑμετέραν ἀλογιστίαν ἐπὶ τὸν κήρυκα τῆς ἀληθείας μετάγετε Tat.*orat*.17(p.18.22; M.6.844A); πάντα εἰς ἀλληγορίαν μ. *ib*.21(p.24. 7; 853B); Clem.*str*.7.16(p.68.11; M.9.533B); Or.*Jo*.20.5(p.333.8; M.14. 584C); **c.** *translate* τὰ ἀφ' ἑτέρας γλώττης εἰς ἑτέραν ~όμενα νοήματα, εἴ τις καὶ τῇ λέξει δουλεύειν, ἀφ' ἧς ἡρμήνευται, πειρῷτο, καὶ ταύτην ~ειν, ἀποσφαλήσεται τῆς διανοίας Diod.*Gen*.1:2(M.33.1563B).

μεταγωγεύς, ὁ, *one who leads to a different state*, name of a Valent. aeon, Iren.*haer*.1.2.4(M.7.460A); Epiph.*haer*.31.4(p.388.10; M.41. 480B); λέγει δὲ αὐτὸς...τὸν κύριον ἡμῶν Ἰησοῦν Χριστόν...Λόγον καὶ Σταυρὸν καὶ Μ. *ib*.31.6(p.396.8; 488A).

***μεταγωγικῶς**, *by transference, metaphorically*, Cosm.Mel.*schol*. (M.38.350) in Gr.Naz.*carm*.2.1.1.329.

***μεταδιδακτέον**, *one must convert* to a better frame of mind, Isid. Pel.*epp*.5.410(M.78.1569D).

μεταδιδάσκω, *teach* something new, Hipp.*haer*.6.21(p.149.9; M. 16.3227A); *teach more correctly*, *ib*.6.9(p.136.4; 3207C); *ib*.6.8(p.135. 8; 3202C); *convert* τοὺς...πρὸς τῆς ἀγνοίας πολεμουμένους μ. καὶ μετάγοντες εἰς εἰρήνην Clem.*str*.1.1(p.6.19; M.8.693B); pass., *learn* the truth about τὴν ἀπάτην μ. Synes.*astrolab*.3(p.136.20; M.66. 1581C).

μεταδίδωμι, A. c. genit. rei; **1.** *give a share of, impart*; of God imparting his divinity, Or.*Jo*.19.4(1; p.303.6; M.14.532B) cit. s. γινώσκω; ref. Gen.1:26 τῆς ἰδίας εἰκόνος αὐτοῖς [sc. ἀνθρώποις] τοῦ κυρίου ἡμῶν Ἰησοῦ Χριστοῦ μεταδίδωσι Ath.*inc*.11.3(M.25.116A); ποιμενικῆς αὐτοῖς ἐπιμελείας μεταδώσω Thdt.*Ezech*.36:37(2.993); id. *Ps*.114:6(1.1419); c. acc. pers. τούτους τῆς ἐντεῦθεν μ. ὠφελείας *ib*. 148:11(1.1580); of Son οὐ γὰρ οἷόν τε τὸν ἐκ μετουσίας ἔχοντα μεταδιδόναι τῆς μεταλήψεως ἑτέροις Ath.*syn*.51(p.274.32; M.26. 784B); ἐν Ἰορδάνῃ λουσάμενος [sc. Χριστὸς] ποταμῷ καὶ τῶν χρώτων τῆς θεότητος μεταδοὺς τοῖς ὕδασιν Cyr.H.*catech*.21.1; of prayer and fasting, personified οὗτος ὁ πόνος τῶν ἀποστολικῶν αὐτῇ μετέδωκε χαρισμάτων Thdt.*h.e*.1.24.1(3.806); **2.** in argument, *concede a share* οὐ δίδωσιν αὐτῷ [sc. Χριστῷ] οὐδὲ τὸ ἄνθρωπον εἶναι· ἀλλὰ τοῖς μὲν πάθεσιν ὑπάγει ὡς ἄνθρωπον, τῆς δὲ ἀνθρωπίνης οὐ μ. φύσεως Gr.Nyss. *Apoll*.25(M.45.1177A); Philost.*h.e*.3.11(M.65.497C); **3.** *distribute* elements in eucharist, Just.*1apol*.66.3(M.6.429A); καὶ τῷ προδότῃ τοῦ τιμίου μετέδωκε σώματός τε καὶ αἵματος Thdt.*1Cor*.11:25(3.238); Συμεώνης [sc. καὶ Δόμνος]...συνηλθέτην, καὶ τὸ ἄχραντον ἱερουργήσαντες σῶμα τῆς ζωοποιοῦ κοινωνίας ἀλλήλοις μετέδοσαν Evagr.*h.e*. 1.13(p.21.8; M.86.245B); abs., Dor.*doct*.9.2(M.88.1717D); CSyr.*act*. (*ACO* 3 p.98.26; H.2.1376A); *Lit.Jac*.(p.232.24); **4.** *infect with*, fig. ἄλλος γὰρ ἄλλῳ τῆς νόσου μεταδόντες συννοσοῦσιν ἀλλήλοις Bas.*hom. in Ps*.1(1.96C; M.29.225B); *Const.App*.6.18.10.

B. c. acc. rei; **1.** *impart* ὁ μὲν θεὸς...μ. ἑκάστῳ ἀπὸ τοῦ ἰδίου τὸ εἶναι Or.*princ*.1.3.5(p.56.1; M.11.150B); **2.** *hand over* τῶν θνησκόντων τὰς ψυχὰς...ὁ μέγας φωστὴρ...μ. τῇ σελήνῃ Hegem.*Arch*.8(p.13.2; M.10.1440B); **3.** *hand down* ὁμολογητὰς καὶ μάρτυρας...ὧν ὁ θεὸς τὴν πίστιν καὶ εἰς τοὺς σοὺς χρόνους τῆς βασιλείας μετέδωκε CArim.*ep. Const*.1(p.237.31; M.26.697B); **4.** *communicate* an order τὸ τοῦ θεοῦ πρόσταγμα Μωσῆς τῷ ἀδελφῷ μετεδίδου Cyr.H.*catech*.21.6; **5.** *give* τὴν ἐλευθερίαν μ. Thdt.*Jer*.34:10(2.559); **6.** freq. = A.1 supra πτωχῷ μ. ἄρτον μου *T.Isach*.7.5; Chrys.*hom.28.7 in Heb*.(12.269B); id.*hom.5.1 in Phil*.(11.228C); ἐκ ταύτης τῆς ὕλης ὁ κύριος ἑαυτῷ διαπλασάμενος σῶμα...τούτῳ δὲ καὶ τὰς ἰδίας ἐνεργείας μεταδεδωκώς, ἐποίει ζῶον θεόν ‡Ath.*dial.Trin*.4.9(M.28.1264C); pass. οὐ μετεδόθη τῷ σώματι εἰς τὸ τελεσιουργηθῆναι ἡ ἐπιθυμία Meth.*lepr*.6(p.459.3); Marc.Er.*opusc*.3.5(M.65.973A); ref. Christ's humanity διὰ τῆς πρὸς τὸν φύσει θεὸν ἑνώσεως αὐτῆς ὑποστατικῆς μεταδιδομένης αὐτῇ τῆς τοῦ ὀνόματος τοῦ υἱοῦ τοῦ θεοῦ καὶ θεοῦ τιμῆς Leont.H.*Nest*.3.5(M.86. 1616A); of H. Ghost, ref. Gen.2:7 ἔστιν ἀεὶ τὸ πνεῦμα, καὶ πρὶν ἐμφυσώμενον αὐτὸ καὶ μεταδιδόμενον ὑπογράψῃ Μωϋσῆς τόπῳ [l. τύπῳ] σωματικῷ τὴν δι' αὐτοῦ ζωοποίησιν ὑπογράφων Didym.(‡Bas.)*Eun*. 5(1.307C; M.29.737A); τὸ πνεῦμα [sc. καλούμενον] κύριος ἀπὸ τοῦ κυρίου τὴν ἐπωνυμίαν ἔχον, ἀφ' οὗ καὶ μεταδίδοται *ib*.(310C; M.744C); ἐκ τοῦ πατρὸς ἐκπορευόμενον [sc. τὸ πνεῦμα], καὶ δι' υἱοῦ μεταδιδόμενον καὶ μεταλαμβανόμενον ὑπὸ πάσης τῆς κτίσεως ‡Cyr.*Trin*.9(6³. 13D; M.77.1140B); ref. Eph.3:15 οὐκ ἐξ ἡμῶν μετηνέχθη ἐπὶ τὴν μακαρίαν θεότητα τὸ τῆς πατρότητος καὶ υἱότητος...ὄνομα· τοὐναντίον δ' ἐκεῖθεν ἡμῖν μ. *ib*.8(12C; M.1137B); eucharistic σῶμα ἡμᾶς ἑαυτοῦ ἐποίησε, σῶμα ἡμῖν τὸ ἑαυτοῦ μετέδωκε Chrys.*hom.3.3 in Eph*.(11. 21D); **7.** = A.3 supra μ. ... αὐτῇ...τὰ μυστήρια Socr.*h.e*.6.9.8(M.67. 693A); τὴν ἀναίμακτον...θυσίαν μ. ... τῷ πιστῷ λαῷ Eustrat.*v.Eutych*. 78(M.86.2364B); σῶμα ἅγιον...Χριστοῦ τοῖς πιστοῖς μεταδιδόμενον εἰς ἄφεσιν ἁμαρτιῶν καὶ εἰς ζωὴν αἰώνιον *Lit.Jac*.(p.234.9); where perh. simply = διδόμενον.

μετάδοσις, ἡ, 1. *imparting*; of H. Ghost, ref. Jo.20:22 τὸ ἐμφύσημα καθαρτικὸν...ἢ καὶ ἐνεργητικὸν τῆς μ. τοῦ ἁγίου πνεύματος Eus.*e.th*.3.5(p.160.17; M.24.1008B); οὔτε ἡ κτίσις οὕτως ἀθλία, οὔτε θεὸς οὕτως ἀδύνατος, ὥστε τὴν ἁγίαν μ. μὴ διαπέμπειν ἐπὶ τὰ ποιήματα Didym.(‡Bas.)*Eun*.5(1.301D; M.29.724B); ἐκπομπῇ καὶ μ. πνεύματος τὰ γινόμενα γίνεται *ib*.(307B; M.737A); Father's creative powers to Son, denied εἰ κατὰ μ. καὶ συγχώρησιν τοῦ πατρὸς καὶ οὐ κατὰ φύσιν δημιουργὸς ὁ υἱός, οὐδὲν ἂν εἴη τῶν ὑπ' αὐτοῦ δημιουργηθέντων κατὰ φύσιν *ib*.4(279C; M.673A); of baptism ἡ μ. τῆς ἀθραύστου σφραγῖδος *Const.App*.3.16.4; of eucharist ἡ τοῦ μυστηρίου μ. ... μεταποιοῦσα πρὸς ἑαυτήν, καὶ ὁμοίους τῷ κατ' αἰτίαν ἀγαθῷ κατὰ χάριν ...ἀποφαίνουσα Max.*myst*.21(M.91.697A) ∞ ‡Bas.*h.myst*.62(p.397.18); **2.** *distribution* of benefits, Clem.*paed*.3.4(p.254.10; M.8.600A); οὐδαμοῦ φιλανθρωπίαν ὠνόμασε τὴν μ., ἀλλὰ χάριν καὶ κοινωνίαν καὶ εὐλογίαν...τῇ ἐξουσίᾳ τῆς γνώμης τὸ τῆς μ. ἐπίστευσε μέτρον Thdt. *2Cor*.9:5(3.334).

μεταδοτέον, *one ought to give a share*, Clem.*paed*.2.1(p.164.25; M.8.401B); *ib*.2.7(p.192.22; 464A); *ib*.3.6(p.256.1; 604B).

***μεταδοτικῶς, 1.** *by imparting, communication*, †Bas.*Chr.generat*. 2(2.596E; M.31.1460C) cit. s. μεταβατικῶς; πάντα...ὅσα ἔχει [sc. ὁ υἱός] οὐ μ. οὔτε διδακτικῶς ἀλλ' ὡς ἐξ αἰτίου ‡Cyr.*Trin*.23(6³.28C; M. 77.1164C); **2.** *by distribution* ὁ θεὸς...ζῶσα ἀρετῇ...καὶ μ. ἐκφοιτᾷ εἰς τὰ ἀπ' αὐτῆς ὡς αἰτίας οὔσης, ὑπάρξαντα νοητά Max.*schol.c.h*.13.3(M. 4.97B).

***μεταδότις, ἡ,** fem. of μεταδότης, *generous giver*, Dion.Ar.*d.n*.1.3 (M.3.589C).

μεταδρομή, ἡ, *change of course*, met. τὴν τῶν τοῖς εἰδώλοις λελατρευκότων εἰς τὸ ἄμεινον μ. Cyr.*Zach*.104(3.798A); *ib*.100(791E v.l. καταδρομή Aubert); id.*Is*.3.2(2.420D).

***μεταζάω**, *convert*, ‡Eus.*ant.mart.coll*.(M.20.1520B).

***μεταζωγραφέω**, *change the likeness of*, Meth.*symp*.2.6(p.23.13; M.18.57A).

***μεταθέσιμος**, *translated*, i.e. from another see; of a bishop, Anast.S.*haer*.(p.265); neut. as subst., *translation* of a bishop, Thphn.*chron*.p.322(M.108.780A).

μετάθεσις, ἡ, 1. *translation* Ἐνὼχ εὐαρεστήσας τῷ θεῷ, ἐν σώματι μετετέθη, τὴν μ. τῶν δικαίων προμηνύων Iren.*haer*.5.5.1(M.7.1134B); Cyr.H.*catech*.14.25 cit. s. ἀνάβασις; of assumption of BMV, *Dorm. BMV* 50(p.112); of death, Chrys.*hom.72.3 in Jo*.(8.426C) cit. s. μετάστασις; τὸν θεὸν ἱκετεύων ταχεῖαν αὐτοῦ τὴν μ. ποιεῖσθαι ‡Pall. *h.mon*.8.17(p.37.16; M.34.1139B); *V.Dan*.(p.58.20); Jo.Eleem.*v.Tych*. 9(p.119.13); of a bishop, Thphn.*chron*.p.322(M.108.780A); **2.** *rapture* τοῦτο οὖν ὁ προφήτης λῆμμα προσηγόρευσε τῆς διανοίας τὴν λῆψιν καὶ τὴν ἀπὸ τῶν ἀνθρωπίνων μ. Thdt.*Nah*.1:1(2.1519); **3.** *change* μεταμέλεια θεοῦ λέγεται τῆς τοῦ θεοῦ οἰκονομίας ἀπὸ πράγματος εἰς πρᾶγμα μ. Or.*fr.5 in 1Reg*.15:11(p.297.9; M.17.45B); *ib*.4(p.296. 15; 44C); Diod.*Gen*.6:6(M.33.1570C) cit. s. μεταμέλεια; Gr.Naz.*or*. 21.25(M.35.1109D) cit. s. μεταποίησις; **4.** rhet., *metathesis est, quae mittit animos judicum in res praeteritas aut futuras*, Isid.H.*etym*.2. 21.34.

***μεταθετικός**, *transferable*, Epiph.*anc*.54(M.43.113A; μεταστατικόν p.63.26).

μεταθέω, *run after*, met., Cyr.*ador*.14(1.489E).

***μεταθρώσκω**, *change one's place*, Cyr.*ador*.17(1.598C).

μεταίρω, 1. *remove* boundaries; fig., of doctrine μὴ μ. ὅρια αἰώνια, μηδὲ ὑπερβαίνοντες τὴν θείαν παράδοσιν Jo.D.*f.o*.1.1(M.94.

792A); **2.** intrans., *depart, migrate* εἰς εὐδαίμονα βίον...μ. Mac.Mgn. *apocr*.3.28(p.119.21).

***μεταίσιος**, *lifted up*, Gr.Nyss.*hom.3 in Cant*.(M.44.812B).

μεταΐσσω, *approach in its radiance* μ. μὲν ἐς ἄργυφον, εἰσέτι δ' οὔπω τρέψεν ὅλην χροιὴν *gleams until* it is *almost* white, Paul.Sil. *ambo*.91(M.86.2255B).

μεταίχμιον, τό, 1. *space between two armies* αὐτὴν τὴν ψυχὴν ποιησάμενοι τοῦ ἐν αὐτῇ πολέμου μ. Gr.Nyss.*hom.2 in Cant*.(M.44. 797B); **2.** *middle, mean* ἐν μ. ... τῶν παρόντων καὶ τῶν μελλόντων Thdt.*Cant*.2:14(2.72); Christol. 'θεανδρικὴν'...οὐ...συνθέτῳ φύσει τινῶν ἄκρων μ. προσήκουσαν, ἀλλ' ἀνδρωθέντι θεῷ Max.*ambig*.(M.91. 1057A); fig. Μωσῆς...μ. ὥσπερ τι κείμενος θεοῦ καὶ ἀνθρώπων τοὺς ἄνωθεν σφίσι διεκόμιζε λόγους Cyr.*ador*.2(1.50C); **3.** *middle* τοῦ παραβάτου πεσόντος ἐν τῷ μ. τοῦ στρατοπέδου ‡Jo.D.*Artem*.70(p.104.23; M.96.1317C); **4.** *uncertainty*, Thdr.Stud.*epp*.2.172(M.99.1540B).

μετακαλέομαι, 1. *summon*, Eus.*h.e*.1.13.13(M.20.125A); Epiph. *haer*.57.1(p.344.4; προσκαλεσάμενοι M.41.996A); pass., Chrys.*hom. 2.2 in Jo*.(8.9E); **2.** *call by a different name* 'Ιεροσόλυμα Αἰλίαν... μετεκαλέσατο Philost.*h.e*.7.11(M.65.549B); pass., Epiph.*haer*.30.25 (p.366.27; M.41.448B); μετακεκλῆσθαι Thdr.Mops.*2Cor*.1:15(M.66. 893D; μεταβεβλῆσθαι p.197.5).

μετακεν-όω, *pour* from one vessel into another, Iren.*haer*.1.13.2 (M.7.581A); fig. ἐπὶ τῆς ψυχῆς, ὅσον ἂν αὐτῇ τῆς ἀγάπης ἐφ' ἃ μὴ προσῆκε, τοσοῦτον ἐνδέειν ἀνάγκη πρὸς τὸν θεόν. ὁ δε ἅπαξ ὁρμήσας ἀγαπᾶν ἀργύριον, πᾶσαν ἐκεῖ μ. τὴν ἀγάπην †Bas.*Is*.51(1.418E; M.30. 213A); Christol ἐπειδὴ ἐκένωσεν ἑαυτὸν μορφὴν δούλου λαβών, οὐ τὸ πλήρωμα ἠλαττώθη· ἀλλ' ἵνα δείξῃ ἀπ' οὐρανοῦ ~ωθέντα εἰς ἀνθρωπότητα τουτέστιν εἰς ἐργαστήριον Μαρίας Epiph.*anc*.40(p.50.9; M.43. 88D); acc. Eunomius εἰ τὸν φαινόμενον Χριστόν τε καὶ κύριον πεποιῆσθαι παρὰ τοῦ θεοῦ πεπιστεύκαμεν, ἀνάγκην εἶναι πάλιν εἰς ἄνθρωπον ~οῦσθαι τὸν κύριον καὶ δευτέραν ὑποδύεσθαι γέννησιν Gr.Nyss.*Eun*.6 (2 p.145.22; M.45.732B).

μετακεράννυμι, 1. *change* one's nature, *transmute*, Gr.Nyss.*v. Mos*.35(M.44.312C); Mac.Mgn.*apocr*.3.23(p.104.1); Christol. φθαρτὸν ἐκ μήτρας λαβὼν τὸ ἐκ τῆς παρθένου σῶμα, εὐθέως αὐτὸ πρὸς ἀφθαρσίαν μετεκεράσατο Leont.B.*Nest.et Eut*.2(M.86.1329B); **2.** met., *work a change in* μ. τὰς τῶν κρατούντων γνώμας, ἐπὶ τὸ χεῖρον διαστρέψας τοὺς πλείονας τοῦ κλήρου Pall.*v.Chrys*.8(p.46.1; M.47.27).

μετακίνησις, ἡ, 1. *translation* of a bishop, *Cod.Afr*.48; **2.** *change* τοῦ λόγου...δόντος μὲν ἑαυτὸν ἀνθρωπίνῃ σαρκὶ...μείναντος δὲ ἐν ταυτότητι καὶ μηδεμίαν θείαν μ. μηδὲ ἀλλοίωσιν ὑποστάντος Apoll.*fid. sec.pt*.2(p.168.8; M.10.1105C); οὔτε γὰρ ἄλλαξις οὔτε μ. οὔτε περικλεισμὸς ἐν νεύματι γέγονεν περὶ τὴν ἁγίαν τοῦ θεοῦ δύναμιν *ib*.11 (p.171.4; 1109A).

μετακινητός, *movable*, Or.*Jo*.10.39(23; p.216.3; M.14.381B).

μετακιρνάω, = μετακεράννυμι, *transmute* ‡Nil.*perist*.4.12(M.79. 840A).

μετακλάω, *subdue*, Gr.Nyss.*v.Mos*.(M.44.388D).

***μετακληρόομαι**, *obtain as a different lot* ὁ 'Ισραὴλ πρωτότοκος ἐν τέκνοις, ἐπειδὴ πεπαρῴνηκεν εἰς Χριστὸν...δευτέραν ὥσπερ μετεκληρώσατο τάξιν Cyr.*Is*.2.4(2.298D).

μετάκλησις, ἡ, 1. *change of name*, *Dial.Tim.et Aquil*.92 r°(p.75); **2.** *naming, calling*, Ath.*apol.sec*.14(p.98.14; M.25.272B); Leont.H. *Nest*.3.8(M.86.1640A); **3.** *recall* to a different frame of mind, Cyr. *ador*.1(1.17A).

μετάκλισις, ἡ, *change of position*; met., of courting popularity ταῖς πρὸς τοὺς πολλοὺς μ. Gr.Naz.*or*.42.24(M.36.488B); ἀπὸ τῶν αἰσχιόνων ἐπὶ τὰ ἀμείνω μ. Cyr.*Abac*.56(3.571C).

μετακομιδή, ἡ, *transporting, conveyance* from one place to another, Ath.*apol.sec*.9(p.95.13; M.25.265A); Chrys.*serm.4.1 in Gen*. (4.659C); Cyr.*Is*.2.4(2.307B); of dead bodies, Eus.*v.C*.4.66 tit.(p.117. 15; M.20.1221A); ‡Just.*qu.et resp*.27(M.6.1273C); *translation* of relics πολλὰ δὲ θαύματα καὶ ἰάσεις ἔν τε τῇ μ. ἔν τε τῇ καταθέσει...διὰ τῶν ὁσίων αὐτοῦ θεραπόντων ἐποίησε κύριος †Jo.D.*B.J*.40(M.96.1240A).

μετακομίζω, 1. lit.; **a.** *transport* from place to place, Bas.*jud*. 5(2.218E; M.31.665A); dead bodies, *T.Neph*.9.1; Isid.Pel.*epp*.5.157 (M.78.1416D); **b.** *translate* relics Ἀνδρέαν τὸν ἀπόστολον ἐκ τῆς Ἀχαΐας μ. ἐπὶ τὸν ναόν Philost.*h.e*.3.2(M.65.481A); Thdt.*h.e*.3.10.2 (3.923); pass., *be translated*, Clem.*str*.7.3(p.10.10; M.9.416C); **2.** met.; **a.** *introduce* practices ἐξ Αἰγύπτου μ. τῇ 'Ελλάδι τῆς Δηοῦς ἑορτάς id. *prot*.2(p.12.14; M.8.73B); **b.** *bring* people from one state of mind to another, Cyr.*Ps*.67:8(M.69.1148A); id.*Abac*.23(3.537C); **c.** *transfer* thought or discourse to a different subject, Bas.*Eun*.1.9(1.222A; M. 29.533B); Cyr.*ador*.10(1.366E); id.*Is*.3.1(2.384D); **d.** *borrow* a metaphor, Bas.*Eun*.2.24(1.260D; M.29.625C).

***μετακομιστέον**, *one must transfer*, Cyr.*Ps*.7:12(M.69.753B).

***μετακύπτω**, *lie down*, Gr.Mag.*dial*.(tr.Zach.)3.16(M.*PL*.77. 258C).

μεταλαγχάν-ω, 1. *have a share allotted* καθ' ὃ ἡ ἑκάστου δύναμις χωρεῖ τῆς αὐτοῦ θεότητος ~ειν Eus.*e.th*.3.16(p.174.22; M.24.1033A); τῆς πρὸς αὐτοῦ [sc. τοῦ 'Εμμανουήλ] οἰκειότητος ἐν πίστει μ. Cyr. *glaph.Gen*.1(1.12A); **2.** *partake* of food, Thdt.*Ps*.79:6(1.1173); of eucharist, *Const.App*.7.40.1; τοῦ δεσποτικοῦ μ. σώματος Thdt.*1Cor*. 8:12(3.218); οὕτω τῶν θείων μυστηρίων μ. ἵνα τὸν ἀγαθὸν δεσπότην ἔνοικον λάβωμεν *ib*.11:34(3.240); *take part* in a festival, id.*ep*.64(4. 1116); **3.** *have assigned in exchange* τὸ πνεῦμα τοῦ θεοῦ διὰ τῆς ὕλης κεχωρηκὸς κατὰ τὰς παραλλάξεις αὐτῆς ἄλλο καὶ ἄλλο ὄνομα ~ειν φατέ Athenag.*leg*.22.3(M.6.937B); ἑτέρας ταῦτα μετὰ τὴν ἀλλοίωσιν μ. προσηγορίας Thdt.*eran*.1(4.12).

μεταλαμβάν-ω, A. *partake of, participate in* μεταληψόμεθα τοῦ ἐλέους 'Ιησοῦ *2Clem*.16.2; τηρήσατε τὴν σάρκα ἵνα τοῦ πνεύματος μεταλάβητε *ib*.14.3; ἡ κτίσις...ὄντως ὄντος ἐκ πατρὸς λόγου ~ουσα καὶ βοηθουμένη δι' αὐτοῦ εἰς τὸ εἶναι Ath.*gent*.41(M.25.84A); οὐδὲ γὰρ ἐν τοῖς πᾶσιν ὤν, τῶν ὄντων ~ει [sc. ὁ λόγος], ἀλλὰ πάντα μᾶλλον ὑπ' αὐτοῦ ζωογονεῖται id.*inc*.17.6(M.25.125C); τὸ πνεῦμα...τοῦ εἶναι τὴν διαμονὴν δωρεῖται ~όμενον Didym.(‡Bas.)*Eun*.5(1.311D; M.29. 748B).

B. *partake* of food; **1.** in gen. μεταλαβὼν ἐκ τοῦ φαρμάκου αὐτῶν οὐκ ἠλλοιώθη ἡ καρδία αὐτοῦ *A.Andr.et Mt*.2(p.66.12); of Christ τροφῆς καὶ ποτοῦ καὶ ὕπνου μεταλαβών *Lit*.ap.*Const.App*.8.12.32; οἱ δὲ τῶν ἐμψύχων ἰχθῦς μόνους ~ουσι Socr.*h.e*.5.22.36(M.67.633A); τῶν μόνοις τοῖς ἱερεῦσιν ἀπονενεμημένων μ. Thdt.*qu.52 in 1Reg*.(1.388); abs., Ath.*v.Anton*.7(M.26.852C); Cyr.H.*catech*.4.27; Pall.*h.Laus*.48 (p.142.19; M.34.1211B); πεποίηκεν [sc. βρώματα] εἰς ἀπόλαυσιν, ὥστε πρόφασιν ἐντεῦθεν τοὺς ~οντας εἰς εὐχαριστίαν λαμβάνειν Thdt.*1Tim*. 4:3(3.659); fig. ἡ νουθέτησις οὖν οἱονεὶ δίαιτά ἐστι νοσούσης ψυχῆς, ὧν χρὴ ~ειν συμβουλευτική, καὶ ὧν οὐ χρὴ ἀπαγορευτική Clem.*paed*.1.8 (p.128.12; M.8.328C); *receive* baptism, Evagr.*h.e*.1.20(p.28.24; M.86. 2473A); **2.** of eucharist οἱ καλούμενοι παρ' ἡμῶν διάκονοι διδόασιν ἑκάστῳ τῶν παρόντων μεταλαβεῖν ἀπὸ τοῦ εὐχαριστηθέντος ἄρτου καὶ οἴνου καὶ ὕδατος Just.*1apol*.65.5(M.6.428B); εἴ τις διακρίνοιτο παρὰ πρεσβυτέρου γεγαμηκότος, ὡς μὴ χρῆναι λειτουργήσαντος αὐτοῦ προσφορᾶς ~ειν, ἀνάθεμα ἔστω CGangr.*can*.4; ~έτω ἑκάστη τάξις καθ' ἑαυτὴν τοῦ κυριακοῦ σώματος καὶ τοῦ τιμίου αἵματος *Const.App*. 2.57.21; ὅτε μετέλαβον οἱ ἀπόστολοι τῶν ἱερῶν δείπνων ἐκείνων Chrys.*hom.27.5 in 1Cor*.(10.248B); πολλοὶ τῆς θυσίας ταύτης ἅπαξ ~ουσι τοῦ παντὸς ἐνιαυτοῦ, ἄλλοι δὲ δίς, ἄλλοι δὲ πολλάκις id. *hom.17.4 in Heb*.(12.169B); ἐξ ἐκείνης [sc. τραπέζης] μ. Thdt.*1Cor*. 11:21(3.237); id.*eran*.3(4.269) cit. s. ἀντίτυπος; Leont.B.*Nest.et Eut*.3(M.86.1385C); ἔδωκεν ὁ θεὸς τὰς ἁγίας ἡμέρας ταύτας [sc. Lent] ἵνα...καθαρθῇ ἀπὸ τῶν ἁμαρτιῶν ὅλου τοῦ ἐνιαυτοῦ, καὶ οὕτως... προσέρχεται τῇ ἁγίᾳ ἡμέρᾳ τῆς ἀναστάσεως καὶ ~ει ἀκατακρίτως τῶν ἁγίων μυστηρίων Dor.*doct*.15.1(M.88.1789A); *Apophth.Patr*.(M. 65.157A); οὐκ εἰμὶ ἄξιος μεταλαβεῖν τῶν ἁγίων καὶ ἀχράντων σου μυστηρίων *Lit.Jac*.(p.232.18); *Lit.Chrys*.(p.395.22); c. acc., Jo.D. *imag*.3.26(M.94.1348A); abs., *communicate* πάντες οἱ κατὰ τὰς ἐρήμους μονάζοντες, ἔνθα μή ἐστιν ἱερεύς, κοινωνίαν οἴκοι κατέχοντες, ἀφ' ἑαυτῶν ~ουσιν Bas.*ep*.93(3.187A; M.32.485A); ψαλμὸς λεγέσθω λγ' ἐν τῷ ~ειν πάντας τοὺς λοιποὺς *Lit*.ap.*Const.App*.8.13.16; σὺ δὲ πρὶν ἢ μὲν μεταλαβεῖν νηστεύεις, ἵνα ὁπωσδήποτε ἄξιος φανῇς τῆς κοινωνίας· ὅταν δὲ μεταλάβῃς, δέον σε ἐπιτεῖναι τὴν σωφροσύνην, πάντα ἀπολλύεις Chrys.*hom.27.5 in 1Cor*.(10.248C); τοὺς κατ' ἀξίαν ~οντας id.*hom.82.6 in Mt*.(7.790C); †Jo.Jej.*poenit*.(M.88.1896A); ὁ θεός, ὁ...ἁγιάζων...τοὺς...ἐν πίστει ~ειν μέλλοντας *Lit.Jac*.(p.230.14); πολλαχοῦ νῦν ~ουσι μετὰ τὸ τέλος τῆς λειτουργίας διὰ τὴν εὐκολίαν *Lit.Chrys*.(p.396.8); **3.** fig. τῇ μυστικῇ τραπέζῃ ἐν ᾗ τῶν οὐρανίων ~ομεν Gr.Nyss.*fr*.3(M.46.1112A); ref. Passover οἱονείπως ἐξοδοιπορεῖν ἐπειγόμενοι τῶν ἐν τῷδε τῷ κόσμῳ περισπασμῶν...μεταληψόμεθα τοῦ Χριστοῦ πολυάγνως καὶ καθαρῶς Cyr.*ador*.17(1.598C); **4.** of Collyridian sacrifice to BMV αἱ πᾶσαι ἀπὸ τοῦ ἄρτου ~ουσιν Epiph. *haer*.79.1(p.476.19; M.42.741A).

C. *suppose* προφῆτιδα ἑαυτὴν μ. Iren.*haer*.1.13.3(M.7.584B); Or. *Jo*.1.21(23; p.25.25; M.14.60B).

D. *receive next, later* καλὸν...καὶ φρένας καλὰς ἐκ μετανοίας αὐτοὺς τῆς εἰς τὴν πίστιν μεταλαβεῖν Clem.*str*.7.14(p.60.33; M.9.517C); ἐπὶ τῶν χειροκμήτων εἰκόνων ὁ διὰ μέσου χρόνος τὴν μεταληφθεῖσαν μορφὴν ἀπὸ τοῦ πρωτοτύπου πάντως διΐστησιν Gr.Nyss.*Eun*.1(1 p.200. 8; M.45.448A).

E. *receive instead* ἄλλον ἐξ ἄλλου μ. δεσπότην Bas.*hom.in Ps*.14 (1.112A; M.29.276C); *understand instead* ὅτι εἰς Βαβυλῶνα ὁ κόσμος μετείληπται δηλοῖ τὸ 'μεγάλη' προστιθέμενον Areth.*Apoc*.14:8(M.106. 688B).

F. *translate* πυνθανόμενος...εἰς τί ~ουσι τὴν σχῖνον τὸ φυτόν, καὶ πῶς τὸ σχίζειν ὀνομάζουσιν Or.*ep*.1.6(M.11.61B); οἱ ~οντες εἰς Ἑλληνισμὸν τὰ Ἑβραίων id.*Jo*.10.40(24; p.218.14; M.14.385D); Eus.*p.e.* 10.5(474B; M.21.788C); ἀπὸ τῆς Ἑλληνικῆς διαλέκτου τὸ κατὰ Ἰωάννην μεταληφθὲν εἰς Ἑβραΐδα Epiph.*haer*.30.3(p.338.5; M.41.409C).

G. *interpret, render,* Or.*Jo*.2.33(27; p.90.19; M.14.172C); *paraphrase* ὀρθῶς...ἐπὶ τὸ σαφέστερον ~οντα φάναι ἀντὶ τοῦ 'ἐν ἀρχῇ ἦν ὁ λόγος' τὸ 'ἐν ἀρχῇ ἦν ὁ υἱός' Eus.*e.th*.2.14(p.116.19; M.24.929D).

H. *transfer* from literal to spiritual level, Or.*Jo*.1.8(10; p.13.14; M.14.37C); εἰ πρὸς τὴν τροπικωτέραν μεταληφθείη θεωρίαν τὸ καθ' ἱστορίαν γεγενημένον Gr.Nyss.*v.Mos*.(M.44.337C); *refer* type to antitype, in exposition Ἀμιναδὰβ...ὃς ~εται εἰς τὸν Χριστόν Or.*schol. in Cant*.6:10(M.17.280B); οἱ...τὴν γυναῖκα πρὸς τὴν ἐκκλησίαν ~οντες Areth.*Apoc*.12:12(M.106.668D).

***μεταλαμπαδεύω**, *hand on the torch to another,* Clem.*str*.2.23(p.189.14; M.8.1088B).

[*]**μετάλειψις, ἡ**, v. μετάληψις.

μεταληπτέον, 1. *one must take in another sense* τὰ περὶ τοῦ δράκοντος...τῇδε μ. Meth.*symp*.8.9(p.91.22, v.l. μεταβλητέον M.18.152C); **2.** *one must transfer* arguments, Cyr.*ador*.15(1.522B); *ib*.16(568C).

μεταληπτικός, 1. *capable of being shared, participated in* οὐ γὰρ ἐφικνεῖταί τι τῶν κτιστῶν...τῆς ἀκτίστου καὶ...μ. καὶ ἀπείρου φύσεως Gr.Naz.*or*.23.11(M.35.1164B, v.l. μεταληπτῆς); ref. H. Ghost, *ib*.41.9(M.36.441B) cit. s. μεταληπτός; ref. Jo.6:52 ἀείζωος ἐστὶν ὁ βιβρωσκόμενος καὶ μ. ἀθανάτου οὐ δεῖται ζωῆς Anast.S.*hex*.12(M.89.1057B); **2.** *involving the use of words in a different sense, allegorical,* cf. παρ' ὧν [sc. pagan writers] τὸν μ. τῶν παρ' Ἕλλησιν μυστηρίων γνοὺς τρόπον [sc. Ὠριγένης] ταῖς Ἰουδαϊκαῖς προσῆψεν γραφαῖς Porphyry ap.Eus.*h.e*.6.19.8(M.20.568A).

μεταληπτικῶς, *by participation* ἐστὶν ἓν πρὸς τὸν ἑαυτοῦ πατέρα, οὐ καθάπερ ἡμεῖς τῇ πρὸς αὐτὸν σχέσει τὴν ἑνότητα κερδαίνοντες μετοχικῶς τε καὶ μ. Cyr.*thes*.12(5^1.119E); εἰ γὰρ οὐκ αὐτουργεῖ τὸ πνεῦμα τὸ ἅγιον ἐν ἡμῖν, οὐδὲ τοῦτό ἐστι κατὰ φύσιν,...μετοχικῶς δὲ καὶ μ., ἁγιασμοῦ πληρούμενον, παρὰ τῆς θείας οὐσίας *ib*.34(352E).

***μεταληπτός**, *shared, participated in,* of H. Ghost ἀεὶ μ., οὐ μεταληπτικόν· τελειοῦν, οὐ τελειούμενον Gr.Naz.*or*.41.9(M.36.441B); v. μεταληπτικός.

***μεταλήπτωρ, ὁ**, *one who participates,* Epiph.*haer*.42.11(p.133.16; M.41.740D).

***μεταληπτῶς**, *by participation* ἔχει δὲ σύμπαν ἐν ἑαυτῷ τὸ τοῦ πατρὸς ἴδιον, οὐ μ., εἰ καὶ δεδωκέναι λέγεται ὁ πατήρ Cyr.*Jo*.2.4(4.170D); χεῖρα ὧδε τὴν δύναμιν καλεῖ, ἣν ἔχει ὁ υἱὸς φυσικῶς καὶ οὐ μ. Ammon.*Jo*.3:35(M.85.1417A).

μετάληψις (once [*]**μετάλειψις**), **ἡ, A.** *participation;* **1.** Christol. θεὸν ἐν σώματι πεφηνότα, σώματος μετάληψιν διδόντα πρὸς μετάληψιν θεότητος Val.Apoll.*apol*.(p.290.8)ap.Leont.B.*Apoll*.(M.86.1957A); of rel. of created world to God τὰ...πλησιάζοντα [sc. τῇ τριάδι]... οὐ φύσει ἀλλὰ μ. Gr.Naz.*or*.23.11(M.35.1164B); cf. οὐ γὰρ οἷόν τε τὸν ἐκ μετουσίας ἔχοντα μεταδιδόναι τῆς μ. ἑτέροις Ath.*syn*.51(p.274.32; M.26.784B); *sharing* κοινωνήσεις εἰς πάντα τῷ ἀδελφῷ σου...κοινὴ γὰρ ἡ μ. παρὰ θεοῦ πᾶσιν ἀνθρώποις παρεσκευάσθη *Const.App*.7.12.5; **2.** *partaking* of food τὴν τοῦ ξύλου μ. Thdt.*Ps*.71:4(1.1103); abs. = *consumption, eating,* cf. *primitivas fructuum quos dedisti nobis ad percipiendum,* Hipp.*trad.ap*.28.3(p.54); cf. ἀπαρχὴν καρπῶν οὓς ἔδωκας ἡμῖν εἰς μ. *Euchol*.(p.522); νηστεία...ποθεινήν σοι τὴν μ. φανῆναι ποιήσει Bas.*hom*.1.8(2.7A; M.30.176C); Chrys.*hom.29.2 in Gen*.(4.282B); in alleged Montanist ritual meal ἀφθόρου παιδὸς κατακεντᾷ τὸ σῶμα καὶ τὸ αἷμα πρὸς μετάληψιν ἀποφέρεται Epiph.*haer*.48.15(p.241.11; M.41.880B); **3.** eucharistic; **a.** *partaking* of elements, Just.*1apol*.67.5(M.6.429C) cit. s. εὐχαριστέω; τῇ μ. τῶν φρικτῶν τούτων καὶ φοβερῶν μυστηρίων Chrys.*prod.Jud*.2.6(2.396B); τοῦτο σημαίνει...ἡ μ. τῶν μυστηρίων, τὸ μεταλαβεῖν τοῦ δεδοξασμένου αὐτοῦ σώματος Cosm.Ind.*top*.5(M.88.308A); ἐμυσταγώγησε τοὺς μαθητὰς διὰ τῆς μ. τῶν ἀπορρήτων μυστηρίων Alex.Sal.*Barn*.1(p.440D); διὰ τῆς ἁγίας μ. τῶν ἀχράντων καὶ ζωοποιῶν μυστηρίων, τὴν πρὸς αὐτὸν κατὰ μέθεξιν ἐνδεχομένην δι' ὁμοιότητος κοινωνίαν τε καὶ ταυτότητα Max.*myst*.24(M.91.704D); ἐξῆλθεν αἷμα καὶ ὕδωρ, τὰ δύο καθάρσια τοῦ τε βαπτίσματος καὶ τῆς μ. τῶν ἀχράντων αὐτοῦ μυστηρίων *Chron. Pasch*.p.220(M.92.536D); *Lit.Jac*.(p.234.22); μετάλειψιν *cat.Lc*.15:20(p.119.35); as participation in Christ ἔλαβεν γὰρ ὁ μὲν υἱὸς τοῦ θεοῦ τὸν ἄνθρωπον ὃν ἐνεδύσατο ἀπὸ τῆς ἐκκλησίας, καὶ ἀνταπέδωκεν αὐτῇ πάλιν εἰς κοινωνίαν αὐτῆς ἁγίαν τὴν σάρκα εἰς μ. Ph.Carp.*Cant*.1:2 ap.Cosm.Ind.*top*.10(M.88.433C); μ. ... τὴν πνευματικὴν τοῦ πάντων ἡμῶν σωτῆρος Χριστοῦ Cyr.*hom.pasch*.19(5^2.249A); ἑνὶ γὰρ σώματι, τῷ ἰδίῳ δηλαδή, τοὺς εἰς αὐτὸν πιστεύοντας εὐλογῶν διὰ τῆς μυστικῆς μ., ἑαυτῷ τε συσσώμους καὶ ἀλλήλοις ἀποτελεῖ Cyr.*Jo*.11.11(4.998D); as spiritual Passover lamb μετὰ τὸ σωτήριον βάπτισμα ἡ του ἀμωμοῦ ἀμνοῦ μ. γίνεται Thdt.*qu.2 in Jos*.(1.305); τὸ βάπτισμα εἰς τὸν θάνατον τοῦ κυρίου...λευκοὺς...ἀποδίδωσι τοὺς βαπτιζομένους ἐν αὐτῷ. ἀλλὰ καὶ ἡ μ. τοῦ ζωοποιοῦ αἵματος τοῦ Χριστοῦ τοῦτο χαρίζεται Oecum. *Apoc*.7:14(p.101); abs. = *Holy Communion* Χριστιανῶν...δοῦλοι... ἤκουον...τὴν θείαν μ. αἷμα καὶ σῶμα εἶναι Χριστοῦ, αὐτοὶ νομίσαντες τῷ ὄντι αἷμα καὶ σάρκα εἶναι Iren.*fr*.13(p.482); μετ' ἐνιαυτὸν τῆς μ. μετέχων, τὰς τεσσαράκοντα ἡμέρας οἴει ἀρκεῖν σοι πρὸς καθαρισμόν; Chrys.*hom.17.4 in Heb*.(12.169D); οἱ πιστοὶ συμβολικῶς τῶν μυστηρίων μεταλαμβάνοντες τοῦ σώματος τοῦ δεσπότου...μετὰ τὸ βάπτισμα, ἵνα μετὰ τὴν ἐκ νεκρῶν ἀνάστασιν προσέχοντες τῷ δεσπότῃ...μεταλαμβάνωμεν τῆς αὐτοῦ δόξης...διὰ τοῦτο καὶ μ. λέγεται Cosm.Ind.*top*.5(M.88.305D); λέγεται μ. μέν, ὅτι δι' αὐτῆς μεταλαμβάνομεν τῆς Ἰησοῦ θεότητος Jo.D.*fr.Mt*.26:27(M.96.1409D); as moment in liturgy πάντας τοὺς εἰσιόντας πιστοὺς καὶ τῶν γραφῶν ἀκούοντας, μὴ παραμένοντας δὲ τῇ προσευχῇ καὶ τῇ ἁγίᾳ μ. *Can.App*.9; οὐ μέχρι τῆς συμπληρώσεως παρίστασθαι ἀξιοῦσιν· ἀλλὰ...ἐρωτῶσι...εἰ ὁ καιρὸς τῆς μ. πάρεστι Anast.S.*synax*.(M.89.829C); **b.** divine *participation* πλήρωσον καὶ τὴν θυσίαν ταύτην τῆς σῆς δυνάμεως καὶ τῆς σῆς μ. Serap.*euch*.13.11.

B. *transference* of meaning μὴ κατὰ ἀποκλήρωσιν ἵστασθαι μὲν ἐπὶ τῆς 'λόγος' ἐννοίας,...χωρὶς μ. τῆς δυναμένης μεταλαμβάνεσθαι, ἀνάγειν δὲ καὶ ἀλληγορεῖν Or.*Jo*.1.26(24; p.33.23; M.14.72C); of words such as 'door' used of Christ πρὸς τὸ ἐνδοξότερον ἡ μ. γινομένη πρὸς τὴν τῆς θείας δυνάμεως ἔνδειξιν ἥρμοσεν Gr.Nyss.*Eun*.3(2 p.45.4; M.45.613A).

μεταλλάσσω, *alter; render* poems into prose, Clem.*str*.6.2(p.443.3; M.9.241B).

μεταλλεία, ἡ, plur., *work in mines, mining operations,* Eus.*v.C*.2.32(p.55.5; M.20.1009B).

***μεταλλευτήρ, ὁ**, *miner,* Paul.Sil.*Soph*.621(M.86.2143A).

μεταλλεύ-ω, 1. *mine* γῆν μ. *Hom.Clem*.3.36; fig., of Bible study, Clem.*str*.4.2(p.249.25; M.8.1217A); Chrys.*hom.31.1 in Rom*.(8.745A); **2.** *dig,* Pall.*v.Chrys*.20(p.127.10; M.47.71); *bore* wells, Bas.Sel.*or*.13.1(M.85.172A); **3.** met., *search out* τὰ ἀπόρρητα...μ. Athenag.*leg*.11.2(M.6.912B); τὸ ἐν γραφῇ μ. βάθος Bas.Sel.*or*.6.1(M.85.85B); **4.** = μεταλλάσσω: πάντα ~εις ὑπάρχοντα καὶ μετασκευάζεις, μόνος ὑπάρχων θεός, ὡς θέλεις Meth.*res*.2.23(p.379.7; M.18.288C); Epiph.*haer*.42.12(p.167.16; M.41.792A).

μεταλλίζομαι, *be condemned to the mines;* for sacrilege, Phot. *nomoc*.2.2(p.500; M.104.581C).

***μετάλλιον, τό**, name of an unguent; prob. for Μεγάλλειον (an unguent named after Megallus, *LS*), Clem.*paed*.2.8(p.196.10; M.8.469B).

***μεταλλόχρυσος**, *possessing gold mines,* ‡Paul.Sil.*therm.Pyth*.(M.86.2263).

***μεταμαραίνω**, *wither,* Gr.Nyss.*v.Mos*.(M.44.332D).

μεταμείβ-ω, intrans., *change* οὔτε...αἱ ψυχαὶ...~ουσιν εἰς ἕτερα σώματα Just.*dial*.4.7(M.6.485B).

μεταμέλεια, ἡ, 1. *repentance, penitence* ὅταν δάκνηται...ἡ ψυχὴ οἷόν τινι μάστιγι τῇ μ. Gr.Nyss.*anim.et res*.(M.46.92B); ἀμέτρητος ἡ τοῦ δεσπότου φιλανθρωπία, μετὰ γὰρ τὴν πολλὴν παρανομίαν μόνην ἐπιζητεῖ μ., διδάσκει δὲ ταύτης τὸν τρόπον Chrys.*fr.in Jer*.3:12(M.64.785A); εὐθὺς τοίνυν ἡμαρτηκόσιν ὁ θεὸς ἐπεφάνη, πρὸς μεταμέλειαν ἕλκων αὐτούς Proc.G.*Gen*.3:6(M.87.196C); φονευθεὶς μὲν ὁ ἀμέμπτως πολιτευόμενος κατέλιπε τοῖς αὐτὸν θανατώσασιν, ἐφ' οἷς εἰς αὐτὸν πεπλημμελήκασι, μ. τὴν κατὰ τὸ παρὸν μὲν τὸ συνειδὸς πλήττουσαν, κατὰ τὸ μέλλον δὲ διηνεκῶς κολάζουσαν ‡Proc.G.*Pr*.11:4(M.87.1324B); possible only in this life, ref. Lc.16:26 ὁ γὰρ ἅπαξ τὸ ἡδὺ κατὰ τὸν βίον τοῦτον ἑλκόμενος [v.l. ἑλόμενος], καὶ μὴ θεραπεύσας ἐκ μ. τὴν ἀβουλίαν, ἄβατον ἑαυτῷ...τὴν τῶν ἀγαθῶν χώραν ἐργάζεται Gr.Nyss.*anim.et res*.(M.46.84B); Bas.*hom*.13.7(2.121B; M.31.441B); ref. heretics οὐδὲν ἕτερον ἐσπουδάκασιν ἢ ἵνα...μηδεμίαν χώραν ἐν τῇ ζωῇ ταύτῃ μ. ἔχωσιν Const.ap.Ath.*apol.sec*.62(p.142.14; M.25.361C); repentance associated with baptism ὕδωρ μυστικόν...ἐπίκλησις θείας δυνάμεως...ἡ ἐκ μ. διόρθωσις Gr.Nyss.*or.catech*.35(p.138.14; M.45.92B); καθαρὸν ἔνδυμα γάμου περιβαλεῖν, ὅπερ ἐστὶ βάπτισμα, ὃ εἰς ἄφεσιν γίνεται τῶν πεπραγμένων ὑμῖν κακῶν, καὶ τοὺς ἀγαθοὺς εἰς τὸ θεοῦ δεῖπνον εἰσάγειν ἐκ τῆς μ., εἰ καὶ τὴν ἀρχὴν ἀπελείφθησαν τῆς εὐωχίας *Hom.Clem*.8.22; dist. from μετάνοια: αὐτοὶ δέ φαμεν εἶναι μετάνοιαν μίαν καὶ διὰ λουτροῦ παλιγγενεσίας ταύτην γίνεσθαι τὴν σωτηρίαν, ἀλλ' οὐκ ἀναιροῦμεν τὴν τοῦ θεοῦ φιλανθρωπίαν...ἡ μὲν τελεία μετάνοια ἐν τῷ λουτρῷ τυγχάνει· εἰ δέ τις παρέπεσεν, οὐκ ἀπόλλει τοῦτον ἡ ἁγία τοῦ θεοῦ ἐκκλησία· δίδωσι γὰρ καὶ ἐπάνοδον καὶ μετὰ τὴν μετάνοιαν τὴν μ. Epiph.*haer*.59.1(p.364.14; M.41.1020A); but usu. identical with it εἰδότες...ὡς οὐ τὴν κόλασιν ἀλλὰ τὴν μ.

τοῦ ἁμαρτωλοῦ ποθῶ, χρήσασθε τῇ μετανοίᾳ Thdt.*Ezech*.18:32(2.815); id.*haer*.4.1(4.381); plur., *Hom.Clem*.3.5; **2.** change of purpose; **a.** for the worse ἄρα...ἐάν τις ποιήσας εὐποιΐαν μεταμεληθῇ, ἐξαλείφει τὸν μισθὸν ὃν ἐποίησε διὰ τῆς μ.; ‡Ath.*qu.Ant*.84(M.28.649B); Thdt.*Jer*.34:10(2.559); **b.** ref. God, ref. 1Reg.15:35 θυμὸς θεοῦ λέγεται παιδεία ἡ κατὰ τῶν πταιόντων, οὐ πάθος θεοῦ, μ. δὲ ἡ ἀπὸ πράγματος εἰς πρᾶγμα μετάθεσις τῆς τοῦ θεοῦ οἰκονομίας Or.*fr.4 in 1Reg*.(p.296.2; M.12.992A); Gr.Nyss.*Eun*.12(1 p.335.18; M.45.1053A); μ. θεοῦ ἡ τῆς οἰκονομίας μεταβολή Thdt.*qu.32 in 1Reg*.(1.375); μ. ἀνθρώπων μέν, πάθος· θεοῦ δέ, ἔργον...οὕτω καὶ μ., ἐφ' ἡμῶν μέν, μετάγνωσις οἷα θνητῶν εἰς κατάγνωσιν ἑαυτῶν, ἐφ' οἷς κακῶς ἢ ἐνεθυμήθημεν ἢ ἐπράξαμεν· ἐπὶ δὲ θεοῦ, μετάθεσις οἰκονομίας εἰς ἕτερον τρόπον Diod.*Gen*.6:6(M.33.1570C); **3.** *retractation* of opinions, Eust.Mon.*ep*.(M.86.936B).

***μεταμελετ-άω**, *repent* μὴ...~ῶμεν ἐπ' ἐσχάτων, πλὴν ἀνωφελῆ καὶ ἀνόνητα ‡Ath.*occurs*.1(M.28.973B).

μεταμελέω, v. μεταμέλω.

μεταμελητικός, *of retractation* μ. λιβέλλους Eust.Mon.*ep*.(M.86.936B).

μετάμελος, ὁ, *repentance* εἰ δὲ ἐκ μ. φαίη τοῦτο πεποιηκέναι τὸν θεὸν ὁ ἀντιλέγων, ἀσθενὴς αὐτῷ ὁ λόγος Meth.*res*.1.39(p.284.1; M.41.1108B).

μετάμελος, *repentant*, †Jo.D.*B.J*.3(M.96.881D); *ib*.35(1193A).

μεταμέλ-ω (μεταμελ-έω), **A.** *cause to change one's mind* εἰ μὴ πρὸς παροξυσμὸν ἁμαρτάνῃ, τάχιστα ~εῖ τὸν κριτήν Ephr.1.138D = id.3.448F.

B. med. and pass.; **1.** *regret, be sorry* ἐὰν μὴ θύσῃς, ~ηθήσῃ *M.Ign.Rom*.4; **2.** *repent* ἐν τελείᾳ ~ουμένους *T.Jud*.23.5; ὅσοι οὖν γνησίως ~ονται CNic.(325)*can*.11; εἰ...βούλοιτο μετανοεῖν, προσλαμβάνου...τοῖς γὰρ ~ομένοις τόπον μετανοίας ὥρισεν ὁ κύριος *Const.App*.2.38.4; **3.** *change one's mind*; not properly applicable to God, *Hom.Clem*.2.43 cit. s. ἔμμονος; sense in which word may be so applied εἰ πάντα πρόοιδεν ὁ θεός, οὐκ ἀφ' ὧν δὲ οἶδε θυμοῦται ἢ ~εῖται, οὐ πάθος ἄρα θεοῦ θυμὸς ἢ μεταμέλεια, ἀλλὰ τοῦ θυμοῦ ἔργον ἡ κόλασις Or.*fr.4 in 1Reg*.(p.296.12; M.12.992A); ref. 1Reg.15:12, Jon.3:10 συγγινώσκει γὰρ ἀτρέπτως τοῖς διορθοῦσι τὰ ἑαυτῶν πταίσματα· τοῖς δὲ ἀδιορθώτως ἔχουσι πρὸς τὰ κακά, ἀτρέπτως οὐ συγγινώσκει. τὸ οὖν 'μεταμέλημαι' τὸ ἄτρεπτον αὐτοῦ ἐμφαίνει τὸ κατὰ τὸ μὴ συγγινώσκειν. τὸ δὲ 'μετενόησεν ὁ κύριος' τὸ ἄτρεπτον αὐτοῦ δηλοῖ τὸ κατὰ τὸ συγγινώσκειν ‡Just.*qu.et resp*.36(M.6.1284A); ὁ δεσπότης θεὸς...παρανομοῦντα τὸν λαὸν παρεδίδου τοῖς ἀλλοφύλοις οἷόν τινι ῥάβδῳ κεχρημένος...καὶ πάλιν ~όμενος ἐλέει Thdt.*qu.12 in Jud*.(1.332); ἡμεῖς γάρ, ὅταν δῶμέν τινι πλοῦτον, καὶ κακῶς ἐκεῖνος χρήσηται, ~ούμεθα. οὕτως τοῦ θεοῦ τὸν ἄνθρωπον ποιήσαντος, καὶ τὸν Σαοὺλ χρίσαντος εἰς βασιλέα, καὶ ἁμαρτησάντων αὐτῶν, ~εῖσθαι λέγεται· οὐ τοῦ θεοῦ ~ηθέντος· προῄδει γὰρ τὸ ἐσόμενον· ἀλλὰ τούτων ἄξια μεταμελείας πραξάντων Jo.D.*Man*.1.80(M.94.1580B); ref. Arian Christology προσάπτειν...τῷ λόγῳ τὰ ἀνθρωποπαθῶς λεχθέντα βουλόμενοι, σάρκα ἄψυχον γεγενῆσθαι αὐτὸν λέγουσιν· καὶ ὡσανεὶ ὑπ' ἀγωνίας ~ομένῳ τῷ ἀτρέπτῳ καὶ ἀκηράτῳ θεῷ Didym.*Trin*.3.21(M.39.900A); pres. ptcpl. as adj., *changeable, unstable* ἄνθρωπον...ὀργίλον καὶ ζηλωτὴν καὶ...~όμενον Arist.*apol*.7(p.103.25).

***μεταμεμελημένως**, *on second thoughts* ὁ θεὸς...οὐ μελλητικῶς οὐδὲ μ. τὸν υἱὸν μετὰ χρόνους ἔχων ἢ τὸ ἅγιον πνεῦμα αὐτοῦ Epiph.*haer*.76.48(p.402.9; M.42.617B).

***μεταμηνίω**, *cease from wrath*, †Apoll.*met.Ps*.29:6(M.33.1349B).

***μεταμορφάζω**, *alter*, Iren.*haer*.1.18.1(M.7.641B).

μεταμορφ-όω, **1.** *transform*, *A.Phil*.60(p.25.18); prayer of the dying apostle κύριέ μου...~ωσον τὴν μορφὴν τοῦ σώματός μου ἐν ἀγγελικῇ δόξῃ *ib*.144(p.87.1); ref. Inc. ἡ μεταμόρφωσις αὐτοῦ, καὶ ἡ κατάβασις αὐτοῦ, καὶ ἡ ἰδέα ἣν δεῖ αὐτὸν ~ωθῆναι, ἐν εἴδει ἀνθρώπου *Ascens.Is*.A 3.13(p.92); διὰ ἡμερότητα καὶ φιλανθρωπίαν ~ούμενος σωματοποιεῖ ἑαυτόν Mac.Aeg.*hom*.4.10(M.34.480B); met., *change* character πρὸς τὴν κακίαν μετεμορφώθημεν Gr.Nyss.*or.catech*.8(p.42.10; M.45.33B); δυνατὸν ἐκ δικαιοσύνης εἰς ἁμαρτίαν μεταπεσεῖν, καὶ ἀπὸ τοῦ πάθους εἰς τὸ ἐμπαθὲς ~ωθῆναι Nil.*epp*.2.140(M.79.261D); τῆς ἁμαρτίας ὁ ῥύπος τὸ τοιοῦτον [i.e. of image of God] ἠμαύρωσε κάλλος· καὶ πρὸς τὸ κτηνῶδες ἡμᾶς μ. εἶδος Procl.CP *annunt*.2(M.85.432A); ~οῦν καὶ μεταρρυθμίζειν πρὸς τὸ βέλτιον τὴν ψυχήν Thdt.*affect*.4(p.100.7; 4.792); τέκνα καλοῦσιν οἱ ἅγιοι τοὺς διὰ τοῦ λόγου αὐτῶν ~ουμένους Dor.*doct*.4.3(M.88.1661B); ὁ ἄνθρωπος...τῷ μὲν θεοειδεῖ τοῦ νοῦ πρὸς τὸ θεῖον κάλλος ~ούμενος Melet.*nat.hom*.synops.(M.64.1101B); **2.** *disguise* oneself ὁ κύριος ἦν μεθ' ἡμῶν ἐν τῷ πλοίῳ καὶ οὐκ ἔγνωμεν αὐτόν· μετεμόρφωσεν γὰρ ἑαυτὸν ὥσπερ πρωρεύς *A.Andr.et Mt*.17(p.85.6); med. ὁ Ζεὺς...μετεμορφοῦτο τὴν ἰδέαν *Hom.Clem*.5.11; **3.** pass., *be transfigured*; of Christ τί ἐστι, μετεμορφώθη; παρήνοιξεν ὀλίγον τῆς θεότητος, καὶ ἔδειξεν αὐτοῖς τὸν ἐνοικοῦντα θεόν Chrys.*ecl*.21(12.566C); μετεμορφώθη γὰρ Χριστός, οὐχ ἁπλῶς, ἀλλ' ἵνα ἡμῖν ἀποδείξῃ τὴν μέλλουσαν τῆς φύσεως μεταμόρφωσιν, καὶ τὴν...δευτέραν ἔλευσιν Procl.CP *or*.8.2(M.65.768B); ~οῦται τοίνυν οὐχ ὃ οὐκ ἦν προσλαβόμενος, ἀλλ' ὅπερ ἦν τοῖς οἰκείοις μαθηταῖς ἐκφαινόμενος Jo.D.*hom*.1.12(M.96.564C); various spiritual interprn. ὁ πάντα τὰ τοῦ κόσμου ὑπερβαίνων πράγματα...βλέπει τὸν Ἰησοῦν τόνδ' οὐδενὶ τῶν κάτω ~ούμενον, ~ωθέντα ἔμπροσθεν αὐτοῦ Or.*schol.in Lc*.9:31(M.17.344C); τότε δέ τις ὁρᾷ τὸν λόγον ~ούμενον ἐνδόξως, ὅτε συνάνεισί τε αὐτῷ καὶ συνυψοῦται καὶ ὁρᾷ αὐτὸν ὡς αὐτολόγον καὶ ὡς ἀρχιερέα κοινολογούμενον καὶ εὐχόμενον τῷ πατρί id.*fr.22 in Lc*.9:28(p.243.10); cf.id.*comm.in Mt*.12.39(p.156.4; M.13.1072B); ὅταν ~ῶθωσιν αὐτῶν [sc. τοῦ νόμου καὶ τῶν προφητῶν] οἱ λόγοι, καὶ κινηθῶσιν αἱ τοῦ νόμου σκιαί, τότε καὶ πιστευθήσεται Μωϋσῆς ὁ θεράπων ὁ πιστὸς περὶ Χριστοῦ γράψας πάντα Anast.Ant.*serm*.1.4(M.89.1369A); ref. post-resurrection appearances μετεμορφώθη ὁ Ἰησοῦς καὶ οὐκ ἦν ὡς τὸ πρότερον πρὶν σταυρωθῆναι αὐτόν, ἀλλ' ἦν διὰ παντὸς φῶς *Narr.Jos*.5(p.469).

μεταμόρφωσις, ἡ, **1.** *transformation*, ref. Christ ἡ ἐξέλευσις τοῦ ἀγαπητοῦ...καὶ ἡ μ. αὐτοῦ *Ascens.Is*.3.13(p.92); of saints into Christ's likeness συμβαλλούσης...τὴν ἐν τῷ λόγῳ τράνωσιν αὐτῶν καὶ μ. τῆς ἐκκλησίας Meth.*symp*.8.8(p.90.19; M.18.149C); **2.** *transfiguration* σώμασι πνευματικοῖς, οὐχὶ τοῦ εἴδους τοῦ προτέρου ἀφανιζομένου, κἂν ἐπὶ τὸ ἐνδοξότερον γένηται αὐτοῦ ἡ τροπή, ὥσπερ ἦν τὸ Ἰησοῦ εἶδος...οὐχ ἕτερον ἐν τῇ μ. παρ' ὃ ἦν Meth.*res*.1.22(p.246.11; M.41.1092B); μ. φρίκης γέμουσα καὶ φῶς ἄκρατον Chrys.*hom.56.4 in Mt*.(7.570D); ἡ δὲ λεγομένη μ. κατὰ τὴν ἔκλαμψιν ἦν...οὐ δὴ τοῦ χαρακτῆρος μεταβολήν τινα προσδοκητέον ἐν τῇ βασιλείᾳ...ἀλλὰ φωτὸς προσθήκην ὑπερλάμπρου Vict.*Mc*.9:3(p.353.8); ἡ μ. καθ' ἣν ὁ ἀναλλοίωτος ὑπὲρ τὸν ἥλιον ἔλαμψε τὸ ὑπὲρ ἡμᾶς καὶ ἡμέτερον Andr.Cr.*or*.7(M.97.941C); ἐν τῷ δὲ ἱστάναι αὐτοὺς [sc. τοὺς ἱερεῖς] ἐν τῷ συνθρόνῳ δεικνύων ὁ ἀρχιερεὺς τῷ λαῷ τὴν θείαν μ. ‡Sophr.H.*liturg*.16(M.87.3997A); *ib*.7(3988C); **3.** *figure* εἰκὼν δὲ τῆς ἀληθείας ἦν [sc. ὁ νόμος] καὶ οἱονεί τις μ. εὐσεβείας διὰ τύπου καὶ σκιᾶς ἀποφέρουσα πρὸς αὐτήν Cyr.*hom.pasch*.30(5^2.339A).

μεταμοσχεύ-ω, *transplant*, Clem.*str*.7.18(p.79.1; M.9.557A); Chrys.*Anna* 3.3(4.725C); Cyr.*Is*.2.3(2.280C); fig. ὁ παράδεισος ὁ πνευματικὸς αὐτὸς ἡμῶν ὁ σωτὴρ ὑπάρχει, εἰς ὃν καταφυτευόμεθα, μετατεθέντες καὶ ~θέντες εἰς τὴν γῆν τὴν ἀγαθὴν ἐκ βίου τοῦ παλαιοῦ Clem.*str*.6.1(p.423.13; M.9.209B); ἕξει...ὁ Ἰσραὴλ τὰ τῆς ἀπονοίας ὀψώνια...τὰ ἔθνη...πρὸς τὸν ἐκείνου ~θήσεται τόπον Cyr.*Jo*.1.9(4.90E); χρῆναι δικαίως ἀπορρίπτεσθαι μὲν τῆς ἐλπίδος τὸν Ἰσραήλ, ~εσθαι δὲ τοὺς ἀλλογενεῖς ἐπ' αὐτήν *ib*.2.5(201C).

***μεταμυέομαι**, s.v.l., *be initiated into new beliefs*, Jo.D.*hom*.8.4(M.96.705C v.l. μεμυη-).

μεταμφιάζομαι, abs., *change one's clothes*; fig. πονηροὺς καὶ ἀγαθοὺς καλεῖσθαι ⟨μὲν ἔ⟩δει, οὐ μὴν ὥστε τοὺς πονηροὺς μένειν πονηρούς, ἀλλὰ μεταμφιασαμένους καὶ ἀποθεμένους τὰ ἀλλότρια τοῦ γαμοῦ ἐνδύματα ἐνδύσασθαι τὰ τοῦ γάμου σπλάγχνα οἰκτιρμοῦ Or.*comm.in Mt*.17.16(p.631.27; M.13.1528B); trans., *put on new* or *different* clothes; fig., of Fall ὁ ἄνθρωπος...ἀπώλεσε μὲν τὸ εἰκὼν εἶναι τοῦ ἀφθάρτου θεοῦ, τὴν δὲ φθαρτὴν καὶ πηλίνην εἰκόνα διὰ τῆς ἁμαρτίας μετημφιάσατο Gr.Nyss.*virg*.12(p.300.2; M.46.372C); of Inc. εἰ προαιώνιος ἡ σάρξ...οὐ μετημφιάσατο τὸ δουλικὸν πρόσωπον id.*Apoll*.14(M.45.1149A); of salvation μετημφιασάμεθα δὲ ὥσπερ εὐφροσύνην καὶ χαράν, θανάτου καὶ ἁμαρτίας ἀπηλλαγμένοι Cyr.*Ps*.31:7(M.69.868B); of metempsychosis σώματα διάφορα μ. CCP(543)*anath*.7(p.228); met., *assume* a new name, Bas.*hom*.21.3(2.166B; M.31.548A).

μεταμφιέννυμαι = foreg., fig., of the earth σκυθρωπὴν καὶ πενθήρη ἀπορρίψασαν περιβολήν, μεταμφιεννυμένην τὴν φαιδροτέραν καὶ...τὰ μυρία γένη τῶν φυομένων προβάλλουσαν Bas.*hex*.5.2(1.41C; M.29.97B); met., of Christ ἔδει πάλιν αὐτὸν...τὴν ἀρχαίαν τε καὶ οὐσιώδη μ. δόξαν Cyr.*Jo*.11.3(4.947C); paraphrase of Col.3:9, id.*ador*.17(1.611A).

***μεταμφιέσκομαι**, = μεταμφιάζομαι, Thdt.*ep*.137(4.1229).

μετανάστασις, ἡ, **1.** *migration*, met. μ. τῆς πρὸς τὸ θεῖον Gr.Thaum.*pan.Or*.2(p.4.3; M.10.1053C); **2.** *removal, overthrow* ἀπείκασεν...σεισμῷ τὴν μ. καὶ κατάλυσιν [sc. τῆς εἰδωλολατρίας] Hipp.*fr.in Is*.19:1(p.180.4; M.10.632A).

μεταναστεύ-ω, intr., *depart*, Synes.*ep*.124(M.66.1504D); from this life μετὰ ἀγαθῆς ἐλπίδος μ. ἀπὸ τοῦ κόσμου τούτου Bas.*ep*.158(3.247C; M.32.620A); Thphyl.*exc.gent*.5(p.483.8; M.113.944B); fig. and met., of Fall τραπέντων ἡμῶν καὶ ~σάντων ἀπὸ τῆς μακαριωτάτης ἐκείνης...ζωῆς εἰς τὸν πολυχειμαστότατον...τοῦτον βίον Meth.*res*.2.25(p.381.8; M.18.328C); Thdt.*Ps*.61:7(1.1014); κατοικήσουσιν εἰς τὴν παγίαν ἕξιν τῶν ἀρετῶν...οὐ ~σουσι ταύτης ‡Proc.G.*Pr.*2:1(M.87.1240D).

μετανάστης, ὁ, *one who has come from one place to another,* Nonn.*par.Jo.*14:16(M.43.869A).

μετανάστιος, *moved from one place to another,* Nonn.*par.Jo.*2:9 (M.43.761B); *ib.*4:11(776A).

[*]**μετανείσσομαι,** = μετανίσομαι, *pass over*; met., of emotions, *pass away,* Nonn.*par.Jo.*16:20(M.43.881A).

μετανέομαι, *pass* from one place *to* another, *arrive at,* c. acc., Nonn.*par.Jo.*6:17(M.43.796C); *ib.*12:11(852B); *ib.*13:5(860C).

μετανίστημι, 1. *remove, cause to depart*; met., of Christianity καινῇ μεθόδῳ πολλῶν κακῶν μ. τοὺς ἀνθρώπους Or.*Cels.*1.64(p.118.2; M.11.781A); **2.** pass. and intrans. tenses, *depart*; ref. death, Tat.*orat.* 16(p.17.18; M.6.840C); fig. μείζω φρονῶν ἢ κατὰ τὰ ἀνθρώπινα καὶ τῶν ἐνθένδε πρὶν ἀποβιῶναι μεταναστάς Gr.Naz.*or.*43.59(M.36.573B).

μετανο-έω, A. *change one's mind* ὅταν αὐτοῖς [sc. would-be catechumens] ἔλθῃ εἰς μνείαν ἡ ἁγνότης τῆς ἀληθείας, μ., καὶ πορεύονται πάλιν ὀπίσω τῶν ἐπιθυμιῶν αὐτῶν τῶν πονηρῶν Herm.*vis.*3.7.3; ὄμοσον τὴν Καίσαρος τύχην, μ. *M.Polyc.*9.2; *ib.*11.2.

B. *repent*; **1.** towards God πᾶσιν οὖν μ. ἀφίει ὁ κύριος, ἐὰν μ. εἰς ἑνότητα θεοῦ καὶ συνέδριον τοῦ ἐπισκόπου Ign.*Philad.*8.1; ἡ γὰρ χρηστότης...τοῦ θεοῦ τὸν ~οῦντα ἀπὸ τῶν ἁμαρτημάτων...ὡς δίκαιον ...ἔχει Just.*dial.*47.5(M.6.580A); ἐὰν ~ήσωσι, πάντες βουλόμενοι τυχεῖν τοῦ παρὰ τοῦ θεοῦ ἐλέους δύνανται *ib.*141.2(797D); with play on words, God 'repenting' if men repent ἐπαγγέλλεται ὅτι ἐὰν ~ήσωσι ~ήσει περὶ τῶν κακῶν ὧν ἐλάλησε τοῦ ποιῆσαι αὐτοῖς Or.*hom.18.5 in Jer.*(p.155.18; M.13.469C,D); cf.*ib.18.6*(p.157.18f.; 473B); Epiph. *haer.*59.6(p.370.13; M.41.1028A); and Christ, Just.*dial.*40.4(M.6.564A) cit. s. ἁμαρτωλός; through baptism typified by Noah's ark δι' ὕδατος καὶ πίστεως καὶ ξύλου οἱ...~οῦντες...ἐκφεύξονται τὴν μέλλουσαν... κρίσιν *ib.*138.3(793C); ὁ φιλάνθρωπος λόγος, ἐλέγχει δέ, ἵνα ~ήσωσιν Clem.*paed.*1.7(p.124.22; M.8.320B); **2.** aspects of repenting τῶν οὖν ~ούντων εὐθὺς δοκεῖς τὰς ἁμαρτίας ἀφίεσθαι; οὐ παντελῶς. ἀλλὰ δεῖ τὸν μ. βασανίσαι τὴν ἑαυτοῦ ψυχὴν...καὶ θλιβῆναι ἐν πάσαις θλίψεσι... καὶ ἐὰν ὑπενέγκῃ τὰς θλίψεις...ὁ τὰ πάντα κτίσας...ἴασίν τινα δώσει· καὶ τοῦτο ὅταν ⟨ὁ θεὸς⟩ τοῦ μ. καθαρὰν ἴδῃ τὴν καρδίαν Herm.*sim.* 7.4,5; τοῦ ~οῦντος δὲ τρόποι δύο, ὁ μὲν κοινότερος φόβος ἐπὶ τοῖς πραχθεῖσιν, ὁ δὲ ἰδιαίτερος ἡ δυσωπία ἡ πρὸς ἑαυτὴν τῆς ψυχῆς ἐκ συνειδήσεως Clem.*str.*4.6(p.265.7; M.8.1249A); τὸν γὰρ μ. οὐκ ὀργίζεσθαι χρὴ οὐδὲ ἀγριαίνειν, ἀλλὰ συντρίβεσθαι ὡς κατεγνωσμένον Chrys. *hom.31.3 in Heb.*(12.288D); τὸν μ. οὐδέποτε χρὴ λήθῃ παραδοῦναι τὴν ἁμαρτίαν, ἀλλὰ τὸν μὲν θεὸν παρακαλεῖν μὴ μνησθῆναι αὐτῆς, αὐτὸν μηδέποτε ἐπιλαθέσθαι αὐτῆς *ib.*(289D); μετενόησε καὶ ὁ Ἰούδας, ἀλλὰ κακῶς *ib.*(288C); **3.** in rel. to salvation, *2Clem.*13.1; *ib.*19.1; βλέπεις δὲ ὅτι οὐδὲ εἷς αὐτῶν μετενόησε, καίπερ ἀκούσαντες τὰ ῥήματα ἃ ἐλάλησας αὐτοῖς...ἀπὸ τῶν τοιούτων ἡ ζωὴ ἀπέστη...ἦσαν γὰρ ὑποκριταί...καὶ ἐκστρέφοντες τοὺς δούλους τοῦ θεοῦ, μάλιστα δὲ τοὺς ἡμαρτηκότας, μὴ ἀφιέντες ~εῖν αὐτούς...οὗτοι οὖν ἔχουσιν ἐλπίδα τοῦ μ. βλέπεις δὲ πολλοὺς ἐξ αὐτῶν καὶ μετανενοηκότας...καὶ ἔτι ~ήσουσιν ὅσοι δὲ οὐ ~ήσουσιν, ἀπώλεσαν τὴν ζωὴν αὐτῶν. ὅσοι δὲ μ. ... ἀγαθοὶ ἐγένοντο Herm.*sim.*8.6.5–7; *ib.*8.7.3; *ib.*9.26.8; εἰ δὲ τῷ τοιούτῳ [sc. David] ἄφεσις πρὶν μ. οὐκ ἐδόθη...πῶς οἱ ἀκάθαρτοι...ἐὰν μὴ...~ήσωσιν, ἐλπίδα ἔχειν δύνανται...; Just.*dial.*141.3(M.6.800A); Clem.*prot.*11(p.82.1; M. 8.236B); id.*str.*2.16(p.151.20; M.8.1012B); ἐὰν μ., ἐλπίδα σωτηρίας ἕξουσιν *Const.App.*2.12.3; αὐτὴν [sc. ψυχήν] πείθωμεν ὅτι ἥμαρτεν, ἵνα καὶ μ., καὶ ἵνα ~ήσασα ἀπαλλαγῇ τῶν κολάσεων Chrys.*hom.31.3 in Heb.*(12.289C); Proc.G.*Is.*59:1–18(M.87.2612C); Jo.Clim.*scal.*5(M. 88.777B); and various blessings ἐὰν δὲ μ. ... δοξάζουσι τὸν θεόν Herm. *sim.*6.3.6; οἱ οὖν μ. ὁλοτελῶς νέοι ἔσονται καὶ τεθεμελιωμένοι id.*vis.*3. 13.4; τὸ ἐν χαρᾷ γεγονέναι τὸν μετανενοηκότα Clem.*str.*2.16(p.151.27; M.8.1012B); ἡ δὲ ~ήσασα οἷον ἀναγεννηθεῖσα...παλιγγενεσίαν ἔχει ζωῆς *ib.*2.23(p.193.25; 1097A); exchange of earthly for heavenly image, Or.*hom.2.1 in Jer.*(p.17.15; M.13.277C); ἀφανισθήσεται [sc. ἁμαρτήματα], ἐὰν θελήσωμεν μ. Chrys.*hom.34.3 in Jo.*(8.199E); **4.** ref. effects of not repenting ἐάν...τις...μὴ μ., ἀπέχου ἀπ' αὐτοῦ καὶ μὴ συνζῆθι αὐτῷ Herm.*mand.*4.1.9; id.*sim.*9.26.8; θεόν...τότε κολάζοντα τοὺς μὴ μ. νῦν...μὴ θέλων μ. ... ἐν ἐκείνῃ τῇ ἡμέρᾳ...τῆς οἰκουμένης ἁπάσης ὁρώσης παραδειγματίζεται Chrys.*hom.34.3 in Jo.*(8.199A,B); **5.** ref. impossibility of repenting in next world ὡς οὖν ἐσμεν ἐπὶ γῆς, ~ῶμεν...ἕως ἐσμὲν ἐν τούτῳ τῷ κόσμῳ, ἐν τῇ σαρκὶ ἃ ἐπράξαμεν πονηρὰ μ. ... ἵνα σωθῶμεν ὑπὸ τοῦ κυρίου...μετὰ γὰρ τὸ ἐξελθεῖν ἡμᾶς ἐκ τοῦ κόσμου, οὐκέτι δυνάμεθα...μ. *2Clem.*8.1–3; ἄπρακτα ~ῶν ἐπὶ τοῖς βουλευθεῖσιν, ὅταν ἴδῃς τὴν φαιδρότητα τῶν δικαίων Bas.*hom.* 13.8(2.122A; M.31.444A); or its futility ~ήσουσιν [sc. Jews], ὅτε οὐδὲν ὠφελήσουσι Just.*1apol.*52.9(M.6.405B); ἐὰν φθάσῃ ὁ Χριστὸς ἐλθεῖν, μάτην ~ήσετε id.*dial.*28.2(M.6.536A); σκώληκα...ἀτελεύτητον τὴν ἐν τῷ μ. τῶν ἰδίων ἁμαρτημάτων συνείδησιν Proc.G.*Is.*64:15–24 (M.87.2716D); **6.** ref. possibility of Devil repenting ὁ δὲ διάβολος αὐτεξούσιος ὢν καὶ ~ῆσαι οἷός τε ἦν καὶ κλέψαι Clem.*str.*1.17(p.54.4; M.8.797C); **7.** ref. eccl. regulations for penitents; penances to be imposed κελεύσεις [sc. bishop] εἰσελθεῖν αὐτόν, καὶ ἀνακρίνας, εἰ μ. ...στιβώσας αὐτὸν ἡμέραις νηστειῶν *Const.App.*2.16.2; *ib.*2.43.1; penitents to be received back into Church, *ib.*2.12.1 cit. s. ἁμαρτάνω; *ib.*2.18.2; ἐὰν δὲ τὸν μ. μὴ προσδέξῃ, ἐπιβούλοις αὐτὸν ἔκδοτον παρέχεις...δέξαι οὖν τὸν μ., μὴ διστάζων ὅλως *ib.*2.14.1,3; ὁ μὴ προσδεχόμενος τοὺς μ. σκορπίζει τὰ τοῦ Χριστοῦ *ib.*2.21.9; *ib.*2.24.4; Epiph. *haer.*61.7(p.388.4; M.41.1049B).

C. *make an inclination, bow*; as a greeting, *Apophth.Patr.*(M. 65.140A); as a sign of penitence, *ask pardon, ib.*(148C); *ib.*(148D).

μετάνοια, ἡ, I. *change of mind, afterthought*;

A. ref. Christian martyrs ἀμετάθετος γὰρ ἡμῖν ἡ ἀπὸ τῶν κρειττόνων ἐπὶ τὰ χείρω μ. *M.Polyc.*11.1; οἱ διάκονοι τῆς τυραννικῆς ὠμότητος ἐπὶ μετάνοιαν ἐκάλουν τὸν πεπονθότα Or.*mart.*24(p.21.29; M.11.593A); *ib.*(p.22.1; M.l.c.).

B. Gnost., ref. birth of aeons ἡ τοῦ πρώτου Χριστοῦ, σὺν τῷ Πνεύματι τῷ ἁγίῳ ἐκ μ. ὑπὸ τοῦ Πατρὸς αὐτῶν μεταγενεστέρα τῶν Αἰώνων γένεσις Iren.*haer.*1.3.1(M.7.468A).

II. *repentance, penitence*;

A. def. and descriptions ἡ μ. σύνεσίς ἐστιν μεγάλη Herm.*mand.* 4.2.2; ἱκανὴ...ἀνθρώπῳ κάθαρσις μ. ἀκριβὴς καὶ βεβαία, εἴγε κατεγνωκότες ἑαυτῶν ἐπὶ ταῖς προγενομέναις πράξεσι προΐεμεν [εἰς] τὸ πρόσθεν, μετὰ ταῦτα νοήσαντες καὶ τὸν νοῦν ἐξαναδύντες τῶν τε κατ' αἴσθησιν τερπόντων καὶ τῶν πρόσθεν πλημμελημάτων Clem.*str.*4.22 (p.311.13; M.8.1352C); βραδεῖα γὰρ γνῶσις μ., γνῶσις δὲ ἡ πρώτη ἀναμαρτησία *ib.*2.6(p.127.14; 961B); ἔστι ἡ μ. καλὴ σφόδρα, παρθένος, καθαρὰ καὶ ἐπιεικὴς καὶ πρᾶος· καὶ διὰ τοῦτο ὁ θεὸς ὁ ὕψιστος ἀγαπᾷ αὐτὴν καὶ πάντες οἱ ἄγγελοι αἰδοῦνται αὐτήν *Asen.*15(p.61.19); δεξώμεθα...μ. ... φάρμακον εἰς σωτηρίαν...μ. δέ ἐστιν, οὐχ ἡ λόγῳ κηρυττομένη, ἀλλ' ἡ πράγμασι βεβαιουμένη· μ. ἡ ἐξ αὐτῆς τῆς καρδίας ἐξαλείφουσα τὸν ῥύπον τῆς ἀσεβείας Chrys.*poenit.*7.3(2.331B,C); μ. δεινὴ καὶ φοβερὰ τῷ ἁμαρτωλῷ, φάρμακον τῶν πλημμελημάτων, δαπάνημα τῶν παρανομιῶν, ἀνάλωμα τῶν δακρύων, παρρησία πρὸς τὸν θεόν, ὅπλον κατὰ τοῦ διαβόλου...σωτηρίας ἐλπίς, ἀπογνώσεως ἀναίρεσις *ib.*8.1(341A); ἰατρεῖον γάρ ἐστιν ἀναιρετικὸν τῆς ἁμαρτίας ἡ μ.· δῶρόν ἐστιν οὐράνιον, δύναμις θαυμαστή, χάριτι νικῶσα τὴν τῶν νόμων ἀκολουθίαν *ib.*7.1(327B); μ. δὲ λέγω, οὐ τὸ τῶν προτέρων ἀποστῆναι κακῶν μόνον, ἀλλὰ καὶ τὸ μείζονα ἐπιδείξασθαι καλά id.*hom.10.6 in Mt.*(7. 146E); ἔστι δὲ μ. τὸ μηκέτι τὰ αὐτὰ ποιεῖν id.*hom.34.3 in Jo.*(8.199E); μ. ῥίζα θεοσεβείας ‡Chrys.*leg.*6(6.413B); μ. ἐστι συνθήκη πρὸς θεὸν δευτέρου βίου. μ. ἐστι ταπεινώσεως ἀγοραστής. μ. ἐστι σωματικῆς κατακλήσεως διηνεκὴς ἀνελπιστία. μ. ἐστι αὐτοματόκριτος λογισμός, καὶ ἀμέριμνος αὐτομέριμνος. μ. ἐστι θυγάτηρ ἐλπίδος, καὶ ἄρνησις ἀνελπιστίας...μ. ἐστι διαλλαγὴ κυρίου, διὰ τῆς τῶν ἐναντίων τοῖς πταίσμασιν ἀγαθῶν ἐργασίας. μ. ἐστι συνειδότος καθαρισμός. μ. ἑκούσιος πάντων τῶν θλιβερῶν ὑπομονή...μ. ἐστι θλίψις γαστρὸς ἰσχυρά, καὶ ψυχῆς πλῆξις ἐν αἰσθήσει κραταιᾷ Jo.Clim.*scal.*5(M.88.764B,C); μ. ἐστιν ἐκ τοῦ παρὰ φύσιν εἰς τὴν κατὰ φύσιν, καὶ ἐκ διαβόλου πρὸς τὸν θεὸν ἐπάνοδος...μ. ἐστι τὸ ἀποστρέψαι ἀπὸ τῆς ἁμαρτίας...μ. ἐστι καταλεῖψαι τὰ πρότερα, καὶ λυπεῖσθαι ὑπὲρ αὐτῶν *Schol.*1 *ib.*5(781B,C); *ib.*7 (801D).

B. ref. God as its author; **1.** in gen., *1Clem.*7.5; πάντας οὖν τοὺς ἀγαπητοὺς αὐτοῦ βουλόμενος μ. μετασχεῖν *ib.*8.5; ὁ θεὸς...μ. διδοὺς ἡμῖν *Barn.*16.9; ἵνα ἴδῃς...τὴν πολυευσπλαγχνίαν τοῦ κυρίου...ἔδωκε πνεῦμα τοῖς ἀξίοις οὖσι μ. διατί...πάντες οὐ μετενόησαν; ὧν εἶδε, φησί, τὴν καρδίαν μέλλουσαν καθαρὰν γενέσθαι...τούτοις ἔδωκε τὴν μ.· ὧν δὲ εἶδε τὴν δολιότητα...ἐκείνοις οὐκ ἔδωκε μ. Herms.*sim.*8.6.1,2; id.*vis.*4.1.3; θέλει γὰρ ὁ πατὴρ ὁ οὐράνιος τὴν μ. τοῦ ἁμαρτωλοῦ Just. *1apol.*15.8(M.6.349C); *ib.*40.7(389B); ὁ κύριος...τὴν μ. ἀπαιτεῖ Clem. *prot.*10(p.67.31; M.8.204C); id.*paed.*1.8(p.130.28; M.8.333B); *ib.*3.12 (p.287.7f.; 672B,C); ἡ μ. ἐστι θυγάτηρ τοῦ ὑψίστου, καὶ αὐτὴ ἐκλιπαρεῖ τὸν θεὸν τὸν ὕψιστον ὑπὲρ...πάντων τῶν μετανοούντων, ἐπειδὴ πατήρ ἐστι τῆς μ. *Asen.*15(p.61.13ff.); *Const.App.*2.22.12; παντοκράτορ θεὲ ...ὁ...ἀμαρτόντι ὑποθήκην δοὺς πρὸς μετάνοιαν τὴν σαυτοῦ ἀγαθότητα *Lit.*ap.*Const.App.*8.9.8; προσάγωμεν...ἑαυτοῖς φάρμακον εἰς σωτηρίαν τὴν μ.· μᾶλλον δὲ δεξώμεθα παρὰ τοῦ θεοῦ τὴν μ. ἰατρεύουσαν ἡμᾶς. οὐ γὰρ ἡμεῖς αὐτῷ ταύτην προσάγομεν, ἀλλ' αὐτὸς ἡμῖν ταύτην ἐχορήγησεν Chrys.*poenit.*7.3(2.331A); **2.** mediated through Christ, *1Clem.* 7.4 cit. s. αἷμα; Ἰησοῦς...ἐξαπέστειλε τὸν λόγον τῆς κλήσεως καὶ τῆς μ. πρὸς τὰ ἔθνη ἅπαντα Just.*dial.*83.4(M.6.673A); ὁ παιδαγωγὸς... ἐπὶ τὴν μ. παρακαλεῖ...καὶ τὸ φιλάνθρωπον τὸ αὐτοῦ τῷ αὐτεξουσίῳ τῆς ψυχῆς ἀφορμὰς μ. χαριζόμενος Clem.*paed.*1.9(p.134.20,26; M.8. 341A); **3.** μ. in rel. to divine foreknowledge ἡ τοῦ θεοῦ πρόγνωσις οὐ βλάπτει τὴν μ., ἐπειδὴ καὶ τοῦτο προγινώσκει, ὅτι καὶ τοῖς ἁμαρτωλοῖς ἔξεστι μεταθέσθαι ‡Chrys.*hom.in Ps.80*(5.742D).

C. ref. preachers of repentance, e.g. Noah, *1Clem.*7.6; *Orac.Sib.*1.129; Jonah ἐβούλετο [sc. Celsus] ἡμᾶς μᾶλλον τὸν Ἰωνᾶν νομίσαι θεὸν ὑπὲρ Ἰησοῦν, Ἰωνᾶν, τὸν κηρύξαντα μ. μιᾷ πόλει τῇ Νινευή, προκρίνων Ἰησοῦ, τοῦ κηρύξαντος μ. ὅλῳ τῷ κόσμῳ Or.*Cels.*7.57(p.206.20f.; M.11.1501C); Jeremiah, *Const.App.*2.14.2; Chrys.*poenit.*3.4(2.300A); Joel, †Jo.Jej.*serm.*(M.88.1920B); Christ, prophets, and apostles οἱ λειτουργοὶ τῆς χάριτος τοῦ θεοῦ διὰ πνεύματος ἁγίου περὶ μετανοίας ἐλάλησαν, καὶ αὐτὸς δὲ ὁ δεσπότης τῶν ἁπάντων περὶ μ. ἐλάλησεν μετὰ ὅρκου *1Clem.*8.1,2; οἱ λόγοι τῶν προφητῶν, οἱ λόγοι τοῦ νόμου, οἱ λόγοι τῶν ἀποστόλων, οἱ λόγοι τοῦ κυρίου...λέγουσιν ἡμῖν περὶ μετανοίας Or.*hom.1.4 in Jer.*(p.3.21; M.13.260A); *Const.App.*2.55.1.

D. in rel. to baptism, v. βάπτισμα, λουτρόν: οὔτε οὖν μ. ἀρκεῖ πρὸς τὸν καθαρισμόν, ἀλλὰ δεῖ τὸ βάπτισμα παραλαβεῖν Chrys.*hom.9.2 in Heb.*(12.95B); ἐν πάσῃ ἐργασίᾳ μετανοίας ἕνα θεμέλιον εἶναι τὸ βάπτισμα Marc.Er.*opusc.*3.7(M.65.976D).

E. ref. question of post-baptismal repentance; **1.** possibility of one repentance asserted ἤκουσα...ὅτι ἑτέρα μ. οὐκ ἔστιν εἰ μὴ ἐκείνη, ὅτε εἰς ὕδωρ κατέβημεν καὶ ἐλάβομεν ἄφεσιν ἁμαρτιῶν ἡμῶν τῶν προτέρων. λέγει μοι· καλῶς ἤκουσας· οὕτω γὰρ ἔχει...οἱ γὰρ νῦν πιστεύσαντες ἢ μέλλοντες πιστεύειν μ. ἁμαρτιῶν οὐκ ἔχουσιν, ἄφεσιν δὲ ἔχουσι τῶν προτέρων ἁμαρτιῶν αὐτῶν. τοῖς οὖν κληθεῖσι πρὸ τούτων τῶν ἡμερῶν ἔθηκεν ὁ κύριος μ. καρδιογνώστης γὰρ ὢν ὁ κύριος ...ἔγνω τὴν ἀσθένειαν τῶν ἀνθρώπων καὶ τὴν πολυπλοκίαν τοῦ διαβόλου...ἐσπλαγχνίσθη ἐπὶ τὴν ποίησιν αὐτοῦ καὶ ἔθηκεν τὴν μ. ταύτην, καὶ ἐμοὶ [sc. angel of repentance] ἡ ἐξουσία τῆς μ. ταύτης ἐδόθη. ἀλλὰ ἐγώ σοι λέγω, φησί· μετὰ τὴν κλῆσιν ἐκείνην τὴν μεγάλην...ἐάν τις ἐκπειρασθεὶς ὑπὸ τοῦ διαβόλου ἁμαρτήσῃ, μίαν μ. ἔχει Herm.*mand.*4.3.1–6; cf.*ib.*4.1.8; id.*vis.*3.7.5; ἐπὶ γὰρ τῇ πρώτῃ καὶ μόνῃ μ. τῶν ἁμαρτιῶν (αὕτη ἂν εἴη τῶν προϋπαρξάντων κατὰ τὸν ἐθνικὸν...βίον, τὸν ἐν ἀγνοίᾳ λέγω) αὐτίκα τοῖς κληθεῖσι πρόκειται μ. ἡ καθαίρουσα τὸν τόπον τῆς ψυχῆς ἀπὸ τῶν πλημμελημάτων, ἵνα ἡ πίστις θεμελιωθῇ... ἔδωκεν οὖν ἄλλην ἔτι τοῖς κἂν τῇ πίστει περιπίπτουσί τινι πλημμελήματι πολυέλεος ὢν μ. δευτέραν, ἵν' εἴ τις ἐκπειρασθείη μετὰ τὴν κλῆσιν... μίαν μ. ἀμετανόητον λάβῃ Clem.*str.*2.13(p.143.16–28; M.8.993B–996A); **2.** in Novatianist controversy; **a.** arising over Novatian's refusal to readmit *lapsi* in Decian persecution agst. policy of Cyprian, Cornelius and in some measure of Dion. Al. and agst. leniency recommended by confessors οἱ θεῖοι μάρτυρες...τῶν παραπεπτωκότων ἀδελφῶν τινας...προσελάβοντο, καὶ τὴν...μ. αὐτῶν ἰδόντες δεκτήν τε γενέσθαι δυναμένην τῷ μὴ βουλομένῳ...τὸν θάνατον τοῦ ἁμαρτωλοῦ ὡς τὴν μ. δοκιμάσαντες, εἰσεδέξαντο...καὶ προσευχῶν αὐτοῖς καὶ ἑστιάσεων ἐκοινώνησαν Dion.Al.ap.Eus.*h.e.*6.42.5(M.20.613C); γράφει [sc. Dion. Al.]...τοῖς κατ' Αἴγυπτον ἐπιστολὴν περὶ μετανοίας, ἐν ᾗ τὰ δόξαντα αὐτῷ περὶ τῶν ὑποπεπτωκότων παρατέθειται Eus.*ib.*6.46.1(633C); δόγμα παρίσταται τοῖς πᾶσιν, τὸν μὲν Νοουάτον...ἐν ἀλλοτρίοις τῆς ἐκκλησίας ἡγεῖσθαι, τοὺς δὲ τῇ συμφορᾷ περιπεπτωκότας...θεραπεύειν τοῖς τῆς μ. φαρμάκοις *ib.*6.43.2(616C); Διονύσιος Ἀλεξανδρείας ἐπίσκοπος, πολλῶν ὑποπεσόντων αὐτῷ τῶν ἐν τῷ διωγμῷ Δεκίου, ὀρέγων αὐτοῖς χεῖρα μετανοίας ἐξευμενίσασθαι τὸν θεόν, πολλοῖς τῶν ἐπισκόπων περὶ αὐτῶν γράφει· ἐν οἷς ἀρθεὶς ὑπερηφανίᾳ Ναύατος...ἔλεγεν μὴ δεῖν αὐτοὺς δεχθῆναι *Chron.Pasch.*p.271(M.92.672B); **b.** developing into Novatianists' refusal to admit any post-baptismal repentance εἰ τῶν μετὰ τὸ λουτρὸν ἁμαρτανόντων...ἀσύγγνωστός ἐστιν ἡ τῶν πλημμελημάτων δίκη...τί δὲ καὶ Νουάτῳ μεμφόμεθα ἀναιροῦντι μ.; Ath.*ep.Serap.*4.13(M.26.653D); μίαν μ., μετὰ δὲ τὸ λουτρὸν μηκέτι δύνασθαί τινα ἐλεεῖσθαι παραπεπτωκότα Epiph.*haer.*59.1(p.364.3; M.41.1017B); Marc.Er.*opusc.*3.7(M.65.976C); Nil.*epp.*3.243(M.79.497B); *ib.*2.155(273A); Thdt.*haer.*3.5(4.345); **c.** orthodox arguments against this; refutation of Novatianist exegesis of Heb.6:4ff. and 12:17 τὸ ἐν τῇ πρὸς Ἑβραίους εἰρημένον οὐκ ἐκκλεῖόν ἐστι τῶν ἁμαρτανόντων τὴν μ., ἀλλὰ δεικνύον ἓν εἶναι τὸ τῆς καθολικῆς ἐκκλησίας βάπτισμα...Ἑβραίοις γὰρ ἔγραφε· καὶ ἵνα μὴ νομίσωσι κατὰ τὴν ἐν τῷ νόμῳ συνήθειαν, προφάσει μ. εἶναι πολλὰ...βαπτίσματα, διὰ τοῦτο μετανοεῖν μὲν παραινεῖ, μίαν δὲ εἶναι τὴν ἀνακαίνισιν διὰ τοῦ βαπτίσματος...οὐδὲ γὰρ ...ἀδύνατον μετανοεῖν· ἀλλ' ἀδύνατον προφάσει μ. ἀνακαινίζειν ἡμᾶς Ath.*ep.Serap.*4.13(M.26.656A); ἀνακαινίζειν, φησίν, εἰς μ.· τουτέστι, διὰ μετανοίας·...ἐκβέβληται ἡ μ.; οὐχ ἡ μ. ... ἀλλ' ὁ διὰ τοῦ λουτροῦ πάλιν ἀνακαινισμός...ἀνακαινισθῆναι, τουτέστιν καινὸν γενέσθαι· τὸ γὰρ καινοὺς ποιῆσαι, τοῦ λουτροῦ μόνον ἐστίν...τῆς δὲ μ. ἐστὶ τό, καινοὺς γενομένους, εἶτα παλαιωθέντας ὑπὸ τῶν ἁμαρτημάτων, ἀπαλλάξαι τῆς παλαιότητος Chrys.*hom.9.3 in Heb.*(12.96C); ποῦ εἰσιν οἱ λέγοντες τὸν ἀπόστολον ἐν ταύτῃ τῇ ἐπιστολῇ ἀναιρεῖν τὴν μ.; ... χωλοῦ δὲ ἴασιν ποίαν βούλεται γενέσθαι ὁ μ. τῶν ἡμαρτηκότων οὐ προσιέμενος; Thdr. Mops.*Heb.*12:12f.(pp.210.27–211.1; M.66.968A); οὐ τὴν μ. ἀνελεῖν διὰ τούτων βούλεται, ἀλλὰ διδάξαι ὡς οὐκ ἔνεστιν ἐν καιρῷ τὴν προσήκουσαν διόρθωσιν ⟨μὴ⟩ ἐπιδειξαμένους ὕστερον αὐτὴν ἀνακτᾶσθαι, ὅταν ὁ τῆς ἀνταποδόσεως καιρὸς καταλλήλως ἐπάγεσθαι τῷ ἑκάστου τρόπῳ μέλλῃ *ib.*12:17(p.211.6; 968A); scriptural proofs λέγομεν δὲ καὶ ἡμεῖς νῦν ἀπὸ παλαιᾶς, εἴπωμεν τί ἀντιλέγουσι πρὸς τὰ ἐκ τῆς παλαιᾶς λεγόμενα. λέγουσι γὰρ ὅτι πρὸ τοῦ πάθους σωτῆρος...ἐὰν ἀπὸ τῆς παλαιᾶς ἀναγνῶτε ἡμῖν περὶ μετανοίας, λέγομεν, ὅτι ἐν τῇ παλαιᾷ συγκεχώρηται· ἐν δὲ τῇ καινῇ διὰ τὸ πάθος οὐκ ἔσται συγχώρησις. ἐὰν δὲ ἀπὸ τῆς καινῆς δείξωμεν, ὅτι καὶ μετὰ τὸ βάπτισμα...ἁμαρτήσας τις ἀνακαλεῖται διὰ μετανοίας τὸ χάρισμα, δῆλον ὅτι ἔστι μ. τοῖς παραπεσοῦσι καὶ μετὰ τὸ βάπτισμα· καὶ τὰ ἐν τῇ παλαιᾷ ἔσται ὑπὲρ τῆς μ. μυρία †Bas.*poenit.*2(2.604A; M.31.1476D–1477A) citing proofs from Ezech.33:11, Jon.3:10, etc.; ἔλθωμεν ἐπὶ τὴν καινήν. ἀφ' ἧς γὰρ μάλιστα θέλουσιν ἀποκλεῖσαι τὴν μ., ἀπ' αὐτῆς μάλιστα κηρύττεται ἡ μ. *ib.*3(605C; M.1480C) citing Mt.9:13, Lc.15:5ff.; δύο, φησίν, ἦσαν...υἱοί· οὐ δύνασαί μοι εἰπεῖν, ὅτι ἡ ἀπὸ Ἑλλήνων ἐστὶν ἡ ὧδε μ., ἀλλ' ἀμφότεροι υἱοί, ἐξ ἴσου μερίσαντες...ἀναλώσας δὲ πάντα, ἦλθεν ἐπὶ μετάνοιαν *ib.*(605D; M.l.c.); from Lord's Prayer εἰ τοίνυν πιστοῖς προσήκει ἡ εὐχή, εὔχονται δὲ οὗτοι ἁμαρτήματα ἑαυτοῖς ἀφεθῆναι δεόμενοι, δῆλον ὅτι οὐδὲ μετὰ τὸ λουτρὸν ἀνῄρηται τῆς μ. τὸ κέρδος Chrys.*hom.19.5 in Mt.*(7.252C); **d.** orthodox position established, esp. ref. distinction between baptismal and other forms of repentance θέλω τοὺς λαμβάνοντας τὸ βάπτισμα μὴ ἁμαρτάνειν. εἰ δὲ παραπίπτοιέν ποτέ τινες μὴ βουλόμενοι, οὐ βούλομαι ὃ βούλονται οἱ τὴν μ. ἀναιροῦντες, μὴ βουλόμενοι συναποθανεῖν ἡμᾶς τῷ σταυρῷ †Bas.*poenit.*6(2.608B; M.31.1485C); Epiph.*haer.*59.1(p.364.14; M.41.1020A) cit. s. μεταμέλεια; μετὰ γὰρ τὴν πρώτην μ. τὴν διὰ λουτροῦ... ἐν ᾗ μ. ἀνεκαινίσθη πᾶς ἄνθρωπος, δευτέρα τις τοιαύτη οὐχ ὑπάρχει... τούτου χάριν ἐπασφαλίσασθαι δεῖ, ἵνα μὴ...τὸν στέφανον τοῦ ἀνακαινισμοῦ ἀπολέσωμεν. ἀλλὰ ἐάν τις παραπέσῃ...μετανοείτω. δέχεται γὰρ ὁ θεὸς τὴν μ. καὶ μετὰ τὸ βάπτισμα *ib.*59.5(pp.369.22–370.3; 1025C,D); and ref. love of God, *ib.*59.2(p.365.27; 1020C); Chrys.*exp.in Ps.*127:1(5.360D).

F. eccl. legislation; **1.** ref. *lapsi* during persecution; **a.** their works of penance οἱ ἀπὸ τοῦ διωγμοῦ παραπεπτωκότες, καὶ αὐτοὶ ἐὰν ἐνδείξωνται τελείαν τὴν μ., ἐν σάκκῳ καὶ σποδῷ...κλαύσαντες ἐνώπιον κυρίου δυνατός ἐστιν ὁ εὐεργέτης καὶ αὐτὸς ἐλεῆσαι· οὐ γάρ τι φαῦλον γίνεται ἀπὸ μ. Epiph.*haer.*59.7(p.372.23,25; M.41.1029D); *ib.*68.2(p.141.26; M.42.185D); **b.** ref. Meletian schism κίνησις ἐγένετο ἀνὰ μέσον τῶν μαρτύρων...τῶν μὲν λεγόντων τοὺς ἅπαξ παραπεσόντας ...μὴ δεῖν ἀξιοῦσθαι εἰς μ. ... ἦσαν δὲ οἱ τοῦτο λέγοντες Μελίτιος καὶ Πηλεὺς καί τινες ἄλλοι πλείους τῶν μαρτύρων καὶ ὁμολογητῶν... ἔφασκον δέ, εἰ ἄρα μετὰ τὸ παύσασθαι τὸν διωγμὸν μετὰ χρόνον ἱκανὸν δίδοσθαι τοῖς προειρημένοις μ. ... ἐάν...καρπὸν τῆς μ. αὐτῶν ἐπιδείξωνται, οὐ μὴν ἵνα ἕκαστος δεξιωθῇ ἐν τῷ ἰδίῳ κλήρῳ *ib.*(p.142.3ff.; M.42.185C); orthodox counter-argument εὔσπλαγχνος ὢν [sc. Petr. I Al.]...καθικέτευε λέγων· δεξώμεθα αὐτοὺς μετανοοῦντας καὶ τάξωμεν αὐτοῖς μ. εἰς τὸ παρακαθέζεσθαι τῇ ἐκκλησίᾳ, καὶ μὴ ἀποστρέψωμεν αὐτοὺς μήτε τῶν κλήρων...μή ποτε...διὰ παρολκὴν τοῦ χρόνου οἱ ἅπαξ ἀπὸ ἀνανδρίας...ὑπὸ διαβόλου ἐπισεισθέντες...τελείως ἐκτραπῶσι καὶ μὴ ἰαθῶσιν *ib.*68.3(p.142.18; 188A); **2.** ref. heretics ἀναθεματίσαντες τὴν Ἀρειανὴν αἵρεσιν ἔγγραφον τὴν μ. αὐτῶν Ath.*h.Ar.*26(p.197.10; M.25.724A); τὴν μ. Οὐρσακίου καὶ Οὐάλεντος στηλιτεύοντες *ib.*34(p.202.17; 733A); τοὺς δὲ ἐπὶ ἐξόδῳ μετανοοῦντας τῶν αἱρετικῶν δέχεσθαι χρή...οὐκ ἀκρίτως, ἀλλὰ δοκιμάζοντας εἰ ἀληθινὴν ἐπιδείκνυνται μ. Bas.*ep.*188 can.5(3.272A; M.32.673B); δέξαι ἡμᾶς [sc. Ursacius and Valens] εἰς κοινωνίαν καὶ μ. καὶ πρὸς αὐτὸν δὲ τὸν Ἀθανάσιον ταῖς αὐτῶν ἐχρήσαντο ἐγγράφοις διὰ μετανοίας συστάσεσιν Epiph.*haer.*68.9(p.149.23,25; M.42.197D); **3.** ref. second marriage μ. αἰτοῦντος τοῦ διγάμου CNeocaes.*can.*7; **4.** ref. class of penitents in Church; **a.** in gen. ἐδέχθησαν εἰς μ. CAnc.(314)*can.*6; πρεσβύτερος... ἐὰν δὲ πορνεύσῃ...ἄγεσθαι αὐτὸν εἰς μ. CNeocaes.*can.*1; *ib.*2; CLaod.*can.*19; εὔξασθε, οἱ ἐν μ. *Lit.*ap.*Const.App.*8.9.2; *ib.*8.12.47; οἱ ἐνεργούμενοι καὶ οἱ ἐν μ. Dion.Ar.*e.h.*3.2(M.3.425C); *ib.*3.3.6(432C); as a special degree dist. from others under discipline χρὴ τῷ πρώτῳ ἐκβάλλεσθαι τῶν προσευχῶν...τῷ δευτέρῳ δεχθῆναι εἰς ἀκρόασιν· τῷ τρίτῳ εἰς μ. Bas.*ep.*199 *can.*22(3.293C; M.32.724A); **b.** their status and treatment in church ὡς τελώνην οὖν ἢ ἐθνικὸν ἔχε τὸν ἐπὶ κακῷ ἔργῳ ἐλεγχθέντα...μέχρις οὗ μ. καρπὸν ἐπιδείξωσιν, ἐπιτρέπομεν εἰσέρχεσθαι...μὴ κοινωνείτωσαν δὲ ἐν τῇ προσευχῇ, ἀλλ' ἐξερχέσθωσαν μετὰ τὴν ἀνάγνωσιν τοῦ νόμου καὶ τῶν προφητῶν καὶ τοῦ εὐαγγελίου *Const.App.*2.39.6; εἰ δὲ ἐπιστραφεὶς μ. καρπὸν ἐπιδείξηται, τότε καὶ εἰς προσευχὴν εἰσδέξασθε αὐτόν...καὶ τοῦτον χειροθετήσας, ὡς ἂν μ. κεκαθαρμένον...ἀποκαταστήσεις αὐτόν *ib.*2.41.1,2; ref. adulterous women αὐτὰς ἄνευ κοινωνίας προσέταξαν, μέχρι τοῦ συμπληροῦσθαι τὸν χρόνον τῆς μ. Bas.*ep.*199 *can.*34(3.295C; M.32.728B); **c.** their penitence to be judged by intensity rather than length of time, *ib.*188 *can.*2(271B; M.672B); *ib.*217 *can.*84(330C; M.808B); **5.** πρεσβύτερος ἐπὶ τῆς μ.: ὑπὸ δὲ τὸν αὐτὸν χρόνον [sc. after Decian persecution] ἔδοξε καὶ τοὺς ἐπὶ τῆς μ. περιελεῖν πρεσβυτέρους τῶν ἐκκλησιῶν δι' αἰτίαν τοιαύτην. ἀφ' οὗ Ναυατιανοὶ τῆς ἐκκλησίας διεκρίθησαν, τοῖς ἐπταικόσιν ἐν τῷ ἐπὶ Δεκίου διωγμῷ κοινωνῆσαι μὴ θελήσαντες, οἱ ἐπίσκοποι τῷ ἐκκλησιαστικῷ κανόνι τὸν πρεσβύτερον τὸν ἐπὶ τῆς μ. προσέθεσαν, ὅπως ἂν οἱ μετὰ τὸ βάπτισμα πταίσαντες ἐπὶ τοῦ προβληθέντος τούτου πρεσβυτέρου ἐξομολογῶνται τὰ ἁμαρτήματα. οὗτος ὁ κανὼν κρατεῖ μέχρι νῦν ἐν ταῖς ἄλλαις αἱρέσεσι· μόνοι δὲ οἱ τοῦ Ὁμοουσίου φρονήματος καὶ οἱ...Ναυατιανοὶ τὸν ἐπὶ τῆς μ. πρεσβύτερον παρῃτήσαντο. Ναυατιανοὶ μὲν γὰρ οὐδὲ τὴν ἀρχὴν τὴν προσθήκην ταύτην ἐδέξαντο· οἱ δὲ νῦν τῶν ἐκκλησιῶν κρατοῦντες ἕως πολλοῦ φυλάξαντες, ἐπὶ Νεκταρίου τοῦ ἐπισκόπου μετέθεσαν, τοιούτου τινὸς ἐπὶ τὴν ἐκκλησίαν συμβάντος...ὅτι καὶ τῇ ἐκκλησίᾳ βλασφημίαν ἡ πρᾶξις καὶ ὕβριν προὐξένησεν...Εὐδαίμων τις τῆς ἐκκλησίας πρεσβύτερος...γνώμην τῷ ἐπισκόπῳ δίδωσι Νεκταρίῳ περιελεῖν μὲν τὸν ἐπὶ τῆς μ. πρεσβύτερον· συγχωρῆσαι δὲ ἕκαστον τῷ ἰδίῳ συνειδότι τῶν μυστηρίων μετέχειν Socr.*h.e.*5.19.1–9(M.67.613A–617A); cf.Soz.*h.e.* 7.16(M.67.1457C–1464A).

G. repentance and confession of sins ἐπεὶ...τῆς ἐπιστροφῆς ὁ τρόπος οἰκεῖος ὀφείλει εἶναι τοῦ ἁμαρτήματος, καὶ καρπῶν δὲ χρεία ἀξίων τῆς μ. ... ἀναγκαῖον τοῖς πεπιστευμένοις τὴν οἰκονομίαν τῶν μυστηρίων τοῦ θεοῦ ἐξομολογεῖσθαι τὰ ἁμαρτήματα Bas.*reg.br.*288(2. 516D; M.31.1284C); ἑπταπλασίονα...τὴν ἀντίδοσιν ἡμῖν χρεωστουμένην τοῖς ἁμαρτωλοῖς συγχωρήσει ὁ κύριος ἐνταῦθα, εἰ διὰ μ. καὶ ἐξομολογήσεως ἐξιλεωθείη παρ' ἡμῶν ‡Bas.*struct.hom.*2.8(1.342D; M.30.52A); ἁμαρτία...κρύπτεται...μ. καὶ ἐξομολογήσει Chrys.*hom.* *48.5 in Mt.*(7.500A); Thdt.*Ps.*6:6(1.642); Proc.G.*Is.*59:1–18(M.87. 2608B); εἰδὼς γὰρ ὁ σωτὴρ...ὅτι νέοι βαπτιζόμενοι καὶ προβαίνοντες ἐν ἡλικίᾳ μολύνομεν διὰ τὰς ἁμαρτίας τὸν...χιτῶνα τῆς ἀφθαρσίας, δέδωκεν ἡμῖν...δι' ἐξομολογήσεως καὶ μ. καθαίρειν τοῦτον †Jo.Jej. *serm.*(M.88.1921B); †Jo.Jej.*poenit.*(M.88.1897A); ὁ κύριος...ἔδωκε νόμον εἰς βοήθειαν...μοναχοὺς δὲ πάλιν ⟨εἰς⟩ τὸ παραινεῖν, ἐπὶ τὸ ἐξομολογεῖσθαι εἰς αὐτοὺς μετὰ μετανοίας †Jo.Jej.*serm.*(1920A).

H. repentance in spiritual life; **1.** causes: prayer of intercession, Ign.*Eph.*10.1; piety ἡ οὖν εὐλάβεια λογικὴ δείκνυται, τοῦ βλάπτοντος ἔκκλισις οὖσα, ἐξ ἧς ἡ μ. προημαρτημένων φύεται Clem.*str.*2.7(p.130. 19; M.8.968C); commandments, *ib.*(p.131.18; 969C); fear of the Lord, *ib.*2.9(p.134.16; 976B); Chrys.*hom.11.3 in Mt.*(7.152E); **2.** importance and universality συνιστῶμεν δὲ μ., οὐχ ἁμαρτίαν ἀδελφοῦ προτρεπόμενοι (οὐ γὰρ ἐλπίδι μ. βουλόμεθα ἐφ' ἁμαρτίαν ἰέναι τὸν ἁμαρτήσαντα), ἀλλ' ἀναστῆσαι τὸν πεσόντα σπεύδοντες...ἡ δὲ προσδοκία τῆς μ. τὸν πεσόντα ἀναστῆναι...προτρέπεται †Bas.*poenit.*1(2.603C; M. 31.1476B); περὶ μετανοίας τὸν λόγον...ἐλέγομεν, ὅτι πολλαὶ καὶ ποικίλαι ὁδοὶ τῆς μ., ἵνα εὔκολος ἡμῖν γένηται ἡ σωτηρία Chrys.*poenit.*3. 1(2.295A); *ib.*3.4(300A); τῇ χειρὶ τῆς μ. ὑμᾶς ἐγχειρίζω, ἵνα μάθητε αὐτῆς τὴν δύναμιν...τὴν ἰσχύν, ἵνα μάθητε ὅτι οὐ περιγίνεται αὐτῆς ἁμάρτημα *ib.*8.3(344D); ὁρᾷς πῶς καὶ ταχίστη καὶ πολλὴ τῆς μ. ὠφέλεια; ὀλίγα κολάσας αὐτὸν ὑπὲρ ἁμαρτημάτων...ἐπειδὴ εἶδον κατηφῆ γενόμενον...καὶ αὐτὴν τὴν μικρὰν ἀνῆκα τιμωρίαν· οὕτω καὶ ἕτοιμός ἐστι πρὸς τὰς ἡμετέρας καταλλαγὰς ὁ θεὸς id.*pan.mart.*1.4(2. 656A); τὸ τῆς μ. φάρμακον, πάντα ἡμῶν τὰ ἁμαρτήματα ἱκανὸν ἀφανίσαι id.*hom.9.4 in Heb.*(12.98C); id.*dimiss.Chan.*2(3.434E); id. *hom.24.3 in Ac.*(9.196B); μεγάλη...τῆς μ. ἡ δύναμις, εἴγε ἡμᾶς ὥσπερ χιόνα ἐργάζεται...κἂν προλαβοῦσα ἡ ἁμαρτία πολλῷ χρόνῳ κατέβλαψε τὴν ψυχὴν φαύλως Nil.*epp.*2.239(M.79.324A); ἡ ποικιλία τῶν ἐντολῶν εἰς ἕνα καταλήγει τὸν τῆς μ. ὅρον Marc.Er.*opusc.*3.1(M. 65.965B); μ. ... οὔτε καιροῖς οὔτε πράγμασι περιώρισται, ἀλλὰ διὰ τῶν τοῦ Χριστοῦ ἐντολῶν ἀναλόγως ἐπιτηδεύεται *ib.*3.6(973D); πᾶσι πάντοτε προσήκειν οἶμαι τὴν μ. ἁμαρτωλοῖς τε καὶ δικαίοις *ib.*3.7 (976B); μικροῖς τε καὶ μεγάλοις ἕως θανάτου ἀτέλεστος ἡ μ. *ib.*3.11 (980D); λέγεις· οὐ δύναμαι τελείαν ἐπιδείξασθαι τὴν μ. ... βέλτιόν σε ἔχειν κἂν ὀλίγα κατορθώματα, ἢ ὅλως μὴ ἔχειν μηδέν †Jo.Jej.*serm.*(M. 88.1956C); Ant.Mon.*hom.*77(M.89.1657C); hence possibility of deathbed repentance, Nil.*epp.*2.229(317D); εἰ μέχρι τῆς ἐσχάτης τοῦ ἀνθρώπου ἀναπνοῆς, τὴν οἰκείαν ἰσχὺν δείκνυσιν ἡ...μ., καὶ ἐν αὐταῖς προσλαμβανομένη ταῖς τοῦ θανάτου πύλαις...καὶ μέλλειν ἐξιέναι τοῦ σταδίου δικαιοῦσα...τὸν ἐξαμαρτήσαντα *ib.*3.270(518D); cf.†Gregent. *leg.Hom.*(M.86.573C); and for Judas to have been saved by repentance, Chrys.*poenit.*1.3(2.284C); **3.** two kinds of repentance; **a.** true, Herm.*mand.*12.3.2; id.*sim.*7.6; ἡ δ' ἀληθινὴ μ. τὸ μηκέτι τοῖς αὐτοῖς ἔνοχον εἶναι, ἀλλὰ ἄρδην ἐκριζῶσαι τῆς ψυχῆς ἐφ' οἷς ἑαυτοῦ κατέγνω θάνατον ἁμαρτήμασιν Clem.*q.d.s.*39(p.185.17; M.9. 644C); Bas.*reg.br.*13(2.419A; M.31.1092A); Chrys.*hom.31.3 in Heb.* (12.287E–288A); θέλει δὲ ὁ ἐν ἀληθείᾳ μετανοῶν ἐφ' οἷς ἔπραξε κακοῖς καὶ ἑαυτὸν ἐπιμέμφεσθαι, καὶ τὰ παρ' ἄλλων ὀνείδη καρτερῶς φέρειν· μ. γάρ ἐστι τὸ ὑπ' ἀφρόνων χλευάζεσθαι...καὶ ὁλοκαρδίως προσφέρειν τῷ θεῷ ἐξομολόγησιν Ant.Mon.*hom.*77(M.89.1661D); **b.** spurious, simulated ἐὰν γὰρ μὴ πορευθῶσιν ἐν αὐταῖς [sc. ἐντολαῖς], εἰς μάτην ἐστὶν ἡ μ. αὐτῶν Herm.*sim.*6.1.3; αἱ δὲ συνεχεῖς καὶ ἐπάλληλοι ἐπὶ τοῖς ἁμαρτήμασι μ. οὐδὲν τῶν καθάπαξ μὴ πεπιστευκότων διαφέρουσιν ἢ μόνῳ τῷ συναίσθεσθαι ὅτι ἁμαρτάνουσι Clem.*str.*2.13(p.144.1; M.8. 996B); *ib.*(p.144.21; 996C); οἶδα πολλοὺς ἐγώ, οἳ λέγουσι μὲν πενθεῖν τὰ ἁμαρτήματα, οὐδὲν δὲ μέγα ἐργάζονται, ἀλλὰ νηστεύουσι μὲν καὶ τραχέα φοροῦσιν ἱμάτια, χρημάτων δὲ μᾶλλον τῶν καπηλευόντων ἐφίενται...καὶ κακηγορίαις χαίρουσι μᾶλλον, ἢ ἐγκωμίοις ἕτεροι. οὐκ ἔστι ταῦτα μ.· εἰκὼν ἐστι μετανοίας ταῦτα καὶ σκιὰ μόνον Chrys.*hom.* *4.5 in 2Cor.*(10.462cf.); **c.** the two contrasted Νινευῖται...πενθοῦντες ἐπὶ τοῖς ἁμαρτήμασιν, ἃ...Ἰωνᾶς ἐξεβόησεν, οὐ τὰ βρέφη μόνον εἰς τὴν μ. προεστήσαντο...ἀλλὰ πρώτους μὲν ἐδάμασε τοὺς πατέρας τοὺς ἡμαρτηκότας ἡ νηστεία...ὢ τῆς ἐμμελοῦς μ. ... τοιαύτη τῶν ἁμαρτίαις ἐνεχομένων ἡ μ. ἡμεῖς δὲ τὴν μὲν ἁμαρτίαν ἐπιτελοῦμεν συντόνως, ὀλιγώρως δὲ...ἀναλαμβάνομεν τὴν μ. Bas.*hom.*8.3,4(2.64E–65D; M.31. 312A–313A); **d.** full and partial repentance ἡ μ. δισσή· ἡ μὲν κοινὴ ἐπὶ τῷ πεπλημμεληκέναι, ἡ δέ, τὴν φύσιν τῆς ἁμαρτίας καταμαθοῦσα, ἀφίστασθαι τοῦ ἁμαρτάνειν αὐτοῦ κατὰ προηγούμενον λόγον πείθει, ᾧ ἕπεται τὸ μὴ ἁμαρτάνειν Clem.*str.*6.12(p.481.2; M.9.320A); **4.** various expressions of repentance; **a.** confession, Chrys.*poenit.*2.1(2.287B); **b.** sorrow, *ib.*2.3(290A); **c.** humility ἔχεις δὲ καὶ τρίτην ὁδὸν μ.· πολλὰς δὲ ὁδοὺς μ. εἶπον, ἵνα τῇ ποικιλίᾳ τῶν ὁδῶν εὔκολόν σοι τὴν σωτηρίαν ἐργάσωμαι. ποία δὲ αὕτη ἡ τρίτη ὁδός; ἡ ταπεινοφροσύνη· ταπεινοφρόνησον, καὶ ἔλυσας τὰς σειρὰς τῶν ἁμαρτιῶν *ib.*2.4(292A); **d.** alms-giving, *2Clem.*16.4; τετάρτην ὁδὸν μ. πράξωμεν...λέγω δὴ τὴν ἐλεημοσύνην Chrys.*poenit.*3.1(2.295C); μ. ἐκτὸς ἐλεημοσύνης νεκρά ἐστι...οὐ δύναται μ. πτερωθῆναι, μὴ ἔχουσα πτερὸν ἐλεημοσύνης *ib.*7. 6(336C); **e.** prayer, *ib.*3.4(299C); **f.** tears, Bas.*moral.*1.2(2.235A; M.31.701A); id.*reg.br.*10(2.417E; M.31.1088C); Chrys.*poenit.*3.4(2. 300C); **g.** outward sign of sackcloth, Bas.*hom.in Ps.*29(1.131B; M.29.321C); †Bas.*Is.*196(1.526A; M.30.457A); **h.** summary βούλεσθε εἴπω καὶ μετανοίας ὁδούς; πολλαί τινές εἰσι...ἔστι πρώτη μ. ὁδὸς ἁμαρτημάτων κατάγνωσις...ὁ γὰρ καταγνοὺς τῶν ἡμαρτημένων, ὀκνηρότερός ἐστι πρὸς τὸ τοῖς αὐτοῖς πάλιν περιπεσεῖν...μία μὲν οὖν μ. ὁδὸς ἀρίστη αὕτη· ἔτι δὲ καὶ ἑτέρα ταύτης οὐκ ἐλάττων, τὸ μὴ μνησικακεῖν τοῖς ἐχθροῖς...βούλει καὶ τρίτην μαθεῖν μ. ὁδόν; εὐχὴ ζέουσα...εἰ δὲ καὶ τετάρτην θέλεις μαθεῖν, τὴν ἐλεημοσύνην ἐρῶ...καὶ τὸ μετριάζειν δὲ καὶ ταπεινοφρονεῖν τῶν εἰρημένων ἁπάντων οὐχ ἧττον δαπανᾷ ἁμαρτημάτων φύσιν...ἰδοὺ πέντε μ. ὁδοὺς ἐδείξαμεν Chrys.*diab.*2.6 (2.266A–E); πρέπον τῇ ἰσχυούσῃ ψυχῇ, δι' ἔργων ποιεῖσθαι τὴν ἐξομολόγησιν, οἷον δὴ νηστείας, καὶ ἀγρυπνίας τε, καὶ σάκκου, καὶ σποδοῦ ὑποστρώσεως καὶ ἐλεημοσύνης ἀφειδοῦς...καὶ τῶν ἄλλων καρπῶν τῶν κεχρεωστημένων τῇ ἀκριβεῖ μ. Nil.*epp.*3.243(M.79.497C); τὸ τῆς μ. ἔργον ἐν ταῖς τρισὶ ταύταις ἀρεταῖς ἐξυφαίνεται· ἐν τῷ λογισμοὺς καθαρεῖν, καὶ ἀδιαλείπτως προσεύχεσθαι, καὶ τὰς ἐπερχομένας θλίψεις ὑποφέρειν...ἄνευ τῶν προειρημένων τριῶν ἀρετῶν οὐ δύναται τελειωθῆναι τὸ τῆς μ. ἔργον *Schol.*29 in Jo.Clim.*scal.*5(M.88.792C,D); πέντε εἰσὶν οἱ τρόποι τῆς μ.· κατάγνωσις τῶν ἡμαρτημένων· τὸ ἀφιέναι τοῖς πλησίον τὰ ἁμαρτήματα· τὸ εὔχεσθαι· τὸ ἐλεεῖν· τὸ ταπεινοφρονεῖν *Schol.*6 *ib.*9(845A); **5.** effects of penitence; **a.** salvation προγινώσκει [sc. ὁ θεὸς] γάρ τινας ἐκ μ. σωθήσεσθαι Just.*1apol.*28.2(M.6.372B); οἱ Νινευῖται...μ. γνησίῳ τὴν...ἀντικατηλλάξαντο σωτηρίαν Clem.*prot.*10 (p.72.16; M.8.213B); διὰ τὰς ἐπὶ τοῖς ἁμαρτήμασιν ἡμῶν μ. τὴν κατὰ θεὸν λύπην λυπούμενοι, μ. εἰς σωτηρίαν ἀμεταμέλητον ἡμῖν ἐργαζομένην Or.*Jo.*10.17(13; p.188.10f.; M.14.336C); id.*or.*13.3(p.327.30; M. 11.456C); ὁ ἁμαρτῶν διὰ μετάνοιαν οὐκ ἀπόλλυται *Const.App.*2.10.4; Proc.G.*Is.*59:1–18(M.87.2612D); and faith, Clem.*str.*7.14(p.60.32; M. 9.517C); ἄνθρωποι μὲν μ. ἐπιδέχονται καὶ ἐξ ἀπιστίας εἰς πίστιν μεταβάλλουσιν Or.*Jo.*13.59(58; p.291.1; 512B); **b.** forgiveness, Clem.*str.* 2.15(p.150.14; M.8.1009A); τοὺς ἐκ πλήθους παραπτωμάτων ἐν μ. εἰληφότας ἄφεσιν *Const.App.*2.21.8; Chrys.*poenit.*5.2(2.311B); *ib.*7.4 (2.332C); and destruction of sin, Clem.*str.*4.6(p.260.12; M.8.1240B); Chrys.*Thdr.*1.19(1.32C); id.*poenit.*1.3(2.284B); **c.** purification ὁ...ἐν ἁμαρτίᾳ τινὶ πεφυρμένος τὴν μὲν εἰς τὸ παρὸν καθαρότητα ἀποβάλλει, τὴν δὲ εἰς τὸ μέλλον ἐκ μ. ἐλπιζομένης καθάρσεως οὐκ ἀποστερεῖται †Bas.*Is.*278(1.591E; M.30.609A); εἴ τις ἅγιος, προσερχέσθω· εἰ δέ τις οὐκ ἔστιν, γενέσθω διὰ μ. *Const.App.*7.26.6; πυρὸς δίκην ὑπὸ τῆς μ. ἀναζέσαντες, χρυσίου καθαροῦ καθαρωτέρας τὰς ἑαυτῶν ἀπεργάζονται ψυχάς Chrys.*Thdr.*1.16(1.27A); id.*poenit.*8.2(2.342E); **d.** life, Herm. *sim.*8.6.6; Clem.*str.*2.23(p.193.28; M.8.1097A); ἡ μ. ζωοποιεῖ τὸν τοῖς παραπτώμασι νεκρωθέντα· αὕτη γὰρ γνώρισμα ὑπάρχει τῆς παλιγγενεσίας, τρόπαιον δὲ ἀναστάσεως Nil.*epp.*1.274(M.79.184A); **e.** παρρησία,

Chrys.*poenit*.8.2(2.342E); **f.** other effects *τίνες εἰσὶν οἱ ἄξιοι καρποὶ τῆς μ., τὰ ἀντικείμενα τῇ ἁμαρτίᾳ ἔργα δικαιοσύνης, ἅπερ ὁ μετανοῶν καρποφορεῖν ὀφείλει;* Bas.*reg.br*.287(2.516B; M.31.1284B); *ἐπαλαιώθης σήμερον ἀπὸ τῆς ἁμαρτίας; ἀνακαίνισον σεαυτὸν ἀπὸ τῆς μ.* Chrys.*poenit*.8.1(2.341B); *προσέλθωμεν οὖν τῇ μ., καὶ αὕτη πρεσβεύῃ ὑπὲρ ἡμῶν πρὸς τὸν θεόν* Ant.Mon.*hom*.77(M.89.1660C); *εἶδον ἀκαθάρτους ψυχὰς περὶ ἔρωτας σωμάτων ἐμμανῶς μαινομένας· καὶ δὴ σκῆ[έ]ψιν μ. προσλαβοῦσαι, ἐκ πείρας ἔρωτος, τὸν αὐτὸν πρὸς κύριον μετενηνόχασιν ἔρωτα· καὶ...ἀπλήστως εἰς ἀγάπην θεοῦ ἐνεγκεντρίσθησαν* Jo.Clim.*scal*.5(M.88.777A); **6.** penitence of the perfect *ἐπιγνώμων ἀνήρ, ὁ μὴ πρὸ τῆς τελείας μ. ἀνασχόμενος τῆς...μνείας τῶν οἰκείων ἁμαρτημάτων* Evagr.Pont.*or*.144(M.79.1197B); *οἱ ἀληθῶς εὐηρεστηκότες τῷ θεῷ...ποίας ἔτι χρήζουσι μ.;...γνώσῃ πῶς καὶ τοιοῦτοι χρήζουσιν αὐτῆς...τίς οὖν ὁ ψεύδους ἀπείραστος...μηδὲ ἀργοῦ ῥήματος ὑπηρέτης εὑρεθείς, ὥστε μὴ χρήζειν μ.; εἰ γὰρ καὶ νῦν οὐκ ἔστι τοιοῦτος, ποτὲ δὲ ἐγένετο, μ. κεχρεώστηκεν ἕως θανάτου* Marc.Er.*opusc*.3.10(M.65.980A,B); *σημεῖον μεμεριμνημένης μ. πασῶν τῶν συμβαινουσῶν ὁρατῶν καὶ ἀοράτων θλίψεων ἀξίους ἑαυτοὺς λογίζεσθαι* Jo.Clim.*scal*.5(M.88.780B); *ἐν τῇ μ. μου ἐκκαυθήσεται πῦρ προσευχῆς καιούσης ὕλην ib.*(780D); *μ. μεμεριμνημένη...καὶ πένθος ἀφηγνισμένον πάσης κηλῖδος, καὶ ἡ πανόσιος εἰσαγομένων ταπείνωσις, τοσαύτην ἀπ' ἀλλήλων τὴν διαφορὰν...κέκτηνται, ὅσην ἔχει παρὰ τὸν ἄρτον ἡ ζύμη καὶ ὁ ἄλευρος. συντρίβεται μὲν γὰρ ψυχὴ...διὰ μ. ἐναργοῦς· ἑνοῦται...θεῷ δι' ὕδατος πένθους ἀψευδοῦς· ἐξ οὗ καὶ ἐξάψασα πῦρ κυρίου ἀρτοποιεῖται...ἡ μακαρία ταπείνωσις ib.*25(989D).

I. those excluded from repentance *ἀπόσταται καὶ βλάσφημοι εἰς τὸν κύριον καὶ προδόται τῶν δούλων τοῦ θεοῦ. τούτοις δὲ μ. οὐκ ἔστι... ὑποκριταὶ καὶ διδάσκαλοι πονηρίας...μὴ ἔχοντες καρπὸν δικαιοσύνης... τούτοις οὖν μ. κεῖται, ἐὰν ταχὺ μετανοήσωσιν...διατί, φημί...διὰ τοῦτο, φησί, τούτοις μ. κεῖται, ὅτι οὐκ ἐβλασφήμησαν τὸν κύριον* Herm. *sim*.9.19.1,2; *ἀδύνατον γάρ ἐστι σωθῆναι τὸν μέλλοντα νῦν ἀρνεῖσθαι τὸν κύριον ἑαυτοῦ, ἀλλ' ἐκείνοις τοῖς πάλαι ἠρνημένοις δοκεῖ κεῖσθαι μ. ib.*9.26.6; *οὕτως ἐπὶ Σοδόμων γέγονε. πολλὰ γὰρ ἁμαρτάνοντες καὶ οὐκ ἐπιστρέφοντες, ὕστερον οὕτω προσέκοψαν ἐπὶ τῇ τῶν ἀγγέλων κακῇ βουλῇ...ὥστε μηκέτι αὐτοὺς ἔχειν μ.* Mac.Aeg.*hom*.4.22(M.34.489B); *τίσιν οὐκ ἔστι μ.; ὁ δ' ἐλπίδι τῆς μ. κακουργῶν, κακουργίας ἔχει τὸν τρόπον, καὶ ἀπεστέρηται μ.* †Bas.*poenit*.6(2.608E; M.31.1488B); *ὁ σπείρων μὲν τὴν διὰ τῶν δακρύων ἐξομολόγησιν, οὐδὲν δὲ ἀπὸ ταύτης προσδεχόμενος κέρδος, οὐδὲ ἀνατρέψαι δυνήσεται τὰ διαφθείροντα τὴν μ. διαφθείρει δὲ τὴν μ. τὸ πάλιν τοῖς αὐτοῖς ἐνέχεσθαι κακοῖς* Chrys. *Thdr*.1.18(1.32B).

J. no repentance after death, *2Clem*.8.2; Clem.*prot*.10(p.67.8; M.8.204A); *ἐν ἁμαρτίᾳ τελευτήσαντι μ. οὐκ ἔστιν Const.App.*2.13.2; Chrys.*Thdr*.1.9(1.11C); ref. Dives and Lazarus *ἕως ἂν ἐνταῦθα ὦμεν, ἐλπίδας ἔχομεν χρηστάς· ἐπειδὰν δὲ ἀπέλθωμεν ἐκεῖ, κύριοι λοιπὸν μετανοίας οὐκ ἐσμέν, οὐδὲ τοῦ τὰ ἡμαρτημένα ἡμῖν ἀπονίψασθαι* id. *Laz*.2.3(1.730C); *νυνὶ* [sc. in next life] *δὲ ἐν ὀδύναις...ὧν ἀπαραιτήτοις, κήδεται τῶν αὐτῷ προσηκόντων...ἀπώνατό τι τῆς μ.;...οὐδαμῶς· ἄκαιρος γὰρ ἡ μ. ἐλύθη τὸ θέατρον, ἀπῆλθε τὰ σκάμματα* id.*grat*.3(2.662D); id.*hom.14.4 in Mt.*(7.183B); ‡Chrys.*prov*.3(2.762E); *ἀποκέκλεισται τοῖς ἐντεῦθεν ἐξιοῦσι τῆς μ. ἡ θύρα, καὶ οὐχ οἷόν τε τοὺς μὴ κατὰ τὸν παρόντα βίον τοῖς τῆς μ. χρησαμένους φαρμάκοις, ἐκεῖ τὴν ὑπὲρ τῆς ἁμαρτίας ἐξομολόγησιν προσενεγκεῖν τῷ θεῷ* Thdt.*Ps*.6:1(1.640); *ib*.6:6(642); *ἐν γὰρ τῷ ᾅδῃ...μ. οὐχ ὑπάρχει* †Jo.D.*B.J*.24(M.66.1084B); except when Christ descended into Hades, Anast.S.*qu. et resp*.111(M.89.764C); but idea of purgatorial repentance of believers *ὁ πιστὸς ἡμῖν μέτεισιν ἐπὶ τὴν βελτίονα τῆς προτέρας μονήν, μεγίστην κόλασιν ἐπιφερόμενος τὸ ἰδίωμα τῆς μ. ὧν ἐξήμαρτεν μετὰ τὸ βάπτισμα* Clem.*str*.6.14(p.486.25; M.9.332A).

K. in relation to the Fall; **1.** repentance would not have sufficed to remedy its consequences, for it would not have brought about cessation of sin for the future, nor mitigated the corruption which ensued from Adam's sin, Ath.*inc*.7.2–4(M.25.108C,D); **2.** Adam's lack of repentance *Ἀδάμ, ποῦ εἶ...καὶ ποῦ ἐστι τὸ συγχώρησον; οὐδαμοῦ μ. ἀλλὰ τὸ ἐναντίον...τί ποιεῖτε, ἄθλιοι; βάλλετε μίαν μ., ἐπίγνωτε τὸ πταῖσμα ὑμῶν* Dor.*doct*.1.8(M.88.1628A,B), v. s. III.

L. Devil and repentance (v. *μετανοέω*); **1.** no repentance for demons, Tat.*orat*.15(p.17.2; M.6.840A) cit. s. *δαίμων*; **2.** Devil's fear of men's repentance *εἴδετε πῶς μ. ἐνεκωμιάζετο, καὶ ὁ διάβολος τὴν πληγὴν οὐκ ἐβάστασεν...τί δέδοικας, ὦ διάβολε, μ. ἐγκωμιαζομένης;... δικαίως ὀδύρομαι...μεγάλα μου σκεύη ἥρπασεν ἡ μ. ... πολλὰ σκεύη αὐτοῦ ἥρπασεν ἡ μ., καὶ αὐτὴν τὴν ἀκρόπολιν αὐτοῦ καθεῖλε, καὶ καιρίαν ἔχει τὴν πληγὴν τῆς μ.* Chrys.*poenit*.2.1(2.287A).

M. scriptural passages attributing repentance to God *περὶ τῆς μ. τοῦ θεοῦ ἀπαιτούμεθα ἀπολογήσασθαι· δοκεῖ γὰρ...ἀνάξιον, οὐ μόνον τοῦ θεοῦ ἀλλὰ καὶ τοῦ σοφοῦ, τὸ μετανοεῖν...ὁ θεὸς δέ, προγνώστης ὢν τῶν μελλόντων, οὐ δύναται...μετανοεῖν...ὅταν δὲ ἐπιπλέκηται ἀνθρωπίνοις πράγμασιν ἡ θεία οἰκονομία, φέρει τὸν ἀνθρώπινον νοῦν... καὶ ὁ θεὸς δὴ λαλεῖ παιδίοις...ἐπεὶ τοίνυν ἡμεῖς μετανοοῦμεν, ὅταν ἡμῖν διαλέγηται μετανοοῦσιν ὁ θεὸς λέγει· μετανοῶ, καὶ ἀπειλῶν ἡμῖν οὐ προσποιεῖται προγνώστης εἶναι, ἀλλ' ὡς βρέφεσι λαλῶν ἀπειλεῖ* Or.*hom.18.6 in Jer.*(p.157.28; M.13.473C); *χαρίζεται* [sc. *ὁ θεός*] *μετανοίᾳ μετάνοιαν οὐχ ὁμοίως ἡμῖν μετανοῶν· οὐ γὰρ νῦν μὲν τοῦτο, νῦν δὲ ἐκεῖνο βούλεται ὁ θεός· ἀλλὰ τὴν μεταβολὴν τῆς ἀπειλῆς μ. προσηγόρευσε* Thdt.*Jon*.3:10(1.1472f.).

N. 'angel of repentance' *οὕτως γράψαι ὁ ποιμὴν ἐνετείλατο, ὁ ἄγγελος τῆς μ.* Herm.*vis*.5.7; id.*mand*.12.4.7; *ib*.12.6.1; id.*sim*.9.1.1; Clem.*q.d.s*.42(p.190.27; M.9.652A); Or.*Jo*.1.17(18; p.22.17; M.14.53B).

O. persons exempted from works of penance *ὁ γὰρ μήπω διὰ τῆς ἡλικίας τὸ ἐν ἀνθρώποις τέλειον ἐσχηκώς, μηδὲ τὸν νοῦν ἀπηρτισμένον ἔχων,...οὐδὲ ἀπαιτεῖται τὰ ἔργα τῆς μ.* †Bas.*Is*.297(1.605B; M.30.640C).

P. *ἡ ἡμέρα μ.* 22nd Oct., observed as day of penitence in Egypt, *POxy*.1357.4.

Q. as name of monastery at Alexandria, *PFlor*.298.54 (saec. vi); Cyr.*hom.div*.18 tit.(M.77.1100D); *ib*.(1101A); another *ἐπιλεγόμενον τῆς Νέας Μ.* Thphn.*chron*.p.250(M.108.628A).

R. as interprn. of name of Abel, Max.*qu.dub*.52(M.90.825B).

III. *prostration*; made as sign of penitence, esp. in religious life for moral faults, ‡Ath.*renunt*.5(M.28.1416A); ‡Jo.Jej.*can*.(p.436); for faults against rule, e.g., being late for choir, ‡Ath.*ep.Cast*.1.8 (M.28.860A); before confession, Jo.Jej.*canonar*.2(p.438); *ὀφείλει δὲ ὁ ἐξαγορευόμενος ποιεῖν τρεῖς μ. ἐν τῇ εἰσόδῳ τοῦ ἁγίου θυσιαστηρίου* †Jo.Jej.*serm*.(M.88.1921C); but not by women in state of penitence, †Jo.Jej.*poenit*.(1904C); in exorcism, *Exorc*.19(p.339); as sign of respect, esp. in religious life *βάλλειν μ. Apophth.Patr.*(M.65.93B); Dor.*doct*.7.1(M.88.1697B); Jo.Mosch.*prat*.39(M.87.2892C); as a sign of worship *βαλὼν μ. τῷ θεῷ* Jo.Mosch.*prat*.11(M.87.2861A); hence as synonym for prayer *δεῦρο βάλωμεν μ. ἵνα ἕως τοῦ Σινὰ μηδεὶς ἡμῶν φάγῃ...καὶ ἔβαλεν ὁ γέρων μ., καὶ ἕως τοῦ Σινὰ οὐ μετέλαβέν τινος ib.*100(2960A).

μεταντλέω, *draw from one vessel to another*; in gen., *transfer*, Clem. *exc.Thdot*.46(p.121.14; M.9.680D); Bas.Sel.*v.Thecl*.2.11(M.85.584A).

***μέταξις**, **ἡ**, *silk*, Cosm.Ind.*top*.11(M.88.445D); *ib*.2(96C, v.l. *μετάξιον* Migne); Thphn.*chron*.pp.153,268(v.l. *μέταξαν* M.108.413A,665A).

μετάξιον, **τό**, = foreg., ‡Jo.D.*Const*.14(M.95.329D).

μεταξύ, **1.** adv., *in the midst*, used elliptically *λῃσταὶ δύο μ. αὐτοῦ ἐσταυρώθησαν* Chrys.*hom.7.3 in Phil.*(11.249B); *in passing ὅταν μνημονεύωμεν μ. χρείας* id.*vid*.1.2(1.340E); *after, afterwards τῷ δὲ ποιήσαντί σε θεῷ ἀπιστεῖς δύνασθαί σε καὶ μ. ποιῆσαι* Thphl. Ant.*Autol*.1.8(M.6.1037B); **2.** prep. c. genit., *in the midst of*, of place *μ. θηρίων, μ. θεοῦ* Ign.*Smyrn*.4.2; *τὸ δὲ κήρυγμα μ. τῆς πλάνης...ἔλαμψε* Chrys.*hom.5.3 in Jo.*(8.40A); of time *μ. τῆς τραπέζης περὶ σταυροῦ διαλέγεται* id.*hom.88.1 in Mt.*(7.782A); *between*, of mediation of Christ *προσάγομεν αὐτῷ* [sc. *εὐχάς*] *ὡς διὰ μ. ὄντος τῆς τοῦ ἀγενήτου καὶ τῆς τῶν γενητῶν πάντων φύσεως* Or.*Cels*.3.34(p.231.7, conjj. *δι' αὐτοῦ ὡς μ.* or *δὴ μ.*; M.11.964B); *before εἰ βουλόμενος ἐγέννησεν, ἄρα ἦν τὸ βούλημα πρὸ τοῦ υἱοῦ, καὶ ἔσται κἂν ῥοπῇ χρόνου μ. υἱοῦ διὰ τοῦ βουλήματος* Epiph.*haer*.69.26(p.177.24; M.42.245A).

***μεταξυλογέω**, *digress*, Oecum.*2Petr*.3:17(M.119.604D).

μεταξυλογία, **ἡ**, *digression*, *cat.Jac*.4:5(p.29.18); Men.*exc.Rom*.3 (p.185.29; M.113.873C).

μεταξύτης, **ἡ**, *mean*, Or.*comm.in Mt*.13.26(p.250.19; M.13.1161C).

μεταπαιδεύ-ω, *educate differently*, *teach a better way*, Ath.*inc*. 14.4(M.25.121A); pass., id.*ep.encycl*.7(p.177.10; M.25.239D); id.*ep. Adelph*.6(M.26.1080C); c. dupl. acc., *teach to reject θείου δὲ νόμου τὸν ἀνθρώπινον ~οντος τὰ αἰσχίω* Cyr.*ador*.1(1.38B).

μεταπαραδίδωμι, *hand over*, *pass on*, Adam.*dial*.1.26(p.50.24; M. 11.1756A); Eus.*v.C*.2.9(p.44.21; M.20.988C); Ast.Am.*hom*.2(M.40. 189C); of the seasons, *cause to give way* to *θέρους ἀκμῇ τοῦτον* [sc. *ἔαρος αἰῶνα*] *μ.* Eus.*l.C*.6(p.209.1; M.20.1345B); intr., *give way* to *καιροὶ...ἐν εἰρήνῃ μ. ἀλλήλοις 1Clem*.20.9.

μεταπαραλαμβάνω, *take over from*, c. acc. pers., Adam.*dial*.1.26 (p.52.8; M.11.1756B).

***μεταπερισπάω**, *draw away* from, Clem.*str*.3.9(p.226.22; M.8. 1168D).

μεταπήγν-υμι, *coagulate*, *harden*; med. in trans. sense, †Apoll. *Ps*.65:6(M.33.1401B); pass. intrans. *αἵματος ὅπερ εἰς σάρκα πέφυκε ~υσθαι* Bas.*hom.in Ps*.29(1.130C; M.29.320D); id.*hex*.7.6(1.68D; M. 29.161A); *ἡ...ἄμμος προσομιλοῦσα πυρὶ...εἰς ὕαλον ~υται* Thdt.*eran*.

1(4.11); fig. ὁ οἶνος εἰς χρυσὸν ∼υται, τὰ ἔριά σοι ἀποχρυσοῦται Bas. *hom.*6.5(2.47C; M.31.269C).

μεταπηδ-άω, *leap from one place to another*; hence gen., *move about*, Chrys.*hom.*9.2 *in Col.*(11.392A); fig. [sc. πλοῦτος] δραπέτου παντὸς ἀγνωμονέστερον ἀπὸ τούτου εἰς ἐκεῖνον μ. id.*hom.*28.3 *in Gen.*(4.274A); τοῦ γάμου...πρὸς ἱερωσύνην...∼ῶντα τὸν ἔρωτα Proc. G.*ep.*78(M.87.2773C); met., *change, change over* συνήθεια τῆς γραφῆς, τὸ ταχέως ∼ᾶν ἀπὸ τοῦ περί τινων λόγου εἰς τὸν περὶ ἑτέρων Or.*comm. min.in Cant.*(M.13.36B); Meth.*symp.*3.2(p.28.14; M.18.61C); Chrys. *hom.*11.1 *in* 1*Tim.*(11.604D); εἰς υἱότητα τὴν θεοῦ καὶ πατρὸς μετέστημεν ἐκ δουλείας, τὸ μὲν οἰκεῖον ἐκβεβηκότες μέτρον, εἰς δὲ τὸ τοῦ χαριζομένου καὶ τοῦτο ἡμῖν ∼ήσαντες Cyr.*thes.*32(5^{1}.315D); id.*Ps.*41:5 (M.69.1004B); μ. ἐπὶ τὰ Θεοδώρου βιβλία τὰ περὶ τῆς ἐνανθρωπήσεως id.*ep.*70(p.16.31; 5^{2}.198D); *shift one's ground* in argument, Bas.*Eun.* 1.5(1.216B; M.29.520B).

μεταπήδησις, ἡ, *interval* between musical notes; fig., of harmony of the different parts of scripture τὴν καθ' ἕκαστον προφήτην κατὰ τὰς μ. τῶν προσώπων συνῳδίαν Clem.*str.*6.11(p.476.12; M.9.309C).

μεταπιπράσκω, *sell to another*, Nil.*Eulog.*4(M.79.1097D); Anast.S. *qu.et resp.*46(M.89.745A).

μεταπίπτ-ω, *undergo change* οὔτε δὲ μεταβάλλει οὔτε ∼ει τὸ θεῖον Athenag.*leg.*22.5(M.6.940A); τὸ ἀθάνατον...μὴ ∼ον ἢ ἐξιστανόμενον εἰς τὴν αἰσχίονα καὶ θνητὴν φύσιν Meth.*res.*1.36(p.275.16; M.41.1101A); οὐκ ἄρα μετέπεσεν ἡ πρὸς θεὸν ἰσότης, ἀλλ' ἀναλλοίωτος ἡ θεότης ἔμεινεν ἐν ταυτότητι Apoll.*corp.et div.*16(p.192.2; M.*PL.*8.875C); Gr. Naz.*or.*39.12(M.36.348C); Chrys.*hom.*11.1 *in Jo.*(8.63E); οὐ γὰρ εἰς ἄνθρωπον μετέπεσεν ὁ θεὸς λόγος, οὐδὲ οὐσία μετεβλήθη id.*hom.*7.3 *in Phil.*(11.248B); ὁ λόγος σὰρξ ἐγένετο οὐ μεταπεπτωκὼς εἰς σάρκα... οὔτε ἡ ἀναληφθεῖσα σὰρξ ἐχώρησεν εἰς τὴν φύσιν τοῦ ἀνειληφότος Paul.Em.*hom.*2(p.12.24; M.77.1440B); οὔτε τοῦ πνεύματος ἢ εἰς πατέρα ∼οντος ἢ εἰς υἱόν, ὅτι ἐκπορεύεται, καὶ ὅτι θεός ‡Cyr.*Trin.*10 (6^{3}.16D; M.77.1144D).

***μεταπλάζω,** *mould anew, refashion*, Clem.*prot.*11(p.79.19; M.8. 229B) cit. s. καινός; Meth.*res.*1.49(M.18.277C; μορφὴν πλασθῆναι p.303.7); Epiph.*haer.*76.20(p.389.32; M.42.596C).

μετάπλασις, ἡ, *remoulding, transformation*, Cyr.*hom.pasch.*10 (5^{2}.134D).

μεταπλασμός, ὁ, **1.** *remoulding, refashioning, transformation*, lit. ποία δ' ἂν γένοιτο καὶ ἡ τοῦ σώματος ἀπολύτρωσις, ἢ τίς ὁ μ., ἀναστοιχειοῦται δὲ ὅπως εἰς ἀφθαρσίαν καὶ δόξαν, αὐτὸς ἂν εἰδείη καὶ μόνος ὁ τούτων τεχνίτης Cyr.*Rom.*8:26(p.219.20; M.74.825B); met., ref. Ps. 50:12, id.*Zach.*86(3.773B); ref. Mt.5:17 μὴ τὴν εἰς ἅπαν ἀνατροπὴν τῶν πάλαι τεθεσπισμένων εἰργάσθαι διανοοῦ· μᾶλλον δὲ μ. ὥσπερ τινὰ καί, ...μεταχάραξιν τῶν ἐν τύποις ἐπὶ τὸ ἀληθές id.*ador.*1(1.5C); **2.** *quando in prosa vitium fit sermonis, barbarismus vocatur; quando in metro, metaplasmus dicitur*, Isid.H.*etym.*1.32.2.

μεταπλάσσ-ω, **1.** *remould, transform*; of resurrection body κἂν γὰρ ἐν πνευματικῷ μεταπλασθῇ σώματι αὐτὸ καὶ ἰδίως τὸ πρῶτον ὑποκείμενον ἐκεῖνο οὐκ ἔσται, ὁμοιότης δέ τις ἐκείνου ἐν λεπτομερεῖ μεταπεπλασμένη σώματι Meth.*res.*3.6(p.398.1; M.18.521C); spiritually πλάσαι μὲν τὸν ἄνθρωπον ἐκ χοός, ἀναγεννῆσαι δὲ ὕδατι, αὐξῆσαι δὲ πνεύματι, παιδαγωγῆσαι δὲ ῥήματι...ἵνα τὸν γηγενῆ εἰς ἅγιον καὶ ἐπουράνιον μεταπλάσας ἐκ προσβάσεως ἄνθρωπον Clem. *paed.*1.12(p.148.21; M.8.368A); ἵππος ἄγεται χαλινῷ,...ὁ δ' ἄνθρωπος ∼εται λόγῳ *ib.*3.12(p.290.11; 680A); Ammon.*Jo.*6:40(M.85.1436C); Cyr.*Jo.*2.1(4.148A); ζωοποιεῖ δὲ λαβὼν ὁ υἱός...καὶ καθάπερ σπινθῆρα πυρὸς ἐγκαταχώσας αὐτοῖς τὴν ζωοποιὸν τοῦ πνεύματος δύναμιν, ὅλους δι' ὅλου ∼ει εἰς ἀθανασίαν *ib.*4.1(340D); ∼εται γὰρ ὥσπερ τῶν πιστευόντων ὁ νοῦς ἐκ νομικῆς εὐμαθείας εἰς παίδευσιν εὐαγγελικήν id. 2*Cor.*3:18(p.338.14; M.74.929C); ∼ομένης...εἰς τὰ ἀμείνω καὶ πνευματικὴν πολιτείαν τῆς τῶν πιστευόντων διανοίας id.*Is.*2.1(2.189C); ref. miracles τοῦ πλάστου μ. ἕκαστον τῶν δημιουργημάτων πρὸς ἣν ἂν ἐθέλῃ χρείαν πολλὴν καὶ ἀκώλυτον ἔχοντος ἐξουσίαν Philost.*h.e.*12. 10(M.65.620B); **2.** pass., *be transfigured*, Cyr.*hom.div.*9(5^{2}.367E); id. *Lc.*9:27ff.(p.79.19; M.72.653A); **3.** in gen., *change*; from types to realities τὴν τοῦ νόμου σκιὰν ∼οντα [sc. τὸν λόγον τοῦ πατρός] ἐπὶ τὸ πνευματικώτερον Ammon.*Jo.*12:5(M.85.1480C); Cyr.*glaph.Gen.*1(1. 2C); id.*Lc.*5:14(M.72.556C); of heretics changing words or sense of scripture, Iren.*haer.*1.8.1(M.7.521A); Meth.*res.*1.58(p.320.9; M.41. 1153C); Bas.*Eun.*2.7(1.243B; M.29.584D); c. dupl. acc., *change into*, Thphyl.*exc.gent.*6(p.483.29; M.113.944D).

***μεταπλέκω,** *unravel*, Gr.Naz.*carm.*1.1.6.13(M.37.431A).

***μεταπληκεύω,** *transfer the camp*, Thphn.*chron.*p.325(M.108.785B).

***μεταπνέω,** *breathe in and out, breathe*, Gr.Naz.*carm.*1.1.8.26(M. 37.448A).

μεταποι-έω, **A.** act.; **1.** *alter the make of, change*; name, Or.*fr.*106 *in Jo.*(p.561.24); Eus.*e.th.*1.16(p.76.19; M.24.857A); τὸ βάπτισμα, τὴν θυσίαν, τὴν ἱερωσύνην, τὴν τοπικὴν λατρείαν ἑτέρως μετεποίησεν [sc. ὁ Χριστός] *Const.App.*6.23.5; ref. Dt.18:15 κἂν τὸν δι' ἐμοῦ [i.e. of Moses] νόμον ἐθέλῃ [sc. ὁ Χριστός] ∼εῖν Proc.G.*Dt.*18:11(M.87.917C); the significance of a word, Ath.*Ar.*2.46(M.26.245C); character after baptism λουσάμενοι τῷ μυστικῷ τούτῳ λουτρῷ κρείττους γεγόναμεν καὶ πρὸς τὸ κρεῖττον μετεποιήθημεν Gr.Nyss.*or.catech.*40(p.160.15; M. 45.101D); this change not an automatic transformation, *ib.*(p.159. 15; 101C); of unconverted soul τὰ μὴ ὄντα λογιζομένη, τὸ ἑαυτῆς δυνατὸν ∼εῖ, καταχρωμένη τούτῳ εἰς ἃς ἐπενόησεν ἐπιθυμίας Ath.*gent.* 4(M.25.9C); **2.** *change* to a different opinion, *convert* ἡ παραίνεσις ∼εῖ καὶ ἡ διδασκαλία μεταβάλλει τὴν διάνοιαν Tit.Bost.*fr.Lc.*6:43 (p.163.10); Philost.*h.e.*2.5(M.65.468C); **3.** *transform* ἵνα τοῦ φωτὸς ἐν τῇ σκοτίᾳ λάμποντος, μεταποιηθῇ πρὸς τὴν ἀκτῖνα τὸ σκότος Gr.Nyss. *hom.*2 *in Cant.*(M.44.797C); τῆς γῆς ∼ουμένης καὶ καινῆς γενομένης Oecum.*Apoc.*16:19(p.182); reflex., Ath.*Ar.*3.49(M.26.428A); met., *change* one's attitude, one's position in argument, *ib.*1.33(80A); ref. miracles τοῦ οἴνου...ὕδατος μὲν τυγχάνοντος ὅτε ἠντλεῖτο πρότερον, οἴνου δὲ γενομένου ὅτε αὐτὸν μετεποίησεν Ἰησοῦς Or.*Jo.*13.62 (60; p.294.33; M.14.517D); Gr.Nyss.*v.Mos.*21(M.44.308A); Bas.Sel. *or.*37.1(M.85.389B); of man's spiritual transformation in eucharist Gr.Nyss.*or.catech.*37(p.143.5; M.45.93B) cit. s. μετατίθημι; ὁ ἀμνὸς τοῦ θεοῦ βιβρώσκεται...∼ῶν πρὸς ἑαυτὸν τῷ πνεύματι τοὺς μεταλαμβάνοντας Max.*ambig.*(M.91.1365C); in future life ∼οῦντος ἡμᾶς πρὸς ἑαυτὸν δηλαδὴ τοῦ θεοῦ καὶ σωτῆρος ἡμῶν Ἰησοῦ Χριστοῦ id. *myst.*24(M.91.705A); explained οὐ τὴν ἑαυτῶν ἀφέντες φύσιν, πρὸς τὴν θείαν ∼ούμεθα ὅταν ἓν γίνεσθαι πρὸς τὸν θεὸν λεγώμεθα, ἀλλ' ὅτι μέτοχοι γεγονότες αὐτοῦ, τοῦτο καλούμεθα Cyr.*thes.*12(5^{1}.122D); **4.** *transmute*; **a.** ref. sacraments; **i.** baptismal water τῆς σωματικῆς ἕνεκεν διακονίας παρείληπται, οὐδὲν παρ' ἑαυτοῦ πρὸς τὸν ἁγιασμὸν εἰσφερόμενον, εἰ μὴ ∼ηθείη διὰ τοῦ ἁγιάσματος Gr.Nyss.*Maced.*19 (M.45.1325A); **ii.** eucharistic elements ∼ούμενον εἰς σάρκα καὶ αἷμα τοῦ κυρίου Thdr.Heracl.ap.*cat.*(*symb.*)*Mt.*26:26(p.349); ὁ ἄρτος... ἁγιάζεται διὰ λόγου θεοῦ καὶ ἐντεύξεως, οὐ διὰ βρώσεως προϊὼν εἰς τὸ σῶμα γενέσθαι τοῦ λόγου ἀλλ' εὐθὺς πρὸς τὸ σῶμα διὰ τοῦ λόγου ∼ούμενος Gr.Nyss.*or.catech.*37(p.150.3; M.45.97A); παρακαλεῖ...γενηθῆναι ἤτοι ∼ηθῆναι τὸν ἄρτον καὶ τὸν οἶνον εἰς σῶμα καὶ αἷμα αὐτοῦ Χριστοῦ ‡Bas.*h.myst.*60(p.395.13); σάρκα θεοῦ ἐκ σίτου καὶ αἷμα θεοῦ ἐξ οἴνου ἀληθῶς τῇ ἐπικλήσει καὶ ἀρρήτως ∼ούμενον Jo.D.*hom.*4.35 (M.96.637C); id.*f.o.*4.13(M.94.1145A); **b.** Christol.; **i.** denied of divine Person οὐ...τῆς θεϊκῆς τελειότητος εἰς ἀνθρωπίνην τελειότητα ∼ηθείσης ‡Ath.*Apoll.*1.16(M.26.1124A); τὸ ὅλως ∼εῖσθαι δυνάμενον καὶ ἀπό τινος εἰς ἕτερόν τι παραφέρεσθαι, τρεπτῆς ἂν εἴη φύσεως Cyr. *thes.*20(5^{1}.199C); οὐ...τὸν ἐκ πατρὸς θεὸν λόγον εἰς τὴν τῆς σαρκὸς ∼ῆσθαι φύσιν, ἤγουν τὴν σάρκα μεταχωρῆσαι πρὸς λόγον id.*Jo.*4.2(4. 363B); id.*ep.*4(p.26.25; 5^{2}.23B); μίαν φύσιν τοῦ θεοῦ λόγου σεσαρκωμένην...κατὰ Εὐτυχέα, ὡς αὐτοῦ τοῦ λόγου εἰς σάρκα ∼ηθέντος ἐκδέχεσθαι Leont.H.*monoph.*(M.86.1853C); **ii.** of Christ's human body τὸ σῶμα τῇ ἐνοικήσει τοῦ θεοῦ λόγου πρὸς τὴν θεϊκὴν ἀξίαν μετεποιήθη Gr.Nyss.*or.catech.*37(p.149.2; M.45.96D); ἡ δεξαμένη τὸν κύριον σὰρξ Χριστὸς καὶ κύριος γίνεται, ὃ μὴ ἦν τῇ φύσει εἰς τοῦτο ∼ουμένη διὰ τῆς ἀνακράσεως id.*Eun.*6(2 p.144.13; M.45.729C); ἡ σὰρξ οὐχ ἡ αὐτὴ τῇ θεότητι, πρὶν ∼ηθῆναι καὶ ταύτην πρὸς τὴν θεότητα *ib.*5(2 p.123. 10; 705A); cf. τῆς παρθένου ἐν τοῖς ἰδιώμασιν τῆς φύσεως μεινάσης ...τῶν παρθενικῶν αἱμάτων...∼ηθέντων ἄφθαρτον γεγενῆσθαι σάρκα Leont.B.*Nest.et Eut.*2(M.86.1325D); **iii.** of Christ after Resurrection μετεποιήθη ἀπὸ θνητοῦ εἰς ἀθάνατον...γέγονε...τὸ σαρκικὸν πνευματικόν, τὸ παθητὸν ἀπαθές Anast.S.*hod.*13(M.89.212C); Anast.Ant. *serm.*1.2(M.89.1365A); **5.** *make instead* ἐξ ὕδατος οἶνον μ. *Const.App.* 5.7.28; in reputed teaching of Apoll. ὅτι οὐκ ἐκ Μαρίας, ἀλλ' ἐκ τῆς ἑαυτοῦ οὐσίας μετεποίησεν ἑαυτῷ σῶμα παθητὸν ὁ λόγος Ath.*ep. Epict.*2(p.5.2; M.26.1053A); εἰ μὲν γὰρ ἐξ ἑαυτοῦ ∼ήσας σάρκα ὁ λόγος μέχρι πάθους κεχώρηκε, μηδὲν παθητικὸν ἢ ἀνάστασιν ἐπιδεχόμενον ἐν ἑαυτῷ προσλαβόμενος, αὐτὸς ἂν εἴη ὁ παθὼν καὶ ἀναστὰς ἐκ νεκρῶν ‡Ath.*Apoll.*2.12(M.26.1152B).

B. med. and pass.; **1.** c. genit., *lay claim to* ὡς οἰκείων ἀλλ' οὐκ ἀλλοτρίων αὐτῶν [sc. τῶν προφητικῶν Ἰουδαίων γραφῶν] ∼ούμεθα Eus.*d.e.*3 proem.(p.94.7; M.22.164A); τὴν Ἀντιοχέων ἐκκλησίαν ὡς οἰκείου ἀγαθοῦ ∼ηθῆναι αὐτοῦ id.*Marcell.*1.4(p.18.5; M.24.752A); Gr. Nyss.*or.catech.*20(p.79.18; M.45.57A); τῆς θείας μ. χάριτος Max.*ambig.* (M.91.1144A); id.*ep.*44(M.91.645B); **2.** c. genit., *seek after* κεκώλυκάς τινας αὐτῶν τῆς ἐκκλησίας ∼ουμένους Const.ap.Ath.*apol.sec.*59(p.140. 9; M.25.357B); τὴν κατὰ λόγον μετάνοιαν ἐπιδεδειγμένοι, καὶ τῆς κοινωνίας ∼οῦνται Mac.Aeg.*carit.*28(M.34.929D); Cyr.*Is.*3.4(2.494A); **3.** c. genit. or acc., *strive for* προσκαίρου τροφῆς...∼ούμενος, τῶν δὲ ἀεὶ παραμόνων οὐκ ἐπιστρεφόμενος; *Const.App.*2.60.1; Ἀβραὰμ

~ουμένου τὴν ὁδὸν τῆς ἀληθείας *ib.*7.33.4; μ. προθύμως τῆς οὐκ ἀθαυμάστου ζωῆς Cyr.*Ps.*36 proem.(M.69.924B); id.*Is.*3.2(2.403C); Sophr.H.*mir.Cyr.et Jo.*16(M.87.3472C); Max.*ambig.*(M.91.1365B); *apply oneself to* εἰσῴχοντο μὲν εἰς τὸν οἶκον τοῦ θεοῦ καὶ μετεποιοῦντο τῶν ἔργων Cyr.*Ag.*11(3.638D); **4.** *support, make common cause with* καταισχύνειν τοὺς Θεοδώρου ~ουμένους Justn.*conf.anath.*(p.104.36; M.86.1029B).

μεταποίησις, ἡ, 1. *changing, alteration* διαφορὰ χειρὸς ἀξία θεοῦ ἡ ἀπὸ κακίας εἰς ἀρετὴν μ. Or.*fr.9 in Jer.*(p.201.17; M.13.556D); ἡ πρὸς τὸ μέλαν τῆς εὐχροίας μ. Gr.Nyss.*hom.2 in Cant.*(M.44.796A); Soz.*h.e.*3.5.2(M.67.1041A); Christol. κύριος καὶ Χριστὸς πεποιῆσθαι λέγεται...διὰ τὴν πρὸς τὸ θεῖον τοῦ ἀνθρωπίνου μεταβολήν τε καὶ μ. ποίησιν γὰρ ὁ ἀπόστολος λέγει τὴν μ. Gr.Nyss.*Eun.*3(2 p.134.2; M.45.717C); this idea rejected εἰ δὲ ὅλως γίνεται θεότης ἐκ μ. ἡ μὴ οὖσα θεότης, τί τοίνυν μέμφεσθε Ἀρειανοῖς; ‡Ath.*Apoll.*1.10(M.26.1109B); ref. Heb.4:15 οὐ τῆς θεότητος μ. ἐπιδειξάμενος ἀλλὰ τῆς ἀνθρωπότητος καινοποίησιν ἐργασάμενος *ib.*2.5(1140B); of elements in eucharist, Ambr.*fr.*ap.Thdt.*eran.*2(4.145) cit. s. διαστίζω; **2.** *reformation, renewal*; **a.** moral and spiritual, at baptism τὸ φώτισμα...δεσμῶν ἔκλυσις, συνθέσεως μ. Gr.Naz.*or.*40.3(M.36.361B); ἡ διὰ τῆς ἀναγεννήσεως γινομένη τῆς ζωῆς ἡμῶν μ. οὐκ ἂν εἴη μ. εἰ ἐν ᾧ ἐσμεν διαμένοιμεν Gr.Nyss.*or.catech.*40(p.159.12; M.45.101B); gen., Proc.G.*Dt.*32:6(M.87.956D); τιμιωτέρα...τῆς φυσικῆς ἀφθαρσίας ἡ ἐν χάριτι πρὸς τὸν θεὸν κατὰ τὴν θέωσιν μ. Max.*ambig.*(M.91.1176A); not possible at day of judgement, Gr.Naz.*or.*16.9(M.35.945B); **b.** of all things, Bas.*hex.*1.3(1.4C; M.29.9B); τὸν τελευταῖον σεισμὸν...τὴν δευτέραν τοῦ Χριστοῦ παρουσίαν καὶ τὴν τοῦδε τοῦ παντὸς μ. καὶ μετάθεσιν εἰς τὸ ἀκίνητον καὶ ἀσάλευτον Gr.Naz.*or.*21.25(M.35.1109D); ἄλογον τὸ πιστεύειν μὲν θεῷ ἐπὶ τῇ ποιήσει τῶν πάντῃ οὐκ ὄντων, ἀπιστεῖν δὲ αὐτῷ ἐπὶ τῇ μ. τῶν φθαρέντων ‡Just.*qu.Gr.*15.29(M.6.1485C); ἡ τῶν ὅλων μεταστοιχείωσις καὶ ἐκ φθορᾶς εἰς ἀφθαρσίαν μ. †Proc.G.*Procl.*(M.87.2792[b]D); ἐλεύσεται ἐπὶ μ. τε καὶ μεταστοιχειώσει τοῦ παντὸς καὶ σωτηρίᾳ τῶν ἡμετέρων ψυχῶν τε καὶ σωμάτων Max.*ambig.*(M.91.1332D); **c.** ὀγδόη ἐστὶν ἡ πρὸς τὴν ἀρχὴν καὶ αἰτίαν τῶν πρακτικῶς πεποιημένων καὶ τῶν θεωρητικῶς ἐγνωσμένων κατὰ τὴν χάριν ἀληθὴς μ. *ib.*(1393A); **3.** *claiming, claiming a share* τῆς τῶν Ἑβραϊκῶν λόγων μ. Eus.*p.e.*7.1(298D; M.21.508C).

***μεταποιητής, ὁ,** *he who refashions*; of Son, Gr.Naz.*or.*30.15(p.132.1; M.36.124A).

***μεταποιητικός,** *able to refashion*, ‡Just.*qu.Gr.*15.18(M.6.1484B).

***μεταποι-όω,** *change the quality of, make of a different quality* θείας ἐστὶ φύσεως...ποιῶσαι καὶ μ. Leont.H.*monoph.*6(M.86.1773A); pass., *be endowed with a different quality* 'τεκνία' μετὰ τὴν τοῦ σωτῆρος ἀνάστασιν, ὡσπερεὶ ~ωθέντες ἀπὸ τῆς ἀναστάσεως Ἰησοῦ, γίνονται τοῦ πρότερον εἰπόντος 'τεκνία' ἀδελφοί Or.*Jo.*32.30(19; p.476.20; μεταποιηθέντος M.14.824A).

***μεταπορθμεύω,** *ferry across*, Hegem.*Arch.*8(p.13.5; M.10.1440B).

μετάπρασις, ἡ, *resale, retail trading*, Meth.*symp.*5.4(p.57.23; M.18.104A); ref. Mt.13:44, Ephr.2.272C.

μεταπρέπω, = πρέπω, *befit*, †Apoll.*met.Ps.*64:2(M.33.1400C).

***μεταπρόσταξις, ἡ,** *permission* μοναχὸς ὁ μὴ εὑρεθὼν [s.v.l.] εἰς τὴν ἀρχὴν τοῦ δόξα ἐν ὑψίστοις...χωρὶς ἀσθενείας...ἡ μ. τοῦ ἡγουμένου †Pach.*poen.*(p.64).

μετάπτωσις, ἡ, 1. *change*, Christol. οὐ τῆς οὐσίας αὐτοῦ μ. εἰς σάρκα *cat.Jo.*1:14(p.186.35) for οὐδὲ γὰρ ἡ οὐσία μετέπεσεν Chrys.*hom.11.1 in Jo.*(8.63E); of change in Christ's natures through confusion postulated by monophysites, ‡Hipp.*Ber.Hel.*5(p.324.26; M.10.837A); of moral reformation τινὲς αἱρετικοὶ...λέγουσιν...ὅτι...ὧδε ἔχει [sc. ἡ ψυχικὴ φύσις] μ. ὅπερ καλεῖται ἔγερσις Didym.ap.*cat.Ac.*24:14(p.378.14); πᾶσαν μ. προαιρετικῇ ῥοπῇ γίνεσθαι *ib.*(p.378.27); **2.** moral *lapse, fall* ἐξ ἰδίας αἰτίας τῶν μὴ προσεχόντων ἑαυτοῖς ἀγρύπνως γίνονται τάχιον ἢ βράδιον μ. καὶ ἐπὶ πλεῖον ἢ ἐπὶ ἔλαττον Or.*princ.*1.6.2(p.81.1; M.11.166C); ἡ ἀπὸ τοῦ πλοίου εἰς τὴν θάλασσαν ἔκριψις τοῦ Ἰωνᾶ γεγενημένη τὴν ἀπὸ τοῦ ζῆν εἰς τὸ τελευτῆσαι τοῦ πρωτοπλάστου δηλοῖ μ. Meth.*res.*2.25(p.381.16; M.18.329A); πρὸς νόσον μ. Chrys.*hom.42.4 in Ac.*(9.324A); of 'lapse' into human condition of Christ's heavenly flesh (Apollinarian) σάρκα ἄκτιστον λέγειν, ὥστε ἢ τὴν θεότητα τοῦ λόγου εἰς μ. σαρκὸς φαντάζεσθαι, ἢ τὴν οἰκονομίαν τοῦ πάθους...καὶ τῆς ἀναστάσεως, ὡς δόκησιν νομίζειν ‡Ath.*Apoll.*1.3(M.26.1097A).

μεταπτωτικός, 1. *liable to change*; neut. as subst., *mutability*, Max.*ambig.*(M.91.1416A); **2.** pass., *that can be changed, removable* ἡ ἄγνοια φαντασία ἐστὶ μ. ὑπὸ λόγου Clem.*str.*2.17(p.152.31; M.8.1013C).

μεταπτωτός, *liable to change*, Or.*comm.in Mt.*13.29(p.260.30; M.13.1172C) cit. s. δίκαιος; ἀμετάπτωτον ἔχει τὴν υἱότητα ὁ μονογενής...τὴν δὲ τῶν λογικῶν υἱοθεσίαν οὐ κατὰ φύσιν αὐτοῖς ὑπάρχουσαν ἀλλὰ... μ. οἶδεν ὁ λόγος Alex.Al.*ep.Alex.*8(p.25.4; M.18.560C); μ. [sc. οἱ ἄρχοντες τούτου τοῦ αἰῶνος] ἔχουσι τὴν ἀρχήν Eus.*Ps.*145:3(M.24.64B); ref. deity of H. Ghost ὁ γὰρ χάριτι θεοποιούμενος τῆς μ. ἐστὶ φύσεως Bas.*Eun.*3.5(1.276E; M.29.665C); denied of Son and H. Ghost, Gr.Nyss.*Eun.*1(1 p.104.11; M.45.337B).

***μεταπύρωσις, ἡ,** *rekindling*, met. καρδίας μ. Ephr.3.320B.

μεταπωλέω, *resell*, *T.Jos.*13.1(vv.ll. ἀπεμπολῶν, μετεμπολῶν, μετεμπωλῶν); Bas.*ep.*53.2(3.147E; M.32.400A).

***μεταρρέπω,** *move to and fro*, Bas.*Eun.*3.2(1.274C; M.29.660C).

μεταρριπίζομαι, *be blown to and fro*; met., of opinions, Gr.Nyss.*Eun.*1(1 p.117.3; M.45.352B).

***μεταρροή, ἡ,** *stream*; of inspiration, Gr.Naz.*carm.*1.2.10.60(M.37.685A).

μεταρρυθμίζ-ω, 1. *change the form* or *fashion of* a thing; *transform*; eucharistic τοῦτο τὸ ῥῆμα [i.e. Mt.26:26] τὰ προκείμενα ~ει Chrys.*prod.Jud.*2.6(2.394B); in day of judgement πάντα ~όμενα id.*hom.76.3 in Mt.*(7.736A); at Pentecost τὴν μίαν ἑκάστου φωνὴν πρὸς τὰς ἁπάντων ἐθνῶν αἰσθήσεις ~ούσης τῆς χάριτος Bas.Sel.*or.*37.1(M.85.389B); *translate* τὸν εἰς τὴν Ῥωμαίων τοὺς σοὺς πόνους ~οντα γλῶτταν Const.ap.Eus.*v.C.*4.35(p.131.9; M.20.1184B); **2.** *reform, amend*; *break in* a horse, Thdt.*provid.*5(4.556).

***μεταρρώνυμαι,** *be restored to strength*, ‡Caes.Naz.*dial.*30(M.38.892).

***μεταρσιολεκτέω,** *prate of high things*, Epiph.*haer.*76.38(p.392.1; M.42.600A).

μεταρσιολέσχης, ὁ, *one who talks of high things*, Isid.Pel.*epp.*5.202(M.78.1453B).

μετάρσιος, A. *raised on high, high in the air*; **1.** lit.; **a.** of *tall* trees, Clem.*str.*4.18(p.299.31; M.8.1325B); neut. plur. as subst., the *heavens*, *ib.*6.11(p.477.8; M.9.312A); πτηνῶν τὰ μ. birds *of the air*, Eus.*l.C.*6(p.208.17; M.20.1345A); **b.** *exalted to heaven* μ. εἰς τὴν πατρῷον ἑστίαν ἀρθεὶς Const.*or.s.c.*1(p.155.7; M.20.1236B); Ἠλίας...ὁ ἐν σώματι μ. Eustrat.*stat.anim.*8(p.368); **c.** *heavenly* ὑψωθεὶς εἰς μ. μονάς Mac.Mgn.*apocr.*2.20(p.40.17); ὁ ἄνθρωπος [sc. ἐνδείκνυται] τὸν ἀέρα, οὐράνιον γὰρ φυτὸν καὶ μ. ὁ ἄνθρωπος διὰ τὴν τοῦ νοῦ λεπτότητα Oecum.*Apoc.*4:7(p.73); **2.** met.; **a.** *exalted, uplifted* μ. ποιησάμενοι τὴν ψυχὴν ἐπτερωμένην τῷ ποθῷ τῶν κρειττόνων Clem.*str.*7.7(p.30.23; M.9.456B); οἱ...ψυχῆς τε αὐτῆς μ. πτερῷ τὸ νοερὸν ἐπερείσαντες Eus.*l.C.*proem.(p.196.4; M.20.1317B); εὐχὴν ἄνω τεθεῖσαν καὶ νοῦν ἀπλανῆ καὶ μ. Gr.Naz.*or.*8.13(M.35.804C); Nil.*Magn.*4(M.79.973C); μ. γίνομαι τὴν ψυχὴν καὶ οὐκ αἰσθάνομαι τῶν βασάνων *M.Thdot.*3(p.133.9); *set on heavenly things* ὅλος μ., ὥσπερ ξένος καὶ ἀλήτης...κατέδραμε ἐπὶ τὰ Ἱεροσόλυμα Bas.*ep.*45.1(3.123D; M.32.365C); **b.** *high* σάββατα πάντα φύλασσε μ. καὶ σκιόεντα Gr.Naz.*carm.*1.1.15.6(M.37.477A).

B. *airy, unsubstantial*, neut. as subst. οἱ οὐράνιοι ῥήτορες πτεροφόροι τῇ γραφῇ ζωγραφοῦνται...ἵνα σημανθῇ τοῖς ἀνθρώποις τὸ ὑψηλὸν καὶ μ. ... τῶν φύσεων ἐκείνων Nil.*epp.*2.224(M.79.360A); τροπικῶς τὴν...γραφὴν τοὺς...ἀγγέλους νεφέλας καλεῖν διὰ τὸ κοῦφον αὐτῶν καὶ μ. Oecum.*Apoc.*1:7(p.37).

μέταρσις, ἡ, 1. *moving from one place to another* μ. λοιμικῆς ἀρρωστίας Geo.Pis.*hex.*412(M.92.1466A); hence gen. *change*; of the seasons, *ib.*280(1456A); **2.** *lifting up*; met., *exaltation*, AQ Is.23:18 ap.Proc.G.ad loc.(M.87.2189B).

***μεταρσίως,** *in mid-air*, Cosm.Ind.*top.*1(M.88.60B).

***μετασαλεύω,** *shake from its position*, *T.Sal.*10.5(p.38.9; M.122.1332B); met., δόγματα, Or.*Cels.*2.2(p.128.26; M.11.797B); Chrys.*hom.4.1 in Col.*(11.351F).

***μετασκέπτομαι,** *change one's views*, Cyr.*Jo.*6.1(4.594C).

μετασκευάζ-ω, 1. *change the fashion of, transform*; **a.** nature, in baptism θείας δυνάμεως παρουσία πρὸς ἀφθαρσίαν ~ει τὸ ἐν τῇ φθαρτῇ φύσει γενόμενον Gr.Nyss.*or.catech.*33(p.126.4; M.45.84D); τοὺς εἰς καινότητα πολιτείας εὐαγγελικῆς μετεσκευασμένους Cyr.*ador.*17(1.613E); med., Dion.Ar.*e.h.*3.3.11(M.3.441B); **b.** elements in eucharist ὁ τότε ταῦτα ποιήσας ἐν ἐκείνῳ τῷ δείπνῳ, οὗτος καὶ νῦν αὐτὰ ἐργάζεται...ὁ ἁγιάζων αὐτὰ καὶ μ., αὐτός Chrys.*hom.82.5 in Mt.*(7.789A); ὁ λόγος...~ει διὰ τῆς θείας ἐνεργείας τὸν ἄρτον καὶ τὸν οἶνον τῆς προσφορᾶς σῶμα αὐτοῦ καὶ αἷμα †Jo.D.*B.J.*19(M.96.1032A); **c.** in gen., ref. ten plagues Μωϋσῆς...μ. τὴν κτίσιν τοῖς θείοις προστάγμασιν Bas.Sel.*or.*25.1(M.85.288A); μετασκευασθὲν τὸ σῶμα Μωϋσέως ὑπὸ τοῦ πνεύματος. πῶς γὰρ ἀνέστη ἐφ' ἡμέρας μ' μὴ φαγών, μὴ πιών, μὴ καθευδήσας, εἴπερ ἔμεινεν ἄνθρωπος; Proc.G.*Dt.*34:6(M.87.992C); in monophysite Christology τὰ τὴν ἡμετέραν φύσιν οὐσιωδῶς χαρακτηρίζοντα καθ' ἡμᾶς τελείως οὐ σώζοντα· ἀλλ' ἢ ταῦτα πρὸς τὴν ἑαυτοῦ θείαν μετασκευάσαντος φύσιν Max.*opusc.*(M.91.93A); **2.** *change* Κωνσταντῖνον...τὸ Βυζάντιον εἰς Κωνσταντίνου πόλιν μ. Philost.*h.e.*2.9(M.65.472B); λύπην...εἰς χαρὰν μ. Hadr.*introd.*88(p.104.

8; M.98.1293A); meanings of words, Gr.Nyss.*Eun*.8(2 p.190.29; M. 45.785B); τὸ μὴ κατ' οὐσίαν ὅμοιον εἰς κατηγορίαν ἀνομοιότητος πατρὸς πρὸς υἱὸν ~οντες Philost.*h.e*.6.1(532B); **3.** *transfer to the class of* μ. [sc. τινά] εἰς ῥήτορας Proc.G.*ep*.23(M.87.2740A); **4.** med., *shift oneself*; fig., of becoming a bishop ὥσπερ εἰς βίον ἀπὸ βίου ~εσθαι Synes.*ep*.105(M.66.1488C).

***μετασκευαστής, ὁ,** *one who rearranges*, in false view of Creation μηκέτι...ποιητὴς ἐκ τοῦ μὴ ὄντος εἰς τὸ εἶναι τὰ ὄντα παράγων, ἀλλ' ἔκ τινος ὑποκειμένης ἀρχῆς τε καὶ ὕλης, ὡς ἄνθρωπος, μ. ... εὑρισκόμενος [sc. ὁ θεός] Cyr.*thes*.4(5^{1}.29C).

μετασκευή, ἡ, *alteration* τὸ δὲ πνεῦμα οὔτε τροπῆς οὔτε μ. ἐστι δεκτικόν Didym.(‡Bas.)*Eun*.5(1.296C; M.29.712A).

***μετάσκεψις, ἡ,** *change of view*, Cyr.*Abac*.12(3.527B).

μετασοβ-έω, *frighten* or *impel by fear* into a *different* course ὁ νόμος παιδαγωγὸν ὥσπερ τινὰ ~οῦντα πρὸς τὸ εὐθὺ τὸν φόβον ἐφίστησιν Cyr.*ador*.7(1.236A); μ. ταῖς θλίψεσι πρὸς τὸ...συμφέρον τε ἡμῖν καὶ ἀναγκαῖον εἰς σωτηρίαν id.*Os*.127(3.160A); ref. Jo.6:53 Χριστὸς κατασμικρύνει τὸν τύπον, ~ῶν εἰς ἀλήθειαν id.*Nest*.4.5(p.87.3; 6. 113A); id.*ador*.6(179D).

μετασπάω, *draw* to a *different* place, Epiph.*haer*.66.48(p.85.27; M.42.101C); Vict.*Mc*.1:12(p.272.28).

μετάστασις, ἡ, 1. *removal, change of place* ὁ θάνατος αὐτοῦ [sc. τοῦ Χριστοῦ] μ. ἐστι καὶ μετάθεσις ἀμείνων, εἰς τόπον σώματα οὐ δεχόμενον φθαρτά Chrys.*hom.72.3 in Jo*.(8.426C); *ib.79.1*(466C); not applicable to divine nature at Inc. τὴν ἐξ οὐρανῶν καταφοίτησιν...μὴ τοπικὴν μ. τῆς ἀχωρήτου αὐτοῦ...θεότητος Gel.Cyz.*h.e*.2.24.9(M.85. 1300D); of assumption of BMV, Jo.Thess.*dorm.BMV* 2.14(p.438.15); Jo.D.*dorm.BMV* 141(p.232; M.94.1365D); of festival of Assumption, *Catech.Stud*.5(M.99.1696C); **2.** *change*; of repentance, Or.*Jo*. 1.11(12; p.16.24; M.14.44B); of effects of baptism τῶν πονηρῶν γνωρισμάτων ἐξαλειφθέντων τῆς φύσεως ἡμῶν ἡ πρὸς τὸ κρεῖττον μ. γίνεται Gr.Nyss.*or.catech*.40(p.160.11; M.45.101D); denied, ref. generation of Son οὐ...μ. καὶ ῥύσιν τῆς τοῦ γεννῶντος οὐσίας Bas. *Eun*.2.6(1.242B; M.29.581B); of change of circumstances, Thdr. Mops.*Ag*.1:1(M.66.477C).

μεταστατικός, 1. *able to move from place to place*, ‡Just.*fr*.16(M. 6.1600A); **2.** *involving motion*, in a *reductio ad absurdum* argument agst. Nest. τὸ θεῖον...ποιεῖσθαι κίνησιν τὴν ἐκ τόπου πρὸς τόπον ἕτερον μ. Cyr.*Nest*.1.2(p.21.4; 6^{1}.13E, cod. μεταστικήν).

μεταστείχω, *go from one place to another*, †Apoll.*met.Ps*.104:13 (M.33.1469A).

***μεταστοιβάζω,** *re-stack* library books, Thdr.Stud.*poen*.1.48(M. 99.1740A).

μεταστοιχει-όω, *change the elementary nature of, transform*; **1.** in gen., Gr.Nyss.*hom.opif*.24.3(M.44.213C); Isid.Pel.*epp*.5.431 (M.78.1580C); Cyr.*Am*.81(3.345D); πότερον...ἆρα τοῦ σώματος τῆς παρθένου ~ωθέντος καὶ τῆς ἰδίας ἐκστάντος φύσεως ὑπὸ τῆς τοῦ λόγου δυνάμεως Leont.B.*Nest.et Eut*.2(M.86.1325D); ref. ten plagues πᾶσαν τὴν κτίσιν μετεστοιχείωσε Chrys.*ep*.2.7(3.542E); Cyr.*Abac*.50(3.563D); id.*ador*.2(1.70A); ‡Nil.*perist*.12.7(M.79.952B); of decomposition after death, Leont.B.*arg.Sev*.(M.86.1941D); **2.** ref. Christ's resurrection body οὐ τὸ ἀπαθὲς τῆς φύσεως εἰς πάθος ἠλλοίωσεν, ἀλλὰ τὸ τρεπτόν τε καὶ ἐμπαθὲς διὰ τῆς πρὸς τὸ ἄτρεπτον κοινωνίας εἰς ἀπάθειαν μετεστοιχείωσεν Gr.Nyss.*v.Mos*.(M.44.336A); τὸ ἴδιον σῶμα...μετὰ ἀναστάσεως ~ωθὲν ἐπὶ τὸ πνευματικὸν καὶ ἐπουράνιον ὑποδεικνύς Anast. Ant.*serm*.1.2(M.89.1365A); ref. men's resurrection bodies, Gr.Nyss. *hom.1 in Cant*.(M.44.777A); ἔξω γεγονότες σαρκὸς καὶ αἵματος, εἰς δὲ τὴν πνευματικὴν ~ωθέντες φύσιν *ib*.9(953C); **3.** of future life in gen. εἰς μακραίωνα βίον ~ούμεθα Cyr.*hom.pasch*.24(5^{2}.294E); of restoration of man ~οῦν δὲ πάλιν εἰς τὴν ἀρχαίαν εἰκόνα τὴν ἀνθρωπότητα διὰ τοῦ πνεύματος ἐδοκίμαζεν Cyr.*Jo*.2.1(4.122E); of all things ἵνα τὴν οἰκουμένην προσκομίσῃ τῷ θεῷ καὶ πατρὶ ~ώσας τὰ πάντα πρὸς τὸ ἀμεινόνως ἔχειν id.*Is*.5.5(2.858B); ref. Ps.67:5 δυσμὴ νοεῖται ἡ ἡμετέρα φύσις...καὶ ὁ ᾅδης· ἐν οἷς τὸ ἄυλον καὶ ἄσκιον φῶς ἐναστράψαν, πάντα πρὸς τὸ κρεῖττον μετεστοιχείωσε, τὴν φύσιν **ἀνεκαίνισε** ‡Caes.Naz.*dial*.30(M.38.893); *cat.Apoc*.7:10(p.293.16); **4.** Christol. ἄυλός τις οὐσία καὶ ἀειδής, ἡ τοῦ ὑψίστου δύναμις, τὴν δουλικὴν μορφὴν τὴν διὰ τῆς παρθένου ὑπόστασιν διαλαβοῦσα, πρὸς τὸ ἴδιον ὕψος ἀνήγαγεν, εἰς τὴν θείαν τε καὶ ἀκήρατον ~ώσασα φύσιν Gr. Nyss.*Apoll*.25(M.45.1177C); ὁ τὴν φύσιν ἡμῶν πρὸς τὴν θείαν δύναμιν ~ώσας, ἄπηρον αὐτὴν καὶ ἄνοσον ἐν ἑαυτῷ διεσώσατο id.*ep*.3(M.46. 1021A); ἔστιν ἰδεῖν ὡς ἐν εἰκόνι τῷ ἄνθρακι ἑνωθέντα μὲν ἀνθρωπότητι τὸν τοῦ θεοῦ λόγον, οὐ μὴν ἀποβεβληκότα τὸ εἶναι ὅ ἐστι, ~ώσαντα δὲ μᾶλλον τὸ προσληφθὲν ἤ γοῦν ἑνωθὲν εἰς τὴν ἑαυτοῦ δόξαν τε καὶ ἐνέργειαν Cyr.*schol.inc*.9(p.221.25; 5^{1}.783E); id.*Nest*.2 proem.(p.33. 34; 6^{1}.32C); ref. Jo.12:27 πρὸς ἀμείνω τινὰ καὶ θειοτέραν κατάστασιν ~ουμένης τῆς φύσεως ἐν πρώτῳ Χριστῷ id.*Jo*.8(4.704A); (Apollinarian) τὴν τοῦ λόγου φύσιν εἰς τὸ σαθρὸν...καὶ γηγενὲς ~ῶσθαι, καὶ τροπὴν φαντάζονται τοῦ τροπὴν οὐκ εἰδότος id.*inc.unigen*.(5^{1}.683B); ref. Son's alleged participation in Spirit ἐδείχθη...πρὸς τὸ ἄμεινον ἢ ἐν οἷοπερ ἦν ἀρχῇ κατὰ χάριν ~ούμενος id.*Jo*.2.1(4.119D); **5.** of elements in eucharist, Gr.Nyss.*or.catech*.37(p.152.7; M.45.97B) cit. s. εὐλογία; **6.** spiritually τοὺς ἐκ παλιγγενεσίας ~ουμένους διὰ τῆς τοῦ λουτροῦ χάριτος id.*ep.can*.(M.45.221B); τῆς εὐαγγελικῆς παιδεύσεως ἡ ζωοποιὸς ἐνέργεια ψυχήν τε καὶ σῶμα καὶ πνεῦμα πρὸς ἰδίαν ὥσπερ ποιότητα ~οῖ Cyr.*ador*.17(1.614B); id.*glaph.Num*.(1.409E); μεταπεπλάσμεθα νοητῶς ἐν Χριστῷ ἤγουν μετεστοιχειώθημεν, οἱ μὲν ἐκ πλάνης Ἑλληνικῆς...οἵ γε μὴν ἐκ περιτομῆς id.*Is*.4.2(2.608A); ~ούμεθα ἐν Χριστῷ εἰς καινότητα ζωῆς ἁγίας καὶ εὐαγγελικῆς *ib*.5.2 (760B); διὰ τοῦ βαπτίσματος...μετεστοιχειώμεθα...εἰς ζωὴν ἑτέραν id. *Rom*.7:1(p.194.12; M.74.800A); ὁ τὴν ἐμὴν ἐσθίων σάρκα, ζήσει δι' ἐμέ...ὅλος εἰς ἐμὲ ~ούμενος, τὸν ζωογονεῖν ἰσχύοντα id.*Jo*.4.3(4. 366E); μετεστοιχειώθητε εἰς τὸν τῆς εὐσεβείας...τρόπον Thdr.Stud. *epp*.2.204(M.99.1620C); of idolaters ὁ τῇ ματαιότητι τῶν εἰδώλων προσανέχων, μετεστοιχειοῦτο πρὸς τὸ βλεπόμενον Gr.Nyss.*hom.5 in Cant*.(M.44.865C); **7.** *change, transfer* in thought ἐκ τύπου πάλιν ἐπὶ τὸ ἀληθὲς ~οῦντες τῶν λεγομένων τὸν νοῦν Cyr.*glaph.Num*.(1.381E); τοὺς τύπους...μ. εἰς πνευματικὴν θεωρίαν *ib*.(432E); id.*Jo*.1.7(4.55B); id.*ador*.14(1.482A).

***μεταστοιχείωσις, ἡ,** *transformation* of elements; of food into human tissue, ‡Nil.*perist*.4.12(M.79.837D); of world at restoration of all things, Gr.Nyss.*virg*.4(p.270.24; M.46.341A); of Christ's body at Resurrection, Anast.S.*hod*.13(M.89.209C); of men's bodies at resurrection τὴν ἰσάγγελον μ. τῶν σωμάτων Meth.*symp*.2.7(p.25.16; M.18.60B); Cosm.Ind.*top*.5(M.88.193D); τὴν ἀπὸ τῶν παχυτέρων ἐπὶ τὰ πνευματικὰ σώματα μ. Anast.Ant.*serm*.1.9(M.89.1376B); Max. *ambig*.(M.91.1332D) cit. s. μεταποίησις; of new life in Christ τὴν σάρκα κατ' οἰκονομίαν ὑπὸ τοῦ μονογενοῦς υἱοῦ προσληφθεῖσαν ἐπὶ μεταστοιχειώσει τῆς φύσεως ἡμῶν Gr.Naz.*ep*.202(M.37.332B); οὐκ ἀριθμὸν Χριστῶν...ἀλλὰ ἕνωσιν τοῦ ἀνθρώπου πρὸς τὸ θεῖον...τὴν τοῦ ἀνθρώπου πρὸς τὸν Χριστὸν μ. Gr.Nyss.*Eun*.5(2 p.126.9; M.45.708D); ἄλλη γέννησις, βίος ἕτερος, ἄλλο ζωῆς εἶδος, αὐτῆς τῆς φύσεως ἡμῶν μ. id.*res*.(M.46.604C); ἀνέστη...ἀντὶ τοῦ πρώτου τοῦ πεπτωκότος Ἀδάμ, πρὸς ἀπολύτρωσιν ἐκείνου...καὶ μ. Gr.Agr.*Eccl*.4.3(M.98.928A); also of *change* for the worse μ. τῶν ἁπάντων ἀθεωτάτη Thdr.Stud. *epp*.2.15(M.99.1164B).

***μεταστοιχίζω,** = μεταστοιχειόω, *transform* εἰς καινότητα ζωῆς ἐν Χριστῷ μετεστοιχίσμεθα Cyr.*ador*.11(1.405D).

***μεταστολιμαῖος,** *sent for*, ‡Nil.*perist*.4.13(M.79.840D).

***μεταστρεπτέος,** *to be turned, directed* from one person to another πρὸς ὑμᾶς...μ. ὁ...λόγος Cael.*ep.CP* 1.5(p.86.23; M.*PL*.50.492B).

***μετασύγκρασις, ἡ,** f.l. for μετασύγκρισις, *recombination* of elements, hence *restoration*, *Hom.Clem*.20.9.

μετασυγκρίνω, *reconstitute, restore*; **1.** pass., of Devil ὁ...πονηρὸς ...μετασυγκριθεὶς ἀγαθὸς γενέσθαι δύναται *Hom.Clem*.20.3; **2.** act. intrans., *return* to a state, *ib*.8.13; med., *recombine*; of atoms, Bas. *hex*.1.2(1.3B; M.29.8A).

μετασχηματίζ-ω, 1. *change the form of* ὁ ἀριστοτέχνας...θεός, τῇ ποιητικῇ δυνάμει τῷ Χριστῷ ~ων καὶ μεταζωγραφῶν τὰς ἰδέας Meth. *symp*.2.6(p.23.12; M.18.57A); τότε μὲν τῆς κτίσεως γενομένης, ὁ ἄνθρωπος ὕστερον πλάττεται· νῦν δὲ...ὁ ἄνθρωπος ὁ νέος δημιουργεῖται ...καὶ τότε ὁ κόσμος ~εται Chrys.*hom.25.2 in Jo*.(8.145C); of star of Epiphany οὐδὲ ἀστὴρ...ἀλλὰ δύναμίς τις ἀόρατος εἰς ταύτην μετασχηματισθεῖσα τὴν ὄψιν id.*hom.6.2 in Mt*.(7.87B); of bodies at resurrection, Anast.Ant.*serm*.1.9(M.89.1376C); met. ὁ τὴν τῆς ἀρχῆς εὐκοσμίαν εἰς τυραννίδα καὶ ἀκοσμίαν μετασχηματίσας Isid.Pel.*epp*. 3.74(M.78.781B); ref. Phil.3:21 σῶμα ἐπιθυμίας...καὶ ταπεινώσεως ...μετασχηματισθήσεται εἰς σῶμα ἀπαθές, οὐ τῇ ἐξαλλαγῇ τῆς διακοσμήσεως τῶν μελῶν, ἀλλὰ τῷ μὴ ἐπιθυμεῖν τῶν ὑλικῶν ἡδονῶν Meth.*res*.3.16(p.412.20; M.18.317A); τὸ 'μετασχηματίσει' οὐκ ἐπὶ τῆς μεταποιήσεως τοῦ χρήματος τέθεικεν, ἀλλ' ἐπὶ τῆς ἀπαλλαγῆς τῆς φθορᾶς Thdt.*Phil*.3:21(3.466); **2.** med., *change one's form*; of demons, *T.Sal*.20.13(M.122.1350B); of phases of moon, Clem.*str*.6. 16(p.505.2; M.9.372A); ptcpl., *in disguise*, Ath.*v.Anton*.28(M.26. 883C); ‡Ath.*dial.Trin*.1.15(M.28.1180D); met., *change one's attitude*, Jul.Papa *ep.Dian*.ap.Ath.*apol.sec*.21(p.103.2; M.26.284A); **3.** *interpret differently* ποικίλαις τισὶν ἑρμηνείαις τοὺς ἐμοὺς λόγους ~ειν εἰς τὴν τοῦ νόμου κατάλυσιν *Clem.ep.Petr*.2(M.2.28A); **4.** *transfer the application* of a saying, Cyr.*Ps*.10:1(M.69.789B).

***μετασχηματικός,** *capable of changing*, Marc.Er.*opusc*.4(M.65. 1012D).

***μετασχημάτισμα, τό,** *change of form*, Nil.*Eulog*.18(M.79.1116D).

μετασχηματισμός, ὁ, **1.** *change of form*, Eus.*e.th.*3.15(p.173.18; M.24.1032A); Anast.Ant.*serm.*1.2(M.89.1365A); moral and spiritual κἂν ὁ κλέπτης καὶ ὁ ψεύστης κατὰ μετασχηματισμὸν ἐνεργείας τὰ ἀληθῆ λέγῃ Clem.*str.*6.8(p.465.14; M.9.288C); ὁ μ. ἡ εἰς τὸ ἀπαθὲς καὶ ἔνδοξόν ἐστιν ἀποκατάστασις Meth.*res.*3.16(p.412.18; M.18.317A); ἐν πράγμασι...καὶ ἐν δυνάμει τῇ κατ' ἐνέργειαν ἀρετῆς ὁ μ. ἐν ἡμῖν γίνεται Cyr.*hom.pasch.*10(5².134C); *different form* οὐ καθ' ὃ εἰσὶν [sc. οἱ ἄγγελοι] ἐπιφαίνονται...ἀλλ' ἐν μ. *cat.Rom.*8:39 suppl.(p.301.22); **2.** *transferred figure*, Or.*comm.in 1Cor.*4:6(*JTS* 9 p.357).

μετάταξις, ἡ, *change of rank, promotion*, Dion.Ar.*e.h.*6.3.4(M.3.536B).

μετατάσσω, **1.** *place among, insert* at a given point in an argument αὗται αἱ ἐπιστολαὶ μετετάγησαν...πρὸς τὸ εἰδέναι... Epiph.*haer.*73.23(p.296.1; M.42.444C); **2.** *transpose*, Proc.G.*Dt.*33:13(M.87.988A); *rearrange*, Synes.*ep.*103(M.66.1476C); **3.** med., *change one's rank* or *status*, Eulog.*fr.Novat.*(M.104.353C); Thphn.*chron.*p.118(M.108.333B); met., *change over*; from law to grace, of the rich young ruler, Clem.*q.d.s.*8(p.165.12; M.9.613A); from paganism to Christianity, Gr.Nyss.*fat.*(M.45.148B); Philost.*h.e.*2.8(M.65.472A); from heresy to orthodoxy, *ib.*1.9(465A); from orthodoxy to heresy, *ib.*9.9(576B); to a holier life, Bas.*ascet.*1.2(2.320B; M.31.873B); ἀπὸ τῆς σκηνῆς καὶ ἀπὸ τῆς ὀρχήστρας πρὸς τὴν ἀγγελικὴν μ. πολιτείαν Chrys.*hom.26.5 in Mt.*(7.321A); Areth.*Apoc.*1:3(M.106.504B); from this world to next; of martyrs, Chrys.*pan.Bern.*4(2.639E).

μετατίθ-ημι, **A.** *transfer a share*, cf.Num.11:17 μετέθηκεν ἐπὶ τὸν Ἰησοῦν ὁ θεὸς ἀπὸ τοῦ ἐν Μωυσεῖ πνεύματος Just.*dial.*49.7(M.6.585A).

B. *place differently*; **1.** *transfer* ἀναστὰς ὁ κύριος εὐηγγελίσατο τοὺς δικαίους τοὺς ἐν τῇ ἀναπαύσει καὶ μετέστησεν αὐτοὺς καὶ μετέθηκεν Clem.*exc.Thdot.*18(p.112.24; M.9.665C); met., *transfer* an argument to a different context τὰ πάλαι ἐν τῷ γένει ὑμῶν ὄντα εἰς ἡμᾶς μετετέθη Just.*dial.*82.1(M.6.669B); ταῦτα εἴπερ εἶδες ἐπὶ τοῦ σώματος, μετάθες ἐπὶ τὴν ψυχήν Or.*hom.6.2 in Jer.*(p.49.14; M.13.525B); an accusation, Chrys.*hom.3.1 in Ac.*(9.24B); affections or energies εἰς ξύλα καὶ εἰς λίθους...τὴν τοῦ θεοῦ τιμὴν μετετίθουν Ath.*inc.*11.4(M.25.116C); οὐδὲν τῷ παρόντι καταλείποντες βίῳ, ἀλλ' εἰς τὴν ἀγήρω πάντα ~έντες Thdt.*qu.1 in Lev.*(1.178); πᾶσαν αὐτοῦ τὴν βουλὴν εἰς τὴν τῶν θείων λογίων ἐκπλήρωσιν ~ησιν id.*Ps.*111:1(1.1403); id.*h.rel.*2(4.1121); persons ἡμᾶς...ἐπὶ τὰ νοητὰ ~ησιν [sc. ἡ ἀστρονομία] ἀπὸ τῶν αἰσθητῶν Clem.*str.*6.11(p.477.19; M.9.312B); τὸ '~εσθε' προστεθεικώς, οὐ 'μετάγεσθε'· ὡς ἐπὶ ἀψύχων φησὶν ~εσθε Thdr.Mops.*Gal.*1:6(p.9.20; M.66.901B); **2.** *translate* persons Ἐνώχ, ὃς ἐν ὑπακοῇ δίκαιος εὑρεθεὶς μετετέθη *1Clem.*9.3; τοὺς μετατεθέντας ἐκεῖσε [sc. εἰς τὸν παράδεισον] μετατεθῆναι...κἀκεῖ μένειν...ἕως συντελείας Iren.*haer.*5.5.1(M.7.1135A); ἀφθαρσίας ἡμῶν ὑπάρχον τὸ σῶμα δεκτικόν, καθάπερ ἐδείχθη καὶ ἐπὶ τοῦ Ἐνὼχ ~εμένου Meth.*res.*3.5(p.396.11; M.18.320C); †Hipp.Th.*fr.*8c 5(p.39.17; M.117.1045B); fig. οὗτος δ' ἂν εἴη ὁ ἐν τῷ θεῷ τέλειος, ὁ τῆς τῶν πολλῶν διατριβῆς μετατεθειμένος Eus.*p.e.*7.8(308B; M.21.521C); a book Σύμμαχος, ὁ τὴν...γραφὴν ἐκ τῆς Ἑβραίων μετατεθεικὼς εἰς τὴν Ἑλλάδα φωνήν Thdt.*haer.*2.1(4.328); **3.** *change*, acc. Origen ἐπὶ τοῦ εἴδους μόνον προσδοκᾶσθαι...τὴν ἀνάστασιν ἐν πνευματικῷ μεταθησομένου σώματι Meth.*res.*3.5(p.394.6; M.18.317C); in eucharist τὸ ἀθανατισθὲν ὑπὸ τοῦ θεοῦ σῶμα ἐν τῷ ἡμετέρῳ γενόμενον ὅλον πρὸς ἑαυτὸ μεταποιεῖ καὶ ~ησιν Gr.Nyss.*or.catech.*37(p.143.5; M.45.93B); τὸν ὅρκον...καὶ τὴν πίστιν...~έναι πειρῶνται Thdt.*Ps.*54:15(1.965); τοὺς παρ' Ἕλλησι νενομισμένους [sc. θεούς] οἳ θυσίαις ~εσθαι λέγονται παρ' αὐτοῖς Proc.G.*Num.*24:11(M.87.868A); *change and direct against* [sc. ὁ θεός]...τοῦ Βαλαὰμ τοῦ μάντεως τὴν γλῶτταν...κατὰ τῆς ἀληθείας λυττῶσαν...κατὰ τοῦ ψεύδους ἄκουσαν μετατέθεικεν Thdt.*affect.*3(p.86.18; 4.777); *convert* to Christianity, Chrys.*laud.Paul.*7(2.516D); Jo.Mosch.*prat.*195(M.87.3077B); **4.** med., *change over from* οὐ γὰρ ἂν ῥαδίως μεταπεισθείη τις προσθέσθαι, τῶν αὐτοῦ ~έμενος, ἑτέροις Gr.Thaum.*pan.Or.*14(p.31.3; M.10.1089B); *change over* to ἐκκέκλικεν εἰς ἡμᾶς καὶ μονονουχὶ μετατέθειται καταλελοιπὼς τὸν Ἰσραήλ Cyr.*Ag.*5(3.632D); abs., *change* one's habits or beliefs, *Const.App.*8.32.14; *repent* τοῖς ἀδίκως ἐχθραίνουσι καὶ μὴ ~εμένοις κόλασιν...ἐργάζεται Just.*1apol.*45.6(M.6.597B); *be converted* τῶν ἐξ Ἑλλήνων ἢ Ἰουδαίων ὀφειλόντων πρὸς τὴν ὀρθὴν μεταθέσθαι πίστιν Chrys.*hom.28.3 in Jo.*(8.162C).

***μετατιτράω**, *pierce*, Nil.*serm.*6(M.79.1273B).

μετατρέπ-ω, **1.** *turn in a different direction*, ref. Mt.25:40 ὁ παιδαγωγὸς τὴν εὐποιΐαν καὶ τῶν ἀδελφῶν...εἰς ἑαυτὸν ~ων Clem.*paed.*3.12(p.287.20; M.8.673A); pass., *turn back, return* μεγάλην...τὴν πτῶσιν τῶν πιστῶν καὶ μετατραπέντων Thdr.Heracl.ap.*cat.Mt.*7:27(p.56.26); Cyr.*glaph.Gen.*5(1.176D); **2.** med., *change oneself* ἄγγελοι...πρὸς πάντα ~εσθαι δυνάμενοι *Hom.Clem.*8.12; pass., *be changed* ὁ φόβος εἰς ἀγάπην μετατέτραπται Clem.*paed.*1.7(p.125.2; M.8.321A); id.*prot.*10(p.74.24; M.8.220B); μετατραπέντι...πρὸς σώφρονα λογισμόν Gel.Cyz.*h.e.*1.11.1(M.85.1213D).

μετατρέχω, *change one's abode*; met., Cyr.*ador.*17(1.598C).

μετατροπή, ἡ, *turning in a different direction, turning away*; met., of Christol. heresies τὰς ἐφ' ἑκάτερα κακίστας μ. Thdr.Raith.*praep.*(p.190.14; M.91.1489C).

μετάτροπος, **1.** *changing* one's *place*, Nonn.*par.Jo.*5:24(M.43.789A); *ib.*13:1(860A); **2.** *liable to change*, *ib.*3:16(769A); **3.** *overthrown*, *ib.*2:15(764A).

***μετατρυπάομαι**, *be pierced*, Nil.*epp.*2.236(M.79.321A).

μετατυπ-όω, **1.** *transform*; fig. and met., of character χρόνῳ καὶ μαθήσει ~ωθῆναι Clem.*str.*4.23(p.314.16; M.8.1357C); of tyrants πρὸς ἀτίθασσον θῆρα ~ούμενοι ‡Caes.Naz.*dial.*19(M.38.873); **2.** *modify* ὁ ἡμέτερος λόγος τῇ προσθήκῃ τῶν σχημάτων πρὸς διαφόρους χρείας ~οῦται Gr.Nyss.*castig.*(M.46.313D).

***μεταύλειος**, *between atrium and vestibule* μ. θύρᾳ Evagr.*h.e.*4.3(p.154.18; M.86.2705B).

μεταύριον, *on the day after tomorrow*, ‡Pall.*h.mon.*12.4(p.63.17; μεθαύριον M.34.1156C).

μεταφέρω, **1.** *move to a different place, transfer*; **a.** lit. εἴ τις...λύσας τὴν ὑποκειμένην τοῦ ἀνθρώπου ἰδέαν, μετενέγκῃ τὰς ψηφῖδας ...καὶ ποιήσει μορφὴν κυνός Iren.*haer.*1.8.1(M.7.521A); of metempsychosis, Hegem.*Arch.*10(p.15.9; M.10.1441C); ‡Just.*qu.Gr.*15.21(M.6.1484D); of soul of Christian μετενεχθεὶς εἰς τὴν μακάρων πόλιν τοὺς οὐρανούς...κατοικισθήσεται Meth.*symp.*6.2(p.65.12; M.18.116A); fig. σαρκὶ μὲν ὀλίγα κατεχομένους, πνεύματι δὲ μετενηνεγμένους, καὶ πρὸ τῆς διαζεύξεως Gr.Naz.*or.*8.5(M.35.793C); *translate* relics, Philost.*h.e.*3.2(M.65.481A); *borrow* from another author, Clem.*str.*6.2(p.442.21; M.9.241B); **b.** met., *transfer* to a different subject; discussion, Or.*Jo.*6.52(34; p.161.19; M.14.292B); words or ideas τὰ περὶ τοῦ σωτῆρος λελεγμένα ἐπὶ τὴν θεότητα τοῦ πατρὸς μεταφέρει Eus.*e.th.*2.1(p.100.8; M.24.900D); τὴν ἐν ταῖς θείαις γραφαῖς περὶ τοῦ μονογενοῦς υἱοῦ τοῦ θεοῦ φερομένην θεολογίαν ἐπὶ τὴν σάρκα μ. id.*Marcell.*2.2(p.43.24; M.24.797A); 'πνεῦμα ὁ θεός' μ. εἰς τὸν θεὸν καὶ πατέρα Didym.*Trin.*2.4(M.39.488A); **2.** *transfer differently, miscopy*, ref. Gen.1:26 ἡ εἰκὼν ἡ δημιουργουμένη, μεταφερομένη ἀπὸ τοῦ πρωτοτύπου Didym.(‡Bas.)*Eun.*5(1.301D; M.29.724B).

***μεταφθάνω**, *attain to*, Ephr.3.348E.

μεταφοιτ-άω, **1.** *go from one place to another*, Men.*exc.Rom.*13(p.201.17; M.113.897B); ref. death of a saint ἐν τῇ τῶν ζώντων μ. χώρᾳ †Jo.D.*B.J.*40(M.96.1237B); fig. μετὰ τὴν τῶν Ἱεροσολύμων πόρθησιν, μεταπεφοίτηκε μὲν ἐπὶ τὰ ἔθνη Χριστός Cyr.*Abac.*28(3.542A); id.*Ps.*49:6(M.69.1081A); ref. Passover ἐξοδοιπορεῖν ἐπειγόμενοι...καὶ εἰς πᾶν ὁτιοῦν τῶν ἀρίστων μ. προθυμούμενοι, μεταληψόμεθα τοῦ Χριστοῦ id.*ador.*17(1.598C); *enter* Church, Isid.Pel.*epp.*5.569(M.78.1644D); met., of change of subject μεταπεφοίτηκεν ὁ λόγος εἰς Χριστόν Cyr.*Ps.*7:7(M.69.749B); **2.** *pass from one state to another* ἀπανίστασθαι μὲν τῶν ἀρχαίων ἀρρωστημάτων, μ. δὲ νεανικῶς εἰς τὸ κατευμεγεθεῖν ἁπάσης φιλοσαρκίας Cyr.*Ps.*6:11(M.69.748C); id.*Zach.*7(3.586D); δουλείας μὲν ἀπηλλάχθαι τῆς ἐν νόμῳ καὶ γράμματι, μ. δὲ μᾶλλον εἰς ἐλευθερίαν id.*Rom.*8:14(p.215.12); ἡμᾶς...οὐ νεκρωθέντας, ἀλλὰ εἰς θειοτάτην ζωὴν ἐκ θανάτου μ. Dion.Ar.*e.h.*3.3.9(M.3.437B); Christol. ὁ μονογενὴς...σεσαρκωμένος...οὐ πέφυρται διὰ τοῦτο...οὔτε μὴν εἰς τὴν τῆς σαρκὸς φύσιν μεταπεφοίτηκεν ἡ τοῦ λόγου φύσις, ἀλλ' οὐδὲ ἡ τῆς σαρκὸς εἰς τὴν αὐτοῦ Cyr.*ep.*46.2(p.159.20; 5².143B); Eust.Mon.*ep.*(M.86.920D); *be converted into* μ. πρὸς τὴν πρᾶξιν ὁ λόγος Thphyl.*exc.gent.*6(p.485.6; M.113.945D); **3.** *go back again* τὰ δι' ὧν ἦν δύνασθαι ~ᾶν εἰς τὸ ἐν ἀρχαῖς τὴν ἀνθρώπου φύσιν Cyr.*hom.pasch.*24(5².286E).

***μεταφοίτησις**, ἡ, *transition* ἡ...τῶν τύπων εἰς ἀλήθειαν μ. Cyr.*Juln.*9(6².319A); id.*glaph.Gen.*5(1.176D); id.*Zach.*23(3.682A).

μεταφράζω, **1.** *paraphrase* τὸ δὲ 'ἐμεγάλυνεν...' μ. εἰς τὸ 'ἐπῆρεν' Or.*Jo.*32.14(8; p.448.24; M.14.777B); **2.** *interpret* ἀπὸ τῆς τῶν πραγμάτων ἐκβάσεως αὐτὸ μ. Chrys.*hom.41.3 in 1Cor.*(10.391A); Cosm.Ind.*top.*5(M.88.256D).

μετάφρασις, ἡ, *paraphrase*, Eus.*p.e.*1.5(474D; M.21.789A); τὴν μὲν ψυχὴν [sc. Χριστοῦ] κατὰ μετάφρασιν, ποτὲ μὲν νοῦν παράφρονα ὀνομάζοντες, ποτὲ δὲ ἁμαρτίαν ἐνυπόστατον, ποτὲ δὲ ὡς ἐργασίαν τῆς ἁμαρτίας, ἐξωθεῖτε ‡Ath.*Apoll.*1.21(M.26.1129B).

***μεταφραστικῶς**, *with a change of expression*, Epiph.*haer.*42.12(p.169.7; M.41.793B).

μετάφρενον, τό, *back*; plur., *shoulders*, ref. Ps.90:4 μ. ... τὰ ὑπαυχένια μέρη...καὶ οὐχὶ δὴ πάντως τὰ νῶτα Cyr.*ador.*11(1.381D).

***μεταφρουρέομαι**, *be transferred to another prison*, Thdr.Stud.*epp.*1.51(M.99.1100A); *ib.*2.67(1293B).

***μεταφρούρησις, ἡ,** *re-imprisonment*, Thdr.Stud.*epp*.1.40(M.99.1052A).

μεταφύομαι, *change* from one nature to another, *become*, c. εἰς, Gr.Nyss.*v.Mos*.(M.44.337B); Cyr.*Nest*.1 proem.(p.15.14; 6¹.4D).

***μεταφυράω,** *knead anew* or *differently*; fig., of effects of good teaching, Gr.Agr.*Eccl*.8.5(M.98.1069A).

***μεταφυσικός,** *metaphysical*; neut. plur. as subst., *metaphysics* τὰ τῆς φυσιολογίας ἀνώτερα..., τὰ καλούμενα παρά τισι μ. †Bas.*Is*.162 (1.494D; M.30.385A).

μεταφύτευσις, ἡ, *transformation* into plants, Cyr.*ador*.17(1.596B).

μεταφυτεύ-ω, *transplant*; fig. and met. ἀνῆλθε...τὸ καλὸν ἔρνος τοῦτο ~ουσα Chrys.*Anna* 3.3(4.725B); διδάσκαλοι...παιδευθέντες... τὸν νόμον τὸν ἔμφυτον ἐντεῦθεν μεταφυτεῦσαι παρασκευάζονται id. *hom.4 in Is.6*:1(6.121C); ref. Inc. ἐρριζόμενος [sc. Christ]...τῶν πατριαρχῶν ῥίζαις, μεταπεφύτευται εἰς τὸ καὶ ἄλλους μεταλαβεῖν αὐτοῦ τῆς εἰκόνος Or.*Ps*.1:3(p.445); ἀπὸ τῶν τῆδε [sc. ὑπὲρ τὰ οὐράνια] μετεφυτεύθη...ἡ βροτοφυὴς πυροφόρος βάτος τῆς θεότητος Mod.*dorm*.3(M.86.3285C); of gift of Spirit τὸ ἅγιον πνεῦμα ταύτῃ πως ~εται διανενεμημένον κατὰ τὴν ἑκάστου περιγραφὴν ἀπεριγράφως Clem.*str*.6.15(p.492.10; M.9.344B); of men at conversion ~ων [sc. Χριστός] τὴν φθορὰν εἰς ἀφθαρσίαν...ὁ τοῦ θεοῦ γεωργός id.*prot*.11 (p.80.28; M.8.232C); Cyr.*hom.div*.12(5².390D); ‡Proc.G.*Pr*.15:6(M.87.1372B).

***μετάφυτον, τό,** *cutting*, Or.*exc.in Ps*.27(M.17.241C).

***μεταχάλκευσις, ἡ,** *re-fashioning of metal*; met., ref. Mal.3:3, Cyr.*ador*.2(1.59E).

***μεταχαλκεύ-ω,** *fashion* metal *anew* μ. ... ἄροτρον εἰς ῥομφαίαν Cyr.*Joel*.41(3.239A); met., *temper anew* or *differently*, *change* to a better state, ref. Ac.10:15 ἐχρῆν [sc. Πέτρον] εἰς ἑτέραν ἕξιν ~εσθαι τῆς ἐνούσης Ἰουδαίοις τὴν ἀμείνω καὶ σοφωτέραν id.*Jo*.10.2 (4.925A); id.*hom.pasch*.10(5².134D); μ. πρὸς εὐανδρίαν id.*Lc*.9:27(p.79.9; M.72.652C); ὁ υἱὸς...~ων ὡς θεὸς τὴν ἀνθρώπου φύσιν εἰς ἀφθαρσίαν id.*Rom*.5:11(p.182.10; M.74.784A).

***μεταχάραξις, ἡ,** *re-engraving, engraving anew*; fig., ref. Mt.5:17 μ. τῶν ἐν τύποις ἐπὶ τὸ ἀληθές Cyr.*ador*.1(1.5C).

μεταχαράσσ-ω, *grave anew, remodel*; fig. and met., of perversion of scripture or Christian doctrine, Cels.ap.Or.*Cels*.2.27(p.156.2; M.11.848A); Gr.Nyss.*Eun*.1(1 p.70.13; M.45.300B); in good sense ὁ Χριστὸς τὰ ὡς ἐν τύπῳ καὶ σκιαῖς μ. εἰς ἀλήθειαν Cyr.*ador*.2(1.50D); τοῦ νόμου...τὰ Ἑλλήνων ἔθη ~οντος...ἐπὶ τὰ πρεπωδέστερα καὶ...εἰς εἰκόνα ζωῆς εὐαγγελικῆς *ib*.16(577D); μέτοχοι γεγονότες τοῦ ἁγίου πνεύματος...εἰς εἰκόνα τὴν πρώτην νοητῶς ~ομεθα id.*Nah*.27(3.496E).

[*]μεταχείρησις, ἡ, v. μεταχείρισις.

μεταχειρίζ-ω, act. and med., *take in hand, have in hand*; met.; **1.** *use* πῇ μὲν ταχύτητα, πῇ δὲ βραδύτητα...μ. Bas.Sel.*or*.19.1(M.85.240A); **2.** *exercise* οὐκ ὀρθῶς αὐτὴν [sc. ἱερωσύνην] ~ουσιν Chrys.*sac*.3.10(p.64.5; 1.387B); Isid.Pel.*epp*.2.52(M.78.493C); *practise* a trade, Chrys.*hom.72.4 in Mt*.(7.706B); **3.** *deal with, treat*, Synes.*Dion* 1 (p.235.7; M.66.1116A).

μεταχείριος, 1. *with the hand*, Nonn.*par.Jo*.13:8(M.43.861A); **2.** *in the hands, in the power* of, *ib*.18:36(896C).

μεταχείρισις (-χείρησις), ἡ, 1. *handling, treatment*; medic.; fig., of baptism, Gr.Nyss.*bapt.diff*.(M.46.417B); **2.** *taking hold, appropriation* οὐ ἡ πρὸς τὴν κλῆσιν ὁρμὴ ἐξαρκεῖ, ἂν μὴ καὶ μ. εὔδρομος ᾖ τῇ προθέσει Areth.*Apoc*.19:9(M.106.740C).

μεταχειρισμός, ὁ, *re-handling, modification* of a statement, Oecum.*Ac*.23:5(M.118.276B).

μεταχθόνιος, *of this world*, Nonn.*par.Jo*.20:18(M.43.912A).

μεταχρόνιος, *later in time, coming afterwards*, †Apoll.*met.Ps*.36:34(M.33.1364A, vv.ll. μετὰ χρόνιον, μεταχθόνιον); *ib*.67:28(1405C); Gel.Cyz.*h.e*.2.22.13(M.85.1293A).

μεταχρώννυμι, 1. *change the colour of*; pass., Cyr.*Joel*.19(3.216A); fig. and met. τῆς ἐκκλησίας...ἀνθούσης, πάσης τῆς πόλεως εἰς εὐσέβειαν μεταχρωσθείσης Pall.*v.Chrys*.5(p.33.9; M.47.21); Cyr.*glaph.Gen*.2(1.26B); **2.** *add colour to, colour in* μ. ὥσπερ τῆς εἰκόνος τὴν γραφήν *ib*.1(17C).

***μεταχρωστέον,** *one must dye*, Clem.*paed*.3.11(p.271.28; M.8.637B).

***μεταχυμίζω,** *change the juice* or *flavour*, Germ.CP *or*.2(M.98.257A).

***μεταχωνεύω,** *recast*, Socr.*h.e*.5.16.11(M.67.605A); met. τὴν τῷ κακῷ μελανθεῖσαν μ. πρὸς τὸ ἀκήρατον Gr.Nyss.*hom.4 in Cant*.(M.44.832B); ἡ ψυχὴ Λαζάρου...τὸ ἴδιον εἰς τὸ ἴδιον μετεχωνεύετο Amph. *hom*.3.5(M.39.65A).

μεταχωρ-έω, *remove, pass over*, ref. death πρὸς...θεὸν μ. Jo.VI H. *v.Jo.D*.13(M.94.449B); met., of Persons of Trin. acc. Sabellians φεύγοι ἂν ἅπερ ἐστίν, εἰς ἄλληλα ~οῦντα καὶ μεταβαίνοντα Gr.Naz.*or*.20.6(M.35.1072B); Christol. σὰρξ ἐγένετο...καὶ οὐκ εἰς σάρκα ~ήσας ἐκ παρατροπῆς Cyr.*Jo*.4.3(4.375E); Heracl.*ecth*.(H.3.793E).

μεταχώρησις, ἡ, *passing over, change* ἀφανισμὸς τοῦ χείρονος...καὶ εἰς τὸ μὴ ὂν μ. Gr.Nyss.*or.catech*.26(p.99.3; M.45.68D).

***μετεγγίζω,** *transfer*; pass., *cat.Apoc*.16:21(p.425.12); *ib*.19:4 (p.451.12).

μετεγγράφω, *inscribe anew upon*, fig. κηρὸν...ὃς τύπους πάλαι τοὺς πρὶν λεανθείς, τοὺς καλοὺς μετεγγραφῇ Gr.Naz.*carm*.2.1.12.456 (M.37.1199A); τὸν θεῖον...νόμον ἐν πτυκτίῳ τῆς καρδίας...μ. Const. Diac.*laud*.33(M.88.517A).

***μετεγείρω (μετέγρω), 1.** pass., *rise again* from the dead, *Apoc. En*.22.13; **2.** ? *rise in pursuit*; met., of persistent prayer μετασπόμενος †Apoll.*met.Ps*.87:14 (v.l. μετεγρόμενος M.33.1441D).

μετεγκεντρίζω, *goad* or *drive elsewhere*, met. ἐξ...φυσικῶν εἰς πνευματικὰ μ. Jo.Clim.*scal*.7(M.88.808C).

***μετεγκεράννυμαι,** *be mingled with*, Max.*ambig*.(M.91.1137C).

μετεγκλίνω, *incline, direct*, Jo.Mal.*chron*.2 p.25(M.97.89C); πρὸς τὰ θεῖα τὴν ῥοπὴν [sc. ψυχῆς]...μ. Max.*ambig*.(M.91.1169A).

***μετεγκλοίω,** *enclose in a collar*, Max.*cap*.4.91(M.90.1344C).

μέτειμι, (εἰμί *sum*), *be concerned with, deal with* ἐν τῷ κεφαλαίῳ ᾧ μέτειμεν Didym.*Trin*.2.6(M.39.521B); c. acc., *ib*.(524C); μέτεστι, *it is possible*, Cyr.*Is*.5.1(2.727C).

μέτειμι (εἶμι *ibo*), **1.** *pursue* ὁ μετιὼν [sc. ἀρετὴν] Chrys.*hom.15.7 in Mt*.(7.196C); *follow, conform to* οὔτε τι τῆς Μωσέως μ. νομοθεσίας Eus.*d.e*.1.6(p.23.33; M.22.49C); *attack* μ. ἀνδρείκελα χαλκοῦ πεποιημένα id.*v.C*.3.54(p.102.23; M.20.1120B); **2.** *move* from one place to another μὴ μετιέναι ἐπίσκοπον ἢ κληρικὸν ἀπὸ πόλεως εἰς πόλιν Phot. *nomoc*.1.26(p.475; M.104.1008C); met., *pass on* to a different subject, Meth.*res*.1.45(p.295.5); Eus.*p.e*.10.11(496C; M.21.825D); Chrys. *hom.4.3 in 2Cor*.(10.458C); *change over* to ὁ γὰρ μέλλων ἐπ' ἀρετὴν μετιέναι, πρότερον τῆς κακίας καταγνῶναι ὀφείλει, καὶ τότε αὐτὴν μετελθεῖν id.*hom.9.2 in Heb*.(12.95A).

μετέκγονοι, οἱ, *great-grandchildren*, Chrys.*hom.4.5 in Heb*.(12.47D, v.l. μετεγγόνων).

μετεκδέχομαι, *follow upon*, Paul.Sil.*Soph*.369(M.86.2133B).

μετεκδύω, *put off* or *change one's clothes*; met., of metempsychosis, Gr.Naz.*carm*.1.1.8.37(M.37.449A).

***μετεκλαμβάνω,** *accept next, in turn*, Leont.H.*Nest*.4.49(M.86.1721A).

μετέλευσις, ἡ, *pursuit*; met., Just.*1apol*.43.5(M.6.393A).

μετεμβιβάζω, *transfer into another* receptacle; of metempsychosis, ‡Jo.D.*Artem*.30(p.161.21; M.96.1280A).

***μετεμπλοκή, ἡ,** *implication, involvement*, Marc.Er.*opusc*.1.160 (M.65.925A); Nil.*Magn*.34(M.79.1009C); plur., *snares* of Devil, *V.Pach.A* 6(p.130.14); *ib.Σ* 47(p.216.1).

***μετέμπτωσις, ἡ,** *transference to new position*, Max.*ambig*.(M.91.1069C).

μετεμψυχόομαι, *be ensouled*; of the body, Max.*ambig*.(M.91.1100D).

μετεμψύχωσις, ἡ, *transmigration of souls* μονογενῆ δὲ λέγει τὴν ψυχὴν ἑαυτοῦ τῷ μόνην αὐτὴν ἐσχηκέναι· οὐ γὰρ προσεκτέον τῇ περὶ μετεμψυχώσεως μυθοποιΐᾳ Didym.*Ps*.34:17(M.39.1332D); ‡Just.*qu.Gr*.15.20(M.6.1484C); ἐξάγει δὲ ψυχὴν ἡ γῆ, ἵνα μάθῃς διαφορὰς ψυχῆς κτήνους καὶ ψυχῆς ἀνθρώπου·...κἂν παῖδες ὑθλῶσιν Ἑλλήνων μ. ἡμῖν φανταζόμενοι Proc.G.*Gen*.1:24(M.87.105D).

***μετενδέομαι,** *be confined in another* body; of souls, Clem.*str*.3.3 (p.201.20; M.8.1116B).

***μετένδεσις, ἡ,** *confinement in another* body, Clem.*str*.7.6(p.24.27; M.9.445A).

***μετενδεσμέω,** *bind* or *attach anew*; money-lenders to oneself, Bas.*hom.in Ps*.14(1.112A; M.29.276C).

***μετενδημέω,** *change residence*, Thdr.Stud.*or*.11.3(M.99.805B).

***μετενδιδύσκ-ω,** *put on in exchange*, Hipp.*haer*.5.26(p.131.15; M.16.3202A); med., met. τὴν κατήφειαν ~όμενοι εὐφροσύνης ἀγαλλιάματι Thdr.Stud.*epp*.2.86(M.99.1329D).

μετενδύ-ω, act., *reclothe*, fig. ἀπεκδύων αὐτὸν ἀπὸ τῆς προϋπούσης αὐτῷ θρησκείας, καὶ μ. αὐτὸν εἰς Χριστόν Ammon.*Ac*.19:5(M.85.1573B); med., *put on instead*, fig. ὁ ἐκ φθαρτοῦ τε καὶ γηΐνου βίου τὴν οὐράνιον ἀφθαρσίαν ~όμενος Gr.Nyss.*hom.9 in Cant*.(M.44.961B); τὰ πρόσκαιρα φύλλα τῆς ὑλικῆς ταύτης ζωῆς, ἅπερ...κακῶς ἑαυτοῖς συνερράψαμεν...ἀντὶ τῶν θείων περιβολῶν μετενδυσάμενοι id.*or.dom*.5 (p.102.4; M.44.1184B); ἐν τῷ βαπτίσματι τοῦ Ἰησοῦ πάντες ἡμεῖς ἐκδυόμενοι τὰς ἁμαρτίας ὡς χιτῶνα πτωχικὸν...τὸν ἱερὸν καὶ κάλλιστον τὸν τῆς παλιγγενεσίας ~όμεθα id.*bapt.Chr*.(M.46.593B); Ast.Am.*hom*.5(M.40.228D).

***μετενεκτέος**, *that must be transferred* ἐπί σε ὁ λόγος μ. Thdr.Stud.*epp*.2.113(M.99.1380A).

***μετένεξις, ἡ**, *translation* of relics, *A.Barth*.9(p.149.26).

***μετενθρονίζω**, *translate* a bishop, Thphn.*chron*.p.110(M.108.316C).

μετενσωματ-όομαι, pass., *be put into another body*; of soul (Gnost.) ∼οῦσθαι...τὰς ψυχάς, ὅσον πάντα τὰ ἁμαρτήματα πληρώσωσιν Iren.*haer*.1.25.4; ἐπιστρέφειν [sc. τὰς ψυχὰς τῶν ἐν ἀγνωσίᾳ ἀνθρώπων] καὶ ∼οῦσθαι εἰς ἕκαστον τῶν ζῴων ἕως ἂν ἐπιγνῷ, καὶ οὕτω καθαρθεῖσα...μεταστῇ εἰς τὰ ἐπουράνια Epiph.*haer*.42.11(p.133.26; M.41.741A); *ib*.27.4(p.305.6; M.41.368C) cit. s. ἀντικαταβάλλω; opposed by Origen, Or.*Cels*.5.49(p.54.2; M.11.1257C); δι' ἁμαρτίαν γενομένη δὶς ἐν σώματι, διὰ τί οὐχὶ καὶ τρὶς καὶ πλεονάκις;...οὐκ ἔσται τάχα ὅτε ψυχὴ οὐ ∼ωθήσεται ἀεὶ γὰρ διὰ τὰ πρότερα ἁμαρτήματα ἐπιδημήσει τῷ σώματι id.*comm.in Mt*.13.1(p.173.27; M.13.1088B); of Christ acc. Callistus τὸν Χριστὸν λέγει ἄνθρωπον κοινῶς πᾶσι γεγονέναι...οὐ νῦν πρώτως ἐκ παρθένου γεγεννῆσθαι, ἀλλὰ...πολλάκις...ἀλλάσσοντα γενέσεις καὶ ∼ούμενον Hipp.*haer*.9.14(p.252.24; M.16.3390B); (Manich.) εἴ τις...γήμῃ γυναῖκα, αὖθις αὐτὸν μετὰ τὴν ἐντεῦθεν ἀπαλλαγὴν ∼οῦσθαι καὶ γίνεσθαι αὐτὸν γυναῖκα Epiph.*haer*.66.9(p.30.1; M.42.41D); *be transferred into a body*; fig., of God as described in anthropomorphic language ὁ δὲ θεὸς ἡμῶν ἀπερίγραφός ἐστι φύσει· περιγράφεσθαι δὲ δοκεῖ ∼ούμενος ‡Ath.*comm.essent*.9(M.28.45A).

μετενσωμάτωσις, ἡ, *transmigration* of souls, *reincarnation*, acc. docetists ἀπὸ τοῦ σωτῆρος μ. πέπαυται, πίστις δὲ κηρύσσεται εἰς ἄφεσιν ἁμαρτιῶν Hipp.*haer*.8.10(p.229.20; M.16.3354C); τὸν ἀθάνατον εἰς θνητὸν ἐρχόμενον σῶμα, οὐ κατὰ τὴν Πλάτωνος μ., ἀλλὰ κατ' ἄλλην τινὰ ὑψηλοτέραν θεωρίαν Or.*Cels*.4.17(p.286.24; M.11.1049A); *ib*.5.29(p.31.8; 1225B); τις ἐρεῖ ὅτι ἑαυτὸν ἠγνόει Ἰωάννης Ἠλίαν ὄντα· καὶ τάχα τούτῳ χρήσονται οἱ ἐκ τούτων τῷ περὶ μετενσωματώσεως παριστάμενοι λόγῳ, ὡς τῆς ψυχῆς...οὐ πάντως μεμνημένης τῶν προτέρων βίων id.*Jo*.6.10(7; p.119.26; M.14.220A); Ἠλίας οὐχ ἡ ψυχὴ ⟨Ἠλίου⟩ δοκεῖ μοι λέγεσθαι, ἵνα μὴ ἐμπίπτω εἰς τὸ ἀλλότριον τῆς ἐκκλησίας τοῦ θεοῦ περὶ τῆς μ. δόγμα id.*comm.in Mt*.13.1(p.173.2; M.13.1088A); οἱ...πρεσβυτέραν τῆς ἐν σαρκὶ ζωῆς τὴν πολιτείαν τῶν ψυχῶν δογματίζοντες, οὔ μοι δοκοῦσι τῶν Ἑλληνικῶν καθαρεύειν δογμάτων τῶν περὶ τῆς μ. αὐτοῖς μεμυθολογημένων Gr.Nyss.*hom.opif*.29(M.44.232A); (Manich.) φάσκοντες ἀνατρέχειν τὰς μεμολυσμένας ψυχὰς ἐπὶ τὰ στοιχεῖα, καὶ συγκαταμίγνυσθαι ἀλλήλαις. πάλιν αὐτὰς ἐν ταῖς μ. φασι τιμωρεῖσθαι κατὰ τὸ μέγεθος τῶν ἁμαρτημάτων Nemes.*nat.hom*.2(M.40.577B); εἰ γὰρ ἡ μὲν ἡμετέρα ψυχὴ τῆς τοῦ θεοῦ οὐσίας ἐστίν, ἡ δὲ μ. καὶ εἰς σικυοὺς καὶ πέπονας ἐκβαίνει...τί φεύγεις τὴν μ. τοῦ θεοῦ; Chrys.*hom.2.5 in Ac*.(9.21B,C).

***μετενταφιάζω**, *prepare anew for burial*, Thdr.Stud.*epp*.2.214(M.99.1644B).

***μετεξορίζω**, *banish from one place to another*, Thphn.*chron*.p.96(M.108.284B).

μετέπειτα, *afterwards; later*, Epiph.*inc*.1(p.227.15; M.41.273C); *then, next in order* πρῶτα θεός, μ. λόγος *Chron.Pasch*.p.46(M.92.168C).

***μετεπινοέομαι**, *be a subsequent concept*, Max.*ambig*.(M.91.1217D).

μετέρχομαι, **1.** *go over* to ἀφιστάμενος ἀπ' αὐτῶν [sc. Israel] ὁ κύριος,...μετελεύσεται ἐπ' ἔθνει ζητοῦντι τὸ θέλημα αὐτοῦ *T.Dan* 6.6; of possessions, *pass* to, Bas.*mor*.11.2(3.535B; M.32.1260B); abs., *change one's place* τὸ πνεῦμα...μὴ μεριζόμενον μήτε μετερχόμενον ἢ μεταβαλλόμενον Didym.*Trin*.2.1(M.39.449B); trans., *change* this life for another, *A.Jo*.65(p.182.24); Philost.*h.e*.10.11(M.65.592B); **2.** *pursue, persecute*, Eus.*v.C*.1.23(p.19.7; M.20.940A); *attack* τὰ...χρύσεα τῶν ἀγαλμάτων...μετήρχετο *ib*.3.54(p.102.1; 1117C); **3.** met., *follow, practise, undergo*, Just.*2apol*.11.6(M.6.461C); μέτελθε τὸν φόβον Cyr.H.*procatech*.13; Chrys.*hom.42.4 in Mt*.(7.457C); ἀμφότερα [sc. τὸ πάσχα καὶ τὸ βάπτισμα] μετελθών, τὸ μὲν ἀνέπαυσε, τῷ δὲ ἀρχὴν δέδωκε *ib.12.3*(164E); Thdt.*qu.18 in Jos*.(1.315); **4.** *go through, discuss, treat of*, Just.*1apol*.4.9(M.6.336A); Eus.Al.*serm*.11(M.86.377B).

μετέχ-ω, *partake of, have a share in*; **1.** in gen. μετανοίας μ. *1Clem*.8.5; ἴδωμεν...τίνες...∼ουσι τῆς ἀληθείας καὶ τίνες τῆς πλάνης Arist.*apol*.3.1; τὰ δὲ τέχνης καὶ σοφίας ∼οντα θεοῦ, ∼ει καὶ τῆς δυνάμεως αὐτοῦ Iren.*haer*.5.3.2(7.130C); θνητοῦ ὄντος τοῦ σώματος καὶ οὐ ∼οντος τῆς ἀληθινῆς ζωῆς Meth.*res*.1.23(p.249.6; M.41.1093D); τῆς τοῦ ἀγαθοῦ πατρὸς οὐσίας πᾶσαν ψυχὴν καὶ πᾶν κινούμενον ζῷον ∼ειν λέγει Hegem.*Arch*.8(p.13.9; M.10.1440C); τῆς δὲ ἀφθαρσίας μεθέξει καὶ τὰ ὁρώμενα Thdt.*Heb*.2:9(3.558); c. acc. τὰ τῆς γνώσεως τὰ μὲν ἤδη ∼ομεν, τὰ δὲ δι' ὧν ἔχομεν βεβαίως ἐλπίζομεν Clem.*ecl*.12(p.139.28; M.9.704B); **2.** *have a right to*, ‡Just.*monarch*.5(M.6.320C); μόνος ὁ ὑπὲρ εὐσεβείας μετεωριζόμενος ∼ει τῆς τοῦ ὑψίστου προσηγορίας Didym.*Ps*.7:18(M.39.1184B); c. infin., ref. Ps.44:8 οἱ βασιλεῖς πάντες καὶ οἱ χριστοὶ ἀπὸ τούτου μετέσχον καὶ βασιλεῖς καλεῖσθαι καὶ χριστοί Just.*dial*.86.3(M.6.681A); **3.** ref. Father and Son τὸ ὅλως ∼εσθαι τὸν θεόν, ἴσον ἐστὶ λέγειν ὅτι καὶ γεννᾷ· τὸ δὲ γεννᾶν τί σημαίνει ἢ υἱόν; αὐτοῦ γοῦν τοῦ υἱοῦ ∼ει τὰ πάντα κατὰ τὴν τοῦ πνεύματος γινομένην παρ' αὐτοῦ χάριν· αὐτὸς μὲν ὁ υἱὸς οὐδενὸς ∼ει, τὸ δὲ ἐκ τοῦ πατρὸς ∼όμενον τοῦτό ἐστιν ὁ υἱός...τὸ ∼εσθαι οὐκ ἄν τις ὑμῶν ἔτι πάθος εἴποι καὶ μερισμὸν τῆς τοῦ θεοῦ οὐσίας Ath.*Ar*.1.16(M.26.45A,B); **4.** of relationship between God and man ἐν ἀμώμῳ ἑνότητι εἶναι, ἵνα καὶ θεοῦ πάντοτε ∼ετε Ign.*Eph*.4.2; ὅπως ἕκαστος τῶν ἁγίων τῷ ∼ειν Χριστοῦ Χριστὸς γεννηθῇ Meth.*symp*.8.8(p.90.14; M.18.149C); ἀπρεπὲς δὲ ἦν πάλιν τὰ ἅπαξ γενόμενα λογικὰ καὶ τοῦ λόγου αὐτοῦ [sc. θεοῦ] μετασχόντα παραπόλλυσθαι Ath.*inc*.6.4(M.25.108A); pass., *be communicated* τὸ πνεῦμα...οὐχ ἑνὶ μέτρῳ ∼όμενον, ἀλλὰ κατ' ἀναλογίαν τῆς πίστεως διαιροῦν τὴν ἐνέργειαν...ἀπαθῶς μεριζόμενον καὶ...∼όμενον Bas.*Spir*.22(3.19D,E; M.32.108C, 109A); αὐτὴ [sc. Trin.] μόνη ὑπὲρ τὸ ἄυλον καὶ ἀόρατον οὖσα, κατ' οὐσίαν ∼εσθαι δύναται...οὐδὲν δὲ κτιστὸν...μετουσίας τρόπῳ ∼εσθαι δύναται, ἢ πληροῦν οὐσιωδῶς τὸν ἄνθρωπον Didym.*Trin*.1.20(M.39.369B); ἡ κτίσις ἀμέθεκτός ἐστιν οὐσιωδῶς τῇ λογικῇ ψυχῇ, ὡς ἐνοικίζεσθαι αὐτήν· μόνου γὰρ θεοῦ ἴδιον τὸ οὕτως ∼εσθαι *ib*.2.6(525A); τὸ μὲν πνεῦμα φύσει εἶναι ἄτρεπτον, οἱ δὲ ∼οντες αὐτοῦ κατὰ μετοχὴν ἄτρεπτοι ‡Ath.*dial.Trin*.1.25(M.28.1153C); οἱ μὲν ἅγιοι μέτοχοι τοῦ λόγου ἦσαν· ἐνταῦθα δὲ ὁ λόγος μέτεσχε τῆς ἀνθρωπότητος. ... τίς ἡ διαφορά; ὅτι οἱ ἅγιοι πρότερον ὑπῆρξαν καὶ τότε μετέσχον θεοῦ λόγου *ib*.4.5(1256C); ὥσπερ γὰρ ἔλαβε σῶμα, οὐ δεόμενος σώματος...οὕτω δὴ καὶ ψυχὴν ἔλαβε...ἵνα πᾶσα ψυχὴ διὰ ταύτης μετάσχῃ τῆς ἀτρεπτότητος Thdt.*ep*.145(4.1249); οὐ μετέσχον ἄγγελοι, οὐ δὲ ἐγένοντο θείας κοινωνοὶ φύσεως...ἄνθρωποι δὲ ∼ουσι καὶ κοινωνοὶ θείας φύσεως γίνονται, ὅσοι μεταλαμβάνουσι τὸ σῶμα...καὶ πίνουσι τὸ αἷμα Jo.D.*imag*.3.26(M.94.1348A); **5.** of eucharist ἡ...εὐχαριστία, ἧς οὐδενὶ ἄλλῳ μετάσχειν ἐξόν ἐστιν ἢ τῷ πιστεύοντι...καὶ λουσαμένῳ τὸ...εἰς ἀναγέννησιν λουτρόν Just.*1apol*.66.1(M.6.428B); τοὺς...τελευτήσαντας διὰ τὸ τῶν μυστηρίων ἀναξίως μ. Chrys.*hom.9.3 in 2Cor*.(10.503C); ἡμεῖς τὸ σῶμα προσκυνοῦμεν, ὡς τὸν λόγον, τοῦ σώματος ∼ομεν ὡς τοῦ πνεύματος Thdt.*eran*.2(4.174); Jo.D.*f.o*.4.13(M.94.1153B) cit. s. ἀντίτυπος; μέχρι τῆς ἐσχάτης ἀναπνοῆς μ. τῶν ἁγιασμάτων σου εἰς ἁγιασμὸν ψυχῶν καὶ σωμάτων *Lit.Jac*.(p.234.24); abs., Chrys.*hom.82.6 in Mt*.(7.790A); ἅπαξ τοῦ ἐνιαυτοῦ μ. πολλάκις δὲ καὶ διὰ δύο ἐτῶν id.*hom.17.4 in Heb*.(12.169B).

μετεωρέω, *lift up* the head, Diod.*Ps*.65:12(M.33.1600B).

μετεωρίζ-ω, **1.** lit., *raise to a height, raise aloft*, Nil.*spir.mal*.19(M.79.1164C); med., *rise aloft*, Chrys.*hom.65.5 in Mt*.(7.651C); pass., *be borne aloft, through the air* Ἀββακοὺμ...μετεωρίσθη ὑπὸ ἀγγέλου Didym.*Ac*.8:39(M.39.1669B); of Ascension, Sev.Ant.ap.*cat.Ac*.8:33(p.145.29); **2.** fig. and met.; **a.** of prayer and aspiration, *lift up* τὸ διορατικὸν...εἰς τὸ πάντελες μ. Or.*Jo*.13.42(p.267.33; M.14.473A); ὑπὲρ τὴν οὐράνιον ἀψῖδα τὴν διάνοιαν μ. Eus.*l.C*.5(p.205.1; M.20.1337A); τὰ...ῥήματα...∼ει τὴν διάνοιαν καὶ πτεροῖ τὸν λογισμόν Chrys.*hom.43.5 in Mt*.(7.465C); πρὸς τὸ θεῖον μ. τὸν νοῦν Aen.*dial*.(M.85.997A); intrans. and med., *rise* ἀνιπταμένους ∼εσθαι καὶ φεύγειν τὰ θέλγητρα [sc. δαιμόνων] Meth.*symp*.8.1(p.81.14; M.18.140A); εὔχεται δοθῆναι αὐτῷ τὰς τοῦ πνεύματος νοήσεις ∼ούσας καὶ ἐπαιρούσας Diod.*Ps*.54:6(M.33.1592C); προστάττομεν τοὺς βουλομένους ∼εσθαι, πνευματικῶς τοῦτο γίνεσθαι ἐν ταῖς ἁγίαις ἐκκλησίαις, οἷον διὰ προσευχῆς, δι' ἀναγνωσμάτων, διὰ ψαλμῳδίας καὶ δι' ἐλεημοσύνης †Gregent.*leg.Hom*.38(M.86.601C); **b.** *exalt, elevate*, Hipp.*fr.4 in Pr*.(p.158.7; M.10.617A); ὁ ὑπὲρ εὐσεβείας ∼όμενος Didym.*Ps*.7:18(M.39.1184B); μετεωρισθέντες τῶν γηΐνων, προσπλάσωσι τῷ οὐρανίῳ id.*2Reg*.22:14(M.39.1117D); πέτραν σημαίνεσθαι...τὸν Χριστὸν...[sc. ὃς] ∼εται κατὰ τὸν νοῦν ὑμνούμενος ὑπὸ τοῦ θεοῦ Diod.*Ps*.60:3(M.33.1596C); pass., *be elated* ἀπέλθωμεν ∼όμενοι ἕως οὗ φθάσωμεν ἐν τῷ οἴκῳ σου, διότι ἠγάπησά σου τὴν ὁμιλίαν *T.Abr*.B 2(p.107.2); **c.** *vaunt oneself, be puffed up* ∼ει τῇ ματαιότητι τοῦ νοός †Bas.*Is*.89(1.441B; M.30.264C); Mac.Aeg.*hom*.5.6(M.34.504D); πῶς γὰρ δυνήσῃ τὸν νέον...σωφρονίσαι, αὐτὸς ἐν πολιᾷ τοιαῦτα ∼ων; Chrys.*Anna* 4.1(4.731A); ∼εσθαι ἐν ἀργολογίᾳ πολλῇ Nil.*epp*.3.323(M.79.540A); **d.** *excite, unsettle, distract* πρὸς ἄλλο τι κάλλος ∼εσθαι Bas.*ascet*.1.2(2.320B; M.31.873B); id.*ep*.22.1(3.99A; M.32.288B); τοῖς...παρὰ τῆς ἰατρικῆς...∼ομένοις ἀπὸ τοῦ ὀρθοῦ λόγου εἰς τὴν τοῦ σώματος ἐπιμέλειαν id.*reg.fus*.55.5(2.400C; M.31.1052A); πρὸς τὰς ἀπάτας τοῦ βίου τούτου ∼εσθαι Gr.Naz.*ep*.238(M.37.381B); δαίμονες...τὴν μνήμην ∼οντες τοῦ νοῦ τῆς πρὸς τὴν χάριν αὐτὸν ὁμιλίας ἀποσπῶσιν Diad.*perf*.81(p.104.22); ὅπως ἂν μὴ ∼ώμεθα ἀπατώμενοι ὑπὸ τῶν αἰσθήσεων περὶ τὴν ματαιότητα Jo.Carp.*cap*.91(M.85.1855); **e.** hence pass., *be* *neglectful* οἱ ∼όμενοι...καὶ ἀμερίμνως βιοῦντες †Cyr.*hom.div*.14(5².408A); ἐὰν θέλῃ τις κτήσασθαι ἀρετήν, οὐκ ὀφείλει ἀδιαφορεῖν οὐδὲ ∼εσθαι Dor.*doct*.10.2(M.88.1725C); *ib*.11.6(1741C).

μετεώρισμα, τό, 1. *height*, Jo.D.*hom*.1.3(M.96.549C); **2.** *assumption* of Elijah, id.*f.o*.4.24(M.94.1208C).

μετεωρισμός, ὁ, A. *prancing* θέατρα καὶ ὀρχήσεις καὶ μ. ‡Hipp.*consumm*.46(p.308.19; M.10.948D).

B. *lifting up* the eyes, *T.Isach*.7.2; *T.Benj*.6.3; ἵνα φυλάττωσιν ἀπὸ μ. τοὺς ὀφθαλμοὺς αὐτῶν *Apophth.Patr*.(M.65.221B); met.; **1.** *distraction, light-mindedness* λόγος ἀνωφελὴς καὶ ὁ διὰ τῆς πρὸς ἀλλήλους ὁμιλίας μ. ἄκαιρος Bas.*ascet*.2.2(2.325E; M.31.885C); γίνεται ὁ μ. ἀπὸ ἀργίας τοῦ νοῦ μὴ ἀσχολουμένου περὶ τὰ ἀναγκαῖα id.*reg.br*.21(2.422C; M.31.1097B); μ. ἀπὸ τῆς πληροφορίας τοῦ παρεῖναι τὸν θεόν id.*ep*.22.2(3.99E; M.32.289C); ἡ αἰχμαλωσία τῶν παθῶν...ἀπόλλυσι τὴν ἐγκράτειαν...διὰ τοῦ μ. καὶ τοῦ κόρου Esias *or*.17.3(p.106); καὶ τῶν ἀκουσίων μ. πάντως λόγον ὑφέξομεν Diad.*perf*.100(p.148.7); **2.** plur., *distractions, things that distract* τῶν τε τοῦ διαβόλου ἐπιθυμιῶν καὶ τῶν τοῦ κόσμου μ. †Bas.*bapt*.1.2.19(2.643D; M.31.1560B); Pall.*h.Laus.* proem.(p.10.14; M.34.1001); δαίμονες...εἰς τὰ πάθη τῆς ἁμαρτίας καὶ εἰς μ. ποικίλους σχηματιζόμενοι Diad.*perf*.81(p.104.21); **3.** *neglect, inattention* ὁ τυχὼν μ. ναυάγιον ἴσως ποιεῖ Nil.*Alb*.(M.79.705D); id.*Magn*.8(M.79.980B).

C. *lifting up* the thoughts to God, Or.*Jo*.2.1(p.53.16; M.14.105C); καρπὸς δὲ τῆς μερίδος τοῦ θεοῦ μ. θεοῦ· οὕτω γὰρ Ἱερεμίας ἑρμηνεύεται id.*fr.60 in Jer*.(p.227.27); †Bas.*ep*.42.2(3.126C; M.32.349B); ἀδολεσχίαν τὸν ἐν θεωρίᾳ μ. λέγει Hesych.H.*fr.Ps*.54:3(M.93.1213B); ἀποκρούεται...τοὺς ἐμπαθεῖς λογισμοὺς...ἡ ψαλμῳδία ἢ προσευχὴ ἢ μ. ἢ ἄλλῳ τινὶ τοπικῷ περισπασμῷ Max.*carit*.4.48(M.90.1057D); Ζαμβρὶ ...ὅπερ ἐστὶν Ἀισμά μου, τουτέστι μ. μου id.*ambig*.(M.91.1201C).

D. *being raised up, swelling*; met., of pride, ref. Ps.130:1 ἁμαρτία ἐστὶ...ὁ μ. †Bas.*Is*.89(1.441D; M.30.265A); ἵνα πάσης κενοδοξίας ἢ μ. ἐκτὸς ὑπάρχωσι Diad.*perf*.94(p.138.8).

***μετεωρόκλαδος,** *with branches pointing skywards*, Ant.Mon.*hom*.45(M.89.1573D).

μετεωρολογία, ἡ, *lofty discourse*, Bas.*hom*.12.6(2.102C; M.31.397B).

μετεωροποιέω, = μετεωροπορέω, *soar*, Proc.G.*Gen*.1:24(M.87.108B); *cat.Apoc*.12:14(p.365.23).

***μετεωροποιός,** *soaring*, Eus.*Is*.35:7(M.24.341B).

μετεωροπορ-έω, 1. *ascend, walk on high*; lit., ‡Meth.*Sym.et Ann*.6(M.18.361A); myst., of contemplation ἐν ἐλευθερίᾳ ∼εῖν τὸν νοῦν Gr.Nyss.*virg*.22(p.331.1; M.46.404A); **2.** *fly away on high*, met. ὁ καιρὸς...∼εῖ γελᾷ τε τοὺς διώκοντας Evagr.*h.e*.3.26(p.123.9; M.86.2649C).

***μετεωροπόρητος,** *who has passed into the heavens*, Thdr.Stud.*nativ.BMV* 7(M.96.692A).

***μετεωροπόρος, 1.** *travelling through the air, soaring aloft*; fig. and met., ref. Mt.13:32 τὰ πετεινὰ τοῦ οὐρανοῦ, ἀγγέλους δηλαδὴ θείους καὶ μ. ψυχάς Clem.*fr*.54(p.226.7; M.9.744B); Gr.Nyss.*hex*.1(M.44.64A); αἱ πτέρυγες τῆς γῆς οἱ διορατικώτεροί εἰσι καὶ μ. παρὰ πάντας τοὺς ἐπὶ τῆς γῆς...καὶ οἱ κατὰ τὸν θεῖον νόμον βιοῦν δεδιδαγμένοι Or.*sel.in Ezech*.7:1(M.13.788C); ἀστρονομίαν τὴν μ. Gr.Thaum.*pan.Or*.8(p.22.18; M.10.1077C); Eus.*Is*.6:2(M.24.125A); τῆς λογικῆς τοῦ λαοῦ τότε τροφῆς, οὐκ ἐσθίοντός τι τῶν καθαρῶν πετεινῶν τοῦ οὐρανοῦ, τρεφομένου δὲ τῷ μὲν δοκοῦντι λόγῳ μ., ἀλλ' οὐ... δυναμένῳ ὑπεραναβῆναι τῆς γῆς Vict.*Mc*.1:4(p.269.11); neut. as subst. ἀετὸς λέγεται ὁ ἅγιος διὰ τὸ μ. Bas.*hom.in Ps*.28(1.121E; M.29.300B); **2.** met., *wandering, distracted* λογισμοὺς...μ. ‡Gr.Nyss.*or.1 in Gen.1:26*(M.44.277A).

μετέωρος, 1. *raised from the ground* θάνατος μ. καὶ ἐν ξύλῳ γινόμενος οὐκ ἄλλος ἂν εἴη εἰ μὴ ὁ σταυρός Ath.*inc*.35.5(M.25.156C); τὸ 'ὑψώσω σε, κύριε'...οὐκ ἐν τόπῳ τινὶ καὶ μ. τὸν κύριον ὄντα παρίστησιν ...ἀλλὰ τὸ μεγαλοπρεπὲς τῆς ἀοράτου θεότητος ὕψος καλεῖ ‡Ath.*Sabell*.15(M.28.120C); Gr.Nyss.*hom.4 in Cant*.(M.44.841A); *high-stepping* φυλάττου δὲ καὶ τῆς ὑπερηφανίας τὰ σύμβολα...βῆμα ποδῶν ἁβρὸν καὶ μ. Clem.*fr*.44(p.221.28); *on higher ground*, fig. σκοπευτήριον ἔχοντες τὴν θεωρητικὴν ψυχήν, ἐκ μ. σκοπεύουσαν ἅπαντα Or.*schol.in Cant*.7:4(M.17.281C); Gr.Thaum.*pan.Or*.14(p.33.8; M.10.1093A); Meth.*symp*.1.1(p.7.19; M.18.37A) cit. s. μετοχετεύω; met., *exalted*, Eus.*h.e*.2.18.1(M.20.184C); id.*d.e*.10.6(p.468.9; M.22.753B); c. genit., *raised above* Ἱερουσαλὴμ μ. θανάτου...ἡρμήνευται Proc.G.*Gen*.14:18(M.87.333D); **2.** *in mid-air, high in the air*, lit. and met. οὗτος τὴν μετάρσιον τῶν κατὰ τὸν ἀέρα συμβαινόντων καὶ τὴν μ. τῶν κατὰ τὸν οὐρανὸν κινουμένων φιλοσοφίαν μετιών, Ἅβραμ ἐκαλεῖτο· ὃ μεθερμηνεύεται, πατὴρ μ. Clem.*str*.5.1(p.331.2; M.9.20A); of angels, Or.*Jo*.1.14(p.18.30; M.14.48B); οἱ γενναῖοι καὶ τοῦ φωτὸς ἐρασταὶ... πρὸς τὰ μ. πέτανται Chrys.*virg*.17(1.281C); Jo.Mosch.*prat*.21(M.87.2862C); *caught up, rapt*, †Marc.Er.*temp*.26(M.65.1065C,D); **3.** *on the high sea*; neut. as subst., *open sea* ἡ ναῦς ἐσάλευεν ἐπὶ μ. Synes.*ep*.4(M.66.1336B); *ib*.130(1513A); **4.** *unsettled, distracted, inattentive*, Clem.*paed*.2.10(p.219.7; M.8.520C); μηδεὶς τοίνυν ἔστω ῥᾴθυμος, μηδεὶς μ., εἰσελθόντων τῶν ἱερέων Chrys.*hom.32.6 in Mt*.(7.373C); Nil.*Eulog*.6(M.79.1101C); of facts, *indeterminate* 'τέξεται'...οὐκ εἶπε 'τέξεταί σοι' διὸ μ. αὐτὸ τέθεικε Chrys.*hom.4.6 in Mt*.(7.58B); neut. as subst., *uncertainty*, Epiph.*anc*.5(p.11.26; M.43.25A); Chrys.*hom.27.2 in 1Cor*.(10.243C).

μετεωροσοφιστής, ὁ, *astronomical sophist*, Isid.Pel.*epp*.5.202(M.78.1453B).

μετεώρως, 1. *at a height*; comp., Clem.*prot*.4(p.46.27; M.8.160A); **2.** *heedlessly, lightly* ᾔτησας...ἀπίστως ἢ μ. ‡Bas.*const*.1.5(2.539E; M.31.1336C).

***μετηλλαγμένως,** *with an alteration, differently*, Epiph.*haer*.42.11(p.121.15, v.l. -νος M.41.724C); *ib*.68.1(p.141.4; -νος M.42.184C).

μέτηλυς, *going from one place to another*, Nonn.*par.Jo*.6:26(M.43.797B); *ib*.6:67(804B).

***μετιστής, ὁ,** *late-comer*, ‡Nil.*perist*.12.2(M.79.941B).

***μετοικείωσις, ἡ,** ? *change of relationship*, *cat.Apoc*.3:8(p.225.18).

μετοικεσία, ἡ, *exile, sojourn* μ. ἐν Αἰγύπτῳ Thphl.Ant.*Autol*.3.24(M.6.1157A); Clem.*str*.1.21(p.76.17; M.8.849B); τὴν εἰς Βαβυλῶνα μ. *Hom.Clem*.16.13.

μετοικία, ἡ, 1. *change of abode*, of death τὴν ἐνθένδε ἐπὶ τὰ κρείττω μετάβασίν τε καὶ μ. Eus.*l.C*.6(p.209.20; M.20.1345C); **2.** *exile* ὅσοι τοῦ μὴ εἰδωλολατρῆσαι χάριν...ἐξορίας καὶ μ. ὑπέμειναν id.*v.C*.2.20(p.49.15; M.20.997B); διετίαν ἔμεινεν ἐν τῇ μ. Ath.*apol.sec*.89(p.167.20; M.25.409A); of Jewish captivity, Or.*hom.4.4 in Jer*.(p.26.7; M.13.289A); Afric.*chron*.13.2(M.10.73C); Eus.*p.e*.10.4(471A; M.21.784B); Thdt.*Dan*.9:1(2.1226).

μετοικίζ-ω, 1. lit., *deport* to another country; ref. Jewish captivity, Clem.*str*.1.21(p.75.9; M.8.848A); *ib*.(p.77.4; 852A); ∼εσθαι κατὰ τὴν ἀξίαν τῶν ἁμαρτημάτων...εἰς Βαβυλῶνα Or.*hom.19.14 in Jer*.(p.170.17; M.13.495A); pass., *be exiled, banished* μετῳκίσθησαν ...οἱ δαίμονες...ἀπ' οὐρανοῦ κατεβλήθησαν Tat.*orat*.20(p.22.15; M.6.852A); Meth.*symp*.4.2(p.46.16; M.18.88C); **2.** fig. οὐκέτι μετοικισθῆναι ἀπὸ τῆς ἀληθείας εἰς τὴν πλάνην ἀνεχόμεθα ‡Hipp.*fr.29 in Pss*.(p.151.20; M.10.724B); of the soul εἰς θεὸν ∼εται Or.*schol.in Cant*.2:16(M.17.265C); pass., *be transported*, Ant.Mon.*hom*.15(M.89.1472D); **3.** met., *transfer* ἡ γνῶσις...[sc. τὸν ἄνθρωπον] εἰς τὸ συγγενὲς τῆς ψυχῆς θεῖόν τε καὶ ἅγιον ∼ει Clem.*str*.7.10(p.41.27; M.9.480C); πρὸς τὸν λαὸν τοῦ θεοῦ μετῳκίσθησαν αἱ δυσφημίαι Const.ap.Ath.*apol.sec*.61(p.141.12; M.25.360C).

μετοίκιον, τό, *colony, settlement abroad* ἡ κάτω Ἱερουσαλήμ, ὥσπερ μ. τῆς ἄνω Areth.*Apoc*.3:12(M.106.560B).

μετοικισμός, ὁ, *deportation*, of the Jewish *captivity* μ. ... εἰς Βαβυλῶνα Cyr.*ador*.1(1.16D).

μετοικονομέω, *alter an arrangement*, Hipp.*haer*.6.14(p.139.14; M.16.3214B).

μέτοικος, ὁ, *one who leaves his home*; *fugitive* in persecution, Eus.*v.C*.2.36(p.56.25; M.20.1013B); *resident alien*, of Jews τῆς οἰκουμένης ...μέτοικοι Thdt.*affect*.11(p.294.23; 4.1007).

μετοίχομαι, *go to something different*; met., Cyr.*glaph.Ex*.1(1.244A); id.Nah.20(3.499B).

μετοκλάζω, *keep changing from one leg to the other*, Gr.Naz.*or*.5.23(M.35.692B); met., *waver*, Clem.*str*.8.7(p.94.1; M.9.588C); Bas.*ep*.71.2(3.165D; M.32.437C).

μετονομασία, ἡ, *change of name*, Chrys.*hom.2.3 in Ac.9:1*(3.111D); μετων-, †Bas.*Is*.227(1.551A; M.30.516A).

μετουσία, ἡ, A. *participation*; **1.** of Christians; **a.** in God, *Hom.Clem*.17.8; διὰ τοῦ πανταχόθεν ἀπείρου νοὸς τὴν μ. ἔχων (l. ἔχειν), ἣν πάντων ἀναπνέουσαι αἱ ψυχαί, τὸ ζῆν ἔχουσιν *ib*.17.10; τὰ γενητά... συμφωνίαν...πρὸς τὸν πεποιηκότα...ἐν κινήσει καὶ μ. καὶ νῷ...ἔχει Ath.*syn*.48(p.273.8; M.26.780B); **b.** in Logos, Just.*2apol*.13.6(M.6.468A); ἵν' ὥσπερ θεὸς εἰς ὕπαρξιν ἤγαγεν τὰ πάντα, οὕτω καὶ ζωοποιηθῇ τὰ πεφυκότα ζῆν μετουσίᾳ αὐτοῦ Or.*fr.2 in Jo*.(p.485.26); κατὰ φύσιν φθαρτοί, χάριτι δὲ τῆς τοῦ λόγου μ., τοῦ κατὰ φύσιν ἐκφυγόντες Ath.*inc*.5.1(M.25.105A); id.*Ar*.1.56(M.26.129B); Gr.Nyss.*hom.1 in Cant*.(M.44.765C); in his glory υἱοὶ θεοῦ κατὰ μετοχὴν τῆς τοῦ μονογενοῦς αὐτοῦ κοινωνίας ἀποτελεσθέντες μετουσίᾳ τῶν τῆς θεότητος αὐτοῦ μαρμαρυγῶν Eus.*e.th*.3.18(p.179.36; M.24.1041C); ref. 2Cor.2:15 ὁ Παῦλος ἐκ τῆς μ. Χριστοῦ εὐώδης γενόμενος Oecum.*Apoc*.1:15(p.42); **c.** in H. Ghost, by baptism χριστῶν γεγονότων τῶν κατὰ μετουσίαν τοῦ πνεύματος εἰς Χριστὸν βεβαπτισμένων Meth.*symp*.8.8(p.90.17; M.18.149C); πᾶσι τοῖς βεβαπτισμένοις ἐπιτιθέντες τὰς χεῖρας εὐχαῖς τὴν τοῦ πνεύματος μ. ἐδωρούμεθα *Const.App.*6.7.2; χλιαρὸν καλεῖ τὸν μ. μὲν λαβόντα πνεύματος ἁγίου διὰ τοῦ βαπτίσματος, σβέσαντα δὲ τὸ χάρισμα διὰ ῥαθυμίας Oecum.*Apoc.*1:16(p.65); at consecration of bishops, *Lit.*ap.*Const.App.*8.5.7; generally τῇ τοῦ πνεύματος μ. τὴν ἀνάστασιν γίγνεσθαι Thdr.Mops.*Rom.*8:2(p.133.17; M.66.817C); **d.** in Trin., Didym.*Trin.*1.20(M.39.369B) cit. s. μετέχω; **e.** in eucharist, Gr.Nyss.*or.catech.*37(p.142.3; M.45.93A) cit. s. ἀνάκρασις; *Lit.Jac.*(p.240.13); **f.** in spiritual blessings ἀναστάσεως μ. Thdr.Mops.*Gal.*1:4(p.8.23; M.66.900C); μ. τῆς πίστεως Thdt.*1Cor.*11:16(3.236); σωτηρίας μ. id.*Rom.*11:11(3.120); χάριτος...μ. id.*Heb.*13:25(3.637); **2.** theol.; **a.** heret., of mutual rel. of divine Persons τὴν δὲ συνάφειαν ἑτέρως πρὸς τὴν σοφίαν νοεῖ, κατὰ μάθησιν καὶ μ. οὐχὶ ⟨κατ'⟩ οὐσίαν, οὐσιωμένην ἐν σώματι Paul.Sam.*fr.*B 13(p.333.27); καθ' ὑμᾶς [sc. Arians] ἐξ οὐκ ὄντων ἐστὶν ὁ υἱός...πάντως που κατὰ μετουσίαν καὶ αὐτὸς υἱὸς καὶ θεὸς καὶ σοφία ἐκλήθη Ath.*Ar.*1.15(M.26.44B); **b.** notion rejected by orthodox; **i.** in rel. to Son υἱὸν θεὸν...οὐκ ἰδιόκτητον καὶ τοῦ πατρὸς ἀφωρισμένην...ἐφελκόμενον θεότητα ἐξ αὐτῆς δὲ τῆς πατρικῆς μ. ὥσπερ ἀπὸ πηγῆς ἐπ' αὐτὸν προχεομένης πληρούμενον Eus.*e.th.*1.2(p.63.25; M.24.832B); εἰ ἦν ἐκ μ. καὶ αὐτός, καὶ μὴ ἐξ αὐτοῦ οἰσιώδης θεότης, καὶ εἰκὼν τοῦ πατρός, οὐκ ἂν ἐθεοποίησε θεοποιούμενος καὶ αὐτὸς Ath.*syn.*51(p.274.30; M.26.784B); τὸ ἀπαύγασμα φῶς ἐστι, οὐ δεύτερον τοῦ ἡλίου...οὐδὲ κατὰ μ. αὐτοῦ, ἀλλ' ὅλον ἴδιον αὐτοῦ γέννημα id.*Ar.*3.4(M.26.329A); ἡ τῆς μ. ἀπαγόρευσις, ὡς ἀκοινωνήτου τῆς τοῦ πατρὸς οὐσίας πρὸς τὴν τοῦ μονογενοῦς ὑπαρχούσης Bas.*Eun.*2.22(1.257D; M.29.620B); ὁ γεννηθεὶς ἐκ τῆς παρθένου Μαρίας υἱὸς θεοῦ φύσει καὶ θεὸς ἀληθινός, καὶ οὐ χάριτι καὶ μ. Apoll.*ep.Jov.*2(p.251.14; M.28.28B); οὐκέτι ἄν τις κατὰ μετουσίαν ζωῆς τὸν λόγον ἐν ζωῇ θεωροίη...ἀνάγκη πᾶσα, τῆς ἁπλότητος ὁμολογουμένης, αὐτοζωὴν εἶναι τὸν λόγον οἴεσθαι, οὐ ζωῆς μετουσίαν Gr.Nyss.*or.catech.*1(p.9.11; M.45.13D); to his attributes ἅγιος, ἀληθινός, ὁ μὴ μετουσίᾳ ἀλλ' οὐσίᾳ ὢν Or.*Apoc.*20(p.29); οὐ κατά τινα μ. ἅγιος ὢν ὥσπερ ἡμεῖς Cyr.*thes.*12(5^1.107E); to his human nature, Leont.H.*Nest.*3.3(M.86.1609B); τοῦ ἐξ αὐτῆς [sc. τῆς θεοτόκου] προελθόντος, τὸ μέν τοι κατ' οὐσίαν, τὸ δὲ κατὰ μ. θεῖον εἰδότες *ib.*4.37(1712B); **ii.** in rel. to H. Ghost φύσις [sc. τῷ μὲν πνεύματι] ἡ ἁγιωσύνη, ταῖς δὲ [sc. ἁγίαις δυνάμεσι] ἐκ μ. ὑπάρχει τὸ ἁγιάζεσθαι Bas.*Eun.*3.2(1.274B; M.29.660C); θεοῦ εἰκών ἐστιν ὁ υἱὸς ...καὶ τὸ πνεῦμα ὁμοίως καλεῖται τοῦ θεοῦ, καὶ τοῦτο φυσικῶς κατ' αὐτὴν τὴν οὐσίαν, οὐ κατὰ μ. θεοῦ Apoll.*fid.sec.pt.*25(p.176.9; M.10.1116A); **3.** *participation in* another's *existence*; of properties opp. essence, *Hom.Clem.*3.22.

B. *communion, fellowship*, Tat.*orat.*20(p.22.14; M.6.852A); Or.*schol.in Cant.*2:16(M.17.265C); *communication* of oneself to others ὁ ἥλιος...τοῦτον ἐκλαμπρύνει, τοῦτον θερμαίνει...τῇ αὐτοῦ μ. *Hom.Clem.*17.8; hence *part, share* τὰ ζ' πνεύματα αἱ μ. τοῦ πνεύματος Or.*Apoc.*19(p.28); υἱός...πρόεισιν μὲν τῆς πατρικῆς θεότητος...ἐπάρδει δὲ τῷ σύμπαντι κόσμῳ τὰς ἐξ αὐτοῦ χορηγίας, ζωῆς τε καὶ λόγου...καὶ παντὸς ἀγαθοῦ μ. ... ἐπιλιμνάζων Eus.*e.th.*2.17(p.121.15; M.24.940A).

***μετουσιόω**, *transform the substance* of a thing θείας ἐστὶ φύσεως...οὐσιῶσαι καὶ μ. Leont.H.*monoph.*6(M.86.1773A); pass., *be transformed in essence, undergo transubstantiation*, acc. Eutychians τοῦ λόγου αὐτοῦ εἰς σάρκα μετουσιωθέντος καὶ οὐδὲν ἔχοντος ἡμῖν ὁμοούσιον τοῦ κυρίου *ib.*(1809C).

***μετουσίωσις, ἡ**, *change of substance, transubstantiation*, ref. Inc. οὔτε κατὰ σύγχυσιν...οὔτε κατὰ μ. ὡς τὸ ὕδωρ τῶν Αἰγυπτίων αἷμα γεγονός· οὔτε κατὰ ἀλλοίωσιν Leont.H.*monoph.*6(M.86.1772D); *ib.*69(1801C).

μετοχετεύ-ω, *convey in a channel, divert*; **1.** lit., Dion.Al.ap.Eus.*h.e.*7.21.7(M.20.685A); ταὐτόν ἐστιν ὕδωρ τὸ ἐκ τῆς πηγῆς εἰς τὸν ποταμὸν ~όμενον Ath.*exp.fid.*2(M.25.204B); Cyr.*Is.*2.5(2.320A); [sc. ἡ βρῶσις ἡ ἀπολλυμένη] χωρήσασα εἰς γαστέρα...ἐκ γαστρὸς αὖθις ~εται id.*Jo.*3.4(4.299D); gen., *convey* from one place to another, Clem.*q.d.s.*1(p.159.17; M.9.605A); **2.** fig. and met. αἵτινες [sc. γενναῖοι φύσεις] τὸ ῥεῦμα ~σασαι τῆς ἡδυπαθείας ἄνω μετέωρον ἀπευθύνουσι τὸ ὄχημα τῆς ψυχῆς Meth.*symp.*1.1(p.7.18; M.18.37A); ταύτην...ὁ διάβολος τὴν [sc. τῆς ὁμιλίας] ἐπιθυμίαν...ἐφ' ἕτερον ~σας τρόπον Chrys.*hom.4.2 in Rom.*(9.456A); ὁ σωτήριος λόγος...πρὸς τὸ κρεῖττον ~ων Isid.Pel.*epp.*3.34(M.78.753D); οἱ ταύτην [sc. διδασκαλίαν] δεξάμενοι μ. εἰς ἅπασαν τὴν οἰκουμένην τὰ νάματα Thdt.*Ps.*2:6(1.620); **3.** *derive* ὁ πλάστης...τηρεῖ τὰ τῆς ἀρχαίας πλάσεως σύμβολα, καὶ τοῖς δευτέροις ἐκ τῶν προτέρων ~ει αὔξησιν Bas.Sel.*or.*6.3(M.85.97A).

***μετοχεύς, ὁ**, *sharer*, name of Gnost. aeon, Hipp.*haer.*6.31(p.159.13; M.16.3242A).

μετοχή, ἡ, *participation*; **1.** essential; within Trinity ὁ Χριστὸς ...τὸ χρῖσμα αὐτῷ δὴ πνεύματι θείῳ τὸ θεοπρεπές, μετοχῇ τῆς ἀγεννήτου καὶ πατρικῆς θεότητος ἀπειλήφει Eus.*h.e.*1.3.13(M.20.73A); regarded by theologians as misleading term ἀληθινὸς υἱὸς ὑπάρχων, δύναμίς ἐστι τοῦ πατρός, καὶ σοφία, καὶ λόγος, οὐ κατὰ μετοχὴν ταῦτα ὤν...ἀλλ' αὐτοσοφία Ath.*gent.*46(M.25.93B); εἰ φύσει θεός ἐστιν ὁ πατήρ, ἀλλ' οὐ μετοχῇ, ἐστὶ δὲ φύσει θεὸς καὶ ὁ υἱός· εἴπερ τῶν κατὰ μετοχὴν ὑπερέχει, τῆς αὐτῆς ἄρα φύσεως ἔσται τῷ πατρί, ἀλλ' οὐ τοῖς κατὰ μετοχήν Cyr.*thes.*10(5^1.82E); cf. ἀγαθοῦ ὄντος τοῦ πατρὸς καὶ τοῦ υἱοῦ καὶ τοῦ ἁγίου πνεύματος οὐ μετοχῇ ἀγαθότητος ἀλλ' οὐσίας ταυτότητι ‡Ath.*dial.Trin.*1.15(M.28.1141A); **2.** by grace; **a.** of men and angels in God υἱοὶ θεοῦ κατὰ μετοχὴν τῆς τοῦ μονογενοῦς αὐτοῦ κοινωνίας ἀποτελεσθέντες Eus.*e.th.*3.18(p.179.35; M.24.1042C); ref. Ps.81:6 μόνον μετοχῇ τοῦ λόγου διὰ τοῦ πνεύματος ταύτην ἔχουσι τὴν χάριν παρὰ τοῦ πατρός Ath.*Ar.*1.9(M.26.29A); ἁγίοις διὰ πίστεως ἡ μ. τοῦ ἁγίου πνεύματος δίδοται Euthal.Diac.*Ac.*11(M.85.656A); ὁ θεὸς αὐτός ἐστιν ἡ ἀθανασία· οἱ δὲ ἄγγελοι μετοχῇ εἰσιν ἀθανασίας ἀθάνατοι ‡Ath.*Maced.dial.*1.9(M.28.1304A); ὁ θεὸς οὐ κατὰ μετοχὴν ἀγαθότητός ἐστιν ἀγαθός, ἀλλ' αὐτός ἐστιν ἀγαθότης· ὁ δὲ ἄνθρωπος μετοχῇ ἀγαθότητός ἐστιν ἀγαθὸς ‡Ath.*dial.Trin.*1.12(M.28.1136B); ἐν τοῖς γεγονόσιν ὁ λόγος ἦν...διὰ μετοχῆς τοῖς οὖσιν ἑαυτὸν ἀναμιγνύς Cyr.*Jo.*1.6(4.50D); id.*Lc.*22:8(M.72.904D) cit. s. βάπτισμα; hence in Apollinarian reference to Christ's human nature τί θαυμαστὸν εἰ ἐν τῷ κατὰ σάρκα δεσπότῃ Χριστῷ ἄμφω [sc. Father and Son] κατ' αὐτὸ νομίζοιντο μένειν, τῆς κατὰ τὴν οὐσίαν κοινωνίας προσιεμένης, ὡς εἰκός, καὶ τὴν τῆς μ. κοινωνίαν; Thdr.Mops.*fr.Apoll.*9(p.317.23; M.66.1000C); **b.** heret., acc. Arians, of Logos in God εἰ δὲ καὶ λέγεται θεός, ἀλλ' οὐκ ἀληθινός ἐστιν· ἀλλὰ μετοχῇ χάριτος, ὥσπερ καὶ οἱ ἄλλοι πάντες...λέγεται ὀνόματι μόνῳ θεὸς Ar.*Thal.fr.*10 ap.Ath.*Ar.*1.6(M.26.24A).

μετοχικός, *able to participate*, Iren.*haer.*5.3.3(M.7.1131C); neut. as subst., Dion.Ar.*c.h.*15.3(M.3.332A).

μετοχικῶς, *by participation* ἰδιάζουσαν ἐκ τοῦ πατρὸς ἔχει τὴν γέννησιν...οὐ καθάπερ ἡμεῖς...ἑνότητα κερδαίνοντες μ. τε καὶ μεταληπτικῶς Cyr.*thes.*12(5^1.119E); *ib.*32(268C); οὐκοῦν μ. ... φυσικῶς δὲ μᾶλλον καὶ οὐσιωδῶς *ib.*34(350D).

μέτοχος, *partaking, sharing*; as subst., *partaker, sharer* τῇ προσευχῇ ὑμῶν...μ. εἶναι Ign.*Eph.*11.2; Herm.*mand.*4.1.9; μ. ... τῆς βασιλείας αὐτοῦ *M.Thdot.*3(p.136.3); ref. Jo.1:4 εἰ οὐδὲν ἑαυτοῦ μ. μέτεχει δὲ ἡ κτίσις, ὡς ζωῆς, τοῦ υἱοῦ Cyr.*Jo.*1.6(4.53B); of relationship with Christ χρῖσαι τὴν κεφαλὴν χρίσματι ἁγίῳ, ἵνα μ. γένῃ Χριστοῦ, καὶ οὕτω πρόσελθε τῇ νηστείᾳ Bas.*hom.*1.2(2.2C; M.31.165A); μορφώσασα [sc. ἡ ἐκκλησία] ἐν ὑμῖν τὸν Χριστόν, οὗ μ. γενόμενοι ἱερὰ μέλη ἐστέ *Const.App.*2.61.5; εἰ μ. αὐτῆς [sc. τῆς τοῦ υἱοῦ οὐσίας] γεγόναμεν, ἀπαθεῖς διαμένομεν ‡Ath.*dial.Trin.*2.23(M.28.1192C); ref. eucharist, *Const.App.*2.33.2; *Lit.ib.*8.6.13; μ. ... τῶν ἁγίων σου μυστηρίων *Lit.Jac.*(p.61.4).

μετρ-έω, **1.** *measure* κατῆλθε...ἵνα πρὸς τὴν ἡμετέραν ἀσθένειαν οὓς ἠγάπησε μετρηθεὶς ἡμᾶς πρὸς τὴν ἑαυτοῦ δύναμιν ἀντιμετρήσῃ Clem.*q.d.s.*37(p.184.7; M.9.641C); **2.** *circumscribe* οἱ τὴν γέννησιν τοῦ υἱοῦ τὴν ἐκ πατρὸς ἀνθρωπίνως περιγράφοντες διαστήματι ~ουμένῳ Apoll.*fid.sec.pt.*1(p.167.12; M.10.1105A); ἡ τοῦ ἁγίου πνεύματος μεγαλωσύνη...πληροῦσα μὲν τὸν κόσμον...~οῦσα μέν, οὐ ~ουμένη δέ Didym.*Trin.*2.6(M.39.509A); οὐ ξένος ὁ υἱός, οὐδὲ ἀλλότριον τὸ πνεῦμα τοῦ θεοῦ καὶ υἱοῦ, οὐ τόποις μεμερισμένα..., οὐ διαστήμασι ~ούμενα id.(‡Bas.)*Eun.*5(1.314C; M.29.753B); met., *include*, Ath.*ep.Marcell.*30(M.27.41C); perf. ptcpl. pass., *limited*, *Hom.Clem.*3.6; εἴπερ ἐστὶν οὐχ ὁ αὐτὸς τῷ μεμετρημένην ἔχοντι γνῶσιν ὁ πάντα εἰδὼς Cyr.*apol.Thdt.*4(p.124.16; 6^1.218B); **3.** *ascribe* τὸ 'δοῦλος' καὶ τὸ 'πέπονθε' μὴ τῇ θεότητι λογίζεσθαι...ἀλλὰ τῇ σαρκὶ ταῦτα ~εῖν Ath.*decr.*14(p.12.22; M.25.'448'(440)C); **4.** *moderate, adapt* τῇ χρείᾳ τῶν ἀκουόντων τὸ φθέγμα μ. Clem.*fr.*44(p.222.1); ~εῖν εἴωθε τοῖς παιδευομένοις ἡ θεία γραφὴ τὰ μαθήματα Thdt.*qu.1 in Gen.*(1.3); id.*1Cor.*4:3(3.186); perf. ptcpl. pass. as adj., *moderate*, Eus.*v.C.*3.11(p.82.10; M.20.1065C); Ath.*gent.*40(M.25.81B); **5.** reflex.; **a.** *size* oneself *up* ἐμαυτὸν ~ῶ, ἵνα μὴ ἐν καυχήσει ἀπόλωμαι Ign.*Trall.*4.1; Or.*Cels.*4.30(p.300.16; M.11.1073B); Thdt.*ep.*42(4.1100); **b.** *esteem* oneself highly τὸ ῥίψαι ἑαυτὸν ἐνώπιον τοῦ θεοῦ, καὶ τὸ μὴ ἑαυτὸν ~εῖν *Apophth.Patr.*(M.65.332B); Bars.*resp.*(M.86.900D); **6.** abs., *write in verse*, Gr.Naz.*ep.*101(M.37.193A).

μετριάζ-ω, **A.** intrans.; **1.** *be moderate, keep measure*; *hold moderate* (i.e. orthodox) *views* οἱ περὶ τὸν υἱὸν ~οντες Gr.Naz.*or.*31.1(p.145.7; M.36.133B); *lack zeal* οἱ μετεωριζόμενοι καὶ ~οντες καὶ ἀμερίμνως βιοῦντες †Cyr.*hom.div.*14(5^2.408A); **2.** *be humble* οὐχ ὅτι ῥυπαροὶ ἦσαν, νίπτει αὐτούς, ἀλλὰ ἵνα διδάξῃ ~ειν Ammon.*Jo.*13:10(M.85.1481C); οὐχ οὕτω τὸν ἁμαρτάνοντα ὡς τὸν κατορθοῦντα σπουδάζειν χρὴ ~ειν Chrys.*hom.33.3 in Jo.*(8.194B); ἑαυτὸν κρύπτει ὁ Ἰωάννης ~ων *ib.*85.2(505E); ~οντα...μᾶλλον ἢ πρὸς ἀλήθειαν ταῦτα φθεγγόμενον id.*sac.*2.5(p.40.13; 1.377D); of a monk's occupations αὐτὰ τὰ ἔργα ~ειν πείθει, καὶ οὐκ ἀφίησι φλεγμαίνειν id.*hom.*72.4 *in Mt.*(7.706B);

Isid.Pel.*epp*.2.232(M.78.668B); of Christ, *manifest humility*, Didym.*Trin*.3.17(M.39.876B).

B. trans.; **1.** *regulate, moderate*, ‡Nil.*perist*.12.11(M.79.961C); **2.** *wear modestly* τὸ...κάλλος μὴ προσεπικαλλώπιζε ἀλλὰ ταπεινοφρόνως μ. αὐτό *Const.App*.1.3.8.

μετριολογέω, *speak moderately, modestly*, Didym.*Trin*.3.17(M.39.876C); Isid.Pel.*epp*.2.232(M.78.668B).

μετριοπαθέω, *be humble*; of Abraham, ref. Gen.18:27, Clem.*str*.4.17(p.294.35; M.8.1313A); of David, ref. Ps.50, *ib*.(p.295.19; 1313C); τοῖς φιλαρέτοις τὸ μ. πρέπει Isid.Pel.*epp*.2.28(M.78.473D).

μέτριος, 1. *moderate*; **a.** *of moderate value* τὰ...φιλοσοφίας ἀπηρτημένα μ. καὶ ἀποδοχῆς ἄξια Just.*dial*.3.3(M.6.481A); in depreciatory sense ὁ...καθ' ὅσον ἐγὼ δύναμαι λόγος ὑπὲρ ἁγνείας...κἂν μ. ᾖ...καὶ ὀλίγος Meth.*symp*.10.6(p.129.10; M.18.204B); **b.** *of low degree, humble, poor*, Tat.*orat*.11(p.12.7; M.6.829B); Meth.*lepr*.12(p.466.17); τὸν βίον τῶν πάλαι θεοφιλῶν Ἑβραίων...οὐκ εἰς βραχεῖς καὶ μ., ἀλλ' εἰς ὅλον ἐφαπλῶσαι τὸν κόσμον ἀποδέδεικται [sc. Christ] Eus.*d.e*.3.3(p.109.14; M.22.188C); ref. Apoc.1:5 ἡμεῖς ὁμόλογοι μ. καὶ ταπεινοί *Ep.Lugd*. ap.eund.*h.e*.5.2.3(M.20.433B); **2.** *proportionate, fitting* τὰ μ. καὶ σεμνὰ νοεῖν *1Clem*.1.3.

μετριότης, ἡ, 1. *modest ability*, Iren.*haer*.1 proem.2(M.7.411B); Or.*ep*.1.1(M.11.49A); hence of the speaker '*your humble servant*' τὴν ἐμὴν μ. ὁ αὐτὸς...θεὸς...ἑαυτῷ κατεδουλώσατο Const.ap.Gel.Cyz.*h.e*.2.7.8(M.85.1233C); CArim.*ep.Const*.2(p.278.18; M.26.792C); *M.Ner. et Ach*.9(p.8.26); **2.** *humility* διὰ μ. ὁ Παῦλος...οὐκ ἐγγράφει ἑαυτὸν Ἑβραίων ἀπόστολον Clem.*fr*.22(p.202.1; M.20.552A); Or.*Jo*.6.49(30; p.159.19; M.14.288C); Chrys.*hom.7.1 in Eph*.(11.45E); ref. Mt.6:12 τοὺς μὲν ἄκρους τὴν ἀρετὴν μετριότητα διδάσκει φρονήματος id.*hom. in Mt.7:14*(3.31B); of God ἐπιμένει τῇ μ.· οὐ γὰρ εἶπε, κρινῶ ὑμᾶς... ἀλλά, κριθήσομαι καὶ πρὸς ὑμᾶς Thdt.*Jer*.2:9(2.412); of Christ, id.*qu. 18 in Jos*.(1.325); of angels ὢ τῆς μ. τῶν ἁγίων ἀγγέλων...ἀδελφοὺς ἑαυτῶν καλοῦσιν τοὺς ἀνθρώπους Oecum.*Apoc*.12:10(p.144).

***μετριοτροφία, ἡ**, *moderation in diet* ὡς ἂν διὰ τῆς ἡσυχίας καὶ μ. καθάρωμεν καρδίαν Thdr.Stud.*epp*.2.147(M.99.1460C).

μετριοφρον-έω, *think modestly, be humble-minded*, ref. Gen.2:7 ὅταν οὖν ἀκούσῃς χοῦν, παιδεύου ~εῖν ‡Bas.*struct hom*.2.10(1.343E; M.30.53B); Mac.Aeg.*or*.11(M.34.861B); Chrys.*hom.1.3 in 1Cor*.(10.7E); ἡ μεγαλοφροσύνη...τῷ μὲν μὴ ἐπαίρεσθαι κατὰ τῶν πέλας ~οῦσα· τῷ δὲ μὴ ὑποκύπτειν τοῖς φόβοις Isid.Pel.*epp*.2.241(M.78.681C); βασιλεῖ...ἔξεστι μετριολογεῖν καὶ ~εῖν· στρατιώτῃ δὲ ἢ στρατηγῷ βασιλικὰς ἀφιέναι φωνάς, οὐ θέμις *ib*.4.166(1260A).

***μετριοφρόνως**, *humbly*, *Hymn*.(*AS* 1 p.481).

μετριοφροσύνη, ἡ, 1. *moderation, restraint* οὗτοι...οἱ πτωχεύοντες τῇ μ. οἱ καὶ εἰς ἄκρον ἐλάσαντες ἀκτημοσύνης Eus.*fr.Lc*.6:20(M.24.533C); in a superior, *considerateness, gentleness, tact* ὅρα σύνεσιν καὶ μ.· οὐ τίθησιν...τοὺς κινδύνους,...τοὺς πόνους...ἀλλὰ τὸ φιλεῖν Chrys.*hom.13.2 in 2Cor*.(10.532C); ἡ ἐξουσία, τὴν μ. καὶ ἐπιείκειαν μέγαν συνεργὸν λαβοῦσα, πάντας εἰκεῖν...πεποίηκεν †Jo.D.*B.J*.33(M.96.1177A); **2.** *humility* πλοῦτος διὰ μετριοφροσύνης καὶ τοῦ προτιμᾶν τῶν δοθέντων τὸν δεδωκότα κατορθώσειεν ἂν τὸ σπουδαζόμενον Tit.Bost.*Man*.2.7(M.18.1145D); ref. 1Cor.15:8, Chrys.*hom.38.4 in 1Cor*.(10.355D); τῶν περὶ τῆς μ. λόγων τούτοις ἁρμοττόντων οἳ τοὺς ἑτέρους ὤφειλον διδάσκειν Thdr.Mops.*Phil*.1:1(p.200.19; M.66.921B); ref. Mt.9:29 μ. ἥντινα καὶ Χριστὸς...ἐνεδείξατο Nil.*epp*.1.326(M.79.200D); of Abraham's courtesy to guests, Isid.Pel.*epp*.3.264(M.78.945A); οὐκ ἔστι φοβερά [sc. πενία], ἀλλὰ καὶ ἀσφαλείας ἁπάσης καὶ μ. ὑπόθεσις *ib*.2.257(692C); **3.** *modesty*, Chrys.*hom.20.3 in Eph*.(11.146A); Thdt.*Cant*.8:12(2.163).

***μετριόφρων**, *modest, humble-minded* πτωχόν, τουτέστι τὸν ἐπιεικῆ καὶ μ. καὶ ταπεινὸν τῇ καρδίᾳ Or.*exc.in Ps*.36:14(M.17.129B); Gr.Nyss.*v.Mos*.(M.44.421C); of Christ on earth ἀνθρωποπρεπῆ καὶ μ. φθέγξασθαι Didym.*Trin*.3.17(M.39.876B); ὅλον αὐτοῦ [sc. θεοῦ] φησιν εἶναι, οὐ τὸ αὐτεξούσιον ἀνατρέπων, ἀλλὰ μ. καὶ εὐγνώμονας κατασκευάζων Chrys.*hom.4.4 in Phil*.(11.223D); τὸ ἄζυμον οὐκ ἀνιστάμενον ...καὶ σημαῖνον τὸν ἐν τῷ μετέρχεσθαι τὴν ἀρετὴν μ. ‡Nil.*perist*.12.10(M.79.960C); οὐ τὸν δουλοπρεπῆ καὶ κόλακα μ. ... οὐδὲ τὸν αὐθάδη καὶ ἀλαζόνα μεγαλόφρονα Isid.Pel.*epp*.2.241(M.78.684A); *ib*.3.264(944D); 'ὁ μικρότερος'...τὸν μ. λέγων καὶ οὐδὲν ὑψηλὸν περὶ ἑαυτὸν λογιζόμενον δι' εὐλάβειαν Cyr.*Lc*.9:46(p.89.29f.; M.72.661A); ref. Mt.11:28 μ. κατ' αὐτὸν οἱ τοῖς αὐτοῦ νόμοις παιδάγωγούμενοι id.*Zach*.41(3.619E).

μετρίως, 1. *moderately, according to measure*; *adequately*, Athenag.*res*.11(p.59.22; M.6.993B); ταῦτα μὲν μ. εἰς ἀπολογίαν Or.*princ*.3.1.14(p.221.3; M.11.277A); Eus.*h.e*.6.23.4(M.20.577A); *considerably* τὸ σῶμά μου συντετριμμένον...καὶ τὴν ψυχὴν μ. κεκακωμένος Bas.*ep*.217(3.324D; M.32.793B); **2.** *keeping a balance* between two opinions, hence *ambiguously*, Didym.(‡Bas.)*Eun*.5(1.316A; M.29.757B).

μέτρον, τό, 1. *measure* μ. ἔχει καὶ σταθμὸν παρὰ θεῷ πᾶσα ἔννοια Marc.Er.*opusc*.1.89(M.65.916C); **2.** *measure* of ability, *capacity* γινώσκω τὰ ἑαυτῆς μ. *Ep.Mar*.5; Ephr.1.307E; Isid.Pel.*epp*.1.175(M.78.297A); of Son, acc. Arius τῇ δυνάμει ᾗ δύναται ὁ θεὸς ἰδεῖν, ἰδίοις τε μ. ὑπομένει ὁ υἱὸς ἰδεῖν τὸν πατέρα Ar.*Thal.fr*.2 ap.Ath.*syn*.15(p.242.22; M.26.758A); *ib*.11 ap.eund.*Ar*.1.6(M.26.24A); **3.** *limit, limitation*, Cyr.*Ps*.7:9(M.69.752B); of Inc. διαλέγεται ἀνθρωπίνως, καὶ κατ' οὐδένα τρόπον ἀπεοικότως τοῖς τῆς κενώσεως μ. id.*Is*.4.5(2.692C); κύριος πάντων ὢν τοῖς τῆς ἀνθρωπότητος ἐμβέβηκε μ. *ib*.5.1(738B); τὸ δουλοπρεπὲς [sc. ὑπελθεῖν] μ. οἰκονομικῶς id.*Soph*.41(3.619E); τὸ ἀνθρώπινον οἰκειώσασθαι μ. id.*apol.Thdt*.3(p.119.5; 6[1].202D); id.*Nest*.1 proem.(p.15.15; 6[1].4E); id.*Heb*.2:7(M.74.961C); τὸ...εὔχεσθαι τῶν τῆς ἀνθρωπότητος μ. ἦν Hypat.*fr*.4(p.152.14); **4.** *degree* εἰ...ἐπίστευσεν τῷ θεῷ, οὐκ ἀκολουθεῖ ὅτι καθόλου ἐπίστευσεν, ἔστιν γὰρ μ. τοῦ πιστεύειν τῷ θεῷ Or.*comm.in Rom*.4:2–3(*JTS* 13 p.357); hence, of persons, *rank* ἐμμενέτωσαν οἱ διάκονοι τοῖς ἰδίοις μ. [i.e. after bishops and presbyters] CNic.(325)*can*.18; Mac.Aeg.*hom*.16.12(M.34.621C); *ib*.18.10(641A); Cyr.*Is*.5.2(2.777B); **5.** *standard, level* νόμος δικαιοσύνης μ. Athenag.*leg*.32.2(M.6.964C); Clem.*paed*.2.6(p.217.20; M.8.517B); μὴ ἐπιθύμει ἀρχὴν ψυχῶν, μήπως οὔπω ἐπέβης τοῖς τῆς ἀπαθείας μ. Ephr.1.267E; ταῦτα τὰ μ. οὐκ εὐθέως καταλαμβάνουσιν οἱ ἄνθρωποι, εἰ μὴ διὰ καμάτου καὶ θλίψεως Mac.Aeg.*hom*.17.4(M.34.625D); **6.** *proportion* τὸ πρόσωπον [sc. θεοῦ] οἱ ἄγγελοι...βλέπουσι...κατὰ τὸ μ. τῆς οἰκείας τάξεως ἕκαστος Cyr.H.*catech*.7.11; **7.** εἰς μ. ἔχω *take into account*, Jo.Clim.*scal*.23(M.88.977B); **8.** πολλῷ τῷ μ. *far, a long way*, fig. and met. ἀρετὴν τοσαύτην [sc. ἔχειν] ὡς καὶ τὸ τῶν ἀνδρῶν γένος ...πολλῷ τῷ μ. κατόπιν ἀφιέναι Chrys.*sac*.6.12(p.166.7; 1.432E); τὴν θεότητα τοῦ Χριστοῦ...καὶ τὴν σάρκα, ψυχῆς καὶ σώματος πολλῷ τινι καὶ ἀπείρῳ μ. τιμαλφεστέραν Thdt.*eran*.2(4.109).

[*]**μετωνομασία, ἡ**, v. μετονομασία.

μετωνυμία, ἡ, *change of name*, Or.*Jo*.6.14(7; p.123.19; M.14.225B); Eus.*p.e*.11.6(514D; M.21.853C); Dion.Ar.*myst*.3(M.3.1033A); Anast.S.*qu.et resp*.51(M.89.612B).

μετωνυμικῶς, *by metonymy*, †Bas.*Is*.12(1.386C; M.30.137C); *ib*.270(585A; M.593B).

μέτωπον, τό, 1. *forehead*, lit. μὴ ἐπαισχυνθῶμεν τῷ σταυρῷ τοῦ Χριστοῦ· ἀλλὰ...φανερῶς ἐπὶ μετώπῳ, σφραγίζου Cyr.H.*catech*.4.14; τὸ τοῦ σταυροῦ προσκυνεῖτε ξύλον, εἰκόνας αὐτοῦ σκιαγραφοῦντες ἐν τῷ μ. Juln.Imp.ap.Cyr.*Juln*.6(6[2].194C); χρίσει...τὸ μ. αὐτῶν τῷ ἁγίῳ ἐλαίῳ *Const.App*.3.16.2; cf.Hipp.*trad.ap*.22.3(p.39); οὗτος ἡμῖν σημεῖον δέδοται ἐπὶ τοῦ μ. ὃν τρόπον τῷ Ἰσραὴλ ἡ περιτομή Jo.D.*f.o*.4.11(M.94.1129B); fig., of Church τὸ μ. [sc. τῆς ἐκκλησίας] ἀστροειδεῖ σφραγῖδι κεκοσμημένον Const.ap.Gel.Cyz.*h.e*.2.7.3(M.85.1232D); σταυρὸν...ἐπὶ τοῦ μ. τῆς ἐκκλησίας ἐκλάμποντα φαίνεσθαι Acac.Mel.*hom*.(p.91.26; M.77.1472A); **2.** *sense of shame* τῶν κακῶς παρατριψάντων ἑαυτῶν τὸ μ. Epiph.*haer*.69.59(p.207.4; M.42.296C); ἀποτριψάμενος τὸ μ. ἐν ἀναισχυντίᾳ *ib*.76.2(p.242.11; 517D).

***μετωποσκοπικός**, *by means of observing the forehead* μ. μαντεία Hipp.*haer*.4.15(p.49.11; M.16.3083A).

μέχρι, *until, as far as*; of place, *even to* ὅτε μ. γῆς πεφανέρωκεν ἑαυτὸν ὁ σωτὴρ Ath.*inc*.46.1(M.25.177C); *at* a certain point in thought or speech οὐ μ. τῶν παρόντων ἱστὰς τὰς ἀμοιβὰς Chrys.*hom.15.3 in Mt*.(7.189A); οὐ μὴν ἀφῆκεν αὐτοὺς πάλιν μ. τῶν σκυθρωπῶν μεῖναι *ib*.82.2(784E); ὁ ἔμπορος θέλει πλουτεῖν, ἀλλ' οὐ μ. τῆς διανοίας τὸ θέλειν ἵστησιν id.*hom.1.3 in Jo*.(8.5C); οὐ λέγει τοῦτο, ἀλλὰ ἵσταται μ. τοῦ ἐγκωμίου τῶν Ἑλλήνων id.*hom.5.5 in Rom*.(9.468A); of feelings, *towards* ἡ [sc. τῶν μακαρίων] μ. τῶν φιλτάτων τελεία διάθεσις Clem.*str*.7.11(p.46.5; M.9.488C); *against* μ. αὐτοῦ τοῦ θεοῦ ἀσεβεῖν *Hom.Clem*.2.22; of time, *during, in the interval of* μ. τοῦ εὔχεσθαι Barth.Edess.*Agar*.(M.104.1428B).

μή, as conjunction *unless* ἄλλως...ὑμᾶς οὐκ ἔνι σωθῆναι, μὴ ἰχθύες ἔχετε γενέσθαι καὶ διὰ θαλάσσης ἀπελθεῖν *Chron.Pasch*.p.395(M.92.1012A).

μηδαμινός, *good for nothing, worthless*, Chrys.*subintr*.8(1.240B); ἡμῶν τῶν μ. Alex.Sal.*Barn*.proem.3(p.437B); ἀνδρὶ...ταπεινῷ καὶ μ. Marc.Diac.*v.Porph*.101; of duties μὴ καταφρονήσωμεν [sc. τῶν μικρῶν] ὡς μ. Dor.*doct*.4.3(M.88.1656A).

§**Μηδικός**, *pertaining to Medea* φαρμάκοις...*M.* Geo.Pis.*carm*.2.23.

μηδοπότερος, = μηδέτερος, *neither of the two*, Jo.D.*haer*.12(M.94.685A).

***μηρεύς, ὁ**, v. *μιρεύς.

μήκοθεν or **μηκόθεν**, *far away*; **1.** as adv., *Chron.Pasch*.p.393(M.92.1009A); Gr.Mag.*dial*.(tr.Zach.)1.4(M.*PL*.77.167C); ἀπὸ μ. Epiph.*exp.fid*.23(p.524.12; M.42.829A); *Apophth.Patr*.(M.65.125B); **2.** as prep., c. genit., Marc.Diac.*v.Porph*.22; †Gregent.*disp*.(M.86.776B).

μῆκος, τό, *length,* in adv. usages ἐκ μήκους *at a distance,* Gr.Mag. *dial.*(tr.Zach.)4.11(M.*PL*.77.335C); ἀπὸ μήκους c. genit., *at a distance from,* Call.*v.Hyp*.(p.11).

***μηκυθμός, ὁ,** *braying,* Gr.Nyss.*v.Mos*.(M.44.421A).

μηκύνω, *lengthen, prolong*; hence *make tall, make to grow up,* Ath.*Ar*.2.21(M.26.192B); pass., *grow tall, grow up,* Serap.*ep.mon*.6 (M.40.932C).

μήλη, ἡ, *sharp instrument, knife,* Cyr.S.*v.Euthym*.60(p.84.12).

μηλοβοτέω, *graze sheep,* †Apoll.*met.Ps*.2:9(M.33.1316A, om. *Teub*., v. not.).

***μηλοβρωτέω,** *eat apples, Hymn.*(*AS* 1 p.577).

μηλοειδής, *like an apple,* met. βίον μ. *life on a bed of roses,* Gr. Nyss.*v.Mos*.(M.44.417C).

μῆλον, τό, *apple-tree*; fig., of Christ, ref. Cant.2:3, Gr.Nyss.*hom. 4 in Cant*.(M.44.844Aff.).

μηλοσσόος, *protecting sheep,* Nonn.*par.Jo*.10:9(M.43.833A).

μηλοσφαγία, ἡ, *sacrifice of sheep,* Cyr.*ador*.2(1.55E); id.*Ps*.34:28 (M.69.912D); id.*Mich*.57(3.449D).

***μηλόσφαγος,** *of slaughtered sheep, Orac.Sib*.8.492.

***μηλοφάγος,** *sheep-eating, who eats sheep, Orac.Sib*.11.111; *ib*.12. 11; of the Passover, a feast *when sheep are eaten,* Nonn.*par.Jo*. 19:31(M.43.904C).

***μηλωτάριος,** *of sheepskin* ἀπὸ ῥακίων τριχίνων καὶ μ. ἢ σεβεννίνων †Jo.D.*B.J*.18(M.96.1020A); neut. as subst., *sheepskin cloak* worn by monks, Esaias *or*.8(p.59); *Apophth.Patr*.(M.65.140B); Cyr.S.*v.Sab*. 13(p.96.14); †Jo.D.*B.J*.29(M.96.1133A).

μηλωτή, ἡ, *sheepskin,* hence *rough hairy cloak* worn by monks, Ath.*v.Anton*.91(M.26.972B); ἕκαστος αὐτῶν ἐχέτω μ. αἰγείαν εἰργασμένην, ἧς ἄνω μὴ ἐσθιέτωσαν. ἀπιόντες δὲ εἰς τὴν κοινωνίαν κατὰ... κυριακὴν...τὴν μ. ἀποτιθέσθωσαν, καὶ μετὰ κουκουλίου μόνου εἰσιέτωσαν Pall.*h.Laus*.32(p.89.10; M.34.1099D); τούτοις ἔστι καὶ μοναστήριον γυναικῶν...τὴν αὐτὴν ἔχον διατύπωσιν...ἐκτὸς τῆς μ. *ib*.33(p.96.8; 1105B); τὴν μ. ἔχουσιν οἱ πάντοτε τὴν νέκρωσιν τοῦ Ἰησοῦ ἐν τῷ σώματι περιφέροντες Evagr.Pont.*cap.pract*.A proem.(M.40.1221B); Isid.Pel.*epp*.1.427(M.78.420A); Gr.Mag.*dial*.(tr.Zach.)2.7(M.*PL*.66. 146C).

μηνίαμα, τό, *anger* αἱρετικῶν μ. Bas.*hom*.23.4(2.189B; M.31.600A).

§μηνιαστής, ὁ, *one who cherishes wrath* ὁ κατὰ τὸ φαινόμενον δοκῶν εἶναι πρᾶος, κατὰ δὲ τὴν ψυχὴν κινούμενος πρὸς θυμὸν...ὑποκριτὴς καὶ μ. Ath.*fr.Lc*.2:22f.(M.27.1396D); τοῦ κατ' ὀργὴν διακειμένου ἐπίμονον αὐτὴν ἔχοντος, ὃν καὶ μ. ἔθος καλεῖν Didym.*Ps*.4:5(M.39. 1168A); Max.*ascet*.32(M.90.937B).

***μήνιος, ὁ,** *honeycomb,* ‡Chrys.*pasch*.6.3(p.147.10; 8.268C).

***μήνισις, ἡ,** = μῆνις, *wrath, Pss.Sal*.2:25; Cyr.*Os*.43(3.74A).

μηνίσκος, ὁ, *neck-ornament,* Cyr.*hom.div*.19(M.77.1108B); ὁ... Σύμμαχος τοὺς μ. μανιάκας καλεῖ Thdt.*Is*.3:16(p.21.2; 2.194).

μήνυμα, τό, 1. *information, message, A.Pil*.B 4(p.296); **2.** *indication,* Bas.*Spir*.74(3.63A; M.32.208A); ref. Lc.2:14 ταῦτα τίνος μηνύματα, σαρκικῆς ἢ θεοπρεποῦς γεννήσεως; Cyr.*apol.orient*.1(p.34.23; 6^1.159C); τῆς...ἀπειρίας...διὰ σαρκὸς θεουργίας ἀνθρώποις παρέχειν ...μηνύματα Max.*ambig*.(M.91.1168A); Jo.VI CP *ep*.(M.96.1416A); **3.** *foreshadowing,* Clem.*str*.5.6(p.348.16; M.9.57C); τίνος ἡ σκηνοπηγία ...μ.; Meth.*res*.2.21(p.375.1; M.18.285C); τῶν προφητῶν τὰ μ. ‡Ath. *Apoll*.1.1(M.26.1093B); Antip.Bost.*Jo.Bapt*.6(M.85.1769A); **4.** plur., *directions, instructions* ὑπὸ νόμον γεγενῆσθαι γράφεται τῷ διὰ τῶν νομικῶν...βαδίσαι μ. Eust.*fr.in Pr*.8:22(M.18.680B); **5.** *meaning, significance* τῆς ὄψεως τὰ μ. Thdt.*h.e*.2.30.10(3.906); **6.** *title,* Chrysipp. *enc.in Mich*.(p.93.26).

***μηνύσιον, τό,** *indication,* Cyr.*ador*.11(1.403C).

μήνυσις, ἡ, *previous information, foreshadowing, A.Xanthipp*.4 (p.60.24); Cyr.*ador*.16(1.583C).

μηνυτής, ὁ, 1. *one who brings information, A.Pil*.B 4(p.296); of prophets, Euthal.Diac.*epp.Paul*.(M.85.773C); Thdt.*Cant*.8:9(2.160); of Jo. Bapt., Cosm.Ind.*top*.5(M.88.277B); **2.** of speech, *that which reveals* thought, Leo Mag.*ep*.2(p.45.9; M.*PL*.54.714A); hence of Son ὁ λόγος ὁ τοῦ πατρῴου μ. ἰδιώματος Clem.*str*.5.6(p.348.11; M.9. 57B).

***μηνυτικῶς,** *indicatively,* Max.*ambig*.(M.91.1244C).

***μηνύτρια, ἡ,** *revealer,* Agath.*v.Gr.Ill*.40.

μηνύω, 1. *disclose, reveal* διὰ Μωυσέως...μ. τὸ προφητικὸν πνεῦμα πῶς...ἐδημιούργησεν ὁ θεός Just.*1apol*.59.1(M.6.416C); τοῦτο προφήτου ἴδιον, τὸ τὴν ἀλήθειαν μ. *Hom.Clem*.2.6; by types, Iren.*haer*.4.31.1 (M.7.1069A); Clem.*str*.7.6(p.24.26; M.9.445A); **2.** *declare, announce* a visitor ἐμήνυσεν ἡμᾶς πρὸς τὴν δέσποιναν, καὶ εἰσήλθομεν πρὸς αὐτήν Marc.Diac.*v.Porph*.52; Jo.Mosch.*prat*.148(M.87.3012C); **3.** *inform* a person; pass., Thphn.*chron*.p.308(M.108.749B).

μήποτε, 1. as adv. = μήπω, *not yet* μετὰ πονηροῦ συνειδότος ζῶντες, κἂν μ. ἀποθάνωσιν, ἀποθανοῦνται πάντως Chrys.*hom.34.3 in Mt*.(7.393D); **2.** as conjunction; **a.** *whether* ἐφίσταμαι μ. εἷς... καταπέμπεται Or.*Jo*.2.31(25; p.88.11; M.14.168B); ἐφίστημι μ. ... ἐστίν Eus.*d.e*.7.3(p.345.28; M.22.564A); ἴδωμεν οὖν μ. καὶ σὺ τὰ... ἐκκαίοντα ποιεῖς Chrys.*hom.7.6 in 2Cor*.(10.488E); ἐννοῶν μ. ἀληθεῖς ὦσιν Max.*schol.e.h*.7.1.2(M.4.176D); **b.** *lest ever,* c. indic. φεῦγε τὴν ὑπερηφανίαν...μ. τὸν θεὸν ἀντιτασσόμενον ἕξεις Nil.*paraen*.128(M.79. 1261A).

μήπως or **μή πως, 1.** *whether* ἐφίστημι δὲ μ. τοὺς τρεῖς τριδύμους ἐγέννησεν Or.*sel.in Gen*.11:26(M.12.112B); ἐπιχειρητέον γὰρ μή πως τὸ ψεῦδος ἰσχύσωμεν...σβέσαι Meth.*symp*.8.14(p.102.16; μήπως M.18. 165B); **2.** *lest in any way* τοὺς λιμένας...τηρεῖσθαι μ. ἐπανέλθωσιν Ath. *h.Ar*.19(p.192.29; M.25.716B); τὸ λεγόμενον ἐξετάσωμεν μ. ... καινότερον ἐπενόησαν λεξείδιον id.*Ar*.3.59(M.26.448A).

***Μηρινθιανοί, οἱ,** *followers of Cerinthus* Κηρινθιανοί, οἱ καὶ *M*. Epiph.*anac*.28(p.236.6; M.41.284B); id.*haer*.28.8(p.320.12; M.41.388A).

***μηρόκλαστος,** *with a broken thigh, Chron.Pasch*.p.270(M.92. 665B).

μήρυγμα, τό, v. μήρυμα.

μηρυκάζω (μαρυκάζω), *chew the cud, ruminate*; met., Clem.*paed*. 3.11(p.278.15; M.8.653A) cit. s. διχηλέω; μαρυκάζει Cyr.*Juln*.9(6^2. 317A,B).

***μηρύκησις, ἡ,** *cud-chewing,* Proc.G.*Ex*.9:3(M.87.557A).

μηρυκίζ-ω, = μηρυκάζω, Bas.*hex*.7.2(1.64E; M.29.152C); †Bas. *hom.in Ps*.115(1.375D; M.30.113A); fig. ὀδόντες εἰσὶ τῆς ἐκκλησίας οἱ τὴν ἀκατέργαστον τῶν θείων λογίων πόαν λεπτοποιοῦντες ἡμῖν καὶ ~οντες Gr.Nyss.*hom.7 in Cant*.(M.44.925D).

μηρυκισμός, ὁ, *chewing the cud,* Clem.*str*.7.18(p.77.5; M.9.556A) cit. s. διχηλέω; τὸ μ. ἔχον ‡Just.*qu.et resp*.35(M.6.1281A); Cyr.*ador*.8 (1.253C).

μήρυμα (μήρυγμα), τό, *that which is drawn out*; **1.** *skein*; fig. ἀπαράλλακτον τὸ μήρυγμα τοῦ υἱοῦ καὶ τοῦ ἁγίου πνεύματος Didym. *Trin*.2.5(M.39.504A); **2.** of time, *extent,* Synes.*hymn*.3.498(p.21; M. 66.1600).

***μητατεύω (*μητεύω, *μιτατεύω),** (cf. Lat. *metatum*) *mark off,* hence *requisition* buildings, Marc.Diac.*v.Porph*.63; μητευέτω οἶκον Ath.Scholast.*coll*.20.5(p.176); τὰς συναγωγὰς [sc. τῶν Ἰουδαίων]... μὴ μιτατεύεσθαι Phot.*nomoc*.12.2(M.104.869D).

μήτειρα, ἡ, = μήτηρ: μ. γαῖα Gr.Naz.*carm*.1.2.1.117(M.37.531A); μάτειρα φύσις Synes.*hymn*.3.334(p.16; M.66.1598).

***μητεύω,** v. *μητατεύω.

μήτηρ, ἡ, *mother*; **1.** of BMV; **a.** partic. ref. Christ's human nature, ref. Jo.2:1 ἐλεγκτέον δὲ καὶ Μανιχαίους λέγοντας μὴ εἶναι τὴν Μαρίαν Ἰησοῦ μ., τοῦ εὐαγγελιστοῦ μαρτυροῦντος ὅτι Ἰησοῦς μ. εἶχεν Or.*fr.28 in Jo*.(p.505.19); ὅτε ἠθέλησεν ὁ πατὴρ ὑπὲρ πάντων λύτρα δοθῆναι,...τότε δὴ ὁ λόγος...ἔλαβε τὴν ἀπὸ γῆς σάρκα, Μαρίαν ἀντὶ τῆς ἀνεργάστου γῆς ἐσχηκὼς μ. τοῦ σώματος Ath.*Ar*.2.7(M.26. 161B); αὐτὸς οὖν μ. ἔχει μόνον ἐπὶ γῆς, καὶ ἡμεῖς πατέρα μόνον ἔχομεν ἐν οὐρανῷ id.*inc.et c.Ar*.8(M.26.996A); ref. separation of the two natures δύο υἱοὺς ἕνα μὲν τὸν ἐκ θεοῦ καὶ πατρός, δεύτερον δὲ τὸν ἐκ μ., ἀλλ' οὐχὶ ἕνα καὶ τὸν αὐτόν Gr.Naz.*ep*.101(M.37.180A); **b.** partic. ref. title Mother of God χωρὶς...γάμου σύλληψις...καὶ θεοῦ μ. κόρη Const.*or.s.c*.11(p.168.25; M.20.1265A); Ephr.3.526E; ὁ...εὔσπλαγχνος θεὸς τῇ...πρεσβείᾳ τῆς ἀχράντου αὐτοῦ μ. *Chron.Pasch*.p.392(M.92. 1005A); ἡ ἁγία ἄμωμος τοῦ θεοῦ μ. καὶ παρθένος *Dorm.BMV* 26(p.103); κυρία ὄντως γέγονε πάντων τῶν ποιημάτων, τοῦ δημιουργοῦ χρηματίσασα μ. Jo.D.*f.o*.4.14(M.94.1157B); ἡ τοῦ μόνου ἀγαθοῦ θεοῦ μ. id. *hom*.8.2(M.96.701B); id.*carm.dorm.BMV* 248(p.232; M.96.1368A); **c.** as source of spiritual life, as antitype of Eve ἀληθῶς ἀπὸ Μαρίας αὐτὴ ἡ ζωὴ τῷ κόσμῳ γεγέννηται, ἵνα ζῶντα γεννήσῃ καὶ γένηται ἡ Μαρία μ. ζώντων Epiph.*ep.Arab*.ap.*haer*.78.18(p.468.28; M.42. 728C); **d.** as mother of the apostles εἶπεν Ἰωάννης, 'εὗρον ὄχλον περὶ τὴν μητέρα ἡμῶν Μαρίαν' Jo.Thess.*dorm.BMV* A 8(p.388.8); **e.** title included in various forms of address ἡ θεία καὶ πανύμνητος παρθενικὴ μ. Thdot.Anc.*hom.BMV et Sym*.13(M.77.1409A); μῆτερ μητέρων *Pers*.(p.17.16; M.10.108A); ζωῆς μ. Jo.Mon.*hymn.Bas*.9 (M.96.1376D); μῆτερ ἄνανδρε, ἡ ἐν μητράσι μόνη ἁγνεύουσα Thdr. Stud.*nativ.BMV* 7(M.96.692A); **2.** mother of the faithful; **a.** of Church; **i.** in gen., cf.Iren.*haer*.3.24.1(M.7.966C) cit. s. ἐκκλησία; μετ' εἰρήνης ἐχώρησαν πρὸς θεόν, μὴ καταλιπόντες πόνον τῇ μητρὶ μηδὲ στάσιν...τοῖς ἀδελφοῖς *Ep.Lugd*.ap.Eus.*h.e*.5.2.7(M.20.436B); ἡ μ. προσάγεται τὰ παιδία καὶ ἡμεῖς ζητοῦμεν τὴν μ., τὴν ἐκκλησίαν Clem.*paed*.1.5(p.102.12f.; M.8.273C); *ib*.3.12(p.290.5; 677B); πατρὸς μὲν ἀκούομεν λόγους, τῆς γραφῆς· μ. δὲ τὰς ἀγράφους παραδόσεις τῆς ἐκκλησίας...ἔστι δὲ καὶ τοὺς φυσικοὺς νοεῖν πατέρας, ἢ καὶ τοὺς πνευματικοὺς νοεῖν διδασκάλους. καὶ γὰρ τούτων μ. ἡ ἐκκλησία Or.*fr.in Pr.*1:8(M.17.157A); ὥσπερ ἐξ ἀποικίας ἐπανιόντες τὴν αὐτῶν ἀπελάμβανον πατρίδα, καὶ τὴν μ., τὴν ἐκκλησίαν, ἐπεγίνωσκον Eus.*v.C.*3.66(p.113.22; M.20.1144B); ἡ καθολικὴ μ. ἡμῶν καὶ ἀποστολικὴ ἐκκλησία ‡Ath.*interpr.*(p.66.32; M.26.1232C); †Bas.*ep.*41.1 (p.284.21; M.32.345A); μιᾶς μ. γεγόνατε υἱοὶ καὶ θυγατέρες Cyr.H. *procatech.*13; id.*catech.*18.26; Epiph.*exp.fid.*18(p.519.13; M.42.817C); ἡ ἐκκλησία μ. ἐστὶ τῶν οἰκείων τέκνων, καὶ τούτους δεχομένη, καὶ τοῖς ξένοις κόλπους ἐφαπλοῦσα Chrys.*pan.Phoc.*2(2.707C); Cyr.*Is.*5.2(2.758A); *ib.*(768E); ζωοτόκος μ. τῶν πιστῶν πολύφατε μ. Χριστοῦ ἐκκλησία, ἡ σύζυγος τοῦ πνευματικοῦ Ἀδὰμ τοῦ θεοῦ Anast.S.*hex.*12 (M.89.1072A); **ii.** ref. Is.54:1 ἔστι δὲ μ. ἡμῶν καὶ ἡ ἐκκλησία ἣν τῷ πνεύματι τῷ ἁγίῳ ἑαυτῷ ὁ θεὸς καὶ πατὴρ ἡρμόσατο εἰς γυναῖκα· τίκτει γὰρ ἀεὶ δι' αὐτῆς ἑαυτῷ υἱοὺς καὶ θυγατέρας· καὶ ἐπὶ τοῖς πεπαιδευμένοις τὴν τοῦ θεοῦ γνῶσιν...εὐφραίνεται καὶ ὁ πατὴρ ἡμῶν θεός, καὶ ἡ μ. ἡ ἐκκλησία Or.*exp.in Pr.*17:21(M.17.201B); ἡ γεννήσασα καὶ γεννῶσα τὸν ἀρρενωπὸν ἐν ταῖς καρδίαις τῶν πιστευόντων λόγον ...ἡ μ. ἡμῶν ἐστιν...ἡ ἐκκλησία Meth.*symp.*8.11(p.93.11; M.18.133C); ἡ ἐκκλησία...ὠδίνουσα καὶ ἀναγεννῶσα τοὺς ψυχικοὺς εἰς πνευματικούς, καθ' ὃν λόγον καὶ μ. ἐστίν *ib.*8.6(p.88.11; 148B); **iii.** as virgin-mother ἐνεγίνετο πολλὴ χαρὰ τῇ παρθένῳ μ. οὓς ὡς νεκροὺς ἐξέτρωσε, τούτους ζῶντας ἀπολαμβανούσῃ *Ep.Lugd.*ap.Eus.*h.e.*5.1.45(M.20.425B); μία δὲ μόνη γίνεται μ. παρθένος· ἐκκλησίαν ἐμοὶ φίλον αὐτὴν καλεῖν Clem.*paed.*1.6(p.115.12; M.8.300B); **b.** of heavenly Jerusalem καταλείπει τὸν πατέρα καὶ τὴν μ. τὴν ἄνω Ἱερουσαλήμ, καὶ ἔρχεται εἰς τὸν περίγειον τόπον καί φησιν [Jer.12:7] Or.*hom.10.7 in Jer.*(p.77.13; M.13.565C); id.*Ps.*44:10(p.42) cit. s. νύμφη; exeg. Lev.21:11, cf. *pater omnium verus dicitur deus. matrem autem apostolus Jerusalem dicit esse coelestem...'in matre contaminamur', si credentes deo...ecclesiam laedimus*, id.*hom.12.4 in Lev.*(p.461.5; M.12.539C); εἰπὼν γάρ, ἡ ἄνω Ἱερουσαλὴμ μ. ἡμῶν ἐστι, καὶ τὴν ἐκκλησίαν οὕτω καλέσας Chrys.*comm.in Gal.*4:26(10.710E); **c.** of Church at Jerusalem τῆς...μ. ἁπασῶν τῶν ἐκκλησιῶν CCP(382)*ep.*ap.Thdt.*h.e.*5.9.17 (3.1033); *Lit.Jac.*(p.206.27); **d.** of font in baptism ἔστιν ἡ κολυμβήθρα τῆς τριάδος, ἐργαστήριον πρὸς σωτηρίαν πιστῶν πάντων ἀνθρώπων· καὶ τοὺς λουομένους ἐν αὐτῇ, τοῦ δήγματος ἀπαλλάττει τοῦ ὄφεως, καὶ μ. πάντων γίνεται, τῷ ἁγίῳ πνεύματι μένουσα παρθένος Didym.*Trin.*2.13(M.39.692A); ref. Ps.26:10 μ. τὴν κολυμβήθραν, πατέρα τὸν ὕψιστον ἀδελφὸν τὸν δι' ἡμᾶς βαπτισθέντα σωτῆρα *ib.* (692B); Thdt.*Cant.*6:7(2.129); Dion.Ar.*e.h.*2.2.7(M.3.396C); of water of baptism καὶ τάφος ὑμῖν ἐγίνετο καὶ μ. Cyr.H.*catech.*20.4; **e.** of saving faith, Polyc.*ep.*3.3; *M.Just.*4.8(M.6.1569B); of Christian religion ἐξ ἑνὸς φύντες πατρὸς ἑνός τε θεοῦ οἷα παῖδες καὶ μητρὸς μιᾶς, τῆς ἀληθοῦς εὐσεβείας Eus.*l.C.*16(p.250.15; M.20.1424D); of knowledge of God, ref. Ex.20:6 πατέρα...τὸν θεὸν λέγει σαφῶς...μ. δὲ οὐχί, ὥς τινες, ἡ οὐσία ἐξ ἧς γεγόναμεν, οὐδ' ὡς ἕτεροι ἐκδεδώκασιν, ἡ ἐκκλησία, ἀλλ' ἡ θεία γνῶσις καὶ ἡ σοφία Clem.*str.*6.16(p.507.3; M.9.377A); of word of God ὁ λόγος τὰ πάντα τῷ νηπίῳ, καὶ πατὴρ καὶ μ. καὶ παιδαγωγὸς καὶ τροφεύς id.*paed.*1.6(p.115.21; M.8.301A); of wisdom of God as source of prophetic inspiration, ref. Jer.15:10 οὐ πρὸς τὴν μ. τὴν σωματικήν, ἀλλὰ πρὸς τὴν μ. τὴν γεννῶσαν προφήτας Or.*hom.14.5 in Jer.*(p.110.10; M.13.409B); **3.** of a spiritual mother πόσαι γυναῖκες ἐμακάρισαν τὴν ἁγίαν παρθένον ἐκείνην...καὶ ηὔξαντο τοιαῦται γενέσθαι μ. ... ἔξεστιν οὐ γυναιξὶ μόνον, ἀλλὰ καὶ ἀνδράσιν ἐπὶ τῆς τοιαύτης γενέσθαι τάξεως...τοῦτο γὰρ πολλῷ μᾶλλον μ. ποιεῖ, ἢ αἱ ὠδῖνες ἐκεῖναι Chrys.*hom.44.2 in Mt.*(7.469C); **4.** of an abbess τῇ μ. τὴν συνήθη διὰ τῶν χειρῶν ὑπηρεσίαν ἐπλήρωσεν Gr.Nyss. *v.Macr.*(p.405.19; M.46.992B); τῇ κατὰ πίστιν μ. πειθαρχεῖν ‡Ath. *v.Syncl.*101(M.28.1549C); τῶν προαναπαυσαμένων ὁσίων μ. καὶ διδασκάλων Serg.*Olymp.*1(p.44.8); κἀγὼ ἡ ἁμαρτωλὸς μ. ὑμῶν Σεργία *ib.* 15(p.51.19); title of nuns, Gr.Mag.*dial.*(tr.Zach.)4.13(M.*PL.*77.342B); **5.** fig. and met., as source ἐκ τῆς πίστεως γεννᾶται ἐγκράτεια, ἐκ τῆς ἐγκρατείας ἁπλότης...ὅταν οὖν τὰ ἔργα τῆς μ. αὐτῶν πάντα ποιήσῃς, δύνασαι ζῆσαι Herm.*vis.*3.8.5; μεγίστη δὲ ἀρετῶν μ. ἡ πίστις Clem.*str.*2.5(p.125.19; M.8.957A); ref. Gen.29:31 κατὰ τὸν πνευματικὸν νόμον ψυχῆς ἀνοίγει [sc. ὁ θεός] μήτραν ἵνα γεννήσῃ θεοῦ λόγον ἡ ἐσομένη αὐτοῦ μ. Or.*sel.in Gen.*(M.12.124C); εὐσεβείας, ἣν μ. φασὶ τῶν ἀρετῶν Gr.Thaum.*pan.Or.*12(p.28.16; M.10.1085C); τὴν πάντων τῶν ἀγαθῶν μ. νηστείαν Cyr.*hom.pasch.*4(5².43C); μ. εὐεργεσίας ἡ ὑπὸ τοῦ θεοῦ ἐπιφερομένη παιδεία Thdt.*Zach.*9:7(2.1632); προσεδρία καὶ σχολὴ τῆς προσευχῆς καὶ τῶν θείων γραφῶν μ. ὑπάρχει πασῶν τῶν ἀρετῶν Anast. S.*synax.*(M.89.825A); of evil things πλεονεξίαν...εἰδωλολατρίας μ. Evagr.Pont.*cap.pract.*A proem.(M.40.1221B); πλεονεξία καὶ ἡ ταύτης μ. ἀσπλαγχνία Marc.Er.*opusc.*3.5(M.65.972C); **6.** Gnost., of Achamoth ταύτην τὴν Μ. καὶ Ὀγδοάδα καλοῦσι, καὶ Σοφίαν καὶ Γῆν Iren. *haer.*1.5.3(M.7.496B); τὸν μὲν Δημιουργὸν υἱὸν τῆς Μ. αὐτῶν λέγουσι *ib.*1.5.4(497B); Σοφία, ἥτις ἐστὶ 'μ. πάντων τῶν ζώντων' Hipp.*haer.*6.34(p.163.1; M.16.3240B); ὁ Ἰησοῦς...ἔχει τὴν...γένεσιν ἀπὸ τῆς μ. τῶν ὅλων *ib.*6.60(p.182.12; 3272B); ἡ μ. αὖθις τὸν τῆς οἰκονομίας προηγάγετο ἄρχοντα εἰς τύπον τοῦ φυγόντος Clem.*exc.Thdot.*33(p.117.26; M.9.676B); ἡ μ. προβαλοῦσα τὸν Χριστὸν ὁλόκληρον καὶ ὑπ' αὐτοῦ καταλειφθεῖσα *ib.*39(p.119.7; 677B); ὃν γεννᾷ ἡ μ. εἰς θάνατον ἄγεται καὶ εἰς κόσμον, ὃν δὲ ἀναγεννᾷ Χριστός, εἰς ζωὴν μετατίθεται *ib.*80(p.131.24; 696A); ἐδόξασαν...σὺν τῷ ζῶντι πνεύματι τὸν πατέρα τῆς ἀληθείας καὶ τὴν μ. τῆς σοφίας *A.Thom.*A 7(p.110.20); ἐλθὲ ἡ μ. ἡ εὔσπλαγχνος...ἡ μ. τῶν ἑπτὰ οἴκων *ib.*27(p.142.15,17); ὑμνοῦμεν σὲ καὶ τὸν ἀόρατόν σου πατέρα καὶ τὸ ἅγιόν σου πνεῦμα καὶ τὴν μ. πασῶν κτίσεων *ib.*39(p.157.17); **7.** Manich. τὸν ἀγαθὸν πατέρα...προβάλλειν ἐξ αὐτοῦ δύναμιν, λεγομένην μ. τῆς ζωῆς, καὶ αὐτὴν προβεβληκέναι τὸν πρῶτον ἄνθρωπον τὰ πέντε στοιχεῖα Hegem.*Arch.*7(p.10.6; M.10.1437A); in gospel of Hebrews, of H. Ghost as mother of Christ, commented ref.Mt.12:50 εἰ ὁ ποιῶν τὸ θέλημα τοῦ πατρὸς...μ. ἐστίν,...οὐδὲν ἄτοπον ἔσται τὸ πνεῦμα τὸ ἅγιον εἶναι μ. Or.*Jo.*2.12(6; p.67.20; M.14.132C).

μήτρα, ἡ, *womb*, fig. μήτρας δίκην, ἐν τῷ δοχείῳ τῆς ψυχῆς τὸ θέλημα τελεσφορήσαντες...τοῦ λόγου Meth.*symp.*3.8(p.37.14; M.18.76A); οἱ πεπλανημένοι ἀπὸ μ. τῆς θείας κολυμβήθρας ‡Jo.D.*ep.Thphl.*15(M.95.365A); name of Gnost. aeon, Iren.*haer.*1.1.1(M.7.445B); Epiph.*haer.*25.5(p.273.1; M.41.328B).

***μητράνοικτος,** *at the opening of the womb*, ‡Epiph.*hom.*2(M.43.444B).

μητρικός, 1. *of a mother*, ref. BMV δέησις μ. πρὸς υἱόν Ephr.3.533B; μ. σου πρεσβείαις Jo.Mon.*hymn.Bas.*(M.96.1377C); ‡Meth. *Sym.et Ann.*3(M.18.356A); **2.** *motherly* μ. σπλάγχνα ἔχοντες καὶ πολλὰ περὶ αὐτῶν [sc. those who refused martyrdom] ἐγχέοντες δάκρυα πρὸς τὸν πατέρα *Ep.Lugd.*ap.Eus.*h.e.*5.2.6(M.20.436B); **3.** name of Gnost. aeon, Iren.*haer.*1.1.2(M.7.449B); μ. ἀγγέλων Hipp.*haer.*5.26(p.127.12; M.16.3194D).

μητρικῶς, *like a mother*, ‡Jo.D.*hom.*5(M.96.653C).

***μητρογαμέω,** *marry* one's *mother*, Eus.*p.e.*1.4(11B; M.21.40A); Gr.Nyss.*fat.*(M.45.169B); ‡Caes.Naz.*dial.*109(M.38.980).

μητρογαμία, ἡ, *marriage with* one's *mother*, Eus.*p.e.*7.2(301A; M.21.512A); id.*d.e.*1.2(p.9.32; M.22.25D); Chrys.*hom.5.4 in Tit.*(11.762B).

***μητροείδωλον, τό,** *image of a mother*; ref. Mother of the gods, Thdr.Stud.*cant.*12.5(p.363); cf.Gr.Nyss.*Thdr.*(M.46.744A).

***μητρόθεος, ἡ,** *mother of God*, Andr.Cr.*or.*12(M.97.1064C); *Hymn.* (*AS* I p.532).

μητροκοίτης, ὁ, *incestuous person*, *Apoc.Esd.*(p.28).

μητροκωμία, ἡ, *mother-village, chief village of a district*, Epiph. *anac.*58(p.213.9; M.41.849A); id.*exp.fid.*11(p.511.11; M.42.801B).

***μητρολέτης, ὁ,** *murderer of* one's *mother, matricide*, *Orac.Sib.*5.386.

μητρομανία, ἡ, *hysteria*, *T.Sal.*18.33(M.122.1345B); Philost.*h.e.*4.7 (M.65.520C).

***μητρόμοιος,** *like that of* one's *mother* μ. σώματι Thdr.Stud. *nativ.BMV* 7(M.96.692B).

***μητρομοιώς,** *through likeness to* one's *mother* ἐκ τῆς μητρὸς περιγραπτός, ἢ εἰκονιζόμενος [sc. Christ] μ. Thdr.Stud.*epp.*2.156(M.99.1488B).

***μητρόνυμφος,** *betrothed and mother*; of BMV, Ephr.3.534F.

***μητροπάρθενος,** *of a virgin-mother*, Ephr.3.534F; Jo.D.*carm. pent.*121(p.217; M.96.840A); as subst., Thdot.Anc.*hom.BMV et Sym.*4(M.77.1396A).

μητροπάτωρ, epithet of Valent. demiurge, as proceeding only from his mother Achamoth, Iren.*haer.*1.5.1(M.7.492B).

μητρόπολις, ἡ, 1. *capital city, chief city*; of Jerusalem, Or.*fr.58 in Jer.*(p.227.11; M.13.584A); of Caesarea, Gr.Naz.*or.*43.13(M.36.512A); of Antioch, Chrys.*stat.*17.2(2.175D); fig., of the heavenly Jerusalem, Gr.Naz.*or.*45.23(M.36.656A); of a person ἀκρόπολις δὲ ἀνδρείας, μ. δὲ δικαιοσύνης Isid.Pel.*epp.*2.151(M.78.605A); **2.** *metropolis, chief see of a province* ἐπειδὴ συνήθεια κεκράτηκε καὶ παράδοσις ἀρχαία, ὥστε τὸν ἐν Αἰλίᾳ ἐπίσκοπον τιμᾶσθαι, ἐχέτω τὴν ἀκολουθίαν τῆς τιμῆς, τῇ μ. [sc. Caesarea] σωζομένου τοῦ οἰκείου ἀξιώματος CNic.(325)*can.*7; τοὺς καθ' ἑκάστην ἐπαρχίαν ἐπισκόπους εἰδέναι χρή, τὸν ἐν τῇ μ. προεστῶτα ἐπίσκοπον καὶ τὴν φροντίδα ἀναδέχεσθαι πάσης τῆς ἐπαρχίας...ὅθεν ἔδοξε καὶ τῇ τιμῇ προηγεῖσθαι αὐτόν, μηδέν τε πράττειν περιττὸν τοὺς λοίπους ἐπισκόπους ἄνευ αὐτοῦ CAnt.(341)*can.*9; μὴ...δίχα γνώμης σου τοῦ τῆς μ. ἐπισκόπου ὅρον τινὰ ἐκφέρειν Arsen.Hyps.ap.Ath.*apol.sec.*69(p.147.19; M.25.372B); Gr.Nyss.*ep.*1 (p.3.3; M.46.1001B); τῆς πατρίδος ἡμῶν εἰς δύο διαιρεθείσης ἡγεμονίας καὶ μ. Gr.Naz.*or.*43.58(M.36.572A); εἰ μακρὰν τῶν Ἀντιοχείων μητροπόλεως ἡ πόλις...ἀπῴκισται, τινὰς τῶν ἀστυγειτόνων...ἐπισκόπων ἀκοῦσαι τῆς ὑποθέσεως· ὑφορᾶται γὰρ τὸν...ἐπίσκοπον τῆς μ. Procl.CP *ep.*(p.68.10; M.65.881D).

μητροπολίτης, ὁ, 1. *citizen of a metropolis* ὁ ἅγιος τοῦ θεοῦ, καὶ τῆς ἄνω Ἱερουσαλὴμ ὄντως μ. Gr.Naz.*or*.43.59(M.36.572C); **2.** *metropolitan* (bishop) τὸ κῦρος τῶν γινομένων δίδοσθαι καθ' ἑκάστην ἐπαρχίαν τῷ μ. CNic.(325)*can*.4; εἴ τις χωρὶς γνώμης τοῦ μ. γένοιτο ἐπίσκοπος...μὴ δεῖν εἶναι ἐπίσκοπον *ib*.6; CLaod.*can*.12; μὴ εἴπῃς· ἐπίσκοπος βαπτισάτω με, καὶ οὗτος μ. ἢ Ἱεροσολυμίτης (οὐ γὰρ τόπων ἡ χάρις, ἀλλὰ τοῦ πνεύματος) Gr.Naz.*or*.40.26(M.36.396B); ἡμεῖς δέ ἐσμεν τεσσαράκοντα ἐκ διαφόρων ἐπαρχιῶν ἐν οἷς ἐσμεν καὶ ἑπτὰ μ. Pall.*v.Chrys*.8(p.48.20; M.47.29); as adj. τούτων τῶν τόπων [sc. Antioch and Alexandria] τῷ σῷ δικαίῳ ὑπαχθέντων, πάντας τοὺς μ. ἐπισκόπους τῆς ἰδίας τιμῆς στερηθῆναι Leo Mag.*ep*.106(p.56.39; M.*PL*.54.1004B).

***μητροπολῖτις,** *metropolitan* μ. ἐκκλησίαν Synes.*ep*.67(M.66.1417A).

***μητροπρεπῶς,** *in a manner befitting a mother*, Thdr.Stud.*nativ. BMV* 7(M.96.689A); ‡Gr.Naz.*Chr.pat*.proem.9(M.38.134A).

***μητρότης, ἡ,** *motherhood*, ‡Just.*qu.et resp*.136(M.6.1389A).

μητρῷος, *of a mother* τὰ μ. τῆς πόλεως...δίκαια Synes.*ep*.66(M.66.1409B).

μηχανάομαι, 1. *construct, prepare* ἐπεὶ δὴ σώματι κοσμικῷ πλησιάζειν...ἔμελλεν...νόθην τινὰ γένεσιν ἑαυτοῦ ἐμηχανήσατο Const. *or.s.c*.11(p.168.23; M.20.1265A); τὴν ἔνδειαν τῶν ἀναγκαίων γυμνάσιον ἡμῖν τῆς διανοίας ἐμηχανήσατο †Bas.*Is*.6(1.382B; M.30.128C); τὴν κοινὴν ἁπάντων ἀνθρώπων ἀνάστασιν μ. Thdt.*Phil*.3:10(3.463); **2.** *contrive, plot*, c. κατά and genit., *M.Polyc*.3.1; Meth.*res*.1.30(p.262.1; M.41.1140B); μ. κατὰ τῆς ἀληθείας Ath.*ep.Aeg.Lib*.8(M.25.556A); c. πρός and acc., Meth.*symp*.11(p.140.14; M.18.220B); c. infin., Gr.Thaum.*pan.Or*.6(p.15.5; M.10.1069A); *Hom.Clem*.3.2; pass., *be plotted against*, Thphn.*chron*.p.126(M.108.349B).

μηχανεύω, = μηχανάομαι 2, abs., Or.*Ps*.72:10(p.95).

μηχανή, ἡ, *contrivance, machine*; in form μηχανίη *engine of war*, *Orac.Sib*.8.25,119; *crane*, fig. ἀναφερόμενοι εἰς τὰ ὕψη διὰ τῆς μ. Ἰησοῦ Χριστοῦ, ὅς ἐστιν σταυρός, σχοινίῳ χρώμενοι τῷ πνεύματι ἁγίῳ· ἡ δὲ πίστις ὑμῶν ἀναγωγεὺς ὑμῶν Ign.*Eph*.9.1; μ. δι' ἧς οἱ εἰς τὴν οἰκοδομὴν εὐθετοῦντες τῆς ἐκκλησίας κάτωθεν, λίθου τετραγώνου δίκην, ἀνέλκονται ἐναρμοσθησόμενοι τῷ θείῳ λόγῳ Meth.*Porph*.1(p.504.25; M.18.400C); of a dredger or water-wheel, fig. (Manich.) μ. ... ἔχουσαν δώδεκα κάδους ἥτις...ἀνιμᾶται τῶν θνησκόντων τὰς ψυχάς Hegem.*Arch*.8(p.12.14; M.10.1440B); of a mill, *ib*.10(p.17.5; 1444B).

μηχάνημα, τό, 1. *mechanical device*; of material equipment of a church, Isid.Pel.*epp*.1.37(M.78.205A); of a spider's web μ. τῆς λεπτουργίας Geo.Pis.*hex*.1175(M.92.1525A); **2.** *engine of war*, fig. Ἰουδαίων...πολλὰ τῇ τῆς ἐκκλησίας ἀσφαλείᾳ προσαγόντων μ. Chrys. *hom.1.3 in Ac.princ*.(3.101D).

[*]**μηχανίη, ἡ,** v. μηχανή.

μηχανοποιΐα, ἡ, *construction of machines*; iron., of Saturninus' account of creation of man, Epiph.*haer*.23.4(p.252.22; M.41.304A).

***μηχανουργέω,** *plot*, Thdr.Stud.*epp*.2.58(M.99.1272C).

μηχανουργία, ἡ, *craftsmanship*, of God, Geo.Pis.*hex*.1199(M.92.1527A); of demons, ‡Jo.D.*Artem*.33(M.96.1282C).

μηχανουργός, ὁ, *craftsman*; of God, Geo.Pis.*hex*.159(M.92.1444A).

***μιαιβαδία, ἡ,** *evil way of life*, ‡Caes.Naz.*dial*.112(M.38.992).

***μιαιβιόω,** *lead an evil life*, ‡Caes.Naz.*dial*.109(M.38.981).

μιαιγαμία, ἡ, *unlawful marriage*, ‡Caes.Naz.*dial*.48(M.38.920); *ib*.110(985).

***μιαιρεύς, ὁ,** v. *μιερεύς.

***μιαιφθορέω,** *pollute*, ‡Caes.Naz.*dial*.109(M.38.981).

μιαιφονία, ἡ, 1. *bloodthirstiness, murderous intent* τὴν κατὰ Χριστοῦ μ. Hipp.*fr.1 in Pr*.(p.157.1; M.10.616D); Vict.*Mc*.7:37(p.339.29); **2.** *murder*, Isid.Pel.*epp*.1.198(M.78.309B); τὴν τοῦ βαπτιστοῦ μ. *ib*. 1.233(328A); Cyr.*Jon*.9(3.374B); **3.** *blood-guiltiness* ἡ τῶν Ἰουδαίων κατὰ τῶν ἁγίων τοῦ θεοῦ μ. Gr.Nyss.*or.catech*.29(p.109.7; M. om.); Thdt.*Is*.1:15(p.8.20; 1.177).

μίανσις, ἡ, *defilement*; of marriage opp. virginity, *M.Ner.et Ach*. 5(p.4.13).

***μιαντικός,** *defiling*, ‡Just.*qu.et resp*.28(M.6.1277A).

***μιαρόθρησκος,** *worshipping abominable deities*, Eudoc.*Cypr*.2. 274(M.85.856C).

***μιαρορρήμων, ὁ,** *one who uses foul language*, Nil.*epp*.1.147(M.79. 144C).

μιαρός, *defiled, polluted, abominable*, of antichrist εἶτα ἐντάλματα ὁ μ. πέμψει κατὰ πᾶσαν ἐπαρχίαν...δεῦτε πάντες εἰς προσκύνησιν...ἡ δὲ σφραγὶς αὐτοῦ...χξϛ'...οὐδὲ ἀκριβῶς ἐπίσταμαι τοῦτο...ἀλλὰ λέγομεν ἴσως γράφειν τὴν αὐτὴν σφραγῖδα *ΑΡΝΟΥΜΕ*, ἐπειδὴ καὶ πρώην... ὁ ἀντίδικος ἐχθρός...τοῖς μάρτυσι τοῦ Χριστοῦ προέτρεπον οἱ ἄνομοι ἄρνησαι, φησίν ‡Hipp.*consumm*.28(p.300.31; M.10.932A); τοῦ μ. ὀνόματος τοῦ ἀντιχρίστου Andr.Caes.*Apoc*.38 tit.(M.106.340B); comp., Isid.Pel.*epp*.2.37(M.78.481A); as subst., *abomination*, of a heathen temple, *Const.App*.2.61.1.

μιαρότης, ἡ, *foulness*, *A.Thom*.A 98(p.211.3).

***μιαρουργία, ἡ,** *foul deed*, Bas.Sel.*v.Thecl*.1(M.85.540C).

***μιαρουργός,** *sacrilegious* τῶν μ. αὐτῶν [sc. Λογγοβάρδων] ἱερέων Gr.Mag.*dial*.(tr.Zach.)3.28(M.*PL*.77.286B).

μιαροφαγέω, *eat polluted meat*, *M.Pion*.3.1; Gr.Naz.*or*.15.6(M.35. 921C); Thdr.Stud.*poen*.2.46(M.99.1753D); Ephr.2.320A.

***μιγαδικός,** *of coenobites*, Thdr.Stud.*cant*.3.9(p.342).

μιγάς, *mixed*, hence *in the world*, opp. monastic τοῦ...ἐρημικοῦ βίου καὶ τοῦ μ. μαχομένων πρὸς ἀλλήλους Gr.Naz.*or*.43.62(M.36.577A); masc. as subst., *ib*.21.10(M.35.1092D) = Eustrat.*v.Eutych*.99(M.86. 2385B); Ephr.3.52B; Thdr.Stud.*epp*.2.66(M.99.1292B).

μ(ε)ίγνυμι (μίγω, σμιγνύω, σμίγω), A. *mix, mingle*; act. trans., pass. intrans.; σμιγνύω, Germ.CP *or*.2(M.98.252A); **1.** fig., of qualities ἡ μακροθυμία γλυκυτάτη ἐστὶν ὑπὲρ τὸ μέλι...ἐὰν οὖν μιγῇ ἡ ὀξυχολία τῇ μακροθυμίᾳ, μιαίνεται ἡ μακροθυμία Herm.*mand*.5.1.6; μεμιγμένη ἡ λύπη μετὰ τῆς ἐντεύξεως οὐκ ἀφίησι τὴν ἔντευξιν ἀναβῆναι καθαρὰν ἐπὶ τὸ θυσιαστήριον *ib*.10.3.3; Clem.*str*.7.13(p.59.5; M.9. 516A); μιγνύμενος γὰρ ὁ λόγος φιλανθρωπίᾳ ἰᾶται τε ἅμα τὰ πάθη καὶ ἀνακαθαίρει τὰς ἁμαρτίας id.*paed*.1.6(p.120.21; M.8.309B); *be compounded* of ἦν γάρ πως καὶ ἡδεία τινὶ χάριτι καὶ πειθοῖ καί τινι ἀνάγκῃ μεμιγμένος Gr.Thaum.*pan.Or*.6(p.16.1; M.10.1069C); **2.** of Inc. as a means of unity with God ὁ λόγος...ἐνεδύσατο τὴν ἁγίαν σάρκα...ὅπως συγκεράσας τὸ θνητὸν ἡμῶν σῶμα τῇ ἑαυτοῦ δυνάμει, καὶ μίξας τὸ φθαρτὸν τῷ ἀφθάρτῳ...σώσῃ τὸν ἀπολλύμενον ἄνθρωπον Hipp.*antichr*.4(p.6.23; M.10.732B); *POxy*.5.14 (saec. iii–iv) cit. s. πνεῦμα; ὁ τοῦ θεοῦ λόγος...σάρκα φορεῖ διὰ τὴν σάρκα, καὶ ψυχῇ νοερᾷ διὰ τὴν ἐμὴν ψυχὴν μίγνυται Gr.Naz.*or*.45.9(M.36.633C); ἦν θεός, ἀλλ' ἐπάγη πατρὸς λόγος ἡμέτερος φῶς, ὥς κε θεὸν μίξῃ, μικτὸς ἐὼν χθονίοις id.*carm*.1.1.11.7(M.37.471A); similarly of eucharist, Chrys.*hom.15.4 in 1Tim*.(11.641D) cit. s. ἀνάκρασις; **3.** in Trin. controversy εἰ...μεμίχθαι τὴν τοῦ πνεύματος φύσιν πρὸς ἑκάτερα λέγουσιν, ἆρα καὶ τοῦ πρεσβυτέρου πρὸς τὸ νεώτερον μίξιν τινὰ ἐννοήσουσι Gr.Nyss.*Maced*.17(M.45.1324A); ὁ τὴν περὶ τοῦ ἀγαθοῦ ἔννοιαν ἐλαττῶν ἔν τινι τῶν ἐν τῇ ἁγίᾳ τριάδι πεπιστευμένων μεμεῖχθαί τι τῆς ἐναντίας ἕξεως τῷ κατὰ τὸ ἀγαθὸν ὑστερουμένῳ πάντως παρασκευάσει id.*Eun*.1(1 p.101.22; M.45.336A); ἆρα μὴ μεμίχθαι πονηρίαν τῇ ἀγαθότητι τοῦ υἱοῦ νομίζεις, καὶ διὰ τοῦτο διαφέρειν τὴν τοῦ πατρὸς ἀγαθότητα; ‡Ath.*dial.Trin*.1.11(M.28.1136A); **4.** in Manich. doctrine of creation ἐν δὲ τοῖς ἄλλοις στοιχείοις καὶ φυτοῖς καὶ ζῴοις... ἀνωμάλως φέρεσθαι τὴν θείαν δύναμιν μεμιγμένην Alex.Lyc.*Man*.3 (p.6.18; M.18.416B).

B. *mate* animals, in form μίγω, Thdr.Stud.*epp*.2.37(M.99.1229B).

C. *bring into contact* [*with oneself*] διὰ τὴν ὑπερηφανίαν μου [i.e. of Devil] πατοῦσιν οἱ πόδες μου τὴν γῆν, ἀλλ' οὖν μᾶλλον, ὅτι καὶ σώματα γηΐνων ἀνθρώπων ἡμᾶς σμίγουσιν *Mir.Geo*.13(p.132.1).

D. ? *set at variance, embroil* οὐαὶ τοὺς μίγοντας...δοῦλον πρὸς τὸν αὐτοῦ δεσπότην *Ep.Chr.dom*.(p.26).

***μιερεύς (*μηερεύς, *μιαιρεύς), ὁ,** *unholy* or *false priest*; of pagan priests, *A.Thom*.B 60(p.42.28); *A.Phil*.125,131(pp.54.8,60.11, v.l. ἱερεῖς); *Const.App*.2.28.8(v.l. μηερεύς); ἱερεῖς Epiph.*haer*.30.33(p.379. 25, v.l. μηερεῖς; μιαιρεῖς M.41.469A); *A.Barth*.8(p.147.32); *ib*.9(p.149. 28); μὴ ἱερεῖς †Jo.D.*B.J*.29(M.96.1132C, v.l. μιερεῖς).

μιερός, = μιαρός, Hipp.*Dan*.3.14.4; *A.Barn*.19(p.299.1).

[*]**Μιθραϊκός,** = Μιθριακός, *of Mithras*, Or.*Cels*.6.22(p.93.16; M. 11.1325B).

μικρο- see also σμικρο-.

μικροθαύμαστος, *admiring trifles*, Hipp.*haer*.4.46(p.68.23; M.16. 3110C); Jo.Clim.*scal*.26(M.88.1064B); neut. as subst., Hipp.*haer*. 4.50(p.74.6; 3118C).

***μικρόκοσμος, ὁ,** *microcosm*; of man, Jo.D.*volunt*.18(M.95.144B).

***μικροκωμία, ἡ,** *hamlet*, Bas.*ep*.190.1(3.282D; M.32.697C).

μικρολογέω (σμικρολογέω), 1. *belittle, disparage*, *cat.Lc*.4:22(p.37. 14); Cyr.*Lc*.4:22(M.72.544A); **2.** *utter platitudes*, Isid.Pel.*epp*.3.195 (M.78.880B); **3.** *concern oneself with trifles*, Chrys.*hom.17.3 in Eph*. (11.125E).

μικρολόγος, *of small account*, Clem.*str*.5.8(p.363.9; M.9.85B); Gr.Naz.*or*.27.10(p.19.2; M.36.24B).

μικρολόγως, *niggardly, parsimoniously* μεταμορφοῦται ἀπὸ τῆς δόξης τοῦ πνεύματος εἰς τὴν οἰκείαν δόξαν, οὐ μ. οὐδὲ ἀμυδρῶς Bas. *Spir*.52(3.45B; M.32.165C); Gr.Naz.*ep*.61(M.37.120D); ref. 2Cor.9:6 οὐκ εἶπε μ., ἀλλ' εὐφημότερον, τὸ τοῦ φειδωλοῦ θεὶς ὄνομα Chrys.*hom. 19.2 in 2Cor*.(10.573C).

***μικρόμασθος**, *small-breasted*, Jo.Mal.*chron.*5 p.100(M.97.188C).

μικρομεγέθης, *modest*, Gel.Cyz.*h.e.*2.1.15(M.85.1228A).

μικρομερῶς, *to a small degree*, Max.*ep.*8(M.91.445A).

***μικροπής**, f.l. for *μικροπρεπής*, Sophr.H.*v.Anast.*(M.92.1693C).

μικροπολιτεία, ἡ, *small town*, Bas.*ep.*190.1(3.282D, M.32.697B).

***μικροπολῖτις**, *of a small town, insignificant*, opp. *μητροπολῖτις*, of a church, Synes.*ep.*58(M.66.1401D).

μικροπρέπεια (σμικρο-), ἡ, *subordination, humble position, low estate*, ref. Jo.8:49 *τοῖς ἐπὶ μικροπρεπείᾳ ἐκδεχομένοις τῆς οἰκονομίας τὰ ῥήματα* Didym.*Trin.*3.18(M.39.385A); Cyr.*Is.*2.1(2.196C); id.*Juln.*2(6^2.70B); esp. of the creature *τῇ τοῦ πεποιῆσθαι σ.* id.*thes.*32 (5^1.320C); *ib.*5(33D); freq. ref. Inc. *ἐν ἀνθρωπίνῃ σ. δόξα θεοπρεπής* id.*Chr.un.*(5^1.753C); id.*Pulch.*3(5^2.130D); id.*Jo.*3.1(4.253D).

***μικροπρεπεύομαι**, v. *σμικροπρεπεύομαι*.

μικροπρεπής (σμικρο-), *petty, insignificant*, †Bas.*hom.in Ps.*28 (1.360A; M.30.77B); neut. as subst.; **1.** *triviality, pettiness*, Synes.*ep.*4(M.66.1332C); Cyr.*Juln.*6(6^2.213E); **2.** *subordinate position, low estate* *ἀδικήσει...οὐδὲν τὴν τοῦ ἀνθρώπου ψυχὴν ἀγαθουργεῖν εἰθισμένην τὸ κατὰ σάρκα σ.* Cyr.*Jo.*5.4(4.512E); esp. of human nature (freq. ref. Inc.) *τῆς ἀνθρωπότητος τὸ σ. ὑποδὺς οἰκονομικῶς* id.*glaph.Gen.*7(1.238B); id.*Is.*2.1(2.193C); id.*Arcad.*25(p.39.23; 5^2.147E); *τὸ σ. ἐν τῷ λόγῳ πολλάκις ἐπιτηδεύοντα τὸν Χριστόν, διὰ τὴν τῶν ἀκροωμένων ἀσθένειαν* id.*Jo.*5.5(4.531E).

μικρός, *small, little*; **1.** exeg. Phil.2:6 acc. Arians *μ. καὶ μέγας θεὸς ἐνὶ;...παρὰ μὲν...ταῖς γραφαῖς...μέγαν μὲν πανταχοῦ, μ. δὲ οὐδαμοῦ* Chrys.*hom.6.2 in Phil.*(11.235C,D); ref. Tit.2:13 *ἰδοὺ καὶ ὁ υἱὸς μέγας. πῶς οὖν λέγεις μ. καὶ μέγαν;...μ. ὤν, φησί, θεός, οὐχ ἥρπασε τὸ εἶναι κατὰ τὸν μέγαν* *ib.*(236A,B); **2.** comp., of *junior* monks, Ephr.2.87F, 1.318C,2.171D; **3.** in adv. phrases *μικρῷ πρός approximately διακοσίων μιλίων μικρῷ πρός* Dam.*troph.*1.2(p.195.5); *κατὰ μικρόν at short intervals*, *Didasc.Jac.*4.1(p.63.10); *πρὸ μικροῦ shortly before*, Ath.*decr.*4(p.3.34; M.25.'429'(421)C).

***μικρόσιμος**, *rather snub-nosed*, Jo.Mal.*chron.*5 p.106(M.97.196C).

***μικρόσχημος**, monk or nun *wearing the lesser habit*, opp. *μεγαλόσχημος*, †Jo.Jej.*poenit.*(M.88.1893B); Thdr.Stud.*poen.*2.47(M.99.1753D); *Nomoc.*147.

***μικροτέχνης**, ὁ, *humble artisan*, Clem.*prot.*10(p.71.16; M.8.212B).

***μικροφανής**, *small in appearance, inconspicuous*; of a planet, Diod.*fat.*(M.103.841B); of a man, Hier.*v.Paul.*B(p.15.3); of rabbits, Cyr.*ador.*14(1.502B).

μικροφυής, *of low growth, short*; met., *stunted, petty* *μ. καὶ χαμαίζηλος...κρίσις* Gr.Nyss.*anim.et res.*(M.46.41A); *μ. διανοίᾳ* id.*Eun.*5(2 p.102.28; M.45.681B); neut. as subst. *τῷ μ. τῆς καρδίας ἡμῶν* id.*hom.opif.*proem.2(p.104; M.44.125D).

μικροφυΐα, ἡ, *insignificance*, Gr.Nyss.*laud.Bas.*(M.46.813B).

μικροφυῶς, *in a stunted way*, Jo.Eleem.*v.Tych.*(p.135).

μικροψυχ-έω, **1.** *be faint-hearted*; **a.** *lack fortitude* *μ. τοῖς διωγμοῖς* Chrys.*comm.in Gal.*4:30(10.711E); abs., id.*paralyt.*2(3.34D); *ὑπὸ...τῶν παθῶν καὶ τῶν θλίψεων...ἐμικροψύχουν καὶ παρεσαλεύοντο* id.*hom.22.1 in Heb.*(12.201C); Pall.*h.Laus.*22(p.71.19; M.34.1081D); *τὸ ~ῆσαι* (of S. Peter's denial) Cyr.*Jo.*9(4.759A); Thphn.*chron.*p.131 (M.108.361B); **b.** *lose heart* *μὴ...δαψιλεστέραν ἔχοντες χορηγίαν τοῦ θεοῦ τὴν πρόνοιαν, πτωχεύωμεν μηδὲ μ.* Chrys.*hom.22.3 in Mt.*(7.278A); id.*hom.26.2 in Heb.*(12.237B); **2.** *be small-minded, petty*, hence *quarrel* *πρὸς τὸν φίλον μ.* Chrys.*hom.16.2 in 1Cor.*(10.137A); id.*hom.19.2 in Heb.*(12.185B); *οὐ περὶ θρησκείας ἀλλὰ περὶ προεδρίας μ.* Socr.*h.e.*5.23.10(M.67.648A).

μικροψυχία, ἡ, **1.** *faint-heartedness, poor-spiritedness* *τὸ διὰ τὰς σωματικὰς ἀλγηδόνας...κακῶν ποιητὴν τὸν θεὸν ὀνομάζειν...τοῦτο τῆς ἐσχάτης μ. ἐστί* Gr.Nyss.*or.catech.*8(p.50.6; M.45.37C); *τὸ πενθεῖν καὶ κόπτεσθαι καὶ ὀδύρεσθαι τοὺς ἀπελθόντας, ἀπὸ μ. γίνεται* Chrys.*hom.26.2 in Heb.*(12.237B); id.*sac.*2.4(p.403.1; 1.377C); Esaias *or.*5.1(p.34; cf.M.40.1121C); Cyr.*Ps.*76:4(M.69.1189D); *ὄκνου τε παντὸς καὶ μ. ἐξῃρημένῳ* id.*Jon.*17(3.380B); id.*Lc.*21:14(M.72.897C); **2.** *small-mindedness, pettiness* *μὴ μ. ἢ φιλονεικία...τοῦ ἐπισκόπου ἀποσυνάγωγοι γεγένηνται* CNic.(325)*can.*5; *χρὴ διαλύειν πᾶσαν ἔχθραν καὶ μ. ἵνα δυνώμεθα προσεύχεσθαι καθαρᾷ τῇ καρδίᾳ καὶ ἀρύπῳ* *Const.App.*2.53.5; *ἡ ἐπιθυμία...καὶ...τὸ πάθος...ἀπὸ μ. ... ἀπὸ ἀτελοῦς διανοίας, ἀπὸ παιδικῆς γνώμης* Chrys.*hom.29.5 in 2Cor.*(10.647E); *καταγέλαστα ...τὰ ῥήματα ταῦτα...καὶ γυναικώδους μ.* *ib.*5.5(472C); Cyr.*ador.*8(1.276C); *χρηστὸς...ὑπάρχων ὁ κύριος ἡμῶν καὶ ἐπιεικής...καὶ τῆς ἐν ἀνθρώποις μ. ἀμείνων ὡς θεὸς εὑρίσκεται* id.*Jo.*5.3(4.499B); hence **3.** *dissension, quarrel*, Serap.Ant.ap.Eus.*h.e.*6.12.4(M.20.545B); Const.ap. Ath.*apol.sec.*70(p.148.15; M.25.373B); Jul.Papa *ep.Dian.ib.*21(p.103.15; 284B); Bas.*ep.*204.7(3.307D; M.32.756B); ref. Mt.18:19 *τὰς μ. ἀναιρεῖ καὶ πρὸς ἀλλήλους συνάγει* Chrys.*hom.60.2 in Mt.*(7.608C); ref. Rom.16:16 *διὰ τῆς εἰρήνης ταύτης πάντα ἐκβάλλων λογισμὸν καὶ μικροψυχίας ἀφορμήν* id.*hom.31.3 in Rom.*(9.749B); **4.** *meanness, parsimony*, Clem.*str.*7.4(p.17.19; M.9.432A); **5.** *limitations of intellect* *ὅταν τούτων* [sc. tangible or visible properties] *μηδὲν εἶναι λέγηται ἄν, εἰς τὸ μηδόλως τι εἶναι οἴεσθαι ὑπὸ μικροψυχίας περιαγόμεθα* Gr.Nyss.*anim.et res.*(M.46.41A).

μικρόψυχος (σμικρόψυχος), **1.** *faint-hearted*, Chrys.*hom.21.3 in Heb.*(12.197D); **2.** *querulous* *ὡς μ. οἱ ἄρρωστοί εἰσιν* id.*anom.*12.2(1.550C); *μικροψύχους...τὸ γῆρας ποιεῖ* id.*hom.4.1 in Tit.*(11.750C); **3.** *small-minded, petty* *τὸ ἐπὶ τοῖς τυχοῦσι παροξύνεσθαι, μ. ἀνδρῶν καὶ...ταλαιπώρων* id.*comm.in Gal.*1:3(10.658B); *ἐν τῇ πρώτῃ ἡλικίᾳ πολὺ τὸ ἀνόητον καὶ μ.* id.*hom.10.1 in Mt.*(7.140A); *ὁ...τὰ βιωτικὰ μεταχειριζόμενος...μ. ... ἐπὶ μικροῖς ἐναβρυνόμενος* Isid.Pel.*epp.*5.500 (M.78.1616C); *σμικρο-*, *cat.Lc.*12:13(p.100.20); **4.** *mean-spirited* *οὐδὲ ...ταπεινόφρονα καὶ μέτριον, ἀλλ' ἀσθενῆ καὶ μ. καὶ ἀνελεύθερον* Chrys.*hom.11.1 in 1Cor.*(10.88C); *niggardly*, id.*hom.18.7 in Rom.*(9.641C); ref. Rom.14:17 *μικρόψυχον ὄντα...μεγάλων ἀπολελαυκότα παρὰ τοῦ θεοῦ καὶ οὐδὲ μικρὰ ἀντιδιδόντα* *ib.26.1*(9.712B); *οἱ μ. ... φίλους καλοῦντες...ἵν' εὐθὺς ἀντικληθέντες, κομίσαιντο τοῦτο* Cyr.*Lc.*14:12(M.72.788B).

μικροψύχως, **1.** *faintheartedly*, Gr.Naz.*ep.*61(M.37.120D); *μ. ἔχειν* *ib.*18(52C); Gr.Nyss.*homm.in Cant.*proem.(M.44.760B); comp., Chrys.*hom.21.2 in Heb.*(12.195D).

μικρύνω, v. *σμικρύνω*.

***μικρυσμός**, ὁ, *depreciation*, Cyr.*Jo.*6.1(4.605C); Jo.Clim.*scal.*24 (M.88.981C).

μιλιαρήσιον (-ρίσιον), τό, (Lat. *milliarense*) a small coin, *-ρίσιον*, Epiph.*mens.*24(M.43.289B); Marc.Diac.*v.Porph.*100.

***μιλιοδρομέω**, *run a mile*, ‡Chrys.*circ.*(8.88A).

μίλιον, τό, **1.** *mile* *ἀπὸ τριῶν μ.* Pall.*h.Laus.*31(p.87.12, v.l. *ἀπὸ τριῶν σημείων* M.34.1099B); **2.** *milestone* *αὗται αἱ ἐντολαὶ...ὥσπερ μ. εἰσὶ στήκοντα καὶ σημεῖα τῆς βασιλικῆς ὁδοῦ* Mac.Aeg.*hom.*27.23(M.34.709C); *ἐν ἀρχῇ...τῶν τρίβων οὐσῶν ἀσήμων, τὰ νῦν προσαγορευόμενα μ. παρὰ Ῥωμαίοις, τότε σημεῖα καλούμενα...ἐτίθεσαν* Didym.*Pr.*1:1(M.39.1621B); *A.Petr.et Paul.*87(p.221.3); Soz.*h.e.*7.24.2(M.67.1489C).

μίλτος, ἡ, = *ἐρυσίβη*, *corn rust*, *Apoc.Dan.*C suppl.(p.123).

***μιλτόχριστος**, *smeared with red*, *Orac.Sib.*3.589.

μιμ-έομαι, **1.** *imitate* *ἐὰν...ἡμᾶς μιμήσεται* [sc. ὁ Χριστός], *καθὰ πράσσομεν, οὐκ ἔτι ἐσμέν* Ign.*Magn.*10.1; *καὶ ἡμεῖς, καίτοι μὴ δυνάμενοι ὅμοιοι κατ' οὐσίαν τοῦ θεοῦ γενέσθαι, ὅμως ἐξ ἀρετῆς βελτιούμενοι, ~ούμεθα τὸν θεόν* Ath.*ep.Afr.*7(M.26.1041B); of God forgiving trespasses *καθάπερ ἐν ἡμῖν τὸ ἀγαθὸν ἐπιτελεῖται τῇ πρὸς τὸ θεῖον μιμήσει, οὕτως ἐλπίσαι ~εῖσθαι τὸν θεὸν τὰ ἡμέτερα* Gr.Nyss.*or.dom.*5 (p.96.15; M.44.1180C); *τὸν σωτήριον αὐτοῦ μ. θάνατον* Thdt.*Phil.*3:11 (3.463); *τὴν τεσσαρακονθήμερον νηστείαν τοῦ κυρίου μ.* Cosm.Ind.*top.*5 (M.88.197B); **2.** of inanimate things, *resemble* *πάντων πανταχόθεν ἀφικνουμένων, καὶ πάσης ὁδοῦ ποταμὸν ~ουμένης* Thdt.*h.rel.*26(3.1272); **3.** of types, *represent, serve as an example of*, ref. Dt.25:5 *τὴν μέλλουσαν ἐπαγγελίαν ἀναστάσει ἐμιμοῦντο θνητῇ* Afric.*ep.Arist.*(p.58.11; M.10.56A); *τῇ ἡμέρᾳ...τῆς ἐνανθρωπήσεως, ὅτε παρθένος οὐρανὸν ἐμιμήσατο* Procl.CP *or.*2.6(M.65.700B); ref. Mt.5:3 *Δαβὶδ...τὸν ἑαυτοῦ υἱὸν...καὶ δεσπότην μ.* Thdt.*Ps.*1:1(1.609).

***μιμηλεύομαι**, *mimic*; of a parrot, Max.*ep.*20(M.91.601B).

***μιμηλόφωνος**, *imitating sounds*, ‡Jo.D.*hom.*5(M.96.652B).

μίμημα, τό, **1.** *copy, image* *μίαν εἶναι τὴν ἀληθῆ ἐκκλησίαν...μ. ὃν ἀρχῆς τῆς μιᾶς* Clem.*str.*7.17(p.76.8; M.9.552A); of candidates at baptism *ἀληθῶς γὰρ μ. ἐφέρετε τοῦ πρωτοπλάστου Ἀδάμ, ὃς ἐν τῷ παραδείσῳ γυμνὸς ἦν, καὶ οὐκ ᾐσχύνετο* Cyr.H.*catech.*20.2; *εἴδωλα καλεῖ τὰ τῶν οὐχ ὑφεστώτων μ.* Thdt.*qu.38 in Ex.*(1.149); ref. Creation *τῶν ἔργων ἀρχετύπων...ἃ δὴ βλέπων ἀτενὲς ἐν τῇ τοῦ πατρὸς διανοίᾳ ὁ υἱὸς μιμήματα ὧν ἑώρα ἐποίει* Eus.*e.th.*3.3(p.155.26; M.24.1000A); ref. creation of man, Meth.*res.*1.34(p.271.8; M.41.1097B); *ὁ ἄνθρωπος ἐκτίσθη μ. καὶ ὑπόδειγμα τῆς ὁρατῆς καὶ ἀοράτου κτίσεως, ὁρατὴν μὲν ἔχων τὴν σάρκα, ἀόρατον δὲ τὴν ψυχήν* Eulog.*fr.Trin.*1 (p.363); fig., of martyrs *τὰ μ. τῆς ἀληθοῦς ἀγάπης* Polyc.*ep.*1.1; **2.** *example, illustration* *μ. τῆς ἐκκλησίας ἐκελεύοντο δαιδάλλειν Ἑβραῖοι τὴν σκηνήν* Meth.*symp.*5.7(p.61.24; M.18.109B); *διηνεκῶς βλέπων τῆς ἀναστάσεως τὰ μ.* [i.e. in plant life] Thdt.*provid.*9(4.650); **3.** = *μίμησις*, *imitation* *ἔνθεον ζῆλον ἀποστολικοῦ μ.* Eus.*h.e.*5.10.2 (M.20.456A); *τὴν τέχνην καὶ οἱ πολλοὶ λέγουσι φύσεως...εἶναι μ.* Ath.*gent.*18(M.25.37B).

μίμησις, ἡ, **1.** *imitation, copying* *καθάπερ ὁ λόγος ἐν ἀρχῇ γεννηθεὶς ἀντεγέννησε τὴν καθ' ἡμᾶς ποίησιν...οὕτω κἀγὼ κατὰ τὴν τοῦ λόγου μ. ἀναγεννηθεὶς...μεταρρυθμίζω τῆς συγγενοῦς ὕλης τὴν σύγχυσιν* Tat.*orat.*5(p.6.10; M.6.817A); ref. Jo.10:30 *πάντας ἡμᾶς κατὰ τὴν αὐτοῦ* μ. τῆς ἑνότητος τῆς αὐτῆς μετασχεῖν Eus.*e.th.*3.19(p.180.4; M.24.1044A); τὸν σωζόμενον ἄνθρωπον διὰ μιμήσεως Χριστοῦ τὴν ἀρχαίαν ἐκείνην υἱοθεσίαν ἀπολαβεῖν...οὐ μόνον ἐν τοῖς κατὰ τὸν βίον ὑποδείγμασιν ἀοργησίας...ἀλλὰ καὶ αὐτοῦ τοῦ θανάτου Bas.*Spir.*35(3.28D; M.32.128D); ἡνίκα αὐτὸς ὁ ἀληθινὸς ποιμὴν παραγένηται διὰ τῆς τῶν εὐαγγελίων...ἀναπτύξεως,...ἀποτίθεται τὸ σχῆμα τῆς μ. ὁ ἐπίσκοπος, αὐτὸν δηλῶν παρεῖναι τὸν κύριον Isid.Pel.*epp.*1.136(M.78.272D); κατὰ μ. τοῦ κατὰ φύσιν υἱοῦ...οἱ κατὰ θέσιν υἱοὶ καλοῦνται Cyr.*thes.*15(5[1].168D); **2.** = μίμημα, *imitation, copy* τὴν ἀρχιερατικὴν τιμήν, ἥτις μίμησιν περιέχει τοῦ μεγάλου ἀρχιερέως Ἰησοῦ Χριστοῦ *Const.App.*8.46.4; ἱερὸν παίγνιον...ἦν μ. ἱερωσύνης καὶ τοῦ καταλόγου τῶν ἱερωμένων ἀνδρῶν Socr.*h.e.*1.15.1(M.67.116A).

μιμητής, ὁ, 1. *imitator* ὁ ἐπίσκοπος...δείκνυσι πᾶσι διὰ τοῦ σχήματος ὅτι μ. ἐστι τοῦ ἀγαθοῦ καὶ μεγάλου ποιμένος Isid.Pel.*epp.*1.136(M.78.272C); fig., *copy* παράδεισος ἡμῖν...οὗτος ἦν, μ. τοῦ μεγάλου παραδείσου τοῦ θεοῦ Gr.Thaum.*pan.Or.*15(p.35.4; M.10.1096B); **2.** *maker of imitations, counterfeiter* τῶν ἑτεροδόξων τοὺς σοφιστὰς μ. εἰδώλων ἀληθείας Meth.*res.*1.28(p.257.4; M.41.1136A).

μιμητικῶς, *repetitively*; superl., Meth.*symp.*3.14(p.45.12; M.18.85C).

***μιμολόγημα, τό,** *mime, farce,* Epiph.*haer.*37.3(p.53.16; M.41.645A).

***μιμολογία, ἡ,** *recitation of mimes*; of teaching of heretics, Epiph.*haer.*24.2(p.258.14; M.41.309D); *ib.*25.5(p.273.9; 328C); *ib.*36.4(p.47.14; 636D).

μιμολόγος, ὁ, 1. *writer of mimes, playwright*; fig., of Basilides, Epiph.*haer.*24.3(p.260.5; M.41.312B); of Manes, *ib.*66.32(p.72.12; M.42.81A); **2.** *actor in mimes, play-actor,* fig. τὴν Ἀρειανὴν ἐκείνην θυμελικὴν ὀρχήστραν...καὶ τοὺς ταύτης μιμολόγους Anast.S.*hod.*4(M.89.96D).

μῖμος, ὁ, *mime*; met., of Gnost. teaching, *farce,* Iren.*haer.*1.9.5(M.7.548A); *play-acting, insincerity, cat.Gal.*proem.(p.1.21).

***μιμώδης, ὁ,** *hypocrite,* ‡Just.*ep.Zen.et Ser.*9(M.6.1193B).

***μίνην,** prob. for μῆνιν, †Gregent.*leg.Hom.*40(M.86.604B).

μινύρισμα, τό, *warbling*; met., of teaching of Gnostics, Clem.*str.*2.8(p.132.18; M.8.972C); *lisping*; of children, *Orac.Sib.*11.110.

μινυώριος, *short-lived, temporal,* Nonn.*par.Jo.*4:10(M.43.776A); *ib.*12:25(853C); *ib.*18:36(896C).

***μινώταυρος, ὁ,** better written *divisim, minotaur,* ref. Apollinarius' coining of word ἀνθρωπόθεος: μινώταυρον ἡμῖν διὰ τῆς αἰσχρᾶς ταύτης ὀνοματοποιΐας τερατεύεται τὸ μυστήριον Gr.Nyss.*Apoll.*49(M.45.1241D).

***μιξανάρρους, ὁ,** *confused flow,* Geo.Pis.*Sev.*91(M.92.1628B).

μίξις (μεῖξις), ἡ, 1. *mingling, mixture* ἦν ποτε ὅτε οὐδὲν ἦν πλὴν χάος καὶ στοιχείων ἀτάκτων ἔτι συμπεφορημένων μ. ἀδιάκριτος *Hom.Clem.*6.3; ἐκ τῆς τῶν δύο μ., ὕδατός τε καὶ γῆς, ὁ πρῶτος, οὐ γεννηθεὶς ἀλλὰ πλασθεὶς *ib.*6.14; Bas.*ascet.*1.2(2.320B; M.31.873B); τῆς ἁγίας τριάδος...περὶ ἣν γὰρ οὐκ ἔστι μεῖξίν τινα ποιοτήτων καὶ συνδρομὴν ἐννοῆσαι Gr.Nyss.*Eun.*1(1 p.89.19; M.45.321B); εἰ δέ τις συκοφαντοίη τὸν λόγον, ὡς ἐκ τοῦ μὴ δέχεσθαι τὴν κατὰ φύσιν διαφοράν, μίξιν τινὰ τῶν ὑποστάσεων καὶ ἀνακύκλησιν κατασκευάζοντα id.*tres dii*(M.45.133B); ref. H. Ghost οὐδὲ γὰρ ἐνδέχεται μίξιν...ἐννοῆσαι τοῦ κτιστοῦ πρὸς τὸ ἄκτιστον id.*Maced.*17(M.45.1324A); *blending* πολλῶν καὶ διαφόρων ἀρωμάτων...τεχνική τις καὶ ἔμμετρος μ. id.*hom.3 in Cant.*(M.44.824A); id.*hom.opif.*5.1(M.44.137B); **2.** *combination*; **a.** in gen., of Pythagorean numbers ὧν καὶ ἐπιπλοκαὶ καὶ μίξεις πρὸς γένεσιν αὐξήσεως γίνονται Hipp.*haer.*1.2(p.6.15; M.16.3024D); τὸ σύνθετον ἁπλῶν τινων μίξιν μηνύει Meth.*arbitr.*12(p.176.4; M.18.260C); ἄνευ...ἔρωτος οὐ στοιχείων οὐ θεῶν οὐκ ἀνθρώπων οὐ ζῴων ἀλόγων οὐ τῶν λοιπῶν ἁπάντων μ. ἢ γένεσις γενέσθαι δύναται *Hom.Clem.*5.10; of physical and spiritual in man, Gr.Naz.*or.*38.11(M.36.321C); Gr.Nyss.*or.catech.*6(p.30.7; M.45.25C); of interprn. of scripture πάντως μ. τις ἐμφαίνεται τοῦ θείου πρὸς τὸ ἀνθρώπινον, τῆς μὲν φωνῆς ἢ τῆς πράξεως ἀνθρωπικῶς διεξαγομένης, τοῦ δὲ κατὰ τὸ κρυπτὸν νοουμένου τὸ θεῖον ἐμφαίνοντος *ib.*32(p.118.4; 80C); of union with Christ in eucharist κάτω πάλιν κατέβην...λεπτύνομαι κατὰ μικρόν, ἵνα πολλὴ ἡ ἀνάκρασις γένηται καὶ ἡ μ. καὶ ἡ ἕνωσις Chrys.*hom.15.4 in 1Tim.*(11.641D); **b.** Christol. ἡ κενωθεῖσα θεότης...ἡ προσληφθεῖσα σάρξ...ἡ καινὴ μ., θεὸς καὶ ἄνθρωπος, ἓν ἐξ ἀμφοῖν καὶ δι' ἑνὸς ἀμφότερα Gr.Naz.*or.*2.23(M.35.432B); τί μεῖζον ἀνθρώπου ταπεινότητι ἢ θεῷ πλακῆναι, καὶ γενέσθαι θεὸν ἐκ τῆς μ. *ib.*30.3(p.112.2; M.36.105C); οὕτω γέγονεν ἡ ἄρρητος ἐκείνη μεῖξις καὶ σύνοδος τῆς ἀνθρωπίνης βραχύτητος πρὸς τὸ θεῖον μέγεθος ἀνακραθείσης Gr.Nyss.*Eun.*6(2 p.150.20; M.45.737A); ὢ καινὴ κτίσις καὶ μ. θεσπεσία· θεὸς καὶ σὰρξ μίαν καὶ τὴν αὐτὴν ἀπετέλεσαν φύσιν Apoll.*fr.*10(p.207.12)ap.Justn.*monoph.*(M.86.1124B); μεσότης δὲ θεοῦ καὶ ἀνθρώπων ἐν Χριστῷ· οὐκ ἄρα οὔτε ἄνθρωπος ὅλος οὔτε θεός, ἀλλὰ θεοῦ καὶ ἀνθρώπου μ. id.*fr.*113(p.234.20)*ib.*(M.86.1140C); this view condemned, ‡Chrys.*ep.Caes.*(3.743A); ὁ ἐκ παρθένου τόκος...ἡ πεῖνα, ἡ δίψα...ὁ θάνατος...ἐν τούτοις...ἅπασιν μ. μὲν ἔστι τοῦ θείου πρὸς τὸ ἀνθρώπινον, πλὴν τοῦ σώματος εἶναι πιστεύεται, οὐδὲν τούτων τοῦ θείου πάσχοντος, δι' αὐτῶν δὲ τὴν ἡμῶν οἰκονομοῦντος σωτηρίαν ‡Cyr.*Trin.*25(6[3].31A; M.77.1168B) = Jo.D.*f.o.*4.18(M.94.1185C); μ. θεότητος καὶ ἀνθρωπότητος, πάθους καὶ ἀπαθείας...ὡς ἂν ἐν πᾶσιν νικηθείη τὸ χεῖρον ὑπὸ τοῦ κρείττονος ‡Jo.D.*hom.*6.5(M.96.668C); **c.** Gnost. αἰῶνας, ὧν τὰ ὀνόματα...Βύθιος καὶ Μ. Iren.*haer.*1.1.2(M.7.449A); Hipp.*haer.*5.21(p.123.8; M.16.3187C); ἡ τοῦ πνευματικοῦ μ. τῷ ψυχικῷ τε καὶ ὑλικῷ Epiph.*haer.*36.5(p.49.3; M.41.640A); Manich. τοῦ μὲν φωτὸς εἶναι μέρος τὴν ἐν ἀνθρώποις ψυχήν, τοῦ δὲ σκότους τὸ σῶμα καὶ τὸ τῆς ὕλης δημιούργημα. μ. δὲ ἤτοι σύγκρασιν τοῦτον λέγει γεγονέναι τὸν τρόπον...καθάπερ δύο βασιλεῖς ἀντιμαχόμενοι πρὸς ἀλλήλους Hegem.*Arch.*7(p.9.16; M.10.1437A); **3.** *composition* πῶς ὁ οὐρανὸς συνέστη, καὶ ἐκ ποίας ὕλης, καὶ τίς ἡ τούτου μ.; Ath.*ep.Serap.*1.18(M.26.572C); ref. Ps.138:6 τίς ἡ μ. ἡμῶν;...πῶς τὸ ἀθάνατον τῷ θνητῷ συνεκράθη; Gr.Naz.*or.*28.22(p.54.10; M.36.56A); **4.** *sexual intercourse*; fig., acc. Naassenes ἀπὸ τῆς Αἰγύπτου...εἰς τὴν ἔρημον, τουτέστιν ἀπὸ τῆς κάτω μ. ἐπὶ τὴν ἄνω Ἱερουσαλήμ...θνητὴ γάρ, φησί, πᾶσα ἡ κάτω γένεσις, ἀθάνατος δὲ ἡ ἄνω γεννωμένη. ... οὗτος, φησίν, ἐστὶν ὁ μέγας Ἰορδάνης, ὃν κάτω ῥέοντα καὶ κωλύοντα ἐξελθεῖν τοὺς υἱοὺς Ἰσραὴλ ἐκ γῆς Αἰγύπτου—ἤγουν ἐκ τῆς κάτω μ.· Αἴγυπτος γάρ ἐστι τὸ σῶμα κατ' αὐτούς—ἀνέστειλεν Ἰησοῦς καὶ ἐποίησεν ἄνω ῥέειν Hipp.*haer.*5.7(p.88.19ff.; M.16.3139A).

μιξόθηρος, *half beast,* met., Athenag.*res.*8(p.57.22; M.6.989B).

***μιξόλεθρος,** *divided between life and death* μ. γνώμην Const.Diac.*laud.*7(M.88.487A).

μιξοπόλιος, *grizzled,* Cyr.S.*v.Euthym.*10(p.20.9); *Chron.Pasch.* p.375(M.92.958D not.).

***μιξοφυσίτης, ὁ,** *one who mixes the natures* of Christ; of Severus, Leont.H.*monoph.*testimonia(M.86.1841B); of his followers, id.*Nest.*1.49(M.86.1512A).

***μισάγαθος,** *hating the good,* Chrys.*exp.in Ps.*7:10(5.62C); Gel.Cyz.*h.e.*3.1.4; Thphn.*chron.*p.376(M.108.900C).

***μισάγιος,** *hating saints,* Steph.Diac.*v.Steph.*(M.100.1100B).

***μισαδελφία, ἡ,** *hatred of one's brother, of the brethren, T.Benj.*7.5; Jul.Papa *ep.Dian.*ap.Ath.*apol.sec.*34(p.112.19; M.25.305B); Cyr.H.*catech.*15.7; Bas.*reg.fus.*34.1(2.377C; M.31.1000C).

***μισάδικος,** *hating injustice,* Ant.Mon.*hom.*106(M.89.1760B).

***μισαρχία, ἡ,** *hatred of rule, rebelliousness* of the Jews, ‡Hesych.H.*m.Long.*7(M.93.1552A).

***μισέργατος,** *hating work, lazy,* Ephr.3.66B.

μίσεργος, = foreg., Leont.et Jo.*sacr.*2(M.86.2026A).

***μισευλαβής,** *hating piety,* Pall.*v.Chrys.*16(p.99.16; M.47.56).

***μισεύω,** *dismiss,* Thphn.*chron.*p.201 (v.l. μησεῦσει M.108.517B).

μισ-έω, *hate,* ref. Lc.14:26, Jo.12:25 ἅγιος ἐμίσει τὰ μίσους ἄξια, τοὺς λόγους τοὺς παρανόμους...κατὰ ταύτην τὴν ἔννοιαν καὶ πατέρα καὶ μητέρα ~εῖν προστετάγμεθα...θεοῦ δὲ προκαλουμένου εἰς τὸ καὶ τὴν ἰδίαν μ. ψυχήν, ὁμοίως καὶ ἀνθρώπους δεῖ παρανόμους ~εῖν, ὡς ἂν αὐτοὺς ἐπιστρέψωμεν βελτιούμενοι τῷ μὴ τούτοις ὁμοιωθῆναι Or.*sel.in Ps.*118:113(M.12.1612cf.); τί δέ ἐστιν 'ὁ ~ῶν αὐτήν' [sc. τὴν ψυχήν]; ὁ μὴ εἴκων αὐτῇ, τὰ βλάπτοντα κελευούσῃ. καὶ οὐκ εἶπεν, ὁ μὴ εἴκων αὐτῇ, ἀλλ', 'ὁ μισῶν αὐτήν'. καθάπερ γὰρ τῶν ~ουμένων οὐδὲ φωνὴν ἀκοῦσαι ἀνεχόμεθα Chrys.*hom.67.1 in Jo.*(8.400D); ὁ κελεύων ἀγαπᾶν τοὺς ἐχθρούς, πῶς ἂν ἠθέλησε ~εῖν τοὺς κατὰ φύσιν οἰκείους;...οὐ...οἰκείους γε ὄντας τῇ πίστει τοὺς οἰκείους μισητέον Cyr.*Lc.*14:26(M.72.793B,C); abs., *feel hatred,* Ign.*Eph.*14.2; Tat.*orat.*17(p.18.25; M.6.844A).

μισητικός, *inclined to hate,* Or.*Cels.*4.47(p.320.12; M.11.1105A).

***μισητικῶς,** *in a state of hatred* μ. διάγουσι πρὸς τὸν δίκαιον Bas.*hom.in Ps.*33(1.157E; M.29.385B).

***μισήτρια,** fem. of μισητής, *hater,* Ephr.2.132C.

μισθαποδοσία, ἡ, *payment of wages, recompense* εἴ τις Χριστιανὸς...κατακριθῇ...εἰς λοῦδον ἢ θηρία ἢ μέταλλον...πέμψατε αὐτῷ εἰς διατροφὴν αὐτοῦ καὶ εἰς μ. τῶν στρατιωτῶν *Const.App.*5.1.1; by God in future life, *Apoc.Bar.rel.*6.2; ‡Bas.*struct.hom.*1.21(1.334D; M.30.33B); Nil.*epp.*2.230(M.79.320A); at general resurrection, *Const.App.*5.7.3; *ib.*6.11.9.

μισθαποδότης, ὁ, *payer of wages, rewarder*; of God, Clem.*str.*6.9(p.469.11; M.9.296B); οἷς ἐντεῦθεν αὐτὴν ὁ δίκαιος μ. ἠμείψατο Gr.Naz.*or.*8.15(M.35.805C); τῶν νόμων δοτὴρ καὶ τῶν φυλαττόντων αὐτοὺς μ. *Lit.*ap.*Const.App.*8.12.22; Leont.N.*v.Jo.Eleem.*22(p.47.14) cit. s. ἀντιμισθία; Jo.D.*f.o.*4.27(M.94.1220C); of Christ τὸν κριτὴν...καὶ μ. τῆς ἀρετῆς Ast.Am.*hom.*1(M.40.176A); *Const.App.*5.6.10;

ref. Mt.20:12, Isid.Pel.*epp*.1.137(M.78.273A); Proc.G.*Is*.62:10(M.87.2661A).

***μισθαποληψία, ἡ,** *receiving payment,* ‡Chrys.*hom*.13(13.253B).

***μισθάργος, ὁ,** *hireling, hired worker,* Barth.Edess.*Agar*.(M.104.1388A).

μισθαρνία, ἡ, 1. *service for hire*; fig., of Christian obedience δουλείαν, μ., υἱότητα Bas.*mor*.7.11(3.512A; M.32.1212D); **2.** *prostitution,* Clem.*str*.2.18(p.160.14; M.8.1029A); Ath.*gent*.26(M.25.52A).

μίσθιος, ὁ, *hireling, hired servant,* Nonn.*par.Jo*.10:13(M.43.833B); Leont.N.*v.Jo.Eleem*.1(p.5.5); in Christian life τὰ ἐκ τοῦ μισθοῦ κέρδη διώκοντες, τῆς ἑαυτῶν ἕνεκεν ὠφελείας πληροῦμεν τὰ προστάγματα, καὶ κατὰ τοῦτο προσεοίκαμεν τοῖς μ. Bas.*reg.fus*. proem.3(2.329E; M.31.896B); ref. Mt.20:12, Max.*myst*.24(M.91.709D).

μισθοδοσία, ἡ, *payment of bribes*; plur., Isid.Pel.*epp*.5.372(M.78.1549C).

μισθοδοτέω, *bribe,* Synes.*ep*.131(M.66.1516A); Gel.Cyz.*h.e*.1.11.20 (M.85.1220A).

μισθοδότης, ὁ, 1. *paymaster*; of Christ, *M.Thdot.2* 3(p.86.31); **2.** *giver of bribes,* Synes.*ep*.2(M.66.1324B).

***μισθοπορία, ἡ,** *reward,* Sophr.H.*mir.Cyr.et Jo*.65(M.87.3648D).

μισθός, ὁ, 1. *hire, wages*; of a prostitute, Eus.*p.e*.4.16(162B; M.21.284C); *fee* μ. λαμβάνει [sc. false prophet] τῆς προφητείας αὐτοῦ· ἐὰν δὲ μὴ λάβῃ, οὐ προφητεύει Herm.*mand*.11.12; Ἀπόλλωνα...μαντευόμενον τοῖς ἀνθρώποις χάριν μισθοῦ Arist.*apol*.11.1(M.96.1116C); Cyr.*Mich*.36(3.423A); of pagan teachers ὁ περιπατητικὸς...ἠξίου με...μ. ὁρίσαι Just.*dial*.2.3(M.6.477A); ῥητορικὴν...ἐπ' ἀδικίᾳ...συνεστήσασθε, μισθοῦ πιπράσκοντες τῶν λόγων ὑμῶν τὸ αὐτεξούσιον Tat.*orat*.1(p.2.14; M.6.805B); σοφισταί, οἳ μισθὸν αἴρονται τῶν λόγων Meth.*res*.1.27 (p.255.15; M.41.1133B); of heret. priests μ. τοῦ λουτροῦ τῆς χάριτος καὶ ἀπὸ τιμῆς ἐκ τῶν λειψάνων τῆς θείας δωρεᾶς Leont.H.*monoph*.(M.86.1892A); kidnapper's *ransom,* Tat.*orat*.18(p.20.18; 848A); **2.** *reward* in gen.; **a.** for Christian in world μ. οὐκ ἔστιν μικρὸς πλανωμένην ψυχὴν...ἀποστρέψαι εἰς τὸ σωθῆναι *2Clem*.15.1; ἐὰν μελήσῃ μοι περὶ ὑμῶν τοῦ μέρος τι μεταδοῦναι ἀφ' οὗ ἔλαβον...ἔσται μοι...εἰς μ. *Barn*.1.5; μείζων ὁ μ. ἐὰν μὴ ἐπ' ἐλπίδι μισθῶν ποιῇς...φιλήσωμεν...αὐτὸν [sc. τὸν Χριστὸν] ὡς φιλεῖν χρή· τοῦτο γὰρ ὁ μέγας μ. Chrys.*hom.5.7 in Rom*.(9.470E); μισθὸν ἡμῖν δίδωσιν ἵνα φιλῶμεν ἀλλήλους, οὗ μ. ὀφείλομεν πράγματος· εὖξαι, φησί, καὶ λάβε μ., ὑπὲρ οὗ μ. ὀφείλομεν, ὅτι αἰτοῦμεν τὰ ἀγαθά id.*hom.2.4 in 1Thess*.(11.439D); εἰ ὄντως φιλάρετος, ᾔδεις ἂν ὅτι καὶ χωρὶς ἀμοιβῆς αὐτὴ ἡ ἀρετὴ μ. ἐστι Isid.Pel.*epp*.2.184(M.78.636A); **b.** in life to come, *2Clem*.3.3; ἐὰν ἐξέλθωμεν τὸν βίον ἔχοντες ἁμαρτήματα...καὶ ἀνδραγαθήματα...κολασθησόμεθα μὲν διὰ τὰ ἁμαρτήματα, οὐδαμοῦ δὲ μ. ληψόμεθα τῶν ἀνδραγαθημάτων; Or.*hom.16.6 in Jer*.(p.137.31; M.13.445B); **c.** given to Christ by Christian μ. γνώσεως τῷ σωτῆρι καὶ διδασκάλῳ...τὴν ἀποχὴν τῶν κακῶν καὶ τὴν ἐνέργειαν τῆς εὐποιΐας Clem.*str*.7.12(p.52.3; M.9.500C); **d.** of punishment as reward for sin, *Barn*.4.12; *Diogn*.9.2.

μισθοφορέω, *take fees,* Cyr.*Mich*.36(3.423A); perf. ptcpl., *mercenary* soldier, id.*Os*.59(3.92C).

μισθοφορία, ἡ, *service for wages*; of a token service performed annually, *Apophth.Patr*.(M.65.301C).

μισθ-όω, 1. act., *let out for hire*; fig., of God τοσαῦτά σοι δημιουργήματα καὶ χαρίσματα ὀλίγης πίστεως μ. Clem.*prot*.11(p.81.14; M.8.233B); **2.** med., *hire,* ref. Mt.20:3, Lc.15:17 'μίσθιοι τοῦ πατρός μου', τουτέστι κατηχούμενοι, καὶ γὰρ ~οῦται ἀεὶ ὁ φιλάνθρωπος θεός *cat.Lc*.15:13(p.118.30).

μισθωμάτιον, τό, *small reward,* Ephr.2.101C.

μισθωτής, ὁ, 1. *tenant,* Chrys.*hom.11.2 in 1Tim*.(11.608B, conj. for μισθωτός Gaume); **2.** *agent* for property; clergy forbidden to be such, CChalc.*can*.3.

μισθωτός, ὁ, *hireling,* ref. Jo.10:12 μ. ... ποιμένας, τοὺς οὐ διὰ τὸ ἀληθὲς ἀλλὰ διὰ τὸ αὐτῶν χρειῶδες τὴν τοῦ ποιμαίνειν ἐξουσίαν λαβόντες Bas.*hom*.23.4(2.187D; M.31.596B); εἰσὶ δέ τινες οἷον μ., τῇ ἐπιθυμίᾳ τῶν μελλόντων ἀγαθῶν τοὺς ὑπὲρ ἀρετῆς ἱδρῶτας φέρειν ἀνεχόμενοι Thdt.*Cant*.6:7(2.127); met. μ. ὀλίγης ἡδονῆς Meth.*symp*.2.4 (p.19.11; M.18.52C).

***μισιεραρχία, ἡ,** *hated hierarchy*; of Jacobites, Anast.S.*serm.imag*.3(M.89.1153B).

***μισόβρωμος,** *hostile to greediness,* Jo.Clim.*scal*.8(M.88.832B).

***μισογείτων, ὁ,** *one who hates his neighbour,* *Ep.Chr.dom*.(p.26).

***μισοδιδασκαλία, ἡ,** *hatred of instruction,* Pall.*v.Chrys*.4(p.25.15; M.47.16).

***μισοδοξία, ἡ,** *hatred of fame,* Ephr.2.394E.

μισόδοξος, *hating fame,* Cyr.S.*v.Euthym*.5(p.13.28); neut. as subst., *ib*.21(p.34.23).

***μισοθεΐα, ἡ,** *hatred of God,* Proc.G.*fr.Cant*.8:7(M.87.1773C).

***μισόθριξ,** *disliking hair,* Clem.*paed*.3.3(p.245.8; M.8.577A).

***μισοϊουδαῖος, ὁ,** *Jew-hater,* *Hom.Clem*.5.2.

***μισόκακος,** *hating evil,* Cyr.*Ps*.14:3(M.69.805C).

μισόκαλος, *hating the good*; as subst., of Devil, Meth.*res*.1.36 (p.276.1; M.41.1101A); Zeno *henot*.(p.53.12; M.86.2621C); Agath.*v.Gr.Ill*.32(p.19).

***μισοκοσμία, ἡ,** *hatred of the world,* Thdr.Stud.*epp*.2.117(M.99.1388C).

***μισόκοσμος,** *hating the world,* Ant.Mon.*hom*.15(M.89.1472D); Thdr.Stud.*epp*.2.118(M.99.1389D); *ib*.1.49(1085A).

***μισόλαγνος,** *hostile to lust,* Jo.Clim.*scal*.8(M.88.832B).

μισόλογος, *who hates talking,* Gr.Naz.*carm*.2.1.34.192(M.37.1321A); *who hates sermons,* Pall.*ep.Laus*.(p.7.16; M.34.1002).

***μισομόναχος,** *hating monks,* †Anast.S.*relat*.59(*OC* 3 p.87).

μισοξενία, ἡ, *inhospitality,* Chrys.*El.et vid*.3(3.330B); id.*hom.37.5 in Mt*.(7.421A); *cat.Lc*.16:22(p.125.18).

μισόξενος, *inhospitable,* Chrys.*hom.1.4 in Rom.16:3*(3.177E).

μισοπαθής, *hating emotion,* Marc.Er.*opusc*.2.140(M.65.952C).

μισοπάτωρ, *hating the Father* μ. ... ὁ χρῆναι δεῖν ἀτιμάζειν οἰόμενος τὸν υἱόν Cyr.*Jo*.10.2(4.903D).

μισοπόνηρος, *hating evil,* Cyr.*Lc*.18:1(M.72.849A); Eus.Dor.*ep.Chalc*.(p.8.39; H.2.312A); neut. as subst., Chrys.*exp.in Ps*.5:5(5.33B); superl., Clem.*str*.7.3(p.14.4; M.9.424B).

μισόπτωχος, *hating the poor,* *Const.App*.2.6.1.

μισοπώγων, ὁ, *beard-hater,* i.e. *hater of bearded philosophers,* title of satire by Julian, Thdt.*h.e*.3.28.3(3.945).

μῖσος, τό, 1. *hate,* ref. Lc.14:26 μ. ... οὐ μελετὴν ἐμποιοῦν ἐπιβουλῆς, ἀλλ' ἀρετὴν θεοσεβείας ἐν παρακοῇ τῶν ἀφελκόντων †Bas.*bapt*.1.1.4(2.628A; M.31.1524A); τὸ μ. κατὰ φύσιν [i.e. unfallen nature] ὅτε εὗρεν...'Ηλίας, ἀπέκτεινε τοὺς προφήτας τῆς αἰσχύνης Esaias *or*.2.2(p.5); personified, Herm.*sim*.9.15.3; of Devil εἰρήνη φυλάξει ἡμᾶς ἀπὸ τοῦ μ. ὅταν ἐξέλθῃ εἰς συνάντησιν ἡμῶν Ammonas *opusc*.4.1(p.474.13); **2.** *hatefulness* τὸ τῆς ἁμαρτίας μ. Nil.*Eulog*.22 (M.79.1121C).

***μισοσύντυχος,** *hating success*; neut. as subst., Cyr.S.*v.Euthym*.21(p.34.23).

***μισοτυφία, ἡ,** *hatred of pride,* Ant.Mon.*hom*.83(M.89.1685A).

***μισόφροντις,** *hating care,* Synes.*ep*.105(M.66.1488B).

***μισοχριστιανός,** *hating Christians,* *Chron.Pasch*.p.336(M.92.872B).

***μισόχριστος,** *hating Christ,* Cyr.H.*catech*.6.12; *A.Thom*.(*consumm*.)(p.290.11); of Jews ὁ μ. δῆμος Procl.CP *or*.19.6(M.65.816A); of S. Paul ἀντὶ μ. γεγονότα φιλόχριστον Jo.VI H.*v.Jo.D*.4(M.94.433B); as subst., *enemy of Christ,* Gr.Naz.*or*.41.5(M.36.436C); of Devil, Gr.Agr.*Eccl*.4.4(M.98.936A); of Jews, Thphn.*chron*.p.284(M.108.700A); superl., Gr.Naz.*or*.43.30(M.36.536C).

***μίσσα, ἡ,** (Lat. *missa*) *dismissal,* *Chron.Pasch*.p.338(M.92.881A).

***μιστυλλεύω,** = μιστύλλω, *chop up*; fig., Gr.Nyss.*Apoll*.42(M.45.1221A).

***μιτατεύω,** v. *μητατεύω.

μιτᾶτον, τό, (Lat. *metatum*) *lodging,* CCP(536)*act*.2(p.159.24; H.2.1233B); CCP(681)*act*.11(H.3.1297B); plur., *billets,* Jo.Mal.*chron*.13 p.347(M.97.517B).

***μιτατώριον (*μεσατώριον), τό,** (cf. μητατεύω) *sacristy,* Thdr.Lect.*h.e*.2.11(M.86.188B); μεσα-, *Euchol*.(p.497).

μίτος, ὁ, *thread,* fig. ὁ ἱστὸς τοῦ κυρίου ὡς τὸ πάθος τὸ ἐπὶ τῷ σταυρῷ γεγενημένον, στήμων δὲ ἐν αὐτῷ ἡ τοῦ ἁγίου πνεύματος δύναμις, κρόκη δὲ ὡς ἡ ἁγία σὰρξ ἐνυφαινομένη ἐν τῷ πνεύματι, μ. δὲ ἡ δι' ἀγάπης Χριστοῦ χάρις σφίγγουσα καὶ ἑνοῦσα τὰ ἀμφότερα εἰς ἕν Hipp.*antichr*.4(p.7.5; M.10.732B); met., *thread of destiny,* proverb ἀπὸ λεπτοῦ...μ. τὸ ζῆν ἠρτῆσθαι Synes.*ep*.4(M.66.1332D).

μίτρα, ἡ, anything which binds or girds; **1.** *breastplate* τὴν περιστήθιον ἐπιβαλὼν αὐτῷ μ. Gr.Nyss.*or.dom*.3(p.46.6; M.44.1148D); **2.** *girdle,* Nonn.*par.Jo*.13:4(M.43.860C); *ib*.21:18(920A); **3.** *headband,* hence *diadem*; fig., *Pss.Sal*.2.22; high priest's *head-dress*; fig., *T.Lev*.8.2; **4.** in building, *tie-beam,* Cyr.*Abac*.26(3.540C); *bonding, bond-stone,* Nonn.*par.Jo*.5:2(M.43.784C).

μιτρ-όω, 1. *surround as with a girdle* πεφόρητο μέσον ~ούμενος ἀνδρῶν Nonn.*par.Jo*.12:14 (v.l. μετρούμενος M.43.852C); *ib*.20:19 (912B); med., *ib*.19:40(908A); **2.** med., *gird,* *ib*.21:7(916B).

μνάομαι, *seek, strive for,* Clem.*paed*.3.5(p.254.30; M.8.601A); Gr.Thaum.*pan.Or*.12(p.28.6; M.10.1085B); Pall.*v.Chrys*.14(p.85.7; M.47.48).

μνασίς, ἡ, a Cypriot corn-measure, Epiph.*mens*.21(M.43.273B).

μνεία, ἡ, *remembrance*, in prayer ἡ πρὸς τὸν θεὸν καὶ τοὺς ἁγίους μετ' οἰκτιρμῶν μ. *1Clem.*56.1; *commemoration* of the departed τῶν ἁγίων μαρτύρων μ. ποιεῖν ἐν τοῖς σαββάτοις καὶ κυριακαῖς CLaod.*can.* 51; πάσης...τῆς ἀποστολικῆς ἁρμονίας τὰς μ. ἐπιτελοῦμεν Gr.Nyss. *Steph.*2(M.46.733A); μ. Ἰωάννου ἐν ταῖς εὐχαῖς ἐκέλευσε ποιεῖσθαι ὡς καὶ τῶν ἄλλων ἐπισκόπων τῶν κεκοιμημένων Socr.*h.e.*7.25.2(M.67.793A); *memorial celebration* ἐν ταῖς μ. [sc. τῶν εὐσεβῶν] καλούμενοι μετὰ εὐταξίας ἑστιᾶσθε *Const.App.*8.44.1; esp. *feast* of a saint μηδεὶς νηστευέτω...ἐν ταῖς τῶν καλλινίκων μαρτύρων μ. Eus.Al.*serm.*1(M.86.324A); *ib.*8(357Aff.); ἐπιτελῶν γὰρ τὰς μ. τῶν ἁγίων, δύο τραπέζας τίθεσθαι προσέταττε, μίαν μὲν πενήτων, καὶ ἑτέραν τοῖς μεγιστᾶσιν αὐτοῦ †Gregent.*leg.Hom.*proem.(M.86.580C); exeg. Rom.12:13 (reading μνείαις for χρείαις), cf. *memini in Latinis exemplaribus magis haberi memoriis sanctorum communicantes. ... nam usibus sanctorum honeste et decenter, non quasi stipem indigentibus praebere, sed censum nostrum cum ipsis...habere communem, et meminisse sanctorum sive in collectis solemnibus, sive pro eo ut ex recordatione eorum proficiamus, aptum...videtur,* Or.*comm.in Rom.*12:13(M.14.1220B); ταῖς μ. τῶν ἁγίων κοινωνεῖν ὁ ἀπόστολος παραινεῖ *M.Pion.* 1.1(p.45.26); ἔνια δὲ τῶν ἀντιγράφων ταῖς μ. ἔχει, τῆς αὐτῆς οὔσης διανοίας· λέγει γὰρ ὅτι δίκαιον ὑμᾶς μνημονεύειν πάντοτε τῶν ἁγίων, κοινάς τε αὐτῶν τὰς χρείας νομίζειν Thdr.Mops.*Rom.*12:13(p.162.2; M.66.861D).

μνῆμα, τό, *tomb* οὔτε ὀστέον νεκροῦ οὔτε μ. ... μιᾶναι δύναται ἀνθρώπου ψυχήν, ἀλλὰ μόνη ἀσέβεια *Const.App.*6.27.8; λέγεται τὸ μ. τοῦ μονάζοντος Ἀμμωνίου νόσους τὰς περὶ ῥῖγος ἐλαύνειν Pall.*v.Chrys.* 17(p.105.7; M.47.59).

μνηματίτης, ὁ, *custodian of a tomb*, Sophr.H.*mir.Cyr.et Jo.*40(M.87.3576D).

μνημεῖον, τό, *tomb*, Or.*hom.10.8 in Jer.*(p.78.8; M.13.368A); πρέπει τῷ θεῷ ἀνοίγειν τὰ μ. ἑκάστου καὶ ἐξάγειν ἐκ τῶν μ. ἡμᾶς ἐζωοποιημένους Meth.*res.*1.23(p.248.6; M.41.1093B); *Hom.Clem.*10.9.

μνήμη, ἡ, A. *memory*; **1.** *remembrance* ἐπὶ τοῦ καλοῦ ἔργου μ. παρὰ θεοῦ ἀγαθή *T.Neph.*8.5; σαββατίζειν ὑμῖν προσέταξεν, ἵνα μ. λαμβάνητε τοῦ θεοῦ Just.*dial.*19.6(M.6.517B); στήλη...ἁλὸς...ἔχουσα τῆς πονηρᾶς προαιρέσεως καὶ ὑποστροφῆς τὴν μ. Cyr.H.*catech.*19.8; in reference to faithful departed, of blessed *memory* μακαρίας μνήμης Ath.*apol.sec.*70(p.148.10; M.25.373A); Thdt.*ep.*81(4.1140); τοῦ ἐν εὐσεβεῖ τῇ μ. Τιβερίου Eustrat.*v.Eutych.*69(M.86.2352C); **2.** *commemoration*; **a.** of the departed ⟨ὑπὲρ⟩ δικαίων ποιούμεθα τὴν μ. καὶ ὑπὲρ ἁμαρτωλῶν· ὑπὲρ μὲν ἁμαρτωλῶν ὑπὲρ ἐλέους θεοῦ δεόμενοι Epiph.*haer.*75.7(p.339.4; M.42.513B); ἐπὶ δὲ τῶν τελευτησάντων ἐξ ὀνόματος τὰς μ. ποιοῦνται, προσευχὰς τελοῦντες id.*exp.fid.*23(p.524.8; M.42.829A); ἐνομοθετήθη ὑπὸ τῶν ἀποστόλων, τὸ ἐπὶ τῶν φρικτῶν μυστηρίων μ. γίνεσθαι τῶν ἀπελθόντων Chrys.*hom.4.4 in Phil.*(11.217E); τῇ τεσσαρακοστῇ ἡμέρᾳ τῆς τοῦ πατρὸς τελευτῆς μ. αὐτῷ τελῶν †Jo.D.*B.J.*36(M.96.1197B); of martyrs ἐπιτελεῖν τὴν τοῦ μαρτυρίου αὐτοῦ ἡμέραν γενέθλιον εἴς τε τῶν προηθληκότων μ. καὶ τῶν μελλόντων ἄσκησιν *M.Polyc.*18.3; τὸ μαρτύριον...ἐπὶ μνήμῃ τῶν ἀποστόλων οἰκοδομεῖν Eus.*v.C.*4.58(p.141.9; M.20.1209A); τῷ τὴν κυριακὴν τῆς ἀναστάσεως ἡμέραν συλλάμψαι τῇ μ. τῶν μαρτύρων Gr.Nyss.*Steph.*2(M.46.728A); ‡Ath.*qu.Ant.*26(M.28.613B); hence *feast day* τέταρτον καθ' ἑκάστην ἑβδομάδα κοινωνοῦμεν...καὶ ἐν ταῖς ἄλλαις ἡμέραις ἐὰν ᾖ μ. ἁγίου τινός Bas.*ep.*93(3.186D; M.32.484B); συνόδου...ἣν δι' ἔτους ἄγομεν ἐπὶ τῇ μ. τοῦ...μάρτυρος *ib.*100(196B; M.505A); ἀναγινωσκομένων τῶν ἐπιστολῶν τοῦ...Παύλου...καθ' ἑκάστην ἑβδομάδα δίς, πολλάκις δὲ καὶ τρὶς καὶ τετράκις, ἡνίκα ἂν μαρτύρων...μνήμας ἐπιτελῶμεν Chrys.*hom.1.1 in Rom.*(9.425A); ἡ ἐτήσιος μ. τοῦ μάρτυρος Chrysipp.*enc.in Thdr.*(p.60.12); τὴν μ. τοῦ ζωοποιοῦ σταυροῦ...ἑορτάσαμεν Eustrat.*v.Eutych.*70(M.86.2353C); **b.** of Christ's sacrifice, in eucharist θῦμα...ἐξαίρετον τῷ πατρὶ καλλιερησάμενος ὑπὲρ τῆς ἁπάντων ἡμῶν ἀνήνεγκε σωτηρίας, μ. καὶ ἡμῖν παραδοὺς ἀντὶ θυσίας τῷ θεῷ διηνεκῶς προσφέρειν Eus.*d.e.*1.10(p.47.16; M.22.89B); τούτου τοῦ θύματος τὴν μ. ἐπὶ τραπέζης ἐκτελεῖν διὰ συμβόλων τοῦ τε σώματος αὐτοῦ καὶ τοῦ σωτηρίου αἵματος *ib.*(p.47.32; 89D); **c.** of Resurrection τρεῖς εὐχὰς ἑστῶτες ἐπιτελοῦμεν μνήμης χάριν τοῦ διὰ τριῶν ἀναστάντος ἡμερῶν *Const.App.*2.59.4; **d.** of Creation κόσμον ἔκτισας διὰ Χριστοῦ καὶ σάββατον ὥρισας εἰς μ. τούτου *ib.*7.36.1; **e.** of Ascension, in foundation of a memorial church τῆς...ἀναλήψεως τὴν ἐπὶ τῆς ἀκρωρείας μ. σεμνύνων Eus.*v.C.*3.41(p.95.8; M.20.1101A); **3.** faculty of *memory* μ. μεγάλας Herm.*sim.*6.5.3; ἕκαστα τῶν ἡμᾶς μὲν λανθανόντων, σοὶ δ' αὐτῷ μόνῳ γνωριζομένων καὶ ταῖς σαῖς βασιλικαῖς μ. οἷα θησαυροῖς ἐν ἀπορρήτοις τεταμιευμένων Eus.*l.C.*18(p.259.20; M.20.1440A); of God τὰ διαβήματά μου ἐν τῇ μ. σου διαφύλαξον *Pss.Sal.* 16.9; Dion.Ar.*e.h.*3.3.9(M.3.437B); plur., *powers of memory*, Gr.Thaum.*pan.Or.*17(p.38.7; M.10.1100C); **4.** *act of memory, recollection* λάβε σπέρματα ἀπὸ τοῦ νόμου...ἀπὸ τῶν προφητῶν...καὶ...σπεῖρον τὴν ψυχὴν διὰ τῆς μ. καὶ τῆς μελέτης Or.*hom.5.13 in Jer.*(p.42.29; M.13.313C); Nil.*exerc.*48(M.79.777C) cit. s. γαλήνη; τῶν ἱερῶν γραφῶν, ὁπόσα εἰς ἀνάγνωσιν καὶ τὴν πρόχειρον μ. ἐτέλει, πολλὴν εἶχον τὴν ἐμπειρίαν Philost.*h.e.*8.11(M.65.628B); **5.** *record* λόγος...κατὰ τὴν ἄγραφον μ. ἐν τῇ ἐκκλησίᾳ διασῴζεται Nil.*epp.*1.2(M.79.84A); Philost.*h.e.*1.2(M.65.461C); **6.** *mention* οἱ προφῆται τὴν τοῦ εὐαγγελίου μ. ἐπὶ τοῦ Χριστοῦ προελάμβανον Eus.*d.e.*3 proem.(p.94.15; M.22.165A); hence *remarks* οἱ μνήμης μοι τῆς περὶ τὴν τριάδα...κοινωνήσαντες Didym.*Trin.*2.27(M.39.761B); **7.** *representation* Ἰωνᾶς ἐποίησε τὴν μ. τοῦ [sc. Χριστοῦ] θανάτου ‡Ath.*comm.essent.*47(M.28.72C); ζῴων μ. ἔχει τὰ οὐράνια, ἤτοι εἰκόνας Max.*schol.c.h.*2.3(M.4.41B).

B. representing Hebr. מָנֶה, *mina* μνᾶς ἥτις τῇ Ἑβραΐδι μ. καλεῖται Epiph.*mens.*24(M.43.289A).

μνημονεῖον, τό, *tomb*, *Ascens.Is.*A 3.14,16.

μνημόνευσις, ἡ, 1. *recollection*, Or.*Jo.*20.24(20; p.358.17; M.14.628A); **2.** *commemoration* of the dead, CCP(381)*can.*21.

μνημονευτικός, *of* or *for remembering* ἡ μ. δύναμις τῆς ψυχῆς Or.*exp.in Pr.*3:8(M.17.168B); Evagr.Pont.*cap.pract.*B 93(M.40.1249C); neut. as subst., *memory*, †Bas.*Is.*43(1.413D; M.30.201B); ‡Proc.G.*Pr.*2:1(M.87.1233C).

μνημονεύ-ω, *make mention of*, in prayer, esp. liturg., Ign.*Magn.* 14.1; μ. ἡμῶν τῷ κυρίῳ Ath.*ep.Adelph.*8(M.26.1084B); ἵνα...λειτουργῶν ἐν ταῖς ἐκκλησίαις ∼σῃς καὶ ὑπὲρ ἡμῶν id.*ep.Drac.*7(M.25.532A); μ. τῶν προκεκοιμημένων Cyr.H.*catech.*23.9; τῶν νηπίων τῆς ἐκκλησίας μ. *Lit.*ap.*Const.App.*8.10.18; τῶν ἁγίων μαρτύρων μ. *Lit.ib.*8.13.6; εἰ μή τινες [sc. αἱ τῶν ἁμαρτωλῶν ψυχαί] εὐεργεσίας μετεῖχον ἐκ τούτου, οὐκ ἂν ἐν τῇ προσκομιδῇ ἐμνημονεύοντο ‡Ath.*qu.Ant.*34(M.28.617B); aor. ptcpl. pass., *said, aforesaid*, Eus.*p.e.*2 proem.(44D; M.21.93B); Euthal.Diac.*epp.cath.*(M.85.672B); Leo Mag.*ep.*23(p.47.3; M.*PL.*54.734B).

μνημονικός, *commemorative*; as subst., *commemorative tablet* or *image*, Dion.Ar.*e.h.*3.3.9(M.3.437B).

μνημόριον, τό, *memorial, tomb*, *IG* 3.3513; *Hesp.*16(p.45).

μνημόσυνον, τό, 1. *memory* ἀπολέσεις τὸ μ. σου ἀπὸ τῆς γῆς *T.Jos.*7.5; *Pss.Sal.*2.19; Gel.Cyz.*h.e.*3.15.9; *recollection* νηφάλιον τὸ τῆς ψυχῆς ἀκριβὲς...καὶ λεπτὸν τοῦ θεοῦ μ. Or.*sel.in Lev.*10:5(M.12.400D); **2.** *memorial* τὴν περιτομὴν...μ. τῆς τε τοῦ Ἀβραὰμ πίστεως καὶ τῆς τοῦ θεοῦ δυνάμεως ‡Just.*qu.et resp.*102(M.6.1348B); ref. Esth. 9:28 κατὰ τὴν ἡμέραν ταύτην...ἑορτάζουσι, μ. οὖσαν σωτηρίας αὐτῶν ‡Ath.*synops.*42(M.28.369B); μ. ἱεροῖς ἀνατίθενται [sc. οἱ ὁσίως βεβιωκότες] Dion.Ar.*e.h.*3.3.9(M.3.437B); of BMV μ. αἰώνιον...εὐσπλαγχνίας [sc. τοῦ θεοῦ]...εἰς ἡμᾶς διὰ σοῦ Mod.*dorm.*10(M.86.3304A); of Lord's day τῆς ἀναστάσεως Χριστοῦ μ. Areth.*Apoc.*1:10(M.106.513D); plur., *memorial rites*, *A.Mt.*31(p.261.9); εἰσέτι μάγοι τὰ μ. τοῦ...Μίθρου τελοῦσιν Dion.Ar.*ep.*7.2(M.3.1081A); περὶ ποιούντων μ. βιοθανούντων †Jo.Jej.*serm.*(M.88.1924B); Jo.D.*imag.*1.21(M.94.1253A); **3.** *reminder* τὴν καθολικὴν διδασκαλίαν...εἰς μ. ἐπιστηρισμοῦ τοῖς πεπιστευκόσι θεοῦ *Const.App.*6.18.11; *record* οἱ ὑπομένοντες...ἔγγραφοι...ἀπὸ τοῦ θεοῦ ἐν τῷ μ. αὐτῶν *1Clem.*45.8.

μνησικακέω, *bear a grudge*; c. acc. pers., *T.Sym.*4.4; fig. τοῖς νόμοις μ. Synes.*regn.*20(p.47.11; M.66.1093C).

μνησικακία, ἡ, *remembrance of injuries* σημεῖον...τὸ φίλημα τοῦ ἀνακραθῆναι τὰς ψυχὰς καὶ πᾶσαν ἐξορίζειν μ. Cyr.H.*catech.*23.3; προσευχὴ...μνησικακίας καθάρσιον Gr.Nyss.*or.dom.*1(p.8.4; M.44.1124A); ref. Eph.4:26 ὅπως μὴ ἡ ἐπίμονος ὀργὴ μ. γένηται *Const.App.* 2.53.2; κατὰ...τοῦ διαβόλου...ἡ μ. ἐπαινετόν Chrys.*hom.22.5 in Eph.*(11.173D); ἡσυχία ἐστὶ τὸ καθεσθῆναι ἐν τῷ κελλίῳ...ἀπεχόμενος μ. καὶ ὑψηλοφροσύνης *Apophth.Patr.*(M.65.389B); ref. Mt.10:39 ὁ εὑρὼν τὴν ψυχὴν αὐτοῦ, τοῦτ' ἔστιν ἐν μ., ἀπολέσει αὐτήν Marc.Er.*opusc.*8.5(M.65.1109B); χωρὶς μ. καθαρὰ ἔστω τοῦ εὐχομένου ἡ διάνοια *cat.1Tim.*2:8(p.19.8); of a demon ὁ ἐπὶ τῆς μ. Jo.Mosch.*prat.*161(M.87.3029A).

***μνησιπονηρέω,** *remember wrongs*, Clem.*str.*2.18(p.160.6; M.8.1028B).

μνηστεία, ἡ, *betrothal*, *A.Pil.*B 2(p.292); ὁ μονάσας ἀζημίως λύει τὴν πρὸς αὐτὸν συστᾶσαν μ. Ath.Scholast.*coll.*1.2(p.14); of Church, Areth.*Apoc.*19:7(M.106.740A) cit. s. γάμος.

μνηστεύ-ω, 1. *woo*; med., *woo for oneself*, fig. φιλοσοφία...σοφίας ἀΐδιον ∼ομένη ἔρωτα Clem.*prot.*11(p.79.26; M.8.229B); *betroth* ἔπεμψεν ὁ θεὸς τοὺς οἰκέτας τοὺς ἑαυτοῦ ∼σομένους τῷ παιδὶ τὴν ἐκκλησίαν Chrys.*hom.23.1 in 2Cor.*(10.596A); c. dat., *arrange a marriage* for, id.*hom.35.5 in 1Cor.*(10.328E); *espouse*, ref. Moses and his second marriage τύπος τοῦ δεσπότου Χριστοῦ ὃς μετὰ τὴν Ἰσραηλῖτιν τὴν ἐξ ἐθνῶν ἐκκλησίαν ἐμνήστευσεν Thdt.*qu.22 in Num.*(1.235); med., of the man, *betroth to oneself*, Just.*dial.*78.3(M.6.657C); Chrys.*hom.3.1 in Mt.*(7.33C); *cat.Lc.*1:24(p.11.12); of the woman, *espouse*, fig. ἡ Θέκλα Χριστοῦ τοῖς νόμοις ~εται Geo.Pis.*carm*.17.2; met., *bring together* τῆς ἱερᾶς γεωμετρίας ἀλλήλους ἡμᾶς ~σάσης Synes.*ep*.93(M.66.1457C); **2.** med.; **a.** *pledge, guarantee* ἡ κλῆσις Ἰουδαίοις σωτηρίαν ἐμνηστεύετο Thdr.Heracl.*Is*.45:22(M.18.1341D); ὁ Χριστὸς...ὁ ἐλευθερίαν τῇ εἰσόδῳ ~όμενος Serap.*Man*.53(p.77; M.18.1256D); τὸ φίλημα ἀνακίρνησι τὰς ψυχὰς ἀλλήλαις, καὶ πᾶσαν ἀμνησικακίαν αὐταῖς ~εται Cyr.H.*catech*.23.3; κοινωνοὺς αὐτοὺς ἐποιεῖτο τοῦ δόγματος, τὸ ἀσφαλὲς ἑαυτῷ ~όμενος καὶ τοῖς μετ' αὐτὸν δεχομένοις αὐτοῦ τὰ διδάγματα Sophr.H.*ep.syn*.(M.87.3152A); met. ἡ συναφὴ τῶν δογμάτων διὰ τῆς ἀντιπαραθέσεως τὴν ἀλήθειαν ~εται Clem.*str*.1.2(p.14.4; M.8.709B); ἡ συμβᾶσά σοι λύπη χαρὰν μεγάλην ~εται Nil.*epp*.1.103(M.79.128B); *have pledged to one* ἀναγεννηθέντες... καὶ τὴν ἁγίαν ~όμενοι τροφήν Clem.*paed*.1.6(p.117.2; M.8.304B); οὐδεὶς ἐν τῷ νόμῳ πλημμελήσας...τῇ μετανοίᾳ τὴν ἄφεσιν ἐμνηστεύσατο Serap.*Man*.49(p.70; 1245A); **b.** *entrust*, Const.ap.Eus.*v.C*.2.68(p.68.17; M.20.1041A); **3.** *secure* for αἱ...στάσεις, τὸ κοινὸν ἀξιοῦσαι σώζειν, τὴν ἡγεμονίαν ἀπὸ τῶν ἐχόντων ἑτέροις ~ουσι Synes.*provid*.2.3(p.120.11; M.66.1269A); Ἀνδρόνικος ἑαυτῷ μνηστεύσας ἀρχήν id.*ep*.58(M.66.1400D); *ib*.67(1428B).

μνηστήρ, ὁ, 1. *betrothed*; of S. Joseph, Ath.*ep.Epict*.5(p.9.3; M.26.1057C); Chrys.*hom.4.4 in Mt*.(7.53C); Isid.Pel.*epp*.1.18(M.78.192B); of Christ τὸν θεῖον μ. Thdt.*h.rel*.9(3.1193); **2.** as adj., *mindful*, Nonn.*par.Jo*.6:26(M.43.797B).

***μνηστηριώδης,** *befitting wooers*, Clem.*paed*.2.5(p.186.4; M.8.449A).

μνηστός, fem., *who is being wooed*, Chrys.*sac*.6.12(p.166.1; 1.432E); *betrothed*, Just.*dial*.78.3(M.6.657C); Jo.Scholast.*coll.cap*.81.

μνῆστρον, τό, plur., *betrothal*, ‡Chrys.*hom.in Lc.2*:1(2.803E); Jo.Scholast.*coll.cap*.tit.81.

μνήστωρ, ὁ, = μνηστήρ, *suitor*, Clem.*paed*.2.8(p.201.12; M.8.481A); *betrothed*, †Gr.Thaum.*annunt*.2(M.10.1164D); Hipp.Th.*fr*.4.1(p.18.9); Ἰάκωβον τὸν ἀδελφὸν τοῦ κυρίου κατὰ σάρκα, υἱὸν ὑπάρχοντα τοῦ μ. Ἰωσὴφ τοῦ τέκτονος *ib*.5.4(p.29.10).

[*]μογγιλάλος, = μογιλάλος, *having an impediment in one's speech*, *A.Thom*.B 29(p.34.26); Hegem.*Arch*.10(p.15.10; μογι- M.10.1441C).

μογγός, *with a hoarse voice*; nickname of Peter, bishop of Alexandria, Evagr.*h.e*.3.11(p.109.21; M.86.2616B); †Leont.B.*sect*.5.2(M.86.1229A).

***μογηροφόρος,** *bearing anxieties*, Gr.Naz.*carm*.2.1.55.24(M.37.1401A).

***μογιβαδής,** *halting*, ‡Caes.Naz.*dial*.140(M.38.1077).

***μογιλαλέω,** *speak with difficulty, stammer*; Germ.CP *or*.2(M.98.280C).

***μογιλαλία, ἡ,** *impediment in speech*, Evagr.Pont.*cap.pract*.B 14(M.40.1265C).

***μοδεράτωρ, ὁ,** (Lat. *moderator*) *governor*, Ath.Scholast.*coll*.4.9(p.55).

***μόδη (μόδια), ἡ,** cf. Hebr. מִדָּה name of a measure μέτρον... κβ' ξέστων, ὃ καλεῖται παρ' Ἑβραίοις μ. παρ' Ἕλλησι δὲ μόδια Epiph.*mens*.23(M.43.280B).

***μοδιάριος, ὁ,** *one who measures out* corn, title of an official in charge of the corn supply, CTyr.(518)*act*.(*ACO* 3 p.87.16; H.2.1357A).

***μόδιον, τό,** = μόδιος 1, *A.Thom*.B 14(p.31.7); ὕδωρ...ἐξιὸν ἐν διαφόροις χεύμασιν...ἅπερ ἐκάλεσεν...διμόδιον, μόδιον Jo.Mal.*chron*.11 p.278(M.97.420C).

μόδιος, ὁ, 1. (Lat. *modius*) a corn measure, Epiph.*mens*.21(M.43.272Bff.); Pall.*h.Laus*.18(p.55.19; M.34.1060B); Cyr.S.*v.Sab*.44(p.134.10); **2.** a vessel of this capacity, hence *bushel*-shaped structure on top of a pillar ἦν δὲ μ. τῷ Συμεὼν ἡ περιβολή, ξύλου καρύας πεποιημένος Niceph.Ur.*v.Sym*.16(M.86.3001B); τὸν γεγλυμμένον μ. *ib*.25(3009A); τινα μηδὲ θυρίδα ἔχοντα μ. *ib*.46(3028C).

μοῖρα, ἡ, 1. *part*, of God μ. ἐσμεν καὶ λεγόμεθα θεοῦ διὰ τὸ τοὺς τοῦ εἶναι ἡμῶν λόγους ἐν τῷ θεῷ προϋφεστάναι Max.*ambig*.(M.91.1081C); acc. Manicheans ὡς ἂν προβάλῃ [sc. θεός] ἐκ τῆς οἰκείας οὐσίας...θείας μ. *Disp.Phot*.1(M.88.536D); **2.** *party*, orthodox or heret., Bas.*Spir*.77(3.65C; M.32.212C); Chrys.*ep.Innoc*.1.3(p.12.6; 3.518B); Philost.*h.e*.4.12(M.65.525B); **3.** *share, portion* ἵνα ὥσπερ ἡ ἀφθαρσία παρὰ τῷ θεῷ, τὸν αὐτὸν τρόπον θεοῦ μοίρας ἄνθρωπος μεταλαβὼν ἔχῃ τὸ ἀθάνατον Tat.*orat*.7(p.7.10; M.6.820B); **4.** *measure*, in phrases ἐκ πλείονος μ., ἐξ ἴσης μ. Chrys.*sac*.3.7(p.59.11; 1.385D); *ib*.6.7(p.156.14; 428C); **5.** appointed *place*, Eus.*h.e*.3.24.1(M.20.264B).

μοιραῖος, *subject to destiny*, i.e. *of this world, mortal*, of BMV νύμφας οὐ νυμφευθείσας ἀνδρῶν μ. κοίταις Synes.*hymn*.5.3(p.35; M.66.1608).

μοιρικός, *ordained by destiny*, Jo.Mal.*chron*.5 p.103(M.97.192B).

μοιρικῶς, 1. *in intervals of one degree*, Synes.*astrolab*.5(p.140.15; M.66.1585A); **2.** *as ordained by destiny, in accordance with destiny* ‡Caes.Naz.*dial*.109(M.38.977).

***μοιχαλλοίωτος,** *who changes adultery* into marriage; of Const. VI and Theodote, Thdr.Stud.*or*.11.29(M.99.832C).

μοιχάομαι, 1. trans., *debauch*, *Pss.Sal*.8:11; fig. μ. τὴν ἐκκλησίαν Synes.*ep*.5(M.66.1341C); *adulterate* τὴν ἀλήθειαν μ. Meth.*symp*.2.3(p.18.17; M.18.52B); **2.** intrans., *commit adultery*, *Hom.Clem*.13.14; *ib*.12.15; met., of idolatry, Herm.*mand*.4.2.9.

μοιχεία, ἡ, *adultery* ὁ...δεύτερος [sc. γάμος] εὐπρεπής ἐστι μ. Athenag.*leg*.33.2(M.6.968A); fig. and met. ἑνὸς μόνου τοῦ τῆς ἀληθείας προφήτου ἀκούειν δεῖ, εἰδότα ὅτι ὁ παρ' ἑτέρου σπαρεὶς λόγος μοιχείας ἔγκλημα λαβὼν...ἐκβάλλεται *Hom.Clem*.3.28; μ. πνευματικῆς, τῆς κατὰ σάρκα χείρονος ὑπαρχούσης *ib*.16.20; ref. Ex.32:19 ἡ νύμφη πρὸ τῆς παστάδος εἰς μ. ἀπέκλινε Thdt.*qu.68 in Ex*.(1.172).

***μοιχειανίζω,** *favour adultery*; pres. ptcpl. plur. as subst. = Μοιχειανοί, Thdr.Stud.*epp*.1.38(M.99.1041B); *ib*.1.51(1097D).

***μοιχειανικός,** *favouring adultery*, of opinion of Μοιχειανοί: τὴν μ. ψευδοδοξίαν Thdr.Stud.*epp*.1.48(M.99.1069C); *ib*.1.34(1025D).

***Μοιχειανοί, οἱ,** *those who favour adultery*; of followers of presbyter Josephus, who performed unlawful marriage between Const. VI and Theodote οἱ τὸ εὐαγγέλιον ἠθετηκότες δυσώνυμοι Μ. Thdr.Stud.*epp*.1.49(M.99.1084D); *ib*.1.35(1029C).

μοιχεύω, *commit adultery with* a woman, fig. οὐ μ. τὴν ἀλήθειαν οὐδὲ...κλέπτειν τὸν κανόνα τῆς ἐκκλησίας Clem.*str*.7.16(p.74.22; M.9.545B); med., of the woman; fig., of soul seduced by false teachers *Hom.Clem*.3.28.

***μοιχιαῖος,** *of adultery*, †Bas.*contub*.7(M.30.821C).

μοιχίδιος, = μοιχικός, Eus.*p.e*.4.16(162B; M.21.284B).

μοιχικός, *adulterous*; of persons, Clem.*paed*.3.2(p.243.23; M.8.573B); of Greek gods opp. Egyptian εἰ καὶ θηρία, ἀλλ' οὐ μ. id.*prot*.2(p.29.16; M.8.120A); ὄργια μ. Eus.*l.C*.7(p.213.16; M.20.1353B); μ. λύσσαν Gr.Nyss.*hom.3 in Cant*.(M.44.813D); neut. as subst., *charge of adultery*, Phot.*nomoc*.13.5(M.104.916A,917A).

***μοιχικῶς,** *adulterously*, Ath.*ep.Amun*.(M.26.1173B); ‡Just.*qu. et resp*.78(M.6.1320B); Thdr.Stud.*epp*.2.218(M.99.1657B).

***μοιχογέννητος,** *begotten in adultery*, Jo.Mal.*chron*.4 p.87(M.97.169C); Thdr.Stud.*epp*.1.31(M.99.1012B).

***μοιχοελέγκτης, ὁ,** *one who reproves adultery*; of Jo. Bapt., Thdr.Stud.*epp*.1.34(M.99.1024C).

***μοιχοζεύκτης, ὁ,** *one who performs an adulterous marriage*, Thdr.Stud.*or*.11.29(M.99.832C); id.*epp*.1.33(M.99.1020A).

***μοιχοζευκτικός,** *of* or *relating to an adulterous marriage*, Thdr.Stud.*epp*.1.33(M.99.1017C).

***μοιχοζευξία, ἡ,** *marriage of adulterers*, Thdr.Stud.*epp*.1.48(M.99.1073B).

***μοιχοκοινωνία, ἡ,** *communion with an adulterer*, Thdr.Stud.*epp*.1.36(M.99.1036A).

***μοιχοκτόνος,** *slaying adulterers*, Gr.Naz.*carm*.1.2.1.669(M.37.573A).

***μοιχοκυρώτης, ὁ,** *one who ratifies adultery*; as adj., Thdr.Stud.*epp*.1.37(M.99.1040D); *ib*.1.53(1105D).

***μοιχολέτης, ὁ,** *destroyer of adulterers*, Gr.Naz.*carm*.1.2.15.70(M.37.771A).

***μοιχομεριδαρχία, ἡ,** *association with adulterous ruler*, Thdr.Stud.*epp*.1.36(M.99.1036B).

μοιχός, ὁ, 1. *adulterer* ὁ ἀποστερῶν ἑαυτὸν τῆς προτέρας γυναικός, καὶ εἰ τέθνηκεν, μ. ἐστιν παρακεκαλυμμένος Athenag.*leg*.33.2(M.6.968A); fig., of a bishop changing his see, CAlex.*ep*.ap.Ath.*apol.sec*.6(p.93.13; M.25.260C); of a usurping bishop, Thphn.*chron*.p.188(M.108.488A); *seducer*, of the Devil μ. ... τῆς τῷ κυρίῳ νενυμφευμένης ψυχῆς Meth.*symp*.6.1(p.65.6; M.18.113C); **2.** as adj., *adulterous*, *T.Lev*.18.3; ‡Caes.Naz.*dial*.108(M.38.976).

***μοιχοσυνδρομία, ἡ,** *association with adulterers*, Thdr.Stud.*epp*.1.34(M.99.1024D); *ib*.1.35(1029C).

***μοιχοσύνδρομος, ὁ,** plur., *followers* or *supporters of adulterers*, Thdr.Stud.*epp*.1.39(M.99.1048B).

***μοιχοσύνοδος, ἡ,** *synod condoning adultery*, Thdr.Stud.*epp*.1.33(M.99.1020D).

***μοιχοσύστατος,** *supporting, countenancing adultery*, Thdr.Stud.*epp*.1.36(M.99.1036B).

***μοιχουργός,** *who makes adulterers* μ. διαβόλου Thdr.Stud.*epp*.1.36(M.99.1032C).

***μοιχόφιλος,** *lover of adulterers*, Thdr.Stud.*epp*.1.31(M.99.1012A).

[*]μολίβδινος, *leaden*, met. μ. ὀργάς Const.ap.Ath.*apol.sec*.62(p.141.30; μολυβδ- M.25.361A).

[*]**μολιβδίς, ἡ,** v. μολυβδίς.

μόλιβδος, ὁ, *lead*; *leaden missile* ὅσον ἀνδρῶν τριακοσίων μόλιβδος ἀκοντίζεται *Apoc.Bar.*5(p.88.15).

***μολιβδοχοέω,** *fix with molten lead*, Gr.Nyss.*Eun.*1(1 p.33.14; M.45.261A).

***μολίβισκος, ὁ,** *lead weight* for use with a pulley, *M.Eleuth.*6 (p.154.7).

***μολοχάς, ἡ,** a name for sardonyx, Epiph.*gemm.*1(M.43.293C).

μολυβδίς (μολιβδίς, μολυβίς), ἡ, 1. *leaden weight* attached to net οὐ καθαρὰν...τὴν ψυχήν, ἀλλ' ὥσπερ μολυβδίδας τὰς ἐπιθυμίας μεθ' ἑαυτῆς φερομένην Clem.*str.*4.4(p.255.10; M.8.1228C); **2.** *whip weighted with lead*, μολυβίς, Bas.*hom.*18.4(2.145E; M.31.500B); μολιβδίς, Petr.II Al.*encycl.*7(M.33.1288B)ap.Thdt.*h.e.*4.22.28; μολυβίς, *M.Ign.Rom.*4; **3.** *leaden holder* for wick, μολυβίς, *Euchol.*(p.346).

μολυβίς, ἡ, v. μολυβδίς.

***μολυντέον,** *one must defile*, Or.*Cels.*8.62(p.278.14; M.11.1609C).

μολύν-ω, *stain, defile, contaminate*, fig. and met. ἵνα μὴ αἰσχρανεῖ τὸ σῶμα καὶ τὴν ψυχὴν ∼εῖ *T.Aser* 4.4; soul by false teaching, Gr.Thaum.*pan.Or.*13(p.29.12; M.10.1088A); ὁ διάβολος...τὸ λογικὸν ἡμῶν...τῆς φρονήσεως κάλλος...μ. ... [sc. τεχναζόμενος] Meth.*symp.* 6.1(p.65.5; M.18.113C); τί ∼εις τὸν σαυτοῦ πλοῦτον, ἐπεισάγων αὐτῷ τὰ μὴ δίκαια κέρδη; †Bas.*miser.*(2 p.1068B; M.31.1709A); μ. θεσπεσία δόγματα Synes.*ep.*143(M.66.1536C); of Christ οὐδὲ ἐν σώματι ὢν ἐμολύνετο ἀλλὰ μᾶλλον καὶ τὸ σῶμα ἡγίαζεν Ath.*inc.*17.5(M.25.125C); οἱ μεμολυσμένοι *sinners*, Cyr.*Os.*3(3.15D); *ib.*130(163C).

[*]**μόλυσις, ἡ,** = μολυσμός, Gr.Mag.*dial.*(tr.Zach.)4.53(M.*PL*.77.415B).

μόλυσμα, τό, 1. *spot, taint, that which defiles*, fig. and met. ὁ παλαιὸς ἄνθρωπος...ἁμαρτήματά τε καὶ μ. ὥσπερ μέλη ἑαυτοῦ δηλοῖ †Bas.*bapt.*1.2.14(2.639E; M.31.1549C); μ. ... περί τε σῶμα καὶ ψυχὴν Gr.Nyss.*v.Mos.*45(M.44.316A); τοῦ ἐκ πονηρίας μ. id.*hom.13 in Cant.*(M.44.1044A); τῶν σαρκικῶν μ. ὧν κατὰ γέννησιν τὴν ἐκ πατέρων διεδεξάμεθα ‡Chrys.*pasch.*4(8.260D); Philost.*h.e.*1.1(M.65.461A); δεύτερόν σοι λουτρὸν...καὶ κολυμβήθραν [i.e. penitence] καθαίρουσάν σου τῶν μ. τὴν συνείδησιν Isid.Pel.*epp.*1.408(M.78.409C); Μαρίας...παντὸς ἐλευθερίας μ. τοῦ τε κατὰ σῶμα καὶ ψυχὴν καὶ διάνοιαν Sophr.H.*ep.syn.*(M.87.3160D); **2.** = μολυσμός, *defilement*, Gr.Naz.*or.*14.12(M.35.872C).

μολυσμός, ὁ, *defilement, pollution*, physical ὕδατος ᾧ μ. σωμάτων πάντως ἀποκαθαίρονται Didym.(‡Bas.)*Eun.*5(1.308C; M.29.740B); of leprosy, Or.*schol.in Lc.*7:22(M.17.333B); ritual τὸν ἐπὶ νεκρῷ μ. Cyr.*Os.*96(3.128C); id.*Ag.*15(3.645D); of idolatry, id.*Os.*20(3.42C); id.*Mich.*25(3.413A); sexual, Clem.*paed.*3.11(p.268.31; M.8.629C); Epiph.*anac.*21(p.234.6; M.41.281A); Jo.Mosch.*prat.*165(M.87.3032C); moral *pollution* in gen., ref. 1Cor.5:11, Clem.*paed.*2.1(p.161.18; M.8.396B); ὥσπερ μέλος ἀνιάτως ἔχον ἀποκοπτέος ἡμῶν...ὁ γὰρ μ. διαδόσιμος γίνεται Synes.*ep.*58(M.66.1401C); Cyr.*Lc.*13:26(M.72.780A); of truth by falsehood τὸ τῶν Ἰσραηλιτῶν ποτὸν τῷ μ. τοῦ ψεύδους αἷμα ποιῆσαι, τουτέστι τὸν ἡμέτερον λόγον Or.*exc.in Ps.*77:44(M.17.147B).

μοναδικός, A. *one, forming a single entity*; **1.** of Godhead σπεύσωμεν εἰς σωτηρίαν...εἰς μίαν ἀγάπην συναχθῆναι οἱ πολλοὶ κατὰ τὴν τῆς μ. οὐσίας ἕνωσιν σπεύσωμεν Clem.*prot.*9(p.65.29; M.8.200B); ὁ μόνος ὑφ' ἑαυτοῦ γινωσκόμενος τρισυπόστατος θεὸς καὶ μ. ‡Gr.Nyss.*hom.1.1 in Jo.*(p.93.9); ref. Dt.6:9 καὶ τὸ τῆς οὐσίας διδάσκει μ. καὶ παραδηλοῖ τῶν προσώπων τὸν ἀριθμόν. ἅπαξ γὰρ 'ὁ θεός', δὶς τὸ 'κύριος' τέθεικεν Thdt.*qu.2 in Dt.*(1.263); ref. Is.6:3 καὶ τῶν τριῶν ὑποστάσεων δηλώσας τὸν ἀριθμόν, καὶ τῆς θεότητος τὸ μ. Cosm.Ind.*top.*5(M.88.312C); τριάδα γὰρ ἐν μονάδι πιστεύομεν...τριάδα μὲν ταῖς τρισὶν ὑποστάσεσι, μονάδα δὲ τῷ μ. τῆς θεότητος Sophr.H.*ep.syn.*(M.87.3152D); τὸ κατ' οὐσίαν ἓν καὶ ταὐτὸν καὶ μ. τῆς θεότητος Max.*ambig.*(M.91.1304A); of Father and Son οὐ γὰρ εἶπε τοῖς δυναμένοις πληθυντικῶς, ἀλλ' ἑνικῷ ὀνόματι τὴν μ. οὐσίαν ἀμφοτέρων ἐσήμανεν εἰπὼν 'τῷ δυναμένῳ' Ammon.*Ac.*20:32(M.85.1584A); **2.** of Christ ὁ Χριστὸς δύο ὑπάρχων φύσεις, ἀλλ' ἐν αὐταῖς ἀληθῶς γνωριζόμενος, μοναδικὸν ἔχει τῆς υἱότητος τὸ πρόσωπον Gr.Nyss.*fr.*(M.46.1112C); †Ath.*fr.*(M.26.1236D); μήτε τὰ τῆς υἱότητος καὶ κυριότητος τέμνηται, μήτε τὰ τῶν φύσεων ἐν τῷ τῆς υἱότητος μοναδικῷ συγχύσεως ἀφανισμῷ κινδυνεύῃ Nest.*ep.Cyr.*2(p.30.4; M.77.52B); οὐδὲν ἡμῖν πρός τε τὸ τὰς δύο φύσεις δεικνύειν τὸ μ. τῆς ὑποστάσεως παρεμποδὼν γέγονεν· οὐδὲ πρὸς τὸ μίαν λέγειν ὑπόστασιν τὸ δυαδικὸν τῶν φύσεων σκληρὸν καθέστηκεν Leont.H.*Nest.*2.5(M.86.1644B); τὴν μὲν [sc. διαφορὰν] ἀδιαιρέτως ἐν τῷ φυσικῷ θεωρουμένην λόγῳ τῶν ἡνωμένων, τὴν δὲ ἀσυγχύτως ἐν τῷ μ. γνωριζομένην τρόπῳ τῶν γιγνομένων Max.*ambig.*(M.91.1052B); πᾶσα μὲν γὰρ εὐαγγελικὴ...παραίνεσις...πῇ μὲν τὸ μ. αὐτοῦ δηλοῦσα πρόσωπον, πῇ δὲ τὰς δύο αὐτοῦ σαφῶς μαρτυροῦσα φύσεις Anast.S.*hod.*10(M.89.181A); **3.** of believer as united to God τὸ εἰς αὐτὸν καὶ τὸ δι' αὐτοῦ πιστεῦσαι μ. ἐστι γενέσθαι, ἀπερισπάστως ἑνούμενον ἐν αὐτῷ Clem.*str.*4.25(p.318.5; M.8.1365B); **4.** speaking *as one, united* τὰς ἄλλας...μ. τῶν ἁγίων πατέρων φωνάς Max.*opusc.*(M.91.88C); **5.** *one, single* ὡς γὰρ εἷς πατήρ, καὶ εἷς υἱός, οὕτω καὶ ἓν πνεῦμα ἅγιον· τῆς μὲν οὖν κτιστῆς φύσεως τοσοῦτον ἀποκεχώρηκεν, ὅσον εἰκὸς τὸ μ. τῶν συστηματικῶν καὶ πληθυσμὸν ἐχόντων Bas.*Spir.*45(3.38D; M.32.152A); τῶν ἐπὶ τῆς παλαιᾶς διαθήκης πνεῦμα μὲν ἅγιον μ. ἐν ὑποστάσει κεχωρισμένως τῶν λοιπῶν, θεοῦ τε ὂν καὶ ἐκ θεοῦ οὐκ ἐπισταμένων Thdr.Mops.*Joel* 2:28(M.66.229B); εἴπερ μ. φύσις ἐστὶν ὁ Χριστός, οὔτε τῷ θεῷ καὶ πατρὶ ὁμοούσιός ἐστιν, οὔτε τοῖς ἀνθρώποις Max.*ep.*13(M.91.520C); ἠρώτησέ τε τὸν βασιλέα περὶ τῆς ἐνεργείας καὶ τῶν θελημάτων, τὸ πῶς δεῖ ταῦτα λέγειν ἐν Χριστῷ, διπλᾶ ἢ μ.; Anast.S.*serm.imag.*3(M.89.1153B); *single, separate* ἔστι [sc. divine nature] τῶν μὲν πάντῃ διαιρετῶν ἑνικωτέρα, τῶν δὲ τελείως μοναδικῶν ἀφθονωτέρα Gr.Naz.*or.*34.8(M.36.249A); συναριθμεῖται...τὰ ὁμοούσια· τὰ δὲ μὴ οὕτως ἔχοντα μοναδικὴν ἔχει τὴν δήλωσιν *ib.*31.11(p.166.12; 152C).

B. *alone, separate*; **1.** *unique* καθόλου γὰρ τὸ παθητικὸν παντὶ γένει ἐπιθυμίας, εἰς δὲ τὴν ἀπάθειαν θεούμενος ἄνθρωπος ἀχράντως μ. γίνεται Clem.*str.*4.23(p.315.26; M.8.1361A); ἵνα...τοῦτο θεϊκὸν ἔχωσι τὸ μ., ὁ μὲν τῆς υἱότητος, τὸ δὲ τῆς προόδου καὶ οὐχ υἱότητος Gr.Naz.*or.*25.16(M.35.1221A); πρωτότοκος ὁ κύριος ἐκ τοῦ πατρὸς καὶ ἐκ τῆς παρθένου καὶ ἐκ τῶν νεκρῶν, ἵνα διὰ πάντων γνωσθῇ τὸ μ. τῆς υἱότητος ἀξίωμα Gr.Nyss.*fr.*(M.46.1112B); ref. Jo.1:3 εἰ γὰρ ἓν πνεῦμα ἅγιον καὶ μόνον, πῶς ὃ τῆς μ. ἐστι φύσεως τοῖς πᾶσι συμπαραλαμβάνεσθαι δύναται; Bas.*Eun.*3.7(1.278D; M.29.669C); ‡Ath.*Maced.*1.8(M.28.1300C); οὐδὲν τῶν ἄλλων πνευμάτων τοιοῦτό ἐστι πνεῦμα· μ. γάρ ἐστι ‡Ath.*dial.Trin.*3.19(M.28.1232D); of God's sovereignty τὴν περιεκτικὴν...τοῦ παντὸς...κόσμου μ. δεσποτείαν Melet.*nat.hom.*1(M.64.1152A); **2.** *solitary* ὅσοι θεῷ ζῶσιν ἐν μ. βίῳ καὶ ἄζυγι Gr.Naz.*or.*18.22(M.35.1012A); Ἀντωνίου...βίον συνέγραφε, τοῦ μ. βίου νομοθεσίαν *ib.*21.5(1088A); πολλοὶ καὶ διάφοροι τῆς εὐσεβείας οἱ βίοι, μ. καὶ κοινωνικοί, ἐρημικοὶ καὶ πολιτικοί Thdt.*Ps.*24:12(1.760); id.*h.rel.*27(3.1283); πρεσβύτεροι μετὰ νεωτέρων, ἱερεῖς καὶ λαός, οἱ μ. καὶ μιγάδες Eustrat.*v.Eutych.*99(M.86.2385B); fig. οἱ ἀρνησίθεοι καὶ μ. λύκοι, οἱ ἀνόσιοι ψευδοχριστιανοί †Cyr.*hom.div.*10(5^2.378A; M.77.1028C); of a group, *solitary, separated* τὴν μοναχικὴν τάξιν...ἐφ' ἑαυτῆς ἑστῶσαν ἐν μ. καὶ ἱερᾷ στάσει Dion.Ar.*e.h.*6.3.1(M.3.533C); **3.** *single, unmarried* μέγα παρθενία,...καὶ τὸ μετ' ἀγγέλων τετάχθαι, καὶ τῆς μ. φύσεως Gr.Naz.*or.*43.62(M.36.576C).

C. = μοναχικός, *monastic*, Synes.*ep.*66(M.66.1408C); τῷ μ. τάγματι Nil.*epp.*2.63(M.79.228D); τοῦ σχήματος τοῦ μ. *ib.*4.38(568A); Cyr.S.*v.Sab.*38(p.128.18); Eustrat.*v.Eutych.*18(M.86.2296A); Thphn.*chron.*p.98(M.108.289B); neut. as subst., *monastic population* τὸ μ. καὶ τὸν δῆμον τῆς βασιλευούσης Evagr.*h.e.*3.7(p.106.24; M.86.2609B); *ib.*3.31(p.127.6; 2657C); *ib.*2.5(p.51.32; 2562B).

D. *concerning the Monad* τῆς μ. γνώσεως Clem.*str.*3.2(p.197.27; M.8.1105A).

μοναδικῶς, 1. *as one, as a unity* μία θεότης οὖσά τε μ. καὶ ὑφισταμένη τριαδικῶς Max.*ambig.*(M.91.1036C); ἑαυτῷ προσφυῶς, μ. ἤγουν ἑνοειδῶς ἐνεργῶν [sc. Χριστός] *ib.*(1052C); τῆς μιᾶς θεότητος τῆς ἐν τριάδι μ. ὑπαρχούσης καὶ διαιρουμένης ἀδιαιρέτως *Lit.Jac.*(p.162.1); **2.** *as one, singly* ἓν...τὸ ἅγιον πνεῦμα καὶ αὐτὸ μ. ἐξαγγελλόμενον Bas.*Spir.*45(3.38C; M.32.149C); δύο τῷ Μωϋσεῖ χερουβὶμ εὑρίσκω μ. ἀριθμούμενα Gr.Naz.*or.*31.10(p.167.8; M.35.153A); ἑκάστην ὑπόστασιν θεὸν καὶ κύριον ὁμολογεῖν ‡Ath.*symb.*(M.28.1581B); *in the singular* τὸ μηδέν τι τῶν θεοπρεπῶν ὀνομάτων πληθυντικῶς ἀριθμεῖν, ἀλλὰ μίαν...τὴν ἀγαθότητα καὶ πάντα τὰ τοιαῦτα μ. ἐξαγγέλλειν Gr.Nyss.*Trin.*3(p.73.23; M.32.688B); ὅταν μὲν μ. ἡ δύναμις λέγηται, πρὸς τὸ θεῖον ἀναπέμπεται διὰ τῆς τοιαύτης φωνῆς ἡ διάνοια· ὅταν δὲ διὰ τοῦ πληθυντικοῦ σχήματος ἐκφωνῆται, τὴν ἀγγελικὴν φύσιν τῷ λόγῳ παρίστησιν id.*hom.5 in Cant.*(M.44.856B); μ. τε τὸ θεῖον ὡς ἕνα θεὸν καὶ μίαν θεότητα λέγεσθαι id.*tres dii*(M.45.125A); ref. Dt.6:4 μ. τὸ θεῖον ἐν τῇ παλαιᾷ προφέρεται ὄνομα Thdt.*qu.2 in Dt.*(1.262); τοὺς τρεῖς ἄνδρας...τύπον...τριάδος, πρὸς οὓς εἰρῆσθαι μ. τὸ 'κύριε' Proc.G.*Gen.*18:1(M.87.364B); **3.** *uniquely* οἰκεῖον ἀποκαλεῖ πατέρα μ. τὸν θεόν, ὡς...μόνος...γεγεννημένος ἀληθῶς Cyr.*Jo.*2.1(4.139B); *ib.*2.5(213D); μεμαρτύρηκε ὅτι οὗτος καὶ μετὰ σαρκὸς καὶ ἐν τῇ τοῦ δούλου μορφῇ μ. τε καὶ ἰδικῶς ἐμὸς ἀληθῶς υἱός id.*inc.unigen.*(5^1.705D); μ. καὶ συνάρθρως ὁ κύριός μου φησὶ καὶ ὁ θεός μου id.*Jo.*12.1(4.1109C); **4.** *once* τὸ μὲν ἅγιος τρὶς...τὸ δὲ κύριος μ. Jo.D.*trisag.*2(M.95.25B).

μονάζ-ω, A. *leave alone*; pass., Jo.Mal.*chron.*14 p.373(M.97.556B).

B. *be apart, keep to oneself*, *Barn.*4.10; οἱ μὴ κολλώμενοι τοῖς δούλοις τοῦ θεοῦ ἀλλὰ ∼οντες ἀπολλύουσι τὰς ἑαυτῶν ψυχάς Herm.*sim.*9.26.3; hence **1.** *be single, unmarried* σωματοθήκη Κόνονος...∼οντος καὶ Μαρίας ἀδελφῖς αὐτοῦ *MAMA* 3.535 (Corycus); ptcpl.

as subst., *celibate* οἱ γενναῖοι ἀπόστολοι καὶ οἱ καθεξῆς παρθένοι καὶ ∼οντες Ἰωάννης μὲν καὶ Ἰάκωβος...μείναντες ἐν τῇ παρθενίᾳ Epiph. *haer*.58.4(p.361.10; M.41.1016A); τινὲς τῶν ∼όντων...κατοικοῦσι τὰς πόλεις, τινὲς δὲ καὶ ἐν μοναστηρίοις καθέζονται, καὶ ἀπὸ μήκοθεν ἀναχωροῦσιν id.*exp.fid*.23(p.524.11; M.42.829A); οὐχὶ ∼ουσιν ἔγραφε ταῦτα οὐδὲ ἀειπαρθένοις, ἀλλὰ...κοσμικοῖς Chrys.*hom.4.5 in Heb.* (12.46D); **2.** *live in solitude* δύσκολον ὁμοῦ καὶ ἐπικίνδυνον τὸ ∼ειν Bas.*reg.fus*.7 tit.(2.345B; M.31.928B); δυνατὸν μετὰ πολλῶν ὄντα ∼ειν τῇ γνώμῃ ‡Ath.*v.Syncl*.97(M.28.1548A); *A.Mt*.1(p.217.1); Leont.N. *v.Sym*.55(M.93.1737C); **3.** *become a monk* ἁρμόζει κατὰ μητέρων ἤτοι γονέων κωλυόντων τοὺς ἑαυτῶν παῖδας ∼ειν Ammon.*Ac*.21:13(M.85. 1584D); Marc.Diac.*v.Porph*.52; *Apophth.Patr*.(M.65.244D); pres. ptcpl. as subst., *monk*, Serap.*euch*.11.5; Ath.*narr.fug*.(M.26.981A); id.*apol.Const*.28(M.25.632A); id.*v.Anton*.86(M.26.964A); τῷ τῶν ∼όντων τάγματι Gr.Nyss.*v.Macr*.(p.407.10; M.46.993A); οὕτως [sc. like pearl divers] καὶ οἱ ∼οντες γυμνοὶ ἐξέρχονται τοῦ κόσμου, καὶ κατέρχονται εἰς βυθὸν θαλάσσης τῆς κακίας...καὶ...ἀναφέρουσι τιμίους λίθους Mac.Aeg.*hom*.15.51(M.34.612A); καλῶς καὶ οἱ ∼οντες καὶ αἱ κανονικαὶ ἀποκείρονται τὴν κόμην Ammon.*Ac*.18:18(M.85. 1569C); Chrys.*sac*.3.15(p.78.13; 1.393D); id.*hom.7.4 in Heb*.(12.80A); ∼ουσα, ἡ, *nun*, Epiph.*haer*.62.8(p.399.3; M.41.1064A); συνέπεται δὲ τῇ αὐτῇ παρθενίᾳ ἡ μονότης, παρὰ πλείοσι τῶν ∼όντων καὶ ∼ουσῶν id.*exp.fid*.21(p.522.1; M.42.824A); Max.*ep*.12(M.91.460B); Thphn. *chron*.p.122(M.108.340C).

***μονάκτινος**, *shining with a single ray*; of Trin., Eulog.*fr.Trin.* 2.1(p.364).

μονάμπυξ, *with no yoke-fellow*; met., *standing alone*, Paul.Sil. *Soph*.893(M.86.2153A).

μονανδρέω, *have only one husband*, Jo.Mal.*chron*.1 p.21(M.97.88A).

***μονανδρία, ἡ**, *having only one husband, not being twice married*, Chrys.*vid*.2 tit.(1.349C).

μόνανδρος, *having only one husband*, *Const.App*.3.3.1; of Church, Ph.Carp.*Cant*.21(M.40.52B); Anast.S.*hex*.12(M.89.1076B).

μοναρχέω, *be sovereign*; of Roman empire, Andr.Caes.*Apoc*.54 (M.106.380D).

μονάρχης, ὁ, *sole ruler*, of God, Gr.Naz.*carm*.1.1.30.1,26(M.37. 508A,509A).

μοναρχία, ἡ, A. *government by a single ruler, monarchy*; of God; **1.** sole supremacy οὐχ οἱ φιλόσοφοι περὶ θεοῦ τὸν ἅπαντα ποιοῦνται λόγον...καὶ περὶ μοναρχίας αὐτοῖς καὶ προνοίας αἱ ζητήσεις γίνονται; Just.*dial*.1.3(M.6.473B); τὴν πολυκοιρανίην μᾶλλον ἤπερ τὴν μ. ἐξησκήσατε Tat.*orat*.14(p.15.9; M.6.836B); εἰ δὲ θεὸς ἀγένητος καὶ ὕλη ἀγένητος, οὐκ ἔτι...μ. θεοῦ δείκνυται Thphl.Ant.*Autol*.2.4(M.6. 1052B); cf. *monarchiam nihil aliud significare scio quam singulare et unicum imperium...eversio enim monarchiae illa est tibi intellegenda, cum alia dominatio...aemula superducitur, cum alius deus infertur adversus creatorem*, Tert.*adv.Praxean* 3(M.*PL*.2.158B,159A); θεὸς...οὐ...ἀδιάδοχος ἡ μ. *Const.App*.7.35.9; **2.** unicity; **a.** opp. polytheism, equivalent of monotheism πρῶτος...αὐτοῖς...τὴν περὶ μοναρχίας θεολογίαν κατήγγειλεν [sc. Moses], τὸν τῶν ἁπάντων δημιουργὸν καὶ ποιητὴν μόνον παραγγείλας σέβειν Eus.*d.e*.3.2(p.97.6; M.22.169A); ἀποκρινέσθω τὰ περὶ ἀνατροπῆς πολυθέου πλάνης, ἀποδεικνύουσα τὸν περὶ μοναρχίας θεοῦ λόγον *Const.App*.3.5.4; ἐν δὲ τῇ μ. πνευματικῶς ἡ τριὰς καταγγελλομένη [i.e. in Pentateuch] Epiph.*haer*.9.2(p.198. 19; M.41.225A); denied by Marcion Μαρκίωνος γὰρ...δίδαγμα εἰς τρεῖς ἀρχὰς τῆς μ. τομὴ καὶ διαίρεσις Dion.R.ap.Ath.*decr*.26(p.22.13; M.25.464A); and by Manicheans, cf. *si enim dicimus monarchiam unius naturae et omnia deum replere et nullum esse extraneum locum, quis erit creaturae susceptor? ubi gehenna ignis?* Hegem. *Arch*.16(p.26.12; M.10.1454A); **b.** in teaching of Sabellian and other 'monarchian' theologians, opp. supposed tritheism of 'pluralists' οὕτως...δοκεῖ [sc. Νοητός] μ. συνιστᾶν, ἓν καὶ τὸ αὐτὸ φάσκων ὑπάρχειν πατέρα καὶ υἱόν...ὀνόματι μὲν πατέρα καὶ υἱὸν καλούμενον κατὰ χρόνων τροπήν, ἕνα δὲ εἶναι Hipp.*haer*.9.10(p.244.23; M.16.3378B); οὐδὲ εἰς τὴν γνώμην τῶν ἀποσχισθέντων ἀπὸ τῆς ἐκκλησίας εἰς φαντασίαν μοναρχίας ἐμπίπτομεν, ἀναιρούντων υἱὸν ἀπὸ πατρός Or.*dial*.4(p.126.17); οἱ ἀπὸ Μαρκέλλου...οἱ τὴν προαιώνιον ὕπαρξιν τοῦ Χριστοῦ καὶ τὴν θεότητα...ὁμοίως Ἰουδαίοις ἀθετοῦσιν ἐπὶ προφάσει τοῦ συνίστασθαι δοκεῖν τῇ μ. *Symb.Ant*.(345)6(p.253.3; M.26.732A); υἱὸν ὑπήκοον... βασιλεύοντα...εἰς τὰς αἰῶνας, σωζομένης ἐν ἅπασι πάντοτε τῆς ὑπεροχῆς τοῦ θεοῦ καὶ μ. Eun.*apol*.27(M.30.865A).

B. = possession of but a single source, *unity* of Godhead as proceeding from Father as sole origin (in early writers esp. idea of supremacy is also present) ἑνὸς ὄντος ἀνάρχου καὶ ἀγεννήτου θεοῦ τοῦ δὲ υἱοῦ ἐξ αὐτοῦ γεγεννημένου, μία ἔσται ἀρχὴ μ. τε καὶ βασιλεία μία, ἐπεὶ καὶ αὐτὸς ὁ υἱὸς ἀρχὴν ἐπιγράφεται τὸν αὐτοῦ πατέρα Eus.*e.th*.2.7 (p.104.6; M.24.908C); cf. *ita trinitas per consertos et connexos gradus a patre decurrens et monarchiae nihil obstrepit et oeconomiae statum protegit*, Tert.*adv.Praxean* 8(M.*PL*.2.164A); μία ἀρχὴ θεότητος, καὶ οὐ δύο ἀρχαί, ὅθεν κυρίως καὶ μ. ἐστίν ‡Ath.*Ar*.4.1(p.44.5; M.26.468B); οὐ γὰρ κατὰ σύνθεσιν ἀριθμοῦμεν...ἓν καὶ δύο καὶ τρία λέγοντες, οὐδὲ πρῶτον καὶ δεύτερον καὶ τρίτον...θεὸν γὰρ ἐκ θεοῦ προσκυνοῦντες...καὶ μένομεν ἐπὶ τῆς μ. ... διὰ τὸ μίαν ἐν θεῷ πατρὶ καὶ θεῷ μονογενεῖ τὴν οἱονεὶ μορφὴν θεωρεῖσθαι Bas.*Spir*.45(3.38A; M.32.149B); περὶ μὲν τῆς τοῦ θεοῦ μ. ... οὐ...μόνον εἰς ἕνα θεὸν δεῖ πιστεύειν· ἀλλὰ καὶ [τὸ] πατέρα τοῦτον εἶναι τοῦ μονογενοῦς...καταδεχώμεθα Cyr.H.*catech*.7.1; ἡμῖν δὲ μ. τὸ τιμώμενον· μ. δέ, οὐχ ἣν ἓν περιγράφει πρόσωπον...ἀλλ' ἣν φύσεως ὁμοτιμία συνίστησι...καὶ ταυτότης κινήσεως Gr.Naz.*or*.29.2 (p.75.1; M.36.76A); ἡ τῆς φύσεως ἑνότης τὸν διαμερισμὸν οὐ προσίεται, ὡς μήτε τὸ τῆς μ. σχίζεσθαι κράτος εἰς θεότητας διαφόρους κατατεμνόμενον Gr.Nyss.*or.catech*.3(p.16.7; M.45.17D); id.*Eun*.1(1 p.171.24; M.45.416A); μ. κηρύττοντες...ὁμολογοῦμεν τὴν τριάδα, μονάδα ἐν τριάδι καὶ τριάδα ἐν μονάδι, καὶ μίαν θεότητα πατρὸς καὶ υἱοῦ καὶ ἁγίου πνεύματος Epiph.*haer*.62.3(p.391.22; M.41.1053B); ὅταν...πρὸς τὴν θεότητα βλέψωμεν, καὶ τὴν πρώτην αἰτίαν, καὶ τὴν μ. καὶ τὸ ἓν καὶ ταὐτὸν τῆς θεότητος...κίνημά τε καὶ βούλημα...ἓν ἡμῖν τὸ φανταζόμενον· ὅταν δὲ πρὸς τὰ ἐν οἷς ἡ θεότης, ἢ τό γε ἀκριβέστερον εἰπεῖν, ἃ ἡ θεότης...τρία τὰ προσκυνούμενα ‡Cyr.*Trin*.10(6^3.16B; M.77.1144C).

***μοναρχίζω**, *rule over as king* πρῶτος ἐμονάρχισε Ῥωμαίων... Ἰούλιος Καῖσαρ Dam.*troph*.4.4(p.268.13).

μοναρχικός, 1. *ruling alone* τῆς μοναρχικῆς θεότητος Eus.*e.th*.2.7 (p.104.4; M.24.908C); neut. as subst. τῶν ὅλων τὸ μ. *omnipotence*, Tat.*orat*.29(p.30.11; M.6.868A); **2.** of Trin., *ruling as one*, Jo.D. *Jacob*.2(M.94.1437A).

μόναρχος, 1. *monarchical* τὴν μόναρχον ... θεότητα Eus.*v.C*.4.29 (p.128.31; M.20.1177C); of Father, *Lit*.ap.*Const.App*.8.11.2; of Trin., Epiph.*haer*.66.3(p.19.3; M.42.33A); **2.** *ruled by one man* ἡ Ῥωμαίων ἀρχὴ μ. Eus.*l.C*.16(p.249.28; M.20.1424B).

μονάς, ἡ, A. *unit*; in abstract, Clem.*str*.5.11(p.374.10; M.9.109A); τέσσαρα μέρη· ἀριθμός, μ., δύναμις, κύβος Hipp.*haer*.1.2(p.6.14; M.16. 3024C); Dion.Ar.*d.n*.5.6(M.3.820D); ref. creation of Eve μ. οὖσα τῷ γένει δυάς ἐστιν *Hom.Clem*.16.12; the number *one*, Clem.*str*.6.11 (p.474.2; M.9.305A); Hipp.*haer*.4.8(p.41.4; 3071A); *ib*.6.24(p.151.19; 3230D); = *one* day πεντηκοστῆς, ἑβδομάσι μὲν ἑπτά, μονάδι δ' ἐπισφραγιζομένης Eus.*v.C*.4.64(p.144.12; M.20.1219B); *single* concrete *object* ἓν καὶ ἓν καὶ ἕν...τὰς τοσαύτας μ. Gr.Naz.*or*.31.18(p.166. 18; M.36.153A).

B. *monad*; **1.** in Pythagorean thought μ. ἐστιν ὁ θεός, τοῦτ' ἔστιν εἷς Athenag.*leg*.6.1(M.6.901A); κόσμον...νοητὸν οἶδεν ἡ βάρβαρος φιλοσοφία...τὸν μὲν ἀνατίθησι μονάδι...τὸν δὲ αἰσθητὸν ἑξάδι Clem. *str*.5.14(p.387.23; M.9.137A); μ. εἶναι ἀπεφήνατο τὸν θεόν Hipp.*haer*.1.2 (p.5.7; M.16.3024A); ἀρχὴν τῶν ὅλων ἀγέννητον ἀπεφήνατο τὴν μ. *ib*.6. 23(p.149.26; 3227B); τῇ μ. ἀγαθοποιῷ οὔσῃ *ib*.4.44(p.67.7; 3107C); Anat.Laod.*decad*.(p.29f.); but cf. ἓν δὲ ὁ θεὸς καὶ ἐπέκεινα τοῦ ἑνὸς καὶ ὑπὲρ αὐτὴν μ. Clem.*paed*.1.8(p.131.19; M.8.336A); Eus.*d.e*.4.1(p.151. 9; M.22.252C) cit. s. ἀρχέγονος; **2.** Gnost., Iren.*haer*.1.16.1(M.7.628B) cit. s. δυάς; as aeon αὕτη ἡ ἑνότης, ἥ τε μονότης...προήκαντο...ἀρχὴν ...νοητὴν...ἣν ἀρχὴν ὁ λόγος μ. καλεῖ. ταύτῃ τῇ μ. συνυπάρχει δύναμις ὁμοούσιος αὐτῇ, ἣν καὶ αὐτὴν ὀνομάζω τὸ ἕν *ib*.1.11.3(563A).

C. *unity*; **1.** in gen., of Church, Clem.*str*.7.7(p.76.18; M.9.552B); ref. Pr.10:19 οὐδεὶς αὐτῶν λόγος, ἀλλ' ἕκαστοι λόγοι· οὐδαμοῦ γὰρ ἡ μ., καὶ οὐδαμοῦ τὸ σύμφωνον καὶ ἓν Or.*Jo*.5.5(4; p.102.34; M.14. 192A); ἡ φύσις μία ἐστίν, αὐτὴ πρὸς ἑαυτὴν ἡνωμένη, καὶ ἀδιάτμητος ἀκριβῶς μ., οὐκ αὐξανομένη διὰ προσθήκης, οὐ μειουμένη δι' ὑφαιρέσεως, ἀλλ' ὅπερ ἐστὶν ἓν οὖσα Gr.Nyss.*tres dii*(M.45.120B); Thdt. *Cant*.8:12(2.163); of monks θεοειδῆ μ. καὶ φιλόθεον τελείωσιν Dion. Ar.*c.h*.6.3(M.3.533A); ἡ σοφία μ. ἐστι, ταῖς ἐξ αὐτῆς διαφόροις ἀρεταῖς ἀτμήτως ἐνθεωρουμένη, καὶ μονοειδῶς ταῖς τῶν ὅλων ἀρετῶν ἐνεργείαις ἐπινοουμένη ‡Proc.G.*Pr*.1:7(M.87.1225D); **2.** of God μὴ μόνοι εἰς μ. τὸν θεὸν κατακλείομεν Athenag.*leg*.6.2(M.6.901B); χρὴν ἕνα ⟨εἶναι⟩... τὸν...τοῦ θεοῦ λόγον, ὡς ἂν κἀν τούτῳ τὸ τῆς εἰκόνος ἐμφερὲς τῷ πατρὶ καὶ κατὰ πάντα ἀποσώζοιτο...κατά τε τὸν τῆς μ. καὶ ἑνάδος ἀριθμόν Eus.*d.e*.4.6(p.158.21; M.22.264C); ὁ...νοῦς ὃν ἀσεβοῦντες λέγουσι κυρίως Χριστόν, τῇ τῆς μ. γνώσει πεποιημένον CCP(543)*anath*.9; **3.** of Trin., cf. ἀδιαίρετος; **a.** in Trin. controversy in gen. εἰς τρεῖς ὑποστάσεις ξένας ἀλλήλων παντάπασι κεχωρισμένας διαιροῦντες τὴν ἁγίαν μ. Dion.R.ap.Ath.*decr*.26(p.22.9; M.25.464A); θειοτάτη...μετὰ τὴν μ. καὶ ἡ τριάς Dion.Al.ap.Bas.*Spir*.72(3.61A; M.32.201C); id. ap.Ath.*Dion*.17(p.58.24; M.25.505A); in views ascribed to Sabellians εἰ ἀεὶ ἦν λόγος καὶ πνεῦμα, ἀεὶ πλατεῖα καὶ οὐ πρῶτον μ. ‡Ath. *Ar*.4.14(p.58.19; M.26.488A); εἰ τοίνυν ἡ μ. πλατυνθεῖσα γέγονε τριάς, ἡ δὲ μ. ἐστιν ὁ πατήρ, τριὰς δὲ πατήρ, υἱός, ἅγιον πνεῦμα...ἡ μ. πάθος ὑπέμεινε *ib*.4.13(p.57.8; 484C); οὐδὲ ὡς Σαβέλλιος τὴν μ. διαιρῶν υἱοπάτορα εἶπεν Ar.*ep.Alex*.(p.12.12; M.26.709A); οἱ...ἐν μ. τὸ τριπλοῦν ἀσεβῶς κατὰ σύνθεσιν φανταζόμενοι καὶ σοφίαν ἐν θεῷ τὸν υἱὸν ...ἡγούμενοι Apoll.*fid.sec.pt*.1(p.167.19; M.10.1105B); Marcellan εἰ ἡ κατὰ σάρκα προσθήκη ἐπὶ τοῦ σωτῆρος ἐξετάζοιτο, ἐνεργείᾳ ἡ θεότης μόνη πλατύνεσθαι δοκεῖ· ὥστε εἰκότως μονὰς ὄντως ἐστὶν ἀδιαίρετος Marcell.*fr*.62 ap.Eus.*e.th*.2.4(p.102.24; M.24.905A); **b.** Arian views μ. μὲν ἦν πρότερον, ἐκ προσθήκης δὲ γέγονεν ὕστερον τριάς Ath.*Ar*. 1.17(M.26.48A); ἡ μ. ἦν· ἡ δυὰς δὲ οὐκ ἦν, πρὶν ὑπάρξῃ· αὐτίκα γοῦν υἱοῦ μὴ ὄντος ὁ πατὴρ θεός ἐστι Ar.*Thal.fr*.2.20 ap.Ath.*syn*.15(p.243. 1; M.26.708A); Cyr.*thes*.9(5^1.66E); μὴ διδοὺς γὰρ ἐκ τῆς μ. εἶναι τὸν λόγον, ἀλλ' ἁπλῶς κεκολλῆσθαι τῷ πατρὶ λόγον, δυάδα οὐσίας εἰσάγει, μηδετέραν τῆς ἑτέρας πατέρα τυγχάνουσαν ‡Ath.*Ar*.4.3(p.47.9; 472B); denied, *ib*.4.1(p.44.3; 468B) cit. s. ἀδιαίρετος; ἐν τῇ τριάδι ὁ τῆς μ. διασωθήσεται λόγος, ἕνα μὲν πατέρα ὁμολογούντων, καὶ ἕνα υἱὸν καὶ ἓν πνεῦμα ἅγιον Bas.*Eun*.3.6(1.277E; M.29.668C); τριάδα τὴν μ. κηρύσσοντες [sc. OT prophets], ἀλλ' ἑνότητα θεότητος εἰδότες, ἐν ἑνὶ προσώπῳ τὰ τρία κηρύσσουσι Didym.(‡Bas.)*Eun*.5(1.315B; M.29. 756B); ref. Jo.17:2 ὁ ζωὴ ὢν ζωὴν θέλει παρὰ πατρὸς λαμβάνειν καὶ διδόναι τοῖς μαθηταῖς...ἵνα μὴ διέλῃ τὴν μ., ἵνα μὴ σκῶλος γένηται τοῖς Ἰουδαίοις Epiph.*haer*.69.29(p.179.10; M.42.249B); **c.** in gen. τριὰς μία καὶ ἀδιαίρετος...συνάπτεται ἀσυγχύτως, ὥσπερ καὶ ἀτμήτως ἡ μ. χωρίζεται Ath.*hom.in Mt.11*:27(M.25.220A); ref. Gen.1:27 ἔφυγεν ἐνταῦθα τὸν πληθυσμὸν τῶν προσώπων...ἀσφαλῶς ἀνέδραμεν ἐπὶ τὴν μ., ἵνα καὶ υἱὸν νοῇς μετὰ πατρός Bas.*hex*.9.6(1.88C; M.29.208A); μ. ἀπ' ἀρχῆς, εἰς δυάδα κινηθεῖσα, μέχρι τριάδος ἔστη Gr.Naz.*or*.29.2 (p.75.7; M.36.76B); τριάδα τελείαν ἐκ τελείων τριῶν, μ. μὲν κινηθείσης διὰ τὸ πλούσιον, δυάδος δὲ ὑπερβαθείσης...τριάδος δὲ ὁρισθείσης διὰ τὸ τέλειον *ib*.23.8(M.35.1160C); ἐκ μ. τριάς ἐστι καὶ ἐκ τριάδος μ. αὖθις id.*carm*.1.1.3.60(M.37.413A); πῶς τὸ αὐτὸ καὶ ἀριθμητόν ἐστι καὶ διαφεύγει τὴν ἐξαρίθμησιν, καὶ διῃρημένως ὁρᾶται καὶ ἐν μ. καταλαμβάνεται Gr.Nyss.*or.catech*.3(p.16.1; M.45.17D); εἷς τοίνυν ἐστὶν ὁ θεός, ἡ τριὰς τῇ μ. τῆς οὐσίας χωρὶς πάσης...διαιρέσεως καὶ διακρίσεως ‡Just.*qu.et resp*.129(M.6.1380D); οὐκ ἔστι κτιστὸν [sc. τὸ πνεῦμα] ὡς τὸ πλῆθος τῶν πνευμάτων, ἀλλὰ τῆς μ. θείας οὐσίας Didym.*Trin*.3.2 (M.39.801B); μ. ἐν τῷ ταὐτῷ τῆς οὐσίας δείκνυται, καὶ ἡ τριὰς οὐκ ἐν ψιλοῖς τοῖς ὀνόμασι, ἀλλ' ἐν ταῖς ὑποστάσεσι γνωρίζεται Thdt.*Trin*.28 (M.75.1188B); ἔνθα δὲ πατὴρ καὶ πνεῦμα ἐνθεωρεῖται τῇ μ. τῇ προσκυνουμένῃ, σὰρξ τῇδε οὐ συμπεριέχεται, ἵνα καὶ ὡς τῆσδε οὖσα τῆς μ. συμπροσκυνῆται Leont.H.*Nest*.1.44(M.86.1504C); τῆς οὖν τριάδος ἀληθῶς ἔφητε ὅτι ἔστι καὶ ἡ σάρξ· μιᾶς γὰρ τῶν τριῶν ὑποστάσεων· ἀλλ' οὐχὶ καὶ τῆς μ. ... πρώτως ἤγουν οἰκείῳ λόγῳ *ib*.7.5(1768^{d}A); ἡ ἁγία τριὰς ἀριθμητὴ ταῖς προσωπικαῖς ἐστιν ὑποστάσεσιν, ἥ τε παναγία μ. πασῆς ἐκτός ἐστιν ἀριθμήσεως Sophr.H.*ep.syn*.(M.87. 3152D); μ. μὲν κατὰ τὸν τῆς οὐσίας, ἤτοι τὸν τοῦ εἶναι λόγον, ἀλλ' οὐ κατὰ σύνθεσιν ἢ...σύγχυσιν· τριάδι δὲ κατὰ τὸν τοῦ πῶς ὑπάρχειν καὶ ὑφεστάναι λόγον, ἀλλ' οὐ κατὰ διαίρεσιν ἢ ἀλλοτρίωσιν. ... οὐ γὰρ μεμέρισται ταῖς ὑποστάσεσιν ἡ μ. Max.*myst*.23(M.91.700D); ἡ μ. μέχρι τριάδος παρ' αὐτοῖς κινουμένη μένει μ. καὶ ἡ τριὰς μέχρι μ. συναγομένη μένει τριάς Thal.*cent*.4.93(M.91.1468D); **4.** Christol. τὸν Χριστὸν...σάρκα γενόμενον λόγον καὶ μείναντα τῆς φυσικῆς αὐτοῦ μ. ἐντός Apoll.*fr*.152(p.248.11)ap.*Doct.Patr*.41(p.307.24); ref. Jo.1:14 διὰ μὲν γὰρ τοῦ 'ἐγένετο', τὸ ἀδιαίρετον τῆς ἄκρας ἑνώσεως ὁ εὐαγγελιστὴς ὑπαινίττεται. ὥσπερ γὰρ ἡ μ. οὐκ ἂν τμηθείη εἰς μονάδας δύο (ἡ γὰρ εἰς ταύτας διαιρουμένη οὐκ ἂν εἴη μ. ἀλλὰ δυάς) οὕτως τὸ ἓν κατὰ τὴν ἄκραν ἕνωσιν οὐκ ἂν διαιρεθείη εἰς δύο Procl.CP *Arm*.6 (p.190.7; M.65.861B); Leont.H.*monoph*.31(M.86.1788D) cit. s. δυάς; κατ' εὐδοκίαν ἡ ἕνωσις, βουλῆς καὶ γνώμης ταυτότητα κρατουμένη, ἵνα καὶ τὸ διάφορον τῶν φύσεων ἀσύγχυτον δείκνυται, καὶ τὸ τῆς εὐδοκίας μυστήριον μονάδι βουλήσεως διαδείκνυται Paul.Pers.*judic.fr*. ap.Max.*opusc*.(M.91.173C).

***μόνασις**, ἡ, *solitude*, ‡Eust.*hex*.(M.18.741A).

μονασμός, ὁ, *solitude* μ. ἡμῶν our *being alone* together, Proc.G. *Gen*.18:16(M.87.381C).

μοναστήριον, τό, **1.** hermit's *cell* ὄντως οἰκία πένθους τὰ μ. ἔνθα σάκκος καὶ σποδός, ἔνθα μόνωσις, ἔνθα γέλως οὐδείς Chrys.*hom.14.3 in 1Tim*.(11.628F); ὥσπερ ἀπὸ γῆς εἰς οὐρανόν, οὕτως ἐστὶν εἰς μ. ἀνδρὸς ἁγίου καταφυγεῖν *ib*.(629C); οὐ γάρ ἐστι κώμη οὔτε πόλις ἐν Αἰγύπτῳ...ἣ οὐχὶ τοῖς μ. καθάπερ τείχεσι περιβέβληται ‡Pall.*h.mon*. proem.(p.3.21; M.65.445B); πρεσβύτερόν τινα...πατέρα πολλῶν μ. καὶ ἡγούμενον πολλῆς ἀδελφότητος *ib*.20.1(p.79.5; M.34.1179B); μ. ... ἐν ᾧ ἀναχωρητής τις ὑπῆρξεν Cyr.S.*v.Sab*.62(p.163.14); κτίσας ἑαυτῷ μικρὸν μ. ... ἀνεχώρει ἐκεῖσε id.*v.Euthym*.37(p.56.8); fig. ὁ ἀκριβὴς φιλόσοφος φροντιστήριον ἔχων τὸ σῶμα...ἐν τῷ φυσικῷ μ. καθίδρυται, ἔνδον συνάγων τὸν νοῦν ‡Bas.*const*.5(2.550D; M.31.1360C); plur., *group of cells* or *monastery*, Gr.Naz.*or*.43.62(M.36.577B); ἵνα μὴ προφάσει ταπεινότητος καὶ πραότητος ἐν συγχύσει τὰ μ. ἦν Mac.Aeg. *perf*.9(M.34.848C); **2.** *monastery* οὔπω ἦν ἐν Αἰγύπτῳ συνεχῆ μ. ... ἕκαστος δὲ τῶν βουλομένων ἑαυτῷ προσέχειν οὐ μακρὰν τῆς ἰδίας κώμης καταμόνας ἠσκεῖτο Ath.*v.Anton*.3(M.26.844B); προέστης μοναστηρίου id.*ep.Drac*.7(M.25.532A); μ. ... εἴτουν μάνδραις Epiph. *haer*.80.6(p.491.20; M.42.765C); ἀνὴρ...καὶ γυνὴ...τέχνην μετεχειρίζοντο, καὶ τῶν ἐν μ. ζώντων ἀκριβεστέραν ἐπεδείξαντο πολλῷ τὴν φιλοσοφίαν Chrys.*hom.1.3 in Rom.16*:3(3.175B); μηδένα...μηδαμοῦ οἰκοδομεῖν μηδὲ συνιστᾶν μ. ἢ εὐκτήριον οἶκον παρὰ γνώμην τοῦ τῆς πόλεως ἐπισκόπου CChalc.*can*.4; χρηματίσας τῷ θείῳ Παχωμίῳ ἐν πρώτοις κοινόβιον συστήσασθαι καὶ τούτῳ συνήργει εἰς τὴν πᾶσαν τοῦ μ. σύστασιν *Apophth.Patr*.(M.65.152B); ἑπτὰ μ. ... συνεστήσαντο...ἐν μὲν λαύραις...ἐν δὲ κοινοβίοις Cyr.S.*v.Sab*.58(p.158.18); τὸν ἡγούμενον τῶν ἐν Ἱεριχῷ μ. *ib*.59(p.161.7); τῶν...τῆς ἐρήμου ὀρθοδόξων μ. *ib*.90 (p.199.21); τὰ...Εὐθυμίου καὶ Θεοκτίστου μ. ἦσαν τότε ἐν ὁμονοίᾳ κοινὸν τὸν βίον ἔχοντα καὶ μίαν διοίκησιν ὑπὸ ἕνα ὄντα οἰκονόμον κατὰ τὴν τοῦ μεγάλου Εὐθυμίου ἐντολήν id.*v.Cyriac*.6(p.226.4); γυναικί τινι ἐναρέτῳ...κτιζούσῃ τὸ τηνικαῦτα περὶ τὸ ὄρος τῶν Ἐλαιῶν μ. καὶ ἐκκλησίαν id.*v.Thgn*.(p.241.20); λαῖλαψ ἀνέμου ἐγείρων κονιορτὸν ἐν πεδίῳ· οὕτως μοναχὸς ὑπερήφανος ἀνεγείρων ὀργὴν ἐν μ. Hyper.*mon*. 68(M.79.1480C); συνασκήσας...αὐτῷ τὸν μονήρη βίον ἐν ἑνὶ καὶ τῷ αὐτῷ μ. Justn.*conf*.(p.108.16; M.86.1031D); ἐγὼ ἐκ μικρᾶς ἡλικίας εἰς τὸ μ. εἰσῆλθον τοῦ ἁγίου Ἰωάννου Eustrat.*v.Eutych*.55(M.86.2337C); of women ἔκβαλλε...αὐτὴν ἀπὸ τοῦ οἴκου σου, καὶ κατάστησον αὐτὴν ἐν μ. Bas.*ep*.55(3.150A; M.32.464A); ἡ γυνὴ ἡ πόρνη...ἔλεγεν...πάντα τὰ ὑπάρχοντά μου δίδωμι τοῖς πτωχοῖς καὶ τὸν οἶκόν μου μ. παρθένων *A.Petr.et Andr*.22(p.126.26); *Apophth.Patr*.(M.65.416B); Pall.*h. Laus*.29(p.85.6; M.34.1098A); γυνὴ χηρὰ ἐπὶ δεύτερον γάμον ὁρμάτω εἴτε ἐν μ. τοῖς παρ' ἡμῶν ἀρτίως συσταθεῖσιν ἀποτασσέσθω, εἰ μὴ βούλοιτο γάμῳ προσορμῆσαι †Gregent.*leg.Hom*.49(M.86.608B).

***μοναστής**, ὁ, *monk*, Bas.*ep*.170(3.259C; M.32.645A); Gr.Naz.*or*. 43.34(M.36.541C); οὗτος μ. ὃς θεῷ ζῇ καὶ μόνῳ id.*carm*.1.2.34.177(M. 37.958A); Cyr.*Is*.5.5(2.867A).

***μοναστικός**, **1.** *solitary* μ. ὁ βίος αὐτοῦ [sc. lion], οὐδενὶ τῶν ζῴων κοινωνῶν ‡Eust.*hex*.(M.18.737D); ἥμερον καὶ κοινωνικὸν ζῷον ὁ ἄνθρωπος, καὶ οὐχὶ μ., οὐδὲ ἄγριον Bas.*reg.fus*.3.1(2.340C; M.31. 917A); κίνδυνος παρέπεται τῇ μ. ζωῇ *ib*.7.3(347B; M.932C); neut. as subst., id.*hex*.9.3(1.82B; M.29.192C); **2.** *proper to a solitary* τὴν μ. σεμνότητα Soz.*h.e*.1.13.10(M.67.900A); μ. τληπαθείας *ib*.1.13.14 (900B); neut. plur. as subst., *life of a solitary* ἐμ' εἶχε τῶν μ. πόθος Gr.Naz.*carm*.2.1.11.327(M.37.1052A).

μονάστρια, ἡ, *nun*, Chrys.*ep*.14.2(3.596A); Isid.Pel.*epp*.1.367 tit. (M.78.389C); μ. ... μετ' ἄλλων...παρθένων ἐποιεῖτο τὴν οἴκησιν. ἐτῶν γὰρ ἦν ὡσεὶ δώδεκα Sophr.H.*mir.Cyr.et Jo*.44(M.87.3589B); μοναχῶν καὶ μ. παρθένων *Chron.Pasch*.p.385(M.92.988B); μὴ ἐχέτω παρρησίαν μοναχὸς πρὸς μονάστριαν ἢ μ. πρὸς μοναχὸν ἰδίᾳ προσομιλεῖν CNic.(787) *can*.20; *woman under religious vows, virgin* μ. τις...ἐκάθητο εἰς τὸν ἴδιον οἶκον, ἡσυχάζουσα καὶ φροντίζουσα τῆς ἰδίας ψυχῆς, ἐν νηστείαις καὶ προσευχαῖς...διατελοῦσα Jo.Mosch.*prat*.60(M.87.2912D).

***μοναύλιος**, *celibate*, Philost.*h.e*.3.4(M.65.484A).

μοναχή, ἡ, *nun*, Thdr.Stud.*poen*.2.54(M.99.1756B).

μοναχικός, *of* or *for monks, monastic*, Nil.*epp*.2.136(M.79.257A); φιλοσοφία Isid.Pel.*epp*.1.1(M.78.177A); γυμνασία *ib*.1.92(245B); κελλίον *Apophth.Patr*.(M.65.148A); σχήματος *ib*.(416D); συνοικιῶν Soz. *h.e*.3.14.38(M.67.1081A); καταγώγιον Thdt.*h.rel*.3(3.1148); ἡ μ. ὑπερηφανία ἐστὶν ὅτε κενοδοξεῖ τις, ὡς ἀγρυπνῶν, ὡς νηστεύων Dor. *doct*.2.5(M.88.1645B); μυστήριον μοναχικῆς τελειώσεως Dion.Ar.*e.h*. 6.2(M.3.533A); τὴν μ. τάξιν οὐκ εἶναι προσαγωγικὴν ἑτέρων, ἀλλ' ἐφ' ἑαυτῆς ἑστῶσαν ἐν μ. καὶ ἱερᾷ στάσει *ib*.6.3.1(533C); neut. as subst., *band* or *body of monks*, *Apophth.Patr*.(M.65.149C); Evagr.*h.e*.2.5 (p.52.9; M.86.2513A); *monastic life*, Jo.Mosch.*prat*.59,69(M.87.2912C, 2921B); *V.Dan*.9(p.258.11); *Schol*. in CNic.*can*.12(*Mon*.2 p.644); as title of book, *Monasticism*, Socr.*h.e*.3.7.22(M.67.396B).

***μοναχικῶς**, *like, in the manner of a monk*, Thdt.*h.rel*.9(3.1191); γυναικῶν καὶ ἀνδρῶν, κοσμικῶς τε καὶ μοναχ⟨ικ⟩ῶς †Jo.Jej.*poenit*. (M.88.1913A).

μοναχός, ὁ, *monk*; **A.** etym. μοναχοὺς ὀνομάζοντες, ἐκ τῆς τοῦ θεοῦ καθαρᾶς ὑπηρεσίας...καὶ τῆς ἀμερίστου καὶ ἑνιαίας ζωῆς, ὡς ἑνοποιούσης αὐτοὺς...εἰς θεοειδῆ μονάδα Dion.Ar.*e.h*.6.1.3(M.3.533A); τῇ μοναδικῇ πολιτείᾳ τοῦτο παρὰ τὰ λοιπὰ οἰκειότερον, τὸ παρθενεύειν, ὃ καὶ βούλεται ἡ τοῦ μ. προσηγορία *Schol*.24 in Jo.Clim.*scal*.15(M.88. 912D).

B. descriptions and characteristics; **1.** in gen. μακάριός ἐστι μ., ὁ πάντων περίψημα ἑαυτὸν λογιζόμενος...ὁ πάντων τὴν σωτηρίαν, καὶ προκοπήν, ὡς οἰκείαν κατὰ πάσης χαρᾶς ὁρῶν...ὁ πάντας ἀνθρώπους ὡς θεὸν μετὰ θεὸν λογιζόμενος. μ. ἐστιν, ὁ πάντων χωρισθείς, καὶ πᾶσι συνηρμοσμένος...ὁ ἑαυτὸν μετὰ πάντων ἡγούμενος διὰ τὸ ἐν ἑκάστῳ ἑαυτὸν ἀπαραλείπτως δοκεῖν ὁρᾶν Evagr.Pont.*or*.121–125(M.79.1193B,C); Chrys.*hom.70.5 in Mt.*(7.693B); διὸ καὶ τοὺς...μ. ἐπαινῶ ...μετὰ τὸ δεῖπνον τοίνυν λέγοντές τινας εὐχαριστηρίους ὕμνους εἰς τὸν θεόν...τοῦ φοβεροῦ δικαστηρίου...ἑαυτοὺς ἀναμιμνήσκουσιν. εἰ δὲ ἐκεῖνοι, οἱ καὶ νηστείαις, καὶ χαμευνίαις, καὶ ἀγρυπνίαις, καὶ σάκκῳ, καὶ μυρίοις ἑαυτοὺς σωφρονίζοντες, ἔτι καὶ ταύτης δέονται τῆς ὑπομνήσεως· πότε δυνησόμεθα ἡμεῖς ἐπιεικῶς ζῆν...μηδὲ ὅλως εὐχόμενοι; *ib.*55.5(560E,561C); τοιαύτην δὲ ὁ μ. ἀρχὴν...κέκτηται, ὥστε δικαιότερον ἄν τις τοῦτον βασιλέα καλέσειεν, ἢ τὸν...στεφάνῳ λαμπόμενον id.*comp.*1(1.117C); συνετὸς μ. τῇ χρείᾳ προσέξει τοῦ σώματος, καὶ τὴν ἔνδειαν τῆς γαστρὸς ἄρτῳ πληρώσει καὶ ὕδατι, οὐ κολακεύσει πλουτοῦντας δι' ἡδονὴν γαστρός, οὐδὲ δουλώσει νοῦν ἐλεύθερον δεσπόταις πολλοῖς· ἱκαναὶ γὰρ αἱ χεῖρες ὑπηρετῆσαι τῷ σώματι...ἀκτήμων μ., ἀθλητὴς ἀμεσολάβητος, καὶ δρομεὺς κοῦφος, ταχέως φθάνων ἐπὶ τὸ βραβεῖον τῆς ἄνω κλήσεως Nil.*spir.mal.*8(M.79.1153A); μ. ἐστιν, τάξις καὶ κατάστασις ἀσωμάτων, ἐν σώματι ὑλικῷ...ἐπιτελουμένη. μ. ἐστιν ὁ μόνον τῶν τοῦ θεοῦ ἐχόμενος ὅρων καὶ λόγων ἐν παντὶ καιρῷ...μ. ἐστιν βία φύσεως διηνεκής, καὶ φυλακὴ αἰσθήσεων ἀνελλιπής. μ. ἐστιν ἡγνισμένον σῶμα, καὶ κεκαθαρμένον στόμα, καὶ πεφωτισμένος νοῦς. μ. ἐστιν κατώδυνος ψυχὴ ἐν διηνεκεῖ μνήμῃ θανάτου ἀδολεσχοῦσα, καὶ ὑπνώττουσα, καὶ γρηγοροῦσα Jo.Clim.*scal.*1(M.88.633B,C); *ib.*4(704D); *ib.*23(969A); μ. ἐστίν, ὁ τῶν ὑλικῶν πραγμάτων τὸν νοῦν ἀποχωρίσας· καὶ δι' ἐγκρατείας καὶ ἀγάπης καὶ ψαλμῳδίας καὶ προσευχῆς προσκαρτερῶν τῷ θεῷ Max.*carit.*2.54(M.90.1001C); ὁ μὲν τοῖς πράγμασιν ἀποταξάμενος, οἷον τῇ γυναικὶ καὶ τοῖς χρήμασι...τὸν ἔξω ἄνθρωπον ἐποίησε μ.· οὔπω δὲ καὶ τὸν ἔσω. ὁ δὲ τοῖς τούτων ἐμπαθέσι νοήμασι, τὸν ἔσω ἄνθρωπον, ὅ ἐστιν ὁ νοῦς. καὶ τὸν μὲν ἔξω ἄνθρωπον, εὐκόλως τις ποιεῖ μ., μόνον ἐὰν θελήσῃ· οὐκ ὀλίγος δὲ ἀγών, τὸν ἔσω ἄνθρωπον ποιῆσαι μ. *ib.*4.50(1060A,B); **2.** special traits: having all things in common, Bas.*ascet.*1.5(2.322C; M.31.880A); but no special friendships, *ib.*(322D; M.880A); poverty, id.*ascet.disc.*1(2.211E; M.31.648C); ἡσυχία Chrys.*hom.70.5 in Mt.*(7.694A); Nil.*inst.*(M.79.1236B); withdrawal τοσαύτην χάριν ὁ θεὸς...τοῖς μ. ἐδωρήσατο, ὥστε τούτους μὲν μὴ θέλειν τὴν ἀνθρωπίνην δόξαν...ἀλλὰ...σπουδάζειν μᾶλλον λανθάνειν τοὺς ἀνθρώπους διὰ τὸ ἐγκαταμίξαι ἑκουσίως ἑαυτοὺς τοῖς εὐτελέσι ...τῶν ἀδελφῶν· πολλοὺς δὲ μεγιστᾶνας...εἴθ' ἑκουσίως, εἴτ' ἀβουλήτως διά τινος περιστάσεως προσφεύγειν τοῖς ταπεινοῖς id.*epp.*1.1(M.79.81A); stability, *ib.*1.295(189D); cf.*ib.*2.72(232D); moderation ἔστι ...τῷ μὲν μ. καὶ ἀμπεχόνη καὶ τράπεζα μετρία Chrys.*comp.*3(1.118D); in speech, Nil.*epp.*3.229(489B); τὸν ἐν φρονήματι μ. δόκιμον εἶναι χρὴ ζυγοστάτην, μηδενὶ μέρει τῶν πλαστίγγων καταρρέπειν παραχωροῦντα, μήτε τῇ ἀσιτίᾳ, εἰς ἀτονίαν, μήτε πολυσιτίαν εἰς ἀσωτίαν *ib.*3.242(496C); ῥήμασι γλυκυτάτοις λαλείτω μ. Hyper.*mon.*113(M.79.1484C); fear of God, *ib.*1(1173A); mercy, *ib.*22(1476B); truthfulness, *ib.*63(1480B); meekness, *ib.*104(1484B); patience, *ib.*135(1485D); obedience, v. ὑπακοή; **3.** tonsure and habit ἡ δὲ τῶν τριχῶν ἀπόκαρσις ἐμφαίνει τὴν καθαρὰν καὶ ἀσχημάτιστον ζωήν...μοναχοῖς εἰς τὸ θεοειδέστατον ἀναγομένην Dion.Ar.*e.h.*6.3.3(M.3.336A); significance of various parts of monastic habit, Dor.*doct.*1.12f.(M.88.1632C–1636A); Max.*qu.dub.*67(M.90.840B–841C).

C. occupations and duties; **1.** to set example χρεωστοῦμεν οἱ μ., ὡς δι' ἑαυτούς, οὕτως καὶ διὰ τοὺς ὁρῶντας ἀνθρώπους φαίνειν τῷ βίῳ, οὐ τῇ σάλπιγγι τῆς ἐπιδείξεως...ἀλλ' ὡς πυρσὸς ἐν σκοτίᾳ *Schol.*27 in Jo.Clim.*scal.*26(M.88.1041D); **2.** prayer τὸν μ. μὲν ὀψόμεθα τῇ τοῦ θεοῦ λατρείᾳ, καὶ ταῖς εὐχαῖς κοσμούμενον, πολὺ πρότερον ᾄδοντα τῶν ὀρνίθων...θεῷ συλλαλοῦντα Chrys.*comp.*3(1.118D); Hyper.*mon.*95(M.79.1481D); and chanting, *ib.*39(1477B); **3.** watching ξίφος κατὰ τῶν παθῶν ἐγρήγορσις μοναχοῦ *ib.*91(1481C); fasting, *ib.*80(1481B); **4.** agriculture τὴν πόλιν ἀφέντα πρὸς τὸ ὄρος φυγεῖν, καὶ φυτεύειν ἐκεῖ, καὶ ἄρδειν, καὶ ὑδροφορεῖν, καὶ τὰ ἄλλα δὴ πάντα τὰ τῶν μ. ποιεῖν Chrys.*oppugn.*2.2(1.59B).

D. cenobites contrasted with solitaries οὐχ οὕτως μ. ὡς μοναχὸς μοναχῷ. ὁ μ. νήψεως πολλῆς, καὶ ἀρεμβάστου νοὸς δέεται· τῷ μὲν προτέρῳ πολλάκις ἐβοήθησεν ἕτερος· τῷ δὲ δευτέρῳ συνήργησεν ἄγγελος Jo.Clim.*scal.*27(M.88.1097C); οἶμαι αὐτὸν τοῦτο λέγειν, ὅτι οὐχ οὕτως σώζεται τοῦ ὀλισθαίνειν ὁ μόνος, ὡς ὁ ἔχων μ. ἕτερον μεθ' ἑαυτοῦ μ. ... διὸ οὐχ οὕτως μ. ὡς μοναχὸς μοναχῷ· τοῦτ' ἔστιν, οὐ καλὸν οὕτως τὸ μόνον εἶναι, ὡς τὸ ἔχειν καὶ ἄλλον ἕνα *Schol.*3 ad loc.(M.88.1101D).

E. grades of perfection τρεῖς εἰσιν ἠθικαὶ καταστάσεις γενικώτεραι ἐν τοῖς μ. καὶ πρώτη μέν, τὸ μηδὲν ἁμαρτάνειν κατ' ἐνέργειαν· δευτέρα δέ, τὸ μὴ ἐγχρονίζειν ἐν τῇ ψυχῇ τοὺς ἐμπαθεῖς λογισμούς· τρίτη δέ, τὸ τὰς μορφὰς τῶν γυναικῶν, καὶ τῶν λυπησάντων ἀπαθῶς θεωρεῖν κατὰ διάνοιαν Max.*carit.*2.87(M.91.1013A).

F. in rel. to angels ἥδιον ἰδεῖν ἐρημίαν σκηνὰς ἔχουσαν μοναχῶν συνεχεῖς...καὶ γὰρ ἄγγελοι κατάγονται πρὸς αὐτούς, καὶ ὁ τῶν ἀγγέλων δεσπότης Chrys.*hom.69.3 in Mt.*(7.684A,B); ἐπὰν...μ. γαυρούμενος τῷ ὕψει τῆς πολιτείας, τὴν ὑπερηφάνειαν ἀσπάσηται...ἀπολείπουσιν οἱ ἄγγελοι τὸν ἀλαζονευόμενον Nil.*epp.*1.326(M.79.200C); ζωὴ τοῦ μ. κατὰ μίμησιν ἀγγέλου γινέσθω καταφλέγουσα ἁμαρτίαν Hyper.*mon.*25(M.79.1476C); ἰσάγγελος ἔσται μ. κοιλίας καταφρονῶν *ib.*53(1480A).

G. in rel. to seculars; **1.** difference of state ἂν εἶ κοσμικός, ἐν τῇ διαγωγῇ τῶν κοσμικῶν ἀγαθῶν ἀναστρέφου. εἰ δὲ μ. εἶ, ἐν τοῖς ἔργοις, ἐν οἷς ἀριστεύουσιν οἱ μ. διάτριψον. εἰ μέντοι ἐν ἑτέροις βούλει ἀναστραφῆναι, ἀπὸ τῶν δύο πεσεῖν μέλλεις *Schol.*13 in Jo.Clim.*scal.*3(M.88.676A); hence τὰ τῶν κοσμικῶν κατορθώματα, πτώματά εἰσι τῶν μ. καὶ τῶν μ. κατορθώματα, πτώματά εἰσι τῶν κοσμικῶν. οἷον, τὰ τῶν κοσμικῶν κατορθώματα πλοῦτός ἐστι καὶ δόξα...εἰς ἅπερ ἐλθὼν ὁ μ., ἀπόλλυται. τὰ δὲ τοῦ μ. κατορθώματα, ἀκτημοσύνη, ἀδοξία...εἰς ἅπερ ἐλθὼν ὁ φιλόκοσμος παρὰ πρόθεσιν, πτῶμα ἡγεῖται μέγα Max.*carit.*3.85(M.90.1044A); **2.** interprn. of difference in dress ἐπείθου μοι...τίνος χάριν οἱ μὲν μ. στολιζόμενοι ἐπὶ τοῦ ἀριστεροῦ ἀναβάλλονται ὤμου, γυμνοῦντες ὅλον τὸ εὐώνυμον μέρος, οἱ δὲ φοροῦντες κοσμικοὶ τὰς χλανίδας τὸ δεξιὸν μέρος τοῦ σώματος τοῖς πᾶσι φανερὸν καθιστῶσιν. ... οἱ μὲν μ. τῷ κυρίῳ πειθόμενοι λέγοντι· 'ὅπερ ποιεῖ ἡ δεξιά σου, μὴ γνώτω ἡ ἀριστερά', τουτέστιν, αἱ ἀγαθαὶ πράξεις... λανθανέτωσαν τὴν λοιμώδη κενοδοξίαν...ἀριστερὰ γὰρ ἀληθῶς ἐστιν ἡ τοιαύτη κατάστασις, δικαίως τὰ μὲν ἑαυτῶν κατορθώματα κρύπτουσιν ἐκ τῶν ἀνθρώπων· τὰ δὲ οἰκεῖα ἐλαττώματα ἐνώπιον ἁπάντων ἐξαγορεύειν εἰώθασιν. οἱ δέ γε βιωτικοὶ κενόδοξοι...τὰ μὲν ἑαυτῶν μυρία κακὰ πράγματα καλύπτουσι, προσποιησάμενοι δὲ μίαν τινὰ ἀρετὴν ἀπεργάσασθαι Nil.*epp.*2.245(M.79.325D); **3.** other differences: monks sin less easily than seculars, Chrys.*oppugn.*3.15(1.104C); id.*hom.68.3 in Mt.*(7.673C); their mouths compared to pure fountains, those of seculars to sewers, *ib.*68.5(677A); παρὰ μὲν κοσμικοῖς ῥίζα πάντων τῶν κακῶν ἡ φιλαργυρία, παρὰ δὲ μ. μᾶλλον ἡ γαστριμαργία ‡Nil.*vit.cog.*(M.79.1444B); obligations of monks much stricter, Dion.Ar.*e.h.*6.3.2(M.3.533D); **4.** but monks and laity must observe same moral principles and devotional practices, and receive same divine blessings, Chrys.*hom.55.6 in Mt.*(7.564C); *ib.*7.7(116B); id.*hom.7.4 in Heb.*(12.80A); **5.** in rel. to women βίος μοναχοῦ ἀκηλίδωτος ἔστω, μὴ χλευαζόμενος ὑπὸ γυναικαρίων σεσωρευμένων ἁμαρτίαις. βέλος γὰρ πειρατηρίου ἐστὶν ἡ γυνή Hyper.*mon.*7(M.79.1473B).

H. monks and vice; for temptations to ἀκηδία v.s.v.; **1.** bad opp. good monks μ. φιλοκτήμων καὶ πλούσιος, κοσμικὸς κτήτωρ· μ. δὲ πένης, οὐράνιος πολίτης Ephr.3.151B, et passim; γαστρίμαργος μ., κοιλίας ὑπόφορος, καὶ μαστιζόμενος ἀπαιτεῖται δασμὸν ἡμερούσιον. ὁδοιπόρος ὀξὺς ταχέως καταλήψεται πόλιν, καὶ μ. ἐγκρατὴς εἰρηνικὴν κατάστασιν· ὁδοιπόρος βραδὺς ἐν ἐρημίᾳ αὐλισθήσεται ὕπαιθρος, καὶ μ. γαστρίμαργος οὐ φθάσει εἰς οἶκον ἀπαθείας Nil.*spir.mal.*2(M.79.1145C–1148A); *ib.*7(1152C); πολυκτήμων μ. χαίρει προσόδοις πολλαῖς, ὁ δὲ ἀκτήμων στεφάνοις κατορθωμάτων. φιλάργυρος μ. ἐργάζεται σφοδρῶς, ὁ δὲ ἀκτήμων προσευχαῖς σχολάζει. ... φιλάργυρος μ. πληροῖ ταμεῖα χρυσοῦ, ὁ δὲ ἀκτήμων θησαυρίζει ἐν οὐρανῷ *ib.*8(1153B); ὁ πανοῦργος ἀνθρωπάρεσκος...καιροὺς θηρεύει, καὶ προσώποις δουλεύει, ὅπως πληροφορήσῃ τὸ πολυτροπώτατον τῆς ἀνθρωπαρεσκείας πάθος· κρύπτειν πειρᾶται τὰ ἑαυτοῦ κακὰ διὰ τῆς τῶν ἀλλοτρίων ἐρωτήσεως. οἱ δὲ ὄντως μ. οὐχ οὕτως, ἀλλὰ τοὐναντίον, τὰ τῶν ἄλλων συμπαθῶς παρορῶσι· τὰ δὲ αὐτῶν τῷ θεῷ φανεροποιοῦσι Marc.Er.*opusc.*7.13(M.65.1089D); μ. φιλόθεος σάλπιγγος προσευχῆς σημαινούσης λέγει· εὖγε, εὖγε· ὁ δὲ ῥᾳθυμὸς λέγει· οἴμοι, οἴμοι Jo.Clim.*scal.*20(M.88.941A); μ. ταπεινόφρων οὐ πολυπραγμονήσει ἄρρητα· ὁ δὲ ὑπερήφανος πολυπραγμονήσει κρίματα *ib.*25(992C); **2.** special faults: vainglory and pride, Nil.*spir.mal.*15(M.79.1160D); *ib.*19(1164C); ‡Nil.*vit.cog.*(M.79.1461A); Jo.Clim.*scal.*23(M.88.969B); Max.*carit.*3.84(M.90.1041D); combined with gluttony, Jo.Clim.*scal.*14(864D); avarice, not natural to monks, but if it takes root in them, all the more difficult to eradicate, ‡Nil.*vit.cog.*(1449B); *ib.*(1452B); laziness, Chrys.*compunct.*1.8(1.132B); wrath, Hyper.*mon.*98(M.79.1484A); evil thoughts, Nil.*inst.*(M.79.1237B).

I. in rel. to devils ἀποτυποῦντες ἑαυτοὺς εἰς σχήματα μοναχῶν, ὡς εὐλαβεῖς προσποιοῦνται λαλεῖν, ἵνα τῷ ὁμοίῳ σχήματι πλανήσωσι, καὶ λοιπὸν ἔνθα θέλουσιν ἑλκύσωσι τοὺς ἀπατηθέντας παρ' αὐτῶν Ath.*v. Anton.*25(M.26.881A); ζέων τῷ πνεύματι μ. ἀποδιώκει τὸν διάβολον· ζηλῶν δὲ μ. ἀδίκως τὸν ἀδελφὸν αὐτοῦ, ἐπισπᾶται τὸν διάβολον Hyper.*mon.*29(M.79.1476D); τῆς καρτερᾶς μάχης τῶν μ., τῆς πρὸς τοὺς ἀλάστορας δαίμονας Nil.*epp.*1.257(M.79.188A); v. δαίμων.

J. comparison with priests and bishops μέγας ὁ τῶν μ. ἀγὼν ...ἀλλ' εἴ τις καλῶς διοικουμένῃ ἱερωσύνῃ τοὺς ἐκεῖθεν ἱδρῶτας παραβάλοι, τοσοῦτον εὑρήσει τὸ διάφορον, ὅσον ἰδιώτου καὶ βασιλέως τὸ μέσον Chrys.*sac.*6.5(p.150.3; 1.425C); bishops more exposed to temptation than monks, hence greater virtue required in them, *ib.*6.8(p.155.8; 427D); monks should help bishops by their prayers, id.*Philogon.*6.3(1.496D).

K. various comparisons: monk's carefree state compared with that of Adam before Fall, Chrys.*hom.68.3 in Mt.*(7.674A); with an altar θυσιαστήριον κυρίου λέγεται ὑπάρχειν ὁ μ.,...ἐν ᾧ καὶ ἐξ οὗ εὐχαὶ καθαραὶ προσφέρονται τῷ...θεῷ, θυσιαστήριον πνευματικῶς ἱδρυμένον Nil.*epp.*3.32(M.79.388A); ἁπλοῦς μ., ἄλογον λογικόν, ὑπήκοον, τὸ οἰκεῖον φορτίον τελείως τῷ ἄγοντι ἀποθέμενος Jo.Clim.*scal.*24(M.88.984C).

L. of order of monks τῶν μ. τάξις Ath.*v.Anton.*44(M.26.908B); highest of non-sacerdotal orders, Dion.Ar.*e.h.*6.1.3(M.3.532C); *ib.* 6.2.5(536D).

M. points of character and conduct; fortitude needed for embracing monastic life, Bas.*renunt.*2(2.204B; M.31.632A); alms not to be exacted by force, Nil.*epp.*1.129(M.79.137C); occasional good food not to be condemned, *ib.*1.287(188B).

N. examples for monks; Jo. Bapt. and Elijah, Hyper.*mon.*48 (M.79.1477D); S. Paul's humility, *ib.*72(1480D); publican in parable, *ib.*73; Moses' meekness, *ib.*74.

O. monk and scripture ἄσκησις μοναχοῦ, μελέτη γραφῶν Hyper. *mon.*4(M.79.1473A); *ib.*42(1477B).

μονάχουσα, ἡ, = μοναχή, †Jo.Jej.*serm.*(M.88.1932C).

μοναχῶς, 1. *alone, uniquely,* of H. Ghost τὸ μὴ ἐν τῷ πλήθει τῆς κτίσεως τετάχθαι, ἀλλὰ μ. ἐκφωνεῖσθαι Bas.*Spir.*45(3.38D; M.32.152A); **2.** *in unity* ἔχει πάντα ἀριθμὸν ἡ μονὰς ἐν ἑαυτῇ μ. Dion.Ar.*d.n.* 5.6(M.3.820D); *in the singular;* of the Godhead, Gr.Nyss.*Trin.*4 (p.74.10; M.32.688C); of Trin., id.*Eun.*1(1 p.113.28; M.45.348D); of collective nouns, id.*tres dii*(M.45.120D); **3.** *in one way,* opp. τετραχῶς, ‡Just.*confut.*54(M.6.1553B); **4.** v. μοναχικῶς.

***μονερημίτης, ὁ,** *hermit, solitary,* †Jo.D.*B.J.*21(M.96.1060B); v. μονηρεμίτης.

μονή, ἡ, 1. *abode, lodging;* **a.** lit., *Hom.Clem.*1.15; Chrys.*stat.*5.2 (2.61E); **b.** fig. and met., of resting places of atoms, Clem.*str.*5.6 (p.349.17; M.9.61A); Dion.Al.ap.Eus.*p.e.*14.25(776D; M.21.1277C); of situation of unregenerate man ἡ ἀνθρωπεία φύσις...ἔχουσα... ἄσεμνον οἰκητήριον, μ. ἀκαλλώπιστον Mac.Mgn.*apocr.*4.18(p.194.10); μ. ... τῆς ἁγίας τριάδος εἰρηνευομένη διάνοια Nil.*spir.mal.*10(M.79.1156A); of BMV εἰς τὴν κρειττοτέραν πασῶν μονῶν μονὴ γενομένη τῆς ὁμοουσίου τριάδος, ἡ ἀκατάλυτος μ. Mod.*dorm.*3(M.86.3285B); **c.** esp. of heaven, ref. Jo.14:2 τὰ βρέφη ἐξαμβλωθέντα...ἀγγέλῳ... παραδίδοσθαι, ἵνα γνώσεως μεταλαβόντα τῆς ἀμείνονος τύχῃ μ. *Apoc. Petr.*B 2; Clem.*str.*4.26(p.322.8; M.8.1376B); *ib.*6.13(p.485.3; M.9.328A); ὠνεῖται χρημάτων τις ἀφθαρσίαν, καὶ δοὺς τὰ διολλύμενα τοῦ κόσμου μ. τούτων αἰώνιον ἐν οὐρανοῖς ἀντιλαμβάνει id.*q.d.s.*32(p.181.7; M.9.637B); μεταρσίους μ. Mac.Mgn.*apocr.*2.20(p.40.18); τὰς ἄνω μ. Cyr.*Is.*2.5(2.340E); id.*Am.*33(3.287A); id.*Mich.*23(3.411E); exeg. Jo. 14:2 ἀγγεῖα αἱ διάφοραι μ. Or.*schol.in Mt.*13:47(M.17.297A); Bas. *Eun.*3.2(1.273C; M.29.657C); μ. εἶπεν τὴν διηνεκῆ τῶν ἀγαθῶν ἀπόλαυσιν, ἀπὸ τοῦ ἐν οἰκίαις ἡμᾶς πᾶσαν ἄνεσιν καὶ ἀπόλαυσιν ἔχειν Thdr.Mops.ad loc.(M.66.776A); τὸ διάφορον τῆς τιμῆς τῷ πολλὰς εἶναι τὰς μ. ὑποσημῆναι βούλεται Cyr.*Jo.*9(4.763D); πολλαὶ μ. ... τουτέστιν ἀξιωμάτων διαφοραί· ἄλλο γὰρ τάγμα πατριαρχῶν, καὶ ἄλλο προφητῶν, ἄλλο ἀποστόλων, καὶ ἄλλο μαρτύρων Thdt.*Cant.*1:3(2.32); id.*1Cor.*16:41(3.278); Gnost. εἰ ὁ τόπος διαφέρει καὶ ἡ μ. τοῦ παντοκράτορος λείπεται ἀπὸ τῆς τοῦ ἀγαθοῦ θεοῦ μ. Clem.*str.*5.1(p.328.17; M.9.13B); αἱ γραφαὶ...ἐκτεθεῖσαι ὑπὸ τῶν αἱρεσιαρχῶν...περὶ τῶν μ. τοῦ στερεώματος Philox.*ep.*36(p.184); **2.** *apartment,* met. ῥοὰ... ἔνδον ἔχει μ. καὶ θήκας πολλὰς διαχωριζομένας διὰ ὑμένων Thphl.Ant. *Autol.*1.5(M.6.1032A); **3.** *hostel, PLond.*1914.16 (335) unless in sense 4; *stopping-place* marking end of a day's journey, Ath.*v.Anton.*86 (M.26.964B); **4.** hence freq., *distance between two stops, stage* ἀπὸ τριάκοντα καὶ ἓξ μ. ἐν Ἀντιοχείᾳ Ath.*apol.sec.*29(p.109.1; M.25.297A); ὁδευσάντων ἡμῶν μ. λε΄ Jo.Disc.*v.Epiph.*14(M.41.40C); Nil. *epp.*4.62(M.79.980C); met., *stage* in progress, Clem.*str.*2.18(p.165.13; M.8.1037B); διὰ...παιδείας ἀπεκδυσάμενος τὰ πάθη ὁ πιστὸς ἡμῖν μέτεισιν ἐπὶ τὴν βελτίονα τῆς προτέρας μονήν *ib.*6.14(p.486.25; M.9.332A; μονῆς MSS); τῷ ἁγίῳ πνεύματι ἑλκόμενοι οἱ μὲν ἐνάρετοι οἰκειοῦνται τῇ πρώτῃ μ.,ἐφεξῆς δ' ἄλλοι μέχρι τῆς τελευταίας *ib.*7.2(p.8.25; 413A); κατὰ προκοπὴν ἀφίξονται [sc. οἱ δίκαιοι] ἐπὶ τὴν πρώτην μ. id.*ecl.*56(p.153.19; M.9.725B); **5.** *dwelling of* one or more *monks* or *nuns;* **a.** *cell* ὑποστρέψαντες εἰς τὰς μ. αὐτῶν, εἴχοντο τῆς προκειμένης ἀσκήσεως Pall.*v.Chrys.*6(p.38.5; M.47.23); περὶ ὥραν ἐννάτην...ἀφ' ἑκάστης μ. ψαλμῳδίαι ἐξέρχονται id.*h.Laus.*7(p.26.7; M.34.1020C); Gr.Nyss.*v.Macr.*(p.388.20; M.46.976D); **b.** *monastery, PLond.*1913.2 (334); Pach.*reg.*B 49(M.40.949A); Ath.*apol.sec.*67(p.145.18; M.25.368C); τὴν τῆς μ. φροντίδα καὶ τῶν ἀδελφῶν Gr.Naz.*ep.*219(M.37.357C); Αὐδιανοί...τὰς ἑαυτῶν μ. ἤτοι μάνδρας ἔχουσιν Epiph.*haer.*70.1 (p.232.18; M.42.340A); Pall.*h.Laus.*21(p.63.20; M.34.1068D); τοῦ τῆς μ. ἡγεμονεύοντος Thdt.*h.rel.*3(3.1149); κατὰ τὴν Θηβαΐδα μ. τινα... χιλίους μοναχοὺς ἔνδον ἔχουσαν ‡Pall.*h.mon.*19(p.78.13; M.34.1175C); Cyr.S.*v.Euthym.*44(p.65.20); v. κοινόβιον; of women's convent, Pach.*reg.*B 49(M.40.952D); Pall.*h.Laus.*11(p.32.19; 1033D); Sergia *Olymp.*2(p.44.15); **c.** met., *monastic life* μ. δέ μοι σύνταγμα πρὸς σωτηρίαν Gr.Naz.*carm.*1.2.34.178(M.37.958A); τρόπων γὰρ εἶναι τὴν μ., οὐ σωμάτων *ib.*2.1.11.329(1052A).

μονήμερος, *of a single day;* neut. as subst. ἐν μ. ‡Pall.*h.mon.*13 (M.34.1161C; ἐν μιᾷ ἡμέρᾳ p.66.5).

***μονηρεμίτης, ὁ,** for μονερημίτης, Nil.*Eulog.*20(M.79.1120B).

μονήρης, 1. *solitary,* epithet of βίος; **a.** *single, unmarried,* Clem. *str.*7.12(p.51.5; M.9.497C); *ib.*3.9(p.226.23; M.8.1169A); **b.** *eremitical,* Bas.*reg.br.*74(2.441B; M.31.1133C); Mac.Aeg.*hom.*45.1(M.34.785C); ἐν τῇ ἀδελφῶν πολιτείᾳ...καὶ τῷ μ. βίῳ Pall.*h.Laus.*proem.(p.10.1; M. 34.1002); *ib.*1(p.16.16; 1010B); *Apophth.Patr.*(M.65.88C); **c.** *monastic* in gen., Ath.*ep.mon.*(M.26.1185C); †Bas.*ep.*42.1(3.125B; M.32.348B); Chrys.*sac.*6.7(p.154.12; 1.427B); Cyr.*ep.*1(p.10.2; 5².1A); τῶν τὸν μ. φιλοσοφούντων βίον Diad.*perf.*9(p.10.24); Thdt.*Ps.*118:108(1.1465); Dor.*doct.*1.10(M.88.1628D); τὸν ἀγγελικὸν καὶ μ. βίον Eustrat.*v.Eutych.* 1.4(M.86.2286A); written as one word μονηρίβιον, Ephr.3.336A; without βίος: μ. σχολή Isid.Pel.*epp.*1.220(M.78.321A); **2.** *sole, unique* ὦ τῆς μ. δυνάμεως πάτερ Const.ap.Gel.Cyz.*h.e.*3.19.26(M.85.1352A).

***μονηρία, ἡ,** *virgin, ascetic,* Mac.Mgn.*apocr.*2.7(p.7.20).

***μονηρίβιος,** v. μονήρης.

***μόνητα (*μόνιτα), ἡ,** (Lat. *moneta*) **1.** *mint,* Jo.Mal.*chron.*12 p.308(M.97.464B); **2.** *coinage, coined money,* μόνιτα, Cosm.Ind.*top.* 11(M.88.448D); Thphn.*chron.*p.18(M.108.104B); *ib.*p.305(741B); **3.** a *coin* of unstated value, †Gregent.*leg.Hom.*43(M.86.605A).

***μονητήριον, τό,** *resting-place,* Mac.Mgn.*apocr.*3.11(p.78.14); *ib.* 3.12(p.82.20); *ib.*4.12(p.176.11).

***μονητικός,** *solitary,* Leont.et Jo.*sacr.*2(M.86.2097D).

μονία, ἡ, 1. *steadfastness, stability,* Ephr.2.109C; **2.** *solitude* τῷ ἐθίσαντι ἐν κοινοβίῳ, δυσχερὴς ἡ μ. id.2.105B; Jo.Clim.*scal.*27(M.88.1112D); †Jo.D.*B.J.*12(M.96.968C); of a widow, Steph.Diac.*v.Steph.* (M.100.1184A); **3.** *independence* μ. καὶ αὐτοβουλία Ephr.3.255F.

***μονίδια, τά,** *group of cells, monastery,* Jo.Mosch.*prat.*151(M.87.3016D); *ib.*152(3017A).

μονιμότης, ἡ, 1. *permanence, eternity;* of God, Dion.Ar.*d.n.*2.4(M.3.640D); Max.*ambig.*(M.91.1288D); of Logos, *ib.*(1317D); id.*ep.*15(M.91.556A); **2.** *fast dye,* fig. ἀνέκπλυτον μονιμότητα ἐμμολυνθεῖσα ψυχή *cat.Apoc.*12:9(p.361.27).

μονιός, ὁ, *solitary wild boar,* ref. Ps.79:14, cited to describe persecution of Church, *M.Pion.*12.3; μ. ... ἄγριον καλεῖ [sc. τὸν Ναβουχοδονόσορ] Thdt.*Ps.*74:19(1.1176); fig., of evil thoughts ὅταν ...καρποφορῇ ἡ ψυχὴ ἄξια τῶν αἰωνίων ἀποθηκῶν...πόρρωθεν ἀπείργει [sc. τὸ πνεῦμα] τὰς τοῦ μ. τοῦ ἀγρίου ἐπιβουλάς †Bas.*Is.*20(1.392E; M.30.153A); Gr.Nyss.*hom.4 in Cant.*(M.44.841D); ‡Max.*cap.al.*232(M.90.1457A).

***μόνιτα, ἡ,** v. *μόνητα.

μονόβολος, *in one piece,* Proc.G.*Jos.*8:29(M.87.1020B).

***μονοβόλως,** *so as to be in one piece,* Epiph.*haer.*61.3(p.383.8; M.41.1041D).

μονογαμ-έω, 1. *be the husband of one wife at a time,* Thdr.Abuc. *opusc.*24(M.97.1556D); **2.** *be married once only to* ~ήσας παρθένον Phot.*nomoc.*1.23(M.104 516A).

μονογαμία, ἡ, *marrying only once,* Thphl.Ant.*Autol.*3.15(M.6.1141B); Clem.*str.*3.1(p.197.11; M.8.1104B); Or.*hom.20.4 in Jer.* (p.182.22; M.13.508C); μ. κατὰ νόμον γινομένη δικαία, ὡς ἂν κατὰ γνώμην θεοῦ ὑπάρχουσα *Const.App.*3.2.2; τὴν μ. ἐκ τῆς πλάσεως ἐδείκνυεν, ὡς μία ἑνὶ ἐπλάσθη ‡Pion.*v.Polyc.*20; Epiph.*haer.*48.9 (p.231.14; M.41.868D).

***μονογαμικός,** *monogamous,* Thdr.Stud.*epp.*1.50(M.99.1093A).

***μονογάμιον, τό,** v. κακογάμιον.

***μονογαμίς, ἡ,** *woman who marries only once,* Meth.*symp.*3.12 (p.40.19; M.18.71A).

μονόγαμος, ὁ, ἡ, *one who marries only once;* of the man, Athenag. *leg.*34.2(M.6.968B); Meth.*symp.*3.12(p.40.18; M.18.71A); ἐπίσκοπον καὶ πρεσβύτερον καὶ διάκονον εἴπομεν μονογάμους καθίστασθαι, κἂν ζῶσιν αὐτῶν αἱ γαμεταὶ κἂν τεθνήκασιν *Const.App.*6.17.1; of the woman, Or. *hom.20.4 in Jer.*(p.182.24; M.13.508C); διακόνισσαι...μ. ἐγκρατευσάμεναι ἢ χηρεύσασαι ἀπὸ μονογαμίας ἢ ἀειπάρθενοι οὖσαι Epiph.*exp. fid.*21(p.522.20; M.42.845A).

μονογενής, A. in gen.; **1.** *only, one and only,* of a child ἡ παιδεία σου ἐφ' ἡμᾶς ὡς υἱὸν πρωτότοκον μ. *Pss.Sal.*18.4; of Isaac τὸν ἴδιον μ. καὶ ἀγαπητόν Iren.*haer.*4.5.4(M.7.986A); καί τις πατὴρ τὸν μ. παῖδα, καὶ μήτηρ τὴν ἀγαπητὴν θυγατέρα προσέθυον τῷ δαίμονι Eus. *p.e.*4.15(154D; M.21.269A); τὰ μ. καὶ ἀγαπητὰ τῶν τέκνων id.*l.C.*13 (p.238.11; M.20.1401A); υἱὸν γνήσιον καὶ μ. Chrys.*fr.Job* 2:8(M.64. 552C); of Isaac as type of Christ ἐκεῖνος μ. καὶ ὁ θεὸς μ. ‡Chrys.*Abr.*2 (2.745D); **2.** equivalent to *beloved* μ. μὲν τὴν ἑαυτοῦ ψυχὴν ὀνομάζει, τὸ μ. τιθεὶς ἀντὶ τοῦ ἠγαπημένου. ἀεὶ γάρ πως ἐστιν ἐν ἀγάπῃ πλείστῃ τὸ μ. ἐν τέκνοις Ath.*exp.Ps.*34:17(M.27.172D); cf. Eus.*l.C.*13 cit. supra; id.*Marcell.*1.1(p.2.13; M.24.713A); **3.** *unique* μ. θυσιαστήριον id.*h.e.* 10.4.68(M.20.877A); μ. τι χρῆμα id.*v.C.*3.50(p.98.30; M.20.1109C); ref. Mt.16:16 ὄντως φωνὴ μ. μαρτυροῦσα μονογενεῖ Mac.Mgn.*apocr.*3. 27(p.117.19); οἱ Ἀρειανοὶ λέγουσιν, ὅτι διὰ τοῦτο καλεῖται ὁ υἱὸς μ., ὅτι μόνος ἐκ θεοῦ γέγονε· πρὸς οὓς λεκτέον, ὅτι καὶ τὸν ἥλιόν τινες λέγουσι μ., καθὸ ἥλιος μόνος ἐστίν· ἀλλ' οὐκέτι καὶ υἱός ἐστιν Ammon.*Jo.*3:16(M.85.1412A); μ. ὅδε κόσμος κατὰ τὸν Πλάτωνα Zach.Mit.*opif.*1(M.85.1072A); τῶν κτισμάτων τὰ μέν εἰσι μ. ... οἷον ἥλιος καὶ σελήνη Olymp.*Eccl.*1:9(M.93.488B); of phoenix, *alone of its kind*, *1Clem.*25.2; ζῷόν τι μ. Or.*Cels.*4.98(p.372.7; M.11.1177C); ὄρνιν...μ. ὄντα τὴν φύσιν Eus.*v.C.*4.72(p.147.18; 1228A); *Const.App.* 5.7.10; of Christ's humanity as σκώληξ (Ps.21:17) used as bait to catch Devil σκώληξ...μυστική, μ., ἀπόρρητος Mac.Mgn.*apocr.*3.9 (p.73.8); of abstracts μ. τῆς ἐκκλησίας τῆς καθολικῆς τὴν ἀλήθειαν Capr.*ep.Eph.*2(p.54.2; M.*PL.*53.848A); τῆς μ. θρησκείας Leo Mag.*ep.* 30.2(p.46.30; M.*PL.*54.790A); in this sense of Father, ref. Son τῆς ἐκ μ. μονότητος καὶ τῆς ἐκ τελείου τελειότητος Acac.Caes.*fr.Marcell.* ap.Epiph.*haer.*72.8(p.262.28; M.42.393A); ὑπὸ τὴν κραταιάν σου χεῖρα τοῦ μ. Serap.*euch.*25.1; and H. Ghost καὶ τὸ πνεῦμα...μ., οὐχ υἱοῦ ἔχον ὄνομα, οὐ πατρὸς τὴν ὀνομασίαν Epiph.*anc.*8(p.15.1; M.43.29A); **4.** *solitary, deserted*, ref. Ps.24:16, Thdt.ad loc.(1.762).

B. partic. of Son, *only, only-begotten*; **1.** coupled with παῖς: διὰ τοῦ παιδὸς αὐτοῦ τοῦ μ. Ἰησοῦ Χριστοῦ *M.Polyc.*20.2; ἐν τῷ ὀνόματι Ἰησοῦ Χριστοῦ τοῦ παιδός σου τοῦ μ. *A.Jo.*11(p.158.10); ref. Sabellianism βλασφημίαν...περὶ τοῦ...θεοῦ πατρὸς τοῦ...Χριστοῦ ἀπιστίαν τε...περὶ τοῦ μ. παιδὸς αὐτοῦ Dion.Al.ap.Eus.*h.e.*7.6(M.20.648A); τὸν δεύτερον μετὰ τὸν πατέρα τῶν ὅλων αἴτιον, τὸν τοῦ θεοῦ παῖδα γνήσιον καὶ μ. Eus.*h.e.*1.2.3(56A); θεὸν...θεοῦ...μόνου μ. παῖδα id.*v.C.* 1.32(p.22.24; M.20.948B); id.*e.th.*1.13(p.73.8; M.24.852A); ὦ μονογενὲς τοῦ θεοῦ παῖ Chrys.*hom.23.7 in Mt.*(7.295A; μονογενῆ Gaume); **2.** with υἱός, Arist.*apol.*15(p.110.31); as antitype of Isaac τὸν ἴδιον μ. καὶ ἀγαπητὸν υἱὸν θυσίαν παρασχεῖν Iren.*haer.*4.5.4(M.7.986A); ὁ...βραβευτὴς ὁ μ. υἱὸς τοῦ θεοῦ Clem.*str.*7.3(p.14.26; M.9.424D); as opp. H. Ghost μόνου τοῦ μ. φύσει υἱοῦ ἀρχῆθεν τυγχάνοντος Or.*Jo.*2.10(p.65. 22; M.14.129A); ὁ τοῦ...θεοῦ τέλειος λόγος, οἷα μ. πατρὸς υἱός Eus. *l.C.*12(p.230.18; M.20.1388C); γῆν ἔκτισεν...ὁ μ. υἱός Mac.Mgn.*apocr.* 3.23(p.105.29); Chrys.*hom.69.2 in Jo.*(8.411B); εἰ καὶ γέγονεν ἀδελφός, καὶ κεχρημάτικεν ἡμῶν πρωτότοκος διὰ τὸ ἀνθρώπινον καίτοι θεὸς ὑπάρχων καὶ υἱὸς μ. Cyr.*Is.*1.5(2.144E); ἄτρεπτον...τοῦ μ. υἱοῦ τὴν θεότητα Thdt.*haer.*proem.(4.4); **3.** with λόγος, Or.*Jo.*32.25(17; p.470.9; M.14.812D); τοῦ μ. σου λόγου τοῦ κυρίου ἡμῶν Ἰησοῦ Χριστοῦ *A.Petr.et Paul.*11(p.184.2); ὁ μ. αὐτοῦ, ὁ ἐν αὐτῷ θεὸς λόγος Gr.Thaum.*pan.Or.*4(p.9.5; M.10.1061A); τῷ μ. καὶ σωτῆρι λόγῳ Eus. *l.C.*2(p.199.11; M.20.1325A); Ath.*gent.*41(M.25.81C); ὁ μ. τοῦ θεοῦ λόγος...γενόμενος ἐκ γυναικός Cyr.*Is.*1.2(2.35C); *ib.*1.4(122D); **4.** with σωτήρ, Eus.*l.C.*10(p.223.10; M.20.1373C); **5.** with θεός, ref. Jo.1:18 οἱ ἀπὸ Οὐαλεντίνου...ἀρχὴν...τὸν Μ. λέγουσιν, ὃν καὶ θεὸν προσαγορεύεσθαι, ὡς καὶ ἐν τοῖς ἑξῆς ἄντικρυς θεὸν αὐτὸν δηλοῖ λέγων· ὁ μ. θεὸς...ἐξηγήσατο Clem.*exc.Thdot.*6(p.107.19; M.9.657A), cf. 10 infra; καταλλήλως δὲ τῷ μ. θεὸν καὶ υἱὸν αὐτὸν εἶναι πατρὸς ὠνομάσθησαν κόλποι...ἀφ' ὧν ἴσμεν σημαίνεσθαι τὴν πρὸς τὸν πατέρα οἰκειότητα Or.*fr.14 in Jo.*(p.495.28); μ. θεός, ἐκ θεοῦ γεγεννημένος λόγος Eus.*l.C.*12(p.231.19; M.20.1389B); Gr.Nyss.*or.catech.*proem. (p.2.13; M.45.9B); id.*ep.*3(M.46.1017D); ἡ...δύναμις, ἥτις ἐστὶν ὁ μ. θεός, πάντα ποιεῖ, οὗ χωρὶς οὐδὲν εἰς γένεσιν τῶν ὄντων ἔρχεται· ἀλλὰ καὶ αὐτὴ πάλιν τῶν ἀγαθῶν ἡ πηγή, ἐκ τοῦ πατρικοῦ βουλήματος ἀφορμᾶται...πᾶν ἀγαθὸν πρᾶγμα...τῆς ἀνάρχου δυνάμεως...ἐξημμένον ἐν τῇ δυνάμει τοῦ πνεύματος διὰ τοῦ μ. θεοῦ ἀχρόνως...εἰς τελείωσιν ἄγεται id.*tres dii*(M.45.129A); id.*Apoll.*5(M.45.1132C); ὁ μ. θεὸς αὐτὸς ἀνίστησι τὸν ἀνακραθέντα ἄνθρωπον αὐτῷ...ἐν γὰρ τῷ ὑπὲρ ἡμῶν ἀποθανόντι...τὸν κόσμον ἑαυτῷ κατήλλαξεν ὁ μ. θεὸς *ib.*17(1156C); μ. θεὸν ἀποκαλεῖ τὸν υἱόν, καὶ ἐν κόλποις εἶναί φησι τοῦ πατρός, ἵνα φαίνηται πάλιν τῆς πρὸς τὴν κτίσιν ὁμοφυΐας ἔξω κείμενος, καὶ ἰδιάζουσαν ἔχων ἐκ πατρὸς καὶ ἐν πατρὶ τὴν ὕπαρξιν. εἰ γὰρ ὄντως θεός ἐστι μ., πῶς οὐκ ἔστι κατὰ φύσιν ἕτερος, ὡς πρὸς ἐκείνους, οἵπερ εἰσὶ κατὰ θέσιν θεοί...; νοηθήσεται γὰρ οὐκ ἐν πολλοῖς ἀδελφοῖς ὁ μ., ἀλλ' ὡς μόνος ὢν ἐκ πατρός. ... θεός ἐστι μ. ὁ υἱός, ἔξω δηλονότι τῶν ἄλλων κείσεται, καὶ οὐκ ἐν τοῖς κατὰ χάριν τετάξεται θεοῖς Cyr. *Jo.*1.10(4.105B); **6.** with εἰκών: τὴν πρωτότυπον τοῦ πατρὸς καὶ μ. εἰκόνα Meth.*res.*1.35(p.274.5; M.18.292C); **7.** abs., Just.*dial.*105.1(M. 6.720C); ὁ τῷ ὄντι μ., ὁ τῆς τοῦ...πατρὸς δόξης χαρακτήρ Clem.*str.* 7.3(p.12.20; M.9.421A); δόξα τῷ μ. τῷ ἀπὸ τοῦ πατρός *A.Thom.*A 60 (p.177.6); περὶ...τοῦ τὸν ἄνθρωπον ὄργανον γεγονότα καὶ ἔνδυμα τοῦ μ. τοῦτο ἀπειργάσθαι Meth.*symp.*3.7(p.33.18; M.18.69C); ὁ πρωτόπλαστος...εἰς αὐτὸν ἀναφέρεσθαι δύναται τὸν Χριστόν, οὐκέτι τύπος ὢν καὶ...εἰκὼν τοῦ μ., ἀλλὰ καὶ αὐτὸ τοῦτο σοφία γεγονὼς καὶ λόγος *ib.*3.8(p.35.6; 72C); ἡ τοῦ μ. αὐτοῦ γέννησις Eus.*e.th.*1.12(p.71.8; M. 24.848A); Mac.Mgn.*apocr.*2.8(p.9.8); †Bas.*hom.in Ps.*28(1.359E; M. 30.77A); Pall.*v.Chrys.*16(p.99.12; M.47.56); Cyr.*Joel.*33(3.226A); τὴν τοῦ μ. σάρκωσιν Thdt.*qu.19 in Gen.*(1.23); **8.** theol. implications and comments, cf. '*unigenitus filius...qui est in sinu patris, ipse enarravit.*' *patrem enim invisibilem existentem, ille qui in sinu ejus est filius omnibus enarrat*, Iren.*haer.*3.11.6(M.7.883B); τό, 'ὡς μονογενοῦς παρὰ πατρός' νοεῖν ὑποβάλλει ἐκ τῆς οὐσίας τοῦ πατρὸς εἶναι τὸν υἱόν. ... εἰ γὰρ καὶ ἄλλα παρὰ πατρὸς εἶχε τὴν ὕπαρξιν, ματαίως ἡ τοῦ μ. ἔκειτο φωνή...οὗτος δὲ μ. παρὰ πατρὸς πλήρης χάριτος καὶ ἀληθείας εἴρηται, οὐκ ἄλλος ὢν τούτων ὧν λέγεται εἶναι πλήρης Or.*fr.9 in Jo.*(p.490.20); cf. *unigenitus filius salvator noster, qui solus ex patre natus est, solus natura et non adoptione filius est, ib.*109(p.562.29); τοῦ μ. παιδὸς...τοῦ πρωτοτόκου πάσης κτίσεως, τοῦ ἐνανθρωπήσαντος λόγου Dion.Al.ap.Eus.*h.e.*7.6(M.20.648A); ὅτι ὁ υἱὸς...οὔτε ἐξ οὐκ ὄντων γεγένηται, οὔτε ἦν ποτε ὅτε οὐκ ἦν, αὐτάρκης ἐπαίδευσεν Ἰωάννης...γράφων...'ὁ μ. υἱός, ὁ ὢν εἰς τὸν κόλπον τοῦ πατρός' Alex.Al. *ep.Alex.*4(p.22.5; M.18.553A); αὐτὸς ὁ μ. τοῦ θεοῦ καὶ πρωτότοκος τῶν ὅλων ἡ πάντων ἀρχή Eus.*p.e.*7.15(327D; M.21.553B); φύσει θεὸς ὁμοῦ καὶ μ. υἱὸς ὢν τυγχάνει, οὐχὶ δὲ ὁμοίως τοῖς ἔξωθεν εἰσποιούμενος...εἰ καὶ φύσει μ. υἱὸς καὶ θεὸς...ἀνευφημεῖται, ἀλλ' οὐχ ὁ πρῶτος θεός, πρωτὸς δὲ τοῦ θεοῦ μ. υἱός, καὶ διὰ τοῦτο θεὸς id.*d.e.*5.4(p.225.27; M.22.372D); ἔπρεπεν...θεῷ πρὸ παντὸς γενητοῦ...τὸ μ. τοῦτο προβαλέσθαι γέννημα, ὥσπερ τινὰ κρηπῖδα καὶ θεμέλιον...τῶν μελλόντων δι' αὐτοῦ γενήσεσθαι id.*e.th.*1.8(p.66.27; M.24.837C); πῶς δ' ἔσται μ. τῷ πλήθει τῶν γεγονότων συναριθμούμενος; *ib.*1.10(p.68.30; 841C); ὁμολογοῦμεν καὶ μ. καὶ πρωτότοκον· ἀλλὰ μ. τὸν λόγον, ὃς πάντοτε ἦν καὶ ἔστιν ἐν τῷ πατρί· τὸ πρωτότοκος δὲ τῷ ἀνθρώπῳ CSard.*ep.cath.* ap.Thdt.*h.e.*2.8.44(3.846); Ath.*Ar.*2.62(M.26.280A) cit. s. πρωτότοκος; μ. γὰρ οὐχ ὁ παρὰ μόνον γενόμενος, ἀλλ' ὁ μόνος γεννηθείς...μ. δέ, ὡς ἔοικεν, ἀνθρώπων οὐδείς, κατά γε τὸν ἡμέτερον λόγον, διὰ τὸ ἐκ συνδυασμοῦ πᾶσιν ὑπάρχειν τὴν γέννησιν. οὐδὲ ἡ Σάρα μήτηρ μονογενοῦς ἦν παιδὸς Bas.*Eun.*2.20–21(1.256A–E; M.29.616A–617A); εἰ δὲ κτιστός ἐστιν, οὐ μ.·...εἰ δὲ μ.,...οὐδεμίαν ἄρα ἔχει πρὸς τὰ κτιστὰ κοινωνίαν Thdt.*haer.*5.2(4.382); οὐκ ἄλλος...ὁ Χριστός, καὶ ἄλλος ὁ θεὸς λόγος...δύο γὰρ υἱοὺς ἡ θεία φύσις οὐκ οἶδεν. ὁ μόνος μ. ἐγέννησεν Procl.CP *Arm.*8(p.190.32; M.65.864A); ἔστι γὰρ εἷς καὶ μόνος μ. υἱὸς καὶ λόγος...οὐ τῶν φύσεων...εἰς δυάδα ὑποστάσεων τεμνομένων id.*fr.* 3(M.65.885D); μόνος μ. ἐκ μόνου πατρός, καὶ μόνος ἐκ μόνης μητρός ‡Jo.D.*hom.*6.10(M.96.677B); **9.** ref. heret. Trin. doctrine πάντα...δι' αὐτοῦ γεγεννῆσθαι...ὁμολογοῦμεν, συναπογεννηθείσης ἄνωθεν αὐτῷ τῆς δημιουργικῆς δυνάμεως, ὥστ' εἶναι θεὸν μ. πάντων τῶν μετ' αὐτὸν καὶ τῶν δι' αὐτοῦ γενομένων Eun.*apol.*15(M.30.849D); οὐκοῦν εἰ μόνος μὲν ἀληθινὸς ὁ θεὸς...ἐπειδὴ καὶ μόνος ἀγέννητος, μ. υἱός, ἐπειδὴ μόνος ἀγεννήτου γέννημα, οὐκ ἂν δέ τι μόνον εἴη, κοινοποιουμένης πρὸς ἕτερον δι' ὁμοιότητα τῆς φύσεως *ib.*22(857B); εἰ τὴν μὲν βούλησιν ἀπέδειξεν ὁ λόγος ἐνέργειαν, οὐκ οὐσίαν δὲ τὴν ἐνέργειαν, ὑπέστη δὲ βουλήσει τοῦ πατρὸς ὁ μ., οὐ πρὸς τὴν οὐσίαν, πρὸς δὲ τὴν ἐνέργειαν, ἥτις ἐστὶ καὶ βούλησις· ἀποσώζειν τὴν ὁμοιότητα τὸν υἱὸν ἀναγκαῖον. ... εἰκόνα τοίνυν φαμέν, οὐχ ὡς ἀγεννήτῳ γέννημα παραβάλλοντες...ἀλλ' υἱὸν μ. καὶ πρωτότοκον πατρί, τῆς μὲν υἱοῦ προσηγορίας τὴν οὐσίαν δηλούσης, τῆς δὲ πατρός, τὴν τοῦ γεννήσαντος ἐνέργειαν *ib.*24(860B,D); διὰ τοῦτο ...μ., ἐπειδή, παρὰ μόνου γεννηθεὶς καὶ κτισθείς, τελειότατος γέγονεν ὑπουργός id.ap.Bas.*Eun.*2.21(1.256D; M.29.617A); εἰ Μωϋσῆς... παραιτεῖται τὸν ἄγγελον,...ἀποδείκνυται...ὅτι ὁ τῇ τοῦ ὄντος ἐπωνυμίᾳ ἑαυτὸν γνωρίσας ὁ μ. ἐστι θεός...εἰ γάρ...ὁ μ. οὐκ ἔστι, καθὼς Εὐνόμιος βούλεται,...τὰ ἐκ τῆς συναγωγῆς δόγματα πρὸς τὴν ἐκκλησίαν... μεταφέρεται Gr.Nyss.*Eun.*11(2 p.263.1,6; M.45.872A); Ἀρείανοι λέγουσιν ὅτι καλεῖται ὁ υἱὸς μ. ὅτι μόνος ἐκ θεοῦ γέγονε Ammon.*Jo.* 3:16(M.85.1412A); **10.** Gnost., of aeon Νοῦς (offspring of Βυθός and Σιγή), Iren.*haer.*1.1.1(M.7.445B); ἑαυτὸν τῆς Σιγῆς μονώτατον γεγονέναι λέγων [sc. Μάρκος] ἅτε μ. ὑπάρχων *ib.*1.14.1(593A); Μωϋσῆς...ἕνα...νεὼν ἱδρυσάμενος τοῦ θεοῦ, μ. τε κόσμον, ὥς φησιν ὁ Βασιλείδης, καὶ τὸν ἕνα...κατήγγελλε θεόν Clem.*str.*5.11(p.376.4; M. 9.112B); [Jo.1:1] ἀρχὴν...τὸν Μ. λέγουσιν [sc. Valentinians], ὃν καὶ θεὸν προσαγορεύεσθαι...τῷ δὴ λόγῳ τῷ ἐν τῇ ἀρχῇ, τουτ' ἔστιν ἐν τῷ Μ., ἐν τῷ Νῷ καὶ τῇ Ἀληθείᾳ, μηνύει τὸν...Χριστόν, τὸν Λόγον...

ἄγνωστος...ὁ πατὴρ ὧν ἠθέλησεν γνωσθῆναι τοῖς αἰῶσι, καὶ διὰ τῆς ἐνθυμήσεως τῆς ἑαυτοῦ...προέβαλε τὸν Μ. ... καὶ ὁ μὲν μείνας 'μ. υἱὸς εἰς τὸν κόλπον τοῦ πατρὸς' τὴν ἐνθύμησιν διὰ τῆς γνώσεως ἐξηγεῖται τοῖς αἰῶσιν...ὁ δὲ ἐνταῦθα ὀφθεὶς οὐκέτι μ., ἀλλ' ὡς μ. πρὸς τοῦ ἀποστόλου προσαγορεύεται, δόξαν ὡς μ. ... εἰκόνα δὲ τοῦ Μ. τὸν Δημιουργὸν λέγουσιν id.*exc.Thdot.*6,7(p.107.19ff.; M.9.657A–C); Epiph.*haer.*31.2 (p.386.5; M.41.477B); *κατὰ τοὺς Βαλεντίνου μύθους...ἄλλον τὸν μ., καὶ ἄλλον τὸν λόγον* Thdt.*haer.*5.2(4.382); **11.** Manichean *εἴθε...μὴ τὸν μ. τὸν ἐκ τῶν κόλπων τοῦ πατρὸς καταβάντα Χριστόν, Μαρίας τινὸς γυναικὸς ἔλεγον* [sc. Christians] *εἶναι υἱόν* Hegem.*Arch.*5(p.7.9; M.10. 1436A).

***μονογλωσσέω**, s.v.l., *sound separately*; intrans., Iren.*haer.*1.14. 1(M.7.597A).

***μονόγραμμον, τό**, *monogram*, CCP(681)*act.*12(H.3.1308C).

***μονόδενδρος**, *having one tree*; of a town, *Apoc.Dan.*C(p.118).

***μονοδέσποτος**, *under a single head*, Leont.H.*Nest.*2.13(M.86. 1561C).

***μονοδιαιτησία, ἡ**, *living alone*, Clem.*str.*2.23(p.191.10; M.8. 1092B).

μονοειδής, **1.** *one in kind μ. ὄχλος A.Jo.*100(p.201.1); *simple*; of the deity, Eus.*e.th.*2.14(p.115.15; M.24.928C); Gr.Nyss.*hom.5 in Cant.*(M.44.873D); of Son, Eus.*d.e.*4.4(p.155.1; M.22.257D); of H. Ghost, Ammon.*Jo.*4:14(M.85.1421A); of Trin., Max.*ambig.*(M. 91.1196B); of Christ's body, Epiph.*exp.fid.*17(p.519.4; M.42.817B); **2.** *unique τέλειον τὸ θεῖον...μ. καὶ ἀσύνθετον* Apoll.*quod un.Chr.*9 (p.300.12; M.28.129A); Mac.Mgn.*apocr.*3.27(p.117.18).

μονοειδῶς, **1.** *as simple*, Dion.Ar.*d.n.*9.4(M.3.912C) cit. s. *ταυτοειδῶς*; *simply, uniformly πῶς...δυνατὸν μ. πάντα μετέχειν τοῦ ἀγαθοῦ, μὴ πάντα ὄντα ταὐτῶς εἰς τὴν ὁλικὴν αὐτοῦ μέθεξιν ἐπιτήδεια*; *ib.*4.20 (720A); *πάντες οἱ λόγοι τῶν ἐντολῶν...ὑπὸ ταύτης* [sc. *τῆς ἀγάπης*] *μ. περιέχονται Schol.* in Max.*ep.*2(M.91.408B); *simply, only ἐκ μητρὸς μ. ἔλαβε τὴν σάρκα* Epiph.*haer.*69.25(p.175.25; M.42.244B); *Χριστὸν... καὶ οὐ μ. τὸν λόγον χθές τε καὶ σήμερον τὸν αὐτὸν εἶναί φησι* Cyr.*inc. unigen.*(5[1].710C); **2.** *uniquely τὸ...πνεῦμα...μ. ἔχον τὸ ἐξ αὐτοῦ* [sc. *τοῦ θεοῦ*] *ἐξαίρετον* Epiph.*haer.*76.24(p.371.14; M.42.564B); *Didasc. Patr.*2(p.13.4); **3.** *in the singular*, Epiph.*anc.*10(p.18.7; M.43.36A); *ib.*22(p.31.23; 57D).

μονοείμων, *with only one garment*, Ast.Am.*hom.*3(M.40.213B).

μονόζυξ, *yoked alone*, hence *solitary*; s.v.l., ?*fighting a lone battle*, Chrys.*pan.Laz.*(2.649A).

μονόζωνος, ὁ, *wearing a belt only* (and not full uniform) i.e., *light-armed soldier*; also, *wearing a special, unique, belt*, i.e. *member of a* corps d'élite, ref. Job 29:25 *οἱ μ. τὰ στρατιωτικὰ τάγματα μηνύουσιν ἢ βαρβαρικὰ στίφη ἢ ληστρικὰ συγκροτήματα* Isid.Pel.*epp.* 3.78(M.78.785B); *μ. εἰσιν οἱ τίμιοι τῶν στρατιωτῶν, οἱ μὴ τὸν αὐτὸν τοῖς ἄλλοις ζωστῆρα φοροῦντες· ἢ οἱ ἀσύντακτοι, καὶ ὡσανεὶ λησταί* Olymp.*Job* 29:25(M.93.308B); *Dial.Tim.et Aquil.*83 v°.

***μονοθεΐα, ἡ**, *single divinity*, *Pers.*(p.13.17; M.10.101C).

***μονοθέλητος**, *of one will μ., μᾶλλον δὲ κακοθέλητον βούλησιν* Taras.*ep.*1(M.98.1432B); *μ. δόγμα* Thphn.*chron.*p.274(M.108.680B).

***μονόθρονος**, *enthroned alone*; of a bishop, Gr.Naz.*carm.*2.1.11. 1586(M.37.1139A).

***μονοκέλλιον, τό**, *solitary cell*, *Apophth.Patr.*(M.65.152B).

μονόκερως, ὁ, *unicorn*, **1.** in gen. *ὁ μ. ... τὴν μὲν κεφαλὴν δράκοντος φέρων,...τὸ δὲ ἄλλο σῶμα ἐλάφῳ προσέοικε μᾶλλον, τοὺς δὲ πόδας λέοντος ἔχει* Philost.*h.e.*3.11(M.65.496B); *ἡνίκα δόξῃ παρὰ πολλῶν διώκεσθαι* [sc. *μ.*]...*εἰς κρημνὸν ἐφάλλεται καὶ ῥίπτει ἑαυτὸν ἐκ τοῦ ὕψους καὶ...τὸ κέρας δέχεται τὴν ὅλην ὁρμήν, καὶ ἀβλαβὲς διαμένει* Cosm.Ind.*top.*11(M.88.444B); *ὁ μ. ὃν δὴ Ἀκύλας ῥινοκέρωτα ἔφη* Olymp.*Job* 39:9(M.93.413A); **2.** as type of Christ, ref. Ps.21:22 *ὁ τοῦ θεοῦ μ., αὐτὸς ὁ κύριος ἡμῶν, μόνον τὸν πατέρα κέρας ἔχων* Eus. *d.e.*10.8(p.489.3; M.22.785B); ref. Ps.28:6 *ὅταν ἀμύνασθαι δέῃ καὶ καθελεῖν τὴν δυναστείαν τὴν ἐπιφυομένην τῷ γένει τῶν ἀνθρώπων... τότε υἱὸς μονοκερώτων ὀνομάζεται* [sc. *ὁ μονογενής*] Bas.*hom.in Ps.* 28(1.120B; M.29.296C); *μ. ζῷον ἀρχικόν, ἀνυπότακτον ἀνθρώπῳ, τὴν ἰσχὺν ἀκαταμάχητον· ἐρημίαις διαιτώμενον, ἑνὶ κερατίῳ πεποιθός. διὰ τοῦτο ἡ ἀκαταγώνιστος τοῦ κυρίου φύσις μονοκέρῳ* [v.l. *-ωτι*] *παρεικάσθη, διά τε τὴν κατὰ πάντων ἀρχήν, καὶ διὰ τὸ μίαν ἔχειν ἑαυτῶν ἀρχήν, τὸν πατέρα* †Bas.*hom.in Ps.*28(1.361A; M.30.80B); *αἱ τῶν προφητῶν καὶ ἀποστόλων σάλπιγγες, ἃς κερατίνας ὁ νόμος φησὶ διὰ τὸ εἶναι αὐτῶν τὴν κατασκευὴν ἐκ τοῦ ἀληθινοῦ μ.* Gr.Nyss.*nativ.*(M.46. 1129A); *περὶ τοῦ μ. ... πῶς οὖν ἀγρεύεται; παρθένον ἁγνὴν...ῥίπτουσιν ἔμπροσθεν αὐτοῦ, καὶ ἅλλεται εἰς τὸ κόλπον αὐτῆς, καὶ ἡ παρθένος θηλάζει τὸ ζῷον καὶ αἴρει αὐτὸ εἰς τὸ παλάτιον τῷ βασιλεῖ Phys.*A 22 (p.78.6); **3.** type of believer in one God, ref. Ps.28:6 *ἔοικε...τὸν υἱὸν μονοκερώτων τὴν Ἱερουσαλὴμ λέγειν,...ἐπεὶ πατέρων γεγόνασιν ἁγίων, οἵτινες ἐλέγοντο μ., διὰ τὸ μόνον θεῷ κέρατι κεχρῆσθαι* Eus.ad loc. (M.23.256C); Thdt.ad loc.(1.783); *ib.*91:11(1267); *ὁ μ. ἐστιν ὁ ἅγιος, ὅτι πρὸς θεὸν μόνον ὁρᾷ καὶ ἐπ' αὐτῷ πέποιθε* Olymp.*Job* 39:9(M.93. 413B); cf. *οἱ θεὸν μόνον ἐγνωκότες πατέρα...οἱ κεράτων μονοκερώτων ἐρασταί* Clem.*paed.*1.5(p.100.4; M.8.269A); **4.** type of Cross, ref. Ps. 21:22 *ὁ ἀντὶ τοῦ ἀμνοῦ παῖς θεοῦ...ὁ ὑψωθεὶς ἐπὶ κεράτων μονοκέρωτος* Claud.*fr.pasch.*(M.5.1297A); ref. Dt.33:17, Just.*dial.*91.2(M.6.692C); **5.** type of Devil *λέοντα καλεῖ...καὶ μ. τὸν τὸ κράτος ἔχοντα τοῦ θανάτου* Thdt.*Ps.*21:21(1.741).

***μονοκιτωνία, ἡ**, v. ***μονοχιτωνία**.

***μονοκρατία, ἡ**, *sole rule*, Gr.Naz.*carm.*1.1.3.79(M.37.414C).

***μονοκρατορέω**, *be sole ruler*, Thphn.*chron.*p.39(M.108.153B).

***μονοκράτωρ, ὁ**, *sole ruler*, *Hom.Clem.*5.23; *Chron.Pasch.*p.278 (M.92.692C); Thphn.*chron.*p.12(M.108.85C).

***μονοκτήτωρ, ὁ**, *sole possessor*; of Godhead, Didym.*Trin.*1.27(M. 39.408A).

***μονόκτιστος**, *only-created*, Bas.*Eun.*2.21(1.256E; M.29.617A); *μ. κυριώτερον ἂν λέγοιτο, κτίσμα μὲν ἀληθῶς κατ' Εὐνόμιον ὤν, γέννημα δὲ ψευδωνύμως καλούμενος* Didym.(‡Bas.)*Eun.*4(1.287C; M.29.689C); Isid.Pel.*epp.*3.31(M.78.752C).

***μονοκώλως**, *as one clause*, Epiph.*haer.*57.2(p.347.3; M.41.997C).

***μονολογία, ἡ**, *single utterance πολυλογία...ἐν προσευχῇ τὸν νοῦν... διέχυσε. μ. δὲ πολλάκις τὸν νοῦν συνάγειν πέφυκε* Jo.Clim.*scal.*28(M. 88.1132B).

***μονολόγιστος**, **1.** *of single thought*, *μ. ἔλπις unwavering* hope, Marc.Er.*opusc.*1.10(M.65.905C); *ib.*2.140(952C); esp. *μ. Ἰησοῦ εὐχή* Jo.Clim.*scal.*15(M.88.889D); *εὐχῇ μ. κτείνει τε καὶ ἐκτεφροῖ τὰς αὐτῶν* [sc. *δαιμόνων*] *ἀπάτας* Hesych.S.*temp.*2.72(M.93.1536B); *ἔξω τοῦ πρώτου καταπετάσματος ἵσταται ὁ ἐν εὐχῇ ῥεμβόμενος· ἔνδοθεν γίνεται ὁ μονολόγιστον ἐξανύων αὐτήν* ‡Max.*cap.al.*102(M.90.1424A); **2.** *in thought alone ἁμαρτία τοῦ πρώτου Ἀδὰμ...ἐστὶ μ. ἐμφάνεια πράγματος πονηροῦ* Marc.Er.*opusc.*4(M.65.1016Aff.).

***μονολογίστως**, **1.** *by a single thought ἀρχὴ μὲν προσευχῆς προσβολαὶ μ. διωκόμεναι ἐκ προοιμίων αὐτῶν* Jo.Clim.*scal.*28(M.88.1132D); **2.** *in thought alone*, Marc.Er.*opusc.*4(M.65.1016B).

μονόλοπος, *with one layer of bark*, Bas.*hex.*5.7(1.46D; M.29.109C).

μονομαχέω, **1.** *fight in single combat*; of the partridge, Or.*hom. 17.1 in Jer.*(p.144.2; M.13.453A); **2.** *fight as a gladiator ὑπὲρ οἰκείου θεοῦ τῆς κοιλίας μ.* Cyr.H.*catech.*19.6.

μονομάχης, ὁ, = *μονομάχος*, *gladiator*, Clem.*paed.*2.1(p.158.15; M. 8.389A).

μονομαχία, ἡ, **1.** *single combat*; of a martyr, *M.Perp.*18(p.89.3); **2.** plur., *gladiatorial show*, *Ep.Lugd.*ap.Eus.*h.e.*5.1.53(M.20.428C); Thdt.*h.e.*5.26.1(3.1067).

μονομάχιον, μονομαχεῖον, τό, **1.** *single combat*; of Passion, Chrys.*hom.2.3 in Col.*(11.369B); **2.** plur., *gladiatorial show*, *Ep. Lugd.*ap.Eus.*h.e.*5.1.40(M.20.424B); **3.** *gladiatorial school*, Jo.Mal. *chron.*9 p.217(M.97.336C); *ib.*13 p.339(505C).

***μονομέρεια, ἡ**, *one sidedness*, *hearing only one party* to a dispute *κατὰ μονομέρειαν* ex parte, Jul.Papa *ep.Dian.*ap.Ath.*apol.sec.*27 (p.107.15; M.25.293B); CSard.*ep.Alex.*ap.Ath.*apol.sec.*37(p.116.13; 313A); Thphn.*chron.*p.25(M.108.121C).

μονομερής, **1.** *consisting of one part, single*, Tat.*orat.*15.1(p.16.7; M.6.837A); **2.** *one-sided*, ex parte, Gr.Nyss.*ep.*16(M.46.1056B); *Const. App.*2.51.1; *ἐκ μ. after hearing only one side*, Socr.*h.e.*1.31.5(M.67. 164A); *Dial.*ap.Thdt.*h.e.*2.16.11(3.866).

μονομερῶς, **1.** *as a single entity, singly*, Ast.Am.*hom.*8(M.40. 268B); **2.** *as one part* of the whole, *particularly*, Epiph.*haer.*25.3 (p.270.3; M.41.324B); Max.*schol.in e.h.*5.1.5(M.4.164D); ref. Persons of Trin., ‡Ath.*disp.*7(M.28.444D); Marc.Er.*opusc.*4(M.65.1009A); Jo. D.*trisag.*3(M.95.28B); Christol. *ἔτη ψηφίζονται οὐκ ἐκ φύσεως μ. ἀλλὰ γεννήσεως τοῦ γενομένου ἀνθρώπου* Marc.Er.*opusc.*10.5(M.65.1124A); *ib.*10.4(1121C); *ἕκαστον καὶ καθ' ἑαυτὸ μ. καὶ κεχωρισμένως...ὑποστῆναι* Jo.D.*fid.Nest.*21(p.568); **3.** *from one point of view τὰ ἀνθρωπολογούμενα οἱ ἀμαθέστατοι τῇ θεότητι ἀσεβῶς προσάπτουσι καὶ τὰς πολυμερῶς καὶ πολυτρόπως ῥηθείσας γραφὰς μ. ἐκλαμβάνοντες πίπτουσιν* Didym.(‡Bas.)*Eun.*5(1.313C; M.29.752A); *μονοτρόπως οὐ χρὴ τὰ πράγματα νοεῖσθαι οὔτε μ.* Mac.Aeg.*hom.*17.5(M.34.628A); *Apophth. Mac.Aeg.*(M.34.208C); of judicial ex parte decisions, *Const.App.*2. 47.3.

μονονουχί, *all but, well nigh ὁ ἐλαιὼν τὸν ἐπὶ νεφέλης ἀναβάντα τοῖς τῶν πιστῶν ὀφθαλμοῖς μ. δεικνύων μέχρι σήμερον καὶ τὴν οὐράνιον τῆς ἀνόδου πύλην* Cyr.H.*catech.*14.23; esp. with verbs of saying, *as if, as much as* to say, ref. Jo.18:6 *ἑαυτὸν παραδίδωσι, μ. λέγων... τὴν δύναμιν ἐξεκάλυψα τὴν ἐμαυτοῦ* Chrys.*prod.Jud.*1.3(2.381A); id.*coemet.*2(2.401A,B); *ἑώρακα, φησίν, ἐν τοῖς υἱοῖς Ἰεσσαὶ ἐμοὶ εἰς* βασιλέα, μ. λέγων, ἐμὴν εἶναι τὴν τοῦ παιδὸς βασιλείαν λογίζομαι Bas.Sel.*or.*14.2(M.85.185A); ἐκάθευδεν ὁ σωτὴρ μ. πρὸς τὴν θάλατταν διαλεγόμενος...ἵνα...μάθωσιν [sc. οἱ μαθηταί] ὡς καὶ θαλάττης δεσπότης ὑπάρχω *ib.*22.2(265C); μονονουχί sts. for οὐ μόνον: [Jo.1:3] ἀποφαίνει αὐτὸν...μ. δημιουργὸν ἀλλ' ὅτι καὶ οὐκ ἐκτίσθη Didym.*Trin.*1.15(M.39.300B); τὸ ἅγιον πνεῦμα μ. δοῦλον οὐ γέγραπται ἀλλὰ καὶ ὡς δεσπότης καὶ φύσει ἐλεύθερον *ib.*2.6(537A); ἀπεδείχθη οὖν μ. θεὸς τὸ ἅγιον πνεῦμα· ἀλλὰ καὶ ἴσος καὶ ὅμοιος τῷ πατρὶ καὶ τῷ υἱῷ *ib.*2.10(636B).

μονόξυλος, *made from a solid trunk*; fig. ἑκάστη...τῶν αἱρέσεων μ. τις οὖσα οὐ τὸν χαρακτῆρα τῆς ἐκκλησίας ὑποφαίνει Epiph.*haer.*61.3 (p.383.12; M.41.1044A).

***μονοούσιος**, **1.** *of one element, simple*, Hipp.*haer.*10.32(p.288.15; M.16.3447A); Max.*schol.c.h.*2.2(M.4.37B); *ib.*15.2(105C); of H. Ghost, ‡Caes.Naz.*dial.*43(M.38.912); *of one substance* ὡς οἱ Σαβέλλιοι λέγοντες μ. καὶ οὐχ ὁμοούσιον †Ath.*exp.fid.*2(M.25.204A); **2.** *alone of its kind, unique*, *Protev.*6.3(p.13).

***μονοπάτιον, τό**, = sq., Jo.Mal.*chron.*18 p.469(M.97.684B).

***μονόπατον, τό**, *single track path*, Thphn.*chron.*p.157(M.108.428A).

***μονόπληξ**, *with one stroke*, *A.Jo.*42(p.171.11); *ib.*71(p.185.26); *ib.*76(p.188.11).

***μονοποδάρενος**, ? *one-legged*, *Exorc.*13(p.336).

***Μονοποδαρία, ἡ**, name of an heretical Jewish festival ἀναθεματίζω...ἀρχιραββίτας καὶ τοὺς νέους τῶν Ἰουδαίων κακοδιδασκάλους, Λάζαρόν φημι, τὸν τὴν ἄθεσμον ἑορτὴν ἐξευρόντα τῆς λεγομένης παρ' αὐτοῖς *Μ.* καὶ...τοὺς λοιποὺς *Clem.recogn.suppl.*2.2(M.1.1457D).

***μονόπορτον, τό**, *single door*, *Chron.Pasch.*p.339(M.92.885B).

***μονοπρόσμονα**, *in private interview*, CQuerc.(M.103.105B).

μονοπρόσωπος, **1.** *always presenting the same aspect*; of persons, *sincere*, *T.Aser* 4.1; of things, *consistent, uniform* τὸ μονότροπον καὶ μ. τῆς ἀληθείας ἀσπασώμεθα Clem.*paed.*3.11(p.267.7; M.8.628A); *ib.*2.3(p.180.13; 437A); ‡Just.*ep.Zen.et Ser.*5(M.6.1188C); **2.** *belonging to* or *consisting of one person, unipersonal* ὁ...θεὸς...οὐδὲ ὅμοιος ἡμῶν ἐστι μ. εἰ γὰρ ἦν μ., ἐγινώσκομεν ἂν αὐτὸν ὡς ἐγινώσκομεν ἀλλήλους ἡμᾶς ‡Ath.*qu.al.*4(M.28.776A); εἰ γὰρ καὶ τὸν θεὸν καὶ πατέρα γινώσκειν καὶ σέβειν ἐλέγοντο...ἀλλὰ τῷ μ. οἴεσθαι καὶ καταγγέλλειν τὴν θεαρχίαν καὶ μήτε τὸν λόγον...μήτε τὸ ἀγαθὸν αὐτοῦ...πνεῦμα τῇ θεολογίᾳ συναριθμεῖν ‡Gr.Nyss.*hom.5.23 in Jo.*(p.181.5); εἴπερ ἓν θέλημα τῆς ὑπερουσίου τριάδος ἐστί, μ. ἔσται θεότης τριώνυμος Max.*opusc.*(M.91.52C); Christol. ἐπειδὴ κατ' οὐσίαν...οὐ γέγονεν ἕνωσις, μία φύσις οὐ γέγονεν, μία μ., ὁ Χριστός, οὐκ ἔστιν ὑπόστασις· οὐκοῦν κατ' εὐδοκίαν ἡ ἕνωσις, βουλῆς καὶ γνώμης ταυτότητι κρατουμένη Paul.Pers.*judic.fr.*(H.3.896D); Anast.S.*hod.*7 (M.89.117C); μὴ οἷόν τε μ. φύσιν γνωρίζεσθαι Thdr.Stud.*epp.*2.170 (M.99.1536D).

μονοπροσώπως, **1.** *without hypocrisy*, *T.Aser* 6.1; **2.** *as one person* διὰ τοῦ βαπτίσματος...διὰ τοῦ πνεύματος τὸν πατέρα καὶ τὸν υἱὸν δεχόμεθα...μ. οὐ λέγομεν εἶναι τὴν τριάδα Marc.Er.*opusc.*4(M.65.1008D); συκοφαντίαν τοῖς σεραφὶμ ὑμῶν παρεισφερόντων ὅτι οἱ οὐ τὴν τριάδα φάσκουσι δοξολογεῖν ἅγιος ἅγιος ἅγιος, ἀλλὰ μ. τὸν υἱόν ‡Felix III Papa *ep.Petr.*2(p.14.20; H.2.825C); **3.** *with reference to one thing only* κρατεῖν μ., τοὺς μὲν κοσμικοὺς τὸ κρέας, τοὺς δὲ μοναχοὺς τὸν τυρὸν καὶ ᾠά †Jo.Jej.*poenit.*(M.88.1913C).

μονόπτερος, *with one wing*, *T.Sal.*25.3(M.122.1356C).

***μονόρραφος**, *having only one suture*, Jo.D.*ep.*(M.95.244C).

[*]**μονόρχης**, *with one testicle*, Cyr.*Mal.*1(3.817D, v.l. μονόρχιον).

μόνος, *alone*;

A. *one only* νομίζομεν [sc. Arians] τὸν υἱόν...μονογενῆ λέγεσθαι, ὅτι μ. μὲν αὐτὸς ὑπὸ μ. τοῦ θεοῦ γέγονε, τὰ δ' ἄλλα πάντα παρὰ τοῦ θεοῦ διὰ τοῦ υἱοῦ ἐκτίσθη Ath.*syn.*7(p.6.25; M.25.'436'(428)B); ὁ θεὸς μ. κατ' οὐσίαν ἐστὶ θεός· μ. δὲ ὅταν εἴπω, τὴν οὐσίαν τοῦ θεοῦ τὴν ἁγίαν καὶ ἄκτιστον δηλῶ...τὸ γὰρ εἷς καὶ μ. ἐπὶ θεοῦ ἐν τῇ γραφῇ οὐ πρὸς ἀντιδιαστολὴν τοῦ υἱοῦ ἢ τοῦ ἁγίου πνεύματος λέγεται, ἀλλὰ πρὸς τοὺς μὴ ὄντας θεούς, ὀνομαζομένους δὲ ψευδῶς Evagr.Pont.*ep.*3(M.32.249Cff.); οὐδὲ γὰρ ἑτέρως ἂν ἦν θεὸς ὁ υἱός, ἑνὸς ὁμολογουμένου καὶ μ. θεοῦ τοῦ πατρός †Apoll.*ep.Bas.*1(M.32.1104A); διὰ τοῦτο...μονογενής, ἐπειδὴ παρὰ μόνου γεννηθεὶς καὶ κτισθεὶς Eun.ap.Bas.*Eun.*2.21(1.256D; M.29.617A); ὁ ἄνω μ. ἐκ μ. πατρὸς καὶ κάτω μ. ἐκ μ. τῆς παρθένου μονογενὴς υἱός *A.Xanthipp.*15(p.69.6); δόξα...τῇ μ. ... καὶ ἀδιαιρέτῳ τριάδι *Lit.Jac.*(p.160.6); *one, a single* εἰ καὶ ἄνδρα μ. αἱ πολλαὶ τῶν χρειῶν ἐπεζήτουν Chrys.*fem.reg.*4(1.256B); neut. as subst., name of a Gnost. aeon, Epiph.*haer.*31.6(p.393.6; M.41.484C).

B. *peculiar to* ἃ μὲν τῆς πενίας δοκεῖ εἶναι κακά, κοινὰ ἑκατέρων ἐστίν· ἃ δὲ τοῦ πλούτου, μόνα ἐκείνου Chrys.*hom.13.4 in 2Cor.*(10.536C).

C. superl. μονώτατος; **1.** *entirely alone*, cf. Gen.2:18 οὐ καλὸν εἶναι τὸν ἄνθρωπον μ. Epiph.*haer.*66.56(p.92.12; M.42.113A); τὴν σάρκα μὴ ἀνίστασθαι τὸ παράπαν, ἀλλὰ τὴν ψυχὴν μονωτάτην *ib.*67.1(p.133.15; 173A); τὴν μὲν αἴσθησιν...ἀπετινάξαντο,...κατὰ δὲ τὸν νοῦν μονωτάτην ἀρρήτως αὐτὴν [sc. τὴν ψυχήν] τῷ θεῷ προσῳκείωσαν Max.*ambig.*(M.91.1193D); **2.** *above all others* τὸν...σωτῆρα Ἰησοῦν...γεραίρωμεν, ὅτι δὴ μόνος, οἷα παναγάθου μονώτατος ὑπάρχων πανάγαθος παῖς Eus.*h.e.*10.4.11(M.20.852C); ὁ μὲν θεὸς αἴτιος τῶν πάντων τυγχάνων, ἔστιν ἄναρχος μ. Ar.*ep.Alex.*(p.13.8; M.26.709B); μ. κατὰ πρόσληψιν σαρκὸς λογικῶς τε καὶ νοερῶς ἐψυχωμένης, θέλων ἀρρήτως γέγονεν ἄνθρωπος Max.*ep.*13(M.91.532B); *ib.*19(596C).

D. neut. as adv., *alone, only*; **1.** emphatic αὐτὸ μόνον: οὐ νοσοῦντας αὐτὸ μ. ... ἀλλὰ καὶ ἐν νεκροῖς κειμένους...αὐτὸς...διεσώσατο Eus.*h.e.*10.4.11(M.20.852C); ἵνα πιστευθῇ ὅτι ἀπέθανεν, οὐ...τῷ σταυρῷ αὐτὸ μ. βεβαιοῦται...ἀλλὰ καὶ τῷ χρόνῳ τῶν ἡμερῶν Chrys.*hom.43.2 in Mt.*(7.459D); **2.** *once*, c. subj., *only* let..., *once* let... μ. ... ἔλθῃ περὶ τῆς...τριάδος πίστις ἐν καρδίᾳ ἡμῶν...εὐθὺς ἵλεως εὑρίσκεται Didym.*Trin.*2.14(M.39.712A); hence μ. or ἢ μ. *as soon as* ἢ μ. δὲ ἐβασίλευσεν, ἐξεζήτησεν τὰ περὶ τοῦ Ἰησοῦ Jo.Mal.*chron.*10 p.250(M.97.381B); *Chron.Pasch.*p.319(M.92.812B); **3.** οὐ μ. or μὴ μ. for οὐ μ. οὐ or μὴ μ. μή: ἀρετὴν...ἣν οὐ μ. σῆτες ἀλλ' οὐδὲ αὐτὸς ὁ θάνατος λυμήνασθαι δύναται Chrys.*hom.23.10 in Mt.*(7.298D); *ib.*4.3(50A); id.*hom.11.4 in 2Cor.*(10.519E); id.*hom.5.5 in 1Cor.*(10.41B).

E. κατὰ μόνας (καταμόνας); **1.** *alone, in solitude*, Ath.*v.Anton.*3,66 (M.26.844B,936C); καλὸν ἀποφυγεῖν ἀπὸ ὄχλου καὶ ἀναχωρεῖν καταμόνας id.*virg.*24(p.59.9; M.28.280C); καταμόνας μονάζων *A.Mt.*1 (p.217.1); **2.** *independently* ὁ ἔχων τὸ πνεῦμα τὸ ἄνωθεν...οὐδὲ κατὰ μ. λαλεῖ...ἀλλὰ τότε λαλεῖ ὅταν θελήσῃ αὐτὸν ὁ θεὸς λαλῆσαι Herm.*mand.*11.8; ἀπόντων δὲ ἡμῶν κατὰ μ. ἔπραξαν ἅπερ ἠθέλησαν Ath.*apol.Const.*1(p.279.13; M.25.596B); σὰρξ ἰδία...ἦν αὐτοῦ [sc. θεοῦ], καὶ οὐχ ἑτέρου τινὸς παρ' αὐτὸν ὄντος υἱοῦ καταμόνας καὶ ἰδικῶς Cyr.*Lc.*13:11(M.72.767A); **3.** *separately, individually* ὁ πλάσας καταμόνας τὰς καρδίας ἡμῶν Thdt.*Am.*proem.(2.1408).

***μονοσέβαστος**, *alone revered*, ‡Chrys.*ador.*2(11.824B).

***μονόσεπτος**, = foreg., Gr.Naz.*carm.*2.1.16.29(M.37.1256A).

***μονοσήμαντος**, *of one significance*, *Disp.Phot.*(M.88.556A).

μονοσιτία, ἡ, *eating alone* φιλοξενίαν ἀθετεῖ, μονοσιτίαν ἐπιτηδεύων CQuerc.(M.103.109D).

***μονοσιτίζω**, = μονοσιτέω *LS*, *have one meal a day*, *Apophth. Patr.*(M.65.361C).

μονόσκηπτρος, *wielding the sceptre alone*, Nonn.*par.Jo.*19:12(M.43.900B).

***μονοσκοπέω**, *concentrate exclusively upon*, Abr.Eph.*occurs.*1 (p.448.27).

[*]**μονοστέλεχος**, *with one stem*, Bas.*hex.*5.7(1.46D; M.29.109B); †Bas.*parad.*5(1.349B; M.30.65C).

***μονοστοιχέω**, *abide, walk by, one* rule *only* μ. τῷ γράμματι of Jewish law, Sophr.H.*or.*7.18(M.87.3349D); Max.*ambig.*(M.91.1145A).

***μονοστράτηγος, ὁ**, *sole commander*, Thphn.*chron.*p.310(M.108.753B); τὸν μ. Συρίας *ib.*p.359(864A); μ. εἴς τε τὴν Θράκην καὶ Μακεδονίαν *ib.*p.401(957A).

***μονοτεῖχος, τό**, *single wall*, Thphn.*chron.*p.310(M.108.753A).

***μονότευχος, ἡ**, *single roll* or *single book* τὴν τοῦ...Παύλου μ. δεκατεσσάρων ἐπιστολῶν ‡Caes.Naz.*dial.*193(M.38.1176).

μονότης, ἡ, **1.** *unity*; **a.** of Father and Son, Epiph.*haer.*69.60 (p.209.9; M.42.300B); Christol. ἀδύνατον τὸν αὐτὸν εἶναι θεόν τε καὶ ἄνθρωπον ἐξ ὁλοκλήρου, ἀλλ' ἐν μ. συγκράτου φύσεως θεϊκῆς σεσαρκωμένης Apoll.*fr.*9(p.206.27)ap.Leont.B.*Apoll.*(M.86.1973B); **b.** ref. origin of Gnost. aeons, acc. Secundus ἔστι τις πρὸ πάντων προαρχὴ ἣν ἐγὼ μ. ἀριθμῶ· ταύτῃ τῇ μ. συνυπάρχει δύναμις ἣν καὶ αὐτὴν ὀνομάζω ἑνότητα· αὕτη ἡ ἑνότης, ἥ τε μ., τὸ ἓν οὖσαι, προήκαντο, μὴ προέμεναι, ἀρχὴν...ἣν...ὁ λόγος μονάδα καλεῖ· ταύτῃ τῇ μονάδι συνυπάρχει δύναμις ὁμοούσιος αὐτῇ ἣν καὶ αὐτὴν ὀνομάζω τὸ ἕν...ἡ μ. καὶ ἑνότης, μονάς τε καὶ τὸ ἕν, προήκαντο τὰς λοιπὰς προβολὰς τῶν Αἰώνων Iren.*haer.*1.11.3(7.563A); **2.** *singleness*, ref. Jo.10:30 ἐπὶ τοῦ πατρὸς καὶ τοῦ υἱοῦ τὸ ἓν οὐκ ἐν μ. καθορᾶται Gr.Nyss.*Eun.*11(2 p.257.14; M.45.864D); *uniqueness* of God, Mac.Mgn.*apocr.*3.27(p.117.27); **3.** *solitude* πτωχεία καὶ μ. καὶ ἐρημία ‡Just.*qu.et resp.*110(M.6.1357C); τὴν μονογενῆ δέ μου ὁ Σύμμαχος τὴν μ. μου εἴρηκεν, ἀντὶ τοῦ, τὴν πάσης ἀνθρωπίνης ἔρημον βοηθείας Thdt.*Ps.*34:18(1.824); *solitary life* συνέπεται δὲ τῇ αὐτῇ παρθενίᾳ ἡ μ. παρὰ πλείοσι τῶν μοναζόντων καὶ μοναζουσῶν Epiph.*exp.fid.*21(p.521.34; M.42.824A); Pall.*h.Laus.*15 (p.39.21; M.34.1041A); **4.** *celibacy* ἡ...ἐκκλησία καὶ παρθενίαν δοξάζει καὶ μ. καὶ ἁγνείαν καὶ χηροσύνην ἐπαινεῖ καὶ γάμον σεμνὸν τιμᾷ Epiph.*haer.*48.9(p.230.26; M.41.868B); *ib.*63.4(p.402.5; 1068B).

***μονοτομία**, error for μονοτονία, Dor.*doct.*4.11(M.88.1673C).

μονοτον-έω, *be obstinate* τῶν ~ούντων (tr. Lat. *contumaces*), *Cod. Afr.*100.

μονοτονία, ἡ, *obstinacy* (tr. Lat. *contumacia*), *Cod.Afr.*48; *ib.*54; Agath.*v.Gr.Ill.*46(p.26).

μονότονος, *steady, unwavering,* Clem.*str.*7.7(p.35.7; M.9.465C).

μονοτροπία, ἡ, 1. *solitary mode of life,* Bas.*ep.*45.1(3.133D; M.32. 365C); **2.** *single mode* of conduct, *consistency, simplicity, Pers.* (p.29.1).

μονότροπος, 1. *of one kind, simple, plain* ἐκ τῆς ἀκροτόμου πέτρας κατειβόμενον...μονότροπον σωφροσύνης ὁ κύριος ἐχορήγει ποτόν Clem. *paed.*2.2(p.167.22; M.8.409A); τὴν μ. τῆς εἰς τὸν θεὸν πίστεως σωτηρίαν *ib.*1.1(p.90.10; 249B); Isid.Pel.*epp.*4.149(M.78.1233D); Max.*ambig.* (M.91.1368B); hence, of persons, *simple, pure,* Jo.Carp.*cap.*37(M. 85.1844); *monotonous*; of a task, Nil.*Magn.*23(M.79.1000B); *unique* τοῦ σαρκωθέντος θεοῦ...μητέρα, μονογενῆ καὶ μ. σύλληψιν δεξαμένην Isid.Pel.*epp.*1.54(M.78.216C); *of one kind only* ἐὰν μ. ἔχῃ τὴν φύσιν ὁ Χριστός, μονοτρόπως ἐστὶν ἀληθὴς καὶ καθ' ἕτερον τρόπον ψευδής Anast.S.*hod.*8(M.89.137C); **2.** *of one way* of life, *single-minded, constant,* ref. Ps.67:6 μ. ... τοὺς αὐτῷ καὶ μόνῳ ἀναθέντας τὴν ἰδίαν ζωήν, πάσης διχοψυχίας...αὐτὴν ἀλλοτριώσαντας Or.*sel.in Ps.*67:6(M. 12.1505D); μ. ἐστιν ὁ τοῦ Χριστιανοῦ βίος, ἕνα σκοπὸν ἔχων, τὴν δόξαν τοῦ θεοῦ Bas.*reg.fus.*20.2(2.365A; M.31.973A); ἡ οἰκειωθεῖσα τῷ θεῷ λόγῳ ἄμωμος ψυχὴ μ. τυγχάνουσα Mac.Aeg.*ep.*(M.34.417B); ‡Ath. *Apoll.*2.6(M.26.1141A); μ. ... οὐχ ἑτερόφρονας Cyr.*ador.*6(1.175D); id.*Os.*58(3.90E); masc. as subst., ref. Ps.67:6, id.*ador.*7(1.246B); neut. as subst., *constant practice* τῷ τῆς ἀπαθείας μ. Nil.*exerc.*6(M. 79.724D); **3.** *living alone, leading solitary life,* Jo.VI H.*v.Jo.D.*8(M. 94.441A); masc. as subst., Gr.Naz.*carm.*1.2.31.37(M.37.943A); *going one's own way, independent* μὴ αὐτόβουλον καὶ μ. ἀρέσκειαν μετέρχου Isid.Pel.*epp.*1.260(M.78.340A).

μονοτρόπως, 1. *in one way, simply* τὰ φανερὰ μ. κατανοεῖσθαι Clem. *str.*5.9(p.364.19; M.9.88B); Hipp.*haer.*7.29(p.212.5; M.16.3326C); τὸν νοῦν...μ. τὸ ὑπὲρ φύσιν καὶ ἀνεξιχνίαστον τῆς θείας φύσεως λογίζεσθαι Max.*schol.epp.Dion.Ar.*9.4(M.4.572C); *in one way only* ἀνὰ μέρος ἐκληπτέον [sc. 2Cor.6:14, Jo.1:5] οὐδὲ μ. Mac.Aeg.*elev.*13(M.34.901C); Χριστὸς μ. οὐ λέγεται, ἀλλ' ἐν αὐτῷ τῷ ὀνόματι ἑνὶ ὄντι...δείκνυται σημασία θεότητός τε καὶ ἀνθρωπότητος ‡Ath.*Apoll.*1.13(M.26.1116B); Jo.D.*f.o.*2.3(M.94.989A); Anast.S.*hod.*8(M.89.137C) cit. s. μονότροπος; of behaviour, *consistently,* Mac.Aeg.*perf.*4(M.34.844D); Cyr.*Ps.*35:1 (M.69.913B); id.*ador.*7(1.194B); *in a unique way* μονογενὴς δέ, οὐχ ὅτι μόνος ἐκ μόνου καὶ μόνον, ἀλλ' ὅτι καὶ μ., οὐχ ὡς τὰ σώματα Gr.Naz. *or.*30.20(p.139.3; M.36.129A); μονογενὴς...καὶ μ. γεννηθεὶς Thdt.*Trin.* 10(M.75.1160A); **2.** *going* one's *own way, separately* οἱ τῆς φυλῆς Ἐφραῒμ...μ. τῶν ἄλλων φυλῶν ἀποσχισθέντων τῆς Ἰούδα φυλῆς †Gregent.*disp.*(M.86.696B); **3.** ἐσθίομεν...μ. *eat* (food) *of one kind, Const.Stud.*(M.99.1716B).

***μονοτύπως,** *in a single form* μ. τὸν αὐτὸν πατέρα θεὸν καὶ υἱὸν καὶ ἅγιον πνεῦμα ἐν σαρκὶ πεπονθότα καὶ γεννηθέντα ἡγησάμενος [sc. Noetus] Epiph.*haer.*57.2(p.347.5; M.41.997C).

***μονοϋπόστατος,** *with one hypostasis,* Thdr.Stud.*icon.*1(M.99. 489A).

μονοφάγος, *eating alone, Const.App.*2.25.3; ‡Nil.*perist.*5.1(M.79. 849D).

μονόφθαλμος, *one-eyed,* met. ἡ μ. Σεβήρου πίστις Anast.S.*hod.*6 tit.(M.89.101C).

μονόφθογγος, *of one sound, on one note, level* μ. φωνῇ διύπνισε τὸν καθεύδοντα [sc. Λάζαρον] Amph.*hom.*3.5(M.39.65A).

μονόφορβος, *feeding alone,* Gr.Naz.*carm.*2.1.1.191(M.37.984A); *ib.*2.1.13.41(1230A).

μονοφυής, *of one nature*; of Son before Inc., Leont.H.*Nest.*2.40 (M.86.1596D); *ib.*4.43(1716D) cit. s. διφυής; wrongly used of Christ incarnate, Anast.S.*hod.*7(M.89.117C); neut. as subst., as attribute of God, Athenag.*leg.*23.4(M.6.944B).

***μονοφωνέω,** *utter once only,* ‡Caes.Naz.*dial.*13(M.38.869).

μονόχειρ, *having one hand,* Mac.Aeg.*hom.*32.6(M.34.737B).

μονοχίτων, ὁ, *one wearing only the tunic,* Max.*ambig.*(M.91.1368A).

***μονοχιτωνέω,** *wear only the tunic,* Thdr.Abuc.*opusc.*24(M.97. 1557A).

***μονοχιτωνία, ἡ,** *wearing of the tunic only,* μονοκι-, Ephr.3.425F = Jo.D.*virt.*(M.95.88A).

***μονόψοφος,** ? *affected by a sound only*; of horses, Ephr.1.58F.

μονόω, *make solitary, isolate*; **1.** med. and pass., *be alone* οὐ δύνασαι νηστεῦσαι, οὐδὲ μονωθῆναι Chrys.*hom.1.2 in Phil.*(11.197B); τὸ δὲ 'ἀφορίσθητε' οἱονεὶ 'μονώθητε' *cat.2Cor.*6:17(p.393.9); **2.** perf. ptcpl. pass. as adj.; **a.** *solitary, alone,* Tat.*orat.*14(p.15.13; M.6.836B); ἐπιτίθεται ὁ διάβολος, ὅταν ἴδῃ μεμονωμένους καὶ καθ' ἑαυτοὺς ὄντας Chrys.*hom.13.1 in Mt.*(7.168C); **b.** *in the singular,* ref. Gen.1:26 μὴ...μεμονωμένον...τὸ πρόσωπον Bas.*hex.*9.6(1.87D; M.29.205A); **c.** *unique* τῇ...μιᾷ μεμονωμένῃ...γεννήσει προόντα τῶν αἰώνων θεὸν λόγον...ὁμολογοῦμεν Leont.H.*Nest.*4.9(M.86.1669B); **d.** masc. as subst., *one who lives the solitary life, monk,* Chrys.*sac.*6.8(p.155.9; 1.427D); **e.** neut. as subst., *solitude,* Ephr.3.425F.

***Μοντήσιοι, οἱ,** name said to be given by Romans to Novatianists Ναυαταῖοι, οἱ καὶ Μ., ὡς ἐν Ῥώμῃ καλοῦνται Epiph.*anc.*13 (p.21.29; M.43.40C) by confusion with Donatists at Rome, cf. Optatus 2.4(M.*PL.*11.955A); *Montenses...eo quod ecclesiam Romae primam in monte habere coeperint,* Hier.*chronicon* anno 358(M.*PL.* 27.687).

μονῳδία, ἡ, *lament, monody,* ref. Gen.4:10 θεὸς ὥσπερ τινὰ μ. ᾄδων Chrys.*hom.23.5 in Rom.*(9.692E); ἔστι ἡ μ. ... θρῆνος μονοειδής, μήτε προσωποποιΐαν μήτε ἠθοποιΐαν ἔχων Isid.Pel.*epp.*5.53(M.78. 1357C).

***μονώνυμος,** *having a unique name, unique* μονογενής, ἵνα μ. ᾖ ὁ υἱός Epiph.*anc.*8(p.14.27; M.43.29A); ἕκαστον τῶν ὀνομάτων μ., μὴ ἔχον δευτέρωσιν *ib.*(p.14.23; 29A); *ib.*(p.15.10; 29B).

***μονωνύμως, 1.** called *by a unique name, by a name all one's own,* Epiph.*anc.*8(p.15.7; M.43.29B); **2.** called *by one name*; of Trin., *ib.*22(p.31.23; 57D).

μονώνυχος, *with uncloven hoof,* Gr.Nyss.*Eun.*10(2 p.227.19; M.45. 828B); neut. as subst., *ib.*7(2 p.160.22; 749B).

***μόνωρος,** *with only one hour to live, A.Jo.*9(p.156.28).

μόνως, *only,* hence *in a unique way* ἀληθῶς υἱὸν τὸν υἱόν, ὅτι μόνος καὶ μόνου καὶ μ. καὶ μόνον Gr.Naz.*or.*25.16(M.35.1221B); of H. Ghost μ. ὑπάρχον Didym.*Trin.*2.4(M.39.484A); irreg. superl. μονωτάτως, *solely,* Epiph.*haer.*37.3(p.55.3; M.41.645C).

μόνωσις, ἡ, 1. *singleness, oneness* τὸ ἄκρως τίμιον κατὰ τὴν μ. ἐπαινεῖται, μίμημα ὂν ἀρχῆς τῆς μιᾶς Clem.*str.*7.17(p.76.8; M.9. 552A); **2.** *solitude, seclusion* ἔχουσι παραπέτασμα τῶν ἰδίων ἁμαρτημάτων τὴν μ. Chrys.*sac.*3.14(p.72.13; 1.391A); καλὸν ἡ ἐρημία καὶ ἡ μ., ὅταν ἐντυγχάνων δέῃ θεῷ id.*hom.50.1 in Mt.*(7.513C); cf. οὐδὲν οὕτως ὡς μ. κακόν, καὶ τὸ ἄσπονδον καὶ ἀπρόσιτον id.*hom.78.4 in Jo.* (8.464B); μηδενὸς ὄντος τοῦ κινοῦντος ἡμᾶς εἰς ὀργήν, εὐκόλως ἐν τῇ μ. ἡ ἀρετὴ τῆς μακροθυμίας κατορθωθήσεται ‡Ath.*ep.Cast.*2.4(M.28. 893A); **3.** c. genit., *absence, lack,* acc. Eunomians μὴ μονώσεως ἀδελφῶν, ἀλλ' ἐρημίας τῶν συντικτόντων δηλωτικὸν εἶναι τοὔνομα [sc. μονογενής] Bas.*Eun.*2.21(1.257A; M.29.617B).

μονωτικός, *solitary,* Esaias *fr.*2(M.40.1213A).

μορέω, *make with pain and toil,* perf. pass. ptcpl. μεμωρημένος *elaborate* τὰς μ. τῶν ἡδυσμάτων περιεργίας Clem.*paed.*2.1(p.159.1, v.l. μεμορημ- M.8.389B); τὰς μ. λεπτουργίας καὶ τὰς ἐν ταῖς ὑφαῖς περιέργους πλοκάς *ib.*2.10(p.221.14; μεμωραμμένας 525A); *ib.*(p.225. 29; μεμωραμμένας 533C).

μόριον, τό, 1. *part* of the body; of eyes and ears, *Const.App.*6.21. 2; **2.** gramm., *particle,* Clem.*paed.*1.8(p.131.19; M.8.336A); *ib.*2.10 (p.218.34; 520B); *cat.Apoc.*9:7(p.317.18).

μορμολύττω, *terrify, scare,* Zach.Mit.*opif.*(M.85.1036A,1092A).

μορμύρω, of waters, *rage*; met., of S. Paul, ref. Ac.9:1, Euthal. Diac.*epp.Paul.*(M.85.696C).

μορφάζ-ω, med., *behave like, imitate* Χριστὸν αὐτὸν ~εσθαι ἐπειρᾶτο [sc. Manes], τότε μὲν τὸν παράκλητον...ἑαυτὸν ἀνακηρύττων ...τότε δέ, οἷα Χριστός, μαθητὰς δώδεκα...αἱρούμενος Eus.*h.e.*7.31.1 (v.l. αὐτὸν μ. M.20.720C).

μορφή, ἡ, *form*;

A. gen.; **1.** outward *form, shape, appearance* φθαρτῆς ὕλης ταῦτα πάντα...ταῖς τέχναις...εἰς τὴν μ. ταύτην ἐκτυπωθῆναι *Diogn.*2.3; οἱ ἀρχάγγελοι...μ. ... [sc. ἔχουσι] ἰδίαν καὶ σῶμα ἀνὰ λόγον τῆς ὑπεροχῆς τῶν πνευματικῶν ἁπάντων...οὐχ ὅμοιον δὲ μ. καὶ σῶμα ἔχουσι τοῖς ἐν τῷδε τῷ κόσμῳ σώμασιν Clem.*exc.Thdot.*10(p.109.18; M.9.660B); ἀντὶ τῆς ἀληθοῦς θεοφανείας δόκησίν τινα...ἐν σωματικῇ μ. κατεσχηματισμένην Gr.Nyss.*ep.*3(M.46.1020D); *face,* facial *expression* ἡ μ. γὰρ αὐτοῦ ἠλλοιώθη, ὥστε μὴ δύνασθαι ἄνθρωπον ὑπενεγκεῖν τὴν ὀργὴν αὐτοῦ Herm.*mand.*12.4.1; Meth.*symp.*8.17(p.112.2; M.18.173D); *pattern,* ref. Rom.2:20, Chrys.*hom.8.1 in 2Tim.*(11.707C); acc. as adv., *like* φέγγος...οἷον...φλὸξ...μηδενὸς ἀστέρος...μ. Philost.*h.e.*12. 8(M.65.616B); **2.** essential *form, character* ὁ δὲ καρπὸς τοῦ δένδρου ἐὰν ἐξεικονισθῇ καὶ τὴν ἑαυτοῦ μ. ἀπολάβῃ, εἰς ἀποθήκην τίθεται Hipp.*haer.*6.9(p.137.12; M.16.3210C); τινῶν εἰς τὰς ἀρχοντικὰς μ. ἐπανερχομένων, ὥστε τινὰς μὲν γίνεσθαι λέοντας Cels.ap.Or.*Cels.*6.33 (p.102.28; M.11.1348A); ἄνθρωπος ἀληθέστατα λέγεται κατὰ φύσιν ...τὸ ἐκ συστάσεως ψυχῆς καὶ σώματος εἰς μίαν τὴν τοῦ καλοῦ μ. συντεθὲν Meth.*res.*1.34(p.272.9; M.18.292B); *ib.*3.7(p.399.12; 324A); τίς...οἶδεν...πῶς ἄστρα φέρεται καὶ τίνας ἔχουσιν τὰς μ., καὶ τοῦ ζῆν τὴν σύστασιν; *Hom.Clem.*3.35; ref. resurrection τὴν ἀνάστασιν ἐπὶ τούτου μὴ χρῆναι παραλαμβάνεσθαι τοῦ σώματος...ἀλλὰ ἐπὶ τοῦ πνευματικοῦ, ἐν ᾧ ὁ αὐτός, ὁ καὶ νῦν ἐν τούτῳ, διασωζόμενος χαρακτὴρ τηρηθήσεται, ἵν' ἕκαστος ἡμῶν καὶ κατὰ τὴν μ. ὁ αὐτὸς ᾖ Meth.*res.*1.25(p.251.6; M.41.1096C); ὁ ἄνθρωπος...οὔποτε μεταβληθήσεται οὔτε εἰς τὴν τῶν ἀγγέλων οὔτε εἰς τὴν τῶν ἑτέρων μ. *ib.*1.49(p.303.4; M.18.277C); χρὴ δὲ οὐδὲ γενείου τρίχα διαφθείρειν καὶ τὴν μ. τοῦ ἀνθρώπου παρὰ φύσιν ἐξαλλάσσειν *Const.App.*1.3.11; ἀναστήσει ἡμᾶς...ἐν τῇ νῦν μ., μηθὲν ἐλλειπὲς ἔχοντας *ib.*5.7.1; **3.** *idea* τὰ ῥήματα...κλίνη καὶ νεάνιδες καὶ τὰ τοιαῦτα· ἡ δὲ διὰ τούτων ἀποτελουμένη μ. μακαριότης Gr.Nyss.*hom.1 in Cant.*(M.44.776B); Nil.*exerc.*48(M.79.780A); **4.** that in which the form is expressed; **a.** *kind, sort* παντοίας φύσεως ζῳοτοκήσας μορφάς, ἄστρα μὲν...καὶ πτηνὰ...τετράποδα δέ Meth.*res.*1.34(p.271.5; M.41.1097B); ἀναπλάττουσι τὰς οὐχ ὑφεστώσας μ., σφίγγας καὶ τρίτωνας καὶ κενταύρους Thdt.*qu.38 in Ex.*(1.149); **b.** Gnost. *embodiment, expression* αὐτὸς τοῦ ἀοράτου μ. φανείς Iren.*haer.*1.14.1(M.7.596A); καὶ εἶναι τούτους μ., ἃς ὁ κύριος ἀγγέλους εἴρηκε *ib.*(597A); τὰ ὑπ' ἄλλου σπαρέντα εἰς μ. καὶ εἰς φωτισμὸν καὶ περιγραφὴν ἰδίαν ἀγαγών Heracleon ap.Or.*Jo.*2.21(15; p.77.28; M.14.149D); τοῦ ἑνὸς θεοῦ τιμᾶν θέλοντες τὴν μ. καὶ μὴ εὑρόντες ποία ἐστίν, πᾶσαν προτιμᾶν εἱλόμεθα *Hom.Clem.*10.17.

B. theol.; **1.** of God ἄρρητον δόξαν καὶ μ. ἔχων Just.*1apol.*9.3(M.6.340B); αὐτὸν μὲν ἐν σχήματι καὶ μ. καὶ κάλλει ὄντα *Hom.Clem.*17.8; cf. ἀδύνατον γὰρ κάλλος ἄνευ μ. εἶναι *ib.*17.10; καλεῖται...μ. ὡς ὅλων τῶν μορφουμένων τῶν ὑπ' αὐτὴν ἤτοι τῶν χαρακτήρων συλληπτική ‡Cyr.*Trin.*13(6^3.19B; M.77.1149A); of the divine substance υἱοῦ μὲν γὰρ καὶ πατρὸς πᾶσα ἀνάγκη τὴν αὐτὴν εἶναι μ., θεοπρεπῶς δηλονότι τῆς μ. νοουμένης, οὐκ ἐν σχήματι σωματικῷ, ἀλλ' ἐν τῷ ἰδιώματι τῆς θεότητος Bas.*hex.*9.6(1.88A; M.29.205C); cf.id.*Eun.*1.18, Gr.Nyss. *Eun.*4 citt. s. 4 infra; ἡ μ. τοῦ θεοῦ οὐσίαν σημαίνει θεοῦ, ὥσπερ καὶ ἡ μ. τοῦ ἀνθρώπου φύσιν ἀνθρωπίνην δηλοῖ *Schol.* in Anast.S.*hod.*10(M.89.181C); **2.** of Persons of Trin. αἱ...ἰδιότητες, οἱονεὶ χαρακτῆρές τινες καὶ μ. ἐπιθεωρούμεναι τῇ οὐσίᾳ, διαιροῦσι μὲν τὸ κοινὸν τοῖς ἰδιάζουσι χαρακτῆρσι, τὸ δὲ ὁμοφυὲς τῆς οὐσίας οὐ διακόπτουσιν Bas.*Eun.*2.28(1.265B; M.29.637B); μία παγά, μία ῥίζα, τριφαὴς ἔλαμψε μ. Synes.*hymn.*2.26(p.44; M.66.1592); **3.** of manifestations of God; **a.** before Inc. διὰ τῆς τοῦ πυρὸς μ. καὶ εἰκόνος ἀσωμάτου τῷ Μωϋσεῖ...ἐφάνη Just.*1apol.*63.16(M.6.425B); ἀρχιστράτηγον ἑαυτὸν λέγει, ἐν ἀνθρώπου μ. φανέντα τῷ τοῦ Ναυῆ Ἰησοῦ id.*dial.*61.1(M.6.613C); *ib.*128.2(776A); **b.** in Christ θεὸν ἐν ἀνθρώπου μ. γεγονέναι καταγγέλλοντες Tat.*orat.*21(p.23.6; M.6.852C); ὥστε ἡ τοῦ υἱοῦ ὑπόστασις οἱονεὶ μ. καὶ πρόσωπον γίνεται τῆς τοῦ πατρὸς ἐπιγνώσεως Gr.Nyss.*diff.ess.*8(M.32.340C); **4.** exeg. Phil.2:7 ὅτι γὰρ δούλου μ. τὸ σαρκικόν, ἐπὶ τοῦ κυρίου φησὶν ὁ ἀπόστολος,...τὸν ἐκτὸς ἄνθρωπον δοῦλον προσειπών Clem.*paed.*3.1(p.237.4; M.8.557A); σωματικῶς λαλούμενος [sc. ὁ λόγος], ἕως ὁ τοιοῦτον αὐτὸν δεξάμενος...δυνηθῇ αὐτοῦ καὶ τήν, ἵν' οὕτως ὀνομάσω, προηγουμένην μ. θεάσασθαι Or.*Cels.*4.15(p.285.22; M.11.1048B); οὐκ ἐκ μέρους δὲ ἡ τῆς θεότητος μ., ἀλλὰ τὸ πλήρωμα τῆς τοῦ πατρὸς θεότητός ἐστι τὸ εἶναι τοῦ υἱοῦ Ath.*Ar.*3.6(M.26.332B); id.*ep.Aeg.Lib.*17(M.25.576C) cit. s. δοῦλος; ὥσπερ γὰρ ἡ μ. τοῦ θεοῦ τὸ πλήρωμα τῆς τοῦ λόγου θεότητος νοεῖται, οὕτως καὶ ἡ μ. τοῦ δούλου ἡ νοερὰ τῆς ἀνθρώπων συστάσεως φύσις σὺν τῇ ὀργανικῇ καταστάσει ὁμολογεῖται ‡Ath.*Apoll.*2.1(M.26.1133A); τὸ ἐν μ. θεοῦ ὑπάρχειν, ἴσον δύνασθαι τῷ ἐν οὐσίᾳ θεοῦ ὑπάρχειν φημί· ὡς γὰρ τὸ μ. ἀνειληφέναι δούλου ἐν τῇ οὐσίᾳ τῆς ἀνθρωπότητος τὸν κύριον ἡμῶν γεγενῆσθαι σημαίνει Bas.*Eun.*1.18(1.230A; M.29.552C); docetic interprn. μ. ... δούλου, καὶ οὐχὶ αὐτὸν τὸν δοῦλον ἀνειληφέναι, καὶ ἐν σχήματι...τὸν κύριον γεγενῆσθαι, ἀλλ' οὐχὶ αὐτὸν τὸν ἄνθρωπον παρ' αὐτοῦ προσειλῆφθαι id.*ep.*261.2(3.402C; M.32.969C); ἡ δὲ μ. τοῦ θεοῦ ταὐτὸν τῇ οὐσίᾳ πάντως ἐστίν· ὡς γὰρ ἐν τῇ μ. τοῦ δούλου γενόμενος τῇ οὐσίᾳ τοῦ δούλου ἐνεμορφώθη, οὐ ψιλὴν ἀναλαβὼν ἐφ' ἑαυτοῦ τὴν μ. οὐδὲ τῆς οὐσίας διεζευγμένην, ἀλλ' ἡ οὐσία τῇ μ. συσσημαίνεται· οὕτως...ὁ εἰπὼν αὐτὸν ἐν μ. θεοῦ εἶναι τὴν οὐσίαν διὰ τῆς μ. ἐνεδείξατο Gr.Nyss.*Eun.*4(2 p.94.16; M.45.672A); ὅταν...ἡ μ. τοῦ θεοῦ τὴν διὰ πάντων καταμηνύῃ ταυτότητα τῷ πάντα δεικνύειν ἐφ' ἑαυτῆς, δι' ὧν ἡ θεότης χαρακτηρίζεται *ib.*8(2 p.192.5; 788A); εἰ ἡ μ. τοῦ θεοῦ τέλειος θεός, καὶ ἡ μ. τοῦ δούλου τέλειος δοῦλος Chrys.*hom.7.3 in Phil.*(11.248C); εἰ...ἄνθρωπος ἦν ψιλός, καὶ διὰ τὰ ἔργα λέγεται μ. θεοῦ, διὰ τί μὴ καὶ ἐπὶ Πέτρου τὸ αὐτὸ ποιοῦμεν; *ib.*7.2(247C); μ. ὅπερ τὴν οὐσίαν ἐμφαίνει, ἢ καὶ οὐσίαν καὶ ὁμοιότητα τὴν κατ' οὐσίαν. ὥσπερ οὖν ἡ μ. τοῦ δούλου οὐδὲν ἄλλο ἐμφαίνει ἢ ἄνθρωπον ἀπαράλλακτον· οὕτω καὶ ἡ μ. τοῦ θεοῦ οὐδὲν ἄλλο ἐμφαίνει ἢ θεόν id.*hom.2.2 in Heb.*(12.17B); cf. *formam autem servi, ut dicat naturam servi, humanam sic vocans naturam...sicut et illud quod dixit in forma dei, in divina dicit natura, hoc est, divinae naturae existens,* Thdr.Mops.*Phil.*2:7(p.217.6); τὸ ληφθὲν οὐχ ὁμοίωμα ἀνθρώπου ἀλλὰ φύσις ἀνθρώπου· μ. γὰρ δούλου ⟨φύσις δούλου⟩, καθάπερ ἡ μ. τοῦ θεοῦ φύσις νοεῖται θεοῦ Thdt.*eran.*1(4.42); hence *nature* ἐνεργεῖ γὰρ ἑκατέρα μ. μετὰ τῆς θατέρου κοινωνίας ὅπερ ἴδιον ἔσχηκεν Leo Mag.*ep.*28.4(p.14.27; M.*PL.*54.768B); οὐκ ἄρα τοῦ θεοῦ λόγου ἡ ἄγνοια, ἀλλὰ τῆς τοῦ δούλου μ., τῆς τοσαῦτα κατ' ἐκεῖνο καιροῦ γινωσκούσης ὅσα ἡ ἐνοικοῦσα θεότης ἀπεκάλυψε Thdt. ap.Cyr.*apol.Thdt.*4(p.122.1; 6^1.215D); εἰ...ἡ κοινωνία τῶν μ. σχετική τίς ἐστι...καθὼς...ἔφη Νεστόριος Sev.Ant.*fr.*(M.86.925C); οὐ δύο οὖν πρόσωπα...τοῦ λόγου καὶ τῆς ἐνσάρκου αὐτοῦ μ. Leont.H.*Nest.*2.16(M.86.1573A); πάντες...οἱ...πατέρες...διδάσκουσιν ἄλλο εἶναι φύσιν ἤτοι οὐσίαν καὶ μ., καὶ ἄλλο...ὑπόστασιν ἤτοι πρόσωπον Justn.*conf.*(p.86.20; M.86.1009C); δούλου μ. = ἄνθρωπος· ὡς δὲ δούλου μ., συγκαταβαίνει τοῖς ὁμοδούλοις Gr.Naz.*or.*30.6(p.116.2; M.36.109C); **5.** *image* of God possessed by man τῇ γὰρ αὐτοῦ μ. ὡς ἐν μεγίστῃ σφραγῖδι τὸν ἄνθρωπον διετυπώσατο *Hom.Clem.*17.7; ὅταν μὴ μόνον τὸ κατὰ θυμὸν αἶσχος ὑβρίζῃ τὴν θείαν μ. Gr.Nyss.*or.catech.*40(p.161.2; M.45.1044A); in the Church, Max.*myst.*1(M.91.665C) cit. s. ἐκκλησία; *likeness* of Christ possessed by Christian ὁ δὲ ἄνθρωπος ἐκεῖνος ᾧ σύνοικος ὁ λόγος...μ. ἔχει τοῦ λόγου, ἐξομοιοῦται τῷ θεῷ Clem.*paed.*3.1(p.236.23; M.8.556C); τῆς καθ' ὁμοίωσιν μ. ἐν αὐτοῖς [sc. τοῖς φωτιζομένοις] ἐκτυπουμένης τοῦ λόγου Meth.*symp.*8.8(p.90.10; M.18.144C); τὴν μ. ἠλλοιώσατε· ἀναγεννήσεως ἑτέρας ὑμῖν δεῖ καὶ ἀναπλάσεως Chrys.*comm.in Gal.*4:19(10.708C).

***μορφίζομαι,** *simulate, make a show of* μ. τὴν εὐσέβειαν Gel.Cyz.*h.e.*3.16.6.

***μορφοεμφερεία, ἡ,** *likeness, shape,* mental *image,* Epiph.*anc.*103(p.123.19; μορφὴν ἐμφερείας M.43.201B).

***μόρφ-ομαι,** *dissemble, prevaricate* προησφαλισάμην τοὺς ~ομένους †Jo.D.*creat.*5(p.127).

μορφοποιέω, = μορφόω, *fashion, form*; of idol-makers, Just.*1apol.*9.2(M.6.340A); ref. Gen.1:26, Meth.*res.*1.34(p.275.9; M.41.1100D); *represent,* Dion.Ar.*c.h.*2.3(M.3.140C).

***μορφοποιΐα, ἡ, 1.** *representation* ὅτι μή, φασί, τιμὴ τοῖς ὑπερκόσμιον εἰληχόσι δόξαν, ὑλικαῖς ἀποτυποῦν μορφοποιΐαις Thdr.Stud.*antirr.*1.17(M.99.348B); in words, Dion.Ar.*c.h.*2.3(M.3.141A); **2.** *shape, form* τῆς πολυειδοῦς τῶν ἀγγελικῶν μ. ποικιλίας *ib.*15.1(328A); **3.** *making like, assimilation,* ref. Os.12:10 ἡ τοῦ θεοῦ πρὸς ἕκαστον, ἐκ τῆς ἐνούσης κατὰ πρᾶξιν ἀρετῆς ἑκάστῳ...μ. χεὶρ γὰρ παντὸς δικαίου, ἡ κατ' ἀρετὴν...πρᾶξίς ἐστιν· ἐν ᾗ...ὁ θεὸς τὴν πρὸς ἀνθρώπους ὁμοίωσιν δέχεται Max.*ep.*2(M.91.401B).

***μορφοποιός,** *making likenesses,* Thdr.Stud.*iamb.*32(M.99.1792D).

***μορφόχροος,** prob. f.l. in ‡Epiph.*phys.*12(M.43.528A) for εὐμορφόχροος, *of beautiful colour, Phys.*B 11(p.204.6).

μορφ-όω, 1. *give shape* or *form to*; pass., *receive shape* or *form*; *Keryg.Petr.*ap.Clem.*str.*6.5(p.451.21; M.9.260A); οὓς ἄνθρωποι ~ώσαντες καὶ ἐν ναοῖς ἱδρύσαντες θεοὺς προσωνόμασαν Just.*1apol.*9.1(M.6.340A); pass., of a child in the womb, Or.*Jo.*20.2(p.328.3; M.14.573B); *ib.*6.49(30; p.157.29; 285A); τοῦ νοητοῦ...σπέρματος, ὃ σπείρει μὲν αὐτὸς...ἐν τῷ βάθει τοῦ νοός, ὑποδέχεται δὲ καὶ ~οῖ δίκην γυναικὸς ἡ ἐκκλησία Meth.*symp.*3.8(p.35.17; M.18.73A); **2.** *express in substantial form* ὅτε...ἠθέλησεν αὐτοῦ τὸ ἄρρητον ῥητὸν γενέσθαι καὶ τὸ ἀόρατον ~ωθῆναι Iren.*haer.*1.14.1(M.7.596A); ἐπειδὴ δὲ...ἐθέμεθα τὸ γένος εἶναι ζῷον, τὸ δὲ ἄνθρωπον εἶδος τῶν πολλῶν ζῴων ἤδη κεχωρισμένον, συγκεχυμένον δὲ ὅμως ἔτι καὶ μήπω μεμορφωμένον εἰς εἶδος οὐσίας ὑποστατῆς, ὀνόματι ~ώσας τὸν ἀπὸ τοῦ γένους ληφθέντα ἄνθρωπον ὀνομάζω Σωκράτην ἢ Διογένην Hipp.*haer.*7.18(p.192.18f.; M.16.3298B); ἐν...ὁμοίῳ σχήματι τοῦ μακαρίου Σαμουὴλ...εἴδωλον ἐκ δαιμονιώδους ἐνεργείας μεμορφωμένον Cyr.*ador.*6(1.191A); of OT theophanies ὄψις αὐτῷ [sc. Μωσεῖ] δείκνυται θεοειδὴς φωτὸς μεμορφωμένου ἐπὶ φλεγομένῳ βάτῳ Clem.*paed.*2.8(p.203.16; M.8.488A); πῶς...ὤφθη ὁ θεὸς τῷ Ἀβραὰμ καὶ Μωσῇ καὶ τοῖς ἁγίοις, μὴ μεμορφωμένος; μεμορφωμένος δέ, κατὰ ποῖον χαρακτῆρα ἢ τὸν ἀνθρώπινον; Or.*sel.in Gen.*(M.12.93B); of the Son εἰκόνα εἶναι τὸν μονογενῆ...οὐχ ὡς ἀψύχῳ ὕλῃ ἀλλ' ὡς ἐν υἱῷ ζῶντι μεμορφωμένην Eus.*e.th.*2.23(p.133.25; M.24.961A); at Inc. αὐτοῦ τοῦ λόγου ~ωθέντος καὶ ἀνθρώπου γενομένου Just.*1apol.*5.4(M.6.336B); τῷ δι' ἡμᾶς ~ωθέντι καὶ βαπτισθέντι καὶ σταυρωθέντι Gr.Naz.*or.*39.17(M.36.353C); of the humanity he assumed, Or.*Jo.*1.28(30; p.36.6; M.14.76C) cit. s. ἄνθρωπος; with reminiscence of Gal.4:19 ἵν' ἐλθὼν ὁ τούτου κῆρυξ ἀντίχριστος, εὕρῃ καὶ ἐν τῇ Αἰγύπτῳ τὰς ἐκκλησίας ἑαυτοῦ γενομένας...καὶ ἐπιγνῷ ἑαυτὸν ἐν ἐκείνοις [sc. τοῖς Πελετιανοῖς] ἤδη ~ωθέντα Ath.*h.Ar.*78(p.227.14; M.25.789A); οὐκ ἀνικάνως ἔχοντος καὶ πάλαι τοῦ νόμου βοηθεῖν ἀρχαιοτέροις· ἐμορφοῦτο γὰρ ἐν αὐτῷ τὸ Χριστοῦ μυστήριον Cyr.*Is.*1.1(2.16B); τοὺς χαρακτῆρας τῆς ὑμετέρας ὁμολογίας...οὓς ἐν ὑμῖν ἐμόρφωσε τὸ πνεῦμα τὸ ἅγιον Martin.*ep.*4(M.*PL.*87.148B); **3.** *form, model* upon a pattern, of the creation of men ζῷα ἐψύχωσεν, ἄνθρωπον πρὸς ἑαυτὸν ἐμόρφωσε Gr.Naz.*or.*5.31(M.35.704B); of the

Son as the image of the Father οὐκ ἄλλῳ τινὶ χαρακτῆρι παρὰ τὸν πατέρα μεμόρφωται Gr.Nyss.*Eun.*4(2 p.94.15; M.45.672A); πρὸς ἐκεῖνο μεμορφωμένος ὁρᾶται τὸ κάλλος οὗ καί ἐστιν εἰκών Cyr.*Jo.*1.1 (4.12A); in moral sense τέλειος, ~ούμενος τῇ τοῦ κυρίου διδασκαλίᾳ Clem.*str.*7.14(p.62.31; M.9.521C); προτρέπεται αὐτὴν ὁ νυμφίος πᾶν νόημα καὶ πρᾶξιν ~ῶσαι τῷ ἑαυτοῦ χαρακτῆρι Or.*schol.in Cant.*8:6 (M.17.285B); ~ούμεθα ἤτοι κατὰ κακίαν ἢ κατὰ ἀρετήν id.*hom.18.1 in Jer.*(p.151.9; M.13.464B); εὐχόμεθα ἕκαστον καὶ ἑκάστην τῷ βίῳ τοῦ μακαρίου ~ωθῆναι Gr.Naz.*ep.*238(M.38.381A); γενοίμεθα τέκνα μεμορφωμένα Ἀβραάμ τε καὶ πατέρων τῶν ἐκλεκτῶν Proc.G.*Jos.* 15:63(M.87.1036C); med. c. acc., *assume a form, conform* or *be conformed to* τῶν πνευματικῶν καὶ μεμορφωμένων τὸν Χριστόν Or. *schol.in Mt.*18:5(M.17.297B); ὁ τῆς ἐπέκεινα βασιλείας τὸ μίμημα...τῇ ψυχῇ μεμορφωμένος Eus.*l.C.*5(p.203.27; M.20.1336A); ὡς δὲ δούλου μορφῇ συγκαταβαίνει...καὶ ~οῦται τὸ ἀλλότριον Gr.Naz.*or.*30.6(p.116. 3; M.36.109C); ~οῦται τὸ ἡμῶν ὁ κατ' οὐσίαν τὴν θείαν ὅσον εἰς σχῆμα καὶ εἶδος ἀμόρφωτος Sophr.H.*ep.syn.*(M.87.3160D); τὸ ἐν αὐτῷ τῆς θείας εἰκόνος κάλλος τὸ ἐξ ἀρχῆς ἐμορφώσατο κάλλιον Jo.VI H.*v.Jo.D.* 33(M.94.477A).

μόρφωμα, τό, 1. *form* φέρων τὰ ὑπὲρ ἀνθρώπων πάθη τῷ ἐξ ἀνθρώπων παθητικῷ μ. ‡Ath.*Apoll.*2.13(M.26.1153A); εἰκὼν ἄγραφος ἀγράφου μ. ‡Gr.Naz.*Chr.pat.*923(M.38.211A); **2.** *kind, specimen* γραφεὺς...πολλὰ μίξας χρωμάτων μορφώματα Gr.Naz.*carm.*2.1.12.561 (M.37.1206A); **3.** *expression of a form, representation, image,* Arist. *apol.*3.2; ἵνα δαιμόνια νοητ⟨αι⟩ τὰ ἐφεδρεύοντα πνεύματα τοῖς ἀψύχοις μ. Or.*Apoc.*35(p.12); id.*comm.in Gen.*ap.*philoc.*23.18(p.207.4; M.12. 80B); ἀνατιθέναι τὰ οὕτως αἰσχρὰ μ. ταῖς θεοειδέσι καὶ ἁγιωτάταις διακοσμήσεσιν Dion.Ar.*c.h.*2.2(M.3.140B).

***μόρφων, ὁ,** *dissembler,* ‡Ign.*Magn.*4.

μόρφωσις, ἡ, 1. *giving of form to, formation, shaping* τὸν μονογενῆ τοῦτον...ἀρχὴν καὶ μ. παντὸς τοῦ πληρώματος Iren.*haer.*1.1.1(M.7. 448A); 'δύναμις δὲ ὑψίστου ἐπισκιάσει σοι' τὴν μ. δηλοῖ τοῦ θεοῦ, ἣν ἐνετύπωσεν τῷ σώματι ἐν τῇ παρθένῳ Clem.*exc.Thdot.*60(p.127.3; M. 9.688B); ὁ Σωτὴρ ἐπιφέρει αὐτῇ [sc. Σοφίᾳ] μ. τὴν κατὰ γνῶσιν καὶ ἴασιν τῶν παθῶν *ib.*45(p.121.5; 680C); ὁ Νοῦς καὶ ἡ Ἀλήθεια [sc. προέβαλον] Χριστὸν καὶ Πνεῦμα ἅγιον εἰς μ. καὶ διαίρεσιν τοῦ ἐκτρώματος Hipp.*haer.*6.31(p.158.25; M.16.3239C); ref. Jo.1:4 αὐτὸς γὰρ τὴν πρώτην μ. ... αὐτοῖς παρέσχε, τὰ ὑπ' ἄλλου σπαρέντα εἰς μορφὴν... ἀγαγών Heracleon ap.Or.*Jo.*2.21(15; p.77.27; M.14.149C); τίς...οὕτω ...σάρκινος τὴν διάνοιαν...ὥστε ἀκούων θείας γεννήσεως, πρὸς τὰς σωματικὰς καταφέρεσθαι φαντασίας, ἐν αἷς...κύησις...καὶ μ.; Bas. *Eun.*2.5(1.241E; M.29.581A); υἱὸς...πνεύματος ἁγίου χορηγός, εἰς...μ. κτίσεως Didym.(‡Bas.)*Eun.*5(1.307B; M.29.736D); cf. *qui nati sunt in Christum...deinde abolere temptaverunt ipsam effigiem veritatis, aliam formationem expectat in illis fieri,* Thdr.Mops.*Gal.*4:19(p.70. 8); ἐν μ. τῶν ἀμορφώτων Dion.Ar.*e.h.*4.3.4(M.3.480A); ref. Inc. κενώσας μὲν ἑαυτὸν κατὰ τὴν μ., ἀκένωτος δὲ...κατὰ τὴν θείαν οὐσίαν Apoll.*corp.et div.*6(p.188.1; M.*PL.*8.874A); πνευματικὴν μὲν ἔχων τὴν ἀνατολήν, σωματικὴν δὲ προσλαμβάνων τὴν μ. ‡Chrys.*pasch.*6.4(p.167. 6; 8.270D); **2.** *form, shape* οὐσίαν ἐργάζεται μορφώσεως Clem.*paed.* 1.6(p.118.29; M.8.308A); τὰς θείας μ. τῶν ἁγίων εἰκόνων Anast.S. *synax.*(M.89.832C); = μορφή: τὴν τοῦ θεοῦ μορφὴν ἡ τοῦ δούλου μ. οὐκ ἐμείωσεν Leo Mag.*ep.*28.3(p.14.2, v.l. μορφὴ M.*PL.*54.766A); **3.** *embodiment, concrete form;* exeg. Rom.2:20, interpreted of 'letter' of Law, cf.Or.*comm.in Rom.*2.11(M.14.896B); ὥσπερ ἂν εἴ τις τὴν βασιλικὴν εἰκόνα ἔχων, μηδὲν πρὸς ἐκείνην γράφοι· οἱ δὲ μὴ πιστευθέντες αὐτήν, καὶ χωρὶς τοῦ πρωτοτύπου μετὰ ἀκριβείας αὐτὴν μιμοῖντο Chrys.*hom.6.2 in Rom.*(9.473E); μ. λέγει οὐ τὴν προτύπωσιν, ἀλλ' αὐτὴν τὴν ὑπόστασιν καὶ τὴν γνῶσιν καὶ τὴν ἀλήθειαν ὡς τὸ 'ὃς ἐν μορφῇ θεοῦ ὑπάρχων' Thdr.Mops.*Rom.*2:20(p.116.12; M.66. 789C); ἔχοντα τὴν μ. τῆς γνώσεως καὶ τῆς ἀληθείας...τούτων γάρ σοι πάντων τοὺς χαρακτῆρας ὁ θεῖος προσέφερε νόμος Thdt.*Rom.*2:20(3. 34); **4.** *expression* ὁ υἱὸς θεός, διὰ τὴν ἐν αὐτῷ τοῦ πατρὸς ὡς ἐν εἰκόνι μ. Eus.*e.th.*1.20(p.93.18; M.24.888B); ταῖς τῶν οὐρανίων νόων μ. Dion. Ar.*c.h.*2.1(M.3.140A); **5.** *likeness, figure* εἶναι μὲν οὖν τὸν 'Ἰησοῦν ὄνομα μὲν τοῦ ἐκ τῆς οἰκονομίας ἀνθρώπου λέγει [sc. Marcus], τεθεῖσθα δὲ ⟨εἰς⟩ ἐξομοίωσιν καὶ μ. τοῦ μέλλοντος εἰς αὐτὸν κατέρχεσθαι Ἀνθρώπου Hipp.*haer.*6.51(p.184.7; M.16.3282B); ἐκεῖνα μὲν τύποι καὶ τῆς ἀληθείας μ. ἦν Cyr.*Zach.*59(3.738D); id.*Juln.*8(6^{2}.258C); **6.** *outward form, appearance* opp. reality, exeg. 2Tim.3:5 ἔχοντες μ. εὐσεβείας ...καὶ ἐν τῇ πρὸς 'Ρωμαίους γράφων, οὕτω πώς φησιν· ἔχοντες τὴν μ. τῆς γνώσεως...ἀλλ' ἐκεῖ μὲν ἐπαινῶν αὐτὸ τίθησιν· ἐνταῦθα δὲ...χαλεπώτερον τοῦτο δείκνυσι τὸ ἁμάρτημα...ἐκεῖ μέν...ὅτι τύπος...καὶ ἀρχέτυπον τῆς εὐσεβείας· ἐνταῦθα δέ, ὅτι...σχῆμα μόνον...δηλοῖ Chrys.*hom.8.1 in 2Tim.*(11.707C); μ. εὐσεβείας...τὸ τῆς εὐσεβείας...πρόσχημα Thdt. *2Tim.*3:5(3.688).

μορφωτικός, 1. *giving shape, formative,* Gnost. ἐν τοῖς γεννητοῖς τὸ μὲν θῆλυ ἐστιν οὐσίας προβλητικόν, τὸ δὲ ἄρρεν μ. τῆς ὑπὸ τοῦ θήλεως προβαλλομένης οὐσίας Hipp.*haer.*6.30(p.158.8; M.16.3239B); met., of scripture μ. καὶ ζωοποιῶν λογίων Dion.Ar.*e.h.*3.3.6(M.3.433A); **2.** *in forms and shapes* τὰς...ἀΰλους ἱεραρχίας ὑλαίοις σχήμασι καὶ μ. συνθέσεσι διαποικίλασα παραδέδωκεν id.*c.h.*1.3(M.3.121C); *ib.*15 tit.(325D).

μορφωτικῶς, *as representations* εἰκόσιν ἱεροπλάστοις μ. ἀποτυποῦσι τὴν θεουργικὴν ὁμοίωσιν Dion.Ar.*c.h.*7.2(M.3.208C).

μοσχάριον, τό, *little calf, T.Lev.*suppl.41(p.251); Clem.*paed.*1.5 (p.102.18; M.8.273C); Pall.*h.Laus.*18(p.51.4; μόσχον M.34.1057B).

μόσχευμα, τό, *sucker,* Cyr.*hom.pasch.*6(5^{2}.63A); fig. ἔρχεται δὲ καὶ ἀναγκαίως μετὰ Αἴγυπτον νόμος, ὑλομανούσης ψυχῆς καὶ αἰγυπτιαζούσης καρδίας ἐκκόπτων τὰ ἀόρατα κακὰ μ. ‡Chrys.*pasch.*6.2(p.137. 14; 8.267B); τὰ ἐκείνων [sc. Paul. Sam. and Lucianus] κεκρυμμένα μ., Ἀρειός τε καὶ Ἀχιλλᾶς Alex.Al.*ep.Alex.*9(p.25.14; M.18.561A); νόθον μ. Nil.*epp.*2.54(M.79.224B); ‡Meth.*Sym.et Ann.*8(M.18.368B).

***μοσχευτός,** *propagated,* Thdot.Anc.*hom.*1.1(p.81.3; M.77.1349A).

μόσχιον, τό, *young shoot,* Cyr.*ador.*9(1.301E); id.*glaph.Gen.*2(1. 38B).

μοσχοποιέω, *make a calf,* ref. Ex.32:4, Just.*dial.*19.5(M.6.517A); Or.*Cels.*1.4(p.58.16; M.11.664A); *Const.App.*1.6.8; τὸν λαὸν μ. τὸν παρ' Αἰγυπτίοις Ἆπιν *ib.*6.20.1; *ib.*6.20.6; Cyr.*ador.*1(1.7D); of Jeroboam, id.*Os.*73(3.108E).

***μοσχοποίησις, ἡ,** = sq., Ast.Am.*hom.*14(M.40.376D).

***μοσχοποιΐα, ἡ,** *making of a calf,* ref. Ex.32:4, Just.*dial.*73.6(M. 6.648C); Clem.*str.*2.15(p.50.16; M.8.1009A); Or.*Jo.*14(11; p.184.25; M.14.329C); Epiph.*haer.*47.2(p.217.16; M.41.852D).

μόσχος, ὁ, *calf, young bullock,* ref. Ps.21:12, Mt.26:47 ἐκύκλωσαν αὐτὸν οὓς μόσχους κερατιστὰς...ὁ λόγος ἔλεγε Just.*dial.*103.1(M.6. 716B); as type of Christ, ref. Lev.16:6 ὁ μ. ὁ 'Ἰησοῦς ἐστιν, οἱ προσφέροντες ἄνδρες ἁμαρτωλοὶ οἱ προσενέγκαντες αὐτὸν τὴν σφαγήν *Barn.*8.2; τίς ὁ μ. ὁ σιτευτός, ἢ πάντως Χριστός, τὸ ἄμωμον ἱερεῖον; Cyr.*Lc.*15:18(M.72.809B); exeg. Dt.25:4, id.*ador.*3(1.99E) cit. s. ἀλωητής; τὸν μ. τὸν σιτευτὸν...τὸν τοῖς μετανοοῦσι μεταδιδόμενον, τὴν μετάληψιν τῶν θείων μυστηρίων *cat.Lc.*15:20(p.119.34).

***μοσχοσφραγιστικός,** *pertaining to* the duties of *a* μοσχοσφραγιστής (one who marks calves destined for sacrifice), Clem.*str.*6.4 (p.449.17, conj. for μοσχοσφαγιστικά M.9.253C).

μοτόω (μωτόω), *plug* a wound with lint, ref. Os.6:1, *Const.App.* 2.41.5; Cyr.*Jo.*2.1(4.137C); μωτόω, id.*Is.*1.6(2.161D); abs., Thdr. Stud.*epp.*1.52(M.99.1100D); *bind up*; met., Pall.*v.Chrys.*7(p.40.18; M.47.24).

***μότωσις, ἡ,** *dressing with lint,* Cyr.*Os.*62(3.96A); id.*Ps.*37:20(M. 69.969A); fig., in form μώτωσις, id.*Is.*1.6(2.160D); ‡Sophr.H.*triod.* (M.87.3841C).

***μουζίκιον, τό,** *box inlaid with mosaic,* Jo.Mosch.*prat.*79(M.87. 2936D); cf.Jo.Mal.*chron.*9 p.220(M.97.341C om.).

[*]μουκίζω, *mock, jeer at,* Leont.N.*v.Sym.*41(M.93.1721A); *ib.*42 (1724A).

***μουλικός,** *like a mule,* Thphn.*chron.*p.358(M.108.860A).

μουλίων, ὁ, (Lat. *mulio*) *muleteer,* as term of abuse, Bas.*ep.*231 (3.354D; M.32.861B).

***μοῦλτος, ὁ,** (Lat. *tumultus*) *riot,* Thphn.*chron.*p.400(M.108.956A).

μουναδόν, = μόνον, Nonn.*par.Jo.*20:7(M.43.909A).

μουνόγονος, *only-begotten,* Nonn.*par.Jo.*1:14(M.43.752B).

***μουρζοῦλιν, τό,** a kind of fish, Thphn.*chron.*p.297(M.108.725B).

§**μοῦσα, ἡ,** *square sponge* λαβὼν τὴν μ. συστέλλει τὰς ἐν τῷ δίσκῳ μερίδας ὑποκάτω τοῦ ἁγίου ἄρτου ὥστε...μὴ ἐκπεσεῖν τι *Lit.Chrys.* (p.359.26).

§**μουσάριον (*μούσαρον), τό,** *mosaic work,* Jo.Mal.*chron.*12 p.302 (M.97.456B); *ib.*14 p.360(536B); Eustrat.*v.Eutych.*53(M.86.2333D).

μουσεῖον (-ιον), τό, *mosaic work, mosaic* κοσμηθεῖσα διαφόροις μαρμάροις καὶ μουσίῳ Jo.Mal.*chron.*18 p.479(M.97.696B); διὰ μουσείων ἐν τοίχοις Jo.Sync.*narr.*(H.4.320E); Thphn.*chron.*p.373(M.108. 893B); fig. τοῦ πολυπηγήτου τῶν ἄστρων μουσείου ἀξιαγαστότερον ἔργον †Hipp.*theoph.*1(p.257.9; M.10.852A).

***μουσηγετέω,** *conduct a choir,* ‡Jo.D.*Artem.*52(p.87.24; M.96. 1300B).

μουσηγέτης, ὁ, *conductor of a choir,* met. οἱ προσεχῶς κρούοντες τὰς ψυχὰς ὑπὸ μουσηγέτῃ τῷ κυρίῳ Clem.*str.*6.11(p.476.7; M.9.309B).

μουσικός, *musical,* as subst.; **1.** *musician, singer,* ref. Lc.15:25, *Const.App.*2.41.1; ἡ γλῶττα, σωφρονοῦντος τοῦ μ., τὴν...ὑμνῳδίαν προσφέρει τῷ...θεῷ Thdt.*Rom.*6:13(3.65); fem., *T.Jud.*23.2; *poetess* Σαπφὼ πρώτη μ. Jo.Mal.*chron.*4 p.72(M.97.152A); **2.** *musical contest* ἱππικοὺς ⟨ἀγῶνας⟩, μουσικούς τε Epiph.*exp.fid.*24(p.525.11; M. 42.832A); **3.** μουσική, ἡ [sc. τέχνη] *music;* **a.** fig. ὁ πεπαιδευμένος τὴν τοῦ θεοῦ μ. ... μαθὼν ἐν καιρῷ κρούειν χορδάς, νῦν μὲν νομικάς, νῦν δὲ συμφώνους αὐταῖς εὐαγγελικάς Or.*comm.in Mt*.2(p.5.22; M.13.832C); **b.** *harmony* ὁ ἥλιος...μέσος τῶν ἄλλων πλανητῶν τεταγμένος τοῖς τε ὑπὲρ αὐτὸν τοῖς τε ὑπ' αὐτὸν κατά τινα θείαν μ. ἐνδίδωσι τοῦ φωτὸς Clem.*str*.5.6(p.349.8; M.9.60A).

***μουσόπνευστος**, *inspired by muses*, Gr.Naz.*carm*.2.1.41.15(M.37.1340A); Cosm.Mel.*schol*.87(M.38.539) in Gr.Naz.*carm*.2.2(epitaph.) 35.1.

***μουσότευκτος**, *equipped by muses*, Cosm.Mel.*schol*.87(M.38.539) in Gr.Naz.*carm*.2.2(epitaph.)35.1.

μουσουργ-έω, **1.** *sing* τὰ μεσημβρινὰ ∼οῦντες [sc. τέττιγες] Gr.Naz.*or*.28.24(p.58.17; M.36.60A); Gr.Nyss.*hom.4 in Eccl*.(M.44.676A); met. οὕτω τοῦ νοῦ διὰ τῆς ὀργανικῆς κατασκευῆς ἐν ἡμῖν ∼οῦντος τὸν λόγον, λογικοὶ γεγόναμεν id.*hom.opif*.10.1(M.44.152A); **2.** *compose*, Jo.VI H.*v.Jo.D*.11(M.94.445C).

***μουσούργημα, τό,** *piece of mosaic*, ‡Jo.D.*ep.Thphl*.30(M.95.384C).

μουσουργικός, *of mosaic* μ. ψηφίσιν ‡Jo.D.*ep.Thphl*.3(M.95.348D).

μουσουργός, ὁ, *musician, composer*, fig. Δαυὶδ...ὁ μ. τῆς σωφροσύνης ‡Chrys.*hom*.1(13.201A).

μουσόω, *adorn with mosaic*, Jo.Mal.*chron*.9 p.223(M.97.345C).

μουστάκιον, τό, dim. of sq., Melet.*nat.hom*.7(M.64.1185A).

[*]**μούσταξ, ὁ,** = μύσταξ, *moustache*, Melet.*nat.hom*.7(M.64.1185A).

***μούσωσις, ἡ,** *mosaic*, Jo.Mal.*chron*.10 p.232(M.97.359A); *ib*.13 p.339(505B).

μουσωτής, ὁ, *worker in mosaic*, Eustrat.*v.Eutych*.53(M.86.2336A).

***μοχθηροποι-έω,** *lay a burden upon* ∼οῦσι τὸν ταύτας [sc. τὰς ἐντολὰς τοῦ κυρίου] φυλάττοντα αἱ ἀντικείμεναι...δυνάμεις ‡Nil.*tract*.2 (M.79.1281C).

μοχθηρῶς, *wickedly*, Tat.*orat*.22(p.25.12; M.6.857A).

***μοχθισμός, ὁ,** = μοχθηρία, *wickedness, depravity*, Ant.Mon.*hom*. 130(M.89.1841C).

μοχλεία, ἡ, 1. *leverage* φυτὸν...χρόνῳ...πολλῷ ῥιζωθὲν...πολλῆς δεῖται τῆς μ. Chrys.*hom.11.5 in 1Cor*.(10.93B); Synes.*insomn*.12 (p.169.23; M.66.1304C); **2.** *pressure, use of* olive *presses*, Cyr.*ador*.9 (1.321E).

μόχλευσις, ἡ, *prising open* of doors, Thphn.*chron*.p.425(M.108.1004D).

μοχλεύω, 1. *move with levers*; pass., *be dislodged, loosened*, met. μοχλευθεῖσα καὶ καταντληθεῖσα ἡ ψυχή [sc. by examples of God's goodness] Bas.*jud*.8(2.222C; M.31.673B); **2.** *bolt, bar*, ref. Pr.18:19 μεμοχλευμένη βασιλεία Chrys.*sac*.1.4(p.16.15; 1.367E); **3.** ? *bind to levers* (s.v.l.), Thphn.*chron*.p.425(M.108.1004D).

***μοχλοποιέω,** *fasten with bolts*, Nil.*epp*.4.1(M.79.545C).

μυάκιον, τό, dim. of μύαξ, *small spoon*, ‡Pall.*h.mon*.31.8(p.94.3; M.34.1082C).

μύαξ, ὁ, *mussel-shell*, hence *conch, domed roof of apse* μ. ὁ ἐπάνω τοῦ βήματος ‡Sophr.H.*liturg*.3(M.87.3984B).

μυελός, ὁ, *marrow* fig. ἡ λογικὴ καὶ οὐρανία ψυχὴ...μυελοῦ γέμουσα πνευματικοῦ Clem.*exc.Thdot*.53(p.124.27; M.9.685A); τοὺς τῆς γῆς μ. ...λέγω...χρυσόν, χαλκὸν...καὶ τὰ ὅμοια *Hom.Clem*.8.14.

μυελώδης, *like marrow*, *Hom.Clem*.6.12; neut. as subst., Meth. *symp*.2.2(p.16.19; M.18.49A).

μυέω, 1. *initiate*; in OT, Gr.Naz.*or*.15.10(M.35.929B); καθαρὸν πάθους προσβῆναι τῷ ὄρει μυηθησόμενον [sc. τὸν λαόν] Gr.Nyss. *v.Mos*.45(M.44.316A); Christian ἵνα...δι' ἐπιγνώσεως τῆς διὰ τοῦ υἱοῦ τοῦ θεοῦ...'πρόσωπον πρὸς πρόσωπον' τὴν μακαρίαν θέαν μυηθῇ [sc. ὁ γνωστικός] Clem.*str*.6.12(p.483.12; M.9.324B); ὅστις ἁγνὸς... μυείσθω τὰ μόνοις ἁγίοις καὶ καθαροῖς εὐλόγως παραδιδόμενα μυστήρια τῆς κατὰ Ἰησοῦν θεοσεβείας Or.*Cels*.3.60(p.254.28; M.11.1000B); Παῦλος ὁ ἐν παραδείσῳ μυηθεὶς τὰ ἀπόρρητα Gr.Nyss.*hom.3 in Cant*. (M.44.820C); ἵνα γένησθε ὡς φωστῆρες ἐν κόσμῳ...καὶ τὴν ἐκεῖσε μυηθῆτε φωταγωγίαν, ἐλλαμπόμενοι τῇ τριάδι Gr.Naz.*or*.39.20(M.36.360A); ref. understanding of allegorical interpretations ἴστε οἱ μεμυημένοι τί λέγω Chrys.*hom.23.3 in Heb*.(12.207D); Thdt.*Ps*.65:6 (1.1045); Gnost. οἱ τὴν τελείαν γνῶσιν ἔχοντες περὶ θεοῦ καὶ τῆς Ἀχαμώθ· μεμυημένους δὲ μυστήρια εἶναι τούτους ὑποτίθενται Iren. *haer*.1.6.1(7.505A); esp. in baptism, Gr.Naz.*or*.5.7(M.35.672C); εὐχὴ καὶ δυνάμεως θείας ἐπίκλησις ἐπὶ τοῦ ὕδατος γινομένη ζωῆς ἀρχηγὸς τοῖς μυηθεῖσι Gr.Nyss.*or.catech*.33(p.124.6, v.l. μυουμένοις M.45.84B); οὔτε μὴν οἱ βαπτισθέντες ὑπ' αὐτῶν [sc. τῶν αἱρετικῶν] μεμύηνται, ἀλλὰ μεμολυσμένοι ὑπάρχουσιν *Const.App*.6.15.3; εἴ τις κατὰ ἄγνοιαν μεταλάβοι, τοῦτον τάχιον στοιχειώσαντες μυήσατε, ὅπως μὴ καταφρονητὴς ἐξέλθοι *ib*.7.25.7; εὔξασθε...ὅπως ὁ κύριος καταξιώσῃ αὐτοὺς [sc. τοὺς φωτιζομένους] μυηθέντας εἰς τὸν τοῦ Χριστοῦ θάνατον, συναναστῆναι αὐτῷ καὶ μετόχους γενέσθαι τῆς βασιλείας αὐτοῦ *Lit*. ap.*Const.App*.8.8.2; ὥσπερ τοίνυν τῶν ἀμυήτων οὐδένα χρὴ παρεῖναι [sc. at eucharist] οὕτως οὐδὲ τῶν μεμυημένων καὶ ῥυπαρῶν Chrys. *hom.3.5 in Eph*.(11.23D); χωρήσας δ' ἔνδον τῶν μακαρίων ὑδάτων ἐπὶ κωλύσει τῶν μυουμένων τὴν ἀνάστασιν τοῦ σωτῆρος Pall.*v.Chrys*.9 (p.57.22; M.47.33); γύναιά τε καὶ παιδία συναρπάζοντες μυεῖσθαι ἠνάγκαζον Socr.*h.e*.2.38.8(M.67.325A); Thphn.*chron*.p.51(M.108.184A); οἱ μυηθέντες, οἱ μεμυημένοι *the baptized*, hence *communicants*, Gr.Naz.*or*.42.16(M.36.477A); Chrys.*hom.16.9 in Mt*.(7.217A); Bas. Sel.*v.Thecl*.1(M.85.501A); Thdt.*Cant*.2:3(2.56); **2.** *instruct* in divine mysteries, c. acc. and infin. ἥλιον αὐτὸν δικαιοσύνης [sc. εἶναι] καὶ φῶς ἐπέκεινα φώτων ἀπάντων λόγων ἀπόρρητοι μυοῦσι θεολογίαι Eus. *l.C*.6(p.211.26; M.20.1349C); c. dupl. acc. οἱ μυοῦντες ἄγγελοι τὰς ἀποκαλύψεις τοὺς προφήτας Max.*schol.c.h*.13.3(M.4.96C); pass. c. acc. ταῦτα πρὸς τῶν θείων λογίων μεμυήμεθα Dion.Ar.*d.n*.1.4(M.3.589D); ‡Proc.G.*Pr*.22:17(M.87.1445B); c. genit. of thing taught ἐμυήθη λόγων θείων Ammon.*Ac*.16:32(M.85.1561B); Jo.D.*hom*.1.5(M.96.553B); abs., Dion.Ar.*d.n*.2.9(M.3.648B); τὴν ὑπερκόσμιον ἐπιστήμην ἠγνοήσαμεν καὶ μᾶλλον...ἡμεῖς ἑτέρου τοῦ φωταγωγοῦντος τοῦ μυοῦντος δεόμεθα Dion.Ar.*c.h*.15.9(M.3.340B).

***μύημα, τό,** *mystery*, Areth.*Apoc*.9:13(M.106.629C).

μύησις, ἡ, 1. *initiation*, in OT τινος ἀπορρητοτέρας μ. ὁ Μωϋσῆς καθηγεῖτο Gr.Nyss.*v.Mos*.45(M.44.316A); Christian ἔνθεος ἐνθέων ἐν μ. γινόμενος Dion.Ar.*c.h*.2.5(M.3.144C); εἰς μ. προβιβάσαι τελεωτέραν, τὸν οὔπω δεδεγμένον τὴν ἥττονα Max.*opusc*.(M.91.57C); esp. of baptism, Gr.Nyss.*or.catech*.40(p.160.17; M.45.101D); ἵνα ἀφέσεως τυχόντες τῶν πλημμελημάτων διὰ τῆς μ. ἀξιωθῶσιν τῶν ἁγίων μυστηρίων *Lit*.ap.*Const.App*.8.6.7; τοὺς ἐν κατηχήσει παίδευσον καὶ τῆς μ. ἀξίους ἀνάδειξον *Lit.ib*.8.15.5; ἐτήσιον ταύτην ἑορτὴν [sc. dedication feast of Church of Holy Sepulchre]...ἄγει ἡ τῶν Ἱεροσολύμων ἐκκλησία ὡς καὶ μυήσεις ἐν αὐτῇ τελεῖσθαι Soz.*h.e*.2.26.4(M.67.1008C); πάροικός ἐστιν ἐκκλησίας, ὅστις...μετὰ...μύησιν ἀποστάτης γενόμενος Proc.G.*Ex*.12:43(M.87.577A); οὐ γάρ ἐστιν τῆς τοῦ ἐσταυρωμένου κυρίου μ. κατευμεγεθῆσαι, μὴ τῇ ὑπερθέῳ τριάδι τὸ εἰσαγώγιμον εἰληχότα Areth.*Apoc*.21:12–14(M.106.769A); ref. ordination as substitute for baptism ἔφησεν ἀρκεῖν αὐτῷ [sc. ἐπισκόπῳ... τοῦ θείου βαπτίσματος ἀμετόχῳ] τὴν τοῦ ἐπισκόπου χειροτονίαν πρὸς ἀναπλήρωσιν τῆς θείας μ. Thdr.Lect.*fr*.(M.86.216D); **2.** *mystery, revelation* Νεστορίου ἐκ τῆς λεγομένης αὐτῷ ἐπιφανοῦς μ. λόγου β' †Nest.*fr*.B 11(p.223)ap.CLater.*act*.5(H.3.896B); Areth.*Apoc*.11:11–14(M.106.653D); fig. τὰς ἀπορρήτους βασιλέως μ. τοῖς τούτων μύσταις διηγείσθων μόνοις Eus.*l.C*.proem.(p.196.2; M.20.1317B); *ib*.11(p.223.24; 1376A); **3.** *instruction* in divine mysteries Χριστιανισμὸς δὲ τοῦ ὄντως ὄντος θεοῦ ἐπίγνωσίς ἐστιν καὶ τοῦ μονογενοῦς υἱοῦ αὐτοῦ καὶ τῆς κατὰ σάρκα οἰκονομίας αὐτοῦ καὶ μ. *M.Ign.Rom*.6; Sophr.H.*ep.syn*. (M.87.3176A); τὴν καθ' ὕπνον μ. id.*mir.Cyr.et Jo*.37(M.87.3564A); Max.*myst*.24(M.91.708D).

μυθάριον, τό, contemptuous dim. of μῦθος *fable*, old wives' *tale*; plur., Nil.*epp*.1.117(M.79.133C); τὰ τῶν...αἱρετικῶν...μ. Cyr.*ador*.9 (1.321C); *ib*.7(251A).

μυθεύω, med., *invent fables*, Didym.*Trin*.2.3(M.39.476A); Mac. Mgn.*apocr*.3.14(p.91.3).

μυθήρια, τά, *hunting fables* πάρεστι...μ. σοι νοεῖν, ἀντιστοιχούντων τῶν γραμμάτων, τὰ μυστήρια Clem.*prot*.2(p.12.3; M.8.73A).

μυθίδιον, τό, = μυθάριον, Ath.*Ar*.1.6(M.26.24C).

μυθίζω, 1. *tell fabulous stories*, Clem.*prot*.6(p.51.14; M.8.172B); **2.** med., *speak, say*, †Apoll.*met.Ps*.34:20(M.33.1357D); Nonn.*par. Jo*.13:13(M.43.861C).

***μυθοθρησκεία, ἡ,** *worship based on fables*, Thdot.Anc.*hom. BMV et Sym*.12(M.77.1408C).

***μυθόλατρις, ὁ,** *slave of fables*, Gr.Naz.*carm*.2.2(poem.)7.159(M.37.1563A).

μυθολέσχης, ὁ, *teller of tales, inventor of fables*, ‡Caes.Naz.*dial*. 107(M.38.976).

μυθολογεύω, *speak, converse*, *Orac.Sib*.2.141.

***μυθομέριμνος,** *paying heed to fables*; of Origenists, Sophr.H.*ep. syn*.(M.87.3181B).

***μυθόπλασμα, τό,** *fiction*, Didym.*Trin*.2.6(M.39.548B).

μυθοπλαστ-έω, *invent* οἱ τὰ ἐπ' αὐτοῖς [sc. τοῖς γίγασιν] ∼εῖν εἰωθότες Cyr.*glaph.Gen*.2(1.30C); id.*ador*.6(1.205D); ἔκγονον ἡλίου τὸν Ἆπιν Αἰγύπτιοι ∼οῦντες ἔλεγον id.*Os*.113(3.145A); ἣν [sc. Cybele] πολύτεκνον ∼οῦσιν οἱ ἄφρονες Jo.D.*hom*.9.15(M.96.741C); of heretics τῇ τῶν δοκητῶν...δόξῃ...οἱ...ὦφθαι μὲν ἐπὶ γῆς ὡς ἄνθρωπον ∼οῦσιν Cyr.*inc.unigen*.(5^1.690E); συγκεχυμένην μίαν φύσιν ἐκ δύο φύσεων ∼οῦσιν Leont.B.*cap.Sev*.15(M.86.1905B); ἀπροαίρετον αἰτίαν...τῇ συστάσει τῶν ὄντων τὸν θεὸν ∼οῦσι Zach.Mit.*opif*.(M.85.1080A).

***μυθοπλαστία, ἡ,** *fabulous invention* ἡ τῶν Ἱπποκενταύρων...μ.

Leont.B.*arg.Sev.*(M.86.1932B); Jo.D.*Jacob.*29(M.94.1452A); of heretics, *invention of fables, invented fables,* Ath.*Ar.*2.44(M.26.240C); *ib.* 3.67(465B); Epiph.*haer.*73.36(p.310.18; M.42.469A); Cyr.*Juln.*2(6². 41C).

μυθοποι-έω, 1. *compose fables,* Athenag.*leg.*10.1(M.6.908B); Or. *Jo.*13.20(p.244.11; M.14.432B); **2.** trans., *invent,* Just.*1apol.*23.2(M. 6.364B); ~*οῦντες ἑαυτοῖς ὑποθέσεις* Or.*princ.*4.2.1(9; p.308.2; M.11. 360A); id.*Cels.*1.32(p.83.20; M.11.721A); *τὰ ~ηθέντα fables composed,* Just.*1apol.*54.1(408C); *ib.*53.1(405C); pres. ptcpl. pass. as adj., *fabled,* Clem.*str.*5.14(p.401.18; M.9.169A); Chrys.*hom.70.3 in Mt.* (7.691C).

***μυθοτόκος,** *fruitful in words,* Nonn.*par.Jo.*16:4(M.43.877C); Jo.D.*hom.*9.1(M.96.724A).

μυΐνος, dim. of *μῦς*: *ὡς μ. εἰσερχόμενον as quietly as a mouse,* Dor. *doct.*5.5(M.88.1681D).

***μυκάζω,** *bleat,* Leont.H.*monoph.*6(M.86.1773A).

***μυκαρός,** *given to bellowing,* ‡Caes.Naz.*dial.*140(M.38.1072).

***μυκαστικός,** *able to bleat, bleating*; neut. as subst., Leont.H. *monoph.*6(M.86.1772D).

μυκηθμός, ὁ, *groaning, Orac.Sib.*8.105.

μύκημα, τό, 1. *roar*; of an angel's voice, Nonn.*par.Jo.*12:29(M. 43.856A); **2.** *groaning, T.Job* 40(p.129.21).

***μυκηματία, ἡ,** *earthquake accompanied by roaring underground,* Or.*Ps.*69:4(p.68, conj. for *μυκοιματίαι, μνηματίαι* codd.).

μυκητής, *resounding, Hymn.*ap.Hipp.*haer.*5.9(p.100.6, conj. for *μύκτητα* M.16.3155A).

μυκητικός, *lowing,* Dion.Ar.*c.h.*2.2(M.3.137C).

μυκτηρισμός, ὁ, 1. *scorn, Pss.Sal.*4.8; plur., *insults,* Marc.Diac. *v.Porph.*2; **2.** *object of scorn μ. τοῖς ἐχθροῖς* Cyr.*Ps.*79:7(M.69.1197D).

***μύκτης, ὁ,** v. *μυκητής.*

μύλη, ἡ, 1. *molar, tooth, Pss.Sal.*13.3; Epiph.*ep.Arab.*ap.*haer.*78. 12(p.463.4; M.42.717A); Thdr.Mops.*Joel* 1:6(M.66.213D); fig., Chrys. *fr.Job* 2:7(M.64.556D); *ὁ φυλάττων σε τὰς...μ. συνθλάσει τῆς πονηρίας* Isid.Pel.*epp.*1.462(M.78.436D); **2.** apptly. of a holy water sprinkler, Dor.*doct.*11.6(M.88.1741A).

μυλιαῖος, *as large as millstones μ. λίθοις* Dion.Al.ap.Eus.*h.e.*6.41. 4(M.20.605C).

μυλικός, *for a mill τὸν μ. λίθον τῆς καταλαλίας* Pall.*v.Chrys.*16(p.93. 29; M.47.53).

***μυλινάριος, ὁ,** (Lat. *molinarius*) *miller, CG–CI* 41 (Corinth, saec. vi).

μυλοειδῶς, *like a millstone,* Thdt.*affect.*4(p.104.16; 4.796).

***μυλοστομίς, ἡ,** *fang,* Epiph.*haer.*35.3(p.43.29; M.41.632D).

μυλωθρίς, ἡ, *girl who turns a mill,* Eus.*Is.*47:2(M.24.424B); Chrys. *hom.24.3 in 2Cor.*(10.609D); ‡Chrys.*hom.*8(13.224A).

μύλων, ὁ, *mill,* ref. Mt.24:41 *μ. νόησον τὴν τοῦδε τοῦ βίου περιφοράν, ἀστάτως ἡμᾶς ἐπιτρέχουσαν* Isid.Pel.*epp.*1.285(M.78.349C).

μυλώνιον, τό, *mill-house,* as place of punishment *μυλωνίῳ ἐμβαλεῖν* Soz.*h.e.*8.6.3(M.67.1529C).

μυξάριον, τό, *little plum, Apophth.Patr.*(M.65.225C).

μυξωτήρ, ὁ, 1. *nostril,* hence *hole* in lamp to hold wick, Oecum. *Apoc.*11:4(p.129); **2.** *nose,* Just.*1apol.*55.4(M.6.412B).

***μυογαλίδιον, τό,** dim. of *μυγαλῆ shrew-mouse,* whose bite was supposed to cause leprosy; met., of heresy, Epiph.*haer.*55.9(p.337. 11,13; *μυογαλλίδιον* M.41.988D).

[*]**μυοξός, ὁ,** v. *μυωξός.*

***μυοφόρος,** prob. for ⟨*μυιοφόρος*⟩ *vexed with flies,* Sophr.H.*mir. Cyr.et Jo.*23(M.87.3489B).

μυραλοιφέω, *anoint with sweet oil,* Synes.*calv.*20(p.226.3; M.66. 1200D); *use perfume,* of excessive use of unguents, contrasted with moderate use permissible to Christians *διαφέρει δὲ ὅλως τὸ μ. τοῦ μύρῳ χρίεσθαι· τὸ μὲν γὰρ θηλυδριῶδες, τὸ δὲ χρίεσθαι τῷ μύρῳ καὶ λυσιτελεῖ ἔσθ' ὅτε* Clem.*paed.*2.8(p.198.22; M.8.476B).

μυρεψεῖον, τό, *perfumery, cosmetic shop,* in simile illustrating pervasive influence of scriptures *εἰ γὰρ μ. τις παριὼν...καὶ ἄκων ἀναχρώννυται ἐκ τῆς εὐωδίας· πολλῷ μᾶλλον εἰς ἐκκλησίαν ἀπιὼν* Chrys.*hom.54.3 in Jo.*(8.313C).

μυρεψ-έω, *make* perfumes, *compound* unguents; met., of formation in soul of image of divine qualities *ἡ δὲ ἐν ἡμῖν διὰ τῆς τῶν ἀρετῶν καθαρότητος ~ουμένη εὐωδία...μιμουμένη τῷ καθ' ἑαυτὴν καθαρῷ τὸ τῇ φύσει ἀκήρατον* Gr.Nyss.*hom.3 in Cant.*(M.44.824A); of formation of spiritual life *τὸν καθαρὸν καὶ εὐώδη ~ῶν βίον, τὸν ἐκ ποικίλων τε καὶ διαφόρων τῶν τῆς ἀρετῆς ἀρωμάτων συγκεραννύμενον* *ib.10*(988D); *ἡ δὲ τῶν ἀρετῶν εὐωδία πᾶν ἄρωμα...νενίκηκε νομικόν, ~ούμενον τοῖς εὐαγγελικοῖς ἐπιτάγμασιν* Proc.G.*Cant.*4:10(M.87. 1657D); cf.Gr.Nyss.*hom.9 in Cant.*(956B); spiritual unguent of Christ as anointed high priest compounded out of virtues, id.*or.dom.*3 (p.48.13; M.44.1149D).

[*]**μυρέψης, ὁ,** *scent-maker, perfumer,* Evagr.*h.e.*2.3(p.41.34; *μυρεψός* M.86.2496C).

μυρεψικός, 1. *of perfumery,* ref. making of unguent for unction of OT priests *χρῖσμα...διὰ μ. τέχνης συνθεῖναι* Eus.*d.e.*4.15(p.174.12; M.22.289D); met., of *μ. τέχνη* with which 'anointed' Christian should treat a brother's *δυσωδία,* Gr.Naz.*or.*32.31(M.36.209A); in comparison of names and definitions of God (which cannot comprehend divine nature but serve to express it) with vase of perfume making scent therein contained available for use, Gr.Nyss. *hom.1 in Cant.*(M.44.784A); exeg. Cant.8:2 *δι' αὐτὴν γὰρ καὶ ἀπὸ οἴνου ἔπιεν· καὶ ταῦτα διὰ τῶν ἀποστόλων προέπιεν τοῦ μ.· ὅπερ ἐστί, τοῦ συγκεκραμένου τῷ ἁγίῳ πνεύματι· ὅνπερ καὶ προέπιεν, ταῦτα λέγων· λάβετε, πίετε,...ποτίζεται ἀπὸ τοῦ οἴνου τοῦ μ. τουτέστιν, ἀπὸ τοῦ μυστηριώδους οὗ εἴληφεν παρ' αὐτοῦ ἡ ἐκκλησία* Ph.Carp.*Cant.*223(M. 40.141A); ref. Cant.5:13 *φύουσαι μ., τὰ ἅγια εὐαγγέλια* *ib.*151(109B); **2.** neut. as subst., *perfume shop ὁ εἰσερχόμενος εἰς μ., κἂν μηδὲν ἀγοράσῃ, ἀλλὰ πάντως μεταλαμβάνει τῆς εὐωδίας· οὕτως καὶ ὁ παραβάλλων τοῖς πατράσιν...ὑποδεικνύουσιν αὐτῷ τὴν ὁδὸν τῆς ταπεινώσεως Apophth.Patr.al.*(M.34.233C).

***μυριάγιος,** *ten thousand times holy,* Jo.D.*trisag.*2(M.95.25D).

***μυριαδικός,** *ten thousand,* Areth.*Apoc.*4:6(M.106.572A).

μυριάκις, *ten thousand times, numberless times,* hence *infinitely μ. ἐν ἀσφαλείᾳ* Chrys.*hom.20.5 in Mt.*(7.267B); *μ. ἐστὶ καθαρὰ ἡ θεοτόκος* Thdt.*Ps.*84:12(1.1207).

***μυρίαμνον, τό,** *ten thousand head of sheep,* ‡Caes.Naz.*dial.*117 (M.38.1004).

***μυριάνθρωπος,** *of countless men μ. δῆμος* Gr.Nyss.*Melet.*(M.46. 861D); Geo.Pis.*Sev.*632(M.92.1669A).

***μυριαρχία, ἡ,** *army of ten thousand men,* Geo.Pis.*bell.Avar.*219 (M.92.1277A).

***μυριαύχενος,** *with countless necks*; of Hydra, Geo.Pis.*Heracl.*1. 75(M.92.1305A).

μυρίζ-ω, *anoint with scent* or *perfumed unguents*;

A. lit.; **1.** in gen., Clem.*paed.*2.8(p.199.5; M.8.477A); *Hom.Clem.* 5.18; ‡Caes.Naz.*dial.*109(M.38.981); **2.** of anointing of dead, Clem. *paed.*2.8(p.194.27; M.8.468A); cf. Gnost. ritual, Iren.*haer.*1.21.5(M. 7.665B); **3.** of anointing of Christ's feet, Mac.Mgn.*apocr.*3.14(p.93. 22); interpreted of apostles *μύρῳ γὰρ εὐώδει ἀλειφόμενοι οἱ πόδες θεϊκὴν αἰνίττονται διδασκαλίαν...καὶ...οἱ πόδες οἱ τοῦ κυρίου οἱ μεμυρισμένοι ἀπόστολοί εἰσιν προφητείᾳ τῆς εὐωδίας τοῦ χρίσματος ἁγίου μεταλαβόντες πνεύματος* Clem.*paed.*2.8(p.194.13; M.8.465C); *ib.*(p.195. 11; 468B); **4.** in Gnost. post-baptismal ritual, Iren.*haer.*1.21.3(M.7. 664B), v. *μύρον*; this rite also practised by some who dispense with water baptism, *ib.*1.21.4(665A).

B. met., *dispense* or *spread abroad sweetness* (*upon*) *ἡ σώφρων γυνὴ τὴν ἐκκλησίαν ἀγαθῇ τιμῇ ~ει Hom.Clem.*13.15; *εὐαγγέλια... ἅπερ οἱ χριόμενοι τὰς τῆς ψυχῆς ~ονται ῥῖνας* Ph.Carp.*Cant.*151(M. 40.109B); of name of Christ *ἀρκεῖ γὰρ ἡ Χριστοῦ προσηγορία οἱονεὶ μυρίσαι, καὶ εὐωδίας ἁπάσης ἐμφορῆσαι τῶν εὐσεβῶν* Thdt.*Cant.*1:2 (2.30); of BMV *χαῖρε, μύρον, τὸ τῶν ἀρετῶν...σύνθημα, ἡ παναγνείας μύροις ~ουσα* Thdr.Stud.*nativ.BMV* 7(M.96.693B).

***μυριόβλαστος,** *with countless shoots,* Geo.Pis.*Sev.*681(M.92. 1673A).

***μυριόγλωσσος,** *of countless tongues,* Sophr.H.*or.*2.5(M.87.3224A); Jo.V H.*icon.*11(M.96.1357C).

***μυριόγνωμος,** *of countless opinions,* Thdr.Stud.*antirr.*2.8(M.99. 352C).

[*]**μυριόδοντος,** = sq., †Nil.*vit.*4(M.79.1144C).

μυριόδους, *with countless teeth,* fig. *κενοδοξία...μ. θηρίον Const. App.*2.41.8.

***μυριόεις,** poet. for *μύριος, Orac.Sib.*1.224; *ib.*11.2.

***μυριοικίς,** *with innumerable houses,* Thdr.Stud.*or.*11.4(M.99. 805D).

***μυριοκέφαλος,** *with countless heads,* Jo.Clim.*scal.*16(M.88.924C).

***μυριομακαριότης, ἡ,** *infinite felicity,* Chrys.*hom.5.7 in Rom.*(9. 471A conj. for *μεγάλη μακαριότης, μυρία μακαριότης* codd.).

***μυριομακάριστος,** *infinitely blessed,* Nil.*epp.*1.27(M.79.96B).

***μυριόμετρος,** *gigantic,* Paul.Sil.*Soph.*457(M.86.2137A).

***μυριόμματος,** *with ten thousand eyes,* Hipp.*haer.*5.9(p.98.15; M. 16.3154B); *ib.*8.12(p.232.25; 3358D).

μυριόμορφος, *of countless shapes*; masc. as subst., fig. *chameleon*; of Severus, Eust.Mon.*ep.*(M.86.929A).

μυριοντάκις, = *μυριάκις,* Ath.*exp.Pss.*proem.(M.27.56A); ‡Ath. *doct.Ant.*94(M.28.656B).

μυριονταπλασίων, *ten thousand times as great*; neut. as adv., *ten thousandfold more, infinitely more*, Epiph.*haer*.69.16(p.165.21; M.42.225C); ὁ θεὸς...μ. παρὰ τὴν ψυχὴν...ἀκατάληπτος *ib*.70.4(p.236.17; 345A); with comp., *infinitely*, Jo.Eub.*concept.BMV* 4(M.96.1464B); μ. μακαριωτέρα *ib*.11(1477B).

***μυριονταπλασίως**, *ten thousandfold, infinitely*, Epiph.*anc*.7(p.14.10; M.43.28C); *ib*.47(p.56.28; 100C).

***μυριοπαθής**, *of countless passions*, Bas.*renunt*.3(2.205A; M.31.632D).

***μυριοπλασιάζω**, *multiply ten thousand times*, *T.Isach*.3.7.

μυρίος, **1.** *countless, infinite*, as name for BMV *M*. δὲ αὐτῆς τοὔνομα, ἥτις ἐν μήτρᾳ ὡς ἐν πελάγει μυριαγωγὸν ὁλκάδα φέρει *Pers*.(p.12.11; M.10.100C); **2.** neut. plur. as adv., *infinitely* κἂν...μ. τις εἴπῃ καλῶς Just.*dial*.115.6(M.6.744A); οἱ...ἀπόστολοι μ. ὑβριζόμενοι Or.*hom.14.14 in Jer*.(p.120.14; M.13.421D); Epiph.*haer*.75.7(p.339.11; M.42.513C).

***μυριόσταχυς**, *with countless ears*, Geo.Pis.*hex*.1323(M.92.1536A).

μυριότιμος, *of infinite value*, Thdr.Stud.*nativ.BMV* 7(M.96.693B).

***μυριότροπος**, *in countless forms*, Gr.Nyss.*hom.8 in Eccl*.(M.44.744B).

***μυριοτρόπως**, *in countless ways*, Gr.Nyss.*Eun*.2(2 p.351.23; M.45.529A).

***μυριοτρόφος**, *feeding countless numbers*, Geo.Pis.*hex*.1793(M.92.1573A).

***μυριόχειλος**, *with ten thousand lips*, Sophr.H.*or*.2.5(M.87.3224A).

μυρίπνοος, *breathing perfume, sweet-scented*, *Orac.Sib*.5.129; Jo.Mon.*hymn.Geo*.9(M.96.1400C).

μύρισμα, τό, *unguent, perfume*, *T.Abr*.A 20(p.103.22).

μυρισμός, ὁ, *ointment, perfume*, ref. Lc.7:37 προσδέχεται γὰρ ὁ κτίσας ἡμᾶς...θρήνου μ., καὶ σταγετὸν δακρύων Nil.*epp*.3.243(M.79.500D).

μυριώνυμος, *of countless names*, *T.Sal*.15.2(M.122.1337A); †Gr.Thaum.*ep.Philagr*.(M.46.1104B).

μυρμηκία, ἡ, *wart*, fig. οἷον μ. τινὲς τοῦ διανοητικοῦ μέρους τῆς ψυχῆς ἐκφυόμεναι Gr.Nyss.*anim.et res*.(M.46.56C).

μυρμηκι-άω, **1.** *be afflicted with warts* δῶρον μνησικάκου ~ῶσα θυσία Nil.*spir.mal*.10(M.79.1156A); **2.** ? *cause to itch*, hence fig., *stimulate* ~ῶντας...λόγους Geo.Pis.*hex*.32(M.92.1429A).

μυρμηκίζω, *become an ant*, ‡Just.*qu.Gr*.15(M.6.1484C).

μυρμήκιον, τό, *ant*, Jo.Mosch.*prat*.184(M.87.3056C).

μυρμηκολέων, ὁ, *ant-lion*, ref. Job 4:11 τὰ μὲν ἐμπρόσθια ἔχει λέοντος, τὰ δὲ ὀπίσθια μύρμηκος. ... δύο φύσεις [sc. ἔχων]...οὐ δύναται φάγειν κρέα διὰ τὴν φύσιν τῆς μητρός, οὐδὲ ὄσπρια διὰ τὴν φύσιν τοῦ πατρός· ἀπόλλυται οὖν διὰ τὸ μὴ ἔχειν τροφήν *Phys*.A 20 (p.73.8); μ. ... τοιοῦτόν τι σημαίνειν ἔοικε. ... αἱ προσβολαὶ τῶν παθῶν ἀπὸ εὐτελῶν ἄρχονται φαντασιῶν, μύρμηκος δίκην λανθανόντως προσέρπουσαι· τὰ δὲ τελευταῖα ἐπὶ μέγαν ἐξαίρεται ὄγκον, ὡς οὐκ ἔλαττον λέοντος ἐπιδρομῆς τῷ παρατυχόντι παρέχειν τὸν κίνδυνον Nil.*exerc*.49(M.79.780C); τῷ δὲ μ. τὸν διάβολον [sc. ἀπεικαστέον] μύρμηκα μὲν ὄντα τοῖς εὐσεβέσι, λέοντα δὲ τοῖς ἀσεβέσιν Olymp.*Job* 4:11(M.93.73A); Germ.CP *or*.1(M.98.236D).

***μυροβαφής**, *dipped in perfume*, Clem.*paed*.2.10(p.222.19; M.8.528A).

***μυρόβλυτος**, *giving forth perfume*, of a saint's relics μύρον ἅγιον ἐκ τοῦ φρέατος ἀντλήσασα, ἐν ᾧ τὸ σῶμα τοῦ μ. θείου Δημητρίου τοῦτο ἀναβλύζον κεῖται *CIG* 8642 [Santinum, saec. vi].

***μυροδοτέω**, *produce unguent*; of a saint's relic, Thphn.*chron*. p.370(M.108.885C).

***μυροδόχος**, *bearing sweet perfume*, Tim.Ant.*nativ.Jo.Bapt*.1 (M.28.908A).

μυροθήκη, ἡ, *vase of perfume*; met., of a saint μ. γενόμενος πνεύματος ἁγίου καὶ εὐωδία Χριστοῦ Jo.Mon.*hymn.Blas*.4(M.96.1401D); of BMV μ. τοῦ πνεύματος πάντερπνε Rom.Mel.(*KlT* p.9).

μύρον, τό, *perfume, unguent, sweet oil*;

A. in gen.; **1.** many kinds employed τῶν μ. ἄπειροι διαφοραί, βρένθιον καὶ μετάλλιον καὶ βασίλειον πλαγγόνιόν τε καὶ ψάγδας Αἰγύπτιος...ἐπιτηδεύουσι δὲ καὶ τὸ ἀπὸ κρίνων μ. καὶ τὸ ἀπὸ τῆς κύπρου, καὶ ἡ νάρδος εὐδοκιμεῖ...καὶ τὸ ἀπὸ τῶν ῥόδων ἄλειμμα...οἷς ἔτι χρῶνται γυναῖκες, ὑγρά τε καὶ ξηρὰ καὶ τὰ ἐπίπαστα καὶ ὑποθυμιώμενα μ. Clem.*paed*.2.8(p.196.7; M.8.469A); **2.** used at festal banquets, *A.Thom*.A 5(p.107.3); at pagan festivals, ‡Just.*coh.Gr*.4 (M.6.236C); **3.** moderate use permissible, Clem.*paed*.2.8(p.198.22; M.8.476B) cit. s. μυραλοιφέω; ὡς μὲν οὖν ἐν φαρμάκου μοίρᾳ ἰάσεως ἕνεκα...οὐκ ἀποβλητέον τὴν ἀπὸ τῶν ἀνθῶν τέρψιν καὶ τὴν ἀπὸ μ. ... ὠφέλειαν *ib*.(p.203.28; 488B); but abstained from by ascetics, Gr.Naz.*or*.44.9(M.36.617B); Chrys.*sac*.6.2(p.143.9; 1.422C); id.*Laz*.1.8(1.718D); **4.** in simile illustrating Trin. doctrine ἡ εὐωδία ἐκ τοῦ μ. ἐστί, καὶ οὔτε μετὰ τὸ μ., οὔτε ἐκτὸς τοῦ μ., ἀλλὰ μετὰ τοῦ μ., καὶ ἐν τῷ μ., καὶ σὺν τῷ μ. ‡Ath.*dial.Trin*.2.1(M.28.1160A); **5.** believed to exude from martyr's relics, *A.Phil*.147(p.89.12); *M.Thdot.2* 3(p.86.24); πολλὰ γὰρ σώματα τῶν ἁγίων μύρον ἔβλυσαν ‡Jo.D.*Const*.2(M.95.312D); cf.*A.Jo*.17(p.160.33); **6.** used in magic, *Hom.Clem*.20.16.

B. use in OT: in consecration of priests, Eus.*d.e*.4.15(p.174.17; M.22.292A); Gr.Nyss.*v.Mos*.(M.44.321B); id.*or.dom*.3(p.46.10; M.44.1149A); Ph.Carp.*Cant*.4(M.40.37C); in unction of kings, *ib*.; described as πιστικὸν ἢ μυστικόν, *Euchol*.(p.509); in comparison of Christ's unction with that of high priests, Eus.*d.e*.4.15(p.176.7; 293B).

C. in Christian ritual; **1.** signifies grace of H. Ghost, Thdt.*Cant*. 1:2(2.28); or Christ τὸ τίμιον μ. τὸ σύμβολον τοῦ δεσπότου Χριστοῦ Dion.Ar.*e.h*.4.3.10(M.3.497A); **2.** freq. employed τῷ θείῳ μ. πρὸς πᾶσαν τελεσιουργίαν χρῆται ἡ ἱεραρχία *ib*.(497B); **3.** in post-baptismal unction (confirmation) ἐβάπτισεν αὐτοὺς...χρίσας αὐτοὺς τῷ ἁγίῳ μ. καὶ μετέδωκεν αὐτοῖς τῶν...μυστηρίων *A.Thadd*.4(p.275.9); Hipp.*Dan*.1.16.3 cit. s. χρίω; exeg. Is.25:7, Eus.ad loc.(M.24.268C); conveying participation in Christ ὑμεῖς δὲ μύρῳ ἐχρίσθητε, κοινωνοὶ καὶ μέτοχοι τοῦ Χριστοῦ γενόμενοι Cyr.H.*catech*.21.2; and sanctification by H. Ghost τῷ μὲν φαινομένῳ μ. τὸ σῶμα χρίεται, τῷ δὲ ἁγίῳ καὶ ζωοποιῷ πνεύματι ἡ ψυχὴ ἁγιάζεται *ib*.21.3; *Const.App*.3.16.4 cit. s. ἔλαιον; associated with consignation τελευταῖον σφραγίσεις μύρῳ, ἵνα...ᾖ...τὸ...μ. σφραγὶς τῶν συνθηκῶν *ib*.7.22.2; ὁ θεός σε μύρῳ ἐτίμησε πνευματικῷ Chrys.*hom.12.7 in 1Cor*.(10.107E); καταχριόμεθα γὰρ μύρῳ κατὰ τὸν καιρὸν μάλιστα τοῦ ἁγίου βαπτίσματος σύμβολον τοῦ μεταλαχεῖν ἁγίου πνεύματος Cyr.*Is*.3.1(2.353E); χριόμεθα...μύρῳ πρὸς ἀνάμνησιν τοῦ τὴν χρίσιν τοῦ μ. ἐνταφιασμὸν ἑαυτοῦ λογιζομένου ‡Just.*qu.et resp*.137(M.6.1389D); οἱ τελούμενοι...οἱονεὶ σφραγῖδα τινὰ βασιλικὴν δέχονται τοῦ πνευματικοῦ μ. τὸ χρῖσμα Thdt.*Cant*.1:2(2.30); πρῶτον μὲν βαπτιζόμεθα, εἶτα τῷ μ. χριόμεθα, ἐκεῖθεν τοῦ τιμίου ἀξιούμεθα αἵματος Job.Mon.ap.Phot.*cod*.222.18(M.103.756C); ἡ δὲ τοῦ μ. τελειωτικὴ χρίσις εὐώδη ποιεῖ τὸν τετελεσμένον Dion.Ar.*e.h*.2.3.8(M.3.404C); διὰ τῆς τοῦ μ. χρίσεως ἐπιφοιτᾷ τὸ πνεῦμα τὸ ἅγιον *ib*.4.3.11(497C); χρίει ὁ ἱερεὺς τοὺς βαπτισθέντας τὸ ἅγιον μ., ποιῶν σταυροῦ τύπον ἐπὶ τοῦ μετώπου...λέγων· σφραγὶς δωρεᾶς πνεύματος ἁγίου *Rit.Bapt*.(p.405); *Euchol*.(p.291); Gnost. μυρίζουσι τὸν τετελεσμένον τῷ ὀπῷ τῷ ἀπὸ βαλσάμου· τὸ γὰρ μ. τοῦτο τύπον τῆς ὑπὲρ τὰ ὅλα εὐωδίας εἶναι λέγουσιν Iren.*haer*.1.21.3(M.7.664B); **4.** in reception of heretics τοῦ αἱρετικοῦ ἐπὶ τὴν ὀρθοδοξίαν ἐρχομένου τὸ σφάλμα διορθοῦται...τοῦ...βαπτίσματος τῇ ἐπιχρίσει τοῦ ἁγίου μ. ‡Just.*qu.et resp*.14(M.6.1261D); CCP(381)‡*can*.7; πρώτη μὲν τάξις ἐστὶ τῶν δεομένων τοῦ ἁγίου βαπτίσματος. δευτέρα δὲ τῶν μὴ βαπτιζομένων, χριομένων δὲ τῷ μ. τῷ ἁγίῳ Tim.CP *haer*.(M.86.13A); **5.** in unction of sick μ., ἢ ἕτερον ἅγιον ἔλαιον, ὁ περιχρίειν θέλων νοσοῦντα ‡Jo.D.*fid.dorm*.18(M.95.264C); cf.‡Jo.D.*Const*.2(M.95.312D); **6.** in consecration of baptismal water τὸ...ὕδωρ ταῖς ἱεραῖς ἐπικλήσεσι καθαγιάσας, καὶ τρισὶ τοῦ παναγεστάτου μ. σταυροειδέσι χύσεσι τελειώσας αὐτό Dion.Ar.*e.h*.2.2.7(M.3.396C); **7.** in consecration of altar τὸ θεῖον θυσιαστήριον ἐν τῷ τιμίῳ τελειοῦμεν μ. *ib*.4.3.12 (497D); **8.** material of its composition ἡ τοῦ μ. σύνθεσις συναγωγή τίς ἐστιν εὐπνόων ὑλῶν ἐν ἑαυτῇ πλουσίως ἔχουσα ποιότητας εὐόσμους *ib*.4.3.4(477C); recipe for its manufacture, and distinction between τὸ ἡμέτερον μ. and τὸ πιστικὸν μ., *Euchol*.(pp.508–9); **9.** its consecration τὸ ἅγιον...μ., οὐκ ἔτι ψιλὸν...μετ' ἐπίκλησιν· ἀλλὰ Χριστοῦ χάρισμα καὶ πνεύματος ἁγίου...ἐνεργητικὸν γινόμενον Cyr.H.*catech*.21.3; consecration prayer, *Const.App*.7.27; τοῦτο τὸ μ. δὸς ἐνεργὲς γενέσθαι ἐπὶ τῷ βαπτιζομένῳ, ὥστε βεβαίαν...ἐν αὐτῷ τὴν εὐωδίαν μεῖναι τοῦ Χριστοῦ σου, καὶ συναποθανόντα αὐτὸν συναναστῆναι...αὐτῷ *ib*.7.44.2; consecrated on altar, Dion.Ar.*e.h*.4.2(M.3.473A); Πέτρον φησὶ τὸν Κναφέα ἐπινοῆσαι τὸ μυστήριον [prob. for μύρον] ἐν τῇ ἐκκλησίᾳ ἐπὶ παντὸς τοῦ λαοῦ ἁγιάζεσθαι Thdr.Lect.*h.e*.2.48(M.86.208A).

D. exeg.; **1.** of Ps.132:2 ἐπεὶ Χριστὸς κεφαλή ἐστι τῆς ἐκκλησίας ...τὸ μ. ἐπὶ κεφαλῆς καταβέβηκεν ἐπὶ τὸν πώγωνα, τὰ σύμβολα τοῦ τελείου ἀνδρὸς Ἀαρών, καὶ ἔφθασε καταβαῖνον τοῦτο τὸ μ. ἐπὶ τὴν ὤαν τοῦ ἐνδύματος αὐτοῦ Or.*Cels*.6.79(p.151.3; M.11.1417D); adduced as argument for wearing of beards, Clem.*paed*.3.3(p.249.32; M.8.588A); **2.** of Cant.1:3 τὸ ὄνομά σου, νύμφιε, μ. ἐστίν, καὶ μ. ... κεκενωμένον. ποῖον δ' ἂν γένοιτο ὄνομα μύρου κεκενωμένου δηλωτικὸν ἢ τὸ τοῦ Χριστοῦ ὄνομα; οὐ γὰρ ἂν ἄλλως...ὀνομασθείη Χριστὸς ἢ μ. προσχυθέντος Eus.*d.e*.4.16(p.195.18ff.; M.22.325A); Gr.Naz.*carm*.1.2.8.107 (M.37.656A); ὡς ἐπὶ τῶν ἀγγείων, ὧν ἂν ἐκκενωθῇ τὸ μ. αὐτὸ μὲν τῇ ἑαυτοῦ φύσει ἀγνοεῖται τὸ μ. τὸ ἐκκενωθὲν τῶν ἀγγείων, οἷόν ἐστιν· ἐξ ἀμυδρᾶς δέ τινος τῆς ὑπολειφθείσης ἐκ τῶν ἀτμῶν τῷ ἀγγείῳ ποιότητος, στοχασμόν τινα περὶ τοῦ ἐκκενωθέντος μ. ποιούμεθα. τοῦτο μανθάνομεν, ὅτι, αὐτὸ μὲν τὸ τῆς θεότητος μ. ὅ τί ποτε κατ' οὐσίαν ἐστίν, ὑπὲρ πᾶν ἐστιν ὄνομα...τὰ δὲ τῷ παντὶ ἐνθεωρούμενα θαύματα, τῶν θεολογικῶν ὀνομάτων τὴν ὕλην δίδωσι, δι' ὧν σοφόν, δυνατόν...κατονομάζομεν Gr.Nyss.*hom.1 in Cant.*(M.44.781Df.); μ. ἐκκενωθὲν ὄνομά σου, δύο ὑποσημαίνει τρόπους. καθάπερ γὰρ μ. ἐκκενωθὲν οἶκον εὐωδιάζει· οὕτω τοῦ κυρίου...ἐπὶ γῆς κατελθόντος...ὅλος ὁ κόσμος τῇ εὐσεβείᾳ εὐωδιάσθη ...ἐν τούτῳ δὲ προφητικὸν σημαίνει τρόπον καὶ τῆς μακαρίας Μαρίας, ἥτις συντρίψασα τὸ ἀλάβαστρον τοῦ μ. ἤλειψε τὸν κύριον Ph.Carp.*Cant.*3(M.40.37C); καθάπερ γὰρ τὸ μ., ἐν ἀγγείῳ κεκρυμμένον, κεκρυμμένην ἔχει καὶ τὴν εὐοσμίαν, εἰ δὲ προχυθείη, καὶ αὐτὸν ἀναπίμπλησι τὸν ἀέρα, οὕτως ὁ...Χριστὸς πρὸ μὲν τοῦ πάθους ὀλίγοις ἦν γνώριμος, ἐπειδὴ δὲ...ὑπέμεινε καὶ τὸν θάνατον, καὶ οἱονεὶ διηνοίγη τὸ τοῦ σώματος ἄγγος, πλήρεις μὲν εὐθὺς οἱ...ἀπόστολοι τῆς εὐοσμίας ἐκείνης ἐγένοντο Thdt.*Cant.*1:2(2.30); interpreted of baptism, *ib.*; ὥσπερ τὸ συνεχόμενον μ. κενούμενον δῆλον γίνεται τῇ εὐωδίᾳ, οὕτω τὸ σὸν ὄνομα...ἔτι σου ὄντος ἐν τοῖς πατρικοῖς κόλποις ἀγνοούμενον, μετὰ τὴν κένωσιν, ἴσα κενωθέντι μύρῳ αὐτόθεν ἔχει τὴν μαρτυρίαν τῇ τῶν σημείων δυνάμει πιστούμενον †Nil.ap.Proc.G.*Cant.*1:2(M.87.1549C, v. not. ad loc. on authorship); cf. ἔχω τι καὶ μ., ἀλλ' ᾧ χρίονται μόνον ἱερεῖς τε καὶ βασιλεῖς...δι' ἡμᾶς κενωθέντι Gr.Naz.*or.*5.35(M.35.709A); typifies BMV, Thdr.Stud.*nativ.BMV* 7(M.96.693B) cit. s. μυρίζω; **3.** of Mt.26:6–13, Jo.12:1–8, cf. διὰ τοῦτο μ. ἔλαβεν ἐπὶ τῆς κεφαλῆς... ὁ κύριος, ἵνα πνέῃ τῇ ἐκκλησίᾳ ἀφθαρσίαν Ign.*Eph.*17.1; Clem.*paed.*2.8(p.194.10,25; M.8.465B,468A) cit. s. ἀλείφω; ὁπηνίκα...γυνή τις ἀλάβαστρον μύρου...κατέχεεν, ὅτε καὶ θρύλλος...ἐγένετο, ὡς ἐχρῆν...πένητας ἐκ τοῦ μ. τραφῆναι, καὶ μὴ τὸν πτωχεύσαντα δι' ἡμᾶς μυρισθῆναι, τοῦτον δὲ τὸν γογγυσμὸν ὁ τῆς προδοσίας ἐργάτης ἀνέκαυσεν, ὁ τριακοσίων μὲν δηναρίων τὸ τῆς βοτάνης μ. ἀποτιμησάμενος, τριάκοντα δὲ τὸ οὐράνιον μ. τὸ κενωθὲν ἐπὶ γῆς ἐν παροινίᾳ πωλῶν Mac.Mgn.*apocr.*3.14(p.93.19); Ph.Carp.*Cant.*3(M.40.37C) cit. s. 2 supra.

E. met.; of H. Ghost γυνὴ δὲ ἀποπνεῖτο Χριστοῦ...ἀεὶ δὲ...ἁγίῳ τερπομένη μ. τῷ πνεύματι. τοῦτο σκευάζει Χριστὸς...ἐκ τῶν οὐρανίων συντιθεὶς ἀρωμάτων τὸ μ. τούτῳ καὶ αὐτὸς ὁ κύριος συναλείφεται τῷ μ. Clem.*paed.*2.8(p.197.1; M.8.472B); χάρισαι καὶ ἡμῖν τῆς εὐωδίας τοῦ παναγίου σου πνεύματος μ. ἄχραντον *Lit.Jac.*(p.236.8); of good report ἡ σώφρων γυνὴ...μύρου...πνέει τῆς ἀγαθῆς φήμης *Hom.Clem.* 13.16; of compunction ἡ ψυχὴ τὸ πολυτελὲς τοῦτο μ. κατασκευάζουσα τὴν κατάνυξιν λέγω Chrys.*compunct.*2.1(1.142B); of episcopal rank ἀντεδώκαμεν...τῆς ἱερατικῆς ἀξίας τὸ μ. ἐξ ἀποστολικῆς αὐθεντίας ἐσφραγισμένον Martin.*ep.*7(M.*PL.*87.165B); as compound substance (opp. simple nature of oil), represents combination of many virtues, Eus.*d.e.*4.15(p.176.7; M.22.293B).

***μυροπνευστός**, *breathing perfume*, of Epiphany σήμερον ῥείθροις μ. πᾶσα ἡ κτίσις ἀρδεύεται *Rit.Epiph.*(p.433.3).

***μυροτόκος**, *bearing perfume*, of S. Paul ἡ μ. πηγή †Cyr.*hom.div.* 11(5^2.383B).

***μυροφορ-έω**, *bear ointment* or *perfume*, ref. Lc.7:38 πόρναι ~οῦσαι †Chrys.*nativ.*1(6.393D).

μυροφόρος, *bearing unguents* or *perfumes*; of S. Paul τὸ σκεῦος τῆς ἐκλογῆς, τὸ μ. ἀγγεῖον ‡Ath.*proph.*1(M.28.1064A); of women at Christ's tomb (Mc.16:1), ‡Ath.*qu.Ant.*11(M.28.697B); εὗρον αἱ μ., ὅπερ διὰ τῆς Εὔας ἀπώλεσαν Hesych.H.*serm.*7(M.93.1477C); ‡Sophr. H.*liturg.*4(M.87.3985A); Gr.Ant.*mul.ung.*tit.(M.88.1848); as title of Mary Magdalene, Mod.*mul.ung.*(M.86.3273A); met. πλησιάζουσι τῷ μ. καὶ γλυκορήμονι, τῷ ἐξερευγομένῳ λόγον ἀγαθὸν Ant.Mon.*hom.*16 (M.89.1476D).

[*]**μυροψός, ὁ**, = μυρεψός, *perfumer*, *MAMA* 3.289 (Corycus).

***μυρσινεών, ὁ**, *myrtle-grove*, name given to fore-court of chapel of S. Thecla, Bas.Sel.*v.Thecl.*2.7(M.85.576B).

μυρώδης, *sweet-scented*, Areth.*Apoc.*2:18(M.106.540A).

***μυρωδία, ἡ**, *unguent*, met., of unction by divine grace, Thdr. Stud.*or.*8.8(M.99.768C) cit. s. ἄπνοος.

μύσαγμα, τό, *defilement*, Eus.*v.C.*3.26(p.90.2; M.20.1088A).

***μυσαροποιΐα, ἡ**, *disgusting activity* τὸ τέλειον τῆς κατ' αὐτοὺς [sc. τοὺς γνωστικούς] μυσταγωγίας ἢ καὶ μᾶλλον μ. Eus.*h.e.*4.7.9(M.20. 320A).

μυσαρός, *loathsome, abominable*; of pagan worship, Eus.*v.C.*3.26 (p.89.34; M.20.1085C); μυσερ-, id.*h.e.*4.11.4 (μυσαρ- M.20.329A); Ath. *gent.*23,24(M.25.45C,49B); ταῖς μυσαρωτάταις τῶν δαιμόνων λατρείαις προσκείμενοι Cyr.*Os.*6(3.26B); Sophr.H.*v.Cyr.et Jo.*24(M.87.3409A); of moral faults μ. ζήλους *1Clem.*14.1; *ib.*30.1; φιλαργυρία...μισάνθρωπός τε καὶ μ. Isid.Pel.*epp.*2.233(M.78.672A); Cyr.*ador.*11(1.397A); μ. ...τὸν γάμον...ἀποκαλοῦσιν, ἵνα τὸν τοιούτων δημιουργὸν ἐνυβρίσωσι Thdt.*1Tim.*4:3(3.659); neut. as subst., id.*Eph.*5:3(3.430); of heresy, Ath.*Ar.*1.55(M.26.125B); ἵνα...παύσωνται τῆς πρὸς ἐκεῖνον μ. κοινωνίας id.*apol.sec.*39(p.118.6; M.25.316C); id.*Dion.*13(p.56.1; M.25.500B).

***μυσαρότης, ἡ**, *foulness*, Cyr.*Jo.*4.5(4.395E).

μυσάττομαι, *feel disgust at, loathe*; in pass. sense, Pall.*h.Laus.*34 (p.98.15; M.34.1106B).

[*]**μυσεράρχης, ὁ**, = μυσάρχης, *source of defilement*; of heresiarchs, Eulog.*fr.Trin.*(M.86.2941C).

μυσερός, = μυσαρός, Thphl.Ant.*Autol.*3.5(M.6.1125C); τὰς ἀτελέστους αὐτῶν [sc. γνωστικῶν] τελετὰς μ. τε μυσταγωγίας Eus.*h.e.*4.11. 4(M.20.329A); id.*d.e.*5 proem.(p.208.21; νοσερῶν M.22.345C).

[*]**μυσερῶς**, = μυσαρῶς, *abominably, disgracefully*, Const.ap.Eus. *h.e.*10.5.22 (v.l. μυσαρῶς M.20.889B).

μῦσος, τό, *pollution, defilement*, hence *polluted thing*; fig., of a heretic, Gel.Cyz.*h.e.*3.13.19.

μύσσω, **1.** = μύω, *close the eyes*, ‡Meth.*Sym.et Ann.*11(M.18. 376C); **2.** sens. dub., *cat.Apoc.*9:3(p.313.10).

μυσταγωγ-έω, **1.** *initiate into mysteries*; of Christian mysteries τῶν ἐν παρθενίᾳ ~ηθέντων αἱ τελεταί Meth.*symp.*6.5(p.69.16; M.18. 120C); προῆλθεν ὁ Ἀντώνιος ὥσπερ ἔκ τινος ἀδύτου μεμυσταγωγημένος καὶ θεοφορούμενος Ath.*v.Anton.*14(M.26.864C); of Christian sacraments: baptism, Or.*Cels.*3.60(p.255.1; M.11.100B); Bas.*hom.*13.5(2. 119B; M.31.436D); φωνῆς...ἣν ἀφῆκας ~ουμένη, Ἀποτάσσομαί σοι, σατανᾶ Chrys.*catech.*2.4(2.242C); Pall.*v.Chrys.*5(p.28.13; M.47.18); id.*h.Laus.*45(p.133.14; M.34.1218A); of eucharist τὸν ἐπίσκοπον τὸν ἐν αὐτῷ [sc. τῷ ποτηρίῳ] ~οῦντα CAlex.*ep.*ap.Ath.*apol.sec.*17(p.100. 7; M.25.276C); τῆς φρικτῆς ταύτης τραπέζης προκειμένης, τῶν ἀδελφῶν σου ~ουμένων ἔτι, αὐτὸς καταλιπὼν ἀποπηδᾷς; Chrys.*bapt.*4(2.374D); Alex.Sal.*Barn.*1(440D); of both sacraments ἴσασιν οἱ ~ούμενοι, δι' ὕδατος μὲν ἀναγεννώμενοι, δι' αἵματος δὲ καὶ σαρκὸς τρεφόμενοι Chrys.*hom.85.3 in Jo.*(8.507E); **2.** abs., *perform sacred rites*; of tribe of Levi, Cyr.*Lc.*20:2(M.72.884A); **3.** *lead into, instruct in, divine mysteries*, exeg. Gen.22:3 καὶ δι' ἀγγέλου προσεχῶς ~εῖται Clem.*str.*5.11(p.375.22; M.9.112A); Or.*Cels.*6.23(p.93.29; M.11.1325C); εἰς τὸν...τῶν προφητῶν κόπον οἱ ἀπόστολοι εἰσεληλύθασιν, Ἰησοῦ ~οῦντος, θερίζοντες...τὸν ἐν ἐκείνοις νοῦν id.*Jo.*13.50(49; p.277.11; M. 14.488D); τῆς εἰς τὸ κοινὸν ἐπιμιξίας, καὶ ὑποχωρήσεως, τῆς μὲν τοὺς ἄλλους παιδαγωγούσης, τῆς δὲ τῷ πνεύματι ~ούσης Gr.Naz.*or.*6.2(M. 35.724B); Μωϋσῆς...ἐπὶ τοῦ ὄρους ~ούμενος Gr.Nyss.*Steph.*1(M.46. 713B); ref. Eph.3:18 Παῦλος ~εῖ τὸν ἐν Ἐφέσῳ λαὸν id.*or.catech.*32 (p.120.15; M.45.81B); Παῦλον...ἐν αὐταῖς ταῖς ἁλύσεσι κατηχοῦντα, ~οῦντα Chrys.*stat.*1.11(2.17E); Pall.*v.Chrys.*9(p.56.10; M.47.33); μ. αὐτοὺς καὶ τὸ βαθὺ καὶ μέγα τῆς ἐνανθρωπήσεως ἐκκαλύπτει μυστήριον Cyr.*Is.*4.4(2.665D); *ib.*5.1(733B); ‡Gr.Nyss.*hom.7 in Jo.*(p.272.6); νοῦν παθῶν γυμνωθέντα εὑρίσκον τὸ πνεῦμα τὸ ἅγιον μ. Thal.*cent.*4.75(M. 91.1465C); ἡ ἀληθὴς ἱερωσύνη...τῆς ἰδίας μεταδίδωσι γνώσεως εἰρήνης τε καὶ ἀγάπης, ἵνα...θεῷ παραστήσῃ διὰ πάντων θεωθέντας τοὺς ὑπ' αὐτῆς ~ουμένους Max.*ep.*31(M.91.625A); *teach in a mystery, in veiled terms*, Didym.*Trin.*2.6(M.39.524B); **4.** *unfold the meaning of* διὰ τούτων ~οῦντος τὴν θέωσιν Gr.Naz.*or.*25.2(M.35.1200B); [Ps.68:14] τοῦτο ~ῶν ὁ ἀπόστολος εἶπεν [Eph.2:5] Diod.*Ps.*68:14(M.33.1604B); med., ref. Ps.109:3 ~εῖται [sc. ὁ ἱερεύς] γαστέρα θεὸν ἀγέννητον, τουτέστι τὸν πατέρα ‡Bas.*h.myst.*60(p.395.9); c. dupl. acc. ὁ...τῷ Ἀβραὰμ παραφανεὶς θεὸς...μ. τὸν θεοφιλῆ τὰς περὶ τοῦ πατρὸς αὐθεντίας Eus.*d.e.*1.5(p.22.18; M.22.48B); τὰ μὲν εἰς ἀκοὰς πάντων ἐκήρυττε, τὰ δὲ μόνους τοὺς αὐτοῦ μαθητὰς ἐμυσταγώγει id.*qu.Steph.*1.1(M.22. 881B); ~εῖ τὸ πάσχα τοὺς μαθητὰς ἐν ὑπερῴῳ Gr.Naz.*or.*40.30(M.36. 401B); Cyr.*Is.*2.1(2.210C); **5.** *lead in mysterious ways, providentially order* ὁ ~ήσας σε [sc. θεοτόκον] θεὸς γενέσθαι πρὸς αὐτόν, τοῦ πρεσβεύειν ὑπὲρ ἡμῶν Mod.*dorm.*10(M.86.3301C); *ib.*14(3312B).

***μυσταγώγημα, τό**, *mystery, thing revealed*, Tim.Ant.*descr.BMV* 1(M.28.944B); *ib.*8(956A).

***μυσταγώγησις, ἡ**, *revelation, new teaching*, Cyr.ap.*cat.Lc.*6:27 (p.52.1) for μυσταγωγοῖς Cyr.ad loc.(M.72.593C).

μυσταγωγία, ἡ, **A.** *initiation into mysteries*; **1.** fig., of Christianity τῶν καλουμένων εἰς ζωὴν καὶ τῆς ἀχράντου μ. εἰς πέρας, δι' ἧς τὸ θεῖον αὐτοῖς ἐνίεται φῶς Cyr.*Is.*5.2(2.785B); τοῖς τῆς ἱερᾶς μ. τὴν τελετὴν ...τετελεσμένοις Dion.Ar.*e.h.*1.1(M.3.372A); **2.** met., of Christian sacraments; **a.** baptism ἡ ἑκάστου ἡμῶν διὰ τῆς τοιαύτης μ. πρὸς τὴν θεογνωσίαν εἰσαγωγή Bas.*Spir.*75(3.64A; M.32.209A); τὰ σῆς μ. ῥήματα *baptismal rite*, Gr.Naz.*or.*40.11(M.36.372C); ὕδωρ ἀναγεννᾷ καὶ ἡ ἐπ' ἐκείνῳ τελουμένη μ. Gr.Nyss.*bapt.Chr.*(M.46.584C); id.*Eun.*11(2 p.272.12; M.45.881C); Chrys.*hom.28.1 in Jo.*(8.159A); οὐ πρὸ τῆς εἰς Χριστὸν μ. ἀλλὰ μετὰ τὸ φώτισμα Pall.*v.Chrys.*15(p.92.19; M.47. 52); τῆς παραδοθείσης αὐτοῖς μ. *Cod.Afr.*72 (Lat. *sacramentum*); **b.** eucharist ἀπὸ τῆς ἀγορᾶς εἰς τὰ ἅγια...καὶ ἀπὸ τῶν θεάτρων ἐπὶ τὴν τοῖς πολλοῖς ἀθέατον μ. Gr.Naz.*or.*36.2(M.36.268A); ταύτην ἐσχάτην ὑμῖν ἔδωκε τὴν μ. Chrys.*hom.27.4 in 1Cor.*(10.246C); τῇ φρικτῇ καὶ θείᾳ ταύτῃ τραπέζῃ καὶ ἱερᾷ μ. id.*nativ.*7(2.364E); ἀναφορᾷ τῆς μ. ἱερουργούμενον Max.*myst.*(M.91.669A); ἐτελεῖτο ἡ θεία μ. κατὰ τὸ σύνηθες ‡Sophr.H.*v.Mar.Aeg.*6(M.87.3701D); **c.** of Marcosian initiations, Eus.*h.e.*4.11.4(M.20.329A) cit. s. μυσερός; esp. sacrament of bridal-chamber, Iren.*haer.*1.21.3(M.7.661A); v. νυμφών; of Montanist practices ἀφθόρου παιδὸς κατακεντᾷ τὸ σῶμα καὶ τὸ αἷμα πρὸς μετάληψιν ἀποφέρεται...εἰς μ. ὀνόματος Χριστοῦ Epiph.*haer.*48.15 (p.241.12; M.41.880B); **3.** *celebration of rites* μὴ κατόπιν ἑορτῆς δραμεῖν, μηδὲ μαρτύρων μυσταγωγίας ἀπολειφθῆναι Gr.Naz.*or.*24.3 (M.35.1173A); **4.** *priesthood* ἔστι καὶ ἱερωσύνη φιλόσοφος καὶ φιλοσοφία δεομένη μυσταγωγίας *ib.*21.19(1104B); χρήμασιν ἀλλ' οὐ πνεύματι τὰς χειροθεσίας τῆς μ. ἐπιτρέποντα Isid.Pel.*epp.*1.26(M.78.200A).

B. *revelation* τὰ λοιπὰ τῆς μ. αὐτῶν [sc. Gnostics] Iren.*haer.*1.15.6 (M.7.628B); τοὺς μέλλοντας εἰς τὸ τέλειον τῆς κατ' αὐτοὺς μ. ... ἐλεύσεσθαι Eus.*h.e.*4.7.9(M.20.320A); τῇ κατὰ τὸ ὄρος [sc. Sinai] μ. Gr. Nyss.*or.dom.*2(p.26.31; M.44.1136D); εἴτε σῶμα ἦν εἴτε νόημα ἐν τῷ καιρῷ τῆς ἐν τῷ παραδείσῳ μ. id.*hom.8 in Cant.*(M.44.940D); προφήταις καὶ ἁγίοις ἀποστόλοις τε καὶ εὐαγγελισταῖς οἱ τῆς ἄνωθεν μ. καταπλουτοῦντες τὴν χορηγίαν Cyr.*Is.*3.1(2.368E); of revelation of mystery of Inc. at Annunciation τῆς γενομένης τῇ παρθένῳ παρὰ τοῦ Γαβριὴλ μ. Gr.Nyss.*Apoll.*21(M.45.1165C); *ib.*43(1225A); at Christ's baptism τὸ πνεῦμα τὸ ἅγιον ἐπισφραγίζον τὴν θεοπρεπῆ μ. Sever. *appar.*8(M.65.21B); hence *mystery* πάντα οἰκονομεῖ τὰ τῆς τοιαύτης μεγάλης μ. ἡ τριάς Epiph.*haer.*69.64(p.213.31; M.42.308B); of mystery of new birth οὐκ ἀφίησι τοῖς ὀφθαλμοῖς τούτοις περιεργάσασθαι τὴν μ. Chrys.*hom.26.1 in Jo.*(8.149C); hence **1.** *explanation of a mystery* διὰ προφήτου Μωϋσέως εἰκόνας καὶ σύμβολα σαββάτου τινὸς γνωστικοῦ καὶ περιτομῆς...ἀλλ' οὐκ αὐτὰς ἐναργεῖς παρεδίδου τὰς μ. Eus.*h.e.*1.2.22(M.20.65A); ταῖς ἑξῆς μ. Cyr.H.*catech.*19.11; αἱ καθ' ἡμέραν μ. καὶ διδασκαλίαι *ib.*20.1; *contemplation of mysteries* τῆς μὲν πρακτικῆς φιλοσοφίας...τῆς δὲ φυσικῆς θεωρίας...τῆς δε θεολογικῆς μ. Max.*cap.*5.94(M.90.1388D); **2.** *institution of a* Christian *mystery*, of baptism τῇ γενομένῃ παρὰ τοῦ σωτῆρος τοῖς μαθηταῖς αὐτοῦ μ. Or. *fr.36 in Jo.*(p.512.15); Didym.*Trin.*2.1(M.39.448C); **3.** *spiritual teaching* in gen. οὐ δεῖ γὰρ ἁπλῶς καὶ ἀκρίτως πᾶσι προθεῖναι τῆς μ. τὸν λόγον Ath.*exp.Ps.*111:5(M.27.465C); τῆς τοῦ εὐαγγελίου μ. Ast. Am.*hom.*8(M.40.272C); Cyr.*Abac.*52(3.567C); of Christ's teaching προσεπάγει ταῖς μ. τὰς μεγαλουργίας id.*Lc.*4:30(M.72.545B); id.*Is.*1.5 (2.150B); οἱ ἑπτὰ τῶν τετρακισχιλίων ἄρτοι τὴν νομικὴν...μ. ὑποτυποῦσιν Max.*ambig.*(M.91.1401D); **4.** *veiled teaching, mystical expression* of a truth τὴν ἁγίαν τοῦ πάσχα ἡμέραν...τῶν ἐκεῖθεν ἀγαθῶν...μ. Gr.Naz.*ep.*120(M.37.213C); εἰς μαρτυρίαν τὴν ἐπὶ Χριστῷ ἥ τε διὰ νόμου καὶ προφητῶν ἁγίων μ. Cyr.*Is.*1.5(2.132E); *symbol conveying mystical truth* ἡ βροντὴ συνίσταται ἐξ ὕδατος καὶ πνεύματος, τοῦτο δέ ἐστιν ἡ τοῦ ἁγίου βαπτίσματος μ. ‡Ath.*dial.Trin.*3.27(M.28.1245A).

***μυσταγωγικός**, **1.** *proper to a* μυσταγωγός: τὸ μ. ἐπιτήδευμα Cyr. *Is.*3.4(2.508C); **2.** *that leads into spiritual truth*, Cyr.H.*catech.*19 tit.; μ. λόγος Cyr.*Am.*46(3.299E); Chrysipp.*enc.in Jo.Bapt.*2(p.31.13).

μυσταγωγός, ὁ, **1.** *initiator into* heathen *mysteries*; of Orpheus, Clem.*prot.*2(p.16.12; M.8.84B); Cels.ap.Or.*Cels.*8.48(p.263.1; M.11. 1588B); fig. αὕτη [sc. ἡ δι' ὀνείρων μαντική] μ. τε καὶ μύστις εὐαγγελίσασθαι τὸ ἀγαθὸν...καταμηνῦσαι τὸ χεῖρον Synes.*insomn.*13(p.171. 1; M.66.1305A); **2.** *spiritual leader* or *teacher*, of God αὐτοῖς [sc. pagans] ὁ μ. ... ὁ ἀναφέρων εἰς ἐπίγνωσιν ἀληθείας Cyr.*Is.*1.2(2.37B); of Christ on earth, ‡Gr.Naz.*Chr.pat.*196(M.38.152A); of Israel τοὺς πάλαι πολεμιωτάτους, φημὶ δὴ τοὺς ἐξ Ἰσραήλ, ἐποιοῦντο μ. καὶ καθηγητὰς ὁδοῦ τῆς ἀποφερούσης εἰς σωτηρίαν Cyr.*Is.*2.1(2.208A); of apostles and evangelists, Or.*exc.in Ps.*36:21(M.17.132B); Ath.*exp. Ps.*97:8(M.27.420D); Cyr.*Is.*3.1(2.358C); opp. prophets, *ib.*(383D); id.*Heb.*2:8(p.383.25); of Christian teachers in gen. παρέδωκε τοῖς μαθηταῖς τὰ οὐράνια μυστήρια καὶ τοῖς τῆς ἐκκλησίας μ. Thdr. Heracl.ap.*cat.Mt.*25:24(p.209.24); Tit.Bost.*fr.Lc.*10:2(p.187); κατὰ καιροὺς καὶ ἐν ἑκάστῃ χώρᾳ τε καὶ πόλει γεγονότες μ. καὶ διδάσκαλοι τῶν ἐκκλησιῶν Cyr.*Is.*3.5(2.530C); id.*Ag.*14(3.643B); ref. Jer.16:16 τοὺς μὲν ἁλιεῖς, τοὺς ἁγίους ἀποστόλους φησί, θηρευτὰς δὲ τοὺς κατὰ καιροὺς τῶν ἁγίων ἐκκλησιῶν ἡγουμένους τε καὶ μ. id. *fr.Lc.*5:2(M.72. 553A); Sophr.H.*ep.syn.*(M.87.3189B); of Gnost. teachers ὅσοι εἰσὶ ταύτης τῆς γνώμης μ., τοσαῦται ἀπολυτρώσεις Iren.*haer.*1.21.1(M.7. 657B); Clem.*str.*7.17(p.75.7; M.9.548A); **3.** c. genit., *expounder of a mystery* τοὺς τῆς σωτηρίας...μ. Gr.Naz.*or.*21.24(M.35.1109B); *ib.*39. 2(M.36.336B); τῆς ἀφθέγκτου οἰκονομίας...μ. Didym.*Trin.*2.8(M.39. 624C).

***μυστήπολος, ὁ**, *initiate*, Taras.*ep.*6(M.98.1477B); ‡Gr.Naz.*Chr. pat.*1167(M.38.229A).

μυστηριάρχης, ὁ, *chief initiate*; fig., of chief disciple of an heresiarch, Sophr.H.*ep.syn.*(M.87.3192B).

μυστηρικός, *secret*, ‡Ath.*synops.*46(M.28.380D).

***μυστηριολογέω**, *celebrate, describe in mysteries*; pagan, *Schol. Clem.prot.*(p.297.19; M.9.777C).

μυστήριον, τό, *mystery*;

A. *secret rite* οὐδὲ ἀνθρωπίνων οἰκονομίαν μ. πεπίστευνται *Diogn.* 7.1; οὐκ ἔστιν ἡμῖν μυστηρίων ἀνέδην μίξις Just.*1apol.*29.2(M.6.373A); fig. ταῦτα τῶν ἡμετέρων, ὦ καλλιπάρθενοι, τὰ ὄργια μυστηρίων Meth. *symp.*6.5(p.69.15; M.18.120C).

B. *oath of secrecy*, CCarth.*act.*(H.1.159–160D); ἡμῶν ἀδελφοῖς τὰς βίβλους μου τῶν κηρυγμάτων δὸς μετὰ τοῦ ὁμοίου τῆς ἀγωγῆς μυστηρίου *Clem.ep.Petr.*2(M.2.25B).

C. *sacred object* τὴν κιβωτὸν μεθ' ὧν μυστηρίων ἐπήγετο Proc.G. *Jos.*3:4(M.87.1004B); of eucharistic vessels, Jul.Papa *ep.Dian.*ap. Ath.*apol.sec.*30(p.109.28; M.25.300B).

D. *secret*; **1.** in gen. τὸ τῆς ἰδίας αὐτῶν [sc. Χριστιανῶν] θεοσεβείας μ. μὴ προσδοκήσῃς δύνασθαι παρὰ ἀνθρώπου μαθεῖν *Diogn.*4.6; κατάσκοπος [sc. Samuel]...τῶν μ. τῶν καταχθονίων Or.*hom.18.2 in Jer.* (p.152.31; M.13.465C); μ. ποίησόν σου τὴν εὐχήν Chrys.*hom.19.3 in Mt.*(7.248B); μ. ἐστιν ἡ ἐλεημοσύνη· κλεῖσον τοίνυν τὰς θύρας *ib.*71.4 (699D); Cyr.*Is.*3.1(2.364A); *secret parts* of the body, ‡Nil.*perist.*9.4 (M.79.869A); of internal organs, ‡Nil.*narr.*1(M.79.596A); ‡Caes. Naz.*dial.*28(M.38.888); ἐν μ. *secretly*, *Diogn.*8.10; Iren.*haer.*1.25.5 (M.7.685A); Clem.*str.*6.15(p.494.26; M.9.348C); τῶν ἐν τῇ ἐκκλησίᾳ πεφυλαγμένων δογμάτων καὶ κηρυγμάτων, τὰ μὲν ἐκ τῆς ἐγγράφου διδασκαλίας ἔχομεν, τὰ δὲ ἐκ τῆς τῶν ἀποστόλων παραδόσεως διαδοθέντα ἡμῖν ἐν μ. παρεδεξάμεθα Bas.*Spir.*66(3.54D; M.32.188A); Thdr.Mops.*2Thess.*2:7(p.54.21; M.66.936A); οὐ τοῦτο λέγει, ὅτι ἐν μ. λαλοῦμεν, ἀλλὰ τὴν ἀποκεκρυμμένην ἐν μ. σοφίαν τοῖς ἀνθρώποις προσφέρομεν ἣν οὐκ ἔκ τινος μεταμελείας νῦν ὁ θεὸς ᾠκονόμησε, ἀλλ' ἄνωθεν καὶ ἐξ ἀρχῆς προώρισε τὴν ἐντεῦθεν ἡμῖν πραγματευόμενος δόξαν Thdt.*1Cor.*2:7(3.175); **2.** *secret purpose* or *activity* τὸν σωτῆρα λέγουσιν...τριάκοντα ἔτεσι κατὰ τὸ φανερὸν μηδὲν πεποιηκέναι, ἐπιδεικνύντα τὸ μ. τούτων τῶν Αἰώνων Iren.*haer.*1.1.3(M.7.449B); μ. δὲ αὐτοὺς [sc. τοὺς αἱρετικούς] ἀνομίας ἐκάλεσεν, ὡς κεκρυμμένην ἔχοντας τῆς ἀνομίας τὴν πάγην Thdt.*2Thess.*2:7(3.534); esp. *secret purpose* of God: in sphere of nature αὐτὸν τὸν τεχνίτην καὶ δημιουργὸν τῶν ὅλων...οὗ τὰ μ. πιστῶς πάντα φυλάσσει τὰ στοιχεῖα *Diogn.* 7.2; and of grace; **a.** to be revealed ἡ παρθενία Μαρίας καὶ ὁ τοκετὸς αὐτῆς ὁμοίως καὶ ὁ θάνατος τοῦ κυρίου, τρία μ. κραυγῆς Ign.*Eph.* 19.1; μεγάλῃ φωνῇ τοῖς πᾶσιν τὸ λεληθὸς καὶ κρύφιον περὶ τοῦ λόγου μ. παραδιδοὺς ἐβόα λέγων [Jo.1:1–3] Eus.*e.th.*2.18(p.122.17; M.24. 941B); μ. ἦν ἀποκεκρυμμένον πρότερον, νυνὶ δὲ φανερωθὲν ὁ υἱὸς τοῦ θεοῦ· τὸ πλῆθος τοῦ Ἰουδαίων ἔθνους ἐν ἀγνοίᾳ ἐτύγχανεν τοῦ κεκρυμμένου μ. ... τοῦτο γὰρ ἐφυλάττετο τῇ ἐξ ἐθνῶν ἐκκλησίᾳ τὸ μ. *ib.*1.20 (p.96.16,23; 893A); ref. Mt.2:2 ἀγνοουμένου τοῦ μ. τῆς γεννήσεως Cyr.H.*catech.*12.9; μ. λέγει πᾶν τὸ ἀγνοούμενον μέν, δυνάμει δὲ πνεύματος ἀποκαλυπτόμενον Sever.*1Cor.*13:2(p.266.1); μ. τοῦ θελήματος αὐτοῦ τὸ κεκρυμμένον προσηγόρευσε θέλημα. ἄνωθεν γάρ, φησί, ταῦτα προορίσας ὕστερον ἀπεκάλυψε Thdt.*Eph.*1:9(3.404); in heaven κατοπτεύσεις τὸν θεόν, καὶ τοῖς ἁγίοις ἐκείνοις τελεσθήσῃ μ. Clem. *prot.*12(p.83.28; M.8.240A); τύπος ἦν...ἡ ἐν τῇ σκηνῇ λατρεία τῶν ἐν οὐρανοῖς μ. Ath.*ep.fest.*45(p.298.28; M.26.1441D); εὔχου...ἵνα ὁ θεός σε καταξιώσῃ τῶν ἐπουρανίων καὶ ἀθανάτων μ. Cyr.H.*procatech.*16; συναναστῆναι αὐτῷ [sc. Χριστῷ] καὶ μετόχους γενέσθαι τῆς βασιλείας αὐτοῦ καὶ κοινωνοὺς τῶν μ. αὐτοῦ *Lit.*ap.*Const.App.*8.8.2; **b.** foreshadowed in OT οὐδεὶς...διὰ τούτου τοῦ μ. ἀποθανών, τουτέστι τοῦ σταυρωθῆναι, εἰ μὴ μόνος οὗτος ὁ Ἰησοῦς Just.*dial.*97.4(M.6.705B); οὐδέπω γὰρ ἀποκεκάλυπτο ἡ τῶν προφητικῶν δήλωσις μυστηρίων πρὸ τῆς τοῦ κυρίου παρουσίας Clem.*str.*5.14(p.385.22; M.9.132B); Hipp. *Dan.*4.24.2; πρὸ τῆς Χριστοῦ ἐπιδημίας ὁ νόμος καὶ οἱ προφῆται, ἅτε μηδέπω ἐληλυθότος τοῦ τὰ ἐν αὐτοῖς μ. σαφηνίζοντος Or.*Jo.*1.6(8; p.11.3; M.14.33D); διακέκραγε ὁ Μωσέως νόμος τὸ τοῦ Χριστοῦ μ., καὶ τῆς εὐαγγελικῆς πολιτείας τὴν δύναμιν ὡς ἐν σκιαῖς εὑρήσομεν Cyr. *Is.*3.3(2.454E); τὸ ὑπὸ τῶν προφητῶν πάλαι βοώμενον φρικτὸν μ. καὶ ἐν τοῖς ἡμετέροις καιροῖς ἀποκαλυφθὲν εἰς σωτηρίαν ἡμῶν Alex.Sal. *Barn.*17(441B); **c.** with emphasis on obscurity rather than revelation περὶ δὲ τοῦ τῆς γενέσεως αὐτοῦ μ. ἤδη λέγειν κατεπείγοντος Just. *dial.*43.3(M.6.568A); τὰ μ. μυστικῶς παραδίδοται, ἵνα ᾖ...οὐκ ἐν φωνῇ ἀλλ' ἐν τῷ νοεῖσθαι Clem.*str.*1.1(p.10.11; M.8.701C); Or.*Jo.*13.24(p.259. 27; M.14.460A); μ. ἓν μέγα καὶ μέγιστον καὶ τοῖς πολλοῖς ἀπόκρυφον ὁ θεός Gr.Naz.*or.*15.5(M.35.920C); ref. sacraments μυστήρια καὶ λέγεται καὶ ἔστιν· ἔνθα δὲ μυστήρια, πολλὴ σιγή Chrys.*bapt.Chr.*4(2. 375C); cf. *mysterium saepe illud dogma dicit quod de Christo est; eo quod deitas unigeniti inerat in homine, et propter hoc facile non ad cognitionem poterat venire multorum*, Thdr.Mops.*1Tim.*3:16(p.134. 15); δυσχερεστάτη λίαν ἐστὶν ἡ περὶ τῶν θείων μ. ἐξήγησις, καὶ τάχα κρείττων ἡ σιωπή Cyr.*Jo.*proem.(4.4D); ref. 1Tim.3:16 ὁ τρόπος τῆς ἑνώσεως, ἀλλ' οὐχ ὁ λόγος τῆς φύσεως, τὸ μέγα τῆς εὐσεβείας περιέχει μ. Leont.B.*arg.Sev.*(M.86.1940B); τὸ πάντων μ. μυστηριωδέστατον, αὐτός ἐστιν ὁ θεός *ib.*(1924A); **d.** secret revealed, *revelation* τουτέστι τὸ μ. ὃ λέγει [sc. ὁ Παῦλος] κατὰ ἀποκάλυψιν ἐγνωρίσθαι αὐτῷ, ὅτι ὁ παθὼν ἐπὶ Ποντίου Πιλάτου, οὗτος κύριος τῶν πάντων Iren.*haer.*3.12.9(M.7.902B); μ. ἐμφανές· θεὸς ἐν ἀνθρώπῳ καὶ ὁ ἄνθρωπος θεός Clem.*paed.*3.1(p.236.27; M.8.557A); ἡ ἀληθὴς...σοφία οὐ λόγοις ψιλοῖς πεποιθυῖα, ἀλλὰ...μ. δραστικοῖς, ταῖς θείαις ἐντολαῖς id.*str.*2.20(p.179.17; M.8.1068A); οὔτε γὰρ ἡ προφητεία οὔτε ὁ σωτὴρ αὐτὸς ἁπλῶς...τὰ θεῖα μ. ἀπεφθέγξατο, ἀλλ' ἐν παραβολαῖς διελέξατο *ib.*6.15(p.494.31; M.9.348C); ὁ διδάσκαλος...παιδεύων μυστηρίοις μὲν τὸν γνωστικόν *ib.*7.2(p.6.8; 409A); τὰ περὶ κοσμοποιΐας καὶ ἄλλα τινὰ μ. Or.*comm.3 in Gen.*ap.*philoc.*23.10 (p.209.20; M.12.84B); Ἡσαΐας τὸ μ. ἑώρα τοῦ ἐπὶ τοῦ θρόνου καθεζομένου id.*Jo.*6.4(2; p.111.11; M.14.205B); of OT βίβλους περιεχούσας τὰ ἀπόρρητα τῆς γνώσεως μ. id.*princ.*4.2.3(p.311.12; M.11.361A); ἡγοῦμαι τὸ μὲν περὶ τῶν φανερῶν εἰδέναι τὴν γνῶσιν εἶναι, γενικωτέραν οὖσαν τῶν μ., ἐν μέρει γὰρ τῆς γνώσεως ἡ τῶν μ. ἐστὶν ἐπιστήμη· τὸ δὲ περὶ τῶν ἀπορρητοτέρων καὶ θειοτέρων εἰδέναι, τοῦτ' εἶναι τὸ μ. γινώσκειν id.*comm.in 1Cor.*13:1–2(*JTS* 10 p.33); *ib.*4:1–5(*JTS* 9 p.354.12); οὐκ ἔστιν αἴνιγμα ἀλλὰ μ. θεῖον Ath.*Ar.*1.41(M.26.96B); ταῦτα τὰ μ. ἃ νῦν ἡ ἐκκλησία διηγεῖταί σοι τῷ ἐκ κατηχουμένων μεταβαλλομένῳ, οὐκ ἔστι ἔθος ἐθνικοῖς διηγεῖσθαι Cyr.H.*catech.*6.29; Gr.Naz.*or.*40.43 (M.36.421A); *ib.*45.24(657A); Ἰωάννης...τὸ τῆς θεολογίας κηρύσσει μ. ὃς καὶ υἱὸν ὀνομάζει θεοῦ Gr.Nyss.*Eun.*4(2 p.53.1; M.45.624A); τὰ...σεραφίμ, παρ' ὧν ἐναργῶς τὸ τῆς τριάδος ἐκηρύχθη μ. *ib.*1(1 p.113.2; 348B); τοῦ θεοῦ τοῦτό ἐστι τὸ μ., τὸ διὰ τοῦ υἱοῦ προσάγεσθαι Chrys.*hom.5.2 in Col.*(11.361A); μ. μέν ἐστιν ἡ οἰκονομία καὶ ἡ ἐνανθρώπησις τοῦ Χριστοῦ, δόξα δὲ τοῦ μ. ἡ ἀνάστασις ἡ ἐκ νεκρῶν, πλοῦτος δὲ ὁ πολὺς ἔλεος ὁ ἐκ τῆς ἀφέσεως τοῦ βαπτίσματος Sever.*Col.*1:26–27 (p.321.13); μ. καλεῖ τὴν περὶ τὰ ἔθνη χάριν, ὡς ἂν ἄδηλον οὖσαν τοῖς πρὸ τούτου, ἐπίγνωσιν δὲ μυστηρίου τὴν μετουσίαν αὐτῆς Thdr.Mops.*Col.*2:2(p.283.20; M.66.929B); μ. λέγεται τὸ μὴ πᾶσι δηλούμενον, ἀλλὰ μόνοις τοῖς φίλοις θαρρούμενον Thdt.*1Cor.*15:51(3.279); οὐκ ἰχνηλατῶ τὰ ἀνεξιχνίαστα, ἀλλὰ τὸ νῦν ἀποκαλυφθὲν μ. τοὺς ἀγνοοῦντας διδάσκειν id.*Eph.*3:9(3.418); of divine nature of Christ τὸ μ. ἐν σαρκὶ ἐφανερώθη Apoll.*fr.*20(p.209.28)ap.Gr.Nyss.*Apoll.*7(M.45.1137A); σὰρξ προκάλυμμα μυστηρίου κρυπτομένου προσείληφεν Val.Apoll.*apol.*5(p.289.13; M.86.1956B); **e.** hence of Christian faith as body of revealed truth διακόνους...μυστηρίων Ἰησοῦ Χριστοῦ Ign.*Trall.*2.3; τὸν ἐξορχησάμενον τὸ μ. καὶ ἐμπομπεύσαντα τῇ μιαρᾷ αἱρέσει τῇ Ἀρτεμᾷ Malch.*ep.*ap.Eus.*h.e.*7.30.16(M.20.716B); τὰ περὶ τῶν μ. γεγραμμένα Cyr.H.*procatech.*6; τῶν ἐξεταστικῶς ζητούντων τοῦ μ. τὸν λόγον Gr.Nyss.*or.catech.*15(p.65.3; M.45.48C); αὕτη [sc. ἡ εἰς πατέρα καὶ υἱὸν καὶ ἅγιον πνεῦμα πίστις] ἐστὶν ἡ μορφὴ τοῦ κατὰ τὸ μ. τῆς ἀληθείας μεμορφωμένου id.*Maced.*15(M.45.1320C); τὸ εὐαγγελικὸν...μ. id.*Pss.titt.*B 8 (M.44.516B); οἱ πρώτως προσιόντες τῷ μ. τῆς εὐσεβείας διὰ τῶν διακόνων προσαγέσθωσαν τῷ ἐπισκόπῳ ἢ τοῖς πρεσβυτέροις *Const.App.*8.32.2; ref. Jacob's blessing ἅπαν ἡμῖν τὸ μ. ἐνταῦθα ᾐνίξατο Chrys.*hom.67.3 in Gen.*(4.638E); ἐπὶ καιροῦ...ἀναγκαίως τῇ τοῦ μ. παραδόσει καὶ ὁ περὶ τῆς ἀναστάσεως τῶν νεκρῶν συνεισκεκόμισται λόγος Cyr.*Is.*3.1(2.354B); ἡ δὲ ἀγάπη τοῦ καθ' ἡμᾶς μυστηρίου ἐστὶ τὸ κεφάλαιον Procl.CP *Arm.*3(p.188.29; M.65.857C); of NT βίβλους νέου μ. Gr.Naz.*carm.*1.1.12.30(M.37.474A); **f.** of mystical truths, Or.*Jo.*13.6(p.230.4; M.14.405B); εὐαγγέλιον σκιὰν μυστηρίων Χριστοῦ διδάσκει *ib.*1.7(9; p.12.11; 36D); αὐτὰ τροπικῶς διὰ δοκούσης ἱστορίας καὶ οὐ σωματικῶς γεγενημένης μηνύειν τινὰ μ. id.*princ.*4.3.1(p.324.4; M.11.377A); εὐλογηθεῖσαν αἱ ψυχαὶ αὐτῶν εἰς μάθησιν καὶ γνῶσιν καὶ τὰ μ. Serap.*euch.*6.2; τὴν ἑνότητα τοῦ πνεύματος...ἡ νόμου καὶ προφητῶν ἐστι μ. εἴτ' οὖν κεφάλαιον Gr.Naz.*or.*24.2(M.35.1172C); ref. Num.20:11 ὁ τοιοῦτος λόγος...ἡμᾶς...διδάξειεν οἷόν ἐστι τὸ τῆς μετανοίας μ. Gr.Nyss.*v.Mos.*(M.44.413A); διὰ τοῦ ᾄσματος τῶν ᾀσμάτων, μυστηρίων μυστήρια διδάσκειν ἡμᾶς ὁ ὑψηλὸς λόγος κατεπαγγέλλεται id.*hom.1 in Cant.*(M.44.773C); ref. 2Cor.12:4 τοῖς ἀπορρήτοις τοῦ παραδείσου μ. ἐναγαλλόμενος id.*hom.5 in Eccl.*(M.44.685A); μ. καλεῖται ὅτι οὐχ ἅπερ ὁρῶμεν βλέπομεν, ἀλλ' ἕτερα ὁρῶμεν καὶ ἕτερα πιστεύομεν Chrys.*hom.7.1 in 1Cor.*(10.51B); πρῶτον τῶν μ. καλεῖται ἡ καθαρότης ἡ συνισταμένη ἐκ τῆς ἐνεργείας τῶν ἐντολῶν Philox.*ep.*25(p.175); **3.** c. genit., also κατά c. acc.; **a.** *secret purpose of God revealed* or *fulfilled* in an event τὸν θεόν...ἐλεῆσαι διὰ τοῦ μ. τοῦ σταυρωθέντος τούτου πᾶν γένος τῶν πιστευόντων ἀνθρώπων Just.*dial.*106.1(M.6.721C); οἱ διὰ τοῦ ἐξουθενημένου καὶ ὀνείδους μεστοῦ μ. τοῦ σταυροῦ κληθέντες ὑπὸ τοῦ θεοῦ *ib.*131.2(780C); ἔστιν δὲ καὶ διὰ προφητικῆς φωνῆς τὸ τοῦ κυρίου μ. κηρυσσόμενον Mel.*pass.*61 p.10.14; Ἰούδαν...τὸ τῆς προδοσίας ἐνεργῆσαι μ. Iren.*haer.*1.31.1(cf.M.7.704B); of whole of Christ's earthly life θεῷ τὰ τῆς ἀγάπης μ., καὶ τοτὲ ἐποπτεύσεις τὸν κόλπον τοῦ πατρός Clem.*q.d.s.*37(p.183.31; M.9.641C); ref. Mc.1:7 λῦσαι ἕκαστον τῶν περὶ τοῦ μ. τῆς ἐνσωματώσεως ἀσαφῶν Or.*Jo.*6.36 (p.143.33; M.14.260A); *ib.*10.36(20; p.210.15; 372C); ἡμεῖς οἱ τὰ ἅγια μ. τῆς εὐμενείας [sc. τοῦ θεοῦ] δοκοῦντες προβάλλεσθαι Const.ap.Ath.*apol.sec.*86(p.165.27; M.25.404C); τὸ μέγα μ. τῆς εἰς τὸν θάνατον αὐτοῦ παρόδου Eus.*d.e.*8.2(p.389.22; M.22.629A); ἐν τῷ νόμῳ μάλιστα τὸ κατὰ τὸν σταυρὸν θεωρεῖται μ. Gr.Nyss.*v.Mos.*(M.44.372C); τὸ κατὰ τὴν παρθενίαν μ. id.*Eun.*3(2 p.20.13; M.45.585A); τὸ κατὰ τὴν σάρκα τοῦ κυρίου μ.· ὅτι ὁ ἄτρεπτος ἐν τῷ τρεπτῷ γίνεται *ib.*5(2 p.119.24; 700D); τὸ πληρῶσαι...τὸ μέγα τοῦ θανάτου μ. *ib.*6(2 p.143.2; 728D); ἡ καθ' ἡμᾶς Ἰησοῦ...ὕπαρξις, καὶ ὅσα τῆς κατ' αὐτὴν ἐστι φιλανθρωπίας οὐσιώδη μ. Dion.Ar.*d.n.*2.3(M.3.640C); ἐν ὅσῳ τῶν συνελθουσῶν φύσεων τὰ ἴδια καὶ τὰ ἀληθῆ συγχεῖ, τὸ μ. τῆς ἡμετέρας λυτρώσεως σβέννυσιν Horm.*ep.cler.*(p.55.6; M.*PL.*63.419B); cf. εἰ δὲ μετὰ τὴν ἕνωσιν ἐν δυσὶ φύσεσι γνωρισθήσεται, λύεται μὲν ἡ ἕνωσις...μερισθήσεται δὲ τὸ μ. Sev.Ant.*fr.*ap.Eust.Mon.*ep.*(M.86.932A); Eulog.*fr.Trin.*2.5(p.365); ‡Bas.*h.myst.*60(p.395.4); c. genit. understood; of Resurrection, Gr.Naz.*or.*1.2(M.35.396B); of Pentecost, *ib.*41.5(M.36.436B); of Inc. ἐν τῷ μ. ὁ θεὸς μορφὴν δούλου ἔλαβε Procl.CP *or.*2.6(M.65.700D); **b.** *secret of God revealed by divine activity* τῆς χάριτος τὸ μ. Meth.*symp.*8.9(p.91.17; M.18.152B); ref. 2Cor.12:2 τὸ τῆς ἁρπαγῆς μ. Gr.Naz.*or.*28.20(p.51.14; M.36.52C); οἱ Χριστιανοὶ ἐν ἐκείνῳ τῷ αἰῶνι, μέλλοντες βασιλεύειν, οὐ ξενίζονται, ἤδη προεγνωκότες τὰ μ. τῆς χάριτος Mac.Aeg.*hom.*17.3(M.34.625B); *ib.*18.11(641C); ἡ χάρις...ἐνεργεῖ τῇ...ψυχῇ τὰ ἑαυτῆς μ. Diad.*perf.*69(p.84.19); **4.** *hidden meaning* ταῦτα μετὰ πολλοῦ νοῦ καὶ μ. γέγονε Just.*dial.*112.3(M.6.733C); τὸ μ. οὖν τοῦ προβάτου ὃ τὸ πάσχα θύειν ἐντέταλται ὁ θεὸς...τύπος ἦν τοῦ Χριστοῦ *ib.*40.1(561B); id.*1apol.*13.4(M.6.348A); Clem.*paed.*1.5(p.103.2; M.8.276A); ἐπεὶ ἐκήρυξεν αὐτὸς ὢν τὸ πάσχα...αὐτίκα ἐδίδαξε τοὺς μαθητὰς τοῦ τύπου τὸ μ. id.*fr.*28(p.216.28; M.9.757A); μὴ εἰδότι τότε Πέτρῳ, ἀλλὰ γνωσομένῳ μετὰ ταῦτα τὸ μ. τῆς νίψεως Or.*Jo.*32.2(p.427.25; M.14.744B); ἡ δὲ εἰς τὸ ὕδωρ κάθοδος...ἕτερον ἐμπεριέχει μ. Gr.Nyss.*or.catech.*35(p.129.10; M.45.85D); id.*Pss.titt.*B 8(M.44.520B); ἐν μ. *with a hidden meaning*, Just.*dial.*68.6(M.6.633D).

E. that by which a secret is conveyed, *object* or *event of mystical significance*; **1.** *symbolic event* πολλοὺς λόγους τοὺς ἐπικεκαλυμμένως καὶ ἐν παραβολαῖς ἢ μ. ἢ ἐν συμβόλοις ἔργων λελεγμένους Just.*dial.*68.6 (M.6.636A); ref. Gen.19:30ff. μυστήρια ταῦτα τυγχάνειν ὑφ' ἡμῶν μὴ νοούμενα Or.*princ.*4.2.2(p.309.7; M.11.360B); ref. Jer.20:8 ὡς μ. ἐστι τὸ συνταφῆναι τῷ Χριστῷ, οὕτω μ. ἐστι...τὸ...ταφῆναι εἰς Βαβυλῶνα id.*hom.19.14 in Jer.*(p.172.25; M.13.493C); *symbolic rite*, of Passover Μωϋσῆς σφάξας τὸ πρόβατον καὶ νύκτωρ διατελέσας τὸ μ. μετὰ τῶν υἱῶν Ἰσραὴλ Mel.*pass.*15 p.3.3; *ib.*16 p.3.11; τὸ τοῦ πάσχα μ. τετέλεσται ἐν τῷ κυρίου σώματι *ib.*56 p.9.26; ἀνάμνησιν τῆς κατ' Αἴγυπτον...σωτηρίας ἡγούμενοι μόνην εἶναι τὸ μ. προβάτου Meth.*symp.*9.1(p.115.17; M.18.180B); of Jewish rites in gen., Gr.Nyss.*Eun.*9(2 p.217.9; M.45.816B); **2.** *foreshadowing* τίς δὲ ἐντολὴ καὶ πρᾶξις ὁμοίως εἴρητο ἢ εἰς μ. τοῦ Χριστοῦ; Just.*dial.*44.2(M.6.569B); ref. Noah's ark ξύλου τοῦ τὸ μ. τοῦ σταυροῦ ἔχοντος *ib.*138.2(793B); τὸ μ. τῶν σωζομένων ἀνθρώπων ἐπὶ τοῦ κατακλυσμοῦ *ib.*138.1(793A); ref. 2Thess.2:6 Νέρωνα...φησιν ὡσανεὶ τύπον ὄντα τοῦ ἀντιχρίστου· καὶ γὰρ ἐκεῖνος ἐβούλετο νομίζεσθαι θεός. καὶ καλῶς εἶπε, τὸ μ.· οὐ γὰρ φανερῶς, ὡς ἐκεῖνος, οὐδὲ ἀπηρυθριασμένως Chrys.*hom.4.1 in 2Thess.*(11.529F); **3.** *symbol, type*, ref. Israel and Amalek ἀμφότερα τὰ μ. ... λέγω τὸν τύπον τοῦ σταυροῦ καὶ τὸν τύπον τῆς τοῦ ὀνόματος ἐπικλήσεως Just.*dial.*111.2(M.6.732B); εἶδες τὸ τοῦ κυρίου μ. ἐν τῷ [τοῦ] προβάτῳ γινόμενον Mel.*pass.*33 p.5.33; εἰ βούλει τὸ τοῦ κυρίου μ. ἰδέσθαι, ἀπόβλεψον εἰς τὸν Ἄβελ τὸν ὁμοίως φονευόμενον *ib.*59 p.10.3; cf. *non igitur manifeste ipsam faciem dei videbant prophetae, sed dispositiones et mysteria per quae inciperet homo videre deum*, Iren.*haer.*4.20.10(M.7.1039A); Cyr.H.*catech.*13.17; ὄρχησαι μέν, ἀλλὰ...τὴν [sc. ὄρχησιν] Δαβὶδ...ἣν ἡγοῦμαι τῆς εὐκινήτου...κατὰ θεὸν πορείας εἶναι μυστήριον Gr.Naz.*or.*5.35(M.35.712A); αἱ λαμπάδες ἅσπερ ἀνάψεις, τῆς ἐκεῖθεν φωταγωγίας μ. *ib.*40.46(M.36.425A); ref. sacrifice of Isaac τύπος ταῦτα τῆς ἀληθείας, ἐν δὲ τῷ τύπῳ σφαγὴν οὐχ ὑπέμεινεν ὁ μονογενής, ἀλλὰ κριὸς ἀντεισήχθη...καὶ τῆς ἱερουργίας πεπλήρωκε τὸ μ. Thdt.*eran.*3 (4.203); ἐν μ. *symbolically, in veiled language* τὸ λίθον τοῦτον εἰπεῖν ...ἐν μ. τὸ αὐτὸ κέκραγε Just.*dial.*76.1(M.6.652C); *ib.*81.3(669A); Hipp.*Dan.*4.36.6.

F. *sacrament*, as revelation of divine operation; **1.** in gen. περὶ τῶν πνευματικῶν τούτων καὶ ἐπουρανίων...μ. Cyr.H.*catech.*19.1; ἐκ τῆς ἁγίας ἀνεστομώθη πλευρᾶς ἡ τῆς σωτηρίας πηγή, ἀφ' ἧς τὰ διπλᾶ τῶν μ. ἐδεξάμεθα νάματα Thdt.*Zach.*14:8(2.1663); αὐτὰ τὰ ἐξ ὕλης τελούμενα θεῖα μ. τὸν ἄρτον, τὸν οἶνον, τὸ τῆς χρίσεως ἔλαιον, τοῦ σταυροῦ τὸ ἐκτύπωμα Jo.D.*imag.*1.27(M.94.1264B); **2.** of baptism, Eus.*d.e.*9.6(p.418.7; M.22.673C); τῆς παλιγγενεσίας μ. id.*e.th.*1.8 (p.66.4; M.24.837A); Ath.*Ar.*2.42(M.26.236C); ὅπως τὸ μ. τὸ νῦν ἐπιτελούμενον μὴ κενὸν εὑρεθῇ ἐν τοῖς ἀναγεννωμένοις Serap.*euch*.19.2; τὴν δύναμιν τοῦ μ. τῆς κολυμβήθρας Ephr.2.378F; Bas.*Spir*.66(3.55A; M.32.188B); ὕδωρ καὶ πίστις ἐστὶ δι' ὧν τὸ τῆς ἀναγεννήσεως πληροῦται μ. Gr.Nyss.*or.catech*.33(p.124.2; M.45.85B); Chrys.*Thdr*.1.17(1.28D); Thdt.*h.e*.3.3.7(3.914); of the various parts of the baptismal rite ἕκαστον τῶν ἁγίων τοῦ βαπτίσματος μ. Cyr.H.*catech*.18.32; **3.** of eucharist; **a.** in gen. οἴνου τοῖς ἔθνεσιν εὐφροσύνην θεσπίζει, τὸ τῆς καινῆς τοῦ Χριστοῦ διαθήκης μ. αἰνιττόμενος Eus.*d.e*.1.10(p.48.1; M.22.92B); πρεσβύτεροι...οἱ καὶ τῶν μ. λειτουργοί Jul.Papa *ep.Dian.* ap.Ath.*apol.sec*.31(p.110.12; M.25.300D); ἐπὶ κατηχουμένων καὶ...ἐπὶ Ἑλλήνων τραγῳδοῦντες τὰ μ. CAlex.*ep*.ap.Ath.*apol.sec*.11(p.96.8; M.25.268A); Serap.*euch*.3.2; Ephr.1.209B; ἀπὸ τοῦ βαπτίσματος πρὸς τὸ ἅγιον τοῦ θεοῦ προσελεύσεσθαι θυσιαστήριον καὶ τῶν αὐτόθι πνευματικῶν καὶ ἐπουρανίων ἀπολαύειν μ. Cyr.H.*catech*.18.32; εὐχαρίστει τῷ θεῷ τῷ καταξιώσαντί σε τῶν τηλικούτων μ. *ib*.23.22; Bas.*ep*.188 *can*.1(3.270D; M.32.669C); σκεῦός τι μυστηρίων [i.e. a chalice] Epiph.*haer*.68.7(p.148.6; M.42.196C); τὰ μ. ... τὰς θύρας κλείοντες ἐπιτελοῦμεν, καὶ τοὺς ἀμυήτους εἴργομεν Chrys.*hom.23.3 in Mt*.(7.288C); id.*hom.23.2 in 1Cor*.(10.203A); τὸ ἐν τῷ πάσχα μ. [i.e. Easter liturgy] id.*hom.5.3 in 1Tim*.(11.577D); ἀπαρχὴ δὲ εἴτε μέλι εἴτε γάλα...προσφερέσθω ἐν μιᾷ ἡμέρᾳ ἐθίμῳ εἰς τὸ τῶν νηπίων μ. *Cod.Afr*.37 (Lat. *mysterio*); φησιν [sc. Nestorius] ὅτι...ἐν τοῖς μ. σῶμά ἐστιν ἀνθρώπου τὸ προκείμενον Cyr.*ep*.11a(p.171.28; M.77.88B); κυριακὸν δεῖπνον καλεῖ τὸ δεσποτικὸν μ. Thdt.*1Cor*.11:20(3.236); δεῖξαι βουλόμενοι τῶν ἡμετέρων μ. τοὺς τύπους, τὸν ἀμνὸν εἰς μέσον φέρομεν, καὶ τὸ αἷμα τὸ ταῖς φλιαῖς ἐπιχριόμενον, καὶ τὴν τῆς θαλάττης διάβασιν *ib*.2:13 (178); ὥσπερ ἡμεῖς πιστοὺς ὀνομάζομεν τοὺς τῶν θείων μ. μετέχοντας, οὕτως τετελεσμένους ἐκάλει τὰ ἔθνη τοὺς δαιμόνων τινῶν διδασκομένους μυστήρια id.*qu.28 in Dt*.(1.278); Hesych.H.*fr.Ps*.104:40(M.93.1297B); Jo.D.*Eph*.5:20(M.95.849A); **b.** with emphasis on *sacramental action* ἐπιτελῶν...τὸ ἅγιον μ., εὐλογήσας εἶπεν, 'πίετε ἐξ αὐτοῦ πάντες' ‡Ath.*serm.fid*.37(p.30; M.26.1289B); ἔλθωμεν ἐπὶ τὴν τελείωσιν τῶν μ.· οὗτος ὁ ἄρτος καὶ τοῦτο τὸ ποτήριον, ὅσον οὔπω εὐχαὶ καὶ ἱκεσίαι γεγόνασι, ψιλά εἰσιν· ἐπὰν δὲ αἱ μεγάλαι εὐχαὶ καὶ αἱ ἅγιαι ἱκεσίαι ἀναπεμφθῶσι, καταβαίνει ὁ λόγος εἰς τὸν ἄρτον καὶ τὸ ποτήριον, καὶ γίνεται αὐτοῦ σῶμα Ath.ap.Eutych.*pasch*.8(M.86.2401B); κἂν πᾶς μὲν ὁ ἐκκλησιαστικὸς κανὼν ἐπιτεθείη, ἡ μυστικὴ δὲ τῆς προσφορᾶς ὑπὸ τοῦ ἱερέως εὐχαριστία καὶ ἡ κοινωνία τοῦ σώματος τοῦ Χριστοῦ μὴ γένηται...ἐλλιπὴς ἐστιν ἡ λατρεία τοῦ μ. Mac.Aeg.*carit*.29(M.34.932C); οὐ...ὁ ἱερεὺς...τὰ τῆς θείας κοινωνίας τελέσει μ., μὴ τῷ θειοτάτῳ θυσιαστηρίῳ τῶν κοινωνικῶν ἐπιτεθέντων συμβόλων Dion.Ar.*e.h*.5.1.5(M.3.505B); **c.** of eucharistic elements δοθῆναι εὐλογίαν τῷ λαῷ τούτῳ διὰ τὴν σὴν φιλανθρωπίαν...καὶ τὰ μ. τὰ παρόντα Serap.*euch*.15.1; παραδοὺς ἡμῖν τὰ ἀντίτυπα μ. τοῦ τιμίου σώματος αὐτοῦ καὶ αἵματος *Const.App*.5.14.7; Μελχισεδὲκ...προτυπῶν τῶν μ. τὰ αἰνίγματα, ἀντίτυπα τοῦ κυρίου ἡμῶν Epiph.*haer*.55.6(p.331.14; M.41.981A); Isid.Pel.*epp*.1.431(M.78.421A); Chrys.*sac*.6.4(p.148.9; 1.424D); τῇ μεταλήψει τῶν ἁγίων καὶ ἀχράντων σου μ. *Lit.Jac*.(p.234.22); **4.** of other religious *rites* τὸ μ. τελετῆς μύρου Dion.Ar.*e.h*.4.1.2 tit.(M.3.473A); τὸ μ. ἱερατικῶν τελειώσεων *ib*.5.7.2(509A); μ. μοναχικῆς τελειώσεως *ib*.6.3.2(533A); μ. ἐπὶ τῶν ἱερῶς κεκοιμημένων *ib*.7.3.2(556B).

***μυστηριοφύλαξ, ὁ,** *guardian of the mysteries*; plur., Thdr.Stud.*epp*.2.11(M.99.1152A).

μυστηριώδης, *concerned with mysteries*; **1.** *of mysteries*; **a.** pagan ἑκάστην φιλόσοφον αἵρεσιν ἐν Ἕλλησιν ἢ βαρβάροις, ἢ μ. ἐπαγγελίαν Or.*Cels*.3.81(p.271.27; M.11.1028A); **b.** Christian; *sacramental* τῆς μ. τροφῆς Eus.*d.e*.8.1(p.366.21; M.22.596A); **2.** *secret, mysterious* τῆς μ. οἰκονομίας τοῦ Χριστοῦ *ib*.1.10(p.46.36; 89A); ἅγια τῶν ἁγίων μείζονά τινα μ. καὶ ἀπόκρυφον ἔχει τὴν τιμήν Ph.Carp.*Cant*.proem.(M.40.29B); comp. οὐδὲν...τῆς θείας ἀγάπης...μ. Max.*ep*.2(M.91.393B); superl. τὸ πάντων μυστηρίων μ., αὐτός ἐστιν ὁ θεός Leont.B.*arg.Sev*.(M.86.1924A); τὸ πάντων μυστηρίων μ. αὐτὸς ὁ θεὸς...γενόμενος ἄνθρωπος Max.*ep*.44(644B); neut. as subst., *secrecy, privacy*, Isid.Pel.*epp*.4.145(M.78.1228B); **3.** *with hidden spiritual meaning, mystical* παραβολὴ μ. Just.*dial*.97.3(M.6.705A); τύπους οὐρανίων καὶ σύμβολα μ. τε εἰκόνας Eus.*h.e*.1.3.2(M.20.69A); ταύτης τῆς ἁγίας καὶ μ. γραφῆς Ph.Carp.*Cant*.8(M.40.45A); ἅπαντα μυστηριώδη καὶ λόγων ἔμπλεα θειοτέρων Sev.Ant.*res*.(p.824.6; M.46.637D); comp. ἀπὸ μυστηρίων εἰς μ. ἀναβαίνουσα Proc.G.*Cant*.8:5(M.87.1772C).

***μυστηριωδῶς, 1.** *mysteriously, as if it were a mystery*, Tat.*orat*.3(p.3.14; M.6.809A); οὐδὲν θαυμαστὸν οἱ...αἱρεσιάρχαι μ. ἐπαγγέλλονται Epiph.*haer*.31.1(p.386.19; M.41.477B); *ib*.62.2(p.391.7; 1052D); **2.** *secretly* τὸ παρ' αὐτοῖς ἀεὶ μ. γινόμενον *ib*.30.9(p.344.16; 420C); **3.** *with hidden spiritual meaning* φανερῶς μὲν μὴ εἰρῆσθαι...μ. δὲ ...διὰ παραβολῶν μεμηνῦσθαι τοῖς συνιεῖν δυναμένοις Iren.*haer*.1.3.1 (M.7.468A); τὴν ἐπὶ τοῦ προφήτου Ἰωνᾶ μ. πεπραγματευμένην οἰκονομίαν Meth.*res*.2.25(p.380.16; M.18.329D); ὡς μ. τὰ πάντα... διηγεῖται ἡ θεία γραφή Epiph.*haer*.57.7(p.353.9; M.41.1005C).

***μυστηρίως,** = μυστικῶς; comp., *with a more profound spiritual meaning* τὸ περὶ τοῦ μονογενοῦς...μ. ὑπ' αὐτῶν [sc. τῶν προφητῶν] παραδιδόμενον Diod.*Rom*.16:25(p.112.8).

μύστης, ὁ, 1. *one initiated into the mysteries, initiate*; Christian ὁ κύριος...τὸν μ. σφραγίζεται φωταγωγῶν Clem.*prot*.12(p.84.25; M.8.241A); Gnost. τελειῶν τοὺς μ. τὰ ἄλαλα μυστήρια Hipp.*haer*.5.24 (p.126.1; M.16.3191D); fig., of one to whom spiritual truth has been revealed ἣν [sc. φιλοσοφίαν ἀληθῆ] εὑρόντες...ἔχουσιν οἱ μ. Clem.*str*.1.5(p.21.23; M.8.728A); of man as a spiritual being ἐπόπτην τῆς ὁρατῆς κτίσεως, μ. τῆς νοουμένης Gr.Naz.*or*.38.11(M.36.324A); of monks μ. κρυπτομένης ζωῆς Χριστοῖο id.*carm*.2.2(poem.)1.47(M.37.1455A); of Adam before Fall μ. τε θεοῦ θείων τε φαεινός *ib*.1.2.1.161(535A); Chrys.*hom.3.6 in Rom*.(9.445C); ἀποκαλῶν...'μύστας' Ἐφεσίους οἷς καὶ ὑψηλότερον ἐπιστέλλει Pall.*v.Chrys*.18(p.119.14; M.47.66); of seraphim οἱ τῶν ἐπουρανίων μ. ‡Meth.*Sym.et Ann*.11(M.18.376B); **2.** of one who has full knowledge, an *expert*: of those who expound inner meaning of scripture, Clem.*str*.1.23(p.96.6; M.8.900B); τοὺς τῶν αὐτοῦ [sc. θεοῦ] λόγων μ. Eus.*v.C*.1.32(p.22.21; M.20.948A); ἐμοί...τῷ μ. καὶ μυσταγωγῷ τῶν τοιούτων Gr.Naz.*or*.39.2(M.36.336B); Didym.*Trin*.1.27(M.39.393B); Pall.*v.Chrys*.18(p.115.32; M.47.64); τῶν ἡττόνων...τοὺς θειοτέρους μ. καὶ χειραγωγοὺς ἐπὶ τὴν θείαν προσαγωγὴν Dion.Ar.*c.h*.4.3(M.3.181A); of priest opp. choir τείχεσιν ὁππόσα μ. ἄνδρα πολυγλώσσοιο διακρίνουσιν ὁμίλου Paul.Sil.*Soph*.686(M.86.2145B); **3.** of one who is privy to a secret, a *confidant* τὰς ἀπορρήτους βασιλέως μυήσεις τοῖς τούτων μ. διηγείσθων μόνοις Eus.*l.C*.proem.(p.196.3; M.20.1317B); Philost.*h.e*.4.8(M.65.521A); of apostles, Eus.*d.e*.3.4(p.119.33; M.22.204C); **4.** *one who is being initiated*; met., *disciple*, Gr.Naz.*or*.15.6(M.35.921B); γνήσιος τοῦ Χριστοῦ μ. Ast.Am.*hom*.9(M.40.305B).

μυστικός, A. in gen., *secret, not easily accessible*; hence also **1.** *sacred* τὸ τετράγραμμον ὄνομα τὸ μ. Clem.*str*.5.6(p.348.17; M.9.60A); τὸν περὶ ἑβδομάδος τε καὶ ὀγδοάδος μ. λόγον *ib*.6.16(p.506.11; 376B); of places μ. ἄντρων Eus.*v.C*.3.43(p.96.7; M.20.1104B); of Easter vigil μ. διανυκτέρευσιν *ib*.4.22(p.125.30; 1169A); ἀπόκρυφον... καὶ μ. λόγον Ammon.*Jo*.19:36(M.85.1513B); *Chron.Pasch*.p.328(M.92.845B); of religious silence εἰσίωμεν...μετὰ σιγῆς μ. Chrys.*hom.1.8 in Mt*.(7.18A); *ib*.2.1(18C); **2.** *secret, esoteric, mysterious*; **a.** of more profound Christian doctrines, e.g. of divinity of Christ τῆς μυστικωτέρας περὶ αὐτοῦ θεολογίας Eus.*d.e*.3.7(p.147.14; M.22.248B); *ib*.4.1(p.150.4; 249D); ἀνθρώπινον τὸ τῆς γεννήσεως ὄνομα, ἀλλὰ μ. τὸ ὑπερχρόνιον γέννημα Gr.Ant.*bapt*.2.2(M.88.1873A); ref. Trin. τὸ τῆς ἁγίας τριάδος ἀπορρητότατον καὶ μυστικώτατον δόγμα Cyr.*syn.def*.(M.76.1424A); Trin. itself called μ., Eus.*Marcell*.1.1(p.3.25; M.24.716C); id.*l.C*.6(p.210.15; M.20.1348B); **b.** ref. *disciplina arcani*, esoteric knowledge to be kept from the profane τὸν ἐλεγκτικὸν λόγον, καὶ τὸν κεκρυμμένον καὶ μ.· καὶ τὸν μὲν ἐλεγκτικὸν ἐν προχείρῳ· τὸν δὲ μ., ἐν ταμιείῳ ἔνδον Thdt.*Cant*.3:8(2.86); τὸ διττὴν εἶναι τὴν τῶν θεολόγων παράδοσιν, τὴν μὲν ἀπόρρητον καὶ μ., τὴν δὲ ἐμφανῆ καὶ γνωριμωτέραν Dion.Ar.*ep*.9.1(M.3.1105D); **c.** *revealed*, as hidden from unaided human reason, Gr.Nyss.*or.catech*.32(p.122.10; M.45.81D); of teaching revealed to Moses on Sinai, id.*v.Mos*.(M.44.319D); **d.** in gen., *spiritual*; of teaching of Christ, Clem.*str*.6.15(p.496.17; M.9.352A); id.*q.d.s*.5(p.163.17; M.9.609C); Eus.*d.e*.1.10(p.46.10; M.22.88C); *ib*.2.3(p.92.4; 161D); Proc.G.*Is*.2:1–4(M.87.1876A); of fraternal kiss ὅπερ ἐχρῆν εἶναι μυστικόν Clem.*paed*.3.11(p.281.9; M.8.660B); περιτομή...μ. Max.*cap*.5.41(M.90.1365A); opp. σαρκικός, Procl.CP *or*.6.14(M.65.748D).

B. *possessing* or *conveying a hidden* (*spiritual*) *meaning* or *reality*; **1.** of hidden *mystical* (i.e. typological or allegorical) sense of scripture πρεσβυτέρα διαθήκη...ἐπαιδαγώγει τὸν λαὸν μετὰ φόβου καὶ λόγος ἄγγελος ἦν, καινῷ δὲ...λαῷ...ὁ μ. ἄγγελος Ἰησοῦς τίκτεται Clem.*paed*.1.7(p.125.2; M.8.321A); id.*prot*.1(p.10.13; M.8.65C); Eus.*h.e*.1.2.22(M.20.65A); used as technical term for *allegorical* sense ἀπόχρη μέχρι τοῦδε προχωρῆσαι τὴν μ. ἑρμηνείαν Clem.*str*.5.6(p.351.8; M.9.64A); esp. in Or. ἀνάπτυξιν τοῦ ἐν ταῖς λέξεσιν ἐναποτεθησαυρισμένου μ. νοῦ *Jo*.1.15(p.19.34; M.14.49B); κρύπτων μὲν τὸ μ., ἐμφαίνων δὲ τὸ ἁπλούστερον *ib*.13.40(p.266.11; 469C); id.*princ*.4.2.9(p.322.1; M.11.376A); ἡ μ. καὶ πνευματικὴ τῶν γραφῶν διάνοια Didym.*Ps*.1:3(M.39.1160A); Cyr.*Is*.1.2(2.53B); *ib*.3.1(353A); Proc.G.*Is*.7:10–17(M.87.1960D); Cosm.Ind.*top*.5(M.88.224A); of Cant. as allegorized book ἐν τῷ μ. τῶν ᾀσμάτων...βιβλίῳ Thdt.*provid*.5(4.550); of scripture in gen. λόγοι δὲ μ. τὸν ἐξηγητὴν ἀναμένουσιν Bas.*ep*.28.2(3.107E; M.32.308C); **2.** of sacraments; **a.** sts. as secret and not to be divulged to uninitiated αἱ διαταγαί...ἃς οὐ χρὴ δημοσιεύειν ἐπὶ πάντων διὰ τὰ ἐν αὐταῖς μ. *Can.App.*85; μυστικῶς τὰ μ. φθέγγεσθαι Gr.Naz.*or.*27.5(p.9.5; M.36.17B); cf.Chrys.*hom.40.1 in 1Cor.*(10.379B); **b.** in gen. τῇ τῶν μ. ἐθῶν τε καὶ συμβόλων κοινωνίᾳ Gr.Nyss.*Eun.*11(2 p.270.13; M.45.880B); τῆς μ. πράξεως id.*bapt.Chr.*(M.46.581A); **c.** ref. baptism; **i.** in gen. τὴν μ. ἀναγέννησιν εἰς ὄνομα τοῦ πατρός, καὶ τοῦ υἱοῦ, καὶ τοῦ ἁγίου πνεύματος Eus.*Marcell.*1.1 (p.8.21; M.24.728C); τοῖς διὰ τῆς μ. ταύτης οἰκονομίας ἀναγεννωμένοις Gr.Nyss.*or.catech.*34(p.129.2; M.45.85C); **ii.** of baptismal water, *ib.* 35(p.138.14; 92C); and chrism, Eus.*d.e.*1.10(p.48.2; M.22.89D); Epiph. *haer.*30.6(p.341.17; M.41.413D); Thdt.*Is.*61:2(p.241.1; 2.383); **iii.** of effects of baptism, e.g. forgiveness of sins διὰ μόνης πίστεως τῶν μ. τετυχήκαμεν ἀγαθῶν Thdt.*affect.*7(p.189.21; 4.892); baptism likened to μ. φίλημα, Gr.Nyss.*hom.11 in Cant.*(M.44.1001B); **d.** ref. eucharist; **i.** of last supper τὸ μ. αὐτοῖς παρέδωκε πάσχα Hesych.H.*qu.ev.*34(M. 93.1421D); *Chron.Pasch.*p.225(M.92.548C); as anticipating sacrifice of Cross, Eutych.*pasch.*4(M.86.2397A); **ii.** of eucharist as antitype of OT sacrifices ἀντὶ θυσίας τῆς δι' αἱμάτων...τὴν μ. τοῦ σώματος αὐτοῦ καὶ τοῦ αἵματος *Const.App.*6.23.4; Philost.*h.e.*3.14(M.65.501B); **iii.** of liturgy περὶ τῆς μ. λατρείας *Lit.*ap.*Const.App.*8.15.11; μ. λειτουργίας Eus.*v.C.*4.71(p.147.14; M.20.1225C); Thdt.*ep.*146(4.1260); μ. ἱερουργίαις Eus.*v.C.*4.45(p.136.18; 1196B); Thdt.*h.rel.*13(3.1208); Eutych.*pasch.*3(M.86.2393D); ἡ μ. τῶν πτυχῶν ἀνάρρησις Dion.Ar. *e.h.*3.2(M.3.425C); **iv.** partic. of Holy Communion ἡ μ. μετάληψις Ammon.*Jo.*6:57(M.85.1440B); μ. ἐκείνην τροφήν Chrys.*hom.54.4 in Mt.*(7.551B); τῶν μ. δείπνων id.*hom.24.5 in 1Cor.*(10.218D); μ. τροφὴ σώματος καὶ αἵματος Χριστοῦ Cosm.Ind.*top.*5(M.88.308B); as μυστικωτέρα than doctrine, Thdt.*Ps.*22:2(1.748); αἰδέσθητι τὴν μ. τράπεζαν Gr.Naz.*or.*40.31(M.36.404A); Thdt.*eran.*1(4.37); Gr.Ant. *bapt.*2.10(M.88.1881D); ἐσθίομεν τὸ σῶμα τὸ μ. Nil.*epp.*2.233(M.79. 320C); of eucharistic bread, Mac.Mgn.*apocr.*3.23(p.106.31); μὴ ὡς ψιλῷ ἄρτῳ προσερχώμεθα τῷ ἄρτῳ τῷ μ. Nil.*epp.*3.39(M.79.405B); and wine, Eus.*d.e.*8.1(p.366.16; M.22.596A); μ. ποτήριον Philost.*h.e.* 2.11(M.65.476B); Thdt.*qu.49 in Gen.*(1.115); id.*Is.*5:2(p.23.32; 2. 198); Proc.G.*Is.*65:13–25(M.87.2689B); cf. αἷμα μ. καὶ ὕδωρ ἀναγεννήσεως Gr.Ant.*mul.ung.*2(M.88.1849D); **3.** of prayers and objects connected with liturgy: Lord's Prayer τῆς εὐχῆς τῆς μ. Chrys.*hom. 14.3 in Rom.*(7.578E); Thdt.*Rom.*8:15(3.86); Cherubic Hymn τὸν μ. ὕμνον *Lit.Bas.* and *Lit.Chrys.*(p.319.3,5); words said by congregation μήποτε φωνὴν αὐτῆς ἐν ἱεροῖς ἀκουσθῆναι...ἔξω τῶν ἀναγκαίων καὶ μ. Gr.Naz.*or.*18.9(M.35.996B); chalice, CAlex.*ep.*ap.Ath.*apol.sec.* 8(p.94.18; M.25.264A); time of communion ἐν τῷ μ. καιρῷ, τοῦ νυμφίου τὰ μέλη δεχόμενοι Thdt.*Cant.*1:1(2.25); id.*Ps.*97:4(1.1303); μ. δὲ ἡμῖν συγγέγραπται βίβλος [i.e. on sacraments] Thdt.*ep.*82(4.1144); μ. παράδοσιν Petr.Laod.*fr.in Mt.*26:26(M.86.3325C); v. εὐλογία; **4.** in teaching of Basilides, Carpocrates, and others μ. κοινωνίαν ὠνόμασαν τὴν ἀσέλγειαν Thdt.*haer.*5.27(4.473); **5.** of ordination τοὺς δὲ ὑπ' αὐτοῦ [sc. Meletius] κατασταθέντος μυστικωτέρᾳ χειροτονίᾳ [Lat. *archana ordinatione* (Opitz 3 p.49)] βεβαιωθέντας κοινωνηθῆναι ἐπὶ τούτοις CNic.(325)*ep.*(p.49.4)ap.Socr.*h.e.*1.9.7(M.67.80A).

C. *mystical*, in technical sense, ref. direct, intuitive experience of God and theology dealing with this experience; esp. of θεωρία: τὸν κατὰ τὴν τάξιν τοῦ Μελχισεδὲκ ἀρχιερέα ὁδηγὸν ἔχοντες τῆς...μ. καὶ ἀπορρήτου θεωρίας Or.*Jo.*13.24(p.248.27; M.14.440C); εὐφραίνοντα καὶ ἐνθουσιᾶν ποιοῦντα ἀπόρρητα καὶ μ. θεωρήματα *ib.*1.30(33; p.37. 29; 80B); τῆς ἐν τῷ ᾄσματι τῶν ᾀσμάτων μ. θεωρίας Gr.Nyss.*hom.1 in Cant.*(M.44.765A); ψυχὴ...τετρωμένη γὰρ τῇ εἰς αὐτὸν [sc. Χριστόν] ἀγάπῃ ἐπιποθεῖ...τὴν πρὸς αὐτὸν...μ. συνουσίαν Mac.Aeg.*ep.*2(M.34. 416D); τέλειος νυμφίος, λαμβάνει αὐτὴν τελείαν νύμφην εἰς τὴν ἁγίαν καὶ μ. ... κοινωνίαν τοῦ γάμου id.*hom.*47.17(M.34.808C); *ib.*15.2(576C); used by Dion. Ar. of 'negative' opp. 'affirmative' theology τούτων μὲν τῶν ἑνώσεών τε καὶ διακρίσεων...ἐξεθέμεθα, τὰ μὲν ἀνελίξαντες τῷ ἀληθεῖ λόγῳ...τοῖς δὲ ὡς μ. κατὰ τὴν θείαν παράδοσιν ὑπὲρ νοερὰν ἐνέργειαν ἐπιβαλόντες *d.n.*2.7(M.3.645A); τριὰς ὑπερούσιε...ἴθυνον ἡμᾶς ἐπὶ τὴν τῶν μ. λογίων ὑπεράγνωστον...κορυφήν id.*myst.*1.1(M.3.997A); εἰς τὸν γνόφον τῆς ἀγνωσίας εἰσδύνει τὸν ὄντως μ. *ib.*1.3(1001A); of mystical contemplation as beyond the senses, imagination, and discursive reason, *ib.*1.1(997B); ref. one with knowledge of divine truths ἔκ τινος...θειοτέρας ἐπιπνοίας, οὐ μόνον μαθών, ἀλλὰ καὶ παθὼν τὰ θεῖα· κἀκ τῆς πρὸς αὐτὰ συμπαθείας...πρὸς τὴν ἀδίδακτον αὐτῶν καὶ μ. ἀποτελεσθεὶς ἕνωσιν καὶ πίστιν id.*d.n.*2.9(648B); *ib.*3.3 (684A); of visions of Moses τοιούτων ὀπτασιῶν μ. ἀξιῶσαι Cosm.Ind. *top.*3(M.88.160C); applied to heavenly realities πάντες δὲ οὗτοι [sc. angels] ἐπιδείκνυνται τὴν εὐταξίαν...τὸ μ. ἐκεῖνο μέλος...ᾄδοντες τῷ ...θεῷ. ... τὸν μ. αὐτῶν ζήλωσον κόσμον Chrys.*hom.19.3 in Mt.*(7. 248C); exeg. 1Thess.4:17 ἁρπαγησόμεθα γὰρ ἐν νεφέλαις νοηταῖς εἰς τὸν μ. ἀέρα Nil.*epp.*3.142(M.79.449B); of resurrection body, Thdt. *provid.*5(4.550) cit. s. σῶμα; ἀναχθῶμεν ἐπὶ τὴν θεοειδεστάτην αὐτῶν [sc. angels] ἁπλότητα, διὰ τῶν μ. ἀναπλάσεων Dion.Ar.*c.h.*4.1(M.3. 177C); τῆς τοῦ κατὰ φύσιν ὀρεκτοῦ [sc. God] μ. ἀπολαύσεως Max. *opusc.*(M.91.24C).

μυστικῶς, **1.** *secretly* ἐν τῷ ταμείῳ μ. προσεύχεσθαι Clem.*paed.*3.11 (p.281.22; M.8.661A); id.*str.*1.1(p.10.12; M.8.701C); ref. sacramental rites ἀξιῶ σε μυστικώτερον ἀποκρίνασθαι. τινὲς γὰρ ἴσως παρεστήκασιν ἀμύητοι Thdt.*eran.*1(4.24); **2.** *'mystically'*, i.e. in types and prophecies ἐγέλα [sc. Isaac] δὲ μ. ἐμπλῆσαι ἡμᾶς προφητεύων χαρᾶς τὸν κύριον Clem.*paed.*1.5(p.103.29; M.8.277A); μ. προφητευομένοις Or.*Jo.* 28.24(19; p.421.8; M.14.733C); οἱ μὲν γὰρ [sc. prophets] προῇδον μ. τὴν θείαν οἰκονομίαν, οἱ δ' [sc. apostles] ᾄδουσιν ἑρμηνεύοντες τὰ ὑπ' ἐκείνων μ. ἀπηγγελμένα Meth.*arbitr.*1(pp.146.19,147.1; M.18.241A,B); Epiph.*haer.*8.7(p.193.12; M.41.216A); Max.*ep.*14(M.91.540C); ref. Pauline teaching, id.*cap.*1.62(M.90.1204B); **3.** *sacramentally* συναποθνήσκει Χριστῷ, μ. εἰπεῖν τῇ ἁμαρτίᾳ κατὰ τὸ βάπτισμα Dion.Ar. *e.h.*2.3.6(M.3.404A); μ. συνταφέντες αὐτῷ διὰ τοῦ βαπτίσματος Marc. Er.*opusc.*4(M.65.985C); διὰ τοῦ βαπτίσματος χάρις δίδοται μ. *ib.*(M. 65.1001B); ὁ κύριος ἡμῶν...μ. πρόκειται εἰς θυσίαν *Lit.Jac.*(p.160.15); *with sacramental reality*, opp. τυπικῶς as relating to OT foreshadowing, Gr.Naz.*or.*41.4(M.36.436A); **4.** liturg., *in a low voice* (Lat. *secrete*), *ib.*27.5(p.9.5; 17B) cit. s. μυστικός; *Lit.Bas.* and *Lit. Chrys.*(p.324.4); **5.** *spiritually*, Clem.*paed.*1.5(p.98.19; M.8.265B); superl., *with deep spiritual significance* μυστικώτατα πέντε ἄρτοι πρὸς τοῦ σωτῆρος κατακλῶνται id.*str.*5.6(p.348.1; M.9.57A); comp., Or.*Jo.*20.4(p.331.16; M.14.581A); Eus.*h.e.*3.39.12(M.20.300A); Chrys. *hom.47.2 in Jo.*(8.278A); **6.** *mysteriously* τὸ μὲν ἀνδρικῶς αὐτὸν [sc. Christ] οὐσιωθῆναι, μ. παρειλήφαμεν Dion.Ar.*d.n.*2.9(M.3.648A); ἐν ἀγγέλοις...ὕλην ἄυλον μ. ἀπειργάσω Geo.Pis.*hex.*881(M.92.1502A); **7.** *mystically* τέλειοι, τῆς θεωρητικῆς ἤδη μ. ἀξιωθέντες θεολογίας Max.*cap.*1.68(M.90.1208A).

***μυστιπολεία**, **ἡ**, *solemnization of rites*, Eudoc.*Cypr.*1.299(M.85. 844B).

μυστιπόλος, **1.** *solemnizing mysteries*; as subst., of Jewish priests, Nonn.*par.Jo.*1:19(M.43.753A); Eudoc.*Cypr.*2.261(M.85.856B) unless as subst. neut. in sense 2; *worshipper*, Nonn.*par.Jo.* 4:23(777B); **2.** *connected with the mysteries, where mysteries are solemnized* ἑορτῆς *ib.*7:14(808A); μελάθρου Paul.Sil.*Soph.*188(M.86. 2127A); hence in gen., *sacred, holy* πίστις Eudoc.*Cypr.*2.2(M.85. 848A); βίβλοις Paul.Sil.*Soph.*585(2142A).

μύστις, **ἡ**, **1.** fem. form of μύστης, *sharer of a secret, confidante* δυνάμεις...ἃς καὶ τῆς οἰκονομίας μ. πεποίητο Gr.Naz.*or.*38.14(M.36. 328B); **2.** as adj., *mystic* μ. ἐδωδήν id.*carm.*1.2.29.299(M.37.906A); Nonn.*par.Jo.*4:21(M.43.777B).

***μυστιφόρος**, *bearing knowledge of mysteries*, Sophr.H.*carm.*8.18 (M.87.3772B).

[*]**μυστοπόλος**, = μυστιπόλος; as subst., *initiator*, of bishops μ. ζωῆς ἀτελευτήτοιο Gr.Naz.*carm.*2.1.13.6(M.37.1228A).

μυτακισμός, **ὁ**, *pronunciation of final M before a vowel*, cf. *motacismus est, quotiens M litteram vocalis sequitur*, Isid.H.*etym.* 1.32.6.

μυχθίζω, trans., *sneer at*, Didym.*Ps.*21:25(M.39.1285D).

μύχιος, *inward*; of rivers, *underground*, Philost.*h.e.*3.9(M.65. 492B).

***μυχοείς**, *lurking in dark corners*, Gr.Naz.*carm.*1.1.7.79(M.37. 444A).

μυχός, **ὁ**, *innermost part* λόγος...μονογενής, οἷα πατρὸς ἐξ ἀδύτου μ. γεγεννημένος Eus.*l.C.*12(p.230.10; M.20.1388B).

μυωξία, **ἡ**, *mouse-hole*, Gr.Naz.*ep.*4(M.37.25A).

μυωξός ([*]**μυοξός**), **ὁ**, *dormouse*, Epiph.*haer.*64.72(p.523.6; M.41. 1197D); id.*anc.*84(p.104.5; M.43.173A); μυοξός, Cyr.H.*catech.*18.7.

μυωπάζ-ω, *be shortsighted*; met., †Bas.*contub.*11(M.30.825B); μὴ ~ωμεν,...μακαρίζοντες ὑπὲρ ἡμᾶς κοσμικούς Jo.Carp.*cap.*suppl.(M. 85.1858); ἡ διδασκαλικὴ ἀκρόασίς ἐστι...~όντων φωτισμός Jo.Clim. *scal.*26(M.88.1064B); c. acc. μικρὰν καὶ...τὸ γραφικὸν ~ειν δοκοῦσαν μετάνοιαν Nil.*epp.*3.254(M.79.509B).

***μύωσις**, **ἡ**, ? *muscular structure* τὸ ἧπαρ...οὐσία ἐστὶν ἐρυθρὰ σαρκώδης μύωσιν ἔχουσα τεταμένην ἐν τοῖς δεξιοῖς μέρεσιν Melet.*nat. hom.*19(M.64.1221C).

§**μῶλος**, **ὁ**, (Lat. *moles*) *mole, breakwater*; μ. Εὐτροπίου name of a port, *Chron.Pasch.*p.380(M.92.976A); Thphn.*chron.*p.367(conj. for μούλῳ codd., M.108.880A).

μωλωπίζω, *scourge*, Gr.Nyss.*Apoll.*21(M.45.1165B).

μώλωψ, **ὁ**, *stripe, weal, bruise*; fig., Gr.Nyss.*virg.*18(p.321.4; M.46. 393A); Marc.Er.*opusc.*3.5(M.65.973A); τούτων οἱ μ. τῷ τῆς μετανοίας ταχυφαρμάκῳ καθαίρονται Chrysipp.*enc.in Mich.*(p.92.32); Max.

ambig.(M.91.1417A); γύμνου σὸν μ. τῷ σῷ ἰατρῷ Thdr.Stud.conf.1 (M.99.1721A).

μωμάομαι, *blame, find fault with*, hence *bring blame upon, discredit* ἐμωμήσω τῆς σωφροσύνης τὸ ἐπάγγελμα Bas.ep.45.2(3.134C; M.32.368B); οὐκ ἐμωμήθη τὰ...φάρμακα ib.(134D; M.368C); ‡Nil. perist.12.13(M.79.968A).

μώμημα, τό, *blemish*, Meth.res.1.43(p.291.7; M.18.272C).

μῶμος, ὁ, 1. *blame, reproach, disgrace*; ὑπὸ μῶμον εἶναι *incur reproach*, Cyr.glaph.Gen.3(1.69D); **2.** physical *blemish, defilement*, Const.App.6.27.7; *taint* γυναῖκα...μὴ ἔχουσαν μ. μήτε βεβηλωμένην T.Lev.9.10; Esaias or.11(p.69); fig. and met., 1Clem.63.1; θεραπευόμενοι τοὺς ψυχικοὺς μ. Thdr.Heracl.Is.30:26(M.18.1324C); τὸ μέγα καὶ ἄθυτον ἱερεῖον...θεραπευτικὸν μώμων...καὶ μολυσμάτων Gr.Naz. or.45.13(M.36.641B); Const.App.2.43.3; τῇ σωφροσύνῃ τοῦ τύφου τὸν μ. ἐντίθησι Thdt.Eph.6:11(3.438); παρθένους ψυχὰς...μὴ ἐχούσας μ. Esaias or.25.20(p.174; cf.M.40.1188A); ref. Inc. καὶ σῶμα λαβὼν καὶ ψυχὴν ὁ μονογενὴς...μώμου ταῦτα παντὸς ἐλεύθερα διεφύλαξε Thdt.ep. 145(4.1249); ἀληθῶς ὑπελθὼν τὰ ὑμέτερα ἔργα καὶ πάθη φυσικὰ...τὰ μώμου μακρὰν καὶ μολύσματος Sophr.H.ep.syn.(M.87.3177D).

***μωμοσκοπ-έω**, *examine* sacrificial victims *for blemishes*, 1Clem. 41.2; Cyr.ador.15(1.521C); id.Mal.proem.(3.817D); *examine* candidates for priesthood, Const.App.2.3.1; fig. γινωσκούσας ὅτι εἰσὶ θυσιαστήριον θεοῦ καὶ ὅτι πάντα ~εῖται, καὶ λέληθεν αὐτὸν οὐδὲν... τῶν κρυπτῶν τῆς καρδίας Polyc.ep.4.3; οὐ τὰ σώματα ~εῖσθαι ἀλλὰ θρησκείαν καὶ βίους Const.App.6.23.5; ref. Rom.12:1 χρὴ πανταχόθεν ~εῖσθαι τὸ σῶμα τὸ ἡμέτερον Chrys.hom.20.2 in Rom.(9.657E); of the formula τὰ ἅγια τοῖς ἁγίοις, id.hom.17.4 in Heb.(12.170B); met., *examine critically, criticize* βαττολογοῦμεν δὲ ὅτε μὴ ~οῦντες ἑαυτοὺς ἢ τούς...τῆς εὐχῆς λόγους λέγομεν τὰ διεφθαρμένα ἔργα ἢ λόγους ἢ νοήματα Or.or.21.1(p.345.4; M.11.480C); Ephr.3.46D; βίον ὑπὸ πάντων ~ούμενον Gr.Nyss.ep.18(M.46.1069C); Marc.Er.opusc.7.13(M.65. 1089D).

μωμοσκόπος, ὁ, *one who looks for blemishes* in sacrificial victims, Clem.str.4.18(p.300.1; M.8.1325B); Cyr.hom.pasch.4(βωμοσκόπους 5². 40D; μωμο- M.77.465D); fig. ἀκριβὴς μ. τῆς ἑαυτοῦ γενέσθω ψυχῆς id.Mal.14(3.832A); met., of *fault-finders*, Thdt.ep.16(4.1077).

μωραίνω, *make foolish, convict of folly*, ref. 1Cor.1:20, Clem.str.1. 18(p.57.17; M.8.804C); Hipp.Dan.3.2.5; πότε τῶν Ἑλλήνων ἡ σοφία μεμώραται, εἰ μὴ ὅτε ἡ ἀληθὴς τοῦ θεοῦ σοφία ἐπὶ γῆς ἑαυτὴν ἐφανέρωσε; Ath.inc.46.4(M.25.177D); Bas.hex.9.1(1.80E; M.29.189A); pass., *become foolish*, ref. Rom.1:20, Arist.apol.8.2; *become insipid*, Chrys. hom.15.6 in Mt.(7.193D); Vict.Mc.9:5(p.369.31); perf. ptcpl. pass. as adj., *foolish*, †Jo.D.B.J.31(M.96.1157C).

μωρίζω, *be foolish*, M.Tar.1(p.453); ib.5(p.460).

***μωρικός**, *foolish*; neut. plur. as subst., Ephr.2.140F.

***μωροπλούσιος, ὁ**, *rich fool*, Jo.Mosch.prat.206(M.87.3097B).

μωροποιέω, *act foolishly*, Nil.epp.3.17(M.79.377C); Apophth.Patr. (PO 11 p.407.2; M.65.121C); Leont.N.v.Sym.47(M.93.1728C).

μωροποιός, *making foolish*, Bas.hom.in Ps.48(1.182C; M.29.444C).

***μωροφανής**, *manifestly foolish*; neut. as subst., *manifest folly*, Gr.Nyss.Apoll.49(M.45.1241C).

μωρῶς, *in folly*, Ign.Eph.17.2.

***Μωσαΐζ-ω**, *speak like Moses* ~οντας μᾶλλον ἢ Πλατωνίζοντας Sophr.H.v.Cyr.et Jo.24(M.87.3409A).

***Μωσαϊκός**, *of Moses* συγγραφή Or.Ps.10:4(2 p.465); εὐλογίας Synes.ep.5(M.66.1344A); γράμματα Cyr.glaph.Gen.2(1.61C); *like that of Moses*; of impassioned prayer, Thdt.h.rel.2(3.1126).

***Μωσαϊκῶς**, *like Moses, as Moses did*, ‡Meth.Sym.et Ann.3(M.18. 353A).

***Μωσῆς**, v. *Μωϋσῆς.

[*]**μωτόω**, v. μοτόω.

[*]**μώτωσις, ἡ**, v. *μότωσις.

***Μωϋσῆς, *Μωσῆς, ὁ**, *Moses*;

A. in gen.; **1.** name explained M. ... διὰ τὸ ἐξ ὕδατος ἀνελέσθαι αὐτό (τὸ γὰρ ὕδωρ μῶυ ὀνομάζουσιν Αἰγύπτιοι),...καὶ γάρ τοι M. τὸν ἀποπνεύσαντα τῷ ὕδατι προσαγορεύουσι Clem.str.1.23(p.95.5; M.8. 897B); cf.Philo v.Mos.1.17; Μεννουθὶμ τοῦτον [sc. Μωϋσέα] ὠνόμασαν, ὅ ἐστιν Αἰγυπτιστὶ ἄνθρωπος τοῦ θεοῦ Hipp.Dan.3.2.6; M. προσεῖπεν ἐπειδὴ διεσώθη ἐκ τοῦ ὕδατος· Αἰγύπτιοι γὰρ τὸ ὕδωρ μῶυ καὶ τὸ σῆς σωθῆναι προσαγορεύουσι ‡Eust.hex.(M.18.780D); **2.** functions and powers ἔστιν οὖν ὁ M. ἡμῖν προφητικός, νομοθετικός, τακτικός, στρατηγικός, πολιτικός, φιλόσοφος Clem.str.1.24(p.99.16; M.8.905B); ἡ...κατὰ Μωϋσέα φιλοσοφία τετραχῇ τέμνεται, εἴς τε τὸ ἱστορικὸν καὶ τὸ κυρίως λεγόμενον νομοθετικόν...τὸ ἱερουργικόν...καὶ...τὸ θεολογικὸν ib.1.28(p.108.24; 921C); **a.** as lawgiver 'ὁ νόμος διὰ M. ἐδόθη' οὐχὶ ὑπὸ Μωσέως, ἀλλὰ ὑπὸ μὲν τοῦ λόγου, διὰ M. δὲ τοῦ θεράποντος αὐτοῦ id.paed.1.7(p.125.19; M.8.321C); M. συνελόντι εἰπεῖν νόμος ἔμψυχος ἦν τῷ χρηστῷ λόγῳ κυβερνώμενος id.str.1.26(p.104.23; 916A); Law of Moses to be interpreted spiritually οὐκ ἔστιν ἐντολὴ θεοῦ τὸ μὴ τρώγειν, M. δὲ ἐν πνεύματι ἐλάλησεν...οὐ κολλήσῃ, φησίν, ἀνθρώποις τοιούτοις οἵτινές εἰσιν ὅμοιοι χοίροις Barn.10.2; Clem.paed.2.10(p.208. 28; 500A); as minister of Christ ἄμφω δὲ τὼ νόμω διηκόνουν τῷ λόγῳ εἰς παιδαγωγίαν τῆς ἀνθρωπότητος, ὁ μὲν διὰ M. ὁ δὲ δι' ἀποστόλων ib. 3.12(p.287.29; 673A); Law imperfect, ref. Jo.4:13 τοῦ νόμου τοῦ διὰ Μωϋσέως τοῦ ὕδατος ὄντος Or.fr.56 in Jo.(p.529.6); οὕτω δὲ M. ἀτελῆ τὴν διδασκαλίαν τοῖς κατ' αὐτὸν παρεδίδου διὰ τὸ ἀτελὲς αὐτῶν τῆς φρονήσεως Eus.e.th.2.20(p.127.28; M.24.949D); Isid.Pel.epp.3.327(M. 78.988A); inspiration questioned by Marcionites, Adam.dial.1.22 (p.42.20; M.11.1749B); defended by Christ, ref. Mt.23:3 σκόπει πόσῃ περὶ τὸν M. κέχρηται τιμῇ, πάλιν τὴν πρὸς τὴν παλαιὰν συμφωνίαν ἐνδεικνύμενος Chrys.hom.72.1 in Mt.(7.701C); ref. Mt.19:8 ὁ Χριστὸς...οὐ μόνον οὐκ ἐμέμψατο τὸν Μωσέα, ἀλλὰ καὶ ὑπεραπελογήσατο Isid.Pel.epp.3.76(784C); **b.** as prophet, 1Clem.43.6; τὸν χορὸν πάντα τὸν προφητικόν, τοὺς συνθιασώτας τοῦ M. Clem.prot.8(p.60.23; M.8.189B); ib.4(p.47.29; 161B); οἱ μὲν γὰρ ἄλλοι προφῆται πάντες ἢ τὰ μετὰ πολὺν ἐσόμενα χρόνον εἶπον, ἢ τὰ κατ' αὐτὸν μέλλοντα συμβήσεσθαι τὸν καιρόν· ὁ δὲ μακάριος οὗτος μετὰ πολλὰς γενεὰς γεγονώς, ὑπὸ τῆς ἄνωθεν δεξιᾶς ὁδηγούμενος, ἐκεῖνα εἰπεῖν κατηξιώθη ἃ πρὸ τῆς αὐτοῦ γενέσεως ὑπὸ τοῦ τῶν ἁπάντων ἐδημιουργήθη δεσπότου Chrys.hom.2.2 in Gen.(4.9B); **c.** as apostle ἐπειδὴ δὲ ἔθετο ὁ θεὸς πρῶτον ἀποστόλους, δεύτερον προφήτας...M. τῶν ἀποστόλων ἐστί †Bas.Is.184(1.515C; M.30.432C); **3.** as author of Pentateuch M. ἀνέγραψεν (αὐτοῦ γάρ ἐστι τὸ Δευτερονόμιον) ὅτι 'οὐδεὶς οἶδε τὴν ταφὴν αὐτοῦ ἕως τῆς ἡμέρας ταύτης' σεμνύνων καὶ ἐπαίρων καὶ τὴν ταφὴν αὐτοῦ ὡς οὐκ ἐγνωσμένην ἀνθρώπων γένει Or.Cels.2.54(p.178.4; M.11.884A); but cf. μετά...τὴν Μωϋσέως ἀνάληψιν ἐγράφη ὑπό τινος, οὐ μὴν ὑπὸ M. Hom.Clem.3.47; and of book of Job, Or.Cels.6.43 (p.114.1; M.11.1365A); Meth.creat.10(p.498.31; M.18.341A); φασὶ δὲ Σολομῶντα συντεταχέναι καὶ τοῦτο τὸ βιβλίον, εἰ μὴ ἄρα Μωϋσέως ἐστὶ σύγγραμμα †Chrys.synops.(6.367B).

B. as type; **1.** of God εἰς τύπον θεοῦ M., προσκομίζουσι μὲν τὴν θυσίαν οἱ ἀμφὶ τὸν Ἀαρών, ὑποδέχεται δὲ αὐτός Cyr.ador.11(1.397E); ref. Ex.7:1, cf. νῦν γὰρ ὑμῖν μὲν ὁ Ἀαρών ἐστιν ὁ διάκονος, M. δὲ ὁ ἐπίσκοπος· εἰ οὖν ἐρρέθη M. ὑπὸ κυρίου θεός, καὶ ὑμῖν ὁ ἐπίσκοπος εἰς θεὸν τετιμήσθω καὶ ὁ διάκονος ὡς προφήτης αὐτοῦ Const.App.2.30.1; **2.** of Christ, ref. Ex.2:1 σεσίγηται δὲ καὶ ἐν τοῖς ἱεροῖς γράμμασιν οἰκονομικῶς ὁ Μωσέως πατήρ...ὅτι καὶ ἀπάτωρ τὸ κατὰ σάρκα Χριστὸς πλαγίως ὑποδηλῶν Cyr.glaph.Ex.1(1.250A); κατατεθηγμένη πρὸς μιαιφονίαν ἡ τεκοῦσα συναγωγή...[sc. Χριστόν] κατέκλεισεν ἐν μνημείῳ· τύπος ἂν γένοιτο...διὰ χειρὸς ὥσπερ τῆς ἰδίας μητρὸς ἐν τῇ καλουμένῃ θίβῃ καθιέμενος ὁ M. ib.(251C); ref. Mt.2:20, Proc.G.Ex. 4:18(M.87.537C); as lawgiver ὁ ἀληθινὸς νομοθέτης οὗ τύπος ἦν ὁ M. ...ἑαυτῷ τὰς τῆς φύσεως ἡμῶν πλάκας ἐλάξευσεν Gr.Nyss.v.Mos.(M. 44.397B); as mediator, Bas.Spir.33(3.27C; M.32.125B); μεσίτης μὲν σαρκικῆς ἐλευθερίας, γράμματός τε καὶ σκιᾶς ὁ ἱεροφάντης Μωσῆς. ὁ δὲ κύριος ἡμῶν...τῶν ὑπὲρ νόμον εἰσηγητής, καὶ τῆς σαρκικῆς ἐλευθερίας τὴν ἀσυγκρίτως ἀμείνω δωρούμενος, τοῦτ' ἔστι τὴν κατὰ πνεῦμα Cyr.ador.2(1.51B); as spouse of Church τὸν Χριστόν, ᾧ...Μωσέως περιθήσομεν πρόσωπον...εἰς τὸ σχῆμα τῆς Ἰουδαίων ἱερωσύνης Ἀαρὼν ληφθήσεται καὶ ἀναπληρώσει τῆς συναγωγῆς τὸ πρόσωπον ἡ Μαριάμ. κατηγόρευσαν τοίνυν τοῦ σωτῆρος ἡμῶν Χριστοῦ...ὅτι τὴν μέλαιναν, τουτέστι τὴν ἐξ ἐθνῶν ἐκκλησίαν, ἐμνηστεύετο id.glaph.Num.(1.380B); his life parallel with Christ's, in fulfilment of Dt.18:18, Eus.d.e.3.2 (pp.97–100; M.24.169–73); as worker of miracles, Chrys.hom.28.2 in Mt.(7.335A); his hand a type of Inc. τοῦ νομοθέτου ἡ χεὶρ προβληθεῖσα τοῦ κόλπου πρὸς τὸ παρὰ φύσιν ἠλλοιώθη χρῶμα· καὶ πάλιν ἐν κόλποις γενομένη, πρὸς τὴν ἰδίαν αὐτῆς καὶ κατὰ φύσιν ἐπανῆλθε χάριν. καὶ ὁ μονογενής...ὁ ὢν ἐν κόλποις τοῦ πατρός, οὗτός ἐστιν ἡ δεξιὰ τοῦ ὑψίστου. ὅτε δὲ ἡμῖν ἐκ τῶν κόλπων ἐφάνη, καθ' ἡμᾶς ἠλλοιώθη· ἐπεὶ δὲ τὰς ἡμετέρας ἀσθενείας ἐκμάξας, πάλιν ἐπανήγαγε τὴν ἐν ἡμῖν γενομένην χεῖρα, καὶ καθ' ἡμᾶς χρωσθεῖσαν ἐπὶ τὸν ἴδιον κόλπον...τότε οὐ τὸ ἀπαθὲς τῆς φύσεως εἰς πάθος ἠλλοίωσεν, ἀλλὰ τὸ τρεπτόν τε καὶ ἐμπαθὲς διὰ τῆς πρὸς τὸ ἄτρεπτον κοινωνίας εἰς ἀπάθειαν μετεστοιχείωσεν Gr.Nyss.v.Mos.(M.44.336A); Cyr.glaph.Ex.2(1.301B); but cf. ὁ δὲ κόλπος Μωϋσέως δύο δυνάμεις ἔχει, τὴν μὲν προτέραν καὶ κατὰ τὰ τοῦ γράμματος νοήματα, ποιοῦσαν τὴν πρᾶξιν τοῦ πράττοντος...λεπρῶσαν· τὴν δὲ δευτέραν καὶ ἀποδεικνύουσαν τὴν πολιτείαν καὶ ἀποκαθισταμένην εἰς τὸ βούλημα τῆς φύσεως τοῦ λόγου Or.Jo. 32.21(13; p.462.22; M.14.800D); first plague a type of Cross ἀρχὴ σημείων ἐπὶ Μωσέως αἷμα καὶ ὕδωρ, καὶ τὸ τελευταῖον πάντων τῶν σημείων Ἰησοῦ τὸ αὐτό Cyr.H.catech.13.21; his outstretched arms a type of Cross τοῦ Μωσέως καὶ ὑπὲρ τούτων [sc. τῶν

Αἰγυπτίων] τὰς χεῖρας ἐκτείναντος, ἀφανισμὸς τῶν βατράχων γίνεται... οἱ γὰρ τὴν ἔκτασιν τῶν χειρῶν τοῦ νομοθέτου κατανοήσαντες (συνήσεις ...διὰ μὲν τοῦ νομοθέτου τὸν ἀληθινὸν νομοθέτην, διὰ δὲ τῆς τῶν χειρῶν ἐκτάσεως, τὸν ἐπὶ τοῦ σταυροῦ τὰς χεῖρας ἐκτείναντα) οἱ...τοῖς ῥυπαροῖς...καὶ βατραχώδεσι λογισμοῖς συζῶντες...ἀπαλλάσσονται τῆς πονηρᾶς αὐτῶν συνοικήσεως Gr.Nyss.*v.Mos.*(M.44.348D); ref. battle with Amalek λέγει εἰς τὴν καρδίαν Μωϋσέως τὸ πνεῦμα, ἵνα ποιήσῃ τύπον σταυροῦ καὶ τοῦ μέλλοντος πάσχειν...σταθεὶς ὑψηλότερος πάντων ἐξέτεινεν τὰς χεῖρας, καὶ οὕτως ἐνίκα ὁ Ἰσραήλ *Barn.*12.2; Just. *dial.*90.5(M.6.692A); ἡ ἔκτασις τῶν χειρῶν τοῦ νομοθέτου γίνεται, ἡ τὸ μυστήριον τοῦ σταυροῦ προδεικνύουσα Gr.Nyss.*v.Mos.*(373B); **3.** of the Christian τῷ μητρῴῳ γάλακτι...τιθηνούμενος [sc. *M.*]. ὅπερ μοι δοκεῖ διδάσκειν ἵν' εἰ τοῖς ἔξωθεν λόγοις καθομιλοίημεν ἐν τῷ καιρῷ τῆς παιδεύσεως, μὴ χωρίζεσθαι τοῦ ὑποτρέφοντος ἡμᾶς τῆς ἐκκλησίας γάλακτος *ib.*(329C); θεὸς ἐξείλετό τε καὶ σέσωκε [sc. ἡμᾶς]...παροίσομεν γὰρ εἰς εἰκόνα καὶ ὑποτύπωσιν τῆς διὰ Χριστοῦ σωτηρίας τὰ ἐπὶ τῷ θεσπεσίῳ *M.* γεγραμμένα Cyr.*glaph.Ex.*1(1.248A); τοῦ *M.* ἡ ἐπὶ τὸ ἐνδοξότερον μεταποίησις...ὁ γὰρ διορθωτὴς τῆς συντετριμμένης ἡμῶν φύσεως πλακὸς...ἐπειδὴ πάλιν εἰς τὸ ἀρχαῖον ἐπανήγαγε τὴν...πλάκα τῷ θείῳ δακτύλῳ...καλλωπισθεῖσαν, οὐκέτι χωρητὸς ταῖς ὄψεσι τῶν ἀναξίων γίνεται Gr.Nyss.*v.Mos.*(M.44.397C); **4.** various moral and spiritual lessons drawn from events in his life ταύτην ἔλαβεν τὴν χάριν [sc. τὴν ἐγκράτειαν] καὶ ὁ *M.* τὸ ἐνδεὲς σῶμα περικείμενος, ἵνα τεσσαράκοντα ἡμέρας μήτε πεινάσῃ μήτε διψήσῃ Clem.*str.*3.7(p.222.20; M.8.1161A); τῷ *M.* ἐκ τῆς δικαιοπραγίας καὶ τῆς κατὰ τὸ συνεχὲς πρὸς τὸν θεὸν τὸν λαλοῦντα αὐτῷ ὁμιλίας ἐπίχροιά τις ἐπεκάθιζε τῷ προσώπῳ *ib.*6.12(p.484.12; M.9.325A); εἰς καθαίρεσιν τῶν τῇ φύσει τοῦ σώματος ἀκολουθησάντων ἁμαρτημάτων τεσσαράκοντα νηστεύει *M.* ἡμέρας, ὁμοίας δὲ καὶ Ἠλίας καὶ ὑπὲρ τῶν ἡμετέρων ἁμαρτημάτων ὁ σωτήρ Or.*fr.79 in Jo.*(p.546.30); ἐπὶ μὲν τῇ πρώτῃ τεσσαρακονταετηρίδι ἐπαιδεύθη τὰ Αἰγυπτίων, ἐπὶ δὲ τῇ δευτέρᾳ τεσσαρακονταετηρίδι ἐπὶ προφάσει τοῦ ποιμαίνειν ἐπὶ τὰς ἐρημίας ἀναχωρήσας, τῇ θεωρίᾳ τῶν ὄντων ἀπεσχόλασε †Bas.*Is.*7(1.382D; M.30.129A); ἡ κατὰ Μωϋσέα παραινίσσεται ἱστορία, τοὺς προκόπτοντας μὴ ἐξομαλίζειν τὰς πράξεις, ἀλλὰ ποτὲ μὲν κρεῖττον βιοῦν, ποτὲ δὲ δι' ἀτονίαν ἐκλύεσθαι καὶ ἀσθενέστερον ἐνεργεῖν *ib.*35(408C; M.189A); ref. Jer.3:1, Ex. 34:34 ὁρᾷς ὡς *M.* ποτε λαμβάνεται καὶ ἐπὶ τοῦ λαοῦ. ὅσον οὐκ ἐπέστρεφεν πρὸς κύριον, σύμβολον ὢν τοῦ λαοῦ τοῦ μὴ ἐπιστρέφοντος πρὸς κύριον, κάλυμμα εἶχεν ἐπικείμενον αὐτοῦ τῷ προσώπῳ Or.*hom.5.8 in Jer.*(p.38.20; M.13.308A); τροπικῶς τὸ δεδοξασμένον πρόσωπον Μωϋσέως, θεοποιηθέντος αὐτοῦ τοῦ νοῦ id.*Jo.*32.27(17; p.472.33; M.14.817A); πρόσωπον Μωϋσέως νόησον εἶναι τὸ φῶς τῆς πεντατεύχου, κάλυμμα δὲ τὸ ἀσαφὲς τῶν μακαρίων λόγων, καὶ τὸ παραβολικόν, ἢ συμβολικόν, καὶ τὸ αἰνιγματῶδες Nil.*epp.*1.119(M.79.136A); ref. Ex.33:7 *M.* ... ἔξω τῆς παρεμβολῆς πηξάμενος ἑαυτοῦ τὴν σκηνήν· τουτέστι τὴν γνώμην καὶ τὴν διάνοιαν ἱδρυσάμενος ἔξω τῶν ὁρωμένων, προσκυνεῖν τὸν θεὸν ἄρχεται· καὶ εἰς τὸν γνόφον εἰσελθών, τὸν ἀειδῆ καὶ ἄυλον, τῆς γνώσεως τόπον, ἐκεῖ μένει τὰς ἱερωτάτας τελούμενος τελετάς Max.*cap.theol.*84(M.90.1117C); μετὰ τὸ προφητεῦσαι Μωϋσῆν οὐκέτι γυναικὶ συνῆπται, οὐκέτι τέκνα κυΐσκει, οὐκέτι γεννᾷ ὁ τοιοῦτος Epiph.*ep.Arab.*ap.*haer.*78.16(p.466.20; M.42.724D); ‡Gr.Naz.*sign.in Ezech.*(M.36.668C); οἱ μὲν τὸ σῶμα τῶν γραφῶν, τὰς λέξεις καὶ τὰ ὀνόματα, καθάπερ τὸ σῶμα τὸ Μωϋσέως, προσβλέπουσιν, οἱ δὲ τὰς διανοίας καὶ τὰ ὑπὸ τῶν ὀνομάτων δηλούμενα διορῶσι, τὸν μετὰ ἀγγέλων *M.* πολυπραγμονοῦντες Clem.*str.*6.15(p.498.30; M.9.357A); ὅταν περὶ τοῦ *M.* ἀκούσῃς σώματος ἐν τῷ νόμῳ, γραφῇ νόμιζέ σοι χαρακτηρίζεσθαι τὸν ὅλον Ἰσραηλίτην λαόν, καὶ περὶ αὐτοῦ γεγονέναι τὴν ἀμφισβήτησιν τοῦ διαβόλου πρὸς τὸν ἀρχάγγελον Chrysipp.*enc.in Mich.*(p.93.9); ref. Jo.4:36 θερισμός πως ἦν ἡ μεταμόρφωσις Ἰησοῦ ἐν δόξῃ φαινομένου οὐ μόνον τοῖς θερισταῖς Πέτρῳ καὶ Ἰακώβῳ καὶ Ἰωάννῃ...ἀλλὰ καὶ τοῖς σπείρασιν *M.* καὶ Ἠλίᾳ Or.*Jo.*13.47(46; p.273.31; M.14.484A); *M.*, νομοθέτης ὁμοῦ καὶ ἀρχιερεὺς καὶ προφήτης καὶ βασιλεύς, καὶ Ἠλίας...συνῆσαν ἐν τῇ μεταμορφώσει τοῦ κυρίου...ὡς φίλοι Χριστοῦ καὶ οἰκεῖοι, ἀλλ' οὐχ ὡς ἐχθροὶ ἢ ἀλλότριοι *Const.App.*6.19.4; ἡ *M.* καὶ Ἡλίου παρουσία τὴν ζώντων καὶ νεκρῶν ἐμαρτύρησεν αὐτῷ δεσποτείαν Isid.Pel.*epp.*1.239(M.78.329B); ἡ Μωσέως καὶ Ἠλία παράστασις...οἰκονομία τις ἦν... καταδεικνύουσα δορυφορούμενον ὑπὸ νόμου καὶ προφητῶν τὸν κύριον ...ὡς καὶ νόμου καὶ προφητῶν δεσπότην Cyr.*hom.div.*9(5².368B); νεκρῶν πιστοῦται ἀνάστασις, καὶ νεκρῶν καὶ ζώντων ἀναδείκνυται κύριος, ἐκ νεκρῶν μὲν τὸν *M.* προηκάμενος, ζῶντα δὲ τὸν Ἠλίαν προσαγόμενος μάρτυρα Jo.D.*hom.*1.3(M.96.549C).

C. Moses = the Law, Or.*comm.in Mt.*12.43(p.168.8; M.13.1084A); id.*Jo.*20.39(31; p.381.17; M.14.665C); Meth.*fr.Job* 9:5(p.511.9); Bas. *Spir.*33(3.27D; M.32.125C); *Const.App.*5.14.9; Cyr.*Is.*1.5(2.133A); Thdt.*qu.1 in Jos.*(1.299); συμμεταμορφωθῶσιν...*M.* καὶ Ἠλίας, τουτέστιν, ὁ νόμος καὶ οἱ προφῆται, ὅταν μεταμορφωθῶσιν αὐτῶν οἱ λόγοι, καὶ κινηθῶσιν αἱ τοῦ νόμου σκιαί, τότε καὶ πιστευθήσεται *M.* ... περὶ Χριστοῦ γράψας πάντα Anast.Ant.*serm.*1.5(M.89.1369B); *M.* καὶ Ἠλίας...ὁ μὲν τὸν γραπτόν,...ὁ δὲ τὸν φυσικὸν νόμον δηλοῖ Andr.Cr. *or.*7(M.97.953C).

D. 'new Moses', 'second Moses'; S. Paul, Eustrat.*stat.anim.*5(p.349); S. Basil, Jo.Mon.*hymn.Bas.*3(M.96.1372C); an abbot of Sinai, †Anast.S.*relat.*32(*OC* 2 p.79.5; M.88.609A).

N

[*]**νά**, **1.** (from ἵνα) conjunction put before subjunctive to express a final clause, *to, in order that* ἐγὼ νὰ ἀναθρέψω τὸν ἀνέψιον Barth.Edess.*Agar.*(M.104.1425D); **2.** emphatic interjection, *lo! verily!* ὁ θεὸς καλὰ νὰ ποιήσει μετὰ τοῦ δεῖνος Eus.Al.*serm.*21.8(M.86.433B); πῶς αὐτοὺς καταλείψω πτωχούς; καὶ νά με καταροῦνται *ib.*21.16(441C).

***νάας (νάς)**, ὁ, (Hebr. נָחָשׁ) *serpent*; **1.** of Devil τὸ γὰρ Σατὰν τῇ Ἰουδαίων καὶ Σύρων φωνῇ ἀποστάτης ἐστί, τὸ δὲ νὰς ὄνομα ἐξ οὗ ἡ ἑρμηνεία ὄφις ἐκλήθη Just.*dial.*103.5(M.6.717B); related to name of Nahash (1Reg.11:2) ὁ ὄφις ὁ νοητός. *ν.* γὰρ ἑρμηνεύεται ὄφις, ὅστις τοῖς Ἰσραηλίταις...ἐπηπείλησε...νικῆσαι τὸν...*ν.* τὸν ἐν σοὶ Ἀμμανίτην Nil.*epp.*2.198(M.79.304C); **2.** in interpretation of Nehushtan Νεεθάν ...χαλκὸς αὕτη. οἱ δὲ λοιποὶ τὸν Νεεθὰν *N.* Thdt.*qu.49 in 4Reg.*(1.543); **3.** source of name Naassene (v. Ναασσηνοί), Hipp.*haer.*5.6(p.78.1; M.16.3126A); *ν.* δὲ ἐστὶν ὁ ὄφις, ἀφ' οὗ φησι πάντας εἶναι τοὺς...προσαγορευομένους ναοὺς ἀπὸ τοῦ *ν.*· κἀκείνῳ μόνῳ τῷ *ν.* ἀνακεῖσθαι πᾶν ἱερὸν καὶ πᾶσαν τελετὴν καὶ πᾶν μυστήριον, καὶ...μὴ δύνασθαι τελετὴν εὑρεθῆναι...ἐν ᾗ ναὸς οὐκ ἔστι καὶ ὁ *ν.* ἐν αὐτῷ, ἀφ' οὗ ἔλαχε ναὸς καλεῖσθαι *ib.*5.9(p.100.19; 3155B); Thdt.*qu.49 in 4Reg.*(1.543); **4.** as angel identified with tree of knowledge in system of Justinus τὸ δὲ ξύλον τοῦ εἰδέναι γνῶσιν καλοῦ καὶ πονηροῦ ὁ τρίτος τῶν μητρικῶν ἀγγέλων, ὁ *N.* Hipp.*haer.*5.26(p.127.25; M.16.3195A); seducer of Adam and Eve, *ib.*(p.130.12; 3199B); responsible for temptation and crucifixion of Jesus, *ib.*(p.131.28; 3202C); identified with eagle, Adam being represented by Ganymede, *ib.*(p.132.11; 3202D).

***Ναασσηνοί (-ινοί)**, οἱ, *Naassenes*, Gnostic sect who revered the serpent (νάας, q.v.) οἱ *N.* ... οἱ ἑαυτοὺς γνωστικοὺς ἀποκαλοῦντες... ἐκεῖνα δογματίζουσιν ἃ πρότερον οἱ Ἑλλήνων φιλόσοφοι ἐδογμάτισαν ...τὰ μυστικὰ παραδόντες Hipp.*haer.*5.2(p.77.4; M.16.3123A); *N.* τῇ Ἑβραΐδι φωνῇ οὕτως ὠνομασμένοι...μετὰ δὲ ταῦτα ἐπεκάλεσαν ἑαυτοὺς γνωστικούς, φάσκοντες μόνοι τὰ βάθη γινώσκειν *ib.*5.6(p.77.30; 3126A); τιμῶσι δὲ οὐκ ἄλλο τι ἢ τὸν νάας οὗτοι, *N.* καλούμενοι *ib.*5.9(p.100.19; 3155B); their doctrine of man and of Jesus, *ib.*10.9(p.268.12; 3419A); ἐκ τῶν Βαλεντίνου σπερμάτων τὸ τῶν...Βορβοριανῶν ἢ Ναασινῶν...μῦσος Thdt.*haer.*1.13(4.304); id.*qu.49 in 4Reg.*(1.543).

νάβλα, ἡ, (Hebr. נֵבֶל, נִבְלָא), a musical instrument of 10 or 12 strings; symbolism and suitability to David discussed, ‡Hipp.*fr. 9 in Pss.*(p.140.21; M.10.716D).

***Ναβουχοδονοσορικός**, *as of Nebuchadnezzar N.* δόγματι Thdr. Stud.*epp.*2.17(M.99.1169D).

***Ναζιραῖος (Ναζαραῖος)**, ὁ, (Hebr. נָזִיר) *Nazirite*; **1.** in gen. ἀπὸ οἴνου καὶ σίκερα ἁγνισθήσεται, καὶ τὰ ἑξῆς περὶ τοῦ καλουμένου *N.* Or. *or.*3(p.306.5; M.11.425D); *N.* τὸ πεφυλαγμένον κατὰ τὴν Σύρων φωνὴν ὀνομάζει id.*sel.in Jud.*16:17(M.12.949B); spiritual interprn. of law against cutting of hair, id.*hom.8.11 in Lev.*(p.413.23; M.12.505B); id.*dial.*22(p.164.6); ἡγιασμένοι γὰρ τὸ Ναζιραῖοι δηλοῖ id.*fr.102 in Lam.*4:7–8(p.271.27; M.13.653A); εἰ δὲ οἴνου οἱ Ναζαραῖοι κατὰ τὸν νόμον ἀπέχονται, θυμοῦ ἄρα τοὺς *N.* ἐκτὸς εἶναι νενομοθέτηται id.*exp.in Pr.*20:1(M.17.209C); τὸ *ν.* ὄνομα σημαίνειν ἤτοι τὸν ἅγιον ἢ τὸν ἀφωρισμένον, ἢ τὸν ἄθικτον Eus.*d.e.*7.2(p.336.26; M.22.549A); of Jo. Bapt., Epiph.*haer.*29.5(p.327.12ff.; M.41.400B); **2.** exeg. Mt. 2:23 κληθεὶς δὲ...*N.* ἀπὸ τῆς Ναζαρέθ,...ἔδει...αὐτὸν...φύσει...*N.* ὄντα, τοῦτ' ἔστιν ἅγιον καὶ ἄθικτον καὶ ἀφωρισμένον ἐξ ἀνθρώπων, κληθῆναι...ἀλλ' ἐπεὶ μὴ ἐκ τοῦ ναζὲρ ἐλαίου ταύτης ἔτυχεν τῆς προσηγορίας, μὴ δεηθεὶς ἀνθρωπίνου χρίσματος, ἐκ τοῦ τόπου τῆς Ναζαρὲθ τὴν ἐπωνυμίαν ἐκτήσατο Eus.*d.e.*7.2(p.336.34; M.22.549B); cf.Tert.*adversus Marcionem* 4.8(M.*PL.*2.372ff.); **3.** '*Christian Nazirite*', *ascetic*, Bas.*ep.*44.1(3.131E; M.32.361C); Ναζαραίων χοροστασίαι Gr.Naz.*or.*42.26(M.36.489C); τοὺς καθ' ἡμᾶς Ναζιραίους *ib.*43.28(533C); Thdr.Stud.*or.*11.17(M.99.820B).

***Ναζωραῖος, ὁ,** *man of Nazareth*; **1.** of Christ *ἐν ὀνόματι Ἰησοῦ Χριστοῦ τοῦ Ν. A.Jo.*47(p.174.33); *ὁ Ν. ἄνθρωπος* Cels.ap.Or.*Cels.* 7.18(p.169.18; M.11.1445C); *A.Phil.*19(p.10.12); *ἐγὼ Ἰουδαῖος...καὶ οὐκ ἄν ποτε τῷ Ν. πιστεύσω A.Phil.epit.*27/28(p.98.17); Juln.Imp. ap.Cyr.*Juln.*3(6².100A); id.*ib.*10(335C); **2.** exeg. Mt.2:23, where interpreted both as *Nazarene* and as *Nazirite* (v. *Ναζιραῖος*) *Ν. κληθήσεται ὁ κυρίως τῷ θεῷ ἀεὶ ἀνακείμενος* Or.*comm.in Mt.*16.19 (p.540.27; M.13.1437C); Eus.*d.e.*7.2(p.336.12ff.; *Ναζαραῖον* M.22. 548D); prophecy cited in Mt. may belong to one of prophetical books lost through Jewish neglect; *οἱ προφῆται, καὶ οἱ ἀπόστολοι πολλαχοῦ Ν. αὐτὸν καλοῦσι* Chrys.*hom.9.4 in Mt.*(7.135C); **3.** as title of Christians *πάντες δὲ Χριστιανοὶ Ν. τότε ὡσαύτως ἐκαλοῦντο· γέγονε δὲ ἐπ' ὀλίγῳ χρόνῳ καλεῖσθαι...Ἰεσσαίους, πρὶν ἢ...ἀρχὴν λάβωσιν... καλεῖσθαι Χριστιανοί* Epiph.*haer.*29.1(p.322.1; M.41.389A); **4.** plur., name of early Judaistic Christian sect, observing sabbath and circumcision, Epiph.*haer.*29.7(p.329.4ff.; M.41.401Bff.); flourishing at Beroea, in Coele-Syria, Decapolis, district of Pella, originating with move of Jerusalem Christians to Pella in A.D. 68, *ib.*(p.330.4; 401D); using Mt. in Hebrew; cursed by orthodox Jews thrice daily, *ib.*29.9(p.332.4ff.; 404Dff.); revering Christ as a righteous man, Thdt.*haer.*2.2(4.329); Jo.D.*haer.*29(M.94.696A); dist. from *Νασαραῖοι* q.v., Epiph.*haer.*29.6(p.327.18; M.41.400B); ass. Elxai and Ebionites, *ib.*19.5(p.222.27; *Ναζαραίοις* 268C).

***Ναζωρικός,** *of a 'Nazirite'* (*Christian ascetic*), Steph.Diac.*v. Steph.*(M.100.1120B).

***ναΐς,** ? *populous ναΐδων πόλεων οἰκήτορες ἔνδοξοι* Mac.Mgn.*apocr.* 2.7(p.7.7).

***νακοτάπητον, τό,** *thick carpet*, Thphn.*chron.*p.268(M.108.665A).

νᾶμα, τό, *stream*; met.; **1.** in gen. *ἔπιες τὸ διειδὲς ν. τοῦ βίου* Bas. *hom.*21.11(2.172D; M.31.561B); **2.** of 'living water' (cf. Jo.4:12) *θείου καὶ καθαροῦ ν. τοῦ ζῶντος ὕδατος* Clem.*str.*2.2(p.116.30; M.8.937C); *νοερὰ...τῆς διδασκαλίας τοῦ Ἰησοῦ ν.* Or.*fr.54 in Jo.*(p.528.27); Meth.*symp.*4.3(p.49.8; M.18.92A); *ζωὴ ὑπῆρχεν ἀληθῶς, καθ' ὃ πᾶσιν τοῖς ζῶσιν τὸ τῆς ἐξ αὐτοῦ χορηγίας παρέχει ν.* Eus.*e.th.*2.14 (p.118.16; M.24.933B); *ζωοποιὰ ν. παρέχεται ὁ Χριστὸς...διὰ τῶν μυστηρίων, οὗ τύπος ἦν ἡ πέτρα* Cosm.Ind.*top.*5(M.88.200C); **3.** of Christian gospel *ἐνθένδε* [sc. Palestine] *τοῦ ζωοποιοῦ ν. ἀνομβρήσαντος εἰς πάντας* Eus.*l.C.*9(p.221.6; M.20.1369B); Thdt.*h.e.*5.31.1 (3.1070); id.*affect.*8(p.196.2; 4.899); **4.** of doctrine *τὰ ὦτα νάμασιν εὐσεβείας καθηράμενοι* Eus.*l.C.*proem.(p.196.4; M.20.1317B); *ἵν'... ἀπονίψωνται τὰς ἑαυτῶν ἀσεβεῖς ἀκοὰς τῷ τῆς ἀληθείας ν. καὶ τοῖς τῆς εὐσεβείας δόγμασιν* Ath.*decr.*2(p.2.34; M.25.'428'(420)B); *τῶν πνευματικῶν Διοδώρου ν. ἀπήλαυον* Thdt.*h.e.*5.40.1(3.1087); **5.** of baptism *σωτηρίων ν.* Cyr.H.*catech.*19.3; *τῆς κολυμβήθρας τοῦ ἁγίου πνεύματος τὰ ἀθάνατα ν.* Didym.*Trin.*2.22(M.39.556C); Chrys.*ep.*2. 2(3.536B); **6.** of eucharist *αἷμα τῆς ἀμπέλου τὸν λόγον τὸν περὶ πολλῶν ...εἰς ἄφεσιν ἁμαρτιῶν, εὐφροσύνης ἅγιον ἀλληγορεῖ ν.* Clem.*paed.*2.2 (p.176.4; M.8.428C); *ὁπόταν μορφωθῇ εἰς τοὺς νεοφωτίστους ὁ Χριστός, δι' αὐτῶν τῶν ἀναγεννωμένων ποτίζεται ἀπὸ τοῦ μυστηριώδους ν.* Ph.Carp.*Cant.*223(M.40.141A); Thdt.*qu.27 in Ex.*(1.144); hence *eucharistic wine*, Anast.*temp.*(p.279); cf.*Lit.Chrys.*(p.357.21); *Nomoc.* 76; *σφραγίζει τὸ ν. καὶ τὸ ὕδωρ Euchol.*(p.86); *ib.*(p.166).

***ναματίζ-ω,** *give to drink*, met. *ἐπιστατεῖ τοῖς λογικοῖς θρέμμασι..., ∼ων κατηχήσεως ῥείθρῳ* Thdr.Stud.*or.*11.24(M.99.825C).

***ναματικός,** *of the spring* or *stream*, Nil.*exerc.*71(M.79.804D).

***ναματοφόρος,** *bearing the stream* (of living water, i.e. Christ); of BMV, *Pers.*(p.15.18; M.10.104C).

[*]**νανούδιον, τό,** *dwarf ὃ ν. καλοῦσιν κατὰ στέρησιν τοῦ ἄνω ἰέναι Schol.Clem.paed.*3.4(p.337.23; *ναννούδιον* M.9.793A).

ναοποι-έω, *make into a temple*; of H. Ghost making faithful into a spiritual temple, Gr.Naz.*or.*31.29(p.184.6; M.36.168A); *ib.*41.9 (441C); *τοῦ τὰς ψυχὰς ∼οῦντος πνευματικοῦ νόμου* ‡Proc.G.*Pr.*5:14 (M.87.1264C).

ναός (νεώς), ὁ, *temple, shrine*;

I. lit.; **A.** of pagan temples; of tombs as *ναοὶ τῶν νεκρῶν* Clem. *prot.*4(p.38.20; M.8.141A); ref. Celsus' complaint that Christians have no temples, Or.*Cels.*8.19(p.236.15; M.11.1545C); of temples at Oxyrhynchus inhabited by monks, ‡Pall.*h.mon.*5.2(p.29.6; M.65. 445D).

B. of Tabernacle, Gr.Nyss.*v.Mos.*(M.44.321); ref. Ps.27:1 *οὐδέπω μὲν ὁ ν. ᾠκοδόμητο· τὴν δὲ σκηνὴν ὀνομάζει ν.* Thdt.ad loc.(1.775).

C. of Jewish Temple; **1.** in gen. *εἰσελεύσεται εἰς τὸν πρῶτον ν. καὶ ἐκεῖ κύριος ὑβρισθήσεται...καὶ ἔσται τὸ ἅπλωμα τοῦ ν. σχιζόμενον καὶ μεταβήσεται τὸ πνεῦμα θεοῦ ἐπὶ τὰ ἔθνη T.Benj.*9.3; *πλανώμενοι* [sc. Jews]*...εἰς τὴν οἰκοδομὴν ἤλπισαν, καὶ οὐκ ἐπὶ τὸν θεὸν...σχεδὸν γὰρ ὡς τὰ ἔθνη ἀφιέρωσαν αὐτὸν ἐν τῷ ν. Barn.*16.2; its destruction due to divine providence, Or.*Cels.*7.26(p.177.20; M.11.1457C); interval of 42 years (between 15th year of Tiberius and Temple's destruction) given to enable some Jews to be converted, id.*hom. 14.13 in Jer.*(p.118.19; M.13.420C); Eus.*h.e.*3.5.4(M.20.224B); in prayer at appointment of deaconesses *θεὸς...ὁ...ἐν τῷ ν. προχειρισάμενος τὰς φρουροὺς τῶν ἁγίων σου πυλῶν Const.App.*8.20.1; **2.** ref. appearance of antichrist, Iren.*haer.*5.30.4(M.7.1207B); **3.** never to be rebuilt, Chrys.*hom.76.2 in Mt.*(7.734A); id.*Jud.*5.4(1.633D); ref. Julian's attempt, Soz.*h.e.*5.22.4(M.67.1284B); Philost.*h.e.*7.14(M.65. 553A); **4.** as symbol of Old Covenant, Oecum.*Apoc.*11:2(p.126).

D. its inner *shrine ἔμπροσθεν τοῦ ν. πρὸς τὸ θυσιαστήριον 1Clem.* 41.2.

E. Christian *church*, Eus.*h.e.*10.2.1(M.20.845B); id.*m.P.*11(p.945. 25; M.20.1456C); id.*v.C.*3.45(p.96.29; M.20.1105B); *ib.*3.50(p.99.2; 1109C); *ib.*4.46(p.136.28; 1197A); Gr.Nyss.*or.catech.*18(p.75.19; M.45. 56A); *εὐκτηρίους...ν.* id.*v.Gr.Thaum.*(M.46.944B); Chrys.*hom.18.5 in Ac.*(9.151A); Thdt.*h.e.*2.12.2(3.853); *ἅγιος ν. ... τῶν...μαρτύρων CIG* 8625 (Bostra, 511).

F. *nave* of church, accessible to laity, unlike *ἱερατεῖον*, Max. *myst.*2(M.91.668D); *Euchol.*(p.2).

II. met.; **A.** of heaven as God's dwelling, Meth.*symp.*9.5(p.120. 5; M.18.188C); Thdt.*Abac.*2:20(2.1549); and as shrine of image of God in righteous who enter it, Meth.*symp.*6.2(p.65.13; M.18.116A).

B. of Church as temple of God (Father, Son, or Holy Ghost), built of living stones *πάντες ὡς εἰς ἕνα ν. συντρέχετε θεοῦ* Ign.*Magn.* 7.2; *ὡς ὄντες λίθοι ναοῦ πατρός* id.*Eph.*9.1; *γενώμεθα πνευματικοί, γενώμεθα ν. τέλειος τῷ θεῷ Barn.*4.11; Clem.*paed.*1.1(p.89.26); id. *str.*7.5(p.21.24; M.9.437C); *ν. δέ ἐστιν ὁ μὲν μέγας, ὡς ἡ ἐκκλησία, ὁ δὲ μικρός, ὡς ὁ ἄνθρωπος ib.*7.13(p.58.30; 516A); id.*fr.*36(p.219.1; M.9. 769A); Or.*Cels.*8.19(p.237.2; M.11.1548A); *παρ' ἡμῖν γὰρ ὁ ἀληθινὸς ν.* id.*hom.26.3 in Jos.*(p.463.15; M.87.1041C); *μᾶλλον γὰρ τοῦ πατρὸς ὁρῶ ἔμψυχον ν., τὸν καλόν τε καὶ ἀγαθόν, ἢ τὸν ν. ἐκεῖνον· ἐξῆλθε γὰρ ἀπὸ τοῦ ν. ἐκείνου εἰπών· ἀφίεται ὑμῖν ὁ οἶκος ὑμῶν, καὶ ἀπῆλθεν ἐπὶ τὸν ν. τοῦ πατρός, τὰς ἐκκλησίας τὰς πανταχοῦ* id.*hom.20 in Lc.* (p.132.17); *ib.38*(p.224.25); of Church as body of Christ, in detailed typological interpretation of Temple, id.*Jo.*10.39–42(p.215.10ff.; M.14.380Cff.); Meth.*symp.*8.5(p.87.3; M.18.145B); *νύμφην ἁγίαν καὶ ν. πανίερον ἑαυτῷ τε καὶ τῷ πατρὶ κατειργάσατο* Eus.*h.e.*10.4.56(M.20. 872A); *ib.*10.4.69(877B); *ἕκαστος ὑμῶν ν. ἐστι, καὶ κοινῇ πάντες, καὶ ὡς ἐν σώματι Χριστοῦ οἰκεῖ* [sc. *θεός*], *καὶ ὡς ἐν ν. πνευματικῷ οἰκεῖ* Chrys.*hom.6.1 in Eph.*(11.40A); to be occupied by antichrist, Thdt.*2Thess.*2:4(3.533).

C. of Church as shrine of virtue, Const.*or.s.c.*1(p.155.9; M.20. 1236B).

D. of individual believer as dwelling of God (Logos, Christ, or H. Ghost) *πάντα...ποιῶμεν...ἵνα ὦμεν αὐτοῦ ναοὶ καὶ αὐτὸς ἐν ἡμῖν θεός* Ign.*Eph.*15.3; *τὴν σάρκα ὑμῶν ὡς ν. τηρεῖτε* id.*Philad.*7.2; *δεῖ... ὡς ν. θεοῦ φυλάσσειν τὴν σάρκα 2Clem.*9.3; *ν. γὰρ ἅγιος...τῷ κυρίῳ τὸ κατοικητήριον ἡμῶν τῆς καρδίας Barn.*6.15; *ib.*16.7,8; *ν. οὐκ ἔχω καὶ ναοὺς ἔχω A.Jo.*95(p.198.10); Clem.*prot.*1(p.6.16; M.8.60A); *λόγος... ὁ ἐν ἀνθρώποις οἰκοδομήσας ν. ib.*11(p.83.1; 237A); *οὐδὲ ν. τῶν παθῶν τῶν αἰσχρῶν τὸν ν. τοῦ θεοῦ ποιητέον* id.*paed.*2.10(p.217.25; M.8. 517B); *τὸν ν. τοῦ πνεύματος ἁγιάζοντες* id.*str.*3.7(p.223.18; M.8. 1164A); *τούτῳ τέθνηκεν ἡ σάρξ, ζῇ δὲ αὐτὸς μόνος ἀφιερώσας τὸν τάφον εἰς ν. ἅγιον κυρίῳ ib.*4.22(p.309.10; 1348B); *τὸ κάλλος τῆς ψυχῆς ν. γίνεται τοῦ ἁγίου πνεύματος, ὅταν διάθεσιν ὁμολογουμένην τῷ εὐαγγελίῳ κατὰ πάντα κτήσηται τὸν βίον ib.*7.11(p.46.21; M.9.489B); *τὰ σώματα ἡμῶν ν. τοῦ θεοῦ ἐστι, καὶ εἴ τις...φθείρει τὸν ν. τοῦ θεοῦ, οὗτος ὡς ἀληθῶς ἀσεβὴς εἰς τὸν ἀληθῆ ν. φθαρήσεται* Or.*Cels.*8.19(p.236. 19; M.11.1545C); *ὁ ἀκολασταίνων...τὸν...ν. τοῦ θεοῦ ὡς Ναβουχοδονόσορ καταστρέφει* id.*hom.12.11 in Jer.*(p.97.23; M.13.393B); *ἀμήχανον...ν. εἶναι τοῦ θεοῦ μετὰ τοῦ ναὸν τυγχάνειν εἰδώλων* id.*Jo.*19.21(5; p.323. 5; M.14.565C); *ἵνα...γένωμαι ν. ἅγιος καὶ κατοικήσῃ ἐν ἐμοὶ αὐτός A.Thom.*87(p.203.3); *τὴν καρδίαν...ἐν ᾗ μάλιστα καὶ τὸ ἅγιον ὡς ἐν ν. κατοικοῦν ἀναπαύεται πνεῦμα* Meth.*symp.*11(p.138.30; M.18.217A); *γινόμεθα ν. θεοῦ, ὅταν μὴ φροντίσι γηΐναις τὸ συνεχὲς τῆς μνήμης διακόπτηται...ἀλλὰ πάντα ἀποφυγὼν ὁ φιλόθεος ἐπὶ θεὸν ἀναχωρῇ* Bas.*ep.*2.4(3.73D; M.32.229B); *διὰ ψυχῆς καὶ σώματος ν. γινόμεθα τοῦ ἐνοικοῦντος ἐν ἡμῖν* Gr.Nyss.*Eun.*2(p.368.18; M.45.548D); *ἡ παρθένος ...ἔστω ἁγία...ὡς ν. θεοῦ, ὡς οἶκος Χριστοῦ, ὡς πνεύματος ἁγίου καταγώγιον Const.App.*4.14.2; *τοὺς...ν. τοῦ θεοῦ καὶ λιμῷ...περιορῶν ἀπολλυμένους* Chrys.*hom.11.6 in Rom.*(9.540B); Anast.*poenit.*4(p.282).

E. of body as temple of soul, Meth.*symp.*1.1(p.8.9; M.18.37B); *τὸν ν. κατέλυσαν καὶ τὴν ψυχὴν οὐκ ἔβλαψαν M.Thdot.*3(p.141.2).

F. of world as temple wherein God has set man as his image, Meth.*res.*1.34(p.271.9; M.41.1097B).

G. of holiness as temple wherein Christ dwells, *A.Thom.*A 86 (p.202.8).

H. of Christ's human nature; **1.** in rel. to character of all believers as temples of God (v. D supra) πάντων δὲ τῶν οὕτως ὀνομαζομένων ν. κρείττων ἦν καὶ διαφέρων ν. τὸ...σῶμα...'Ιησοῦ, ὅστις ἐπιστάμενος ἐπιβουλεύεσθαι μὲν δύνασθαι ὑπὸ τῶν ἀσεβῶν τὸν ν. τοῦ ἐν αὐτῷ θεοῦ, οὐ μὴν ὥστε ἰσχυροτέραν εἶναι τὴν τῶν ἐπιβουλευόντων προαίρεσιν τῆς τὸν ν. οἰκοδομούσης θειότητος, φησὶ...λύσατε τὸν ν. τοῦτον Or.*Cels.*8.19(p.236.22; M.11.1545D); εἰ θεοῦ ν. ἐγεννήθη ἐκ τῆς Μαρίας, περιττὴ ἡ καινότης τῆς ἐκ παρθένου γεννήσεως· ν. γὰρ θεοῦ καὶ ἄνευ ταύτης ἄνθρωποι Apoll.*anac.*22(p.244.19; M.28.1276C); εἰ δέ τινες ἄνθρωποι ναοί, ἀλλ' οὐχ οὕτω, ὡς καὶ Χριστοί· οὐδεὶς δὲ αὐτῶν συντεθεὶς τῷ θεῷ λόγῳ Χριστός ‡Ath.*dial.Trin.*5.22(M.28.1276C); οὐκ ἐν μόνῃ τῇ μήτρᾳ Μαριὰμ ἔπλασεν ἑαυτῷ ν. τὸ θεῖον, ἀλλὰ καὶ ἐν πάσῃ τῇ μήτρᾳ γυναικός, ἡ σοφία πλάττει καὶ ἁγιάζει τοὺς ἀνθρώπους *Dial. Ath.et Zacch.*22(p.18); **2.** in gen., of Christ's humanity τὸ τοῦ Χριστοῦ πρόσωπον εἰσιδὼν ἔργῳ μὲν ἔνδοθεν ἑώρα καὶ πράξει θεὸν καὶ φύσει θεοῦ γνήσιον υἱόν, ἄνθρωπον δὲ καθαρόν, ἄχραντον,...ἐξωτάτω περικείμενον ἐποπτεύων καὶ ναοῦ χρῆμα περικαλλές, ἀφιερωμένον Eust.*engast.*10(p.31.14; M.18.633B); ν. γὰρ κυρίως ὁ καθαρὸς καὶ ἄχραντος, ἡ κατὰ τὸν ἄνθρωπόν ἐστι περὶ τὸν λόγον σκηνή id.*fr.in Pr.* 8:22(M.18.677B); συνεχώρει μὲν αὐτοῖς λύειν ἀβούλως τὸν ν. ἐγχειροῦσιν *ib.*(681C); τὴν ἀσώματον σοφίαν οἰόμεθα...μεταλλάττειν τὴν φύσιν, εἰ ὁ ν. αὐτῆς σταυρῷ προσηλοῦται...; ἀλλὰ πάσχει μὲν ὁ ν., ἡ δὲ ἀκηλίδωτος οὐσία...ἄχραντος τὴν ἀξίαν καθέστηκεν *ib.*(684C); τοῦ λόγου τε καὶ θεοῦ τὸν ἑαυτοῦ ν. ἀξιοπρεπῶς ἀναστήσαντος id.*fr.*(p.72; M.18.685C); ν. πανάγιον αὐτὸς αὐτῷ σωματικὸν ὄργανον κατεσκευάσατο, λογικῆς δυνάμεως αἰσθητικὸν οἰκητήριον Eus.*l.C.*14(p.241.28; M.20. 1409A); ἐν τῇ παρθένῳ κατασκευάζει ἑαυτῷ ν. τὸ σῶμα, καὶ ἰδιοποιεῖται τοῦτο ὥσπερ ὄργανον Ath.*inc.*8.3(M.25.109C); τὸν ἑαυτοῦ ν. καὶ τὸ σωματικὸν ὄργανον προσάγων ἀντίψυχον *ib.*9.2(112A); *ib.*20.2(132A); αὐξάνοντος ἐν ἡλικίᾳ τοῦ σώματος, συνεπεδίδοτο ἐν αὐτῷ καὶ ἡ τῆς θεότητος φανέρωσις, καὶ ἐδείκνυτο παρὰ πᾶσιν, ὅτι ν. θεοῦ ἐστι, καὶ θεὸς ἦν ἐν τῷ σώματι id.*Ar.*3.53(M.26.433C); ν. δὲ τοῦ λόγου τυγχάνον [sc. τὸ σῶμα], πεπληρωμένον ἦν τῆς θεότητος id.*ep.Epict.*10(p.16.9; M.26.1068A); Gr.Nyss.*Eun.*2(2 p.368.19; M.45.548D); εἴ τις βούλοιτο καταχρηστικῶς καὶ τὸν υἱὸν τοῦ θεοῦ τὸν θεὸν λόγον, υἱὸν Δαβὶδ ὀνομάζειν, διὰ τὸν ἐκ σπέρματος Δαβὶδ τοῦ θεοῦ λόγου ν., ὀνομαζέτω Diod.*synous.*1(M.33.1560B); *ib.*(1560C); οὐκ εἰς σάρκα μεταβέβληται οὐδὲ ἀπέστη τοῦ εἶναι θεός, ἀλλ' ἐκεῖνο μὲν ἦν ἀιδίως, τοῦτο δὲ γέγονεν οἰκονομικῶς, αὐτὸς οἰκοδομήσας τὸν ἑαυτοῦ ν. καὶ ἐνοικήσας Flav. Ant.*fr.*4(p.106)ap.Thdt.*eran.*1(3.46); ὁ γὰρ σὸς δημιουργὸς τὸν σωματικὸν ν. παρὰ σοῦ τικτόμενον δημιουργεῖ *ib.*2(p.105; 1.66); ἕτερον ἡ σκηνὴ καὶ ἕτερον ὁ λόγος, ἕτερον ὁ ν. καὶ ἕτερον ὁ ἐνοικῶν αὐτῷ θεός Gel.Caes.*fr.*(p.47.19)ap.Thdt.*eran.*1(4.46); τὸν μὲν λόγον ὡς θεόν, τὴν δὲ σάρκα ὡς ν. τιμήσωμεν θεοῦ *ib.*(p.46.11)ap.Leont.B. *Nest.et Eut.*1(M.86.1313B); ἔπλασε...τὸ πνεῦμα τὸν ν. Chrys.*hom.4.3 in Mt.*(7.51A); οὐδὲ ἁπλῶς ν. πλάττεται, ἀλλὰ κύησις γίνεται *ib.*7.3 (123C); ν. ἑαυτῷ κατασκευάσας ὁ θεὸς ζῶντα ἐκ πνεύματος ἁγίου id. *nativ.*6(2.363B); ‡Chrys.*mart.*2(3.813C); ὁ γε...ὁμοούσιος τῷ πατρί, τῷ μὲν ἐκ τῆς παρθένου ν. ὃν ἐγὼ κτίσας ἐμαυτῷ περιέθηκα ‡Chrys. *serm.pasch.*19; ἀνέστησε...τὸν ἑαυτοῦ ν. ὁ ἐνοικήσας θεός ‡Chrys. *serm.ascens.*1.11; γεννηθέντι...καὶ...ἀναπλασθέντι...ἐνῆν· ἐπειδὴ ἅμα τῷ διαπλασθῆναι καὶ τὸ εἶναι ν. θεοῦ εἰλήφει. οὐ μὴν τὸν θεὸν γεγεννῆσθαι ἡγητέον ἡμῖν ἐκ τῆς παρθένου, εἰ μὴ ἄρα ταὐτὸν ἡγητέον ἡμῖν τό τε γεννηθὲν καὶ τὸ ἐν τῷ γεννηθέντι, τὸν ν. καὶ τὸν ἐν τῷ ν. θεὸν λόγον Thdr.Mops.*fr.Apoll.*3.1(p.312.14; M.66.997B); τῷ θεῷ λόγῳ συναφθεὶς...ἐξ αὐτῆς τῆς μήτρας ὁ τεχθεὶς ἐκ τῆς παρθένου ν. μεμένηκεν ἀδιαίρετος id.*ep.Domn.*(p.339.7; M.66.1013A); γέγονε σὰρξ ὁ λόγος, καὶ κατῴκησε καθάπερ ἐν ν., τῷ ἐκ τῆς...παρθένου...σώματι· ἥγουν ἀνθρώπῳ τελείῳ, τῷ ἐκ ψυχῆς λέγω, καὶ σώματος ἀμέσως τε καὶ οἰκονομικῶς ἡνῶσθαι πεπιστευμένῳ Cyr.*Mal.*32(3.850A); τὸν ἐκ τῆς... παρθένου ν. λαβὼν ἄνθρωπος γέγονε id.*Jo.*1.1(4.13C); σοφία...τὴν ἀληθεστέραν ἔστησε σκηνήν, τουτέστι, τὸν ἐκ παρθένου ν. *ib.*4.4(384E); τριήμερον δὲ τὸν ἑαυτοῦ ν. ἀναστήσας id.*hom.pasch.*1(5^2.16A); θεοποιουμένου τοῦ ἀναληφθέντος ν. id.*thes.*20(5^1.196E); *ib.*21(214E); φασὶ παραιτητέον εἰκότως, ἄνθρωπον δοῦναι τέλειον, τὸν συνενωθέντα τῷ λόγῳ ν., ἵνα καὶ ἡ σύνθεσις, ἥπερ ἂν ἐπὶ Χριστῷ νοοῖτο τυχόν, ἀκριβῆ... τὸν ἐπ' αὐτῆς ἀποσῴζοι λόγον id.*Thds.*17(p.53.5; 5^2.15D); υἱοὺς δὲ οὔτι πω δύο προσκυνήσομεν, ἀλλ' οὐδὲ Χριστοὺς ἐροῦμεν δύο, κἂν ἐψυχῶσθαι πιστεύωμεν ψυχῇ λογικῇ τὸν ἑνωθέντα τῷ λόγῳ ν. *ib.*18(p.53.21; 16B); χρῆναι...φημί, μήτε τὸν ἐκ θεοῦ λόγον ἀνθρωπότητος δίχα, μήτε μὴν τὸν ἐκ γυναικὸς ἀποτεχθέντα ν., ὡς μὴ ἑνωθέντα τῷ λόγῳ, Χριστὸν 'Ιησοῦν ὀνομάζεσθαι *ib.*28(p.60.19; 25B); ὁμολογοῦμεν τὴν...παρθένον θεοτόκον, διὰ τὸ τὸν θεὸν λόγον σαρκωθῆναι...καὶ ἐξ αὐτῆς τῆς συλλήψεως ἑνῶσαι ἑαυτῷ τὸν ἐξ αὐτῆς ληφθέντα ν. episcopi orientales ap.eund.*ep.*39(p.17.17; 5^2.106C); εἶναι μὲν οὖν τῆς τοῦ υἱοῦ θεότητος τὸ σῶμα ν., καὶ ν. κατὰ ἄκραν τινὰ καὶ θείαν ἡνωμένον συνάφειαν, ὡς οἰκειοῦσθαι τὰ τούτου τὴν τῆς θεότητος φύσιν, ὁμολογεῖσθαι καλόν Nest. *ep.Cyr.*2(p.31.26; M.77.56A); cf. *Christi appellatio modo templum, modo inhabitantem deum in illo demonstrat,* id.*fr.*C 10(p.270.8); *non dixi alterum filium aut alterum deum verbum; sed dixi deum verbum naturaliter et templum naturaliter aliud, filium conjunctione unum,* *ib.*18(p.308.10); οὐκ αὐτὸς φύσει ἐκ τῆς παρθένου γεγέννηται...ἀρχὴν ἐκεῖθεν τοῦ εἶναι λαβὼν...ἀλλ' ἑαυτῷ ν. ἐν τῇ...γαστρὶ διαπλάσας συνῆν τῷ πλασθέντι Thdt.ap.Cyr.*apol.Thdt.*1(p.109.16; 6^1.204D); ἐπειδὴ δὲ οὐ γυμνὴ ἦν [sc. ἡ τοῦ δούλου μορφή] τῆς τοῦ θεοῦ μορφῆς, ἀλλὰ ν. ἦν θεὸν ἔνοικον ἔχων...οὐκ ἀνθρωποτόκον, ἀλλὰ καὶ θεοτόκον τὴν παρθένον προσαγορεύομεν id.*ib.*(p.109.26; 205A); ἀπαθὴς μὲν ὁ... λόγος..., παθητὸς δὲ ὁ ν. id.*ep.*171(p.163.31; 4.1355); ν. γὰρ τὴν ἀνθρωπείαν ὠνόμασε φύσιν, ἣν ὁ...λόγος ἀνέλαβεν id.*Mal.*3:1(2.1685); views of Ibas τὴν ἀσεβῆ ἐπιστολὴν περιέχουσαν, ὅτι ὁ λέγων αὐτὸν τὸν θεὸν λόγον σαρκωθῆναι καὶ ἐνανθρωπῆσαι τὴν διαφορὰν ἀναιρεῖ τοῦ ν. καὶ τοῦ ἐνοικοῦντος ἐν τῷ ν. Justn.*ep.Thdr.Mops.*(p.50.20; M. 86.1051A); condemnation by Justn. διαφορὰν δὲ τοῦ ν. καὶ τοῦ ἐνοικοῦντος ἐν αὐτῷ οὐδεὶς τῶν...πατέρων ἐδίδαξεν, ἀλλὰ μόνοι οἱ ἀσεβεῖς Νεστόριος καὶ Θεόδωρος εἰρήκασι δύο ἐντεῦθεν πρόσωπα εἰσάγειν βουλόμενοι· κἂν γὰρ αἱ γραφαὶ καὶ οἱ πατέρες τῇ τοῦ ν. ὀνομασίᾳ κέχρηνται, ἀλλὰ τὸ σῶμα τοῦ μονογενοῦς υἱοῦ...σημαίνοντες τοῦτο λέγουσιν *ib.* (p.50.22,25; M.l.c.); φανερός ἐστι...δύο πρόσωπα εἰσάγων, ὅτι εἶπεν· πῶς δυνατὸν ληφθῆναι τὸν...λόγον ἐπὶ τοῦ ν. τοῦ ἐκ Μαρίας γεννηθέντος; δι' ὧν ῥημάτων δείκνυται φανερῶς ὅτι οὐ τὸν θεὸν λόγον σαρκωθῆναι...ἐκ τῆς...Μαρίας λέγει, ἀλλὰ ψιλὸν ἄνθρωπον τὸν Χριστὸν ὃν ν. ἀποκαλεῖ *ib.*(p.53.6,8; 1057A); λέγων· ὅτι δεῖ ὁμολογεῖν εἰς τὸν ν. καὶ εἰς τὸν ἐνοικοῦντα ἐν τῷ ν. ... ἡ γὰρ καθολικὴ ἐκκλησία ἕνα κύριον ...Χριστὸν...ὁμολογεῖ, καὶ οὐχὶ εἰς τὸν ν. καὶ εἰς τὸν ἐνοικοῦντα ἐν τῷ ν. πιστεύειν...διδάσκει [a doctrine which implies a fourth Person of the Trinity] *ib.*(p.62.14ff.; 1077B,C); ref. Mt.8:25ff. οὐδὲ καθεύδοντα ἑώρακέ ποτε [sc. τὸν θεόν]...καθεύδει τοίνυν ὁ τοῦ...λόγου ν. Bas.Sel. *or.*22.1(M.85.265B); περὶ τοῦ ἁγίου αὐτοῦ ν., ὃς ἔσται ἐκ σπέρματος αὐτοῦ τοῦ Δαυίδ, καὶ τῆς συναφθείσης τῷ ν. θεότητος ‡Bas.Sel.*or.*38. 2(M.85.405C); εἰ μὴ εἰς ν. ἢ φόρημα ἔχει ὁ λόγος τὸν ἄνθρωπον, ἐξ ἀνάγκης εἰς οὐσίαν ἔχει· ὁ δὲ λαμβάνων τὴν σάρκα εἰς οὐσίαν τοῦ Χριστοῦ, αὔξησιν ποιεῖ τῆς οὐσίας τοῦ υἱοῦ, τρέπων...αὐτὴν εἰς ἕτερον. ἀλλ' ἔστι μὲν καὶ ὡς εἰς ν. καὶ ὡς εἰς σκηνὴν καὶ ὡς εἰς φόρημα κατὰ ἀναλογίαν τινὰ ὁ λόγος ἐν τῇ σαρκί· οὐ μέντοι κατὰ ἀπαραλλαξίαν ὡς ἐν ἑνὶ τούτων ἐστίν· εἴπερ γὰρ μὴ ταὐτόν ἐστιν, οὐδὲ ὡσαύτως τὸ ἐν τοῖσδε αὐτοῖς πᾶσιν ἓν εἶναι, πολλῷ μᾶλλον τὸ μηδὲ ὡς ἓν τῶνδε πάντῃ εἶναι, τὸ ἐχόμενον πρὸς τὸν ἔχοντα ἕξει ἐν Χριστῷ τὴν διαφοράν· εἰ δὲ τὸ παρὰ τάδε ὄν, εὐθὺς εἰς οὐσίαν προσληφθῆναι καὶ οὐκ εἰς ὑπόστασιν μᾶλλον, διὰ τῆς πρὸς οὐσίαν συνελεύσεως οὐσίας δηλοῖ, ἆρα γε...τῆς ψυχῆς πρὸς τὸ σῶμα ἐν τῷ ἀνθρώπῳ Leont.H.*Nest.*7.4(M.86.1756A,B).

I. BMV Χαῖρε, ὁ ἔμψυχος ν. τοῦ θεοῦ ‡Gr.Thaum.*annunt.*3(M.10. 1177A); ‡Epiph.*hom.*5(M.43.496D); †Cyr.*hom.div.*11(5^2.380D); οὐκ αὐτὴ θεός, ἀλλὰ θεοῦ ν. Procl.CP *or.*2.6(M.65.700D); *ib.*6.17(753B); Mod.*dorm.*10(M.86.3301B); Jo.Eub.*concept.BMV* 14(M.96.1481A); *ib.*16(1485A); Thdr.Stud.*nativ.BMV* 1(M.96.680D).

***ναουργ-έω,** *make into a shrine,* Christol. τὸν ἄνθρωπον ~ήσας ἐφόρεσεν ὁ λόγος Eust.*fr.in Pr.*8:22(M.18.677C); ~ῶν Χριστὸς ἑαυτῷ τὸ σῶμα Thdr.Stud.*nativ.BMV* 7(M.96.689C).

***ναουργία, ἡ,** *construction of a shrine, making into a shrine,* Christol. φύσει θεὸς...γεννηθεὶς ὁ χρίσας· ὁ δὲ χρισθεὶς ἐπίκτητον εἴληφεν ἀρετήν, ἐκκρίτῳ ν. κοσμηθεὶς ἐκ τῆς τοῦ κατοικοῦντος ἐν αὐτῷ θεότητος Eust.*fr.in Ps.*(p.69; M.18.688B).

***ναοφόρος, ὁ,** *shrine-bearer*; met., of Christians θεοφόροι καὶ ν., Χριστοφόροι, ἁγιοφόροι Ign.*Eph.*9.2.

***ναργέλλιον, τό,** *coconut,* Cosm.Ind.*top.*11 (v.l. ἀργέλλια M.88. 445C); *ib.*(conj. for ἀργελλίων codd., 445A).

***νάρδιον, τό,** ? *receptacle for unguent* (or ? = νάρδος, *spikenard*), *Euchol.*(p.503).

νάρθηξ, ὁ, 1. *giant fennel,* used as thyrsus, Clem.*prot.*2(p.17.8; M.8.89A); **2.** *forecourt* of church; **a.** in gen., long and narrow vestibule along west end of church, Paul.Sil.*Soph.*428(M.86.2136A); with seven gates at S. Sophia, *ib.*440(2136B); Cyr.S.*v.Jo.Hes.* 17(p.214.24); also extending along sides of nave, hence ἐν τῷ τρίτῳ ν. τῆς ἁγιωτάτης μεγάλης ἐκκλησίας Const.Pogon.*edict.*tit. (H.3.1445C); **b.** used in penitential discipline ἡ ἀκρόασις ἔνδοθι τῆς πύλης ἐν τῷ ν., ἔνθα ἑστάναι χρὴ τὸν ἡμαρτηκότα ἕως τῶν κατηχουμένων, καὶ ἐντεῦθεν ἐξέρχεσθαι Gr.Thaum.*ep.can.*11(M.10.1048A); †Jo.Jej.*poenit.*(M.88.1912D); for psalm-singing at vigils, Paul.Sil. *Soph.*428ff.(M.86.2136A,B); as repository for corpse at funerals, Cyr.S.*v.Jo.Hes.*17(p.215.5); *Euchol.*(p.424); for confessions of women, *Nomoc.*40; as place of congregation, esp. in monastic churches *v.* ἐστὶ διὰ τὸ ἑστάναι τὸν λαὸν ἔξω ἐν τῇ τοῦ θυμιάματος ὥρᾳ ‡Sophr.H.*liturg.*4(M.87.3985A).

ναρκ-άω, *be numb, be stiff*; met.; **1.** *be torpid, slack,* mentally or spiritually ψυχὴν...~ῶσαν *A.Jo.*69(p.184.18); Chrys.*hom.*25.4 *in Mt.*(7.312B); *ib.*57.4(582A); id.*hom.*9.1 *in Eph.*(11.68D); εἰς βασιλείαν κέκλησαι...καὶ ~ᾷς; id.*hom.*2.4 *in Col.*(11.338B); Isid.Pel.*epp.*1.13 (M.78.188B); Cyr.*Jo.*1.9(4.88A); **2.** *shrink, lose heart* βίαν πάσχων, καὶ οὐδὲ οὕτως ἐνάρκα Chrys.*hom.*36.2 *in Jo.*(8.208D); οὐ ~ᾷ πρὸς τὸ μῆκος id.*hom.*39.1 *in Gen.*(4.396A); οὐδὲ πρὸς τοῦτο ἐνάρκησεν id. *hom.*8.3 *in Mt.*(7.123A); *ib.*25.1(306C); id.*hom.*7.7 *in 1Cor.*(10.61D); ~ᾷ ἡ ψυχὴ καὶ τὸ σῶμα *ib.*22.4(197E); id.*hom.*7.5 *in Col.*(11.378A); **3.** *shrink from,* c. infin. οὐδὲ...ἀπογεύσασθαι ~ήσαντες Evagr.*h.e.* 2.8(p.56.25; M.86.2524A); **4.** *be shocked, horrified* ἀπὸ τῆς ὄψεως μόνης εἰκὸς ἦν ~ῆσαι λοιπόν Chrys.*hom.*48.4 *in Mt.*(7.499C); **5.** *be amazed, stupefied,* ‡Caes.Naz.*dial.*48(M.38.920); *ib.*183(1157); **6.** *be bewildered* ~ᾷ πρὸς τὰς τῶν προφητῶν πολυσήμους φωνάς *Clem.ep. Petr.*1(M.2.25B); μὴ συγχέῃς τὰς φύσεις καὶ οὐ ~ήσεις περὶ τὴν οἰκονομίαν Ant.Ptol.*fr.*ap.Leont.B.*Nest.et Eut.*1(M.86.1316A); Procl.CP *or.* 18.3(M.65.821A); **7.** *slacken, grow feeble, A.Andr.fr.*5(p.40.9); ἀνθρακίαν ~ήσασαν ‡Nil.*perist.*10.5(M.79.893C); *ib.*11.6(912C); Procl.CP *or.*18.3(M.65.821B).

[*]**ναρκ-ιάω,** = ναρκάω; **1.** *be numb, paralysed, A.(Pass.)Andr.*14 (p.32.12, v.l. ἐνάρκουν M.2.1244B); met. οὐ ~ιᾷ τὴν χεῖρα Ephr.*Abr. et Is.* (v.l. ναρκεῖ M.56.541); ~ιᾷ μου ἡ ψυχή Rom.Mel.(*ABAW* 24^3 p.26); **2.** *be slack*; met., Tim.Ant.*nativ.Jo.Bapt.*(M.28.908C).

ναρκ-όω, *hesitate, shrink from* μὴ ~οῦντες λέγειν *Mir.Artem.*40 (p.70.12).

νάρκωσις, ἡ, *insensibility* (to passion, bodily desire); of Adam and Eve before Fall, Gennad.*fr.Gen.*3:8(M.85.1637A).

***νάς, ὁ,** v. νάας.

***Νασαραῖοι (Νασαρηνοί), οἱ,** name of a Jewish sect, mentioned with Essenes, etc., Epiph.*haer.*1 proem.5(p.159.29; M.41.164C); *N.* ἑρμηνευόμενοι ἀφηνιασταί, οἳ πᾶσαν σαρκοφαγίαν ἀπαγορεύουσιν, ἄχρι δὲ Μωϋσέως καὶ Ἰησοῦ τοῦ Ναυῆ τοῖς ἐν τῇ πεντατεύχῳ ἁγίοις ὀνόμασι πατριαρχῶν κεχρημένοι τε καὶ πιστεύοντες...τὰς δὲ τῆς πεντατεύχου γραφὰς οὐκ εἶναι Μωϋσέως δογματίζουσιν, ἄλλας δὲ παρ' αὐτὰς ἔχειν διαβεβαιοῦνται id.*anac.*19(p.168.4; M.41.172C); *N.* οἵτινες Ἰουδαῖοί εἰσι τὸ γένος, ἀπὸ τῆς Γαλααδίτιδος καὶ Βασανίτιδος καὶ τῶν ἐπέκεινα τοῦ Ἰορδάνου ὁρμώμενοι id.*haer.*18.1(p.215.15; Ναζαραῖοι M.41.257A); dist. from Christian *Ναζωραῖοι, ib.*29.6(p.327.18; 400B); a few surviving in upper Thebaid and Arabia, *ib.*20.3 (*Νασαρηνοί* p.226. 21; 273A).

***νάτιβος, ὁ,** (Lat. *nativus*) a gem, one of the varieties of the hyacinth stone (identified by Epiph. with the lyncurium or tourmaline), so called prob. because of its natural colour, Epiph. *gemm.*7(M.43.300A).

ναυάγιον, τό, *shipwreck*; met., *disaster*; financial, Chrys.*hom.* 56.6 *in Mt.*(7.574D); *ib.*61.3(614B); of troubles of Job, id.*hom.*28.3 *in 1Cor.*(10.253D); of Flood κοινὸν τῆς οἰκουμένης *v.* id.*hom.*6.6 *in Mt.*(7.98C); *ib.*12.3(163E); Bas.Sel.*or.*14.1(M.85.185B); Cosm.Ind. *top.*5(M.88.220D); moral τὰ τῆς μέθης *v.* Clem.*paed.*2.2(p.169.21; M.8. 413C); *ib.*(p.173.14; 424A); τρυφὴ...ἀνθρώποις *v.* γίνεται *ib.*3.7(p.258.4; 608B); Chrys.*hom.*26.7 *in Mt.*(323D); *ib.*55.5(561D); *ib.*57.4(582B).

***ναυάγιος,** *shipwrecked, T.Abr.*A 19(p.102.5).

***ναυαγιοφόρρς,** *bringing shipwreck,* ‡Chrys.*hom.in Mt.*12:14 (10.759E).

***Ναυαταῖος,** v. *Ναυατιανός.

***Ναυατιανικός,** *Novatianist N.* ἀπανθρωπίας Thdr.Stud.*epp.*2. 162(M.99.1512A).

***Ναυατιανός (*Ναυαταῖος, *Νοουατιανός),** (Lat. *Novatianus*); **1.** *Novatianist, N.* ἀπόνοια Eulog.*fr.Novat.*(M.104.329C); **2.** masc. plur. as subst., *followers of Novatian, Novatianists,* Νοουατιανοί Const.ap.Eus.*v.C.*3.64(p.111.17; Ναυατιανοί M.20.1140B); Νοουατιανοί Ath.*Ar.*1.3(M.26.17A); otherwise known as καθαροί, Epiph.*haer.*59.13 (p.379.2; M.41.1037B); Ναυαταῖοι id.*anc.*13(p.21.29; M.43.40C) cit. s. Μοντήσιοι; Ναυᾶτοι id.*rescr.*4(p.158.24; M.41.161D); similar to Donatists except in their Trin. orthodoxy, *ib.*; persecuted by Valens, Socr.*h.e.*4.9.4–6(M.67.477D); refusing post-baptismal repentance, *ib.*6.22.10(729A); for mortal sins in addition to apostasy, *ib.*7.25.18–19(796C,D); their observance of Easter *N.* δοκοῦσιν ἄλλως πως τὰ καθ' ἡμᾶς ἠρέμα μιμεῖσθαι· δουλεύουσι μὲν καὶ αὐτοὶ τῇ προθεσμίᾳ τῶν Ἰουδαίων καὶ πρῶτον μῆνα καὶ αὐτοὶ νομίζουσι, καὶ τεσσαρακαιδεκάτην κατὰ σελήνην τὴν παρ' ἐκείνοις μεταδιώκοντες ἀλλ' οὐχὶ ἕως τούτου γε ἵστανται, ἀλλ' ὅταν ἐν τούτοις γένωνται, καὶ ἐπὶ τὴν τριήμερον ἔρχονται, εἰ καὶ μάλιστα ἀκύρως, καὶ οὐ καθ' ἁρμονίαν ἐκκλησιαστικήν ‡Chrys.*pasch.*7(8.276B); attitude to re-baptism, Bas. *ep.*199 *can.*47(3.296D; M.32.732A) cit. s. ἀναβαπτίζω; ποῦ εἰσιν οἱ *N.*; Oecum.*2Cor.*12:21(p.446.1).

***Ναυᾶτοι, οἱ,** v. foreg.

***ναύκλα, ἡ,** *ship, Vaticin.*2(p.54).

***ναυλομάχος, ὁ,** s.v.l., ? nickname for ναυλοδόκ(χ)ος, *receiver of freights,* Sophr.H.*mir.Cyr.et Jo.*6(M.87.3433D), perh. error for ναυλοδόχος.

***ναυμάχης, ὁ,** = ναυμάχος, *one who fights on shipboard, marine,* Chrys.*sac.*4.4(p.111.20; 1.408D); cf. ναυμαχῶν *ib.*6.12(p.167.3; ναυμάχων 433B).

***ναυμάχιον, τό,** a *lake* at Rome *for exhibition of sea-fights,* near Vatican ὁ Νέρων εἶπεν...κελεύω αὐτοὺς ἐν τῷ *v.* τόπῳ ἀναλωθῆναι *A.Petr.et Paul.*79(p.212.12); ἦραν δὲ τὸ σῶμα τοῦ...Πέτρου...καὶ ἔθηκαν αὐτὸ ὑπὸ τὴν τερέβινθον πλησίον τοῦ *v.* εἰς τόπον καλούμενον Βατικάνον *ib.*84(p.216.16).

ναῦς, ἡ, *ship*; met.; **1.** of man in voyage of life, Clem.*q.d.s.*34 (p.182.29; M.9.640C); ‡Just.*ep.Zen.et Ser.*4(M.6.1188B); **2.** of Church, Hipp.*antichr.*59(p.39.13; M.10.777C); *Clem.ep.*14(M.2.49A); of assembled congregation where bishop acts as captain of ship, *Const. App.*2.57.2; of heretical sect as *v.* πειρατική, Clem.*str.*3.8(p.224.14; M.8.1164C); **3.** Pythagorean name for unity ἔτι ἐπενόουν...ναῦν, ἅρμα, φίλον Anat.Laod.*decad.*(p.30).

***ναυσηρός,** *nauseous*; met., of heret. dogma, Ath.*Ar.*2.43(M.26. 240A).

***ναυσιασμός, ὁ,** *nausea*; met., ‡Chrys.*circ.*(8.89A).

***ναυσιπορ-έομαι,** *be navigable* ~εῖται...τούτων ἕκαστος μυριοφόροις ὁλκάσιν ‡Caes.Naz.*dial.*147(M.38.1096).

ναυστολία, ἡ, *fleet,* Thphn.*chron.*p.285(M.108.701A).

ναυστολόγος, ὁ, *ship's steward* who assigned passengers their places and directed them; hence, met., of catechists in comparison of Church with a ship, *Clem.ep.*14(M.2.49A); and of deaconesses showing women members of congregation to their places, *Const. App.*2.57.10.

***ναυταρίδιον, τό,** *lubber,* contemptuous term for *sailor,* Gr.Naz. *carm.*2.1.11.841(M.37.1087A).

***ναυτηλόγος, ὁ,** = ναυστολόγος, *A.Phil.epit.*30–33(p.92.17).

ναύτης, ὁ, *sailor,* in comparison of Church with a ship ἔχει δὲ καὶ ναύτας δεξιᾷ καὶ εὐωνύμῳ ὡς ἁγίους ἀγγέλους παρέδρους Hipp. *antichr.*59(p.40.4; M.10.780A); παρεικάσθω ὁ μὲν...πρωρεὺς ἐπισκόπῳ, οἱ *v.* πρεσβυτέροις *Clem.ep.*14(M.2.49A).

***ναυτίασις, ἡ,** *nausea,* Epiph.*exp.fid.*1(p.496.27; M.42.776A).

ναυτιασμός, ὁ, = foreg.; met., Isid.Pel.*epp.*1.143(M.78.280A); Nest.*ep.Cyr.*2(p.29.9; M.77.49B); Thdr.Stud.*epp.*2.7(M.99.1129A).

ναυτιλία, ἡ, *fleet,* Thphn.*chron.*p.239(M.108.601A).

ναυτίλλω, 1. *sail, navigate,* Thdr.Stud.*epp.*1.11(M.99.945B); **2.** med., c. acc., *sail on, navigate,* Philost.*h.e.*3.11(M.65.496A).

***ναυφράγιον, τό,** (Lat. *naufragium*) *shipwreck, Hom.Clem.*12.10; ναυάγιον *ib.*12.16,25 (v.l. ναυφράγιον).

νεάζ-ω, 1. *be young*; hence *be junior, inferior* ὁ γὰρ ἐλθὼν [sc. Χριστὸς] πρεσβυτέρας ἀξίας ὢν τοὺς ~οντας ἐν αὐτῇ σείσει *Pers.*(p.14. 9; M.10.104A); **2.** = νεάω, *plough up,* met. νόμος...~ων τὴν ψυχὴν εἰς ὑποδοχὴν τοῦ...λόγου ‡Chrys.*pasch.*6(p.137.17; 8.267B); Rom. Mel.(*AS* 1 p.66).

***νεαλογέω,** *teach innovations,* Didym.*Trin.*2.1(M.39.617C); *ib.* 2.24(745C).

νέαμα, τό, *fallow land, Nomoc.*516.

νεανίας, ὁ, *young man,* of Christ as revealed in visions ὤφθη αὐτοῖς *v.* λαμπάδα ἀνημμένην κατέχων *A.Thom.*A 27(p.143.5); with angels ἔρχεται πρός με *v.* τις εὐμορφώτατος...ἐξαστράπτων, καὶ ἕτεροι μετ' αὐτοῦ *v.* ὡραῖοι *M.Perp.*10(p.77.13); *v.* εὐειδής, ἔχων κυκλόθεν ἀκτῖνας *A.Xanthipp.*15(p.68.20).

***νεανιότης, ἡ,** *youthfulness*; hence **1.** *freshness, vigour,* met. *v.* πίστεως Ph.Carp.*Cant.*4(M.40.41A); **2.** *ardour,* Epiph.*exp.fid.*13 (p.513.9; M.42.805A); **3.** *impetuosity, wilfulness, ib.*9(p.504.28; 788C); **4.** exeg. Is.7:14 τὸ τῆς *v.* ὄνομα ἐπὶ τῆς παρθενίας εἴωθεν ἡ γραφὴ τιθέναι, οὐκ ἐπὶ γυναικῶν μόνον, ἀλλὰ καὶ ἐπὶ ἀνδρῶν Chrys.*hom.*5.3 *in Mt.*(7.76A).

νεᾶνις, ἡ, *young woman, girl*; **1.** in gen. (unmarried or married) οὔ μοι δοκεῖς Ἀττικῆς ἐπαΐειν φωνῆς, παρ' ἧς ἔστιν ἐκμαθεῖν τὰς καλὰς καὶ ὡραίας, ἔτι δὲ καὶ ἐλευθέρας *v.* παιδίσκας καλουμένας, παιδισκάρια δὲ τὰς δούλας, καὶ *v.* δὲ καὶ αὐτάς Clem.*paed.*1.5(p.98. 3; M.8.265A); νέοι μὲν καὶ *v. ib.*2.7(p.190.4; 457A); *M.Perp.*20(p.91. 9); Meth.*symp.*proem.(p.6.18; M.18.36A); **2.** exeg. Is.7:14 [AQ, THDN, SM], cited in this form, *Pers.*(p.40.16); ὑμεῖς [sc. Jews] καὶ οἱ διδάσκαλοι ὑμῶν τολμᾶτε λέγειν μηδὲ εἰρῆσθαι...ἰδοὺ ἡ παρθένος ἐν γαστρὶ ἕξει, ἀλλ', ἰδοὺ ἡ ν. ἐν γαστρὶ λήψεται...καὶ ἐξηγεῖσθε τὴν προφητείαν ὡς εἰς Ἑζεκίαν Just.*dial.*43.8(M.6.569A); *ib.*67.1(629A); *ib.*71.3(644A); ὑμεῖς δὲ...παραγράφειν τὰς ἐξηγήσεις, ἃς ἐξηγήσαντο οἱ πρεσβύτεροι ὑμῶν παρὰ Πτολεμαίῳ...τολμᾶτε, λέγοντες μὴ ἔχειν τὴν γραφὴν ὡς ἐκεῖνοι ἐξηγήσαντο, ἀλλ', ἰδοὺ ἡ ν. ... ὡς μεγάλων πραγμάτων σημαινομένων, εἰ γυνὴ ἀπὸ συνουσίας τίκτειν ἔμελλεν, ὅπερ πᾶσαι αἱ ν. γυναῖκες ποιοῦσι *ib.*84.3(673C); οὐχ ὡς ἔνιοί φασι τῶν νῦν μεθερμηνεύειν τολμώντων τὴν γραφήν· ἰδοὺ ἡ ν. ... ὡς Θεοδοτίων... καὶ Ἀκύλας...οἷς κατακολουθήσαντες οἱ Ἐβιωναῖοι, ἐξ Ἰωσὴφ αὐτὸν γεγενῆσθαι φάσκουσι Iren.*haer.*3.21.1(M.7.946A); ἡ μὲν λέξις ἡ ἀαλμά (Hebr. עַלְמָה), ἣν οἱ μὲν ἑβδομήκοντα μετειλήφασι πρὸς τὴν παρθένον ἄλλοι δ' εἰς τὴν ν. κεῖται...καὶ ἐν τῷ Δευτερονομίῳ ἐπὶ παρθένου [Dt.22:23–26]...ποῖον οὖν σημεῖον τὸ ν., μὴ παρθένον τεκεῖν; Or.*Cels.*1.34–35(p.86.3; M.11.725C); Eus.*d.e.*7.1(p.303.20; M.22.497A); *ib.*(p.305.1; 500A); οὐδὲν δὲ ἡμᾶς κωλύει, εἰ καὶ ν. κατ' αὐτοὺς περιέχει τὸ Ἑβραϊκόν, ὡς περὶ παρθένου δηλοῦσθαι νομίζειν τὰ εἰρημένα· καὶ γὰρ οὖν ἐν τῷ Λευιτικῷ εὕροις ἂν τὴν...παρθένον...ν. ὑπὸ τῆς γραφῆς ὀνομαζομένην [i.e. Dt.22:27] id.*ecl.*4.4(M.22.1204Af.); Cyr.H.*catech.* 12.21; ἀνθίστανται οἱ Ἰουδαῖοι τῇ ἐκδόσει τῶν ἑβδομήκοντα, λέγοντες μὴ κεῖσθαι παρὰ τῷ Ἑβραίῳ τό, ἡ παρθένος, ἀλλ', ἡ ν., ὡς δυναμένης νεάνιδος ὀνομάζεσθαι τῆς ἀκμαζούσης καθ' ἡλικίαν, οὐχὶ δὲ τῆς ἀπειρογάμου γυναικός· πρὸς οὓς ῥᾳδία...ἡ ἀπάντησις. εἰ γὰρ σημεῖόν ἐστι τεραστίου τινὸς...τί θαυμαστὸν ἦν, μίαν τῶν πολλῶν γυναῖκα...μητέρα γενέσθαι παιδίου;...εἰ μὲν σημεῖόν ἐστι τὸ διδόμενον παράδοξος ἔστω καὶ ἡ γέννησις...ὅτι μέντοι ἡ ν. ἐπὶ παρθένων ἰδίως ὠνομάσθη, δῆλον ἐκ τῶν...οὕτως εἰρημένων [Dt.22:25ff.]. ἡ τοίνυν βοῶσα πρὸ τῆς φθορᾶς παρθένος ἦν, δηλονότι. ἴσον οὖν δύναται εἰπεῖν, ἐβόησεν ἡ παρθένος καὶ ἐβόησεν ἡ ν. ... καὶ...ἡ Σωμανῖτις, ἡ συνθάλπουσα τὸν Δαβίδ, παρθένος οὖσα...ν. προσαγορεύεται †Bas.*Is.*201(1.528E–529C; M.30.464A–C); cf.Chrys.*hom.5.3 in Mt.*(7.76A); *Dial.Ath.etZacch.*32(p.22); εἰ μέντοι ν. εἶπε, ν. ἐν τῷ Ἑβραϊκῷ ἐστιν· ἵνα δὲ καὶ οὕτως συμπεριενεχθῶ σοι, ἡ ν. παρθένος ἑρμηνεύεται· φησὶ γὰρ ἐν τῷ Δευτερονομίῳ [22:25ff.]... γνῶθι οὖν...ὅτι ἡ ν. καὶ ἡ παρθένος ἕν ἐστιν *Dial.Tim.et Aquil.*111 r°; **3.** exeg. Cant.1:3,6:7; cf. *adulescentulae vero, quae nondum in id beatitudinis venerant neque summam perfectionis acceperant neque usu et operibus fructus perfectae caritatis expleverant,* Or.*comm.in Cant.*1(p.110.31; M.13.100A); ἑτέραις δὲ ψυχαῖς κοινωνεῖ [sc. ὁ λόγος] παιδαγωγουμέναις φόβῳ θεοῦ· αὗταί εἰσιν αἱ παλλακίδες· εἰσί τινες καὶ ἄλλαι ψυχαὶ ὑποδεέστεραι, ἐλάττονα φόβον ἔχουσαι· αὗταί εἰσιν αἱ ν. id.*schol.in Cant.*6:7(M.17.277D); αὗταί εἰσιν αἱ...ν., διὰ τὸ νέαν ἄγειν τὴν πνευματικὴν ἡλικίαν, αἳ γεννηθεῖσαι μὲν τῷ λόγῳ τῆς πίστεως, οὐδέπω διὰ τῆς προσηκούσης αὐξήσεως τοιαῦται γεγόνασιν ὡς ἐπὶ γάμων ἀκμὴν προελθεῖν Gr.Nyss.*hom.15 in Cant.*(M.44.1112B); ν. δὲ...ἐν ταῖς λοιπὸν κατὰ πάντα κόσμον φιλοσοφίαις καὶ ἑκάστης ψυχῆς πολιτείαις, τῆς μὲν οὔσης ἐπαινετῆς, τῆς δὲ οὒ Epiph.*exp.fid.*9(p.504.23; M.42.788C); *ib.*13(p.513.4; 804D); ν. ... αἱ διά τινας προφάσεις κοσμικὰς σωφρονοῦσαι Isid.Pel.ap.Proc.G.*Cant.*6:7–8(M.87.1721C); ν. ... τὰ ἔθνη τὰ ἀπηλλοτριωμένα τοῦ θεοῦ καὶ ξένα τῶν διαθηκῶν Nil. *ib.*(1720C); ν. ... αἱ ψυχαὶ τῶν δικαίων Ph.Carp.*Cant.*4(M.40.40B); **4.** as adj., *fresh, youthful,* Just.*dial.*84.3(M.6.673C); *A.Jo.*20 (p.162.6).

νεανίσκος, ὁ, A. *young man*; **1.** in gen., of one described as παῖς ἐτῶν κγ' *A.Phil.*29(p.15.22); cf.*ib.*28(p.15.7); **2.** of Christ in visions ὁ κύριος ὤφθη...ὡς ν. *A.Jo.*87(p.193.24); ἀρχιγένειος ν. *ib.*89(p.194.23); *A.Andr.*6(p.71.4); ἐξαστράπτων ὥσπερ τις ν. εὔμορφος *A.Mt.*17 (p.238.5); in gen., description, *M.Ner.et Ach.*8(p.7.23); **3.** of angels in a vision, Herm.*vis.*3.4.1; **4.** met.; **a.** ref. Lam.1:18 παρθένους νόει τοὺς ἐν ἀφθαρσίᾳ βιοῦντας, ν. δὲ τοὺς ἐν ἀρετῇ εὐδοκίμους Or.*fr. 39 in Lam.*(p.253.13; M.13.629C); **b.** as adj., *vigorous, active* οἱ σφόδρα ν. πρὸς εὐσέβειαν Cyr.*ador.*4(1.130E).

B. *slave, A.Jo.*19(p.161.26); *ib.*111(p.210.2); *A.Thom.*A 64(p.181.1).

***νεαρότης, ἡ,** *freshness, new vigour,* Chrys.*hom.15.6 in Mt.*(7.194A).

***νεαρότμητος,** *freshly cut,* Pall.*h.Laus.*36(p.107.13; M.34.1179D).

***νέβελ,** (Hebr. נֶבֶל) a Hebrew measure = 150 ξέσται, about 18 gallons, Gr.Nyss.*Eun.*2(1 p.283.19; M.45.992B); Epiph.*mens.*21(M.43.272B).

***νεελαία, ἡ,** *young olive,* met. ὦ τοῦ Χριστοῦ ν. (cf. Ps.127:3), ‡Ign.*Ant.*6 (v.l. νεολαία).

[*]**νεήκονος,** *newly whetted,* Isid.Pel.*epp.*5.479(M.78.1605C).

νέηλυς, ὁ, *newcomer, novice*; **1.** in gen., Jo.VI H.*v.Jo.D.*23(M.94.464A); of university freshmen τῶν ν. συστέλλειν τὸ φρόνημα Gr.Naz.*or.*43.16(M.36.516C); *ib.*43.17(517C); of catechumens, Cyr.H.*catech.* 12.17; **2.** as adj., of Church as new people of God opp. Jews λαοῖο Gr.Naz.*carm.*1.1.9.30(M.37.459A); of Arian Christ οὔτε ν. οὔτε πρόσφατον σέβοντες θεόν Petr.II Al.*encycl.*5 ap.Thdt.*h.e.*4.22.17(M.33.1284A).

***νεήπιος,** *newly gentle* νήπιος δὲ ὁ ν., ὡς ἤπιος ὁ ἁπαλόφρων, οἷον ἤπιος νεωστί Clem.*paed.*1.5(p.101.7; M.8.272A).

νεῖκος, τό, *strife*; hence *the separative principle* in the cosmos, acc. Empedocles, Clem.*prot.*5(p.49.6; M.8.165A); whose doctrine Marcion borrowed, Hipp.*haer.*6.25(p.152.1; M.16.3231A); *ib.*7.29 (p.210.12; 3323B).

***Νειλαγαθίον, τό,** a kind of fruit growing by the Nile and Indus, Cosm.Ind.*top.*2(M.88.117B).

***νεκρεγερσία, ἡ,** *raising of the dead,* ‡Chrys.*Marth.*(10.754E); Germ.CP *or.*2(M.98.277C).

***νεκρέγερσις, ἡ,** *resurrection from the dead,* ‡Gr.Naz.*Chr.pat.*239 (M.38.136A).

***νεκρέγερτος, ὁ,** *one risen from the dead,* ‡Gr.Naz.*Chr.pat.*239(M.38.136A); *ib.*780 (νεκρεγέρτην 198A).

***νεκρικός,** *putting to death, fatal* ἀγνωσία θεοῦ νεκρικῆς ἀναισθησίας ὁμοίωμα Nest.*hom.tent.*1(p.339, v.l. νεκρωτικῆς M.61.683).

νεκροβόρος, *devouring the dead* or *corpses*; **1.** lit., Or.*hom.10.8 in Jer.*(p.78.8; M.13.368A); Eus.*fr.Lc.*12:22(M.24.557A); *ib.*17:37(588B); Gr.Nyss.*v.Mos.*(M.44.409D); of flesh-eating birds proscribed as unclean by Law, signifying duty to abstain from greed, Thdt.*qu.11 in Lev.*(1.190); **2.** met., *battening on the dead* by hunting legacies, Gr.Naz.*carm.*2.1.17.33(M.37.1264A).

***νεκροδρομία, ἡ,** *escape of the dead,* i.e. the delivery of the righteous souls at Christ's descent into Hades, Ephr.3.472A.

***νεκροειδής,** *corpse-like,* ‡Chrys.*hom.in Ps.100*(5.639E).

***νεκροκόμος, ὁ,** *one who attends to corpses, undertaker*; of those who honour martyrs only by external devotion to their tombs, Gr.Naz.*carm.*2.2(epigr.)48.18(M.38.109A).

***νεκρολατρεία, ἡ,** *worship of the dead,* ref. hero cults προσκυνητέον...θεῷ μόνῳ τῷ κατὰ φύσιν...καὶ λόγος ἔστω μηδεὶς τῶν... ἀνθρώπων οἷς ἐπεγράφη τὸ θεῶν ὄνομα. ν. γὰρ τοῦτο Cyr.*Is.*3.5(2.515D).

***νεκρολάτρης, ὁ,** *worshipper of a dead man* οὐ καθ' ἑαυτὸ θεὸς τὸ ταφὲν ἐπὶ μνήματος· οὕτω γὰρ ἂν ἦμεν ἀνθρωπολάτραι καὶ ν. σαφεῖς Nest.*fr.*C 9(p.262.10)ap.Cyr.*Nest.*2.13(p.51.7; 6[1].58B).

νεκρομαντεία, ἡ, *necromancy* ψυχῆς ἀναπομπήν, τὴν λεγομένην ν. *Hom.Clem.*1.5; μὴ κατὰ νεκρομαντείαν ὁ τρόπος αὐτῷ [sc. Apollonius of Tyana] τῆς φανείσης ὄψεως γένοιτο. οὔτε γὰρ βόθρον...Ὀδυσσέως ὀρυξάμενος, οὐδ' ἀρνῶν αἵμασι ψυχαγωγήσας Eus.*Hierocl.*28(529A; M.22.836B); forbidden to Christians, *Const.App.*2.62.2.

***νεκροπαθεία, ἡ,** *mortification of the passions, Hymn.*(*AS* 1 p.607).

***νεκροποιέω,** *put to death,* Iren.*haer.*5.12.1(M.7.1151C).

νεκροποιός, *death-dealing,* Eus.*h.e.*10.4.14(M.20.853C); *Const. App.*2.61.3.

***νεκροπρεπής,** *befitting the dead,* ‡Gr.Naz.*Chr.pat.*2145(M.38.305A); *ib.*2159(306A).

***νεκροπρεπῶς,** *in a manner befitting the dead,* ‡Epiph.*hom.*2(M.43.448D); Germ.CP *or.*2(M.98.253B).

νεκρός, ὁ, I. *corpse, dead body*;

A. lit.; of serpent in the wilderness as type of Christ ὢν ν. δύναται ζωοποιῆσαι *Barn.*12.7; ref. difference between Christ's body and other νεκροί in that blood and water flowed therefrom, and of appropriateness that being καινὸς ν. it should be laid ἐν καινῷ...μνημείῳ, Or.*Cels.*2.69(p.191.8; M.11.904C); applied contemptuously by Jews to Christ's body εἰώθασι τὸν ἐσταυρωμένον ν. καλεῖν Thdt.*Ps.*17:47(1.714).

B. met.; **1.** of false teachers τάφοι νεκρῶν, ἐφ' οἷς γέγραπται μόνον ὀνόματα ἀνθρώπων Ign.*Philad.*6.1; τοὺς γὰρ ἐν ἀγνοίᾳ τῆς ἀσεβείας ὄντας ν. ὑπὸ τοῦ ᾅδου καταπίνεσθαί φησιν ἡ γραφή· ν. γάρ, καὶ ζῆν δοκοῦντες, ἐτύγχανον ὄντες Marcell.*fr.*88 ap.Eus.*Marcell.*1.4 (p.27.12; M.24.768B); **2.** of pagans and non-Christians in gen. πρὶν ...φορέσαι τὸν ἄνθρωπον τὸ ὄνομα τοῦ υἱοῦ τοῦ θεοῦ, ν. ἐστιν. ... εἰς τὸ ὕδωρ οὖν καταβαίνουσι ν., καὶ ἀναβαίνουσι ζῶντες Herm.*sim.*9.16.3,4; ἀθεωτάτους ὄντας καὶ ν. τῶν ἀνθρωπίνων λογισμῶν *A.Jo.*39(p.170.16); νεκροί, τῆς ὄντως οὔσης ἀμέτοχοι ζωῆς Clem.*prot.*1(p.5.31; M.8.57C); πάντας εἶναι ν. τοὺς μὴ ζῶντας θεῷ Or.*Jo.*2.16(10; p.73.17; M.14.144A); id.*fr.14 in Lc.*8:39(p.239.16); **3.** of men as sinful ἔγραψας νεκροῦ νεκρὰν εἰκόνα *A.Jo.*29(p.167.6); Clem.*str.*3.5(p.215.4; M.8.1145A); **4.** of actual sinners τίς ὁ ν.; ὁ ἁμαρτωλός, ὁ μὴ ἔχων τὸν εἰπόντα· ἐγώ εἰμι ἡ ζωή Or.*hom.9.3 in Jer.*(p.67.25; M.13.353A); among Pythagoreans, of those who offend against tenets of their philosophy, Clem.*str.*5.9(p.364.29–31; M.9.88C–89A); Or.*Cels.*3.51 (p.247.22; M.11.988B); **5.** Gnost.; of χοϊκοί, opp. πνευματικοί, who are not reborn so as to enter gate of heaven, Hipp.*haer.*5.8(p.93.

20; M.16.3146C); Or.*Cels*.6.35(p.105.3; M.11.1349C); **6.** of one to whom life is worthless σύ με ν. ἐποίησας γενέσθαι τοῦτό μοι παρασχομένη *A.Jo*.20(p.162.10).

II. plur., *the dead*;

A. lit.; **1.** in gen., of resurrection from the dead τὸν κύριον...ἐκ νεκρῶν ἀναστήσας *1Clem*.24.1; ἠγέρθη ἀπὸ νεκρῶν Ign.*Trall*.9.2; ὑπέσχετο ἡμῖν ἐγεῖραι ἡμᾶς ἐκ ν. Polyc.*ep*.5.2; *Barn*.15.9; Marcell.*ep*.ap.Epiph.*haer*.72.3(p.258.10; M.42.385D), et freq.; ἀνάστασις νεκρῶν *Did*.16.6; *Barn*.5.6; *Symb*.ap.Epiph.*anc*.118(p.147.16; M.43.232D); *Symb*.ap.Epiph.*anc*.119(p.149.3; 236B); *Symb.Nic.–CP*(p.80.16; H.2.288B); **2.** of judgement of quick and dead, *Barn*.7.2; *2Clem*.1.1; cf.*Symb*.ap.Hipp.*trad.ap*.21.15; Marcell.*ep*.ap.Epiph.*haer*.72.3(p.258.11; M.42.385D); *Symb.App*.(p.30); *Symb.Caes*.(p.43.15; M.20.1537B); *Symb.Nic*.(325)(Hahn p.161); *Symb.Hier*.(M.33.533B); *Symb*.ap.*Const.App*.7.41.6; *Symb*.ap.Epiph.*anc*.118(p.147.11; M.43.232D); *Symb*.ap.Epiph.*anc*.119(p.148.25; 236A); Gr.Naz.*or*.40.45(M.36.425C); *Symb.Nic.–CP*(p.80.12; H.2.288B); 2Tim.4:1 and 1Petr.4:5 also interpreted so that ζῶντες = righteous and νεκροί = sinners, Chrys.*hom.9.1 in 2Tim*.(11.715A); Sev.Ant.ap.*cat.1Petr*.4:5(p.73.18); or ζῶντες = souls and ν. = bodies, *ib*.(p.73.15); **3.** of patriarchs and prophets visited at *descensus ad inferos* προφῆται ...ὡς διδάσκαλον αὐτὸν προσεδόκων, καὶ διὰ τοῦτο, ὃν δικαίως ἀνέμενον, παρὼν ἤγειρεν αὐτοὺς ἐκ ν. Ign.*Magn*.9.2; ἐμνήσθη δὲ κύριος ...ἀπὸ Ἰσραὴλ τῶν ν. αὐτοῦ, τῶν κεκοιμημένων...καὶ κατέβη πρὸς αὐτοὺς εὐαγγελίσασθαι αὐτοῖς τὸ σωτήριον αὐτοῦ 'Jer.'ap.Just.*dial*.72.4(M.6.645B); id.ap.Iren.*haer*.4.22.1(M.7.1046C); cited anonymously, *ib*.4.33.1(1072B); *ib*.4.33.12(1081B); *ib*.5.31.1(M.7.1208C); ascribed to Isaiah, *ib*.3.20.4(M.7.945A); μέχρι...νεκρῶν οἱ τῆς φιλανθρωπίας αὐτὸν ἐκάλουν νόμοι, ὡς ἂν καὶ τῶν πάλαι τεθνεώτων τὰς ψυχὰς ἀνακαλέσοιτο Eus.*d.e*.4.12(p.169.13; M.22.281C); cf. Marcion's theory that Cain, Sodomites, and Egyptians were so saved, but patriarchs and prophets suspected a trick, Iren.*haer*.1.27.3(M.7.689A); Thdt.*haer*.1.24(4.316); 1Petr.4:6 referred either to sinners νενεκρωμένους τὴν ψυχὴν ταῖς ἁμαρτίαις, or to those who through good works mortified body from sinful passions; but also understood with special reference to dead in Hades, Sev.Ant.ap.*cat.1Petr*.4:6(p.76.5–34); **4.** of preaching to, and baptizing of, dead in Hades by departed apostles and teachers, Herm.*sim*.9.16.5–6; Clem.*str*.2.9(p.136.15; M.8.980B); **5.** exeg. Rom.11:15; interpreted of gen. resurrection to follow conversion of Israel, cf.Or.*comm.in Rom*.8.9(M.14.1185A); but, though coinciding with Israel's conversion, it is not caused by this, Chrys.*hom.19.4 in Rom*.(9.647D); εἰ πάντες οὗτοι πιστεῦσαι θελήσαιεν, οὐδὲν ἕτερον ὑπολείπεται ἢ τὸ γενέσθαι τῶν ν. τὴν ἀνάστασιν Thdt.*Rom*.11:15(3.121); **6.** exeg. 1Thess.4:16 ν. ἐν Χριστῷ...τουτέστι τὰ σκηνώματα Meth.*symp*.6.4(p.69.8; M.18.120B); ὅταν εἴπῃ, οἱ ν. ἐν Χριστῷ ἀναστήσονται πρῶτον, οὐκ ἀναιρῶν τοὺς πρὸ τῆς Χριστοῦ παρουσίας δικαίους λέγει *cat.1Thess*.4:17(p.365.12); ν. τοὺς πιστοὺς λέγει, οὐ μόνον τοὺς τῷ εὐαγγελίῳ πεπιστευκότας, ἀλλὰ καὶ τοὺς ἐν νόμῳ, καὶ τοὺς πρὸ νόμου διαλάμψαντας Thdt.*1Thess*.4:15(3.520); **7.** exeg. Apoc.14:13 οὐ πάντας μακαρίζει τοὺς ν., ἀλλὰ τοὺς ἐν κυρίῳ ἀποθανόντας, τοὺς νεκρωθέντας τῷ κόσμῳ καὶ τὴν νέκρωσιν τοῦ κυρίου...ἐν τῷ σώματι περιφέροντας Areth.*Apoc*.14:13(M.106.692B); **8.** exeg. 1Cor.15:29; interpreted: **a.** of vicarious baptism undertaken on behalf of unbaptized dead, and likened to Marcionite practice ἐπειδὰν γάρ τις κατηχούμενος ἀπέλθῃ...τὸν ζῶντα ὑπὸ τὴν κλίνην τοῦ τετελευτηκότος κρύψαντες, προσίασι τῷ ν. καὶ...πυνθάνονται, εἰ βούλοιτο λαβεῖν τὸ βάπτισμα· εἶτα ἐκείνου μηδὲν ἀποκρινομένου, ὁ κεκρυμμένος...ἀντ' ἐκείνου φησίν, ὅτι δὴ βούλοιτο βαπτισθῆναι· καὶ οὕτω βαπτίζουσιν αὐτὸν ἀντὶ τοῦ ἀπελθόντος Chrys.*hom.40.1 in 1Cor*.(10.378C); cf.Epiph.*haer*.28.6(p.318.23; M.41.384D) on Cerinthian practice; **b.** to mean 'those on point of death' who, if catechumens, are baptized, Chrys.*hom.40.1 in 1Cor*.(378C); **c.** to mean 'dead bodies', i.e. bodies of the baptized, which are dead if there is no bodily resurrection εἰ μὴ ἔστιν ἀνάστασις, τί καὶ βαπτίζῃ ὑπὲρ τῶν ν.; τουτέστι τῶν σωμάτων. καὶ γὰρ ἐπὶ τούτῳ βαπτίζῃ, τῇ τοῦ ν. σώματος ἀναστάσει, πιστεύων ὅτι οὐκέτι μένει ν. *ib*.(379B,C); ὁ βαπτιζόμενος...τῷ δεσπότῃ συνθάπτεται, ἵνα...τῆς ἀναστάσεως γένηται κοινωνός. εἰ δὲ ν. ἐστι τὸ σῶμα, καὶ οὐκ ἀνίσταται, τί δήποτε καὶ βαπτίζεται; Thdt.*1Cor*.15:29(3.275); ἐπειδὴ βαπτιζόμεθα...ὑπὲρ τῶν ἡμετέρων ν. σωμάτων...μιμούμενοι θάνατον καὶ ἀνάστασιν, ἐλπίδι καὶ ἐπαγγελίᾳ τῆς ἐκ ν. ἀναστάσεως· τί μάτην...ταῦτα ποιοῦμεν, μὴ στοιχοῦντες οἷς ποιοῦμεν Cosm.Ind.*top*.7(M.88.352A); **d.** of angels who are baptized on men's behalf, Clem.*exc.Thdot*.22(p.113.29; M.9.668C).

B. met.; exeg. Mt.8:22; **1.** interpreted of sinful selves, Clem.*str*.3.4(p.207.16; M.8.1129A); ὅτε ἐτεθνήκει τῷ νεανίσκῳ ὁ πατὴρ [i.e. Devil] καὶ ἦν ν., τότε ὑπὸ τοῦ σωτῆρος ἐκλήθη. ... ὥσπερ ὁ κόσμος Παύλῳ...ν. ἦν...οὕτως ἑκάστῳ δικαίῳ τέθνηκεν ὁ διάβολος...τὸ δὲ τοὺς ν. θάψαι τοὺς ἑαυτῶν ν. ἀλληγορεῖται μόνον· θάπτουσι γάρ πως νεκροὶ τοὺς ἑαυτῶν ν. ἐν ἑαυτοῖς, τάφοι καὶ μνημεῖα αὐτῶν γενόμενοι. τέλεον δὲ καταλείπει τὸν ν. καὶ οὐδαμῶς ἔτι αὐτοῦ ἅπτεται ὁ πειθόμενος τῷ Ἰησοῦ· οἶδε γὰρ ὅτι ὁ ἁπτόμενος νεκροῦ μολύνεται Or.*fr.29 in Lc*.9:60(p.246); **2.** of those who persist in 'dead works', Cyr.*ador*.16(1.580C); **3.** of heathen εἰπὼν δέ, 'τοὺς ἑαυτῶν ν.', δείκνυσιν ὅτι οὗτος οὐκ ἔστιν αὐτοῦ νεκρός. καὶ γὰρ τῶν ἀπιστῶν, ὡς...οἶμαι, ἦν ὁ τετελευτηκὼς Chrys.*hom.27.3 in Mt*.(7.330B).

III. adj. *dead*;

A. lit.; **1.** in gen. τὴν ἐκ τῶν ν. σωμάτων...τροφήν Clem.*paed*.2.10(p.210.27; M.8.504A); ἀνθρώπου ν. Or.*Cels*.4.57(p.330.16; M.11.1124B); Chrys.*hom.73.3 in Mt*.(7.711B); **2.** of flesh of animal that has died natural death ν. μὴ γεύεσθαι σαρκός *Hom.Clem*.7.4.

B. *inanimate, material*, in interprn. of scourge used by Christ in Temple as H. Ghost οὐ γὰρ ἐκ δέρματος ν. ἐποίησεν αὐτό Heracleon ap.Or.*Jo*.10.33(19; p.207.21; M.14.368A); Μωϋσέα τοῖς ν. ὑποδήμασι βεβαρημένον Gr.Nyss.*v.Mos*.20(M.44.305D); τῆς ν. τῶν δερμάτων περιβολῆς ἐλευθερώσας τοὺς πόδας id.*hom.11 in Cant*.(M.44.1005C).

C. met.; *dead* because; **1.** powerless χεῖρες...ν. τυγχάνουσαι *Hom.Clem*.12.13; **2.** barren; of land, Arist.*apol*.4.3; νεκρὰς δὲ φλογεροῦ πυρὸς φέρουσαι λαμπάδας Meth.*symp*.11(p.133.26; M.18.209C); spiritually ν. καθέστηκεν [sc. πίστις], ἐάν τις αὐτὴν ἄπρακτον ἔχῃ †Chrys.ap.*cat.Jac*.2:19(p.16.4); νεκρὸς τοῦ βίου Tit.Bost.*Man*.2.9(M.18.1152B); **3.** lifeless; **a.** of idols οἱ ζῶντες τοῖς ν. θεοῖς οὐ θύομεν *2Clem*.3.1; λατρεία...θεῶν ν. *Did*.6.3; Arist.*apol*.3.2; Clem.*paed*.2.8(p.202.1; M.8.484B); ἀψύχοις καὶ ν. εἰδώλοις Or.*Jo*.2.3(p.57.19; M.14.113C); id.*Cels*.6.14(p.84.14; M.11.1312A); *Hom.Clem*.10.9; *ib*.11.12; **b.** of pagan philosophy ν. σοφίας Clem.*q.d.s*.11(p.167.8; M.9.616B); **c.** of bequests to poor by the dead, which involve no personal sacrifice and are ν. θυσίαι, ‡Ath.*qu.Ant*.91(M.28.653C); **d.** of things done of necessity and ἀπροαιρέτως, Nil.ap.Proc.G.*Cant*.5:3(M.87.1684A); **e.** of what is dead through sin, Herm.*sim*.8.8.1; τὰ ῥήματα αὐτῶν μόνα ζῶσι, τὰ δὲ ἔργα αὐτῶν ν. ἐστιν *ib*.9.21.2; Clem.*paed*.2.2(p.172.30; M.8.421B); ν. περιφέρων ψυχήν Chrys.*hom.73.3 in Mt*.(7.711A); id.*hom.6.3 in 2Cor*.(10.477C); καθεύδοντα καὶ ν., τὸν ἐν ἁμαρτίαις id.*hom.18.1 in Eph*.(11.128B); Cyr.*Ag*.15(3.646A); hence τὰ ν. *sins*, Or.*hom.8.14 in Lev*.(p.412.31); **4.** insensitive ἡμεῖς τέφρας ψυχρότεροι...καὶ τῶν τεθνηκότων νεκρότεροι Chrys.*hom.6.5 in Mt*.(7.94B); id.*hom.6.3 in 2Cor*.(10.477D); **5.** mortified πᾶς ζῶν ἐν Χριστῷ...ἔζη ποτὲ τῇ ἁμαρτίᾳ, καὶ ὕστερον ν. γενόμενος αὐτῇ ἔζησεν τῷ θεῷ Or.*comm.in Rom*.6:11(*JTS* 13 p.366); ἐν ν. ἀνθρώπῳ βούλεται [sc. εὐαγγέλιον] νεκρῶσαι τὴν ἁμαρτίαν Ephr.3.211A; ἵνα...τὰ μέλη...ν. ταῖς κακαῖς ἀποφήνωμεν ἐνεργείαις Thdt.*Cant*.7:11–13(2.151); πάντα ἔχων τὰ πάθη ν. Marc.Diac.*v.Porph*.8; v. infra D.2.b.

D. exeg.; **1.** Eph.2:1,5 θάνατος τῆς ψυχῆς εἶναι λέγεται τὰ ἁμαρτήματα Or.*comm.in Eph*.2:1–5(p.403); Chrys.*hom.4.1 in Eph*.(11.25B); τοὺς ν., τοὺς ὀργῆς υἱούς, τούτους ἐζωοποίησεν *cat.Eph*.2:5(p.140.12); **2.** Rom.8:10 interpreted; **a.** of body being dead because belonging to sin, Cyr.*Rom*.8:10(p.214.15ff.); **b.** of body as mortified οὐδὲ...εἶπεν, ἀργεῖν τὸ σῶμα...τῇ ἁμαρτίᾳ, ἀλλὰ καὶ ν. εἶναι ...ὅτι τὴν πονηρίαν, ἀλλ' οὐ τὴν φύσιν τοῦ σώματος καθάπαξ ἀνεῖλεν Chrys.*hom.13.8 in Rom*.(9.570A); οὐ τῆς σαρκὸς κατηγορεῖ, ἀλλὰ τῆς ἁμαρτίας. τῇ γὰρ ἁμαρτίᾳ προσέταξε τοῦτο γενέσθαι ν., ἀντὶ τοῦ, τὴν ἁμαρτίαν μὴ ἐνεργεῖν Thdt.*Rom*.8:10(3.83); ν. τοὺς...διὰ τῶν τῆς δικαιοσύνης ἔργων τὸ σῶμα νεκροῦντας ἀπὸ τῶν τῆς ἁμαρτίας παθῶν...κατὰ τὸ εἰρημένον...τὸ μὲν σῶμα ν. δι' ἁμαρτίαν Sev.Ant.ap.*cat.1Petr*.4:6–7(p.76.11); **3.** Rom.7:8 πᾶς...ἄνθρωπος ἔζη χωρὶς νόμου ποτέ, ὅτε παιδίον ἦν...ἅμα δὲ τῷ ἐλθεῖν τὴν ἐντολὴν...ὑφίσταται ἡ κακία...ἀναζῇ ἡ ἁμαρτία, τέως οὖσα ν. Or.*comm.in Rom*.7:8(*JTS* 14 p.14); 'χωρὶς γὰρ νόμου ἡ ἁμαρτία ν.'· τουτέστιν, οὐχ οὕτω γνώριμος. ᾔδεσαν μὲν γὰρ καὶ οἱ πρὸ τοῦ νόμου, ὅτι ἡμάρτανον, ἀκριβέστερον δὲ ἔμαθον μετὰ τὴν τοῦ νόμου δόσιν Chrys.*hom.12.5 in Rom*.(9.550A); Isid.Pel.*epp*.4.62(M.78.1120B); εἰ γάρ ἐστιν ἀληθῶς ἁμαρτία ν. χωρὶς νόμου, πῶς οὐ πιθανὸν ἐννοεῖν ζωοποιεῖσθαι τρόπον τινὰ διὰ τοῦ νόμου τὴν ἁμαρτίαν τοῦ καὶ ἐμφανῆ καθιστάντος αὐτήν, καὶ οἷον ἔμπνουν ἀποτελοῦντος, καίτοι πάλαι μὴ ἐγνωσμένην, εἰ καὶ ἦν ἐν ἡμῖν; Cyr.*Rom*.7:8(p.199.9; M.74.804C); ἁμαρτία ν. νόμου γὰρ οὐκ ὄντος, τοῦ τὸ πρακτέον ὑποδεικνύντος, καὶ τὸ οὐ πρακτέον ἀπαγορεύοντος, οὐκ ἔχει χώραν ἡ ἁμαρτία Thdt.*Rom*.7:8(3.72); **4.** Heb.6:1, 9:4; **a.** of works that are dead because sinful ὁ ἔχων ν. ἔργα, ὁ μηδέπω μετανοήσας ἀπὸ ν. ἔργων Or.*hom.9.3 in Jer*.(p.68.1; M.13.353B); καλῶς εἶπεν, 'ἀπὸ ν. ἔργων'· εἴ τις ἥψατο νεκροῦ, ἐμιαίνετο· καὶ ἐνταῦθα εἴ τις ἅψαιτο ν. ἔργου, μολύνεται διὰ τῆς συνειδήσεως Chrys.*hom.15.2 in Heb*.(12.153A); ν. ... τοὺς...τῶν τῆς νεκρότητος ἔργων οὐκ ἀπεχομένους Cyr.*ador*.16(1.580C); ἔργα...τὰ ν. τῆς σαρκὸς δηλονότι τὰ μυσαρὰ καὶ βέβηλα πάθη id.*glaph.Lev.*1(1.354B); ἀποστῆναι τῶν ἁμαρτημάτων...τουτέστιν ἀναχωρεῖν τῶν ν. ἔργων Eulog.*fr.Novat.*(M. 104.336B); Sev.Ant.ap.*cat.1Petr.*4:5(p.73.19); **b.** of Judaistic works as ν. καὶ ψευδῆ, Chrys.*hom.15.2 in Heb.*(12.153A).

E. ν. θάλασσα *Dead Sea*, Afric.*chron.*9(M.10.69B); Pall.*h.Laus.*50 (p.144.11; M.34.1212C); Thdt.*Ezech.*25:11(2.886).

νεκροσυλία, ἡ, *robbery of the dead*, †Bas.*Is.*272(1.586B; M.30. 596C); Thdt.*ep.*145(4.1245).

***νεκροτάφιον, τό, 1.** *tomb, burial place*, Nil.*epp.*1.26(M.79.92D); *CIG* 8846 (Hieracium); **2.** plur., *grave-clothes*, Amph.*hom.*3(M.39. 65B); ‡Pall.*h.mon.*1.37(p.15.1, v.l. νεκροτάφοις M.34.1122C).

***νεκρότης, ἡ,** *state of death*;

A. four kinds defined διάφοροι νεκρότητός εἰσι τρόποι· καὶ ἔστιν εἷς μὲν ὁ τοῦ σώματος, καθ' ὃν ὁ Ἀβραὰμ νεκρὸς ὤν, οὐκ ἦν νεκρός· ὁ γὰρ θεὸς...οὐκ ἔστι νεκρῶν, ἀλλὰ ζώντων· ἕτερος ὁ τῆς ψυχῆς..., ἄλλος ὁ καὶ ἐπαινετός, ὁ διὰ τῆς φιλοσοφίας γινόμενος..., ἕτερος...ὁ ἐπὶ τοῦ βαπτίσματος· ὁ γὰρ παλαιὸς ἡμῶν ἄνθρωπος...νενέκρωται Chrys.*hom. 11.5 in Rom.*(9.536D).

B. *physical death*; **1.** in gen., Or.*Jo.*28.8(7; p.398.35; M.14.697A); Ephr.3.211A; συνταφέντες τῷ Χριστῷ...οὐ νεκρότητος φθορὰν ἐκδεχόμεθα, ταφὴν δὲ καὶ ὥσπερ φυτείαν σπερμάτων μιμούμεθα †Bas.*bapt.* 1.2.13(2.638E; M.31.1548B); ὕπνος...νεκρότητος εἰκὼν Chrys.*hom.27. 5 in 1Cor.*(10.249C); **2.** of Christ's death τὸν...ζωτικὰ σημεῖα καὶ ἐν τῇ ν. δείξαντα τὸ ὕδωρ καὶ τὸ αἷμα Or.*Cels.*2.69(p.191.9; M.11.904C); γευσαμένῳ δι' ἡμᾶς νεκρότητος Gr.Naz.*or.*19.12(M.35.1057C); ἡ ν. δέ, τῆς ἐμῆς ἀναίρεσις id.*carm.*1.2.34.219(M.37.961A); ref. Cant.2:1 ταῖς κοιλᾶσι, ταῖς ἐν ᾅδου ψυχαῖς, κρίνον, νεκρότητα ἀναδεξάμενος Diod. *Ps.*64:14(M.33.1599C).

C. *mortality* κατέβη ἐπὶ τὴν ν. ἡμῶν, ἵνα...τὴν μετὰ τὴν ν. ζωὴν αὐτοῦ...χωρῆσαι δυνηθῶμεν Or.*Jo.*1.31(35; p.40.15; M.14.84C); θεὸς ...τοὺς δερματίνους χιτῶνας διὰ τοῦτο κατεσκεύασεν, οἱονεὶ νεκρότητι περιβαλὼν αὐτόν, ὅπως διὰ τῆς λύσεως τοῦ σώματος πᾶν τὸ ἐν αὐτῷ γεννηθὲν κακὸν ἀποθάνῃ Meth.*res.*1.38(p.281.14; M.18.293B); μὴ εἶναι τοὺς δερματίνους χιτῶνας τὰ σώματα, ἀλλὰ τὴν ἀπὸ τοῦ ἀλόγου τῶν ζῴων ν. κατεσκευασμένην *ib.*1.39(p.283.11; M.41.1108A); ἐκ τῆς τῶν ἀλόγων φύσεως ἡ ν. οἰκονομικῶς περιετέθη τῇ εἰς ἀθανασίαν κτισθείσῃ φύσει Gr.Nyss.*or.catech.*8(p.43.16; M.45.33C).

D. *corruption* of living but decayed body, *T.Job* 30(p.122.9).

E. *atrophy, paralysis* ἐν τοῖς σώμασιν μερῶν τινων νεκρότητες καὶ ξηρότητες. ... οὐκ αἰσθάνεται ἐκεῖνος, ὅταν ᾖ ν. περὶ αὐτό Or.*hom.6.2 in Jer.*(p.49.9; M.13.325A); of leprosy, Cyr.*ador.*15(1.541D).

F. *spiritual deadness*; **1.** in gen. ἀπὸ τῆς ἀναισθησίας καὶ ν. ἀναστησομένους Or.*Jo.*6.28(14; p.137.19; M.14.248C); *ib.*28.8(7; p.398. 35; 697A); opp. ζωή, *ib.*2.6(4; p.61.2; 120C); *ib.*6.19(11; p.128.27; 233C); Ephr.3.210F; **2.** caused by sin ἔργοις τῆς ν. Or.*hom.9.3 in Jer.*(p.68.6; M.13.353B); Bas.*Spir.*35(3.29C; M.32.129D); Gr.Naz. *carm.*1.2.8.108(M.37.657A); Chrys.*hom.70.3 in Mt.*(7.690E); id.*hom. 6.2 in Col.*(11.367F); Cyr.*ador.*7(1.228B); and typified by shoes removed by Moses, id.*glaph.Ex.*1(1.263E); **3.** from which Christ delivers man, Or.*Jo.*1.9(11; p.14.23; M.14.40C); of Lazarus as typical of sinners ἀξίους τῆς ν. δεσμοὺς ἐκ τῶν προτέρων ἁμαρτημάτων περικείμενος...μήτε...δυνάμενος...τι ἐνεργῆσαι διὰ τῆς ν. δεσμούς, ἕως Ἰησοῦς κελεύσῃ τοῖς λῦσαι αὐτὸν δυναμένοις *ib.*28.7(6; p.397.20; 693C); Meth.*res.*1.23(p.248.3; M.41.1093A); Agath.*v.Gr.Ill.*136; **4.** from which baptism is resurrection, Bas.*Spir.*35(3.29C; M.32.129D); Chrys.*hom.6.3 in 2Cor.*(10.476E); cf.*ib.*(476C).

G. *mortification*, Tit.Bost.*Man.*2.9(M.18.1152B); τὴν ν. τὴν μακαριζομένην καὶ θαυμαζομένην Chrys.*hom.11.5 in Rom.*(9.537B); ν. ... ζωῆς αἰτία γενομένη id.*hom.10.1 in 1Cor.*(10.80E).

***νεκροτοκέω,** *bear a still-born child*, ‡Caes.Naz.*dial.*102(M.38. 968).

***νεκροτόκιον, τό,** *still-born child*, Max.*schol.e.h.*3.3.6(M.4.141C).

***νεκροφανῶς,** *like a corpse*, ‡Ath.*occurs.*12(M.28.988C).

***νεκροφόνος, ὁ,** *murderer of the dead*, i.e. robber of graves, Gr. Naz.*carm.*2.2(epigr.)57(M.38.112A).

νεκροφορέω, 1. *bear about a dead body*; of souls doomed to wear physical bodies as penalty of Fall, Meth.*res.*1.29(p.258.7; M. 41.1136C); *ib.*(p.260.2; M.41.1137B); *ib.*1.54(p.312.3; M.41.1145C); **2.** *bear a mortified body*, Thdr.Stud.*nativ.BMV* 7(M.96.689B).

νεκροφόρος, 1. *bearing a corpse*; met., of docetist who denies reality of Christ's flesh μὴ ὁμολογῶν αὐτὸν σαρκοφόρον, ὁ δὲ τοῦτο μὴ λέγων τελείως αὐτὸν ἀπήρνηται, ὢν ν. Ign.*Smyrn.*5.2; δερματίνους δὲ χιτῶνας ἐφέσσατο σάρκα βαρεῖαν ν. Gr.Naz.*carm.*1.1.8.116(M.37. 455A); ψυχή,...τίς δέ σε ν. θήκατο; *ib.*1.2.14.64(760A); in allegorical interprn. of Lc.7:12ff. οἱ βαστάζοντες στήσονται, τουτέστι παύσονται τοῦ δρόμου τῆς ν. κακίας Nil.*epp.*4.12(M.79.556B); **2.** as subst., *tomb*, Amph.*hom* 3.4(M.39.64C); ἡ νεκροφόρου δυσίνιος [l. δυσήνιος] ἀποφορά *ib.*(64D).

***νεκρόφρων,** *with mind set on the dead*, ‡Gr.Naz.*Chr.pat.*2153(M. 38.306A).

***νεκροφῶρ, ὁ,** *corpse-stealer*, ‡Gr.Naz.*Chr.pat.*1895(M.38.287A).

***νεκροχειροτόνητος,** *ordained by a dead man* αὐτῶν μὲν [sc. Ἡσαϊανιστῶν] διαβεβαιουμένων, ὑπὸ τοῦ Ἐπιφανίου τοῦ Παμφύλου τοῦ χειροτονήσαντος πρεσβύτερον Σεβῆρον, καὶ αὐτὸν κεχειροτονῆσθαι· τῶν δὲ λοιπῶν μὴ συντιθεμένων, ἀλλὰ ν. αὐτὸν εἶναι λεγόντων, ὡς νεκρᾶς ἐπιτεθείσης αὐτῷ τῆς Ἐπιφανίου χειρός Tim.CP *haer.*(M.86.45B).

νεκρ-όω, *make dead*;

A. lit.; **1.** *kill*, ‡Just.*coh.Gr.*3(M.6.236A); Or.*enarr.in Job* 40:26 (M.17.101A); **2.** pass.; **a.** *be made dead* τὰ ~ούμενα...σώματα Just. *1apol.*18.6(M.6.356B); τὰ ~ωθέντα τῶν σωμάτων Athenag.*res.*2(p.50. 9; M.6.977B); θεάσῃ αὐτὸν νενεκρωμένον, ἀνιστάμενον δὲ τῇ τοῦ θεοῦ... δυνάμει *A.Jo.*23(p.164.6); in interprn. of raising of Lazarus οὐ ταὐτόν ἐστιν τὴν ἀρχὴν τοῦ δεδέσθαι ἐκ τοῦ νενεκρῶσθαι εἰληφέναι Or.*Jo.*28.8(7; p.398.34; M.14.697A); νεκροὶ ἐν Χριστῷ ἀναστήσονται πρῶτον (τουτέστι τὰ σκηνώματα· ἐνεκρώθησαν γὰρ ἀπαμφιασθέντα τῶν ψυχῶν) Meth.*symp.*6.4(p.69.8; M.18.120B); in interprn. of δερμάτινοι χιτῶνες as τὴν πρὸς τὸ ~οῦσθαι δύναμιν Gr.Nyss.*or.catech.*8(p.43. 10; M.45.33C); Chrys.*hom.24.4 in 1Cor.*(10.216E); **b.** *be as good as dead*, *A.Thom.*A 33(p.150.1); *ib.*75(p.190.4); cf.*A.Andr.*B 3(p.60.3); **3.** *paralyse, render ineffective*, Or.*hom.6.2 in Jer.*(p.49.10; M.13. 325A); *Hom.Clem.*12.15; Chrys.*hom.55.2 in Jo.*(8.324E); Thdt.*h.e.* 1.7.5(3.755); met. ψυχὴ ~ουμένη τὰ μέλη Or.*hom.6.2 in Jer.*(p.49.15; M.13.325B); ~οῖ τὴν...ὄψιν id.*Jo.*20.39(p.382.28; M.14.668D); λόγους ...τῇ τῶν ἀγαθῶν ἔργων ἀπραξίᾳ νενεκρωμένους Max.*ep.*20(M.91.597C); πίστιν...~ωθεῖσαν τοῖς πάθεσιν *ib.*25(613C); **4.** *deaden* (through effects of cold), *numb*, *Hom.Clem.*17.8; met. ἀχαρίστου γὰρ ἔλπις ὡς πάχνη χειμέριος...ναρκᾶν καὶ ~οῦσθαι τὴν ψυχὴν ποιεῖ, ὥσπερ ἐκείνη τὰ σώματα Chrys.*hom.25.4 in Mt.*(7.312B); ἐν ἀκμῇ τοῦ χειμῶνος τῆς... ἁμαρτίας...ὅτε...ἀγάπη...ἡ πρὸς θεὸν ψυγήσασα ἐνενέκρωτο Hesych.H. *fr.Ps.*35:9(M.93.1189D).

B. met.; **1.** *kill, make dead* sin, Devil, etc. κυρίου τὰ πάθη νεκρώσαντος Clem.*str.*3.4(p.207.17; M.8.1129A); ~οῦμεν...τὸν διάβολον Or. *enarr.in Job* 40:26(M.17.101A); καταγωνισαμένη τὸν διάβολον...καὶ ~ώσασα τὰς ἑπτὰ κεφαλὰς τῶν ἑπτὰ στεφάνων τῆς ἀρετῆς ἐγκρατὴς γίνεται Meth.*symp.*8.13(p.97.19; M.18.160B); id.*res.*1.60(p.324.5; M. 41.1157A); ἔδει...~ωθῆναι...θανάτῳ τὴν ἁμαρτίαν, ἵν' ἐκτακείσης τῆς ἁμαρτίας...ὁ ἄνθρωπος καθαρὸς φάγῃ τῆς ζωῆς *ib.*1.39(p.284.6; M.41. 1108C); **2.** *destroy* τῶν κοσμοκρατόρων ~ωθῆναι τὴν βίαν Mac.Mgn. *apocr.*4.30(p.221.33); **3.** *reduce to condition of spiritual death*, *A.Jo.* 112(p.211.8); νεκροὶ δὲ ἡμεῖς οἱ ~ωθέντες τῇ συστάσει ταύτῃ, ζῶντες δὲ οἱ ἄρρενες οἱ μὴ μεταλαβόντες τῆς συστάσεως ταύτης Clem.*exc. Thdot.*22(p.114.1; M.9.669A); αὐτὸν μὴ δεξαμένων καὶ ἑαυτοὺς μᾶλλον ἢ τὸν Ἰησοῦν ~ωσάντων Or.*hom.26.3 in Jos.*(p.462.30; M.87.1041B); τῆς οἱονεὶ νεκρότητος ἣν νενέκρωνται Meth.*res.*1.23(p.248.3; M.41. 1093A); δόξα δὲ πατρός ἐστι τὸν...ἄνθρωπον...~ωθέντα ζωοποιηθῆναι Ath.*Ar.*1.42(M.26.100B); *ib.*2.65(285A); ὁ ταῖς ἁμαρτίαις νενεκρωμένος πρὸς τὸ ἀγαθὸν ἀκίνητος μένει ‡Ath.*qu.script.*111(M.28.764A); Gr.Naz.*or.*30.20(p.141.11; M.36.132A); Gr.Nyss.*virg.*13(p.304.16; M. 46.376D); Epiph.*haer.*9.4(p.202.12; M.41.229C); ἐν τάφῳ τῷ σώματι νενεκρωμένην ψυχὴν περιφέρων Chrys.*hom.27.4 in Mt.*(7.331E); *ib.73.3* (711B); ἡ μὲν ταῖς ἁμαρτίαις νενεκρωμένης ψυχῆς ἀνάστασις...τελεῖται, ὅταν ταῖς τῆς δικαιοσύνης πράξεσιν εἰς ζωὴν ἀναστοιχειωθῇ Isid.Pel. *epp.*5.179(M.78.1432B); Cyr.*Ps.*29:8(M.69.856C); τὰ τοῦ σώματος πάθη ~ωσον, ~οῦντα τὸν νοῦν μου Jo.Mon.*hymn.Bas.*9(M.96.1376D); produced by heret. beliefs, Gr.Naz.*or.*31.13(p.162.4; M.36.148C); *ib.*38.16(329C); **4.** *mortify* ~ῶσαι τὰς ἐπιθυμίας Clem.*str.*4.12(p.286.2; M.8.1293C); ὁ γνωστικὸς...ζῇ...~ώσας τὰς ἐπιθυμίας καὶ οὐκέτι συγχρῆται τῷ σώματι *ib.*6.9(p.469.17; M.9.296C); id.*exc.Thdot.*52(p.124. 12; M.9.684C); σῶμα...ἐσταύρωσαν καὶ οἷον ἐνέκρωσαν ἀπὸ τῶν σωματικῶν παθῶν id. *fr.*7(p.197.5); Or.*or.*25.3(p.359.1; M.11.500A); id.*schol. in Cant.*8:4(M.17.285B); Ephr.3.255F; ~ωθῆναι τῷ κόσμῳ, ζῶσαι τῇ ἀρετῇ id.3.549C; ἡ ἐλπὶς ἐν τῷ ~ῶσαι μὲν πάντα τὰ σεαυτοῦ, ζητῆσαι δὲ τὴν ἐν Χριστῷ ζωὴν τὴν μέλλουσαν Bas.*hom.*20.3(2.159A; M.31. 532A); βαπτισθέντα εἰς τὸν θάνατον τοῦ κυρίου συνδιατεθῆναι τῷ θανάτῳ, ὅπερ ἐστὶ ~ωθῆναι τῇ ἁμαρτίᾳ ἑαυτῷ τε καὶ τῷ κόσμῳ †Bas. *bapt.*1.2.10(2.636D; M.31.1541D); *ib.*1.2.13(638E; M.1548C); Diod. *Rom.*7:9–11(p.88.12); θεῷ γὰρ οὐκ ἔστιν ἄλλως ζῆν, ἀλλ' ἢ ~ωθέντα τῇ ἁμαρτίᾳ Chrys.*comm.in Gal.*2:20(10.692E); ἄνθρωπος ἐὰν μὴ ~ώσῃ τὰ θελήματα τῆς σαρκὸς πάντα,...οὐ δύναται γενέσθαι μοναχὸς *Apophth. Patr.*(M.65.340C); μέτοχοι γὰρ γεγονότες αὐτοῦ διὰ τοῦ πνεύματος... ἐνεκρώθημεν τῷ κόσμῳ, ζῶμεν δὲ τὴν ἀρίστην ζωὴν τῷ θεῷ Cyr.*Jo.*4.7 (4.432D).

***νεκρώσιμος**, **1.** *of* or *concerned with death* τί δηλοῦσιν οἱ δερμάτινοι χιτῶνες...; τὰ δέρματα νεκρωθέντων ἀλόγων εἰσί, ν. οὖν σύμβολον τοῦτο περιέθηκε Ephr.3.477E; **2.** *funeral* ἀκολουθία ν. *Euchol.*(p.451); κανόνας ν. *Const.Stud.*7(M.99.1708A).

νέκρωσις, **ἡ**, *state of death*;

I. lit.; **A.** *death, condition of death*; **1.** in gen. νέκρωσιν αὐτοῖς [sc. Adam and Eve] ὁρίσας Meth.*res.*1.38(p.281.12n.); τὰ νεκρὰ σώματα ...μυσάττονται διὰ τὴν...δυσωδίαν, καὶ οὐ διὰ τὴν ν. ‡Just.*qu.et resp.* 28(M.6.1276B); **2.** of Christ's death; **a.** in gen. ἐπὶ...τῆς ἀνθρωπότητος αὐτοῦ, καὶ τῆς ν. Iren.*haer.*3.18.3(M.7.933B); ‡Hipp.*fr.24 in Pr.* (p.165.19; M.10.621D); εἰ γὰρ κατὰ μετάστασιν θεότητος ὁ θάνατος γέγονε καὶ ἡ τοῦ σώματος ν., ἴδιον ἄρα θάνατον ἀπέθανε, καὶ οὐ τὸν ἡμέτερον ‡Ath.*Apoll.*1.18(M.26.1125B); ν. δὲ θεὸς οὐκ ἐπιδέχεται *ib.* 2.7(1144B); τριήμερον ν. Gr.Nyss.*or.catech.*35(p.132.10; M.45.88C); **b.** ref. 2Cor.4:10, interpreted; **i.** of 'dying daily', Chrys.*hom.9.1 in 2Cor.*(10.498D); Thdt.*2Cor.*4:10(3.310); **ii.** of mortification (v. infra IV) ὅτε τὴν ν. Ἰησοῦ ἐν τῷ σώματι περιφέρομεν, καὶ οὐκέτι ζῶμεν κατὰ σάρκα ζῇ δὲ τὸ πνεῦμα Or.*hom.11.2 in Jer.*(p.80.2; M.13.369A); id.*Jo.*1.31(35; p.40.15; M.14.84C); Cyr.*ador.*11(1.407E); **iii.** of baptism, Bas.*Spir.*32(3.27A; M.32.125A); Cyr.*ador.*11(1.407D); cf. ref. Mc.10:38, Lc.12:50, Max.*cap.*2.98(M.90.1220C) cit. s. βάπτισμα.

B. *mortality* τινες δερματίνους χιτῶνας τὴν ν., ἣν ἀμφιέννυνται ὁ Ἀδὰμ καὶ ἡ Εὔα, διὰ τὴν ἁμαρτίαν θανατωθέντες, ἀπεφήναντο τυγχάνειν. οὐ πάνυ τι οὐδὲ αὐτοὶ εὐχερῶς δυνάμενοι παραστῆσαι, πῶς ὁ θεός, καὶ οὐχὶ ἁμαρτία, ν. ἐμποιεῖ τῷ παραβεβηκότι Or.*sel.in Gen.*3:21(M.12.101B); ἡ σὰρξ ἀναστᾶσα, καὶ ἀποθεμένη τὴν ν. καὶ θεοποιηθεῖσα Ath. *Ar.*3.48(M.26.425B); ‡Chrys.*pasch.*2(8.257A); Proc.G.*Gen.*3:21(M. 87.220A).

C. *deadness, paralysis, uselessness*; **a.** lit., of effects of illness ποίμνιον ἀποίμαντον...διὰ τὴν ἡμετέραν ν. Gr.Naz.*ep.*152(M.37.257B); of leprosy ν. ἐν ζώσῃ σαρκί Cyr.*ador.*15(1.541A); **b.** met., ref. Rom. 3:26 διὰ τὴν πάρεσιν, τουτέστι, τὴν ν. Chrys.*hom.7.3 in Rom.*(9. 486A); Sev.Ant.*res.*(p.836.3; M.46.644A).

II. *spiritual death*;

A. as state of man before Inc. τὴν ἡμετέραν ν. διὰ τῆς πρὸς ἑαυτὸν ἀνακράσεως εἰς ζωτικὴν μεταποιῆσαι χάριν καὶ δύναμιν Gr.Nyss. *Eun.*5(2 p.119.22; M.45.700D); Nest.*hom.tent.*1(p.338; M.61.685).

B. as state of unbaptized, Herm.*sim.*9.16.3; Chrys.*hom.6.3 in 2Cor.*(10.476C).

C. of those who do not hear God's word or are in state of sin, †Bas.*Is.*165(1.497A; M.30.389D); *ib.*166(497E; M.392C); Μωσῆς ἐν τῇ τῆς ἁγίας γῆς ἐπιβάσει τὴν δερματίνην ν. τῶν ποδῶν ἐκβαλών Gr.Nyss. ap.Proc.G.*Cant.*5:3(M.87.1680A); cf.id.*hom.11 in Cant.*(M.44.1005C); Chrys.*hom.6.3 in 2Cor.*(10.477D); ἡ ν. ἡ ψυχική, προαιρέσεως οὖσα, ἔγκλημα ἔχει καὶ λύσιν οὐδεμίαν id.*hom.4.1 in Eph.*(11.25B); τί δὲ ν. ψυχῆς; ὥσπερ γὰρ τὸ σῶμα τότε νεκροῦται, ὅταν ἔρημον αὐτὸ καταλίπῃ τῆς...ἐνεργείας ἡ ψυχή· οὕτω καὶ ἡ ψυχὴ τότε νεκροῦται, ὅταν ἔρημον αὐτὴν καταλίπῃ τῆς...ἐνεργείας τὸ πνεῦμα τὸ ἅγιον *ib.18.3*(130C); ν. ...ψυχῆς τὴν κακοπραγίαν Isid.Pel.*epp.*5.179(M.78.1432B).

III. of death of the 'old man', sin etc. in baptism τῆς μὲν ν. ἐν τῷ ὕδατι τελουμένης, τῆς δὲ ζωῆς ἡμῶν ἐνεργουμένης διὰ τοῦ πνεύματος Bas.*Spir.*35(3.29D; M.32.129D); ἐν τῇ τῆς ν. εἰκόνι τῇ γενομένῃ διὰ τοῦ ὕδατος Gr.Nyss.*or.catech.*35(p.134.10; M.45.89B); δύο...ν. εἶναί φησι ...καὶ τὴν μὲν ὑπὸ τοῦ Χριστοῦ γεγενῆσθαι ἐν τῷ βαπτίσματι, τὴν δὲ ὑφ' ἡμῶν ὀφείλειν γίνεσθαι διὰ τῆς μετὰ ταῦτα σπουδῆς Chrys.*hom.11.1 in Rom.*(9.530B); Cyr.*ador.*11(1.408A).

IV. *mortification*, ref. Rom.4:19 οὐ διὰ τὸ γῆρας λέγεται τὸ σῶμα τοῦ Ἀβραὰμ νενεκρωμένον...ὥστε ἐν ἐπαίνῳ λέγεται ἡ τοιαύτη ν. τοῦ τὰ μέλη τὰ ἐπὶ τῆς γῆς νεκρώσαντος Or.*comm.in Rom.*4:18–22(*JTS* 13 p.361); μία γὰρ θυσία, ὁ Χριστός, καὶ ἡ κατ' αὐτὸν ν. τῶν ἁγίων †Bas. *Is.*26(1.400B; M.30.169B); Gr.Nyss.*v.Mos.*(M.44.349A); *ib.*(385D); ref. Cant.5:5 αὐτάς φησι τὰς χεῖρας (σημαίνει δὲ τὰς ἐνεργητικὰς τῆς ψυχῆς κινήσεις) ἀφ' ἑαυτῶν στάξαι τὴν σμύρναν, τὴν οἰκόθεν ἐκ προαιρέσεως τῶν σωματικῶν γινομένην ν.· διὰ τούτου σημαίνων τὴν ἐν πᾶσι τοῖς δακτύλοις πεπληρωμένην. λέγει δὲ τὰ καθ' ἕκαστον εἴδη τὰ διῃρημένως δι' ἀρετῆς σπουδαζόμενα, τῷ τῶν δακτύλων διερμηνεύων ὀνόματι, ὡς εἶναι πάντα τὸν νοῦν τῶν λεγομένων τοιοῦτον· ὅτι ἔλαβον δύναμιν ἀναστάσεως διὰ τοῦ νεκρῶσαι τὰ μέλη μου τὰ ἐπὶ τῆς γῆς, ἑκουσίως μοι τῆς τῶν μελῶν τῶν τοιούτων ἐνεργηθείσης ν. id.*hom. 12 in Cant.*(M.44.1017A); Chrys.*hom.11.1 in Rom.*(9.530B); λῃστὴς ἐστιν εὐγνώμων, ὁ διὰ τῆς παντελοῦς τῶν παθῶν ν. καταξιωθεὶς συσταυρωθῆναι Χριστῷ, τουτέστι μετὰ λόγου καὶ γνώσεως πᾶσαν διεξιὼν ἀρετήν ‡Ammon.*Mt.*27:44(M.85.1389B); in monastic life, Sophr.H.*v.Anast.*(M.92.1689B); Jo.Mon.*hymn.Blas.*6(M.96.1404C).

νεκρωτικός, **1.** *mortifying* τῆς ν. τῶν παθημάτων σμύρνης πλήρεις Gr.Nyss.*hom.14 in Cant.*(M.44.1068B); ὕπνον πάσης ἁμαρτίας ν. Nil. *epp.*3.180(M.79.469A); τὴν ν. τῶν παθῶν πρᾶξιν, τὴν ἀγαθότητα καὶ τὸ τῆς ἀφθονίας καλόν Max.*ambig.*(M.91.1284D); νοητῷ... σταυρῷ, τῇ ν. ... τῶν παθῶν ἐνεργείᾳ Thdr.Stud.*icon.*5(M.99.496B); **2.** v. νεκρικός.

***νεκταριώδης**, *like nectar*, †Gr.Thaum.*ep.Philagr.*(M.46.1105D).

νεκταρώδης, = foreg., Jo.VI H.*v.Jo.D.*31(M.94.472C).

νεκυομαντεία, **ἡ**, *divination by the dead, necromancy*, Just.*1apol.* 18.3(M.6.356A); Clem.*prot.*2(p.11.6; M.8.69A); Eust.*engast.*3(p.19. 12; M.18.617C); τὰ νεκυομαντειῶν παρανομώτατα πράγματα, μηδὲ μέχρις ἀκοῆς παραδέχου Cyr.H.*catech.*4.37; Chrys.*hom.24.4 in Rom.* (9.699D); Cyr.*ador.*6(1.186A); id.*Is.*1.5(2.146D); ἔθυον...ἐν μνήμασι... ν. τὰς καλουμένας ἐπιτηδεύοντες *ib.*5.6(893D); used in attempt to divine succession to throne in reign of Valens, Socr.*h.e.*4.19.1(M. 67.505A); ἐπὶ νεκυομαντείας οἱ δαίμονες ψυχὰς τὰς καλουμένας ὑποκρινόμενοι Proc.G.*Is.*29:1–8(M.87.2252D).

***νεκυοσσόος**, *raising the dead to life*, Nonn.*par.Jo.*5:25(M.43. 789A); *ib.*11:44(845C); *ib.*12:18(853A).

νεκυοστόλος, *bearing the dead*, Nonn.*par.Jo.*19:38(M.43.905C).

***νεκυοφάγος**, *feeding on corpses*, Epiph.*exp.fid.*10(p.509.27; M. 42.797C).

νέκυς, **ὁ**, *corpse*, ref. ideal man, Papa, in Naassene system λέγουσι δὲ...τὸν αὐτὸν τοῦτον καὶ ν., οἱονεὶ ἐν μνήματι καὶ τάφῳ ἐγκατωρυγμένον ἐν τῷ σώματι Hipp.*haer.*5.8(p.93.13; M.16.3146B); Naassene hymn ap.Hipp.*haer.*5.9(p.99.20; 3155A).

νεμεσήμων, *exciting indignation*, Nonn.*par.Jo.*15:22(M.43.876C).

νεμεσίζω, *be angry with* ἐνεμέσιζε τοῖς...στρατιάρχαις Men.*exc. gent.*17(p.460.5; M.113.821A).

***νενοθευμένως**, *in an irregular* or *illegitimate manner*, Bas.Sel.*or.* 36.2(M.85.385B).

***νεοβάπτιστος**, *newly baptized*, Job.Mon.*inc.*2(M.86.3316C); *Didasc.Jac.*tit.(p.745.2).

***νεόβουλος**, **ὁ**, *newly appointed member of municipal council* ἐπειδὴ γέγονεν ἡγεμών, ἀξιοῦται συντελεῖν ὥσπερ οἱ ν. Synes.*ep.*38(M. 66.1364B).

***νεογενία**, **ἡ**, *new, strange birth*, Thdot.Anc.*hom.BMV et Sym.* 3(M.77.1393B).

***νεόγληνος**, *provided with new eyes*, Nonn.*par.Jo.*9:8(M.43. 825A).

νεόγραπτος, *newly inscribed*, Gr.Naz.*carm.*2.2(poem.)4.110(M.37. 1513A).

νεόγραφος, *newly-written* δέλτοις ὀλίγῃσι ν. αἷμα λελογχώς (of a brand-new title of nobility) Gr.Naz.*carm.*2.1.32.30(M.37.1302A).

νεοθλιβής, *newly pressed* or *squeezed*; of wine, fig. ὁ ν. οὗτος οἶνος, ὁ ἐκ τῆς ληνοῦ προχυθείς, ἣν ἐπάτησε διὰ τοῦ εὐαγγελίου ὁ κύριος, ἵνα σοι πότιμον τοῦ ἰδίου βότρυος τὸ αἷμα ποιήσῃ Gr.Nyss. *Spir.*(M.46.701A).

***νεοκαής**, *newly lit*, Jo.Mon.*hymn.Geo.*6(M.96.1397B).

***νεοκαλλιγράφος**, *latter-day artist*; of women who paint their faces, Gr.Naz.*carm.*1.2.29.332(M.37.908A).

νεοκατασκεύαστος, **1.** *newly made*, Chrys.*hom.15.4 in 1Tim.*(11. 640C); ‡Proc.G.*Pr.*21:9(M.87.1432C); **2.** *newly appointed* ν. ἄρχοντι id.*Num.*27:21(M.87.877B).

***νεοκατήχητος**, *newly instructed*, of those who have recently become catechumens σαρκικοὺς δὲ τοὺς ν. καὶ μηδέπω κεκαθαρμένους Clem.*paed.*1.6(p.111.22; M.8.293A); id.*str.*6.15(p.497.25; M. 9.353B); Acac.et Paul.*ep.*(p.154.14; M.41.157A); Chrys.*hom.10.2 in 1Tim.*(11.600F); Pall.*h.Laus.*41(p.129.9; M.34.1234B); in gen. sense of new converts, Chrys.*hom.1.1 in 1Thess.*(11.426A); of religious novices, Ephr.1.318B cit. s. ἀσυστρόφημα.

***νεοκῆρυξ**, **ὁ**, *preacher of novelties*, Jo.V H.*icon.*2(M.96.1349C); *ib.*(1352A); *ib.*16(1361A).

***νεοκληρονόμος**, **ὁ**, *new heir*; of one who has despoiled another man's tomb, Gr.Naz.*carm.*2.2(epigr.)61.2(M.38.114A).

***νεόκλητος**, *newly called, called by a new name* εἰ ὁ νεόπλαστος καὶ νεότοκος καὶ ν. ὁ αὐτὸς οὗτος καὶ θεός, ἐξ ἀνάγκης καὶ νέος θεός Leont.H.*Nest.*5.47(M.86.1720B).

***νεόκοσμος**, *of a new world*, *Orac.Sib.*11.241.

νεόκτιστος, **1.** *newly created*, Cosm.Ind.*top.*2(M.88.93C); of the new creation τῆς ν. ψυχῆς, ἣν τὸ πνεῦμα δι' ὕδατος ἀνεμόρφωσεν Gr. Naz.*or.*7.15(M.35.773C); οὐ βούλεταί σε ὁ λόγος ποτὲ ἐν ταὐτῷ μένειν, ἀλλὰ ἀεικίνητον εἶναι, εὐκίνητον, πάντως ν. *ib.*44.8(M.36.616D); **2.** *newly appointed* ν. καθηγεμόνι Thdr.Stud.*epp.*2.126(M.99.1409B); **3.** *novel in creation*, ref. Arian conception of Christ νεογενῆ καὶ ν. οὐσίαν Χριστοῦ Const.*ep.*ap.Gel.Cyz.*h.e.*3.19.29(M.85.1352C).

***νεόκτυπος**, *newly pealing*; of thunder, Gr.Naz.*carm.*2.2(epitaph.)5.5(M.38.13A).

νεολαία, ἡ, *band of youths, youth* (collectively); hence *youthfulness, freshness*, in interprn. of the 'fresh colt' of Zech.9:9 τὴν ἐν Χριστῷ ν. τῆς ἀνθρωπότητος Clem.*paed.*1.5(p.99.6; M.8.268A); v. νεελαία.

νεολαμπής, *newly illumined*, i.e. baptized, Gr.Naz.*carm.*2.1.13.87 (M.37.1234A).

νεόλεκτος, *newly enlisted*; met., of converts to Christianity, Eus.*p.e.*1.5(16B; M.21.45C); Gr.Nyss.*Thdr.*(M.46.740C); Bas.Sel. *pasch.*2.4(M.28.1085C); σφραγισθέντων ν. στρατιωτῶν Χριστοῦ *Rit. Bapt.*(p.392); Thdr.Stud.*epp.*2.21(M.99.1181B).

***νεόλοχος**, ἡ, *woman who has just brought forth a child*, ‡Caes. Naz.*dial.*139(M.38.1044).

***νεομάρτυς**, ὁ, *recent martyr*, *Exorc.*31(p.342).

***νεομάχος**, ὁ, *one who is new to battle*, Jo.Mal.*chron.*8 p.209(M.97. 325A), but prob. for ναυμάχος.

νεόνυμφος, *newly betrothed*; of couple at beginning of marriage service, *Euchol.*(p.310).

[*]**νεόξυστος**, *newly scraped*, Gr.Nyss.*hom.14 in Cant.*(M.44. 1073A), but prob. for νεόξεστος.

νεοπαγής, *newly fixed*; **1.** *newly built*, Eus.*h.e.*10.3.1(M.20.848A); id.*v.C.*3.47(p.97.31; M.20.1108B); Bas.*ep.*94(3.188A; M.32.488A); of CP ν. Χριστοῦ πόλιν Soz.*h.e.*2.3.7(M.67.940B); met., of Church πόλει ...ν. καὶ θεοτεύκτῳ Eus.*h.e.*10.4.7(849C); of 'foundation' of instruction, Chrys.*hom.7.1 in Jo.*(8.44D); **2.** *newly made*, Eus.*theoph.*3 (p.14*.10; M.24.620A); Chrys.*hom.85.5 in Jo.*(8.580E); *ib.10.2*(59E); **3.** *newly constituted* ν. βίον Eus.*v.C.*3.1(p.77.25; M.20.1056B); ν. λαόν Gr.Naz.*or.*36.6(M.36.272C); of church at CP on its return to orthodoxy, CCP(381)*ep.*ap.Thdt.*h.e.*5.9.15(3.1032); of a new bishop, Gr. Naz.*ep.*121(M.37.216B); of new converts, Gr.Nyss.*v.Mos.*(M.44. 360D); Ast.Am.*hom.*8(M.40.272D); Proc.G.*Gen.*12:17(M.87.320C); Jo.Clim.*scal.*1(M.88.641A); of religious novices, Isid.Pel.*epp.*1.258 (M.78.337B); Nil.*Eulog.*23(M.79.1124C); **4.** *newly found*, of a convert ν. παιδίῳ Clem.*paed.*1.6(p.114.28; M.8.300A); ‡Gr.Nyss.*or.1 in Gen. 1:26*(M.44.269D); **5.** = νέος, Thdr.Stud.*or.*11.6(M.99.808C); **6.** of Lazarus, *newly compacted* (i.e. restored from corruption), Eust. *Laz.*9(p.34.9).

***νεοπειθής**, *recently converted*, Nonn.*par.Jo.*6:37(M.43.800C); *ib.*8:31(817B).

νεοπενθής, *in new sorrow, fresh-mourning*, Nonn.*par.Jo.*11:33(M. 43.844C).

νεοπηγής, *newly made* or *fashioned*, Gr.Naz.*carm.*1.1.8.70(M.37. 452A); Nonn.*par.Jo.*7:8(M.43.805B).

νεόπηκτος, = foreg., Gr.Naz.*carm.*1.2.1.378(M.37.550A).

***νεόπηξ**, *newly framed* ν. ... νόμον Gr.Naz.*carm.*1.1.1.20(M.37. 400A).

νεόπιστος, *recently converted to the faith*, Anon.ap.Eus.*h.e.*5.16.7 (M.20.465B).

***νεοπλανήτης**, ὁ, *new heretic*, Dam.*troph.*suppl.(p.280.13).

[*]**νεόπλαστος**, *newly formed* εἰ ὁ ν. καὶ νεότοκος καὶ νεόκλητος ὁ αὐτὸς οὗτος καὶ θεός, ἐξ ἀνάγκης καὶ νέος θεός Leont.H.*Nest.*5.47(M. 86.1720B).

***νεόπληκτος**, *newly wounded*, Anast.S.*haer.*(p.258).

***νεοπροσήλυτος**, *newly converted*, Ast.Am.*hom.*8(M.40.272D).

***νεοπτερίζ-ω**, *furnish with new wings*, met. ~ων ὡς ἀετὸν τοὺς ἀγαπητούς σου Agath.*v.Gr.Ill.*38.

***νεόπτητος**, *newly baked*, Leont.H.*monoph.*(M.86.1900B).

νέος, **I.** *young*;

A. lit.; **1.** as subst., *young man* ν. καὶ πρεσβύτην καὶ τέκνα *Pss. Sal.*2.8; *T.Neph.*5.4; Clem.*prot.*4(p.45.9; M.8.156B); *A.Thom.*A 51 (p.167.14); Thdt.*h.e.*3.14.1(3.927); of God ἐν ταῖς ἱεραῖς τῶν μυστικῶν ὁράσεων θεοφανείαις καὶ πάλιος καὶ ν. πλάττεται...τοῦ νεωτέρου...τὸν ἀγήρω σημαίνοντος Dion.Ar.*d.n.*10.2(M.3.937B); **2.** comp. in positive sense τῇ δὲ τρίτῃ ὁράσει ὅλη νεωτέρα...μόνας δὲ τὰς τρίχας πρεσβυτέρας εἶχεν Herm.*vis.*3.10.5; τὸν μᾶλλον νεώτερον *Const.App.*2.58. 5; μᾶλλον ἐμεῖο νεώτερος Nonn.*par.Jo.*5:7(M.43.785B); masc. as subst., *T.Reub.*2.9; *T.Lev.*2.2; *A.Thom.*A 54(p.170.11); *Const.App.* 1.3.6; fem. as subst., name of Egyptian goddess, Ath.*gent.*10(M. 25.21C); **3.** comp., *junior* Σοφοκλῆς ὁ νεώτερος Clem.*prot.*2(p.22.17; M.8.104A); of Jacob as younger son of Isaac typifying Christ opp. Judaism, Hipp.*ben.Jac.*8(p.21.3); of Ephraim as younger son of Jacob typifying Church opp. old Israel, *ib.*11(p.24.23); **4.** comp., *too young*, for episcopal orders, *Cap.*6 ap.CBeryt.*act.*(*ACO* 2.1.3 p.25.6; H.2.520A); **5.** comp. as subst., of class of younger men in Church ὁμοίως διάκονοι ἄμεμπτοι...ὁμοίως καὶ νεώτεροι ἄμεμπτοι Polyc.*ep.*5.3.

B. *young* in the faith; of new converts, Herm.*vis.*3.5.4; Meth. *res.*1.28(p.256.19; M.41.1133D).

C. of Logos ὁ...πάντοτε ν. ἐν ἁγίων καρδίαις γεννώμενος ‡*Diogn.* 11.4.

D. of Christians, Herm.*vis.*3.13.4; νέοι τοίνυν ὁ λαὸς ὁ καινὸς πρὸς ἀντιδιαστολὴν τοῦ πρεσβυτέρου λαοῦ, τὰ νέα μαθόντες ἀγαθά. καὶ ἔστιν ἡμῖν τὸ οὖθαρ τῆς ἡλικίας ἡ ἀγήρως αὕτη νεότης, ἐν ᾗ πρὸς νόησιν ἀεὶ ἀκμάζομεν, ἀεὶ ν. καὶ ἀεὶ ἤπιοι καὶ ἀεὶ καινοί Clem.*paed.*1.5(p.101.33; M.8.273B); ἐτήρει γὰρ τὸ ὄνομα τὸ καινὸν τῷ ν. λαῷ τῷ νηπίῳ *ib.*1.7 (p.123.33; 317C); id.*str.*1.29(p.110.16; M.8.925C).

II. *new*;

A. *renewed*; of new Jerusalem in Jewish thought, *T.Dan* 5:12.

B. *new*, of additions to an existing class διδάσκει θεὸν ν. ἕνα *A.Thom.*A 20(p.130.10); ἀπόστολε τοῦ ν. θεοῦ *ib.*42(p.159.15); Marcell.*fr.*74 ap.Eus.*Marcell.*1.4(p.28.20; M.24.769C); τὰ ν. *new crops, first-fruits*, *Const.App.*6.5.3.

C. *fresh, new*; **1.** of Christ as new leaven, Ign.*Magn.*10.2; **2.** of Christians λαὸν ν. καὶ λαὸν καινόν Clem.*paed.*1.5(p.98.22; M.8. 265B); *ib.*1.7(p.125.1; 321A); ν. τέκνα βιαρκέος...τοκῆος Nonn.*par. Jo.*8:47(M.43.821A); Thdt.*Ps.*70:5(1.1092) cit. s. νεότης; διδάσκει... τὸν ν. λαόν, ὡς οὐκ ἀδίκως τὸν ἀχάριστον...λαὸν τῆς οἰκείας κηδεμονίας ἐγύμνωσεν *ib.*104 proem.(1343); ν. λαόν...τὴν ἐξ ἐθνῶν ἐκκλησίαν *ib.* 105:4(1355); id.*affect.*10(p.269.27; 4.980); **3.** ν. διαθήκη; **a.** of New Covenant, v. διαθήκη; **b.** of NT, v. διαθήκη; ἡ νέα *the NT*, ‡Petr.I Al.*phys.*12; Cosm.Ind.*top.*proem.(M.88.56C); Jo.Mosch.*prat.*171(M. 87.3040A); τὰ ν. opp. τὰ παλαιά, Cyr.H.*catech.*19.3; cf.Ath.*exp.Ps.* 67:27(M.27.301B) cit. s. διαιρέω; **4.** of new dispensation of Inc. εὐαγγελιστὴς...τῆς ἄνωθεν μνημονεύων ἀρχῆς καὶ μηδενὸς νεωτέρου, ἐν ἀρχῇ ἦν ὁ λόγος ἔφη...ἵνα δείξῃ ὅτι, εἴ τι καινὸν καὶ νεώτερον ὄνομα, τοῦτ' ἀπὸ τῆς καινῆς αὐτῷ καὶ ν. ὑπῆρξε κατὰ σάρκα οἰκονομίας Marcell.*fr.*37 ap.Eus.*e.th.*1.20(p.89.11; M.24.880B); **5.** of Christ as the new bread, opp. manna, Or.*Jo.*6.45(26; p.154.33; M.14.280A); **6.** of the new man put on in Christ, as one of the two χιτῶνες, παλαιός and ν., of which only one is to be possessed (ref. Mt.10:10), Or.*hom.23 in Lc.*(p.152.18); **7.** of gospel as ν. καὶ καινὰ...μυστήρια, Eus.*e.th.*2.18(p.122.27; M.24.941C); **8.** of new life in Christ, Nonn. *par.Jo.*4:21(M.43.777A); **9.** of age to come as ὁ ν. καὶ καινὸς αἰών, Eus.*e.th.*3.17(p.178.33; M.24.1040D); Manich., Hegem.*Arch.*13(p.21. 7; M.10.1448C); **10.** of BMV as ν. μήτηρ καὶ νεογενίας τὸ πλαστήριον Thdot.Anc.*hom.BMV et Sym.*3(M.77.1393B).

III. *recent*;

A. in gen. τεσσαράκοντα μὲν γενεαῖς νεώτερα τὰ Ἀττικά Clem.*str.* 1.21(p.65.15; M.8.821A); τὰ νεώτερα καὶ ὑπὸ Ἑλλήνων ἐπιτετηδευμένα *ib.*1.29(p.110.17; 925C); ref. Pr.8:22 ἦν γὰρ ἀκόλουθον...πάντα ἃ εἰς γένεσιν ἦλθον εἶναι ταύτης [sc. σοφίας] νεώτερα, ἐπεὶ καὶ δι' αὐτῆς γεγόνασιν Meth.*creat.*11(p.499.5; M.18.341B); ἀρχήν τε πρόσκαιρον καὶ νεωτέραν τῇ βασιλείᾳ τοῦ Χριστοῦ διδοὺς καὶ ταύτης τέλος ὑφιστάμενος Eus.*Marcell.*2.4(p.56.19; M.24.820A); ἠρεύξαντό τινες...ἀσέβειαν...ὥστε εἰπεῖν μὴ νεώτερον εἶναι τὸ σῶμα τῆς τοῦ λόγου θεότητος Ath.*ep.Epict.*2(p.5.9; M.26.1053B); of an historian writing after the event διαστέλλει δὲ τὸν Ἰούδαν...ὁ συγγραφεὺς ὡς νεώτερος Proc.G. *Jos.*11:8(M.87.1024A).

B. *later, second*; **1.** of emperors, *junior, second* Θεοδόσιος ν. Αὔγουστος *Chron.Pasch.*p.307(M.92.780C); *ib.*p.376(964A); **2.** of a later saint of same name as an earlier, Steph.Diac.*v.Steph.*tit.(M. 100.1069A); **3.** of one who resembles an earlier person, e.g. Judas as διάβολος ν., Nonn.*par.Jo.*6:70(M.43.804C); of Celestine and of Cyril as 'second Paul', CEph.(431)*act.*2(*ACO* 1.1.3 p.57.24; H.1.1472A).

IV. ν. κυριακή *Sunday after Easter, Low Sunday* (cf. καινὴ κυριακή Gr.Naz.*or.*44 tit.(M.36.608A)); CSyr.*act.*(H.2.1365B); *ib.* (1376D); Evagr.*h.e.*1.3(p.8.30; M.86.2428A).

***νεόσοφος**, ὁ, *professor of the new learning, wiseacre*, Jo.V H. *icon.*2(M.96.1349D).

***νεόσπαρτος**, *newly sown*, Andr.Cr.*Agath.*(M.97.1440C).

νεόσπορος, *newly sown* ν. ... ἄτη Gr.Naz.*carm.*1.1.8.128(M.37. 450A).

νεοσσοποιέω, *hatch*; met., *Phys.*A 8(pp.29.5,30.1); intrans., ‡Epiph.*phys.*8(M.43.525B).

νεοσσός, ὁ, *nestling, chick*; met., of man in relation to God's loving care, Clem.*prot.*10(p.67.21; M.8.204B); id.*paed.*1.5(p.98.17; M.8.265B); Or.*schol.in Cant.*5:11(M.17.276A); in simile of antichrist as a partridge who decoys other birds' broods away by imitating their parent's call, Hipp.*antichr.*55(p.36.19ff.; M.10.775B); of the creative principles productive of earth and water, as ν. of the dove (Holy Spirit or Achamoth), *A.Thom.*A 50(p.166.13).

***νεοστράτευτος**, *newly enlisted*, Pall.*v.Chrys.*9(p.57.18; M.47.33).

***νεοσύντακτος**, *lately enrolled*, Nil.*Magn.*65(M.79.1057A).

νεοτελής, **1.** *newly initiated*, of newly baptized τοὺς ν. βεβαίωσο

Lit.ap.Const.App.8.15.5; Bas.Sel.v.Thecl.2.18(M.85.596C); Dion.Ar. d.n.3.2(M.3.681B); in gen. of one recently converted, Gr.Naz.ep.217 (M.37.353C); ib.228(372B); **2.** s.v.l., recently finished, Max.ambig. (M.91.1325A).

νεότευκτος, newly made, Nonn.par.Jo.19:41(M.43.908A); met., of heresy ν. ... βλασφημίαν Procl.CP Arm.13(p.193.27; M.65.869B).

νεότης, ἡ, 1. youth, ref. Ps.70:5 νεότητα καλεῖ τὸν ἐπὶ...Μωσέως χρόνον, ὅτε καὶ τῆς ἐλευθερίας ἀπήλαυσαν...ὁ δὲ νέος λαὸς νεότητα λέγει ἧς τετύχηκε νεουργίας διὰ τῆς τοῦ λουτροῦ παλιγγενεσίας Thdt. ad loc.(1.1092); of eternal youth spiritually possessed by Christians, Clem.paed.1.5(p.102.3; M.8.273B); **2.** youthful folly ὁ γὰρ δίκαιος οὐκ ἔστιν ἐν ν. Or.fr.1 in Jer.(p.199.6; M.13.545A); **3.** youthful indulgence, Tit.Bost.fr.Lc.7:44(p.170.8); **4.** newness οὐκ ἄρα ἡ ν. τοῦ λόγου ὀνειδιστέα Clem.paed.1.7(p.125.8; M.8.321B).

***νεοττοκομέω**, rear nestlings, Cyr.Is.3.3(2.439D).

νεουργ-έω, 1. restore, renovate, IGC As.Min.215 bis (Naxos saec. vii–ix); ~ηθεῖσαν...ἐκκλησίαν †Jo.D.B.J.33(M.96.1177B); of temple of Christ's body renewed at Resurrection, Eust.fr.in Pr.8:22(M.18.681B); **2.** renew, recreate; **a.** lit., Geo.Pis.hex.1057(M.92.1515A); **b.** of physical and mental refreshment, Thdt.qu.7 in Gen.(1.11); **c.** of spiritual renewal, symbolized by renewal of mankind after Flood, id.Ps.28:10(1.785); ἐπειδὴ τὸ γῆρας ἐδεξάμην τῆς ἁμαρτίας, τῇ σῇ με φιλανθρωπίᾳ ~ησον ib.50:12(1.940); id.Rom.12:2(3.130); λόγῳ θείῳ ~εῖται...ὁ νοῦς ‡Proc.G.Pr.24:3–4(M.87.1460D); esp. of renewal by gift of H. Ghost in baptism, Thdt.1Cor.12:13(3.247); id.Heb.3:14(3.565); id.Tit.3:5(3.708); by baptismal invocation of Trin. whose recreative function corresponds to original work of Creation, id.haer.5.3(4.392); **3.** plough up fallow land, id.Mich.3:12 (2.1492); **4.** build something new ~ῆσαι μονήν Thdr.Stud.epp.2.159 (M.99.1500A).

***νεούργημα, τό**, novelty ὀπτασίας τὸ ν. μὴ φέρων Gr.Mag.dial.(tr. Zach.)4.12(M.PL.77.339A).

***νεούργητος**, newly built, IGC As.Min.215 bis (Naxos, saec. vii–ix).

***νεουργία, ἡ**, renewal, restoration; **1.** lit. πόλεως ν. Thdt.Ps. 101:17(1.1320); id.Ezech.48:35(2.1045); id.eran.2(4.81); **2.** spiritual ἀνθρωπίνης φύσεως ν. ἣν ὁ...Χριστὸς ἐπετέλεσε id.Ps.29:1(1.786); in baptism, id.Ps.70:5(1.1092).

νεουργός, as subst., renovator, renewer; of H. Ghost, Jo.D. carm.pent.90(p.216; M.96.837A).

***νεοφανής, 1.** newly come to light, recently appeared, Cyr.ador.17 (1.594E); Thphn.chron.p.299(M.108.729C); Thdr.Stud.antirr.2.10 (M.99.357B); id.epp.2.73(M.99.1305C); **2.** newly appointed ν. ... ἰατροῦ Mir.Artem.40(p.66.7).

***νεοφανῶς**, as recently appearing, Jo.Clim.scal.15(M.88.896D).

***νεοφοίτητος**, newly frequenting, i.e. of prayers, newly offered μνημονεύσατε ἐν ταῖς ν. ὑμῶν προσευχαῖς Agath.v.Gr.Ill.146.

νεοφυής, newborn, Clem.paed.1.6(p.114.28; M.8.300A).

***νεοφυΐα, ἡ**, new growth, Clem.paed.2.10(p.209.10; M.8.500B).

νεόφυτος, A. lit.; **1.** newly planted, Clem.str.2.18(p.156.2; M.8. 1020C); ib.3.3(p.207.3; 1128A); Chrys.hom.2.3 in Ac.princ.(3.64E); **2.** neut. as subst., young tree, Clem.str.2.18(p.165.1; M.8.1037A); Chrys.hom.in Gal.2:11(3.372A); met., ref. Is.5:7 ν. γὰρ παρὰ θεοῦ ἠγαπημένον, μοναχὸς σωφροσύνῃ ἀρδευόμενος Hyper.mon.79(M.79. 1481A).

B. met., newly converted, neophyte (adj. and subst.); **1.** of newly converted in gen. ἡμεῖς ν. ἐσμεν A.Andr.et Mt.32(p.114.15); Ath. h.Ar.75(p.225.4; M.25.784C); τῶν ν. ἦσαν οἱ ἀκούοντες ἔτι Chrys.hom. 3.1 in Rom.(9.448E); **2.** partic. ref. prohibition against neophyte's consecration to bishopric; **a.** exeg. 1Tim.3:6 'μὴ ν.', φησίν. οὐ τὸν νεώτερον ἐνταῦθα λέγει, ἀλλὰ τὸν νεοκατήχητον...μὴ εὐθέως, φησί, ν. εἰς τὸν τῆς ἀρχῆς ὄγκον ἄγετε, τουτέστι, νεοκατήχητον Chrys.hom.10.2 in 1Tim.(11.600F); cf. οὐδὲ τὸν νέον πάντως ἀπείργειν τῆς τοιαύτης διακονίας, ἀλλὰ τὸν ν. id.sac.2.8(p.46.22; 1.380B); ν. τὸν εὐθὺς πεπιστευκότα καλεῖ...οὐ γάρ, ὥς τινες ὑπέλαβον, τὸν νέον τῆς ἡλικίας ἐκβάλλει Thdt.1Tim.3:6(3.655); μὴ παρέχειν ταχέως ἀξίαν νεοφύτῳ, ὡσανεὶ νεωστὶ προσελθόντι τῇ πίστει Cosm.Ind.top.3(M.88.148D); **b.** in canons ἐπειδὴ πολλὰ...ἐγένετο...ἅμα τῷ βαπτισθῆναι προάγειν εἰς ἐπισκοπὴν ἢ πρεσβυτερεῖον,...ἔδοξεν μηδὲν τοιοῦτο γίνεσθαι. καὶ γὰρ καὶ χρόνου δεῖ τῷ κατηχουμένῳ, καὶ μετὰ τὸ βάπτισμα δοκιμασίας πλείονος· σαφὲς γὰρ τὸ ἀποστολικὸν γράμμα τὸ λέγον· μὴ ν. CNic.(325) can.2; οὔτε ἡ ἀγαθὴ ἀναστροφὴ ἐπιδέχεται...ὥστε ἢ ἐπίσκοπον ἢ πρεσβύτερον ἢ διάκονον προχείρως καθίστασθαι· οὕτω γὰρ ἂν εἰκότως ν. νομισθείη, ἐπειδὴ...ὁ...ἀπόστολος...φαίνεται κωλύσας ταχείας γίνεσθαι τὰς καταστάσεις CSard.can.10.

***νεοφωστικός**, = sq. ἔνδυμα τὸ ν. †Anast.S.relat.51(OC 3 p.75).

***νεοφωτιστικός**, of or belonging to newly baptized persons ἐβάπτισαν αὐτὴν...ἐνδύσαντες αὐτὴν καὶ τὰ ν. ἐνδύματα Jo.Mosch.prat.208 (M.87.3100B); καθεζομένου...Φιλίππου ἐν τῷ παστῷ τῷ ν. †Anast.S. relat.51(OC 3 p.74).

νεοφώτιστος, newly illuminated, newly baptized; **1.** with retention of idea of illumination; of newly baptized as lights in spiritual firmament, Meth.symp.8.6(p.88.20; M.18.148C); διὰ τοῦτο καὶ ν. μέλλεις καλεῖσθαι, ὅτι νέον σοι τὸ φῶς ἀεί Chrys.catech.5.1(2. 236A); διὰ...τὸν...ἥλιον Χριστὸν οὐρανὸς ἡ ἐκκλησία γεγένηται...οὐκ ἀστέρας τινὰς πλανήτας ἀνατέλλουσα, ἀλλ' ἀστέρας ν. ἐκ κολυμβήθρας ἀναφέρουσα ‡Epiph.hom.3(M.43.465C); **2.** in gen. as synonym for νεοβάπτιστος; **a.** of newly baptized opp. Christians of long standing Μάτουρον, ν. μέν, ἀλλὰ γενναῖον ἀγωνιστήν Ep.Lugd.ap.Eus.h.e.5. 1.17(M.20.416A); αἱ προσευχαὶ τῶν ν. A.Phil.142(p.81.25); ref. Arian baptism τί με ποιεῖς...ν. καὶ ἀφώτιστον; Gr.Naz.or.33.17(M.36.236C); ν. καὶ κατηχουμένοις Const.App.2.10.1; ib.5.6.4; Chrys.hom.24.3 in Ac.(9.195E); Ast.Soph.hom.5 in Ps.5(M.40.433C); ν. ... καὶ μήπω ἐστηριγμένους ἐν τῇ...πίστει Marc.Diac.v.Porph.85; of those baptized but not yet confirmed, Rit.Bapt.(p.404); **b.** spiritual condition of ν. to be emulated by senior Christians ν. δὲ λέγω, οὐχὶ τοὺς πρὸ δύο καὶ τριῶν, οὐδὲ πρὸ δέκα ἡμέρων φωτισθέντας μόνον, ἀλλὰ καὶ τοὺς πρὸ ἐνιαυτοῦ, καὶ τοὺς πρὸ πλείονος χρόνου...εἰ γὰρ πολλὴν σπουδὴν ἐπιδεικνύμεθα περὶ τὴν ἑαυτῶν ψυχήν, ἔξεστι καὶ μετὰ δέκα ἔτη εἶναι ν. ἐὰν τὴν νεότητα τὴν ἀπὸ τοῦ φωτίσματος ἐγγινομένην ἡμῖν διασώσωμεν Chrys.hom.1.5 in Ac.princ.(3.58B); καὶ μετὰ δέκα καὶ εἴκοσι ἔτη δυνατὸν ν. καλεῖν τοὺς μεμυημένους, ἐὰν νήφωσι ib.3.6(80C); ‡Chrys.Thom.1.3(8.213A); **c.** ν. as one in whom Christ has been formed, Ph.Carp.Cant.223(M.40.141A); ν. dist. from catechumens, Eus.h.e.6.4.3(M.20.532A); Cyr.H.catech.19 tit.; **d.** as subject of liturg. prayer, Lit.ap.Const.App.8.10.13; Lit.ib.8.13.8; **e.** ref. Cant. 7:12 ἤνθησεν ὁ κυπρισμός interpreted as τοὺς ν. ... τοὺς διὰ λουτροῦ παλιγγενεσίας λελευκανθισμένους Ph.Carp.Cant.214(M.40.133C); **f.** consecration of ν. to bishopric advised as emergency measure ἡγεῖσθαι χρὴ ταῦτα μὲν τῆς ἀνάγκης εἶναι τὰ ῥήματα...εἰ δέ ἐστί τις τῶν ν. ... ἐκεῖνος προβληθήτω Bas.ep.217 can.50(3.325B; M.32.796A); **3.** neut. as subst., newly baptized child ῥίψαντες τὰ ν. Jo.Mosch.prat.265(M. 87.3032C); **4.** of baptismal robes τὰς ν. ἐσθῆτας Jo.Disc.v.Epiph.52 (M.41.88D)? for νεοφωτιστικούς.

***νεοχειροτόνητος**, newly appointed; of bishops, Pall.v.Chrys.9 (p.52.4; M.47.30).

***νεόχνοος**, with first down on cheeks, beardless, Gr.Naz.carm.2.1. 51.6(M.37.1394A); id.carm.2.2(epitaph.)125.3(M.38.78A).

νεόχριστος, 1. newly plastered; of walls, Philost.h.e.8.8(M.65. 561B); **2.** newly anointed (with post-baptismal unction), ‡Jo.D. Const.1(M.95.309B).

***νέρβος, ὁ**, (Lat. nervus) stocks; as instrument of punishment, M.Perp.8(p.75.4); εἰς τὸ ξύλον, ὡς ἂν εἴποι τις, εἰς τὸν ν. Chrys.hom. 35.2 in Ac.(9.271E).

[*]νερόν, τό, v. νηρός.

***νεροφόρος ἡ**, cold bath, Ephr.2.131C; Thdr.Lect.fr.4(M.86. 224A); Thphn.chron.p.122(M.108.341A).

***Νεστοριανίζ-ω**, adopt the views of Nestorius, be a Nestorian μηδεὶς...προσαπτέτω ἄγνοιαν ἢ τῇ ἀνθρωπότητι αὐτοῦ Παυλιανίζων ἢ ~ων Steph.Hier.agn.(p.156.17).

***Νεστοριασμός, ὁ**, Nestorianism, Thdr.Lect.exc.Vat.55(p.68n.).

νεῦμα, τό, 1. sign; of actions that are empty signs without significance αὐτοῖς [sc. Jews] περιτομὴ χωρὶς λόγου νεύματα, καὶ πάσχα καὶ προσευχαί Or.hom.5 in Lc.(p.32.9); of a signal conveyed in speech, Nonn.par.Jo.13:27(M.43.864C); **2.** command; **a.** in gen., Ath.gent.32(M.25.65A); **b.** of rulers βασιλικῷ ν. Eus.h.e.8.6.6(M.20. 753A); id.v.C.3.6(p.79.29; M.20.1060B); ἕπεσθαι νεύμασιν ἰθυνόμενοι Thdt.h.e.4.6.3(3.953); **c.** of a bishop πατρικὸν ν. Euthal.Diac.Ac. (M.85.629C); ποιμένα ἔχειν καὶ τοῖς ἐκείνου ν. ἕπεσθαι Thdt.h.e.4.18.4 (3.977); **d.** of divine commands; **i.** of Father πατέρα...πανηγεμόνα βασιλικῷ ν. προστάττοντα Eus.h.e.1.2.5(M.20.56B); θεοῦ τοῦ παμβασιλέως ν. ib.10.4.54(869D); πάντων ἑνὶ ν. διαφθείρεσθαι μελλόντων id.p.e.7.8(308D; M.21.524A); τὰς...νίκας νεύματι καὶ συνεργείᾳ τοῦ κρείττονος ἠράμην Const.ap.Eus.v.C.3.12(p.82.27; M.20.1068B); τοῖς τοῦ πατρὸς ἐξυπηρετούμενος [sc. Logos] ν. Eus.e.th.3.3(p.155.1; M.24. 997C); ἴσως...θελήσουσι...λέγειν ὅτι ἔδει τὸν θεόν,...σῶσαι θέλοντα τοὺς ἀνθρώπους, νεύματι μόνον ποιῆσαι, καὶ μὴ σώματος ἅψασθαι τόν... λόγον Ath.inc.44.1(M.25.173B); Chrys.ep.1.1(3.528C); Cyr.Is.2.2(2. 222E); Thdt.h.e.3.25.7(3.943); **ii.** of Son ὁ...λόγος τῷ ἑαυτοῦ ν. κινεῖ Ath.gent.44(M.25.88C); πάντα αὐτὸς ἐδημιούργησεν ὁ υἱὸς τὰ γεγενημένα νεύματι πατρικῷ οὐκ ὀφθαλμῶν βλέμματι, ἀσύνθετος γὰρ ὁ θεός, ...ἀλλὰ νεύματι Gel.Cyz.h.e.2.19.20(M.85.1280B); **iii.** of H. Ghost δεσπότῃ γὰρ ὑποτέτακται παρακλήτῳ, καὶ τῷ αὐτοῦ ν. εἴκειν ἀναγκάζεται *cat.2Cor.*1:17(p.355.4); **3.** *inclination*; **a.** lit. τὸ τῶν ὀφθαλμῶν ...πρὸς τὸ κάτω ν. Ath.*gent.*8(M.25.17A); **b.** met. ψυχῆς νεύματι Const.ap.Eus.*v.C.*2.67(p.67.30; M.20.1040A).

***νευρίζω,** *nerve, strengthen,* ‡Dion.Al.*fr.in Lc.22:43*(p.243.4; M.10.1593A).

νευρικός, *made of sinew* κατάφρακτα ν. Thphn.*chron.*p.266(M.108.660B).

νευροκοπ-έω, 1. *hamstring, hough,* ref. Gen.49:6, of Simeon and Levi representing Jewish people and priests ἀπεκτόνασι μὲν...τοὺς ἀνθρώπους, ἐνευροκόπησαν δὲ τὸν ταῦρον. θανάτῳ γὰρ περιβεβλήκασι τοὺς ἁγίους...ἀλλ' οἷά τις μόσχος ὑπὸ ἀετοῦ ∼ούμενος, ὤκλασε μὲν οἱονεί πως εἰς γῆν ὁ Χριστός, ἑκὼν ὑπομείνας τὸν τῆς σαρκὸς θάνατον· πλὴν οὐ γέγονε τῷ θανάτῳ κάτοχος Cyr.*glaph.Gen.*7(1.218E f.); id.*glaph.Dt.*(1.412C); of punishment inflicted on Paphnutius in persecution, Gel.Cyz.*h.e.*2.9.1(M.85.1245B); **2.** *cut string* of a bow, Ast.Soph.*hom.in Ps.*7(M.40.464A); **3.** met. ∼οῦσι γάρ μου τὴν ψυχήν Hermias *irris.*6(M.6.1176A).

νευρορραφέω, *stitch with sinews*; met., ref. forming of child in womb, Dion.Al.ap.Eus.*p.e.*14.26(779A; M.21.1281B).

***νευροστασία, ἡ,** *nervous system,* Amph.*hom.*3.1(M.39.60D).

***νευρότμητος,** *with sinews cut,* †Gregent.*leg.Hom.*5(M.86.584C).

νευροτομέω, *cut the sinews of*; met., *maim the vigour of,* Jo.D.*hom.*11.11(M.96.773C).

νευροχονδρώδης, *neuro-cartilaginous,* Melet.*nat.hom.*28–29(M.64.1265C).

νευρ-όω, *innervate, strengthen, brace,* met. ψυχῆς ∼ῶσαι τὰς δυνάμεις Eus.*l.C.*17(p.257.9; M.20.1436B); ν. τὴν διάνοιαν Cyr.H.*procatech.*17; ἐλπίδα...∼οῦσαν Chrys.*hom.26.7 in Mt.*(7.323C); id.*hom.8.7 in Rom.*(9.507D); ∼ούμενοι...παρὰ τῶν γραφῶν *ib.27.2*(721C); Cyr.*ador.*1(1.39A); id.*Is.*3.3(2.440A); Thdt.*1Tim.*1:12(3.642); τὸ νενευρωμένον *strength, robustness* δεῖξον ἐν ἀσκήσει τῆς καρδίας σου τὸ ν. Cyr.H.*catech.*1.5.

***νεύρωσις, ἡ, 1.** *strengthening, bracing* πολυετὴς μὲν ἡ πάρεσις, ὀξυτάτη δὲ ἡ ν. Cyr.H.*hom.*13; **2.** *muscular system,* Geo.Pis.*hex.*1337(M.92.1537A).

νεύ-ω, *nod, beckon*; hence **1.** *bow,* at liturgy ἀγγέλων...θυσιαστήριον κυκλούντων, καὶ κάτω ∼όντων Chrys.*sac.*6.4(p.148.5; 1.424D); ∼ει πρὸς τὸν ἀρχιδιάκονον *Lit.Jac.*(p.212.1); **2.** *command* αὐτῷ γὰρ ἔξεστι ν. μόνον Chrys.ap.Jo.D.*parall.*(M.95.1112B); Thdt.*qu.3 in 1Reg.*(1.356); **3.** *decline, descend* ψυχὴ...διαιτωμένη πρὸς τὴν ὕλην ∼ει κάτω συναποθνήσκουσα τῇ σαρκί Tat.*orat.*13(p.14.22; M.6.833B); *ib.*16(p.17.21; 840C); Clem.*q.d.s.*17(p.170.16; M.9.621A); εἰ νένευκέ σου ἡ ψυχὴ περὶ τὰ τῇδε πράγματα Or.*hom.17.4 in Jer.*(p.148.3; M.13.460A); τοῖς καταβεβλακευμένοις καὶ κάτω ∼ουσιν Gr.Naz.*or.*28.4(p.27.5; M.36.32A); **4.** *incline,* met. πρὸς δόγμα ἓν ∼ουσαν ἀεί Clem.*str.*1.25(p.103.11; M.8.912B); *ib.*4.5(p.257.15; 1233A); Or.*Cels.*4.87(p.358.6; M.11.1161C); οὐ γάρ...θέμις τοὺς ἄνω ∼οντας...ἀφανίσαι Meth.*symp.*8.10(p.92.15; M.18.153A); θεὸν ἐνδελεχῶς ὑμνοῦντες, καὶ πρὸς ἑαυτοὺς ∼οντες Thdt.*Eph.*5:18(3.432); πάσης ἑαυτὸν ἀνθρωπίνης συνουσίας χωρίζων, καὶ εἰς ἑαυτὸν ∼ων id.*h.rel.*2(3.1122); *ib.*15(1219); πολλὰ ν. *lean many ways*; of scripture as involving apparent contradictions, *Clem.ep.Petr.*1(M.2.25B).

νεφέλη, ἡ, *cloud*;

A. lit.; **1.** in gen. προσκρουομένων τῶν ν. ... γίνεται ἡ ἀστραπή Or.*hom.8.4 in Jer.*(p.60.5; M.13.341C); δεσμεύων ὕδωρ ἐν νεφέλαις, καὶ τὸ μὲν ἱστὰς ἐπὶ τῶν ν. ... λόγῳ κρατουμένην φύσιν τὴν ῥέουσαν, τὸ δ' ἐκχέων Gr.Naz.*or.*28.28(p.65.13; M.36.65C); Manich. ὁ ἄρχων ὁ μέγας προβάλλει τὰς ν. ἐξ αὐτοῦ, ὅπως σκοτίσῃ τῇ ὀργῇ αὐτοῦ τὸν κόσμον Hegem.*Arch.*9(p.14.8; M.10.1441A); in simile of man's inconstancy ἄνθρωποι δὲ ταῖς ν. ἐοίκασι Bas.*ep.*244.9(3.381D; M.32.924A); **2.** as dwelling of God, *Pap.Chr.*(p.447); **3.** of cloud of Exodus ν. εἰς σκιὰν ἀπὸ καύματος καὶ φυλακὴν ἀπὸ κρύους εἵπετο, ἄλλου οὐρανοῦ καινοῦ τρόπον καὶ προαγγελίαν ἀπαγγέλλουσα Just.*dial.*131.6(M.6.781B); τῆς ἀκολουθούσης χάριτι φιλανθρωπίας θεραπαίνης δίκην Ἑβραίοις νεφέλης Clem.*prot.*1(p.8.20; M.8.64B); cf. *ibi nubes eos praecesserit...nobis autem qualem tradiderit de his Paulus intelligentiae regulam videamus...quam illi aestimant nubem, Paulus spiritum sanctum ponit,* Or.*hom.5.1 in Ex.*(p.184.1; M.12.326B); cf. id.*comm.in Cant.*2(p.163.1; M.13.137C); symbol of H. Ghost, cf.id.*comm.ser.50 in Mt.*(p.112.2; M.13.1678B); ὁ στῦλος τῆς φωτεινῆς ν. Ἰησοῦ, προάγων ἡμᾶς id.*Jo.*32.1(p.425.6; M.14.740B); ἡ δὲ ν. σκιὰ τῆς ἐκ τοῦ πνεύματος δωρεᾶς τοῦ τὴν φλόγα τῶν παθῶν διὰ τῆς νεκρώσεως τῶν μελῶν καταψύχοντος Bas.*Spir.*31(3.26D; M.32.124B); ν. δὲ τοῦ λαοῦ θείᾳ δυνάμει καθηγουμένης, οὐ κατὰ τὴν κοινὴν φύσιν...ἀλλὰ κρεῖττόν τι καὶ ὑψηλότερον τῆς ἀνθρωπίνης καταλήψεως—ἐκείνης τῆς ν. ... τοιοῦτον τὸ θαῦμα ἦν, ὡς...διατείχισμα πρὸς τὸν λαὸν εἶναι, σκιάζουσάν τε τὸ ὑποκείμενον Gr.Nyss.*v.Mos.*32(M.44.309C); ὁ ὁδηγὸς ἡ ν. (τοῦτο γὰρ ὄνομα τῷ ὁδηγοῦντι, ὅπερ καλῶς τοῖς πρὸ ἡμῶν εἰς τὴν τοῦ ἁγίου πνεύματος μετελήφθη χάριν) *ib.*(361B); *Const.App.*6.3.1; *Lit.ib.*8.12.26; ἐν στύλῳ νεφέλης καὶ πυρός· ἐγράφετο δι' ἀμφοῖν ὁ Χριστός Cyr.*ador.*3(1.84B); ἐν εἴδει νεφέλης, ὡς ἐν τύπῳ τοῦ ἁγίου βαπτίσματος καὶ τῆς δι' ὕδατος σωτηρίας. ἡ οὐχ ὕδωρ, ἡ ν.; *ib.*(85A); ἐν στύλῳ...νεφέλης προβιβάζοντος...θεοῦ, οὐ γὰρ ἔστιν...εἰς τὴν ἄνω...ἀφικνεῖσθαι πόλιν, μὴ οὐχὶ καθηγουμένου Χριστοῦ *ib.*(85E); cloud and sea signifying justification and sanctification in baptism, id.*Is.*2.4(2.283A); ἡ θάλασσα γὰρ ἐμιμεῖτο τὴν κολυμβήθραν, ἡ δὲ ν. τὴν χάριν τοῦ πνεύματος Thdt.*1Cor.*10:1–4(3.225); cf. *nubes erat corporeum quoddam domini organum, quo interveniente, cum ipse foret incorporeus et excederet omnem sensilem et compositam substantiam, per sensilem vocem compellabat...Mosen,* Proc.G.*Ex.*13:21(M.87.581B); τῇ μὲν ν. τὸ πνεῦμα, τῇ δὲ θαλάσσῃ τὸ ὕδωρ τυπῶν, ἐξ ὧν καὶ δι' ὧν ἡ πηγὴ βαπτίσματος Andr.Cr.*or.*7(M.97.953A); intervention of cloud between camp of Egyptians and Israel signifies ὁ σωματικὸς γνόφος which prevents man from contemplating things of God, Gr.Naz.*or.*28.12(p.40.19; M.36.41A); or Christ as protector of his people, Cyr.*ador.*3(1.86E); **4.** of cloud in Tabernacle and at Sinai, ref. Ps.98:7 τὸν σταυρωθέντα...γεγενῆσθαι μετὰ Μωϋσέως καὶ Ἀαρὼν καὶ λελαληκέναι αὐτοῖς ἐν στύλῳ ν. Just.*dial.*38.1(M.6.557A); Clem.*str.*6.3(p.448.11; M.9.252C); cf. *quod dicit: nubes recessit a tabernaculo et...Maria facta est leprosa...ut ostendatur quia, etiam si est in aliquo gratia sancti spiritus et obtrectat ac detrahit, recedit ab eo post obtrectationem, et sic lepra repletur anima ejus,* Or.*hom.7.2 in Num.*(p.41.5; M.12.614B); ὁ γάρ...ἐν τῷ στύλῳ τῆς ν. λαλήσας θεός, μετὰ ταῦτα ἐφανερώθη ἐν σαρκί...εἰ δὲ πιστὸν τοῖς Ἰουδαίοις ἐστὶ τὸ ἐν στύλῳ ν. τὸν θεὸν λαλῆσαι, μηδὲ τὸ ἐν σαρκὶ αὐτὸν λελαληκέναι ἄπιστον ἔστω Gr.Nyss.*Pss.titt.*A 9(M.44.532D); ἀναδεδειγμένης...τῆς...ἀληθεστέρας σκηνῆς...τῆς...ἐκκλησίας, φῶς περιελάμπετο Χριστοῦ, καὶ ἡ ν. ... τὸν θεῖον ναὸν ἀναπίμπλησι...ν. γὰρ ἦν...ἐπὶ τῆς σκηνῆς τὴν ἡμέραν, καὶ πῦρ τὴν νύκτα. καταπιαίνει...ὁ Χριστὸς χαρίσμασι τοὺς πνευματικούς, τοὺς ὥσπερ ἐν ἡμέρᾳ...γεγονότας Cyr.*ador.*10(1.353C,E); ἐν τῷ ἱλαστηρίῳ τὴν οἰκείαν ἐπιφάνειαν...ἐποιεῖτο θεός· καὶ τὴν οἰκείαν ἐμφαίνων ἀγαθότητα, οὐκ ἐν γνόφῳ...καθάπερ τῷ Ἰσραήλ, ἀλλ' ἐν ν. φωτοειδεῖ ἑωρᾶτο Thdt.*qu.22 in Lev.*(1.199); symbolizing glory of God, ‡Epiph.*v.proph.Jer.*(p.22; M.43.400D); **5.** of cloud at Transfiguration, cf. *postquam in verum Moysen,...Christum, extenderunt linguas blasphemiae suae, discessit ab illis nubes, et transivit ad nos in montem excelsum cum salvator...transformatus est et nubes refulgens obumbravit discipulos,* Or.*hom.7.2 in Num.*(p.41.12; M.12.614C); θεὸς...δείκνυσι...κρείττονα...σκηνὴν τὴν ν. εἰ γὰρ ἔργον ἐστὶ σκηνῆς τὸ ἐπισκιάσαι τὸν ἐν αὐτῇ καὶ σκεπάσαι, ἡ δὲ φωτεινὴ ν. ἐπεσκίασεν αὐτούς, οἱονεὶ σκηνὴν θειοτέραν...τυγχάνουσαν πεποίηκεν αὐτοῖς εἰς παράδειγμα μελλούσης ἀναπαύσεως ὁ θεός. ... τίς δ' ἂν εἴη ἡ φωτεινὴ ν. ... ἢ τάχα μὲν πατρικὴ δύναμις...τάχα δὲ καὶ τὸ ἅγιον πνεῦμα ἡ φωτεινή ἐστι ν. ... τολμήσας δ' ἂν εἴποιμι καὶ τὸν σωτῆρα ἡμῶν εἶναι φωτεινὴν ν. ... φωτεινὴ γὰρ πατρός, υἱοῦ καὶ ἁγίου πνεύματος ν. ἐπισκιάζει τοὺς Ἰησοῦ γνησίους μαθητάς id.*comm.in Mt.*12.42(p.165.15; M.13.1081A); foreshadowing second advent on clouds, id.*comm.ser.50 in Mt.*(p.108.24); φωνὴ πατρικὴ διὰ νεφέλης, οὕτως γὰρ φαίνεται ὁ θεός Eus.*fr.Lc.*9:34(M.24.549C); ν. ... ἐστι φωτεινή... ἡ ἐπὶ τὸν Ἰορδάνην μικρὸν ἔμπροσθεν καταπτᾶσα περιστερά Andr.Cr.*or.*7(M.97.952D); πάλιν μαρτυρεῖται [sc. ἡ τριάς] τῷ κηρύττοντι, τῷ κηρυττομένῳ, τῇ ν. τῷ πνεύματι Jo.D.*fr.Mt.*17:5(M.96.1409B); **6.** of cloud at Ascension, Clem.*prot.*10(p.68.6; M.8.205A) cit. s. ἀεροβατέω; cf.Or.*comm.ser.50 in Mt.*(p.111.5; M.13.1677C); ὀμβροτόκοι ν. μαρτυροῦσι, δεξάμεναι τὸν δεσπότην Cyr.H.*catech.*10.19; Ἠλίας μὲν οὖν ὡς εἰς τὸν οὐρανὸν ἀνελήφθη, δοῦλος γὰρ ἦν· ὁ δὲ Ἰησοῦς εἰς τὸν οὐρανόν, δεσπότης γὰρ ἦν· ἐκεῖνος ἐν ἅρματι πυρίνῳ, οὗτος ἐν ν. ὅτε μὲν γὰρ τὸν δοῦλον ἔδει κληθῆναι, ἅρμα ἐπέμπετο· ὅταν δὲ τὸν υἱόν, θρόνος βασιλικός· καὶ...αὐτὸς ὁ πατρικός· καὶ γὰρ περὶ τοῦ πατρὸς φησιν ὁ Ἡσαΐας, ἰδοὺ κύριος κάθηται ἐπὶ ν. κούφης. ἐπεὶ οὖν ὁ πατὴρ ἐπὶ ν. κάθηται, διὰ τοῦτο καὶ τῷ υἱῷ τὴν ν. ἔπεμψε Chrys.*ascens.*5(2.455B); νεφέλην αὐτοῦ ὑπηρετήσασθαι οἱ προφῆται προεῖπον, ἵνα σωματώδης τις καὶ ἐλαφρὴ οὐσία τὸν σεσωματωμένον φανείη πάλιν βαστάζουσα κύριον. βαστάζει μὲν γὰρ ἐν τῇ αὐτοῦ βουλήσει...τὰ σύμπαντα ὡς θεός· ὑπὸ δὲ τῆς ν. βασταχθήσεται ὡς ἄνθρωπος Diad.*ascens.*5(M.65.1145C); Cosm.Ind.*top.*2(M.88.121D); **7.** ref. second advent ὄψεται ὁ κόσμος τὸν κύριον ἐρχόμενον ἐπάνω τῶν ν. *Did.*16.8; ἰδοὺ ὡς υἱὸς ἀνθρώπου ἔρχεται ἐπάνω τῶν ν. Just.*1apol.*51.9(M.6.404C); id.*dial.*14.8(M.6.505C); *ib.*31.1(540B); *ib.*120.4(753D); cf. *si ...ut ne terram calcaret filius dei...straverunt vestimenta sua in via ...quid mirum si pater...nubes sternat caelestes sub corpore filii* *descendentis ad opus consummationis? ... intellegat autem qui potest, utrum id ipsum est super nubibus caeli venire eum et cum nubibus eum venire, aut aliae quidem sunt nubes super quibus veniet, aliae autem cum quibus veniet. ... si beati homines in nubibus rapientur in aerem, quid mirum est in nubibus filium dei venire...? ...quomodo non consequens est domino...vehiculum fieri nubes...ut sedeat super eis? ... dicet aliquis quoniam nubes super quibus videbunt...venientem, virtus altissimi est et spiritus sanctus, quae fient ei in nubibus caeli, ut veniat illis invectus. ... ratio haec qui vult quidem secundum utrumque modum suscipere...non reprobabit, et si dixerit quis intelligibiles nubes in quibus veniet...sive sanctas et divinas virtutes sive beatissimos prophetas*, Or.*comm.ser.50 in Mt.*(p.110.6ff.; M.13.1677Aff.); *ἐν συσσεισμῷ ἐπάνω τῶν ν. Const.App.*7.32.4; *τὴν ν. πάλιν προσδοκώμενος σχεῖν τὴν προφητικὴν εἰς τὴν ἑαυτοῦ κάθοδον ὑπηρέτην* Diad.*ascens.*5(M.65.1145C); **8.** exeg. Is.19:1, cf. *considera...Esaiam dicentem: ecce dominus sedet super nubem levem, et veniet in Aegyptum, utrum Aegyptum dicit hanc quae communiter intellegitur, aut totum mundum...qui autem super nubem levem veniet in Aegyptum primum ascensionem faciet in Judaeam*, Or.*comm.ser.50 in Mt.*(p.111.13; M.13.1677D); interpreted as signifying Christ's body, formed from H. Ghost and earthly substance, in which he took flight into Egypt, Eus.*Is.*19:1(M.24.220B,C); Ath.*inc.*37.6(M.25.161A); *ν. τὴν ἁγίαν...σάρκα, τουτέστι τὸν ἐκ τῆς παρθένου ληφθέντα ναόν* Cyr.*Is.*2.4(2.282B); or interpreted as BMV, *ib.*(282C), as signifying Christ's presence in baptism, *ib.*(283A–D); as Christ's body, Proc.G.*Is.*19:1–15(M.87.2144B); as BMV, *ib.*(2144D); as baptism, *ib.*(2145A,B); **9.** exeg. Eccl.11:3 *ὥσπερ ὅταν τὰ νέφη τὰ αἰσθητὰ πληρωθῶσι...τὸν ὑετὸν ἐπὶ τὴν γῆν ἀφιᾶσιν· οὕτω...καὶ τὰ πνευματικὰ νέφη, ἤτοι αἱ ν. ... αἳ ὅταν πληρωθῶσι τῶν νοερῶν τοῦ...πνεύματος ὑδάτων...ῥαίνουσι νοητὸν ὄμβρον ἐπὶ τὴν γῆν...προσημαίνων τὴν ἐπὶ τοὺς...ἀποστόλους γεγονυῖαν τοῦ...πνεύματος παρουσίαν...κατὰ τὴν ἡμέραν τῆς...πεντηκοστῆς* Gr.Agr.*Eccl.*9.21(M.98.1129A); **10.** clouds sent by God to convey saints *ἦλθεν ν. καὶ ἥρπασέν με καὶ ἀπήνεγκέν με πάλιν εἰς τοὺς οὐρανούς Apoc.Esd.*(p.29); *ἐπέταξεν Ἀνδρέας ν., καὶ ἦρεν ἡ ν. Ματθείαν καὶ τοὺς μαθητὰς...καὶ ἀπέθετο αὐτοὺς ἡ ν. ἐν τῷ ὄρει ὅπου ἦν ὁ Πέτρος διδάσκων A.Andr.et Mt.*21(p.94.6); *ἀπόστειλον Μιχαὴλ... ἐν ν. πυρός, καὶ περιτείχισον τὴν πόλιν ib.*30(p.110.16); *1 Apoc.Jo.*2(p.71); *ἀποστελῶ τοὺς ἀγγέλους...καὶ ἀροῦσιν ἀπὸ τῆς γῆς...τὰς σεπτὰς ...εἰκόνας, καὶ...σταυρούς, καὶ...βίβλους· καὶ τὰ τίμια...ἀρθήσονται ὑπὸ νεφελῶν ἐν τῷ ἀέρι ib.*13(p.80); *Dorm.BMV* 6(p.97); Jo.Mon.*hymn.Petr.*3(M.96.1392B); **11.** cloud of fire in vision signifies iniquity of mankind, *Apoc.Paul.*13(p.41); **12.** personified *αἱ ν. εὐφρανθήσονται T.Lev.*18.5; controlled by angels, Epiph.*mens.*22(M.43.276C); *ταῖς ν. ἐντελοῦμαι* (Is.5:6) interpreted of angelic powers, Cyr.*Is.*1.3(2.81E); symbolize angels *νεφέλης αὐτοῖς ἰδέαν ἡ θεολογία περιπλάττει, σημαίνουσα...τοὺς ἱεροὺς νόας τοῦ...κρυφίου φωτὸς...ἀποπληρουμένους* Dion.Ar.*c.h.*15.6(M.3.336A).

B. met.; **1.** as designation of H. Ghost, Jo.Mon.*hymn.Bas.*3(M.96.1372C); **2.** and of BMV; exeg. Is.19:1 v. supra A.8; hence in gen., *Pers.*(p.15.19; M.10.104C); ‡Gr.Thaum.*annunt.*3(M.10.1183D); *ἡ ὄντως κούφη ν.* Procl.CP *or.laud.BMV* 1(p.103.15; M.65.681A); *ν. τῶν ὑετῶν χωρὶς φθορᾶς συλλαμβάνουσαν* Hesych.H.*serm.*5(M.93.1461A); Chrysipp.*enc.in BMV* 1(p.337.17); *ἡ ἐνεγκαμένη αὐτὸν παμφαὴς ν.* Mod.*dorm.*3(M.86.3285A); *τὴν ἔμψυχον ν. θεοῦ* Jo.Mon.*hymn.Petr.*3(M.96.1392B); **3.** of prophets, Hipp.*ben.Jac.*10(p.23.7); cf.Or.*comm.in Cant.*3(p.221.25; M.17.264C); id.*comm.ser.50 in Mt.*(p.112.7; M.13.1678C); Ath.*exp.Ps.*35:6(M.27.176A); Cyr.H.*catech.*13.29; Chrys.*Is.interp.*5.3(6.54B); Cyr.*Is.*1.3(2.81E); id.*Jo.*1.9(4.103A); *καθάπερ γὰρ ἡ ν. ἑτέρωθεν ὑποδέχεται τῶν ὄμβρων τὰς ἀφορμάς, οὕτω καὶ προφῆται...ὑπὸ τῆς θείας χάριτος ἐνεργούμενοι, τὴν πνευματικὴν ἀρδείαν προσήνεγκαν ταῖς...ψυχαῖς* Thdt.*Ps.*56:11(1.982); Proc.G.*Is.*5:1–8(M.87.1909A); of saints *ἡ ἀλήθεια τοῦ θεοῦ ἕως τῶν ν. ἐστιν, αἵτινες ἀκούουσιν ἐντολῆς θεοῦ...ἕκαστος τῶν ἁγίων ν. ἐστίν. Μωσῆς ν. ἦν καὶ ὡς ν. ἔλεγεν· πρόσεχε, οὐρανέ, καὶ λαλήσω* Or.*hom.8.3 in Jer.*(p.58.19; M.13.340B); *ἀπὸ τῶν ἐσχάτων ἀνάγει ὁ θεὸς καὶ σωματοποιεῖ τὰς ν. διὰ τοῦτο εἰ βουλόμεθα γενέσθαι ν., ἐφ' ἃς φθάνει ἡ ἀλήθεια τοῦ θεοῦ, ἔσχατοι πάντων γενώμεθα ib.8.4*(p.59.28; 341B); hence converse of Moses with Joshua, Jeremiah with Baruch, Paul with Silvanus produces 'lightning' of their teaching, as clashing of clouds effects physical lightning, *ib.8.5*(p.60.10; 341C); *ν. ἐστὶ φύσις λογική, τοὺς περὶ προνοίας λόγους πεπιστευμένη· ἀστραπὴ δέ ἐστι διδασκαλία πνευματική* id.*sel.in Ps.*134:7(M.12.1653C); Proc.G.*Dt.*32:2(M.87.953A); **4.** of idolatry as cloud which produces shadow of death, Proc.G.*Is.*9:1–7(M.87.2001A).

C. name given to third of the veils of the oblation, covering chalice and paten *εἰς τὸ βάλλειν τὴν ν. καὶ ν. φωτεινὴ ἐπεσκίασεν αὐτούς Euchol.*(p.90).

νεφεληδόν, *in the manner of clouds*, Nonn.*par.Jo.*3:26(M.43.772A); *ib.*4:31(780B); *ib.*11:44(848A).

***νεφελόδρομος,** *borne upon clouds*, Jo.Mon.*hymn.Petr.*3(M.96.1392B).

***νεφελοσύστατος,** *cloudlike*, Tim.Ant.*nativ.Jo.Bapt.*2(M.28.909B).

***νεφελοχυσία, ἡ,** *film over the eyes, cataract*, Leont.B.*mesopent.*(M.86.1984C).

***νεφηδόν,** *in a cloud*, Gr.Nyss.*v.Mos.*(M.44.324A).

***νεφοδιώκτης, ὁ,** *one who impels the clouds* towards or away from a selected place by magic; question how *ν.* can produce storms at will, if God controls clouds, dismissed on ground that evidence for activities of *ν.* rests on hearsay, ‡Just.*qu.et resp.*31(M.6.1277D); penalties imposed on Christians becoming *ν.*, CTrull.*can.*61(interpreted by Balsamon (M.137.721A) as *one who divines by shapes of clouds*).

***νεφομήκης,** *cloud-piercing*, ‡Caes.Naz.*dial.*117(M.38.1004).

***νεφόομαι,** *be clouded over*, Clem.*str.*6.3(p.444.22; M.9.245A); Bas.*hex.*3.7(1.29B; M.29.69A); Chrys.*hom.14.1 in Eph.*(11.104D).

νέφος, τό, *cloud*;

A. lit. *ἀτμοῦ σύστασις τὸ ν. ἐστίν* Gr.Nyss.*hex.*(M.44.97D); *ἵνα...ὁ κύριος διὰ λαίλαπος καὶ ν. λέγῃ* Or.*Jo.*1.17(p.21.16; M.14.52B).

B. met.; **1.** *cloud λόγων εὐτεχνίᾳ ἐπισκιάζειν ὡς ν. ... τὸ τῆς γραφῆς ...φέγγος* Gel.Cyz.*h.e.*2.20.1(M.85.1281A); of idolatry as cloud obscuring man's perception of God's will, *2Clem.*1.6; **2.** *storm* of trouble; of a famine, Thdt.*qu.22 in 4Reg.*(2.526); of political disturbance, id.*h.e.*3.9.2(3.922); **3.** *cloud* of men, *great crowd*; ref. Heb.12:1, gen. interpreted as *large number*, e.g. Thdt.*Heb.*12:1(3.624) but also as cloud of shade and refreshment provided by memory of saints, Chrys.*hom.28.2 in Heb.*(12.256B); **4.** of body of Christ *ἔλαβε ν. ὁ θεὸς λόγος τὸ σῶμα, ἵνα μὴ καταφλέξῃ τὰς κτιστὰς φύσεις τὰς ἐν τῷ κόσμῳ* Gel.Cyz.*h.e.*2.19.24(M.85.1280C); **5.** exeg. Eccl.12:2 *ν.* interpreted as *διδάσκαλοι τῆς ἐκκλησίας* Gr.Agr.*Eccl.*10.6(M.98.1152A).

***νεφοφανής,** *like a cloud in appearance*, Agath.*v.Gr.Ill.*113.

νέφρησις, ἡ, *pain in the kidney*, Isid.H.*etym.*4.7.24.

νεφρός, ὁ, *kidney*, as seat of *πανουργία* (in good sense), *T.Neph.*2.8; *ν. ἐν τῇ γραφῇ τὸ ἐπιθυμητικόν* Or.*fr.73 in Lam.*(p.264.11; M.13.644C); Cyr.*Os.*53(3.84A); *ν. ... εἰς τύπον...τῆς εἰς νοῦν ἔσω διακριτικῆς ἐνεργείας· καθ' ἣν ἀπόβλητον...τὸ πεφυκὸς ἀδικεῖν, αἱρετὸν δὲ... ποιεῖται τὸ ὠφελοῦν* id.*ador.*16(1.568B); *ν. ... τοὺς λογισμούς* Thdt.*Ps.*7:9(1.648); plur. *τὰ ν. Exorc.*5(p.334).

νεφύδριον, τό, *little, passing cloud*, met. *ν. γάρ ἐστι, καὶ παρέρχεται* Socr.*h.e.*3.14.1(M.67.416A); Soz.*h.e.*5.15.3(M.67.1256B); Thphn.*chron.*p.41(M.108.157B).

***νεφώθ,** v. **ἐφώθ.*

νεωκορέω, *be a devotee of*; c. dat., Synes.*ep.*32(M.66.1360C).

νεωκόρος, ὁ, *temple-keeper*, in sense of menial official; ass. pagan priests as minor cultic official, Or.*Cels.*8.73(p.290.30; M.11.1628B); Ath.*ep.encycl.*5(p.174.24; M.25.233B); id.*h.Ar.*54(p.214.8; M.25.760A); Thdt.*affect.*10(p.244.16; 4.952); of assistant priests substituted by Juln. for Christian clergy *ἀντ' ἐπισκόπων καὶ πρεσβυτέρων καὶ διακόνων καταστήσας ζακόρους καὶ ν.* ‡Jo.D.*Artem.*22(p.82.14; M.96.1272C); *οἱ...ἱερεῖς καὶ τῶν ν. τὸ πλῆθος ib.*56(p.93.9; 1304A); of Kohathite Levites (Num.3:5ff.) as parallel to order of subdeacons, *Const.App.*8.21.3; of Samuel as *παιδόθεν ν.*, Thdt.*Dan.*proem.(2.1058); of member of a minor order in Church, concerned with menial work, Gr.Naz.*or.*24.12(M.35.1184B); ‡Nil.*narr.*6(M.79.676B).

νέωμα, τό, *fallow ground just broken up*; in simile of catechists' duty to prepare minds of hearers before sowing spiritual seed, Or.*hom.5.13 in Jer.*(p.42.26; M.13.313C); Gr.Naz.*or.*28.1(p.21.9; M.36.25C); Chrys.*hom.1.4 in Jo.*(8.6A); Cyr.*Is.*3.3(2.450E); as myst. interprn. of name Horeb, exeg. 3Reg.19, Max.*cap.theol.*174(M.90.1160A).

***νέωσις, ἡ,** *breaking up of fallow ground*, Chrys.*hom.18.1 in Jo.*(8.104B); hence *instruction*, Gr.Agr.*Eccl.*2.12(M.98.836B).

***νεωστός,** error for *νεωστί*, ‡Jo.D.*conf.*13(M.95.300A; *νεωστί* p.123.7).

νεωτερίζω, 1. *make innovations*; of heretics introducing newfangled doctrine, Eus.*h.e.*5.15(M.20.464A); *ib.*5.28.2 (v.l. *μετεωρισθεῖσαν* 512B); id.*Marcell.*2.4(p.56.18; M.24.820A); id.*e.th.*1.19(p.80.14; M.24.864C); of Const.'s religious policy acc. Juln., ‡Jo.D.*Artem.*43(p.14.27; M.96.1292A); **2.** *have recourse to violent measures περὶ τούτων ν.* Mel.*fr.*3(M.5.1212B); **3.** pass., *be violently changed, be* *disrupted*, Philost.*h.e.*12.10(M.65.617B); **4.** *play the youth, behave with youthful folly*, Or.*exc.in Ps.*36:25(M.17.136B); Ephr.1.271E; Chrys.*hom.7.3 in Heb.*(12.78A).

νεωτερικός, 1. *youthful* πρεσβυτέρους οὐ προσειληφότας τὴν φαινομένην ν. τάξιν [sc. of a bishop] Ign.*Magn.*3.1; ἐπίσκοπον...οὐκ ἔλαττον ἐτῶν πεντήκοντα, ὅτι...τὰς ν. ἀταξίας...ἐκπεφευγὼς ὑπάρχει *Const.App.*2.1.1; Chrys.*sac.*1.1(p.3.12; 1.363A); φεῦγε παίγνια...ν. Thdr.Stud.*epp.*2.114(M.99.1381B); τὰ ν. *youthful follies*, Chrys.*hom.11.3 in 1Thess.*(11.506E); **2.** *recent* σύγγραμμα ν. καὶ πεπλασμένον Afric.*ep.Or.*1(p.79.1; M.11.44A); ψαλμοὺς...ν. ἐπλάσατο [sc. Hieracas] Epiph.*haer.*67.3(p.136.12; M.42.176D).

νεωτεροποιία, ἡ, 1. *innovation*; of introduction of heresies or schisms, Eus.*h.e.*1.1.1(M.20.48C); τὴν κατὰ Νοουάτον...ν. *ib.*7.4 (641B); Bas.*ep.*265.2(3.409B; M.32.985B); Thdt.*h.e.*1.9.1(3.764); **2.** *revolutionary movement*, Eus.*h.e.*2.6.8(M.20.156A); Chrys.*hom.10.5 in Mt.*(7.145D); Gel.Cyz.*h.e.*1.4.2(M.85.1201B).

***νηάριον, τό,** *small boat*; fig., Thdr.Stud.*epp.*1.11(M.99.944D).

νήδυμος, *sweet, delightful*; neut. plur. as adv., Paul.Sil.*ambo.* 216(M.86.2260A); *ib.*269(2261B).

***νηδυπόρος,** *going on its belly* ν. δράκοντος Eudoc.*Cypr.*2.14(M.85. 845A).

νηκτικός, *able to swim*, Bas.*hex.*7.1(1.63B; M.29.148C); neut. as subst., *faculty of swimming*, ‡Eust.*hex.*(M.18.724B).

***νηοπέδη, ἡ,** *anchor*, Gr.Naz.*carm.*1.2.2.226(M.37.596A).

νηπιάζ-ω, 1. *be a babe*; **a.** in gen., Clem.*prot.*10(p.66.9; M.8.201A); Eus.*v.C.*12(p.13.9; M.20.925A); **b.** of Christ, ref. Is.8:4 ∼οντι σώματι τοσαῦτα...οἰκονομούμενον Eus.*d.e.*7.1(p.319.10; M.22.521B); θεὸς...νηπιάσας ἐπέφανεν ‡Amph.*circ.*(p.12B); Mod.*dorm.*4(M.86. 3289A); ‡Ath.*occurs.*12(M.28.989A); **2.** met.; **a.** *be like a child, be innocent*; of Adam before Fall, Thphl.Ant.*Autol.*2.25(M.6.1092B); of Christian τὸν...τῇ κακίᾳ ∼οντα Chrys.*hom.36.1 in 1Cor.*(10. 332E); Isid.Pel.*epp.*1.442(M.78.425B); Cyr.*glaph.Gen.*1(1.19C); **b.** *be a beginner*; of Israel under Law, Eus.*Marcell.*1.1(p.3.16; M.24. 716B); id.*e.th.*2.18(p.122.33; M.24.941D); of beginners in spiritual life, Ephr.3.339C; Gr.Nyss.*hom.1 in Cant.*(M.44.768B); ∼ομεν πρὸς τὸ τῆς εὐκτικῆς ἀρετῆς τέλειον Diad.*perf.*61(p.70.13); τῶν ἔτι ∼όντων τῇ ψυχῇ *ib.*79(p.100.17); **c.** *be childish, behave foolishly*, Jo.D.*hom.* 2.1(M.96.576D).

***νηπίασις, ἡ,** *infancy*, Andr.Cr.*or.*2(M.97.820B).

***νηπιόθεν,** *from infancy*, †Cyr.*coll.VT*(6^4.70C; M.77.1280D); ἀπὸ ν. Hesych.H.*Ps.tit.*119(M.27.1220D, v.l. ἀπενοήθην); Gel.Cyz.*h.e.*2. 33.4(M.85.1337B); Jo.Mal.*chron.*5 p.117(M.97.212A).

νηπιοκτόνος, *infant-slaying*, ‡Ign.*Phil.*8.

***νηπιοπρεπής,** *suited to, fit for, children*; **1.** lit., Cyr.*ador.*16(1. 575A); id.*Ps.*90:12(M.69.1224A); of Christ's infancy ν. πολιτεία ‡Amph.*circ.*(p.12C); **2.** met., *fit for beginners, elementary*; of Law, Cyr.*ador.*1(1.7A); *ib.*2(56C); id.*hom.pasch.*23(5^2.281B); of elementary instruction in spiritual life, id.*Joel.*44(3.243C); id.*hom.pasch.*16(5^2. 215A).

***νηπιοπρεπῶς,** *like a child*, Anast.S.*hod.*13(M.89.221A).

νήπιος, *infant, child*;

A. lit.; **1.** as adj., of Christ ἐπεὶ γὰρ ἄρνας ὀνομάζει ἡ γραφὴ τοὺς παῖδας τοὺς ν., τὸν...λόγον...ἄνθρωπον γενόμενον, κατὰ πάντα ἡμῖν ἀπεικάζεσθαι βουλόμενον, ἀμνὸν κέκληκεν τοῦ θεοῦ, τὸν υἱὸν τοῦ θεοῦ, τὸν ν. τοῦ πατρός Clem.*paed.*1.5(p.104.20; M.8.280A); **2.** neut. as subst.; **a.** in gen. ἔσῃ ὡς τὰ ν. τὰ μὴ γινώσκοντα τὴν πονηρίαν Herm. *mand.*2.1; τῶν ν. τῆς ἐκκλησίας μνημονεύσωμεν, ὅπως ὁ κύριος τελειώσας αὐτὰ ἐν φόβῳ αὐτοῦ εἰς μέτρον ἡλικίας ἀγάγοι *Lit.*ap.*Const.App.* 8.10.18; **b.** of Holy Innocents ἐν σχήματι τῶν ψαλλόντων ἐν τῷ παραδείσῳ ν. ἦλθεν πρὸς τὸν Ματθαῖον ὁ Ἰησοῦς *A.Mt.*1(p.217.5); ἔψαλλες μετὰ τῶν ἄλλων ν. τῶν ἀναιρεθέντων ἐν Βηθλεέμ *ib.*3(p.219. 12); ἔνθα ἐστὶν ὁ ποταμὸς τοῦ γάλακτος, καὶ ἐκεῖ πάντα τὰ ν. ἅπερ ἀπέκτεινεν...Ἡρώδης *Apoc.Paul.*26(p.54); μηδὲν δυνάμενος κατὰ τοῦ κυρίου ὁ διάβολος, ἐπὶ τοὺς ν. καὶ ἀτελεῖς τῶν βρεφῶν παῖδας κατατρέχει ...ἀπὸ διετοῦς καὶ κατωτέρω· τοὺς δὲ τὴν τριάδα τῶν ἐτῶν ζήσαντας οὐ κατασφάζει. ν. γὰρ οἱ τὴν δυάδα ὁμολογοῦντες, καὶ τῇ τριάδι μὴ πιστεύσαντες ‡Chrys.*infant.*(10.750D).

B. met.; **1.** of those uninstructed in full mysteries of Christian faith, or beginners in Christianity μὴ οὐ δύναμαι ὑμῖν τὰ ἐπουράνια γράψαι; ἀλλὰ φοβοῦμαι, μὴ ν. οὖσιν ὑμῖν βλάβην παραθῶ Ign.*Trall.* 5.1; πῶς ἡ τοῦ τελείου καὶ γνωστικοῦ μετὰ τὴν βρῶσιν ἀνάπαυσις αὖθις νηπίῳ τετίμηται γάλακτι; Clem.*paed.*1.6(p.110.35; M.8.292B); Or.*princ.*3.1.12(p.216.13; M.11.272A); id.*comm.in Eph.*4:14(p.415); Meth.*res.*1.48(p.301.1; M.18.276C); Gr.Nyss.*hom.1 in Cant.*(M.44. 784B); Isid.Pel.*epp.*1.445(M.78.428A); Thdt.*1Cor.*13:11(3.254); **2.** of those who lived under dispensation of Law opp. gospel ν. μὲν τοὺς ἐν νόμῳ λέγει, οἳ τῷ φόβῳ, καθάπερ οἱ παῖδες τοῖς μορμολυκείοις, ἐκταράττονται Clem.*paed.*1.6(p.110.1; M.8.289B); Cyr.*ador.*2(1.56B); Isid.Pel.*epp.*1.445(M.78.428A); Dion.Ar.*e.h.*5.1.2(M.3.501B); **3.** of the innocent and simple ὡς ν. βρέφη εἰσίν, οἷς οὐδεμία κακία ἀναβαίνει ἐπὶ τὴν καρδίαν Herm.*sim.*9.29.1; Clem.*paed.*1.5(p.101.1; M.8.269C); οὐκ ἐπὶ ἀφρόνων τάττεται τὸ ν.· νηπύτιος μὲν γὰρ οὗτος, ν. δὲ ὁ νεήπιος, ὡς ἤπιος ὁ ἁπαλόφρων, οἷον ἤπιος νεωστὶ καὶ πρᾶος τῷ τρόπῳ γενόμενος *ib.*(p.101.5; 272A); *ib.*1.6(p.109.8; 288C); *ib.*3.12(p.287.27; 673A); Or.*fr.35 in Lc.*10:21(p.250.9); τί δέ ἐστι ν. εἶναι κακίᾳ; τὸ μηδὲ εἰδέναι τί ποτέ ἐστι κακία Chrys.*hom.36.1 in 1Cor.*(10.333A); of Adam in his original state, Thphl.Ant.*Autol.*2.25(M.6.1092A); cf. Iren.*haer.*3.22.4(M.7.959A); *ib.*4.38.1(1105C); Clem.*str.*3.17(p.243.19; M.8.1205B); of Christians as possessing newness of life, id.*paed.* 1.5(p.98.21; 265B); *ib.*(p.99.8; 268A); *ib.*(p.101.19; 272B); neut. as subst., *infantile state*, ref. Inc. συνενηπίαζεν υἱὸς τοῦ θεοῦ, τέλειος ὤν, τῷ ἀνθρώπῳ...διὰ τὸ τοῦ ἀνθρώπου ν. οὕτω χωρούμενος, ὡς ἄνθρωπος αὐτὸν χωρεῖν ἠδύνατο Iren.*haer.*4.38.2(M.7.1107B); ὁ θεὸς φειδόμενος ἡμῶν ἀπατᾷ ἡμᾶς...ἵνα μὴ ὡς ὑπερβεβηκότες τὸ ν., μηκέτι δι' ἀπάτης παιδευώμεθα, ἀλλὰ διὰ τῶν πραγμάτων Or.*hom.19.15 in Jer.*(p.174.8; M.13.496D); **4.** *feeble, in rudimentary state*; in Gnost. theory of salvation οὐ γὰρ πρᾶξις εἰς πλήρωμα εἰσάγει, ἀλλὰ τὸ σπέρμα τὸ ἐκεῖθεν ν. ἐκπεμπόμενον, ἐνθάδε τελειούμενον Iren.*haer.*1.6.4(M.7. 512A); ἄχρι μὲν γὰρ ἦμεν τῆς θηλείας μόνης τέκνα...ἀτελῆ καὶ ν. καὶ ...ἄμορφα, οἷον ἐκτρώματα προενεχθέντα, τῆς γυναικὸς ἦμεν τέκνα, ὑπὸ δὲ τοῦ σωτῆρος μορφωθέντες ἀνδρὸς καὶ νυμφῶνος γεγόναμεν τέκνα Clem.*exc.Thdot.*68(p.129.12; M.9.692A); **5.** *foolish, unstable* δι' ἀφροσύνην οἱ ν. ἀπιστοῦντες id.*str.*1.23(p.98.24; M.8.904B); *Hom.Clem.*2. 29; ν. ἡμᾶς φησι, καὶ ὅταν τέλειοι ὦμεν, ἀλλὰ πρὸς ἕτερον ὁρῶν. ἐκεῖ μὲν γὰρ πρὸς τὴν μέλλουσαν γνῶσιν ν. ἐκάλεσεν...ἐνταῦθα δὲ πρὸς ἕτερον εἶπε, πρὸς τὸ εὐμετάπτωτον Chrys.*hom.11.3 in Eph.*(11.84A); Nonn. *par.Jo.*18:28(M.43.896A).

νηπιότης, ἡ, A. lit., *childhood, infancy*; of Christ τὸν ἐν ν. προαιώνιον ‡Meth.*Sym.et Ann.*6(M.18.360C); τὸν ἐν ν. παλαιὸν τῶν ἡμερῶν *ib.*8(365B).

B. *childishness, childlike condition*; **1.** of those who are beginners or imperfect in spiritual life and knowledge, Clem.*q.d.s.*4(p.162.18; M.9.608C); Or.*Cels.*5.16(p.17.22; M.11.1204C); id.*hom.19.15 in Jer.* (p.174.3; M.13.496C); who require τὸ λογικὸν ἄδολον γάλα id.*Jo.*13. 33(p.258.14; M.14.456D); καταρτίζειν σπουδάζετε τὴν τῶν ἀδελφῶν ν. Ephr.3.339C; τοὺς μηδέπω οὕτως δυναμένους διὰ τὴν ν. τῇ εὐχῇ προσκαρτερεῖν id.346D; ὥσπερ ὑλικὸς ἔρως τῶν ἔτι νηπιαζόντων οὐχ ἅπτεται (οὐ γὰρ χωρεῖ τὸ πάθος ἡ ν.)...οὕτω καὶ ἐπὶ τοῦ θείου κάλλους ...μόνη δὲ ἡ τοιαύτη ψυχὴ ἡ διαβᾶσα τὴν νηπιώδη κατάστασιν...μήτε ὑπὸ νηπιότητος ἀναισθητοῦσα...πείθεται τῇ...πρώτῃ ἐντολῇ τοῦ νόμου Gr.Nyss.*hom.1 in Cant.*(M.44.784B,C); ‡Gr.Nyss.*imag.*(M.44.1337C); Isid.Pel.*epp.*1.445(M.78.428A); **2.** ref. state of those under Law opp. gospel πῶς...εἰ ὁ νόμος νηπιώδης ὡς νηπίοις δεδομένος, καὶ ἡ κατὰ Χριστὸν στοιχείωσις πάλιν τυγχάνει ν. ... οὕτως γάλα ποτίζει Παῦλος τὸν νεογνὸν τοῦ κυρίου λαόν, σοφῶς αὐτὸν διὰ τῆς νόμου ν. παιδεύων τὴν τελειότητα *ib.*(428A,B); †Marc.Er.*temp.*11(M.65.1057C); **3.** *innocence*, Herm.*sim.*9.24.3; *ib.*9.29.1; **4.** ref. newness of life enjoyed by Christians, Clem.*paed.*1.5(p.101.26; M.8.273A); ἡ δὲ ἐν Χριστῷ ν. τελείωσίς ἐστιν, ὡς πρὸς τὸν νόμον. ἐνταῦθα γενομένοις τῇ ν. ἡμῶν συνηγορητέον *ib.*1.6(p.110.25; 292A).

***νηπιοφανής,** *appearing as an infant*; of Christ, Tim.Ant.*Sym.* (M.86.240C); Andr.Cr.*or.*11(M.97.1044B); ‡Jo.D.*hom.*5(M.96.652C).

***νηπιοφρόνως,** *childishly, foolishly*, ‡Gr.Nyss.*occurs.*(M.46. 1157A).

νηπιοφροσύνη, ἡ, *childishness, foolishness*, Philox.*ep.*39(p.186).

νηπιόφρων, *of childish mind, foolish*, Ephr.3.538B; ‡Amph.*circ.* (p.12A); ‡Caes.Naz.*dial.*13(M.38.869).

***νηπιώδης, A.** *of* or *belonging to a child, infantile* ν. ἡλικίαν Ephr. 3.326D; ἐκ τῆς ν. ὀλιγωρίας Bas.*hom.*8.2(2.63D; M.31.308C); Diad. *perf.*65(p.78.12).

B. *childish*; **1.** in sense of *imperfect, incomplete*; **a.** of those under Law opp. gospel, Or.*exp.in Pr.*9:8(M.17.185D); ἀκοὰς τὰς ν. τῶν σωματικῶν Ἰουδαίων Eus.*Is.*60:6–7(M.24.492C); Chrys.*hom.8.3 in 1Thess.*(11.482D); ὁ νόμος ν. ὡς νηπίοις δεδομένος Isid.Pel.*epp.*1.445 (M.78.428A); Cyr.*Ps.*68:31(M.69.1176B); Thdt.*affect.*proem.(p.3.9; 4.692); **b.** of novices in Christian life and understanding ὁ γενόμενος ἄνωθεν ἐξ ὕδατος καὶ πνεύματος οὐκ εἰς ν. τῆς νοητῆς ἡλικίας ἐξανίστασθαι ὀφείλει Ephr.3.326E; ἡ...ψυχὴ ἡ διαβᾶσα τὴν ν. κατάστασιν, καὶ διὰ τῆς πνευματικῆς ἡλικίας ἀκμάσασα Gr.Nyss.*hom.1 in Cant.*(M.44.784B); Chrys.*hom.21.1 in Eph.*(11.158E); Isid.Pel.*epp.*1. 211(M.78.316C); Max.*opusc.*(M.91.184B); **c.** in gen., of the less fully instructed, Gr.Nyss.*comm.not.*(M.45.181C); ‡Amph.*circ.*(p.12B);

2. in sense of *innocent* ν. ἁπλότητα καὶ ἀνενδοίαστον συγκατάθεσιν ἔχοντας Isid.Pel.*epp*.1.440(M.78.425A).

C. *fit for children, elementary*, Eus.*h.e*.4.23.8(M.20.388A); Cyr.H. *catech*.4.3.

D. *foolish*, Gr.Nyss.*or.dom*.1(p.14.18; M.44.1128C); Jo.D.*Man*.1. 10(M.94.1516A); †Jo.D.*B.J*.24(M.96.1073B).

[*]**νηποινί**, = νηποινεί, *with impunity*, Cyr.*ador*.11(1.410B).

νηπτικῶς, *soberly*, Meth.*res*.1.28(p.256.20; M.41.1133D); Chrys.*fr. in Jer*.1:17(M.64.753D).

νηρός (νερός), = νεαρός, *fresh*; neut. as subst., *fresh* or *cold water*, Thdr.Stud.*iamb*.13(M.99.1785A); νερόν *Apophth.Patr*.(M.65. 205B); Leont.N.*v.Sym*.35(M.93.1713C).

νῆσις, ἡ, ? *web*; met., Dan.Raith.*v.Jo.Clim*.(M.88.600B).

νῆσος, ἡ, *island*; **1.** ref. punishment of *relegatio*, Or.*hom.12.3 in Jer*.(p.90.19; M.13.384B); CSard.*can*.7; **2.** of Sirens' island likened to force of habit, Clem.*prot*.12(p.83.15; M.8.237B); **3.** of churches as islands affording refuge from shipwreck, and heret. congregations as rocky islands whereon those who frequent them are wrecked, Thphl.Ant.*Autol*.2.14(M.6.1076B); **4.** exeg. Is.41:1, of gentile churches as islands in sea of infidelity, Gr.Naz.*or*.44.1(M. 36.608A); of souls surrounded by worldly distractions but not submerged, Thdr.Heracl.*Is*.41:1(M.18.1332D); either of churches as islands in worldly society, or of *oases* where Edomite or Moabite idolaters dwell, which thus signify sinners, Cyr.*Is*.3.5(2.521Aff.); **5.** exeg. Jer.38:10, interpreted of humanity, far from truth and beaten by waves of this world, Or.*fr.54 in Jer*.(p.225.13; M.13. 580C); **6.** *people of an island* τὴν Κυπρίων ν. ... μετοικίσαι ἐσπούδασε Thphn.*chron*.p.304(M.108.741A).

νηστεία, ἡ, *fast*;

A. in gen., defined ν. ἐστὶν οὐ μόνον ἡ παντελὴς ἕωθεν μέχρι ἑσπέρας ἀσιτία, ἀλλὰ καὶ ἡ τινῶν βρωμάτων ἀποχή Jo.D.*jej*.3(M.95. 69A); **1.** spiritual significance ν., ἡ τῶν ἀγγέλων ὁμοίωσις, ἡ τῶν δικαίων ὁμόσκηνος, ὁ τοῦ βίου σωφρονισμός Bas.*hom*.2.6(2.14B; M.31. 193A); ν. θεμέλιος ἀρετῆς Gr.Nyss.*paup*.1(M.46.456C); τὴν μητέρα τῶν ἀγαθῶν ἁπάντων, καὶ τῆς σωφροσύνης, καὶ τῆς ἄλλης ἁπάσης ἀρετῆς διδάσκαλον, τὴν ν. λέγω Chrys.*hom.1.1 in Gen*.(4.3A); *ib*.1.2(3E); ν. γάρ ἐστιν γαλήνη τῶν ἡμετέρων ψυχῶν, ἡ τῶν γεγηρακότων εὐκοσμία, ἡ τῶν νέων παιδαγωγός, ἡ τῶν σωφρονούντων διδάσκαλος, ἡ πᾶσαν ἡλικίαν καὶ φύσιν καθάπερ διαδήματί τινι κατακοσμοῦσα *ib*.2.1(8A); φιλῶ μὲν τὴν ν., ὅτι μήτηρ σωφροσύνης ἐστίν, καὶ πηγὴ φιλοσοφίας ἁπάσης id.*serm.6.1 in Gen*.(4.670D); ν. ἐστὶν εἰρήνη κοινὴ ψυχῆς καὶ σώματος, ἀτάραχος ζωή, εὐσταθὴς πολιτεία Ast.Am.*hom*.14(M.40. 372D); ν. τῆς μελλούσης ζωῆς εἰκών· τῆς ἀφθάρτου διαγωγῆς μίμημα *ib*.(373D); ν. τῶν ἁγίων σύντροφος· ν. πάσης ἀγαθῆς πράξεως ἀρχηγός *ib*.(377B); οὐχὶ ν., πάσης ἡμῖν ἀρετῆς ἰδέαν ἀποτίκτουσα; ν., τῆς ἰσαγγέλου πολιτείας τὸ μίμημα, σωφροσύνης πηγή, ἐγκρατείας ἀρχή Cyr.*hom.pasch*.1(5^2.8B); τοιαύτη ἐστὶν ἡ ν. ὡς καὶ δι' ἡμᾶς ἐνανθρωπήσας νηστεύσας κατεδέξατο. ν. ἀγγέλων ἐστὶν μίμημα, ν. ἀπὸ πολλῶν γέγονε σωτηρία. ὦ νηστείας δύναμις· τοὺς ἀνθρώπους εἰς οὐρανοὺς ἐνεκόμισεν, καὶ μετὰ ἀγγέλων πολιτεύεσθαι παρεσκεύασεν Eus.Al. *serm*.1(M.86.317D); ν. ἐστὶ βία φύσεως, καὶ περιτομὴ ἡδύτητος λάρυγγος, πυρώσεως ἐκτομή, πονηρῶν ἐννοιῶν ἐκκοπή, ἐνυπνιασμῶν ἐλευθερία, προσευχῆς καθαρότης· ψυχῆς φωστήρ, νοὸς φυλακή Jo. Clim.*scal*.14(M.88.869A); **2.** of fasting in Eden νόμου πρεσβυτέρα ν. ...δυσωπήθητι τὴν πολιὰν τῆς ν.· συνηλικιῶτίς ἐστι τῆς ἀνθρωπότητος· ν. ἐν τῷ παραδείσῳ ἐνομοθετήθη. τὴν πρώτην ἐντολὴν ἔλαβεν Ἀδάμ· 'ἀπὸ τοῦ ξύλου τοῦ γινώσκειν...οὐ φάγεσθε.' τὸ δὲ 'οὐ φάγεσθε', ν. ἐστι...νομοθεσία. εἰ ἐνήστευσεν ἀπὸ τοῦ ξύλου ἡ Εὔα, οὐκ ἂν ταύτης νῦν ἐδεόμεθα τῆς ν. ... ἡ ἐν παραδείσῳ διαγωγή, ν. ἐστιν εἰκών Bas. *hom*.1.3(2.2E–3B; M.31.165C–168A); νεαρώτερον παραδείσου τὸ εὕρημα τῆς οἰνοποσίας, καὶ οὕτως ἀρχαῖον τὸ τῆς ν. σεμνόν *ib*.1.5(2.4C; M. 169C); ὁ θεὸς τὸν ἄνθρωπον ποιῶν ἐξ ἀρχῆς, εὐθέως αὐτὸν ταῖς τῆς ν. φέρων παρακατέθετο χερσίν...τὸ γάρ...ἀπὸ δὲ τοῦ ξύλου τοῦ γινώσκειν ...οὐ φάγεσθε, νηστείας εἶδός ἐστιν. εἰ δὲ ἐν παραδείσῳ ἀναγκαία ἡ ν., πολλῷ μᾶλλον ἐκτὸς τοῦ παραδείσου Chrys.*poenit*.5.1(2.310C); Ast. Am.*hom*.14(M.40.373C); **3.** other fasting in scripture; **a.** of Moses, *1Clem*.53.2; Μωσέα διὰ νηστείας ἔγνωμεν προσλαβόντα τῷ ὄρει... οὐδ' ἂν ἐθάρσησεν εἰσελθεῖν εἰς τὸν γνόφον, εἰ μὴ νηστείᾳ καθώπλιστο. διὰ ν. τὴν ἐντολὴν ὑπεδέξατο...καὶ ἄνω μὲν ἡ ν. νομοθεσίας πρόξενος ἦν, κάτω δὲ ἡ γαστριμαργία εἰς εἰδωλολατρείαν ἐξέμηνεν...ἃς γὰρ ἡ ν. ἔλαβε πλάκας...ταύτας ἡ μέθη συνέτριψεν Bas.*hom*.1.5(2.4C,D; M.31. 169C); Moses and Elijah, Chrys.*poenit*.5.1(2.310B); id.*hom.1.3 in Gen*.(4.4D,E); and Samuel, Bas.*hom*.2.6(2.14B; M.31.193B); **b.** of Daniel οὐδ' ἂν ὁ σοφὸς Δανιὴλ τὰς ὀπτασίας εἶδεν, εἰ μὴ ν. διαυγεστέραν ἐποίησε τὴν ψυχὴν *ib*.1.9(8D; M.180C); Eus.Al.*serm*.1(M. 86.317A); and Elijah, Pall.*v.Chrys*.12(p.76.8ff.; M.47.43); **c.** of Samuel and Samson τὸν δὲ Σαμουὴλ οὐχ ἡ μετὰ νηστείας προσευχὴ ἐχαρίσατο τῇ μητρί; τί τὸν...Σαμψὼν ἀκαταγώνιστον ἀπειργάσατο; οὐχ ἡ ν., μεθ' ἧς ἐν τῇ γαστρὶ τῆς μητρὸς συνελήφθη; ν. αὐτὸν ἐκύησε· ν. αὐτὸν ἐτιθηνήσατο· ν. αὐτὸν ἤνδρωσεν, ἣν ὁ ἄγγελος διετάξατο τῇ μητρί Bas.*hom*.1.6(2.4E–5A; M.31.172A); **d.** of Esther, *1Clem*.55.6; Clem.*str*.4.19(p.300.22; M.8.1329A); other OT saints, Eus.Al.*serm*.1 (317B–D); **e.** of NT saints τί τὸν Λάζαρον ἐνανέπαυσε τοῖς κόλποις τοῦ Ἀβραάμ; οὐχὶ ν.; Ἰωάννου δὲ ὁ βίος μία ν. ἦν...Παῦλον μετὰ τῶν ἄλλων καὶ ἡ ν. ... εἰς τὸν τρίτον οὐρανὸν ἀνήγαγε. κεφάλαιον δὲ ἐπὶ τοῖς εἰρημένοις, ὁ κύριος ἡμῶν νηστείᾳ τὴν σάρκα...ὀχυρώσας οὕτως ἐν αὐτῇ τοῦ διαβόλου τὰς προσβολὰς ὑπεδέξατο, ἡμᾶς τε παιδεύων νηστείαις ἀλείφειν...ἑαυτοὺς πρὸς τοὺς ἐν τοῖς πειρασμοῖς ἀγῶνας Bas.*hom*.1.9(2.7E–8A; M.31.177C); **4.** the true moral fast; **a.** abstinence from evil ὁ θεὸς οὐ βούλεται...ν. ματαίαν· οὕτω γὰρ νηστεύων τῷ θεῷ οὐδὲν ἐργάσῃ τῇ δικαιοσύνῃ. νήστευσον...ν. τοιαύτην· μηδὲν πονηρεύσῃ ἐν τῇ ζωῇ σου, καὶ δούλευσον τῷ κυρίῳ ἐν καθαρᾷ καρδίᾳ· τήρησον τὰς ἐντολὰς αὐτοῦ πορευόμενος ἐν τοῖς προστάγμασιν αὐτοῦ, καὶ μηδεμία ἐπιθυμία πονηρὰ ἀναβήτω ἐν τῇ καρδίᾳ σου...ταῦτα ἐὰν ἐργάσῃ, μεγάλην ν. τελέσεις καὶ δεκτὴν τῷ θεῷ Herm.*sim*.5.1.4,5; ν. δὲ ἀποχὰς κακῶν μηνύουσιν πάντων ἁπαξαπλῶς· τῶν τε κατ' ἐνέργειαν καὶ κατὰ λόγον καὶ κατὰ τὴν διάνοιαν αὐτήν Clem.*str*.6.12(p.483.13; M.9.324B); μὴ νομίσῃς...ὅτι οὕτως ἁπλῶς ἐστιν ἡ ν.· οὐ γὰρ ὁ νηστεύων ἀπὸ βρωμάτων μόνον ἐκεῖνος κατώρθωσεν ἀλλ' ὁ ἀπεχόμενος ἀπὸ παντὸς πονηροῦ πράγματος, τούτῳ λογίζεται ἡ ν.· ἐὰν γὰρ νηστεύσῃς καὶ μὴ τηρήσῃς τὸ στόμα σου λαλῆσαι λόγον πονηρόν...ἐὰν ταῦτα ἐξέλθῃ ἐκ τοῦ στόματος τοῦ νηστεύοντος, οὐδὲν ὠφέλησεν Ath.*virg*.7 (p.41.23ff.; M.28.260C); Bas.*hom*.1.10(2.9B; M.31.181B); οὐ...ἐξαρκεῖ καθ' ἑαυτὴν ἡ ἀποχὴ τῶν βρωμάτων πρὸς τὴν ἐπαινετὴν ν., ἀλλὰ νηστεύσωμεν ν. δεκτήν, εὐάρεστον τῷ θεῷ. ἀληθὴς ν., ἡ τοῦ κακοῦ ἀλλοτρίωσις, ἐγκράτεια γλώσσης, θυμοῦ ἐποχή,...ἡ τούτων ἔνδεια ν. ἐστιν ἀληθής. ἐν τούτοις...ἡ ν. καλόν *ib*.2.7(15D,E; M.196D); ν. δὲ οὐ ταύτην λέγω τὴν τῶν πολλῶν, ἀλλὰ τὴν ἀκριβῆ ν., οὐ τὴν τῶν βρωμάτων ἀποχὴν μόνον, ἀλλὰ καὶ τὴν τῶν ἁμαρτημάτων· οὐ γὰρ ἀρκεῖ τῆς ν. ἡ φύσις ἐξελέσθαι τοὺς μετιόντας, ἐὰν μὴ μετὰ τοῦ προσήκοντος γένηται νόμου...ἵνα οὖν μὴ πόνον ὑπομείναντες νηστείας ἐκπέσωμεν τοῦ στεφάνου τῆς ν., μάθωμεν πῶς...τὸ πρᾶγμα μετιέναι χρή. ἐπεὶ καὶ ὁ Φαρισαῖος ἐκεῖνος ἐνήστευσεν, ἀλλὰ μετὰ τὴν ν. ἐκείνην κατῆλθεν ἔρημος...τῶν ἀπὸ τῆς ν. καρπῶν· ὁ τελώνης οὐκ ἐνήστευσε, καὶ ἔμπροσθεν γέγονεν ἐκείνου τοῦ νηστεύσαντος ὁ μὴ νηστεύσας, ἵνα μάθῃς ὅτι ν. ὄφελος οὐδέν, ἂν μὴ καὶ τὰ λοιπὰ ἕπηται πάντα...ἐπεὶ οὖν τοσοῦτος ὁ κίνδυνος τοῖς οὐκ εἰδόσιν ὅπως χρὴ νηστεύειν, μάθωμεν τῆς ν. τοὺς νόμους, ἵνα μὴ τρέχωμεν ἀδήλως...φάρμακόν ἐστιν ἡ ν., ἀλλὰ τὸ φάρμακον...πολλάκις ἄχρηστον γίνεται διὰ τὴν ἀπειρίαν τοῦ χρωμένου Chrys.*stat*.3.3(2.39E–40B); *ib*.3.4(41C); τοῖς ἐχθροῖς καταλλαττέσθω, πᾶσαν μνησικακίαν ἐξοριζέτω τῆς ἑαυτοῦ ψυχῆς. ἂν ταῦτα κατορθοῦν βούληται, τὴν ἀληθῆ ν. ἐπεδείξατο id.*hom.10.2 in Gen*.(4.73A); οὐ...μόνων βρωμάτων ἀποβολαῖς τὴν...τῆς ν. εὑρήσομεν χάριν,...ἀλλ' ἐκεῖνα τῆς ἑαυτῶν διανοίας ἀποπεμπόμενοι, δι' ἃ καὶ τὸ τῆς ν. ἐξεύρηται φάρμακον Cyr.*hom.pasch*.1(5^2.7B,C); ὥσπερ ἐστὶ βρωμάτων ν., οὕτω καὶ θυμοῦ ν. ἐστί, καὶ φιλαρχίας ν., καὶ βασκανίας κτλ. Nil.*epp*.2.28(M.79.212B); Eus.Al.*serm*.1(M.86.317D–320A); **b.** from pleasures of sense and worldliness ἡ ν. ἀποχὴ τροφῆς ἐστι κατὰ σημαινόμενον, τροφὴ δὲ οὐδὲν δικαιοτέρους ἡμᾶς ἢ ἀδικωτέρους ἀπεργάζεται, κατὰ δὲ τὸ μυστικὸν δηλοῖ ὅτι ὥσπερ τοῖς καθ' ἕνα ἐκ τροφῆς ἡ ζωή, ἡ δ' ἀτροφία θανάτου σύμβολον, οὕτως καὶ ἡμᾶς τῶν κοσμικῶν νηστεύειν χρή, ἵνα τῷ κόσμῳ ἀποθάνωμεν καὶ μετὰ τοῦτο τροφῆς θείας μεταλαβόντες θεῷ ζήσωμεν, ἄλλως τε κενοῖ τῆς ὕλης τὴν ψυχὴν ἡ ν. καὶ καθαρὰν...σὺν καὶ τῷ σώματι παρίστησι τοῖς θείοις λόγοις Clem.*ecl*.14(p.140.23ff.; M.9.704D–705A); διὰ καθαρότητα ψυχῆς ἐνομοθετήθη ν. εἰ δὲ ἐκείνη τῇ προαιρέσει...μολύνεται, τί μάτην προσδαπανῶμεν τὸ πινόμενον ὕδωρ;...τίς ὄνησις τῆς σωματικῆς ν., ἂν μὴ καθαρεύῃ ὁ νοῦς; Gr.Nyss.*paup*.1(M.46.456C); τῶν ἀτοπωτάτων ἂν εἴη ἐπὶ μὲν βρωμάτων...ἀφίστασθαι...διὰ τὴν ν., ἐπὶ δὲ τῶν ὀφθαλμῶν ἀκολασίαν διὰ τῶν ὀφθαλμῶν. νηστευέτω καὶ ἀκοή. ν. δὲ ἀκοῆς μὴ δέχεσθαι κακηγορίας Chrys.*stat*.3.4(2.41E–42A); οὐδὲν οὖν ν. βρωμάτων ὀνίνησι τοὺς μὴ πάσαις νηστεύοντας αἰσθήσεσιν Isid.Pel. *epp*.1.403(M.78.408B); καλὸς ὁ τῆς ν. ἄρτος, ἐπειδὴ τῆς ζύμης ἐστὶ τῶν ἡδονῶν ἐλεύθερος Nil.*sent*.39(M.79.1244C); **c.** exeg. Is.58:1ff., Just. *dial*.15.1(M.6.505D); cf.Clem.*paed*.3.12(p.285.19; M.8.668C); τοιαύτην ν. ἀγαπᾷ ὁ θεός...τί γὰρ ὄφελος ὅτι εἰ κοιμήσῃ ἐπὶ σποδοῦ...καὶ ὁ πένης πεινᾷ; διὰ τοῦτο προσετάγης νηστεύειν, ἵνα ὅτε σὺ πεινᾷς, οἱ πένητες χορτασθήσονται Eus.Al.*serm*.1(M.86.316C); Joel 1:14 ἡμεῖς δὲ ν. ὄντες ἁγίας θρέμματα, καὶ ἐν ἀτροφίᾳ σωμάτων τρυφήσαντες τὰ οὐράνια, σπουδάσωμεν τὴν ν. ἁγίαν φυλάξαι· 'ἁγιάσατε' γάρ, φησί, 'ν.' ἡμεῖς αὐτὴν ἁγιάζομεν, ἢ ὑπ' αὐτῆς ἁγιαζόμεθα; ἀλλὰ ἀντὶ τοῦ ἁγίαν αὐτὴν φυλάξαι, τοῦτο εἴρηκεν ὁ προφήτης Sever.*creat.*1.7(M.56.437); 'ἁγιάσατε ν.' τουτέστιν, ὡς ἐν ἀναθήματος ποιεῖσθε τάξει, καὶ ὡς ἐν θυσίας τρόπῳ τὴν...ν. ... εἰ γὰρ μέλλοιμεν ἐν καιρῷ ν. τῶν ἰδίων ἀποπαύεσθαι θελημάτων...οὔπω νενηστεύκαμεν ἁγίως Cyr.*Joel.*11(3.209E); **5.** fasting in rel. to various groups: ἀγαπήσωμεν [sc. virgins] σφόδρα τὴν ν.· μέγα γὰρ φυλακτήριόν ἐστιν ἡ ν. ... Χριστὸς...χρῄζει παρὰ σοῦ...σῶμα ἀμόλυντον ὑπωπιαζόμενον ὑπὸ νηστείας Ath.*virg.*6 (pp.39.27–40.11; M.28.257B,C); οἱ παῖδες, ὥσπερ τῶν φυτῶν τὰ εὐθαλῆ, τῷ τῆς ν. ὕδατι καταρδευέσθωσαν. τοῖς πρεσβυτέροις κοῦφον ποιεῖ τὸν πόνον ἡ ἐκ παλαιοῦ πρὸς αὐτὴν οἰκείωσις...τοῖς ὁδοιπόροις εὐσταλὴς ἐστι συνέμπορος ἡ ν. ... κούφους αὐτοὺς καὶ εὐζώνους ἡ ν. παρασκευάζει Bas.*hom.*2.2(2.11E; M.31.188B); ὁ τῶν χηρῶν τάγμα...παρῄνει [sc. Chrys.] ἢ ν. ἀναλαβεῖν ἀπεχομένας βαλανείων...ἢ θᾶττον χωρεῖν ἐπὶ δεύτερον γάμον Pall.*v.Chrys.*5(p.32.20; M.47.20); **6.** necessity and motives εἰ μετὰ νηφούσης διανοίας τὸν ἑαυτῶν βίον οἰκονομῶμεν... καὶ τῇ τροφῇ οὕτω προσίωμεν, ὡς τὴν χρείαν μόνον πληροῦν...οὐδὲ χρεία ἡμῖν ἦν τῆς βοηθείας τῆς ἀπὸ τῆς ν. ἀλλ' ἐπειδὴ ῥᾴθυμός ἐστιν ἡ φύσις ἡ ἀνθρωπίνη, καὶ...τῇ τρυφῇ μᾶλλον ἑαυτὴν ἐπιδίδωσι, διὰ τοῦτο ...τὴν ἀπὸ τῆς ν. ἡμῖν ἰατρείαν ἐπενόησεν ὁ...δεσπότης Chrys.*hom.10.1 in Gen.*(4.72D,E); id.*poenit.*5(2.310D); τὴν ν. ἡδέως καταδεχόμεθα, κελευσάντων ἡμῖν τῶν τὸν βίον προοδευκότων...πλεῖον γὰρ τῆς ν. ἡ καθ' ὑπακοὴν μετάληψις μαστίζει τοὺς δαίμονας Nil.*epp.*1.307(M.79.193B,C); ἡ ν. ἔχει μὲν καθ' ἑαυτὴν καύχημα, ἀλλ' οὐ πρὸς θεόν...οὐ δεῖ οὖν ἐπ' αὐτῇ μεγάλα φρονεῖν τοὺς τῆς εὐσεβείας ἀγωνιστάς Diad.*perf.*47(p.52.18); ref. Mt.6:17f. πολλοί εἰσιν οἱ νηστεύοντες...καὶ θέλουσιν προσκυνεῖσθαι ὑπὸ πάντων ὡς εὐλαβεῖς· καὶ ταύτην ν. οὐ φιλεῖ ὁ θεός...ἡ γὰρ κατὰ ἀνθρωπαρέσκειαν γινομένη ν. μισθὸν οὐκ ἔχει Eus.Al.*serm.*1 (M.86.321B,C); **7.** effects; **a.** physical and material οὐ πρὸς τὰ μέλλοντα μόνον ὠφέλιμος ἡ ν., ἀλλὰ καὶ αὐτῇ τῇ σαρκὶ λυσιτελεστέρα Bas.*hom.*1.9(2.7C; M.31.177A); *ib.*(9A; M.181A); ἐρώτησον τοὺς ἰατρούς, καὶ ἀναγγελοῦσί σοι, ὅτι σφαλερώτατόν ἐστι πάντων ἡ ἐπ' ἄκρον εὐεξία. διόπερ διὰ νηστείας ὑφαιροῦσι τὸ πλεονάζον οἱ ἐμπειρότατοι, ὡς μὴ τῷ βάρει τῆς πολυσαρκίας ὑποκλασθῆναι τὴν δύναμιν *ib.*2.7(14E; M.193D); τὴν τῶν βρωμάτων ἀπόλαυσιν ν. φαιδρύνει...ὥστε εἰ βούλει σεαυτῷ ἐπιθυμητὴν κατασκευάσαι τὴν τράπεζαν, δέξαι τὴν ἐκ τῆς ν. μεταβολήν *ib.*1.8(7A; M.176C); ἡ ν. χαρίζεται, τὴν ἐκ τῆς γαστριμαργίας πύρωσιν τῶν σωμάτων ἀποδιώκουσα Ast.Am.*hom.*14(M.40.372B); Nil.*epp.*1.168(M.79.149B); id.*inst.*(M.79.1236A); δύο εὐεργεσίας κέκτηται ἡ ν., ἵνα δι' αὐτῆς ταπείνωσιν κτήσωνται σώματος· τοῖς δὲ γεγαμηκόσιν ν. ἐπετέθη ἵνα μετάδοσιν ποιήσωνται τοῖς πτωχοῖς ἄρτου καὶ οἴνου Eus.Al.*serm.*1(M.86.316D); **b.** spiritual ἁμαρτίαν, ὑποικουροῦσαν τῷ βάθει, ἐναποκτείνει τῇ ψυχῇ εἰσελθοῦσα ν. Bas.*hom.*1.1(2B; M.164B–165A); *ib.*1.2(2E; M.165C); ν. θεῷ προσάγει *ib.*1.5(4E; M.169D); οὐκ ἐπιθυμίαν λήψῃ τῆς ἐν τῇ βασιλείᾳ τραπέζης, ἣν πάντως ἡ ἐνθάδε ν. προευτρεπίσει; *ib.*1.9(8C; M.180B); strengthens spiritual athlete, *ib.*2.1(11B; M.185B); defeats passions, *ib.*2.3(12D; M.189B); *ib.*1.9(8B; M.180A); ν. γὰρ τῆς ψυχῆς ἐστι τροφή, καὶ καθάπερ αὕτη ἡ σωματικὴ τροφὴ πιαίνει τὸ σῶμα, οὕτω καὶ ἡ ν. τὴν ψυχὴν εὐτονωτέραν ἐργάζεται, κοῦφον αὐτῇ τὸ πτέρον κατασκευάζει, μετάρσιον αὐτὴν ποιεῖ, τὰ ἄνω φαντάζεσθαι προξενεῖ, ἀνωτέραν αὐτὴν τῶν ἡδονῶν...τοῦ παρόντος βίου ἀπεργαζομένη...ἡ μὲν ν. κουφότερον ἐργαζομένη τὸν λογισμόν, παρασκευάζει μετ' εὐκολίας τὸ πέλαγος τοῦ παρόντος βίου διαπερᾶν Chrys.*hom.1.4 in Gen.*(4.5D,E); *ib.10.2*(73C); ἡ δὲ ν. δουλεύοντας ἡμᾶς, καὶ δεδεμένους εὑροῦσα, ἀνίησι τῶν δεσμῶν, ἀπαλλάττει τῆς τυραννίδος, καὶ πρὸς τὴν ἐλευθερίαν ἐπανάγει τὴν προτέραν id.*poenit.*5.1(2.309E); id.*Anna* 1.1(4.700A); purifies souls, id.*hom.31.2 in Ac.*(9.242E); pacifies, Eus.Al.*serm.*1(316D); ν., τὴν μὲν ἐπιθυμίαν μαραίνει Max.*carit.*1.79(M.90.977C); makes men to be like angels, Ath.*virg.*7(p.41.21; M.28.260C); Chrys.*poenit.*5.1(2.310B); πολλοὶ διὰ νηστείας ὑπερέβησαν τὰ οὐράνια, καὶ μετὰ ἀγγέλων ἔσχον τὴν ἅμιλλαν Eus.Al.*serm.*1 (317A); **c.** social ν. οἴκων αὔξησις, ὑγείας μήτηρ, νεότητος παιδαγωγός, κόσμος πρεσβύταις, ἀγαθὴ συνέμπορος ὁδοιπόροις, ἀσφαλὴς ὁμόσκηνος τοῖς συνοίκοις. οὐχ ὑποπτεύει γάμων ἐπιβουλὴν ὁ ἀνήρ, νηστείαις ὁρῶν τὴν γυναῖκα συζῶσαν. οὐ τήκεται ζηλοτυπίαις γυνή, τὸν ἄνδρα βλέπουσα ν. καταδεχόμενον. τίς τὸν ἑαυτοῦ οἶκον ἠλάττωσεν ἐν ν.;...οὐδὲν διὰ τὴν ν. λείψει τῶν ἐν τῷ οἴκῳ Bas.*hom.*1.7(2.6B; M.31.173C–176A); ν. φυλάσσει νήπια, σωφρονίζει τὸν νέον, σεμνὸν ποιεῖ τὸν πρεσβύτην ...γυναιξὶ κόσμος ἁρμοδιώτατος...συζυγίας φυλακτήριον, παρθενίας τροφός *ib.*2.5(13C; M.192B); **d.** on demons; in exorcism, Or.*comm. in Mt.*13.7(p.198.25; M.13.1112B); πρὸς τὴν τῶν δαιμόνων φυγὴν...ἡ ν. ... βοήθημα *Hom.Clem.*9.10; πᾶς οὖν ὑπὸ πνεύματος ἀκαθάρτου ὀχλούμενος, ἐὰν...χρήσηται τῷ φαρμάκῳ τούτῳ, λέγω δὴ τῇ ν., εὐθὺς τὸ πνεῦμα τὸ πονηρὸν στενοχωρούμενον ἀναχωρεῖ, φοβούμενον τὴν ν. Ath.*virg.*7(p.41.14; M.28.260B); Bas.*hom.*2.2(2.11B; M.31.185C); Chrys.*poenit.*5.1(2.309D); exeg. Mt.17:21 ὁρᾷς πῶς αὐτοῖς ἤδη τὸν περὶ τῆς ν. προκαταβάλλεται λόγον; μὴ γάρ μοι ἀπὸ τῶν σπανιζόντων λέγε, ὅτι τινὲς καὶ χωρὶς ν. ἐξέβαλον. εἰ γὰρ περὶ τῶν ἐπιτιμώντων τοῦτο ἂν εἴποι τις ἑνός που καὶ δευτέρου, ἀλλὰ πάσχοντα ἀμήχανόν ποτε τρυφῶντα ἀπαλλαγῆναι τῆς μανίας ταύτης...καὶ μὴν εἰ πίστεως χρεία...τί δεῖ νηστείας; ὅτι μετὰ τῆς πίστεως κἀκεῖνο οὐ μικρὰν εἰσάγει τὴν ἰσχὺν id.*hom.57.4 in Mt.*(7.581A); **e.** summaries ὁρᾷς τί ποιεῖ ἡ ν.; καὶ νόσους θεραπεύει καὶ ῥεύματα σωματικὰ ξηραίνει καὶ δαίμονας ἐκβάλλει καὶ λογισμοὺς πονηροὺς ἀποδιώκει καὶ τὸν νοῦν λαμπρότερον ποιεῖ καὶ καρδίαν καθαρὰν καὶ σῶμα ἡγιασμένον καὶ τῷ θρόνῳ τοῦ θεοῦ παρίστησι τὸν ἄνθρωπον...ἔχεις μαρτυρίαν ἐν τοῖς εὐαγγελίοις...[Mt.9:29] Ath.*virg.*7(p.41.3; M.28.260A); δέομαι πάντων ὑμῶν...εἰς τὸ συνειδὸς ἕκαστος αὐτοῦ ἀναλογιζέσθω τὴν ἀπὸ τῆς ν. πραγματείαν, κἂν μὲν εὕρῃ κέρδος πολὺ γεγενημένον, προστιθέτω τῇ πραγματείᾳ· ἂν δὲ μηδὲν ᾖ συνειλεγμένον, τῷ λειπομένῳ τοῦ χρόνου κεχρήσθω πρὸς τὴν ἐμπορίαν Chrys.*poenit.*6(2.317C); μνήσθητι ποταπὸς ὑπῆρχες πρὸ τῆς ν. τί θλίβῃ ὅταν νηστεύεις; ὅτι ἡ κεφαλή σου οὐ βαρεῖται, καὶ οἱ ὀφθαλμοί σου οὐκ εἰσὶν τεθολωμένοι καὶ αἱματώδεις...ὅτι οὐ περικρούεις εἰς τοὺς τοίχους...διὰ τοῦτο λυπήσῃ; μέγα κτῆμα ἡ ν. Eus.Al.*serm.*1(M.86.317A); **f.** scriptural illustrations, ref. Three Children οὐδὲ γὰρ τῶν τριχῶν τὸ πῦρ κατετόλμησε, διὰ τὸ ὑπὸ νηστείας αὐτὰς ἐκτραφῆναι Bas.*hom.*1.6(6A; M.173B); ref. Dan.10:2ff. Δανιὴλ...ὁ τρεῖς ἑβδομάδας ἄρτον μὴ φαγών...καὶ τοὺς λέοντας νηστεύειν ἐδίδαξε...οὕτως οἱονεὶ βαφῇ σιδήρου τὸ σῶμα τοῦ ἀνδρὸς ἡ ν. στομώσασα, ἀδάμαστον ἐποίει τοῖς λέουσιν...ν. ἔσβεσε δύναμιν πυρός· ἔφραξε στόματα λεόντων *ib.*1.7(6A; M.173C); *ib.*1.9(8D; M.180C); **8.** coupled with other good works; **a.** prayer, Polyc.*ep.*7.2; *T.Jos.*4.8; Iren.*haer.*2.31.2(M.7.825A); Clem.*q.d.s.*42(p.190.15; M.9.649C); ν. προσευχὴν εἰς οὐρανὸν ἀναπέμπει, οἱονεὶ πτερὸν αὐτῇ γινομένη πρὸς τὴν ἄνω πορείαν Bas.*hom.*1.7(2.6B; M.31.173C); *ib.*2.4(12E; M.189C); τῇ ν. τὴν προσευχὴν ἀεὶ συνεζεῦχθαι δεῖ...εἶδες πῶς δεῖται τῆς ἐντεῦθεν συμμαχίας ἡ ν.; τότε γὰρ μάλιστα καὶ μετὰ νήψεως αἱ προσευχαὶ γίνονται, κουφοτέρας τῆς διανοίας τυγχανούσης Chrys.*hom.30.5 in Gen.*(4.300E–301A); id.*poenit.*5.1(2.309E); ὁ εὐχόμενος μετὰ νηστείας διπλᾶς ἔχει τὰς πτέρυγας id.*hom.57.4 in Mt.*(7.581C); Pall.*v.Chrys.*3(p.16.22; M.47.12); ἡμέρας μὲν σύμβολον ἡ ν. διὰ τὸ ἔκδηλον· νυκτὸς δὲ διὰ τὸ ἄδηλον, ἡ εὐχή ‡Max.*cap.al.*84(M.90.1420A); **b.** μετάνοια, Bas.*hom.*1.3(3B; M.168A); *ib.*2.7(15D; M.196C); **c.** prayer and almsgiving, *2Clem.*16.4; Ath.*virg.*6(p.40.1; M.28.257B); τῇ ν. τὴν ἐλεημοσύνην συζεύξωμεν, ἵνα οἷα πτεροῖς γῆθεν ἡμῶν ἡ ψυχὴ πρὸς τὰ οὐράνια αἴρηται Nect.*Thdr.*22(M.39.1837C); κἂν νηστεύσῃς χωρὶς ἐλεημοσύνης, οὐδὲ ν. τὸ πρᾶγμα λογίζεται Chrys.*hom.57.6 in Mt.*(7.749E); ‡Chrys.*eleem.*1(1.818B); νηστεύων δὲ ὀφείλει μεταδοῦναι τῷ μὴ ἔχοντι· ὁ γὰρ νηστεύων καὶ μὴ μεταδιδοὺς πεινῶντι τὸν ἄρτον αὐτοῦ, ματαιοῖ τὴν ν. αὐτοῦ. ἄκαρπός ἐστιν, ἀμετάδοτος ἡ ν. Eus.Al.*serm.*1(M.86.316A,B); cf. τὴν ν. τῆς τροφῆς προαιρούμεθα...ἀλλ' ἴσμεν ὅτι τῆς ἀγάπης τὸ χρῆμα τῆς ν. ἐστὶ τιμιώτερον Thdt.*h.rel.*3(3.1145); **d.** humility, *1Clem.*53.2; *ib.*55.6; **e.** patience and prayer, *T.Jos.*10.1; **f.** watching, Max.*carit.*2.70(M.90.1005D); ‡Max.*cap.al.*60(M.90.1413C).

B. Christ's fast ἐνήστευσεν οὐκ αὐτός...ν. χρείαν ἔχων...ὁ τῇ φύσει καθαρὸς...ἀλλ' ἵνα καὶ Ἰωάννῃ ἀλήθειαν μαρτυρήσῃ καὶ ἡμῖν ὑπογραμμὸν παράσχηται *Const.App.*7.22.5; ὁ γὰρ κύριος...αὐτὸς τεσσαράκοντα ἡμερῶν ν. ἐπιδειξάμενος, οὕτω τῆς πρὸς τὸν διάβολον ἥψατο πάλης, πᾶσιν ἡμῖν ὑπογραμμὸν διδούς, ὥστε διὰ ταύτης καθοπλίζεσθαι Chrys.*hom.1.3 in Gen.*(4.5A); οὐδὲ γὰρ νηστεύοντι, ἀλλὰ πεινῶντι προσέρχεται [sc. διάβολος]· ἵνα σὺ μάθῃς, ἡλίκον ἡ ν. καλόν, καὶ πῶς ὅπλον ἐστὶ κατὰ τοῦ διαβόλου...καὶ ὅτι μετὰ τὸ λουτρὸν οὐ τρυφῇ... ἀλλὰ ν. προσέχειν δεῖ. διὰ γὰρ τοῦτο καὶ αὐτὸς ἐνήστευσεν, οὐκ αὐτὸς ταύτης δεόμενος, ἀλλ' ἡμᾶς παιδεύων...οὕτω...αὐτὸς μετὰ τὸ λουτρὸν ν. εἰσήγαγε id.*hom.13.1 in Mt.*(7.168D–169A).

C. Lenten fast; **1.** in gen.; **a.** reasons for observance προσελαύνουσι νηστεῖαι, κοῦφα μὲν τῆς ψυχῆς ἐργαζόμεναι τὰ πτερά, κοῦφον δὲ τῆς σαρκὸς κατασκευάζουσαι τὸ φορτίον...ἀλλ' ὁ μὲν τῆς ν. ἀναμενέτω λόγος, ὁ δὲ τῶν μυστηρίων ἤδη κινείσθω, δι' ἃ καὶ αἱ ν. ... τῆς ν. τέλος ἡ καθαρὰ κοινωνία· ὡς ἐὰν μὴ τοῦτο κατορθώσωμεν διὰ τῶν ἡμερῶν τούτων, εἰκῇ...κατακόψαντες ἑαυτούς, ἀστεφάνωτοι...ἀπὸ τοῦ σκάμματος τῆς ν. ἀναχωρήσομεν. διὰ τοῦτο καὶ οἱ πατέρες ἐξέτειναν τῆς ν. τὸ στάδιον, προθεσμίαν μετανοίας διδόντες ἡμῖν, ἵνα καθηράμενοι... οὕτω προσίωμεν Chrys.*hom.6.3 in Is.6:1*(6.141E–142A); **b.** proper preparation for it μὴ μυσταγωγείτω σε ἐπὶ νηστείαν ἡ μέθη. οὐκ ἔστι διὰ μέθης εἴσοδος εἰς ν. ... ἄλλη θύρα ἐπὶ ν. μέθη εἰς ἀκολασίαν εἰσάγει, ἐπὶ ν. αὐτάρκεια Bas.*hom.*1.10(2.9D; M.31.181C); *ib.*2.4(13A; M.189C); τὴν...ν., καὶ διὰ τὴν συνήθειαν, καὶ διὰ τὴν πρὸς ἀλλήλους αἰδῶ, οἱ πολλοὶ καταδέχονται. φοβοῦμαι δὲ τὴν μέθην, ἥν, ὥσπερ τινὰ κλῆρον πατρῷον, οἱ φίλοινοι διασώζουσιν. ὡς γὰρ οἱ πρὸς τὰς μακρὰς ἀποδημίας ἀπαίροντες, οὕτω τινὲς τῶν ἀνοήτων σήμερον πρὸς τὰς πέντε τῶν ν. ἡμέρας οἰνίζονται *ib.*2.7(15B; M.196B); μὴ...διὰ μέθης ἴωμεν εἰς τὴν ν., μηδὲ ἀπὸ ν. εἰς μέθην καταλύσωμεν πάλιν...κἂν μὲν ἐρωτήσω, τίνος ἕνεκεν εἰς βαλανεῖον τρέχεις σήμερον; ἵνα καθαρῷ τῷ σώματι τὴν ν. ὑποδέξωμαι, φήσεις· ἂν δὲ ἐρωτήσω, τίνος ἕνεκεν μεθύεις; ἐπειδὴ εἰς ν. μέλλω εἰσιέναι, πάλιν ἐρεῖς. καὶ πῶς οὐκ ἄτοπόν ἐστι, σώματι μὲν καθαρῷ, ψυχῇ δὲ ἀκαθάρτῳ καὶ μεθυούσῃ, τὴν καλλίστην ταύτην ἀρετὴν ὑποδέχεσθαι; Chrys.*poenit*.5.5(2.316A,B); **c.** conditions for fruitfulness δευτέραν ἑβδομάδα τῆς ν. παρήλθομεν, ἀλλὰ μὴ τοῦτο σκοπῶμεν· οὐ γὰρ τοῦτό ἐστι παρελθεῖν νηστείαν, ἐὰν τὸν χρόνον παρέλθωμεν, ἀλλ' ἐὰν μετὰ κατορθωμάτων παρέλθωμεν. τοῦτο λογισώμεθα, εἰ σπουδαιότεροι γεγόναμεν...εἰ τὰ ἁμαρτήματα ἀπενιψάμεθα. ἔθος ἅπασιν ἐρωτᾶν κατὰ τὴν τεσσαρακοστήν, πόσας ἕκαστος ἑβδομάδας ἐνήστευσε· καὶ ἔστιν ἀκοῦσαι λεγόντων τῶν μέν, ὅτι δύο, τῶν δέ, ὅτι τρεῖς, τῶν δέ, ὅτι πάσας ἐνήστευσαν τὰς ἑβδομάδας. καὶ τί τὸ κέρδος, ἐὰν ἔρημοι κατορθωμάτων παρέλθωμεν τὴν ν.; ἐὰν ἕτερος λέγῃ, ὅτι πᾶσαν ἐνήστευσα τὴν τεσσαρακοστήν, σὺ εἰπέ, ὅτι ἐχθρὸν εἶχον, καὶ κατηλλάγην· ἔθος εἶχον κακηγορεῖν, καὶ ἐπαυσάμην...οὐδὲν ὄφελος τῆς ν. ἡμῖν, ἂν παρέλθωμεν αὐτὴν ἁπλῶς, εἰκῇ καὶ μάτην. ἂν τὴν τῶν βρωμάτων νηστεύωμεν ν., παρελθουσῶν τῶν τεσσαράκοντα ἡμερῶν παρέρχεται καὶ ἡ ν.· ἐὰν δὲ ἁμαρτημάτων ἀπεχώμεθα, καὶ τῆς ν. παρελθούσης ταύτης, ἐκείνη πάλιν μένει id.*stat*.16.6(2.168D–169A); μὴ διὰ τοῦτο χαίρειν, ὅτι ἐδαπανήθη τῆς ν. τὸ ἥμισυ, ἀλλ' ἐκεῖνο σκοπεῖν, εἰ τῶν ἁμαρτημάτων ἐδαπανήθη τὸ ἥμισυ *ib*.18.1(2.180B); **d.** other practices of abstinence and piety to accompany it τί δήποτε, εἴπερ τίμιος ὁ γάμος...οὐκ ἀφίησιν αὐτὸν χώραν ἔχειν ἐν τῷ τῆς ν. καὶ τῆς προσευχῆς καιρῷ; ὅτι τῶν σφόδρα ἀτόπων ἦν, Ἰουδαίους μὲν...ὡς μέλλοντας θείων ἀκούειν λόγων, ἀποστῆναι καὶ τῆς κατὰ νόμον μίξεως...ἡμᾶς δὲ...μηδὲ εἰς τὴν αὐτὴν ἀφικέσθαι...σπουδήν...οὐ χρὴ συνιέναι κατὰ τὸν τῆς ν. καιρόν...διὰ τοῦτο καὶ ἡ ν. καλόν, ὅτι περικόπτει τὰς τῆς ψυχῆς φροντίδας id.*virg*.30(1.290A–C); αἱ τῆς ν. ἡμέραι, καὶ οἱ σύλλογοι, καὶ αἱ διατριβαὶ αἱ κοιναί, καὶ τὰ ἄλλα ἃ παρ' ἐκείνης ἐκαρπούμεθα καλά id.*Anna* 1.1(4.699C); *ib*.(700D); **e.** effects on community ν. ... δημοσίᾳ δὲ πῶς τῷ βίῳ ἡμῶν ἐμπολιτεύεται; πᾶσαν ἀθρόως τὴν πόλιν, καὶ πάντα τὸν δῆμον μεθαρμόζει πρὸς εὐταξίαν, κοιμίζει κραυγήν...τίνος διδασκάλου παρουσία παίδων θόρυβον οὕτως...καθίστησιν, ὡς ἡ ν. παραφανεῖσα ταραχὴν πόλεως καταστέλλει; ποῖος κωμαστὴς ἐν ν. προῆλθε; ποῖος χορὸς ἀσελγὴς ἀπὸ ν. συνέστη; ἁπαλοὶ γέλωτες...ἐξαπίνης τῆς πόλεως ὑπεξέρχονται, ὥσπερ ὑπὸ δικαστοῦ τινος αὐστηροῦ τῆς ν. φυγαδευθεῖσαι Bas.*hom*.2.5(2.13D; M.31.192B); ν. πόλεως εὐσχημοσύνη, ἀγορᾶς εὐστάθεια, οἴκων εἰρήνη, σωτηρία τῶν ὑπαρχόντων...ὄψει τὴν πόλιν ἐκ ταραχῆς καὶ ζάλης εἰς γαλήνην βαθεῖαν μεταβαλοῦσαν *ib*.1.11(10B; M.184B); *ib*.2.6(14A; M.193A); **f.** fruits should be lasting μένωμεν...ἅπερ ὑπεδεξάμεθα τηροῦντες μετὰ ἀκριβείας, ἵνα καὶ τῆς ν. ἀπελθούσης ὁ τῆς ν. βρύῃ καρπός, καὶ διὰ τῶν ἀγαθῶν, ὧν ἐκαρπωσάμεθα ἀπὸ τῆς ν., καὶ αὐτῆς μνημονεύωμεν τῆς ν. Chrys.*stat*.18.1(2.180D); τοῦτο...ἐπὶ τῆς ν. ποιήσωμεν. καὶ γὰρ κατήχθη πρὸς ἡμᾶς ἡμέρας τεσσαράκοντα, ὑπεδεξάμεθα αὐτὴν φιλοφρόνως, καὶ ἀπεπέμψαμεν· ἐπεὶ οὖν μέλλομεν παρατιθέναι τράπεζαν νῦν πνευματικήν, ἀναμνησθῶμεν αὐτῆς, καὶ τῶν ἐξ αὐτῆς ...ἀγαθῶν. οὐ γὰρ δὴ παρουσία νηστείας μόνον, ἀλλὰ καὶ μνήμη νηστείας τὰ μέγιστα ὠφελῆσαι δύναιτ' ἂν id.*Anna* 1.1(4.699B); ἀπεθέμεθα τῆς ν. τὸ φορτίον, ἀλλὰ μὴ ἀποθώμεθα τῆς ν. τὸν καρπόν· ἔστι γὰρ φορτίον ἀποθέσθαι ν., καὶ καρπὸν δρέπεσθαι ν. ... ἀπῆλθεν ἡ ν., ἀλλὰ μενέτω ἡ εὐλάβεια· μᾶλλον δὲ οὐδὲ ἡ ν. ἀπῆλθεν...παρῆλθεν ἡ ν. ἡ σωματική, ἀλλ' οὐ παρῆλθεν ἡ ν. ἡ πνευματική id.*res.Chr*.1(2.437Aff.); Dor.*doct*.15.1(M.88.1789A); **g.** proper attitude to it ὁρῶ πολλοὺς μικροψύχως ἔχοντας, ὡς ἐν τῷ παρόντι περὶ τῆς μελλούσης μεριμνᾶν τεσσαρακοστῆς, καὶ πολλῶν ἤκουσα λεγόντων, ὅτι μετὰ τὴν τῆς ν. ἀπαλλαγὴν οὐκ αἰσθάνονται τῆς ἡδονῆς τῆς ἐκ τῆς ἀνέσεως διὰ τὴν φροντίδα τοῦ μέλλοντος ἐνιαυτοῦ...τί δὲ τὸ αἴτιον τούτου ἐστίν; ὅτι ν. παραγενομένης οὐχ ὅπως τὰ κατὰ ψυχὴν εὖ διατεθείη σπουδάζομεν, ἀλλ' ἐν τῇ τῶν σιτίων ἀποχῇ μόνον αὐτὴν ὁριζόμεθα. ὡς εἰ μέγα εἰς τὴν τῶν τρόπων διόρθωσιν ἀπ' αὐτῆς ἐκαρπωσάμεθα, κἂν ηὐξάμεθα καθ' ἑκάστην ἡμέραν παραγίνεσθαι τὴν ν. Chrys.*stat*.18.1(2.180E–181A); λέγω οὐκ ἀναγκάζων νηστεύειν, ἀλλὰ πείθων μὴ τρυφᾶν, μηδὲ κατὰ τοὺς πολλοὺς τῶν ἀνθρώπων διακεῖσθαι...οἳ καθάπερ ἐκ δεσμῶν ἀφεθέντες...λέγουσι· μόλις ποτὲ τὸ χαλεπὸν τῆς ν. διηνύσαμεν πέλαγος· ἄλλοι δὲ...καὶ ὑπὲρ τῆς μελλούσης δεδοίκασι τεσσαρακοστῆς. τοῦτο δὲ γίνεται ἐκ τοῦ τὸν ἄλλον ἅπαντα καιρὸν τρυφῇ...ἑαυτοὺς ἐκδιδόναι. ὡς εἴγε μεμελετήκειμεν τὰς ἄλλας ἡμέρας σεμνῶς...ζῆν, καὶ ἀπελθοῦσαν ἂν ἐποθήσαμεν τὴν ν., καὶ παραγίνεσθαι μέλλουσαν μετὰ πολλῆς ἂν ὑπεδεξάμεθα τῆς ἡδονῆς id.*Anna* 1.1(4.700A); **h.** comparison with various seasons: summer ἔχωμεν καὶ τὴν ν. ... σύμμαχον...καθάπερ οὖν...θέρους φανέντος, ἕλκει μὲν πρὸς τὸ πέλαγος τὸ πλοῖον ὁ ναύτης...καὶ γεωργὸς ἀκονᾷ δρέπανον...οὕτω...ἡμεῖς καθάπερ θέρους πνευματικοῦ τινος τῆς ν. φανείσης...ὡς γεωργοὶ τὴν δρεπάνην ἀκονήσωμεν id.*stat*.3.3(2.39A); winter ὑετῶν συνεχῶν καὶ ἐπαλλήλων ἀπελαύσαμεν ἐν τῷ χειμῶνι κατὰ τὸν τῆς ν. καιρὸν διηνεκοῦς μετασχόντες διδασκαλίας, καὶ σπέρματα ἐδεξάμεθα πνευματικά *ib*.18.1(180D); spring ἡδὺ τὸ τῆς ν. ἔαρ, ὅτι κύματα ἡμῖν, οὐχ ὑδάτων, ἀλλ' ἐπιθυμιῶν ἀλόγων καταστέλλειν εἴωθε, καὶ στέφανον ἡμῖν...τὸν ἀπὸ τῶν χαρίτων περιτίθησι τῶν πνευματικῶν...οὐχ οὕτω χελιδὼν φανεῖσα τὸν χειμῶνα ἀπελαύνειν εἴωθεν, ὡς ν. φανεῖσα τὸν χειμῶνα τῶν παθῶν τῆς διανοίας ἐκβάλλει id.*serm*.*1*.*1 in Gen*.(4.645B,C); **2.** regulations for observance; **a.** variations in length: originally lasting only during Holy Week, Iren.*ep.Vict*.ap.Eus.*h.e*.5.24.12,13(M.20.500A–504A); one day εἴ τις ἐν ἡμέρᾳ τοῦ πάσχα καὶ τῆς ν. ἐπισφαλῶς νοσηλευομένῳ προσέφερε τροφὴν Meth.*symp*.3.12(p.41.9; M.18.80B); general Lenten preparation dist. from Holy Week fast, cf. *sanctum jejunium exordientes die v Pharmuthi; et huic consequenter adjungentes sex illos dies... finem jejunii faciemus die decimo ejusdem Pharmuthi in Sancto hebdomadae Sabbato*, Ath.*ep.fest*.1.10(M.26.1366A); *quadragesimale tempus exordiemur die xiii mensis Phamenoth. deinde ex ordine jejunii abstinentiam prosequentes, sanctam Paschatis hebdomadam incipiemus die xviii mensis Pharmuthi: et die xxiii jejunia finientes*, *ib*.2.8(1371C); five days, Bas.*hom*.2.4(2.12D; M.31.189B); forty days, Chrys.*Anna* 1.1(4.699B); Pall.*v.Chrys*.9(p.56.7; M.47.32); **b.** discussion when Holy Week fast is to end ἐπεὶ μηδὲ τὰς ἓξ τῶν ν. ἡμέρας ἴσως μηδὲ ὁμοίως πάντες διαμένουσιν· ἀλλ' οἱ μὲν καὶ πάσας ὑπερτιθέασιν ἄσιτοι διατελοῦντες, οἱ δὲ δύο, οἱ δὲ τρεῖς, οἱ δὲ τέσσαρας, οἱ δὲ οὐδεμίαν. καὶ τοῖς μὲν πάνυ διαπονηθεῖσιν ἐν ταῖς ὑπερθέσεσιν, εἶτα ἀποκάμνουσι καὶ μόνον οὐκ ἐκλείπουσι, συγγνώμη τῆς ταχυτέρας γεύσεως Dion.Al.*ep.can*.(p.101.9; M.10.1277A); μηδ' ἑτέρᾳ προσήκειν παρὰ τὴν τῆς ἀναστάσεως...ἡμέρᾳ τὰς ν. ἐπιλύεσθαι Eus.*h.e*.5.23.1(M.20.492A); **c.** inconveniences resulting from different Easter dates ἀπρεπὲς κατὰ τὰς αὐτὰς ἡμέρας ἑτέρους μὲν ταῖς ν. σχολάζειν, ἑτέρους δὲ συμπόσια συντελεῖν, καὶ μετὰ τὰς τοῦ πάσχα ἡμέρας ἄλλους μὲν ἐν ἑορταῖς...ἐξετάζεσθαι, ἄλλους δὲ ταῖς ὡρισμέναις ἐκδεδόσθαι ν. Const.ap.Eus.*v.C*.3.18(p.86.12ff.; M.20.1077A); **d.** food not to be taken before evening, v. ἑσπέρα; **e.** summary of later local divergences τὰς πρὸ τοῦ πάσχα ν., ἄλλως παρ' ἄλλοις φυλαττομένας ἐστὶν εὑρεῖν· οἱ μὲν γὰρ ἐν Ῥώμῃ, τρεῖς πρὸ τοῦ πάσχα ἑβδομάδας, πλὴν σαββάτου καὶ κυριακῆς, συνημμένας νηστεύουσιν. οἱ δὲ ἐν Ἰλλυριοῖς καὶ ὅλῃ τῇ Ἑλλάδι, καὶ οἱ ἐν Ἀλεξανδρείᾳ, πρὸ ἑβδομάδων ἓξ τὴν πρὸ τοῦ πάσχα ν. νηστεύουσι, τεσσαρακοστὴν αὐτὴν ὀνομάζοντες. ἄλλοι δὲ παρὰ τούτους, ἄλλοι πρὸ ἑπτὰ τῆς ἑορτῆς ἑβδομάδων τῆς ν. ἀρχόμενοι, καὶ τρεῖς μόνας πενθημέρους ἐκ διαλειμμάτων νηστεύοντες... ἔστι δὲ εὑρεῖν οὐ μόνον περὶ τὸν ἀριθμὸν τῶν νηστείων διαφωνοῦντας, ἀλλὰ καὶ τὴν ἀποχὴν τῶν ἐδεσμάτων οὐχ ὁμοίαν ποιουμένους· οἱ μὲν γὰρ πάντῃ ἐμψύχων ἀπέχονται· οἱ δὲ τῶν ἐμψύχων ἰχθῦς μόνους μεταλαμβάνουσι. τινὲς δὲ σὺν τοῖς ἰχθύσι καὶ τῶν πτηνῶν ἀπογεύονται...ἕτεροι δὲ ἄχρις ἐννάτης ὥρας νηστεύοντες διάφορον ἔχουσι τὴν ἑστίασιν...τοιαύτη...περὶ νηστειῶν διαφωνία κατὰ τὰς ἐκκλησίας ἐστὶ Socr.*h.e*.5.22.32–41(M.67.632B–636A); **f.** later rationalization of its duration οἱ ἅγιοι ἀπόστολοι ἐβουλεύσαντο πρὸς βοήθειαν...τῶν ψυχῶν ἡμῶν...τὰς ἡμέρας τῆς ζωῆς ἡμῶν ἀποδεκατῶσαι...ἡγίασαν ἡμῖν ἀπὸ τῶν τριακοσίων ἑξήκοντα πέντε ἡμερῶν τοῦ ἐνιαυτοῦ, ταύτας ἑπτὰ ἑβδομάδας τῶν ν.· οὕτω γὰρ ἀφώρισαν ἑπτὰ ἑβδομάδας. ἀλλὰ οἱ πατέρες τῷ χρόνῳ συνεῖδον προστεθεῖναι αὐταῖς καὶ ἄλλην μίαν ἑβδομάδα, ἅμα μὲν διὰ τὸ προγυμνάζεσθαι, καὶ οἷον προομαλίζεσθαι τοὺς μέλλοντας εἰσελθεῖν εἰς τὸν κόπον τῶν ν., ἅμα δὲ καὶ τιμῶντες τὰς ν. τῷ ἀριθμῷ τῆς ἁγίας τεσσαρακοστῆς ἣν ἐνήστευσεν ὁ κύριος ἡμῶν. αἱ γὰρ ἑπτὰ ἑβδομάδες ὑφαιρουμένων τῶν σαββάτων καὶ τῶν κυριακῶν, τεσσαράκοντα ἡμέραι γίνονται, τιμωμένης καθ' ἑαυτὴν τῆς ν. τοῦ ἁγίου σαββάτου, διὰ τὸ εἶναι αὐτὴν ἱερωτάτην καὶ μόνην ν., ἀπὸ πάντων τῶν σαββάτων τοῦ ἐνιαυτοῦ Dor.*doct*.15.1(M.88.1788C); **g.** Lenten fast dist. from that of Holy Week φυλακτέα ἡ ν. τῆς τεσσαρακοστῆς, μνήμην περιέχουσα τῆς τοῦ κυρίου πολιτείας τε καὶ νομοθεσίας. ἐπιτελείσθω δὲ ἡ ν. αὕτη πρὸ τῆς ν. τοῦ πάσχα, ἀρχομένη μὲν ἀπὸ δευτέρας, πληρουμένη δὲ εἰς παρασκευὴν *Const.App*.5.13.3; τὴν δὲ τεσσαρακοστὴν τὴν πρὸ τῶν ἑπτὰ ἡμερῶν τοῦ ἁγίου πάσχα ὡσαύτως φυλάττειν εἴωθεν ἡ αὐτὴ ἐκκλησία ἐν νηστείαις διατελοῦσα, τὰς δὲ κυριακὰς οὐδ' ὅλως, οὔτε ἐν αὐτῇ τῇ τεσσαρακοστῇ· τὰς δὲ ἓξ ἡμέρας τοῦ πάσχα ἐν ξηροφαγίᾳ διατελοῦσι πάντες οἱ λαοί Epiph.*exp.fid*.22(p.523.18; M.42.828B); Anast.S.*qu.et resp*.64(M.89.664B); **h.** fast relaxed on Saturday and Sunday, Chrys.*hom*.*11*.*2 in Gen*.(4.84B); Roman custom of fasting on Saturday in Lent condemned ἐπειδὴ μεμαθήκαμεν ἐν τῇ Ῥωμαίων πόλει ἐν ταῖς...ν. τοῖς...σάββασι νηστεύειν παρὰ τὴν παραδοθεῖσαν ἐκκλησιαστικὴν ἀκολουθίαν, ἔδοξε τῇ ἁγίᾳ συνόδῳ, ὥστε κρατεῖν καὶ ἐπὶ τῇ Ῥωμαίων ἐκκλησίᾳ ἀπαρασαλεύτως τὴν κανόνα [sc. *Can.App*.64] τὸν λέγοντα· εἴ τις κληρικὸς εὑρεθείη...νηστεύων...τὸ σάββατον πλὴν τοῦ ἑνὸς καὶ μόνου, καθαιρείσθω CTrull.*can*.55; cf.Eus.Al.*serm*.1(M.86.313A); **i.** kept more strictly than other fasts, Nect.*Thdr*.9(M.39.1829A); μὴ θήσῃς νόμον ὥστε ἄλυτον ἔχειν τὴν ν., ἀλλὰ τὴν μὲν τεσσαρακοστὴν κτῆσαι ἑαυτῷ, καὶ μὴ χάριν παρουσίας φίλου λύσῃς τὴν ν. ὁ γὰρ τῆς τεσσαρακοστῆς κανὼν τοῖς πᾶσιν ἐπίκειται νηστεύειν· τὰς δὲ ἄλλας ἡμέρας τετράδας καὶ παρασκευὴν ἐπὶ φίλου μηδὲν διακρίνειν Eus.Al.*serm.*1(M.86.321D–324A); Dor.*doct.*15.2(M.88.1789B); **j.** alleviations εἰ δὲ ἀσθενές σοι τὸ σῶμα, ὥστε νηστεύειν διηνεκῶς, ἀλλ' οὐκ εἰς εὐχὴν ἀσθενές, οὐδὲ πρὸς ὑπεροψίαν γαστρὸς ἄτονον. εἰ γὰρ νηστεύειν οὐ δύνασαι, ἀλλὰ μὴ τρυφᾶν δύνασαι· οὐ μικρὸν δὲ καὶ τοῦτο, οὐδὲ πολὺ νηστείας ἀπέχον Chrys.*hom.57.4 in Mt.*(7.581D); cf.id.*hom.27.2 in Ac.*(9.207C,D).

D. Wednesday and Friday fasts; **1.** in gen., *Did.*8.1 cit. s. νηστεύω; *Const.App.*5.20.18; Eus.Al.*serm.*1(M.86.313A); **2.** reasons and regulations; myst. interprn., Clem.*str.*7.12(p.54.4; M.9.504B); τετράδι δὲ καὶ [ἐν] προσαββάτῳ ἐν ν. ἕως ὥρας ἐνάτης, ἐπειδήπερ ἐπιφωσκούσῃ τετράδι συνελήφθη ὁ κύριος καὶ τῷ προσαββάτῳ ἐσταυρώθη. καὶ παρέδωκαν οἱ ἀπόστολοι ἐν ταύταις νηστείας ἐπιτελεῖσθαι...οὐχ ἵνα χάριν ποιήσωμεν τῷ ὑπὲρ ἡμῶν πεπονθότι, ἡ ν. ἡμῖν προστέτακται, ἀλλ' ὅπως ὁμολογήσωμεν εἰς ἡμῶν σωτηρίαν ⟨γενόμενον⟩ τὸ τοῦ κυρίου πάθος...καὶ ὅπως ὑπὲρ τῶν ἡμῶν ἁμαρτιῶν αἱ ν. ἡμῖν εὐλόγιστοι θεῷ γένωνται. καὶ δι' ὅλου μὲν τοῦ ἔτους ⟨οὕτως⟩ ἡ ν. φυλάττεται ἐν τῇ...ἐκκλησίᾳ, φημὶ δὲ τετράδι καὶ προσαββάτῳ ἕως ὥρας ἐνάτης, δίχα μόνης τῆς πεντηκοστῆς ὅλης τῶν πεντήκοντα ἡμερῶν, ἐν αἷς οὔτε γονυκλισίαι γίνονται οὔτε ν. προστέτακται...ἔτι δὲ ἐν ταῖς ν' ἡμέραις ...τῆς πεντηκοστῆς οὐκ ἔστιν οὔτε ν. ... οὔτε ἐν τῇ ἡμέρᾳ τῶν ἐπιφανείων...ἔξεστι νηστεῦσαι, κἂν τε περιτύχῃ τετρὰς ἢ προσάββατον Epiph.*exp.fid.*22(pp.522.28–523.10; M.42.825B–828B); **3.** in monasteries τὰς δὲ καθολικὰς ν. ... μὴ ἐξὸν λύειν ἄνευ πάσης ἀνάγκης· ἐν γὰρ τετράδι ὁ σωτὴρ παρεδόθη, ἐν δὲ τῇ παρασκευῇ σταυροῦται. ὁ οὖν ταύτας λύων συμπαραδίδωσι τὸν σωτῆρα καὶ συσταυροῖ· ἀλλ' ἐὰν ἥκῃ πρὸς ὑμᾶς ἀδελφὸς ἀναπαύσεως δεόμενος ν. οὔσης, παραθήσεις αὐτῷ μόνῳ τὴν τράπεζαν ‡Pall.*h.mon.*8.58(p.48.21,24; M.34.1148B).

E. special fasts of Eastern Church defended ὑπεισῆλθέ τινας τῶν ἡμετέρων...οἳ...ἀναιδῶς διδάσκουσι μόνην εἶναι ν., ἔκ τε τῶν...πατέρων παραδεδομένην τὴν λεγομένην μεγάλην, τὴν δέ γε τῶν Χριστοῦ γέννων, ἣν καὶ τοῦ ἁγίου Φιλίππου τινὲς ὀνομάζουσι...καὶ τὴν πρὸ τῆς μνήμης τῶν ἁγίων...Πέτρου καὶ Παύλου, μὴ εἶναι, μήτε ἐξ ἀποστολικῆς καὶ πατρικῆς διαταγῆς, ἀλλὰ τινων εὑρέματα μοναχῶν...τῶν ταύτας...δύο νηστευόντων ν. ‡Anast.Ant.*serm.*4(M.89.1392A,B); regulations ἐνηστεύετο...ἡ τοιαύτη ν. [sc. after Pentecost] μέχρι τῆς κοιμήσεως τῆς θεοτόκου· ὑπὸ δὲ τῶν ἁγίων πατέρων δι' οἰκονομίαν ἐξεκόπη...ἐτυπώθη γάρ, ἄχρι τῆς ἑορτῆς τῶν ἁγίων ἀποστόλων νηστεύειν· εἶθ' οὕτως ἐπιλύειν· εἶτα ἀπ' ἀρχῆς Αὐγούστου νηστεύειν, ἄχρι τῆς κοιμήσεως τῆς θεοτόκου, καὶ πάλιν διαλύειν *ib.*(1397C); τὴν...ν. τῆς τοῦ Χριστοῦ γεννήσεως, τὰς τρεῖς ἡμέρας διαφυλαττέσθω τῆς ἑβδομάδος, ἤτοι β', δ', καὶ ς', ἰχθύας καὶ ἔλαιον, καὶ ν. ἐνθέως ποιείτω· ὡσαύτως καὶ τῶν... ἀποστόλων ποιείτω, καὶ τὴν τῆς θεομήτορος ἁγίαν ν. *Catech.Stud.*6(M.99.1696D–1697A); *Nomoc.*429–433; cf.*Const.Stud.*5(1696C,D).

F. other fasts; **1.** baptismal, Clem.*exc.Thdot.*84(p.132.20; M.9.696D); οὐκ ἔστι τοῦτο ν. βαπτίσματος, ὃ μὴ δι' αὐτὸ γέγονεν *Hom.Clem.*13.11; διαμείνωμεν τὴν σήμερον ἐν ν., καὶ αὔριον βαπτισθήσεται *ib.*13.12; **2.** eucharistic παρέμεινεν [sc. Thomas] τῇ ἑαυτοῦ ν., ἔμελλεν γὰρ ἡ κυριακὴ ἐπιφέρειν *A.Thom.*A 29(p.146.4); **3.** before ordination, Chrys.*hom.31.2 in Ac.*(9.242E); **4.** as eccl. penance, *Const.App.*2.16.2; *ib.*2.17.5.

G. heret. fasts; Montanist πλανῶνται, ν. καινὰς καὶ παραδόξους ὁρίζοντες Hipp.*haer.*10.25(p.282.21; M.16.3439C); Apollon.ap.Eus.*h.e.*5.18.2(M.20.476B); Thdt.*haer.*3.2(4.341); Messalian ν. δὲ οὐδ' ὅλως οἴδασιν Epiph.*haer.*80.3(p.488.4; M.42.761A); Thdt.*h.e.*4.11.7(3.967); dualist (Marcion, Valentinus, Manes) ἡ γὰρ ν. καὶ ἡ παρθενία οὔτε καλὸν καθ' ἑαυτό, οὔτε κακόν, ἀλλ' ἀπὸ τῆς τῶν μετιόντων προαιρέσεως ἑκάτερον γίνεται...ὑμεῖς δέ, ὅτι τῷ θεῷ μαχόμενοι καὶ διαβάλλοντες αὐτοῦ τὰ κτίσματα, οὐ μόνον ἀπέχετε τὸν μισθὸν ὑμῶν, ἀλλὰ καὶ κολασθήσεσθε Chrys.*virg.*4(1.271B); Eustathian ν. τε ἐν κυριακῇ ποιούμενοι καὶ τῆς ἁγιότητος τῆς ἐλευθέρας ἡμέρας καταφρονοῦντες καὶ τῶν ν. τῶν ἐν ταῖς ἐκκλησίαις τεταγμένων ὑπερφρονοῦντες CGangr.*ep.*(H.1.531A); Eudoxian ὅτι τῆς τετράδος καὶ παρασκευῆς τὴν ν. ὁ Φιλοστόργιός φησι οὐκ ἐν μόνῃ τῇ τῶν κρεῶν ἀποχῇ περιορίζεσθαι, ἀλλὰ καὶ τὸ μηδὲ τροφῆς ὅλως ἅπτεσθαι μέχρι τῆς ἑσπέρας κανονίζεσθαι Philost.*h.e.*10.12(M.65.592C).

H. Jewish fasts τὴν τῆς ν. καὶ νουμηνίας εἰρωνείαν *Diogn.*4.1; Just.*dial.*40.4(M.6.564A); *ib.*46.2(573B); ὅσοι τὴν ν. τὴν Ἰουδαϊκὴν ὡς μὴ νοοῦντες τὴν τοῦ ἱλασμοῦ ἡμέραν τηρεῖτε [τὴν] μετὰ τὴν Ἰησοῦ Χριστοῦ ἐπιδημίαν, οὐκ ἠκούσατε τοῦ ἱλασμοῦ κεκρυμμένως Or.*hom.12.13 in Jer.*(p.100.15; M.13.397A); ref. Pr.10:3, Ps.36:25, Am.8:11 ἀπὸ μέντοι τῆς ἐν τῷ κρυπτῷ ν. φυλαξώμεθα, περὶ ἧς καὶ ὁ προφήτης ἀπεύχεται λέγων·...μὴ ἔλθῃ καὶ ἐφ' ἡμᾶς ἡ τοῖς Ἰουδαίοις ἀπειληθεῖσα ν. Bas.*hom.*2.8(2.15E–16A; M.31.197A); εἰ δὲ ὅτε τοὺς συνδούλους ἔτυπτες, βδελυκτή σου ἦν ἡ ν., ὅτε τὸν δεσπότην κατέσφαξας, τότε σου προσδεκτὴ ἡ ν. γίνεται; Chrys.*Jud.*1.2(1.590A); *ib.*2.1(601B); ref. Ac.23:14 ἰδοὺ ν. ἀνδροφονίας μήτηρ id.*hom.49.2 in Ac.*(9.366D).

***νηστευτής, ὁ,** *one who fasts*, Bas.*hom.*1.6(2.5D; M.31.172D); Chrys.*hom.2.2 in Tit.*(11.739D); ‡Chrys.*hom.*3(13.209B); τῆς τοῦ ν. οἰκίας ἀγγέλους εἶναι φύλακας Ast.Am.*hom.*14(M.40.373A); Jo.Mosch.*prat.*174(M.87.3041D); as nickname of an ascetic, *Apophth.Patr.*(M.65.177C); of John IV CP, †Jo.Jej.*poenit.*tit.(M.88.1890); ‡Jo.Jej.*can.*(p.432); Thphn.*chron.*p.213(M.108.544B).

***νηστευτικός,** *given to fasting*, Philost.*h.e.*10.12(M.65.592C).

νηστεύ-ω, *fast, abstain*;

A. in gen.; **1.** reasons for fasting; **a.** Passion of Christ διὰ τοῦτο ∼ομεν, ὅτι τὸν ἀμνὸν τὸν ἡμέτερον, λοιδορίαι καὶ ῥαπίσματα...καθύβρισαν Gr.Nyss.*paup.*1(M.46.456D); ἐγὼ...ὁ Χριστιανός, καὶ τοῦ σταυρωθέντος δοῦλος, ν. καλῶς, εἴτε πρὸς τὴν ἐλπίδα τῆς ἀναστάσεως ἐμαυτὸν ἐκκαθαίρων, εἴτε ἐπιστυγνάζων ὡς φιλοδέσποτος δοῦλος τοῖς τοῦ κυρίου μου πάθεσι Ast.Am.*hom.*14(M.40.385D); μνημόνευσον...ῥητοῦ τοῦ Μωσαϊκοῦ τοῦ λέγοντος, τῇ δεκάτῃ τοῦ ἑβδόμου μηνὸς χρῆναι ν. δηλοῖ γὰρ ὁ ἕβδομος μὴν τὴν ἑβδόμην ἡμέραν· ἡ δὲ δεκάτη ἡμέρα, τὴν δεκάτην ὥραν, ἐν ᾗ ὁ κύριος ἐπὶ τοῦ σταυροῦ ἀφῆκε τὸ πνεῦμα *ib.*(388B); **b.** for benefit of the poor, *Const.App.*5.1.3; **2.** right dispositions μέλλων τοίνυν ν., μὴ σκυθρωπάσῃς Ἰουδαϊκῶς, ἀλλ' εὐαγγελικῶς σεαυτὸν καταφαίδρυνον· μὴ πενθῶν τῆς γαστρὸς τὴν ἔνδειαν, ἀλλὰ συνηδόμενος τῇ ψυχῇ τῶν πνευματικῶν ἀπολαύσεων Bas.*hom.*2.3(2.12C; M.31.189A); *ib.*2.4(13B; M.192A); Chrys.*stat.*3.3(2.40A,B); τὸν ∼οντα κατεσταλμένον εἶναι χρή, ἡσύχιον, ἥμερον, ταπεινὸν id.*hom.8.6 in Gen.*(4.63C); **3.** bodily fasting to be supported by moral and spiritual fasting, Sever.*creat.*1.7(M.56.437); *ib.*(438); σῶμα ∼ον ἁγιάζεται, ψυχὴ μὴ τρεφομένη φθείρεται. γένοιτο δὲ τὸ μὲν σῶμα ν. ἀπὸ ἁμαρτημάτων, τὴν δὲ ψυχὴν ἐντρυφᾶν τοῖς θείοις δόγμασιν *ib.*; ∼εις; δεῖξόν μοι διὰ τῶν ἔργων αὐτῶν. ... ἐὰν ἴδῃς πένητα, ἐλέησον· ἐὰν ἴδῃς ἐχθρόν, καταλλάγηθι...μὴ γὰρ δὴ στόμα ∼έτω μόνον, ἀλλὰ καὶ ὀφθαλμός, καὶ ἀκοή...καὶ πάντα τὰ τοῦ σώματος ἡμῶν μέλη κτλ. Chrys.*stat.*3.4(2.41D); θέλεις ∼σαι καλῶς; δίδαξον ∼ειν τὴν γλῶσσαν καὶ τοὺς ὀφθαλμοὺς καὶ τὰς χεῖρας καὶ τοὺς πόδας Eus.Al.*serm.*1(M.86.320C,D); τί σοι ὄφελον ∼σασθαι; δίδαξον καὶ ὅλον τὸ σῶμά σου, καὶ τὴν ψυχὴν καὶ τὸ πνεῦμα *ib.*(321A); χρήζομεν δὲ μὴ μόνον τὴν δίαιταν ἑαυτῶν φυλάττειν, ἀλλὰ καὶ πάσης ἄλλης ἁμαρτίας ἀπέχεσθαι, ἵνα ὥσπερ ∼ομεν τῇ κοιλίᾳ, οὕτως ν. καὶ τῇ γλώττῃ, ἀπεχόμενοι ἀπὸ καταλαλίας ...ὁμοίως ∼ειν τοῖς ὀφθαλμοῖς τὸ μὴ βλέπειν μάταια Dor.*doct.*15.4(M.88.1792D); **4.** spiritual fasting possible without bodily fast ὥσπερ, ὅτε ἐνηστεύετε, ἔλεγον ὑμῖν ὅτι ἐστὶ ∼οντα μὴ νηστεύειν, οὕτω καὶ νῦν λέγω ὅτι ἐστὶ μὴ ∼οντα ν. ... πῶς ἔστι ∼οντα μὴ ν.; ὅταν τις...τροφῆς μὲν ἀπολαύῃ, ἁμαρτίας δὲ μὴ γεύηται Chrys.*res.Chr.*(2.437B–438A); cf. ὁ...ν. μὴ δυνάμενος, δαψιλεστέραν τὴν ἐλεημοσύνην ἐπιδεικνύσθω, εὐχὰς ἐκτενεῖς id.*hom.10.2 in Gen.*(4.73A); **5.** effects; **a.** aid to prayer, *Const.App.*5.20.17; ὁ ∼ων κοῦφός ἐστι καὶ ἐπτερωμένος, καὶ μετὰ νήψεως εὔχεται, καὶ τὰς ἐπιθυμίας σβέννυσι τὰς πονηράς Chrys.*hom.57.4 in Mt.*(7.581B); ∼οντος προσευχή, νεοσσὸς ἀετοῦ ἀνιπτάμενος...∼οντος νοῦς, ἀστὴρ ἐν αἰθρίᾳ λαμπρὸς Nil.*spir.mal.*1(M.79.1145B); **b.** restoration to paradise, Bas.*hom.*1.4(2.3C; M.31.168B) **c.** union with Christ, *ib.*2.4(12E; M.189C); **d.** effect on outward appearance ∼οντος σεμνὸν τὸ χρῶμα, οὐκ εἰς ἐρύθημα ἀναιδὲς ἐξανθοῦν ...ὀφθαλμὸς πραΰς...πρόσωπον σύννουν *ib.*1.9(7D; M.177B); **e.** in working of miracle ∼σας Ἠλίας ἀπέκλεισε τὸν οὐρανὸν Bas.*hom.*2.6(2.14D; M.31.193B); **6.** various aspects: as sign of repentance, Or.*hom.20.9 in Jer.*(p.191.25; M.13.521B); undertaken for persecutors, *Did.*1.3; privacy in fasting impossible for bishop, cf.Hipp.*trad.ap.*25.2; advisability of fasting in temptations, Chrys.*hom.31.2 in Ac.*(9.243E); as universal obligation, Ast.Am.*hom.*14(M.40.376B); false pretence of fasting οἶδα πολλούς, οὐχὶ ∼οντας καὶ ἐπιδεικνυμένους μόνον, ἀλλὰ καὶ μὴ ν., καὶ τὰ τῶν ∼όντων προσωπεῖα περικειμένους, καὶ ἀπολογίαν χείρονα τῆς ἁμαρτίας προβαλλομένους. ἵνα γὰρ μὴ σκανδαλίσω, φησί, τοὺς πολλούς, τοῦτο ποιῶ Chrys.*hom.20.1 in Mt.*(7.259B,C); enjoined esp. on women, cf. χῆραι καὶ παρθένοι πολλάκις ∼έτωσαν Hipp.*trad.ap.*25.1; τὰς γυναῖκας ἁρμόζῃ ἵνα πάντοτε ∼ωσι ‡Ath.*exhort.*2(M.28.1112A); γυναιξὶ δὲ ὥσπερ τὸ ἀναπνεῖν, οὕτω καὶ τὸ ν. οἰκεῖόν ἐστι καὶ κατὰ φύσιν Bas.*hom.*2.2(2.11E; M.31.188B).

B. ref. fasting of Christ εἰ μηδὲν εἰλήφει παρὰ τῆς Μαρίας...οὐδ' ἂν εἰς τεσσαράκοντα ἡμέρας, ὁμοίως ὡς Μωϋσῆς καὶ Ἠλίας, ∼σας ἐπείνησε Iren.*haer.*3.22.2(M.7.957A); ἀπ' ἐξουσίας μετὰ τὸ βάπτισμα ∼ει ὡς κύριος Ἰωάννου· ὁ δὲ εἰς τὸν αὐτοῦ μυούμενος πρότερον ὀφείλει ∼σαι καὶ τότε βαπτίσασθαι *Const.App.*7.22.6; διὰ δὴ τοῦτο καὶ αὐτὸς ∼ει τεσσαράκοντα ἡμέρας, ἡμῖν τὰ φάρμακα τῆς σωτηρίας δεικνύς, καὶ οὐ προέρχεται περαιτέρω, ὥστε μὴ πάλιν τῇ ὑπερβολῇ τοῦ θαύματος ἀπιστηθῆναι τῆς οἰκονομίας τὴν ἀλήθειαν Chrys.*hom.13.2 in Mt.*(7.169B).

C. fasting as special feature of ascetic life, ref. consecrated virgins, Ath.*virg.*6(p.40.12; M.28.257C); ∼σον ὅλον τὸν ἐνιαυτὸν χωρὶς πάσης ἀνάγκης· ὥρᾳ δὲ ἐνάτῃ...μεταλάμβανε τὸν ἄρτον σου ἐν λαχάνῳ ἀναπεποιημένῳ ἐλαίῳ *ib.*8(p.43.1; 261B); προαιρέσει δὲ ἀγαθῇ οἱ...ἀσκηταὶ διὰ παντός, χωρὶς κυριακῆς καὶ πεντηκοστῆς, ν. ... τὰς δὲ κυριακὰς ἁπάσας τρυφερὰς ἡγεῖται ἡ...ἐκκλησία...οὐ ν. ⟨δὲ⟩· ἀνακόλουθον γάρ ἐστιν ἐν κυριακῇ ν. Epiph.*exp.fid.*22(p.523.13ff.; M.42.828B); κάτοπτρον κάλλιστον τῇ...παρθένῳ τὸ ν., ἐν τούτῳ γὰρ καὶ θεὸν κατοπτρίζεται Nil.*epp.*1.163(M.79.148D).

D. fasting in Lent and Holy Week; **1.** gen. obligation, Ath.*ep. encycl.*4(p.173.13; M.25.232A); μηδεὶς ἑαυτὸν ἔξω ποιείτω τοῦ καταλόγου τῶν ∼όντων...ἄγγελοί εἰσιν οἱ καθ' ἑκάστην ἐκκλησίαν ἀπογραφόμενοι τοὺς ν. Bas.*hom.*2.2(2.11C; M.31.185D–188A); ἕκαστος γὰρ Χριστιανὸς ὑπόκειται ν. ἐν ταῖς ἡμέραις τῆς τεσσαρακοστῆς· ὀφείλουσιν δὲ ν. ὡς ταγμάτων μοναχῶν, οὕτω καὶ τῶν λαϊκῶν Eus.Al.*serm.*1(M.86.316A); together with Wednesday and Friday fasts εἴ τις ἐπίσκοπος, ἢ πρεσβύτερος...τὴν ἁγίαν τεσσαρακοστὴν οὐ ν., ἢ τετράδα ἢ παρασκευήν, καθαιρείσθω, ἐκτὸς εἰ μὴ δι' ἀσθένειαν σωματικὴν ἐμποδίζοιτο· ἐὰν δὲ λαϊκὸς ᾖ, ἀφοριζέσθω *Can.App.*69; **2.** reasons; **a.** for its duration τίνος οὖν ἕνεκεν ∼ομεν...τὰς τεσσαράκοντα ταύτας ἡμέρας; πολλοὶ τὸ παλαιὸν τοῖς μυστηρίοις προσῄεσαν ἁπλῶς καὶ ὡς ἔτυχε, καὶ μάλιστα κατὰ τὸν καιρὸν τοῦτον, καθ' ὃν ὁ Χριστὸς αὐτὰ παρέδωκε. συνειδότες οὖν οἱ πατέρες τὴν βλαβὴν τὴν γινομένην ἐκ τῆς ἠμελημένης προσόδου, συνελθόντες ἐτύπωσαν ἡμέρας τεσσαράκοντα νηστείας, εὐχῶν Chrys.*Jud.*3.4(1.611C); **b.** for abstinence during Holy Week παρήγγειλεν...ν. τὰς ἓξ ἡμέρας ταύτας διὰ τὴν τῶν Ἰουδαίων δυσσέβειαν *Const.App.*5.14.20; ἂν οὖν ἔρηταί σε Ἰουδαῖος καὶ Ἕλλην, τίνος ἕνεκεν ∼εις, μὴ εἴπῃς, ὅτι διὰ τὸ πάσχα, μηδὲ ὅτι διὰ τὸν σταυρόν...οὐ γὰρ διὰ τὸ πάσχα ∼ομεν, οὐδὲ διὰ τὸν σταυρόν, ἀλλὰ διὰ τὰ ἁμαρτήματα τὰ ἡμέτερα, ἐπειδὴ μέλλομεν μυστηρίοις προσιέναι· ἐπεὶ τό γε πάσχα οὐ νηστείας ἐστὶν...ἀλλ'...χαρᾶς ὑπόθεσις Chrys.*Jud.*3.4(1.611E); **c.** evidence for this view ὁ γοῦν κατηχούμενος οὐδέποτε πάσχα ἐπιτελεῖ, καίτοι ∼ων κατ' ἐνιαυτόν, ἐπειδὴ προσφορᾶς οὐ κοινωνεῖ, ὥσπερ οὖν καὶ ὁ μὴ ν., ἂν μετὰ καθαροῦ προσέλθῃ συνειδότος, πάσχα ἐπιτελεῖ *ib.*3.5(612B); **3.** regulations for Holy Week fast ἐν ταῖς ἡμέραις οὖν τοῦ πάσχα ∼ετε, ἀρχόμενοι ἀπὸ δευτέρας μέχρι τῆς παρασκευῆς καὶ σαββάτου, ἓξ ἡμέρας, μόνῳ χρώμενοι ἄρτῳ καὶ ἁλὶ καὶ λαχάνοις καὶ ποτῷ ὕδατι...τὴν μέντοι παρασκευὴν καὶ τὸ σάββατον ὁλόκληρον ∼σατε, οἷς δύναμις πρόσεστιν τοιαύτη, μηδενὸς γευόμενοι μέχρις ἀλεκτοροφωνίας νυκτός· εἰ δέ τις ἀδυνατεῖ τὰς δύο συνάπτειν ὁμοῦ, φυλασσέσθω κἂν τὸ σάββατον *Const.App.*5.18.1,2; *ib.*5.19.2.

E. ref. Wednesday and Friday fast αἱ δὲ νηστεῖαι ὑμῶν μὴ ἔστωσαν μετὰ τῶν ὑποκριτῶν. ∼ουσι γὰρ δευτέρᾳ σαββάτων καὶ πεμπτῇ· ὑμεῖς δὲ ∼σατε τετράδα καὶ παρασκευήν *Did.*8.1; τετράδα καὶ παρασκευὴν ∼οντες...εἴ τις κυριακὴν ἢ σάββατον ν., πλὴν ἑνὸς σαββάτου [τοῦ πάσχα], οὗτος Χριστοκτόνος ἐστίν ‡Ign.*Phil.*13; τετράδα δὲ καὶ παρασκευὴν προσέταξεν ἡμῖν ν., τὴν μὲν διὰ τὴν προδοσίαν, τὴν δὲ διὰ τὸ πάθος *Const.App.*5.14.20; *ib.*5.20.18; ἡ ἐκκλησία τὴν τετράδα φυλάττει διὰ τὴν τοῦ κυρίου σύλληψιν, ∼ουσα δι' ὅλου τοῦ ἔτους πάρεξ μόνον πεντηκοστῆς καὶ ἐπιφανίων Epiph.*ep.fr.*(p.206.4); Friday because of Crucifixion, *ib.*(p.207.15); Socr.*h.e.*7.22.3(M.67.785A); Soz.*h.e.*7.19.9(M.67.1477C).

F. Sunday fasting forbidden, CGangr.*can.*18; *Const.App.*5.20.19; Epiph.*exp.fid.*22(p.523.13; M.42.828B); to which Saturday was added later, cf. σάββατον καὶ κυριακὴν μὴ ∼σῃς ‡Ath.*syntag.*2.13(p.123; M.28.840A); Eus.Al.*serm.*1(M.86.324A).

G. fasting after octave of Pentecost μετὰ οὖν τὸ ἑορτάσαι ὑμᾶς τὴν πεντηκοστὴν ἑορτάσατε μίαν ἑβδομάδα, καὶ μετ' ἐκείνην ν. μίαν· δίκαιον γὰρ καὶ εὐφρανθῆναι...καὶ ν. μετὰ τὴν ἄνεσιν *Const.App.*5.20.14.

H. fasting before baptism πρὸ δὲ τοῦ βαπτίσματος προνηστευσάτω ὁ βαπτίζων καὶ ὁ βαπτιζόμενος καὶ εἴ τινες ἄλλοι δύνανται· κελεύεις δὲ ∼σαι τὸν βαπτιζόμενον πρὸ μιᾶς ἢ δύο *Did.*7.4; cf.*Const.App.*7.22.4,6; ὅσοι ποτὲ βαπτισθῆναι θέλετε, ἀπὸ τῆς αὔριον ν. ἄρξασθε *Hom. Clem.*4.73; *ib.*11.35; *ib.*13.9.

I. at ordination, Chrys.*hom.27.2 in Ac.*(9.217C).

J. *abstain (from)* ἐὰν μὴ νηστεύσητε τὸν κόσμον, οὐ μὴ εὕρητε τὴν βασιλείαν τοῦ θεοῦ *Agraph.*48(p.68); οἱ τοῦ κόσμου ∼οντες Clem.*str.*3.15(p.242.2; M.8.1200B); *ib.*7.12(p.54.7; M.9.504B).

νήστης, *fasting, Asen.*13(p.57.16); Pall.*v.Chrys.*16(p.95.23; M.47.54); ref. fasting Communion as unwritten tradition, ‡Jo.D.*Const.*5(M.95.320B).

νηστικός (A), *fasting* ἅγια θυσιαστηρίου, εἰ μὴ ἀπὸ ν. ἀνθρώπων, μὴ ἐπιτελεῖσθαι ἐξῃρημένης μιᾶς ἐτησίας ἡμέρας, ἐν ᾗ τὸ κυριακὸν δεῖπνον ἐπιτελεῖται *Cod.Afr.*41; CTrull.*can.*29; τὸ κοινωνεῖν νηστικόν as one of unwritten traditions of Church, Anast.S.*hod.*1(M.89.40C).

νηστικός (B), *of* or *for spinning* ἡ ν. [sc. τέχνη] *the art of spinning*, Or.*Cels.*4.76(p.346.17; M.11.1148C).

νήστιμος, *of* or *belonging to a fast*, Thphl.Al.*theoph.*(M.65.33B).

[*]**νηφάλαιος,** v. νηφάλιος.

νηφαλέος, = νηφάλιος; **1.** of persons, *temperate, sober, A.(Pass.) Andr.*12(p.28.6); **2.** of things, *sober* ἔξοδον...ν. ... ἔχουσα *A.Jo.*69(p.184.10); v.l. for νηφαλίου, Cyr.H.*catech.*4.1.

***νηφαλεόω,** *waken, rouse*, Thdr.Stud.*epp.*1.37(M.99.1041A).

νηφαλέως, *soberly, with a sober mind*, Didym.*Trin.*2.27(M.39.765B); ref. prayer, Mac.Aeg.*hom.*33.1(M.34.741B); ref. behaviour in church, *Const.App.*2.57.13.

νηφάλιος (νηφάλαιος), 1. *without wine, temperate*, Clem.*prot.*12(p.84.9; M.8.240B); ν. ποτὸν...ὕδωρ id.*paed.*2.2(p.167.20; M.8.409A); *ib.*2.4(p.182.7; 440C); Or.*Jo.*10.12(10; p.183.5; M.14.328B); πνευματικοῦ...πιεῖν οἴνου, καὶ μεθυσθῆναι μέθην ν. Mac.Aeg.*carit.*15(M.34.921A); **2.** *sober*, opp. drunken, Thdt.*1Tim.*3:11(3.656); -αιος id. *qu.10 in Lev.*(1.188); **3.** τὸ ν. *temperance*, Clem.*paed.*2.9(p.206.21; M.8.493C); **4.** *sober-minded* ν. φρονήματι θεοῦ γνῶσιν ἀναλαβεῖν Eus. *d.e.*10.8(p.473.9; M.22.761B); χρεία...ν. διανοίας Cyr.H.*catech.*4.1; Nil.ap.Proc.G.*Cant.*4:13–15(M.87.1673B); Cyr.*Lc.*6:41(M.72.604A); **5.** *vigilant, alert*, Ephr.1.100F; -αιος id.1.221C; ν. ... τουτέστι, διορατικόν,...ὀξὺ βλέποντα Chrys.*hom.10.1 in 1Tim.*(11.599B).

***νηφαλιότης, ἡ,** *vigilance, perspicacity*, Constantius Imp.ap.Ath. *h.Ar.*23(p.195.26; M.25.720C); Ephr.1.94F; †Gr.Thaum.*ep.Philagr.*(M.46.1101A).

***νηφόντως, 1.** *soberly*, Gr.Nyss.*Eun.*1(1 p.197.16; M.45.444B); Isid.Pel.*epp.*1.392(M.78.404A); Jo.Clim.*scal.*1(M.88.641B); **2.** *vigilantly, alertly*, Ephr.1.272E; †Bas.*hom.in Ps.*37(1.362B; M.30.81D); Chrys.*hom.27.4 in Heb.*(12.251B).

νήφ-ω, 1. *be temperate, drink no wine* ὅμοιον ποιεῖν τὸν διδάσκαλον [sc. Christian], ⟨ὡς⟩ εἴ τις μεθύων εἰς μεθύοντας παριὼν κακηγορεῖ τοὺς ∼οντας ὡς μεθύοντας Cels.ap.Or.*Cels.*3.76(p.268.13; M.11.1020C); met. ∼ε ὡς θεοῦ ἀθλητής Ign.*Polyc.*2.3; τοῦ διὰ τὴν κακίαν μεθυσθέντος καὶ τὸ ν. ἀπολωλεκότος Or.*Jo.*6.58(37; p.166.22; M.14.300C); **2.** *be sober, sober-minded*, Meth.*symp.*8.13(p.97.14; M.18.160A); Gr.Nyss.*or.catech.*39(p.155.14; M.45.100B); Cyr.*Ps.*35:12(M.69.921C); **3.** *recover one's senses, become sane*, Or.*Cels.*8.66(p.282.6; M.11.1616A); *A.Thom.*A 63(p.180.10); *Hom.Clem.*11.3; Call *v.Hyp.*(p.88); **4.** *be sane*, Phot.*nomoc.*13.30(M.104.965A); **5.** *be vigilant, alert* ∼οντες πρὸς τὰς εὐχάς Polyc.*ep.*7.2; ∼ωμεν ἐπὶ τὸ ἀγαθόν *2Clem.*13.1; Ephr.1.94F; *Const.App.*2.20.5; περὶ τὰ τοιαῦτα ∼οντες *ib.*2.50.3; ν. ἐν κυρίῳ *ib.*3.6.5; Chrys.*stat.*4.1(2.50C); ν. εἰς τὰ ἔργα *Apophth.Patr.*(M.65.101A); Thdt.*Cant.*7:2–5(2.145).

νήχ-ομαι, *swim*; met., *be tossed about* μίαν οὐκ ἔχουσι τὴν γνώμην, ἀλλὰ ποικίλαις...∼ονται μεταβολαῖς Ath.*syn.*14(p.241.30; M.26.705B); Cyr.*Ag.*11(3.639B); id.*apol.Thdt.*4(p.125.5; 6^1.218E); Andr. Caes.*Apoc.*55.19(M.106.392D).

νῆψις, ἡ, 1. *sobriety, temperance*, Chrys.*hom.18.2 in Jo.*(8.106B); id.*hom.13.3 in 1Tim.*(11.621B); *ib.13.4*(622D); **2.** *sobriety, sober-mindedness*, Meth.*symp.*11(p.129.17; M.18.205A); Mac.Aeg.*hom.*4.2(M.34.473B); Cyr.*Ps.*37:11(M.69.964A); id.*Jo.*1.2(4.15A); **3.** plur., *sober counsels*, id.*ador.*6(1.199E); id.*Am.*59(3.316C); **4.** *recovery of senses*, Isid.Pel.*epp.*1.240(M.78.329C); Cyr.*Lc.*6:37(M.72.600B); **5.** *vigilance, alertness*, Ath.*decr.*1(p.1.3; M.25.416A); Ephr.1.237E; as monastic virtue, id.1.479D; Chrys.*sac.*6.8(p.155.8; 1.427D); Cyr. *Abac.*17(3.532C).

[*]**νίβω,** v. νίπτω.

νικ-άω, A. *conquer*; **1.** in gen., ref. meaning of name Israel ἄνθρωπος ∼ῶν δύναμιν· τὸ γὰρ ἴσρα ἄνθρωπος ∼ῶν ἐστι, τὸ δὲ ἢλ δύναμις Just.*dial.*125.3(M.6.765D); **2.** of Christ's victory παθεῖν ὑπέμεινεν, ἵνα ἀποθανὼν καὶ ἀναστὰς νικήσῃ τὸν θάνατον id.*1apol.*63.16(M.6.425B); ἥνωσεν οὖν...τὸν ἄνθρωπον τῷ θεῷ· εἰ γὰρ μὴ ἄνθρωπος ἐνίκησε τὸν ἀντίπαλον τοῦ ἀνθρώπου, οὐκ ἂν δικαίως ἐνικήθη ὁ ἐχθρός Iren.*haer.*3.18.7(M.7.937A); τοῦ λόγου...συγγινομένου τῷ ἀνθρώπῳ ἐν τῷ ν. *ib.*3.19.3(941A); βούλεται...∼ῆσαι θάνατον Clem.*prot.*1(p.6.30; M.8.60B); Or.*engast.*6(p.289.2; M.12.1020D); ὁ κύριος, ἡ ἀφθαρσία ∼ήσασα τὸν θάνατον Meth.*symp.*3.7(p.34.25; M.18.72B); Cosm.Ind. *top.*2(M.88.124B); κύριε...νίκα *Inscr.*(*Hesp.*16 p.49, Athens [post saec. vi]); the Temptations, Or.*hom.32 in Lc.*(p.193.1); **3.** of victory over spiritual enemies οὗτος τὸ ἀγαθὸν ποιῶν ∼ᾷ τὸ κακόν *T.Benj.*4.3; συμπαλαίσαντες τῷ διαβόλῳ ἐνίκησαν αὐτόν Herm.*sim.*8.3.6; ἄνθρωποι...θανάτῳ τῷ διὰ πίστεως τὸν θάνατον νενικήκασιν... δυνατὸν δὲ παντὶ τῷ νενικημένῳ πάλιν ∼ᾶν, τοῦ θανάτου τὴν σύστασιν παραιτούμενον Tat.*orat.*15(p.17.6,9; M.6.840B); ἐὰν ἐθέλῃς μόνον νενίκηκας τὴν ἀπώλειαν Clem.*prot.*12(p.83.24; M.8.240A); τοῦ...κατ' ἀρετὴν ~ῶντος id.*str.*1.24(p.100.14; M.8.908A); ref. proverbial sporting expression ἐκεῖνος 'ἄνδρας νικᾷ' ὁ γάμῳ...καὶ τῇ τοῦ οἴκου προνοίᾳ...ἀλυπήτως ἐγγυμνασάμενος...ἀδιάστατος τῆς τοῦ θεοῦ γενόμενος ἀγάπης *ib.*7.12(p.51.6; M.9.497C); ~άτω γὰρ ἡ πίστις πάντῃ Meth. *symp.*8.4(p.85.10; M.18.144B); ψυχὴ ~ῶσα τὰ πάθη *ib.*9.4(p.118.9; 185A); **4.** νίκα and νικᾷ in special cases; **a.** of Const.'s vision τούτῳ νίκα Eus.*v.C.*1.28(p.21.17; M.20.944B); Socr.*h.e.*1.2.7(M.67. 37A); **b.** in acclamations νικᾷ ἡ πίστις τῆς τριάδος...νικᾷ ἡ πίστις τῆς Αὐγούστας *Libell.*ap.CCP(518)*act.*(*ACO* 3 p.72.10ff.; H.2.1333D); νικᾷ Ἰουστῖνος CTyr.(518)*act.*(*ACO* 3 p.87.4; H.2.1356E); *ib.*(p.88.27; 1357E); νικᾷ ἡ πίστις τοῦ βασιλέως CCP(536)*act.*4(*ACO* 3 p.181.26; H.2.1261D); **c.** watchword in rebellion against Justn. in 532, hence τὸ Νίκα...ἐπίκλησιν καλοῦσιν Evagr.*h.e.*4.13(p.163.11; M.86.2728A); *Chron.Pasch.*p.336(M.92.873A); Thphn.*chron.*p.154(M.108.417A).

B. *excel, surpass* τοῖς ἰδίοις βίοις ~ῶσι τοὺς νόμους *Diogn.*5.10; ~ῶμεν ἐκεῖνον...τῇ πονηρίᾳ τὸν πλούσιον Bas.*hom.*21.8(2.169B; M.31. 553B); ἀνθρώπους θηρίων ὠμότητα ~ῶντας Chrys.*hom.19.9 in Mt.*(7. 258C); τὸν κακίᾳ νικήσαντα πάντας ἀνθρώπους Νέρωνα *ib.33.4*(383A); ὁ πάντας ἀσεβείᾳ νικήσας Ἰουλιανός *ib.43.3*(462E); θεὸς...τὴν ἀνθρώπου φύσιν ~ῶν, ~ήσει πάντως αὐτὴν καὶ περὶ τὸν τοῦ γεννᾶν τρόπον Cyr.*thes.*6(5[1].43E).

C. *exceed* λοιδορίᾳ...~ώσῃ τὸ μέτριον Didym.*Trin.*2.8(M.39.613D); Chrys.*stat.*21.1(2.214A); id.*hom.3.3 in Eph.*(11.20D); ἀριθμὸν ~ῶντας Thdt.*Os.*1:10(2.1317); id.*haer.*5.11(4.425).

D. *prevail over, overcome* τὴν ψυχὴν ἡμῶν ~ήσωμεν *2Clem.*16.2; Clem.*prot.*4(p.44.34; M.8.156A); Thdt.*Ps.*18:13(1.723); pass. c. genit. κλέπτης ἦν, κτεάνων ~ώμενος Nonn.*par.Jo.*12:6(M.43.852A).

E. *prevail* to, *succeed* in after a struggle ἐνίκησε σκορπίσαι *Pss. Sal.*4.13.

F. *get the better of*, hence *do away with, annul*, Thdt.*Jer.*27:18 (2.531); ~ῆσαι ἄρα φιλονεικοῦσι τοῦ πατρὸς τὴν προσφωνίαν κτίσμα τὸν υἱὸν προσαγορεύειν τολμῶντες id.*haer.*5.2(4.384).

νίκη, ἡ, 1. *victory*; **a.** Christ's Χριστὸν...κατὰ τοῦ θανάτου νίκας ἐπιδειξάμενον Ath.*inc.*29.1(M.25.145B); λαβὼν τὴν κατὰ τῶν ἀντικειμένων δαιμόνων ν. *ib.*37.5(160D); Eus.*v.C.*1.32(p.22.25; M.20.948B); id.*l.C.*18(p.259.24; M.20.1440B); Chrys.*coemet.*2(2.400C); τὴν ν. τοῦ δευτέρου Ἀδάμ Cosm.Ind.*top.*2(M.88.121C); ἀνέστην...τὴν ν. ἔχων κατὰ τοῦ θανάτου, καὶ πάσῃ τῇ ἀνθρωπείᾳ φύσει πρόξενος τῆς ν. γεγένημαι, δι' ἐμοῦ εἰς πᾶσαν τὴν ἀνθρωπότητα τῆς ν. διαδραμούσης *ib.*(124B); *CIG* 8922 (Antioch); **b.** in spiritual warfare ἔργον δὲ τὸ ἀγώνισμα καὶ τέλος ἡ ν. Clem.*str.*1.8(p.26.8; M.8.736B); ἀθλητὴς ἀληθῶς ὁ ἐν τῷ μεγάλῳ σταδίῳ, τῷ...κόσμῳ τὴν ἀληθινὴν ν. κατὰ πάντων στεφανούμενος τῶν παθῶν *ib.*7.3(p.14.24; M.9.424C); οὗτος νόμος τῆς ἐν Χριστιανοῖς ν., καὶ ὁ ἔλαττον ἔχειν καταδεξάμενος στεφανοῦται Bas.*ep.*191(3.284B; M.32.701B); ἐν τῷ παθεῖν κακῶς ἡ ν. Chrys.*hom.33.2 in Mt.*(7.380B); *ib.84.4*(802D); **c.** in acclamations τὴν ν. τοῦ Αὐγούστου CTyr.(518)*act.*(*ACO* 3 p.86.24; H.2.1356C); *ib.* (p.89.5; 1360B); **2.** *superiority, gaining of advantage* τὴν ἐν τοῖς φιλικοῖς ἧτταν νίκης ἔχειν δύναμιν Bas.*ep.*65(3.158A; M.32.421B); Marc. Er.*opusc.*3.3(M.65.969A); *ib.*3.4(1021B); **3.** *advantage, gain* ἱερεῖς οἱ ζητοῦντες ν. ἐνταφιασμοῦ *Nomoc.*85.

νικητήριος, *of* or *belonging to victory*; neut. plur. as subst.; **1.** *reward* or *prize of victory*, in spiritual warfare αἱ...παρθενεύσασαι τῷ Χριστῷ τὰ ν. φέρονται τῶν ἄθλων Meth.*symp.*8.2(p.83.11; M.18. 141A); Bas.*hom.in Ps.*28(1.116C; M.29.288A); of crown of martyrdom, Eus.*h.e.*4.16.1(M.20.364B); **2.** *victory*, id.*v.C.*2.6(p.44.4; M.20. 988A); *ib.*2.23(p.50.19; 1000D); Bas.*hom.*12.10(2.106C; M.31.408A); Gr.Nyss.*hom.12 in Cant.*(M.44.1017D); **3.** *memorial of victory*, Eus. *v.C.*3.50(p.98.26; M.20.1109B); **4.** sing. as subst., *conqueror*, Thdr. Stud.*epp.*2.18(M.99.1173B).

νικητής, ὁ, *conqueror*; **1.** in gen. νικηταὶ τῆς πλάνης *M.Ner.et Ach.*14(p.13.29); **2.** as imperial title αὐτοκράτορι καίσαρι σεβαστῷ ν. τροπαιούχῳ [i.e. Domitian: perh. late passage] *A.Jo.*3(p.152.23); devised by Const., Eus.*v.C.*2.19(p.48.22; M.20.996B); ν. Κωνσταντῖνος μέγιστος σεβαστός Const.*ib.*2.24(p.51.3; M.20.1001B); Eus.*h.e.* 10.9.6(M.20.904A); Κωνστάντιος ν. αὔγουστος Constantius Imp.ap. Ath.*apol.sec.*51(p.132.11; M.25.341A); **3.** of Christ, Const.ap.Gel. Cyz.*h.e.*2.7.19(M.85.1236C); νικητῇ γὰρ ἀκολουθεῖς βασιλεῖ, τῆς νίκης αὐτοῦ βουλομένῳ σε γενέσθαι κοινωνόν Bas.*inst.ascet.*2(2.200E; M.31. 624A); **4.** of victors in spiritual warfare, ref. Const.'s title ν. δὲ ἡδονῶν...ν. ἐτύμως ὁ τὴν νίκην τῶν καταπαλαιόντων θνητὸν γένος παθῶν ἀράμενος Eus.*l.C.*5(p.204.16; M.20.1336C); of writers as conquerors of opposing vices, Gr.Nyss.*v.Mos.*(M.44.332A); *Const.App.* 2.14.6; Ἰὼβ ν. τοῦ...ὄφεως *Lit.*ap.*Const.App.*8.12.23.

νικητικός, *of victory, victorious* ν. τρόπαιον Eus.*l.C.*6(p.212.6; M. 20.1352A); Thdr.Stud.*epp.*1.22(M.99.977A); ἀπόλλυσι τὸ παρθενικὸν μέρος τὸν ν. στέφανον *ib.*1.50(1096B); neut. as subst. τὸ...κατὰ τῶν ἐχθρῶν ν. Eus.*p.e.*1.4(10A; M.21.36D).

νικητικῶς, *as a victor* ν. στεφανοῦντές σε Isid.Pel.*epp.*1.75(M.78. 236A).

νικηφόρος, A. *victorious*; **1.** in gen., of Const. πανταχοῦ...ν. ὁ βασιλεὺς ἀνεδείκνυτο Thdt.*h.e.*1.25.13(3.812); of Ath., *ib.*1.30.11 (820); **2.** of Christ κάλλιστον θέαμα τῷ πατρὶ υἱὸς ἀΐδιος ν. Clem. *prot.*12(p.85.23; M.8.244A); διὰ ξύλου ν. εὑρίσκεται Hipp.*cant.Mos.* (p.83.15; M.10.612A); ὁ στρατηλάτης ἡμῶν ὁ ἅγιος καὶ ν. *A.Thom.*A 39(p.157.11); πορεύεται ν. καὶ τροπαιοφόρος μετὰ τοῦ ἐκ νεκρῶν ἀναστάντος σώματος Or.*Jo.*6.56(37; p.164.29; M.14.297B); ἐπειδὴ κατάρας ἦν ἡ ἄκανθα γεώργιον, ἣν ἡ γῆ κατεδικάσθη μετὰ τὴν...παράβασιν,...τούτου χάριν ἀκάνθας ὡς ν. ἐστεφανώσατο, ὥσπερ οἱ δόκιμοι ποιοῦσι τῶν νικητῶν, αὐτὸ τὸ ὅπλον...θριαμβεύοντες, δι' οὗ τὴν νίκην εἰργάσαντο Isid.Pel.*epp.*1.95(M.78.248C); ref. Ascension ὡς ἐν θριάμβῳ ν. ἀναφερόμενος Cosm.Ind.*top.*2(M.88.121D); **3.** of Christians as included in Christ's victory, Or.*schol.in Cant.*7:1(M.17. 281A); **4.** of martyrs, *Ep.Lugd.*ap.Eus.*h.e.*5.1.55(M.20.429B); Eus. *h.e.*8.6.4(752C); Gr.Naz.*carm.*1.2.10.743(M.37.734A); τὸν ν. ἀγωνιστήν [sc. Petr. I Al.] Thdt.*h.e.*1.2.8(3.725); *ib.*3.10.2(923); of S. Paul γενναίου...παλαιστοῦ καὶ ν. Isid.Pel.*epp.*1.212(M.78.317A); **5.** of victors in spiritual warfare, likened to victorious athletes, Clem.*str.* 2.20(p.173.16; M.8.1056A); id.*ecl.*28(p.145.23; M.9.713A); id.*q.d.s.*3 (p.162.7; M.9.608B); Didym.*Trin.*3.1(M.39.776C); ἡμᾶς ἄγγελοι νικηφόρους ἰδόντες Mac.Mgn.*apocr.*2.7(p.5.9); **6.** of Church ἐκκλησίαν ...ν. ... πάσης τῆς τῶν ἑτεροδόξων ἀσεβεστάτης ἐπαναστάσεως Alex. Al.*ep.Alex.*53(p.28.12; M.18.568C); **7.** of things ν. ... βοαῖς Meth. *symp.*11(p.135.2; M.18.212A); ν. εἰκόνας καὶ στήλας Chrys.*exp.in Ps.* 3(5.1A); ν. ... στεφάνοις Thdt.*Ps.*50:7(1.937); ν. τέλος Eustrat.*stat. anim.*11(p.398).

B. as subst., *victor*, Geo.Pis.*Heracl.*1.217(M.92.1315A).

***Νικολαΐτης, ὁ,** *Nicolaitan*, member of licentious early Gnost. sect said by some to have been founded by Nicolas of Antioch (Ac.6:5), cf.Apoc.2:6,15; cf. *Nicolaitae autem magistrum habent Nicolaum unum ex vii..., qui indiscrete vivunt. plenissime...per ...Apocalypsim manifestantur qui sint, nullam differentiam esse docentes in moechando, et idolythyton edere*, Iren.*haer.*1.26.3(M.7. 687A); ass. Cerinthus, cf.*ib.*3.11.1(880A); οἱ φάσκοντες ἑαυτοὺς Νικολάῳ ἕπεσθαι, ἀπομνημόνευμά τι τἀνδρὸς φέροντες ἐκ παρατροπῆς τὸ δεῖν παραχρῆσθαι τῇ σαρκί Clem.*str.*2.20(p.177.2; M.8.1061B); sexual licentiousness, *ib.*3.4(p.207.18ff.; 1129B); Hipp.*haer.*7.36(p.223.7; M. 16.3343B); ἡ λεγομένη τῶν Ν. αἵρεσις Eus.*h.e.*3.29.1(M.20.276C); ass. Barbeloite Gnostics and 'Προύνικος', Epiph.*haer.*25.2(pp.268–9; M. 41.321C–324D); οἱ δὲ ἀναίδην ἐκπορνεύουσιν, οἷοι οἱ νῦν ψευδώνυμοι *N. Const.App.*6.8.2; φεύγετε καὶ τοὺς ἀκαθάρτους Ν., τοὺς ψευδωνύμους, τοὺς φιληδόνους, τοὺς συκοφάντας· οὐ γὰρ ἦν τοιοῦτος ὁ τῶν ἀποστόλων Νικόλαος ‡Ign.*Trall.*11; Thdt.*haer.*3.1(4.340).

***νικοποιέω,** *bring victory*, Ephr.3.372D.

νικοποιός, 1. of God; *causing, giving victory* τῷ ν. τε καὶ ἀγωνοθέτῃ τῆς νίκης ἀναθεὶς τὰς ἐλπίδας Gr.Nyss.*Eun.*3(2 p.1.15; M. 45.573A); Epiph.*haer.*64.63(p.500.15; M.41.1177B); **2.** of Christ as giver of victory in spiritual warfare, ‡Meth.*palm.*1(M.18.384B); τροπαιοφόρος ἀθλητὴς...δεξιᾷ νικοποιῷ στεφθησόμενος Jo.Mon.*hymn. Geo.*9(M.96.1400D); **3.** of Cross βασιλεὺς [sc. Const.]...τῇ τοῦ ν. σταυροῦ ὁμολογίᾳ λαμπρυνόμενος Eus.*v.C.*1.41(p.26.27; M.20.956B); τὸ ν. ἀνεκήρυττεν σημεῖον id.*l.C.*9(p.219.13; M.20.1365A); Ἰακὼβ προσεκύνησεν ἐπὶ τὸ ἄκρον τῆς ῥάβδου...ἐκμηνύων...τὸν ν. ... σταυρόν ‡Ath.*proph.*1(M.28.1064B); **4.** ref. Ps.4:1 tit. τοῦτον τὸν ψαλμὸν μετὰ τὸ νικῆσαι...ἀνατίθησι τῷ ν. ἀντὶ τοῦ, εἰς τὸ τέλος, ὁ Ἀκύλας καὶ ὁ Θεοδοτίων, τῷ ν., ἡρμήνευσαν· ὁ δὲ Σύμμαχος, ἐπινίκιον †Ath.*exp. Ps.*4:1(M.27.72B); Cyr.*Ps.*4:1(M.69.733A); Thdt.*Ps.*4:1(1.629).

νῖκος, τό, 1. *victory* (tr. לַמְנַצֵּחַ) ψαλμὸς τῷ Σαλωμὼν εἰς ν. *Pss. Sal.*8.1; of BMV χαίροις τὸ ν. τοῦ βασιλέως τε καὶ θεοῦ Ephr.3.534F; **2.** εἰς ν. *utterly*, hence *for ever* (tr. נֵצַח), cf.*T.Dan* 5.10; ἄχρι τέλους τὴν αὐτὴν...ἐπιδειξάμενοι γνώμην· τὸ γάρ, ἐφύλαξεν εἰς ν., τοῦτο λέγει Thdr.Mops.*Am.*1:11–12(M.66.252D); interpreted as meaning *to victory*, Cyr.*Ps.*48:9–11(M.69.1069D); Olymp.*fr.Lam.*5:10(M.93.761B); cf.Meth.*res.*1.44(p.292.2; M.18.273A).

[*]**νικοφόρος,** for νικηφόρος, metri gr., *IGC As.Min.*104[Ephesus].

νίμ(μ)α, τό, 1. *water that has been used for washing*, Dor.*doct.*1. 17(M.88.1640B); **2.** *washing* of disciples' feet, †Cyr.*hom.div.*10(5[2]. 376E).

νιπτήρ, ὁ, 1. *basin* for washing; **a.** in gen. ν. τῶν ποδῶν *T.Job* 25 (p.118.19); Pall.*h.Laus.*55(p.148.20; M.34.1244A); *Apophth.Patr.*(M.

65.301C); **b.** at church door δύο ν. εἰσι πρὸ τῶν πυλῶν τῆς ἐκκλησίας· μία τοῦ ὕδατος, ἐν ᾗ νίπτεις τὰς χεῖρας, καὶ μία ἡ χεὶρ τοῦ πένητος, ἐν ᾗ ἀποσμήχεις τὴν ψυχήν σου ‡Chrys.*eleem.*2(9.792A); **2.** name of episode of washing of disciples' feet (Jo.13), Eutych.*pasch.*1(M.86.2392A); περὶ τοῦ ν. Cosm.Ind.*top.*5(M.88.292C); ‡Germ.CP *contempl.*(M.98.396B); **3.** name of ceremony of foot-washing on Maundy Thursday, *Euchol.*(p.591).

***νιπτικός,** *for washing* ὕδωρ νιπτικὸν τῶν ὀμμάτων Gr.Nyss.*hom. 13 in Cant.*(M.44.1060A).

***νιπτοποδέω,** *have one's feet washed,* Rom.Mel.(*SBBAW* 1901 p.740).

νίπτρον, τό, *wet cloth, Euchol.*(pp.656,659).

νίπτ-ω ([*]νίβω), **I.** *wash* hands or other parts of body (but not the whole [λούω]);

A. lit.; **1.** in gen. τὸ πρόσωπόν σου ~ων *A.Jo.*29(p.166.29); ~ε τεὸν ῥέθος Nonn.*par.Jo.*9:7(M.43.825A); **2.** of washing of disciples' feet by Christ, cf.Iren.*haer.*4.22.1(M.7.1046B); τοὺς πόδας ἔνιπτεν αὐτῶν...ὁ ἄτυφος θεὸς καὶ κύριος τῶν ὅλων, οὐκ ἀργυροῦν δὴ ποδονιπτῆρα περιφέρων ἀπ' οὐρανοῦ Clem.*paed.*2.3(p.179.30; M.8.436B); cf.Or.*hom.8.5 in Jud.*(p.514.15; M.12.985B); id.*Cels.*2.7(p.133.4; M.11.804C); id.*Jo.*32.6ff.(5; p.434.27ff.; M.14.756Aff.); *ib.*32.7(6; p.436.30; 760A) cit. s. ποῦς; ὁ θεὸς ὁ πλάστης, ὁ πλάσας ἀπὸ χοὸς ἄνθρωπον ἐν χάριτι, αὐτὸς ~ει τοὺς πόδας τοῦ ἑαυτοῦ πλάσματος Ephr.3.423B; Chrys.*hom.70.2 in Jo.*(8.416A); Cyr.*Jo.*9(4.726A) cit. s. ποῦς; Ammon.*Jo.*13:4(M.85.1481B); related to baptism, Or.*Jo.*32.7(6; p.436.17; 757C) cit. s. πούς; **3.** med., in Peratic conjurings τῷ γὰρ λέβητι τῆς πίσσης ὡς ἐμβράσσοντι καθίησι τὰς χεῖρας...φθάνει δὲ καὶ τὰς χεῖρας πολλάκις ἅλμῃ νιψάμενος δι' ὃ οὐ πάνυ τι καίει, κἂν ἀληθῶς ζέῃ Hipp.*haer.*4.33(p.59.18; M.16.3098A); before eating, *A.Jo.*6 (p.154.20); after meal, *Apophth.Patr.*(M.65.137B); Dor.*doct.*1.17(M.88.1640B); before morning prayer, *Const.App.*8.32.18; in healing, *A.Thom.*A 52(p.168.22); ref. fasting before Communion ἐὰν...νιβομένου εἰσέλθῃ ὕδωρ ἐν τῷ στόματι,...μὴ ἀποστραφῇ τῆς κοινωνίας *Nomoc.*505; **4.** of ritual washings; **a.** Jewish, of priest before sacrificing πρὸ τοῦ εἰσελθεῖν σε εἰς τὰ ἅγια, λούου· καὶ ἐν τῷ θύειν σε, νίπτου· καὶ ἀπαρτίζων πάλιν τὴν θυσίαν, νίπτου *T.Lev.*9.11; **b.** Christian, of priest before anaphora ἑωράκατε τοίνυν τὸν διάκονον τὸν νίψασθαι διδόντα τῷ ἱερεῖ, καὶ τοῖς κυκλοῦσι τὸ θυσιαστήριον τοῦ θεοῦ πρεσβυτέροις. ... σύμβολόν ἐστι τοῦ δεῖν ὑμᾶς καθαρεύειν πάντων ἁμαρτημάτων ...τὸ νίψασθαι. ἐπειδὴ γὰρ αἱ χεῖρες σύμβολον πράξεως· ⟨τῷ⟩ νίψασθαι ταύτας, τὸ καθαρὸν...τῶν πράξεων αἰνιττόμεθα Cyr.H.*catech.*23.2; cf. *Lit.*ap.*Const.App.*8.11.12; Dion.Ar.*e.h.*3.2(M.3.425D); *ib.*3.3.10(437D); ‡Germ.CP *contempl.*(M.98.424C); before beginning service, *Lit. Chrys.*(p.356.5); of people before entering church, as sign of cleansing of soul by prayer, Nil.*epp.*1.24(M.79.89D); **c.** ref. washing of Pilate's hands in token of innocency τῶν δὲ Ἰουδαίων οὐδεὶς ἐνίψατο τὰς χεῖρας, οὐδὲ Ἡρώδης οὐδὲ [ε]ἷς [τ]ῶν κριτῶν αὐτοῦ. κ[αὶ μὴ] βουληθέντων νίψασθαι ἀνέστη Πειλᾶτος *Ev.Petr.*1(p.202); *A.Pil.* B 9.4(p.301); παρὰ δὲ τὰ νῦν ἔθη Ῥωμαίων ἐνίψατο τὰς χεῖρας, ἴσως Ἰουδαϊκὸν ἔθος ποιῶν Or.*comm.ser.124 in Mt.*(p.259.19); *Const.App.* 5.19.4.

B. met., of penitential tears τούτῳ τῷ ὕδατι, ὁ χοῦς ~εται Ephr. 3.368E; of cleansing of soul from sin, Bas.*hom.*1.2(2.2C; M.31.165A).

II. *wash off,* met. μετανοίῃ ἀμπλακίας ~οντες Nonn.*par.Jo.*3:23 (M.43.769C).

***νίτρος, ἡ,** *tax on nitre,* Epiph.*haer.*76.1(p.341.13; M.42.516D).

νιτρόω, *cleanse with nitre*; pass., Synes.*ep.*44(M.66.1368D).

νιτρώδης, *impregnated with nitre, nitrous,* ‡Paul.Sil.*therm.Pyth.* 113(M.86.2265).

νιφάς, ἡ, *snowflake*; hence *thick shower,* met. ὅρκων τὰς ν. Chrys. *stat.*4.6(2.58B); βελῶν...ν. id.*sac.*6.12(p.168.7; 1.433D); ν. λυπηρῶν id. *hom.15.3 in Mt.*(7.188A); πειρασμῶν ν. *ib.33.7*(387A); ν. γραμμάτων Constantius Ant.*ep.*3(M.52.745); λίθων ν. Thdt.*h.e.*5.4.9(3.1021).

νίψις, ἡ, *washing*; **1.** of Christ's washing of disciples' feet οἱ μὲν οὖν πολλοὶ καὶ μετὰ τὸ λουτρὸν κονιορτοῦ τῶν ἁμαρτημάτων πληροῦνται κατὰ τὴν κεφαλὴν...οἱ δὲ γνησίως τῷ Ἰησοῦ μαθητευθέντες...μόνους τοὺς πόδας δεομένους ἔχουσιν τῆς ὑπὸ τοῦ λόγου ν. Or.*Jo.*32.2(p.427.18; M.14.744A); *ib.*32.4(p.432.27; 752C); *ib.*32.7(6; p.436.16; 757C); καὶ ἅγιον ὄντα ἐνδέχεται δεῖσθαι τῆς ν. τῶν ποδῶν *ib.*32.12(7; p.444.15; 769D); *ib.*32.13(8; p.446.8; 773B); **2.** of washing of celebrant's hands at eucharist, referred to Jo.13:10, Dion.Ar.*e.h.*3.3.10(M.3.440A); ἡ δὲ ν. τῶν χειρῶν, ἀντὶ τοῦ νίψαντος, καὶ 'ἀθῷός εἰμι' φωνήσαντος. καθ' ἡμᾶς δὲ τοὺς ἱερεῖς δηλοῖ, ἵνα καθαριεύοντες τὸ συνειδός, νοῦν καὶ διάνοιαν, ἅτινά εἰσι χεῖρες τῶν...ψυχῶν,...προσίωμεν τῇ ἁγίᾳ τραπέζῃ ‡Germ.CP *contempl.*(M.98.424C).

***νοβελ(λ)ήσιμος, *νοβελ(λ)ίσιμος,** v. *νωβελ(λ)ίσ(σ)ιμος.

***Νοέμβριος,** (Lat. *Novembris*) *of November, A.Andr.*A 19(p.57.22); *A.Andr.*B 11(p.64.6); *M.Das.*12.1; βαπτισθέντος αὐτοῦ [sc. Χριστοῦ] κατ' Αἰγυπτίους Ἀθὺρ δωδεκάτῃ...πρὸ ἓξ εἰδῶν Ν. Epiph. *haer.*51.16(p.270.15; M.41.920A); Socr.*h.e.*5.18.14(M.67.613A); Jo. Mal.*chron.*11 p.279(M.97.421A); Thphn.*chron.*p.45(M.108.169B).

***νοερητόκος,** *parent of intellectual things,* Synes.*hymn.*3.167(p.12; M.66.1596).

***νοερηφόρος,** *bearing towards intelligible, spiritual things,* Synes. *hymn.*1.121(p.63; M.66.1592).

***νοερόομαι,** *be inspired* ἐκ θεοῦ νοὸς ἡμῖν νοερωθεῖσα [sc. ψυχή] Anast.S.*serm.imag.*3(M.89.1165A).

νοερός, I. *intellectual* (often scarcely to be dist. from *spiritual* (v. II infra); hence often joined with λογικός, λογικός meaning strictly *rational, intellectual,* ν. (more widely), *belonging to the unseen, intellectual,* or *spiritual order*; sometimes equivalent to πνευματικός);

A. τὸ ν. *intellectual part* of man, in tripartite division (cf. Plato *Rep.*441A) τὸ ν., ὃ δὴ λογιστικὸν καλεῖται Clem.*paed.*3.1(p.236.4; M.8.556A); ὁ...ὄφις...διαβιβρώσκων τὸ ν. *ib.*3.2(p.238.28; 561A); μεταρσίῳ πτερῷ τὸ ν. ἐπερείσαντες Eus.*l.C.*proem.(p.196.5; M.20.1317C); Ath.*v.Anton.*20(M.26.873A); ‡Bas.*const.*2.1(2.541B; M.31.1340A); καταμιχθέντα δὲ πρὸς ἑκάτερον τούτων, πρός τε τὸ αἰσθητὸν... καὶ τὸ ν. τοῦ ἀνθρωπίνου συγκρίματος Gr.Nyss.*or.catech.*16(p.70.12; M.45.52B); id.*Eun.*12(1 p.361.13; M.45.1084C); theory that possession of τὸ ν. or τὸ λογικόν constitutes divine image in man refuted, Thdr.Mops.ap.Thdt.*qu.20 in Gen.*(1.31); ὁ θεὸς τῇ φύσει ἐνέπηξε τῇ ν. τοῦ ἀνθρώπου οὐσίᾳ τὸ κατ' εἰκόνα αὐτοῦ...ἵν' ἅπερ ἐστὶν ὁ θεὸς τῇ φύσει, ταῦτα κατὰ τὴν αὐτοῦ χάριν ἔχειν δυνηθῇ καὶ ὁ...ἄνθρωπος, τοῦτ' ἔστι τὸ ν. αὐτοῦ Gel.Cyz.*h.e.*2.15.8(M.85.1260A).

B. *intelligent, rational*; **1.** in gen. ἀριθμὸν...ν. οὐσιῶν Or.*princ.*2.9.1(p.164.2; M.11.225C); Eus.*p.e.*11.20(541C; M.21.901B); λόγος... ἀρχιερεὺς πάσης ν. καὶ λογικῆς κτίσεως id.*d.e.*1.10(p.47.4; M.22.89A); id.*e.th.*1.8(p.66.34; M.24.837D); δυνάμει ν. καὶ λογικῇ τὰς κατ' εἰκόνα ...πεποιημένας ψυχὰς ν. καὶ λογικὰς ἀπειργάζετο *ib.*1.20(p.81.31; 868A); †Ath.*exp.fid.*3(M.25.204C); τὴν λογικὴν ψυχήν, πνεῦμα οὖσαν ν. ‡Just.*qu.Gr.*2(M.6.1469C); Dion.Ar.*d.n.*4.1(M.3.693B); **2.** of the will αὐτεξουσιότης ἐστὶ νοῦς κατὰ φύσιν κινούμενος ἢ νοερὰ τῆς ψυχῆς κίνησις αὐτοκρατής Clem.*fr.*40(p.220.17; M.9.752B); ψυχῆς νοερᾶς αὐτεξούσιος κίνησις ‡Ath.*serm.fid.*(M.26.1292D)ap.*Doct.Patr.* 40(p.298.18); ἡ δὲ λογικὴ καὶ ν. φύσις, ἐὰν τὸ κατ' ἐξουσίαν ἀπόθηται, καὶ τὴν χάριν τοῦ ν. συναπώλεσεν Gr.Nyss.*or.catech.*31(p.113.13,14; M.45.77C); **3.** of actions, *intelligent,* Or.*fr.81 in Lam.*(p.266.20; M.13.645D); **4.** of man's nature, *rational* (but freq. combined with notion of man as a spiritual being, v. infra) ὁ...τοῦ θεοῦ λόγος, ὁ τῆς ἐν ἀνθρώποις λογικῆς καὶ ν. πατὴρ οὐσίας Eus.*l.C.*4(p.202.32; M.20.1333A); τῇ τῶν ἀνθρώπων λογικῇ καὶ ν. δυνάμει id.*d.e.*1.10(p.44.18; M.22.85A); Gel.Cyz.*h.e.*2.15.8(M.85.1260A); **5.** of human soul; **a.** in gen. τοῖς...τὴν ψυχὴν ἢ τὸν νοῦν (εἴτε πνευματικὸν τοῦτον ἐθέλουσι καλεῖν εἴτε πνεῦμα ν. ἅγιον καὶ μακάριον εἴτε ψυχὴν ζῶσαν εἴτε θείας ...φύσεως ἔκγονον...) τοῖς τοῦτο ἐλπίζουσιν ἕξειν αἰώνιον σὺν θεῷ, τούτοις διαλέξομαι Cels.ap.Or.*Cels.*8.49(p.264.7; M.11.1589A); Or. *mart.*47(p.42.30; M.11.629B); ἄφθαρτον γὰρ φύσιν πεποίηκε τὴν ν. καὶ αὐτῷ συγγενῆ, καὶ οὐκ ἀποκλείεται ὥσπερ ἐπὶ τῆς ἐνταῦθα ζωῆς ἡ λογικὴ ψυχὴ τῆς θεραπείας id.*princ.*3.1.13(p.218.11; M.11.273A); Eus.*v.C.*4.64(p.144.18; M.20.1220B); id.*l.C.*5(p.205.31; M.20.1340A); τὴν ν. τοῦ ἀνθρώπου φύσιν, ἥτις νοεῖται ψυχή ‡Ath.*Apoll.*2.8(M.26.1144C); οὐδὲ γὰρ ἐπὶ τῆς ἡμετέρας ζωῆς ἐντὸς κατακλείεται τῶν τῆς σαρκὸς ὅρων ἡ ν. φύσις Gr.Nyss.*or.catech.*10(p.54.13; M.45.41C); id. *Apoll.*8(M.45.1140B); **b.** of Christ's human soul ψυχῆς ν. ἐστερημένην αὐτῷ σάρκα διδούς [sc. Ἄρειος], φύσει παθητὸν αὐτὸν δείκνυσι ‡Ath. *serm.fid.*(M.26.1292D)ap.*Doct.Patr.*40(p.298.13); μορφὴ τοῦ δούλου, ἡ ν. τῆς ἀνθρώπων συστάσεως φύσις σὺν τῇ ὀργανικῇ καταστάσει ‡Ath. *Apoll.*2.1(M.26.1133A); ἄνθρωπος γέγονε...κατὰ πρόσληψιν πάσης τῆς ἀνθρωπείας φύσεως, τουτέστι ψυχῆς λογικῆς καὶ ν. καὶ σαρκὸς ἀνθρωπίνης Photinus et al.*ep.*ap.Epiph.*haer.*72.12(p.266.19; M.42.400A); Gr.Nyss.*Apoll.*35(M.45.1201A–C); ὁ...λόγος...ἥνωσεν ἑαυτῷ σῶμα ἐμψυχωμένον ψυχῇ ν. ... ἑνοῦντες...τῇ ἁγίᾳ σαρκὶ ψυχὴν ἐχούσῃ τὴν ν. ... τὸν ἐκ θεοῦ...λόγον Cyr.*ep.*45(p.153.3; 5^2.136E); ἐμψυχωμένον... ψυχῇ λογικῇ καὶ ν. Vict.*Mc.*7:32(p.339.2); εἴ τις λέγει, ὅτι οὐχ ὁ λόγος ...σαρκωθεὶς σαρκὶ ἐμψυχωμένῃ ψυχῇ λογικῇ καὶ ν. κατελήλυθεν...ἀ. ἔ. CCP(543)*anath.*9(Hahn p.229); **6.** of the cosmos (Stoic), cf.Clem. *str.*8.2(p.82.6; M.9.564A); denied by Aristotle, Cyr.*Juln.*2(6^2.60B).

C. *intellectual* ἀντίληψις δὲ νοερὰ πίστεως ἔχεται Clem.*str.*6.17(p.510.6; M.9.384A); ἀγάπη...αἰσθήσει ν. τὸν ἀόρατον ἐξιχνεύουσα Diad.*perf.* 1(p.6.5); of God νοῦς καὶ νοερός, καὶ τὸ νοητόν, καὶ πρὸ νοητοῦ Synes. *hymn.*3.177(p.12; M.66.1596).

D. *of* or *belonging to the mind* ν. ... ὀφθαλμοῖς v.l. in *A.Thom.*A 65 (p.182.7n.); ν. ἀρετῆς *Hom.Clem.*6.16; Dion.Al.ap.Eus.*p.e.*14.27 (783C; M.21.1288C); *Lit.Jac.*(p.196.7); Jo.D.*hom.*1.6(M.96.553C).

E. *understanding, with knowledge* of Χριστὲ νοερὲ τῆς εὐσπλαγχνίας *A.Thom.*A 39(p.156.24).

F. *skilful* μιῆς παλάμης νοερῷ κεχαραγμένον ὁλκῷ Nonn.*par.Jo.* 19:20(M.43.901C).

II. *spiritual, belonging to spiritual world* or *order*;

A. of God, who is ν., like human soul, Or.*mart.*47(p.42.30; M.11. 629B); Nonn.*par.Jo.*1:33(M.43.756B); *ib.*15:26(877A); ὁ δὲ θεὸς ἀσώματόν τι χρῆμα καὶ ν. Zach.Mit.*opif.*(M.85.1101A); of Logos, Clem.*str.*6.9(p.468.4; M.9.293B); Wisdom τὴν πρὸ αἰώνων ν. καὶ οὐσιώδη σοφίαν Eus.*h.e.*1.2.3(M.20.53B); σοφίαν, ὅλην δι' ὅλου ν. καὶ λογικὴν καὶ πάνσοφον id.*d.e.*4.2(p.151.31; M.22.253A); ν. τι χρῆμα καὶ ἀσώματον Gr.Nyss.*or.catech.*1(p.9.4; M.45.13C); of H. Ghost τὸ τῆς σοφίας ν. πνεῦμα καὶ ἅγιον Meth.*symp.*7.1(p.71.3; M.18.121C); Gr.Naz.*or.*31.29(p.184.10; M.36.168A); τοῦ ν. καὶ θείου πνεύματος Thdt.*h.rel.*1(3.1108).

B. Gnost.; **1.** of three ἀρχαί (Sethian), Hipp.*haer.*5.19(p.118.1; M. 16.3182A); of primordial fire (Simonian), *ib.*6.11(p.138.1; 3211A); **2.** of μονογενὴς καὶ ἰδίως ν. Clem.*exc.Thdot.*10(p.109.24; M.9.660C).

C. of heavenly beings; angels (v. ἄγγελος) σώματα...εὔμορφα καὶ ν. Clem.*exc.Thdot.*11(p.110.13; M.9.661B); ἀγγέλων καὶ τῶν ν. οὐσιῶν οἰκητήριον Or.*exp.in Pr.*3:19(M.17.168D); Meth.*res.*3.15(p.411. 25; M.18.317A); Eus.*l.C.*1(p.196.28; M.20.1320B); δυνάμεις ἀσωμάτους ...καὶ ν. id.*d.e.*3.3(p.113.10; M.22.193C); *ib.*4.1(p.150.21; 252A); Gr. Naz.*or.*31.29(p.185.3; M.36.168A); *ib.*45.6(629C); Gr.Nyss.*hom.7 in Cant.*(M.44.912C); †Diad.*Ar.*9(M.65.1165B); οὐκ ἄγγελος, οὐκ ἀρχάγγελος, οὐκ ἄλλη τις δύναμις ν. καὶ ἀσώματος Jo.Eleem.*v.Tych.* (p.138); *Rit.Bapt.*(p.400); Gnost. οὐδὲ τὰ πνευματικὰ καὶ νοερά, οὐδὲ οἱ ἀρχάγγελοι, οὐδὲ οἱ πρωτόκτιστοι Clem.*exc.Thdot.*10(p.109. 16; M.9.660B); *ib.*12(p.110.26; 664A); Gnost. aeons, *ib.*64(p.128.18; 689C).

D. of the heavens, Synes.*hymn.*9.48(59; p.55; M.66.1613); Gnost., Iren.*haer.*1.5.2(M.7.493B).

E. of evil spirits μὴ...ἐλαφρότητι διανοίας...σεαυτὸν ἐμπάρεχε ταῖς τῶν ν. ἐπιστασίαις εἰς ἀπάτην σου Mac.Aeg.*pat.*13(M.34.876B).

F. of human soul, Or.*mart.*47(p.42.30; M.11.529B); ἄυλος ὑπάρχεις...ν.,...οὐράνιος *A.Andr.fr.*6(p.40.33); ψυχαὶ...σώματα ν. ὑπάρχουσαι Meth.*res.*3.18(p.415.14; M.18.328A); ψυχαῖς νοερὰν οὐσίαν κεκτημέναις Eus.*p.e.*1.1(2A; M.21.24B); id.*d.e.*1.7(p.38.31; M.22.76A).

G. in gen. of what is spiritual, opp. material νοερῷ καταβληθεῖσα χωρίῳ Clem.*paed.*1.1(p.90.1); τὰ ν. καὶ οὐράνια τῆς διδασκαλίας τοῦ Ἰησοῦ νάματα Or.*fr.54 in Jo.*(p.528.26); Ἰωάννης ν. σπινθῆρας ἰάλλων Nonn.*par.Jo.*5:35(M.43.789C); πνεῦμα...πάντας ἔχον νοερὸν δόμον *ib.*14:17(869B); ἄξια τοῦ ν. νυμφῶνος...ἐνδύματα Isid.Pel.*epp.*1.74(M. 78.233C); ὁ μέγας ἀρχιερεὺς τοῖς ἐκ τοῦ ν. πολέμου...ἀναστρέφουσι δίδωσιν ἄρτον καὶ οἶνον Marc.Er.*opusc.*10.8(M.65.1132A); τῷ ἀχράντῳ αἵματι τὰς ν. ἐπιχρίσει φλιάς Const.Diac.*laud.*37(M.88.521C); of divine light, Clem.*str.*2.20(p.175.27; M.8.1060B); *ib.*6.12(p.484.17; M. 9.325B); id.*exc.Thdot.*12(p.110.27; M.9.664A); *A.Thom.*A 170(p.287. 3); Eus.*p.e.*1.3(8B; M.21.33B); *ib.*1.5(14B; M.44A); πνεύματα νοεροῦ φωτὸς ἔκγονα id.*l.C.*1(p.198.18; M.20.1324A); ὁ τοῦ μέλλοντος αἰῶνος τὴν ἀνάπαυσιν εὐτρεπίσας τῷ ν. καὶ ἀπαύστῳ φωτί Bas.*hex.*2.8 (1.21E; M.29.52B); Thdt.*Is.*2:21(p.117.8; 2.189); id.*Eph.*1:19(3.407); φῶς ν. τε καὶ ἀληθινὸν εἶναι τὸν θεόν id.*eran.*3(4.184); of Christ, Nonn.*par.Jo.*1:8(M.43.749B); of Church τῶν ἐπέκεινα οὐρανίων ἁψίδων...ν. ... ἐπὶ γῆς εἰκόνα Eus.*h.e.*10.4.69(M.20.877B); of worship οὔτε τὴν...ἔνυλον ἐζήτει λατρείαν· ἀλλὰ...ν. Cyr.*Juln.*4(6^2.126C); τὸ ἐπουράνιον καὶ ν. θυσιαστήριον ‡Sophr.H.*liturg.*3(M.87.3984B); of priesthood ν. καὶ ἅγια ‡Chrys.*sac.*7(1.805A); Proc.G.*Is.*40:1–8(M.87. 2332A); of gospel as ν. φῶς, Thdt.*h.e.*1.23.8(3.805); of Inc. ν. ... οἰκονομίαν Eus.*e.th.*2.18(p.122.3; M.24.941A); in gen. of spiritual persons ν. ἦμεν τῇ καρδίᾳ *A.Phil.*143(p.82.20); ἡ ν. φύσις Gr.Nyss.*or. catech.*8(p.44.12); Diad.*perf.*78(p.98.4).

***νοερότης, ἡ,** *pure spirituality* ψυχὴ...ἑνικῇ ν. κινουμένη Dion.Ar. *d.n.*4.9(M.3.705B); τὰ δὲ καὶ νοήσεως, ἢ καὶ ν. Max.*schol.d.n.*11.6(M.4. 401B).

νοερῶς, *intellectually, with the mind* σαρκὸς...ἐψυχωμένης ν. Oecum.*Apoc.*1:1–2(p.32); Eustrat.*stat.anim.*5(p.351); Thdr.Stud. *antirr.*3.4.12(M.99.436A).

νοέω, A. *think about, have in mind* σεμνὰ νοεῖν *1Clem.*1.3; τὰ αὐτὰ...νοοῦντες Clem.*str.*7.12(p.54.30; M.9.505A); νοοῦντες τὰς ἔξω τοῦ βίου ὁδοὺς Or.*mart.*20(p.19.1; M.11.589A); περὶ τῆς ἀναστάσεως νοεῖν Meth.*res.*1.45(p.295.9; M.41.1116C).

B. *apprehend spiritually* δύναμαι νοεῖν τὰ ἐπουράνια Ign.*Trall.*5.2; Herm.*mand.*6.2.5; ὑπὸ ἀπίστων μὴ νοούμενος ‡*Diogn.*11.2; ν. ... τὸν θεόν Clem.*prot.*1(p.10.13; M.8.68A); *ib.*2(p.18.13; 92A); id.*str.*7.1(p.4. 11; M.9.404C); τοῦ ἀκούειν ἐν τῷ νοεῖν καὶ γινώσκειν κρινομένου Or. *princ.*4.2.6(p.317.7; M.11.369B); ἐν τῷ νοεῖν ὁ πατὴρ μειζόνως... νοεῖται ὑφ' ἑαυτοῦ ἢ ὑπὸ τοῦ υἱοῦ *ib.*4.4.8(p.360.6; 410B); ἀνάλογον... τῇ μύσει τῶν ὄψεων τῆς αἰσθήσεως νοεῖται καὶ θεωρεῖται ἑκάστῳ ὁ ἐπὶ πᾶσι θεός id.*Cels.*7.39(p.190.15; M.11.1477A); Eus.*l.C.*11(p.226.23; M.20.1380D); Nonn.*par.Jo.*10:14–15(M.43.833C); esp. of apprehension of spiritual sense of scripture or allegories in gen., Clem.*str.*1.1 (p.10.13; M.8.701C); *ib.*1.24(p.103.3; 912A); Or.*Cels.*7.38(p.188.21; M. 11.1473C); id.*fr.87 in Lc.*24:50(p.275.13); id.*Jo.*13.19(p.243.20; M. 14.429D); ἀπὸ τῶν ῥητῶν ἀναβαίνειν καὶ νοητῶς νοεῖν τὰ...τῆς ψυχῆς βρώματα *ib.*32.4(p.431.21; 749B); Meth.*symp.*10.3(p.125.5; M.18. 197A); ἔοικε γὰρ τὸ μὲν κῆτος νοεῖσθαι ὁ χρόνος id.*res.*2.25(p.380.19; M.18.328C); Eus.*d.e.*6.18(p.276.31; M.22.456A); οὐχ ἡ φύσις τῆς ὁρωμένης πέτρας, ἀλλ' ἡ δύναμις τῆς νοουμένης, τοὺς ποταμοὺς ἠφίει τῶν ὑδάτων Chrys.*anom.*11.1(1.542A); Cyr.*ador.*5(1.164D); id.*Is.*3.4 (2.491B); and of apprehension of spiritual reality made intelligible or represented on earth by an earthly being, Heracleon ap.Or.*Jo.* 6.39(23; p.148.16; M.14.268B); τοὺς διὰ τῶν μαθητῶν νοουμένους ἀγγέλους *ib.*13.49(48; p.276.34; 488C).

C. *be understanding, be wise* λεχθείη ἂν ὑπὸ τοῦ νοοῦντος τῷ θεῷ Or. *hom.*6.2 *in Jer.*(p.50.9; M.13.328A); *ib.16.6*(p.139.8; 448B); id.*Jo.*1.7 (9; p.12.14; M.14.36D).

D. *mean, signify*; hence τὸ νοούμενον *the sense, meaning,* Clem. *str.*1.10(p.31.18; M.8.745A); τὸ νενοημένον Or.*or.*11(p.323.17; M.11. 449D).

[*]**νοηθός,** = νοητός, *intelligent,* Philox.*ep.*31(p.179).

νόημα, τό, 1. *thought* ἐγείρας τὸ διανοίας ν. Iren.*haer.*1.14.3(M.7. 601B); ὅταν ἀποβάλλῃ φαῦλον ν. καὶ γνωστικὸν προσλάβῃ Clem.*str.*7.12 (p.54.19; M.9.505A); Or.*princ.*4.2.3(p.311.4; M.11.361B); πολὺ βάθος νοημάτων ἔχει Chrys.*hom.1.3 in Ac.princ.*(3.54C); ἅμα νοήματι Clem. *str.*6.16(p.504.10; 369B); Eus.*l.C.*6(p.206.20; M.20.1341A); **2.** *mental representation, idea* ἀσώματόν τέ ἐστι καὶ λεκτὸν καὶ πρᾶγμα καὶ ν. καὶ πάντα μᾶλλον ἢ ζῷον Clem.*str.*8.4(p.87.25; M.9.576C); ὀνόματα σύμβολα ὄντα τῶν ν. ... τὰ ν. ὁμοιώματα καὶ ἐκτυπώματα τῶν ὑποκειμένων ὄντα...τὰ ὑποκείμενα πράγματα, ἀφ' ὧν ἡμῖν τὰ ν. ἐκτυποῦνται *ib.*8.8(p.94.6; 588D); τὸ ἐγκάρδιον ν. Bas.*Spir.*61(3.51E; M.32.181A); **3.** *notion,* Or.*princ.*4.2.4(p.314.2; M.11.365B); ἀφανίζουσι τὰ ὑλικώτερα τῶν ν. id.*Jo.*2.7(4; p.61.31; M.14.121B); Diod.*Gen.*1:2(M.33. 1563C); **4.** more strictly, *conception, definition* ἔχοντες...ζῴου τι ν. Clem.*str.*8.4(p.85.18; M.9.572A); Gr.Nyss.*Eun.*12(1 p.265.26; M. 45.969C); **5.** *point* under discussion, Thdt.*Rom.*9:5(3.101); **6.** *sense* of passage, Or.*princ.*4.2.4(p.312.8; M.11.364B); τὸ ν. ... τὸ βαθύ id.*hom.19.11 in Jer.*(p.166.32; M.13.485C); τὰ τοῦ γράμματος ν. id.*Jo.*32.21(13; p.462.23; M.14.800D); id.*fr.12 in Lc.*8:16(p.238); Thdt.*qu.2 in Ruth*(1.352); **7.** *understanding, mind, A.Phil.*100(p.39. 11).

νοηματικός, 1. *of* or *belonging to thought* ἕτερός ἐστιν ὁ υἱὸς παρὰ τὸν ἐνδιάθετον, ἤτοι τὸν ἐν κινήσει νοηματικῇ λόγον Eun.ap.Cyr.*Jo.*1.4 (4.31A); **2.** *spiritual, to be understood spiritually* οὐχ ὡς σωματικοὺς ἔχων ὄγκους, ν. δὲ παρέχων λόγους Epiph.*haer.*65.4(p.6.20; M.42.17A).

***νοηματικῶς,** *in a spiritual, mystical sense,* Epiph.*anc.*19(p.28. 11; M.43.52C).

νοήμων, 1. *wise, discreet,* Meth.*fr.14 in Job*(p.515.8); Nonn.*par. Jo.*15:19(M.43.876B); iron. of wiseacres ν. αὐτοδίδακτοι Gr.Naz.*carm.* 1.1.1.38(M.37.401A); **2.** *aware of* ν. τῶν θείων...μυστηρίων Chrysipp. *enc.in Jo.Bapt.*6(p.37.10); **3.** *significant,* Nonn.*par.Jo.*4:32(M.43. 780B); **4.** *spiritual* ν. καρπὸν ἀγείρει *ib.*4:36(780C); ν. πώεα *ib.*21:16 (917C).

νόησις, ἡ, *thought, conception*; hence *sense, interpretation,* Clem. *str.*1.28(p.110.8; M.8.925B); τὴν ν. ἀναλαβὼν τὴν μεγαλοπρεπῆ *ib.*6.15 (p.489.27; M.9.340A); Or.*fr.43 in Jo.*(p.518.18); Didym.*Trin.*3.3(M. 39.805C); Chrys.*hom.32.3 in Jo.*(8.188C).

νοητέον, *one must conceive, understand, think of* ἀναζωπυρεῖσθαι τὸ...ἀγαθὸν ν. Clem.*str.*1.6(p.23.5; M.8.729B); πῦρ δὲ τὸ ὑλικὸν ν. id. *ecl.*25(p.144.1; M.9.709C); ν. ... ὅτι ὁ λόγος φησίν Or.*Jo.*1.37(42; p.48.7; M.14.97B); ν. τὸν λόγον...ἀεὶ εἶναι *ib.*1.39(42; p.51.8; 101C); ν. τὸ πάντα δι' αὐτοῦ ἐγένετο *ib.*2.12(6; p.68.3; 133B); οὕτω καὶ πρότερον ν. *ib.*2.34(28; p.92.29; 176B); ν. ὅτι ἡ αὐτοαλήθεια...ἐγένετο *ib.*6.6(3; p.114.21; 209D); Meth.*res.*1.22(p.246.1; M.41.1092B); τὰ ὀστᾶ ταῦτα ν. *ib.*1.23(p.247.13; 1093A); ἐκεῖνο δὲ...ν. θεῖον Const.ap. Eus.*v.C.*2.28(p.53.4, v.l. ἐννοητέον M.22.1005B); Chrys.*hom.8.2 in 2Cor.*(10.494C); ἑτέρως...τοῦτο ν. ἡμῖν id.*comm.in Gal.*2:20(10.692A); πῶς...ν. τὸ κατ' εἰκόνα Gel.Cyz.*h.e.*2.15.1(M.85.1257B).

***Νοητιανοί, οἱ,** *followers of Noetus* τινὲς δὲ αὐτῶν [sc. Montanists] τῇ τῶν N. αἱρέσει συντιθέμενοι τὸν πατέρα αὐτὸν εἶναι τὸν υἱὸν λέγουσι Hipp.*haer*.8.19(p.238.18; M.16.3367A); *ib*.(p.239.18; 3367D); Epiph. *haer*.57.2(p.345.11; M.41.996D); Σαβέλλιος...παραπλησίως τῶν N. ἐδίδασκε *ib*.62.1(p.389.7; 1052A); Thdt.*haer*.3.3(4.343); Jo.D.*haer*.57 (M.94.712B).

νοητός, I. *intelligible, falling within the sphere of* νοῦς, *apprehended by the intellect*;

A. in gen., opp. αἰσθητός: διακρίνοντες...τὸ ν. καὶ τὸ αἰσθητόν Athenag.*leg*.15.1(M.6.920A); νοῦς καὶ λόγος δέδοται τοῖς ἀνθρώποις πρὸς διάκρισιν νοητῶν, οὐκ οὐσιῶν μόνον, ἀλλὰ καὶ τῆς τοῦ δόντος ἀγαθότητος id.*res*.15(p.66.21; M.6.1004D); ἐν ἡμῖν...τρία κριτήρια μηνύεται, αἴσθησις μὲν αἰσθητῶν, λεγομένων δὲ ὁ λόγος, νοητῶν δὲ νοῦς Clem.*str*.2.11(p.139.16; M.8.985B); τῶν μὲν αἰσθητῶν διὰ σώματος ἀντιλαμβανόμεθα, τῶν δὲ ν. δι' αὐτῆς τῆς λογικῆς ἐφαπτόμεθα δυνάμεως *ib*.5.1(p.330.4; M.9.17A); ὁ ἐλπίζων, καθάπερ ὁ πιστεύων, τῷ νῷ ὁρᾷ τὰ ν. καὶ τὰ μέλλοντα *ib*.5.3(p.336.1; 32A); ὡς αἴσθησις πρὸς τὸ αἰσθητόν, οὕτως νόησις πρὸς τὸ ν. *ib*.6.16(p.501.7; 361A); *ib*.6.11 (p.477.19; 312B); ἡ γὰρ τῶν ν. γνῶσις...βεβαία δεόντως ἂν λέγοιτο ἐπιστήμη *ib*.7.3(p.12.29; 421B); ἀναβαίνοντας ἀπὸ τῶν ὁρατῶν ἐπὶ τὰ ν. Or.*Cels*.3.47(p.244.4; M.11.981C); οὐχὶ ἐπεὶ οὐκ ἀληθινὸν τὸ αἰσθητόν, ψεῦδος τὸ αἰσθητόν· δύναται γὰρ ἀναλογίαν ἔχειν τὸ αἰσθητὸν πρὸς τὸ ν., οὐ μὴν τὸ ψεῦδος ὑγιῶς παντὸς κατηγορεῖσθαι τοῦ οὐκ ἀληθινοῦ id.*Jo*.1.26(24; p.31.32; M.14.69A); ὑπεράνω μὲν τῶν αἰσθητῶν...γινόμενος, πρὸς δὲ τὰ ἐν οὐρανοῖς θεῖα καὶ ν. τῇ δυνάμει τοῦ νοῦ συναπτόμενος Ath.*gent*.2(M.25.8A); διϊστῶν [sc. Plato] τὰ πάντα εἰς δύο εἴδη, ν. τε καὶ αἰσθητόν,...τὸ μὲν νῷ καταληπτόν, τὸ δὲ δόξῃ μετ' αἰσθήσεως δοξαστόν Const.*or.s.c*.9(p.164.9; M.20.1256C); Gr.Naz.*or*. 23.11(M.35.1164A); διχῇ τέτμηται...ἡ τῶν ὄντων φύσις. τὸ μὲν γάρ ἐστιν αἰσθητὸν καὶ ὑλῶδες· τὸ δὲ ν. καὶ ἄυλον. ... ν. δὲ τὸ ὑπερπίπτον τὴν αἰσθητικὴν κατανόησιν· ἐκ τούτων τὸ μὲν ν. ἄπειρόν ἐστι καὶ ἀόριστον Gr.Nyss.*hom.6 in Cant*.(M.44.885C); id.*Eun*.1(1 p.100.1; M.45.333B); αἰσθητὴ μὲν ἡ ὑπόσχεσις, ν. δὲ ἡ ἐπιθυμία τοῦ δικαίου Chrys.*serm.9.4 in Gen*.(4.694E); of monks ἀπὸ τῶν αἰσθητῶν ἐπὶ τὰ ν. ἀναχωρεῖν ‡Pall.*h.mon*.15.9(p.71.4, v.l. νόησιν M.34.1164A); in rel. to νοερός: οἷς ὑγιαίνουσι τὸ νοερὸν ὄμμα φῶς ἀνάπτει συγγενὲς ὁ θεός, ὃ τοῖς τε νοεροῖς τοῦ νοεῖν, καὶ τοῖς ν. αἴτιον τοῦ νοεῖσθαι Synes.*ep*.154 (M.66.1556C); ἕτερόν ἐστι ν., καὶ ἕτερον νοερόν. τὸ γὰρ ν. τροφὴ οἷά τις τοῦ νοεροῦ ἐστιν, εἴπερ τὸ νοούμενον, ὅ ἐστι ν., μεῖζόν ἐστι καὶ προεπινοούμενον τοῦ νοοῦντος, ὅ ἐστι νοερόν Max.*schol.d.n*.4.1(M.4.230B); τὰ ν. opp. both αἰσθητά and διδακτά, Clem.*str*.7.1(p.4.5; M.9.404C); as second in series πνευματικά, ν., αἰσθητά, id.*exc.Thdot*.8(p.108.23; M.9.657C); of οὐσία as object of νόησις opp. γένεσις as object of δόξα, Cels.ap.Or.*Cels*.7.45(p.196.19; M.11.1488A).

B. κόσμος ν. in Platonist thought κόσμον...τὸν μὲν ν. οἶδεν ἡ βάρβαρος φιλοσοφία [cf.Philo *opif.mund*.13–16] τὸν δὲ αἰσθητόν, τὸν μὲν ἀρχέτυπον, τὸν δὲ εἰκόνα τοῦ...παραδείγματος Clem.*str*.5.14(p.387.21; M.9.137A); *ib*.(p.388.7; 140A) cit. s. αἰσθητός; *ib*.4.25(p.319.1; M.8.1368B); equated with heaven εἰς δὲ τὸν ν. κόσμον μόνος ὁ κύριος... εἴσεισι *ib*.5.6(p.348.20; M.9.60A); τά τε ἐπὶ τῆς ἁγίας κιβωτοῦ ἱστορούμενα μηνύει τὰ τοῦ ν. κόσμου τοῦ ἀποκεκρυμμένου...τοῖς πολλοῖς *ib*. (p.350.1; 61A); κόσμον γάρ φησιν εἶναι ὁ Ἐμπεδοκλῆς τὸν ὑπὸ τοῦ νείκους διοικούμενον...καὶ ἕτερον ν. τὸν ὑπὸ τῆς φιλίας Hipp.*haer*.7.31 (p.216.23; M.16.3334C); equated with spiritual world in gen. ὁ δὲ σωτὴρ...τοῦ ν. κόσμου ἐστὶ φῶς Or.*Jo*.1.25(24; p.31.1; M.14.68B); *ib*. 19.22(5; p.323.34; 568B); id.*Cels*.6.5(p.74.27; M.11.1296B); Const.*or. s.c*.11(p.169.7; M.20.1265B); οὐδ' ἂν...συγκριθείη...ὁ αἰσθητὸς κόσμος τῷ ν. οὐδ' αἱ εἰκόνες τοῖς παραδείγμασιν *ib*.14(p.173.22; 1273C); Gr. Naz.*or*.45.6(M.36.629B).

C. ν. κτίσις preceding material Creation, Bas.*Spir*.49(3.41A; M. 32.156D); consisting of angelic powers, Gr.Nyss.*or.catech*.6(p.31.11; M.45.28A).

D. of God, Clem.*prot*.4(p.40.11; M.8.145A); ἡ ὑπὲρ πᾶσαν ἐπίνοιαν αὐτοῦ παρουσία...ταῖς ν. ἀκρότησι τῶν ἁγιωτάτων αὐτοῦ τόπων ἐπιβατεύουσα Dion.Ar.*myst*.1.3(M.3.1001A); but God is ἐπέκεινα τοῦ ν. Clem.*str*.5.6(p.352.14; M.9.65A).

II. *spiritual, belonging to the supra-sensible and spiritual order* (a sense often combined with or scarcely differentiated from I supra);

A. of God τὴν ν. οὐσίαν δι' ὕλης σεβάζεσθαι ἀτιμάζειν ἐστὶν αὐτήν Clem.*str*.5.5(p.344.12; M.9.49B); *ib*.7.7(p.30.22; 456B); τοὺς μὴ δυναμένους ἐπὶ τὴν ν. ἀναδραμεῖν φύσιν, δι' αἰσθητῶν θεῶν κινουμένους περὶ θεότητος Or.*Jo*.2.3(p.56.19; M.14.112C); id.*Cels*.6.70(p.140.3; M.11. 1404C); ὁ τῆς ν. καταφρονῶν φύσεως, περὶ δὲ τὰ αἰσθητὰ καταφιλοσοφῶν id. *fr.69 in Lc*.14:18(p.268.12; M.17.364B); τὴν αἰώνιον...φύσιν καὶ ν., ἧς καὶ χαρακτήρ ἐστιν ὁ ἄνθρωπος Meth.*symp*.6.2(p.65.10; M. 18.116A); ref. Inc. αἰωνίου φύσεως ἀρχὴ χρόνιος καὶ ν. οὐσίας αἴσθησις Const.*or.s.c*.11(p.168.25; M.20.1265A); τὴν ἐπέκεινα οὐρανοῦ τε καὶ κόσμου θείαν καὶ ν. οὐσίαν Eus.*l.C*.13(p.238.8; M.20.1401A); τὴν... κατάστασιν τοῦ θεοῦ, ἥτις οὐχ ἑτέρα τῆς ν. αὐτοῦ οὐσίας τυγχάνει Didym.ap.*cat.Jo*.6:58(p.255.34).

B. of Μονάς in Gnost. system of Secundus ν. ἀγέννητόν τε καὶ ἀόρατον Iren.*haer*.1.11.3(M.7.565A).

C. of angels οὔτε γὰρ αἱ ν. φύσεις ἐκ τῆς τῶν ἀνθρώπων ἀναστάσεως ἀδικηθεῖεν ἂν Athenag.*res*.10(p.58.14; M.6.992B); Or.*Cels*.7.37(p.187.29; M.11.1473A) cit. s. ἀόρατος; Cyr.H.*catech*.4.16; ἔστι δὲ ἀγγελικὴ μὲν ἡ ἀσώματος [sc. φύσις]...ἡ μὲν οὖν ν., ἅτε δὴ τοῦ βαροῦντος κεχωρισμένη σώματος Gr.Nyss.*or.dom*.4(p.74.14; M.44.1165B); id.*or. catech*.6(p.31.11; M.45.28A); ἵνα...αἱ...ν. φύσεις ἐν τῇ περὶ τοῦτον [sc. τὸν ἄνθρωπον] κηδεμονίᾳ τὴν περὶ τὸν πεποιηκότα δεικνύωσιν εὔνοιαν Thdt.*qu.20 in Gen*.(1.26); οὐ πολύμορφοι δέ, ἀλλ' ἀσώματοι αἱ ν. φύσεις id.*Zach*.1:8–11(2.1598); id.*affect*.4(p.115.25; 4.809); τὰ μὲν οὖν ὑπερκείμενα καὶ προσεχῆ τῷ θεῷ τάγματα ν. κυρίως λεκτέον· τὰ δὲ ὑποβεβηκότα νοερά, ἅτε νοοῦντα τὰ ὑπερκείμενα· οὐχ ὅτι δὲ ν. ἐστι τὰ νοούμενα, νομιστέον αὐτὰ μὴ νοεῖν Max.*schol.d.n*.4.1(M.4.240C).

D. of spiritual beings in gen., Hipp.*haer*.8.9(p.228.7; M.16.3351B); πρὸς γὰρ ἀντιδιαστολὴν τῶν αἰσθητῶν ἔθος τῇ γραφῇ τὰ ν. ὀνομάζειν πνεύματα καὶ πνευματικά Or.*Cels*.6.70(p.140.13; M.11.1404D); Eus. *e.th*.3.3(p.147.10; M.24.985A); Gr.Nyss.*hom.6 in Cant*.(M.44.885D); id.*or.catech*.6(p.29.9; M.45.25C); *Const.App*.7.42.3; of demons, Eus. *d.e*.2.3(p.81.31; M.22.145C).

E. in gen.; **1.** opp. physical or material τῷ...τοῦ ν. φωτὸς ἡλίῳ Clem.*str*.5.5(p.345.9; M.9.52B); γῆν ἀειδῆ καὶ φῶς ν. *ib*.5.14(p.388.2; 137B); φωνὴν τὴν ν. *ib*.7.7(p.32.31; 461A); id.*exc.Thdot*.81(p.132.4; M.9.696B) cit. s. αἰσθητός; ἀνάγκη καὶ τοῦ ὕδατος τὸ μέν τι ν., τὸ δὲ αἰσθητὸν ὑπάρχειν...καὶ τὸ μὲν ἐπίγειον ὕδωρ τὸ σῶμα ἀπορρύπτει, τὸ δὲ ἐπουράνιον ὕδωρ διὰ τὸ εἶναι ν. καὶ ἀόρατον πνεῦμα ἀλληγορεῖται ἅγιον id.*ecl*.8(p.139.3; M.9.701B); of spiritual riches, id.*q.d.s*.20(p.172.28; M.9.625A); Or.*mart*.15(p.15.5; M.11.584A); νοητὸν γνώσεως φῶς id.*Cels*.5.10(p.11.9; M.11.1196B); ἄρτος...ν. id.*or*.27.9(p.369.1; M.11. 512C); τὸ ν. τοῦ χρόνου πλήρωμα id.*Jo*.1.7(9; p.11.29; M.14.36C); *ib*.13.22(p.246.4; 436B) cit. s. ἀόρατος; ἐὰν δέ τις ᾖ λογικώτερος καὶ διὰ τοῦτο καὶ ν. ἄνθρωπος, τὸν ν. ἄρτον ἐσθίει *ib*.13.33(p.258.31; 457B); τὸ ν. γαζοφυλάκιον *ib*.19.7(2; p.307.8; 540A); ἐπὶ τῆς ν. καταβάσεως τῆς ψυχῆς...καὶ ν. ἀναβάσεως *ib*.19.22(5; p.323.24; 568A); ἐπαγγελία ἐστὶν μὴ γεύσεσθαι θανάτου τινὰ τῶν ἑστώτων ἐν τῷ δεικνυμένῳ...ν. τόπῳ *ib*.20.43(33; p.387.6; 676C); ὀστᾶ ν. Meth.*res*. 1.39(p.282.13; M.18.268B); τῷ ν. καὶ λογικῷ ἄρτῳ Eus.*d.e*.10.8(p.491.33; M.22.789B); καταφυτεύῃ λοιπὸν εἰς τὸν ν.· παράδεισον Cyr.H. *catech*.1.4; τὰ χερουβὶμ συνέτριψεν. οὐ λέγω τὰ ν. ... ἀλλὰ τὰ γλυπτά *ib*.2.17; ἐκεῖνος ἐλαίῳ ν. ἀγαλλιάσεως ἐχρίετο...ὑμεῖς δὲ μύρῳ ἐχρίσθητε *ib*.21.2; Gr.Nyss.*hom.1 in Cant*.(M.44.780C); ὕδωρ, οὐκ αἰσθητόν τε καὶ ἔνυλον, θεῖον δὲ μᾶλλον καὶ ν. Cyr.*Is*.3.2(2.427D); φῶς ν. Dion.Ar. *d.n*.4.6(M.3.701B); πρῶτος μέν ἐστιν ὁ αἰσθητὸς [sc. θάνατος]...δεύτερος δὲ ὁ ν. ὁ τῆς ἁμαρτίας Oecum.*Apoc*.20:6(p.221); Χριστὸν... ἐποίησεν ὁ πατήρ, ν. χρίσει χρίσας †Diad.*Ar*.4(M.65.1157C); **2.** opp. literal in exegesis, cf. αἰσθητός, Or.*princ*.4.2.9(p.321.16; M.11.376A); γράμμα μὲν τὴν αἰσθητὴν ὠνόμασεν ἐκδοχὴν τῶν...γραμμάτων, πνεῦμα δὲ τὴν ν. id.*Cels*.6.70(p.140.18; M.11.1405A); id.*Cant*.3(p.220.31; M. 13.181D); id.*Jo*.1.8(10; p.13.12; M.14.37C), *ib*.13.9(p.233.22; 412C) citt. s. αἰσθητός; παραστατέον δὲ τὴν περὶ τούτων ἀλήθειαν ἀποκεῖσθαι ἐν τοῖς ν. *ib*.10.3(2; p.172.20; 309A); οὐ γὰρ νομιστέον τὰ ἱστορικὰ ἱστορικῶν εἶναι τύπους καὶ τὰ σωματικὰ σωματικῶν, ἀλλὰ τὰ σωματικὰ πνευματικῶν καὶ τὰ ἱστορικὰ νοητῶν *ib*.10.18(13; p.189.29; 337D); ν. εἶναι λέγεις τὰς γραφὰς ἢ ψιλάς; Adam.*dial*.1.7(p.14.6; M.11.1725C); Eus.*h.e*.10.4.55(M.20.872A); οὐ περὶ αἰσθητοῦ μᾶλλον ἀμπελῶνος, ἀλλὰ περὶ ν. Cyr.*Is*.1.3(2.83C); ἐν αἰχμαλωσίᾳ τῇ ν. *ib*.1.5(135E); εἰς τὴν ν. Σιὼν *ib*.2.1(205D); ν. μυστήριον id.*Abac*.24(3.538A); εἰκόνες εἰσὶν ὥσπερ αἱ παραβολαὶ πραγμάτων οὐχ ὁρατῶν, ν. δὲ μᾶλλον καὶ πνευματικῶν id.*Lc*.8:4(M.72.624C); hence τὸ ν. *the spiritual sense* of a passage or event ὅρα, εἰ δύναται κατὰ τὸ ν. ταῦτα...παρίστασθαι Or.*Jo*.2.7(4; p.61.18; M.14.121A); *ib*.13.30(29; p.255.10; 452C); Bas.*hom.in Ps*.29 (1.124D; M.29.305C); Didym.*Trin*.3.25(M.39.941B); **3.** of a spiritual reality, opp. type or image διὰ τοῦ γάμου Μωϋσέως ὁ τοῦ Ἰησοῦ ν. γάμος ἐδείκνυτο Iren.*haer*.4.20.12(M.7.1042C); τοῦ ν. Αἰθίοπος Or.*or*. 27.12(p.370.30; M.11.516A); οἱ ν. Βαβυλώνιοι id.*hom.1.4 in Jer*.(p.3. 18; M.13.257D); τὴν ν. νεφέλην *ib*.8.5(p.60.9; 341C); ν. Ἰσραὴλ id. *hom.8 in Lc*.(p.61.13); id.*Jo*.20.10(p.338.25; M.14.593B); κἀκεῖνος μὲν ἐβλήθη εἰς κοιλίαν κήτους· οὗτος δὲ κατῆλθεν...ὅπου τὸ ν. τοῦ θανάτου κῆτος Cyr.H.*catech*.14.17; Chrys.*hom.27.2 in Jo*.(8.155C); Cyr.*ador*.10(1.356C); τῆς ν. ἤγουν τῆς ἐν πνεύματι περιτομῆς ἡ δύναμις id.*Ps*.11:1(M.69.796B); id.*Joel*.14(3.213E); Χριστός, ὁ ν. Νῶε Procl. CP *or*.7.3(M.65.760C); ν. Φαραὼ *ib*.14.2(797A); ν. ἀμνὸς *ib*.14.3(800A);

ὁ ν. Ἐλισσαῖος [i.e. Χριστός] Bas.Sel.*or*.10.1(M.85.140B); Proc.G. *Is*.13:12–16(M.87.2085D); Dor.*doct*.13.9(M.88.1772B); ἀπὸ τῆς ν. Αἰγύπτου...τῆς ἁμαρτίας *ib*.22.1(1821C).

III. *intelligent, thinking* οὐκ ἔστι τελεία προσευχὴ χωρὶς ν. ἐπικλήσεως Marc.Er.*opusc*.2.31(M.65.936A).

IV. *belonging to the mind* διὰ τῆς αἰσθήσεως ἢ ν. δύναμις Gr.Nyss. *anim.et res*.(M.46.29B).

νοθεύ-ω, 1. *corrupt, seduce*; c. infin., *corrupt so as to, lead astray into* οὓς δὲ τρεῖς...ὑποστάσεις...σέβειν ἐνόθευσε Jo.D.*imag*.2.2(M.94. 1285B); **2.** *adulterate*; **a.** *water down, weaken* μὴ ~σῃς τὴν ἀρετήν ‡Chrys.*pseud*.12(8.86B); Nil.*sent*.94(M.79.1249A); Bas.Sel.*or*.6.4(M. 85.97C); **b.** *falsify* writings κλεψισόφοις ~οντες δόγμασι τὰς γραφάς Meth.*symp*.2.3(p.18.17; M.18.52B); *Clem.contest*.2(M.2.29B); *ib*.5 (32C); Const.*or.s.c*.19(p.181.9; M.20.1289C); of 'Gospel according to the Hebrews' used by Ebionites τῷ παρ' αὐτοῖς εὐαγγελίῳ κατὰ Ματθαῖον ὀνομαζομένῳ...ἀλλὰ νενοθευμένῳ Epiph.*haer*.30.13(p.349.3; M.41.428C); and Περιόδοι Πέτρου *ib*.30.15(p.352.5; 429D); **3.** *regard as spurious*, ref. books, e.g. Epistle of James, Eus.*h.e*.2.23.25(M.20. 205B); Apoc., Areth.*Apoc*.1 proem.(M.106.500A); **4.** *disown, reject*, Sophr.H.*v.Anast*.(M.92.1684B); *ib*.(1717B).

***νοθηφορέω,** *bastardize, turn into bastardy*; fig., Cyr.*ador*.14(1. 485E).

νόθος, A. *bastard*; met.; **1.** *counterfeit, not genuine* (with idea of birth and illegitimate descent retained); ref. Anomoean doctrine of Son ν. τὸν γεγεννημένον ὡς πρὸς τὴν τοῦ γεγεννηκότος φύσιν ἀποφαινόμενος Gr.Nyss.*Eun*.1(1 p.84.20; M.45.316C); ref. teaching that title μονογενής ought to be used to the exclusion of Χριστός: μερίζει τὸν ἕνα κύριον...καὶ τὸν μονογενῆ...υἱὸν ὑπολαμβάνει γνήσιον... τὸν δὲ Χριστὸν...ν. Thdt.*ep*.146(4.1258); consequence of Marcion's teaching οὐ δύναται αὐτοῦ ὁ ν. πατὴρ καλούμενος ἐν αὐτῷ εἶναι οὐδὲ αὐτὸς ἐν τῷ πατρί Epiph.*haer*.42.16(p.186.3; M.41.817A); of those who are 'bastard' children of God and in fact children of destruction, Clem.*prot*.10(p.69.9; M.8.208A); of union of sons of God and daughters of man ἐκ δὲ τῆς ν. μίξεως αὐτῶν ἄνθρωποι ἐγένοντο ν. *Hom.Clem*.8.15; **2.** *cross-bred*; of trees, Gr.Thaum.*pan.Or*.7(p.19. 8; M.10.1073C); **3.** of Christ's birth as wholly *novel* ν. τινὰ γένεσιν... ἐμηχανήσατο [sc. Χριστός] Const.*or.s.c*.11(p.168.23; M.20.1265A).

B. *counterfeit, adulterated*, met.; **1.** in gen., *spurious, not genuine*, of crown of thorns στέμμα ν. βασιλῆος Nonn.*par.Jo*.19:2(M.43. 897B); of Christ's disciples as νόθοι κόσμοιο πολῖται *ib*.17:14(885C); **2.** of the elements in man foreign to his true spiritual nature (Basilidean), Clem.*str*.2.20(p.174.9; M.8.1056B); ἵνα μηδὲν ἔχῃ ν. ἐπιπροσθοῦν τῇ δυνάμει ἑαυτοῦ τὸ ἡγεμονικόν *ib*.4.6(p.266.4; 1252A); **3.** of Epicureans νόθοι τῆς θεόθεν δωρηθείσης γεωργίας Ἕλλησιν ὑπάρχουσι καρποί Clem.*str*.6.8(p.465.29; M.9.289A); of bogus philosophers in gen., Or.*Cels*.4.27(p.296.8; M.11.1065D); of spurious teachers in Church, Chrys.*hom.21.4 in 1Cor*.(10.184D); iron. of converted Jews, Nonn.*par.Jo*.9:27(M.43.829B); **4.** of spurious books and hence uncanonical literature, e.g. Πέτρου Κήρυγμα, Or.*Jo*.13.17 (p.241.15; M.14.424C); *Acts of Paul, Shepherd, Apoc. Petr., Barn., Did.*, and possibly Apoc., Eus.*h.e*.3.25.4(M.20.269A); dist. from heretical works, *ib*.3.25.7(272A); but elsewhere the παντελῶς ν. described as alien to apostolic orthodoxy, *ib*.3.31.6(281B); Susannah so described by Afric., *ib*.6.31.1(589C); accepted by Audians, Thdt.*haer*.4.10(4.365); of heterodox material in αἱ τῶν ἁγίων ἀποστόλων διὰ Κλήμεντος διατάξεις CTrull.*can*.2.

C. *false*; **1.** morally εὐσεβείᾳ νόθῳ Clem.*prot*.2(p.17.3; M.8.88A); id.*paed*.2.10(p.222.2; M.8.525B); οὐδὲν γὰρ ν. χρὴ ἐνυπάρχειν ἐν τῇ ψυχῇ τοῦ ἀληθῶς...εὐσεβοῦς Or.*Cels*.7.66(p.215.22; M.11.1513C); Gr. Thaum.*pan.Or*.7(p.20.15; M.10.1076B); οἱ μὲν νόθῳ φρονήματι τὴν ἐκκλησίαν ὑπεδύοντο Eus.*v.C*.3.66(p.113.7; M.20.1144A); **2.** intellectually; **a.** in gen., Nonn.*par.Jo*.2:25(M.43.765A); ν. βουλεύμασι Geo.Pis.*Pers*.2.348(M.92.1234A); **b.** of heret. teaching ν. ἐκφωνημάτων Anon.ap.Eus.*h.e*.5.16.8(M.20.468A); ἀποστὰς τοῦ κανόνος ἐπὶ κίβδηλα καὶ ν. διδάγματα μετελήλυθεν Hymen.*ep*.(p.330.12); Chrys. *comm.in Gal*.4:17(10.708A); id.*hom.8.4 in Heb*.(12.89C); Thdt.*h.e*. 1.7.15(3.758); Oecum.*Apoc*.2:2(p.48).

D. *substitute, makeshift* Nonn.*par.Jo*.2:15(M.43.764A); *ib*.13:4 (860C); ἱστίον ἕτερον ν. Synes.*ep*.4(M.66.1336A).

[*]**νοθρός,** = νωθρός, *sluggish*, *M.Thdot.1* 1(p.58); Sophr.H.*mir. Cyr.et Jo*.51(M.87.3612B).

***νοϊκός,** *intellectual* ἦν δὲ...ἡ ν. βούλησις πνεῦμα τὸ ἅγιον Val.Gn. ap.Epiph.*haer*.31.6(p.394.11; M.41.485A); τοῦ νοϊκοῦ *ib*.(p.394.5; οὖν μικροῦ 485A).

νομαδίτης, ὁ, *nomad*; as adj., *nomad, pastoral*, Synes.*catast*.2 (p.289.2; M.66.1569A).

***νομαρείτης, ὁ,** *market-gardener*, ‡Dor.Tyr.*disc.Dom*.(M.92. 1076A).

***νομεγκλάτωρ, ὁ,** (Lat. *nomenclator*) slave responsible for telling master names of those he met while canvassing, etc.; name applied to Chryseros, freedman of M. Aurelius and chronographer of Rome, Thphl.Ant.*Autol*.3.27(M.6.1161C).

νομεύς, ὁ, 1. *herdsman*; **a.** of guardian angel, Bas.*Eun*.3.1(1. 272D; M.29.656B); **b.** of bishop, Gr.Naz.*carm*.2.2(epitaph.)59.2(M. 38.41A); *Const.App*.2.20.8; Thdt.*h.e*.2.12.4(3.854); *ib*.2.17.3(870); Sophr.H.*ep.syn*.(M.87.3189A); **2.** *distributor* θεὸς ἀγαθῶν...ν. Synes. *ep*.8(M.66.1345C); **3.** *possessor* τῷ βόνα φίδε ν. Ath.Scholast.*coll*.10.10 (p.131).

νομικός, *relating to law, forensic*; **1.** *relating to*, or *consisting in the Law* of Moses ἐκ τῆς Ἑλληνικῆς παιδείας, ἀλλὰ καὶ ἐκ τῆς ν. Clem.*str*.6.5(p.452.25; M.9.261B); ἀκούειν τῶν ν. γραμμάτων Or. *Cels*.2.76(p.198.5; M.11.913C); *ib*.7.20(p.172.14; 1449D); διαιρούντων τὴν κατὰ τὸ εὐαγγέλιον θεότητα ἐκ τῆς ν. θεότητος *ib*.7.25(p.176.18; 1456D); ἐντεθραμμένος τῇ ν. κατηχήσει id.*or*.2.4(p.302.19; M.11. 421C); ἀπὸ τῶν ν. στοιχείων ἐπὶ τὴν εὐαγγελικὴν τελειότητα id.*hom. 12.12 in Jer*.(p.100.10; M.13.396D); id.*Jo*.1.3(5; p.6.21; M.14.28B); ὁ πίνων ἐκ τοῦ ὕδατος τοῦ ν. διψήσει πάλιν, ὄρεξιν ἔχων τοῦ εὐαγγελικοῦ πόματος id.*fr.56 in Jo*.(p.529.12); id.*fr.30 in Lc*.9:62(p.247); of legal Passover opp. Christ as true Passover, Petr.I Al.*fr*.(M.18. 518B,C); ν. βάπτισμα (ref. 1Cor.10:2) Bas.*Spir*.33(3.27D; M.32.125C); μετὰ φυσικὸν νόμον, μετὰ ν. παραίνεσιν *Lit*.ap.*Const.App*.8.12.30; ν. πολιτεία Chrys.*hom.3.3 in Mt*.(7.38A); νομικωτάτη...ἡ ἐρώτησις Cyr. *Ag*.15(3.644C); ν. τινα διατύπωσιν id.*Jo*.3.1(4.249E); στοιχεῖα γὰρ τοῦ κόσμου τὰς ν. παρατηρήσεις ἐκάλεσεν Thdt.*Gal*.4:1–3(3.381); Max. *ambig*.(M.91.1164A); neut. plur. as subst.; **a.** *provisions* or *teaching of the Law*, Or.*Cant*.1(p.111.30; M.13.99D); Chrys.*hom.10.1 in Mt*. (7.140B); Vict.*Mc*.1:9(p.271.12); **b.** *books of the Law*, Clem.*str*.5.6 (p.346.28; M.9.56B); Or.*Jo*.13.48(46; p.275.20; M.14.485B); **2.** *observing the Law, devoted to the Law* Ἰωσίας ὁ...νομικώτατος Clem. *str*.1.21(p.75.22; M.8.848B); *ib*.4.21(p.305.25; 1340C); ἐάν τε ν. ᾖ ἐάν τε Ἕλλην *ib*.6.6(p.455.20; M.9.269B); ὁ σπείρων and ὁ θερίζων (Jo. 4:37) interpreted as ὁ ν. and ὁ εὐαγγελικός, Or.*Jo*.13.49(47; p.276. 15; M.14.488A); id.*sel.in Jos*.6:26(M.12.824B); Thdr.Stud.*epp*.2.8(M. 99.1133D); **3.** as subst., *lawyer, one learned in law*; in gen., Or.*ep*. 2.1(p.64.17; M.11.88A); Gr.Thaum.*pan.Or*.5(p.13.19; M.10.1068A); *A.Thom*.B 11(p.30.15); of Jewish Scribes, freq.; *treasurer* of church, Jo.Mosch.*prat*.193(M.87.3073A).

νομικῶς, *in accordance with* Mosaic *Law*, Clem.*str*.6.14(p.486.17; νομικοῖς M.9.329B); Max.*ambig*.(M.91.1152B).

νόμιμος, *pertaining to law, legal, of the* Mosaic *Law* τὰς ν. ἐντολάς Clem.*q.d.s*.8(p.165.1; M.9.612C); ν. καὶ προφητικαῖς γραφαῖς Or. *Cels*.2.76(p.197.2; M.11.912D); Chrys.*hom.49.3 in Jo*.(8.292D); neut. plur. as subst., *ordinances* of God, *1Clem*.1.3; Herm.*vis*.1.3.4; *Const.App*.1.21.1; *provisions of* Mosaic Law, *Hom.Clem*.11.28; Gr. Nyss.*v.Mos*.(M.44.321B); ref. Christ's baptism ἔσχατον ἦν αὐτῷ κατόρθωμα τῶν ν. Chrys.*hom.10.1 in Mt*.(7.140B).

νομίμως, *lawfully, according to the law*; **1.** ref. Mosaic Law, Meth. *symp*.9.2(p.116.20; M.18.181B); *Const.App*.6.10.3; **2.** ref. 1Tim.1:8 ὅταν ἐξηγῶνται...αὐτὸν διὰ ῥημάτων, διὰ δὲ τῶν ἔργων παραβαίνωσι, τοῦτό ἐστιν ἀνόμως χρῆσθαι. χρῆται μὲν γάρ, ἀλλ' οὐκ εἰς οἰκείαν ὠφέλειαν. ... ἐὰν ν. χρήσῃ, παραπέμπει σε πρὸς τὸν Χριστόν...καὶ νόμῳ ν. χρῆται ὁ μὴ διὰ τὴν ἐκ τῶν γραμμάτων ἀνάγκην σωφρονῶν...ὁ γὰρ πρὸς τοσοῦτον ἀρετῆς φθάσας, ὥστε μὴ διὰ τὸν ἐκείνου φόβον αὐτὸν κατορθοῦν, ἀλλὰ διὰ τὴν ἀρετήν, οὗτος ν. χρῆται αὐτῷ Chrys.*hom. 2.1 in 1Tim*.(11.556Ef.); ἐάν...ν. χρῆται, τοῦτο δηλοῖ, ἐάν τις ἀκολουθῇ αὐτοῦ τῷ σκοπῷ· σκοπὸς δὲ τῷ νόμῳ προσαγαγεῖν ἡμᾶς τῷ δεσπότῃ Χριστῷ Thdt.*1Tim*.1:8(3.641).

νόμισις, ἡ, *belief, opinion* (religious), Or.*Cels*.5.27(p.28.15; M.11. 1221B); Evagr.*h.e*.3.30(p.126.8; M.86.2656C); Μανιχαϊκῆς ν. *ib*.3.32 (p.130.11; 2665A); τῆς εἰς τὸν θεὸν ν. *ib*.4.11(p.161.5; 2721B).

νόμισμα, τό, A. *current coin, currency*; met. ν. δύο, ὃ μὲν θεοῦ, ὃ δὲ κόσμου, καὶ ἕκαστον αὐτῶν ἴδιον χαρακτῆρα ἐπικείμενον ἔχει, οἱ ἄπιστοι τοῦ κόσμου τούτου, οἱ δὲ πιστοὶ ἐν ἀγάπῃ χαρακτῆρα θεοῦ πατρός Ign.*Magn*.5.2.

B. *a coin*; **1.** in gen. ὀλίγου ν. ὠνοῦνται θάνατον Clem.*paed*.3.3 (p.249.17; M.8.585A); Or.*Jo*.19.9(2; p.308.28; M.14.541C); *Const.App*. 2.37.2; **2.** *aureus* or *solidus*, Gr.Naz.*test*.(M.37.392C); Epiph.*mens*. (M.43.285A); ἑξακισχιλιοστὸν ταλάντου, ὅπερ γίνεται ἐν ἥμισυ ν. *cat. Mt*.10:24(p.80.10); its superiority in appearance as compared with Persian μιλιάρισιν, Cosm.Ind.*top*.11(M.88.448D); *Chron.Pasch*.p.389 (M.92.997A); **3.** met. σοφία...πιπράσκεται νομίσματι δικαίῳ, τῷ λόγῳ τῷ ἀφθάρτῳ Clem.*paed*.2.3(p.181.13; M.8.440A); ὁ δίκαιος, ν. κυρίου γενόμενος καὶ χάραγμα βασιλικὸν ἀναδεξάμενος id.*str*.6.7(p.462.2; M.9.281B); *ib*.6.10(p.472.11; 301B); *ib*.7.15(p.64.18; 525B); of spiritual 'pounds' of Lc.19:12ff., Or.*fr*.79 *in Lc*.19:22(p.272); ref. Eph.6:12 πνευματικὰ τῆς πονηρίας ἐν τοῖς ἐπουρανίοις compared with money-changers in Temple, as those who defile heavenly sanctuary by giving spurious money, id.*Jo*.10.29(18; p.203.11; M.14.360D); φερέτω δόκιμα ν., ῥήματα ζωῆς αἰωνίου, ἐπὶ τὸ γαζοφυλάκιον *ib*.19.10(2; p.309.19; 544B); of heresy as κίβδηλον ν., Eus.*e.th*.1.14(p.74.11; M.24.853A); exeg. Mt.22:20ff.; coin's image interpreted of H. Ghost in believer, superscription of name of God which he bears through Christ, Clem.*exc.Thdot*.86(p.133.1; M.9.697B); ὥσπερ γὰρ τὸ ν. εἰκόνα ἔχει τοῦ βασιλεύοντος τῶν ἐθνῶν, οὕτως ὁ ποιῶν τὰ ἔργα τοῦ κοσμοκράτορος τὴν εἰκόνα αὐτοῦ φορεῖ Or.*hom*.39 *in Lc*.(p.229.16).

νομιστεύ-ω, *ordain, prescribe* θεὸς...φιλανθρωπίαν ~ων *Hom. Clem*.2.45; *ib*.3.26.

***νομμοκλάριος, ὁ**, (Lat. *nummularius*) *banker, money-changer, MAMA* 3.302 [Corycus].

νομοδιδάσκαλος, ὁ, 1. *doctor of the* Mosaic *Law*, Iren.*haer*.1.3.2 (M.7.469A); Clem.*str*.7.3(p.11.7; M.9.417B); id.*exc.Thdot*.5(p.107.16; M.9.656D); Or.*Jo*.28.20(15; p.414.28; M.14.724B); of Symeon, ‡Meth. *Sym.et Ann*.12(M.18.377A); **2.** of apostles as doctors of new Law, Eus.*l.C*.17(p.256.25; M.20.1433C).

νομοδότης, [*]νομοδώτης, ὁ, *lawgiver*; of God, Jo.D.*imag*.3.4(M.94.1321B, v.l. -θέτης); -ώτης (metri gr.) Eudoc.*Cypr*.1.116(M.85.836D); of Christ, Andr.Cr.*can.Ann*.3(M.97.1308B); Jo.D.*hom*.1.2(M.96.548A); ref. BMV as ark containing Christ as the ν., Mod.*dorm*.4 (M.86.3288C); ‡Meth.*Sym.et Ann*.5(M.18.360A).

***νομοδόχος,** *receiving the Law*, of ark of covenant ἐκείνη γὰρ ν., αὕτη δὲ θεοδόχος [sc. BMV] Jo.Eub.*concept.BMV* 4(M.96.1465A); as type of BMV, ‡Meth.*Sym.et Ann*.9(M.18.369C); of Symeon receiving Christ as new Law, Andr.Cr.*or*.9(M.97.988D); *ib*.13(1076A).

[*]νομοδώτης, ὁ, v. νομοδότης.

νομοθεσία, ἡ, A. *legislation*; **1.** in gen. Πλάτων...ἐκ τῶν Μωϋσέως τὰ περὶ τὴν ν. ὠφεληθεὶς Clem.*str*.1.25(p.103.9; M.8.912B); Thdt.*Jer*. 35:1–2(2.561); **2.** of divine law in gen. τῇ μὲν ν. τοῦ θεοῦ...συνηδόμεθα Meth.*res*.2.6(p.340.10; M.18.304C); Ath.*gent*.27(M.25.53B); *Const.App*.7.39.2; τῆς σῆς δέομαι φωταγωγίας καὶ ν. Thdt.*Ps*.118:33 (1.1446); as due to work of H. Ghost from Father through Son, Didym.(‡Bas.)*Eun*.5(1.311B; M.29.745C); opp. counsels which are αὐθαιρέτου γνώμης, Thdt.*Eph*.2:15(3.414); **3.** of Mosaic Law, Iren. *haer*.3.21.2(M.7.949A); Clem.*prot*.11(p.79.11; M.8.229A); ἡ ν. τὴν τοῦ θεοῦ δικαιοσύνην ἅμα καὶ ἀγαθότητα καταγγέλλει id.*str*.2.18(p.158.11; M.8.1025A); Hipp.*haer*.9.27(p.261.9; M.16.3406B); ref. Col.2:16–17 τὸ βούλημα τῆς πάσης ἐπιτεμνόμενος ν. Or.*princ*.4.2.6(p.317.9; M.11.369B); id.*Cels*.2.75(p.196.12; M.11.912B); ἐν τῇ θείᾳ ν. προστέτακται *ib*.8.38(p.253.5; 1573B); id.*Jo*.10.13(11; p.184.11; M.14.329A); ref. Zach.4:1ff. ἡ ἐλαία τὴν ἐπὶ Μωσέως αἰνίσσεται ν. Meth.*symp*.10.6 (p.128.13; M.18.201C); Eus.*h.e*.1.2.23(M.20.65A); *Const.App*.8.46.5; partic. of decalogue, Clem.*str*.6.16(p.500.6; M.9.360A); Jo.D.*f.o*.1.5 (M.94.800C); of Pentateuch ἡ δευτέρα βίβλος κατὰ τὴν ν. Epiph.*haer*. 8.4(p.190.10; M.41.212A); **4.** of Christ's teaching as new Law, Clem.*paed*.2.8(p.203.18; M.8.488A); προπαιδείας [sc. Mosaic Law] ἐπὶ τὴν τοῦ Ἰησοῦ ν. id.*q.d.s*.9(p.165.21; M.9.613A); ἀρχὴ μὲν γὰρ νομοθεσίας, ἐπὶ Μωϋσέως ἦν...ἀρχὴ δὲ νομοθεσίας καὶ διαθήκης δευτέρας κατὰ τὸν Ἰησοῦν...γεγονέναι ὁμολογεῖται Or.*Cels*.2.75(p.196.14; M.11.912C); *ib*.3.7(p.208.10; 929A); ἡ κατὰ τὸ εὐαγγέλιον...ν. Meth.*symp*.10.3(p.125.4; M.18.197A); *Const.App*.5.13.3; πνευματικὴ ν. Thdt.*h.e*.5.13.3(3.1042); ref. Elisha's refusal of riches τὴν εὐαγγελικὴν ν. πρὸ τῆς ν. πεπλήρωκε id.*qu*.19 *in 4Reg*.(1.523); id.*affect*.9 (p.220.23; 4.925); ἀκριβεστέρα τοῦ νόμου ἡ ν. τῆς χάριτος id.*Rom*.6:14 (3.65); **5.** of eccl. law, *Const.App*.8.46.12; **6.** *rule*; **a.** monastic, Thdt.*h.rel*.3(3.1138); **b.** of any rule of conduct ὁ ἀνὴρ ν. ἑαυτῷ ἦν δεδωκώς, ἵνα ἐξερχόμενος...μηδαμῶς μεταλάβῃ τροφῆς, μέχρις ἂν τῆς ὁτοῦ ἁγίου ἀξιωθῇ εὐχῆς Gr.Mag.*dial*.(tr.Zach.)2.13(M.*PL*.66.157C); **7.** *statement of doctrine* καινὴ...τῶν δογμάτων ν. Bas.*Eun*.2.26(1.263A; M.29.632C); ἡ δὲ τῶν ἐναντίων ν. καὶ τοῖς γεγραμμένοις ἀπ' ἀρχῆς ἀπειθεῖ Euther.*confut*.5(M.28.1352C); *ib*.8(1361C).

B. *precept, ordinance*; **1.** in gen.; of Tatian's precepts against marriage, Hipp.*haer*.10.18(p.279.20; M.16.3435C); of apostolic precepts, Thdt.*qu*.1 *in Lev*.(1.178); id.*1Cor*.6:6(3.195); id.*1Thess*.4:4 (3.516); **2.** of imperial constitutions, Const.ap.Eus.*h.e*.10.5.14(M.20.885A); Const.ap.Eus.*v.C*.3.64(p.111.17; M.20.1140B); Thdt.*h.e*.4.17.6 (3.976); **3.** of divine precepts, Clem.*str*.3.18(p.246.17; M.8.1212B); Or.*princ*.4.3.5(p.331.1; M.11.385A); Meth.*symp*.9.1(p.114.1; M.18.177A); Bas.*hom*.1.2(2.2C; M.31.165A).

νομοθετ-έω, A. *legislate, lay down law*; trans., *frame* or *ordain* laws; **1.** of God as lawgiver; **a.** in gen. ἢ...μόνον ὑποληψόμεθα τὸ πνεῦμα ~εῖν ἡμῖν...καὶ μὴ ἐκ τοῦ πατρὸς δι' υἱοῦ τὴν νομοθεσίαν... κατάρχεσθαι; Didym.(‡Bas.)*Eun*.5(1.311B; M.29.745C); of law of nature, Or.*Cels*.5.37(p.40.18; M.11.1237B); cf. εὔλογον...τὸν τῆς φύσεως προτιμᾶν νόμον, ὄντα νόμον τοῦ θεοῦ, παρὰ τὸν...ὑπὸ τῶν ἀνθρώπων...νενομοθετημένον *ib*.(p.41.6; 1237C); **b.** in Mosaic and other OT Law ὁ...κύριος...ὁπήνικα ~εῖν ἤρχετο τῷ λόγῳ Clem.*paed*. 2.8(p.203.14; M.8.488A); id.*str*.3.10(p.227.29; M.8.1172B); docetic οὐ μόνον δὲ ὁ λόγος ἡμῖν ἀπὸ τοῦ βάτου, τουτέστιν ἀέρος, ~εῖ, ἀλλὰ γὰρ καὶ ὀσμαὶ καὶ χρώματα διὰ τοῦ ἀέρος ἡμῖν τὰς δυνάμεις τὰς ἑαυτῶν ἐμφανίζουσιν Hipp.*haer*.8.9(p.229.5; M.16.3354A); κατὰ τὴν ἐπαγγελίαν τῶν γραμμάτων ὁ πρῶτος αὐτὰ ~ήσας Or.*Cels*.1.18(p.70.13; M.11.693A); δεκάλογος, ἣν...θεὸς αὐτοῖς ἐνομοθέτησεν *Const.App*.6.20.1; κρεωφαγίαν ἐνομοθέτησεν Thdt.*qu*.55 *in Gen*.tit.(1.66); **2.** of Moses, *Barn*.10.11; and scriptures in gen., *Const.App*.5.12.1; ref. scripture literally interpreted ἄλλοτε καὶ ἀδύνατα ~εῖται Or.*princ*. 4.2.9(p.322.8; M.11.376A); **3.** divine legislation through Christ, id.*Cels*.3.73(p.265.1; M.11.1016B); of Christ in his precepts, opp. counsels, Thdt.*Eph*.2:15(3.414); id.*h.e*.2.31.13(3.910); **4.** ref. apostolic legislation, Or.*princ*.3.1.19(p.233.12; M.11.292B); Meth.*symp*. 3.12(p.40.20; M.18.80A); inspired by H. Ghost, Thdt.*1Cor*.7:12(3.204); **5.** of conciliar decisions, id.*h.e*.1.9.1(3.764).

B. *furnish with laws* ἐνομοθέτησεν...Ἀλέξανδρος τὴν χώραν Jo. Mal.*chron*.8 p.194(M.97.305B); pass. ὑπὸ...ὄφεως ~ουμένων Ἰουδαίων *A.Jo*.94(p.197.12); Or.*Cels*.1.17(p.69.18; M.11.692B); id.*hom*.28 *in Lc*.(p.175.13); id.*Jo*.10.13(11; p.184.21; M.14.329B).

C. *instruct* παρ' ἑτέρου ~ούμενος Cyr.*Jo*.2.4(4.177A).

D. *prescribe, lay down, ordain*; Tat.*orat*.8(p.8.23; M.6.824A); Clem.*paed*.1.5(p.101.3; M.8.272A); μετριάζειν ~οῦσα *ib*.2.7(p.193.4; 464B); οὗτος...νενομοθέτηται καλεῖσθαι Hipp.*haer*.1.2(p.6.3; M.16.3024C); Eus.*e.th*.3.3(p.154.27; M.24.997B); ~εῖ ῥήματα Bas.*Eun*.2.6 (1.242D; M.29.584B); παρθενίαν ~ῶν [sc. Χριστός] Gr.Naz.*or*.43.62 (M.36.576C); Gr.Nyss.*tres dii*(M.45.132B); Chrys.*hom*.70.4 *in Mt*.(7.693A); οὐχὶ ~ῶν τὸ πορεύεσθαι λέγει, ἀλλ' οὐκ ἐπέχων id.*hom*.36.3 *in 1Cor*.(10.337E); οἴκημα τὸ νενομοθετημένον id.*hom*.16.2 *in 1Tim*. (11.646A); Thdt.*Ps*.104:4(1.1344); of counsels of perfection, id.*Ps*. 111:3(1.1403); id.*2Thess*.3:12(3.540); c. ἵνα, Maximinus Daia ap. Eus.*h.e*.9.10.8(M.20.833B); c. genit. τῶν...ἡμερῶν τῶν ἀζύμων αὐτοῖς ~εῖ †Chrys.*synops*.(6.327D).

νομοθέτης, ὁ, *lawgiver*; **1.** of God εἰ δὲ σεαυτὸν ἀναγράφεις τοῦ θεοῦ, οὐρανὸς μέν σοι ἡ πατρίς, ὁ δὲ θεὸς ν. Clem.*prot*.10(p.77.16; M.8.225A); id.*str*.3.12(p.232.22; M.8.1181A); ὁ αὐτὸς ν. ἅμα καὶ εὐαγγελιστής *ib*.(p.234.19; 1184C); Or.*Cels*.5.37(p.40.24; M.11.1237B) cit. s. νόμος; Meth.*symp*.3.2(p.29.10; M.18.64B); εἰ μὲν οὖν ν. ἐστίν, δίκαιος τυγχάνει *Hom.Clem*.18.1; Cyr.H.*catech*.2.15; διὰ Χριστοῦ ποιητήν,...ν. δι' αὐτοῦ *Const.App*.6.11.3; Thdt.*eran*.1(4.35); τὸν τῶν καινῶν καὶ τῶν παλαιῶν...ν. id.*Hebr*.13:25(3.637); εἷς παλαιᾶς καὶ καινῆς διαθήκης ν. id.*qu*.52 *in Ex*.(1.158); **2.** of Christ, esp. as institutor of new Law, Just.*dial*.12.2(M.6.500B); ὁ καινὸς ν. *ib*.14.3 (505A); ποιμήν τε καὶ ν. ἀγαθός Clem.*str*.1.26(p.105.16; M.8.916C); as ἀρχιερεύς and ν., *ib*.2.5(p.123.27; 953B); Gr.Nyss.*Maced*.20(M.45.1325D); τῆς φύσεως δημιουργὸς καὶ τῆς διατάξεως ν. *Const.App*.3.9.4; ἐγένετο ὁ ν. αὐτὸς πλήρωμα τοῦ νόμου, οὐκ ἀνελὼν τὸν φυσικὸν νόμον, ἀλλὰ παύσας τὰ διὰ τῆς δευτερώσεως ἐπείσακτα, εἰ καὶ πάντα *ib*.6.22.5; ref. Jo.14:10 ἀνθρωπίνως ὁ λόγος πρόεισιν. οὐ γὰρ...ὁ ν. ὑπὸ ἐντολὰς ἔμελλε κείσεσθαι Chrys.*hom*.76.2 *in Jo*.(8.448D); Cyr.*Jo*.1.4(4.33B) cit. s. νομοφύλαξ; τὰ περιττὰ τοῦ νόμου μετὰ τὴν τοῦ ν. παρουσίαν ἐπαύσατο, τὰ δέ γε φυσικῶς προηγορευμένα, καὶ μετὰ τὴν καινὴν διαθήκην κρατεῖ Thdt.*Eph*.6:3(3.436); ὁ ἀληθινὸς ν., οὗ τύπος ἦν ὁ Μωϋσῆς id.*eran*.1(4.64); **3.** of Moses, Clem.*str*.2.15(p.149.18; M.8.1008A); Or.*princ*.4.1.1(p.293.6; M.11.344A); *Hom.Clem*.2.16; **4.** of Jewish rabbis, *Pers*.(p.27.24); of a Scribe, Cyr.ap.*cat.Mt*.22:32 (p.183.18) for νομομαθής id.*fr.Mt*.22:46(M.72.437A); **5.** of S. Paul, Thdt.*1Thess*.5:28(3.526); **6.** of leaders of Church, *Barn*.21.4; **7.** of teachers of doctrine, ‡Just.*qu.Gr*.15(M.6.1484A).

νομοθέτησις, ἡ, *enactment of laws, legislation*, ‡Bas.*struct.hom*.2.7 (1.341E; M.30.49A).

νομοθήκη, ἡ, *treasury of laws*, †Nil.*vit*.4(M.79.1144C).

νομοΐστωρ, ὁ, ἡ, *one learned in* Mosaic *Law*, Cyr.*Is*.3.2(2.432B); *ib*.4.1(2.577E).

***νομοκάνονον, τό,** = sq., *Schol*. in CTrull.*can*.2(*Mon*.2 p.651).

***νομοκανών, ὁ,** *compilation of canons, Nomoc*.tit.

***νομομάθεια, ἡ,** *knowledge of* Mosaic *Law*, Cyr.*Is*.3.2(2.411D); id. *Jo*.2.1(4.149A); *ib*.3.1(251E).

***νομομαθέω,** *be learned in the Law* *Chron.Pasch*.p.184(M.92.452B).

νομομαθής, *learned in the law*; **1.** in gen.; of Persian sages, *Pers.*(p.11.4; M.10.97C); of those learned in Roman law, Gennad.*fr. Rom.*7:4(p.368.27; M.85.1677D); **2.** of those learned in Mosaic Law; in gen., Hipp.*Dan.*1.29.2(νομοθέτῃ M.10.697A); ‡Ath.*Sabell.*11(M.28.113C); comp., Cyr.*hom.pasch.*23(5^2.282B); Dam.*troph.*1.8(p.214.7); of the Scribes, Cyr.*Jo.*11.12(4.1025C); Levites, id.*Os.*67(3.102A); of Symeon and others who understood Messianic prophecies, id.*Is.*5.5(2.861B); superl., of Symeon, ‡Meth.*Sym.et Ann.*7(M.18.364C); of Christ's disciples, Or.*fr.59 in Jo.*(p.531.21); of S. Peter, Adam.*dial.*2.13(p.84.6; M.11.1781A); S. Paul, ‡Ath.*serm.fid.*20(p.20; M.26.1273A); Didym.*Trin.*2.8(M.39.624C); Chrys.*hom.7.3 in 1Cor.*(10.54A); Cyr.*ador.*10(1.339A); Sophr.H.*mir.Cyr.et Jo.*27(M.87.3497D).

νόμος, ὁ, **I.** *established principle, custom*, religious ν. ἱερωσύνης, θυσιῶν *T.Lev.*9.7; ἀγάλματα...ἐθεράπευε κατὰ τοὺς πατρίους...ν. *V.Const.*19(p.556.8); ‡Jo.D.*Artem.*43(p.14.27; M.96.1292A).

II. *law*; **A.** def. ν. δέ ἐστιν οὐ τὰ νομιζόμενα...οὐδὲ δόξα πᾶσα... ἀλλὰ ν. ἐστὶ χρηστὴ δόξα, χρηστὴ δὲ ἡ ἀληθής,...ᾗ τινες ἀκολούθως δηλονότι τῇ χρηστῇ δόξῃ λόγον ὀρθὸν τὸν ν. ἔφασαν, προστακτικὸν μὲν ὧν ποιητέον, ἀπαγορευτικὸν δὲ ὧν οὐ ποιητέον Clem.*str.*1.25(p.104.6; M.8.913B); Eus.*p.e.*7.9(313C; M.21.529B); ν. κανὼν δικαίων ἐστὶ καὶ ἀδίκων, προστακτικὸς μὲν ὧν ποιητέον, ἀπαγορευτικὸς δὲ ὧν οὐ ποιητέον· οὗ φυλακτικός ἐστιν ὁ πολύς, κἂν τὸ ἐν αὐτῷ ὠφέλιμον ἀγνοῇ †Bas.*Is.*23(1.397B; M.30.164A).

B. of human or secular law in rel. to Christianity πείθονται τοῖς ὡρισμένοις ν., καὶ τοῖς ἰδίοις βίοις νικῶσι τοὺς ν. *Diogn.*5.10; ἐὰν δέ τις τοὺς διαφόρους ν. τῶν ἀνθρώπων προβάληται, λέγων ὅτι παρ' οἷς μὲν ἀνθρώποις τάδε καλά, τὰ δὲ αἰσχρὰ νενόμισται, παρ' ἄλλοις δὲ τὰ παρ' ἐκείνοις αἰσχρὰ καλά, καὶ τὰ καλὰ αἰσχρὰ νομίζεται, ἀκουέτω...καὶ νόμους διατάξασθαι τῇ ἑαυτῶν κακίᾳ ὁμοίους τοὺς πονηροὺς ἀγγέλους ἐπιστάμεθα, οἷς χαίρουσιν οἱ ὅμοιοι γενόμενοι ἄνθρωποι, καὶ ὀρθὸς λόγος παρελθὼν οὐ...πάντα δόγματα καλὰ ἀποδείκνυσιν, ἀλλὰ τὰ μὲν φαῦλα, τὰ δὲ ἀγαθά Just.*2apol.*9.4(M.6.460A); οὐ γὰρ πρὸς ἀνθρωπικοὺς ν. ὁ λόγος ἡμῖν, οὓς ἄν τις γενόμενος πονηρὸς καὶ λάθοι...ἀλλ' ἔστιν ἡμῖν ν. ⟨ὁ θεοῦ δεσπότης καὶ ἡ τοῦ παρ' αὐτοῦ λόγου ἐντολή⟩ ἢ δικαιοσύνης μέτρον ἐποίησεν Athenag.*leg.*32.2(M.6.964B); contrast between secular laws peculiar to individual nations, and laws of Moses and Christ which are accepted universally, Or.*princ.*4.1.1(p.293.17; M.11.344B); δύο...νόμων προκειμένων γενικῶς, καὶ τοῦ μὲν ὄντος τῆς φύσεως ν., ὃν θεὸς ἂν νομοθετήσαι, ἑτέρου δὲ τοῦ ἐν ταῖς πόλεσι γραπτοῦ· καλόν, ὅπου μὲν μὴ ἐναντιοῦται ὁ γραπτὸς ν. τῷ τοῦ θεοῦ, μὴ λυπεῖν τοὺς πολίτας προφάσει ξένων ν.· ἔνθα δὲ τὰ ἐναντία τῷ γραπτῷ ν. προστάσσει ὁ τῆς φύσεως τουτέστι τοῦ θεοῦ, ὅρα εἰ μὴ ὁ λόγος αἱρεῖ μακρὰν μὲν χαίρειν εἰπεῖν τοῖς γεγραμμένοις...ἐπιδιδόναι δὲ ἑαυτὸν τῷ θεῷ νομοθέτῃ id.*Cels.*5.37(p.40.17ff.; M.11.1237B); οἱ θαυμαστοὶ ἡμῶν ν., οἷς νῦν τὰ πάντων τῶν ὑπὸ τὴν Ῥωμαίων ἀρχὴν ἀνθρώπων κατευθύνεται πράγματα, οὔτε συγκείμενοι οὔτε καὶ ἐκμανθανόμενοι ἀταλαιπώρως· ὄντες μὲν αὐτοὶ σοφοί τε καὶ ἀκριβεῖς καὶ ποικίλοι καὶ θαυμαστοί, καὶ συνελόντι εἰπεῖν Ἑλληνικώτατοι Gr.Thaum.*pan.Or.*1(p.2.23; M.10.1052C).

C. of divine law; **1.** in gen., of God's moral law, *T.Gad* 3.1; *T.Neph.*2.6; κατά τινα θεῖον ν. καὶ λόγον Athenag.*leg.*31.1(M.6.961B); Clem.*str.*7.2(p.8.29; M.9.413B); παντὸς μὲν ἁγίου ὑπὸ θεοῦ βασιλευομένου καὶ τοῖς πνευματικοῖς ν. τοῦ θεοῦ πειθομένου Or.*or.*25.1(p.357.4; M.11.496C); id.*Jo.*2.16(10; p.73.1; M.14.141C); ἐπαναπαύεσθαι τοῖς σοῖς ἁγίοις ν. Const.ap.Eus.*v.C.*2.56(p.64.11; M.20.1032A); Thdt.*ep.*7(4.1066); ὁ δὲ ν. τοῦ θεοῦ θέλημα αὐτοῦ ἐστιν Jo.D.*Man.*1.43(M.94.1545D); **2.** its three divisions τρεῖς ν., τόν τε φυσικὸν καὶ τὸν Μωσαϊκὸν καὶ τὸν εὐαγγελικόν †Cyr.*coll.VT*(6^4.52D; M.77.1253B); τῶν θείων ν. εἴδη τρία παρὰ...Παύλου· τὸν μὲν γὰρ δίχα γραμμάτων...διὰ τῆς κτίσεως καὶ τῆς φύσεως τοῖς ἀνθρώποις δεδόσθαι...τὸν δὲ διὰ... Μωσέως ἐν γράμμασι...καὶ τρίτον...τὸν τῆς χάριτος Thdt.*Ps.*18:1(1.716); two divisions δύο ν., τόν τε φυσικὸν καὶ τὸν γραπτόν, καὶ μηδέτερον θατέρου ἔχοντα πλέον ἢ ἔλαττον Max.*ambig.*(M.91.1128C); numerous divisions, viz. Mosaic Law; other parts of OT; and ἡ μυστικωτέρα καὶ θειοτέρα τοῦ ν. ἐκδοχή, ὡς ἐν τῷ 'οἴδαμεν γὰρ ὅτι ὁ ν. πνευματικός ἐστι'.... ν. ὁ κατὰ τὰς κοινὰς ἐννοίας ἐνεσπαρμένος τῇ ψυχῇ καὶ...ἐγγεγραμμένος τῇ καρδίᾳ λόγος, προστακτικὸς μὲν ὧν ποιητέον, ἀπαγορευτικὸς δὲ ὧν οὐ ποιητέον Or.*comm.in Rom.*7:7(*JTS* 14 p.11); **3.** of natural law, Athenag.*leg.*3.1(M.6.896C); ἐποίησεν ἄνθρωπον ἐκ ψυχῆς ἀθανάτου καὶ σώματος νοῦν τε συγκατεσκεύασεν αὐτῷ καὶ ν. ἔμφυτον ἐπὶ σωτηρίᾳ καὶ φυλακῇ τῶν παρ' αὐτοῦ διδομένων id.*res.*13(p.63.19; M.6.1000B); Clem.*paed.*3.3(p.249.27; M.8.585B); ἐκ θεοῦ ὅ τε τῆς φύσεως ὅ τε τῆς μαθήσεως ν., εἷς ὤν id.*str.*1.29(p.111.19; M.8.929A); *ib.*3.11(p.228.29; 1173B); ὁ γὰρ γραπτὸς ἐν ταῖς καρδίαις ν. καὶ ἐν ἐθνικοῖς φύσει τὰ τοῦ ν. ποιοῦσιν οὐκ ἄλλος ἐστὶ τοῦ κατὰ τὰς κοινὰς ἐννοίας φύσει ἐγγεγραμμένου τῷ ἡγεμονικῷ ἡμῶν, καὶ τρανωτέρου μετὰ τῆς συμπληρώσεως τοῦ λόγου ὁσημέραι γινομένου. τοῦτο τὸ σημαινόμενον ἦν τοῦ ν. καὶ ἐν τῷ 'ἁμαρτία οὐκ ἐλλογεῖται μὴ ὄντος ν.' ... πρὸ γὰρ τοῦ κατὰ Μωσέα ν. ἐλλελόγηται ἁμαρτία...πολλοί τε ἔγνωσαν τὴν ἁμαρτίαν καὶ πρὸ τοῦ Μωσέως ν. Or.*comm.in Rom.*7:7(*JTS* 14 p.12); contrasted with written civil law, id.*Cels.*5.37(p.40.21; M.11.1237B); ἡ ἀνομία δὲ τῆς Ἱερουσαλὴμ ὑπὲρ τὴν Σοδόμων ἐμεγαλύνθη· οἱ μὲν τὸν φυσικὸν ν. εἶχον μόνον, οἱ δὲ καὶ γραπτὸν καὶ προφήτας id.*fr. 101 in Lam.*(p.271.16; M.13.562D); δισσὰ γὰρ ἐν ἡμῖν λογισμῶν γένη, τὸ μὲν ἀπὸ τῆς ἐπιθυμίας...ἥτις ἐξ ἐπιπνοίας...ἐγενήθη τοῦ ὑλικοῦ πνεύματος, τὸ δὲ ἀπὸ τοῦ ν. κατὰ τὴν ἐντολήν, ὃν ἔμφυτον ἐλάβομεν ἔχειν καὶ φυσικὸν ν., πρὸς τὸ καλὸν ἐξεγείροντα...τὸν λογισμόν Meth.*res.*2.6(p.340.8; M.18.304C); τρεῖς γὰρ ν. ὑποτιθέμενος...ὁ Παῦλος... ἕνα μὲν κατὰ τὸ ἔμφυτον ἐν ἡμῖν ἀγαθόν, ὃν καὶ ν. σαφῶς νοὸς ἐκάλεσεν *ib.*2.7(p.341.1; 304D); ἁπάσῃ ψυχῇ φυσικὸν ν. βοηθὸν αὐτῇ καὶ σύμμαχον ἐπὶ τῶν πρακτέων ὁ τῶν ὅλων δημιουργὸς ὑπεστήσατο Eus.*p.e.*6.6(250B; M.21.425A); δικαιωθέντων ἐν τῷ φυσικῷ ν. ‡Ath.*Apoll.*2.9(M.26.1148B); δοὺς [sc. θεός] ἐπὶ πᾶσι ν. προφήτας, καὶ πρὸ τούτων τὸν φυσικὸν ν. ἄγραφον, τῶν πραττομένων ἐξεταστὴν Gr.Naz.*or.*14.27(M.35.893A); Ἄβελ καὶ Νῶε...φυσικῷ ν. κινηθέντας ἀφ' ἑαυτῶν προσενέγκαι θυσίαν θεῷ *Const.App.*6.20.4; τόν τε γὰρ φυσικὸν ν. οὐκ ἀνεῖλεν, ἀλλ' ἐβεβαίωσεν *ib.*6.23.1; *ib.*7.26.3; ἐξ ἀρχῆς πλάττων ὁ θεὸς τὸν ἄνθρωπον, ν. αὐτῷ φυσικὸν ἐγκατέθηκε. καὶ τί ποτέ ἐστι ν. φυσικός; τὸ συνειδὸς ἡμῖν διήρθρωσε, καὶ αὐτοδίδακτον ἐποίησε τὴν γνῶσιν τῶν καλῶν καὶ τῶν οὐ τοιούτων Chrys.*stat.*12.3(2.127E); αὐτοδίδακτον εἶχον ν. *ib.*12.4(130A); διδάσκαλον αὐτῷ τὸν ἔμφυτον ἐναπέθετο ν., ὥσπερ πλοίῳ κυβερνήτην καὶ ἡνίοχον ἵππῳ id.*scand.*8(3.482C); id.*hom.12.6 in Rom.*(9.550E); dist. from γραπτὸς ν., Isid.Pel.*epp.*4.9(M.78.1057A); τῇ φύσει τοὺς ἀναγκαίους τέθεικε νόμους ὁ ποιητής. οὕτω τὸν Κάϊν κατέκρινεν, ἐπειδήπερ αὐτὸν ἡ φύσις ἐδίδασκεν, ὡς ὁ φόνος παράνομος Thdt.*qu.57 in Gen.*(1.68); ὁ δὲ ν. ὁ ἐν ἡμῖν τῆς ἐμφύτου θεογνωσίας, ἐκάλει τοὺς ἄνδρας πρὸς τὸ δεῖν ἀνάπτειν τὰ χαριστήρια τῷ...δοτῆρι θεῷ Proc.G.*Gen.*4:2(M.87.236A); ‡Jo.D.*Artem.*45(p.16.34; M.96.1293B); **4.** of laws of nature εὐφημοῦμεν οὖν Ἥλιον ὡς καλὸν θεοῦ δημιούργημα καὶ τοὺς ν. φυλάσσον τοῦ θεοῦ Or.*Cels.*8.66(p.282.21; M.11.1616C); Gr.Naz.*or.*28.6(p.29.5; M.36.32C); ταῦτα τῷ ν. τῆς φύσεως ὑποτεταγμένα καρποῖς διετρέφετο ‡Gr.Nyss.*or.2 in Gen.1:26*(M.44.284B); ref. Inc. Κύριλλος εἰρηκώς,...ἐφιέναι αὐτὸν τῇ ἰδίᾳ σαρκί, διὰ τῶν τῆς ἰδίας φύσεως ἰέναι ν. †Leont.B.*sect.*10(M.86.1260D); *ib.*(1260C); τὴν τοῦ κυρίου νόει μοι σάρκα τῶν τῆς φύσεως ν., καὶ μετὰ τὴν...ἕνωσιν, ἀλωβήτων αὐτῆς συντηρηθέντων *ib.*(1333D); ref. Virgin Birth νόμοι γὰρ φύσεως καταλύονται ῥᾷστα τῷ νομοθέτῃ ἐν καιρῷ Leont.H.*Nest.*1.10(M.86.1444A); οὐ θεοφιλὴς ἡ ἀπόφασις, θεὸν ποιεῖν τῶν οἰκείων ν. ὑπόδουλον, θεὸν δουλεύειν τοῖς τῶν δούλων ἐθέλειν ἐθίσμασι Sophr.H.*or.*2.35(M.87.3264C); **5.** of law given to Adam, Meth.*res.*1.58(p.320.15; M.41.1153D); *Hom.Clem.*8.10; ἠσφαλίσατο ν. καὶ τόπῳ τὴν δοθεῖσαν αὐτοῖς χάριν Ath.*inc.*3.4(M.25.101C); ὁ πλάσας...τὸν ἄνθρωπον, ἐλεύθερον ἀφῆκε καὶ αὐτεξούσιον, ν. τῷ τῆς ἐντολῆς μόνῳ κρατούμενον Gr.Naz.*or.*14.25(M.35.892A); μὴ διὰ φωνῆς...δέδωκε τῷ Ἀδὰμ τὴν ἐντολὴν ὁ θεός, ἀλλ' ὥστε ἐντυπῶσαι μὲν αὐτῷ κατὰ τὴν οἰκείαν ἐνέργειαν τήν τε γνῶσιν τοῦ ν. καὶ τὴν ἀκοὴν Diod.*Gen.*2:7(M.33.1567C); ref. Rom.7:12 τινὲς...οὐ περὶ τοῦ ν. Μωϋσέως αὐτόν φασι λέγειν...ἀλλ' οἱ μὲν περὶ τοῦ φυσικοῦ, οἱ δὲ περὶ τῆς ἐντολῆς τῆς ἐν τῷ παραδείσῳ δοθείσης...τὴν δὲ ἐντολὴν τὴν ἐν τῷ παραδείσῳ οὐδὲ ν. φαίνεται ποτε καλέσας, οὔτε αὐτὸς οὔτε ἄλλος οὐδεὶς Chrys.*hom.12.6 in Rom.*(9.550E); Thdt.*haer.*5.17(4.440); **6.** of Gen.2:24 as ν. γάμου, id.*qu.7 in 2Reg.*(1.406); id.*Cant.*2:4–5(2.57); **7.** of laws given to Adam, Noah, Abraham, Moses, as continuous series completed by Christ's teaching, id.*haer.*5.17(4.440); **8.** of Mosaic Law; **a.** known also as Μωσῆς q.v.; **b.** its scope; **i.** Pentateuch, opp. 'prophets', *T.Lev.*16.2; Ign.*Smyrn.*5.1; ‡*Diogn.*11.6; Clem.*paed.*3.12(p.284.16; M.8.665C); id.*str.*3.10(p.228.3; M.8.1172B); exeg. Cant.2:9 λέγοις δ' ἂν καὶ ὄρη τὰ ἐν ν. νοήματα, βουνοὺς δὲ τὰ τῶν λοιπῶν προφητῶν Or.*Cant.*3(p.201.27; M.13.167D); id.*hom.5.13 in Jer.*(p.42.10; M.13.313A); εἰς τὰς αὐτὰς σκηνὰς ἀνάγουσι ν. καὶ προφῆται καὶ εὐαγγέλιον, τρεῖς μὲν ἀριθμούμεναι, πρὸς ἓν δὲ τέλος ὁρῶσαι id.*fr.24 in Lc.*9:33(p.246); Cyr.H.*catech.*4.35; Gr.Nyss.*Eun.*5(2 p.101.15; M.45.680A); *Const.App.*2.5.4; *ib.*2.25.3; μετὰ τὴν ἀνάγνωσιν τοῦ ν. καὶ τῶν προφητῶν καὶ τοῦ εὐαγγελίου *ib.*2.39.6; **ii.** esp. decalogue, dist. from δευτέρωσις, *ib.*2.5.6; *ib.*6.20.1; δέδωκεν ν. εἰς βοήθειαν τοῦ φυσικοῦ, καθαρόν, σωτήριον, ἅγιον...δέκα λογίων πλήρη *ib.*6.19.2; dist. from law of circumcision, Chrys.*hom.49.3 in Jo.*(8.292A); **iii.** including whole OT, Thphl.Ant.*Autol.*1.11(M.6.1041B); προφήτας, ὧν τὰ ῥήματα...ν. λέγεται Or.*Jo.*19.3(p.301.19; M.14.529B); incl. Pss., id.*comm.in Rom.*7:7(*JTS* 14 p.11); *Const.App.*1.6.3; **iv.** including all Jewish λατρεία and πολιτεία, ‡Just.*qu.et resp.*92(M.6.1333B); **v.** ἐντολαὶ αἱ κατὰ νόμον dist. from αἱ πρὸ τοῦ ν.,

Clem.*str.*7.2(p.8.29; M.9.413B); and from ἐντολὴ ἡ ἐν τῷ παραδείσῳ, Chrys.*hom.12.6 in Rom.*(9.550E); **c.** division of Law; **i.** into historical, moral, and ceremonial; historical Law, Or.*comm.in Rom.* 7:7(p.11); moral law, including τὰ φύσει καλὰ καὶ εὐσεβῆ καὶ δίκαια, observed by patriarchs, dist. from later ceremonial Law, Just.*dial.* 45.3ff.(M.6.572Cff.); moral law of decalogue dist. from laws given on account of sin after making of golden calf, cf.Iren.*haer.*4.15.1(M.6.1012B); latter not to be observed by Christians, *Const.App.*1.6.9; *ib.*6.20.1; Thdt.*Gal.*2:15–16(3.370); **ii.** literal and spiritual, v. infra i and j; **iii.** Law consists in μαρτυρία...ὡς τοὺς ἁμαρτάνοντας διαμαρτυρόμενος καὶ...τὴν τιμωρίαν ὑποδεικνύς· δικαιώματα δέ, ὡς διδάσκων τὸ δίκαιον...· ἐντολὴ δέ, ὡς τὸ πρακτέον ἐντελλόμενος Thdt.*Ps.*18:8–11(1.721); **d.** given by Logos through (not by) Moses, Clem.*paed.*1.7(p.125.19; M.8.321C); through Moses by God, Eus.*e.th.*2.14(p.116.5; M.24.929B); through mediation of Moses as type of Christ, Bas.*Spir.*33(3.27C; M.32.125B); through angels, Or.*hom.13.1 in Jer.*(p.102.27; M.13.400C); id.*Jo.*13.50(49; p.277.30; M.14.489B); ἀγγέλους...καὶ τὸν θεόν· ὧν μέσον ὄντα τὸν υἱὸν τοῦ θεοῦ τὸν ν. χειρὶ μὲν ἰδίᾳ εἰληφέναι φησὶν παρὰ τοῦ πατρός, δι' ἀγγέλων δὲ τῷ πρώτῳ διατεταχέναι λαῷ· ἦν ἄρα...ὁ υἱὸς μεσίτης θεοῦ τε καὶ ἀγγέλων, πρὶν ἢ γενέσθαι μεσίτης θεοῦ καὶ ἀνθρώπων Eus.*Marcell.*1.1(p.7.29; M.24.725B); **e.** transmitted orally by Moses to 70, to be administered by them in succession; written down by someone other than Moses after latter's death, and found in Temple 500 years later, *Hom.Clem.*3.47; cf.*ib.*2.38; **f.** divine, *A.(Pass.)Petr.et Paul.*39(p.152.13); Or.*ep.*2.3(p.66.5; M.11.89C); *Hom.Clem.*2.52; **g.** prior in time to Greek philosophy and to poets, cf.Tat.*orat.*40(p.41.12; M.6.884C); cf.Thphl.Ant.*Autol.*3.17ff.(M.6.1144Cff.); cf.Or.*Cels.*4.11(p.281.25; M.11.1040D); ὅτι δὲ παλαιὸς καὶ πρῶτος ὁ Μωϋσέως ν., καὶ ἐκ τῆς Διοδώρου καὶ τῶν λοιπῶν ἱστοριῶν ἱκανῶς ἡμῖν ἐν τοῖς προάγουσιν ἀποδέδεικται ‡Just.*coh.Gr.*26(M.6.288B); source of Plato's philosophy, Clem.*str.*1.25(p.103.14; M.8.912B); and Pythagoras', *ib.*2.18(p.162.14; 1032B); **h.** its purpose; **i.** morality, Clem.*str.*3.6(p.217.11; 1149A); ‡Gr.Nyss.*or.2 in Gen.1:26*(M.44.288A); through fear, Clem.*str.*2.7(p.130.21; 968C); *ib.*2.18(p.157.6; 1021C); *ib.*2.20(p.178.11; 1065A); οὔκουν πάθος ὁ φόβος οὗ γεννητικὸς ὁ ν. ὥστε ὁ ν. ἅγιος καὶ τῷ ὄντι πνευματικός ἐστι κατὰ τὸν ἀπόστολον *ib.*4.3(p.253.6; 1224B); **ii.** to dist. Israel from gentiles, Chrys.*dimiss.Chan.*7(3.438E); ref. Eph.2:14–15 τινὲς μέν φασιν ὅτι...μεσότοιχον τῶν Ἰουδαίων πρὸς τοὺς Ἕλληνας, ὅτι οὐκ ἀφίησιν αὐτοὺς ἀναμίγνυσθαι. ἐμοὶ δὲ οὐ τοῦτο δοκεῖ· ἀλλὰ...τὸ μεσότοιχον τοῦτο κοινὸν εἶναι, τὴν ἔχθραν ἐν τῇ σαρκί. ... φραγμὸς ὁ ν. ἦν, ἀλλ' οὗτος ἐγένετο μὲν ἀσφαλείας ἕνεκεν id.*hom.5.2 in Eph.*(11.34C,D); **iii.** as temporary dispensation, ending with Jo. Bapt. and fulfilled in advent of Christ, Iren.*haer.*4.4.2(M.7.982A); cf.*ib.*4.15.2(1013B); cf.Or.*hom.10.1 in Lev.*(p.441.4; M.12.525B); Jo.Philop.*pasch.*(p.209.26); **iv.** as pedagogue to bring men to Christ ὁ γὰρ ν. παιδαγωγία παίδων ἐστὶ δυσηνίων...διὰ τοῦτο αὐτοῖς καὶ ὁ ν. καὶ ὁ φόβος εἵπετο εἰς ἀνακοπὴν ἁμαρτημάτων καὶ προτροπὴν κατορθωμάτων, καταρτίζων εὐηκοΐαν αὐτοῖς τοῦ ἀληθοῦς παιδαγωγοῦ, τὴν εὐπείθειαν Clem.*paed.*1.11(p.147.19; M.8.365B); id.*str.*1.26(p.104.13ff.; M.8.916A); *ib.*7.14(p.61.29; M.9.520C); its significance being revealed by Christ's advent, Or.*princ.*4.1.6(p.301.14; M.11.352B); when Law ceased, cf.id.*hom.14.2 in Ezech.*(p.452.33; M.13.766D); ἐκ τοῦ παρ' ἐκείνοις ν. ... ἡ ἐξ ἡμῶν εἰς εὐσέβειαν ὑπῆρξε προαγωγή id.*Cant.*2(p.169.27; M.13.141D); Eus.*d.e.*1.6(p.27.22; M.22.56B); id.*e.th.*2.14(p.117.11; M.24.932B); Cyr.*ador.*1(1.5A); *ib.*6(173C); id.*Is.*1.1(2.20B); ὅσιος δὲ λόγος ὁ ν. ἦν, ὅτι καὶ θεοῦ, καὶ...παιδαγωγὸς εἰς εὐσέβειαν id.*Am.*47(3.301D); **v.** prophetic and typical, cf.Just.*dial.* 42.4(M.6.565C); cf.Mel.*pass.*3 p.1.9; cf. *lex...erat...prophetia futurorum*, Iren.*haer.*4.15.1(M.7.1012B); ν. καθ' ὃν ὑποδείγματι καὶ σκιᾷ ἐλάτρευον τῶν ἐπουρανίων οἱ Ἰουδαίων ἱερεῖς, ἐν ἀπορρήτῳ διηγούμενοι τὸ τοῦ ν. περὶ τῶν θυσιῶν βούλημα καὶ ὧν σύμβολα ἦσαν αὗται Or.*Cels.*5.44(p.47.24; M.11.1249B); τυπικῶς ἐποίουν τὰ προσταττόμενα ὑπὸ τοῦ ν. *ib.*6.70(p.140.21; 1405A); cf. *Christum autem tamquam verbum dei non solum in evangeliis loqui, sed et in lege certum est...verum in lege incipientes, in evangeliis perfectos docet*, id.*hom.14.1 in Gen.*(p.122.21; M.12.237A); cf.id.*hom.10.1 in Lev.*(p.441.12; M.12.525C); id.*hom.7.1 in Jer.*(p.52.12; M.13.329C); id.*Jo.*1.6(8; p.11.11; M.14.36A); τυπικῶς...καὶ αἰνιγματώδως ἀναφερόμενα εἰς τὸν Χριστὸν τῶν ἀναγεγραμμένων ἐν τῷ ν. πλεῖστα ὅσα ἔστιν εὑρεῖν *ib.*13.26(p.251.7; 445A); ὁ ν. ἐστὶ...πνευματικός, τὰς εἰκόνας ἐμπεριέχων τῶν μελλόντων ἀγαθῶν Meth.*symp.*5.7(p.61.21; M.18.109B); Gr.Naz.*or.*6.4(M.35.728A); τύπος γὰρ ὁ ν. καὶ σκιά, καὶ τῆς εὐσεβείας ἡ μόρφωσις ὡς ἐν ὠδῖσιν ἔτι, καὶ κεκρυμμένον ἐν ἑαυτῇ τὸ τῆς ἀληθείας ἔχουσα κάλλος Cyr.*ador.*1(1.3E); hence Law not abolished but completed by Christ, *ib.*(5C); id.*Is.*1.1(2.20B); ἔργα λέγει τοῦ ν. τούτων δὲ ἡ μὲν παράβασις ἁμαρτία, ἡ δὲ φυλακὴ οὐ δικαιοσύνης τελείας κατόρθωσις· ταῦτα γὰρ ἑτέρων αἰνίγματα Thdt.*Gal.*2:16(3.370); **vi.** conveys allegorical meaning, cf.*Barn.*10; cf.Just.*dial.*41(M.6.564Bff.); ref. food laws, cf. *praedixit autem figuraliter omnia haec lex, de animalibus delineans hominem...immunda...quae neque duplicem ungulam habent,...hoc est, qui neque in deum fidem habent*, Iren.*haer.*5.8.3(M.7.1143A); Clem.*paed.*2.1(p.166.7; M.8.405B); *ib.*3.11(p.267.13; 628B); cf.id.*str.*5.6(p.346.28ff.; M.9.56Bff.); αἱ μὲν γὰρ κατὰ τὸν ν. θυσίαι τὴν περὶ ἡμᾶς εὐσέβειαν ἀλληγοροῦσι *ib.*7.6(p.24.22; M.9.445A); Or.*Jo.*6.4(2; p.111.7; M.14.205A); Mac.Aeg.*hom.*47.16(M.34.808A); **i.** hence to be spiritually interpreted, cf.*Barn.*7ff.; Just.*dial.*12.2(M.6.500B); διὰ γραπτῆς νομοθεσίας οἱ τῆς ἀληθείας ν. προφητεύονται. ... προέκειτο γὰρ καὶ τὸ ἔνδυμα τῶν πνευματικῶν, λέγω δὲ τὸ σωματικὸν τῶν γραφῶν Or.*princ.*4.2.8(p.320.13; M.11.373A); ἐὰν ἀκούω τοῦ ν., ἤτοι κεκρυμμένως ἀκούω ἢ οὐκ ἀκούω κεκρυμμένως· ὁ Ἰουδαῖος οὐκ ἀκούει κεκρυμμένως τοῦ ν. id.*hom.12.13 in Jer.*(p.99.22; M.13.396B); ὁ γὰρ μὴ πιστεύσας τῇ ἐκδοχῇ τοῦ γράμματος, διὰ μεγαλόνοιαν πιστεύει τῇ πνευματικῇ τοῦ ν. διηγήσει id.*Jo.*32.21(13; p.462.32; M.14.801A); ἀπεδράσαμεν μὲν τὰς Ἰουδαίων μυθολογίας σωφρονιζόμεθα δὲ...τῇ τοῦ ν. ... μυστικῇ θεωρίᾳ id.*Cels.*2.6(p.132.24; M.11.804B); *ib.*7.20(p.171.31ff.; 1449Bff.); ὁ τοίνυν νοήσας τὸν πνευματικὸν ν. καὶ τὴν ἐν τοῖς προφήταις...ἀποκεκρυμμένην σοφίαν ὁρᾷ Μωϋσῆν καὶ Ἡλίαν ἐν δόξῃ id.*fr.22 in Lc.*9:28(p.243; M.17.344D); τῇ...δικαιοσύνῃ τοῦ θεοῦ...μαρτυρεῖ οὐδαμῶς μὲν ὁ τῆς φύσεως ν. ... ὁ δὲ Μωσέως ν., οὐ τὸ γράμμα ἀλλὰ τὸ πνεῦμα id.*comm.in Rom.*7:7(*JTS* 14 p.12); Meth.*symp.*5.7(p.61.21; M.18.109B); αἰσχυνέσθωσαν οἱ Ἰουδαῖοι, τὰ βάθη τῶν γραφῶν μὴ συνησθημένοι καὶ πάντα σωματικὰ τὸν ν. ἡγούμενοι...εἰρηκέναι *ib.*9.1(p.115.7; 180A); Gr.Nyss.*Eun.*7(2 p.154.16; M.45.741D); Cyr.*ador.*7(1.225C); v. θεωρία, γραφή; **j.** hence literal observance of Law not required, cf. *Barn.*3.6; *ib.*10.12; literal observance being *cultus angelorum et non dei*, Arist.*apol.*14.4; and ν. ἐντολῶν opp. true law of δόγματα, Or.*comm.in Eph.*2:15(p.406); τὴν συναγωγὴν...καὶ τὴν σωματικὴν τοῦ ν. λατρείαν τῶν πάλαι ἐν τῷ γράμματι συμβόλων, παντελῶς ἀδιάγνωστον ἔχουσαν τὸ φῶς τῆς ἐν νοήμασιν ἀληθοῦς ἐπιγνώσεως id.*fr.12 in Lc.*8:16(p.238); †Cyr.*coll.VT*(6[4].52D; M.77.1253C); **k.** Saul represents those who interpret Law literally, Gibeonites those who interpret it spiritually, *ib.*(51D; M.1251D); **l.** Law and grace, v. χάρις; **m.** Law and faith, v. πίστις; **n.** Law and gospel, cf.Clem.*paed.*1.6(p.110.1; M.8.289B); οὐ δὴ μάχεται τῷ εὐαγγελίῳ ὁ ν., συνᾴδει δὲ αὐτῷ. πῶς γὰρ οὐχί, ἑνὸς ὄντος ἀμφοῖν χορηγοῦ τοῦ κυρίου; id.*str.*2.23(p.193.23; M.8.1096D); *ib.*4.21(p.305.29; 1341A); ἡ τοῦ εὐαγγελίου γνῶσις ἐξήγησίς ἐστι τοῦ ν. καὶ πλήρωσις *ib.*(p.307.34; 1345A); *ib.*7.14(p.61.29; M.9.520C); Or.*Cels.*7.25(p.176.25; M.11.1457A); Law sweetened by gospel of Cross as bitter water by wood (Ex.15:25), id.*hom.10.2 in Jer.*(p.73.4; M.13.360C); id.*Jo.*1.6(8; p.11.2; M.14.33D); *ib.*1.7(9; p.12.10; 36D); ὁμοίως τῷ εὐαγγελίῳ στοιχείτωσαν αἱ ἐκ ν. καὶ προφητῶν ἑρμηνεῖαι *Const.App.*2.5.4; Chrys.*exp.in Ps.*48:2(5.203C); Mac.Aeg.*hom.*32.4(M.34.736C); Cyr.*glaph.Ex.*3(1.326A); id.*Jo.*3.2(4.258C,D); τί γάρ ἐστιν ὁ ν.; εὐαγγέλιον προκατηγγελμένον. τί δὲ τὸ εὐαγγέλιον; ν. πεπληρωμένος ‡Just.*qu.et resp.*101(M.6.1345D); **o.** Law and H. Ghost, Cyr.H.*catech.*17.29; Apoll.*Rom.*7:7(pp.63–65); Chrys.*hom.6.2 in 2Cor.*(10.475E); Thdt.*Rom.*7:14(3.75); id.*2Cor.*3:7–8(3.303); v. πνεῦμα; Law contrasted with πνευματικὴ πολιτεία of Christianity, Jo.Philop.*pasch.*(p.210.8); **p.** Jewish-Christian observance of Law, Just.*dial.*47.3(M.6.577B); cf. *Ebionaei...Paulum recusant, apostatam eum legis dicentes...ac perseverant in his consuetudinibus, quae sunt secundum legem*, Iren.*haer.*1.26.2(M.7.687A); Ἐβιωναῖοι...κατὰ νόμον φάσκοντες δικαιοῦσθαι καὶ τὸν Ἰησοῦν λέγοντες δεδικαιῶσθαι ποιήσαντα τὸν ν. Hipp.*haer.*7.34(p.221.10; M.16.3342B); Eus.*h.e.*3.27.3(M.20.273B); Epiph.*haer.*30.26(p.368.10; M.41.449B); (Cerinthus) *ib.*28.5(p.317.19; 384B); **q.** other heret. attitudes to Law; **i.** Tatian, ref. marriage χωρίζει δὲ καὶ τὸν παλαιὸν ἄνδρα καὶ τὸν καινὸν ὁ Τατιανός, ἀλλ' οὐχ ὡς ἡμεῖς φαμεν· παλαιὸν μὲν ἄνδρα τὸν ν., καινὸν δὲ τὸ εὐαγγέλιον συμφωνοῦμεν αὐτῷ καὶ αὐτοὶ λέγοντες, πλὴν οὐχ ᾗ βούλεται ἐκεῖνος καταλύων τὸν ν. ὡς ἄλλου θεοῦ Clem.*str.*3.12(p.233.19; M.8.1184A); **ii.** Simon Magus δύο...θεούς, ἀφ' ὧν ὁ μὲν εἷς ἐστιν ὁ κόσμον κτίσας, ὁ δὲ ἕτερος ὁ τὸν ν. δοὺς *Hom.Clem.*3.2; *ib.*18.12; Epiph.*haer.*21.4(p.243.15; M.41.292A); **iii.** rejection of Law by Marcion, Iren.*haer.*3.12.12(M.7.905C); and Apelles, Hipp.*haer.*10.20(p.281.1; M.16.3438B); Clem.*str.*2.7(p.131.7; M.8.969B); regarding it as just, but not good, *ib.*2.8(p.133.28; 973C); Μαρκιωνιστῶν παράνοια...οἳ τὸν ν. ἀλλότριον εἶναί φασι Χριστοῦ Or.*fr.78 in Lc.*18:20(p.271; M.17.365D); Epiph.*haer.*42.4(p.99.8; M.41.700C); Thdt.*haer.*1.24(4.314); **iv.** Basilides τὸν ν. ὑπὸ τοῦ ἄρχοντος τεθῆναι τῶν Ἰουδαίων *ib.*1.4(292); **v.** Valentinian, Or.*hom.20.1 in Lc.*(p.131.15; M.13.1851C); **vi.** Montanist; prophecies superior to Law, prophets and gospels, Hipp.*haer*.8.19(p.238.12; M.16.3366C); **9.** of Christian law; **a.** Christ's teaching as law ὑποτάσσεται...τῷ πρεσβυτερίῳ ὡς ν. Ἰησοῦ Χριστοῦ Ign.*Magn*.2; ὁ καινὸς ν. τοῦ κυρίου ἡμῶν Ἰησοῦ Χριστοῦ, ἄνευ ζυγοῦ ἀνάγκης ὢν *Barn*.2.6; δοὺς αὐτοῖς τὸν ν. ὃν ἔλαβε παρὰ τοῦ πατρὸς αὐτοῦ Herm.*sim*.5.6.3; *ib*.8.3.4; Athenag.*leg*.32.2(M.6.964C); ὁ ν. αὐτοῦ τὸν φόβον ὑπεκλύειν βούλεται τὸ ἑκούσιον ἐλευθερώσας εἰς πίστιν Clem.*paed*.3.12(p.284.4; M.8.665B); οἱ λογικοὶ ν. *ib*.(p.287.23; 673A); id.*str*.1.26(p.105.26; M.8.917A); Thdt.*Ps*.116:1(1.1424); id.*affect*.11(p.288.51; 4.1001); ὁ Χριστὸς ν. ἔδωκεν ἡμῖν, τὴν διαθήκην τῶν ἁγίων εὐαγγελίων *Didasc.Jac*.1.50(p.774.28); hence **b.** εὐαγγελικοὶ νόμοι Or.*mart*.30(p.26.22; M.11.601A); Thdt.*Ps*.118:134(1.1471); content of gospel as εὐαγγελικὸς ν., id.*Mich*.4:1–3(2.1493); cf.Meth.*res*.2.8(p.345.2; M.41.1176C); **c.** gospels as νόμοι, Meth.*symp*.10.2(p.124.3; M.18.196B); ref. Fourth Gospel ἀπὸ τοῦ ὄρους κάτεισιν ὁ Ἰωάννης τὸν ν. ἐγχειρισθείς, ὡς ὁ θεόπτης πλάκας Μωσῆς ‡Hipp.Th.*fr*.14(p.46.17); **d.** apostolic ν., Clem.*paed*.3.12(p.287.28; M.8.673A); Thdt.*Ps*.118:136(1.1472); οἱ τοῦ ἀποστόλου νόμοι, τοῦ δεσπότου Χριστοῦ ν. id.*1Cor*.7:12(3.204); *ib*.10:24(230); **e.** Christianity as ν., *A.Petr.et Paul*.60(p.205.4); Const. ap.Eus.*h.e*.10.5.19(M.20.888B); *ib*.10.7.1(893B); Const.II Imp.*ep*.ap. Thdt.*h.e*.2.2.1(3.825); Dam.Papa *ep.Illyr*.ap.Thdt.*h.e*.2.22.5(3.882); **f.** contrasted with Mosaic Law, Just.*dial*.11.2(M.6.497B); as spiritual law of which Mosaic was a shadow, Or.*Jo*.6.51(32; p.160.24; M.14.289C); *ib*.13.13(p.238.11; 420B); Meth.*symp*.10.1(p.122.8; M.18.193A); *Const.App*.2.5.7; Cyr.*Lc*.6:29(M.72.597A); **g.** its obligations compared with those of secular law, Herm.*sim*.1.5–7; Clem.*str*.7.12(p.49.23; M.9.496C); **h.** Christ as law νόμος οὗτος υἱὸς θεοῦ ἐστι κηρυχθεὶς εἰς τὰ πέρατα τῆς γῆς Herm.*sim*.8.3.2; αἰώνιός τε ἡμῖν ν. καὶ τελευταῖος ὁ Χριστὸς ἐδόθη καὶ ἡ διαθήκη πιστή, μεθ' ἣν οὐ ν., οὐ πρόσταγμα, οὐκ ἐντολή Just.*dial*.11.2(M.6.497B); *ib*.43.1(568A); *A.Jo*.112(p.211.9); ἐν δὲ τῷ Πέτρου Κηρύγματι εὕροις ἂν ν. καὶ λόγον τὸν κύριον προσαγορευόμενον Clem.*str*.1.29(p.112.3; M.8.929A); id.*paed*.1.3(p.95.21; M.8.260B); likened to Stoic ν. ἔμψυχος, id.*str*.2.4(p.122.19; M.8.952A); ψυχή, ἐν ᾗ...ἐνιδρύεται ὁ...βασιλεύς τε καὶ γεννήτωρ τῶν καλῶν, ν. ὢν ὄντως καὶ θεσμὸς καὶ λόγος αἰώνιος...εἷς ὢν σωτήρ *ib*.7.3(p.12.18; M.9.421A); Or.*Jo*.1.7(9; p.12.10; M.14.36D); ἵνα...ζῶντι καὶ ἐμψύχῳ ν. τε καὶ λόγῳ ἐν πᾶσιν ὄντι καὶ διὰ πάντων ἥκοντι τὰ πάντα συναρμόζοιτο ὑφ' ἑνὶ πανσόφῳ δεσμῷ, αὐτῷ δὴ τῷ τοῦ θεοῦ λόγῳ τε καὶ ν. συναγόμενά τε καὶ συνδούμενα Eus.*d.e*.4.2(p.152.7; M.22.253C); Thdt.*eran*.2(4.136); **i.** hence of Christian believers as a law οἱ ἅγιοι οὓς προέγνω...ν. εἰσὶ καὶ οὐκ ἐν ν. Or.*comm.in Rom*.3:19,20(*JTS* 13 p.220); Meth.*symp*.11(p.131.4; M.18.208A); *Hom. Clem*.13.15; **10.** of eccl. laws or canons, CNic.(325)*can*.13 cit. s. κανονικός; τοῦ ν. τοῦ κελεύοντος, παρὰ γνώμην τοῦ ἐπισκόπου Κωνσταντινουπόλεως χειροτονίαν ἐπισκόπου μὴ γίνεσθαι· ἠμέλησαν δὲ τοῦ ν. τούτου Socr.*h.e*.7.28.2(M.67.801B); εἶναι γὰρ ν. ἱερατικόν, ὃς ἄκυρα ἀποφαίνει τὰ παρὰ γνώμην πραττόμενα τοῦ Ῥωμαίων ἐπισκόπου Soz.*h.e*.3.10.1(M.67.1057A); of Nicene canons, Thdt.*h.e*.1.8.18(3.764).

D. met., of practice so firmly established as to become a regular principle τὸ λάγνον πᾶν ἐπικέχυται ταῖς πόλεσι ν. γενόμενον Clem.*paed*.3.3(p.248.33; M.8.584C); hence of 'law' of sin (Rom.7:23 etc.), id.*str*.4.6(p.266.11; M.8.1252B); Or.*Cels*.7.69(p.218.15; M.11.1517C); *ib*.8.56(p.273.16; 1601C); Meth.*res*.2.7(p.342.1; M.41.1173B); ν. ἁμαρτίας τὰ ἐν τῇ σαρκὶ πρὸς τὰς ἐκτόπους ἡδονὰς κινήματα Cyr.*thes*.34(5^{1}.354C); and of death, Tat.*orat*.15(p.17.4; M.6.840A); Meth.*res*.2.8(p.345.5; M.41.1176D).

III. *rule* or *standard* of any kind μετροῦντες τὴν εὐσέβειαν θυσιῶν νόμῳ Athenag.*leg*.13.1(M.6.916A); κατὰ τὸν ν. τῆς ἰατρικῆς Gr.Nyss.*or.dom*.4(p.70.6; M.44.1164A); Chrys.*hom.81.2 in Jo*.(8.481A); ἀλληγορίας δὲ νόμῳ ποιμήν ἐστιν ὁ Ἄβελ ζῴων, ὅ ἐστι τῶν αἰσθήσεων Proc.G.*Gen*.4:2(M.87.237A); of rules of a game, Clem.*str*.2.6(p.126.18; M.8.960B).

νομοφύλαξ, ὁ, *keeper, observer, of laws*; civil, Cyr.*ador*.6(1.199D); divine, id.*Am*.14(3.265B); of Christ τῷ κατὰ φύσιν μὲν νομοθέτῃ, διὰ δὲ τὴν πρὸς ἡμᾶς ὁμοίωσιν ν. id.*Jo*.1.4(4.33B); esp. Mosaic, Chrys.*comm.in Gal*.2:6(10.683B).

[*]**νόνα**, ἡ, v. νόννος.

***νόναι** (*νόνναι), αἱ, v. *νῶναι.

νόννος, ὁ, (Lat. *nonnus*) *father*; fem. νόνα perh. in sense of *maternal aunt*, *IGC As.Min*.16 [Cyzicus], cf. νέννος, *uncle*.

[*]**νονοράριος**, v. *ὀνοράριος.

***νοοβλαβής**, *injured in mind, deluded*, Nonn.*par.Jo*.12:14(M.43.857A).

***Νοουατιανοί**, οἱ, v. *Ναυατιανός.

νοσ-έω, *be ill, be sick of, suffer from*, a disease; **1.** ref. mental illness, esp. of heathen, etc., Clem.*str*.7.15(p.64.13; M.9.525B); Eus.*v.C*.3.54(p.101.30; M.20.1117B); εἰδωλολατρείαν ~οῦσιν id.*e.th*.2.21(p.131.20; M.24.957A); πολιτείαν ~εῖν Ἰουδαϊκήν Chrys.*hom.4.5 in Ac.princ*.(3.88A); Diod.*Ex*.20:5(M.33.1583C); Thdt.*1Cor*.7:15(3.205); of heretics τὰ Ἀρείου ~ούντων Chrys.*hom.8.5 in Mt*.(7.128C); id.*hom.38.2 in 1Cor*.(10.352E); Thdt.*Ps*.57:6(1.985); id.*Heb*.1:3(3.547); **2.** ref. moral infirmity οἱ ἐν τῷ βίῳ ~οῦντες Clem.*paed*.1.9(p.138.23; M.8.349B); *ib*.3.3(p.248.19; 584A); Eus.*v.C*.4.25(p.126.22; M.20.1173A); †Bas.*Is*.114(1.458E; M.30.304C); Epiph.*mens*.16(M.43.264B); τοῖς ἀδικοῦσιν· ἐκεῖνοι γάρ εἰσι μάλιστα οἱ ~οῦντες Chrys.*hom.18.4 in Mt*.(7.240A); Thdt.*Rom*.11:29(3.125); **3.** ref. spiritual sickness ἐπῳδὸς [sc. ὁ λόγος]...~ούσης ψυχῆς Clem.*paed*.1.2(p.93.12; M.8.256A); Or.*Cels*.8.62(p.278.23; M.11.1609D); τὸ δὲ ἐπιθυμεῖν ν. ἐστι Meth.*res*.1.47(p.296.21; M.41.1117B); *Const.App*.2.20.3; ἄγνοιαν~οῦσα θεοῦ Thdt.*Ezech*.28:2(2.908).

νόσημα, τό, *sickness, disease*, spiritual παθῶν καὶ νοσημάτων Clem.*paed*.1.2(p.92.1; M.8.253A); id.*q.d.s*.1(p.160.3; M.9.605A); ψυχικὰ ν. *ib*.21(p.174.5; 625D); Gr.Nyss.*or.dom*.4(p.70.9; M.44.1164A); Isid.Pel.*epp*.1.142(M.78.277C); μὴ περιφρονῶμεν τοῦ μεγάλου ν. [sc. of drunkenness] *ib*.2.279(345D).

[*]**νοσιλεύομαι**, = νοσηλεύομαι, *be ill*, Thphn.*chron*.p.231(M.108.584C).

νοσοκομεῖον, τό, *hospital, infirmary*, cf. *Fabiola prima omnium v. instituit, in quo aegrotantes colligeret de plateis, et consumpta languoribus atque inedia miserorum membra foveret*, Hier.*ep*.73.6(M.*PL*.22.694A); Pall.*h.Laus*.68(p.164.2; M.34.1219B); ἔρχεται εἰς τὸ μέρος τοῦ ἀναλώματος τοῦ ἐπισκοπείου καὶ...κελεύει μετενεχθῆναι τὴν πολυτέλειαν τούτων εἰς τὸ ν. ... κτίζει πλείονα ν., προσκαταστήσας δύο τῶν...πρεσβυτέρων, ἔτι μὴν καὶ ἰατροὺς καὶ μαγείρους καὶ χρηστοὺς τῶν ἀγάμων ἐργάτας τούτοις εἰς ὑπηρεσίαν· ὥστε τοὺς ἐπιχωριάζοντας ξένους καὶ ὑπὸ νόσου ληφθέντας...τυγχάνειν ἐπιμελείας id.*v.Chrys*.5(p.32.12; M.47.20); †Gregent.*leg.Hom*.proem.(M.86.580B); ἐν τῷ ν. τοῦ πατριάρχου ἐν τῇ ἁγίᾳ πόλει Jo.Mosch.*prat*.42(M.87.2896C); Max.*ep*.44(M.91.648A); in monastery, Dor.*doct*.4.10(M.88.1669D); τὴν διακονίαν τοῦ ν. *ib*.11.8(1745A); ἐν τῷ ν. τῷ λεγομένῳ τοῦ Σαμψῶ Anast.S.*Ps*.6(M.89.1112B); met. ἐν τῷ ν. τοῦ παρόντος αἰῶνος Nil.*epp*.2.110(M.79.248D); ἐν τῷ τῆς ἀναλγησίας...ν. ‡Max.*cap.al*.29(M.90.1408B).

νοσοκόμος, ὁ, **1.** *sick-nurse*; in gen., Gr.Naz.*ep*.147(M.37.252B); Nonn.*par.Jo*.5:7(M.43.785B); Thdt.*serm.Chrys*.(5.99); of superintendent of monastic infirmary, Thdr.Stud.*poen*.1.69(M.99.1741C); **2.** as adj., *tending the sick*, Nonn.*par.Jo*.5:15(M.43.788A).

νοσοποιός, *causing sickness*; **1.** lit., Clem.*paed*.3.10(p.266.8; M.8.625A); Or.*or*.27.9(p.369.16; M.11.513A); Chrys.*hom.17.4 in Heb*.(12.169D); **2.** of moral disease, Clem.*str*.1.17(p.55.22; M.8.801A); Or.*exc.in Ps*.77:31(M.17.145B); νοσοποιοῦ τῶν ψυχῶν τυραννικῆς ἐξουσίας Jo.VI CP *ep*.(M.96.1417A).

νόσος, ἡ, *disease, sickness*; **1.** physical; effected by demons, Tat.*orat*.16(p.18.6; M.6.841B); beneficial as discipline for sinner, Bas.*hom.in Ps*.45(1.171A; M.29.417A); Gr.Naz.*ep*.31(M.37.68B); *ib*.34(76B); cf.Bas.*reg.fus*.55.4(2.399D,E; M.31.1049A); ἱερὰ ν. *leprosy*, Gr.Naz.*or*.14.6(M.35.865A); ‡Chrys.*poenit*.1.3(9.768C); Jo.Clim.*scal*.5(M.88.776A); **2.** mental; of heathenism, Eus.*d.e*.1.6(p.27.23; M.22.56C); Thdt.*1Cor*.7:14(3.205); *ib*.12:1(240); of heresy, id.*h.e*.5.31.3(3.1070); id.*ep*.113(4.1190); *ib*.145(1246); **3.** moral, Herm.*sim*.6.5.5; Clem.*prot*.3(p.33.30; M.8.129B); παθῶν, ἃ δὴ ψυχῆς νόσοι *ib*.11(p.81.17; 233B); id.*q.d.s*.11(p.166.28; M.9.616A); νόσοι ἦσαν ἐν τῷ λαῷ...ἔπεμπεν αὐτοῖς ἰατροὺς ὁ θεὸς τοὺς προφήτας Or.*hom.14.2 in Jer*.(p.107.4; M.13.405B); Meth.*symp*.3.12(p.41.20; M.18.81A); Bas.*hom.in Ps*.7(1.100E; M.29.236C); ν. τῆς πλεονεξίας Gr.Nyss.*or.dom*.1(p.6.5; M.44.1121C); *Const.App*.6.18.10; Thdt.*Ps*.52:5(1.952); ἀχαριστίας ν. *ib*.77:18(1153).

***νοσουργός**, *baneful*, Geo.Pis.*carm*.4.104.

νοστέω, *season, make palatable*, ‡Chrys.*hom.in Mt.26:39*(10.806C).

νόστος, ὁ, *taste, flavour*, Mac.Aeg.*hom*.27.12(M.34.701B); Rom.Mel.(*SBBAW* 1898^{2} p.118); ‡Barth.Edess.*Muham*.(M.104.1456C).

***νοταρικός**, *secretarial*, Thdr.Stud.*or*.11.5(M.99.808B).

***νοτάριος**, ὁ, (Lat. *notarius*) *shorthand writer, secretary*; **1.** in gen., Call.*v.Hyp*.(p.83); Jo.Mal.*chron*.18 p.449(M.97.660C); ν., Ῥωμαῖα ἡ λέξις· νότα γὰρ τὰ γράμματά εἰσι Ῥωμαϊστί Anast.S.*hod*.2(M.89.85A); **2.** of bishops' secretaries, Bas.*ep*.333 tit.(3.451E; M.32.1076C); βούλομαι...τὸν ν. μου ἐλεύθερον εἶναι Gr.Naz.*test*.(M.37.392C); ἀναγνώστης καὶ ν. τοῦ...ἐπισκόπου CEph.(431)*act*.1(*ACO* 1.1.2 p.10.3; H.1.1360A); CCP(536)*act*.5(*ACO* 3 p.52.27; H.2.1305B); Soz.*h.e*.4.3 tit.(M.67.1113C); Jo.Mosch.*prat*.34(M.87.2884A); νωτάριος τῆς τῶν Ῥωμαίων ἐκκλησίας Gr.Mag.*dial*.(tr.Zach.)1.8(M.*PL*.77.186B);

3. attached to Councils, Ath.*syn*.29(p.257.30; M.26.744B); διάκονος ν. CCP(536)*act*.5(*ACO* 3 p.52.30; H.2.1305B); **4.** of secretary of monastic steward, Sophr.H.*mir.Cyr.et Jo*.39(M.87.3576A); **5.** of clerk who recorded proceedings in court of law, *M.Pion*.9.1; **6.** of clerks of senate, *Chron.Pasch*.p.384(M.92.985B); **7.** of imperial notaries; **a.** *tribuni et notarii*; staff of imperial chancery, Eus.*v.C*.4.44 tit.(p.116.14; M.20.1146B); Ath.*h.Ar*.29(p.198.23; M.25.725C); id.*apol.Const*.22(M.25.621D); Pall.*v.Chrys*.4(p.23.12; M.47.15); **b.** *domestici et notarii*, personal secretarial staff of emperor ν. τοῦ βασιλέως Epiph.*haer*.71.1(p.250.26; M.42.376C); Pall.*v.Chrys*.2(p.11.19; M.47.10); Jo.Mal.*chron*.18 p.449(M.97.660C).

νοτιαῖος, *southern*, Cosm.Ind.*top*.proem.(M.88.53A); *Chron. Pasch*.p.29(M.92.127A).

νότιος, *southern*; τὸ ν. *the south*, ref. Manich. doctrine that north, east, west are assigned to the good God, the south to ὕλη, Jo.D.*Man*.2(M.96.1321B).

νοτίς, ἡ, *moisture*; met., *trace* οὐδὲ νοτίδα κακίας ἔστιν εὑρεῖν Serap.*Man*.44(p.62; M.18.1229C).

***νοτωρία, ἡ,** *indictment*, *M.Agap*.3.1.

***νουβίτισσα, ἡ,** (Lat. *novitia*) *novice*, Thphn.*chron*.p.381(M.108.912C).

νουθεσία, ἡ, *admonition*; **1.** in gen. ν. πατέρων *T.Reub*.3.8; Ign.*Eph*.3.1; Clem.*paed*.1.8(p.128.18; M.8.329A); id.*str*.5.1(p.329.10; M.9.16A); Const.*or.s.c*.23(p.189.3; M.20.1305B); id.ap.Eus.*v.C*.2.71(p.70.13; M.20.1045A); **2.** divine τὰς πρὸ τῆς κρίσεως πατρῴας ν. ὑπομένοντες Clem.*str*.7.16(p.72.13; M.9.541B); by Christ, id.*paed*.1.8(p.133.23; M.8.340A); Eus.*d.e*.1.6(p.23.13; M.22.49A); **3.** in scriptures Μωσῆς καὶ προφῆται, γράψαντες τὰ πρὸς νουθεσίαν ἡμῶν Or.*Jo*.13.46(p.272.35; M.14.481B); Meth.*lepr*.14(p.469.20); †Bas.*bapt*.2.2(2.653D; M.31.1581C); **4.** by bishops ὁ προεστὼς διὰ λόγου τὴν ν. ... ποιεῖται Just.*1apol*.67.4(M.6.429B); *Clem.ep*.12(M.2.48A); ἔστω [sc. ἐπίσκοπος]...μακρόθυμος ἐν ταῖς ν. *Const.App*.2.5.4; *ib*.2.16.2; διὰ παρακλητικῆς ν. *ib*.2.20.4; *ib*.6.18.10.

νουθετητέος, *to be admonished*, Synes.*ep*.58(M.66.1401C).

***νουθετικῶς,** *by way of admonition*, Clem.*paed*.2.2(p.172.23; M.8.421A); Thdr.Stud.*epp*.2.122(M.99.1400A); *ib*.2.152(1473A, v.l. νομοθετικῶς).

***νουμεράριος, ὁ,** (Lat. *numerarius*) *accountant* (*tabularius*), Bas.*ep*.142 tit.(3.235A; M.32.592B); *ib*.143 tit.(235C; M.592C); Nil.*epp*.1.130 tit.(M.79.137D).

***νουμέραρχος, ὁ,** *captain of a detachment of troops*, Agath.*v.Gr.Ill*.15; *ib*.19 (νουμένaρχος cod.).

***νουμέριος,** *of* or *belonging to a detachment of troops*, Thphn.*chron*.p.185 (v.l. νουμέροις M.108.482B).

***νούμερος, ὁ (νούμερον, τό),** (Lat. *numerus*) *independent cohort*, *M.Acac*.3(p.762C); *M.Seb*.1(p.171.10); σπεῖρά ἐστιν, ὃ καλοῦμεν νυνὶ ν. Chrys.*hom.22.1 in Ac*.(9.177D); Cyr.S.*v.Sab*.1(p.87.11); ἀπὸ νουμέρων *ex-soldier*, Nil.*epp*.2.67 tit.(M.79.229D).

***νουμίον, τό,** (= Lat. *nummus*, sc. *assarius*), a Roman coin τὸ δὲ ν. τετύπωται ἀπὸ τοῦ Νουμᾶ τινος βασιλέως τῶν Ῥωμαίων Epiph.*mens*.24(M.43.289A); *Apophth.Patr*.(M.65.253C); Zos.*alloquia* 14(M.78.1700C); Jo.Mosch.*prat*.127(M.87.2992A).

νουνεχής, *sensible, intelligent*; neut. as subst., *good sense*, Men.*exc.Rom*.19(p.216.22; M.113.920B).

νοῦς, ὁ, [discussion of declension of word, Max.*schol.c.h*.1.2(M.4.32B)]; **I.** *mind*;

A. in gen.; descriptions of mind and its functions; **1.** ref. man's distinctive nature ἔστι γὰρ ἄνθρωπος οὐχ, ὥσπερ οἱ κορακόφωνοι δογματίζουσι, ζῷον λογικὸν ν. καὶ ἐπιστήμης δεκτικόν· δειχθήσεται γὰρ κατ' αὐτοὺς καὶ τὰ ἄλογα ν. καὶ ἐπιστήμης δεκτικά· μόνος δὲ ὁ ἄνθρωπος εἰκὼν...τοῦ θεοῦ Tat.*orat*.15(p.16.11ff.; M.6.837A,B); τῇ τοῦ δημιουργήσαντος ἡμᾶς γνώμῃ, καθ' ἣν ἐποίησεν ἄνθρωπον ἐκ ψυχῆς ἀθανάτου καὶ σώματος νοῦν τε συγκατεσκεύασεν αὐτῷ Athenag.*res*.13(p.63.18; M.6.1000B); ταὐτὸ γάρ ἐστιν ἐκ νοερᾶς ψυχῆς καὶ σώματος τὸν ἄνθρωπον λέγειν, καὶ ἰδιαζόντως τὸν ν. ἐφ' ἑαυτοῦ ἀριθμήσαντα, τριχῇ διελεῖν τὴν περὶ τὸν ἄνθρωπον θεωρίαν Gr.Nyss.*Apoll*.8(M.45.1140B); **2.** in rel. to other faculties ν. καὶ λόγος δέδοται τοῖς ἀνθρώποις πρὸς διάκρισιν νοητῶν Athenag.*res*.15(p.66.20; M.6.1004C); τεσσάρων δὲ ὄντων ἐν οἷς τὸ ἀληθές, αἰσθήσεως, ν., ἐπιστήμης, ὑπολήψεως, φύσει μὲν πρῶτος ὁ ν., ἡμῖν δὲ καὶ πρὸς ἡμᾶς ἡ αἴσθησις, ἐκ δὲ αἰσθήσεως καὶ τοῦ ν. ἡ τῆς ἐπιστήμης συνίσταται οὐσία, κοινὸν δὲ ν. τε καὶ αἰσθήσεως τὸ ἐναργές Clem.*str*.2.4(p.119.21ff.; M.8.944B,C); ψυχὴ...εἶναι πέφυκε τόν γε πρῶτον λόγον, οὗπερ ἂν ὁ ν. ᾖ Gr.Thaum.*pan.Or*.6(p.17.20; M.10.1072C); ἀναθεὶς ἐμοὶ καὶ τὴν ψυχὴν καὶ τὴν αἴσθησιν καὶ τὸν ν. Meth.*symp*.5.2(p.54.13; M.18.100A); dist. from ψυχή and σῶμα, id.*lepr*.9(p.463.2); τὴν ἑκάστου ψυχὴν εἶναι, καὶ τὸν ἐν αὐτῇ ν. Ath.*gent*.30(M.25.61A); λογισμοὶ τῆς ψυχῆς· λέγω δέ, τὸ θέλημα, ἡ συνείδησις, ὁ ν., ἡ ἀγαπητικὴ δύναμις Mac.Aeg.*hom*.1.3(M.34.452C); *ib*.7.8(528B); εἰς...τὸ βάθος τῆς ψυχῆς, τοῦτ' ἔστιν, εἰς τὸν ν. Diad.*perf*.79(p.100.11); cf. *ib*.33(p.38.15); τὸ φρόνημα, καὶ αἱ μνῆμαι, καὶ ὁ ν. Nil.*epp*.1.34(M.79.140B); **3.** partic. in rel. to sense perception, v. αἴσθησις; ὁ τὸν φαινόμενον κόσμον νοῶν, θεωρεῖ τὸν νοούμενον· τυποῖ γὰρ τῇ αἰσθήσει τὰ νοητὰ φανταζόμενος, καὶ κατὰ νοῦν σχηματίζει τοὺς θεαθέντας λόγους· καὶ μεταφέρει, πρὸς μὲν αἴσθησιν πολυειδῶς, τοῦ νοητοῦ κόσμου τὴν σύστασιν, πρὸς δὲ νοῦν, τοῦ αἰσθητοῦ κόσμου πολυπλόκως τὴν σύνθεσιν· καὶ νοεῖ, ἐν μὲν τῷ νοητῷ, τὸν αἰσθητόν, μετενέγκας πρὸς τὸν ν. τοῖς λόγοις τὴν αἴσθησιν, ἐν δὲ τῷ αἰσθητῷ, τὸν νοητόν, πρὸς τὴν αἴσθησιν ἐπιστημόνως τοῖς τύποις μετεγκλοιώσας τὸν ν. Max.*cap*.4.91(M.90.1344C); ref. trees of knowledge and life ἀμφότερα τὰ ξύλα κατὰ τὴν γραφήν, τινῶν εἰσι διακριτικά, ἤγουν ὁ ν., καὶ ἡ αἴσθησις· οἷον, ὁ μὲν ν. ἔχει δύναμιν διακριτικήν, νοητῶν καὶ αἰσθητῶν, προσκαίρων καὶ αἰωνίων...ἡ δὲ αἴσθησις ἔχει δύναμιν διακριτικὴν ἡδονῆς σωμάτων καὶ ὀδύνης *ib*.2.33(1233A); **4.** its various processes, cf. *prima etiam motio ejus* [sc. Nus] *de aliquo, ennoia appellatur; perseverans autem et aucta...enthymesis vocatur. haec autem enthymesis multum temporis faciens in eodem...sensatio nominatur...unum autem et idem est omnia quae praedicta sunt, a No initium accipientia, et secundum augmentum assumentia appellationes*, Iren.*haer*.2.13.2(M.7.743A); **5.** as guiding principle in man; **a.** in gen., cf. *animum, sive mens est, νοῦς apud Graecos, non aliud quid intelligimus quam suggestum animae ingenitum et insitum...quo agit, quo sapit, quem secum habens ex semetipsa se commoveat in semetipsa, atque ita moveri videatur ab illo tanquam substantia alia*, Tert.*de anima* 12(M.*PL*.2.666A); ὁ δὲ κυβερνήτης, ὁ ν. ὁ ἀνθρώπινος Clem.*paed*.2.2(p.173.18; M.8.424A); ὡς γὰρ ἡ κεφαλὴ τὸ κυριώτατον μέρος ἐστὶν ἐν τῷ σώματι, οὕτω τῆς ψυχῆς ἡμῶν τὸ κυριώτατόν ἐστιν ὁ ν. Meth.*fr.12 in Job*(p.514.14f.); **b.** owing to its power of discernment τοῦτο δ' ἐστὶ ν. ἀνθρώπου, καὶ κριτήριον ἐλεύθερον ἔχων ἐν ἑαυτῷ καὶ τὸ αὐτεξούσιον τῆς μεταχειρίσεως τῶν δοθέντων Clem.*q.d.s*.14(p.169.4; M.9.617C); ταύτῃ καὶ τὸν ν. εἰλήφαμεν, ἵνα εἰδῶμεν ὃ ποιοῦμεν, καὶ τὸ 'γνῶθι σαυτὸν' ἐνταῦθα, εἰδέναι ἐφ' ᾧ γεγόναμεν id.*str*.7.3(p.15.8; M.9.425A); ἔχειν ἐν ψυχῇ τὸν ν. διορατικώτατον Or.*fr.11 in Lc*.8:16(p.237; M.17.336B); *ib.53 in* 11:34(p.258); ἄλλος παρὰ τὰς σωματικὰς αἰσθήσεις ἐστὶν ὁ τῶν ἀνθρώπων ν.· διὰ τοῦτο γοῦν ὡς ἄλλος ὤν, αὐτῶν τῶν αἰσθήσεων γίνεται κριτής· καὶ ὧν ἐκεῖναι ἀντιλαμβάνονται, ταῦτα οὗτος διακρίνει...καὶ δείκνυσιν αὐταῖς τὸ κρεῖττον Ath.*gent*.31(M.25.61C); *ib*.(64A) cit. s. αἴσθησις; ν. ἐστι φύσις ἐπινοητικὴ παντὸς πράγματος. ν. ἐστι ὅρασις ἀσώματος εἰς πᾶν ἐκτεινομένη. ν. ἐστι ὥσπερ ὄψις τις ὑπὸ τοῦ δημιουργοῦ ἐν τῇ ψυχῇ ἀποκείμενος ἤτουν ὀφθαλμός *Doct.Patr*.33(p.263.15ff.); but καλὸν τοῦ ν. ἡ ἐνέργεια· καὶ ὅτι ἀεικίνητος ὢν οὗτος, πολλάκις μὲν φαντασιοῦται περὶ τῶν οὐκ ὄντων ὡς ὄντων Bas.*ep*.233.1(3.355E; M.32.864D); **c.** hence compared to an eye or a light ὀφθαλμὸν...κυρίως φησὶν τὸν ἐν ἡμῖν ν., περὶ ὃν ἐστιν ἡ ἀρχὴ ἐν μόνῳ τῷ σπουδαίῳ τῆς ἁπλότητος, μηδεμίαν ἔχοντι διπλοὴν καὶ δόλον...νοῦν γὰρ ἐν ψυχῇ ἀνθρώπου ὁ θεὸς ἐποίησεν Or.*fr.53 in Lc*.11:34(p.258); *ib*.(p.259); *ib.59 in* 12:35(p.261); exeg. Mt.5:8 ἡ γὰρ καρδία ὀφθαλμός ἐστιν, ὁ δὲ ὀφθαλμὸς ἡ φύσις τοῦ ν. id.*fr.in Mt*.5:8(p.50); ὅρασις δὲ τῆς ψυχῆς, ὁ συμφυὴς αὐτῇ ν.· ἀλλ' οὐχ ὡς ἕτερον ἐν ἑτέρῳ, ἀλλὰ ταὐτὸν ψυχή τε καὶ ν. ‡Bas.*const*.2.1(2.541B; M.31.1340A); Nil.*epp*.1.135(M.79.140B); **d.** in metaphor of charioteer ὁ ν. ἡνίοχός ἐστι καὶ ζεύγνυσι τὸ ἅρμα τῆς ψυχῆς κατέχων ἡνίας τῶν λογισμῶν Mac.Aeg.*hom*.40.5(M.34.765B); Gr.Nyss.*virg*.22(p.332.22; M.46.404D); *Const.App*.7.34.6 cit. s. αἴσθησις; ὁ ἡνίοχος ν. τὸν μὲν εὐθύνει τῶν ἵππων, τὸν δὲ ἀνακόπτει, τὸν δὲ καθικνεῖται διὰ τῆς μάστιγος...μέχρις ἂν τοῖς πᾶσι μίαν σύμπνοιαν πρὸς τὸν δρόμον ἐμποιήσῃ Nil.*epp*.3.268(M.79.517A); **e.** other comparisons τὸν τοῦ σκηνώματος ἡμῶν οἰκοδεσπότην καὶ οἰκονόμον, τὸν ν. λέγω, πάντα τὰ ἐν ἡμῖν εὖ διατίθεσθαι ἑκάστῃ τε τῶν τῆς ψυχῆς δυνάμεων...πρὸς τὸ καλὸν κεχρῆσθαι Gr.Nyss.*virg*.18(p.317.24; M.46.389C); = ἁρμοστής, id.*hom.opif*.9.3(M.44.149C); ἀνάπτυξόν μοι τούτου τὸ συνειδός, καὶ ὄψει πολὺν ἔνδοθεν θόρυβον τῶν ἁμαρτημάτων...καθάπερ ἐν δικαστηρίῳ τὸν ν. ἐπὶ τὸν θρόνον ἀναβάντα τὸν βασιλικὸν τοῦ συνειδότος, καὶ ὥσπερ τινὰ δικαστὴν καθήμενον Chrys.*Laz*.1.11(1.723E); τὸ μὲν σῶμα πολλῷ φαυλοτέρᾳ περίβαλε στολῇ, τὸν δὲ ν. ἁλουργίδα ἔνδυσον, καὶ στέφανον ἐπίθες αὐτῷ ...νῦν γὰρ τοὐναντίον ποιεῖς, τὴν μὲν πόλιν καλλωπίζων ποικίλως, τὸν δὲ βασιλέα ν. ἀφεὶς σύρεσθαι δεδεμένον ὀπίσω τῶν ἀλόγων παθῶν id.*hom.69.2 in Mt*.(7.682D); **6.** in teaching of Or. and his followers διὰ τὸν μιασμὸν τοῦ ν., σώματι ταπεινώσεως ἀνθρώπων ἐνδεδεμένου Or.*Cels*.6.17(p.88.6; M.11.1316C); cf. *νοῦς, id est mens, corruens facta est anima, et rursum anima instructa virtutibus mens fiet*, id.*princ*.2.8.3(p.161.6; M.11.223C); γεγόνασιν ἀπὸ νόων ἄγγελοι, ἀρχάγγελοι καὶ τὰ ἑξῆς Antip.Bost.*fr*.(M.96.504A); εἴ τις λέγει, πάντων τῶν λογικῶν τὴν παραγωγὴν νόας ἀσωμάτους καὶ ἀΰλους γεγονέναι δίχα παντὸς ἀριθμοῦ καὶ ὀνόματος...ἀ. ἔ. CCP(543)*anath*.2(Hahn p.227); πρὸ τῶν αἰώνων ν. ἦσαν πάντες καθαροί, καὶ οἱ δαίμονες καὶ ψυχαὶ καὶ οἱ ἄγγελοι, λειτουργοῦντες τῷ θεῷ †Leont.B.*sect*.10.5(M.86.1264D).

B. in pagan philosophy θεὸν μὲν τὸν ν. τοῦ κόσμου ἄγει [sc. Thales] Athenag.*leg*.23.2(M.6.941B); ἔφη [sc. Anaxagoras] τὴν τοῦ παντὸς ἀρχὴν ν. καὶ ὕλην, τὸν μὲν ν. ποιοῦντα, τὴν δὲ ὕλην γινομένην. ὄντων γὰρ πάντων ὁμοῦ, ν. ἐπελθὼν διεκόσμησεν Hipp.*haer*.1.8(p.13.8ff.; M.16.3032C); ἐδογμάτισαν [sc. Plato and Aristotle] τὴν τῶν πάντων γένεσιν...οἱ δὲ περὶ τὸν Πλάτωνα ἐκ τριῶν· εἶναι ταῦτα λέγουσι θεὸν καὶ ὕλην καὶ παράδειγμα...θεὸν δὲ τὸν ταύτης εἶναι δημιουργόν, τὸ δὲ παράδειγμα ν. *ib*.10.7(p.268.4; 3419A); Ἑλλήνων δὲ οἱ θεολογικώτεροι, καὶ μᾶλλον ἡμῖν προσεγγίσαντες, ἐφαντάσθησαν μέν, ὡς ἐμοὶ δοκεῖ· περὶ δὲ τὴν κλῆσιν διηνέχθησαν, ν. τοῦ παντός, καὶ τὸν θύραθεν ν., καὶ τὰ τοιαῦτα προσαγορεύσαντες Gr.Naz.*or*.31.5(p.150.5; M.36.137B).

C. ref. spiritual life; **1.** God as object of the mind; **a.** ref. mind's capacity for knowing God ἔστιν οὖν...τῷ ν. ἡμῶν τοιαύτη τις καὶ τοσαύτη δύναμις, ἢ μὴ τὸ ὂν δι' αἰσθήσεως ἔλαβεν; ἢ τὸν θεὸν ἀνθρώπου ν. ὄψεταί ποτε μὴ ἁγίῳ πνεύματι κεκοσμημένος; φησὶ γὰρ Πλατών, ἦν δ' ἐγώ, αὐτὸ τοιοῦτον εἶναι τὸ τοῦ ν. ὄμμα καὶ πρὸς τοῦτο ἡμῖν δεδόσθαι, ὡς δύνασθαι καθορᾶν αὐτὸ ἐκεῖνο τὸ ὂν εἰλικρινεῖ αὐτῷ ἐκείνῳ Just.*dial*.4.1(M.6.481D–484A); τὸ...θεῖον ἀγένητον εἶναι καὶ ἀΐδιον, ν. μόνῳ καὶ λόγῳ θεωρούμενον Athenag.*leg*.4.1(M.6.897B); *ib*.10.1(908B); οἱ ὀφθαλμοὶ πρὸς τὰ ὁρατὰ καὶ ὦτα πρὸς τὰ ἀκουστά, οὕτω ν. πρὸς τὰ νοητὰ καὶ τὸν ἐπέκεινα τῶν νοητῶν θεόν Or.*mart*.47(p.43.7; M.11.629B); ὁ θεὸς καθ' ἡμᾶς τῷ μὲν μὴ εἶναι σῶμα ἀόρατός ἐστιν· τοῖς δὲ θεωρητικοῖς καρδίᾳ θεωρητός, τουτέστι νῷ id.*Cels*.6.69(p.139.11; M.11.1404A); τὸν μηκέτι σώματος ὀφθαλμοῖς μόνῳ δὲ νῷ διαυγεῖ καὶ καθαρῷ νοούμενον τὸν...θεοῦ λόγον Eus.*l.C*.11(p.226.22; M.20.1380D); τὴν ἑκάστου ψυχὴν εἶναι, καὶ τὸν ἐν αὐτῇ ν. δι' αὐτοῦ γὰρ μόνου δύναται θεὸς θεωρεῖσθαι καὶ νοεῖσθαι...οὐ γὰρ ἐχόντων ἔστι ν. ἀρνεῖσθαι τὸν τούτου ποιητὴν...θεόν Ath.*gent*.30(M.25.61A); **b.** ref. creation of mind κατ' εἰκόνα: καθαρὸς γὰρ ὢν...ὁ ν. δεκτικός πως ὑπάρχει τῆς τοῦ θεοῦ δυνάμεως, ἀνισταμένης ἐν αὐτῷ τῆς θείας εἰκόνος Clem.*str*.3.5(p.215.24; M.8.1145C); *ib*.5.14(p.388.16; M.9.140A) cit. s. εἰκών; Or.*Cels*.7.33 (p.184.3; M.11.1468B); Eus.*p.e*.7.10(316C; M.21.536A); Bas.*ep*.233.1 (3.355D; M.32.864C); τὸ δέ, 'κατ' εἰκόνα', ὡς ἐμοὶ δοκεῖ, νοητέον, ὅτι ἐκ τοῦ θεϊκοῦ φυσήματος τὸ πνεῦμα τὸ ἀθάνατον ἔχομεν, καὶ ν. ἀεὶ θέοντα, καὶ κυβερνῶντα, ἐφ' ὃ χρή Didym.*Trin*.2.7(M.39.565C); δέδωκεν ὁ θεὸς καὶ τῷ ἀνθρώπῳ τῷ ὑπ' αὐτοῦ κτισθέντι ἐν τῷ νοερῷ ταμείῳ τῆς ψυχῆς, τοῦτ' ἔστι τῷ νῷ, ἔχειν διὰ τῶν ἀρετῶν τὸ 'κατ' εἰκόνα αὐτοῦ καὶ ὁμοίωσιν' Gel.Cyz.*h.e*.2.15.9(M.85.1260B); **2.** mind and body; **a.** mind enslaved by senses, Clem.*paed*.2.1(p.157.7; M.8.385B); λύπαις καὶ ἡδοναῖς...συνδεσμοῦσι τὸν ν. τοῖς αἰσθητοῖς οἱ δαίμονες Thal.*cent*.2.17(M.91.1440A); ἡ πρὸς τὴν αἴσθησιν σχέσις τοῦ ν., δοῦλον αὐτὸν καθίστησι τῶν τοῦ σώματος ἡδονῶν *ib*.2.55(1444A); σαλεύεται ὁ ν. ἐκ τοῦ τόπου τῆς γνώσεως, ὅτε τὸ παθητικὸν αὐτοῦ κινηθῇ ἐκ τῶν ἰδίων ἀρετῶν *ib*.2.56(1444A); **b.** mind controlling senses ὅταν ὁ ν. πλουτήσῃ τὴν τῆς μονάδος γνῶσιν, τότε καὶ τὴν αἴσθησιν πάντῃ δεδουλωμένην ἔχει *ib*.2.47(1441C); ἀδύνατον τὸν ν. τῇ γνώσει ποιωθῆναι, εἰ μὴ πρότερον τὸ παθητικὸν ταῖς οἰκείαις ἀρεταῖς ἐξ αὐτοῦ πελάσει *ib*.2.50(1441D); **3.** mind and sin; **a.** mind's responsibility for sin οὐ γὰρ τὰ ὄργανά εἰσιν βλαστικά, ἀλλὰ ὁ ν. ὁ συγκαταβαίνων τῇ ἁμαρτίᾳ *A.Jo*.54(p.178.22); but cf. τὰ ὄργανα τὰ παιδογόνα ...βρίθοντα τὸν ν. Meth.*symp*.4.4(p.49.17; M.18.92A); **b.** mind obscured and coarsened by sin, *T.Reub*.3.8; ποία δὲ χείρων ταλαιπωρία τοῦ τετυφλῶσθαι τὸν ν. καὶ μὴ βλέπειν τὸν παντὸς ν. δημιουργόν; Or.*Cels*.8.38(p.253.19; M.11.1573D); καταπεπτώκασι τῇ διανοίᾳ καὶ ἐσκοτίσθησαν τὸν ν., ὥστε καὶ τὰ μηδ' ὅλως μηδαμῶς ὑπάρχοντα... θεοποιῆσαι Ath.*gent*.9(M.25.20A); τί βούλεται τοῖς δαίμοσι ἐνεργεῖν ἐν ἡμῖν γαστριμαργίαν, πορνείαν, φιλαργυρίαν...; ἵνα παχυνθεὶς ὁ ν. ἐξ αὐτῶν, μὴ δυνηθῇ ὡς δεῖ προσεύξασθαι Evagr.Pont.*or*.50(M.79.1177B); Marc.Er.*opusc*.2.72(M.65.941A); **c.** various faults ἀρχὴ πλάνης, νοῦ κενοδοξία, ἐξ ἧς κινούμενος ὁ ν., ἐν σχήματι καὶ μορφαῖς περιγράφειν πειρᾶται τὸ θεῖον Evagr.Pont.*or*.116(M.79.1193A); νοός ἐστι ἀκαθαρσία, πρῶτον μέν, τὸ γνῶσιν ἔχειν ψευδῆ· δεύτερον δέ, τὸ ἀγνοεῖν τι τῶν καθόλου· ὡς πρὸς ἀνθρώπινον ν. λέγω· ἀγγέλου γάρ ἐστι τὸ μηδὲν τῶν ἐπὶ μέρους ἀγνοεῖν· τρίτον δέ, τὸ ἐμπαθεῖς ἔχειν λογισμούς· τέταρτον δέ, τὸ συγκατατίθεσθαι τῇ ἁμαρτίᾳ Max.*carit*.3.34(M.90.1028B); **d.** mind between good and evil τρεῖς οὖν εἰσιν οἱονεὶ βίων καταστάσεις· καὶ ἰσάριθμοι τούτοις, αἱ τοῦ ν. ἡμῶν ἐνέργειαι. ἡ γὰρ πονηρὰ ἡμῶν τὰ ἐπιτηδεύματα...οἷον μοιχεῖαι, κλοπαί, εἰδωλολατρίαι... ἡ μέση τίς ἐστι τῆς ψυχῆς ἡ ἐνέργεια, οὔτε κατεγνωσμένον τι ἔχουσα, οὔτε ἐπαινετόν·...ποία γὰρ κακία κυβερνητικῆς ἢ ἰατρικῆς...ὁ μέντοι τῇ θεότητι τοῦ πνεύματος ἀνακραθεὶς ν., οὗτος ἤδη τῶν μεγάλων ἐστὶ θεωρημάτων ἐποπτικός Bas.*ep*.233.1(3.356B,C; M.32.865B); ὁ ν. ἡμῶν μέσος ἐστὶ δύο τινῶν, ἑκάστου τὰ ἴδια ἐνεργοῦντος· τοῦ μέν, τὴν ἀρετήν· τοῦ δέ, τὴν κακίαν· τουτέστι ἀγγέλου καὶ δαίμονος. ἐξουσίαν δὲ ἔχει ὁ ν., καὶ δύναμιν ᾧ θέλει εἴτε ἕπεσθαι, εἴτε ἀντιστῆναι Max.*carit*.3.92 (M.90.1045B); id.*cap*.2.35(M.90.1233C); Thal.*cent*.1.58(M.91.1433A); **4.** mind's way to perfection; **a.** struggle against temptation, Clem.*fr*.44(p.221.18,22); ὅταν μὴ δυνηθῇ τὴν μνήμην κινῆσαι ἐν τῇ προσευχῇ ὁ...δαίμων, τότε τὴν κρᾶσιν τοῦ σώματος ἐκβιάζεται εἰς τὸ ποιῆσαι ξένην τινὰ φαντασίαν τῷ νῷ Evagr.Pont.*or*.68(M.79.1181B); Marc.Er.*opusc*.2.68(M.65.940C); ὅταν ὁ ν. ἡμῶν ἄρξηται τῆς τοῦ ἁγίου πνεύματος αἰσθάνεσθαι παρακλήσεως, τότε καὶ ὁ σατανᾶς ἐν ἡδυφανεῖ τινι αἰσθήσει ἐν ταῖς νυκτεριναῖς ἡσυχίαις...τὴν ψυχὴν παρακαλεῖ. ἐὰν οὖν εὑρεθῇ ἐν θερμῇ μνήμῃ λίαν κρατῶν ὁ ν. τὸ ὄνομα τὸ ἅγιον τοῦ...Ἰησοῦ καὶ ὥσπερ ὅπλῳ κέχρηται κατὰ τῆς ἀπάτης...ἀναχωρεῖ μὲν ὁ πλάνος τοῦ δόλου...ὅθεν ἐπιγιγνώσκων ὁ ν. τὴν ἀπάτην τοῦ πονηροῦ πλέον εἰς τὴν πεῖραν προκόπτει τῆς διακρίσεως Diad.*perf*.31(p.34.18ff.); οὐ πρὸς τὰ πράγματα ὁ ν. πολεμεῖ τοῦ θεοφιλοῦς, οὐδὲ πρὸς τὰ τούτων νοήματα· ἀλλὰ πρὸς τὰ πάθη τὰ τοῖς νοήμασι συνεζευγμένα Max.*carit*.3.40(M.90.1028D); **b.** stages of progress ἀναβῆναι τῷ νῷ ἀπὸ ὁρατῶν καὶ πάντων αἰσθητῶν ἐπὶ τὸν ὅλων δημιουργόν Or.*Cels*.6.66(p.136.21; M.11.1400A); κἂν ὑπὲρ τὴν θεωρίαν τῆς σωματικῆς φύσεως ὁ ν. γένηται, οὔπω τέλεον τὸν τοῦ θεοῦ τόπον ἐθεάσατο· δύναται γὰρ ἐν τῇ τῶν νοητῶν εἶναι γνώσει, καὶ ποικίλλεσθαι πρὸς αὐτήν Evagr.Pont.*or*.57(M.79.1180A); ἡ θεαρχία τοὺς ἐν οἷς ἂν ἐγγένηται ν. ἀποκαθαίρει πρῶτον, εἶτα φωτίζει, καὶ φωτισθέντας ἀποτελειοῖ πρὸς θεοειδῆ τελεσιουργίαν Dion.Ar.*e.h*.5.1.7(M.3.508D); διὰ μὲν τῆς ἐργασίας τῶν ἐντολῶν, τὰ πάθη ὁ ν. ἀποδύεται· διὰ δὲ τῆς τῶν ὁρατῶν πνευματικῆς θεωρίας, τὰ ἐμπαθῆ τῶν πραγμάτων νοήματα. διὰ δὲ τῶν ἀοράτων γνώσεως, τὴν τῶν ὁρατῶν θεωρίαν· ταύτην δέ, διὰ τῆς γνώσεως τῆς ἁγίας τριάδος Max.*carit*.1.94 (M.90.981B); *ib*.1.97–100(981D–984A); *ib*.3.97(1045D); threefold way in rel. to angelic hierarchies καθ' αὐτὸν ἕκαστος οὐράνιός τε καὶ ἀνθρώπειος ν. ἰδικὰς ἔχει καὶ πρώτας καὶ μέσας καὶ τελευταίας τάξεις τε καὶ δυνάμεις, πρὸς τὰς εἰρημένας τῶν καθ' ἕκαστον ἱεραρχικῶν ἐλλάμψεων οἰκείας ἀναγωγὰς ἀναλόγως ἐκφαινομένας, καθ' ἃς ἕκαστος ἂν μετουσίᾳ γίνεται κατὰ τὸ αὐτῷ θεμιτόν τε καὶ ἐφικτὸν τῆς ὑπεραγνοτάτης καθάρσεως, τοῦ ὑπερπλήρους φωτός Dion.Ar.*c.h*.10.3(M.3.273C); ascent from sensible to intellectual ὅταν δὲ ὁ ν. διὰ τῶν αἰσθητῶν ἀνακινεῖσθαι σπεύδῃ πρὸς θεωρητικὰς νοήσεις, τιμιώτεραι...εἰσὶν αἱ ἐπιδηλότεραι τῶν αἰσθήσεων διαπορθμεύσεις, οἱ σαφέστεροι λόγοι, τὰ τρανέστερα τῶν ὁρατῶν, ὡς ὅταν ἀτράνωτα ᾖ τὰ παρακείμενα ταῖς αἰσθήσεσιν, οὐδὲ αὐταὶ τῷ νῷ παραστῆσαι τὰ αἰσθητὰ καλῶς δυνήσονται id.*d.n*.4.11(M.3.708D–709A); **c.** qualities and virtues of progressing mind αἴσθησίς ἐστι νοὸς γεῦσις ἀκριβὴς τῶν διακρινομένων. ὃν γὰρ τρόπον τῇ γευστικῇ ἡμῶν αἰσθήσει τοῦ σώματος τὰ καλὰ ἐκ τῶν φαύλων ...διακρίνοντες τῶν χρηστῶν ὀρεγόμεθα, οὕτω καὶ ὁ ν. ἡμῶν, ὅταν εὐρώστως καὶ ἐν πολλῇ ἀμεριμνίᾳ κινεῖσθαι ἄρξοιτο, δύναται καὶ τῆς θείας παρακλήσεως πλουσίως αἰσθάνεσθαι καὶ ὑπὸ τῆς ἐναντίας μηδεπώποτε συναρπάζεσθαι Diad.*perf*.30(pp.33.24–34.2); τρεῖς ἀρεταί εἰσι προνοοῦσαι τοῦ ν. διὰ παντός, καὶ χρείαν αὐτῶν ἔχει. ἡ κατὰ φύσιν ὁρμή, καὶ ἡ ἀνδρεία, καὶ ἡ ἀοκνησία. τρεῖς εἰσιν ἀρεταὶ ἃς ἐὰν ἴδῃ ὁ ν. μετ' αὐτοῦ, πιστεύει ὅτι ἔφθασεν εἰς τὴν ἀθανασίαν. ἡ διάκρισις, τὸ ἀφορίσαι ἕκαστον ἀπ' ἀλλήλων, καὶ τὸ προβλέπειν πάντα πρὸ καιροῦ, καὶ τὸ μὴ συμπείθεσθαι μετά τινος ἀλλοτρίου. τρεῖς ἀρεταί εἰσιν ἐπιχορηγοῦσαι φῶς τῷ νῷ διαπαντός. τὸ μὴ εἰδέναι πονηρίαν τινὸς ἀνθρώπου, καὶ τὸ ἀγαθοποιῆσαι τοὺς κακοποιοῦντάς σε, τὸ ὑποφέρειν τὰ ἐπερχόμενα ἀταράχως...ὁ ν. χρῄζει τῶν τεσσάρων ἀρετῶν πάντοτε τούτων—τὸ εὔχεσθαι τῷ θεῷ προσπίπτοντα ἀδιαλείπτως, καὶ τὸ παραρίπτεσθαι ἐνώπιον τοῦ θεοῦ, καὶ τὸ ἀμεριμνῆσαι ἀπὸ παντὸς ἀνθρώπου τοῦ μὴ κρῖναι αὐτόν, καὶ τὸ κωφεῦσαι πρὸς τὰ λαλοῦντα αὐτῷ πάθη Esaias *or*.7.1(cf.M.40.1126Cff.); **d.** divine assistance, Just.*dial*.121.2(M.6.757B); λόγος ὁ ὑγιής, ὅς ἐστιν ἥλιος ψυχῆς, δι' οὗ μόνου ἔνδον ἀνατείλαντος ἐν τῷ βάθει τοῦ ν. αὐτῆς καταυγάζεται τὸ ὄμμα Clem.*prot*.6(p.52.16; M.8.173B); *ib*.11(p.79.32; 229C); τοῦ λόγου ...χειραγωγήσαντος τὸν τοῦ βουλομένου σώζεσθαι ν. πρὸς τὸν ἀγένητον ...θεόν Or.*Cels*.6.66(p.136.26; M.11.1400A); id.*or*.2.4(p.302.1; M.11.421A); πρὸς ὑποδοχὴν τοῦ νοητοῦ...σπέρματος, ὃ σπείρει μὲν αὐτὸς ὑπηχῶν καὶ καταφυτεύων ἐν τῷ βάθει τοῦ ν. Meth.*symp*.3.8(p.35.17; M.18.73A); *ib*.8.10(p.92.8; 153A); οἱ μὲν λοιποὶ διὰ τῆς ἀλλοιώσεως τοῦ σώματος ἐμποιοῦσι τῷ νῷ λογισμούς...ὁ δέ γε θεὸς τοὐναντίον δρᾷ, αὐτῷ τῷ νῷ ἐπιβαίνει, καὶ ἐντιθεὶς αὐτῷ γνῶσιν,...καὶ διὰ τοῦ ν. τὴν τοῦ σώματος ἀκρασίαν κατευνάζων Evagr.Pont.*or*.63(M.79.1180D); ἡ τοῦ λόγου νόησις, ἀρίδηλος τοῦ γεννήσαντος αὐτὸν ν. καθέστηκε γνῶσις, ὡς ἐν ἑαυτῷ δεικνύντος ὑφιστάμενον κατ' οὐσίαν τὸν ν., πρὸς ὃν ἀνάγει τὸν ἐφιέμενον τῆς πρὸς θεὸν κατὰ χάριν ταυτότητος νοῦν Max.*qu.Thal*.25(M.90.332Df.); **e.** ascent of the mind, exeg. 1Cor.11:3ff. τῷ τῆς ἀναγωγῆς προσβαίνοντες λόγῳ, φαμὲν ἄνδρα εἶναι τὸν πρακτικὸν ν., κεφαλὴν ἔχοντα τὸν λόγον τῆς πίστεως· πρὸς ὃν ὡς Χριστὸν ἀφορῶν...

τὸν οἰκεῖον συνίστησι βίον ὁ ν., μὴ καταισχύνων τὴν κεφαλὴν αὐτοῦ, τουτέστι τὴν πίστιν *ib.*(329D); rel. of mind to action γυναῖκα δὲ τοῦ... ν. εἶναί φαμεν, αὐτὴν τὴν ἕξιν τῆς πράξεως...κατακεκαλυμμένην πρακτικοῖς τε λογισμοῖς καὶ ἤθεσι· μᾶλλον δὲ αὐτὸν τὸν ν., ὡς κεφαλὴν ἰδίαν κατὰ τὴν τῶν τοιούτων λογισμῶν...πύκνωσιν...εὐπρέπειαν ἔχοντα κεκαλυμμένην *ib.*(332A); ἀνήρ ἐστιν ὁ τῆς φυσικῆς ἐν πνεύματι θεωρίας ἐπιμελούμενος ν., κεφαλὴν ἔχων τὸν κατὰ πίστιν ἐκ τῆς τῶν ὁρωμένων διακοσμήσεως γενεσιουργὸν τοῦ παντὸς λόγον διαδεικνύμενον...γυνὴ δὲ τοῦ τοιούτου ν. ἐστιν ἡ σύνοικος αἴσθησις, δι' ἧς ἐπιβατεύει τῇ φύσει τῶν αἰσθητῶν *ib.*(332A,B); πᾶς...πρακτικὸς ν. προσευχόμενος ἢ προφητεύων...μόνον ὁρᾶν ὤφειλε γυμνὸν τὸν τῆς πίστεως λόγον, μηδὲν ...ποιῶν κατὰ πρόσκλισιν ἐπικαλύπτων τὴν κεφαλήν...καὶ πᾶσα γυνή, τουτέστι πρακτικοῦ ν. ἕξις, προσευχομένη ἢ προφητεύουσα...ἄνευ λογικῆς διακρίσεως, καταισχύνει τὴν κεφαλὴν αὐτῆς...καὶ πᾶς ν. τὴν φυσικὴν ἀσκούμενος θεωρίαν, προσευχόμενος ἢ προφητεύων, κατὰ κεφαλῆς ἔχων, τουτέστι, γνωστικῶς τοὺς τῶν ὄντων λόγους ἐπιζητῶν, ἢ...ἄλλοις παραδιδούς...ἄνευ τοῦ κατ' εὐσέβειαν σκοποῦ, καταισχύνει τὴν κεφαλὴν αὐτοῦ...καὶ πᾶς ν. μυστικῆς...ἐραστὴς θεολογίας, προσευχόμενος ἢ προφητεύων, κατὰ κεφαλῆς ἔχων, τουτέστι ταῖς ἀδύτοις ἐμβατεύων...θεωρίαις...εἴ τινα μορφὴν σχοίη νοήσεως, τὸν ὑπὲρ νόησιν λόγον μυσταγωγούμενος...καταισχύνει τὴν κεφαλὴν αὐτοῦ *ib.*(333A–C); **5.** mind in prayer and contemplation; **a.** in gen. τῇ αὐξήσει τοῦ ν. ἐπὶ τὸ διορατικόν Or:*hom.11 in Lc.*(p.78.30); *ib.27*(p.171.11); βασιλείαν δὲ Χριστοῦ...θεωρήσας ὁ ν. πῶς οὐ καταφρονήσει...πάσης τῆς ἐπὶ γῆς βασιλείας; στρατιάν τε ἀγγέλων...ὡς χωρεῖ ὁ ἔτι δεδεμένος σώματι ἀνθρώπινος ν. id.*or.*17.2(p.339.22; M.11.472D); Evagr.Pont.*or.*83,84 (M.79.1185B); ὥσπερ ὁ ἄρτος τροφή ἐστι τῷ σώματι, καὶ ἀρετὴ τῇ ψυχῇ, οὕτω καὶ τοῦ ν. ἡ πνευματικὴ προσευχὴ τροφὴ ὑπάρχει *ib.*101 (1189B); *ib.*110(1192B); αἱ κατὰ φύσιν ἐφέσεις τῶν ν., ἐρωτικῶς ἀεὶ γλιχόμεναι τῆς ἐγχωρούσης τῶν ὑπερφυῶν θεωρίας Dion.Ar.*d.n.*3.3(M. 3.684C); ἴδιον ἔργον ὑπάρχει τοῦ ν., τὸ λόγοις θεοῦ σχολάζειν ἀεί Thal. *cent.*1.30(M.91.1429D); κατὰ φύσιν ὁ ν. ἐνεργεῖ, ὅταν...τοὺς λόγους τῶν ὄντων θεωρῇ, καὶ πρὸς τὸν θεὸν διάγῃ Max.*carit.*4.45(M.90.1057C); **b.** mind as instrument of contemplation ἡ μέν [sc. ποιότης] τις τῆς ψυχῆς, καθ' ἣν τοιάδε ἐστίν, ἡ δέ τις τοῦ ν., καθ' ἣν τοιῶνδέ ἐστι θεωρητικός Or.*or.*24.2(p.353.25; M.11.492B); ἥκειν ἐπὶ τὴν εὐχήν...τὸν ν. πρὸς τὸν θεὸν ἐκτείναντα *ib.*31.2(p.396.4; 549C); δι' αὐτῆς [sc. ἀρετῆς] ὁδεύσας ὁ ν. τυχεῖν ὧν ὀρέγεται καὶ καταλαβεῖν δυνηθῇ, καθ' ὅσον ἐφικτόν ἐστι τῇ ἀνθρώπων φύσει περὶ τοῦ θεοῦ λόγον μανθάνειν Ath. *inc.*57.1(M.25.196C); Evagr.Pont.*or.*28(M.79.1173A) cit. s. εὐχή; cf. προσευχή ἐστιν ἀνάβασις νοῦ πρὸς θεόν *ib.*35(1173D); πρὸς θεωρητικὴν ἕξιν...ἐν...νοὸς ὀφθαλμοῖς ἀναγομένους Dion.Ar.*c.h.*3.3(M.3.165D); **c.** necessity of its purification ἀσκήσεσι καθαιρόμενος ὁ ν. τῶν ἐπικαλυπτόντων αὐτὸν ἀλλοίων διανοημάτων ὀξυδερκεῖ πρὸς τὴν ἀλήθειαν Meth.*symp.*9.4(p.118.13; M.18.185B); Ath.*gent.*2(M.25.8A) cit. s. ἄνω; Marc.Er.*opusc.*2.81(M.65.941B); ἀγωνίζου στῆσαι τὸν ν. σου, κατὰ τὸν καιρὸν τῆς προσευχῆς κωφόν, καὶ ἄλαλον Evagr.Pont.*or.*11' (M.79.1169C); ἡ καθαρθεῖσα πάσης ἀνιέρου κηλῖδος, καὶ πάναγνον ἐσχηκυῖα τὴν τοῦ οἰκείου ν. ἀκίνητον ἵδρυσιν, ἐπὶ τὴν θεωρητικὴν ἕξιν... μετάγεται Dion.Ar.*e.h.*6.1.2(M.3.532B); διὰ πολλὴν καθαρότητα νοῦ πρὸς θεοπτείαν ἐπιτηδειότατος id.*ep.*8.6(M.3.1097B); οἱ διὰ πολλὴν τῶν ἀρετῶν ἐπιμέλειαν, τῆς τῶν παθῶν αἰθάλης τὸν ν. ἐκκαθάραντες, ἐσόπτρου δίκην καθαροῦ...τὴν τῶν θείων ὑποδέχονται γνῶσιν Max.*qu. Thal.*65(M.90.737A); ὅτε ν. τελείως τῶν παθῶν ἐλευθερωθῇ, τότε καὶ ἐπὶ τὴν θεωρίαν τῶν ὄντων...ὁδεύει, ἐπὶ τὴν γνῶσιν τῆς ἁγίας τριάδος id.*carit.*1.86,87(M.90.980C); οὐ δυνήσῃ σωμάτων καὶ χρημάτων...ὑπέρτερον ποιῆσαι τὸν ν., εἰ μὴ ἐν τῇ καθαρᾷ τῶν δικαίων χώρᾳ εἰσάξῃς αὐτόν ‡Max.*cap.al.*118(M.90.1428A); **d.** effects of prayer on mind τὸ ἅγιον πνεῦμα συμπάσχον τῇ ἡμετέρᾳ ἀσθενείᾳ...εἰ εὕροι τὸν ν. ἡμῶν φιλαλήθως αὐτῷ προσευχόμενον, ἐπιβαίνει αὐτῷ Evagr.Pont.*or.*62(M. 79.1180C); νοῦν δὲ λαμπρύνει προσευχὴ καθαρά Thal.*cent.*1.11(M.91. 1429A); ῥώννυσι...ν. δὲ προσευχὴ καθαρά, καὶ θεωρία πνευματική *ib.*1. 81(1436A); ν. διὰ προσευχῆς τῷ θεῷ ἐγχρονίζων, καὶ τὸ παθητικὸν τῆς ψυχῆς τῶν παθῶν ἀπαλλάττει *ib.*1.94(1436D); **e.** mystic union as surpassing capacities of mind δέον εἰδέναι τὸν καθ' ἡμᾶς ν., ἔχειν τὴν μὲν δύναμιν εἰς τὸ νοεῖν, δι' ἧς τὰ νοητὰ βλέπει, τὴν δὲ ἕνωσιν ὑπεραίρουσαν τὴν τοῦ ν. φύσιν, δι' ἧς συνάπτεται πρὸς τὰ ἐπέκεινα ἑαυτοῦ Dion.Ar.*d.n.*7.1(M.3.865C); εἰς τὸν ὑπὲρ νοῦν εἰσδύνοντες γνόφον id. *myst.*3(M.3.1033B); εἴ τις ἰδὼν θεόν, συνῆκεν ὃ εἶδεν, οὐκ αὐτὸν ἑώρακεν...αὐτὸς δὲ ὑπὲρ νοῦν ὑπεριδρύμενος...καὶ ὑπὲρ ν. γινώσκεται id. *ep.*1(M.3.1065A); **6.** perfect mind; **a.** separated from sensible world and passions, Evagr.Pont.*or.*61(M.79.1180C); ὁ ν. εἰς ἄκρον καθαρθεὶς στενοχωρεῖται τοῖς οὖσι· καὶ ἔξω θέλει γίνεσθαι πάντων τῶν γεγονότων Thal.*cent.*1.55(M.91.1433A); ὅταν ὁ ν. πλουτήσῃ τὴν τῆς μονάδος γνῶσιν, τότε καὶ τὴν αἴσθησιν πάντῃ δεδουλωμένην ἔχει *ib.*2.47(1441C); ἡ παντελὴς ἀπάθεια, καθ' ἣν γενόμενος ὁ ν. ἀναχωρεῖ τῶν ἐνταῦθα *ib.*2.90 (1445D); **b.** enjoying perfect knowledge ἔστιν...ἡ θειοτάτη τοῦ θεοῦ γνῶσις, ἡ δι' ἀγνωσίας γινωσκομένη, κατὰ τὴν ὑπὲρ νοῦν ἕνωσιν, ὅταν ὁ ν., τῶν ὄντων πάντων ἀποστάς, ἔπειτα καὶ ἑαυτὸν ἀφείς, ἑνωθῇ ταῖς ὑπερφαέσιν ἀκτῖσιν Dion.Ar.*d.n.*7.3(M.3.872B); Thal.*cent.*1.50(M.91. 1432D); ν. παθῶν ἐλευθερωθείς, ψιλὰ βλέπει τὰ νοήματα, καὶ ἐγρηγορότος τοῦ σώματος, καὶ κατὰ τοὺς ὕπνους αὐτοῦ *ib.*1.54(1432D); τέλειός ἐστιν ὁ ν. ὁ ποιωθεὶς τῇ γνώσει *ib.*2.54(1444A); Max.*carit.*1.34(M.90. 968A); τὸν καθαρὸν ν., ποτὲ μέν, αὐτὸς ὁ θεὸς αὐτῷ ἐπιβαίνων διδάσκει· ποτὲ δέ, αἱ ἅγιαι δυνάμεις τὰ καλὰ ὑποτίθενται· ποτὲ δέ, ἡ φύσις τῶν πραγμάτων θεωρουμένη *ib.*3.94(1045B); ν. ἐστι τέλειος, ὁ διὰ πίστεως ἀληθοῦς, τὸν ὑπεράγνωστον ὑπεραγνώστως ὑπερεγνωκώς *ib.*3.99 (1048A); εἰς ἑαυτὸν ὁ ν. συναγόμενος, οὐδὲν οὔτε τῶν κατὰ τὸν λογισμὸν θεωρεῖ· γυμνοὺς δὲ ν. καὶ θείας αὐγάς ‡Max.*cap.al.*111(M.90.1425A); **c.** in rel. to Christ and H. Ghost θεὸς δὲ δῴη μὴ ψιλῷ καὶ γυμνῷ θειότητος τῷ ἡμετέρῳ νῷ...⟨πρὸς⟩ τὸ προκείμενον γενέσθαι...ν. δὲ Χριστοῦ λαβόντες ἀπὸ τοῦ μόνου διδόντος αὐτὸν πατρὸς αὐτοῦ καὶ πρὸς τὴν μετοχὴν τοῦ λόγου τοῦ θεοῦ βοηθηθέντες Or.*Cels.*5.1(p.2.8,10; M. 11.1181B); id.*mart.*4(p.5.18; M.11.568A); τὸν ἐν Χριστῷ κτισθέντα καὶ ἀνακαινισθέντα ν. ... ἀναλαβεῖν Ath.*ep.Serap.*1.9(M.26.553C); ὁ ν., ὅτε ἐπάνω τοῦ τῆς σαρκὸς καυχᾶται φρονήματος, δύναται γεύεσθαι τῆς παρακλήσεως ἀπλανῶς τοῦ ἁγίου πνεύματος Diad.*perf.*30(p.34.7); **d.** blessedness of mind in myst. prayer μακάριός ἐστιν ὁ ν., ὃς ἀπερισπάστως εὐχόμενος, πλείονα πόθον ἀεὶ πρὸς θεὸν προσλαμβάνει. μακάριός ἐστιν ὁ ν., ὁ κατὰ τὸν καιρὸν τῆς προσευχῆς ἄυλος καὶ ἀκτήμων γίνεται. μακάριός ἐστιν ὁ ν., ὁ κατὰ τὸν καιρὸν τῆς προσευχῆς τελείαν ἀναισθησίαν κτησάμενος Evagr.Pont.*or.*118–120(M.79.1193A,B); **e.** myst., exeg. 1Cor.11:3 ἀνήρ ἐστιν ὁ τῆς μυστικῆς θεολογίας ἐντὸς γενόμενος ν., κεφαλὴν ἔχων ἀκατακάλυπτον τὸν Χριστόν· τουτέστι, τὸν ταῖς ἀναποδείκτοις μυσταγωγίαις ἀγνώστως νοούμενον...ὁ τὴν... ὑπερέχουσαν ἑαυτοῦ τε καὶ τῶν ὄντων...θεοποιὸν στέρησιν συνασκούμενος ν. γυνὴ δὲ τοῦ τοιούτου ν. ἐστιν, ἡ πάσης αἰσθητῆς φαντασίας καθαρεύουσα διάνοια, καθάπερ κεφαλὴν ἔχουσα τὸν ν. Max.*qu.Thal.*25 (M.90.332C,D); exeg. 1Cor.2:16 τουτέστι, τὰ ἐν τῷ νῷ Χριστοῦ ταῦτα ἡμεῖς ἴσμεν, καὶ ἅπερ αὐτὸς βούλεται καὶ ἀπεκάλυψεν. ... οὐ τοῦτο λέγων, ὅτι πάντα ἃ οἶδεν ἴσμεν, ἀλλ' ὅτι πάντα ἃ οἴδαμεν, οὐκ ἀνθρώπινα ...ἀλλὰ τοῦ ν. ἐκείνου καὶ πνευματικά. τὸν γὰρ ν., ὃν ἔχομεν περὶ τούτων, τοῦ Χριστοῦ ἔχομεν· τουτέστι, τὴν γνῶσιν...πνευματικὴν ἔχομεν. ... τὸν ἡμέτερον ν. τὸν περὶ τούτων, ἐκείνου λέγων εἶναι ν. ... 'ἡμεῖς δὲ ν. Χριστοῦ ἔχομεν'. τουτέστι, πνευματικόν, θεῖον, οὐδὲν ἀνθρώπινον ἔχοντα. οὐ γὰρ Πλάτωνος οὐδὲ Πυθαγόρου, ἀλλ' ὁ Χριστὸς τὰ ἑαυτοῦ τῇ ἡμετέρᾳ ἐνέθηκε διανοίᾳ Chrys.*hom.*7.5,6 *in 1Cor.*(10. 58B–E).

D. human mind in life after death; **1.** its perfect illumination ἐν φωτὶ τῷ ἀληθινῷ καὶ ἀλήκτῳ τῆς γνώσεως τὸν ν. καταλαμπόμενοι πρὸς τὴν θέαν τῶν δι' ἐκείνου τοῦ φωτὸς θεωρεῖσθαι πεφυκότων Or.*mart.*47 (p.43.16; M.11.632A); id.*or.*25.2(p.358.11; M.11.497B); τῆς δὲ νοητῆς αὐτοῦ [sc. of God] φωτοδοσίας ἐν ἀπαθεῖ καὶ ἀΰλῳ τῷ νῷ μετέχοντες, καὶ τῆς ὑπὲρ νοῦν ἑνώσεως ἐν ταῖς τῶν ὑπερφανῶν ἀκτίνων ἀγνώστοις ...ἐπιβολαῖς, ἐν θειοτέρᾳ μιμήσει τῶν ὑπερουρανίων ν. Dion.Ar.*d.n.*1.4 (M.3.592C); *ib.*1.5(593C,D); **2.** condemnation of Origenist teaching εἴ τις λέγει, ὅτι ἡ μέλλουσα κρίσις ἀναίρεσιν παντελῆ τῶν σωμάτων σημαίνει· καὶ ὅτι τέλος ἐστὶ τοῦ μυθευομένου ἡ ἄυλος φύσις...γυμνὸς ὁ ν.· ἀ. ἔ. CCP(543)*anath.*11.

E. of angelic intelligences; **1.** νοῦς as name of angelic powers τῶν οὐρανίων ν. ἱεραρχίας Dion.Ar.*c.h.*1.2(M.3.121A); *ib.*1.3(124A); ν. καλοῦσι καὶ οἱ παρ' Ἕλλησι φιλόσοφοι τὰς νοεράς, ἤτοι ἀγγελικὰς δυνάμεις· ἐπειδὴ τὸ πᾶν ν. ἐστιν ἕκαστος αὐτῶν, καὶ τὴν οὐσίαν ἅπασαν ν. ζῶντα εἰς τὸ εἶδος τὸ ἑαυτῶν οὐσιωμένον ἔχει Max.*schol.c.h.*1.2(M.4. 32A,B); **2.** their hierarchical orders and divisions εἰς τρία διῄρηνται τῷ κατ' αὐτοὺς ὑπερκοσμίῳ λόγῳ πάντες θεῖοι ν., εἰς οὐσίαν, καὶ δύναμιν, καὶ ἐνέργειαν Dion.Ar.*c.h.*11.2(M.3.284D); *ib.*13.3(301D); **3.** their intellectual processes αἱ μὲν [sc. angelic powers] ὡς ν., νοοῦσαι κατὰ τὸ αὐταῖς θεμιτόν· ἡμεῖς δὲ αἰσθηταῖς εἰκόσιν ἐπὶ τὰς θείας, ὡς δυνατόν, ἀναγόμεθα θεωρίας Dion.Ar.*e.h.*1.2(M.3.373B); ἡ...τῶν ὑπερκοσμίων ν. γνῶσις ἀκάματός τέ ἐστι, καὶ ἀκατάληκτον ἔχει τὸν θεῖον ἔρωτα *ib.*4. 3.5(480C); κινεῖσθαι μὲν οἱ θεῖοι λέγονται νόες, κυκλικῶς μὲν ἑνούμενοι ταῖς ἀνάρχοις καὶ ἀτελευτήτοις ἐλλάμψεσι τοῦ καλοῦ καὶ ἀγαθοῦ· κατ' εὐθεῖαν δέ, ὁπόταν προΐωσιν εἰς τὴν τῶν ὑφειμένων πρόνοιαν, εὐθείᾳ τὰ πάντα περαίνοντες· ἑλικοειδῶς δέ, ὅτι καὶ προνοοῦντες τῶν καταδεεστέρων, ἀνεκφοιτήτως ἐν ταυτότητι περὶ τὸ τῆς ταυτότητος αἴτιον καλὸν καὶ ἀγαθόν, ἀκαταλήκτως περιχορεύοντες id.*d.n.*4.8(M.3.704D).

F. God and mind; **1.** God as *Νοῦς*: Πλάτων τὸν τῶν ἰδεῶν θεωρητικὸν θεὸν ἐν ἀνθρώποις ζήσεσθαί φησι· ν. δὲ χώρα ἰδεῶν, ν. δὲ ὁ θεός Clem.*str.*4.25(p.317.11; M.8.1364C); ὁ θεός, ν. ἀΐδιος ὤν Athenag. *leg.*10.2(M.6.900A); οὐκ ἄφρων ὁ τῶν ὅλων πέφυκεν ν. †Just.*fr.res.*8 (p.45; M.6.1585B); ὁ ν. ὁ ὑπερύψωτος ἐν τῇ αὐτοῦ δόξῃ *A.Phil.*132

(p.63.17); νοῦν...ἢ ἐπέκεινα νοῦ καὶ οὐσίας λέγοντες εἶναι...τὸν τῶν ὅλων θεόν, οὐκ ἐν ἄλλῳ τινὶ ἢ τῷ κατὰ τὴν ἐκείνου τοῦ ν. εἰκόνα γενομένῳ φήσομεν καταλαμβάνεσθαι τὸν θεόν Or.*Cels*.7.38(p.188.11ff.; M.11.1473B); μονὰς εἶ μονάδων...ν. καὶ νοερός Synes.*hymn*.3.177(p.12; M.66.1596A); God called ν. ἀνόητος, Dion.Ar.*d.n*.1.1(M.3.588B); ὁ θεῖος ν. πάντα συνέχει τῇ πάντων ἐξῃρημένῃ γνώσει, κατὰ τὴν πάντων αἰτίαν ἐν ἑαυτῷ τὴν πάντων εἴδησιν προειληφώς...οὐ γὰρ ἐκ τῶν ὄντων τὰ ὄντα μανθάνων, οἶδεν ὁ θεῖος ν., ἀλλ' ἐξ αὐτοῦ, καὶ ἐν αὐτῷ...οὐ κατ' εἰδέαν ἑκάστοις ἐπιβάλλων, ἀλλὰ κατὰ μίαν τῆς αἰτίας περιοχὴν τὰ πάντα εἰδὼς καὶ συνέχων *ib*.7.2(869A); *ib*.(869C); Max.*schol.d.n*.5.6(M.4.320B); in rel. to εἰκών in man νοερὸς γὰρ ὁ λόγος τοῦ θεοῦ, καθ' ὃ ὁ τοῦ ν. εἰκονισμὸς ὁρᾶται ἐν μόνῳ τῷ ἀνθρώπῳ...τὸ γὰρ εἶδος ἑκάστου ὁ ν., ᾧ χαρακτηριζόμεθα Clem.*str*.6.9(p.468.5ff.; M.9.293B); **2.** Father as ν.; Son as Logos ὁ θεὸς δὲ ἄναρχος...ἀρχῆς ποιητικός. ἧ μὲν οὖν ἐστιν οὐσία...ᾗ δ' αὖ ἐστι ν., τοῦ λογισμοῦ καὶ κριτικοῦ τόπου· ὅθεν καὶ διδάσκαλος μόνος ὁ λόγος, υἱὸς τοῦ ν. πατρός, ὁ παιδεύων τὸν ἄνθρωπον Clem.*str*.4.25(p.320.18f.; M.8.1372B); δύναται...ὁ λόγος ὁ υἱὸς εἶναι παρὰ τὸ ἀπαγγέλλειν τὰ κρύφια τοῦ πατρός...ἀνάλογον τῷ καλουμένῳ υἱῷ λόγῳ νοῦ τυγχάνοντος. ὡς γὰρ ὁ παρ' ἡμῖν λόγος ἄγγελός ἐστι τῶν ὑπὸ τοῦ ν. ὁρωμένων, οὕτως ὁ τοῦ θεοῦ λόγος...ἀποκαλύπτει ὃν ἔγνω πατέρα Or.*Jo*.1.38(42; p.49.5f.; M.14.100A); αὐτοῦ τοῦ πρώτου ν. λόγος ἔμψυχος ὤν Gr.Thaum.*pan.Or*.4(p.9.14; M.10.1061B); πηγὴ τῶν ἀγαθῶν...ὁ θεός· ποταμὸς δὲ ὑπ' αὐτοῦ προχεόμενος ὁ υἱὸς ἀναγέγραπται. ἀπόρροια γὰρ νοῦ λόγος καί, ὡς ἐπ' ἀνθρώπων εἰπεῖν, ἀπὸ καρδίας διὰ στόματος ἐξοχετεύεται, ἕτερος γινόμενος τοῦ ἐν καρδίᾳ λόγου ὁ διὰ γλώσσης ν. προπηδῶν...ὡς γὰρ ὁ ἡμέτερος ν. ἐρεύγεται μὲν ἀφ' ἑαυτοῦ τὸν λόγον...καὶ ἔστι μὲν ἑκάτερος ἕτερος θατέρου...ὁ μὲν ἐν τῇ καρδίᾳ, ὁ δὲ ἐπὶ τῆς γλώττης...οἰκῶν...οὐδέ ἐστιν οὔτε ὁ ν. ἄλογος οὔτε ἄνους ὁ λόγος, ἀλλ' ὅ γε ν. ποιεῖ τὸν λόγον ἐν αὐτῷ φανεὶς καὶ ὁ λόγος δείκνυσι τὸν ν. ἐν αὐτῷ γενόμενος, καὶ ὁ μὲν ν. ἐστιν οἷον λόγος ἐγκείμενος, ὁ δὲ λόγος ν. προπηδῶν· καὶ μεθίσταται μὲν ὁ ν. εἰς τὸν λόγον, ὁ δὲ λόγος τὸν ν. εἰς τοὺς ἀκροατὰς ἐγκυκλεῖ. καὶ οὕτως ὁ ν. διὰ τοῦ λόγου ταῖς τῶν ἀκουόντων ψυχαῖς ἐνιδρύεται συνεισιὼν τῷ λόγῳ· καὶ ἔστιν ὁ μὲν οἷον πατὴρ ὁ ν. τοῦ λόγου ὢν ἐφ' ἑαυτοῦ, ὁ δὲ καθάπερ υἱὸς ὁ λόγος τοῦ ν., πρὸ ἐκείνου μὲν ἀδύνατον ἀλλ' οὐδὲ ἔξωθέν ποθεν σὺν ἐκείνῳ γενόμενος, βλαστήσας δὲ ἀπ' αὐτοῦ. οὕτως ὁ πατήρ, ὁ...καθόλου ν. πρῶτον τὸν υἱὸν λόγον...ἔχει Dion.Al.ap.Ath.*Dion*.23(p.63.7ff.; M.25.513B–516A); *ib*.24(p.64.12; 516B); εἰ...λόγου προϊόντος παρὰ ἀνθρώπων, ἐνθυμούμεθα τὴν τούτου πηγὴν εἶναι τὸν ν., καὶ τῷ λόγῳ ἐπιβάλλοντες, τὸν ν. σημαινόμενον ὁρῶμεν τῷ λογισμῷ· πολλῷ πλέον μείζονι φαντασίᾳ...τοῦ λόγου τὴν δύναμιν ὁρῶντες, ἔννοιαν λαμβάνομεν καὶ τοῦ...πατρὸς αὐτοῦ Ath.*gent*.45(M.25.89A); ὥσπερ δὲ ἐπὶ τοῦ καθ' ἡμᾶς παραδείγματος ὁ μὲν ἀόρατος...ἐν ἡμῖν ν., ὃν ὅστις...ὢν...οὐδεὶς πώποτε ἀνθρώπων ἔγνω, βασιλεὺς...ἐν ἀπορρήτοις εἴσω τοῖς αὐτοῦ ταμείοις καθιδρυμένος τὰ πρακτέα βουλεύεται, λόγος δ' ἐξ αὐτοῦ πρόεισι μονογενής...οἱ μὲν τῆς ἐκ τοῦ λόγου μεταλαμβάνουσιν ὠφελείας, τὸν δ' ἀφανῆ...ν., τὸν τοῦ λόγου πατέρα, οὐδεὶς πώποτε εἶδεν ὀφθαλμοῖς· κατὰ ταῦτα δὴ μᾶλλον δὲ ἐπέκεινα πάσης εἰκόνος...ὁ τοῦ παμβασιλέως θεοῦ...λόγος Eus.*theoph*.(p.3*.3ff.; M.24.609A); id.*e.th*.2.17(p.121.1ff.; M.24.937D–940A); μίαν...φύσιν θεότητος, ἀνάρχῳ, καὶ γεννήσει, καὶ προόδῳ γνωριζομένην, ὡς νῷ τῷ ἐν ἡμῖν, καὶ λόγῳ, καὶ πνεύματι Gr.Naz.*or*.23.11(M.35.1161C); γεννᾷ μὲν ὁ ν. τὸν λόγον, συμπρόεισι δὲ τῷ λόγῳ πνεῦμα...ταῦτα ὡς ἐν εἰκόνι πρόσεστι τῷ ἀνθρώπῳ Thdt.*qu.20 in Gen*.(1.28); τὸν γὰρ ν. τοῦ παντοκράτορος, ὡς αἴτιον πάντων, πατέρα ὀνομάζομεν· τὸν δὲ λόγον, ὡς ἀπὸ τοῦ ν. γενόμενον, υἱὸν...προσαγορεύομεν· τὸ δὲ πνεῦμα τὸ ἅγιον ὡς ἐκ τοῦ ν. ἐκπορευόμενον...πνεῦμα ὀνομάζομεν †Gregent.*disp*.(M.86.625B); ν. Χριστοῦ τὸν πατέρα καλεῖ. ἔχομεν, φησίν, ἐν ἑαυτοῖς τὸν τοῦ Χριστοῦ πατέρα...ν. γὰρ τὸν πατέρα λέγειν ἔθος τοῖς ἁγίοις, ὡς Γρηγόριος· καὶ νῷ καὶ λόγῳ καὶ πνεύματι τῇ μιᾷ συμφυΐᾳ καὶ θεότητι Oecum.*1Cor*.2:16(pp.432.23–433.1); exeg. 1Cor.11:3 κεφαλὴ δὲ Χριστοῦ, τουτέστι τοῦ κατὰ πίστιν διὰ τῆς κατὰ φύσιν τῶν γεγονότων θεωρίας...δημιουργικοῦ λόγου ἐστίν, ὁ κατ' οὐσίαν αὐτὸν γεννῶν ἀπόρρητος ν. ... κεφαλὴ δὲ Χριστοῦ, τουτέστι τοῦ καθ' ὑπεροχὴν μυστικῶς ἀποπεφασμένου λόγου, ἐστὶν ὁ...ἀπείρως ἐξῳκισμένος ν.· ὃν ὡς φύσει νοῦ λόγος ὑπάρχων ὁ Χριστὸς νοούμενος, ποιεῖ γνωστὸν τοῖς ἀξίοις Max.*qu.Thal*.25(M.90.332B–D); **3.** Son as νοῦς; **a.** in gen. ν. ... τοῦ πατρὸς ὁ υἱὸς τοῦ θεοῦ Athenag.*leg*.10.2(M.6.909A); πρὸ γάρ τι γίνεσθαι τοῦτον [sc. λόγον] εἶχε σύμβολον, ἑαυτοῦ ν. καὶ φρόνησιν ὄντα Thphl.Ant.*Autol*.2.22(M.6.1088B); τὸ δὲ πᾶν πατήρ, ἐξ οὗ δύναμις λόγος· οὗτος δὲ ν., ὃς προβὰς ἐν κόσμῳ ἐδείκνυτο παῖς θεοῦ Hipp.*Noët*.11(p.253.12; M.10.817C); νοηθῆναι θέλω ν. ὢν ὅλος *A.Jo*.95(p.198.2); ὁ σταυρὸς οὗτος ὁ τοῦ φωτὸς ποτὲ μὲν λόγος καλεῖται ὑπ' ἐμοῦ δι' ὑμᾶς, ποτὲ δὲ ν., ποτὲ δὲ Ἰησοῦς *ib*.98(p.200.6); αὐτὸς Ἰησοῦς ὁ θεαρχικώτατος ν. Dion.Ar.*e.h*.1.1(M.3.372A); **b.** λόγος in rel. to νοῦς: ὥσπερ ὁ ν., δι' ὅλου τοῦ ἀνθρώπου ὤν, ἀπὸ μέρους τοῦ σώματος, τῆς γλώττης λέγω, σημαίνεται, καὶ οὐ δήπου τις ἐλαττοῦσθαι τὴν οὐσίαν τοῦ ν. διὰ τοῦτο λέγει· οὕτως ὁ λόγος, διὰ πάντων ὤν, εἰ ἀνθρωπίνῳ κέχρηται ὀργάνῳ, οὐκ ἀπρεπὲς ἂν φαίνοιτο τοῦτο Ath.*inc*.42.7(M.25.172A); **c.** Origenist teaching condemned ἕνα δὲ ν. ἐκ πάσης τῆς δῆθεν ἑνάδος τῶν λογικῶν ἀκίνητον μεῖναι...ὃν Χριστὸν καὶ βασιλέα γεγονότα πάντων τῶν λογικῶν παραγαγεῖν πᾶσαν τὴν σωματικὴν φύσιν CCP(543)*anath*.6; εἴ τις λέγει, ὅτι οὐχ ὁ λόγος τοῦ θεοῦ σαρκωθεὶς σαρκὶ ἐμψυχωμένῃ ψυχῇ λογικῇ...κατελήλυθεν εἰς τὸν ᾅδην ...ἀλλ' ὁ παρ' αὐτοῖς λεγόμενος ν., ὃν ἀσεβοῦντες λέγουσι κυρίως Χριστόν...ἀ. ἔ. *ib*.9; *ib*.12.

G. Christol.; **1.** arguments of Apoll. against Christ's having a human ν.; **a.** trichotomy of man ἀπόδειξιν [sc. of Apoll.]...τοῦ συνιστάναι τὸν ἄνθρωπον ἀπὸ σαρκός τε καὶ ψυχῆς καὶ ν., ἅπερ οὐ πόρρω τοῦ καθ' ἡμᾶς ἐστι λόγου Gr.Nyss.*Apoll*.8(M.45.1140B); Apoll.*fr*.25(p.210.24)*ib*.9(1140D); **b.** Logos as ν. ἔνσαρκος: εἰ μὴ ν. ἔνσαρκός ἐστιν ὁ κύριος, σοφία ἂν εἴη φωτίζουσα ν. ἀνθρώπου. αὕτη δὲ καὶ ἐν πᾶσιν ἀνθρώποις· εἰ δὲ ταῦτα, οὐκ ἦν ἐπιδημία θεοῦ ἡ Χριστοῦ παρουσία, ἀλλ' ἀνθρώπου γέννησις Apoll.*fr*.70(p.220.28f.)*ib*.36(1204C); εἰ μὴ ν. ἔνσαρκος γέγονεν ὁ λόγος, ἀλλὰ σοφία ἦν τῷ νῷ, οὐ κατέβη ὁ κύριος οὐδὲ ἐκένωσεν ἑαυτόν Apoll.*fr*.71(p.221.14)*ib*.37(1205C,1208A); as ν. οὐράνιος: ζῶν δὲ Χριστὸς σῶμα θεόπνουν καὶ πνεῦμα ἐν σαρκὶ θεϊκόν, ν. οὐράνιος Apoll.*fr*.155(p.249.4)ap.Leont.B.*Apoll*.(M.86.1964B); **c.** assumption of human ν. would introduce change into the Godhead πῶς...θεὸς ἄνθρωπος γίνεται μὴ μεταβληθεὶς ἀπὸ τοῦ εἶναι θεός, εἰ μὴ ν. ἐν ἀνθρώπῳ κατέστη; Apoll.*fr*.97(p.229.31)ap.Gr.Nyss.*Apoll*.56(M.45.1260C); Apoll.*fr*.151(p.247.30)ap.*Doct.Patr*.41(p.307.12) cit. s. αὐτοκίνητος; **d.** would affect the completeness of Inc. εἰ μετὰ τοῦ θεοῦ...ν. ὄντος καὶ ἀνθρώπινος ἦν ἐν Χριστῷ ν.—οὐκ ἄρα ἐπιτελεῖται ἐν αὐτῷ τὸ τῆς σαρκώσεως ἔργον· εἰ δὲ μὴ ἐπιτελεῖται τὸ τῆς σαρκώσεως ἔργον ἐν τῷ αὐτοκινήτῳ καὶ μὴ ἀναγκαστῷ ν., ἐν τῇ ἑτεροκινήτῳ καὶ ὑπὸ τοῦ θείου ν. ἐνεργουμένῃ σαρκὶ τελεῖται τὸ ἔργον, ὅ ἐστι λύσις ἁμαρτίας· μεταλαμβάνει δὲ τῆς λύσεως ὁ ἐν ἡμῖν αὐτοκίνητος ν., καθ' ὅσον οἰκειοῖ ἑαυτὸν Χριστῷ Apoll.*fr*.74(p.222.7ff.)ap.Gr.Nyss.*Apoll*.38(M.45.1209C); **e.** assumption of flesh alone necessary for salvation, Apoll.*fr*.76(p.222.21ff.)*ib*.40(1213C) cit. s. ἐπιστημοσύνη; **f.** in confession of faith ὁμολογοῦμεν οὐκ εἰς ἄνθρωπον ἅγιον ἐπιδεδημηκέναι τὸν τοῦ θεοῦ λόγον ὅπερ ἦν ἐν προφήταις, ἀλλ' αὐτὸν τὸν λόγον σάρκα γεγενῆσθαι μὴ ἀνειληφότα ν. ἀνθρώπινον, ν. τρεπόμενον καὶ αἰχμαλωτιζόμενον λογισμοῖς ῥυπαροῖς, ἀλλὰ θεῖον ὄντα ν. ἄτρεπτον οὐράνιον id.*ep.Diocaes*.2(p.256.5ff.)ap.Leont.B.*Apoll*.(M.86.1969D); **2.** orthodox reply; **a.** denies possibility of separating ν. from ψυχή: ὁ λογικὴν ψυχὴν εἰπών, καὶ διανοητικὴν ὡμολόγησεν· ἡ δὲ διάνοια, ν. κίνησίς ἐστι καὶ ἐνέργεια. πῶς ἂν ὁ ν. μὴ παρὼν ἐνεργήσειεν, εἴπερ ἀμέτοχον τοῦ ν. τὴν τοῦ κυρίου ψυχὴν διορίζοιντο; Gr.Nyss.*Apoll*.29(M.45.1188C); **b.** denies possibility of ν. ἔνσαρκος: λέγω ν. ἔνσαρκον ὄντα τὸν υἱὸν ἐκ γυναικὸς τεχθῆναι· οὐκ ἐν τῇ παρθένῳ σάρκα γενόμενον, ἀλλὰ παροδικῶς δι' αὐτῆς διεξελθόντα...σάρκινον ὄντα θεόν, ἢ καθὼς αὐτὸς ὀνομάζει, ἔνσαρκον ν. *ib*.24(1173B); εἰ γὰρ ὡς ἀληθὲς προτείνεται τό, εἰ μὴ ν. ἐστιν ἔνσαρκος, σοφία ἂν εἴη· ἀληθὲς καὶ τὸ ἐκ τοῦ ἀντιστρόφου ἀναφαινόμενον, ὅτι εἰ σοφία ἐστί, ν. ἔνσαρκος οὐκ ἔστιν. ἀλλὰ μὴν σοφίαν εἶναι τὸν Χριστόν, πᾶς ὁ παραδεξάμενος τὴν πίστιν συντίθεται. ἄρα κατὰ τὴν τοῦ σοφοῦ πρότασιν, τὸ μὴ εἶναι αὐτὸν ν. ἔνσαρκον ὁμολογεῖται *ib*.36(1204B); *ib*.37(1205D); denies ν. ἐπουράνιος: εἰ γὰρ ἕτερός ἐστιν ὁ Χριστὸς παρὰ τὸν ἐπουράνιον ν. τὸν ἐν αὐτῷ γενόμενον, τέλειος δὲ καὶ ὁ ν., δύο ἄρα καθ' ὑμᾶς...ν. δὲ ἐπουράνιον καὶ οἱ προφῆται ἐσχήκασιν, οἱ τὰ ἐπουράνια...λαλήσαντες ‡Ath.*Apoll*.1.13(M.26.1116C); cf.*ib*.1.2(1096B); *ib*.1.16(1121B); *ib*.2.16(1157Df.); **c.** defence against Apollinarian allegation that orthodox teaching impairs divinity of Christ ἀλλά φησι λέγειν ἡμᾶς ὅτι ὁ σταυρωθεὶς οὐδὲν εἶχε θεϊκὸν ἐν τῇ ἑαυτοῦ φύσει...ὅ ἐστι πνεῦμα...εἰ γὰρ τὸ πνεῦμα ν. ὁ Ἀπολινάριος οἴεται, οὐδεὶς τῶν Χριστιανῶν λέγει τὸν ἀνακραθέντα τῷ θεῷ ἄνθρωπον ἥμισυν εἶναι,...οὐκοῦν οὐ πρὸς ἡμᾶς ἂν βλέποι ἡ λοιδορία, ὡς τὸν ἄνθρωπον ἐκεῖνον οὐκ ἔχοντα ἐν ἑαυτῷ τὸ πνεῦμα, ὅ ἐστιν ὁ ν., γεγενῆσθαι λέγοντας· ἀλλὰ πρὸς αὐτὸν ἐκεῖνον... τὸν τοῖς ἰδίοις ὀνείδεσιν ἡμᾶς βάλλοντα. ὁ γὰρ πνεῦμα τὸν ν. ὀνομάζων, μὴ ἔχειν δὲ ν. τὸν κατὰ Χριστὸν ἄνθρωπον λέγων, ἐκεῖνός ἐστιν, ὁ μὴ ἔχειν πνεῦμα κατασκευάζων τὸν κύριον Gr.Nyss.*Apoll*.27(M.45.1181B,C); **d.** Apollinarian argument would equate the divinity with ν., *ib*.38(1209A,B); πῶς οὖν λέγεις τέλειον γεγονέναι ἄνθρωπον [sc. Χριστόν];...ἐκ σαρκὸς καὶ ψυχῆς καὶ θεότητος ἀντὶ τοῦ νοῦ Epiph.*haer*.77.23(p.436.13; M.42.673C); **e.** assumption of flesh alone insufficient ἤρκει, φησίν, ἡ θεότης ἀντὶ τοῦ ν. ... θεότης γὰρ μετὰ σαρκὸς μόνης οὐκ ἄνθρωπος, ἀλλ' οὐδὲ ψυχῆς μόνης, οὐδὲ ἀμφοτέρων χωρὶς τοῦ ν. Gr.Naz.*ep*.101(M.37.184B); Ἀπολινάριος δὲ ἔμψυχον μὲν τὸ δεσποτικὸν σῶμα καλεῖ, τὸν δὲ ν. τῆς γεγενημένης σωτηρίας ἀποστερεῖ, οὐκ οἶδα πόθεν μαθὼν ψυχῆς καὶ ν. διαίρεσιν. ἡ δὲ τῶν...ἀποστόλων διδασκαλία ψυχὴν λογικήν τε καὶ νοερὰν μετὰ σαρκὸς προσειλῆφθαι διδάσκει, καὶ τελείαν τοῖς πιστεύουσιν ὑπισχνεῖται τὴν σωτηρίαν Thdt. *ep*.104(4.1174); **f.** assumption of human ν. does not involve sin ν. καὶ λόγος λέγεται ὁ Χριστός. οὕτω δὲ ν. ἀνθρώπινον λέγω ἐν ᾧ ἦν ὁ λόγος, ὡς...εἴπομεν σῶμα ἀνθρώπινον τῇ φύσει, τῇ δὲ οἰκονομίᾳ θεοῦ. καὶ ὥσπερ ἡ σὰρξ αὐτοῦ οὐκ εἶδε διαφθοράν, οὕτως οὐδὲ ὁ ν. αὐτοῦ ἐποίησεν ἁμαρτίαν...ὁ ν. φύσει μὲν ἀνθρώπινος, τῇ δὲ ἑνώσει τῆς οἰκονομίας θεοῦ ν. ‡Ath.*dial.Trin*.4.2(M.28.1253A); v. ἁμαρτία; **g.** orthodox counter-argument from ν. being created κατ' εἰκόνα: τὸ οὖν κατ' εἰκόνα ἀνακαινίσαι βουλόμενος ὁ θεὸς λόγος, γέγονεν ἄνθρωπος. τί δὲ τὸ κατ' εἰκόνα, εἰ μὴ ὁ ν.; τὸ κρεῖττον οὖν παρείς, τὸ χεῖρον ἀνέλαβε; ν. γὰρ ἐν μεταιχμίῳ ἐστὶ θεοῦ καὶ σαρκός, τῆς μὲν ὡς σύνοικος, τοῦ θεοῦ δέ, ὡς εἰκών. ν. οὖν νοΐ μίγνυται, καὶ μεσιτεύει ὁ ν. θεοῦ καθαρότητι καὶ σαρκὸς παχύτητι Jo.D.*f.o*.3.18(M.94.1073A); **h.** ref. Apoll.'s exegesis of 1Cor.2:16 ν. Χριστοῦ τὴν θεότητα λέγοντες, οὐχ, ὅπερ ἡμεῖς, ὑπολαμβάνοντες, ὅτι οἱ τὸν ἑαυτῶν ν. καθήραντες μιμήσει τοῦ ν. ἐκείνου, ὅνπερ ἡμῶν ὁ σωτὴρ ἀνεδέξατο, καὶ πρὸς αὐτὸν ῥυθμίζοντες, ὡς ἐφικτόν, οὗτοι ν. Χριστοῦ ἔχειν λέγονται Gr.Naz.*ep*. 102(M.37.197A); 1Cor.15:47 εἶτα κατασκευάζει τὸν ἄνθρωπον ἐκεῖνον τὸν ἄνωθεν ἥκοντα τὸν ν. μὴ ἔχειν, ἀλλὰ τὴν θεότητα τοῦ μονογενοῦς τὴν τοῦ ν. φύσιν ἀναπληρώσασαν, μέρος γενέσθαι τοῦ ἀνθρωπείου συγκράματος τὸ τριτημόριον, ψυχῆς τε καὶ σώματος κατὰ τὸ ἀνθρώπινον περὶ αὐτὸν ὄντων, ν. δὲ μὴ ὄντος, ἀλλὰ τὸν ἐκείνου τόπον τοῦ θεοῦ λόγου ἀναπληροῦντος *ib*.203(333A); **3.** other references to Apollinarian controversy φησὶν οὗτος, τὸν σαρκωθέντα τῇ ἀνθρωπίνῃ σαρκὶ Χριστὸν ἐν ἑαυτῷ θεόν, τὸ πνεῦμα, τουτέστι τὸν ν., ἔχειν Gr.Nyss.*Apoll*.9(M.45. 1141B); *ib*.10(1141D); *ib*.40(1216Bf.); *ib*.56(1261Bf.); παρεκβάλλειν τὸν ν. ἀπὸ τῆς τοῦ Χριστοῦ ἐνσάρκου παρουσίας, καὶ λέγειν ὅτι σάρκα ἔλαβεν ὁ Χριστός...ν. δὲ οὐκ ἔλαβε τουτέστι τέλειον ἄνθρωπον Epiph. *haer*.77.1(p.416.18ff.; M.42.641B); οὐκ ἔστιν ὑπόστασις ὁ ν., ἀλλὰ κίνησις τῆς ἡμῶν πάσης ὑποστάσεως *ib*.77.24(p.437.6; 676B); id.*anc*. 78(p.97.29; M.42.164B); Tim.CP *haer*.(M.86.40A); **4.** Christ's ν. symbolized by salt used in eucharist, ‡Jo.D.*azym*.proem.(M.95. 388A).

H. as Gnost. aeon ταύτην [sc. Σιγήν] δὲ ὑποδεξαμένην τὸ σπέρμα τοῦτο [sc. of Βύθος] καὶ ἐγκύμονα γενομένην, ἀποκυῆσαι Ν., ὅμοιόν τε καὶ ἴσον τῷ προβαλόντι, καὶ μόνον χωροῦντα τὸ μέγεθος τοῦ Πατρός· τὸν δὲ Ν. τοῦτον καὶ Μονογενῆ καλοῦσι Iren.*haer*.1.1.1(M.7.445B); counterpart of Ἀλήθεια, *ib*.(448A); τὸν...Προπάτορα αὐτῶν γινώσκεσθαι μόνῳ λέγουσι τῷ ἐξ αὐτοῦ γεγονότι Μονογενεῖ, τουτέστι τῷ Νῷ...μόνος δὲ ὁ Ν. κατ' αὐτοὺς ἐτέρπετο θεωρῶν τὸν Πατέρα, καὶ τὸ μέγεθος τὸ ἀμέτρητον αὐτοῦ κατανοῶν ἠγάλλετο· καὶ διενοεῖτο καὶ τοῖς λοιποῖς αἰῶσιν ἀνακοινώσασθαι τὸ μέγεθος τοῦ Πατρὸς *ib*.1.2.1(452B); cf. *Nus enim est ipsum quod est principale, et summum, et velut principium, et fons universi sensus*, *ib*.2.13.1(742A); cf.*ib*.(742A,B); *Aeones a Logo, Logos autem a Nu, et Nus a Bytho*, *ib*.2.17.4(763A); refutation of Gnost. teaching that Logos, offspring of Nus, was blind, *ib*.2.17.9,10(766A,B); νόμος ἦν γενικὸς τοῦ παντὸς ὁ πρωτότοκος νόος *Ps.Naas*.ap.Hipp.*haer*.5.10(p.102.23; M.16.3159A); *ib*.5. 19(p.120.19; 3183C).

II. *sense, meaning* of scripture, esp. of non-literal sense ἐν τοῖς ὑμετέροις [sc. of Jews] ἀπόκεινται γράμμασι...ὑμεῖς δὲ ἀναγινώσκοντες οὐ νοεῖτε τὸν ἐν αὐτοῖς ν. Just.*dial*.29.2(M.6.537B); μὴ σαρκίνων ἀκροᾶσθαι τῶν λεγομένων, ἀλλὰ τὸν ἐν αὐτοῖς κεκρυμμένον ν. μετὰ τῆς ἀξίας ζητήσεως καὶ συνέσεως ἐρευνᾶν Clem.*q.d.s*.5(p.163.19; M.9. 609C); opp. λέξις, id.*str*.7.1(p.3.20; M.9.404B); ὁ ν. γε τοῦ προφητικοῦ ...πνεύματος ἐπικεκρυμμένως λαλούμενος διὰ τὸ μὴ πάντων εἶναι τὴν συνιεῖσαν ἀκοήν,...ἀσφαλῶς γὰρ ἐγνώκεσαν τὸν ν. ἐκεῖνον οἱ προφῆται *ib*.1.9(p.30.2,6; M.8.741B); ἐχρήσατο ἀποκρύπτων ἀπὸ τῶν πολλῶν τὸν βαθύτερον ν. Or.*princ*.4.2.9(p.321.15; M.11.376A); ὁ ἀκριβὴς ν., ἅτε ν. ὢν Χριστοῦ *ib*.4.2.3(p.310.9; 361B); εὑρήσεις τινὰ ἄξιον ν. βάθους προφητικοῦ id.*hom.14.16 in Jer*.(p.122.10; M.13.424D); λέγεσθαι τῇ γραφῇ τὸν ἐν αὐτῇ τοῦ ἁγίου πνεύματος ν. id.*Jo*.10.43(27; p.221.24; M.14.392C); μυστικὸς ν. *ib*.1.15(p.19.34; 49B); of sense of a passage dist. from actual words ἔν τισι τὸν ν. μόνον, ἔν τισι δὲ καὶ ῥήματα σὺν τῷ ν. κρατῶ Gr.Mag.*dial*.(tr.Zach.)1 proem.(M.*PL*.77. 154B).

III. phrases: ἐν νῷ ἔχω *have in mind*, Clem.*paed*.3.11(p.267.1; M.8.628A); ἐν νῷ or εἰς νοῦν λαμβάνω *pay attention to, think about* οὐδὲ ἐκεῖνο ἐν νῷ λαβόντες τὸ Μωυσέως Clem.*paed*.3.3(p.249.21; M.8. 585B); id.*str*.2.8(p.132.7; M.8.972B); κατενόουν τὰ ὑπὸ τοῦ ἐπισκόπου ...γινόμενα, εἰς ν. τε ἔλαβον καὶ παρ' ἐμαυτῷ ἐταμιευόμην Epiph.*haer*. 30.6(p.341.2; M.41.413C); *ib*.31.2(p.384.14; 476A); Chrys.*hom.15.3 in 1Tim*.(11.638F); id.*hom.43.4 in Mt*.(7.464E); λαμβάνω κατὰ νοῦν *recall to memory*, id.*carit*.4(6.292A); Gel.Cyz.*h.e*.2.22.15(M.85.1293A); εἰς ν. βάλλω *lay to heart*, Chrys.*hom.3.5 in Mt*.(7.41A).

***νουσαλέος**, **1.** *sick*, Nonn.*par.Jo*.5:9(M.43.785B); *ib*.6:26(797B); Paul.Sil.*Soph*.799(M.86.2149B); **2.** *pertaining to disease*, Nonn.*par. Jo*.11:2(810A); *ib*.11:16(810B).

***νυγματίζομαι**, *be stung, roused*, Gel.Cyz.*h.e*.2.17.6(M.85.1265D).

***νυκταγεῖς**, **οἱ**, *heretics who repudiate night vigils*, cf. *nyctages a somno nuncupati, quod vigilias noctis respuant, superstitionem esse dicentes jura temerari divina, qui noctem ad requiem tribuit*, Isid.H.*etym*.8.5.62 (? l. *nystages* (cf. νυστάζω), i.e. *sleepy-heads*, as nickname).

***νυκταυγία**, **ἡ**, *twilight*, Thdr.Stud.*epp*.1.37(M.99.1040A).

νυκτέπαρχος, **ὁ**, *praefectus vigilum, chief of the watch*, Pall. *v.Chrys*.16(p.97.10; M.47.55); Jo.Mal.*chron*.16 p.396(M.97.588A); *Chron.Pasch*.p.321(M.92.821A).

νυκτερεία, **ἡ**, *darkness* Ζαβουλὼν μὲν ῥῦσις νυκτερείας ἑρμηνευόμενος, σημαίνει τοὺς ἀπὸ Ἰσραὴλ πιστεύσαντας· οὓς ἡ νὺξ πρὸ Χριστοῦ ῥεύσασα Thdt.*Is*.9:2(2.232).

***νυκτερικῶς**, *by night*, *Lit.Gr.Naz*.(M.36.729A).

***νυκτερινῶς**, = foreg., ‡Epiph.*hom*.3(M.43.469A).

νυκτερόβιος, *of nocturnal habits*; of species of birds, Bas.*hex*.8.7 (1.77B; M.29.181A).

[*]**νυκτεροφοῖτις**, *roaming by night*; of Hecate, *Hymn*.ap.Hipp. *haer*.4.35(p.62.2; M.16.3102A).

***νυκτιαῖος**, *nightly*, ‡Caes.Naz.*dial*.118(M.38.1005A).

νυκτικόραξ, **ὁ**, *long-eared owl*; of Devil, Nil.*Eulog*.2(M.79.1096C).

νυκτιλόχος, *lying in wait by night*; of robbers, Nonn.*par.Jo*. 19:18(M.43.901B); *ib*.19:32(905A); of Satan, Germ.CP *or*.1(M.98. 228C).

***νυκτίπερ**, *by night*, ‡Paul.Sil.*therm.Pyth*.50(M.86.2264).

νυκτιφανής, **1.** *shining by night*; of a star, Nonn.*par.Jo*.20:1(M. 43.908B); **2.** *appearing by night*; of Nicodemus, *ib*.3:2(765B).

***νυκτίχρους**, *of the colour of night*, Nil.*epp*.3.129(M.79.444C).

***νυκτίωρος**, *nocturnal*, Thdr.Stud.*or*.11.36(M.99.840B).

***νυκτοειδῶς**, *like night*, Thdr.Stud.*epp*.2.21(M.99.1181C).

***νυκτοκλοπία**, **ἡ**, *theft by night*, *Orac.Sib*.3.238; *ib*.3.380.

***νυκτόναρ**, **τό**, *dream by night*; met., Thdr.Stud.*iamb*.21(M.99. 1788C).

***νυκτοπόρος**, *moving by night*, Chrys.*hom.in Ps.115:1–3*(p.357.7).

***νυκτοτριήμερος**, *of three days and nights* ν. ταφῇ Bas.Sel.*pasch*. 1.3(M.28.1076D).

νυκτοφαής, *shining by night*, Ophites ap.Or.*Cels*.6.31(p.101.14; M.11.1344A).

***νυκτόχρους**, *of the colour of night*, Hipp.*haer*.5.14(p.109.8; M.16. 3167C).

νυμφαγωγέω, *lead* a bride to the bridegroom's house; met., ref. virgin souls being espoused to Christ, Meth.*symp*.6.2(p.65.16; M. 18.116A); *ib*.8.5(p.87.17; 145D); *ib*.10.6(p.129.6; 204B); ref. a bishop being 'espoused' to his see, Gr.Naz.*or*.36.6(M.36.273A).

νυμφαγωγία, **ἡ**, *leading of the bride to the bridegroom's house, bridal procession*; met.; **1.** of marriage between God or Christ and Church δείκνυσιν, ἡ ν. πῶς γίνεται, ὅτι διὰ φωνῆς καὶ διδασκαλίας. οὕτω γὰρ καὶ ἡ ἐκκλησία ἁρμόζεται τῷ θεῷ Chrys.*hom.29.3 in Jo*. (8.168B); id.*exp.in Ps*.5:1(5.31D); **2.** ref. candidates for baptism νυμφαγωγίας λαμπάδες Cyr.H.*procatech*.1; **3.** of espousals of virgin souls μυστικὴ ν. †Bas.Anc.*virg*.50(M.30.769C); τῆς πρὸς αὐτὴν [sc. Thecla] ν. τὸν δεσπότην Χριστὸν ἐξ οὐρανοῦ δεξιὰν δεδωκότα ‡Chrys. *Thecl*.(2.749E).

***νυμφαγωγικός**, *bridal*, Thdr.Stud.*epp*.2.132(M.99.1425C).

νυμφαγωγός, **ὁ**, **ἡ**, *leader of the bride*; **1.** of God, ref. Adam and Eve, Bas.Sel.*or*.29.1(M.85.328B); **2.** of angels, ref. virgins, †Bas. Anc.*virg*.29(M.30.729A); of apostles, ref. Church or ref. individual souls whom they lead to Christ, the spouse, Cyr.*Ps*.44:11(M.69. 1041C); of S. Paul, Chrys.*exp.in Ps*.5:1(5.31A); partic. ref. virgins, ‡Chrys.*hom*.10(13.239C); of S. Philip, *A.Phil*.97(p.37.36); of Jo. Bapt., Gr.Naz.*or*.45.26(M.36.660A); Cyr.*Jo*.2.1(4.159C); of priests leading virgins to Christ, †Bas.Anc.*virg*.37(M.30.744B); of scripture and theology leading to Christ, *ib*.50(769A); τὴν ἀρετὴν πορευθῶμεν...τὴν τῷ θεῷ λόγῳ...τὴν λογικὴν ψυχὴν...πρὸς κοινωνίαν ἁρμοσαμένην ἀχώριστον, ἵνα καὶ παρὰ ἀνθρώποις...τοὺς θεοειδεῖς φθόγγους ἡ ν. [sc. theology] ἐναρμόσῃ Diad.*perf*.67(p.82.16); of Devil τῆς μοιχείας ν. ὁ διάβολος Gr.Nyss.*hom.in 1Cor.6:18*(M.46. 496A); Bas.Sel.*or*.8(M.85.124A).

νύμφευσις, **ἡ**, *marriage, espousal*; **1.** lit., †Bas.Anc.*virg*.50(M.30. 769C); **2.** met.; **a.** of marriage between Christ and Church ἡμέραι δὲ νυμφεύσεως αὐτοῦ αἱ τρεῖς εἰσι τοῦ πάθους· τότε γὰρ τὴν ἁγίαν ταύτην ἐκκλησίαν ἐνυμφεύσατο Ph.Carp.*Cant*.90(M.40.88A); Vict.*Mc*. 2:18ff.(p.290.22); **b.** of spiritual marriage between Christ and virgins, †Bas.Anc.*virg*.37(M.30.745B); ‡Gr.Nyss.*hom.10.36 in Jo.* (p.306.5); Thdr.Stud.*epp*.2.150(M.99.1468B).

νυμφευτήριον, τό, *bridal chamber,* Bas.Sel.*v.Thecl*.2.10(M.85.581A).

νυμφευτής, ὁ, *groomsman*; met., of God becoming ν. to Adam after having created Eve, Thdt.*haer*.5.25(4.464).

νυμφεύτρια, ἡ, 1. *she who escorts the bride* (to her husband), *bridesmaid,* exeg. 1Cor.7:4f. δόξει νυμφευτρίας εἶναι μᾶλλον ἢ ἀποστόλου τὰ ῥήματα Chrys.*virg*.29(1.289B); id.*hom.20.8 in Eph.*(11.155A); id.*hom.5.3 in 1Thess.*(11.462F); **2.** *bride,* Synes.*ep*.3(M.66.1324B).

νυμφεύ-ω, *marry, espouse*; **1.** of Christ espousing Church; through baptism, Ammon.*Jo*.3:29(M.85.1413C); through Passion τὴν ἡμέραν τοῦ πάθους...καθ' ἣν ἐνυμφεύσατο τὴν ἐκκλησίαν διὰ τοῦ αἵματος αὐτοῦ Cyr.*fr.Cant*.3:11(M.69.1288B); ἀνδρωθεὶς Χριστὸς... τὴν...ἐκκλησίαν ἐνυμφεύσατο, ὑπὲρ ἧς καὶ τὸ τίμιον αἷμα ἐξέχεε Mod.*dorm*.3(M.86.3288B); Andr.Caes.*Apoc*.67(M.106.429B); **2.** of mankind being espoused to Christ μαθηταί, τὴν ~ομένην ἀνθρωπότητα τῷ Χριστῷ πρὸς αὐτὸν ἰοῦσαν ὁρῶντες Cyr.*Jo*.2.1(4.159D); med., of Christ ἐν ᾗ [sc. BMV] ὁ λόγος ἐνυμφεύσατο τὴν σάρκα Procl.CP *or. laud.BMV* 1(p.103.14; M.65.681A); **3.** of virgins espoused to Christ ~ομαι τῷ λόγῳ καὶ τὸν ἀΐδιον τῆς ἀφθαρσίας προῖκα λαμβάνω στέφανον Meth.*symp*.6.5(p.69.17; M.18.120C); ἡ δὲ τῷ κυρίῳ ~ομένη, οὐ δυναμένη οὔτε τὴν ὄψιν, οὔτε τὴν ἀκοήν, οὔτε τὴν παρουσίαν φυγεῖν, ἐν ὄψει αὐτοῦ ἅπαντα πράττει †Bas.Anc.*virg*.27(M.30.725C); τὴν Χριστῷ διὰ τῆς κατὰ τὴν παρθενίαν ὑποσχέσεως ἁρμοσθεῖσαν, ὡς ἂν σοφίᾳ καὶ λόγῳ ἑαυτὴν διὰ βίου ~ουσαν *ib*.50(768D); **4.** souls espoused through ecstasy of Christ on Cross, Meth.*symp*.3.8(p.36.19; M.18.73D) cit. s. ἔκστασις; apostles εὑρίσκεις ἐκείνους παρανύμφους, ~οντας ψυχὰς Χριστῷ Mac.Aeg.*hom*.28.6(M.34.713D); fruit in good works, Clem.*str*.3.12(p.235.2; M.8.1185B); espousal perfected after death, Ammon.*Jo*.3:29(M.85.1416A).

νύμφη, ἡ, *bride*;

A. of Church as bride of Christ; **1.** justification of title οὐκ ἴσασι τὴν αἰτίαν τοῦ μὴ γῆμαι τὸν κύριον· πρῶτον μὲν γὰρ τὴν ἰδίαν ν. εἶχεν, τὴν ἐκκλησίαν Clem.*str*.3.6(p.218.27; M.8.1152C); ν. λέγων τὴν ὅλην ἐκκλησίαν, τυγχάνουσαν ἁγνὴν παρθένον διὰ τὴν τῶν δογμάτων καὶ ἠθῶν ὀρθότητα Or.*fr.45 in Jo.*(p.520.15); ἡ [sc. ἐκκλησία]...ἐστὶν ἡ ὑπερβάλλουσα ν. τῷ κάλλει τῆς ἀκμῆς καὶ τῆς παρθενίας πάσας...διὸ ...αἰνεῖται Meth.*symp*.7.7(p.78.4; M.18.133B); παρθένος δ' ἐστί [sc. ἡ ἐκκλησία], καὶ ἁγνή, καὶ ν. διὰ τὴν τῶν δογμάτων ὀρθότητα Ammon.*Jo*.3:29(M.85.1413C); νύμφην ἐκάλεσεν,...ὅτι καὶ πάντας ἓν σῶμα εἶναι βούλεται καὶ μίαν ψυχήν,...καὶ ὅτι καθάπερ ἡ ν. πάντα ποιεῖ πρὸς ἀρέσκειαν τοῦ ἀνδρός, οὕτω καὶ ἡμᾶς διὰ παντὸς τοῦ βίου τοιούτους εἶναι χρή. οἵα ἡ ν. κατὰ τὴν ἡμέραν ἐκείνην ἐπὶ τῶν παστάδων καθέζεται, ἓν μεριμνῶσα μόνον ὅπως ἀρέσῃ τῷ νυμφίῳ· οὕτω δὴ καὶ ἡμεῖς ἐπὶ τοῦ βίου τούτου προκαθήμενοι ἓν σκοπῶμεν, τοῦ νυμφίου τὴν ἀρέσκειαν, καὶ τὴν τῆς ν. εὐταξίαν διατηρῶμεν Chrys.*exp.in Ps*.5:1(5.30E); ν. ... διὰ τὴν πρὸς τὸν λόγον συνάφειαν Cyr.*fr.Cant*.4:9(M.69.1288D); also of various local churches, id.*glaph.Gen.*(1.153B); of Church as likened to heavenly Jerusalem ἡ...βασίλισσα, ἡ μήτηρ τῶν θυγατέρων, παρέστη ἐκ δεξιῶν, ἡ καθολικὴ ἐκκλησία. κυριώτερον δὲ εἴποις ἐπουράνιον, ἥτις ἐστὶ μήτηρ τῶν ἐπὶ γῆς ἁγίων...αὕτη μὲν οὖν ἡ τελεία Χριστοῦ ν., ἧς οὐκ ἂν ἁμάρτοις θυγατέραν λέγων τὴν ἐπὶ γῆς ἐκκλησίαν Or.*Ps*.44:10(p.42); *1Apoc.Jo*.17(p.85); **2.** her origin and development, from old dispensation to new ὁρῶμεν τοίνυν ὥσπερ τὰ ἐν βαθμῶν ἀναβάσει χειραγωγουμένην διὰ τῶν τῆς ἀρετῆς ἀνόδων ἐπὶ ὕψη παρὰ τοῦ λόγου τὴν ν. ... ἐνίησι πρῶτον διὰ τῶν προφητῶν θυρίδων, καὶ τῶν δικτύων τῶν τοῦ νόμου παραγγελμάτων τὴν ἀκτῖνα ὁ λόγος, καὶ προσκαλεῖ αὐτὴν ἐγγίσαι φωτὶ...εἶτα μετασχοῦσαν τῶν καλῶν, ...πρὸς τοῦ ὑπερκειμένου κάλλους μετουσίαν ἐφέλκεται Gr.Nyss.*hom.5 in Cant.*(M.44.876B); Thdt.*Cant*.proem.(2.16); from idolatry διδάσκει ἡμᾶς πόθεν ἡ ν., καὶ ὅτι ἐξ εἰδωλολατρείας ἔρχεται Cyr.*fr.Cant*.4:8(M.69.1288C); birth from side of Christ ἐκ τοῦ στάξαντος ὕδατος, καὶ αἵματος, καὶ πνεύματος τοῦ ἐκ πλευρᾶς αὐτοῦ, αὐτὸς γέγονέ μοι νυμφίος, κἀγὼ αὐτοῦ ν. Ph.Carp.*Cant*.26(M.40.56A); ῥευσάσης αἷμα καὶ ὕδωρ οἰκοδομηθῇ ἡ νοητὴ ν. αὐτοῦ, τουτέστιν ἡ καθολικὴ ἐκκλησία Nil.*epp*.1.26(M.79.92C); **3.** in relationship with bridegroom ν. πολλοῖς...οἴνοις εὐφρανθεῖσα καὶ ἔχουσα παρασκευὴν εἰς τὸ δέξασθαι τοὺς κρείττονας τούτων τοῦ νυμφίου μαστοὺς τοῦτό φησι προτιμῶσα τούτους, οἴνου τοῦ ἐν νόμῳ τε καὶ προφήταις Or.*Cant*.1(p.96.30; M.13.89D); ἔπρεπε τῇ ν. τοῦ κάλλους ὅλῃ τοῦ νυμφίου γεγενημένῃ περὶ ἑαυτῆς μὲν λέγειν οὐδέν *ib*.3(p.179.31; M.13.151C); ἡ νῦν ἐκκλησία, ἡ ν. τὸν νυμφίον ἐφίλει Gr.Nyss.*hom.1 in Cant.*(M.44.777C); ὁ ἄνω ἀντάρτης κάτω ἀντίδικος τῆς ν. σου γέγονεν Ast.Soph.*hom.2 in Ps*.5(M.40.412A); ἀναδιπλασιάζει τῆς ν. ὁ νυμφίος τὸν ἔπαινον, τό τε θεωρητικὸν αὐτῆς ἐπαινῶν καὶ τὸ πρακτικόν...λέγει οὖν ὡς ἐδέξατο νοῦν ἡ ν. μόνον ὁρῶντα θεόν. ὀφθαλμοί...τῆς ἐκκλησίας διδάσκαλοι Cyr.*fr.Cant*.1:14(M.69.1281A,B); νύμφην δὲ προσαγορεύει τοὺς ἐν ἐκείνοις τοῖς ᾄσμασι τῆς αἰχμαλωσίας ἀπαλλαγέντας, καὶ τῆς ἐλευθερίας τετυχηκότας, καὶ προσοικειωθέντας τῷ βασιλεῖ Thdt.*Cant*.1(2.23); **4.** in relationship with others; **a.** as instrument of salvation ἀγαλλιώμενος σὺν τῇ ν. τῇ εἰς σωτηρίαν ἡμῶν βοηθῷ, τῇ ἐκκλησίᾳ Clem.*paed*.1.5(p.103.12; M.8.276B); τὸ δ' ἀνάλογον σελήνῃ καὶ ἄστροις ὑπολαμβάνομεν εἶναι περὶ τὴν ν. ἐκκλησίαν καὶ τοὺς μαθητάς, ἔχοντας οἰκεῖον φῶς,...ἵνα φωτίσωσι μὴ δεδυνημένους πηγὴν ἐν αὐτοῖς κατασκευάσαι φωτὸς Or.*Jo*.1.25(24; p.31.11; M.14.68C); **b.** as assembly of the faithful, guided by priests and bishops, *Clem.ep*.7(M.2.41B); *Hom.Clem*.3.72; **c.** persecuted by Devil, *Clem.ep*.4(M.2.37B).

B. of virgins as brides of Christ, ref. Cant.4:9ff. ταῦτα Χριστὸς ταῖς ἐπὶ πέρατα παρθενίας ἐλθούσαις τὰ ἐγκώμια ψάλλει, πάσας ἑνὶ περιγράψας τῷ νύμφης ὀνόματι, ἐπειδὴ τὴν ν. ἡρμόσθαι μὲν δεῖ καὶ κατωνομάσθαι τῷ μνηστευσαμένῳ, ἄχραντον δὲ ἔτι καὶ ἀμιγῆ τυγχάνειν Meth.*symp*.7.1(p.72.10f.; M.18.125B); *ib*.7.3(p.74.15; 129A); δοκιμαζέτω τοίνυν τὸ ἑαυτῆς βλέμμα τοῦ κυρίου ἡ ν.· καὶ εἰ μὲν ὁρῶν ἀρεσθήσεται, καὶ δὴ τοῦτο θαρροῦσα κινείτω †Bas.Anc.*virg*.27(M.30.728A); τῇ τοῦ Χριστοῦ μάλιστα ν. ἁρμόττει, τὰς διὰ τῶν αἰσθήσεων τῆς ψυχῆς ἐνεργείας ἀπὸ τῶν ἔξωθεν ἐπὶ τὰ ἔσω ὅλας συνήθως ἐπιστρέψασαν, τῷ μὲν νυμφίῳ ἐν ἀπορρήτοις κατὰ τὸν νοῦν παστοῖς, ὡς θεῷ λόγῳ ἀεὶ ὁμιλεῖν *ib*.50(768D); σοὶ λοιπὸν τοῦτο πρέπει, μηδὲ ὅλως ἐγγίζειν ἀνδρί, εἰ ἐνδέχεται, μηδὲ ὅλως βλεπέτω ἀνὴρ τὸ πρόσωπόν σου. ν. γὰρ Χριστοῦ εἶ· οὕτω προέρχου, ὡς ν. κεκοσμημένη, ἐσκεπασμένη τῷ περιβολαίῳ τὴν ὄψιν ‡Chrys.*ascet.facet*.(1.810D).

C. of individual saints; **1.** esp. of BMV, ‡Epiph.*hom*.5(M.43.489B); Procl.CP *or*.6.17(M.65.756B); ‡Serg.*acath*.(p.140); τριετὴ ὡς τριάδος ἀχωρίστου ν. Jo.Eub.*concept.BMV* 14(M.96.1481A); ‡Jo.D.*hom*.5(M.96.656A); ν., ἧς νυμφοστόλος τὸ πνεῦμα τὸ ἅγιον Thdr.Stud.*nativ.BMV* 7(M.96.693A); **2.** of S. Paul ν. τοῦ λόγου Meth.*symp*.3.9(p.37.21; M.18.76B); Gr.Nyss.*hom.3 in Cant.*(M.44.824C).

D. of flesh of Christ as an alternative to Church in interprn. of Cant. δυνήσεται δέ τις καὶ ἑτέρως τὴν ν. φάναι τὴν σάρκα τὴν ἀμόλυντον εἶναι τοῦ κυρίου Meth.*symp*.7.8(p.78.17; M.18.136A).

E. of soul; **1.** reasons for title ἡ λογικὴ οὐσία, ἧς μέρος ἐστὶ καὶ ἡ ἀνθρώπου ψυχή, ἐξ ἑαυτῆς οὐδενός ἐστι τῶν ἀγαθῶν γεννητική, εἰ καὶ δεκτική ἐστι τούτων. αὕτη τοιγαροῦν γυναικὸς τρόπῳ ἐξ ἄλλου γεννᾶν πέφυκεν ἃς δύναται τίκτειν ἀρετὰς πρακτικάς τε καὶ διανοητικάς. διὸ ν. αὐτὴν ἐρῶ, οὐ τοῦ τυχόντος ἀλλὰ μόνου τοῦ σπορέως τῶν ἀγαθῶν Or.*fr.45 in Jo.*(p.519.21); **2.** esp. of perfect souls ταύτῃ γὰρ ἠθέλησεν ὁ θεὸς κοινωνῆσαι, καὶ ταύτην ἡρμόσατο ἑαυτῷ εἰς ν. βασιλέως, καὶ ταύτην καθαρίζει ἀπὸ τοῦ ῥύπου...κτίσμα γὰρ οὖσα εἰς ν. τῷ υἱῷ τοῦ βασιλέως ἡρμόσθη...τείνει γὰρ αὐτὴν...εἰς ἀπέραντον καὶ ἀμέτρητον αὔξησιν, ἕως ἂν ἄμωμος καὶ ἀξία αὐτοῦ νύμφη γένηται...αὐτὸς γὰρ ὢν τέλειος νυμφίος, λαμβάνει αὐτὴν τελείαν ν. εἰς τὴν ἁγίαν καὶ μυστικήν, καὶ ἄχραντον κοινωνίαν τοῦ γάμου Mac.Aeg.*hom*.47.17(M.34.808B,C); δεῦρο τοίνυν ἀπὸ Λιβάνου, φησίν, οὐκέτι μνηστή, ἀλλὰ ν. οὐ γάρ ἐστι δυνατὸν ἐμοὶ συζῆσαι τὸν μὴ ἀλλοιωθέντα διὰ τῆς τοῦ θανάτου σμύρνης πρὸς τὴν τοῦ λιβάνου θεότητα Gr.Nyss.*hom.8 in Cant.*(M.44.944C); ὁ αὐτὸς [sc. Χριστὸς] καὶ νυμφίος καὶ τοξότης ἡμῶν ἐστι, ν. τε καὶ βέλος ἡ κεκαθαρμένη ψυχή·...ὡς νύμφην εἰς κοινωνίαν ἀναλαμβάνει τῆς ἀφθάρτου ἀϊδιότητος Cyr.*fr.Cant*.2:6(M.69.1281D); τὰς τετελειωμένας ἐν ἀρετῇ ψυχὰς αὐτὴν νοεῖν τὴν ν. τὰ θεῖα ἡμᾶς ἐδίδαξε λόγια Thdt.*Cant*.proem.(2.17); **3.** spiritual ascent of soul as bride ἐκεῖνα φωνῆς ἦχος ἐνομίσθη, πρὸς τὴν τῶν μυστικῶν θεωρίαν τὴν ψυχὴν διὰ τῆς ἀκοῆς ἐπιστρεφούσης...πάλιν ἐν μείζονι καταστάσει ἡ ν. γίνεται, φωνῆς δευτέρας πρὸς αὐτὴν ἐλθούσης...δι' ὧν πάλιν τελειοτέρα γινομένη ἡ ν., αὐτὴν ἀξιοῖ τοῦ φθεγγομένου τὴν ὄψιν ἰδεῖν ἐκφανῶς Gr.Nyss.*hom.6 in Cant.*(M.44.889B,C); **4.** its obligations to Christ ψυχὴ ἣν ἂν μνηστεύσηται ν. ὁ ἐπουράνιος νυμφίος Χριστός, πρὸς τὴν ἑαυτοῦ μυστικὴν καὶ θείαν κοινωνίαν,...ἐν πολλῇ σπουδῇ γνησίως ἀρέσκειν ὀφείλει τῷ αὐτῆς μνηστῆρι Χριστῷ, καὶ τὴν τοῦ πνεύματος διακονίαν...ἁρμοζόντως ἐκπληροῦν, τῷ ἀρέσκειν τῷ θεῷ ἐν πᾶσι, καὶ τὸ πνεῦμα ἐν μηδενὶ λυπεῖν Mac.Aeg.*hom*.15.2(M.34.576D); **5.** called ἀδελφή; v.s.v.

F. wider applications ν. γάρ ἐστι ὁ πᾶς ἄνθρωπος, ὁπόταν τοῦ ἀληθοῦς προφήτου λευκῷ λόγῳ ἀληθείας σπειρόμενος φωτίζηται τὸν νοῦν *Hom.Clem*.3.27; πᾶσα οὖν λογικὴ φύσις ἀγγέλων τε καὶ ἀνθρώπων ν. ἐστίν Ammon.*Jo*.3:29(M.85.1413D).

G. Gnost., of souls οὐκέτι ν. [sc. ψυχή] ἀλλ' ἤδη λόγος γενόμενος Clem.*exc.Thdot*.27(p.116.10; M.9.673A); τοὺς δὲ πνευματικοὺς ἀποδυσαμένους τὰς ψυχὰς...νύμφας ἀποδοθήσεσθαι τοῖς περὶ τὸν Σωτῆρα ἀγγέλοις Iren.*haer*.1.7.1(M.7.512B); of Achamoth as bride of Saviour, *ib.* cit. s. νυμφών.

νυμφικός, *bridal*, ref. Mt.22:11ff. *ἔμειναν ἔξω οἱ μηδὲ ἴχνος πώποτε πίστεως μηδὲ αἴσθησιν ἐνδύματος ν. μηδὲ ἔννοιαν φόβου θεοῦ σχόντες Ep.Lugd.*ap.Eus.*h.e.*5.1.48(M.20.428A); *Βλανδῖνα...ἀγαλλιωμένη ἐπὶ τῇ ἐξόδῳ ὡς εἰς ν. δεῖπνον κεκλημένη ib.*5.1.55(429B); Meth. *symp.*4.5(p.51.23; M.18.96A); Cyr.H.*procatech.*3; ref. Cant. *μή... ἐρωτικὰ νομίσῃς εἶναι καὶ ἐμπαθῆ τὰ Ἄισματα· ἀλλὰ ν. τὰ ῥήματα, σωφροσύνης πεπληρωμένα* id.*hom.*10(M.33.1144A); *οὐ κατὰ τὴν ἀνθρωπίνην συνήθειαν...εὐχὴν ποιουμένη τοῦ ν. ποτε κατατρυφῆσαι φιλήματος* Gr.Nyss.*hom.1 in Cant.*(M.44.772B); *ἡ λογικὴ ψυχή, τῇ πρὸς τὸν θεὸν λόγον ν. κοινωνίᾳ...ἀπαθείας τῆς ἀληθοῦς ἀπολαύσειεν ἐν πνεύματι* †Bas.Anc.*virg.*50(M.30.768C).

νυμφικῶς, *bridally, in bridal fashion*; **1.** lit. *σὺ* [sc. S. Luke] *τὴν κεχαριτωμένην παρθένον* [i.e. BMV] *ἐκόσμησας, ν. ἀναδήσας* Ephr.3. 465C; ref. Macrina's body adorned for funeral, Gr.Nyss.*v.Macr.* (p.406.12; M.46.992C); **2.** met., ref. Christ's appearance at Transfiguration *ὦ μακαρίων ὀμμάτων, ν. τὸν Χριστὸν ἐστολισμένον θεωρούντων* Bas.Sel.*or.*40.3(M.85.460B); ref. heavens decked with stars, Geo.Pis.*hex.*139(M.92.1443A); ref. union of soul with virtue of humility, Jo.Clim.*scal.*25(M.88.992B); ref. union between Son and human nature *τοῦ πατρὸς υἱὸν...κάτω παρθενικῆς παστάδος ν. ἑνώσαντα ἑαυτῷ τὸν Ἀδὰμ ἀτρέπτως* ‡Meth.*Sym.et Ann.*3(M.18.356A).

***νυμφιοκλεῶς**, ? *in bridal glory*, of a convent *παρθένους φέρουσα ν.* Thdr.Stud.*iamb.*120(M.99.1809C).

νυμφίος, ὁ, *bridegroom, spouse*;

A. reasons for applying term to Christ *διὰ τοῦτο ν. ὁ ἐν ταῖς Παροιμίαις ὀνομάζεται υἱός, καὶ ἡ σοφία εἰς νύμφης τάξιν ἀντιμεθίσταται, ἵνα μνηστευθῇ τῷ θεῷ ὁ ἄνθρωπος ἁγνὴ παρθένος, καὶ κολληθεὶς τῷ κυρίῳ γένηται πνεῦμα ἕν* Gr.Nyss.*hom.1 in Cant.*(M.44.772A); *διὰ τί ἐκλήθη ν.; ὅτι νύμφην με ἡρμόσατο* Chrys.*Eutrop.*2.8(3.393C); difference between lit. and met. use of term *ἡ δὲ εἰκὼν γαμική τίς ἐστι κατασκευή, ἐν ᾗ κάλλους ἐπιθυμία μεσιτεύει τῷ πόθῳ, οὐ κατὰ τὴν ἀνθρωπίνην συνήθειαν τοῦ ν. τῆς ἐπιθυμίας κατάρξαντος, ἀλλὰ προλαμβάνει τὸν ν. ἡ παρθένος ἀνεπαισχύντως τὸν πόθον δημοσιεύουσα* Gr. Nyss.*hom.1 in Cant.*(M.44.772B); *ὁ μὲν ν. μετὰ τὰς πρώτας ἡμέρας καταλύει τὸ σφοδρὸν τοῦ ἔρωτος· ὁ δὲ ἡμέτερος ν. μένει διηνεκῶς ἡμᾶς ἀγαπῶν, καὶ ἐπιτείνων τὸν πόθον· ὅπερ δηλῶν ὁ Ἰωάννης νυμφίον καλεῖ, ὅτε ἀκμάζοντες οἱ πόθοι* Chrys.*exp.in Ps.*5:1(5.30D).

B. Christ as bridegroom of Church; **1.** in gen. *ὁ ν., λόγος ὁ οὐράνιος, αὐτὸς Ἰησοῦς Χριστός* Eus.*h.e.*10.4.49(M.20.869A); *ib.*10.4. 54(869D); Gr.Nyss.*hom.1 in Cant.*(M.44.777C) cit. s. *νύμφη*; Ammon. *Jo.*3:29(M.85.1413D); Cyr.*glaph.Gen.*(1².112D); *περὶ τοῦ Χριστοῦ καὶ τῆς ἐκκλησίας, ὡς ἐπὶ βασιλέως ν. καὶ νύμφης βασιλίδος* Cosm.Ind. *top.*5(M.88.253D); *ὁ ἄχραντος τῆς ἐκκλησίας ν.* ‡Gr.Nyss.*hom.10.42 in Jo.*(p.307.29); **2.** as teacher *διδασκαλεῖον δὲ ἡ ἐκκλησία ἥδε καὶ ὁ ν. ὁ μόνος διδάσκαλος* Clem.*paed.*3.12(p.289.27; M.8.677A); Or.*Cant.*1 (p.96.32; cf.M.13.89D) cit. s. *νύμφη*; *ib.*(p.109.24; M.17.256A); *γέγονε τοίνυν ἡ τοῦ ν. φωνὴ ἡ διὰ τῶν προφητῶν ἐν οἷς ἐλάλησεν ὁ θεός* Gr. Nyss.*hom.5 in Cant.*(M.44.861D); **3.** in his human nature *οὐκ ἦλθε τὴν δόξαν αὐτοῦ ἐπιδεικνύμενος, ἵνα μὴ τῇ ὑπερβολῇ τοῦ κάλλους ἐπιπλήξῃ αὐτήν, καὶ παράφρονα ἐργάσηται, ἀλλ' ἔρχεται ἱμάτιον περιβεβλημένος, οἷον ἡ νύμφη· μετέχεται γὰρ αἵματος καὶ σαρκὸς παραπλησίως αὐτῇ· καὶ οὐκ αὐτὴν ἄνω καλεῖ, ἀλλ' αὐτὸς πρὸς αὐτὴν παραγίνεται, τηρῶν κἀνταῦθα τοῦ ν. τὸν νόμον τὸν πρὸς τὴν νύμφην αὐτὸν ἄγοντα* Chrys. *exp.in Ps.*5:1(5.31B); **4.** union with bride; **a.** effected by baptism, exeg. Jo.3:29 *ἐστὶ τοίνυν, φησί* [sc. Jo. Bapt.], *ν. ... ὁ Χριστός... ὑμεῖς δέ, ὦ σοφώτατοι μαθηταί, τὴν νυμφευομένην ἀνθρωπότητα τῷ Χριστῷ πρὸς αὐτὸν ἰοῦσαν ὁρῶντες, καὶ εἰς πνευματικὴν ἀναβαίνουσαν οἰκειότητα διὰ τοῦ ἁγίου βαπτίσματος τὴν ἀποκεκομμένην καὶ δραπετεύσασαν τῆς εἰς αὐτὸν ἀγάπης καταθεώμενοι φύσιν, μὴ ἀσχάλλετε, φησίν, ὅτι μὴ μᾶλλον ἐμοὶ πρέπει, προστρέχει δὲ λίαν εὐπετῶς τῷ κατὰ πνεῦμα ν. ... μὴ ἐν ἐμοὶ ζητεῖτε τοῦ ν. τὸν στέφανον* Cyr.*Jo.*2.1(4.159C–E); **b.** by becoming her food *ὁ δὲ ν. ... ἐσθίεται καὶ γίνεται τροφὴ τῇ νύμφῃ* Thdt.*Cant.*2:3(2.55); **c.** vicissitudes of life of bride dependent on her relation to spouse *δι' ὅλου δὲ τοῦ λόγου* [sc. Cant.], *τινὰ μὲν ὡς παρόντι λέγεται τῷ ν.· τινὰ δὲ ὥσπερ ζητουμένου παρὰ τῆς νύμφης· ἐπεὶ καὶ τῶν προβλημάτων ποτὲ μέν τινα ζητοῦμεν ἀποροῦντες τῆς λύσεως· ποτὲ δὲ τῆς λύσεως ἀπολαύομεν, τοῦ ν. λόγου καταυγάζοντος ἡμῶν τὰς καρδίας. εἶτα πάλιν ἀποροῦμεν ἐν ἑτέροις, καὶ πάλιν ἡμῖν ἐπιφαίνεται· καὶ τοῦτο πολλάκις, μέχρι τελειωθέντες τοῦ ν. τύχωμεν οὐ μόνον ἐρχομένου πρὸς ἡμᾶς, ἀλλὰ καὶ μονὴν ποιουμένου. καὶ ἡ ἐκκλησία ποθεῖ μὲν ἐγκαταλειπομένη τοῖς πειρασμοῖς, ἐπιφαίνεται δὲ αὐτῇ τοῖς χαρίσμασι* Cyr.*fr.Cant.*2:9(M.69.1284D)—though Church in this passage not always clearly dist. from soul; cf. identification of both *δῆλον ὡς ἡ νύμφη τοῦ λόγου ψυχή, ἤγουν ἐκκλησία Χριστοῦ ib.* (1284C); cf. term *ἐκκλησιαστικὴ ψυχή, ib.*3:6(1285D,1288A); **d.** esp. in connexion with parousia, Ephr.2.230A.

C. Christ as bridegroom of virgins; **1.** in gen., Meth.*symp.* proem.(p.5.18; M.18.32C); *ib.*11(p.131.18; 208C); *ἡ δὲ φροντίζουσα τὸ ἔργον τοῦ θεοῦ, ν. αὐτῆς ὁ Χριστός ἐστιν* Ath.*virg.*2(p.37.12; M.28. 253D); †Bas.Anc.*virg.*21(M.30.713A); ref. BMV *νύμφη, ἧς...ν. ὁ Χριστός* Thdr.Stud.*nativ.BMV* 7(M.96.693A); **2.** his demands *διὰ νηστείας καὶ ὑπακοῆς...ὦ παρθένε,...ἀρέσεις τῷ ἐπουρανίῳ ν.* Ath. *virg.*6(p.40.6; M.28.257C); *ib.*24(p.59.5; 280C); *δεῖ...τὴν παρθένον... τὸ...σῶμα, ὥσπερ τινὰ ναὸν ἢ παστὸν τοῦ ν., ἔχειν εὐτρεπισμένον, τὴν δὲ ψυχὴν ἐν τούτῳ αὐτῷ νύμφην καθαρὰν συνευνάζειν* †Bas.Anc.*virg.*27 (M.30.725B); *κἂν μόνη αὐτὴ ᾖ* [sc. *παρθένος*], *μηδενὸς ἀνθρώπων παρόντος...πράττειν τι τῶν μὴ ἀξίων τοῦ ν. οὐκ ἀνεχομένη ib.*29(729A); *ib.*27(725C); *ἐὰν...ὅλη θεῷ συναφθῇς, ἄνω χωρίσῃς, οὐ μὴ κάτω πέσῃς, οὐ μὴ διαχυθῇς, ὅλη Χριστοῦ μενεῖς, μέχρις ἂν καὶ Χριστὸν ἴδῃς τὸν σὸν ν.* Gr.Naz.*or.*37.12(M.36.297A); **3.** love of bridegroom and fraternal charity *ἀγαπᾶν οὖν δεῖ τοὺς πρὸς τὸν ν. παρακαλοῦντας, ἀλλὰ δεῖ τὴν ἀγάπην δικαίαν καὶ μὴ συγκεχυμένην ποιεῖσθαι, ἵνα μὴ τοὺς ὑπηρέτας τοῦ ν., ἀπὸ τοῦ συνεχῶς ἀκούειν αὐτῶν τὰ περὶ τοῦ ν. λαλούντων, ἴσους τοῦ ν. ἀγαπήσασά ποτε, καθέλῃ μὲν τὸ ἀξίωμα τοῦ ν.* †Bas.Anc.*virg.* 37(M.30.744B); *ἕως ἂν διὰ τὴν πρὸς τὸν ν. ἀγάπην ἀγαπῶσα φαίνῃ τοὺς ἀδελφούς, σώζεις καὶ τὸ πρὸς ἐκεῖνον καὶ τὸ πρὸς αὐτοὺς τὸ τῆς ἀγάπης σεμνόν ib.*(745A).

D. Christ as bridegroom of soul; **1.** non-myst. (though distinction between myst. and non-myst. use is not always clear cut); **a.** in gen. *μακάριός ἐστιν ὁ κεκλημένος ὑπὸ τοῦ ν. A.Phil.*135(p.67. 20); *ζηλοῖ...ἐπὶ ψυχῆς ἐχούσης ἕνα λόγον ἕνα ν. ... ὁ δὲ ν. καὶ καλὸς ζηλωτής* Or.*hom.8.5 in Ex.*(p.227.31ff.); *ἡ σώφρων γυνὴ ὡς νυμφίῳ τῷ υἱῷ τοῦ θεοῦ κοσμεῖται...ἔστι δὲ αὐτῇ κάλλος ἡ ἐν τῇ ψυχῇ εὐνομία Hom.Clem.*13.16; **b.** by baptism *ἔκδυσαί μοι πορνείαν καὶ ἀκαθαρσίαν, καὶ ἔνδυσαί μοι σωφροσύνης λαμπροτάτην στολήν. ἐγὼ παραγγέλλω, πρὶν ὁ ν. τῶν ψυχῶν εἰσέλθῃ Ἰησοῦς* Cyr.H.*procatech.*4; *αἱ δὲ μέλλουσαι ψυχαὶ τῷ νοητῷ ν. συνάπτεσθαι, παρασκευαζέσθωσαν* id.*catech.* 3.1; **c.** after resurrection of body *ἡ σὰρξ...ἣν ἡ ψυχὴ βαστάζουσα δαδὸς δίκην τῷ ν. παρίσταται Χριστῷ τῇ ἡμέρᾳ τῆς ἀναστάσεως* Meth. *symp.*6.3(p.67.13; M.18.117B); **2.** myst.; **a.** description of mystical relationship between bridegroom and bride *νῦν ἔοικε πρότερον ἐνεωρακέναι τρανότερον τῷ τοῦ ν. κάλλει ἡ νύμφη...τάχα δὲ κλίνην κοινὴν ἑαυτῆς καὶ τοῦ ν. τὸ σῶμα αἰνίττεται, ἐν ᾧ ἔτι οὖσα ἡ ψυχὴ ἀξιοῦται τῆς τοῦ λόγου κοινωνίας...σύσκιον δέ φησι τὸν ν. διὰ τὴν πυκνότητα τῶν ἐν τῷ λόγῳ καὶ τῇ σοφίᾳ θεωρημάτων* Or.*Cant.*3(pp.174. 28–175.27; M.13.147D); *ψυχὴ...ἔρωτι πνεύματος οὐρανίου τετρωμένη, καὶ πόθον ἔμπυρον διὰ τῆς χάριτος ἀεὶ ἐν αὐτῇ πρὸς τὸν οὐράνιον ν. ἀνακινοῦσα, ἐπιθυμοῦσα τελείως καταξιωθῆναι τῆς πρὸς αὐτὸν μυστικῆς καὶ ἀρρήτου ἐν ἁγιασμῷ πνεύματος κοινωνίας ἀποκεκαλυμμένῃ τῷ τῆς ψυχῆς προσώπῳ, καὶ ἐνατενίζουσα τῷ ἐπουρανίῳ ν. πρόσωπον ἐν φωτὶ πνευματικῷ* Mac.Aeg.*hom.*10.4(M.34.544A,B); *ὡς γὰρ ὁ ν. αὐτῆς καταλιπὼν θρόνους καὶ κυριότητας κατὰ τὸ θνητὸν ἐκολλήθη, ἵνα ἐν αὐτῇ κατὰ συμπάθειαν γεγονώς, εἰς ἀπάθειαν αὐτὴν τὴν ἑαυτοῦ μεταβάλῃ· οὕτω καὶ αὐτὴ τῷ δι' αὐτὴν ἀπεκδυσαμένῳ τὰς ἀρχὰς καὶ ἐξουσίας, καὶ ἑαυτὸν ἀπὸ μορφῆς θεοῦ εἰς μορφὴν δούλου διὰ τὸ περὶ τὴν νύμφην φίλτρον κενώσαντι, κατὰ τὸ ἀθάνατον κεκολλῆσθαι ὀφείλει, ἵνα καὶ εἰς τὸν οὐράνιον παστὸν αὐτῷ πρὸς τὸν πατέρα ἀνιόντι συνανέλθῃ* †Bas.Anc.*virg.*50(M 30.769A); **b.** effects of this relationship *ἁρμοσθεῖσα εἰς νύμφην ἡ ψυχὴ τῷ ἐπουρανίῳ ν., λαμβάνει ἀρραβῶνα ἐκ τοῦ πνεύματος, εἴτε χαρίσματα ἰαμάτων, εἴτε γνώσεως, εἴτε ἀποκαλύψεως* Mac.Aeg.*hom.*45.7(M.34.792B); *ὁ ν. τοῦ περὶ αὐτὸν ἔρωτος αὐτὴν ἀμειβόμενος, κἂν δούλη...διὰ τὴν πρὸς αὐτὸν κοινωνίαν ἐξευγενίζων βασιλίδα οὐρανῶν ποιεῖ* †Bas.Anc.*virg.*26(M.30.724C); *ἡ νύμφη, συνιστῶσα τοῦ ν. τὴν ἀγαθότητα, ὅτι κἂν μέλαινάν τινα λάβοι ψυχήν, τῇ πρὸς ἑαυτὸν κοινωνίᾳ καλὴν ἀπεργάζεται* Gr.Nyss.*hom.2 in Cant.*(M. 44.792C); *πλεονασμὸν τῆς ἐν τοῖς ἀγαθοῖς εὐφροσύνης οἰκονομῶν ὁ ἀγαθὸς ν. τῇ πρὸς αὐτὸν ἀνιούσῃ ψυχῇ ib.*8(845B); *οὐδ' ἑνὸς ἐπιβουλεύειν δυναμένου τῇ περιληφθείσῃ ὑπὸ τοῦ ν. ψυχῇ* Cyr.*fr.Cant.*2:6 (M.69.1284C).

E. Gnost., of Valent. Saviour, becoming spouse of Achamoth, when she will finally enter into Pleroma, Iren.*haer.*1.7.1(M.7.512A); *Ἱερουσαλὴμ ἡ ἔξω Σοφία, καὶ ὁ ν. αὐτῆς ὁ κοινὸς τοῦ πληρώματος Καρπός* Hipp.*haer.*6.34(p.163.4; M.16.3246B); cf. *τὸ δὲ ἐντεῦθεν ἀποθέμενα τὰ πνευματικὰ τὰς ψυχὰς ἅμα τῇ μητρὶ κομιζομένῃ τὸν ν., κομιζόμενα καὶ αὐτὰ τοὺς νυμφίους τοὺς ἀγγέλους ἑαυτῶν, εἰς τὸν νυμφῶνα ἐντὸς τοῦ Ὅρου εἰσίασι* Clem.*exc.Thdot.*64(p.128.16; M.9. 689B).

F. other met. applications; **1.** of lawful bishop as 'bridegroom' of his see, *Supplicatio* ap.Evagr.*h.e.*2.8(p.58.14; M.86.2525A); **2.** in pagan mysteries; in ritual cry of devotees at Eleusis *χαῖρε νυμφίε, χαῖρε νέον φῶς* Firmicus Maternus *de errore profanarum religionum* 20(M.*PL.*12.1025A).

***νυμφιοφόρος**, *representing the bridegroom*, Thdr.Stud.*epp*.2.150 (M.99.1469B).

***νυμφίωσις, ἡ**, *wedding*; spiritual, Thdr.Stud.*epp*.2.150(M.99. 1469A) ? f.l. for νύμφευσις.

***νυμφοδόχος**, *receiving the bride*, Andr.Cr.*or*.12(M.97.1065A).

νυμφοστολ-έω, *act as escort of* bride or bridegroom; **1.** lit., of Christ joining Adam and Eve ἐμοὶ [sc. Jo. Bapt.] τὴν κεφαλὴν ὑποκλίνεις, ὁ τὸν Ἀδὰμ καὶ τὴν Εὔαν ἐν τῷ παραδείσῳ, καθάπερ ἐν θαλάμῳ, νυμφοστολήσας; ‡Chrys.*praecurs*.1(2.806A); νύμφην [sc. Eve] χειρὶ πλαττομένην θεοῦ...~οῦντα θεόν Bas.Sel.*or*.3.3(M.85.53C); Anast.S.*hex*.12(M.89.1052B); **2.** met.; *lead* the soul as bride to God or Christ ~εῖται τρόπον τινὰ ἡ ψυχὴ πρὸς τὴν ἀσώματον...τοῦ θεοῦ συζυγίαν Gr.Nyss.*hom.1 in Cant*.(M.44.765A); *ib*.(769B); τοῖς μὲν γὰρ ἀρχομένοις τὸ βασιλεύεσθαι πρέπει, τοῖς δὲ τετελειωμένοις ~εῖσθαι Thdt.*Cant*.3:9f.(2.87); μακάριος ὁ ~ούμενος καὶ διακρίνειν ἐπιστάμενος φωνὴν μοιχοῦ καὶ νυμφίου [sc. Christ] *ib*.5:2(109); ref. union of Christ's human soul with his body ἡ ἁγία παρθένος... ψυχῆς αὐτοῦ [sc. Χριστοῦ] μήτηρ ἐστίν, αὐτῆς πρὸς τὴν φυσικὴν τοῦ ἰδίου ἐνδύματος συζυγίαν ~ουμένης Leont.H.*Nest*.3.2(M.86.1609A); of leading Christ as bridegroom to Church as bride, Gr.Nyss.*hom. 7 in Cant*.(M.44.916C).

***νυμφοστολία, ἡ**, *nuptials*, Bas.Sel.*v.Thecl*.1(M.85.484B).

***νυμφοστολίζω**, *espouse*, met. νυμφοστολισθῆναι τῷ Χριστῷ Bas. Sel.*v.Thecl*.1(M.85.501C); of bishop in rel. to his see ἦλθε νύμφοστολίσων ὑμᾶς Gr.Nyss.*Melet*.(M.46.860A).

***νυμφοστολικός**, *like a groomsman*; met., ref. God's dealings with Adam πατρικὴν καὶ ν. τῶν χιτώνων περιβολήν Anast.S.*hex*.12 (M.89.1056B).

νυμφοστόλος, ὁ, *one who escorts the bride* κύριος...τὴν γυναῖκα δημιουργήσας, καὶ οἱονεὶ ν. γενόμενος, προσάγει...αὐτὴν τῷ ἀνδρί Thdt.*Mal*.2:14f.(2.1682); id.*haer*.5.25(4.464); νύμφη [sc. BMV] ἧς νυμφοστόλος τὸ πνεῦμα τὸ ἅγιον Thdr.Stud.*nativ.BMV* 7(M.96. 693A); of those who lead Church or individual souls to Christ: S. Paul, Gr.Nyss.*virg*.21(p.327.16; M.46.400B); Thdt.*carit*.(3.1302); id.*ep*.146(4.1268); S. Luke τοὺς τῷ παρθενικῷ τῷδε νυμφῶνι...παραστάντας ἡμᾶς ὁ μυστικὸς ν. Λουκᾶς πρὸς τὴν τῶν ἐν αὐτῷ καλῶν κατανόησιν τῷ λόγῳ χειραγωγείτω ‡Ath.*occurs*.1(M.28.973A); ref. function of λόγος ἐνδιάθετος in the soul τὰς γνωστικὰς ἡ θεωρητικὴ ἀρετὰς ἐφιστῶσα...ὡς ν. λόγον τὸν ἐνδιάθετον ‡Max.*cap.al*.166(M.90. 1440C).

***νυμφοτόκος, ἡ, 1.** *mother of the bridegroom*, of BMV χαῖρε τοῦ χηρεύσαντος κόσμου ν. ἀμίαντε ‡Gr.Thaum.*annunt*.3(M.10.1177A); **2.** *mother of the bride*; of S. Anne, Andr.Cr.*can.BMV* 9(M.97.1328D).

***νυμφοφυλακτήριον, τό**, *house of brides*, of a convent ν. τοῦ βασιλέως τῶν οὐρανῶν Thdr.Stud.*epp*.2.150(M.99.1468B).

νυμφών, ὁ, *bridechamber*; met.; **1.** of heaven, ref. Mt.25:1–13 ζητῶ προσαρμοσθῆναί σοι εἰς τὸν ν. τὸν μέλλοντα *A.Xanthipp*.36 (p.140); ὁ ν. μου [i.e. Christ] ἕτοιμός ἐστιν, ἀλλὰ μακάριός ἐστιν ὁ εὑρεθεὶς ἐν αὐτῷ ἔχων τὸ ἔνδυμα λαμπρόν *A.Phil*.135(p.67.5); κύριος... τὸν χορὸν τὸν ἅγιον αὐτῷ τῶν παρθένων ὥσπερ εἰς ν. τὴν ἀνάπαυσιν τῶν καινῶν αἰώνων ἐφομαρτοῦντα συνεισελεύσεσθαι χρησμῳδεῖ Meth. *symp*.7.3(p.74.7; M.18.128D); *ib*.8.12(p.96.21; 157C); κατὰ γὰρ τὸν θνητὸν τοῦτον βίον...μήπω τοῦ ν. ἠξιωμένοι...ἀλλ' ἐπὶ τέλει αὐξήσαντας αὐτοὺς καὶ τελειωθέντας παραλήψεσθαι ἐπαγγέλλεται, καὶ εἰς τὸν αὐτοῦ συνεισάξειν ν. Eus.*fr.Lc*.12:36(M.24.561C,D); συνάξωμεν τοίνυν εἰς ἀγγεῖα τὸ ἔλαιον...εἴ γε βουλόμεθα μετὰ τοῦ νυμφίου εἰσελθεῖν· εἰ δὲ μή, ἔξω μένειν τοῦ ν. ἀνάγκη Chrys.*hom.23.3 in Jo*.(8.136E); **2.** in connexion with Church 'ἐκκλησία θεοῦ, στῦλος καὶ ἑδραίωμα' [1Tim. 3:15] τοῦ ν. *Const.App*.3.16.3; νυμφίος ἐστὶν ὁ Χριστὸς καὶ ἡ ἐκκλησία νύμφη, καὶ ὁ ν. ὁ τόπος τοῦ βαπτίσματος Ammon.*Jo*.3:29(M. 85.1413D); **3.** of spiritual sense of Cant. ὑμεῖς ἀκούσατε τοῦ μυστηρίου τοῦ ᾄσματος τῶν ᾀσμάτων. ὑμεῖς ἐντὸς γίνεσθε τοῦ ἀκηράτου ν. Gr. Nyss.*hom.1 in Cant*.(M.44.765A); **4.** Gnost. τὴν μὲν Ἀχαμὼθ... λέγουσι...ἐντὸς πληρώματος εἰσελθεῖν, καὶ ἀπολαβεῖν τὸν νυμφίον αὐτῆς τὸν Σωτῆρα...καὶ τοῦτο εἶναι νυμφίον καὶ νύμφην, ν. δὲ τὸ πᾶν πλήρωμα Iren.*haer*.1.7.1(M.7.512B); Clem.*exc.Thdot*.64(p.128.17; M. 9.689B) cit. s. νύμφιος; *ib*.68(p.129.14; 692A); ref. Marcosian sacramental rite of the bridechamber οἱ μὲν γὰρ αὐτῶν ν. κατασκευάζουσι καὶ μυσταγωγίαν ἐπιτελοῦσι, μετ' ἐπιρρήσεών τινων τοῖς τελειουμένοις Iren.*haer*.1.21.3(661A); cf. *Evangelium Philippi* pp.115.30,117.25; of BMV θάλαμος, ὡς ἐν ν. γὰρ ὁ θεὸς λόγος κατεσκήνωσεν Procl.CP *or*.5.3(M.65.720C); Abr.Eph.*occurs*.9(p.454.4); Geo.Pis.*carm*.40.1.

νύξ, ἡ, [acc. νύκταν *Didasc.Jac*.1.14(p.752.4)] *night*; **A.** lit.; **1.** etym. ν. λέγεται ἐπειδὴ νύττει τὸν ἄνθρωπον...λέγουσα·...ὕπνῳ δουλεύεις, διατί τὰ ὑπέρ σε φαντάζῃ; ἡ γὰρ ν. κατανυγή ἐστιν †Jo.D. *creat*.1(p.61); **2.** purpose; **a.** night and day, in their respective spheres and order, glorify God, Chrys.*hom.in Is.45*:7(6.147D); and manifest his providence, Thdt.*Ps*.18:3(1.719); **b.** provides rest and enables man to enjoy the light, Chrys.*hom.in Is.45*:7(6.156A); providentially designed for rest, id.*scand*.1.7(3.480C); id.*compunct*. 2.5(1.148C); **c.** for meditation and spiritual training, Or.*fr.60 in Lam*.(p.260.23; M.13.640B); Cyr.H.*catech*.9.7; **3.** of night of Resurrection, Cosm.Ind.*top*.2(M.88.128A); night of Easter Eve τῇ κυριακῇ ν. Sev.Ant.*res*.(p.794.7; M.46.628C); **4.** ἱερὰ ν.; **a.** of night of Holy Thursday, Chrys.*anom*.7.5(1.507E); **b.** of Easter Eve, *Libell*.ap. CEph.(449)ap.CChalc.*act*.1(*ACO* 2.1.1 p.187.15; H.2.233E).

B. met.; **1.** of ignorance of God and spiritual darkness before Inc., Clem.*prot*.11(p.80.19; M.8.232B); id.*str*.5.5(p.345.9; M.9.52B); Eus.*theoph.fr*.6(p.19*.7; M.24.625D); Cyr.*ador*.3(1.84D); Thdt.*Rom*. 13:12(3.139); **2.** of spiritual darkness and sin in gen., Clem.*paed*.2. 10(p.217.2; M.8.516C); Chrys.*hom.56.3 in Jo*.(8.330B); **3.** of state after death, *ib.56.2*(329C); **4.** of sorrows and misfortunes, Thdt. *Ps*.3:6(1.627); *ib*.16:4(696); **5.** of uncertainty and doubt, *T.Jud*. 18.6; Gr.Thaum.*pan.Or*.16(p.37.7; M.10.1097C); **6.** of present life in gen., Or.*fr.60 in Lam*.(p.261.2; M.13.640C); Chrys.*hom.56.3 in Jo*. (8.330B).

νύσσα, ἡ, 1. *turning-post*; fig., of mid-day as turning-post in sun's course, Nonn.*par.Jo*.4:8(M.43.773C); **2.** *winning-post* (also *starting-post*); met., Gr.Naz.*or*.38.10(M.36.321B); *ib*.43.22(525B); Evagr.*h.e*.1.11(p.20.18; M.86.2452C); κατάγχων τῶν παθῶν τοὺς ἱππέας εἰς ν. ἤρθης τῆς ἄνω θεωρίας (with pun on Gregory of Nyssa), Geo.Pis.*carm*.14.2; **3.** met., *course* of time, Nonn.*par.Jo*.2:20(M.43. 764C); *ib*.6:35(800B); *ib*.7:14(808A).

νύσσ-ω (νύττω), 1. *pierce, prick*, of piercing the side of Christ (Jo.19:34) τῷ κάτω ὄχλῳ...λόγχαις ~ομαι...σοὶ δὲ λαλῶ *A.Jo*.97 (p.199.15); ἀκούεις με...νυγέντα καὶ οὐκ ἐπλήγην *ib*.101(p.201.20); εἰ μηδὲν εἰλήφει παρὰ τῆς Μαρίας...οὐδ' ἂν νυγείσης αὐτοῦ τῆς πλευρᾶς ἐξῆλθεν αἷμα καὶ ὕδωρ Iren.*haer*.3.22.2(M.7.957B); Or.*Jo*.2.8(4; p.62. 23; M.14.121D); ὁ κύριος...ἐξ ἑνὸς ὢν ἐξ ἑνὸς ἐνύγη, ἐγὼ δὲ [sc. S. Thomas] ἐκ τεσσάρων [sc. elements] ὑπάρχων ἐκ τεσσάρων ~ομαι *A.Thom*.A 165(p.279.18); Ath.*ep.Epict*.10(p.16.8; M.26.1065D); Nonn. *par.Jo*.19:34(M.43.905B); **2.** *nudge*, Chrys.*hom.8.2 in Eph*.(11.55C); *ib.8.5*(61B); **3.** *stir, move*, Thdt.*provid*.3(4.519); Jo.Mosch.*prat*.43 (M.87.2897B); **4.** met.; **a.** *prick, stab* λόγοι...τὴν συνείδησιν ~οντες †Bas.*hom.in Ps*.37(1.364E; M.30.89A); cf.Chrys.*hom.64.5 in Mt*.(7. 643A); Pall.*v.Chrys*.20(p.139.14; M.47.78); Marc.Diac.*v.Porph*.4; Diad.*perf*.92(p.132.10); †Jo.D.*creat*.1(p.61); **b.** *urge, incite*, Or.*fr. 66 in Lc*.13:6(p.265); Thdt.*h.e*.1.2.10(3.726); Gel.Cyz.*h.e*.3.10.17.

νυσταγμός, ὁ, *drowsiness*, *A.Jo*.32(p.168.4); ref. Mt.25:5 ὁ... χρονισμός ἐστι τὸ πρὸ τῆς παρουσίας διάστημα τοῦ Χριστοῦ, ὁ δὲ ν. καὶ ἡ κοίμησις τῶν δέκα παρθένων ἡ ἔξοδος ἀπὸ τοῦ βίου Meth.*symp*.6.4 (p.68.21; M.18.120A); ὕπνος βαρεῖα τίς ἐστιν ἀναισθησία· ὁ δὲ ν. μῖγμά ἐστιν ἐγρηγόρσεως καὶ ὕπνου †Bas.*hom.in Pr.6*:4(2.618B; M. 31.1500C); Pall.*h.Laus*.2(p.17.18; M.34.1011C); plur., Clem.*paed*.2.9 (p.207.18; M.8.496C); met., of spiritual torpor, Bas.*hom*.10.6(2.79A; M.31.344C); Gr.Nyss.*hom.11 in Cant*.(M.44.996A); Pall.*h.Laus*. proem.(p.10.10; M.34.1001).

νυστάζ-ω, *be drowsy, doze*; **1.** lit., prevented among church congregation by deacons, *Const.App*.2.57.13; proverb φαλακρὸς ὢν κατὰ κριοῦ μὴ ~ειν Gr.Naz.*ep*.191(M.37.313B, v.l. νευστάζειν); **2.** ref. mental and spiritual torpor, *Pss.Sal*.16.1; Hipp.*haer*.proem.(p.3.5; M. 16.3020C); ~οντες φανταζέσθωσαν Ath.*ep.Aeg.Lib*.23(M.25.592A).

***νυχαλία, ἡ**, *night*, Gr.Nyss.*v.Ephr*.(M.46.836B).

νυχθημερινός, *of a night and a day*, ‡Chrys.*hom*.13(13.253D); *Schol.Clem.prot*.9(p.316.5; M.9.788A).

νύχος, τό, *night, darkness* λύχνος γάρ, παρὰ τὸ λύειν τὸ ν. λέγεται. ν. δὲ καλοῦσι τὸ σκότος οἱ περὶ λόγους σπουδάζοντες Max.*qu.Thal*.63 (M.90.668C); intellectual, id.*opusc*.(M.91.72A).

***νωβελ(λ)ίσ(σ)ιμος (*νοβελ(λ)-, *νοβελ(λ)ή-)**, (Lat. *nobilissimus*) *most noble*, highest title next to that of Caesar, restricted to imperial family, Philost.*h.e*.8.8(M.65.561B); ‡Jo.D.*Artem*.7(p.27.18; M.96.1257C); Thphn.*chron*.p.374(M.108.896B).

νωδός, *dumb*, *Orac.Sib*.4.9; Epiph.*ep.Arab*.ap.*haer*.78.3(p.454.13; M.42.704B); Isid.Pel.*epp*.1.54(M.78.217A).

***Νῶε, ὁ**, *Noah*; **1.** as antitype of Adam; **a.** as renewing human race, Thdt.*qu.53 in Gen*.(1.66); cf.Ath.*Ar*.2.51(M.26.256A); **b.** as preserving divine image, Bas.Sel.*or*.5.2(M.85.84B); Cosm.Ind.*top*.5(M. 88.236C); and also as having dominion over lower creatures, Chrys. *hom.25.5 in Gen*.(4.238B,C); Bas.Sel.*or*.6.3(96B); **c.** exeg. Gen.9:20–21 τοιοῦτος ἦν ὁ καρπὸς τοῦ ξύλου τοῦ γνωστοῦ καλοῦ καὶ πονηροῦ, οἷος ὁ οἶνος, ὁ τὸν Ν. γυμνώσας Or.*sel.in Gen*.9:20(M.12.109C); but Noah sinned in ignorance οὐκ ᾔδει Ν. τὴν τοῦ οἴνου φύσιν, ὅτι μεθύσκει *ib.*; Chrys.*hom.29.2 in Gen.*(4.282B); Thdt.*qu.56 in Gen.* (1.68); **2.** as type of Christ; **a.** in gen. *ὁ δίκαιος γὰρ N. μετὰ τῶν ἄλλων ἀνθρώπων ἐπὶ τοῦ κατακλυσμοῦ...οἵτινες ἀριθμῷ ὄντες ὀκτώ, σύμβολον εἶχον τῆς...ὀγδόης ἡμέρας, ἐν ᾗ ἐφάνη ὁ Χριστὸς...ἀναστάς. ...ὁ γὰρ Χριστὸς...ἀρχὴ...ἄλλου γένους γέγονε, τοῦ ἀναγεννηθέντος ὑπ' αὐτοῦ δι' ὕδατος καὶ πίστεως καὶ ξύλου, τοῦ τὸ μυστήριον τοῦ σταυροῦ ἔχοντος, ὃν τρόπον καὶ ὁ N. ἐν ξύλῳ διεσώθη ἐποχούμενος τοῖς ὕδασι μετὰ τῶν ἰδίων* Just.*dial.*138.1–2(M.6.793A,B); **b.** ref. Christ's baptism *ταύτης ἔφερε τύπον μερικῶς...ἡ ἐπὶ N. περιστερά. ὥσπερ γὰρ ἐπ' ἐκείνου διὰ ξύλου καὶ ὕδατος αὐτοῖς μὲν ἐγένετο ἡ σωτηρία, καινῆς δὲ γενέσεως ἀρχή, καὶ ἡ περιστερὰ ἀνέστρεψε πρὸς αὐτὸν τὸ πρὸς ἑσπέραν...οὕτω...καὶ τὸ πνεῦμα τὸ ἅγιον κατῆλθεν ἐπὶ τὸν ἀληθινὸν N., τὸν τῆς δευτέρας γενέσεως ποιητὴν...ἵνα δείξῃ ὅτι οὗτός ἐστιν ὁ διὰ ξύλου σταυροῦ σώζων τοὺς πιστεύοντας, ὁ μέλλων πρὸς ἑσπέραν διὰ τοῦ θανάτου αὐτοῦ χαρίζεσθαι τὴν σωτηρίαν* Cyr.H.*catech.*17.10; ref. Christian baptism *ἐπεὶ οὖν πρώτη ἀνάστασις τοῦ γένους μετὰ τὸν κατακλυσμὸν διὰ ὀγδοάδος ἀνθρώπων ἐγένετο, διὰ τοῦτο καὶ ὁ κύριος πρῶτος τὴν ἀνάστασιν τῶν νεκρῶν ἐν τῇ ὀγδόῃ ἄρχεται. ὅτε καθάπερ ἐν κιβωτῷ τῷ τάφῳ ὡς ὁ N. ἔμεινεν...καὶ τὸ βάπτισμα τῆς παλιγγενεσίας ἐπέδωκεν· ἵνα συνταφέντες αὐτοῦ τῷ βαπτισμῷ, κοινωνοὶ τῆς ἀναστάσεως αὐτοῦ γενώμεθα* Ast.Soph.*Ps.6*(M.40.448C); **c.** ref. name Noah (= *ἀνάπαυσις*) *ὁ λόγος...ἐστιν ὁ κατ' ἀλήθειαν N., τουτέστιν, ἡ δικαιοσύνη καὶ ἡ ἀνάπαυσις. ἑρμηνεύεται γὰρ ὧδε τὸ ὄνομα* Cyr.*glaph.Gen.2*(1^2.33B); Proc.G.*Gen.*9:3(M.87.297D); cf. *quomodo enim verum erit quod ille Noe requiem dederit...ubi potius et iracundia divina major ostenditur?...si vero respicias ad...Christum...huic ergo spiritali Noe qui requiem dedit hominibus...dicitur 'facies tibi arcam'*, Or.*hom.2.3 in Gen.*(p.31.19ff.; M.12.169A,B); **d.** as eleventh from Adam *ἑνδέκατος μὲν ἐξ Ἀδὰμ ὁ N. Χριστὸς δὲ...ὡς ἐν ἐσχάτῳ τε καὶ ἑνδεκάτῳ καιρῷ γεγένηται κατὰ σάρκα* Cyr.*glaph.Gen.2*(1^2.32E); **e.** as inaugurating new dispensation, *Lit.*ap.*Const.App.*8.12.22; **f.** as foreshadowing salvation, Cyr.*glaph.Gen.*2.(1^2.32C); Cosm.Ind.*top.* 5(M.88.236C); **3.** as moral example; of faith, Gr.Naz.*or.*43.70(M. 36.592B); Cyr.*fr.Ezech.*14:14(M.70.1460A); Bas.Sel.*or.*5.2(M.85.84C); Proc.G.*Is.*24:1–23(M.87.2192C); of monastic poverty, *Apophth. Patr.*(M.65.336C); **4.** as preacher of repentance *N. ἐκήρυξεν μετάνοιαν* *1Clem.*7.6; Thphl.Ant.*Autol.*3.19(M.6.1145C); *Apoc.Paul.*50(p.68).

νωθροκάρδιος, *slow, indifferent, of heart*, Pall.*v.Chrys.*4(p.25.14; M.47.16); Thdr.Stud.*or.*2(M.99.696A).

νωθρώδης, *senseless, stupid*, †Gregent.*disp.*4(M.86.752C).

***νωμεύς, ὁ**, *governor*, Gr.Naz.*carm.*1.1.1.34(M.37.401A); *ib.*2.2 (poem.)3.4(1480A).

***νωμητής, ὁ**, = foreg., Gr.Naz.*carm.*2.1.38.11(M.37.1320A).

***νῶναι (*νόναι, *νόνναι), αἱ**, (Lat. *Nonae*) *Nones* *νόναις φευρουαρίαις* *M.Perp.*proem.(p.61.5); *νωνῶν Ἀπριλλίων* Eus.*m.P.*7(p.921. 22; M.20.1484A); *ib.*(p.923.6; 1484B); *νόνναις Μαίαις* Cyr.H.*ep. Const.*4(M.33.1169A); CCP(536)*act.*1(p.126.1; H.2.1188C); Thphn. *chron.*p.72(M.108.229A).

§**νῶσις, ἡ**, f.l. for *οἴνωσις*, Proc.G.*Gen.*9:21(M.87.305A).

***νωτάριος, ὁ**, v. **νοτάριος*.

νωτοφόρος, *carrying on the back*; **1.** of beasts *of burden v. ζῷα* Melet.*nat.hom.*14(M.64.1208C); **2.** as subst.; **a.** neut., *beast of burden*, Eus.*v.C.*3.6(p.79.30; M.20.1060B); Bas.*ep.*94(3.188B; M.32. 488C); Soz.*h.e.*4.19.10(M.67.1172B); **b.** masc., *carrier*, Or.*Jo.*10.39 (p.217.6; M.14.384B).

***νωτοφύλαξ, ὁ**, *one of the rearguard*, *Chron.Pasch.*p.397(M.92. 1016B); Thphn.*chron.*p.331(M.108.797C).

***νωχελῶς**, *sluggishly*, Eus.*Is.*48:15–20(M.24.428B); Horm.*ep.cler.* (p.55.13; M.*PL.*63.419C).

Ξ

ξανθίζω, *dye fair*; hair, Clem.*paed.*3.2(p.239.9; M.8.561B).

Ξανθικός ([*]**Ξαντικός**), **ὁ**, Macedonian month, *M.Polyc.*21; *ἔστι μὴν πρῶτος Ξ., ὁ καλούμενος Ἀπρίλλιος, ὅπερ ἐστὶν ἡ ἡμέρα τῆς ἀναστάσεως* Mac.Aeg.*hom.*5.9(M.34.513C); *ὁ πρῶτος μὴν τῆς συλλήψεως τοῦ δεσπότου, Ἀπρίλλιος, ὅς ἐστι Ξαντικός* Chrys.*nativ.*1.5(2.362B); *Ἑβραῖοι δὲ τὸν Ξ. πρῶτον ἴσασι μῆνα* Thdt.*Zach.*1:7(2.1596).

ξάνθισμα, τό, *dyeing fair*; of hair, Clem.*paed.*3.3(p.246.1; M.8. 577C).

***ξανθοαρχιγένειος**, *having the beginnings of a fair beard*, Jo.Mal. *chron.*5 p.104(M.97.193A).

***ξανθογένειος**, *fair-bearded*, *A.Barth.*2(p.131.20).

***ξανθόμματος**, *with tawny eyes*, ‡Hipp.Th.*fr.*17(p.50.9).

***ξανθόπλοκος**, *yellow-twining*; poet., Geo.Pis.*hex.*1387(M.92. 1541A).

***ξανθοποιέω**, *dye fair*; of hair, *Const.App.*1.3.10.

***ξάνθοφρυς**, *having fair eyebrows*, Jo.Mal.*chron.*5 p.104(M.97. 193A).

ξανθοχολικός, *containing* or *consisting of yellow bile*, Melet.*nat. hom.*synops.(M.64.1128A).

[*]**Ξαντικός, ὁ**, v. *Ξανθικός*.

***ξεινηδόκος, ὁ**, *host*, Nonn.*par.Jo.*11:11(M.43.840C).

***ξεινήϊος**, *provided for a guest* *ξ. ὕδωρ* Nonn.*par.Jo.*4:7(M.43. 773C).

[*]**ξεινιτεία, ἡ**, v. *ξενιτεία*.

ξεινοδόκος, *hospitable*, Nonn.*par.Jo.*8:39(M.43.820A).

ξεναγ-έω, **1.** *guide*, met. *ἐπὶ ταύτην ἅπαντας τὴν ἀλήθειαν* ~*ῶν* Thdt.*h.e.*1.13.18(3.787); pass., ref. God's guidance, id.*provid.*5(4. 555); ~*εῖσθαι ὑπὸ τῆς πίστεως* id.*affect.*1(p.26.1; 4.716); *lead* into Arianism, id.*h.e.*4.11.4(968); *act as cicerone to*, id.*provid.*1.15(490); **2.** *introduce a stranger*, Bas.*ep.*319(3.446C; M.32.1065C); **3.** *shew hospitality to, receive as a guest*, Thdr.Stud.*epp.*2.111(M.99.1373A).

ξεναγός, ὁ, ἡ, 1. *guide, cicerone* *ξ. ἡμῶν...θεόν* Thdt.*Bar.*5:9(2. 646); **2.** fem., *hostess*; of Sarah, ‡Caes.Naz.*dial.*31(M.38.896).

ξεναγωγέω, 1. *guide strangers*, Bas.*hex.*7.4(1.66E; M.29.157A); Thdt.*h.rel.*6(3.1168); met., id.*provid.*1(4.497); pass., *be led as strangers*, Tit.Bost.*Man.*1.18(M.18.1092D); **2.** *entertain as guest*, Dion.Ar.*ep.*8.6(M.3.1097B); pass., Bas.Sel.*v.Thecl.*1(M.85.481D).

***ξενακούω**, *ξενηκούσθησαν* Jo.D.*carm.pent.*88(M.96.837A; corrected to *ξέναι ἠκούσθησαν* p.216).

ξενεών, ὁ, *hostel*, Isch.*libell.*(p.18.2; H.2.327A); *ib.*(p.19.6; 329A).

ξένη, ἡ, [sc. *γῆ*] *foreign land*; met., of earth opp. heaven, Herm. *sim.*1.1; *ib.*1.6; ‡Epiph.*hom.*2(M.43.448A).

ξενηλατέω, 1. *banish foreigners*, *T.Lev.*6.10; **2.** *disturb*, Athenag. *leg.*24.1(M.6.945A).

ξενία, ἡ, 1. *place where hospitality is offered, hostel, lodging*, *Hom. Clem.*8.2; *τὸν εὐρύτατον τῆς ξ. οἶκον εἰσελθόντες* *ib.*10.26; *cat.Mt.*2:7 (p.15.14); theol., met. *εἰ 'τὴν τοῦ σώματος ξ. πρὸς οἰκονομίαν τῶν θείων ἐνεργειῶν' παραλαμβάνεις, οὐκ ἀποδοκιμάζω* Const.ap.Gel.Cyz. *h.e.*3.19.14(M.85.1348C); **2.** monk's *cell* *ᾠκοδόμησεν ἑαυτῷ ἐκεῖ ξ. μικράν* Pall.*h.Laus.*47(p.136.16; M.34.1196A); *ib.*16(p.41.5; 1041D); †Jo.D.*B.J.*21(M.96.1045A).

ξενίδιον, τό, *guest-chamber, lodging*, Pall.*v.Chrys.*20(p.138.19; M. 47.77); id.*h.Laus.*26(M.34.1073C; *ξένιον* p.65.2); *ξ. λαβεῖν* Call. *v.Hyp.*(p.73).

ξενίζ-ω, 1. *entertain as guest*, Chrys.*hom.45.3 in Ac.*(9.341D); Nil. *epp.*1.61(M.79.109B); met., the truth, *Hom.Clem.*1.11; **2.** *greet*, Gr. Naz.*or.*34.6(M.36.245B); ~*ων* ⟨*ὑμᾶς*⟩...*τῷ τῆς εἰρήνης προσ⟨ρήματι⟩* Anast.Ant.*redit.*(p.251); **3.** *astonish, dismay, shock*, Gr.Nyss.*fat.*(M. 45.149D); Didym.(‡Bas.)*Eun.*5(1.316D; M.29.760A); of BMV *αὕτη καὶ τὰς τῶν οὐρανῶν δυνάμεις ἐξένισεν* ‡Epiph.*hom.*5(M.43.488B); pass., *be astonished, be shocked*, Alex.Al.*ep.syn.*4(p.8.17; M.18.573D); c. *περί*, Ath.*v.Anton.*20(M.26.872C); c. *ἐπί*, id.*decr.*23.2(p.19.18; M. 25.456D); c. *πρός*, Bas.*ep.*266(3.412A; M.32.992B); **4. a.** trans., *make strange* *συνθέσει λέξεων...*~*ούσῃ τὴν διάλεκτον* Or.*Cels.*7.60(p.210.6; M.11.1505D); **b.** intrans., *be strange* or *new*; of words and doctrines, Ath.*decr.*18(p.15.29; M.25.448C); Bas.*Spir.*3(3.3D; M.32.72C); *ib.*17 (14E; M.97A); *κατὰ τὸ ξενίζον* *in a strange manner*, Philost.*h.e.*3.11(M. 65.497D); **5.** *use strange* or *unfamiliar language* *ξ. καὶ καινοτομεῖν* Chrys.*hom.16.7 in Mt.*(7.214B); id.*hom.7.6 in 1Cor.*(10.59D); Gr. Nyss.*Eun.*1(1 p.202.10; M.45.449B).

ξένιον, τό, 1. *gift, reward* *τὰ τῆς ἑορτῆς ξ.* *Can.App.*70; *οἱ...προφῆται...οὐ προσήκαντο ξ.* *Const.App.*4.7.2; *ξ. εὐπειθίας* Cyr.*Is.*5.2 (2.764A); **2.** *guest-chamber, lodging*, Pall.*h.Laus.*26(p.65.2; *ξενίδιον* M.34.1073C).

ξενισμός, ὁ, 1. *astonishment*, ‡Ign.*Eph.*19; Serap.*Man.*17(p.36; M.40.913B); Gr.Nyss.*or.catech.*25(p.95.3; M.45.65C); **2.** *injurious effect, hardship*; of journeys, *T.Abr.*B 13(p.117.20); Bas.*ep.*198(3. 290B; M.32.716A); **3.** *entertainment of a stranger, hospitality* *ξ. λαχάνων* Hyper.*mon.*92(M.79.1481C); met., of BMV *ὅτι τῷ δημιουργῷ λόγῳ καταγώγιον ξενισμοῦ ἡτοίμασται* Thdr.Stud.*nativ.BMV* 1(M.96.681A); **4.** *differentiation*, Cyr.*thes.*9(5^1.70D).

ξενιτεία (**ξεινιτεία**), **ἡ, 1.** *sojourn* or *travel in a foreign land, exile* *'Ιησοῦ, ὃν ἡ θλῖψις τῶν ἐν ξ. κινεῖ πρὸς εὐσπλαγχνίαν* *A.Xanthipp.*24 (p.75.16); Max.*ep.*30(M.91.624C); met., of saints on earth, Clem. *q.d.s.*36.2(p.183.25; M.9.642B); **2.** *solitude, isolation from world* as religious person, *Apophth.Mac.Aeg.*2.7(M.34.236A); *πρώτη τῶν* λαμπρῶν ἀγωνισμάτων ἐστὶ ξ. Nil.*Eulog.*2(M.79.1096B); ξεινιτεία Esaias *or.*9(p.17); φύλαξον τὴν ξ. σου *Apophth.Patr.*(M.65.109A).

ξενιτεύ-ω, 1. *be away from home*, Iren.*haer.*4.5.3(M.7.985B); ‡Epiph.*hom.*3(M.43.473C); †Bas.Sel.*or.*41(M.85.473A); **2.** *live in separation from the world* νηστεύων πολύ, ~ων, εὐχόμενος Mac.Aeg. *cust.cor.*10(M.34.829B); μεῖζόν ἐστι τὸ ξ. παρὰ τὸ ξενοδοχεῖν *Apophth. Patr.*(M.65.232B); Pall.*h.Laus.*4(p.20.11; M.34.1017B).

***ξενοβόρος, ὁ,** *one who eats strangers, cannibal*, ‡Caes.Naz.*dial.* 109(M.38.980).

ξενοδοχεῖον, τό, *guest-house* or *hospice*; for travellers, sick, and poor εἰ δεῖ τὸν ἐν ἀδελφότητι ζῶντα, καὶ ἀσθενείᾳ σωματικῇ περιπεσόντα, εἰς ξ. ἀπάγειν Bas.*reg.br.*286 tit.(2.516A; M.31.1284B); τὸ ξ. ... ὅπερ ἐν τῷ Πόντῳ καλεῖται πτωχοτροφεῖον Epiph.*haer.*75.1(p.333. 24; M.42.504B); πρόσκειται δὲ τῇ ἐκκλησίᾳ ξ., εἰς ὃ τὸν ἀπελθόντα ξένον...δεξιοῦνται Pall.*h.Laus.*7(p.25.21; M.34.1020B); ὁ δὲ μέγας Κωνσταντῖνος σιτομέτριον...ἐχαρίσατο ξενοδοχείοις Thphn.*chron.*p.23 (M.108.117B); ξενοδόχεν *MAMA* 3.347 (Corycus); ξενοδοκεῖον *CIG* 8645 (Smyrna, ? saec. v–vi).

ξενοδοχ-έω, 1. trans., *entertain* or *receive as guest*, Bas.Sel.*or.* 6.3(M.85.96A); Nil.*epp.*3.145(M.79.452A); Jo.Mosch.*prat.*87(M.87. 2944C); myst. ἐν ἁγναῖς...~οῦμεν ψυχαῖς τὸν θεόν Clem.*prot.*9(p.63. 32; M.8.196C); αὐτὸν ξ. Ἰησοῦν Nil.*epp.*1.61(M.79.109B); **2.** intrans., *entertain guests* or *strangers* μὴ ἁπλῶς ~εῖτε, ἀλλὰ μετὰ τοῦ φιλεῖν τοὺς ξένους Chrys.*hom.33.3 in Heb.*(12.305B); as a pious duty, Gr. Naz.*carm.*2.1.11.1219(M.37.1113A).

ξενοδοχία, ἡ, *exercise of hospitality* οὐκ εἶπε, τῆς ξ. μὴ ἐπιλανθάνεσθε, ἀλλά, τῆς φιλοξενίας Chrys.*hom.33.3 in Heb.*(12.305B); Bas. *ascet.disc.*1(2.212C; M.31.649B); Pall.*h.Laus.*40(p.127.7; ξενοδοχείαν M.34.1209A); ὅσον γὰρ διαφέρει τοῖς ἀτονοῦσιν ὕδατος ὁ οἶνος, τοσοῦτον ὑπερβάλλει ξενοδοχίας διδασκαλία id.*v.Chrys.*12(p.72.17; M.47.41).

ξενοδόχος, ὁ, ἡ, 1. *one who entertains guests, host, hostess*; masc., Chrys.*hom.79.2 in Mt.*(7.761A); id.*hom.32.2 in Rom.*(9.756C); fem., *Hom.Clem.*12.33; *ib.*13.9; **2.** *guest-master*; **a.** in a church Ἰσιδώρῳ πρεσβυτέρῳ ὄντι ξενοδόχῳ τῆς Ἀλεξανδρέων ἐκκλησίας Pall.*h.Laus.*1 (p.15.9; M.34.1009A); ξ. Ἀλεξανδρείας id.*v.Chrys.*6(p.35.10; M.47.22); **b.** in a monastery, Dor.*doct.*11.7(M.88.1741C); **3.** neut., *hospitality*, Pall.*v.Chrys.*20(p.131.12; M.47.73).

***ξενοεποῦντες,** s.v.l., ? *using strange language*, Cyr.*ep.*8(p.111.32, vv.ll. ἐξενοεποῦντες, ξενοποιοῦντες 5^2.35A).

***ξενοκομεῖον, τό,** *strangers' hostel*, Max.*ep.*44(M.91.648A).

***ξενολεκτέω,** *use strange language*; med., Epiph.*haer.*66.4(p.22. 1; M.42.36B); pass., *ib.*66.70(p.111.6; 140C); *ib.*32.1(p.439.8; M.41. 544C).

***ξενολεξία, ἡ,** *strange* or *heretical saying*, Epiph.*haer.*42.11(p.107. 15; M.41.709D); *ib.*(p.124.6; 725C); κατὰ τῆς ἀληθείας ξ. *ib.*57.10(p.357. 19; 1009D).

ξενολογία, ἡ, *strange* or *heretical talk*, Epiph.*haer.*69.53(p.200.29; M.42.285B); *ib.*77.2(p.417.11; 644A).

***ξενοπαγής,** *made of strange* or *alien substance*; ref. Christ's physical body, Procl.CP *or.*4.2(M.65.712A).

ξενοπαθέω, 1. *be perturbed, distressed* (at); c. dat., Gr.Nyss.*diff. ess.*(M.32.336B); c. genit., *mourn* τοῦ ἡμετέρου πατρὸς ξ. Thdr.Stud. *epp.*2.126(M.99.1409A); intrans., Chrys.*hom.5.4 in Heb.*(12.58C); **2.** *be affected in a strange manner, undergo a strange experience*, Chrys.*hom.3.4 in 1Thess.*(11.445C); id.*hom.1.1 in 2Tim.*(11.658B).

ξενοπολίτης, ὁ, *naturalized alien*, Eustrat.*v.Eutych.*61(M.86. 2344C).

ξενοπρεπής, *strange, extraordinary*, comp. ξενοπρεπεστέρα...τῆς Εὔας ἢ τοῦ Ἀδὰμ γέννησις Tim.Ant.*nativ.Jo.Bapt.*3(M.28.913B).

***ξενοπρόσωπος,** *of strange features*, ‡Chrys.*hom.*13(13.252E).

***ξενορρυής,** *of strange flow*, Tim.Ant.*descr.BMV* 1(M.28.945A).

ξένος, A. *extraneous* τῶν ξ. ἐπισκόπων ἢ πρεσβυτέρων ἢ διακόνων *Can.App.*33; of a visiting bishop, *Const.App.*2.58.3; *strange* to, *alien* from, c. genit. ξένοι δέ, ὧν ξ. τὰ κοσμικά Clem.*str.*2.9(p.134.25; M.8.976C); *ib.*4.26(p.321.31; 1376A); *excommunicate from* ξ. τῆς Ῥωμαίων ἐκκλησίας Tim.CP *haer.*(M.86.25A).

B. *of different nature*; **1.** in gen., ‡Ath.*serm.fid.*25(p.22; M.26. 1280B); of metals of various kinds, Ath.*decr.*23(p.19.24; M.25.457A); **2.** theol., *separate, alien, foreign*, abs. and c. genit. οἱ δὲ τρεῖς θεοὺς...κηρύττουσιν, εἰς τρεῖς ὑποστάσεις ξ. ἀλλήλων...κεχωρισμένας Dion.R.ap.Ath.*decr.*26(p.22.8; 464A); Gr.Naz.*or.*20.6(M.35.1072B) cit. s. ἀνόμοιος; οὐ ξ. ἂν εἴη τῆς οὐσίας τοῦ πατρὸς Dion.Al.ap.Ath. *Dion.*20.2(p.61.17; M.25.509B); Ath.*Ar.*2.32(M.26.216B); ref. Jo. 14:28 οὐκ εἴρηκεν· ὁ πατήρ μου κρείττων...ἵνα μὴ ξένον τις τῆς ἐκείνου φύσεως αὐτὸν ὑπολάβῃ, ἀλλὰ μείζων εἶπεν...διὰ τὴν ἐξ αὐτοῦ τοῦ πατρὸς γέννησιν Cyr.*Heb.*1:4(p.372.26; M.74.957B); in Arianism ξ. καὶ ἀλλότριος, καὶ ἀπεσχοινισμένος ἐστὶν ὁ λόγος τῆς τοῦ θεοῦ οὐσίας Alex.Al.*ep.encycl.*3(p.8.3; M.18.573B); Ath.*decr.*6(p.5.26; M.25.425A) cit. s. ἀνόμοιος; ὁ λόγος οὐκ ἔστιν ἴδιος τοῦ πατρός, ἀλλ' ἄλλος μέν ἐστιν ὁ ἐν τῷ θεῷ λόγος, οὗτος δὲ ὁ κύριος ξ. μὲν καὶ ἀλλότριός ἐστι τῆς τοῦ πατρὸς οὐσίας, κατ' ἐπίνοιαν δὲ μόνον λέγεται λόγος καὶ οὐκ ἔστι μὲν κατὰ φύσιν...τοῦ θεοῦ υἱός Ar.*Thal.fr.*16 ap.Ath. *Dion.*23(p.62.29; M.25.513A); τὸ δὲ 'πεποιῆσθαι'...διὰ τὸ ἀλλοτρίου καὶ ξ., καὶ πάντη ἀνοικείου πρὸς τὸν ποιήσαντα τὴν ἔννοιαν παριστᾶν Bas.*Eun.*2.6(1.242C; M.29.584A); of H. Ghost οὐ ξ. τοῦ θεοῦ Ath. *ep.Serap.*1.25(M.26.588C); οὐ ξ. τῆς τοῦ υἱοῦ φύσεως, οὔτε τῆς τοῦ πατρὸς θεότητος *ib.*4.3(641B); of Father in rel. to humanity of Son ὁ γεωργὸς ξ. ἐστὶ κατ' οὐσίαν τῆς ἀμπέλου id.*Dion.*10(p.53. 12; M.25.493C); of God in rel. to creatures ξ. τὰ γενητὰ κατὰ φύσιν ἐστὶ τοῦ θεοῦ *ib.*26(p.66.3; 520B); χωρὶς τοῦ πνεύματος ξ. καὶ μακρὰν ἐσμεν τοῦ θεοῦ id.*Ar.*3.24(M.26.373C); ξ. τῶν προσταγμάτων σου κατέστην Anast.*poenit.*7(p.284); ref. Marcionites πῶς οὗτοι ξένην τοῦ πατρὸς τὴν κτίσιν εἰσάγουσιν; Ath.*inc.*2.6(M.25.100C); of Arian heresy ξ. τῆς ἐκκλησιαστικῆς πίστεως id.*h.Ar.*66(p.219. 19; M.25.772B); Thdt.ap.Cyr.*apol.Thdt.*2(p.114.12; 6^1.208B) cit. s. ἀλλόφυλος.

C. *strange, unusual, novel* ξ. διδαχάς Herm.*sim.*8.6.5 (v.l. ἑτέρας p.103); ξ. ἀποδείξεις Just.*dial.*55.3(M.6.596C); ὁ κύριος...ξ. ἀστὴρ καὶ καινός Clem.*exc.Thdot.*74(p.130.18; M.9.693A); ξ. ... παραβολάς Eus. *h.e.*3.39.11(M.20.300A); in derisive sense, *unheard of*, Clem.*prot.*6 (p.51.11; M.8.172B); ξ. λατρείας Apoll.*fid.sec.pt.*1(p.167.14; M.10. 1105B); ξ. κολάσεις Jo.D.*parall.*tit.(M.96.205D); *strange, repugnant* to, c. genit. τῆς ἐκκλησίας ξένων Ἑλληνικῶν μαθημάτων ‡Proc.G. *Pr.*5:15(M.87.1264D); c. dat. τῆς ἀλλοτρίας καὶ ξ. τοῖς ἐκλεκτοῖς... στάσεως *1Clem.*1.1; hence **1.** *wonderful, marvellous*, Just.*1apol.*16. 4(M.6.352D); of Zacharias' speech (Lc.1:64), ‡Thdt.*nativ.Jo.Bapt.* 7(5.91); of curious wonders, Philost.*h.e.*3.11(M.65.497D); *ib.*12.8 (617B); τὸ ξένον *novelty*, *ib.*3.11(497A); **2.** *peculiar to itself* ὁ λόγος ...ἔχει ξένον, τὸ εἶναι θεός Or.*hom.20.1 in Jer.*(p.176.23ff.; M.13. 500C,D).

D. masc. as subst., *stranger*; as object of Christian charity, *Const.App.*4.2.1; ξ. καὶ πένης θεοῦ κολλούριον Evagr.Pont.ap.Jo.D. *parall.*(M.96.289C); Pall.*h.Laus.*14(p.38.7; M.34.1036A); of one devoted to separation from the world, *Apophth.Patr.*(M.65.256C); met., of Christ incarnate, ‡Epiph.*hom.*2(p.15 passim; M.43.445C); of Christian as living on earth, *Diogn.*5.5; ὁ ἐκλεκτὸς ὡς ξ. πολιτεύεται Clem.*str.*4.26(p.321.32; M.8.1376B); of Abraham's life, Chrys.*hom.45.3 in Ac.*(9.342D).

***ξενόσπορος,** *of strange seed*, Geo.Pis.*bell.Avar.*87(M.92.1270A); fig. τῶν ξ. λόγων id.*hex.*77(M.92.1435A).

ξενοτάφιον τό, *strangers' burial-place*, Jo.Mosch.*prat.*88(M.87. 2945B); Max.*ep.*44(M.91.648A); Leont.N.*v.Sym.*61(M.93.1744D).

***ξενοτόκος, ἡ,** *mother in a strange way* ἡ θεοτόκος ἡ ξ. Ant.Ptol. *fr.*ap.Cyr.*Arcad.*(p.66.33; 5^2.49E).

ξενότροπος, *of strange fashion*, Geo.Pis.*hex.*1481(M.92.1548A).

***ξενοτρόπως,** *in strange* or *wondrous fashion*, *A.Pil.*B 10.4(p.306).

***ξενοτρόφος,** *showing hospitality to strangers*, Max.*ep.*44(M.91. 645D).

***ξενουργέω,** *bring about as a strange* or *new thing*, Geo.Pis.*hex.* 532(M.92.1476A); *ib.*1187(1526A).

***ξενοφανής,** *of strange appearance*, Germ.CP *or.*2(M.98.277D); ‡Jo.D.*ep.Thphl.*16(M.95.365D).

ξενοφωνέω, 1. *speak strange things*; of Montanus, Anon.ap.Eus. *h.e.*5.16.7(M.20.465C); med., *A.Phil.*124(p.53.4); *innovate in speech*, Chrys.*hom.15.4 in Mt.*(7.189A); **2.** *startle, perturb, astonish by strange words* or *teaching*, Eus.*d.e.*3.7(p.143.21; M.22.241B); Gr.Nyss.*fat.* (M.45.149B); Socr.*h.e.*4.7.10(M.67.473B); *ib.*7.2.3(741B); Tim.Ant. *nativ.Jo.Bapt.*(M.28.913A).

***ξενοχαρής,** *taking pleasure in strange things*; neut. as subst., *delight in strange things*, Gr.Naz.*ep.*101(M.37.193A).

ξενόω, pass., *be exiled, live in exile*; of Christ in Egypt, ‡Epiph. *hom.*2(M.43.448A).

ξενών, ὁ, *hostel, hospice*, e.g. for sick people ἔστιν οἴκημα κοινὸν ἡ ἐκκλησία, ὃν ξ. καλοῦμεν Chrys.*hom.45.4 in Ac.*(9.342E); ἄπιθι πρὸς τὸν ἐπιτραπέντα τὴν τοῦ ξ. ἐπιστασίαν id.*Stag.*3.13(1.223B); τῶν ἐκκλησιῶν τοὺς ξ. περινοστοῦσα, τοὺς κλινοπετεῖς δι' ἑαυτῆς ἐνοσήλευεν Thdt.*h.e.*5.19.3(3.1053).

ξένως, *strangely, marvellously, in unwonted fashion*; ref. Mt. 26:29 καινῶς, τουτέστι ξ., οὐ σῶμα παθητὸν ἔχων, ἀλλ' ἀθάνατον...καὶ οὐ δεόμενον τροφῆς Chrys.*hom.82.2 in Mt.*(7.784A); Cyr.*Is.*4.4(2. 658D); ἐξ ὕδατος οἰνοποιήσῃς ξ. ‡Gr.Naz.*Chr.pat.*457(M.38.173A).

[*]**ξεράω,** for ἐξεράω, *vomit*, Sophr.H.*conf.*(M.87.3369C).

ξέσις, ἡ, *scraping*; as torture, Eus.*m.P.*11.1(p.933.16; M.20.1445B).

ξέσμα, τό, 1. *abrasion, scratch*; by a needle, Marc.Diac.*v.Porph.* 82(p.65); **2.** met., *irritation, provocation*, Nil.*Eulog.*5(M.79.1100C).

ξεσμός, ὁ, *scraping*; as torture, Eus.*h.e.*8.3.1(M.20.748B); *ἐπεδείκνυντο ξ. πλευρῶν ἐπὶ ξύλου* Pall.*v.Chrys.*3(p.20.17; M.47.14); *ib.*20 (p.129.2; M.47.72).

***ξεσμοσαρκία, ἡ,** *flesh-wound*, Thdr.Stud.*epp.*1.51(M.99.1097C).

ξέω, 1. *carve, fashion by carving τὴν ὕλην ξ.* Just.*1apol.*9.2(M.6.340A); *engrave* letters, Ath.*gent.*21(M.25.44A); met., *set forth* a subject, Gr.Naz.*carm.*1.2.10.265(M.37.699A); **2.** *shave, shave off νεκρῶν τρίχας* Gr.Naz.*carm.*1.2.28.134(866A); pass., of priests, Ph.Carp. *Cant.*196(M.40.124A); **3.** *scratch off* or *out τὸν ἰχῶρα* Chrys.*hom.8.3 in Phil.*(11.259E); *τὴν ὄψιν* Jo.Mosch.*prat.*77(M.87.2932C); *γράμμα* Geo.Pis.*carm.*28.1; **4.** *sharpen*; met., wits *τῆς ἐξεσμένης τῶν εὐαγγελιστῶν, τάχα δὲ καὶ ἀγγέλων καταλήψεως* Alex.Al.*ep.Alex.*19(p.22.23; M.18.553C); **5.** *lacerate, tear* flesh, Ath.*ep.encycl.*4(p.173.9; M.25.229C); id.*apol.Const.*33(M.25.640B) cit. s. *πλευρά*.

ξηρά, ἡ, [sc. *γῆ*] **1.** *dry land*, opp. *ὁ βυθός*, Herm.*vis.*3.2.7; **2.** *earth*, opp. heaven, Eus.*h.e.*7.24.1(M.20.692C).

ξηραίν-ω, *dry up*; met., *destroy*; ref. sin, Meth.*res.*1.41(p.286.9; M.18.269B); *ξ. Ἰουδαίους* Vict.*Mc.*11:13(p.391.11); *αἱρέσεων ∼ον τὰ ὀμβρήματα* Jo.Mon.*hymn.Chrys.*(M.96.1380B).

ξηραντικός, *causing to dry up*; neut. as subst., *faculty of drying*, Bas.*hex.*3.7(1.30A; M.29.72A).

***ξηρένυδρος,** *dry yet giving water τὴν ξ. πέτραν* Leont.N.*serm.*3 (M.93.1608A).

***ξηροβάτραχος, ὁ,** kind of *frog*, dist. from *ὑγροβάτραχος*, ‡Epiph. *phys.*22(M.43.532C); cf.*Phys.*B 26 (*ξηρὸς βάτραχος* p.253.8).

***ξηρόκηπος, ὁ,** *area, yard ἐν ξ. τριγχίῳ πλησίον τῆς οἰκίας* Chrysipp.*enc.in Jo.Bapt.*15(p.46.18).

***ξηροκοιτία, ἡ,** *sleeping on the ground* or *floor*, Eus.Al.*serm.*21.14 (M.86.440D); *ξ. καὶ ἀγρυπνία Mir.Mich.*4(p.552.2).

***ξηρόλιθος, ὁ,** *dry stone*, i.e. stone without mortar, Thphn.*chron.* p.331(M.108.797C); plur., Anton.Hag.*v.Sym.Styl.*12(p.34.20).

ξηροποιός, *drying, making dry*, Anast.S.*qu.et resp.*114(M.89.765D).

ξηρός, 1. *dry*; of physical element, *τὸ ξ. what is dry* Meth.*res.*2.9 (p.348.2; M.18.309A); *θερμοῦ καὶ ψυχροῦ, ὑγροῦ καὶ ξ. Hom.Clem.*19.12; of elements of eucharist *τῆς τροφῆς...ξ. καὶ ὑγρᾶς* Just.*dial.*117.3 (M.6.745C); ref. ascetic practices *ξ. ἄρτῳ* Pall.*h.Laus.*57(p.151.2; M.34.1250); Socr.*h.e.*5.22.38(M.67.633B); **2.** *dried up, withered*, Herm. *sim.*8.6.4; of one cut off from Christ, Apoll.ap.*cat.Jo.*15:4ff.(p.355.9); **3.** *austere*, ‡Chrys.*ascet.facet.*(1.809D); superl., Ephr.1.203A; **4.** *bare*, of the letter of a text *ἐὰν κατὰ ξηροῦ τὰς λέξεις ἐκλάβωμεν* ‡Ath. *comm.essent.*49(M.28.73A); using the *bare* phrase, Anast.S.*hod.*13 (M.89.205B); *ib.*(213A).

***ξηροστομία, ἡ,** *arid utterance*, Gr.Nyss.*Eun.*12(1 p.386.7; M.45.1116A).

ξηροφαγέω, *eat dry food* as a religious discipline *νηστεύειν ∼οῦντας* CLaod.*can.*50; †Jo.Jej.*serm.*(M.88.1933A); Thdr.Stud. *conf.*2(M.99.1721C).

ξηροφαγία, ἡ, *eating of dry food*; technical term for this kind of abstinence, cf. *Xerophagiam dicunt, abstinentiam...ciborum humentium*, Isid.H.*etym.*6.19.70; ‡Jo.Jej.*exc.poenit.*(M.88.1932D); ref. Holy Week spent in abstinence of this kind *τῆς ἑβδομάδος τῆς ξ. καὶ πάσχα καλουμένης ἁγίας* Epiph.*haer.*70.12(p.245.24; M.42.365A); *τὰς δὲ ἓξ ἡμέρας τοῦ πάσχα ἐν ξηροφαγίᾳ διατελοῦσι πάντες οἱ λαοί, φημὶ δὲ ἄρτῳ καὶ ἁλὶ καὶ ὕδατι μόνον χρώμενοι πρὸς ἑσπέραν* id.*exp.fid.*22(p.523.20; M.42.828B); *τῇ δὲ τοῦ πάθους ἑβδομάδι ξ. νενομοθέτητο* Jo.D.*jej.*5(M.95.69D).

***ξηροφορέω,** s.v.l., *speak aridly*, Iren.*haer.*1.11.1(M.7.560A), *ἐξεφόρησεν* ap.Epiph.*haer.*31.32(p.434.10; *ἐξηφόρησεν* M.41.537A).

***ξηρόχειρ,** *with a withered hand*, Thdr.Stud.*or.*9.6(M.99.777C).

***ξήροψις,** *of withered countenance*, Jo.Mal.*chron.*12 p.306(M.97.461B).

ξηρῶς, *drily*, superl. *ξηρότατα in the most arid way*, Epiph.*anac.* 70(p.230.11; M.42.336B).

***ξιφηρέω,** s.v.l., *carry a sword*, Socr.*h.e.*7.33.2(M.67.813A, perh. f.l. for *ξιφηφοροῦντες*).

***ξιφοδότης, ὁ,** *giver of a sword*, Thdr.Stud.*epp.*2.39(M.99.1237A).

ξιφοκτονέω, *slay with the sword*; pass., ‡Jo.D.*hom.*5(M.96.657B).

ξίφος, τό, 1. *sword*; met., in spiritual warfare *ξ. τοῦ πνεύματος* Cyr.H.*procatech.*10; of *ψαλμῳδία*, Hyper.*mon.*88(M.79.1481C); *ἐγρήγορσις μοναχοῦ ib.*91(1481C); **2.** *death by the sword τῷ παιδίῳ τοῦ ξίφους διδόντα Κωνσταντῖνον τὴν δίκην* Philost.*h.e.*2.4(M.65.468B).

ξιφουλκία, ἡ, *sword-drawing*, Synes.*provid.*2(p.110.4; M.66.1260A).

ξόανον, τό, 1. *statue, form*, ref. creation of man *καθάπερ ἐν ξ. καλλωπισθέντι* Bas.Sel.*or.*1.3(M.85.33B); ref. foetus in womb *γλύφει τὸ ὕδωρ εἰς ἔμψυχον ξ.* ‡Nil.*fr.pasch.*2(M.79.1496C); **2.** *ancient monument* of wood or stone, Clem.*prot.*4(p.35.17; M.8.133B); **3.** ? *hewn* or *polished wood* or *stone ποιήσας...στήλην ἀπὸ ξ. Chron.Pasch.*p.285 (M.92.712A); **4.** *image, idol*; inhabited by a demon, Or.*Cels.*8.43 (p.258.20; M.11.1581B); Eus.*d.e.*6.20(p.287.7; M.22.472B); by a god, *Hom.Clem.*10.23; *εἰς λίθους καὶ ξύλα καὶ εὐτελῆ ξ.* †Chrys.*nativ.* 6(2.363B); object of false worship *οἵτινες ξ. ἐποίησαν Apoc.Petr.* A 33; *τοῦ νεοπαγοῦς ξ. προφήτας καὶ ἱερεῖς* Eus.*h.e.*9.11.6(M.20.840A); *τὰ ξ. θεοὺς ὀνομάζοντος* Thdt.*qu.86 in Gen.*(1.95); *ἐκ χαλκοῦ καὶ ἐκ ξύλων κενὰ...ξ.* id.*h.e.*5.22.2(3.1059).

ξυλάριον, τό, *small stick*; used as a discipline, ‡Nil.*vit.cog.*(M.79.1448C).

***ξυλέλαιον, τό,** s.v.l., '*wood-oil*', perh. wood and oil paid as tribute, Jo.Mal.*chron.*18 p.437(M.97.645B).

***ξυλέμπορος, ὁ,** *timber-merchant*, CCP(518)*act.*(*ACO* 3 p.86.25; H.2.1356C).

ξυλεύομαι, 1. *cut wood*, Gr.Naz.*carm.*2.1.11.374(M.37.1055A); **2.** met., *gather for firewood*, Germ.CP *or.*2(M.98.248B).

***ξυλή, ἡ,** *wood ξ. κυπαρισσίνην* Thphn.*chron.*p.322(M.108.780B).

***ξυληγία, ἡ,** *carrying of wood*, Gr.Naz.*ep.*6(M.37.29D).

***ξυλόγλυπτος,** *carved out of wood εἰκόνας ξ.* Agath.*v.Gr.Ill.*34.

***ξυλόθεος, ὁ,** *one who worships a wooden god*, Leont.N.ap.Jo.D. *imag.*3(M.94.1384B).

[*]ξυλοκασσία, ἡ, *an inferior kind of cassia*, Philost.*h.e.*3.6(M.65.488B).

***Ξυλοκερκῆται, οἱ,** *followers of S. John Chrysostom*, so called because, upon his expulsion from his church, they met together in the Xylocircus, *Chron.Pasch.*p.307(M.92.871A).

ξυλοκοπέω, *cut wood*, Isid.Pel.*epp.*1.72(M.78.232C).

***ξυλοκόπι(ο)ν, τό,** *bill-hook σιδηροῦν ἐργαλεῖον, ὅπερ ἐπιχωρίως ὀνομάζεται ξυλοκόπιν* Gr.Mag.*dial.*(tr.Zach.)2.6(M.*PL.*66.143C).

***ξυλοκούκουδον, τό,** ? a kind of *hard seed*, Thphn.*chron.*p.238 (M.108.600A).

***ξυλολάτρης, ὁ,** *wood-worshipper*, ‡Jo.D.*ep.Thphl.*14(M.95.364A); Steph.Diac.*v.Steph.*(M.100.1121A).

***ξυλολογέω,** *gather wood*, Isid.Pel.*epp.*1.181(M.78.300C); ‡Caes. Naz.*dial.*195(M.38.1185).

ξύλον, τό, A. *wood*, as abode of Jesus *σχίσον τὸ ξ., κἀγὼ ἐκεῖ εἰμι Agraph.*(p.69).

B. of things made of wood; **1.** *walking-stick, staff*; carried by philosophers, Tat.*orat.*25(p.26.23; M.6.860B); **2.** *sounding-board κρούσαντος τοῦ κανονάρχου τὸ ξ.* Jo.Mosch.*prat.*11(M.87.2860C); *τὸ ξ. τὸ νυκτερινόν ib.*104(2961B); Leont.N.*v.Sym.*19(M.93.1693D); **3.** *fuller's implement*, Clem.ap.Eus.*h.e.*2.1.5(M.20.136B); Chrys.*hom. 2.3 in 1Tim.*(11.559D); **4.** *instrument of torture* or *death*; **a.** *stake ξύλῳ ἐμπαγῆναι* Just.*2apol.*3.1(M.6.448A); **b.** *post ξ. ὄρθια, οἷς ἐντεινόμενα τῶν ἐνισταμένων τὰ σώματα* Gr.Nyss.*v.Gr.Thaum.*(M.46.945A); **c.** *wooden ? horse*, to which victims were bound *ἐπὶ τοῦ ξύλου στρεβλούσθω* Bas.*hom.*18.4(2.145E; M.31.500B); *ξεσμὸν πλευρῶν ἐπὶ ξύλου* Pall.*v.Chrys.*3(p.20.18; M.47.14); *ib.*(p.129.12; M.47.72); **d.** *wooden bonds, stocks* for stretching the feet, Eus.*h.e.*5.1.27(M.20.417C); **e.** s.v.l., executioner's *block*, *T.Sal.*9.6; **5.** of Noah's *wooden ark*, compared with Cross, Just.*dial.*138.2(M.6.793B); Pall.*v.Chrys.* 12(p.74.22; M.47.42); *διασώσαντα ἐν ξ. δίκαιον γένος* Chrysipp.*enc.in Jo.Bapt.*8(p.40.6); **6.** *lump of wood* venerated in idolatrous worship, *2Clem.*1.6; *λίθοις καὶ ξ.* Clem.*prot.*1(p.4.27; M.8.56B); Const. ap.Gel.Cyz.*h.e.*2.7.31(M.85.1240A); ref. Ex.15:25, compared with Cross, cf. *si quis sine ligno vitae, id est sine mysterio crucis...bibere voluerit de legis littera, per amaritudinem nimiam morietur*, Or.*hom. 7.1 in Ex.*(p.206.9; M.12.342B); *οὕτως τὸ ξ. τοῦ πάθους...ἐλθὸν εἰς τὸν λόγον πεποίηκε τὸν ἄρτον αὐτοῦ γλυκύτερον* id.*hom.10.2 in Jer.*(p.72.23; M.13.360B); *δηλοῖ γὰρ τὸ ξ., τὸν τοῦ σωτῆρος σταυρόν, ἤτοι τὸ ἐπ' αὐτῷ μυστήριον* Cyr.*glaph.Ex.*2(1.284A); *τοῦτο γὰρ τὴν ἡμετέραν προεδήλου σωτηρίαν. τὸ γὰρ σωτήριον τοῦ σταυροῦ ξ. τὴν πικρὰν τῶν ἐθνῶν ἐγλύκανε θάλατταν* Thdt.*qu.26 in Ex.*(1.143); cf. *Christi...mysterium, quod per lignum in aquam conjectum significatur*, Proc.G. *Ex.*(M.87.587); **7.** *wooden representation of Cross τὸ ξ. ... τὸν τύπον τοῦ σταυροῦ* Marc.Diac.*v.Porph.*61(p.49.4); the *labarum*, Geo.Pis. *Pers.*2.253(M.92.1227A).

C. *wood, tree*; **1. a.** of Cross *ἐπὶ ξύλου πολυκάρπου Orac.Sib.*5.257; *ib.*6.26; *διὰ τοῦ ξ. τοῦ σταυροῦ ζωοποιηθέντος A.Phil.*140(p.74.6); *A.(Pass.)Andr.*3(p.5.27; M.2.1221A); *τὸ σωτήριον ξ.* Thdt.*Ps.*95:12 (1.1294); pl. *τῆς ἀποκαταστάσεως τῶν τιμίων ξ.* Geo.Pis.*carm.*2 tit.; *τοῖς τιμίοις καὶ ζωοποιοῖς ξ.* Thphn.*chron.*p.272(M.108.673A); ref.

Exaltation by Heraclius, *ib*.p.273(676A); exeg. Jer.11:19, Just.*dial.* 72.2(M.6.645A); ὅταν γὰρ τῷ λόγῳ τῆς Ἰησοῦ διδασκαλίας προσάπτηται τὸ σταυρῶσαι τὸν διδάσκαλον, εἰς τὸν ἄρτον αὐτοῦ ξ. ἐμβέβληται Or. *hom.10.2 in Jer.*(p.72.18; M.13.360B); Chrys.*fr.in Jer.*(M.64.869C); τοῦτον τὸν ἄρτον ξύλῳ προσήλωσαν Thdt.*Jer.*12:19(2.473); Olymp. *fr.Jer.*(M.93.652A); ref. Gal.3:13, Jo.D.*Gal.*3:13(M.95.795B); exeg. Jer.11:19, ‡Germ.CP *contempl.*(M.98.397A); hence **b.** of Christian's cross, Clem.*prot.*12(p.83.25; M.8.240A); *ib.*(p.84.19; 240C); **c.** of the Cross in devotion, Juln.Imp.ap.Cyr.*Juln.*6(6².194C,195D,E) cit. s. σταυρός; liturg., in rite of veneration διὰ τῆς προσψαύσεως τοῦ ζωοποιοῦ ξ. Sophr.H.*or.*5(M.87.3312C,3313B); τὸ ξ. ... προσκυνητέον Jo.D.*f.o.*4.11(M.94.1129C); **2.** *tree*; **a.** met., of Christ ξ. ὑγρὸν... ἔγκαρπον opp. τῷ ξηρῷ καὶ ἀκάρπῳ ξ., τῷ λαῷ τῶν Ἰουδαίων *cat.Lc.* 23:31(p.166.26); of believers and unbelievers, Vict.*Mc.*11:20(p.395.6); of a heavenly-minded monk, Hyper.*mon.*87(M.79.1481C); **b.** of tree of knowledge of good and evil, Chrys.*hom.16.6 in Gen.*(4.131D); Pall.*v.Chrys.*12(p.73.12; M.47.41); Thdt.*qu.26 in Gen.*(1.41); Thdt.*pentat.*(5.131); contrasted with Cross, *A.*(*Pass.*)*Andr.*5(pp.11, 12); Jo.Eub.*concept.BMV* 21(M.96.1496B) cit. s. ἀνάκλησις; **c.** of tree of life (v. ζωή) οἷόν τι ἔπαθλον προὔκειτο τετηρηκότι τὴν ἐντολήν Thdt.*qu.26 in Gen.*(1.41); compared with Cross, Just.*dial.*86.1(M.6.680B); met. 'τὸ ξ.' ... νῦν δὲ πᾶσιν ἀνεβλάστησεν ἡ ἐκκλησία Meth. *symp.*9.3(p.117.14; M.18.184A); (Gnost.) description of Ophite rite, Cels.ap.Or.*Cels.*6.27(p.97.5; M.11.1333A) cit. s. ζωή; **d.** the two trees, found in paradise alone, Thphl.Ant.*Autol.*2.24(M.6.1089B); Clem.*str.*3.17(p.244.7ff.; M.8.1208A,B); (Gnost.) ἐκ δὲ τοῦ Ἀνθρώπου καὶ τῆς Γνώσεως βεβλαστηκέναι Ξ. Iren.*haer.*1.29.3 ap.Thdt.*haer.*1.13 (4.305); the two trees equated with angels in Gnost. system of Justinus, Hipp.*haer.*5.26(p.127.22; M.16.3195A); ref. pagan divination ξύλῳ μαντικῷ Tat.*orat.*19(p.21.24; M.6.849B).

***ξυλοπάνδουρον, τό,** a kind of *wooden fetter*, Thphn.*chron.*p.364 (M.108.873A).

ξυλοπέδη, ἡ, *wooden fetter*, Olymp.*Job* 13:26(M.93.164D); Thphn. *chron.*p.215(M.108.552A).

***ξυλοποτήριον, τό,** *wooden chalice*, Leont.H.*monoph.*(M.86.1900B).

***ξυλοπρατικός,** *pertaining to a woodseller* or *selling of wood*, *Mir. Artem.*7(p.8.13).

ξυλοφόρος, ὁ, *wood-carrier*, ‡Pion.*v.Polyc.*8.

***ξυλοφορτηγός, ὁ,** = foreg., ref. Jos.9:27, Gr.Naz.*carm.*2.1.13.187(M.37.1242A).

ξυλώδης, *wooden, hard as wood*, met. τῆς ψυχῆς τὸ ἀναίσθητον καὶ ξ. καὶ πρὸς καῦσιν ἐπιτήδειον Oecum.*Apoc.*8:7(p.106).

ξύλωσις, ἡ, *making woody* λέγεται πύρωσις τοῦ ξύλου, καὶ οὐ ξ. τοῦ πυρός †Jo.D.*fr.*(M.95.413D).

ξυν- v. συν-.

ξυνήων, *common, shared*, Nonn.*par.Jo.*4:9(M.43.776A); *ib.*11:16 (841B).

ξυν-όω, 1. *cause to participate* in, *associate* with ἐμὲ...φιλίης ἀλύτῳ ~ώσατε θεσμῷ Nonn.*par.Jo.*8:42(M.43.820B); *ib.*14:15(869A); λόγος...~ώσας ζαθέην βροτοειδέϊ σύζυγα μορφήν *ib.*1:14(752B); Paul.Sil.*Soph.*996(p.255; M.86.2157A); **2.** *communicate* to ξ. ἔπος... Φιλίππῳ Nonn.*par.Jo.*1:47(M.43.757C); *ib.*6:61(801B); med. ἀμφοτέροισιν...φωνὴν ξ. *ib.*1:40(756C); *ib.*20:2(908C); **3.** *hold communion* with Χριστῷ ~ούμενος Gr.Naz.*carm.*2.1.50.43(M.37.1388A).

***ξύνω,** s.v.l., *sharpen* ἧλοι οὓς ἔξυνας Mel.*pass.*93 p.15.23.

***ξυραίνω,** s.v.l., *shave*, aor. infin. pass. ξυρανθῆναι Or.*schol.in Lc.* 7:22(M.17.333B).

***ξυραῖος,** *shaven*, Synes.*calv.*7(p.204.16; M.66.1181A).

ξυρίζω, *shave*, ‡Ath.*Melch.*(M.28.529A).

ξύριον, τό, *razor*, Epiph.*haer.*27.5(p.308.4; M.41.372A).

***ξυσπλενδία, ἡ,** internal organ of body, ‡Caes.Naz.*dial.*7(M.38.865).

ξυστήρ, ὁ, *flesh-scraper*, an instrument of torture, Dion.Al. ap.Eus.*h.e.*6.41.17(M.20.609C); Eus.*m.P.*7.6(p.924.6; M.20.1485A); Const.Diac.*laud.*6(M.88.485C).

ξυστήριον, τό, = foreg., Eus.Al.*serm.*6(M.86.352A).

§**ξυστόν, τό,** *a species of fish*, Thphn.*chron.*p.297(M.108.725B).

ξυστός, ὁ, *a place for walking*, Just.*dial.*1.1(M.6.472A).

***ξυφοίνικον,** v. ὀξυφοίνικος.

O

ὀαρίζω, *say*, Nonn.*par.Jo.*6:20(M.43.796C); *ib.*8:54(821C).

ὀαριστής, ὁ, *familiar friend*, Clem.*str.*2.20(p.170.12; M.8.1049A).

ὀβελίζω, *mark with a critical obelus* τινὰ ὠβελίσαμεν ⟨ὡς⟩ ἐν τῷ Ἑβραϊκῷ μὴ κείμενα Or.*comm.in Mt.*15.14(p.388.17; M.13.1293B); τὰ τοίνυν ἀκριβῆ τῶν ἀντιγράφων ὠβέλισται· ὁ δὲ ὀβελός, ἀθετήσεως σύμβολον Bas.*hex.*4.5(1.37C; M.29.89A); διὸ καὶ ὠβέλισται, ὡς οὐδένα νοῦν ἐμφαῖνον †Bas.*Is.*129(1.469C; M.30.328C).

ὀβελός, ὁ, 1. *critical mark*, Epiph.*mens.*3(M.43.241A,B); **2.** *arrow*, Isid.H.*etym.*1.21.3.

ὄβρυζος, *pure, refined*, of gold ἄπεφθον, ὃ νῦν οἱ πολλοὶ ὄ. ὀνομάζουσιν Thdt.*Is.*13:12(p.67.20, v.l. εὔρυζον 2.262); *of pure gold*, Cosm.Ind.*top.*11 (conj. for εὔροιζος M.88.448D); Jo.Mal.*chron.*16 p.395(M.97.585A).

ὀγδοαδικός, *connected with the eighth day* εἰς ὀγδοαδικῆς εὐεργεσίας κληρονομίαν ὑπερκύψαντες Clem.*str.*6.14(p.486.7; M.9.329B).

ὀγδοάς, ἡ, *ogdoad*; **1.** Gnost.; primary series of emanations or aeons ὀ. μία ἡμῖν συμψάλλει *A.Jo.*95(p.198.5); (Valent.) εἶναι ταύτην ἀρχέγονον ὀ. Iren.*haer.*1.1.1(M.7.448A); τῆς Ἐνθυμήσεως...ἣν δὴ καὶ δευτέραν ὀ. καλοῦσι *ib.*1.3.4(473A); *ib.*1.1.3(449B); διὰ τοῦτο Ἑβδομάδα καλοῦσιν αὐτόν, τὴν δὲ μητέρα τὴν Ἀχαμὼθ Ὀ. *ib.*1.5.2 (493B); containing Christ, *ib.*1.9.3(544A); Σεκοῦνδος...λέγει εἶναι τὴν πρώτην ὀ. τετράδα δεξιὰν καὶ τετράδα ἀριστεράν, οὕτως παραδιδοὺς καλεῖσθαι τὴν μὲν μίαν φῶς, τὴν δὲ ἄλλην σκότος *ib.*1.11.2(564B); acc. Colorbasius τὴν Πρώτην Ὀ. οὐ καθ' ὑπόβασιν ἄλλων ὑπὸ ἄλλου Αἰῶνα προβεβλῆσθαι, ἀλλ' ὁμοῦ καὶ εἰς ἅπαξ τὴν τῶν ἓξ Αἰώνων προβολὴν ὑπὸ τοῦ Προπάτορος καὶ τῆς Ἐννοίας αὐτοῦ τετέχθαι *ib.*1.12.3 (573A); ἐγένοντο οἱ τρεῖς τόποι ὅμοιοι τοῖς ἀριθμοῖς, ὀ. ὄντες *ib.*1.14.5 (605A); ἡ καλουμένη κατ' αὐτοὺς Ὀ., ἥτις ἐστὶν ἡ ἐκτὸς πληρώματος Σοφία Hipp.*haer.*6.31(p.159.17; M.16.3242B); ἐὰν ἐξομοιωθῇ τοῖς ἄνω, τῇ ὀ. ἀθάνατος ἐγένετο καὶ ἦλθεν εἰς τὴν ὀ., ἥτις ἐστίν, φησίν, Ἱερουσαλὴμ ἐπουράνιος *ib.*6.32(p.161.17; 3243C); γένηται λόγος ἐπουράνιος ἀπὸ τῆς ὀ. γεννηθεὶς διὰ Μαρίας *ib.*6.35(p.165.2; 3247C); Δημιουργὸν καλοῦσι...ἀφ' οὗπερ πάλιν καὶ ὑστέραν Ὀ. μετὰ ἑπτὰ οὐρανοὺς καλοῦσι κατὰ τὴν πρώτην Ὀ. ἀφομοιωθεῖσαν ἐκτίθεται, αὐτοῦ ὄντος ἐν τῇ Ὀ. Epiph.*haer.*31.4(p.388.2ff.; M.41.480A); τὰς θηλείας· Δυάδα Τετράδα Ἑξάδα Ὀ. *ib.*31.5(p.393.7; 484C); βολὴν ὑπὸ τοῦ Προπάτορος καὶ τῆς Ἐννοίας αὐτοῦ τετέχθαι... *ib.*35.1(p.40.1; 628B); (Basilidean) αὕτη ἐστὶν ἡ κατ' αὐτοὺς ὀ. λεγομένη, ὅπου ἐστὶν ὁ μέγας ἄρχων καθήμενος Hipp.*haer.*7.23(p.201.15; 3310D); τῶν ὅλων ὁ μέγας ἄρχων, ἡ ὀ. ... ἄρρητος *ib.*7.25(p.203.9ff.; 3314A,B); ἡ τῆς ὀ. κτίσις *ib.* 7.26(p.204.18; 3315A); *ib.*7.27(p.207.14; 3319B) cit. s. ἑβδομάς; ὁ μέγας ἄρχων...γεννᾷ υἱὸν...καὶ τοῦτον ἐκ δεξιῶν αὐτοῦ ἐκάθισε· καὶ ταύτην οὗτοι φάσκουσι τὴν ὀ. *ib.*10.14(p.275.23; 3430C); **2.** ref. circumcision on eighth day (Valent.) καὶ ὅσα εὑρίσκεται ἐν ταῖς γραφαῖς, ὑπάγεσθαι δυνάμενα εἰς τὸν ἀριθμὸν τῶν ὀκτώ, τὸ μυστήριον τῆς ὀ. ἐκπληροῦν λέγουσιν Iren.*haer.*1.18.3(M.7.645B); ἡ τῆς πνευματικῆς ὀ. χαρὰ καὶ γνῶσις κηρυχθήσεται ἀφέσεως ἁμαρτημάτων οὖσα καὶ ἀναστάσεως παρεκτική· περιτμηθήσεσθαι γὰρ δι' αὐτῆς τῶν ἀνθρώπων τὰ πάθη καὶ τὴν φθοράν Meth.*symp.*7.6(p.77.12; M.18.133A); **3.** ref. eighth (Lord's) day ἡ ὀ. ... κυρίως εἶναι σάββατον Clem.*str.*6.16(p.502.13; M.9.364C); ἡ τῶν πνευματικῶν ἀνάπαυσις ἐν κυριακῇ, ἐν ὀ., ἣ κυριακὴ ὀνομάζεται id.*exc.Thdot.*63(p.128.9; M.9.689B); cf. ὃν δὲ ἀναγεννᾷ Χριστός, εἰς ζωὴν μετατίθεται, εἰς ὀ. *ib.*80.1 (p.131.25; 696A); **4.** *eighth sphere* of heavens, region of the fixed stars τήν τε ὀ. κύβον καλοῦσι, μετὰ τῶν ἑπτὰ πλανωμένων τὴν ἀπλανῆ συγκαταριθμοῦντες σφαῖραν Clem.*str.*6.16(p.503.7; M.9.368A); εἴτε καὶ ἡ ἀπλανὴς χώρα ἡ πλησιάζουσα τῷ νοητῷ κόσμῳ ὀ. λέγοιτο *ib.*4.25(p.319.1; M.8.1368B); cf. εἴτ' οὖν ὀ. καὶ ὁ νοητὸς κόσμος εἴτε ὁ ⟨περὶ⟩ πάντων περιεκτικὸς...δηλοῦται θεός *ib.*5.6(p.350.18; M.9.61B); **5.** the number *eight* κατὰ τοὺς ἀριθμοὺς αὐτοὺς σώζεται τῇ τάξει ἑκάστη μονὰς εἰς ἑβδομάδα τε καὶ ὀ. Clem.*str.*6.16(p.503.21; M.9.369A); signifying Christ incarnate ὁ δὲ...ὀ. ὑπάρχων, φανῇ θεὸς ἐν σαρκίῳ *ib.*(p.503.16; 368B); and glorified by Father ἐπὰν ἑβδομὰς δοξάζῃ τὴν ὀ. *ib.*(p.503.30; 369A); **6.** *period of eight years*, Or.*Jo.*10.39(23; p.217.15; M.14.385A); **7.** *group of eight* πρώτη ὀ. ἀνθρώπων, ἐπὶ τοῦ Νῶε Ast.Soph.*Ps.*6(M.40.447B); **8.** *eighth part* τῆς ὀκτάβης ...(τέλος τοῦτο κατ' ὀγδοάδα) Sophr.H.*mir.Cyr.et Jo.*1(M.87.3424C).

ὀγδοατικός, *of the eighth day* ὀγδοατικῆς ἐνεργείας, εἴτουν μυστικῆς ἀναστάσεως Max.*cap.theol.*1.60(M.90.1105A).

ὀγδοήκοντα, *eighty* εἰκότως ὀ. εἶναι λέγονται [sc. αἱ παλλακαί]· ὁ μὲν γὰρ ὀκτὼ ἀριθμὸς τὴν ὀγδόην σημαίνει Thdt.*Cant.*6:7(2.128f.); v. παλλακή, ὄγδοος.

***ὀγδοηκοντάς**, ἡ, *unit of eighty*, Epiph.exp.fid.6(p.502.20; M.42.784C); of years, Mod.occurs.(M.86.3276C).

ὀγδοηκοντοῦτις, fem. of ὀγδοηκοντούτης, *eighty years old*, Eus. v.C.3.46 tit.(p.74.14; M.20.1106C).

ὄγδοος, **A.** *eighth*; **1.** [sc. ἡμέρα] *eighth day*, of Jewish circumcision, Resurrection, and age to come οὐ τὰ νῦν σάββατα ἐμοὶ δεκτά, ἀλλὰ ὃ πεποίηκα, ἐν ᾧ καταπαύσας τὰ πάντα ἀρχὴν ἡμέρας ὀ. ποιήσω, ὅ ἐστιν ἄλλου κόσμου ἀρχήν. διὸ καὶ ἄγομεν τὴν ἡμέραν τὴν ὀ. εἰς εὐφροσύνην, ἐν ᾗ καὶ ὁ Ἰησοῦς ἀνέστη ἐκ νεκρῶν, καὶ φανερωθεὶς ἀνέβη εἰς οὐρανούς *Barn.*15.8,9; ὅτι ἡ ἡμέρα ἡ ὀ. μυστήριόν τι εἶχε κηρυσσόμενον διὰ τούτων ὑπὸ τοῦ θεοῦ μᾶλλον τῆς ἑβδόμης Just.dial. 24.1(M.6.528B); ἡ δὲ ἐντολὴ τῆς περιτομῆς, κελεύουσα τῇ ὀ. ἡμέρᾳ ἐκ παντὸς περιτέμνειν τὰ γεννώμενα, τύπος ἦν τῆς ἀληθινῆς περιτομῆς, ἣν περιετμήθημεν ἀπὸ τῆς πλάνης καὶ πονηρίας διὰ τοῦ ἀπὸ νεκρῶν ἀναστάντος τῇ μιᾷ τῶν σαββάτων ἡμέρᾳ Ἰησοῦ Χριστοῦ τοῦ κυρίου ἡμῶν ib.41.4(564D); ref. those saved in the ark οἵτινες ἀριθμῷ ὄντες ὀκτώ, σύμβολον εἶχον τῆς ἀριθμῷ μὲν ὀ. ἡμέρας ib.138.1(793B); τῇ ἑβδόμῃ γὰρ ἡ ἀνάπαυσις θρησκεύεται, τῇ δὲ ὀ. ἱλασμὸν προσφέρει Clem.str.4.15(p.318.23; M.8.1368A); connected with eight heavenly spheres (cf. ὀγδοάς) ἡ δὲ μετὰ τοὺς πλανωμένους πορεία, ἐπὶ τὸν οὐρανὸν ἄγει, τουτέστι τὴν ὀ. κίνησίν τε καὶ ἡμέραν ib.5.14(p.397.15; M.9.161B); cf. *in septimana namque dierum consummatus est mundus...nisi octava venerit dies, id est nisi futuri saeculi tempus affuerit*, Or.hom.8.4 in Lev.(p.399.14; M.12.497A); ὥσπερ ἡ ὀ. σύμβολόν ἐστι τοῦ μέλλοντος αἰῶνος, δύναμιν ἀναστάσεως περιέχουσα id. sel.in Ps.118:164(M.12.1624B); exeg. Ps.6:1 ὀ. ἡ ἀναστάσιμος τοῦ σωτῆρος ἡμέρα κτλ. Eus.Ps.6:1(M.23.120A); ἀνέσπερον καὶ ἀδιάδοχον καὶ ἀτελεύτητον τὴν ἡμέραν...ὀ. Bas.hex.2.8(1.21D; M.29.52A); πρὸς τὸν ἐφεξῆς αἰῶνα βλέπει. οὗ ἡ ἀρχὴ ὀ. λέγεται, τὸν αἰσθητὸν διαδεξαμένη χρόνον, τὸν ἐν ἑβδομάσιν ἀνακυκλούμενον Gr.Nyss.Pss.titt.B 5(M.44.504D); ἡ ὀ. ..., ἥτις ἐστὶν ὁ ἐφεξῆς αἰών, ὅλος μία ἡμέρα γενόμενος, καθώς φησί τις τῶν προφητῶν, 'μεγάλην ἡμέραν' τὴν ἐλπιζομένην ὀνομάσας ζωήν ib.(505A); also Day of Judgement ἡ δὲ κληρονομία ἐν τῇ ὀ. τοῖς ἀξίοις ἀπόκειται, ἐν ταύτῃ δὲ καὶ ἡ δικαία τοῦ θεοῦ γίνεται κρίσις, ἑκάστῳ τὸ κατ' ἀξίαν νέμουσα id.Ps.6(M.44.612A); ἡ ὀ., τὸν τῆς κρίσεως ἐφανέρωσε φόβον ib.(613D); εἰς δὲ τὸ τέλος ᾄδεται τῷ τελεώτατα εἶναι τὰ περὶ τῆς ὀ. θεωρήματα Didym.Ps.6:1(M.39.1173D); ἐν ὀ. δὲ ἡμέρᾳ ἡ τοιαύτη κατορθοῦται περιτομή· δεῖ γὰρ ὑπερβάντα τὸν ἐν ς' ἡμέραις γενόμενον κόσμον, ἐν τῇ ἑβδόμῃ γενέσθαι...δεῖ προσλαβεῖν τὴν ὑπερκόσμιον ὑπὲρ ταύτην κατάστασιν οὖσαν ὀ. ib.(1176A); ὀ. οἶδεν ἡ μὲν παλαιὰ διαθήκη τὴν περιτομήν· ἡ δὲ καινὴ τὴν ἐκ νεκρῶν ἀνάστασιν, ἐν ᾗ ὁ θάνατος περιτέμνεται Ast.Soph.Ps.6(M.40.444C); ἐπεὶ οὖν πρώτη ἀνάστασις τοῦ γένους μετὰ τὸν κατακλυσμὸν διὰ ὀγδοάδος ἀνθρώπων ἐγένετο, διὰ τοῦτο καὶ ὁ κύριος πρῶτος τὴν ἀνάστασιν τῶν νεκρῶν ἐν τῇ ὀ. ἄρχεται ib.(448C); καλῶς ὑπὲρ τῆς ὀ. προσηύχετο, ὁ ὀ. τοῦ Ἰεσσαὶ υἱός ib.(448D); ἑαυτοὺς τοίνυν περιτέμνωμεν τῇ μαχαίρᾳ τοῦ πνεύματος, ἀποβλέποντες εἰς τὴν ὀ. ἡμέραν, τουτέστιν εἰς τὸν μέλλοντα αἰῶνα Nil.epp.1.13(M.79.88B); ᾄδεται δὲ περὶ τῆς ὀ. καθ' ἣν ἡ ἀνάστασις, καὶ ἡ τῶν ἐθνῶν γέγονε κλῆσις, καὶ ἡ τοῦ ἁγίου πνεύματος δόσις, καὶ τῆς νοητῆς ἤγουν τῆς ἐν πνεύματι περιτομῆς ἡ δύναμις Cyr.Ps.11:1(M.69.796B); exeg. Ps.11 tit. ὑπὲρ τῆς ὀ. ... τῷ δὲ ὀ. [sc. ἔτει] τοὺς μὲν παραδίδωσιν εἰς κόλασιν αἰώνιον, τοὺς δὲ εἰς ζωὴν αἰώνιον Hesych.H.Ps.tit.11(M.27.685D); συνέκλεισε γὰρ ὁ θεὸς ἐνταῦθα μὲν βίον καὶ πρᾶξιν, ἐκεῖ δὲ τὴν τῶν πεπραγμένων ἐξέτασιν. καίγε ἴδιον τοῦτο τῆς ὀ., τὸ μηκέτι καιρὸν εἰς παρασκευὴν ἀγαθῶν ἢ κακῶν διδόναι, τοῖς ἐν αὐτῇ γινομένοις Thdt.Ps.6:6(1.642) ∞ Gr.Nyss.Pss.titt.B 11(M.44.548C); ὑπὲρ δὲ τῆς ὀ. τὴν ἐπιγραφὴν ἔχει· ἅτε δὴ τῆς δικαίας τοῦ θεοῦ κρίσεως μεμνημένος Thdt.Ps.11:1(1.674); τὸν γὰρ τῆς κρίσεως καιρὸν ὀγδόην ἡ θεία προσαγορεύει γραφή id.Cant. 6:7(2.128); exeg. Eccl.11:2 ὁ δὲ τὴν νέαν [sc. προσιέμενος] καθ' ἣν ἡ κυριακὴ τοῦ σωτῆρος ἀνάστασις, ἡ ὀ. καὶ πρώτη ἀρχὴν ἔχουσα τοῦ μέλλοντος αἰῶνος, δέδωκε μερίδα τοῖς ὀκτὼ Olymp.Eccl.11:2(M.93.605C); τὴν μέλλουσαν ζωὴν ὀνομάσας ὀ. ἅτε δὴ μετὰ τὴν ἑβδοματικὴν ταύτην πολιτευθησομένην ἐν τοῖς ἀνθρώποις Gr.Agr.Eccl.9.20(M.98.1128B); ὁ μέλλων αἰών, καθ' ὃν τῆς ἐν φθορᾷ δουλείας ἐλευθερούμεθα *Schol.*20 in Jo.Clim.scal.5(M.88.790A); ἡ δὲ ὀ. τῆς ὑπὲρ φύσιν καὶ χρόνον ὑποδηλοῖ καταστάσεως τὸν τρόπον Max.cap.theol.1.51(M.90.1101C); ὀ. δέ, ἡ πρὸς θέωσιν τῶν ἀξίων μετάταξίς τε καὶ μετάβασις...τὴν ἑβδόμην καὶ τὴν ὀ. ... ὁ κύριος προσηγόρευσεν ἡμέραν συντελείας καὶ ὥραν ib.1. 55(1104B); ἡ δὲ ὀ., τὸ τοῦ ἀεὶ εὖ εἶναι τῶν ὄντων ἄρρητον μυστήριον ὑπαγορεύει ib.1.56(1104C); ref. Apoc.20:4 ὀ. ὀφείλει ἡ γραφὴ ὀνομάζειν τὴν κατὰ τὴν ἑβδόμην τοῦ παρόντος αἰῶνος ζωὴν καὶ διαγωγήν· ἣν προεμήνυσεν ἡ ὀκταήμερος περιτομή...[ref. Eccl.11:2]...χιλιοντάδος ἀγαθῆς τῆς μελλούσης καὶ μενούσης ζωῆς αἰωνίου Anast.S.Ps.6(M.89. 1080B); cf.Hesych.H.Ps.tit.11 cit. supra; ref. eighth day of Creation (Marcosian) ἐν τῇ ὀ. τῶν ἡμερῶν πεπλάσθαι λέγουσι τὸν ἄνθρωπον... εἰ μὴ τὸν μὲν χοϊκὸν ἐν τῇ ἕκτῃ...ἐροῦσι πεπλάσθαι, τὸν δὲ σαρκικὸν ἐν τῇ ὀ. Iren.haer.1.18.2(M.7.645A,B); **2.** of eighth heaven corresponding to eighth aeon (Marcosian), ib.1.17.1(637A); cf. ἐλθὲ ἡ μήτηρ τῶν ἑπτὰ οἴκων, ἵνα ἡ ἀνάπαυσίς σου εἰς τὸν ὀ. οἶκον γένηται *A.Thom.* A 27(p.142.18); **3.** of soul or life-principle as eighth element in constitution of man ἔστι καὶ δεκάς τις περὶ τὸν ἄνθρωπον...τοῦτο δὴ ὀ. τὸ κατὰ τὴν πλάσιν πνευματικόν. ἔννατον δὲ τὸ ἡγεμονικὸν τῆς ψυχῆς Clem.str.6.16(p.500.3; M.9.360A); **4.** of eighth of the spirits which provide occasions for sin ὄ. πνεῦμα τοῦ ὕπνου ἐστί, μεθ' οὗ ἐκτίσθη ἔκστασις φύσεως καὶ εἰκὼν τοῦ θανάτου *T.Reub.*3.1.

B. *eight*, Nonn.par.Jo.5:5(M.43.785A).

ὀγκηρός, *solid*; of Christ's body, ref. docetism, Epiph.haer.42.11 (p.128.9; M.41.732C); ib.(p.154.16; 772C).

ὀγκία, ἡ, (Lat. *uncia*) *ounce* ἀσσάριόν ἐστιν, ὀγκίας τὸ τέταρτον *cat.Mt.*10:29(p.80.7).

***ὀγκινάρα**, ἡ, s.v.l., *claw* made of iron and used in torture, *A.Petr.et Paul.*79(p.212.11).

***ὀγκινίσκος**, ὁ, *hook*, †Jo.D.B.J.23(M.96.1069B).

ὄγκινος, ὁ, = foreg., *A.Phil.*23(p.12.23); ib.140(p.73.10).

***ὀγκόμασθος**, *with prominent breasts*, Jo.Mal.chron.5 p.106(M. 97.196C).

ὀγκοποιέω, *puff out* hair *by way of adornment*, *Const.App.*1.3.10.

ὄγκος, ὁ, **1.** *mass*; name for atoms in science of Heraclides, Dion.Al.ap.Eus.p.e.14.23(773B; M.21.1272C); ἀτόμων ἢ ὄ. ἢ ἀμερῶν ἢ ὁμοιομερῶν Meth.res.2.10(p.350.2); *mass, great sum* of money, *PLond.*1915.20; Chrys.hom.83.2 in Mt.(7.793E); *lump*; of a bodily tumour, Bas.hom.in Ps.32(1.135A; M.29.332B); theol., *bulk, mass* μείζων ὁ πατὴρ τοῦ υἱοῦ γέγραπται, οὔτε δὲ ὄγκῳ ‡Ath.dial.Trin.2.7,8 (M.28.1165Cff.); οὐχὶ δὲ καὶ σὺ τὸν υἱὸν παραπλησίως ἐρεῖς...μήτε ὄ. ... ἔχειν ἐν ἑαυτῷ; Bas.Eun.1.22(1.234B; M.29.561C); Eun.apol.19(M.30. 856A); of Christ's body σωματικὸν ὄ. Dion.Ar.d.n.2.9(M.3.648A); **2.** met.; **a.** *swelling* of pride ὁ δὲ ὄ. φλέγμα ἐστί Gr.Nyss.Eun.12(1 p.310.21; M.45.1024B); θεραπεία δέ ἐστιν τὸ...διαστεῖλαι τὸν διάκενον ὄ. id.ep.1.35(M.46.1009A); **b.** *weight, burden*, Synes.ep.105(M.66. 1484B); τῶν πειρασμῶν Nil.epp.4.30(M.79.564C); ὄ. τῶν ἁμαρτημάτων Tit.Bost.fr.Lc.7:44ff.(p.170.13); **c.** *weight* of dignity, Bas.hom.7.6 (2.58B; M.31.296B); Chrys.hom.10 in 1Tim.(11.601A); plur., Geo. Pis.carm.vit.81; **d.** *weight, sublimity* of speech, Didym.Trin.3.17 (M.39.876A); of inflated phrases in prayer of Pharisee ὁ τῶν ῥημάτων ὄ. κενὸς περὶ τὰ χείλη κατέρρει Sev.Ant.ap.cat.Lc.18:12ff.(p.133.31).

ὀγκόω, **1.** *swell*, physically; of pregnancy, *T.Lev.*6.9; met. τὴν ὠγκωμένην γαστέρα τοῦ θανάτου *cat.Ac.*2:24(p.43.33); **2.** *puff up*; with vanity or pride, Clem.paed.2.12(p.233.20; M.8.552B); ἐπιχειρημάτων ὠγκωμένων id.str.1.1(p.6.30; M.8.693C); ὀγκῶσαι τὸ φρόνημα Thdt.Eph.4:1(3.422); Sophr.H.v.Anast.(M.92.1701B); **3.** *exaggerate*, Cyr.Ps.50:8(M.69.1096B); Malchus exc.Rom.1(p.163. 15; M.113.769A).

ὀγκύλλ-ομαι, *be puffed up* τῇ ἀθέῳ σοφίᾳ ὡς ξένῃ ὀγκύλλωνται αἱρέσει Clem.str.7.7(p.31.6; M.9.457A); κύριε, ὁ τοὺς ~ομένους... πίπτειν ποιῶν Didym.Ps.9:20(M.39.1197C).

ὄγκωσις, ἡ, *bulk* of body τὰς ἐν ὀ. φύσεις Geo.Pis.hex.982(M.92. 1510A).

***ὁδευτέον**, **1.** *one must proceed*, Or.Cels.8.1(p.221.15; M.11.1521B); ἐπὶ τὸν προκείμενον λόγον...ὁ. id.Jo.13.34(p.259.7; M.14.458C); **2.** *one must proceed by* πάσας οὖν ὁ., ἢ τινὰς τῶν ὁδῶν τούτων; Gr. Naz.or.27.8(p.14.8; M.36.21B).

ὁδεύ-ω, *go, travel, journey*; met., c. acc., by the way of light, *Barn.*19.1; ἡ πίστις δὲ διὰ τῶν αἰσθητῶν ὁδεύσασα ἀπολείπει τὴν ὑπόληψιν Clem.str.2.4(p.119.25; M.8.944C); *go by, follow*, Or.Jo.32.7 (6; p.437.8; M.14.760B); ib.13.52(51; p.280.15; 493C); *pass through*, Chrys.hom.10 in Heb.(12.107B); Σολομών, καίτοι διὰ πάσης εὐημερίας ὁδεύσας Thdt.Ps.115:2(1.1421); *proceed* ἐπὶ τὴν τελειότητα Or.Jo.32. 15(6; p.449.34; 780B); ~ει πρὸς τὸ τέλος ἤδη, καθάπερ ἐπὶ τὸν καρπὸν ἡ συκῆ Cyr.Lc.21:29ff.(M.72.900C); *proceed, occur* τὸ κατὰ φύσιν ~ον Thdt.Is.7:14(p.38.32; 2.218).

ὁδηγ-έω, *lead, guide* ~ούμενος ὑπὸ τοῦ θείου πνεύματος Or.Cels.7.44 (p.196.3; M.11.1485B); ~ήσει σε αὐτῇ ἡ ἀλήθεια Gel.Cyz.h.e.2.20.8 (M.85.1284A); met. γνώμας...ἐπὶ τὸν σώφρονά τε καὶ κόσμιον βίον ~ούσας Const.or.s.c.19(p.181.12; M.20.1289C).

ὁδηγητικός, *leading, guiding* κατὰ προφητικὴν χάριν καὶ ὁ. Or. sel.in Dt.9:10(M.12.805B); ἡμεῖς ὁ. λέγομεν τὸ πνεῦμα τὸ ἅγιον ‡Ath.Maced.dial.1.12(M.28.1308C).

ὁδηγία, ἡ, *guidance* διὰ τῆς τῶν γραφῶν ὁ. Gr.Nyss.tres dii(M.45. 125D); τὸ δὲ πνεῦμα τὴν ὁ. χαρίζεται ib.(141C); of Trin., Didym.Trin. 2.8(M.39.629B) cit. s. γαληνότης; c. genit., *guidance in* εἰς ὁ. τοῦ κρείττονος Gr.Naz.or.24.4(M.35.1173C).

ὁδηγός, ὁ, *guide*; of the Lord as man's guide, Clem.*exc.Thdot.* 74(p.130.21; M.9.693A); †Bas.*bapt.*1.2.5(2.633A; M.31.1533C); of guardian angels ἕκαστος τῶν ἀνθρώπων ἔχει ὁ. Ammon.*Ac.*12:15 (M.85.1540C).

[*]**ὁδηποτοῦν,** = ὁ δή ποτ' οὖν, *whatever it may be*, Clem.*str.*6.18 (p.515.30; M.9.396B).

ὀδμή, ἡ, *smell, odour*, met. ὀ. ἀφθαρσίας Iren.*haer.*1.4.1(M.7. 480A).

ὁδοιπορ-έω, *journey, travel*, Gr.Thaum.*pan.Or.*16(p.38.12; M.10. 1100C); ‡Meth.*palm.*3(M.18.389A); met. ἡμῖν ἄρα ἀνάγκη πρὸς ἀλήθειαν ~οῦσιν εὐζώνοις γενέσθαι Clem.*paed.*3.7(p.258.28; M.8. 609A).

ὁδοιπορία, ἡ, *journey, way*, Nil.*epp.*2.322(M.79.357B); met. ἡ πρὸς δικαιοσύνην ὁ. Clem.*paed.*2.12(p.233.31; M.8.552C); τὴν εἰς τὸ ἐξώτερον σκότος ὁ. ἐπανῃρημένοι id.*str.*3.18(p.247.1; M.8.1212C); ὀρθὴ πρὸς οὐρανὸν καὶ σύντομος ὁ. Meth.*symp.*5.6(p.61.2; M.18.108C).

ὁδοιπορικῶς, *for a journey*, Clem.*paed.*3.7(p.259.10; M.8.610B).

***ὁδοιπόριστος,** *able to be crossed by road*, †Bas.*ep.*365(3.467B; M. 32.1109A).

ὁδοιπόρος, ὁ, *wayfarer, traveller* Χριστὸς ἐγὼ ταχύγουνος ὁ. εἰμὶ θαλάσσης Nonn.*par.Jo.*6:20(M.43.796C); fig., Clem.*paed.*3.7(p.259.9; M.8.610B).

ὁδοποι-έω, 1. *make a way*, met. φόβος θεοῦ ~ῶν εἰς σοφίαν Clem. *str.*2.7(p.130.21; M.8.968C); Or.*Jo.*19.20(5; p.322.11; M.14.565A); *make one's way, pass*, id.*engast.*9(p.293.24; M.12.1028A); med., *proceed*, Bas.*jud.*2(2.214E; M.31.656B); *make into a way* or *road*, met. ~ήσας πάσῃ σαρκὶ τὴν ἐκ νεκρῶν ἀνάστασιν *Lit.Bas.*(p.327.7); pass., Just.*dial.*131.3(M.6.780D); *prepare as a way* for ~εῖν δὲ ἑαυτοὺς τῷ κυρίῳ ‡Caes.Naz.*dial.*30(M.38.893); **2.** *make* or *prepare a way for*, c. acc., ‡Nil.*perist.*6.1(M.79.856A); *ib.*11.18(930B).

ὁδός, ἡ, *way, road*; met.; **1.** in gen. ὁ. δικαιοσύνης *Barn.*1.4; εὐσεβείας Gr.Thaum.*pan.Or.*4(p.9.8; M.10.1061A); τοῦ πνεύματος Meth.*symp.*3.1(p.27.8; M.18.61A); τῆς εὐθείας καὶ βασιλικῆς ὁ. Eus. *e.th.*3(p.148.4; M.24.985C); ὁδοὶ κυρίου καὶ τρίβοι...τὰ σωτήρια τῶν ἁγίων προφητῶν συγγράμματα Cyr.*Jo.*9(4.766A); of evil ways τῆς πλάνης Just.*dial.*39.2(M.6.560B); τῆς ἀπωλείας Chrys.*hom.44.3 in Mt.*(7.471E); two ways: ὁ. δύο εἰσί, μία τῆς ζωῆς καὶ μία τοῦ θανάτου *Did.*1.1; τοῦ φωτὸς καὶ τοῦ σκότους *Barn.*18.1; of Adam and of Christ contrasted, Ath.*Ar.*2.65(M.26.285A,B); the 'gnostic' way, Clem.*ecl.*28.2(p.145.24; M.9.713A); **2.** of the Christian *way* (cf. Ac. 9:2,22:4,24:14) βλασφημοῦντες τὴν ὁ. *Ep.Lugd.*ap.Eus.*h.e.*5.1.48(M. 20.428A); ὁδὸν τοὺς πιστεύοντας καλεῖ Chrys.*hom.19.2 in Ac.*(9. 155E); ὁ. λέγει τὴν πίστιν ἤτοι τὴν παράδοσιν Ammon.*Ac.*24:14(M.85. 1592C); fig. προσπταίειν εἰώθασιν οἱ ἑτέρως τὴν διάνοιαν ἔχοντες, καὶ τὴν ὁ. προσκοπεῖν οὐκ ἐθέλοντες. τοῦτο πεπόνθασιν Ἰουδαῖοι Thdt. *Rom.*9:33(3.110); **3.** of Christ, the *Way* ποτὲ μὲν ποιμένα λέγουσα... καὶ ὁ. καὶ θύραν Bas.*Spir.*17(3.14D; M.32.97A); *ib.*(15A; M.97B); ἀγαθὴ γὰρ ὄντως ὁ., ἀπαρεξόδευτος καὶ ἀπλανής, ὁ κύριος ἡμῶν, πρὸς τὸ ὄντως ἀγαθόν, τὸν πατέρα, φέρων *ib.*18(16B; M.100C); τὴν ὁ. εὑρήσει τὴν ἀγαθήν, τουτέστι Χριστόν Cyr.*Jo.*9(4.766A); τοῦτον Ἰησοῦν καλοῦμεν καὶ θύραν καὶ φῶς καὶ ὁ. *V.Aberc.*16(p.14.16); exeg. Pr.8:22 οὐκ οὖσαν γὰρ τὴν σάρκα, ἣν ἀνείληφεν ὁ λόγος, ἀλλὰ μὴ οὖσαν 'ἔκτισεν ἀρχὴν ὁδῶν αὐτοῦ' Marcell.*fr.*10 ap.Eus.*e.th.*3.2(p.145.9; M.24.981B); 'ἀρχὴν' δὲ 'ὁδῶν' διὰ τοῦτο εἰκότως εἴρηκεν τὸν δεσπότην ἡμῶν τὸν σωτῆρα *ib.*12(p.145.23; 981C); ἔκτισέν με δηλονότι διὰ τῆς παρθένου Μαρίας *ib.*9 ap.eund.*Marcell.*2.3(p.46.20; M.24.801C); of the flesh or human nature of Christ τῷ μὲν οὖν ὀνόματι τῆς ὁ. τὴν κατὰ ἄνθρωπον δηλοῖ περιβολήν Eust.*fr.in Pr.8:22*(p.77); ὁ. δὲ σωματικόν τί ἐστι θέαμα, ἥτις ἐστὶν ὁ κυριακὸς ἄνθρωπος †Ath.*exp.fid.*4(M.25. 205C); ὡς εἶναι ἐναντίον τὸ μὲν 'ἔκτισε' τῷ γεννήματι, τὸ λεγόμενον ἀρχὴν ὁδῶν τῷ εἶναι αὐτὸν μονογενῆ λόγον Ath.*Ar.*2.47(M.26.248C); ὁ λόγος...ὕστερον κτίζεται ἀρχὴ τῶν ὁ. εἰς ἔργα διὰ τὴν ἐνανθρώπησιν *ib.*2.60(276C); ἐπιβαίνων ὁ λόγος εἰς τὴν ἡμετέραν σάρκα, καὶ ἐν αὐτῇ κτιζόμενος ἀρχὴ ὁδῶν εἰς ἔργα αὐτοῦ *ib.*2.76(309A); **4.** of God ὁ θαιὸς γένηται ἡμεῖν ὁδὸς εὐθεῖα *Pap.Chr.*(p.393).

***ὁδοστασία, ἡ,** *insurrection on the highway*, Zach.H.*ep.*(M.86. 3232C); Leont.N.*v.Jo.Eleem.*41(p.80.12).

***ὁδοστατ-έω, 1.** *waylay*, †Gregent.*leg.Hom.*(M.86.589C); Thphn. *chron.*p.304(M.108.740B); met., ref. Lc.10:30 [sc. Christ] κατερχόμενος ὡδοστατήθη τοῖς πάθεσι Germ.CP *or.*2(M.98.268C); **2.** *obstruct*, Geo.Pis.*hex.*996(M.92.1511A v.l.); met. ~ῶν δὲ τὴν ἁμαρτίαν φόβῳ *ib.*406(1465A); ~οῦσι τῇ γραφῇ id.*Sev.*358(M.92.1648B).

***ὁδοστάτης, ὁ, 1.** *highwayman*, *Didasc.Jac.*3.1(p.52.13); Jo. Mosch.*prat.*189(M.87.3068C); fig. τὸν ὁ. ἐχθρὸν...τὴν ἀρετὴν ὑποκλέψαντα CTrull.*or.imp.*(H.3.1653B); **2.** *obstructor of the highway, adversary*, Germ.CP *or.*2(M.98.253A); fig. ὁ τῆς ἀπαρχῆς ἐντολῆς ὁ. Geo.Pis.*res.*44(M.92.1377B); ὁ κρυπτὸς τῶν φρενῶν ὁ. id.*hex.*760(M.92. 1492A).

ὁδοστρωσία, ἡ, *paving of roads* αἱ ἐκκλησίαι μόναις ὑποκείμεναι ὁ. καὶ γεφυροποιΐαις Justn.*cod.*1.4.26(p.42).

ὀδούς, ὁ, *tooth*, derivation ὀδόντες...ἐκ τοῦ ἔδω...ὀνομαζόμενοι Melet.*nat.hom.*10(M.64.1192D); σῖτός εἰμι θεοῦ, καὶ δι' ὀδόντων θηρίων ἀλήθομαι Ign.*Rom.*4.1; fig. δεινή τις βιαία τόλμα βρυχᾶται ἐπιπρίουσα τὸν ὀδόντα Const.ap.Gel.Cyz.*h.e.*3.19.3(M.85.1345B); spiritual powers τῆς ψυχῆς δύναμιν μασητικὴν ἐχούσης, ἥτις...βρύξει τοὺς ὀδόντας Meth.*res.*1.24(p.248.21; M.41.1093C); τοὺς ὀδόντας δέ, τὸ διαιρετικὸν τῆς ἐνδιδομένης τροφίμου τελειότητος Dion.Ar.*c.h.*15.3 (M.3.332B); phrase ὑπ' ὀδόντα, *secretly* ὑπ' ὀ. τέως λαλουμένην τὴν βλασφημίαν ἐπήρθη δημοσιεῦσαι Bas.*Eun.*1.1(1.208B; M.29.501A); id. *ep.*204.4(3.305A; M.32.749B).

***ὀδυνοποιός,** *causing pain*, Epiph.*haer.*41.3(p.93.12; M.41.693D).

ὀδυρτικός, *sad*, opp. περιχαρής, Thdr.Stud.*epp.*2.16(M.99.1165C).

ὀδωδή, ἡ, *scent*, Clem.*paed.*2.8(p.201.9; M.8.481A).

[*]**ὀδώνιον, τό,** *long cloth boot* or *sock* (cf. οὐδών, Lat. *udo*) τὰ δὲ ἄλλα πέδιλα...τὰ ἐξ ἱματίων γεγενημένα, ἃ παρά τισιν ὀ. κέκληται ἢ βράκαι Epiph.*haer.*59.11(p.376.15; M.41.1033C).

***ὀζοδία, ἡ,** = ὀζωδία, met. ὀζοδίας γέμοντα ἔργα *Pers.capt.*(M.86. 3244C).

***ὀζοθήκη, ἡ,** *latrine*, †Cyr.*hom.div.*14(5^2.412A); Jo.Clim.*scal.*18 (M.88.933A).

ὀζομενία, ἡ, *stench*, met. τῆς ὀ. τῶν ψυχῶν τῶν ἁμαρτωλῶν ὀσφραινόμεθα μόνον ‡Mac.Al.*serm.*(M.34.388A).

ὄζω, 1. *smell* of, met. ὀ. τρυφῆς Clem.*paed.*2.10(p.224.13; M.8. 532A); c. acc. τὴν εὐωδίαν ὀ. ἅμα τὴν Χριστοῦ *Ep.Lugd.*ap.Eus.*h.e.* 5.1.35(M.20.421B); **2.** *smell, stink*, abs., met. μύθων ὀδωδότων Cyr. *Is.*2.3(2.276C).

***ὀζωδία, ἡ,** *stench*, met. τὴν τῶν κακῶν πράξεων ὀ. ‡Mac.Al.*serm.* (M.34.388B); fig., Nil.*epp.*4.26(M.79.561C); met., Jo.Clim.*scal.*25(M. 88.993B).

ὅθεν, *whence*; in phrase ὅθεν καὶ πόθεν, *from this place and that*, Iren.*haer.*1.8.1(M.7.524A).

ὁθενοῦν, *whencesoever*, Clem.*q.d.s.*12.5(p.167.30; M.9.616D).

ὀθνεῖος, *foreign, strange*, of marriage with foreigners λύσις ὀ. ἐπιγαμβρείας Clem.*str.*1.21(p.77.26; M.8.853A); *not one's own* ὀ. τε ἐπισκευάζεσθαι τῇ κεφαλῇ τὰς κόμας ἀθεώτατον id.*paed.*3.11(p.271. 19; M.8.637B); γάμοις ὀ. Cyr.*hom.pasch.*8(5^2.95C); *alien* τῶν ὀ. ἐνθυμημάτων Meth.*res.*2.3(p.334.2; M.41.1165D); theol. Μακεδονιανοί... φάσκοντες τὸ ἅγιον πνεῦμα μὴ μνημονεύεσθαι, ὡς δῆθεν ὀ. τῇ φύσει Didym.*Trin.*3.36(M.39.965B); οὐ γὰρ ἐπ' ὀ. πλεονεκτήμασιν, ἀλλὰ τοῖς ἐμοὶ προσοῦσιν οὐσιωδῶς, σεμνύνομαι [sc. Χριστός] Cyr.*Jo.*5.2(4.492E).

ὀθόνη, ἡ, *fine linen*; *handkerchief*, Malch.*ep.*ap.Eus.*h.e.*7.30.9(M. 20.713A); *tent-cloth* σκηνὴν ἐκ ποικίλης ὀ. Gel.Cyz.*h.e.*3.10.26; *linen garment* οὐκ ὀ. ἐφόρεσεν ἐκτὸς φακιολίου Pall.*h.Laus.*1(p.15.14; M.34. 1009B); *linen grave-clothes*; plur., Nonn.*par.Jo.*19:40(M.43.908A); *ib.*20:5(908C); liturg., originally a *linen vestment* worn by deacons on the left shoulder ταῖς λεπταῖς ὀ. ταῖς ἐπὶ τῶν ἀριστερῶν ὤμων κειμέναις ‡Chrys.*prodig.*1.3(8.37A); a reminder of Christ washing and wiping dry the feet of his disciples ἡ ὀ. μεθ' ἧς λειτουργοῦσιν ἐν τοῖς ἁγίοις οἱ διάκονοι Isid.Pel.*epp.*1.136(M.78.272C); linen material used in construction of a fan, *Lit.*ap.*Const.App.*8.12.3.

***ὀθονοειδής,** *like a sheet*, Ammon.*Ac.*10:13(M.85.1537A).

οἰακίζ-ω, *steer*; hence *govern, guide, manage*, met. τὸν βίον ἡμῶν ~εσθαι τῆς εἱμαρμένης ταῖς ἀνάγκαις λέγειν Meth.*symp.*8.13(p.99.4; M.18.161A); of God ~ει τὸ ὕδωρ ὡς ἂν βούληται Cyr.H.*catech.*9.9; τῶν ὄντων αἴτιον...πᾶν τό τε κινούμενον ~οντα Gr.Nyss.*Eun.*6(2 p.138. 9; M.45.724A); διδάξαντες, καὶ διὰ τοῦ νοῦ καὶ τοῦ λόγου, ὥσπερ ναῦν, τὴν ψυχὴν σοφῶς οἰακίσαντες Max.*ambig.*(M.91.1116D).

***οἰακισμός, ὁ,** *guidance*, Gr.Naz.*carm.*1.2.34.265(M.37.964A).

οἰακοστροφ-έω, = οἰακίζω: τῷ ἀγαθῷ καὶ φιλανθρώπῳ θεῷ τὰ καθ' ἡμᾶς ~εῖν ἐπιτρέπωμεν Cyr.*Jo.*3.1(4.247B).

οἴαξ, ὁ, *tiller, helm*; plur. (Greek ships having a pair of rudders), met. τῆς Ἀντιοχέων ἐκκλησίας κατέχων τοὺς οἴ. Thdt.*h.e.*2.7(3.849); ref. government of God ὁ θεὸς . . . ὥσπερ σκάφος τῷ τῆς σοφίας οἴ. διευθύνων ἀκλινῶς τὸ πᾶν Meth.*res.*1.37(p.278.7; M.41.1104A); τὸν θεὸν...σοφῶς κατέχειν τοὺς τῆς κτίσεως οἴ. Thdt.*Rom.*1:20(3.24).

οἰάπερ, *though*, Malchus *exc.Rom.*1(p.156.9; M.113.757C).

οἶδα, A. *know*, theol.; **1.** of man's knowledge: of the Word οὗ βασιλικώτατον καὶ δικαιότατον ἄρχοντα μετὰ τὸν γεννήσαντα θεὸν οὐδένα οἴδαμεν ὄντα Just.*1apol.*12.7(M.6.344B); of God ὁμοίως ἐστὶν ἄνθρωπον εἰδέναι καὶ θεόν, ὡς μουσικὴν καὶ ἀριθμητικήν; id.*dial.*3.6(M.6.481B); Iren.*haer.*1.9.2(M.7.541A); Const.ap.Ath.*apol. sec.*86(p.165.26; M.25.404C); Ath.*decr.*17(p.14.4; M.25.444B); *ib.*(p.14.

34; 445B); of God's attributes τὴν μεγαλειότητα τοῦ θεοῦ εἰδέναι λέγομεν, καὶ τὴν δύναμιν Bas.*ep.*234.1(3.357B; M.32.868C); πίστις δὲ αὐτάρκης εἰδέναι ὅτι ἐστὶ θεός, οὐχὶ τί ἐστι *ib.*234.2(358A; M.32.869B); οὔτε ὑμεῖς ἴστε τί τὴν οὐσίαν ὁ θεός Chrys.*hom.77.2 in Mt.*(7.742B); ὅτι μὲν ἔστιν, ἴσμεν, τί ποτε δέ ἐστι τὴν οὐσίαν, οὐκέτι id.*hom.34.2 in 1Cor.*(10.312D); **2.** ref. Christ's ignorance as man, exeg. Mt. 24:36, Mc.13:32 οὐκ οἶδε γὰρ σαρκί, καίπερ ὡς λόγος γινώσκων Ath.*Ar.*3.45(M.26.420A); ὡς ἄνθρωπος, οὐκ οἶδε· θεϊκῶς δὲ...οἶδε *ib.* 3.46(421A); τὸ μὴ εἰδέναι, καθὸ ἄνθρωπος Cyr.*fr.Mt.*24:36(M.72. 441C); σκήπτεται χρησίμως τὸ μὴ εἰδέναι *ib.*(444B); ψευδομυθήσει οὐδαμῶς ὅταν λέγῃ καὶ μὴ εἰδέναι *ib.*(445A); **3.** of divine knowledge; **a.** of Father, exeg. Mt.11:27 μόνος ὁ πατὴρ οἶδε τὸν υἱὸν τὸν ἴδιον *ib.*11:27(404D); πάντως δήπου καὶ ὁμοούσιον, καὶ τῆς ἐνούσης αὐτῷ δόξης οἶδεν ὄντα κατ' οὐδὲν ὅλως χείρονα id.*Jo.*5.2(4.496B); **b.** of Son, exeg. Mc.13:32 ἵνα δείξῃ, ὅτι, εἰδὼς ὡς θεός, ἀγνοεῖ σαρκικῶς Ath. *Ar.*3.43(M.26.416A); οἶδε δὲ ὁ πατὴρ τὴν ἡμέραν...φανερόν, ὅτι καὶ ὁ υἱὸς ἐν τῷ πατρὶ ὢν καὶ εἰδὼς τὰ ἐν τῷ πατρί, οἶδε *ib.*3.44(417A); τὸν μὲν πατέρα οἶδε σαφῶς, καὶ οὕτω σαφῶς, ὡς ἐκεῖνος τὸν υἱόν Chrys. *hom.77.1 in Mt.*(7.742A); exeg. Jo.16:30 τὸ γὰρ εἰδέναι, φησί, τὰ ἐν τῷ παραβύστῳ καὶ λεληθότα, τοῦ πάντων ἂν εἴη θεοῦ Cyr.*Jo.*11.2(4. 942A); ἡ αἰτία τοῦ εἰδέναι τὸν υἱὸν παρὰ τοῦ πατρός Bas.*ep.*236.2(3. 362C; M.32.880B); (Arian) ὁ υἱὸς τὴν ἑαυτοῦ οὐσίαν οὐκ οἶδεν Ar. *Thal.fr.2* ap.Ath.*syn.*15(p.243.18; M.26.708B); **c.** of H. Ghost εἰ τὸ πνεῦμα τὸ ἅγιον οἶδε πάντα τὰ τοῦ θεοῦ Ath.*inc.et c.Ar.*7(M.26.993C); μόνον τὸ ἅγιον πνεῦμα οἶδε τὰ βάθη τοῦ θεοῦ, ὅ ἐστι τὰς ἐννοίας τοῦ πατρὸς καὶ τοῦ υἱοῦ Cyr.*fr.Mt.*11:27(M.72.404D); οὕτως οἶδε τὰ τοῦ θεοῦ, ὡς ἡμεῖς τοὺς οἰκείους λογισμοὺς ἐπιστάμεθα Thdt.*1Cor.*2:11 (3.177); **4.** of angelic knowledge οὐδὲ οἱ ἄγγελοι, φησίν, ἴσασιν· τουτέστιν, οὐδὲ ἡ ἐν αὐτοῖς θεωρία καὶ οἱ λόγοι τῶν διακονιῶν εἰσι τὸ ἔσχατον ὀρεκτόν Evagr.Pont.*ep.*7(M.32.257A); εἰ δὲ ἄγγελος οὐκ οἶδεν, οὐδὲ ἄνθρωπος εἴσεται Cyr.*fr.Mt.*24:36(M.72.444A); **5.** of knowledge of inferior created beings, met. ἥλιος, σελήνη...εἰδότες τὸν ἑαυτῶν δημιουργὸν καὶ βασιλέα λόγον Ath.*inc.*43.3(M.25.172C); θέλεις δὲ γνῶναι, ὅτι τὰ θηρία καὶ τὰ κτήνη οἴδασι τὸν θεόν; id.*virg.* 15(p.50.26; M.28.269C).

B. *acknowledge, recognize*, theol. ὁ πατὴρ...ἐγέννησε τὸν υἱόν, καὶ οὐκ ἔκτισεν, ὡς ποταμὸν ἀπὸ πηγῆς, καὶ ὡς βλαστὸν ἀπὸ ῥίζης, καὶ ὡς ἀπαύγασμα ἀπὸ φωτός, ἃ οἶδεν ἡ φύσις ἀδιαίρετα †Ath.*exp.fid.*4(M.25. 208A); cf.Ath.*Dion.*24(p.64.23; M.25.516C); τὸ γὰρ ἔκ τινος φύσει γεννώμενον, καὶ μὴ ἔξωθεν ἐπικτώμενον, υἱὸν οἶδεν ἡ φύσις id.*decr.* 10(p.9.22; M.25.434B); Χριστιανῶν δὲ ἡ πίστις...τὴν μακαρίαν οἶδε τριάδα id.*Ar.*1.18(M.26.49B); in Arian creed οἴδαμεν ἕνα θεόν Ar.*ep. Alex.*ap.eund.*syn.*16(p.243.28; M.26.708D); of BMV οἶδα σεβασμίαν τὴν δεξαμένην θεόν Nest.*fr.*C 11(p.277.20)ap.Cyr.*Nest.*1.1(p.18.25; 6^{1}.10A); met. ἡ διδασκαλία ἕνα υἱὸν οἶδε Thdt.*ep.*125(4.1209); οἶδε γὰρ οὐ μόνον ἡ καινή, ἀλλὰ καὶ ἡ παλαιὰ γραφή, περιτομὴν καρδίας id.*Ezech.*31:18(2.944).

C. *know how, be able* οἶδεν ὁ θεὸς καὶ δικαίους μετὰ ἀσεβῶν τιμωρεῖσθαι Chrys.*hom.6.4 in Eph.*(11.44E); Cyr.*fr.2Reg.*5:6(M.69.684A) cit. s. ὀρθοποδέω; θεότης...πάσχειν οὐκ εἰδυῖα τὰ τῆς κτίσεως ἴδια Sophr.H.*ep.syn.*(M.87.3157C); met. οἶδε [sc. ἡ γραφή]...υἱὸν ἀληθινὸν λέγειν Bas.*Spir.*17(3.14C; M.32.96C).

D. *recognize as acceptable, accept* οὐ γὰρ μόνον παρθένους οἶδεν, ἀλλὰ γνωρίζει καὶ ἐγγάμους Cyr.H.*catech.*17.7; ταύτην οἶδε θυσίαν ὁ τῶν ὅλων δεσπότης Thdt.*Ps.*53:9(1.957); *allow, permit* οὐχ ἵνα τῇ φύσει γενώμεθα κτήνη...οὐδὲ τοῦτο οἶδεν ἡ φύσις Ath.*Ar.*3.18(M.26. 361B); id.*ep.Max.*3(M.26.1088C).

οἰδαίν-ω, *swell*; **1.** intrans., met., Chrys.*sac.*3.14(p.72.4; 1.390D); ἀλλ' οἰ., φησίν, ἡ καρδία, καὶ ταῖς ὕβρεσι δάκνεται; id.*hom.4.5 in Jo.* (8.33C); δαίμονες...οἰ. ἐδόκουν Synes.*provid.*1.7(p.77.6; M.66.1224C); **2.** trans., *make to swell*, Nonn.*par.Jo.*18:1(M.43.888C); met. ∼ομαι κακουργίαν ἀνθρώπων *T.Sal.*5.7.

οἴδημα, τό, *swelling, tumour*, met. οἰ. τῆς καρδίας ‡Gr.Nyss.*or.2 in Gen.1:26*(M.44.289D); οἰ. τῆς ὀργῆς Chrys.*prod.Jud.*1.1(2.377D); ὑπερηφανία ἐστίν, οἰ. ψυχῆς ‡Nil.*vit.cog.*(M.79.1464A).

οἴδησις, ἡ, *swelling*, Sophr.H.*mir.Cyr.et Jo.*16(M.87.3469D); met. οἰ. τῆς ψυχῆς ‡Caes.Naz.*dial.*121(M.38.1009).

οἴδιον, τό, *lamb*; fig., *M.Pion.*18.13.

Οἰδιπόδειος, *Oedipodean, incestuous*, ref. accusations against Christians Οἰ. μίξεις Athenag.*leg.*3.1(M.6.896C); *Ep.Lugd.*ap.Eus. *h.e.*5.1.14(M.20.413B).

οἶδμα, τό, *swelling* as of wind; met., *Orac.Sib.*3.72.

***οἰηκοφόρος, ὁ,** *helmsman*, Synes.*hymn.*3.288(p.15; M.66.1598).

οἴημα, τό, *self-conceit* περὶ τοῦ καυχησαμένου μετά τινος μοχθηροῦ οἰ. φαρισαίου Or.*Cels.*3.64(p.258.11; M.11.1004D); *ib.*5.1(p.2.13; 1181C).

οἰηματίας, ὁ, *conceited person*, Arsen.*tent.*(M.66.1624C); Ἀβεσσαλώμ ἐστι, πᾶς οἰ. καὶ ὑπερήφανος †Cyr.*coll.VT*(6^{4}.29E).

***οἰηματικός,** *conceited*, Jo.Carp.*cap.*49(M.85.1847); Jo.Clim.*past.* 7(M.88.1181D).

***οἰησικοπία, ἡ,** *imagination, fancy*, Eust.*engast.*9(p.28.13; M.18. 629B); *ib.*27(p.59.31; 669D).

οἴησις, ἡ, *conceit* ἡ οἰ. βδέλυγμα κυρίῳ Mac.Aeg.*carit.*3(M.34. 909B); οἰ. καὶ ἀλαζονεία βλασφημίας εἰσὶν αἴτια Marc.Er.*opusc.*2.80 (M.65.941B); οἰ., ἥτις ἐστὶ μήτηρ πάντων τῶν κακῶν Diad.*perf.*81 (p.104.25).

***οἰησισοφία, ἡ,** *conceit of wisdom*, Chrys.*hom.5.2 in 1Cor.*(10. 35B).

οἰησίσοφος, *wise in one's own conceit*, Iren.*haer.*1.16.3(M.7. 633B); Eust.Mon.*ep.*(M.86.908B).

***οἰησίφρων,** *wise in one's own opinion*, Cyr.*Jo.*5.2(4.484B); *ib.*3.1 (249E); *ib.*6.1(627E).

***οἰκαρχία, ἡ,** *government of a house*, Gr.Naz.*ep.*203(M.37.336B).

οἰκειακός, 1. *domestic* οἰ. ὑπηρεσίας Ath.*h.Ar.*38(p.204.34; M.25. 737C); Bas.*ep.*98.2(3.192E; M.32.497A); **2.** theol., *personal*, opp. δουλικός: ἡ...οἰ. [sc. δόξα], παρὰ τοῦ πνεύματος ἐκπληροῦται Bas. *Spir.*46(3.39B; M.32.152C).

***οἰκειόγραφος,** *autograph*, Jo.VI H.*v.Jo.D.*15(M.94.453B).

***οἰκειόπιστος,** *self-confident* βάρος τῷ ταπεινῷ τὸ οἰ. Jo.Clim. *scal.*25(M.88.1000C).

οἰκειοποιέω, *make one's own*, theol., med. ὡς εἷς ὢν ἡμῶν ὁ Χριστὸς μετὰ τῆς ἰδίας σαρκός, οἰ. τὰ τῆς ἀνθρωπότητος πάθη Ammon. *Jo.*4:6(M.85.1420C); οἱ προφῆται...οἰ. τὰ διὰ τὰς αὐτῶν ἁμαρτίας συμβάντα κακά Cyr.*Ps.*43:19(M.69.1024B).

***οἰκειοπραγέω,** *mind one's own affairs*, Synes.*ep.*103(M.66.1476D).

οἰκεῖος, 1. *belonging to the house* or *home*; **a.** οἱ οἰ. *servants*, Thdt. *qu.19 in 4Reg.*(1.523); **b.** *homely*, Thdt.*2Tim.*1:5(3.677); **2.** *of one's own country*; plur. as subst., *fellow countrymen*; as spurning prophets, Or.*Jo.*13.55(54; p.285.16; M.14.504A); *one's own people* ἀμελεῖν ἐπειθόμην πατρίδος τε καὶ οἰ. Gr.Thaum.*pan.Or.*6(p.17.8; M. 10.1072B); s.v.l., c. dat., one's *own* κατὰ τὸν οἰ. ὑμῖν σοφιστήν Tat. *orat.*35(p.37.17; M.6.877C); **3.** *kinsman, associate*, met. οἰ. τῆς πίστεως Socr.*h.e.*5.21.15(M.67.624B); *akin* (to), met. τι τῶν οἰ. τῇ ὕλῃ καὶ τῇ φθορᾷ Or.*Jo.*20.36(29; p.377.21; M.14.660C); of Christ as Word, and Jo. Bapt. as Voice, Heracleon ap.Or.*Jo.*6.20(12; p.129. 21; M.14.236B); τίς τοῦ κτίσαντος οἰκειότερος; Bas.*hom.*13.3(2.116C; M.31.429C); of Son's kinship and unity with Father τῷ οἰ. πέφυκε τὸ οἰ. ἐπιγινώσκεσθαι Bas.*Eun.*1.17(1.229D; M.29.552B); by analogy from natural kinship, *ib.*2.30(267C; M.644A); ὁ Χριστὸς...οἰ. ἄρα καὶ προσήκων τῇ οὐσίᾳ ἔσται τοῦ θεοῦ *ib.*2.31(268D; M.645B); **4.** masc. as subst., *friend*, Clem.*str.*7.2(p.8.3; M.9.412C); *ib.*7.12(p.55.32; 508B); εἰ δ' οἰ. τοῦ σωτῆρος ἦσαν..., πῶς ἐζήτουν αὐτὸν ἀποκτεῖναι; Or.*Jo.*20. 8(p.336.10; M.14.589B); Gr.Thaum.*pan.Or.*16(p.36.9; M.10.1097A); **5.** *personal, private, one's own*, in phrase τὰ οἰκεῖα, *one's own affairs*, Chrys.*hom.10.4 in 2Tim.*(11.725B); οὐδεὶς τῶν τῆς εὐσεβείας τροφίμων τὰ οἰ. προτίθησι τοῦ θεοῦ Thdt.*Eph.*5:24(3.433); theol. τὸ οἰ. σῶμα (σὰρξ γὰρ Χριστοῦ τὸ ἡμέτερον σῶμα) ἐσταύρωσαν Clem.*fr.* 7(p.197.3); τὰ οἰ. κτίσματα Bas.*Eun.*1.27(1.237E; M.29.572A); διὰ τῆς οἰ. εἰκόνος τοῦ θεοῦ λόγου *ib.*2.21(257C; M.620A); ἐκκλησίαν καὶ τὸν ταύτην δι' αἵματος οἰ. ... ἁρμοσάμενον κύριον Max.*opusc.*(M.91. 92D); reflexively, *of himself* τὴν οἰ. ποιούμενος ἐπιφάνειαν Thdt.*qu. 60 in Ex.*(1.161); τὴν οἰ. ἐπίγνωσιν id.*Ps.*65:7(1.1046); *of its own* ἡ γνῶσις...διά τινος οἰ. φωτὸς διαβιβάζει Clem.*str.*7.10(p.41.28; M.9. 480C); **6.** *belonging* to τὸ Σιὼν...οἰ. τοῦ θεοῦ Or.*Jo.*13.12(p.237.7; M. 14.417B); **7.** *appropriate, fitting, suitable* ἑκάστη οἰ. τι ἔργον ἀπονέμει Or.*hom.5.17 in Jer.*(p.55.6; M.13.336A); ποία δὲ οἰκειοτέρα πατρὶς τῇ...Μαριάμ; id.*Jo.*6.40(24; p.149.28; M.14.270C); Bas.*Eun.*1.21(1. 233A; M.29.560B); τὰς οἰ. λέξεις τῶν σπερμάτων Chrys.*hom.41.1 in 1Cor.*(10.387A); theol. οἰ. ἑαυτῷ...προσηγορίαν...'ὁ ὤν' Bas.*Eun.*2.18 (253D; M.609A); εἰ οἰ. τῷ θεῷ ἡ φωνή *ib.*2.24(260D; M.625C); **8.** *in common with, relevant to, to do with* οὐδὲν συγγενὲς καὶ οἰ. ἐκείνῳ τῷ φωτὶ καὶ τῇδε τῇ σαρκί Clem.*exc.Thdot.*5(p.107.6; M.9.656C); Bas. *Eun.*2.2(1.239B; M.29.576A); τὰ οἰ. τοῦ τέλους id.*reg.fus.*5(2.341D; M. 31.920B); **9.** *proper*; **a.** *characteristic of* ὅσα θεῷ οἰ. ἐστι Just.*1apol.* 10.1(M.6.340C); ὁ θεῖος λόγος...τῇ οἰ. δὲ αὐτῷ δυνάμει Gr.Thaum. *pan.Or.*5(p.11.18; M.10.1064C); τροπῆς γὰρ ἤδη τοῦτο οἰ. Eus.*d.e.*5.1 (p.212.15; M.22.352D); τῶν οἰ. τῷ θεῷ Bas.*Eun.*1.10(1.223A; M.29. 536B); οὐδὲν αὐτῷ τῆς τῶν ἀνθρώπων σωτηρίας εἰς δόξης λόγον ἐστὶν οἰκειότερον Max.*ep.*44(M.91.644B); **b.** *proper* to τὴν οἰ. τῶν ὑποθέσεων ἀκολουθίαν *Hom.Clem.*2.8; **c.** *proper, appointed* ἡ θάλασσα...οὐχ ὑπερβαίνουσα τὸν οἰ. τόπον Meth.*arbitr.*2.3(p.148.13; M.18.244A); of Christ's obedience, Thdt.*Is.*49:4(p.194.4; 2.348).

οἰκειότης, ἡ, 1. *relationship* τὴν σαρκικὴν οἰ. διὰ τὴν πνευματικὴν ἔχθραν διαλυσάτω Clem.*q.d.s*.22(p.174.30; M.9.628B); *kinship, affinity* with τὴν οἰ. ἔχει πρὸς τὸ φῶς id.*exc.Thdot*.41.2(p.119.19; M.9.677C); ἕκαστον μέλος ἡμῶν πρός τι πέφυκεν οἰ. σώζειν Or.*mart*.47 (p.43.6; M.11.629B); between soul and body, Jo.D.*f.o*.3.23(M.94.1088C); *likeness* of scriptural passages, Or.*exc.in Ps*.17:6(M.17.109D); **2.** *appositeness* of language 'νῦν ὀστοῦν ἐκ τῶν ὀστῶν μου', διαφόρῳ οἰ. τὸ ὁμοούσιον τῆς γυναικὸς παριστῶν Proc.G.*Gen*.2:18ff.(M.87.173D); *seemliness* δεινὸς τύραννος τῇ τῶν λόγων οἰ. προσσαίνων Gr.Naz.*or*.7.12(M.35.769B); **3.** *synthesis* of ideas πάντα κατά τινα θαυμαστὴν οἰ. συμπεριγράφων Meth.*symp*.3.2(p.28.24; M.18.61D); **4.** *friendliness*, *Ep.Lugd*.ap.Eus.*h.e*.5.1.15(M.20.413C); *friendship*, Gr.Naz.*ep*.208(M.37.345A); **5.** *kinship, friendship, intimacy*, theol.; **a.** between man and God, Clem.*str*.4.7(p.267.10; M.8.1253B); τὴν πρὸς τὸν δίκαιον τοῦ θεοῦ οἰ. Or.*Cels*.1.22(p.72.30; M.11.700A); ἵνα... τὴν τοῦ πνεύματος ἐνοίκησιν καὶ οἰ. κατασκευάσῃ Ath.*Ar*.1.46(M.26.108B); τὴν πρὸς αὐτὸν οἰ. πεπλουτηκότων Cyr.*Os*.6(3.26D); Ἰσραὴλ...οὐ γὰρ ἠθέλησεν ἐν οἰ. διαμεῖναι τῇ πρὸς θεόν id.*Jo*.1.9(4.90D); **b.** within Godhead αὐτὸς ὁ θεός...οἰ. τῇ πρὸς ἑαυτὸν νόησιν ἔχει περὶ ἑαυτοῦ Or.*fr.13 in Jo*.(p.495.23); παραστατικὸν οἰκειότητος τοῦ πατρὸς πρὸς τὸν υἱόν *ib*.50(p.525.2); ἕν εἰσιν αὐτὸς [sc. υἱός] καὶ ὁ πατὴρ τῇ ἰδιότητι καὶ οἰ. τῆς φύσεως Ath.*Ar*.3.4(M.26.329A); τοῦ γὰρ ἑνὸς ἴδιος καὶ ἀδιαίρετός ἐστιν ὁ υἱός, κατὰ τὴν ἰδιότητα καὶ οἰ. τῆς οὐσίας *ib*.3.16 (357A); τῆς κατὰ τὴν οὐσίαν οἰ. Bas.*Eun*.2.25(1.262A; M.29.629B); denied by Eunomius ὅτι ὁ θεὸς τῶν ὅλων οὐδὲ βουλόμενος ἐδύνατο πρὸς τὴν τῆς οὐσίας οἰ. τὸν μονογενῆ παραδέξασθαι *ib*.2.30(267A; M.641B); τῆς φυσικῆς οἰ. ἀμέτοχον εἶναι τοῦ πατρὸς τὸν υἱόν Gr.Nyss.*Eun*.1(1 p.86.6; M.45.317C).

***οἰκειοχείρως, 1.** *with one's own hand* ἔθαψεν...οἰ. v.l. *T.Abr*.B 14 (p.118.26n.); **2.** *of one's own accord* οἰ. τὰ ὀνόματα...παρεδώκαμεν *T.Sal*.C 12.4(p.85.B6).

οἰκει-όω, A. act. and pass.; **1.** *claim as a friend*, Chrys.*poenit*.7.6(2.336C); id.*hom.20.1 in Ac*.(9.162E); *make one's friend*, Isid. Pel.*epp*.3.219(M.78.904A); *win over* as a convert, Chrys.*hom.3.1 in 2Tim*.(11.673C); met., *make one's ally*, id.*hom.3.1 in Ac*.(9.24A); *recommend as a friend*, id.*hom.14.2 in 2Cor*.(10.540A); *ib.16.3*(556B); *join* as foster-father, of S. Joseph σε καὶ ἀπὸ τῆς τοῦ ὀνόματος θέσεως εὐθέως ~ῶ τῷ τικτομένῳ id.*hom.4.6 in Mt*.(7.58B); pass., myst. τοῖς νοητοῖς καὶ πνευματικοῖς ὡς ἔνι μάλιστα γνωστικῶς οἰ. Clem.*str*.7.7(p.34.7; M.9.465A); ὅτε πᾶς τόπος οἰ. τῷ ὄρει Σιών †Bas. *Is*.138(1.475E; M.30.342C); **2.** pass.; **a.** *be made friendly* towards, Chrys.*hom.29.2 in Heb*.(12.273A); ptcpl., *friend*, id.*hom.65.3 in Mt*.(7.647D); **b.** *be made familiar to*, Or.*Cels*.5.45(p.48.13; M.11.1249C); **3.** *make a kinsman* to Christ ὅτι καὶ μητέρα ἑαυτοῦ καὶ ἀδελφοὺς ὁ κύριος τοὺς ἐκ τῶν ἔργων τῆς ἀρετῆς ~ωθέντας προσαγορεύει Bas.*Eun*.2.23(1.259C; M.29.624B); **4.** *reconcile* to, *make friendly*; **a.** men towards God, Clem.*str*.7.7(p.28.2; M.9.452A); Or. *Cels*.3.54(p.250.10; M.11.992C); *ib*.4.26(p.295.22; 1065B); *ib*.8.4(p.224.4; 1525A); τοσαύτην ἔχοντι πρὸς θεὸν οἰκειότητα, ὥστε καὶ ἄλλους οἰ. δύνασθαι Gr.Naz.*ep*.66(M.37.132A); in prayer, Chrys.*hom.19.4 in Mt*.(7.249C); *ib.22.3*(278E); πρὸ γὰρ τῶν ἄλλων ἁπάντων τοὺς ~ωθέντας αὐτῷ διὰ πίστεως δεῖ ἀναστήσεσθαι λέγει Cyr.*Jo*.4.7(4.435D); med., Chrys.*hom.1.6 in Ac.9:1*(3.105E); **b.** pass., of God towards man ~ωθεὶς τοῖς ἁγίοις...πνεῦμα ~ωθὲν τοῖς προφήταις Or.*Jo*.6.11(7; p.120.23; M.14.221A); **c.** *draw* towards, *bring* to οἱ μὲν ἐνάρετοι ~οῦνται τῇ πρώτῃ μονῇ Clem.*str*.7.2(p.8.24; M.9.413A); **d.** *make* oneself *ready* for, *join* oneself to; spiritual life, Gr.Nyss.*v.Mos*.(M.44.337D).

B. med.; **1.** *claim as one's own* ὁ διάβολος ~οῦται αὐτὸν ὡς ἴδιον σκεῦος *T.Neph*.8.6; Thdr.Heracl.*Is*.45:14(M.18.1340D); Chrys.*hom. 52.3 in Gen*.(4.510A); ~ώσεται γὰρ ὡς ἐξ ἀνάγκης τὰ ἐν τῇ εἰκόνι τὸ ἀρχέτυπον Cyr.*Jo*.2.2(4.163E); of God and Israel, Proc.G.*Is*.65:1 (M.87.2685B); in gen. τί οὖν ὁ ὢν οὐκ ~οῦται τὸ εἶναι...; τὸ γὰρ μὴ ~οῦσθαι τῷ ἀλλοτριοῦσθαι ταὐτὸν σημαίνει Gr.Nyss.*Eun*.8(2 p.248.14; M.45.852C); **2.** *identify oneself with* κατεργάζομαί τι πολλάκις οὐκ ~ούμενος Gennad.*fr.Rom*.7:15(p.372.26; M.85.1685A); Justn.*conf*. (p.104.5; M.86.1027C); **3.** *assimilate* food; met., of doctrine, Gr. Naz.*or*.2.45(M.35.453A); **4.** *make one's own* ᾠκειοῦτο τὰ ἡμέτερα ‡Chrys.*caec.Zacch*.4(8.125D); ref. pastoral care, Didym.*Trin*.1.28 (M.39.412B); Jo.Clim.*past*.6(M.88.1177C); *take upon oneself*, Thdt. *Is*.9:11(p.51.18; 2.238); ~οῦται γὰρ [sc. Christ] τὸ πρόσωπον τῶν ἀνθρώπων, ὡς γενόμενος ἄνθρωπος ‡Dion.Al.*fr.in Lc.22:42*(p.233.8; M.10.1589A); of Inc. ᾠκείωται τὰ τοῦ σώματος ‡Ath.*Apoll*.2.16(M.26.1160A); Nil.*epp*.3.7(M.79.369A); τὴν καθ' ἡμᾶς ἀνθρωπίνως ἀπότεξιν οἰ. Cyr.*ep*.50(p.95.15; 5².164C); id.*Heb*.1:9(p.379.14); τὸ τῆς ἀνθρωπίνης φύσεως θέλημα...οὐσιωδῶς ᾠκειώσατο ‡Cyr.*Trin*.20(6³.26B; M.77.1160C); πῶς δυνατόν, πλέον οἰ. τὸν θεὸν λόγον τῆς σαρκός, οὗ οἰ. τὰ τοῦ θεοῦ λόγου ὁ πατήρ; ‡Quint.*ep*.(p.16.23; M.85.1737B); of Christ's sufferings, Thdr.Heracl.*Is*.53:10(M.18.1357C); οἰ. τοῦ ἰδίου σώματος τὰ πάθη ὁ...λόγος Paul.Em.*hom*.2(p.12.16; M.77.1440A); τὰ τῆς ἀνθρωπότητος εἰς ἑαυτὸν οἰ. πάθη Cyr.*Jo*.2.4(4.178C); τὰ τῆς ἰδίας σαρκὸς ἀπαθῶς οἰ. πάθη id.*ep*.17(p.37.11; 5².72A); Thdt.*Ps*. 40:5(1.866); of Christ bearing man's sin τὴν ἀφροσύνην ἡμῶν, καὶ τὸ πλημμελὲς οἰ. Gr.Naz.*or*.30.5(p.115.10; M.36.109B); Gennad.*fr. Rom*.15:3(p.413.21; M.85.1725A); τὰς τοῦ παντὸς κόσμου ἀναλαβὼν καὶ οἰ. ἁμαρτίας Oecum.*Heb*.9:28(p.466.10; M.119.384C); pass. τὰ πάθη ~ωθέντα θεῷ Thdot.Anc.*hom*.1.4(p.83.7; M.77.1353C).

οἰκείως, 1. *properly, rightly, correctly*, of faring well after a cure οἰ. ἔχει Heracleon ap.Or.*Jo*.13.60(59; p.292.23; M.14.516A); ὡς ἄρα ὁ πρωτόπλαστος οἰ. εἰς αὐτὸν ἀναφέρεσθαι δύναται τὸν Χριστόν Meth. *symp*.3.8(p.35.4; M.18.72C); Bas.*Eun*.1.6(1.217E; M.29.524B); *ib*.1.11 (224A; M.537C); **2.** *appropriately, suitably* οἰ. ἂν λεχθησόμενον πνευματικόν Or.*Jo*.1.7(9; p.12.13; M.14.36D); Eus.*h.e*.4.22.8(M.20.384A); Bas.*Eun*.1.23(1.234C; M.29.564A); *in a manner appropriate* to, c. dat., Chrys.*hom.41.1 in 1Cor*.(10.387A); σφραγιζομένην τὴν θείαν ὑπεροχὴν οἰ. θεῷ νοεῖν *cat.Jo*.15:16(p.357.18); *appositely*, *Hom. Clem*.18.13; **3.** οἰ. ἔχω *be conformable, be of one kind*, theol. τοῦ γεννηθέντος οἰ. ἔχειν ὀφείλοντος πάντως καὶ ἀπαραλλάκτως πρὸς τὸν γεννήσαντα Bas.*Eun*.2.6(1.242C; M.29.581C); τὴν ὑπερκειμένην οὐσίαν ...οἰ. ἔχειν αὐτὴν πρὸς ἑαυτήν Gr.Nyss.*Eun*.1(1 p.90.22; M.45.321D).

οἰκείωσις, ἡ, 1. *propensity, inclination, tendency* τῇ τῶν παθῶν οἰ. Clem.*paed*.2.10(p.217.23; M.8.517B); πρὸς τὰ καλά id.*str*.6.9(p.468.15; M.9.293C); *desire*, Nil.*Magn*.1(M.79.969B); **2.** *appropriation* ἔπαινος τοῦ καλοῦ καὶ τοὺς ὀκνηρῶς ἔχοντας διεγείρει πρὸς τὴν τούτου οἰ. *ib*.(969A); **3.** *restoration to home* τῷ Ἰσραὴλ οἰ. Thdt.*Ezech*.28:25f. (2.920); **4.** *kinship, affinity* ἐν τοῖς ζῴοις πρὸς τὰς ἰδιότητας τῶν δαιμονικῶν σωμάτων οἰ. †Bas.*Is*.25(1.399A; M.30.168A); exeg. Phil. 3:8 τὴν οἰ. τῆς γνώσεως Chrys.*hom.11.1 in Phil*.(11.284F); *friendship, fellowship, communion* ἐν τῇ τῆς πίστεως οἰ. Apoll.*fid.sec. pt*.2(p.168.16; M.10.1105C); φιλία καὶ οἰ. Gr.Naz.*ep*.100(M.37.173B); τὴν οἰ.· ὅσην μέλος πρὸς μέλος Chrys.*hom.15.3 in Jo*.(8.88E); ἔχομεν γὰρ καὶ φυσικήν τινα πρὸς ἀλλήλους οἰ., ἣν καὶ θηρία πρὸς ἄλληλα κέκτηνται id.*hom.5.1 in Rom*.(9.461B); **5.** *familiarity* with, Bas. *hom*.2.2(2.11E; M.31.188B); **6.** theol.; **a.** *kinship, relationship* bet. Father and Son, Bas.*Eun*.2.23(1.260A; M.29.625A); *ib*.2.28(265A; M.637A); bet. Father, Son, and H. Ghost, *ib*.3.3(274E; M.661A); Didym.*Trin*.2.2(M.39.461C); of men with God ὁ θεὸς πατήρ ἐστιν οὐ κατὰ τὴν φυσικὴν συγγένειαν ἀλλὰ κατ' οἰ. πίστεως Or.*comm. in Rom*.4:15ff.(*JTS* 13 p.360); κυρίως καὶ προσηκόντως πατὴρ λέγεται ὁ θεός...οἰκειώσεώς ἐστιν ὄνομα Bas.*Eun*.2.24(1.260B; M.625B); ὁ τῆς πνευματικῆς οἰ. τρόπος Cyr.*Is*.4.1(2.558D); κατὰ τὸν τῆς πνευματικῆς οἰ. τρόπον id.*Am*.25(3.275C); **b.** *relation, application* οὐδὲ γὰρ τὰ Ἰουδαίων ἀλλότρια Χριστοῦ, τυπικὴν δὲ καὶ σκιώδη τὴν πρὸς Χριστὸν εἶχεν οἰ. ‡Chrys.*pasch*.5.1(8.261A); **c.** *friendship, fellowship* with God οἰ. καὶ ἡ πρὸς αὐτὸν ἀγάπη Clem.*q.d.s*.7(p.164.2; M.9.612B); διὰ τοῦ Χριστοῦ...ἀναλαμβάνειν ἡμᾶς τὴν πρὸς αὐτὸν οἰ. Or. *Cels*.4.6(p.279.3; M.11.1036D); βασιλείας τοῦ θεοῦ δύο οἶδεν ἡ γραφή, τὴν μὲν κατ' οἰ., τὴν δὲ κατὰ δημιουργίαν Chrys.*hom.39.6 in 1Cor*.(10.371E); πάντες...ἄνθρωποι τοῦ θεοῦ, ἀλλὰ κυρίως οἱ δίκαιοι...κατὰ τὸν [sc. λόγον] τῆς οἰ. id.*hom.17.2 in 1Tim*.(11.649C); δύο [sc. τρόπους] παιδαγωγικοὺς πρὸς ἀρετὴν καὶ τὴν πρὸς θεὸν οἰ. Max.*ambig*.(M.91.1133B); between God and angels, Chrys.*hom.16.3 in Heb*.(12.161A); **d.** *reconciliation*, Euthal.Diac.*epp.Paul*.(M.85.764B); exeg. Col. 1:9ff. σὺν εὐχαριστίᾳ τῆς οἰ., τῆς ἐν καθάρσει *ib*.(768B); Oecum.*Apoc*. 6:7(p.88); *ib*.6:9(p.90); παράθεσις...οἷον οἰ. τοῦ τελευτήσαντος *Schol*. in CCarth.*can*.41(*Mon*.2 p.650); **7.** Christol.; **a.** *appropriation* of human flesh by Logos, Cyr.*Juln*.6(6².197A); and of its sufferings, id.*ep*.39(p.19.11; 5².108A); id.*ep*.50(p.95.11; 5².164C); ‡Quint.*ep*. (p.16.24; M.85.1737C); οὔτε...κατ' οἰκείωσιν ἐκ θεοῦ γέγονεν ἄνθρωπος Anast.S.*hod*.10(M.89.157B); **b.** (Nestorian) *association* ἄνθρωπον, καὶ θεὸν ἀπεκάλει τὸν Χριστόν...τῇ σχέσει καὶ τῇ οἰ. ὥσπερ λέγομεν περὶ δύο τινῶν φίλων, πάνυ ἀλλήλους ἀγαπώντων †Leont.B.*sect*.4.4(M.86.1221C); εἰ οὖν τῇ οἰ. τοῦ παθόντος ὑπὸ Ἰουδαίων παθητὸς ὁ θεός... ἀλλ' ἡμεῖς ὄντως, οὐχ ἁπλῶς οἰκειώσει τῆς σαρκὸς παθεῖν ἢ γεννηθῆναι τὸν λόγον φαμέν Leont.H.*Nest*.7.10(M.86.1768ᵇB); διὰ τὴν ἕνωσιν· οὐ δι' οἰ. μόνον *ib*.(1768ᵇC); ἀλλὰ δύο υἱοὺς λέγοντας, ἄλλον μέν..., ἄλλον δὲ...χάριτι δὲ καὶ σχέσει καὶ οἰ. τῇ πρὸς τὸν θεὸν λόγον καὶ θεὸν αὐτὸν γεγενῆσθαι Justn.*cod*.1.1.6(p.8); **c.** in monothelite controversy, *appropriation, claiming as one's own* τὴν ἡμῶν αὐτῶν προαίρεσιν τῷ σαρκωθέντι θεῷ κατ' οἰκείωσιν ἐνυπάρχουσαν Max.*opusc*.(M.91.29C); τίς τῶν ἁγίων κατ' ἀναφορὰν ἢ κατ' οἰ. τὰς ἐπὶ Χριστοῦ τοῦ θεοῦ διεπρέσβευσε φύσεις; *ib*.(128A); δύο συνιστῶντες θελήματα, τό τε κατὰ φύσιν λέγω, καὶ τὸ κατ' οἰ. ... οἱ δέ, ποίαν ἄρα φασί; τὴν οὐσιώδη...

ἢ τὴν σχετικήν; *ib.*(220B); κατ' οἰκείωσίν φασιν εἰρηκέναι τοὺς πατέρας ἔχειν τὸν κύριον τὸ ἀνθρώπινον θέλημα id.*Pyrr.*(M.91.304A).

***οἰκειωτέον**, **1.** *one must be friendly with*, Clem.*paed.*3.11(p.278.12; M.8.653A); **2.** *one must join* 'τὸ δὲ σῶμα' τοῦτο τὸ πνευματικόν... 'οὐ τῇ πορνείᾳ'...οἰ. id.*str.*7.14(p.62.24; M.9.521B).

οἰκειωτικός, *friendly* τοὺς κατ' οἰ. διάθεσιν προσλαμβανομένους τὸν Χριστόν ‡Just.*qu.et resp.*110(M.6.1357C).

οἰκέτης, ὁ, 1. *household servant* or *slave*, employed on the estate τῆς τῶν οἰ. γεωργίας, τῆς οἰκοδομῆς Cyr.*Ps.*15:2(M.69.808B); ref. their admission to clerical orders, *Can.App.*82; fig., *servant* of God; of people of Israel, *Const.App.*6.20.10; of Moses, exeg. Dt.34:5, Gr.Nyss.*v.Mos.*(M.44.428A); in gen., Clem.*str.*7.2(p.6.7; M.9.409A); **2.** s.v.l., *citizen* (cf. οἰκητής), Marc.Diac.*v.Porph.*32.

οἰκετία, ἡ, 1. *servitude*, Clem.*str.*2.18(p.161.6; M.8.1029B); **2.** *household* τῆς βασιλικῆς οἰ. Eus.*h.e.*8.6.5(M.20.753A); τῆς ἡγεμονικῆς οἰ. id.*m.P.*11.24(p.943.15; M.20.1509A); Chrys.*hom.12.7 in 1Cor.*(10.106D); fig. τὴν τοῦ θεοῦ οἰ. Gr.Nyss.*hom.12 in Cant.*(M.44.1017D); in phrase οἱ ἐν οἰκετίαις, *small men, private citizens* or *persons* opp. men of public distinction, Eus.*h.e.*8.2.4(748A) = *Chron.Pasch.*p.277 (M.92.689A).

οἰκετικός, 1. *of a household slave, menial*; ref. origin, Pall.*h.Laus.*49(p.143.18; M.34.1212A); ἀπὸ οἰ. ῥίζης ὁρμώμενος Isid.Pel.*epp.*5.59(M.78.1361C); fig., of Moses and prophets μέτρον ἔχοντες τὸ οἰ. Cyr.*Is.*5.2(2.777B); of Christ οὐκ ἀξίωσις οἰ. id.*Lc.*8:22(M.72.632C); ὡς οἰ. ἔχοντα τάξιν id.*Jo.*1.1(4.13E); τῆς οἰ. φιλοσοφίας τὴν αἴγλην Thdt.*h.rel.*21(3.1250); οἱ οἰ. *menials*, Cyr.*ador.*1(1.10A); **2.** *of a household*, Alex.Sal.*Barn.*13(p.440D).

οἰκέτις, ἡ, *maid-servant*, *Const.App.*6.17.3, cf.*Can.App.*18; fig., *Pers.*(p.15.20; M.10.104C); met. τὴν τιμὴν οἰ. ἐποίησε βρώσεως Isid.Pel.*epp.*1.192(M.78.305C).

οἰκέω, *dwell in, inhabit* οἰκεῖ μὲν ἐν τῷ σώματι ψυχή, οὐκ ἔστι δὲ ἐκ τοῦ σώματος· καὶ Χριστιανοὶ ἐν κόσμῳ οἰκοῦσιν, οὐκ εἰσὶ δὲ ἐκ τοῦ κόσμου *Diogn.*6.3; τὸ δὲ θυμικὸν...πλησίον μανίας οἰκεῖ Clem.*paed.*3.1(p.236.7; M.8.556B); ὑμῖν δωρήσεται πτερὸν...ἵνα...οἰκήσητε τοὺς οὐρανούς id.*prot.*10(p.76.10; M.8.221C); of fear of God dwelling in a holy man, *T.Gad* 5.4; of God's indwelling ταύτην γὰρ ὁ θεὸς ὁρᾷ καὶ οἰκεῖ τὴν εὐθύτητα Cyr.*Ps.*10:7(M.69.793D; perh. l. οἰκονομεῖ).

οἴκημα, τό, *house* ἔστιν οἰ. κοινὸν ἡ ἐκκλησία Chrys.*hom.45.4 in Ac.*(9.342E).

οἰκημάτιον, τό, *little house*; of a hovel, *Ep.Mareot.*2 ap.Ath.*apol.sec.*76(p.156.11; M.25.385B); met. ἀρεταὶ μὲν γὰρ τὰ οἰ., ὑπ' αὐτῶν γὰρ σκεπόμεθα Or.*fr.*47 *in Lam.*(p.256.10; M.13.633B).

οἴκησις, ἡ, 1. *house, dwelling*; of a church, *IGC As.Min.*215 [Naxos, saec. vii–ix]; of Inc., ‡Ath.*Ar.*4.34(p.83.10; M.26.520C); of future life εἰς καθαρὰν οἰ. ἀδύτων φώτων Meth.*symp.*4.5(p.51.21; M.18.96A); τῆς κατὰ τὸν οὐρανὸν οἰ. *ib.*5.7(p.62.4; 109B); ἡ γὰρ ἐπουράνιος ἡμῶν προηγουμένως οἰ. ἐστιν Didym.*2Cor.*5:1(p.27.9; M.39.1704A); **2.** s.v.l., *administration* τῆς ὑπὲρ ἡμῶν τοῦ θεοῦ οἰ. Sever.ap.*cat.Heb.*1:1(p.123.25) for διοικήσεως id.*Heb.*1:1(p.346.9).

***οἰκήτειρα, ἡ,** *inhabitant*, *Orac.Sib.*3.442.

οἰκητήριον, τό, *dwelling-place, abode* ἐστὶν ἄνω τὸ οἰ. [sc. of H. Ghost] Tat.*orat.*13(p.14.25; M.6.833B); στῆθος οἰ. καρδίας καὶ ψυχῆς Clem.*str.*5.6(p.351.16; M.9.64A); εἶναί φησι [sc. Empedocles] τὰ σώματα τῶν ζῴων τὰ ἐσθιόμενα ψυχῶν κεκολασμένων οἰ. Hipp.*haer.*7.29(p.214.13; M.16.3330C); ἡ ἀνθρωπεία φύσις...ἔχουσα...ἄσεμνον οἰ. Mac.Mgn.*apocr.*4.18(p.195.6); ἡ σὰρξ οἰ. ἐστι τῆς ψυχῆς ‡Proc.G.*Pr.*17:13(M.87.1397B); of the soul as God's chosen abode, Clem.*ecl.*12 (p.140.18; M.9.704C); 'ποιήσωμεν ἄνθρωπον', θεοῦ μονογενοῦς οἰ. Bas.Sel.*or.*1.3(M.85.33C); of Inc. ἁγνοῦ σώματος οἰ. κατηξίωσεν ἐκ παρθένου λαβεῖν Const.ap.Gel.Cyz.*h.e.*2.7.13(M.85.1236A); ἡ ἀληθινὴ σοφία...ἑαυτῇ τὸ οἰ. ἐκ τοῦ παρθενικοῦ σώματος ἐδομήσατο Gr.Nyss.*Eun.*3(2 p.16.14; M.45.580D); of Church τῆς πίστεως τὸ κυριακὸν οἰ. Const.ap.Gel.Cyz.*h.e.*2.7.1(1232C); exeg. Cant.1:5 κἂν τις σκήνωμα ᾖ Κηδάρ, φωτὸς οἰ. γίνεται τοῦ ἀληθινοῦ Σολομῶντος Gr.Nyss.*hom.2 in Cant.*(M.44.792D); of place of eternal punishment for blasphemers, *Apoc.En.*27.2; of hell, *A.Mt.*3(p.219.16); exeg. 2Cor.5:2, of heavenly abode of departed soul ποῖον οἰ. ...; τὸ σῶμα τὸ ἄφθαρτον Chrys.*hom.10.1 in 2Cor.*(10.506C); ἐξ οὐρανοῦ οἰ., τουτέστι τὴν ἀφθαρσίαν Cyr.*2Cor.*5:2(p.350.7; M.74.940B); ἀείδιον οἰ. *CG–CI* 1 p.51; of tomb as abode of dead body, *IG* 3.3503,3504; *MAMA* 1.243.

οἰκητικός, *habitable, inhabited*, *Ep.Mareot.*2 ap.Ath.*apol.sec.*76 (p.156.11; M.25.385B).

οἰκία, ἡ, *house*, fig. σκοτεινῆς τῆς τοῦ θανάτου οἰ. Or.*mart.*41(p.38.25; M.11.617A); exeg. 2Cor.5:1 οἰ. δὲ ἀχειροποίητον οὖσαν ἐν τοῖς οὐρανοῖς, τὸν κόσμον τὸν ἄλλον παρὰ τοῦτον Didym.*2Cor.*5:1(p.26.27; M.39.1701C); τινὲς μὲν τὴν οἰ. τὴν ἐπίγειον τὸν κόσμον τοῦτόν φασιν· ἐγὼ δὲ τὸ σῶμα μᾶλλον ἂν φαίην αὐτὸν αἰνίττεσθαι Chrys.*hom.10.1 in 2Cor.*(10.506A); ἀχειροποίητον οἰ. ... τὴν ἀφθαρσίαν Cyr.*2Cor.*5:1 (p.350.2; M.74.940B); ἐν δὲ τῇ οἰ. τοῦ θεοῦ...δέδεκται...ἡ θεότευκτος οἰ. [sc. BMV] τοῦ υἱοῦ Mod.*dorm.*3(M.86.3285B); exeg. Mt.8:11, Jo.14:2 'ἐν τῇ βασιλείᾳ τῶν οὐρανῶν', τυγχανούσῃ οἰκίᾳ τοῦ πατρὸς ἐν ᾗ πολλαὶ μοναί εἰσιν Or.*Jo.*10.44(28; p.223.26; M.14.396B).

οἰκιακός, *domestic* οἰ. πολεμίους Chrys.*exp.in Ps.*3:1(5.3D).

οἰκίδιος, *domestic, private*, Gr.Naz.*carm.*2.2(poem.)6.67(M.37.1547A).

οἰκίζ-ω, *settle, stay*; **1.** act. ἔν τινι τῶν ἱερῶν οἰ. Sophr.H.*v.Anast.*(M.92.1696A); **2.** pass. intrans. θεὸς...ταῖς τῶν ἀγαθῶν ψυχαῖς ∼όμενος *Hom.Clem.*2.45; of righteousness εἴσω οἰκισθεῖσα Const.ap.Gel.Cyz.*h.e.*2.7.6(M.85.1233B).

οἰκίσκος, ὁ, *small room, chamber*, sometimes *hut, cottage*, or *house*; of pagan shrines, Ath.*gent.*22(M.25.45A); of a sepulchre, id.*v.Anton.*9(M.26.857A); Chrys.*hom.24.4 in 2Cor.*(10.611E); ref. Jer.18:2, id.*hom.3.4 in Gal.*(10.701C); of a small building, Synes.*ep.*67 (M.66.1420C); of monks' cells, Isid.Pel.*epp.*1.327(M.78.372A); of oratories, Nil.*epp.*4.61(M.79.580A); οἰ. τινὰ βραχὺν σφίσιν δείμασθαι Thdt.*h.rel.*2(3.1122); prob. of caverns, id.*eran.*2(4.115); met., of the Father's house, Chrys.*hom.11.2 in Col.*(11.407A).

οἰκοδεσποτέω, *rule as a household*; of God ruling the universe, Eus.*p.e.*7.8(306D; M.21.520B).

οἰκοδεσπότης, ὁ, *master of a house*; of God, Ign.*Eph.*6.1; Herm.*sim.*5.2.9; Or.*hom.4.5 in Jer.*(p.28.25; M.13.293A); of Adam, †Bas.*parad.*10(1.350F; M.30.69C).

οἰκοδεσποτικός, *of the master of a house*, Or.*comm.in Mt.*14.10 (p.299.17; M.13.1208B).

οἰκοδομ-έω, 1. *build, build up*, fig. τὸ βάπτισμα...οὐ μὴ προσδέξονται, ἀλλ' ἑαυτοῖς ∼ήσουσιν *Barn.*11.1; πνευματικὸς ναὸς ∼ούμενος τῷ κυρίῳ *ib.*16.10; ∼εῖσθαι εἰς τὴν δοθεῖσαν ὑμῖν πίστιν Polyc.*ep.*3.2; Iren.*haer.*3.3.3(M.7.849A) cit. s. ἀπόστολος; Or.*princ.*3.1.19(p.231.5; M.11.289A); Meth.*symp.*3.8(p.36.5; M.18.73B); of S. Paul ᾠκοδομήθη ἤδη εἰς τελειότητα πνευματικὴν ἀναπλασθείς *ib.*3.9(p.37.20; 76B); ∼εῖ...ὁ Μωσῆς, τουτέστιν, ἡ διὰ νόμου παίδευσις, τὴν ἐκκλησίαν Χριστοῦ Cyr.*ador.*10(1.329D); of Christ's flesh, likened to Solomon's Temple, Clem.*fr.*36(p.218.27; M.9.768D); identified with house of Wisdom, ‡Ath.*dial.Trin.*3.28(M.28.1245D); ref. Jo.2:21 τὴν ἐκ τῆς ἁγίας παρθένου σάρκα καὶ αὐτὸς ᾠκοδόμησε Thdt.*qu.21 in 2Reg.*(1.418); **2.** *edify* οὐδὲν...οὕτως ∼εῖ τοὺς βιωτικούς, ὡς τὸ μὴ λαμβάνειν Chrys.*hom.23.5 in 2Cor.*(10.602B); τοὺς παρατυγχάνοντας οἰ. Pall.*h.Laus.*40(p.126.7; M.34.1204C); Thdt.*1Cor.*10:23(3.230); **3.** *encourage* ὁ ἁμαρτάνων ∼ηθήσεται εἰς τὸ τὰ αὐτὰ ποιεῖν *Const.App.*2.17.3; οἰ. αὐτοὺς διὰ τῆς ἀναξίου δόσεως *ib.*3.8.3.

οἰκοδομή, ἡ, 1. *building, edifice*, fig. ἡτοιμασμένοι εἰς οἰ. θεοῦ πατρός Ign.*Eph.*9.1; αὐτοῦ γὰρ καὶ οἰ. ἦμεν *M.Perp.*4(p.67.18); ἡ οἰ. 'ἐπὶ τὴν πέτραν' τοῦ θεοῦ ἐστιν Or.*hom.1.15 in Jer.*(p.13.27; M.13.273A); Χριστὸς...τὰς οἰ. τῆς κακίας κατέσκαψε *ib.*14.5(p.110.28; 409D); **2.** *act* or *process of building, building up*, fig. τὴν γνωστικὴν οἰ. Clem.*str.*5.4(p.342.16; M.9.45B); οὐκ ἐπὶ οἰ. τῆς ἐκκλησίας, ἀλλ' ἐπὶ καθαιρέσει Jul.Papa *ep.Dian.*ap.Ath.*apol.sec.*34(p.112.8; M.25.304C); οἰ. εἶναι τὴν κατήχησιν Cyr.H.*procatech.*11; ref. building of Church on S. Peter, v. ἐκκλησία; *edification* πᾶσαν οἰ. τὴν εἰς τὸν κύριον ἡμῶν ἀνήκουσαν Polyc.*ep.*13.2; πρὸς οἰ. τῆς σῆς ψυχῆς *A.(Pass.)Andr.*4(p.10.11); εἰς οἰ. τοῦ λαοῦ σου *Const.App.*8.16.3; εἰς οἰ. τῶν ἀπίστων Gr.Naz.*or.*8.15(M.35.805C); ἱκανῆς οὔσης καὶ πρὸς οἰκοδομὴν τῆς ἀληθείας Marc.Diac.*v.Porph.*1.

οἰκοδόμημα, τό, *building, edifice*, fig. τοῦ θεοῦ ἐστιν ἔργον τόδε τὸ οἰ. Or.*princ.*3.1.19(p.231.10; M.11.289B); of Church, Chrys.*hom.2.2 in Ac.princ.*(3.62D); τῶν ἐν ψυχῇ θείων οἰ. Max.*opusc.*(M.91.69C).

***οἰκοδομητέος,** *that must be built up*, Gr.Mag.*dial.*(tr.Zach.)3.1 (M.*PL.*77.215D).

οἰκοδομητός, *built*, Pall.*h.Laus.*32(p.89.7; M.34.1099D); fig. οἰ. ναός *Barn.*16.7; ref. formation of Eve, Ant.Ptol.*hom.Adam*(p.651.31).

οἰκοδομικός, 1. *connected with building*, Or.*Jo.*28.13(12; p.405.17; M.14.708C); neut. as subst., *ability to edify*, Dion.Ar.*c.h.*15.5(M.3.333C) cit. ap.Max.*ambig.*(M.91.1213C); **2.** *suitable for building purposes* σπαρτίον οἰ. Thdt.*Ezech.*40:3(2.1021).

οἰκοδόμος, ὁ, *builder, architect*; fig., of a bishop, *Const.App.*2.57.1.

οἴκοθεν, 1. *from home*; also *at home*, Eus.*d.e.*1.6(p.32.7; M.22.64A); θεόν, οἴ. ἕκαστον σέβειν *ib.*(p.33.19; 65B); **2.** met., *by* or *from oneself*, or *one's own will, mind*, or *nature*; so *spontaneously, of one's own accord* οὐδὲ οὕτως ἦν ἡμῖν ἀσφαλὲς αὐτοὺς οἴ., καὶ παρ' ἑαυτῶν προσηγορίαν ἐπιτιθέναι τῇ τοῦ δεσπότου οὐσίᾳ Chrys.*incomprehens.*5.4 (1.486D); πόθεν οὖν τοιοῦτος ἦν; καὶ οἴ., καὶ παρὰ θεοῦ id.*laud.Paul.*7

(2.513D); οἰ. καὶ ἀπὸ τῆς τοῦ θεοῦ χάριτος id.*hom.18.1 in 2Cor.*(10.564D); id.*hom.2.2 in 2Tim.*(11.666F); Nil.*Magn.*40(M.79.1017C); Cyr.*glaph.Gen.*1(1.14E).

οἴκοι, 1. *at home*, i.e. *of one's own* συνηγόρους τοὺς οἰ. κέκτησθε Tat.*orat.*1(p.1.19; M.6.805A); *from home*, *ib.*31(p.31.12; 869A); **2.** ? *homewards, home*, Pall.*h.Laus.*40(p.127.10; M.34.1209A).

***οἰκοκυρός, ὁ,** *paterfamilias, head of the household, householder*, *Nomoc.*274.

***οἰκονομεῖον, τό,** *storeroom* of monastery, Cyr.S.*v.Sab.*58(p.160.6ff.); Jo.Mosch.*prat.*5(M.87.2857A).

οἰκονομ-έω, A. in gen.; **1.** *govern, supervise, manage (the affairs of), administer*, Ath.*gent.*43(M.25.85C); τῷ νόμῳ τῆς φύσεως, καὶ τῷ πολιτικῷ τούτῳ καθ' ὃν ~ούμεθα Bas.*ep.*276(3.421A; M.32.1011B); ref. pastoral care and eccl. administration, *Hom.Clem.*3.60; γενέσθω ἐν αὐτῷ [sc. a presbyter] πνεῦμα θεῖον πρὸς τὸ δύνασθαι αὐτὸν ~ῆσαι τὸν λαόν σου Serap.*euch.*27.1; οἱ κατὰ διαδοχὴν τὰς ἐκκλησίας ~ήσαντες Bas.*Spir.*74(3.63B; M.32.208A); τὸν μὲν Ἀλεξανδρείας ἐπίσκοπον τὰ ἐν Αἰγύπτῳ μόνον ~εῖν CCP(381)*can.*2; Chrys.*laud.Paul.*2(2.485E; perh. interpolated); *administer* as οἰκονόμος, CChalc.*can.*26 cit. s. οἰκονόμος; ~εῖν τεταγμένος τὸν σεβάσμιον νεὼν τοῦ ἁγίου προδρόμου καὶ βαπτιστοῦ Ἰωάννου Evagr.*h.e.*3.12(p.109.27; M.86.2618A); τὸν ~οῦντα τὸ τέμενος Sophr.H.*mir.Cyr.et Jo.*35(M.87.3545B); Niceph.Ur.*v.Sym.*220(M.86.3188D); *act as treasurer*; of Judas, Chrys.*hom.65.2 in Jo.*(8.391D); *manage, administer* money, Or.*princ.*4.3.8(p.335.6; M.11.389B); **2.** *regulate, control* ἡ...~οῦσα τὸ ζῷον δύναμις Bas.*hom.*1.4(2.4A; M.31.169A); ἐπὶ τῶν χερσαίων ψυχὴν ~οῦσαν σώματα Proc.G.*Gen.*1:24(M.87.105C); *order, discipline, control*, Gr.Nyss.*anim.et res.*(M.46.84A); οὕτω τὰ καθ' ἑαυτοὺς ~ῶμεν Chrys.*hom.57.3 in Jo.*(8.336C); *discipline* by penance ὁ τὴν ἀσχημοσύνην ἐν τοῖς ἄρρεσιν ἐπιδεικνύμενος, τὸν χρόνον τοῦ ἐν τῇ μοιχείᾳ παρανομοῦντος ~ηθήσεται Bas.*ep.*217 *can.*62(3.327A; M.32.800A); ὁ γοητείαν ἢ φαρμακείαν ἐξαγορεύων...οὕτως ~ούμενος *ib.can.*65(327C; M.800B); *ib. can.*72(328A; M.801B); ἔξεστι τῷ ~οῦντι...συντεμεῖν τὸν χρόνον τῆς ἀκροάσεως Gr.Nyss.*ep.can.*4(M.45.229B); *administer* as penance τὰ δὲ εἴκοσιν ἔτη οὕτως ~ηθήσεται ἐπ' αὐτῷ Bas.*ep.*217 *can.*56(3.326B; M.797A); **3.** *support, sustain* with necessities of life, Jo.Mosch.*prat.*9(M.87.2860A); ref. God's providence, *A.Thom.*A 28(p.145.2); ref. Ex.34:38 ἐτρέφετο γὰρ ὑπὸ τοῦ θεοῦ, καὶ ᾠκονομεῖτο αὐτοῦ τὸ σῶμα ἄλλῃ τροφῇ ἐπουρανίῳ Mac.Aeg.*hom.*12.14(M.34.565B); ἐκ σοῦ τρέφομαι, καὶ ἀπὸ σοῦ ~οῦμαι εἰς πᾶσαν χρείαν *ib.*33.8(740A); *furnish with*, Gr.Nyss.*Eun.*10(2 p.227.6; M.45.828A); **4.** *dispense, distribute* τὰ εἰσφερόμενα...καλῶς ~είτω ὀρφανοῖς *Const.App.*2.25.2; Pall.*h.Laus.*10(p.30.12; M.34.1028C); *show forth, exhibit* τὴν ἑαυτοῦ δόξαν οἰ. Cyr.*Is.*3.4(2.500E); *administer* a rebuke, Chrys.*hom.4.2 in 2Cor.*(10.457C); **5.** *plan, dispose affairs beforehand* ᾠκονόμει γὰρ καὶ παρεσκεύαζεν Dion.Al.ap.Eus.*h.e.*7.11.14(M.20.668A); **6.** *effect, bring about, contrive*, *T.Sal.*D 4.15; Chrys.*hom.49.1 in Jo.*(8.287E); med., Eus.*h.e.*7.32.8(724B).

B. theol.; **1.** ref. God's providence; **a.** *dispense, bestow* τῆς ἡμέρας ἐκείνης τῆς μεγάλης καὶ φοβερᾶς, ἣν μέλλω οἰ. εἰς τὸν κόσμον *Apoc.Mos.*37(p.20); κἂν...οἱ λόγοι τῶν παρὰ θεοῦ ~ουμένων διαφεύγωσιν ἡμᾶς Bas.*ep.*5.2(3.78A; M.32.240C); δεόμεθα τοῦ ἁγίου θεοῦ ~ηθῆναι δεύτερον ἡμῖν τὴν συντυχίαν ὑμῶν *ib.*314(444E; M.1061C); exeg. Jo.1:14 τὰ διὰ σαρκὸς ~ηθέντα κατ' ἰδίαν ὁρῶμεν Gr.Nyss.*Eun.*5(2 p.123.2; M.45.704D); Epiph.*haer.*64.9(p.418.12; M.41.1084C); ἡ Μαρία...κατ' ἐπαγγελίαν δέ, ὥσπερ ὁ Ἰσαάκ ~ηθεῖσα id.*ep.Arab.ib.*78.23(p.474.14; M.42.737B); Chrys.*hom.12.7 in Col.*(11.422C); **b.** *provide, care, have a regard* for δόξα κ(υρί)ῳ τῷ ~οῦντι ὑπὲρ ὑγίας Νόννου *IG* 12.1.1038 [Carpathus, ? date]; **c.** *effect, bring about* ~ήσαντι...σωτηρίαν καὶ ἀνάστασιν *A.Jo.*79(p.190.20); Or.*princ.*4.2.9(p.321.6; M.11.373B); δι' ἀνθρώπου τὴν ἐπὶ σωτηρίᾳ πάντων ᾠκονομήσατο ἔκβασιν Meth.*Porph.*1(p.504.5; M.18.400A); Bas.*ep.*214.1(3.321A; M.32.785A); **d.** *dispatch, dispose of, settle* affairs, ref. Christ's descent into hell ἡ ψυχὴ ~ησαμένη δέ τινα ἔξω αὐτοῦ Or.*Cels.*2.16(p.145.26; M.11.832A); εἰς τὰ καταχθόνια κατελθόντα καὶ τὰ ἐκεῖσε ~ήσαντα *Symb.Sirm.*3(p.236.1; M.26.693A); **e.** *plan, ordain, arrange beforehand*, *Diogn.*9.1; ἐὰν δέ τι περὶ τῆς ὑμετέρας ζωῆς ὁ κύριος ~ήσῃ Bas.*ep.*81(3.174A; M.32.456C); ταῦτα ᾠκονόμησε γενέσθαι *ib.*101(196D; M.505B); ref. prophecy ἀσφαλῶς τὸ παρὰ τοῦ θεοῦ ~ηθὲν ὡς ἤδη τετελειωμένον ἐκηρύττετο Epiph.*haer.*79.6(p.481.4; M.42.749A); **f.** *ordain, direct, appoint*, *M.Perp.*6(p.73.1); τὴν τῶν σωμάτων διάλυσιν...τῇ τῶν στοιχείων μεταβολῇ ᾠκονόμησε γίνεσθαι Clem.*fr.*42(p.221.2; M.9.768C); Or.*Jo.*10.41(25; p.219.9; M.14.388C); ὁ θεὸς...τὸν πρῶτον Κωνσταντῖνον εἰς ὑποδοχὴν τῆς βασιλείας παρεῖναι ~ησάμενος Eus.*v.C.*1.18(p.17.16; M.20.936A); τοῦ ἁγίου πνεύματος χάρις πολλαχόθεν ἡμῖν ἐγγενέσθαι τὰς θείας περὶ τοῦ μονογενοῦς ὑπολήψεις ᾠκονομήσατο Gr.Nyss.*Eun.*8 (2 p.189.12; M.45.784B); pass. ἡ ~ηθεῖσα ὑπὸ θεοῦ εἰς ἀνθρώπων σωτηρίαν δοθῆναι γραφή Or.*princ.*4.2.4(p.313.3; M.11.365A); *ib.*4.3.10(p.337.2; 392C); ὁ κύριος Ἰησοῦς...προσηλώθη τῷ σταυρῷ ~ούμενος Meth.*Porph.*1(p.503.15; M.18.397D); ἐπὶ τὴν ἀσπόρως ~ηθεῖσαν σύλληψιν Leont.B.*Nest.et Eut.*2(M.86.1328A); of angelic direction, ref. Mt.1:20,2:13, Or.*Cels.*1.66(p.119.25; M.11.784B); **g.** *administer, regulate* τὸ πνεῦμα τὸ ἅγιον, τὴν διανομὴν τῶν χαρισμάτων...~οῦν Bas.*Spir.*37(3.31B; M.32.133C); **h.** *rule, govern, dispose* τοῖς ~ουμένοις καὶ ἀγομένοις ἀνθρώποις ὑπὸ τοῦ λόγου αὐτοῦ Or.*Cels.*2.76(p.199.2; M.11.916B); ὁ θεὸς...~εῖ ὅλους τοὺς αἰῶνας *ib.*4.69(p.339.13; 1137D); κατὰ τὸ βούλημα τοῦ τὰ πάντα ἐπὶ σωτηρίᾳ καὶ συστάσει τῶν ὅλων ~οῦντος Bas.*Eun.*3.7(1.278B; M.29.669A); id.*ep.*193(3.286B; M.32.705C); πῶς τὰ μέσα καὶ τὰ ἀδιάφορα περὶ ἡμᾶς ~εῖται, εἴτε συντυχίᾳ τινὶ αὐτομάτῳ, εἴτε τῇ δικαίᾳ τοῦ θεοῦ προνοίᾳ; *ib.*236.7(364C; M.884C); τινα πράγματα, ἃ ~εῖ ὁ κύριος ἵνα μὴ ἁμάρτυρον ἑαυτὸν ποιήσῃ...καὶ ἔστι τινὰ πράγματα, ἃ οὕτως ~εῖ κατὰ παραχώρησιν Mac.Aeg.*hom.*15.29(M.34.596A); πάντα γὰρ δι' ἡμᾶς καὶ ὑπὲρ ἡμῶν ᾠκονομεῖτο σαφῶς Cyr.*glaph.Ex.*3(1.328E); **2.** *administer, dispense*; so, *utter, interpret* doctrine, *with discretion, accommodate, adapt* to men's condition, or to circumstances, exeg. Jer.20:7 θεὸς ἀπατᾷ; πῶς ~ήσω τὸν λόγον, ἀπορῶ Or.*hom.19.5 in Jer.*(p.173.27; M.13.496B); ref. Christ's ignorance (Mc.13:32) τοῦτο οἰ. διὰ τὴν σὴν ἀσθένειαν Evagr.Pont.*ep.*6(M.32.256A); οὕτω καὶ περὶ τῆς ἡμέρας καὶ τῆς ὥρας κἂν λέγῃ μὴ εἰδέναι, χρήσιμόν τι καὶ ἀγαθὸν ~ῶν, τοῦτο ποιεῖ Cyr.*thes.*22(5[1].221E); *ib.*(222B); ~ῶν τι χρήσιμον μὴ εἰδέναι λέγῃ τὴν ἡμέραν ὡς ἄνθρωπος, καίτοι πάντα εἰδὼς ὡς σοφία τοῦ πατρὸς *ib.*(223A); *ib.*(223E); τοῖς ~ήσασι τὰ καθ' ἡμᾶς πατράσιν ἀκολουθητέον Bas.*ep.*188 *can.*1(3.270C; M.32.669B); Gr.Naz.*or.*43.68(M.36.588A); exeg. Jo.7:8–10 παιδεύων ἡμᾶς τὰ πράγματα ~εῖν Chrys.*hom.49.1 in Jo.*(8.288A); connected with μυστήριον, cf.1Cor.2:7,4:1, Eph.3:9 δι' αὐτοῦ [sc. Moses] πάλιν ὡς ἐν τύπῳ τὸ καλῶς ~ηθὲν μυστήριον Cyr.*glaph.Num.*(1.380A); ἀφ' ὧν ἦν ἀναγκαίως ἄνθρωπον ὄντως ὁρᾶσθαι, ταῦτα ποιεῖ καὶ λέγει, ~ῶν τῷ μυστηρίῳ τὴν ἀλήθειαν id.*thes.*23(5[1].228A); κἂν εἰ πανσόφως αὐτὸς ~ῶν τὸ μυστήριον ἑαυτῷ προσνέμων ὁρῷτο τὰ τῇ ἰδίᾳ σαρκὶ συμβεβηκότα πάθη id.*ep.*39(p.19.8; 5[2].108A); διὰ τούτους...καὶ ἐν τῇ Λυκαονίᾳ τὸν Τιμόθεον περιέτεμε, καὶ ἄλλα μυρία παραπλήσια ᾠκονόμησε Thdt.*1Cor.*9:20(3.223); **3.** med., *effect, contrive* by accommodation ~ούμενός τι θεοσόφως καὶ συμπεριφερόμενος ἐνεργήσει Clem.*str.*1.1(p.12.23; M.8.708A); ἐὰν...ὁ Ἰησοῦς ὑπὲρ ἐπιστροφῆς τῶν ἀκουόντων λέγῃ τὸ 'οὐαὶ' καὶ ἃς νομίζεις λοιδορίας, οὐδὲν ~εῖται πρὸς τοὺς ἀκούοντας; Or.*Cels.*2.76(p.198.25; M.11.916A); οὐδὲν οὖν θαυμαστόν, ᾠκονομηκέναι τοὺς ἑρμηνεύσαντας τὰ περὶ τὴν Σωσάνναν ἀνευρεῖν ἤτοι σύμφωνον τῷ Ἑβραϊκῷ id.*ep.*1(M.11.77A); *contrive in adaptation* τὸ 'πρῶτον' εἴτε μὴ νοήσαντες ἐξεῖλάν τινες τῶν γεγραμμένων εἴτε καὶ ~ήσαντες ἐξελεῖν οἱ Ἑβδομήκοντα, θεὸς ἂν εἰδείη id.*hom.16.5 in Jer.*(p.137.15; M.13.445A); καὶ ᾔδει τὴν προαίρεσιν τοῦ προφήτου μὴ βουλομένου τὰ χείρονα προφητεῦσαι τῷ λαῷ Ἰσραήλ, διὰ τοῦτο ᾠκονόμησεν εἰπεῖν *ib.*20.2(p.178.30; 504A); **4.** *use concealment* in a matter, Dor.*doct.*9.3(M.88.1721B); ref. 1Reg.16:1,2 ἐντεῦθεν διδασκόμεθα ἐν ἐνίοις ~εῖν χρείαν εἶναι τὰ πράγματα Jo.D.*parall.*(M.95.1228A); pass., *be concealed* βέλτιον οὖν ~ηθῆναι τὴν ἀλήθειαν ...ἢ καταλυθῆναι τῷ φανερῷ τοῦ κηρύγματος Gr.Naz.*ep.*58(M.37.116C); **5.** *manage diplomatically, handle with care* τοὺς μὲν οἰ. τοὺς δὲ καθησυχάσαι Bas.*ep.*66.2(3.159D; M.32.425B); **6.** esp. ref. Inc.; **a.** *handle by divine accommodation*, i.e. *by condescension* to human weakness ἄνθρωπος δὲ γενόμενος καὶ ~ήσας τὰ ἀνθρώπινα Ath.*ep.Serap.*2.7(M.26.620C); τὸ βάπτισμα καὶ πάντα τὰ πρέποντα ~ῶν κατεδέχετο Cyr.*deip.BMV* 28(p.31.26; M.76.288C); **b.** *teach by condescension*, ref. Lc.2:51 ~ῶν τὸ ἡμᾶς πατράσι πείθεσθαι Didym.*Trin.*3.20(M.39.893D); **7.** *provide for, have consideration for* ὁ θεός, οὐχ ἕνα ἄνθρωπον ~εῖ, ἀλλ' ὅλον τὸν κόσμον Or.*hom.12.5 in Jer.*(p.92.26; M.13.385D); ἑκατέρους τοίνυν διὰ τῆς προσποιητῆς ἀγνοίας ~εῖ Evagr.Pont.*ep.*6(M.32.256B); μηκέτι τὴν ἐμὴν δειλίαν ~ῶν Gr.Naz.*or.*21.34(M.35.1124B); τὸ μὴ εἰδέναι ~εῖν τὰ τῶν πλησίον Chrys.*hom.36.2 in 1Cor.*(10.335E); ταῦτα...ἀνθρωπίνως ἐφθέγγετο...~ῶν τὴν τῶν Ἰουδαίων ἀσθένειαν Thdr.Mops.*Ps.*54(M.66.677B); pass., ref. flight into Egypt τί οὖν ἄτοπον τὸν ἅπαξ ἐνανθρωπήσαντα...~εῖσθαι πρὸς τὸ ἐκκλίνειν κινδύνους; Or.*Cels.*1.66(p.120.9; M.11.783C).

***οἰκονομητέον,** *one must use accommodation* or *concealment* in doctrine, Gr.Naz.*ep.*58(M.37.117B); cf. οἰκονομέω.

οἰκονομία, ἡ, A. *ministration*; **1.** *management, charge, office* ὃν πέμπει ὁ οἰκοδεσπότης εἰς ἰδίαν οἰ. Ign.*Eph.*6.1; οὐδὲ ἀνθρώπων οἰκονομίαν μυστηρίων πεπίστευνται *Diogn.*7.1; δύναμιν μὲν ἰδίαν ἔχει ἕκαστον τῶν πνευματικῶν καὶ ἰδίαν οἰ. Clem.*exc.Thdot.*11(p.110.20; M.9.661B); ἐπίσκοπος τελευτᾷ, δέκατον τῆς οἰ. ἀποπλήσας ἔτος Eus.*h.e.*4.4(M.20.308C); τοὺς ἐπὶ ταύτην ἥκοντας τὴν οἰ. Chrys.*sac.*3.11

(p.66.25; 1.388D); πρὶν ἐπὶ τὸ χεῖρον τραπῆναι τὴν τοῦ ἀέρος οἰ. ἐπεπίστευτο [sc. Devil] Thdt.*haer*.5.8(4.407); **2.** *direction, governance* over persons ὁ Ῥαφαὴλ φανερῶν ἑαυτοῦ ὡς ἀγγέλου τὴν...πρὸς ἀμφοτέρους οἰ. Or.*or*.11.1(p.321.24; M.11.448C); τῆς αὐτῶν οἰκονομίας *Hom.Clem*.3.64; οἰ. πολλῶν ψυχῶν *A.Andr.et Mt*.3(p.67.13); Chrys.*hom.24.2 in Mt*.(7.301A); **3.** abstract for concrete, *ministry*, ref. appointment of deacons to assist bishops τῆς ἐκκλησίας λαβούσης τὰ πληρώματα τῆς οἰ. Epiph.*haer*.75.4(p.336.28; M.42.509B); **4.** *good management, thrift* ἔστιν οἰ. ἀρετὴ καὶ τὸ οἰκονομικὸν εἶναι· παρυφέστηκεν ἡ φειδωλία καὶ ἡ μικρολογία Chrys.*hom.48.3 in Ac*.(9.362D); cf.Philo ap.Eus.*p.e*.8.12(382D; M.21.648A); **5.** *operation, business, occupation*, *A.Jo*.113(p.213.14); οὐκέτι περὶ τὸν οἶκον εἴη ἂν μόνον ἡ οἰ. ἀλλὰ καὶ περὶ τὴν ψυχήν Clem.*str*.1.6(p.22.17; M.8.728C); οὐκ ἐδύναντο ἕπεσθαι τῷ λόγῳ ἀπιόντι εἰς τὰς ἑαυτοῦ οἰ. Or.*Jo*.32.31(19; p.479.13; M.14.828A); εἰσιέναι δὲ ἐν τῷ ἱερῷ καὶ τὰς ἀτόπους οἰ. ἐξωθεῖν Serap.*Man*.36(p.54; M.18.1216B); πρὸς οἰκονομίαν θεοῦ ἕτοιμος Epiph.*ep.Arab*.ap.*haer*.78.16(p.466.24; M.42.725A); Thdt.*1Cor*.11:1(3.232); **6.** *function*; **a.** in gen. θάτερον δὲ θατέρου [sc. parts of body] ὂν διάφορον κατ' οἰκονομίαν συμφωνίας ἐστὶν ἁρμονία Tat.*orat*.12(p.13.8; M.6.832A); μὴ ἐπιβαίνειν ἐπὶ χειροτονίαις ἢ τισιν ἄλλαις οἰ. ἐκκλησιαστικαῖς CCP(381)*can*.2; of Christ ποιμένα ἑαυτὸν λέγει καὶ πρόβατον καὶ διαφόρως τὰς οἰ. κηρύττει τὰς ἑαυτοῦ Chrys.*hom.59.2 in Jo*.(8.347D); θεὸς ἦν ὁ αὐτὸς καὶ ἄνθρωπος καὶ ἄγγελος...ἀλλὰ τὸ μὲν τῆς ἐνανθρωπήσεως, τὸ δὲ τῆς οἰ., τὸ δὲ τῆς φύσεως Thdr.Mops.*Gen*.32:27(M.66.645A); **b.** Trin. τὸ γὰρ ἀποτμηθὲν τοῦ πρώτου κεχώρισται, τὸ δὲ μερισθὲν οἰκονομίας τὴν διαίρεσιν προσλαβὸν οὐκ ἐνδεᾶ τὸν ὅθεν εἴληπται πεποίηκεν Tat.*orat*.5(p.5.26; M.6.816A); **c.** of one's life's work or career, *Apoc.Bar.rel*.9.29; *ib*. 9.31; ἐν ᾗ...ἡμέρᾳ νοσήσας ἐξετέλει αὐτοῦ τὴν οἰ. *T.Job* 1(p.104.2); hence *destiny* τελείως...ἤκουσας τὴν οἰ. σου *T.Abr*.B 7(p.112.5); **7.** of administrative action, *arrangement, procedure, system* τὰς πολιτικὰς οἰ., τὰς τῶν στρατοπέδων διοικήσεις Eus.*l.C*.18(p.259.17; M.20.1440A); τῇ καινῇ ταύτῃ τῶν πραγμάτων οἰ. Bas.*ep*.76(3.171C; M.32.452A); Thdt.*provid*.7(4.602); of eccl. discipline, Bas.*ep*.217 *can*.60(326E; M.800A); τὴν...κανονικὴν ἐπὶ τῶν πεπλημμεληκότων οἰ. Gr.Nyss.*ep.can*.1(M.45.221B); ἔξεστι τῷ οἰκονομοῦντι πρὸς τὸ συμφέρον τὴν ἐκκλησιαστικὴν οἰ. συντεμεῖν τὸν χρόνον τῆς ἀκροάσεως *ib*.4 (229B); of Mosaic Law, Cyr.*ador*.12(1.444D); hence **8.** *ordinance, provision* τὰς οἰ. τοῦ προεστῶτος Nil.*epp*.2.65(M.79.229A); μὴ οὖν ἐναντιοῦσθε ταῖς ἐμαῖς οἰ. ὡς οὐδὲ πηλὸς κεραμεῖ Proc.G.*Is*.45:9ff. (M.87.2421B); συμπαθητικαῖς οἰ. †Jo.Jej.*poenit*.(M.88.1916C); **9.** *administration*, of alms νομισμάτων εἰς...οἰ. ἀναπαύσεως πενήτων προσφερομένων Or.*Jo*.19.7(2; p.306.32; M.14.537D); τοῦ ἐπιτεταγμένου εἰς οἰ. εὐποιΐας CGangr.*can*.8; Bas.*ep*.236.7(3.364D; M.32. 884D); hence **a.** *relief, support* παρ' ἐμοῦ λαμβάνουσιν εἰς οἰ. τῶν πτωχῶν *T.Job* 11(p.110.15); Bas.*ep*.31(110D; M.313C); τῆς τῶν πτωχευόντων ἐν τῇ ἐκκλησίᾳ οἰ. †Bas.*Is*.50(1.418A; M.30.212A); πεποιηκὼς αὐτῷ οἰκονομίαν Thphn.*chron*.p.118(M.108.332C); **b.** *alms* οἰκονομίας πτωχῶν εἰς ἰδίας ἀπολαύσεις...παραναλισκόντων Bas.*ep*. 92.2(184E; M.480B); cf. εἰ χρὴ ἀπὸ τῆς οἰ. [i.e. monastic funds] διδόναι τοῖς ἐνδεέσι τῶν ἔξωθεν id.*reg.br*.302 tit.(2.522A; M.31.1296C); Diad.*perf*.43(p.50.12); **10.** of eccl. administration in gen., Bas.*ep*. 144(3.236B; M.32.593C); *ib*.188 *can*.1(270B; M.669B); Leont.N.*v.Jo. Eleem*.1(p.5.15); **11.** *tenure of office of* οἰκονόμος: ἐπὶ τῇ οἰ. κυριακοῦ διακόνου...ἐγένετο τὸ ἔργον τοῦτο *IGC As.Min*.238 (Caria, saec. vi–vii).

B. *disposition, organization, constitution*; **1.** physical μέχρι τῶν ἔσω φλεβῶν καὶ ἀρτηριῶν τὴν τῆς σαρκὸς οἰ. θεωρεῖσθαι *M.Polyc*.2.2; τριχῶν διακόσμησις καὶ ἐντοσθίων οἰ. Tat.*orat*.12(p.13.6; M.6.832A); ὀστέων τε καὶ νεύρων...καὶ τῆς λοιπῆς τῆς κατὰ τὸν ἄνθρωπον οἰ. Iren.*haer*.5.3.2(M.7.1130A); τὴν μὲν κατὰ σὲ γέννησιν [MS διήγησιν] ...οὐ δύνῃ ἐξειπεῖν, καίτοι ἑκάστης ἡμέρας ὁρῶν τὴν κατὰ ἄνθρωπον αἰτίαν, καὶ τὴν περὶ τοῦτον οἰ. ... ἐξειπεῖν οὐ δύνασαι...ἀλλ' ἢ μόνον ὁρῶντα...πιστεύειν ὅτι ἔργον θεοῦ ἄνθρωπος Hipp.*Noët*.16(p.261.2; M.10.825B); κατεσθίει τὸ ἧπαρ καὶ πᾶσαν αὐτῶν τὴν οἰ. Jo.D.*drac*. (M.94.1604A); τὴν οἰ. τῆς ἀνθρωπίνης φύσεως ἐκ τοῦ περιέχοντος σώματος ἐξελθοῦσαν παραδεικνύς ‡Jo.D.*Artem*.61(M.96.1309A); **2.** mental *disposition* τῆς δεούσης κατὰ τὴν γνωμὴν οἰ., ἤγουν διακρίσεως Max.*cap*.2.70(M.90.1245C); **3.** Trin., *functional organization, distribution of function*, cf. *unicum quidem deum credimus, sub hac tamen dispensatione, quam oeconomiam dicimus, ut unici dei sit et filius*, Tert.*adversus Praxeam* 2(M.*PL*.2.156B); *quasi non sic quoque unus sit omnia, dum ex uno omnia, per substantiae scilicet unitatem, et nihilominus custodiatur oeconomiae sacramentum, quae unitatem in trinitatem disponit*, *ib*.(157B); *simplices enim quique..., non intellegentes unicum quidem, sed cum sua oeconomia esse credendum, expavescunt, quod oeconomiam numerum et dispositionem trinitatis divisionem praesumunt unitatis, quando unitas, ex semetipsa derivans trinitatem, non destruatur ab illa sed administretur*, *ib*.3 (158A); *ib*.8(164A) cit. s. μοναρχία; *ib*.13(169B); τίς γὰρ οὐκ ἐρεῖ ἕνα θεὸν εἶναι; ἀλλ' οὐ τὴν οἰ. ἀναιρήσει Hipp.*Noët*.3(p.239.11; M.10. 808A); εἰ δὲ βούλεται μαθεῖν πῶς εἷς θεὸς ἀποδείκνυται, γιγνωσκέτω ὅτι μία δύναμις τούτου [sc. θεοῦ], καὶ ὅσον μὲν κατὰ τὴν δύναμιν εἷς ἐστιν θεός, ὅσον δὲ κατὰ τὴν οἰ. τριχῆς ἡ ἐπίδειξις [perh. l. τριχῇ ἐστι τάξις] *ib*.8(p.249.22; 816B); ταύτην τὴν οἰ. παραδίδωσιν ἡμῖν καὶ ὁ μακάριος Ἰωάννης...καὶ τοῦτον τὸν λόγον θεὸν ὁμολογεῖ οὕτως λέγων· [Jo.1:1]...δύο μὲν οὐκ ἐρῶ θεούς, ἀλλ' ἢ ἕνα, πρόσωπα δὲ δύο οἰκονομίᾳ [MS οἰκονομίαν], ⟨τὴν⟩ τε τρίτην τὴν χάριν τοῦ ἁγίου πνεύματος· πατὴρ μὲν γὰρ εἷς, πρόσωπα δὲ δύο ὅτι καὶ ὁ υἱός, τὸ δὲ τρίτον τὸ ἅγιον πνεῦμα. ... οἰκονομία συμφώνως [MS συμφωνίας] συνάγεται εἰς ἕνα θεόν *ib*.14(p.255.26; 821A); of relation of Father to Son in Inc. ἐν τίνι δὲ ὁ θεός, ἀλλ' ἢ ἐν Χριστῷ Ἰησοῦ τῷ πατρῴῳ λόγῳ καὶ τῷ μυστηρίῳ τῆς οἰ.;...τὸ δὲ εἰπεῖν ὅτι 'ἐν σοὶ ὁ θεός ἐστιν' ἐδείκνυεν μυστήριον οἰκονομίας, ὅτι, σεσαρκωμένου τοῦ λόγου καὶ ἐνανθρωπήσαντος, ὁ πατὴρ ἦν ἐν τῷ υἱῷ καὶ ὁ υἱὸς ἐν τῷ πατρί, ἐμπολιτευομένου τοῦ υἱοῦ ἐν ἀνθρώποις *ib*.4(p.241.12; 808D).

C. *dispensation, ordering*; **1.** in gen., of the natural order or natural laws, Clem.*str*.2.18(p.162.21; M.8.1033A); **2.** of divine dispensation in creation and providential ordering of world θείας οἰ. ἡ περίπτωσις Clem.*str*.1.19(p.60.13; 809B); Or.*princ*.3.1.14(p.220.13; M.11.277A); θεία τις ὑπάρχει οἰ. καὶ δύναμις κρειττόνων ἡ συνέχουσα τὰ ὅλα, ἣν καὶ θεὸν δικαίως ἂν εἴποιμεν Meth.*arbitr*.2(p.149.18; M.18. 244C); υἱόν...ὑπηρετήσαντα πρὸς τὴν τῶν ὄντων σύστασιν...πρὸς οἰ. καὶ πᾶσαν πρόνοιαν Eun.*apol*.27(M.30.864C); τὴν τοῦ παντὸς οἰ. καὶ σύστασιν Gr.Nyss.*tres dii*(M.45.126C); Max.*qu.dub*.20(M.90.801B); **3.** of God's special dispensations or interpositions, esp. of grace and mercy οἰκονομίας εἰς τὸν καινὸν ἄνθρωπον...Χριστόν Ign.*Eph*. 20.1; διὰ τῆς οἰ. τοῦ...ἀνατεῖλαι αὐτῷ [sc. Jonah] σικυῶνα Just.*dial*. 107.3(M.6.725A); ἐνταῦθα δὴ μεγάλη τις οἰ. θεοῦ ἐγίνετο *Ep.Lugd*.ap. Eus.*h.e*.5.1.32(M.20.420C); Clem.*str*.1.11(p.34.8; M.8.749C); διηγεῖσθαι τὴν θαυμαστὴν περὶ ἡμᾶς οἰ. τοῦ θεοῦ Dion.Al.ap.Eus.*h.e*.7.11.2 (664A); ἐξ οἰ. τῆς τοῦ θεοῦ προνοίας ἀβλαβῆ Eus.*m.P*.11(p.945.11; M. 20.1509C); οἰ. τις γέγονεν ἐκ θείας προνοίας Ephr.2.187D; οἰ. γὰρ ἦν μεγάλη τὸ μηδαμόθεν πειθόμενον ἄνωθεν καλέσαι [sc. S. Paul] Chrys. *hom.6.2 in Eph*.(11.40E); κατ' οἰκονομίαν δὲ θεοῦ ἀπῆλθεν ὁ γέρων εἰς τὰ μέρη ἐκεῖνα Jo.Mosch.*prat*.83(M.87.2940C); in revelations, prophecies, and types οἰκονομίαι τινὲς μεγάλων μυστηρίων... ἀπετελοῦντο· ἐν γὰρ τοῖς γάμοις τοῦ Ἰακὼβ τίς οἰ. καὶ προκήρυξις ἀπετελεῖτο ἐρῶ Just.*dial*.134.2(M.6.785C); Thphl.Ant.*Autol*.2.12(M. 6.1069B); ref. Gen.19:33 οἰ. ἐπετελεῖτο, δι' ἧς αἱ δύο συναγωγαὶ ἀπὸ ἑνὸς καὶ τοῦ αὐτοῦ πατρὸς τεκνοποιησάμεναι ἐμηνύοντο ἄνευ σαρκὸς ἡδονῆς Iren.*haer*.4.31.1(M.7.1068C); οἰ. τινές εἰσι μυστικαὶ δηλούμεναι διὰ τῶν θείων γραφῶν Or.*princ*.4.2.2(p.309.1; M.11.360B); τὴν ἐπὶ τῇ κιβωτῷ...ἀπόρρητον οἰ. Cyr.*glaph.Gen*.2(1.32C); id.*hom. pasch*.5(5^2.55B); **4.** of divine grace or operation in sacraments: baptism, Or.*hom.16.5 in Jer*.(p.137.24; M.13.445B) cit. s. παλιγγενεσία; προηγεῖσθαι τὴν διὰ τῆς εὐχῆς κλῆσιν τῆς θείας οἰ. Gr. Nyss.*or.catech*.34(p.128.1; M.45.85B); τοῖς διὰ τῆς μυστικῆς ταύτης οἰ. ἀναγεννωμένοις *ib*.(p.129.2; 85C); κατὰ γὰρ τὴν διάθεσιν τῆς καρδίας τοῦ προσιόντος τῇ οἰ. καὶ τὸ γινόμενον τὴν δύναμιν ἔχει *ib*.39(p.156. 4; 100B); eucharist, Epiph.*haer*.75.3(p.334.30; M.42.505C); λατρεία οἰκονομίας ἐν τῇ πέμπτῃ γίνεται id.*exp.fid*.22(p.524.1; M.42.828C); προσευχὰς τελοῦντες καὶ λατρείαν οἰκονομίας *ib*.23(p.524.9; M.l.c.); **5.** of the OT dispensation as a whole, Or.*Cels*.4.9(p.280.15; M.11. 1037D); **6.** of Inc.; **a.** as dispensation of divine purpose ὁ γὰρ θεὸς ἡμῶν...ἐκυοφορήθη ὑπὸ Μαρίας κατ' οἰκονομίαν Ign.*Eph*.18.2; Ath. *decr*.25(p.21.10; M.25.461A); μετὰ τὴν μεγίστην ἐκείνην...οἰ. τοῦ κυρίου, τῆς ἐνσάρκου αὐτοῦ παρουσίας Epiph.*ep.Arab*.ap.*haer*.78.23(p.473.1; M.42.736A); Chrys.*hom.44.3 in Mt*.(7.470C); πῶς μὲν ἄνθρωπος γεννᾶται, νοῆσαι οὐ δύνασαι, θεοῦ δὲ οἰ. ζητήσειν δύνῃ; Procl.CP *or*.2.4 (M.65.697B); **b.** ref. fact of Inc., virtually synonymous with ἐνανθρώπησις: ἐξ ὧν ἔμελλεν ἔσεσθαι, κατὰ τὴν οἰ. τὴν διὰ τῆς παρθένου Μαρίας, ὁ Χριστός Just.*dial*.120.1(M.6.753B); (Valent.) φάσκουσιν ἀπὸ μὲν τῆς Ἀχαμὼθ τὸ πνευματικὸν...ἀπὸ δὲ τῆς οἰ. περιτεθεῖσθαι σῶμα ψυχικὴν ἔχον οὐσίαν Iren.*haer*.1.6.1(M.7.504B); οὐχ ὁ λόγος σὰρξ ἐγένετο, ὅς γε οὐδὲ ἦλθέ ποτε ἐκτὸς πληρώματος, ἀλλὰ ὁ τῆς οἰ. μεταγενέστερος τοῦ λόγου σωτήρ *ib*.1.9.2(541A); (Marcosian) ὁ κατ' οἰκονομίαν διὰ τῆς Μαρίας...ἄνθρωπος *ib*.1.15.3(620B); ἐν γὰρ μάλιστα μετὰ τὴν οἰ. γεγένηται πρὸς τὸν λόγον τοῦ θεοῦ ἡ ψυχὴ καὶ τὸ σῶμα Ἰησοῦ Or.*Cels*.2.9(p.136.31; M.11.809D); id.*fr.18 in Jo*.(p.498.15); Didym.*Trin*.1.15(M.39.328C); ὁ κατ' οὐσίαν ἀμήτωρ καὶ κατ' οἰκονομίαν ἐπὶ γῆς ἀπάτωρ Procl.CP *or.laud.BMV* 4(p.104.24; M.65.

685A); ἀνάγκη διὰ τὴν οἰ. ἴδιον αὐτοῦ σῶμα νοεῖσθαι τὸ πεπονθὸς τὸν θάνατον, ἵνα καὶ αὐτὸς ἀναστῆναι λέγοιτο Cyr.*Pulch.*(p.32.31; 5^{2}.137E); τὴν ἐνανθρώπησιν δὲ τοῦ θεοῦ λόγου καλοῦμεν οἰ. Thdt.*eran.*2(4.93); ἡ εἴσοδος τοῦ εὐαγγελίου τὴν ἔλευσιν τῆς οἰ. μηνύει Jo.Jej.*liturg.*(p.441); ἐκεῖνος [sc. S. Luke] τὸν τῆς οἰ. λόγον δοκεῖ πως λεπτομερέστερον ὑφηγεῖσθαι τῶν ἄλλων εὐαγγελιστῶν Abr.Eph.*annunt.*2(p.443.23); **c.** partic. ref. 'accommodation' or voluntary and contingent self-limitation of Son ἐπὶ τοῦτό γε τέλος τὴν πᾶσαν οἰ. τῆς ἑαυτοῦ κενώσεώς τε καὶ ταπεινώσεως στήσας Eus.*d.e.*10.8(p.489.15; M.22.785C); πρότερον μὲν θεὸς λόγος ὤν, γενόμενος δὲ δεύτερον υἱὸς ἀνθρώπου δι' ἣν ἀνεδέξατο ὑπὲρ ἡμῶν οἰ. *ib.*8.1(p.364.9; 592B); πᾶσάν τε αὐτοῦ τῆς σωτηρίου οἰ. καὶ δι' ἡμᾶς ταπεινώσεως φωνὴν ἐκλεξάμενοι Alex.Al.*ep.Alex.*1(p.20.8; M.18.549A); τῇ μὲν οὐσίᾳ γέννημα τοῦ πατρός, τῇ δὲ οἰ. κατ' εὐδοκίαν τοῦ πατρὸς ἐποιήθη δι' ἡμᾶς ἄνθρωπος Ath.*Ar.*2.11(M.26.169A); εὐλογημένος ὁ ἐλθὼν κατ' οἰ. καὶ δι' ἡμᾶς πτωχεύσας πλούσιος ὤν ‡Ath.*palm.*(M.26.1313A); Bas.*hom. in Ps.*44(1.163D; M.29.400B) cit. s. συγκατάβασις; οἰκονομίᾳ γὰρ ἐδάκρυσεν δι' ἐμέ, καὶ ἐξουσίᾳ τεταρταῖον νεκρὸν ἤγειρέν με ‡Bas.*inc.*53(p.247.5); Gr.Naz.*or.*29.18(p.102.6; M.36.97C); ref. Jo.17:5 οὐ προσθήκην οὖν δόξης αἰτεῖ, ἀλλὰ τῆς οἰ. τὴν φανέρωσιν γενέσθαι Didym.(‡Bas.)*Eun.*4(1.292B; M.29.701A); καὶ πολλὰ τοιαῦτα ἐγένετο, οὐδὲν τούτων τῇ φύσει ὤν, ἀλλὰ δι' ἡμᾶς κατ' οἰκονομίαν γενόμενος Gr.Nyss.*fid.*(M.45.137B); τῆς μετὰ σαρκὸς οἰ. ὁ λόγος καὶ ἡ διὰ τοῦτο λεγομένη ταπείνωσις Cyr.*Jo.*1.3(4.22C); οὐ γὰρ φύσεως ἔχει λόγον ἡ τοῦ θεοῦ λόγου σάρκωσις, ἀλλ' οἰκονομίας ὑπὲρ φύσιν πραττομένης ὑπὸ θεοῦ ἐκ μὲν τῆς κοινῆς καὶ ἀνθρωπίνης ἡμῶν φύσεως ἤτοι οὐσίας· διὸ καὶ...ὁμοούσιος ἡμῖν λέγεται κατὰ τὸν τῆς οἰ. λόγον...οὔτε δὲ φύσις οὔτε οὐσία κοινοῦ τινος ἀνθρώπου προσηγόρευται πώποτε τὸ...σῶμα τοῦ θεοῦ λόγου Tim.II Al.*fr.*(M.86.273D); **d.** Christol.; ref. Person of Word incarnate εἰ οὖν φύσει μεσίτης Χριστὸς θεοῦ καὶ ἡμῶν καὶ οὐ κατ' οἰκονομίαν Didym.(‡Bas.)*Eun.*4(1.288A; M.29.692C); συνενώσας τὴν πᾶσαν οἰ. [sc. of body, soul, and deity] εἰς μίαν ἕνωσιν πνευματικὴν Epiph.*haer.*69.65(p.214.26; M.42.309A); cf. *si tu attribues à dieu le verbe deux natures: dieu et l'homme, et que l'homme ne soit rien...ou bien tu dis seulement le nom et l'apparence de l'homme sans nature qui aurait servi à désigner dieu le verbe; ou (tu fais) comme si l'humanité a été inutile en nature au* prosopon *de l'économie pour nous,* Nest.*Heraclid.*2.1(p.194); τοὺς δὲ λέγοντας ὅτι οὐ χρὴ κοινοποιεῖν τὴν σάρκα τῇ θεότητι...οὐδὲ τὴν θεότητα τῇ σαρκὶ...φαμὲν...τῆς μετὰ σαρκὸς οἰ. ἀγνοῆσαι τὸ μυστήριον Cyr.*resp.*(6^{2}.390B); Leont.B.*Nest.et Eut.*1(M.86.1276C); πρὸς ἀνατροπὴν τῶν συγχεόντων καὶ τεμνόντων τὸ τῆς θείας οἰ. μυστήριον εἰκότως ἐγράψαμεν, καὶ οὐ...σύγχυσιν ἢ διαίρεσιν τῇ θείᾳ οἰ. εἰσάγομεν Justn.*conf.*(p.88.30; M.86.1013A); ταὐτὸν εἶναι φάσκων [sc. Severus] ἐπὶ τῆς οἰ. τῇ φύσει τὴν ὑπόστασιν Max.*opusc.*(M.91.40B); Νεστορίου...τὴν μίαν ὑπόστασιν εἰς ὑποστάσεις δύο μερίζοντος καὶ τὴν ὅλην οἰ. ἀρνουμένου id.*ep.*13(M.91.524A); οἱ διαιροῦντες καὶ οἱ συγχέοντες τὴν...οἰ. id.*Pyrr.*(M.91.316B); τὰς τῶν ἐν αὐτῷ οὐσιῶν ἰδιότητας ἀρνούμενοι φυρμὸν τὸ τῆς οἰ. μυστήριον ἀπεργάζονται Dam.*troph.*suppl.(p.280.8); **e.** partic. ref. human nature alone; Gnost. [sc. Σωτῆρα] εἰληφέναι...ἀπὸ μὲν τῆς Ἀχαμὼθ τὸ πνευματικόν, ἀπὸ δὲ τοῦ Δημιουργοῦ ἐνδεδύσθαι τὸν ψυχικὸν Χριστόν, ἀπὸ δὲ τῆς οἰ. περιτεθεῖσθαι σῶμα ψυχικὴν ἔχον οὐσίαν Iren.*haer.*1.6.1(M.7.504B); τὸ μὲν τῆς οἰ. ἦν τὸ πέταλον περικεῖσθαι καὶ μανθάνειν εἰς γνῶσιν, τὸ δὲ δυνάμεως τὸ θεοφόρον γίνεσθαι τὸν ἄνθρωπον Clem.*exc.Thdot.*27(p.116.14; M.9.673B); τῆς κατὰ τὸν Χριστὸν οἰ. τε καὶ θεολογίας Eus.*h.e.*1.1.7(M.20.49A); οἱ δὲ τὴν ἔνσαρκον οἰ. παραδεδεγμένοι τὸν δὲ πρόοντα τοῦ θεοῦ υἱὸν ἀρνησάμενοι id.*e.th.*1.7(p.65.14; M.24.836B); ὅτε δὲ ὁ κύριος ἐπεδήμησε καὶ πεῖραν ἔσχεν ὁ ἐχθρὸς τῆς ἀνθρωπίνης οἰ. αὐτοῦ, μὴ δυνηθεὶς ἀπατῆσαι τὴν ὑπ' αὐτοῦ φορουμένην σάρκα Ath.*ep.Aeg.Lib.*2(M.25.541A); οὐχὶ θεολογίας ἡμῖν παραδίδωσι τρόπον ἀλλὰ τοὺς τῆς οἰ. λόγους παραδηλοῖ Bas.*Eun.*2.3(1.240A; M.29.577A); ἵνα μὴ...τῇ θεολογίᾳ προσέχοντες τῆς οἰ. καταφρονῶμεν Evagr.Pont.*ep.*3(M.32.252C); ἵνα...ἡ...ἔνσαρκος οἰ. ... συνενωθῇ ἄνω τῷ ἀκτίστῳ λόγῳ Epiph.*haer.*69.42(p.190.11; M.42.268C); τὴν ἔνσαρκον οἰ. σὺν τῷ θεῷ λόγῳ ἡνωμένην εἰς μίαν θεότητα *ib.*69.56(p.204.8; 292A); cf. *dimidiatam Christi introducit* [sc. Apoll.] οἰκονομίαν, Hier.*ep.*84.2(M.*PL.*22.744); Thdr.Mops.*Gen.*32:27(M.66.645A); τὸ γὰρ τῆς οἰ. οὐδὲν ἔβλαψε τὴν θεότητα Thdot. Anc.*hom.*3.4(M.77.1389A); ἡ σμύρνα καὶ ὁ λίβανος, τουτέστιν ἡ θεολογία τε καὶ οἰ. Thdt.*Cant.*3:6(2.83); ref. Mc.4:38 οἰ. καθεύδουσαν βλέπετε...καθεύδει τοίνυν ὁ τοῦ θεοῦ λόγου ναός...ἐφ' ὅσον ἡ τῆς οἰ. βούλεται χρεία Bas.Sel.*or.*22.1(M.85.265B); τὰ περὶ τῆς οἰ. καὶ τῆς θεολογίας ὑπὲρ νοῦν δόγματα ‡Proc.G.*Pr.*31:22(M.87.1540D); Max.*Pyrr.*(M.91.348C); Jo.D.*f.o.*1.2(M.94.792B); **f.** ref. Christ's incarnate life and work, in gen., Just.*dial.*87.5(M.6.684C); ref. acts of Christ πνεῦμα ἅγιον, τὸ διὰ τῶν προφητῶν κεκηρυχὸς τὰς οἰ. ... τοῦ...Χριστοῦ Iren.*haer.*1.10.1(M.7.549A); τὸν Ἰησοῦν τοιαῦτα παρὰ τῇ οἰ. λελαληκέναι Or.*Cels.*2.26(p.155.26; M.11.845C); τὴν ἔνσαρκον ἐπιδημίαν τοῦ λόγου...καὶ τὴν τότε παρ' αὐτοῦ γενομένην οἰ. Ath.*Ar.*1.59(M.26.133C); πᾶσαν τὴν οἰ. πληρώσαντα *Symb.Sirm.*3(p.235.33; M.26.693A); ἐξήγησιν οἰκονομίας τῆς μετὰ σαρκὸς ἣν ἐποιήσατο δι' ἡμᾶς ὁ υἱός Cyr.*Jo.*1.9(4.89B); partic. of Passion and of Christ's redeeming activity in death and Resurrection, Just.*dial.*30.3(540B); τὴν οἰ. ... ἐν τῇ ἕκτῃ τῶν ἡμερῶν...ἧς οἰ. ἀρχὴν καὶ τέλος καὶ τὴν ἕκτην ὥραν ἐν ᾗ προσηλώθη τῷ ξύλῳ Iren.*haer.*1.14.6(M.7.608A); γέγονεν ἄρα τις καθολικὴ κίνησις...κατὰ τὴν οἰ. τοῦ σωτῆρος Clem.*str.*6.6(p.455.18; M.9.269A); ἐπεγράφη τὴν ὑπὲρ ἀνθρώπων οἰ. τελοῦντι· οὗτός ἐστιν ὁ βασιλεὺς τῶν Ἰουδαίων Or.*fr.in Pr.*1:1(p.524); τὸ μετὰ τὴν οἰ. ἐμφύσημα Gr.Naz.*or.*41.11(M.36.444B); τὸ περὶ Ἰωνᾶ...ὃ τὴν οἰ. σημαίνει τοῦ σωτῆρος Epiph.*haer.*42.11(p.135.9; M.41.744A); ὁ σωτὴρ ἐπὶ τοῦ σταυροῦ τὴν ἔνθεον οἰ. ἐπλήρου Ant.Ptol.*Adam*(p.652.13); of other actions or events in Christ's life τὴν περὶ τὸ ποτὸν οἰ. Or.*Jo.*13.32(31; p.256.3; M.14.453B); τῆς κατὰ τὸν ἐν Κανᾷ...γάμον οἰ. *ib.*10.3(2; p.172.30; 309B); μετὰ τὴν ἐν τῷ ὄρει οἰ. id.*comm.in Mt.*12.43(p.169.19; M.13.1084B); Eus.*h.e.*10.4.46(M.20.868B).

D. *adaptation of means to ends, prudent handling* of any matter; **1.** in gen., *prudence, discretion* μετ' οἰκονομίας περιϊστάμενον τοὺς κινδύνους μὴ ὁμόσε αὐτοῖς χωρεῖν Or.*Cels.*1.61(p.112.29; M.11.773A); **2.** *consideration* for special circumstances, *concession* τὸ ἐν φανερῷ εἶναι Ἰουδαῖοι διὰ τὴν τῶν πολλῶν σωτηρίαν κατ' οἰκονομίαν οὐ μόνον λόγοις ὁμολογοῦντες ἀλλὰ καὶ διὰ τῶν ἔργων δεικνύντες Or.*Jo.*1.7(9; p.12.22; M.14.37A); τὰ ὑποπτευθέντα κατ' οἰκονομίαν ἔγραψεν. οὐ δεῖ δὲ τὰ κατ' οἰ. γραφόμενα...ταῦτα κακοτρόπως δέχεσθαι...καὶ διδασκάλου δὲ φρονίμου τρόπος οὗτος πρὸς τὰ τῶν διδασκομένων ἤθη διατίθεσθαι καὶ λαλεῖν Ath.*Dion.*6(p.50.7; M.25.488B); διὰ τὴν οἰ. καὶ τὴν ἐν καιρῷ διδασκαλίαν *ib.*9(p.52.8; 492C); οὐδὲ γὰρ ὑπόκρισις τὸ πρᾶγμά ἐστιν, ἀλλ' οἰκοδομὴ καὶ οἰ. Chrys.*hom.26.2 in Rom.*(9.714A); ὁ μὲν γὰρ ὀφείλων μεγάλα περὶ ἑαυτοῦ φθέγγεσθαι, ὅταν μικρόν τι εἴπῃ καὶ ταπεινόν, πρόφασιν εὐπρόσωπον ἔχει οἰκονομίας τινὸς ἕνεκεν τοῦτο ποιῶν· ὁ δὲ εὐτελῆ λέγειν ὀφείλων περὶ ἑαυτοῦ, ἂν μέγα τι εἴπῃ, τίνος ἕνεκεν τὰ ὑπερβαίνοντα αὐτοῦ τὴν φύσιν φθέγγεται; τοῦτο γὰρ οὐκ ἔτι οἰκονομίας τινὸς ἀλλ' ἐσχάτης ἀσεβείας ἐστίν id.*hom.39.1 in Jo.*(8.227A); οἰκονομίας ἕνεκα μὴ ἀκριβολογεῖσθαι σφόδρα περὶ τοὺς μεταγινώσκοντας· οἰκονομίας γὰρ...δεῖται τὸ πρᾶγμα πολλῆς Cyr.*ep.*57(p.21.25; 5^{2}.192D); οὐδὲ αὐτὸν ὑπέθηκεν ὀνομαστὶ τῷ ἀναθεματισμῷ δι' οἰκονομίαν, ἵνα μή τινες τῇ ὑπολήψει τοῦ ἀνδρὸς προσεσχηκότες ἀποβάλωσιν ἑαυτοὺς τῶν ἐκκλησιῶν· ἡ δὲ ἐν τούτοις οἰ. ἄριστόν τι χρῆμα καὶ σοφόν id.*ep.*72(p.18.18; 200B); ἀφεκτέον συνεσθίειν [sc. with those conforming to heresies], εἰ μή τι οἰκονομίας τρόπῳ, καὶ τοῦτο σπανιώτερον Thdr.Stud.*epp.*2.219.5(M.99.1661C); **3.** *accommodation*, ref. attribution to God of ὀργή, θυμός etc. οἰκονομίαι χρήσεως λέξεών εἰσι...ἐπεὶ καὶ ἡμεῖς τοῖς παιδίοις πρόσωπον ποιοῦμεν οὐκ ἀπὸ διαθέσεως ἀλλὰ κατ' οἰκονομίαν φοβερόν Or.*hom.18.6 in Jer.*(p.160.15; M.13.477C); ταῦτα δὲ πάντα, τὸ κατελθεῖν λέγων ἐξ οὐρανοῦ τὸ πνεῦμα..., οἰκονομίας ἕνεκεν γέγραπται, οὐχ ἱστορικὴν διήγησιν ἔχοντα ἀλλὰ θεωρίαν νοητήν id.*fr.20 in Jo.*(p.501.17); οὐ δεῖ οὖν τὰ κατ' οἰκονομίαν ὡς ἁπλῶς εἰρημένα ἐκδέχεσθαι Didym.(‡Bas.)*Eun.*4(1.290D; M.29.697B); καὶ γὰρ καὶ τὸ ἐπὶ τῆς ἐγγαστριμύθου τούτῳ προσέοικε τῆς οἰ. τῷ τρόπῳ Chrys.*hom.6.3 in Mt.*(7.91B); εἰπεῖν δὲ τοῖς μαθηταῖς οὐ θελήσας διά τινα λόγον οἰκονομίας ἀπόρρητον...καὶ τὸν υἱὸν ἔφησε μὴ εἰδέναι, ἀνθρωπινώτερον μὲν περὶ ἑαυτοῦ λέγων ὥσπερ περὶ ἀνθρώπου, φυλάττων δὲ ἑαυτῷ τὸ εἰδέναι πάλιν πάντα ὡς θεός Cyr.*thes.*22(5^{1}.219C); οἰ. τινὸς ἕνεκεν τὸ μὴ εἰδέναι ποῦ κεῖται Λάζαρος ἔφασκεν *ib.*(221E); ref. Gen.3:9;4:9 εἰ δὲ τρόπον οἰκονομίας εἰσάγεσθαί τινα διὰ τοῦτο δώσετε, μὴ ξενίζεσθε κἂν ὁ τοῦ θεοῦ λόγος ...οἰκονομῶν τι χρήσιμον μὴ εἰδέναι λέγῃ τὴν ἡμέραν ὡς ἄνθρωπος *ib.*(223A); εἰ ἀληθεύει λέγων ὁ σωτὴρ 'πάντα μοι παρεδόθη ὑπὸ τοῦ πατρός μου'...οὐκ ἐξ ἀσθενείας ἔφησεν 'οὐκ ἔστιν ἐμὸν δοῦναι', ἀλλ' ἔχει λόγον οἰκονομίας τὸ ῥῆμα *ib.*26(244C); πολλάκις καὶ ἅπερ οἶδεν ὡς θεός, ἀγνοεῖν ὡς ἄνθρωπος σχηματίζεται...ὅρα μοι τὴν ἐν τῷ πράγματι πεπλασμένην οἰ.· εἰδὼς γὰρ ὅτι τέθνηκε Λάζαρος...ἀντεπύθετο 'ποῦ τεθείκατε;' id.*Jo.*5.5(4.529C); ref. Christ's prayer in Gethsemane οὐκ ἀπότευξιν γενέσθαι φαμὲν ἐν τῇ τοῦ σωτῆρος προσευχῇ, οἰ. δὲ μᾶλλον id.*Is.*4.4(2.669A); ref. S. Paul's difference of manner in addressing various audiences ἔστι δὲ αὐτοῦ τὰς παντοδαπὰς οἰ. ἰδεῖν Thdt.*1Cor.*9:21(3.223); **4.** *prudent handling* or *explanation* of text οἰ. δεῖται γενναίας τὰ λεχθησόμενα Or.*hom.19.15 in Jer.*(p.173.28; M.13.496B); ἔχει τινὰ σοφὴν καὶ ἀναγκαίαν οἰ. ὁ λόγος Cyr.*Ps.*62:12(M.69.1124D); **5.** *prudent reserve* ἐκεῖνα μὲν κατ' οἰκονομίαν, ταῦτα δὲ ὡς ὁ τῆς εὐσεβοῦς πίστεως βούλεται λόγος, εἴρηκε Ath.*Dion.*24(p.64.12; M.25.516B); ref. Basil's reticence on deity of H. Ghost ἀποβλέποντες εἰς τὸν σκοπὸν τῆς ἀληθείας αὐτοῦ καὶ τὴν οἰ., δοξαζέτωσαν τὸν κύριον τὸν δεδωκότα τῇ

Καππαδοκίᾳ τοιοῦτον ἐπίσκοπον id.*ep.Pall.*(M.26.1168D); *οὐ παρρησιάζονται, εἴτε οἰ. τινὶ χρώμενοι περὶ τὸν λόγον, εἴτε δειλίᾳ* Gr.Naz.*or.* 42.14(M.36.473C); *ib.*43.68(588B); Chrys.*hom.1.1 in Ac.*(9.2E) cit. s. *συγκατάβασις*; *συμβουλῆς...σιγὴν παραινεσάσης καὶ τὴν καλουμένην οἰ.* Thdt.*ep.*122(4.1204); **6.** *diplomacy, management, strategy ἔδοξέ τισι τῶν κατὰ τὴν Ἀσίαν, οἰκονομίας ἕνεκα τῶν πολλῶν, δεχθῆναι αὐτῶν τὸ βάπτισμα* Bas.*ep.*188.*can.*1(3.270B; M.32.669A); *ib.*199 *can.* 47(296E; M.732A); *περιέτεμεν ἵνα καθέλῃ περιτομήν· διὰ τοῦτο οὐκ εἶπεν "Ἰουδαῖος" ἀλλ' "ὡς Ἰουδαῖος", ὅπερ οἰ. ἦν* Chrys.*hom.22.2 in 1Cor.*(10.195A); *εἶτα ἡ οἰ. αὐτοῦ· 'γέγονα τοῖς Ἰουδαίοις ὡς Ἰουδαῖος* id.*hom.6.3 in Eph.*(11.42D); *manœuvre, stratagem* involving 'pious deception' *ποικίλας καὶ πολλὰς συντίθησιν ἀπολογίας...τοσαύτῃ κέχρηται λόγων οἰ. ἵνα μὴ πλήξῃ τοὺς ἀκούοντας* id.*hom.16.2 in Mt.* (7.205B); ref. Gal.2:14 *οὐ μάχης ἦν τὰ ῥήματα ἀλλ' οἰκονομίας* id. *comm.in Gal.*2:11f.(10.688A); cf. *ἀκούων ταῦτα Πέτρος συνυποκρίνεται ὡς ἁμαρτάνων ib.*2:13(688D); *πολλὴ γὰρ ἡ τῆς ἀπάτης ἰσχύς, μόνον μὴ μετὰ δολερᾶς προσαγέσθω τῆς προαιρέσεως. μᾶλλον δὲ οὐδὲ ἀπάτην τὸ τοιοῦτον δεῖ καλεῖν, ἀλλ' οἰ. τινὰ καὶ σοφίαν καὶ τέχνην ἱκανὴν πολλοὺς πόρους ἐν τοῖς ἀπόροις εὑρεῖν* id.*sac.*1.5(p.23.23; 1.370D); *ὅτι μὲν οὖν ἔστι καὶ ἐπὶ καλῷ τῇ τῆς ἀπάτης κεχρῆσθαι δυνάμει, μᾶλλον δὲ ὅτι μηδὲ ἀπάτην δεῖ τὸ τοιοῦτον καλεῖν, ἀλλ' οἰ. τινὰ θαυμαστήν, ἐνῆν μὲν καὶ πλείονα λέγειν ib.*2.1(p.25; 371D); *ἔστι γὰρ καὶ καλὴ ἀπάτη...ἣν οὐδὲ ἀπάτην δεῖ καλεῖν· περὶ ἧς φησιν ὁ Ἱερεμίας, ἠπάτησάς με κύριε ...ἐπεὶ καὶ τὸν πατέρα ἠπάτησεν ὁ Ἰακώβ, ἀλλ' οὐκ ἀπάτη ἀλλ' οἰ. ἦν* id.*hom.6.1 in Col.*(11.365E); Philost.*h.e.*4.12(M.65.528A); †Leont.B. *sect.*6.6(M.86.1237D); ‡Cyr.*Trin.*17(6^{3}.23E; M.77.1156C); †Jo.D.*B.J.* 30(M.96.1148C); *trick,* Jo.D.*parall.*(M.95.1225B); *connivance* at evil, †Jo.D.*B.J.*30(1148B); v. *συγκατάβασις.*

οἰκονομικός, 1. *concerned with management γραφικήν, οἰ., ἰατρικήν* [sc. *τέχνην*] Juln.ap.Cyr.*Juln.*7(6^{2}.235C); hence *belonging to a steward οἰ. προστασία* Isid.Pel.*epp.*3.216(M.78.900A); **2.** *careful, prudent τὸ τῶν ἀνθρώπων περὶ τὴν τροφὴν οἰ.* Or.*Cels.*4.83(p.353. 4; M.11.1156C); *νοήσωμεν τὸ οἰ. τῆς γραφῆς φόβον θεοῦ γεννῆσαι βουλομένης* †Bas.*Is.*265(1.581B; M.30.585A); *οὐκ οἰκονομικοί, πηλῷ μαργαρίτην πιστεύοντες* Gr.Naz.*or.*41.6(M.36.437B); esp. ref. expenditure, *economical ὁ...δίκαιος...οὐ...ἀπολαυστικός ἐστι τῶν δεδομένων, ἀλλὰ οἰ.* Bas.*ep.*236.7(3.364E; M.32.885A); id.*hom.*7.3(2.54E; M.31. 288B); Chrys.*sac.*3.16(p.87.15; 1.397D); **3.** *accommodating, politic εἶναι οἰκονομικὸν τῷ εἰδέναι πῶς δεῖ ἑνὶ ἑκάστῳ ἀποκρίνασθαι* Chrys. *hom.6.3 in Eph.*(11.43A); *γέγονεν οἰ. καὶ λοιπὸν ἤσθιε πάντα τὰ παρατιθέμενα Apophth.Patr.*(M.65.172A); *τὸν τῆς οἰ. καὶ κατὰ περίστασιν συμβάσεως τρόπον* Jo.VI CP *ep.*(M.96.1428A); *πάντα τὰ ἀνθρώπινα τοῦ Χριστοῦ τὰ ἐν εὐαγγελίοις ἀναγεγραμμένα ἐν δοκήσει... καὶ σκιᾷ τινι οἰκονομικῇ ἤτοι προσποιητῇ πεπράχθαι τε καὶ λελέχθαι διδάσκων* Anast.S.*haer.*(p.260); **4.** *relative, conditional ἐν τῇ παλαιᾷ διαθήκῃ οὐκ ἦν ἡ κλῆσις δικαία, ἀλλ' οἰ., προκατασκευάζουσα ὁδὸν τῇ δικαιοσύνῃ* ‡Chrys.*leg.*2(6.406D); **5.** *voluntary, deliberate ὡσάν τις... ἐλεύθερος ὢν δοῦλον ἑαυτὸν παραδίδωσιν...ἵνα...ἐλευθερώσῃ τῇ ἑαυτοῦ οἰ. δουλείᾳ τοὺς πολίτας* Or.*comm.in Rom.*6:8ff.(*JTS* 13 p.365); Max.*carit.*4.96(M.90.1072B); **6.** *providential, by* divine *dispensation*; **a.** in gen. *κατὰ τὴν οἰ. προδιατύπωσιν* Clem.*paed.*1.6(p.105.12; M.8. 280C); *οὐ κατὰ τὴν τῶν ἀνθρώπων βούλησιν ἡ ἀλήθεια ἔχει τὴν δύναμιν, ἀλλὰ κατὰ τὴν αὐτῆς διακυβερνητικὴν σοφίαν καὶ οἰ. ἀκαταληψίαν* Epiph.*haer.*77.25(p.438.11; M.42.677A); *οἰ. ἐπιφορᾶς διὰ τῆς προνοίας ἐπαγομένης* Max.*carit.*2.41(M.90.997B); **b.** esp. of Inc., *dispensational, pertaining to the dispensation of the Incarnation* (sts. = *incarnational*) *τὴν οἰ. αὐτοῦ πρὸς ἀνθρώπους ἐπιδημίαν* opp. *τὴν αἰώνιον τοῦ μονογενοῦς ὕπαρξιν,* Bas.*ep.*210.3(3.315A; M.32.772B); *περὶ τῆς...οἰ. τοῦ θεοῦ λόγου δι' ἡμᾶς κενώσεως* Didym.*Trin.*3.10(M. 39.853C); *τὴν...οἰ. γέννησιν* Cyr.*Is.*2.1(2.192D); *ὁ...λόγος...προῆλθεν ἄνθρωπος...οὐ μεταβολῇ φύσεως...ἀλλ' εὐδοκίᾳ μᾶλλον οἰκονομικῇ* id. *ep.*45(p.153.4; 5^{2}.137A); *κένωσις δὲ τῷ θεῷ λόγῳ...τὸ δρᾶσαί τι καὶ εἰπεῖν τῶν ἀνθρωπίνων διὰ τὴν πρὸς σάρκα σύνοδον οἰ.* id.*apol.Thdt.*4 (p.125.26; 6^{1}.219C); *γέγονεν ἴδιον τῆς ἀνθρωπότητος ἐν Χριστῷ τὸ μονογενὲς διὰ τὸ ἡνῶσθαι τῷ λόγῳ κατὰ σύμβασιν οἰ.* id.*inc.unigen.*(5^{1}. 700B); *ἀνθρωπότητι γὰρ καθ' ἕνωσιν οἰ. ἀπορρήτως συνενηνεγμένος ὁ ἐκ θεοῦ λόγος νοεῖται Χριστός, ἀνωτέρω μὲν ἀνθρωπότητος ὡς φύσει θεός..., οὐκ ἀτιμάζων δὲ καὶ τὸ ἐν ὑφέσει γενέσθαι δοκεῖν διὰ τὸ ἀνθρώπινον ib.*(698C); *Χριστὸν Ἰησοῦν ὀνομάσας, δι' αὐτοῦ τὰ πάντα γενέσθαι φησίν, ὡς ἑνὸς ὄντος υἱοῦ καθ' ἕνωσιν οἰ.* id.*Arcad.*(p.76.10; 5^{2}.63C); *εἷς γὰρ κύριος Ἰησοῦς Χριστὸς καθ' ἕνωσιν οἰ., τὴν πρὸς...τὸν ἐκ θεοῦ λόγον ib.*(p.86.2; 78B); *Χριστὸς καὶ κύριος εἷς καθ' ἕνωσιν οἰ. συνενεχθέντος τοῦ λόγου πρὸς τὸ ἀνθρώπινον ib.*(p.106.1; 107E); *οὐκ ἄρα ψιλῇ συναφείᾳ τῇ πρὸς θεὸν λόγον τετιμημένος ἄνθρωπος ὁ Χριστός, συνόδῳ δὲ μᾶλλον τῇ πρὸς τὸ ἀνθρώπινον καθ' ἕνωσιν οἰ. υἱὸς εἷς καὶ κύριος* id.*Pulch.*(p.44.3; 5^{2}.154C); id.*apol.Thdt.*1(p.212.15; 6^{1}.206B); *ib.*6(p.129.27; 224A); *ἔστιν οὖν ὁ λόγος οὐκ ἀσθενείας ἀπόδειξις, ἀλλ' οἰ. ἀσθενείας* [i.e. in respect of the Incarnation] id.*thes.*26(5^{1}.243E).

οἰκονομικῶς, 1. *prudently οἰκονομικώτατα δὲ περιέκρυβεν ἑαυτὴν ἡ Ἐλισάβετ* Or.*schol.in Lc.*1:24(M.17.320A); **2.** *relatively, conditionally τὸ...ἁρμόζον τοῖς πολλοῖς μετὰ τοῦ οἰ. ἀληθοῦς* opp. *τὰ βαθύτερα,* Or. *Cels.*5.19(p.20.23; M.11.1209A); Cyr.*Abac.*35(3.549E); *κἂν τῇ παλαιᾷ οἰ. ἡ θεία γραφὴ λέγει πολλά* Thdt.*eran.*2(4.110); hence in various senses opp. absolutely; *progressively, according to capacity καθ' ἡλικίαν καὶ προκοπὴν οἰ. δεδομέναι* [sc. *διαθῆκαι*], *δυνάμει μία οὖσαι* Clem.*str.*2.6(p.128.24; M.8.964C); *ἡ χάρις οἰ. παιδεύει ἕως ὅτε φθάσῃς εἰς τέλειον ἄνδρα* Mac.Aeg.*hom.*32.10(M.34.740D); *with accommodations, in a modified form,* Or.*ep.*1.12(M.11.77B); Cyr.*Juln.*10(6^{2}. 360A); *for a particular purpose, in special circumstances οἰ. ἐν αὐτοῖς* [sc. Balaam and Caiaphas] *ὁ λόγος οὐ κατὰ τὴν ἀξίαν, ἀλλὰ πρὸς τὸν καιρόν* †Bas.*Is.*4(1.381A; M.30.125A); *οὐ γὰρ ἔδει πρόφασιν αἰσχρᾶς...ζωῆς γενέσθαι πολλοῖς τὸ οἰ. πρὸς ἕνα κατὰ καιροὺς εἰρημένον* Cyr.*Os.*2(3.11A); *κηρύττεται δὲ καὶ διὰ τῶν...γραμμάτων, ποτὲ μὲν ὡς ὅλος ὢν ἄνθρωπος, σεσιωπημένης αὐτοῦ τῆς θεότητος οἰ.· ποτὲ δὲ αὖ πάλιν ὡς θεός, σεσιωπημένης αὐτοῦ τῆς ἀνθρωπότητος* id.*Thds.*29(p.60.27; 5^{2}.25D); **3.** *deliberately, voluntarily ταύτην* [sc. wealth] *οἰ. ἀποθέσθαι βέλτιον* Mac.Mgn.*apocr.*3.12(p.83.21); Cyr. *Jo.*2.5(4.210D); *ἔστιν ὅτε πτωχοτέρως τῶν καθ' ἡμᾶς δείκνυσιν ὁ Χριστὸς ἐν ἑαυτῷ τὰ καθ' ἡμᾶς ἑκουσίως καὶ οἰ.* Anast.S.*hod.*13(M. 89.221C); **4.** *diplomatically, by way of accommodation,* Clem.*paed.* 2.1(p.166.6; M.8.405B); *τυπικά τινα ποιεῖν, ἵνα τοὺς τῷ τύπῳ δεδουλωμένους οἰκονομικώτατα ἐλευθερώσας τῶν τύπων προσαγάγῃ τῇ ἀληθείᾳ* Or.*Jo.*13.18(p.242.26; M.14.429B); *ἀπολογίαν πιθανὴν ἐπορίσαντο, καὶ ἔδοξε τοῦτό πως οἰ. γενέσθαι* Ath.*ep.Rufin.*(M.26. 1180C); Chrys.*hom.65.3 in Mt.*(7.648B); *οἰ. οὐκ ἐμνημόνευσεν τοῦ ἀνδρὸς...ὀνομαστί* Cyr.*ep.*72(p.18.17; 5^{2}.200B); *οἰ. τοίνυν ἀγνοεῖν ὑπεκρίνετο πάσης ἅμα κτίσεως γινώσκων ἀπόρρητα* ‡Caes.Naz.*dial.*30 (M.38.893); **5.** *providentially, by* divine *dispensation*; **a.** in gen. *οἰ. ἐποίησε γενέσθαι τὸν λιμὸν ἵνα δι' αὐτὸν κατελθόντες εἰς Αἴγυπτον* Ath.*exp.Ps.*104:16(M.27.444C); Gr.Nyss.*or.catech.*8(p.43.16; M.45. 33D); Chrys.*hom.18.4 in 1Cor.*(10.157D); *οἰ. συμβέβηκέ σοι τοῦτο* Nil.*epp.*2.283(M.79.341B); **b.** esp. ref. Inc., *according to the dispensation of the Incarnation, incarnately,* with additional sense of *by way of accommodation* or *limitation*; hence freq. = *ἀνθρωπίνως*: *ταῦτα δὲ πάντα Χριστὸς οἰ. ὡς ἄνθρωπος ηὔχετο, θεὸς ὢν ἀληθινός* Hipp. *Jud.*4(p.20.11; M.10.789C); id.*theoph.*2(p.258.10; M.10.853B) cit. s. *φυσικῶς*; *ἅπερ οἶδε φυσικῶς ὡς θεός, ταῦτα πάλιν ἀκούειν λέγεται διὰ τὸ ἀνθρώπινον οἰ.* Ath.*exp.Ps.*44:2(M.27.208C); *οἰ. ὁ σεσαρκωμένος θεὸν ἑαυτοῦ τὸν πατέρα καλεῖ ib.*88:27(389C); *τὴν μὲν φύσιν νόει θεοπρεπῶς, τὰ δὲ ταπεινότερα τῶν ῥημάτων δέχου οἰ.* Bas.*hom.*15.2(2.132D; M.31. 468C); *τὸ τῆς ἀγνοίας ἐπὶ τὸν οἰ. πάντα καταδεξάμενον, καὶ προκόπτοντα...σοφίᾳ καὶ χάριτι, λαμβάνων τις* id.*ep.*236.1(3.361D; M.32. 877C); *οὐκ ἄλλου καὶ ἄλλου θελήματος ἔμφασιν ἔχει...ἀλλ' ἑνὸς καὶ τοῦ αὐτοῦ, θεϊκῶς μὲν ἐνεργουμένου οἰ. δὲ παραιτουμένου τὸν θάνατον* Apoll.*fr.*109(p.233.6)ap.Max.*opusc.*(M.91.169D); *ἡ δόξα οἰ. κατασκηνοῖ ἐν τῇ γῇ ἡμῶν* Gr.Nyss.*Apoll.*17(M.45.1157A); Epiph.*haer.*69. 61(p.209.24; M.42.300C); *τεταπείνωκεν ἑαυτὸν καθεὶς οἰ. ἐν τοῖς τῆς ἀνθρωπότητος μέτροις* Cyr.*Chr.un.*(5^{1}.742B); *ὁ κένωσιν τὴν ἐθελούσιον οἰ. δι' ἡμᾶς ὑπομείνας* id.*Pulch.*3(p.27.29; 5^{2}.130C); *θεὸς μὲν τῇ φύσει, ἄνθρωπος δὲ καθ' ἡμᾶς ὁ αὐτὸς οἰ., ὅτε γέγονεν ἐκ γυναικὸς κατὰ σάρκα* id.*Arcad.*(p.82.30; 5^{2}.73C); *τὰ πρέποντα σῴζειν βουλόμενος πάντα οἰ. ἐποίει, καὶ συνεχώρει τῇ σαρκὶ δεικνύειν τὰ αὐτῇ ἀκόλουθα* id.*deip. BMV* 28(p.31.21; M.76.288C); *ἣν* [sc. *ἡμέραν*] *ἀγνοεῖν ἔφησεν οἰ., ἀποσῴζων πάλιν τῇ ἀνθρωπότητι τὴν αὐτῇ πρέπουσαν τάξιν· ἀνθρωπότητος γὰρ ἴδιον τὸ μὴ εἰδέναι τὰ μέλλοντα* id.*thes.*22(5^{1}.218C); *οὐ κατὰ φύσιν ὁ πατὴρ τοῦ υἱοῦ θεὸς λέγεται, ἀλλὰ καθὸ γέγονεν ἄνθρωπος οἰ. ib.*9(71E); *ἔκλαυσεν ἀνθρωπίνως ἵνα τὸ σὸν περιστείλῃ δάκρυον... ἐδειλίασεν οἰ. ... ἵν' ἡμᾶς εὐτολμωτάτους ἀποφήνῃ* id.*apol.Thdt.*10 (p.139.19; 6^{1}.234A); *ἀλώβητον...ἐν ἑαυτῷ τὸ τῆς ἰδίας φύσεως ἀνασῴζων ἀξίωμα, προσλαβὼν δὲ τὸ ἀνθρώπινον οἰ.* id.*dial.Trin.*1(5^{1}.405A); *τὰ μὲν θεολογικῶς, τὰ δὲ οἰ. ἡ θεία λέγει γραφή...οὐ χρὴ τὰ οἰ. εἰρημένα τοῖς θεολογικοῖς συναρμόττειν* Thdt.*eran.*2(4.110); *ἀκούων τόν... υἱὸν προσευχόμενον, κατὰ τὸν τῆς ἐνανθρωπήσεως λόγον λάμβανε· προσεύχεται γὰρ οἰ., θαυματουργεῖ δὲ θεοπρεπῶς...εἷς καὶ ὁ αὐτός* Leont.B.*parasc.*(M.86.1997B); *φαίνεται γὰρ ὁ αὐτὸς ὡς ἄνθρωπος, καὶ τὸ κατὰ φύσιν ὑπάρχων θεός, θέλων οἰ. παρελθεῖν τὸ ποτήριον* Max. *opusc.*(M.91.84B); *ὅ τε λόγος θεός ἐστι κατὰ φύσιν καὶ οὐ σάρξ, εἰ καὶ οἰκείαν ἐποιήσατο τὴν σάρκα οἰ.* id.*ep.*12(M.91.472C); *τὰ μὲν γάρ... κατὰ φύσιν οἰ. πέπρακταί τε καὶ λέλεκται, οἷον ὁ ἐκ παρθένου τόκος...ἡ πεῖνα, ἡ δίψα...τὰ δὲ κατὰ προσποίησιν, οἷον τὸ ἐρωτᾶν ποῦ τεθείκατε Λάζαρον* Jo.D.*f.o.*4.18(M.94.1185B).

οἰκονόμος, ὁ, A. *steward*; **1.** ref. spiritual things *συγκοπιᾶτε* ἀλλήλοις...ὡς θεοῦ οἰκονόμοι Ign.*Polyc*.6.1; ὁ ἐμὸς κύριος...τὸν οἰ. τὸν ἑαυτοῦ οὐ καταδικάσει Just.*dial*.125.2(M.6.765C); exeg. 1Cor.4:1 οἰκονόμους δὲ εἶπε, δεικνὺς ὡς οὐχ ἅπασιν αὐτὰ χρὴ διδόναι Chrys.*hom.10.2 in 1Cor*.(10.83A); λάβωμεν τὸν μισθὸν τῶν πιστῶν καὶ φρονίμων οἰ. *Lit.Jac*.(p.194.19); of pastors ὡς κακοὶ οἰ. τῶν ψυχῶν Bas.*reg.br*.149(2.465D; M.31.1181A); πᾶσι τοῖς ψυχῶν οἰ., καὶ τοῦ λόγου ταμίαις Gr.Naz.*or*.42.13(M.36.473A); of administrator of penance ἐπισκοποῦντος δηλαδὴ τοῦ οἰ. ἐξ αὐτοῦ τοῦ βίου τὴν ἰατρείαν Gr.Nyss.*ep.can*.8(M.45.236A); **2.** of a state official; also of a city official, Thdt.*Rom*.16:23(3.162); **3.** of an eccl. administrator, local official having charge of revenues and property τοὺς οἰ. τῆς ἐκκλησίας Bas.*ep*.237.1(3.365B; M.32.885B); ὥστε γνώμῃ παντὸς ἱερατείου οἰ. ἀποδειχθῆναι ἕτερον Thphl.Al.*common*.9(M.65.41D); οἰ. γὰρ εἴρηται παρὰ τὸ οἰκεῖα αὐτῶν νέμειν τοῖς πένησιν Isid.Pel.*epp*.1.269 (M.78.341C); *ib*.2.127(568B); βούλονται γὰρ τοὺς μὲν οἰ. τῆς ἐκκλησίας, ἤτοι τοὺς τῶν ἐκκλησιαστικῶν πραγμάτων χειριστὰς ἐκβαλεῖν Cyr.*ep*. 77(p.66.34; 5².209A); περὶ δὲ τῆς ἐκκλησιαστικῆς προσόδου καὶ τῶν ἐξ οἱασδήποτε αἰτίας προσποριζομένων τῇ ἁγιωτάτῃ ἐκκλησίᾳ...διοικεῖται τὰ πράγματα διὰ οἰ. ἐκ τοῦ κλήρου προβαλλομένων Phot.Tyr.*libell*. (p.16.1; H.2.505C); τὴν μέντοι πρόσοδον τῆς χηρευούσης ἐκκλησίας σώαν παρὰ τῷ οἰ. τῆς αὐτῆς ἐκκλησίας φυλάττεσθαι CChalc.*can*.25; πᾶσαν ἐκκλησίαν ἐπίσκοπον ἔχουσαν καὶ οἰ. ἔχειν ἐκ τοῦ ἰδίου κλήρου οἰκονομοῦντα τὰ ἐκκλησιαστικὰ κατὰ γνώμην τοῦ ἰδίου ἐπισκόπου *ib*.26; οἰ...οἰ. δαπάνην ἐκ τῶν ἐκκλησιαστικῶν ἐπιδοῖεν πόρων Justn.*nov*.3.2 (p.22.36); πρεσβύτερος καὶ οἰ. *Chron.Pasch*.p.378(M.92.968B); περὶ τοῦ χρῆναι τὸν οἰ. ἐκ τοῦ κλήρου τῆς ἐκκλησίας εἶναι Phot.*nomoc*.10.1 tit.(p.456; M.104.1144B); τῶν τῆς ἐκκλησίας ἀρχόντων...πρῶτός ἐστιν ὁ μέγας οἰ. *Euchol*.(p.226); duties, *ib*.(p.228); rite of institution in office, *ib*.(p.232); διακόνου [κ]αὶ οἰ. *CIG* 4.8822 (Phrygia, ? date); **4.** of a monastic official [οἰ]κονόμους τῆς μονῆς *PLond*.1913.13; τοῦ οἰ. ἐζήτησα χρείαν Ephr.2.124F; Pall.*h.Laus*.10(p.30.11; M.34.1028C); Dor.*doct*.9.2(M.88.1720A); ὁ τῆς Μεγίστης λαύρας οἰ. Cyr.S.*v.Sab*.58 (p.159.25); Jo.Mosch.*prat*.5(M.87.2856D); Thdr.Stud.*epp*.2.50(M.99. 1260C); **5.** of dispensers of alms in gen., exeg. 1Cor.16:2 γενοῦ φύλαξ χρημάτων ἱερῶν, αὐτοχειροτόνητος οἰ. πενήτων Chrys.*hom.43.1 in 1Cor*.(10.401B).

B. *administrator, governor*; met., of God πάντων...οἰκονόμον Ar. *ep.Alex*.(p.243.30; M.26.709A); ἕνα τὸν τῆς δημιουργίας ἁπάσης οἰ. Eus.*d.e*.4.1(p.151.4; M.22.252B); ὁ σοφὸς τῆς ζωῆς ἡμῶν οἰ. Bas.*ep*. 263.1(3.405A; M.32.976C); ὁ τῶν ὅλων ἀγαθὸς οἰ. Gr.Nyss.*bapt.diff*. (M.46.416C); of Christ ὁ ἡμέτερος καλὸς οἰ. *A.Phil*.18(p.10.5); οἰ. πάντων Didym.*Trin*.3.4(M.39.836D); of H. Ghost εἷς οἰ., ἓν γὰρ τὸ πνεῦμα τοῦ θεοῦ, τὸ διέπον τὰ πάντα Iren.*haer*.4.36.6(M.7.1098A); pagan Κρόνος...τῆς εἱμαρμένης οἰ. Tat.*orat*.9(p.10.24; M.6.828A); of invisible agents assisting in government of Nature, Or.*Cels*.8.31 (p.246.27; M.11.1561D).

***οἰκοπαῖς**, ὁ, *house-servant*, v.l. *T.Abr*.B 14(p.118.26n.).

***οἰκοποι-έω**, *build a temple*, met. ὁδοποιεῖν...ἑαυτοὺς τῷ κυρίῳ παιδευόμεθα, καὶ ~εῖν δι' ἐναρέτου πολιτείας ‡Caes.Naz.*dial*.30(M.38.893).

οἶκος, ὁ, **1.** *house, dwelling-place*; hence *household* ἀσπάζομαι τοὺς οἰ. τῶν ἀδελφῶν μου σὺν γυναιξὶ καὶ τέκνοις Ign.*Smyrn*.13.1; of a bishop's household (ref. 1Tim.3:2,4) οἰ. δὲ κυριακὸν 'μιᾶς γυναικὸς' συνίστησι συζυγία Clem.*str*.3.18(p.246.19; M.8.1212B); **2.** *house, lineage*, ref. Mt.21:9,15 ζητήσεις δὲ πότερον ταυτόν ἐστιν οἰ. Δαυίδ, καὶ υἱὸς Δαυίδ. καὶ εἰ μὴ ταυτόν ἐστιν, ἡμάρτηται τὸ κατὰ Ματθαῖον γραφικῶς ὀφεῖλον ἔχειν ἤτοι δὶς τῷ οἴκῳ Δαυίδ, ἤτοι τῷ υἱῷ Δαυίδ Or.*sel.in Ps*.9:2(M.12.1184C); **3.** *house* of God or of prayer, *shrine, (church-)building* ἐπεισελθόντες εἰς τὸν οἰ. τοῦ θεοῦ προσευχομένων ἐκεῖ πάντων Hipp.*Dan*.1.20.3(M.10.693D); μήτε τῶν ἐκκλησιῶν τοὺς οἰ. καθελὼν Eus.*h.e*.8.13.13(M.20.780B); cf. οἰ. ἐκκλησιῶν οἰκοδομεῖν *ib*.9.9a.11(829A); ἵνα αὖθις ὦσιν Χριστιανοὶ καὶ τοὺς οἰ. ἐν οἷς συνήγοντο, συνθῶσιν Galerius *ib*.8.17.9(793B); οἰ. εὐκτήριον θεοπρεπῆ ἀμφὶ τὸ σωτήριον ἄντρον Eus.*v.C*.3.29(p.91.9; M.20.1089A); *ib*.3.43(p.96.1; 1104A); τῶν αἱρετικῶν τοὺς εὐκτηρίους, εἴ γε εὐκτηρίους ὀνομάζειν οἴκους προσήκει Const.*ib*.3.65(p.112.29; 1141C); εἴ τις διδάσκοι, τὸν οἰ. τοῦ θεοῦ εὐκαταφρόνητον εἶναι..., ἀνάθεμα ἔστω CGangr.*can*.5; περὶ τοῦ μὴ συγχωρεῖν τοῖς αἱρετικοῖς εἰσιέναι εἰς τὸν οἰ. τοῦ θεοῦ ἐπιμένοντας τῇ αἱρέσει CLaod.*can*.6; ὁ οἰ. ἔστω ἐπιμήκης, κατὰ ἀνατολὰς τετραμμένος *Const.App*.2.57.3; μήτε γὰρ εἶναί τι κοινὸν τάφοις καὶ εὐκτηρίοις οἰ. Bas.Sel.*v.Thecl*.2.15(M.85.592C); ἐποίησε... εὐκτήριον οἰ. μέγαν τῆς δεσποίνης ἡμῶν τῆς θεοτόκου, ἀνανεώσας καὶ τὸν οἰ. τοῦ ἁγίου Προκοπίου *Chron.Pasch*.p.327(M.92.841A); οἰ. τῶν ἁγίων Μακκαβαίων *ib*.392(1005D); in conjunction with various adjs.: *basilica* τοῦ βασιλείου οἰ. Eus.*v.C*.3.36(p.94.8; 1096C); *ib*.4.59 (p.141.22; 1209B); *oratory* τὰς πάντων ἔκρουε κέλλας, συνάγων αὐτοὺς εἰς τοὺς εὐκτηρίους οἰ. Pall.*h.Laus*.43(p.130.16; M.34.1210C) v. supra; *vestibule* εἰς τὸν προαύλιον τοῦ βαπτιστηρίου οἶκον Cyr.H.*catech*.19.2; of a martyr's shrine ἀνεδομήσατο αὐτῶν [sc. relics of the forty martyrs] οἶκον *Chron.Pasch*.p.319(813A); οἰ. σωμάτων παλαιῶν ἀνδρῶν καὶ ἐνίων γε ἐπ' εὐσεβείᾳ μαρτυρουμένων ‡Jo.D.*Artem*.55 (p.92.15; M.96.1301D); of any grave or tomb οἰ. αἰώνιος *CG–CI* 1 pp.93 (Salamis, ? date) and 101 (Athens, ? saec. iv); οἰ. δὲ τοῦτον ἐδωρήσατό μοι πατὴρ Διονύσιος *BCH* 7 p.239 (Corycus, saec. iv–v); τετράσωμον δὲ ὗκον *MAMA* 1.235 (Phrygia, ? date); **4.** met.; **a.** of Church τὸν οἰ. τοῦ θεοῦ Herm.*sim*.9.14.1; Const.*ep*.ap.Eus.*v.C*.2.55 (p.63.36; M.20.1029D); τὸν φαιδρότατον τῆς σῆς ἀληθείας οἰ. *ib*.2.56(p.64. 13; 1032B); Bas.*hom.in Ps*.29(1.124E; M.29.308A) cit. s. ἐγκαινισμός; **b.** of individuals τὸ γὰρ ἔνοικον πνεῦμα, λοιπὸν οἰ. θεῖον τὴν διάνοιάν σου ἐργάζεται Cyr.H.*procatech*.6; ἡ παρθένος...ἔστω ἁγία σώματι καὶ ψυχῇ..., ὡς οἰ. Χριστοῦ *Const.App*.4.14.2; οἰ. γὰρ θεοῦ ἑαυτὸν ἐτέλεσας *BCH* 7 p.239 (Corycus, ? date); of unregenerate heart οἰ. δαιμονίων *Barn*.16.7; **c.** of Christ's body, exeg. Pr.9:1 τὸν οἰ. τὴν τῆς σαρκὸς τοῦ κυρίου κατασκευὴν διὰ τοῦ λόγου αἰνίσσεται Gr.Nyss.*Eun*.3(2 p.16. 12; M.45.580D); κατεσκεύασεν οἰ. τὴν ἐκ παρθένου σάρκα...ἢ καὶ οἰ. τὴν ἐκκλησίαν...ἢ τὸν σοφὸν ἄνδρα Chrys. *fr.in Pr*.9:1(p.166; M.64. 679A); exeg. Ps.29:1 v. s. ἐγκαινισμός; exeg. Cant.2:4 'εἰς οἰ. τοῦ οἴνου': εἰς τὸ τοῦ κυρίου σῶμα συγκεράσατέ με Ph.Carp.*Cant*.40(M. 40.61C); **d.** of heaven τῆς κλήσεως χάριν καὶ τῆς εἰς οἰ. ἀνακομιδῆς Clem.*str*.7.11(p.46.3; M.9.488C); *A.Petr.et Paul*.82(p.215.16); **e.** of God, exeg. Jer.12:7 ἴδε αὐτοῦ οἰ. ὄντα τὸν θεόν Or.*hom.10.7 in Jer*. (p.77.12; M.13.365C); **5.** met., a kind of *hymn* as a building composed of praises, *Euchol*.(pp.54,57,531,541); **6.** astrol. τὰς δὲ δεκαδύο θύρας τοὺς δώδεκα οἰ. ἱστόρησε τοῦ ζωδιακοῦ Jo.Mal.*chron*.p.175(M. 97.280D); of planetary houses or spheres, followed by that of the fixed stars ἔλθε ἡ μήτηρ τῶν ἑπτὰ οἰ., ἵνα ἡ ἀνάπαυσίς σου εἰς τὸν ὄγδοον οἰ. γένηται *A.Thom*.A 27(p.142.18).

οἰκουμένη, ἡ, [sc. γῆ]; **1.** *inhabited land*, of Judaea τὴν οἰ. τὴν ἀοίκητον Chrys.*hom.7.1 in Mt*.(7.104A); of scenes of S. Paul's preaching, id.*hom.32.4 in Rom*.(9.759C); **2.** *world*; of Roman empire; also οἰ. ... τὴν Βαβυλῶνα λέγει Thdt.*Is*.13:9(p.67.3; 2.262); roughly, of Mediterranean world, Chrys.*hom.div*.8.1(12.372C); of Western world, Bas.*ep*.243.1(3.373A; M.32.904B); **3.** *earth, world*, loosely or generally σύ, κύριε, τὴν οἰ. ἔκτισας *1Clem*.60.1; ref. Sap.1:7 εἰ τὴν οἰ. πληροῖ Didym.*Trin*.3.2(M.39.804C); σὺ γὰρ ὁ σταυρωθεὶς... ἀνεφάνης τῆς οἰ. δημιουργός Chrys.*exp.in Ps*.8:4(5.86B); τῷ ἐνδύσαντι τὴν οἰ. ἀθανασίαν, τούτῳ προσπέσωμεν Sever.*creat*.5.9(M.56. 483); as scene of life and activity of Christ and Church τῶν κατὰ τὴν οἰ. ἐκκλησιῶν *M.Polyc*.5.1; Just.*dial*.53.5(M.6.593B); ἡ μὲν γὰρ ἐκκλησία, καίπερ καθ' ὅλης τῆς οἰ. ἕως περάτων τῆς γῆς διεσπαρμένη Iren.*haer*.1.10.1(M.7.549A); εἰ μὴ τὰ τῆς οἰ. τῇ Ἰησοῦ ἐπιδημίᾳ μετεβέβλητο πανταχοῦ ἐπὶ τὸ ἡμερώτερον Or.*Cels*.2.30(p.158.19; M.11. 852A); Χριστὸν Ἰησοῦν, ἵνα συναναγραφεὶς τοῖς ἐν τῇ οἰ. ἁγιάσῃ τὴν οἰ. id.*hom.11 in Lc*.(p.82.8f.); κατῆλθεν εἰς τὴν καθ' ἡμᾶς οἰ. ὁ λόγος καὶ ἐσαρκώθη Meth.*res*.2.24(p.380.13; M.18.329D); Eus.*h.e*.4.15.15(M.20. 348B); τὰς καθ' ὅλης τῆς οἰ. ἐκκλησίας *ib*.5.21.1(485D); πάσης τῆς οἰ. τὴν ἀποστολικὴν πίστιν κρατούσης Ath.*ep.Jov*.2(M.26.817A)ap.Thdt. *h.e*.4.3.9; id.*ep.Afr*.1(M.26.1029A); ἐκ τοῦ πλήθους τῶν κατὰ τὴν οἰ. ἐπισκόπων Bas.*ep*.204.7(3.307A; M.32.753C); διδάσκαλος τῆς οἰ. ... ὁ Χριστός Ammon.*Jo*.15:13(M.85.1496B); ἐπὶ σωτηρίᾳ τῆς οἰ. Chrys. *hom.32.4 in Rom*.(9.759C); διδασκάλῳ [sc. Basil] τῆς οἰ. Thdt.*h.e*. 4.19.12(3.982); so of Chrysostom, id.*ep*.151(4.1313); in connexion with primacy of Roman see τὴν τῆς οἰ. προκαθημένην id.*Rom*. 16:16(3.160); and city, id.*ep*.113(1187); of see of Constantinople Νεστόριος...τῆς κατὰ Κωνσταντινούπολιν τῶν ὀρθοδόξων καθολικῆς ἐκκλησίας τὴν προεδρίαν πιστεύεται, οὐδὲν δὲ ἧττον καὶ τῆς οἰ. ἁπάσης id.*haer*.4.12(4.370); Eustrat.*v.Eutych*.10(M.86.2285C); **4.** *the whole world*, i.e. *everybody*, colloquially ὅταν ἡ οἰ. πᾶσα παρῇ Chrys.*hom. 87.1 in Mt*.(7.818C); **5.** of inhabited world opp. desert, ‡Pall.*h.mon*. 1.54(p.21.2,4; M.34.1124D); *ib*.2.5(p.25.20; 1027C); **6.** of another world, CAlex.*ep*.ap.Ath.*apol.sec*.8(p.94.25; M.25.264B); Chrys.*hom. 69.4 in Mt*.(7.685B); of world to come, exeg. Heb.2:5, id.*hom.4.1 in Heb*.(12.39C); οἰ. μέλλουσαν τὸν μέλλοντα βίον ἐκάλεσε Thdt.*Heb*. 2:5(3.556); **7.** of world as fallen into sin πέπτωκεν ἡ οἰ. καὶ δεῖται ἀνορθώσεως Or.*hom.8.1 in Jer*.(p.56.29; M.13.337B); τὴν οἰ. ἐπ' ὄψιν κειμένην Chrys.*pan.Bab*.1.1(2.532C).

οἰκουμενικός, *of the whole world, world-wide, universal*; **1.** in gen. ἀγὼν ἰσελαστικὸς ἔσται εἰς πόλιν οὐράνιον, οἰ. δέ τε πᾶσιν *Orac.Sib*. 2.40; of Flood, Or.*sel.in Gen*.(M.12.109A); ἵνα καθολικὸν γεῦμα παράσχῃ τῆς οἰ. σωτηρίας Tit.Bost.*fr.Lc*.11:14(p.203); Ἰησοῦς τὰς οἰ. ἁμαρτίας ἀναλαβὼν ἀπέθανεν Cyr.H.*catech*.3.12; εἰ ὁ πρωτόπλαστος ἀπὸ γῆς ἤνεγκεν οἰ. θάνατον *ib*.13.2; ἡ οἰ. γῆ *ib*.15.24; ref. Ac.15:29 ἐξ ἁγίου πνεύματος οἰκουμενικόν ἐστι τὸ διάταγμα *ib*.17.29; ref. Mal.

1:11,14 θεῷ τῷ εἰπόντι περὶ τῆς οἰ. αὐτοῦ ἐκκλησίας *Const.App.*7. 30.2; ὁ τῆς οἰ. νηστείας δημιουργός Pall.*v.Chrys.*12(p.76.8; M.47.43); ἡμέραν τῆς οἰ. διαγνώσεως Nil.*epp.*3.133(M.79.445A); τῆς οἰ. χάριν εἰρήνης Attic.*ep.Cyr.*(p.24.24; M.77.352B); κριτὰς ἐσχήκαμεν οἰ. τοὺς ἁγίους μαθητὰς Cyr.*glaph.Gen.*7(1.229C); of apostles ἰατροὺς ἀπέδειξεν οἰ. id.*glaph.Dt.*(1.426D); οἰ. ὀνομάζει φθορὰν τὴν κατὰ πολλῶν ἐθνῶν γενομένην Cyr.*Is.*2.5(2.335C); τῇ οἰ. καὶ τῇ ἡμετέρᾳ εὐπραγίᾳ Basilisc. *encycl.*(p.51.14; M.86.2601C); of acknowledged doctors, e.g. Ath., Cyr.ap.Jo.D.*Jacob.*(M.94.1497A); Chrys., *Theodori lapsi responsio* tit.(int. opp. ‡Chrys.; Gaume 1.801A); **2.** of councils, *general, oecumenical*; **a.** of Nicaea (325), Eus.*v.C.*3.6(p.79.26; M.20.1060B); ἡ οἰ. σύνοδος...τὸν Ἄρειον ἐξέβαλε τῆς ἐκκλησίας Ath.*Ar.*1.7(M.26.25B); id.*syn.*33.1(p.260.31; M.26.752A); id.*ep.Afr.*2(M.26.1032B); Epiph. *haer.*70.9(p.242.4; M.42.353C); cf. τῆς κατὰ Νίκαιαν ὁρισθείσης οἰ. καὶ ἐκκλησιαστικῆς πίστεως Marcell.*ep.ib.*72.11(p.265.25; M.42.397B); **b.** of other specified councils, Sardica, Justn.*conf.*(p.106.2)ap. *Chron.Pasch.*p.369(M.92.944C); CP(381), CCP(382)*ep.*ap.Thdt.*h.e.*5. 9.13(3.1032); Eph.(431), CEph.(431)*can.*proem.(*ACO* 1.1.3 p.26.8; H.1.1621A); Chalc., Thdr.Al.*libell.*(p.15.32; H.2.321D); Nic. (787), Thdr.Stud.*epp.*2.162(M.99.1516A); **c.** of councils specified by number τῶν ἐγκρίτων οἰ. πέντε συνόδων CLater.*can.*17; μνήσθητι, κύριε, τῶν ἁγίων μεγάλων καὶ οἰ. ἓξ συνόδων *Lit.Jac.*(p.216.18); τῶν ζ′ οἰ. συνόδων ‡Anast.Ant.*serm.*4(M.89.1397A); **d.** in gen. ἄνευ ἐπικρίσεως συνόδου οἰ. ἀναβαπτίζειν τοὺς ἐρχομένους...ἀπὸ Ἀρειανῶν Epiph.*exp. fid.*13(p.513.24; M.42.808A); ἢ οἰ. σύνοδον ταράττειν CCP(381)*can.*6; ἕως ἂν δῷ κύριος χώραν οἰ. συνόδου Pall.*v.Chrys.*20(p.140.20; M.47. 78); **3.** as title, *universal, oecumenical*, of pope of Rome οἰ. ἀρχιεπισκόπῳ καὶ πατριάρχῃ Thdr.Al.*libell.*(p.15.31; H.2.321D); *Libell.* ap.CCP(536)*act.*1(*ACO* 3 p.136.30; H.2.1204A); Const.Pogon.*sacr.*1 (M.*PL.*87.1147A); of patriarch of CP Μηνᾶς ἀρχιεπίσκοπος...καὶ οἰ. πατριάρχης Menas *ep.Anthim.*(H.2.1253E; v.l. p.176.31); Const. Pogon.*sacr.*2(H.3.1049A); of Dioscorus of Alexandria, cf. *universalis archiepiscopus Dioscurus*, Olympius Evazensis ap.CEph.(449)(H. 2.229B); of patriarchal sees τῶν μεγάλων καὶ οἰ. θρόνων, Ῥώμης τε, φημί, καὶ Κωνσταντινουπόλεως, Ἀλεξανδρείας τε καὶ Ἀντιοχείας καὶ Ἱεροσολύμων Thphn.*chron.*p.2(M.108.60A).

***οἰκουργέω**, *keep house, perform household tasks*, *1Clem.*1.3.

οἰκουρ-έω, *keep house*, fig. ~εῖ γὰρ ἐν τῷ νῷ τούτων ἡ κακία πολλάκις Mac.Aeg.*elev.*20(M.34.905C); exeg. Cant.2:9 ἔνδον ~οῦσαν τὴν νύμφην Gr.Nyss.*hom.5 in Cant.*(M.44.864C).

οἰκουρία, ἡ, *housekeeping*, Clem.*str.*4.8(p.275.26; M.8.1272C); Chrys.*hom.20.7 in Eph.*(11.154B).

οἰκουρικός, *home-made*, Clem.*paed.*3.11(p.273.17; M.8.641B).

οἰκοφθορία, ἡ, 1. *ruin of property*, Dionysius Halicarnassensis ap.Eus.*p.e.*4.16(158D; M.21.277B); **2.** *corruption of homes*, Bas.*ep.* 289(3.427C; M.32.1025B).

οἰκοφθόρος, ὁ, *corrupter of a home*, Ign.*Eph.*16.1; *Orac.Sib.*2.257.

***οἰκτείρησις, ἡ**, *mercy*, Clem.*paed.*1.9(p.141.12; M.8.353C).

οἰκτείρ-ω (οἰκτειρ-έω), 1. *pity, have compassion on*, of Logos ὁ δὲ οὐ νῦν γε πρῶτον ᾤκτειρεν ἡμᾶς τῆς πλάνης Clem.*prot.*1(p.8.1; M.8. 61C); ὁ θεὸς ~ήσας ἡμᾶς...κατέπεμψεν βοήθημα Meth.*symp.*4.2(p.47. 9; M.18.88D); ὁ τοῦ θεοῦ λόγος...τὴν ἀσθένειαν ἡμῶν ~ήσας...λαμβάνει ἑαυτῷ σῶμα Ath.*inc.*8.2(M.25.109B); pass. οἰκτίρμων καρδία δῆλον ὅτι ~ήσεται Marc.Er.*opusc.*1.27(M.65.909A); **2.** *lament*, *Pers.*208ᵃ (p.3.24).

οἰκτιρμός, ὁ, *mercy, pity, compassion*, plur. ἀθετήσας γάρ τις νόμον Μωσέως, χωρὶς οἰ. ... ἀποθνήσκει Cyr.*Ps.*6:2(M.69.744A); of God ἔδωκέ με ὁ κύριος εἰς οἰ. ἐνώπιον τοῦ δεσμοφύλακος *T.Jos.*2.3; τοὺς προσπεφευγότας τοῖς οἰ. αὐτοῦ *1Clem.*20.11; λυτήριοι δὲ καὶ οἱ τοῦ θεοῦ πάντως οἰ. θανάτου καὶ ἁμαρτημάτων Meth.*symp.*10.2(p.123. 14; M.18.196A); τὸ πλῆθος τῶν οἰ. τοῦ θεοῦ Cyr.H.*catech.*2.6; ὁ νόμος τῆς ἐλευθερίας...πληροῦται διὰ τῶν οἰ. τοῦ κυρίου ἡμῶν Ἰησοῦ Χριστοῦ Marc.Er.*opusc.*1.30(M.65.909B); τεθαρρηκὼς εἰμὶ εἰς τοὺς οἰ. τοῦ υἱοῦ Jo.Mosch.*prat.*36(M.87.2885B).

***οἰκτός**, *open*; of ears, Gr.Naz.*carm.*2.2(poem.)6.76(M.37.1548A).

οἰκτρός, 1. *pitiable, lamentable* οἰκτρότατον δὲ τὸ στέρεσθαι τῆς παρὰ τοῦ θεοῦ ἐπικουρίας Clem.*prot.*10(p.75.7; M.8.220C); **2.** *mean, base* ὁ Χριστὸς καὶ ἐνεπτύετο καὶ ἐρραπίζετο παρὰ ἀνδραπόδων οἰ. Chrys.*hom.33.2 in 1Cor.*(10.301B); **3.** *lowly* ὁ τῶν ὅλων...κύριος, οἰκτροτάτην οὕτω τὴν δουλείαν πρὸς τοὺς ἑαυτοῦ μαθητὰς ἐπεδείξατο Cyr.*Jo.*9(4.722C).

***οἰκτροφανής**, *miserable in appearance*, ‡Nil.*perist.*9.6(M.79.873D).

οἰκωφέλεια, ἡ, *housekeeping*, Gr.Naz.*or.*18.8(M.35.993C); id.*ep.*12 (M.37.45A).

***οἰκωφελ-έω**, met., *benefit spiritually, edify* οἱ σοφοὶ οἴδασι... ~εῖν τοὺς ἀκούοντας ‡Proc.G.*Pr.*15:2(M.87.1369C).

οἶμος, ὁ, *path*; fig., Dion.Ar.*c.h.*15.9(M.3.337D).

[*]**οἰμόσσω**, for οἰμώσσω, = οἰμώζω, *wail*, Anast.S.*hex.*12(M.89. 1073C).

οἰνάριον, τό, *wine*; plur. with sing. meaning βρώσιμά τινα καὶ οἰ. *Chron.Pasch.*p.396(M.92.1013B).

[*]**οἰνεών, ὁ**, *wine harvest*, Mac.Aeg.*hom.*26.11(M.34.681B).

οἰνηγία, ἡ, *conveyance of wine*, Clem.*paed.*2.2(p.174.21; M.8. 425A).

οἰνίζ-ω, 1. *indulge in wine*, med. τινὲς τῶν ἀνοήτων σήμερον πρὸς τὰς πέντε τῶν νηστειῶν ἡμέρας ~ονται Bas.*hom.*2.7(2.15B; M.31.196B); **2.** *resemble wine*; in colour of eyes, Isid.Pel.*epp.*4.114(M.78.1188A).

οἰνοβαρέω, *be heavy with wine*, Clem.*paed.*2.2(p.169.9; M.8. 413B); *ib.*2.9(p.206.29; 496A).

[*]**οἰνοβραχής**, *wetted with wine* σεμίδαλις οἰ. Cyr.*ador.*17(1.623B).

οἰνοδοσία, ἡ, *bestowing of wine*, of miracle at Cana τὴν ἀγεώργητον οἰ. ‡Meth.*palm.*3(M.18.389A).

***οἰνοδυνάστης, ὁ**, *one powerful in drinking wine*, Isid.Pel.*epp.*1. 359(M.78.384A).

***οἰνολίβανος, ὁ**, *wine mingled with frankincense*; as diet for elephants, *Chron.Pasch.*p.176(M.92.432C).

οἰνομανής, *mad for* or *with wine*, Pall.*v.Chrys.*4(p.25.15; M.47. 16).

***οἰνόμαχλος**, *lustful for* or *with wine*, Clem.*paed.*2.2(p.176.24; M. 8.429B).

***οἰνοπαής**, *wine-coloured*; of eyes, Jo.Mal.*chron.*5 p.105(M.97. 196A); *ib.*10 p.259(393C); *ib.*11 p.280(424A).

***οἰνόπληκτος**, *drunken with wine*, Bas.*hom.*13.5(2.126D; M.31. 453B).

***οἰνόπολος**, *concerned with wine*, *Orac.Sib.*3.442.

οἰνοποσία, ἡ, *drinking of wine* ἐν τῷ παραδείσῳ...οὔπω οἰ. Bas. *hom.*1.3(2.3C; M.31.168B); ref. 1Tim.5:23 μέτρα καὶ ὅρους ἡμῖν τίθησι τῆς οἰ. Chrys.*stat.*1.4(2.6E); Pall.*h.Laus.*proem.(p.13.6; M.34.1004).

οἰνοποτ-έω, *drink wine* οὐ κωλυτέον...οἰ. Clem.*str.*3.12(p.235.16; M.8.1185C); μετ' Ἰησοῦ ἐν σοφίᾳ ~ήσωμεν, εἰ χρῄζει τὸ σῶμα Pall. *h.Laus.*proem.(p.13.15; M.34.1003).

οἰνοπωλεῖον, τό, *wine-shop*, †Bas.*Is.*154(1.488C; M.30.372A).

οἶνος, ὁ, *wine*; **1.** in gen.; **a.** temperate use prescribed or allowed in moral teaching ὀλίγῳ δὲ τῷ οἴνῳ [ref. 1Tim.5:23] κἀνταῦθα· οὐ γὰρ μέχρι τῶν ὕβρεως προϊτέον κρατήρων Clem.*paed.*2.2(p.169. 15; M.8.413B); used by Christ, *ib.*(p.176.8; 429A); εὐλόγησέν γε τὸν οἰ.·...αἷμα τῆς ἀμπέλου τὸν λόγον...ἀλληγορεῖ *ib.*(p.176.1; 428B); οὐ γὰρ εἶπεν ἡ γραφὴ μὴ πίνειν οἰ., ἀλλὰ τί φησιν; 'μὴ πίνε οἰ. εἰς μέθην' *Const.App.*8.44.3; οἰ. τὸ παρὰ θεοῦ δῶρον εἰς παραμυθίαν τῆς ἀσθενείας δεδομένον τοῖς σωφρονοῦσιν Bas.*hom.*14.1(2.123D; M.31. 448A); οἰ. γὰρ ἐδόθη παρὰ θεοῦ, οὐχ ἵνα μεθύωμεν, ἀλλ' ἵνα νήφωμεν, ἵνα εὐφραινώμεθα, οὐχ ἵνα ἀλγῶμεν Chrys.*stat.*1.4(2.7B); οὐ κακὸν ὁ οἰ., ἀλλὰ κακὸν ἡ μέθη *ib.*2.5(26E); οὔτε ὁ οἰ. πονηρόν, ἀλλ' ἡ παρὰ τὸ δέον χρῆσις id.*hom.29.3 in Gen.*(4.284A); πίνε τὸν οἰ. ἐλάχιστον· ὅσον γὰρ κολοβοῦται, εὐεργετεῖ τοὺς πίνοντας Nil.*paraen.*(M.79.1253C); **b.** in rel. to fasts νηστεύομεν γὰρ οἴνου...ἀπεχόμενοι, οὐχ ὡς βδελύγματα μισοῦντες, ἀλλὰ τὸν μισθὸν προσδοκῶντες Cyr.H.*catech.*4.27; ἐν ταῖς ἡμέραις οὖν τοῦ πάσχα νηστεύετε...οἴνου δὲ...ἀπέχεσθε ἐν ταύταις *Const.App.*5.18.1; and feasts εἴ τις ἐπίσκοπος ἢ πρεσβύτερος...οὐ μεταλαμβάνει κρεῶν καὶ οἴνου, καθαιρείσθω ὡς 'κεκαυτηριασμένος τὴν συνείδησιν' καὶ αἴτιος σκανδάλου πολλοῖς γινόμενος *Can.App.*53; **c.** use forbidden in heret. teaching, e.g. of Marcion and Encratites, Bas.*ep.*199 *can.*47(3.297A; M.32.732A); *Const.App.*6.10.2; of Severiani, Epiph.*haer.*45.1(p.200.14; M.41.833B); of Encratites οἶ. δὲ ὅλως οὐ μεταλαμβάνουσι· φάσκοντες εἶναι διαβολικὸν *ib.*47.1(p.216.11; 852B); Τατιανὸς...ἠρανίσατο...ἀπὸ Σατορνίλου καὶ Μαρκίωνος τὸ βδελύττεσθαι...τὴν τοῦ οἴνου μετάληψιν. τοῦτον ἔχουσιν ἀρχηγὸν οἱ λεγόμενοι ὑδροπαραστάται καὶ ἐγκρατῖται Thdt.*haer.*1.20(4.312); hence wrongful abstinence condemned εἴ τις ἐπίσκοπος...οἴνου οὐ δι' ἄσκησιν ἀλλὰ διὰ βδελυρίαν ἀπέχεται...ἢ διορθούσθω ἢ καθαιρείσθω *Can.App.*51; οἴνου δὲ...ἀποχὴν...οὐ τοῖς αἱρετικοῖς παραπλησίως ἀσπάζεται Thdt.*haer.*5.29(4.479); **2.** liturg.; **a.** not used by Encratites in eucharist, water being used instead, Epiph.*haer.*47.1(p.216. 11; M.41.852B); practice condemned, Chrys.*hom.82.2 in Mt.*(7. 784A); **b.** in orthodox use and interprn. of liturgy οἱ καλούμενοι παρ' ἡμῖν διάκονοι διδόασιν ἑκάστῳ τῶν παρόντων μεταλαβεῖν ἀπὸ τοῦ εὐχαριστηθέντος ἄρτου καὶ οἰ. καὶ ὕδατος Just.*1apol.*65.5(M.6.428B); *ib.*67.5(429C); τὸ ποτήριον κεράσας ἐξ οἰ. καὶ ὕδατος *Lit.*ap.*Const. App.*8.12.36,37; ref. Pr.9:2 ὁ υἱὸς τοῦ θεοῦ 'ἐκέρασε' τὸ 'ἑαυτοῦ' αἷμα ἀντὶ τοῦ οἰ. ἐκείνου ‡Bas.*h.myst.*53(p.391.23); ref. change in elements ὥσπερ γὰρ ὁ ἄρτος καὶ ὁ οἰ. τῆς εὐχαριστίας, πρὸ τῆς ἁγίας ἐπικλήσεως τῆς προσκυνητῆς τριάδος, ἄρτος ἦν καὶ οἰ. λιτός· ἐπικλήσεως δὲ γενομένης, ὁ μὲν ἄρτος γίνεται σῶμα Χριστοῦ, ὁ δὲ οἶ. αἷμα Χριστοῦ Cyr.H.*catech*.19.7; ἐν τύπῳ οἴνου, δίδοταί σοι τὸ αἷμα *ib*.22.3; *ib*.22.9 cit. s. αἷμα; effected by descent of H. Ghost παρακαλοῦμεν τὸν φιλάνθρωπον θεόν, τὸ ἅγιον πνεῦμα ἐξαποστεῖλαι ἐπὶ τὰ προκείμενα· ἵνα ποιήσῃ...τὸν δὲ οἶ. αἷμα Χριστοῦ *ib*.23.7; hence as instrument of salvation, Chrys.*hom.29.3 in Gen*.(4.284B); τὸν οἶ. πιστευέτω προσφερόμενον μεταβάλλεσθαι εἰς...αἷμα Χριστοῦ ‡Sophr.H.*liturg*.3(M.87.3894D); νῦν ἐρωτᾷς, πῶς ὁ ἄρτος γίνεται σῶμα Χριστοῦ, καὶ ὁ οἶ. καὶ τὸ ὕδωρ, αἷμα Χριστοῦ·...πνεῦμα ἅγιον ἐπιφοιτᾷ, καὶ ταῦτα ποιεῖ τὰ ὑπὲρ λόγον καὶ ἔννοιαν Jo.D.*f.o*.4.13(M.94.1141A); ἐπειδὴ ἔθος τοῖς ἀνθρώποις ἄρτον ἐσθίειν, ὕδωρ τε καὶ οἶ. πίνειν, συνέζευξεν αὐτοῖς τὴν αὐτοῦ θεότητα, καὶ πεποίηκεν αὐτὰ σῶμα καὶ αἷμα αὐτοῦ, ἵνα διὰ τῶν συνήθων καὶ κατὰ φύσιν, ἐν τοῖς ὑπὲρ φύσιν γενώμεθα *ib*.(1144A); ὁ τῆς προθέσεως ἄρτος, οἶ. τε καὶ ὕδωρ διὰ τῆς ἐπικλήσεως καὶ ἐπιφοιτήσεως τοῦ ἁγίου πνεύματος, ὑπερφυῶς μεταποιοῦνται εἰς τὸ σῶμα τοῦ Χριστοῦ καὶ τὸ αἷμα, καὶ οὐκ εἰσὶ δύο, ἀλλ' ἓν καὶ τὸ αὐτό *ib*.(1145A); not a mere symbol, *ib*.(1148A) cit. s. τύπος; though some have called the elements before consecration ἀντίτυπα, *ib*.(1153A); **c.** quality of wine to be used; σίκερα ἐπιτηδευτά forbidden, *Can.App*.2; complaint about poor and insufficient supplies, cap.10 ap.CBeryt.*act*.(p.25.17; H.2.520B); **d.** use in Marcosian rite, Iren.*haer*.1.13.2(M.7.580A); **e.** in pagan libations, *A.Thom*.A 77(p.192.10); καὶ ἡ τῶν οἴνων σπονδὴ καὶ αὐτὰ κορεῖ τὰ ἀκάθαρτα πνεύματα *Hom.Clem*.11.15; **3.** exeg. Gen.49:11, as symbolizing Christ's blood, Just.*dial*.54.1(M.6.593C); cf.Or.*hom.17.8 in Gen*.(M.12.260B); Thdt.*eran*.1(4.25); Pr.9:2,5, as knowledge of Christ, mingled by prophets, Or.*exp.in Pr*.9:2(M.17.185B); οἶνον τὴν ἐκ μελέτης τῶν θείων γραφῶν ἐπίγνωσιν αὐτοῦ [sc. τοῦ θεοῦ]...καὶ τίμιον αἷμα αὐτοῦ Didym.*Pr*.9:5 (M.39.1633A); τὰ θεῖα, φωναῖς ἀνθρωπίναις ἐκέρασεν, ὅ ἐστιν σοφίᾳ ἀνθρώπων Chrys.*fr.in Pr*.9:2(M.64.680B); πίετε τὸ κατὰ γνῶσιν δίκην οἴνου εὐφραῖνον ὑμᾶς, καὶ πρὸς θέωσιν ἐξιστῶν αἷμά μου, ὃ τῇ θεότητι παραδόξως κεκέρακα ‡Proc.G.*Pr*.9:5(M.87.1301D); Cant.1:2,4, as doctrines of Law and prophets, cf.Or.*hom.1 in Cant*.(p.94.8; M.13.87D); cf.id.*Cant*.1(p.111.29; M.13.99D); Cant.2:4, as mystical wine of true Vine, Christ, drawn from doctrines of truth and mingled by Wisdom (ref. Pr.9:2), cf.id.*hom.3 in Cant*.(pp.185.14–186.2; M.13.155A–C); Cant.4:10 ἐκαλλιώθησαν γὰρ αἱ δύο διαθῆκαι καὶ ἀπὸ τοῦ πνευματικοῦ οἶ.· ὅπερ ἐστίν, ἀπὸ τοῦ αἵματος τοῦ Χριστοῦ Ph.Carp.*Cant*.119(M.40.96B); Cant.8:2, as sacred doctrine, Thdt.*Cant*.8:2(2.153) v. ἄμπελος; Lc.10:34, as Christ's teaching, applied to the wounds of fallen man caused by sin, *cat.Lc*.10:30ff.(p.88.22); Jo.2:1–11 πρὸ μὲν Ἰησοῦ ἡ γραφὴ ὕδωρ ἦν, ἀπὸ δὲ τοῦ Ἰησοῦ οἶ. ἡμῖν γεγένηται Or.*Jo*.13.62(60; p.295.1; M.14.517D); ὑστέρησεν ὁ πρότερος οἶ. διὰ τὸ 'ὁ νόμος καὶ οἱ προφῆται μέχρι Ἰωάννου', τὸ καλοῦ οἶ. εὐπορηκέναι ἡμᾶς οἷς συνανάκειται Ἰησοῦς id.*fr.74 in Jo*.(p.541.27f.); *ib*.30(p.506.15); τὸ ὕδωρ ποτὲ εἰς οἶ. οἰκείῳ νεύματι μεταβέβληκεν...καὶ οὐκ ἀξιόπιστός ἐστιν οἶ. εἰς αἷμα μεταβαλών; Cyr.H.*catech*.22.2; wine which failed representing Law, miraculous wine Christ's doctrine, Cyr.*Jo*.2.1(4.137D–138A); Jo.15:1 τὰ...μυστικὰ θεωρήματα...ἔστιν ἀπὸ τῆς 'ἀληθινῆς ἀμπέλου' ἐρχόμενα, 'οἶνος' καλούμενα Or.*Jo*.1.30(33; p.37.32; M.14.80B); σὺ γὰρ εἶ ἀληθινὴ ἄμπελος, ἀφ' ἧς ὁ σωτήριος οἶ. γεωργούμενος ἐν ταῖς πνευματικαῖς ἀποθλίβεται ληνοῖς Thdt.*Cant*.7:9(2.149); Jo.19:34, Thdt.*eran*.1(4.25); ὁ δὲ οἶ. καὶ τὸ ὕδωρ [i.e. of eucharist] ἐστὶ τὸ ἐξελθὸν ἐκ τῆς πλευρᾶς αὐτοῦ αἷμα καὶ ὕδωρ ‡Bas.*h.myst*.31a(p.264.10); ‡Germ.CP *contempl*.(M.98.397B); Ac.2:13 νέος γὰρ ἦν ἀληθῶς ὁ οἶ. καινῆς διαθήκης ἡ χάρις· ἀλλ' ὁ νέος οὗτος οἶ. ἀπὸ νοητῆς ἀμπέλου Cyr.H.*catech*.17.18; Ps.103:15 ἐὰν ᾖ ὁ πατὴρ οἶ. εὐφραίνων καρδίαν καὶ ὁ υἱὸς οἶ. ..., καὶ τὸ πνεῦμα οἶ. ‡Ath.*dial.Trin*.1.27(M.28.1157B); **4.** in interprn. of Nazirite vow, Or.*exp.in Pr*.20:1(M.17.209C) cit. s. Ναζιραῖος; ref. abstinence of Jo. Bapt. μήτε ἐσθίων μήτε πίνων—δηλαδὴ κρέα καὶ οἶ. Pall.*h.Laus*.proem.(p.13.8; M.34.1003); drunk by Christ after Resurrection, Chrys.*hom.82.2 in Mt*.(7.784A); **5.** met., of H. Ghost ἀναλόγως τοίνυν κιρνᾶται ὁ μὲν οἶ. τῷ ὕδατι, τῷ δὲ ἀνθρώπῳ τὸ πνεῦμα Clem.*paed*.2.2(p.168.3; M.8.409B); exeg. Gen.49:11 οἶνον δὲ τὸ καταβὰν ἐπ' αὐτὸν ἐν τῷ Ἰορδάνῃ πατρικὸν πνεῦμα Hipp.*ben.Jac*.18(p.34.17); οἶ. δὲ ἡ τοῦ ἁγίου πνεύματος δύναμις *ib*.25(p.39.3); exeg. Mt.9:17, cf. *ut vinum novum, id est spiritus sancti gratiae susciperent novitatem*, Or.*princ*.1.3.7(p.59.2; M.11.153A); τοῦ πνευματικοῦ τούτου διάπλεοι γεγονότες οἶ., μυστηρίων θείων λαλήσωμεν διηγήματα Mac.Aeg.*carit*.15(M.34.921A); **6.** in payment of first-fruits ὡσαύτως κεράμιον οἴνου...ἀνοίξας, τὴν ἀπαρχὴν λαβὼν δὸς τοῖς προφήταις *Did*.13.6; to bishop διδόντες αὐτῷ ὡς ἱερεῖ θεοῦ, ἀπαρχὴν...οἴνου *Const.App*.2.34.5; κεραμίου οἴνου...τὴν ἀπαρχὴν δώσεις τοῖς ἱερεῦσιν *ib*.7.29.3.

***οἰνοσσόος**, *wine-preserving*, Nonn.*par.Jo*.2:7(M.43.761A).

***οἰνότευκτος**, *caused by wine*, Jo.D.*carm.pent*.87(p.216; M.96.837A).

***οἰνόφιλος**, *fond of wine*, Pall.*h.Laus*.47(p.139.21; M.34.1201D).

οἰνοφλυγέω, *make drunk*, Pall.*v.Chrys*.7(p.39.10; M.47.24).

οἰνοφλυγία, ἡ, *bout of drunkenness*, Bas.*hom*.1.5(2.4D; M.31.169C); plur., Thdr.Mops.*Os*.7:5ff.(M.66.165D).

οἰνοχο-έω, *pour out wine*, met. τὸν οἶνον τὸν ἐμποιοῦντα εὐφροσύνην αἰώνιον ~οῦντος τοῦ πνεύματος Proc.G.*Is*.1:21ff.(M.87.1860A).

οἰνοχοΐα, ἡ, *pouring out of wine*; met., of S. Paul πρὸς τὴν οἶ. τοῦ λόγου φιάλη γενόμενος Gr.Nyss.*hom.14 in Cant*.(M.44.1065A).

οἰνόω, *turn into wine* νάματος οἰνωθέντος Nonn.*par.Jo*.2:9(M.43.761B); *ib*.4:54(784C).

οἰνώδης, **1.** *affected by wine*, Chrys.*hom.in 1Cor*.7:2(3.195D); **2.** *of wine*, of miracle at Cana ἡ ἐξ ὑδάτων οἰνώδης ἐμφόρησις Sophr.H.*ep.syn*.(M.87.3176A).

οἰόβιος, *living alone*; of ascetics, Gr.Naz.*carm*.1.2.1.46(M.37.525A); *ib*.1.2.5.11(643A).

***οἰόγονος**, ὁ, *only-begotten*, Gr.Naz.*carm*.2.1.38.6(M.37.1326A).

οἰόκερως, ὁ, *unicorn*, †Apoll.*met.Ps*.28:6(M.33.1348D).

οἱοσδήποτε, *any whatsoever* οὐδὲ οἱ. πρόφασιν Chrys.*hom.16.4 in Jo*.(8.95A); *ib.18.4*(108D); *Dial.Christ.et Jud*.15(p.78.10).

οἱοσδηποτοῦν, *any whatsoever*, Just.*dial*.125.2(M.6.765D); *of whatever kind*, Jo.D.*disp*.(M.96.1345C).

***οἱοσδήτις**, *any whatever*, ‡Jo.Jej.*can*.(p.432); s.v.l., *any* person, *whoever he may be*, Heracl.*nov*.24(p.42).

οἱοσδητισοῦν, *any whatsoever*, Hipp.*haer*.6.24(p.151.11; M.16.3230C).

οἱοσποτοῦν, *any whatsoever*, Or.*Cels*.6.61(p.131.31; M.11.1392B).

οἰοχίτων, *possessing* or *wearing only a tunic*, Gr.Naz.*carm*.2.2 (poem.)5.147(M.37.1532A).

ὀΐσσομαι, = οἴομαι, *think*, Paul.Sil.*Soph*.1022(M.86.2158A).

ὀϊστεύω, *shoot at*, Nonn.*par.Jo*.10:31(M.43.837A); *ib*.11:8(840C).

οἰστός, *that can be borne, tolerable*, Cyr.*Os*.39(3.70B); id.*Juln*.9 (6^2.325B); in Christol. allusion to burning bush οὐ γὰρ ἦν ἀμήχανον τῷ φιλανθρώπῳ θεῷ, οἰστὸν ἑαυτὸν ἀποφῆναι τοῖς τῆς ἀνθρωπότητος μέτροις...οἰστὴ δὲ ὅπως ταῖς τῆς φλογὸς ἐμβολαῖς ἡ εὐκατάπρηστος ὕλη id.*Chr.un*.(5^1.737B,C).

οἰστρηλασία, ἡ, *mad passion*, Isid.Pel.*epp*.1.423(M.78.417B); Cyr.*hom.div*.19(M.77.1108C).

οἰστρηλατ-έω, **1.** *be mad*, intrans. παιδεύουσα ἡμᾶς μὴ ~εῖν ὀπίσω σαρκός Chrysipp.*enc.in Jo.Bapt*.(p.46.22); **2.** pass.; **a.** *be maddened, driven mad*, ref. sexual passion ἀσχημονῶσιν ~ούμενοι τὴν ψυχήν Meth.*symp*.3.14(p.44.5; M.18.85A); of Julian ταῖς κατὰ μικρὸν μανίαις ~ούμενος Gr.Naz.*or*.5.8(M.35.672C); δεινοτάτῃ φιλίᾳ οἱ. Ph.Carp.*Cant*.1:1(M.40.33B); ref. discontinued concubinage ἵνα μηκέτι ~ῶνται *A.Petr.c.Sim*.4(p.84.26); **b.** *be stung, goaded*, or *maddened into* or *towards* πονηρῷ συνειδότι οἱ. πρὸς τὴν βάσανον Or.*fr.in Ps*.1:5(p.71.13); Meth.*symp*.5.5(p.59.13; M.18.105C); ~ούμενοι γὰρ ὑπὸ τοῦ ἐνεργοῦντος ἐν αὐτοῖς διαβόλου εἰς...ἡδονήν Alex.Al.*ep.Alex*.1 (p.19.4; M.18.548A).

***οἰστρηλάτημα**, τό, *madness*, ‡Nil.*narr*.3(M.79.621B).

οἴστρημα, τό, *goading, incitement*; of demons, Ath.*inc*.11.5(M.25.116C).

οἰστρομανής, *raging, furious*, *Orac.Sib*.1.114; *ib*.1.363; *ib*.3.810.

οἰστρομανία, ἡ, *insane passion*, Bas.Sel.*v.Thecl*.1(M.85.529A).

οἰστρώδης, *frenzied*, ‡Just.*or.Gr*.4(M.6.236C).

οἰφι, τό, *ephah*, Clem.*str*.2.11(p.140.9; M.8.988A).

οἰωνίζομαι, **1.** intrans., *divine by means of omens*; forbidden in Mosaic law, †Bas.*Is*.77(1.433D; M.30.248B); Chrys.*hom.6.4 in Eph*.(11.44C); **2.** trans., *regard as an omen* οἰωνισαμένου τινός, ὅτι κατέφαγεν ὗς τὰ δελφάκια Clem.*str*.7.4(p.17.18; M.9.432A); *regard as unfortunate, deplore, abhor*; widowhood, Gr.Nyss.*virg*.3(p.262.16; M.46.332C); lamentation, Chrys.*hom.15.4 in Heb*.(12.156D); poverty, *ib.18.3*(178B,C); *regard as bringing ill fortune*, id.*hom.70.2 in Mt*.(7.689D); *regard as accursed*; the Cross. id.*hom.85.1 in Jo*.(8.504A).

οἰώνισμα, τό, **1.** *taking omens by watching birds* οἰ. δὲ ἡ [sc. παρατήρησις] διὰ πτηνῶν Thdt.*qu.53 in 4Reg*.(1.548); φαρμακείαις καὶ δαιμονιώδεσιν οἰ. ‡Jo.D.*ep.Thphl*.9(M.95.356C); **2.** *omen, portent* τῶν νομικῶν οἰ. †Cyr.*coll.VT*(6^4.69B; M.77.1277D).

οἰωνισμός, ὁ, *observation of omens*, esp. from birds, *augury* φεύγετε...οἰωνισμούς *Const.App*.2.62.2; Gr.Nyss.*fat*.(M.45.172C); Chrys.*hom.4.6 in 1Cor*.(10.32B); οἰ. ... καὶ τοῖς ὁμοίοις μύθοις ἀσεβῶν Jo.D.*haer*.94(M.94.757C).

οἰωνός, ὁ, *omen*; of a ship's grounding, Synes.*ep*.4(M.66.1328B).

οἰωνοσκοπία, ἡ, *practice of augury* οὐ μυσερά τις ἡγεῖται τὰ τῆς οἰ. αἴτια; Eust.*engast*.24(p.54.16; M.18.664B); οἰ., μαντεία,...λατρεῖαι εἰσι διαβόλου Cyr.H.*catech*.19.8; condemned as idolatry, Cyr.*Os*.44 (3.75B).

οἰωνοσκοπική, ἡ, [sc. *τέχνη*], *art of augury*, Thdt.*affect*.1(p.10. 2; 4.699).

οἰωνοσκόπος, ὁ, *augur μὴ γίνου οἰ. Did*.3.4; *βουληθεὶς δέ ποτε ὁ θεὸς δι' οἰωνοσκόπου ἀποτρέψαι ἀπὸ τῆς οἰωνιστικῆς πεποίηκε πνεῦμα ἐν τῷ οἰ. εἰπεῖν* Or.*Cels*.4.95(p.368.11,12; M.11.1173B).

***οἰωσδήποτε,** *in any way whatsoever*, †Leont.B.*sect*.7.6(M.86. 1248A).

ὀκλάζ-ω, 1. *kneel* in prayer *ἐν γόνασιν ὀ.* Just.*dial*.90.5(M.6. 692B); *sink down*; in supplication, Nonn.*par.Jo*.4:20(M.43.777A); **2.** *faint, tire, collapse*; of body in death, Meth.*res*.1.51(p.307.1; M. 18.281D); from exhaustion, Pall.*h.Laus*.18(p.50.11; M.34.1057A); morally *fail οὐδὲ πρὸς ὀλίγον ~όντων τὴν παρρησίαν* Const.*or.s.c*.22 (p.188.21; M.20.1304C); Ath.*h.Ar*.41(p.206.11; M.25.741B); *τοὺς πρὸς τὴν ἀληθῆ πίστιν ~οντας φανεροὺς πᾶσι ποιῆσαι* Bas.*ep*.69.2(3.163A; M.32.432C); Cyr.*Ps*.90:6(M.69.1220A); id.*Juln*.9(6²·325B); *περὶ τὴν μαρτυρίαν ὀκλάσαντες* Thphn.*chron*.p.425(M.108.1004D); met., of hopes, Bas.Sel.*or*.30.1(M.85.336A); of doctors, failing before a disease, Sophr.H.*mir.Cyr.et Jo*.51(M.87.3613D); c. dat. *στηρίζειν με μικροψυχίαις ~οντα* id.*ep.syn*.(M.87.3149C).

ὀκνηρία, ἡ, *sluggishness, laziness*; of soul, Bas.*reg.br*.174(2.473E; M.31.1197B); *μὴ ἀγαπήσῃς τὴν ὀ.* Esaias *or*.16.2(p.88); Eustrat.*stat. anim*.1(p.337); as work of Devil, Dor.*doct*.2.2(M.88.1641C).

ὀκνηρός, 1. *reluctant, hesitant ὀ. πρὸς τὴν ὁδοιπορίαν* Gr.Thaum. *pan.Or*.5(p.14.1; M.10.1068B); *ἵνα...ὀκνηρότερος γένηται ὁ ἀνὴρ* [sc. Pilate] *περὶ τὸν φόνον* Chrys.*hom.86.1 in Mt*.(7.812B); *sluggish, lazy*, *Hom.Clem*.11.30; Chrys.*sac*.3.16(p.84.17; 1.396B); id.*stat*.1.2(2.4A); Cyr.*Lc*.19:15(M.72.876A); **2.** *troublesome, burdensome ταῦτα λέγειν ...οὐκ ὀκνηρόν* ‡Ath.*dial.Trin*.3.28(M.28.1245C).

***ὀκνοποιέω,** *make sluggish, idle*, Or.*exp.in Pr*.31:27(M.17.252B).

ὄκνος, ὁ (A), *sluggishness, laziness, sloth οἴγε μὴν ὄ. καὶ ἀργίᾳ δεδουλωμένοι ἐν ἐσχάτοις ἔσονται κακοῖς* Cyr.*fr.Mt*.25:14ff.(M.72. 448D); *τὸν ἀκερδῆ καὶ ἐπάρατον ὄ.* id.*Lc*.19:15ff.(M.72.873B); *ἀτιμία δὲ ἔσται τοῖς ὄκνῳ νενικημένοις cat.Lc*.19:13(p.139.15).

§ὄκνος, ὁ (B), part of equipment of a ship, perh. for securing the steering-oar in position *ὄκνων τε καὶ αὐχενίων* Epiph.*haer*.61.3(p.383. 10; M.41.1044A).

***ὀκνόφιλος,** *inclined to idleness*, Cyr.*Jo*.2.5(4.194A).

***ὀκτᾶβα, ἡ,** (Lat. *octava*) *tax of 12½ per cent.*, Sophr.H.*mir.Cyr. et Jo*.1(M.87.3424C).

***ὀκταβάριος, ὁ,** (Lat. *octavarius*) *collector of the* octava, Sophr.H. *mir.Cyr.et Jo*.1 tit.(M.87.3424B); cf.*IGC As.Min*.10 (Hellespont, saec. iv–v).

ὀκταετηρίς, ἡ, *period of eight years*, Afric.*chron*.16(M.10.84A).

ὀκταετία, ἡ, = foreg., Afric.*chron*.16(M.10.84B); Epiph.*haer*.16.1 (p.210.13; M.41.248B); ‡Epiph.*epit.haer*.16(p.351.23).

***ὀκταζύξ,** *eightfold*, Paul.Sil.*Soph*.732(M.86.2147A).

ὀκταήμερος, 1. *eight days old τὸ παιδίον* [sc. Christ]...*τὸ ὀ. περιτεμνόμενον* Amph.*hom*.2.6(M.39.52D); Jo.D.*f.o*.4.23(M.94.1204A); **2.** *of the eighth day*; of circumcision, Iren.*haer*.1.17.3(M.7.645B); Epiph.*haer*.30.26(p.369.24,28; M.41.452B); Jo.D.*jej*.3(M.95.69B).

***ὀκτάηχος, ἡ,** *office-book* containing troparia and other chants, according to eight tones, *Nomoc*.120.

ὀκτάμηνος, ὁ, ἡ, *child born in the eighth month of gestation*, or [sc. *περίοδος*] *period of gestation lasting eight months*, in title of medical book, Clem.*str*.6.16(p.502.21; M.9.365A).

***ὀκτάπλευρος,** *eight-sided*, Paul.Sil.*Soph*.728(M.86.2147A).

ὀκταπλοῦς, *eight-fold*; neut. plur., *Octapla*, title of Origen's arrangement of OT text *τοῖς λεγομένοις ὑπ' αὐτοῦ Ἑξαπλοῖς ἢ Ὀ., τὰς μὲν δύο Ἑβραϊκὰς σελίδας καὶ τὰς ἓξ τῶν ἑρμηνευτῶν ἐκ παραλλήλου ἀντιπαραθείς, μεγάλην ὠφέλειαν γνώσεως ἔδωκε τοῖς φιλοκάλοις* Epiph.*mens*.7(M.43.248A).

ὀκτάπους, *eight-footed*, Gr.Naz.*carm*.1.2.1.714(M.37.576A); as subst., ? *crab*, Max.*schol.d.n*.4.2(M.4.244B).

***ὀκταπτερυγός,** *eight-winged*, *cat.Apoc*.4:6ff.(p.244.10).

ὀκτάς, ἡ, *octad ἐπαγαγὼν* [sc. Eunomius]...*ἀσυναρτήτους τινὰς καὶ ἀναρμόστους ὕβρεων τε καὶ λοιδορημάτων ὀ.* Gr.Nyss.*Eun*.9(2 p.212. 17; M.45.809D).

***ὀκτάστιχος,** *of eight lines* or *verses*, Synes.*astrolab*.(p.141.15; M. 66.1585C).

Ὀκτάτευχος, ἡ, *Octateuch*, name for first eight books of OT, †Gregent.*disp*.(M.86.621A); Proc.G.*Gen*.proem.(M.87.21A); name of work on Persian religion *τὰ δ' αὐτὰ καὶ Ὀστάνης φησὶ περὶ αὐτοῦ ἐν τῇ ἐπιγραφομένῃ Ὀ.* Eus.*p.e*.1.10(42B; M.21.88D) citing Philo of Byblos.

ὀκτάτομος, *cut eight times*, Paul.Sil.*Soph*.609(M.86.2142B).

***Ὀκτώβριος,** (Lat. *October*) *of October*, Agath.*v.Gr.Ill*.142(p.72); *V.Aberc*.80(p.55.11); Ath.Scholast.*coll*.1.17(p.24).

ὀκτωκαιδέκατος, *eighteenth*, [sc. *σημεῖον*], a place eighteen miles distant from Alexandria, Jo.Mosch.*prat*.110(M.87.2973A); *ib*.162 (3029B).

***ὀκτωκαιεικοσαετηρίς, ἡ,** *cycle of twenty-eight years*, *Chron. Pasch*.p.10(M.92.88A); *ib*.p.12(89C); *ib*.pp.13,14(93A).

***Ὀκτώμβριος,** = *Ὀκτώβριος*, *M.Ariadn*.18(p.133.12); Abr.Eph. *annunt*.2(p.443.38).

[*]ὀκύμωρος, = *ὠκύμορος*, *soon to die*, Olymp.*Job* 7:21(M.93. 105A).

[*]ὀκύπτερα, τά, = *ὠκύπτερα*, *long quill-feathers in a wing*, Olymp.*Job* 9:26(M.93.125A).

***ὁλαίματος,** *all bloody*; of hands, *Apoc.Paul*.36(p.59).

ὀλβιόδωρος, *bestowing bliss*; of Christ, Gr.Naz.*carm*.2.1.38.9(M. 37.1326A).

***ὀλεάριος, ὁ,** *bath cloakroom attendant*, Epiph.*haer*.30.24(p.365. 17; M.41.445B).

ὀλεθρίως, *in pernicious fashion*, Dion.Ar.*e.h*.3.3.6(M.3.432C); *ib*. 7.1.2(556A).

***ὀλεθροποιός,** *bringing destruction*; of Devil, Cyr.H.*catech*.4.1; of sin, Cyr.*Is*.4.4(2.664C).

ὄλεθρος, ὁ, *destruction*, i.e. of a moral or spiritual nature *καθαιροῦνται αἱ δυνάμεις τοῦ σατανᾶ, καὶ λύεται ὁ ὄ. αὐτοῦ* Ign.*Eph*.13. 1; of sentence passed on fallen man, Meth.*symp*.3.6(p.33.8; M.18. 69B); as punishment for cupidity, *Hom.Clem*.6.15; *ὁ θεὸς...δέδωκέ σοι χρήματα, οὐχ ἵνα κατακλείσῃς ἐπ' ὀλέθρῳ τῷ σῷ* Chrys.*stat*.2.7(2. 30D).

***ὀλεθροτόκος,** *producing destruction*, Jo.D.*hom*.4.23(M.96.621B); †Jo.D.*B.J*.39(M.96.1232B); ‡Sophr.H.*triod*.(M.87.3897D).

ὀλεθροφόρος, *bringing ruin*, ‡Ath.*v.Syncl*.82(M.28.1536C); *ib*.99 (1548D); of teachings, Olymp.*Eccl*.5:8(M.93.544B).

[*]ὀλεσίκαρπος, = *ὠλεσίκαρπος*, *losing its fruit*, †Apoll.*met.Ps*. 136:2(M.33.1520B).

ὀλέσκω, = *ὀλέκω*, *destroy*, imperf. *ὤλεσκον*, *Orac.Sib*.1.108; of anger, *ὀλέσκων*, Hesych.S.*temp*.1.31(M.93.1492A).

ὀλετήρ, ὁ, *destroyer*, of Christ *τῶν ἀσεβῶν ὀ.* Eus.*h.e*.10.4.10(M.20. 852B); *ὀ. τῆς Ἀρείου αἱρέσεως* CArim.*ep.Const*.1 ap.Ath.*syn*.10(p.237. 14; M.26.696C); *τοὺς ἄλλους θεοὺς ὀ. ἐκάλει* Philost.*h.e*.7.15(M.65. 553C); of demons, ‡Jo.D.*Artem*.54(p.91.5; M.96.1301B).

***ὀλετήριος,** *destructive, deadly*, Epiph.*haer*.45.4(p.202.23; M.41. 836D); *ib*.51.2(p.249.25; 889C).

ὀλιγάκις, *now and then*, Cyr.*Ps*.4:2(M.69.733C).

***ὀλιγαμάρτητος,** *guilty of little*, †Jo.Jej.*serm*.(M.88.1925D).

ὀλιγανδρ-έω, *contain few people ἡ ἐκκλησία κατ' ἀρχὰς ~οῦσα* Proc.G.*Is*.52:6ff.(M.87.2513B).

ὀλιγάνθρωπος, *of few people*, Chrys.*hom.1.1 in Ac.princ*.(3.50C).

ὀλιγαρκής, *content with little*, ‡Bas.*struct.hom*.2.4(1.340C; M.30. 45C); neut. as subst., = *ὀλιγαρκία*, Gr.Nyss.*or.dom*.4(p.78.14; M. 44.1168D).

ὀλιγαρκία (-εια), ἡ, *contentment with little*, Bas.*hom*.13.3(2.3B; M.31.168B); *θαυμαστὸν ἡ ἐγκράτεια, καὶ ὀ.* Gr.Naz.*or*.43.61(M.36. 576A); *τὸ περὶ τὴν ὀ. αὐθαίρετον* Nil.*Magn*.2(M.79.969D); *ζωὴν...τὴν ἐμφερῶς δι' ὀλιγαρκείας τὸ ἀπροσδεὲς τῶν ἀγγέλων μιμουμένην* Max. *ambig*.(M.91.1160A).

[*]ὀλιγηπελεέσκω, = *ὀλιγηπελέω*, *be wanting, fail*, †Apoll.*met. Ps*.63:7(M.33.1400A).

ὀλιγηπελίη, ἡ, *weakness*, *Orac.Sib*.5.474.

***ὀλιγηφρενίη, ἡ,** s.v.l., *faint-hearted* or *weak-minded woman*, *Orac.Sib*.7.63.

[*]ὀλιγοαμάρτητος, = *ὀλιγαμάρτητος*, Jo.Jej.*canonar*.2(p.438); †Jo.Jej.*serm*.(M.88.1932B).

ὀλιγόβιος, *short-lived*; neut. as subst., *shortness of life*, Gr.Nyss. *fat*.(M.45.157B); Thdt.*1Cor*.4:3(3.187).

ὀλιγογνώμων, 1. *feeble-witted, stupid*, Synes.*regn*.14(p.30.10; M. 66.1078B); of idolaters, Cyr.*Is*.4.3(2.628E); of pagan gods, id.*Juln*.7 (6²·226C); **2.** *simple-minded*, id.*Is*.3.2(430C).

ὀλιγογράμματος, *of little education*, Ath.Scholast.*coll*.14.3(p.151).

ὀλιγοδάπανος, *costing little*, Bas.*reg.fus*.22.1(2.366E; M.31.977A); Pall.*h.Laus*.66(p.163.4; but *spending little*, M.34.1218D).

ὀλιγοδεής, 1. *needing, lacking little ὁ γὰρ τοῦ δικαίου ζηλωτής, ὡς ἂν τοῦ ἀνενδεοῦς ἐραστής, ὀ.* Clem.*prot*.10(p.75.21; M.8.221A); neut. as subst., id.*str*.2.18(p.155.16; M.8.1020B); Chrys.*hom.19.2 in Eph*. (11.135D); **2.** *in a little need*; of one desiring some small thing, Nil. *Magn*.45(M.79.1025B).

ὀλιγόδεια, ἡ, *contentment with little* πλοῦτον νόμιζε γνήσιον καὶ βέβαιον τὴν ὀ. Gr.Naz.*ep*.244(M.37.388A); ἐκ τῆς ὀ. προκόψαντες πλησίον τῶν ἀσωμάτων ἔστησαν δυνάμεων Nil.*exerc*.18(M.79.741D); τὸ σῶμα...τροφῆς δεῖται οὐ τρυφῆς, ὀ. οὐ πλησμονῆς Isid.Pel.*epp*. 2.57(M.78.500B).

ὀλιγοδίαιτος, *frugal*, Nil.*epp*.4.41(M.79.569C).

ὀλιγοδρανέω, *be weak*, Gr.Naz.*carm*.2.1.87.10(M.37.1434A); *ib*.2.2 (poem.)1.2(1451A).

[*]**ὀλιγοήμερος**, *short-lived*, Nil.*epp*.1.319(M.79.198B).

***ὀλιγόθριξ**, *with little hair*; in description of Justinian, *Chron. Pasch*.p.375(M.92.957n.; one MS).

ὀλιγοθυμέω, *become weak*, Barth.Edess.*Agar*.(M.104.1436A).

***ὀλιγοκτήμων**, *possessing little*, Cyr.*Juln*.7(6^2.226B).

***ὀλιγόλαλος**, *saying little*, ‡Hipp.Th.*fr*.17(p.50.3).

ὀλιγομαθής, *of little learning*, Iren.*haer*.2.26.1(M.7.800A); Socr. *h.e*.2.35.10(M.67.300A); Euthal.Diac.*Ac*.(M.85.629B).

***ὀλιγομαθῶς**, *ignorantly*, Socr.*h.e*.4.7.6(M.67.473A).

***ὀλιγόνοια**, ἡ, *limited intelligence*, Thdr.Stud.*antirr*.2 proem.(M. 99.353A).

ὀλιγοπαιδία, ἡ, *fewness of children*, Cyr.*Is*.4.4(2.674B).

***ὀλιγοπιστέω**, *have little faith*, Cyr.*hom.div*.12(5^2.391B); id.*Lc*. 9:52ff.(p.92.26; M. om.).

***ὀλιγοπιστία**, ἡ, *lack of faith*, *A.Thom*.A 65(p.182.10); Chrys. *hom.50.2 in Mt*.(7.516A); Nil.*epp*.3.33(M.79.396A).

ὀλιγόπιστος, *of little faith*, *A.Phil*.144(p.85.8); *M.Perp*.1(p.63.8); Pall.*h.Laus*.39(p.125.7; M.34.1195D).

***ὀλιγορημοσύνη**, ἡ, *fewness of words*, Ast.Am.*hom*.8(M.40.280B).

ὀλιγόσιτος, *eating little*; neut. as subst., *frugality*, Gr.Nyss.*laud. Bas*.(M.46.805B).

ὀλιγόστιχος, *consisting of few lines*; of Epistle of Jude, Or. *comm.in Mt*.10.17(p.22.15; M.13.877B); Max.*schol.myst*.3(M.4.425B).

ὀλιγοστός, = ὀλίγιστος, *smallest*, *Trad.Pil*.6(p.453); *briefest*, Euthal.Diac.*Ac*.(M.85.633C); ὀ. χρόνῳ Cyr.*Os*.147(3.181B); plur., *very few*, *T.Sym*.5.6; Just.*dial*.136.1(M.6.789C); Cyr.*Os*.42(73C).

***ὀλιγοστῶς**, *to a very small extent*, Ath.*Ar*.2.32(M.26.216B).

ὀλιγοτεκνία, ἡ, *fewness of children*, Chrys.*hom.8.3 in Ac*.(9.68D).

ὀλιγοτιμία, ἡ, *worthlessness* ταῖς ἡμετέραις ὀ. συσχηματίζεται κύριος Cyr.*Jo*.2.4(4.172E).

***ὀλιγοτίμως**, *cheaply*, ‡Ath.*syntag*.3.10(p.124; M.28.840C) = *Didasc.Patr*.3(p.13.23).

ὀλιγοφρενία, ἡ, *little understanding*, Gr.Naz.*carm*.1.2.14.126(M. 37.765A).

***ὀλιγοχειρία**, ἡ, *fewness of troops*, Men.*exc.Rom*.20(p.220.20; M. 113.925C).

***ὀλιγοχρηματία**, ἡ, *slenderness of means*, Clem.*str*.2.5(p.124.17; M.8.956A).

ὀλιγοχρόνιος, *short-lived, ephemeral* ἡ ἐπιδημία ἡ ἐν τῷ κόσμῳ τούτῳ...ὀ. *2Clem*.5.5; ζωαὶ δύο, ἡ μὲν ὀ., ἡ δὲ αἰώνιος *M.Ign.Rom*.3 (p.503.12); τὸ ὀ. τῆς ζωῆς Bas.*hex*.5.2(1.41D; M.29.97C); comp., Or. *comm.in Ex*.(p.246.9; M.12.269C); id.*hom.16.1 in Jos*.(p.394.24; M. 87.1024B).

ὀλιγοψυχέω, **1.** *faint*, *A.Pil*.B 10.2(p.303); *feel faint*, *V.Zos*.6 (p.100.9); **2.** *be discouraged, become faint-hearted*, *Const.App*.2.40. 3; Chrys.*hom.22.1 in Heb*.(12.201C); ὀλιγοψυχοῦσαν τῷ μεγέθει τῶν θλίψεων καρδίαν Nil.*epp*.4.30(M.79.564C); Cyr.*Jo*.3.4(4.280A); *Apophth.Patr*.(M.65.221A); **3.** *become desolate of soul*; of Christ on the Cross, *A.Andr.et Mt*.28(p.107.10).

ὀλιγοψυχία, ἡ, **1.** *faint-heartedness, pusillanimity* γογγυσμὸν καὶ ὀ. ἐν θλίψει μάκρυνον ἀπ' ἐμοῦ *Pss.Sal*.16.11; opp. μακροθυμία, *T.Gad* 4.7; Chrys.*hom.11.1 in Heb*.(12.112A); Isid.Pel.*epp*.1.301(M.78. 357B); **2.** *desolation of soul, temptation to despondency*, plur. ἔθος δὲ τοῖς ἁγίοις ἐν ταῖς οὕτω πικραῖς ὀ. τὸ ἀναλῦσαι ζητεῖν Cyr.*Abac*.4(3. 519E); ὁ πονηρὸς ἔρχεται καὶ βαρεῖ τὴν ψυχὴν...ἐν ὀλιγοψυχίαις *Apophth.Patr*.(M.65.201C).

ὀλιγόψυχος, *faint-hearted, dispirited*; of penitents, Eus.*Is*.57:15 (M.24.476C); παραμυθεῖσθαι τοὺς ὀ. Bas.*ascet.disc*.1(2.212C; M.31. 649B); μὴ γινώμεθα...ὀ. Chrys.*hom.16.6 in 1Cor*.(10.143D); Jo. Mosch.*prat*.164(M.87.3032A).

ὀλιγωρ-έω, **1.** *neglect*; c. genit., Clem.*q.d.s*.2(p.161.5; M.9.605C); *be negligent, neglect one's duty*, abs., Meth.*symp*.2(p.66.3; M.18. 116B); Ephr.1.322F; c. περί, id.2.80B,81F; *be inattentive* in prayer, Chrys.*Anna* 2.2(4.714C); †Jo.Jej.*serm*.(M.88.1944B); *be contemptuous* of, *esteem lightly*, c. πρός, Cyr.*Mich*.69(3.465D); Dor.*doct*. 14.3(M.88.1777C); pass., Clem.*paed*.1.9(p.140.27; M.8.353A); **2.** *be faint-hearted, discouraged* πῶς ἡμεῖς ~οῦμεν, ὡς μόνοι θλιβόμενοι; Ephr.2.125E; Marc.Diac.*v.Porph*.19; μὴ γένοιτο ἵνα...ὀλιγωρήσωμεν ταῖς βασάνοις Agath.*v.Gr.Ill*.74(p.38); τὸ μὴ ~εῖν τινα πρὸς τὴν θλῖψιν Dor.*doct*.13.6(M.88.1768A); *feel faint*, *Chron.Pasch*.p.155(M. 92.381A); Thphn.*chron*.p.277(M.108.685B).

ὀλιγωρία, ἡ, **1.** *negligence, neglect of duty* ἵνα...ῥαθυμότερος γένηται, καὶ ταύτην ἀποτειχίζει τὴν ὀ. Chrys.*hom.28.1 in Jo*.(8.160A); *ib. 36.2*(210C); **2.** *neglect*, c. genit. τῆς βραδυτῆτος καὶ ὀ. τῶν ὑπεσχημένων Philost.*h.e*.6.1(M.65.532B); **3.** *diminution* τὸ τῶν ψαλμῶν πλῆθος εἰς ὀ. ἄγων †Thdt.*Pss.proem*.(5.77).

***ὀλίγωσις**, ἡ, *dwindling*, Diod.*Gen*.49:16(M.33.1580B).

ὁλικός, **1.** *complete, entire, perfect*, †Marc.Er.*temp*.5(M.65.1056B); ἡ ὀ. εἰς ἐμὲ ἀγάπη Proc.G.*fr.Cant*.8:6(M.87.1773A); προσάγων ὀ. μεταποίησιν Max.*opusc*.(M.91.72A); of perfect likeness, Thdr.Stud. *antirr*.3.4.6(M.99.432A); plur. τῆς χορηγοῦ τῶν ὁ. ἀγαθῶν ὁμοουσίου τριάδος Didym.*Trin*.2.4(M.39.485A); ὁ. δυνάμεσιν Dion.Ar.*c.h*.7.1 (M.3.205D); **2.** Christol., *general, universal*, opp. μερικός, individual, particular τίνες ἂν εἴησαν αἱ παρ' αὐτῶν λεγόμεναι φύσεις, ὁ. ἢ μερικαί; Leont.H.*Nest*.2.6(M.86.1548B).

ὁλικῶς, **1.** *altogether, completely, fully* μόνον τὸν θεὸν κατ' ἐρωτικὴν ἔκστασιν ὁ. ἐνδυσάσης †Marc.Er.*temp*.2(M.65.1053D); Dion.Ar.*c.h*. 15.3(M.3.332A); Χριστοῦ τοῦ θεοῦ ἐν αὐτῇ ὁ. καὶ ἀληθῶς κυοφορηθέντος Mod.*dorm*.3(M.86.3285C); Trin. μιᾶς...θεότητος...ἐν ἑκάστῳ οὔσης ὁλοτελῶς καὶ ὁ. Sophr.H.*ep.syn*.(M.87.3157C); ὁ. πρὸς θεὸν συναχθέντες, ὅλοι ὅλῳ θεῷ ἐγκραθῆναι Max.*ambig*.(M.91.1113B); ἐκ θεοῦ τοῦ ἀεὶ ὄντος τὰ πάντα ἐκ τοῦ μὴ ὄντος γενέσθαι παντελῶς τε καὶ ὁ., ἀλλ' οὐ μερικῶς τε καὶ ἀτελῶς *ib*.(1188B); ἰστέον δὲ ὅτι τὸ θεῖον ἀμερές ἐστιν, ὅλον ὁ. πανταχοῦ ὄν Jo.D.*f.o*.1.13(M.94.852C); **2.** *in general*, Didym.*Trin*.2.27(M.39.768B).

ὀλισθάνω, **1.** met.; **a.** *slip, lapse, fall*; spiritually and morally, *Pss.Sal*.16.1; Clem.*str*.3.12(p.231.19; M.8.1177C); of angels τινὰς ὑπὸ ῥαθυμίας ὀλισθήσαντας *ib*.7.7(p.35.2; M.9.465C); Σαβέλλιος...τῆς ὀρθῆς ὀλισθήσας πίστεως Marcell.*fr*.38 ap.Eus.*e.th*.1.15(p.74.33; M. 24.853C); ὠλίσθησε τῶν αἱρετικῶν ἡ διάνοια ‡Ath.*Apoll*.2.19(M.26. 1165A); **b.** *lapse* from faith in time of persecution, Petr.I Al.*ep.can*. 6(M.18.477C); περὶ Νωβατιανοῦ καὶ τῶν ὀλισθησάντων Hier.*vir.ill*. (tr.Sophr.Pal.)66(p.42.13; M.*PL*.23.678A); **c.** *cause to slip* or *err* οὐδεμία πλάνη αὐτὸν ὀλισθήσει Const.ap.Gel.Cyz.*h.e*.2.7.12(M.85. 1236A); **2.** *fall* in ruin; of Jewish race, Nonn.*par.Jo*.11:50(M.43. 848C).

ὀλίσθημα, τό, *slip, fall* ὀ. γὰρ ἀπὸ ἐδάφους μᾶλλον, ἢ ἀπὸ γλώσσης Isid.Pel.*epp*.1.459(M.78.436A); moral, Cyr.*Ps*.4:2(M.69.733C); of S. Peter's denial, Eulog.*fr.Novat*.(M.104.328D); ἐκτροπὴ καὶ ὀ. Max. *opusc*.(M.91.192A).

ὀλισθηρός, **1.** *slippery*, fig. ὀ. ... παρεκτροπαὶ καὶ κρημνώδεις Clem.*str*.7.12(p.53.2; M.9.501B); **2.** *liable to slip* or *fall*, met. ὀ. γὰρ εἰς ἀκολασίαν ἡ τῆς χορηγίας ἑτοιμότης Isid.Pel.*epp*.5.186(M.78. 1440D); *liable to slip* or *err* spiritually or morally τίνες αἱ τῶν ὀ. ὀφθαλμῶν παιδαγωγήσεις; Clem.*paed*.2.6(p.187.28; M.8.453A); id. *str*.7.18(p.78.1; M.9.556A).

ὀλισθηρῶς, *in* moral or spiritual *instability*, Clem.*paed*.2.1(p.159. 21; M.8.392B); ὀ. ἔζησε Gr.Mag.*dial*.(tr.Zach.)4.52(M.*PL*.77.414B); ὀ. ἔχω *be liable to fall* ὀ. ἔχοντι πρὸς εἰδωλολατρείαν Eus.*e.th*.2.22 (p.132.34; M.24.900B).

ὄλισθος, ὁ, **1.** *slip, fall*; lit., Or.*comm.in Gen*.ap.Eus.*p.e*.6.11 (287D; M.12.64B); Geo.Pis.*hex*.644(M.92.1485A); met., moral τὸν εἰς μαγείαν ὄ. Or.*Cels*.8.60(p.276.9; M.11.1605D); of Eve, Isid.Pel.*epp*. 1.330(M.78.373A); ref. 2Reg.11:2ff., Thdt.*qu.24 in 2Reg*.(1.423); **2.** *cause of* moral *lapse, temptation* or *danger*; of custom, Clem. *paed*.2.1(p.160.14; M.8.393A); τοῖς τῆς ἡδονῆς ὄ. Eus.*d.e*.4.9(p.163.24; M.22.273A); γλῶσσα γὰρ ὄ. ἀνθρώποις μὴ λόγῳ κυβερνωμένη Gr.Naz. *or*.3.7(M.35.524B); τὸν ἐκ τῆς ἀνθρωπίνης δόξης παρεισδύνοντα ὄ. Gel. Cyz.*h.e*.3.10.5; **3.** *liability to slip* or *fall* morally τότε γὰρ ὁ πολὺς εἰς ἁμαρτίαν ὄ. γίνεται Synes.*hom*.1(p.279.14; M.66.1561A).

ὁλκάς, ἡ, *trading-ship, merchantman* ὥσπερ εἰς ὁλκάδας..., τὰς τῶν πενήτων μετατεθέντα γαστέρας Bas.*hom*.21.7(2.168D; M.31.552D); fig., of Christ, borne in womb of BMV as in a sea, *Pers*.(p.12.12; M.10. 100C); καταπαύσωμεν τὴν σταυροφόρον ὁ. τοῦ λόγου ‡Meth.*Sym.et Ann*.13(M.18.377D); of BMV, Mod.*dorm*.4(M.86.3288C), cit. s. θεοφερής.

ὁλκή, ἡ, **1.** *attraction* τῆς τοῦ πατρὸς πρὸς αὐτὸν ὁλκῆς Clem.*str*.5.1 (p.330.2; M.9.16C); οὐδὲ γάρ ἐστι τὰ Χριστιανῶν...ὥσπερ ὁλκαῖς τισὶ φυσικαῖς, ἀκολουθῆσαι τὸ θεῖον Synes.*ep*.67(M.66.1421A); *force, power*; of chastity, Meth.*symp*.8.4(p.85.6; M.18.144B); **2.** *enticement*; of a bribe, Isid.Pel.*epp*.1.145(M.78.280B); **3.** *drawing in* of breath, fig. τῇ τοῦ πνεύματος ὁ. τὴν τοῦ Χριστοῦ συνεφελκομένης εὐωδίαν Gr.Nyss.*hom.1 in Cant*.(M.44.780D).

ὁλκός, ὁ, **1.** *dragging, drawing*; **a.** *tugging* of pitch-plasters on the body, Clem.*paed*.3.3(p.245.19; M.8.577B); of a wave, Nonn.*par.Jo.* 21:8(M.43.916C); **b.** *trailing*, fig. τοὺς ὁ. τοὺς ἐρπηστικούς Clem.*prot.* 10(p.76.4; M.8.221B); **c.** *impulsion* of a hand in writing, Nonn.*par. Jo.*19:20(M.43.901C); **d.** *attraction*; spiritual, *cat.Jo.*10:22(p.302.16); **2.** *what is dragged along* or *trailed*; **a.** *trail* of a beard, Nonn.*par.Jo.* 18:19(conj. for ἄκρον M.43.893A); **b.** *body* of a serpent, *Orac.Sib.*13. 161; Gr.Nyss.*or.catech.*30(p.110.5; M.45.76C); **3.** *channel, stream*, Bas. *renunt.*6(2.208A; M.31.640B); id.*ep.*134(3.225D; M.32.569C); Philost. *h.e.*7.3b(p.80.24; M.65.627A); ὁ. ὅλων παθέων ἐλατήριον Paul.Sil.*Soph.* 579–601(M.86.2142A,B); blood-*vessel*, Geo.Pis.*carm.vit.*42; **4.** *course* of years; plur., Paul.Sil.*ambo*.93(M.86.2255B).

ὁλκός, 1. *drawing, attracting* ὁλκὰ πρὸς αἰσχρουργίαν Eus.*p.e.*2.6 (74D; M.21.141B); **2.** *heavy* ἐπιπολάσασα τῇ κάτω ὁλκοτάτῃ φύσει *Hom.Clem.*6.12; *ib.*9.15.

ὁλκότης, ἡ, *heaviness*, *Hom.Clem.*6.6.

***ὁλόαγνος,** *perfectly holy*, Jo.Jej.*canonar.*1(p.113C) ∞ †Jo.Jej. *poenit.*(M.88.1913D); *ib.*(1916C).

***ὁλοαπόλυτος,** *quite free*, Jo.Jej.*canonar.*2(p.438); †Jo.Jej. *poenit.*(M.88.1913C).

***ὁλοβαθύς,** *very deep*, *Apoc.En.*22.2.

***ὁλόβολος,** *beaten solid* (from a play on Arabic ṣamad(u), *unchanging*, ṣâmit(u), *firm, solid*, in the given context), Barth.Edess. *Agar.*(M.104.1385C).

***ὁλοβρύχιος,** *completely overwhelmed by the sea*, Cosm.Mel.*schol.* (M.38.490) in Gr.Naz.*carm.*2.2(poem.)7.152.

ὁλόγραφος, *written entirely* or *fully written out* λίβελλον ὁ. ἐν χειρὶ ἐμῇ Thdr.Scyth.*libell.*12(M.86.236B); Eus.*h.e.*6.24.3(M.20. 580A); τοῦ...Ἰσχύρα...χεῖρα ὁ. αὐθεντικήν Jul.Papa *ep.Dian.*ap. Ath.*apol.sec.*28(p.107.34; M.25.296A): πίστιν ὁ. ... Λουκιανοῦ Soz. *h.e.*3.5.9(M.67.1044B).

***ὁλόγυμνος,** *stark naked*, Gr.Nyss.*mart.*3(M.46.777B); *Chron. Pasch.*p.383(M.92.981A); Jo.D.*hom.*12.16(M.96.804B).

ὁλόγυρος, *completely round*, Melet.*nat.hom.*7(M.64.1184A).

***ὁλόδοξος,** *all-glorious*, Ephr.3.545D; Gr.Naz.*or.*6.22(M.35.749C).

ὁλοήμερος, *lasting the whole day*, *Apoc.Bar.*8(p.90.25).

***ὁλοθανής,** *completely dead*, Anast.S.*Ps.*6(M.89.1088B).

***ὁλόθεος,** *wholly divine*, Anast.S.*hod.*21(M.89.281B).

ὀλοθρευτής, ὁ, *destroyer*; ref. Assyria, Cyr.*Os.*98(3.130C); perh. of Devil, *A.Phil.*130(p.59.9); ref. Ex.12:23 ὅτε ὁ. εἰσέρχεται εἰς πᾶσαν οἰκίαν τῆς ἐν κόσμῳ Αἰγύπτου Or.*schol.in Lc.*11:5ff.(M.17.353C); ὁ ὁ. ἄγγελος Meth.*symp.*6.4(p.68.23; M.18.120A); Cyr.H.*catech.*19.3; ἐσφάγη γὰρ ὁ νοητὸς ἀμνός, ὁ υἱὸς τοῦ θεοῦ...λυτρωσάμενος ἡμᾶς τοῦ ὁ. Procl.CP *or.*14.3(M.65.800A).

ὀλοθρεύ-ω, *destroy*, *Pss.Sal.*15.7; *T.Lev.*13.7; Or.*exc.in Ps.*36:22 (M.17.132D); ref. Ex.12:23 τῶν πρωτοτόκων ~ομένων τέκνων τοῦ σατανᾶ Meth.*symp.*9.1(p.115.19; M.18.180B); Bas.*Spir.*31(3.26C; M. 32.124A).

***ὀλοθροτόκος,** *producing destruction*; of Satan, Ephr.3.546B.

***ὁλοθύμως,** *whole-heartedly*, Agath.*v.Gr.Ill.*106(p.53).

[*]**ὀλοίιος,** = ὀλοός, *destructive*, *Orac.Sib.*5.33 ∞ *ib.*12.85.

ὁλόκαλος, *all-beautiful*, for LXX ὅλη καλή (Cant.4:7) cit. ap. Thdr.Stud.*nativ.BMV* 7(M.96.693B).

***ὁλοκάρδιος, 1.** *whole-hearted*, Petr.I Al.*ep.can.*8(M.18.481A); Sophr.H.*or.*5(M.87.3313B); **2.** *of sound heart*; of trees and men, *Phys.*B 19(pp.232.3,233.5; M.43.533B,C).

***ὁλοκαρδίως,** *whole-heartedly*, Nil.*epp.*3.33(M.79.400C); *ib.*3.125 (441A); Ant.Mon.*hom.*77(M.89.1661D).

[*]**ὁλοκαρπεύω,** *offer as a whole (burnt-)offering*, *Orac.Sib.*3.579.

ὁλοκαρπόω, = foreg., *Orac.Sib.*3.565.

ὁλοκάρπωμα, τό, *whole (burnt-)offering*, Or.*Cels.*5.44(p.47.19; M. 11.1249B); Meth.*symp.*1.1(p.9.2; M.18.40A); met. ὁ. γὰρ ὑπὲρ ἡμῶν ἄπυρον θῦμα ὁ Χριστός Clem.*str.*5.11(p.373.12; M.9.108A); τὴν ἄτυφον καρδίαν μετ' ἐπιστήμης ὀρθῆς ὁ. τοῦ θεοῦ *ib.*7.3(p.10.29; 417B).

ὁλοκάρπωσις, ἡ, *sacrifice of a whole (burnt-)offering*, Mac.Aeg. *hom.*1.6(M.34.456C); Gr.Nyss.*hom.9 in Cant.*(M.44.957A); διὰ τὴν ἀμώμητον αὐτοῦ ὁ. Ephr.3.4A = ‡Chrys.*sac.*7(1.806C); ὡς προσεδέξω ...Ἀβραὰμ τὰς ὁ. *Lit.Jac.*(p.194.11); met., of Christ τὴν ὁ. τοῦ ἰδίου σώματος...θυσίαν προσήνεγκεν *A.Petr.et Paul.*30(p.192.14); typified in Isaac ὁ δὲ μονογενὴς βαστάζει ἐφ' ἑαυτοῦ τὰ τῆς ὁ. ξύλα Gr.Nyss. *res.*1(M.46.601C).

ὁλόκαυστος, *completely burnt*, *T.Job* 7(p.108.10).

ὁλοκαυτ-όω, 1. *offer as a whole burnt-sacrifice*, Clem.*prot.*3(p.32. 8, v.l. -καεῖν M.8.125B); of Isaac θῦμα...~ούμενον Gr.Nyss.*deit.*(M. 46.568C); ὡς κριὸς...~ούμενος Cyr.*ador.*11(1.402D); Jo.Mon.*hymn. Blas.*5(M.96.1404A); met. ὅλον σαυτὸν ἀνάθες τῷ θεῷ καὶ ὁλοκαύτωσον Chrys.*hom.33.2 in Jo.*(8.192A); of Church ἅτε δὴ τῷ καινῷ πυρὶ τὴν τῶν ἀνθρώπων θυσίαν ὁλοκαυτώσασαν Thdt.*Cant.*7:1(2.141); μυστικῶς ~ούμενοι Dion.Ar.*e.h.*4.3.12(M.3.484D); **2.** intrans., *offer whole burnt-sacrifice*, Cyr.*Os.*proem.(3.5A).

ὁλοκαύτωμα, τό, *whole burnt-offering*, ref. Is.1:11ff., *Barn.*2.4; θυσία δὲ αἰνέσεως ὑπὲρ ὁλοκαυτώματα Clem.*str.*2.18(p.165.15; M.8. 1037B); Chrys.*hom.33.2 in Jo.*(8.192A); met., of Polycarp ὁ. δεκτὸν τῷ θεῷ *M.Polyc.*14.1; γενώμεθα ὁ. λογικά, θύματα τέλεια Gr.Naz.*or.* 40.40(M.36.417A); μόνοι διεσώθησαν οἱ οἶκοι, ὁ. γενόμενοι τῷ κυρίῳ Pall.*h.Laus.*54(p.148.12; M.34.1227D).

***ὁλοκαύτως,** *by complete, fiery consumption*, Dion.Ar.*c.h.*7.1(M.3. 205C).

ὁλοκαύτωσις, ἡ, *sacrifice of a whole burnt-offering* τί δεῖ μοι ὁλοκαυτώσεων, ὧν μὴ δεῖται ὁ θεός; Athenag.*leg.*13.2(M.6.916C); ref. 3Reg.18:31ff., Iren.*haer.*1.18.4(M.7.649A); of sacrifice of Isaac, typifying that of Christ, Jo.D.*hom.*4.25(M.96.624C); met., of Christ αὐτὸς ἡ ὁ. ‡Cyr.H.*occurs.*5(M.33.1192B); ὁ. ἑαυτὴν τῷ θεῷ προσκομίσασαν Thdt.*Cant.*3:6(2.82).

***ὁλόκεντρος,** *covered with spines*, ‡Petr.A Al.*phys.*17(p.47); ‡Eust.*hex.*(M.18.745A).

ὁλόκληρος, 1. *whole, healthy*, Clem.*q.d.s.*24(p.175.26; M.9.629A); ὁλόκληρος τὸ σῶμα ἢ σεσινωμένος Or.*comm.in Gen.*ap.Eus.*p.e.*6.11 (291B; M.12.72B); ὁ. ἐκ πάσης αἰτίας *Pers.*(p.25.1); **2.** *complete*; **a.** *whole, entire* τὰ φώρια ὁ. Clem.*str.*6.2(p.442.3; M.9.241A); ὁ. ἔθνη Thdt.*Abac.*1:15f.(2.1542); ἐπὶ ὁλοκλήρῳ τετραμήνῳ †Gregent.*leg. Hom.*31(M.86.597C); κοιμηθέντες ὁλόκληροι ‡Nil.*narr.*2(M.79.605A); theol. ἡ μονὰς ἀδιαίρετος καὶ ὁ. μένει ‡Ath.*Ar.*4.2(p.45.25; M.26. 469C); οὐ μερικῶς, ἀλλ' ἐπὶ τῆς...ὁ. καὶ πλήρους θεότητος Dion.Ar.*d.n.* 2.1(M.3.636C); of the fountain of the Spirit παρὰ πᾶσιν ὁλόκληρος, καὶ ἐν ἑκάστῳ ὁ. Chrys.*hom.3.1 in Ac.princ.*(3.72B); ref. resurrection of body ὁ. αὐτὸν ἐν τῇ δευτέρᾳ αὐτοῦ παρουσίᾳ...ἀναστήσει Just. *dial.*69.7(M.6.640A); εἰ ὁ. ἀναστήσεται τὸ σῶμα, καὶ τὰ μόρια αὐτοῦ πάντα ἕξει †Just.*fr.res.*3(p.38; M.6.1576B); of Christ's body, Ath. *inc.*21.7(M.25.133C); **b.** *perfect* ἡ μακροθυμία κατοικεῖ μετὰ τῶν τὴν πίστιν ἐχόντων ὁ. Herm.*mand.*5.2.3; Ath.*Dion.*14(p.56.26; M.25. 501A); of Son οὔσης ὑποστάσεως, ἔστι ταύτης ὁ χαρακτὴρ ὁ. Ath. *Ar.*1.20(M.26.53B); **3.** in phrase ἐξ ὁλοκλήρου, *completely, entirely* οὐ γὰρ ἐξ ὁ. συγκατέθου πάσῃ τῇ παλαιᾷ διαθήκῃ Or.*fr.*57 *in Jo.*(p.530. 14); ἐλευθερώσῃ δι' ἑαυτοῦ ἐξ ὁ. τὸν ἄνθρωπον ‡Ath.*Apoll.*1.14(M.26. 1117B); †Ath.*fr.Mt.*(M.27.1372C); Didym.*Ac.*2:5(M.39.1656A).

ὁλοκλήρως, *wholly, completely, perfectly, in their entirety* or *completeness* αἱ ψυχαὶ...ὁ. ἀναστᾶσαι, τουτέστι σωματικῶς Iren. *haer.*5.31.2(M.7.1209C); οὐδεὶς γὰρ τὰ ἔργα τοῦ θεοῦ ὁ. καταλαβεῖν δύναται †Dion.Al.*fr.Eccl.*3:11(p.226.13; M.10.1588C); τελείως, καὶ ὁ. τὸ ἀνθρώπινον γένος ἐλευθερούμενον ἀπὸ τῆς ἁμαρτίας Ath.*tom.*7 (M.26.804B); ὁ ἱερεὺς...τὸ τρισάγιον ὁ. φθεγγόμενος *Lit.Praesanct.* (p.345.2).

***ὁλοκότινος, ὁ (-τίνον, -τίνι(ο)ν, τό),** a coin, prob. *solidus*, Thdt. *h.e.*2.16.27(v.l. χρυσίνους 3.869); *Apophth.Patr.*(M.65.237A); *V.Pach.* A 21(p.148.17); ὁλοκοτίνα Leont.N.*v.Sym.*44,52(M.93.1725A,1733C); ὁλοκοτίνιν Thphn.*chron.*p.345(M.108.832B).

ὁλολαμπής, *wholly bright*, Thdt.*Cant.*2:17(2.75); Dion.Ar.*d.n.*4.4 (M.3.697C); Max.*myst.*6(M.91.684C).

***ὁλόλαμπρος,** = foreg., Mac.Aeg.*hom.*16.8(M.34.620B).

***ὁλόλεπρος,** *full of leprosy*, Or.*schol.in Lc.*7:22(M.17.333C).

ὁλόλευκος, *entirely white* or *bright*, *Phys.*A 3(pp.11.3,13.5; cf.M. 43.533A).

***ὁλόλοξος,** *all crooked*; met., *A.Phil.*110(p.42.19).

***ὁλομανέω,** *rave*, Gr.Nyss.*anim.et res.*(M.46.65A).

***ὁλομαργαραργυρόχρους,** *wholly of the colour of silver and pearls*, Sophr.H.*carm.*20.24(p.46; ὁλομαργαρογυρόχρουν M.87.3817B).

***ὁλομόχθηρος,** *wholly vile*, Nil.*epp.*2.189(M.79.297C).

ὁλονύκτιος, *continuing all night* ὁ. ἀγρυπνιῶν Marc.Er.*opusc.*5.7 (M.65.1040A).

[*]**ὁλόνυκτος,** = foreg., Ephr.3.298A; †Jo.D.*B.J.*22(M.96. 1056C); *ib.*30(1141C).

ὁλόξηρος, *quite dry*; met., of one devoid of charity, Anast.S.*qu. et resp.*109(M.89.761B).

***ὁλόξυλος,** *entirely covered with wood*, Thphn.*chron.*p.332(M.108. 801A).

***ὁλοπαγής,** *completely solid*, Jo.D.*dialect.*68(M.94.676A).

***ὁλοπίστως,** *with complete confidence*, Jo.Clim.*past.*7(M.88. 1184B).

ὁλοποιός, *whole-making*, Leont.H.*Nest.*1.52(M.86.1525A).

***ὁλοπόλιος,** *entirely grey-headed*, *Apophth.Patr.*(M.65.108A); Jo. Mal.*chron.*10 p.250(M.97.381B); *ib.*12 p.290(437B).

ὁλοπόρφυρος, *all of porphyry*, Jo.Mal.*chron.*13 p.320(M.97.480B).

***ὁλοπράκτως**, *entirely*, Nil.*epp*.3.294(M.79.529C).

§**ὁλόπυρος**, *all of fire*, Anast.S.*hod*.21(M.89.281B).

ὁλόρριζος (ὁλόριζος), **1.** *with all its roots*, lit. ὁλόριζον σέλινον Clem.*prot*.2(p.15.7; M.8.81A); **2.** *perfect* τῆς παρθενίας ὁλόρριζον δόξαν ‡Meth.*Sym.et Ann*.1(M.18.348A); **3.** adverbially, *completely, utterly, root and branch* ἵνα μὴ ὁ. ἐκ γῆς ἀπολῇ Cyr.*Ps*.36:8(M.69.928D); id.*Is*.2.3(2.255B); ἵν' ὁ. ἀνέλῃ τὴν τοιαύτην πλάνην id.ap.*cat.Jo*.1:9 (p.183.20).

***ὁλόρρυπος**, *completely foul*, ‡Chrys.*hom*.13(13.255F).

***ὁλορύπαρος**, *utterly defiled*, Ant.Mon.*hom*.77(M.89.1660A).

ὅλος, **1.** *whole, entire*; **a.** adverbially ὅλη ἦν ἀσθενὴς τῷ σώματι Ath.*v.Anton*.61(M.26.932B); ὅλος πρὸς ἀρετὴν βλέπων †Bas.Sel.*or*.41 (M.85.464B); ὅλος ἔπνευσε *with all his might*, Chrys.*hom.81.3 in Mt*. (7.776E); **b.** *full of, entirely devoted to* ὅ. τῆς περὶ τὸ μαρτύριον ὁρμῆς Eus.*h.e*.6.2.5(M.20.524B); ὅ. τοῦ λήμματος Chrys.*hom.81.3 in Mt*. (7.776D); ὅ. ἦν τοῦ καλέσαντος Vict.*Mc*.2:14(p.288.16); ὅ. γέγονε τῆς ἐφέσεως· ὅ. τῆς ἐλπίδος· ὅ. τῆς χαρᾶς ‡Meth.*Sym.et Ann*.6(M.18. 360D); **c.** with numbers, *as many as, in all, all told*, Eus.*d.e*.7.3 (p.338.21; M.22.552C); ἐν εἴκοσι ἢ καὶ τριάκοντα ὅλοις ἔτεσι Chrys. *hom.75.2 in Mt*.(7.726A); Socr.*h.e*.1.1.1(M.67.33A); **2.** *all*; **a.** τὰ ὅ. *the universe* τὸν ποιητὴν τῶν ὅλων θεόν Just.*dial*.7.3(M.6.492B); τῶν ὅ. ἀρχή Tat.*orat*.4(p.5.2; M.6.813A); Clem.*prot*.10(p.70.23; M.8.209C); ὁ τῶν ὅ. δημιουργός *ib*.(p.71.21; 212B); κύριος τῶν ὅ. id.*paed*.2.3 (p.179.31; M.8.436B); Cyr.H.*procatech*.9; **b.** ref. Persons of Trin. ὅλαι αἱ τρεῖς ὑποστάσεις διαιωνίζουσαι ἑαυταῖς εἰσι καὶ ἴσαι ‡Ath.*symb*. (p.266; M.28.1584A); **3.** *whole, complete*; theol.; **a.** wholeness not properly predicated of God, who is beyond magnitude, Clem.*str*. 5.12(p.380.20; M.9.121A); nevertheless phrase τὸ ἀπερίγραπτον ὅ. is used, Leont.H.*Nest*.1.1(M.86.1408C,D) v. infra d; **b.** being, in its entirety, is the peculiarity of God τὸ δὲ ὄν, ἴδιον ὄντως θεοῦ, καὶ ὅλον Gr.Naz.*or*.30.18(p.137.1; M.36.128A); θεὸς...ὅλον ἐν ἑαυτῷ συλλαβὼν ἔχει τὸ εἶναι *ib*.38.7(317B); **c.** God is not divided ὅλος ἔννοια ὤν, ὅ. θέλημα, ὅ. νοῦς, ὅ. φῶς, ὅ. ὀφθαλμός, ὅ. ἀκοή, ὅ. πηγὴ πάντων τῶν ἀγαθῶν Iren.*haer*.1.12.2(M.7.573A); cf.Cyr.H.*catech*.6.7; **d.** ref. relationship between Father and Son ὁ υἱός, ἐκ τοῦ θεοῦ τοῦ πατρὸς γεννηθεὶς ὅλος ἐξ ὅλου ‡Ath.*dial.Trin*.3.4(M.28.1208C); υἱὸν...ὅλον δεικνύντα ἐν ἑαυτῷ τὸν πατέρα Bas.*ep*.105(3.200A; M.32.513A); ref. Jo.1:1 ὅλῳ γὰρ τῷ θεῷ ὅλως συνθεωρεῖται ὁ λόγος. εἰ γὰρ ἐλλιπὴς ἦν ἐν τῷ ἰδίῳ μεγέθει ὁ λόγος, ὥστε μὴ δύνασθαι πρὸς ὅλον τὸν θεὸν εἶναι Gr.Nyss.*fid*.(M. 45.141A); οὐ μέρος φαμὲν τὸν υἱὸν τοῦ πατρὸς...ἀλλ' ὅλον ὅλου γεννητὸν ἐξ ἀγεννήτου Didym.(‡Bas.)*Eun*.4(1.285B; M.29.685B); συνεῖναι δὲ τῷ υἱῷ τὸν πατέρα νοοῦμεν...ὡς ὅλον ὄντα ἐν αὐτῷ διὰ τὸ ἀπαράλλακτον τῆς οὐσίας Cyr.*Jo*.1.5(4.45D); **e.** of H. Ghost ὅλον ἑκάστῳ παρὸν καὶ ὅλον ἁπανταχοῦ ὄν Bas.*Spir*.22(3.19D; M.32.108C); ὡς μέρη δὲ ἐν ὅλῳ, οἱ καθ' ἕνα ἐσμὲν ἐν τῷ πνεύματι *ib*.61(52B; M.181B); **f.** Christol. θεὸς λόγος ὤν, ἐγένετο ἄνθρωπος, ὅ. ἀνθρωπότητα λαβών. ἡ γὰρ μορφὴ τοῦ δούλου ὅ. ἐστὶν ἀνθρωπότης, ὡς ἡ μορφὴ τοῦ θεοῦ ὅ. θεότης ‡Ath.*dial. Trin*.5.28(M.28.1281C); ὅ. ἄνθρωπον, τὸν αὐτὸν καὶ θεόν, ὑπὲρ ὅλου τοῦ πεπονθότος, ἵνα ὅλῳ σοι τὴν σωτηρίαν χαρίσηται, ὅ. τὸ κατάκριμα λύσας τῆς ἁμαρτίας Gr.Naz.*or*.40.45(M.36.424B); ὅλον οὖν ὅλῃ συνηνῶσθαι φαμὲν τῇ καθ' ἡμᾶς ἀνθρωπότητι τὸν...λόγον Cyr.*Thds*.21(p.55.14; 5². 18C); ὅλον γὰρ ὅλος ἀνέλαβέ με, καὶ ὅλος ὅλῳ ἡνώθη, ἵνα ὅλῳ τὴν σωτηρίαν χαρίσηται Jo.D.*f.o*.3.6(M.94.1005B); κηρύττοντες...ὅ. θεὸν καὶ ὅ. ἄνθρωπον *ib*.3.7(1012A); **g.** eucharistic φάγωμεν...τὸ πάσχα, ἔχοντες μεθ' ἑαυτῶν τὸν ὑπὲρ ὑμῶν τυθέντα Χριστόν, ὅ. αὐτὸν ὡς ζωὴν ἐσθίοντες Thphl.Al.*fr.ep.pasch*.1(p.300.7; M.65.53A); **4.** in phrases, *entirely, altogether, completely* ὅλη δι' ὅλης ἡ ἐπιστολή Chrys.*hom. 1.1 in Tit*.(11.731B); ἡ τοῦ Χριστοῦ ἀνθρωπότης, ὅλη δι' ὅλου ὁλόθεος Anast.S.*hod*.21(M.89.281B); ἐξ ὅλου φθείρεσθαι Ath.*gent*.22(M.25. 44D); τῶν ἐξ ὅλου τὴν σύνοδον ἀρνουμένων id.*syn*.41(p.266.27; M.26. 764D); μέχρις ὅλου σκληροκαρδίων Just.*dial*.95.4(M.6.701D).

ὁλοσηρικός (ὁλοσήρικος), *all of silk* ὁλοσηρικήν Jo.Mal.*chron*.12 p.287(M.97.433B); *ib*.17 p.413(612B); neut. as subst., *garment all of silk*, Mac.Aeg.*hom*.17.9(M.34.629C); *Apophth.Patr*.(M.65.104A); *Chron.Pasch*.p.394(1012A).

***ὁλόστατος**, *full-length, life-size*, ‡Ath.*imag.Beryt*.(M.28.797B).

***ὁλόστερνος**, *wholly beloved*, Thdr.Stud.*or*.11.13(M.99.816A).

ὁλόστημον, τό, *garment consisting all of warp-threads* θέριστρον δέ φασι τὸ ὁ. Proc.G.*Gen*.24:65(M.87.404A).

***ὁλοσυμπαθής**, *wholly sympathetic*, Sophr.H.*carm*.10.92(M.87. 3784C).

ὁλοσφύρατος (-ητος), *made of solid beaten metal*, Ephr.3.174C; met., ref. unity of body and soul in man ἕν τι εἶναι ὁλοσφύρητον τὸν ἄνθρωπον Epiph.*anc*.35(p.45.23; M.43.81B).

ὁλόσφυρος, *made of solid beaten metal*, Jo.Mal.*chron*.10 p.265 (M.97.401B); hence *entire, being a compact whole*; of God acc. Mohammedans, Barth.Edess.*Agar*.(M.104.1385C); εἷς θεὸς ὁ. οὐκ ἐγέννησεν οὔτ' ἐγεννήθη ‡Barth.Edess.*Muham*.(M.104.1453C); v. ὁλόβολος.

ὁλοσχερῶς, **1.** *entirely, completely* ὁ σατανᾶς...ὁ. αὐτοῦ περιγέγονε Chrys.*hom.81.3 in Mt*.(7.776E); τῶν μὴ ὁ. ἑαυτοὺς προσαγόντων τῷ θεῷ Ammon.*Ac*.5:1f.(M.85.1525C); τοῖς ὁ. τε καὶ ὁλοτρόπως ἀκολουθοῦσι θεῷ Cyr.*ador*.1(1.22A); **2.** *while remaining complete*, of H. Ghost ὁ. μετεχόμενον Bas.*Spir*.22(3.19D; M.32.108C); **3.** *coarsely*, of heretics πρὸς δὲ καὶ τὰ ἔργα τῆς δικαιοσύνης ὁλοσχερέστερον, οὐχὶ δὲ ἀκριβέστερον μετερχομένους Clem.*str*.7.18(p.78.9; M.9.556B).

***ὁλόσχοινος**, *of wicker*, Soz.*h.e*.5.10.12(M.67.1245A).

ὁλοσώματος, **1.** *of the whole body*, of Church ὁλοσώματον ποιεῖται αὐτῆς τὸ ἐγκώμιον Gr.Nyss.*hom.7 in Cant*.(M.44.940A); **2.** *entire, wholesale* ὁ. αὐτὰς καταπίνοντες †Gregent.*leg.Hom*.42(M.86.604C).

***ὁλόσωμος**, **1.** *with the entire body*, Eust.*engast*.5(p.22.20; M.18. 621C); Alex.Sal.*Barn*.42(450F); **2.** *complete, utter* ὁ ὁ. τοῦ σατανᾶ ὑπηρέτης Thdr.Stud.*epp*.2.75(M.99.1312A); ὁλόσωμος ἡ ἁμαρτία καὶ ἡ ἄρνησις *ib*.2.95(1348B).

ὁλοτελής, **1.** *perfect*; of faith, Clem.*paed*.1.6(p.107.18; M.8. 285A); Meth.*symp*.8.3(p.84.5; M.18.141B); of love towards God, Cyr.*Is*.5.3(2.807A); **2.** *complete*, Herm.*vis*.3.10.9; of human salvation, Gr.Nyss.*ep*.3(M.46.1021D); Cyr.*Am*.63(3.320E); τῆς ὁ. καὶ πάσης θεότητος Dion.Ar.*d.n*.2.1(M.3.636C).

ὁλοτελῶς, *completely, fully* οἱ μετανοήσαντες ὁ. Herm.*vis*.3.13.4; ὁ. ἀδιάφθοροι Meth.*symp*.11(p.137.18; M.18.213C); ὁ. ἁγιασθῆναι Gr. Nyss.*Apoll*.46(M.45.1236A); ref. Godhead as fully in each of the three Persons, Sophr.H.*ep.syn*.(M.87.3157C).

ὁλότης, ἡ, *totality, entirety* τὰ μέρη πάντα τῆς ὁ. Mac.Aeg.*pat*.12 (M.34.873D); αἱ τελειότητες τῶν ὁ. Dion.Ar.*d.n*.4.10(M.3.705C); τὰ μέρη ἐν ταῖς ὁ. Max.*ambig*.(M.91.1189D); theol. ἁπάσῃ τῇ ὁ. τῆς... θεότητος Dion.Ar.*d.n*.2.1(M.3.636C); of Christ, called God and man ἰδοὺ τὴν ὁ. τῇ τῶν ἀποτελεστικῶν αὐτῆς μερῶν ἐπωνυμίᾳ προσαγορεύεις Leont.H.*monoph*.54(M.86.1800A); κατὰ τὴν προσωπικὴν αὐτοῦ ὁ. Anast.S.*hod*.13(M.89.221D).

***ὁλοτρόπως**, *in every way, completely, entirely* πεπάτηκε ὁ. τὴν ἁμαρτίαν Cyr.*glaph.Gen*.5(1.143A); οὐχ ὁ. τῆς εἰς θεὸν ἀγάπης ἐξείχοντο id.*Os*.proem.(3.5B); id.*Abac*.28(3.541E); Christol. φασὶ...ὁ. ἀποφοιτᾶν τὰς φύσεις id.*apol.Thdt*.3(p.118.18; 6¹.212A).

***ὁλοφαής**, *all bright*, †Bas.Sel.*or*.41(M.85.461C).

***ὁλοφανῶς**, *quite openly*, Thdr.Stud.*epp*.2.83(M.99.1325A).

***ὁλόφθαλμος**, *full of eyes*, Mac.Aeg.*hom*.1.3(M.34.452D).

***ὁλόφλογος**, *all of flame*, Anast.S.*hod*.21(M.89.281B).

***ὁλοφυρτέον**, *one must lament*, Isid.Pel.*epp*.2.285(M.78.716B).

ὁλοφυρτικός, *to be lamented*, Marc.Er.*opusc*.5.12(M.65.1048D).

***ὁλόφωτος**, *all of light, all bright*, Andr.Cr.*or*.14(M.97.1100C); Gr.II Papa *ep.Germ*.(M.98.152B); ‡Sophr.H.*triod*.(M.87.3864C).

ὁλόχαλκος, *all of bronze*, ‡Pall.*h.mon*.30.2(p.92.13; M.34.1050C).

ὁλόψυχος, *of one's whole soul*, Clem.*fr*.44(p.223.6).

ὁλοψύχως, *with one's whole soul*, Leont.N.*v.Sym*.12(M.93.1684D); Anast.S.*Ps*.6(M.89.1084B); *cat.Lc*.14:31(p.116.20).

ὀλυμπικός, ὁ, *one who participates in the Olympic games*; condemned, *Const.App*.8.32.9.

ὄλυνθος, ὁ, **1.** *wild fig*, Bas.*hex*.5.7(1.47C; M.29.112B); Isid.Pel. *epp*.3.84(M.78.789D); **2.** *early fig*; fig., of apostles, exeg. Cant.2:13, Ph.Carp.*Cant*.58(M.40.69C).

[*]**ὄλυρα, τά**, = ὄλυραι, αἱ, a form of *wheat*, Thphn.*chron*.p.168 (M.108.448A).

ὀλυρίτης, ὁ, *bread* or *cake* made of ὄλυρα, ref. 3Reg.19:6, Or.*fr. 20 in Reg*.(p.302.11; M.17.57B); Gr.Nyss.*laud.Bas*.(M.46.805B).

ὅλως, in various constructions, *at all* οὐδὲ γὰρ εἶναι τὸ σύνολον ὅ. ἐκ παντὸς τὸ παράπαν ἕτερος δημιουργὸς δύναται πλὴν αὐτοῦ Meth.*res*. 1.36(p.277.3; M.41.1101C); *ib*.1.38(p.281.2; M.18.265D); οὐδὲν ὅ. *ib*. 1.46(p.296.2; M.41.1117A); κατὰ ὅ. τινός *anyone at all*, Chrys. *hom.15.2 in 1Tim*.(11.637B); τίς δὲ ὅ. ...; Gel.Cyz.*h.e*.2.21.2(M.85. 1284B).

***ὁμάγαθος**, *of equal goodness*, of Logos ὁ. τῷ γεννήσαντι πατρί Alex.Sal.*cruc*.(M.87.4017A).

***ὁμαδήν**, *briefly*, Ph.Carp.*Cant*.106(M.40.93C).

***ὁμαδικῶς**, *in united fashion, as one* of Christ speaking as man and God ὁ., τοῦτ' ἔστι θεανδρικῶς Anast.S.*hod*.13(M.89.221D); *ib*.16 (261D).

***ὁμαδόν**, *together*, Rom.Mel.(*AS* 1 p.156).

ὁμακοεῖον, τό, *school* of Pythagoras; said to foreshadow Church, Clem.*str*.1.15(p.42.2; M.8.768B).

ὁμαλίζ-ω, **1.** *make smooth*, met. ὁ κύριος...ὁδὸν τῷ εὐαγγελίῳ ~ων ἀπρόσκοπον Isid.Pel.*epp*.1.145(M.78.280C); **2.** *make homogeneous*,

Or.*Cels*.2.30(p.158.10; M.11.849C); **3.** *render free from difficulties, resolve* a question, Max.*ambig*.(M.91.1265D); *ib*.(1273A).

ὁμαλισμός, ὁ, 1. *levelling*, *Pss.Sal*.11.5 (cf. Bar.5:7); **2.** *resolution* of a difficulty, Max.*ambig*.(M.91.1244B).

ὁμαλός, 1. *level, even, smooth* εἰς τὰ ὁ. *on to level ground*, Herm. *vis*.1.1.3; id.*mand*.2.4; ref. Mt.7:13 ἡ τῶν ἀπολλυμένων ὁδὸς... ὁμαλωτάτη *Hom.Clem*.7.7; **2.** in phrase καθ' ὁμαλοῦ, *likewise*, Didym.*Trin*.3.28(M.39.945B); **3.** *equable* τὸ ἐν σκυθρωπότητι ὁ. Bas.*ep*.173(3.261D; M.32.649B); Melit.Ant.*hom*.ap.Epiph.*haer*.73.33 (p.308.28; M.42.465C).

ὁμαλότης, ἡ, *equability*, Max.*ambig*.(M.91.1248D).

ὁμαλῶς, *easily*, Herm.*mand*.6.1.4.

ὁμάς, ἡ, *sum, total* κατὰ τὴν ὁ. τοῦ ἀριθμοῦ Epiph.*haer*.8.8(p.195. 4; M.41.220B); Leont.B.*arg.Sev*.(M.86.1920B); cf.Jo.D.*Jacob*.50(M. 94.1460A); Leont.H.*Nest*.2.15(M.86.1569D); Jewish *community*, Phot.*nomoc*.6.3(p.517; M.104.636A); phrases: καθ' ὁμάδα *general* bequests, *ib*.2.1(p.489; 569C); ἐν ὁ. *all together* τῆς ἐν ὁ. μεθεκτῆς οὐσίας τῆς ἁγίας τριάδος Didym.*Trin*.2.2(M.39.456B).

ὀμβρ-έω, 1. *shower down like rain*, fig. τὴν ἄνω 'Ιερουσαλὴμ...ἐν ᾗ μέλι καὶ γάλα ~εῖν ἀναγέγραπται Clem.*paed*.1.6(p.117.1; M.8.304B); ref. 3Reg.17:16 ὤμβρει τὸ ἄλευρον ‡Nil.*perist*.11.17(M.79.928C); **2.** *soak*, *Orac.Sib*.3.392; **3.** *pour forth*; intrans., Or.*Cels*.8.31(p.246. 30; M.11.1564A); trans., *Orac.Sib*.3.461; Jo.D.*carm.pasch*.18(p.218; M.96.840C).

***ὀμβρήεις,** *making wet as with rain*, *Orac.Sib*.11.218; *ib*.12.153.

ὄμβρημα, τό, 1. *shower*; fig., Eus.*l.C*.12(p.231.24; M.20.1389B); **2.** *standing water*; of heresy, Jo.Mon.*hymn.Chrys*.(M.96.1380B).

ὀμβριμαῖος, *rain-swollen*, Cyr.S.*v.Jo.Hes*.26(p.221.12).

ὀμβροβλυτέω, *shed forth like rain*, Jo.D.*carm.pent*.3.38(p.214; M. 96.833C).

***ὀμβρόθεος,** *divinely pouring forth water*, Leont.N.*serm*.3(M.93. 1608B); cf.Gr.II Papa *ep.Germ*.(M.98.153B).

ὄμβρος, ὁ, 1. *shower*, met. πατρῴης σοφίης...ὁ. Nonn.*par.Jo*.3:34 (M.43.772C); *ib*.8:14(813C); of tears, *ib*.20:11(909B); of blood, Geo. Pis.*carm.vit*.34; **2.** *flood*; met., Const.ap.Gel.Cyz.*h.e*.3.19.40(M.85. 1356); **3.** *stream, brook* Κεδρὼν...ὁ. Nonn.*par.Jo*.18:1(888C).

***ὀμβροτοκία, ἡ,** *production of rain*, met. κατὰ τὴν νοητὴν ὁ. Dion. Ar.*c.h*.15.6(M.3.336B).

ὁμηγύριος, *festive*, Isid.Pel.*epp*.3.286(M.78.961B).

ὁμήγυρις, ἡ, 1. *assembly*, Thdt.*h.e*.5.35.4(3.1077); of CChalc., Thdr.Abuc.*opusc*.4(M.97.1512B); **2.** *company* τῆς ὁ. τῶν ἀρχαγγέλων Meth.*symp*.6.5(p.69.23; M.18.121A); ἡ θεία τῆς ἐκκλησίας ἡμῶν ὁ. ‡Caes.Naz.*dial*.122(M.38.1012A).

ὁμῆλιξ, 1. *of the same age* as; c. dat., Nonn.*par.Jo*.8:21(M.43. 816B); *co-eternal* with God οὐ γὰρ ὁ. αὐτῷ ὁ αἰών Didym.*Trin*.1.15 (M.39.312C); wrongly predicated of evil, Chrys.*hom.59.3 in Mt*.(7. 596D); of Logos, Nonn.*par.Jo*.1:1(749A); **2.** as subst., *contemporary*, Just.*dial*.115.5(M.6.744A).

ὅμηλυς, ὁ, *companion*, Nonn.*par.Jo*.1:19(M.43.753A); *ib*.11:33 (844C).

ὁμηρεύ-ω, 1. *join in agreement*, intrans. ~έτωσάν σοι αἱ σωματικαὶ ἀρεταὶ πρὸς τὰς ψυχικάς Evagr.Pont.*or*.132(M.79.1196A); Nil.*exerc*.75 (M.79.809B); trans. εἰς φιλικὴν ὁ. συμφωνίαν τοὺς ἐπουρανίους πρὸς τοὺς γηγενεῖς ‡Meth.*Sym.et Ann*.6(M.18.361A); **2.** *give pledge* or *promise of* μὴ ~έτω σου ἡ διάνοια βαθμὸν ἱερωσύνης Nil.*epp*.4.1(M.79.544C).

ὁμηρία, ἡ, = ὁμηρεία, *condition of being a hostage* καθ' ὁμηρίαν *as a hostage*, Philost.*h.e*.3.4(M.65.484A).

ὁμιλ-έω, A. of association in gen.; **1.** *come into contact* with; c. dat., things, Chrys.*hom.18.3 in Mt*.(7.237B); id.*hom.13.8 in Rom*. (9.569B); Thdt.*h.rel*.17(3.1227); **2.** *approach*, c. dat. οὐκ εἶπεν, ὅτι ἥψατο τῆς ῥίζης ἀλλ' ὅτι...~εῖ τῇ ῥίζῃ Chrys.*hom.11.3 in Mt*.(7. 152D); **3.** *meet* with ὁ. ὀλέθρῳ Nonn.*par.Jo*.8:22(M.43.816C); *ib*.8:24 (816C); **4.** *consort* in marriage, Chrys.*hom.37.6 in Mt*.(7.423C); id. *hom.7.4 in 2Tim*.(11.704E); Thdt.*1Tim*.5:9(3.664); **5.** *be acquainted* with or *accustomed* to, *hold converse* with νάπαις ~οῦντες καὶ ὄρεσι ...καὶ πρὸ τούτων ἁπάντων τῷ θεῷ Chrys.*hom.68.3 in Mt*.(7.673E); μήπω...ἀνδρείῳ ~ήσασα λογισμῷ Nil.*epp*.2.68(M.79.232B); **6.** *busy oneself* with, *become acquainted* with ἐπὶ πλεῖον ὡμιληκέναι τῇ κακίᾳ Or.*or*.29.15(p.391.2; M.11.544B); Meth.*symp*.11(p.130.9; M.18.205B); Chrys.*hom.68.4 in Mt*.(7.676D); ὀνησιφόροις ἱδρῶσιν ~εῖν Cyr.*Ps*. 32:20(M.69.881D); **7.** *pay attention* to ὁ. τοῖς ἐγγεγραμμένοις Meth. *symp*.3.14(p.45.2; M.18.85B); ὁ τοῖς εὐαγγελικοῖς συγγράμμασιν ~ῶν Cyr.*Ps*.34:16(M.69.904D); **8.** *consort* with, *associate* with ὅταν ἐνδιατρίψῃ τῇ θεωρίᾳ, τῷ θείῳ καθαρῶς ~ῶν Clem.*str*.4.6(p.266.6; M.8. 1252A); id.*ecl*.37(p.148.10; M.9.717A); of Inc. διὰ μέσου νοὸς ~ήσας σαρκί Gr.Naz.*or*.29.19(p.103.1; M.36.100A); Ast.Am.*hom*.1(M.40. 173D); ἡμῖν ὁ τοῦ πατρὸς υἱὸς ~ήσας διὰ σαρκός Const.Diac.*laud*.13 (M.88.496A); **9.** *meet* with, *come across* οὐδέ ποτε τούτοις ὡμιλήσαμεν Or.*Cels*.5.62(p.66.5; M.11.1284A); **10.** *address, communicate* with in writing, Eus.*h.e*.3.38.2(M.20.293C).

B. of communication by speech or utterance; **1.** *speak* τὰς διανοήσεις...~ούσας παλίμφημα Meth.*res*.1.62(p.329.1; M.41.1162C); οἱ δαίμονες...τοιαῦτα ~οῦντες Nil.*epp*.2.103(M.79.245B); φιλικὰ ὁ. Thdr.Stud.*epp*.2.63(M.99.1284A); of speaking unknown tongues, Nil.*epp*.2.204(M.79.308C); *speak* to or with; c. dat., Or.*hom.8.5 in Jer*.(p.60.10; M.13.341C); Ath.*Ar*.3.12(M.26.348B); abs. εἴ τις ἑσπέρας, μετὰ τὸ Πάτερ ἡμῶν, εὑρεθῇ ~ῶν, ἀφοριζέσθω ‡Bas.*poen. mon*.26(2.528C; M.31.1309B); of conversation between God and man; as a strength to martyrs, *M.Polyc*.2.2; of Jesus speaking with the patriarchs, Just.*dial*.113.4(M.6.737A); of Adam τῷ θεῷ μετὰ παρρησίας ὡμίλει Chrys.*hom.68.3 in Mt*.(7.674A); of addressing God in prayer, ‡Pall.*h.mon*.1.25(p.11.10; M.34.1116C); ὁ ἱερεὺς καθ' ἑαυτὸν τῷ θεῷ ~εῖ λέγων οὕτως *Lit.Jac*.(*NBP* 10 p.98); of converse between Father and Logos ᾧ καὶ ~ῶν ἐποίει τὰ ὅλα Ath.*gent*. 46(M.25.93A); met., of the gospel ἐσφαλμένοις ὡμίλει Serap.*Man*.50 (p.71; M.18.1245D); abs., of voice of Father, *ib*.48(p.67; 1240B); **2.** *teach* οὐ ξένα ~ῶ ‡*Diogn*.11.1; ὅλῳ ἐνιαυτῷ...ὡμίλησεν ὁ διδάσκαλος *Hom.Clem*.17.19; Εὔα ἡμῖν ὁ. τὸ τοιοῦτον Diad.*perf*.56(p.62.6); **3.** *preach* 'Ιουδαίοις ~οῦντας περὶ τῆς εἰς τὸν 'Ιησοῦν πίστεως Or.*Cels* 1.62(p.114.12; M.11.776B); τὸ παρόντων ἐπισκόπων λαϊκοὺς ~εῖν Alex.H.ap.Eus.*h.e*.6.19.17(M.20.569C); presbyters who have sacrificed to idols as forbidden to, CAnc.(314)*can*.1; ὅταν ~ῇ [sc. ὁ τῆς ἐκκλησίας προεστὼς] Chrys.*hom.3.3 in Col*.(11.348C); ὡμίλησεν εἰς τὸ μὴ δεῖν μνησικακεῖν id.*hom.6.3 in 1Tim*.(11.581E); ὡμίλει ταύτας [sc. ὁμιλίας] Phot.*cod*.172–4(M.103.501D); pass. ὡμίληται αὐτῷ...εἰς τὸν σταυρόν *ib*.(504A); ὡμίλησεν αὐτῷ τὰ τῆς θρησκείας τῶν Χριστιανῶν †Jo.D.*B.J*.22(M.96.1057D).

ὁμιλητέον, *one must talk*, Clem.*paed*.2.7(p.192.21; M.8.461C).

ὁμιλητής, ὁ, 1. *one who converses with*, hence *disciple* τῶν ἀποστόλων ὁ. Πολύκαρπος Eus.*h.e*.3.36.1(M.20.288B); ὁ. ... τοῦ τῆς οἰκουμένης δεσπότου Chrys.*hom.31.3 in Jo*.(8.179D); τῶν Λουκιανοῦ τοῦ μάρτυρος ὁ. εἷς Philost.*h.e*.3.15(M.65.505B); **2.** *speaker, preacher* ἐπειδὴ γὰρ διαλεκτικὸς ἐδόκει τις εἶναι, Μάνην ἑαυτὸν ἐπωνόμασεν, οἱονεὶ ὁ. τινα ἄριστον Cyr.H.*catech*.6.24; Chrys.*hom.3.4 in 2Thess*.(11.528B).

ὁμιλητικός, *sociable*, Chrys.*sac*.6.12(p.164.8; 1.432A).

ὁμιλία, ἡ, A. *association*; **1.** *contact*; of forehead with ground in prayer, Chrys.*hom.5.3 in Mt*.(7.78A); of wood with fire, Thdt. *provid*.7(4.593); **2.** social *intercourse*; also **a.** sexual, ref. virgin birth δίχα ὁ. ἀνδρός *Const.App.epit*.1.10; λογισμὸς...τὴν ὄρεξιν ἄγχων ὁρμῶσαν πρὸς γαμικὴν ὁ. ‡Nil.*narr*.2(M.79.601B); τῆς πρὸς γυναῖκας ὁ. πάλαι κεκαθαρμένους Procl.CP *annunt*.1(M.85.428B); **b.** spiritual, of converse or communion with God τῆς κατὰ τὸ συνεχὲς πρὸς τὸν θεὸν τὸν λαλοῦντα αὐτῷ [sc. Moses] ὁ. Clem.*str*.6.12 (p.484.13; M.9.325A); as def. of prayer, v. εὐχή; subject to H. Ghost, Serap.*Man*.43(p.61; M.18.1229A); ποῦ σοι [sc. Adam] τῆς ἐμῆς ὁ. ἡ παρρησία; Bas.Sel.*or*.3.3(M.85.60B); of the mind with grace, Diad. *perf*.81(p.104.23); fig. ἀγνότης...ἥτις ἐκ τῆς ἁγιωτάτης ὁ. μετὰ τῆς πηγῆς τῆς δικαιοσύνης προελήλυθε Const.ap.Gel.Cyz.*h.e*.2.7.25(M.85. 1237A); **3.** *occupation* in, *attention* to pursuit of divine studies, c. πρός, Euthal.Diac.*Ac*.(M.85.633A).

B. verbal *communication*; **1.** *word, utterance* καὶ λόγον καλοῦσιν, ἐπειδὴ καὶ τὰς παρὰ τοῦ πατρὸς ὁμιλίας φέρει τοῖς ἀνθρώποις Just.*dial*. 128.2(M.6.776A); **2.** *speech, language, type of utterance*; used by each nature in Christ, Hil.Pict.*fr*.2(p.21.1)ap.Thdt.*eran*.2(4.163); ἀνάγκη γὰρ κατὰ τὴν ποιότητα τῶν γενῶν καὶ τῶν φύσεων ἄλλην μὲν αὐτοῦ [sc. Christ] γεγενῆσθαι τὴν ὁ. μηδέπω κατὰ τὸ τοῦ ἀνθρώπου τεχθέντος μυστήριον, ἄλλην δὲ ἔτι προσελαύνοντος τῷ θανάτῳ καὶ ἄλλην ἤδη τυγχάνοντος αἰωνίου *ib*.(p.21.19)ap.Thdt.l.c.(4.164); of Pentecost συνιέσαν ὁμιλίαν οἱ Γαλιλαῖοι Πάρθων Didym.*Trin*.2.18(M.39.729A); **3.** *teaching*, *Clem.ep*.2(M.2.36A); ταῖς τῶν πλάνων καὶ τῶν ψευδοπροφητῶν ὁ. *ib*.14(49B); of Law πατρὸς ὁ. φήσωμεν Serap.*Man*.43 (p.61; M.18.1228D); **4.** *colloquy*; **a.** *conversation* ἡ περὶ 'Αρείου πρὸς αὐτὴν ὁ. Gel.Cyz.*h.e*.3.12.3(p.158.29); Dor.*doct*.9.1(M.88.1716C); **b.** *discussion* τὴν γραφὴν ταύτην, περὶ ἧς ἡ νῦν ὁ. ἐστίν Just.*dial*.68.8 (M.6.636B); *ib*.137.3(792B); ἐν ταῖς πρὸς τοὺς γραμματεῖς καὶ Φαρισαίους ὁ. Or.*Cels*.2.73(p.195.2; M.11.909B); Meth.*symp*.proem.(p.4. 16; M.18.29C); **5.** *exhortation*, Eus.*v.C*.3.13(p.83.21; M.20.1069B); Serap.*Man*.50(p.71; M.18.1245D); **6.** *discourse*; of unprofitable words, Esaias *or*.27.15(p.193; cf.M.40.1197B); of valedictory address, Eus.*v.C*.3.21(p.87.26; M.20.1080B); of exposition, sermon, for purposes of instruction or exhortation τὰς κακοτεχνίας φεῦγε, μᾶλλον δὲ περὶ τούτων ὁ. ποιοῦ Ign.*Polyc*.5.1; Just.*dial*.85.5(M.6.677B);

πυθομένου σου τίς μου ὁ θεὸς καὶ δι' ὀλίγου παρασχόντος σου τὰ ὦτα τῇ ὁ. ἡμῖν Thphl.Ant.*Autol.*2.1(M.6.1048A); Οὐαλεντῖνος δὲ ἔν τινι ὁ. ...γράφει Clem.*str.*4.13(p.287.11; M.8.1296C); Or.*Jo.*32.2(p.426.9; M.14.741A); of bishop's sermon, CLaod.*can.*19; as translation of name 'Manes', Cyr.H.*catech.*6.24; ἐν ὁμιλιῶν εἴδει τὴν ὑπηγορίαν πεποίημαι Gr.Nyss.*homm.in Cant.*proem.(M.44.764B); cf. *homiliae, quas Latini verbum appellant,...proferuntur in populis...ad vulgus loquuntur,* Isid.H.*etym.*6.8.2; dist. from λόγοι by rhetorical and spontaneous style, Phot.*cod.*172–4(M.103.501C,D).

ὅμιλος, ὁ, *multitude, throng, company,* Meth.*symp.*3.6(p.33.3); *ib.*6.5(p.69.24; M.18.121A); Gel.Cyz.*h.e.*1.10.4(M.85.1212C); plur., cf.Philo ap.Eus.*p.e.*8.11(379B; M.21.641A); cf.*ib.*8.14(394B; M.665C).

ὁμιχλήεις, *gloomy,* Paul.Sil.*Soph.*191(M.86.2127A).

ὁμιχλώδης, 1. *misty,* Gr.Nyss.*v.Mos.*32(M.44.310C); **2.** *dark,* spiritually ἡ ὁ. δύναμις Mac.Aeg.*hom.*27.2(M.34.693D); τὸ ὁ. τοῦ πνεύματος Synes.*insomn.*10(p.163.15; M.66.1300A).

ὄμμα, τό, 1. *eye* τοῦ...Διὸς τὸ ὄ. Clem.*paed.*3.2(p.244.12; M.8.573C); fig. τοῖς ὄ. τῆς ψυχῆς *1Clem.*19.3; Clem.*paed.*2.9(p.207.1; M.8.496A) cit. s. διορατικός; διανοίας ὄ. Eus.*m.P.*13.7(p.948.21; M.20.1516C); ἔοικε...ὁ...Ἡσαΐας τοῖς τῆς διανοίας ὄ. τὰ κατὰ καιροὺς ἐσόμενα...τεθεᾶσθαι Cyr.*Is.*1.1(2.****E); οἱ τοῖς τῆς διανοίας ὄ. ὁρῶντες θεόν id.*Nah.*13(3.491C); τοῖς νοητοῖς τῆς καρδίας ὄ. id.*Jo.*4.1(4.343C); Max.*ambig.*(M.91.1140A) cit. s. ἀνεπίμυστος; in phrase ἀπὸ ὀμμάτων *blind,* Pall.*h.Laus.*4(p.19.19; M.34.1012D); Jo.Mosch.*prat.*96(M.87.2953C); met., of enlightenment ἀνεῴχθαι τὰ ὄ. Just.*dial.*123.2(M.6.761A); **2.** *source of light,* Nonn.*par.Jo.*12:42(M.43.857B); τῆς γραφῆς τῶν ὄ. Geo.Pis.*carm.*107.23.

***ὀμματίζω,** *engraft,* Anast.S.*hex.*(M.89.1076C).

***ὀμματολαμπής,** *with brilliant eyes,* Synes.*hymn.*3.272(p.14; M.66.1597D); *ib.*4.217(p.32; 1607A).

***ὀμματόπλουτος,** *rich with eyes* ἡ τῶν χερουβὶμ ὀ. φύσις Geo.Pis. *hex.*1492(M.92.1549A).

ὀμματ-όω, 1. *give sight to,* Chrys.*hom.*3.6 *in Heb.*(12.35D); Isid. Pel.*epp.*3.335(M.78.996C); Gr.II Papa *ep.Germ.*(M.98.152B); pass., Bas.Sel.*or.*26.2(M.85.305B); **2.** *enlighten, instruct* ∼οῖ τὴν Ἱερουσαλὴμ πρὸς κατανόησιν τῆς αὐτῆς πλάνης Thdr.Heracl.*Is.*30:21(M.18.1324A); τὰ νοερὰ αὐτῆς [sc. soul] αἰσθητήρια τῷ θείῳ πάλιν φωτὶ τῆς χάριτος ∼οῖ Mac.Aeg.*libert.ment.*26(M.34.960A); ὀ. τὴν ψυχὴν τῶν παρόντων Pall.*v.Chrys.*20(p.137.1; M.47.76); Cyr.*hom.div.*14(5².415B); Dor. *doct.*2.8(M.88.1649C); pass., Thdr.Heracl.*Is.*30:12(M.18.1321B); Bas. Sel.*or.*25.1(M.85.288C).

ὀμμάτωσις, ἡ, 1. *giving of sight,* Jo.D.*disp.*(M.94.1597B); τὴν τῶν τυφλῶν ὀ. ‡Ath.*occurs.*18(M.28.997A); **2.** *enlightenment* ὀ. καὶ διδασκαλίαν Thdr.Heracl.*Is.*63:1(M.18.1369A).

ὄμνυ-μι, *swear;* **1.** exegetical; Gen.22:16 ἔθος ∼ναι τῷ πατρὶ ὡς κατ' ἰδίας δυνάμεως τοῦ υἱοῦ Proc.G.*Gen.*17:22(M.87.360A); Ps.109:4 θεὸς ἀληθεύων ∼ναι λέγεται, οὐκ ἀπομοτικῷ ἢ κατομοτικῷ χρησάμενος Didym.*Ps.*109:4(M.39.1540D); οὐ γὰρ ∼σι θεός, ἀλλὰ τὸ πάντως ἐσόμενον λέγει Chrys.*exp.in Ps.*109:4(5.262C); Jer.4:2 τάχα γὰρ πρῶτον δεῖ ὀμόσαι 'ἐν ἀληθείᾳ...', ἵνα μετὰ τοῦτο προκόψας τις ἄξιος γένηται τοῦ μὴ ὀ. ὅλως Or.*hom.*5.12 *in Jer.*(p.41.3,5; M.13.312A); Ἰουδαίοις δέ, ὡς ἀσθενῶς διακειμένοις, παρακελεύεται κατ' αὐτοῦ [sc. God] ὀ. Thdt.*Jer.*4:2(2.430); οὐκ ∼ναι προστάττει, ἀλλ' εἰ ἄρα τις ὀ., βούλεται ἑαυτῶν μὴ τὰ εἴδωλα ὅρκια ποιεῖσθαι Olymp.*fr.Jer.*(M.93.636A); as reason why Jews might swear ἵνα μὴ κατὰ τῶν εἰδώλων ὀ. ὀμεῖσθε γάρ, φησί, τὸν θεὸν τὸν ἀληθινόν Chrys.*hom.*17.6 *in Mt.*(7.230D); ref. passages where God is said to swear ὅρκῳ ὤμοσέ μοι ὁ κύριος μὴ ἐξαλεῖψαι *T.Jud.*22.3; ἡ διαθήκη, ἣν ὤμοσεν τοῖς πατράσιν δοῦναι τῷ λαῷ *Barn.*14.1; Herm.*vis.*2.2.5,8; but no excuse here for wrong swearing, *Hom.Clem.*3.55; **2.** pagan oaths forbidden to Christians εἰ κενοδοξεῖς, ἵνα ὀμόσω τὴν Καίσαρος τύχην,...ἄκουε· Χριστιανός εἰμι *M.Polyc.*10.1; Or.*mart.*7(p.8.21; M.11.572B); τύχην βασιλέως οὐκ ∼μεν...ἀποθανετέον ἐστὶ μᾶλλον ἡμῖν ὑπὲρ τοῦ μὴ ὀμόσαι μοχθηρὸν δαίμονα id.*Cels.*8.65(p.281.20ff.; M.11.1613D,1616A); swearing by idols, *Const.App.*5.11.1; by sun, moon, or stars, *ib.*5.12.5; ὀ. ὅρκους Ἑλληνικούς Bas.*ep.*217 *can.*81(3.329E; M.32.805C); **3.** in gen., all swearing forbidden (cf. Mt.5:34), Clem.*str.*7.8(p.38.25; M.9.473B); cf.Or.*comm.ser.*17 *in Mt.*(p.32.21; M.13.1623D); Bas.*ep.*22.1(3.99A; M.32.288C); Chrys.*hom.*17.4 *in Mt.*(7.228C); τί γὰρ εὐκολώτερον τοῦ μὴ ὀ.; id.*stat.*5.7(2.70C); ὁ ὀμόσας, κἂν δοκῇ ζῆν, ἤδη τετελεύτηκε *ib.*15.5(158E); those who go to altar and swear, touching gospels, condemned, *ib.*(159B); ἂν τοίνυν...μηδὲ ∼ωμεν τὰ νεῦρα ἐξεκόψαμεν τοῦ θυμοῦ id.*hom.*9.5 *in Ac.*(9.76D); an exception, for avoidance of blasphemy μηδέποτε...ὀμόσῃς τὸν θεόν· εἰ δὲ καὶ ἀνάγκη σοι γίνεται τοῦ ὀμόσαι, κατ' ἐμοῦ τοῦ ταπεινοῦ ∼ε Anton.Hag. *v.Sym.Styl.*13(p.36.15ff.); **4.** of oaths to commit wrong which do not bind, Bas.*ep.*199 *can.*29(3.294Cff.; M.32.725A,B); **5.** exeg. Mt. 23:16ff., one ought not to 'swear by' non-Scriptural interpretations, Or.*comm.ser.*18 *in Mt.*(p.33.5; M.13.1624B).

***ὁμοάγαθος,** *of the same goodness;* of Trin., Dion.Ar.*d.n.*1.5(M.3.593B).

***ὁμόαρχος,** *of the same sovereignty;* of Trin., Anast.*fid.*(p.272).

***ὁμοβασίλειος,** *of the same majesty;* of Trin., Andr.Cr.*can.mag.* 144(p.151; M.97.1353A).

ὁμόβιος, *mate* [sc. ὄρνις], Ast.Am.*hom.*5(M.40.237A).

***ὁμόβουλος,** *of the same will,* Thdr.Abuc.*opusc.*3(M.97.1501C).

ὁμογάστριος, *from the same womb* as ὁ. ... Πέτρου Nonn.*par.Jo.* 21:2(M.43.913C).

ὁμογένεια, ἡ, *kinship* with πρὸς αὐτὸν ὁ. Cyr.*thes.*15(5¹.171D); c. genit., *ib.*32(315A); *ib.*(327E).

ὁμογενής, A. *akin* or *alike;* **1.** of fellow countrymen, Or.*Cels.*3.5(p.207.2; M.11.925D); Cyr.*Os.*102(3.134E); **2.** of fellow men, Meth. *arbitr.*3.3(p.151.7; M.18.245B); Ath.*gent.*25(M.25.49B); id.*virg.*3(p.38.11; M.28.256B); Cyr.*ador.*8(1.270A).

B. *of the same genus* or *class* ὁ κανὼν τῆς συγκρίσεως τοῖς ὁ. ἁρμόζει Isid.Pel.*epp.*1.422(M.78.417B); ὁ. εἰσιν, ὅσα ὑπὸ τὴν αὐτὴν κατηγορίαν τάσσονται Jo.D.*dialect.*48(M.94.621C,D); *ib.*(624A); κατὰ τὸ ζῶόν εἰσιν ἴσοι, ἄνθρωπος, ἵππος, βοῦς...ὄντες ὁ. Thdr.Abuc.*opusc.* 2(M.97.1473A).

C. *akin, of the same kind* or *character* (cf. ὁμοούσιος); **1.** in gen., Eus.*d.e.*1.10(p.45.10; ὁμοιογενῆ M.22.85C); ἡμεῖς δὲ ἀλλήλων ὄντες ὁ. (ἐκ γὰρ ἑνὸς οἱ πάντες γεγόναμεν, καὶ μία πάντων ἀνθρώπων ἡ φύσις) Ath.*Ar.*3.20(M.26.365A); Bas.*hex.*2.4(1.16C; M.29.37C); τὸ τέκνον γενόμενόν τινος ὁ. πάντως ἐστὶ τῷ γεννήσαντι Gr.Nyss.*or.catech.*40(p.162.6; M.45.104B); **2.** theol.; **a.** of Christ's body and blood with mankind ἡμεῖς ὁ. τὰ σώματα ἔχοντες τῷ σώματι τοῦ κυρίου Ath. *Dion.*10(p.53.23; M.25.496A); ἵνα διὰ τοῦ ὁ. ἡμῖν αἵματος τὸ μὴ ὁ. ἡμῖν πνεῦμα τὸ ἅγιον λαβεῖν δυνηθῶμεν ‡Chrys.*pasch.*2(8.254E); cf. of Inc. ὁ. ἡμῖν καθίσταται ἵνα καὶ ὡς ὁ. ἡμῖν μεταδῷ τῆς δόξης τῆς ἑαυτοῦ Gel.Cyz.*h.e.*2.24.12(M.85.1301A); Dion.Ar.*e.h.*3.3.11(M.3.441B); ref. Christ's soul ἡ ψυχὴ τοῦ Χριστοῦ...τὴν ὁ. τοῦ ἀνθρώπου ψυχὴν εἰς τὸν παράδεισον εἰσήγαγεν Eust.*fr.*56(p.91; M.18.689D); **b.** ref. difference bet. Christ and angels, exeg. Heb.1:4, Ath.*Ar.*1.55(M.26.128A); οὐχ ὁ. ἄρα τοῖς ἀγγέλοις ἐστίν, ὁ τῷ πατρὶ συμβασιλεύων Cyr.*thes.* 20(5¹.203E); **c.** of Father and Son, by analogy ἀνθρωπείαν γονὴν παρεθέμην δῆλον ὡς οὖσαν ὁ. Dion.Al.ap.Ath.*Dion.*18(p.59.11; M.25.505B); ὁ. ἐστιν ὁ υἱὸς τῷ πατρί, τουτέστιν ὁμοούσιος Cyr.*Jo.*10.1(4.849C); οὕτω λέγομεν τὸν πατέρα, πάντα ὅσα ποιεῖ, διὰ τοῦ ὁ. υἱοῦ αὐτοῦ ποιεῖν ‡Cyr.*Trin.*8(6³.12E; M.77.1137D); contrast ὁμοούσιος...οὐχ ὡς τὰ ὁ. ... ἀλλ' ὡς ἐκ τοῦ ἑνὸς γένους καὶ εἴδους τῆς θεότητος †Apoll.*ep. Bas.*1(M.32.1104D); in anti-Arian argument εἰ ποίημά ἐστιν ὁ λόγος... ὁ. τῇ φύσει τοῖς ποιήμασι Ath.*syn.*48(p.272.24; M.26.777C); Gr.Nyss. *or.catech.*39(p.157.10; M.45.100D); **d.** in Valentinian Gnosticism ὁ. Ἀγγέλους συμπροβεβλῆσθαι Iren.*haer.*1.2.6(M.7.465A); λέγειν...τὰ συγκρινόμενα ὁ., ὥστε τὸν υἱὸν τῆς τῶν ἀγγέλων εἶναι φύσεως...ὁ μὲν [sc. Valentinus] τοὺς ἀγγέλους ὁ. εἴρηκε τῷ Χριστῷ Ath.*Ar.*1.56(M.26.129C).

ὁμόγλωσσος, 1. *united in utterance* πᾶς ὁ. αὐτῷ [sc. Moses]...τῶν προφητῶν χορός Meth.*res.*2.10(p.349.14); of Christians, Mac.Aeg. *hom.*12.4(M.34.560A); Nonn.*par.Jo.*7:12(M.43.805C); ὁ. μύθῳ *ib.* 12:34(856B); **2.** *speaking the same tongue,* of apostles at Pentecost ὁ. πᾶσι τοῖς ἔθνεσιν Gr.Nyss.*or.catech.*30(p.112.4; M.45.77A).

ὁμογνήσιος, *of the same parentage,* Isid.Pel.*epp.*5.423(M.78.1576C).

ὁμόγνητος, *of the same people,* Nonn.*par.Jo.*4:44(M.43.781B).

ὁμόγνιος, 1. *akin,* Nonn.*par.Jo.*18:26(M.43.893C); χθονίοισι ὁμόγνια Eudoc.*Cypr.*2.86(M.85.848D); Dion.Ar.*d.n.*11.2(M.3.952A); neut. as subst., *kinship,* Philost.*h.e.*4.1(M.65.517B); **2.** *of kinsmen* ὁ. λύθρῳ *ib.*5.4(532A).

ὁμογνωμον-έω, 1. *agree, be of one mind* οὔτε ∼οῦντας ἐφ' οἷς κακῶς ἐφρόνουν CArim.*ep.Const.*1 ap.Ath.*syn.*10(p.238.4; M.26.697C); *Const. App.*2.44.2; οὔτε πρὸς ἀλλήλους...∼οῦν Chrys.*sac.*3.15(p.76.24; 1.393A); **2.** *consent* τοῖς πρὸς κακίαν ∼οῦσιν *Hom.Clem.*11.19.

ὁμογνωμόνως, *with unanimity, with one accord,* Hermias *irris.*3(M.6.1172B); CChalc.*act.*6(*ACO* 2.1.2 p.156.2; H.2.488C); ‡Jo.D.*ep. Thphl.*1(M.95.345C).

***ὁμόγνωμος,** *like-minded,* Gr.Nyss.*Steph.*2(M.46.733A); neut. as subst., *unanimity,* of Trin. τὸ ἑαυτῶν ὁ. καὶ ὁμόδοξον ‡Caes.Naz. *dial.*126(M.38.1021).

ὁμογνωμοσύνη, ἡ, *agreement in opinion, unanimity* ἡ ὁ. συμφωνία γνωμῶν Clem.*str.*2.9(p.135.12; M.8.977B); ταυτοβουλίαν καὶ ὁ. Leont.H.*Nest.*2.1(M.86.1525C); of Father and Son, Chrys.*hom.*64.3 *in Jo.*(8.386B); *cat.Mt.*12:18(p.91.17); of Trin., Oecum.*Phil.*3:20f.

(p.453.17; M.118.1313C); ref. Inc. συνδεσμῶν εἰς ὁ. ὁ...θεὸς ἦν ἐδημιούργησε φύσιν Procl.CP *ep.*(p.67.20; M.65.881A).

ὁμογνώμων, *like-minded, of one mind* ὁ. ἐν τοῖς κυριακοῖς *Hom. Clem.*2.58; *ib.*6.1; c. dat., Dion.Al.ap.Eus.*h.e.*6.42.6(M.20.616A); *Hom.Clem.*15.2; of Father and Son ὁ. κατὰ πάντα Cyr.*Jo.*2.6(4.215C); neut. as subst., ‡Caes.Naz.*dial.*126(M.38.1021); met., *united* judgement, Const.ap.Eus.*v.C.*4.42(p.135.5; M. om.); the *same* faith, Socr.*h.e.*5.8.8(M.67.577A).

***ὁμογνώμως**, *with the same purpose*, ‡Caes.Naz.*dial.*140(M.38.1068).

ὁμόδελφος, *from the same womb*, Melet.*nat.hom.*synops.(M.64.1085A).

***ὁμοδέσποτος**, *under the same master*, Tim.Ant.*cruc.*(M.86.264A).

ὁμοδίαιτος, **1.** *eating with* τῷ ἄρχοντι αὐτῶν [sc. demons] ὁ. *Hom. Clem.*7.3; of Judas, Chrys.*hom.in Mt.26:39*(3.17D); id.*hom.59.4 in Jo.*(8.351A); **2.** *sharing the life*; of man with angels, in Eden, Bas.*hom.1.3*(2.3B; M.31.168A); ‡Bas.*struct.hom.*2.4(1.340C; M.30.45C); in heaven, Cyr.*hom.pasch.*1.6(5^{2}.15D); †Jo.D.*B.J.*12(M.96.964B); hence **3.** *being, acting as a friend* οἱ μισάλληλοι...νῦν μετὰ τὴν ἐπιφάνειαν τοῦ Χριστοῦ ὁ. γινόμενοι Just.*1apol.*14.3(M.6.348C); τῶν ταπεινῶν ὁ. Mac.Mgn.*apocr.*2.20(p.41.10); **4.** *living together* ὁ. συζυγία Procl.CP *or.*17.3(M.65.812C).

ὁμοδοξ-έω, *agree* with, *be of the same opinion* as, Clem.*str.*4.9(p.281.3; M.8.1284A); Eus.*h.e.*5.24.8(M.20.497A); εἰ φανεῖεν τοῖς Ἑβραίων προφήταις...οἱ παρ' Ἕλλησιν ~οῦντες id.*p.e.*10.8(482D; M.21.804B); of things, *accord, be in harmony* with ~εῖ δὲ αὐτῷ [sc. τῷ εὐαγγελίῳ] καὶ ἡ προφητεία Clem.*paed.*1.5(p.97.27; M.8.264C); *consent* ~ούσης ἡμῖν εἰς τοῦτο τῆς σαρκός Meth.*res.*1.31(p.267.8; M.41.1141D).

ὁμοδοξία, ἡ, 1. *unanimity*, Const.*or.s.c.*17(p.178.9; M.20.1284B); **2.** *agreement* with, Philost.*h.e.*4.12(p.64.13; M.65.525A).

ὁμόδοξος, 1. *of the same view* or *belief, like-minded, unanimous*, Or.*Cels.*3.9(p.210.11; M.11.932B); τοῖς πιστοῖς τε καὶ ὁ. *Const.App.* 1.5.1; Chrys.*ep.Innoc.*1.3(3.519B); αὐτοῖς...ὡς ὁ. ἐκοινωνεῖτε Socr.*h.e.*3.10.6(M.67.408A); περὶ τὴν πίστιν ὁ. Sophr.H.*mir.Cyr.et Jo.*36(M.87.3552B); c. genit., Ath.*Dion.*1(p.46.14; M.25.480B); Eus.Dor.*ep.imp.*(*ACO* 2.1.1 p.67.2; M.86.2500A); c. dat., Eus.*e.th.*1.1(p.62.25; M.24.829B); Ath.*ep.Aeg.Lib.*8(M.25.557A); met. ἡ πίστις ὁ. Gr.Nyss.*Steph.*2(M.46.733A); ὁ βίος ὁ. *ib.*(736A); **2.** *equal in glory*; **a.** of Father and Son ὁ. ὢν τῷ ἰδίῳ πατρί Gr.Nyss.*Eun.*5(2 p.114.12; M.45.693C); Didym.(‡Bas.)*Eun.*5(1.317A; M.29.760B); Thdr.Stud.*cant.* 1.2(p.337); neut. as subst., ‡Caes.Naz.*dial.*126(M.38.1021) cit. s. ὁμόγνωμος; **b.** of H. Ghost οὔτ' ἐκτὸς θεότητος ἀειδέος, ἀλλ' ὁ. Gr.Naz.*carm.*1.1.3.9(M.37.409A); **c.** of Trin., id.*or.*42.16(M.36.476C); Alex.Sal.*cruc.*(M.87.4088A); Max.*ambig.*(M.91.1348B); Jo.D.*haer.* epilog.(M.94.777B); Arian denial ὁ θεὸς...οὐδὲ ὅμοιον, οὐχ ὁ. ἔχει μόνος οὗτος Ar.*Thal.fr.*2 ap.Ath.*syn.*15(p.242.10; M.26.705D); **d.** of 'kings' of present and future world-order οὐ μὴν ἀπὸ τοῦ θεοῦ ὡς ζῷα προεβλήθησαν, ὁ. γὰρ αὐτῷ ἦσαν *Hom.Clem.*20.3.

***ὁμοδόξως, 1.** *with the same belief*, Ar.*Thal.fr.*1 ap.Ath.*Ar.*1.5(M.26.21A); **2.** *with* or *in respect of equal glory*, of Trin. τὴν τριάδα ὁ. ... δοξάζοντες Epiph.*anc.*26(p.34.22; M.43.64C); ‡Cyr.*Trin.*10(6^{3}.16C; M.77.1144C); ὅπως...ὁμοτίμως καὶ ὁ. παρὰ πάσης κτίσεως συμπροσκυνηθῇ ‡Meth.*palm.*7(M.18.397B).

***ὁμοδόρπιος**, *dining together*, Nonn.*par.Jo.*6:10(M.43.793C); *ib.* 6:71(804C).

ὁμόδουλος, ὁ, *fellow-slave, fellow-servant* ὁ πονηρὸς...μετὰ τῶν ὁ. ἀγγέλων *Hom.Clem.*20.9; ref. Arian doctrine ὁ. ποιῶν τὸ ὁμόθεον Gr.Naz.*or.*25.17(M.35.1224A); Christol.: ref. Phil.2:7 συγκαταβαίνει τοῖς ὁ. Nil.*epp.*1.102(M.79.128B); ref. Nestorian teaching ἐν ὁ. σεσώσμεθα; *cat.Heb.*2:9(p.154.32); as adj., *sharing the same bondage* πρὸς τὴν ὁ. κτίσιν ἑαυτὸν ἀπάγοι Gr.Nyss.*or.catech.*39(p.159.2; M.45.101A); met., of stars, Gr.Naz.*carm.*1.2.10.191(M.37.694A); of sun, Thdt.*Ezech.* 8:16(2.735); of Hades, Andr.Cr.*or.*14(M.97.100B); ὁ. τῷ ἀγρῷ ? *colonus*, Soz.*h.e.*9.17.1(M.67.1628C).

***ὁμοδύναμος, 1.** *of the same* or *like significance, of like force*; of expressions, Dion.Ar.*d.n.*4.11(M.3.708C); ταύταις ὁμοδύναμοι θεωνυμίαι *ib.*9.1(909B); id.*c.h.*15.9(340B); Thdr.Stud.*antirr.*2.27,28(M.99.372A,C); **2.** *of the same power* or *authority*; **a.** of Trin., Cyr.*apol.orient.*9(p.51.27; 6^{1}.182B); Anast.*fid.*(p.272); Max.*ambig.*(M.91.1304A); Jo.D.*haer.*epilog.(M.94.777B); **b.** of Father and Son, ‡Cyr.H.*occurs.*8(M.33.1196A); Alex.Sal.*cruc.*(M.87.4017A); ‡Meth.*Sym.et Ann.*8(M.18.368D); *cat.Mt.*16:19(p.132.13).

ὁμοειδής, 1. *of like form* or *aspect*, Meth.*res.*3.18(p.416.18); Areth.*Apoc.*9:7(M.106.625C); of Christ's humanity δείκνυσι ταύτην ἀνθρώποις ὁμοειδεῖ θέᾳ Bas.Sel.*or.*25.3(M.85.293B); **2.** *of the same kind* or *species* φιλοῦσι...ἐν τοῖς ὁ. αἱ συγκρίσεις γίνεσθαι Cyr.*thes.*20(5^{1}.202E); τὰ γὰρ ἀλλήλοις ὁ. κἂν ἔχῃ τινὰ πρὸς ἄλληλα τὴν διαφοράν, ἀλλὰ τῆς αὐτῆς ἔχεται φύσεως *ib.*(203C); ὁ. εἰσιν, ὅσα ὑπὸ τὸ αὐτὸ εἶδος τάσσονται Jo.D.*dialect.*48(M.94.621D); of Son in rel. to angels ἑτεροειδὴς μᾶλλον ἢ ὁ. Cyr.*thes.*20(5^{1}.203B); Christol. εἰ ὁ. ἀμφοῖν τοῖς συντεθεῖσι κατὰ πάντα τὸ τοῦ συνθέτου εἶδος Leont.H.*monoph.*4(M.86.1772B); of Father and Son ἐν ὁ. μέν, ὑφειμένῳ δὲ φωτὶ νοεῖν τὸν υἱόν †Apoll.*ep.Bas.*1(M.32.1104C).

ὁμοειδία, ἡ, *sameness of kind* τῆς δὲ τῶν γενητῶν ἀποδιορίζοντες φύσεώς τε καὶ ὁ. Cyr.*Jo.*1.5(4.45A); of angels διὰ τῆς πρὸς ἀλλήλους ὁ., εἰς μίαν ἅπαντες ἀναδεσμούμενοι φύσιν *ib.*2.1(117C).

ὁμοειδῶς, *as the same kind*, Clem.*str.*6.15(p.490.32; M.9.341A).

***ὁμοεργής, 1.** *following the same profession*, Epiph.*haer.*51.14(p.267.28; M.41.916A); **2.** *performing the same operations*, Christol.; wrongly predicated of divine and human natures in rel. to each other, ‡Hipp.*Ber.Hel.*5(p.324.20; M.10.837A); τίνι...ὁ. ... ὁ σαρκωθεὶς...λόγος; Max.*opusc.*(M.91.116A); ἡμῖν ὁ.,...τῷ πατρὶ ὁ. *ib.*(209C).

***ὁμοεργία, ἡ,** *identity of operation*, ref. Father τῇ πρὸς τὸν υἱὸν ὁ. Max.*opusc.*(M.91.116B).

[*]**ὁμοεργός**, = ὁμοεργής 2, of Son εἴπερ καὶ μετὰ σάρκωσιν ὁ. ἐστι τῷ οἰκείῳ γεννήτορι Max.*Pyrr.*(M.91.344C).

ὁμόζηλος, *of like zeal*, met. ὁ τρόπος ὁ. Gr.Nyss.*Steph.*2(M.46.736A); ὁ. ... λαιμῶν Nonn.*par.Jo.*10:21(M.43.836A).

ὁμοζυγέω, *be yoked together*; met., Clem.*prot.*11(p.82.27; M.8.236D).

ὁμοζυγής, 1. *joined together*, Nonn.*par.Jo.*18:3(M.43.889B); **2.** *banded together, assembled*, *ib.*4:30(780A); *ib.*7:14(808A); *ib.*13:22(864B).

ὁμοζυγία, ἡ, *union in marriage*, Thdr.Stud.*epp.*2.159(M.99.1497B).

ὁμόζυγος, (ὁ, ἡ), subst. or adj.; *yoke-fellow*; **1.** lit., of oxen, Ephr.3.262C; **2.** met., *husband*, Clem.*paed.*3.4(p.253.24; M.8.597A); Bas.*ep.*6.2(3.79E; M.32.244C); *Const.App.*8.25.3; Bas.Sel.*v.Thecl.*2.4(M.85.572B); *wife*, Just.*1apol.*27.4(M.6.372A); Hipp.*fr.in Pr.*5:19(p.160.2); Thdr.Stud.*epp.*2.137(M.99.1437B); exeg. Ex.2:21,4:24ff., interpreted of moral and natural philosophy, Gr.Nyss.*v.Mos.*(M.44.336D); *companion*, Thdt.*carit.*(3.1309); τὰ...τῶν ἱερῶν ψυχῶν ὁ. ...σώματα Dion.Ar.*e.h.*7.1.1(M.3.553A); c. dat., Nonn.*par.Jo.*6:56(M.43.801A); c. genit., *ib.*10:38(837C); *bride, spouse*; met., of avarice, Pall.*v.Chrys.*20(p.133.5; M.47.74); of truth, *ib.*(p.137.21; M.47.77); of virginity, Gr.Naz.*carm.*1.2.1.33(M.37.523A); ἀζυγίῃ Χριστοῦ...ὁ. *ib.*1.2.1.708(576A); ref. Cant.4:10ff. τοῦ κυρίου...ὁ. Gr.Nyss.*hom.9 in Cant.*(M.44.961C).

ὁμόζυξ, ὁ, ἡ, 1. *husband*, Gr.Naz.*carm.*2.2(poem.)6.77(M.37.1548A); Thdt.*provid.*8(4.615); *wife*, Bas.*hex.*7.5(1.68B; M.29.160C); Thdt.*2Cor.*13:2(3.354); id.*Philm.*2(3.712); **2.** *companion*; met., of soul to body, Thdt.*eran.*3(4.222); of night to day, id.*provid.*1(4.492); **3.** *spouse*; of Christ ὁ. δὲ οἷον ἐδέγμην Χριστόν Gr.Naz.*carm.* 1.2.1.597(M.37.567A); **4.** *assembled*, Nonn.*par.Jo.*2:6(M.43.761A); *ib.* 6:22(797A); *ib.*10:24(836B); **5.** *united*, *ib.*17:11(885B); *ib.*17:21(888A).

***ὁμοζῶος**, *sharing the same life*, ‡Ath.*dial.Trin.*5.29(M.28.1284A).

ὁμοήθεια, ἡ, *similarity in character* or *disposition* ὁ. θεοῦ λαβόντες Ign.*Magn.*6.2; κατὰ ὁμοήθειαν θεοῦ id.*Polyc.*1.3; Clem.*str.*7.12(p.54.29; M.9.505A); c. πρός, Cyr.*Juln.*10(6^{2}.338D).

ὁμόηχος, *producing one* or *the same sound*; fig., Procl.CP *or.*17.3(M.65.812C); ‡Jo.D.*ep.Thphl.*13(M.95.361C).

***ὁμοθελής**, *of the same will*; of Son with Father, ‡Proc.G.*Pr.* 8:31(M.87.1297C); c. genit., Andr.Cr.*or.*5(M.97.889A).

***ὁμοθελητός**, *of the same will*; of Trin., Anast.*fid.*(p.272).

***ὁμόθεος**, *of the same Godhead, identically God*; **1.** of Son, Gr.Naz.*or.*25.17(M.35.1224A) cit. s. ὁμόδουλος; of Trin., Leont.H.*Nest.* 2.21(M.86.1584A); Dion.Ar.*d.n.*1.5(M.3.593B); Max.*ambig.*(M.91.1348B); **2.** Christol.; of Christ's humanity as wholly one with God, Gr.Naz.*or.*45.13(M.36.641A); ἡ σὰρξ τεθεῶσθαι λέγεται, καὶ θεὸς γενέσθαι, καὶ ὁ. τῷ λόγῳ ‡Cyr.*Trin.*24(6^{3}.29E; M.77.1165C); ‡Gr.Nyss.*hom.2.18 in Jo.*(p.117.23); Anast.S.*hod.*21(M.89.281C); Jo.D.*f.o.*3.17(M.94.1069A); id.*Jacob.*83(M.94.1481C); Thdr.Stud.*antirr.*2.41(M.99.381C).

***ὁμόθεσμος**, *subject to the same law*, *Orac.Sib.*5.265.

***ὁμοθέωρος**, *apparent, visible as the same*, of Christ ὁ. ... θνητοῖς ἀθάνατος ‡Caes.Naz.*dial.*38(M.38.904).

***ὁμόθρησκος**, *of the same religion*, Socr.*h.e.*5.24.3(M.67.648C); Sophr.H.*or.*2.5(M.87.3221C); ἔδει τοὺς γάμῳ συναπτομένους ὁ. εἶναι Phot.*nomoc.*12.13(M.104.885A).

ὁμόθρονος, *sharing the same throne*; of Trin., Gr.Naz.*or.*6.22(M.

35.749C); Didym.*Trin*.3.28(M.39.797B); Alex.Sal.*cruc*.(M.87.4088A); Bas.Anc.al.*libell*.(H.4.41A); of Father and Son, Gr.Nyss.*Eun*.5(2 p.114.12; M.45.693C); Cyr.*thes*.20(5^{1}.200E); id.*Is*.4.4(2.656A); Andr. Cr.*or*.5(M.97.889C).

*ὁμόθροος, *as with one voice*, Nonn.*par.Jo*.1:39(M.43.756C); *ib*. 7:3(805A).

ὁμοθυμαδόν, *with one consent*, ‡Jo.D.*icon*.11(M.96.1357C); met., Gr.Mag.*dial*.(tr.Zach.)3.29(M.*PL*.77.286C); *simultaneously, at the same time*, Just.*dial*.81.4(M.6.669A); Jo.Clim.*scal*.8(M.88.833B); *together*, *Orac.Sib*.3.458; †Dion.Al. *fr.4 in Job*(p.207.2).

*ὁμοίθεος, *like to God*; of H. Ghost, Gr.Naz.*carm*.1.1.3.3(M.37.408A).

ὁμοιογενής, *of like kind* or *character*, Eus.*d.e*.1.10(M.22.85C; ὁμογενῆ p.45.10); εἰ κατὰ τοὺς Χριστομάχους ὁ. τοῖς ἀγγέλοις ὁ υἱός *cat. Heb*.2:4(p.388.31).

ὁμοιογενῶς, *so as to be of like kind* εἴπερ ὁ. ἔχοι [sc. Son] τῷ κόσμῳ Gr.Nyss.*Eun*.4(2 p.59.4; M.45.629C).

*ὁμοιογνώμων, **1.** *of like opinion*, Epiph.*haer*.35.1(p.39.21; M.41.628A); **2.** *of like mind*, Synes.*provid*.13(p.93.1; M.66.1241B).

ὁμοιογραφέω, **1.** *write alike*, Leont.H.*Nest*.5.16(M.86.1737D); **2.** *paint*, Diad.*perf*.89(p.126.11); Agath.*v.Gr.Ill*.59; Jo.D.*f.o*.4.16(M.94.1173A).

ὁμοιόγραφος, ὁ, *painter*, Agath.*v.Gr.Ill*.59.

[*]ὁμοιογράφω, *paint*, Diad.*perf*.89(pp.124.17,126.13).

*ὁμοιόδοξος, *of like glory*, ‡Ath.*Maced.dial*.2(M.28.1336C).

ὁμοιοειδής, *bearing resemblance*, of appearance of soul after death ὁ. ὂν τῷ πάχει καὶ γηΐνῳ σώματι Or.ap.Meth.*res*.3.17(p.414.7; M.18.325A); Meth.*ib*.3.18(p.414.19; 325B); †Juln.Imp.*ep*.205(p.283.6; M.32.344A).

ὁμοιοκατάληκτος, *ending alike*, Gr.Nyss.*Eun*.1(1 p.25.7; M.45.253A).

*ὁμοιοκαταλήκτως, for ὁμοιοκαταλήπτως, *with a similar meaning*, Epiph.*mens*.24(M.43.280C).

*ὁμοιόλεκτος, *similarly expressed*, Didym.*Trin*.1.15(M.39.316B); c. dat., *ib*.2.5(500C); c. genit., *ib*.2.6(521A).

*ὁμοιολέκτως, *in similar terms* ὁ. τὸν υἱὸν τῷ πατρὶ θεολογοῦντες Didym.*Trin*.1.27(M.39.405B).

*ὁμοιολεξία, ἡ, *similarity of expression*, ‡Ath.*sem*.10(M.28.156B); Didym.*Trin*.2.3(M.39.476A,C).

*ὁμοιομερῶς, *homogeneously*, Ath.*syn*.35(p.262.25; M.26.756A).

ὁμοιοπάθεια, ἡ, **1.** *similarity of passions*, Christol.; of Christ with men, Eus.*d.e*.4.11(p.169.7; M.22.281C); τοῦ σωματικοῦ ὀργάνου τὴν πρὸς ἡμᾶς ὁ. ὑποδεικνύς id.*l.C*.14(p.244.5; M.20.1412D); *ib*.(p.242.7; 1409B); ἄνθρωπος δεικνύμενος τῇ τῆς φύσεως ὁ. Thdt.*rect.conf*.11(M.6.1228B); Leont.B.*Nest.et Eut*.2(M.86.1337A); **2.** *similarity of suffering*; of Christ and S. Peter, Nil.*epp*.2.306(M.79.349D).

ὁμοιοπαθέω, *be affected in sympathy*, Synes.*insomn*.2(p.147.13; M.66.1285B).

ὁμοιοπαθής, **1.** *of like passions*, Just.*dial*.93.3(M.6.697C); Meth.*lepr*.12(p.466.16); Nil.*epp*.2.261(M.79.333B); theol. θεὸς...οὐδὲ ὁ. ... καθάπερ τὰ γενητά Clem.*str*.7.6(p.22.7; M.9.440B); Christol. γεννηθῆναι ἄνθρωπος ὁ. ἡμῖν, σάρκα ἔχων...ὑπέμεινεν Just.*dial*.48.3(580B); τὸν ἡμῖν ἄνθρωπον ὁ. ὑπέδυ Eus.*h.e*.1.2.1(M.20.53A); Cyr.H.*catech*.4.9; ἀληθῶς ἐγεννήθη ὁ θεὸς λόγος ἐκ τῆς παρθένου σῶμα ὁ. ἡμῖν ἠμφιεσμένος ‡Ign.*Trall*.10; διὰ τί οὖν πεινᾷ; ἵνα δείξῃ ὅτι κατ' ἀλήθειαν ἔλαβε σῶμα ὁ. ἀνθρώποις ‡Ign.*Phil*.9; ref. Passion, Bas.Sel.*or*.13.3(M.85.180D); Jo.D.*hom*.2.1(M.96.576B); **2.** *sympathetic*, *A.Mt*.6(p.233.11).

*ὁμοιοπαθῶς, *so as to suffer in the same way*, Thdr.Stud.*epp*.2.21.1(M.99.1637C).

*ὁμοιόπιστος, *of like faith*, Just.*dial*.119.6(M.6.753A).

*ὁμοιοπλάστως, *with a similar appearance*; c. genit., Steph.Diac.*v.Steph*.(M.100.1076C).

ὁμοιοπρόσωπος, *of similar appearance*, Cyr.H.*catech*.12.14.

ὁμοιόπτωτον, τό, rhetorical figure in which words of similar inflexion are used, Isid.H.*etym*.1.36.15.

*ὁμοιοπτώτως, *similarly inflected*, Areth.*Apoc*.1:5(M.106.508D, 509A).

ὅμοιος, *like*;

A. denied of God in rel. to creatures; ref. Son, Eus.*ep.Caes*.11(p.45.17; M.20.1541B); ἄφρονες οἱ Ἀρειανοί· τί γὰρ ὅ. υἱὸς καὶ ποίημα; Ath.*Ar*.1.29(M.26.72A); ὁ Παῦλος ὅμοια τῷ σωτῆρι διδάσκων, οὐκ ἦν κατ' οὐσίαν ὅ. αὐτῷ *ib*.3.11(344B); hence denied of Son in rel. to angels, Cyr.*thes*.20(5^{1}.203B); and of H. Ghost in rel. to 'the multitude of spirits', Didym.*Trin*.2.5(M.39.492B); contrast Arian assertion that many spiritual powers are like Son, Ar.*Thal.fr*.8 ap.Ath. *Ar*.1.5(M.26.21C); cf. ὅ. τὸ γενητὸν τῷ ἀγενήτῳ θέλουσιν Ath.*Ar*.1.31(76C); *ib*.3.18(360B).

B. Christol., of Christ's human nature in rel. to mankind in gen. ἀπὸ τῶν ἡμετέρων τὸ ὅ. λαβών Ath.*inc*.8.4(M.25.109C); ἀπὸ πάντων τῶν ὅ. ἠφάνιζε τὸν θάνατον *ib*.9.1(112A); ὅ. κατὰ τὴν φύσιν τοῖς ἀνθρώποις *ib*.37.2(160B); ὅ. ἡμῖν σῶμα id.*Ar*.2.10(M.26.168C); *ib*.2.74(304B).

C. Trin., in 4th-cent. controversy, ref. Son in rel. to Father; **1.** asserted τί γὰρ ἂν εἴη ὅ. τῷ θεῷ, ἢ τὸ ἐξ αὐτοῦ γέννημα; Ath.*decr*.17(p.14.19; M.25.444C); ἔχει πάντα τὰ τοῦ πατρός...τὸ κατὰ πάντα καὶ ἐν πᾶσιν ὅ. ... ὅ. ὢν κατὰ τὴν οὐσίαν τοῦ πατρός id.*ep.Aeg.Lib*.17(M.25.577A,B); ὅ. κατὰ πάντα id.*Ar*.2.18(M.26.184C); ἡμῶν μὲν οὖν ἀνόμοιός ἐστιν ὁ λόγος, τοῦ δὲ πατρὸς ὅ.· διὰ τοῦτο ἐκεῖνος μέν ἐστι φύσει καὶ ἀληθείᾳ ἓν μετὰ τοῦ ἑαυτοῦ πατρός *ib*.3.20(365A); explained ὅ. τε καὶ ἀπαράλλακτον...ὁμοούσιον...ἵνα μὴ μόνον ὅ. τὸν υἱόν, ἀλλὰ ταὐτὸν τῇ ὁμοιώσει ἐκ τοῦ πατρὸς εἶναι σημαίνωσι. ... οὐ μόνον ὅ., ἀλλὰ καὶ ἀδιαίρετός ἐστι τῆς τοῦ πατρὸς οὐσίας id.*decr*.20(pp.16.28,17.8,16; 449C–452C); οὐδὲ ἔξωθεν ἁπλῶς ὅ., ἵνα μὴ καθ' ἕτερον ἢ ὅλως ἑτεροούσιος φαίνηται *ib*.23(p.19.23; 457A); ref. Nicene definition, id.*ep.Jov*.4(M.26.817C)ap.Thdt.*h.e*.4.3.13 cit. s. ἁπλῶς; εἰ γὰρ οὐκ ἔστι κατ' οὐσίαν ὅ. ὁ υἱὸς τῷ πατρί, πῶς ἀπαράλλακτος τῆς οὐσίας εἰκών ἐστιν;...εἰ γὰρ οὐχ ὅ. κατ' οὐσίαν πάντως ἀνόμοιός ἐστι...τὸ δὲ ἀνόμοιον οὐχ οἷόν τε ὅ. λέγεσθαι. ποίᾳ τοίνυν μηχανῇ τὸ ἀνόμοιον ὅ. λέγετε...; εἰ γὰρ οὐκ ἔστι κατ' οὐσίαν ὅ. ὁ υἱὸς τοῦ πατρός, λείπει τι τῇ εἰκόνι id.*syn*.38(p.264.25; M.26.760C,D); τὸ ὅ. οὐκ ἐπὶ τῶν οὐσιῶν, ἀλλ' ἐπὶ σχημάτων καὶ ποιοτήτων λέγεται ὅ. ... διὸ καὶ ὁ λέγων ὅ. κατ' οὐσίαν ἐκ μετουσίας τοῦτο λέγει ὅ. τὸ γὰρ ὅ. ποιότης ἐστίν, ἥτις τῇ οὐσίᾳ προσγένοιτ' ἄν. τοῦτο δὲ τῶν ποιημάτων ἴδιον ἂν εἴη *ib*.53(p.276.24; 788B,C); ὅλος ἐξ ὅλου, ὅ. τῷ πατρὶ ὢν †Ath.*exp.fid*.1(M.25.201A); κατὰ πάντα ὅ. *Symb.Ant*.(345)6 ap.Ath.*syn*.26(p.253.12; 732C); τὸν ὅ. κατὰ πάντα Cyr.H.*catech*.4.7; ἐν πᾶσιν ὅ. *ib*.11.4; *ib*.11.18; ὅ. κατ' οὐσίαν CAnc.(358)*ep.syn*.ap.Epiph.*haer*.73.5(p.275.12; M.42.412C); ὅ. κατὰ τὴν θεότητα καὶ ἀσωματότητα καὶ τὰς ἐνεργείας *ib*.73.9(p.279.29; 420B); τῆς ὁμοίου ἐννοίας οὐκ ἐπὶ τὴν ταυτότητα τοῦ πατρὸς ἀγούσης τὸν υἱόν *ib*.(p.280.13; 420C); CAnc.(358)*anath*.12,13 *ib*.73.11(p.283.2; 424B); ὅ. κατὰ τὰς γραφὰς...ὅ. κατὰ πάντα *Symb.Sirm*.3 ap.Ath.*syn*.8(pp.235.29,236.14; 693A,C); τὸ δὲ ὅ. ... σαφῶς ὁμολογοῦμεν *Symb.Sel.ib*.29(p.258.4; 745A); ὅ. ... κατὰ τὰς γραφάς *Symb.Nic*.(359)ap.Thdt.*h.e*.2.20.3(3.879); cf. τὰ ἐν Σαρδικῇ καὶ ἐν Σιρμίῳ καὶ ταῖς ἄλλαις συνόδοις κεκριμένα, ἐν αἷς συνεδόκει ὅ. κατ' οὐσίαν Soz.*h.e*.4.13.4(M.67.1145B); ὁμολογίαν ἐκομίσαντο παρὰ Λιβερίου ἀποκηρύττουσαν τοὺς μὴ κατ' οὐσίαν καὶ κατὰ πάντα ὅ. τῷ πατρὶ τὸν υἱὸν ἀποφαίνοντας *ib*.4.15.3(1152A); purpose and scope of term explained νῦν αἵρεσις κατὰ μὲν τὴν βούλησιν καὶ τὴν ἐνέργειαν ἀποφαίνεται εἶναι ὅ. ... κατὰ δὲ τὸ ⟨εἶναι⟩ ἀνόμοιον Geo.Laod.*ep.dogm*.ap.Epiph.*haer*.73.13(p.286.2; 428D); εἰ γὰρ κατὰ πάντα, ὡς ὡμολόγησαν, ἐστιν ὅ. ... ἐστιν ὅ. οὐ κατὰ τὴν βούλησιν καὶ τὴν ἐνέργειαν μόνην, καθὰ αὐτοὶ διορίζονται, ἀλλὰ κατὰ τὴν ὕπαρξιν καὶ κατὰ τὴν ὑπόστασιν καὶ κατὰ τὸ εἶναι ὡς υἱός *ib*.73.15(p.288.7; 432C); ὅ. κατὰ τὴν φύσιν *ib*.73.19(p.292.14; 437D); ὅ. οὐ κατὰ μίμησιν μόνον, ἀλλὰ καὶ κατ' οὐσίαν *ib*.73.22(p.294.23; 441B); in profession of Bas. Anc., ap. Geo.Laod.*ib*.73.22(p.295.21; 444B); ὅ. κατ' οὐσίαν put forward in explanation of ὁμοούσιος, CAnt.(363)*ep*.ap.Socr.*h.e*.3.25.14(M.67.453B); in teaching of Macedonius ὅ. κατὰ πάντα ‡Ath.*Maced.dial*.1.11(M.28.1305B); Thdt.*h.e*.2.6.2(3.831); of Basil ἐγὼ δὲ...τὸ ὅ. κατ' οὐσίαν, εἰ μὲν προσκείμενον ἔχει τὸ ἀπαραλλάκτως, δέχομαι τὴν φωνήν, ὡς εἰς ταὐτὸν τῷ ὁμοουσίῳ φέρουσαν. ...εἰ δέ τις τοῦ ὅ. τὸ ἀπαράλλακτον ἀποτέμνοι, ὅπερ οἱ κατὰ τὴν Κωνσταντινούπολιν πεποιήκασιν, ὑποπτεύω τὸ ῥῆμα Bas.*ep*.9.3(3.91A; M.32.272A); τὸ ὅ., μὴ κατὰ τὴν τοῦ εἴδους ταυτότητα...ἀλλὰ κατ' αὐτὴν τὴν οὐσίαν id.*Eun*.1.23(1.234D; M.29.564A); τὸ ἀγαθὸν τοῦ θελήματος, ὅπερ σύνδρομον ὂν τῇ οὐσίᾳ ὅ. καὶ ἴσον, μᾶλλον δὲ ταὐτὸν ἐν πατρὶ καὶ υἱῷ id.*Spir*.21(3.18B; M.32.105B); δοκεῖ μοι ἡ τοῦ ἀπαραλλάκτως ὅ. φωνὴ μᾶλλον ἤπερ τοῦ ὁμοουσίου ἁρμόττειν...ὅ. δὲ κατ' οὐσίαν ἀκριβῶς ἀπαραλλάκτως, ὀρθῶς ἂν οἶμαι λέγεσθαι †Bas.*ep*.361(3.463D; M.1101B); εἰ ὅ. ἐστιν ὁ υἱὸς τῷ πατρί, οὐ κατ' οὐσίαν δέ, λείπεται ἢ κατὰ μορφήν, ἢ κατ' ἐνέργειαν· ἀλλὰ μορφῇ μὲν ἀδύνατον... καὶ κατὰ ἐνέργειαν ὅ., ἐξ ἀνάγκης καὶ κατ' οὐσίαν ὅ. εἶναι Didym.(‡Bas.)*Eun*.4(1.288A; M.29.692C); formula ὅ. κατὰ τὰς γραφάς declared inadequate, Gr.Naz.*or*.21.22(M.35.1108A); so with ὅ. itself ἡμεῖς...οὔτε ὅ., οὔτε ἀνόμοιον λέγομεν τὸν υἱὸν τῷ πατρί...ὅ. γὰρ καὶ ἀνόμοιον, κατὰ τὰς ποιότητας λέγεται· ποιότητες δὲ τὸ θεῖον ἐλεύθερον Evagr.Pont.*ep*.3(M.32.249B); ἀντεισαγωγὴ τοῦ ὁμοουσίου τὸ ὅ. κατ' οὐσίαν...κακοήθως νοηθὲν...ὅτι οὐχ ὅ. θεῷ, ἀλλὰ θεὸν δηλοῖ τὸ ὁμοούσιον †Apoll.*ep.Bas*.2(M.32.1108A); together with ὁμοιούσιος, Epiph.*haer*.73.36(p.311.10; M.42.469C); οὐ τὸ ὅ. μόνον,...ἀλλὰ ταὐτὸν καὶ ἴσον *ib*.76.2(p.342.24; 520A); τὸ ἴσον...καὶ τὸ ὅ. οὐ μόνον, ἀλλὰ καὶ ταὐτὸν ἐν ἅπασι καὶ μὴ παρηλλαγμένον *ib*.76.6(p.346.30; 525C); **2.** Arian attitude οὔτε ὅ. κατ' οὐσίαν τῷ πατρί ἐστιν Alex.Al.*ep.encycl*.7(p.7.21; M.18.573A); Ath.*Ar*.1.21(M.26.56A); attack on phrase ὅ. κατὰ πάντα *ib*.(56B); cf. Οὐάλεντος...προστεθεικότος τῇ ὑπογραφῇ, ὅ. τὸν υἱὸν τῷ πατρί, μὴ προστεθεικότος δέ, κατὰ πάντα Epiph.*haer*.73.22(p.295.12; M.42.444A); πῶς ὅ. τῷ ἀτρέπτῳ ὁ τρεπτὸς εἶναι δυνήσεται; Ath.*Ar*.1.35(84C); *ib*.3.11(344B); id.*syn*.45(p.271.1; M.26.773C); πῶς ὅ.;...ἀρετῇ τελείᾳ καὶ συμφωνίᾳ τὸ αὐτὸ θέλειν τῷ πατρί id.*ep.Afr*.7(M.26.1041A); only a very reduced likeness (at most) admitted by Anomoeans τοῦτον ὅ. ... μόνον κατ' ἐξαίρετον ὁμοιότητα καὶ τὴν ἰδιάζουσαν εὔνοιαν· οὐχ ὡς πατρὶ πατέρα Eun.*exp.fid*.2(p.256); idea of a substantial likeness attacked on ground that distinction between Father and Son is thereby abolished, id.*apol*.24(M.30.861A); cf.Bas.*Eun*.2.31(1.267D; M.29.644B); acceptance of ὅ. κατὰ τὰς γραφὰς Philost.*h.e*.6.1(M.65.532C); cf. Acacius and his followers ἔλεγον κατὰ τὴν βούλησιν μόνον, οὐ μὴν κατὰ τὴν οὐσίαν ὅ., though Acacius alleged to have formerly accepted ὅ. κατὰ πάντα Socr.*h.e*.2.40.31(M.67.341C); extreme Anomoean position κατ' οὐδένα τρόπον ὅ. Ath.*syn*.31(p.259.24; 748C); Ἀετίῳ οὐδὲ τοῦ ὅμοιον πρὸς πατέρα τὸν υἱὸν ἀξιοῦν ἔδοξεν Epiph.*haer*.76.2(p.342.28; M.42.520B); contrast reply of Aëtius to emperor ἀπαραλλάκτως ὅ. Philost.*h.e*.4.12(528A); πολλοὶ τῶν αἱρετικῶν λέγουσιν, ὅτι οὐχ ὅ. ὁ υἱὸς τῷ πατρί. διὰ τί; ὅτι ἐδεήθη, φησί, προσευχῆς ὁ Χριστὸς εἰς τὸ ἐγεῖραι τὸν Λάζαρον Chrys.*anom*.9.1(1.525A); orthodox counter-arguments: like operations imply like nature, Gr.Nyss.*Eun*.1(1 p.147.28; M.45.388B); like begets like, *ib*.(p.149.24; 389B); definition of Eun. discussed ref. various kinds of similarity, *ib*.2(2 p.355.29; 533B); Eun. really attached to notion of unlikeness, *ib*.(p.357.30; 536C); ποίοις ἔργοις τοῦ πατρός ἐστιν ὅ.; τὸν κόσμον πάντως ἐρεῖ *ib*.(p.362.15; 541B).

D. of Godhead ὅ. [sc. τριάς] ἑαυτῇ Ath.*ep.Serap*.1.17(M.26.569C); *ib*.1.28(596A); three Persons said to be of like (not of one) nature, as of 'gold compared with gold', ‡Ath.*Maced.dial*.1.12(M.28.1309C); ὅ. [sc. ὑπόστασις] ἐξ ὅ. Epiph.*anc*.67(p.82.6; M.43.137C); ἀνατέθειται τῷ πάντων αἰτίῳ...καὶ τὸ ὅ. καὶ τὸ ἀνόμοιον. ... ὁ θεὸς...ὅ., ὡς ὁμοίων καὶ ὁμοιότητος ὑποστάτης Dion.Ar.*d.n*.9.1(M.3.909B); ὅ. δὲ τὸν θεὸν εἰ μὲν ὡς ταὐτὸν εἴποι τις, ὡς ὅλον διόλου ἑαυτῷ μονίμως καὶ ἀμερίστως ὄντα ὅ., οὐκ ἀτιμαστέον ἡμῖν τὴν τοῦ ὅ. θεωνυμίαν. οἱ δὲ θεολόγοι τὸν ὑπὲρ πάντα θεόν, ᾗ αὐτός, οὐδενί φασιν εἶναι ὅ. *ib*.9.6(913C); οὐ τρεῖς ὅμοιαι ἀλλήλαις, ἀλλὰ μία καὶ ἡ αὐτὴ κίνησις τῶν τριῶν ὑποστάσεων ‡Cyr.*Trin*.10(6³.15D; M.77.1144A); τὴν μίαν καὶ ὅ. θέλησιν καὶ ἐνέργειαν Dam.*troph*.suppl.(p.281.9); three Persons being compared with three similar eyes sharing a common vision, *ib*.(p.281.16); Arian τριὰς ἐστι δόξαις οὐχ ὁμοίαις Ar.*Thal.fr*.2 ap.Ath.*syn*.15(p.242.24; M.26.708A).

***ὁμοιοσχημάτιστος**, *similarly formed*, Gr.Nyss.*Eun*.12(1 p.237.17; M.45.936A).

ὁμοιότεχνος, ὁ, *fellow craftsman*, Ephr.3.36C.

ὁμοιότης, ἡ, A. *image, copy* ὅ. ... ἐν λεπτομερεῖ μεταπεπλασμένη σώματι Meth.*res*.3.6(p.398.3; M.18.321C); *appearance*, *ib*.1.20(p.243.4; M.41.1088D).

B. in phrases καθ' ὁμοιότητα, c. genit., *as in the case of*, ‡Ath.*Melch*.(M.28.529D); *like*, Chrys.*hom.in Mt*.7:14(3.27A); αὐτῷ ἐν ὁμοιότητι *like him*, Ign.*Eph*.1.3.

C. *likeness, resemblance*; **1.** in gen., of Son, ruling all things like Father κατὰ τὴν τοῦ πατρὸς ὅ. Ath.*decr*.30(p.26.19; M.25.472B); ref. virgin birth ὁμοιότητι γεννήσεως *in the likeness* of a (human) birth, Leont.H.*Nest*.4.9(M.86.1669B); εἰ καθ' ὁμοιότητα τοῦ ἡμετέρου πνεύματος, καὶ τὸ πνεῦμα ὑπονοοῖτο Jo.D.*f.o*.1.7(M.94.805B); as Logos in being a Person, *ib*.; **2.** of man to God, v. εἰκών; Clem.*str*.4.6(p.261.22; M.8.1241B); *Hom.Clem*.10.6f.; *ib*.11.4; τῷ...πατρὶ διὰ τῆς εὐποιΐας τὴν ὅ. δείξας *ib*.11.27; διὰ τὴν πρὸς τὸν ὄντα ὅ., ἣν εἰ ἐφύλαττε διὰ τῆς πρὸς αὐτὸν κατανοήσεως...ἔμεινεν ἄφθαρτος Ath.*inc*.4.6(M.25.104C); Gr.Nyss.*virg*.12(p.298.13; M.46.369C); Chrys.*hom*.9.2 *in Gen*.(4.67B); ὁ ἄνθρωπος ἐκπεσὼν τῆς ὅ. τῆς θείας Didym.(‡Bas.)5(1.303A; M.29.728A); Cyr.*ep.Calos*.(pp.604f.; 6².364A,E); **3.** ref. dissimilarity between God and creatures ποία ὅ. ... ἡμῶν πρὸς τὸν υἱόν; Ath.*Ar*.3.24(M.26.373C); ποία ὅ. τῷ κτίσματι πρὸς τὸν κτίστην; id.*ep.Serap*.1.9(M.26.552B); *ib*.1.24(588A); *ib*.1.26(592B); ποία ὅ. τῷ πνεύματι πρὸς τὰ γενητά; *ib*.1.27(593B); *ib*.2.3(612B); Cyr.*Heb*.1:4(p.372.24; M.74.957B); **4.** of likeness between men and human nature assumed by Son τὴν ὅ. τῆς σαρκός Ath.*Ar*.2.63(M.26.281A); *ib*.3.53(433B); **5.** between Father and Son, v. ὅμοιος, ἀπαράλλακτος; Or.*princ*.4.4.1(p.349.16; M.11.401C); τὴν κατὰ πάντα ὅ. Ath.*Ar*.2.22(M.26.192D); διὰ τὴν ὅ. τοῦ πατρός *ib*.3.36(400C); φυσικὴν ὅ. *ib*.(401A); αὐτοαληθὴς ὅ. τοῦ γεννήσαντος id.*syn*.45(p.270.8; M.26.772D); ἡ οὐσία αὕτη τῆς οὐσίας τῆς πατρικῆς ἐστι...ὅ. *ib*.48(p.272.29; 777D); ἐπὶ τῶν οὐσιῶν οὐχ ὅ., ἀλλὰ ταυτότης ἂν λεχθείη *ib*.53(p.276.26; 788C); τὴν δὲ ἀνείδεον καὶ ἀσχημάτιστον φύσιν ἐν αὐτῇ τῇ οὐσίᾳ λείπεται ἔχειν τὴν ὅ. Bas.*Eun*.1.23(1.234D; M.29.564A); Anomoean assertion of likeness merely according to will and operation confuted, *ib*.1.24(235D; M.565B); likeness being in substance and nature, *ib*.2.22(258C; M.621A); id.*hex*.9.6(1.88D; M.29.208B); ἡ κατὰ τὴν φύσιν ὅ. Gr.Nyss.*Eun*.1(1 p.148.19; M.45.388D); likeness not like an illusion of the senses, nor like that subsisting between God and man, but resembles that of a human father to his son, where the nature is the same, *ib*.2(2 pp.355ff.; 533Bff.); Eun. attacked for suggesting the safeguard, 'not like as a Father to a Father', *ib*.(p.358.13; 536D); ὅπερ ἐμφαίνει ...ὅ. τὴν κατ' οὐσίαν Chrys.*hom*.2.2 *in Heb*.(12.17B); εἰς ἀπαράλλακτον ἀναβαίνουσιν ὅ. Cyr.*Jo*.1.2(4.15E); *ib*.5.5(525D); φυσικὴ πάντως ἡ ὅ. id.*Heb*.1:8(M.74.960B); τὸ ἀκριβὲς τῆς ὅ. Thdt.*haer*.5.2(4.387); τὴν ὅ. τῆς οὐσίας Bas.Sel.*or*.24(M.85.280C); in Arian teaching γεγονὸς ὁλοσχερῶς ἕτερον τῇ φύσει καὶ τῇ δυνάμει, πρὸς τελείαν ὅ. διαθέσεώς τε καὶ δυνάμεως τοῦ πεποιηκότος γενόμενον Eus.Nic.*ep.Paulin*.(p.16.5; M.82.913C); Eun.*exp.fid*.2(p.257), v. ὅμοιος; argument of Eun. that substantial likeness would make the Son unbegotten, id.*apol*.11(M.30.845D); τὴν κατ' οὐσίαν ὅ. ἀνελόντες *ib*.22(857B); οὐ πρὸς τὴν οὐσίαν, πρὸς δὲ τὴν ἐνέργειαν, ἥτις ἐστὶ καὶ βούλησις, ἀποσώζειν τὴν ὅ. τὸν υἱὸν ἀναγκαῖον *ib*.24(860B); διὰ τὸ ἀκολουθεῖν, φησί, τῷ τῆς γεννήσεως τρόπῳ τὸν τρόπον τῆς ὅ. Gr.Nyss.*Eun*.1(1 p.148.26; M.45.389A); argument from Christ's apparent ignorance, Bas.*ep*.236.1(3.360D; M.32.876B); in Homoeousian doctrine; earthly fathers have sons καθ' ὁμοιότητα τῶν οἰκείων οὐσιῶν and Father has Son καθ' ὅ. τῆς ἑαυτοῦ οὐσίας CAnc.(358)*ep.syn*.ap.Epiph.*haer*.73.5(p.274.27,29; M.42.412B); ὥστε καὶ ἀπὸ τῶν ἀποστολικῶν μαρτυριῶν τὴν κατ' οὐσίαν ὅ. ... κηρύττεσθαι *ib*.73.8(p.279.14; 417D); οὐδὲ ὁ υἱὸς...εἰς ταυτότητα ἄξει τοῦ πατρὸς τὴν ἑαυτοῦ οὐσίαν, ἀλλ' ἐπὶ τὴν ὅ. *ib*.73.9(p.280.20; 420D); id.*anath*.1,11 *ib*.73.10,11(pp.280.23,282.18; 421A,424A); Geo.Laod.*ep.dogm.ib*.73.17(p.289.18; 433C); Anomoean opponents' views quoted, *ib*.73.21(pp.293ff.; 440Dff.); ἀναθεματίσατε τοὺς διαφορὰν λέγοντας ὁμοιότητος *ib*.73.22(p.294.28; 441C); **6.** of Godhead οὐκ εἶπον ὅ., ἀλλὰ ταυτότητα ‡Cyr.*Trin*.10(6³.15C; M.77.1141D); v. ὅμοιος; Dion.Ar.*d.n*.9.1(M.3.909B); ἔστιν ἡ τῆς θείας ὅ. δύναμις, ἡ τὰ παραγόμενα πάντα πρὸς τὸ αἴτιον ἐπιστρέφουσα...καὶ τὸ ἐν πᾶσιν ὅμοιον ἴχνει τινὶ τῆς θείας ὅ. ὁμοιόν ἐστι *ib*.9.6(913C,916A); τῇ κατὰ πάντα ὅ. Anast.*fid*.(p.272); Arian τὸν λόγον εἰς ὅ. δόξης καὶ οὐσίας ἀλλότριον εἶναι παντελῶς ἑκατέρων τοῦ τε πατρὸς καὶ τοῦ ἁγίου πνεύματος Ar.*Thal.fr*.14 ap.Ath.*Ar*.1.6(M.26.24B).

D. *simile, similitude* διαφέρει ὅ. παραβολῆς Or.*comm.in Mt*.10.4(p.4.29; M.13.844C); *ib*.10.16(p.20.13; 873B).

ὁμοιοτροπία, ἡ, *similarity of character, way of life* or *customs* τῆς τῶν φαύλων ὅ. Eus.*p.e*.7.7(305B; M.21.517B); τῇ παρ' Αἰγυπτίοις ὅ. *ib*.7.8(312C; M.528C); ταῖς Αἰγυπτιακαῖς ὅ. ἀπαχθέντες id.*d.e*.1.6(p.27.28; M.22.56C); Tit.Bost.*fr.Lc*.6:43(p.163.17); Cyr.*Ps*.48:20(M.69.1073A).

***ὁμοιοτύπωτος**, *similarly fashioned*, Dion.Ar.*c.h*.2.3(M.3.141B).

ὁμοιούσιος, *of like substance* or *essence*; **1.** Trin., ref. Eusebius of Nicomedia, Theognis, and Maris at Nicaea ἐν δόλῳ μὲν καὶ τὸ ὅ. ἐν τῇ τοῦ ὁμοουσίου φωνῇ ὑποκλέψαντες Philost.*h.e*.1.9(M.65.465A); excluded together with ὁμοούσιον, *Symb.Sirm*.2(p.257.4; M.26.741B); by Acacian party at Seleucia τὸ μὲν ὁμοούσιον καὶ τὸ ὅ. ἐκβάλλομεν, ὡς ἀλλότριον τῶν γραφῶν...τὸ δὲ ὅμοιον τοῦ υἱοῦ πρὸς τὸν πατέρα ὁμολογοῦμεν *Symb.Sel*.(p.258.2; M.26.744B); Socr.*h.e*.2.45.3(M.67.360A); orthodox objection εἰ μὲν οὖν καὶ τὸν υἱὸν ἐκ μετουσίας λέγετε, λεγέσθω μὲν παρ' ὑμῶν ὅ.· οὐκ ἔστι μέντοι λεγόμενος οὕτως ἀληθείᾳ οὐδὲ ὅλως φῶς οὐδὲ φύσει θεός...φύσει δὲ ὢν καὶ οὐ μετοχῇ οὐκ ἂν κυρίως λεχθείη ὅ., ἀλλ' ὁμοούσιος Ath.*syn*.53(p.276.34; M.26.788D); but maintained as watchword of 'Semiarian' party, Epiph.*anac*.73(p.231.3; M.42.872A); rejected by Aëtius, id.*haer*.76.12(p.353.10; M.42.536C); and Eunomius μήτε μὴν ὁμοούσιον, μηδὲ ὅ., ἐπείπερ τὸ μὲν γένεσιν καὶ μερισμὸν σημαίνει τῆς οὐσίας, τὸ δὲ ἰσότητα Eun.*apol*.26(M.30.864C); asserted by Macedonians, Didym.*Trin*.1.34(M.39.437A); implications of term τί ἐλύπει λέγειν τὸ ὅ. ὁμοούσιον;...δύναται γὰρ καὶ ὅ. εἶναι πρὸς χρυσὸν χαλκὸς Epiph.*haer*.73.36(p.310.16; 469A); *ib*.(p.311.7; 469C); Orth.: οὕτως λέγεις ὅμοιον τῷ πατρὶ τὸν υἱόν, ὡς ἄγγελον ἀγγέλῳ·...τῶν δὲ ἀγγέλων ἡ αὐτή ἐστιν οὐσία; Maced.: ἡμεῖς τοιαύτην λέγομεν καὶ ὁμοίαν, οὐ τὴν αὐτήν· διὸ καὶ ὅ. λέγομεν καὶ οὐχ ὁμοούσιον ‡Ath.*dial.Trin*.3.1(M.28.1204C); τὸ ὅ. ... ἄγροικος σοφία ἐστίν· ὡς ἐὰν λέγῃ τις τὸν ὁμότροπον ὁμοιότροπον... Maced.: οὔκ· ἀλλὰ τὸ ὅ. ἐπὶ τῶν ἀσωμάτων· τὸ δὲ ὁμοούσιον ἐπὶ τῶν σωμάτων Euther.*confut*.(M.28.1336C); **2.** Christol. οὐ γὰρ ὅ., ὡς ἔδοξε τισὶ τῶν αἱρετικῶν, ἀλλ' ὁμοούσιον, τουτέστιν ἐκ τῆς ἡμετέρας οὐσίας Cyr.*hom.div*.15(p.14.30; M.77.1093B).

ὁμοιοφανής, *similar in appearance,* Thdr.Stud.*epp.*2.84(M.99.1328C).

***ὁμοιόφρων,** *of a similar mind,* ‡Ath.*Maced.dial.*2(M.28.1336C).

***ὁμοιόφωνος,** *of similar sound,* Gr.Nyss.*Eun.*1(1 p.25.7; M.45.253A).

ὁμοι-όω, 1. *liken,* Or.*hom.18.9 in Jer.*(p.162.31; M.13.481A); Ath.*ep.Serap.*4.22(M.26.673B); **2.** pass., *be made like, become* or *be like*; ref. Inc., Ath.*Ar.*2.9(M.26.165A); τότε δὴ καὶ ὁ λόγος δέδωκεν ἑαυτὸν εἰς τὸ συγκαταβῆναι καὶ ~ωθῆναι τοῖς ἔργοις *ib.*2.51(256B); ὡμοιώθη ἡμῖν κατὰ πάντα χωρὶς ἁμαρτίας id.*inc.et c.Ar.*11(M.26.1004A); εἰ γὰρ μὴ αὐτὸς ὡμοίωτο πρὸς ἀνθρώπους, οὐκ ἠδύναντο οἱ ἄνθρωποι ~οῦσθαι πρὸς θεόν †Ath.*fr.*(M.26.1240D); ἀδύνατον ἦν θεὸν ~ωθῆναι ἡμῖν μὴ σαρκωθέντα Gel.Cyz.*h.e.*2.24.11(M.85.1300D); of creatures in rel. to God ~οῦταί τις θεῷ Clem.*str.*2.9(p.137.11; M.8.981A); ἐκ μετοχῆς ~οῦται τῷ θεῷ Ath.*syn.*53(p.276.31; M.26.788C); ἐὰν γένῃ φιλάδελφος...ὡμοιώθης θεῷ ‡Bas.*struct.hom.*1.21(1.334B; M.30.33A); Gr.Nyss.*hom.opif.*16(M.44.181B); Trin., ref. objection to ὁμοούσιον: ἀντεισαγωγὴ δὴ τοῦ ὁμοουσίου τὸ ὅμοιον κατ' οὐσίαν...κακοήθως νοηθέν· ἐπειδὴ ἡ ὁμοιότης τῶν ἐν οὐσίᾳ ἐστίν, τῶν οὐσιωδῶν· ἵνα δὴ οὕτως ὡμοιωμένη οὐσία νοῆται, οἷος ἂν εἴη καὶ ἀνδριὰς πρὸς βασιλέα †Apoll.*ep.Bas.*2(M.32.1108A); ποῖος ἔτι συγχωρήσει λόγος πρὸς τὸν ἀγέννητον ~οῦν τὴν γεννητήν [sc. οὐσίαν]; τῆς ...συγκρίσεως...μετὰ τῆς ἰσότητος ἀγέννητον ἀποφαινούσης τὸν ~ούμενον Eun.*apol.*11(M.30.845D); Arian view being that Son is ἐξ ἀρετῆς καὶ τοῦ θέλειν ~ούμενος τῷ θεῷ Ath.*ep.Afr.*7(M.26.1041B); of H. Ghost πάρεστι πανταχοῦ τῷ ἐκπέμποντι αὐτὸ θεῷ ~ούμενον Didym.(‡Bas.)*Eun.*5(1.321D; M.29.772A).

ὁμοίωμα, τό, 1. *likeness, image*; **a.** of Son in rel. to Father οὐχ ὅτι ἡμεῖς τῷ ὁ. ἐπερειδόμεθα·...ταὐτὸν τῇ θεότητι Epiph.*haer.*76.2(p.342.15; M.42.517D); τὸ ὁ. ... αὐτὸ τὸ γεννητῶς αὐτὸν ἐκ τοῦ πατρὸς ὑποστῆναι Gr.Nyss.*Eun.*1(1 p.160.12; M.45.401B); ὁ. τῆς ἰδιότητος αὐτοῦ Cyr.*thes.*6(5^{1}.48A); **b.** of man in rel. to God, Bas.*hom.*9.9(2.81E; M.31.349C); Gr.Nyss.*virg.*12(p.298.10; M.46.369C); **c.** exeg. Ex. 20:4, distn. between idols and images, Or.*hom.8.3 in Ex.*(p.221.24ff.; M.12.353Bf.); εἴδωλα καλεῖ τὰ τῶν οὐχ ὑφεστώτων μιμήματα· ὁ. δὲ τὰ τῶν ὑφεστώτων εἰκάσματα Thdt.*qu.38 in Ex.*(1.149); Proc.G.*Lev.*2:11ff.(M.87.704C); Cant.1:11, ref. Jewish religion, cf.Or.*hom.2 in Cant.*(p.160.8ff.; M.13.135D–136B); cf.Cyr.*fr.Cant.*1:9(M.69.1281A); Thdt.*Cant.*1:11(2.47); πᾶσα ἡ περὶ τῆς ἀρρήτου φύσεως διδασκαλία ...ὁ. χρυσίου ἐστίν, οὐκ αὐτὸ τὸ χρυσίον. οὐ γὰρ ἔστι παραστῆσαι δι' ἀκριβείας τὸ ὑπὲρ ἔννοιαν ἀγαθόν Gr.Nyss.*hom.3 in Cant.*(M.44.820C); ὁ. ... τοὺς ἁγίους μάρτυρας Ph.Carp.*Cant.*23(M.40.53A); Rom. 6:5 ἐπὶ ὑμῶν θανάτου μὲν καὶ παθημάτων ὁ.· σωτηρίας δὲ οὐχ ὁ., ἀλλὰ ἀλήθεια Cyr.H.*catech.*20.7; Rom.8:3, of Inc.; in likeness of (not in) sinful flesh itself (i.e. in true flesh but without sin), Bas.*ep.*261.3(3.403A; M.32.972B); Ammon.*Jo.*3:14(M.85.1409D); Thdt.*Rom.*8:3(3.81); Jo.D.*Rom.*8:3(M.95.500A); Phil.2:7, purpose of Inc. ἵνα γενώμεθα οἱ πάντες εἰς υἱοὺς θεοῦ, ἐν ὁ. τοῦ υἱοῦ τοῦ θεοῦ Ath.*inc.et c.Ar.*8(M.26.997A); against Marcionites ἰδού, φασίν, οὐκ ἐγένετο ἄνθρωπος, ἀλλ', ἐν ὁ. ἀνθρώπου γενόμενος. ... ἀνθρώπου ὁ., ἄνθρωπος ἕτερος Chrys.*hom.2 in Phil.*(11.246B); reason for 'likeness' only, explained πολλὰ μὲν εἶχεν ἡμέτερα, πολλὰ δὲ οὐκ εἶχεν· οἷον ἀπὸ συνουσίας οὐκ ἐτέχθη, οἷον ἁμαρτίαν οὐκ ἐποίησε...οὐκ ἦν ψιλὸς ἄνθρωπος *ib.*(247D,E); **d.** of God as known from likenesses, Dion.Ar.*d.n.*7.3(M.3.869D); **2.** *symbol, token, sign* κατὰ τὸ τῆς κηρύξεως ὁ. Clem.*str.*7.9(p.39.11; M.9.473C); τὴν ἀφέλειαν καὶ τὸ πρᾶον τῆς νέας ἐπιφανείας τοῦ πνεύματος ἐβούλετο δεῖξαι τῷ τῆς περιστερᾶς ὁ. id.*fr.*57(p.226.26; M.9.765C); liturg. σοὶ προσηνέγκαμεν τὸν ἄρτον τοῦτον, τὸ ὁ. τοῦ σώματος τοῦ μονογενοῦς·... καὶ τὸ ποτήριον τὸ ὁ. τοῦ αἵματος Serap.*euch.*13.12,14; **3.** in phrases, *in like fashion* κατὰ τὸ ὁ. Ign.*Trall.*9.2; *in likeness* ὑμεῖς δὲ κατὰ τὸ βάπτισμα, ἐν ὁ. καὶ συσταυρωθῆναι Cyr.H.*catech.*21.2; **4.** verbal *figure, illustration,* Hipp.*antichr.*55(p.37.3); Dion.Al.ap.Ath.*Dion.*18(p.59.16; M.25.505C); †Ath.*fr.*(M.26.1241B); μὴ γάρ μοι πρὸς τὰ ἀνθρώπινα καταπέσῃς ὁ. Didym.(‡Bas.)*Eun.*5(1.304E; M.29.732A); **5.** *example,* ref. Adam and Christ τῷ ὁ. τῆς αὐτοῦ παραβάσεως...τῷ ὁ. τῆς αὐτοῦ ὑπακοῆς Max.*ambig.*(M.91.1276C).

ὁμοιωματικός, 1. *denoting resemblance,* Chrys.*hom.47.1 in Jo.*(8.276A); κατὰ ἀναφορὰν ὁμοιωματικὴν τῆς οὔσης εἰδωλολατρείας Thdr.Stud.*epp.*2.162(M.99.1513D); **2.** *comparative,* gram. δίχα τοῦ ὁ. ἐπιρρήματος Gennad.*fr.Rom.*7:14(p.372.8; M.85.1684C); Thdr.Stud.*epp.*2.212(M.99.1640A); τὸ ὁ. 'ὡς' *cat.Apoc.*6:6(p.267.23).

ὁμοιωματικῶς, *by way of comparison* ἢ τό, 'ὡς', οὐχ ὁ. εἴρηται Olymp.*Job* 42:18(M.93.468A); *in likeness*; ref. Christ in an image, Thdr.Stud.*epp.*2.65(M.99.1288B).

ὁμοίως, *in similar fashion* ἵνα μὴ νομίσῃς, ὅτι ὁ. τοῦ υἱοῦ καὶ τῶν κτισμάτων ἐστὶ πατήρ Cyr.H.*catech.*11.19; ἔχει ὁ. πάντα κατ' οὐσίαν ...ὡς ὁ πατήρ CAnc.(358)*ep.syn.*ap.Epiph.*haer.*73.8(p.279.6; M.42.417C); ὁ πατὴρ...αὐθεντικῶς ποιεῖ, ὁ δὲ υἱός...οὐκ αὐθεντικῶς...ἀλλ' ὁ. Geo.Laod.*ep.dogm.*ap.eund.73.18(p.290.13; 436C); οὐχ οὕτως...ἀλλ' ὁ. *ib.*(p.291.7; 436D); οὐκ ἄλλως θεὸς ὁ υἱός, ἑτέρως δὲ ὁ πατήρ, ἀλλ' ὁ. Didym.(‡Bas.)*Eun.*4(1.279B; M.29.672A); ὁ. ἡμῶν id.*Trin.*2.12(M.39.685A); in phrase ὁ. ἔχω *be similar,* Gr.Nyss.*Eun.*2(2 p.356.7; M.45.533C); c. πρός, *ib.*1(1 p.149.11; 389A); c. dat., *ib.*(1 p.151.25; 392C).

ὁμοίωσις, ἡ, (cf. εἰκών); **A.** *likeness*; **1.** of man created after likeness of God; **a.** ref. man's soul, Clem.*prot.*10(p.71.28; M.8.213A); Or.*hom.1.13 in Gen.*(p.15.15; M.12.156A); τῆς ψυχῆς τὸ λογικόν τε καὶ νοερόν...ὡς ἂν τοῦ ἐπὶ πάντων θεοῦ τὴν ὁ. φέρον Eus.*p.e.*7.4(303A; M.21.513B); **b.** ref. free will καὶ τῷ αὐτεξουσίῳ τῆς προαιρέσεως τὴν πρὸς τὸ θεῖον διασώζων ὁ. Gr.Nyss.*or.catech.*21(p.81.7; M.45.57D); **c.** ref. man's governance of creation, Chrys.*hom.23.5 in Gen.*(4.212D); **d.** of corrupted likeness restored in Inc., †Ath.*fr.*(M.26.1245B); ἀποδιδοὺς ἡμῖν τὴν πρὸς ἑαυτὸν ὁ. ὁ αὐτὸς τοῦ θεοῦ λόγος εἰς ὁ. ἡμῶν κατῆλθεν Gel.Cyz.*h.e.*2.24.10(M.85.1300D); through baptism, Didym.*Trin.*2.12(M.39.680A); Jo.D.*f.o.*4.9(M.94.1121A); cf. τῆς καθ' ὁμοίωσιν μορφῆς ἐν αὐτοῖς [sc. the baptized] ἐκτυπουμένης τοῦ λόγου Meth.*symp.*8.8(p.90.9; M.18.149C); **e.** ὁ. dist. from εἰκών and related to perfection, Clem.*str.*2.22(p.185.27; M.8.1080C); ἔτι γὰρ ἔχρῃζε, 'κατ' εἰκόνα' θεοῦ γεγονώς, καὶ τὸ 'καθ' ὁ.' ἀπολαβεῖν ὅπερ τελεσιουργῆσαι καταπεμφθεὶς ὁ λόγος εἰς τὸν κόσμον Meth.*symp.*1.4(p.12.23; M.18.44C); ‡Gr.Nyss.*hom.1 in Gen.1:26*(M.44.273A); Chrys.*hom.9.3 in Gen.*(4.67C); πάντες ἄνθρωποι κατ' εἰκόνα ἐσμὲν τοῦ θεοῦ· τὸ δὲ καθ' ὁ. ἐκείνων μόνων ἐστὶ τῶν διὰ πολλῆς ἀγάπης τὴν ἑαυτῶν ἐλευθερίαν δουλωσάντων τῷ θεῷ Diad.*perf.*4(p.6.26); Jo.D.*f.o.*2.12(M.94.920B); cf. ὁ μὲν χοϊκός ἐστι 'κατ' εἰκόνα', ὁ δὲ ψυχικὸς 'καθ' ὁ.' θεοῦ Clem.*exc.Thdot.*54(p.125.2; M.9.685A); **f.** ὁ. perfected by means of virtue; **i.** in gen., cf. *apostoli se ad ejus similitudinem reformarunt...semper ergo intueamur istam imaginem dei, ut possimus ad ejus similitudinem reformari,* Or.*hom.1.13 in Gen.*(p.17.21,26; M.12.157B); καθ' ὁμοίωσιν ἀκριβωθῆναι τότε πάρεστι θεοῦ, ὁπότε δὴ τοὺς αὐτοὺς αὐτῷ χαρακτῆρας τῆς κατὰ ἄνθρωπον πολιτείας ...ἐν ἑαυτοῖς...κατέχωμεν Meth.*symp.*1.4(p.13.3; M.18.44D); in good works, Bas.*Eun.*1.27(1.238A; M.29.572B); id.*hom.*3.7(2.24A; M.31.216B); ἡ ἀποταγή...ἀρχὴ τῆς πρὸς Χριστὸν ὁ. id.*reg.fus.*8.3(2.350D; M.31.940C); Gr.Nyss.*hom.opif.*5(M.44.137B); ὁ φωτισμὸς τῆς ἀγάπης προστεθεὶς εἰς τὴν τοῦ καθ' ὁ. ὁλοκλήρως εὐπρέπειαν δηλοῖ γενέσθαι τὸ κατ' εἰκόνα Diad.*perf.*89(p.126.16); **ii.** ref. intellectual virtue ψυχῆς ἀγαθὸν γνῶσις, ὑγεία τις οὖσα ψυχῆς, καθ' ἣν πρὸς θεὸν ὁ. γίνεται †Just.*fr.*18(p.52; M.6.1600B); ὁ. οὐκ ἄνευ γνώσεως Bas.*Spir.*2(3.2C; M.32.69B); ἐξ ὧν ἡ θεία ὁ. δείκνυται, γνώσεώς τέ φημι καὶ ἀρετῆς Max.*ambig.*(M.91.1140B); **g.** of Persons of Trin. as portrayed in man, Nil.*epp.*1.174(M.79.152A); Bas.Sel.*or.*1.3(M.85.36A); ‡Gr.Nyss.*imag.*(M.44.1333B,C); cf.Anast.S.*serm.imag.*3(M.89.1161C); **h.** likeness of God not found in irrational animals, but only in man, Tat.*orat.*15(p.16.13ff.; M.6.837Bf.); **2.** likeness to angels achieved by Adam through temperance, Bas.*hom.*1.3(2.3B; M.31.168B); **3.** man's likeness assumed in Inc. τὰ ἡμῶν ἀναδεχόμενος, ἵνα ἡμεῖς ...συνδεθέντες ἐν αὐτῷ διὰ τῆς ὁ. τῆς σαρκός Ath.*Ar.*2.74(M.26.305A); προῆλθεν ἄνθρωπος καθ' ὁ. ἡμετέραν id.*ep.Max.*2(M.26.1088B); τὸν εἰς ὁ. ἡμῶν καταβαίνοντα †Ath.*fr.*(M.26.1240D); τὴν πρὸς ἡμᾶς ὁ. ὑφελών Cyr.*Ps.*9:4(M.69.764B); id.*thes.*32(5^{1}.303B); **4.** likeness of Son to Father; **a.** asserted, Eus.*d.e.*5.4(p.225.23; M.22.372C); Ath.*decr.*20(p.17.10; M.25.452B) cit. s. ἀρετή; *ib.*30(p.26.31; 472D); ἀνάγκη τὴν ὁ. ... ἐπ' αὐτὴν τὴν οὐσίαν τοῦ θεοῦ φέρειν id.*Ar.*3.11(M.26.344A); cf. ὑπὲρ τὴν ὁ. οἴδαμεν τὸν υἱόν...ὡς ταυτὸν τῇ θεότητι Epiph.*haer.*76.2(p.342.15; M.42.517D); ὁ. φυσικῆς Cyr.*thes.*32(5^{1}.301C); **b.** Arian denial, at least of essential likeness μᾶλλον οὐδὲ ὅλως...ὁ. τινα τοῦ πατρὸς ἔχων φανήσεται Ath.*Ar.*3.11(M.26.344B); cf. τήν τε τῆς ὁ. ἑνότητα τοῦ υἱοῦ...οὐκ ἔλεγον [sc. Arians] κατὰ τὴν οὐσίαν id.*syn.*45(p.270.30; M.26.773C); cf. τὴν ὁ. ἔξωθεν φέροντες τῷ υἱῷ προστιθέασιν †Apoll.*ep.Bas.*1(M.32.1104C); οὐδὲν ἔχοντα τῆς οὐσίας αὐτοῦ, ἀπολαύσαντα δὲ μόνης τῆς ἀκριβοῦς ὁ. Cyr.*Jo.*3.5(4.302E); γυμνός ποτε τῆς ὁ. ὁ υἱός *ib.*(303C); κατὰ μόνην τὴν ταυτοεργίαν εἰς ὁ. ἀναβαίνοντα *ib.*(304C); **5.** of H. Ghost in rel. to Son ὁ. ἀκραιφνής τε καὶ φυσικὴ τοῦ υἱοῦ, τὸ πνεῦμά ἐστι Cyr.*dial.Trin.*7(5^{1}.639B,D).

B. *form, appearance* ἠλλάγη ἡ ὁ. τοῦ σώματος αὐτῆς *A.Phil.*126(p.55.10); ἀνθρωπίνην ὁ. Clem.*fr.*57(p.226.24; M.9.765C).

C. *likeness, portrait, Pers.*(p.18.1); εἰκὼν γάρ ἐστιν...ὁ. τοῦ ἐν αὐτῇ γραφέντος Steph.Bost.*fr.*(p.668; M.94.1376D).

D. verbal *figure, simile, comparison* ἐν παραβολαῖς καὶ ὁ. πολλάκις λαλοῦν τὸ ἅγιον πνεῦμα Just.*dial.*77.4(M.6.657A); ὁ. πρὸς τὴν τῶν οὐρανῶν βασιλείαν Or.*comm.in Mt.*10.4(p.4.17; M.13.844A); διαφορὰν εἶναι ὁμοιώσεως καὶ παραβολῆς. ἔοικεν οὖν ἡ μὲν ὁ. εἶναι γενική, ἡ δὲ παραβολὴ εἰδική. τάχα δὲ καὶ ἡ ὁ. γενικωτάτη οὖσα τῆς παραβολῆς ἔχει ἐν εἴδει, ὥσπερ τὴν παραβολήν, οὕτω καὶ ὁμώνυμον τῷ γενικῷ τὴν ὁ. *ib.*(p.5.2ff.; 844C); οὕτω μοι νόει καὶ ἐπὶ τῶν κατὰ τὸ εὐαγγέλιον ὁ. τὴν βασιλείαν τῶν οὐρανῶν ὁμοιουμένην τινὶ ὁμοιοῦσθαι οὐ διὰ πάντα τὰ προσόντα τῷ εἰς ὃ ἡ ὁ., ἀλλὰ διά τινα ὧν χρῄζει ὁ παραληφθεὶς λόγος *ib.* 10.11(p.12.5f.; 860A); τὴν κατὰ τὰς παρθένους ὁ. Ath.*Ar.*3.46(M.26.420B); †Ath.*fr.*(M.26.1241B); cf. *homoeosis est...similitudo, per quam minus notae rei per similitudinem ejus, quae magis nota est, panditur demonstratio. hujus species sunt tres: icon, parabolae, paradigma, id est imago, conparatio, exemplum*, Isid.H.*etym.*1.37.31; τό, ὡς, πῇ μὲν ἐπὶ ὁμοιώσεως εἴληπται παρὰ τῇ θεοπνεύστῳ γραφῇ· ...οὐ γὰρ ταὐτὸν εἰκὼν καὶ ἀρχέτυπον τῇ φύσει, ἀλλὰ...τῇ ὁ. Thdr.Stud.*epp.*2.65(M.99.1288A,B).

***ὁμοιωτέον**, *one must make like* οὐχ ὁ. ἐστὶ τὰς εὐχὰς ἡμῶν τοῖς ἐθνικοῖς Or.*or.*21.2(p.346.1; M.11.481B).

ὁμοιωτικός, **1.** *demonstrating similarity*; of a comparison, Gr.Nyss.*Apoll.*11(M.45.1144D); **2.** *capable of becoming like* δυνάμει ἡμᾶς ἐποίησεν ὁ. θεοῦ ‡Gr.Nyss.*or.1 in Gen.1*:26(M.44.273A); **3.** *figurative, allegorical* 'ὁμοιότητας' δέ φησι τὰς ὁ. ὑπονοίας Max.*schol.c.h.*2.2(M.4.37D).

***ὁμοκάρδιος**, *of one heart*, Thdr.Stud.*epp.*2.180(M.99.1556D).

***ὁμοκλεής**, *of like renown*, Thdr.Stud.*epp.*2.21(M.99.1180D).

ὁμοκλητήρ, *rebuking*, Paul.Sil.*Soph.*1023(M.86.2158B).

[*]**ὁμοκλινής**, *reclining together* at table, Nonn.*par.Jo.*2:2(M.43.760C).

***ὁμοκοίλιος**, *from the same womb*, Eust.*engast.*20(p.47.8; M.18.653B).

ὁμόκοιτος, *sharing the same bed*, Just.*2apol.*2.6(M.6.444B); fem. as subst., *wife*, Gr.Thaum.*pan.Or.*5(p.13.17; M.10.1068A).

***ὁμόκρηνος**, *flowing from the same source*, ‡Caes.Naz.*dial.*147(M.38.1096).

***ὁμόκτιστος**, *created together*, Didym.(‡Bas.)*Eun.*5(1.308D; M.29.740B).

***ὁμόλεκτος**, *sharing the same couch* at table, Pall.*v.Chrys.*20 (p.143.1; M.47.79).

***ὁμολεξία, ἡ**, **1.** *equivocal, ambiguous word*, Epiph.*haer.*64.8 (p.417.8; M.41.1081D); **2.** *identity of utterance*, Cyr.H.*catech.*6.27.

ὁμολογ-έω, **1.** *confess, acknowledge*, c. dat. ὁ. καὶ ταῖς ἐντολαῖς καὶ τῷ θεῷ Clem.*str.*4.9(p.282.10; M.8.1285A); προσκυνοῦσι Χριστόν, θεὸν αὐτὸν ~οῦντες Ath.*inc.*53.2(M.25.189D); c. ὅτι, *Lit.Chrys.*(p.394.17); pass., c. ptcpl. ~εῖται μὴ ὢν κτίσμα Ath.*ep.Serap.*1.24(M.26.588B); c. ὅτι, id.*inc.*48.9(M.25.184A); **a.** in gen., ref. articles of faith ὃς ἂν μὴ ~ῇ τὸ μαρτύριον τοῦ σταυροῦ Polyc.*ep.*7.1; τὸ ἀποθανεῖν σταυρωθέντα ~ῶ ὑπομεῖναι αὐτὸν καὶ τὸ ἄνθρωπον γενέσθαι Just.*dial.*67.6(M.6.629D); πατέρα καὶ υἱὸν ὁ. Ath.*syn.*52(p.275.27; M.26.785B); ~οῦμεν ἕνα...θεὸν καὶ πατέρα Bas.*fid.*4(2.227B; M.31.685A); τὰς τρεῖς ὑποστάσεις ὁ. Gr.Naz.*or.*20.6(M.35.1072C); τὸ ὁμοούσιον ὁ. Thdt.*Ps.*109:3(1.1395); *Symb.Chalc.*(p.129.23; H.2.456B); ἀνθρώπῳ ἐνὶ [i.e. Christ] πάντα προσενέγκαντες τὰ ὡμολογημένα *Pers.*(p.3.1); Thdr.Stud.*antirr.*2.26(M.99.369D); **b.** partic., in time of persecution ὁ. εἶναι Χριστιανούς, γινώσκοντες τῷ ~οῦντι θάνατον τὴν ζημίαν κεῖσθαι Just.*1apol.*11.1(M.6.341B); Clem.*str.*4.9(p.281.6; 1284A); ὡμολόγησα καὶ τὸ πρῶτον, ὅτε διωγμὸς γέγονεν Hos.*ep.* ap.Ath.*h.Ar*44(p.207.20; M.25.744D); **2. a.** *profess* Christian faith, Or.*princ.*4.1.2(p.295.1; M.11.345A); *M.Das.*8.2; Ath.*ep.Afr.*11(M.26.1048B); **b.** *vow* ὁ. μὴ γῆμαι Clem.*str.*3.15(p.241.4; M.8.1197A); παρθενίαν ὡμολόγησαν Bas.*ep.*199 *can.*20(3.292D; M.32.720C); *ib.* 217 *can.*60(326D; M.797C); *V.Olymp.*1.1(p.410.8); πῶς τὰ ὡμολογημένα θεῷ διαλῦσαι τολμήσω; †Jo.D.*B.J.*30(M.96.1148A); **3.** *confess* sins ὁ. ἁμαρτάνειν Clem.*paed.*2.10(p.217.4); *Const.App.*2.50.3; Bas.*ep.*217 *cann.*70,71(3.327E,328A; M.32.801A); αἰσχύνῃ ὁ. ἁμαρτήματα; Chrys.*grat.*3(2.663C); τὸ ~ῆσαι τὰ ἐπταισμένα id.*hom.10.2 in Gen.*(4.74A); πῶς γὰρ ἂν τις ἀφήσει τῷ μηδὲ ἡμαρτηκέναι ~οῦντι, μηδὲ μετανοοῦντι; id.*exp.in Ps.*49:18(5.235A); Isid.Pel.*epp.*3.230 (M.78.912C); **4.** ὁ. χάριν *acknowledge gratitude, give thanks*, also χάριν εἰδέναι ὁ. Just.*2apol.*2.19(M.6.448A); ὁ. τὴν μεγίστην χάριν Clem.*paed.*1.12(p.150.7; M.8.369C); χάριτας ὁ. τῷ θεῷ Or.*Jo.*32.29(18; p.475.32; M.14.821C); Const.ap.Eus.*v.C.*2.72(p.71.22; M.20.1048B); εἰδέναι τῷ βασιλεῖ τῶν ὅλων τὴν χάριν ὁ., ὅτι...id.*ib.*3.12(p.82.18; 1068A); ὁ. τῷ θεῷ χάριν, ὅτι... Chrys.*hom.23.3 in 2Cor.*(10.593E); Thdr.Stud.*epp.*2.212(M.99.1637D); **5.** pass. ptcpl., *acknowledged, accepted, received*, of sacred writings Πέτρος...μίαν ἐπιστολὴν ~ουμένην καταλέλοιπεν Or.*Jo.*5.3(p.101.26; M.14.188D); τῶν ἀποστολικῶν ὁ. γραμμάτων id.*fr.in Heb.*(M.14.1309A)ap.Eus.*h.e.*6.25.12; ταῖς ὁ. τῶν ἀποστόλων Πράξεσιν Eus.*h.e.*2.17.6(M.20.177A); τῶν ἐνδιαθήκων καὶ ὁ. γραφῶν *ib.*3.3.3(217A); of *1Clem.*, *ib.*3.16(249A); of the NT writings, *ib.*3.25.3(268D); **6.** *declare, assert* συνιέναι τὰ ἐν τῇ πίστει λεγόμενα οὐχ οἷόν τε μὴ μαθόντα ~οῦμεν Clem.*str.*1.6(p.23.8; M.8.729B); ἀκρασίαν...καὶ πορνείαν διαβολικὰ εἶναι πάθη καὶ ἡμεῖς ~οῦμεν *ib.*3.12(p.233.3; 1181B); τὴν ἔνστασιν ὁ. Eus.*h.e.*6.5.5(M.20.533B); ~εῖται ὁ τόπος [i.e. to be what it is] Chrys.*hom.53.1 in Mt.*(7.538D); ~ῶ σοι,...παντὶ ξένῳ ἄνοιγε τὴν θύραν σου Call.*v.Hyp.*(p.23).

***ὁμολογησία, ἡ**, *confession* πεποιήμεθα...τῆς ὀρθῆς πίστεως τὴν ὁ. Cyr.*Is.*2.2(2.224D).

ὁμολόγησις, ἡ, = foreg., Herm.*sim.*9.28.7.

ὁμολογητέον, **1.** *one must acknowledge*, Clem.*paed.*1.12(p.150.11; M.8.369C); **2.** *one must confess*, Synes.*ep.*44(M.66.1369D).

ὁμολογητής, ὁ, *confessor* of the faith; **1.** under persecution ὑπὲρ τοῦ ὀνόματος αὐτοῦ διαμείνω ἐν βασάνοις ὁ. *A.(Pass.)Andr.*8(p.21.17); ἐπὶ τοῦ κρατηθέντος ὁ., πότερον μαρτυρήσει καὶ κολασθήσεται Clem.*str.*4.12(p.285.9; M.8.1293A); τῶν ἐν ταῖς φυλακαῖς γενομένων ὁ. Dion.Al.ap.Eus.*h.e.*7.11.24(M.20.672B); of one under sentence of death τὸν ὁ. τοῦ Χριστοῦ *M.Niceph.*5; ἀμφὶ τὰ ἐν Παλαιστίνῃ χαλκοῦ μέταλλα οὐκ ὀλίγης ὁμολογητῶν συγκεκροτημένης πληθύος Eus.*m.P.*13.1(p.947.16; M.20.1513C); Jul.Papa *ep.Dian.*ap.Ath.*apol.sec.*33 (p.111.20; M.25.304A); Ath.*v.Anton.*46(M.26.909C); Epiph.*haer.*68.3 (p.143.25; M.42.189A); Hier.*vir.ill.*(tr.Sophr.Pal.)54(p.36.25; M.*PL.*23.668A); Ἀπολλώνιος...ἐν τῷ καιρῷ τοῦ διωγμοῦ παραθαρσύνων τοὺς τοῦ Χριστοῦ ὁ. πολλοὺς μάρτυρας ἀπετέλεσε ‡Pall.*h.mon.*21.2(p.80.6; M.34.1171A); suffering mutilations and forced labour, Soz.*h.e.*1.10 (M.67.885B); ἐξῆλθεν ὁ ὁ. ἐκ τῆς φυλακῆς καὶ μάρτυς τοῦ Χριστοῦ Γρηγόριος Agath.*v.Gr.Ill.*110; Mac.Aeg.*hom.*27.15(M.34.704C); ὁ. τὰ στίγματα τοῦ Ἰησοῦ ἐν τῷ σώματι βαστάζοντες Alex.Sal.*cruc.*(M.87.4060B); in this sense as a title or rank of honour δύνανται εἶναι ἐν τῇ λειτουργίᾳ ταχθέντες ἐν τοῖς ὁ. Petr.I Al.*ep.can.*14(M.18.505B); παρὰ τοῦ μεγάλου καὶ ὁ. Ὁσίου Ath.*ep.Aeg.Lib.*8(M.25.556C); id.*fug.*3(p.70.1; M.25.648B); ὁ. οὐ χειροτονεῖται, γνώμης γὰρ τοῦτο καὶ ὑπομονῆς· τιμῆς δὲ μεγάλης ἐπάξιος ὡς ὁμολογήσας τὸ ὄνομα τοῦ θεοῦ *Const.App.*8.23.2; ὁ ὁ. Μελίτιος καὶ μάρτυς Epiph.*haer.*69.4(p.155.19; M.42.208C); τὸν μέγαν ὁ. ἀββᾶν Ἀνούφ ‡Pall.*h.mon.*12.1(p.63.4; M.34.1156A); *M.Ner.et Ach.*12(p.11.5); τοῦ ἁγίου καὶ ὁ. Μαξίμου CNic.(787)*act.*4(H.4.188E); confessors associated with martyrs, apostles, etc., *M.Seb.test.*(p.116.10); Epiph.*haer.*64.2(p.404.13; M.41.1072B); *ib.*72.12(p.267.13; M.42.400B); Chrys.*exp.in Ps.*109:3(5.259E); Thal.CP *Thds.*(p.7.13,18; M.91.1472A,B); liturg., *Lit.*ap.*Const.App.*8.12.43; *Lit.Jac.*(p.212.17); *Lit.Chrys.*(p.331.17); as glorified οἱ χοροὶ τῶν ὁ. Bas.*ep.*139.2(3.231D; M.32.584B); ὁ ὑπομένων τοὺς πειρασμούς, ὡς ὁ. στεφανοῦται ἐνώπιον τοῦ βήματος τοῦ Χριστοῦ †Cyr.*hom.div.*14(5^2.413B); *V.Olymp.*11(p.418.9); derisively, of bogus confessors among Montanists, Eus.*h.e.*5.18.5(M.20.477A); **2.** of monks τοιοῦτοι...ὁ. εἰσιν, ἐὰν εἰς τὸ τέλος φυλάξωσιν *Apophth.Patr.*(M.65.369B).

***ὁμολογητικός**, neut. as subst., *affirmation*, Epiph.*haer.*76.41 (p.395.23; M.42.605C).

***ὁμολογήτρια, ἡ**, female *confessor*, *M.Pion.*2.1; Epiph.*haer.*68.5(p.145.20; M.42.192B); *V.Olymp.*16(p.422.6) ∞ Pall.*h.Laus.*56(M.34.1250A; ὁμολογηταῖς p.150.10).

ὁμολογία, ἡ, **1.** *confession, profession* of the faith; **a.** in gen. τῇ τοῦ νικοποιοῦ σταυροῦ ὁ. Eus.*v.C.*1.41(p.26.28; M.20.956B); τῇ ὁ. τῆς ὀρθοδοξίας ὑπογεγραφέναι Epiph.*haer.*75.2(p.334.16; M.42.505B); ὁμοούσιόν ἐστι τὸ τῆς ὁ. ἡμῶν ἔρεισμα *ib.*76.33(p.382.18; 584B); ἕψεται πάντως ταῖς τοῦ πιστεύειν ὁ. ἡ χάρις, καὶ τῶν πλημμελημάτων ἡ ἄφεσις *cat.Heb.*13:11f.(p.273.28); τὴν τῆς ἁγίας καὶ ὁμοουσίου τριάδος σεπτὴν ὁ., ὡς εἰς οὐρανοὺς ἀνάγουσαν, περιέθαλπε Jo.D.*hom.*12.7(M.96.792A); ἐν τῇ ὀρθοδόξῳ σου ὁ. ... τὸν δρόμον τελέσαι †Jo.D.*B.J.*39(M.96.1232A); of a written creed, Bas.Anc.al.*libell.*(H.4.40E); δεξάμενος δὲ ὁ ἄγγελος τῆς παναγίας παρθένου τὴν ὁ. τῆς πίστεως *cat.Lc.*1:38(p.13.25); liturg. ὁ ἱερεὺς λέγει τὴν ὁ. *Lit.Bas.*(M.31.1652A); ἡ δὲ τοῦ θείου συμβόλου τῆς πίστεως...ὁ. ‡Bas.*h.myst.*57(p.392.16); ἡ...παρὰ παντὸς τοῦ λαοῦ γινομένη τοῦ εἷς ἅγιος καὶ τῶν ἑξῆς ὁ. *ib.*62(p.397.13); **b.** partic. ref. Christ, ‡Eust.*Laz.*26(p.48.10); Epiph.*haer.*76.1 (p.341.9; M.42.516D); πάντα δεύτερα τίθεσθαι τῆς ὁ. τῆς εἰς Χριστὸν Chrys.*hom.17.1 in Jo.*(8.96B); Cyr.*Jo.*1.9(4.80D); ref. Mt.16:16 ἐπὶ ταύτῃ τῇ πέτρᾳ..., τουτέστι, τῇ πίστει τῆς ὁ. Chrys.*hom.54.2 in Mt.*(7.548A); cf. Πέτρος...ὁ τῆς ὁ. θεμέλιος id.*hom.in Mt.18*:23(3.4E); Proc.G.*Ex.*33:21(M.87.680A); **c.** at baptism, Dion.Al.ap.Eus.*h.e.*7.8(M.20.653A); CNeocaes.*can.*6; involving renunciation of Satan, Ephr.2.216F; πιστεύομεν δὲ ὡς βαπτιζόμεθα—σύμφωνον γὰρ εἶναι προσήκει τῇ ὁ. τὴν πίστιν Gr.Nyss.*ep.*24(M.46.1092B); *Const.App.*7.22.3; *ib.*7.42.3; τί χαριέστερον...τῆς ὁ. ἐκείνης τῆς πρὸ τοῦ λουτροῦ; τῆς μετὰ τὸ λουτρόν; Chrys.*hom.1.3 in Eph.*(11.6E); ἔθος δὲ γέγονεν ἐκ τούτου, τρεῖς ὁ. ἀπαιτεῖσθαι τοὺς μέλλοντας βαπτισθῆναι Ammon. *Jo.*21:17(M.85.1521B); εἰ μὴ πρῶτον ὁμολογήσειέν τις τὴν τῆς ἁγίας τριάδος ὁ.,...οὐ βαπτίζεται Cosm.Ind.*top.*5(M.88.221B); **d.** under persecution, Just.*1apol.*4.6(M.6.333A); *Ep.Lugd.*ap.Eus.*h.e.*5.1.12 (M.20.413A); Θεμίσων...ὁ μὴ βαστάσας τῆς ὁ. τὸ σημεῖον Apollon.*ib.* 5.18.5(477A); τῆς ὁ. τῆς μέχρι θανάτου Or.*Jo.*6.54(36; p.163.14; M.14. 293D); Eus.*h.e.*6.39.2(M.20.600B); πρὸς τὰς βασάνους ἐν τῷ καιρῷ τῆς ὁ. Gr.Nyss.*ep.can.*3(M.45.228A); δι' ὁμολογίας ποιούμενος τὴν ἔξοδον τοῦ βίου *Const.App.*5.6.8; οἱ διὰ...τὴν εἰς Χριστὸν ὁ. πάσχοντές τι δεινὸν καὶ ὑβριζόμενοι, οὗτοι μάλιστά εἰσιν οἱ τιμώμενοι Chrys.*hom.* *59.1 in Jo.*(8.344C); Στέφανος, ὁ τῆς ὁ. ἀκαθαίρετος πύργος Procl.CP *or.*17.2(M.65.812A); Socr.*h.e.*3.19.7(M.67.428B); ὅσοι διὰ τὴν...ὁ. κατεδικάσθησαν μετοικεῖν,...ἢ μετάλλοις ἐμπονεῖν, ἢ δημοσίοις ἔργοις Soz. *h.e.*1.8.3(M.67.876D); Thphn.*chron.*p.19(M.108.108C); **e.** ref. its reward τοῦ στεφάνου τῆς κατὰ Χριστὸν ὁ. Bas.*ep.*221(3.334B; M.32.816C); τῷ κόσμῳ τῆς ὁ. καλλωπιζομένη Chrys.*pan.Pelag.Ant.*3(2.588E); **f.** true confession being not only in belief or word, but in works, Bas.*ep.*295(3.433D; M.32.1040A); Chrys.*hom.14.1 in 1Tim.*(11.625D); Cyr.*Jo.*10.2(4.866E); cf.Heracleon ap.Clem.*str.*4.9(p.280.12ff.; M.8. 1281B); **g.** confession not giving automatic right to clerical office εἰ δέ τις ὁμολογητὴς μὴ χειροτονηθεὶς ἁρπάσῃ ἑαυτῷ ἀξίωμά τι τοιοῦτον ὡς διὰ τὴν ὁ., οὗτος καθαιρείσθω *Const.App.*8.23.4; **2.** *profession, vow*; monastic, Bas.*reg.br.*2 tit.(2.415A; M.31.1081C); of virginity τὰς δὲ ὁ. τότε ἐγκρίνομεν, ἀφ' οὗπερ ἂν ἡ ἡλικία τὴν τοῦ λόγου συμπλήρωσιν ἔχῃ id.*ep.*199 *can.*18(3.292A; M.32.720B); ἀνδρῶν δὲ ὁμολογίας οὐκ ἔγνωμεν, πλὴν εἰ μή τινες ἑαυτοὺς τῷ τάγματι τῶν μοναζόντων ἐγκατηρίθμησαν *ib.*199 *can.*19(292C; M.720C); **3.** *confession* of sins μέγα κακίας φάρμακον, καὶ ὁ., καὶ φυγὴ τοῦ πταίσματος Gr.Naz.*or.* 16.17(M.35.957B); ἡ ὁ. τῶν ἡμαρτημένων ἀφανισμὸς γίνεται τῶν πλημμελημάτων Chrys.*hom.20.3 in Gen.*(4.175C); ἵνα ἡ ὁ. κώλυμα αὐτοῖς γένηται πρὸς τὸ μὴ τοῖς αὐτοῖς περιπεσεῖν *ib.44.2*(450B); Socr.*h.e.*5. 19.6(M.67.616B); ‡Jo.D.*conf.*3(p.111.12; M.95.285A); **4.** *acknowledgement* of gratitude τὴν τῆς χάριτος ὁ. προσφέρουσιν Thdt.*affect.*8(p.217. 12; 4.921); **5.** legal *recognizance, undertaking*, Jo.Scholast.*coll. cap.*55,59(p.401); Ath.Scholast.*coll.*1.2(p.10); **6.** *agreement, correspondence* ὁμολογιῶν τε καὶ ἀναλογιῶν Clem.*str.*6.11(p.477.16; M.9. 312B).

ὁμόλογος, ὁ, *confessor, Ep.Lugd.*ap.Eus.*h.e.*5.2.3(M.20.433B).

ὁμονο-έω, 1. *be of one mind, agree*; of Son with Father, Chrys. *hom.82.2 in Jo.*(8.486A); as duty of all believers, Isid.Pel.*epp.*4.103 (M.78.1169D) cit. s. ὁμόπιστος; Thdt.*1Cor.*1:2(3.166); of the natures in Christ δύο ὑπεναντία οὐσιωδῶς ὡμονόησαν Ephr.Ant.*fr.*(M.86. 2109A); ὁ. σὺν θεῷ περὶ τὴν ὀρθὴν πίστιν *Ep.*ap.Evagr.*h.e.*3.33(p.133. 11; M.86.2672A); **2.** *agree in* οἱ τὴν κακὴν ~οῦντες ὁμόνοιαν Andr. Caes.*Apoc.*54(M.106.384C).

ὁμονοητικός, *conducing to harmony*; of government of H. Ghost, Didym.*Trin.*2.4(M.39.485A); neut. as subst., *harmony*, Chrys.*hom.* *82.2 in Jo.*(8.485A).

ὁμόνοια, ἡ, *unanimity, concord*; **1.** in natural order, *1Clem.*20.3; Ath.*gent.*29(M.25.60A); **2.** of angels, *A.(Pass.)Andr.*13(p.30.27; M. 2.1241C); **3.** as characteristic of Christian society ἐν τῇ ὁ. ὑμῶν... Χριστὸς ᾄδεται Ign.*Eph.*4.1; ἐν ὁ. θεοῦ σπουδάζετε πάντα πράσσειν id. *Magn.*6.1; Herm.*sim.*9.15.2; τὴν ὁ. τῆς πίστεως Iren.*ep.Vict.*ap.Eus. *h.e.*5.24.13(M.20.504A); as object of religious policy of Constantine, ref. Council of Arles ὡς ἂν...καὶ τοῦτο ὅπερ...φαύλως δι' αἰσχράς τινας ζυγομαχίας παραμεμένηκεν...δυνηθῇ εἰς τὴν ὀφειλομένην θρησκείαν καὶ πίστιν ἀδελφικήν τε ὁ. ... ἀνακληθῆναι Const.*ib.*10.5.24(892A); ἀνοίξατε δή μοι λοιπὸν ἐν τῇ καθ' ὑμᾶς [sc. Alexander and Arius] ὁ. τὸ ἔφας τὴν ὁδόν, ἣν ταῖς πρὸς ἀλλήλους φιλονεικίαις ἀπεκλείσατε id.ap.eund. *v.C.*2.72(p.71.17; M.20.1048B); ἐγώ εἰμι ὁ ὑμέτερος συνθεράπων, ὃς πᾶσαν τὴν περὶ τῆς...ὁ. ἐπανῄρημαι φροντίδα id.ap.Gel.Cyz.*h.e.*3.15. 4; ἐπικουρήσατε οὖν, παρακαλῶ, τῇ ὁ. ... ποιήσατέ με ἀκοῦσαι ταῦτα, ἅπερ βούλομαι...τὴν τῶν πάντων ὑμῶν εἰρήνην καὶ ὁ. id.*ib.*3.15.5; cf. ὅπως καὶ ὑμεῖς [sc. council of Nicaea] τῆς ὑμετέρας ἀδελφότητος εὐθὺς συγχωρῆσαι τὴν εὔνοιαν καταξιώσητε εἰς μίαν ὁ. καὶ εἰρήνην τῆς καθολικῆς πίστεως βλέψαντες id.*ib.*2.7.39; παντὶ σθένει διώξατε τοὺς τὴν τῆς ἡμετέρας ὁ. χάριν ἀφανίζειν ἐπιθυμοῦντας id.ap.Ath.*apol.sec.* 62(p.142.15; M.25.361C); εἰς ὁ. ἐπαναγαγεῖν τὰ διεστῶτα τῶν μελῶν id.ap.Eus.*v.C.*4.42(p.134.12; 1192A); cf. τὴν ὑμῖν τε πρέπουσαν καὶ ἡμῖν ἀρίστην ὁ. ... κατὰ τὸν τῆς ἐκκλησίας θεσμὸν διαρκῆ φυλάττειν σπουδάσατε Constantius ap.Ath.*apol.sec.*55(p.135.26; 348D); τὴν θεῷ φίλην...ὁ. Thdt.*Col.*3:15(3.495); ὁ. τῶν ἐκκλησιῶν ἐπὶ ὀρθοδοξίᾳ CNic. (787)*act.*1(H.4.73C); **4.** theol., between Father and Son, Or.*Cels.*8. 12(p.230.2; M.11.1533C) cit. s. βούλημα; Gr.Naz.*or.*6.13(M.35.740A) cit. s. ταυτότης; Chrys.*hom.54.1 in Mt.*(7.546B); *ib.71.2*(697B); id. *hom.70.1 in Jo.*(8.414B); **5.** as name of church in CP, so named from concord prevailing at Council of 381, Thdr.Lect.*fr.*(M.86. 225A); Evagr.*h.e.*2.13(p.65.8; M.86.2541A).

ὁμόνυμφος, *allied by marriage, Orac.Sib.*1.290.

***ὁμοουσιαστής, ὁ,** *supporter of doctrine of consubstantiality of Son with Father, champion of the* ὁμοούσιον (term coined by its opponents) παρ' ὀλίγον με πείθεις ὁ. γενέσθαι ‡Ath.*dial.Trin.*1.10(M.28. 1133A); Bas.*ep.*226.3(3.348A; M.32.848B); ἡμεῖς μὲν ὡς ὁ. διωκόμεθα *ib.*244.7(380E; M.921A); this name, derived from orthodox faith, contrasted with names of heresies derived from individual teachers, Sever.*creat.*4.10(M.56.470).

***ὁμοουσιοκόρυφος,** *consubstantially highest* τὴν τρισυπόστατον ὁ. δόξαν Jo.V H.*icon.*3(M.96.1352C).

ὁμοούσιος, *of the same substance* or *stuff*;

I. in gen. ὁ θεὸς δὲ οὐδεμίαν ἔχει πρὸς ἡμᾶς φυσικὴν σχέσιν...εἰ μή τις μέρος αὐτοῦ καὶ ὁ. ἡμᾶς τῷ θεῷ τολμήσει λέγειν Clem.*str.*2.16 (p.152.10; M.8.1021C); *ib.*4.13(p.288.14; 1300A); ὁ. τῇ ἀγεννήτῳ φύσει τοὺς προσκυνοῦντας ἐν πνεύματι τῷ θεῷ [Heracleon's doctrine] Or. *Jo.*13.25(p.249.5; M.14.441A); δῆλός ἐστιν [sc. Heracleon] ὁ. τινὰς τῷ διαβόλῳ λέγων ἀνθρώπους, ἑτέρας...οὐσίας τυγχάνοντας παρ' οὓς καλοῦσι ψυχικοὺς ἢ πνευματικούς *ib.*20.20(18; p.352.33; 617A); where equivalent to ἐκ τῆς οὐσίας...τοῦ διαβόλου, *ib.*20.24(20; p.359.4; 628C); *ib.*(p.358.15; 628A); ὧν [sc. ἀγγέλων]...καὶ τοὺς πόδας ὡς ὁ. ἀνθρώπων ἄνθρωποι ἔνιψαν *Hom.Clem.*20.7; πᾶν γὰρ τὸ ἐκ καθαροῦ ἀέρος καὶ...πυρὸς συνιστάμενον σύγκριμα, καὶ τοῖς ἀγγελικοῖς ὁ. ὑπάρχον Meth.*res.*2.30(p.388.12; M.18.316C); φατὲ ἀγενήτους εἶναι καὶ ἀφθάρτους τὰς δύο οὐσίας· ἀνάγκη καὶ ὁ. ταύτας ὑπάρχειν καὶ ὁμοίας, ὅπερ ἀδύνατον Adam.*dial.*3.7(p.122.32; M.11.1797C); τό τε ἀγαθὸν...ἐπέκεινα τῆς οὐσίας...ὥστε μὴ ὁμοούσια [sc. with τὸ ἀγαθόν] αὐτὰ [sc. τὰς νοητὰς οὐσίας] τίθεσθαι Eus.*p.e.*11.21(542D; M.21.904B); ὥστε ὁμογενῆ καὶ ὁμοφυῆ καὶ ὁ. εἶναι ἡγεῖσθαι τοῖς ἀπὸ γῆς βλαστήμασι καὶ φυτοῖς τὰ ἄλογα id.*d.e.*1.10(p.45.11; M.22.85C); οὐδὲ τὰ φυσικὰ τοῖς ἠθικοῖς ὁ., οὐδὲ τὰ τοῦ σώματος παθήματα τοῖς τῆς ψυχῆς πάθεσι τὰ αὐτά Const.*or.s.c.*13(p.172.13; M.20.1273A); ἐκ πηλοῦ...τὸ ὁ. πάντων ἀνθρώπων ἀποσημαίνοντος [sc. τοῦ λόγου] Bas.*Eun.*2.4(1. 241B; M.29.580B); in refutation of argument that γέννησις is an element of οὐσία: εἴ τι γέννημα, τοῦτο οὐσία, ὁ. τὰ γεννήματα πάντα ἀλλήλοις ἔσται *ib.*2.10(245B; M.589A); ἄνθρωποι γὰρ τέχνῃ μὲν ὑπερέχουσι τῶν οἰκείων ἔργων ὁμοούσιοι δὲ ὅμως αὐτοῖς καθεστήκασιν, ὡς ὁ κεραμεὺς τῷ πηλῷ...σώματα γὰρ ὁμοίως ἀμφότερα *ib.*2.19(255D; M.613C); οὐσία δὲ πάσαις [sc. souls] ὑπόκειται μία καὶ τὸ ὁ. ὑποκείμενον ἐν αὐταῖς τῆς σωματικῆς διαφθορᾶς ἠλλοτρίωται Gr.Nyss.*Eun.*7 (p.173.6); θνητὸς γὰρ θνητὸν γεννᾷ κατὰ φύσιν καὶ σῶμα τὸ ὁ. Diod. *synous.*1.4(M.33.1561A); ὁ τῆς κατ' οὐσίαν ἑνώσεως ἐπὶ μόνων τῶν ὁ. ἠλήθευται λόγος, ἐπὶ δὲ τῶν ἑτεροουσίων διέψευσται, συγχύσεως εἶναι καθαρὸς οὐ δυνάμενος Thdr.Mops.*ep.Domn.*(p.339.1; M.66.1013A); τὸ μεῖζον καὶ τὸ ἔλαττον ἐπὶ τῶν ὁ. ζητεῖται καὶ κρίνεται, ὡς ἄνθρωπος ἀνθρώπου μείζων, καὶ βοῦς βοός Isid.Pel.*epp.*1.422(M.78.417A); ἄνθρωπος, ἵππος, βοῦς, λέων, εἴπερ ὄντες ὁμογενεῖς [i.e. as living creatures] οὐκ εἰσὶν ὁμοφυεῖς, οὐδὲ ὁ. Thdr.Abuc.*opusc.*2(M.97. 1473A); cf.Jo.D.*dialect.*48(M.94.624A); but ἐλυπήθην τοὺς ὁ. καὶ ὁμογενεῖς μου ὁρῶν εἰς βάθος κακίας πεσόντας Diod.*Ps.*54:4(M.33. 1592A); οὐ θεσμῷ τῆς ἀκολουθίας τῶν ὁ. ἄρξας, ἀλλ' ἀνάγκῃ καὶ βίᾳ τοὺς ὁμογενεῖς ἐδουλώσατο Mac.Mgn.*apocr.*4.26(p.212.10); for ὁμοούσιοι = *fellow-men*, cf. Chrys.*hom.16.2 in 1Tim.*(11.646C); in sense of, *of same* metaphysical *essence* τῆς γὰρ ὑποστάσεως ἡ ὑπογραφὴ ἐξ ἰδιοτήτων τινῶν παρὰ τὰ ὁ. ἔν τινι...συνίσταται Leont.H. *Nest.*1.6(M.86.1421A); ὧν δὲ κοινὸς ὁ λόγος, καὶ ἡ ὕπαρξις ὁ. Leont.B. *cap.Sev.*2(M.86.1901B); ὁ. ἐστι τὸ τῆς αὐτῆς οὐσίας ἄλλῳ τυγχάνον, διάφορον δὲ πρὸς τὸ αὐτὸ κατὰ τὴν ὑπόστασιν ὄν, ὡς ἐπί τε ἀνθρώπου καὶ τῶν ἄλλων ἔχει εἰδῶν Max.*opusc.*(M.91.149C).

II. theol.; **A.** Gnost. τοῦ ἀγαθοῦ φύσιν ἔχοντος τὰ ὅμοια ἑαυτῷ καὶ ὁ. γεννᾶν τε καὶ προφέρειν Ptol.*ep.*ap.Epiph.*haer.*33.7(p.457.13; M.41. 568B); βασιλέα πάντων, τῶν τε ὁ. αὐτῷ, τουτέστι τῶν ψυχικῶν...καὶ τῶν ἐκ τοῦ πάθους καὶ τῆς ὕλης Iren.*haer.*1.5.1(M.7.492B); κατ' εἰκόνα μὲν τὸν ὑλικὸν ὑπάρχειν, παραπλήσιον μὲν ἀλλ' οὐχ ὁ. τῷ θεῷ *ib.*1.5. 5(500B); cf. *et cui credibile est, deum non apparuisse materiae? vel qua consubstantiali suae per aeternitatem?* Tert.*adversus Hermogenem* 44(M.*PL.*2.236C); ψυχὴν γεώδη καὶ ὑλικὴν ἐτεκτήνατο, ἄλογον καὶ τῇ τῶν θηρίων ὁ. Clem.*exc.Thdot.*50(p.123.11; M.9.684A); ὁ. τι αὐτῷ δι' ἀγγέλων ἐνθεὶς *ib.*(p.123.13; M.l.c.); τοῦ ἀρχανθρώπου καὶ τοῦ ἀναγεννωμένου πνευματικοῦ κατὰ πάνθ' ὁ. ἐκείνῳ τῷ ἀνθρώπῳ Hipp.*haer.*5. 8(p.91.5; M.16.3142C); ὑπὸ τοῦ ὄφεως ἄγεται ἀπὸ τοῦ κόσμου τὸ ἐξεικονισμένον τέλειον γένος ὁ. *ib.*5.17(p.115.24; 3178B); σωματοποιηθείς, ὥσπερ ἐγκίσσημά τι ἀπὸ τῆς ῥάβδου λευκὸν γέγονεν, ὁ. τῷ πατρὶ τῷ ἐν τοῖς οὐρανοῖς ὅλως *ib.*(p.115.4; 3178A); ταύτῃ τῇ δυνάμει συνυπάρχει δύναμις ὁ. αὐτῇ *ib.*6.37(p.168.16; 3254B); υἱότης τριμερής, κατὰ πάντα τῷ οὐκ ὄντι θεῷ ὁ., γενητὴ ἐξ οὐκ ὄντων *ib.*7.22(p.198. 26; 3306C); Manich. μέρος ὁ. τοῦ πατρὸς τὸ γέννημα Ar.*ep.Alex.* (p.12; M.26.709A).

B. Trin.; **1.** in pre-Nicene usage, expressive of belief that what the Father is, that also the Son is, cf.Hipp.*trad.ap.*21.11b(baptismal creed; Arabic, Ethiopic, and Sahidic versions, prob. not original); ὁ υἱὸς τοῦ πατρός, ὁ ὁ. βασιλεύς, ἀλλὰ δούλου μορφὴν φέρων Or.*Ps.*54:4(p.56); cf. *communionem substantiae esse filio cum patre. aporrhoea enim ὁ. videtur, id est, unius substantiae cum illo corpore ex quo est vel aporrhoea vel vapor*, id.ap.Pamph.Caes.*apol.Or.*5(M. 17.581C); προφέρουσιν ἔγκλημα κατ' ἐμοῦ, ψεῦδος ὄν, ὡς οὐ λέγοντος τὸν Χριστὸν ὁ. εἶναι τῷ θεῷ...καὶ γὰρ ἀνθρωπείαν γονὴν παρεθέμην δῆλον ὡς οὖσαν ὁμογενῆ...καὶ φυτὸν εἶπον...ἕτερον εἶναι τοῦ ὅθεν ἐβλάστησε, καὶ πάντως ἐκείνῳ καθέστηκεν ὁμοφυές. καὶ ποταμὸν ἀπὸ πηγῆς ῥέοντα Dion.Al.ap.Ath.*Dion.*18(p.59.8; M.25.505Bff.); use of term condemned by CAnt.(269) ὡς αὐτοί [i.e. Bas. Anc. and others at CAnc.(358)] φασι (τὴν γὰρ ἐπιστολὴν οὐκ ἔσχον ἐγώ), οἱ τὸν Σαμοσατέα κατακρίναντες ἐπίσκοποι γράφοντες εἰρήκασι μὴ εἶναι ὁ. τὸν υἱὸν τῷ πατρί Ath.*syn.*43(p.268.17; M.26.768C); reason for this οἱ μὲν γὰρ τὸν Σαμοσατέα καθελόντες, σωματικῶς ἐκλαμβάνοντες τὸ ὁ., τοῦ Παύλου σοφίζεσθαί τε θέλοντος καὶ λέγοντος, εἰ μὴ ἐξ ἀνθρώπου γέγονεν ὁ Χριστὸς θεός, οὐκοῦν ὁ. ἐστι τῷ πατρί, καὶ ἀνάγκη τρεῖς οὐσίας εἶναι, μίαν μὲν προηγουμένην, τὰς δὲ δύο ἐξ ἐκείνης· διὰ τοῦτ' εἰκότως εὐλαβηθέντες τὸ τοιοῦτον σόφισμα τοῦ Σαμοσατέως, εἰρήκασι μὴ εἶναι τὸν Χριστὸν ὁ.... λογισάμενοι μὴ οὕτως καὶ ἐπὶ τῶν ἀσωμάτων, καὶ μάλιστα ἐπὶ θεοῦ τὸ ὁ. σημαίνεσθαι *ib.*45(p.269.38; 772C); οἱ ἐπὶ Παύλῳ τῷ Σαμοσατεῖ συνελθόντες, διέβαλον τὴν λέξιν ὡς οὐκ εὔηχον· ἔφασαν γὰρ ἐκεῖνοι τὴν τοῦ ὁ. φωνὴν παριστᾶν ἔννοιαν οὐσίας τε καὶ τῶν ἀπ' αὐτῆς, ὥστε καταμερισθεῖσαν τὴν οὐσίαν παρέχειν τοῦ ὁ. τὴν προσηγορίαν τοῖς εἰς ἃ διῃρέθη· τοῦτο δὲ ἐπὶ χαλκοῦ μὲν καὶ τῶν ἀπ' αὐτοῦ νομισμάτων ἔχει τινὰ λόγον τὸ διανόημα· ἐπὶ δὲ θεοῦ πατρὸς καὶ θεοῦ υἱοῦ οὐκ οὐσία πρεσβυτέρα, οὐδ' ὑπερκειμένη ἀμφοῖν θεωρεῖται Bas.*ep.* 52.1(3.145B; M.32.393A) (this account based on Ath.; cf.*ep.*52.2 with *syn.*51); but contrast Hilary's view that term was rejected at CAnt. on ground that it implied Sabellianism, *per hanc unius essentiae nuncupationem solitarium atque unicum sibi esse patrem et filium praedicabat* [sc. Paul. Sam.], Hil.Pict.*de synodis* 81(M.*PL.*10.534A,B); cf. *quis secundum Samosateum...quod Christus in se sibi et pater et filius sit confitebitur? ib.*82 (term possibly used by Paul to imply that pre-existent Logos is latent in God and impersonal and also employed by him as argument against view that Logos as an οὐσία (hypostasis) is ὁ. with God); **2.** in 4th-cent. controversies; **a.** understood by Arians in material sense, Ar.*ep.Alex.*(p.12; M.26.709A); εἰ δὲ τό, ἐξ αὐτοῦ, κτλ. [Jo.8:42]...ὡς μέρος αὐτοῦ ὁ. καὶ ὡς προβολὴ ὑπό τινων νοεῖται, σύνθετος ἔσται ὁ πατὴρ καὶ διαιρετὸς καὶ τρεπτὸς καὶ σῶμα κατ' αὐτοὺς...τὰ ἀκόλουθα σώματι πάσχων ὁ ἀσώματος θεός *ib.* (p.13; 709C); hence οὐδὲ γάρ ἐστιν ἴσος, ἀλλ' οὐδὲ ὁ. αὐτῷ Ar.*Thal. fr.*2 ap.Ath.*syn.*15(p.242.17; M.26.708A); **b.** affirmed at Nicaea γεννηθέντα ἐκ τοῦ πατρὸς μονογενῆ, τουτέστιν ἐκ τῆς οὐσίας τοῦ πατρός, θεὸν ἐκ θεοῦ, φῶς ἐκ φωτός,...ὁ. τῷ πατρί *Symb.Nic.*(325)(p.51; M.20. 1540B); use explained at Council ἑνὸς μόνου προσεγγραφέντος ῥήματος τοῦ ὁ., ὃ καὶ αὐτὸς [sc. Constantine] ἑρμήνευε λέγων· ὅτι μὴ κατὰ τῶν σωμάτων πάθη λέγοιτο ὁ. ⟨ὁ υἱός⟩, οὔτ' οὖν κατὰ διαίρεσιν οὔτε κατά τινα ἀποτομὴν ἐκ τοῦ πατρὸς ὑποστῆναι· μηδὲ γὰρ δύνασθαι τὴν ἄυλον ...φύσιν σωματικόν τι πάθος ὑφίστασθαι Eus.*ep.Caes.*4(p.44.4; M.20. 1540A); hence τῇ διανοίᾳ καὶ ἡμεῖς συνετιθέμεθα οὐδὲ τὴν φωνὴν τοῦ ὁ. παραιτούμενοι τοῦ τῆς εἰρήνης σκοποῦ πρὸ ὀφθαλμῶν ἡμῖν κειμένου καὶ τοῦ μὴ τῆς ὀρθῆς ἐκπεσεῖν διανοίας *ib.*5(p.45.12; 1541A); on ground that οὕτω δὲ καὶ τὸ 'ὁ. εἶναι τοῦ πατρὸς τὸν υἱόν' ἐξεταζόμενος ὁ λόγος συνίστησιν, οὐ κατὰ τὸν τῶν σωμάτων τρόπον οὐδὲ τοῖς θνητοῖς ζῴοις παραπλησίως, οὔτε γὰρ κατὰ διαίρεσιν τῆς οὐσίας οὔτε κατὰ ἀποτομήν, ἀλλ' οὐδὲ κατά τι πάθος ἢ τροπὴν ἢ ἀλλοίωσιν τῆς τοῦ πατρὸς οὐσίας τε καὶ δυνάμεως. τούτων γὰρ πάντων ἀλλοτρίαν εἶναι τὴν ἀγέννητον τοῦ πατρὸς φύσιν. παραστατικὸν δὲ εἶναι τὸ 'ὁ. τῷ πατρὶ' τοῦ μηδεμίαν ἐμφέρειαν πρὸς τὰ γενητὰ κτίσματα τὸν υἱὸν τοῦ θεοῦ φέρειν, μόνῳ δὲ τῷ πατρὶ τῷ γεγεννηκότι κατὰ πάντα τρόπον ἀφωμοιῶσθαι καὶ μὴ εἶναι ἐξ ἑτέρας τινὸς ὑποστάσεώς τε καὶ οὐσίας, ἀλλ' ἐκ τοῦ πατρὸς *ib.* 7(p.45.21; 1541B); thus term was used as definition of full and absolute deity of Son; but acc. Athanasius it implied also substantial identity of Father and Son as solution of problem of divine unity οἱ ἐπίσκοποι...θεωρήσαντες τὴν ὑπόκρισιν ἐκείνων [i.e. Arians in sophistic treatment of declaration that Logos is ὅμοιόν τε καὶ ἀπαράλλακτον...κατὰ πάντα τῷ πατρί]...ἠναγκάσθησαν...λευκότερον εἰπεῖν καὶ γράψαι, ὁ. εἶναι τῷ πατρὶ τὸν υἱόν, ἵνα μὴ μόνον ὅμοιον τὸν υἱόν, ἀλλὰ ταὐτὸν τῇ ὁμοιώσει ἐκ τοῦ πατρὸς εἶναι σημαίνωσι καὶ ἄλλην οὖσαν τὴν τοῦ υἱοῦ ὁμοίωσιν καὶ ἀτρεψίαν δείξωσι παρὰ τὴν ἐν ἡμῖν λεγομένην μίμησιν, ἣν ἐξ ἀρετῆς διὰ τὴν τῶν ἐντολῶν τήρησιν ἡμεῖς προσλαμβάνομεν. τὰ μὲν γὰρ τῶν σωμάτων ὅμοια πρὸς ἑαυτὰ τυγχάνοντα δυνατόν πως διΐστασθαι...οἷοί εἰσιν οἱ τῶν ἀνθρώπων υἱοὶ πρὸς τοὺς γεννήσαντας...ἐπειδὴ δὲ ἡ ἐκ πατρὸς τοῦ υἱοῦ γέννησις ἄλλη παρὰ τὴν ἀνθρώπων φύσιν ἐστὶ καὶ οὐ μόνον ὅμοιος, ἀλλὰ καὶ ἀδιαίρετός ἐστι τῆς τοῦ πατρὸς οὐσίας καὶ ἕν μέν εἰσιν αὐτὸς καὶ ὁ πατήρ...ἀεὶ δὲ ἐν τῷ πατρί ἐστιν ὁ λόγος καὶ ὁ πατὴρ ἐν τῷ λόγῳ, ὡς ἔστι τὸ ἀπαύγασμα πρὸς τὸ φῶς—τοῦτο γὰρ καὶ ἡ λέξις σημαίνει—, διὰ τοῦτο ἡ σύνοδος... καλῶς ὁ. ἔγραψεν Ath.*decr.*20(p.17.8; M.25.452B), thus Ath. balances two senses of ὁ.: *of one stuff* as against Arius, and *of one content* as against objection that former means existence of two gods; cf. for emphasis on former τὸ μὲν ὁμοφυὲς καὶ ὁ., τὸ δὲ ἑτεροφυὲς καὶ ἑτεροούσιον id.*syn.*53(p.276.29; M.26.788C); ὧν ἐσμεν ὅμοιοι, καὶ τὴν ταυτότητα ἔχομεν τούτων, καὶ ὁ. ἐσμεν· ἄνθρωποι γοῦν ὅμοιοι καὶ ταυτότητα ἔχοντες, ὁ. ἐσμεν ἀλλήλων, τὸ αὐτὸ γὰρ πᾶσι, τὸ θνητόν, τὸ φθαρτόν, κτλ. ... καὶ ἄγγελοι...καὶ τὰ ἄλλα πάντα ὡσαύτως ὁμοφυῆ ἐστιν ἀλλήλων id.*ep.Serap.*2.3(M.26.612B); term is not confined to collaterals (ἀδελφά) but applies equally to derivation and derived; hence denial of theory that if Father and Son are ὁ. they must be collateral, requiring assumption of antecedent common source, id.*syn.* 51(p.275.1ff.; 784B,C); material analogies not to be pressed in use and understanding of ὁ., *ib.*42(p.268.2; 768A); ποταμὸς θεοῦ ὁ μονογενής. ὡς γὰρ ἀπὸ πηγῆς ἔρχεται ποταμός, οὕτω καὶ ἐκ τῆς τοῦ τεκόντος οὐσίας, καὶ ἔστιν ὁ. αὐτῷ id. *fr.Pss.comm.*64:11(p.18; M.27.580B); cf. for emphasis on substantial identity εἰ μὲν ποίημά ἐστιν ὁ λόγος καὶ ἀλλότριος τῆς τοῦ πατρὸς οὐσίας, ὥστε καὶ χωρίζεσθαι αὐτὸν ἀπὸ τοῦ πατρὸς τῷ ἑτεροφυεῖ χωρισμῷ, οὐκ ἂν εἴη ὁ. τῷ πατρί, ἀλλὰ μᾶλλον ὁμογενὴς τῇ φύσει τοῖς ποιήμασι...εἰ δὲ ὁμολογοῦμεν μὴ εἶναι αὐτὸν ποίημα, ἀλλὰ γνήσιον ἐκ τῆς οὐσίας τοῦ πατρὸς γέννημα, ἀκόλουθον ἂν εἴη καὶ ἀχώριστον αὐτὸν εἶναι τοῦ πατρός, ὁμοφυῆ ὄντα...τοιοῦτος δὲ ὢν εἰκότως καὶ ὁ. ἂν λέγοιτο. ἔπειτα εἰ...τῇ οὐσίᾳ λόγος ἐστί...ἡ δὲ οὐσία αὕτη τῆς οὐσίας τῆς πατρικῆς ἐστι γέννημα...λέγει δὲ ὁ υἱός, ἐγὼ καὶ ὁ πατὴρ ἕν ἐσμεν...πῶς...σώσομεν τὸ ἓν εἶναι τὸν πατέρα καὶ τὸν υἱόν; εἰ μὲν οὖν τῇ συμφωνίᾳ τῶν δογμάτων καὶ τῷ μὴ διαφωνεῖν πρὸς τὸν πατέρα...οἱ ἅγιοι καὶ...ἄγγελοι...τὴν τοιαύτην ἔχουσι πρὸς τὸν θεὸν συμφωνίαν...ὁ δὲ υἱὸς ἐκ τῆς οὐσίας ὢν γέννημα τῇ οὐσίᾳ ἕν ἐστιν αὐτὸς καὶ ὁ γεννήσας αὐτὸν πατήρ id.*syn.*48(p.272.24; 777C); τὸ δὲ τῆς τοῦ πατρὸς οὐσίας ἴδιον, καὶ ἐξ αὐτῆς γέννημα, τί ἂν εἴη, ἢ πῶς ἄν τις ὀνομάσειεν αὐτό, ἢ ὁ.; ἃ γὰρ βλέπει τις ἐν τῷ πατρί, ταῦτα βλέπει καὶ ἐν τῷ υἱῷ· υἱῷ δὲ οὐκ ἐκ μετουσίας, ἀλλὰ κατ' οὐσίαν. ... τὸ δὲ ἴδιον καὶ ταὐτὸν τῇ τοῦ θεοῦ οὐσίᾳ καὶ ἐξ αὐτῆς γέννημα φύσει τυγχάνον τί ἂν εἴη ἢ πάλιν καὶ κατὰ τοῦτο ὁ. τῷ γεννήσαντι id.*ep.Afr.*8 (M.26.1041A,C); doctrine dist. from Sabellianism οὔτε γὰρ υἱοπάτορα φρονοῦμεν ὡς οἱ Σαβέλλιοι, λέγοντες μονοούσιον καὶ οὐχ ὁ., καὶ ἐν τούτῳ ἀναιροῦντες τὸ εἶναι υἱόν †Ath.*exp.fid.*2(M.25.204A); and guarded against Christol. misunderstanding οἱ πατέρες οἱ ἐν Νικαίᾳ συνελθόντες οὐ τὸ σῶμα, ἀλλ' αὐτὸν τὸν υἱὸν εἰρήκασιν ὁ. τοῦ πατρός Ath.*ep.Epict.*4(p.7.9; M.26.1056B); with Ath.'s emphasis on ὁ. as expressing identity of substance, cf.Hil.Pict.*de synodis* 88(M. *PL.*10.540Aff.); **c.** after Nicaea; **i.** term rejected entirely by Arians, e.g. μήτε μὴν ὁ. μηδὲ ὁμοιούσιον, ἐπείπερ τὸ μὲν γένεσιν καὶ μερισμὸν σημαίνει τῆς οὐσίας, τὸ δὲ ἰσότητα Eun.*apol.*26(M.30.864C); cf. εἰ μὲν οὖν ὁ. ἐστι τῷ πατρὶ τῶν ὅλων ἡ πᾶσα κτίσις, τοῦτο καὶ τὸν πρωτότοκον αὐτῆς εἶναι οὐκ ἀρνησόμεθα· εἰ δὲ διαφέρει κατὰ τὴν οὐσίαν τῆς κτίσεως ὁ τῶν ὅλων θεός, ἀνάγκη πᾶσα μηδὲ τὸν πρωτότοκον ταύτης κοινωνεῖν τῷ θεῷ τῆς οὐσίας λέγειν [Eunomian objection] Gr.Nyss. *Eun.*4(2 p.62.7; M.45.633B); cf. condemnation of ὁ. and ὁμοιούσιον, *Symb.Sirm.*2(p.257.4; M.26.741B) cit. s. οὐσία; **ii.** accepted in orthodox sense by followers of Marcellus ἀναθεματίζοντες...τὴν... αἵρεσιν...Σαβελλίου καὶ...Παύλου...καὶ τοὺς μὴ λέγοντας τὴν ἁγίαν τριάδα τρία πρόσωπα ἀπερίγραφα καὶ ἐνυπόστατα καὶ ὁ. καὶ συναΐδια καὶ αὐτοτελῆ Photinus et al.ap.Epiph.*haer.*72.11(p.266.4; M.42. 397B); but Sabellianism of Marcellus increased dislike of term among 'conservative' theologians; hence condemned by 'Semi-Arians' in sense disclaimed by †Ath.*exp.fid.*2 (v. supra 2.b ad fin.); εἴ τις...ὁ. ... ἢ ταυτοούσιον λέγοι τὸν υἱὸν τῷ πατρί, ἀνάθεμα ἔστω CAnc.(358)*anath.*ap.Epiph.*haer.*73.11(p.284.5; M.42.425A); οἱ περὶ Βασίλειον καὶ Γεώργιον οἱ τῆς Ἡμιαρείων ταύτης αἱρέσεως προστάται, φασίν, οὐ λέγομεν ὁ., ἀλλὰ ὁμοιούσιον Epiph.*haer.*73.1(p.268.15; 401B); rejecting it also as unscriptural, *ib.*(p.268.11; M. l.c.); cf. objection of Arius ap.Ath.*syn.*36(p.263.13; M.26.757A); cf. 'Semi-arian' condemnation of use of οὐσία and endorsement of 'ὅμοιος', v. ὅμοιος and οὐσία; **iii.** reconciliation of conservative theologians to use of term, e.g. Bas. who uses it occasionally as safeguard against Arianism and Sabellianism ἀπαύγασμα εἴρηται, ἵνα τὸ συνημμένον νοήσωμεν, καὶ χαρακτὴρ τῆς ὑποστάσεως, ἵνα τὸ ὁ.

ἐκμανθάνωμεν Bas.*Eun*.1.20(1.231D; M.29.556C); ἐπήγαγον [sc. Nicene Fathers] τὸ ὁ.· *παραδεικνύντες ὅτι ὅνπερ ἂν τις ἀποδῷ φωτὸς λόγον ἐπὶ πατρός, οὗτος ἁρμόσει καὶ ἐπὶ υἱοῦ. ... οὐ γὰρ τὰ ἀδελφὰ ἀλλήλοις ὁ. λέγεται...ἀλλ' ὅταν, καὶ τὸ αἴτιον καὶ τὸ ἐκ τοῦ αἰτίου τὴν ὕπαρξιν ἔχον, τῆς αὐτῆς ὑπάρχῃ φύσεως, ὁ. λέγεται* id.*ep*.52.2(3.145D,E; M.32.393B,C); *οὐ γὰρ αὐτό τί ἐστιν ἑαυτῷ ὁ. ἀλλ' ἕτερον ἑτέρῳ* *ib*.52.3 (146A; M.393C); *ἵνα καὶ ὁ τοῦ ὁ. λόγος διαφυλαχθῇ ἐν τῇ ἑνότητι τῆς θεότητος, καὶ ἡ τῆς εὐσεβείας ἐπίγνωσις, πατρὸς καὶ υἱοῦ καὶ...πνεύματος, ἐν τῇ...ὁλοτελεῖ ἑκάστου τῶν ὀνομαζομένων ὑποστάσει κηρύσσηται* *ib*.214.4(322E; M.789B); *ὡς μὲν εἰκών, τὸ ἀπαράλλακτον ἔχει. ὡς δὲ γέννημα, τὸ ὁ. διασώζει* id.*hom*.24.4(2.192C; M.31.608A; *πῶς ἂν ὑγιῶς λέγοιτο* [sc. τὸ ὁ.], *ἐφ' ὧν οὔτε γένος κοινὸν ὑπερκείμενον θεωρεῖται, οὔτε ὑλικὸν ὑποκείμενον προϋπάρχον, οὐκ ἀπομερισμὸς τοῦ προτέρου εἰς τὸ δεύτερον. πῶς οὖν χρὴ λέγειν ὁ. τὸν υἱὸν τῷ πατρί, εἰς μηδεμίαν ἔννοιαν τῶν εἰρημένων καταπίπτοντας;...δοκεῖ μοι ἡ τοῦ ἀπαραλλάκτως ὁμοίου φωνὴ μᾶλλον ἤπερ ἡ τοῦ ὁ. ἁρμόττειν* †Bas.*ep*. 361(3.463Cf.; M.32.1101A); *οὗτος ὁ., ἐξῃρημένως παρὰ πάντα καὶ ἰδιαζόντως· οὐχ ὡς τὰ ὁμογενῆ, οὐχ ὡς τὰ ἀπομεριζόμενα, ἀλλ' ὡς ἐκ τοῦ ἑνὸς γένους καὶ εἴδους τῆς θεότητος, ἓν καὶ μόνον ἀπογέννημα, ἀδιαιρέτῳ καὶ ἀσωμάτῳ προόδῳ* †Apoll.*ep.Bas*.1(M.32.1104D); *οὐχ ὅμοιον θεῷ, ἀλλὰ θεὸν δηλοῖ τὸ ὁ.* *ib*.2(1108A); *ὁ. δὲ ταῦτα ἢ τί; πῶς δ' οὔ; ὡμολόγηται οὖν καὶ τὰ διαφόρως ὑποστάντα τῆς αὐτῆς εἶναι οὐσίας ἐνδέχεσθαι* Gr.Naz.*or*.31.11(p.158.10; M.36.145A); *ταυτότητα δὲ τῆς φύσεως ὁμολογοῦντες, καὶ τὸ ὁ. ἐκδεχόμεθα, καὶ τὸ σύνθετον φεύγομεν...ἐκ γὰρ τούτου τὸ ὁ. δείκνυται. ὁ γὰρ κατ' οὐσίαν θεὸς τῷ κατ' οὐσίαν θεῷ ὁ. ἐστιν* Evagr.Pont.*ep*.3(M.32.249C); *υἱὸς ὁ. τῷ πατρί, οὐ συνούσιος, ἀλλ' ὁ., τουτέστιν οὐκ ἔξωθεν τοῦ πατρὸς γεννηθείς. ... σύνδεσμος δὲ τῆς πίστεως ὁ. λέγειν* Epiph.*anc*.6(p.12. 14; M.43.25B); term opposes both Sabellianism and division of Godhead, *ib*.(p.12.17ff.; 25B,C); *οὐ δύναται δὲ εἶναι ἑτεροούσιος τῷ γεγεννηκότι οὐδὲ ταυτοούσιος, ἀλλὰ ὁ.* id.*haer*.65.8(p.11.11; M.42. 25A); *τὸ δὲ ὁ. οὐχ ἕνα...σημαίνει, ἀλλ' ἀπὸ τοῦ ὁμο δύο σημαίνει τέλεια· ἀλλ' οὐκ ἀλλοῖα ἀλλήλων ἐστὶν οὐδὲ ἀλλότρια τῆς αὐτῶν ἑνότητος... ὥσπερ γὰρ μισεῖ ὁ ὄφις τὴν ὀσμὴν τῆς ἀσφάλτου...οὕτω καὶ Ἄρειος καὶ Σαβέλλιος μισεῖ τὸν λόγον τῆς...ὁμολογίας τοῦ ὁ.* *ib*.69.72(p.220.16; 320A); *οὐ γὰρ εἴπομεν ἁμαούσιον, ἀλλ' ὁ.* *ib*.73.36(p.310.22; 469A); cf. *οὐ λέγομεν ταυτοούσιον, ἵνα μὴ ἡ λέξις παρά τισι λεγομένη Σαβελλίῳ ἀπεικασθῇ* *ib*.76.7(p.348.13; 528C); Didym.*Trin*.1.16(M.39.332C); **3.** in later writers *ὁ. μὲν οὖν ὁ υἱὸς τῷ πατρὶ καὶ ὁ πατὴρ τῷ υἱῷ, διὸ δὴ καὶ εἰς ἀπαράλλακτον ἀναβαίνουσιν ὁμοιότητα* Cyr.*Jo*.1.2(4.15E); *οὐκ ἐλάττονα...ἀλλ' ἐξ αὐτοῦ καὶ ἐν αὐτῷ καὶ ὁ.* *ib*.5.5(525C); *ὁμογενής ἐστιν ὁ υἱὸς τῷ πατρί, τουτέστιν, ὁ.* *ib*.10.1(849C); *ὁ. τε αὐτῷ, σύμμορφός τε καὶ ὁ.* id.*dial.Trin*.1(5^1.391C); *ib*.(408B); *ὡς κατὰ φύσιν υἱός, ἔσται δὲ ὁ.* id.*thes*.9(5^1.71D); Maced.: *τὸ ὁμοιούσιον ἐπὶ τῶν ἀσωμάτων, τὸ δὲ ὁ. ἐπὶ τῶν σωμάτων.* Orth.: *μᾶλλον...τὸ ὁμοιούσιον ἔδει λέγεσθαι...ἐπὶ τῶν σωμάτων, ἐφ' ὧν καὶ ὁμοιότης· τὸ δὲ ὁ. ἐπὶ τῶν ἀσωμάτων, ἐφ' ὧν ἡ ταυτότης. τὸ γὰρ ὁ. ἐστι τὸ ταυτοούσιον* ‡Ath. *Maced.dial*.2(M.28.1336C); as subst. *οὐ λειτουργὸν τὸν ὁ. ἐστηλίτευσε* Procl.CP *or*.2.1(M.65.692C); **4.** of H. Ghost *οὐκ ἔστι τῶν πολλῶν τὸ πνεῦμα...ἀλλ' ἓν ὄν, μᾶλλον δὲ τοῦ λόγου ἑνὸς ὄντος ἴδιον, καὶ τοῦ θεοῦ ἑνὸς ὄντος ἴδιον καὶ ὁ. ἐστι* Ath.*ep.Serap*.1.27(M.26.593C); *ἐπαρασάμενος* [sc. Basil] *ἑαυτῷ τὸ φρικωδέστατον, αὐτοῦ τοῦ πνεύματος ἐκπεσεῖν, εἰ μὴ σέβοι τὸ πνεῦμα μετὰ πατρὸς καὶ υἱοῦ ὡς ὁ. καὶ ὁμότιμον* Gr.Naz.*or*.43.69(M.36.589A); *θεὸς τὸ πνεῦμα; πάνυ γε· τί οὖν, ὁ.; εἴπερ θεός* *ib*.31.10(p.156.12; 144A); *ὄντως ἐκ θεοῦ ὂν καὶ οὐκ ἀλλότριον πατρὸς καὶ υἱοῦ, ἀλλ' ὁ. πατρὶ καὶ υἱῷ* Epiph.*haer*.74.11 (p.328.30; M.42.496C); *ὁ...λόγος...διὰ τοῦ ἁγίου καὶ ὁ. πνεύματος... δημιουργήσας ναόν* Cyr.*ep*.50(p.92.23; 5^2.161A); id.*Is*.5.5(2.882D); in liturg. epiclesis *τὸ ὁ. καὶ συναΐδιον* *Lit.Jac*.(p.204.26); **5.** of Trin. *βαπτίζομεν εἰς τριάδα ὁ.* Bas.*fid*.4(2.228A; M.31.688A); Didym.*Trin*.2. 6(M.39.536A); Epiph.*haer*.36.6(p.49.30; M.41.640C); CCP(381)*ep*.ap. Thdt.*h.e*.5.9.11(3.1032); *δόξα τῇ ὁ. τριάδι* Mac.Aeg.*hom*.18.15(M.34. 633D); Cyr.*Is*.1.5(2.132A); *θεὸς ἐν ἁγίᾳ τε καὶ ὁ. τριάδι προσκυνούμενος* id.*Jo*.10.1(4.852C); Cosm.Ind.*top*.6(M.88.333C); Max.*ep*.15(M.91. 552B); id.*ambig*.(M.91.1036B); id.*opusc*.(M.91.148C); *Lit.Jac*.(p.226.15).

C. Christol.; **1.** denial that Christ's body is ὁ. with God *ποίος ᾅδης ἠρεύξατο ὁ. εἶναι τὸ ἐκ Μαρίας σῶμα τῇ τοῦ λόγου θεότητι;...τίς τοσοῦτον ἠσέβησεν, ὥστε εἰπεῖν...ὅτι ἡ θεότης...ἡ ὁ. τῷ πατρὶ περιετμήθη;* Ath.*ep.Epict*.2(p.4.11; M.26.1052C); **2.** teaching of Apoll.: Christ's humanity, in so far as it is admitted, is ὁ. with human nature *σάρκα ὁ. τῇ ἡμετέρᾳ σαρκὶ προσείληφεν ἀπὸ τῆς Μαρίας ὁ...λόγος* Apoll.*tom.syn*.(p.262.29)ap.Leont.B.*Apoll*.(M.86. 1952A); *φύσει μὲν ὁ. ἡμῖν σάρκα προσείληφεν, ἑνώσει δὲ θείαν ἀπέδειξεν ...καὶ διὰ τῆς ἑνώσεως ἔχουσαν τὸ διάφορον* id. *fr*.161(p.254.22)*ib*.(M. 86.1960B); *οὐ γὰρ αὐτὸ ἑαυτῷ συνάπτεται οὐδὲ ὁμοούσιον ὁμοουσίῳ... εἰ δὲ ὁ. μὲν ὁ λόγος τῷ σώματι, ὁ. δὲ τὸ σῶμα τῷ λόγῳ...οὐκ ἄρα ἐφανερώθη κατὰ τοῦτο...οὐδὲ ἀληθὴς Ἰωάννης λέγων, ἐθεασάμεθα* *ib*. 162(p.255.1; M.86.1949C); *εἰ δέ τις...λέγει...τὴν σάρκα ὁ. τῷ θεῷ καὶ οὐ τῇ ἡμετέρᾳ σαρκὶ...παθητὴν λέγων τὴν θεότητα, ἀναθεματιζέσθω* *ib*.163(p.255.12; 1949C); *οὕτως καὶ θεῷ ὁ. κατὰ τὸ πνεῦμα τὸ ἀόρατον, συμπεριλαμβανομένης τῷ ὀνόματι καὶ τῆς σαρκός, ὅτι πρὸς τὸν θεῷ ὁ. ἥνωται, καὶ πάλιν ἀνθρώποις ὁ., συμπεριλαμβανομένης καὶ τῆς θεότητος τῷ σώματι, ὅτι πρὸς τὸ ἡμῖν ὁ. ἡνώθη, οὐκ ἀλλαττομένης τῆς τοῦ σώματος φύσεως ἐν τῇ πρὸς τὸν θεῷ ὁμοούσιον ἑνώσει καὶ τῇ κοινωνίᾳ τοῦ ὁ. ὀνόματος* id.*corp.et div*.8(p.188.10; M.*PL*.8.874Af.); but *οὐκ ἄνθρωπος (φησίν), ἀλλ' ὡς ἄνθρωπος, διότι οὐχ ὁ. τῷ ἀνθρώπῳ κατὰ τὸ κυριώτατον* id. *fr*.45(p.214.29)ap.Gr.Nyss.*Apoll*.23(M.45.1172B); in teaching of his followers *τέλειος θεὸς κατὰ τὴν θεότητα καὶ ὁ. τῷ πατρὶ καὶ τέλειος ἄνθρωπος...καὶ ὁ. ἀνθρώποις κατὰ τὴν σάρκα. εἴ τις δὲ...λέγει...ὁ. τῷ θεῷ κατὰ τὴν σάρκα, ἔστω ἀνάθεμα. εἴ τις μὴ ὁμολογεῖ τὴν τοῦ κυρίου σάρκα...ἀνθρώποις ὁ. ἔστω ἀνάθεμα* Vital. *fr*.ap.Cyr.*Arcad*.17(p.68.2; 5^2.51C); *κύριος...καὶ πρὸ σαρκὸς ὁ. τῷ πατρί· οὐκ ἦν ἡ σὰρξ ὁ., στολὴ γὰρ καὶ περιβόλαιον...πάλιν δὲ καὶ ἡμῖν ὁ. ὁ κύριος κατὰ σάρκα· οὐ γὰρ κατὰ τὴν θεότητα· οὐδὲ γὰρ ἡ θεότης ἐκ γυναικός...· οὐδὲ ἡ σὰρξ ἄνωθεν* Val.Apoll.*apol*.4(p.289.11; M. 86.1956A); Tim.Beryt.*ep.Homon*.(p.278.8; M.86.1960C); but Tim. Beryt. objected to view that flesh united to the Lord is not *καθ' οἷον δήποτε λόγον ὁ. τῷ θεῷ* *ib*. and was denounced by Valentinus for declaring *ὅτι τῇ ἑνώσει τῇ πρὸς τὸν θεὸν λόγον θεολογουμένη καὶ τῷ θεῷ ὁ. ὁμολογουμένη ἡ τοῦ κυρίου σὰρξ τῇ φύσει μένει ἀνθρωπίνη καὶ ἡμῖν ὁ.* Val.Apoll.*apol*.1(p.287.27; M.86.1953A); hence comment *οὐ χρὴ...ἡμᾶς θαυμάζειν, εἰ καὶ οἱ περὶ Οὐαλεντῖνον, καὶ οἱ περὶ Τιμόθεον...οἱ μὲν τὸ ὁ. ὁμολογοῦσιν, οἱ δὲ ἀθετοῦσι, καὶ ἀμφότεροι ἐκ τοῦ διδασκάλου ἀλλήλους καταγωνίζονται* Leont.B.*Apoll*.(M.86. 1973C); **3.** in Eutyches' teaching *τέλειον θεὸν εἶναι καὶ τέλειον ἄνθρωπον τὸν γεννηθέντα ἐκ τῆς παρθένου Μαρίας μὴ ἔχοντα σάρκα ὁ. ἡμῖν* CCP(448)*act*.3(p.124.34; H.2.141B); *περὶ τοῦ ὁ. εἶπεν ὅτι τῇ μητρί ἐστιν ὁ., οὐκ εἶπεν ἡμῖν τοῖς ἀνθρώποις. ... ὁ. τῇ μητρὶ ἐστιν καὶ οὐκ ἔχει ἡμῖν ὁ. τὴν σάρκα* CCP(449)*act*.(p.162.2; H.2.189B); *λόγου... εἰς σάρκα μετουσιωθέντος, καὶ οὐδὲν ἔχοντος ἡμῖν ὁ. τοῦ κυρίου λέγει τὸ μίαν φύσιν τοῦ θεοῦ λόγου σεσαρκωμένην* Leont.H.*monoph*.(M.86. 1809C); **4.** affirmation of consubstantiality with common human nature of Christ's complete humanity *ὅνπερ γὰρ τρόπον λυτρούμενος τὰ σώματα τῶν ἀνθρώπων, σῶμα ὁ. αὐτὸς ὑπὲρ αὐτῶν δέδωκεν, οὕτως λυτρούμενος λογικὰς ψυχάς, λογικὴν ψυχὴν ὑπὲρ αὐτῶν ἔθηκεν* Diod. *Ps*.70:23(M.33.1611A); Ambr.*fr*.ap.Thdt.*eran*.2(4.139); *λογικὴ* [sc. *ψυχή*]...*ταῖς ψυχαῖς τῶν ἀνθρώπων ὁ. ὥσπερ καὶ ἡ σὰρξ ὁ. τῇ τῶν ἀνθρώπων σαρκὶ τυγχάνει ἐκ τῆς Μαρίας προελθοῦσα* Didym.*Ps*.15:9 (M.39.1233C) cit. ap. Thdt.*eran*.1(4.56) as Eust.; *ἀπόστολος ὁ ἡμῖν ὁ.* Nest.*hom.in Heb*.3:1(p.235.2; M.64.484B)ap.Cyr.*Nest*.3.2(p.62.27; 6^1.75D); *ἀπέσταλται τε καὶ γέγονεν ἡμῖν ὁ., τουτέστιν ἄνθρωπος, ὁ. δὲ μεμενηκὼς καὶ αὐτῷ τῷ θεῷ...ἔχων δὲ τὴν ταυτότητα τῆς οὐσίας πρὸς τὸν...πατέρα...ἐπελάβετο...καὶ τῆς πρὸς ἡμᾶς ὁμοιότητος* [where ὁ. expresses, in same context, *identity of substance* with God and *similarity* to men] Cyr.*Nest*.3.3(p.65.26; 6^1.80B); *ὁ. τῷ πατρὶ τὸν αὐτὸν κατὰ τὴν θεότητα καὶ ὁ. ἡμῖν κατὰ τὴν ἀνθρωπότητα* *Symb.Ant*. (433)(p.9.1; M.77.172D); *κατὰ μὲν τὴν θεότητα...ὁ. τῷ πατρί, κατὰ δὲ τὴν ἀνθρωπότητα τὸν αὐτὸν ἡμῖν ὁ.* Paul.Em.*hom*.2(p.12.7; M.77. 1437D); Flav.CP *ep.Thds*.(p.35.16; M.65.892B); *Symb.Chalc*.(p.129. 26; H.2.456C); Procl.CP *annunt*.5(M.85.445C); discussed, Leont.H. *monoph*.1ff.(M.86.1770Aff.); *ib*.36(1792Bf.); Sophr.H.*or*.2.47(M.87. 3281B); accepted by most monophysites, but rejected by Eutychians followed by Severus and others *Χριστὸν...μηδενὶ εἶναι ὁ.* Eust.Mon.*ep*.(M.86.913A).

ὁμοουσιότης, ἡ, *consubstantiality, identity of substance*, Trin. *τὸν...υἱὸν...ἀποστερεῖν τῆς ὁ. τοῦ πατρὸς οὐκ ἐντρέπεται* ‡Eust.*alloc*. (M.18.676A); *οὐχ ἑνὸς προσώπου ὁ. ἀλλὰ τριῶν* Amph.*fr*.15(M.39. 112C); ‡Ath.*Apoll*.2.12(M.26.1152A); Gr.Naz.*or*.40.41(M.36.417B); Didym.*Trin*.2.13(M.39.689C); *ib*.3.7(849A); Epiph.*haer*.76.19(p.364. 32; M.42.552D); Cyr.*Jo*.1.4(4.36B); *ib*.10.2(871B); id.*Is*.3.5(2.540A) cit. s. *ὑπόστασις*; of H. Ghost with Father, id.*Jo*.1.9(93C); *ἡ ἐπὶ τῶν θεαρχικῶν ὑποστάσεων ὁ.* ‡Gr.Nyss.*hom.6.58 in Jo*.(p.220.18).

***ὁμοουσίως, 1.** *consubstantially* *υἱὸς ἐκ πατρὸς...ὁ. γεγεννημένος* Epiph.*ep.Arab*.ap.*haer*.76.3(p.343.18; M.42.520C); *ib*.76.19(p.365.8; 553A); *λόγου...ἀνάρχως ὁ. τε γεγεννημένου* id.*haer*.76.29(p.378.32; 576D); *τοῦ ἐν ἐμοὶ* [i.e. Wisdom] *ὁ. ἀναπαυομένου...πνεύματος* ‡Proc.G. *Pr*.8:27(M.87.1297A); **2.** *as being consubstantial* *τιμῶντας ὁ. τὴν τριάδα* Epiph.*haer*.78.24(p.475.6; M.42.740A).

ὁμοπάθεια, ἡ, *sameness of calamity* or *misfortune*, Eus.*l.C*.11 (p.224.21; M.20.1377A).

ὁμοπαθής, *subject to the same passions*, Eus.*e.th*.1.12(p.72.33; M. 24.849B).

ὁμοπάτριος, *by the same father* τῆς ὁμοπατρίου ἀδελφῆς Isid.Pel. *epp*.4.35(M.78.1088A); theol. ὁ γὰρ μονογενὴς...οὐκ ἔχει φύσει ὁ. ἀδελφόν Didym.*Trin*.3.2(M.39.788C).

***ὁμοπιστία,** ἡ, *unity of faith* ὁ τίμιος σταυρὸς γέγονε πρόξενος τοῦ συνενεχθῆναι πρὸς ὁμοπιστίαν τοὺς ἀνὰ πᾶσαν τὴν γῆν Cyr.*Is*.2.1(2. 205E); id.*Soph*.2(3.624C); συντίθεμαι τῇ ὁ. CEph.(431)*act*.1(*ACO* 1. 1.2 p.28.20; H.1.1385A); Thdr.Stud.*epp*.2.53(M.99.1264C).

***ὁμόπιστος,** *of the same faith* τοῖς ὁ. τοῖς τὴν οἰκοῦσι σκηνήν Or. *exc.in Ps*.77(M.17.144D); οὐχ ὁ. τῷ αἱρετικῷ Ath.*h.Ar*.65(p.219.6; M. 25.772A); *Const.App*.4.12.3; πρὸς πάντας τοὺς κατὰ τὴν οἰκουμένην ὁ. ὁμονοεῖν Isid.Pel.*epp*.4.103(M.78.1169D); τοὺς ὁ. ἡμῶν Χριστιανούς Thphn.*chron*.p.387(M.108.925A); of doctrines ὁμόπιστα τῶν ἁγίων πατέρων CEph.(431)*act*.1(*ACO* 1.1.2 p.26.10; H.1.1381C).

***ὁμοπλεκής,** 1. *twined together*; of fish in a net, Nonn.*par.Jo*. 21:11(M.43.917A); 2. *fastened together*, *ib*.19:18(901B).

***ὁμόπλεκτος,** *bound together*, Nonn.*par.Jo*.11:44(M.43.845C).

ὁμόπλοκος, 1. *woven together* στέφος...ὁμόπλοκον εἶχεν ἀκάνθης Nonn.*par.Jo*.19:5(M.43.897C); 2. *fastened together* πᾶς βροτὸς...ὁ. εἰς ἐμὲ μίμνων *ib*.15:5(873A); 3. *twisted up* σουδάριον...ὁ. εἰν ἑνὶ χώρῳ *ib*.20:7(909A).

ὁμόπνοια, ἡ, *unity of spirit*, ‡Eust.*Laz*.23(p.45.6).

***ὁμοπόρευτος,** ὁ, *fellow-traveller*; of body with soul, Dion.Ar.*e.h*. 7.1.1(M.3.553A); *ib*.7.3.9(565B); Eustrat.*v.Eutych*.98(M.86.2385A).

***ὁμοπροσκύνητος,** *worshipped with the same adoration*; of Christ's image and Christ, Thdr.Stud.*antirr*.3.3.8(M.99.424C) cit. s. ἑτεροπροσκύνητος; of Son and Father, *ib*.3.3.12(425C).

***ὁμοπρόσωπος,** *of the same person* εἰ ταὐτόν ἐστιν ἡ οὐσία καὶ τὸ πρόσωπον, εἴπατε αὐτὸν ὁ. τοῦ πατρὸς κατὰ τὴν θεότητα καὶ ὁ. ἡμῶν κατὰ τὴν ἀνθρωπότητα Anast.S.*hod*.9(M.89.144C).

ὁμόπτολις, *from the same town*, Nonn.*par.Jo*.12:22(M.43.853B).

ὄμοργμα, τό, *defilement*, Synes.*ep*.44(M.66.1369A).

***ὁμόρρητος,** *spoken in agreement*, Nonn.*par.Jo*.1:46(M.43.757C).

***ὁμόρριζος,** *from the same root*, Procl.CP *or*.17.3(M.65.812C).

ὁμόρροθος, *rushing together*, *Orac.Sib*.14.327.

***ὁμόρροπος,** neut. as subst., *sameness of weight*, Epiph.*haer*.76. 37(p.388.11; M.42.593A).

[*]**ὁμορρόφιος,** = ὁμωρόφιος, *sharing the same roof*, Thdt.*h.rel*. 10(3.1199).

ὁμόρροφος, = foreg., v.l. for ὁμώροφος, Synes.*ep*.148(M.66. 1548B).

***ὁμόσαρκος,** *of one flesh* with; c. dat., Cyr.*Mal*.28(3.845E); Ant. Mon.*hom*.53(M.89.1596A); c. genit., Thdr.Stud.*epp*.2.10(M.99. 1144A).

***ὁμόσεπτος,** *worshipped equally with*, Gr.Naz.*carm*.1.1.3.42(M. 37.411A).

***ὁμοσθενής,** 1. *of the same strength*, Nonn.*par.Jo*.21:11(M.43. 917A); 2. *of equal might* or *power* τριάδος...ὁ. Gr.Naz.*carm*.2.2 (epitaph.)119.14(M.38.73A); Chrys.*hom*.*59.3 in Mt*.(7.596D); Jo.D. *hom*.4.4(M.96.605A).

ὁμοσκηνία, ἡ, 1. *living together*, Chrys.*subintr*.1(1.229B); id.*fem. reg*.5(1.258E); 2. *company* ἡ ἀσκητῶν ὁ. Thdr.Stud.*epp*.2.29(M.99. 1200A).

ὁμόσκηνος, 1. *living together, dwelling with*, †Bas.*contub*.9(M.30. 824D); Gr.Nyss.*hom.14 in Cant*.(M.44.1084A); Chrys.*stat*.2.5(2.28C); 2. *who is a comrade* or *companion* τοὺς ὁ. καὶ συμψύχους ἀδελφούς Dion.Al.ap.Eus.*h.e*.7.21.3(M.20.684B); fig. νηστεία...ἡ τῶν δικαίων ὁ. Bas.*hom*.2.6(2.14B; M.31.193A); ἡ...ὁ. τῶν μοναζόντων εἰρήνη Nil. *epp*.2.96(M.79.244C).

***ὁμόσκοτος,** *in the same darkness*, Gr.Naz.*carm*.2.1.18.4(M.37. 1270A).

ὁμόσπονδος, *who is a friend* or *ally*, Gr.Naz.*carm*.1.2.10.145(M. 37.691A); Pall.*v.Chrys*.20(p.142.29; M.47.79); Thdt.*Abd*.1:7(2.1452); fig. ἀκτῖνος ὁ. προφητῶν *Orac.Sib*.5.239.

ὁμοστεγέω, *dwell with*, Bas.Sel.*v.Thecl*.2.15(M.85.592D).

***ὁμόστεγος,** *sharing the same roof*, Gr.Naz.*or*.43.19(M.36.520D); id.*carm*.1.2.8.168(M.37.661A); *ib*.2.1.11.477(1062A).

***ὁμοστεφής,** *sharing the same crown*, Andr.Cr.*or*.16(M.97.1168B).

***ὁμοστιβής,** *in step with*; met., Cyr.*Jo*.11.12(4.1024B).

***ὁμοστιχής,** *proceeding together*, Nonn.*par.Jo*.10:41(M.43.837C).

***ὁμοστίχως,** *line by line*, Leont.Abb.*v.Gr.Agr*.52(M.98.641A).

ὁμόστοιχος, 1. *of the same rank*, Dion.Ar.*d.n*.4.7(M.3.704B); *ib*. 4.10(708A); theol. ὁ. ... ἡ ἁγία τριάς Epiph.*anc*.64(p.77.6; M.43. 132A); id.*haer*.62.4(p.393.9; M.41.1056B); *ib*.66.57(p.94.11; M.42. 116B); *conferring the same rank* οὐδὲ ταῖς ὁ. συλλαβαῖς τὸ ποιοῦν τοῖς γιγνομένοις ὀνομάσαι τολμήσας Alex.Al.*ep.Alex*.19(p.22.21; M.18. 553C); 2. *of the same kind*, Epiph.*haer*.66.76(p.118.1,7; M.42.149B,C); ὁμόστοιχον γνῶσιν...εἰδωλολατρείας *ib*.4.2(p.183.7; M.41.201A); Mac. Mgn.*apocr*.4.12(p.176.17); Thdr.Stud.*epp*.2.84(M.99.1328B).

***ὁμοστοίχως,** 1. *in respect of equal rank*; ref. Trin., Epiph.*anc*.26 (p.34.22; M.43.64C); 2. *in accordance* with, *Const.App*.proem.; ὁ. τοῖς προφήταις καὶ τῷ νόμῳ τὸ εὐαγγέλιον ἑρμηνεύων *ib*.2.5.4; 3. *so as to be of the same kind*, Synes.*astrolab*.5(p.140.19; M.66.1585A).

ὁμόστοργος, 1. *of the same love*, Nonn.*par.Jo*.14:21(M.43.869C); 2. *united in love*, met. ὁ. τραπέζης *ib*.13:12(861B).

***ὁμοσύμφωνος,** *in perfect agreement*, Ath.*virg*.9(p.43.11; M.28. 261B).

***ὁμόσχημος,** *wearing the same* religious *habit*, Thdr.Stud.*epp*.1. 31(M.99.1009D); μοναχοὶ...κατὰ τῶν ὁ. φερόμενοι *ib*.2.16(1168A); *ib*. 2.183(1565A).

ὁμοσχήμων, *of the same appearance*, Nemes.*nat.hom*.42(M.40. 792A).

***ὁμόσωμος,** *of the same body*; met., Ant.Mon.*hom*.73(M.89. 1645C); c. genit., Thdr.Stud.*epp*.1.28(M.99.997D).

ὁμοταγής, *of the same order* or *rank*; eccl., Dion.Ar.*ep*.8.4(M.3. 1093C); Thdr.Stud.*epp*.2.10(M.99.1141C); Πέτρος ἢ Παῦλος σὺν τοῖς ὁ. *ib*.2.21(1180D); angelic τὸν τριαδικὸν οὖν τοῦτον διάκοσμον, ὡς ἕνα καὶ ὁ. ... ἱεραρχίαν Dion.Ar.*c.h*.6.2(M.3.201A); *ib*.8.1(240A).

***ὁμοταγία,** ἡ, *same series*; of angels, Max.*schol.d.n*.1.3(M.4. 196B).

ὁμοτιμία, ἡ, *equality of honour* πάντων τῶν ἐν τῇ κτίσει νοουμένων ...τὴν ὁ. ἐχόντων Gr.Nyss.*Maced*.18(M.45.1324B); of Eve ἐπειδὴ οὐκ ἐχρήσω εἰς δέον τῇ ὁ., διὰ τοῦτό σε ὑποτάττω τῷ ἀνδρί Chrys.*hom.17.8 in Gen*.(4.145D); c. genit., ‡Jo.D.*Artem*.38(M.96.1288A); theol., of Persons of Trin. φύσεως ὁ. Gr.Naz.*or*.29.2(p.75.3; M.36.76B); *ib*.43. 30(537B); of Son τὴν πρὸς τὸν γεγεννηκότα ὁ. Chrys.*hom.15.5 in Mt*. (7.191E); *ib.29.1*(343A); τῆς οὐσίας τὴν ὁ. id.*hom.29.3 in 1Cor*.(10. 262D); of H. Ghost ἀνάξιον δὲ τῆς πρὸς τὸν πατέρα καὶ υἱὸν ὁ. φασί Gr.Nyss.*Maced*.2(M.45.1304B).

ὁμότιμος, 1. *equal in honour* πάντες υἱοὶ καὶ ὁ. Just.*dial*.134. 4(M.6.788A); ἀνθρώπους ὄντας ἐν ὁ. τῇ φύσει Gr.Nyss.*ep*.1(M.46. 1004C); Chrys.*hom.26.2 in 1Cor*.(10.229E) cit. s. γυνή; theol., of Trin. βαπτίζειν...εἰς τρεῖς ὁ. ‡Ign.*Phil*.2; τὸ τῆς τριάδος...ὁ. Cyr. *apol.orient*.9(p.51.27; 6[1].182B); Gel.Cyz.*h.e*.2.19.21(M.85.1280C); of Father and Son ἡ ἐκ δεξιῶν τοῦ πατρὸς ἀφωρισμένη τῷ υἱῷ καθέδρα, τί ποτε ἕτερον, καὶ οὐχὶ τὸ ὁ. τῆς ἀξίας ἀποσημαίνει; Bas.*Eun*. 1.25(1.236B; M.29.568B); τὸ ὁ. τὸ πρὸς τὸν πατέρα Chrys.*hom. 71.2 in Mt*.(7.696B); c. dat., *ib.29.1*(7.342E); c. genit., Thdt.*Zach*. 2:8f.(2.1605); ref. Eunomian doctrine ἵνα...εἰς τὸ ὁ. τῇ κτίσει τὸν μονογενῆ καταγάγῃ Bas.*Eun*.1.26(1.237A; M.29.569B); 2. *paying* or *which pays the same honour* ἕως ἂν...τὸ πνεῦμα τὸ ἅγιον ἐν ὁ. τῇ προσκυνήσει δοξάζηται Gr.Nyss.*ep*.3(M.46.1017D); ἡ ὁ. πίστις Thdot. Anc.*exp.symb*.24(M.77.1348C); 3. *equal in value*, Gr.Nyss.*hom.2 in Cant*.(M.44.788B); of a garment after washing ὁ. ἑαυτῷ δι' ὅλου id.*or. catech*.27(p.101.16; M.45.69D); 4. *of the same intensity* κοινήν τε καὶ ὁ. τὴν τῆς ἀγάπης ἀκτῖνα ἐπὶ πάντας φερέτωσαν Bas.*ascet*.2(2.325C; M. 31.885B); μανίαν ὁ. id.*mor*.17.4(3.566E; M.32.1336A); 5. *equal* ὁ. ἐπὶ πάντας ἡ κλῆσις Gr.Nyss.*or.catech*.30(p.112.1; M.45.76D); in phrase κατὰ τὸ ὁ. *equally*, *ib*.6(p.31.9; 28A).

ὁμοτίμως, 1. *with* or *in respect of equal honour*; of Trin. ἵνα... ὁ. ... προσκυνηθῇ ‡Meth.*palm*.7(M.18.397A); *with the same honour*, Dion.Ar.*c.h*.9.4(3.261B); 2. ὁ. ἔχω *be of equal value*, Gr.Nyss.*or. catech*.28(p.106.14; M.45.73B); *be equivalent*, *ib*.40(p.163.7; 104D); *be equal in honour* ὡς τοῦ παιδὸς ὁ. [sc. ἔχοντος] πρὸς τὸν γεγεννηκότα Chrys.*hom.26.2 in 1Cor*.(10.230B); 3. *equally*, †Bas.*Is*.118(1.461A; M. 30.309A); Gr.Nyss.*or.catech*.27(p.104.5; M.45.72C); Chrys.*hom.15.3 in Jo*.(8.89B).

ὁμοτράπεζος, ὁ, *table-companion* ὁ. τοῦ πάντων δεσπότου Isid. Pel.*epp*.2.5(M.78.461B); τοῖς ἱεροῖς συλλόγοις ὁ. *ib*.3.376(1024C); at eucharist, Gr.Ant.*bapt*.2.10(M.88.1884A).

***ὁμότρητος,** *pierced together*, Nonn.*par.Jo*.19:18(M.43.901B).

***ὁμοτροπέω,** *be of the same disposition* or *way of life* as; c. genit., Cyr.*glaph.Gen*.2(1.32C); abs., id.*Jo*.10(4.833C).

ὁμοτροπία, ἡ, *sameness of disposition* or *way of life*, Gr.Naz.*ep*. 230(M.37.373A); Dion.Ar.*e.h*.3.3.1(M.3.428B); *ib*.7.1.3(556B).

ὁμοτρόπως, *with the same disposition*, Dion.Ar.*e.h*.3.3.1(M.3. 428B).

ὁμότροφος, *nourished with the same food*; ref. eucharist, Dion.Ar. *e.h*.3.3.1(M.3.428B).

ὁμοῦ, *together*, in phrases ὁ. μὲν...ὁ. δὲ..., *both...and, at once...and* ὁ. μὲν διδασκάλους ἀποστέλλων...ὁ. δὲ ἐκκόπτων Chrys.*hom.8.1 in Mt*.(7.120B); *ib.14.1*(178B); ὁ. τε...ὁ. τε... *ib*.9.4(134E); ὁ. τε...καὶ..., *immediately, as soon as* ὁ. τε γὰρ ἐτέχθη τὸ παιδίον, καὶ ἡ μαῖα...

Bas.*hex*.6.5(1.54E; M.29.129A); Chrys.*hom.4.9 in Mt*.(7.64B); id. *hom.7.5 in 2Cor*.(10.486D,E); with ptcpl., *as soon as* ὁ. φανεὶς id. *hom.8.4 in Mt*.(125C).

***ὁμοϋπόστατος**, *united in one person* ὁ. δὲ οὔτε πρὸ σαρκὸς ὁ λόγος γέγονε τῷ πατρί Leont.H.*Nest*.2.1(M.86.1533B); οὐ γάρ ἐστιν ἡμῖν ὥσπερ ὁμοφυής, οὕτω καὶ ὁ. Anast.Ant.*fr*.(p.135.2; M.89.1281C); ὁ. ἐστι, τὸ εἰς μίαν καὶ τὴν αὐτὴν ὑπόστασιν ἄλλῳ συντεθειμένον Max. *opusc*.(M.91.152A); id.*ep*.15(M.91.552C); ὁ. εἰσιν, ὅτε δύο φύσεις ἐν μιᾷ ὑποστάσει ἑνωθῶσι, καὶ μίαν σχῶσιν ὑπόστασιν σύνθετον, καὶ ἓν πρόσωπον, ὡς ψυχὴ καὶ σῶμα Jo.D.*dialect*.48(M.94.624A); id.*Jacob*. 10(M.94.1440B); id.*fid.Nest*.46(p.578).

[*]**ὁμοφόριος**, for ὁμορόφιος Firm.*ep*.27(M.77.1501A).

ὁμοφραδής, *talking* or *agreeing together*, Nonn.*par.Jo*.4:40(M.43. 781A); *ib*.7:40(812B).

***ὁμοφρονία**, ἡ, *concord*, Hipp.*Noët*.7(p.247.19; M.10.813B).

***ὁμοφρόνως**, *in unity of mind, in concord*, *Const.App*.2.44.2; *ib*. 3.19.2; ὁ. τῇ ἁγίᾳ θεοῦ ἐκκλησίᾳ Epiph.*haer*.77.19(p.434.1; M.42. 669B); σὲ τὴν...μητέρα θεοῦ...οἱ πιστοὶ ὁ. μεγαλύνομεν Jo.D.*carm. assumpt.Chr*.84(p.228; M.96.845D); ‡Jo.D.*ep.Thphl*.1(M.95.345C).

ὁμοφροσύνη, ἡ, *concord, unanimity, agreement*, Clem.*str*.4.21 (p.307.6; M.8.1344B); Meth.*symp*.3.14(p.45.4; M.18.85B); Eus.*e.th*.1. 15(p.75.12; M.24.856A); συντρέχουσι τοῖς διωκομένοις...τῇ ὁ. Ath.*h. Ar*.79(p.228.7; M.25.792A); ἔστω πάντων ὁ. ... τὰ δὲ τῶν πατέρων φυλάξωμεν id.*syn*.9(p.236.26; M.26.696A); Chrys.*hom.3.1 in 1Cor*.(10. 15C); τὴν πρὸς τὰ θεῖα καὶ ἑαυτοὺς καὶ ἀλλήλους ὁ. Dion.Ar.*e.h*.3.3. 5(M.3.432A); Max.*opusc*.(M.91.113A); of Father and Son εὕροις ἂν τοὺς ἑκατέρους ἓν κατ' οὐσίαν καὶ ὁ. ‡Gr.Nyss.*Ar.et Sab*.12(M.45. 1300A).

ὁμόφρων, *of one mind, agreeing* with, Dion.Al.ap.Eus.*h.e*.7.5.1 (M.20.641B); Ath.*Dion*.1(p.46.14; M.25.480B); ὁ. ὄντες πρὸς ἀλλήλους *Const.App*.2.44.2; c. genit., Eus.Dor.*contest*.(p.101.8; M.89. 277C); Gel.Cyz.*h.e*.3.12.2; c. dat., *Hom.Clem*.15.1; Cyr.*Mich*.28(3. 414D).

ὁμοφυής, *of the same nature*; **1.** in gen., Eus.*d.e*.1.10(p.45.11; M. 22.85C); of men τῇ οὐσίᾳ ὁ. εἰσι Ath.*syn*.53(p.276.28; M.26.788C); ἄγγελοι πρὸς ἑαυτούς, καὶ τὰ ἄλλα πάντα, ὡσαύτως ὁ. ἐστιν ἀλλήλων id.*ep.Serap*.2.3(M.26.612B); of soul and body, Thdt.*provid*.9(4. 644); Dion.Ar.*d.n*.11.2(M.3.952A); of things of same genus, but not necessarily those of same species, Thdr.Abuc.*opusc*.2(M.97. 1472D); **2.** theol.; **a.** ref. Trin. τὸ...ὁ. τῆς ἁγίας τριάδος Ath.*ep.Serap*. 1.17(M.26.572B); Thdt.ap.Cyr.*apol.Thdt*.9(p.134.10; 6¹.228C) cit. s. ἐκπορεύω; Max.*ep*.15(M.91.552C); ‡Jo.D.*hom*.5(M.96.661A); **b.** of Father and Son, in illustration φυτὸν εἶπον ἀπὸ σπέρματος...ἀνελθὸν ἕτερον εἶναι τοῦ ὅθεν ἐβλάστησε, καὶ πάντως ἐκείνῳ καθέστηκεν ὁ. Dion.Al.ap.Ath.*Dion*.18(p.60.1; M.25.505C); τῆς τοῦ πατρὸς οὐσίας ἴδιος καὶ ὁ. Ath.*Ar*.1.58(M.26.133B); ὁ. ὄντα διὰ τὸ ἐξ αὐτοῦ γεγεννῆσθαι id.*syn*.48(p.272.27; M.26.777C); *ib*.52(p.276.12; 788A); αἱ ἰδιότητες...τὸ ὁ. τῆς οὐσίας οὐ διακόπτουσιν Bas.*Eun*.2.28(1.265B; M. 29.637B); Didym.*Trin*.2.6(M.39.524B); ὁ. τε καὶ ἐξ αὐτοῦ Cyr.*thes*.32 (5¹.295E); id.*dial.Trin*.1(5¹.391D); id.*Jo*.1.4(4.36B); τῷ πυρὶ δὲ ὁ. τὸ ἀπαύγασμα· οὐκοῦν καὶ ὁ υἱὸς τῷ πατρί Thdt.*Heb*.1:3(3.547); ὁ... θεός, ὁμοφυοῦς ὑπάρχει λόγου πηγαστικός ‡Cyr.*Trin*.13(6³.20A; M.77. 1149C); Jo.D.*Jacob*.25(M.94.1449C); Arian denial οὐχ ὁ. ὁ υἱὸς τῷ πατρί Didym.(‡Bas.)*Eun*.4(1.291B; M.29.700A); **c.** Christol., denied of Son in divine nature in rel. to creatures πῶς ὁ. ἔσται τοῖς ἀγγέλοις ὁ υἱός; Cyr.*thes*.20(5¹.204D); οὐκ ἄρα ὁ. τοῖς πεποιημένοις ὁ υἱός id.*Jo*.1.7(4.55A); Arian ὁ υἱὸς...τοῖς ἄλλοις ἅπασιν ὁ., οἷς ἐξ οὐκ ὄντων ἡ γένεσις *ib*.1.1(13D); asserted of Christ's humanity in rel. to men ὁ. ἡμᾶς εἶναι τῇ ἀμπέλῳ κατὰ τὴν σάρκα *ib*.10.2.(864B); ὁ. ... τῶν ἀνθρώπων τὸ θεωρούμενον Bas.Sel.*or*.25.3(M.85.293B); Anast. Ant.*fr*.(p.135.2; M.89.1281C) cit. s. ὁμοϋπόστατος; τοῦ γηΐνου σώματος τοῦ ἡμῖν ὁ. Max.*ambig*.(M.91.1309B).

ὁμοφυΐα, ἡ, *identity of nature*, Cyr.*ador*.6(1.210E); Max.*ambig*.(M. 91.1312D); of Father and Son, Gr.Naz.*or*.29.16(p.98.11; M.36.96A); Proc.G.*Is*.11:10(M.87.2049B).

ὁμοφυῶς, *in identity of nature* πάντα τὰ φυσικὰ τῆς τριάδος ἰδιώματα...ὁ. ὁρᾶται ἐν τῷ υἱῷ, ὥσπερ καὶ ἐν τῷ πατρί, καὶ ἐν τῷ ἁγίῳ πνεύματι Anast.S.*hod*.17(M.89.264C).

ὁμόφωνος, *speaking the same language*, hence *in agreement*, Eust. *engast*.25(p.55.24; M.18.665A); Eus.*v.C*.3.14(p.83.26; M.20.1069C); Gr. Nyss.*or.catech*.26(p.100.8; M.45.69B); CEph.(431)*act*.1(p.28.9; H.1. 1384E); c. dat., Didym.*Trin*.3.2(M.39.788C); Socr.*h.e*.2.26.4(M.67. 268A).

ὁμοφώνως, *with one voice* or *accord*, Gr.Nyss.*anim.et res*.(M.46. 72B); ref. witness of evangelists, Chrys.*hom.17.3 in Jo*.(8.101A); Isid.Pel.*epp*.4.55(M.78.1108A); ‡Jo.D.*hom*.5(M.96.653D).

***ὁμόφωτος**, *shining with the same light*; of Persons of Trin., ‡Caes.Naz.*dial*.3(M.38.860).

***ὁμοχορέω**, for ⟨ὁμοχωρέω⟩, *go forward together*, Alex.Sal.*Barn*. 22(p.443B).

***ὁμόχριστος**, *anointed with the same unction*, Ant.Mon.*hom*.49 (M.89.1585C).

***ὁμοχρόνιος**, *contemporary*, *Ep.Her*.(p.69.17).

ὁμόχρονος, **1.** *contemporary, contemporaneous*, Afric.*chron*.13.1 (M.10.73B); Gr.Naz.*or*.15.5(M.35.920C); *ib*.45.28(M.36.661C); **2.** *of the same age, coeval* τὰ κακά...ὁ. αὐτῷ [sc. God]...λέγουσι Chrys.*hom. 2.5 in Ac*.(9.21A); ὁ λόγος...οὐδὲ ὁ. τῇ σαρκὶ τὴν ὕπαρξιν ἔχων Cyr. *inc.unigen*.(5¹.694C); ἡ χάρις...οὐχ ὁ. ἔχει τῇ ἁμαρτίᾳ τὴν βασιλείαν, ἀλλ' αἰώνιον Thdt.*Rom*.5:21(3.60); of soul and body, id.*ep*.130(4. 1216); of Trin., †Alex.Sal.*cruc.epit*.(M.87.4088A); οὐ...πᾶσα σύνθετος ὑπόστασις ἀλλήλοις ὁ. κατὰ τὴν γένεσιν ἔχει τὰ μέρη Max.*ep*.13(M.91. 525D); ὁ. τῇ σαρκὶ τὸν λόγον ὄντα ὑποτιθέμενος *ib*.12(489B).

***ὁμοχρόνως**, *at the same time*, Gr.Nyss.*hom.7 in Cant*.(M.44. 937C); Jo.Clim.*scal*.5(M.88.780C).

[*]**ὁμόχρος**, f.l. for ὁμόχωρος, Thdr.Stud.*epp*.2.213(M.99.1641C).

ὁμόχωρος, *living in the same place*, Epiph.*haer*.51.14(p.267.27; M. 41.916A).

ὁμόψηφος, **1.** *agreeing* with, Const.ap.Gel.Cyz.*h.e*.2.4.5 for ὁμοψύχους id.ap.Eus.*v.C*.2.71(p.70.2; M.20.1044C); **2.** *expressing the same opinion* ὁ. γράμματα Socr.*h.e*.4.12.38(M.67.496A).

***ὁμοψυχέω**, *be of one soul* τῶν πιστευσάντων εἰς Χριστὸν ὁμοψυχησάντων ἀλλήλοις Cyr.*Jo*.11.11(4.997D); Thdr.Stud.*epp*.2.59(M. 99.1273B).

ὁμοψυχία, ἡ, *unity of soul, concord, unanimity* γενώμεθα ἓν πρὸς ἀλλήλους τῇ ὁ. Ath.*Ar*.3.20(M.26.364C); id.*ep.Afr*.10(M.26.1045D); Chrys.*hom.20.6 in Eph*.(11.152D); συνειρόντος εἰς ὁ. αὐτοὺς τοῦ... σωτῆρος Cyr.*Is*.2.1(2.200B); συνθήκας ὁμοψυχίας ποιήσασθαι πρὸς αὐτόν id.*Am*.6(259A); ὁ Χριστός...συλλέγων ἡμᾶς εἰς ἕνωσιν...ἐν ὁ. id.*ador*.15(1.532D); as style of address (cf. Lat. *vestra unanimitas*) ὑμῶν ἡ ὁ. CSard.*ep.Alex*.ap.Ath.*apol.sec*.39(p.118.1; M.25.321D); ἡ ὑμετέρα ὁ. *Cod.Afr*.57.

ὁμόψυχος, **1.** *united in soul, agreeing together*, Const.ap.Eus.*v.C*. 2.71(p.70.2; M.20.1044C); τὸν ὁ. ἡμῶν Ἄνθιμον Bas.*ep*.210.5(3.316C; M.32.776A); *Const.App*.6.18.11; Chrys.*sac*.1.4(p.15.22; 1.367C); τοὺς ἐχθροὺς οὕτως ἠγάπησαν, ὡς οὐκ ἄν τις ἀγαπήσειε τοὺς ὁ. id.*hom.19.2 in Heb*.(12.184B); τὸν ὁμοψυχότατον ἡμῖν Γάϊον Synes.*ep*.4(M.66. 1341B); in polite address ὁ. συλλειτουργῷ...χαίρειν Alex.Thess.*ep. Ath*.ap.Ath.*apol.sec*.66(p.145.1; M.25.368A); CAnc.(358)*ep.syn*.ap. Epiph.*haer*.73.2(p.268.31; M.42.404A); **2.** met.; **a.** *unanimous* ὁ. ἀγχίνοιαν Const.ap.Eus.*v.C*.2.68(p.68.9; M.20.1040B); τῇ εἰς Χριστὸν ὁμοψύχῳ...πίστει Ath.*ep.encycl*.7(p.177.9; M.25.237D); **b.** *united* βασιλικὸν χρῖσμα ὁ. τῆς πάντων συνέσεως Const.*or.s.c*.11(p.169.2; M.20. 1265B); ὁ. συζυγίαν Gr.Naz.*or*.8.5(M.35.793C); **3.** *having the same soul* or *spiritual nature* δούλων τῶν ὁ. ὑπεροράς; Chrys.*hom.12.7 in 1Cor*.(10.106E).

ὁμοψύχως, *unanimously, with one accord, in harmony*, *Const. App*.3.19.2; Nil.*Magn*.64(M.79.1056D); Leo Mag.*ep*.35.1(p.40.21; M.*PL*.54.804A).

ὀμφακίζ-ω, **1.** *bear unripe grapes*, Or.*fr.in Mt*.21:33ff.(M.17. 301B); **2.** *be sour*, met. τὰ νοήματά σου...οὐδαμῶς ~οντα Or.*schol.in Cant*.7:6f.(M.17.284B); **3.** *be unripe*, met. μὴ θελήσωμεν ~οντες ἔτι... διδάσκειν Nil.*epp*.2.103(M.79.245C).

ὀμφάκινος, *of the colour of unripe grapes*, Clem.*paed*.2.10(p.222. 14; M.8.528A).

ὀμφή, ἡ, *voice*, Cyr.*glaph.Gen*.6(1.181A); κατὰ θείαν ὀ. id.*Os*.20(3. 42C); ὑποκάρδιον ὀ. Nonn.*par.Jo*.6:15(M.43.796B).

ὀμφήεις, *oracular*, Nonn.*par.Jo*.1:49(M.43.760A); *ib*.13:21(864B); Paul.Sil.*Soph*.997(M.86.2157A).

ὁμωνυμέω, **1.** *have the same name*, Clem.*str*.8.8(p.95.19; M.9.592B); Or.*dial*.16(p.154.21); Leont.H.*Nest*.3.8(M.86.1636D); **2.** *be equivocal*; of words which are the same but have different meanings when applied to God or man (e.g. 'good'), Isid.Pel.*epp*.3.92(M.78.796D, 797A,B).

ὁμωνυμία, ἡ, **1.** *a having the same name, verbal identity*; **a.** in gen. πότερον δὲ ὁ. ἐστὶ δύο ὄντων Λαζάρων...; Or.*fr.77 in Jo*.(p.544.3); τῇ τοῦ πάππου κοσμούμενος ὁ. Κωνστάντιος Eus.*v.C*.4.40(p.133.6; M.20. 1188C); Gr.Nyss.*or.catech*.1(p.8.6; M.45.13B); exeg. Mc.9:48 σκώληκά τις ἀκούσας μὴ διὰ τῆς ὁ. πρὸς τὸ ἐπίγειον τοῦτο θηρίον ἀποφερέσθω *ib*.40(p.163.16; 105A); Chrys.*hom.14.1 in Jo*.(8.79C); Isid.Pel.*epp*.3. 31(M.78.752D,753A); **b.** in theol. controversy; **i.** with Eunomians, Gr.Naz.*or*.29.14(p.94.18ff.; M.36.92Df.) v. ὁμώνυμος; **ii.** with Macedonians τὸ ἅγιον πνεῦμα τὴν ὁ. ... πρὸς τὸν θεὸν ἔχει Didym.*Trin*.2.3

(M.39.476C); **iii.** with Nestorians, who concealed their doctrine of two sons under a merely verbal identity of the name son, or Christ, Cyr.*Pulch*.18(p.35.24; 5^{2}.141E); Thdot.Anc.*hom*.3.4(p.72.34; M.77.1388D); Justn.*conf.anath*.4(p.90.30; M.86.1015A); **2.** *ambiguity*, Isid.Pel.*epp*.3.92(M.78.797A); Thdt.*Ezech*.13:2(2.757); Thdr.Abuc. *opusc*.2(M.97.1473C,D); **3.** καθ' ὁμωνυμίαν *equivocally, so as to convey a double meaning*; of naming Christ's image 'Christ', Thdr. Stud.*epp*.2.162(M.99.1513D); **4.** *ambiguous, equivocal word*, Epiph. *haer*.64.8(p.417.9; M.41.1081D); Didym.*Trin*.2.3(M.39.476A,B).

***ὁμωνυμικός**, *equivocal, bearing a twofold meaning*; of worship of Christ's image, Thdr.Stud.*epp*.2.85(M.99.1329A).

***ὁμωνυμικῶς**, *by the use of the same term*, Epiph.*haer*.35.2(p.42.29; M.41.632A).

ὁμώνυμος, *having the same name*; **1.** masc. as subst., *namesake*, ὁ τοῦ σωτῆρος ἡμῶν ὁ. [i.e. Joshua] Thdt.*qu.34 in Ex*.(1.146); **2.** *equivocal, ambiguous* τῶν ὁ. λέξεων Just.*dial*.34.1(M.6.548A); Or.*comm. in Gen.*ap.*philoc*.14.2(p.69.7,28; M.12.89B,C); id.*comm.in Mt*.10.16 (p.20.20; M.13.873C); †Leont.B.*sect*.10.2(M.86.1261C); **3.** neut. plur. as subst., *things denoted by ambiguous or equivocal words, things having the same name but different definitions*; **a.** def., Clem.*str*.8.8 (p.95.17; M.9.592A); Or.*hom.20.1 in Jer*.(p.177.17; M.13.501A); Isid. Pel.*epp*.3.92(M.78.796C); Jo.D.*dialect*.31(M.94.596Af.); **b.** theol., exeg. 1Reg.15:11 ἡ μεταμέλεια αὐτοῦ [sc. of God] ὁμώνυμόν ἐστι τῇ ἡμετέρᾳ μεταμελείᾳ [i.e. has same name, but different nature] Or.*hom.20.1 in Jer*.(p.177.17; M.13.501A); (Eunomian), of Father and Son as ὁ., Gr.Naz.*or*.29.13(p.93.7; M.36.92A); Leont.H.*monoph*. 2(M.86.1769A); **4.** *having only the same name*, ref. Nestorian nominal unity of Christ πῶς οὐχὶ κατὰ τὴν τῶν ὁ. ἕνωσιν, τὴν κατὰ τοὔνομα μόνον ἔσται ἔχων τὴν πρὸς θεὸν κοινωνίαν ὁ Χριστός, οὐχὶ δὲ κατὰ τὸ ὑποκείμενον τῷ ὀνόματι πρᾶγμα; Leont.H.*Nest*.3.8(M.86.1636C); cf. Thdot.Anc.*exp.symb*.7(M.77.1324A).

ὁμωνύμως, *by* or *under the same name(s)*, Iren.*haer*.1.8.5(M.7.536A); Clem.*str*.1.10(p.31.15; M.8.744C); ὁ. πᾶσι τοῖς σωματικοῖς ὀνομαζόμενα οὐ σωματικά Or.*dial*.11(p.146.7); Gr.Nyss.*or.catech*.1(p.7.10; M.45.13A); Thdt.*qu.98 in Gen*.(1.104); πῶς οὐχὶ ἐν τῇ εἰκόνι ὁ εἰκονιζόμενος ὁ. ὁρᾶται; Thdr.Stud.*epp*.1.17(M.99.961C); Christol. ὁ μὲν γὰρ φύσει...υἱὸς ὁ ἐκ θεοῦ πατρός ἐστι λόγος· ὁ δὲ ὁ. τῷ υἱῷ υἱός... ὃν δὲ ἀνέλαβεν ἄνθρωπον, οὐ φύσει θεὸς ὢν διὰ τὸν ἀναλαβόντα αὐτὸν ἀληθῶς θεοῦ υἱὸν ὁ. αὐτῷ χρηματίζει Nest.*fr*.B 5(pp.217.19,218.2)ap. Cyr.*Thds*.6(p.46.1,6; 5^{2}.5Ef.).

ὁμώροφος, *being under the same roof*; met., Gr.Naz.*carm*.1.2.5.4 (M.37.642A).

ὁμῶς, *like* λέοντος ὁ. βωστρεῖν Eudoc.*Cypr*.2.294(M.85.857A).

ὄναρ, τό, *dream*, also adverbially *in a dream* (treated together with ὄνειρος, ὁ), **1.** in gen. τῶν ὀνείρων οἱ ἀληθεῖς...νηφούσης εἰσὶ ψυχῆς λογισμοί Clem.*paed*.2.9(p.207.23; M.8.496C); τήν τε ἀλήθειαν αὐτὴν ἐποπτεύσαντες...τοὺς ἀληθεῖς τῶν ὀνείρων ἐναργῶς καὶ φρονίμως ἀποκαλυπτώμεθα *ib*.(p.206.28; 496A); ref. true 'gnostic' προορατικὸς ὢν καὶ ἄκαμπτος ἡδοναῖς ταῖς τε ὕπαρ ταῖς τε δι' ὀνειράτων id.*str*.6.10 (p.471.12; M.9.300B); καὶ ὀνείρους βλέπων τὰ ἅγια ποιεῖ καὶ νοεῖ *ib*. 7.12(p.56.5; 508C); in rel. to prophetic revelations ὥσπερ ὄναρ πεπίστευται πολλοὺς πεφαντασιῶσθαι τινὰ μὲν θειότερα τινὰ δὲ περὶ μελλόντων βιωτικῶν ἀναγγέλλοντα..., καὶ τοῦτ' ἐναργές ἐστι παρὰ πᾶσι τοῖς παραδεξαμένοις πρόνοιαν, οὕτως τί ἄτοπον τὸ τυποῦν τὸ ἡγεμονικὸν ἐν ὀνείρῳ δύνασθαι αὐτὸ τυποῦν καὶ ὕπαρ πρὸς τὸ χρήσιμον τῷ ἐν ᾧ τυποῦται...; καὶ ὥσπερ φαντασίαν λαμβάνομεν ὄναρ ἀκούειν...καὶ ὁρᾶν...οὕτως οὐδὲν ἄτοπον τοιαῦτα γεγονέναι ἐπὶ τῶν προφητῶν, ὅτε ἀναγέγραπται...αὐτοὺς...ἀκηκοέναι λόγους κυρίου Or.*Cels*.1.48(p.97.24; M.11.748A); ref. Montanist ecstasy αὐτὴ δὲ ἡ ψυχὴ οὐκ ἐξέστη τοῦ ἡγεμονικοῦ...πολλάκις γὰρ φαντάζεται...δι' ὀνειράτων ἑαυτὴν θεωμένη Epiph.*haer*.48.5(p.227.10; M.41.864A); **2.** as means of divine revelation, *Apoc.En*.13.8; ὄναρ γὰρ τῷ Ἰωσὴφ...λέγεται ἄγγελος ταῦτ' εἰρηκέναι· τὸ δὲ ὄναρ δηλοῦσθαί τισι τάδε ποιεῖν καὶ ἄλλοις πλείοσι συμβαίνει, εἴτ' ἀγγέλου εἴθ' οὑτινοσοῦν φαντασιοῦντος τὴν ψυχήν Or. *Cels*.1.66(p.120.5; M.11.784C); *Hom.Clem*.14.7; ἴσμεν πολλοὺς...ἁμαρτάνοντας...ἀληθεῖς ὀνείρους ὁρῶντας *ib*.17.16; εἰ συμβῇ ποτε ὀνείρατα θεάσασθαι...καυχώμεθα Cyr.H.*hom*.16(M.33.1149B); *M.Thdot.1* 12 (p.68.11); ref. Ac.16:9 ὅπου γὰρ κηρύξαι ἠπείγετο μόνον, εἰς τοῦτο ὄναρ φαίνεται αὐτῷ· ὅπου δὲ μὴ κηρύξαι οὐκ ἠνείχετο, εἰς τοῦτο πνεῦμα ἅγιον ἀποκαλύπτει [ref. Ac.10:20]. οὐ γὰρ δὴ καὶ τὰ εὔκολα εἰργάζετο τὸ πνεῦμα, ἀλλ' ἤρκει καὶ ὄναρ αὐτῷ. καὶ τῷ Ἰωσὴφ δὲ ῥᾳδίως πειθομένῳ ὄναρ φαίνεται, τοῖς δὲ ἄλλοις ὕπαρ Chrys.*hom.34.4 in Ac*.(9.265C); οὕτως αἰτήσομεν ὄνειρον, ὥσπερ ἴσως Ὅμηρος ᾔτησε. κἂν ἐπιτήδειος ᾖς, πάρεστιν ὁ πόρρω θεός Synes.*insomn*.12(p.167.11; M.66.1301C); ἀλλὰ τῆς γε δι' ὀνείρων μαντικῆς αὐτός τίς ἐστιν ἕκαστος ὄργανον· ὥστε οὐδὲ βουλομένοις ἔξεστιν ἀπολιπεῖν τὸ χρηστήριον *ib*.(p.170.6; 1304C); **3.** ref. pagan divination ἐξεπόνησαν...Τελμησεῖς τὴν δι' ὀνείρων μαντικήν Clem.*str*.1.16(p.48.8; M.8.784B); forbidden to Christians παρατηρήσεις ἡμερῶν...κληδονισμοὺς καὶ ὄνειρα ‡Chrys. *pseud*.7(8.80E); as source of superstition, Cyr.H.*catech*.19.8; **4.** as means of diabolical deception ποτὲ μὲν δι' ὀνείρων ἐπιφανείας, ποτὲ δ' αὖ διὰ μαγικῶν στροφῶν χειροῦνται [sc. demons] πάντας τοὺς οὐκ... ὑπὲρ τῆς αὐτῶν σωτηρίας ἀγωνιζομένους Just.*1apol*.14.1(M.6.348B); οἱ νομιζόμενοι θεοὶ τοῖς τινων ἐπιφοιτῶντες μέλεσιν, ἔπειτα δι' ὀνείρων τὴν εἰς αὐτοὺς πραγματευόμενοι δόξαν Tat.*orat*.18(p.20.20; M.6.848A); demons appearing in dreams in form of pagan images, *Hom.Clem*.9.15.

ὀνειδίζω, **1.** *reproach, rebuke* ὀ. ὑμᾶς τὸ πνεῦμα Just.*dial*.37.2(M.6.556B); *ib*.82.4(672A); ὀ. τῷ λαῷ ὡς μὴ ἀξίῳ *ib*.135.5(789A); *reproach* with ὀ...Κέλσος ὀ. τῷ σωτῆρι ἐπὶ τῷ πάθει Or.*Cels*.1.54(p.105.4; M.11.760C); *reproach* for ὀ. τῆς δειλίας Thphn.*chron*.p.164(M.108.440B); **2.** *utter reproaches*, *Ep.Lugd*.ap.Eus.*h.e*.5.1.60(M.20.432B); Or.*Cels*.2.34(p.161.4; M.11.856B); περὶ ἀναστάσεως δὴ εἰ...πολλάκις ὀ. *ib*.8.49(p.264.16; 1589B).

ὀνειδισμός, ὁ, **1.** *reproach* φαρμακείᾳ δὲ ἔοικεν ὁ ὀ. Clem.*paed*.1.8 (p.128.8; M.8.328C); of Christ ὑπομείνας...ὀ. καὶ ἐμπαιγμόν *Const. App*.5.5.3; τοῦ κυρίου βουλομένου ἡμᾶς ὑπομένειν ὀνειδισμοὺς καὶ κακοπάθειαν Marc.Er.*opusc*.8.2(M.65.1104B); ζηλώσωμεν...ἐπὶ πᾶσιν τὸν ὀ. τοῦ Χριστοῦ Jo.D.*hom*.2.6(M.96.585D); **2.** *insult* ὀ. τοῦ Χριστοῦ Synes.*ep*.58(M.66.1400C).

ὀνειδιστέον, *one must rebuke*, Clem.*paed*.3.4(p.251.18; M.8.592B).

***ὀνειδιστέος**, *to be made a ground for reproach*, Clem.*paed*.1.7 (p.125.9; M.8.321B).

ὄνειδος, τό, or **ὁ**, **1.** *reproach* τοῦ...ὀνείδους μεστοῦ μυστηρίου τοῦ σταυροῦ Just.*dial*.131.2(M.6.780C); σιωπῇ τῶν ἐμῶν ὕβρεων πνίγων τὸν ὄ. Bas.*ep*.115(3.207E; M.32.529B); **2.** *disgrace* Νῶε...τὸν ὄ. ἐκαρπώσατο Pall.*v.Chrys*.12(p.78.12; M.47.44).

***ὀνειράζομαι**, *have sexual dreams*, Tim.I Al.*resp*.(M.33.1304C); Phot.*nomoc*.3.19(p.507; M.104.1053D).

ὀνειροκριτικός, *worthy of an interpreter of dreams*, Gr.Naz.*or*.45.12(M.36.637D); Chrys.*fr.Job* 1:3(M.64.520D).

***ὀνειρολύτης, ὁ**, *interpreter of dreams*, Eus.Al.*serm*.21.4(M.86.428B).

[*]ὀνειρόμενος, for ὁμειρόμενος (or ὀμ-) Thdr.Stud.*epp*.2.97(M.99.1349A).

***ὀνειρόομαι**, = ὀνειράζομαι, Sophr.H.*conf*.(M.87.3369B).

ὀνειροπολ-έω, **1.** *dream (of), imagine* δόξῃ, οὐκ ἐπιστήμῃ, ~οῦντας τοῦ καλοῦ τὴν φύσιν Clem.*paed*.2.10(p.220.18; M.8.524A); id.*str*.7.6 (p.24.27; M.9.445A); πῶς τὴν αἰώνιον ζωὴν ἄνευ τοῦ πνεύματος ~εῖς; Didym.(‡Bas.)*Eun*.5(1.310E; M.29.745A); δοῦλον ἀντ' ἐλευθέρου... ~οῦντες τὸν υἱόν Cyr.*Jo*.1.5(4.47E); c. infin., Dion.Al.ap.Eus.*h.e*.3.28.5(M.20.276A); Isid.Pel.*epp*.5.393(M.78.1561D); θεὸς ἔσεσθαι ὀ. ἐξέπεσε Thdt.*Ezech*.31:10f.(2.938); med. Φιλιππικὸν...ἐξώρισεν, ὡς ~ούμενον βασιλεύειν Thphn.*chron*.p.311(M.108.756B); pass. ptcpl., *dreamt of* τὴν ~ουμένην ἐλπίδα Gr.Nyss.*or.dom*.4(p.90.3; M.44.1176C); Nil.*Magn*.56(M.79.1041D); ‡Nil.*narr*.6(M.79.665B); **2.** pass., *be haunted in dreams* ὑπὸ θεοῦ...~εῖσθαι *Hom.Clem*.17.15; **3.** *interpret dreams*, *ib*.9.18; so perh. *interpret* ὀ. τὰ πετεινά i.e. *practise augury*, *Orac.Sib*.1.95.

***ὀνειροπόλημα, τό**, *dream*, Clem.*q.d.s*.25(p.176.9; M.9.629C); *A.Pil*.A 2.1(p.223).

ὀνειροπολία, ἡ, *dreaming*, ref. Gnostics τῆς αὐτῶν ὀ. συζυγιῶν τε καὶ ὀγδοάδων Epiph.*haer*.31.1(p.382.19; M.41.473B); ἡ...ληρολόγος ὀ. *ib*.32.7(p.447.10; 553C).

ὀνειροπομπεία, ἡ, *sending of dreams*, Eus.*d.e*.5 proem.(p.203.7; M.22.336D).

***ὀνειροπομπεῖον, τό**, *vision sent in a dream*, Cyr.*Is*.5.6(2.893D).

ὀνειροπομπός (ὀνειρόπομπος), ὁ, *dream-sender* οἱ λεγόμενοι παρὰ τοῖς μάγοις ὀ. Just.*1apol*.18.3(M.6.356A); Iren.*haer*.1.23.4(M.7.673A); of a kind of demon, *ib*.1.25.3(681B); τοὺς λεγομένους ὀ. δαίμονας ἐπιπέμπουσι [sc. followers of Simon Magus] πρὸς τὸ ταράσσειν οὓς βούλονται Hipp.*haer*.6.20(p.148.2; M.16.3226A); Eus.*h.e*.4.7.9(M.20.317B).

ὄνειρος, ὁ, v. ὄναρ.

***ὀνειροσκόπος, ὁ**, *interpreter of dreams*, Bas.*ep*.210.2(3.314A; M.32.769B); id.*hom.in Ps*.45(1.171D; M.29.417C).

ὀνειρώδης, *dreamy*, Gr.Nyss.*hom.9 in Cant*.(M.44.973C); of Origen's doctrine, *fantastic*, Sophr.H.*ep.syn*.(M.87.3185C); τὸ ὀ. *dream-like nature* τὸ τοῦ κόσμου μάταιον καὶ ὀ.· ὡς οὐδὲν μόνιμον ἐν αὐτῷ, ἀλλὰ παρατρέχον ἴσα καὶ σκιαῖς Thdr.Stud.*epp*.2.51(M.99.1261B).

ὀνησιφόρως, *profitably*, Cyr.*Ps*.32:8(M.69.873B).

ὀνίνημι (also forms as from ὀνέω), **1.** trans., *benefit, help* τὸ μὲν βάπτισμα φασὶ μηδὲν ὀνεῖν τοὺς προσιόντας Thdt.*haer*.4.11(4.366); **2.** intrans., *profit, benefit*, i.e. *be benefited* οὐδὲν ὤνησαν Chrys.*hom.* 78.2 *in Mt.*(7.752D); id.*hom.9.3 in 1Cor.*(10.77B); οὐδὲν μέγα ὀνήσει *ib.32.6*(294B); ὀνοῦντος οὐδέν Thdr.Lect.*fr.*(M.86.225A).

ὀνοειδής, *in the shape of an ass*; of an 'archon' as represented in Ophite diagram, Or.*Cels*.6.30(p.100.22; M.11.1341A); *ib*.7.40(p.191.10; 1477C).

***ὀνοζύγιον, τό,** *yoke-ass*, Pall.*v.Chrys*.10(p.61.18; ὑποζύγιον M.47.35); *ib*.20(p.129.20; M.47.72).

ὀνοκένταυρος, ὁ, *ass-centaur*; attempts to interpret or explain this obscure word: ἀντὶ τοῦ, 'ὀ.', 'σείειν', ἀνέγραψαν, αὐτῇ χρησάμενοι τῇ Ἑβραΐδι φωνῇ διὰ τὸ ἄδηλον τῆς ἑρμηνείας Eus.*Is*.13:22(M.24.189D); τοὺς τῶν ὄνων ἀγρίους ὀ. ὠνόμασεν Cyr.*Is*.2.2(2.226D); καλεῖ ὀ. μὲν ἃς οἱ παλαιοὶ μὲν ἐμπούσας οἱ δὲ νῦν ὀνοσκ⟨ελίδας⟩ προσαγορεύουσι Thdt.*Is*.13:22(p.69.17; 2.265); *ib*.34:11(p.139.1; 2.315).

ὄνομα, τό, A. *name*; **1.** of God; **a.** no name can express essential nature ὀ. τῷ ἀρρήτῳ θεῷ οὐδεὶς ἔχει εἰπεῖν Just.*1apol*.61.11(M.6.421B); οὐδὲν ὀ. ἐπὶ θεοῦ κυριολογεῖσθαι δυνατόν ‡Just.*coh.Gr*.21(M.6.277A); ἡ θεία φύσις ἐν πᾶσι τοῖς ἐπινοουμένοις ὀνόμασι, καθὸ ἐστι, μένει ἀσήμαντος Gr.Nyss.*Trin*.(p.80.16; M.32.696A); ὀ. τῆς θείας φύσεως σημαντικὸν οὐκ ἐμάθομεν id.*Eun*.7(2 p.169.26; M.45.760D); λεγόμενος...ὢν δὲ ὡς οὐκ ἔχων ὀ. γνωριστικὸν τῆς οὐσίας, ἀλλὰ πάσης ὑπερκείμενος τῆς ὀνοματικῆς σημασίας *ib*.11(2 p.264.29; 873A); πᾶν ὀ. εἴτε παρὰ τῆς ἀνθρωπίνης συνηθείας ἐξεύρηται, εἴτε παρὰ τῶν γραφῶν παραδέδοται, τῶν τι περὶ τὴν θείαν φύσιν νοουμένων ἑρμηνευτικὸν εἶναι λέγομεν, οὐκ αὐτῆς δὲ τῆς φύσεως περιέχειν τὴν σημασίαν id.*tres dii* (M.45.121A); οὐδὲ τό, θεός, ὀ. οὐσίας ἐστίν, οὐδὲ ἔστιν ὅλως τῆς οὐσίας ἐκείνης ὀ. εὑρεῖν Chrys.*hom.2.2 in Heb.*(12.17B,C); οὐδὲν οὐδαμῇ πω πέφηνεν ὀ. τῆς οὐσίας ἁπτόμενον τοῦ θεοῦ Synes.*regn*.9(p.18.12; M.66.1065C); τῆς οὐσίας αὐτοῦ μὴ ἐκζητήσωμεν ὀ. Jo.D.*f.o*.1.12(M.94.845B); **b.** God being named from his operations τὸ δὲ πατὴρ καὶ θεὸς...οὐκ ὀνόματά ἐστιν, ἀλλ' ἐκ τῶν εὐποιϊῶν καὶ τῶν ἔργων προσρήσεις Just.*2apol*.6.2(M.6.453A); κατὰ τὴν τῶν ἐνεργειῶν διαφοράν, καὶ τὴν πρὸς τὰ εὐεργετούμενα σχέσιν, διάφορα ἑαυτῷ καὶ τὰ ὀ. τίθεται. φῶς μὲν γὰρ ἑαυτὸν τοῦ κόσμου λέγει...ἄμπελον δέ...ἄρτον δέ Bas.*Eun*.1.7(1.218D; M.29.525A); ὁ ὑπὲρ πᾶν ὀ. ὢν ἡμῖν πολυώνυμος γίνεται κατὰ τὰς τῶν εὐεργεσιῶν ποικιλίας ὀνομαζόμενος, φῶς...ζωή...ὁδός Gr.Nyss.*Eun*.10(2 p.230.7; M.45.832A); ἄλλο μέν τί ἐστιν ἡ οὐσία...ἑτέρα δὲ τῶν περὶ αὐτὴν ὀνομάτων ἡ σημασία ἐξ ἐνεργείας τινὸς ἢ ἀξίας ὀνομαζομένων id.*Trin*.8(p.80.25; M.32.696B); Thdt.*Ps.* 17:2f.(1.702); **c.** various instances of divine names: God named by negation, or affirmation ἐν τοῖς περὶ θεοῦ λεγομένοις ὀνόμασι, τὰ μέν, τῶν προσόντων τῷ θεῷ δηλωτικά ἐστι· τὰ δέ, τὸ ἐναντίον, τῶν μὴ προσόντων...ἄφθαρτον...ἀόρατον...ἀγαθόν...δίκαιον Bas.*Eun*.1.10(1.222C; M.29.533C); ὅτι καὶ τόπος γίνεται ὁ θεὸς τοῖς ἀξίοις, καὶ οἶκος, καὶ ἔνδυμα...καὶ πᾶν νόημά τε καὶ ὀ. τῶν πρὸς τὴν ἀγαθὴν ἡμῖν συντελούντων ζωήν Gr.Nyss.*anim.et res*.(M.46.104B); id.*Eun*.1(1 pp.182.15–183.2; M.45.428A,B); τούτων δέ φαμεν τῶν ὀ. οὐ μονοειδῆ πάντων εἶναι τὴν σημασίαν, ἀλλὰ τὰ μὲν τῶν προσόντων τῷ θεῷ, τὰ δὲ τῶν ἀποπεφυκότων ἔχει τὴν ἔμφασιν *ib*.12(1 p.252.17; 953B); id.*tres dii*(M.45.133A); id.*nativ*.(M.46.1149A); τοῦτο γοῦν εἰδότες οἱ θεολόγοι, καὶ ὡς ἀνώνυμον αὐτὴν [sc. deity] ὑμνοῦσι, καὶ ἐκ παντὸς ὀ. ἀνώνυμον μὲν...πολυώνυμον δέ, ὡς ὅταν αὖθις αὐτὴν εἰσάγωσι φάσκουσαν· ἐγώ εἰμι ὁ ὤν· ἡ ζωή, τὸ φῶς...καὶ ὅταν αὐτοὶ τὸν πάντων αἴτιον οἱ θεόσοφοι πολυωνύμως ἐκ πάντων τῶν αἰτιατῶν ὑμνῶσιν, ὡς ἀγαθόν, ὡς καλόν...ὡς θεὸν θεῶν Dion.Ar.*d.n*.1.6(M.3.596A); δοκεῖ μὲν οὖν κυριώτερον πάντων τῶν ἐπὶ θεοῦ λεγομένων ὀ. εἶναι ὁ ὤν Jo.D.*f.o*.1.9(M.94.836A); διὸ τῶν θείων ὀ., τὰ μὲν ἀποφατικῶς λέγεται, δηλοῦντα τὸ ὑπερούσιον· οἷον ἀνούσιος, ἄχρονος, ἄναρχος...τὰ δὲ καταφατικῶς λεγόμενα, ὡς αἰτίου τῶν πάντων κατηγορεῖται. ὡς γὰρ αἴτιος πάντων τῶν ὄντων καὶ πάσης οὐσίας, καὶ ὢν λέγεται, καὶ οὐσία *ib*.1.12(845C); **d.** name or names of Trin. οὕτως ὁ εἰπὼν ὄνομα πατρὸς καὶ υἱοῦ καὶ ἁγίου πνεύματος, τρία εἰπών, συνέπλεξεν αὐτὰ τῷ συνδέσμῳ, ἑκάστῳ ὀνόματι ἴδιον ὑποβεβλῆσθαι τὸ σημαινόμενον ἐκδιδάσκων· διότι πραγμάτων ἐστὶ σημαντικὰ τὰ ὀ. ... φύσις μὲν ἡ αὐτή...ὀνόματα δὲ διάφορα, περιωρισμένας καὶ ἀπηρτισμένας τὰς ἐννοίας ἡμῖν παριστῶντα Bas.*ep*.210.4(3.315E,316A; M.32.773B,C); ταῦτα μὲν οὖν ἔτι κοινὰ θεότητος τὰ ὀ. ἴδιον δὲ τοῦ μὲν ἀνάρχου, πατήρ· τοῦ δὲ ἀνάρχως γεννηθέντος, υἱός· τοῦ δὲ ἀγεννήτως προελθόντος, ἢ προϊόντος, τὸ πνεῦμα τὸ ἅγιον Gr.Naz.*or.* 30.19(p.138.9; M.36.128C); ἡ τριὰς οὐκ ἐν ψιλοῖς τοῖς ὀ., ἀλλ' ἐν ταῖς ὑποστάσεσι γνωρίζεται Thdt.*Trin*.28(M.75.1188C); τὰ δὲ διακεκριμένα, τὸ πατρὸς ὑπερούσιον ὀ. καὶ χρῆμα, καὶ υἱοῦ, καὶ πνεύματος, οὐδεμιᾶς ἐν τούτοις ἀντιστροφῆς, ἢ ὅλως κοινότητος ἐπεισαγομένης Dion.Ar.*d.n*.2.3(M.3.640C); ἐν ὀ. μὲν εἰπών, εἰς τρεῖς δὲ ὑποστάσεις διελών Cosm.Ind.*top*.5(M.88.312C); partic.; **i.** of Father ὅτι οὔτε οὐσίας ὀ. ὁ πατήρ...οὔτε ἐνεργείας, σχέσεως δὲ καὶ τοῦ πῶς ἔχει πρὸς τὸν υἱὸν ὁ πατήρ, ἢ ὁ υἱὸς πρὸς τὸν πατέρα Gr.Naz.*or*.29.16(p.98.6; M.36.96A); **ii.** of Son οἴδαμεν γὰρ ὅτι πάντων τῶν ὀ., δι' ὧν τὸ θεῖον διασημαίνεται, τινὰ μὲν ἐνδεικτικὰ τῆς θείας μεγαλωσύνης ἐστίν, αὐτὰ ἐφ' ἑαυτῶν λεγόμενά τε καὶ νοούμενα, τινὰ δὲ ταῖς ὑπὲρ ἡμᾶς τε καὶ πᾶσαν τὴν κτίσιν ἐνεργείαις ἐπονομάζεται. ... ἀφθάρτῳ, ἀοράτῳ. ... ἀληθινὸς χρηστὸς [v.l. Χριστὸς] κύριος ἰατρὸς ποιμὴν ὁδὸς ἄρτος Gr.Nyss.*Eun*.2(2 p.346.15; M.45.524A); ἀλλ' ἔστιν...διχῇ διελέσθαι τῶν θείων ὀ. τὴν σημασίαν. τὰ μὲν γὰρ τῆς ὑψηλῆς τε καὶ ἀφράστου δόξης τὴν ἔνδειξιν ἔχει, τὰ δὲ τὸ ποικίλον τῆς προνοητικῆς οἰκονομίας ἐνδείκνυται·...ἄμπελος...ποιμήν...ἰατρός...υἱὸς δὲ καὶ δεξιὰ καὶ μονογενὴς καὶ λόγος καὶ σοφία καὶ δύναμις καὶ τὰ τοιαῦτα πάντα, ὅσα πρός τι λέγεται, καθάπερ ἐν συζυγίᾳ τινὶ σχετικῇ τῷ πατρὶ πάντως συνονομαζόμενος λέγεται *ib*.3(2 p.43.31; 612B); ὀνόματα δὲ τὰ πρὸ τῆς ἐνανθρωπήσεως οἰκείως πως ἔχοντα τῇ αὐτοῦ φύσει, θεός, καὶ σοφία... ἐπειδὴ δὲ καθῆκεν ἑαυτὸν εἰς κένωσιν ἐν ὁμοιώματι ἀνθρώπου γενόμενος...ὄνομα δέχεται τὸ κοινόν, τοῦτ' ἔστι, τὸ Χριστός τε καὶ Ἰησοῦς, ἤτοι τό, Μεθ' ἡμῶν ὁ θεός...ἀνάρμοστον οὖν ἄρα τῷ θεῷ λόγῳ πρὸ τῆς γεννήσεως τῆς κατὰ σάρκα φημὶ τὸ Χριστοῦ ὀ.· κεχρισμένος γὰρ οὔπω, πῶς ἂν λέγοιτο Χριστός; Cyr.*Is*.4.4(2.656A–E); **iii.** of H. Ghost ἐγὼ μὲν φρίττω τὸν πλοῦτον ἐννοῶν τῶν κλήσεων, καὶ καθ' ὅσων ὀνομάτων ἀναισχυντοῦσιν οἱ τῷ πνεύματι ἀντιπίπτοντες. πνεῦμα θεοῦ λέγεται, πνεῦμα Χριστοῦ...ἀγαθόν...ἁγιάζον...δάκτυλος θεοῦ, πῦρ...ποιοῦν ἀποστόλους Gr.Naz.*or*.31.29(p.183.2; M.36.165B); **iv.** names of Father and Son confused (Patripassian and Sabellian) ἓν καὶ τὸ αὐτὸ φάσκων ὑπάρχειν...ὀνόματι μὲν πατέρα καὶ υἱὸν καλούμενον κατὰ χρόνων τροπήν Hipp.*haer*.9.10(p.245.2; M.16.3378B); in teaching of Marcellus λόγον αὐτὸν μόνον διδοὺς...ὀνόμασιν μὲν διαφόροις πατρὸς καὶ υἱοῦ χρηματίζοντα οὐσίᾳ δὲ καὶ ὑποστάσει ἓν ὄντα, πῶς οὐ δῆλος ἂν γένοιτο τὸν μὲν Σαβέλλιον ὑποδυόμενος Eus.*Marcell*.1.1(p.4.25; M.24.720A); διὰ τοῦτο Σαβέλλιος ἀλλότριος τῆς ἐκκλησίας ἐκρίθη, τολμήσας εἰπεῖν ἐπὶ τοῦ πατρὸς τὸ υἱός, καὶ ἐπὶ τοῦ υἱοῦ τὸ τοῦ πατρὸς ὀ. Ath.*ep.Serap*.4.5(M.26.644D); μαίνεται δὲ καὶ Σαβέλλιος λέγων τὸν πατέρα εἶναι υἱόν, καὶ ἔμπαλιν τὸν υἱὸν εἶναι πατέρα, ὑποστάσει μὲν ἕν, ὀνόματι δὲ δύο ‡Ath.*Ar*.4.25(p.72.22; M.26.505C); **v.** different names of Father and Son not implying different essences ἐπὶ πατρὸς καὶ υἱοῦ οὐχὶ οὐσίαν παρίστησι τὰ ὀ., ἀλλὰ τῶν ἰδιωμάτων ἐστὶ δηλωτικά· ὥστε μηδεμίαν εἶναι χώραν τῷ λόγῳ, ἐκ τῆς τῶν ὀ. παραλλαγῆς τὴν τῶν οὐσιῶν ἐναντίωσιν παρεισάγοντι Bas.*Eun*.2.5(1.241C; M.29.580C); οὐκ οὐσίας ἡμεῖς ταῦτα [sc. ἀγέννητος and γεννητός] λέγομεν, ὀνόματα δὲ δηλοῦντα τὴν ἑκάστου αὐτῶν ὕπαρξιν. οὐδὲν δὲ κωλύει διαφόρων ὀνομάτων μίαν οὐσίαν εἶναι Didym.(‡Bas.)*Eun*.4(1.285A; M.29.685A); **e.** name of God in baptism; **i.** of Trin., *Did*.7.1; Just.*1apol*.61.3 (M.6.420C); *A.Phil*.86(p.34.5); *A.Xanthipp*.21(p.73.6,13); *Const.App*.7.44.1; Ath.*decr*.31(p.27.24; M.25.473C); Bas.*Eun*.3.5(1.276E; M.29.665C); Thdr.Stud.*epp*.2.24(M.99.1192A); in a baptism by means of sand, Jo.Mosch.*prat*.176(M.87.3045A); in self-baptism, *A.Paul.et Thecl*.34(p.260.7); **ii.** of the Lord or Christ, *Did*.9.5; Herm.*vis*.3.7.3; cf.Or.*comm.in Rom*.5.8(M.14.1039C); baptism in name of the Lord only held to be insufficient, Bas.*Spir*.28(3.23B; M.32.116C); cf. ὁ δὲ ὑπεξαιρούμενός τι τῆς τριάδος, καὶ ἐν μόνῳ τῷ τοῦ πατρὸς ὀ. βαπτιζόμενος, ἢ ἐν μόνῳ τῷ ὀ. τοῦ υἱοῦ, ἢ χωρίς γε τοῦ πνεύματος ἐν πατρὶ καὶ υἱῷ, οὐδὲν λαμβάνει Ath.*ep.Serap*.1.30(M.26.597C); **iii.** mere repetition of names insufficient without right faith, id.*Ar*.2.43(M.26.237B); **iv.** Elchezaite βαπτισάσθω...ἐν ὀ. τοῦ μεγάλου καὶ ὑψίστου θεοῦ Hipp.*haer*.9.15(p.254.15; M.16.3391C); **f.** in Lord's Prayer ἅγιόν ἐστι τῇ φύσει τὸ τοῦ θεοῦ ὀ. ... εὐχόμεθα ἐν ἡμῖν ἁγιασθῆναι τὸ ὀ. τοῦ θεοῦ Cyr.H.*catech*.23.12; τὸ μὴ βλασφημεῖσθαι ἐν τῷ ἐμῷ βίῳ τὸ ὀ. τοῦ θεοῦ, ἀλλὰ δοξάζεσθαι καὶ ἁγιάζεσθαι Gr.Nyss.*or.dom*.3(p.54.5; M.44.1153C); Sever.*creat*.1.7(M.56.437); τὸ ὀ. ἐστι τοῦ υἱοῦ τοῦ θεοῦ τὸ ἐπικληθὲν ἐφ' ἡμᾶς, Χριστός ‡Bas.*h.myst*.61 (p.396.23); **g.** in other prayers; eucharistic prayer εὐχαριστοῦμέν σοι, πάτερ ἅγιε, ὑπὲρ τοῦ ἁγίου ὀ. σου *Did*.10.2; δόξαν τῷ πατρὶ...διὰ τοῦ ὀνόματος τοῦ υἱοῦ καὶ τοῦ πνεύματος τοῦ ἁγίου ἀναπέμπει καὶ... εὐχαριστίαν...ποιεῖται Just.*1apol*.65.3(M.6.428A); ἐπιφημιζόμέν σε τὸ τῆς μητρὸς ὀ. ... ἐπιφημιζόμέν σε ὀνόματί σου Ἰησοῦ *A.Thom*.A 133(p.240.12); *Lit.Jac*.(p.238.19); at the dismissal, *Lit.Chrys*.(p.343.14); *Lit.Praesanct*.(p.352.10); at anointing, *A.Thom*.A 27(pp.142.13,143.3); *ib*.157(p.267.11,13); in blessing of oil, *Const.App*.7.42.3; of oil and water, Serap.*euch*.17.1,2; of sick persons ἐν τῷ ὀ. τοῦ μονογενοῦς σου θεραπευθήτωσαν, γενέσθω αὐτοῖς φάρμακον τὸ ἅγιον αὐτοῦ ὀ. εἰς ὑγείαν *ib*.8.2; at ordination of bishop, *Lit*.ap.*Const.App*. 8.5.6; **h.** name or names of Christ; **i.** as God and man ἀληθὲς γάρ ἐστιν ἐπ' ἀμφοτέρων τὸ ἓν ὀ., ἔν τε τῇ θεότητι καὶ ἐν τῇ ⟨ἐν⟩ανθρωπήσει Epiph.*haer*.69.42(p.190.5; M.42.268B); ἐν αὐτῷ τῷ ὀ. ἑνὶ ὄντι ἑκατέρων τῶν πραγμάτων δείκνυται σημασία, θεότητός τε καὶ ἀνθρωπότητος ‡Ath.*Apoll*.1.13(M.26.1116B); διὸ καὶ τὰ μεγάλα καὶ θεοπρεπῆ τῶν ὀ. τῷ ἀνθρωπίνῳ κυρίως ἐφήρμοσται καὶ τὸ ἔμπαλιν διὰ τῶν ἀνθρωπίνων ἡ θεότης κατονομάζεται Gr.Nyss.*Eun*.6(2 p.150.22; M. 45.737A); **ii.** name Jesus, v. Ἰησοῦς; Just.*1apol*.33.7(M.6.381C); its letters, taken numerically, add up to 888, Iren.*haer*.1.15.2(M.7. 616A); **iii.** power of Christ's name, in Church's missionary enterprise, Eus.*d.e*.3.7(p.142.20; M.22.240B); in expulsion of demons, Just.*dial*.30.3(M.6.540B); ὁ ἡμέτερος Ἰησοῦς, οὗ τὸ ὄ. μυρίους ἤδη ἐναργῶς ἑώραται δαίμονας ἐξελάσαν ψυχῶν καὶ σωμάτων Or.*Cels*.1.25 (p.76.13; M.11.708A); ἔνθα γὰρ ὀνομάζεται τὸ ὄ. τοῦ σωτῆρος, ἐκεῖθεν πᾶς δαίμων ἀπελαύνεται Ath.*inc*.50.4(M.25.185B); in gen. ἔτι γε τὸ ὄ. τοῦ Ἰησοῦ ἐκστάσεις μὲν διανοίας ἀνθρώπων ἀφίστησι καὶ δαίμονας ἤδη δὲ καὶ νόσους, ἐμποιεῖ δὲ θαυμασίαν τινὰ πρᾳότητα καὶ καταστολὴν τοῦ ἤθους καὶ φιλανθρωπίαν Or.*Cels*.1.67(p.121.23; M.11. 785C); ἐν τῷ ὀ. τούτῳ θάνατος ἐλύθη, δαίμονες ἐδέθησαν, οὐρανὸς ἀνεῴχθη...πνεῦμα κατεπέμφθη Chrys.*exp.in Ps*.8:2(5.78B); πῶς δὲ τὸ ὄ. αὐτοῦ ἅγιον καὶ φοβερόν; δαίμονες αὐτὸ τρέμουσι, νοσήματα αὐτὸ δέδοικε, τούτῳ κεχρημένοι τῷ ὀ. οἱ ἀπόστολοι τὴν οἰκουμένην κατώρθωσαν ἅπασαν *ib*.110:9(275D); **iv.** ref. entrance into kingdom εἰς τὴν βασιλείαν τοῦ θεοῦ οὐδεὶς εἰσελεύσεται, εἰ μὴ λάβοι τὸ ὄ. τοῦ υἱοῦ αὐτοῦ Herm.*sim*.9.12.4; **v.** ref. persecution δεδεμένον...ὑπὲρ τοῦ κοινοῦ ὀ. καὶ ἐλπίδος Ign.*Eph*.1.2; *ib*.3.1; ἀρνεῖσθαι ἡμᾶς τὸ ὄ. τοῦ Χριστοῦ ἀγωνιζομένων, θανατοῦσθαι μᾶλλον αἱρούμεθα καὶ ὑπομένομεν Just. *dial*.96.2(M.6.704B); διώκοντας τοὔνομα Clem.*str*.7.1(p.3.6; M.9. 401B); *Const.App*.4.9.2; εἴ τις Χριστιανὸς διὰ τὸ ὄ. τοῦ Χριστοῦ... κατακριθῇ ὑπὸ ἀσεβῶν εἰς λοῦδον ἢ θηρία ἢ μέταλλον... *ib*.5.1.1; *Lit*. *ib*.8.10.15; **vi.** ref. nominal Christians δόλῳ πονηρῷ τὸ ὄ. περιφέρειν Ign.*Eph*.7.1; τῶν ἐν ὑποκρίσει φερόντων τὸ ὄ. τοῦ κυρίου Polyc.*ep*. 6.3; ἐὰν τὸ ὄ. φορῇς, τὴν δὲ δύναμιν μὴ φορῇς αὐτοῦ, εἰς μάτην ἔσῃ τὸ ὄ. αὐτοῦ φορῶν Herm.*sim*.9.13.2; μὴ τοίνυν ὑποδυόμενοι τὸ ὄ. τοῦ Χριστοῦ καὶ τῶν ἐν ἔθνεσιν ἀκρατεστάτων ἀκολαστότερον βιοῦντες βλασφημίαν τῷ ὀ. προστριβέσθωσαν Clem.*str*.3.1(pp.196.22f.; M.8. 1104A); ὀνομάζουσι τὸ Ἰησοῦ ὄ., οὐκ ἔχουσι δὲ τὸν Ἰησοῦν Or.*hom*. *10.5 in Jer*.(p.75.24; M.13.364C); διαφέρει γὰρ τὸ πιστεύειν εἰς αὐτὸν τοῦ πιστεύειν εἰς τὸ ὄ. αὐτοῦ...διὰ τοῦτο τῷ πιστεύοντι εἰς τὸ ὄ. αὐτοῦ ἑαυτὸν οὐ πιστεύει ὁ Ἰησοῦς id.*Jo*.10.44(28; p.223.1ff.; M.14.393C); καὶ ὅρα ⟨εἰ⟩ οἱ εἰσαγόμενοι εἰς εὐλάβειαν σημαίνονται τῷ φοβεῖσθαι τὸ ὄ. τοῦ θεοῦ, οἱ δὲ αὐτὸν καὶ μὴ τὸ ὄ. αὐτοῦ ἔτι φοβούμενοι τῇ τῶν ἁγίων προσηγορίᾳ id.*Apoc*.37(p.14); **2.** of BMV τοῦτο γὰρ τὸ ὄ. [sc. Theotokos] οὐδεὶς τῶν ἐκκλησιαστικῶν διδασκάλων παρῄτηται Jo.Ant. *ep.Nest*.4(p.95.19; M.77.1456A); in arithmetical sum of letters of *Μαρία*: οὔνομα δὲ αὐτῆς δὶς ἑβδομήκοντα ἕξ *Pers*.(p.9.3); **3.** efficacy of invocation of saint's name, Niceph.Ur.*v.Sym*.50(M.86.3033A); **4.** name of Christian τὸ πρῶτον καὶ ἐξαίρετον ὄ. Χριστιανός *M.Carp*. 3; ἔτι δὲ φῂς με καὶ Χριστιανὸν ὡς κακὸν τοὔνομα φοροῦντα, ἐγὼ μὲν οὖν ὁμολογῶ εἶναι Χριστιανός, καὶ φορῶ τὸ θεοφιλὲς ὄ. τοῦτο Thphl. Ant.*Autol*.1.1(M.6.1025A); *Dial.Ath.et Zacch*.57(p.35); δότε μοι τὰ ὀ., ἵνα ἐγὼ μὲν αὐτὰ ταῖς αἰσθηταῖς ἐγχαράξω βίβλοις...θεὸς δὲ ταῖς ἀφθάρτοις πλαξὶν ἐνσημήνηται Gr.Nyss.*bapt.diff*.(M.46.417B); **5.** scriptural names treated as edifying puns, Or.*Jo*.2.33(27; p.90. 12,18; M.14.172B,C); †Cyr.*coll.VT*(6^4.62D; M.77.1268D).

B. *person*, Ign.*Rom*.10.1; ἀσπάζομαι Ἄλκην, τὸ ποθητόν μοι ὄ. id.*Polyc*.8.3; Epiph.*haer*.26.17(p.298.16; M.41.360D); Chrys.*hom.11. 1 in Eph*.(11.80E); Cyr.S.*v.Sab*.16(p.100.3); ὀνόματα ἀρρενικῶν τε καὶ θηλυκῶν Jo.Mal.*chron*.3 p.60(M.97.137B); *ib*.11 p.276(417B); μοναστήριόν ἐστι παρθένων ὡς ὀνομάτων τεσσαράκοντα Jo.Mosch. *prat*.135(M.87.2997D).

C. in phrases; **1.** εἰς ὄνομα; **a.** *in the name* of, Just.*dial*.53.6(M.6. 593C); Epiph.*haer*.14.3(p.208.14; M.41.241A); ἄρτον προτιθέασι καὶ ἀναφέρουσιν εἰς ὄ. τῆς Μαρίας *ib*.79.1(p.476.18; M.42.741A); ref. heret. baptism οὐκ εἰς ὄ. ἀγενήτου καὶ γενητοῦ...ἀλλ' εἰς ὄ. πατρὸς κτλ. Ath.*decr*.31(p.27.24; M.25.473C); εἰ εἰς ὄ. πατρὸς καὶ υἱοῦ δίδοται ἡ τελείωσις, οὐ λέγουσι δὲ πατέρα ἀληθινὸν...ἀρνοῦνται...τὸν υἱόν id.*Ar*.2.42(M.26.236C); **b.** *after the name* of (cf. Gen.4:17), Jo. Mal.*chron*.proem.p.4(M.97.65B); **2.** ἐν ὀ. *in the name* of, Ign.*Eph*.1. 3; *Did*.12:1; Arsen.Hyps.*ep*.(p.147.15; M.25.372B); **3.** ἐξ ὀνόματος, *by name* ἀσπάζομαι πάντας ἐξ ὀ. Ign.*Polyc*.8.2; Clem.*str*.7.11(p.46.4; M.9.488C); *Const.App*.3.4.3; **4.** ἐπ' ὀνόματι *in the name* of ἐπ' ὀ. εἰδώλων Athenag.*leg*.23.1(M.6.941B); ἐπ' ὀ. τοῦ θεοῦ Cosm.Ind.*top*. 3(M.88.140A); *under the false name* of ὁ ἐπ' ὀ. προσφορῶν τὴν δωροληψίαν ἐπιτεχνώμενος Apollon.ap.Eus.*h.e*.5.18.2(M.20.476B); *under a pretence* of τοὺς ἁρπάζοντας γυναῖκας ἐπ' ὀ. συνοικεσίου CChalc.*can*. 27; **5.** μέχρι ὀνόματος, *in name and nothing else, so-called* αἱ δημοτελεῖς μέχρι ὀ. ἑορταί Or.*Cels*.8.21(p.238.27; M.11.1549B).

ὀνομάζ-ω, *call by name* κἂν ~ωμεν αὐτό ποτε [sc. τὸ θεῖον] οὐ κυρίως καλοῦντες Clem.*str*.5.12(p.380.25; M.9.121B); *call on, worship*, id.*prot*.2(p.17.25; M.8.89B); οὐ δεῖ Χριστιανοὺς ἐγκαταλείπειν τὴν ἐκκλησίαν τοῦ θεοῦ...καὶ ἀγγέλους ~ειν CLaod.*can*.35; pass., *be called by the name* of, *dedicated* to, Chrys.*hom.15.1 in 1Tim*. (11.634C); *term* κακία...ἣν ὠνόμασε λιθίνην καρδίαν Or.*princ*.3.1.15 (p.222.17; M.11.280B); *assert, profess*, id.*Cels*.8.65(p.281.21; M.11. 1616A); τὸν...ἐν τῷ πατρὶ ὄντα...~ειν ὑπό τινος ἔξωθεν βελτιοῦσθαι, πᾶσαν ὑπερβάλλει μανίαν Ath.*decr*.16(p.13.26; M.25.441D); προσποιούμενοι...~ειν τὴν...ἐν Νικαίᾳ πίστιν id.*tom*.3(M.26.800A); pass. μίαν ὑπόστασιν ~εσθαι *Symb.Nic*.(359)ap.Thdt.*h.e*.2.21.7(3.881); *mention*, Just.*dial*.53.4(M.6.593A); *put forward* ~ειν...σύνοδόν τινα ὡς ἐν Ἀριμήνῳ γενομένην Ath.*ep.Afr*.1(M.26.1032A); *nominate* for office, id.*apol.sec*.29(p.109.2; M.25.297B).

ὀνομασία, ἡ, 1. *naming, giving of name*, Just.*dial*.130.4(M.6. 780A); of Adam naming animals and Eve, Clem.*str*.1.21(p.84.7; M. 8.869C); of naming of Christ, Or.*Jo*.1.20(22; p.25.12; M.14.57C); of pagan gods, Ath.*gent*.16(M.25.33A); **2.** *name, designation* τῶν αἱρέσεων ἀνάγκη τὴν ὀ. πρὸς ἀντιδιαστολὴν τῆς ἀληθείας λέγεσθαι Clem.*str*.7.15(p.65.32; M.9.528C); Or.*or*.3(p.304.20; M.11.424C); εἴτε βάπτισμα εἴτε φώτισμα...βούλοιτό τις ὀνομάζειν, οὐδὲν πρὸς τὴν ὀ. διαφερόμεθα Gr.Nyss.*or.catech*.32(p.122.13; M.45.84A); Diod.*Gen*.2:7 (M.33.1565D); Cyr.*Os*.40(3.81A); ref. God οὐδεὶς τῆς αὐτοῦ κοινωνεῖ ὀ., τοῦτο δὴ λέγεται θεός *Hom.Clem*.3.37; τοῦ πατρὸς ὄνομα ἅμα τῷ τῆς ὀ. προσρήματι νοεῖν παρέχει καὶ τὸν υἱόν Cyr.H.*catech*.7.4; τοῦ θεοῦ τιμὴν καὶ ὀ. Thdr.Mops.*Os*.5:10(M.66.157B); ref. humanity assumed in Inc. συναναφέρεται τῇ τε ὀ. καὶ τῇ τιμῇ τοῦ τε υἱοῦ καὶ τοῦ κυρίου id.*symb*.(p.99.3; M.66.1017D); of H. Ghost ἄλλας πολλὰς ὀ. τοῦ ἁγίου πνεύματος εὑρήσεις Cyr.H.*catech*.17.5; **3.** *mention, ib*.; **4.** *classification*, Or.*or*.27(p.371.23; M.11.516C).

***ὀνομαστήρια, τά**, *name-giving day*, Gr.Naz.*or*.40.1(M.36.360B).

ὀνοματίζ-ω, *make idle use of a name* Ἰσραὴλ παιδὸς αὐτοῦ· οὐκ ~ει, τὸν ἀληθινὸν [sc. Ἰσραήλ] σημαίνει Antip.Bost.*annunt*.25(M.85. 1792B).

***ὀνοματογραφέω**, *enter names in a list, enrol*; newly baptized, Cyr.H.*catech*.3.2; Max.*schol.e.h*.2.2(M.4.125A).

ὀνοματογραφία, ἡ, *registration, enrolment*; for baptism, Cyr.H. *procatech*.1.

ὀνοματοθέτης, ὁ, *framer of words*, ‡Ath.*def*.(M.28.533C).

ὀνοματομάχος, ὁ, *fighter about the use of a term*, Leont.B.*Nest.et Eut*.1(M.86.1304A); cf.id.*fr*.(M.86.2008D).

ὀνοματοποιΐα, ἡ, *coining names* or *words*; of Gnost. appellations of aeons, Iren.*haer*.1.11.4(M.7.565A); Epiph.*haer*.31.3(p.387.2; M. 41.477B); *ib*.76.15(p.361.27; M.42.548B); μὴ κατατολμᾶν ἐπὶ τῶν θείων δογμάτων τῆς ὀ. Gr.Nyss.*Eun*.4(2 p.52.6; M.45.621C); τῷ θεῷ τὴν ὀ. ἡμέρας τε καὶ νυκτὸς ὁ Μωϋσῆς ἀνατίθησιν id.*hex*.15(M.44. 77B); id.*Apoll*.2(M.45.1125C); of use by Bible of foreign words, Isid.Pel.*epp*.4.28(M.78.1080D); Max.*opusc*.(M.91.225B).

***ὀνοράριος**, (Lat. *honorarius*) honorary, Ath.Scholast.*coll*.7.3 (p.93); cf. νονοράρια *ib*.18 paratit.6(p.169).

ὀνοσκελίς, ἡ, *she with ass's legs*; of female demon, *T.Sal*.4.2(p.18. 6; M.122.1320D); Thdt.*Is*.13:22(p.69.18; 2.265) cit. s. ὀνοκένταυρος; *ib*.34:11(p.139.1; 2.315).

ὀντότης, ἡ, *principle of being, reality*, in gen. ἡ οὐσία τοῦ τε εἶναι καὶ ζῆν...ὀρέγεται, τῆς οἰκείας ἐφιεμένη φυσικῆς καὶ πλήρους ὀ. Max. *opusc*.(M.91.12C); οὐσία ἐστὶ...ἡ κατὰ πολλῶν καὶ διαφερόντων ταῖς ὑποστάσεσιν ὀ. φυσική *ib*.(276A); τῆς τοῦ ἀνθρώπου ἀληθοῦς ὀ. ... ἔκπτωσις id.*ep*.10(M.91.449C); τὸ...θεωθῆναι τῇ πρὸς θεὸν ἑνώσει... τῆς κατ' οὐσίαν ὀ. οὐκ ἐξίστησιν id.*opusc*.(189C); of God ὁ ὢν... ἐστι...χρόνων ὀ. καὶ αἰὼν τῶν ὄντων Dion.Ar.*d.n*.5.4(M.3.817C); οὐκ ἔστιν ὁ θεὸς οὐσία...ἀλλὰ οὐσιοποιὸς καὶ ὑπερούσιος ὀ. Max.*cap.theol*. 1.4(M.90.1084C); id.*ambig*.(M.91.1172C); μονὰς...οὐ...ἔστιν ἀρχὴ τῶν μετ' αὐτήν,...ἀλλ' ἐνυπόστατος ὀ. τῆς ὁμοουσίου τριάδος *ib*.(1036B); οὐχ ὁρᾶται τὸ ὁλικὸν τῆς τριαδικῆς ὀ. ἐν τῇ ἰδικῇ ὑποστάσει τοῦ λόγου Anast.S.*hod*.17(M.89.264B); ἡ οὐσία τοῦ...εἶναι ὀρέγεται, τῆς οἰκείας ἐφιεμένη φύσεως, καὶ πλήρους ὀντότητος Jo.D.*volunt*.28(M.95.161A); ἐγὼ εἰμὶ ὁ ὤν, οὐχὶ ὀ. Thdr.Stud.*epp*.2.67(M.99.1296A).

ὄντως, *essentially, really, truly* προστάγματι τοῦ ὄ. θεοῦ Arist. *apol*.4.1(M.96.1109A); ὅταν τὸν ὄ. θάνατον φοβηθῇς, ὃς φυλάσσεται τοῖς κατακριθησομένοις εἰς τὸ πῦρ τὸ αἰώνιον *Diogn*.10.7; υἱὸν αὐτοῦ τοῦ ὄ. θεοῦ Just.*1apol*.13.3(M.6.348A); id.*dial*.74.2(M.6.649A); τῇ περὶ τὸ ὄ. θεῖον εὐσεβείᾳ Athenag.*leg*.7.2(M.6.904C); *ib*.15.3(920B); θεὸν...τὸ ὄ. ὂν...τὸ ἀγαθὸν ἀπ' αὐτοῦ ἀποχεόμενον *ib*.23.4(944B); μόνος ὁ θεὸς ἐποίησεν ἐπεὶ καὶ μόνος ὄ. ἐστὶ θεός Clem.*prot*.4(p.48.17; M.8.164A); ὁ ὄ. πατήρ *ib*.10(p.68.28; 208A); περὶ τὸν ὄ. ὄντα βασιλέα τὰ ὄ. ὄντα ἀγαθὰ ὄντα id.*paed*.3.12(p.283.26; M.8.665A); τὸν ἀπόρρητον τῆς ὄ. φιλοσοφίας λόγον id.*str*.1.2(p.14.14; M.8.709C); ἀγάπη...τοῦ ὄ.

ἐραστοῦ ἑλκόμενος *ib.*4.22(p.312.24; 1356A); ἀλήθειαν ἡ μόνη περὶ τὸν ὄ. ὄντα θεὸν καταγίνεται *ib.*7.15(p.64.27; M.9.525C); ἐμπόδιον πρὸς τὴν κατάληψιν ἡμῖν τὸ σῶμα τῶν ὄ. ὄντων Meth.*res.*1.29(p.258.13; M.41.1136C); of Son τὸν ὄ. ὄντα...τὸν πᾶσι τοῖς οὖσι τοῦ εἶναι παρεκτικόν Bas.*Eun.*2.18(1.253D; M.29.609A); ἐκ τῆς ὄ. ζωῆς ἡ ζωοποιὸς προῆλθε πηγή *ib.*2.27(264B; M.636A); of Son ὄ. ὢν εἰκὼν εἰκονοποιός Didym.(‡Bas.)*Eun.*5(1.302A; M.29.724C); τῆς πηγῆς τῆς ὄ. ζωῆς, τῆς...τριάδος Gel.Cyz.*h.e.*2.23.6(M.85.1296D); ὄ. οὖσαν ὕπαρξιν καὶ τῆς τῶν ὄντων ὑπάρξεως αἰτίαν ἀληθινήν Dion.Ar.*c.h.*2.3(M.3.140C); τὴν τοῦ ὄ. ἔρωτος γνῶσιν id.*d.n.*4.12(M.3.709C); ἔκπτωσις τοῦ ὄ. ἔρωτος *ib.*

ὄνυξ, ὁ, *claw, nail*; **1.** in phrases; **a.** ἐξ ἁπαλῶν ὀ. *from earliest infancy*, Eus.*e.th.*2.25(p.136.27; M.24.965D); Pall.*v.Chrys.*16(p.95.7; M.47.54); Evagr.*h.e.*6.23(p.239.4; M.86.2880A); or ἐξ ὀ. Gr.Naz.*or.* 40.17(M.36.380D); **b.** ἐξ ὀνύχων *deeply* στενάζουσι...ἐξ ὀ. †Anast.S. *relat.*40(*OC* 2 p.86.4); ἐπ' ἄκρων ὀ. *on tiptoe*; as sign of pride, Thdt. *provid.*7(4.587); **2.** *instrument* of torture *with teeth* or *claws*, Eus.*h.e.* 8.9.1(M.20.760A); Soz.*h.e.*6.19.4(M.67.1340B); *M.Thdot.1* 27(p.77.24); in hell, †Cyr.*hom.div.*14(5^2.411C).

***ὀνυχοκοπέω,** *cut the nails of* ὀ. σε ‡Ath.*Melch.*(M.28.529A).

***ὀνυχώδης,** *furnished with nails*, Nil.*epp.*4.44(M.79.572B).

***ὀξέω** (or **ὀξάω**), *turn sour*, Ath.*fr.Cant.*6(M.27.1360A).

ὄξινος, = ὀξίνης, *sour*, Pall.*h.Laus.*35(p.104.11; M.34.1114C).

***ὀξυγραφέω,** *write fast*, Rom.Mel.(*AS* 1 p.142).

ὀξυγράφος, ὁ, *shorthand writer*, Epiph.*haer.*64.3(p.406.8; M.41.1073B); Socr.*h.e.*6.4.9(M.67.672C); *ib.*2.30.44(222A).

ὀξυδερκέω, *be sharp-sighted*, Meth.*symp.*9.4(p.118.14; M.18.185B); ‡Nil.*perist.*4.15(M.79.844B).

ὀξυδερκής, *clear-sighted*; neut. as subst., Jo.D.*hom.*1.7(M.96.557B); met. ψυχῆς ὄψιν...ὀξυδερκῆ Clem.*str.*5.4(p.338.23; M.9.37B); ref. Ps.18:9 κατὰ τὸν νοῦν ὀξυδερκέστεροι Or.*dial.*16(p.156.7); τὸ ἡγεμονικὸν...ὀξυδερκέστατον id.*schol.in Cant.*4:5(M.17.272C).

ὀξυδερκῶς, *with keen discernment*, *V.Pach.A* 6(p.130.14).

***ὀξύδορκος,** *keen-sighted*, Ath.*virg.*17(p.52.16; M.28.272C).

***ὀξυδρομεύς, ὁ,** *swift runner*, †Hipp.*Laz.*(p.226.31; M.62.778).

***ὀξυδρομέω, 1.** *run swiftly*, Cyr.*hom.pasch.*7(5^2.83D); Sophr.H. *or.*7.6(M.87.3333B); **2.** *make haste*, Didym.*Trin.*3.21(M.39.908B).

ὀξυδρόμος, *swift-running*, †Nil.*vit.*3(M.79.1141D); masc. as subst., Ephr.1.50C.

***ὀξυδρόμως,** *by running swiftly*; met., †Jo.D.*B.J.*20(M.96.1040B).

***ὀξυθέριστος,** *soon cut down*, Geo.Pis.*carm.vit.*26.

ὀξυκίνητος, *quickly moving* τὸ πνεῦμα...τὸ σαρκικόν, ὀ. ὄν Clem. *str.*6.16(p.500.18; M.9.360B); Meth.*symp.*6.3(p.67.17; M.18.117B); ὠνομάσαμεν...ἐκ τῶν ἡμετέρων τὰ τοῦ θεοῦ...ὀ. πτῆσιν Gr.Naz.*or.*31.22(p.173.1; M.36.157C); τὸ πρὸς τὰ θειότερα τῶν νοημάτων ὀ. Nil. *epp.*2.188(M.79.297C); id.*exerc.*15(M.79.737C); ὀ. καὶ καθαρὰν...ὑποδοχὴν τῶν θεαρχικῶν ἐλλάμψεων Dion.Ar.*c.h.*15.3(M.3.332A).

***ὀξυκόρυμβος, ὁ,** *sharp point*, Paul.Sil.*Soph.*729(M.86.2147A).

ὀξύκραμα, τό, *sour wine and water*, Pall.*h.Laus.*57(p.151.1; M.34.1250C).

ὀξυλάβη, ἡ, *forceps, tongs*, Jo.Mal.*chron.*1 p.21(M.97.88A).

***ὀξύμορφος,** v. σύμμορφος.

ὀξύνω, *sharpen*, met. γλῶτταν ὀ. Eus.*Marcell.*1.1(p.2.11; M.24.713A); Diod.*fat.*(M.103.868C).

[*]**ὀξυοπέω,** = ὀξυωπέω, *gaze keenly*, ‡Eust.*hex.*(M.18.732B).

***ὀξυπαθέω,** *suffer acute pain*, Thphn.*chron.*p.298(M.108.729A).

***ὀξυπετεστέρως,** *more rapidly, with a swifter movement* ἡ ψυχὴ περισσοτέρως ὀχλουμένη καὶ ὀ. ὑπ' αὐτῶν [sc. παθῶν] ὑποσυρομένη Marc.Er.*opusc.*5.1(M.65.1029B).

ὀξυπετής, *flying swiftly*; of time, Evagr.*h.e.*3.26(p.123.7; M.86.2649B).

ὀξυποδέω, *hasten*, *M.Pers.*4.1(p.446.10); Ephr.3.478E; ‡Chrys. *anim.*(9.821B).

***ὀξυποδίζω,** = foreg., Ephr.1.44E; id.3.311F.

§**ὀξύπορος,** *quick-moving*, Dion.Ar.*c.h.*15.2(M.3.329B).

***ὀξυπτέρυξ, ὁ,** *hawk*, Jo.Carp.*cap.*25(M.85.1842D).

ὀξυρρεπής, *ready to change* προαίρεσις...ὀ. ... πρὸς κακίαν Chrys. *hom.12.2 in Heb.*(12.124B); id.*pan.Lucn.*2(2.526E); Nil.*epp.*2.224(M.79.317B); superl., Philost.*h.e.*6.4(M.65.536A).

***ὀξυρρεπῶς,** *changeably* εὐολίστως καὶ ὀ. πρὸς αὐτὸ ἔχοντα τὸ πάθος Marc.Er.*opusc.*5.8(M.65.1041B); comp., Chrys.ap.Jo.D.*parall.* (M.95.1133B).

[*]**ὀξύρυγχος,** *sharp-pointed*; of a style of handwriting, Pall.*h. Laus.*38(p.120.12; M.34.1194A); Andr.Cr.*Agath.*9 (conj. for ὀξυρύχων M.97.1437C).

ὀξύς, 1. *keen, sharp*; of persons, *clear-sighted*; met., Chrys.*hom.* *3.8 in 2Cor.4:13*(3.285E); **2.** *swift* ὀ. ... πρὸς ἐναντίωσιν *Pers.*(p.39.8); neut. as subst., Hadr.*introd.*4(p.72.18; M.98.1276A).

***ὀξυτικός,** *swift*, comp., †Hipp.*theoph.*1(p.257.7; M.10.852A).

ὀξυτόμος, *sharp-cutting*, Nonn.*par.Jo.*19:2(M.43.897B).

ὀξυτόρος, *sharply-piercing*, Nonn.*par.Jo.*20:25(M.43.912C).

ὀξυφαής, *keen-sighted*, Gr.Naz.*carm.*1.2.9.50(M.37.671A); Nonn. *par.Jo.*9:39(M.43.832A).

ὀξυφοίνικος, *bright red*, Epiph.*gemm.*4 (conj. for ξυφοίν- M.43.296D).

***ὀξυχολέω,** *be enraged*, Herm.*mand.*10.2.3; †Gregent.*disp.*(M.86.765B).

***ὀξυχολία, ἡ,** *hot temper, irascibility* ἐὰν...ὀ. ἐπέλθῃ, εὐθὺς τὸ πνεῦμα τὸ ἅγιον στενοχωρεῖται...μιαινόμενον ὑπὸ τῆς ὀ. ἐν γὰρ τῇ μακροθυμίᾳ ὁ κύριος κατοικεῖ, ἐν δὲ τῇ ὀ. ὁ διάβολος Herm.*mand.*5.1.3; ἡ μακροθυμία γλυκυτάτη ἐστὶν...ἡ δὲ ὀ. πικρὰ...ἐὰν οὖν μιγῇ ἡ ὀ. τῇ μακροθυμίᾳ, μιαίνεται ἡ μακροθυμία *ib.*5.1.6; ἀδελφή ἐστι [sc. λύπη] ...τῆς ὀ. *ib.*10.1.1; as demonic, Or.*Jo.*20.36(29; p.376.4; M.14.657B) cit. s. δαιμόνιον; as a πάθος of soul, Ephr.3.426C; identified with θυμός, Dor.*doct.*8.2(M.88.1709A); Jo.D.*spir.neq.*7(M.95.81B); warning to bishop against its influence in exercise of discipline, Jo. Scholast.*nomoc.*15(p.14.30); remedies ὥσπερ ἐστὶ βρωμάτων νηστεία, οὕτω καὶ...ὀ. Nil.*epp.*2.28(M.79.212B); ὀφείλεις νηστεύων ἀποθέσθαι ...τὴν ὀ. Eus.Al.*serm.*1(M.86.320A).

***ὄπεραι, οἱ,** (Lat. *operae*) *workmen*, Thphn.*chron.*p.306(M.108.745A); *ib.*p.370(888B).

ὀπή, ἡ, *opening*; met., of Inc., ref. Ex.33:22 ὄψει τὴν ὀ. κατὰ τὴν ἐπιδημίαν αὐτοῦ, δι' ἧς ὀ. θεωρεῖται τὰ μετὰ τὸν θεόν· τοιοῦτον γὰρ νοεῖται ἐν τῷ 'καὶ ὄψει τὰ ὀπίσω μου' Or.*hom.16.2 in Jer.*(p.134.21; M.13.441A).

§**ὀπίζομαι,** (from ὀπή) *make passage, pass through*, Melet.*nat. hom.*2(M.64.1173A).

ὀπισθάγκωνα, *with the hands tied behind the back*, Nil.*epp.*4.62(M.79.580C); Jo.Mal.*chron.*14 p.370(M.97.552B); cf.*Chron.Pasch.*p.322(M.92.825A).

***ὀπισθαγκώνων,** *with the arms behind the back*, Barth.Edess. *Agar.*(M.104.1441B).

***ὀπισθάμβωνος,** *behind the ambo*; ὀ. εὐχή last prayer of liturgy said by the priest behind, i.e. to the west of, the ambo in the middle of the church, *Lit.Bas.*(p.343.15); *Lit.Chrys.*(p.343.15); cf. εὐχὴ ὀ. ἐκφωνουμένη παρὰ τοῦ ἱερέως ἔξω τοῦ βήματος *ib.*(p.397.28); ἡ ὀ. εὐχὴ οἱονεὶ σφραγίς ἐστι πάντων τῶν αἰτημάτων καὶ ἀνακεφαλαίωσις τακτική ‡Germ.CP *contempl.*(M.98.452C).

ὀπίσθιον, τό, *hinder part, back*, Jo.Mosch.*prat.*181(M.87.3053B); exeg. Ex.33:23; **1.** not to be taken in lit. sense, cf. *manifestum est... quia faciem, inquit, meam non videbis,...sed posteriora mea. quae utique cum eo sunt intelligenda sacramento, quo intellegi convenit dicta divina, abjectis profecto illis...anilibus fabulis, quae de anterioribus dei ab imperitis posterioribusque finguntur*, Or.*princ.* 2.4.3(p.131.7; M.11.202B); εἰ...τις τὸ ὀ. τοῦ θεοῦ κατὰ τὸ γράμμα νοήσειεν, εἰς ταύτην τὴν ἀτοπίαν...ἀπαχθήσεται· τὸ γὰρ ἐμπρόσθιόν τε καὶ ὀ. ἐν σχήματι πάντως· τὸ δὲ σχῆμα ἐν σώματι...ἀλλὰ μὴν ἄφθαρτος ὁ θεὸς καὶ ἀσώματος Gr.Nyss.*v.Mos.*(M.44.400B); ὀνομάζουσι τὴν... ὑπερώνυμον ἀγαθότητα καὶ μορφὰς αὐτῇ...περιτιθέασι...καὶ ὀπίσθια Dion.Ar.*d.n.*1.8(M.3.597B); **2.** interpreted of divine attributes or energies, opp. incomprehensible and incommunicable essence, Or. *hom.16.2 in Jer.*(p.134.21; M.13.441A); ταῦτα θεοῦ τὰ ὀ. ... ὅσα μετ' ἐκεῖνον ἐκείνου γνωρίσματα, ὥσπερ αἱ καθ' ὑδάτων ἡλίου...εἰκόνες ταῖς σαθραῖς ὄψεσι παραδεικνῦσαι τὸν ἥλιον Gr.Naz.*or.*28.3(p.25.9; M.36.29B); ἰδεῖν τὴν οὐσίαν ἀδύνατον...τὰς δὲ θείας οἰκονομίας καὶ ἐνεργείας (οὕτω γὰρ προσήκει νοεῖν τοῦ θεοῦ τὰ ὀ.) θεωρῆσαι δυνατὸν τοῖς... τελείοις τὴν ἀρετήν Thdt.*qu.68 in Ex.*(1.173); **3.** of revelation of God in Inc., cf. *ibi* [sc. at Transfiguration] *ei completur illa promissio...vidit ergo posteriora ejus, vidit enim quae in posterioribus et novissimis diebus facta sunt*, Or.*hom.12.3 in Ex.*(p.265.15; M.12.384D); *ponam te in foramine petrae, petra autem erat Christus, per foramen...videas posteriora mea, hoc est, ut ea quae in novissimis temporibus implebuntur per assumptionem carnis, agnoscas*, id. *hom.4.1 in Ps.36*(M.12.1350C); Gr.Naz.*or.*28.3(p.24.13; M.36.29A); ‡Meth.*Sym.et Ann.*6(M.18.360C); **4.** as signifying that to follow God is to see God, Gr.Nyss.*v.Mos.*(M.44.405A); id.*hom.12 in Cant.*(M.44.1025D); **5.** as denoting τὰ κτίσματα καὶ οἱ λόγοι αὐτῶν, ‡Ath. *qu.Ant.*62(M.28.633A).

***ὀπισθοβατικός,** *mounting from behind*, Clem.*paed.*2.10(p.210.32; M.8.504A).

ὀπισθόδομος, ὁ, *back* or *inner chamber*; of Tabernacle, Proc.G. *Num.*1:3ff.(M.87.800A); of temple of Athena at Athens where treasury was kept; hence *public record office*, Apollon.ap.Eus.*h.e.* 5.18.6(M.20.477B).

ὀπισθοκέλευθος, *following behind*, Nonn.*par.Jo.*1:44(M.43.757B); *ib.*13:36(865B); *ib.*18:15(892B).

ὀπισθόκομος, *wearing the hair long behind*, Nonn.*par.Jo.*2:2(M. 43.760C).

***ὀπισθομερής,** *situated behind* ὁ. ... τὸν ναὸν ἐτίθει τοῦ ἰδίου σώματος Cyr.*Jo.*4.5(4.396E).

ὀπισθοπόρος, *following*, Nonn.*par.Jo.*10:4(M.43.832C); *ib.*6:66 (804A); *ib.*11:31(844B).

ὀπισθόρμητος, *speeding back*; of an arrow, *Mir.Geo.*2(p.11.6).

***ὀπισθοτέλεια, ἡ,** *arrears of taxes*, Thphn.*chron.*p.414(M.108.984A).

ὀπισθότονος, *drawn backwards*, Nonn.*par.Jo.*18:24(M.43.893B).

ὀπισθοφανής, *appearing behind* ὁ...νοεῖται...ὀπισθοφανὲς τοῖς τῆς ἑσπέρας ἐνορῶντος μέρεσιν Cyr.*Jo.*4.5(4.397A).

ὀπισθοφανῶς, *backwards*; ref. Gen.9:23, Mac.Aeg.*hom.*20.1(M. 34.649C); *looking backwards*; ref. covering a dead body, ‡Sophr.H. *v.Mar.Aeg.*39(M.87.3725A).

ὀπίσω, *backwards, back*; **1.** τὰ ὀ. *hinder parts*, of God (cf. Ex. 33:23) ἡ μὲν προκόσμιος ὕπαρξίς τε καὶ θειότης δηλοῦται διὰ τοῦ προσώπου, ἡ δὲ δημιουργία καὶ πρόνοια διὰ τῶν ὀ. Didym.*Gen.*33:23 (M.39.1116A); **2.** *above*, i.e. *previously, supra*, Cyr.*ador.*4(1.132E); Ammon.*Ac.*20:26(M.85.1580C); **3.** as prep. c. genit.; **a.** *pursuing after, in quest of* οἱ...Χαλδαῖοι...ἐπλανήθησαν ὀ. τῶν στοιχείων Arist. *apol.*3.1; Serap.*ep.mon.*9(M.40.936A); Mac.Aeg.*elev.*3(M.34.892C); **b.** of time, *after*, Thphn.*chron.*p.105(M.108.305C).

***ὀπίτιον, τό,** *awl*, Nil.*exerc.*53(M.79.784D).

ὁπλίζω, *cultivate*, met. ὁπλίσατε τὴν εἰρήνην ἀποχειροτονοῦντες τὸν πόλεμον Thphyl.*exc.gent.*3(p.479.16; M.113.937B).

***ὁπλοδεξιά, ἡ,** *handling of arms*, Chrys.*hom.3.6 in 2Cor.*(10.451E).

ὁπλομανέω, *be mad on using arms*, Synes.*ep.*105(M.67.1488B).

ὁπλομάχος, ὁ, *warrior*, Gr.Nyss.*hom.7 in Cant.*(M.44.904A); fig., of a martyr ὁ ἀνδρειότατος ὁ. τοῦ θεοῦ Dion.Al.ap.Eus.*h.e.*6.41.16 (M.20.609B); of heavenly host, †Bas.*Is.*261(1.577E; M.30.576E); *ib.* 268(583E; M.592A).

ὁπλοποιητική, ἡ, [sc. τέχνη] *the art of forging arms*, Gr.Naz.*or.*43. 57(M.36.569A).

ὁπλότερος, *younger*, hence *new* ὁ. ... ἄσπορον ἀρχήν Nonn.*par.Jo.* 3:5(M.43.765C); *ib.*13:34(865B); *ib.*2:20(764C).

***ὁπλοφορία, ἡ,** *bearing of arms*, Isid.Pel.*epp.*1.180(M.78.300B); ἐν ὁ. *under arms*, *Chron.Pasch.*p.287(M.92.717A).

***ὁποιοσποτοῦν,** *of whatever kind*, Or.*comm.in Mt.*16.4(p.485.8; M.13.1381B).

***ὁποσαπλασιόνως,** *as many times*, Or.*Jo.*20.34(27; p.372.15; M. 14.652A).

ὁπόταν, *when*, *Barn.*12.2; Mel.*pass.*11 p.2.27.

ὀπτάν-ομαι, 1. med.; **a.** *see an appearance*, Eus.*qu.Marin.suppl.* 8(M.22.1012D); **b.** *look upon*, Thdr.Stud.*epp*:2.207(M.99.1628A); **2.** pass., *be seen, appear* ὁ θεὸς ὤφθη...ἑκάστῳ τῶν προφητῶν, σμικρύνων ἑαυτὸν καὶ σωματοποιῶν...μεταμορφούμενός τε καὶ ~όμενος Mac.Aeg.*elev.*8(M.34.896B); of Christ after Resurrection, Jo.D.*hom.* 9.4(M.96.729B).

ὀπτασία, ἡ, A. *vision, apparition*; **1.** of God or Christ; **a.** in OT: Just.*dial.*56.5(M.6.597C); δεῖ ἀποδιδράσκειν τοὺς ἐπιβουλεύοντας καὶ διωγμοὺς φεύγειν, εἰ καὶ ὀπτασιῶν καταξιωθῶμεν ὡς ὁ Ἰακὼβ Or.*sel. in Gen.*27:42(M.12.124B); cf. ὁ Ἰακὼβ φεύγων πλειόνων ὀ. καὶ τούτων θείων κατηξιοῦτο Ath.*fug.*20(p.81.23; M.25.669A); ἐμεσίτευε [sc. Aaron] τῇ ὀ. τοῦ θεοῦ καὶ ταῖς τῶν ἀνθρώπων θυσίαις id.*Ar.*2.7(M.26. 161B); of vision at burning bush, Just.*dial.*128.1(773C); Cyr.*glaph. Ex.*1(1.260A); *ib.*(262A); Proc.G.*Dt.*33:13(M.87.988A); Cosm.Ind. *top.*3(M.88.140A); v. βάτος; of theophany at Sinai, Gr.Nyss.*hex.*5(M. 44.68B); Cosm.Ind.*top.*3(141A); of prophets' visions, Hipp.*Dan.*4. 36.1; Ath.*ep.Serap.*1.11(M.26.557C); **b.** in NT: of appearance of Christ at Transfiguration, Meth.*res.*1.52(p.308.11; M.41.1128B); cf. *ib.*3.5(p.394.8; M.18.317C); after Resurrection, Eus.*qu.Marin.suppl.* 1.7(M.22.993D); Cyr.ap.*cat.Mt.*28:20(p.243.16); ref. 2Cor.12:2ff., Ath.*Ar.*3.47(421C); of S. Paul's vision on Damascus road, †Leont.N. *laud.Barn.*(p.144.20); of S. John ὀ. ἐν ᾗ τὸν Ἰησοῦν ἐθεάσατο ἐν μέσῳ λυχνιῶν ἑπτά Andr.Caes.*Apoc.*2 tit.(M.106.228A); **c.** in Church πρόγνωσιν ἔχουσιν [sc. Christians] τῶν μελλόντων καὶ ὀ. καὶ ῥήσεις προφητικάς Iren.*haer.*2.32.4(M.7.829B); **2.** of angels, Clem.*str.*6.15(p.499. 9; M.9.357B); Bas.*Eun.*3.1(1.273A; M.29.657A); ὁ βλέπων ἀγγέλων ὀ. οἶδεν, ὅτι τὸν ἄγγελον εἶδε καὶ οὐ τὸν θεόν Ath.*Ar.*3.14(M.26.349D); ἀνὴρ [sc. Pachomius]...ὡς καταξιωθῆναι προρρήσεων καὶ ὀ. ἀγγελικῶν Pall.*h.Laus.*32(p.88.2; M.34.1099C); Proc.G.*Dt.*33:13(M.87.988A); **3.** of saints ὀ. εἶδον, ἄνδρα ὑπερμεγέθη ὡπλισμένον...οὗτος...ἦν ὁ ἅγιος ...μάρτυς Σώσανδρος *M.Thdot.1* 19(p.73.12); **4.** of light; denoting presence of Christ, Ath.*v.Anton.*10(M.26.860A); of a saint appearing as transfigured in light, *A.Phil.*61(p.25.33); **5.** ref. nature and effects of visions ἡ...ὀ. ... τῷ ὀφθέντι πίστιν παρέχει τῷ ὁρῶντι, ὅτι θειότης ἐστίν *Hom.Clem.*17.13; τούτῳ τῷ ἀδελφῷ...νηστεύσαντι ἡμέρας τεσσαράκοντα θεόθεν ὀ. γίνεται Jo.Mosch.*prat.*56(M.87.2909D); conveying prophetic message, *M.Polyc.*5.2; cf.*ib.*12.3; of prophetic dreams, *M.Thdot.1* 12(p.68.11); of visions of things happening at a distance, Ath.*v.Anton.*82(M.26.957B); consciousness of recipient of vision οἶδεν ὁ ἀπόστολος ὃ πέπονθεν ἐν τῇ ὀ., κἂν λέγει οὐκ οἶδα id. *Ar.*3.47(M.26.421C); reception of visions as consolation in labours of ascetic life, id.*v.Anton.*66(937B); **6.** ref. good and evil apparitions ἀσφαλέστερός ἐστιν ὁ ὑπ' ὀπτασίας ἀκούων τοῦ παρ' αὐτῆς ἐνεργείας ἀκούοντος *Hom.Clem.*17.14; ὁ...ὀπτασίᾳ πιστεύων ἢ ὁράματι καὶ ἐνυπνίῳ ἐπισφαλής ἐστιν *ib.*; εἰ φῄς τὰς ὀ. μὴ πάντως ἀληθεύειν, ἀλλ' οὖν γε τὰ ὁράματα καὶ τὰ ἐνύπνια θεόπεμπτα ὄντα οὐ ψεύδεται *ib.*17. 15; true visions may be seen by the impious, *ib.*17.17; of demonic apparitions ἴσμεν πολλοὺς...κατὰ πάντα ἁμαρτάνοντας ὁράματα καὶ ἀληθεῖς ὀνείρους ὁρῶντας, ἐνίους δὲ καὶ δαιμόνων ὀπτασίας *ib.*17.16; ἄσαρκον...δύναμιν οὐ μόνον υἱοῦ, ἀλλ' οὐδ' ἀγγέλου ἰδεῖν τις δύναται· εἰ δὲ ἴδῃ τις ὀπτασίαν, κακοῦ δαίμονος ταύτην εἶναι νοείτω *ib.*; criteria of good and evil apparitions ἡ...τῶν ἁγίων ὀ. οὐκ ἔστι τεταραγμένη... ἡσύχως δὲ καὶ πράως γίνεται...ἐὰν δὲ καὶ ὡς ἄνθρωποι τινὲς φοβηθῶσι τὴν τῶν καλῶν ὀ., ἀφαιροῦσιν οἱ φαινόμενοι τὸν φόβον παρ' αὐτὰ τῇ ἀγάπῃ...τοιαύτη...οὖν ἡ τῶν ἁγίων ὀ. Ath.*v.Anton.*35(M.26.896A); ὅταν τις φαντασία γένηται...ἐρώτα πρῶτον· τίς εἶ καὶ πόθεν; καὶ ἐὰν μὲν ᾖ ἁγίων ὀ., πληροφοροῦσί σε καὶ τὸν φόβον σου εἰς χαρὰν μεταβάλλουσιν· ἐὰν δὲ διαβολική τις ᾖ, εὐθὺς ἐξασθενεῖ *ib.*43(908A).

B. *manifestation, appearance, becoming visible* ὁ θεὸς ἡμῶν ἐπὶ γῆς ὤφθη...ὀπτασίαν...φησι τὴν κατὰ σάρκα φανέρωσιν Procl.CP *Arm.*8(p.191.3; M.65.864B).

ὀπτήρ, ὁ, *one who regards* or *oversees*, c. genit. τὸν τῶν ὅλων ὀ. [i.e. God] Thdt.*qu.in 2Par.*(1.580).

ὀπτικός, *of* or *for seeing*; **1.** *keen-sighted* ἡ τῶν χερουβὶμ ὀπτικωτάτη φύσις Geo.Pis.*carm.*35.1; met., *acute, profound* ὀπτικωτέρων νοῶν Dion.Ar.*e.h.*7.3.11(M.3.568D); ἡ τῶν προφητῶν ὀπτικωτάτη κάρα Geo.Pis.*carm.*8.1; εἰ...τι ὀπτικώτερον ἐξενεχθείη Thdr.Stud. *epp.*2.168(M.99.1532C); **2.** as subst.; **a.** ἡ ὀ. *power of sight*, Thdt.*Ps.* 5:2,3(1.635); **b.** τὸ ὀ.; **i.** *organ of sight, eye*, Max.*Pyrr.*(M.91.292C); esp. ref. spiritual sight τὸ ὀ. τῆς διανοίας Thdt.*Ps.*6:8(1.643); τὸ... τῆς ψυχῆς ὀ. id.*Ezech.*proem.(2.669); id.*Cant.*4:7(2.96); **ii.** *power of sight*, Max.*ambig.*(M.91.1116C) cit. s. συνεπιτείνω.

ὀπτικῶς, *profoundly*; comp., Dion.Ar.*d.n.*3.2(M.3.681A).

***ὀπτιμάτοι, οἱ,** (Lat. *optimates*) body of soldiers called *optimates*, Thphn.*chron.*p.377(M.108.901C); *ib.*p.400(953A).

***ὀπτρίζ-ομαι,** med., *behold as in mirror* μακαρίους τίθεμαι τοὺς κατηκόους τῶν...λόγων...δι' αὐτῶν μυστήρια ~ομένους περὶ τὴν ἰδίαν φύσιν *A.Andr.fr.*15(p.44.15; perh. for κατοπτρίζομαι).

ὀπωδής, *bitter*; superl., Synes.*provid.*6(p.126.18; M.66.1276B).

ὀπώρα, ἡ, *fruit*, met. τὰς ὀ. τῶν διδασκάλων Geo.Pis.*carm.*46.7.

ὀπωρικός, *of fruit*; neut. plur. as subst., *fruits*, ‡Pall.*h.mon.*13.16 (p.68.14; M.34.1162D).

***ὀπωροβόρος,** *fruit-eating*, ‡Caes.Naz.*dial.*148(M.38.1100A).

ὀπωροφυλάκιον, τό, *crop-watcher's hut*, *T.Jos.*19.12; Just.*dial.* 52.4(M.6.592B); Ath.*exp.Ps.*78:2(M.27.357C); Thdt.*Ps.*78:2(1.1166).

ὅπως, 1. *in order that*; c. ἄν and pres. indic., Nil.*epp.*1.232(M.79. 168C); c. infin., ‡Caes.Naz.*dial.*140(M.38.1077); **2.** *so that, with the result that*, exeg. Ps.50:6 τὸ τοίνυν ὅ. οὐκ ἔστιν ἐνταῦθα αἰτίας δηλωτικόν...ἀλλὰ τοὐναντίον Thdt.*Ps.*50:6(1.935); **3.** in phrase οὐχ ὅ. ...ἀλλὰ καί *not only...but also*, Dion.Al.ap.Eus.*h.e.*7.21.3(M.20.684B).

***ὁπωσποτανοῦν,** *in any way whatever*, Or.*Cels.*7.42(p.193.17; M. 11.1481C).

ὁπώσποτε, *absolutely, necessarily*, Didym.*fr.Ps.*5:6(M.39.1172A).

***ὁραΐζ-ομαι,** (for ὡρ-) *be stocked with* ἀγρὸν...παντοίοις καρπίμασιν ~όμενον Alex.Sal.*Barn.*9(439A).

ὅραμα, τό, *vision*, Herm.*vis.*3.2.3; ἀξιῶ τὸν κύριον, ἵνα τὰς ἀποκαλύψεις καὶ τὰ ὁ. ἅ μοι ἔδειξεν διὰ τῆς...ἐκκλησίας αὐτοῦ τελειώσῃ *ib.*4.1.3; Just.*dial.*78.3(M.6.657C); ὑπὸ τοῦ πνεύματος δι' ὁραμάτων ἀπεκαλύφθη τῷ...προφήτῃ Hipp.*Dan.*4.1.2(M.10.680C); δι' ὁράματος πολλάκις ἐνουθετεῖτο ὑπὸ τοῦ κυρίου †Hipp.*Artem.*ap.Eus.*h.e.*5.28.11 (M.20.513C); ὅ. θεόπεμπτον προσελθὸν ἐπέρρωσέν με...ἀπεδεξάμην τὸ ὅ., ὡς ἀποστολικῇ φωνῇ συντρέχον Dion.Al.ap.Eus.*h.e.*7.7.3(648B); μόνος ὁ δίκαιος ὅ. ἀληθὲς ἰδεῖν δύναται *Hom.Clem.*17.15; ὁρᾷς πῶς τὰ τῆς ὀργῆς δι' ὁραμάτων καὶ ἐνυπνίων; τὰ δὲ πρὸς φίλον, στόμα κατὰ στόμα, ἐν εἴδει καὶ οὐ δι' αἰνιγμάτων ἢ ὅ. ... ὡς ἐχθρόν *ib.*17.18.

ὁραματισμός, ὁ, *vision*, *Const.App.*7.33.4.

ὀράριον, τό, v. *ὠράριον.

ὅρασις, ἡ, 1. *seeing, act of sight*; of physical sight likened to spiritual vision as one of spiritual senses, Or.*Jo.*20.43(33; p.386.24; M.14.676B); of spiritual vision οὔσης...θείας τινὸς γενικῆς αἰσθήσεως ...καὶ ὄντων εἰδῶν ταύτης τῆς αἰσθήσεως, ὁ. πεφυκυίας βλέπειν τὰ κρείττονα σωμάτων πράγματα, ἐν οἷς δηλοῦται τὰ χερουβὶμ καὶ τὰ σεραφίμ id.*Cels.*1.48(p.98.12; M.11.749B); ἐὰν μὴ καθαρισθῇ ἡ ὁ. τοῦ νοὸς ἐν τῇ ἐργασίᾳ τῶν ἐντολῶν...οὐ δύναται θεωρητικὸς ἀληθινὸς γενέσθαι τῆς θείας θεωρίας Philox.*ep.*32(p.180); ref. vision of God ὁ θεῖος γνόφος ἐστὶ τὸ ἀπρόσιτον φῶς, ἐν ᾧ κατοικεῖν ὁ θεὸς λέγεται. ... ἐν τούτῳ γίγνεται πᾶς ὁ θεὸν γνῶναι καὶ ἰδεῖν ἀξιούμενος, αὐτῷ τῷ μὴ ὁρᾶν μηδὲ γινώσκειν ἀληθῶς ἐν τῷ ὑπὲρ ὁ. καὶ γνῶσιν γιγνόμενος Dion.Ar.*ep.*5(M.3.1073A); **2.** *vision*; **a.** of prophetic visions Ἡσαΐας... πυρὶ καθαίρεται τὴν γλῶτταν, ὡς εἰπεῖν δυνηθῆναι τὴν ὁ. Clem.*str.*1.12 (p.35.19; M.8.753A); Hipp.*Dan.*4 tit.; πολλοὶ...τῶν προφητῶν καὶ... ἁγίων ἀνδρῶν ὀπτασίας καὶ ὁ. ἑωρακότες ἀνεγράφησαν τεθεωρηκέναι Or.*fr.20 in Jo.*(p.500.10); id.*hom.18.1 in Jer.*(p.150.22; M.13.464A); Μωσῆς...ὅτε ἔφευγε, τότε καὶ τὴν μεγάλην ὁ. εἶδε Ath.*fug.*20(p.81.27; M.25.669A); σημεῖον...τῆς τοῦ θεοῦ λόγου παρουσίας τὸ μηκέτι... προφήτην ἐγερθῆναι, μήτε ὁ. ἀποκαλύπτεσθαι id.*inc.*40.1(M.25.165A); cf.*ib.*39.3(164C); ὁ. καλεῖ τῶν μελλόντων τὴν πρόγνωσιν. ὥσπερ γὰρ οἱ τοῦ σώματος ὀφθαλμοὶ...τὰ προκείμενα ὁρῶσιν, οὕτω τὸ ὀπτικὸν τῆς διανοίας ὑπὸ τοῦ θειοῦ φωτιζόμενον πνεύματος, ὡς παρόντα βλέπει τὰ μὴ παρόντα Thdt.*Is.*1:1(p.2.26; 2.167); **b.** of apocalyptic visions, *Apoc.En.*1.2; in dreams, *ib.*13.18; cf.*ib.*13.10; **c.** opp. revelations by angels, Hipp.*fr.in Eccl.*(p.179.6); **d.** mediated by angels, Dion.Ar. *c.h.*4.2(M.3.180B); *ib.*9.4(261B); ὁ τὴν ὁ. διαπλάσας ἄγγελος *ib.*13.3 (300C); **e.** of manifestation of the divine in visions αὐτὸ μὲν ὅτι ποτέ ἐστι τὸ τοῦ θεοῦ κρύφιον οὐδεὶς ἑώρακεν, οὐδὲ ὄψεται. θεοφάνειαι δὲ τοῖς ὁσίοις γεγόνασι κατὰ τὰς πρεπούσας θεῷ διὰ...τινων ἱερῶν καὶ τοῖς ὁρῶσιν ἀναλόγων ὁράσεων ἐκφαντορίας *ib.*4.3(M.3.180C); *ib.* cit. s. θεοφάνεια; ἐν ταῖς ἱεραῖς τῶν μυστικῶν ὁ. θεοφανείαις ὁ θεὸς καὶ πολιὸς καὶ νέος πλάττεται id.*d.n.*10.2(M.3.937B); τὴν θεαρχίαν ἐν μιᾷ τῶν μυστικῶν τῆς συμβολικῆς θεοφανείας ὁ. *ib.*1.6(596A); τὴν ἑτερότητα τῶν ποικίλων τοῦ θεοῦ κατὰ τὰς πολυειδεῖς ὁ. σχημάτων ἕτερά τινα τοῖς φαινομένοις παρ' ὃ φαίνονται σημαίνειν οἰητέον *ib.*9.5(912D); **f.** of visions of saints, id.*ep.*8.5(M.3.1097B); *ib.*8.6(1097C); **3.** *manifestation*; in gen., Or.*fr.11 in Mt.*(p.19.12; M.17.289B); **4.** *appearance* ἡ ὁ. αὐτοῦ [sc. Michael] ὑπερφέρει πάντας τοὺς υἱοὺς τῶν ἀνθρώπων *T.Abr.*A 4(p.80.27); Gr.Naz.*or.*45.1(M.36.624A); *Apoc.Paul.*48(p.65); ‡Chrys.*ascet.facet.*(1.810E).

ὁρατικός, *able to see*, met. τοῦ σωτῆρος τοῦ καταγαγόντος...τῷ θείῳ λόγῳ τοῦ ὁ. τῆς ψυχῆς τὴν...ἄγνοιαν Clem.*str.*1.28(p.109.22; M.8.924C); ἄλλη μέν τις εἴη ⟨ἡ⟩ ὁ. τῆς ψυχῆς δύναμις καὶ θεωρητική, ἄλλη δὲ ἡ γνωστικὴ καὶ ἀντιληπτικὴ τῆς ποιότητος τῶν νοητῶν τροφῶν Or.*Jo.*20.43(33; p.386.26; M.14.676B).

ὁρατός, *visible*; **1.** of material things opp. spiritual; of body opp. soul, *Diogn.*6.4 cit. s. ἀόρατος; ref. Apollinarianism, ‡Ath.*Apoll.*1.13(M.26.1117A); ἄστρα...οὐχ ὁποῖα...ἐν τῷ ὁ. κείμενα τόπῳ, ἀλλά τινα κρείττω Meth.*symp.*8.5(p.88.2; M.18.148A); id.*res.*35(p.274.3; M.41.1100B); φιλόσοφοι...ἐκ στοχασμῶν...ἐπιβάλλοντες τοῖς ὁ. περὶ τῶν ἀδήλων ἀπεφήναντο *Hom.Clem.*2.7; πρὸ οὐρανοῦ καὶ γῆς...καὶ οὐ πρὸ τῶν ὁ. μόνον, ἀλλὰ καὶ πρὸ τῶν νοητῶν ἔργων τοῦ θεοῦ...ἦν [sc. Logos] καὶ προῆν Eus.*e.th.*3.3(p.147.10; M.24.985A); ὁ...λόγος... τόν τε ὁ. κόσμον καὶ τὰς ἀοράτους δυνάμεις κινεῖ καὶ συνέχει Ath.*gent.*44(M.25.88C); Bas.*ep.*97(3.191B; M.32.493B); ἀνατίθεμεν...τὸν ἀναφῆ καὶ ἀόρατον γνόφον τῷ φωτὶ τῷ ἀπροσίτῳ καθ' ὑπεροχὴν τοῦ ὁ. φωτὸς Dion.Ar.*d.n.*7.2(M.3.869A); κατὰ πᾶσαν ὑπερούσιον ὑπεροχὴν ἀσυγκρίτως ὑπερίδρυτο τὸ θεῖον ἁπάσης ὁ. καὶ ἀοράτου δυνάμεως id.*c.h.*13.4 (M.3.304C); *ib.*7.2(208A); *ib.*9.4(261D); ἡ πάσης εὐκοσμίας ὁ. καὶ ἀοράτου ταξιαρχία *ib.*13.3(301C); id.*e.h.*5.1.4(M.3.504D); **2.** of the visible as image of the invisible; **a.** man as image of God αὐτὸς ἀόρατος, ἡ δὲ αὐτοῦ εἰκὼν ὁ ἄνθρωπος ὁ., ὁ αὐτὸν σέβειν θέλων τὴν ὁ. αὐτοῦ τιμᾷ εἰκόνα, ὅπερ ἐστὶν ἄνθρωπος *Hom.Clem.*17.7; **b.** of symbols and representations of God θεολόγοι τὴν ὑπερούσιον...οὐσίαν ἐν πυρὶ...διαγράφουσιν, ὡς ἔχοντα πολλὰς τῆς θεαρχικῆς...ἰδιότητος ὡς ἐν ὁρατοῖς εἰκόνας Dion.Ar.*c.h.*15.2(M.3.329A); ἀληθῶς ἐμφανεῖς εἰκόνες εἰσὶ τὰ ὁ. τῶν ἀοράτων id.*ep.*10(M.3.1117B); **3.** denied of God ἀνθρωπίνοις οὐκ ἔστιν ὁρατὸς ὀφθαλμοῖς Tat.*orat.*4(p.4.26; M.6.813A); ref. pagan gods οὐ χρὴ...θεοὺς ὀνομάζειν ὁ. καὶ μὴ ὁρῶντας Arist.*apol.*13.8; **4.** ref. Inc., Ign.*Polyc.*3.2 cit. s. ἀόρατος; ἐπὶ Ἰησοῦ τοῦ ὁ. Or.*Jo.*1.37(42; p.48.12; M.14.97B); ὁ μὲν ἀόρατος θεὸς οὐκ ἐξηγήσατο, ὁ δὲ μονογενὴς υἱὸς ὁ. γενόμενος τὴν περὶ τοῦ πατρὸς ἀνθρώποις ἐξήγησιν ἐποιήσατο, ἕτερος ὢν...παρὰ τὸν ἀόρατον θεόν Eus.*e.th.*1.20(p.83.25; M.24.869C); Χριστός...ἀόρατος τὸ πρὶν καὶ ταῖς ἐν οὐρανῷ δυνάμεσιν... ὁ. νυνὶ διὰ τὴν πρὸς τὸν ὁρώμενον ἄνθρωπον ἕνωσιν ‡Ath.*Ar.*4.36(p.86.18; M.26.524C); πῶς ἀπέθανεν ὁ κύριος, εἰ καὶ ὁ ἄκτιστος ἀκτίστως ἐπεδήμησεν ἐπὶ γῆς; ἢ πῶς ὁ. καὶ ψηλαφητὸς γέγονεν; ‡Ath.*Apoll.*1.6 (M.26.1101B); τὸ ἓν καὶ ἁπλοῦν καὶ κρύφιον Ἰησοῦ τοῦ θεαρχικωτάτου λόγου τῇ καθ' ἡμᾶς ἐνανθρωπήσει πρὸς τὸ σύνθετόν τε καὶ ὁ. ἀναλλοιώτως...προελήλυθε Dion.Ar.*e.h.*3.3.12(M.3.444A); of Christ's humanity καλεῖ αὐτοὺς ἐπὶ τὸ ἰδεῖν ἄνθρωπον...τὸ γὰρ ὁρατὸν ὀφθαλμοῖς αὐτοῦ ἄνθρωπος ἦν Or.*Jo.*13.29(p.253.18; M.14.449A); of body, ref. teaching ascribed to Apollinarians σάρκα...ὁ. γενομένην, ἄκτιστον λέγοντες, δυσὶ περιπίπτετε πτώμασιν· ἢ φαντασίαν...τὴν ἀνοχὴν τοῦ παθοῦς ὑπολαμβάνοντες...ἢ τοιαύτην ὑποτίθεσθε τῆς...θεότητος τὴν οὐσίαν ‡Ath.*Apoll.*1.3(M.26.1097B); ἐξ οὐρανῶν ἐπὶ γῆς κατενέγκῃ σῶμα καὶ τὸ ἀόρατον ὁ. ποιήσῃ *ib.*1.7(1104B); **5.** of divine appearances in mystical life ὅταν ἄφθαρτοι...γενώμεθα...τῆς...ὁ. ... θεοφανείας...ἀποπληρούμενοι, φανοτάταις μαρμαρυγαῖς ἡμᾶς περιαυγαζούσης, ὡς τοὺς μαθητὰς ἐν ἐκείνῃ τῇ θειοτάτῃ μεταμορφώσει Dion. Ar.*d.n.*1.4(M.3.522C); **6.** of revelation in gen. δώσω σοι θησαυροὺς... ἀποκρύφους, ἀοράτους ἔθνεσιν, ἡμῖν δὲ ὁ. Clem.*paed.*3.12(p.284.13; M.8.665C); of prophecy ἐμφανῆ...τοῖς...προφήταις κατέστησεν ὁ θεὸς ὁμοῦ ταῖς ἀποκαλύψεσι μονονουχὶ καὶ αὐτὰ παρόντα τὰ πράγματα, ὥστε δοκεῖν καὶ ὁρατοὺς ἤδη πως γενέσθαι τοὺς λόγους Cyr.*Am.*2(3.248A, Aubert ὁρᾶν αὐτοὺς ἤδη πρὶν γενέσθαι κτλ.); **7.** ref. life after death θεὸς...ὅτε βούλεται, τὴν ὁρατὴν αὐτῷ μόνον ὑπόστασιν ἀποκαταστήσει πρὸς τὸ ἀρχαῖον Tat.*orat.*6(p.7.4; M.6.820A); Σαμουὴλ φαινόμενος... ὁ. ὢν παρίστησιν ὅτι σῶμα περιέκειτο Meth.*res.*3.17(p.414.10; M.18.325A); **8.** of Christ καθ' ὃ μὲν ἄρτος...γευστός ἐστιν...καθ' ὃ δὲ σοφία ἐστίν, ὁ. ἐστιν Or.*Jo.*20.43(33; p.386.29; M.14.676B); ὥσπερ...ὁ κύριος γευστὸς καὶ ὁ., οὕτως καὶ ὁ ἐχθρὸς αὐτοῦ θάνατος γευστός ἐστι καὶ ὁ. *ib.*(p.386.33; 676C); **9.** neut. plur. as subst.; **a.** *visible world, creatures*, gen. connected with ἀόρατα as sum of creation μηθέν με ζηλώσαι τῶν ὁ. καὶ ἀοράτων, ἵνα...Χριστοῦ ἐπιτύχω Ign.*Rom.*5.3; Tat.*orat.*5(p.5.19; M.6.813C); Or.*fr.1 in Jo.*(p.484.18) cit. s. ἀόρατος; πάντα τὰ ὁ. καὶ τὰ ἀόρατα δι' αὐτοῦ γέγονε Ath.*Ar.*2.39(M.26.229C); ὁ κόσμος οὗτος, τὸ ἐξ ὁ. ... καὶ ἀοράτων σύστημα Gr.Naz.*ep.*101(M.37.184C); in creeds, *Symb.Nic.*(325)(p.44.11; M.20.1540B) cit. s. ἀόρατος; cf. ἡμῶν ἡ πίστις...εἰς ἕνα θεὸν πατέρα παντοκράτορα, πάντων ὁ. τε καὶ ἀοράτων ποιητήν Ath.*ep.Afr.*11(M.26.1048B); *Symb.Ant.*(341)1 (p.249.3; M.26.721A); *Symb.Ant.*(341)4(p.251.5; M.26.725C); *Symb. Ant.*(345)1(p.251.6; M.26.728B); *Symb.Sirm.*1(p.254.21; M.26.736B); *Symb.Sel.*(p.258.6; M.26.745A); *Symb.CP*(360)(p.258.28; M.26.748A); *Symb.Nic.-CP*(p.80.3; H.2.288B); cf.Ath.*virg.*1(p.35.5; M.28.252A); ‡Ath.*interpr.*(p.66.11,15; M.26.1232A); **b.** *eyes*, Ephr.2.231D; Gr. Naz.*ep.*101(M.37.184C); **10.** neut. as subst., *capacity of seeing*, Dion. Ar.*e.h.*2.3.3(M.3.400A); *ib.*2.3.4(400B).

ὁράω, [1st sing. aor. act. εἶδα *Mir.Geo.*6(p.77.10)]; **1.** *see* God τίς ...σὰρξ δύναται...ὀφθαλμοῖσιν ἰδεῖν θεόν; *Orac.Sib.fr.*1.11; ἕως τοῦ νῦν οὐδεὶς εἶδεν τὸν υἱὸν τοῦ θεοῦ ὡς ἔστι...ὃν δὲ ἐφόρεσεν δι' ἡμᾶς υἱὸν τοῦ ἀνθρώπου εἴδομεν ‡Ath.*serm.fid.*26(p.11; M.26.1272B); exeg. Jo.1:18 συγκαταβαίνοντα τὸν θεὸν ἰδεῖν οὐκ ἤνεγκαν Chrys.*incomprehens.*4(1.475C); of heavenly vision, id.*Philogon.*(1.494B); of the vision of God ἐκεῖ δὲ διηνεκῶς οἱ παρόντες ὁρῶσιν ὡς αὐτοῖς ἰδεῖν δυνατὸν *ib.* (494C); πλῆθος ἀγγέλων ἰδεῖν id.*sac.*6.4(p.148.3; 1.424D); **2.** *have reference to*; of prophecies, etc. προρρήσεις...αἱ...ὁρῶσαι τὸν ἡμέτερον σωτῆρα Eus.*d.e.*7.3(p.347.16; M.22.565B); οὐκ αὐτὸν ἐκεῖνον ἑώρα τὸν ἄνδρα τὰ...εἰρημένα *ib.*8.1(p.355.23; 577D); *ib.*9.17(p.440.23; M.22.709B); **3.** *regard, attend to, be concerned with* ὁρῶν δ' οἶμαι ὁ θεὸς καὶ τὴν ἀλαζονείαν ἢ τὴν πρὸς τοὺς ἄλλους ὑπεροψίαν Or.*Cels.*7.44(p.195.13; M.11.1484D); Chrys.*hom.3.2 in Tit.*(11.745F); Thdt.*1Cor.*3:8(3.181); **4.** *regard as*, c. dupl. acc. φοβερὸν τὸν θάνατον ὁρῶσι καὶ δειλιῶσιν αὐτὸν Ath.*inc.*27.3(M.25.144A); οὐδὲ ἀνθρώπους ἑώρων τοὺς ἀνθρώπους Chrys.*hom.8.2 in 1Thess.*(11.479F); id.*hom.26.7 in Mt.*(7.323E); **5.** med.; **a.** *see* εἴ τις μὴ τὸν υἱὸν λέγοι τὸν Ἀβραὰμ ἑωρᾶσθαι, ἀλλὰ τὸν ἀγέννητον θεόν, ἢ μέρος αὐτοῦ, ἀ. ἔ. *Symb.Sirm.*1 *anath.*15; **b.** *provide for* τὸν ἐπὶ τῷ πάσχα νόμον ἀνανεώσασθαι ὁρᾶται Cyr.*Is.* proem.(2.***E); **6.** pass.; **a.** *show oneself, appear* Ἰσχύρας λαϊκὸς ὤφθη Ath.*apol.sec.*76(p.156.10; M.25.385B); ὤφθη ἄνθρωπος ὁ Χριστός ‡Ath.*Apoll.*1.13(M.26.1116B); χρὴ τοὺς ἁγίους πανταχῇ μονοτρόπους ὁρᾶσθαι Cyr.*ador.*5(1.147B); *ib.*8(269B,275B); ὦπται...Νεστόριος... ὑπεναντία τῆς ὀρθοδόξου πίστεως φρονῶν CEph.(431)*act.*1(*ACO* 1.1.2 p.34.34; H.1.1393C); ‡Jo.D.*Artem.*7(ὤφθη M.96.1257B; ἔφθη p.26.7); **b.** *be perceived* τοὺς ἔξω...τῷ σωτῆρι...ἑωραμένους οὐ βεβαίους ἔσεσθαι ἐν τῇ ἐπιστροφῇ Or.*princ.*3.1.17(p.226.6; M.11.284A); **c.** *be represented* ὁρῶ τὸν χῶρον, ἐφ' ᾧ ὁ στῦλος τοῦ πυρὸς τῷ στύλῳ τῶν ἀρετῶν ὦπται Thdr.Stud.*epp.*2.16(M.99.1165B).

ὀργανικός, *serving as an instrument* or *organ* φυσικὰ καὶ ὁ. σώματα Const.*or.s.c.*3(p.156.21; M.20.1240A); ψυχή ἐστιν...οὐσία...νοερά, σώματι ὁ. καὶ αἰσθητικῷ δύναμιν ζωτικὴν...ἐνιοῦσα [v.l. ἐνιεῖσα] Gr.Nyss.

anim.et res.(M.46.29B); Christol. ὥσπερ...ἡ μορφὴ τοῦ θεοῦ τὸ πλήρωμα τῆς τοῦ λόγου θεότητος νοεῖται, οὕτως ἡ μορφὴ τοῦ δούλου ἡ νοερὰ τῆς ἀνθρώπων συστάσεως φύσις σὺν τῇ ὀ. καταστάσει ὁμολογεῖται ‡Ath.*Apoll.*2.1(M.26.1133A); κἂν εἴπερ τι τῶν θεοπρεπεστάτων ἐνεργῆσαι λέγοιτο διὰ τοῦ ἰδίου σώματος ὀργανικὴν αὐτῷ πληροῦντος τὴν ὑπουργίαν, οὐδὲν ἧττον ὁ τῶν δυνάμεων κύριος ὁ ἐνεργῶν ἐστιν Cyr.*apol.Thdt.*7(p.130.16; 6[1].224D); Apollinarian ἀντὶ τοῦ ἔσωθεν ἐν ἡμῖν ἀνθρώπου νοῦς ἐπουράνιος ἐν Χριστῷ· ὡς γὰρ ὀ. κέχρηται σχήματι τῷ περιέχοντι ‡Ath.*Apoll.*1.2(1096B).

ὀργανικῶς, *as an instrument*, Or.*fr.*53 *in Lc.*11:34(p.259); δύο φύσεις φέρων μετὰ τὴν ἕνωσιν...ὁ εἷς Χριστὸς...τῆς μὲν ὀ. λειτουργησάσης, τῆς δὲ δεσποτικῶς ἐνεργησάσης Jo.D.*hom.*11.3(M.96.765B).

ὄργανον, τό, 1. *instrument, tool*; of instruments of martyrdom, *M.Polyc.*13.3; *Ep.Lugd.*ap.Eus.*h.e.*5.1.51(M.20.428B); met. ἔτι ὢν ἐν μέσοις τοῖς ὀ. τοῦ διαβόλου *2Clem.*18.2; *machine* of war λιθοβόλον ὄ. Thdt.*h.e.*5.37.8(3.1080); **2.** *musical instrument*; use by Christians deprecated, Clem.*paed.*2.4(p.182.7; M.8.440C); use in OT dispensation replaced by active praise to God through bodily service, Chrys.*exp.in Ps.*150:6(5.502B); *ib.*(502D); *ib.*143:9(465A); ref. human voice as archetypal instrument, Thdt.*provid.*3(4.516); κιθάραις καὶ κυμβάλοις...καὶ ἑτέροις μουσικοῖς ὀ. ἐκέχρηντο...ἁρμόττει δὲ καὶ ἡμῶν τὰ εἰρημένα πνευματικῶς νοούμενα καὶ δυνατὸν ἡμᾶς εὔηχον καὶ παναρμόνιον ὄ. ἡμᾶς αὐτοὺς ἀποφῆναι id.*Ps.*32:3(1.806); τοῖς νηπίοις ἁρμόδιον...τὸ μετὰ τῶν ἀψύχων ὀ. ᾆσαι...διὸ ἐν ταῖς ἐκκλησίαις προαίρεται ἐκ τῶν ᾀσμάτων ἡ χρῆσις τῶν τοιούτων ὀ. ... καὶ ὑπολέλειπται τὸ ᾆσαι ἁπλῶς ‡Just.*qu.et resp.*107(M.6.1353C); met., of universe εἰ...ὁ κόσμος ὄ. κινούμενον ἐν ῥυθμῷ, τὸν ἁρμοσάμενον καὶ πλήσσοντα τοὺς φθόγγους...οὐ τὸ ὄ. προσκυνῶ Athenag.*leg.*16.2(M.6.920D); of Christ ref. creation of man καλὸν ὁ κύριος ὄ. ἔμπνουν τὸν ἄνθρωπον ἐξειργάσατο κατ' εἰκόνα τὴν ἑαυτοῦ· ἀμέλει καὶ αὐτὸς ὄ. ἐστι τοῦ θεοῦ παναρμόνιον, ἐμμελὲς καὶ ἅγιον Clem.*prot.*1(p.6.22; M.8.60B); ref. inspiration τῷ παρὰ τοῦ θεοῦ πνεύματι ὡς ὄργανα κεκινηκότι τὰ τῶν προφητῶν στόματα Athenag.*leg.*7.2(M.6.904C); ὥσπερ ἐπὶ τῶν προφητῶν...ἄνθρωπος μὲν ἦν τὸ ὁρώμενον, θεὸς δὲ ὁ διὰ τοῦ φαινομένου ὡς ἂν δι' ὀργάνου θεσπίζων Eus.*d.e.*5.13(p.236.20; M.22.389D); Ἡσαΐας...καθάπερ ὄ. τοῦ ἐν αὐτῷ φθεγγομένου γενόμενος Gr. Nyss.*Eun.*8(2 p.177.2; M.45.769B); of scripture ὄ. τοῦ θεοῦ εἶναι πᾶσαν τὴν γραφήν, μίαν ἀποτελοῦν ἐκ διαφόρων φθόγγων σωτήριον...φωνήν Or.*comm.in Mt.*2(p.5.28; M.13.832C); Christol., v. infra 6; **3.** *means, instrument*, in gen. παρασύρων τῷ χρυσῷ τὴν ἀλήθειαν, ὃν δι' εὐσέβειαν συναγόμενον, ὄ. ἀσεβείας οἱ πονηροὶ πεποίηνται Gr.Naz. *or.*21.21(M.35.1105B); of living beings, *agent, instrument*, in gen. λιτανεύσατε...ἵνα διὰ τῶν ὀ. τούτων [sc. lions] θεοῦ θυσία εὑρεθῶ Ign. *Rom.*4.2; βέλτιον...ἐστιν αὐτόπτην γενέσθαι τοῦ λόγου καὶ χωρὶς ὀργάνων διδάσκοντος ἀκούειν αὐτοῦ...ἤπερ...διὰ διακόνων τῶν ἑωρακότων αὐτὸν ἀκούειν τὸν περὶ αὐτοῦ λόγον Or.*Jo.*13.53(52; p.281.33; M.14.496D); of Logos as agent in creation αὐτὸν πρῶτον πάντων ὑπὸ τοῦ πατρὸς οἷόν τι μονοειδὲς πάσης οὐσίας καὶ φύσεως προβεβλῆσθαι ὄ. ἔμψυχον καὶ ζῶν, μᾶλλον δ' ἔνθεον καὶ ζωοποιόν Eus.*d.e.*4.4(p.155.2; M.22.257D); καθάπερ...οὐ τιθέμεθα ὄ. ὑπουργικὸν εἶναι τοῦ πυρὸς τὸ ἐξ αὐτοῦ φῶς, δύναμιν δὲ μᾶλλον φυσικήν· οὕτω λέγομεν τὸν πατέρα πάντα ὅσα ποιεῖ διὰ τοῦ...υἱοῦ...ποιεῖν· οὐχ ὡς δι' ὀργάνου λειτουργικοῦ, ἀλλὰ φυσικῆς καὶ ἐνυποστάτου δυνάμεως ‡Cyr.*Trin.*8(6[3].12E; M. 77.1137D); εἰρήκατε [sc. Ἀρειανοί]...ὄ. ἑαυτῷ τὸν υἱὸν ἐκ τοῦ μὴ ὄντος κατεσκεύασε, ἵνα δι' αὐτοῦ ποιήσῃ τὰ πάντα...τοιαῦτα...λέγοντες τοῦ κατασκευάσαντος μᾶλλον ἀσθένειαν δεικνύετε, εἰ μὴ καὶ μόνος ἴσχυσε δημιουργῆσαι τὰ πάντα, ἀλλ' ἔξωθεν ἑαυτῷ ὄ. ἐπινοεῖ Ath.*Ar.*1.26(M. 26.65A); ἐκ θεοῦ λόγος καθ' ἡμᾶς οὐκ εἰς τὸ εἶναι, ἀλλ' εἰς τὴν ἡμῶν χρείαν ὡς ὄ. πεποίηται...ὥστε κατὰ τοὺς ἀσεβοῦντας περιττὸν εἶναι λοιπὸν τὸν υἱόν, τὸν γενόμενον ὡς ὄ., γενομένων ὧν ἕνεκα καὶ ἐκτίσθη *ib.*2.30(209B); οὐδὲ εἴρηκε...ὅτι διὰ τὸ ποιῆσαί με ἔργα ἔκτισεν, ἵνα μὴ πάλιν κατὰ τὴν κακόνοιαν τῶν ἀσεβῶν ὡς ὄ. δι' ἡμᾶς γενόμενος νομισθῇ *ib.*2.71(297A); ὁ...λόγος...οὐδὲ διὰ τὴν ἡμῶν ἀσθένειαν οὗτος...ὑπὸ μόνου τοῦ πατρὸς γέγονεν, ἵν' ἡμᾶς δι' αὐτοῦ ὡς δι' ὀργάνου δημιουργήσῃ *ib.*2.31(212B); εἰ ⟨μὴ⟩ γὰρ τὸ μὴ ἐκ τοῦ θεοῦ, ἀλλ' ὡς ὄ. ἑτεροφυὲς καὶ ἑτεροούσιον δείκνυται, καλῶς ἄρα ἡ σύνοδος ἔγραψε id.*decr.*23(p.19.29; M.25.457B); denial that H. Ghost is inferior agent ὡς περὶ ὀ. καὶ ὑπηκόου καὶ ὁμοτίμου τῇ κτίσει καὶ ἡμῶν ὁμοδούλου Bas.*Spir.*50 (3.42C; M.32.160B); of heretics as agents of Devil, Thdt.*haer.*4.12 (4.368); *ib.*4.13(372); **4.** physical *organ*, Pythagorean γνώσεως ὄ. Hipp.*haer.*6.24(p.151.8; M.16.3230C); Clem.*str.*6.16(p.505.9; M.9. 373A); Meth.*symp.*2.2(p.16.22); οὐκ ἔστιν ἁμαρτία...ἡ ἀληθὴς χρῆσις, εἰ τὰ ὄ. παρὰ τοῦ δημιουργοῦ διαπέπλασται Ath.*ep.Amun.*(M.26. 1173A); ὅτε ἀποκάμῃ τὰ ὄ., τότε προσάγεις αὐτὰ τῷ θεῷ Bas.*hom.*13.5 (3.118D; M.31.436B); **5.** of body as *organ* of soul τὰ...σώματα αὐτῶν μέρη αὐτῶν οὐδέποτε γίνεται τῶν ψυχῶν, ὄ. δὲ ὧν μὲν ἐνίζηματα, ὧν δὲ ὀχήματα Clem.*str.*6.18(p.516.13; M.9.396C); ψυχὴν...λογικὴν τιμᾶν ἡμεῖς ἴσμεν καὶ τὰ ταύτης ὄ. παραδιδόναι κατὰ τὰ νενομισμένα ταφῇ Or.*Cels.*8.30(p.245.28; M.11.1561A); δεξάμενον καλῶς ἀγωνισαμένην διὰ τοιούτου ὀ. ψυχήν *ib.*(p.246.5; 1561B); id.*fr.*36 *in Jo.*(p.512.10); τὸ ἁμαρτῆσαι καὶ τὸ μὴ ἁμαρτῆσαι διὰ τοῦ σώματος γίγνεται, τῆς ψυχῆς ἢ πρὸς ἀρετὴν ἢ πρὸς κακίαν ὀργάνῳ χρωμένης αὐτῷ Meth.*res.* 1.60(p.324.11; M.41.1157A); τῆς ψυχῆς...ἐστὶν ἡ ἡγεμονία· κέχρηται γὰρ...ὡς ὀ. τῷ σώματι, ἄγουσα τοῦτο καὶ ἰθύνουσα Jo.D.*f.o.*3.15(M. 94.1049A); of body as organ of demons πνεύματα ὄντες...διὰ τὸ...δεῖσθαι ὀ. τῶν πρὸς τὴν χρῆσιν ἐπιτηδείων εἰς τὰ ἀνθρώπινα εἰσίασιν σώματα, ἵνα...ὑπουργούντων ὀ. τυχόντες, ὧν θέλουσιν ἐπιτυχεῖν δυνατοὶ ὦσιν *Hom.Clem.*9.10; **6.** of Christ's humanity as *organ* of deity ἐκ τῆς παρθένου τὸ ἀνθρώπινον ὄ. ἀναλαβὼν ἐφόρεσε καὶ ὑπὸ νόμον ἐγένετο Hipp.*pasch.*2(p.297.13; M.10.701A) = Eust.*fr.in Pr.* 8:22(M.18.680C); ἔδει ποτὲ καὶ αὐτῷ ὀ. ἀνθρωπείου, ὡς ἂν καὶ ἀνθρώποις ἑαυτὸν φήσειεν...θεὸν δι' ἀνθρώπου μέγα θαῦμα τοῖς πᾶσιν ἐπιδεικνύμενος...θεῖόν τε ὡς ἀληθῶς καὶ παράδοξον χρῆμα Eus.*d.e.*4.10 (p.168.15; M.22.280D); ἐχρῆν ἀνθρώποις θεοῦ λόγον ὁμιλεῖν μέλλοντα...μὴ ἄλλως ἢ διὰ τοῦ συνήθους ἡμῖν ὀ. τοῦτο πρᾶξαι *ib.*7.1(p.301. 31; 493D); δι' ὀ. θνητοῦ τὰς πρὸς τοὺς θνητοὺς ὁμιλίας...ὑπήει, τὸ θνητὸν διὰ τοῦ ὁμοίου σῶσαι προμηθούμενος id.*l.C.*13(p.241.13; M.20. 1408B); νεὼν πανάγιον αὐτὸς αὐτῷ σωματικὸν ὄ. κατεσκευάσατο, λογικῆς δυνάμεως αὐτῷ σωματικὸν ὄ. κατεσκευάσατο, λογικῆς δυνάμεως αἰσθητικὸν οἰκητήριον *ib.*14(p.241.29; 1409A); ἑκὼν παρεδίδου τὸ αὐτὸ ὄ. τοῖς ἐπιβουλεύουσι, τὸ μὲν ἀπὸ γῆς ἀνωρθοῦτο αὐτίκα id.*theoph.*3 (p.4*.18; M.24.612A); ἐν τῇ παρθένῳ κατασκευάζει ἑαυτῷ ναὸν τὸ σῶμα καὶ ἰδιοποιεῖται τοῦτο ὥσπερ ὄ., ἐν αὐτῷ γνωριζόμενος καὶ ἐνοικῶν Ath.*inc.*8.3(M.25.109C); ὧν ὁ λόγος τοῦ θεοῦ εἰκότως τὸν ἑαυτοῦ ναὸν καὶ τὸ σωματικὸν ὄ. προσάγων ἀντίψυχον, ὑπὲρ πάντων ἐπλήρου τὸ ὀφειλόμενον ἐν τῷ θανάτῳ *ib.*9.2(112A); εἰ τὸ μέρος ἀπρεπὲς ἐστιν ὀ. αὐτοῦ γίνεσθαι πρὸς τὴν τῆς θεότητος γνῶσιν, ἀτοπώτατον ἂν εἴη καὶ δι' ὅλου τοῦ κόσμου γνωρίζεσθαι τοῦτον *ib.*41.7(169A); ἐν ᾧ ἔστιν ὁ λόγος, τούτῳ πρὸς φανέρωσιν ὡς ὀ. κέχρηται ὁ λόγος *ib.*42.5 (169C); ὀ. κέχρηται ἀνθρώπου σώματι πρὸς φανέρωσιν ἀληθείας καὶ γνῶσιν τοῦ πατρός *ib.*42.6(172A); τῷ σώματι ὀ. χρώμενος οὐδενὸς τῶν τοῦ σώματος μετεῖχεν, ἀλλὰ μᾶλλον αὐτὸς ἡγίαζε τὸ σῶμα *ib.*43.6 (173A); ἐπειδὴ...ἐν τῷ ὅλῳ αὐτὸν...οὐκ ἠδυνήθησαν...γνῶναι οἱ ἄνθρωποι, μέρος τοῦ ὅλου λαμβάνει ἑαυτῷ ὄ. τὸ ἀνθρώπινον σῶμα...ἵνα...κἂν ἐν τῷ μέρει μὴ ἀγνοήσωσιν αὐτόν *ib.*43.4(172C); διατί...οὐχὶ...καλλίονι ὀ. οἷον ἡλίῳ...κέχρηται, ἀλλὰ ἀνθρώπῳ μόνον;...οὐκ ἐπιδείξασθαι ἦλθεν ὁ κύριος, ἀλλὰ θεραπεῦσαι καὶ διδάξαι *ib.*43.1(172B); θεὸς ὤν, ἴδιον ἔσχε σῶμα καὶ τούτῳ χρώμενος ὀ., γέγονεν ἄνθρωπος δι' ἡμᾶς id.*Ar.*3.31(M.26.389A); ἵνα ἐὰν ἴδωμεν αὐτὸν δι' ὀργάνου τοῦ ἰδίου σώματος θεϊκῶς πράττοντά τι ἢ λέγοντα, γινώσκωμεν ὅτι θεὸς ὤν, ταῦτα ἐργάζεται *ib.*3.35(397B); τὸ ἀνθρώπινον ἐν τῇ σοφίᾳ προέκοπτεν, ...ὄ. αὐτῆς πρὸς τὴν ἐνέργειαν τῆς θεότητος...γινόμενον *ib.*3.53(436A); θεὸς ἀναλαβὼν ὄ. καὶ θεός ἐστι καθὸ ἐνεργεῖ καὶ ἄνθρωπος κατὰ τὸ ὄ. ...ὄ. καὶ τὸ κινοῦν μίαν πέφυκεν ἀποτελεῖν τὴν ἐνέργειαν...μία ἄρα οὐσία γέγονε τοῦ λόγου καὶ τοῦ ὀ. Apoll.*fr.*117(p.235.24ff.)ap.CCP(681) *act.*10(H.3.1248D); σὰρξ...θεοῦ ζωῆς ὄ. ἁρμοζόμενον τοῖς πάθεσι πρὸς τὰς θείας βουλάς id.*anac.*29(p.246.3; M.28.1284A); μέγα τῇ Χριστοτόκῳ παρθένῳ τὸ τεκεῖν ἀνθρωπότητα, τῆς τοῦ θεοῦ λόγου θεότητος ὄ. Nest.*fr.*C 8(p.247.6); οὐκ ἔτεκεν Μαρία τὴν θεότητα...ἀλλ' ἔτεκεν ἄνθρωπον, θεότητος ὄ. *ib.*C 9(p.252.11)ap.Thdt.*haer.*4.12(4.372); cf. ἡ παρθένος...τέξεται υἱόν...οὐ κατά σε...θεότητος ὄ., ἀλλὰ θεὸν μεθ' ἡμῶν, καθ' ἡμᾶς γενόμενον ἄνθρωπον †Thdt.*Nest.*(4.1048); ὄ. εἴη [sc. ἡ σάρξ] τῆς ἐν αὐτῇ θεότητος κατὰ βραχὺ πρὸς τὴν ἔκφρασιν αὐτῆς διὰ τῶν ἔργων ὑπηρετοῦν Cyr.*thes.*28(5[1].252E); ὁ εἷς τε καὶ μόνος Χριστὸς ...ὡς δι' ὀργάνου τοῦ ἰδίου σώματος ἐνήργηκεν τὰς θεοσημείας καὶ οὐκ ἐνηργῆσθαι φαμὲν αὐτὸν καθ' ὁμοιότητα τῶν ἁγίων id.*apol.Thdt.*7 (p.131.6; 6[1].225B); πολλάκις διὰ τῆς σαρκὸς αὐτοῦ ἐνεργεῖ ὁ λόγος θαυματουργῶν, ὡς φυσικοῦ ὀ. λοιπὸν νοουμένης αὐτῷ προσιέναι τῆς σαρκός Leont.H.*Nest.*6.9(M.86.1757C); ref. healings ἰᾶτο...δι' ὀργάνου οὐ προυβέβλητο ἀνθρωπίνου, οἷά τις μουσικὸς ἀνὴρ διὰ τῆς λύρας τὴν σοφίαν ἐπιδεικνύμενος Eus.*d.e.*4.13(p.171.25; M.22.285C); Ath.*inc.*44. 2(173C); cf. ἀπρεπὲς μὲν ἦν τὸν τῶν ἄλλων τὰς νόσους θεραπεύοντα παρορᾶν τὸ ἴδιον ὄ. ἐν νόσοις τηκόμενον *ib.*22.5(136B); ref. human mind of Christ in simile of ὄ. as musical instrument ὥσπερ μουσικὸς καὶ τὸ ὄ. οὐ δύο μουσικοί, οὕτως θεὸς λόγος καὶ νοῦς ἀνθρώπινος οὐ δύο ἡγεμονικά. ἀντὶ γὰρ ὀ. τῷ νῷ ἀνθρωπίνῳ κέχρηται ὁ λόγος ‡Ath.*dial. Trin.*4.5(M.28.1257A); ἀλλὰ τὸ ὄ. τοῦ μουσικοῦ ἄνουν ἐστίν. Orth.: καὶ ὁ μουσικὸς θνητός ἐστιν. ἐνταῦθα δὲ ὁ λόγος ἀθάνατος ὤν, τῷ νῷ κέχρηται ὀ. ... καὶ ἐν μὲν τῷ ἑκουσίῳ πάθει τῷ νῷ κέχρηται...ὀ., ἐν δὲ τοῖς σωματικοῖς τῷ σώματι *ib.*(1257A,B); **7.** of physical *organs* in representations of God ὑμνήσαμεν...ἐν...τῇ συμβολικῇ θεολογίᾳ...τίνα τὰ θεῖα σχήματα καὶ μέρη καὶ ὄ. ... καὶ ὅσαι ἄλλαι τῆς συμβολικῆς εἰσι θεοτυπίας ἱερόπλαστοι μορφώσεις Dion.Ar.*myst*.3(M.3.1033B); and angels ἔστι δὲ ὅτε καὶ τῶν εἰς ἡμᾶς θεοκρισιῶν ἐστι σύμβολα τὰ πλαττόμενα τῶν ἁγίων ἀγγέλων ὄ. id.*c.h*.15.5(M.3.333C).

ὀργανοποιΐα, ἡ, *organization*, Clem.*str*.4.26(p.320.24; M.8.1373A).

ὀργή, ἡ, *wrath, anger*;

A. of man; **1.** ref. moral and spiritual life; **a.** in gen. ἐπαρᾶται... τοῖς πονηροῖς...πάθεσι, τῇ ὀ., τῇ μήνιδι· ἐπιθυμίαν δὲ τὴν ὀ. ἐκάλεσεν· ἐκ ταύτης γὰρ καὶ ἡ ὀ. τὴν ἐτυμολογίαν ἔχει· ὀρέγεται γὰρ ὁ ὀργιζόμενος ἀμύνασθαι τὸν ἐχθρόν Thdt.*qu.110 in Gen*.(1.112); ὀ. ἐστιν ὑπόμνησις κεκρυμμένου μίσους ἤγουν μνησικακίας. ὀ. ἐστιν ἐπιθυμία κακώσεως τοῦ παροξύνοντος Jo.Clim.*scal*.8(M.88.828C); **b.** as vice and sin βαπτίσθητε τὴν ψυχὴν ἀπὸ ὀ. καὶ ἀπὸ πλεονεξίας...καὶ ἰδοὺ τὸ σῶμα καθαρόν ἐστι Just.*dial*.14.2(M.6.504D); ἡ ἀκολασία φύσει κακόν, κατὰ ἀκολασίαν δὲ μοιχεῖαι γίνονται καὶ...ὀργαί Meth.*symp*.8.16(p.106.7; M.18.169B); ὁ θεὸς...τὴν πρὸς τὸν πλησίον ὀ. φόνῳ παρείκασε Marc.Er.*opusc*.3.10(M.65.980B); **c.** as disposition of mind ὀκτώ εἰσι πάντες οἱ γενικώτατοι λογισμοί...πέμπτος ὁ τῆς ὀ. Evagr.Pont.*vit.cog*.1(M.40.1272A); μὴ δῷς ἑαυτὸν τῷ τῆς ὀ. λογισμῷ, κατὰ διάνοιαν τῷ λελυπηκότι μαχόμενος id.*cap.pract*.A 14(M.40.1225A); ἀπόστησον λογισμοὺς ὀργῆς ἀπὸ σῆς ψυχῆς καὶ θυμὸς μὴ αὐλιζέσθω ἐν σῇ καρδίᾳ Nil.*spir.mal*.10(M.79.1156A); *ib*.9(1153C); **d.** as passion ἡ ὀ. πάθος ἐστὶν ὀξύτατον Evagr.Pont.*vit.cog*.1(M.40.1273A); ποία μανία οὕτως ἐκστήσειεν ἂν τῶν κατὰ φύσιν φρενῶν ὡς ὀ. καὶ παραπληξία; Chrys.*hom.6.4 in Ac*.(9.54C); οὐδὲν ὀ. χεῖρον...διὸ παρακαλῶ πάντα ποιεῖν, ὥστε τὸ θηρίον τοῦτο χαλινοῦν *ib*.(54D); ὀ. πάθος ἐστὶ μανιῶδες καὶ τοὺς ἔχοντας γνῶσιν ἐξίστησιν εὐχερῶς Nil.*spir.mal*.9(M.79.1153C); τοῦ ἀλόγου τῆς ὀ. πάθους...τοῦ πᾶσαν ψυχὴν ἐρημοῦντος...καὶ θηρίοις ὅμοιον τὸν ἄνθρωπον ἀποδεικνύντος Marc.Er.*opusc*.5.8(M.65.1041A); **e.** origin ἐκ τῆς ἀφροσύνης γίνεται πικρία, ἐκ δὲ τῆς πικρίας θυμός, ἐκ δὲ τοῦ θυμοῦ ὀ., ἐκ δὲ τῆς ὀ. μῆνις Herm.*mand*.5.2.4; from Devil, Chrys.*hom.16.10 in Mt*.(7.218A); ἕως ἂν ὑπονοτίζηται τὸ τῆς πικρίας ...καὶ ὀ. καὶ θυμοῦ διαβολικὸν δένδρον τῷ φαύλῳ τῆς ὑπερηφανίας ὕδατι Marc.Er.*opusc*.5.8(M.65.1041B); cf.*ib*.5.10(1045A); **f.** compared or connected with other passions: τῦφος, Meth.*symp*.5.4(p.58.7; M.18.104B); λύπη, Marc.Er.*opusc*.2.156(M.65.953D); ὀξυχολία, Clem.*fr*.44(p.221.24); θυμός: γενικὸν μέν τινες πάθος ᾠήθησαν εἶναι τὴν ὀ., καὶ αὐτὴν τάξαντες ὑπὸ γένος τὴν ἐπιθυμίαν·...τὴν πικρίαν μὲν εἶναι ὀ. δυσπαράδεκτον...θυμὸν δὲ ὀ. ἐναρχομένην Or.*comm.in Eph*.4:31(p.556); *ib*.(p.557); διαφέρει...θυμὸς ὀργῆς, τῷ θυμῷ μὲν εἶναι ὀ. ἀναθυμιωμένην καὶ ἔτι ἐκκαιομένην, ὀ. δὲ ὄρεξιν ἀντιλυπήσεως ‡Ath.*fr.Ps*.2:5(M.27.65C); ἔστι γὰρ θυμὸς μὲν οἷον ἔξαψίς τις καὶ ἀναθυμίασις ὀξεῖα τοῦ πάθους· ὀ. δὲ ἔμμονος λύπη καὶ ὁρμὴ διαρκὴς πρὸς τὴν τῶν ἠδικηκότων ἀντίδοσιν Bas.*hom*.10.6(2.90A; M.31.369A); ἔστι...θυμὸς ζέσις τοῦ περὶ καρδίαν αἵματος παρὰ τὸ οἱονεὶ ἐξ ἀναθυμιάσεως τῶν χυμῶν συνιστάμενον οἴδημα περὶ τὴν καρδίαν ὠνομασμένος· ὀ. δέ ἐστιν ὄρεξις ἀντιλυπήσεως †Bas.*Is*.180(1.511B; M.30.424A); ὀργή...θυμὸς ἐμμένων Gr.Naz.*carm*.1.2.34.44(M.37.948A); ὀ. ... καὶ μῖσος αὔξει θυμόν, ἐλεημοσύνη δὲ καὶ πραΰτης καὶ τὸν ὄντα μειοῖ Evagr.Pont.*cap.pract*.A 11(M.40.1224C); ἀδικούμενοι γάρ, ἢ νομίζοντες ἀδικεῖσθαι, θυμούμεθα, καὶ γίνεται τότε μικτὸν τὸ πάθος ἐξ ἐπιθυμίας καὶ θυμοῦ. εἴδη δὲ τοῦ θυμοῦ τρία· ὀ. ἡ καὶ χολὴ καὶ χόλος καλεῖται, μῆνις καὶ κότος. θυμὸς μὲν γὰρ ἀρχὴν καὶ κίνησιν ἔχων, ὀ. καὶ χολὴ καὶ χόλος λέγεται Nemes.*nat.hom*.21(M.40.692A) = Jo.D.*f.o*.2.16(M.94.933A); Isid.Pel.*epp*.4.223(M.78.1317B); ἄσειστον...τὸν νοῦν ἡμῶν ἀπεργάζεται [sc. fear of God] πρὸς ὀ. καὶ θυμὸν καὶ μνησικακίαν *V.Pach.A* 12(p.136.19); **g.** its products: μισαδελφία Marc.Er.*opusc*.5.3(1032C); μνησικακία Jo.Clim.*scal*.9(M.88.841B); **h.** as barrier to effective prayer, Chrys.*hom.17.3 in Ac*.(9.140D); **i.** humility, after example of Christ's humility, as its remedy, Marc.Er.*opusc*.5.10(1045B); **j.** in good sense οὐ πρότερον προσεύξῃ πειραζόμενος πρὶν εἰπεῖν τινα ῥήματα μετ' ὀργῆς πρὸς τὸν θλίβοντα· τῆς γὰρ ψυχῆς πεποιωμένης τοῖς λογισμοῖς συμβαίνει μηδὲ καθαρὰν γενέσθαι τὴν προσευχήν. ἐὰν δὲ μετ' ὀργῆς εἴπῃς τι πρὸς αὐτούς,...ἐξαφανίζεις τῶν ἀντικειμένων τὰ νοήματα Evagr.Pont.*cap.pract*.A 30(M.40.1229B); οὐ καθόλου τὴν ὀ. ἀπεῖπεν· ἔστι γὰρ καὶ ἐπὶ καλῷ ποτε τῇ τοιαύτῃ τῆς ψυχῆς χρήσασθαι ὁρμῇ Gr.Nyss.*beat*.6(M.44.1276A); **2.** of persons, *object of wrath*, Synes.*ep*.47(M.66.1376B); Dor.*doct*.6.4(M.88.1689C).

B. of pagan gods ἔχειν...πάθη ὀ. καὶ ἐπιθυμίας Athenag.*leg*.21.1(M.6.932C).

C. of God; **1.** not to be understood lit. as passion, Athenag.*leg*.21.1(M.6.933A); οὐ τ⟨ὸ⟩ συμβεβηκὸς πάθος ὀνομάζεται θεοῦ ὀ. ... ἔξω ὑπάρχ⟨ο⟩ν αὐτοῦ πλὴν εἰς χρείαν κατατασσόμενον τοῖς δεομένοις, ᾧ καὶ παραδίδονται ὡς ἀνάξιο⟨ι⟩ θεοῦ Or.*Apoc*.30(p.5); id.*hom.20.1 in Jer*.(p.176.12; M.13.500B); θεὸς οὔτε κινεῖται πάθει ὀργῆς...οὔτε ἀλλοιοῦται πρὸς τὴν ἑκάστου ἀξίαν Marc.Er.*opusc*.8.3(M.65.1105C); **2.** in Christian understanding ηὐλαβεῖσθε...ἂν τὴν τοῦ θεοῦ ὀ. Just.*dial*.123.3(M.6.761B); as opp. χάρις, Clem.*prot*.9(p.63.31; M.8.196C); ref. Cross σταυρός, τρόπαιον κατὰ τῆς ἀδικίας...τεθείς, ὥστε μηκέτι τῇ ὀ. ὑπεύθυνον εἶναι ἀπεντεῦθεν τὸν ἄνθρωπον Meth.*Porph*.1(p.504.13; M.18.400B); kindled by impenitence, Chrys.*sac*.3.10(p.66.4; 1.388B); to be understood met., Dion.Ar.*ep*.9.1(M.3.1105B); **3.** as chastisement θεοῦ...ὀ. ... οὐκ ἄκαρπός ἐστιν, ἀλλ' ὡς ὁ λόγος αὐτοῦ παιδεύει, οὕτως καὶ ἡ ὀ. αὐτοῦ παιδεύει· τοὺς γὰρ μὴ παιδευθέντας λόγῳ παιδεύει ὀργῇ Or.*hom.20.1 in Jer*.(p.176.16; M.13.500C); τὸ...κολάζειν ὀργίζεσθαι πεποιήκαμεν· οὕτω γὰρ ἡμῖν ἐξ ὀ. ἡ κόλασις Gr.Naz.*or*.31.22(p.172.14; M.36.157B); as future punishment of wicked, Thdt.*Rom*.5:9(3.54); Oecum.*Apoc*.10:11(p.125); and punishment of ungodly in present life, Ath.*v.Anton*.86(M.26.964A); v. infra 4; **4.** in rel. to θυμός: ὀ. ... ἐστιν ὁ ἑπόμενος τοῖς ἁμαρτάνουσιν ἐπὶ τιμωρίᾳ πόνος· θυμὸν δὲ ὁρίζονται ὀργὴν ἀναθυμιωμένην καὶ διοιδαίνουσαν Or.*comm.in Rom*.2:7–9(*JTS* 13 p.215); εἰ οὖν παιδεύει μὲν ὀ., ἐλέγχει δὲ θυμός, ἀνυσιμώτερον ἡ ὀ. τοῦ θυμοῦ †Bas.*Is*.180(1.511D; M.30.424B); θυμὸς... ἐστιν ἡ κρίσις τοῦ ἐπαχθῆναι τάδε τινὰ τὰ σκυθρωπὰ τῷ ἀξίῳ· ὀ. δὲ ὁ πόνος ἤδη καὶ κόλασις ἡ ἀπὸ τοῦ δικαίου κριτοῦ κατὰ τὸ μέτρον τῆς ἀδικίας ἐπαγομένη Bas.*hom.in Ps*.29(1.127C; M.29.313B); τὴν...ὀ. ἀπένειμε τῷ θυμῷ· ὀργὴν γὰρ τὴν παιδείαν καλεῖ Thdt.*Ps*.29:5(1.788); **5.** two modes of divine wrath γίνεται...δικαίως ἐπὶ τὸν ὑψηλόφρονα νοῦν ὀ.· τουτέστιν, ἐγκατάληψις· ἤγουν ἡ τοῦ διοχληθῆναι αὐτὸν...ὑπὸ δαιμόνων συγχώρησις ἵνα...ταπεινωθῇ Max.*qu.Thal*.52(M.90.493D); ὀ. θεοῦ ἐστιν...ἡ τῶν παιδαγωγουμένων ἐπίπονος αἴσθησις...ἡ τῶν ἀκουσίων πόνων ἐπαγωγὴ δι' ἧς τὸν ἐπ' ἀρετῇ καὶ γνώσει φυσιούμενον νοῦν ὁ θεὸς...ἄγει πρὸς...ταπείνωσιν *ib*.(489D); ἢ πάλιν ὀ. κυρίου ἐστίν, ἡ ἀνακωχὴ τῆς τῶν θείων χαρισμάτων χορηγίας· ἥτις συμφερόντως ἐπὶ πάντα γίνεται νοῦν ὑψηλόν *ib*.(492A); ὁ...μὴ σωφρονισθεὶς τῷ πρώτῳ εἴδει τῆς ὀ. ..., ἐλθεῖν πρὸς ταπείνωσιν, τὴν ἄλλην δέχεται σαφῶς ἐπ' αὐτὸν ἐρχομένην ὀ., ἀφαιρουμένην αὐτοῦ τὴν τῶν χαρισμάτων ἐνέργειαν καὶ ἔρημον αὐτὸν καθιστῶσαν τῆς...φρουρούσης δυνάμεως *ib*.(496B); **6.** of Devil as instrument of God's wrath ὀ. θεοῦ ὁ διάβολος...καί ἐστιν ἡ ὀ. τοῦ θεοῦ ἡ ἐπισείσασα τὸν Δαυῒδ...ἐφ' ᾗ κόλασις ἀπὸ θεοῦ ἀκολουθεῖ τῷ π⟨ε⟩ισθέντι τῇ τοιάδε εἰρηκυ⟨ί⟩ᾳ ὀ. Or.*Apoc*.30(pp.5f.); cf.id.*comm.in Rom*.1:18(*JTS* 13 p.214); ἔοικε...λέγεσθαι ὀ. καὶ ὁ διάκονος τῶν ἐπὶ τοῖς ἡμαρτημένοις πόνων *ib*.; **7.** of divine wrath expressed in rise of heresy, Ath.*v.Anton*.82(M.26.957B).

ὀργίζ-ω, pass., *be angry*, of God πῶς οὖν, φασί, εἰ φιλάνθρωπός ἐστι καὶ ἀγαθὸς ὁ κύριος, ∼εται; Clem.*paed*.1.8(p.128.1; M.8.328B); τὸ τὸν πατέρα ∼εσθαι ὑπὲρ τῶν εἰς τὸν υἱὸν γεγενημένων, τοῦτο τῆς πολλῆς περὶ τὸν υἱὸν ἀγάπης καὶ τιμῆς Chrys.*hom.3.2 in Heb*.(12.27C); c. κατά, Thdt.*Soph*.1:3(2.1561); Thphn.*chron*.p.140(M.108.380B).

***ὀργιστικῶς**, *angrily*, Gr.Nyss.*beat*.6(M.44.1276A).

***ὀρδιναῖος**, (Lat. *ordinarius*) *arranged in order*, Steph.Diac.*v.Steph*.(M.100.1124B).

***ὀρδινάριος**, ὁ, (Lat. *ordinarius*) *magistrate* elected regularly at beginning of the year, Synes.*ep*.144(M.66.1537D); Jo.Mal.*chron*.13 p.345(M.97.516A); Thphn.*chron*.p.125(M.108.348A).

***ὀρδινεύω**, (cf. Lat. *ordino*), **1.** *arrange, bring about*, *A.Petr.et Paul*.16(p.186.9); **2.** *ordain* ὀ. ... ἐπίσκοπον *ib*.7(p.182.4).

***ὄρδινος**, ὁ, (cf. Lat. *ordo*), **1.** *right order, turn* εἴ τις οὐκ αἱρεῖ εὐλογίαν εἰς τὸν ὄ. αὐτοῦ, γενέσθω ἀπευλογίας ‡Bas.*poen.mon*.22(2.528B; M.31.1309A); Gr.Mag.*dial*.(tr.Zach.)1.8(M.*PL*.77.186C); **2.** *row, line*, *ib*.3.37(311A).

***ὀρδίνως**, (cf. Lat. *ordine*) *in line*, ‡Petr.I Al.*phys*.15(p.44).

***ὀρειάριος**, ὁ, (Lat. *horrearius*) *store-keeper*, Eustrat.*v.Eutych*.17(M.86.2293B).

***ὀρειβατικός**, *of mountain travel*, Clem.*paed*.2.11(p.226.30; M.8.537A).

[*]**ὀρεινοβατής**, *walking on, living in mountains*, Eus.*Ps*.17:33f.(M.23.181A).

[*]**ὀρεῖον**, τό, v. §ὅριον.

***ὀρεκτέον**, *one should offer*, Clem.*str*.5.3(p.338.10; M.9.37A).

ὀρεκτιάω, *desire eagerly*; of physical desires, Cyr.*ador*.2(1.56E); *ib*.14(516E); id.*Am*.64(3.321C); of spiritual desires, id.*Jo*.10.2(4.879A).

ὀρεκτικός, *desiring*, c. genit. προαίρεσις...ὀρεκτική τινος οὖσα Clem.*str*.2.2(p.117.15; M.8.940B); *ib*.6.15(p.491.11; M.9.341B); id.*fr*.40(p.220.13; M.9.752A).

ὀρεκτικῶς, *with desire* ὀ. ... διακειμένους Nil.*perist*.4.9(M.79.836A).

ὄρεξις, ἡ, *desire, appetite*; **1.** of natural desire ὄρεξιν ἐπιθυμίας διακρίνουσιν...καὶ τὴν μὲν ἐπὶ ἡδοναῖς καὶ ἀκολασίᾳ τάττουσιν ἄλογον οὖσαν, τὴν δὲ ὀ. ἐπὶ τῶν κατὰ φύσιν ἀναγκαίων λογικὴν ὑπάρχουσαν κίνησιν Clem.*str*.4.18(p.300.3; M.8.1325B); τὸ μὲν ἀστεῖον βούλησιν ὀνομάσαι, ἣν ὁρίζονται εὔλογον ὄ., τὸ δὲ φαῦλον ἐπιθυμίαν, ἣν φασιν εἶναι ἄλογον ὄ. ἢ σφοδρὰν ὄ. Or.*Jo*.20.22(20; p.355.21; M.14.621C); τί

...ἐστιν ἕτερον ὄ. ἡ ἐπιθυμία τοῦ ἐλλείποντος πρὸς ἀναπλήρωσιν τοῦ ὑπεκρεύσαντος; Leont.B.*Nest.et Eut.*2(M.86.1345B); ref. Manich. doctrine εἰ κακὸν ἡ ὕλη, πάντως πού εἰσιν αὐτῆς καὶ ὀρέξεις τοιαῦται. ἔστι δὲ ἡ μὲν τοῦ κακοῦ ὄ. φαύλη, ἡ δὲ τοῦ καλοῦ πάνυ σπουδαία Alex.Lyc.*Man.*9(p.15.10; M.18.424D); **2.** in good sense; of desire for righteousness, Clem.*ecl.*14(p.141.2; M.9.705A); for instruction, Chrys.*diab.*1.1(2.247A); for good, Dion.Ar.*d.n.*4.19(M.3.716C); **3.** in bad sense τὴν ἄλογον τῆς σωματικῆς ὄ. ἐπικράτειαν, ἅπαν τὸ ζῷον ὠθούσης ἐπὶ τὸ κατ' αἴσθησιν ἐπιθυμητόν id.*c.h.*2.4(M.3.144A); ἐμφαίνει...ἡ σταυροειδὴς...σφραγὶς τὴν...τῶν σαρκικῶν ὄ. ἀνενεργησίαν [ref. ordination] id.*e.h.*5.3.4(M.3.512A); as being worldly, Meth. *symp.*11.3(p.138.27; M.18.217A); partic. of sexual desire, Or.*Jo.*20. 27(22; p.363.11; M.14.636A); Meth.*symp.*2.5(p.22.14; 56B); *Hom. Clem.*3.68; Eus.*d.e.*3.6(p.132.31; M.22.224B); Thdt.*Ps.*7:11(1.648); of desire for money, Clem.*q.d.s.*12(p.167.25; M.9.616C); **4.** denied of God, Athenag.*leg.*21.1(M.6.933A); and, in bad sense, of heavenly beings, Meth.*symp.*8.16(p.105.4; M.18.168C).

***ὀρεόμονες, οἱ,** s.v.l., *mountain-dwellers* οἱ...σπηλοδίαιτοι καὶ ὀ. Steph.Diac.*v.Steph.*(M.100.1113C).

ὀρεσίτροφος, *growing on mountains* ὀ. ῥίζης Cyr.*ador.*2(1.61E).

ὀρθοβατ-έω, *walk straight,* met. τῷ γήρᾳ συγκύπτουσα, ∼οῦσα τῇ γνώσει Amph.*hom.*2.5(M.39.52A).

***ὀρθόβυθος,** *straight into the depths,* Jo.Mosch.*prat.*76(M.87. 2929C).

***ὀρθόγραμμος,** *rectilinear,* Dion.Ar.*d.n.*4.11(M.3.708C).

ὀρθόδικος, *judging rightly,* Gr.Naz.*carm.*1.2.2.200(M.37.594A); *ib.* 2.1.13.217(1244A).

***ὀρθοδοξαστής, ὁ,** *one of right opinion,* Clem.*str.*1.9(p.30.17; M.8. 743A).

ὀρθοδοξαστικῶς, *as men of right opinion should* ὀ. τὴν θείαν ἀποθαυμαζόντων πρόνοιαν Olymp.*Job* 38 proem.(M.93.396B).

ὀρθοδοξ-έω, 1. *hold right belief, be orthodox* Ὠριγένης εὐθύνας μὴ ∼οῦντα [sc. Βήρυλλον]...ἐπὶ...τὴν ὑγιῆ δόξαν ἀποκαθίστησιν Eus.*h.e.* 6.33.2(M.20.593A); Ath.*h.Ar.*35(M.25.733C); Bas.*ep.*69.2(3.163B; M. 32.433A); Epiph.*haer.*73.28(p.302.27; M.42.457A); πᾶς ∼ῶν...πάντα αἱρετικὸν δυνάμει, κἂν οὐ ῥήματι ἀναθεματίζει Thdr.Stud.*epp.*1.49(M. 99.1088B); **2.** *become orthodox* ὁ πατριάρχης...ὠρθοδόξησε...ἐκ τῆς τῶν μονοθελητῶν κακοδοξίας Thphn.*chron.*p.349(M.108.840B).

ὀρθοδοξία, ἡ, A. *right opinion, sound doctrine;* **1.** in gen. ὀ. ἐστὶν ἀψευδὴς περὶ θεοῦ καὶ κτίσεως ὑπόληψις ἢ ἔννοια περὶ πάντων ἀληθὴς ἢ δόξα τῶν ὄντων καθάπερ εἰσίν Anast.S.*hod.*2(M.89.76D); opp. absurdity in doctrine ὁ θεὸς...πάλιν τὰς ψυχὰς...ὡς εἰς παγίδα τὴν σάρκα, δίκην ὑφεξούσας των ἡμαρτημένων, ἐμβιβάζει, ὅπερ ἀτοπίας μᾶλλον ἢ ὀρθοδοξίας ἐστίν Meth.*res.*1.54(p.310.16; M.41.1145A); ὀρθοδοξίας κατηχητική, εἰρήνης τε καὶ ἑνώσεως ὑποθετική [i.e. of a letter] Eus.*h.e.*4.23.2(M.20.384B); **2.** ref. apocryphal writings τῶν... παντελῶς νόθων καὶ τῆς ἀποστολικῆς ὀ. ἀλλοτριῶν *ib.*3.31.6(281B); ἥ τε γνώμη καὶ ἡ τῶν ἐν αὐτοῖς φερομένων προαίρεσις πλεῖστον ὅσον τῆς ἀληθοῦς ὀ. ἀπᾴδουσα *ib.*3.25.7(272A); *ib.*3.38.5(296A).

B. partic., *orthodoxy,* the traditional and universal doctrine of the Church; **1.** of official teaching opp. heresy τῆς ἐκκλησιαστικῆς... ὀ. Eus.*h.e.*3.23.2(M.20.257A); *ib.*4.23.8(388A); Ἀμβρόσιος, τὰ τῆς Οὐαλεντίνου φρονῶν αἱρέσεως, πρὸς τῆς ὑπὸ Ὠριγένους πρεσβευομένης ἀληθείας ἐλεγχθείς..., τῷ τῆς ἐκκλησιαστικῆς ὀ. προστίθεται λόγῳ *ib.*6.18. 1(560B); CAlex.*ep.*ap.Ath.*apol.sec.*6(p.92.9; M.25.257C); ὡμολόγησε [sc. Marcell.] φρονεῖν, ὥσπερ καὶ ἡ καθολικὴ ἐκκλησία φρονεῖ... ὥσπεροῦν καὶ οἱ ἡμέτεροι πρεσβύτεροι...ἐμαρτύρησαν αὐτοῦ τῇ ὀ. Jul. Papa *ep.Dian.ib.*32(p.110.26; 301B); cf.Jul.Papa *ib.*(p.111.1; 301B); Ath.*h.Ar.*78(p.227.11; M.25.788D); id.*ep.Pall.*(M.26.1168B); id.*ep. Aeg.Lib.*8(M.25.556B); Bas.*ep.*25.2(3.104E; M.32.301A); προσεποιεῖτο εἰρωνείᾳ τὰ τῆς ὀ. ῥήματα Epiph.*haer.*68.4(p.144.25; M.42.192A); κατὰ τῆς ὀ. λέγειν *ib.*73.36(p.311.2; 469B); τοῖς τὰ τῆς ὀ. φρονοῦσι CEphr.(431)*can.*1; ref. θεοτόκος as symbol of orthodoxy χαίροις ...Μαρία θεοτόκε...τὸ σκῆπτρον τῆς ὀ. Cyr.*hom.div.*4(p.102.21; 5[2]. 355E); τὸ τῆς ὀ. δόγμα CCP(448)*act.*2(*ACO* 2.1.1 p.113.28; H.2.128D); ἀρνούμενος [τε] τὰ εὐσεβῆ τῆς ὀ. δόγματα, διασύρων δὲ καὶ τοὺς ἁγίους πατέρας Eus.Dor.*libell.*(p.100.28; H.2.112A); ὀρθοδοξίαν αὐτῷ μαρτυρῶν CChalc.*act.*1(*ACO* 2.1.1 p.70.7; H.2.73C); ref. emperors ὡς οἱ ἀπόστολοι οὕτω πιστεύετε...ὑμεῖς φωστῆρες τῆς ὀ. *ib.*6(*ACO* 2.1.2 p.155.17; H.2.488A); τῇ ὀ. καὶ ταῖς ἄλλαις ἀρεταῖς διαπρέπουσα Cyr.S. *v.Sab.*53(p.145.12); Λέοντος τόμον, ὀρθοδοξίας ὅρον Evagr.*h.e.*2.2 (p.38.31; M.86.2489C); ὁμοίως τοῖς...Κυρίλλου...χαράγμασιν ὡς...ὁμότιμον δέχομαι καὶ τῆς αὐτῆς ὀ. γεννητρίαν καὶ τὴν...ἐπιστολὴν...τοῦ... Λέοντος...ἣν καὶ στήλην ὀρθοδοξίας καλῶ...ὡς πᾶσαν μὲν ὀ. ἡμᾶς ἐκδιδάσκουσαν, πᾶσαν δὲ κακοδοξίαν αἱρετικὴν...ἀπελαύνουσαν Sophr.H. *ep.syn.*(M.87.3188D); Geo.Pis.*hex.*187(M.92.1447A); CTrull.*can.*1; ἰθύνας...κλυδωνιζομένην τὴν ἐκκλησίαν τῷ...χειμῶνι τῶν αἱρέσεων πρὸς ὀρθοδοξίας ὅρμον ἄκλυστον Jo.Mon.*hymn.Bas.*4(M.96.1373A); ψυχὴ ἐν σκοτομήνῃ αἱρέσεως οὖσα τὸ φῶς τῆς ὀ. δυσχερῶς ἐπιγινώσκει Taras.ap.CNic.(787)*act.*1(H.4.48E); τῷ αὐτῷ στοιχεῖν κανόνι τῆς ὀ. Thdr.Stud.*epp.*2.171(M.99.1537D); ἐκκλησία...ὡς νίκης βραβεῖα δεξαμένη...ὀρθοδοξίας σύμβολα [sc. icons] id.*can.imag.*1(M.99.1769A); cf. Θεοδώρας...βασιλίδος τῆς τὴν ὀ. καὶ προσκύνησιν τῶν...εἰκόνων... ἀναστηλωσάσης *Triodion*(Rome 1879, p.246); Γερμανοῦ, Ταρασίου... τῶν...τῆς ὀ. προμάχων *ib.*(p.241); ref. reception of heretics διὰ τί οἱ ὀρθόδοξοι τὸν προσφεύγοντα τῇ ὀ. αἱρετικὸν οὐ βαπτίζουσιν;...τοῦ αἱρετικοῦ ἐπὶ τὴν ὀ. ἐρχομένου τὸ σφάλμα διορθοῦται, τῆς μὲν κακοδοξίας τῇ μεταθέσει τοῦ φρονήματος, τοῦ δὲ βαπτίσματος τῇ ἐπιχρίσει τοῦ ἁγίου μύρου, τῆς δὲ χειροτονίας τῇ χειροθεσίᾳ ‡Just.*qu.et resp.*14 (M.6.1261C); CCP(381)‡*can.*7; CTrull.*can.*95; **2.** ref. faith εἰς ἡμᾶς τῆς ἀποστολικῆς παραδόσεως ἢ τῆς ὑγιοῦς πίστεως ἔγγραφος κατῆλθεν ὀ. Eus.*h.e.*4.21(M.20.377B); *ib.*6.2.14(525C); Παύλου σὺν καὶ τῇ τῆς πίστεως ὀ. τῆς ἐπισκοπῆς ἀποπεπτωκότος, Δόμνος...τὴν λειτουργίαν ...διεδέξατο *ib.*7.30.18(717A); Bas.*ep.*129.2(3.221D; M.32.561A); τὴν πίστιν τῆς ὀ. Epiph.*haer.*30.5(p.339.24; M.41.412C); *ib.*73.23(p.296. 32; M.42.448A); οἷα διὰ τὴν ἀληθῆ πίστιν τῆς ὀ. ... ὑπομένομεν Memn. *ep.*(p.46.7; M.77.1464A); **3.** ref. credal professions ὑποτάξας τοῖς ἑαυτοῦ γράμμασιν ἔγγραφον τὴν ἀνδρῶν ὀ. CHier.(335)*ep.*ap.Ath.*syn.* 21(p.248.5; M.26.720A); αὐτοὶ [sc. 150 fathers at CCP(381)] τὸ τῆς ὀ. ἐκραταίωσαν σύμβολον *Chron.Pasch.*p.304(M.92.769A); τῷ τῆς ὀ. λιβέλλῳ ‡Jo.D.*ep.Thphl.*21(M.95.372D).

C. phrase, κυριακὴ τῆς ὀ., *Sunday of orthodoxy,* first Sunday in Lent when second restoration of icons by Theodora and Methodius (842) is celebrated, champions of orthodoxy commemorated, and heretics anathematized, ‡Ath.*imag.Beryt.*tit.(M.28.797C); cf.*Triodion*(Rome 1879, p.223); *ib.*(p.240).

ὀρθόδοξος, A. as adj., *of right belief, orthodox,* i.e. expressing or holding faith and doctrine of Church; **1.** of interpretation of scripture παρὰ τὸν ὀ. βιάζεσθαι τολμῶσι λογισμὸν τὰς γραφάς Meth.*symp.* 3.10(p.38.13; M.18.76C); φέρε κατὰ τὸν ἀληθῆ πάλιν καὶ ὀ. ... τοῦτο διαλάβωμεν λογισμόν id.*res.*1.35(p.273.14; M.41.1100A); *ib.*1.45(p.294. 16; 1116B); νικώσης τῆς ὀ. διανοίας τὴν ἁπλουστέραν τῶν ῥημάτων προφοράν Ath.*Ar.*3.59(M.26.448A); **2.** of faith of Church opp. heresy τῆς εὐσεβοῦς καὶ ὀ. πίστεως id.*ep.Epict.*13(p.427.26; M.26. 1069A); ἀναθεματίζουσι τὴν Ἀρείου πίστιν...καὶ ὁμολογοῦσι τὴν τῶν πατέρων ὀ. πίστιν...ἀπὸ τῶν ἀποστόλων καὶ προφητῶν παραδοθεῖσαν Epiph.*haer.*69.11(p.160.30; M.42.220A); τὴν [sc. πίστιν] ὑπὸ τῶν πατέρων ταχθεῖσαν ἐν τῇ Νικαίᾳ τῇ πόλει, τὴν ὀ. καὶ καλῶς τεταγμένην *ib.*73.23(p.297.5; 448B); πολλὰ...λύσας τῶν γραφῶν κεφάλαια καὶ τὴν ὀ. πίστιν παραδούς ‡Pall.*h.mon.*2.7(p.26.3; M.34.1027C); πάντες οἱ πανταχοῦ τῆς ὀ. πίστεως ἱερεῖς Thds.Imp.*ep.Jo.Ant.*(p.4.5; M.77. 1460C); ταῖς...ἐκκλησίαις ταῖς πανταχοῦ τῆς ὀ. πίστεως *ib.*(p.4.11; 1460D); τὴν ὀ. φυλάττων πίστιν CEph.(431)*act.*1(*ACO* 1.1.2 p.18.8; H.1.1369D); *ib.*(p.29.11; 1385C); Νεστόριος...ἀπεναντία τῆς ὀ. πίστεως φρονῶν *ib.*(p.34.34; 1393C); τὰς ἐπεισαχθείσας αἱρέσεις τῇ ὀ. πίστει καὶ τῇ εὐαγγελικῇ καὶ ἀποστολικῇ διδασκαλίᾳ Jo.Ant.*ep.Ruf.*(p.40.1; M.83.1476B); *ib.*(p.42.3; 1481A); ἐπὶ καθαρότητι βίου καὶ ὀ. πίστει εὐδοκιμοῦντα Thds.Imp.*ep.Diosc.*2(p.71.7; H.2.76A); τοῦ καθολικοῦ καὶ ἀποστολικοῦ δόγματος τῆς ἡμετέρας ὀ. πίστεως *ib.*(p.68.11; 72B); τὸ τῆς ὀ. ... πίστεως δόγμα *ib.*(p.68.28; 72D); τὰ ὀ. δόγματα τῆς ἐκκλησίας CCP(448)*act.*2(*ACO* 2.1.1 p.103.11; H.2.113C); ἀρκεῖν ἡμῖν τὴν παραδοθεῖσαν παρὰ τῶν ἁγίων πατέρων τῶν ἐν Νικαίᾳ ὀ. πίστιν Thds.Imp.*sacr.*7(p.73.29; H.2.77E); τὰ τῆς ὀ. καὶ ἀληθοῦς πίστεως Marcian.Imp.*ep.Nic.*2(p.30.13; H.2.52C); τὰ περὶ τῆς ἁγίας καὶ ὀ. πίστεως παρὰ τῶν ἁγίων ἡμῶν πατέρων πάλαι ὁρισθέντα *ib.*(p.30.8; 52C); μήτε...συνάπτειν πρὸς γάμον αἱρετικῷ ἢ Ἰουδαίῳ ἢ Ἕλληνι, εἰ μὴ ἄρα ἐπαγγέλλοιτο μετατίθεσθαι εἰς τὴν ὀ. πίστιν τὸ συναπτόμενον πρόσωπον τῷ ὀ. CChalc.*can.*14; εἰ...αἱρετικὸς...λάθῃ κοινωνῶν τῇ ἐκκλησίᾳ...καὶ μετὰ θάνατον ἐκ τῶν συγγραμμάτων αὐτοῦ...αἱρετικὸς εἶναι φανῇ, ὅμως οὐκ ἐκ τούτου ἡ ὀ. βλάπτεται πίστις Justn.*ep.Thdr. Mops.*(p.67.29; M.86.1089C); Κωνσταντῖνος...ἐσπούδασε τὴν ὀ. κρατῦναι πίστιν id.*typ.Thdr.Mops.*(M.86.1035B); βοηθῆσαι τῇ καθολικῇ ὀ. πίστει...κινδυνευούσῃ Cyr.S.*v.Sab.*50(p.141.14); εἰς ἐκκλησίαν καθολικὴν καὶ πίστιν ὀ. ... τὴν νόσον ἀπέβαλεν Sophr.H.*mir.Cyr.et Jo.*39(M. 87.3572C); μνήσθητι, κύριε,...τῶν ἐν ὀ. πίστει καὶ εὐλαβείᾳ σου οἰκούντων *Lit.Jac.*(p.208.23); τὸν ἀποστολικὸν καὶ εὐαγγελικὸν τῆς ὀ. πίστεως λόγον *Chron.Pasch.*p.8(M.92.84C); of orthodox faith as attested by scripture, Marc.Er.*Nest.*9(p.12.15); *ib.*27(p.26.19); **3.** of Church's θρησκεία, Meth.*symp.*8.10(p.92.24; M.18.153B); Marcian. Imp.*ep.episc.*(p.27.25; H.2.45D); τῆς ὀ. θρησκείας διδασκαλίαν *ib.* (p.28.2; 45E); Φλαβιανὸς ἔσωσεν τὴν ὀ. καὶ καθολικὴν θρησκείαν CChalc.*act.*1(*ACO* 2.1.1 p.114.17; H.2.129A); **4.** of decisions or opinions οἱ κατὰ τὴν Γαλλίαν ἀδελφοὶ τὴν ἰδίαν κρίσιν...εὐλαβῆ καὶ ὀρθοδοξοτάτην ὑποτάττουσιν Eus.*h.e.*5.3.4(M.20.437B); τὴν ὀ. γνώμην ‡Chrys.*hom.*13(13.255F); Nest.*ep.Cyr.*2(p.30.21; M.77.52D); **5.** of writings, Eus.*h.e.*5.27(M.20.512A); of letters, Justn.*ep.Thdr.Mops.*(p.48.9; M.86.1045B); Sophr.H.*ep.syn.*(M.87.3188D); of a confession of faith, †Jo.D.*B.J.*39(M.96.1232A); **6.** of Church πίστις τῆς καθολικῆς καὶ ἀποστολικῆς καὶ ὀ. ἐκκλησίας Epiph.*rescr.*4(p.157.23; M.41.161B); Basilisc.*encycl.*(p.50.27; M.86.2601A); Cyr.S.*v.Sab.*52(p.144.15); **7.** of persons: bishops, *Ep.Dion.*2(p.160.18; M.25.393B); Ath.*ep.Aeg.Lib.*7(M.25.553B); Εὐστάθιον τὸν ὁμολογητὴν καὶ ὀ. id.*fug.*3(p.70.2; M.25.648B); id.*h.Ar.*19(p.192.20; M.25.716A); CCP(381)*can.* 6; αὕτη...τῆς καθολικῆς καὶ ἀποστολικῆς ἐκκλησίας ἡ πίστις ᾗ συναινοῦσιν ἅπαντες οἵ τε κατὰ τὴν ἑσπέραν καὶ τὴν ἑῴαν ὀ. ἐπίσκοποι Cyr.*ep.*17(p.34.25; 5^2.69B); ἀναθεματισθέντος Παύλου τοῦ Σαμοσατέως...ὑπὸ τῶν ὀ. πατέρων ἐπισκόπων Eus.Dor.*contest.*(p.101.9; M.89.277C); τῶν...τεσσάρων μεγάλων ὀ. πατριαρχῶν *Lit.Jac.*(p.220.20); Church fathers πάντας...τοὺς ἁγίους πατέρας...ὀ. ἔσχον CEph.(449) *act.*(*ACO* 2.1.1 p.92.5; H.2.100B); *Lit.Jac.*(p.218.12); laity, Thds. Imp.*sacr.*3(p.71.3; H.2.76A); *Lit.Jac.*(p.218.22); *Ep.*ap.CChalc.*act.*4 (*ACO* 2.1.2 p.117.32; H.2.425D); comp., Gr.Naz.*or.*23.13(M.35.1165A); Thphn.*chron.*p.123(M.108.344A); superl., *ib.*p.115(328A); emperors, CEph.(449)*act.*(*ACO* 2.1.1 p.138.29; H.2.160D); CChalc.*act.*1(*ACO* 2.1.1 p.70.18; H.2.73D); *ib.*(p.91.32; 100A); *ib.*(p.112.1; 125C); ἡ αὐγούστα Νεστόριον ἐξέβαλεν, πολλὰ τὰ ἔτη τῆς ὀ. *ib.*(p.69.33; 73B); Justn.*typ.Thdr.Mops.*(M.86.1035B); in prayer for emperors, *Lit. Jac.*(p.186.17); of councils, CEph.(431)*can.*3(p.28.5).

B. as subst. masc., *adherent of the orthodox faith*; **1.** in gen., opp. heretics, *Ep.Aeg.*ap.Ath.*apol.sec.*77(p.156.30; M.25.388A); CAlex.*ep. ib.*7(p.93.24; 261A); CSard.*ep.cath.ib.*42(p.119.9; 324B); Ath.*h.Ar.*3 (p.184.12; M.25.697A); εἰ...παρὰ ὀρθοδόξων ἦν τὰ γραφόμενα..., οὐδὲν ἦν ἐν τοῖς γραφομένοις ὑποπτεύειν· ἄδολος γὰρ...ἐστιν ὁ τῶν ἀποστολικῶν ἀνδρῶν τρόπος id.*ep.Aeg.Lib.*8(M.25.556B); Epiph.*haer.*73.23 (p.296.32; M.42.448A); οὐδεὶς τῶν ὀ. θεοτόκον αὐτὴν δέδιεν εἰπεῖν Cyr. *ep.*14(*ACO* 1.1.1 p.98.18; 5^2.44D); ἀξιοῦμεν...κωλύεσθαι τοὺς κατὰ τῶν ὀ. ἐπανισταμένους Thal.CP *Thds.*5(p.9.40; M.91.1477C); εἴ τις αἱρετικὸς κατὰ αἱρετικοῦ, οὐ διὰ τοῦτο αὐτὸς ὀ. δείκνυται Justn.*ep.Thdr. Mops.*(p.53.1; M.86.1055D); of BMV as protectress of orthodox, ‡Rom.Mel.(*AS* 1 p.225); Θεοδόσιος...ἔδωκε τὰς ἐκκλησίας τοῖς ὀ. ... διώξας ἐξ αὐτῶν τοὺς...Ἀρειανοὺς *Chron.Pasch.*p.303(M.92.764A); of bishops τὸν ὀ. τῇ συνόδῳ CChalc.*act.*1(*ACO* 2.1.1 p.70.14; H.2.73C); ὁ ὀ. τῇ συνόδῳ, ὁ πατὴρ τοῖς πατράσι, τοῖς ὀ. ὁ θεὸς καλῶς ἤνεγκε CNic. (787)*act.*1(H.4.48A); of congregations, Gr.Naz.*or.*21.34(M.35.1124B); ὁ λαὸς τῶν ὀ. Pall.*v.Chrys.*5(p.29.23; M.47.19); *ib.*15(p.91.26; M.47.52); τῇ τῶν ὀ. ἐγκαταλεγέντες ποίμνῃ CTrull.*can.*72; **2.** ref. schismatics who are not excused by their orthodoxy, Chrys.*hom.11.5 in Eph.* (11.87A); cf.Epiph.*exp.fid.*13(p.513.22; M.42.808A); **3.** partic. ref. faith τετολμήκασι τὸν αἱρετικὸν λογισμὸν τῇ τῶν ὀ. πίστει συνάψαι CArim.*decr.*(p.238.38; M.26.700C); CEph.(431)*act.*1(*ACO* 1.1.2 p.31.2; H.1.1388D); αὕτη ἡ πίστις τῶν πατέρων· αὕτη ἡ πίστις τῶν ἀποστόλων· αὕτη ἡ πίστις τῶν ὀ. CChalc.*act.*6(*ACO* 2.1.2 p.155.10; H.2.485E); and ref. θρησκεία, Isid.Pel.*epp.*1.300(M.78.357A); Διόσκορος... τὴν...εὐσεβῆ θρησκείαν τῶν ὀ. ... ἐλυμήνατο Eus.Dor.*ep.imp.*(p.67.4; M.86.2549C); **4.** partic. ref. Church πρεσβύτερος τῆς ἁγίας ἐκκλησίας τῶν ὀ. *MAMA* 1.290 [Phrygia, saec. iv]; Pall.*v.Chrys.*16(p.97.4; M.47.55); διαμαρτύρεται...ὁ θεὸς ἐκείνων εἶναι τὰς ἐκκλησίας δι' ὧν θαύματα ἐκτελεῖται, τουτέστι τῶν ὀ. ‡Just.*qu.et resp.*100(M.6.1345A); Cyr.*ep.*14(p.98.18; 5^2.44C); *ib.*45(p.151.16; 135D); μὴ παριδεῖν...τὴν τῶν ὀ. ἐκκλησίαν μοιχευομένην παρὰ αἱρετικῶν Thal.CP *Thds.*4(p.9.5; τὴν ὀ. ἐκκλησίαν M.91.1476C); ἐκκλησία λέγεται ὡς ἐν ταύτῃ συναγειρομένων καὶ καλουμένων τῶν ὀ. ‡Sophr.H.*liturg.*2(M.87.3984A).

C. neut. as subst., *orthodoxy*, Philost.*h.e.*10.5(M.65.585C).

***ὀρθοδόξως**, *in an orthodox manner, with right belief* ἐπισκεψώμεθα πῶς ὀ. ἀνήγαγε [sc. Παῦλος] τὸν Ἀδὰμ εἰς τὸν Χριστόν Meth.*symp.*3.4 (p.30.16; M.18.65A); περὶ τὰς ἐξηγήσεις τῶν γραφῶν εἰς τὸ ὀ. ὑμνῆσαι καὶ μεγαλοπρεπῶς...τὸν θεόν *ib.*5.4(p.57.7; 101C); id.*res.*2.5(p.338.18; M.41.1172B); τὴν μὲν διάνοιαν ὑγιαίνοντες,...ὀ. πρεσβεύοντες τὸν λόγον ...οἰδῶσι δὲ τὴν ψυχὴν ὑπὸ φιλαρχίας id.*lepr.*12(p.466.6); Epiph.*haer.* 73.23(p.296.33; M.42.448A); περὶ τοῦ υἱοῦ ὀ. ἔχοντες *ib.*74.1(p.313.20; 473C); CEph.(431)*act.*1(*ACO* 1.1.2 p.19.28; H.1.1372E); CChalc. *act.*1(*ACO* 2.1.1 p.94.1; H.2.101C); *Lit.Jac.*(p.208.4); οὐ πᾶς ὁ βαπτιζόμενος, ἀλλὰ πᾶς ὁ ὀ. φωτιζόμενος θεοῦ υἱὸς ἀναδείκνυται Dam.*troph.* suppl.(p.277.1); CTrull.*can.*1; *ib.*32; superl., Epiph.*haer.*70.2(p.233.30; 341A).

ὀρθοεπέω, *say the right word*, Cyr.*ador.*8(1.280A).

***ὀρθοκρισία, ἡ**, *right judgement*, Cyr.*Is.*5.3(2.786C).

ὀρθολεκτ-έω, *speak correctly, uprightly*, ‡Gr.Nyss.*occurs.*(M.46. 1164C); βούλομαί σε τῷ τρόπῳ καὶ τῇ πράξει ~εῖν Nil.*epp.*2.191(M.79. 345A).

ὀρθοποδ-έω, *walk straight, walk correctly*; met., of moral conduct ἐν...τῇ ἐκκλησίᾳ οὐ πάντες εἰσὶ βλέποντες οὐδὲ...~οῦντες Or.*comm. in Mt.*16.24(p.557.7; M.13.1456B); Bas.*ep.*204.7(3.307A; M.32.753C); Epiph.*haer.*42.11(p.145.6; M.41.756D); ἀντέστησαν τῷ...σωτῆρι...οἱ τῆς Ἱερουσαλὴμ οἰκήτορες χωλοὶ καὶ τυφλοί· οὐ γὰρ ᾔδεσαν ~εῖν Cyr. *fr.2Reg.*5:6(M.69.684A); ~εῖν ἔμαθον οἱ πάλαι χωλεύοντες id.*Ps.*39:6 (M.69.985C); Ἰουδαῖοι...τὸ ~εῖν δύνασθαι λαχόντες ἀπό γε τῆς ἐν νόμῳ παιδαγωγίας id.*Is.*3.3(2.465B); ὡς ἀπατεῶνες...ἀποπεμπέσθωσαν ἵνα μὴ ταράττωσι τοὺς ἐθέλοντας ~εῖν id.*ep.*50(*ACO* 1.1.3 p.101.3; 5^2.171C).

***ὀρθοπόδησις, ἡ**, *straight walking*, hence, *righteous behaviour*, Thdr.Stud.*epp.*2.10(M.99.1141B).

ὀρθός, A. as adj.; **1.** *upright* τὸ ἀνθρώπινον σχῆμα οὐδενὶ ἄλλῳ τῶν ἀλόγων ζῴων διαφέρει ἢ τῷ ὀ. ... εἶναι Just.*1apol.*55.4(M.6.412B); liturg., in deacon's cry at special moments in service, telling people to stand, and to elevate their thoughts ὀ. πρὸς κύριον...ἑστῶτες ὦμεν προσφέρειν *Lit.*ap.*Const.App.*8.12.2; παρακελεύεσθαι τὸν διάκονον...καὶ λέγειν· ὀρθοί, στῶμεν καλῶς,...νενομοθέτηται...ἵνα τοὺς... λογισμοὺς ἀνορθώσωμεν, ἵνα...ὀ. ἔμπροσθεν τοῦ θεοῦ παραστῆσαι δυνηθῶμεν...τὴν ψυχήν Chrys.*incomprehens.*4.5(1.478C); *Lit.Jac.*(p.176.16); *Lit.Chrys.*(p.368.24); ὀ., μεταλαβόντες τῶν...τοῦ Χριστοῦ μυστηρίων...εὐχαριστήσωμεν τῷ κυρίῳ *ib.*(p.397.7); **2.** *straight*, fig. τὸ δίκαιον ὀ. ὁδὸν ἔχει, τὸ δὲ ἄδικον στρεβλήν Herm.*mand.*6.1.2; Just. *dial.*8.2(M.6.492D); παιδαγωγία...ἀγωγὴ...ὀ. ἀνάγουσα εἰς οὐρανόν Clem.*str.*1.7(p.122.5; M.8.313A); ὀ. ὁδὸν τοῦ βίου Const.ap.Ath.*apol. sec.*68(p.146.9; M.25.369B); **3.** *true, right, correct*; of mind and reason, *T.Benj.*3.2; Ign.*Eph.*1.1; ἄνευ...φιλοσοφίας καὶ ὀ. λόγου Just. *dial.*3.3(M.6.480B); id.*2apol.*9.4(M.6.460B); Clem.*paed.*1.13(p.150.21; M.8.372A); ἐννοιῶν τῶν παρὰ τὸν ὀ. λόγον id.*ecl.*62(p.155.2; M.9. 728C); ἁμαρτωλοὶ...καὶ παρὰ τὸν ὀ. λόγον πράττοντες Or.*hom.9.4 in Jer.*(p.68.29; M.13.353D); πίστιν οὐκ οὖσαν κατὰ τὸν ὀ. λόγον Hegem.*Arch.*6(p.6.4; M.10.1433B); Ath.*h.Ar.*32(p.200.28; M.25. 729B); ὅτι ἀγένητός ἐστιν ὁ θεός, πάντες...οἱ νοῦν ὀ. ἔχοντες ὁμολογοῦσιν ‡Ath.*dial.Trin.*2.5(M.28.1164A); **4.** *righteous*; of life, Clem. *paed.*1.12(p.150.10; M.8.369C); id.*str.*1.5(p.18.8; M.8.720A); μέγα... ὅπλον ἐστὶ κατ' αὐτῶν [sc. demons] βίος ὀ. Ath.*v.Anton.*30(M.26. 889A); **5.** *straightforward* οὐ γὰρ ὀ. διανοίᾳ λαλοῦσιν, ἀλλ' ὡς ἔνδυμα προβάτου τὰ ῥήματα περιβαλλόμενοι id.*ep.Aeg.Lib.*8(M.25.556B); *true, genuine* ἀρχήν, ἀφ' ἧς ἀνεβλάστησεν ὁ ὀρθότατος λόγος Meth. *creat.*11(p.499.9; M.18.341B); ὀ. καὶ εἰλικρινῆ τὴν θεότητα τοῦ μονογενοῦς ‡Ath.*Ar.*4.35(p.85.15; M.26.521B); Dion.Ar.*d.n.*4.32(M.3. 732C); **6.** of faith and doctrine, *orthodox*, def. ἡ πίστις ἐστὶν ὀ. ... ἐκ διδασκαλίας ἀποστολικῆς ὁρμωμένη καὶ παραδόσεως τῶν πατέρων, βεβαιουμένη ἔκ τε νέας καὶ παλαιᾶς διαθήκης Ath.*ep.Adelph.*6(M.26. 1080A); in gen. προτρεπόμεθα ὑμᾶς...τὴν ὀ. πίστιν τῆς καθολικῆς ἐκκλησίας κατέχειν CSard.*ep.Alex.*ap.Ath.*apol.sec.*38(p.117.12; M.25. 316A); id.*ep.cath.ib.*45(p.121.39; 332B); τῆς ὀ. ... δόξης *ib.*46(p.122.28; 333B); ἀδελφοὶ...τῆς ὀ. δόξης ὄντες Ath.*ep.Aeg.Lib.*5(M.25.548C); διδασκαλία...διανοίας ἐστὶν οὐκ ὀ. id.*v.Anton.*84(M.26.960B); ἵν' ἐκ τῆς μαθήσεως ἡ πίστις ὀ. γένηται id.*Ar.*2.42(M.26.237B); κρατείτω... τὰ ἐν Νικαίᾳ...ὁμολογηθέντα· ὀ. γάρ ἐστι καὶ ἱκανὰ πᾶσαν...αἵρεσιν ἀνατρέψαι id.*ep.Max.*5(M.26.1089C); ταῦτα...διανοίας ἀλλότρια...τῆς ὀ. Gr.Nyss.*Eun.*12(1 p.310.17; M.45.1024B); ἀποδραμοῦνταί τινες... τῆς ὀ. καὶ ἀδιαβλήτου πίστεως Cyr.*Lc.*18:8(M.72.852A); id.*expl.xii cap.*2(p.18.12; 6^1.148E); *Chron.Pasch.*p.8(M.92.84B); neut. plur. ὀρθὰ ...αὐτὸν φρονοῦντα [sc. Marcell.]...ἔδει μὴ ἀποβάλλειν τῆς κοινωνίας Jul.Papa *ep.Dian.*ap.Ath.*apol.sec.*32(p.110.29; 301B); Ath.*Ar.*1.8 (28A); of writings πολλὰ αὐτοῦ [sc. Irenaeus] συγγράμματα κάλλιστα καὶ ὀρθότατα φέρεται *M.Polyc.*epilog.2; ref. interprn. of scripture, esp. texts used by Arians ἔχει...τὴν διάνοιαν εὐσεβῆ καὶ λίαν ὀ. Ath.*decr.*13(p.11.22; M.25.437B); id.*Ar.*1.46(M.26.105C); τὸ ἐν ταῖς Παροιμίαις ῥητόν, ὀ. ἔχον καὶ αὐτὸ τὴν διάνοιαν *ib.*2.44(240C); *ib.*2.81 (317C); *ib.*3.1(321B); *ib.*3.37(404A); id.*ep.Serap.*1.3(M.26.536C).

B. as subst. masc., *person of orthodox faith* ἡ ἐπισκοπὴ...ὑπὸ πολλῶν ἁρπαγήσεται...οὐκ ὀρθῶν Ath.*ep.Drac.*1(M.25.524B); Bas.*ep.* 125(3.214E; M.32.545B).

ὀρθοτενής, *straight*, Cyr.*Jo.*8:19(4.494D); Paul.Sil.*Soph.*741(M.86. 2147B).

ὀρθότης, ἡ, *uprightness, correctness*; **1.** moral, Athenag.*leg.*31.2 (ὁσιότητα M.6.961B); Cyr.*Lc.*18:28(M.72.860A); **2.** of faith and doctrine, Clem.*paed.*1.13(p.151.2; M.8.372B); *orthodoxy*, Gr.Naz.*carm.* 2.1.11.1187(M.37.1110A); Cyr.*Lc.*18:18(M.72.856D); τοῖς τῆς ὀ. ... δόγμασιν id.*ador.*11(1.397A); δογματικῆς ὀ. *ib.*(397B); οὔτε...εἰς υἱοὺς καταμερίζειν δύο τὸν ἕνα Χριστὸν...ἐφίησι...ὁ τῆς ὀ. λόγος id.*apol.*

*Thdt.*3(p.120.17; 6[1].214A); *Chron.Pasch.*p.8(M.92.84B); **3.** of persons, *orthodoxy*, in complimentary address ἐλύπησέ σου τὴν ὀ. Bas. *ep.*25.2(3.104D; M.32.301A).

ὀρθοτομ-έω, 1. *cut in a straight line*, met. αἱ...ὁδοὶ σοφίας ποικίλαι ~εῖν ἐπὶ τὴν ὁδὸν τῆς ἀληθείας Clem.*str.*2.2(p.114.30; M.8.933C); τὴν εὐθεῖαν καὶ βασιλικὴν ὁδὸν ~οῦσα ἡ ἐκκλησία Eus.*e.th.*1.8(p.66.1; M.24.837A); ὀρθοτόμησον ἡμῶν τὴν ὁδόν *Lit.Jac.*(p.240.23); **2.** *expound rightly, in an orthodox way*; exeg. 2Tim.2:15 ~οῦντα· τουτέστι, τέμνε τὰ νόθα Chrys.*hom.5.2 in 2Tim.*(11.687D); ἐπαινοῦμεν τῶν γεωργῶν τοὺς εὐθείας τὰς αὔλακας ἀνατέμνοντας. οὕτω καὶ διδάσκαλος ἀξιέπαινος, ὁ τῷ κανόνι τῶν θείων λογίων ἑπόμενος Thdt.*2Tim.*2:15(3.684); in gen. προχειρίσασθε...ἐπισκόπους...~οῦντας ἐν τοῖς τοῦ κυρίου δόγμασιν *Const.App.*7.31.1; ὠρθοτόμησαν [sc. Nicene fathers] τὴν πίστιν ‡Ath. *Melch.*(M.28.529D).

***ὀρθοτομία, ἡ,** *cutting straight*; met., *correctness* of doctrine, *orthodoxy* ὁ γνωστικὸς...τὴν ἀποστολικὴν καὶ ἐκκλησιαστικὴν σῴζων ὀ. τῶν δογμάτων, κατὰ τὸ εὐαγγέλιον ὀρθότατα βιοῖ Clem.*str.*7.16(p.73.16; M.9.544A); Eus.*h.e.*4.3.1(M.20.308B); ἐμαρτύρει...τοῖς ἀνδράσιν...πίστεως ὀρθοτομίαν...ὑποτάξας...ἔγγραφον τὴν τῶν ἀνδρῶν ὀρθοδοξίαν CHier.(335)*ep.*(p.248.3; M.26.717C); ὁ. ἐκάλεσε τὴν τῆς ἀληθείας διδασκαλίαν Thdt.*2Tim.*2:15(3.684); τὸ...ἀντιλέγειν τῇ ἀληθείᾳ τῆς ὁδοῦ εἰσι παραλλαγαὶ καὶ οὐκ ὀρθοτομίαι Marc.Er.*opusc.*4(M.65.993D); Max.*ambig.*(M.91.1301C); Thdr.Stud.*epp.*2.138(M.99.1441B).

***ὀρθοτόμος, 1.** *rightly expounding* κατὰ πίστιν ἐκλεκτῶν θεοῦ... παίδων ἁγίων, ὀ. Ar.*Thal.fr.*1 ap.Ath.*Ar.*1.5(M.26.20C); **2.** *orthodox* ὀ. λάτρης τῆς ἁγίας...τριάδος Jo.D.*haer.*(M.94.780C); id.*ep.Thphl.*14 (M.95.364A); οὐκ ἐξ ἑτέρας θρησκείας μεταθεμένῳ εἰς τὴν ὀ. Jo.VI H. *v.Jo.D.*4(M.94.433C).

***ὀρθοφρονέω,** *hold orthodox views, be orthodox*, Thdr.Stud.*epp.*2.171(M.99.1537A).

ὀρθόφρων, *orthodox*, Geo.Pis.*Sev.*141(M.92.1632B); Thdr.Stud. *epp.*2.4(M.99.1121D); *ib.*2.76(1313B).

ὀρθρίζ-ω, *rise early, at dawn*, *A.Thom.*A 93(p.206.9); *A.Pil.*A 12.2 (p.253); Eus.*h.e.*1.13.14(M.20.125B); Or.*enarr.in Job* 2:13(M.17.63C); τὸ ~ων ἀντὶ τοῦ μετὰ σπουδῆς Olymp.*fr.Jer.*25:3(M.93.677C); esp. for morning prayer, *T.Jos.*3.6; ~ων ἀντιφώνους ὕμνους εἰς τὸ θεῖον ἔλεγε Socr.*h.e.*7.22.5(M.67.685A); ἐκ νυκτὸς ~οντα, φιλάνθρωπε, φώτισον Andr.Cr.*can.mag.*153(p.152; M.97.1353B); Jo.D.*carm.anast.* 48(p.219; M.96.841B).

ὀρθρινός, *of the morning, early*, Herm.*sim.*5.1.1; πρὸς ὀ. δοξολογίαν Pall.*h.Laus.*104(M.34.1210C); μετὰ τὸ ῥηθῆναι τὸν ὀ. [sc. ψαλμόν] *Const.App.*8.38.1; neut. plur. as subst., *matins*, ‡Bas.*poen. mon.*54(2.530B; M.31.1313B); Call.*v.Hyp.*(p.54).

ὄρθρος, ὁ, *day-break, dawn*, as time of prayer; **1.** in gen., Bas. *reg.fus.*37.5(2.384B; M.31.1016B); αἰτησώμεθα τὸν ὄ. ... καὶ τὴν ἡμέραν εἰρηνικὴν καὶ ἀναμάρτητον *Const.App.*8.38.2; ὄρθρου *at dawn*, *ib.*2.59.1; συναθροίζεσθε ὄ. καὶ ἑσπέρας ψάλλοντες *ib.*2.59.2; εὐχὰς ἐπιτελεῖτε ὄ. ... εὐχαριστοῦντες ὅτι ἐφώτισεν ἡμῖν ὁ κύριος...ἐπαγαγὼν τὴν ἡμέραν *ib.*8.34.1; **2.** esp. ref. early morning service, matins, as one of regular hours of prayer τοὺς διατετυπωμένους καιροὺς τῶν προσευχῶν...τὸν μὲν ὄ. ὥστε πρῶτα κινήματα τῆς ψυχῆς...ἀναθήματα εἶναι θεοῦ Bas.*reg.fus.*37.3(2.383B; M.31.1013A); ἀπερχομένους ἐν τῇ ἁγίᾳ ἐκκλησίᾳ...ἔν τε τῷ σαββάτου ἑσπερινῷ καὶ ἐν τῷ ὄ. τῆς κυριακῆς καὶ ἐν τῇ λειτουργίᾳ αὐτῆς †Gregent.*leg.Hom.*64(M.86.616B); penitents admitted to this service, †Jo.Jej.*poenit.*(M.88.1913A); εἰς τὸν ὄ. μετὰ τὸ ἑξάψαλμον τὸ θεὸς κύριος λέγομεν *Const.Stud.*9(M.99.1708B).

ὀρθῶς, *rightly* ἐὰν...δουλεύσητε αὐτῷ ὀ. κατὰ τὸ θέλημα αὐτοῦ Herm. *mand.*12.6.2; ἐτέλεσε τὴν δικαιοσύνην τοῦ κυρίου ὀ. id.*sim.*2.7; τῆς Ἰουδαίων...ἀλαζονείας ὀ. ἀπέχονται Χριστιανοί *Diogn.*4.6; παρέχει ὁ θεὸς τοῖς ἀγαπῶσιν ὀ. ‡*Diogn.*12.1; ἐν πενίᾳ βίου ὀ. ἐστι βιοῦν Clem. *str.*1.6(p.23.12; M.8.729B); *ib.*4.21(p.305.31; 1341A); τούτους μόνους ζῆν...τοὺς ὀ. βιοῦν ἐπιτηδεύοντας Gr.Thaum.*pan.Or.*6(p.15.11; M.10.1069A); comp. ὀρθοτέρως, Didym.(‡Bas.)*Eun.*5(1.312B; M.29.749A); superl. ὀρθότατα, Meth.*symp.*3.7(p.33.23; M.18.69C).

***ὀριγνώμων, ὁ,** v. *ὁριογνώμων.

ὁρίζ-ω, 1. *divide, separate*; abs.; **a.** τὸ ~ον *the horizon* τοῦ ἀνατολικοῦ...ὁ. Or.*comm.in Gen.*ap.Eus.*p.e.*6.11(291A; M.12.72A); Or.*ib.* (294B; M.12.80A); τοῦ δ' ἡλίου...πρὸς τῷ ὁ. τῆς δύσεως πλησιάζοντος ‡Nil.*narr.*5(M.79.644A); *ib.*7(684C); **b.** ὁ ~ων; **i.** *the horizon* τὸν καθ' ἡμᾶς ὁ. Bas.*hom.in Ps.*45(1.174A; M.29.424C); **ii.** name of meridian which cuts another meridian at right angles ὁ μεσημβρινὸς [sc. κύκλος]...καὶ...ὁ εἰς ἴσα τέμνων μέρη καλούμενος ὁ. Meth. *symp.*8.14(p.101.7; M.18.164C); **2.** *determine, define* μὴ παρεκβαίνειν τὸν ὡρισμένον τῆς λειτουργίας αὐτοῦ κανόνα *1Clem.*41.1; esp. of conciliar decisions φρονεῖν...ἅπερ ἐν τῇ κατὰ Νίκαιαν συνόδῳ...ὡρίσθη Const.ap.Gel.Cyz.*h.e.*3.15.2; Ath.*decr.*2(p.2.25; M.25.'428'(420)A); CSard.*ep.Alex.*ap.Ath.*apol.sec.*40(p.118.24; M.25.324A); Constantius Imp. *ib.*54(p.135.8; 348B); ἡ...σύνοδος ἡ ἐν Σαρδικῇ...ὥρισε μηδὲν ἔτι περὶ πίστεως γράφεσθαι, ἀλλ' ἀρκεῖσθαι τῇ ἐν Νικαίᾳ...πίστει Ath. *tom.*5(M.26.800C); τὰ δοκοῦντα τοῖς...κανόσιν...ὁρίσαι CEph.(431)*act.* 1(*ACO* 1.1.2 p.11.19; H.1.1361A); ~ομεν...περὶ τῶν πρεσβείων τῆς... ἐκκλησίας Κωνσταντινουπόλεως CChalc.*can.*28; **3.** *appoint, ordain* ἐπίσκοποι οἱ κατὰ τὰ πέρατα ὁρισθέντες ἐν Ἰησοῦ Χριστοῦ γνώμῃ εἰσίν Ign. *Eph.*3.2; προαιώνιος ὢν ὁ υἱός, ἐν ἐσχάτοις...καιροῖς εἰς υἱὸν ὡρίσθαι λέγεται θεοῦ, τῆς ἰδίας σαρκὸς τὴν γέννησιν οἰκειούμενος οἰκονομικῶς Cyr.*hom.pasch.*17.3(5[2].230B); cf.id.*inc.unigen.*(5[1].695E); of fixing fasts in OT opp. NT οἱ μὲν ὡρισμένας ἔχοντες νηστείας...οἱ δὲ γνώμῃ μᾶλλον...νηστεύουσιν...εἰ δὲ καὶ ὡρίσθαι ὁ τῆς τεσσαρακοστῆς δοκεῖ καιρὸς δι' ὑπόμνησιν τῶν ῥαθύμων, ἀλλὰ καὶ ταύτην γνώμῃ μᾶλλον τὴν νηστείαν μέτιμεν Vict.*Mc.*6:21(p.291.30); med., *Hom.Clem.*3.36.

ὀρικόν, τό, *mule-cart*, Synes.*ep.*3(M.66.1325A).

ὁρικός, *defining*, Eus.*e.th.*1.20(p.93.13; M.24.888A).

[*]**ὀρινός,** = ὀρεινός, *hilly*, *M.Ariadn.*15(p.132.16).

***ὁριογνώμων, ὁ,** *one who sets boundaries, surveyor*, Epiph.*haer.*42.7(p.103.2; M.41.705A); iron. ὁ ὁρι⟨ο⟩γνώμων τῶν ἐπουρανίων...καὶ γεωμέτρης τῆς...εἰς Χριστὸν σωτηρίας *ib.*76.8(p.348.22; ὁριγνώμων M.42.529A).

§ὅριον ([*]**ὅριον,** [*]**ὀρίον,** [*]**ὀρεῖον,** [*]**ὡρίον,** §**ὠρεῖον, ὡρεῖον,** ***ὡραῖον**), **τό,** (Lat. *horreum*) *granary*, Jo.Eleem.*v.Tych.*(p.150); plur., *Chron.Pasch.*p.314(M.92.800B); *ib.*p.329(852B); ὀρίον Jo. Mosch.*prat.*85(M.87.2941D,2944A); ὅρια Thphn.*chron.*p.322 (ὡραῖα M.108.777C); ὀρεῖον Eustrat.*v.Eutych.*17(M.86.2293B,C); ὠρείων Socr. *h.e.*7.39.2(v.l. ὡρίων M.67.828A); ὡρεῖον Jo.Mal.*chron.*3 p.60(M.97.137A); *M.Pers.*1.12(p.431.8).

ὀριπλανής, *mountain-roaming*, Nonn.*par.Jo.*6:58(M.43.801A).

ὅρισις, ἡ, *limitation* ὅρασις ὅ. τις εἶναι δοκεῖ Melet.*nat.hom.*2(M.64.1173B).

ὅρισμα, τό, *definition* τὰ παρὰ τοῦ...Λέοντος...ὁ. Horm.*ep.cler.* (p.54.35; M.*PL*.63.419A); νεωτέροις ὁ. *ib.*(p.55.27; 419D).

ὁρισμός, ὁ, *decree*; of God, *Hom.Clem.*7.6.

***ὁριστίζω,** *pronounce, decide*, ‡Ath.*doct.mon.*(M.28.1421B,C).

ὁριστικός, 1. *of one who makes a decree* ὁ. ... προσώπῳ Flav.Ant. *anath.*3(M.48.948); **2.** *determining*, c. genit. αἰτίαν ὁριστικὴν τοῦ ἀγνώστου Max.*ambig.*(M.91.1113A); *ib.*(1140A); *ib.*(1217C); abs., neut. as subst., *determining factor* οὐχ ἡ φύσις ἀλλ' ἡ προαίρεσις τὸ ὁ. ἔχει Serap.*Man.*25(p.41; M.40.921B); **3.** gram., *indicative*; neut. as subst., *indicative mood* τὸ ὁ., ὑπό τινων καλούμενον διαβεβαιωτικόν Or.*sel.in Ps.*4:5(M.12.1141D).

ὁριστικῶς, *definitely, clearly, expressly*, Clem.*str.*1.19(p.60.27; M.8.812A); Bas.*jud.*3(2.216C; M.31.660B); †Bas.*bapt.*1.1.2(2.625D,E; M.31.1517A,B).

ὀριτρεφής, *mountain-grown* κώνοισιν ὀ. Paul.Sil.*Soph.*874(M.86.2152B).

***ὀρκεύω,** sens. dub., ? *swell* μὴ ὀρκεύσῃς, μὴ φλεγμαίνῃς *Exorc.*3 (p.334).

ὁρκίζω, 1. *administer an oath*, Or.*schol.in Cant.*8:4(M.17.285A); *Clem.contest.*1(M.2.29A); *Hom.Clem.*2.30; **2.** *adjure*, Herm.*sim.*9.10.5; *A.Petr.et Paul.*77(p.211.4); Jo.Mosch.*prat.*75(M.87.2928B); ὁ. ὑμᾶς εἰς τὸν θεόν Dam.*troph.*3.6(p.246.12); pass., c. acc. of ground of oath, Chrys.*hom.11.3 in 1Thess.*(11.506B).

ὁρκισμός, ὁ, *taking of an oath*, Eus.*onomast.*(p.50.5); *Hom.Clem.* 9.4; Gr.Nyss.*hom.6 in Cant.*(M.44.889A); Chrys.*hom.11.3 in 1Thess.* (11.506A).

ὅρκος, ὁ, *oath*; **1.** in gen. ὅ. ... ἐστιν ὁμολογία καθοριστικὴ μετὰ προσπαραλήψεως θείας Clem.*str.*7.8(p.37.20; M.9.472A); *ib.*(p.38.12; 472B); ἡ...τῶν ὅ. παράβασις ἀσεβείας ἐστὶ τὸ κεφάλαιον Thdt.*Zach.* 5:4(2.1616); διδάσκει...ὁ λόγος μὴ παραβαίνειν τὰς ἐπὶ θεοῦ μεθ' ὅρκων γινομένας συνθήκας id.*qu.42 in 2Reg.*(1.444); **2.** in OT ὁ ὅ., τὸ παλαιὸν διὰ τοῦτο ἐνομοθετήθη, ἵνα μὴ κατὰ τῶν εἰδώλων ὀμνύωσιν Chrys.*hom.17.6 in Mt.*(7.230C); Ἰουδαίοις...παρακελεύεται κατ' αὐτοῦ ὀμνύναι, ἵνα τῇ τοῦ ὅ. συνηθείᾳ αὐτὸν μόνον προσκυνεῖν διδαχθῶσιν Thdt.*Jer.*4:2(2.430); **3.** as forbidden to Christians ὅ. ... μέγας ἐστὶν ἡ ἐν τῷ 'ναί' ἀλήθεια, καὶ διὰ τοῦτο Χριστιανῷ ὀμνύναι αἰσχρόν· ἐκ γὰρ ψεύδους ἀπιστία καὶ δι' ἀπιστίαν πάλιν ὅ. *M.Apollon.* 5; Bas.*ep.*199 *can.*29(3.294D; M.32.725A); τοὺς ὅ. ἐπὶ τοῖς δημοσίοις τελέσμασι μὴ ἐπάγεσθαι id.*ep.*85(178A; M.465A); τί οὖν, ἂν ἀπαιτῇ τις ὅ. ... ἀνάγκην ἐπάγῃ; ὁ τοῦ θεοῦ φόβος τῆς ἀνάγκης ἔστω δυνατώτερος Chrys.*hom.17.5 in Mt.*(7.229B); αὐτὸ τὸ βιβλίον αἰδέσθητι, ὃ προτείνεις εἰς ὅ. καὶ τὸ εὐαγγέλιον...ἀνάπτυξον καὶ ἀκούσας τί περὶ ὅρκων ὁ Χριστὸς ἐκεῖ διαλέγεται, φρίξον id.*stat.*15.5(2.159A); Isid.Pel.*epp.* 1.155(M.78.288A); Cyr.*ador.*6(1.212C); **4.** of God's oath, *1Clem.*8.2; *Hom.Clem.*16.7; οὐ γὰρ ὡς ἄνθρωπος ὀμνύει ὁ θεός, ἀλλ' ἡμῖν ὁ λόγος αὐτοῦ ἀντὶ ὅρκου πρὸς ἀλήθειαν γίνεται…ὡς γὰρ ἀνθρώπων τὸν λόγον ὁ. βεβαιοῖ, οὕτως ἃ λαλεῖ ὁ θεὸς ἀνθ᾽ ὅρκου λογιζέσθω διὰ τὸ βέβαιον καὶ ἀμετάθετον τῆς βουλῆς αὐτοῦ ‡Ath.*pass*.6(M.28.193A); **5.** of pagan oaths in magical conjurations, *Hom.Clem*.2.26; οἱ…προδόντες τὴν…πίστιν καὶ ὀμόσαντες ὁ. Ἑλληνικοὺς ἐκβάλλεσθαι…ἐν γ᾽ ἔτεσι Bas.*ep*.217 *can*.81(3.329E; M.32.805C).

ὁρκωμοσία, ἡ, *swearing, oath,* Eus.*h.e*.10.8.3(M.20.896B); *Dial. Tim.et Aquil*.89 v°; Jo.Mosch.*prat*.97(M.87.2956B).

***ὅρκωσις, ἡ,** *exorcism,* Or.*Cels*.7.4(p.156.15; M.11.1425C).

ὁρμάζω, = ἁρμόζω, **1.** *betroth*; pass., Epiph.*haer*.78.13(p.464.11; M.42.720A); **2.** med., *take to wife,* Thphn.*chron*.p.250 (ἁρμοσάμενος M.108.628A).

[*]**ὁρμαστός, ὁ, ἡ,** = ἁρμοστός, *betrothed, A.Thom*.A 43(p.160.12); *M.Ner.et Ach*.18(p.17.8); Epiph.*ep.Arab*.ap.*haer*.78.16(p.467.8; M.42.725B); οὐκ ἔστιν ἀπὸ Μαρίας μόνον ὁ θεὸς λόγος…οὐκ ἔστιν ἀπὸ τῶν χρόνων Ἰωσὴφ τοῦ ταύτης ὁ. …, ἀλλὰ 'ἐν ἀρχῇ ἦν ὁ λόγος' id.*haer*.69.23(p.173.3; 237C); Mac.Aeg.*hom*.51.1(p.20).

[*]**ὅρμαστρον, τό,** = ἅρμοστρον, *betrothal gift, A.Pil*.A 2.4(p.225); Ephr.2.352C.

ὁρμ-άω, 1. *start,* c. genit. ὥρμησεν…τοῦ ἐξιέναι *Mir.Artem*.40 (p.66.26); **2.** *have an impulse* μὴ ∼ᾶν παρὰ τὸν ὀρθὸν λόγον Clem.*str*.2.18(p.155.6; M.8.1020A); *ib*.4.19(p.303.6; 1333B); Max.*opusc*.(M.91.24A); **3.** med.; **a.** *be disposed* τῶν ὡρμωμένων κακῶς Bas.*hom.in Ps*.45(1.171A; M.29.417B); **b.** *come, originate* ὁπόθεν τε καὶ ἀφ᾽ οἵου γένους ὡρμᾶτο Eus.*h.e*.3.9.1(M.20.240C); *Pers*.(p.17.17; M.10.105C); Philost.*h.e*.8.15(M.65.568A).

ὁρμή, ἡ, *origin* ἐλάττων ὁρμή σου [sc. BMV] τῆς ἀξίας Chrysipp. *enc.in BMV* 2(p.339.20, conj. for cod. ἐλάττων ὅμησον τῆς ἀξίας).

***ὁρμητιαῖος,** *raging,* Mac.Aeg.*hom*.43.6(M.34.776C).

ὁρμητίας, ὁ, *impetuous person,* Chrys.*hom.81.5 in Mt*.(7.780B); Cyr.*glaph.Gen*.7(1.214D); id.*Is*.2.1(2.198D); *enthusiast, zealot,* Chrys. *laud.Paul*.7(2.515A).

***ὀρνατόριον (-ούριον), τό,** (cf. Lat. *urna*) *place for keeping urns* at the Hippodrome, Thphn.*chron*.p.321 (v.l. ὀρνατούριον M.108.777A).

***ὀρνεοβατία, ἡ,** *immoral act with birds,* †Jo.Jej.*serm*.(M.88.1921D).

ὀρνεόβρωτος, *eaten by birds, Pers*.(p.43.3).

ὀρνεοθυσία, ἡ, *sacrifice of birds,* Jo.Mal.*chron*.8 p.202(M.97.317A).

***ὀρνεοπάτακτος,** *killed by birds,* †Jo.Jej.*poenit*.(M.88.1896A).

***ὀρνεοσκοπία, ἡ,** *observation of the movement of birds, divination by flight of birds,* Cyr.*catech*.4.37; Ephr.2.196A; ἀπόστηθι…τῆς ὁ. … τῆς παρατηρήσεως τῆς βδελυρᾶς Nil.*epp*.2.151(M.78.269D).

***ὀρνεοφθορία, ἡ,** *immoral act with birds,* Jo.Jej.*canonar*.1(106D).

***ὀρνεύω,** (Lat. *orno*) *ornament, adorn, Apoc.Dan*.A(p.36).

ὀρνιθιακός, *of* or *for birds* τὰ ὀ. *books about birds,* Olymp.*Job* 39:13–15(M.93.413C).

ὀρνιθοσκοπία, ἡ, *observation of the movement of birds, divination by the flight of birds,* †Bas.*Is*.77(1.433D; M.30.248B).

***ὀρνιθοφασιανός, ὁ,** *pheasant,* Leont.H.*Nest*.2.47(M.86.1600B).

***ὀρνοσκόπος, ὁ,** *diviner by birds, augur,* Jo.Mal.*chron*.8 p.199(M.97.313A).

ὀρογλυφέω, *remove and alter marks* or *boundary stones, Const. App*.1.1.5.

ὀροθεσία, ἡ, 1. *boundary,* †Hipp.*theoph*.2(p.258.14; M.10.853B); Eus.*d.e*.4.9(p.162.28; M.22.272B); ref. three independent principles in Marcion's doctrine οὐκέτι τὸ περιεχόμενον θεός…ἀλλά…ἡ περιεκτικὴ ὁ. Epiph.*haer*.42.7(p.102.21; M.41.704C); Cyr.*Ps*.15:6(M.69.812B); **2.** *fixed limit of time,* ‡Jo.D.*ep.Thphl*.20(M.95.372A); **3.** *determination of date* (of Easter), Petr.I Al.*fr*.(M.18.513A).

ὀροθέσιον, τό, *fixing of boundaries,* Jo.D.*dialect*.8(M.94.553C).

ὀροθετ-έω, 1. *fix boundaries,* Tim.Ant.*nativ.Jo.Bapt*.1(M.28.908D); of Gnostics τὰ ἐπουράνια ἐπαγγελλόμενοι μέτροις τισὶν ὁ. Epiph.*haer*.33.8(p.458.10; M.41.569A); *ib*.66.14(p.38.12; M.42.52A); **2.** *define, fix, prescribe,* Dion.Ar.*d.n*.2.4(M.3.640D); πάντα…ἡ θεία δικαιοσύνη τάττει καὶ ∼εῖ *ib*.8.7(896A); id.*ep*.9.2(M.3.1108D); pass. περιπατῶν κατὰ τὴν ∼ηθεῖσαν ἀσφαλῆ πίστιν Procl.CP *or*.6.6(M.65.732C); Areth.*Apoc*.4:10(M.106.576A).

ὀροθέτης, ὁ, 1. *one who determines boundaries* τὸν δημιουργὸν καὶ ὁ. Cyr.H.*catech*.9.7; Epiph.*haer*.66.14(p.38.8; M.42.52A); φύσεως ὀροθέτην κύριον ‡Chrys.*nat.Jo.Bapt*.(10.815C); name of Valent. aeon also called Ὅρος, Val.Gn.ap.Epiph.*haer*.31.6(p.395.7; M.41.485B); Iren.*haer*.1.2.4(M.7.460A); *ib*.1.3.1(468A); Epiph.*haer*.31.4 (p.388.9; 480B); *ib*.31.35(p.437.18; 541A); **2.** *one who defines* Ἀέτιος …ὁ διαστολεὺς καὶ ὁ. περὶ φύσεως θεοῦ *ib*.76.28(p.376.29; M.42.573A).

***ὀροθέτις,** *acting as a boundary, bounding* τῇ ὁ. ψάμμῳ ‡Chrys. *hom*.6(13.214C).

ὀροπέδιον, τό, *mountain plain, table-land*; plur., Thdr.Mops. *Joel* 1:17–20(M.66.217D).

ὄρος, τό, *mountain*; **1.** in gen.; of Sinai, *1Clem*.53.2; ἡ λεγομένη κατάβασις ἐπὶ τὸ ὄ. θεοῦ ἐπίφασίς ἐστι θείας δυνάμεως Clem.*str*.6.3 (p.447.9; M.9.249B); ref. Transfiguration πρὸ τοῦ σταυροῦ σου, κύριε, ὄ. οὐρανὸν ἐμιμεῖτο Cosm.Mel.*od*.11(M.98.521B); ὄ. τὸ ποτὲ ζοφῶδες καὶ καπνῶδες νῦν τίμιον καὶ ἅγιόν ἐστιν *ib*.(521D); of Sion θεοῦ ὄ. τὸ ἅγιον …, ἴδε…τέκνα σου id.*hymn*.11(7.82,p.185; M.98.500C); **2.** as region inhabited by monks ἔχαιρεν ἀποδημῶν ὡς εἰς τὸν ἴδιον οἶκον εἰς τὸ ὄ. Ath.*v.Anton*.71(M.26.944B); ἦν εἰς τὸ ἔσω ὄ., ταῖς εὐχαῖς καὶ τῇ ἀσκήσει σχολάζων *ib*.50(917A); ἐλυπεῖτο…διοχλούμενος ὑπὸ πολλῶν καὶ ἑλκόμενος εἰς τὸ ὄ. τὸ ἔξω *ib*.84(961A); τὰ ὄ. καταλαμβάνειν καὶ μοναχοὺς γίνεσθαι Chrys.*hom.7.7 in Mt*.(7.116B); id.*hom.6.4 in Eph*.(11.44A); Pall.*v.Chrys*.7(p.39.26; M.47.24); Διόσκορον…ἐπίσκοπον ὄντα τοῦ ὄ. *ib*.(p.39.12; M.47.24); σῶζε τὴν σεαυτοῦ ψυχὴν πρὸς τὸ ἡμέτερον ὄ. Isid.Pel.*epp*.1.213(M.78.317B); **3.** in allegorical interpretation, of prophets ὁ ἰχθύς, ὁ ὑπὸ τῶν ἁλιέων Ἰησοῦ συλληφθείς, καταλιπὼν τὰς ἐν θαλάσσῃ διατριβάς, διατριβὰς ποιεῖται ἐν ὄρεσιν Or.*hom.16.1 in Jer*.(p.133.9; M.13.440B); μετάβαλε ἀπὸ τῆς θαλάσσης…ἧκε ἐπὶ τὰ ὄ., τοὺς προφήτας *ib*.(p.133.15; 440B); of synagogue, ref. Abac.3:3 ὄ. … δασὺ καὶ κατάσκιον ἡ συναγωγή Cyr.*Abac*.38(3.554B); of Jerusalem, Thdr.Mops.*Abac*.3:3(M.66.444A); cf.Thdt.ad loc.(2.1550); ref. Heb.12:22 οἶδεν…τὴν ἐπουράνιον Ἱερουσαλὴμ ὁ…ἀπόστολος καὶ τὸ οὐράνιον ὄ. ἐφ᾽ ᾧ ταύτην εἶναί φησιν Eus.*e.th*.3.3 (p.150.28; M.24.993C); of Church ὄ. ἐστὶ τοῦτο θεῷ πεφιλημένον…ὄ. νηφάλιον, ἁγναῖς ὕλαις σύσκιον Clem.*prot*.12(p.84.7; M.8.240B); id. *paed*.1.9(p.139.21; M.8.352A); of Christ εἰς τὸ ὄ. σώζου…ἐκεῖ γὰρ ἔστι μόνον σωθῆναι. ἔστι δὲ τὸ ὄ. κύριος Ἰησοῦς Or.*hom.13.3 in Jer*.(p.105.20; M.13.404B); *ib.18.5*(p.157.3; 473A); τοῦ μὲν ὄ. τὴν προΰπαρξιν τῆς θεότητος αὐτοῦ σημαίνοντος, τοῦ δὲ λίθου τὴν ἀνθρωπότητα Eus.*e.th*.1.20(p.94.25; M.24.889B); διὰ τοῦτο ὄ., ὅτι τὰ πάντα συνέχει Chrys.*Dan*.2:35(6.215B); of BMV οὗτος [sc. Christ]…ἐτμήθη ἀπὸ ὄρους ἄνευ χειρῶν, γεννηθεὶς ἐκ παρθένου γαμικῆς κοινωνίας χωρίς Thdt.*Dan*.2:35(2.1093); χαῖρε τὸ ὄ., ὅθεν ὁ ἀκρογωνιαῖος ἄνευ χειρῶν ἀπετμήθη λίθος Chrysipp.*enc.in BMV* 1(p.337.12); χαίροις, τὸ ἐκ τοῦ θεοῦ πιότατον καὶ κατάσκιον ὄ. Germ.CP *or*.3(M.98.308A); *ib*.5(321B); Cosm.Mel.*hymn*.1(2.56,p.166; M.98.461B); ὄ. ἅγιον ἔμψυχον θεοῦ ἡ ἁγία θεοτόκος Jo.D.*imag*.3.34(M.94.1353C); Δανιήλ σε ὄ. καλεῖ νοητόν ‡Jo.D.*carm.annunt*.174(p.242; M.96.853A); of spiritual beings φωτεινὰ ὄ. οἱ…ἄγγελοι…, οἱ προφῆται…οἱ ἀπόστολοι…ὁ διάβολος ὄ. σκοτεινόν ἐστιν…τὸ δαιμόνιον, ὁ σεληνιασμός, ὄ. ἦν καὶ σκοτεινὸν ὄ. ἦν περὶ οὗ ἔλεγεν ὁ σωτήρ· ἐρεῖτε τῷ ὄ. τούτῳ κτλ. Or.*hom.12.12 in Jer*.(p.98.11; 393C); ὄ. καὶ βουνοὺς τὰς θείας…δυνάμεις αἰνιττόμενος Eus.*e.th*.1.11(p.70.24; M.24.845B); ὄ. … κατωνόμασται ὁ σατανᾶς Cyr.*Abac*.46 (3.560D); of apostles, Or.*hom.12.12 in Jer*.(p.98.12; 393C) cit. supra; Marcell.*fr.22* ap.Eus.*e.th*.3.3(p.150.19; M.24.989C); cf.Eus. *e.th*.3.3(pp.150.30,153.4; 993D,996A); ὄρη θεοῦ λογικὰ οἱ ἀπόστολοι Jo.D.*imag*.3.34(M.94.1353C); of heights of contemplation, Clem. *str*.5.12(p.377.28; M.9.116B); *ib*.7.18(p.78.25; 557A); of spiritual, opp. worldly, life in gen., Or.*hom.16.2 in Jer*.(p.133.26; 440C); cf. *ib.16.4*(p.135.19; 441C); Andr.Cr.*can.mag*.71(p.149; M.97.1341C).

ὅρος, ὁ, A. *boundary, limit*; **1.** in Creation τὴν θάλασσαν ἰδίοις ὅ. ἐνέκλεισεν *Diogn*.7.2; Arist.*apol*.4.2; Clem.*prot*.1(p.6.3; M.8.57C); Ath.*gent*.2(M.25.808A); met. ἐντὸς ὅρων εὐσεβείας ὄντος *Hom.Clem*.3.6; εἴσω τῶν ἡμετέρων ὅ. φιλοσοφῶμεν καὶ μὴ εἰς Αἴγυπτον ἐκφερώμεθα Gr.Naz.*or*.27.5(p.8.2; M.36.17A); *ib*.29.2(p.76.8; 76C); βασιλεία …ἡ παντὸς ὅ. … διανέμησις Dion.Ar.*d.n*.13.3(M.3.980C); of God ὡς ἐν ἀπείρῳ μέσος ἐστίν, τοῦ παντὸς ὑπάρχων ὅ. *Hom.Clem*.17.9; ref. iniquity ἐν τοῖς πλημμελήμασιν οἱ ἄνθρωποι οὐκ ἄχρις ὅ. ὡρισμένων εἱστήκεισαν Ath.*inc*.5.3(M.25.105A); ὅ. ἔσχατος ἀσεβείας Thdt.*Ezech*.23:39(2.871); id.*Phil*.3:19(3.465); **2.** in time, *term* τὸν τῆς ἀναστάσεως διαπηξάμενος ὅ. ‡Ath.*Apoll*.1.14(M.26.1117B); **3.** Valent.; name of an aeon, *Horus,* the limit of the Pleroma, identified with Σταυρός: ὁ…Πατὴρ τὸν…Ὅ. … διὰ τοῦ Μονογενοῦς προβάλλεται ἐν εἰκόνι ἰδίᾳ Iren.*haer*.1.2.4(M.7.457A); cf. ὁ Πατὴρ ἐπιπροβάλλει αἰῶνα ἕνα τὸν Σταυρόν, ὅς…ὅ. γίνεται τοῦ πληρώματος, ἔχων ἐντὸς ἑαυτοῦ πάντας ὁμοῦ τοὺς τριάκοντα αἰῶνας. … καλεῖται δὲ Ὅ. … ὅτι ἀφορίζει ἀπὸ τοῦ πληρώματος ἔξω τὸ ὑστέρημα…ἔξω οὖν τοῦ Ὅ. … ἐστὶν ἡ…Ὀγδοάς, ἥτις ἐστὶν ἡ ἐκτὸς πληρώματος Σοφία Hipp. *haer*.6.31(p.159.10; M.16.3242A); ἡ Σοφία…τῇ στηριζούσῃ καὶ… φυλασσούσῃ τὰ ὅλα συνέτυχε δυνάμει. ταύτην δὲ τὴν δύναμιν καὶ Ὅ. καλοῦσιν Iren.*haer*.1.2.2(456A); τὸν…Ὅ. τοῦτον καὶ Σταυρὸν καὶ Λυτρωτὴν καὶ Καρπιστὴν…καὶ Μεταγωγέα καλοῦσιν. … διὰ δὲ τοῦ Ὅ. τούτου φασὶ…ἐστηρίχθαι τὴν Σοφίαν καὶ ἀποκατασταθῆναι τῇ συζυγίᾳ …τὴν δὲ ἐνθύμησιν αὐτῆς…ὑπὸ τοῦ Ὅ. ἀφορισθῆναι *ib*.(460A); Hipp. *haer*.10.13(p.274.5; 3427B); ὁ Χριστὸς…ἐντὸς τοῦ ὅ. μετὰ τῶν ἄλλων *αἰώνων δοξάζων τὸν Πατέρα* ib.6.31(p.159.25; 3242B); ib.6.37(p.168.2; 3254A); *εἰκόνα λέγουσιν αὐτὸν* [sc. *τὸν ὑπερθεν οὐρανὸν*] *τοῦ Ὅ.* ib.6.53 (p.188.2; 3290A); *οἱ ἄγγελοί εἰσιν οἱ ὑπὲρ ἡμῶν βαπτιζόμενοι, ἵνα...μὴ ἐπισχεθῶμεν κωλυθέντες εἰς τὸ πλήρωμα παρελθεῖν τῷ Ὅ. καὶ τῷ Σταυρῷ* Clem.*exc.Thdot.*22(p.114.8; M.9.669A); *ὁ Σταυρὸς τοῦ ἐν πληρώματι Ὅ. σημεῖόν ἐστιν· χωρίζει γὰρ τοὺς ἀπίστους τῶν πιστῶν ὡς ἐκεῖνος τὸν κόσμον τοῦ πληρώματος* ib.42(p.120.1; 680A).

B. *limitation*, *T.Gad* 7.4; Tat.*orat.*2(p.2.23; M.6.808A); of passions, Clem.*paed.*2.1(p.155.24; M.8.384A); Bas.*ep.*227(3.350A; M.32.852B).

C. *definition, determining*; **1.** in gen. *τὸ κεφαλαιωθὲν ἐκ τῆς διαιρέσεως ὅ. γίνεται* Clem.*str.*8.6(p.90.22; M.9.581C); *ἐξηγητικὸς...ὁ ὅ. ὧν τῆς τοῦ πράγματος οὐσίας περιλαβεῖν...τὴν φύσιν...ἀδυνατεῖ* ib.(p.93.15; 588A); ‡Just.*coh.Gr.*23(M.6.284A); Jo.D.*dialect.*8(M.94.552D); *ἔστιν...ὁ μὲν ὅ. ὄνομα ἐξηπλωμένον, ὄνομα δὲ ὅ. κατὰ σύναψιν* ib.(553A); **2.** partic. of God *τὸ ἀγέννητον οὔτε ὅ. ἐστὶ θεοῦ, οὔτε ἴδιον* Didym.(‡Bas.)*Eun.*4(1.286B; M.29.688B); *τὸν ὑπὲρ πάντα θεὸν...τὸν ὑπὲρ πάντα καὶ ὅ. καὶ λόγον* Dion.Ar.*d.n.*9.6(M.3.913C); ib.8.5(892C); *τὸ πάντων αἴτιον...ἀρχὴ...ἐστι τῶν ὄντων, ἀφ' ἧς καὶ αὐτὸ τὸ εἶναι καὶ... πᾶσα διάκρισις, πᾶς ὅ.* ib.5.7(821B); *ὑμνεῖν τὴν...θεότητα, τὸ πάντων αἴτιον ἕν, τὸ πρὸ παντὸς...ὅ. καὶ ἀοριστίας* ib.13.3(980C); of the gospel, Or.*Jo.*1.5(7; p.10.1; M.14.33A); ib.1.6(8; p.10.31; 33C); of prayer, id.*or.*14.4(p.332.11; M.11.461D); of man, Gr.Nyss.*or.catech.*33(p.123.13; M.45.84C); *μετανοίας ὅ. οὐ τὸ στένειν μόνον ἐπὶ ταῖς ἁμαρτίαις, ἀλλὰ καὶ τὸ φεύγειν ταύτας* Thdt.*Is.*30:15(p.123.3; 2.306); cf.id.*Jon.*3:9(2.1472); id.*Heb.*10:39(3.613); **3.** *law* or *condition of existence* *ἀδύνατον...ἐν κόσμῳ σωθῆναι τοῦ εἰδώλου τὸν λόγον ἢ τὸν ὅ.* Mac.Mgn.*apocr.*3.42(p.147.5); ib.(p.147.1); *ὁ θεὸς λόγος...εἰς σάρκα κατελθὼν...εἰς θείαν ἔστησε λῆξιν...ὡς ἂν ἡ σὰρξ...τὸν ὅ. σώσῃ καὶ τὸν θόρυβον τοῦ ὅ. καταβάλῃ* ib.4.28(p.216.18); *τὸ πνεῦμα...οὐκ ἔστιν... θεός· πῶς οὖν ἔσται προσκυνητόν, μὴ ὂν ἐν τῷ τῆς προσκυνήσεως ὅ.;* ‡Ath.*Maced.dial.*1.4(M.28.1293D); ib.1.6(1297C); of God, Ath.*gent.*29(M.25.57B); *τὸ κακὸν...παρὰ τὴν φύσιν...καὶ παρὰ τὸν ὅ. ... καὶ παρὰ τὴν ὑπόστασιν* Dion.Ar.*d.n.*4.32(M.3.732D); Christol. *οὐσίαι ἡνωμέναι καθ' ὑπόστασιν καὶ διῃρημέναι ὅσον ἐπινοίᾳ μόνῃ, ταῖς τε ποιότησι καὶ ἐνεργείαις, ὅ. τε καὶ θελήσεσιν* *Lit.Jac.*(*NBP* 10[2] p.37); ref. dogmatic terms, hypostasis, nature, etc. *καινοτομεῖσθαι τοὺς ὅ. τούτων ὀνομάτων ἐπὶ τῆς οἰκονομίας* Leont.B.*arg.Sev.*(M.86.1924D); **4.** *law, order of nature* *σώζειν τὸν ὅ. τῆς φύσεως* ‡Ath.*fr.*(M.26.1233A); *ἀκοσμία...τῶν θειοτάτων ἐστὶ καὶ ὅρων καὶ θεσμῶν ἔκβασις* Dion.Ar.*ep.*8.1(M.3.1088C); *νενίκηνται τῆς φύσεως οἱ ὅ. ἐν σοί, παρθένε ἄχραντε* Cosm.Mel.*can.dorm.*153(p.183); **5.** *decision, decree, order*; **a.** in gen.; of God, Meth.*res.*1.38(p.281.6; M.18.268A); Eus.*d.e.*4.16(p.190.5; M.22.317A); Thdt.*qu.9 in Jos.*(1.309); of apostles, id.*Tit.*1:5(3.700); of emperor, Const.ap.Eus.*v.C.*4.42(p.135.3; M.20.1192C); Eus.*h.e.*5.21.3(M.20.488A); **b.** of councils; **i.** of dogmatic decisions: Nicene creed, Philost.*h.e.*1.9(M.65.464C); *οἱ...πατέρες...ἐν τῇ Νικαέων πόλει συναγηγερμένοι καὶ τὸν τῆς...πίστεως ὅ. ἐκτιθέμενοι* Cyr.*expl.xii cap.*1(p.17.2; 6[1].147B); Socr.*h.e.*2.20.10(M.67.237B); *τὸ σύμβολον τῶν τιη' ἁγίων πατέρων...κρατεῖν...ὡς μόνον κυρίως τῆς ἀπλανοῦς πίστεως ὅ.* Basilisc.*encycl.*(p.50.9; M.86.2600C); Chalcedonian definition, CChalc.*act.*5(*ACO* 2.1.2 p.123.21; H.2.448B); ib.(p.130.12; 456E); Basilisc.*encycl.*(p.50.18; 2600D); Justn.*ep.Thdr.Mops.*(p.64.16; M.86.1081C); ref. prohibition against innovations in doctrine, denied by orthodox *οὐκ ἔστιν ὅ. τοιοῦτος, οὐκ ἔστιν κανὼν τοῦτο διαγορεύων* CChalc.*act.*1(*ACO* 2.1.1 p.91.16; H.2.97E); asserted by Dioscorus *ὃν ὥρισαν οἱ ἐπίσκοποι, οὐκ ἔστιν ὅ.;... ἄλλο ἐστὶν κανών, ἄλλο ὅ.* ib.(p.91.18f.; 97E); **ii.** of canons, CAnc.*can.*19,21,23; CNic.(325)*can.*15; ib.17; *τὸν ὅ. τῆς...συνόδου τῆς ἐν Νικαίᾳ...περὶ τῆς... ἑορτῆς τοῦ...πάσχα* CAnt.(341)*can.*1; ib.6; CSard.*can.*15; CLaod.*can.*proem.; CChalc.*can.*10; *ἀμετατρέπτους...εἶναι τῶν συνόδων τοὺς ὅρους* Soz.*h.e.*1.9.5(M.67.884C); **iii.** of liturgical decisions *ἀναθεματίζομεν τοὺς ἔτι μετὰ τὸν παρόντα ὅ. παραδεχομένους τὴν τοιαύτην φωνὴν* [sc. *ὁ σταυρωθεὶς δι' ἡμᾶς κτλ.*]...*ἢ ἄλλως πως τῷ τρισαγίῳ ὕμνῳ συνάπτοντας* CTrull.*can.*81; **c.** of eccl. decisions in gen. *Ζεφυρῖνον, ἄνδρα...ἄπειρον τῶν ἐκκλησιαστικῶν ὅ.* Hipp.*haer.*9.11(p.245.15; M.16.3378C); Ath.*syn.*13(p.240.19; M.26.704B); *τοῖς τῶν ἁγίων πατέρων ὅ. ἑπόμενοι...ὁρίζομεν...περὶ τῶν πρεσβείων τῆς...ἐκκλησίας Κωνσταντινουπόλεως* CChalc.*can.*28; CTrull.*can.*40; ‡Jo.D.*ep.Thphl.*31(M.95.385A); of episcopal decisions, Eus.*h.e.*5.23.4(M.20.493A); id.*v.C.*4.27(p.127.31; M.20.1176B); Arsen.Hyps.*ep.*(p.147.19; M.25.372C); **d.** of disciplinary decisions, hence *penalty* *καυτήρ ἐστιν ὅ. καὶ ἐπιτίμιον εἰς μετάνοιαν πρὸς χρόνον διδόμενον φιλανθρώπως* Jo.Clim.*past.*2(M.88.1169B); **e.** of judicial decisions, *ruling*, Eus.*h.e.*6.5.3(M.20.533A); Jo.Mal.*chron.*13 p.340(M.97.508A); ib.15 p.384(569C); *sentence*, Bas.*ep.*2.5(3.74B; M.32.232A); *τῷ ὅ. σου...τοὺς ἀνθρώπους παραπέμπεις θανάτῳ* Thdt.*Ps.*16:14(1.700); *τῆς...ἑνώσεως λυομένης, τὸ μὲν θνητὸν δέχεται τοῦ θανάτου τὸν ὅ., μένει δὲ ἀθάνατος ἡ ψυχή* id.*eran.*3(4.177); **f.** monastic *rule*, Bas.*reg.fus.*tit.(2.335; M.31.905A); cf.id.*reg.br.*tit.(2.401A; M.31.1052C); **6.** *statement* *τοῦ εὐαγγελίου ὁ ὅ.* ‡Ath.*Apoll.*2.4(M.26.1137C); ib.2.5(1140A); Didym.(‡Bas.)*Eun.*5(1.307A; M.29.736B); **7.** *dogma* *τότε...⟨τὰ⟩ τῆς πλάνης...σοφίσματα ἀσύστατα φανερωθήσεται, ἐπὰν ὁ τῆς ἀληθείας ὅ. ἐπιδειχθῇ* Hipp.*haer.*10.5(p.265.10; M.16.3414A); ‡Ath.*Apoll.*2.15(M.26.1157B); ‡Jo.D.*ep.Thphl.*3(M.95.349A); statement of doctrine, Thgn.*hypot.fr.*1(p.75; M.10.240A); **8.** liturg. *formula* *ὁ δεσπότης τὸν περὶ τὸ βάπτισμα δίδωσιν ὅ.* Didym.*Trin.*2.6(M.39.548B); **9.** *expression* *ἡ ἀπαράλλακτος εἰκών, ὁ τοῦ πατρὸς ὅ. καὶ λόγος* Gr.Naz.*or.*38.13(M.36.325B); **10.** *standard, pattern*, Const.ap.Eus.*h.e.*10.5.14(M.20.885A); *ὅρον... ἐπισκοπῆς εἶναι τὸν ἐκείνου βίον καὶ τρόπον* Gr.Naz.*or.*21.37(M.35.1128A); *κανὼν καὶ ὅ. τῆς εὐζωΐας* Chrys.*hom.13.1 in 1Tim.*(11.618A); id.*hom.3.1 in 2Tim.*(11.672E); **11.** *appointed condition* *γνῶσιν καὶ ἀγνωσίαν ὅρους εὐδαιμονίας κακοδαιμονίας τε...ἐδήλωσεν* Clem.*str.*5.14 (p.421.3; M.9.205B); plur., *terms* *ἐπὶ τοῖς προειρημένοις ὅ. εἰρηνεύσαντες τῇ...ἐκκλησίᾳ* Arsen.Hyps.*ep.*(p.148.2; M.25.372C); **12.** *appointed place of refuge, sanctuary*, Ath.Scholast.*coll.*4.3(p.52); **13.** *aim*, Clem.*q.d.s.*22(p.174.23; M.9.628B).

ὅρουσις, ἡ, *eagerness, vitality*, Clem.*paed.*2.10(p.214.8; M.8.509B).

ὀρούω, *rise, tower*, Paul.Sil.*Soph.*837(M.86.2151A); id.*ambo.*240 (M.86.2260B).

***ὀροφανής,** *mountain-like, huge*, Thphn.*chron.*p.365(M.108.876A).

ὀρόφιον, τό, *roof, canopy* *οὐρανὸν...τὸ ἐπάνωθεν τῆς ἁγίας τραπέζης ὀ. ἀπαρτίζουσιν* ‡Germ.CP *contempl.*(M.98.421B).

ὄροφος, ὁ, *roof*, met. *ὁ γεννώμενος τέκτων* [sc. Christ]...*τὸν τρισύστατον οὐράνιον ὄ. ἐτεκτόνησε πανσόφοις τέχναις* *Pers.*(p.12.19; M.10.101A); *ὁ στῦλος καὶ ὄ. τῆς πίστεως* Alex.Sal.*Barn.*proem.6 (438D).

ὀροφόω, *cover with a roof*, Melet.*nat.hom.*1(M.64.1156D); fig. *κατοικητήριόν σου...ὃ τοῖς σταυρικοῖς...ὠρόφωσας* [sc. Christ] *ξύλοις* Germ.CP *or.*2(M.98.284B).

ὀρόφωσις, ἡ, *vaulting*, Epiph.*exp.fid.*4(p.500.26; M.42.781A).

ὄρπηξ, ὁ, *sapling, shoot*; met., *scion, descendant*, Thdr.Stud.*epp.*1.18(M.99.694B).

ὀρρωδέω, *terrify*, Thdr.Stud.*epp.*2.134(M.99.1432B).

ὀρύγιον, τό, *digging implement*, Jo.Mosch.*prat.*90(M.87.2948A).

[*]**ὀρυγμαδός, ὁ,** = *ὀρυμαγδός*, cf. *ὀρυγμάδες*, *hubbub, noisy crowd* *φεύγετε...Βασιλίδην καὶ ὅλον αὐτοῦ τὸν ὀ. τῆς κακίας* ‡Ign.*Trall.*11.

***ὀρυκτήριον, τό,** *digging implement*, Sophr.H.*v.Mar.Aeg.*4.39 (M.87.3725A).

***ὀρύκτωρ, ὁ,** *one who breaks into graves*, Gr.Naz.*carm.*2.2(epigr.) 34.4(M.38.102A).

ὄρυξ, ὁ, *pickaxe* or any sharp iron tool for digging, Pall.*h.Laus.*39(p.125.9; M.34.1195D).

***ὀρφανικῶς,** *in the manner of orphans*, Gr.Naz.*ep.*86(M.37.160B); Thdr.Stud.*epp.*2.200(M.99.1613D).

ὀρφανόομαι, *be orphaned*, Eus.*v.C.*1.43(p.28.7, v.l. *ὀρφανισθείσας* M.20.957B).

ὀρφανοτροφεῖον, τό, *orphanage*, *Chron.Pasch.*p.395(M.92.1012C).

ὀρφανοτρόφος, *caring for orphans*, Max.*ep.*44(M.91.645D); masc. as subst. *τότε ἐλεηθήσονται...οἱ ὀ.* Eus.Al.*serm.*21.3(M.86.425D); *περὶ ἐπισκόπων καὶ ὀ. ... καὶ οἰκονόμων* Jo.Mal.*chron.*18 p.430(M.97.633C); cf.Thphn.*chron.*p.176(M.108.408B).

***ὀρφνῆθεν,** *from the dark*, †Apoll.*met.Ps.*10:2(M.33.1325A).

ὀρχέομαι, *dance*, hence met.; **1.** *jeer* *θέλοντα κατὰ τοῦ σωτῆρος ὀρχήσασθαι* Ath.*Ar.*1.4(M.26.20B); **2.** c. *εἰς*, *leap* upon, *seize* upon, Chrys.*stat.*2.1(2.20D).

***ὀρχηστομανία, ἡ,** *dancing madness*, Or.*Cels.*3.56(p.251.28, v.l. *ὀρχηστρομανίας* M.11.996A).

ὀρχήστρια, ἡ, *dancing girl*, †Gregent.*leg.Hom.*(M.86.601A).

[*]**ὀρχισμός, ὁ,** = *ὀρχησμός*, *dance*, Thdt.*Dan.*5:10(2.1163).

ὁσαχῶς, *in how many ways?, in what ways?*, Anast.S.*hod.*2(M.89.52C).

ὁσία, ἡ, **1.** *piety, reverence*; towards God, Eus.*v.C.*3.45(p.96.26; M.20.1105B); ib.2.20(p.49.10; 997B); ib.2.45(p.60.15; 1021C); towards the dead, ib.3.47(p.97.18; 1108A); **2.** *funeral service*, Gr.Naz.*ep.*63 (M.37.125A); *σώματα...οὐδ' ὁσίᾳ κοινωνήσαντες* Petr.II Al.*encycl.*ap. Thdt.*h.e.*4.22.29(3.997); *τὸ...ὅσιον τί ἐστιν; τὸ καθαρόν, τὸ ὀφειλόμενον. διὰ τοῦτο καὶ τὴν ὁ. ἐπὶ ἀπελθόντων φαμέν· τουτέστιν οὐδὲν ὀφείλω αὐτοῖς λοιπόν* Chrys.*hom.13.2 in Eph.*(11.98F); Isid.Pel.*epp.*4.157(M.78.1241D).

***ὁσιομάκαρ,** *holy and blessed* *εἴληφας τριάδος...γνῶσιν, ὁ. τὴν ἔνθεον* *Hymn.*(*AS* 1 p.584).

***ὁσιομάρτυς, ὁ,** *holy martyr*, *Mir.Geo.*6(p.86.18); Steph.Diac. *v.Steph.*(M.100.1108B).

ὅσιος, *holy*, *God-fearing*, *religious*;

A. in gen.; **1.** of persons δικαιώσαιεν οἱ ὅ. τὸ κρίμα τοῦ θεοῦ αὐτῶν *Pss.Sal.*4.9; *T.Gad* 5.4; *T.Benj.*3.1; δίκαιοι καὶ ὅ., ἵνα μετὰ παρρησίας αἰτῶμεν τὸν θεόν *2Clem.*15.3; ὅ., ὡς ἀληθῶς, οὗτοί εἰσιν οἱ φιλοσοφίᾳ τὸν νοῦν προσεσχηκότες Just.*dial.*2.1(M.6.476B); *ib.*96.3(704B); of the wise, Clem.*str.*1.26(p.105.5; M.8.916B); of the 'gnostic' ὅ. τε καὶ εὐσεβῆ, θεοπρεπῶς τὸν τῷ ὄντι θεὸν θρησκεύοντα *ib.*7.1(p.3.27; M.9.404B); μόνον ὄντως ὅ. ... τὸν τῷ ὄντι κατὰ τὸν ἐκκλησιαστικὸν κανόνα γνωστικόν *ib.*7.7(p.31.11; 457A); ὁ...ἐγνωκὼς τὸν θεὸν ὅσιος καὶ εὐσεβής *ib.*(p.35.19; 468A); of David, *ib.*6.6(p.456.29; 272B); of S. Paul, *M.Scill.*12; οἱ...μὴ μετανοήσαντες διὰ τῆς τοῦ πυρὸς κολάσεως...τὸ τέλος ἕξουσιν, κἂν ἐν τοῖς λοιποῖς ἅπασιν ὁσιώτατοι ὦσιν *Hom.Clem.*3.6; ὅσιον ἀντὶ τοῦ τὸν ἀθῷον τέθεικε Thdt.*Ps.*4:5(1.631); **2.** of actions δίκαιον καὶ ὅ. ... ὑπηκόους...γενέσθαι τῷ θεῷ *1Clem.*14.1; *2Clem.*6.9; τὸ...ὅ. τὰ πρὸς θεὸν δίκαια κατὰ πᾶσαν οἰκονομίαν μηνύει Clem.*str.*7.12(p.57.23; M.9.512B); πατέρα τῆς σαρκὸς τὸν θεὸν λέγειν ὅσιον Eus.*e.th.*1.20(p.88.16; M.24.877C); ὁσιώτατόν ἐστι βούλεσθαι... ὅπερ...οὐδεμίαν μετὰ τῆς Ἰουδαίων ἐπιορκίας ἔχει κοινωνίαν Const.ap. Eus.*v.C.*3.19(p.87.1; M.20.1077C); Thdt.*haer.*5.20(4.478); of divine activity παιδεύει...διὰ τῆς ὁ. παιδείας αὐτοῦ *1Clem.*56.16; of prayer, Clem.*str.*7.6(p.24.18; 445A); of spiritual exercises, Jo.Clim.*scal.*4(M.88.685B); neut. plur. as subst., *holy acts* πόσα...αὐτῷ [sc. Christ] ὀφείλομεν ὅσια *2Clem.*1.3; **3.** of doctrine, Clem.*str.*4.23(p.314.5; M.8.1357B); **4.** of mental and moral conditions ὁ. βουλῆς *1Clem.*2.3; Meth.*symp.*3.7(p.33.21; M.18.69C); Cyr.*ador.*4(1.122B).

B. as regular epithet, *holy*, *sainted*; of name of God; superl., *1Clem.*58.1; of prophets, Mac.Mgn.*apocr.*3.8(p.64.15); of BMV ἡ ὁ. μήτηρ τοῦ σωτῆρος ‡Epiph.*hom.*5(M.43.492D); ἡ ὁ. παρθένος *ib.*(496A); of bishops ὁ ὅ. ἐπίσκοπος *Πορφύριος* Marc.Diac.*v.Porph.*65; superl., *ib.*68; of monks, *V.Pach.Γ* tit.(p.407.2); τοῦ ὁ. πατρὸς ἡμῶν *Σάβα* Cyr.S.*v.Sab.*tit.(p.85.11); *Lit.Jac.*(p.218.11); of a monastery, Jo.Clim.*scal.*4(M.88.697B); superl. as title of address to bishops, Cyr. *ep.*11(p.10.14; 5^{2}.36B); Procl.CP *ep.*(p.67.18; M.65.881A); Eustrat. *v.Eutych.*41(M.86.2324A); Gennad.*encycl.*tit.(p.79.3; M.85.1613); Petr.Full.*ep.Acac.*(p.115.30; M.86.2629C); iron. μὴ γίνου πρεσβυτέρου πρεσβύτερος καὶ ἐπισκόπου ὁσιώτερος Pall.*v.Chrys.*10(p.60.5; M.47.34).

C. masc. as subst., *saint*; in gen., Or.*Cels.*8.58(p.275.15; M.11.1605B); Thdt.*affect.*8(p.212.17; 4.916); Proc.G.*Gen.*4:2(M.87.241A); esp. of ascetics, Pall.*h.Laus.*144(M.34.1249C); Thdt.*h.rel.*26.16(p.13.6; 3.1277); Jo.Clim.*scal.*4(M.88.697C); *Lit.Jac.*(p.212.18); Jo.Mosch. *prat.*69(M.87.2920A).

D. neut. as subst., *the divinity*, Const.ap.Gel.Cyz.*h.e.*2.7.29(M.85.1240A).

ὁσιότης, ἡ, *holiness*, *sanctity*; **1.** in gen., as divine quality opp. human righteousness ἡ δικαιοσύνη, ἀνθρωπίνη οὖσα...ὑποβέβηκε... τὴν ὁ., θείαν δικαιοσύνην ὑπάρχουσαν Clem.*str.*6.15(p.495.14; M.9.349A); Meth.*res.*2.4(p.336.4; M.41.1168D); not relative εἴπερ...ἡ ὁ. ...τῶν πρός τι ἐστίν, ὡς τὸ αὐτὸ εἶναι ὅσιον καὶ ἀνόσιον παρὰ τὰς διαφόρους σχέσεις..., ὅρα εἰ μὴ καὶ ἡ σωφροσύνη...ὧν οὐδὲν ἂν εἴη ἀτοπώτερον Or.*Cels.*5.28(p.29.7; M.11.1224A); **2.** in OT ἦν καὶ ὁ. ἐπὶ Ἰουδαίων, ἀλλ' οὐ τῆς ἀληθείας, ἀλλὰ τοῦ τύπου Chrys.*hom.13.2 in Eph.*(11.98C); **3.** Christian προσέλθωμεν...αὐτῷ ἐν ὁ. ψυχῆς *1Clem.*29.1; *ib.*49.4; συμπλακεῖσα τῇ...προνοίᾳ ἡ τοῦ γνωστικοῦ ὁ. ... τελείαν τὴν εὐεργεσίαν ἐπιδείκνυσι τοῦ θεοῦ Clem.*str.*7.7(p.31.28; M.9.457C); δι' ὁσιότητα ἀποθνήσκειν εὐλόγως εἶναι νενομίκαμεν Or.*Cels.*8.54(p.271.10; M.11.1600A); id.*hom.12.11 in Jer.*(p.97.19; M.13.393A); τὰς πέντε τῆς αἰσθήσεως...φαντασίας, ἀφ' ἑκάστης αὐτῶν οἷα λαμπτὴρ τὴν ὁ. λάμπουσα Meth.*symp.*6.3(p.67.11; M.18.117A); ὑπέταξεν αὐτοῦ τὸ σῶμα...εἰς ὁ. id.*res.*1.59(p.323.17; M.41.1156D); δὸς ἡμῖν...ὁ. Serap. *euch.*12.1; πεπλουτήκαμεν...τὴν...ἐν ἁγιασμῷ καὶ ὁ. πολιτείαν Cyr. *Joel.*34(3.226C); **4.** as complimentary title of address: to emperor, CArim.*ep.Const.*1(p.238.12; M.26.700A); *ib.*(p.238.32; 700B); to bishops, Const.ap.Eus.*v.C.*2.46(p.61.7; M.20.1024B); Ath.*ep.Serap.*1.1(M.26.532B); Bas.*ep.*48(3.141E; M.32.385A); Gr.Naz.*ep.*202(M.37.332A); collectively in address to council, Const.ap.Eus.*v.C.*2.46(p.86.10; M.20.1072A); Const.*ib.*3.32(p.93.2; 1093A); Photinus et al. *ep.*ap.Epiph.*haer.*72.11(p.265.17; M.42.397A); to priests, Nil.*epp.*2.215(M.79.312D); Thdt.*ep.*20(4.1082); to monks, Philox.*ep.*1(p.157); *ib.*36(p.184).

ὁσιουργέω, *do holy works*, Cyr.*ador.*7(1.247B); *ib.*(248E).

***ὁσιουργός,** *working holiness*, Cyr.*Is.*5.2(2.776B).

***ὁσίωμα, τό,** *act of piety*, Thdr.Stud.*epp.*2.25(M.99.1192C).

ὅσος, 1. *all over, entire* ἐσθὴς ὅση ποικίλη τε καὶ λεπτὴ καὶ πολύτιμος Bas.Sel.*v.Thecl.*2.5(M.85.573A); **2.** adv.; **a.** ὅσον...τοσούτῳ *as* (much)...*so* (much); with comps., *the more...the more...* ὅσον... ψυχὴ τιμιωτέρα σώματος, τοσούτῳ χαλεπωτέρα ἡ ταύτης βλάβη Chrys. *comm.in Gal.*5:15(10.719C); cf. τοσούτῳ μείζονα, ὅσον γῆς οὐρανός id. *hom.63.2 in Mt.*(7.629D); so also **b.** ὅσα ἄν...τοσούτῳ: ὅσα ἂν δεινὰ πάθης ἐπιεικῶς ζῶν, τοσούτῳ γέγονας ἰσχυρότερος *ib.24.4*(305B); *ib.61.5*(617D); **c.** ὅσον ἄν *however much* ὅσον ἂν γένηται ἀκέραιος ἡ περιστερά, τί ὠφελήσει; *ib.33.2*(379B); **d.** ὅσον εἰς...ἧκει *as far as concerns* ...ὅσον εἰς τὴν αὐτῶν ἧκεν ἀρετήν *ib.32.2*(367B); without ἧκει: ὅσον εἰς ἀνθρώπινον λογισμόν *ib.*2.2(22A); cf. ὅσον πρὸς Ἰουδαίους *ib.*2.3(25A); **e.** ὅσον ὅσον *a little* ἐμαυτὸν ὅσον ὅσον Rom.Mel.*hymn.*(*AS* 1 p.145).

ὁσπίτι(ο)ν (ὀσπίτι(ο)ν, ὀσπήτιον), τό, (Lat. *hospitium*); **1.** *poor-house*, Pall.*h.Laus.*6(p.24.7; M.34.1019B); Jo.Mal.*chron.*13 p.345(M.97.516B); **2.** *lodging*, CChalc.*act.*1(*ACO* 2.1.1 p.176.3; H.2.208E); *ib.*11(*ACO* 2.1.3 p.49.10; 553A); **3.** *building, house*, Jo.Disc.*v.Epiph.*35(M.41.69A); Leont.N.*v.Sym.*5(M.93.1676A).

***ὀσπρίδιον, τό,** *vegetable*, Pall.*h.Laus.*38(p.122.14; ὀσπρίων M.34.1194D).

ὀσπριοπώλης, ὁ, *one who deals in pulse*, Nil.*epp.*2.263 tit.(M.79.333C).

***ὀσπριοφάγος,** *pulse-eating*, ‡Eust.*hex.*(M.18.745A).

***Ὀσσαῖοι (Ὀσσηνοί), οἱ,** *Ossaeans*, members of a Jewish sect connected with Elchezaites, Epiph.*haer.*19.1(p.217.19; M.41.261A); ἡ αἵρεσις...τῶν Ὀσσηνῶν...ἡ πολιτευομένη...τὴν τῶν Ἰουδαίων πολιτείαν...μόνον δὲ ⟨τῷ⟩ ἀπαγορεύειν τὰς βίβλους ⟨Μωυσέως⟩...σχίσμα ...ἐργάζεται *ib.*19.5(p.222.14; 268B); Ὀ. μετέστησαν ἀπὸ Ἰουδαϊσμοῦ εἰς τὴν τῶν Σαμψαίων αἵρεσιν *ib.*20.3(p.227.6; 275A); *ib.*19.2(p.219.6; 264B); τὸ γένος τῶν Ὀ. ἑρμηνεύεται...στιβαρὸν γένος *ib.*(p.218.1, v.l. Ὀσσηνῶν 261A); Ὀσσηνοί, οἱ...ἰταμώτατοι ἑρμηνεύονται id.*anac.*18(p.168.1; M.41.472C).

***ὀστέωσις, ἡ,** *bony substance* τῶν ποδῶν τὴν ὀ. Sophr.H.*v.Anast.*(M.92.1720B); plur. (rendering עַצְמוֹת, *proofs*, as though עֲצָמוֹת, *bones*), AQ ap.Proc.G.*Is.*41:21(M.87.2361B).

ὀστιάριος, (Lat. *ostiarius*) *of a door*; **1.** masc. as subst., *porter*, *door-keeper*, CCP(536)*act.*4(*ACO* 3 p.176.8; H.2.1253C); CNic.(787) *act.*1(H.4.33B); of monastery, Leont.N.*v.Sym.*8(M.93.1680A); Thdr. Stud.*poen.*1.63(M.99.1741A); **2.** neut. as subst., *porter's lodge*, ‡Bas. *poen.mon.*48(2.529E; M.31.1312C).

***ὀστογλύφος,** *bone-carving* γυψὶν ὀ. Pall.*v.Chrys.*19(p.124.6; M.47.69).

***ὀστρακάριος, ὁ** *tile-maker*, Thphn.*chron.*p.371(M.108.888B).

ὀστράκινος, *of earthenware*, *Diogn.*2.7; τεῖχος...ὀ. τὴν τῶν ἐπὶ σοφίᾳ φυσώντων ἐκάλεσε διαλεκτικήν Proc.G.*Is.*16:6ff.(M.87.2116A); Jo.Mosch.*prat.*196(M.87.3081A); fig. (cf. Jud.7:16, 2Cor.4:7) εἴη δ' ἂν λύχνος αὐτοῦ [sc. Christ]...τὸ ἀνθρώπειον σκῆνος, δι' οὗ δίκην ὀ. σκεύους...τὰς τοῦ ἰδίου φωτὸς ἀκτίνας...ἐξέλαμψεν Eus.*d.e.*7.2(p.335.29; M.22.548B); οἷόν τι σκεῦος ὀ. ... ὁ ἄνθρωπος εἰς γῆν ἀναλύεται Gr. Nyss.*or.catech.*8(p.42.11; M.45.33B); ‡Nil.*narr.*6(M.79.660B); of man after Fall ἡμᾶς...ἡ παρακοὴ...ὀ. ἐποίησεν Gr.Nyss.*hom.7 in Cant.*(M.44.912C).

ὀστρακίτης, ὁ, a kind of snake, Epiph.*haer.*40.8(p.90.5; M.41.692A); *ib.*57.10(p.357.14; 1009C).

***ὀστρακοειδής,** *like oyster-shell*, Sophr.H.*mir.Cyr.et Jo.*34(M.87.3537B).

ὀστρακόεις, poet. for ὀστράκινος, *like earthenware*, Gr.Naz.*carm.*1.2.1.535(M.37.562A).

ὄστρακον, τό, *shell-fish*, Or.*comm.in Mt.*10.7(p.9.6; M.13.852B).

ὀστρακώδης, *testaceous*, hence τὸ ὀ. *shell* of an almond, Olymp. *Eccl.*12:5(M.93.617C).

***ὄστωσις, ἡ,** *formation of bone*, Geo.Pis.*hex.*1230(M.92.1529A).

ὀσφραντικός, *olfactory* τῆς ὀ. αἰσθήσεως Gr.Nyss.*hom.3 in Cant.*(M.44.821C); Max.*ambig.*(M.91.1248B).

ὄσφρησις, ἡ, 1. *sense of smell*, spiritual τῶν Χριστοῦ μύρων ἀντιλαμβάνεται ἡ τῆς ψυχῆς ὄ. Hipp.*fr.7 in Pr.*(p.159.10; M.10.617B); εἰκὼν...τοῦ δὲ θυμοῦ ἐστιν ἡ ὄ. Max.*ambig.*(M.91.1248C); **2.** *smell*, *odour*, Clem.*paed.*2.8(p.197.18; M.8.473A); Chrysipp.*enc.in Jo.Bapt.*5(p.35.6); Cyriac.*Laz.*(*SBBAW* p.732; *AS* 1 p.286); met. θανάτου λύσιν καὶ ἀναστάσεως ὄσφρησιν τοῖς ἀνθρώποις εὐαγγελίζονται [sc. δικαῖοι] Bas.Sel.*or.*4.1(M.85.64D).

ὀσφρητικός, *olfactory* αἰσθήσεσι ταῖς ὀ. Cyr.*ador.*12(1.415B); τὸ ὀ. *olfactory organ*, Chrys.*hom.5.5 in 2Thess.*(11.544E).

ὅταν, 1. *whenever*, c. opt. οἱ...τρυγῶντες ὅταν εἰς τοῦτο καταλήξειαν πόνων χαίροντες ἀλαλάζουσιν Cyr.*Is.*2.5(2.340D); c. pres. indic., Ath.*v.Anton.*20(M.26.873A); Chrys.*hom.3.2 in Tit.*(11.746D); id.

hom.17.2 in 1Tim.(11.649F); c. aor. indic. id.*hom.12.3 in Col.*(11. 416F); **2.** = ὅτε, *when*; c. indic., Diod.*Gen.*1:14(M.33.1564A); Gr. Nyss.*hom.3 in Cant.*(M.44.816C); *ib.*7(912D).

ὅτε, *since*, Chrys.*hom.28.4 in Heb.*(12.261B).

ὅτι, 1. *that*, introducing an objective clause, after a noun of saying followed by τοῦ: δοθείσης τῆς ἐπαγγελίας τοῦ ὅτι σωθήσεται κατὰ καιροὺς ὁ Ἰσραὴλ Cyr.*Is.*5.4(2.839C); *ib.*(843C); **2.** used elliptically; **a.** = δῆλον ὅτι *it is plain that* εἰ γὰρ μὴ ἐγένετο τὰ γεγενημένα,...ὅτι ταῦτα πλάττειν φιλονεικοῦντες...τῷ θεῷ προσκρούειν ἔμελλον Chrys. *hom.5.4 in 1Cor.*(10.38B); *ib.*(38D); **b.** = αἴτιον ὅτι *it is because* εἰ δὲ οὐκ αἰσθάνῃ τῆς κουφότητος, ὅτι προθυμίαν...οὐκ ἔχεις *ib.14.4*(10. 122, v.l. δῆλον ὅτι); **c.** *to show that, as evidence that* ὅτι γὰρ καὶ ἀποπνεῖν ἔμελλεν, ὁ Λουκᾶς φησιν ὅτι καὶ 'ἔμελλε τελευτᾶν' id.*hom. 26.1 in Mt.*(7.313C); *ib.82.3*(786B); id.*hom.42.2 in 1Cor.*(10.397E); cf.Gal.4:6 ὅτι δέ ἐστε υἱοί, ἐξαπέστειλεν ὁ θεὸς τὸ πνεῦμα, commented: πόθεν δῆλον ὅτι γεγόναμεν υἱοί;...ὅτι τὸ πνεῦμα...ἐλάβομεν id.*comm.in Gal.*4:6(10.705B); οὐ γὰρ ἂν ἐτολμήσαμεν προσαγορεῦσαι τὸν θεὸν...μὴ τοῦ τῆς υἱοθεσίας ἀξιωθέντες χαρίσματος. ἀναντίρρητος δὲ ἡ ἀπόδειξις Thdt.*Gal.*4:6(3.382); **d.** πόθεν ὅτι *how we know that* τοῖς ζητοῦσι μαθεῖν πόθεν ὅτι ἀπόστολός εἰμι Chrys.*hom.21.2 in 1Cor.* (10.181B); id.*hom.2.4 in Mt.*(7.27B); id.*hom.2.3 in 2Tim.*(11.670A); **3.** inserted pleonastically after various conjunctions and adverbs: πῶς ὅτι Or.*Cels.*4.86(p.357.14, v.l. ἔτι M.11.1161A); πόθεν ὅτι *ib.*(p.357.21; 1161B); ἐπειδὴ ὅτι Mac.Aeg.*hom.*12.6(M.34.560C); πλὴν ἀλλ' ὅτι Bas.*hex.*3.1(1.22A; M.29.52C); πάντως ὅτι *Const.App.*5.7. 23; Gr.Nyss.*Eun.*3(2 p.13.10; πάντως M.45.577A); Epiph.*haer.*66.82 (p.124.11; M.42.157C); Chrys.*hom.4.2 in Phil.*(11.221C); **4.** = ὥστε, *so that*; c. infin., Cyr.*hom.pasch.*15(5^2.200E); c. indic., after οὕτως, Chrys.*hom.24.2 in Heb.*(12.222B); id.*hom.26.6 in Mt.*(7.322C); id. *hom.1.4 in Phil.*(11.200C); after τοσοῦτον, id.*hom.12.2 in Mt.*(7. 162D,E); *ib.30.3*(351B); **5.** *for*, introducing a main clause, *Pers.* (p.10.20).

ὅτιπερ, 1. introducing an objective clause, *that* μανθάνομεν ὅ. ... προνοεῖ Chrys.*hom.28.3 in Mt.*(7.337E); Philost.*h.e.*9.13(M.65.577A); inserted pleonastically in introducing a quotation, Pall.*h.Laus.*18 (p.48.11, v.l. ὅτι M.34.1051B); *ib.*36(p.107.4; 1179C); *ib.*47(p.138.2; 1196D); **2.** *because, since*, Eus.*h.e.*1.1.8(M.20.52B); Philost.*h.e.*9.6(M. 65.572C); *ib.*9.15(580C); Jo.D.*f.o.*3.10(M.94.1020C).

***ὁτιποτοῦν,** *at any time*, Or.*comm.in Mt.*16.6(p.484.29; M.13. 1384B).

ὀτραλέος, *sharp* ὀ. δρεπάνοιο tr.Vergil *ecl.*4.41 ap.Const.*or.s.c.*20 (p.186.4; M.20.1300A).

οὐ, *not*; **1.** used instead of μή in the protasis of a conditional clause εἰ γὰρ βασιλεὺς...τὸ σύνολον οὐ παρορᾷ... Ath.*inc.*10.1(M.25. 112C); Bas.*Eun.*2.11(1.246C; M.29.592C); Cyr.*ador.*7(1.239E); **2.** used instead of μή with a ptcpl. which can be resolved into the protasis of a conditional clause εἰ γάρ, οὐ γινομένων σημείων, οἱ πλεονεκτήμασιν ἑτέροις κομῶντες... Chrys.*hom.32.7 in Mt.*(7.375E); Cyr.*ador.*1 (1.17C); Max.*schol.d.n.*7.1(M.4.341C); **3.** used with the ptcpl. as subst. where there is distinct reference to a fact τὸν υἱὸν ἀναγκάσεις ἐξ οὐκ ὄντων εἰς τὸ εἶναι παρεληλυθέναι Gr.Naz.*or.*20.8(M.35. 1073C); ἐξ οὐκ ὄντων τὰ πάντα γεγένηται Epiph.*haer.*69.59(p.208.3; M.42.297B); Chrys.*hom.4.3 in Heb.*(12.43C); *ib.22.1*(202B); **4.** used instead of μή in a prohibition οὔ με ἐπιχλευάσητε Ephr.2.107A; **5.** used elliptically instead of οὐ μόνον: ὥστε ἀναβῆναί σε ἐκεῖ· καὶ τὸ δὴ μεῖζον, οὐχ ὥστε ἀναβῆναι, ἀλλ' ὥστε καὶ ἑτέρους ἀνάγειν Chrys. *hom.12.4 in Mt.*(7.166B); *ib.68.1*(670B); id.*hom.11.4 in Eph.*(11. 85C); **6.** inserted pleonastically before μετ' οὐ πολύ: ὅπερ καὶ γέγονεν οὐ μετ' οὐ πολὺ *Chron.Pasch.*p.128(M.92.325D); *ib.*p.258(629A); *ib.* p.277(689B).

οὐαί, exclamation of pain and anger, *ah! woe!*; as subject of sentence οὐαὶ ἔχει τὸν δεχόμενον αὐτόν *Didasc.Jac.*5.1(p.70.19).

οὖας, τό, poet. for οὖς *ear* δεξιὸν οὖας Nonn.*par.Jo.*18:10(M.43. 882A).

οὐδαμινός, *worthless, good for nothing*; of persons, Epiph.*anc.*89 (p.110.10; M.41.181A); Chrys.*hom.11.6 in Eph.*(11.88F); Cyr.*Ps.*8:5 (M.69.760A); of things, Nil.*epp.*2.141(M.79.264D); Eus.Al.*serm.*21. 12(M.86.437D); τὰ...οὐ. τῶν ἀφθάρτων προκρῖναι καὶ αἰωνίων †Jo.D. *B.J.*24(M.96.1085A); of abstracts, Nect.*Thdr.*3(M.39.1824C); Chrys. *hom.23.1 in Mt.*(7.284E); Isid.Pel.*epp.*2.156(M.78.609B); comp. οὐδαμινέστερος Chrys.*hom.2.4 in Tit.*(11.742C); id.*hom.9.5 in Heb.*(12. 100D); *ib.32.3*(300D); neut. as subst., *worthlessness* λόγισαι τὸ οὐ. τῶν παρόντων πραγμάτων id.*hom.1.2 in 2Thess.*(11.513D); ‡Caes. Naz.*dial.*140(M.38.1048A).

οὐδενία, ἡ, *nothingness, worthlessness*, as polite form of self-depreciation οὐ παρακούσῃ τῆς ἡμῶν οὐ. Nil.*epp.*4.1(M.79.552A); Max.*ep.*45(M.91.649C); liturg. ὑπὲρ τῆς ἐμῆς τοῦ προσφέροντός σοι οὐ. καὶ παντὸς τοῦ κλήρου *Lit.*ap.*Const.App.*8.12.41.

οὐδέπω, 1. *never yet at any time*; inserted pleonastically after οὔπω, Chrys.*hom.68.4 in Mt.*(7.676B); **2.** *by no means*, Or.*Cels.*2.72 (p.194.13; M.11.909A).

***οὐδόλως,** for οὐδ' ὅλως, *not at all*, Ath.*ep.Aeg.Lib.*7(M.25.536A); Barth.Edess.*Agar.*(M.104.1429A).

***οὐδοπόθεν,** *from no place*, Euthal.Diac.*epp.Paul.*(M.85.721C).

***οὐετρανίζω,** (cf. sq.) *retire from duty*, Epiph.*mens.*20(M.43.269C).

οὐέτρανος, ὁ, (Lat. *veteranus*) *veteran*, Epiph.*haer.*66.1(p.13.21; M.42.29A).

***οὐθενής,** *worthless, insignificant*, Thdr.Stud.*epp.*2.79(M.99. 1317C).

[*]οὐθενία (οὐθένεια), ἡ, = οὐδενία, Eus.*Ps.*38:6(M.24.40C); κατά γε τὴν ἐμὴν οὐθένειαν Ath.*Ar.*2.15(M.26.177B).

***οὐθενότης, ἡ,** *nothingness, worthlessness*; as polite term of self-depreciation, Leont.N.*v.Jo.Eleem.*3(p.9.22); †Jo.Jej.*poenit.*(M.88. 1896C); Thdr.Stud.*epp.*1.33(M.99.1020D).

***οὐικάριος, ὁ,** (Lat. *vicarius*) *deputy*; **1.** of deputy of a *praefectus praetorius*, *vicar* of an imperial diocese, Const.ap.Eus.*h.e.*10.6.4(M. 20.892B); *Chron.Pasch.*p.297(M.92.745A); **2.** of deputy of a *priest* τοῦ καβιδαρίου Ἀναστασίου οὐ. πρεσβυτέρου *MAMA* 3.226; v. *βικάριος.

οὔλιμος, *baneful*, *Orac.Sib.*12.221 (conj. for οὔλαμος).

οὐλόθριξ, *with curly hair*, acc. οὐλόθριξιν; of Christ, ‡Jo.D.*ep. Thphl.*3(M.95.349C).

***οὐλοξανθόκομος,** *with fair curly hair*, *Chron.Pasch.*p.312(M.92. 793D).

***οὐλόξανθος,** *with fair curls*, Jo.Mal.*chron.*12 p.283(M. om.).

οὖλος, *woolly*, hence, of hair, *crisp, curly*; fem. as subst., *curly hair*, *Const.App.*1.3.10.

***οὐλωτικός,** *causing cicatrization*, Sophr.H.*conf.*(M.87.3365B).

***οὐραλύφιος,** *anointed with urine*; of Constantine Copronymus, Thdr.Stud.*epp.*2.77(M.99.1316C).

οὐρανίδης, *heavenly*, Gr.Naz.*carm.*1.1.29.15(M.37.508A).

οὐράνιος, A. *heavenly, pertaining to the sky*; of elements, Just. *2apol.*5.2(M.6.452B); of heavenly bodies ἄστρα...σὺν τῷ οὐ. κόσμῳ Arist.*apol.*4.2; Or.*hom.10.6 in Jer.*(p.76.22; M.13.365A).

B. *heavenly, divine, spiritual*, opp. earthly, material; **1.** pagan; of gods, Athenag.*leg.*23.6(M.6.945A); in address to Persian king ἡ οὐ. σου θειότης *Pers.*(p.2.20); **2.** of God, *Orac.Sib.*3.247; τὸ οὐ. μὴ καθορῶντες φῶς...τὸ γήϊνον ἐπιζητοῦσιν οὐδεμίαν ἔχον δυναστείαν τῆς οὐ. θεότητος Const.ap.Gel.Cyz.*h.e.*2.7.30(M.85.1237D); **3.** of Logos, Clem.*paed.*1.1(p.90.12; M.8.249B); of Christ's birth Χριστοῖο γενέθλης οὐ. *Orac.Sib.*8.484; and teaching οὐ. διδασκαλίᾳ θεοποιῶν τὸν ἄνθρωπον Clem.*prot.*11(p.81.1; M.8.233A); **4.** of spiritual beings, Just.*dial.*131.3(M.6.781A); ζωὴ τὸ πνεῦμα, τὸ τῶν οὐ. δυνάμεων ἀποτελεστικόν Didym.(‡Bas.)*Eun.*5(1.303D; M.29.728C); τοῖς οὐ. πυλωροῖς προμηνύοντες τοῦ παμβασιλέως...τὴν εἴσοδον Procl.CP *hom.* 1.3(M.65.836C); θεῖα καὶ οὐ. τάγματα Dion.Ar.*c.h.*4.3(M.3.196B); τῶν οὐ. νόων ἱεραρχίας *ib.*1.2(121A); *ib.*2.2(140A); αἱ...ἅγιαι τῶν οὐ. οὐσιῶν διακοσμήσεις *ib.*4.2(180A); θεολόγοι πάσας...τὰς οὐ. οὐσίας ἀγγέλους καλοῦσι *ib.*5.1(196B); τῶν οὐ. ἀρχῶν καὶ ἀποπερατώσεων αἰτία τἀγαθόν id.*d.n.*4.4(M.3.697B); τῶν οὐ. ἱεραρχιῶν μίμησιν id.*c.h.* 1.3(121C); *ib.*(124C); id.*e.h.*6.3.5(M.3.537A); **5.** of heavenly or future life, other world, *Orac.Sib.*8.475; μεταβᾶσα [sc. ἡ ψυχή]...τῆς οὐ. συνουσίας τῶν ἐλαττόνων μετουσίαν ἐπεπόθησεν Tat.*orat.*20(p.22.14; M.6.852A); Meth.*symp.*4.5(p.50.2; M.18.93B); Eus.*v.C.*1.2(p.7.24; M. 20.912C); ‡Just.*monarch.*6(M.6.325B); **6.** of heavenly bread: ref. manna τῆς οὐ. καὶ θείας τροφῆς τὸ μνημόσυνον Clem.*str.*2.11(p.139. 12; M.8.985A); as body of Christ, interpreted of Church ἡ σὰρξ τὸ σῶμα αὐτοῦ ἐστιν, 'ὅπερ ἐστὶν ἡ ἐκκλησία', 'ἄρτος οὐ.', συναγωγὴ εὐλογημένη Clem.*exc.Thdot.*13(p.111.11; M.9.664B); of Christ's words αὐτὰ εἶναι τὰ ῥήματα...τὴν σάρκα καὶ τὸ αἷμα, ὧν ὁ μετέχων...ὡσανεὶ ἄρτῳ οὐ. τρεφόμενος τῆς οὐ. μεθέξει ζωῆς Eus.*e.th.*3.12(p.168.34; M. 24.1024A); eucharistic, Iren.*haer.*4.18.5(M.7.1028B) cit. s. εὐχαριστία; ἡ τροφὴ...τουτέστιν ὁ λόγος τοῦ θεοῦ, πνεῦμα σαρκούμενον, ἁγιαζομένη σὰρξ οὐ. Clem.*paed.*1.6(p.116.4; M.8.301B); ἀλλαχοῦ τὸ ἅγιον πνεῦμα καλεῖ ἄρτον οὐ. λέγων· τὸν ἄρτον ἡμῶν τὸν ἐπιούσιον δὸς ἡμῖν σήμερον. ἐδίδαξε γὰρ ἡμᾶς ἐν τῇ εὐχῇ ἐν τῷ νῦν αἰῶνι αἰτεῖν τὸν ἐπιούσιον ἄρτον, τουτέστι τὸν μέλλοντα, οὗ ἀπαρχὴν ἔχομεν ἐν τῇ νῦν ζωῇ, τῆς σαρκὸς τοῦ κυρίου μεταλαμβάνοντες. ... πνεῦμα γὰρ ζωοποιοῦν ἡ σάρξ ἐστι τοῦ κυρίου Ath.*inc.et c.Ar.*17(M.26.1012B); cf. ἐπὶ δεῖπνον...τὸ μέγα καὶ οὐ. ... κληθέντες id.*ep.fest.*40(p.296.27; M.26.1440A); cf. ἵνα...τὴν σάρκα βρῶσιν ἄνωθεν οὐ. καὶ πνευματικὴν τροφὴν...μάθωσιν id.*ep. Serap.*4.19(M.26.668A); *Lit.Jac.*(p.180.15); *ib.*(p.232.17); ref. BMV, Procl.CP *annunt.*6(M.85.449B), Mod.*dorm.*2(M.86.3285A) citt. s.

ἄρτος; **7.** of baptism, ref. Heb.6:4 ἐπὶ μὲν τοῖς ἀτελέσιν ἐστὶ συγγνώμη· ἐπὶ δὲ τοῖς γευσαμένοις τῆς οὐ. δωρεᾶς...οὐδεμία περιλείπεται συγγνώμης ἀπολογία Thgn.*hypot.fr.*1(p.76.19; M.10.241A); **8.** of divine grace, Or.*princ.*3.1.12(p.216.6; M.11.272A); *ib.*4.1.6(p.302.3; 353A); id.*hom.1.7 in Jer.*(p.5.18; M.13.261B); Const.ap.Thdt.*h.e.*1.10.11(1.773); **9.** of spiritual light, Const.ap.Eus.*v.C.*3.60(p.108.27; M.20.1133A); Didym.*Trin.*2.1(M.39.452B); **10.** of spiritual men ἡ σὰρξ τοῦ κυρίου...τοὺς οὐ. τῶν ἀνθρώπων εἰς ἀφθαρσίαν ἐκτρέφων Clem.*paed.*1.6(p.118.8; M.8.305B); οὐρανίους...πατέρας τοὺς πνευματικοὺς καλεῖ Thdt.*Eph.*3:15(3.420); of man opp. irrational creatures, Cosm.Ind.*top.*3(M.88.156D); μόνος ὁ ἄνθρωπος...ὡς λογικὸς καὶ οὐ. μέλλων εἶναι, ἀναλόγως τὸ σχῆμα παρὰ τοῦ δημιουργοῦ ἐδέξατο *ib.*(157B); **11.** of Christian πολιτεία, Or.*fr.102 in Lam.*(p.272.6; M.13.653B); Ath.*ep.Aeg.Lib.*1(M.25.540A); Cyr.H.*procatech.*1; **12.** in gen. μελετήσας ἐνθένδε ἁγίαν συνήλυσιν ἀγάπης, οὐ. ἐκκλησίαν Clem.*paed.*2.1(p.157.25; M.8.388A); οὐ. ἐστι πόμα [sc. virginity]...ὁ νυμφίος ὅπερ τέθεικε Meth.*symp.*11(p.133.31; M.18.209C); τὴν καρδίαν τῶν κακῶν οὐρανίῳ καθάρατε λογισμῷ *Hom.Clem.*11.28; Μωυσῆς...ποιμαίνων...τῆς ὁμιλίας τῆς οὐ. ἠξιώθη Bas.*hom.*23.3(2.187A; M.31.593B); εὐχώμεθα...τῆς οὐ. ἐλπίδος, εὐέλπιδες, Χριστῷ πιστεύοντες Procl.CP *hom.*1.5(M.65.837A); ἡ ἀγαθὴ πάντων αἰτία...πάντα θεῖα φῶτα καὶ...λόγους οὐ. ἀπολιμπάνουσα Dion.Ar.*myst.*1.3(M.3.1000C); of heavenly Jerusalem, Cosm.Ind.*top.*2(M.88.72C); v. οὐρανόπολις; **13.** neut. as subst., of things in heaven as created by God who made earthly things also τὸν ποιητὴν τῶν οὐ. καὶ γηΐνων ἁπάντων Just.*1apol.*58.1(M.6.416A); Iren.*haer.*1.10.3(M.7.556A); Clem.*str.*3.7(p.224.8; M.8.1164B); Procl.CP *hom.*1.3(M.65.836C); as object of contemplation, Just.*1apol.*44.9(M.6.396A); of spiritual things in gen. ἐργάζεται...ὁ σωτὴρ...εἰς πόθον τῶν οὐ. ἀνάγων Ath.*inc.*31.2(M.25.149B); id.*ep.Jov.*1(M.26.813B)ap.Thdt.*h.e.*4.3.1; Chrys.*hom.63.1 in Jo.*(8.376A); ἀντίδος αὐτοῖς ἀντὶ τῶν ἐπιγείων τὰ οὐ., ἀντὶ τῶν φθαρτῶν τὰ ἄφθαρτα *Lit.Jac.*(p.212.12).

οὐρανίων, ὁ, *heavenly being*, *Orac.Sib.*5.76; Gr.Naz.*carm.*1.2.2.680(M.37.681A).

οὐρανίως, *in a heavenly way* ἱεραρχικῶς καὶ οὐ. τελεσιουργεῖν Dion.Ar.*e.h.*5.3.5(M.3.513A).

οὐρανοβάμων, *traversing, scaling heaven* τοῦ...οὐ. Διονυσίου *Lit.Jac.*(p.178.3); *cat.Apoc.*16:16(p.420.21).

οὐρανοβατ-έω, *walk in heaven, scale heaven* δίπους [sc. ὁ ἄνθρωπος]...ὡς μέλλων ἵπτασθαι καὶ ~εῖν Cosm.Ind.*top.*3(M.88.157B); of Elijah, *ib.*5(260C); spiritually, Chrys.*bapt.*4(2.374C); ~εῖτε τῇ διανοίᾳ Nil.*epp.*2.199(M.79.305A); Isid.Pel.*epp.*2.151(M.78.604D).

***οὐρανοβάτης**, ὁ, *one who traverses heaven* οὐ. ... εἰρωνευόμενος τοὺς ἀμφὶ τὸν Ἀέτιον Philost.*h.e.*9.3(M.65.569A).

***οὐρανοβλέπτης**, ὁ, *one who sees heaven*, Chrysipp.*enc.in Jo.Bapt.*2(p.31.17).

***οὐρανογεώργητος**, *cultivated in heaven*; of manna, Mart.Ant.*pan.*6(M.47.xlviii).

***οὐρανοδρομ-έω**, *traverse the heavens*; of Elijah, Cosm.Ind.*top.*5(M.88.260B); δυνατὸν τοῖς ἀνθρώποις, θεοῦ θέλοντος, ~εῖν *ib.*(M.88.260C, v.l. οὐρανοβατεῖν Migne).

οὐρανοδρόμος, *traversing the heavens*; of stars, Eust.*engast.*19(p.46.21; M.18.653A); of Elijah, Isid.Pel.*epp.*2.37(M.78.481A); Tim.Ant.*Sym.*(M.86.240A); met. λόγοι...οὐ. Geo.Pis.*carm.*48.6; of S. Paul τὸν οὐ. Jo.VI H.*v.Jo.D.*4(M.94.433B); in spiritual sense ὦ μύστα..., ὦ οὐ. Jo.Clim.*past.*15(M.88.1205D).

***οὐρανοδύναμος**, *powerful in heaven*, *Pers.*(p.18.8; M.10.108B).

οὐρανοειδής, *of heavenly appearance*, Gr.Nyss.*hom.14 in Cant.*(M.44.1076B).

***οὐρανομέτρης**, ὁ, *heavenly measurer* τὸ πνεῦμα τὸ ἅγιον φησὶν [sc. Photinus]...μεῖζον εἶναι τοῦ Χριστοῦ...ὡς οὐ. τῶν ἀνεκδιηγήτων Epiph.*haer.*71.1(p.250.3; M.42.376A).

οὐρανομίμητος, *imitating heaven* οὐ. βίωσιν Jo.Clim.*scal.*4(M.88.688D); οὐ. ἐκκλησία ‡Jo.D.*hom.*6.11(M.96.677C).

***οὐρανόμορφος**, *with heavenly shape, heaven-like*, Agath.*v.Gr.Ill.*118(p.60); Proc.G.*Cant.*7:13(M.87.1737B).

***οὐρανοπεμπής**, *sent from heaven*, *Pers.*(p.9.1).

οὐρανοπετής, *flying through the heavens*; of Const., Eus.*v.C.*3.55(p.102.27; οὐρανοπέτης M.20.1120); of angels, Eust.*engast.*20(p.47.23; M.18.653D); *ib.*23(p.52.15; 660D).

***οὐρανόπνοος**, *heavenly scented* ἡ ῥοδωνιὰ τῶν οὐ. ἀρετῶν Alex.Sal.*Barn.*6(p.438D).

***οὐρανοπόθητος**, *desired, beloved by heaven*, *Pers.*(p.15.14).

***οὐρανοποίησις**, ἡ, *making heavenly* ἵνα καὶ ἐπὶ τῆς γῆς ὁμοίως τῷ οὐρανῷ...πληρωθῇ τὸ θέλημα θεοῦ εἰς τὴν...οὐ. αὐτῆς Or.*or.*26.6(p.363.9; M.11.504C).

***οὐρανοπολέω**, v. *οὐρανοπορέω.

οὐρανόπολις, ἡ, *heavenly city*; of heavenly Jerusalem, Clem.*paed.*2.12(p.228.11; M.8.540C); τῆς οὐ. Ἱερουσαλήμ, ἥν...φασιν...εἶναι τὸ ἄθροισμα τῶν ψυχῶν Meth.*symp.*4.5(p.51.17; M.18.96A); id.*lepr.*10(p.464.15); Eus.*d.e.*4.12(p.169.28; M.22.284A); ‡Chrys.*hom.*6(13.215C).

οὐρανοπολίτης, ὁ, *citizen of heaven*, of Christians in gen. ἠλευθερώθημεν ἀπὸ τοῦ κόσμου, οὐ. γεγόναμεν *cat.1Petr.*2:16(p.56.11); Germ.CP *or.*2(M.98.260B); ref. baptism ἐν ὕδασι μήτρα κατεσκευάζετο οὐ οὐρανοπολίτας ὠδίνουσα Bas.Sel.*or.*34.1(M.85.369B); in life after death καταλιπὼν τὸ σῶμα, οὐ. ἐγένετο ‡Pall.*h.mon.*16.22(p.76.11; M.34.1170D); of monks οἱ μὲν οὐ., ἡμεῖς δὲ οὐδὲ τῆς γῆς ἄξιοι Chrys.*hom.69.4 in Mt.*(7.685D); cf.Isid.Pel.*epp.*3.234(M.78.916A); as adj., of the soul, Hyper.*mon.*62(M.79.1480B); of life, †Jo.D.*B.J.*12(M.96.972B).

***οὐρανοπορέω**, *traverse heaven*; of Elijah, Cosm.Ind.*top.*5(M.88.260B) cf. οὐρανοπολῶν *ib.*ap.*Chron.Pasch.*p.147(M.92.361A); met., Gr.Nyss.*v.Ephr.*(M.46.845A); Cosm.Mel.*schol.*proem.(M.38.346).

***οὐρανοπορία**, ἡ, *traversing of heaven*, Dion.Ar.*d.n.*4.4(M.3.697B).

***οὐρανοπόρος**, *traversing heaven*, Meth.*symp.*8.12(p.96.15; M.18.157B).

***οὐρανοπράτης**, ὁ, *one who sells heaven*, of God τοῖς λαβεῖν θέλουσιν οὐρανοπράτης Geo.Pis.*hex.*475(M.92.1472A).

***οὐρανοπρεπής**, *befitting heaven* τὴν ὁ...εὐπρέπειαν τῆς Ἱερουσαλὴμ Olymp.*fr.Lam.*2:1(M.93.736B).

***οὐρανοπρόβλητος**, *put forward, proposed by heaven* οὐ. καὶ ἅγιον σταυρόν ‡Chrys.*ador.*2(11.824B).

***οὐρανόπτης**, ὁ, *one who sees the sky*, ‡Caes.Naz.*dial.*140(M.38.1073).

οὐρανός, ὁ, *sky, heaven*; **1.** of visible heaven in gen. ἐν ὅλῳ τῷ κόσμῳ...παντὶ τῷ συστήματι τῷ ἐξ οὐ. καὶ γῆς ἢ ἐξ οὐρανῶν καὶ γῆς Or.*Jo.*1.15(p.19.22; M.14.49A); οὐ. καὶ ἡλίῳ...τὴν τοῦ θεοῦ τιμὴν ἀνέθηκαν Ath.*gent.*9(M.25.17C); *ib.*27(52C); ἄρτος οὐρανοῦ [i.e. manna]...οὐκ ἐξ αὐτοῦ τοῦ οὐ., ἀλλ' ἐκ τοῦ ἀέρος Thdt.*qu.29 in Ex.*(1.144); as element Μωσέως...τεττάρων...στοιχείων...μνημονεύσαντος, οὐ. καὶ γῆς καὶ ἀβύσσου καὶ ὕδατος Eus.*e.th.*3.2(p.143.30; M.24.980B); ὁ οὐ. τοῦτο γὰρ πέμπτον σῶμά φασι Jo.D.*f.o.*1.4(M.94.797C); order and composition, Ath.*ep.Serap.*1.18(M.26.572C); εἴτε...τις ἀναβλέπειν εἰς τὸν οὐ. βούλεται, ὁρᾷ τὴν τούτου διακόσμησιν id.*inc.*45.3(M.25.177A); τινὲς Χριστιανίζειν νομιζόμενοι...σφαιρικὸν εἶναι τὸ σχῆμα τοῦ οὐ. ὑπολαμβάνουσι, ἐκ τῶν ἡλιακῶν...ἐκλείψεων πλανώμενοι Cosm.Ind.*top.*arg.(M.88.56A); ἀνομία...μεγάλη τὸ ἀθετεῖν τὰ λόγια τοῦ θεοῦ, καὶ ἄντικρυς αὐτῶν τὸ σφαιρικὸν σχῆμα τῷ οὐ. δωρεῖσθαι *ib.*2(128C); τὸν οὐ. σῶμα λέγοντες εἶναι, περιέχειν λέγουσι τὸν πάντα κόσμον *ib.*1(69D); not infinite οὐκ ἔστι...ἄπειρος ὁ οὐ. ... πεπερασμένος δὲ καὶ ἐν τέρματι· τὰ δὲ ὑπὲρ τοῦτον αἰῶνες οἱ κρείττονες...Tat.*orat.*20(p.22.20; M.6.852A); κατὰ ἀνατολὰς κεῖται ὁ παράδεισος, ἔνθα καὶ τὰ ἄκρα τοῦ οὐ. τοῖς ἄκροις συνδέδενται τῆς γῆς Cosm.Ind.*top.*2(92B); **2.** ref. number of heavens: unity of the whole, Or.*Cels.*1.48(p.98.8; M.11.749A); two heavens, visible and invisible μήτε τῷ ὁρωμένῳ, μήτε τῷ ὑπερτέρῳ χειρούμενος [sc. God] οὐ. Thdt.*qu.27 in 3Reg.*(1.474); εἷς οὐ. ἢ δύο εἰσίν;...ὁ μὲν οὐκ ἔκ τινος, ὁ δὲ ἐξ ὑδάτων id.*qu.11 in Gen.*(1.14); ὁ ὁρώμενος οὐ. ὄροφον ἔχει τὸν ὑπερκείμενον οὐ. *ib.*(1.15); δύο οὐ. γενομένων παρὰ θεοῦ...καὶ συνδουμένων ἀλλήλοις, ποτὲ μὲν πληθυντικῶς ἡ...γραφὴ περὶ αὐτῶν ποιεῖ τὸν λόγον, ποτὲ δὲ ἑνικῶς Cosm.Ind.*top.*7(M.88.341D); οὐρανὸν οὐρανοῦ καλέσας τὸν πρῶτον καὶ ἀνώτερον οὐ., ὅς οὐ. ἐστι τούτου τοῦ ὁρωμένου οὐ. ὑπεράνω αὐτοῦ κείμενος *ib.*(341C); μύαξ ὁ ἐπάνω τοῦ βήματος τύπος τοῦ πρώτου οὐ., τὸ δὲ λοιπὸν στέγος τῆς ἐκκλησίας εἰς τύπον τοῦ φαινομένου οὐ. ‡Sophr.H.*liturg.*3(M.87.3984B); ref. 2Cor.12:2 ὁ...ἁρπαγεὶς εἰς τρίτον οὐ. ἐξιχνίασε...τὰ ἐν τοῖς τρισὶν οὐ. Or.*or.*1(p.297.18; M.11.416B); μὴ πλάνην ὑπομείνῃς ἀκούων τοῦ...Παύλου ἡρπάχθαι ἕως τρίτου οὐ. οὐκ εἰσὶ γὰρ τρεῖς οὐ., οὔτε πλείους, οὔτε τοῦτο βούλεται λέγειν...ἀλλ' ὅτι ἡρπάχθαι λέγει ἀπὸ τῆς γῆς ὅλον τὸ διάστημα τοῦ ὕψους τοῦ οὐ., παρὰ τὸ τρίτον αὐτοῦ Cosm.Ind.*top.*7(341D); three heavens, *T.Lev.*2.7–9; Gnost. ἄνθρωπος...ἐν τῷ παραδείσῳ, τῷ τετάρτῳ οὐ., δημιουργεῖται Clem.*exc.Thdot.*51(p.123.19; M.9.684A); theory of seven heavens, declared unscriptural ἑπτὰ...οὐ. ... αἱ φερόμεναι ἐν ταῖς ἐκκλησίαις οὐκ ἀπαγγέλλουσι γραφαί, ἀλλ' οὐρανούς, εἴτε τὰς σφαίρας τῶν...πλανητῶν, εἴτε καὶ ἄλλο τι ἀπορρητότερον ἐοίκασι διδάσκειν οἱ λόγοι Or.*Cels.*6.21(p.91.15; M.11.1321B); οὐδαμοῦ τῶν γνησίων...γραφῶν ἑπτὰ εἴρηνται οὐ. *ib.*6.23(p.94.11; 1328A); cf. explanation of plural usage οὐ...ὡς πολλῶν ὄντων οὐρανῶν...πληθυντικῶς εἶπε γραφή, ἀλλὰ τὸ ἰδίωμα φυλάξασα τῆς Ἑβραΐδος φωνῆς Thdt.*qu.11 in Gen.*(1.15); theory asserted ἑπτὰ...οὐ. κατεσκευακέναι, ὧν ἐπάνω τὸν δημιουργὸν εἶναι λέγουσι...τοὺς δὲ ἑπτὰ οὐ. οὐκ εἶναι νοητούς φασιν, ἀγγέλους δὲ αὐτοὺς ὑποτίθενται...καὶ τὸν παράδεισον ὑπὲρ τρίτον οὐ. ὄντα, τέταρτον ἄγγελον λέγουσιν Iren.*haer*.1.5.2(M.7.493B); created by Demiurge at instigation of Achamoth, *ib*.1.5.3(496A); ὁ Ἰαλδαβαὼθ ἦλθεν εἰς τὰ κατώτατα καὶ ἐποίησεν ἑαυτῷ ἑπτὰ υἱούς, οἵτινες ἑαυτοῖς οὐ. ἑπτὰ ἐποίησαν Epiph.*haer*.37.3(p.55.1; M.41.645C); ἔστη ὁ ἄνθρωπος ἐπὶ τοὺς πόδας καὶ ὑπερβέβηκε τῇ διανοίᾳ τοὺς ὀκτὼ οὐ. καὶ ἐπέγνω...τὸν ἄνω πατέρα τὸν ἐπάνω τοῦ Ἰαλδαβαώθ *ib*.37.4(p.56.4; 648A); fig., ref. BMV ὦ γαστὴρ ἑπτάκυκλος οὐ. καὶ μειζοτέρως αὐτῶν τυγχάνουσα. ὦ γαστὴρ ἑπτὰ οὐ. ὑψηλοτέρα...ὦ γαστὴρ ὁ ὄγδοος οὐ. στερεωμάτων ἀνωτέρα ‡Epiph.*hom*.5(M.43.497A); in apocalyptic cosmology σαλευθήσονται τὰ ἐννέα πέταλα τοῦ οὐ. *1Apoc.Jo*.17(p.85); ref. firmament dividing heaven from earth ἔστι γῆ καὶ οὐ. καὶ μέσον διάφραγμα τὸ στερέωμα τοῦτο Chrys.*nativ*.3(2.359A); Cosm.Ind.*top*. arg.(56D); οὐρανοῦ τούτου τοῦ ὁρωμένου, τουτέστι τοῦ στερεώματος *ib*.7(341B); **3.** as created together with the earth, by Logos, Or. *fr.1 in Jo*.(p.484.13); Ath.*Ar*.1.62(M.26.141B); by Trin., Evagr. Pont.*ep*.11(M.32.264B); by Father πιστεύομεν εἰς ἕνα θεόν, πατέρα παντοκράτορα· ποιητὴν οὐ. καὶ γῆς *Symb.Hier*.(M.33.533A); *Symb*. ap.Epiph.*anc*.118(p.146.22; M.43.232B); *Symb.Nic.–CP*(p.80.3; H.2. 288B); *Symb.App*.(p.30); hence, as creature, dist. from God, cf. *1Clem*.20.1; φανερόν ἐστι μὴ εἶναι τὸν οὐ. θεόν, ἀλλ' ἔργον θεοῦ Arist. *apol*.4.2; πῶς ἐστι θεὸς ὁ οὐ., ὁ μὴ βουλήσει τὴν ἀθανασίαν ἐνεργῶν, ἀλλὰ τῇ κινήσει...τῶν ἑαυτοῦ μερῶν; ‡Just.*confut*.52(M.6.1545A); **4.** as abode of the divine; of pagan gods, Ath.*gent*.16(M.25.36A); hence as divine realm, sphere of God's particular presence and his manifestations; **a.** in gen. ὁ γνωστικὸς...τέμνει διὰ τῆς ἐπιστήμης τὸν οὐ. καὶ ἅπτεται τῶν θρόνων τῶν ἄκρων Clem.*str*.7.13(p.59.2; M.9. 516A); ὁ παντοδύναμος θεός, ὁ τὸν οὐ. οἰκῶν Const.ap.Gel.Cyz.*h.e*. 2.7.21(M.85.1236D); ἐν νόοις αὐτὸν εἶναί φασι...καὶ ἐν οὐ. καὶ ἐν γῇ Dion.Ar.*d.n*.1.6(M.3.596B); but not containing God, Thdt.*qu.27 in 3Reg*.(1.474); **b.** 'kingdom of heaven', v. βασιλεία; **c.** ref. God as king of heaven, *T.Benj*.10.7; or God of heaven, *T.Reub*.1.6; cf. *T.Benj*.3.1; **d.** hence as periphrasis for θεός: πέπτωκεν ὁ ἄνθρωπος... ὁ παράδεισος ἐκλείσθη, ὁ οὐ. ἐθυμώθη Ath.*hom.in Mt*.11:27(M.25. 209D); **e.** as sphere of worship of Trin., Didym.*Trin*.2.8(M.39. 593A); **f.** ref. Son's descent in Inc. ἔδει γὰρ ἀπὸ οὐ. κατερχόμενον τὸν λόγον, ἐξ οὐ. καὶ τὴν σημασίαν ἔχειν Ath.*inc*.37.7(M.25.160C); ὁ δεσπότης τῶν οὐ. ἐν ὁμοιώματι ἡμῶν γέγονε id.*inc.et c.Ar*.20(M.26. 1021A); ὁ λόγος ἐξ οὐρανῶν ἐπιδημήσας ‡Ath.*Apoll*.1.4(M.26.1097C); Χριστὸς ἐξ οὐρανῶν Gr.Naz.*or*.38.1(M.36.312A); in creeds, *Symb. Ant*.(341)2(p.249.23; M.26.721C) citing Jo.6:38; τὸν ἐπ' ἐσχάτων τῶν ἡμερῶν κατελθόντα ἐξ οὐρανῶν *Symb*.ap.*Const.App*.7.41.6; διὰ τὴν ἡμετέραν σωτηρίαν κατελθόντα ἐκ τῶν οὐ. *Symb*.ap.Epiph.*anc*.118 (p.147.6; M.43.232C); *Symb.Nic.–CP*(p.80.8; H.2.288B); **g.** ref. Ascension ἀνέβη εἰς οὐρανοὺς *Barn*.15.9; ἀναβάντα εἰς τοὺς οὐ. *Symb.Rom*. (p.23); ἀνελθόντα εἰς οὐρανούς *Symb.Nic*.(325)(p.52.1; M.20.1540C); εἰς οὐρανοὺς ἀνεληλυθέναι *Symb.Ant*.(341)1(p.249.5; M.26.721A); ἀνελθόντα εἰς οὐρανούς *Symb.Ant*.(341)2,3(pp.249.25,250.14; 724A,D); ἀναληφθέντα εἰς οὐ. *Symb.Ant*.(341)4(p.251.8; 725C); *Symb.Ant*.(345)(p.251. 29; 728B); ἀνελθόντα εἰς τοὺς οὐ. *Symb.Hier*.(M.33.533A); *Symb*.ap. *Const.App*.7.41.6; *Symb*.ap.Epiph.*anc*.118(p.147.9; 232C); *Symb. Nic.–CP*(p.80.10; H.2.288B); Χριστὸς οὐ μόνον εἰς τὸν ὁρώμενον οὐ. ἀνελήλυθεν, ἀλλὰ καὶ εἰς τὸν ὑπέρτερον Thdt.*Ps*.67:34(1.1074); ὡς ἀέρα τὸν οὐ. διεπέρα ὁ τῶν οὐ. ποιητής Procl.CP *hom*.1.3(M.65.836C); πρὸς τὸν οὐ. τῆς σαρκὸς...ὑψουμένης...αἱ τῶν ἐν οὐρανοῖς ἀσωμάτων δυνάμεις ἐξ οὐρανοῦ πρὸς οὐρανὸν ἐκεχήνουν *ib*.(836D); βασιλέα τῆς δόξης, τὸν εἰς οὐρανοὺς ἀνθρωποπρεπῶς ἀναληφθέντα Dion.Ar.*c.h*.7.3 (M.3.209B); cf. ἐκ γὰρ θανάτου πρὸς ζωὴν καὶ ἐκ γῆς πρὸς οὐ. Χριστὸς ...ἡμᾶς διεβίβασεν Jo.D.*carm.pasch*.3(p.218; M.96.840C); **h.** Christol., ref. Logos acc. Paul. Sam. λόγον...ἐνεργῆ ἐξ οὐ. καὶ σοφίαν ἐν αὐτῷ ὁμολογεῖ ‡Ath.*Apoll*.1.20(M.26.1128B); cf.*ib*.2.3(1136B); ref. Christ's flesh acc. Marcion ἐξ οὐρανοῦ ὀφθεῖσαν καὶ εἰς οὐρανοὺς χωρήσασαν καὶ θεότητα ὅλην οὖσαν *ib*.(1136C); in alleged Apollinarian teaching πῶς ὑμεῖς...λέγετε ἐξ οὐ. τὸ σῶμα; *ib*.1.7(1104B); μάτην...φαντάζονται...ἐξ οὐ. λέγοντες τὸ τοῦ κυρίου σῶμα. καίτοι ὁ Ἀδὰμ ἐξ οὐ. ἐπὶ τὴν γῆν κατενήνοχε, Χριστὸς ἀπὸ γῆς εἰς οὐρανοὺς ἀνενήνοχε *ib*. (1105A); διὰ τί...οὐχὶ ἄνθρωπος...λέγεται ὁ Χριστὸς ὡς καινός τις ἐξ οὐρανῶν ἐπιδημήσας, ἀλλὰ υἱὸς ἀνθρώπου γέγονεν; *ib*.1.8(1105C); οὐχ ...ἕτερός τις ἀναγέγραπται ἄνθρωπος ἐν οὐ. ὑπάρξας παρὰ τὸν ἐκ γῆς Ἀδάμ, ἵνα καὶ ἐξ οὐρανῶν ἔχῃ τὸ σῶμα καὶ υἱὸς ἀνθρώπου ᾖ *ib*.(1108A); εἴπερ ἐξ οὐ. καὶ οὐκ ἐξ αὐτῆς τὸ...σῶμα γεγενῆσθαι...φαμὲν τοῦ Χριστοῦ, πῶς ἂν ἔτι νοοῖτο θεοτόκος; Cyr.*ep*.39(p.18.5; 5².107A); but cf. οὐδὲ ἐξ οὐ. τὴν σάρκα τοῦ κυρίου...λέγομεν, ἀλλ' ἐκ τῆς...παρθένου Apoll.*fid.inc*.3(p.194.19; M.*PL*.8.876C); τὸ δὴ πνεῦμα τουτέστι τὸν νοῦν θεὸν ἔχων ὁ Χριστὸς μετὰ ψυχῆς καὶ σώματος εἰκότως ἄνθρωπος ἐξ οὐ. λέγεται id. *fr*.25(p.210.24)ap.Gr.Nyss.*Apoll*.9(M.45.1140D); orthodox ἀναβαίνων ὡς ἄνθρωπος καὶ ἀναφέρων εἰς τὸν οὐ. ἣν ἐφόρει σάρκα Ath.*Ar*.3.48(M.26.425B); ἡ σὰρξ τοῦ κυρίου...λαμβάνει δόξαν συναναβαίνουσα αὐτῷ εἰς οὐ. id.*inc.et c.Ar*.3(M.26.989B); ἐπουράνιος... ἄνθρωπος ὁ κύριος οὐχὶ ἐξ οὐ. τὴν σάρκα ἐπιδειξάμενος, ἀλλὰ τὴν ἐκ γῆς ἐπουράνιον συστησάμενος ‡Ath.*Apoll*.2.17(1160A); ὅταν...λέγωμεν ἐξ οὐ. ... τὸν...Χριστόν, οὐχ ὡς...ἐξ οὐ. κατενεχθείσης τῆς...αὐτοῦ σαρκὸς τὰ τοιαῦτα φαμέν...ἐπειδὴ...ἐξ οὐ. καταφοιτήσας θεὸς λόγος... κεχρημάτικεν υἱὸς ἀνθρώπου...ὡς εἷς ἤδη νοούμενος μετὰ τῆς ἰδίας σαρκός, ἐξ οὐ. λέγεται κατελθεῖν, ὠνόμασται δὲ καὶ ἄνθρωπος ἐξ οὐ. Cyr.*ep*.39(p.18.15; 5².107B); of Christ's flesh as bread from heaven (eucharistic), Clem.*paed*.1.6(p.118.8; M.8.305B); Gr.Nyss.*v.Mos*.(M. 44.368C); v. ἄρτος, οὐράνιος; **5.** as source of visions and revelations ἤνοιξέ μοι ὁ ἄγγελος τὰς πύλας τοῦ οὐ. *T.Lev*.5.1; ἀνοιγήσονται ἐπ' αὐτῷ οἱ οὐ. ἐκχέαι πνεῦμα πατρὸς ἁγίου *T.Jud*.24.2; προσευχομένου μου ἠνοίγη ὁ οὐ. Herm.*vis*.1.1.4; cf.*Diogn*.7.2; ἐγὼ οὐχ ὑπολαμβάνω τὸν αἰσθητὸν οὐ. ἀνεῷχθαι Or.*Cels*.1.48(p.98.3; M.11. 749A); cf. δυνάμενος ἀπὸ τοῦ οὐ. λαλῆσαι τὸν νόμον, εἶδε ὅτι λυσιτελεῖ ...ἀπὸ τοῦ Σινᾶ λαλῆσαι Ath.*Ar*.2.68(M.26.292B); ὁ...πατὴρ ἀποκαλύπτων ἀπ' οὐ. τὸν ἑαυτοῦ λόγον *ib*.3.59(448B); Dion.Ar.*ep*.8.6 (M.3.1100A); *ib*.(1100D); of gospel, cf.Or.*Jo*.1.11(12; p.16.32; M.14. 44C); τὸ ἐξ οὐρανῶν εὐαγγέλιον διὰ τῆς φωτεινῆς νεφέλης...ἐκήρυξεν Gr.Nyss.*Eun*.4(2 p.56.1; M.45.625D); **6.** as sphere of eternal or divine opp. earthly, future opp. present, life Χριστιανοὶ παροικοῦσιν ἐν φθαρτοῖς, τὴν ἐν οὐρανοῖς ἀφθαρσίαν προσδεχόμενοι *Diogn*.6.8; Meth.*symp*.1.1(p.8.4; M.18.37B); Ath.*v.Anton*.17(M.26.868C); Chrys. *hom.76.3 in Jo*.(8.449E); *ib*.(450B); αὐτὸς [sc. Christ]...ἡμῖν τὸν οὐ. ἐπαγγέλλεται *ib*.77.5(457A); ἐκερδάναμεν οὐ. ζημιωθέντες παράδεισον Procl.CP *hom*.1.1(M.65.833B); [Ps.113:24] νῦν δὲ...καὶ τὴν γῆν ἔδωκεν τοῖς ἀνθρώποις καὶ ὁ οὐ. τοῦ οὐ. τῷ ἀνθρώπῳ *ib*.1.5(837B); ὁ οὐ. μέγας καὶ ἀχειροποίητος...ἔνθα γίνεται ἡ αἰωνία λύτρωσις Cosm.Ind.*top*.7 (M.88.344D); hence sphere of true, opp. typical, worship, Ath.*ep. fest*.45(p.298.28; M.26.1441D); **7.** as abode of angels, Or.*Cels*.4.92 (p.365.10; M.11.1169C); *Apoc.Paul*.10(p.40); τῶν ἐν οὐρανοῖς δυνάμεων ἀγγέλων τε καὶ ἀρχαγγέλων ἀεὶ προσκυνούντων...τὸν κύριον Ath.*Ar*. 1.42(M.26.100B); ‡Ath.*Ar*.4.36(p.86.18; M.26.524C); **8.** ref. eschatological descent of the heavenly to the earthly τότε σχισθήσονται οἱ οὐ. ... καὶ ἀνοιχθήσονται οἱ θησαυροὶ τῶν οὐ. ... καὶ τότε μείνῃ ὁ οὐ. κενὸς *1Apoc.Jo*.17(p.85); **9.** ref. BMV as mediating between heaven and earth τὸν θεὸν τὸν ἐν οὐ. ἐπὶ γῆς κυήσασα...αὕτη οὐ. καὶ γῆς μεσίτης πέφυκεν ‡Epiph.*hom*.5(M.43.492B); cf. ἡ φωτεινὴ νεφέλη... ἀστράπην ἐξ οὐ. ... καταλάμψασα Χριστόν *ib*.; ἡ πύλη τῶν οὐρανῶν *ib*. (492C); ἡ τὴν πεσοῦσαν Εὔαν ἀναστήσασα καὶ τὸν...Ἀδὰμ εἰς οὐρανοὺς ἀποστείλασα *ib*.(501B); διὰ σοῦ...δοξολογία...εἰς οὐρανοὺς ἀναπέμπεται, διὰ σοῦ παρρησίαν ἄνθρωποι ἐν οὐ. πρὸς τὸν ὕψιστον ἔχουσι *ib*.(497A,B); cf. ὑπὲρ ὕψους οὐρανοῦ σε σκήνωμα ὁ δημιουργὸς οὐρανοῦ, θεομήτωρ, εὑρών Jo.Mon.*hymn.Blas*.(M.96.1404D); **10.** some allegorical usages; **a.** various οἱ οὐ. λέγονται πολλαχῶς, καὶ οἱ κατὰ διάστημα καὶ περίοδον καὶ ἡ κατὰ διαθήκην τῶν πρωτοκτίστων ἀγγέλων ἐνέργεια προσεχής... καλοῦνται δὲ οὐρανοὶ κυρίως μὲν ὁ κύριος, ἔπειτα δὲ καὶ οἱ πρωτόκτιστοι, μεθ' οὓς καὶ οἱ ἅγιοι...καὶ προφῆται, εἶτα καὶ οἱ ἀπόστολοι Clem.*ecl*. 51–52(p.151.11,20; M.9.721B); **b.** of Christ ἀλληγορῶν τὸν οὐ. καὶ φάσκων αὐτὸν εἶναι τὸν Χριστόν, γῆν δὲ τὴν ἐκκλησίαν Or.*or*.26.3(p.360. 23; M.11.501A); *ib*.26.4(p.361.20; 501C); **c.** of BMV Μαρία...ἡ παρθένος καὶ οὐ. Procl.CP *or.laud.BMV* 1(p.103.17; M.65.681B); ἐπειδὴ σὺ τυγχάνεις ἥλιος, οὐ. ἀναγκαίως ἡ παρθένος κληθήσεται Hesych.H.*serm*.5 (M.93.1464D); θρόνον χερουβικὸν καὶ οὐ. ἐπίγειον Jo.Thess.*dorm. BMV* 1.14(p.404.17); Χριστὸν...ἀναδείξαντα αὐτὴν ἐνδοξοτέραν τοῦ οὐ., οὐρανὸν τῆς θεότητος αὐτοῦ Mod.*dorm*.2(M.86.3284A); Geo.Pis. *carm.vit*.37; χαῖρε...ὁ λαμπρὸς οὐ., ἡ τὸν ἀχώρητον ἐν οὐρανοῖς ἔχουσα θεόν ‡Epiph.*hom*.5(M.43.489D); *ib*.(492B); *ib*.(497C); Cosm.Mel.*can. dorm*.47(p.181); Jo.Eub.*concept.BMV* 12(M.96.1477B); ὡς ἔμψυχον σὲ οὐ. ὑπεδέξατο οὐράνια, πάναγνε, θεῖα σκηνώματα Jo.D.*can.dorm. BMV* 12(p.229; M.96.1364A); ‡Jo.D.*hom*.6.2(M.96.664B); οὐρανὲ πολύφωτε Jo.Mon.*hymn.Chrys*.(M.96.1381C); **d.** of cave of Christ's nativity οὐ. τὸ σπήλαιον, θρόνον χερουβικὸν τὴν παρθένον Cosm.Mel. *hymn*.1(2.178, p.168; M.98.465A); ὁ ἀστὴρ...ἔστη ἐπάνω...ἐν τῷ σπηλαίῳ ἢ μᾶλλον ἐν τῷ οὐ. ὅπου γὰρ Χριστός, ἐκεῖ ὁ οὐ. τὸ γὰρ σπήλαιον οὐ. ὤφθη ἐπὶ γῆς ‡Epiph.*hom*.5(M.43.501A); **e.** of angels, Clem.*ecl*.51–52(p.151.11,20; M.9.721B) cit. s. 10. a supra; *Lit.Jac*. (p.198.23); and saints, Andr.Cr.*idiomel*.1(p.97; M.97.1433C); **f.** of those who do God's will (ref. Lord's Prayer), Or.*or*.26.6(p.363.3,11; M.11.504C); ἐάν...τὸ θέλημα τοῦ θεοῦ γένηται καὶ ἐπὶ γῆς, ἐσόμεθα πάντες οὐρανός *ib*.(p.363.19; 505A); **g.** of churches as heaven on earth, Didym.*Trin*.2.8(M.39.589C); ‡Bas.*h.myst*.1(p.257); **11.** symbolized by Temple veil, ref. Heb.10:20, Chrys.*nativ*.3(2.359B); **12.** phrases: ὑπὸ τὸν οὐ. *in all the world, everywhere*, in gen., Herm.

*sim.*9.17.4; ref. preaching of gospel, Or.*Cels.*2.13(p.143.7; M.11.824A); Mac.Mgn.*apocr.*2.19(p.34.15); Didym.*Ac.*4:12(M.39.1661D); of catholic Church *τὴν...πᾶσαν τὴν ὑπὸ τὸν οὐ. ἐκκλησίαν* Anon. ap.Eus.*h.e.*5.16.9(M.20.468B); Eus.*h.e.*3.24.2(264B); *ib.*7.29.1(708B); Ath.*ep.Serap.*1.28(M.26.596C); Pall.*v.Chrys.*16(p.99.12; M.47.56); of whole creation *οὐρανὸς καὶ γῆ* Or.*fr.1 in Jo.*(p.484.13); Ath.*gent.*46(M.25.93B); id.*Ar.*1.62(M.26.141B); *εἰς οὐ. ... καὶ γῆν ἡ τῆς κτίσεως διανέμεται φύσις* Procl.CP *hom.*1.1(M.65.833A).

***οὐρανοτίμητος,** *honoured in heaven γένοισθε θεοῦ θυγατέρες, βασιλίδες οὐ.* Thdr.Stud.*epp.*2.123(M.99.1404A).

οὐρανοῦχος, *holding heaven, Orac.Sib.*8.430.

***οὐρανοφανής,** *appearing from heaven*; of Christ's flesh, ‡Ath. *Apoll.*1.12(M.26.1116A); ‡Jo.D.*ep.Thphl.*3(M.95.348C).

οὐρανοφάντωρ, *revealing heaven,* ‡Amph.*v.Bas.*2(168D).

***οὐρανόφθαστος,** *reaching to heaven*; fig., of BMV *οὐ. κλίμαξ* ‡Jo.D.*hom.*5(M.96.649B).

οὐρανοφοίτης, ὁ, *one who enters heaven*; of S. John, Gr.Naz. *carm.*1.1.12.33(M.37.474A); *ib.*1.2.2.652(629A); id.*carm.*2.2(poem.)5.146(1532A); of Elijah, Jo.D.*f.o.*4.24(M.94.1208C).

οὐρανοφόρος, prob. *bearing to heaven,* †Bas.*ep.*42.5(3.129D; M.32.357B).

***οὐρανόφρων,** *heavenly minded,* Ast.Am.*hom.3.2 in Ps.*5(M.40.413C); *Hymn.*(*AS* 1 p.607).

***οὐρανοφυής,** *heaven-born, of heavenly origin, Pers.*(p.23.7).

***οὐρανόχρως,** *sky-blue, sky-coloured,* Agath.*v.Gr.Ill.*121(p.62).

οὐρανόω, *make heavenly,* Const.Diac.*laud.*39(M.88.524B); ‡Sophr. H.*triod.*(M.87.3840A).

οὐρίαχος, ὁ, *support* or *shaft* bearing a light, Paul.Sil.*Soph.*825 (M.86.2150B).

οὐροδόχη, ἡ, *chamber-pot,* Clem.*paed.*2.3(p.180.28; M.8.437C).

οὖρος, ὁ, (Lat. *urus*) *wild ox,* ‡Epiph.*phys.*3(M.43.520C).

οὐσία, ἡ, I. in gen.; etym. *ἰσία λέγεται κατ' ἐτυμολογίαν, τροπῇ τοῦ ι εἰς ο, καὶ πλεονασμῷ τοῦ υ στοιχείου, οὐ. διερμηνεύεται, ὡς οὐσά τις συστατικὴ ὕπαρξις, τῶν ἐκ πλειόνων ἐπὶ μίαν μονάδα ἐχόντων τὸ ἄθροισμα* ‡Ath.*annunt.*3(M.28.921A).

A. *being*; **1.** *reality*; **a.** def. *οὐ. ἐστὶν τὸ δι' ὅλου ὑφεστός* Clem.*fr.*37(p.219.17; M.9.752A); *ἡ...κυρίως οὐ. τοῖς μὲν προηγουμένην τὴν τῶν ἀσωμάτων ὑπόστασιν εἶναι φάσκουσι νενόμισται κατὰ τὰ ἀσώματα, τὸ εἶναι βεβαίως ἔχοντα...τοῖς δὲ ἐπακολουθητικὴν αὐτὴν εἶναι νομίζουσι προηγουμένην δὲ τῶν σωμάτων ὅροι αὐτῆς οὗτοί εἰσιν· οὐ. ἐστὶν ἡ πρώτη τῶν ὄντων ὕλη...ἢ...ἢ...ἢ τὸ ὑπομένον πᾶσαν ἀλλοίωσιν καὶ μεταβολήν. κατὰ τούτους δὲ ἡ οὐ. ἐστὶν ἄποιός τε καὶ ἀσχημάτιστος* Or.*or.*27(pp.367.13,368.2,8; M.11.512Af.); *ἡ...ὑπόστασις οὐ. ἐστί, καὶ οὐδὲν ἄλλο σημαινόμενον ἔχει ἢ αὐτὸ τὸ ὂν...ἡ γὰρ ὑπόστασις καὶ ἡ οὐ. ὕπαρξίς ἐστιν* Ath.*ep.Afr.*4(M.26.1036B); *κατὰ... τὴν θύραθεν σοφίαν...ἡ...οὐ. τὸ ὂν σημαίνει* Thdt.*eran.*1(4.7); *εἰ...οὐ. ἁπλῶς ὁριζόμενοι, εἴποιμεν τήν τινος ὕπαρξιν δηλοῦν...ὑπάρχειν... φαμὲν οὐ. καὶ θεόν...καὶ ζῷον καὶ φυτόν, καὶ κοινὸς ἐπὶ πάντων ὁ τῆς οὐ. ἀποδίδοται λόγος, τὸ ὑπάρχειν τούτων δηλῶν οὐ τὸ τί αὐτῶν ἢ τὸ πῶς* Leont.B.*arg.Sev.*(M.86.1921C); **b.** opp. *γένεσις* and *τὸ μὴ εἶναι*: *εἰς οὐ. ἤγαγε αὐτά* Clem.*exc.Thdot.*45(p.121.9; M.9.680C); Or. *fr.1 in Jo.*(p.485.3); *τῶν πάντων ἀθέων καὶ τὴν οὐ. τοῦ θεοῦ ἀρνουμένων* id. *or.*5(p.308.14; M.11.429A); *οἴεσθαι ὅτι ἡ τῆς ἀληθείας οὐ. πρὸ τῶν χρόνων τῆς τοῦ Χριστοῦ ἐπιφανείας οὐκ ἦν* id.*Cels.*8.12(p.229.30; M.11.1533B); *μόνος ὢν...αἴτιος τοῦ εἶναι κατέστη τῷ θέλειν καὶ τῷ δύνασθαι, καὶ τὴν οὐ. τοῖς πᾶσι καὶ τὰς δυνάμεις καὶ τὰ εἴδη...ἀνεπιφθόνως ἐξ αὐτοῦ κεχαρισμένος* Eus.*d.e.*4.1(p.151.27; M.22.253A); *κατ' αὐτοὺς ἡ κακία ὑπόστασιν ἔχει καθ' ἑαυτὴν καὶ οὐ.* Ath.*gent.*6(M.25.13A); *εἰ πᾶν τὸ γεγονὸς ὑφ' ἑτέρου γέγονεν, ἡ δὲ ἀγέννητος ὑπόστασις οὔτε ὑφ' ἑαυτῆς οὔτε ὑφ' ἑτέρας γέγονεν, ἀνάγκη οὐ. δηλοῦν τὸ ἀγέννητον* Aët. *synt.*28(p.358.2; M.42.541C); *ὁ...λέγων πᾶσαν οὐ. εἶναι ἀγέννητον...οὐκ ἔστι Χριστιανός* ‡Ath.*dial.Trin.*2.23(M.28.1192D); *οἱ μὲν πάντῃ τὸ θεῖον ἀρνησάμενοι...ὑπόκενον δὲ εἶναι τοὔνομα, καὶ κατὰ μηδεμίας οὐ. ὑποκείμενον τεταγμένον* Thdt.*Ps.*13:1(1.681); *τῆς οὐ. τὴν ὕπαρξίν τε καὶ φύσιν παραστῆσαι καθώς ἐστι, μεῖζόν ἐστιν ἢ καθ' ἡμᾶς, μᾶλλον δὲ καὶ τὴν τῶν πολλῶν ὑπερβαίνει κατάληψιν* Pamph.H.*panopl.*2.1 (p.601); **2.** *ultimate reality* in rel. to God *φησὶ...Πλάτων...τι ὂν... ἐπέκεινα πάσης οὐ., οὔτε ῥητὸν οὔτε ἀγορευτόν* Just.*dial.*4.1(M.6.484A); *τί θεός; θεός ἐστι...πνεῦμα. πνεῦμα δέ ἐστι κυρίως οὐ.* Clem. *fr.*39(p.220.7; M.9.769B); *οὐ. καὶ γένεσις νοητόν, ὁρατόν· μετὰ οὐσίας μὲν ἀλήθεια, μετὰ δὲ γενέσεως πλάνη...ὅπερ ἐν τοῖς ὁρατοῖς ἥλιος... ὀφθαλμῷ...τοῦ ὁρᾶν αἴτιος...τοῦτο ἐν τοῖς νοητοῖς ἐκεῖνος, ὅσπερ οὔτε νοῦς οὔτε νόησις...ἀλλὰ νῷ...τοῦ νοεῖν αἴτιος...καὶ νοητοῖς ἅπασι καὶ αὐτῇ ἀληθείᾳ καὶ αὐτῇ οὐ. τοῦ εἶναι, πάντων ἐπέκεινα ὤν, ἀρρήτῳ τινὶ δυνάμει νοητός* Cels.ap.Or.*Cels.*7.45(pp.196.20,197.2; M.11.1485Cf.); *νοῦν...ἢ ἐπέκεινα νοῦ καὶ οὐ. λέγοντες εἶναι...τὸν...θεόν* Or.*ib.*7.38 (p.188.11; 1473B); *ἀλλ' οὐδ' οὐ. μετέχει ὁ θεός· μετέχεται γὰρ μᾶλλον ἢ μετέχει...ὁ περὶ τῆς οὐ. λόγος...δυσθεώρητος...ἐὰν ἡ κυρίως οὐ. ἡ ἑστῶσα καὶ ἀσώματος ᾖ· ἵν' εὑρεθῇ, πότερον ἐπέκεινα οὐ. ἐστὶ πρεσβείᾳ καὶ δυνάμει* [Plato *Rep.*509B]*...ὁ θεὸς μεταδιδοὺς οὐσίας...κατὰ τὸν ἑαυτοῦ λόγον καὶ αὐτῷ λόγῳ, ἢ καὶ αὐτός ἐστιν οὐ. ... ζητητέον δὲ καί, εἰ οὐσίαν μὲν οὐσιῶν λεκτέον...τὸν μονογενῆ...ἐπέκεινα δὲ πάντων τούτων τὸν πατέρα* Cels.*ib.*6.64(p.134.24ff.; 1396Bf.); *πρότερον* [sc. *νοεῖ τις ἢ θεωρεῖ*] *τὴν ἀλήθειαν, ἵν' οὕτως ἔλθῃ ἐπὶ τὸ ἐνιδεῖν τῇ οὐ. ἢ τῇ ὑπερέκεινα τῆς οὐ. δυνάμει καὶ φύσει τοῦ θεοῦ* Or.*Jo.*19.6(p.305.16; M.14.536C); *ὁ ὑπὲρ τὴν οὐ. θεὸς ὢν ἀεί* Const.*or.s.c.*3(p.156.9; M.20.1237C); *οὐ...τὸ μὴ γενέσθαι τὸν θεὸν τῶν οὐ. αἴτιον· ἀλλ' ἡ οὐ. τῶν οὐ. αἰτία* ‡Ath.*dial.Trin.*2.23(M.28.1193B); *θεὸν μὲν τὴν ἀΐδιον γνωρίζοντες οὐ. καὶ πάντων αἰτίαν* Thdr.Mops.*Zach.*1:7ff.(M.66.504A); *τί ἐστι θεός; οὐ. ἀναίτιος* Anast.Ant.*fid.*(M.89.1400A); *πῶς ποτὲ μὲν οὐ. τὸ θεῖον καλεῖ, ποτὲ δὲ ὑπερούσιον, ὥσπερ νοῦν ἀνόητον, καὶ ὄνομα τὸ ὑπὲρ πᾶν ὄνομα, οὕτω καὶ οὐ. ὑπερούσιον* Max.*schol.d.n.*1.2 (M.4.192A); *οὐ. τοίνυν ἐστὶ θεός, καὶ πᾶν κτίσμα, εἰ καὶ ὁ θεὸς οὐ. ἐστὶν ὑπερούσιος* Jo.D.*dialect.*4(M.94.537B); *ὁ θεὸς πάντων ἐστὶν...ἀρχὴ· τῶν ὄντων οὐ.* id.*f.o.*1.12(M.94.844C); *ὡς αἴτιος πάντων τῶν ὄντων καὶ πάσης οὐ., καὶ 'ὢν' λέγεται, καὶ οὐ. ib.*(848A); **3.** *existent object, reality, thing* opp. name or idea or other representation *ἡ...τῆς ἀληθείας πρωτότυπος οὐ. ἐν τῷ Ἰησοῦ μόνῳ λέγοντι* [Jo.14:6] Or. *comm.in Eph.*4:20(p.418); *τίς ἡ αὐτὴ οὐ. ἐν Ἡλίᾳ καὶ Ἰωάννῃ* [i.e. *πνεῦμα καὶ δύναμις*] id.*comm.in Mt.*13.2(p.178.4; M.13.1092C); *γέγραφεν* [sc. Eus.] *δ' αὐταῖς λέξεσιν οὕτως· οὐ δήπου δὲ ἡ εἰκὼν καὶ τὸ οὗ ἐστιν ἡ εἰκὼν ἓν καὶ ταὐτὸν ἐπινοεῖται, ἀλλὰ δύο μὲν οὐ. καὶ δύο πράγματα καὶ δύο δυνάμεις* Marcell. *fr.*72 ap.Eus.*Marcell.*1.4(p.26.20; M.24.765C); *οὓς ἐχρῆν...παρηλλαγμένων τῶν ὀνομάτων, παρηλλαγμένας ὁμολογεῖν καὶ τὰς οὐ.* Eun.*apol.*18(M.30.853B); Gr.Nyss. *Eun.*4(2 p.82.6; M.45.656D); *ἐπὶ Χριστοῦ τῆς ὄντως οὐ. τῶν ἀγαθῶν καὶ πηγῆς* Max.*opusc.*(M.91.33A); opp. *σχῆμα*: *οὐ γὰρ ἡ ὑπόστασις οὐδὲ ἡ οὐ. τῆς κτίσεως ἐξαφανίζεται...ἀλλὰ τὸ σχῆμα παράγει τοῦ κόσμου τούτου* Iren.*haer.*5.36.1(M.7.1221B); Mac.Mgn.*apocr.*4.30 (p.222.13); **4.** *κατ' οὐσίαν* and *οὐσίᾳ, in reality, in actuality, truly* *οὐσίᾳ* opp. *ὀνόματι,* Hipp.*haer.*10.27(p.283.16ff.; M.16.3442Af.); *κατ' οὐ. ὑφεστηκέναι* Or.*Cels.*1.23(p.73.15f.; M.11.700Bf.); Gr.Nyss.*Eun.*7 (2 p.171.25; M.45.761D); *ὁ δὲ θεὸς μόνος κατ' οὐ. ἐστὶ θεός* Evagr. Pont.*ep.*3(M.32.249C); cf. *συντίκτεται μετ' ἐμοῦ οὐκ ἐν ὑποστάσεως οὐ. γενόμενος, ἀλλ' ἐν θελήματος ἑνούμενος χάριτι* Mac.Mgn.*apocr.*2.8(p.11.3).

B. *substance*; **1.** *essence*; **a.** def. *φύσις λέγεται παρὰ τὸ πεφυκέναι, πρώτη οὐ. ἐστὶ πᾶν τὸ καθ' ἑαυτὸ ὑφεστός, οἷον λίθος· δευτέρα δὲ οὐ. αὐξητική...τρίτη δὲ οὐ. ἔμψυχος αἰσθητική...τετάρτη δὲ οὐ.· ἔμψυχος αἰσθητικὴ λογική* Clem.*fr.*38(p.219.26ff.; M.9.769C); †Gr.Thaum. *anim.*(M.10.1140D) cit. s. *παραμερός*; *οὐ. ... ἐστὶ...πᾶν τὸ κατ' ἰδίαν ὕπαρξιν ὑφεστώς, καὶ μὴ ἐν ἄλλῳ τὸ εἶναι ἔχον· τοῦτο δὲ εἴρηται πρὸς ἀντιδιαστολὴν πάντων τῶν συμβεβηκότων...καὶ τῶν...ποιοτήτων* Pamph.H.*panopl.*2.2(p.601); *οὐ. ἐστὶ πρώτως τε καὶ κυρίως πᾶν, ὅτι αὐθυπόστατον ὑπάρχει, τουτέστιν ὃ καθ' ἑαυτό ἐστι καὶ οὐ δι' ἄλλο οὐδὲ ἐν ἑτέρῳ ἔχει τὸ εἶναι* Thdr.Raith.*praep.*(p.201.13); *οὐ. ἐστί, κατὰ μὲν φιλοσόφους, αὐθυπόστατον πρᾶγμα μὴ δεόμενον ἑτέρου πρὸς σύστασιν· κατὰ δὲ τοὺς πατέρας, ἡ κατὰ πολλῶν καὶ διαφερόντων ταῖς ὑποστάσεσιν ὀντότης φυσική* Max.*opusc.*(M.91.276A); *οὐ. ἐστὶ πρᾶγμα αὐθύπαρκτον, καὶ μὴ δεόμενον ἑτέρου πρὸς ὕπαρξιν* Jo.D.*dialect.*4(M.94.537B); Thdr.Abuc.*opusc.*2(M.97.1472f.); **b.** opp. *ποιότης* and *συμβεβηκός*: *Ἀριστοτέλης...τὰ μὲν στοιχεῖα τῶν πάντων ὑποθέμενος οὐσίαν καὶ συμβεβηκός· τὴν μὲν οὐ. μίαν τὴν πᾶσιν ὑποκειμένην* Hipp.*haer.*1.20(p.24.3; M.16.3045D); *οὐ...ποιότητος ἁπλῶς ἀλλ' οὐσίας μεταβολὴ τὸ ἐξ ὕδατος οἶνον γενέσθαι* Or.*fr.30 in Jo.* (p.506.14); Ath.*syn.*53(p.276.25ff.; M.26.788Bf.) cit. s. *ποιότης*; *ἐν τῇ οὐ. τὸ συμβεβηκός* id.*decr.*22(p.18.21; M.25.453C); *ὄχημα γὰρ ὥσπερ ἐστὶν ὑποβεβλημένον τοῖς συμβεβηκόσιν ἡ οὐ.* Alex.Lyc.*Man.*8(p.13.20; M.18.424A); *εἰ...σκιὰ τὸ σκότος ἐστί, καὶ οὐκ οὐ., ἀλλὰ πρᾶγμά ἐστι συμβεβηκός* Thdt.*Dan.*3:59ff.(2.1124); *ἡ μὲν γὰρ ὑπόστασις τὸν τινὰ δηλοῖ, τὸ δὲ ἐνυπόστατον τὴν οὐ. ... τὸ μὴ εἶναι αὐτὸ συμβεβηκὸς δηλοῖ ὃ ἐν ἑτέρῳ ἔχει τὸ εἶναι...τοιαῦται δὲ πᾶσαι αἱ ποιότητες...ὧν οὐδετέρα ἐστὶν οὐ., τουτέστι πρᾶγμα ὑφεστός, ἀλλ' ὃ ἀεὶ περὶ τὴν οὐ. θεωρεῖται* Leont.B.*Nest.et Eut.*1(M.86.1277D); **c.** dist. from *ἐνέργεια* (v.s.v.), *πρᾶξις,* and *ἕξις*: *κατ' ἀλλήλους...τὰς οὐ. καὶ τὰς πράξεις εἶναι χρή, ἵνα καὶ ἐκ τῆς ἐνεργείας ὁ πράξας μαρτυρηθῇ, καὶ ἐκ τῆς οὐ. πρᾶξις γνωσθῆναι δυνηθῇ* Ath.*gent.*16(M.25.33C); *περὶ τῆς σοφίας, ἥτις ἐστὶν ἕξις, καὶ οὐκ οὐ.* Thdt.*Cant.*2:6(2.57); **d.** in gen. contexts *νοῦς καὶ λόγος δέδοται τοῖς ἀνθρώποις πρὸς διάκρισιν νοητῶν, οὐκ οὐσιῶν μόνων ἀλλὰ καὶ τῆς τοῦ δόντος ἀγαθότητος* Athenag.*res.*15 (p.66.21; M.6.1004D); *οὐσίαν ἑκάστῳ δεῖ πάντως τῶν ὄντων ὑπάρχειν* Clem.*str.*8.6(p.92.5; M.9.585A); *ἐπιούσιος...ἄρτος ὁ τῇ φύσει τῇ* λογικῇ καταλληλότατος καὶ τῇ οὐ. αὐτῇ συγγενής...τῆς ἰδίας ἀθανασίας ...μεταδιδούς Or.*or.*27(p.369.19; M.11.513A); τῆς...γραφῆς διαφόρως τὴν τοῦ ἀγαθοῦ οὐ. διδασκούσης Eus.*p.e.*11.21(524A; M.21.901D); οὗτοι [sc. everyday meanings of the word λόγος]...πάντες τῶν πρός τι ὄντες ἐν ἑτέρᾳ προϋποκειμένῃ νοοῦνται οὐ. id.*e.th.*2.14(p.114.23; M. 24.928B); ὁ υἱός...ὡς ἀγαθὸς γραφεὺς τὰς ἀρχετύπους ἰδέας ἐκ τῶν πατρικῶν λογισμῶν ἀπολαμβάνων ἐπὶ τὰς τῶν ἔργων μετέφερεν οὐ. *ib.*3.3(p.155.14; 997D); τίς δὲ ἰδὼν καὶ τὴν ὑδάτων ἀλλασσομένην οὐ., καὶ εἰς οἶνον μεταβαλοῦσαν, οὐκ ἐννοεῖ τὸν τοῦτο ποιήσαντα κύριον εἶναι καὶ κτιστὴν τῆς τῶν ὅλων ὑδάτων οὐ.; Ath.*inc.*18.6(M.25. 128D); ὥσπερ ἡμεῖς τὸ πνεῦμα λαμβάνοντες οὐκ ἀπόλλυμεν τὴν ἰδίαν ἑαυτῶν οὐ. id.*decr.*14(p.12.28; M.25.'448'(440)D); ἴδιόν ἐστι τῆς τοῦ πυρὸς οὐ. ἡ ἐπὶ τὸ ἄνω φορά Gr.Nyss.*or.catech.*24(p.92.2; M.45.64C); ἤρκεσεν αὐτῷ [sc. τῷ θεῷ] πρὸς ὑπόστασιν τῆς τῶν γεγονότων οὐ. ἡ βούλησις id.*Eun.*4(2 p.58.2; M.45.628D); Mac.Mgn.*apocr.*4.30(p.222. 13); ἐπιστήμης μέν ἐστι τὸ ἐφάπτεσθαι οὐσίας τε καὶ ἀληθείας γνώσεως, αἰσθήσεως δὲ οὐκ ἔστι ‡Just.*qu.Gr.*2(M.6.1469B); διαιρεῖται...ἡ οὐ. ... εἰς σῶμα καὶ ἀσώματον *ib.*; Chrys.*hom.41.2 in 1Cor.*(10.388C); ἐκ... τῆς μιᾶς τῶν ὑδάτων οὐ. γίνεται μὲν χρύσταλλος...χιὼν...καὶ κόνις ὑγρά Thdt.*Ps.*147:6f.(1.1574); ὁ...αἰὼν οὐκ οὐ. τίς ἐστιν, ἀλλ' ἀνυπόστατον χρῆμα id.*Heb.*1:1f.(3.546); ἡ...γυνὴ οὐ ποίημα τοῦ ἀνδρός, ἀλλ' ἐκ τῆς οὐ. τοῦ ἀνδρός id.*1Cor.*11:3(3.233); Cosm.Ind.*top.*5(M.88.309D) cit. s. ἐκπορευτικῶς; **e.** of the rational and incorporeal creation τοῖς ἀναιροῦσι νοητὰς οὐ. Στοϊκοῖς Or.*Cels.*7.37(p.187.23; M.11.1472D); τὸν υἱόν...πάσης νοερᾶς καὶ λογικῆς οὐ. φωτιστικόν Eus.*e.th.*1.8(p.66. 34; M.24.837D); †Ath.*exp.fid.*3(M.25.204C); αἱ λογικαὶ πᾶσαι οὐ. Leont.B.*Nest.et Eut.*1(M.86.1284A); of demons, Athenag.*leg.*23.2(M. 6.941B); of angels, Eus.*d.e.*4.5(p.157.24; M.22.261D); περὶ τοῦ...θεοῦ, περί τε τοῦ δευτέρου αἰτίου [i.e. Son] τῶν τε μετ' αὐτὸν λογικῶν καὶ νοερῶν οὐ. *ib.*5 proem.(p.206.11; 341C); Chrys.*Stag.*1.2(1.157E); Dion.Ar.*c.h.*5(M.3.196B); *ib.*4.4(181C); ἄγγελός ἐστι οὐ. νοερά Jo.D. *f.o.*2.3(M.94.865B); **f.** ref. problem of evil τὰ κακὰ πότερον οὐσίαι σοι δοκοῦσιν εἶναι ἢ ποιότητες οὐσιῶν Meth.*arbitr.*8.1(p.164.16; M.18. 256B); τὸ κακὸν οὐ παρὰ θεοῦ...οὔτε ἐξ ἀρχῆς γέγονεν, οὔτε οὐ. τίς ἐστιν αὐτοῦ Ath.*gent.*7(M.25.16A); μὴ οὐ. εἶναί τινα τοῦ κακοῦ ἢ ἄναρχον, ἢ παρ' ἑαυτῆς ὑποστᾶσαν...ἀλλ' ἡμέτερον ἔργον εἶναι τοῦτο καὶ τοῦ πονηροῦ Gr.Naz.*or.*40.45(M.36.424A); cf. τὸ ἁμαρτάνειν ⟨ἐν⟩ ἐνεργείᾳ κεῖται, οὐκ οὐσίᾳ Clem.*str.*4.13(p.289.21; M.8.1300D); ἡ... ἁμαρτία...δύναμίς τις οὖσα λογικὴ τοῦ σατανᾶ καὶ οὐ., ἐνέσπειρε τὰ κακὰ πάντα Mac.Aeg.*hom.*15.49(M.34.609B); τὸν θάνατον οὐκ οὐ. ὄντα τινὰ ἀλλὰ πρᾶγμα συμβαῖνον ὡς ἐνυπόστατον εἰσάγει Thdt.*Is.* 14:9(p.71.3; 2.267); **g.** of man's soul τὴν...τοῦ σώματος φύσιν καὶ τὴν τῆς ψυχῆς οὐ. Clem.*str.*4.3(p.253.8; M.8.1224B); Or.*Cels.*4.17(p.286. 22; M.11.1049A); οὐσίας λογικῆς ψυχῆς ὡς ἐχούσης τι συγγενὲς θεῷ id. *mart.*47(p.42.20; M.11.629A); αὐταὶ φύσει αἱ ψυχαί, παντὸς ἀπογυμνωθεῖσαι περιβλήματος, τοιαῦται κατὰ τὴν οὐ. ὑπάρχουσιν Meth. *res.*3.18(p.416.2; M.18.328A); ἐν ψυχῇ μὲν ὁρίζεται τὸν ἀληθῆ ἄνθρωπον, νοερᾶς οὐ. καὶ ἀσωμάτου καὶ λογικῆς μέτοχον, ὡς ἂν κατ' εἰκόνα θεοῦ δεδημιουργημένον Eus.*p.e.*7.10(316A; M.21.533D); id.*d.e.*1.7(p.38. 31; M.22.76A); ὁποῖον...αὐτῆς τὸ εἶδος, τί τὸ σχῆμα, τίς ἡ μορφή, τίς ἡ οὐ. id.*e.th.*1.12(p.71.22; M.24.848B); Ath.*fr.*(*AP* p.7.28); ψυχή ἐστιν οὐ. γεννητή, οὐ. ζῶσα νοερά Gr.Nyss.*anim.et res.*(M.46.29B); id. *or.catech.*6(p.30.10; M.45.25D); ἄρτος...ἡμῶν τῆς ψυχῆς ὁ...λόγος· ὥσπερ...ὁ ἄποιος ἄρτος τὸ σῶμα τρέφει, οὕτως ὁ ἐξ οὐρανοῦ λόγος τὴν οὐ. τῆς ψυχῆς Thdt.*Ps.*101:6(1.1317); cf.Jo.D.*f.o.*4.13(M.94.1152Af.); Cosm.Ind.*top.*3(M.88.149C); and body παρακαλοῦμέν σε ἁρμόδιον τοῦτον [sc. eucharist] γενέσθαι καὶ εὐφραντικὸν τῇ ἡμετέρᾳ οὐ. τοῦ σώματος Ath.*virg.*13(p.47.9 not.); τὴν νοερὰν οὐ. τῇ αἰσθητῇ συγκατέμιξεν Gr.Nyss.*or.catech.*16(p.72.1; M.45.52C); δείκνυσι καὶ ψυχῆς καὶ σωμάτων αὐτὸν ὄντα δημιουργόν. ἑκατέρας...οὐ. τὴν παράλυσιν ἰᾶται Chrys.*hom.29.3 in Mt.*(7.345B); **2.** *secondary substance, substance* as common to members of a kind; **a.** def. and descriptions οὐ. δὲ καὶ ὑπόστασις ταύτην ἔχει τὴν διαφορὰν ἣν ἔχει τὸ κοινὸν πρὸς τὸ καθ' ἕκαστον Bas.*ep.*236.6(3.363E; M.32.884A); οὐ. ... ἐστιν ἤτοι φύσις, παρ' αὐτοῖς [sc. τοῖς πατράσιν], ὅπερ οἱ φιλόσοφοι λέγουσιν εἶδος...τὸ κατὰ πολλῶν καὶ διαφερόντων τῷ ἀριθμῷ λεγόμενον †Leont.B.*sect.*1.1(M.86. 1193A); Pamph.H.*panopl.*2.3(pp.602–3); οὐ. ἐστὶν ἡ κατὰ πολλῶν καὶ διαφερόντων τῷ ἀριθμῷ ἐν τῷ τί ἐστι κατηγορουμένη. ἢ οὕτως· οὐ. ἐστὶν ἡ καθ' ὑποκειμένων τῶν ὑποστάσεων λεγομένη καὶ ἐν πάσαις αὐταῖς ἐπίσης...θεωρουμένη Thdr.Raith.*praep.*(p.209.19ff.); ὃ κοινῶς καὶ ἐν πολλοῖς θεωρεῖται, οὐ τινὶ μὲν πλέον, τινὶ δὲ ἔλαττον, ὑπάρχον, οὐ. ὀνομάζεται Eulog.*fr.dogm.*(M.86.2953D); οὐ. μὲν αὐτὸ τὸ εἶδος καὶ τὴν φύσιν, ὅπερ ἐστὶ καθ' ἑαυτήν, δηλοῖ, ὑπόστασις δέ, τόν τινα τῆς οὐ. ἐμφαίνει Max.*opusc.*(M.91.260Df.); ἡ μὲν οὐ., τὸ κοινὸν καὶ περιεκτικὸν εἶδος τῶν ὁμοειδῶν ὑποστάσεων σημαίνει Jo.D.*f.o.*3.4(M.94.997A); **b.** opp. ὑπόστασις, v.s.v.; // φύσις, v.s.v.; // μορφή (ref. Phil.2:6) ἐγὼ γὰρ καὶ τὸ ἐν μορφῇ θεοῦ ὑπάρχειν ἴσον δύνασθαι τῷ ἐν οὐ. θεοῦ ὑπάρχειν φημί Bas.*Eun.*1.18(1.230A; M.29.552C); ἡ δὲ μορφὴ τοῦ θεοῦ ταὐτὸν τῇ οὐ. πάντως ἐστίν. ὡς γὰρ ἐν τῇ μορφῇ τοῦ δούλου γενόμενος τῇ οὐ. τοῦ δούλου ἐνεμορφώθη, οὐ ψιλὴν ἀναλαβὼν ἐφ' ἑαυτοῦ τὴν μορφὴν οὐδὲ τῆς οὐ. διεζυγμένην, ἀλλ' ἡ οὐ. τῇ μορφῇ συσσημαίνεται Gr. Nyss.*Eun.*4(2 p.94.16ff.; M.45.672A); Thdt.*Phil.*2:11(3.456); **c.** in gen. τὰ προηγούμενα τῶν...εἰδῶν...τὴν οὐ. καὶ φύσιν διασημαίνει τοῦ πράγματος Clem.*str.*8.6(p.93.9; M.9.585D); οὐσίας ζῴων καὶ φυτῶν Or. *Cels.*5.38(p.42.28; M.11.1241A); πᾶς...ὁρισμὸς οὐσίας πρὸς τὸ ἴδιον τοῦ ὑποκειμένου βλέπει Gr.Nyss.*anim.et res.*(M.46.53A); οὐκ ἦν δὲ ἑτεροούσιος ἀναγκαίως ὁ Σὴθ τῷ Ἀδάμ. καὶ ὅμως εἰκόνα τὴν εἰδέαν καὶ ὁμοίωσιν τῆς οὐ. ἐκάλεσεν Didym.*Trin.*1.16(M.39.337A); [ref. Mc.5:2, Mt.8:28] ὁ μέν...τὴν οὐ. ἐμήνυσεν, ὡς ἀνθρωπεία φύσις ἦν ἡ τυραννουμένη· ὁ δὲ τὴν ὑπόστασιν, ὡς οὐχ εἷς, ἀλλὰ δύο τὸν ἀριθμὸν ἐτύγχανον Mac.Mgn.*apocr.*3.11(p.76.21f.); πᾶν γένος ζῴων φυλάττει τὸν τῆς οἰκείας οὐ. νόμον Euther.*confut.*8(M.28.1361B); τὸ Χριστὸς ὄνομα οὔτε ὅρου δύναμιν ἔχει οὔτε μὴν τήν τινος οὐ., ὅ τί ποτέ ἐστι, σημαίνει, καθάπερ ἀμέλει καὶ τὸ ἄνθρωπος ἢ ἵππος ἢ βοῦς Cyr.*schol.inc.*1(p.219. 9; 5[1].779A); Leont.B.*Nest.et Eut.*1(M.86.1280B) cit. s. οὐσιωδῶς; ψυχὴ ...πρὸς ψυχὴν τῷ ταὐτῷ τῆς οὐ. ἡνωμένη, τῷ διαφόρῳ τῆς ὑποστάσεως διακέκριται *ib.*(1288D); τὰ τὴν φύσιν χαρακτηρίζοντα συστατικὰ τῆς οὐ. εἰσί, τὰ δὲ τὴν ὑπόστασιν οἷον συμβεβηκότων λόγον ἐπέχει...ὥσπερ ἐπὶ ἀνθρώπου...τὴν μὲν οὐ. αὐτοῦ χαρακτηρίζει τὸ ζῷον, τὸ λογικόν, τὸ θνητόν...τὴν δὲ ὑπόστασιν σχῆμα, χρῶμα, μέγεθος...οἱ γονεῖς ἢ ἀνατροφὴ ἢ ἀγωγή id.*arg.Sev.*(M.86.1945B); ἀνυπόστατος...φύσις, τουτέστιν οὐ., οὐκ ἂν εἴη ποτέ Leont.B.*Nest.et Eut.*1(M.86.1280A); cf. πολλῷ γὰρ μᾶλλον οὐκ ἔστιν ὑπόστασις ἀνούσιος ἤπερ οὐ. ἀνυπόστατος Leont.H.*monoph.*51(M.86.1797C); οὐδέ...ἐστι τὸ παράπαν γεννητὸν κυρίως ἁπλοῦν, ὅτι μὴ τόδε μόνον ἐστὶν ἢ τόδε, ἀλλ' ὡς ἐν ὑποκειμένῳ τῇ οὐ. ἔχει τὴν συστατικήν τε καὶ ἀφοριστικὴν διαφορὰν συνεπιθεωρουμένην Max.*ambig.*(M.91.1400C); **3.** of actual individual substances, *subsistence*, esp. of persons, *being*, addressed to a soul ὦ φύσις μὴ καταβαλλομένη πρὸς τὸ κρεῖττον...ὦ οὐ. φθορᾶς σκότους πλήρης *A.Jo.* 84(p.192.18); ὡς ἐν ἰδιαζούσῃ τινὶ οὐ. συμβεβηκέναι τινὰ χάριν καὶ ἕξιν ἀρετῆς Ath.*Ar.*1.36(M.26.88A); εἰ δὲ φαίη τις ὅτι Πέτρον καὶ Παῦλον καὶ Βαρνάβαν φαμὲν τρεῖς οὐ., μερικὰς δηλονότι, τουτέστιν ἰδικάς...ὅτι μερικὴν οὐ., τουτέστιν ἰδικὴν λέγοντες, οὐδὲν ἕτερον σημᾶναι βουλόμεθα, ἢ ἄτομον ὅπερ ἐστὶ πρόσωπον Gr.Nyss.*comm.not.*(M.45.177C); ὑπόστασις δὲ καὶ πρόσωπόν ἐστιν οὐσία ἡ τίς, μερική, ἄτομος, ἡ μήτε καθ' ὑποκειμένου τινὸς λεγομένη μήτε ἐν ὑποκειμένῳ τινὶ οὖσα...σημειωτέον δὲ ὅτι οὐκ ἀντιστρέφει ὁ λόγος. οὐ γὰρ ἐπειδὴ ἡ ὑπόστασις οὐσία ἐστίν, ἤδη καὶ ἡ οὐ. ὑπόστασις Thdr.Raith.*praep.*(p.212.15ff.); this usage not approved for formal statements οὐκοῦν οὐκ ἔστι κυρίως εἰπεῖν ὅτι Ἀδὰμ οὐσίαν παρ' αὐτὸν ἄλλην ἐγέννησεν, ἀλλὰ μᾶλλον ὅτι ἐξ ἑαυτοῦ ἐγέννησεν ἄλλον ἑαυτόν Gr.Nyss.*Eun.*3(2 p.27.14; M.45.592D); Στοϊκοὶ...μερίζουσι...τὴν μίαν θεότητα εἰς πολλὰς μερικὰς οὐ., εἰς ἥλιον κτλ. Epiph.*haer.*5.1(p.183.15; M.41.201A); τοῦτο εἶναι ὑπόστασιν ἐλέγετε μόνον, τὴν ἰδικὴν οὐ. Leont.H.*Nest.*7.2(M.86.1760A); ἡ ὑπόστασις τὴν τινὰ οὐ. δηλοῖ μετὰ τῶν προσόντων αὐτῇ ἰδιωμάτων Pamph.H.*panopl.*1.2(p.598).

C. *material*; **1.** substance from which a thing is made or in which it exists, *stuff*, *matter*; **a.** incorporeal or supra-sensible εἶναι μὲν πνευματικὴν οὐ. ... τυγχάνουσαν, ἄμορφον δὲ καὶ ἀνείδεον Iren. *haer.*1.2.4(M.7.461A); *ib.*1.5.1(492A); προβάλλει...τοὺς...ἀγγέλους... ἐκ τῆς ψυχικῆς καὶ φωτεινῆς οὐ. Clem.*exc.Thdot.*47(p.122.1; M.9. 681B); σαρκὸς καὶ ...αἵματος μὴ δυναμένων κληρονομεῖν βασιλείαν θεοῦ, κληρονομεῖν δ' ἂν λεχθησομένων, ἐὰν μεταβάλωσιν ἀπὸ σαρκὸς καὶ γῆς καὶ χοῦ καὶ αἵματος ἐπὶ τὴν οὐράνιον οὐ. Or.*or.*26(p.363.22; M.11. 506A); id.*Cels.*6.71(p.141.26; M.11.1405D); πρὸς τοὺς ἀγγέλους, πρὸς τῶν ἀνθρώπων ψυχὰς...ὧν διὰ τὸ λεπτὸν τῆς οὐ. ἀκώλυτος ἡ...διάβασις Euther.*confut.*14(M.28.1384A); **b.** material *substance*, *matter* γενέσθαι [sc. τροφήν] πρόσληψιν εἰς οὐ. [sc. τοῦ σώματος] Athenag.*res.*6(p.54.6; M.6.984C); of *material* of which a statue is made, Clem.*prot.*4(p.44. 17; M.8.153B); μὴ πάντες ἓν σῶμά ἐσμεν κατὰ τὴν οὐ., ἢ τῇ δυνάμει καὶ τῇ διαθέσει τῆς ὁμοφρονίας ἓν γινόμεθα; Hipp.*Noët.*7(p.247.18; M.10. 813B); τὸν αἰθέρα, τὸν ἥλιον...ἅτινα εἰς ὑπηρεσίαν ἀνθρώπου γενόμενα καὶ κατ' οὐσίαν κρείττονα ὄντα *Hom.Clem.*16.19; αἱ προσηγορίαι οὐχὶ τῶν οὐ. εἰσι σημαντικαί, ἀλλὰ τῶν ἰδιοτήτων...(οὐ. δὲ λέγω νῦν τὸ ὑλικὸν ὑποκείμενον) Bas.*Eun.*2.4(1.240D; M.29.577C); ἡ φύσις καὶ ἡ τέχνη ἐκ τῶν οὐ. ποιοῦσιν ἅπερ ποιοῦσιν· οἷον ἐκ σπέρματος ποιεῖ ἡ φύσις τὸν ἄνθρωπον, καὶ ἐξ ἀνθρώπου τὸ σπέρμα· οὐσίαι δέ εἰσι τό τε σπέρμα καὶ ὁ ἄνθρωπος. ὡσαύτως καὶ αἱ τέχναι ποιοῦσιν ἐκ τοῦ χαλκοῦ ...καὶ ἐκ πλίνθων...οὐσίαι δέ εἰσιν ὅ τε χαλκὸς καὶ οἱ πλίνθοι ‡Just.*c. Gr.*5(M.6.1460A); Chrys.*hom.13.4 in Rom.*(9.563E); εἴδωλα· ἐκ μὲν τῆς ὕλης τὴν οὐ. ἐκ δὲ τῆς τέχνης τὸ εἶδος Thdt.*Is.*17:10(p.80.14; 2. 280); ref. Creation, Clem.*str.*5.14(p.385.16; M.9.132B); ὡς ἄρα ἐξ ὑποκειμένης τινὸς οὐ. ταῦτα ἐδημιούργησεν Meth.*arbitr*.4.1(p.155.5; M.18.248C); ὕλην ὥσπερ τινὰ καὶ οὐ. τῆς τῶν ὅλων γενέσεώς τε καὶ συστάσεως τὴν ἑαυτοῦ βουλὴν καὶ δύναμιν προβεβλημένος Eus.*d.e*.4.1 (p.151.20; M.22.252D); id.*l.C*.12(p.232.1; M.20.1389C) cit. s. ἄψυχος; **2.** *element* Ζεὺς ἡ ζέουσα οὐ. κατὰ τοὺς Στοϊκούς Athenag.*leg*.22.2(M.6. 937A); αἱ...πρῶται οὐ. ἐξ οὐκ ὄντων γενόμεναι, πῦρ καὶ πνεῦμα, ὕδωρ καὶ γῆ Hipp.*haer*.10.33(p.289.14; M.16.3447C); τὴν ὑγρὰν οὐ. *ib.* (p.289.22; 3450A); πέμπτη τις...οὐ., φυσικῶν ἀπηλλαγμένη στοιχείων πάντων...οἱονεὶ οὐ. τις ὑπερκόσμιος *ib*.7.19(p.194.9ff.; 3299B); Thdt. *Ps*.94:5(1.1286); id.*provid*.1(4.489).

D. *essential element* or *feature, special character* τὸ...ἀεὶ νοεῖν, οὐ. τοῦ γινώσκοντος κατὰ ἀνάκρασιν ἀδιάστατον γενομένη Clem.*str*.4.22 (p.308.26; M.8.1345C); ἡ...τῆς ἀληθείας ἐπίγνωσις ἐκ τῶν ἤδη πιστῶν τοῖς οὔπω πιστοῖς ἐκπορίζεται τὴν πίστιν, ἥτις οὐ. ... ἀποδείξεως καθίσταται *ib*.7.16(p.69.24; M.9.536C); Eus.*d.e*.4.5(p.157.27; M.22.264A).

E. *property, possessions, substance* κέχρηται...τῷ προσρήματι...τῆς οὐ. ἡ...συνήθεια ἐπὶ τῷ σημαινομένῳ τῶν κτήσεων, ὧν τις κέκτηται Thdr.Raith.*praep*.(p.201.3); of capital opp. income ἕτερος ἀναθεῖναι τὴν δεκάτην τῶν καρπῶν, ἄλλος τῆς οὐ. Meth.*symp*.5.1(p.53.16; M.18. 97B); met. οὐσίᾳ μὲν ὑπέθετο τὴν ἀρετὴν ὁ ἀπόστολος...χρῆσιν δὲ αὐτῆς οὐκ εἰς δέον, τῷ τἀναντία διαπραττομένους ἀφανίζειν αὐτῆς τὴν ὑπόστασιν Thdr.Mops.*Gal*.4:1ff.(p.61.24; M.66.905D); τῶν εἰς τὸν κύριον πεπιστευκότων τὰς οὐ. διήρπασαν οἱ τοῖς εὐαγγελικοῖς ἀντιλέγοντες δόγμασιν Thdt.*Is*.5:17(p.27.1; 2.202).

II. theol.; **A.** *being* of God; **1.** opp. activity, Athenag.*res*.1(p.48. 13; M.6.976A); cf.Or.*princ*.1.1.6(p.21.7; M.11.124C) cit. s. 5 infra; **2.** as identical with God himself οὐ. ... ἐστιν ἐπὶ θεοῦ θεός Clem. *fr*.37(p.219.17; M.9.749D); ἡ δὲ οὐ. οὐχ ἕν τι τῶν μὴ προσόντων ἐστίν, ἀλλ' αὐτὸ τὸ εἶναι τοῦ θεοῦ Bas.*Eun*.1.10(1.223B; M.29.536C); cf. ‡Just.*qu.Chr*.3.1(M.6.1432A) cit. s. βουλή; **3.** as ultimate reality v. I.B.2; **4.** as incomprehensible ἀσθενὴς...φύσει ὁ ἀνθρώπειος λόγος καὶ ἀδύνατος φράσαι θεόν, οὐ τοὔνομα λέγω...οὐδὲ τὴν οὐ. (ἀδύνατον γάρ), ἀλλὰ τὴν δύναμιν καὶ τὰ ἔργα τοῦ θεοῦ Clem.*str*.6.18(p.517.22; M.9.397C); νοῦν τοίνυν ἢ ἐπέκεινα νοῦ καὶ οὐ. λέγοντες εἶναι...τὸν... θεόν, οὐκ ἐν ἄλλῳ τινὶ...φήσομεν καταλαμβάνεσθαι τὸν θεόν...ἀλλὰ κατὰ τροπολογίαν Or.*Cels*.7.38(p.188.11; M.11.1473B); cf. *nos autem mensurae quidem ipsius, id est substantiae, nomen vel rationem comprehendere aut invenire non possumus, confitentes tamen patrem et filium unum*, id.*hom.13.4 in Lev*.(p.474.1; M.12.549A); Eus.*e.th*. 1.20(p.86.2; M.24.873C); Ath.*syn*.35(p.262.11; M.26.753C); τῆς ἁπλῆς καὶ ἀπεριλήπτου οὐ. Evagr.Pont.*ep*.2(M.32.249A); Gr.Naz.*or*.30.17 (p.135.7; M.36.125B); οὐ μόνον τοῖς ἀνθρώποις, ἀλλὰ καὶ πάσῃ νοητῇ φύσει τῆς θείας οὐ. τὴν γνῶσιν ἀνέφικτον εἶναι...διοριζόμενος Gr.Nyss. *v.Mos*.(M.44.377A); id.*Eun*.1(1 p.213.16; M.45.461B); τὸν μονογενῆ θεόν...θεὸν κατὰ ἀλήθειαν ἀεὶ ὄντα...οὐ τὸ εἶναι ὅ τι ποτὲ κατ' οὐσίαν ἐστὶ πᾶσαν ἐκφεύγει καταληπτικὴν ἔφοδον *ib*.12(1 p.220.25; 913D); *ib*.11(2 p.264.29; 873A); ὑπὲρ νοῦν καὶ οὐ. ἵδρυται...τὸ ἕν...τὸ ὑπερούσιον Dion.Ar.*d.n*.1.5(M.3.593B); τὴν...ὑπερουσιότητα τὴν θεαρχικὴν ὅ τί ποτέ ἐστιν ἡ τῆς ὑπεραγαθότητος ὑπερύπαρξις, οὔτε ὡς λόγον...ἢ οὐ. ὑμνῆσαι θεμιτὸν...ἀλλ' ὡς πάσης...οὐ. ... ὑπεροχικῶς ἀφῃρημένην *ib*.(593C); τῷ λόγῳ σκοπὸς οὐ τὴν ὑπερούσιον οὐ., ᾗ ὑπερούσιος, ἐκφαίνειν (ἄρρητον γὰρ τοῦτο καὶ ἄγνωστόν ἐστι) *ib*.5.1(816B); υἱός ἐστιν...ἀπαράλλακτος οὐ., φύσις ἀνεπιχείρητος Anast.Ant.*fid*.(M.89. 1404C); cf. ὁ Εὐνόμιος...ἐτόλμησε εἰπεῖν, ὡς οὐδὲν τῶν θείων ἠγνόησεν, ἀλλὰ καὶ αὐτὴν ἀκριβῶς ἐπίσταται τοῦ θεοῦ τὴν οὐ. Thdt.*haer*.4.3(4. 357); cf.Epiph.*haer*.76.4(p.344.20; M.42.521C); **5.** in what sense knowable γάλα μὲν ἡ κατήχησις...βρῶμα δὲ ἡ ἐποπτικὴ θεωρία· σάρκες αὗται καὶ αἷμα τοῦ λόγου, τουτέστι κατάληψις τῆς θείας δυνάμεως καὶ οὐ. [Ps.33:9], φησίν· οὕτως γὰρ ἑαυτοῦ μεταδίδωσι τοῖς πνευματικώτερον τῆς τοιαύτης μεταλαμβάνουσι βρώσεως...βρῶσις γὰρ καὶ πόσις τοῦ θείου λόγου ἡ γνῶσίς ἐστι τῆς θείας οὐ. Clem.*str*.5.10 (p.370.17,21; M.9.101A); cf. *quasi radii quidam sunt dei naturae opera divinae providentiae et ars universitatis hujus ad comparationem ipsius substantiae ejus ac naturae. quia ergo mens nostra ipsum per se ipsam deum sicut est non potest intueri*, Or.*princ*.1.1.6(p.21.7; M. 11.124C); αἱ μὲν γὰρ ἐνέργειαι ποικίλαι, ἡ δὲ οὐ. ἁπλῆ. ἡμεῖς δὲ ἐκ μὲν τῶν ἐνεργειῶν γνωρίζειν λέγομεν τὸν θεὸν ἡμῶν, τῇ δὲ οὐ. αὐτῇ προσεγγίζειν οὐχ ὑπισχνούμεθα. αἱ μὲν γὰρ ἐνέργειαι αὐτοῦ πρὸς ἡμᾶς καταβαίνουσιν, ἡ δὲ οὐ. αὐτοῦ μένει ἀπρόσιτος Bas.*ep*.234.1(3.357D; M. 32.869A); τὸ δὲ κατ' οὐσίαν ὅ τί ποτέ ἐστιν, οὐδὲν ἧττον ἐν ἀδήλῳ μένει ...πᾶν γὰρ ὅ τί περ ἂν εἴπῃς ὄνομα, περὶ τὸ ὄν ἐστιν, οὐκ ἐκεῖνό ἐστιν Gr. Nyss.*Eun*.7(2 p.171.29; M.45.761Df.); τί κωλύει καὶ ἡμᾶς ἀνθρώπους ὄντας, ἔλαττον μὲν εἰδέναι θεοῦ, ἢ ὡς αὐτὸς ἑαυτὸν οἶδε τί ποτέ ἐστι κατ' οὐσίαν, μὴ μὴν ψευδῶς τε καὶ διεστραμμένως; Cyr.*thes*.31(5^1.265E); **6.** in rel. to created things εἴτε...τέχνη τοῦ θεοῦ [sc. ὁ κόσμος]... εἴτε οὐ. καὶ σῶμα...εἴτε δυνάμεις τοῦ θεοῦ τὰ μέρη τοῦ κόσμου νοεῖ τις Athenag.*leg*.16.2(M.6.921A); τῷ πάτερ ἡμῶν ἐν τοῖς οὐρανοῖς, οἱονεὶ ἀφιστάντι τὴν οὐ. τοῦ θεοῦ ἀπὸ πάντων τῶν γεννητῶν· οἷς γὰρ οὐ κοινωνεῖ, αὐτοῖς δόξα τις θεοῦ καὶ δύναμις αὐτοῦ, καὶ...ἀπορροὴ τῆς θεότητος ἐγγίνεται αὐτοῖς Or.*or*.23(p.353.10; M.11.492A); μένων...τῇ οὐ. ἄτρεπτος συγκαταβαίνει τῇ προνοίᾳ καὶ τῇ οἰκονομίᾳ τοῖς ἀνθρωπίνοις πράγμασιν id.*Cels*.4.14(p.284.18; M.11.1045A); *ib*.4.15(p.285.17; 1048A); Eus.*e.th*.2.9(p.108.32; M.24.917A) cit. s. ἀπαραλλάκτως; τὴν μὲν οὐ. ἤμην [sc. Wisdom] σὺν τῷ πατρί, τῇ δὲ πρὸς τὰ γενητὰ συγκαταβάσει, ἥμην ἁρμόζουσα τὸν παρ' ἐμοὶ τύπον τοῖς ἔργοις Ath. *Ar*.2.81(M.26.317B); id.*ep.Serap*.2.5(M.26.616B); τὸ...'ἐξ αὐτοῦ τὰ πάντα' οὐ τὴν οὐ. δηλοῖ—οὐ γὰρ ἐκ τῆς οὐ. τοῦ θεοῦ τὰ δημιουργήματα Sever.*1Cor*.8:6(p.255.1f.); τὸ ἐν πᾶσιν ὂν καὶ διὰ πάντων διῆκον, συμπλέκεσθαι τοῖς πᾶσιν ἀναγκαῖον...ἀλλ' οὐ συμπεπλέχθαι μὲν τὴν οὐ. τοῦ θεοῦ τῇ ποικιλίᾳ τῶν ἐν κόσμῳ σωμάτων ὁμολογήσομεν... διήκει δὲ ὁ μὲν διὰ πάντων παραδόξως καὶ ἀρρήτως Cyr.*thes*.6(5^1.44A); id.*Is*.5.3(2.809E) cit. s. ἐκπόρευσις; μακρυνθῆναι δὲ αὐτοῦ, οὐ τὴν οὐ. λέγει τοῦ θεοῦ· πανταχοῦ γὰρ πάρεστι...ἀλλὰ τὴν πρόνοιαν, καὶ τὴν τῆς βοηθείας ἐνέργειαν Thdt.*Ps*.70:12(1.1095); **7.** as incorporeal, v. ἀσώματος, the mode of Son's eternal generation according therewith τὴν δύναμιν ταύτην γεγεννῆσθαι ἀπὸ τοῦ πατρὸς...ἀλλ' οὐ κατὰ ἀποτομήν, ὡς ἀπομεριζομένης τῆς τοῦ πατρὸς οὐ. Just.*dial*.128.4(M.6. 776B); Or.*Jo*.20.18(16; p.351.5ff.; M.14.613cf.) cit. s. B.1.a infra; κατὰ τὴν οἰκείαν φύσιν τῶν ἀσωμάτων ἀσυγχύτως τὴν ἕνωσιν γίνεσθαι τῶν οὐ. Nemes.*nat.hom*.3(M.40.605B); οὐ...κατὰ σῶμα γέγονεν, ἀλλ' ὡς ἂν πρέποι τῇ νοερᾷ τε καὶ ἀσωμάτῳ φύσει. φῶς γὰρ ἐξέλαμψεν ἐκ φωτός, ἀνέφυ δὲ καὶ ζωὴ ἐκ ζωῆς· καὶ ὅτι μὲν ἐγεννήθη κατὰ ἀλήθειαν ἐκ τῆς οὐ. τοῦ...πατρός, ἀνενδοιάστως πιστεύομεν. τὸ δὲ ὅπως, εἰπεῖν ἢ νοεῖν οὐκ ἔστι Cyr.*Is*.5.1(2.748A); rendering possible an incarnation without detriment ἡ ἀσώματος τοῦ θεοῦ δύναμις οὔτ' ἂν πάθοι τὴν οὐ. οὔτ' ἂν βλαβείη...σώματος ἀσωμάτως ἐπαφωμένη Eus.*d.e*.4.13 (p.171.2; M.22.285A).

B. of the divine *essence* in Father and Son; **1.** in pre-Nicene period; **a.** of Father and Son as related essentially λόγος...οὐ. ὑπάρχων θεοῦ Hipp.*haer*.10.33(p.290.8; M.16.3450B); cf. *qui filium non aliunde deduco, sed de substantia patris...quomodo possum de fide destruere monarchiam quam, a patre filio traditam, in filio servo?* Tert.*adversus Praxean* 4(M.*PL*.2.182A); ὁ...σωτὴρ οὐ κατὰ μετουσίαν, ἀλλὰ κατ' οὐ. ἐστὶ θεός Or.*sel.in Ps*.135:2(M.12.1656A); ᾤοντο...παρίστασθαι μὴ διαφέρειν τῷ ἀριθμῷ τὸν υἱὸν τοῦ πατρός, ἀλλ' ἓν οὐ μόνον οὐσίᾳ ἀλλὰ καὶ ὑποκειμένῳ τυγχάνοντας ἀμφοτέρους, κατά τινας ἐπινοίας διαφόρους, οὐ κατὰ ὑπόστασιν λέγεσθαι πατέρα καὶ υἱόν id.*Jo*.10.37(21; p.212.14; M.14.376B); cf. *quae imago etiam naturae ac substantiae patris et filii continet unitatem*, id.*princ*.1.2.6(p.35.1; M.11.134C); *unus quidem est panis—una enim voluntas est et una substantia—sed duae sunt positiones, id est duae personarum proprietates*, id.*hom. 13.4 in Lev*.(p.474.11; M.12.549B); Thgn.*hypot.fr*.2(p.76; M.10.240A) cit. s. ἀπόρροια; Origen was suspicious of words ἐκ τῆς οὐ. as introducing a materialistic note ἄλλοι δὲ τὸ 'ἐξῆλθον ἀπὸ τοῦ θεοῦ' διηγήσαντο ἀντὶ τοῦ 'γεγέννημαι ἀπὸ τοῦ θεοῦ', οἷς ἀκολουθεῖ ἐκ τῆς οὐ. φάσκειν τοῦ πατρὸς γεγεννῆσθαι τὸν υἱόν, οἱονεὶ μειουμένου καὶ λείποντος τῇ οὐ. ᾗ πρότερον εἶχεν τοῦ θεοῦ, ἐπὰν γεννήσῃ τὸν υἱόν... ἀκολουθεῖ δὲ αὐτοῖς καὶ σῶμα λέγειν τὸν πατέρα καὶ τὸν υἱὸν καὶ διῃρῆσθαι τὸν πατέρα, ἅπερ ἐστὶν δόγματα ἀνθρώπων μηδ' ὄναρ φύσιν ἀόρατον καὶ ἀσώματον πεφαντασμένων, οὖσαν κυρίως οὐ. Or.*Jo*.20.18 (16; p.351.5ff.; 613cf.); hence ἕτερος κατ' οὐσίαν καὶ ὑποκείμενόν ἐστιν ὁ υἱὸς τοῦ πατρός id.*or*.15(p.334.5; M.11.465A); μονογενῆ υἱόν... πρὸ αἰώνων ὄντα οὐ προγνώσει, ἀλλ' οὐ. καὶ ὑποστάσει θεόν Hymen.*ep*. (p.324.24); θεὸν οὐ. καὶ δυνάμει ὑφεστῶτα τὸν τοῦ θεοῦ λόγον Eus. *Marcell*.1.4(p.29.30; M.24.772C); **b.** objections to this view ἡ μὲν αὐγὴ οὐ κατὰ προαίρεσιν τοῦ φωτὸς ἐκλάμπει, κατά τι δὲ τῆς οὐ. συμβεβηκὸς ἀχώριστον, ὁ δὲ υἱὸς κατὰ γνώμην καὶ προαίρεσιν εἰκὼν ὑπέστη τοῦ πατρὸς Eus.*d.e*.4.3(p.153.13; M.24.256B); εἰκών [sc. Son] ...μὴ μόνον τῆς οὐ. ... ἀλλὰ καὶ τοῦ κατὰ τὸ ποσὸν ἀριθμοῦ *ib.* (p.153.20; 256C); ξένος τοῦ υἱοῦ κατ' οὐσίαν ὁ πατήρ, ὅτι ἄναρχος ὑπάρχει Ar.*Thal.fr*.2 ap.Ath.*syn*.15(p.242.27; M.26.708A); *ib*.10 ap. Ath.*Ar*.1.6(M.26.24A) cit. s. ἀνόμοιος; Alex.Al.*ep.encycl*.3(p.8.4; M.18.573B) cit. s. ξένος; Ath.*decr*.6(p.5.27; M.25.'433'(425)A) cit. s. ἀνόμοιος; τὴν...τῆς ὁμοιώσεως ἑνότητα τοῦ υἱοῦ πρὸς τὸν πατέρα οὐκ ἔλεγον κατὰ τὴν οὐ., οὐδὲ κατὰ τὴν φύσιν...ἀλλὰ διὰ τὴν συμφωνίαν τῶν δογμάτων καὶ τῆς διδασκαλίας id.*syn*.45(p.271.1; M.26. 773C); κτιστὸν εἶναι καὶ θεμελιωτὸν καὶ γεννητὸν τῇ οὐ. ...τῇ πρὸς τὸν πεποιηκότα μεμαθήκαμεν Eus.Nic.*ep.Paulin*.(p.16.9,13; M.82. 913C); **c.** legitimacy of speaking of the οὐ. of any one Person οἰόμενοι προφορὰν πατρικὴν...εἶναι τὸν υἱὸν τοῦ θεοῦ, καὶ κατὰ τοῦτο ὑπόστασιν αὐτῷ...οὐ διδόασιν οὐδὲ οὐσίαν αὐτοῦ σαφηνίζουσιν Or. *Jo*.1.24(23; p.29.25; M.14.65B); cf.Apoll.*fr*.110(p.233.16)ap.Anast.S.

monoph.(M.89.1184B); ‡Ath.*dial.Trin.*3.24(M.28.1240B); *τὴν...περὶ τῆς τοῦ πνεύματος οὐ. παραδοθεῖσαν διδασκαλίαν Symb.Chalc.*(451) (p.129.3; H.2.453E); but to speak of two or three *οὐ.* never condoned, cf. *Ὁσίου τοῦ ἐπισκόπου ἐρωτήσαντος αὐτόν, εἰ, ὥσπερ Εὐσέβιος ὁ τῆς Παλαιστίνης δύο οὐ. εἶναί φησιν, οὕτως καὶ αὐτὸς λέγοι, ἔγνων αὐτὸν ἀπὸ τῶν γραφέντων τρεῖς εἶναι πιστεύειν οὐ. ἀποκρινόμενον* Marcell.*fr.* 71 ap.Eus.*Marcell.*1.4(p.26.8; M.24.765Bf.); Marcell.*fr.72 ib.*(p.26.15; 765C) cit. s. *λόγος*; *τοῦ ἑνὸς θεοῦ τὸ μέν τι πατέρα καλεῖ* [sc. Marcell.], *τὸ δὲ υἱόν, ὡς διπλῆν τινα καὶ σύνθετον οὐ. ἐν αὐτῷ εἶναι* Eus.*e.th.*1.5 (p.64.24; M.24.833B); *οὐ...δύο οὐ. ... εἰσάγει* [sc. *ἡ ἐκκλησία*] *διὸ οὐδὲ δύο θεούς ib.*2.23(p.133.13; M.24.960D); cf. *μεμερισμέναι τῇ φύσει, καὶ ἀπεξενωμέναι...καὶ ἀμέτοιχοί εἰσιν ἀλλήλων αἱ οὐ. τοῦ πατρὸς καὶ τοῦ υἱοῦ καὶ τοῦ ἁγίου πνεύματος, καὶ...ἀνόμοιοι πάμπαν ἀλλήλων ταῖς τε οὐ. ... εἰσίν* Ar.*Thal.fr.*13 ap.Ath.*Ar.*1.6(M.26.24B); *διαιρεῖ* [sc. *ὁ Ἄρειος*] *τὰς οὐ.* Thdt.*eran.*2(4.78); **2.** Nicene and post-Nicene usage; **a.** Son declared to be *ἐκ τῆς οὐ. τοῦ πατρός Symb.Nic.*(325)(p.44.13; M.20.1540B); *οὔτε γὰρ τὰ πάντα ὡς ὁ υἱὸς οὔτε ὁ λόγος εἷς τῶν πάντων ἐστί· τῶν γὰρ πάντων κύριος καὶ δημιουργός ἐστι. διὰ τοῦτο...ἡ... σύνοδος λευκότερον εἴρηκεν ἐκ τῆς οὐ. αὐτὸν εἶναι τοῦ πατρός* Ath.*decr.* 19(p.16.23; M.25.449C); *οἱ ἐν Νικαίᾳ συνελθόντες οὐ τὸ σῶμα, ἀλλ' αὐτὸν τὸν υἱὸν εἰρήκασι...ἐκ τῆς οὐ. τοῦ πατρός, τὸ δὲ σῶμα ἐκ Μαρίας ὡμολόγησαν εἶναι* id.*ep.Epict.*4(p.7.10; M.26.1056C); *οὐκ ἀρέσκεσθε τῷ ἐκ τῆς οὐ. ὀνόματι...ὑμεῖς* [sc. Arians] *ἐγράψατε ἐκ τοῦ πατρὸς... εἰ μὲν οὖν τὸν πατέρα ὀνομάζοντες ἢ τὸ θεὸς ὄνομα λέγοντες οὐκ οὐσίαν σημαίνετε οὐδὲ αὐτὸν τὸν ὄντα ὅπερ ἐστὶ κατ' οὐσίαν νοεῖτε...ἔδει... γράφειν ὑμᾶς...'ἐκ τῶν περὶ αὐτὸν ἢ τῶν ἐν αὐτῷ'* id.*syn.*34(p.261.31ff.; M.26.753A); *ib.*35(p.262.14; 753D); id.*tom.*6(M.26.801C) cit. s. *φύσις*; Bas.*hom.*15.2(2.132B; M.31.468B) cit. s. *υἱός*; *Symb.*ap.Epiph.*anc.*118, (p.147.2; M.43.232C); *Symb.ib.*119(p.148.7; 233B); *εἴ τις μὴ εἴπῃ τὸν υἱὸν γεννηθέντα ἐκ τοῦ πατρός, τουτέστιν ἐκ τῆς οὐ. τῆς θείας αὐτοῦ* Dam.Papa *anath.*ap.Thdt.*h.e.*5.11.7(3.1038); ‡Ath.*dial.Trin.*2.9(M. 28.1169Cff.); expression persisting in orthodox use, Cosm.Ind.*top.* 5(M.88.309B); *ib.*(256B); ‡Meth.*Sym.et Ann.*3(M.18.353C); **b.** *κατ' οὐσίαν* and other expressions specifying *οὐσία*: *λόγος...ὅμοιος...ὢν κατὰ τὴν οὐ. τοῦ πατρός* Ath.*ep.Aeg.Lib.*17(M.25.577B); id.*syn.*38 (p.264.25; M.26.760C); *τὴν...ἑνότητα τοῦ υἱοῦ πρὸς τὸν πατέρα οὐχ ὁμοιώσει διδασκαλίας, ἀλλὰ κατὰ τὴν οὐ. καὶ ἀληθείᾳ φρονοῦμεν ib.*52 (p.275.33; 785B); *εἰ...ὁ λόγος...οὔτε ἐκ τῆς οὐ. ἐστὶ τοῦ πατρός, οὔτε αὐτὸς ὁ υἱὸς κατ' οὐ. ἐστιν υἱός, ἀλλ' ἐξ ἀρετῆς, ὡς ἡμεῖς οἱ κατὰ χάριν καλούμενοι υἱοί* id.*decr.*22(p.19.6f.; M.25.456C); *σύμπαν τὸ εἶναι τοῦ υἱοῦ, τοῦτο τῆς τοῦ πατρὸς οὐ. ἴδιόν ἐστι* id.*Ar.*3.8(M.26.328A); cf. Or.*princ.*1.2.10(p.43.10; M.11.141B); *τὸ κατ' οὐ. κοινὸν τε καὶ γνήσιον...τοῦ λόγου πρὸς τὴν ἀρχήν* Gr.Nyss.*Eun.*4(2 p.53.20; M.45. 624B); *κατ' οὐ. δὲ καὶ κατὰ πάντα εἰκών ἐστιν* [sc. *ὁ θεὸς λόγος*]...*τοῦ πατρός, καὶ οὐ κατὰ μορφὴν καὶ σχῆμα* Didym.*Trin.*1.16(M.39.336B); *προεϊστήκεισαν...τῶν κατ' οὐ. ὅμοιον πρεσβευόντων Βασίλειός τε καὶ Εὐστάθιος* Philost.*h.e.*4.12(M.65.525A); **c.** ambiguities of usage, Ast.Soph.*fr.*21 ap.Eus.*Marcell.*1.4(p.25.7; M.24.764C) ∞ *Symb.Ant.* (341)2(p.249.17; M.26.721C) cit. s. *εἰκών*; *ὁ δὲ* [sc. *Εὐδόξιος*] *τῆς Ἀρειανῆς μὲν δόξης ἦν, πλὴν ἐκ τῶν Ἀστερίου γραμμάτων εἰς τὸ κατ' οὐ. ὅμοιον ὑπενήνεκτο* Philost.*h.e.*4.4(M.65.520A); and avoidance of term *οὐ.*: *περὶ τῆς λεγομένης 'Ῥωμαϊστὶ μὲν 'σουβσταντίας', 'Ἑλληνιστὶ δὲ λεγομένης 'οὐσίας', τουτέστιν ἵνα ἀκριβέστερον γνωσθῇ τὸ ὁμοούσιον ἢ τὸ λεγόμενον ὁμοιούσιον, οὐ χρή τινα τούτων παντελῶς μνήμην γίνεσθαι οὐδὲ περὶ τούτων ἐξηγεῖσθαι ἐν τῇ ἐκκλησίᾳ...ὅτι ἐν ταῖς θείαις γραφαῖς οὐ γέγραπται περὶ τούτων Symb.Sirm.*2(p.257.3; M.26.741B); *Symb.Sirm.*3(p.236.10; 693B); *Symb.Nic.*(359)ap.Thdt.*h.e.*2.21.7(3. 880); *Symb.CP*(360)(p.259.13; M.26.748B); Philost.*h.e.*4.8(M.65. 521B); *ἡ δὲ ἐν Ἀριμήνῳ συνελθοῦσα* [sc. *σύνοδος*] *τὸ...τῆς οὐ. ὄνομα εἰς τὸ παντελὲς διώσατο ib.*4.10(M.65.524B); **d.** Eun. wholly opposed to its use *μόνος αὐτός ἐστιν ἀγέννητος· αὐτὸ* [? l. *αὐτὸς*] *ἂν εἴη οὐ. ἀγέννητος* Eun.*apol.*8(M.30.844B); *τὸ πρὸς τὸν υἱὸν ἀκοινώνητον τῆς τοῦ πατρὸς οὐ. κατασκευάσας* Bas.*Eun.*1.19(1.230D; M.29.554C); *τὸ μηδὲν οἴεσθαι διαφέρειν κατ' οὐ. αὐτόν τε τὸν κύριον καὶ τὰ παρ' αὐτοῦ γεγονότα πλὴν τῆς κατὰ τὴν τάξιν διαφορᾶς* Gr.Nyss.*Eun.*4(2 p.58.19; M.45.629B); *φάσκουσιν· ὧν τὰ ὀνόματά ἐστι διάφορα, τούτων παρηλλάχθαι καὶ τὰς οὐ. ἀνάγκη* Didym.*Trin.*1.11(M.39.293B); *τὸν Εὐνόμιον τινες...διαβάλλουσιν...τὸ μὴ κατ' οὐ. ὅμοιον εἰς κατηγορίαν ἀνομοιότητος πατρὸς πρὸς υἱὸν μετασκευάζοντες* Philost.*h.e.*6.1(M.65.532B); ‡Ath.*Maced.dial.*2(M.28.1329C).

C. of the divine *essence* in Trin.; **1.** in doctrine prior to Cappadocian fathers, *est ergo haec trium distinctio personarum in patre et filio et spiritu sancto...sed...unus est fons; una enim substantia est et natura trinitatis,* Or.*hom.12.1 in Num.*(p.95.13; M.12.657B); *εἰ ...ὁ υἱὸς...ἴδιος τῆς οὐ. αὐτοῦ ἐστιν, ἀνάγκη καὶ τὸ πνεῦμα ἐκ τοῦ λόγου λεγόμενον, ἴδιον εἶναι κατ' οὐ. τοῦ υἱοῦ* Ath.*ep.Serap.*1.25(M.26.588Cf.); id.*tom.*3(M.26.800A) cit. s. *διαιρέω*; *τὸ πνεῦμα ὁμοίως καλεῖται τοῦ θεοῦ, καὶ τοῦτο φυσικῶς κατ' αὐτὴν τὴν οὐ.* Apoll.*fid.sec.pt.*25(p.176. 8; M.10.1116A); *πνεῦμα...ἐκ τῆς οὐ. τοῦ θεοῦ ὑπάρχον ib.*27(p.177.1; 1116B); cf. *Ἀπολινάριος...ὁμοίως ἡμῖν καὶ τὴν μίαν τῆς θεότητος οὐ., καὶ τὰς τρεῖς ὑποστάσεις ἐκήρυξεν* Thdt.*haer.*4.8(4.362); **2.** development of orthodox doctrine up to Chalcedon; **a.** Persons in Godhead united by *οὐ.* opp. *ποιότης, συμβεβηκός, δύναμις, μορφή,* etc. *ἡ θεία μονὰς ἀδιαίρετος οὖσα, σύνθετος φανήσεται* [sc. on Arian premisses], *τεμνομένη εἰς οὐ. καὶ συμβεβηκός* ‡Ath.*Ar.*4.2(p.45.19; M.26.469B); *οὐ γὰρ ἐκ τῆς οἰκίας τὴν οὐ. τοῦ οἰκοδόμου καταλαβεῖν δυνατόν· ἐκ μέντοι τοῦ γεννήματος νοῆσαι ῥᾴδιον τοῦ γεγεννηκότος τὴν φύσιν. ὥστε εἰ μὲν δημιούργημα ὁ μονογενής, οὐ παρίστησιν ἡμῖν τοῦ πατρὸς τὴν οὐ.* Bas. *Eun.*2.32(1.269E; M.29.648D); *οὔτε ὅμοιον οὔτε ἀνόμοιον λέγομεν τὸν υἱὸν τῷ πατρί. ... ὅμοιον γὰρ καὶ ἀνόμοιον κατὰ τὰς ποιότητας λέγεται· ποιότητος δὲ τὸ θεῖον ἐλεύθερον. ταυτότητα δὲ τῆς φύσεως ὁμολογοῦντες, καὶ τὸ ὁμοούσιον ἐκδεχόμεθα, καὶ τὸ σύνθετον φεύγομεν, τοῦ κατ' οὐ. θεοῦ καὶ πατρὸς τὸν κατ' οὐσίαν θεὸν καὶ υἱὸν γεγεννηκότος...ὁ γὰρ κατ' οὐσίαν θεὸς τῷ κατ' οὐ. θεῷ ὁμοούσιός ἐστιν...ὁ δὲ θεὸς μόνος κατ' οὐ. ἐστὶ θεός. μόνος δὲ ὅταν εἴπω, τὴν οὐ. τοῦ θεοῦ τὴν ἁγίαν καὶ ἄκτιστον δηλῶ* Evagr.Pont.*ep.*3(M.32.249C); *κατ' οὐ. ... εἰκών ἐστιν* [sc. *ὁ θεὸς λόγος*]...*τοῦ πατρός, καὶ οὐ κατὰ μορφὴν καὶ σχῆμα, ὡς ὁ πλαστουργηθεὶς...ἀνδριάς· οὐδὲ κατὰ εἶδος καὶ χρῶμα ὡς ἡ τεχνητὴ... εἰκών* Didym.*Trin.*1.16(M.39.336B); *οὕτως ἐστὶν υἱὸς τοῦ θεοῦ, ὥσπερ ἐκεῖνος υἱὸς 'Ιωνᾶ, τῆς αὐτῆς οὐ. τῷ γεγεννηκότι* Chrys.*hom.54.2 in Mt.*(7.547E); *οὐ.* not admitting of degrees *ἐπὶ μὲν τῆς οὐ. ἐδείχθη παρὰ τῶν τὰ τοιαῦτα φιλοσοφεῖν εἰδότων, μηδεμίαν δύνασθαι διαφορὰν ἐννοῆσαι, ἐάν τις αὐτὴν ψιλώσας καὶ ἀπογυμνώσας τῶν ἐπιθεωρουμένων ποιοτήτων τε καὶ ἰδιωμάτων αὐτὴν ἐφ' ἑαυτῆς ἐξετάζῃ, κατὰ τὸν τοῦ εἶναι λόγον* Gr.Nyss.*Eun.*1(1 p.104.5; M.45.337B); *τὰ...τῆς αὐτῆς οὐ. ὄντα καὶ φύσεως οὐκ ἂν ὅλως ἔχοι καθ' ἑαυτῶν τὸ μεῖζον, κατά γε τὸν τοῦ πῶς εἶναι λόγον* Cyr.*Jo.*1.3(4.22E); or difference *οὐ. ... οὐσίας οὐδὲν διαφέρει, ᾗ οὐ. ἐστίν* ‡Ath.*dial.Trin.*2.25(M.28.1196B); hence *μεσολαβοῦν...ὁρῶμεν οὐδέν, ὅσον ἧκεν εἰς οὐσίας ὑφεστώσης λόγον* Cyr.*Jo.*2.2(4.164B); cf. *εἰ δὲ μὴ κτίσμα, ὁμοούσιος τῷ πατρί* Evagr. Pont.*ep.*9f.(261Bf.); Son does not partake of essence of even the most exalted of creatures, CCP(543)*anath.*2(Hahn p.228; H.3. 284C) cit. s. *ἑνάς*; *εἴ τις λέγει, ὡς...ἕξει ὁ Χριστὸς πρὸς οὐδὲ ἓν τῶν λογικῶν διαφορὰν οὐδὲ τῇ οὐ. οὐδὲ τῇ γνώσει οὐδὲ τῇ...δυνάμει ἢ ἐνεργείᾳ...ἀ. ἔ. ib.*13(Hahn p.229; H.3.285E); cf. *οὐ κοινοποιοῦμεν οὐδὲ τοῦ μονογενοῦς τὴν οὐ. πρὸς τὰ ἐκ μὴ ὄντων γενόμενα ἐπείπερ οὐκ οὐ. τὸ μὴ ὄν...τοσαύτην αὐτῷ νέμομεν ὑπεροχήν, ὅσην ἔχειν...τῶν ἰδίων ποιημάτων τὸν ποιητήν* Eun.*apol.*15(M.30.849C); *οὐκ ἐκ τῆς οὐ. εἶναι τοῦ πεποιηκότος, οὔτε τὴν ἀγγελικὴν κτίσιν, οὔτε τὴν ἐγκόσμιον πεπιστεύκαμεν* Gr.Nyss.*Eun.*4(2 p.59.17; 629D); **b.** *οὐ.* of Trin. is not a prior substance of which each Person forms a part *ὅταν...εἴπω μίαν οὐ., μὴ δύο ἐξ ἑνὸς μερισθέντα νόει, ἀλλ' ἐκ τῆς ἀρχῆς τοῦ πατρὸς τὸν υἱὸν ὑποστάντα, οὐ πατέρα καὶ υἱὸν ἐκ μιᾶς οὐ. ὑπερκειμένης...τὸ δὲ τῆς οὐ. ταυτόν, ἐπειδὴ ἐκ τοῦ πατρὸς ὁ υἱός...οὐκ ἀπομερισθεὶς τοῦ πατρὸς ἀλλὰ μένοντος τελείου τέλειος ἀπολάμψας* Bas.*hom.*24.4(2. 191E; M.31.605B); id.*ep.*52.1(3.145B; M.32.393A) cit. s. *ὁμοούσιος*; *τινὲς...ταῖς προσηγορίαις ὁμοῦ καὶ τὴν οὐ. παχυμερῶς συνδιαιρεῖσθαι δοξάζοντες* †Gr.Thaum.*ep.Philagr.*(M.46.1104C); *οὐκ ἔστιν ἔμπροσθεν τοῦ υἱοῦ ὁ...πατήρ, οὐ τῷ ἀνάρχῳ, οὐ τῇ οὐ.* Didym.*Trin.*1.15(M.39. 296B); **c.** relation of genus and species as mere illustration *ἐπειδὴ ὥσπερ ὁ πατὴρ συνθήκης ἐστὶ πάσης ἐλεύθερος, οὕτω καὶ ὁ υἱὸς ἁπλοῦς παντελῶς, καὶ ἀσύνθετος, καὶ τὸ ὅμοιον, μὴ κατὰ τὴν τοῦ εἴδους ταυτότητα θεωρεῖσθαι, ἀλλὰ κατ' αὐτὴν τὴν οὐ. ὅσοις μὲν γὰρ μορφὴ καὶ σχῆμα περίκειται, τούτοις, κατὰ τὴν ταυτότητα τοῦ εἴδους, ἡ ὁμοιότης· τὴν δὲ ἀνείδεον καὶ ἀσχημάτιστον φύσιν ἐν αὐτῇ τῇ οὐ. λείπεται ἔχειν τὴν ὁμοιότητα· καὶ τὸ ἴσον μὴ ἐν τῇ τῶν ὄγκων παραμετρήσει, ἀλλ' ἐν τῇ ταυτότητι τῆς δυνάμεως* Bas.*Eun.*1.23(1.234D; M.29.564A); †Apoll.*ep.Bas.*1(M.32.1104A); *τὸ ἴδιον τῆς τοῦ πατρὸς οὐ. ἐν υἱῷ κείμενον καὶ τῆς θεότητος, ἵν' οὕτως εἴπω, τὸ εἶδος, δεικνύει πᾶσιν αὐτὸν ἐν αὐτῷ...εἰ πᾶς ὁ...προσκυνῶν τῷ πατρί, προσκυνεῖ τῷ υἱῷ, πῶς οὐχ οὗτος ἐν ἐκείνῳ, κἀκεῖνος ὢν ἐν τούτῳ δειχθήσεται κατὰ τὸ τῆς οὐ. ἀπαράλλακτον;...ἐν ταυτότητι τῆς οὐ. ὄντων καὶ οὐδὲν ἐχόντων ὃ τῆς φυσικῆς ἰδιότητος ἀποτέμνει τὸν ἕτερον* Cyr.*thes.*12(5[1]. 109D–112C); **d.** the one *οὐ.* fully and equally possessed by each Person, Bas.*hom.*24.4(2.191E; M.31.605B) cit. s. b supra; *τὸ ὅμοιον κατ' οὐσίαν, εἰ μὲν προσκείμενον ἔχει τὸ ἀπαραλλάκτως, δέχομαι τὴν φωνήν, ὡς εἰς ταὐτὸν τῷ ὁμοουσίῳ φέρουσαν...οὔτε τῆς τοῦ μονογενοῦς οὐ. πρὸς τὴν τοῦ πατρὸς ἐπινοῆσαί τινα παραλλαγὴν δυνατόν* id.*ep.*9.3(3.91Af.; M.32.272A); *τὴν μίαν θεότητά τε καὶ δύναμιν ἐν τοῖς τρισὶν εὑρισκομένην ἑνικῶς καὶ τὰ τρία συλλαμβάνουσαν μεριστῶς, οὔτε ἀνώμαλον οὐ. ἢ φύσεσιν, οὔτε αὐξομένην ἢ μειουμένην...τριῶν ἀπείρων ἄπειρον συμφυΐαν* Gr.Naz.*or.*40.41(M.36.417B); *ib.*34.13(M.

36.253A); Gr.Nyss.*comm.not.*(M.45.177A); id.*Eun.*1(1 p.164.6; M.45.405B); *ib.*2(2 p.301.19; 472D) cit. s. διαφορά; id.*ep.*24(M.46.1092A); δυναμένης μὲν ἑκάστης θείας ὑποστάσεως ἀπροσδεῶς πάντα ποιῆσαι τελείως· ἵνα δὲ δειχθῇ τὸ...ἀπαράλλακτον τῆς τε οὐ. αὐτῶν...διὰ τοῦτο κοινῇ παρὰ τῆς ἁγίας τριάδος τῆς κτίσεως πληρωθείσης Didym.*Trin.*2.1(M.39.452A); πατὴρ καὶ υἱός...ἰδιοσύστατοι καὶ ἐν ἀλλήλοις θεωρούμενοι, κατὰ τὴν ταυτότητα τῆς οὐ. Cyr.*Jo.*1.2(4.16E); *ib.*5.5(525D); *ib.*10(832C); οὐ γὰρ ἀλλότριον τῆς οὐ. τοῦ μονογενοῦς τὸ ἅγιον νοεῖται πνεῦμα, πρόεισι δὲ φυσικῶς ἐξ αὐτῆς, οὐδὲν ἕτερον παρ' αὐτὸν ὑπάρχον, ὅσον εἰς ταυτότητα φύσεως, εἰ καὶ νοοῖτο τυχὸν ἰδιοσυστάτως *ib.*10.2(4.925C); **e.** plurality of hypostases consistent with unity of οὐ.: οὔτε τῆς τῶν ὑποστάσεων διαφορᾶς τὸ τῆς φύσεως συνεχὲς διασπώσης, οὔτε τῆς κατὰ τὴν οὐ. κοινότητος τὸ ἰδιάζον τῶν γνωρισμάτων ἀναχεούσης Gr.Nyss.*diff.ess.*4(M.32.333A); πλημμελεῖν δοκεῖ, 'οὐ.' ἀντὶ 'ὑποστάσεων' ὀνομάζων. οὐ γὰρ ὅσα τὸν τῆς οὐ. λόγον τὸν αὐτὸν ἔχει, ὁμοίως καὶ ἐπὶ τῇ ὑποστάσει τῇ ἀποδόσει τοῦ λόγου συνενεχθήσεται. Πέτρος γὰρ καὶ Ἰάκωβος καὶ Ἰωάννης ἐν μὲν τῷ λόγῳ τῆς οὐ. οἱ αὐτοὶ ἦσαν ἀλλήλοις id.*Eun.*1(1 p.87.24ff.; M.45.320B); ὁ μὲν προσώπων συγχέων ὑπόστασιν, ὁ δ' αὖ μερίζων δυσσεβῶς τὴν οὐ. Amph.*Seleuc.*207(M.37.1599A); ἵνα τριῶν ὑποστάσεων ἐν οὐ. μιᾷ γνωρισθῇ τὸ ὄνομα Mac.Mgn.*apocr.*4.25(p.209.31); θεότητος καὶ δυνάμεως καὶ οὐ. μιᾶς τοῦ πατρὸς καὶ τοῦ υἱοῦ καὶ τοῦ ἁγίου πνεύματος πιστευομένης... ἐν τρισὶ τελείαις ὑποστάσεσιν CCP(381)*ep.*ap.Thdt.*h.e.*5.9.11(3.1031); ἐκεῖνος [sc. Δάμασος]...μίαν τὴν τῆς τριάδος οὐ. ὁμολογῶν τὰς τρεῖς ὑποστάσεις διαρρήδην κηρύττει Flav.Ant.ap.Thdt.*h.e.*5.3.10(3.1018); **f.** different modes of being not excluding consubstantiality ὡμολόγηται οὖν [sc. by illustration of Adam, Eve, and Seth] καὶ τὰ διαφόρως ὑποστάντα τῆς αὐτῆς εἶναι οὐ. ἐνδέχεσθαι· λέγω δὲ ταῦτα οὐκ ἐπὶ τὴν θεότητα φέρων τὴν πλάσιν ἢ τὴν τομήν...ἐπὶ δὲ τούτων θεωρῶν ὡς ἐπὶ σκηνῆς, τὰ νοούμενα Gr.Naz.*or.*31.11(p.158.12; M.36.145A); ἐδείχθη...πρῶτον μὲν ἕτερον εἶναι τὸ τῆς οὐ. καὶ ἄλλο τὸ τῆς γεννήσεως ὄνομα· ἔπειτα δὲ ὅτι οὐκ οὐ. τις καινὴ καὶ παρηλλαγμένη παρὰ τὴν τοῦ πατρὸς οὐ. ἐν τῷ υἱῷ ὑπέστη Gr.Nyss.*Eun.*3(2 p.29.21; M.45.596A); ὑπάρξεως...τρόπος τὸ ἀγέννητος, καὶ οὐκ οὐσίας ὄνομα Didym.(‡Bas.)*Eun.*4(1.283B; M.29.681A); τῶν θείων ὑποστάσεων τὸ μὲν τῆς οὐ. ἕν ἐστιν ἀδιαίρετον, τὸ δὲ αὐτῶν τρεῖς ἐστι διαιρετόν...εἷς ἐστιν ὁ θεὸς τῷ ἑνὶ καὶ ἀδιαιρέτῳ τῆς οὐ. ‡Just.*qu.et resp.*17(M.6.1264C); εἷς ἐστιν ὁ θεὸς τῇ συνυπάρξει τῶν τριῶν θείων ὑποστάσεων, τῶν διαφερουσῶν ἀλλήλων οὐ τῇ οὐ. ἀλλὰ τοῖς τῆς ὑπάρξεως τρόποις. ἡ διαφορὰ δὲ τῶν τῆς ὑπάρξεως τρόπων οὐ διαιρεῖ τὸ ἓν τῇ οὐ. *ib.*139(1392Cf.); τὰ μὲν οὖν ἐπὶ τῶν θείων τριῶν ὑποστάσεων ὡσαύτως ἀπαραλλάκτως λεγόμενα, ἐν τούτοις νόει τὸ ἓν τῆς οὐ.· τὰ δὲ μὴ ὡσαύτως, ταῦτα νόει τῷ τρόπῳ τῆς τῶν προσώπων ὑπάρξεως *ib.*(1393A); ‡Ath.*dial.Trin.*2.10(M.28.1172D); *ib.*2.24f.(1193Df.); τὸ μὲν 'ἀγέννητον' καὶ 'γεννητὸν' καὶ 'ἐκπορευτὸν' οὐκ οὐσίας ὀνόματα ἀλλὰ τρόποι ὑπάρξεως...ὡς εἶναι τὴν διαφορὰν τῷ πατρὶ πρὸς τὸν υἱὸν καὶ τὸ πνεῦμα κατὰ τὸν τῆς ὑπάρξεως τρόπον, τὸ δὲ ταὐτὸν κατὰ τὸν τῆς οὐ. λόγον Thdt.*rect.conf.*3(M.6.1209B); **g.** consubstantiality implying a mutual interpenetration ὥσπερ ἀνθρώπου ψυχῇ δύο ἐπιστῆμαι ἢ πλείους συνελθοῦσαι...ὑπ' ἀλλήλων οὐ στενοχωροῦνται ἐν νῷ καὶ ψυχῆς χώρῳ, αἱ πολλαὶ τὸν ἀριθμὸν εὐρυχωρούμεναι καὶ ἀλλήλαις ἐνδιδοῖαι [? l. ἐνδίδουσαι] τὸ πᾶν· καίτοιγε πληροῦσαι τὴν ψυχὴν καὶ μὴ ὑπεξιοῦσαι ἑτέρα τῆς ἑτέρας, ὡς μίαν οὐσίας φαντασίαν παρέχειν...ἐπεὶ καθ' ἑνὸς καὶ ταὐτοῦ ἵδρυνται νοῦ, διενηνόχασιν ἀλλήλων καθότι ἄλλον μὲν ἰατρικὴ ἕτερον δὲ φιλοσοφική· οὕτω δὴ καὶ ὁ πατὴρ καὶ ὁ υἱός ‡Gr.Nyss.*Ar.et Sab.*12(M.45.1297C); Cyr.*thes.*12(5^1.109E); αὐτὸ τῆς πατρικῆς οὐ. τὸ ἴδιον ὑπάρχων ὁ υἱός, ὅλον ἐν ἑαυτῷ φορεῖ τὸν πατέρα, καὶ ὅλος ἐστὶν ἐν πατρὶ κατὰ τὴν ταυτότητα τῆς οὐ. *ib.*(111E); ἔχει...ὁ υἱὸς ἐν ἑαυτῷ τὸν γεννήτορα, μιᾶς πρὸς αὐτὸν ὑπάρχων οὐ., ἔστι δὲ καὶ αὐτὸς ἐν πατρὶ φυσικῶς id.*Jo.*10(4.831C); *ib.*1.10(105E); id.*dial.Trin.*6(5^1.621A); *ib.*(618E); **h.** inadequacy of human analogies ἀναγκαζόμεθα καὶ πολλοὺς λέγειν ἀνθρώπους καὶ ὀλίγους, τῇ τροπῇ καὶ ἀλλοιώσει τῶν προσώπων ἐκκρουσθείσης τῆς κοινῆς συνηθείας, καὶ παρὰ αὐτὸν τὸν τῆς οὐ. λόγον· ὥστε συναριθμεῖν τοῖς προσώποις τινὰ τρόπον καὶ οὐσίας. ἐπὶ δὲ τῆς ἁγίας τριάδος οὐδὲν τοιοῦτον συμβαίνει ποτέ, διὰ τὸ τὰ αὐτὰ πρόσωπα... λέγεσθαι κατὰ τὸ αὐτὸ καὶ ὡσαύτως ἔχοντα, μήτε προσθήκην τινὰ δέχεσθαι αὐτήν...μήτε μείωσιν Gr.Nyss.*comm.not.*(M.45.180A); αἱ μὲν ...ὑποστάσεις...διακεχωρισμέναι εἰσί...ἡ δὲ οὐ. αὐτῶν ἥτις ποτὲ αὕτη ἐστὶν (ἄφραστος γάρ ἐστι λόγῳ καὶ νοήματι ἄληπτος) εἰς ἑτερότητά τινα φύσεως οὐ διαμερίζεται id.*ep.*24(M.46.1089C); οὐδὲ τὸ θεὸς ὄνομα οὐσίας ἐστίν, οὐδὲ ἔστιν ὅλως τῆς οὐ. ἐκείνης ὄνομα εὑρεῖν Chrys.*hom.*2.2 *in Heb.*(12.17C); Cyr.*resp.*(p.580.22; 6^2.388A); **3.** post-Chalcedonian usage in light of Christological definition ἐπὶ τούτων μὲν τὸ ταὐτὸν τῆς οὐ. συνάπτων τὸ ἑτεροῖον τῆς ὑποστάσεως διαιρεῖ· ἐνταῦθα δὲ [sc. in Inc.] τὸ ἑτεροῖον τῆς οὐ. χωρίζων, τὸ ταὐτὸν συνάπτει τῆς ὑπόστασεως Leont.B.*arg.Sev.*(M.86.1917D); οὐ. δέ ἐστιν, ἤτοι φύσις...ὅπερ οἱ φιλόσοφοι λέγουσιν εἶδος...μία οὐ. ἡ τῶν τριῶν...τοῦτο μόνον διαφέρουσιν, ὅτι ὁ μὲν υἱὸς γεννᾶται ἐκ πατρός, τὸ δὲ πνεῦμα ἐκπορεύεται †Leont.B.*sect.*1.1(M.86.1193Af.); ὁ...Ἀριστοτέλης φησίν, ὅτι εἰσὶ τῶν ἀτόμων καὶ μερικαὶ οὐ., καὶ μία κοινή. οὕτως οὖν καὶ ὁ Φιλόπονος ἔλεγεν, ὅτι εἰσὶ τρεῖς μερικαὶ οὐ. ἐπὶ τῆς...τριάδος, καὶ ἔστι μία κοινή *ib.*5.6(1233B); ἰδικάς τε...καὶ τρεῖς τὰς οὐ. τῆς τριάδος ὑμεῖς ἐδώκατε Leont.H.*Nest.*7.1(M.86.1760A); οὐκ ἀνουσίους...τὰς ὑποστάσεις δοξάζομεν...οὔτε δὲ οὐ. ... ἡ ὑπόστασις ἐστιν...ἐνυπόστατόν τι καὶ οὐσιῶδες πρᾶγμα Pamph.H.*panopl.*16.2(p.643); θεὸς εἷς ἐστιν, ἤγουν μία θεότης, οὐ. ἄναρχος...ἁπλοῦς, ἀσύνθετος...ἐν τρισὶ τελείαις ταῖς ὑποστάσεσι ‡Cyr.*Trin.*1(6^3.1A; M.77.1120A); *ib.*7(8D; M.1132B) = Jo.D.*f.o.*1.8(M.94.809A); καλεῖται δὲ καὶ οὐ., καὶ φύσις, καὶ μορφή, τὸ ἓν καὶ ταὐτόν· καὶ οὐ. μέν, ὡς τὸ καθ' αὑτὸ εἶναι ἔχουσα...ἐπὶ τῆς θεότητος μίαν οὐ. δογματίζομεν *ib.*13(19B,D; M.1149A); ‡Gr.Nyss.*hom.*1.12 *in Jo.*(p.97.10); *ib.*9.9(p.285.27); Jo.D.*fo.*1.2(792C).

D. of Persons, *subsistent reality*, *real* or *independent entity*; **1.** claimed for Son as for Father οὐ. ... οὖσα τοῦ θεοῦ σοφία, πρὸ αἰώνων γεγένηται Or.*exp.in Pr.*8:22(M.17.185A); ἐντεῦθεν [sc. Jo.1:4ff. and 1Jo.1:5] κατασκευάζεσθαι τῇ οὐ. μὴ διεστηκέναι τοῦ υἱοῦ τὸν πατέρα id.*Jo.*2.23(18; p.80.3; M.14.376B); terminology of Pierius περὶ μὲν πατρὸς καὶ υἱοῦ εὐσεβῶς πρεσβεύει πλὴν ὅτι οὐ. δύο καὶ φύσεις δύο λέγει τῷ τῆς οὐ. καὶ φύσεως ὀνόματι, ὡς δῆλον ἔκ τε τῶν ἑπομένων καὶ προηγουμένων τοῦ χωρίου, ἀντὶ τῆς ὑποστάσεως ...χρώμενος Phot.*cod.*119(M.103.400B); μετὰ τὴν ἄναρχον καὶ ἀγένητον τοῦ θεοῦ...οὐ. ... δευτέραν οὐ. καὶ θείαν δύναμιν...πρώτην...ὑποστᾶσαν κἀκ τοῦ πρώτου αἰτίου γεγεννημένην, εἰσάγουσι, λόγον...αὐτὴν προσαγορεύοντες Eus.*p.e.*7.12(320C; M.21.541B); id.*d.e.*6 proem.(p.251.4; M.22.412C); *ib.*5 proem.(p.202.5; 336A); ἠναγκάσθησαν οἱ πατέρες [i.e. CAnt.(269)]...ἵνα δείξωσιν ὅτι ὁ υἱὸς ὑπόστασιν ἔχει καὶ ὑπάρχων ἐστὶ καὶ ὤν ἐστιν...οὐ. εἰπεῖν καὶ τὸν υἱόν, τὴν διαφορὰν τοῦ τε καθ' ἑαυτὸν ἀνυπάρκτου καὶ τοῦ ὑπάρχοντος τῷ τῆς οὐ. ὀνόματι ἐπιδεικνύντες...παριστῶντες, ὅτι ὁ θεὸς ὤν ἐστιν, καὶ οἱ λόγοι, οὓς λαλεῖ, ὄντες ⟨εἰσίν⟩, ἀλλ' οὐκ οὐσίαι τοῦ θεοῦ, λεκτικαὶ δὲ ἐνέργειαι. ὁ δὲ υἱός, λόγος ὤν, οὐχὶ ἐνέργεια λεκτική ἐστι...ἀλλ' υἱὸς ὢν οὐ. ἐστίν Geo.Laod.*ep.dogm.*ap.Epiph.*haer.*73.12(p.285.6ff.; M.42.428Bf.); Bas.*Eun.*2.17(1.252B; M.29.605B) cit. s. ἐπιτηδειότης; Gr.Nyss.*or.catech.*5(p.21.9; M.45.21A); *ib.*4(p.19.14; 20C); Μάρκελλος καὶ Φωτεῖνος ...τὸν λόγον ἐνέργειαν εἶναί φασι...οὐκ οὐ. ἐνυπόστατον Chrys.*hom.*6.1 *in Phil.*(11.234D); ἡ βούλησις αὕτη τοῦ πατρὸς...πότερόν ποτε οὐ. τίς ἐστι καὶ ὑπέστη αὐτὴ καθ' ἑαυτὴν ἢ οὐχί; εἰ μὲν γὰρ οὐσιώδη καὶ ὑποστατικὴν εἶναι δώσετε... Cyr.*thes.*8(5^1.61B); **2.** claimed for H. Ghost ἔσται δέ τις κατὰ τρίτον...δογματίζων μηδὲ οὐ. τινὰ ἰδίαν ὑφεστάναι τοῦ ἁγίου πνεύματος ἑτέραν παρὰ τὸν πατέρα καὶ τὸν υἱόν Or.*Jo.*2.10(6; p.65.8; M.14.128A); σημαίνει...τοῦτο καὶ οὐ. εἶναι τὸ πνεῦμα· οὐ γὰρ...ἐνέργειά ἐστι θεοῦ οὐκ ἔχον, κατ' αὐτούς, ὑπάρξεως ἰδιότητα id.*fr.37 in Jo.*(p.513.12); Bas.*Spir.*46(3.38E; M.32.152B); cf. τρίτης δὲ ἤδη μετὰ τὴν δευτέραν οὐ. ... τοῦ ἁγίου πνεύματος Eus.*p.e.*7.13(325B; M.21.549B); **3.** Arian terminology ταύτην ἔχομεν τὴν καθολικὴν παράδοσιν...μίαν εἶναι ὑπόστασιν, ἣν αὐτοὶ οἱ αἱρετικοὶ οὐ. προσαγορεύουσι CSard.*ep.cath.*ap.Thdt.*h.e.*2.8.39(3.844); οἱ Ἀρειανοὶ ...ταῖς ὑποστάσεσιν ἐνουσίοις οὔσαις, τὰς οὐ. ἐπεφήμιζον, ταύτῃ τὸ ἑτεροούσιον συμπλέκοντες Leont.B.*arg.Sev.*(M.86.1921A); cf. B.1.c supra.

III. Christol.; **A.** ref. Christ's body as of one *substance* with men's bodies ὁ...λόγος, δι' ἀνθρώπου κατὰ μηδὲν σώματος οὐσίᾳ τὴν ἡμετέραν φύσιν διαλλάττοντος...ἐπιφανείς Eus.*h.e.*1.2.23(M.20.65B); τὸ...σῶμα...κοινὴν ἔχον τοῖς πᾶσι τὴν οὐ. (σῶμα γὰρ ἦν ἀνθρώπινον) Ath.*inc.*20.4(M.25.132A); denied by Gnostics σῶμα...αὐτῷ ὑφαίνεται ἐκ τῆς ἀφανοῦς ψυχικῆς οὐ. Clem.*exc.Thdot.*59(p.126.24; M.9.688B).

B. of Christ's *divinity* as that which he possesses by nature as God ἡγοῦμαι...βασιλέα μὲν λέγεσθαι τὴν προηγουμένην τοῦ πρωτοτόκου πάσης κτίσεως φύσιν...τὸν δὲ ἄνθρωπον, ὃν ἀνείληφεν...υἱὸν τοῦ βασιλέως...μηδεὶς δὲ προσκοπτέτω διακρινόντων ἡμῶν τὰς ἐν τῷ σωτῆρι ἐπινοίας, οἰόμενος καὶ τῇ οὐ. ταὐτὸν ἡμᾶς ποιεῖν Or.*Jo.*1.28(30; p.36.26; M.14.77B); τῇ οὐ. μένων λόγος οὐδὲν...πάσχει id.*Cels.*4.15(p.285.17; M.11.1048A); εἰ δέ τι θεῖον ἐν τῷ κατ' αὐτὸν νοουμένῳ ἀνθρώπῳ ἐτύγχανεν, ὅπερ ἦν ὁ μονογενὴς τοῦ θεοῦ...ἄλλος δήπου ὁ περὶ τούτου καὶ τῆς οὐ. αὐτοῦ λόγος ἐστὶ παρὰ τὸν περὶ τοῦ νοουμένου κατὰ τὸν Ἰησοῦν ἀνθρώπου *ib.*7.16(p.167.27; 1444C); πάσχει μὲν ὁ νεώς, ἡ δὲ ἀκηλίδωτος οὐ. παντάπασιν ἄχραντος τὴν ἀξίαν καθέστηκεν Eust.*fr.in Pr.*8:22(M.18.684C); εἰ καὶ σῶμά μοι ὅμοιον ἀνθρώποις ἦν, ἀλλ' οὐ καὶ τὴν δύναμιν οὐδὲ τὴν οὐ. τοῖς πολλοῖς ὢν ἐμφερής Eus.*d.e.*10.8(p.481.28; M.22.773D); ref. Pr.8:22 οὐ τὴν οὐ., ἀλλὰ τὸ ἀνθρώπινον τοῦ λόγου σημαίνει Ath.*Ar.*2.51(M.26.256A); *ib.*2.11(169A); οὐ τὴν οὐ. τῆς θεότητος αὐτοῦ...ἀλλὰ...τὸ ἀνθρώπινον καὶ τὴν εἰς ἡμᾶς οἰκονομίαν αὐτοῦ...ἡ δὲ τοῦ 'ἔκτισε'...λέξις λεγομένη οὐ πάντως τὴν οὐ. ... σημαίνει

...καὶ οὐ πάντως τὸ λεγόμενον κτίζεσθαι ἤδη καὶ τῇ φύσει καὶ τῇ οὐ. κτίσμα ἐστί *ib.*2.45(241Cf.); ὅτε ὅλον ἄνθρωπος καλεῖται, μή τις ἀρνήσηται τὴν θείαν οὐ. Apoll.*corp.et div.*4(p.186.16; M.*PL*.8.873C); id.*quod un.Chr.*11(p.302.2; M.28.129D); Gr.Nyss.*Eun.*6(2 p.134.14; M.45.717D); οὐ γὰρ διὰ τοῦτο ἔλαβε κρίσιν ὅτι ἄνθρωπός ἐστιν...ἀλλ' ἐπειδὴ τῆς ἀρρήτου οὐ. ἐκείνης ἐστὶν υἱός Chrys.*hom.39.3 in Jo.*(8.230A); τὸ δὲ ἱερὸν σκεῦος ὡς θεοῦ οὐ. τιμᾶται, καθὸ καὶ ἡνώθη σκεύει ἡ θεία οὐ. κατὰ τὴν σάρκωσιν Proc.G.*Num.*3:45(M.87.801B).

C. of human *nature* assumed by Christ, cf.Clem.*exc.Thdot.*19 (p.113.12f.; M.9.668B) cit. s. δραστήριος; καθὸ ἄνθρωπος τὴν ἀνθρωπείαν οὐ. συμπλέξας θεότητι Mac.Mgn.*apocr.*2.20(p.40.16); ἐγεννήθη ἐκ τῆς ἡμετέρας οὐ. Chrys.*hom.82.5 in Mt.*(7.788C); ὑποστάσει...ὁ λόγος λέγεται παθεῖν· προσελάβετο γὰρ παθητὴν οὐ. εἰς τὴν ἑαυτοῦ ὑπόστασιν ...καὶ τὰ τῆς οὐ. κατηγορήματα εἰώθει τῆς ὑποστάσεως κατηγορεῖσθαι ὀρθῶς Leont.H.*Nest.*7.9(M.86.1768^{h}A); οὐκ ἀποθέμενος μὲν [sc. at Transfiguration] τὴν οὐ. τὴν δουλικήν· φαιδρύνας δὲ αὐτὴν τοῖς θεϊκοῖς ἰδιώμασι Anast.Ant.*serm.*1.4(M.89.1368B).

D. ref. Person of Christ; **1.** Apollinarian: one οὐ. of Christ οὐκ ἐν δύο οὐ. ἀλλ' ἐν μιᾷ Apoll.*fr.*158(p.249.29)ap.Justn.*monoph.*(p.39.22; M.86.1140C); μία...ἡ προσκύνησις τοῦ Χριστοῦ...οὐκ ἄρα ἄλλη καὶ ἄλλη οὐ. θεὸς καὶ ἄνθρωπος, ἀλλὰ μία κατὰ σύνθεσιν θεοῦ πρὸς σῶμα ἀνθρώπινον Apoll.*fr.*119(p.236.26; M.86.1125C); *ib.*117(p.236.1)ap. CCP(681)*act.*10(H.3.1248D); οὐ γὰρ αὐτοῦ κατὰ μὲν τὸ ἀόρατον ἡ θεότης, κατὰ δὲ τὸ ὁρατὸν ἡ σάρξ id.*fid.inc.*7(p.199.18; M.*PL*.8.877C); **2.** orthodox: natures of Christ as two, either explicitly or by implication θεὸς...ὢν ὁμοῦ τε καὶ ἄνθρωπος τέλειος ὁ αὐτὸς τὰς δύο αὐτοῦ οὐ. ἐπιστώσατο ἡμῖν Mel.*fr.*6(p.310; M.5.1221A); τῶν...οὐ. αὐτοῦ ἡ μέν ἐστιν ἄναρχος...ἡ δὲ ἐν χρόνῳ γέγονε...ποιηθεῖσα ὑπὸ τοῦ δημιουργοῦ δι' ἀγαθότητα ‡Ath.*fr.*ap.*Doct.Patr.*2(p.11.15); τοὺς... λέγοντας...τὰς δύο οὐ. τοῦ Χριστοῦ κατὰ ἀνάκρασιν συγχυθείσας μίαν γεγενῆσθαι οὐ., καὶ μὴ ὁμολογοῦντας τὸν...Χριστὸν δύο εἶναι οὐσίας ἀσυγχύτους, ἓν δὲ πρόσωπον...τούτους ἀναθεματίζει ἡ...ἐκκλησία Ambr.*fr.*ap.Doct.*Patr.*2(p.15.17ff.)et ap.Thdt.*eran.*2(4.141 reading throughout φύσις for οὐ.); Bas.*Eun.*1.18(1.230Af.; M.29.552C) cit. s. ἀνθρωπότης; λέγεται...παρὰ...τοῖς Εὐνομιανοῖς, ἡνῶσθαι τὸν θεὸν λόγον τῷ σώματι, οὐ κατ' οὐσίαν, ἀλλὰ κατὰ τὰς ἑκατέρου δυνάμεις. οὐ γὰρ εἶναι τὰς οὐ., τὰς ἑνωθείσας ἢ κραθείσας, ἀλλὰ τὰς δυνάμεις τοῦ σώματος ταῖς δυνάμεσι ταῖς θείαις συγκεκρᾶσθαι...βελτίον...κατὰ τὴν οἰκείαν φύσιν τῶν ἀσωμάτων ἀσυγχύτως τὴν ἕνωσιν γίνεσθαι τῶν οὐ. Nemes.*nat.hom.*3(M.40.605Af.); κοινὰ...τῶν δύο οὐ. τὰ ὀνόματα [sc. Χριστός, υἱός, Ἰησοῦς, κύριος] ‡Chrys.*ep.Caes.*(3.743D); Gel.Cyz.*h.e.* 2.19.25(M.85.1280D) cit. s. διαφορά; τέλειος ἐν ἀμφοτέραις ταῖς οὐ. ὁ Χριστός· ὁμοούσιος τῷ θεῷ καὶ πατρὶ καὶ ὁμοούσιος τῇ παρθένῳ καὶ μητρί Cyriacus Paphius ap.Leont.B.*Nest.et Eut.*1(M.86.1312C); **3.** Nestorian τῆς ἀπαθοῦς καὶ παθητῆς οὐ. ἐν μοναδικῷ προσώπῳ Nest.*ep.Cyr.*2(p.30.12; M.77.52B); **4.** against Nestorians σύνθετον μέν, κατ' οὐσίαν τὴν αὐτοῦ πρὸς τὴν ἡμετέραν οὐ. φαμὲν τὸν λόγον· καὶ ὡς μέρος τοῦ συνθέτου ὅλου Χριστοῦ διαστέλλομεν· σύνθετον δὲ οὐ., ἀπὸ τῆς αὐτοῦ τε καὶ τῆς ἡμετέρας, οὐ φαμέν ποτε Leont.H.*Nest.*1.10 (M.86.1444D); ἔχει [sc. ὁ λόγος]...τὴν σάρκα...εἰς οὐ. τὴν ὡς μίαν τῶν τῆς ὑποστάσεως αὐτοῦ, τοῦ καὶ διουσίου ὄντος Χριστοῦ *ib.*1.24(1492B); **5.** against monophysites ἄλλο...ἐστι τὸ ἀναπληροῦσθαι οὐ. ἐκ δύο μερῶν, καὶ ἄλλο τὸ ἑνοῦσθαι δύο οὐ. †Ath.*fr.*(M.26.1233B); ἀδύνατον τὰς δύο οὐ. γενέσθαι μίαν *ib.*(1237B); ἀμφοτέρας τε καὶ δι' ἀμφοῖν καὶ ἄμφω, φύσεις τε καὶ οὐ., οὔσας τε καὶ φυλαττομένας Leont.B. *Nest.et Eut.*1(M.86.1308C); *ib.*(1281D); ἡ αὐτὴ...ὑπόστασις τοὺς ὅρους τῶν δύο φύσεων ἐπιδέχεται· καὶ ὃν δ' ἂν λόγον ἀποδῷ τις τῆς θεότητος, τὸν αὐτὸν εὑρίσκει καὶ ἐπὶ τοῦ Χριστοῦ· καὶ ὃν δ' ἂν ἀποδῷ τῆς ἀνθρωπότητος, τὸν αὐτὸν εὑρίσκει καὶ ἐπὶ τῆς οὐ. τοῦ Χριστοῦ κατ' οὐσίαν ἁρμόζοντα †Leont.B.*sect.*7.8(M.86.1249C); πῶς ἄνευ προσθέσεως ἢ λείψεως ἢ ἀλλοιώσεως φύσεως τὸ κατ' ἀριθμὸν ποσὸν τῶν ἡνωμένων φύσεων πλέον ἢ ἔλαττον φανήσεται, ἵνα ἢ τρεῖς ἢ μίαν τὰς οὐ., δύο οὔσας, μεταποιήσῃ; Leont.H.*monoph.*7(M.86.1773B); ἐπεὶ οὖν καὶ οὐσιώδης μὲν τοῖς συνελθοῦσιν ἡ διαφορά, ἐπίκτητος δὲ ταῖς οὐ. ἡ ἕνωσις, καλῶς τὰς μὲν οὐ. τῷ ἰδίῳ αὐτῶν λόγῳ διακρίναντες δύο φαμέν, ἤγουν τῇ διαφορᾷ· τὸ δὲ πρόσωπον, αὐταῖς ἐν τῇ ἑνώσει δοξάζομεν *ib.*30 (1788C); ἡ αὐτὴ φύσις ἤγουν οὐ. κτιστὴ καὶ ἄκτιστος; Pamph.H. *panopl.*11.1(p.639); διπλοῦν τὴν φύσιν, ἤτοι τὴν οὐ. Max.*ep.*12(M.91.468C); ‡Gr.Nyss.*hom.7.154 in Jo.*(p.279.18); *Lit.Jac.*(*NBP* 10^{2} p.37) cit. s. διαιρέω; divine and human elements as οὐσίαι opp. ὑποστάσεις: τίνα τρόπον τοῦ τε θεοῦ λόγου, καὶ τῆς κατ' αὐτὸν ἀνθρωπότητος...οὐχ ὑποστάσεις, ἀλλ' οὐσίας, εἰς τὴν τῶν ἑνωθέντων συνδρομήν, οἱ πατέρες παραλαμβάνουσιν Leont.B.*arg.Sev.*(M.86.1936C); εἰ οὖν τις ἐνυποστάτους κατὰ τοῦτον τὸν λόγον εἴποι τὰς οὐ., ὅ ἐστιν ὑπαρχούσας οὐδὲ ἡμεῖς ἀρνηθείημεν...τὴν δὲ ὑπόστασιν [sc. φημί] ἰδικῶς, ὅταν μετὰ τῶν καθόλου καὶ ἰδικόν τι ἔχοι. οὐ κατὰ τοῦτο οὖν φαμεν τὴν ἡμετέραν ἐν Χριστῷ οὐ. ἐνυπόστατον εἶναι, οἷον ὑπόστασιν καθ' ἑαυτὴν...οὖσαν Eulog.*fr.dogm.*(M.86.2953Bf.); and opp. συμβεβηκότα: τίνα δὲ ταῦτά [sc. τὰ διαφέροντα ἐν Χριστῷ] ἐστιν εἰσπραττόμενοι, θεότητα καὶ ἀνθρωπότητα ὀνομάσοιτε ὡς οἶμαι· τί δὲ τάδε...εἴπερ μὴ εἴη ποιά, ἢ ποσά, ἢ σχέσεις, ἤ τι τοιόνδε, οὐ. ὁμολογήσοιτε πάντως· δύο ἄρα οὐ. λέγειν ὑμᾶς...ἐπὶ Χριστῷ σαφῶς συνάγεται Leont.H.*monoph.*17(M.86.1780A); Max.*opusc.*(M.91.41A); **6.** against monothelites τὰς ἑκατέρας φυσικῶς οὐ. εἰργάζετο κατὰ τὴν ἑκατέρᾳ προσοῦσαν οὐσιώδη ποιότητα, ἢ καὶ φυσικὴν ἰδιότητα Sophr.H.*ep.syn.*(M.87.3168B); τέλειον τὸν αὐτὸν κατὰ πάντα θεὸν ὁμοῦ καὶ ἄνθρωπον...θείαν ὁμοῦ καὶ ἀνθρωπίνην ἔχειν κυρίως οὐ. καὶ θέλησιν καὶ ἐνέργειαν Max.*opusc.* (M.91.80B); φρονησάντων [sc. at CCP(681)] ἓν θέλημα καὶ μίαν ἐνεργείαν ἐπὶ τῶν δύο οὐ. τοῦ Χριστοῦ *CIG* 8964 [Bethlehem].

E. for union of natures as ἕνωσις κατ' οὐσίαν, v. ἕνωσις; cf. τὴν... συνάφειαν ἑτέρως πρὸς τὴν σοφίαν νοεῖ, κατὰ μάθησιν καὶ μετουσίαν, οὐχὶ ⟨κατ'⟩ οὐ. οὐσιωμένην ἐν σώματι Paul.Sam.*fr.*B 13(p.333); ἀληθῆ τῶν πραγμάτων κατ' οὐ. γεγενῆσθαι τὴν σύνοδον λέγειν οὐκ ἀνεχόμενος [sc. Nestorius] Max.*opusc.*(M.91.41D).

IV. eucharistic: of *substance* of bread remaining after consecration, cf. *dignus habitus dominici corporis appellatione, etiamsi natura panis in ipso permansit, et non duo corpora, sed unum corpus filii praedicamus*, ‡Chrys.*ep.Caes.*(3.744C); μετὰ τὸν ἁγιασμὸν τὰ μυστικὰ σύμβολα...μένει...ἐπὶ τῆς προτέρας οὐ. καὶ τοῦ σχήματος, καὶ τοῦ εἴδους, καὶ ὁρατά ἐστι, καὶ ἁπτά...νοεῖται δὲ ἅπερ ἐγένετο Thdt.*eran.*2(4.126).

V. ref. union of man with the divine ὁ δίκαιος...λέγεται...πρὸς τὸν Χριστὸν εἶναι ἕν...οὐκ ἔστιν ὃς μὲν οὐ. ὑποδεεστέρας...καὶ ἐλάττονος, Χριστὸς δὲ θειοτέρας καὶ...μακαριωτέρας; Or.*dial.*3(p.126.5); ἵνα... ὦμεν...οἱ πάντες εἷς, ἑνωθέντες αὐτοῦ τῇ θεότητι...οὐ κατὰ συναλοιφὴν μιᾶς οὐ. κατὰ δὲ τελείωσιν τῆς...ἀρετῆς Eus.*e.th.*3.18(p.179.30; M.24.1041C); ref. Mt.12:49f. συντίκτεται μετ' ἐμοῦ οὐκ ἐν ὑποστάσεως οὐ. γενόμενος ἀλλ' ἐν θελήματος ἑνούμενος χάριτι Mac.Mgn.*apocr.*2.8 (p.11.3).

οὐσιακός, = οὐσιώδης, *real, essential*; of the hypostatic union, Leont.H.*Nest.*1.46(M.86.1505A).

***οὐσιαρχία, ἡ**, *source of being*, Dion.Ar.*d.n.*5.1(M.3.816B).

***οὐσιαστής, ὁ**, *author of essence* οὐ. καὶ φυσικὸς εἰδοποιός Leont.H. *Nest.*1.52(M.86.1524A).

***οὐσιοποι-έω**, *make a reality of*, of idolaters ὡς θεοποιούντων ἤτοι ~ούντων τὰ μακρὰν ἀπέχοντα τῇ φύσει ἀπὸ τῶν πρωτοτύπων Thdr. Stud.*epp.*2.167(M.99.1532A).

οὐσιοποιός, **1.** *bestowing being* or *essence*, of God ταῖς πρώταις οὐσίαις, αἱ μετὰ τὴν ὁ. αὐτῶν θεαρχίαν ἱδρυμέναι Dion.Ar.*c.h.*7.2(M.3.208A); id.*d.n.*1.4(M.3.592A); *ib.*2.7(645A); ‡Gr.Nyss.*hom.2 in Jo.* (p.120.10); **2.** *determinative of essence* αἱ οὐ. ἰδιότητες τὴν φύσιν τοῦ ὑποκειμένου δηλοῦσιν, αἷς προστιθέμενον τὸ ἰδίως ἀφοριστικὸν ἑκάστου τὴν ὑπόστασιν τοῦ τινος χαρακτηρίζει Leont.B.*arg.Sev.*(M.86.1928C).

οὐσιότης, ἡ, *quality of being* ἐκεῖνα [sc. θύρα, ὁδός κτλ.] καταχρηστικῶς εἴρηται, οὐδὲν εἰς τὴν θεότητα τοῦ υἱοῦ ἐνσκήπτοντα, οὔτε ἐλλιπῆ ποιούμενα πρὸς τὸν πατέρα τῆς αὐτοῦ οὐ. Epiph.*haer.*69.35 (p.183.22; M.42.256D).

οὐσι-όω, *invest with being*;

A. in gen.; **1.** *give substance to, cause to exist as a substance* ἣν [sc. τὴν ὕλην]...ὁ τεχνίτης...ἐμόρφωσε, καὶ εἰς τάξιν ἤγαγε, καὶ οὕτω δι' αὐτῆς ~ωσε τὰ ὁρώμενα Bas.*hex.*2.2(1.13B; M.29.32A); pass.; **a.** *become a substance* ὁ...Πλάτων...τῷ εἴδει...ἀρχὴν ἰδίαν...δεδωκώς, καὶ καθ' ἑαυτὸ ~ῶσθαι ἀποφήσας ‡Just.*coh.Gr.*7(M.6.256A); **b.** *be fulfilled* or *realized* μετὰ τὸν προορισμὸν τὴν πρόθεσιν γίνεσθαι· ὥστε οἷον κατὰ μὲν τὰ ἐννοήματα τοῦ θεοῦ γίνεσθαι τὸν προορισμόν, κατὰ δὲ ταῦτα ἤδη τὴν περὶ ὧν προώρισε πρόθεσιν ~ωμένων πως ἐπακολουθεῖν καὶ εἰς ἔργον ἐρχομένων τοῦ προορισμοῦ Or.*comm.in Eph.*1:9(p.241); Gr.Nyss.*Eun.*1(1 p.136.22; M.45.376A); **2.** *invest with existence*, esp. of God as Creator τὰ λογικὰ...μετὰ τὸ ~ωθῆναι καὶ εἶναι δέχονται τὸ κτισθῆναι Or.*Apoc.*26(p.32); Ath.*gent.*41(M.25.84A); ~οῖ τὰ μὴ ὄντα, τὰ κτισθέντα συνέχει Bas.*Spir.*19(3.16D; M.32.101B); Gr.Agr.*Eccl.*6.2 (M.98.981B); Max.*carit.*4.4(M.90.1048D); τὰ ~ωθέντα ὑπ' αὐτοῦ νοητά Max.*schol.c.h.*13.3(M.4.97B); of H. Ghost πνεῦμα ἅγιον...δι' αὐτοῦ [sc. τοῦ υἱοῦ] κτίζον καὶ ~οῦν τὰ σύμπαντα ‡Cyr.*Trin.*9(6^{3}.13D; M.77.1140B); of Christ τὴν...θείαν ἐνέργειαν· ᾗ τὸ πᾶν ὁ Χριστὸς ~ώσας, καθὸ νοεῖται θεός, συνέχει κρατούμενον ‡Hipp.*Ber.Hel.*8(M.10.837D)ap.*Doct.Patr.*44(p.325.18); met. 'ἀρχὴν τῆς ὑποστάσεως' τὴν πίστιν, δι' ἧς ὑπέστημεν καὶ γεγενήμεθα καὶ ~ώθημεν Chrys.*hom.6.2 in Heb.*(12.64B); **3.** *invest with a particular character* or *specific essence*, Or.*Jo.*20.24(20; p.357.35; M.14.625C); pass., *derive one's substance, be constituted, inhere* ἐπειδὴ πᾶσα κίνησις ἀπό τινός ἐστι δυνάμεως, τίς ἡ δύναμις αὕτη, καὶ τίνι ~ωται; Nemes.*nat.hom.*2(M.40.

540B); τὸν μὲν ἐκ τῆς ἀγεννησίας τὸν δὲ ἐκ τῆς γεννήσεως ~ῶσθαι λέγων Gr.Nyss.*Eun.*1(1 p.203.13; M.45.449D); ὁ σοφὸς...πραγματεύεται περὶ νόησιν, ᾗ τὸ θεῖον ~ωται Synes.*insomn.*1(p.145.17; M.66.1284C); *ib.*7(p.155.19; 1292D); id.*calv.*7(p.204.14; M.66.1180D); exeg. Gal.3:13 οὐ τοῦτό φησιν, ὅτι ἡ οὐσία αὐτοῦ, τῆς οἰκείας ἀποστᾶσαν δόξης, εἰς κατάραν ~ώθη Chrys.*hom.11.2 in Jo.*(8.64B); Thdt.*eran.*1(4.47); **4.** pass., *assume a particular character* or *essence*; met., *make oneself one with, share the lot of,* Geo.Pis.*carm.*4.91(p.13).

B. Trin.; **1.** mentally *invest with substantive existence, attribute personality to,* Gr.Naz.*or.*31.32(p.188.1; M.36.169B) cit. s. ἐνυπάρχω; pass., *have substantive existence, exist as a Person* λόγον...ἤτοι οὐ κεχωρισμένον τοῦ πατρὸς καὶ κατὰ τοῦτο τῷ μὴ ὑφεστάναι οὐδὲ υἱὸν τυγχάνοντα ἢ καὶ κεχωρισμένον καὶ ~ωμένον Or.*Jo.*1.24(23; p.29.30; M.14.65B); εἰ ὁ πατὴρ ὑποκειμένου καὶ οὐσιώδους ἐστὶ πατήρ, λέγεται δὲ καὶ τῆς δόξης πατήρ. δηλονότι ἡ δόξα ὑποκείμενόν τί ἐστι καὶ ~ωμένον id.*comm.in Eph.*1:15(p.398); *ib.*1:1(p.235); ὁ δέ γε τοῦ θεοῦ λόγος καθ' ἑαυτὸν ~ωταί τε καὶ ὑφέστηκεν Eus.*d.e.*5.1(p.213.20; M.22.353C); *ib.*4.3(p.153.4; 256A); εἰκὼν ἄρα ἐστὶν ὁ...λόγος, ζῶσα σοφία, ὑποστατική, λόγος ἐνεργὴς καὶ υἱός, αὐτὴ ~ωμένη Acac.Caes.*fr.Marcell.*ap.Epiph.*haer.*72.7(p.262.16; M.42.392D); οὐκ ἐν τοῖς γενομένοις ἡ τοῦ θεοῦ βούλησις ~ωμένη φαίνεται Cyr.*thes.*7(5[1].51E); **2.** pass., *be existent, possess being* θεοῦ λόγον προόντα καὶ πρὸ αἰώνων ἁπάντων ~ωμένον Eus.*h.e.*1.3.19(M.20.76A); οὐδὲ γὰρ ἐξ οὐσίας τῆς ἀγενήτου κατά τι πάθος ἢ διαίρεσιν ~ωμένος id.*d.e.*5.1(p.213.27; M.22.353D); ὁ θεὸς...ὑπερουσίως ~ωται Max.*schol.c.h.*13.3(M.4.97B); **3.** pass., *derive from the essence* οὐ γὰρ...ἀπόβλητον ἔχει [sc. ὁ υἱός] τὴν ἀρχὴν ἀλλὰ φύσει καὶ ~ωμένην Chrys.*hom.3.3 in Jo.*(8.21B).

C. Christol.; **1.** *invest with substance* ὁ θεὸς λόγος...ἐνυπόστατόν τι μέρος λαβὼν τῆς ἐκείνης [sc. BMV] φύσεως καὶ εἰς τὴν ἰδίαν ὑπόστασιν ~ώσας Pamph.H.*panopl.*7.3(p.625); pass. θεοῦ δ' ὅλου μέτεσχεν ἀνθρώπου φύσις, οὐχ ὡς προφήτης ἤ τις ἄλλος ἔνθεων ὃς οὐ θεοῦ μετέσχε, τῶν θεοῦ δέ γε, ἀλλ' ~ωθεὶς Gr.Naz.*carm.*2.1.11.645(M.37.1073A); **2.** *invest with an* [other] *essence* ὦ ἀνθρωπότης, ἡ τὸν τοῦ θεοῦ λόγον σωματικῶς ~ώσασα Amph.*hom.*1.4(M.39.41A); pass., *assume an* [other] *essence* τὴν δὲ συνάφειαν ἑτέρως πρὸς τὴν σοφίαν νόει, κατὰ μάθησιν καὶ μετουσίαν, οὐχὶ οὐσίαν ~ωμένην ἐν σώματι Paul.Sam.*fr.*B 13(p.333.27; M.86.1393B); οὐ δίδως ~ῶσθαι ἐν τῷ ὅλῳ σωτῆρι τὸν υἱὸν τὸν μονογενῆ τὸν...ἀϊδίως ὑπάρχοντα Malch.*fr.*(p.337.9); τὸ καθ' ἡμᾶς ἐξ ἡμῶν ὁλικῶς...~ωθῆναι τὸν ὑπερούσιον λόγον Dion.Ar.*d.n.*2.6(M.3.644C); *ib.*2.9(648A); ἄνθρωπος ἀληθῶς...ἐκ τῆς τῶν ἀνθρώπων οὐσίας ὁ ὑπερούσιος ~ωμένος id.*ep.*4(M.3.1072B); ἐν...τῇ οἰκονομίᾳ ὡς κατὰ τὴν οὐσίαν ὅλην ~ωθεὶς ἄνθρωπος λέγεται [sc. Logos] Max.*schol.epp.Dion.Ar.*4(M.4.532B); id.*ambig.*(M.91.1048B); οὐκ αὐθυπόστατον φανεῖσαν [sc. the manhood]...ἀλλ' ἐν αὐτῷ τῷ κατ' ἀλήθειαν αὐτὴν ~ωθέντι θεῷ λόγῳ τὸ εἶναι λαβοῦσαν *ib.*(1052B); Jo.D.*f.o.*3.11(M.94.1025C); **3.** pass., *be made* a particular substance οἱ...τῆς ἀπὸ σώματος εἰς θεότητα μεταβολῆς...πραγματευόμενοι· οἱ...λέγοντες...τὴν σάρκα εἰς λόγον ~ωθῆναι Thdt.*rect.conf.*15(M.6.1233B); cf. exeg. Gal.3:13 s. A.3.

οὐσιώδης, *essential*;

A. in gen.; **1.** *of existence, of being* οὗ [sc. τοῦ ἀγαθοῦ] ἐφίεται πάντα, τὰ μὲν νοερὰ...γνωστικῶς, τὰ δὲ αἰσθητικὰ αἰσθητικῶς...τὰ δὲ ἄζωα καὶ μόνον ὄντα, τῇ πρὸς μόνην τὴν οὐ. μέθεξιν ἐπιτηδειότητι Dion.Ar.*d.n.*4.4(M.3.700B); **2.** *having ultimate reality, ultimate, real* ἡ αὐτοαλήθεια ἡ οὐ. καὶ...πρωτότυπος τῆς ἐν ταῖς λογικαῖς ψυχαῖς ἀληθείας Or.*Jo.*6.6(3; p.114.22; M.14.209D); τὸν σοφὸν κατὰ μετοχὴν τῆς οὐ. σοφίας, οὐκ αὐτὸν σοφίαν ὄντα Meth.*creat.*3(p.495.29; M.18.336A); Ath.*Ar.*2.28(M.26.208A); ὁ...θεὸς λόγος σοφία ὑπάρχων οὐ. Nil.*epp.*1.205(M.79.160A); οὐ. καὶ φυσικὴν ἀγαθότητα ‡Gr.Nyss.*hom.3.2 in Jo.*(p.135.19); **3.** *proper to the essence, intrinsic* ἐνέργειά ἐστι φυσική, ὁ πάσης φύσεως οὐ. καὶ γνωστικὸς λόγος Alex.Al.*ep.Aegl.*(M.18.584A); οὐκ ἔστι καθ' ἑαυτὴν ἰδεῖν ψυχὴν οὐ. καλήν, οὕτω πεφυκυῖαν καὶ οὖσαν Serap.*Man.*5(p.31; M.40.904C); οὐ. διαφορὰ Gr.Nyss.*comm.not.*(M.45.185A); ἐν τοῖς οὐ. οὐ παραλαμβάνεται προαίρεσις. οὐδεὶς γὰρ λέγει προαιρετικῶς ζῷον εἶναι, ἢ λίθον· ταῦτα γὰρ οὐ. Didym.*Man.*12(M.39.1100D); Epiph.*anc.*66(p.79.22; M.43.136A); esp. of qualities, characteristics, properties οὔτε γὰρ ἀκτίς, οὔτε φῶς, ἄλλος ἥλιος, ἀλλ' ἡλιακαί τινες ἀπόρροιαι, καὶ ποιότητες οὐ. Gr.Naz.*or.*31.32(p.188.4; M.36.169B); Cyr.*Jo.*1.1(4.12C); Leont.B.*Nest.et Eut.*1(M.86.1277D) cit. s. ἐπουσιώδης; οὐ. ... ποιότητας, ἐν μὲν ψυχῇ, τὸ λογικόν· ἐν δὲ πυρί, τὸ θερμὸν καὶ ξηρόν...ταῦτα συμπληρωτικά εἰσιν, εἴτουν συστατικὰ τῆς ὑποκειμένης αὐτοῖς φύσεως ἤγουν οὐσίας, ὅθεν καὶ τῆς τοιαύτης ἔτυχον ὀνομασίας Pamph.H.*panopl.*2.2(p.602); Sophr.H.*ep.syn.*(M.87.3148B); with φυσικός: οὗτος [sc. ἄνθρωπος] ὁ οὐ. καὶ φυσικός Chrys.*hom.13.2 in Eph.*(11.97D); Cyr.*thes.*13(5[1].128D); cf. id.*Pulch.*57(p.60.7; 5[2].178A) cit. s. εἰσκεκριμένως; ‡Gr.Nyss.*hom.1.44 in Jo.*(p.108.25); Jo.D.*Man.*1.10(M.94.1513C); v. B and C infra; opp. ἐκ μετουσίας, κατὰ μετοχήν, or similar expressions εἰ ἦν ἐκ μετουσίας καὶ αὐτὸς καὶ μὴ ἐξ αὐτοῦ οὐ. θεότης καὶ εἰκών Ath.*syn.*51(p.274.30; M.26.784B); εἰ...ἐπείσακτον ἤτοι κατὰ μετοχήν, καὶ οὐκ οὐσιῶδες ἔχει τὸ εἶναι ζωή Cyr.*thes.*14(5[1].143E); Proc.G.*Is.*49:7(M.87.2469B); **4.** *concerned with essence* or *being,* ref. knowledge, *of essences* κατὰ τὴν οὐ. αὐτοῦ θεογνωσίαν καὶ κατάληψιν Clem.*fr.*42(p.221.2; M.9.768C); πάντα οἶδε τὰ ὄντα [sc. ὁ θεός]...οὐ. γάρ ἐστι γνῶσις, καὶ πάντας ὁμοίως ἐπίσταται Proc.G.*Ex.*33:17(M.87.673A); id.*Dt.*18:11(M.87.917D); **5.** *existing as a substance, with real existence* σκότος...παρακολούθημα μόνον ἐστίν, οὐ μὴν δημιουργήματος τρόπον οὐσιῶδες κατεσκεύασται Tit.Bost.*Man.*2.17(M.18.1168D); καπνὸς...οὐκ ἔστι...ἐν ὑποστάσει ἰδίᾳ, οὐδὲ οὐ. αὐτοῦ καὶ σεσωματωμένη ἡ φύσις ἡ τοῦ καπνοῦ †Bas.*Is.*289(1.598E; M.30.625A); ἐνύπαρκτόν...ἐστι τὸ οὐσιώδους καὶ φυσικῆς μετέχον ὑπάρξεως Max.*opusc.*(M.91.205B); *concrete, actual* πνεύματος ἁγίου οὐ. ἐπιφοίτησις αὐτῷ [sc. Christ] ἐγίνετο Cyr.H.*catech.*21.1; ἱεροφόρε σκίμπου...τὸ ὑπ' αὐτοῦ κτισθὲν εἰς τὴν οὐ. ... ἐνοίκησιν τῆς αὐτοῦ σαρκώσεως Mod.*dorm.*(M.86.3309A); *personal, in person* ὅταν κατὰ οὐ. συμβολὴν τῇ ψυχῇ καὶ τῷ σατανᾷ ἡ μάχη γένηται Diad.*perf.*87(p.120.19); **6.** *true, genuine* τὸν δαίμονα...εἰς λογισμὸν μορφοῦντα τὸν νοῦν κοῦφον γνωμόνως πρὸς τὸν ἀναπλασμὸν τῆς θείας καὶ οὐ. γνώσεως Evagr.Pont.*or.*73(M.79.1184A); τὸν οὐ. λόγον...εἴπομεν Mac.Mgn.*apocr.*2.17(p.28.3).

B. Trin.; **1.** *substantial*; **a.** *proper to essence, intrinsic,* Ath.*syn.*51(p.274.30; M.26.784B); ref. Phil.2:6 ἐκ φύσεως ἴσος ἦν, καὶ οὐ. εἶχεν τὴν εὐγένειαν Isid.Pel.*epp.*4.22(M.78.1072B); πῶς...οὐκ ἂν εἶεν ἀλλήλοις ὁμοφυῆ τὰ τῆς αὐτῆς ὄντα φύσεως τε καὶ οὐ. ἐνεργείας; Cyr.*thes.*32(5[1].293B); **b.** *in terms of essence* ἡ αὐτὴ ἐν τοῖς τρισὶ νοουμένη οὐ. θεότης ‡Bas.*struct.hom.*1.3(1.325E; M.30.13C); ἐν οὐ. ταυτότητι ‡Gr.Nyss.*hom.6.1 in Jo.*(p.204.8); *ib.*6.8(p.206.3); μιᾷ καὶ ἑνιαίᾳ θεότητι, καὶ τῷ ταὐτῷ τῆς οὐ. τε καὶ φυσικῆς θεότητος Sophr.H.*ep.syn.*(M.87.3153D); **2.** *really existing*; *substantive*; *personal,* Or.*comm.in Eph.*1:15ff.(p.398) cit. s. οὐσιόω; λόγον...θεῖον, ἀσώματον, καὶ οὐ. Eus.*p.e.*11.23(546E; M.21.909B); οὐ. λόγον ζῶντα καὶ ὑφεστῶτα id.*e.th.*1.20(p.87.28; M.24.877A); οὐχ...ἁπλῶς φωνὴ σημαντική, ἀλλὰ οὐ. λόγος καὶ οὐ. σοφία...ἐξ οὐσίας οὐ. καὶ ἐνούσιος ‡Ath.*Ar.*4.1(p.44.18f.; M.26.468C); ὥσπερ...μία οὐσία ἡ ἀρχή, οὕτως εἷς οὐ. καὶ ὑφεστὼς ὁ ταύτης λόγος καὶ ἡ σοφία· ὡς γὰρ ἐκ θεοῦ θεός ἐστι...οὕτως ἐξ ὑποστάσεως ὑπόστατος καὶ ἐξ οὐσίας οὐ. καὶ ἐνούσιος καὶ ἐξ ὄντος ὤν. ἐπεὶ εἰ μὴ οὐ. σοφία καὶ ἐνούσιος λόγος καὶ ὢν υἱός, ἀλλ' ἁπλῶς σοφία καὶ λόγος καὶ υἱὸς ἐν τῷ πατρί, εἴη ἂν αὐτὸς ὁ πατὴρ σύνθετος *ib.*4.1f.(p.45.1ff.; 469A); *ib.*4.3(p.47.4; 472C); οὐσίας καὶ βουλῆς καὶ δυνάμεως καὶ δόξης εἰκόνα λέγομεν, οὐκ ἄψυχον καὶ νεκράν, ἀλλ' οὐ. καὶ βουλητικὴν καὶ δυνατὴν καὶ ἔνδοξον Acac.Caes.*fr.Marcell.*ap.Epiph.*haer.*72.7(p.262.11; M.42.392C); δύναμιν οὐ. αὐτὴν ἐφ' ἑαυτῆς ἐν ἰδιαζούσῃ ὑποστάσει θεωρουμένην Gr.Nyss.*or.catech.*2(p.15.2; M.45.17C); cf.id.*Eun.*1(1 p.93.24; M.45.325C); βασιλεὺς μὲν γὰρ ὁ υἱός· βασιλεία δὲ ζῶσα καὶ οὐ. καὶ ἐνυπόστατος τὸ πνεῦμα id. *Maced.*16(M.45.1321A); τὸ 'θεὸς ἦν ὁ λόγος' συνιστᾷ τὸ οὐ. εἶναι τὸν λόγον Didym.*Trin.*1.15(M.39.300B); τὸ οὐ. καὶ ἐνυπόστατον θεῖον γέννημα Epiph.*haer.*76.19(p.365.8; M.42.553A); οὐ. ἡ τοῦ γεννήματος ὕπαρξις Cyr.*dial.Trin.*2(5[1].453D); ὁ δέ γε υἱὸς τὴν ἐκ πατρὸς ὕπαρξιν οὐ. τε καὶ φυσικὴν κατασημήνειεν ἂν id.*Pulch.*8(p.29.30; 5[2].133C); οὐ. καὶ ὑποστατικὴν id.*thes.*8(5[1].61B); πατὴρ λόγον γεννήσας...οὐ. τε καὶ ἐνυπόστατον, καὶ τῆς αὐτῆς οὐσίας αὐτῷ Zach.Mit.*opif.*(M.85.1116C); τῆς ἐνυποστάτου καὶ οὐ. ἀληθείας Χριστοῦ τοῦ θεαρχικοῦ λόγου ‡Gr.Nyss.*hom.5.2 in Jo.*(p.174.10); τῆς ἐνυποστάτου καὶ οὐ. ἀληθείας Χριστοῦ *ib.*5.5(p.175.22); ὁ λόγος ὁ ἐνυπόστατος, ἡ οὐ. καὶ τελεία καὶ ζῶσα εἰκὼν τοῦ...θεοῦ ‡Cyr.*Trin.*7(6[3].9B; M.77.1132D) = Jo.D.*f.o.*1.8(M.94.812A); Jo.D.*Man.*1.9(M.94.1513B); id.*trisag.*5(M.95.17A).

C. Christol.; **1.** *having real existence, substantial, real*; **a.** ref. Inc. πῶς οὐ ψιλῇ τῇ ἐννοίᾳ καὶ οὐχ ὑπάρξει οὐ. λέγετε γεγενῆσθαι τὴν ἐνανθρώπησιν τοῦ κυρίου; Leont.H.*Nest.*2.6(M.86.1544D); οὐκοῦν τὸ μὴ ἀνυποστάτους ἢ ἀνενεργήτους ἐπὶ Χριστοῦ τὰς φύσεις ὁμολογεῖν, οὐκ ἔστιν ὑποστάσεις ἢ ἐνεργοῦντας συνάγειν, ἀλλὰ τὰς οὐ. αὐτῶν καὶ φυσικὰς ὑπάρξεις τε καὶ ἐνεργείας ὀρθοδόξως ὁμολογεῖν Max.*opusc.*(M.91.205B); **b.** of hypostatic union, Leont.B.*Nest.et Eut.*2(M.86.1353B) cit. s. ἕνωσις; Sophr.H.*ep.syn.*(M.87.3168A) cit. s. ἀνάκρασις; opp. φαντασιώδης, Eust.Mon.*ep.*(M.86.909D); οὐ. ἕνωσις, v. ἕνωσις; **2.** *proper to the essence* or *nature,* in Nestorius signifying that flesh of Christ is properly human, cf. *non que l'essence de Dieu le Verbe se fût changée en l'essence de la chair, mais (il avait) une chair essentielle et une chair naturelle,* Nest.*Heracl.*1.3.266(p.160); ref. either nature of Christ οὔτ' ἂν ἡ φθαρτή τε καὶ ἀλλοιουμένη φύσις, τουτέστιν ἡ γενητή, καταπλουτήσειεν ἂν οὐ. τὴν ἀτρεψίαν Cyr.*Thds.*

10(p.49.2, v.l. οὐσιωδῶς 5^{2}.9E) = id.*inc.unigen.*(5^{1}.683E); ἑκατέραν τῶν φύσεων μένειν ἀμειώτως ἐπὶ τῇ οὐ. αὐτῆς ὅρῳ καὶ λόγῳ Thdr. Raith.*praep.*(p.191.27; M.91.1492C); τὰς ἑκατέρας φυσικῶς οὐσίας εἰργάζετο κατὰ τὴν ἑκατέρᾳ προσοῦσαν οὐ. ποιότητα, ἢ καὶ φυσικὴν ἰδιότητα Sophr.H.*ep.syn.*(M.87.3168B); κατ' οἰκείωσίν φασιν...ἔχειν τὸν κύριον τὸ ἀνθρώπινον θέλημα...ἆρα τὴν οὐ., καθ' ἣν τὰ φυσικῶς προσόντα ἕκαστος ἔχων, διὰ τὴν φύσιν οἰκειοῦται· ἢ τὴν σχετικήν; Max.*Pyrr.*(M.91.304A); ὧν...αὐτὸς φύσεων ὑπόστασις ἦν, τούτων καὶ τοὺς οὐ. φυσικῶς ἐπεδέχετο λόγους. εἰ δὲ τοὺς οὐ. ... ἐπεδέχετο λόγους, καὶ φυσικὴν ἔμψυχον σαρκὸς εἰκότως εἶχεν ἐνέργειαν, ἧς οὐσιώδης τῇ φύσει κατέσπαρται λόγος id.*opusc.*(M.91.36B); τοὺς οὐ. τε καὶ φυσικοὺς τῶν ἑνωθέντων νόμους τε καὶ λόγους, θελήματα καλῶς προσαγορεύσαντες *ib.*(45C); τῇ ἀναιρέσει τοῦ τε φυσικοῦ θελήματος καὶ τῆς οὐ. ἐνεργείας *ib.*(76A); ref. differences *of essence, in the sphere of essence* οὐ. μὲν τοῖς συνελθοῦσιν ἡ διαφορά, ἐπίκτητος δὲ ταῖς οὐσίαις ἡ ἕνωσις Leont.H.*monoph.*30(M.86.1788C); [sc. in monophysite teaching] ὡς μιᾶς φύσεως γενομένων τῶν δύο καὶ τῆς οὐ. διαφορᾶς ἀμφοῖν μηκέτι γινωσκομένης Thdr.Raith.*praep.*(p.196.21; 1497D); *ib.*(p.199.8; 1501B); τὴν οὐ. διαφορὰν προσωπικὴν ποιεῖται [sc. Nest.] διαίρεσιν... διὰ τὴν διαίρεσιν τὴν οὐ. μὴ λέγων [sc. Sev. Ant.] διαφορὰν τὴν... ἕνωσιν ἐργάζεται σύγχυσιν Max.*opusc.*(M.91.56C).

οὐσιωδῶς, A. in gen.; 1. *in essence, in terms of* or *in virtue of essence* μὴ οὐ. ἔχειν ὡς ἀχώριστον συμβεβηκὸς τὴν μακαριότητα Or.*Jo.* 2.18(12; p.75.8; M.14.145C); τῷ οὐ. ἀγαθῷ opp. ἀγαθὸν τὸ κατὰ συμβεβηκός id.*Cels.*6.44(p.114.18; M.11.1365B); πάσης ἀρετῆς...πηγὴν οὐ., ἀλλὰ μὴ ἐπικτήτως...τὸν θεόν Meth.*creat.*3(p.494.32; M.18.333C); ἡ ...αὐγή...οὐ. συνυπάρχουσα τῷ φωτί, οὐκ ἂν δύναιτο ἐκτὸς ὑφεστάναι τοῦ ἐν ᾧ ἐστιν Eus.*d.e.*5.1(p.213.18; M.22.353C); παντοκράτωρ...ἀπὸ γὰρ τοῦ κυριεύειν οὐ. ... οὕτως ὠνόμασται Cyr.*Am.*81(3.345E); id.*Is.* 3.5(2.539E); τῶν ἰδίων καὶ οὐ. αὐτῇ [sc. divine nature] προσπεφυκότων ἀγαθῶν id.*Nest.*1 proem.(p.15.13; 6^{1}.4E); ‡Gr.Nyss.*hom.1.29 in Jo.*(p.103.13); Jo.D.*Jacob.*21(M.94.1448B) cit. s. ἐπουσιωδῶς; ref. ποιότητες: ποιότητας ὅσαι οὐ. συμπεφύκασιν Gr.Nyss.*Eun.*1(1 p.100. 5; M.45.333B); συμπληρωτικὰ τῆς ἀλλήλων οὐσίας, ὅπερ ἐστὶν ἰδεῖν ἐπὶ τῶν οὐσιῶν καὶ τῶν οὐ. κατ' αὐτῶν κατηγορουμένων, ποιότητες δὲ αὗται καλοῦνται Leont.B.*Nest.et Eut.*1(M.86.1280B); *by nature*, ‖ φυσικῶς: ἡ...θεία...φύσις...φυσικῶς καὶ οὐ. ἀπειθοῦσα τῇ πονηρίᾳ Cyr.*Is.*1.4(2.123B); id.*glaph.Gen.*7(1.238A); v. B, C infra; ref. a mode of knowledge, of knowing something *in [its] essence* τὸν θεὸν οὐδεὶς ἔγνω οὐ. μετὰ ἀκριβείας ἁπάσης Chrys.*incomprehens.*4.3(1. 475C); ref. a mode of existence, *substantially, in [one's] essence, as an essence*, ref. Ac.13:47 ὃν τρόπον...τεθεὶς φῶς εἶναι ἐθνῶν, οὐκ οὐ. ἐγένετο φῶς, ἀλλ' ᾧ φωτίζονται οἱ ἐπιγινώσκοντες αὐτόν Didym. *Trin.*3.6(M.39.846B); οὐδὲν κτίσμα μεθεκτόν ἐστι τῇ λογικῇ ψυχῇ, ὡς ἐνοικίζεσθαι αὐτῇ οὐ. τὸ δὲ πνεῦμα τὸ ἅγιον ἐνοικίζεται ἐν αὐτῇ id. (‡Bas.)*Eun.*5(1.297A; M.29.713A); Cyr.*Juln.*8(6^{2}.265D); τὸν θεὸν τῶν ἐν οὐσίᾳ φαιδροτέρων κατάρχεσθαι, ἀλλ' οὐ τῶν σκοτίων...καὶ οἷς τὸ εἶναι οὐκ ἐστὶν οὐ. Proc.G.*Gen.*1:5(M.87.56D); ref. a mode of origin, *from the essence* εἰ γενητός ἐστιν [sc. ὁ πονηρός] ὑπ' αὐτοῦ...γέγονεν θεοῦ, ἢ ὡς ζῷον γεννηθεὶς ἢ οὐ. προβληθεὶς καὶ ἔξω τῇ κράσει συμβεβηκὼς *Hom.Clem.*19.4; Cyr.*Is.*5.3(2.810A); 2. *concretely, in actuality*, ref. Pentecost οὐκ ἔτι ἐνεργείᾳ παρὸν...οὐ. δὲ...συγγινόμενόν τε καὶ συμπολιτευόμενον. ἔπρεπε γάρ, υἱοῦ σωματικῶς ὑμῖν ὁμιλήσαντος, καὶ αὐτὸ φανῆναι σωματικῶς Gr.Naz.*or.*41.11(M.36.444C); ref. BMV αὕτη ...οὐκ ἐνεργείας θεοῦ ὑπῆρξε δοχεῖον, ἀλλ' οὐ. τῆς τοῦ υἱοῦ καὶ θεοῦ ὑποστάσεως ‡Jo.D.*hom.*6.6(M.96.672A); 3. *genuinely, in fact* πῶς... ἀνενέργητοι...οἱ...ἅγιοι μάρτυρες;...οὐ. ὑπὸ θεοῦ στελλόμενοι Eustrat. *stat.anim.*12(p.403).

B. Trin.; 1. *by virtue of essence, by nature*, ref. relation of Son to Father ἡ ...σοφία...οὐ. πρὸ αἰώνων παρὰ τῷ θεῷ ὑπάρχουσα Or.*exp.in Pr.*8:22(M.17.185A); τὰ μὲν περὶ τῆς θεότητος οὐ. ... προσφέρων Ἰησοῦ Χριστῷ τὴν θεότητα id.*dial.*5(p.132.1); οὕτως ἔχει τὴν ζωὴν ὁ υἱὸς ὥσπερ καὶ ὁ πατήρ, τουτέστιν ἐν ἑαυτῷ, δι' οὗ τὸ οὐ. σημαίνεται Cyr.*thes.*14(5^{1}.140E); πάντων...ὅσα...πρόσεστι τῷ πατρὶ κατὰ φύσιν καὶ ἐν υἱῷ κειμένων φυσικῶς τε καὶ οὐ. *ib.*32(5^{1}.293B); of H. Ghost to Father τοῦ πνεύματος τοῦ θεοῦ...τῶν ἄλλων [sc. πνευμάτων] μὴ οὐ. ὄντων αὐτοῦ Didym.*Trin.*2.2(M.39.461B); ἐστι [sc. τὸ πνεῦμα] φυσικῶς ἐνυπάρχον αὐτῷ καὶ οὐ. ἐμπεπηγός Cyr.*thes.*33(5^{1}.333D); Max.*qu. Thal.*63(M.90.672C) cit. s. ἐκπορεύω; ref. presence of H. Ghost in Son ὁ κύριος ἦν ὁ λύχνος ὁ καιόμενος, διὰ τὸ πνεῦμα τῆς θεότητος τὸ μένον οὐ. ἐν αὐτῷ, καὶ ἐκκαῖον αὐτοῦ τὴν καρδίαν κατὰ τὸ ἀνθρώπινον Mac.Aeg.*hom.*43.2(M.34.772D); cf. ‡Gr.Nyss.*hom.1.44 in Jo.*(p.108. 25); ἄνθρωπος γεγονὼς ὁ...λόγος ἀπομεμένηκεν καὶ οὕτω θεός, πάντα ὑπάρχων ὅσα καὶ ὁ πατήρ...καὶ ἴδιον ἔχων τὸ...οὐ. ἐμπεφυκὸς αὐτῷ πνεῦμα ἅγιον Cyr.*expl.xii cap.*9(p.23.22; 6^{1}.155A); τὸ πνεῦμα ἐν ἑαυτῷ οὐ. εἶχεν ἀεί Vict.*Mc.*1:10(p.272.1); Ammon.*Jo.*3:34(M.85.1416D); [Jo.5:22] συμπαρόντος αὐτῷ...φυσικῶς καὶ οὐ. τοῦ ζωοποιοῦ πνεύματος Oecum.*Apoc.*18:1ff.(p.194); 2. *from one's essence* εἰ...ὅλος [sc. ὁ θεός]...ἐστιν ἀγέννητος, οὐκ οὐ. εἰς γένεσιν διέστη, ἐξουσίᾳ δὲ ὑπέστησε γέννημα Aët.*synt.*7(p.353.20; M.41.536D); *ib.*8(p.353.22; 537A); οὐ κτιστήν φαμεν τὴν οὐσίαν, οὐδὲ ἀλλοτρίαν ὡς ποιητήν, ἀλλὰ γεννητὴν οὐ. καὶ οὐκ ἀλλοίαν παρὰ τὸν γεγεννηκότα Epiph.*haer.*76.22 (p.370.14; M.42.561B); ἐξ αὐτοῦ ἐγέννησεν οὐ. πνεῦμα ἐκ πνεύματος καὶ οὐ σῶμα ἐκ σώματος *ib.*76.46(p.400.1; 613B); Cyr.*Nest.*2 proem. (p.32.33; 6^{1}.30E); 3. *substantivally*; *as a Person* οὐ. ὑφεστῶτος τοῦ υἱοῦ τοῦ θεοῦ Or.*or.*27(p.271.7; M.11.516B); τοῦ υἱοῦ τοῦ θεοῦ... ὑφεστηκότος οὐ. κατὰ τὸ ὑποκείμενον, τοῦ αὐτοῦ ὄντος τῇ σοφίᾳ id. *Jo.*6.38(22; p.146.14; M.14.264C); Gr.Nyss.*or.catech.*2(p.14.14; M.45. 17B); *ib.*4(p.18.4; 20B).

C. Christol.; 1. *in essence, substantially, really*; a. ref. Inc. τῇ μὲν γὰρ φυσικῇ ταυτότητι ἕν ἐστιν ὁ...λόγος πρὸς τὸν...πατέρα...πῶς δὲ καὶ ἐν ἡμῖν γέγονε κατὰ τὸν ἴσον τρόπον, οὐ. δὴ λέγω καὶ φυσικῶς; Cyr. *Arcad.*(p.91.16; 5^{2}.86A); μηδεὶς...ὑπολαμβανέτω τὴν πυκνότητα τῆς ἀνθρώπου φύσεως ἥνπερ οὐ. κοινωνήσας ὁ...λόγος ἐγνώρισται...ἠλλοιῶσθαι Diad.*ascens.*6(M.65.1145D); πῶς...Ἰησοῦς, ὁ πάντων ἐπέκεινα, πᾶσιν ἐστιν ἀνθρώποις οὐ. συντεταγμένος; Dion.Ar.*ep.*4(M.3. 1072A); τὰ...τῆς ἡμῶν ἐπιτιμίας δι' αὐτῆς τῆς πείρας, οὐ. ... τὰ πάθη δεχόμενος Max.*opusc.*(M.91.29D); οὐ. ... ἀλλ' οὐχ ὡς ἀνθρώπων αἰτίου ἐπ' αὐτοῦ τοῦ φύσει θεοῦ καθ' ἡμᾶς ἀληθῶς οὐσιωθέντος τὸ ἄνθρωπος ὄνομα λέγομεν id.*ambig.*(M.91.1048B); οὐ. καὶ ἀληθῶς γενόμενος ἄνθρωπος Jo.D.*f.o.*3.12(M.94.1029B); b. ref. hypostatic union, opp. σχετικῶς: τῶν οὐ. ἡνωμένων φύσεων...ὁ τρόπος...τῆς ἑνώσεως, οὐ. ἀλλ' οὐ σχετικῶς γεγονώς...περὶ...τῆς...ἑνώσεως...ἣν οἱ πατέρες οὐ. γεγενῆσθαι ἐφρόνησαν, ὑμεῖς δὲ [sc. Νεστοριανοί] σχετικὴν καὶ γνωμικὴν ταύτην εἰσάγετε Leont.B.*Nest.et Eut.*3(M.86.1380A,C,D); κατὰ Παῦλον καὶ Θεόδωρον καὶ Νεστόριον δύο φύσεις ἁπλῶς ἐπὶ Χριστοῦ λέγειν ἀποδεδοκίμακεν ὁ λόγος ὁ ἐκκλησιαστικός, ἀλλὰ δύο φύσεις οὐ. ἡνωμένας, διὰ τῆς ἐπαγωγῆς ταύτης ἀποβάλλων πᾶσαν διαιρετικὴν ἔννοιαν Thdr.Raith.*praep.*(p.191.7; M.91.1492A); in Paul. Sam. of manner in which Logos dwelt in human body of Christ ἐκείνους μὲν [sc. prophets] μετεσχηκέναι σοφίας ἐμπνεούσης ἔξωθεν καὶ ἄλλης οὔσης παρ' αὐτούς, αὐτὴν δὲ τὴν σοφίαν δι' ἑαυτῆς ἐπιδεδημηκέναι οὐ. ἐν τῷ ἐκ Μαρίας σώματι Paul.Sam.*fr.*B.9(p.332.23)ap.Leont.B.*Nest.et Eut.* 3(1393B); c. for exegesis of Col.2:9 v. σωματικῶς; 2. *in conformity with* one's *essence* τὸν...ὅρον τῆς καθ' ἡμᾶς τελειότητος οὐ. κεκτημένη [sc. humanity of Christ] Leont.B.*Nest.et Eut.*2(M.86.1337A); Sophr.H.*ep.syn.*(M.87.3168B); τοὺς οὐ. προσούσας ταῖς αὐτοῦ φύσεσι κινήσεις Max.*Pyrr.*(M.91.337C); ref. divine and human elements as opposed *in essence* δύο ὑπεναντία οὐ. ὡμονόησαν, τῆς ὑποστάσεως δεικνυμένης ἐπὶ ἑκάστης φύσεως Ephr.2.263E.

***οὐσιωμένως**, *in essence* περὶ τῶν ἀγγέλων οὓς εἴωθεν ὀνομάζειν... νόας...ὡς τὸ πᾶν νοῦς οὐ. ὄντες Max.*schol.d.n.*1.1(M.4.188C); cf. τὸ πᾶν νοῦς ἐστιν ἕκαστος αὐτῶν, καὶ τὴν οὐσίαν ἅπασαν νοῦν ζῶντα εἰς τὸ εἶδος τὸ ἑαυτῶν οὐσιωμένον ἔχει id.*schol.c.h.*1.2(M.4.32B).

***οὐσιωνυμία**, ἡ, *name of Being* τὴν...τοῦ ὄντως ὄντος θεολογικὴν οὐ. Dion.Ar.*d.n.*5.1(M.3.816B).

[*]**οὐσιωποιός**, for οὐσιοποιός, Jo.D.*rect.sent.*1(M.94.1424C).

οὐσίωσις, ἡ, A. in gen.; 1. *bringing into being, origination*, of Creation ἐν τῇ τούτων οὐ. αὐτὸς ἦν κτίστης αὐτῶν Or.*fr.1 in Jo.* (p.484.14); Alex.Al.*ep.Alex.*4(p.22.19; M.18.553B) cit. s. δημιουργέω; Μωυσῆς...τὴν τοῦ παντὸς...οὐ. τε καὶ διακόσμησιν ὑπογράφων Eus. *h.e.*1.2.4(M.20.56A); τῆς τῶν γενητῶν ἁπάντων οὐ. τε καὶ ὑπάρξεως αἴτιον id.*d.e.*4.1(p.151.14; M.22.252C); id.*l.C.*13(p.240.14; M.20. 1405C); Gr.Naz.*or.*30.20(p.140.12; M.36.129C); κτίσις καὶ ἐπὶ μεταποιήσεως λέγεται χωρὶς τῆς ἐξ ἀρχῆς οὐ. Proc.G.*Dt.*32:6(M.87.956D); ref. Heb.1:4 οὐ περὶ οὐσιώσεως...ὁ λόγος Chrys.*hom.1.2 in Heb.*(12. 9A); 2. opp. ὕπαρξις, *subsistence, existence as a substance* or *entity* τὸν ὕπαρξιν τοῖς ὅλοις, καὶ τοῖς λογικοῖς οὐ. καὶ ἀθανασίαν δεδωκότα Didym.*Trin.*1.15(M.39.300B); adopted as equivalent of *subsistentia* by Boethius, *est igitur et hominis quidem essentia i.e.* οὐσία, *et subsistentia i.e.* οὐσίωσις, *et* ὑπόστασις *i.e. substantia et* πρόσωπον *i.e. persona:* οὐσία *quidem atque essentia, quoniam est;* οὐ. *vero atque subsistentia, quoniam in nullo subjecta est;* ὑπόστασις *vero atque substantia, quoniam subest ceteris, quae subsistentiae non sunt i.e.* οὐσιώσεις: *est* πρόσωπον *atque persona, quoniam est rationabile individuum. deus quoque et* οὐσία *est et essentia; est enim et maxime ipse est, a quo omnium esse proficiscitur. est* οὐ., *i.e. subsistentia; substitit enim nullo indigens, et* ὑφίστασθαι, *substat enim. unde etiam dicimus unam esse* οὐσίαν *vel* οὐ. *i.e. essentiam vel subsistentiam deitatis; sed tres* ὑποστάσεις *i.e. tres substantias*, Boethius *contra Eutychen et Nestorium* (M.*PL.*64.1345Af.); 3. *realization*, ref. Eph. 4:24 κτίσιν καλεῖ τὴν οὐ. τῆς ἀρετῆς Chrys.*hom.13.2 in Eph.*(11.98B);

κατ' οὐσίωσιν *in fact* in illustration to show ἐποίησε not always synonymous with ἔκτισεν: τὸν ἤδη ὄντα κατ' οὐ. διδάσκαλον, τότε ποιεῖ τις τῶν ἑαυτοῦ παίδων διδάσκαλον, ὅταν διδάσκειν τοὺς παῖδας ὁ διδάσκαλος ἄρξηται Didym.*Trin*.3.6(M.39.845A); **4.** *essence, constitution* τῷ ἀντιχρίστῳ πᾶν τὸ πλήρωμα τῆς σατανικῆς οὐ. προσγενήσεται *cat.Apoc*.16: 2(p.410.22).

B. theol.; **1.** ref. generation of Son περὶ τῆς τοῦ δευτέρου αἰτίου συστάσεώς τε καὶ οὐ. Eus.*p.e*.11.19(541A; M.21.901A); id.*d.e*.4.15 (p.182.2; M.22.304B); τὰ περὶ τῆς πρώτης οὐ. τοῦ σωτῆρος *ib*.5.1 (p.213.26; 353D); τὴν ἔνθεον...προϋπαρξίν τε καὶ οὐ. *ib*.6.13(p.266.18; 437B); but ὁ κύριος οὐχ ἀρχὴν οὐσιώσεως δέχεται, ἀΐδιος γάρ...ἐστι Didym.*Ps*.117: 14(M.39.1560C); **2.** Christol., in sense A.1 applicable only to the humanity καὶ ἡ οὐ. τοῦ σώματος ἐκ πνεύματός ἐστιν ἁγίου Leont.B.*Nest.et Eut*.2(M.86.1352D); τὴν μὲν τῶν αὐτοῦ φύσεων ἀρχὴν οὐ τῆς οὐ. ἀλλὰ τῆς συνουσιώσεως μόνον ἐν τῇ ἁγίᾳ παρθένῳ λαβεῖν. τὴν δὲ ἑτέραν τῶν ἐν αὐτῷ φύσεων, ἤγουν τὴν τῆς σαρκός, ἀρχὴν τῆς τε οὐ. καὶ συνουσιώσεως ἐν αὐτῇ λαβεῖν Leont.H.*Nest*.4.17 (M.86.1684B); οὐκ ἀρνούμεθα τὴν ἕνωσιν, παραιτούμεθα δὲ τὴν οὐ. †Ath. *fr*.(M.26.1237B); **3.** *assumption of essence* ὅλην ὅλου τὴν φύσιν οὐσιωθέντος τοῦ λόγου, καὶ ὅλην τῇ οὐ. θεώσαντος Max.*opusc*.(M. 91.68C).

***οὐσούσφρουκτος, ὁ,** (Lat. *ususfructus*) *usufruct*, Ath.Scholast. *coll*.2.1(p.28).

οὔτε, *not even* τὰ γὰρ τοιαῦτα οὔτε βαρβάροις ἄγνωστα Chrys.*hom. 26.5 in 1Cor*.(10.235A); id.*hom.15.2 in Eph*.(11.112C).

***οὐτίλιος,** (Lat. *utilis*) *useful, proper*, Phot.*nomoc*.9.27(M.104. 776D).

οὕτως, *so, thus*, as antecedent to ὅτι: οὕτω θαρρῶ...ὅτι καὶ περαιτέρω πρόειμι Chrys.*hom.26.6 in Mt*.(7.322C); id.*hom.5.5 in 2Thess*.(11.545A); id.*hom.24.2 in Heb*.(12.222B).

***οὔφ,** exclamation of disgust or reprobation, †Anast.S.*relat*.17 (*OC 2* p.69).

ὀφειλέτης, ὁ, *debtor*, met. πάντες ὀφειλέται ἐσμὲν ἁμαρτίας Polyc. *ep*.6.1; ἕκαστος δὲ ἡμῶν ὀ. ἐστὶ ταῖς ἁμαρτίαις καὶ ὀ. ἐστιν ἔχων χειρόγραφον Or.*hom.15.5 in Jer*.(p.129.5,6; M.13.433C); τοῦ κολάσεως ὀφειλέτην εἶναι τὸν...κακόν *cat.Ac*.23: 3–5(p.366.31).

ὀφειλή, ἡ, 1. *debt*, Meth.*arbitr*.16(p.187.17; M.18.264C); περιτέθεται [sc. Logos] σῶμα...ἵνα, ἀνθ' ἡμῶν τὴν ὀ. ἀποδιδούς, τὰ λείποντα τῷ ἀνθρώπῳ δι' ἑαυτοῦ τελειώσῃ Ath.*Ar*.2.66(M.26.288B); Gr.Nyss. *or.dom*.5(p.108.28; M.44.1188C); Chrys.*hom.3.4 in Philm*.(11.784F); **2.** one's *due*, Pall.*h.Laus*.20(p.63.15; M.34.1068D); αὐτῷ τῆς δεήσεως ἀποδιδόναι τὴν ὀ. *Lit*.ap.*Const.App*.8.10.5.

ὀφείλημα, τό, *that which is owed*, hence *duty* τὸ ὀ. τοῦ γάμου, τὴν παιδοποιΐαν Clem.*str*.3.18(p.246.7; M.8.1212A).

***ὀφειλομένως,** *duly, rightly* προσκυνεῖται [sc. God] ὀ., καὶ θεϊκῶς προσκυνεῖται ‡Ath.*Apoll*.1.6(M.26.1101C); Epiph.*haer*.76.42(p.396. 24; M.42.608B); οἰκειοπαθοῦμέν σοι ὀ. Thdr.Stud.*epp*.2.53(M.99. 1265B); *ib*.2.180(1556B).

ὀφείλ-ω, 1. *owe*; hence pass. ptcpl. ~όμενος *appointed, deserved* τὸν ὀ. τόπον τῆς δόξης *1Clem*.5.4; τὰς ὀ. ἐνθέους προκοπάς τε καὶ διοικήσεις Clem.*str*.7.7(p.35.31; M.9.468B); πρὸς τὴν ὀ. εἰρήνην CArim. *ep.Const*.1(p.237.26; M.26.697A); **2.** *be bound to, be obliged to*, c. infin., hence used like μέλλω *be about to, be going to* ὡς θνητός...μᾶλλον δέ, ὡς ~ων ἀθανάτου ζωῆς...ἀπολαύειν Chrys.*hom.18.7 in Rom*.(9.641D); ἔβαλεν αὐτόν ποτε εἰς πλοῖον ὡς ~οντα πλεῦσαι ἐπὶ τὴν Ῥώμην Pall.*h.Laus*.37(p.112.13; M.34.1186B); τὸν ~οντα τὴν Ἀλεξανδρέων ἐκκλησίαν ἐπιτροπεύειν Soz.*h.e*.2.17.4(M.67.977A); πέμπει τὸν Νάρσην, ~οντα μαθεῖν τίς ἐκ τῶν δύο ~ει εἶναι ἐπίσκοπον †Leont.B.*sect*. 5.5(M.86.1232B); **3.** ὄφελον ἦν introducing a wish that something had taken place in the past, *would that*, c. acc. et infin. ἦν ὄ. γε ἦν μὴ γενέσθαι Eus.Dor.*ep.imp*.(p.68.25; M.86.2549B); ὄφελον without ἦν introducing a wish that something were so in the present, *would that*, c. imperf. indic. ὄ. πάντες αὐτὸν ἐμιμοῦντο Ign.*Smyrn*. 12.1; Gr.Thaum.*pan.Or*.16(p.35.18; M.10.1096C); Gr.Naz.*or*.26.15 (M.35.1248C); Socr.*h.e*.4.26.19(M.67.533A); c. subj. ὄ. κἀγὼ τοιοῦτος γένωμαι Or.*hom.20.7 in Jer*.(p.188.8; M.13.516D).

***ὀφεοδαίμων, ὁ,** *serpent-like Devil*, ‡Gr.Thaum.*annunt*.2(M.10. 1157B).

***ὀφθαλμιαῖος,** *of the eyes*, Sophr.H.*mir.Cyr.et Jo*.(M.87.3661A).

ὀφθαλμίζω, *engraft*; met., Anast.S.*hex*.12(M.89.1076C).

ὀφθαλμοδουλεία, ἡ, *eye-service* i.e. service performed only to attract attention, Chrys.*hom.19.4 in 1Cor*.(10.164D).

***ὀφθαλμόδουλος, ὁ,** *one who performs eye-service*, *Const.App*. 4.12.3.

***ὀφθαλμοπλανία, ἡ,** *deceit, illusion of the eyes*, Nil.*epp*.3.252(M. 79.505B); Leont.N.*v.Sym*.56(M.93.1740B).

***ὀφθαλμορρεπής,** *with eyes cast down*; met., *downward gazing*, ‡Chrys.*hom*.10(13.238C).

ὀφθαλμός, ὁ, *eye*;

A. lit.; denied ref. God, Gel.Cyz.*h.e*.2.19.20(M.85.1280B); of 'evil eye', *T.Isach*.4.6; ὅταν...ἀκούσῃς...ὀ. πονηρόν...μὴ τοῦτο νομίσῃς, ὅτι ἡ τῶν ὀ. βολὴ τοὺς ὁρῶντας βλάπτειν πέφυκεν. ὀ. γὰρ οὐκ ἂν εἴη πονηρός, αὐτὸ τὸ μέλος, ἀλλ'...ὁ Χριστὸς οὕτω τὸν φθόνον λέγει Chrys. *comm.in Gal*.3: 1(10.695C); ὀφθαλμῶν...τὸ ἁπλῶς ὁρᾶν μόνον, τὸ δὲ πονηρῶς ὁρᾶν τῆς ἔνδον διεστραμμένης γίνεται γνώμης *ib*.; id.*hom. 8.5 in Col*.(11.388B); id.*hom.12.7 in 1Cor*.(10.107C).

B. met.; **1.** of capacity to see spiritual things: of 'eyes of the heart', opened by Christ, *1Clem*.36.2; cf. *ib*.59.3; Thdt.*Cant*.1: 1(2. 25); darkened by Devil, Gr.Mag.*dial*.(tr.Zach.)2.8(M.*PL*.66.147B); of 'eyes of soul' διηνοίχθησαν...αὐτῶν [sc. Adam and Eve] οἱ ὀ. τῆς αἰσθήσεως, οὓς καλῶς ἦσαν μύσαντες, ἵνα μὴ περισπώμενοι ἐμποδίζωνται βλέπειν τῷ τῆς ψυχῆς ὀ.· οὓς δὲ τέως εἶχον βλέποντας τῆς ψυχῆς ὀ. καὶ εὐφραινομένους ἐπὶ τῷ θεῷ...τούτους...διὰ τὴν ἁμαρτίαν ἔμυσαν Or. *Cels*.7.39(p.189.32; M.11.1476D); μηδὲν ἐπισκοτοῦν...τὸν ὀ. τῆς ψυχῆς πρὸς τὴν θείαν...θεωρίαν Meth.*symp*.11.3(p.138.26; M.18.217A); Gr. Nyss.*hom.5 in Cant*.(M.44.864B), *ib.8*(952A) citt. s. διορατικός; cf. Didym.*Trin*.3.16(M.39.873A); ἡ ψυχὴ ἡ βαστάζουσα τὸν θεόν, μᾶλλον δὲ βασταζομένη ὑπὸ τοῦ θεοῦ, γίγνεται...ὅλη ὀ. Mac.Aeg.*hom*.33.2(M. 34.741D); of 'eyes of the mind' ἐπὶ τὸν οὐράνιον βασιλέα τοὺς τῆς διανοίας παραπέμποντας ὀ. Eus.*v.C*.4.19(p.125.3; M.20.1168A); id.*l.C*. 16(p.251.2; M.20.1425B); Cyr.*Lc*.14: 7(M.72.785C); Gr.Mag.*dial*.(tr. Zach.)3.7(M.*PL*.77.230B); as synon. with mind, Meth.*symp*.7.2(p.72. 21; M.18.128A); of the 'eye of faith', Chrys.*comm.in Gal*.3: 1(10. 696A); **2.** of 'eye of God' ὅλος...ἀκοὴ καὶ ὅλος ὀ. ... ὁ θεός Clem.*str*.7.7 (p.29.14; M.9.453B); πάντα πράττειν ὡς ἐν ὀφθαλμοῖς θεοῦ Or.*Cels*.7.51 (p.202.14; M.11.1496B); id.*hom.6.1 in Jer*.(p.48.7; M.13.524B); ἐπὶ...θεοῦ ὀφθαλμὸς...τὸ ἐποπτικόν id. *fr.4 in 1Reg*.(p.295.26; M.17.44B); of divine providence, Eus.*v.C*.1.58(p.35.15; M.20.973A); cf.id.*l.C*.17 (p.255.26; M.20.1433A); ref. Christ ποιμένος ἁγνοῦ...ὀφθαλμοὺς ὃς ἔχει μεγάλους πάντη καθαρεύοντας Aberc.*epitaph*.5; **3.** of spies, Const. ap.Thdt.*h.e*.1.20.2(3.797); **4.** of deacons as 'eyes' of bishop, *Const. App*.2.44.4; Isid.Pel.*epp*.1.29(M.78.200C); **5.** of persons capable of illuminating and guiding others, also of exercising oversight ὀ. ἦν Σαμουὴλ ὁ βλέπων...ὀ. Μιχαῖος ὁ ὁρῶν καὶ Μωϋσῆς ὁ θεώμενος... ὀφθαλμοὶ πάντες...οἱ εἰς ὁδηγίαν τοῦ λαοῦ τεταγμένοι...καὶ νῦν οἱ...ἐπισκοπεῖν τεταγμένοι ὀ. κυρίως κατονομάζονται Gr.Nyss.*hom.7 in Cant*. (M.44.920A); χρὴ ὅλον εἶναι ὀ. πάντα ὁρῶντα καὶ μηδὲν παρορῶντα Isid. Pel.*epp*.1.149(M.78.284A); **6.** of eye as most precious part of body, hence of leading or important persons, in Church as body ἓν σῶμα οἱ πάντες..., ἀλλ' οἱ μὲν ὡς κεφαλή, οἱ δὲ ὡς ὀφθαλμοί...ἐν ἡλίῳ τεθήσονται φωτεινοί Clem.*ecl*.56(p.153.10; M.9.725A); ἕκαστος...ἢ ὀ. τοῦ σώματος τῆς ἐκκλησίας γινόμενος ἢ εἰς χεῖρα τασσόμενος Gr.Nyss. *hom.7 in Cant*.(M.44.913A); of individuals, *leading light* ὁ...Ἰωάννης, ὁ τῆς ἐν Βυζαντίῳ ἐκκλησίας καὶ πάσης ὀφθαλμός Isid.Pel.*epp*.1. 156(M.78.288B); ὁ μέγας τῆς ἐκκλησίας ὀ. Βασίλειος Max.*Pyrr*.(M.91. 309A); ὀ. ὤφθης, Γρηγόριε, ⟨τῶν⟩ δογμάτων Geo.Pis.*carm*.10.1; of a focus or central point τὰ Ἱεροσόλυμα ὀ. εἶναι τῆς γῆς Ath.*exp. Ps*.67: 12(M.27.336C).

C. *source*, fig. τὸ...κακὸν ὥσπερ πηγῆς ὀ. ἐστι πάντοτε βρύων Mac. Aeg.*hom*.15.48(M.34.609A); Trin. ὃν...τρόπον...ῥεῦμά τι...μίαν ἐξ ἑνὸς ὀ. τῆς πηγῆς τὴν ῥοὴν ἐσχηκός, δίρρυτον...τῶν ποταμῶν σχηματισθέντων,...παραπλησίως...καὶ ὁ...θεὸς...δίρρυτόν τινα τοῦ τε υἱοῦ καὶ τοῦ...πνεύματος...ἀποστείλας χάριν †Gr.Thaum.*ep.Philagr*.(M.46. 1105D); ὀ. τινα καὶ πηγὴν καὶ ποταμὸν ἐνενόησα...τῷ μὲν ὁ πατήρ, τῷ δὲ ὁ υἱός, τῷ δὲ τὸ πνεῦμα τὸ ἅγιον ἀναλόγως ἔχῃ...ἀλλ' ἔδεισα...μὴ τὸ ἐν τῷ ἀριθμῷ εἰσάγεται· ὀ. γὰρ καὶ πηγὴ καὶ ποταμὸς ἕν ἐστιν ἀριθμῷ Gr.Naz.*or*.31.31(p.186.15; M.36.169A); cf.Anast.*fid*.(p.272).

***ὀφθαλμοφάνεια, ἡ,** *outward aspect*, Proc.G.*Is*.1: 20(M.87.1852C).

ὀφθαλμοφανῶς, 1. *so as to be seen with the eyes, so as to be actually visible*, Hipp.*haer*.1.24(p.29.4; M.16.3052C); σταυρὸς ἐκ φωτὸς... ὑπὲρ γῆν ὀ. θεωρούμενος Cyr.H.*ep.Const*.4(M.33.1169A); φαίνεται... αὐτῷ ὁ δαίμων ὀ. Jo.Mosch.*prat*.45(M.87.2900B); ἀπαντήσασα...ἡ... θεοτόκος ὀ. *ib*.48(2904A); **2.** *with one's own eyes* ἀπόστολοι...ὀ. ἰδόντες τὸν προφητευόμενον Eus.*d.e*.6.24(p.293.7; M.22.481B); οἱ...ὀ. αὐτόπται...τοῦ σωτῆρος id.*Is*.52: 8(M.24.453C); ἐζήτει...ὀ. τὴν δόξαν ταύτην ἰδεῖν Chrys.*hom.7.2 in 2Cor*.(10.482A); ὀ. ... οὐκ εἶδον, διὰ δὲ τῆς πίστεως ἀκριβέστερον εἶδον id.*comm.in Gal*.3: 1(10.696A); id. *sac*.6.13(p.170.8; 1.434C); οἰόμενος τάχα ὀ. δύνασθαι ἰδεῖν τὸν θεόν Ammon.*Jo*.14: 12(M.85.1488D); **3.** *clearly, plainly* κατανοήσωμεν αὐτὰ [sc. prophecies] ὀ. Hipp.*antichr*.27(p.19.7; M.10.749A); ref. scriptural exegesis, ‡Pion.*v.Polyc*.18.

***Ὀφιανοί, οἱ, 1.** *serpent-worshippers*, Clem.*str*.7.17(p.76.28; M.9.

553A); *A.Phil.*96(p.37.26); **2.** *Ophites*, Gnost. heretics called also Ὀφῖται, Or.*Cels.*6.28(p.98.16; M.11.1336A); *ib.*(p.98.26; 1337A); Proc.G.*Gen.*3:1(M.87.184A); v. Ὀφῖται, ὄφις.

***ὀφιγέννημα, τό,** *serpent's offspring*, Anast.S.*hex.*12(M.89.1073A).

***ὀφιείκελος,** *serpent-like*, Epiph.*haer.*45.1(p.200.1,5; M.41.833A).

***ὀφιογνώμων,** *with the mind of a serpent*; met., Jo.VI H.*v.Jo.D.*17(M.94.456B); Thdr.Stud.*epp.*1.9(M.99.937C).

ὀφιοειδής, *in serpentine form*, Epiph.*haer.*37.5(p.56.15; M.41.648B).

***ὀφιοκέφαλος,** *serpent-headed*; of Egyptian gods, Ath.*gent.*9(M.25.20B).

ὀφιοκτόνος, *killing serpents*; of deer, Eus.*Is.*34:15(M.24.337B); Cyr.*Ps.*17:34(M.69.824D).

ὀφιομάχος (-ης), ὁ, *enemy of serpents*; **1.** *locust* or *grasshopper* [in form ὀφιομάχης, LXX Lev.11:22; Hebr. חַרְגֹּל], symbolically interpreted of ἀγάπη: ταύτην καὶ Μωσῆς...ἐν τοῖς φυσικοῖς συμβολικῶς ὀ. ὠνόμασεν Evagr.Pont.*cap.pract.*A 26(M.40.1228D, v.l. ὀφιομάχην); **2.** ὄφεις τοὺς λεγομένους ἀργόλας, ὅ ἐστιν ὀφιομάχους a kind of snake introduced by Jeremiah into Egypt to destroy poisonous serpents, ‡Epiph.*v.proph.Jer.*6(p.21; M.43.422A); ἀργόλας [חַרְגֹּל] perh. a nickname given to *mongoose* on account of its rapid movement, LXX and ‡Epiph. supra having misunderstood the true meaning; ὀ. prob. in fact = *mongoose*.

***ὀφιόμορφος,** *snake-like, in the form of a snake*; **1.** Ophite; of son generated by Ialdabaoth, Iren.*haer.*1.30.5(M.7.697D); ὁ Ἰαλδαβαὼθ ...γεγέννηκε δύναμιν ὀ. ἰδέαν ἔχουσαν, ὃν καὶ υἱὸν αὐτοῦ καλοῦσι καὶ ...οὗτος...ἠπάτησε τὴν Εὔαν Epiph.*haer.*37.4(p.56.7; M.41.648A); τὸν ὀ. ... ἐκεῖνον Μιχαὴλ καὶ Σαμαννὰ ὀνομάζουσι Thdt.*haer.*1.14(4.308); **2.** met., of heresy of Alogoi, Epiph.*haer.*51.1(p.249.20; M.41.889B); ὀ. πρόσφθεγμα Sophr.H.*or.*2.23(M.87.3244A).

***ὀφιότης, ἡ,** *form proper to a serpent* ὥσπερ...διαβολότης καὶ ὀ. δύο φύσεις ἐν ἑνὶ προσώπῳ ἡνώθησαν καὶ ἡ μὲν...ὀ. ἐφαίνετο, ἡ δὲ... διαβολότης οὐκ ἐφαίνετο...οὕτως καὶ ἐπὶ τοῦ Χριστοῦ ‡Ath.*qu.al.*20 (M.28.793D).

***ὀφιοτρόφος,** *nourishing a serpent*; met., Thdr.Stud.*epp.*2.156 (M.99.1489A).

***ὀφιόφωνος,** *with a serpent's voice*; met., Thdr.Stud.*epp.*1.49(M.99.1088D).

ὄφις, ὁ, *serpent*; **1.** in Eden, *Barn.*12.5; as instrument of Devil, cf. *initio per serpentem seduxit hominem, quasi latens deum*, Iren.*haer.*5.26.2(M.7.1194B); Or.*or.*29.18(p.392.11; M.11.545A); Dion.Al.*fr.Gen.*(p.200.4; M.89.541C); οὐκ ἦν...αἴτιος ὁ φαινόμενος τότε ὄ., ἀλλ' ὁ ἐν τῷ ὄφει ὄφις λαλήσας (φημὶ δὲ ⟨ὁ⟩ διάβολος) Epiph.*haer.*37.1 (p.51.17; M.41.641D); ὁ κύριος...τὸν ὄ. εἰς ἔχθρίαν κατέστησε τῷ τῶν ἀνθρώπων γένει, ἐπειδὴ ὅλως σκεῦος διαβόλου γέγονεν κτῆνος ὢν καὶ δι' αὐτοῦ ἠπάτησεν ὁ διάβολος τὸν ἄνθρωπον ἐν τῷ παραδείσῳ *ib.*37.2 (p.53.8; 645A); Thdt.*qu.32 in Gen.*(1.45); ὁ διάβολος...τὸν ὄ. ... ἐργαστήριον τῆς ἰδίας πλάνης λαβόμενος δι' αὐτοῦ ὡμίλησε τῇ γυναικί †Jo.D.*B.J.*7(M.96.908B); **2.** of Devil in gen. ὁ πονηρευσάμενος τὴν ἀρχὴν ὄ. καὶ οἱ ἐξομοιωθέντες αὐτῷ ἄγγελοι Just.*dial.*45.4(M.6.573A); σατὰν...ἀποστάτης ἐστί, τὸ δὲ νὰς ὄνομα ἐξ οὗ ἡ ἑρμηνεία ὄ. ἐκλήθη· ἐξ ὧν ἀμφοτέρων...ἓν ὄνομα γίνεται σατανᾶς *ib.*103.5(717B); τὰ παρὰ θεοῦ ποθούμενα, ὧν ὄ. οὐχ ἅπτεται ‡*Diogn.*12.8; ζιζάνιον...καὶ σπέρμα τοῦ διαβόλου...καὶ ὄ. Clem.*exc.Thdot.*53(p.124.17; M.9.684C); as vanquished by martyrs, *Ep.Lugd.*ap.Eus.*h.e.*5.1.42(M.20.424C); Ἰησοῦ ...συνοδεύοντος ὑμῖν ἐπὶ τὸν παράδεισον, καταφρονήσατε τοῦ ὄ., νενικημένου καὶ συντριβέντος ὑπὸ τοῦ Ἰησοῦ πόδας Or.*mart.*36(p.34.5; M.11.612A); ὦ ἔργον ὄφεως *A.Thom.*A 52(p.168.12); τὸν...κατάρξαντα τῆς πτώσεως...δράκοντα καὶ ὄ. ... ἀποκαλεῖν εἴωθεν Eus.*p.e.*7.16(328D; M.21.556A); in baptismal renunciation ἀποτάσσομαί σοι τῷ...πανουργοτάτῳ ὄ. Cyr.H.*catech.*19.4; μὴ μιμήσῃ τῆς Εὔας τὴν παρακοήν, μὴ πάλιν σύμβουλον παραδέξῃ τὸν ὄ. Bas.*hom.*1.4(2.3C; M.31.168B); ὄ. ἡ γραφὴ καλεῖ τὸν διάβολον, οὐ πάντως ὄντα τοιοῦτον τῇ μορφῇ, ἀλλὰ διὰ τὸ φαίνεσθαι τοῖς ἀνθρώποις σκολιώτατον καὶ τὸ ἐν πρώτοις ἐν ὄ. ἐνεργηθὲν τῆς ἀπάτης Epiph.*haer.*37.2(p.52.23; M.41.644C); δίκην...ὄφεως ἀτιμάσαντες τὸν σωτῆρα ἀπὸ ἐπιβουλῆς τῆς τοῦ ὄ. ἠδικοῦντο, φημὶ δὲ τοῦ διαβόλου *ib.*37.7(p.59.20; 652A); Cosm.Ind.*top.*2(M.88.124B); γνωσθήσεται ἐπὶ τέλει κύριος, ὅτι φωτίσουσι τοὺς διωκομένους ὑπὸ τοῦ ὄ. ‡Epiph.*v.proph.Abac.*14(p.29; ὄφιος M.43.409D); **3.** of evil principle concealed in the depth of the soul ὁ παλίμβολος ὄ. ἐκεῖνος διαβιβρώσκων τὸ νοερὸν τοῦ ἀνθρώπου...χηραμὸν ἔχει τὴν ψυχὴν Clem.*paed.*3.2(p.238.28; M.8.561A); τῷ ἐμφωλεύοντι ἐν τῇ...καρδίᾳ δεινῷ ὄ. ὥσπερ ἐπᾴδοντες *Hom.Clem.*10.5; *A.Phil.*111 (p.43.12); ὁ δεινὸς ὄ. τῆς ἁμαρτίας σύνεστι τῇ ψυχῇ...γαργαρίζων· καὶ ἐὰν συνθῆται, κοινωνεῖ ἡ...ψυχὴ τῇ...κακίᾳ...καὶ μοιχεύει Mac.Aeg. *hom.*15.28(M.34.593D); ἡ ἀσώματος ψυχὴ τῷ ἐνδομυχοῦντι ὄ. κοινωνοῦσα, τῷ πονηρῷ πνεύματι, πορνεύει ἀπὸ θεοῦ *ib.*26.13(684A); hence slaying of serpent as object of ascetic struggle, *ib.*18.15(633B); εἴσελθε...πρὸς τὸν αἰχμάλωτόν σου...τῆς ἁμαρτίας νοῦν καὶ ἴδε ἔτι τούτου κατώτερον καὶ βαθύτερον τῶν λογισμῶν τὸν εἰς τὰ λεγόμενα τῆς ψυχῆς σου ταμιεῖα ἐμφωλεύοντα ὄ. καὶ ἀναιροῦντά σε διὰ τῶν καιριωτάτων τῆς ψυχῆς σου μελῶν id.*elev.*20(M.34.908A); ὁ...αὐτὸς ὄ., ὁ ἐκβαλὼν τὸν Ἀδὰμ διὰ τῆς ὑψηλοφροσύνης...οὗτος καὶ νῦν ἐν ταῖς καρδίαις ὑποβάλλει ὑψηλοφροσύνην id.*hom.*27.6(697A); μὴ ἀκούων τοῦ ἔνδον εἰλισσομένου ὄ. συμβουλεύοντος τὰ πρὸς ἡδονήν *ib.*37.1(749C); wise of this world dominated by serpent, *ib.*45.2(788B); equated with sin, Chrys.*exp. in Ps.*41:2(5.138A) cit. s. ἔλαφος; ἐκβάλλεσθαι...πιστεύομεν ἐκ τῶν ταμιείων τοῦ νοῦ διὰ τοῦ λουτροῦ τῆς ἀφθαρσίας...τὸν πολύμορφον ὄ. Diad.*perf.*78(p.98.24); λέγουσι [sc. Messalians] ὅτι μόνη ἡ ἐκτενὴς προσευχὴ διώκειν δύναται...τὸν δαίμονα...φυγαδευομένου...ὡς ὄφεως ἐν τῷ ἐκπορεύεσθαι Tim.CP *haer.*(M.86.48C); **4.** Gnost. (Ophite and Peratic) in explanation of Ophite belief τινὲς δὲ αὐτὸν τὸν ὄ. τῇ Σοφίᾳ συνεῖναι φασί, καὶ ὡς ἐναντίῳ θεῷ τῷ ποιητῇ πολεμοῦντα, τὸν Ἀδὰμ ἐξαπατῆσαι, καὶ δεδωκέναι τὴν γνῶσιν, καὶ τούτου χάριν εἰρῆσθαι φρονιμώτατον εἶναι πάντων τὸν ὄ. Thdt.*haer.*1.14(4.308); οὐδεὶς...ὁ δυνάμενος σῶσαι καὶ ῥύσασθαι τοὺς ἐκπορευομένους ἐκ τῆς Αἰγύπτου, τουτέστιν ἐκ σώματος καὶ τοῦδε τοῦ κόσμου, εἰ μὴ μόνος ὁ τέλειος, ὁ πλήρης τῶν πληρῶν ὄ. ... οὗτος...ὁ ὄ. ἐστὶν ἡ δύναμις ἡ παρακολουθήσασα Μωσεῖ, ἡ ῥάβδος ἡ στρεφομένη εἰς ὄ. ... ὁ καθολικὸς ὄ. ... οὗτός ἐστιν ὁ σοφὸς τῆς Εὔας λόγος...τούτου κατ' εἰκόνα γέγονεν ὁ ἐν τῇ ἐρήμῳ ὁ χαλκοῦς...οὗτος ἦν ἐν ἀρχῇ πρὸς τὸν θεόν...καὶ εἴ τινος οἱ ὀφθαλμοὶ μακάριοι, οὗτος ὄψεται ἀναβλέψας εἰς τὸν οὐρανὸν τοῦ ὄ. τὴν καλὴν εἰκόνα ἐν τῇ μεγάλῃ ἀρχῇ τοῦ οὐρανοῦ στρεφομένην καὶ γινομένην ἀρχὴν πάσης κινήσεως Hipp.*haer.*5.16(p.112.12; M.16.3174Aff.); καθέζεται...μέσος τῆς ὕλης καὶ τοῦ πατρὸς ὁ υἱός, ὁ λόγος, ὁ ὄ., ἀεὶ κινούμενος πρὸς ἀκίνητον τὸν πατέρα *ib.*5.17(p.114.18; 3175B); οὐδεὶς δύναται σωθῆναι δίχα τοῦ υἱοῦ, οὐδὲ ἀνελθεῖν, ὅς ἐστιν ὁ ὄ. *ib.*(p.115.14; 3178B); ὥσπερ ἄγεται ὑπὸ τοῦ ἠλέκτρου τὸ ἄχυρον, οὕτω... ὑπὸ τοῦ ὄ. ἄγεται πάλιν ἀπὸ τοῦ κόσμου τὸ ἐξεικονισμένον τέλειον γένος ὁμοούσιον *ib.*(p.115.23; 3178B); οἱ τὰ τοῦ ὄ. ἑλόμενοι ὡς καλῶς τοῖς πρώτοις ἀνθρώποις συμβουλεύσαντος...καὶ Ὀφιανοὶ διὰ τοῦτο καλούμενοι Or.*Cels.*6.28(p.98.14; M.11.1336A); ἀπὸ τοῦ πολεμιωτάτου ἀνθρώποις ὄ. ..., ὡς οὐκ ἄνθρωποι, ὧν ἐχθρός ἐστιν ὄ., σεμνύνονται ἐπὶ τῷ Ὀφιανοὶ καλεῖσθαι *ib.*(p.98.30; 1337A); Ὀφῖται καλοῦνται δι' ὃν δοξάζουσιν ὄ. Epiph.*haer.*37.1(p.50.24; M.41.641B); ἀποδιδόασι...οἱ Ὀφῖται...τούτῳ τῷ ὄ. τὴν πᾶσαν γνῶσιν, λέγοντες ὅτι οὗτος ἀρχὴ γνώσεως γέγονεν τοῖς ἀνθρώποις *ib.*37.3(p.53.14; 645A); λέγει...ἑαυτὸν εἶναι Χριστὸν ὁ παρ' αὐτοῖς ὄ. *ib.*37.2(p.53.4; 644D); πῶς οὖν βασιλεὺς ἐπουράνιος ὁ ὄ., εἴπερ κατὰ τοῦ πατρὸς ἐγήγερται; *ib.*37.6(p.58.29; 649C); ἡ τῶν Ὀφιανῶν...αἵρεσις θεοποιούντων τὸν ὄ., ὡς ἄν ἀγαθόν τι προξενεῖν ἡμῖν ἐθελήσαντα Proc.G.*Gen.*3:1(M.87.184A); Anast.S.*hex. fr.*(M.89.963C); **5.** of brazen serpent as type of Christ, Just.*dial.*112.2(M.6.733B); διὰ τοῦ σταυροῦσθαι μέλλοντος θάνατος γενήσεσθαι ἔκτοτε προεκηρύσσετο τῷ ὄ. *ib.*91.4(693B); Bas.*ep.*260.8(3.400C; M.32.965B); καθάπερ ἐν τῷ ὑψώματι τοῦ ὄ. ἴασις ἐγίνετο τοῖς δηγμένοις, οὕτω ἐπὶ τῇ τοῦ Χριστοῦ σταυρώσει λύτρα γέγονε ταῖς ἡμῶν ψυχαῖς ἀπὸ τῶν... δηγμάτων τῆς ἁμαρτίας Epiph.*haer.*37.7(p.59.22; M.41.652A); τί... ἐστιν ὁ νεκρὸς ὄ., ὁ προσπεπηγμένος εἰς τὸ ἀκρότατον τοῦ ξύλου, ἰᾶτο τοὺς πεπληγμένους; ὁ νεκρὸς ὄ. τοὺς ζῶντας ἐνίκα, ὥστε τύπος ἐστὶ τοῦ σώματος τοῦ κυρίου. τὸ σῶμα γὰρ...ἀνήνεγκεν...ἐπὶ τοῦ σταυροῦ... καὶ τὸν ἐν τῇ καρδίᾳ ἕρποντα νεκρὸν σῶμα...ἀπέκτεινεν Mac.Aeg. *hom.*11.9(M.34.549C); Germ.CP *or.*1(M.98.229C); **6.** as symbol: of wisdom, ref. Mt.10:16, Clem.*str.*7.13(p.59.5; M.9.516A); of pleasure, id.*prot.*11(p.78.27; M.8.228C); of envy, Pall.*v.Chrys.*11(p.66.24; M.47.38); descriptive of Chosroes, Geo.Pis.*carm.*2.20; in prophecies on fate of Byzantium ἐγερθήσεται ὁ ὄ. ὁ κοιμώμενος καὶ πατάξει τὸν μείρακα...καὶ οὕτως δώσει ὁ ὄ. ὁ κοιμώμενος θάνατον ὁσίων *Apoc.Dan.* C(p.116).

Ὀφῖται, οἱ, *Ophites*, Gnostic heretics worshipping the serpent, Epiph.*haer.*37.1(p.50.24; M.41.641B); *ib.*37.3(p.53.14; 645A); Anast.S.*hex. fr.*(M.89.963C); cf.Isid.H.*etym.*8.5.10; v. Ὀφιανοί.

ὄφλημα, τό, *that which is owed*; hence **1.** *due* μικρόν ἐστί σοι τὸ τῆς φύσεως ὄ.· τροφὴν χρεωστεῖς τῷ σαρκίῳ σου, πρᾶγμα μέτριον Gr.Nyss. *or.dom.*4(p.80.9; M.44.1169B); Chrys.*hom.in Rom.*8:28(3.150C); Isid.Pel.*epp.*1.387(M.78.401A); ὡς ὄ. λήψεται τιμήν· ἀκούσεται γάρ... 'προσανάβηθι ὧδε' Cyr.*Lc.*14:7(M.72.785C); **2.** *wage*, ‡Chrys.*pasch.*1 (8.250A).

ὀφρυόω, *make conceited*, Gr.Naz.*carm.*1.2.10.26(M.37.682A); Diod.*Rom.*8:9(p.91.30); Nil.*Eulog.*33(M.79.1137A); pass., Cyr.*Nah.*29(3.507A); id.*ep.*11(5^2.38E, v.l. ὀφρύεται Aubert); ‡Nil.*perist.*4.14(M.79.841D); Nil.*Magn.*64(M.79.1056B).

ὀφρυώδης, *proud,* Gr.Naz.*carm.*2.1.11.707(M.37.1078A).

ὀφρύωσις, ἡ, *pride, superciliousness,* Or.*sel.in Lev.*14:9(M.12.404B).

***ὀφφικιάλιος, ὁ,** (Lat. *officialis*) *dignitary, official,* Maximinus Daia ap.Eus.*h.e.*9.10.8(M.20.833A); Bas.*ep.*198.1(3.289B; M.32.713A); Mac.Aeg.*cust.cor.*12(M.34.833D).

***ὀφφίκιον, τό,** (Lat. *officium*); **1.** *office, V.Aberc.*49; *ἐν ἀξιώματι τοῦτ' ἐστὶν ὀ. ἐκκλησιαστικῷ* CTrull.*can.*7; *αἱρετικὸς...μηδὲ πολιτευέσθω, μηδὲ ὀ. μετίτω* Ath.Scholast.*coll.*2.6(p.39); **2.** government *bureau μάγιστρος τῶν θείων ὀ.* CChalc.*act.*1(*ACO* 2.1.1 p.55.12; H.2.53C); **3.** *business, trade,* Thphn.*chron.*p.316(M.108.765A).

***ὀχεικός,** *salacious, T.Sal.*17.1(conj. for *ὀχικόν* cod., M.122.1340D).

[*]**ὀχετέω,** *convey in a channel,* Gr.Nyss.*hom.15 in Cant.*(M.44.1092D).

ὀχετηγέω, *conduct,* Gr.Nyss.*anim.et res.*(M.46.37D); ‡Nil.*perist.*4.12(M.79.837C).

ὀχετηγία, ἡ, *irrigation by ditches,* Gr.Naz.*ep.*6(M.37.29D).

ὀχετηγός, 1. *conducting*; lit., ‡Nil.*perist.*2.4(M.79.821A); met., Nonn.*par.Jo.*4:21(M.43.777B); *ib.*16:13(880A); Synes.*hymn.*3.168 (p.12; M.66.1596); **2.** as subst., *navvy, canal maker,* Ephr.3.455E.

ὀχή, ἡ, *prop, support,* Melet.*nat.hom.*28–29(M.64.1265C).

[*]**ὄχθα, ἡ,** = *ὄχθη, bank* of river, *Mir.Geo.*11(p.111.5).

ὄχθος, τό, = foreg., *Mir.Geo.*11(p.111.6).

***ὀχικός,** v. **ὀχεικός.*

ὀχλαγωγ-έω, *lead the mob, attract a crowd οὐ...δόξαν καρπώσασθαι ἐβούλετο* [sc. Christ], *οὐδὲ ∼εῖν* Chrys.*hom.57.2 in Jo.*(8.333E); *ib.*64.3(386E); *ib.84.2*(501B); id.*hom.in 1Cor.*proem.(10.2C); Isid.Pel.*epp.*1.482(M.78.444D); *ἀνεφάνη...δογματίζων Μάνης, διδάσκων καὶ ∼ῶν Chron.Pasch.*p.251(M.92.605B); pass., Steph.Diac.*v.Steph.*(M.100.1077A).

ὀχλαγώγιον, τό, *assemblage, mob,* CChalc.*act.*6(*ACO* 2.1.2 p.156.20; H.2.488D).

ὀχλάζω, = *ὀκλάζω, Asen.*16(p.64.1).

ὀχλέω, *trouble, importune*; c. dat., Ath.*v.Anton.*6(M.26.849B); *Hom.Clem.*11.13; Jo.Mal.*chron.*14 p.352(M.97.525B).

***ὀχληδόν,** *in a crowd,* Ph.Carp.*Cant.*197(M.40.124B).

ὀχλίζω, *gather together*; pass., Meth.*symp.*1.5(p.14.17; M.18.45D).

ὀχλοκρασία, ἡ, *mob-rule,* Clem.*str.*7.7(p.28.10; M.9.452B).

[*]**ὀχλοκράτεια, ἡ,** = foreg., met. *τὴν ὀ. τῶν παθῶν* Evagr.*h.e.*3.1 (p.100.1; *ὀχλοκρατίαν* M.86.2596A); *ib.*6.1(p.223.9; *ὀχλοκρατίαν* 2845B).

ὀχλοχαρής, *liking to be in a crowd,* Bas.*ep.*42.3(3.127D; M.32.353A).

ὀχλώδης, *turbulent, unruly δῆμος...ὀ.* Gr.Naz.*or.*34.7(M.36.248B).

ὀχυρότης, ἡ, *firmness πίστεως ὀ.* Eust.*engast.*7(p.25.4; M.18.625B).

ὀχυρ-όω, *fortify*; met., *confirm τὴν ∼οῦσαν τὴν πίστιν ἡμῖν θεωρίαν* Clem.*str.*1.11(p.33.26; M.8.749B); Cyr.H.*catech.*5.12; *παρρησιαστικοῖς γράμμασιν ὠχύρωσεν αὐτούς* Socr.*h.e.*2.15.3(M.67.212B); med. in act. sense, Chrys.*hom.9.3 in 2Tim.*(11.719C).

ὀχύρωμα, τό, *stronghold, fortress,* met. *ὀ. δογμάτων* Bas.*Spir.*77 (3.65D; M.32.213A); *τὰ ἔργα τῆς σαρκός, ὀ. ὄντα τῆς ἁμαρτίας* Epiph.*anc.*66(p.81.5; M.43.137A); Ast.Am.*phar.*(p.118.7).

ὀχύρωσις, ἡ, *strengthening,* †Bas.*Is.*92(1.443E; M.30.269C); Cyr.*thes.*34(5^{1}.350A); Proc.G.*Is.*2:10ff.(M.87.1889B).

ὀψάρι(ο)ν, τό, *fish, Chron.Pasch.*p.391(M.92.1004B); Leont.N.*v.Sym.*49(M.93.1729D); Thphn.*chron.*p.297(M.108.725B).

***ὀψεδύ-ω,** *set late,* better written *divisim ∼οντα Βοώτην* Paul.Sil.*Soph.*854(M.86.2151B).

***ὀψέποτε,** *at last,* Thdr.Stud.*epp.*2.105(M.99.1364A).

ὀψιγάμιον, τό, *late marriage ἐπιτίμιον...ὀψιγαμίου* Clem.*str.*2.23 (p.191.10; M.8.1092A).

ὀψίγαμος, *late-married,* Gr.Naz.*carm.*1.2.1.660(M.37.572A).

ὀψιγενής, 1. *born late in time*; of Logos acc. Arians, Cyr.*inc.unigen.*(5^{1}.679B); *ὀ. καὶ τῶν ἐν χρόνῳ πεποιημένων εἷς* id.*Jo.*1.1(4.14A); of Christ as man *εἰ γάρ ἐστιν ὀ. καθὸ ἄνθρωπος ὁ Ἐμμανουήλ, ἀλλ' ἦν πρὸ παντὸς αἰῶνος ὡς θεός* id.*Chr.un.*(5^{1}.748B); of Isaac, id.*glaph.Gen.*3(1.88B); **2.** *produced* or *made lately*; of idols, id.*Is.*4.3(2.629E).

ὀψίζω, 1. impers., *get late,* Jo.Clim.*scal.*26(M.88.1016A); med. *Ἰωάννης...τὸ ὀψισμένον...τῆς αὐτῆς νυκτὸς ὠνόμασε 'πρωΐ'* Eus.Em.*fr.Jo.*20:1–2(M.86.549A); **2.** pass., *be performed late θυσίαν ὀψισθεῖσαν Const.App.*4.10.2.

***ὀψικέλευθος,** *coming* or *going late,* Nonn.*par.Jo.*5:15(M.43.788A); *ib.*11:17(841B).

***ὀψικεύ-ω,** (cf. Lat. *obsequor*) *escort in procession,* esp. with lights, *T.Abr.*A 10(p.87.26); *ib.*20(p.103.26); Leont.N.*v.Sym.*13(M.93.1688A); *τὰ κηρία ∼οντα ἐν τῇ εἰσόδῳ δεικνύουσιν τὸ θεῖον φῶς* ‡Sophr.H.*liturg.*13(M.87.3993C).

***ὀψίκιον, τό,** (Lat. *obsequium*) *retinue, escort, A.Phil.*66(p.27.14); Jo.Mosch.*prat.*151(M.87.3016D); Leont.N.*v.Jo.Eleem.*5(p.11.11); *ib.*12(p.25.5); id.*v.Sym.*13(M.93.1685C); CCP(681)*act.*2(H.3.1061D); Gr.Mag.*dial.*(tr.Zach.)3.7(M.*PL.*77.280C).

ὀψίμορος, *dying slowly ὀ. δύο φωτῶν* Nonn.*par.Jo.*19:31(M.43.905A).

ὀψίνοος, *late-observing ὀ. μετανοίῃ* Nonn.*par.Jo.*3:23(M.43.769C).

ὀψινός, *late ὀ. ὥραν* Eus.*qu.Marin.*2.2(M.22.944A); fem. as subst., *evening,* Jo.Mal.*chron.*2 p.31(M.97.100A).

***ὀψίπλουτος,** *becoming rich late,* Bas.*hom.*7.4(2.56A; M.31.289D).

ὄψις, ἡ, 1. *pomp πᾶσαν δημοσίαν ὄ.* Marc.Diac.*v.Porph.*27; **2.** *status, condition*; of a thing, Ath.Scholast.*coll.*2.1(p.27).

***ὄψις, ὁ,** (Lat. *obses*) *hostage,* Thphn.*chron.*p.329(M.108.793B); *ib.* p.330(796C).

***ὀψιτόκος,** *bearing children late in life*; of Sarah, Gr.Naz.*carm.*2.1.1.442(M.37.1003A).

***ὀψιφανής,** *appearing late,* Nonn.*par.Jo.*7:14(M.43.808A); *ib.*20:20(912B).

***ὀψόβαφος,** ? *for dipping food τρυβλίον, ὀψόβαφόν ἐστι τὴν πλάσιν* Epiph.*mens.*24(M.43.284B).

ὀψοποιΐα, ἡ, *cooked dainty,* Chrys.*hom.in Mt.7:14*(3.30B).

ὀψοφαγία, ἡ, *dainty meal,* Gr.Nyss.*or.catech.*23(p.88.13; M.45.61D).

ὀψωνάτωρ, ὁ, (Lat. *obsonator*) *caterer,* Ast.Soph.*Ps.*7(M.40.473B).

ὀψώνιον, τό, 1. *wages,* †Gregent.*leg.Hom.*45(M.86.605B); met., *reward,* exeg. Rom.6:23 *ὀψωνίου μὲν ἐπὶ τῆς ἁμαρτίας τεταγμένου, χαρίσματος δὲ ἐπὶ τοῦ θεοῦ· οὔτε γὰρ ὀψώνια, εἰς ὀφειλόμενα δίδωσιν ὁ θεός, ἀλλὰ χάρισμα, οὐδὲ χάρισμα ἡ ἁμαρτία ἀλλ' ὀφειλόμενα ὀψώνια* Or.*comm.in Rom.*6:23(*JTS* 13 p.368); *εὐνοίας ὀ.* Cyr.*Abac.*19(3.533D); *ἀπειθείας ὀ.* id.*Zach.*4(3.657C); *κενοδοξίας ὀ.* Jo.Mosch.*prat.*110(M.87.2973B); **2.** *gratuity, gift,* Hipp.*Dan.*3.8.8.

Π

***παγανεύω,** *live as a civilian, M.Tar.*1(p.452); Ephr.2.244D.

παγανικός, *pagan,* of those who deny orthodox Christology *παγανικώτατοι φιλόσοφοι* Honor.*ep.Serg.*1(H.3.1324B).

παγανός, 1. *civilian π. δέ εἰμι, Χριστιανὸς...ῶν M.Tar.*2(p.454); *βασιλεύς τις ἐν τῇ αὐτοῦ βασιλείᾳ πάντας εἶχεν ἐστρατευομένους, π. δὲ οὐκ εἶχεν ἀλλ' ἢ...δύο* Epiph.*haer.*64.70(p.516.3; M. om.); opp. person in official position, Dor.*doct.*2.6(M.88.1648A); neut. as subst., *civilian clothes, M.Artem.*18(p.21.5); **2.** masc. as subst., *outsider, stranger ἡ διάταξις κελεύουσα ἀντὶ τῶν ἐλλειπόντων κληρικῶν τῷ... κλήρῳ τῆς μεγάλης ἐκκλησίας Κωνσταντινουπόλεως μὴ ἀντεισάγεσθαι π., ἀλλὰ σουπερνουμέρουμ ἐκ τῶν ἄλλων ἐκκλησιῶν* Ath.Scholast.*coll.*1.10(p.19).

πάγαρχος, ὁ, *local governor,* Bas.*ep.*3.2(3.76B; M.32.236C); Isid.Pel.*epp.*2.91(M.78.536C).

***παγγάληνος, 1.** *all-serene*; of emperor, CCP(681)*act.*18(H.3.1393D); **2.** *perfectly calm,* of future abode of blessed *π. ... λιμένας* Ephr.3.261C; Anast.S.*defunct.*(M.89.1193A).

***παγγέλαστος,** *ridiculous,* Epiph.*haer.*52.3(p.314.19; M.41.957D); ‡Sophr.H.*triod.*(M.87.3948A).

παγγενεί (παγγενεῖ), *with the whole race, including the whole tribe πολεμίους...π. κτείνειν* Cels.ap.Or.*Cels.*7.18(p.169.15; M.11.1445C); Dion.Al.ap.Eus.*h.e.*7.23.1(M.20.692A); Gr.Nyss.*v.Mos.*(M.44.324C).

***παγγενής,** *of all kinds πᾶσα σὰρξ διεφθάρη ἐκ...π. ἁμαρτίας* Geo.Pis.*Heracl.*1.90(M.92.1306A); *τίς ἐκστρατεύει παγγενῆ τὴν ἀκρίδα;* id.*hex.*1236(*παγκενῆ* M.92.1529A); hence *π. νικηφόρος victor in every kind of contest,* id.*Heracl.*1.217(1315A).

***παγγενναῖος,** *wholly noble,* Ephr.3.141F.

***παγγέραστος,** *renowned by all,* Nect.*Thdr.*23(M.39.1840A); Geo.Pis.*carm.*21.1.

παγγέωργος, *cultivating all things,* met. *ὁ π. λογισμὸς καὶ ἀποκνίζων* Melet.*nat.hom.*synops.(M.64.1113C).

παγίδευμα, τό, *snare, Clem.ep.*7(M.2.41A).

***παγιδευτήριον, τό,** *snare,* Eus.Al.*serm.*5(M.86.348B).

παγιδεύ-ω, *lay a snare for, entrap*; met., of snares of sin, Devil, etc., *T.Jos.*7.1; ∼εται...ἡ ψυχὴ ἀπὸ τῶν συμβεβηκότων αὐτῷ Or. *enarr.in Job* 22:10(M.17.84B); ∼οντες αὐτοὺς ἐν συνειδήσει Thdr. Heracl.*Is.*42:18(M.18.1337A); *Const.App.*1.3.4; *ib.*1.8.19; Nil.*epp.*2. 167(M.79.284C); φυλάσσουσιν ἡμῶν τὰς ψυχὰς...εἰς κακὸν οἱ δαίμονες ...ὥστε καὶ ∼ειν ἐνεδρεύοντες Hesych.H.*fr.Ps.*70:10(M.93.1236B); ὁ κόσμος...αὐτοὺς ∼ων †Jo.D.*B.J.*17(M.96.1021A).

πάγιος, **1.** of persons, *firm, steadfast* παγίους τῇ πίστει Thdt. *Cant.*2:15(2.73); **2.** *stable, established*, of things οὐδὲν...ὑγιὲς...οὐδὲ π. Meth.*res.*1.27(p.255.7; M.41.1133A); Gr.Nyss.*hom.4 in Cant.*(M. 44.856A); Chrysipp.*enc.in Mich.*(p.88.22); medic., *chronic* παγίαν... λέπραν Thdt.*qu.18 in Lev.*(1.195); of abstracts, Clem.*paed.*1.5(p.103. 13; M.8.276B); ἀπὸ δὲ τοῦ ξηροῦ τὸ ἀνδρῶδες καὶ π. *ib.*3.11(p.272.15; 640B); Gr.Nyss.*hom.4 in Cant.*(848B); πάγιον γνώμην Gel.Cyz.*h.e.*3. 10.14.

παγιότης, ἡ, **1.** *firmness, solidity*, Gr.Nyss.*hom.opif.*1.1(M.44. 128D); **2.** *steadfastness* τὸ δὲ σχῆμα τοῦ τετραγώνου, ἔνδειξίς σοι ἔστω τῆς ἐν τῷ καλῷ π. id.*v.Mos.*(M.44.392C); id.*Eun.*12(1 p.335.24; M.45. 1053A).

παγιόω, **1.** *fix, establish*, conj. for ἀποπετρωθῆναι Meth.*symp.* 3.5(p.31.17; M. om.); ref. Arians βουλόμενοι δὲ π. τὰ ζιζανιώδη φυτουργήματα Eust.*fr.in Pr.8*:22(M.18.676D); Didym.*Trin.*3.22 (M.39.917C); Jo.Clim.*scal.*4(M.88.685B); Thal.*cent.*3.7(M.91.1448D); *establish* in a treaty, Men.*exc.Rom.*3(p.182.22; M.113.868B); **2.** *confirm* πεπαγιωμένη ἔστω ἡ καθαίρεσις ‡Felix III Papa *ep.Petr.*2(H.2. 825B); **3.** *take firm hold of* ἐμὲ πεπαγίωκε συνήθεια πονηρά Jo.Clim. *scal.*18(M.88.933C).

παγίς, ἡ, *snare*; met., of snares of sin, Devil π. γὰρ θανάτου ἡ διγλωσσία *Did.*2.4; Clem.*prot.*12(p.83.10; M.8.237B); of temptation to apostatize as π. τοῦ διαβόλου *M.Sab.*3.2(p.120.22); Thdt.*Ps.*17:6 (1.703).

πάγκακος, *utterly evil*; superl., of antichrist ὁ...π. ... ὥσπερ δράκων ἀνήμερος πᾶσι τοῖς ἀνθρώποις ὡς ἐχθρὸς ἐπελεύσεται, τοῖς δικαίοις δὲ μάλιστα Rom.Mel.(*SBBAW* 1898² p.172); id.(p.171) cit. s. δολιότης.

***παγκάλλινος**, *all-beautiful*; of BMV, ‡Jo.D.*hom.*5(M.96.653C).

***παγκενής**, v. *παγγενής.

παγκοίρανος, *who is supreme ruler*; of BMV, ‡Gr.Naz.*Chr.pat.* 634(M.38.187A).

παγκόσμιος, **1.** *common to, shared by all the world* π. βήματος τοῦ δεσπότου *M.Just.*5.6(p.17.22); τὴν π. τοῦ...διαβόλου πλάνην ‡Hipp. *consumm.*2(p.290.2; M.10.905C); π. δικαστήριον ‡Chrys.*ascens.*1(3. 777E); Sophr.H.*or.*7.7(M.87.3332D); ref. Noah π. ... ναυάγιον Jo.D. *f.o.*4.24(M.94.1208C); ἐκκλησίας π. id.*hom.*1.16(M.96.569D); title of sun as worshipped by Julian, ‡Jo.D.*Artem.*31(p.81.26; M.96. 1280B); of BMV, *Hymn.*(*AS* 1 p.519); in address to saint πάτερ π. *universal father*, *ib.*(p.566); **2.** *for the whole world* τὸ π. πάθος ὑπέμεινεν ‡Chrys.*pasch.*7.2(8.279A).

***παγκοσμίως**, *universally, in all the world*, Apoll.*fr.*106(p.232.1) ap.*Doct.Patr.*12(p.77.4); ‡Ath.*fr.Ps.*39:10(p.47).

***παγκράτεια**, ἡ, *'all in' contest*, ‡Caes.Naz.*dial.*29(M.38.889).

παγκρατιάζ-ω, *fight in 'all in' boxing and wrestling match*; **1.** lit., in a martyr's vision, *M.Perp.*10(p.79.1); **2.** of spiritual warfare πρὸς τὸν διάβολον π. Chrys.*stat.*1.11(2.17D) etc.; **3.** *strive for mastery* ∼ων μοναχὸς βδελυχθήσεται Ephr.2.361A; οἱ δὲ ∼ουσιν ὑπὲρ χρημάτων Nil. *Magn.*31(M.79.1008A).

***παγκράτιστος**, *most excellent* or *powerful*, epithet of high official, Pall.*h.Laus.*proem.(p.3.8; M.34.995).

***παγκρατορικός**, *all-ruling*, Didym.*Trin.*1.32(M.39.425C); *ib.*2.5 (577A); Dion.Ar.*d.n.*8.5(M.3.893A).

***πάγκρυφος**, *completely hidden* Ἄκμωνος μὲν ἐν τοῖς περὶ αὐτοῦ λόγοις π. τὸν θεὸν ὀνομάζοντος ‡Just.*coh.Gr.*38(M.6.312A) perh. citing Hermetic document (? corruption of Ἀγαθοδαίμονος).

***παγκτήμων**, *possessing all*, Clem.*paed.*3.6(p.257.30; M.8.608A).

παγκτησία, ἡ, *full ownership*, Clem.*q.d.s.*25(p.176.20; M.9.629D); Dion.Ar.*d.n.*12.2(M.3.969B); ‡Nil.*perist.*9.8(M.79.880B).

***παγόω**, *freeze*, intrans., Chrys.*hom.9.6 in Phil.*(11.273A); Thphn.*chron.*p.249(M.108.624C).

παγχάλεπος, *most grievous*, Cyr.*Lc.*9:26(p.78.18; M.72.652B).

[*]**παγχάλκειος**, *all of brass*, †Apoll.*met.Ps.*103:5(M.33.1465B).

***πάγχαρτος**, *all-gladdening*, ‡Gr.Naz.*Chr.pat.*2182(M.38.308A).

***παγχρησίμως**, *very usefully*, Eus.*qu.Steph.*1.2(M.22.881D).

***παγχρυσόομαι**, *be made all of gold*, Jo.Mon.*hymn.Chrys.*6(M.96. 1381C).

πάθησις, ἡ, *suffering, passion*; of a martyr, *A.*(*Pass.*)*Andr.*1 (p.2.26; M.2.1217A); *ib.*9(p.23.22; 1236A); *ib.*(p.23.13).

***παθητής**, ὁ, *slave to passion*, Ast.Am.*hom.*2(M.40.181A).

παθητικός, **1.** *subject to change*; of matter, Ath.*decr.*10(p.9.26; M.25.'411'(433)A); Gr.Nyss.*Eun.*12(1 p.321.12; M.45.1036D); **2.** *capable of sense-experience* νοῦν πρὸς τῷ νοητῷ τὸν π. (ὃν καὶ φαντασίαν καλοῦσι τοῦ ζῴου, καθ' ὃν καὶ τὰ λοιπὰ ζῷα...ἐπιγινώσκουσι, περὶ ἣν συνίστασθαι τὴν αἴσθησίν φασιν) Max.*ambig.*(M.91.1116A); τοῦ π. τῆς ψυχῆς μέρους *ib.*(1196A); **3.** *passible, liable to suffering* μὴ δεῖν σωματικήν τινα καὶ π. ὑπολαμβάνειν τὴν τῆς θεότητος τοῦ υἱοῦ γέννησιν Eus.*Marcell.*1.4(p.22.4; M.24.760A); of man in gen. opp. God, id.*e.th.*1.12(p.72.32; M.24.849B); ref. natures of Christ, Leont.B. *Nest.et Eut.*1(M.86.1305A); δύναμις π. *faculty* or *potentiality of passibility* ἀναγκαίως ἔχει σχέσιν τινὰ...πρὸς ἄλληλα, ἡ ἐνεργητικὴ καὶ ἡ π. δύναμις, ὧν εἰ χωρισθείη τῷ λόγῳ τὸ ἕτερον, οὐκ ἂν ἐφ' ἑαυτοῦ συσταίη καὶ τὸ λειπόμενον...ὁ πατὴρ δὲ...οὐδὲν ἕτερόν ἐστιν ἢ ἐνέργεια, π. ἄρα διὰ τούτων ὁ...υἱός Gr.Nyss.*Eun.*12(1 p.321.2; M.45. 1036C); τὰ...θαύματα παθητά, τῇ κατὰ φύσιν τοῦ αὐτὰ θαυματουργοῦντος π. δυνάμει συμπληρούμενα τῆς σαρκός Max.*ambig.*(M.91.1056B); *ib.*(1060B); **4.** *pertaining to, connected with passions* or *emotions* [sc. σοφία] ἡ μὲν ἄνευ π. τινος κινήσεως, ἡ δὲ μετὰ π. ὀρέξεως Clem.*str.*6.7 (p.459.16; M.9.277A); οὐδὲν...κίνημα π. οὔτε ἡδονὴ οὔτε λύπη *ib.*6.9 (p.467.14; 292C); ὁ ἄνθρωπος ἀπὸ τῶν π. τὴν ἀρχὴν τοῦ ζῆν λαμβάνει *ib.*6.16(p.500.13; 360B); ἥ γε πρακτική ἐστι διδασκαλία πνευματική, τὸ π. μέρος τῆς ψυχῆς ἐκκαθαίρουσα Or.*Ps.*2:12(p.449); Gr.Nyss.*hom.1 in Cant.*(M.44.776C); οὐ τὸν π. φόβον ἔχειν προστάττει πρὸς τοὺς δεσπότας τοῖς οἰκέταις, ἄλογος γὰρ οὗτος *cat.1Petr.*2:18(p.56.27); νοῦς διὰ προσευχῆς τῷ θεῷ ἐγχρονίζων, καὶ τὸ π. τῆς ψυχῆς τῶν παθῶν ἀπαλλάττει Thal.*cent.*1.94(M.91.1436D); *ib.*2.49(1441D); **5.** *subject to passion*, of pagan gods ἐρωτικοὺς...καὶ π. Clem.*prot.*2(p.27.1; M.8. 113B); **6.** *emotional, pathetic*; of oratory, etc., Isid.Pel.*epp.*2.146(M. 78.592A); Philost.*h.e.*11.6(M.65.600B).

***παθητοαπαθής**, *both passible and impassible* εἰ μία φύσις σύνθετος ἐπὶ τοῦ Χριστοῦ, ἢ παθητὴ ἔσται μόνον, ἢ ἀπαθής, ἢ π. Jo.D.*Jacob.*43 (M.94.1456B) = id.*nat.*8(M.95.121D).

παθητός, *passible*;

A. *liable to change* (to process of becoming and of decay) ὡς οἱ ἀπὸ τοῦ Περιπάτου, οὐ παραλιπόντες προσκυνεῖν τὸν αἴτιον τῆς κινήσεως τοῦ σώματος θεὸν ἐπὶ τὰ πτωχὰ...στοιχεῖα καταπίπτομεν, τῷ ἀπαθεῖ ἀέρι κατ' αὐτοὺς τὴν π. ὕλην προσκυνοῦντες Athenag.*leg.*16.9 (M.6.921A); οὐδ' ἐκεῖνοι μὲν γὰρ ὅσιοι, οἱ τὴν ὕλην ὡς ἀγέννητον ὑποχείριον εἰς διακόσμησιν διδόντες τῷ θεῷ· π. γὰρ αὐτὴν καὶ τρεπτὴν ὑπάρχουσαν, εἴκειν ταῖς θεοποιήτοις ἀλλοιώσεσι Dion.Al.ap.Eus.*p.e.* 7.19(333D; M.21.564A); πῶς...ἀγήρως ἔμεινεν ὁ οὐρανός, οὐδεμίαν μεταβολὴν ἐκ τοῦ χρόνου δεξάμενος, καὶ...π. ἔχων τὴν φύσιν, ὡς... διδάσκει Δαβίδ· αὐτοί, φησίν, ἀπολοῦνται Thdt.*provid.*1(4.488).

B. *passible, liable to suffering and death*; **1.** of man, esp. of human body ἡ κοινωνία ἡ πνευματικὴ πρὸς τὸν π. ἄνθρωπον Clem.*paed.*1.6 (p.120.29; M.8.312A); τῷ σώματι τῷ φύσει π. ἐνδεδεμένος id.*str.*7.11 (p.45.5; M.9.488A); ἐν ἀνθρωπίνῳ σώματι καὶ παθητῷ ἀπάθειαν ἅπασαν κατορθοῦντες Chrys.*hom.18.3 in Mt.*(7.237D); τὸ σῶμα αὐτοῦ [sc. Ἀδάμ] γέγονε θνητὸν καὶ π. id.*hom.12.3 in Rom.*(9.547A); 'ἔχομεν τὸν θησαυρὸν...ἐν ὀστρακίνοις σκεύεσι', τουτέστι, π. ... σώμασι...εἰ μὴ π. ἦν τὰ σώματα, αὐτοῖς ἂν ἐπεγράφετο ἅπαντα id.*hom.10.3 in 2Tim.* (11.724A); **2.** denied of God, ‡Cyr.*Trin.*3(6.3E; M.77.1124C); v. ἀπαθής, ἀπαθῶς; asserted of God by Sabellians τὸν...ἀπαθῆ πατέρα ...π. διὰ τῆς ἐνανθρωπήσεως ὑποτίθενται *Symb.Ant.*(345)7(p.253.17; M.26.732C); ref. doctrine of Noëtus ἀπαθῆ καὶ ἀθάνατον, καὶ πάλιν αὖ π. καὶ θνητόν Thdt.*haer.*3.3(4.343); asserted by Manicheans π. μὲν...ὁ θεός, ἀπαθὴς δὲ ὁ σατανᾶς Serap.*Man.*34(p.51; M.18.1129C); **3.** of Christ in his humanity τὸν ἀπαθῆ, τὸν δι' ἡμᾶς π. Ign.*Polyc.*3.2; πρῶτον π. καὶ τότε ἀπαθής id.*Eph.*7.2; δύο γὰρ αὐτοῦ παρουσίας... μίαν μέν,...ὡς ἀτίμου καὶ π. ἀνθρώπου Just.*1apol.*52.3(M.6.405A); ὁ... π. ἡμῶν καὶ σταυρωθεὶς Χριστός id.*dial.*111.2(M.6.732C); acc. Valentinians σῶμα ψυχικὴν ἔχον οὐσίαν, κατεσκευασμένον δὲ...πρὸς τὸ...π. γεγενῆσθαι Iren.*haer.*1.6.1(M.7.505A); ὁ δι' ἡμᾶς τὴν π. ἀναλαβὼν σάρκα Clem.*str.*7.2(p.6.23; M.9.409B); ἡ μὲν γένεσις τὸ ἄφθαρτον ἔχει καὶ ἀναμάρτητον, ἡ δὲ γέννησις τὸ π. καὶ ἁμαρτητικόν, ὁ μὲν οὖν κύριος τῆς μὲν γενέσεως τὸ ἀναμάρτητον φυσικῶς λαβὼν τὸ ἄφθαρτον οὐ προσέλαβε, τῆς δὲ γεννήσεως τὸ π. εἰληφὼς τὸ ἁμαρτητικὸν οὐ προσέλαβε Or. *fr.in Mt.*1:18(*GCS* p.19.17; M.17.289B); ἦν ἐν τῷ π. μένων ἀπαθής Meth.*Porph.*3(p.507.3; M.18.401C); ὁ τὰ ἔργα ποιῶν ὁ αὐτός ἐστιν ὁ καὶ τὸ σῶμα π. δεικνύς Ath.*Ar.*3.55(M.26.437C); αὐτὸς μὲν ὁ ἀσώματος ἦν ἐν τῷ π. σώματι· τὸ δὲ σῶμα εἶχεν ἐν ἑαυτῷ τὸν ἀπαθῆ λόγον id.*ep. Epict.*6(p.10.19; M.26.1060C); οὔτε τὸ π. σῶμα ὃ ἐφόρεσεν διὰ τὴν τοῦ παντὸς σωτηρίαν, ἀνατίθεμεν τῷ πατρί ‡Ath.*serm.fid.*14(p.10; M.26. 1269D); ἀπαθῆ θεότητι, π. τῷ προσλήμματι Gr.Naz.*or.*40.45(M.36. 424B); ἔλαβε τὸ ἡμέτερον π. σῶμα,...ἵνα ἐν αὐτῷ συνευδοκήσῃ τοῦ παθεῖν καὶ ἀναδέξηται τὰ ἡμέτερα πάθη ἐν σαρκί, συνούσης τῆς θεότητος Epiph.*haer*.69.24(p.174.21; M.42.241A); μετὰ τὴν ἔνσαρκον παρουσίαν, τοῦ αὐτοῦ ἀπαθοῦς ὄντος καὶ π. *ib*.69.38(p.186.25; 261A); monoph. assertion διὰ τοῦ π. τὸ ἀπαθὲς ὑπομείνῃ τὸ πάθος Thdt.*eran*.3(4.176); answered τοῦ π. σώματος τὸ πάθος εἶναι φαμέν, τὴν ἀπαθῆ δὲ φύσιν ἐλευθέραν μεμενηκέναι τοῦ πάθους ὁμολογοῦμεν *ib*.(190); ἡ θεία φύσις ἡνώθη τῇ φύσει τῇ π. Leo Mag.*ep*.28.3(p.13.14; M.*PL*.54.764A); ὁ ἀπαθὴς θεὸς οὐκ ἀπηξίωσε π. εἶναι ἄνθρωπος *ib*.28.4(p.14.18; 768A); agst. monoph. doctrine εἰ ἡ φύσει π. σὰρξ τοῦ λόγου οὐκ ὤφθη ἀπαθὴς διὰ τὴν πρὸς αὐτὸν ἕνωσιν, πόσῳ γε μᾶλλον ὁ φύσει ἀπαθὴς λόγος, αὐτὸς οὐ γέγονε π., διὰ τὴν πρὸς τὸ π. ἕνωσιν; Leont.H.*monoph*.46(M.86.1796D); λέγει...ἡ ἐκκλησία ὅτι εἰ λέγετε ἀσύγχυτα τὰ ἑνωθέντα, καὶ τὸ μὲν π., τὸ δὲ ἀπαθὲς...ἐξ ἀνάγκης δύο φύσεις εἰσάγετε· ἀντιλέγουσι πρὸς ταῦτα, ὅτι οὐδὲν ἄτοπον, καὶ ἀσύγχυτα ὁμολογῆσαι τὰ ἑνωθέντα· καὶ τὸ μὲν π., τὸ δὲ ἀπαθές, καὶ μίαν φύσιν ἐπὶ αὐτῶν †Leont.B.*sect*.7.5(M.86.1245A); agst. Nestorian teaching δεδοίκατε γὰρ αὐτὸν σαρκὶ συνάπτειν καὶ ὅλῳ ἀνθρώπῳ, ὡς ἐξ ἀνάγκης περιγραφησόμενον καὶ πεισόμενον. εἰ μὲν οὖν φύσει π. ὁ λόγος, ἢ τὴν ἐν τόπῳ δέχεται περιγραφήν, ἔσται ταῦτα ἐν αὐτῷ δι' αὐτόν, ἀλλ' οὐ διὰ τὴν πρὸς τὸ περιγραπτὸν καὶ π. σῶμα ἕνωσιν· καὶ ἔσται οὕτως π. περιγραπτός, κἂν μὴ πέπονθε μηδὲ περιγέγραπται Leont.B.*Nest.et Eut*.1(M.86.1284B); π. σαρκί, ἀπαθὴς ὁ αὐτὸς θεότητι Justn.*conf*.(p.74.1; M.86.995C); **4.** of Christ (heret.); of Word in divine nature: Valent. μορφὴν δούλου λαβεῖν εἴρηται, οὐ μόνον τὴν σάρκα κατὰ τὴν παρουσίαν, ἀλλὰ καὶ τὴν οὐσίαν ἐκ τοῦ ὑποκειμένου, δούλη δὲ ἡ οὐσία, ὡς ἂν π. καὶ ὑποκειμένη τῇ δραστηρίῳ καὶ κυριωτάτῃ αἰτίᾳ Clem.*exc.Thdot*.19(p.113.13; M.9.668B); Eunomian, Gr.Nyss.*Eun*.12(1 p.321.9; M.45.1036D); ‡Ath.*dial.Trin*.2.23(M.28.1192D); Cyr.*Jo*.2.1(4.120D); ref. monophysitism π. τοῦ μονογενοῦς τὴν θείαν φύσιν τῇ συγχύσει τερατευόμενοι *Symb.Chalc*.(p.128.22; H.2.453E); ‡Quint.*ep*.(p.17.20; M.85.1740C); Leont.H.*monoph*.44(M.86.1796B); ref. Arius and Apollinarius ἑκάτερος γὰρ π. φύσει θεότητος, ἀλλ' οὐ φύσει σαρκὸς εἶπον τὸν μονογενῆ Max.*opusc*.(M.91.97C); cf.‡Caes.Naz.*dial*.26(M.38.885).

***παθοκίνητος**, *moved by passion* or *emotion*, Anast.S.*hod*.3(M.89.92A).

παθοκρατέομαι, *be swayed by emotion*, Const.Diac.*laud*.10(M.88.489D).

***παθοκρατορικός**, *able to govern the passions*, †Ath.*fr.Mt*.(M.27.1369B).

***παθόκτονος**, *passion-destroying*, ‡Sophr.H.*triod*.(M.87.3893B); *Apophth.Patr*.(M.65.368A); Germ.CP *or*.1(M.98.240B); π. παθήμασιν Andr.Cr.*Geo*.(p.xxiv A).

[*]**παθολογ-έομαι**, *be spoken of as suffering, have suffering ascribed to one* ὥσπερ γὰρ θεολογεῖται ἡ σὰρξ διὰ τὴν...ἕνωσιν, οὕτω...ἀνθρωπολογεῖται καὶ ~εῖται, καὶ θανατολογεῖται Anast.S.*hod*.12(M.89.200D).

παθοποιός, *producing suffering*; of demons, *Hom.Clem*.9.21; ref. passibility of Christ τό, σαρκί, οὔτε ὡς δι' ὀργάνου π. εἴρηται, οὔτε...ὥσπερ φαμὲν ὅτι ὁ δεῖνα προσέπταισε τῷ ποδί, ἢ ἐκρεμάσθη τῇ χειρί Leont.H.*Nest*.7.2(M.86.1764A).

πάθος, τό, **I.** *incident, accident, change*;

A. in nature οὐκ ἔστι θεὸς ἡ ἅλως...οὐκ ἔστι θεὸς ἡ ἶρις, ἀλλὰ π. ἀέρος καὶ νεφῶν Clem.*prot*.10(p.73.20; M.8.217A); ὕπνος καὶ θάνατος ...π. ταῦτα περὶ τὰ ζῷα *ib*.(p.73.29; 217B); τὸ γὰρ κατὰ φύσιν ἢ κατὰ π. θερμὸν ἢ ψυχρόν ‡Just.*qu.Chr*.5(M.6.1460B); ἔγνως σελήνης φύσιν, καὶ πάθη Gr.Naz.*or*.28.30(p.69.6; M.36.69B); Gr.Nyss.*or.catech*.23(p.87.7; M.45.61C); οὐ τῆς τοῦ μάννα φύσεως ἦν τὸ π. Thdt.*qu.31 in Ex*.(1.145); φροῦδον γίνεται τοῦ ἡλίου τὸ φῶς; ταὐτὸ δὲ τοῦτο καὶ τῇ σελήνῃ νύκτωρ τὸ π. προσγίνεται id.*affect*.3(p.71.8; 4.762).

B. in men; **1.** *calamity* τὸ Σοδομιτῶν π. κρίσις μὲν ἀδικήσασι Clem.*paed*.3.8(p.262.5; M.8.616A); id.*prot*.3(p.33.16; M.8.129A); **2.** *disease*, Cyr.H.*catech*.19.8; Gr.Nyss.*or.catech*.29(p.108.12; M.45.76A); Thdt.*2Tim*.2:17(3.684); of spiritual disease, Clem.*str*.1.8(p.27.1; M.8.737A).

II. of the soul, *emotion, passion*;

A. in man; **1.** def. π., ἃ δὴ ψυχῆς νόσοι Clem.*prot*.11(p.81.17; M.8.233B); π. δὲ πλεονάζουσα ὁρμὴ ἢ ὑπερτείνουσα τὰ κατὰ τὸν λόγον μέτρα, ἢ ὁρμὴ ἐκφερομένη καὶ ἀπειθὴς λόγῳ· παρὰ φύσιν οὖν κίνησις ψυχῆς κατὰ τὴν πρὸς τὸν λόγον ἀπείθειαν τὰ π. id.*str*.2.13(p.145.3,6; M.8.997A,B); ὁ...λόγος τῆς καθ' ἡμᾶς φιλοσοφίας τὰ π. πάντα ἐναπερείσματα τῆς ψυχῆς φησιν εἶναι τῆς μαλθακῆς καὶ εἰκούσης καὶ οἷον ἐναποσφραγίσματα τῶν 'πνευματικῶν' δυνάμεων *ib*.2.20(p.173.7; 1053C); *ib*.6.14(p.488.8; M.9.336B); τῶν δὲ ψυχικῶν π. ὅρος οὗτος· π. ἐστὶ κίνησις τῆς ὀρεκτικῆς δυνάμεως αἰσθητὴ ἐπὶ φαντασίᾳ ἀγαθοῦ ἢ κακοῦ. καὶ ἄλλως· π. ἐστὶ κίνησις ἄλογος τῆς ψυχῆς δι' ὑπόληψιν καλοῦ ἢ κακοῦ. τὸ δὲ γενικὸν π. οὕτως ὁρίζονται· π. ἐστὶ κίνησις ἐν ἑτέρῳ ἐξ ἑτέρου...π. δέ, τῶν δύο μερῶν τῆς ψυχῆς, καὶ προσέτι τοῦ σώματος ἡμῶν παντός, ὅταν ὑπὸ τοῦ θυμοῦ βιαίως ἄγηται πρὸς τὰς πράξεις. ἐξ ἑτέρου γὰρ ἐν ἑτέρῳ γέγονεν ἡ κίνησις, ὅπερ ἐλέγομεν εἶναι π. καὶ καθ' ἕτερον δὲ τρόπον, ἡ ἐνέργεια π. λέγεται, ὅταν ᾖ παρὰ φύσιν. ἐνέργεια μὲν γάρ ἐστι κατὰ φύσιν κίνησις, π. δὲ παρὰ φύσιν. καὶ κατὰ τοῦτον οὖν τὸν λόγον ἡ ἐνέργεια, ὅταν μὴ κατὰ φύσιν κινῆται, λέγεται π., εἴτε ἐξ ἑαυτοῦ κινοῖτο, εἴτε ἐξ ἑτέρου. τῆς γοῦν καρδίας ἡ μὲν κατὰ τοὺς σφυγμοὺς κίνησις ἐνέργειά ἐστιν· ἡ δὲ κατὰ τοὺς παλμούς, π. Nemes.*nat.hom*.16(M.40.673B,C); Gnost. οἱ δ' ἀμφὶ τὸν Βασιλείδην προσαρτήματα τὰ π. καλεῖν εἰώθασι, πνεύματά τέ τινα ταῦτα κατ' οὐσίαν ὑπάρχειν προσηρτημένα τῇ λογικῇ ψυχῇ κατά τινα τάραχον Clem.*str*.2.20(p.174.6; M.8.1056B); **2.** rel. to soul ταῦτα τὰ π. τῆς φύσεως ὄντα καὶ οὐκ οὐσία...τοῦ δὲ ὁρισμοῦ τοῦ περὶ ψυχῆς οὐ προσάπτεται Gr.Nyss.*anim.et res*.(M.46.56A); ὕστερον ἐπεισήχθη τὸ π. αὐτῷ [sc. ἀνθρώπῳ] μετὰ τὴν πρώτην κατασκευήν id.*virg*.12(p.298.8; M.46.369B); τὰ π. αὐτὰ...τῇ φύσει τῶν ἀνθρώπων προηγουμένως οὐ συνεκτίσθη· ἐπεὶ καὶ εἰς τὸν ὅρον ἂν συνετέλουν τῆς φύσεως. λέγω δέ, παρὰ τοῦ Νυσσαέως μεγάλου Γρηγορίου μαθών, ὅτι διὰ τὴν τῆς τελειότητος ἔκπτωσιν, ἐπεισήχθη αὐτὰ τῷ ἀλογωτέρῳ μέρει προσφυέντα τῆς φύσεως· δι' ὧν, ἀντὶ τῆς θείας...εἰκόνος, εὐθὺς ἅμα τῇ παραβάσει διαφανὴς...ἐν τῷ ἀνθρώπῳ γέγονεν, ἡ τῶν ἀλόγων ζῴων ὁμοίωσις Max.*qu.Thal*.1(M.90.269A); but cf. μάθετε θείων δογμάτων ἀλήθειαν...ψυχῆς φύσιν ἀθάνατον, καὶ τὸ ταύτης λογικὸν ἡγούμενον τῶν π., καὶ τὰ π. ἀναγκαῖα τῇ φύσει Thdt.*affect*.5(p.146.13; 4.843); **3.** rel. to sin and evil πᾶν τὸ παρὰ τὸν λόγον τὸν ὀρθὸν τοῦτο ἁμάρτημά ἐστιν. αὐτίκα γοῦν τὰ π. τὰ γενικώτατα ὧδέ πως ὁρίζεσθαι ἀξιοῦσιν οἱ φιλόσοφοι Clem.*paed*.1.13(p.150.22; M.8.372B); οὐδὲ γὰρ τὰ π., οὐδὲ τὰ ἁμαρτήματα κακίαι, καίτοι ἀπὸ κακίας φερόμενα id.*str*.7.11(p.47.20; M.9.492A); τῶν ἁμαρτημάτων...αἴτια, ἢ τὰ π. τῆς ψυχῆς καὶ αἱ διὰ σώματος ἐπιθυμίαι Meth.*symp*.8.16(p.109.13; M.18.172C); ἡ ψυχὴ ὅλη ἔπαθε τὰ τῆς κακίας π. Mac.Aeg.*hom*.2.1(M.34.464B); *ib*.4.8(477C); ταῦτα δέ ἐστιν ὅσα ἐν ἡμῖν γινόμενα π. λέγεται, ἃ οὐχὶ πάντως ἐπὶ κακῷ τινι τῇ ἀνθρωπίνῃ συνεκληρώθη ζωῇ· ἢ γὰρ ἂν ὁ δημιουργὸς τῶν κακῶν τὴν αἰτίαν ἔχῃ, εἰ ἐκεῖθεν αἱ τῶν πλημμελημάτων ἦσαν ἀνάγκαι συγκαταβεβλημέναι τῇ φύσει· ἀλλὰ τῇ ποιᾷ χρήσει τῆς προαιρέσεως, ἢ ἀρετῆς, ἢ κακίας ὄργανα τὰ τοιαῦτα τῆς ψυχῆς κινήματα γίνεται Gr.Nyss.*anim.et res*.(M.46.61A); ὥσπερ διάφορα π. τῷ σώματι...συμβαίνειν πέφυκεν, κἂν μὴ πάντα πᾶσιν μηδὲ πάντοτε ἐγγίνεται, οὕτω καὶ ἁμαρτιῶν διάφορα π. πέφυκεν ἡμῖν ἐνοχλεῖν, κἂν μὴ πάντα παρὰ πάντων ἐπιτελεῖται μηδὲ πάντοτε· ὡς γὰρ κατὰ τὸ σῶμα ὁ μὲν ἧττον ὁ δὲ μᾶλλον τοῖς π. περιπίπτει, οὕτω καὶ ἐπὶ τῶν ἁμαρτημάτων ὁ μὲν πλείονα ὁ δὲ ἐλάττονα ἁμαρτάνει. ἐπειδὴ τοίνυν νόμῳ τινὶ τὰ ἁμαρτήματα κρίνεται, εἴτε κατὰ τὴν φυσικὴν διάκρισιν εἴτε κατὰ τὰς δεδομένας ἔξωθεν διατάξεις, τοῦτο λέγει ὅτι πάντα τῶν ἁμαρτιῶν τὰ π., ὁσάπερ νόμῳ τινὶ διακρινόμενα ἐγγίνεσθαι ἡμῖν συμβαίνει...ἐπράττετο παρ' ἡμῶν Thdr.Mops.*Rom*.7:5(p.123.13ff.; M.66.808A,B); ἡ ἁμαρτία...εἰς ἀμετρίαν ἐκκαλουμένη τὰ π. Thdt.*Rom*.5:21(3.60); τῶν γὰρ π. πεπαυμένων, οὐχ ἕξει χώραν ἡ ἁμαρτία *ib*.(61); ἄλλα γάρ εἰσι τὰ π., καὶ ἄλλαι εἰσὶν αἱ ἁμαρτίαι· τὰ π. εἰσί, θυμός, κενοδοξία, μῖσος...καὶ ὅσα τοιαῦτα· αἱ δὲ ἁμαρτίαι εἰσίν, αὗται αἱ ἐνέργειαι τῶν π. ὅτε τις ἐνεργῶς ποιεῖ αὐτά Dor.*doct*.1.4(M.88.1621D); **4.** associated with corruption τὰ χαμαιπετῆ καὶ τὰ διαφθορᾶς...π. Just.*dial*.134.2(M.6.785C); Meth.*symp*.7.6(p.77.14; M.18.133A); φθοροποιοῖς π. Dion.Ar.*e.h*.3.3.12(M.3.444B); *ib*.7.1.2(556A); and the flesh, Max.*qu.Thal*.47(M.90.425A); therefore where π. is absent, as in faith of Christ, there is also no corruption, Gr.Nyss.*or.catech*.13(p.60.5; M.45.45A); **5.** and with Devil ἡ δαίμονος φύσις ἐμπαθὴς οὖσα, μᾶλλον δὲ π. οὖσα ζῶν καὶ κινούμενον, πελάσασα ψυχῇ τὸ ἐν αὐτῇ π. κινεῖ, καὶ προάγει τὴν δύναμιν εἰς ἐνέργειαν Synes.*provid*.10(p.84.3f.; M.66.1232A); δαίμονας εἶναί τινας τοὺς τοῖς π. ἀκολουθοῦντας καὶ τὰ π. ἡμῶν πολλάκις ἐπὶ τὸ κακὸν μετατρέποντας· ὅστις οὖν...βούλεται τοὺς δαίμονας ἀπελαύνειν, πρότερον τὰ π. δουλώσηται. οἵου γὰρ ἂν πάθους τις περιγένηται, τούτου καὶ τὸν δαίμονα ἀπελαύνει. καὶ δεῖ κατὰ μικρὸν ὑμᾶς νικῆσαι τὰ π., ἵνα τούτων τοὺς δαίμονας ἀπελάσητε ‡Pall.*h.mon*.17.2f.(p.77.11ff.; M.34.1178C,D); Max.*carit*.2.31(M.90.993C) cit. s. ἁμαρτία; **6.** origin; **a.** from within πεπληρωμένος τῆς ἐν τῷ ἡγεμονικῷ ἑαυτοῦ στάσεως τῶν π. Or.*Jo*.20.37(29; p.378.29; M.14.661C); Gr.Thaum.*pan.Or*.9(p.23.15; M.10.1080A); dating from Adam, Mac.Aeg.*hom*.5.3(M.34.496D); **b.** from without, Clem.*paed*.2.5(p.187.4; M.8.452A); Nil.*exerc*.49(M.79.781A); αἴσθησις ἐπιρεμβομένη τοῖς αἰσθητοῖς ὕλας κατὰ τῆς ψυχῆς τοῖς π. δίδωσι πρὸς τὸ βλάψαι ταύτην id.*praest*.7(M.79.1068D); παντὸς πέφυκε πάθους ἄρχειν τὸ προσφυὲς αἰσθητόν. ἄνευ γάρ τινος ὑποκειμένου, καὶ τὰς δυνάμεις τῆς ψυχῆς διὰ μέσης τινὸς αἰσθήσεως ἐπικινοῦντος πρὸς ἑαυτό, π. οὐκ ἂν συσταίη ποτέ. χωρὶς γὰρ αἰσθητοῦ πράγματος, π. οὐ συνίσταται. μὴ γὰρ οὔσης γυναικός, οὐκ ἔστι πορνεία Max.*cap*.3.3(M.90.1260C); πρὸς ἅπερ τὰ π. κεκτήμεθα πράγματα, εἰσὶ ταῦτα, οἷον, γυνή, χρήματα, δῶρα, καὶ τὰ ἑξῆς id.*carit*.4.49(M.90.1057D); πολλὰ π. ἐν ταῖς ψυχαῖς ἡμῶν κέκρυπται· τότε δὲ ἐλέγχονται, ὅταν τὰ πράγματα ἀναφαίνωνται. δύναταί τις μὴ ὀχλεῖσθαι ὑπὸ παθῶν ἐν τῇ τῶν πραγμάτων ἀπουσίᾳ...ἐὰν δὲ ἀναφανῶσι τὰ πράγματα, εὐθὺς τὰ π. τὸν νοῦν περισπῶσι *ib*.4.52f.(1060B); **7.** effects; **a.** darkening of the understanding, Clem.*str*.2.16(p.151.12; M.8.1012A); τοῦ ὑπὸ τῶν π. ἐμποδιζομένου βλέπειν ἀλήθειαν Or.*Cels*.6.67(p.137.24; M.11.1400D); Meth.*symp*.9.4(p.118.17; M.18.185B); οὐδὲ π. ἔχοντα θεολογίας ἅπτεσθαι Jo.Clim.*scal*.27(M.88.1097C); **b.** prevention of virtue and spiritual peace αἱ γὰρ αἰσθήσεις τῆς ψυχῆς,...ἐπειδὰν τῶν ἔξωθεν προσπιπτόντων π. ἡττηθεῖσαι προσδέξωνται τὰς ἐπιφορὰς τοῦ τῆς ἀνοίας ἐπικλύσαντος εἴσω κύματος, εὐθέως τῆς εὐθείας ὁρμῆς ἐμποδίζουσι σκοτωθεῖσαι Meth.*symp*.4.2(p.47.6; M.18.88D); Chrys.*hom*.55.2 *in Jo*.(8.324E); **8.** hence incompatible with life of perfection and prayer ἐξαιρετέον ἄρα τὸν γνωστικὸν ἡμῖν καὶ τέλειον ἀπὸ παντὸς ψυχικοῦ π. ... οὐδὲ ἐκείνων τῶν θρυλουμένων ἀγαθῶν, τουτέστι τῶν παρακειμένων τοῖς π. παθητικῶν ἀγαθῶν, λαμβάνει ὁ γνωστικός Clem. *str*.6.9(p.468.28,32; M.9.296A); οὗτος ὁ τῷ ὄντι ἀγαθὸς ἀνὴρ ὁ ἔξω τῶν π. *ib*.7.11(p.47.1; 489C); προσεύχου πρότερον περὶ τοῦ καθαρθῆναι τῶν π. Evagr.Pont.*or*.37(M.79.1176A); τί βούλεται τοῖς δαίμοσι ἐνεργεῖν ἐν ἡμῖν γαστριμαργίαν...καὶ τὰ λοιπὰ π.; ἵνα παχυνθῇς ὁ νοῦς ἐξ αὐτῶν, μὴ δυνηθῇ ὡς δεῖ προσεύξασθαι *ib*.50(1177B); ὁρᾶτε, μὴ π. ὑμῖν ἐνοχλήσῃ...λοιπὸν πρὸς τὰ π. διαμαχόμενος οὐ δύναται ὁρᾶν τὸν θεόν ‡Pall.*h.mon*.1.25f.(p.11.5,15; M.34.1116C,D); ἄσχετος γεγονὼς ἐκ π., καὶ ἐπὶ τὸ ἁρπάζεσθαι πρὸς κύριον ἥξει ἐν τῷ προσεύχεσθαι ‡Max. *cap.al*.178(M.90.1441C); οὐ καθαρῶς δύναται προσεύξασθαι, ὁ φιλοκάλῳ π. ... κρατούμενος *ib*.220(1453A); **9.** of the fight against passions; its necessity, Clem.*str*.7.12(p.52.8; M.9.500C); id.*q.d.s*.14(p.169.6,10; M.9.617D–620A); Or.*hom*.5.16 *in Jer*.(p.45.22; M.13.320C); *Const. App*.8.25.3; κατὰ φύσιν ὁ νοῦς ἐνεργεῖ, ὅταν τὰ π. ἔχῃ ὑποτεταγμένα Max.*carit*.4.45(M.90.1057C); maintained by education and virtue θεραπεύεται δὲ πολλὰ τῶν π. τιμωρίᾳ καὶ προστάξει αὐστηροτέρων παραγγελμάτων...ἔστι δὲ οἱονεὶ χειρουργία τῶν τῆς ψυχῆς π. ὁ ἔλεγχος, ἀπόστασις δὲ τὰ π. τῆς ἀληθείας Clem.*paed*.1.8(p.128.7ff.; M.8.328B); τῆς ψυχῆς π., ὧν ἐπικρατοῦμεν τῇ ἀρετῇ id.*str*.1.24(p.100.17; M.8.908A); id.*q.d.s*.40(p.187.5; M.9.645C); τὴν ἄσκησιν τῶν θείων μαθημάτων, οἷς ἐκκαθαίρεται...ψυχὴ νικῶσα τὰ π. Meth.*symp*.9.4 (p.118.9; M.18.185A); Thal.*cent*.2.13(M.91.1437D); v. ἀγάπη; by ascetical practices ὁ κρατῶν γαστρός, ἐλαττοῖ π. Nil.*spir.mal*.1 (M.79.1145A); methodical combat, id.*exerc*.24(M.79.752A); ἡσυχία, id.*praest*.11(M.79.1073C); ταπεινώσεως εἰσαγωγικῆς αὔξησις,...παθῶν ἀλλοτρίωσις Jo.Clim.*scal*.27(M.88.1108C); εἰσί τινα ἱστῶντα τὰ π. τῆς κινήσεως, καὶ μὴ ἐῶντα προβῆναι εἰς αὔξησιν· καὶ εἰσὶν ἕτερα ἐλαττοῦντα, καὶ εἰς μείωσιν ἄγοντα. οἷον, νηστεία καὶ κόπος καὶ ἀγρυπνία, οὐκ ἐῶσιν αὔξειν τὴν ἐπιθυμίαν· ἀναχώρησις δὲ καὶ θεωρία καὶ προσευχή, καὶ ἔρως εἰς θεόν, ἐλαττοῦσιν αὐτήν Max.*carit*.2.47(M. 90.1000C); constancy γίνεται γὰρ τοῦτο τοῖς ἀμελέστερον τῇ διανοίᾳ προσέχουσι τῇ ἑαυτῶν μετὰ τὴν τῶν π. ἐκκοπήν, ὥσπερ βλαστοί τινες παρακύπτειν ἄρχονται αἱ εἰκόνες τῶν παλαιῶν φαντασιῶν, αἷς εἴ τις δῷ χώραν...αὖθις εἰσοικίσει τὰ π. ἑαυτῷ ἐναγώνιον μετὰ τὴν νίκην... ἔστι γὰρ τῶν π. ἐξημερωθέντων, καὶ χόρτον ἴσα βουσὶν ἐσθίειν δεδιδαγμένων ἀμελείᾳ τοῦ τιθασεύοντος πάλιν ἐξαγριωθῆναι Nil.*exerc*.37 (M.79.765B); τὰ π. ταῖς συνεχέσι συντυχίαις παρακύπτειν εἰς φανερὸν κωλυόμενα, ἀλκιμώτερα γίνεται, καὶ ἡσυχίας εὐπορήσαντα...ἐπικίνδυνον τοῖς ἐν ἀρχῇ τῆς πρὸς αὐτὰ μάχης ἀμελήσασι ποιοῦντα τὸν πόλεμον ...αἱ μὲν γὰρ προσβολαὶ τῶν π. ἀπὸ εὐτελῶν ἄρχονται φαντασιῶν...τὰ δὲ τελευταῖα ἐπὶ μέγαν ἐξαίρεται ὄγκον...διὸ χρὴ τὸν ἀγωνιστὴν τότε παλαίειν πρὸς τὰ π., ὅταν, ὡς μύρμηξ, προσέρχωνται δέλεαρ τὴν εὐτέλειαν προσελόμενα. ἐὰν γὰρ ἐπὶ τὴν τοῦ λέοντος φθάσωσιν ἰσχὺν προελθεῖν, δυσκαταγώνιστα γίνεται *ib*.49(780B,D); various modes of combat οἱ μὲν τῶν ἀγωνιζομένων, ἀποκρούονται μόνον τοὺς ἐμπαθεῖς λογισμούς· οἱ δὲ καὶ αὐτὰ τὰ π. περικόπτουσι. καὶ ἀποκρούεται μέν τις τοὺς ἐμπαθεῖς λογισμούς· οἷον, ἢ ψαλμῳδία, ἢ προσευχή... ἐκκόπτει δὲ τὰ π., τῶν πραγμάτων ἐκείνων περιφρονῶν, πρὸς ἅπερ αὐτὰ κέκτηται Max.*carit*.4.48(M.90.1057C,D); τὰ μὲν σωματικὰ π. θηρίοις ἐοίκασι· πτηνοῖς δέ, τὰ ψυχικά· ἀλλὰ τὰ μὲν ἀπὸ τοῦ λογικοῦ δύναται ἀμπελῶνος ἀποτειχίζειν ὁ πρακτικός· οὐκέτι δὲ καὶ τὰ πετεινά, εἰ μὴ ἐν θεωρίᾳ πνευματικῇ γένηται, κἂν ὅτι μάλιστα ποιήσεται σπουδὴν πρὸς τὴν τῶν ἔνδοθεν φυλακήν ‡Max.*cap.al*.163(M.90.1440A); ἄλλα τὰ σωματικὰ π., καὶ ἄλλα εἰσὶ τὰ ψυχικά· ἄλλα τὰ κατὰ φύσιν, καὶ ἄλλα τὰ παρὰ φύσιν. ὁ γοῦν τὰ μὲν ἀπωθούμενος, τῶν δὲ πρόνοιαν μὴ ποιούμενος, ὅμοιός ἐστιν ἀνθρώπῳ φραγμὸν μὲν ὑψηλὸν...κατὰ τῶν θηρίων ἱστῶντι, συνηδομένῳ δὲ τοῖς πτηνοῖς ἐσθίουσιν τὰς τοῦ λογικοῦ ἀμπελῶνος περιφανεῖς σταφυλάς *ib*.226(1456A); struggle easier while passions are still slight, Dor.*doct*.11.3(M.88.1737C); **10.** assumed and healed by Christ ὅπως καὶ τῶν π. τῶν ἡμετέρων συμμέτοχος γενόμενος καὶ ἴασιν ποιήσηται Just.*2apol*.13.4(M.6.468A); λόγος...πάθη ...ἰᾶται Clem.*paed*.1.1(p.90.8; M.8.249A); ὁ λόγος...τῶν ἐν ἡμῖν π. ὑπισχνούμενος τὴν ἴασιν *ib*.(p.90.18; 249B); ἔστιν οὖν ὁ παιδαγωγὸς ἡμῶν λόγος διὰ παραινέσεων θεραπευτικὸς τῶν παρὰ φύσιν τῆς ψυχῆς π. *ib*.1.2(p.93.9; 256A); τὰ ἡμέτερα π. ἰδιοποιούμενος Eus.*d.e*.10.1(p.450. 27; M.22.725A); ἰώμενος τὰ ἀνίατα π. Mac.Aeg.*hom*.5.27(M.34.493B); cf.Ath.*Ar*.2.16(M.26.181A); ἀπέστειλεν τὸν υἱὸν αὐτοῦ...πάντα τὰ ἀνθρώπινα π. ἀναδέξασθαι χωρὶς ἁμαρτίας *Const.App*.7.43.4; σταυρῷ προσηλώθη ὁ ἀπαθής,...ἵνα πάθους λύσῃ...τούτους, δι' οὓς παρεγένετο *Lit.ib*.8.12.33; Dion.Ar.*e.h*.3.3.11(M.3.441B); Bas.Sel.*or*.35.2(M.85. 377A); τὰ δὲ ἀνθρώπινα π. καὶ φυσικὰ τῆς σαρκός, ἅπερ ὁ κύριος κατεδέξατο, πέφυκέ πως καὶ τὴν σάρκα καταμαραίνειν...τὰ τοίνυν ἀνθρώπινα π. λυπεῖν οἶδεν τὴν φύσιν...καὶ φθορᾷ ὑποβάλλειν, ὥσπερ ὁ κύριος παραπλησίως ἡμῖν πάντων μετέσχηκεν Leont.B.*Nest.et Eut*. 2(M.86.1337D); **11.** remedied through sacraments: baptism τὸ δεῖν πάντας τοὺς διερχομένους τὸ μυστικὸν ὕδωρ ἐν τῷ βαπτίσματι, πᾶσαν τὴν τῆς κακίας παρεμβολὴν νεκρὰν ποιεῖν ἐν τῷ ὕδατι· οἷον τὴν πλεονεξίαν...τὸ κατὰ τὸν τύφον καὶ ὑπερηφανίαν π. ... ἐπειδή πως πέφυκεν ἕπεσθαι τῇ φύσει τὰ π., νεκρὰ ποιεῖν ἐν τῷ ὕδατι Gr.Nyss.*v. Mos*.(M.44.364A); eucharist τῆς Χριστοῦ διαίτης μεταλαμβάνοντας... ἵνα καταργήσωμεν τῆς σαρκὸς ἡμῶν τὰ π. Clem.*paed*.1.6(p.115.29; M. 8.301A); **12.** exeg.: Gal.5:24 οἵτινες τὴν σάρκα τοῦ Χριστοῦ, τουτέστι τὸ οἰκεῖον σῶμα...ἐσταύρωσαν καὶ οἷον ἐνέκρωσαν ἀπὸ τῶν σωματικῶν π., καὶ οὐ μόνον τὸ σῶμα, ὅσον ἧκεν εἰς τὰ π., ἐσταύρωσαν, ἀλλὰ καὶ αὐτὰ τὰ π. Clem.*fr*.7(p.197.6f.; M.9.745B); Ex.14:9 στρατὸς Αἰγύπτιός ἐστι τὰ ποικίλα τῆς ψυχῆς π., οἷς καταδουλοῦται ὁ ἄνθρωπος...τὸ δὲ περὶ τὰς ἡδονὰς π., οἱ ἵπποι νοείσθωσαν Gr.Nyss.*v.Mos*.(M.44.361C).

B. theol.; **1.** absent from God; **a.** in gen. τὸ ἔξω παντὸς π. εἶναι τὸν θεόν Or.*Cels*.6.65(p.136.6; M.11.1397C); τὸ δὲ θεῖον...οὐ δόξης ὀρέγεται, οὐκ ἐπιθυμεῖ. ταῦτα γὰρ π. ἐστί, π. δὲ τὸ θεῖον ἀνεπίδεκτόν ἐστιν Adam.*dial*.4.14(p.170.19; M.11.1829A); τὸ δὲ θεῖον παθῶν [v.l. κακῶν] ἀσύμπλοκον. οὐκ ἄρα γένεσις...χαίρει δὲ ὁ θεὸς τῇ σωφροσύνῃ, παθῶν ἀνεννόητος ὢν Meth.*symp*.8.16(p.106.9; M.18.169B); Gr.Nyss. *prof.Chr*.(p.134.14; M.46.241D); Epiph.*haer*.76.35(p.384.28; M.42. 588A); Cyr.*inc.unigen*.(5[1].683E); Procl.CP *Arm*.10(p.192.7; M.65. 865C) cit. s. ἀνεπίδεκτος; **b.** ref. certain scriptural expressions ὀργὰς καὶ ἀπειλὰς μὴ π. θεοῦ τις ὑπολάβῃ παρὰ Ἑβραίοις λέγεσθαι Clem.*str*.5.11(p.371.19; M.9.104B); ὀργὴν...ὀνομάζομεν θεοῦ, οὐ π. δ' αὐτοῦ αὐτὴν εἶναί φαμεν Or.*Cels*.4.72(p.341.9; M.11.1141A); id.*hom*. 18.6 *in Jer*.(p.160.13; M.13.477B) al.; οὐδὲ γὰρ π. ἐστιν ὁ ζῆλος ἐπὶ θεοῦ Chrys.*fem.reg*.5(1.258A); Jo.D.*f.o*.1.1(M.94.792A); **2.** not involved in generation of Son οὐ δεῖ τὴν τοῦ θεοῦ γέννησιν παραβάλλειν τῇ τῶν ἀνθρώπων φύσει,...ἢ ὅλως τι π. σημαίνειν τὴν γέννησιν Ath.*Ar*. 1.28(M.26.69A); λόγος δὲ καὶ σοφία...οὔτε κατὰ πάθος ἐστὶ γέννημα *ib*. (69B); τὸ ἐκ τοῦ θεοῦ γέννημα οὐκ ἔστι π. ... δέδεικται δὲ καὶ ἰδίᾳ νῦν ὁ λόγος οὐ κατὰ πάθος γεννώμενος *ib*.(69C); *ib*.1.16(M.26.45B); εἰ δὲ π. ἐν θεῷ γεννῶντι φοβεῖταί τις, ἔστι καὶ κτίζοντος φοβηθῆναι κίνησιν, καὶ κάματον...εἰ δὲ ταῦτα οὐ πρόσεστι θεῷ, οὐδὲ π. ἐν τῷ γεννᾶν Didym. (‡Bas.)*Eun*.5(1.316D,E; M.29.760A); doctrine elaborated in controversy with Aëtius; his contention: εἰ μὴ εἴκει ἡ ἀγέννητος φύσις γενέσει, τοῦτ' ἔστιν ὃ λέγεται· εἰ δὲ εἴκει γενέσει, τὰ τῆς γενέσεως π. τῆς ὑποστάσεως τοῦ θεοῦ εἴη ἀμείνω Aët.*synt*.14 ap.Epiph.*haer*.76.31 (p.379.29; M.42.577D); its refutation: π. ὅλως ἐν θεῷ διηγεῖσθαι ἀσεβέστατον· εἴσω γὰρ π. οὐδ' ὅλως περιέχεται τὸ θεῖον, ἀνωτάτω [δὲ] ὂν τῶν τοιούτων τῶν ἐν ἡμῖν εἰς μεριστικὰς ἐννοίας ὑποπιπτόντων, κατὰ πάντα δὲ τρόπον ὁ Ἀετίου λόγος ἀνατραπήσεται...ἐν ἡμῖν γὰρ κατά τι μέρος τὸ θέλειν ἐστὶ π.,...ὅσον δέ ἐστιν ἐν ἐμοὶ παθητικῶς συνεχόμενον, τοσοῦτον ἐν τῷ θεῷ ἀπαθῶς ἐστιν ὑπάρχον Epiph.*haer*.76.31(pp.379. 31–380.4; 577D); π. γεννῶμεν καὶ γεννώμεθα...ἐν θεῷ δὲ οὐδὲν τούτων ἐν τῷ τὸν υἱὸν γεγεννηκέναι ἐνυπῆρξεν...ἐν ἡμῖν τοῖς ἐν π. γεννῶσί τε καὶ γεννωμένοις π. ἐστὶ δεύτερον ἐν τῷ κτίζειν καὶ πάσχομεν ἐν τῷ γεννᾶν τε καὶ γεννᾶσθαι, θεὸς δὲ ὁ παρ' ὑμῖν κτίστης καὶ οὐ γεννήτωρ ἐπινοούμενος, ᾧ διὰ μὲν τὸ γεννᾶν ἀνατρεπτικῶς τὸ π. παραφέρετε, ἵνα τὴν υἱοῦ γνησιότητα ἀρνήσησθε, λήθῃ δὲ παραδιδόατε τὸ ἐπὶ τῷ κτίζειν π., ὅπερ καὶ αὐτὸ ἐν θεῷ οὐ π. ὑπάρχει (μὴ γένοιτο). οὔτε γὰρ ἡμεῖς π. αὐτῷ προσάπτομεν, ὁμολογοῦντες αὐτὸν κτίστην ὄντα τῶν ἁπάντων, οὐδὲ πάλιν π. ⟨ἕτερ⟩ον περὶ αὐτὸν διανοούμεθα, γεγεννηκότα τὸν ἀληθινὸν υἱόν...ἀχρόνως ὁμολογοῦντες. διὸ τὴν φύσιν αὐτοῦ γινώσκομεν ἀκατάληπτον οὖσαν καὶ π. μὴ συνεχομένην *ib*.(pp.380.21–381.3; 580B–D); *ib*.76.44(p.398.21ff.; 612A,B); **3.** discussion how far πάθος was involved in Inc. ἡ τροπὴ τοῦ ἡμετέρου σώματος π. ἐστίν. ὁ δὲ ἐν τούτῳ γεγονὼς ἐν π. γίνεται· ἀπαθὲς δὲ τὸ θεῖον. οὐκοῦν ἀλλοτρία περὶ θεοῦ ἡ ὑπόληψις, εἴπερ τὸν ἀπαθῆ κατὰ τὴν φύσιν πρὸς κοινωνίαν πάθους ἐλθεῖν διορίζονται...τὸ π. τὸ μὲν κυρίως, τὸ δὲ ἐκ καταχρήσεως λέγεται. τὸ μὲν οὖν προαιρέσεως ἁπτόμενον καὶ πρὸς κακίαν ἀπὸ τῆς ἀρετῆς μεταστρέφον ἀληθῶς π. ἐστί, τὸ δ' ὅσον ἐν τῇ φύσει κατὰ τὸν ἴδιον εἱρμὸν πορευομένῃ διεξοδικῶς θεωρεῖται, τοῦτο κυριώτερον ἔργον ἂν μᾶλλον ἢ π. προσαγορεύοιτο, οἷον ἡ γέννησις, ἢ αὔξησις...τίνος οὖν λέγει τὸ μυστήριον ἡμῶν ἧφθαι τὸ θεῖον; τοῦ κυρίως λεγομένου π., ὅπερ κακία ἐστίν, ἢ τοῦ κατὰ τὴν φύσιν κινήματος; εἰ μὲν γὰρ ἐν τοῖς ἀπηγορευμένοις γεγενῆσθαι τὸ θεῖον ὁ λόγος διϊσχυρίζετο, φεύγειν ἔδει τὴν ἀτοπίαν τοῦ δόγματος...εἰ δὲ τῆς φύσεως ἡμῶν αὐτὸν ἐφῆφθαι λέγει ἧς καὶ ἡ πρώτη γένεσίς τε καὶ ὑπόστασις παρ' αὐτοῦ τὴν ἀρχὴν ἔσχε, ποῦ τῆς θεῷ πρεπούσης ἐννοίας διαμαρτάνει τὸ κήρυγμα, μηδεμιᾶς παθητικῆς διαθέσεως ἐν ταῖς περὶ θεοῦ ὑπολήψεσι τῇ πίστει συνεισιούσης; οὐδὲ γὰρ τὸν ἰατρὸν ἐν π. γίνεσθαι λέγομεν, ὅταν θεραπεύῃ τὸν ἐν π. γινόμενον· ἀλλὰ κἂν προσάψηται τοῦ ἀρρωστήματος, ἔξω π. ὁ θεραπευτὴς διαμένει. εἰ ἡ γένεσις αὐτὴ καθ' ἑαυτὴν π. οὐκ ἔστιν, οὐδ' ἂν τὴν ζωήν τις π. προσαγορεύσειεν, ἀλλὰ τὸ καθ' ἡδονὴν π. τῆς ἀνθρωπίνης καθηγεῖται γενέσεως...εἰ οὖν ἡδονῆς μὲν ἡ γένεσις ἠλλοτρίωται, κακίας δὲ ἡ ζωή, ποῖον ὑπολείπεται π., οὗ τὸν θεὸν κεκοινωνηκέναι φησὶ τὸ τῆς εὐσεβείας μυστήριον; Gr.Nyss.*or.catech.*16(p.67.1ff.; M.45.49B–D); id. *Eun.*6(2 p.137.2ff.; M.45.721B,C); **4.** Christ's freedom from passions υἱὸς...ἀπόλυτος εἰς τὸ παντελὲς ἀνθρωπίνων π., διὰ τοῦτο γὰρ καὶ μόνος κριτής, ὅτι ἀναμάρτητος μόνος Clem.*paed.*1.2(p.91.27; M.8.252C); Ath.*Ar.*3.41(M.26.412A) cit. s. ἀληθής; *ib.*3.32(392B) cit. s. ἅπτω; οὐδὲ γὰρ ὡς π. ὑπομένων ζηλοτυπίας, χωρήσει κατὰ ἐχθροῦ... ἀλλ' ἐλεύθερος ὢν παντὸς π. ἀνθρωπίνου ἅτε θεὸς ἑαυτὸν κινήσει πρὸς ἄμυναν...δάκρυον γὰρ ἐξέχεε, καὶ κάματον ὑπέμενε σωματικόν, τὰ π. οὐκ ἀκουσίως ὑπομένων, ἀλλ' ἐπ' ἐξουσίας τῷ σώματι ἐπιτάττων Thdr. Heracl.*Is.*42:13(M.18.1336C); σωτὴρ...κατ' οἰκείωσιν οἰκονομικὴν εἰς ἑαυτὸν...τὰ τῆς ἰδίας σαρκὸς ἀναφέρει π. Cyr.*ep.*39(p.19.12; 5².108B); **5.** ref. H. Ghost π. καὶ ἀδυναμία ἐν τῷ ἑνὶ ἁγίῳ πνεύματι οὐχ εὑρίσκεται Didym.*Trin.*2.3(M.39.477A).

III. *Passion* of Christ;

A. in gen. ἐπιτρέψατέ μοι μιμητὴν εἶναι τοῦ π. τοῦ θεοῦ μου Ign. *Rom.*6.3; ὁ πατὴρ τὸν ἑαυτοῦ υἱὸν καὶ ἐν τοιούτοις π. ἀληθῶς γεγονέναι δι' ἡμᾶς βεβούληται Just.*dial.*103.8(M.6.720A); contrasted with sufferings of sons of Zeus in pagan mythology, id.*1apol.*22.4(M.6.361B); ὁ λόγος...ὕπνωσε τὴν ἔκστασιν τοῦ π. Meth.*symp.*3.8(p.35.13; M.18.73A); as voluntary τὸ π. ἑκούσιον Chrys.*hom.50.3 in Jo.*(8.297B); *ib.55.2*(8.324B); ref. controversy with Patripassians ἑνὸς ⟨θεοῦ⟩ ὁμολογουμένου, τοῦτον ὑπὸ πάθος φέρειν Hipp.*Noët.*2(p.237.28; M.10.805C); cf.Hipp.*haer.*8.19(p.238.20; M.16.3367A); τοῦτον πάθει ξύλου προσπαγέντα...τοῦτον τὸν τῶν ὅλων θεὸν καὶ πατέρα εἶναι λέγει Κλεομένης *ib.*9.10(p.245.6; 3378B); cf.Epiph.*haer.*57.2(p.346.16; M.41.997B).

B. as means of salvation τὸ σωτήριον τοῦτο μυστήριον, τοῦτ' ἔστι τὸ π. τοῦ Χριστοῦ Just.*dial.*74.3(M.6.649B); αὐτὸς γὰρ τῷ ἰδίῳ π. ῥυσάμενος ἡμᾶς ἀπὸ σκανδάλων καὶ ἁμαρτιῶν Clem.*paed.*2.8(p.203.7; M.8.488A); ἐπεὶ...Κέλσος ὀνειδίζει τῷ σωτῆρι ἐπὶ τῷ π. ὡς μὴ βοηθηθέντι ὑπὸ τοῦ πατρὸς ἢ μὴ δυνηθέντι ἑαυτῷ βοηθῆσαι, παραθετέον ὅτι τὸ π. αὐτοῦ ἐπροφητεύετο μετὰ τῆς αἰτίας, ὅτι χρήσιμον ἦν ἀνθρώποις τὸ ἐκεῖνον ὑπὲρ αὐτῶν ἀποθανεῖν Or.*Cels.*1.54(p.105.4,6; M.11.760C); τὸ σωτήριον π. Pall.*v.Chrys.*20(p.129.15; M.47.72); Cyr.*Zach.*100(3.792B); π. κόσμου καθάρσιον Procl.CP *or.*11.4(M.65.785C).

C. as endured in human, not divine, nature; **1.** in gen. εἰ γὰρ ὁ Παῦλος ἔφρασε, τὸν κύριον τῆς δόξης ἐσταυρῶσθαι, σαφῶς εἰς τὸν ἄνθρωπον ἀφορῶν, οὐ παρὰ τοῦτο δεήσει π. τῷ θείῳ προσάπτειν Eust. *fr.in Pr.8*:22(M.18.681C); εἴ τις τὸν...υἱὸν τοῦ θεοῦ ἐσταυρωμένον ἀκούων, τὴν θεότητα αὐτοῦ...π. ... ὑπομεμενηκέναι λέγοι, ἀνάθεμα ἔστω *Symb.Sirm.*1 *anath.*13; ὁ υἱός, παθὼν ἐξ ἀσθενείας, τουτέστιν, ἐκ τῆς σαρκικῆς συμπλοκῆς· καὶ παραιτούμενος τὸ π., ὡς ἄνθρωπος· ζῶν δὲ διὰ τῆς ἑαυτοῦ δυνάμεως Ath.*inc.et c.Ar.*21(M.26.1024A); οὔτε τὸ παθεῖν τὸν μονογενῆ ἐν σαρκὶ π. περιποιεῖται τῇ αὐτοῦ θεότητι Epiph.*haer.*76.39(p.393.1; M.42.601A); διὰ τοῦτο...ἐν τῷ π. πολὺ τὸ ἀνθρώπινον αὐτῷ προσάπτουσιν, ἀπὸ τούτου δηλοῦντες ὅτι ἀλήθεια τὰ τῆς οἰκονομίας Chrys.*hom.63.2 in Jo.*(8.377D); οὐχ ὅτι πάντως αὐτὸς ὁ ἐκ θεοῦ κατὰ φύσιν γεννηθεὶς λόγος ἀπέθανεν,...ἀλλ' ὅτι ἑνωθεὶς τῇ σαρκί...αὐτὸς πρὸς ἑαυτὸν οἰκειοῦται τὸ π. Cyr.*ep.*10(p.110.16; 5².33A); φρίξον τὸ π. τοῦ ἑκουσίως παθόντος σαρκί, ἀπαθοῦς ὄντος θεοῦ λόγου Procl.CP *or.*11.2(M.65.784C); **2.** orthodox view defended in controversy with Apollinarians, Apoll.: ἄνθρωπος οὖν ἐσταυρώθη ὑπὲρ ἡμῶν; Orth.: ψιλός, οὔ· ἀλλὰ θεὸς ὢν ὁ τοῦ θεοῦ υἱός, βουληθεὶς σταυρωθῆναι ὑπὲρ ἡμῶν, ἥνωσεν ἑαυτῷ σῶμα ἔμψυχον λογικόν, τὸ δυνάμενον σταυρωθῆναι μετὰ ἑκουσίου π. Apoll.: διὰ τί λέγεις, σταυρωθῆναι μετὰ π.; ἄλλο ἐστὶ σταύρωσις, καὶ ἄλλο π.;...Orth. ὅτι σῶμα ἔμψυχον σταυρωθῆναι δύναται, παθεῖν δὲ ἑκουσίως οὐ δύναται, μὴ ὂν ἔμψυχον λογικόν. καὶ τοῦτό ἐστι τὸ ἀσέβημα τῶν λεγόντων, ὅτι ψυχὴν οὐκ εἶχεν. τοῦ γὰρ σώματος μὴ δυναμένου αἰσθηθῆναι ἑκουσίου π. ἄνευ ψυχῆς, ἀνάγκη τὸν λόγον ἀντὶ ψυχῆς ὄντα παθεῖν, ἢ μηδ' ὅλως εἶναι αἴσθησιν π. ἑκουσίου...ἑνώσας ἑαυτῷ σῶμα τὸ δυνάμενον παθεῖν· ὡς εἶναι τὸ π. τῆς οἰκονομίας, καὶ οὐχὶ τῆς φύσεως τοῦ λόγου ‡Ath. *dial.Trin.*4.3,4(M.28.1253C,D); αὐτοῦ πάθος τὸ π. οὐ τῇ φύσει (ἀπαθὴς γὰρ ἡ φύσις), ἀλλὰ τῇ οἰκονομίᾳ τῆς ἑνώσεως. διὰ γὰρ τὸ π. καὶ ἡ ἕνωσις· καὶ διὰ τὴν σωτηρίαν τὸ π. *ib.*4.4(1256A); ἅπας γὰρ αὐτῷ [sc. Apollinarius] τῆς λογογραφίας ὁ σκοπὸς πρὸς τοῦτο βλέπει, τὸ θνητὴν τοῦ μονογενοῦς υἱοῦ τὴν θεότητα, καὶ οὐχὶ τῷ ἀνθρωπίνῳ τὸ π. δέξασθαι, ἀλλὰ τὴν ἀπαθῆ...φύσιν πρὸς πάθους μετουσίαν ἀλλοιωθῆναι Gr.Nyss.*Apoll.*5(M.45.1132B); εἰ οὖν τὸ θεῖον οὔτε γεννήσεως, οὔτε ἀναστάσεως δέεται, δηλονότι καὶ τὸ π., οὐχ ὡς τῆς θεότητος πασχούσης, ἐπιτελεῖται, ἀλλ' ὡς ἐν τῷ πάσχοντι οὔσης, καὶ διὰ τῆς πρὸς τὸν πεπονθότα ἑνώσεως, τὸ ἐκείνου π. οἰκειουμένης *ib.*54(1256C).

D. effects (salvation, v. III.B supra); **1.** ref. Church τῇ προωρισμένῃ...εἰς δόξαν παράμονον, ἄτρεπτον ἡνωμένην καὶ ἐκλελεγμένην ἐν π. ἀληθινῷ ἐν θελήματι τοῦ πατρὸς καὶ Ἰησοῦ Χριστοῦ, τοῦ θεοῦ ἡμῶν, τῇ ἐκκλησίᾳ Ign.*Eph.*proem.; ἀφ' οὗ καρποῦ ἡμεῖς ἀπὸ τοῦ...αὐτοῦ π. id.*Smyrn.*1.2; ἐκκλησίᾳ...εἰρηνευούσῃ ἐν σαρκὶ καὶ πνεύματι τῷ π. Ἰησοῦ Χριστοῦ id.*Trall.*proem.; *ib.*11.2; **2.** reproduction of Passion in Christians διὰ Ἰησοῦ Χριστοῦ, δι' οὗ ἐὰν μὴ αὐθαιρέτως ἔχωμεν τὸ ἀποθανεῖν εἰς τὸ αὐτοῦ π., τὸ ζῆν αὐτοῦ οὐκ ἔστιν ἐν ἡμῖν Ign.*Magn.*5.2; τίνος ἕνεκεν...οὐ μιμούμεθα αὐτοῦ τὰ π. *Const.App.*5.5.4; **3.** (with play on words) subjection of the passions ἐλευθερῶσαι τὰς ψυχὰς παθῶν ἐβουλήθη...τούτῳ τὰ π. τῷ σχήματι ἤμβλυνται, π. παθῶν διὰ τοῦ παθεῖν γενόμενος...οὐδὲ ἀλγυνθεὶς ὑπὸ πάθους· οὔτε γὰρ π. ὅλως αὐτὸν ἐξέστησεν Meth.*Porph.*3(pp.506.20–507.2; M.18.401B,C); διὰ πάθους σώζει τοὺς τὰ π. ἔχοντας τοῦ θανάτου Epiph.*haer.*76.39(p.393.5; M.42.601A); Thdt.*Ps.*108:26f.(1.1389); τῷ παλαιῷ π. τῶν πρωτοπλάστων ἀντεισήχθη τὸ νέον π. Χριστοῦ· καὶ ὁ παθὼν Ἀδὰμ ἐκεῖνος, διὰ τοῦ θείου π. τοῦ νέου Ἀδὰμ ἀνακέκληται id.*pental.*(5.130); Sev. Ant.ap.*cat.1Petr.*4:1(p.71.17); **4.** other effects τὸ π., ὅ ἐστιν ἡμῶν ἀνάστασις Ign.*Smyrn.*5.3; ὁ Χριστὸς...ἐβαπτίσθη ἵνα τῷ π. τὸ ὕδωρ καθαρίσῃ id.*Eph.*18.2; τὰ δαιμόνια ὑποτάσσεσθαι τῷ ὀνόματι αὐτοῦ καὶ τῇ τοῦ γενομένου π. αὐτοῦ οἰκονομίᾳ Just.*dial.*30.3(M.6.540B); cf. *passio ejus expergefactio est dormientium discipulorum*, Iren. *haer.*4.22.1(M.7.1047A); πεπλήρωκεν τὸ π. τοῦ κυρίου ἡμᾶς μὲν εὐωδίας, Ἑβραίους δὲ ἁμαρτίας Clem.*paed.*2.8(p.195.17; M.8.468C); τὸ ξύλον τοῦ π. Ἰησοῦ Χριστοῦ ἐλθὸν εἰς τὸν λόγον πεποίηκεν τὸν ἄρτον αὐτοῦ [i.e. his doctrine] γλυκύτερον Or.*hom.10.2 in Jer.*(p.72.24; M.13.360B); τῷ καιρῷ τοῦ σωτηρίου π. ἔμελλεν ὁ τύραννος [sc. Devil] καθαιρεθήσεσθαι id.*fr.90 in Jo.*(p.553.13).

E. ref. BMV ταύτην δὲ εἶναι τὴν θεοτόκον πιστεύειν ἀκόλουθον ὅτι μηδὲ ἀπελείφθη τοῦ π., ἀλλ' ἵστατο παρὰ τῷ σταυρῷ Sev.Ant.*res.* (p.810.2; M.46.633A).

F. ref. eucharist εἴ τις ἐν ἀλλοτρίᾳ γνώμῃ περιπατεῖ, οὗτος τῷ π. οὐ συγκατατίθεται Ign.*Philad.*3.3; τοῦ ἄρτου τῆς εὐχαριστίας, ὃν εἰς ἀνάμνησιν τοῦ π. ... ὁ κύριος ἡμῶν παρέδωκε ποιεῖν Just.*dial.*41.1(M.6.564B); *ib.*117.3(745C).

G. in scripture; **1.** types and symbols: paschal lamb, Just.*dial.* 40.3(M.6.561C); touching of Jacob's thigh, *ib.*125.5(768B); sacrifice of Isaac, Clem.*paed.*1.5(p.104.2; M.8.277B); oil, *ib.*2.8(p.194.23; 468A); **2.** exeg.: Ps.21:17ff. ἐν σαρκὶ οὖν αὐτοῦ μέλλοντος φανεροῦσθαι καὶ πάσχειν, προεφανερώθη τὸ π. *Barn.*6.7; Δαυεὶδ εἰς τὸ π. καὶ τὸν σταυρὸν ἐν παραβολῇ μυστηριώδει οὕτως εἶπεν... Just.*dial.*97.3(M.6.705A); *ib.*105.2(721A); Gen.49:11 τὸ γὰρ 'πλύνων τὴν στολὴν αὐτοῦ ἐν αἵματι σταφυλῆς' προαγγελτικὸν ἦν τοῦ π. οὗ πάσχειν ἔμελλε, δι' αἵματος καθαίρων τοὺς πιστεύοντας αὐτῷ id.*1apol.*32.7(M.6.380B); Is.53:7, id.*dial.*114.2(M.6.740A); Pr.1:10ff., Clem.*paed.*1.10(p.146.14; M.8.364A); Lev.14:51ff. τοῦ σωτηρίου π. περιέχει τὸν τύπον Thdt. *qu.19 in Lev.*(1.195).

H. in liturg. and other eccl. observance ἡ νηστεία ἡμῖν προστέτακται...ὅπως ὁμολογήσωμεν εἰς ἡμῶν σωτηρίαν ⟨γενόμενον⟩ τὸ τοῦ κυρίου π. Epiph.*exp.fid.*22(p.523.2; M.42.828A); παρασκευὴν προσέταξεν ἡμῖν νηστεύειν...διὰ τὸ π. *Const.App.*5.14.20; τὴν μεγάλην ἑβδομάδα πᾶσαν...ἀργείτωσαν οἱ δοῦλοι, ὅτι ἡ μὲν πάθους ἐστίν...καὶ χρεία διδασκαλίας, τίς ὁ παθών *ib.*8.33.3; commemoration in some places on same day as Resurrection κατ' αὐτήν γε τὴν τοῦ σωτηρίου π. ἡμέραν, ἐν ᾗ καὶ τοῦ π. καὶ τῆς δεσποτικῆς ἀναστάσεως τὴν μνήμην πανηγυρίζομεν Thdt.*affect.*9(p.227.4; 4.932); ἡνίκα μὲν τὸ σωτήριον π. ὑπὲρ τοῦ γένους τῶν ἀνθρώπων ὁ δεσπότης ὑπέμεινεν, ἠθύμει λίαν ὁ τῶν...ἀποστόλων χορός. οὐ γὰρ ᾔδεσαν ἀκριβῶς τὸν τοῦ π. καρπόν, ἐπειδὴ δὲ ἔγνωσαν τὴν ἐντεῦθεν βλαστήσασαν σωτηρίαν, εὐαγγέλιον ἐκάλεσαν τὸ τοῦ π. κήρυγμα...οἱ δὲ πεπιστευκότες...ἑορτάζουσι τοῦ π. τὴν μνήμην, καὶ τὸν θανάτου καιρὸν δημοθοινίας ἔχουσι καὶ πανηγύρεως ἀφορμὴν id.*ep.*64(4.1116); elsewhere the two are distinguished ἡ τοῦ σωτηρίου π. ἡμέρα, καὶ νὺξ ἱερά, καὶ ἡ τῆς ἀναστάσεως ἑορτή *Libell.*ap. CEph.(449)*act.*(*ACO* 2.1.1 p.187.15; H.2.233E); τὰς τοῦ σωτηρίου π. ἡμέρας ἐν νηστείᾳ καὶ προσευχῇ καὶ κατανύξει καρδίας ἐπιτελοῦντας χρὴ τοὺς πιστοὺς περὶ μέσας τῆς περὶ τὸ μέγα σάββατον νυκτὸς ὥρας ἀπονηστίζεσθαι CTrull.*can*.89; τῇ δὲ τοῦ π. ἑβδομάδι ξηροφαγία νενομοθέτητο, οὐ μέντοι προηγιασμένων τελετή Jo.D.*jej*.5(M.95.69D).

I. Gnost., ref. passibility of aeons, Iren.*haer*.2.17.6,7(M.7.764A–C); 'passion' of Sophia contrasted with Passion of Christ, cf. *neque Christi passio similis est passioni Aeonis, neque in similibus facta. Aeon enim passus est passionem dissolutionis et perditionis, ita ut periclitaretur ipse qui patiebatur et corrumpi: dominus autem noster Christus passus est passionem validam, et quae non accederet; non solum ipse non periclitatus corrumpi, sed et corruptum hominem firmavit robore suo, et in incorruptionem revocavit. et Aeon quidem passus est passionem ipse requirens Patrem, et non praevalens invenire: dominus autem passus est, ut eos qui erraverunt a patre, ad agnitionem, et juxta eum adduceret. et illi quidem inquisitio magnitudinis Patris fiebat passio perditionis: nobis autem dominus passus, agnitionem patris conferens, salutem donavit. et illius quidem passio fructificavit fructum foemineum, sicut dicunt, invalidum, et infirmum, ...istius autem passio fructificavit fortitudinem et virtutem. ... et dominus quidem per passionem mortem destruxit; et solvit errorem, corruptionemque exterminavit*, *ib*.2.20.3(777C–778A); discussion of Gnost. connexion of passion of twelfth aeon with treachery of twelfth apostle and other biblical types or analogies, *ib*.1.3.3(472A–473A); refutation, *ib*.2.23.1,2(786B–787A).

IV. *suffering, passion* of martyrs; as means of remission of sins, parallel to baptism, †Mel.*fr*.(p.313); *story of martyrdom* ἀναγινώσκεσθαι τὰ π. τῶν μαρτύρων *Cod.Afr*.46(Lat. *passio*).

***παιγνιάζω**, *play*, †Gregent.*leg.Hom*.40(M.86.604A).

***παιγνίδιον, τό, 1.** *plaything*, Leont.N.*v.Sym*.35(M.93.1713A); **2.** *jesting*, *ib*.37(1716C); *comic performance*, Jo.Mal.*chron*.12 p.314 (M.97.473A); Gr.Mag.*dial*.(tr.Zach.)1.9(M.*PL*.77.194A); *ib*.4.17(347C, cod. παιγνίου).

***παιγνικός**, *serving for entertainment*, Dam.*troph*.2.2(p.218.9); Phot.*nomoc*.13.21(p.626; M.104.953D).

***παιγνικῶς**, *in jest*, Leont.N.*v.Sym*.30(M.93.1708B).

παίγνιον, τό, 1. *plaything, toy*, met. π. γέγονεν ὁ δυστυχὴς τοῦ περιβοήτου *Hom.Clem*.20.16; εἱμαρμένης...μοιρῶν π. Eus.*Hierocl*.46(542B,C; M.22.865A); Ἡρώδης μέθης γενόμενος π. Isid.Pel.*epp*.1.203(M.78.312C); Bas.Sel.*v.Thecl*.1(M.85.489C); Dor.*doct*.5.3(M.88.1680B); **2.** *trifle, contemptible thing*, Clem.*q.d.s*.32(p.181.12; M.9.637C); τοῖς π. τοῦ αἰῶνος τούτου Or.*hom.14.15 in Jer*.(p.121.15; M.13.424C); βίος...τὸ ἐπὶ γῆς π. Gr.Naz.*or*.7.19(M.35.777C); id.*ep*.204 (M.37.337C); **3.** *foolish thing, farce*, Ath.*ep.Aeg.Lib*.11(M.25.561B); **4.** *game, sport*, of events at pagan festivals π. δαιμόνων Nil.*epp*.3.252(M.79.505B); of rites of Priapus equated with Beelphegor, Cyr.*Os*.46(3.77E); τὰ τῆς εἰδωλολατρίας π. *ib*.133(166C); περὶ χορευόντων καὶ τραγῳδούντων, περὶ τῶν ποιούντων π. σατανικά †Jo.Jej.*serm*.(M.88.1924B).

***παιγνιωδῶς**, *lightly, flippantly*, Innoc.*fr.ep*.(p.17.6; M.47.13A).

παιδαγωγ-έω, 1. *teach, instruct*, Clem.*paed*.3.8(p.260.24; M.8.612C); ἄσκησις ἐκ πίστεώς τε καὶ φόβου ~ουμένη id.*str*.7.16(p.72.6; M.9.541A); φρόνημα...τὰ ἐκεῖ βλέπειν...~ούμενον Meth.*symp*.8.10 (p.92.14; v.l. ~ουμένων M.18.153A); τὸ ἀτελὲς τῶν δι' αὐτοῦ ~ουμένων Eus.*e.th*.3.2(p.143.29; M.24.980B); ~εῖ αὐτοὺς...χάριν εἰδέναι *cat. 2Cor*.4:15(p.378.2); **2.** *train, lead on by instruction*; **a.** by Mosaic Law, Gr.Nyss.*or.dom*.5(p.100.2; M.44.1181C); id.*v.Mos*.(M.44.321A); ὁ ὑπὲρ τὸν νόμον, οὐ ~εῖται τῷ νόμῳ Chrys.*hom.2.2 in 1Tim*.(11.557B); ἡ δοθεῖσα χάρις διὰ Μωσέως, τουτέστιν ἡ ἐν νόμῳ γνῶσις ~οῦσα πρὸς ἀλήθειαν Cyr.*ador*.13(1.471A); *ib*.(474E); ref. Gal.3:24, id.*Os*.20(3.43C); ὁ νόμῳ ~ούμενος Ἰούδας id.*Am*.14(3.264C); **b.** by OT doctrine in gen. Μωσῆς καὶ οἱ...προφῆται...τέως ~οῦντες αὐτοὺς διὰ τοῦ...ἐπάγειν...ἐπὶ τὴν εἰσαγωγὴν τοῦ ἑνός [i.e. preparatory to revelation of Trin.] Eus.*e.th*.2.20(p.127.26; M.24.949D); Cyr.*Is*.3.2 (2.417C); id.*Jo*.1.9(4.89D); **c.** of training of Israel contrasted with that of fully instructed Christians, Or.*hom.19.15 in Jer*.(p.175.31; M.13.497B); **d.** of elementary training and discipline of Christians; **i.** in gen., by upbringing and education, Bas.*hom*.12.9(2.105A; M.31.404B); τὰ πάθη τῆς σαρκὸς ~οῦντα τῷ λόγῳ id.*ep*.146(3.237A; M.32.596B); *ib*.150.1(239D; M.601B); κεχρῆσθαι...ὀφθαλμῷ πεπαιδαγωγημένῳ *ib*.173(261B; M.649A); Cyr.*Is*.1.1(2.22D); *ib*.(27B); **ii.** by scriptures τοῦ θεοῦ...~ήσαντος τέσσαρσι νόμοις [i.e. gospels] Meth.*symp*.10.2(p.124.2; M.18.196B); γραφαὶ ὥσπερ...νηπίους ~οῦσαι Eus.*Marcell*.1.1(p.5.7; M.24.720B); id.*e.th*.2.18(p.122.20; M.24.941B); **iii.** by fear of God φόβος...εἰς ἀγαθὸν ~ῶν εἰς Χριστὸν ἄγει καὶ ἔστι σωτήριος Clem.*ecl*.20(p.142.18; M.9.708B); πᾶς μὲν ὁ...μηκέτι ὑπὸ φόβου ~ούμενος ἀλλὰ δι' αὐτὸ τὸ καλὸν αἱρούμενος υἱός ἐστι θεοῦ Or.*Cels*.1.57(p.108.7; M.11.764D); id.*schol.in Cant*.6:7–8(M.17.277D); Gr.Naz.*ep*.206(M.37.341C); by fear and grace, Clem.*prot*.10(p.69.21; M.8.208C); **e.** of preliminary training of gentiles, philosophy being a propaedeutic for them as Mosaic Law was for Israel, id.*str*.1.5(p.18.2; M.8.717D).

παιδαγώγημα, τό, *method of education*, Clem.*paed*.1.9(p.137.1; M.8.345B).

***παιδαγώγησις, ἡ,** *education*, Clem.*paed*.2.6(p.187.28; M.8.453A); Gennad.*fr.Heb*.(p.421.2; M.85.1733A).

***παιδαγωγητέον,** *one must train*, Nil.*epp*.4.41(M.79.569B).

παιδαγωγία, ἡ, *elementary* or *preparatory training* π. δὲ ὁμολογοῦμεν εἶναι ἀγωγὴν ἀγαθὴν ἐκ παίδων πρὸς ἀρετήν Clem.*paed*.1.5 (p.99.20; M.8.268B); of elementary instruction opp. more profound religious truth, Eus.*e.th*.3.3(p.151.30; M.24.992D); of Law ὅτε ἡ τοῦ εὐαγγελίου σοφία ἐξέλαμψεν, ἡ τοῦ νόμου π. ἐσχόλασεν Isid.Pel.*epp*.1.257(M.78.337A); ἡ τοῦ νόμου π., ὁδὸς καὶ τρίβος τοῦ κυρίου λέγεται ἄγουσα ἐπὶ τὴν ἀλήθειαν Cyr.*Ps*.24:4(M.69.848B); id.*Is*.1.1(2.20B); *ib*.3.1(351A).

παιδαγωγικός, *instructive*, Cyr.*Jo*.1.10(4.110E); Max.*ambig*.(M.91.1133B).

παιδαγωγικῶς, *in the manner of a teacher*, Clem.*paed*.3.3(p.245.22; M.8.577C); superl., *ib*.1.7(p.123.19; 317B).

παιδαγωγός, ὁ, 1. *instructor, teacher*; of Moses in his writings, Eus.*e.th*.3.3(p.152.5; M.24.993A); of Logos ὁ δὲ ἡμέτερος π. ἅγιος θεὸς Ἰησοῦς, ὁ πάσης τῆς ἀνθρωπότητος καθηγεμὼν λόγος, αὐτὸς ὁ φιλάνθρωπος θεός ἐστι π. Clem.*paed*.1.7(p.123.5; M.8.316B); *ib*.1.9 (p.133.28; 340B); ἀξιόπιστος ὁ θεῖος π. τρισὶ τοῖς καλλίστοις κεκοσμημένος, ἐπιστήμῃ, εὐνοίᾳ, παρρησίᾳ *ib*.1.11(p.148.3; 365C); *ib*.3.11 (p.271.32; 637C); of godparent as τὰ θεῖα π. Dion.Ar.*e.h*.7.3.11(M.3.568B); guardian angel, Bas.*Eun*.3.1(1.272D; M.29.656B); as title of book, Clem.*str*.6.1(p.422.14; M.9.208A); **2.** *elementary instructor, preparatory trainer*; of Law, Eus.*Marcell*.1.1(p.3.16; M.24.716B); ὁ μὲν οὖν π. νόμος διὰ Μωσέως id.*e.th*.2.14(p.117.10; M.24.932B); Cyr.*ador*.13(1.468D); id.*Is*.3.2(2.413B); ὁ νόμος...π. εἰς εὐσέβειαν id.*Am*.47 (3.301D); of prophets, Or.*Jo*.7(9; p.12.6; M.14.36C).

παιδαριεύομαι, *behave childishly*, Nil.*epp*.2.49(M.79.220C).

παιδαρικός, *of childhood*, Epiph.*haer*.51.20(M.41.925A; v.l. for παιδικά p.278.3).

***παιδαριογέρων, ὁ,** *one young in years but old in wisdom*; description of Mac. Aeg., Pall.*h.Laus*.17(p.43.16, v.l. παιδιο- M.34.1043B); Soz.*h.e*.3.14.2(M.67.1069A); of Sabas, Cyr.S.*v.Sab*.11(p.94.16).

παιδάριον, τό, *little boy*; met., *babe* in sense of one who is humble, Dam.*troph*.2.2(p.219.5).

παιδαρίσκος, ὁ, *little boy*, Pall.*h.Laus*.20(p.54.22; M.34.1059D).

***παιδαρύλλιον, τό,** *infant, little boy*; as term of contempt, Cyr.*ep*.10(p.111.23; 5².34D).

παιδεία, ἡ, A. *training, teaching, education*; **1.** of children; **a.** pagan; opposed and interfered with by Christians, Cels.ap.Or.*Cels*.3.55(p.250.29; M.11.993B); ἔλαττον οἱ κατ' ἀγρὸν βιοῦντες ἐξαμαρτάνουσιν, οὐκ εἰσηγμένοι πονηρῶς...ἐκ π. κακῆς ἀσεβεῖν μεμαθηκότες *Hom.Clem*.4.18; **b.** Christian τὰ τέκνα ἡμῶν τῆς ἐν Χριστῷ π μεταλαμβανέτωσαν· μαθέτωσαν, τί ταπεινοφροσύνη παρὰ θεῷ ἰσχύει, τί ἀγάπη...δύναται, πῶς ὁ φόβος αὐτοῦ καλός *1Clem*.21.8; τὰ τέκνα παιδεύειν τὴν π. τοῦ φόβου τοῦ θεοῦ Polyc.*ep*.4.2; Herm.*vis*.2.3.1; τὸν...παιδευόμενον παιδείᾳ...κυρίου ἕως γήρους...οὐ μὴ ἐγκαταλίπῃ ὁ θεός Ant.Mon.*hom*.82(M.89.1681A); **2.** *higher* or *adult education, training in philosophy* (pagan), *learning* or *philosophical study*, in gen. Λουκίῳ, ἐραστῇ παιδείας Just.*1apol*.1.1(M.6.328A); τὴν διὰ γραμμάτων π. [sc. ἐξεῦρον] Φοίνικες Tat.*orat*.1(p.1.8; M.6.804A); ἀπὸ φιλοσοφίας καὶ π. πάσης ὁρμώμενοι Athenag.*leg*.2.2(M.6.893C); οὐδ' αὐτὸς τὴν ἐγκύκλιον π. συντελεῖν πρὸς τἀγαθὸν δίδωσι, συνεργεῖν δὲ πρὸς τὸ διεγείρειν καὶ συγγυμνάζειν πρὸς τὰ νοητὰ τὴν ψυχήν Clem.*str*.1.19(p.60.9; M.8.809B); φιλοσοφίας τε γὰρ τῆς ἐγκυκλίου καὶ π. οὐδενὸς ὑστερήσεις· τῆς εὐαγγελικῆς τε αὖ καὶ θείας Meth.*symp*.8.1 (p.80.19; M.18.137B); γεγόνασι δὴ παρ' ἡμῖν λόγιοι ἄνδρες, καὶ τῶν ἀπὸ π. οὐδενὸς δεύτεροι Eus.*p.e*.10.9(487A; M.21.809D); Φίλων...ἀνὴρ οὐ μόνον τῶν ἡμετέρων, ἀλλὰ καὶ τῶν ἀπὸ τῆς ἔξωθεν ὁρμωμένων π. ἐπισημότατος id.*h.e*.2.4.2(M.20.148A); Μελέτιος (τὸ μέλι τῆς Ἀττικῆς ἐκάλουν αὐτὸν οἱ ἀπὸ π.) *ib*.7.32.27(733A); cf.Bas.*leg.lib.gent*.8(2.184B; M.31.588B); classical education for Christians defended, Socr.*h.e*.3.16.8(M.67.420Bff.); of Egyptian sacred learning, Clem.*str*.6.4 (p.449.25; M.9.256A); **3.** of Christian learning and wisdom τὰ...τῆς ἡμετέρας π. ἐστὶν ἀνωτέρω τῆς κοσμικῆς καταλήψεως Tat.*orat*.12(p.14.8; M.6.833A); μὴ γὰρ δυσχεράνητε τὴν ἡμετέραν π. ... λέγοντες· Τατιανὸς ὑπὲρ τοὺς Ἕλληνας...καινοτομεῖ τὰ βαρβάρων δόγματα *ib*.35 (p.37.12; 877C).

B. *discipline, disciplined mode of life*; **1.** of pagan moral discipline, Clem.*str.*1.5(p.18.27; M.8.720C); **2.** Christian, *godly discipline* π. ἐστὶ μετριοπαθεία παθῶν· ὅπερ συμβαίνειν πέφυκεν ἐκ τῆς πρακτικῆς· ἥ γε πρακτική ἐστι διδασκαλία πνευματική, τὸ παθητικὸν μέρος τῆς ψυχῆς ἐκκαθαίρουσα Or.*Ps.*2:12(p.449); Meth.*res.*1.31(p.264.9; M.41.1141A); Mac.Aeg.*ep.*(M.34.416B).

C. *chastisement, corrective training* νουθετήσει δίκαιον ὡς υἱὸν ἀγαπήσεως, καὶ ἡ π. αὐτοῦ ὡς πρωτοτόκου *Ps.Sal.*13.8; εἰ...ἥμαρτον, ἐν π. παιδεύσατέ με *T.Zab.*2.3; Herm.*sim.*6.3.6; Or.*hom.*12.3 *in Jer.*(p.91.3; M.13.384C); εἰς π. ὑπομένετε...οὐκ εἰς κόλασιν, οὐδὲ εἰς τιμωρίαν *cat.Heb.*12:6(p.261.27); εἰ...τὸ μὴ παιδεύεσθαι τῶν νόθων ἐστί, δεῖ χαίρειν ἐπὶ τῇ π. *ib.*12:8(p.262.5); Jo.Mosch.*prat.*135(M.87.3000A); ἡ γὰρ κατὰ θεὸν π. ἐπ' ἐσχάτων παρρησιασθήσεται ἐν πολλῇ ἀνέσει...καὶ ὁ ἐπαγαγὼν ἡμῖν τὰ κακά, αὐτὸς ἐπάξει ἡμῖν τὴν αἰώνιον εὐφροσύνην Ant.Mon.*hom.*82(M.89.1681A); μηδὲ βαρυτέρας τῆς ἡμετέρας δυνάμεως π. ἐπαγάγῃς ἡμῖν *Lit.Jac.*(p.168.8).

παίδευμα, τό, *subject of study*; **1.** of pagan learning ὅσον δὲ σκιαγραφίαν τινὰ τῆς ἀρετῆς...ἐκ τῶν ἔξωθεν π. περιγραψώμεθα Bas.*leg.lib.gent.*8(2.184B; M.31.588B); **2.** ref. 'psychic' man's inferior mode of perception in Valent. teaching ἔδει γὰρ τῶν ψυχικῶν [l. τῷ ψυχικῷ] καὶ αἰσθητῶν π. Iren.*haer.*1.6.1(M.7.504B); **3.** of Christian doctrine ἐγὼ διδάσκαλος ὑπερουρανίων π. Clem.*q.d.s.*23(p.175.14; M.9.628D); πρὸ τῆς τῶν Ἑλληνικῶν μαθημάτων μελέτης...τοῖς ἱεροῖς ἐνασκεῖσθαι π. Eus.*h.e.*6.2.8(M.20.524C); *ib.*6.3.8(529A); id.*l.C.*1(p.196.15; M.20.1320A); id.*e.th.*1.13(p.73.33; M.24.852C); τῶν εὐαγγελικῶν...π. Cyr.*Lc.*13:26(M.72.780B); of heret. teaching Μαρκίωνος...δίδαγμα ...π. ὂν διαβολικόν Dion.R.ap.Ath.*decr.*26(p.22.13; M.25.464A).

παίδευσις, ἡ, A. *teaching, instruction, education*; **1.** pagan ἔξω π. Clem.*fr.*7(p.224.17)ap.Max.*ambig.*(M.91.1085A); influence on Origen's thought, Marcell.*fr.*78 ap.Eus.*Marcell.*1.4(p.23.4; M.24.760C); ἡ μὲν γὰρ ἔξωθεν π. πολὺν ἀνελίττουσα λῆρον Chrys.*stat.*1.1(2.2E); id.*hom.*1.4 *in Ac.princ.*(3.56D); ἡ Ἑλληνικὴ π., οὔτε παρὰ τοῦ Χριστοῦ, οὔτε παρὰ τῶν αὐτοῦ μαθητῶν, ἢ ὡς θεόπνευστος ἐδέχθη, ἢ ὡς ἐπιβλαβὴς ἐξεβλήθη Socr.*h.e.*3.16.9(M.67.420B); ὁ ἀπόστολος οὐ μόνον οὐ κωλύει μανθάνειν Ἑλληνικὴν π. ἀλλὰ γὰρ φαίνεται καὶ αὐτὸς μὴ ἀμελήσας αὐτῆς *ib.*3.16.23(421C); **2.** Christian, Or.*princ.*3.1.15(p.222.11; M.11.280B); τοσοῦτον γνώσεως τοῖς ἐν σοὶ διδασκάλοις περίεστι χάρις, ὡς μὴ μόνον τοὺς παρὰ σοὶ ἀπολαύειν αὐτῶν τῆς π., ἀλλ' ἤδη καὶ τῆς ἔξωθεν καὶ πόρρωθεν τῆς αὐτῶν ἀπολαύειν ὠφελείας id.*schol.in Cant.*7:4(M.17.281C); χάριν τε καὶ ἀλήθειαν τὴν διὰ τῶν εὐαγγελικῶν θεσπισμάτων ἀποκαλεῖ π. Cyr.*Is.*5.2(2.775E); **3.** in complimentary address ἵνα τὴν σὴν διδάξωσιν π. Thdt.*ep.*10(4.1068); *ib.*124(1207).

B. *corrective discipline, chastening*, Clem.*str.*7.2(p.10.2; M.9.416B); Or.*hom.*12.6 *in Jer.*(p.93.4; M.13.388A); τῆς ἐν νόμῳ π. ἀμείνων ἐστίν...ἡ διὰ Χριστοῦ· ἡ μὲν γὰρ εἰς ἔλεγχον ἐκεῖτο τῶν ἠσθενηκότων καὶ εἰς κατάκριμα...ἡ δὲ εἰς δικαίωσιν τῶν ἠσθενηκότων Cyr.*Ps.*6:2(M.69.744B).

παιδευτήριον, τό, A. *school*; **1.** plur., of schools of secular learning, grammatical, rhetorical, legal, and philosophical education, Gr.Thaum.*pan.Or.*5(p.13.6; M.10.1065C); Eus.*m.P.*7(p.934.27; M.20.1540B); id.*h.e.*7.29.2(M.20.708C); Jo.Mosch.*prat.*195(M.87.3077B); **2.** met., of this world or life τὸ κοινὸν τοῦτο π. Clem.*q.d.s.*33(p.182.14; M.9.640B); ψυχῶν λογικῶν διδασκαλεῖον καὶ θεογνωσίας ἐστὶ π. Bas.*hex.*1.6(1.6E; M.29.16C); Cosm.Ind.*top.*5(M.88.220C); of Israel's probation in wilderness ὥσπερ π. ἡσύχῳ τῇ ἐρήμῳ χρησάμενος ὁ θεός *ib.*(217A).

B. *lesson, means of instruction*, Mac.Mgn.*apocr.*3.11(p.78.24); τὸ ...γενόμενον αὐτῷ κατὰ τὸν Ἀνανίαν καὶ Σάπφειραν κριτήριον... καθολικὸν ὄντως...π. φανεῖταί σοι τὸ πραχθὲν *ib.*3.28(p.119.2); ‡Caes.Naz.*dial.*192(M.38.1172).

παιδευτής, ὁ, **1.** *instructor, teacher*, Tat.*orat.*22(p.25.1; M.6.856B); of S. Paul φιλανθρώπου καὶ φιλοθέου π. Clem.*str.*7.9(p.40.2; M.9.477A); of Solomon, ‡Hipp.*fr.*38 *in Pr.*(p.172.10); **2.** *chastiser*, *Pss.Sal.*8.35.

παιδευτικός, **1.** *of* or *concerned with teaching* ὁ...παιδευτικὴν ἡγεμονίαν κεκληρωμένος λόγος Clem.*paed.*1.12(p.149.19; M.8.369A); πάρεστιν ἀεὶ τῇ...π. ἁπτομένη ἡμῶν δυνάμει δύναμις τοῦ θεοῦ id.*str.*2.2(p.115.26; M.8.936B); **2.** *of* or *concerned with discipline* or *correction*, fem. as subst., *discipline* αὐτῷ ῥάβδον περιτίθησιν ἡ προφητεία, ῥάβδον π. id.*paed.*1.7(p.126.5; M.8.324A); δύο...τρόποι τῆς ἐπανορθώσεως, ὃ μὲν διδασκαλικός, ὃ δὲ κολαστικός, ὃν καὶ π. εἰρήκαμεν id.*str.*4.24(p.316.27; M.8.1364A); σωτήριοι καὶ π. αἱ κολάσεις τοῦ θεοῦ *ib.*6.6(p.455.4; M.9.268C); χρήσιμος...ἡ ἀλγηδὼν...κατά τε τὴν...π. *ib.*7.3(p.13.15; 421C); πῦρ ἦλθον βαλεῖν...δηλονότι δύναμιν...π. id.*ecl.*26(p.144.24; M.9.712A); Or.*princ.*3.1.5(p.200.6; M.11.253C); πάντων μὲν ἡ ὀργὴ χαλεπὴ ἡ δὲ καλουμένη τοῦ θεοῦ π. id.*hom.*20.1 *in Jer.*(p.177.29; M.13.501B); †Bas.*Is.*146(1.482A; M.30.357A); π. συμβάσεις Marc.Er.*opusc.*7.17(M.65.1096C).

***παιδεύτρια, ἡ,** *instructress*, Geo.Pis.*hex.*620(M.92.1483A).

παιδεύ-ω, **1.** *instruct, educate*; **a.** of pagan education, Tat.*orat.*42(p.43.11; M.6.888A); Or.*Cels.*6.14(p.84.11; M.11.1309D); Ἰουλιανὸς... τοὺς Χριστιανοὺς ἀπέτρεπε τὰ Ἑλλήνων ~εσθαι Socr.*h.e.*3.16.19(M.67.421B); **b.** of Christian teaching μὴ ἀναξιοπαθήσητε παρὰ τοῖς βαρβαρικῇ νομοθεσίᾳ παρακολουθοῦσι ~εσθαι Tat.*orat.*12(p.14.4; M.6.833A); Or.*Cels.*3.29(p.226.30; M.11.957A); Cyr.H.*catech.*19.1; Gr.Naz.*or.*21.7(M.35.1088C); of parents' duty τὰ θεῖα ~ειν Thdt.*Eph.*6:4(3.436); **2.** *train, discipline*, *1Clem.*57.1; Clem.*str.*7.9(p.39.5; M.9.473C); Or.*Cant.*1(p.142.29; M.17.257A); of ascetic discipline τὴν ἀθλητικὴν ταύτην ἄριστα παιδευθεὶς Thdt.*h.rel.*3(3.1139); **3.** *chastise*, *Pss.Sal.*7.3; *ib.*16.11; τοὺς μετὰ τὸ λουτρὸν τοῖς ἁμαρτήμασι περιπίπτοντας τούτους εἶναι τοὺς ~ομένους Clem.*str.*4.24(p.316.29; M.8.1364A); θεὸς διὰ τρεῖς ταύτας ~ει αἰτίας...ἵν'...ἀμείνων αὐτοῦ γένηται ὁ ~όμενος...ὅπως οἱ δι' ὑποδειγμάτων σωθῆναι δυνάμενοι προανακρούωνται νουθετούμενοι, καὶ...ὡς μὴ ὁ ἀδικούμενος εὐκαταφρόνητος ᾖ *ib.*(p.316.22; 1364A); Gr.Naz.*or.*5.33(M.35.708A); Cyr.*Ps.*4:2(M.69.736B).

παιδικῶς, *like a child* λαλοῦντι πρὸς τὸ παιδίον π. Or.*hom.*18.6 *in Jer.*(p.159.16; M.13.476C); Thphn.*chron.*p.306(M.108.745B).

παιδίον, τό, *child*; **1.** in gen., of the Innocents τὰ μνημεῖα τῶν π. εἰσὶ φανερὰ ἕως τῆς ἡμέρας ταύτης *Dial.Ath.et Zacch.*76(p.44); of child representing Christ in a vision, *A.Mt.*24(p.250.10,251.2); **2.** of Christ; **a.** in gen., Just.*dial.*88.1(M.6.685A); ὁ ἄνω υἱὸς κάτω π. Acac.Mel.*hom.*(p.91.8; M.77.1469B); **b.** exeg. Is.7:16 σημαίνει δὲ ὁ λόγος, ὅτι καὶ παρ' αὐτὴν τὴν γέννησιν διακριτικός τις ἦν καὶ ἀγαθῶν ποιητικὸς Eus.*Is.*7:15(M.24.137A); ὁ κύριος ἐν μὲν τῇ παιδικῇ διαθέσει τὸ ἀκέραιον καὶ ἄτρωτον ἔτι τοῦ Ἀδὰμ ἐμιμήσατο· ἐν δὲ τῷ ἀθετεῖν τὴν πονηρίαν, τὴν ἐκ τῆς παρακοῆς παρανομίαν ἐπηνωρθώσατο †Bas.*Is.*202(1.530B; M.30.456C) = Proc.G.*Is.*7:10–17(M.87.1965B); προϊὼν ᾐνίξατο εἰπών, πρὶν ἢ γνῶναι τὸ π.· καὶ ἐπεξηγήσει κέχρηται πάλιν λέγων· ἀγαθὸν ἢ κακόν, ἀπειθεῖ πονηρίᾳ, τοῦ ἐκλέξασθαι τὸ ἀγαθόν. τούτου γὰρ αὐτοῦ μόνου ἦν τὸ ἐξαίρετον. διὸ καὶ ὁ...Ἰωάννης...ἀνεκήρυξε λέγων· ἴδε ὁ ἀμνὸς τοῦ θεοῦ Chrys.*Is.interp.*7:16(6.84A); ἡ δέ γε θεία... φύσις, οὐκ ἔν γε τοῖς καθ' ἡμᾶς, ἀλλ' ἐν ἰδίοις...ἄβατος ἀεὶ πονηρίας ἐστὶν...οὐ πειραζομένη ποθὲν Cyr.*Is.*1.4(2.123A); τῶν γὰρ ἀνθρώπων ἡ φύσις οὐκ εὐθὺς τικτομένη τὴν διάκρισιν δέχεται τοῦ ἀγαθοῦ...ὁ δὲ Ἐμμανουὴλ εὐθὺς ἀπὸ σπαργάνων ἀπώσατο τὴν τοῦ χείρονος αἵρεσιν Thdt.*Is.*7:15(p.39.8; 2.219); **c.** exeg. Is.9:6 τίς δ' ἐστὶν οὗτος ὃς καὶ... υἱὸς ἀνθρώπου διὰ Δανιήλ, καὶ π. διὰ Ἡσαίου...κέκληται; Just.*dial.*126.1(M.6.768C); Eus.*Is.*9:6(M.24.152B); †Bas.*Is.*226(1.549E; M.30.512C); τὸ μὲν γεννηθὲν π. δεικνὺς ἐν ἀληθείᾳ, ὅπως σημάνῃ τὴν ἀληθινὴν ἐνανθρώπησιν, τὸ δὲ υἱὸς ἐδόθη ἡμῖν, ὅπως δείξῃ τὸν ἄνωθεν θεοῦ λόγον καὶ υἱὸν θεοῦ δοθέντα καὶ...ἐνανθρωπήσαντα...αὐτὸν υἱὸν ἄνωθεν δοθέντα, αὐτὸν π. γεννηθέντα Epiph.*haer.*30.27(p.370.25; M.41.453A); π. ἡμῖν ἐγεννήθη υἱὸς καὶ ἐδόθη...οὐ μόνον ἐγεννήθη, ἀλλὰ καὶ ἐδόθη· ὁ γὰρ ὢν ἐδόθη Acac.Mel.*hom.*(p.91.9; M.77.1469B); π. ... λέγων γεγενῆσθαι, διελέγχει σαφῶς τῆς τῶν Μανιχαίων δόξης τὸ ἀδρανές, οἳ παραιτοῦνται λέγειν ὅτι γέγονε σὰρξ ὁ λόγος Cyr.*Is.*1.5(2.154E); θελήσουσι...εἰ ἐγενήθησαν πυρίκαυστοι, ὅτι π. ἐγεννήθη ἡμῖν...τῷ φθόνῳ πυρπολοῦντες...θεώμενοι ...τὸ π. τὸ δι' ἡμᾶς γεννηθὲν Thdt.*Is.*9:6(p.50.11; 2.234); ὁ αὐτὸς...ὁ νῦν υἱὸς καὶ π. λεγόμενος Proc.G.*Is.*9:1–7(M.87.2004D); **3.** exeg. Is.8:18, cf. *quia accepit donum a patre eos, qui credunt, idcirco prophetans de iis ait, ecce, ego et pueri, quos mihi dedit deus*, Or.*hom.*7.1 *in Is.*(p.281.2; M.13.247D); βούλεται... ἡμᾶς οὕτω γενέσθαι ὡς τὰ π. ... ὁμοιωθέντα τῷ ἁγίῳ πνεύματι· ἅτινα π. ἔδωκεν ὁ θεὸς τῷ σωτῆρι κατὰ τὸ ἐν Ἡσαΐᾳ λελεγμένον id.*comm.in Mt.*13.18(p.227.2; M.11.1141B); τὰ μὲν οὖν Ἰουδαϊκὰ π. σωματικὰ...τὰ δὲ αὐτὰ τοῦ ταῦτα χρηματίζοντος κυρίου οὐκ ἐξ αἵματος...ἀλλ' ἐκ θεοῦ ἐγεννήθησαν, τοῦ πατρὸς τοιαῦτα αὐτῷ δεδωρημένου τέκνα Eus.*Is.*8:18(M.24.145C) ∾ Proc.G.*Is.*8:16–18(M.87.1992A); τοὺς εἰς ἐμὲ πεπιστευκότας, ἄρτι ἀναγεννηθέντας...οἱονεὶ παῖδας ἀρτιγενεῖς...προσάγω τῷ πατρί...ἐκ προσώπου τοῦ Χριστοῦ εἰσιν οἱ λόγοι †Bas.*Is.*216(1.541C; M.30.492D); ὀνομάζει...ἡμᾶς π. τοῦ πατρός, ὡς τὴν διὰ πνεύματος ἔχοντας ἀναγέννησιν Cyr.*Is.*1.5(2.144E); interpreted of apostles, Thdt.*Is.*8:18(p.46.5; 2.229); π. ... τοὺς πιστούς, ὡς ἀναγεννηθέντας τῷ πνεύματι Proc.G.*Is.*8.16–18(1992A); **4.** exeg. Mt.18:2–3 ἡ πρωτότοκος ἐκκλησία ἡ ἐκ πολλῶν ἀγαθῶν συγκειμένη π. Clem.*prot.*9(p.62.26; M.8.193B); οὐκ ἄρα κατακέχρηται τῇ τῶν π. προσηγορίᾳ ὡς ἀλογίστων ἡλικίᾳ, ᾗ τισιν ἔδοξεν id.*paed.*1.5(p.99.26; M.8.268C); τοῖς περὶ πρωτείων φιλονικοῦσι γνωρίμοις μετὰ ἁπλότητος τὴν ἰσότητα παρεγγυᾷ λέγων ὡς τὰ π. αὐτοὺς γενέσθαι δεῖν id.*str.*5.5(p.345.23; M.9.53A); οἷον ἵνα στραφῇ τις καὶ ὁποῖόν ἐστι τὸ βραχὺ π. πρὸς ὀργὴν τοιοῦτος γένηται ὢν ἀνήρ, καὶ ὁποῖόν ἐστι τὸ π. πρὸς λύπην (ἔσθ' ὅτε παρὰ τὸν καιρὸν τοῦ τεθνηκότος πατρὸς...ὡς γελᾶν καὶ παίζειν κατ' ἐκεῖνον τὸν χρόνον), τοιοῦτος ἂν γένοιτο ὁ στραφεὶς ὡς π. καὶ ἕξιν ἀναλαβὼν ἐκ λόγου τῆς λύπης ἀπαράδεκτον, ὥστε ὁποῖόν ἐστι πρὸς λύπην τὸ βραχὺ π. αὐτὸν γενέσθαι, τὸ δ' ὅμοιον φήσεις περὶ τῆς καλουμένης ἡδονῆς,...ἣν οὐ πάσχει τὰ π. οὐδ' οἱ...γενόμενοι ὡς τὰ π. ... ὅτι οὐδὲν τῶν παθῶν πίπτει εἰς τὰ μηδέπω συμπεπληρωκότα τὸν λόγον π. ... οὐ γὰρ πίπτει ὑψηλοφροσύνη καὶ οἴησις...εἰς π. Or.*comm.in Mt.* 13.16(p.220.17; M.13.1136B); οὐ πάντες οἱ στραφέντες πρὸς τὸ γενέσθαι ὡς τὰ π., ἐφθάκασιν ὡς ἐπὶ τὸ ἐξομοιωθῆναι τοῖς π.· ἀλλ' ἕκαστος τοσοῦτον ἀπολείπεται τῆς πρὸς τὰ π. ὁμοιώσεως, ὅσον ἀπολείπεται τῆς ἀποδεδομένης τῶν π. πρὸς τὰ πάθη ἕξεως *ib.*13.17(p.224.3; 1140A); ζητήσωμεν ποῖον προσκαλεσάμενος π. ὁ Ἰησοῦς ἔστησεν ἐν μέσῳ...ὅρα δὲ...τὸ ταπεινῶσαν ἑαυτὸ πνεῦμα ἅγιον, ὑπὸ τοῦ σωτῆρος προσκληθὲν καὶ σταθὲν ἐν μέσῳ τῷ ἡγεμονικῷ τῶν μαθητῶν Ἰησοῦ...μείζων οὖν ἐν τῇ βασιλείᾳ τῶν οὐρανῶν ὁ ταπεινώσας ἑαυτὸν...μιμητικῶς ἐκείνου τοῦ π. *ib.*13.18(p.226.23; 1141B); τὰ μὲν π. οὐκ ἀμύνεται τοὺς ἠδικηκότας, οὐ λυπεῖται ἐπὶ τῇ ἀποβολῇ τῶν ἡδέων, οὐ προσπάσχει...τοῖς οὖσι προσηνέσι. βούλεται τοίνυν τοιούτους εἶναι ἡμᾶς ἐκ διαθέσεως οἷα τυγχάνει τὰ π. ἐξ ἡλικίας id.*fr.35 in Jo.*(p.511.3); ἐὰν τοιοῦτοι γενώμεθα πρὸς τὴν διδασκαλίαν τοῦ κυρίου, οἷόν ἐστι τὸ π. ἐν τοῖς μαθήμασι ...εὐπειθῶς δεχόμενον τὰ διδάγματα Bas.*reg.br.*217(2.487E; M.31.1225C); φθόνου καθαρὸν τὸ π. ... καὶ τὴν μεγίστην κέκτηται ἀρετήν, τὴν ἀφέλειαν καὶ τὸ...ταπεινόν Chrys.*hom.58.2 in Mt.*(7.587C).

***παιδιστί**, *in children's language*, Or.*hom.1.9 in Jer.*(p.8.4; M.13.265A).

***παιδογον-έω**, *beget children* οὐ ζήτει...καταλιπεῖν παῖδας, ἀλλὰ... ~εῖν πνευματικῶς Bas.*inst.ascet.*2(2.200B; M.31.621B).

παιδογόνος, **1.** *reproductive*; of sexual organs, Meth.*symp.*3.12 (p.41.21; M.18.81A); Thdr.Mops.*Gen.*3:7(M.66.640B); Thdt.*qu.28 in Gen.*(1.42); **2.** *sexual* π. ἡδοναῖς Meth.*symp.*2.2(p.16.15; M.18.49A).

παιδοκομ-έω, *look after children*; **1.** lit., ref. Pharaoh's daughter hiring Moses' mother to care for her own child, as type of Jews who will ultimately accept Christ at the hands of gentiles, Cyr. *glaph.Ex.*1(1.252B); **2.** met. ὁ νόμος...γάλακτι καὶ ὥσπερ νηπίους ὄντας ~εῖ id.*ador.*8(1.285B); ~εῖ ὁ νόμος, τελειοῖ δὲ...τὸ Χριστοῦ μυστήριον id.*glaph.Gen.*2(1.46A); ἔδει διὰ...Μωσέως ~εῖσθαι τὸν Ἰσραήλ id.*Juln.*9(6^2.322B).

παιδοκόμος, **ὁ**, *one who looks after children*, Proc.G.*Gen.*24:1(M.87.396B); met. π. ... ὥσπερ τοῖς ἐξ ἐθνῶν γεγόνασιν οἱ...μαθηταί Cyr. *Is.*4.4(2.680D); π. ... ὁ νόμος εἰς Χριστὸν ἀναφέρων id.*dial.Trin.*4(5^1.514A).

παιδοκτόνος, **ὁ**, *slayer of children*, Clem.*str.*2.18(p.163.12; M.8.1033B); ref. Abraham τί...με καὶ πατέρα δείξας π. ἐργάζῃ; Bas.Sel. *or.*7.2(M.85.105C); of Herod, Gr.Naz.*carm.*1.2.1.454(M.37.556A); of Simon Magus π. τε καὶ φαρμακόν *M.Ner.et Ach.*12(p.11.14).

***παιδομανέω**, *be mad after boys*, Evagr.*h.e.*5.3(p.197.21; M.86.2793B).

παιδονόμος, **ὁ**, *tutor*, παιδαγωγούς...ἢ π. ἐπιτεταγμένους [sc. angels] τοῖς ἀνθρώποις Bas.*Spir.*30(3.25B; M.32.120C); of prophets and holy men of OT, Thdt.*Ps.*65:9(1.1047).

παιδοποιέω, *beget children*, theol. ἀεὶ τὸν Χριστὸν εἶναι, λόγον ὄντα καὶ σοφίαν καὶ δύναμιν, οὐ γὰρ δὴ τούτων ἄγονος ὢν ὁ θεὸς εἶτα ἐπαιδοποιήσατο Dion.Al.ap.Ath.*Dion.*15(p.57.3; M.25.501C); fig. τῷ φόβῳ τοῦ κυρίου δύνασθαι κυοφορῆσαι, καὶ πνεῦμα σωτηρίας παιδοποιήσασθαι Gr.Nyss.*hom.15 in Cant.*(M.44.1112B).

παιδοποιητέον, *one must beget children*, Clem.*prot.*11(p.79.21; M.8.229B).

***παιδοσπορία**, **ἡ**, *begetting of children* παρὰ τοῖς θεοῖς γάμοι π. τε ἐνομίσθησαν Const.*or.s.c.*4(p.157.23; M.20.1241B); οὐκ ἐξ ἀνδρικῆς π. γενήσεται ἡ σύλληψις Procl.CP *annunt.*5(M.85.444D).

***παιδοσφαγία**, **ἡ**, *slaughter of children*; in magical rites, ‡Caes. Naz.*dial.*118(M.38.1005A); of massacre of Innocents, *Pers.*(p.35.5); ‡Anast.S.*Jud.disp.*3(M.89.1248A).

παιδοτριβ-έω, *train*, met. τὴν...ψυχὴν πρὸς ἀνδρείαν ~ήσασα Gr. Nyss.*v.Macr.*(p.380.22; M.46.969A); in ascetic life, Thdt.*h.rel.*3(3.1139); ref. Abraham πολλαῖς γυμνασίαις ἀρετῆς αὐτὸν καθάπερ ἐν παλαίστρᾳ ~ήσας Bas.Sel.*or.*7.1(M.85.101C).

παιδοτρίβης, **ὁ**, **1.** *trainer* of athletes; met., of God τῶν εὐσεβῶν παιδοτρίβης Thdt.*Cant.*3:1(2.77); **2.** *teacher, instructor* Παῦλος, ὁ τῆς οἰκουμένης π. Chrys.*hom.in Rom.*5:3(3.143A); Thdt.*Ps.*65:9(1.1047).

***παιδοτρίβιον**, **τό**, *gymnasium* οἱ ἐν παιδοτριβίοις γυμνασθέντες Isid.Pel.*epp.*5.334(M.78.1529B, v.l. παιδοτρίβου).

***παιδοφαγία**, **ἡ**, *eating of children*, Chrys.*hom.76.1 in Mt.*(7.733A).

***παιδοφθορ-έω**, *corrupt boys* δευτέρα δὲ ἐντολὴ τῆς διδαχῆς· οὐ φονεύσεις, οὐ μοιχεύσεις, οὐ ~ήσεις *Did.*2.2; *Barn.*19.4; Clem.*prot.*10 (p.77.17; M.8.225A); Μωυσῆς...οὐ πορνεύσεις, οὐ μοιχεύσεις, οὐ π. λέγων id.*paed.*2.10(p.211.11; M.8.504B); ‡Ath.*syntag.*1.5(M.28.836A).

***παιδοφθορία**, **ἡ**, **1.** *corruption of boys*, Clem.*paed.*2.10(p.211.8; M.8.504B); in list of σωματικὰ πάθη, Jo.D.*spir.neq.*(M.95.88C); ascribed to gods by pagans, Thphl.Ant.*Autol.*1.9(M.6.1037B); ὁμολογοῦντες εἶναι κακὸν τὴν π., τοὺς ἐπὶ ταύτῃ διαβαλλομένους θρησκεύουσι Ath.*gent.*12(M.25.28B); id.*v.Anton.*74(M.26.945B); *M.Thdot.*1 24(p.76.9); **2.** *destruction of children* by abortion, ‡Jo.Jej.*can.*(p.443).

***παιδοφθόρος**, *corrupting boys*, *T.Lev.*17.11; τὸν δασύποδα οὐ μὴ φάγῃ· πρὸς τί; οὐ μὴ γένῃ...π., οὐδὲ ὁμοιωθήσῃ τοῖς τοιούτοις *Barn.* 10.6; Or.*sel.in Ex.*12:15(M.12.284D).

παιδοφονεύς, **ὁ**, *slayer of children*, †Apoll.*met.Ps.*134:11(M.33.1516D).

παιδοφονία, **ἡ**, *murder of children*, Gr.Nyss.*virg.*3(p.266.4; M.46.336C); of massacre of Innocents, id.*or.catech.*29(p.109.7; M.45.76B).

παιήων, *healing* π. μύθῳ Nonn.*par.Jo.*3:2(M.43.765B); *ib.*12:40 (857A).

***παίκτος**, *to be trifled with* παίζεις ἐν οὐ παίκτοις Chrys.*hom.31.5 in Rom.*(9.753B); id.*hom.22.3 in 2Cor.*(10.592E); id.*hom.27.5 in Heb.*(12.253C).

παῖς, **ὁ**, [acc. παίν tr.Vergil *ecl.*4.8 ap.Const.*or.s.c.*19(p.182.11; M.20.1292C); Gr.Naz.*carm.*1.1.2.32(M.37.404A); *ib.*1.1.27.82(504A)];

A. *child, son*; **1.** in gen. π. ... ὁ δωδεκαέτης λέγεται Chrys.*incomprehens.*1.3(1.447A); οἱ ῥαντιζόμενοι π. (cf. Num.19) interpreted of apostles, *Barn.*8.3; of the 'Three Children', Or.*fr.66 in Jer.* 47:5(p.230.16); met. π. ἐν πίστει...οὐδέπω δὲ ἄνδρες ἐν ἀγάπῃ Clem.*str.*7.11(p.48.14; M.9.493A); Eus.*p.e.*1.4(13D; M.21.41C); **2.** of David as son of God (or perh. *servant*, v. B infra), *Did.*9.2; **3.** Christol.; **a.** of pre-existent Son, *Diogn.*8.9; Gr.Naz.*carm.*2.1.2.32 (M.37.404A); οὐκ ἦν δέ, ὅτε οὐκ ἦν ὁ πατήρ, ἀεὶ συνὼν τῷ π. καὶ γὰρ ἀεὶ συνυπῆρχον ἀλλήλοις, ὁ πατὴρ τῷ π., ὁ π. τῷ πατρί Bas.Sel.*v.Thecl.*1 (M.85.481A); as πρωτόγονος π., Hipp.*haer.*10.33(p.290.25; M.16.3450C); as μονογενὴς π., *M.Polyc.*20.2; Clem.*str.*7.1(p.5.11; M.9.408A); τοῦ μονογενοῦς π. αὐτοῦ, τοῦ πρωτοτόκου πάσης κτίσεως Dion. Al.ap.Eus.*h.e.*7.5.6(M.20.648A); Eus.*v.C.*1.32(p.22.24; M.20.948B); Chrys.*sac.*3.15(p.80.6; 1.394B); as πρωτότοκος π. typified by Jacob/Israel, Hipp.*ben.Jac.*14(p.30.15); as ἀγαπητὸς π., *M.Polyc.*14.1; in rel. to Christ as priest τοῦ αἰωνίου...ἀρχιερέως...ἀγαπητοῦ σου παιδός *ib.*14.3; *Diogn.*8.11; *A.Paul.et Thecl.*24(p.252.7); ‡Pion.*v.Polyc.*5; **b.** explicitly in rel. to incarnate life, *Did.*9.2; cf.*Barn.*9.2 (but v. B infra); ὁ ἀντὶ τοῦ ἀμνοῦ π. θεοῦ Claud.*fr.pasch.*(M.5.1297A); Χριστόν, π. θεοῦ, θεὸν καὶ ἄνθρωπον Hipp.*antichr.*61(p.41.21; M.10.781A); ἃ πάλαι τοῖς...προφήταις ἀπεκάλυψεν ὁ τοῦ θεοῦ λόγος, νῦν αὐτὸς πάλιν ὁ τοῦ θεοῦ π., ὁ πάλαι μὲν λόγος ὤν, νυνὶ δὲ καὶ ἄνθρωπος *ib.*3(p.5.23; 729C); τὸν κατὰ σάρκα γενόμενον π. θεοῦ *ib.*8(p.9.10; 736A); ἔδει γὰρ ἐκεῖ [sc. at Jordan] τὸν π. δείκνυσθαι id.*Dan.*4.36.4(M.10.657B); ὃς προβὰς ἐν κόσμῳ ἐδείκνυτο π. θεοῦ id.*Noët.*11(p.253.12; M.10.817C); αἵματι θεοῦ παιδός Clem.*q.d.s.*34(p.182.22; M.9.640C); Eus.*l.C.*17 (p.258.15; M.20.1437A); ‡Pion.*v.Polyc.*27; Diod.*Ps.*68:17(M.33.1604D); σωτῆρος π. ἐκ παρθένου γενομένου *Chron.Pasch.*p.157(M.92.385B).

B. *servant*; of David, *Did.*9.2 (but perh. = *son*, v. supra); of Christ as 'servant of the Lord', *1Clem.*59.2; *Did.*9.2; *Barn.*6.1; cf. *ib.*9.2 (but in these cases perh. = *son*, v. supra).

C. *disciple, follower*, Didym.*Trin.*1.34(M.39.436C); *Pers.*(p.10.5); Thdt.*h.e.*2.18.3(3.872); Leont.B.*arg.Sev.*(M.86.1940C).

***πάκης**, transliteration of *pacis* ἐν Ἱππῶνι Ῥεγίῳ εἰς τὸ σήκρητον τῆς ἐκκλησίας πάκης (tr. Lat. *basilicae Pacis*) *Cod.Afr.*(H.1.881A).

πακτεύ-ω, *contract* ~ει καθιεροῦν τὸν...τόπον Phot.*nomoc.*2.1 (p.485; M.104.565D).

πάκτον, **τό**, (Lat. *pactum*) **1.** *agreement* ἠγόρασαν...ἀγράφῳ π. Jo.Mal.*chron.*12 p.286(M.97.432B); Phot.*nomoc.*13.18(p.624; M.104.932C); **2.** plur.; **a.** *terms* π. εἰρήνης Jo.Mal.*chron.*10 p.232(357C); *ib.*11 p.271(409B); *Chron.Pasch.*p.299(M.92.749C); *ib.*p.396(1013A); **b.** *agreed tribute* τῷ Χαγάνῳ τὰ π. ἐπαυξήσας Thphn.*chron.*p.245(M.108.616C).

[*]**παλαιορράφος**, **ὁ**, *cobbler* αἱρεσιάρχαι δίκην π. συγκαττύσαντες... τὰ τῶν παλαιῶν σφάλματα Hipp.*haer.*5.6(p.77.23; M.16.3123B).

παλαιός, *ancient*; **1.** of pre-Christian beliefs, life, and institutions contrasted with new dispensation of gospel, Ign.*Eph.*19.3; οἱ ἐν π. πράγμασιν ἀναστραφέντες εἰς καινότητα ἐλπίδος ἦλθον id.*Magn.* 9.1; μὴ τὰ π. τῆς κακῆς ζύμης ἔργα πράττητε Just.*dial.*14.2(M.6.504D); θάνατος καὶ τέλος λέγεται τοῦ π. βίου τὸ βάπτισμα Clem. *exc.Thdot.*77(p.131.8; M.9.693C); τῆς π. ἀπάτης ἔοικεν εἶναι ταῦτα πλημμελήματα Gr.Thaum.*pan.Or.*16(p.35.22; M.10.1096C); **2.** personal, of men of old, ancients παραιτουμένους δόξαις παλαιῶν ἐξακολουθεῖν, ἂν φαῦλαι ὦσιν Just.*1apol.*2.1(M.6.329A); ἴστε δὲ καὶ ὑμεῖς ταῦτα ...ὡς ἂν...ὑπὲρ πάντας τοῖς π. συγγινόμενοι Athenag.*leg.*17.1(M.6.921C); μὴ...ὡς ἐχώρουν οἱ π., σῶμα τὸν θεὸν νομίζωμεν Or.*fr.4 in 1Reg.*15:9–11(p.296.23); τὸ γνῶθι σεαυτόν...τὸ δὲ εἶναι ὄντως ἔργον φρονήσεως...καλῶς τοῖς π. λέγεται Gr.Thaum.*pan.Or.*11(p.27.11; M.10.1084C); Meth.*symp.*1.2(p.9.25; M.18.40C); τὴν...σοφίαν τοῦ θεοῦ... ἥν τε π. ἄνδρες φύσιν ἐκάλεσαν καὶ πρόνοιαν id.*res.*2.9(p.348.21; M.18.288C); Eus.*e.th.*2.18(p.122.12; M.24.941B); id.*v.C.*3.54(p.101.22; M.20.1117B); **3.** of Son ὁ μὲν υἱὸς...τῆς κτίσεως αὐτοῦ προγενέστερός ἐστιν ...διὰ τοῦτο καὶ π. ἐστιν Herm.*sim.*9.12.2; ὁ καινὸς φανεὶς καὶ π. εὑρεθεὶς *Diogn.*11.4; τὸν π. καὶ νεώτερον, τὸν χρόνῳ φαινόμενον καὶ ἀεὶ ὄντα *V.Aberc.*16(p.14.7); **4.** of God as π. τῶν ἡμερῶν (Dan.7), Just.*dial.*32.1(M.6.541D); ἄφθαρτον...καὶ ἀτελεύτητον οὐ τοῦ λόγου τοῦ ἐν τῷ θεῷ τὴν βασιλείαν ἔσεσθαι, ἀλλὰ τοῦ υἱοῦ τοῦ ἀνθρώπου παρίστησιν ὁ προφήτης, ἕτερόν τε παρὰ τὸν π. τῶν ἡμερῶν σαφῶς διδάσκει τὸν υἱὸν εἶναι...τὸν τὴν...βασιλείαν παρὰ τοῦ π. τῶν ἡμερῶν...ὑποδεξάμενον Eus.*e.th.*3.17(p.177.2; M.24.1037B); ἡμερῶν δὲ π. ὁ θεὸς ὑμνεῖται διὰ τὸ πάντων αὐτὸν εἶναι καὶ αἰῶνα, καὶ χρόνον, καὶ πρὸ ἡμερῶν, καὶ πρὸ αἰῶνος, καὶ χρόνου Dion.Ar.*d.n.*10.2(M.3.937B); **5.** π. διαθήκη; v. διαθήκη; abs. ἡ π. *the Old Testament* Ἰωσὴφ ἐν τῇ π. τύπος διὰ τῶν ἐνυπνίων χρηματίζεται Hipp.*ben.Jac.*1(p.13.5) (passage prob. interpolated, v. θεοτόκος); Anon.ap.Eus.*h.e.*5.17.3(M.20.473B); ἡ π. μὲν οὐκ εὐαγγέλιον, οὐ δεικνύουσα τὸν ἐρχόμενον, ἀλλὰ προκηρύσσουσα, πᾶσα δὲ ἡ καινὴ τὸ εὐαγγέλιόν ἐστιν Or.*Jo.*1.3(5; p.7.2; M.14.28C); Ath.*Ar.*1.4(M.26.20A); ἔστιν ἄρα καὶ ἐν τῇ π. φανερῶς περὶ υἱοῦ κείμενα ‡Ath.*Ar.*4.29(p.77.12; M.26.512C); εἰ...ἐπὶ τῆς π. τοῦτο ἦν, πολλῷ μᾶλλον ἐπὶ τῆς καινῆς Chrys.*hom.4.4 in Eph.*(11.30F); id.*hom.17.6 in Mt.*(7.230B); id.*hom.47.1 in Jo.*(8.276E); Jo.Mosch.*prat.*171(M.87.3040A); ἐν τῇ π., ἢ ἐν τῷ εὐαγγελίῳ Jo.D.*imag.*3.11(M.94.1333B); **6.** of OT writings in gen., without mention of διαθήκη: π. βιβλίων Mel.*fr.*3(p.309; M.5.1213); τὰ π. καὶ τὰ καινὰ γράμματα Or.*Jo.*10.30(18; p.203.24; M.14.361A); Ath.*exp.Ps.*67:27(M.27.301B) cit. s. διαιρέω; π. παραδείγματος Thdt.*1Cor.*15:20(3.269); π. προρρήσεων *cat.Lc.*24:13(p.171.34); ‡Petr.I Al.*phys.*12(p.42); Dam.*troph.*1.4(p.201.8); **7.** of OT history, etc. ἀναγνῶναι τὰ π. Or.*hom.*4.6 *in Jer.*(p.29.23; M.13.293C); π. ἱστορίᾳ Cyr.H.*catech.*19.2; Chrys.*hom.16.4 in Rom.*(9.608D); id.*hom.6.4 in Phil.*(11.44E); **8.** of Israel as π. λαός, Eus.*e.th.*2.22(p.132.32; M.24.960B); Cyr.H.*catech.*19.3, v. λαός; **9.** of earthly Jerusalem, Thdt.*Is.*60:16(p.238.26; 2.381); **10.** of Melchizedek, opp. Christ Μελχισεδὲκ...ὁ π. id.*haer.*5.4(4.395); **11.** of π. ἐκκλησία at Antioch, Chrys.*stat.*1 tit.(2.1A); **12.** ἡ π., a quarter of Antioch, Thdt.*h.e.*1.3.1(3.727).

παλαι-όω, A. trans.; **1.** *make old* τοῦ πάντα ~οῦντος χρόνου Nil.*praest.*19(M.79.1084B); **2.** pass., *grow old, be worn out, become inveterate* τὴν κακὴν ζύμην, τὴν ~ωθεῖσαν Ign. *Magn.*10.2; Herm.*vis.*3.11.3; Iren.*haer.*5.36.1(M.7.1221B); Arist.*apol.*13.2; Just.*dial.*131.6(M.6.781C); Ath.*Ar.*2.76(M.26.309A); οὐ ~ούμενον...ἀλλὰ ἀνανεούμενον Bas.*hom.*1.2(2.2E; M.31.165C); καινὴ...κτίσις μεταλαμβάνουσα τοῦ πνεύματος, οὗπερ ἐστερημένη πεπαλαίωτο Didym.(‡Bas.)*Eun.*5(1.303A; M.29.728A); ὑπὸ τῆς ἁμαρτίας ~ωθέντας Thdt.*Cant.*5:16(2.118); τὸ 'γεννᾷ με' νόει...τῆς αὐτῆς φύσεως ~ουμένης καὶ ἀνανεουμένης ἄχρι συντελείας Gel.Cyz.*h.e.*2.17.26(M.85.1272A); Anast.S.*serm.*2.8(M.89.1385A).

B. intrans., *grow up*, Clem.*paed.*2.6(p.187.14; M.8.452B).

***παλαιστημαῖος,** *a hand's-breadth in size*, Anast.S.*hod.*13(M.89.233A).

***παλαιστήριον, τό,** *wrestling school*, met. μοναχικὰ π. Isid.Pel.*epp.*1.262(M.78.340B).

παλαί-ω, *wrestle, contend*; of Jacob's wrestling ἄγγελος καὶ θεὸς [sc. Son]...ἐν ἰδέᾳ ἀνθρώπου...τῷ Ἰακὼβ ~σας Just.*dial.*58.10(M.6.609B); *Hom.Clem.*16.14; of Christ grappling with Satan in Hades, Or.*engast.*6(p.289.4; M.12.1021A); in Temptations, Cosm.Ind.*top.*2(M.88.121C); of Christians' struggle against evil powers ὅταν τῆς χάριτος [sc. of baptism] καταξιωθῇς, τότε σοι πρὸς τὰς ἀντικειμένας δυνάμεις ~ειν δίδωσι τὴν ἐξουσίαν Cyr.H.*catech.*3.13; Thdt.*1Cor.*15:19(3.269).

***παλαμοφλεκτ-έω,** *apply fire to the hands* τὸν βαπτιστὴν...τὸν ~ούμενον καὶ μὴ καιόμενον Chrysipp.*enc.in Jo.Bapt.*(p.33.17).

παλατῖνος, *belonging to the palace* or *court*; **1.** title of officials belonging to various branches of civil *militia*, Nil.*epp.*3.69 tit.(M.79.421A) etc.; of *agentes in rebus* π. ... ἦσαν οἱ κομίσαντες τὰ γράμματα Ath.*apol.sec.*59(p.140.5; M.25.357B); οὐ π. ἢ νοταρίων ἀποσταλέντων id.*h.Ar.*29(p.198.23; M.25.725C); **2.** ἄρτος π., *bread distributed by emperor*, Jo.Mal.*chron.*13 p.322(M.97.484A).

παλάτιον, τό, *palace*; **1.** *imperial residence, court*, *A.Jo.*11(p.158.3); *A.Petr.et Paul.*84(p.219.4); Eus.*v.C.*3.54(p.101.26; M.20.1117B); Ath.*h.Ar.*14(p.189.31; M.25.708C); Pall.*v.Chrys.*7(p.42.3; M.47.25); id.*h.Laus.*44(p.131.5; M.34.1209C); ἐν τῷ θείῳ ἡμῶν π. Justn.*ep. Thdr.Mops.*(p.66.17; M.86.1087A); Jo.Mal.*chron.*4 p.89(M.97.173A); Jo.Mosch.*prat.*186(M.87.3064C); **2.** ref. officials of imperial court and administration γενόμενοι Χριστιανοὶ οὐκ ἔτι ἠθέλησαν στραφῆναι ἐν τῇ στρατιᾷ οὔτε ἐν τῷ π. *A.(Pass.)Petr.et Paul.*10(p.128.23); *A.Petr.et Paul.*31(p.193.7); ὁ...τοῦ π. μάγιστρος Ath.*apol.Const.*10(M.25.608B); ἀπὸ παλατίου *ex-official*, id.*v.Anton.*57(M.26.925B); Ἀρσένιος, ἔτι ὢν ἐν τῷ π. *Apophth.Patr.*(M.65.88B); ὑπὲρ τῶν...βασιλέων, παντὸς τοῦ π. καὶ τοῦ στρατοπέδου αὐτῶν *Lit.Jac.*(p.186.17); τῶν ἐν π. ἀδελφῶν *Lit.Bas.*(p.333.28); **3.** of residences of non-Roman kings: in Edessa, *Ep.Abg.*7(p.283.8); India, *A.Thom.*A 17(p.125.7); Persia, *M.Pers.*3.1(p.439.19); Ptolemaic Egypt, Epiph.*mens.*3(M.43.241C); **4.** of royal palaces in gen. οἱ εἰσερχόμενοι εἰς τὸ π. πρὸς τὸν βασιλέα...ὑπὸ φόβον πολύν εἰσι Mac.Aeg.*hom.*15.19(M.34.588C); ἄνθρωπον...ἐν παλατίοις ἐξεταζόμενον τρυφερόν Ph.Carp.*Cant.*139(M.40.105B); **5.** *governor's residence* ὁ Πιλᾶτος ἐν τῷ π. *A.Pil.*B 3.2(p.294); *M.Agap.*5.8(p.99.9); **6.** ? *church* [ἀνήγειρε Θεό]δοτος τὸ π. τοῦ ἀρχαγγέλου ἔτους ἑξακοσιοστοῦ ἑβδομικοστοῦ *MAMA* 4.225 (Phrygia, saec. vii); **7.** of heavenly palace as abode of God, *A.Thom.*A 17(p.124.14); Nil.*epp.*2.170(M.79.285C); ἀπάθειαν μὲν νοήσεις, τὸ τοῦ ἐπουρανίου βασιλέως ἐν οὐρανοῖς π. Jo.Clim.*scal.*29(M.88.1149D); **8.** of the heart as the π. of Christ, Mac.Aeg.*hom.*15.33(M.34.597C); **9.** of BMV τὸ ἔμψυχον τοῦ βασιλέως τῶν ἀγγέλων π. ‡Gr.Thaum.*annunt.*3(M.10.1172B); Mod.*dorm.*13(M.86.3309A); Germ.CP *hymn.BMV*(M.98.453C); ἰδοὺ π. τοῦ ἐπουρανίου βασιλέως ἄνευ χειρῶν...κατασκευάζεται, καὶ τοῦτο τὸ π. ἐν Ἐδὲμ κατὰ ἀνατολὰς τὴν πύλην ἔχον Jo.Eub.*concept.BMV* 17(M.96.1488A); ‡Sophr.H.*triod.*(M.87.3972B).

παλαχή, ἡ, *anything acquired by lot*; ἐκ π. *from the beginning*, †Apoll.*met.Ps.*75:9(M.33.1420D); *ib.*77:2(1424A).

παλιγγενεσία, ἡ, I. in gen., *renewal of life, revival*; of miraculous resuscitation of a corpse, *A.Jo.*11(p.158.11); of renewal after Flood, *1Clem.*9.4; Epiph.*anc.*94(p.115.24; M.43.189A); met. τὰ Ἰουδαϊκὰ πράγματα τέλεον οἴχεται, καὶ π. οὐχ ἕξει Isid.Pel.*epp.*4.17(M.78.1064C).

II. *restoration* (Stoic); of successive renewals of universe after conflagration ἀπείρους φθορὰς κόσμου καὶ π. εἰσάγουσιν Bas.*hex.*3.8(1.31A; M.29.73C).

III. *rebirth, regeneration*;

A. eschatol. (cf. Mt.19:28); **1.** of general rebirth and new creation in age to come ἡ π. καινή τις γένεσις οὖσα, ὅτε οὐρανὸς καινὸς καὶ γῆ καινὴ τοῖς ἑαυτοὺς ἀνακαινώσασι κτίζεται καὶ καινὴ διαθήκη παραδίδοται καὶ τὸ ποτήριον αὐτῆς Or.*comm.in Mt.*15.22(p.416.27; M.13.1320B); ἀνανεώσεώς τε καὶ π. αἰῶνος ἑτέρου Eus.*d.e.*1.9(p.40.23; M.22.77C); ἡμῶν περὶ συντελείας τοῦ κόσμου τούτου καὶ π. αἰῶνος ἀπαγγελλόντων Bas.*hex.*1.4(1.5B; M.29.12C); Ph.Carp.*Cant.*24(M.40.53B); ἕως οὗ ὁ βασιλεὺς ἐν τῇ π. παραγένηται id.ap.Proc.G.*Cant.*1:11(M.87.1564B); τὸ κατὰ ἀνατολὰς εὔχεσθαι...ὡς ἐκδεχομένους τὴν ἀνατολὴν τῆς φωτοφανείας...τοῦ κυρίου παρουσίας καὶ π. ‡Germ.CP *contempl.*(M.98.392B,C); ἠξίωσεν ἡμᾶς...ἐν τῇ π. σὺν αὐτῷ αὐλισθῆναι...τί δέ ἐστι π.; τὸ ἐκ δευτέρου γεννηθῆναι, καὶ ἀνακαινισθῆναι *ib.*(452B); **2.** of bodily resurrection φανήσεται δυνατὴ ἡ τῆς σαρκὸς ὑπάρχειν παλιγγενεσία †Just.*fr.res.*(p.42; M.6.1581B); τὰ οὖν σώματα τῶν μαρτύρων ...καέντα...κατεσαρώθη εἰς τὸν Ῥοδανὸν...καὶ ταῦτ' ἔπραττον ὡς δυνάμενοι...ἀφελέσθαι αὐτῶν τὴν π. *Ep.Lugd.*ap.Eus.*h.e.*5.1.62–63(M.20.432C); Clem.*q.d.s.*42(p.190.19; M.9.649D); τῆς σαρκὸς τὴν π. Meth.*res.*2.18(p.371.2; M.18.313B); τῆς ἐκ νεκρῶν π. Chrys.*fr.Job* 7:9(M.64.600C); Proc.G.*Is.*65:13ff.(M.87.2696A); †Jo.D.*B.J.*9(M.96.928C); **3.** of future life, ‡Hipp.*fr.47 in Pr.*(p.174.10); Eus.*l.C.*15(p.246.19; M.20.1417A); *Const.App.*7.34.6; αἱ μὲν γὰρ ἱεραὶ ψυχαί...ἐν τῇ π. τὴν ἐπὶ τὸ ἄτρεπτον ἕξουσι...μετάταξιν Dion.Ar.*e.h.*7.1.1(M.3.553A); *ib.*7.1.3(556B); in which man lives the angelic life, Gr.Nyss. ap.Proc.G.*Cant.*2:7(M.87.1592A); in which man's state of life will be directly related to life he has lived on earth, Dion.Ar.*e.h.*7.3.1(557A); in Indian theology Βραχμᾶναι...οὐδὲν ἡγοῦνται τὸ ζῆν· πείθονται γὰρ εἶναι π. Clem.*str.*2.7(p.224.1; M.8.1164B).

B. (pagan) of transmigration of souls Κρόνιος μὲν γὰρ ἐν τῷ Περὶ παλιγγενεσίας (οὕτω δὲ καλεῖ τὴν μετενσωμάτωσιν) Nemes.*nat.hom.*2(M.40.581B).

C. *spiritual rebirth, regeneration*, = ἀναγέννησις, Chrys.*hom.5.3 in Tit.*(11.761A); **1.** in gen. σπεύσωμεν εἰς σωτηρίαν, ἐπὶ τὴν π. Clem.*prot.*9(p.65.28; M.8.200B); of Romans under Const. πάντες...οἱ τὴν πόλιν οἰκοῦντες...φωτὸς ἀπολαύειν ἐδόκουν καθαρωτέρου αὐγῶν καινοῦ τε καὶ νέου βίου παλιγγενεσίας μετέχειν Eus.*v.C.*1.41(p.27.4; M.20.956B); Gr.Nyss.*hom.7 in Cant.*(M.44.913A); Didym.*Trin.*2.1(M.39.453A); **2.** as closely connected with baptism, Eus.*e.th.*3.5(p.163.23; M.24.1013A); and generally effected by it, v. βάπτισμα; **a.** as result of baptism; **i.** in gen., Eus.*qu.Steph.suppl.*2(M.22.960A); Cyr.H.*procatech.*16; ἐβαπτίσθησαν...εἰς τὸν Μωϋσῆν. τί οὖν τὸ καύχημα τῆς ἐλπίδος ἡμῶν, καὶ τὴν...τοῦ θεοῦ καὶ σωτῆρος ἡμῶν δωρεάν, τοῦ διὰ τῆς π. ἀνακαινίζοντος ἡμῶν...τὴν νεότητα εὐκαταφρόνητον δεικνύουσιν; Bas.*Spir.*33(3.27D; M.32.125C); τὸ βάπτισμα τῆς π. *Const.App.*7.43.3; Isid.Pel.*epp.*3.195(M.78.880C); ‡Germ.CP *contempl.*(M.98.385D); **ii.** normally partic. ass. baptismal washing, esp. in phrase λουτρὸν παλιγγενεσίας (Tit. 3:5): τὴν οἰκονομίαν τοῦ λουτροῦ τῆς π. Or.*hom.16.5 in Jer.*(p.137.24; M.13.445B); id.*Jo.*6.33(17; p.143.14; M.14.257B); Eus.*h.e.*10.4.34(M.20.864A); Didym.(‡Bas.)*Eun.*5(1.303A; M.29.725D); Marc.Er.*opusc.*2.22(M.65.933B); **iii.** but also ass. chrismation οἱ...τοῦ ἁγίου τῆς ἐν τῷ Χριστῷ π. χρίσματος κατηξιωμένοι Eus.*d.e.*4.16(p.190.27; M.22.317C); **b.** παλιγγενεσία, λουτρὸν παλιγγενεσίας as synonyms for βάπτισμα, Gr.Nyss.*Eun.*11(2 p.269.13; M.45.877C); Pall.*v.Chrys.*5(p.28.13; M.47.18); Evagr.*h.e.*1.15(p.25.19; M.86.2464B); **c.** nature and effects of baptismal παλιγγενεσία; **i.** as part of double regeneration wrought by Christ through baptism and resurrection, Gr.Nyss.*Eun.*4(2 p.64.23; M.45.636D); **ii.** prelude to future παλιγγενεσία: ἐκείνης δὲ τῆς π. προοίμιόν ἐστι τὸ καλούμενον παρὰ τῷ Παύλῳ λουτρὸν παλιγγενεσίας Or.*comm.in Mt.*15.23(p.416.32; M.13.1320C); **iii.** cleansing, *ib.*(p.417.4; 1321A); Chrys.*hom.4.7 in Ac.princ.*(3.93A); Marc.Er.*opusc.*2.22(M.65.933B); and sprinkling, †Bas.*Is.*26(1.400B; M.30.169B); **iv.** remission of sins, cf.Hipp.*trad. ap.*22.1; Chrys.*hom.28.1 in Jo.*(8.158E); and justification, id.*hom.15.2 in Rom.*(9.595D) cit. s. δικαιόω; Thdt.*Rom.*5:1f.(3.53) cit. s. δίκαιος; **v.** sealing σφράγισόν με καθάπερ Παῦλος σφραγίζει διὰ λουτρὸν παλιγγενεσίας *A.Xanthipp.*28(p.78.34); **vi.** re-creation, Chrys.*Eutrop.*2(3.396D); and beginning of a second life, Bas.*Spir.*35(3.28E; M.32.129A); **vii.** means whereby Church regenerates men, Meth.*symp.*3.8(p.35.24; M.18.73B); **viii.** adoptive sonship, Didym.(‡Bas.)*Eun.*5(1.303A; M.29.725D); Chrys.*sac.*3.5(p.56.6; 1.384B); making men brothers of Christ the first-born, Gr.Nyss.*Eun.*4(2 p.64.16; M.45.636C); **ix.** gift of H. Ghost, Chrys.*hom.24.2 in Jo.*(8.140C); **x.** union of Church with heavenly Wisdom, Ph.Carp.*Cant.*181(M.40.117B); **xi.** in λουτρὸν παλιγγενεσίας wiping away of tears from all faces, Cyr.H.*catech.*19.10; **3.** achieved through repentance, Clem.*str.*2.23(p.193.25; M.8.1097A).

***παλιγγενέσιος**, *of* or *pertaining to regeneration* παραπέμπομαι γὰρ νῦν τῆς π. οἰκονομίας τὴν ἐξήγησιν Clem.*paed.*2.9(p.207.6; M.8.496A).

παλιγγενής, *reborn, regenerate*, ref. effect of baptism τοῖς ῥα λοετροῖς λύματ' ἀπωσάμενοι, ζῆτε παλιγγενέες Gr.Naz.*carm.*2.2 (epitaph.)24.6(M.38.22A); Nonn.*par.Jo.*1:33(M.43.756B); *ib.*5:25 (789A); in transferred sense βλάστημα παλιγγενέος τοκετοῖο *ib.*3:6 (768A).

παλιγκάπηλος, ὁ, *retailer, huckster*, Isid.Pel.*epp.*2.127(M.78.568C); *ib.*3.326(985D).

***παλίζωος**, *reviving, returning to life* π. σελήνη Gr.Naz.*carm.*1.2.14.115(M.37.764A).

***παλιλλεξία**, ἡ, *repetition*, Cosm.Mel.*schol.*proem.(M.38.344).

παλιμβόλως, *craftily, so as to deceive*, Epiph.*haer.*64.63(p.502.7: M.41.1177D); *ib.*76.21(p.368.10; M.42.557C); *ib.*76.45(p.399.9; 612C).

παλίμπλαγκτος, *returning, retracing one's steps*, met. π. στρέψας θεὸν ἱλάσκοιο *Orac.Sib.*3.625.

παλίμφημος, **1.** *inconsistent, contradictory*, Meth.*res.*1.62(p.329.1; M.41.1162C); Serap.*Man.*14(p.35; M.40.912B); ἄτοπα καὶ π. Gr.Agr.*Eccl.*7.4(M.98.1033A); **2.** *abusive, insulting*, ‡Nil.*perist.*9.4(M.79.869D); Cyr.*ador.*1(1.18E); id.*Is.*3.4(2.490A); id.*Am.*62(3.320A); id.*Juln.*1(6².6A); Olymp.*Job* 3:2(M.93.52C).

παλιμφυής, *revived, renewed* π. ... ὕδωρ Nonn.*par.Jo.*4:14(M.43.776B); *ib.*7:38(812A).

παλινδρομ-έω, *run back again, return, revert*; **1.** of man's return from sin to grace, death to life, etc., Clem.*prot.*2(p.20.6; M.8.97A); ~οῦμεν εἰς ἀφθαρσίαν Cyr.*glaph.Gen.*3(1.79A); π. πρὸς ζωήν id.*Os.*9(3.30C); id.*Jo.*4.2(4.354C); Bas.Sel.*or.*11.3(M.85.156B); Cosm.Ind.*top.*5(M.88.228C); **2.** of repentance, esp. from paganism ἐκ τῆσδε τῆς ἀπάτης π. Clem.*str.*7.16(p.67.14; M.9.532B); Hipp.*haer.*10.34(p.293.9; M.16.3454C); Or.*Jo.*28.6(5; p.396.34; M.14.693A); Cyr.*Os.*158(3.191A); Jo.Carp.*cap.*4(M.85.1838); **3.** of reversion to sin and paganism, Clem.*str.*2.13(p.144.9; M.8.996B); ~εῖν...ἐπὶ τὴν Ἑλληνικὴν φιλοσοφίαν *ib.*6.8(p.463.3; M.9.284B); ἐπὶ τὰ κοσμικὰ ~εῖν ἀγαθά *ib.*6.9(p.469.8; 296B); id.*ecl.*24(p.143.13; M.9.709A); μετὰ τὸ προτραπῆναι εἰς φιλοσοφίαν π. ἐπὶ τὸν ἰδιωτικὸν βίον Or.*Cels.*2.12(p.141.17; M.11.817C); id.*or.*6(p.314.20; M.11.437C); οἱ καταξιωθέντες...τῆς δωρεᾶς τοῦ...πνεύματος ~ήσωσιν εἰς τὸ ἁμαρτάνειν Ath.*ep.Serap.*4.9 (M.26.649B); Gr.Naz.*or.*6.19(M.35.748A); Cyr.*Os.*proem.(3.6E); Nil.*exerc.*37(M.79.765C); **4.** of Christ's return to heaven, Or.*or.*23(p.350.24; M.11.488C); **5.** ref. emission and return of Logos acc. Sabellians ὥσπερ γὰρ προελθόντος τοῦ λόγου γέγονεν ἡ κτίσις...οὕτω ~οῦντος τοῦ λόγου, οὐχ ὑπάρξει ἡ κτίσις ‡Ath.*Ar.*4.12(p.56.19; M.26.484B).

***παλινδρομητέον**, *one must return*, Clem.*paed.*3.4(p.251.17; M.8.592B).

***παλινδρόμως**, *running back* π. ᾔεσαν *Mir.Geo.*4(p.35.12).

***παλινδωμήτωρ**, *concerned with rebuilding*, Paul.Sil.*Soph.*218(M.86.2128A).

***παλινζωΐα**, ἡ, *restoration to life*; of resurrection life in gen., Or.*fr.in Ps.*1:4(p.71.16); τοῦ φωνοῦντος πρὸς π. τοὺς νεκρούς ‡Caes.Naz.*dial.*30(M.38.893); δι' αὐτὸν ἐλπιζομένης ἀτελευτήτου καὶ αἰωνίου π. Areth.*Apoc.*1:4f.(M.106.508A); of assumption of BMV τὸ τῆς π. σου μυστήριον Thdr.Stud.*or.*5.5(M.99.728C).

παλίνζωος, *of renewed life*, Nonn.*par.Jo.*2:22(M.43.764C).

παλινοδία, ἡ, *return*, Jo.VI H.*v.Jo.D.*26(M.94.468A).

παλιντοκία, ἡ, *rebirth*, ref. Mt.11:11 ἐν τῇ βασιλείᾳ τῶν οὐρανῶν, τουτέστιν ἐν τῇ κατὰ Χριστὸν π. Isid.Pel.*epp.*1.68(M.78.228C); ἑνὸς σώματος ὑποστάσει...τὴν ἀπ' αἰῶνος ἀνθρωπότητα εἰς π. ἀνακαινισάσῃ *ib.*1.201(312B).

***παλιντραπέλως**, *by recantation*, Philost.*h.e.*2.7(M.65.469C).

παλινῳδία, ἡ, **1.** *repetition*, Clem.*paed.*3.11(p.270.26; M.8.636A); Eus.*h.e.*8.13.8(M.20.776B); **2.** *phrase constantly repeated*, Clem.*paed.*3.11(p.280.30; 660A); **3.** *recantation*; **a.** of palinode of Stesichorus, Iren.*haer.*1.23.2(M.7.672A); Hipp.*haer.*6.19(p.146.1; M.16.3223A); **b.** in gen. of any change of front, change of attitude, Clem.*prot.*7 (p.56.16; M.8.181B); Or.*Cels.*8.63(p.278.29; M.11.1612A); of Galerius' toleration rescript, Eus.*h.e.*8.16.1(M.20.789A) = *m.P.*13(p.950.5; M.20.1517D); Ath.*h.Ar.*27(p.197.28; M.25.724C); τὴν τῶν περὶ τὸν Εὐσέβιον πρὸς τὴν ἀσέβειαν π. Philost.*h.e.*2.1(M.65.465B); **c.** of expression of repentance for sin, *Lit.*ap.*Const.App.*8.9.2; ‡Nil.*perist.*9.6 (M.79.873B).

παλίρροια, ἡ, *reflux, ebb and flow*, Gr.Naz.*or.*6.19(M.35.748A); Diod. *fat.*ap.Phot.*cod.*223(M.103.845A); of reflection of light, ‡Bas.*struct.hom.*1.1(1.324B; M.30.12A); met. π. τῶν πραγμάτων Hermias *irris.*2(M.6.1172A); π. τῆς...ζωῆς Evagr.*h.e.*6.17(p.234.10; M.86.2869C).

παλλακή, ἡ, *concubine*, dist. from παράκοιτις, Phot.*nomoc.*13.5 (p.618; M.104.917B) cit. s. παράκοιτις; ὀγδοήκοντα π. (Cant.6:7) interpreted of those who act virtuously through fear of punishment, opp. souls who spontaneously desire to follow Christ (βασιλίσσαι), Gr.Nyss.*hom.15 in Cant.*(M.44.1112D); Thdt.*Cant.*6:7(2.127).

***παλλακισμός**, ὁ, *concubinage*, Phot.*nomoc.*1.23(p.473; M.104.1001D).

παλ(λ)ικάριον, τό, *boy camp-follower*, *Chron.Pasch.*p.392(M.92.1005C); of an angelic escort, †Anast.S.*relat.*51(*OC* 3 p.72); ἀγγελικαὶ δυνάμεις, ἃς αὐτὸς π. ὠνόμαζεν *ib.*(p.73).

πα(λ)λίον, τό, (Lat. *pallium*) *cloak*, *Ev.Thom.*A 11.2(p.151); *A.Jo.*5(p.154.21); *ib.*6(p.154.33); *A.Barth.*2(p.131.23); Gr.Naz.*test.*(M.37.393B); Epiph.*haer.*68.3(p.143.4; M.42.188B); Thphn.*chron.* p.353(M.108.848A); esp. of monk's cloak, ‡Pall.*h.mon.*5.6(p.30.4; M.65.448B); for sleeping, Esaias *or.*3(p.8; cf.M.40.1109A); Cyr.S.*v.Euthym.*43(p.64.1,5,7); Jo.Mosch.*prat.*18(M.87.2865A); its four corners symbolizing cardinal virtues, Max.*qu.dub.*67(M.90.841C); Leont.N.*v.Sym.*33(M.93.1709C); ὁ ἀδελφὸς...λαμβάνει τὸ π. τὸν ἀρραβῶνα τοῦ...ἀγγελικοῦ σχήματος *Euchol.*(p.386).

παλμός, ὁ, *vibration, palpitation*; of bodily palpitations as means of divination, Eus.*d.e.*5 proem.(p.203.8; M.22.336D); παλμῶν ἑρμηνεύς *Const.App.*8.32.11; Epiph.*exp.fid.*24(p.525.9; M.42.829D); reason for prohibition discussed, ‡Just.*qu.et resp.*19(M.6.1265A,B).

πᾶλος, ὁ, (Lat. *palus*) *stake*, used in execution of martyrs, *M.Bon.*6(p.327); *M.Tar.*6(p.461); *M.Pers.*3.5(p.443.9); Philost.*h.e.*12.9(M.65.617C; πάτων p.147.1).

παμβασιλεύς, ὁ, *king of all, universal sovereign* (often as adj.); **1.** of God, Clem.*str.*7.3(p.12.20; M.9.421A); *ib.*7.9(p.40.19; βασιλέα 477B); Eus.*d.e.*3.2(p.97.13; M.22.169B); id.*e.th.*2.17(p.121.9; M.24.940A); Cyr.H.*ep.Const.*5(M.33.1169C); Epiph.*haer.*8.5(p.190.29; M.41.212C); Isid.Pel.*epp.*4.73(M.78.1133A); Thdt.*Ps.*46:9(1.906); **2.** of Christ, Eus.*h.e.*10.4.16(M.20.856A); Ath.*ep.Aeg.Lib.*23(M.25.593A); id.*apol.Const.*26(M.25.628B); id.*Ar.*2.18(M.26.184C); Didym.*Trin.*1.15(M.39.300A); Μαρίαν...ἐν κόλποις...ὑποδέξασθαι τὸν π. Epiph.

haer.79.3(p.477.30; M.42.744B); Thdt.*Ps*.44:17(1.896); ἀρχιερέως καὶ π. καὶ κυρίου Cosm.Ind.*top*.5(M.88.208D); μήτηρ τοῦ π. θεοῦ ‡Jo.D.*hom*.6.9(M.96.476A).

***παμβέβηλος**, *wholly profane*, Cyr.*Is*.5.5(2.860C); π. αἵρεσιν Sophr.H.*ep.syn*.(M.87.3196A); Jo.Mon.*hymn.Nic.Myr*.5(M.96.1385B).

***παμβλάσφημος**, *wholly blasphemous*, Cyr.*Os*.1(3.9D).

***παμβόητος**, *all-renowned*; of Moses, ‡Jo.D.*hom*.5(M.96.649B).

πάμμακαρ, *wholly blessed*, Leont.N.*v.Jo.Eleem*.1(p.5.17); Thdr.Stud.*epp*.2.16(M.99.1164D).

***παμμακάριος**, = foreg. ἀσεβὲς ὁμοουσίους τῇ ἀγεννήτῳ φύσει καὶ παμμακαρίᾳ λέγειν εἶναι τοὺς προσκυνοῦντας Or.*Jo*.13.25(p.249.6; M.14.441A); π. ... Σιών Cyr.*Is*.1.1(2.8E); π. τῶν ἀγγέλων...πληθύς id.*Am*.46(3.299E); κοινωνοὶ...τῆς...ἀπαλαιώτου καὶ π. ... ζωῆς Gennad.*fr.Rom*.6:3(p.365.31; M.85.1673C); π. κοίμησις τῆς...θεοτόκου Mod.*dorm*.7(M.86.3296A).

παμμακάριστος, = foreg., Eus.*p.e*.1.1(2D; M.21.24C); τὴν παμμακάριστον μητέρα αὐτοῦ Mod.*dorm*.2(M.86.3281C); Max.*ambig*.(M.91.1097C).

***παμμάχως**, *with all one's fighting power*, Just.*2apol*.13.2(M.6.465B); Clem.*paed*.3.2(p.241.15; M.8.569A).

παμμεγέθης, *very large*; comp., *V.Mac*.A(p.148); superl., Thphn.*chron*.p.89(M.108.268C).

***παμμεδέων**, *all-ruling*; of God, Nonn.*par.Jo*.6:23(M.43.797B); Jo.D.*carm.theoph*.acrostic(p.209; M.96.825A); of Christ, Nonn.*par.Jo*.5:26(789A); *CIG* 8639 [CP, saec. vi].

***παμμέδων**, *carefully, with careful* (*devout*) *thought* ἵνα π. ... σέβας εἰκόνι προσοίσω Sophr.H.*carm*.20.39(p.46; M.87.3820A).

παμμήτωρ, *which is universal mother* τῆς π. καὶ γενεσιουργοῦ φύσεως Clem.*paed*.2.10(p.209.26; M.8.500C); π. φύσιν Or.*Cels*.4.83(p.354.8; M.11.1157A); παμμήτορα κόσμου ζωήν Nonn.*par.Jo*.5:26(M.43.789A); of Simon's Helen as π. οὐσίαν καὶ σοφίαν *Hom.Clem*.2.25.

παμμίαρος, *utterly abominable*, of antichrist ἥξει ὁ π. ... ταπεινός, καὶ ἥσυχος...ἀποστρέφων εἴδωλα Ephr.3.137F; ὁ π. οὐ παύεται ἐκζητῶν τοὺς ἁγίους ἔν τε γῇ καὶ θαλάσσῃ id.2.223F; Rom.Mel.(*SBBAW* 1898² p.168).

παμμιγής, *mixed of all kinds*, dat. as adv. τοὺς...π. περιεστῶτας Eus.*m.P*.8(p.927.8; codd. παμμιγῇ M.20.1489B).

***παμμιγῶς**, *so as to mix thoroughly*, Max.*ambig*.(M.91.1212C).

***παμμισής**, *full of hatred*, Isid.Pel.*epp*.1.281(M.78.348B).

***παμμίσητος**, *universally detested*, Thphn.*chron*.p.89(M.108.268A).

πάμμορος, *all-hapless*, *Orac.Sib*.5.65.

πάμμουσος, *wholly musical* π. φθόγγῳ *Orac.Sib*.5.141; π. φύλλων v.l. in *Hom.Clem*.4.10(παμμήνων M.2.104C).

***παμμόχθηρος**, **1.** *wholly wretched*, Cyr.*Is*.1.1(2.8B); id.*Os*.128(3.160C); **2.** *wholly wicked*, id.*ador*.7(1.228B); id.*Joel*.31(3.223B); id.*hom.pasch*.15(5².202A).

***πάμπιστος**, *wholly faithful*, Ephr.3.141F.

***πάμπλανος**, *wholly erring* γυναικῶν π. ... φύσις ‡Jo.D.*hom*.5(M.96.657B).

***πάμπλεως**, *packed full* πλοῦς...κινδύνων...π. Euthal.Diac.*Ac*.(M.10.1557B; ἔμπλεως M.85.661B).

παμπληθής, **1.** *very abundant* τροφήν...π. *1Clem*.20.4; **2.** of the moon, *quite full*, *Anaph.Pil*.B 7(p.447).

***πάμπληξ**, *utterly smitten* with madness; of Nestorius, Max.*opusc*.(M.91.177D); Anast.S.*haer*.(p.259).

***παμπόθητος**, *wholly desired*; of BMV, Ephr.3.528D; of day of Christ's release of souls from Hades, Mod.*dorm*.7(M.86.3296A); of a saint, Jo.D.*hom*.12.2(M.96.784D); *Mir.Geo*.4(p.42.1); in form of address τὴν...π. σου ὑπεροχήν Thdr.Stud.*epp*.2.129(M.99.1416A).

πάμπολις, *greatest of cities*, *Orac.Sib*.5.436.

***παμπρίκιλος**, prob. for παμποίκιλος, *Asen*.18(p.68.12).

πάμφαγος, *all-devouring*; of gluttons, Clem.*paed*.2.1(p.155.21; M.8.384A); met. πάμφαγος...τῆς βασκανίας...φλόξ Chrys.*sac*.3.14(p.73.23; 1.391D); of death, Germ.CP *or*.2(M.98.285B).

παμφαής, *all-shining, radiant*, met. παμφαέος Χριστοῖο...μαθηταί Nonn.*par.Jo*.14:35(M.43.865B); superl. π. λόγος Jo.D.*carm.theoph*.36(p.210; M.96.828A); of angelic powers τὰς δοθείσας αὐτοῖς [sc. τοῖς δαίμοσι] ἀγγελικὰς δωρεάς, οὐ μήποτε αὐτὰς ἠλλοιῶσθαί φαμεν·... παμφαεῖς εἰσι, κἂν αὐτοὶ μὴ ὁρῶσιν Dion.Ar.*d.n*.4.23(M.3.725C).

παμφανής, *most bright, most glorious*; superl., ‡Gr.Naz.*Chr.pat*.1799(M.38.280A); -ώτατος, ‡Meth.*Sym.et Ann*.6(M.18.361C).

***πάμφαυλος**, *wholly worthless*, Gr.Nyss.*res*.5(M.46.685D); Nil.*epp*.2.178(M.79.292B); Isid.Pel.*epp*.1.281(M.78.348B).

***παμφιλεῖ**, *with all one's friends*, Didym.*Trin*.2.8(M.39.593A).

***πάμφρων**, *wise in all things*, *Pers*.(p.3.5).

[*]**παμφύλιος**, *of all nations* or *tribes*, *Orac.Sib*.11.228.

πάμφυλος, **1.** = foreg., *Orac.Sib*.11.185; *Hom.Clem*.6.2; **2.** *consisting of a mixed mob, mongrel assortment* τὸ λεγόμενον, πάμφυλοι γεγόνατε ‡Ath.*Apoll*.2.3(M.26.1137A); **3.** *filled with people, crowded*, *Chron.Pasch*.p.178(M.92.437A).

***πάμφυτος**, *with every kind of plant*, Hipp.*haer*.5.9(p.102.4; M.16.3158C).

***πάμφωτος**, *full of light, glorious*, ‡Chrys.*hom*.10(13.239D); of Christ's baptism, Max.*comput*.32(M.19.1249B).

παμψηφεί, *by unanimous vote*, Thdot.Anc.*exp.symb*.12(M.77.1329D).

πάν, ὁ, *a goat-like ape* in India, supposed to have been taken by Greeks for a god (Pan), Philost.*h.e*.3.11(p.41.5; M.65.496D).

πανάγαθος, *all-good*; of God, Ath.*inc*.10.1(M.25.112D); Eus.*d.e*.1.7(p.35.24; M.22.69B); Jo.D.*f.o*.4.13(M.94.1136B); of divine attributes ἡ π. πρόνοια Mac.Mgn.*apocr*.4.18(p.195.9); and gifts, Dion.Ar.*d.n*.3.1(M.3.680B); of Christ, Isid.Pel.*epp*.1.83(M.78.240C); παναγάθου πατρὸς π. υἱός Gel.Cyz.*h.e*.2.22.18(M.85.1293C).

***πανάγαστος**, *wholly admirable*, ‡Jo.D.*Artem*.40(M.96.1288D); Thdr.Stud.*cant*.10.3(p.356).

***παναγένητος**, *wholly unoriginate*, Dion.Ar.*d.n*.9.4(M.3.912C).

***παναγήραος**, *never growing old*, †Apoll.*met.Ps*.104:1(M.33.1468D).

***παναγήρατος**, v. πανακήρατος.

παναγής, **1.** *all-hallowed* π. ποίμνης Clem.*paed*.3.12(p.291.22; M.8.681C); of affusion of oil in consecrations, Dion.Ar.*e.h*.4.3.12(M.3.484C); of teaching of apostles and prophets, Thdt.*affect*.1(p.20.27; 4.710); id.*ep*.4(4.1065); of mysteries, id.*affect*.1(p.33.4, v.l. ~ίων 4.722); **2.** *wholly accursed* π. ... κακῷ Gr.Thaum.*pan.Or*.3(p.7.23; M.10.1060A); παναγεστάτου Μαξιμίνου Eus.*m.P*.13(p.949.14; M.20.1517B); Synes.*ep*.67(M.66.1420D); ‡Jo.D.*Artem*.43(p.15.27; M.96.1292B).

***παναγιόριστος**, *defined as most holy* π. σταυρόν ‡Chrys.*ador*.2(11.824B).

πανάγιος, *all-holy*; **1.** of God, *1Clem*.35.3; Ath.*gent*.40(M.25.80C); Didym.(‡Bas.)*Eun*.5(1.313D; M.29.752B); Epiph.*haer*.26.17(p.297.24; M.41.360C); ἅγιος...καὶ π. καὶ ἁγίων ἁγιώτατος Chrys.*hom.in Mt.7:14*(3.29D); τρεῖς ὑποστάσεις τῆς π. μονάδος Max.*ambig*.(M.91.1397C); **2.** of Logos, Clem.*paed*.1.9(p.139.11; M.8.349C); Son τὸ π. τῆς τοῦ πατρὸς καὶ υἱοῦ θεότητος Gel.Cyz.*h.e*.2.14.6(M.85.1257A); ὁ παναγιώτατος Ἰησοῦς Dion.Ar.*e.h*.4.3.12(M.3.485A); **3.** of H. Ghost, in doxology σὺν τῷ π. ... πνεύματι †Hipp.*theoph*.10(p.263.20; M.10.861B); *M.Eupl*.2.3(p.101.18); Ath.*decr*.32(p.28.26; M.25.476C); Gr.Naz.*carm*.1.1.31.2(M.37.511A); Mac.Aeg.*carit*.25(M.34.928B); Chrys.*hom.1.4 in Jo*.(8.7A); Thdt.*Trin*.2(M.75.1149C); ‡Gr.Nyss.*hom.2.67 in Jo*.(p.134.6); Sophr.H.*ep.syn*.(M.87.3157D); Jo.Eub.*concept.BMV* 10(M.96.1476A); *Lit.Jac*.(p.226.13,22); **4.** of Trin. τὴν π. καὶ τρισμακαρίαν...τριάδα Eus.*e.th*.proem.(p.60.14; M.24.825A); id.*l.C*.6(p.210.15; M.20.1348B); *cat.Lc*.11:5(p.91.17); Sophr.H.*ep.syn*.(M.87.3157D); **5.** of Christ's human body, Eus.*l.C*.16(p.249.3; M.20.1421C); Chrys.*hom.32.5 in Mt*.(7.788B); **6.** of BMV, Or.*hom.7 in Lc*.(p.50.3,8); *ib.19*(p.129.3; M.17.329C); Ephr.3.526E; Eulog.*palm*.10(M.86.2933A); †Jo.Jej.*poenit*.(M.88.1913C); Jo.Mosch.*prat*.180(M.87.3052A); Jo.D.*hom*.9 tit.(M.96.721B); Jo.Eub.*concept.BMV* 15(M.96.1484A); Jo.Mon.*hymn.Bas*.10(M.96.1377B); ‡Meth.*Sym.et Ann*.10(M.18.373B); **7.** of saints, Evagr.*h.e*.1.13(p.22.20; M.86.2456C); *ib*.2.3(p.40.30; 2493B); of ascetics, Eus.*v.C*.4.28(p.128.13; M.20.1177A); of eccl. leaders, *PLond*.1916.1 s.v.l.; π. τῆς ἁγίας...ἐκκλησίας πρεσβύτεροι Epiph.*haer*.42.2(p.96.4; M.41.697A); bishops in council, Thds.Am.*libell*.(H.4.45C); **8.** of baptism, Thdt.*qu.4 in Jos*.(1.307); Sophr.H.*v.Anast*.(M.92.1685C); **9.** of relics of Cross, *ib*.(1685B); bodies of saints, Evagr.*h.e*.1.13(p.23.5; M.86.2457A); **10.** of sacred places π. τῆς...ἀναστάσεως μαρτύριον Eus.*v.C*.3.28(p.91.1; M.20.1088D); π. τούτῳ Γολγοθᾷ Cyr.H.*catech*.13.22; church building (baptistery), Evagr.*h.e*.2.8(p.56.19; M.86.2524A); **11.** of festivals; Easter, Epiph.*haer*.70.12(p.245.7; M.42.364B); *Chron.Pasch*.p.8(M.92.84C); **12.** of see of Rome, Thdt.*ep*.116(4.1197); **13.** of virtues, etc.; ascetic life, Eus.*v.C*.4.26(p.127.10; M.20.1173C); π. ἡδονῆς ἀπόλαυσις id.*l.C*.6(p.211.18; M.20.1349B); Christian faith, Cyr.H.*catech*.4.18; τὸν π. ὕμνον Chrys.*incomprehens*.4.5(1.478E).

παναγιστία (-εία), ἡ, *all-holiness*, as courtesy title of address τῇ ὑμετέρᾳ π. CLater.*act*.2(H.3.720D); *Libell.ib*.(724C); Cyrus Al.*ep*.1(H.3.804C); Gr.Mag.*dial*.(tr.Zach.)1.4(M.*PL*.77.171B).

***παναγίως**, *all-holily*, Hipp.*haer*.8.9(p.228.3; M.16.3351A).

***παναγλαής**, *wholly bright*, Jo.D.*hom*.10.2(M.96.756B).

***παναγνεία, ἡ**, *complete purity*, Thdr.Stud.*nativ.BMV* 7(M.96.693B).

πάναγνος, *perfect in purity*; of God, Cyr.*Os.*4(3.20C); *ib.*11(32D); of Christ as π. ἱερεύς, id.*ador.*12(1.431D); of H. Ghost, Amph.*Seleuc.* 194(M.37.1590A); as π. δόξα, Didym.*Trin.*2.1(M.39.452C); of Christ's body as temple κατῴκησε καθάπερ ἐν ναῷ, τῷ ἐκ τῆς...παρθένου π. σώματι Cyr.*Mal.*32(3.850B); of BMV, Oecum.*Apoc.*12:17(p.146); Χριστὸν γεννᾶν ἡ π. ἔμελλε Sophr.H.*or.*2.45(M.87.3277B); Jo.D. *hom.*8.14(M.96.721A); id.*carm.dorm.BMV* 71(p.230; M.96.1364D); Jo.V H.*icon.*5(M.96.1353C); σάρκα λαβὼν...ἐκ π. αἱμάτων σου Jo. Mon.*hymn.Geo.*8(M.96.1400B); id.*hymn.Blas.*5(1404B); of Church as π. παρθένος Cyr.*Nest.*1 proem.(p.16.2; 6^{1}.6A); of priests, id.*Mal.*34 (3.853A); of Christian life, id.*Lc.*9:1(M.72.640B).

***πανάγνως**, *with perfect purity*, Dion.Ar.*e.h.*3.3.7(M.3.436A).

***πανάδηλος**, *altogether mysterious*; of God's counsels, Anast.S. *hod.*4(M.89.93B).

***πανάθεος**, *utterly godless*, Leont.N.ap.Jo.D.*imag.*3(M.94.1384B); *Chron.Pasch.*p.392(M.92.1005B).

***παναθλίως**, *altogether wretchedly*, Philost.*h.e.*7.13(M.65.552A).

***πάναθλος**, *victorious in every contest*, ‡Pion.*v.Polyc.*16.

***πανάϊστος**, *altogether unseen*, *Orac.Sib.*3.393; Eudoc.*Cypr.*2.244 (M.85.856A).

πάναισχρος, *utterly shameful*, Cyr.*ador.*6(1.204D); id.*Am.*19(3. 269C).

παναίτιος, *who is the cause of all things*; of God and his attributes, Dion.Ar.*d.n.*2.5(M.3.644A); id.*c.h.*4.1(M.3.177C); id.*ep.*7.2(M. 3.1080C).

πανακήρατος, *wholly inviolate*, Ephr.3.528C; †Apoll.*met.Ps.*103:1 (v.l. παναγήρατον M.33.1345A); Nonn.*par.Jo.*12:25(M.43.853C); Jo.D. *hom.*8.12(M.96.720A).

παναλκής, *all-powerful*; of God and his attributes, Eus.*p.e.*6.6 (249C; M.21.424C); id.*d.e.*4.15(p.175.13; M.22.292C); Didym.*Trin.* 2.12(M.39.537C); παναλκεστάτη τριάς *ib.*2.27(764C); Cyr.*Is.*4.5(2. 717A); id.*Os.*105(3.137E); Thdt.*qu.18 in Gen.*(1.20); Mod.*dorm.*4(M. 86.3289B); Jo.D.*hom.*10.2(M.96.756D); of Solomon, Cyr.*Am.*5(3. 256E); of law and prophets as remedies for Israel's sin, Thdt.*affect.*6 (p.178.15; 4.880); π. κρίσις Geo.Pis.*Heracl.*1.150(M.92.1310B).

***παναμόλυντος**, *wholly undefiled*; of BMV, Ephr.3.528C.

***παναμώματος**, = sq., Ephr.3.547F.

***παναμώμητος**, = sq., Ephr.3.528C; *ib.*535A.

πανάμωμος, *wholly without blemish*; of Christ as sinless, Cyr.*Is.*5. 1(2.750C); αὐτὸς τὸ π. ἱερεῖον id.*Jo.*11.8(4.966C); of BMV, †Or.ap. *cat.Lc.*1:24(p.11.11); ‡Ath.*occurs.*16(M.28.993C); Jo.D.*carm.dorm. BMV* 15(p.229; M.96.1364A); Jo.Mon.*hymn.Bas.*5(M.96.1373C); Jo.Eub.*concept.BMV* 13(M.96.1480A); as π. θυσιαστήριον, ‡Meth. *Sym.et Ann.*7(M.18.364B); of Christians ἵνα π. ... ἐξεργασθῶμεν Meth.*res.*1.42(p.289.7; M.41.1112C); of virtuous conduct, *ib.*2.3(p.334. 19; M.18.300D).

***πανάνθρωπος**, *of all men* πανάνθρωπον ἀνάστασιν ‡Caes.Naz.*dial.* 187(M.38.1164).

πανaοίδιμος, *sung by all*; met., *renowned*, Cyr.*ador.*17(1.619D); †Bas.Sel.*or.*41(M.85.465D); Jo.Mon.*hymn.Geo.*4(M.96.1396C).

[*]**παναπείρατος**, *wholly limitless*, Didym.*Trin.*2.16(M.39.721B).

***πανάπειρος**, *quite indefinite*, Leont.H.*Nest.*1.48(M.86.1508A).

παναπήμων, *wholly unharmed*, Synes.*hymn.*8.7(p.50; M.66.1612).

πανάπορος, *quite destitute*, Anast.S.*qu.et resp.*127(M.89.777A).

***παναρά**, ἡ, *total curse*, *Inscr.*(*Hesp.*16 p.30.12) (Athens, saec. iv–vi).

***παναργαλέος**, *wholly mischievous*, †Bas.Sel.*or.*41(M.85.464D).

πανάρετος, *all-virtuous, all-perfect, excellent*; **1.** of what pertains to God τῷ π. ὀνόματι αὐτοῦ *1Clem.*45.7; τὸν...καρπὸν τῆς π. θεολογίας Eus.*d.e.*1.10(p.49.4; M.22.92D); and Christ: words, *ib.*1.1(p.3.29; 17A); *ib.*8 proem.(p.350.25; 569C); power, *ib.*4.6(p.159.3; 265A); way of life instituted by him, *ib.*1.6(p.34.26; 68B); *ib.*3.6(p.131.29; 224A); *ib.*4.12(p.170.27; 284D); **2.** as title of Wisdom Books (as enshrining revelation of divine wisdom): Proverbs οὕτως...λέγει ἡ π. σοφία *1Clem.*57.3; Clem.*str.*2.22(p.188.11; M.8.1085A); καὶ Εἰρηναῖος δὲ καὶ ὁ πᾶς τῶν ἀρχαίων χορὸς π. Σοφίαν τὰς Σολομῶνος Παροιμίας ἐκάλουν Heges.ap.Eus.*h.e.*4.22.9(M.20.384A); Ecclesiasticus Ἰησοῦς ὁ τοῦ Σιρὰχ...ὁ τὴν καλουμένην π. Σοφίαν συντάξας Eus.*d.e.*8.2(p.380.15; M.22.616C); Isid.Pel.*epp.*3.66(M.78.776A); Wisdom of Solomon, Meth.*symp.*1.3(p.12.5; M.18.44B); τῆς Σοφίας Σολομῶντος τῆς λεγομένης π. ‡Ath.*synops.*45(M.28.376D); Gr.Nyss.*Eun.*8(2 p.198.22; M. 45.793D); δύο βίβλοι ἦτε τοῦ Σολομῶντος, ἡ π. λεγομένη, καὶ ἡ τοῦ Ἰησοῦ τοῦ υἱοῦ Σιράχ Epiph.*mens.*4(M.43.244C); Nil.*epp.*1.293(M.79. 189B); Jo.D.*f.o.*4.17(M.94.1180B); **3.** of angels ἀσωμάτους τὴν φύσιν καὶ νοεράς, λογικάς τε καὶ π. Eus.*d.e.*3.3(p.113.9; M.22.193C); of Michael, *T.Abr.*A 5(p.82.4); **4.** of Christian virtues: faith, *1Clem.* 1.2; humility, Bas.*renunt.*9(2.210D; M.31.645B); Christian life τῇ π. ...πολιτείᾳ κεκοσμημένοι *1Clem.*2.8; *M.Perp.*21(p.95.12); 'λαμπάδες' ἡ π. πρᾶξις Or.*fr.in Mt.*25:1(M.17.304B); Eus.*h.e.*6.9.5(M.20.540B); virginity, ‡Chrys.*hom.*10(13.239D); **5.** of Easter τὴν ἁγίαν θεοῦ π. ἡμέραν Epiph.*haer.*69.11(p.161.2; M.42.219A).

πανάριον, τό, (= Lat. *panarium*) *medicine-chest*; as title of book of remedies against poisons of heresy, Epiph.*rescr.*1(p.155. 15; M.41.157D); plur. Ἐπιφάνιος...ἐν τοῖς π. ... γράφει *Chron.Pasch.* p.23(M.92.109A).

παναρκής, *all-sufficient*; **1.** of God as creator Ἕλληνες...εἶπαν ὅτι οὐκ ἂν εἴη δημιουργός, μὴ ὑποκειμένης ὕλης...ἀλλὰ μὴ προσέχωμεν, εἰδότες θεοῦ δύναμιν π. Chrys.*hom.66.3 in Jo.*(8.398D); contrasted with sun as a god, id.*hom.12.2 in Eph.*(11.92B); Cyr.*hom.pasch.*22 (5^{2}.271E); **2.** of Logos παναρκέστατος καὶ δημιουργός Mac.Mgn. *apocr.*4.28(p.216.3); **3.** of H. Ghost π. θεός Didym.*Trin.*3.46(M.39. 804B); **4.** in gen., of a human benefactor, Isid.Pel.*epp.*1.178(M.78. 297D).

***παναρρεπής**, *wholly immutable*, Dion.Ar.*c.h.*7.2(M.3.208D).

***πανάρρητος**, *wholly unutterable* τοῦ π. θαύματος [i.e. Inc.] Thdr. Stud.*epp.*2.121(M.99.1397C).

***πανάσπιλος**, *wholly unspotted*; of BMV, Ephr.3.528C; Jo.V H. *icon.*13(M.96.1360B); *Hymn.*(*AS* 1 p.536).

***πανάσωτος**, *altogether abandoned* morally, Ephr.3.548A; ‡Sophr.H.*v.Mar.Aeg.*23(M.87.3713C).

***πανάφθορος**, *wholly uncorrupt*; of BMV, Ephr.3.528C; ‡Ath. *occurs.*16(M.28.993C); of Church as bride of Christ, Anast.S.*hex.*12 (M.89.1072C).

***πανάχραντος**, *wholly undefiled*; of hands of Christ crucified, *A.Pil.*B 10.3(p.305n.); of altar, Paul.Sil.*Soph.*720(M.86.2147A); of God, Gr.Ant.*mul.ung.*12(M.88.1865A); of Logos, Jo.D.*carm.theoph.* 78(p.211; M.96.829A); of Christ, *Hymn.*(*KlT* p.19); of Inc., †Gregent. *disp.*(M.86.745A); Jo.Mon.*hymn.Geo.*2(M.96.1392A); of Christ's body, †Anast.S.*relat.*49(*OC* 3 p.69); ‡Bas.*h.myst.*50(p.391.14); of BMV, ‡Hipp.*consumm.*1(p.289.12; M.10.905A); Thdot.Anc.*hom.BMV et Sym.*3(M.77.1393B); Mod.*dorm.*3(M.86.3288B); Jo.Eub.*concept. BMV* 2(M.96.1464A); Jo.Thess.*dorm.BMV* B 13(p.431.15); ‡Hipp. Th.*fr.*17(p.49.8); Thphn.*chron.*p.332(M.108.801B); of womb of BMV, Jo.D.*haer.Nest.*43(M.95.221C); of Anna and Joachim, ‡Jo.D. *hom.*6.5(M.96.668B).

***πανγνώστης**, ὁ, *one who has entire knowledge* π. τῆς οὐσίας ὁ θεός *Disp.Phot.*45(M.88.569D).

πανδαισία, ἡ, *feast of all good things, banquet*, ref. 1Cor.11:22ff., Cyr.*Nest.*4.5(p.86.8; 6^{1}.111D) cit. s. δημοθοινία; of divine teaching πνευματικῆς π. Gr.Nyss.*hom.9 in Cant.*(M.44.976D); of banquet provided by Christ for the soul, *ib.10*(985B); of heavenly banquet, Bas.Sel.*v.Thecl.*1(M.85.553B); Jo.D.*hom.*9.6(M.96.732A); πολλῶν δὲ ὄντων τοῦ μέλλοντος αἰῶνος ἀγαθῶν,...πολυωνύμως ἡ τούτων μετοχὴ προφέρεται·...ποτὲ...ὡς παράδεισος, διὰ τὴν...τῶν ἀγαθῶν π. Andr. Caes.*Apoc.*57(M.106.397D).

πανδαμάτωρ, *all-subduing* λόγε π. Clem.*paed.hymn.*12(p.291; M. 8.681B); ὃς [sc. ᾅδης] ταῖς σαῖς π. μύλαις τὰς τῶν ἀνθρώπων πανσπερμίας ἀλήθων Germ.CP *or.*2(M.98.280B).

πανδέκτης, ὁ, *receiver of all*; **1.** *book of the universal dictionary* or *encyclopedia* compiled by Dorotheus, Clem.*str.*1.21(p.82.22; M.8. 868B); **2.** of persons, ? *learned person*, Synes.*ep.*101(M.66.1472C); **3.** sens. dub. παρέκειτο ἡμῖν π. *A.Thom.*A 91(p.205.11).

πανδερκής, *all-seeing*, ref. Isaiah's vision ὀφθαλμῷ κραδίης πανδερκέι Nonn.*par.Jo.*12:41(M.43.857B); of eye of God, Cyr.*ador.* 14(1.493B); id.*Am.*89(3.343A); Olymp.*Job* 34:23(M.93.361C); of Logos in creation, Cyr.*Ps.*32:1(M.69.869B).

πανδεχής, *capable of receiving all forms* ἡ π. ὕλη ἄνευ τοῦ θεοῦ τοῦ δημιουργοῦ διάκρισιν καὶ σχῆμα...οὐκ ἐλάμβανεν Athenag.*leg.*15.2(M. 6.920B).

πανδήμιος, **1.** *public* π. ὕδωρ *water for common* or *public use*, Nonn.*par.Jo.*9:7(M.43.825A); ἦμαρ...π. *festal day*, *ib.*10:22(836A); **2.** *of all people* τὸν π. [sc. κατακλυσμόν] Bas.Sel.*or.*7.4(M.85.100B).

πάνδημος, *common, belonging to all the people*; of Egyptian demotic script, *litteras...pandēmous*... Isid.H.*etym.*1.3.5.

***πανδόκιμος**, *thoroughly tested* or *approved*, Cyr.*Is.*3.5(2.520D).

πανδοκίον, τό, v. πανδοχεῖον.

πάνδοξ, ὁ, *innkeeper*, Ephr.2.15B.

πανδοῦρις, ἡ, *three-stringed lute*, Leont.N.*v.Sym.*42(M.93.1721B); perh. also a wind-instrument, cf. πανδοῦροι...ηὔλουν Jo.Mal.*chron.*7 p.179(M.97.288A).

πανδοῦρος, ὁ, *player of* πανδοῦρις, Jo.Mal.*chron.*7 p.179(M.97. 288A).

πανδοχεῖον, τό, *inn*, in comparison of this world with temporary lodging-place, Chrys.*Stag*.3.1(1.204B); -δοκίον Didym.*Trin*.3.1(M. 39.780D); ref. hospitality to poor ἔστω τὸ τοῦ Χριστοῦ π. ἡμῶν ἡ οἰκία Chrys.*hom.45.4 in Ac*.(9.344B); in Valent. analogy ἔστι...ὁ ὑλικὸς ἄνθρωπος οἱονεὶ...π. ἢ κατοικητήριον ποτὲ μὲν ψυχῆς μόνης, ποτὲ δὲ ψυχῆς καὶ δαιμόνων, ποτὲ δὲ ψυχῆς καὶ λόγων, οἵτινές εἰσι λόγοι ἄνωθεν κατεσπαρμένοι...κατοικοῦντες ἐν σώματι χοϊκῷ μετὰ ψυχῆς Hipp.*haer*.6.34(p.163.14; M.16.3246C).

***πανδοχικός,** *all-embracing*, *M.Thdot.1* 32(p.81.17).

[*]**πάνδοχος,** 1. *receiving everything*, Gr.Naz.*carm*.1.2.8.143(M. 37.659A); 2. *all-embracing, wholly inclusive*, Eus.*l.C*.6(p.207.9; M.20. 1341B); *ib*.11(p.227.29; 1381C).

πανδύναμος, *all-powerful* π. θεϊκῆς ἰσχύος Didym.*Trin*.2.6(M.39. 537C).

***πανέγκλητος,** *universally blamed*; of Arius' *Thalia*, Ath.*Ar*.1.9 (M.26.29A).

***πάνεθνος,** *comprising all nations*; of Church, ‡Caes.Naz.*dial*.192 (M.38.1172).

πανείδεος, *of every form* or *kind*; of God, Dion.Ar.*d.n*.5.8(M.3. 824B) cit. s. ἀκαλλής.

***πανεκκλήσιος,** *of the whole Church* π. συνόδῳ Leont.H.*monoph*. (M.86.1845A).

πανελεήμων, *all-merciful*; of God, *M.Tar*.11(p.475); Chrys.*hom. 2.5 in 2Cor*.(10.435D).

πανελεύθερος, *completely free* βίος π. ... δεσμῶν Gr.Naz.*carm*.1.2. 30.313(M.37.907A).

***πανέμφυτος,** *universally inborn*, of 'law of sin' in the flesh, Cyr. *Ps*.36:10(M.69.932A).

πανένδοξος, *altogether glorious* π. τῆς ἀγάπης ὁδόν Max.*ep*.2(M.91. 404C); π. ... ἀνάπαυσιν Mod.*dorm*.10(M.86.3301B); π. ... κατὰ σάρκα ἐπίγνωσιν τοῦ...σωτῆρος ‡Meth.*Sym.et Ann*.4(M.18.357A); of BMV, Max.*ep*.12(M.91.509B); Anast.S.*hod*.5(M.89.100C); Jo.Thess.*dorm. BMV* A 1(p.376.1); of S. Barbara, Jo.D.*hom*.12.9(M.96.793B); of S. George, *Mir.Geo*.4(p.18.4).

***πανέντιμος,** *held in all honour*; of Dormition, Mod.*dorm*.1(M.86. 3280B); of BMV, *Lit.Jac*.(*NBP* 10² p.106); of Cross, *Apoc.Dan*.A (p.35).

πανέορτος, *wholly festal, kept as high festival*, ‡Jo.D.*hom*.5(M.96. 649A).

πανεπίσκοπος, *all-surveying*; of God, *Orac.Sib*.1.152; ὕψιστος πάντων π. *ib*.2.177; *ib*.5.352; οὔ φασιν εἶναι θεόν, ἢ ὄντα μὴ εἶναι π. Clem.*str*.7.3(p.11.27; M.9.420B); Gr.Naz.*carm*.1.1.35.1(M.37.517A); Cyr.*Ps*.32:1(M.69.869B); Olymp.*Job* 34:24(M.93.361D); of eye of God, *ib*.25:4(M.93.268C); of power of God, Clem.*str*.2.10(p.227.13; M.8.1169C); of Logos, id.*paed*.3.12(p.291.14; M.8.681A).

πανεπόπτης, *all-observing*; of God, *Orac.Sib.fr*.1.4; ὁ π. ὀφθαλμός Isid.Pel.*epp*.2.199(M.78.644C); *ib*.3.247(925A).

[*]**πανεργάτης,** *working all things*; of Logos, Geo.Pis.*hex*.1262(M. 92.1531A).

πανέρημος, *totally desolate*; ἡ π. *absolute desert*, *Apophth.Patr*. (M.65.261A); Pall.*v.Chrys*.17(p.106.9; M.47.59); id.*h.Laus*.7(p.25.3; M.34.1020A); *ib*.23(p.75.6; 1084B); plur., ‡Chrys.*Petr.et El*.4(2. 739D).

πανέστιος, *with all one's household*, Olymp.*Job* 4:7(M.93.69D).

πανετήτυμος, *all-true* ἦμαρ ἐλευθερίης πανετήτυμον *very day of freedom*, Nonn.*par.Jo*.8:36(M.43.817C).

πανευγενής, *wholly noble*, of BMV δέσποινα...πανευγενεστάτη Ephr.3.527B.

[*]**πανεύδαιμος,** = πανευδαίμων, *wholly fortunate* τῇ π. ... πόλει ‡Jo.D.*Artem*.67(M.96.1316A).

***πανευκλεής,** *full of all praise* π. ἐγκώμιον Jo.D.*hom*.9.1(M.96. 721C); *ib*.10.2(756B); *Hymn*.(*AS* 1 p.544).

***πανευλαβῶς,** *most reverently*, *Mir.Geo*.6(p.69.11).

***πανευμενής,** *altogether gracious*; of BMV, Ephr.3.526E.

***πανευπρόσδεκτος,** *altogether acceptable*, *Hymn*.(*AS* 1 p.536).

πανευσεβής, *most pious* δόγμα...π. Cyr.H.*ep.Const*.4(M.33.1169B); superl., in address to emperor, *ib*.3(1168B); *ib*.7(1173A); *Ep*.tit.ap. CCP(536)*act*.1(*ACO* 3 p.131.9; H.2.1193B).

πανεύφημος, *wholly blessed*, Thdt.*haer*.5.9(4.414); ὁ...πατήρ ἐστιν ἐν τοῖς π. κόσμοις *Pap.Chr*.(p.446); Chrysipp.*enc.in Jo.Bapt*.15 (p.46.21); εὐφημείσθω ἡ π., ὡς εὔφημος π. εὐφημίαις ‡Jo.D.*hom*.5(M. 96.648B).

***πανευώδης,** *wholly fragrant*, Jo.D.*hom*.10.4(M.96.760C).

πανηγεμών, ὁ, *ruler of all*; of God, Clem.*str*.7.9(p.40.18; M.9. 477B); Eus.*p.e*.11.16(535A; M.21.888B).

[*]**πανηγυραρχέω,** *preside at festival*, Cyr.*hom.pasch*.9(5².108B).

[*]**πανηγυράρχης, ὁ,** *president of festal assembly*, Eus.*h.e*.10.4.72 (M.20.880A); of Christ, Cyr.*thes*.11(5¹.98E); id.*hom.pasch*.26(5².304C).

πανηγυριάρχης, ὁ, = foreg., †Leont.N.*laud.Barn*.(p.144.30).

πανηγυρίζ-ω, A. *celebrate, hold festival*; 1. pagan, cf. Πλάτων, οὗ τὴν ἐπώνυμον ἑορτὴν σήμερον ~ομεν Porphyry ap.Eus.*p.e*.10.3(468A; M.21.780A); 2. Jewish ἐν μόνῳ τῷ δηλουμένῳ τόπῳ ~ειν Eus.*d.e*.1.3 (p.14.7; M.22.33B); τῆς ἐν ἐρήμῳ διαγωγῆς ~ειν τὴν μνήμην Thdt.*Os*. 12:9(2.1369); id.*Zach*.14:16(2.1666); 3. Christian ἐν ᾠδαῖς πνευματικαῖς...~ειν δεῖ *M.Ariadn*.(p.124.13); Chrys.*anom*.10.1(1.529C); Euthal.Diac.*epp.Paul*.proem.(M.85.701A); ἡ τοῦ...πάσχα...ἑβδομάς, τὴν...σωτηρίαν ~ουσα Niceph.Ur.*v.Sym*.99(M.86.3077D); Gr.Ant. *mul.ung*.1(M.88.1848A); 4. in gen. ψαλμὸς...ᾠδῆς, ὅτι ~ων Cyr.*Ps*. 4:1(M.69.733B).

B. *rejoice*, †Dion.Al.*fr.Eccl*.3:4(p.225.7; M.10.1588B); Cyr.H. *catech*.19.10; Gr.Naz.*or*.40.12(M.36.373B); Chrys.*hom.88.4 in Mt*. (7.829D); οὐσίαν, τῷ τῆς ἀθανασίας λόγῳ ~ουσαν Mac.Mgn.*apocr*.4.27 (p.214.11); Jo.D.*hom*.1.1(M.96.545A).

C. *pronounce a panegyric, make an oration*, Gr.Naz.*ep*.10(M. 37.37A); Mac.Mgn.*apocr*.2.19(p.35.13); Thdt.*ep*.151(4.1304); οὔτε ῥητορικὸν λέγομεν τὸν μήτε ~οντα Zach.Mit.*opif*.(M.85.1068A).

πανηγυρικός, 1. *festal* μετὰ τιμῆς π. Clem.*prot*.4(p.37.17; M.8. 140A); 2. *pertaining to a festival* π. θεσμῶν Bas.*hex*.6.1(1.49E; M.29. 117A); of Easter letters of bishop of Alexandria ἑορταστικὰς [sc. ἐπιστολάς]...πανηγυρικωτέρους ἐν αὐταῖς περὶ τῆς τοῦ πάσχα ἑορτῆς ἀνακινῶν λόγους Eus.*h.e*.7.20(M.20.681B); Synes.*ep*.8(M.66.1345B); π. γραμμάτων, ἃ καταγγέλλει τὴν κυρίαν τῆς ἑορτῆς ἡμέραν *ib*.13 (1349B); 3. *suitable for a festival*, Dion.Al.ap.Eus.*h.e*.7.22.4(M.20. 688A); 4. *of* or *belonging to a panegyric*, Gr.Thaum.*pan.Or*.1(p.2.3; M.10.1052A); Philost.*h.e*.6.2(M.65.533B).

πανηγυρικῶς, 1. *suitably to a panegyric*, Synes.*Dion* 3(p.242.17; M.66.1121C); hence *rhetorically*, Thdt.*eran*.3(4.202); id.*ep*.151(4. 1304); Gel.Cyz.*h.e*.2.36.3; 2. *with pomp and ceremony* ἑορτάσωμεν... μὴ π., ἀλλὰ θεϊκῶς Eulog.*palm*.13(M.86.2936D).

***πανηγύριον, τό,** *fair, market*, Ephr.1.74D; Thphn.*chron*.p.396 (M.108.945A).

πανήγυρις, ἡ, 1. *festal assembly, festival*; a. pagan, Tat.*orat*. 19(p.21.13; M.6.849A); δημοτελεῖς ὑμῶν π. *ib*.22(p.24.19; 856A); Athenag.*leg*.14.2(M.6.917A); of imperial cult, at which martyrdoms took place, *Ep.Lugd*.ap.Eus.*h.e*.5.1.47(M.20.425B); π. Ἑλληνικὴ ἐπὶ νεκρῷ δράκοντι συνεκροτεῖτο Πυθοῖ Clem.*prot*.1(p.3.10; M.8.52A); Or.*Cels*.6.8(p.78.8; M.11.1301A); τὰ ἐν εἰδωλικαῖς π. κρεμώμενα, ἔσθ' ὅτε κρέα...ἢ ἄλλα τοιαῦτα μιανθέντα...τῇ τοῦ διαβόλου πομπῇ ἐγκαταλέγεται Cyr.H.*catech*.19.7; Mac.Mgn.*apocr*.2.21(p.43.16); οὐδέποτε δημοτικὴν π. ἀνέχῃ, οὐδὲ σπουδάζεις παιγνίοις δαιμόνων Nil.*epp*.3.252 (M.79.505B); b. Jewish; of sabbath, Or.*Cels*.6.61(p.131.23; 1392B); τὰς κατὰ Μωσέα π. Eus.*d.e*.1.6(p.28.16; M.22.57A); of σκηνοπηγία· ἑορτὴ δὲ ἦν αὕτη καὶ π. καὶ εὐχή Ath.*apol.Const*.18(M.25.617C); Cyr.*Os*.113(3.124D); c. Christian; i. of dedication-festival, Eus.*h.e*. 10.4.72(M.20.880A); Ath.*apol.sec*.84(p.162.33; M.25.397C); ii. of annual commemorations of saints, esp. martyrs, Bas.*ep*.176(3.263B; M.32.653B); Gr.Nyss.*mart*.2.9(M.46.784D); τρίτην...μετὰ τοῦ Χριστοῦ γέννησιν Στεφάνῳ...πανήγυριν Sophr.H.*or*.8.6(M.87.3361B); †Leont.N. *laud.Barn*.(p.144.25); iii. of major feasts, e.g., Easter π. τῶν π. Eustrat.*v.Eutych*.92(M.86.2377B); *Supplic*.ap.Evagr.*h.e*.2.8(p.58.28; M.86.2525B); Annunciation, Abr.Eph.*annunt*.1(p.442.13); Transfiguration, Jo.D.*hom*.1.1(M.96.545A); Exaltation of Cross, Sophr.H. *v.Anast*.(M.92.1713A); 2. *time of rejoicing, festivity*, in gen., Gr. Thaum.*pan.Or*.16(p.37.8; M.10.1100A); of entire life of primitive Church, Mac.Mgn.*apocr*.3.28(p.119.22); πανηγύρεως ἀρχὴν ἔχοντας τὸν Ἐμμανουήλ Cyr.*ador*.17(1.591A); id.*Jo*.2.1(4.134E); Eustrat.*v. Eutych*.74(M.86.2357D); of Christian life ὁ βίος αὐτοῦ π. ἁγία Clem. *str*.7.7(p.37.3; M.9.469B); π. τὸν βίον ἡμῶν σοφῶν παῖδες εἰρήκασιν εἶναι Meth.*symp*.8.1(p.81.10; M.18.140A); 3. *festal oration, laudatory speech*, Clem.*paed*.3.12(p.290.29; M.8.680B); 4. *assembly* μεγάλης π. ἀποκειμένης ἐν τοῖς μέλλουσιν ‡Hipp.*fr.9 in Ps*.(p.138.13; M.10. 713C); Or.*Jo*.10.18(13; p.189.30; M.14.340A); τὴν ἄνω π. Mac.Mgn. *apocr*.3.12(p.83.25); Ἱερουσαλὴμ ἡ ἐπουράνιος, π. ἐκλεκτῶν *Lit.Jac*. (p.198.25); exeg. Heb.12:22–23; heavenly Jerusalem described as π. both because it consists of assembly of saints and because it provides a rich feast, Chrys.*Philogon*.1(1.494A); 5. *market, trading-fair*, id.*poenit*.3.2(2.296D); *Chron.Pasch*.p.254(M.92.613B); met. ὁδός ἐστιν ὁ παρὼν βίος, καὶ...π. τὰ παρόντα· ἠγοράσαμεν, ἐπωλήσαμεν, καταλύομεν Pall.*v.Chrys*.8(p.46.22; M.47.28); π. γάρ ἐστιν ὁ βίος...καὶ ἐπὰν λύθῃ ἡ π., οὐδεὶς οὐκέτι ἐκεῖ πραγματεύσασθαι δύναται Anast.S. *Ps*.6(M.89.1096D).

***πανηγύρισμα, τό,** *festival*, ‡Chrys.*pasch*.6(p.189.15; 8.273D).

πανήλιος, *of the sun in his might*, ‡Ath.*annunt*.5(M.28.924C).

πανῆμαρ, *all day*, Just.*dial*.90.4(M.6.692A); *Orac.Sib.fr*.3.44.

***πανθαμάρτητος**, **ὁ**, *total sinner*, *Did*.5.2 = *Barn*.20.2.

***πανθαμαρτωλός**, **ὁ**, = foreg., *2Clem*.18.2.

πανθάνω, = *πάσχω*, *suffer*, Thdr.Stud.*epp*.2.37(M.99.1228A).

πανθαύμαστος, *wholly marvellous*, *T.Abr*.A 11(p.89.19); *ib*.13(p.91.28); Nect.*Thdr*.23(M.39.1840A); of BMV, Thdr.Stud.*nativ. BMV* 4(M.96.684C); ‡Jo.D.*Artem*.52(p.87.20; M.96.1300A).

πανθελγής, *all-comforting*, Nonn.*par.Jo*.1:32(M.43.756A); *ib*. 18:37(896C).

[*]**πάνθεον**, **τό**, *temple of all the gods*; near Gaza, Soz.*h.e*.5.15.14(M.67.1260A); at Antioch, Jo.Mal.*chron*.10 p.242(M.97.372A).

πανίερος, *all-holy*; of Abraham, *T.Abr*.A 1(p.77.8); of Church, Eus.*h.e*.10.4.56(M.20.872A); of Christ's earthly body, id.*l.C*.15(p.247.29; M.20.1420B); *π. γνῶσις τῶν...ἑορτῶν τῆς θεομήτορος* Mod.*dorm*.(M.86.3277B); of prayers, Max.*ep*.19(M.91.597B); *ἡ π. μετάστασις τῆς θείας...μητρός* Jo.D.*carm.dorm.BMV* 109(p.231; M.96.1365B); *τὸ π. πνεῦμα* [i.e. of BMV] *ib*.128(p.231; 1365D); as complimentary address, Sophr.H.*ep.syn*.(M.87.3149C); Thds.Am.*libell*.ap.CNic.(787)*act*.1(H.4.44C).

***πανιέρως**, *all-holily*, Dion.Ar.*c.h*.8.2(M.3.242A).

πανίλαος, *all-gracious*, *all-kindly* *π. ὄμμα* Nonn.*par.Jo*.6:40(M.43.800C).

παν(ν)ίον, **τό**, *piece of cloth*, Jo.Mosch.*prat*.27(M.87.2873C); *ib*.107(2968A).

***παννόητος**, *wholly belonging to the intelligible order*, of God *ἡ ἀγνωσία, τὸ π.* Dion.Ar.*d.n*.2.4(M.3.641A).

***πάννυκτος**, *lasting all night*, Eust.*engast*.13(M.18.640C; *πάννυχος* p.36.30).

***παννυξία**, **ἡ**, *total darkness*, ‡Epiph.*hom*.2(M.43.453B).

παννυχεύω, *keep vigil*, Chrys.*hom.div*.2.2(12.332D); *Mir.Artem*.41(p.69.22); Thphn.*chron*.p.373(M.108.892C).

παννύχιος, *lasting all night*; *π. εὐχή night office*, Thdr.Lect.*fr*.(M.86.225B) cit. as *π. ἔχειν*, Jo.D.*imag*.3(M.94.1392C).

παννυχίς, **ἡ**, **1.** *all-night watching*, *vigil*; of Easter vigil, celebrated, acc. mistaken interpretation of Philo by Eus., by Therapeutae, Eus.*h.e*.2.17.22(M.20.181C); *ἐν ἡμέρᾳ τῆς ὑστάτης τοῦ πάσχα π.* *ib*.6.34.1(596A); *π. τῆς ἐσομένης συνάξεως* Ath.*apol.Const*.25(M.25.625C); Gr.Naz.*or*.5.31(M.35.704B); *δεῖ* [sc. *παρθένον*]...*ἐκφορῶν καὶ π. ἀπείργειν* Chrys.*sac*.3.17(p.91.17; 1.399C); id.*hom.8.5 in Mt*.(7.127C); Isid.Pel.*epp*.4.4(M.78.1052C); **2.** *night office*, comprising twelve prayers acc. Pachomian rule, Pall.*h.Laus*.32(p.92.5; M.34.1100B); and psalmody, ‡Chrys.*hom*.1(13.202D); **3.** *night festival* (pagan) *διαβολικαὶ π.* Chrys.*kal*.1(1.698C).

πανόδυρτος, *wholly wretched*, *Orac.Sib*.5.394.

***πανοικτίρμων**, *all-merciful*; of God, Chrys.*hom.34.4 in Gen*.(4.345C); Max.*ambig*.(M.91.1277D); ‡Jo.D.*fid.dorm*.11(M.95.256B).

πανόλβιος, *wholly happy* or *blessed* *Γάζα πανολβίστη* *Orac.Sib*.3.345; *π. θαλάμων* Meth.*symp*.11(p.132.14; M.18.208D); *π. θεοφιλίας* Eus.*p.e*.1.1(2C; M.21.24C); of lips of S. Peter when confessing Christ, Jo.D.*hom*.1.6(M.96.556A); *νύμφης...τὸν π. τόκον* id.*carm. theog*.21(p.205; M.96.820B).

***πανολεθρία**, **ἡ**, *total destruction*, *A.Jo*.41,42(p.171.23,37); Gr. Nyss.*hom.14 in Cant*.(M.44.1069D); Bas.Sel.*or*.6.3(M.85.97A); of Flood, Jo.D.*Man*.1.41(M.94.1545A).

***πανολέθριος**, *utterly destructive*, *Hom.Clem*.12.8; of heret. exegesis, Didym.*Trin*.1.35(M.39.437C); of Flood, †Gregent.*disp*.1(M.86.636C); Thphn.*chron*.p.415(M.108.984B).

***πανομβρία**, **ἡ**, *flood*, *constant pouring*; of fluid, Sophr.H.*mir. Cyr.et Jo*.36(M.87.3549B).

***πανόμματος**, *all-seeing*; of God, Geo.Pis.*hex*.1477(M.92.1548A).

πανοπλία, **ἡ**, *suit of armour*, met. *περιαμφιάσας ἡμᾶς* [sc. *ὁ υἱός*] *ἀφθάρτῳ π.* †Hipp.*theoph*.8(p.262.9; M.10.860A); Mac.Mgn.*apocr*.3.23(p.103.8); *σκεύη γὰρ αὐτοῦ* [sc. *τοῦ Δαβίδ*] *καὶ π., ἡ πνευματικὴ δωρεά* Thdt.*qu.53 in 1Reg*.(4.389); *τῇ τοῦ...βαπτίσματος π. φραξάμενον* id.*h.e*.4.12.2(3.968); exeg. *τὴν δὲ δύναμιν...εἰκάζει πανοπλίᾳ, δηλῶν, ὅτι καθάπερ ὁ γυμνὸς οὐ δυνατός ἐστιν εἰς πόλεμον, οὕτως ὁ πνεύματος ἀμέτοχος, οὐ δυνατὸς πρὸς τὸν τὴν κακίαν ἐξεργαζόμενον τὸν διάβολον* Jo.D.*Eph*.6:11(M.95.853B); in Manich. system *οἱ τοῦ σκότους ἄρχοντες...ἔφαγον ἐκ τῆς π. αὐτοῦ* [sc. *τοῦ πρώτου ἀνθρώπου*] *ὅ ἐστιν ἡ ψυχή* Hegem.*Arch*.7(p.10.10; M.10.1437B); *ib*.10(p.15.13; 1441C); Epiph.*haer*.66.24(p.52.4,8; M.42.69B,C).

***πανόπτριος**, *all-seeing*, Geo.Pis.*hex*.218(M.92.1450A).

***πανόργιλος**, *thoroughly evil-tempered*, Nil.*epp*.2.77(M.79.233D).

πάνορμος, ?*fitted for entering any harbour*, Geo.Pis.*hex*.505(M.92.1475A).

πανόσιος, *all-holy*, *saintly*; of Abraham, *T.Abr*.A 13(p.92.4); Jo. Clim.*scal*.4(M.88.685A); ‡Jo.D.*fid.dorm*.27(M.95.273B); superl., as title of Cyril, Justn.*typ.Thdr.Mops*.(M.86.1037A).

***πανούκλα**, **ἡ**, *total ulceration*, Anton.Hag.*v.Sym.Styl*.17(p.44.1).

πανούργευμα, **τό**, *trick*, *villainy* *τοῦ δράκοντος τὸ π.* †Hipp. *theoph*.4(p.259.13; M.10.856A); Didym.*2Cor*.2:10–11(p.19.8; M.39.1689B); Cyr.*hom.pasch*.6(5[2].63C).

πανουργεύομαι, *contrive a stratagem*, *plot*, Epiph.*haer*.66.44(p.82.3; M.42.96D); c. infin., *Apophth.Patr*.(M.65.304A); c. acc., *contrive*, *T.Reub*.5.4; pass. *τὸ...πεπανουργευμένον* ‡Proc.G.*Pr*.6:13(M.87.1273B).

πανουργία, **ἡ**, **1.** *cleverness*, *astuteness*, in neutral sense *ἔστιν οὖν ἡ π. ἐνέργεια πάντων κατ' ἐπιτήδευσιν τεχνικήν· ὥσπερ ἡ κακουργία ἡ μόνου ἐστὶ τοῦ κακοῦ ἐργασία* Bas.*hom*.12.11(2.107E; M.31.409B); in good sense, *T.Neph*.2.8; Or.*hom.12.6 in Jer*.(p.93.10; M.13.388A); Ephr.1.190A; **2.** in bad sense, *cunning*, *craftiness*, *T.Jud*.10.3; *T. Isach*.1.11; †Hipp.*Artem*.ap.Eus.*h.e*.5.28.15(M.20.516B); Gr.Thaum. *pan.Or*.10(p.25.22; M.10.1081B); Ath.*decr*.28(p.25.16; M.25.469B); *π. καὶ ἡ δαιμονιώδης σοφία* Esaias *or*.5.3(p.36; cf.M.40.1122D).

πανοῦργος, **1.** *clever*, *astute*; in good sense, ref. Ecclus.21:20 *φρόνιμον λέγει τὸν π. ... τὸν ἐναντίως τῷ μωρῷ διακείμενον* Clem. *paed*.2.5(p.186.7; M.8.449A); id.*str*.6.4(p.450.14; M.9.256B); *νοῦς παθῶν γυμνωθεὶς καὶ γνώσεως μέτοχος γεγονὼς πανουργότερος γίνεται τῶν δαιμόνων* Or.*sel.in Ps*.118:98(M.12.1605D); Ephr.1.204D; Thdt. *Pss*.proem.(1.603); **2.** *cunningly*, *artificially contrived*; of hair-dressing style, Clem.*paed*.3.11(p.271.15; M.8.637A); **3.** in bad sense; **a.** in jesting reproof, *inquisitive*, Herm.*vis*.3.3.1; id.*sim*.5.5.1; **b.** *crafty*, *deceitful*, *cunning*, Just.*dial*.123.4(M.6.761C); of evil spirits, Or.*Cant*.3(p.235.28; M.17.265B); *Hom.Clem*.1.10; of Arianism, Ath.*Ar*.1.1(M.26.13A); of Satan in baptismal renunciation *πανουργοτάτῳ ὄφει* Cyr.H.*catech*.19.4.

πανούργως, *craftily*, *wickedly*, Herm.*mand*.3.3; Clem.*str*.6.10(p.473.12; M.9.304B).

***πανσάλευτος**, *thoroughly unstable* *γυναικῶν...π. φύσις* ‡Jo.D. *hom*.5(M.96.657C).

***πανσεβάσμιος**, *wholly august*; of festivals, Amph.*hom*.1.1(M.39.36A); Epiph.*haer*.70.12(p.245.7; -*μος* M.42.364B); *ib*.70.14(p.247.22; 372A); Jo.Eub.*concept.BMV* 10(M.96.1476A); of Christ's birth, ‡Jo. D.*hom*.5(M.96.657C); of God *π. πάτερ* Thdr.Stud.*epp*.1.11(M.99.949B); in gen., *Mir.Geo*.4(p.43.17); *ἡ τῶν ἀποστόλων π. δυάς, Πέτρος καὶ Παῦλος* *Hymn*.(*AS* 1 p.549).

πάνσεμνος, **1.** *all-holy*, *wholly consecrated* *π. πνεῦμα καὶ...δεδοκιμασμένον* Herm.*vis*.1.2.4; **2.** *wholly sacred*; of festival of Pentecost, Eus.*v.C*.4.64(p.144.11, v.l. *πανσέπτου* M.20.1220B); of chrismation, Dion.Ar.*e.h*.4.3.12(M.3.485A); **3.** *all-revered*; of BMV, Gel.Cyz.*h.e*.1 proem.17(M.85.1196C); Jo.V H.*icon*.14(M.96.1360C).

πάνσεπτος, *all-sacred*, *all-holy*; **1.** of persons; saints, Cyr.*Ps*. 18:8(M.69.832B); BMV, Leont.H.*Nest*.4.37(M.86.1712B); of Trin., Sophr.H.*ep.syn*.(M.87.3160B); **2.** of saint's body, Evagr.*h.e*.1.13(p.23.1; M.85.2457A); **3.** of sanctuaries, *Mir.Anast.Pers*.7(p.22.25); **4.** of festivals, Sergia *Olymp*.3(p.46); Jo.Eub.*concept.BMV* 10(M.96.1476A); *ib*.22(1497B); **5.** of dormition of BMV, Mod.*dorm*.2(M.86.3281C); of conception of BMV, Jo.Eub.*concept.BMV* 13(M.96.1480B).

***πανσθενεί**, *with all one's power*, Gr.Naz.*carm*.2.1.11.1372(M.37.1123A).

***πανσθενής**, *all-powerful*, of divine Persons *πνεῦμα...π.* Gr.Naz. *carm*.1.1.3.5(M.37.408A); *σωτῆρα...π.* Cyr.*Abac*.32(3.547D); of divine nature, id.*Nest*.5(p.101.8; 6[1].135A); Dion.Ar.*d.n*.6.2(M.3.857A); of divine power, Clem.*str*.7.7(p.33.19; M.9.464B); 'hand' equated with Christ, Cyr.*Is*.2.1(2.203E); id.*Am*.80(3.344D); id.*Lc*.20:37(M.72.892D); of hand of Christ in healing, *ib*.5:12(556B); of Christ's will, *ib*. 5:2(553B); Anast.S.*haer*.(p.269); of divine activity in creation, Geo.Pis.*hex*.1199(M.92.1527A); of stability of created order, id.*bell. Avar*.520(M.92.1293A); *τὴν αὐτοῦ* [sc. Holy Cross] *π. συμπόρευσιν* Sophr.H.*or*.4(M.87.3305B).

***πανσθενουργός**, *all-powerful in operation*; of Trin., ‡Jo.D.*fid. dorm*.13(M.95.257D).

***πανσθενουργόφωτος**, *illuminating with all-powerful operation*; of H. Ghost, Jo.D.*carm.pent*.27(p.214; M.96.833B).

***πανσθενῶς**, *all-powerfully*, Jo.D.*carm.theog*.98(p.208; M.96.824A); Thdr.Stud.*antirr*.1.4(M.99.332D).

***πανσκευεί**, *with all one's gear*, Cyr.*ador*.1(1.23A).

πάνσοφος, *all-wise*; of God, Clem.*prot*.1(p.3.15; M.8.52A); id. *paed*.3.11(p.278.5; M.8.652B); Eus.*d.e*.1.7(p.37.6; M.22.72D); Cyr.H. *catech*.9.4; Bas.Sel.*or*.1.3(M.85.33B); Leont.N.*v.Jo.Eleem*.1(p.5.12);

of H. Ghost, Nil.*epp*.2.140(M.79.260D); of providence, Cyr.H. *catech*.8.4; of Creation, Gr.Thaum.*pan.Or*.8(p.22.3; M.10.1077B); Cyr.H.*catech*.9.5; of Christ's teaching, Eus.*h.e*.1.2.17(M.20.61B); of apostles' doctrine, Thdt.*qu.2 in Jos*.(1.301); of moral conduct, Cyr.*Os*.87(3.118C); of men: Moses, prophets, apostles, Clem.*prot*.1 (p.8.21; M.8.64B); Nil.*epp*.1.127(M.79.137A); Cyr.*Os*.4(3.20C); id. *Nest*.5(p.102.20; 6¹.137A); Thdt.*qu.Jos*.proem.(1.299); bishops and holy men, Eustrat.*stat.anim*.10(p.387); Leont.N.*v.Jo.Eleem*.31(p.64. 5); id.*v.Sym*.2(M.93.1672B).

πανσόφως, *all-wisely*, Isid.Pel.*epp*.1.46(M.78.440B); Cyr.*Os*.4(3. 20C).

πανσπερμία, ἡ, 1. *mixture of all seeds* ᾄδῃ, ὃς ταῖς...μύλαις τὰς τῶν ἀνθρώπων π. ἀλήθων, τρέφεις τὴν μισανθρωπίαν Germ.CP *or*.2(M.98. 280B); **2.** *mixture of all the elements*, in system of Basilides σπέρμα τι ἓν ἔχον πᾶσαν ἐν ἑαυτῷ τὴν τοῦ κόσμου π. Hipp.*haer*.7.21(p.197.9; M. 16.3303C); *ib*.7.22(p.198.17; 3306B); *ib*.(p.200.16; 3310A).

πανστρατεί (πανστρατί), *with all one's forces*, ref. Ps.2:2 τοῦ πονηροῦ π. ἀγωνιζομένου κατ' αὐτοῦ [sc. Χριστοῦ] Or.*Jo*.32.23(15; p.466.15; M.14.805D); Men.*exc.gent*.4(p.444.12; M.113.796C); ἀπώλετο πανστρατί Thphn.*chron*.p.105(M.108.305B).

***πανσύνετος**, *wholly prudent* πανσύνετος οὖσα ἡ σὴ θεοσέβεια Cyr. *ep*.82(p.20.10; M.77.376A).

***πάνσχημος**, *of every form*; of God, Dion.Ar.*d.n*.5.8(M.3.824B) cit. s. ἀκαλλής.

***πανσώμως**, *over the whole body*; of pre-baptismal anointing, Dion.Ar.*e.h*.2.2.7(M.3.396C).

***πανσωτήριος**, *all-saving*; of name of Christ, Agath.*v.Gr.Ill*.152 (p.77).

παντάγαθος, *wholly good* τὸν...περὶ ἡμᾶς παντάγαθον τοῦ θεοῦ σκοπόν Max.*ambig*.(M.91.1097C).

[*]πανταδύναμος, = παντοδύναμος, *all-powerful*, of Son as πανταδύναμος...χεὶρ τοῦ πατρός Meth.*creat*.9(p.498.28; παντο- M.18.341A).

[*]πανταίσχης, = παναίσχης, *wholly shameful*, Gr.Naz.*carm*.1.2. 1.661(M.37.572A).

[*]πανταίτιος, = παναίτιος, *causing all things*; of Wisdom, Proc.G.*fr.Cant*.6:8(M.87.1756A); ‡Proc.G.*Pr*.30:17(M.87.1528D).

παντακύριος, *who is lord of all*, Ephr.2.344D.

***πανταληθινός**, *wholly true*, Diad.*perf*.74(p.92.11).

***παντάναξ, ὁ**, *lord of all*; of God, *CIG* 8672; ‡Gr.Naz.*Chr.pat*.878 (M.38.207A); of Christ, Sophr.H.*carm*.20.10(p.45; M.87.3817A); Jo.D. *hom*.12.2(M.96.784D); id.*carm.theog*.81(p.207; M.96.821C).

***παντάνασσα, ἡ**, *queen of all*; of BMV, Sophr.H.*carm*.19.42(M.87. 3813A); Germ.CP *hymn.BMV*(M.98.453B); ‡Gr.Naz.*Chr.pat*.2600 (M.38.338A).

***πανταπλασιάζω**, *cat.Lc*.19:13(p.139.11) for πεντα-, Cyr.*Lc*.19:15 (M.72.872B).

***πανταπώλεια, ἡ**, *total destruction*, Anast.S.*hod*.7(M.89.121D).

πανταπώλης, ὁ, *tradesman, shopkeeper*, *A.Petr.et Andr*.16(p.124. 14; codd. παντάπολις, πατάπιος) perh. l. παντο-.

παντάριστος, *most excellent*; of the patriarchs, Thdt.*qu.17 in Jos*.(1.314).

παναρκής, *all-sufficient*, of Son θησαυρὸς σοφίας...παναρκής Didym.*Trin*.1.28(M.39.409A).

παναρχ-έω, *be sovereign ruler* ~οῦντος μὲν καθόλου πάντων καὶ αὐτοῦ τοῦ υἱοῦ μόνου τοῦ πατρός, τοῦ δὲ υἱοῦ ὑποτεταγμένου τῷ πατρί *Symb.Ant*.(345)9(p.254.2; M.26.733C).

πάνταρχος, *all-sovereign*; of Logos, Jo.D.*carm.pent*.63(p.215; M. 96.836B).

παντάσκιος, *wholly without shadow*, Gr.Naz.*carm*.2.1.12.742(M.37. 1220A).

***παντάχρηστος**, *wholly useless, unprofitable*, Dor.*doct*.6.4(M.88. 1689B).

***παντεκνεί**, *with all one's children*, Didym.*Trin*.2.7(M.39.593A).

[*]παντελεήμων, = πανελεήμων, *all-merciful* θεοῦ τοῦ π. Max. *ambig*.(M.91.1332B).

παντέλειος, *quite perfect*, of number ten ἡ δεκὰς...ὁμολογεῖται π. εἶναι Clem.*str*.6.11(p.473.31; M.9.305A); Eus.*l.C*.6(p.210.20; M.20. 1348C); Cyr.*Os*.33(3.60C); of Trin., *Symb.Ant*.(345)9(p.253.40; M.26. 733B); Cyr.*glaph.Gen*.2(1.37C); of divine being τῆς μιᾶς θεότητος... τὸ εἰς πᾶν ὁτιοῦν π. *ib*.2(37A); of Son, Ath.*gent*.42(M.25.84B); π. γὰρ ὁ Ἐμμανουήλ Cyr.*ador*.17(1.594D); ἐν αὐξήσει σώματος ὁ π. ὡς θεός id. *Lc*.2:40(M.72.508A); ἐν πᾶσι π. εἶναι...τὸν υἱόν id.*Jo*.1.9(4.100B); id. *inc.unigen*.(5¹.690A); *Chron.Pasch*.p.47(M.92.172A); of Christ's divine nature, Cyr.*Jo*.2.6(219A); of his human virtue, Leont.H. *Nest*.2.21(M.86.1581D); of man who partakes of Logos, Ath.*Ar*.3.51 (**M.26.429C**).

[*]παντελεύθερος, *wholly free*, ‡Jo.D.*fid.dorm*.11(M.95.256C).

παντελής, *complete* π. τῆς ἀληθείας γνῶσιν Clem.*paed*.1.1(p.91. 5; M.8.252A); θεὸς..., ἀρχὴ τῶν ὅλων π. id.*str*.4.25(p.320.16; M.8. 1372B); Eus.*h.e*.4.6.4(M.20.313A); κυρίων καὶ π. καὶ ἁπλῶν ὀνομάτων Dion.Ar.*d.n*.5.9(M.3.824D); Jo.D.*f.o*.1.1(M.94.789B); εἰς τὸ π. *completely*, Tat.*orat*.6(p.6.20; M.6.817B); Clem.*paed*.1.2(p.91.27; M.8. 252C); Meth.*res*.1.39(p.284.1; M.41.1108B).

***παντελικός**, *all-effecting*; of divine providence, Athenag.*leg*. 24.3(M.6.948A); Meth.*res*.1.44(p.293.16; M.41.1113C).

παντελῶς, *completely*, οὐ (μή) π. *not at all*, Herm.*sim*.7.4; Cyr. *ador*.1(1.12C); Esaias *or*.3.4(p.13; cf.M.40.1111D).

***παντεξάκουστος**, *all-famous*, *Mir.Geo*.4(p.43.13).

***παντεξάλειπτος**, *wholly wiped away*; of antediluvian world, Tim.Ant.*Sym*.(M.86.237C).

***παντεξούσιος**, *with complete authority*, of God π. ... αὐτοῦ δυνάμει Clem.*fr*.42(p.220.32; M.9.768B); τὸν μὲν γὰρ θεὸν π. φημι, τὸν δὲ ἀποστάτην ἄγγελον...αὐτεξούσιον λέγω Adam.*dial*.3.9(p.128.7; M.11. 1801A); τῆς αὐτεξουσίου καὶ π. μονάδος οὐσίας Didym.*Trin*.1.15(M. 39.325B).

***παντεξουσίως**, *as being possessed of complete authority*, of Christ's divine nature θεότητος αὐτεξουσίως καὶ π. διὰ τῆς ἀνθρωπότητος αὐτοῦ ἐνεργούσης Jo.D.*rect.sent*.4(M.94.1429B).

***παντεπαίνετος**, *worthy of all praise*, Thdr.Stud.*epp*.2.187(M.99. 1573B).

[*]παντεπήκοος, = πανεπήκοος, *all-hearing*, Didym.*Trin*.2.1(M. 39.449A).

[*]παντεπίσκοπος, = πανεπίσκοπος, *all-surveying*; of Trin., Didym.*Trin*.2.1(M.39.449A); of divine nature, Areth.*Apoc*.4:8ff. (M.106.573C); of Christ ὁ π. πάντων *A.Phil*.132(p.63.17).

[*]παντεπόπτης, = πανεπόπτης, *overseeing all things*; **1.** of God, *1Clem*.55.6; Polyc.*ep*.7.2; Hipp.*antichr*.49(p.33.9; M.10.769B); *Hom. Clem*.4.14; Nil.*epp*.2.140(M.79.260B); ὁ π. ὀφθαλμός Isid.Pel.*epp*.5. 16(M.78.1333C); Marc.Er.*opusc*.2.176(M.65.957B); **2.** of Logos, Clem. *paed*.3.8(p.262.8; M.8.616A); of Christ, Cyr.*Is*.5.2(2.767A); Proc.G. *Is*.54:1–17(M.87.2541A); Sym.Styl.J.*ep.Just*.(M.86.3217D).

***παντεποπτικός**, *overseeing all things*; of eye of God, Jo.D.*f.o*.1. 14(M.94.860D); of Christ's divinity, id.*volunt*.11(M.95.141B).

[*]παντεργάτης, = πανεργέτης, *working all things, all-accomplishing*; of God, *CIG* 8794 (Ancyra, saec. ix); ‡Gr.Naz.*Chr.pat*. 1098(M.38.224A).

[*]παντέρημος, *utterly destitute* or *deserted* ὀρφανὸς...π. Thdr. Stud.*epp*.1.3(M.99.913D).

***πάντερπνος**, *all-delightful*, of BMV μυροθήκη τοῦ πνεύματος πάντερπνε *Hymn*.(*KlT* p.9).

***παντευεργέτης, ὁ**, *benefactor to all*, ‡Gr.Naz.*Chr.pat*.145(M.38. 149A).

***παντευλόγητος**, *blessed by all*; of BMV, Ephr.3.534E; ‡Meth. *Sym.et Ann*.10(M.18.372C).

παντευχία, ἡ, *complete armour*, ref. spiritual warfare οὐ γὰρ ἡ σκέπη μόνη τῆς π. ... ἱκανὴ πρὸς τελείωσιν, εἰ μὴ προσλάβοι τὸ ἔργον τῆς δικαιοσύνης Clem.*str*.6.12(p.484.1; M.9.324C); Chrys.*sac*.6. 13(p.171.17; 1.435B); Cyr.*glaph.Dt*.(1.422D); ἔχοντες τὴν νοητὴν π., ἀντεξάγουσι τῷ σατανᾷ id.*Is*.5.1(2.737C); of God's armour, ref. Is.59:17, *ib*.5.4(829D).

παντέφορος, *overseeing all things*; of God, Const.ap.Eus.*v.C*.3.17 (p.84.31; M.20.1073C); Nil.*epp*.1.139(M.79.141A); Thdr.Stud.*epp*.1. 25(M.99.989A); of H. Ghost, Didym.*Trin*.2.17(M.39.721B); of providence, eye of God, etc., Mac.Mgn.*apocr*.4.14(p.183.7); *ib*.4.30(p.227. 2); ‡Proc.G.*Pr*.5:21(M.87.1268A); Sophr.H.*mir.Cyr.et Jo*.32(M.87. 3525A); †Jo.D.*B.J*.36(M.96.1205B).

***παντεχνήμων**, *devising all things*; of Logos, ‡Jo.D.*hom*.6.3(M.96. 665A).

πάντεχνος, *all-contriving* τῆς π. ... σοφίας [sc. of God] ‡Chrys. *hom*.7(13.217E).

***παντήκοος**, *hearing all things*; neut. as subst., as attribute of God, Cyr.*Juln*.5(6².173C).

***παντογείτων**, *near to, being neighbour to all*; of Danube as boundary of Empire, Geo.Pis.*bell.Avar*.30 (cj. for ποντο-, M.92. 1266A).

***παντοδαίμων, ὁ**, *supreme god*; of Zeus, Agath.*v.Gr.Ill*.132 (p.67).

παντοδαπής, = παντοδαπός, *of all sorts*, Thdt.*Joel* 1:5(2.1384); Jo.D. *f.o*.4.13(M.96.1152A); π. ἱστορία rendering *omnimoda historia* (ascribed to Dexter), Hier.*vir.ill*.(tr.Sophr.Pal.)132(p.61.17; M.*PL*. 23.716A) and *chronicon omnimodae historiae* (of Hier.), *ib*.135(p.62. 8; 718A).

παντοδαπία, ἡ, *abundance of all kinds*, ref. Is.66:12(AQ.), Nil. *epp*.3.191(M.79.473A).

***παντοδότης,** *giving all things* τῷ ἀπροσδεεῖ καὶ π. θεῷ Didym. *Trin*.2.7(M.39.580A).

***παντοδόχος,** *receiving all*; of earth which receives bodies of all men, typified by sea-monster of Jonah, Meth.*res*.2.25(p.381.20; M. 18.329A).

παντοδύναμος, *almighty*; **1.** of God, Const.ap.Gel.Cyz.*h.e*.2.7.1 (M.85.1232C); π., καὶ πάντα ἰσχύων Eus.*p.e*.11.6(517D; M.21.857D); π. θεότητι Gr.Nyss.*Eun*.12(2 p.289.5; M.45.901B); μόνος ὁ θεὸς π. id. *usur*.(M.46.441B); Cosm.Ind.*top*.3(M.88.149A); παντόκρατορ, π. *Lit. Jac*.(p.200.14); π., παντοκράτωρ Jo.D.*f.o*.1.2(M.94.792C); of divine operation π. νεύματι Jo.D.*carm.dorm.BMV* 31(p.229; M.96.1364B); **2.** of Son, Gr.Nyss.*or.catech*.2(p.14.15; M.45.17B); ‡Gr.Nyss.*hom. 5.30 in Jo*.(p.183.12); Ἰησοῦς...θεὸς π. ἐστιν Heracl.*ep*.(M.92.1020B); Max.*ambig*.(M.91.1117A); τοῦ σταυρωθέντος ἡ π. δύναμις Jo.D.*f.o*. 4.4(M.94.1109A); Jo.V H.*icon*.7(M.96.1356B); κύριος...ὁ παντοδυναμώτατος ἰατρός Jo.VI H.*v.Jo.D*.20(M.94.460B); ‡Meth.*Sym.et Ann*. 10(M.18.373A); **3.** of Christ's divine nature, Gr.Nyss.*Eun*.5(2 p.124. 9; M.45.705C); id.*or.catech*.24(p.91.5; M.45.64B); Thdt.*eran*.1(4.20); **4.** of H. Ghost, Nil.*epp*.2.140(M.79.260D); ‡Cyr.*Trin*.9(6^3.13C; M.77. 1140B).

***παντοδωροδότης, ὁ,** *giver of all gifts*, Agath.*v.Gr.Ill*.102(p.51); *ib*.110(p.56).

***παντόθυρος,** *wholly shut in, completely barred* τὰ π. ... τοῦ ᾅδου δεσμωτήρια ‡Epiph.*hom*.2(M.43.456D).

***παντοιοτρόπως,** *in every kind of way*, Ephr.3.514A; *Schol*. in Bas.*ep.can*.88(*Mon*.2 p.654).

***παντοκήρυκτος,** *universally renowned*, *Mir.Artem*.32(p.46.18).

***παντοκράτητος,** *wholly dominating*, †Jo.Jej.*poenit*.(M.88.1908A).

παντοκρατορία, ἡ, *authority over all, supreme power* μιᾶς οὔσης οὐσίας τοῦ πατρὸς καὶ τοῦ υἱοῦ τῆς θεότητος, καὶ μία π. τυγχάνει ‡Ath. *disp*.37(M.28.488C); τὸ ἀπαράλλακτον τῆς φύσεως καὶ δόξης καὶ π. Didym.*Trin*.3.2(M.39.789D).

***παντοκρατορικός,** *possessing universal sovereignty* τῷ π. καὶ παναρέτῳ ὀνόματί σου *1Clem*.60.4; divine essence, Didym.*Trin*.3.2 (M.39.800A); Jo.D.*volunt*.11(M.95.141B); of will of God, *1Clem*.8.5; Clem.*str*.4.17(p.295.25; M.8.1316A); *ib*.5.1(p.329.23; M.9.16B); divine glory, Or.*Jo*.13.25(p.249.32; M.14.444A) cit. s. δόξα; wisdom and other attributes, Dion.Ar.*d.n*.4.5(M.3.700B); *ib*.10.1(936D); ‡Meth. *palm*.6(M.18.393C); of Logos as π. δύναμις τοῦ θεοῦ Proc.G.*Is*.11:1–10(M.87.2040C); ‡Proc.G.*Pr*.10:3(M.87.1309D); of Son's power, Jo.V H.*icon*.7(M.96.1356B); of H. Ghost πνεῦμα...παντοκρατορικῆς φύσεως Didym.*Trin*.2.17(M.39.724C); πνεῦμα...π. Jo.D.*f.o*.1.8(M.94. 821B).

παντοκράτωρ, *all-sovereign, controlling all things*;

A. apptly. as subst. (but often hard to distinguish from adjectival use); **1.** of God in gen. ὁ π. *Orac.Sib*.1.66; *ib*.2.220; π. καὶ ποιητὴν τῶν ὅλων Just.*dial*.16.4(M.6.512A); π. δέ, ὅτι αὐτὸς τὰ πάντα κρατεῖ καὶ ἐμπεριέχει Thphl.Ant.*Autol*.1.4(M.6.1029B); Clem.*str*.1.17(p.55. 19; M.8.801A); ἡ υἱοῦ φύσις ἡ τῷ μόνῳ π. προσεχεστάτη *ib*.7.2(p.5.22; M.9.408B); ὡς ἄρχοντα δὲ στρατοπέδων, δυνάμεων ἐκάλεσαν κύριον, ὅπερ ἐν τῷ Ἑβραϊκῷ Σαβαὼθ εἴρηται. τοῦτο δὲ καὶ κύριον στρατιωτῶν οἱ ἑβδομήκοντα καὶ π. ... ἑρμηνεύουσι Or.*sel.in Ps*.23:10(M.17.116B); id.*dial*.1(p.120.7); Σαβέλλιος αὐτὸν τὸν π. λέξας πεπονθέναι Meth. *symp*.10(p.93.3; M.18.153B); θεὸν τὸν π. τὸν τὴν βασιλείαν τοῦ... Κωνσταντίνου διαφυλάττοντα *Ep.Dion*.2(p.160.6; M.25.393A); *Lit*.ap. *Const.App*.8.5.1 cit. s. δεσπότης; †Bas.*Is*.240(1.562A; M.30.540B); π. τί ἐστιν;...ἐκ τοῦ πάντων κρατεῖν ‡Ath.*disp*.37(M.28.488C); συνάπτει τῷ ἀγεννήτῳ τὸ τοῦ π. ὄνομα, [ὃ] οὐκ εἰς προνοητικὴν ἐνέργειαν...ἀλλ' εἰς τυραννικὴν ἐξουσίαν μεταλαμβάνων τὴν ἑρμηνείαν τοῦ π., ὡς μέρος τῆς ἀρχομένης...φύσεως καὶ τὸν υἱὸν ποιῆσαι, μετὰ πάντων δουλεύοντα τῷ διὰ τῆς τυραννικῆς ἐξουσίας κρατοῦντι Gr. Nyss.*Eun*.2(2 p.359.17; M.45.537C); Didym.(‡Bas.)*Eun*.4(1.281C; M.29.677B); id.*Trin*.3.2(M.39.805B); νοῦν αὐτοκράτορα ἔχων τῶν ὀρέξεων...τῷ κοσμοκράτορι ἐχθρῷ ἀντέστης...βοηθὸν πλουτήσας τὸν π. Jo.Mon.*hymn.Nic.Myr*.9(M.96.1389C); **2.** title of each Person of Trin., Thdt.*eran*.1(4.8); **3.** ref. eternity of creation, *ne omnipotens quidem deus dici potest, si non sint in quos exerceat potentatum; et ideo ut omnipotens ostendatur deus, omnia subsistere necesse est*...εἰ δὲ οὐκ ἔστιν ὅτε π. οὐκ ἦν, ἀεὶ εἶναι δεῖ ταῦτα, δι' ἃ π. ἐστί, καὶ ἀεὶ ἦν ὑπ' αὐτοῦ κρατούμενα Or.*princ*.1.2.10(p.42.1ff.; M.11.139A); Ὠριγένης... ἔφασκε...εἰ οὐκ ἔστι...π. ἄνευ τῶν κρατουμένων (τὸν γὰρ...π. διὰ τὰ κρατούμενα λέγεσθαι), ἀνάγκη ἐξ ἀρχῆς αὐτὰ...γεγενῆσθαι...εἰ γὰρ ἦν χρόνος ὅτε οὐκ ἦν τὰ ποιήματα ...ὅρα οἷον ἀσεβὲς ἀκολουθεῖ. ἀλλὰ καὶ ἀλλοιοῦσθαι...τὸν...ἀναλλοίωτον συμβήσεται θεόν Meth.*creat*.2(p.494. 19; M.18.333B); Jo.D.*Man*.2(M.96.1325C); **4.** closely ass. with πατήρ, *M.Polyc*.14:1; in credal forms, *Lit.Marc*.(p.32); *Symb.Nic*. (325)(p.43.9; M.20.1540B); Marcell.*ep*.ap.Epiph.*haer*.72.3(p.258.6; M.42.385D); *Symb.Hier*.(M.33.533A); *Symb*.ap.Epiph.*anc*.118(p.146. 22; M.43.232B); *Symb*.ap.Epiph.*anc*.119(p.148.4; 233B); *Symb.Nic.– CP*(p.80.3; H.2.288B); *Symb.App*.(p.30) etc.; cf.Eus.*e.th*.1.12(p.72. 7; M.24.848D); **5.** of Son π. ἐκ π. †Ath.*exp.fid*.1(M.25.201A) v. infra.

B. as adj.; **1.** of God χάρις...ἀπὸ π. θεοῦ *1Clem*.proem.; *ib*.62.2; ἔλεος...παρὰ θεοῦ π. Polyc.*ep*.proem.; *Did*.10.3; ὁ π. καὶ παντοκτίστης καὶ ἀόρατος θεός *Diogn*.7.2; Just.*dial*.38.2(M.6.557A); ἕνα θεὸν π. Iren.*haer*.1.9.2(M.7.540A); ἕνα π. ἀόρατον...θεόν *A.(Pass.) Petr.et Paul*.37(p.150.17); *Lit.Marc*.(p.20); Const.ap.Eus.*v.C*.3.53 (p.101.9; M.20.1117A); θεὸς ἀγαθός, καὶ δίκαιος, καὶ π. Cyr.H.*catech*. 5.1; μία τριὰς γάρ, εἷς θεὸς π. Amph.*Seleuc*.198(M.37.1590A); Jo.D. *Man*.2(M.96.1325B); **2.** of Logos τοῦ π. καὶ πατρικοῦ λόγου Clem. *paed*.1.9(p.139.12; M.8.349C); τὸν π. θεὸν λόγον *ib*.3.7(p.259.24; 609C); *A.Andr*.A 12(p.53.13); Christ, ref. Apoc.1:8 καλῶς εἶπεν π. Χριστόν...καὶ π. παρὰ πατρὸς κατεστάθη Χριστός Hipp.*Noët*.6 (p.245.15ff.; M.10.812B); εἰκότως ἡ π. φωνὴ τοῦ σωτῆρος κατηγορηθείη· εἰ γὰρ...κρατεῖ...προνοητικῶς τῶν δι' αὐτοῦ πάντων γεγενημένων ...ἀκολούθως π. λέγεται...π. γὰρ ὑπὸ π. ἀποστελλόμενος ὁ υἱός ἐστιν ...ἀριδηλότατα δὲ ἐν τῇ...Ἀποκαλύψει π. ὁ σωτὴρ λέγεται Or.*Ps*.23:10 (p.482); πάντων γὰρ κρατεῖ καὶ π. ἐστὶν ὁ υἱός, ὥσπερ καὶ ὁ πατήρ ‡Ath.*disp*.37(M.28.488C); **3.** of H. Ghost, ref. Am.4:13 εἰ δὲ δὴ καὶ δοθείη αὐτοῦ εἶναι ἡ φωνή, τὸ πνεῦμα τὸ ἅγιον ἀναφαίνεται θεὸς π. Didym.*Trin*.3.31(M.39.952B); **4.** of Valent. demiurge ὑστέρημα καὶ π. καὶ δημιουργόν Epiph.*haer*.31.4(p.388.1; M.41.480A); cf.Iren.*haer*. 1.16.3(M.7.636A); **5.** of divine name, Herm.*vis*.3.3.5.

***παντοκτίστης,** *all-creating*, *Diogn*.7.2.

***παντολέτης, ὁ,** *destroyer of all*, Gr.Naz.*carm*.1.2.15.88(M.37.772A).

***παντολμία, ἡ,** *complete audacity*, Isid.Pel.*epp*.1.326(M.78.372A); Areth.*Apoc*.8:11(M.106.617C).

***παντόλμως,** *with complete audacity*, Sophr.H.*ep.syn*.(M.87. 3173C).

παντομέδων, ὁ, *universal ruler*; of God, Eudoc.*Cypr*.1.229(M.85. 841A).

[*]**παντομιγής,** = παμμιγής, *embracing all* natures *in itself* τὰν π. φύσιν Synes.*hymn*.7.14(p.48; M.66.1612).

***παντομνημόνευτος,** *to be commemorated by all*; of BMV, Ephr. 3.528D; ‡Meth.*Sym.et Ann*.10(M.18.372C).

***παντομώμητος,** *wholly disgraceful*, ‡Chrys.*ep.mon*.(9.837B).

***παντόνως,** *with all diligence*, *A.Thadd*.5(p.275.18n.).

***παντοπάθεια, ἡ,** *universal suffering*, Areth.*Apoc*.8:9(M.106. 617B).

παντοπαθής, *subject to all passions*; of pagan gods, *Hom.Clem*.4. 12; *ib*.5.29.

***παντόπωλις, ἡ,** fem. of παντοπώλης, *general dealer*, Chrys.*hom. 12.5 in Col*.(11.419A).

παντοτρόφος, *giving food to all*, *Orac.Sib.fr*.1.5.

***παντοτύραννος,** *wholly tyrannical*, Nil.*epp*.2.178(M.79.292B).

***παντουργέτης, ὁ,** *worker of all things*; of Christ, El.H.*cant*.1.2 (p.289).

***παντουργέω,** *do everything*, Leont.H.*Nest*.1.48(M.86.1509A).

***παντούργητος,** *universally effective*; of Trin., ‡Jo.D.*Const*.2(M. 95.312A).

***παντουργία, ἡ,** *universal operation*, Geo.Pis.*hex*.57(M.92.1430A).

***παντουργικός,** *universally effective* θεὸς δυνάμει...παντουργικῇ, τουτέστι τῷ υἱῷ,...χρώμενος Cyr.*glaph.Gen*.1(1.4A); ἔχει...ὁ Χριστὸς ...τὸ π. ὡς θεὸς id.*Jo*.5.2(4.493A); *ib*.9(778A); βουλὴ δὲ καὶ θέλημα τὸ π. τοῦ...πατρὸς ὁ υἱός id.*hom.pasch*.29(5^2.337E); of H. Ghost, Jo.Mon.*hymn.Petr*.3(M.96.1392B).

παντουργός, 1. *accomplishing* or *effecting all things*; of God, Const.ap.Gel.Cyz.*h.e*.3.3.2; of Christ χεῖρα...τοῦ πατρὸς τὴν π. εἶναί φαμεν τὸν υἱόν Cyr.*Is*.4.2(2.611A); of H. Ghost, ‡Cyr.*Trin*.9(6^3.13C; M.77.1140B); of divine attributes, Cyr.*ador*.2(1.70E); id.*Jo*.11.4(4. 951B); Jo.D.*hom*.4.24(M.96.621C); of divine command, Max.*ambig*. (M.91.85D); of Christ's human will, Jo.D.*volunt*.32(M.95.169A); **2.** *wholly efficient*; of human body, Dion.Al.ap.Eus.*p.e*.14.26(780C; M.21.1284B).

παντοφαγία, ἡ, *indiscriminate eating, gluttony*, Melet.*nat.hom*. synops.(M.64.1113B).

***παντοφάγος,** *all-devouring*; of fire, Gr.Naz.*carm*.2.2(epigr.)83. 2(M.38.123A).

***παντοφίλητος,** *beloved of all*, Thdr.Stud.*epp*.2.29(M.99.1197D).

***παντωφελής,** *beneficial to all*, Sophr.H.*mir.Cyr.et Jo*.37(M.87. 3565B).

***πανυβρίζω,** *insult thoroughly*, Eus.Al.*serm*.9(M.86.364B).

***πανύμνητος,** *praised by all, worthy of all praise*; **1.** of God ἡ πανύμνητος...τριάς Ath.*hom.in Mt.11*:27(M.25.220A); τρεῖς π. ὑποστάσεις Didym.*Trin*.3.23(M.29.924C); Oecum.*Apoc*.19:6(p.201); Jo.Mon.*hymn.Petr*.3(M.96.1392C); **2.** of BMV, Ephr.3.526F; Cyr.S. *v.Sab*.32(p.117.9); Mod.*dorm*.9(M.86.3301A); Jo.Mosch.*prat*.187(M. 87.3064D); Anast.S.*hod*.20(M.89.272A); Jo.D.*hom*.9.18(M.96.748A); **3.** of fathers of Chalcedon, Sophr.H.*ep.syn*.(M.87.3185A); **4.** of a saint, Jo.Eleem.*v.Tych*.12(p.122); **5.** of Inc., ‡Meth.*Sym.et Ann.* 2(M.18.352B).

***πανυπέρτερος,** *wholly superior*, †Apoll.*met.Ps*.37 tit.(M.33. 1364B; πανυπέρτατος Teub. p.78).

***πανυπηκόως,** *in all obedience*, Thdr.Stud.*epp*.1.8(M.99.936B).

πανυστάτιος, *last of all*, Nonn.*par.Jo*.19:30(conj. for καὶ ὑστατίῳ M.43.904C).

***πανύψιστος,** *most high above all*, of Christ ὄνομα...Χριστοῦ τοῦ π. θεοῦ Nil.*epp*.2.140(M.79.261D); εὐχαριστεῖν...τῷ π. θεῷ *ib*.3.33(389B); *ib*.(389D); σκήνωμα...ἐξ οὗπερ ὁ π. ... θεὸς προσέλαβε τὸ...σῶμα Mod. *dorm*.13(M.86.3309B); of Zeus in formula prescribed to martyr εἰπέ· Δίε π., σῶζε τὸ πλῆθος τοῦτο *M.Con*.4.4.

***πανώνυμος,** *bearing every name*; of God, Gr.Naz.*carm*.1.1.29.13 (M.37.508A).

πανωφελής, *altogether beneficial*, Didym.*Trin*.3.38(M.39.972C).

***πανωφέλιμος,** = foreg., Mac.Aeg.*hom*.27 tit.(M.34.693A).

παξαμᾶς ([*]-μάτης, [*]-μήτης), ὁ, [*]παξαμίς, ἡ, *biscuit* -μητῶν Ephr.1.228D; Pall.*h.Laus*.22(p.72.4; -μάτας M.34.1081D); -μίδας *ib*.71(1258B; -μάτας p.168.2n.); *Apophth.Patr*.(M.65.276C); -μάτης *ib*.(241A); Jo.Mosch.*prat*.184(M.87.3056C).

παξαμάτιον (παξαμάδιον), τό, = foreg., *Apophth.Patr*.(M.65. 113C); παξαμάδιον Pall.*h.Laus*.22(p.72.12; M.34.1082B).

***παπαδία, ἡ,** *priest's wife*, †Jo.Jej.*serm*.(M.88.1921D); ἱερεὺς δείρας τὴν π. αὐτοῦ, μὴ λειτουργείτω αὐτῇ τῇ ἡμέρᾳ *Nomoc*.137(p.91).

***παπαδίτζης, ὁ,** *boy being trained by priest*, †Jo.Jej.*poenit*.(M.88. 1909B).

πάπας (παπᾶς, πάππας), ὁ, *papa, father*;

A. as title of respect; **1.** of priests τὸν π. Ἡραείσκον *PLond*.1914. 25 (unless Heraiscus is Meletian 'antipope' of Alexandria); Καὸρ π. Ἑρμουπόλεως *PLond*.417.3; *M.Thdot.1* 12(p.68); cf.Call.*v.Hyp*. (p.110); Jo.Mal.*chron*.14 p.362(M.97.537C); π. τῆς μεγάλης ἐκκλησίας *ib*.p.361(537A); Cyr.S.*v.Sab*.54(p.147.2); †Anast.S.*relat*.51(p.72); **2.** of bishops; **a.** in gen. σὺ [sc. Ὀπτάτος ὁ ἐπίσκοπος] π. ἡμέτερος εἶ, καὶ σὺ πρεσβύτερος *M.Perp*.13(p.83.5); παρακαλῶ σε, π. Ἡρακλεῖδα Or. *dial*.1(p.120.7); ἱερώτατε πάππα Gr.Thaum.*ep.can*.1(M.10.1020A); Lucn.*fr*.ap.*Chron.Pasch*.p.277(M.92.689B); ‡Pion.*v.Polyc*.27; Bas. *ep*.120(3.212B; M.32.540B); *ib*.121(212D; M.541A); ‡Just.*ep.Zen.et Ser*.1(M.6.1184A); **b.** of bishop of Alexandria, Dion.Al.ap.Eus.*h.e*. 7.7.4(M.20.648C); μακαρίῳ π. καὶ ἐπισκόπῳ ἡμῶν Ar.*ep.Alex*.(p.13. 2; M.26.708C); id.*ep.Eus*.(p.1.2; M.42.209C); Ischyras *ep*.(p.143.15; M.25.364C); Ath.*tom*.10(M.26.808B); Bas.*ep*.258.3(3.394B; M.952A); Epiph.*haer*.68.9(p.149.18; M.42.197D); Pall.*v.Chrys*.1(p.7.16; M.47. 8); τοῦ μακαρίου π. Ἀθανασίου Cyr.*ep*.44(p.36.4; 5².133D); Sophr.H. *epigr*.2 tit.(M.87.4009B); Ἰωάννης ὁ π. Ἀλεξανδρείας Max.*Pyrr*.(M. 91.333A); *Chron.Pasch*.p.382(M.92.977B); Jo.Mosch.*prat*.147(M.87. 3012A); προσεύξασθε ὑπὲρ τοῦ π. καὶ τοῦ ἐπισκόπου *Lit.Marc*.(p.115. 2); **c.** of bishop of Rome, Ursac.*ep.Jul*.(p.138.3; M.25.353B); Dam. Papa *anath*.ap.Thdt.*h.e*.5.11.1(3.1036); ὁ π. Ἰννοκέντιος Pall.*v. Chrys*.3(p.16.17; M.47.12); τοῦ μακαριωτάτου π. τῆς πόλεως Ῥώμης Petr.Rav.*ep*.(p.46.11; M.*PL*.54.744A); CChalc.*act*.3(*ACO* 2.1.2 p.79. 31; H.2.288A) al.; Δαμάσου τοῦ...π. τῆς πρεσβυτέρας Ῥώμης Justn. *conf*.(p.106.2; M.86.1029C); Jo.Mal.*chron*.18 p.483(M.97.700B); Cyr.S. *v.Sab*.32(p.118.12); Μαρτῖνος ὁ ἁγιώτατος...π. τῆς τῶν Ῥωμαίων ἁγίας τοῦ θεοῦ καθολικῆς καὶ ἀποστολικῆς ἐκκλησίας CLater.*act*.1(H. 3.705C); Jo.Mosch.*prat*.147(M.87.3012A).

B. name of archetypal Man in 'Phrygian' mysteries τὸ γὰρ ὄνομα τοῦ π. πάντων ὁμοῦ ἐστι τῶν ἐπουρανίων καὶ ἐπιγείων Hipp. *haer*.5.8(p.93.8; M.16.3146B).

παπ(π)ίας, ὁ, *little father*; in colloquial address to one's elders, *M.Con*.2(p.65.1); Pall.*h.Laus*.22(M.34.1081D); παπία (v.l. παππία) *ib*.(p.72.13; 1082B).

πάππος, ὁ, *grandfather*, in argument of 'tropici' that if H. Ghost is not a creature he is a son εἰ ἐκ τοῦ υἱοῦ λήψεται τὸ πνεῦμα... οὐκοῦν π. ὁ πατήρ, καὶ ἔκγονόν ἐστιν αὐτοῦ τὸ πνεῦμα Ath.*ep.Serap*. 4.1(M.26.637C); εὑρεθήσεται τοῦ μὲν υἱοῦ πατὴρ ὁ πατήρ, τῆς δὲ κτίσεως π. ‡Ath.*dial.Trin*.1.8(M.28.1129A).

παππῷος, *ancestral*, CCP(449)*act*.(*ACO* 2.1.1 p.151.23; H.2.176D).

παπυλιών (παπυλεών), ὁ, *pavilion, tent*, Cosm.Ind.*top*.5(v.l. παπυλεώνων M.88.212D); παπυλέων Jo.Mal.*chron*.5 p.114(M.97. 205C); *ib*.6 p.159(261C); *ib*.12 p.307(464B); *Chron.Pasch*.p.268(M.92. 660B).

παρά, A. c. genit.; **1.** *issuing* from; theol. τὸ πνεῦμα ἐκ τοῦ Χριστοῦ ἢ π. ἀμφοτέρων (ὥς φησιν ὁ Χριστός, 'ὃ π. τοῦ πατρὸς ἐκπορεύεται' καὶ 'οὗτος ἐκ τοῦ ἐμοῦ λήψεται') Epiph.*anc*.67(p.81.15; M.43.137B); *ib*.70(p.88.5; 148A); τὸν μὲν υἱὸν καλεῖ τὸν ἐξ αὐτοῦ, τὸ δὲ ἅγιον πνεῦμα τὸ π. ἀμφοτέρων *ib*.71(p.88.14; 148B); **2.** π. αὐτοῦ ἀγνοούμενος *unknown to him*, Thdt.*qu.39 in Num*.(1.246); **3.** *in the power of* ἄλλοι π. ὧν πλουτῆσαι οὐκ ἦν Chrys.*vid*.1.6(1.346B); **4.** *against* εἴ τις διακρίνοιτο π. πρεσβυτέρου γεγαμηκότος CGangr.*can*.4.

B. c. dat.; **1.** *in* writings π. τῇ θείᾳ γραφῇ Thdt.*Ps*.5:1(1.635); id.*Cant*.5:16(2.117); Olymp.*fr.Pr*.1:6(M.93.472A); π. τῷ Ἑβραίῳ *in the Hebrew text*, Thdt.*qu.61 in Gen*.(1.74); id.*Ps*.100:1(1.1312); *ib*.117:26(1435); *in* the Hebrew tongue, id.*Is*.8:9(p.43.15; 2.225); **2.** *by* ὁ π. αὐτῷ καλούμενος id.*qu.39 in Num*.(1.246); **3.** *at the hands of* π. τοῖς ἀλλοφύλοις ἔτισε...ποινήν id.*Ps*.26:2(1.769); **4.** = π. c. genit., *from* ζητῶν δὲ π. ἐμαυτῷ τί ἄρα ἦν τὸ ἐκπλῆξαν τοὺς πολλοὺς Eus.*d.e*.9.5(p.415.19; M.22.669B).

C. c. acc.; **1.** *on, upon* τρίχες...αἱ π. ὅλον τὸ σῶμα Clem.*paed*.3.3 (p.248.1; M.8.581C); **2.** *into* π. τὴν γῆν ὀρύττων Thdt.*h.rel*.19(3.1231); **3.** *in accordance with, because of*, Eus.*d.e*.5.2(p.217.33; M.22.360B); π. τοῦτο *by this statement*, *Hom.Clem*.18.18; **4.** *short of, without* π. ἐνίους τῶν δακτύλων ἐγένετο Synes.*ep*.79(M.66.1445B).

παραβαίν-ω, 1. *transgress*; **a.** natural laws, divine arrangement οὐ ~ουσι [sc. stars] τοὺς ἰδίους ὅρους κατὰ ἀπαραίτητον φύσεως ἀνάγκην Arist.*apol*.4.2; τῶν...περὶ τὴν τοῦ παντὸς κόσμου σύστασιν οὐδὲν ἄτακτον..., ἀλλ' ἕκαστον...γεγονὸς λόγῳ, διὸ οὐδὲ τὴν ὡρισμένην ἐπ' αὐτοῖς ~ουσι τάξιν Athenag.*leg*.25.3(M.6.949C); ἐπὰν δὲ παραβῇ τις τὸν λόγον καὶ διὰ τούτου τὸν θεόν Clem.*str*.7.16(p.70.22; M.9.537B); **b.** law ὅσοι...παρέβησαν τὸν νόμον ὃν ἔλαβον παρ' αὐτοῦ Herm.*sim*. 8.3.5; Mosaic law (ref. Christ healing on sabbath) οὐ ~ων, ἀλλ' ὑπερβαίνων τὸν νόμον Chrys.*hom.37.2 in Jo*.(8.314B); ἐγὼ μὲν οὖν εἰ καὶ ἔλυσα τὸν νόμον, φησίν, ἀλλὰ ἄνθρωπον σώσας· ὑμεῖς δὲ ~ετε ἐπὶ κακῷ *ib*.49.2(8.291B); τὰ πλείονα ~ομεν τῶν ἐπιταγμάτων *ib*.*87.3* (523E); pass. πολλοὺς...ἱερατικοὺς...παραβαθέντας θεσμούς CCP(536) *act*.4(p.180.21; H.2.1260D); **c.** oaths, promises, agreements πεποίθαμεν τῷ μόνῳ θεῷ, ὃν γιγνώσκομεν ὅτι οὐ παραβήσεται τὰ καλῶς ἡμῖν ἐπηγγελμένα Clem.*str*.2.6(p.128.6; M.8.964B); *ib*.7.8(p.38.16; M.9. 473A); *ib*.7.15(p.64.1,4; 525A); παραβεβηκέναι τὸν ὅρκον κυρίου καὶ τὴν διαθήκην Hipp.*Dan*.1.3.6(M.10.640C); **d.** social institution μοιχός ἐστι παρακεκαλυμμένος [sc. one who takes a second wife], ~ων... τὴν χεῖρα τοῦ θεοῦ, ὅτι ἐν ἀρχῇ ὁ θεὸς ἕνα ἄνδρα ἔπλασεν καὶ μίαν γυναῖκα Athenag.*leg*.33.2(M.6.968A); **e.** eccl. ἡμᾶς κατὰ μηδένα τρόπον τὸν ἐκκλησιαστικὸν ~ειν προσήκει κανόνα Clem.*str*.7.15(p.64.5; M.9.525A); pass. ἵνα μὴ τῶν πατέρων οἱ κανόνες ~ωνται CEph.(431) *act*.7(*ACO* 1.1.7 p.122.15; H.1.1620E); **2.** *disobey*, commands, esp. divine τοὺς ~οντας τὰ διατεταγμένα καλά Just.*2apol*.9.1(M.6.460A); τοῦ θεοῦ μὴ παραβὰς τὸ βούλημα Tat.*orat*.7(p.7.18; M.6.820B); ἡ...θεία γραφὴ τοὺς παραβάντας τὰς ἐντολὰς πεπρᾶσθαι λέγει τοῖς ἀλλογενέσι Clem.*str*.2.23(p.192.22; M.8.1096A); π. αὐτάς [sc. τὰς ἐντολάς] Or. *princ*.3.1.7(p.204.8; M.11.260A); παραβεβήκαμεν τὴν ἐντολὴν μὴ φυλαξάμενοι ποιῆσαι βιβλία πολλά id.*Jo*.5.1(p.100.10; M.14.188A); of fallen angels, Just.*2apol*.5.3(M.6.452B); Ἐνὼχ φησιν τοὺς παραβάντας ἀγγέλους διδάξαι τοὺς ἀνθρώπους ἀστρονομίαν καὶ μαντικὴν καὶ τὰς ἄλλας τέχνας Clem.*ecl*.53.4(p.152.8; M.9.724A); of Fall παραβάσῃ [sc. τῇ ψυχῇ]...τὴν ἐντολήν,...δεσμὸν αὐτῇ τὸ σῶμα διδόσθαι τιμωρόν Meth.*res*.1.29(p.260.10; M.41.1137C); μετὰ τὸ παραβῆναι τὸν ἄνθρωπον *ib*.1.44(p.292.1; M.18.273A); ὁ ἄνθρωπος μετὰ τὸ πεσεῖν ἤθελε... τῆς ἀφθαρσίας τοῦ παραδείσου τῆς τρυφῆς μὴ ἀποβληθῆναι, ἀλλ' ἀπεκρούσθη παραβάς id.*symp*.10.3(p.125.8; M.18.197A); ὁ Ἀδὰμ τὴν ἐντολὴν παραβάς, κατὰ δύο τρόπους ἀπώλετο· ἕνα μέν, ὅτι ἀπώλεσε τὸ κτῆμα τὸ καθαρὸν τῆς φύσεως αὐτοῦ,...ἕτερον δέ, ὅτι ἀπώλεσεν αὐτὴν τὴν εἰκόνα Mac.Aeg.*hom*.12.1(M.34.557A); ἓν οἶδα, ὅτι, εἰ μὴ ὁ Ἀδὰμ παρέβη, ἐγὼ τῆς τοῦ κακοῦ προσβολῆς πεῖραν οὐκ ἐλάμβανον Marc.Er. *opusc*.4(M.65.1013C); **3.** abs., *be a transgressor, do wrong* παρέβησαν, ὅτι ἄγγελος πονηρὸς ἐσόφιζεν αὐτούς *Barn*.9.4; Just.*dial*.141.1(M.6. 797B); Clem.*paed*.3.4(p.252.5; M.8.593A); ἀκρασίᾳ γνώμης παραβῆναι id.*q.d.s*.(p.171.18; M.9.621D); pass. δίκην εἰσπράττεται τῶν παραβαθέντων Olymp.*fr.Job* 33:30(M.93.356A); **4.** *desert, betray* διὰ τὸ ὑπὸ Σαβελλίου συχνῶς κατηγορεῖσθαι ὡς παραβάντα τὴν πρώτην πίστιν, ἐφεῦρεν αἵρεσιν τοιάνδε Hipp.*haer*.9.12(p.248.24; M.16.3383C); πρὸς αὐτοὺς οὓς παρέβη θεοὺς ἀράμενος τὰ ὅπλα Eus.*v.C*.2.5(p.43.4; M.20.984B); μικρὸν γάρ, ἐὰν ἀνδρωθῇ ὁ υἱὸς αὐτοῦ ὁ Καῖσαρ, πάντως καὶ ἐμὲ ~ει. ἐγὼ δὲ οὐ παρέβην αὐτόν, ἀλλὰ καὶ αὐτὸν ἐποίησα ἐπὶ τόπῳ πατρίκιον καὶ στρατηλάτην Jo.Mal.*chron*.15 p.382(M.97.568A);

μὴ ~ῶμεν τὸν Χριστόν *Didasc.Jac.*5.4(p.74.12); **5.** *lapse* from the faith (cf. παραπίπτω) περὶ τῶν παραβάντων χωρὶς ἀνάγκης CNic.(325) *can.*11.

παράβακχος, *disorderly* π. ... τὴν ἡμετέραν εὑρόντες παράταξιν, τέλεον ταύτην κατέβαλον †Jo.D.*B.J.*29(M.96.1133C).

παραβαλανεύς, ὁ, *sick-nurse* οἱ μονάζοντες καὶ οἱ παραβαλανεῖς CChalc.*act.*1(*ACO* 2.1.1 p.179.28; H.2.213D); cf. *LS* s. παραβολᾶνοι.

παραβάλλ-ω, A. trans.; **1.** *throw* at λόγους ψευδεῖς σοι παραβαλών Or.*hom.5.17 in Jer.*(p.47.11; M.13.321C); esp. of throwing to wild beasts, *M.Polyc.*11.1; pass. ὁρᾷς ~ομένους θηρίοις, ἵνα ἀρνήσωνται τὸν κύριον, καὶ μὴ νικωμένους; *Diogn.*7.7; hence *feed* τοὺς λέοντας... ὑποδέχεσθαι αὐτόν, καὶ ἐν τῷ κόλπῳ αὐτοῦ ~ειν αὐτοῖς Jo.Mosch. *prat.*2(M.87.2853C); λεοπάρδῳ ἀπὸ χειρὸς παρέβαλεν Jo.Clim.*scal.*7 (M.88.812D); **2.** *expose*, esp. to danger πρὸς πάντα...τὰ δεινὰ παρέβαλλον αὐτούς *Ep.Lugd.*ap.Eus.*h.e.*5.1.54(M.20.429A); reflex. κινδύνῳ ἑαυτὴν παρέβαλεν *1Clem.*55.6; κινδύνῳ παραβαλοῦμεν ἑαυτούς Or.*Jo.*20.2(p.328.23; M.14.576A); Chrys.*hom.3.6 in Heb.*(12.37C); pass., id.*hom.44.1 in 1Cor.*(v.l. for παρεμβεβλημένος 10.406E); πρὸς τὴν Θρᾳκῶν χιόνα ~όμενον Synes.*ep.*61(M.66.1404D); ~όμενος ἐπὶ βασκάνων μαρτύρων *ib.*131(1513D); *hazard* καθάπερ καὶ αὐτὸς ὁ κύριος διασαφήσας...τὰς γραφὰς καὶ οἱ τούτου γνώριμοι οἱ κηρύξαντες τὸν λόγον ὡσαύτως μετ' αὐτὸν τὸ ζῆν παρεβάλοντο Clem.*str.*6.15 (p.496.24; M.9.352B); **3.** med., *incite* ἐπὶ ἀπροαιρέτῳ καὶ πράγματι ἀδιαφόρῳ ἐπαιρούμενοι, οὐδὲ πιθανότητα εὔλογον ἔχουσι τὴν ~ομένην αὐτοὺς ἐπὶ τὸ ἐπαίρεσθαι Or.*hom.12.8 in Jer.*(p.94.20; M.13.389A); **4.** *submit* for examination συνόδους δὲ γενέσθαι προστάξαι [sc. τὸν Κωνστάντιον] δύο,...αἳ τὰ παρ' ἑκατέρου μέρους λεγόμενα δοκιμασίαις ἔμελλον ~ειν Philost.*h.e.*4.10(M.65.524B); **5.** *put side by side, identify* τὰ οἰκεῖα καὶ πατρικὰ ~ων Max.*qu.Theop.*(M.90.1397A); *compare* or *contrast*, Or.*Cant.*3(p.179.24; M.13.149D); ἀσεβὲς...τὸ τὸν κτίστην τοῖς δι' αὐτοῦ κεκτισμένοις δημιουργήμασι ~ειν Ath.*syn.*26.8(p.253.31; M.26.733A); ref. entombment of Christ μὴ ~ε ταῦτα τοῖς ἀνθρωπίνοις Chrys.*hom.85.5 in Jo.*(8.510E); Philost.*h.e.*8.18(M.65.568B); pass. οὐχ οὕτως ἔσται εὐαγγέλιον τὸ κατὰ τὰς ἐπιστολὰς πᾶν γράμμα, ὅταν ~ηται τῇ διηγήσει τῶν περὶ Ἰησοῦ πράξεων καὶ παθημάτων καὶ λόγων αὐτοῦ Or.*Jo.*1.3(5; p.7.24; M.14.29A); id.*Cant.*1:4 (p.liii, cf.p.113.24ff.; M.17.256B); *be comparable* οὐδὲ γὰρ ῥύπῳ ~εται id.*hom.2.2 in Jer.*(p.18.29; M.13.230C); Meth.*symp.*3.3(p.30.2; M.18.64C); idea of contrast predominant τὴν γῆν ἔτι περικείμενοι καὶ [γῆ] πρὸς τὸ μέγεθος ~όμενοι τοῦ κυρίου Clem.*fr.*36(p.219.2; M.9.769A); ἵνα μικρὰ καὶ ἐπίκηρα μεγάλοις καὶ ἀφθάρτοις παραβάλωμεν id.*q.d.s.*3(p.161.22; M.9.608A); οὐ τὴν ἱστορίαν ἐκβάλλων, ἀλλὰ τῇ ἀληθείᾳ ~ων τὸν τύπον Thdt.*qu.Jos.*proem.(1.299); pass., *be equivalent* to 'ἀρχήν' δὲ λέγω οὐ τὴν ~ομένην ἐξουσίᾳ ἀλλὰ τὴν ἀντιδιαστελλομένην τέλει καὶ παρακειμένην πρώτῳ Or.*Jo.*13.37(p.263.1; M.14.464C); *represent by a parable* τῷ ᾆδη προσεοικέναι τὸν...ἔρωτα [sc. τῆς πόρνης] παρέβαλεν ὁ Σολομῶν Chrys.*hom.87.4 in Jo.*(8.525A); σκιᾷ καὶ τροχῷ τὰ λυπηρὰ τοῦ βίου καὶ τὰ φαιδρὰ ~ε· ὡς γὰρ σκιὰ οὐ μένει, καὶ ὡς τροχὸς κυλίεται Nil.*paraen.*123(M.79.1260D); ζύμην δοκεῖ μοι διδασκαλίαν καὶ τὴν εἰς αὐτὸν πίστιν ~ειν ὁ κύριος ‡Caes.Naz.*dial.*180(M.38.1152); pass. ὄψιμον...σῦκον οὐκ ἔστιν ᾧ ~εται ὁ σωζόμενος Or.*fr.22 in Jer.*(p.209.19).

B. intrans.; **1.** *arrive* παρέβαλον ἀδελφοὶ ἀπὸ κοινοβίου τῆς Αἰγύπτου *Apophth.Patr.*(M.65.236C); by sea εἰς Σελεύκειαν παρεβάλομεν *Hom.Clem.*14.7; **2.** *enter* οὔτε...εἰς κώμην, οὔτε εἰς πόλιν, οὔτε εἰς κοινὸν σύλλογον ἀνδρῶν παρέβαλεν Eus.*d.e.*9.5(p.415.28; M.22.669C); οὐκ ἐπέτρεπον...ὅλως εἰς τὴν ἐκκλησίαν τοῦ θεοῦ ~ειν Ath. *apol.sec.*46(p.122.19; M.25.333A); Nil.*epp.*1.41(M.79.101C); **3.** *visit* ἀδελφὸς παρέβαλε τῷ ἀββᾷ Ἀκμώνῃ, αἰτούμενος παρ' αὐτοῦ λόγον *Apophth.Patr.*(M.65.128A); *have audience* with, Dor.*doct.*16 tit.(M.88.1793C); Leont.H.*monoph.*(M.86.1900B); **4.** *attend* a meeting ὁ μὲν ὄκνῳ, ὁ δὲ δειλίᾳ, οὐ ~ουσι τῇ συνάξει Chrys.*ep.*210(3.717A); εἰ τελεῖται σύναξις ἐν ἐκκλησίᾳ παράβαλε Nil.*paraen.*105(M.79.1260A); Thdt.*ep.*160(4.1330); **5.** *break in* upon ἐπὰν τῇ συντόνῳ σου νηστείᾳ ἀδελφὸς παραβάλῃ Nil.*Eulog.*25(M.79.1125D); **6.** *have access to* πῶς ἄγγελοι μὲν καὶ δαίμονες τῷ ἡμετέρῳ ~ουσι κόσμῳ, ἡμεῖς δὲ τοῖς αὐτῶν κόσμοις οὐ ~ομεν; †Nil.*mal.cog.*20(M.79.1222D–1224A); **7.** *associate with* ~ειν τῇ τοῦ σωτῆρος διατριβῇ Eus.*d.e.*10.1(p.451.12; M.22.725B); σπανίως ~όντων τοῖς ἀδελφοῖς †Nil.*mal.cog.*11(M.79.1213B); καθίσαι εἰς τὸ κελλίον ἥμισύ ἐστι, καὶ τὸ παραβαλεῖν γέρουσι ἥμισύ ἐστι Dor.*doct.*16.1(M.88.1793C); Jo.D.*spir.neq.*4(M.95.80B).

***παράβαμα, τό,** *transgression*, Ephr.3.329D.

παραβαπτίζω, *baptize in separation from the Church, perform schismatic baptism*; practice prohibited by law, Justn.*nov.*42.3.1 (p.268.8); τοῦ...βασιλέως κελεύσαντος μήτε παρασυνάξαι μήτε π. CCP (536)*act.*1(*ACO* 3 p.139.1; H.2.1205E).

***παραβάπτισμα, τό,** *separate baptism, baptism by those in schism*, Thdr.Lect.*exc.Vat.*44(p.59 not.2) cit. s. παρασύναγμα; *Ep.*ap.CCP (536)*act.*1(*ACO* 3 p.132.32; H.2.1196D); *Libell.ib.*(*ACO* 3 p.137.11; H.2.1204C); *ib.act.*5(*ACO* 3 p.43.10; 1292C); Epiph.CP *sent.*(*ACO* 3 p.111.25; M.86.785D); Max.*ep.*12(M.91.464B); Ath.Scholast.*coll.*1.5 (p.16); *ib.*3 paratit.1(p.48).

παραβαπτιστής, ὁ, *administrator of schismatic baptism*, CCP (536)*act.*4(*ACO* 3 p.181.19; H.2.1261C).

παραβασία, ἡ, *dishonesty*, *Libell.*ap.CCP(536)*act.*5(*ACO* 3 p.41.6; H.2.1288D); *Chron.Pasch.*p.333(M.92.864C).

παράβασις, ἡ, I. *transgression*;

A. in gen. μεγάλας θλίψεις ἔσχες...διὰ τὰς π. τοῦ οἴκου σου Herm. *vis.*2.3.1; π. ἐντολῶν Clem.*q.d.s.*18(p.171.27; M.9.624A); *A.Phil.*143 (p.84.1); Bas.*reg.fus.*11(2.353E; M.31.948B); Chrys.*hom.57.2 in Jo.* (8.334A).

B. ref. original sin; **1.** Adam's sin as ἡ τῆς ἐντολῆς π. Marc.Er. *opusc.*4(M.65.1616A); **2.** ref. man's state before Adam's transgression τὸν ἄνθρωπον πρὸ μὲν τῆς π. πῇ μὲν βλέποντα πῇ δὲ μὴ βλέποντα Or.*Cels.*7.39(p.189.24; M.11.1476B); συκῇ διὰ τὴν γλυκασίαν καὶ τὸν ὡραϊσμὸν τὴν τρυφὴν τὴν πρὸ τῆς π. ἐν παραδείσῳ τοῦ ἀνθρώπου παρίστησι γεγενημένην Meth.*symp.*10.2(p.124.5; M.18.196B); τὸ σῶμα σῶμα δόξης ἦν πρὸ τῆς π., καὶ οὕτως ἔνδοξον ἦν, ὅτι νῦν μετὰ τὴν π. σῶμα ταπεινώσεως λέγεται id.*res.*3.14(p.410.32ff.); Messalian καὶ πρὸ τῆς π. ἀπαθῶς ἐκοινώνησεν ὁ Ἀδὰμ τῇ Εὔᾳ Jo.D.*haer.*80(M.94.732A); v. Ἀδάμ; **3.** causes of transgression ἡ π. διὰ τοῦ ὄφεως ἐν Εὔᾳ ἐγένετο *Barn.*12.5; θηρίον, δι' οὗ ἡ π. ... τὴν ἀρχὴν ἔλαβεν Just.*dial.* 112.3(M.6.733C); τὴν π. ὑπὸ τοῦ Ἀδὰμ γενέσθαι ἐργασαμένου *ib.*94.2 (700B); ἡ προκατάρξασα τῆς π. [sc. Eve] Clem.*str.*3.9(p.225.30; M.8.1168A); v. ἁμαρτία; **4.** universality κατεδικάσθησαν ἐν τῷ ὁμοιώματι τῆς π. Ἀδάμ, οὐχ οὕτως περὶ ἑνός τινος ὡς περὶ ὅλου τοῦ γένους ταῦτα φάσκοντος τοῦ θείου λόγου Or.*Cels.*4.40(p.313.21; M.11.1093B); **5.** effects; **a.** death, *Barn.*12.5; ἦν γὰρ ἡμῶν καὶ πρόσθεν ἄπτωτος ἡ σκηνή· ἀλλὰ διὰ τὴν π. ἐσαλεύθη καὶ ἐκλίθη Meth.*symp.*9.2(p.116.12; M.18.181A); id.*res.*2.21(p.375.3; M.18.285C); **b.** expulsion from paradise, id.*symp.*3.3(p.29.24; 64C); *ib.*4.2(p.46.16; 88C); Cyr.H.*catech.* 19.9; **c.** loss of grace and glory οὐδέπω γὰρ τῆς ἁμαρτίας ὑπεισελθούσης...τῇ ἄνωθεν ἦσαν δόξῃ ἠμφιεσμένοι...μετὰ δὲ τὴν π. τῆς ἐντολῆς, τότε καὶ ἡ αἰσχύνη ἐπεισῆλθε, καὶ ἡ γνῶσις τῆς γυμνότητος Chrys.*hom.15.4 in Gen.*(4.120D); ἐπειδὴ δὲ διὰ τὴν π. ἐκολάζετο... ἀπεγυμνώθη τῆς χάριτος Cyr.*Jo.*1.9(4.95A); **d.** ref. view that material human bodies are consequence of sin committed by souls in a purely spiritual state τοὺς δερματίνους...χιτῶνας, οὓς διὰ τὴν π. τῶν ἀνθρώπων ἐποίησε τοῖς ἁμαρτήσασιν ὁ θεός Or.*Cels.*4.40(p.313.27; M.11.1093B); δερμάτινοι χιτῶνες being interpreted by Or. as bodies—v. χιτών; ἀνάγκη γάρ μοι (δεδωκότι τοὺς δερματίνους χιτῶνας εἶναι τὰ σώματα) ὁμολογεῖν, καὶ πρὶν εἰς τὸ σῶμα τὴν ψυχὴν ἐληλυθέναι ἡμαρτηκέναι, ἀνθ' ὧν πρὸ τῆς κατασκευῆς αὐτῶν ἡ π. ἐγένετο (διὰ τὴν π. γὰρ οἱ χιτῶνες αὐτοῖς κατασκευάζονται, καὶ οὐχ ἡ π. διὰ τοὺς χιτῶνας γίγνεται) Meth.*res.*1.29(p.261.4ff.; M.41.1137D); stating view of Or. οὐ δεσμὸν τὸ σῶμα διὰ τὴν π. δέδωκας εἶναι τῆς ψυχῆς; *ib.*1.31 (p.266.19; M.41.1141D); refuted ἤρκει...ἀπὸ τῆς γραφῆς αὐτῆς ἀποδείξαντα πρὸ τῆς π. τὸν πρωτόπλαστον ἐκ ψυχῆς καὶ σώματος ὄντα *ib.*1.58(p.319.20; M.41.1153C); **e.** marriage and unlawful pleasure as consequence of π.: ἡ δὲ π. τῆς ἐντολῆς τὸν γάμον εἰσήγαγε διὰ τὸ ἀνομῆσαι τὸν Ἀδάμ Ath.*exp.Ps.*50:7(M.27.240C), cit. Max.*qu.dub.*3 (M.90.788A,B); ἀναίτιον δέ φημι τὴν ἐκ τῆς π. ἡδονήν, ὡς μὴ γενομένην δηλονότι προλαβόντος πόνου διάδοχον. οὐκοῦν...μετὰ τὴν π. πάντες οἱ ἄνθρωποι τὴν ἡδονὴν εἶχον τῆς ἰδίας φυσικῶς προκαθηγουμένην γενέσεως id.*qu.Thal.*61(M.90.628C); ἀρχὴν ἔσχε μετὰ τὴν π. ἡ τῶν ἀνθρώπων φύσις τῆς ἰδίας γενέσεως τὴν καθ' ἡδονὴν ἐκ σπορᾶς σύλληψιν id.*cap.*4.46(M.90.1325B); **f.** other effects εἰς μόχθους καὶ πόνους διὰ τὴν π. τέξεσθαι τὴν γυναῖκα Clem.*str.*5.14(p.414.9; M.9.192B); κατηραμένη ἐν τοῖς ἔργοις τῆς π. τοῦ Ἀδὰμ γῇ Or.*Cels.*7.28(p.179.21; M.11.1461A); τὸ σκότος τοῦ αἰῶνος τούτου ἐπικείμενον πάσῃ τῇ κτίσει καὶ πάσῃ φύσει ἀνθρώπου ἀπὸ τῆς π. Mac.Aeg.*hom.*43.7(M.34.777A); estrangement from God, *ib.*24.2(664A); Ammonas *ep.*1(p.432.5); δεσπότης γὰρ ἦν ὁ ἄνθρωπος, ἀπὸ τοῦ οὐρανοῦ καὶ τῶν κάτω,...διὰ δὲ τῆς π. ἀπολωλώς ἐστι, καὶ τετραυματισμένος Mac.Aeg.*hom.*26.1(676B); passibility, Max.*ambig.*(M.91.1041C); division, id.*cap.theol.*2.8(M.90.1128C); **g.** discussion of consequences of Adam's transgression for his descendants εἰ τὴν τοῦ Ἀδὰμ π. κατὰ ἀνάγκην οὐ παρεδεξάμεθα;...οὐκ ἔστι τοῦ Ἀδὰμ π., ἀλλ' ἔλεγχος τῆς ἑκάστου ἡδυπαθείας. ἀλλ' οὐδὲ τὴν π. διεδεξάμεθα...οὐδὲ γὰρ πάντες παραβαίνομεν τὴν ἐντολήν, οὐδὲ πάντες φυλάττομεν. ὅθεν δῆλον, ὅτι οὐ κατὰ ἀνάγκην ἐστίν, ἀλλ' ἡδυπάθεια ἡ π. εἰ δὲ λέγεις διὰ ταύτην ἐληλυθέναι τὸν κύριον· διὰ τί ταύτην οὐκ ἀνῄρει ἐν τῷ βαπτίσματι, ἀλλ' ἔτι καὶ νῦν ἕκαστος ἐξουσίαν ἔχει παραβῆναι, ἢ μὴ παραβῆναι; οὐκοῦν τὴν π. προαιρετικὴν οὖσαν...οὐδεὶς ἐξ ἀνάγκης διεδέξατο· τὸν δὲ ἐκ ταύτης θάνατον ἀναγκαστικὸν ὄντα διεδεξάμεθα...οὐκοῦν οὐ τὴν π. διεδεξάμεθα, ἐπειδὴ κἀκεῖνον ἐξ ἀνάγκης ἐκράτησεν, ὃς ἐβασίλευσε καὶ ἐπὶ τοὺς μὴ ἁμαρτήσαντας ἐπὶ τῷ ὁμοιώματι τῆς π. Ἀδάμ Marc.Er.*opusc.*4(M.65.1017B–D); **6.** of Adam's sin as healed τοῦ πρώτου ἀνθρώπου...διὰ τοῦ ξύλου τοῦ σταυροῦ ζωοποιηθέντος ἐκ τοῦ θανάτου τῆς π. *A.Phil.*140 (p.74.7); ἡ ἡμῶν π. τοῦ λόγου τὴν φιλανθρωπίαν ἐξεκαλέσατο, ὥστε καὶ εἰς ἡμᾶς φθάσαι Ath.*inc.*4.2(M.25.104A); **7.** as foreseen by God τῶν ὅλων ποιητὴς προεώρα τοῦ Ἀδὰμ τὴν π. Thdt.*Rom.*8:20(3.88); **8.** as taking place on day of his creation, Cosm.Ind.*top.*2(M.88.124D).

II. *betrayal, desertion*; of apostasy π. τοῦ Χριστιανισμοῦ καὶ τροπὴν εἰς εἰδωλολατρείαν Gr.Nyss.*Eun.*8(2 p.178.29; M.45.772B).

III. *going bad* οἴνου γὰρ π. τὸ ὄξος Diod.*Ps.*67:20(M.33.1605B).

IV. *approach, coming forward* συνέρρει πάντα [sc. ζῷα] πρὸς τὸν Ἀδὰμ τῇ π. τὴν δουλείαν ὁμολογοῦντα Bas.Sel.*or.*2.3(M.85.41A); but cf. οὐκ ἴσχυσεν οὐδὲ π. σαλεῦσαι τὰς κλήσεις [sc. τῶν ζῴων] *ib.*(41B).

παραβάτης, ὁ, 1. *one who steps aside, transgressor* (of) ὧν ἤδη π. Apollon.ap.Eus.*h.e.*5.18.9(M.20.477C); ἀλάστορά τε καὶ π. Meth. *symp.*2.4(p.20.21; M.18.53B); π. τοῦ νόμου Eus.*d.e.*1.7(p.35.13; M.22.70B); Μωσέως π. *Const.App.*5.4.9; π. τῆς πατρίας διδασκαλίας Gr. Nyss.*v.Mos.*(M.44.329D); π. τοῦ νόμου Chrys.*hom.52.1 in Jo.*(8.305C); **2.** *renegade, apostate* π. μὲν γενόμενος, πατριώτης δὲ ὢν τοῦ Γρηγορίου Ath.*ep.encycl.*3(p.171.27; M.25.228B); π. ἐκ Χριστιανῶν *ib.*5(p.174.23; 233B); id.*h.Ar.*9(p.188.17; M.25.705A); esp. of Julian, *V.Aberc.*66(p.47.10); Philost.*h.e.*7.15(M.65.553A); *Chron.Pasch.*p.295 (M.92.740A); ‡Jo.D.*Artem.*7,8(M.96.1257Cf.).

παραβατικός, *perverting, being a perversion of* Κέλσου νομίζοντος Ἰουδαϊκὸν εἶναι τὸ προσκυνεῖν οὐρανῷ καὶ τοῖς ἐν αὐτῷ ἀγγέλοις, οὐκ Ἰουδαϊκὸν μὲν τὸ τοιοῦτον, παραβατικὸν δὲ Ἰουδαϊσμοῦ Or.*Cels.*5.8 (p.8.8; M.11.1192A).

παραβατός, *to be traversed,* hence *to be accomplished* ὅσα κατὰ τοῦτον ἔστιν ἡδέα τὸν π. βίον εὑρεῖν Gr.Nyss.*infant.*(M.46.180B); τὰς συνθήκας παραβάτους τηρεῖτε Thdr.Mops.*Mal.*2:16(M.66.617B) error for ἀπαρα-.

παραβιάζ-ομαι, 1. *force* to do, *M.Polyc.*4.1 cit. s. ἑκών; **2.** *persuade, prevail upon* παρεβιασάμην αὐτοὺς ἵνα...ἀναπαύσονται *A.Petr. et Andr.*7(p.121.7); παρεβιάσατο ἡμᾶς καὶ ἐπεμείναμεν *A.Xanthipp.* 38(p.84.26); ~ομένου αὐτὸν τοῦ μεῖναι *Mir.Artem.*40(p.66.22); **3.** *strengthen, bolster up* τοῦ λαοῦ ~ομένους τὴν ἀσθένειαν Pall.*v. Chrys.*18(p.112.12; M.47.62).

παραβιβάζω, 1. *corrupt* τί πρὸς τὸ χεῖρον παρεβιβάσθη; Cyr.*Juln.* 10(6^2.327D); **2.** abs., *act unjustly* 'οὐ μὴ ἀδικήσω', ἀντὶ τοῦ 'οὐ μὴ παραβιβάσω' Thdt.*Ps.*88:34(1.1242).

παραβλάπτ-ω, 1. *injure*; **a.** abs. οὐ πρὸς τὰ μέλλοντα ~ουσι μόνον Chrys.*hom.26.5 in Mt.*(7.321B); pass., Iren.*haer.*1.6.2(M.7.508A); τῆς κεφαλῆς παραβλαβείσης, ὅλον τὸ σῶμα ἄχρηστον γίνεται Chrys. *stat.*1.3(2.6A); **b.** with object τοὺς φθονουμένους παραβλάψειε id. *hom.16.1 in Jo.*(8.89E); pass. εἰς τὴν περὶ τῆς ἀναστάσεως ~ονται πίστιν id.*hom.40.3 in 1Cor.*(10.382E); c. ἀπό, id.*hom.9.5 in Heb.*(12.100C); c. ἐκ, id.*hom.1.3 in Rom.*(9.434D); c. παρά, id.*hom.13.2 in Phil.*(11.300D); **c.** of spiritual injury τοὺς βαπτιζομένους [sc. ὑπὸ τοῦ Ζωσίμου] εἰς τὰ καίρια καὶ ἀναγκαιότατα ἡγῇ ~εσθαι. ὁ τελούμενος οὐδὲν ~εται εἰς τὰ σωτηριώδη σύμβολα, εἰ ὁ ἱερεὺς μὴ εὖ βιοὺς εἴη Isid. Pel.*epp.*2.37(M.78.480C); esp. of damage to εὐσέβεια, Gr.Nyss.*Eun.*3 (2 p.33.9; M.45.600A); τι τῶν τὴν εὐσέβειαν ~όντων Chrys.*hom.5.4 in Heb.*(12.59A); μηδὲν τὴν εὐσέβειαν ~ων *ib.30.1*(280B); **2.** *be a disadvantage to,* Diod.*fat.*ap.Phot.*cod.*223(M.103.857C); οὐκ ἄρα παραβλάψει τὸν ἀλλογενῆ τὸ νόθον τοῦ γένους Proc.G.*Is.*56:1(M.87.2565D); **3.** *impair* οἱ ἀστέρες...οὐδὲν εἰς τὸ οἰκεῖον ~ονται κάλλος Chrys.*hom. 8.4 in Phil.*(11.261E); Melet.*nat.hom.*synops.(M.64.1129D); *cat.Gal.* 3:18(p.53.29) for βλαβῆς, Chrys.*comm.in Gal.*3:16ff.(10.701E; λάβης Gaume); **4.** *prevent, hinder* μηδὲν...πρὸς τὸ γενέσθαι κρίνον παραβλαβεῖσα Gr.Nyss.*hom.4 in Cant.*(M.44.841C); Chrys.*comm.in Gal.* 1:7(10.667D); **5.** *rob* τὸ θεῖον ἴσθι τοι ~ων ἀνάθημα, καὶ χρήμασιν ἱεροῖς τὰς χεῖρας ἐπάγων Cyr.*ador.*7(1.239A); pass., *be cheated of* οὐδὲ μέλλων αὐτὸς εἰς τὸν τοῦ κόπου τούτου ~εσθαι μισθόν Chrys.*hom.13.1 in Jo.*(8.71E).

***παραβλεπτέον,** *one must neglect* οὐ π. ... τὰ αὐτὰ πάλιν διαγορεῦσαι Gel.Cyz.*h.e.*2.17.9(M.85.1268A).

παραβλέπ-ω, 1. *see wrongly, distortedly* οἱ ~οντες,...τῇ διεφθαρμένῃ ὄψει Chrys.*hom.10.1 in 1Cor.*(10.81B); οὕτω ~ει καὶ οὕτω παρακούει Bas.*hom.*14.3(2.124C; M.31.449A); **2.** *look askance at, despise* χήραν παρορῶσι...καὶ πρεσβύτην ~ουσι δίκαιον Clem.*paed.*3.4(p.253.27; M.8.597B); Serap.*Man.*52(p.75; M.18.1253B); **3.** *look away from, neglect, ignore* χήρας ἐπισκέπτεσθε καὶ μὴ ~ετε αὐτάς Herm.*sim.*1.8; τὰς...σπουδὰς ~ων, πρὸς ἓν ἀφεώρα μόνον Gr.Nyss.*v.Gr.Thaum.*(M.46.933D); †Jo.D.*B.J.*9(M.96.933B); med., Mac.Mgn.*apocr.*2.8(p.10.10).

παράβλεψις, ἡ, 1. *carelessness,* Cyr.*ador.*1(1.17B); **2.** *ignoring* of περὶ π. ἐνδεοῦς †Jo.Jej.*poenit.*(M.88.1924C).

παραβλήδην, *by way of parable* Χριστὸς...μύθους δ' ἀγόρευε π. Gr.Naz.*carm.*1.1.25.2(M.37.476A); Nonn.*par.Jo.*16:25(M.43.881B).

***παράβλησις, ἡ,** *presentation* ἡ π. τῆς ὁμοιώσεως οὐ δι' ἕτερόν τι... ἐξείληπτο, ἢ διὰ μόνην ἀναίρεσιν τῶν ἐγνωσμένων ἑτέρων συνθέσεως Leont.H.*Nest.*1.14(M.86.1456B).

***παραβλώπισμα, τό,** *distorted view,* Leont.H.*monoph.*(M.86.1861C).

***παραβόλαιον, τό,** ? *border,* hence *district, Vaticin.*1(p.47).

παραβολεύ-ομαι, 1. *expose oneself to* danger, *venture* οἱ ἐν τῷ κόσμῳ ἔμποροι διὰ τὸ κέρδος...ἕως θανάτου ~ονται *V.Alex.Acoem.*5 (p.660.2); **2.** *give in parable form,* pass. τῆς τότε παραβολευθείσης ἀληθείας Epiph.*haer.*64.71(p.519.21; M.41.1197A).

παραβολή, ἡ, 1. *comparison,* Gr.Thaum.*pan.Or.*10(p.25.22; M.10.1081B); τὰ περὶ θεοῦ...ἐκ τῆς πρὸς τὴν κτίσιν π. ἔστι νοῆσαι *Hom. Clem.*3.48; cf.*ib.*3.42; **2.** *illustration, simile,* Chrys.*hom.79.1 in Jo.*(4.466A); προσέθηκε τὴν π. ... τεθνηκότα κύνα...ἑαυτὸν ὀνομάζει Thdt.*qu.57 in 1Reg.*(1.392); **3.** *narrative composed to illustrate an argument, hypothetical case* συσκευασάμενοι τὴν κατὰ τὴν γυναῖκα καὶ τοὺς ἕπτα ἀδελφοὺς π. Meth.*res.*1.51(p.305.1; M.18.281A); **4.** *saying* or *narrative illustrating a truth external to itself* (esp. a spiritual truth), or *expressing spiritual truth in form of a story, parable*; **a.** def. τοιοῦτον γὰρ ἡ π., λόγος ἀπό τινος οὐ κυρίου μέν, ἐμφεροῦς δὲ τῷ κυρίῳ ἐπὶ τἀληθὲς καὶ κύριον ἄγων τὸν συνιέντα, ἤ, ὥς τινές φασι, λέξις δι' ἑτέρων τὰ κυρίως λεγόμενα μετ' ἐνεργείας παριστάνουσα Clem.*str.* 6.15(p.495.30; M.9.349C); πολυσήμαντον τὸ ὄνομα τῆς π. ἔστι γὰρ π. λάλημα καὶ ἀπόδειγμα καὶ ὀνειδισμός. καὶ π. ἐστι λόγος παραβάλλων τὰ νοητὰ τοῖς αἰσθητοῖς καὶ παριστῶν ἐκ τῶν ἐγκοσμίων καὶ ὁρατῶν τὰ ὑπερκόσμια καὶ ἀόρατα ‡Hipp.*fr.32 in Pr.*(p.169.1); π. ἐστι λόγος ὡς περὶ γενομένου τοῦ μὴ γενομένου κατὰ τὸ ῥητόν, δυναμένου δὲ γενέσθαι, τροπικῶς δηλωτικὸς τῶν πραγμάτων ἐκ μεταλήψεως τῶν ἐν τῇ π. λεγομένων· ἢ λόγος ἀπό τινος οὐ κύριον μὲν ἐμφορῶν τῷ κυρίῳ, ἐπὶ δὲ τὸ ἀληθὲς καὶ κύριον ἄγων τὸν συνιέντα Or.*Ps.*77:2(p.111); ἡ μὲν π. ἐστι λόγος ὁμοιότητα περιέχων τοῦ γεγονότος πράγματος πρὸς τὸ ἐσόμενον ‡Just.*qu.et resp.*60(M.6.1301D); **b.** opp. saying or narrative that is literally true μὴ νομίζειν αἴνιγμα εἶναι τὸ εἰρημένον καὶ π., ἀλλ' εἰδέναι ὅτι πάντως δεῖ φαγεῖν τὸ σῶμα Chrys.*hom.47.1 in Jo.*(8.275D); π., ἀλλ' οὐκ ἀλήθειαν Thdt.*Ezech.*20:49(2.838); οὐ γὰρ ἐν πράγματι γέγονεν ἡ τοῦ Λαζάρου π. διότι οὐχ ὁρῶσιν οἱ ἁμαρτωλοὶ ἐν γεέννῃ τοὺς δικαίους ‡Ath.*qu.Ant.*21(M.28.609C); **c.** in gen., Herm. *vis.*3.3.2; id.*mand.*11.18; ταύτας τὰς π. οὐ γινώσκω οὐδὲ δύναμαι νοῆσαι, ἐὰν μή μοι ἐπιλύσῃς αὐτάς id.*sim.*5.3.1; ἐδεήθην...ἵνα μοι δηλώσῃ τὴν π. τοῦ ἀγροῦ καὶ τοῦ δεσπότου *ib.*5.4.1; **d.** of Christ's parables ἐπὶ τῆς π. τῶν ...ἐργατῶν Iren.*haer.*1.1.3(M.7.452A); question why Christ spoke in parables 'that seeing they might not see', etc. (Mc.4:12), discussed in relation to problem of free will, Or. *princ.*3.1.16(p.223.12ff.; M.11.280Cff.); κατ' ἰδίαν τοῖς ἰδίοις μαθηταῖς ἐπέλυεν τὰς π., μετ' ἐπικρύψεως τοῖς ἔξω ὄχλοις εἰρημένας, ὥσπερ ταῖς ἀκοαῖς ἦσαν κρείττους οἱ ἀκούοντες τῆς λύσεως τῶν π. παρὰ τοὺς ἀκούοντας τῶν χωρὶς λύσεων π. id.*Cels.*2.64(p.186.13; M.11.897A); τοὺς μὲν ὄχλους τῶν πιστευόντων τῶν π. ἀκούοντας ὡς ἔξω τυγχάνοντας καὶ ἀξίους μόνον τῶν ἐξωτερικῶν λόγων, τοὺς δὲ μαθητὰς κατ' ἰδίαν τῶν π. μανθάνοντας τὰς διηγήσεις...προτιμῶν παρὰ τοὺς ὄχλους τοὺς τῆς σοφίας αὐτοῦ ἐπιδικαζομένους *ib.*3.46(p.242.14; 980B); *ib.*6.5(p.75.23; 1297A); αἱ π. καὶ αἱ ὁμοιώσεις οὐκ εἰς πάντα, οἷς παραβάλλονται ἢ ὁμοιοῦνται, παραλαμβάνονται ἀλλ' εἴς τινα id.*comm.in Mt.*10.13(p.15.31; M.13.865B); χρὴ φρονεῖν περὶ πάσης π., ἧς μὴ ἀναγέγραπται ἡ διήγησις...ὅτι καὶ Ἰησοῦς τοῖς...μαθηταῖς...ἐπέλυε πάντα, καὶ διὰ τοῦτο ἀπέκρυψαν οἱ τὰ εὐαγγέλια γράφοντες τὴν σαφήνειαν τῶν π., ἐπεὶ μείζονα ἦν τὰ κατ' αὐτὰς δηλούμενα τῆς τῶν γραμμάτων φύσεως... γένοιτο δ' ἀνευρεθῆναι καρδίαν ἐπιτηδείαν καὶ διὰ τὴν καθαρότητα χωροῦσαν τὰ γράμματα τῆς σαφηνείας τῶν π., ὥστε ἐν αὐτῇ γραφῆναι πνεύματι θεοῦ ζῶντος *ib.*14.12(p.304.9; 1212C); *Hom.Clem.*17.5; εἰ δὲ καὶ κατὰ λέξιν ἐθέλοις τὴν π. ἐξετάζειν, οὐδὲν κωλύει θυρωρόν [Jo. 10:3]...νοεῖν τὸν Μωϋσέα Chrys.*hom.59.2 in Jo.*(8.347C); **5.** *saying containing an inner* or *hidden meaning and requiring interpretation*; **a.** in gen. περὶ πάσης γραφῆς τῆς καθ' ἡμᾶς ἐν τοῖς ψαλμοῖς γέγραπται ὡς ἐν π. εἰρημένης·...'ἀνοίξω ἐν παραβολαῖς τὸ στόμα μου...' καὶ ὁ... ἀπόστολος τὰ ὅμοια...λέγει· σοφίαν δὲ λαλοῦμεν ἐν τοῖς τελείοις Clem. *str.*5.4(p.341.10; M.9.44B); id.*ecl.*32(p.146.26; M.9.716A); τινες...τὰ ἐν π. σκοτεινῶς δι' αἰνίγματος εἰρημένα ψιλὰ καὶ ἀνερμήνευτα πρὸς ἀνατροπὴν τῆς ἀληθείας προφέροντες Gr.Nyss.*Eun.*1(1 p.108.23; M.

45.341D); **b.** of prophetic utterances λέγει γὰρ ὁ προφήτης π. κυρίου *Barn.*6.10; ὅσα εἶπον καὶ ἐποίησαν οἱ προφῆται...π. καὶ τύποις ἀπεκάλυψαν Just.*dial.*90.2(M.6.689B); *ib.*97.3(705A); Ζαχαρίᾳ ἐν π. δεικνύντι τὸ μυστήριον τοῦ Χριστοῦ [Zach.2:10–3:2] *ib.*115.1(741A); Clem.*str.*6.15(p.495.24; M.9.349B); οἱ...προφῆται...εἰδότες αὐτὰ οὐκ ἠθέλησαν παρρησίᾳ κηρῦξαι...ἀλλὰ μυστικῶς διηγήσαντο διὰ π. καὶ αἰνιγμάτων Hipp.*antichr.*29(p.19.20; M.10.749B); Or.*fr.22 in Jer.*24:1–3(p.208.22; M.13.576A); *Dial.Ath.etZacch.*35(p.24); **c.** of typological imagery, *Barn.*17.2; κύριος τῶν δυνάμεων ὁ Χριστὸς καὶ Ἰακὼβ καλεῖται ἐν π. ὑπὸ τοῦ πνεύματος...[Ps.23:1–10] Just.*dial.*36.2 (M.6.553B); Μωϋσῆς...αἵματι σταφυλῆς, ἐν π. εἰπών, τὴν στολὴν αὐτοῦ πλύνειν ἔφη, ὡς τοῦ αἵματος αὐτοῦ οὐκ ἐξ ἀνθρωπείου σπέρματος γεγεννημένου ἀλλ' ἐκ θελήματος θεοῦ *ib.*63.2(620C); λίθος καὶ πέτρα ἐν παραβολαῖς ὁ Χριστὸς...ἐκηρύσσετο *ib.*113.6(737B); ἐν π. λίθον... καλεῖν...Χριστὸν καὶ ἐν τροπολογίᾳ Ἰακὼβ *ib.*114.2(740A); ref. Heb. 11:19 ἐν π. ἐκομίσατο, τουτέστιν ὡς ἐν αἰνίγματι· ὥσπερ γὰρ π. ἦν ὁ κριὸς τοῦ Ἰσαάκ· ἢ ὡς ἐν τῷ τύπῳ· ἐπειδὴ γὰρ ἀπήρτιστο ἡ θυσία καὶ ἐσφακτο ὁ Ἰσαὰκ τῇ προαιρέσει, διὰ τοῦτο αὐτὸν χαρίζεται τῷ πατριάρχῃ Chrys.*hom.25.1 in Heb.*(12.229C); ἐν π. ... τουτέστιν ὡς ἐν συμβόλῳ καὶ τύπῳ τῆς ἀναστάσεως Thdt.*Heb.*11:19(3.619); **6.** *riddle, enigma, M.Thdot.1* 31(p.82); **7.** Hebr. מָשָׁל, any *wise saying*, not necessarily involving an illustration or parable, hence *proverb* π. τὸν σοφὸν λόγον εἴωθεν ἡ γραφὴ λέγειν Proc.G.*Num.*23:3 (M.87.864B); π. εἴρηται παρὰ γραφῇ οὐ μόνον ὁ καθ' ὁμοίωσιν εἰσαγόμενος λόγος, ἀλλὰ καὶ πᾶς λόγος σοφός...οὐχ ὁμοιώματα διεξιών, ἀλλὰ λόγους σοφοὺς Olymp.*fr.Pr.*1:6(M.93.472A); but cf. *Masloth, quem Graeci Parabolas, Latini Proverbiorum nominant, eo quod in ipso sub comparativa similitudine figuras verborum et imagines veritatis ostenderit*, Isid.H.*etym.*6.2.18; **8.** *interposition* μὴ εἰς τέλος ὑπομείναντες διὰ τὴν π. τοῦ χρόνου Mac.Aeg.*hom.*29.2(M.34.716D); **9.** *refuse* οὗτοι γάρ εἰσι τὰ λείψανα καὶ ἡ π. τῆς Καππαδοκίας *Pet.Ar.*1(M.26. 820B).

παραβολικός, *parabolic, containing spiritual* (opp. literal) *meaning, figurative* π. ... ὁ χαρακτὴρ τῶν γραφῶν Clem.*str.*6.15(p.495.24; M.9.349B); τὸ π. εἶδος τῆς γραφῆς *ib.*(p.496.12; 352A); Thdt.*1Thess.* 5:3(3.522); ἐπειδὴ π. τοῦ λόγου τὸ σχῆμα, ἀναγκαίως αὐτὸν διήγειρεν εἰς κατανόησιν τοῦ κεκρυμμένου νοήματος id.*2Tim.*2:7(3.682); τὸ π., ἡ συμβολικόν, καὶ τὸ αἰνιγματῶδες Nil.*epp.*1.119(M.79.136A); ἡ π. θεηγορία ‡Caes.Naz.*dial.*180(M.38.1152).

***παραβολικῶς**, **1.** *indirectly, in riddles, obscurely* τὰ μὲν πρῶτα τυπικῶς καὶ μυστικῶς, τὰ δ' ὕστερα π. καὶ ᾐνιγμένως διδάσκειν Clem. *exc.Thdot.*66(p.128.25; M.9.689C); τοῦ π. καὶ ⟨ἀ⟩σαφῶς λεχθέντος id.*q.d.s.*20(p.173.3; M.9.625A); ταυτὶ...παραβολικώτερον εἰπεῖν ὁ κύριος ἐδικαίωσεν Thdr.Mops.*Jo.*10:6(p.349.17; M.66.757C); **2.** *as consisting in an image* or *comparison, figuratively* ἵνα τὰ ἀπαράβλητα π. πως παραδειχθείη Didym.*Trin.*1.15(M.39.308A); π. νοουμένης Thdt.*Ps.*109:3(1.1395); ‡Just.*qu.et resp.*94(M.6.1336C bis); **3.** *in the form of a parable* π. τοῖς ὄχλοις..., τοῖς ἀποστόλοις κατ' οἶκον... ἑρμηνείας προσέφερεν Or.*Ps.*48:5(p.49).

παράβολος, ὁ, *fighter* in the arena, Socr.*h.e.*7.22.12(M.67.785C).

***παραβομβέω**, *remain on a constant note*, Synes.*Dion* 18(p.278. 20; M.66.1164A).

παραβόσκω, med., *prey upon*, *cat.Lc.*9:46(p.79.25) for περιβόσκεται, Cyr.*Lc.*9:46(M.72.660C).

παραβουλεύ-ομαι, *venture, risk oneself*, Chrys.*hom.56.3 in Mt.* (7.569A); id.*hom.22.1 in 1Cor.*(10.192C); id.*hom.9.3 in Phil.*(11. 267D); ζήσεται...μὴ ~σάμενος, τεθνήξεται...τολμῶν id.*hom.9.2 in 1Thess.*(11.487C); ἐάν τις...~σηται...ὡς θέλων ἐπιδείξασθαι αὐτὸν ὡς γενναῖον, καὶ...ἀποθάνῃ, μετὰ τῶν παραβούλων κρίνεται ἡ ψυχὴ αὐτοῦ Eus.Al.*serm.*6(M.86.349D; cf.352C).

παράβουλος, *foolhardy*, Eus.Al.*serm.*6(M.86.352C); as subst., *adventurer* καὶ φύεται ἐκεῖσε παράβουλος..., καὶ πολλοὺς τῶν Ἀράβων ἀπέκτεινε Thphn.*chron.*p.306(M.108.744C).

παραβραβεύ-ω, **1.** *fail to give one credit for* οὐδείς σου τὴν πάλην ~σει Procl.CP *or.*17(M.65.817B); **2.** *distort, pervert* ὡς εἰς μυθολογίαν τὴν ἀλήθειαν ~ωσι Tat.*orat.*40(p.41.10; M.6.884C); ~σαι τὴν ἀλήθειαν Eus.*h.e.*3.29.4(M.20.277B); Isid.Pel.*epp.*3.119(M.78.824A); **3.** *deprive of good fortune* τὸ ἐπικρατῆσαν...ἑνὸς αὐτῶν φῶς τοὺς πλείονας ~ει, καὶ ὁ νικώμενος εἰσαῦθις νῦν ἐπικρατεῖν εἴωθεν Tat.*orat.*9(p.10.5; M.6.825B); **4.** pass., *be misdirected*; of justice, Nil.*exerc.*61(M.79. 793C).

παράβυστος, *pushed aside*; phrase ἐν π. adverbial or adjectival: **1.** *secret(ly)*, Isid.Pel.*epp.*2.127(M.78.569D); Cyr.*Jo.*5.1(4.463E); τὸ ἐν π. *ib.*5(448A); *hidden* πῦρ...τὴν λαμπηδόνα...οὐκ ἐν τῷ π. κατέχειν δύναται Jo.D.*hom.*12.5(M.96.788C); **2.** *in private*, opp. ἐν συλλόγοις, Isid.Pel.*epp.*4.145(M.78.1228B); κεκρυμμένον καὶ ἐν π. λόγον Cyr. *ador.*16(1.597C).

παραβύω, **1.** *stanch*, Bas.*hex.*9.3(1.82D; M.29.193A); **2.** *stuff in* to conceal ἐνθεῖναι τῇ χειρὶ τοῦ νεκροῦ καὶ παραβῦσαι τοῖς ἱματίοις Philost.*h.e.*2.16(M.65.477C); **3.** fig., *smuggle in* ὡς ἐπεισόδιον παραβυσθῆναι τῷ λόγῳ *cat.Apoc.*16:19(p.424.1).

παραβώμιον, τό, *chant by the altar* μετὰ μέθην παραβώμιον ἐπολολύζουσιν *Hom.Clem.*9.7.

***παραγανακτ-έω**, *feel uneasy* about ἐπὶ τῆς τοῦ κόσμου προθεσμίας ~εῖ πᾶσα ἡ κτίσις *Hom.Clem.*11.10.

***παραγαύδιος**, *with a purple border*, Jo.Mal.*chron.*17 p.413(M.97. 612B).

παραγγελία, ἡ, **1.** *precept, maxim* παραγγελίας...λαβόντες καὶ πληροφορηθέντες...καὶ πιστωθέντες...ἐξῆλθον, εὐαγγελιζόμενοι *1Clem.* 42.3; Clem.*paed.*1.10(p.146.7; M.8.364A); ἀποστολικῇ...π. id.*prot.*1 (p.8.15; M.8.64A); ἡ...παραίνεσις τοῦ θεοῦ καὶ π. ἡ δοθεῖσά μοι αὕτη εἰς ζωὴν καὶ ἀφθαρσίαν Meth.*res.*2.2(p.331.14, v.l. ἐπαγγ- M.18.297C); *ib.*2.6(p.339.17; M.41.1172C); **2.** of one in custody, *subjection* ἐν πολλῇ στενοχωρίᾳ καὶ π. καὶ ἀσφαλείᾳ Thdr.Stud.*epp.*1.48(M.99. 1072B); **3.** *muster-roll*, Evagr.*h.e.*2.1(p.37.11; M.86.2488B).

παραγγέλλ-ω, **1.** trans., *ask, enjoin*, ethical ~ω ὑμῖν, ἀγαπᾶτε τὸν Λευί *T.Jud.*21.1; *1Clem.*1.3; Ign.*Polyc.*5.1; Χριστοῦ...παραγγείλαντος ἡμῖν εὔχεσθαι...ὑπὲρ τῶν ἐχθρῶν Just.*dial.*133.6(M.6.785B); ritual, *ib.*14.3(505A); *ib.*112.1(733B); pass. τὰ παραγγελθέντα Clem. *str.*3.4(p.214.1; M.8.1144A); *ib.*6.17(p.515.10; M.9.393C); **2.** intrans.; **a.** *enlist*, Evagr.*h.e.*2.1(p.37.5; M.86.2488B); **b.** *enter* the ranks εἰς βαθμὸν διακόνων παραγγεῖλαι Philost.*h.e.*3.4(M.65.484A); παραγγείλας εἰς φαλακρούς Synes.*calv.*7(p.204.5; M.66.1180D); id.*ep.*57(M. 66.1388B); **c.** *come as spectator*, Pythagorean view παραγγεῖλαι... αὐτὸν [sc. τὸν σοφὸν] εἰς τὸν κόσμον, ὥσπερ εἰς ἀγῶνα ἱερόν, ἐφ' ᾧ θεάσασθαι τὰ γινόμενα id.*provid.*8(p.130.1; M.66.1280A).

παράγγελμα, τό, **1.** *rule* or *precept*; from God, Tat.*orat.*32(p.33. 3; M.6.872B); combated by the serpent, Cels.ap.Or.*Cels.*4.39(p.311. 5; M.11.1089B); given by Christ, *1Clem.*49.1; τῷ π. τῆς ζωῆς Clem. *q.d.s.*10(p.166.10; M.9.613C); Cels.ap.Or.*Cels.*7.58(p.207.11; M.11. 1504A); in NT τὸ τοῦ ἀποστόλου π. [Tit.3:10] Ath.*ep.Serap.*4.1(M.26. 637A); in Fathers τῶν πατέρων τὰ π. ‡Ath.*Apoll.*1.1(M.26.1093B); tending to salvation, Meth.*symp.*7.5(p.76.10; M.18.132A); but simple observance of precepts not sufficient, *Hom.Clem.*11.15; ref. church discipline, *Const.App.*3.12.2; **2.** medical *prescription*, Bas. *hom.*10.1(2.83A; M.31.353A); cf. θεραπεύεται...τῇ προστάξει αὐστηροτέρων π. Clem.*paed.*1.8(p.128.5; M.8.328B).

***παραγγελτικός**, *exhorting* to τοὺς π. τῶν πρακτέων λόγους ἀπὸ τῆς θείας...γραφῆς Eus.*e.th.*2.24(p.134.27; M.24.964C); λόγους...ἐν ταῖς προφητικαῖς γραφαῖς...ὁσίων ἔργων παραγγελτικούς *ib.*2.25(p.136.26; 965D).

***παραγεννάω**, *produce in error*, Max.*ambig.*(M.91.1100A).

παραγίν-ομαι, *come, arrive*, of Christ's first coming παραγενόμενον θεὸν ἐν σαρκί, οὐκ ἐπίστευσαν αὐτῷ *T.Benj.*10.8; ὁ σωτὴρ... ~εται Clem.*q.d.s.*8(p.164.31; M.9.612C); Proc.G.*Dt.*32:43(M.87.976A); πρὸς ἡμᾶς παραγέγονε, καὶ παραγενήσεται πάλιν Jo.D.*f.o.*1.2(M.94. 793A); of his second coming, Just.*1apol.*52.1(M.6.401B); id.*dial.*38. 2(M.6.557A); *ib.*52.1(589B); μέχρις ἂν ὁ κόσμος πέρας λαβὼν ἀναλυθῇ, καὶ ὁ δικαστὴς παραγένηται Tat.*orat.*12(p.13.25; M.6.832C); ἐπειδὰν ὁ τοῦ θεοῦ υἱὸς παραγένηται ἀγαθὰ τοῖς ἰδίοις ἀποκαθιστῶν Clem.*fr.* 44(p.223.19).

παραγινώσκω, *make known in company*, by scripture reading ἡ ἀρτίως ἡμῖν παραγνωσθεῖσα, Ἄννα ἡ προφῆτις Amph.*hom.*2.4(M.39. 49C).

παραγκωνίζω, med.; **1.** *thrust aside, supplant*, Eus.*l.C.*17(p.258. 10; M.20.1437A); Ath.*gent.*13(M.25.29A); *ib.*29(57C); παράφρονες, παραγκωνισάμενοι...γνῶσιν καὶ εὐσέβειαν *ib.*47(96A); Nil.*epp.*2.101 (M.79.245B); **2.** esp. with contempt, *put away, reject* τὸν υἱὸν τοῦ θεοῦ παραγκωνισάμενοι Eus.*e.th.*1.7(p.65.27; M.24.836C); Mac.Mgn. *apocr.*2.7(p.4.6); Nil.*epp.*2.268(M.79.336D).

***παραγνωρίζ-ω**, **1.** *ignore* τοῦτό τινες δι' ἀπάτην ~οντες ‡Proc.G. *Pr.*27:20(M.87.1497D); **2.** *mistake for, misunderstand as* εἰς θεὸν τὴν κτίσιν ~ειν *ib.*20:28(1429A); κατορθώματα...εἰς ἐλάττονα ~ει Thal. *cent.*1.83(M.91.1436B); τὰς ἀρετὰς οἱ πονηροὶ εἰς κακίας ~ουσι *ib.*1. 89(1436C).

***παραγονάτιον, τό,** *space on either side of a node*, of cane τὰ... Αἰγύπτια...τοῖς γόνασιν οἰδοῦντα τοῖς π. συνιζάνει [i.e. becomes concave] Synes.*ep.*133(M.66.1520C).

παραγραφή, ἡ, **1.** *misstatement, perversion* τί τὸ ψεῦδος; αὐτῆς τῆς ἀληθείας π. Gr.Nyss.*Eun.*1(1 p.55.27; M.45.284C); **2.** *impugning, contradiction* παρατίθενται ἐπὶ παραγραφῇ τῆς ἀνωτάτω καὶ ἀρχῆθεν αὐτοῦ θεότητος Alex.Al.*ep.Alex.*9(p.25.19; M.18.561B); **3.** *marginal note,* Cosm.Ind.*top.*arg.(M.88.57B); **4.** *section* περὶ τὸ τέλος τοῦ πρώτου κεφαλαίου, ἐν τῇ ἕκτῃ π. Max.*schol.d.n.*4.1(M.4.241A).

παραγράφ-ω, rarely act. **1.** *write beside, in the margin, annotate* ἀναντιρρήτως ἔστι λαβεῖν, ὅτι ἀληθῆ πρὸ μικροῦ παρεγράψαμεν Max. *schol.c.h.*10.3(M.4.92B); ταῦτα μὲν ὁ παραγράψας ἐνόησεν *ib.*13.3 (97C); ὁ...τὴν γυναῖκα ~όμενος *cat.Apoc.*12:6(p.358.11); pass. τὰ παραγεγραμμένα τῷ σταυρῷ τοῦ Χριστοῦ Synes.*ep.*58(M.66.1401A); **2.** *pervert, twist* ἔστι...ὁ τρόπος λέξις παραγεγραμμένη ἀπὸ τοῦ κυρίου ἐπὶ τὸ μὴ κύριον Clem.*str.*6.15(p.497.13; M.9.353A); ταῦτα πάντα ἐξετέθησαν ὅσον πρὸς εἴδησιν, παραγεγραμμένα δέ εἰσι πάντως καὶ νόθα, καὶ ἀπόβλητα ‡Ath.*synops.*76(M.28.432C); **3.** *defraud, cheat of* τῆς ἐν στιγμῇ ἀντιλογίας παραγραψαμένης αὐτοῦ τὴν εἰς τὴν γῆν τῆς ἐπαγγελίας εἴσοδον †Bas.*ep.*42(3.126B; M.32.349B); cf. μόνος Ἀμάραντος εὔθυμος ἦν, ὡς αὐτίκα περιγράψων τοὺς δανειστάς Synes.*ep.*4 (αὐτίκα ἂν παραγ- M.66.1333A); **4.** *cross through, cancel, discount; invalidate* δυνάμει γὰρ ἐὰν τόδε μὲν δυνατὸν εἶναι φῇς, τόδε δὲ ἀδύνατον, τοῦ εἶναι αὐτὴν δύναμιν παραγράφῃ, ἀσθενοῦσαν περὶ ἃ μὴ δύναται Meth. *Porph.*2(p.505.16; M.18.401D); Bas.*Eun.*2.22(1.258B; M.29.620D); σπουδὴ δὲ...πᾶσα καθελεῖν καὶ παραγράψασθαι καὶ ἀνατρέψαι παντελῶς τὰς περὶ τοῦ μονογενοῦς θεοῦ...εὐσεβεῖς ὑπολήψεις Gr.Nyss.*Eun.*1(1 p.67.15; M.45.296D); τὴν καθαράν τε καὶ θείαν καὶ ἀπαθῆ τοῦ κυρίου ~όμενος γέννησιν *ib.*2(2 p.52.23; 621D); τῶν...Ἑλληνιζόντων ἐξαφανίζεται πλάνη, τῆς κατὰ φύσιν ἑνότητος ~ομένης τὴν πληθυντικὴν φαντασίαν id.*or.catech.*3(p.17.6; M.45.20A); **5.** *remove* from canon of scripture εἰ μὲν...παρέγραψάν τι ἀπὸ τῶν γραφῶν οἱ ἄρχοντες τοῦ λαοῦ, θεὸς δύναται ἐπίστασθαι Just.*dial.*73.5(M.6.648B); ἀξιοῦμεν εἰπεῖν σε ἡμῶν καί τινας ὧν λέγεις τέλεον παραγεγράφθαι γραφῶν *ib.* 71.4(644B); hence pass., *be suspect* γραφὴ δέ ἐστιν αὕτη μαρτυρουμένη, οὐ ~ομένη Sever.*creat.*3.5(M.56.453); **6.** *reject;* **a.** fig., *take* legal *exception to* ὁ τοὺς μὲν δικαστὰς...παραγραψάμενος, περὶ δὲ τὴν κρίσιν ...σιγήσας Gr.Nyss.*Eun.*1(1 p.41.22; M.45.269A); προὔλαβε...ὁ μονογενὴς παραγράψαι τὴν δικαστικὴν αὐτοῦ ταύτην φωνήν Epiph.*haer.*76. 49(p.404.12; M.42.621A); **b.** a ruler παραγραψαμένη [sc. Jerusalem] τὸν ἄρχειν παρ' ἐμοῦ τεταγμένον ὑμῶν Thdr.Mops.*Mich.*4:10(M.66. 368D); id.*Os.*8:4(M.66.172C); ref. Christ ὅς με παραγράψαιτο Nonn. *par.Jo.*12:48(M.43.857C); **c.** *disregard* custom, law, ordinance, Hipp. *Dan.*4.20.2; Gr.Nyss.*Trin.*3(p.73.15; M.32.688A); ὁ...τὴν περιτομὴν ...~όμενος Mac.Mgn.*apocr.*3.30(p.125.23); pass. τὰς μὲν αὐτῶν φυλάττεσθαι, τὰς δὲ θείας ~εσθαι *cat.Mt.*12:1(p.120.24) for παραβαίνεσθαι Chrys.*hom.51.1 in Mt.*(7.520D); scripture φοβοῦμαι...μήπως ὡς Μανιχαῖος ~ῃ τὴν παλαιὰν διαθήκην ‡Ath.*dial.Trin.*3.8(M.28.1216A); texts of scripture π. τὸν κύριον λέγοντα· ἐγώ εἰμι ἡ ζωή, π. δὲ Παῦλον τὸν εἰπόντα· Χριστὸς θεοῦ δύναμις Bas.*Eun.*2.27(1.264A; M.29.633C); ~έσθω τὴν εὐαγγελικὴν μαρτυρίαν Gr.Nyss.*Apoll.*45(M.45.1232C); Didym.*Trin.*3.20(M.39.893C); ὁ Ἰουδαῖος ~εται τὴν μαρτυρίαν πάντως Chrys.*Jud.*5.1(1.628E); τὰς ἱερὰς ~ονται γραφάς [sc. οἱ Ἕλληνες] Isid. Pel.*epp.*2.43(M.78.485A); Thdt.*Ps.*21:2(1.733); traditional interprn. ὑμεῖς...~ειν τὰς ἐξηγήσεις, ἃς ἐξηγήσαντο οἱ πρεσβύτεροι ὑμῶν παρὰ Πτολεμαίῳ..., τολμᾶτε Just.*dial.*84.3(M.6.673C); the faith, Gr.Nyss. *Eun.*2(2 p.36.8; M.45.489A); **7.** *gloss over* οὐδὲν τῶν εἰρημένων ~όμενοι ‡Caes.Naz.*dial.*166(M.38.1125); *scorn, make light of* τοῦ ἀκροατοῦ ~εσθε τὴν εὐτέλειαν Isid.Pel.*epp.*1.93(M.78.248A); τὸ παρὸν ~ομαι παῖσμα, τὸ ἐσόμενον ἐλπίζων κατόρθωμα Bas.Sel.*or.*29.2(M.85.329B); *ib.*30.1(333B).

παραγρυπνέω, *be alert all the time,* Gr.Nyss.*instit.*(p.55.2; M.46. 293B).

***παραγύμνωσις, ἡ,** *exposure,* Clem.*paed.*2.6(p.188.8; M.8.1453A).

παράγ-ω, 1. *lead astray, pervert,* Clem.*prot.*2(p.19.10; M.8.96A); id.*str.*7.11(p.44.20; M.9.485B); Chrys.*hom.32.1 in Rom.*(9.755D); **2.** *introduce, bring in beside;* as character in drama, Clem.*str.*7.6 (p.22.22; M.9.441A); as candidate for office τὸν ἐπιτήδειον [i.e. ordination candidate]...κἂν ἅπαντες ἀντιπίπτωσι, ~ειν Chrys.*sac.*3.16 (p.83.6; 1.395D); id.*hom.5.1 in 1Tim.*(11.574B); into argument, Meth.*symp.*3.11(p.39.15; M.18.77B); Didym.(‡Bas.)*Eun.*5(1.302C; M.29.725A); Leont.B.*Nest.et Eut.*3(M.86.1388D); **3.** *adduce,* Chrys. *hom.42.3 in Mt.*(7.456B); σημεῖον τοῦ εἰδέναι τὸν θεὸν...~ει τοῦτο αὐτό, τὸ θεοὺς ἐγνωκέναι id.*hom.3.2 in Rom.*(9.450C); **4.** *produce, create, bring into being* στοιχεῖα...ἐκ τοῦ μὴ ὄντος παραχθέντα Arist. *apol.*4.1; δοῦλον γὰρ πᾶν τὸ παραχθὲν τοῦ παραγαγόντος Didym.*Trin.* 1.7(M.39.276B); Chrys.*hom.23.8 in Mt.*(7.295E); τὰ μὴ ὄντα ὡς ὄντα ~αγεῖν id.*hom.8.5 in Rom.*(9.503E); Zach.Mit.*opif.*(M.85.1076B); ‡Cyr.*Trin.*7(6^3.10C; M.77.1133D); Χριστὸς κατὰ σάρκα ἀσπόρως... παρήχθη Cosm.Ind.*top.*5(M.88.224B); **5.** *withdraw, make to pass away* παρήγαγες ταχέως τὴν θλίψιν Chrys.*hom.1.3 in 2Cor.*(10. 421C).

παραγωγεύς, ὁ, *one who brings into being, creator* ὁ τῆς ἀνθρωπίνης φύσεως π. ‡Chrys.*ascens.*3(3.783A); δημιουργὸς καὶ π. Cosm. Ind.*top.*3(M.88.149A); Max.*schol.d.n.*11.6(M.4.400C).

παραγωγή, ἡ, 1. *bringing forward* as proof, Chrys.*hom.19.4 in Rom.*(9.636B); **2.** *derivation,* Clem.*str.*5.8(p.359.9; M.9.77A); †Proc.G. *Procl.*(M.87.2792^hB); **3.** *bringing into being, creation;* **a.** esp. with stress on previous non-existence κτίσις...ἡ ἐκ τοῦ μὴ ὄντος ἐπὶ τὸ εἶναι π. Cyr.*Ps.*50:12(M.69.1097C); ἡ τῶν μὴ ὄντων π. καὶ γένεσις Max. *ep.*24(M.91.609D); **b.** simply τοῦ ὁρωμένου κόσμου π. Sophr.H.*ep.syn.* (M.87.3181B); Max.*ep.*16(577D); id.*schol.d.n.*1.4(M.4.200B); **c.** ref. source of existence εἴ τις λέγει, πάντων τῶν λογικῶν τὴν π. νόας ἀσωμάτους καὶ ἀΰλους γεγονέναι... CCP(543)*anath.*2(p.227; H.3. 284C); **d.** ref. Inc. ἤδη καὶ αὐτῆς [sc. τῆς σαρκός] ὑπ' αὐτοῦ θεωθείσης ἅμα τῇ εἰς τὸ εἶναι ταύτης π. Jo.D.*Jacob.*83(M.94.1481D).

παράγωγος, neut. as subst., *derivative;* **1.** etym. ἀπὸ...τοῦ εἶναι καὶ τοῦ ὄντος ἡ οὐσία, καὶ τὸ π. οὖσα ἡ ὕπαρξις Max.*schol.c.h.*2.3(M.4. 40C); **2.** of the will of God, Max.*Pyrr.*(M.91.308B) cit. s. πρωτότυπος; **3.** in sense of subsequent copy πρωτότυπον...ἐστι τὸ εἰκονιζόμενον, ἐξ οὗ τὸ π. γίνεται Jo.D.*f.o.*4.16(M.94.1169A); Thdr.Stud.*epp.*2.26 (M.99.1193B).

παράδειγμα, τό, 1. *pattern,* of heavenly reality opp. earthly copy, ref. Ex.25:40 τὸ γὰρ ἐν τῷ ὄρει π. παρενεχθέν...ἰδέα τις ἦν τῆς κατὰ τὸν οὐρανὸν οἰκήσεως Meth.*symp.*5.7(p.62.3; M.18.109B); ὄντα δέ φημι τὰ καλά, καθότι ἐκ τοῦ ὄντος θεοῦ τὰ π. ἔχει Ath.*gent.*4(M.25.9C); ‡Just.*qu.Chr.*4.3(M.6.1449B); προυφεστάναι τὰ πάντα τῶν ὄντων π. ... π. δέ φαμεν εἶναι τοὺς ἐν θεῷ τῶν ὄντων οὐσιοποιοὺς καὶ...προυφεστῶτας λόγους, οὓς ἡ θεολογία προορισμοὺς καλεῖ Dion.Ar.*d.n.*5.8 (M.3.824C); *ib.*7.3(869D); **2.** *example, illustration,* in gen., Or.*princ.* 3.1.19(p.232.14; M.11.292A); id.*or.*2(p.299.19; M.11.417B); μικρῶν... καὶ παρὰ πόδας νουθετούντων π. Dion.Al.ap.Eus.*p.e.*14.24(773D; M. 21.1275A); Meth.*symp.*2.4(p.19.7; M.18.52C); ref. relation of emperor to subordinate governors as illustration of pagan theory of supreme and lesser gods, *Hom.Clem.*10.15; ἀνθρωπίνοις χρώμενος π. *ib.*19.9; of simile of light and ray in Trin. doctrine, Eus.*d.e.*4.3 (p.152.30; M.22.256A); τὰ...τῆς...θεολογίας, ἐπέκεινα παντὸς ὄντα π. *ib.*(p.154.12; 257A); id.*e.th.*1.12(p.72.24; M.24.849A); of H. Ghost as ῥῆμα of Son τὸ...ἐπὶ θεοῦ πρὸς τὴν τῆς μιᾶς ἀπόδειξιν ἐνεργείας λαμβάνω τὸ τοῦ λόγου π. Didym.(‡Bas.)*Eun.*5(1.304E; M.29.732A); ἄρα γὰρ...ἀνάγκη...τὸ κατά τι πρὸς ὁμοίωσίν τινος παραλαμβανόμενον, καὶ κατὰ πάντα τὸν ἑαυτοῦ λόγον ἐοικέναι τῷ π.; καὶ πῶς ἂν ἔτι μένοι λεγόμενον π.; ἔσται γὰρ καὶ τοῦτο πρωτότυπον, τῷ ἀνελλιπεῖ τῆς ὁμοιώσεως Leont.H.*Nest.*1.14(M.86.1453B); of simile of soul and body in Christology, †Leont.B.*sect.*7.5(M.86.1245A); *ib.*7.7(1248C); of illustrations from scripture, Or.*princ.*3.1.10(p.210.2; M.11. 265A); Eus.*d.e.*1.7(p.36.16; M.22.72A); Cyr.H.*catech.*23.17; ἀπὸ γραφικῶν π. πείθεις Pall.*v.Chrys.*19(p.120.29; M.47.67); **3.** *public shame,* Jo.Thess.*dorm.BMV* 1.13(p.399.20).

***παραδεικτικός,** *indicating, pointing the way* χεὶρ ἠγιάζετο, πρακτικῆς ἐνεργείας π. Cyr.*ador.*11(1.397B); id.*glaph.Gen.*6(1.95B); id.*Is.*1.1(2.20B); νουθεσίαι...τῆς ἀληθοῦς εὐζωΐας π. id.*Ps.*22:5(M. 69.841C).

***παραδεισιακός,** *of paradise* βίου οἱονεὶ π. ἐκπεπτωκέναι Thdr. Stud.*epp.*2.50(M.99.1261A).

***παραδεισιάς,** adj. fem., *of paradise,* Eudoc.*Cypr.*1.73(M.85.836A).

***παραδείσιον, τό,** *little garden* ποιήσας ἰχθυοτροφεῖα καὶ π. ἔνδοθεν Thphn.*chron.*p.229(M.108.580C); met., one of several titles given to *pratum spirituale* of Jo.Mosch. νέον π. Phot.*cod.*199(M.103.668A).

***παραδεισογενής,** *paradise-born;* of Christ as new Adam, Anast. S.*hex.*12(M.89.1064A).

παράδεισος, ὁ, *paradise;*

A. ref. Gen.2:8; **1.** situation and description; **a.** in gen. ἐκεῖ οὖν ἐφύτευσεν ὁ θεὸς τὸν π., ὅπου οὐκ ἀνέμων βία, οὐκ ἀμετρία ὡρῶν...οὐχ ὑγρότης ἠρινή, οὐ θερινὴ πύρωσις...ἀλλ' εὔκρατος καὶ εἰρηνικὴ συμφωνία τῶν ὡρῶν †Bas.*parad.*2(1.348B; M.30.64B); situated in the east, Sever.*creat.*5.6(M.56.478f.); Philost.*h.e.*3.10f.(M.65.493Aff.); beyond Ocean, Cosm.Ind.*top.*2(M.88.84C); Anast.S.*qu.et resp.*127 (M.89.780B); **b.** location on earth affirmed ὅτι...ὁ π. γῆ ἐστιν καὶ ἐπὶ τῆς γῆς πεφύτευται, ἡ γραφὴ λέγει...τὸ οὖν ἔτι ἐκ τῆς γῆς καὶ κατὰ ἀνατολὰς σαφῶς διδάσκει ἡμᾶς ἡ θεία γραφὴ τὸν π. ὑπὸ τοῦτον τὸν οὐρανόν Thphl.Ant.*Autol.*2.24(M.6.1089B); ὁ π., ὅθεν καὶ ἐξεβλήθημεν ἐν τῷ πρωτοπλάστῳ, ἐκ ταύτης ἐστὶ τῆς γῆς προδήλως τόπος ἐξαίρετος, πρὸς ἄλυπον ἀνάπαυσιν...τοῖς ἁγίοις ἀφωρισμένος, ⟨ὡς⟩ δῆλον ἀπὸ τοῦ καὶ τὸν Τίγριν καὶ Εὐφράτην καὶ τοὺς λοιποὺς ποταμοὺς τοὺς ἐκεῖθεν προχεομένους ἐνταῦθα φαίνεσθαι τῶν ῥευμάτων τὰς διεκβολὰς εἰς τὴν καθ' ἡμᾶς ἤπειρον ἐπικλύζοντας Meth.*res.*1.55(p.313.6; M.41.1148B); ὁ δὲ π., φησίν, 'ἐν Ἐδὲμ κατὰ ἀνατολάς'· 'πηγὴ δὲ ἀνέβαινεν ἐξ Ἐδέμ', καὶ οὐκ εἶπε 'κατέβαινεν', ἵνα μὴ νομίσωμεν ἐν οὐρανῷ εἶναι τὴν 'Εδέμ. εἰ γὰρ ἐν οὐρανῷ ἦν, ἄνωθεν ἂν εἶπε 'κατέρχεται' πηγή Epiph.*anc*.58 (p.67.11; M.43.117B); διὰ τοῦτο καὶ τὸ ὄνομα τοῦ τόπου ἐντίθησιν ἐν τοῖς γράμμασιν ὁ...Μωϋσῆς, ἵνα μὴ ἐξῇ τοῖς φλυαρεῖν μάτην βουλομένοις ἀπατᾶν τῶν ἀφελεστέρων τὰς ἀκοάς, καὶ λέγειν, μὴ εἶναι ἐν τῇ γῇ τὸν π., ἀλλ' ἐν οὐρανῷ Chrys.*hom.13.3 in Gen.*(4.103A); ποῦ σοι δοκεῖ ὑπάρχειν ὁ π.;...οἱ μὲν γὰρ αὐτὸν λέγουσιν ὑπάρχειν ἐπουράνιον νοητόν, οἱ δὲ ἐπίγειον αἰσθητόν. ἐμοὶ αἰσθητὸς δοκεῖ ὑπάρχειν, καὶ ἐπὶ γῆς· σαφῶς...τοῦτο βοώσης τῆς θείας γραφῆς ‡Caes.Naz.*dial*.141(M. 38.1089); cf. Clem.*str*.5.11(p.374.24f.; M.9.109B); **2.** man not created in it μετέθηκεν δὲ αὐτὸν ὁ θεὸς ἐκ τῆς γῆς, ἐξ ἧς ἐγεγόνει, εἰς τὸν π. Thphl.Ant.*Autol*.2.24(M.6.1089D); so that he should appreciate the difference and fear to lose π., †Bas.*parad*.10(1.351A; M.30.69C); **3.** man's happy state in it contrasted with his life after Fall, Or.*schol.in Cant*.6:10(M.17.280A); Bas.*reg.fus*.55.1(2.397D; M. 31.1044C); Chrys.*hom.36.2 in Jo*.(8.209A); cf.‡Ath.*diab*.5(p.6.33); **4.** necessity of both lit. and spiritual interpretation τὸν π. νοοῦμεν μὲν καὶ σωματικῶς, ἀλληγοροῦμεν δὲ καὶ πνευματικῶς †Bas.*parad*.7 (1.350B; M.30.68C); ἂν μὲν οὖν σάρκινος εἶ...ἔχεις τὴν ὑπογραφὴν ἐκείνην τοῦ σωματικοῦ π. ... εἰ δὲ πνευματικὸς εἶ...ἀνάβα τῇ διανοίᾳ πρὸς τὰ κάλλη τῶν ἀγγέλων, κατάμαθε τοὺς ἐν αὐτοῖς τῆς δικαιοσύνης καρπούς *ib*.12(351D; M.72B); allegorical exegesis necessitated by heresies, e.g. those of Anthropomorphites and Ophites, based on lit. exegesis of paradise stories, Anast.S.*hex*.7(M.89.963C); but lit. exegesis upheld against Origenists, cf.*ib*.(968A–C); distn. bet. paradise of Gen. and that of Ezech.28:13 οὐχ ἁπλῶς π. λέγεται οὗτος ὁ παρὰ τῷ προφήτῃ, ἀλλὰ π. θεοῦ. ὁ δὲ Μωσαϊκὸς π. οὐ θεώνυμος, ἀλλ' ἁπλῶς π. ὅθεν καὶ ὁ...Ἀμβρόσιος, καὶ Ἰουστῖνος...ἐν τοῖς εἰς τὴν Ἑξαήμερον αὐτῶν ὑπομνήμασι τὰ περὶ παραδείσου διεξιόντες, μετὰ τὸ εἰπεῖν περὶ τῶν αἰσθητῶν δένδρων καὶ ὑδάτων, καὶ γηγενοῦς π. παρήγαγον ἐν μέσῳ τὰ προκείμενα τοῦ θείου Ἰεζεκιὴλ περὶ π. οὐρανίου ῥήματα...λέγοντες, ὡς αἴσχιστον...τὸ φάσκειν,...τὴν μακαρίαν...τοῦ θεοῦ λόγου θεότητα σὺν τῷ δικαίῳ λῃστῇ εἰς...ὑλικὸν π. εἰσελθεῖν *ib*. (966B,C); τινὲς μὲν οὖν αἰσθητὸν τὸν π. ἐφαντάσθησαν, ἕτεροι δέ, νοητόν. πλὴν ἔμοιγε δοκεῖ, ὅτι ὥσπερ ὁ ἄνθρωπος αἰσθητὸς ἅμα καὶ νοητὸς δεδημιούργητο, οὕτω καὶ τὸ τούτου ἱερώτατον τέμενος, αἰσθητὸν ἅμα καὶ νοητόν, καὶ διπλῆν ἔχον τὴν ἔμφασιν· τῷ γὰρ σώματι ἐν τῷ θειοτάτῳ χώρῳ...αὐλιζόμενος· τῇ δὲ ψυχῇ ἐν ὑπερτέρῳ...τόπῳ διέτριβε, θεὸν ἔχων οἶκον τὸν ἔνοικον...οὕτω διπλοῦν οἶμαι τὸν θεῖον π., καὶ ἀληθῶς οἱ θεοφόροι πατέρες παρέδωκαν, οἵ τε οὕτως, οἵ τε ἐκείνως διδάξαντες Jo.D.*f.o*.2.11(M.94.917A); Manich. περὶ δὲ τοῦ π. ὃς καλεῖται κόσμος. ἔστι δὲ τὰ φυτὰ τὰ ἐν αὐτῷ, ἐπιθυμίαι καὶ ἄλλαι ἀπάται διαφθείρουσαι τοὺς λογισμοὺς τῶν ἀνθρώπων ἐκείνων. τὸ δὲ ἐν π. φυτὸν ἐξ οὗ γνωρίζουσι τὸ καλόν, αὐτός ἐστι ὁ Ἰησοῦς Hegem. *Arch*.11(p.18.1ff.; M.10.1445A); **5.** ref. parallelism between Fall and redemption ἐν π. ἡ ἀπόπτωσις, καὶ ἐν κήπῳ ἡ σωτηρία...δειλινὸν τοῦ κυρίου περιπατοῦντος ἐκρύβησαν, καὶ δειλινὸν ὑπὸ τοῦ κυρίου εἰς π. ὁ λῃστὴς εἰσάγεται Cyr.H.*catech*.13.19; ἐκεῖνος [sc. Adam] διὰ τοῦ ξύλου ἀπέπεσε, καὶ σὺ διὰ τοῦ ξύλου εἰσάγῃ εἰς τὸν π. *ib*.13.31; *ib*.17. 15; ὥσπερ οὖν ἐν τῇ ἕκτῃ ἡμέρᾳ ἡμαρτηκὼς ὁ Ἀδὰμ...ἐξεβλήθη τὸ δειλινόν, οὕτως καὶ τῇ ἕκτῃ ἡμέρᾳ, ὥρᾳ ς' τὸν σωτήριον σταυρὸν ὁ δεσπότης...ὑπέμεινεν. καὶ ὥσπερ ἀπὸ τῆς παραβάσεως ἕως τῆς ἐκβολῆς τοῦ π., πάντες οἱ ἄγγελοι ἠθύμουν σφόδρα...οὕτως καὶ ἐπὶ τοῦ πάθους ἀπὸ ὥρας ἕκτης ἕως ἐννάτης ἡ κτίσις πᾶσα ἐμελανειμόνει...καὶ ὥσπερ ἐννάτην ὥραν οἱ δύο ἐξεβλήθησαν τοῦ π. ... οὕτως καὶ ὥραν ἐννάτην ὁ...Χριστὸς κατὰ τὴν ψυχὴν καὶ ὁ λῃστὴς εἰσέβησαν ἐν τῷ π. Cosm.Ind.*top*.2(M.88.124C); cf.Germ.CP *or*.2(M.98.256C); **6.** exeg. Cant.1:5 ταὐτὸν χρὴ νοεῖν τῷ π. τὸν ἀμπελῶνα. καὶ γὰρ κἀκεῖ φυλάσσειν ἐτάχθη ὁ ἄνθρωπος τὸν π.· ἡ δὲ τῆς φυλακῆς ἀμέλεια ἐκβάλλει τοῦ π. τὸν ἄνθρωπον, καὶ οἰκήτορα τῶν δυσμῶν ποιεῖ τῆς ἀνατολῆς ἀποστήσασα...ἐπειδὴ ἔθετο ὁ θεὸς ἄνθρωπον ἐργάζεσθαι...τὸν π., τουτό φησιν ἡ νύμφη, ὅτι τοῦ θεοῦ [τοῦ] θεμένου τὴν ψυχήν μου εἰς ζωὴν (ζωὴ γὰρ ἦν ἡ τοῦ π. τρυφή, ἐν ᾧ ἔθετο ὁ θεὸς τὸν ἄνθρωπον...) οἱ ἐχθροὶ μετέστησαν αὐτὴν ἐκ τῆς τοῦ π. τρυφῆς Gr.Nyss.*hom.2 in Cant*. (M.44.797B–D); cf.*ib*.5(869C); **7.** (Origenist) as state of souls without bodies, before supramundane Fall ἡ νύμφη [sc. soul]...ἐκπεσοῦσα τὰ [l. τοῦ] π. πρὸς τὴν ἐπίμοχθον ταύτην ζωὴν Or.*schol.in Cant*.6:10f. (M.17.280A); εἰπὼν [sc. Or.] ἐν τῷ π. πρὸ τοῦ σώματος τὴν ψυχὴν Meth.*res*.1.29(p.260.9; M.41.1137B); cf.*ib*.2.1(p.329.12; M.18.297A); **8.** Gnost., = μήτρα: ἔστω, φησί [sc. Simon Magus], π. ἡ μήτρα, καὶ ὅτι τοῦτό ἐστιν ἀληθὲς ἡ γραφὴ διδάξει ὅτε λέγει· 'ἐγώ εἰμι ὁ πλάσσων σε ἐν μήτρᾳ μητρός σου'...τὸν π., φησίν, ἀλληγορῶν ὁ Μωσῆς τὴν μήτραν εἴρηκεν...εἰ δὲ πλάσσει ὁ θεὸς ἐν μήτρᾳ μητρὸς τὸν ἄνθρωπον, τουτέστιν ἐν π., ὡς ἔφην, ἔστω π. ἡ μήτρα, 'Εδὲμ δὲ τὸ χόριον, 'ποταμὸς ἐκπορευόμενος ἐξ 'Εδὲμ ποτίζειν τὸν π.' ὁ ὀμφαλός Hipp.*haer*.6.14 (p.140.8ff.; M.16.3214D–3215A).

B. in rel. to heaven; **1.** identified, esp. by Gnostics cf. τὸν π. ὑπὲρ τρίτον οὐρανὸν ὄντα, τέταρτον ἄγγελον λέγουσι δυνάμει ὑπάρχειν Iren. *haer*.1.5.2(M.7.496A); ἦραν τὰς ψυχὰς ἡμῶν καὶ ἀπήγαγον ἐν τῷ π. τῷ ἐν τῷ οὐρανῷ *A.Andr.et Mt*.17(p.86.2); ἄνθρωπος ἐν τῷ π., τῷ τετάρτῳ οὐρανῷ, δημιουργεῖται· ἐκεῖ γὰρ χοϊκὴ σὰρξ οὐκ ἀναβαίνει Clem.*exc.Thdot*.51(p.123.19; M.9.684A); τὴν εἰρηνευομένην Ἱερουσαλὴμ...ἔνθα καὶ ὁ π. Mac.Aeg.*hom*.25.7(M.34.672C); ref. Lc.10:20 οὗτινος ὁ βίος...ἀναγέγραπται ἐν τῷ π. τῆς τρυφῆς Marc.Diac.*v.Porph*. 20; cf. μίαν πατρίδα ἀνθρώπων, τὸν π. εἶναι λέγων, πᾶσαν δὲ τὴν γῆν ὡς κοινὴν τῆς φύσεως ἐξορίαν βλέπειν Gr.Nyss.*laud.Bas*.(M.46. 797A); id.*v.Gr.Thaum*.(M.46.896B); **2.** ref. 2Cor.12:2f.: **a.** interpreted as not identifying π. with third heaven but asserting its location on earth οὐδὲ ὁ ἀπόστολος ὑποτίθεται τὸν π. εἶναι ἐν τρίτῳ οὐρανῷ τοῖς λεπτῶν ἀκροᾶσθαι λόγων ἐπισταμένοις...δύο ἀποκαλύψεις μεγάλας ἑωρακέναι μηνύει, δὶς ἀναληφθεὶς ἐναργῶς, ἅπαξ μὲν ἕως τρίτου οὐρανοῦ, ἅπαξ δὲ εἰς τὸν π. Meth.*res*.1.55(pp.313.14–314.4; M. 18.296A); περὶ παραδείσου πολλοὶ ἀλληγοροῦσιν, ὡς ὁ...Ὠριγένης...καί φησιν· οὐκ ἔστι π. ἐπὶ τῆς γῆς· δῆθεν ἀπὸ τοῦ ῥητοῦ τοῦ παρὰ τοῦ ἁγίου ἀποστόλου εἰρημένου ὅτι 'οἶδα ἄνθρωπον...κτλ.'...οὐ γὰρ ἐν μιᾷ συντομίᾳ τὸν οὐρανὸν καὶ τὸν π. συνῆψεν...τὸ δὲ μετὰ τοῦ ἄρθρου ἑτέρου προσώπου ἐστὶ διαληπτικὸν καὶ ἑτέρου τόπου μεταστατικόν Epiph.*anc*.54(p.63.10ff.; M.43.112B,C); *ib*.55(p.64.9; 113B); **b.** as identifying the two ταῦτα δὲ ὑπὸ τῶν ψυχῶν [acc. Or.] εἴρηται τῶν εἰς τὴν παγίδα τὸ σῶμα, ὡς εἰς ἀγώνισμα, κατενεχθεισῶν ἐκ τοῦ τρίτου οὐρανοῦ, ἔνθα ὁ π. Meth.*res*.1.54(p.312.18; M.41.1148A); ridiculing idea that S. Paul should have heard ineffable words in an earthly paradise, which he heard neither in second nor in third heaven, Anast.S.*hex*.7(M.89.967A); **c.** as distinct from earth, but not identified with heaven, cf. τὸ χωρίον ὁ π., ὡς πρὸς καλλονήν, μέσος τοῦ κόσμου καὶ τοῦ οὐρανοῦ γεγένηται Thphl.Ant.*Autol*.2.24(M.6. 1092A); cf. *Paulus...usque ad tertium coelum raptum se esse significans; et rursum, delatum esse in paradisum*, Iren.*haer*.2.30.7(M.7. 818C); Ἠλίας εἰς οὐρανὸν μόνον· Παῦλος δὲ καὶ εἰς οὐρανόν, καὶ εἰς π., ἔπρεπε γὰρ τοὺς μαθητὰς τοῦ Ἰησοῦ, πολυπλασίονα λαβεῖν τὴν χάριν Cyr.H.*catech*.14.26; Cosm.Ind.*top*.3(M.88.168A); *ib*.5(297D); cf. ἐξ ὧν δηλοῦται ἐν οὐρανοῖς ὑπάρχειν τὸν π.· οὐ γὰρ εἶπεν, ἁρπαγέντα εἰς τρίτον οὐρανόν, κἀκεῖθεν καταβάντα εἰς τὸν π.· ἀλλ' ἐν τῇ ἁρπαγῇ ἀμφοτέρων ἐμνήσθη. ἀλλ' οὐκ ἐν μιᾷ συντομίᾳ τὸν οὐρανὸν καὶ τὸν π. συναπεφήνατο...φατὲ γὰρ μὴ εἰρηκέναι αὐτόν, καταβάντα, ἀλλ' ἁρπαγέντα εἰς τὸν π., ἐκ τούτου ἀποσειόμενον, ὡς ἔοικε, τὰς τῶν ἀοιδίμων πατρῶν παιδείας. ἐπεὶ γὰρ οὐκ ἔφη ἀναβάντα, ἀλλ' ἁρπαγέντα, παρὰ τοῦτο ἆρ' οὐκ ἀναβέβηκεν; εἰ δὲ ἀναβέβηκεν ἁρπαγείς, δηλονότι καὶ καταβέβηκεν ἁρπαγείς ‡Caes.Naz.*dial*.142(M.38.1089–1092); *ib*.143(1092); **3.** superiority of heaven over paradise ὁ ἐκ τοῦ π. πεσὼν μεῖζον ὑπακοῆς ἆθλον, οὐρανούς, ἀπολαμβάνει Clem. *prot*.11(p.79.5; M.8.229A); τὸν δὲ π. καὶ ὀφθαλμὸς εἶδε τοῦ Ἀδάμ, καὶ οὖς ἤκουσε...οὐ γὰρ εἰς π. ἐπαγγέλλεται εἰσαγαγεῖν ἡμᾶς ὁ θεός, ἀλλ' εἰς αὐτὸν τὸν οὐρανόν· οὐδὲ βασιλείαν π., ἀλλὰ βασιλείαν οὐρανῶν ἐκήρυξεν...ἀπωλέσας μὲν γὰρ π., ἔδωκε δέ σοι ὁ θεὸς τὸν οὐρανόν... ἔπλασεν ὁ θεὸς τὸν ἄνθρωπον...καὶ ἔθετο αὐτὸν ἐν τῷ π. οὐκ ἐγένετο χρήσιμος ὁ πλασθείς, ἀλλὰ διεστράφη. οὐκέτι λοιπὸν ἀπὸ γῆς καὶ ὕδατος αὐτὸν ἀναπλάττει, ἀλλ' ἐξ ὕδατος καὶ πνεύματος· καὶ οὐκέτι π. ἐπαγγέλλεται πρὸς αὐτόν, ἀλλὰ βασιλείαν οὐρανῶν Chrys.*serm.7.5 in Gen*.(4.681A–D); id.*hom.25.2 in Jo*.(8.145D).

C. as place of life after death; **1.** place of judgement, *T.Abr*.B 10 (p.114.12); Hipp.*antichr*.64(p.44.15; M.10.784C); **2.** intermediate state, where souls of just await general resurrection; ἆρον αὐτὸν εἰς τὸν π. ἕως τρίτου οὐρανοῦ, καὶ ἄφες κἀκεῖσε ἕως τῆς ἡμέρας ἐκείνης τῆς μεγάλης *Apoc.Mos*.37(p.20); Ἀβραάμ, οὗ τὸ σῶμα ἐν τῷ μνημείῳ, ἡ δὲ ψυχὴ ἐν τῷ π. *A.Andr.et Mt*.15(p.82.11); ποῦ οὖν ἐτέθη ὁ πρῶτος ἄνθρωπος; ἐν τῷ π. ... καὶ ἐκεῖθεν ἐξεβλήθη εἰς τόνδε τὸν κόσμον, παρακούσας. διὸ καὶ λέγουσιν οἱ πρεσβύτεροι,...τοὺς μετατεθέντας ἐκεῖσε μετατεθῆναι. δικαίοις γὰρ ἀνθρώποις...ἡτοιμάσθη ὁ π., ἐν ᾧ καὶ Παῦλος ἀπόστολος εἰσκομισθεὶς ἤκουσεν ἄρρητα ῥήματα ...κἀκεῖ μένειν τοὺς μετατεθέντας ἕως συντελείας, προοιμιαζομένους τὴν ἀφθαρσίαν Iren.*haer*.5.5.1(M.7.1135A,B); cf. *puto enim quod sancti quique discedentes ex hac vita permanebunt in loco aliquo in terra posito, quem paradisum dicit scriptura divina, velut in quodam eruditionis loco...vel schola animarum, in quo de omnibus his, quae in terris viderant, doceantur*, Or.*princ*.2.11.6(p.190.3; M. 11.246A); cf.id.*engast*.9(p.294.8; M.12.1028B); ἄγονται γὰρ ὑπὸ τῶν ἀγγέλων...αἱ μὲν τῶν δικαίων ψυχαὶ εἰς τὸν π., ἔνθα συντυχία...ἀγγέλων ...κατ' ὀπτασίαν δὲ καὶ τοῦ σωτῆρος Χριστοῦ ‡Just.*qu.et resp*.75(M.6. 1317A); cf.*ib*.85(1328A); αἱ ψυχαὶ τῶν δικαίων...ἐν τῷ π. ἐναποτίθενται ...ἄχρι τῆς ἀναστάσεως, ὡς ἐν...τιμίῳ χωρίῳ ὑπὸ τῶν ἀοράτων δυνάμεων διατηρούμεναι Cosm.Ind.*top*.9(M.88.412A); identified with

Abraham's bosom, *T.Abr.*A 11(p.90.1); *ib.*20(p.104.1); *Lit.Jac.* (p.220.11); **3.** where body of BMV awaits resurrection *ἀπὸ τοῦ νῦν ἔσται τὸ τίμιόν σου σῶμα μετατιθέμενον ἐν τῷ π., ἡ δὲ ἁγία σου ψυχὴ ἐν τοῖς οὐρανοῖς* *Dorm.BMV* 39(p.108); *ib.*48(p.111); *Χριστὸν ...τὸν τῷ σώματι ἀφθάρτῳ κατασκηνοῦντά σε ἐν π.* Mod.*dorm.*10 (M.86.3305B); **4.** exeg. Lc.23:43 (v. *λῃστής*); **a.** dist. from heaven *ὁπηνίκα μὲν εἰς τοὺς καταχθονίους ἀφικνεῖτο τόπους, ἐν ταὐτῷ δὲ καὶ τὴν τοῦ λῃστοῦ ψυχὴν αὐθήμερον εἰσῆγεν εἰς τὸν π. ... ἅμα μὲν εἰς τὰ καταχθόνια κατιοῦσα μέρη τοῦ χάους, ἅμα δὲ καὶ τῇ ἀρχαιοτάτῃ τοῦ π. πάλιν ἀποκαθιστῶσα νομῇ τὸν ὑπεισδύντα τῷ κράτει τῆς ἀηττήτου βασιλείας* Eust.*engast.*18(p.45.15ff.; M.18.652B); *εἰ πρὸ τῆς ἀναστάσεως οὐκ ἔστιν ἡ τῶν ἔργων ἀντίδοσις, ποῖον τῷ λῃστῇ προσγέγονεν ὄφελος, πρὸς τὸν π. αὐτοῦ τῆς ψυχῆς εἰσαχθείσης, καὶ μάλιστα ὅτι ὁ μὲν π. αἰσθητός, οὐκ αἰσθητὴ δέ ἐστι τῆς ψυχῆς ἡ οὐσία; ὄφελος γέγονε τῷ λῃστῇ εἰς τὸν π. εἰσελθόντι τὸ ἔργοις μαθεῖν τῆς πίστεως τὸ ὠφέλιμον...ἔχει δὲ τοῦ π. τὴν αἴσθησιν, καὶ τὴν ἐννοηματικὴν λεγομένην αἴσθησιν, καθ' ἣν ὁρῶσιν αἱ ψυχαὶ ἑαυτάς τε καὶ τὰ ὑπ' αὐτάς* ‡Just.*qu.et resp.*76(M.6.1317B); **b.** equated with it *τὸν π. ... ἐνταῦθα οὐ τὸν π. εἶπεν, ἀλλὰ τῷ τοῦ π. ὀνόματι τὴν βασιλείαν τῶν οὐρανῶν ὠνόμασεν. ἐπειδὴ γὰρ πρὸς λῃστὴν διελέγετο, ἄνθρωπον οὐδὲν ἀκηκοότα τῶν ὑψηλῶν δογμάτων...τῷ γνωριμωτέρῳ...ὀνόματι τοῦ π. τὴν βασιλείαν τῶν οὐρανῶν δηλοῖ* Chrys.*serm.7.5 in Gen.*(4.681E–682A); esp. ref. Christ *πῶς κατὰ ταὐτὸν καὶ ἐν τῷ ᾅδῃ καὶ ἐν τῷ π. ὁ κύριος; οὗ ζητήματος λύσις ἐστὶ μία, τὸ μηδὲν ἄβατον εἶναι θεῷ...ἑτέρα δὲ...διὰ...τοῦ σώματος, ἐν ᾧ τὴν ἐκ τοῦ θανάτου καταφθορὰν οὐκ ἐδέξατο, κατήργησε τὸν ἔχοντα τοῦ θανάτου τὸ κράτος, διὰ δὲ τῆς ψυχῆς πρὸς τὴν ἑστίαν ἐπειγομένης, τὴν ἐπὶ τὸν π. τῶν ἀνθρώπων ἐπάνοδον... εἰ δὲ ζητεῖς πῶς ἐν τῷ π. ὤν, ἐν ταῖς χερσὶ τοῦ πατρὸς ἑαυτὸν παρατίθεται, ἑρμηνεύσει σοι ὁ...Ἡσαΐας...εἶπε γὰρ ἐκεῖνος ἐκ προσώπου τοῦ θεοῦ περὶ τῆς ἄνω Ἱερουσαλήμ, ἣν οὐκ ἄλλην παρὰ τὸν π. εἶναι πιστεύομεν, ὅτι 'ἐπὶ τῶν χειρῶν μου ἐζωγράφησά σου τὰ τείχη'. εἰ οὖν ἐν ταῖς χερσὶ τοῦ πατρὸς περιγέγραπται ἡ Ἱερουσαλήμ, ἥτις ἐστὶν ὁ π., δηλονότι ὁ ἐν π. γενόμενος ταῖς πατρῴαις πάντως ἐνδιαιτᾶται παλάμαις* Gr.Nyss.*res.*1(M.46.616D–617C); as present there only in his Godhead, not with body or soul, Anast.S.*hod.*13(M.89.225A); ‡Caes.Naz. *dial.*143(M.38.1093); for gen. exegesis cf.Or.*Jo.*32.32(19; p.497.32ff.; M.14.828C); **5.** as state of final bliss after general resurrection *πλασθέντος τοῦ ἀνθρώπου ἐν τῷ κόσμῳ...δὶς αὐτοῦ ἐν τῷ π. τεθέντος· ἵνα τὸ μὲν ἅπαξ πεπληρωμένον ὅτε ἐτέθη, τὸ δὲ δεύτερον μέλλῃ πληροῦσθαι μετὰ τὴν ἀνάστασιν καὶ κρίσιν* Thphl.Ant.*Autol.*2.26(M.6.1093A); *ὡς οἱ πρεσβύτεροι λέγουσι, τότε καὶ οἱ μὲν καταξιωθέντες τῆς ἐν οὐρανῷ διατριβῆς, ἐκεῖσε χωρήσουσιν, οἱ δὲ τῆς τοῦ π. τῆς τρυφῆς ἀπολαύσουσιν* Iren.*haer.*5.36.1(M.7.1222B); *οἱ μὲν δίκαιοι κληρονομήσουσι τὴν* [sic] *π., οἱ δὲ ἁμαρτωλοὶ...τὴν αἰώνιον κόλασιν* *Apoc. Dan.*C 116(p.120); *1Apoc.Jo.*25(p.91); ‡Ath.*qu.Ant.*19(M.28.609A); **6.** summary of patristic opinions, cf. *ὅτι μετὰ τὴν ἀνάστασιν ἐν π. τῶν δικαίων ἔσται ἡ διατριβή, καὶ ὅτι οὐκ ἐν π., ἀλλ' ἐν τοῖς οὐρανοῖς, καὶ ὡς ὁ π. οὔτε ἐν τῷ οὐρανῷ οὔτε ἐπὶ τῆς γῆς, ἀλλὰ τούτων μεταξύ.— ὡς ὁ π. ἡ ἄνω ἐστὶν Ἱερουσαλήμ, καὶ ἐν τῷ τρίτῳ ἐστὶν οὐρανῷ, καὶ τὰ ἐν αὐτῷ ξύλα νοερά τέ εἰσι καὶ σύνεσιν ἔχουσι καὶ λόγον, καὶ ὡς ὁ ἄνθρωπος μετὰ τὴν παράβασιν ἐκεῖθεν ἐπὶ τὴν γῆν κατηνέχθη. εἶτα καὶ τὸ ἀντικείμενον, ὅτι ὁ π. οὐκ ἔστιν ἐν τῷ τρίτῳ οὐρανῷ, ἀλλ' ἐπὶ τῆς γῆς* Steph.G.*fr.*ap.Phot.*cod.*232(M.103.1093D–1096A).

D. as regained; **1.** through Christ; **a.** in gen., cf. *αὐτὸς* [sc. Messiah] *ἀνοίξει τὰς θύρας τοῦ π.* *T.Lev.*18.10; *Apoc.Bar.*4(p.87.33); ref. Mt.6:25 *ὁ κύριος εἰς τὴν ἐν τῷ π. ζωὴν ἡμᾶς ἀνακαλούμενος, ἐκβάλλει τὴν μέριμναν τῶν ψυχῶν* Bas.*hom.*9.9(2.81C; M.31.349B); Chrys. *hom.in Rom.5:3*(3.145C); **b.** through Passion, esp. ref. the good thief (v. *λῃστής*) *ἀρχὴ ὁδῶν κτισθεὶς ἡμῖν...εἴσοδον ἐν τῷ π., ἐξ οὗ ἐκβέβληται Ἀδάμ, εἰς ὃν πάλιν εἰσῆλθε διὰ τοῦ λῃστοῦ* Ath.*exp.fid.*1 (M.25.201B); *ὅτε ἐξωρίσθη τοῦ π. ὁ ἄνθρωπος, ἐτάχθη φρουρεῖν τὴν εἴσοδον φλογίνη ῥομφαία...ζητούμενον τοῦτο ἦν· εἰ καὶ τοῖς ἁγίοις ἄβατός ἐστιν ὁ π. ... καὶ εἰ τοῦ π. οἱ ἀθληταὶ ἀποκλείονται...ὁ λῃστὴς... μὲν ἀξιοῦται τοῦ π.· ἐπὶ δὲ τῶν ἁγίων ἡ φλογίνη ῥομφαία διακωλύει τὸν εἴσοδον;...τοῖς μὲν ἀναξίοις κατὰ στόμα προφαίνηται, τοῖς δὲ ἀξίοις στρεφομένη κατὰ νώτου γίνηται* Gr.Nyss.*mart.*2(M.46.772A,B); *Ἀδὰμ δὲ διὰ τὴν παρακοὴν ἐκ τοῦ π. ὁ θεὸς δικαίως ἔρριψε· τὸν δὲ λῃστήν, καὶ σὺν αὐτῷ τὸν Ἀδὰμ καὶ τὸ κοινὸν ἡμῶν ὅλον γένος ὁ υἱὸς εἰσήγαγεν* Didym.*Trin.*1.16(M.39.337C); *τὸν π. πεντακισχίλια ἔτη καὶ πλείω κεκλεισμένον σήμερον ἡμῖν ἠνέῳξεν. ἐν ταύτῃ γὰρ τῇ ἡμέρᾳ...τὸν λῃστὴν εἰσήγαγεν ὁ θεός, δύο κατορθώματα ἐργασάμενος. ἓν μέν, ὅτι π. ἠνέῳξεν, ἕτερον δέ, ὅτι λῃστὴν εἰσήγαγε...καίτοι τὰ χερουβὶμ ἐτήρει τὸν π.· ἀλλ' οὗτος καὶ τῶν χερουβὶμ δεσπότης...τιμὴ γὰρ π. τὸ τοιοῦτον ἔχειν δεσπότην, ὡς καὶ λῃστὴν ἄξιον ποιῆσαι τῆς τρυφῆς τῆς ἐν τῷ π.* Chrys.*cruc.*1.2(2.404C–405B); Procl.CP *or.*11.1(M.65.784B); Jo.D. *hom.*3.8(M.96.600B); cf.*ib.*4.21(620B); **c.** through sacraments; ref. baptism, Cyr.H.*catech.*19.9 cit. s. *ἀνατολή*; *ὁ γὰρ τῆς χάριτος ποταμὸς...εἰσβάλλων εἰς τὸν π. ... εἰσάγων εἰς τὸν π. ... γεννήματα πνεύματος* Gr.Nyss.*bapt.diff.*(M.46.420C,D); *ἐξώρισας τοῦ π., καὶ πάλιν ἀνεκαλέσω...ἐρράντισας ὕδατι καθαρῷ, καὶ τῶν ῥύπων ἐκάθαρας* id. *bapt.Chr.*(M.46.600A); *τῶν αὐτοῦ* [sc. *θεοῦ*] *μετέχειν μυστηρίων ἐξουσίαν ἔλαβον, καὶ ἡ τοῦ π. θύρα ἀνέῳκται* †Jo.D.*B.J.*16(M.96.1005B); **2.** through human virtue: virginity *τῆς εἰς τὸν π. ἀποκαταστάσεως...οὐδὲν αἴτιον οὕτως ἄλλο γέγονε...ὡς ἁγνεία* Meth. *symp.*4.2(p.46.9; M.18.88B); *οὐ πρότερον αὐτὴν* [sc. Eve] *ἔγνω, πρὶν ἐξορισθῆναι τοῦ π. ... δι' ἧς τοίνυν ἀκολουθίας ἔξω τοῦ π. γεγόναμεν τῷ προπάτορι συνεκβληθέντες, καὶ νῦν διὰ τῆς αὐτῆς ἔξεστιν ἡμῖν παλινδρομήσασιν ἐπανελθεῖν ἐπὶ τὴν ἀρχαίαν μακαριότητα...ἐπεὶ οὖν τοῦ χωρισμοῦ τῆς ἐν τῷ π. ζωῆς τὸ τελευταῖον ὁ γάμος ἐστί, τοῦτον πρῶτον καταλιπεῖν...ὑφηγεῖται ὁ λόγος...καὶ...τάχα οὕτως ἄν τις ἀπὸ τοῦ κόσμου τούτου...ἁρπαγείη πάλιν εἰς τὸν π., ἐν ᾧ καὶ Παῦλος γενόμενος ἤκουσε...τὰ ἄρρητα* Gr.Nyss.*virg.*12f.(pp.302.15–304.12; M.46.373D–376C); temperance, Bas.*renunt.*7(2.208E; M.31.641B); Thdr. Stud.*or.*1(M.99.689B); obedience, †Cyr.*hom.div.*10(5².373C); martyrdom, Gr.Nyss.*mart.*2(M.46.764D).

E. met.; **1.** of God [*πατὴρ τ*]*οῦ κυρίου ἡμῶν Ἰ*(*ησο*)*ῦ...ὁ π.* [*τῆ*]*ς τρυφῆς* *Pap.Chr.*(p.431); and Christ *ὁ π. ὁ πνευματικὸς αὐτὸς ἡμῖν ὁ σωτὴρ ὑπάρχει* Clem.*str.*6.1(p.423.12; M.9.209B); *A.Mt.*2(p.219.2); **2.** of BMV *Μαρία...ὁ λογικὸς τοῦ δευτέρου Ἀδὰμ π.* Procl.CP *or.laud. BMV* 1(p.103.12; M.65.681A); Mod.*dorm.*10(M.86.3305A); Jo.Eub. *concept.BMV* 12(M.96.1480A); *σήμερον* [sc. on day of Dormition] *ἡ Ἐδὲμ τοῦ νέου Ἀδὰμ τὸν λογικὸν π. ὑποδέχεται, ἐν ᾧ τὸ κατάκριμα λέλυται, ἐν ᾧ τὸ τῆς ζωῆς ξύλον πεφύτευται* Jo.D.*hom.*9.2(M.96.725A); Thdr.Stud.*nativ.BMV* 7(M.96.696D); **3.** of saints *ὅσιοι κυρίου...ὁ π. κυρίου* *Pss.Sal.*14.2; Alex.Sal.*Barn.*proem.5(437C); **4.** of Church; **a.** in gen., cf. *plantata est enim ecclesia paradisus in hoc mundo.* Iren.*haer.*5.20.2(M.7.1178A); *τὸ ξύλον τῆς ζωῆς, ὃ πρόσθεν μὲν ὁ π. ἔφερε, νῦν δὲ...ἡ ἐκκλησία* Meth.*symp.*9.3(p.117.14; M.18.184A); Ath. *Ar.*1.1(M.26.13B); cf.Hipp.*Dan.*1.18(M.10.693A); *καταφυτεύῃ* [sc. catechumen]...*εἰς τὸν νοητὸν π.* Cyr.H.*catech.*1.4; *ib.*5.10; Amph. *exerc.*(p.28.1); Gr.Nyss.*hom.9 in Cant.*(M.44.977C); Epiph.*exp.fid.* 2(p.497.27; M.42.776C); Chrys.*poenit.*8.1(2.340D); *ἡ ἐκκλησία...π. ἐστι τρυφῆς*, with detailed description of difference between paradise and Church, ‡Chrys.*caec.*2(8.63Cff.); *ib.*(8.64B); as symbol of Church, Niceph.Ur.*v.Sym.*172f.(M.86.3145A,B); **b.** entered through baptism *ἀναγεννώμενοι διὰ τοῦ θείου βαπτίσματος ἐν τῷ π. τίθενται, τουτέστιν ἐν τῇ ἐκκλησίᾳ* Or.*sel.in Gen.*2:13(M.12.100B); Cyr.H.*catech.*19.9; **c.** parallelism between Church and paradise *ὁ μὲν πνευματικὸς οὗτος...λειμὼν...τύπον ἔχειν τοῦ θείου π. μοι φαίνεται. ὃν γὰρ τρόπον ὁ αἰσθητὸς ἐκεῖνος...χορὸς...μυρίοις...φαιδρύνεται κάλλεσιν· οὕτω δὴ καὶ...ἐκκλησίας θίασος* Amph.*hom.*1.1(M.39.36A); Bas.Sel.*or.*34.1(M. 85.365D); *κῆπος...κεκλεισμένος καὶ π. ἡ ἐκκλησία...π. δὲ λέγω οὐ κατὰ τὸν ἀρχαῖον ἐκεῖνον, ἀλλὰ πολὺ ἐκείνου ἀνώτερον. ἐκεῖ μὲν ἐβασίλευσεν ὄφις, ἐνταῦθα δὲ βασιλεύει ὁ Χριστός* ‡Chrys.*caec.*1(8.63A); exclusion from Church compared with expulsion from *π.*, *ib.*2(64B); Marc.Er.*opusc.*4(M.65.1025B); cf.Meth.*symp.*9.3(p.117.14; M.18. 184A); **d.** authors who equated the two *οἱ...ἀρχαιότεροι τῶν ἐκκλησιῶν· λέγω δὴ Φίλων ὁ φιλόσοφος...καὶ Παπίας...Εἰρηναῖος...καὶ Ἰουστῖνος ὁ μάρτυς...Πανταίνετός τε ὁ Ἀλεξανδρεύς, καὶ Κλήμης ὁ Στρωματεύς, καὶ οἱ ἀμφ' αὐτούς, πνευματικῶς τὰ περὶ π. ἐθεωρήθησαν εἰς τὴν Χριστοῦ ἐκκλησίαν ἀναφερόμενα. ἐξ ὧν εἰσι καὶ οἱ...δύο Καππαδοκαὶ Γρηγόριοι* Anast.S.*hex.*7(M.89.962A,B); *ib.*(969C); **e.** Adamite *ἡγοῦνται γὰρ τὴν ἑαυτῶν ἐκκλησίαν εἶναι τὸν π.* Epiph.*haer.*52.2(p.313.12; M.41.957A); **5.** of spiritual state; ref. souls *οἱ γενόμενοι π. τρυφῆς, πάγκαρπον ξύλον εὐθαλοῦν ἀνατείλαντες ἐν ἑαυτοῖς* ‡*Diogn.*12.1; *καρποφορῶμεν τοὺς καρποὺς τοῦ πνεύματος, ἵνα ὡς ἐν π. πνευματικῷ κύριος ἡμῖν ἐμπεριπατῇ* Or.*or.*25.3(p.359.3; M.11.500A); id.*hom.1.16 in Jer.* (p.16.10; M.13.276C); *τὴν ἑαυτοῦ καρδίαν...ὡς π. φυλάσσων ἐν αὐτῇ τὸν λόγον...μὴ ἀκούων τοῦ ἔνδον εἰλισσομένου ὄφεως συμβουλεύοντος τὰ πρὸς ἡδονὴν...εἰς τοῦτον τὸν π. εἰσῆλθε Νῶε, τὴν ἐντολὴν φυλάσσων... τοῦτον φυλάσσων Ἀβραὰμ φωνὴν θεοῦ ἤκουσε* Mac.Aeg.*hom.*37.1(M. 34.749C,D); ref. reading of scripture *π. τρυφῆς ἡ τῶν θείων γραφῶν ἐστιν ἀνάγνωσις, π. δὲ τρυφῆς ἐκείνου τοῦ π. βελτίων. τοῦτον τὸν π. οὐκ ἐν τῇ γῇ, ἀλλ' ἐν ταῖς τῶν πιστευόντων ψυχαῖς ἐφύτευσεν ὁ θεός· τοῦτον τὸν π. οὐκ ἐν Ἐδέμ...ἔθετο ἐν ἑνὶ περιγράψας χωρίῳ, ἀλλὰ πανταχοῦ τῆς γῆς ἐξήπλωσε* Chrys.*hom.3.1 in Ac.princ.*(3.71C); ref. contemplation *πειράθητι...ἐν περινοίᾳ γενέσθαι τοῦ π. ἐκείνου, καὶ φθάσαι...εἰς τὰς αὐγὰς τοῦ θείου φωτός· ἔνθα τὸ φῶς τῆς γνώσεως ἀνατέλλει· ἔνθα ὁ π. τῆς τρυφῆς πεφύτευται* †Bas.*parad.*11(1.351C; M.30.72A); *αὕτη* [sc. *παρθενία*] *ὁ λογικὸς τοῦ θεοῦ π., ἐν ᾧ πᾶν ξύλον ὡραῖον εἰς ὅρασιν, τουτέστιν πνευματικὴν θεωρίαν* Procl.CP *or.*6.3 (M.65.725A); *π., ἡ θεωρία τῶν νοητῶν ἐστιν* ‡Max.*cap.al.*162(M.90.

1440A); 6. ref. books; a. scripture ἐν τῷ π. τῆς γραφῆς Chrys.*hom.3.1 in Ac.princ.*(3.71C); cf.id.*stat.*1.1(2.2B); Cyr.*Jo.*proem.(4.2C); Jo.Mon.*hymn.Bas.*9(M.96.1376C); b. as title of books on Egyptian monks ἡ κατὰ Αἰγύπτων τῶν μοναχῶν ἱστορία, ἤτοι π. ‡Pall.*h.mon.* tit.(M.65.441; p.1n.); ἀναγινωσκόντων ἡμῶν εἰς τὸν π. τὰ ἀποφθέγματα τῶν ἁγίων πατέρων Jo.Mosch.*prat.*212(M.87.3104C); in variant title of Pall.*h.Laus.*(p.9n.).

παραδεκτέον, *one must interpret* ἀλληγορικῶς...π. Eus.*Is.*12:3(M.24.181D).

***παραδεκτικός,** *receptive* of, Clem.*str.*2.4(p.121.16; M.8.948B); *ib.*7.3(p.13.23; M.9.424A).

παραδεκτός, 1. *accepted* τὸ...ἄγνωμον...μηδὲ ὑφ' ἡμῶν π. Tat.*orat.*31(p.31.13; M.6.869A); Or.*hom.14.8 in Jer.*(p.113.12; M.13.413A); **2.** *acceptable* οὐδεὶς τὸ τῶν δεισιδαιμόνων ὄνομα ποιεῖται π. Cyr.*Is.*5.6(2.899B).

παραδέχ-ομαι, 1. *accept*; pass., *be acceptable*; **a.** of God accepting man ἐπιστρέψωμεν ἐπὶ τὸν καλέσαντα ἡμᾶς θεόν, ἕως ἔτι ἔχομεν τὸν ~όμενον ἡμᾶς *2Clem.*16.1; **b.** of men accepting Christ: in the flesh τῆς τῶν Γαλιλαίων παραδοχῆς, ἣν παρεδέξαντο τὸν σωτῆρα ἐλθόντα Or.*Jo.*13.56(55; p.286.5; M.14.504C); as Son of God εἰς ἑαυτοὺς ~όμενοι τὸν υἱὸν τοῦ θεοῦ id.*comm.in Rom.*8:4(*JTS* 14 p.17); τοῦ ἐν Μωϋσεῖ θεοῦ ἀκούομεν καὶ τὸν μαρτυρούμενον ὑπ' αὐτοῦ θεὸν Ἰησοῦν ὡς υἱὸν θεοῦ παρεδεξάμεθα id.*Cels.*5.51(p.55.13; M.11.1261A); Eus.*Is.*12:2(M.24.181D); τοῦτον...αὐτοὶ οὐ παραδεξάμενοι, ἔξω που τῆς ἑαυτῶν σωτηρίας ἀπήλασαν Cyr.*Ps.*68:27(M.69.1173A); of accepting foreign gods Σκύθαι μὲν τοὺς Περσῶν, Πέρσαι δὲ τοὺς Σύρων οὐ ~ονται θεούς Ath.*gent.*23(M.25.45B); οὐδὲ πρόσφατόν τινα παραδέξασθαι θεὸν παρακελευόμεθα Didym.(‡Bas.)*Eun.*5(1.317A; M.29.760C); **2.** *accept* as a fact τὸ...τῶν ὑπὸ τοῦ θεοῦ κτισθέντων...ἃ μὲν ὡς καλῶς κτισθέντα ~εσθαι *Diogn.*4.2; Eus.*e.th.*1.17(p.78.26; παραδεδειγ- M.24.861A); φύσει ἀγαθοὺς καὶ κακοὺς ἀνθρώπους παρεδέξαντο Diod.*Ps.*63:8(M.33.1598C); of uncritical acceptance ματαίαν ἀκοὴν παραδεξάμενοι Just.*dial.*8.4(M.6.493B); Athenag.*leg.*30.2(M.6.960B); of acceptance with discrimination, Or.*princ.*3.1.3(p.197.11; M.11.252A); **3.** *receive* teaching, Ign.*Eph.*9.1; Or.*Cels.*6.57(p.127.30; M.11.1385B); τοὺς μακρὰν τῆς ἀληθείας δυνάμει τινὶ θείᾳ ~εσθαι αὐτήν *ib.*8.43(p.257.24; M.11.1580C); καλὴ δὲ διὰ τὸν λόγον ὃν παρεδέξατο id.*schol.in Cant.*1:4(p.liii; M.17.256B); cf. τὸν σπόρον τῆς αὐτοῦ διδασκαλίας ~ομένων Eus.*theoph.*14(p.33*.7; M.24.680A); **4.** *receive as* canonical *scripture* οἱ μόνου...Μωϋσέως ~όμενοι τὰς βίβλους Σαμαρεῖς ἢ Σαδδουκαῖοι Or.*Cels.*1.49(p.100.25; M.11.753A); οὐδὲ γὰρ ~ονται [sc. Marcionites] τοὺς εὐαγγελιστὰς ἅπαντας, ἀλλ' ἕνα μόνον Chrys.*comm. in Gal.*1:6(10.667C); *accept as authoritative* τοῦτον ἠτιμώσατε τὸν νόμον καὶ τὴν καινὴν ἁγίαν αὐτοῦ διαθήκην ἐφαυλίσατε, καὶ οὐδὲ νῦν ~εσθε Just.*dial.*12.2(M.6.500B); τὰς καλουμένας τοῦ θεοῦ διαθήκας ἐπὶ συνθήκαις παρεδεξάμεθα αἷς πρὸς αὐτὸν ἐποιησάμεθα Or.*mart.*12(p.11.24; M.11.577C); τὸ...ὅλως πίστει παραδεχθὲν πολυπραγμονεῖν οὐκ ἀζήμιον Cyr.*hom.pasch.*24.3(5^2.289C); **5.** of accepting persons; **a.** upon letters of introduction τὸν ἀδελφὸν ἡμῶν Ἡρακλῆν παράδεξαι [κ]ατὰ τὸ ἔθος *Pap.Chr.*(p.386); **b.** for church membership τοὺς ἐξ ἁρπαγῆς ἔχοντας γυναῖκας...οὐ πρότερον χρὴ ~εσθαι, πρὶν ἢ ἀφελέσθαι αὐτῶν Bas.*ep.*199 *can.*22(3.293B; M.32.721B); *Const.App.*2.16.2; Philost.*h.e.*10.1(M.65.584B); *retain as a member* πᾶσιν ἐπιπλήσσει ὡς κακῶς αὐτὸν παραδεξαμένοις Or.*comm.in 1Cor.*5:1(*JTS* 9 p.363); for priesthood, Gr.Nyss.*v.Gr.Thaum.*(M.46.936A); **6.** of receiving as a wife ἐὰν οὖν, φημί, κύριε, μετὰ τὸ ἀπολυθῆναι τὴν γυναῖκα μετανοήσῃ [ἡ γυνὴ] καὶ θελήσῃ ἐπὶ τὸν ἑαυτῆς ἄνδρα ὑποστρέψαι, οὐ παραδεχθήσεται; καὶ μήν, φησί, ἐὰν μὴ παραδέξηται αὐτὴν ὁ ἀνήρ, ἁμαρτάνει..., ἀλλὰ δεῖ παραδεχθῆναι τὸν ἡμαρτηκότα καὶ μετανοοῦντα Herm.*mand.*4.1.7–8; **7.** of things, *admit, be liable to* ἰὸν οὐ παραδέχεται [sc. χρυσός] Meth.*symp.*5.8(p.63.5; M.18.112B).

παραδέω, pass., *be bound by, in the grip of* παρεδέθησαν καὶ αὐτοὶ [sc. οἱ Ἰουδαῖοι] ταῖς τῶν Ῥωμαίων στρατιαῖς Cyr.ap.*cat.Lc.*22:66(p.163.7) for παρεδόθησαν, Cyr.*Lc.*23:1(M.72.932C).

παραδηλ-όω, 1. *indicate, signify*; **a.** directly δύο στοιχεῖα τὸ Χριστοῦ ~οῦντα ὄνομα Eus.*v.C.*1.31(p.22.2; M.20.945A); Bas.*Eun.*2.3(1.240A; M.29.577A); σημαίνεται...~οῦται Thdt.*rect.conf.*3(M.6.1209B); *ib.*4(1213B); **b.** by false pretences τὰ ὑπὲρ φύσιν τὴν ἑαυτοῦ ~ῶν Cyr.*ador.*1(1.10C); **c.** indirectly, Just.*dial.*106.4(M.6.724B); *mean to say*, Chrys.*hom.34.2 in Mt.*(7.391B); ὃ καὶ αὐτὸ παρεδήλωσε λέγων... id.*hom.15.3 in 2Cor.*(10.548A); **d.** by way of enigma, parable, Gr.Nyss.*v.Mos.*(M.44.333D); καὶ ἄλλο τι...ᾐνίξατο,...καὶ γὰρ τὴν μετασχημάτισιν...παρεδήλωσε Chrys.*hom.3.2 in Heb.*(12.26D); θηρία...~οῦσθαι πλαγίως...τοὺς ἐχθρούς Cyr.*Os.*27(3.50D); **e.** by symbolism, ‡Sophr.H.*liturg.*9(M.87.3989A); **2.** *display, point out, comment on*, Bas.*Eun.*1.2(1.210C; M.29.505B); ~οῦντος τοῦ τύπου τὴν ἀστειότητα Cyr.*ador.*2(1.80A).

παραδιατάσσομαι, *range oneself in opposition* ἅπαξ ὑπὸ ζυγὸν εἰσῆλθες, τί παραδιατάσσῃ; Ephr.1.115E.

παραδιδάσκ-ω, *teach falsely*, Iren.*haer.*1 proem.2(M.6.441B); Chrys.*hom.5.2 in 1Tim.*(11.575E); ‡Chrys.*pasch.*1(8.253A); ποτὲ μὲν συνὼν...ποτὲ ~ων *Chron.Pasch.*p.256(M.92.620B).

***παραδιδράσκω, 1.** *pass by, omit*, Paul.Sil.*Soph.*703(M.86.2146A); **2.** *surpass* Λυδὸν...παρέδραμες ὄλβον *ib.*1012(2158A).

παραδιδῶ, = παραδίδωμι, †Gregent.*leg.Hom.*34(M.86.600B).

παραδίδ-ωμι, A. *give, hand over* ἡ γραφή [sc. *Apoc. Petr.*] φησι τὰ βρέφη τὰ ἐκτεθέντα τημελούχῳ ~οσθαι ἀγγέλῳ ὑφ' οὗ παιδεύεσθαι Clem.*ecl.*41(p.149.1; M.9.717C); τημελούχοις ἀγγέλοις...τὰ ἀποτικτόμενα ~οσθαι παρειλήφαμεν ἐν θεοπνεύστοις γράμμασιν Meth.*symp.*2.6(p.23.14; M.18.57A).

B. *teach, impart* as instruction, Just.*dial.*41.1(M.6.564B); *ib.*69.7(640A); Or.*hom.6.2 in Jer.*(p.50.2; M.13.325D); ὁ ~ούς μοι τὸν τόπον [i.e. exegesis of scriptural passage] *ib.20.5*(p.184.22; 512A).

C. *transmit, hand on*, as tradition; **1.** pagan teaching ~όντες τὰ μυθοποιηθέντα ὑπὸ τῶν ποιητῶν Just.*1apol.*54.1(M.6.408C); τὸ Ἡρακλείτειον σκότος τοῖς σπουδαίοις παραδεδωκέναι Tat.*orat.*3(p.3.17; M.6.809A); ~όντων τοῖς ὑποχειρίοις μυστήρια Or.*Cels.*8.67(p.283.12; M.11.1617B); traditional doctrine of philosophical schools, Just.*dial.*2.2(M.6.477A); **2.** oral tradition of Mosaic Law, handed down in succession from Seventy Elders until committed to writing after Moses' assumption, *Hom.Clem.*3.47; **3.** ref. authoritative tradition of Christian teaching ἀπολιπόντες τὴν ματαιότητα τῶν πολλῶν...ἐπὶ τὸν ἐξ ἀρχῆς ἡμῖν παραδοθέντα λόγον ἐπιστρέψωμεν Polyc.*ep.*7.2; διδάξας ἀεὶ [sc. Polycarp] ἃ καὶ παρὰ τῶν ἀποστόλων ἔμαθεν, ἃ καὶ ἡ ἐκκλησία ~ωσιν Iren.*haer.*3.3.4(M.7.852A); Clem.*str.*1.12(p.35.32; M.8.753B); τὰ προσφυῆ τοῖς θεοπνεύστοις λόγοις ὑπὸ τῶν μακαρίων ἀποστόλων τε καὶ διδασκάλων ~όμενα *ib.*7.16(p.73.6; M.9.544A); Or.*Cels.*4.32(p.302.12; M.11.1076C); ref. tradition of scriptural exegesis, Meth.*symp.*5.6(p.61.5; M.18.108C); κίνδυνος ἀφελεῖν τι ἢ προσθεῖναι τοῖς ~ομένοις ὑπὸ τοῦ πνεύματος Bas.*Eun.*2.8(1.243E; M.29.585B); Serap.*Man.*40(p.58; M.18.1224C); ref. written and unwritten apostolic tradition τὰ μὲν ἐν γραφαῖς, τὰ δὲ ἐν παραδόσεσιν παρέδωκαν οἱ ἀπόστολοι Epiph.*haer.*61.6(p.386.18; M.41.1048B); οὐ πάντα δι' ἐπιστολῆς παρεδίδοσαν, ἀλλὰ πολλὰ καὶ ἀγράφως Chrys.*hom.4.2 in 2Thess.*(11.532B); ἕνα καὶ τὸν αὐτὸν...Χριστόν· καθάπερ...τὸ τῶν πατέρων ἡμῖν παραδέδωκε σύμβολον *Symb.Chalc.*(p.130.3; H.2.456D); οὐ δεῖ...περιεργάζεσθαι τὰ μὴ παραδεδομένα ἡμῖν Jo.D.*f.o.*1.1 tit.(M.94.789A); τὰ παραδεδομένα ἡμῖν διά τε νόμου καὶ προφητῶν καὶ ἀποστόλων καὶ εὐαγγελιστῶν δεχόμεθα...ἐν αὐτοῖς μείνωμεν, μὴ μεταίροντες ὅρια αἰώνια, μηδὲ ὑπερβαίνοντες τὴν θείαν παράδοσιν *ib.*1.1(792A); **4.** ref. tradition of canonical scriptures, Meth.*symp.*10.2(p.124.1; M.18.196B); of eccl. practice, Eus.*h.e.*5.24.1(M.20.493B); of Christ's visual appearance reproduced in pictures, etc., ‡Jo.D.*ep.Thphl.*3(M.95.348D) v. παράδοσις.

D. *deliver*, Tat.*orat.*15(p.17.4; M.6.840B); τὰ μόνοις ἁγίοις...~όμενα μυστήρια τῆς...θεοσεβείας Or.*Cels.*3.60(p.254.29; M.11.1000B); Gr.Thaum.*pan.Or.*1(p.3.2; M.10.1053A).

E. *deliver up, give up*; **1.** in gen., *1Clem.*55.1; *Barn.*12.5; καρδίας ...παραδεδομένας τῇ...ἀνομίᾳ *ib.*14.5; π. ἑαυτοὺς εἰς τὰς ἀκηδίας Herm.*vis.*3.11.3; εἰς θάνατον ~όναι...τοὺς Ἰησοῦ μαθητάς Or.*Cels.*1.63(p.116.9; M.11.777C); ἑαυτὴν...~όναι...ψεύδεσι λόγοις Gr.Thaum.*pan.Or.*13(p.30.9; M.10.1088C); θανάτῳ διὰ παιδείαν παρεδόθη Meth.*res.*2.18(p.368.17; M.18.313A); **2.** of Christ παραδοῦναι τὴν σάρκα εἰς καταφθοράν *Barn.*5.1; **3.** exeg. Rom.1:24, problem of free will presented by 'παρέδωκεν αὐτοὺς ὁ θεὸς...εἰς ἀκαθαρσίαν' discussed, Or.*or.*29(p.386.31ff.; M.11.537Cff.); οὐκ εἶπεν, ἐπειδὴ παρεδόθησαν ἐπληρώθησαν, οὔτε μήν, παρεδόθησαν πληρωθησόμενοι, ἀλλά, πεπληρωμένους παρέδωκε τουτέστιν ἀφῆκε, γυμνώσας τῆς ἑαυτοῦ βοηθείας Isid.Pel.*epp.*4.59(M.78.1117A); τὸ παρέδωκεν ἀντὶ τοῦ συνεχώρησε τέθεικε Thdt.*Rom.*1:24(3.25); ἢ τάχα ἑαυτοὺς παρέδωκαν ἐπειδὴ τοῦτο ἐπεθύμουν Oecum.*Rom.*1:24(p.423.1).

F. *hand over by treachery, betray*; ref. Christ, Eus.*d.e.*10.1(p.452.6; M.22.728A); Cyr.H.*catech.*22.1; ref. Polycarp περιέμενεν γάρ, ἵνα παραδοθῇ, ὡς καὶ ὁ κύριος *M.Polyc.*1.2.

G. *commend* παρέδοτο ἡμᾶς τῷ θεῷ *V.Mac.*B(p.165).

***παραδικάζω,** *pervert justice*, *Chron.Pasch.*p.301(M.92.757A).

***παράδικος,** *unrighteous*, Jo.Eub.*innoc.*1(M.96.1504A).

παραδιοικέω, 1. *mismanage* οὐδὲ διοικεῖν ἡμᾶς, ἀλλὰ π. ἀξιοῖς Synes.*ep.*57(M.66.1396B); **2.** *be meddlesome*, *ib.*103(M.66.1476D).

παραδοξάζω, 1. pass., *appear strange* ἀλλ' εἰσὶν οἷς καὶ ὑπὲρ ἡμᾶς ὁ τόκος [sc. of Christ] παρεδοξάσθη Germ.CP *or.*2(M.98.260D);

2. *discredit* παρεδόξασε κύριος τὰς ἐπαγωγάς Martin.*ep*.13(M.*PL*.87.195A).

***παραδόξασμα, τό,** *strange happening, marvel*; of Inc., Germ.CP *or*.2(M.98.260D).

παραδοξασμός, ὁ, *wonder, glory* ἐν τῷ π. αὐτοῦ, κατὰ τὸν Σύμμαχον Eus.*Ps*.45:4(M.23.408C, cf. LXX κραταιότητι).

***παραδοξοποι-έω, 1.** *work miracles*; of God ὡς εἴωθεν ἐν γενεᾷ καὶ γενεᾷ π. Epiph.*haer*.68.6(p.146.31; M.42.193C); τῆς ἄνωθεν ῥοπῆς ~ούσης τὰ θαύματα Chrys.*exp.in Ps*.135:13(5.400A); τὰ εἴδωλα... οὐδὲν εἶχον ὅμοιον τῷ ~οῦντι θεῷ Ath.*exp.Ps*.113:4(M.27.469A); of Christ ~ῶν ὡς θεός Eus.*d.e*.4.11(p.169.8; M.22.281C); *ib*.9.16(p.438.31; 708A); Chrys.*hom.29.1 in Mt*.(7.342C); *ib.68.2*(672E); **2.** *work magic* μάγος...ἄνθρωπος...~ῆσαι βουληθείς, ἐπ' ἀνδροφονίας τε καὶ ζωοκτονίας...πρότερον ἵεται Bas.Sel.*v.Thecl*.1(M.85.540C); **3.** pass., *happen extraordinarily*, Philost.*h.e*.7.8(M.65.545B).

***παραδοξοποιΐα, ἡ, 1.** *wonder-working*; of pagan oracles, Eus. *p.e*.4.3(139C; M.21.244C); πάντων ὁρώντων τὸ θαῦμα ἐγένετο, καὶ μετὰ πολλῆς τῆς π. Chrys.*hom.66.1 in Jo*.(8.395B); Thdr.Mops.*Am*.9:7 (M.66.300D); ref. Exodus παραδοξοποιΐας...ἐπίδειξις τῆς πανσθενεστάτης δεξιᾶς Cyr.*Is*.4.5(2.711D); ἥκει καιρὸς παραδοξοποιΐας τοῦ κρείττονος Nil.*epp*.3.2(M.79.364D); **2.** *miracle*; in OT, e.g. of Moses, Eus.*d.e*.3.2(p.97.25; M.22.169C); in NT and after: why those of Christ kept within bounds εἰ ὡς ἐν ἀληθείᾳ θεὸς πάντα ἐνήργει, ἠγνοήθη ⟨ἂν⟩ ἄνθρωπος γεγονώς Or.*fr.53 in Jo*.(p.527.12); αὐτὸς... ψιλῷ ῥήματι καὶ ἐξουσίᾳ θεραπεύσας, ἔδειξε διὰ τῆς π. ὅτι καὶ τοῦ σαββάτου κύριος ὑπῆρχε Thdr.Heracl.*fr.Jo*.7:23(p.265.17); Cyr.H.*catech*.22.2; performed by followers of Christ τὰς ὑπὸ τοῦ Φιλίππου δυνάμει θείᾳ τελουμένας...π. Eus.*h.e*.2.1.11(M.20.137B); *ib*.2.3.2 (144A); παραδοξοποιΐαι τοῦ θείου χαρίσματος *ib*.5.3.4(457A); of exotic magicians παραδοξοποιΐαι τοῦ Βραχμᾶνος id.*Hierocl*.23(526A; M.22.829B); methods contrasted with Christ's πῶς βοηθοὺς δαίμονας ἐπεκαλέσατο ἐν ταῖς π., ὁπότε εἰσέτι δεῦρο πᾶς δαίμων...τοῦ Ἰησοῦ τὸ ὄνομα φρίττει; id.*d.e*.3.6(p.139.4; 233D); **3.** *divine mystery*, of Crucifixion τὸν...δεσπότην ἐπὶ τῷ τοιούτῳ σκάμματι καὶ π. ἑστῶτα Epiph.*haer*.69.60(p.211.19; M.42.304B).

παραδοξοποιός, 1. adj.; **a.** *doing unexpected things*, Cyr.*Is*.3.4 (2.499C); **b.** *working wonders*; of God, ‡Pall.*h.mon*.8.29(p.41.9; M.34.1140D); ὁ π. θεοῦ λόγος Eus.*l.C*.11(p.228.16; M.20.1384B); π. δύναμις id.*Is*.7:12(M.24.133B); Ath.*gent*.44(M.25.88C); θείας τινὸς καὶ π. δυνάμεως Chrys.*hom.9.1 in Mt*.(7.131A); cf. τὴν χεῖρα αὐτοῦ τὴν π. διὰ Μωϋσέως προστησάμενος Eus.*Is*.11:11(176B); of power of Christ, id.*d.e*.3.7(p.144.22; M.22.244A); id.*h.e*.1.13.1(M.20.120B); transmitted to his followers, *ib*.3.24.3(264B); **c.** *marvellous* τὰς ὑπ' αὐτοῦ πραχθείσας π. ἱστορίας id.*d.e*.3 arg.(p.93.9; 164); **2.** as subst.; **a.** *wonder-worker*; so some regarded Christ, Cyr.*Jo*.3.4(4.294E); of Devil's disciples, Mac.Aeg.*pat*.3(M.34.868C); **b.** *conjuror* τῶν ἐπὶ σκηνῆς π. Nil.*Magn*.65(M.79.1057B).

παράδοξος, *varying from common experience* or *belief*; **1.** *with wrong beliefs* οἱ π. τῆς Ἀρείου θυμέλης μεσόχοροι τὸ μὲν ἁμαρτίαν πεποιηκέναι τὸν Χριστὸν φράζουσι Eust.*fr*.61(p.92; M.18.692B); **2.** *beyond reason* ὅπως τὰ π. ἡμῶν ταῦτα νοήσαντες, εἰ δὲ μή..., ἔτι γὰρ καὶ παραδοξοτέρους δοκοῦντας ἄλλους λόγους ἀκούσετε Just.*dial*.38.2(M.6.557A–B); π. ... τις...καὶ μὴ δυνάμενος [sc. λόγος] ὅλως ἀποδειχθῆναι *ib*.48.1(580A); τῆς π. ἀπὸ ἁγίου πνεύματος συλλήψεως Or.*Cels*.1.32(p.83.22; M.11.721A); τῇ π. γενέσει τοῦ Ἰησοῦ *ib*.(p.83.22; M.l.c.); π. ... ἡ ἕνωσις γέγονεν...μὴ τοίνυν ζήτει λόγον τῶν ὑπὲρ λόγον γενομένων Thdot.Anc.*exp.symb*.4(M.77.1317D); μονάδα...ἐν τριάδι καὶ τριάδα ἐν μονάδι προσκυνοῦμεν π. ἔχουσαν καὶ τὴν διαίρεσιν καὶ τὴν ἕνωσιν Just.Imp.*edict*.ap.Evagr.*h.e*.5.4(p.198.19; M.86.2796B); ἀσυγχύτως ἡνωμέναις [sc. ὑποστάσεσι] καὶ ἀδιαστάτως διαιρουμέναις· ὃ καὶ π. Jo.D.*f.o*.1.8(M.94.809A); **3.** *unexpected, novel* π. ἐπιδείκνυνται [sc. Christians] τὴν κατάστασιν τῆς ἑαυτῶν πολιτείας *Diogn*.5.4; τὸ π. καὶ ἐκβεβηκὸς τὴν συνήθειαν Or.*Jo*.13.64(60; p.296.22; M.14.521B); π. τὸ γέννημα τοῦ χειμῶνος id.*schol.in Cant*.6:10–11 (M.17.280A); Chrys.*hom.2.1 in Ac.princ*.(3.60D); εἰθισμένον αὐτοῖς [sc. τοῖς Ἕλλησι] τὰ π. θεοποιεῖν Philost.*h.e*.3.11(M.65.497A); πάντας ἐκίνει τὸ...π. εἰ καὶ τὴν πίστιν οὐκ ἔφθασαν Vict.*Mc*.8:27–29(p.345.24); **4.** *astounding* τὸ π. τῆς ἐπιβουλῆς αὐτῶν CAlex.*ep*.ap.Ath.*apol.sec*.10(p.95.29; M.25.265C); Chrys.*hom.in Mt.26:39*(3.19D); phrase τὸ δὲ παράδοξον *and what is strange, surprising,...*, Ath.*decr*.3(p.3.12; M.25.'428'(420)D); id.*ep.Serap*.3.1(M.26.625B); comp., id.*ep.Adelph*.3(M.26.1067B); comp. τὸ δὲ πάντων παραδοξότερον τοῦτο ἦν, ὅτι Evagr.*h.e*.4.29(p.177.26; M.86.2753B); superl., Ath.*h.Ar*.2(p.184.6; M.25.696D); **5.** *miraculous*, Or.*Cels*.4.80(p.350.7; M.11.1152D); *ib*.5.8(p.8.23; 1192C); τοῖς π. τοῦ Ἰησοῦ ἔργοις *ib*.7.54(p.204.24; 1500B); neut. as subst., *miraculous character* τῷ π. ἐκπλῆξαι καὶ βιάσασθαι τὸν ἄνθρωπον Clem.*fr*.29(p.217.14); Hipp.*haer*.4.36(p.62.9; M.16.3102A); hence *miracle*; of Christ, Or.*Cels*.8.9(p.227.24; M.11.1532A); Bas.*hex*.8.5(1.76A; M.29.177B); ὅτι μὴ κατὰ γοητείαν ἐνθέῳ δὲ ἀρετῇ καὶ δυνάμει τὰ π. διεπράξατο Eus.*d.e*.3 arg.(p.93.10; M.22.164); τὸ τῶν πέντε ἄρτων π. ‡Nil.*perist*.11.20(M.79.932A); Cyr.*Lc*.9:42(p.85.1; M.72.657B); ἀμείνων εἰς γνῶσιν τὴν τοῦ θεοῦ ἢ τῶν παραδόξων ἐπίδειξις τοῦ σωτῆρος ἡμῶν Χριστοῦ τῆς ἐν τῷ ὄρει Σινᾷ, χρῆναι δεῖν ὑπολαμβάνω...ἡμᾶς ἀοκνότατα λέγειν id.*Jo*.9(4.779E); θεῖος λόγος... ἐκτελεῖ τὰ π. Vict.*Mc*.8:23f.(p.344.13); necessary for apostles in their work οὐκ ἂν...χωρὶς δυνάμεων καὶ π. ἐκίνουν τοὺς...ἀκούοντας Or.*Cels*.1.46(p.96.2; 744D); of miracles as signs ἴδωμεν τὸ π. σημεῖον [sc. phoenix] τὸ γινόμενον ἐν τοῖς ἀνατολικοῖς τόποις *1Clem*.25.1; Or.*Jo*.13.64(60; p.296.30; M.14.521B) cit. s. αἰσθητῶς; εἰ...σύγχυσις φύσεων ἐποίει τὴν ἕνωσιν, οὐκ ἦν θαῦμα τὸ γεγενημένον· νῦν δὲ σημεῖόν τι καὶ π. δείκνυσι Thdot.Anc.*exp.symb*.4(M.77.1320A); in paraphrase of Jo.2:11 ταύτην ἀρχὴν ἐποίησε τῶν π. ὁ Ἰησοῦς Eus.*h.e*.3.24.11(M.20.265C); **6.** neut. as subst. as t.t., *paradox* τινὰ δόγματα παρὰ τοῖς Ἕλλησι καλούμενα π. Or.*Jo*.2.16(10; p.72.29; M.14.141C); *ib*.20.34 (p.371.32,33; 649C); ἐπιλυόμεθα τῷ π. †Leont.B.*sect*.7.9(M.86.1249D); **7.** *champion* π. ἀγωνιστῶν Or.*mart*.18(p.16.26; M.11.585B); fig. of martyrs τῶν ὡς ἀληθῶς π. τῆς θεοσεβείας ἀθλητῶν Eus.*h.e*.8.7.1(M.20.756B); so perh. τὸ μὲν π. [? *glorious*], μηδὲ δέχεσθαι ταύτην [sc. ἐπιθυμίαν πονηράν] ἀλλὰ σβεννύναι, εἰ δὲ τοῦτο οὐ δυνατόν, κἂν παλαίωμεν καὶ διαπαντὸς κατέχωμεν Chrys.*hom.22.5 in Eph*.(11.172D).

***παραδοξοσημεία, ἡ,** *miraculous sign, portent* καὶ οἱ βέβαιοι τὴν πίστιν ταῖς π. νευρωθεῖεν *cat.Apoc*.16:3(p.411.19).

παραδόξως, 1. *unexpectedly*, Eus.*h.e*.6.3.5(M.20.528B); Philost.*h.e*.1.5(M.65.464B); **2.** *paradoxically* ἵνα π. εἴπω Or.*Cels*.8.42(p.257.12; M.11.1580B); **3.** *miraculously*; ref. influence from on high, Clem.*str*.6.3(p.444.4; M.9.244B); divine omnipresence in creation, Cyr.*thes*.6(5^1.44A); Christ's power, Ath.*ep.Serap*.4.14(M.26.657A); Jonah's ordeal, Or.*Cels*.7.57(p.206.23; M.11.1501C); the escape from Egypt, Cyr.H.*catech*.19.2; Cyr.*Am*.57(3.312B); mystery of Inc. πατρὸς υἱόν,...πάσης γενόμενον ἥττονα βραχύτητος π. ‡Meth.*Sym.et Ann*.14(M.18.381B).

παράδοσις, ἡ, A. *handing over, delivery*, hence *teaching* committed to a pupil; **1.** of teaching in gen., Or.*hom.6.2 in Jer*.(p.50.4; M.13.328A); τῆς εἰς τὴν πίστιν π. Cyr.H.*catech*.4.3; Bas.*Spir*.35 (3.29D; M.32.132A); **2.** of teaching by example π. τὴν διὰ τῶν ἔργων φησί· καὶ κυρίως ταύτην ἀεὶ λέγει π. Chrys.*hom.5.1 in 2Thess*.(11.538B); Gr.Mag.*dial*.(tr.Zach.)2.12(M.*PL*.66.155C); **3.** of scriptural doctrine πεπίστευται γὰρ ἔκ τε τῆς κοινῆς ὑπολήψεως, καὶ ἐκ τῆς τῶν γραφῶν π. Gr.Nyss.*anim.et res*.(M.46.72A); τὰς...ἐκ τῆς...γραφῆς... ὑποθήκας ἔξεστιν...ἐξ ἀμφοτέρων τῶν διαθηκῶν ἀναλέξασθαι· πολλὰ μὲν γὰρ ἐν προφήταις καὶ νόμῳ, πολλὰ δὲ ἐν εὐαγγελικαῖς τε καὶ ἀποστολικαῖς π. πάρεστιν...λαβεῖν id.*virg*.12(p.297.21; M.46.369A); Cyr.*Is*.5.6(2.909C); τὰ παραδεδομένα ἡμῖν διά τε νόμου καὶ προφητῶν καὶ ἀποστόλων καὶ εὐαγγελιστῶν δεχόμεθα...μὴ...ὑπερβαίνοντες τὴν θείαν π. Jo.D.*f.o*.1.1(M.94.792A); **4.** of Christ's institution of eucharist, Thdt.*eran*.1(4.26); Eutych.*pasch*.6(M.86.2397D).

B. *transmission, handing down*, hence *that which is received, tradition*; **1.** of historical tradition κατὰ τὴν Ἑλλήνων π. οὐδ' ἱστορίας τις ἦν παρ' αὐτοῖς ἀναγραφή Tat.*orat*.39(p.39.25; M.6.881B); ὁ δὲ Ῥωμαίων βασιλεύς (ὡς ἡ π. διδάσκει) κατεδίκασε τὸν Ἰωάννην Or.*comm.in Mt*.16.6(p.486.7; M.13.1385A); Διονύσιος...περὶ τῆς Ἰωάννου ἀποκαλύψεως εἰπών τινα ὡς ἐκ τῆς ἀνέκαθεν π. τοῦ αὐτοῦ μέμνηται ἀνδρός Eus.*h.e*.3.28.3(M.20.276A); of reminiscences handed on to Papias by Aristion and John the Elder, *ib*.3.39.7(297C); of tradition of later activities of the Twelve, *ib*.3.1.1(216A); of reminiscences of 'elders' collected by Clement of Alexandria, *ib*.6.13.9(549A); of tradition of miracles wrought by Narcissus of Jerusalem πολῖται ὡς ἐκ π. τῶν κατὰ διαδοχὴν ἀδελφῶν...μνημονεύουσιν *ib*.6.9.1(537C); **2.** of accepted tradition of Church order and usage, as derived from apostles and handed on as norm of practice μία γὰρ ἡ πάντων γέγονε τῶν ἀποστόλων ὥσπερ διδασκαλία, οὕτως δὲ καὶ ἡ π. Clem.*str*.7.17(p.76.24; M.9.552C); Μοντανοῦ...παρὰ τὸ κατὰ π. καὶ κατὰ διαδοχὴν ἄνωθεν τῆς ἐκκλησίας ἔθος...προφητεύοντα Anon.ap.Eus.*h.e*.5.16.7(M.20.465C); cf.Hipp.*trad.ap*.1.2; *ut ii qui bene docti sunt eam quae permansit usque nunc traditionem...custodiant*, *ib*.1.3; πατρὸς μὲν ἀκούομεν λόγους, τῆς γραφῆς· μητρὸς δὲ τὰς ἀγράφους π. τῆς ἐκκλησίας· ὁποῖον τὸ νηστεύειν ἐν παρασκευαῖς, καὶ ἕτερα τοιαῦτα Or.*fr.in Pr*.3:8(M.17.157A); κεκράτηκε...π. ἀρχαία, ὥστε τὸν ἐν Αἰλίᾳ ἐπίσκοπον τιμᾶσθαι CNic.(325)*can*.7; ref. Quartodeciman observance in Asia, Eus.*h.e*.5.23.1(M.20.492A); of Stephen's practice in reception of those baptized in schism, opp. Cyprian's practice of rebaptism, *ib*.7.3(641A); ὁρίσαι ταῦτα ἃ τῇ τῶν ἀποστόλων π. σύμφωνα ἂν εἴη...δυνήσεται ὑμῶν ἡ σύνεσις κατὰ τὸν τῆς ἐκκλησίας κανόνα καὶ τὴν ἀποστολικὴν π. οὕτω ῥυθμίσαι τὴν...χειροτονίαν, ὡς ἂν ὁ τῆς ἐκκλησιαστικῆς ἐπιστήμης ὑφηγῆται λόγος Const.ap.Eus.*v.C.*3.62(p.110.25; M.20.1137B); Jul.Papa *ep.Dian.*30 ap.Ath.*apol.sec.*30(p.109.9; M.25.297C); μήτε ἐκκλησιαστικῷ κανόνι τὴν κατάστασιν εἶχε μήτε ἀποστολικῇ π. κληθεὶς ἦν ἐπίσκοπος Ath.*h.Ar.*14(p.189.31; M.25.708C); *Const.App.*8.46.6; ζητήσεως...περὶ Καικιλιανοῦ...κινηθείσης, ὡς τῆς ἐκκλησιαστικῆς παρατραπέντος π. Justn.*conf.*(p.108.29; M.86.1033A); ἡ τῆς...μεσοπεντηκοστῆς ἡμέρα οὐκ ἀργῶς...ἐπιτελεῖσθαι παραδέδοται, ἀλλὰ θεία τις ὑπάρχει π. Leont.N.*serm.*2(M.93.1584B); παραδόσεις καὶ ἀγράφως παρέλαβεν ἡ ἐκκλησία· οἷον τὸ κοινωνεῖν νηστικόν. καὶ τὸ προσεύχεσθαι κατὰ ἀνατολάς Anast.S.*hod.*1(M.89.40C); συνήθειαν τῆς ἐκκλησίας ἐξ ἀγράφου π. ἐπιστάμεθα, μίαν προνήστιμον ἑβδομάδα, ἐν ᾗ...κρεῶν ἀποχή Jo.D.*jej.*5(M.95.69D); **3.** partic. of liturg. usage or institutions, e.g. method of receiving Communion, Cyr.H.*catech.*23.23; scriptural baptismal formula τοῦτο δὲ [i.e. Eunomian doctrine]...μάχεται τῇ π. τοῦ...βαπτίσματος. πορευθέντες, φησί, βαπτίζετε εἰς τὸ ὄνομα κτλ. Bas.*Eun.*3.5(1.276E; M.29.665C); id.*ep.*105(3.200B; M.32.513B); ref. making sign of cross, praying towards east, words of eucharistic epiclesis, blessing of baptismal water, oil of unction, and candidate, as traditional practices ἀπὸ τῆς σιωπωμένης καὶ μυστικῆς π.; so also unction, triple immersion, renunciation and credal profession of faith at baptism, Bas.*Spir.*66(3.54D–57A; M.32.188A–193A); baptismal formula ἡ τῆς θείας μυσταγωγίας π. Gr.Nyss.*Eun.*11(2 p.272.12; M.45.881C); id.*ep.*24(M.46.1089A); ἡ π. δὲ τοῦ...βαπτίσματος ἕνα υἱὸν...εἶναι διδάσκει Thdt.*ep.*84(4.1153); Dion.Ar.*e.h.*7.3.9(M.3.568A); Jo.D.*f.o.*4.16(M.94.1172C); as title of work of Hipp., *CIG* 8613A 10; **4.** *tradition of doctrinal teaching* (after combining meanings A and B, i.e. teaching *authoritatively delivered* and subsequently *transmitted* as received doctrine); **a.** of rabbinical interpretation of scripture τῆς π. τῶν ὑμετέρων διδασκάλων [which is to be rejected as uninspired] Just.*dial.*38.2(M.6.557B); τῶν πρεσβυτέρων π. Hipp.*Dan.*4.20.2; Eus.*Is.*22:10–11(M.24.249A); Proc.G.*Is.*22:1–14(M.87.2176C); **b.** of pagan religion, *V.Aberc.*13(p.11.15); τῆς μὲν κατὰ παράδοσιν τῶν ἔξωθεν πλάνης ῥυσθεὶς Bas.*jud.*1(2.213E; M.31.653A); **c.** of false doctrine among Christians ταῖς μὲν γραφαῖς ἀκριβῶς οὐ προσέχουσιν, ταῖς δὲ ἀνθρωπίναις π. καὶ ταῖς ἑαυτῶν πλάναις...πείθονται Hipp.*Dan.*4.20.1; in form of written documents τοῖς συντάγμασι καὶ ταῖς π. τῶν αἱρετικῶν ἐνέτυχον Dion.Al.ap.Eus.*h.e.*7.7.1(M.20.648B); of unwritten tradition supposed by heretics to have been committed by Christ to apostles and held to be superior to scripture, Or.*comm.in 1Cor.*4:6(*JTS* 9 p.357); **d.** of orthodox doctrine ἀπολίπωμεν τὰς κενὰς...φροντίδας, καὶ ἔλθωμεν ἐπὶ τὸν εὐκλεῆ καὶ σεμνὸν τῆς π. ἡμῶν κανόνα *1Clem.*7.2; εὐαγγελίων πίστις ἵδρυται καὶ ἀποστόλων π. φυλάσσεται ‡*Diogn.*11.6; maintained universally in Church, Iren.*haer.*1.10.2(M.7.552B); safeguarded by succession of bishops in churches founded by apostles Κλήμης...τὴν π. πρὸ ὀφθαλμῶν ἔχων...ἔτι γὰρ πολλοὶ ὑπελείποντο τότε ὑπὸ τῶν ἀποστόλων δεδιδαγμένοι...νεωστὶ ἀπὸ τῶν ἀποστόλων παράδοσιν εἰλήφει *ib.*3.3.3(849B); cf. *traditionem itaque apostolorum in toto mundo manifestatam, in omni ecclesia adest perspicere..., et habemus annumerare eos qui ab apostolis instituti sunt episcopi..., et successiones eorum usque ad nos, qui nihil tale docuerunt...quale ab his* [sc. Gnostics] *deliratur*, *ib.*3.3.1(848A); ἡ ἐν Ἐφέσῳ ἐκκλησία...μάρτυς ἀληθής ἐστι τῆς ἀποστόλων π. *ib.*3.3.4(855A); Ptol.*ep.*ap.Epiph.*haer.*33.7(p.457.14; M.41.568B) cit. s. διαδοχή; Clem.*str.*1.1(p.9.5; M.8.700A) cit. s. διδασκαλία; τῆς γνωστικῆς π. *ib.*(p.11.19; 704C); ὃ ἀκούετε εἰς τὸ οὖς...κηρύξατε ἐπὶ τῶν δωμάτων, τὰς ἀποκρύφους τῆς ἀληθοῦς γνώσεως π. ὑψηλῶς...ἑρμηνευομένας ἐκδέχεσθαι κελεύων...καὶ παραδιδόναι οἷς δέον *ib.*1.12(p.35.32; 753B); *ib.*5.10(p.368.14; M.9.96C); *ib.*6.7(p.462.20; 284A); ἡ κατὰ τὸν τῆς ἀληθείας κανόνα γνωστικῆς π. φυσιολογία *ib.*4.1(p.249.11; M.8.1216C); ἀναλακτίσας τὴν ἐκκλησιαστικὴν π. καὶ ἀποσκιρτήσας εἰς δόξας αἱρέσεων ἀνθρωπίνων *ib.*7.16(p.67.13; M.9.532B); αἱρετικοὺς κενοὺς τῶν...τοῦ Χριστοῦ π. *ib.*(p.70.12; 537A); δόξης δὲ ἐπιθυμοῦσιν ὅσοι τὰ προσφυῆ τοῖς θεοπνεύστοις λόγοις ὑπὸ τῶν...ἀποστόλων τε καὶ διδασκάλων παραδιδόμενα ἑκόντες εἶναι σοφίζονται δι' ἑτέρων παρεγχειρήσεων, ἀνθρωπείαις διδασκαλίαις ἐνιστάμενοι θείᾳ π. ὑπὲρ τοῦ τὴν αἵρεσιν συστήσασθαι *ib.*(p.73.7; 544A); cf. *illa sola credenda est veritas, quae in nullo ab ecclesiastica et apostolica traditione discordat*, Or.*princ.*1 proem.2(p.8.28; M.11.116B); τῆς τε σωτηρίου πίστεως τὴν μυστικὴν ἀναγέννησιν...παρεχούσης, καὶ πρὸς τοῖς θείοις ἐγγράφοις τῆς ἀπὸ περάτων γῆς ἕως περάτων καθολικῆς τοῦ θεοῦ ἐκκλησίας τὰς ἀπὸ τῶν θείων γραφῶν μαρτυρίας ἐξ ἀγράφου π. ἐπισφραγιζομένης Eus.*Marcell.*1.1(p.8.24; M.24.728C); esp. of doctrine established by early fathers ταύτην [sc. Nicene faith] εἶναι τῆς ἐκκλησίας τὴν πίστιν καὶ τῶν πατέρων τὴν π. Ath.*decr.*3(p.3.14; M.25.'429'(421)A); πιστεύομεν ἀκολούθως τῇ εὐαγγελικῇ καὶ ἀποστολικῇ π. *Symb.Ant.*(341)2 ap.Ath.*syn.*23(p.249.11; M.26.721B); Ath.*ep.Serap.*1.28(M.26.593D), id.*ep.Adelph.*6(M.26.1080A) citt. s. διδασκαλία; οὐδὲ τῶν θείων δυνάμεων ταῦτα [sc. τὰ ἐν τῷ θεῷ] δυναμένων εἰδέναι, εἰ μὴ π. μαθημάτων ἐκ τῆς τοῦ μονογενοῦς ἐξηγήσεως παραδοθῇ Serap.*Man.*40(p.58; M.18.1224B); ἀλλ' οὐ τοῦτο ἡμῖν ἐξαρκεῖ, ὅτι τῶν πατέρων ἡ π.· κἀκεῖνοι γὰρ τῷ βουλήματι τῆς γραφῆς ἠκολούθησαν, ἐκ τῶν μαρτυριῶν, ἃς μικρῷ πρόσθεν ὑμῖν ἐκ τῆς γραφῆς παρεθέμεθα, τὰς ἀρχὰς λαβόντες Bas.*Spir.*16(3.13D; M.32.96A); *ib.*25(21C; M.112C); Gr.Nyss.*Eun.*1(1 p.80.8; M.45.312A); πατρόθεν ἥκειν πρὸς ἡμᾶς τὴν π., οἷόν τινα κλῆρον δι' ἀκολουθίας ἐκ τῶν ἀποστόλων διὰ τῶν ἐφεξῆς ἁγίων παραπεμφθέντα *ib.*4(2 p.79.22; 653B); ref. 2Thess.2:14 οὐ πάντα δι' ἐπιστολῆς παρεδίδοσαν, ἀλλὰ πολλὰ καὶ ἀγράφως· ὁμοίως δὲ κἀκεῖνα...ἐστιν ἀξιόπιστα, ὥστε καὶ τὴν π. τῆς ἐκκλησίας ἀξιόπιστον ἡγώμεθα. π. ἐστι, μηδὲν πλέον ζήτει Chrys.*hom.4.2 in 2Thess.*(11.532B); τῆς πίστεως τὴν...ἀρχαιοτάτην καὶ ἐξ αὐτῶν τῶν ἁγίων ἀποστόλων διήκουσαν εἰς ἡμᾶς π. Cyr.*Thds.*(p.53.11; 5^2.15E); opp. doctrines of heretics, id.*hom.pasch.*8(5^2.94D); τὰ ἐκ τῆς θεοπνεύστου γραφῆς ἀντανιστάντες ἐμφρόνως καὶ τῆς ἀποστολικῆς τε καὶ εὐαγγελικῆς πίστεως τὴν π. καὶ τὴν τῶν πατέρων ὁμολογίαν τῶν...ἐν τῇ Νικαέων συνειλεγμένων ἀντεξάγοντες id.*apol.Thdt.*1(p.112.1; 6^1.205E); περὶ δὲ τῆς θεοτόκου...ὅπως καὶ φρονοῦμεν...τοῦ τε τρόπου τῆς ἐνανθρωπήσεως...ὡς ἄνωθεν ἔκ τε τῶν θείων γραφῶν ἔκ τε τῆς π. τῶν ἁγίων πατέρων παρειληφότες ἐσχήκαμεν...ἐροῦμεν Jo.Ant.*ep.Cyr.*2(p.8.21; M.77.172C); τῆς ὀρθοδόξου πίστεως κηρύκων, κατὰ τὴν ἀποστολικὴν π., θεοτόκον διδαξάντων ὀνομάζειν...τὴν τοῦ κυρίου μητέρα Thdt.*haer.*4.12(4.371); ἡ τῶν πατέρων π. Thdot.Anc.*exp.symb.*12(M.77.1329D); ref. 'negative theology' ἡ κρυφία καὶ ἡ ἱερατικὴ π. Dion.Ar.*c.h.*2.3(M.3.140D); ref. doctrine of redemption ἡ κρυφία π. id.*e.h.*3.3.11(M.3.441B); ref. Christology ἡ τῶν ἐνθέων...καθηγεμόνων κρυφία π. Pamph.H.*panopl.*3.3(p.610); ἡμᾶς ἐξακολουθοῦντας ταῖς ἀποστολικαῖς π. καὶ διατάξεσι, καὶ ταῖς τῶν ἁγίων πατέρων...ἐγγράφοις νομοθεσίαις ‡Anast.Ant.*serm.*4(M.89.1389C); Anast.S.*hod.*6(M.89.109B); ref. doctrine of veneration of images ἡ τῶν...πατέρων διδασκαλία, εἴτουν π. τῆς καθολικῆς ἐκκλησίας *Symb.Nic.*(787)(H.4.456C); **e.** as title of Gnostic apocryphal work, *Traditions of Matthias*, Clem.*str.*2.9(p.137.2; M.8.981A); *ib.*7.13(p.58.20; M.9.513B); **f.** doctrinal tradition in rel. to scripture; **i.** π. consisting in interprn. of scripture διδάξαντος τοῦ σωτῆρος τοὺς ἀποστόλους ἡ τῆς ἐγγράφου [sc. OT] ἄγραφος ἤδη καὶ εἰς ἡμᾶς διαδίδοται π., καρδίαις καιναῖς κατὰ τὴν ἀνακαίνωσιν τοῦ βιβλίου [ref. Is.8:1] τῇ δυνάμει τοῦ θεοῦ ἐγγεγραμμένη Clem.*str.*6.15(p.498.17; M.9.356B); πρώτῳ τοι χρήσομαι π. Ἑβραϊκῇ [sc. of exegesis]...ἔλεγεν οὖν μοι ἡ π. καὶ τοιοῦτόν τι Or.*hom.20.2 in Jer.*(p.178.9; M.13.501C); εἰ...αἱρετικοὶ φυλάττουσι...τὴν...περὶ τὸ βάπτισμα τοῦ υἱοῦ π. Didym.*Trin.*3.2(M.39.805B); Proc.G.*Gen.*9:18–19(M.87.301B); Dion.Ar.*e.h.*2.3.7(M.3.404C); of tradition of allegorical exegesis, Gr.Nyss.*or.catech.*32(p.118.1; M.45.80C); **ii.** church tradition, maintained *per successionem*, a safeguard of scriptural revelation against *secretae scripturae* of heretics, Or.*comm.ser.46 in Mt.*(p.94.28; M.13.1667D); **iii.** unwritten tradition of Catholic Church sets seal upon scriptural evidence for truth of its doctrine, Eus.*Marcell.*1.1(p.8.24; M.24.728C); tradition given by Christ, preached by apostles, guarded by fathers, Ath.*ep.Serap.*1.28(M.26.593D); faith being derived from apostolic doctrine and tradition of fathers, confirmed by scripture, id.*ep.Adelph.*6(M.26.1080A); tradition of fathers adhering to the sense of scripture and derived from it, Bas.*Spir.*16(3.13D; M.32.96A); tradition of teaching, maintained by bishops, to be set alongside scripture ἐν μιᾷ τάξει θετέον τήν τε ἁγίαν γραφὴν καὶ τὰς τῶν ἐπισκόπων π. Max.*schol.d.n.*1.4(M.4.197B); **iv.** apostolic tradition as source of Church's doctrine and preaching additional to scripture; ref. fasting etc., Or.*fr.in Pr.*3:8(M.17.157A); τῶν ἐν τῇ ἐκκλησίᾳ πεφυλαγμένων δογμάτων καὶ κηρυγμάτων, τὰ μὲν ἐκ τῆς ἐγγράφου διδασκαλίας ἔχομεν, τὰ δὲ ἐκ τῆς τῶν ἀποστόλων π. διαδοθέντα ἡμῖν ἐν μυστηρίῳ παρεδεξάμεθα, ἅπερ ἀμφότερα τὴν αὐτὴν ἰσχὺν ἔχει πρὸς τὴν εὐσέβειαν: this tradition being concerned with rites and ceremonies, and kept secret in order to enhance the dignity of the mysteries οὗτος ὁ λόγος τῆς τῶν ἀγράφων π., ὡς μὴ καταμεληθεῖσαν τῶν δογμάτων τὴν γνῶσιν εὐκαταφρόνητον τοῖς πολλοῖς γενέσθαι διὰ συνήθειαν Bas.*Spir.*66(3.54Dff.; M.32.188Aff.); apostles' tradition of ethical teaching entrusted to Church independently of their writings δεῖ δὲ καὶ π. κεχρῆσθαι· οὐ γὰρ πάντα ἀπὸ τῆς θείας γραφῆς δύναται λαμβάνεσθαι. διὸ τὰ μὲν ἐν γραφαῖς, τὰ δὲ ἐν π. παρέδωκαν οἱ...ἀπόστολοι. ... παρέδωκαν...ἀπόστολοι...ἁμαρτὲς εἶναι τὸ μετὰ τὸ ὁρίσαι παρθενίαν εἰς γάμον τρέπεσθαι Epiph.*haer.*61.6(p.386.16; M.41.1048B); much unwritten teaching, which must be obeyed, transmitted by apostles, Chrys. *hom.4.2 in 2Thess.*(11.532B); scope of unwritten tradition including both practice (τὸ κοινωνεῖν νηστικόν...τὸ προσεύχεσθαι κατὰ ἀνατολάς) and accretions to scriptural narratives οἷον...ὅτι παρθένος ἔμεινε μετὰ τόκον ἡ θεοτόκος. καί, ὅτι ἐν σπηλαίῳ ἔτεκε, καὶ ἕτερα πολλά Anast.S.*hod.*1(M.89.40C); **v.** of tradition concerning the origins of the four gospels, Or.*comm.in Mt.*1(p.3.1; M.13.829A); **g.** of textual tradition κατὰ τὴν τῶν ἑβδομήκοντα καὶ τοῦ Ἀκύλα π. Phot.*nomoc.*12.3(p.604; M.104.872D).

C. *surrender, handing over*; of betrayal of Christ, Gr.Naz.*or.*30.16 (p.134.6; M.36.124D); ἡ τῆς π. ἡμέρα Chrys.*hom.33.1 in Gen.*(4.331B); id.*hom.84.1 in Mt.*(7.797D).

***παραδότως**, s.v.l., *according to tradition*, ‡Hipp.*fr.22 in Pss.* (p.148.20; παραδόξως M.10.613A).

παραδοχή, ἡ, 1. *reception*; **a.** of 'taking' of dye by wool, Clem. *paed.*1.9(p.135.28; M.8.344A); **b.** of knowledge π. τῆς τοῦ πατρὸς γνώσεως Eus.*h.e.*1.2.23(M.20.65A); id.*p.e.*1.1(4C; M.21.28A); οἱ γινόμενοι ἐν αὐτῷ [sc. Christ] ἐπὶ τῷ λούσασθαι τὸν ὀνειδισμὸν ἀποτίθενται τῆς Αἰγύπτου...καὶ καθαρίζονται...καὶ ἕτοιμοι πρὸς πνεύματος ἁγίου παραδοχὴν γίνονται, ἄλλῳ ποταμῷ οὐκ ἐφιπταμένης τῆς πνευματικῆς περιστερᾶς Or.*Jo.*6.48(29; p.157.21; M.14.285A); αἱ τῶν ἁγίων δυνάμεων ἀγγελοπρεπεῖς ἑνώσεις, ἃς εἴτε ἐπιβολάς, εἴτε παραδοχὰς χρὴ φάναι τῆς...ὑπερφανοῦς ἀγαθότητος Dion.Ar.*d.n.*1.5(M.3.593B); of tradition, Clem.*str.*1.1(p.11.18; M.8.704C); **2.** *apprehension, understanding* τυφλώττων περὶ τὴν π. τοῦ λεγομένου Or.*Cels.*6.76(p.145.25; M.11.1413B); **3.** *acceptance* τήρησιν τῶν νόμων καὶ π. τῶν μαθημάτων Or.*princ.*4.1.1(p.294.4; M.11.344B); π. ... δογμάτων Bas.*Eun.*1.19(1.231A; M.29.556A); ἐκ τοῦ θαύματος ἀναγκαία ἡ π. τῆς θεότητος τοῦ μονογενοῦς...ἐγίνετο †Bas.*hom.in Ps.*115(1.371C; M.30.104B); διὰ τῆς τοῦ λόγου π. καὶ τοῦ πνεύματος, τῶν Ἰουδαίων καθαιρεῖται τὸ δόγμα Jo.D.*f.o.*1.7(M.94.808A); **4.** *reception* of a person, Or.*Jo.*13.56(55; p.286.4; M.14.504C) cit. s. παραδέχομαι; **5.** *means of receiving* αἰσθήσεων αἱ π. τινές εἰσι τῶν ἔξωθεν Gr.Naz.*or.*28.22(p.56.11; M.36.57A); *ib.*32.27(205A).

παραδρομή, ἡ, *passage* of time, Men.*exc.Rom.*3(p.175.20; M.113.857C); *Mir.Geo.*4(p.44.7); Heracl.*nov.*23(p.39).

παραδυναστεύω, *have great authority* with, c. dat.; also c. πρός, Anast.S.*haer.*(p.261); abs., Thdt.*h.e.*2.12.1(3.853).

παραδύομαι, *put on, assume*, Philost.*h.e.*12.8(M.65.616B).

***παραδυσσεβέω,** παραδυσσεβεῖ: f.l. for παρὰ δυσσεβεῖ, Sophr.H. *v.Anast.*(M.92.1717A).

[*]**παράδ-ω,** *make discordant* καὶ τὰς ἄλλας [sc. ῥήσεις τάς] προφητικὰς ὁμοίως ∼ουσι διὰ πλειόνων βιβλίων Hipp.*haer.*5.27(p.133.17; M.16.3203B).

παραζεύγνυμι, *join together*, Just.*dial.*91.2(M.6.693A); Christol. ἄνθρωπος θεῷ παραζευχθείς, ἕτερος παρὰ τὸν θεόν ἐστι ταῖς ζωτικαῖς κινήσεσι, λογιστικαῖς τε καὶ παθητικαῖς ‡Ath.*dial.Trin.*5.29(M.28.1284A); *ib.*(1284B).

***παραζῆλον, τό,** *perverted zeal*, i.e. zeal of the wrong kind or for the wrong objects, Thdr.Stud.*epp.*1.22(M.99.976B).

παραζηλ-όω, 1. *provoke to jealousy, stir up to emulation*, Chrys. *hom.67.3 in Mt.*(7.665B); *incite*, *M.Carp.*8; *stir up, kindle* to bravery and endurance, *M.Perp.*20(p.91.10); **2.** *be vexed at* ∼ῶν ὁ κύριος τὸν ἀχάριστον δῆμον Isid.Pel.*epp.*1.147(M.78.281A); **3.** *be jealous* of, Clem.*str.*1.5(p.21.6; M.8.725A); *ib.*2.8(p.133.16; 973B); **4.** *be zealous for besides* or *in addition* ∼οῦν λέγεται τὸ ἀπό τινων δύο ποτὲ μὲν τοῦτον θαυμάζειν, ποτὲ δὲ ἐκεῖνον Thdr.Mops.*1Cor.*10:22 (p.186.26; M.66.888B).

παραζήλωσις, ἡ, 1. *zeal*; for God, *T.Zab.*9.8; **2.** *jealousy, spite*, Epiph.*haer.*24.2(p.259.18; M.41.312B); **3.** in trans. sense, *provocation to rivalry* ὅπερ οὐκ ἴσχυσεν ἡ παράκλησις, τοῦτο ἐποίησεν ἡ π. Chrys.*hom.18.3 in Rom.*(9.634B); τοὺς πολλῷ καταδεεστέρους...(ὃ μάλιστα ποιεῖ π.) εἰσάγων *ib.*(634C); cf.*ib.*8.5(637B).

παράθεσις, ἡ, 1. *juxtaposition*; *moving up to, contact*, Hipp.*haer.* 5.19(p.118.3; M.16.3182A); cf. ἡ δαίμονος φύσις...τὸ ἐν αὐτῇ [sc. τῇ ψυχῇ] πάθος κινεῖ, καὶ προάγει τὴν δύναμιν εἰς ἐνέργειαν· παραθέσει γὰρ ἕκαστον δρᾷ Synes.*provid.*1.10(p.84.5; M.66.1232A); Christol. οὔτε μὴν κατὰ παράθεσιν τὸν τῆς συναφείας νοοῦμεν τρόπον Cyr.*ep.*17 (p.36.17; 5².71A); rel. of H. Ghost to soul ἐμοί...δοκεῖ κατὰ παράθεσιν τοῦτο γενέσθαι ἀλλ' οὐ κατὰ κρᾶσιν Clem.*exc.Thdot.*17(p.112.14; M.9.665B); **2.** *available supply* τῷ...μὴ ἔχειν ἐργαλείων παράθεσιν Tit. Bost.*Man.*2.26(M.18.1185B); **3.** *presentation* of ideas τὴν τῶν νοημάτων...π. Cyr.*Os.*proem.(3.2A); id.*Pulch.*(p.61.25; 5².180C); of evidence, Or.*Jo.*6.60(38; p.168.29; M.14.304C); of good example τῇ τῶν ἐθνῶν π. φλεγμαίνουσαν τὴν ψυχὴν ἐντρέπων Chrys.*hom.65.4 in Mt.* (7.649B); **4.** *citation, adducing* of parallels, Athenag.*leg.*6.2(M. 6.901B); Clem.*str.*2.11(p.139.6; M.8.985A); π. ... παραδειγμάτων Or. *Jo.*6.59(38; p.167.19; M.14.301C); Eus.*d.e.*2.2(p.60.24; M.22.112B); **5.** *statement* of accounts, Jo.Scholast.*coll.cap.*60; **6.** *comparison* or *contrast* Ἀζώτιοι...κατέκριναν ἐκ π. τοὺς υἱοὺς Ἰσραὴλ Or.*fr.in 1Reg.* 5:3(M.17.44A); ἵνα τῇ π. ἡ διαφορὰ νοηθῇ id.*Jo.*1.28(30; p.35.15; M. 14.76A); Eus.*d.e.*4.16(p.188.31; M.22.316A); Tit.Bost.*Man.*2.3(M.18. 1137B); of (alleged) incomparables, such as Father and Son acc. Eunomius ὧν...ἀμήχανος ἡ π. Bas.*Eun.*1.25(1.236A; M.29.568A); κατὰ παράθεσιν φανῆναι τὰ κατὰ Χριστὸν...ὑπερέχοντα τοῦ νόμου Thdr.Mops.*Rom.*8:5–6(p.134.17; M.66.820C); ὧν [sc. τῶν ἁγίων] ἡ ἀρετὴ πάντα κρίνει τὸν κόσμον, οὐ κατ' ἐξέτασιν, ἀλλὰ κατὰ π. id. *1Cor.*6:1(p.179.16; M.66.881D); ἐν παραθέσει *by comparison*, Vict. *Mc.*3:30(p.300.16); *ib.*8:1(p.340.22); **7.** *commendation* to God, as a pious farewell, *blessing* λαβὼν εὐχὴν μετὰ παραθέσεως ἐξῆλθεν Marc. Diac.*v.Porph.*14; *ib.*30; ὑποχωρῆσαι χωρὶς τῆς τοῦ ἁγίου π. Cyr.S. *v.Euthym.*19(p.30.9); Dor.*doct.*1.15(M.88.1637B); ἔβαλλον αὐτῷ [sc. τῷ ἀββᾷ] μετάνοιαν ἵνα λάβω π. παρ' αὐτοῦ καὶ ἀναχωρήσω *ib.*4.9 (1669B); Jo.Clim.*scal.*4.61(M.88.697D); Gr.Mag.*dial.*(tr.Zach.)3.31 (M.*PL.*77.291D); **8.** *permission*, ref. 2Cor.12:4 ὁ...νοῦς, ἡνίκα ἐν τῷ πνεύματι τῆς ἀποκαλύψεως εἶδεν αὐτὰ ἐν τῷ τόπῳ αὐτῶν, οὐκ ἐδέξατο π. λαλῆσαι αὐτὰ ἐν τῷ τόπῳ τῷ μὴ ἰδίῳ αὐτῶν Philox.*ep.*3(p.183); Gr.Mag.*dial.*(tr.Zach.)2.24(M.*PL.*66.179C); **9.** rhet. t.t., *putting aside* until later, cf. *parathesis est cum quasi deponimus aliquid imperfectum apud memoriam iudicum, repetituros nos dicentes, cum oportunum fuerit*, Isid.H.*etym.*2.21.46.

***παραθετέος,** *to be set before, to be presented*, Clem.*paed.*3.8(p.260.22; παράθετα M.8.612C).

***παραθετικός,** *commendatory, of introduction*, Bas.*ep.*23 tit.(3.101A; M.32.293B); συστατικῶν, τουτέστι π., ἐπιστολῶν *cat.2Cor.*3:1 (p.364.23).

παραθεωρέω, *digress*, Thdr.Stud.*nativ.BMV* 6(M.96.688C).

παραθήγω, 1. *sharpen*; teeth, *gnash*, ‡Bas.*Lac.*18.5(2.589D; M. 31.1444C); fig., the tongue, *make incisive*, Isid.Pel.*epp.*1.351(M.78.384A); Thdt.*eran.*1(4.46); **2.** *incite*; to acts, Synes.*Dion* 9(p.255.17; M.66.1136C); Cyr.*ador.*3(1.106B); *ib.*16(581C); to (courageous) frame of mind εἰς ἀνδρείαν...π. φρονήματα Thdt.*eran.*2(4.94); †Jo.D.*B.J.*23 (M.96.1065B); *ib.*(1069C); pass., Cyr.*Pss.*proem.(M.69.717A); id.*Os.* 56(3.86E); Jo.D.*hom.*1.14(M.96.568B).

παραθήκη, ἡ, 1. *deposit*, of traditions ἀσεβεῖς μέλλομεν, ἐὰν τὰ παραδοθέντα ἡμῖν ἐκ πατέρων σεβάσματα καταλείψωμεν· ὅμοιον γάρ ἐστι τῷ παραθήκην φυλάξαι *Hom.Clem.*11.13; of one entrusted to another's care, Clem.*q.d.s.*42(p.189.10; παρακαταθήκην M.9.649A); **2.** *coffin*, *T.Benj.*12.2.

***παραθηκοφύλαξ, ὁ,** *keeper of a deposit*, Eus.*e.th.*1.20(p.86.7; M. 24.873C); id.*v.C.*1.14(p.15.9; M.20.929A).

παράθηξις, ἡ, *incitement* ἅμιλλαν ἀρετῆς καὶ παράθηξιν Gr.Naz. *ep.*6(M.37.29C).

***παραθίγω,** = -θιγγάνω, *attain, reach* προσεύχου τῆς...στάσεως σου ἐγγύθεν [sc. με] παραθίγειν Thdr.Stud.*epp.*2.45(M.99.1248D).

παραθλίβ-ω, 1. *constrict* the breath in speech ἢ τοῖς ὀδοῦσιν ἢ τῇ ὑπερῴᾳ τὸ δι' αὐτῆς παριὸν πνεῦμα...∼ουσα Gr.Nyss.*Eun.*12(1 p.271.20; M.45.977B); **2.** *press, force* facts πανταχῇ τὸν τῆς ἱστορίας ∼οντες λόγον Cyr.*glaph.Gen.*6(1.190C).

***παραθολόω,** *besmirch*, Athenag.*leg.*32.3(M.6.964C).

***παραθρηνέω,** *keep on wailing*, Bas.*hom.*4.6(2.31A; M.31.232C).

***παραθρύπτω,** ptcpl. pass., *mincing, affected* τὰ βλακώδη ταῦτα καὶ παρατεθρυμμένα σωτάδεια Gr.Nyss.*Eun.*1(1 p.25.10; M.45.253A).

***παραθυμία, ἡ,** *outburst of anger*, Jo.Mosch.*prat.*171(M.87.3040A).

***παραθυρίδιον, τό,** *little window by door*, ‡Ath.*qu.al.*19(M.28. 789B,C).

παράθυρος, ἡ, *side entry*, Clem.*str.*7.17(p.75.5; παράθυμον M.9. 548A); διὰ τῶν π. ἐπὶ τὴν καρδίαν ὁδεῦσαν τὸ πνεῦμα Hipp.*haer.*6.14 (p.140.26; M.16.3215B); διὰ μὲν τῆς πλατείας θύρας ἐξελθὼν τοῦ κόσμου, διὰ δὲ τῆς π. εἰσελθών Mac.Aeg.*hom.*43.3(M.34.773B); ἔχεις τὴν θύραν τοῦ νόμου, φύγε τὴν π. τῆς ἀνομίας Ast.Soph.*hom.5 in Ps.5* (M.40.444A).

παραίνεσις, ἡ, 1. *spoken exhortation, preaching*, ref. Jo. Bapt. καθολικὴν ἐποιήσατο τὴν π. Cyr.ap.*cat.Jo.*3:36(p.214.24); of Christian preaching ὁ λόγος ἐντρέπει καὶ ἡ π. μεταποιεῖ Tit.Bost.*fr.Lc.* 6:43(p.163); of written, scriptural injunctions, Oecum.*Apoc.*1:3 (p.33); of law μετὰ φυσικὸν νόμον, μετὰ νομικὴν π. *Lit.*ap.*Const.App.* 8.12.30; of counsels opp. law περὶ ἀγαμίας...οὐ νόμους ἀλλὰ π. εἰσενεγκών [sc. ὁ Παῦλος] Thdt.*affect.*9(p.238.18; 4.945); ἵνα μὴ νόμος ἡ π. γένηται id.*1Cor.*7:26(3.208); cf. τὴν π. τοῦ Παύλου Meth. *symp.*3.13(p.43.19; M.18.84B); imparted by God ἡ π. τοῦ θεοῦ καὶ παραγγελία id.*res.*2.2(p.331.13; M.41.1164B); of evil counsel, Const.

ep.(Opitz p.63; M.85.1357D); perh. as title of philosophical work, *Precepts* Ἰσίδωρον φάσκουσιν ἐν παραινέσεσιν τῆς αὐτοῦ μοχθηρίας γεγενῆσθαι Epiph.*haer*.32.4(p.443.1; M.41.548C); **2.** *assurance, encouragement* τῇ π. τοῦ λόγου ὑγιάζειν *Const.App*.2.14.11; τὰ...ἐκείνων ῥύπη ἡμετέρα π. *ib*.2.18.5; Chrys.*hom.80.1 in Jo*.(8.472D).

παραινέτης, ὁ, *adviser, counsellor,* Gr.Naz.*ep*.33(M.37.73B); παράκλητον ἔχομεν...Χριστόν, οὐχ ὡς ὑπὲρ ἡμῶν προκυλινδούμενον τοῦ πατρός, καὶ προσπίπτοντα δουλικῶς...ἀλλ' οἷς πέπονθεν, ὡς ἄνθρωπος, πείθει καρτερεῖν, ὡς λόγος καὶ παραινέτης. τοῦτο νοεῖταί μοι ἡ παράκλησις id.*or*.30.14(p.131.10; M.36.121C); *exhorter,* Isid.Pel.*epp*.2. 168(M.78.620C).

παραινετικός, *hortatory,* of a type of literature τὸ π. εἶδος Clem. *paed*.1.1(p.90.28; M.8.252A); Isid.Pel.*epp*.3.84(M.78.792A); πρὸς παρθένους π. [sc. λόγος] Gr.Naz.*carm*.1.2.3 tit.(M.37.632); of spoken word, or message, Socr.*h.e*.1.8.18(M.67.64C); of address (in synagogue), Ammon.*Ac*.13:14(M.85.1541B); in gen. γυναιξὶ τὸν π. ἐπιτρέπει λόγον ἐπ' οἰκίας Chrys.*hom.4.1 in Tit*.(11.750F); τοῦ... νομοθετικοῦ τὸ μὲν π. τὸ δὲ ἀπαγορευτικόν Proc.G.*Gen*.proem.(M.87. 24C); of persons ὁ ἐπίσκοπος, ἔσο...π. *Const.App*.2.57.1; π. τις καὶ αὐτὸς ὑπῆρχεν Epiph.*haer*.32.4(p.443.4; M.41.548C).

παραιτ-έομαι, 1. *refrain from, avoid* τὰ ὀνόματα καταλέγειν... ∼ούμεθα Just.*1apol*.46.3(M.6.397C); Meth.*symp*.9.1(p.113.3; M.18. 176C); π. τὰ...πρὸς θάνατον ἄγοντα τῶν πλημμελημάτων Cyr.*Ps*.33:23 (M.69.893C); **2.** *reject, repudiate* τὸν διάκονον τοῦ πεπονθότος θεοῦ π. Tat.*orat*.13(p.15.6; M.6.836A); μηδαμῶς ∼ώμεθα ἐλέγχοντα τὸν θεόν Nil.*epp*.2.3(M.79.204B); ref. Montanism ὅταν ἴδω τὴν προφῆτιν εἰληφυῖαν...χρυσὸν...πῶς αὐτὴν μὴ ∼ήσωμαι; Apollon.ap.Eus.*h.e*.5.18.4 (M.20.477A); esp. demons and heathenism τοὺς...διὰ τῆς παρὰ τῶν ἀποστόλων...διδαχῆς πεισθέντας καὶ ∼ησαμένους τὰ παλαιά Just. *1apol*.53.3(M.6.405D); δαίμονας...φαύλους...∼εῖσθαι τοὺς ἀνθρώπους ἐδίδαξε id.*2apol*.10.6(M.6.461A); ἀπόθνησκε τῷ κόσμῳ ∼ούμενος τὴν ἐν αὐτῷ μανίαν. ζῆθι τῷ θεῷ...τὴν παλαιὰν γένεσιν ∼ούμενος Tat. *orat*.11(p.12.11; M.6.829B); τοῦ θάνατον τὴν σύστασιν π. *ib*.15(p.17. 9; 840B); τούτους δὲ [sc. demons] νικᾶν ἄν τις θελήσῃ, τὴν ὕλην ∼ησάσθω *ib*.16(p.18.4; 841A); τὴν φαυλοτέραν ὕλην π. *ib*.18(p.19.30; 845A); ∼ησάμενοι τοὺς δαίμονας θεῷ...κατακολουθήσατε *ib*.19(p.22.4; 849B).

παραίτησις, ἡ, 1. *rejection,* Eus.*d.e*.6.1(p.252.20; M.22.413D); *ib*. 6.13(p.267.13; 440A); *refusal,* Chrys.*dimiss.Chan*.10(3.441C); to admit ἀλόγιστος παντάπασιν ἡ τοῦ κτίσματος [sc. of Son] π. Eun.*apol*.18 (M.30.853A); to have dealings with παραιτήσεως τῶν ἀργῶν καὶ περιέργων Euthal.Diac.*epp.Paul*.(M.85.773B); **2.** *thing to be avoided* οἱονεὶ μίσημα καὶ π. Cyr.*ador*.1(1.41B); **3.** *penalty, satisfaction* τίμημα, ὃ πᾶν τῷ χρέει ὑπῆρχε δικαίωμα πρὸς παραίτησιν Procl.CP *or.laud.BMV* 5(p.105.7; M.65.685C).

***παραιτία, ἡ,** *cause,* Areth.*Apoc*.1:5(M.106.505B).

παραίτιος, ? *weak, faulty* ἵνα εὕρωσιν [sc. δαίμονες] ἀγγεῖον παραίτιον, λακίσουσιν αὐτό, τουτέστι, ψυχὴν ἄπιστον καὶ διστάζουσαν Ephr.2.83F, perh. l. πάρετον.

παραιφασίη, ἡ, *advice,* Gr.Naz.*carm*.1.2.1.717(M.37.576A).

παραίφασις, ἡ, = foreg., Gr.Naz.*carm*.1.2.2.5(M.37.578A).

παρακαθέζ-ομαι, 1. lit.; **a.** *be near,* of spirit hovering near dead body; idea rejected, Or.*Jo*.28.6(5; p.396.3,6; M.14.689D–692A); **b.** *invest, besiege,* ‡Epiph.*v.proph.Is*.4(p.20; παρακαθίζοντο M.43. 397B); Thphn.*chron*.p.216(M.108.553B); **2.** fig., *hold fast* by ∼εσθαι τῷ γράμματι τοῦ νόμου Euthal.Diac.*epp.Paul*.(M.85.756D); τάξωμεν αὐτοῖς μετάνοιαν εἰς τὸ ∼εσθαι τῇ ἐκκλησίᾳ Epiph.*haer*.68.3(p.142. 18; M.42.188A); οὐ...ἔδει ∼εσθαι τοῖς τύποις, οὐδὲ προσεδρεύειν ταῖς σκιαῖς, ἀλλὰ τῆς ἀληθείας ἔχεσθαι Chrys.*hom.3.4 in Tit*.(11.749A).

παρακάθημαι, = παρακαθέζομαι, *hold fast by* τῷ νόμῳ κατὰ τὸ γράμμα παρακαθήμενος Euther.*confut*.12(M.28.1373D).

παρακαθίζω, 1. *set beside, call in* doctors ἐπίδειξον αὐτὴν [sc. τὴν ψυχήν] Παύλῳ νοσοῦσαν· εἰσάγαγε Ματθαῖον· παρακάθισον Ἰωάννην Chrys.*hom.74.4 in Mt*.(7.720B); cf.*ib.20.4*(265A); **2.** *sit by* παρεκάθισέν μοι Herm.*vis*.5.2; παρακάθισον...αὐτοῖς [sc. τοῖς ἰατροῖς] καὶ μάθε παρ' αὐτῶν τοῦ νοσήματός σου τὴν φύσιν Chrys.*hom.74.4 in Mt*.(7. 720D); **3.** *besiege* (cf. παρακαθέζομαι) Νισίβιν παρεκάθισεν Thphn. *chron*.p.31(M.108.136B); *ib*.p.382(913B).

***παρακαινοτομέω,** *introduce as novel* ἐν τῷ σώματι ἡμετέρῳ γενόμενος [sc. ὁ λόγος] οὐκ ἄλλην τινὰ παρεκαινοτόμησε τῇ ἀνθρωπίνῃ φύσει τὴν σύστασιν Gr.Nyss.*or.catech*.37(p.148.5; M.45.96C).

παρακαίριος, *out of season, Orac.Sib*.12.200.

παρακαλ-έω, 1. *call in, summon* ἑξῆς ∼είτωσαν οἱ πρεσβύτεροι τὸν λαόν *Const.App*.2.57.9; Valentinian μόνος ὁ ἀρχάγγελος εἰσέρχεται πρὸς αὐτόν [sc. τὸν Τόπον], οὗ κατ' εἰκόνα καὶ ὁ ἀρχιερεὺς ἅπαξ τοῦ ἐνιαυτοῦ εἰς τὰ ἅγια τῶν ἁγίων εἰσῄει. ἔνθεν καὶ ὁ Ἰησοῦς παρακληθεὶς συνεκαθέσθη τῷ Τόπῳ, ἵνα μένῃ τὰ πνεύματα καὶ μὴ προαναστῇ αὐτοῦ Clem.*exc.Thdot*.38(p.119.3; M.9.677B); **2.** *call on, invoke,* Meth. *symp*.9.1(p.113.2; M.18.176B); δείκνυσι τοῦ ὀνόματος τὴν δύναμιν, εἴ γε μὴ ὁρώμενος μηδὲ ∼ούμενος, ἀλλ' ὀνομαζόμενος μόνον...ποιεῖ θαυμαστούς Chrys.*hom.79.1 in Jo*.(8.466D); **3.** *comfort* καίγε πολλὰ παρεκάλεσέν με ὁ πατήρ μου *T.Reub*.4.4; ὁ θεὸς παρεκάλεσέ με *T.Jos*. 1.6; *soothe* ∼οῦντες τοὺς ὑβρισμένους Chrys.*hom.79.4 in Jo*.(8. 469D); of Father and Son, Gr.Nyss.*Eun*.2(2 p.370.23; M.45.552A); of H. Ghost, Cyr.H.*catech*.16.16, etc., v. παράκλητος, παράκλησις; ref. Christian conduct, *be gentle to, address gently* τοὺς ἀδικοῦντας αὐτοὺς ∼οῦσι καὶ προσφιλεῖς αὐτοὺς ἑαυτοῖς ποιοῦσι Arist.*apol*.15.5; διωχθήσεται; ἀνέξεται· βλασφημηθήσεται; παρακαλέσει Gr.Naz.*or*.26.12(M. 35.1244C); **4.** *exhort* δι' ὀλίγων ὑμᾶς γραμμάτων παρεκάλεσα Ign. *Polyc*.7.3; ἡμεῖς οὐ πανσόμεθα τὰ αὐτὰ ἐνηχοῦντες, ἀναμιμνήσκοντες, διδάσκοντες, ∼οῦντες Chrys.*hom.51.3 in Jo*.(8.303C); id.*stat*.6.1(2. 73B); Thphyl.*exc.gent*.6(p.485.11; M.113.948A); **5.** *entreat, beseech* ἀποβλήτους γίνεσθαι τῆς ἐκκλησίας, ἕως ἂν ἐξομολογησάμενοι καὶ δείξαντες καρποὺς μετανοίας, καὶ παρακαλέσαντες, τυχεῖν δυνηθῶσι συγγνώμης CAnt.(341)*can*.2; δέομαι καὶ ∼ῶ μὴ ζημιοῦν ἑαυτούς Chrys. *hom.81.3 in Jo*.(8.481E); Call.*v.Hyp*.(p.92); c. genit. and infin., Hier.*v.Paul*.2(p.27.7); *intercede, pray* (for) ∼οῦμεν ὑπὲρ πάντων ἀνθρώπων τῆς ἐκκλησίας ταύτης Serap.*euch*.10.3; *ib*.11.2,4; ὑπὲρ τούτων ∼εῖν τὸν δεσπότην Chrys.*hom.19.5 in Mt*.(7.251B); *offer prayer* ∼οῦμεν διὰ τῆς θυσίας ταύτης Serap.*euch*.13.13; Chrys.*hom.82.1 in Jo*.(8.483B); parenthetical, *please, pray* μή, ∼ῶ, μηδεὶς ταύτην ζητείτω τὴν παραμυθίαν id.*hom.43.4 in Mt*.(7.464C); cf.*ib.35.5*(404D); id.*hom.8.2 in 1Tim*.(11.591C); pass., *'be pleased to'* παρακλήθητε... οἱ...ἐντυγχάνοντες...συγγνῶναι ἡμῖν Epiph.*rescr*.(p.156.6; M.41.160B); *be so kind as to* τὰ περὶ τῆς ὑγιείας δηλῶσαι ἡμῖν παρακλήθητι Synes. *ep*.157(*EG* p.738C); *Didasc.Jac*.3.2(p.53.8).

παρακαταθήκη, ἡ, 1. lit., *something laid by,* of grave-goods ἐγὼ δὲ...τὸ παλαμναῖον βαλάντιον, τὴν π. τοῦ ξένου, ἔκλαον Synes.*ep*.4 (ἔκλαιον M.66.1333C); θεοῦ...τῇ γῇ κελεύοντος ἀφεῖναι τὴν π. [i.e. at resurrection] Chrys.*hom.8.1 in 1Thess*.(11.479A); **2.** *person* or *thing entrusted*; **a.** in gen. τοὺς τιμιωτάτους υἱοὺς ἡμῶν...ἔχε ἐν π. Bas.*ep*. 200(3.298C; M.32.733C); Nil.*epp*.3.14(M.79.377A); lost property, e.g. stray donkey, to be so regarded φυσικὴν κοινωνίαν διδάσκει τὸ εὕρημα π. λογίζεσθαι Clem.*str*.2.18(p.160.1; M.8.1028B); μίμημα τῆς οἰκουμένης ἡ κιβωτός, τὴν τῶν ζῴων π. φυλάττουσα Bas.Sel.*or*.6.4(M. 85.97C); **b.** ref. Lc.23:46 εἰ παρέθετο τὸ πνεῦμα τῷ πατρί, π. δέδωκεν τὸ πνεῦμα. ἄλλο ἐστὶν χαρίσασθαι, καὶ ἄλλο παραδοῦναι, καὶ ἄλλο τὸ παρακαταθέσθαι. ὁ παρακατατιθέμενος παρακατατίθεται ἵνα ἀπολάβῃ τὴν π. τί οὖν ἔδει τὴν π. παραθέσθαι τὸ πνεῦμα τῷ πατρί; ὑπὲρ ἐμέ ἐστιν καὶ τὴν ἐμὴν ἕξιν καὶ τὸν ἐμὸν νοῦν Or.*dial*.7(p.138.6ff.); **c.** *tradition* ἡ τῶν πρεσβυτέρων π. διὰ τῆς γραφῆς λαλοῦσα Clem.*ecl*.27(p.145. 3; M.9.712C); τὴν καλὴν π., ἣν παρὰ τῶν πατέρων εἰλήφαμεν Gr.Naz. *or*.6.22(M.35.749B); cf.Justn.*conf*.(p.78.1; M.86.999D); **d.** of the self surrendered in martyrdom οἷον π. εὐγνωμόνως καὶ ἀγαπητικῶς ἀποδιδοὺς τὸν ἀπαιτούμενον ἄνθρωπον Clem.*str*.4.9(p.282.13; M.8.1285A); Chrys.*pan.Lucn*.3(2.528C); **e.** associated with ἀγάπη: ἡ γνῶσις δὲ ἐκ παραδόσεως διαδιδομένη κατὰ χάριν θεοῦ τοῖς ἀξίους σφᾶς αὐτοὺς τῆς διδασκαλίας παρεχομένοις οἷον π. ἐγχειρίζεται, ἀφ' ἧς τὸ τῆς ἀγάπης ἀξίωμα ἐκλάμπει Clem.*str*.7.10(p.41.5; M.9.480A); μακάριοι δὲ καὶ ὑμεῖς, ὅτι τῆς ἀγάπης δεξάμενοι τὴν π. ἀκέραιον αὐτὴν τῷ παρακαταθεμένῳ μέχρι νῦν φυλάττοντες διεμείνατε Chrys.*pan.Melet*.1(2.518A); **f.** of gift of H. Ghost οἱ...ψευδόμενοι ἀθετοῦσι τὸν κύριον καὶ γίνονται ἀποστερηταὶ τοῦ κυρίου, μὴ παραδιδόντες αὐτῷ τὴν π. ἣν ἔλαβον. ἔλαβον γὰρ παρ' αὐτοῦ πνεῦμα ἄψευστον Herm.*mand*.3.2; ὥσπερ τινὰ π. μοι δεδωκὼς ἐπὶ τῷ τὴν ὁλοτελῆ...τότε τοῦ πνεύματος κομίσασθαι χάριν Thdr.Mops.*2Tim*.1:12(p.200.15; M.66.945B); φυλάξαντες τὴν δωρεὰν τοῦ ἁγίου πνεύματος, καὶ αὐξήσαντες τὴν π. τῆς χάριτος *Rit. Bapt*.(p.401); **g.** *mission* ἄσυλον τὴν ἀποστολικὴν π. διαφυλάξαντας Bas.*ep*.242.3(3.372B; M.32.901B); **h.** spiritual *advice* παρατίθημί σοι π. ἐν κυρίῳ, ὡς ἀνθρώπῳ τοῦ θεοῦ καὶ σωθῆναι βουλομένῳ Ephr.1. 215B; cf.id.2.77D.

παρακατακλίνω, fig., of burial, *lay to rest* beside, Gr.Nyss.*v. Macr*.(p.409.24; M.46.996B).

***παρακατάσχει,** v. παρακατέχω.

παρακατατίθ-ημι, 1. *present* to μετὰ τῆς ἐπιστολῆς πέμπων αὐτὸν ∼έναι τῇ ἐκκλησίᾳ Or.*comm.in 1Cor*.16:10ff.(*JTS* 10 p.50); **2.** med., fig., *set before* τὴν ἐν παισὶν ἁπλότητα εἰς ἐξομοίωσιν ∼έμενος ἡμῖν Clem.*paed*.1.5(p.97.9; M.8.264A); ταῦτα μετὰ πολλῆς σαφηνείας ὁ Δανιὴλ ἡμῖν ∼εται Chrys.*hom.4.1 in 2Thess*.(11.530B).

παρακατέχ-ω, 1. ref. one type of avarice, *keep back* part when the whole has been promised, ‡Nil.*vit.cog*.(παρακατάσχει M.79. 1452A); *withhold* information about μηδὲν τῶν κρυφῇ πεπραγμένων

~ων Niceph.Ur.*v.Sym.*221(M.86.3189C); **2.** *retain* in memory ἐπειδὰν ...ψευδῶν ἀναπλασμῶν...ἡ ψυχὴ πληρωθεῖσα, παρακατάσχῃ τῇ μνήμῃ Bas.*Eun.*1.6(1.217B; M.29.521B); ὧν οὐδ' ἴχνος τῇ μνήμῃ ~ομεν Max. *ambig.*(M.91.1104C); in supposed etym. of μῆνις: παρὰ τὸ μένειν καὶ τῇ μνήμῃ ~εσθαι *ib.*(1197C); **3.** *restrain, make ineffective* ~ει δέ πως ἡ βλασφημία τὸν λόγον Gr.Nyss.*Eun.*11(2 p.267.16; M.45.876C).

παρακάτω (παρὰ κάτω), *below*; **1.** adv., *Apophth.Patr.*(M.65.261A); **2.** prep. παρὰ κάτω τῶν...μοναστηρίων Cyr.S.*v.Sab.*72(p.175.18).

παράκειμαι, 1. *be similar, correspond* τὰ παρακείμενα...συνεξεταστέον, δόξαντα ἄν τισιν οὐχὶ παρακείμενα μόνον ἀλλὰ καὶ τὰ αὐτά Or. *Jo.*1.25(24; p.30.18,19; M.14.68A); κακίαν ἐκ τῆς παρακειμένης ἀρετῆς Bas.*hom.in Ps.*61(1.195D; M.29.476B); **2.** *coexist* παράκειται...τὸ πνεῦμα τῷ πνεύματι, ὡς τὸ πνεῦμα τῇ ψυχῇ Clem.*exc.Thdot.*17(p.112.17; M.9.665B); **3.** *be relevant* to παράκειται...τῷ ἐξετάζειν...καὶ τὸ ἰδεῖν Or.*Jo.*20.26(21; p.362.8; M.14.633A); παρακείμενα...τῇ ἐξετάσει *ib.*20.44(33; p.388.12; 677B); **4.** *be exposed* to εὐαλωτότατοι λίαν παρακείσονται τοῖς διώκειν αὐτοὺς ᾑρημένοις Cyr.*ador.*5(1.142B).

παρακεκαλυμμένως, *in a veiled manner* ἐν παραβολῇ καὶ π. Just. *dial.*52.1(M.6.589B); π. προπεφητευκέναι *ib.*76.2(653A); Clem.*str.*1.1 (p.10.7; M.8.701B); Or.*Jo.*20.16(14; p.347.5; M.14.608B).

παρακεκινδυνευμένως, *daringly, with danger*, Clem.*prot.*7(p.56.13; M.8.181A); Chrys.*hom.23.2 in Jo.*(8.133E).

παρακελεύ-ομαι, 1. *advise* ~εται αὐτοῖς καὶ φυγήν Thdt.*Jer.*48:3 (2.594); **2.** *command, impose* course of action, virtuous practice etc. ὁ κύριος ἡμῶν ἐν εὐαγγελίοις ~εται...ὧδε νομοθετῶν Meth.*symp.* 5.2(p.54.19; M.18.100A); *ib.*11.1(p.129.18; 205A); Thdt.*1Cor.*7:36(3.211); pass., *be* divinely *ordered*, Didym.(‡Bas.)*Eun.*5(1.317A; M.29.760C); ὁ προφήτης ~εται Thdt.*Jer.*3:11(2.425); fig. ὀχετοὶ...ὕδωρ... κατιέναι...~ονται id.*provid.*3(4.523).

παρακελευστικῶς, *by way of injunction*, Thdt.*haer.*2 proem.(4.326).

παρακεν-όω, *disclose, give away* to φοβοῦμαι μήποτε...~ώσῃς με τοῖς Χριστιανοῖς καὶ...καύσωσίν με *Didasc.Jac.*1.55(p.779.23).

παρακεντ-έω, of cataract, *couch*, fig. ~ήσει σου τοὺς ὀφθαλμοὺς τῆς ψυχῆς καὶ τῆς καρδίας Thphl.Ant.*Autol.*1.7(M.6.1036A); Nil.*Eulog.*25 (M.79.1128A).

παρακέντησις, ἡ, *mark at the side*, Hipp.*can.pasch.*(M.10.879).

***παρακενωτή, ἡ,** plur., *ordure*, *Chron.Pasch.*p.337(M.92.880A).

παρακερδαίνω, *filch, embezzle*, Niceph.Ur.*v.Sym.*186(M.86.3157A).

παρακιν-έω, trans.; **1.** *move* ἐάν, φησίν, ἄλλον ~ήσῃ ἡ χάρις τοῦ πνεύματος, παραχωρείτω ὁ τοῦ λέγειν ἀρξάμενος Thdt.*1Cor.*14:30(3.262); **2.** *alter* μηδὲν αἱρεῖσθαι τῶν ὀρθῶς ἐγνωσμένων ~εῖν Bas.*leg.lib. gent.*8(p.59; M.31.588A); of divine scripture τὰ θεῖα λόγια ~οῦντες Dion.Ar.*d.n.*4.11(M.3.709A); ‡Chrys.*pasch.*7(8.277A); **3.** *violate* ὁ ~ήσας τι τῶν ἀπειρημένων Eus.*p.e.*13.21(711C; M.21.1176A).

***παρακιόνιον, τό,** *pillar* supporting canopy of altar τὰ δὲ π. κατὰ μίμησιν τῶν τεσσάρων ζῴων ‡Sophr.H.*liturg.*2(M.87.3984B).

[*]παρακιρν-άω, *mix, dilute*, Bas.*hom.in Ps.*14(1.354E; M.29.257A); τῷ φαύλῳ...τῶν οἰκείων δογμάτων ~ῶντες ὕδατι, τὰ θεῖα καπηλεύειν τολμῶσι Isid.Pel.*epp.*3.125(M.78.825D).

παρακλέπτ-ω, 1. *steal*; lit., Cyr.*ador.*16(1.573D); met. ~ουσι τῶν ἀκεραίων τὸν νοῦν id.*Ps.*9:28(M.69.784A); **2.** *assume falsely* τὴν τῆς ἐπιεικείας δόκησιν ~οντες id.*Is.*1.1(2.18E); **3.** *evade* ~ουσι τὸν νόμον, ἀποδιδράσκοντες τὰ καλά Clem.*str.*7.11(p.48.32; M.9.493C); **4.** pass., *be robbed of*, c. dat. μηδὲν τῇ πίστει παρακλοπέντες...ἀλλ' ἐπὶ κύριον τὰς ἐλπίδας θέμενοι *Mir.Geo.*9(p.101.15).

παράκλησις, ἡ, A. *comfort, consolation*; **1.** in gen., Just.*dial.*78.8 (M.6.660C); ἐν τῷ μέλλοντι αἰῶνι τὴν π. ὑπισχνούμενος *Hom.Clem.* 3.26; Chrys.*stat.*1.6(2.9B); **2.** of spiritual comfort; **a.** in gen. ὁ θεὸς ὁ πατὴρ τῆς π. *T.Sal.*D 4.11(p.93*.11); καταλήγει...πᾶσα ἀρετὴ εἰς π. πνευματικήν Marc.Er.*opusc.*1.48(M.65.912B); **b.** as activity of whole Trin., Gr.Nyss.*Eun.*2(2 p.370.19; M.45.552A), v. παράκλητος; **c.** as operation of H. Ghost as παράκλητος, cf. *paracletus...a consolatione dicitur* (π. *enim Latine consolatio appellatur*), Or.*princ.*2.7.4(p.151.12; M.11.218A); τὸ πνεῦμα τὸ ἅγιον, τὸ εἰς π. καὶ ἁγιασμὸν...τοῖς πιστεύουσι διδόμενον *Symb.Ant.*(341)2 ap.Ath.*syn.*23(p.249.26; M.26.724A); Isid.H.*etym.*7.3.10, v. παράκλητος; **3.** *refreshment* ἀπὸ π. ... ἀνιστάμενος...ἡσύχαζε ἐν τῷ σῷ κελλίῳ Ephr.1.215C; Zos.*alloquia* 13 (M.78.1700B).

B. *exhortation* (to) ἀρετῆς π. Gr.Naz.*or.*8.4(M.35.793B); τῶν ξένων π. καὶ νουθεσία *Const.App.*2.58.3; διδασκαλίαν φησὶ τὴν ἀπόλυτον ἐξήγησιν, π. δὲ τὴν ἀπὸ τινῶν συμβεβηκότων νουθεσίαν τε καὶ ὑπόμνησιν Thdr.Mops.*1Tim.*4:13(p.149.19; M.66.941D).

C. *entreaty*; **1.** in gen., Or.*mart.*26(p.23.2; M.11.596A); Eus.*h.e.* 2.15.1(M.20.172B); *ib.*3.36.6(288C); Bas.*ep.*82(3.175D; M.32.460B); **2.** of prayer to God π. καὶ λιταῖς ἵλεω τὸν πατέρα...καταστησάμενος Eus.*h.e.*10.4.36(M.20.864B); εἰσάκουσον τῶν π. καὶ τῶν προσευχῶν ἡμῶν Serap.*euch.*9.3; Ammon.*Jo.*20:21(M.85.1517C); Thphn.*chron.* p.398(M.108.949C); **3.** *intercession, advocacy* on behalf of someone Ῥουφίνῳ...εἰς π. ἐλθόντι δεινῶς ἐπέπληξεν Ἀμβρόσιος *ib.*p.62(208B).

παρακλητικός, 1. *comforting, consolatory*, Hipp.*Dan.*3.7.8; as description of H. Ghost, Epiph.*haer.*74.7(M.42.489A, v.l. for παράκλητον p.324.3); **2.** *hortatory* φωνὴ π. Clem.*prot.*1(p.9.20; M.8.65A); id.*paed.*1.7(p.126.20; M.8.324B); *ib.*1.8(p.128.25; 329A); Isid.Pel.*epp.* 5.394(M.78.1564A); **3.** neut. as subst., *office-book* containing troparia of ferial office for the year, so called either because of consolatory character of its material or because consisting largely of invocations, *Nomoc.*120.

***παρακλητικῶς,** *by way of exhortation*, Clem.*str.*7.11(p.46.3; M.9.488C); †Bas.*bapt.*1.2.17(2.641E; M.31.1556A).

παράκλητος, (adj. and subst.); **A.** *advocate, intercessor, spokesman on* someone's *behalf*; **1.** in gen. πλουσίων παράκλητοι, πενήτων ἄνομοι κριταί *Did.*5.2 = *Barn.*20.2; τίς ἡμῶν π. ἔσται, ἐὰν μὴ εὑρεθῶμεν ἔργα ἔχοντες ὅσια *2Clem.*6.9; *Ep.Lugd.*ap.Eus.*h.e.*5.1.10 (M.20.412B); **2.** of Son σωτῆρα...τὸν τῆς σῆς συνήγορον καὶ π. ψυχῆς Clem.*q.d.s.*25(p.176.23; M.9.629D); Or.*princ.*2.7.4(p.151.27; M.11.218C); πρὸς τὸν πατέρα π. ἐστιν ὁ υἱὸς τοῦ θεοῦ, εὐχόμενος ὑπὲρ τῶν εὐχομένων id.*or.*10(p.320.21; M.11.445D); ὁ π. ἐγώ *A.Mt.*2(p.219.2); Gr.Naz.*or.*30.14(p.131.4; M.36.121C) cit. s. παραινέτης; π. μὲν καὶ ἱλαστήριον ὁ υἱὸς ὠνόμασται· καθίστησι γὰρ τοῖς ἐπὶ τῆς γῆς εὐμενῆ τὸν πατέρα Cyr.*Pulch.*(p.54.7; 5².169C); Ammon.*Jo.*14:16(M.85.1489A); *paracletus id est advocatus, quia pro nobis intercedit apud patrem...paracletus autem graecum est, quod latine dicitur advocatus, quod nomen et filio et spiritui sancto adscribitur*, Isid.H.*etym.*7.2.27–28; **3.** of H. Ghost, v. infra; **4.** of saints τεσσαράκοντα γὰρ μάρτυρες ...ἀξιόπιστοι...τῆς πρὸς τὸν δεσπότην ἱκεσίας π. Gr.Nyss.*mart.*2.9(M.46.788B).

B. *comforter, consoler*; **1.** of Persons of Trin. ὁ γὰρ υἱὸς ἐπίσης ἑαυτόν τε καὶ τὸ πνεῦμα...ὀνομάζει π.· ὁ δὲ πατὴρ δι' ὧν ἐνεργεῖ τὴν παράκλησιν, οἰκειοῦται πάντως τοῦ π. τὸ ὄνομα...διπλῆς δὲ οὔσης τῆς τοῦ παρακαλεῖν σημασίας, μιᾶς μὲν διὰ τῶν τιμητικῶν ῥημάτων τε καὶ σχημάτων, ὑπὲρ ὧν, ἄν τινος δεόμενοι τύχωμεν, εἰς συμπάθειαν αὐτὸν ἐπαγόμεθα, ἑτέρας δὲ τῆς θεραπευτικῆς τῶν ψυχικῶν τε καὶ σωματικῶν παθημάτων ἐπινοίας, τῶν καθ' ἑκάτερον σημαινομένων ἐπίσης ἡ... γραφὴ προσμαρτυρεῖ τῇ θείᾳ φύσει τοῦ π. τὴν ἔννοιαν...τούτων οὖν οὕτως ἐχόντων, ὅπως ἂν ἐπὶ τοῦ πνεύματος νοήσῃς τοῦ π. τὸ ὄνομα, τῆς τοῦ πατρός τε καὶ τοῦ υἱοῦ κοινωνίας καθ' ἑκάτερον τῶν σημαινομένων οὐκ ἀποστήσεις Gr.Nyss.*Eun.*2(2 p.370.18ff.; M.45.552Aff.); **2.** of Son Χριστὸς π. ἐκ τοῦ παρακαλεῖσθαι ἐκλήθη Didym.*Trin.*2.6(M.39.548C); Ammon.*Jo.*14:16(M.85.1489A); **3.** of H. Ghost, v. infra.

C. as description of H. Ghost; **1.** in sense of *advocate, supporter*, cf.Tert.*de monogamia* 3(M.*PL.*2.934A); Ἐπάγαθος...π. Χριστιανῶν χρηματίσας, ἔχων δὲ τὸν π. ἐν ἑαυτῷ *Ep.Lugd.*ap.Eus.*h.e.*5.1.10(M.20.412B); cf. *paracletus enim latine dicitur advocatus*, Aug.*tractatus 74.4 in Jo.*(M.*PL.*35.1828); π. ὡς τὰς τῶν ὅλων παρακλήσεις δεχόμενον ‡Cyr.*Trin.*9(6³.13C; M.77.1140B) = Jo.D.*f.o.*1.8(M.94.821C); **2.** combining senses of *advocate* and *comforter* or *consoler*, Cyr.H. *catech.*16.20; cf.Gr.Nyss.*Eun.*2(2 p.371.2; M.45.552B); cf. *spiritus sanctus...paracletus ab eo quod consolatur in tristitia positos, nuncupatus est...in alio loco reperitur paracletus spiritus, legati ad patrem persona fungi*, Didym.*Spir.*27(M.39.1058A); π. καλεῖται ὁ υἱὸς καὶ τὸ πνεῦμα, ὡς παραμυθίαν ἡμῖν ἐμποιοῦντες, καὶ ὡς παρακαλοῦντες ὑπὲρ ἡμῶν τὸν πατέρα Ammon.*Jo.*14:16(M.85.1489A); cf. *consolator ergo ille vel advocatus (utrumque enim interpretatur quod est graece paracletus)* Aug.*tractatus 94.2 in Jo.*(M.*PL.*35.1868); **3.** together with sense of *exhorter, spokesman*, cf. *paracletus pro eo quod consolationem praestet animabus quae gaudium temporale amittunt. alii paracletum latine oratorem vel advocatum interpretantur. ipse enim spiritus...dicit, ipse docet, per ipsum datur sermo sapientiae*, Isid.H.*etym.*7.3.12; cf.†Jo.D.*B.J.*5(M.96.889D); **4.** in sense of *comforter* only, cf. *paracletus vero quod dicitur spiritus...a consolatione dicitur* (παράκλησις *enim latine consolatio appellatur*). *si quis namque de spiritu...participare meruerit, cognitis ineffabilibus sacramentis consolationem sine dubio et laetitiam cordis assumit*, Or.*princ.*2.7.4(p.151.12; M.11.218A); this meaning, as applied to H. Ghost, dist. from sense of *deprecator* properly applied to Son as Paraclete, *ib.* (p.152.4; 218C); ὁ σωτὴρ ἀποστέλλει τοῖς...μαθηταῖς τὸ πνεῦμα...τὸ π., πρὸς τὸ παρακαλεῖν αὐτοὺς καὶ παραμυθεῖσθαι ἐφ' οἷς κηρύττοντες τὸ εὐαγγέλιον ὑπὸ τῶν ἐλαυνόντων αὐτοὺς ἔπασχον Eus.*e.th.*3.5(p.161.26; M.24.1009B); συνεχῶς δὲ π. καλεῖ, διὰ τὰς συνεχούσας αὐτοὺς τότε θλίψεις Chrys.*hom.*75.3 *in Jo.*(8.443A); ref. comfort of Paraclete as given in response to penitence, hence 'blessed are they that mourn', Proc.G.*Is.*32:9–20(M.87.2284D); *ib.*40:1–8(2329A,C); *spiritus*

...*quod dicitur paracletus a consolatione dicitur; παράκλησις enim graece, latine consolatio appellatur. Christus enim apostolis lugentibus misit,* Isid.H.*etym*.7.3.10; **5.** in sense of *instructor* ἄλλον δὲ π. λέγει ἀντὶ τοῦ ἄλλον διδάσκαλον, π. λέγων τὴν ἐν τοῖς δεινοῖς διδασκαλίαν Thdr.Mops.*Jo*.14:15(p.391.12f.; M.66.777A); **6.** as title, without definition of meaning, distinguishing H. Ghost from other πνεύματα, Eus.*e.th*.3.5(p.163.15; M.24.1012D); τὸ πνεῦμα..., τὸν π., τὸ πνεῦμα τῆς ἀληθείας *Symb.Ant.*(341)3 ap.Ath.*syn*.24(p.250.16; M.26.724D); τὸ ἅγιον πνεῦμα, τουτέστι τὸν π. *Symb.Ant.*(341)4(p.251.12; 725C); εἰς τὸ πνεῦμα...τουτέστι τὸν π. *Symb.Ant.*(345)(p.252.1; M.26.728C); *Symb.Sirm*.1(p.254.19; M.26.736C); ὁ δὲ π. τὸ πνεῦμα τὸ ἅγιον δι' υἱοῦ ἀποσταλέν *Symb.Sirm*.2(p.257.26; 744A); **τὸν π. κατὰ τὸ** γεγραμμένον *Symb.Sirm*.3(p.236.7; 693B); τὸν π., καθὼς γέγραπται, τὸ πνεῦμα τῆς ἀληθείας *Symb.Nic.*(359)ap.Thdt.*h.e*.2.21.6(3.880); πνεῦμα, ὃ καὶ π. ὠνόμασεν ὁ σωτήρ *Symb.Sel*.ap.Ath.*syn*.29(p.258.14; M.26.745B); πνεῦμα, ὅπερ...ὁ κύριος...ἐπηγγείλατο πέμπειν τῷ γένει τῶν ἀνθρώπων π. *Symb.CP*(360)*ib*.(p.259.11; M.26.748B); ὅτε γοῦν ἐκπίπτει τις ἀπὸ τοῦ πνεύματος...οὐκέτι ἐν τῷ θεῷ ἐστιν ἐκεῖνος ὁ πεσών, διὰ τὸ ἀποστῆναι ἀπ' αὐτοῦ τὸ ἐν τῷ θεῷ ἅγιον καὶ π. πνεῦμα Ath.*Ar*.3.25(M.26.376C); Eun.*apol*.25(M.30.861B); τοὺς γάρ τοι πεπιστευκότας ἐνέργειαν εἶναί τινα τοῦ θεοῦ τὸν π. ... διελέγχειν, μακρᾶς ἂν εἴη σχολῆς *ib*.(861D); πιστεύομεν...εἰς τὸν π., τὸ πνεῦμα τῆς ἀληθείας [evading, acc. Gr. Nyss., title πνεῦμα ἅγιον] id.ap.Gr.Nyss.*Eun*.2 (2 p.369.10; M.45.549B); ἐν...πνεῦμα ἅγιον τὸ π. Bas.*fid*.4(2.227D; M.31.685B); ὁ θεὸς τοῦ π. καὶ τῶν ὅλων κύριος *Lit*.ap.*Const.App*.8.6.11; ‡Ign.*Philad*.2; Mac.Aeg.*hom*.6.6(M.34.521C); Chrys.*hom.46.4 in Jo*.(8.273E); †Jo.D.*B.J*.1(M.96.861C); reference of Christ to π. as ἄλλος (Jo.14:15f.) proves distn. bet. Son and H. Ghost, Eus.*e.th*.3.5(p.160.5; M.24.1008A); delay in sending of π. after Resurrection intended to prevent disciples from expecting a second incarnation, Chrys. *hom.75.1 in Jo*.(8.439E); **7.** Montanist; **a.** as inspiring prophetesses Priscilla and Maximilla ἐν ταύταις τὸ π. πνεῦμα κεχωρηκέναι Hipp. *haer*.8.19(p.238.7; M.16.3366C); **b.** as identified with Montanus ἐγώ εἰμι ὁ πατὴρ καὶ ὁ υἱὸς καὶ ὁ π. Mont.*fr*.ap.Didym.*Trin*.3.41(M.39.984B); *Dial.Mont.et Orth*.(p.452.13); τὸν μὲν δὴ π. Μοντανόν Eus. *h.e*.5.14(M.20.464A); and Priscilla, Bas.*ep*.188 *can*.1(3.269C; M.32.668A); Thdt.*haer*.3.2(4.341); **8.** applied by Manes to himself τὸν π. καὶ αὐτὸ τὸ πνεῦμα τὸ ἅγιον αὐτὸς ἑαυτὸν ἀνακηρύττων Eus.*h.e*.7.31.1(M.20.720C); Hegem.*Arch*.11(p.19.4; M.10.1445B); ‡Chrys.*Spir*.10(3.808D); Socr.*h.e*.1.22.8(M.67.137B).

D. title of Valent. aeon, Iren.*haer*.1.1.2(M.7.449B); identified with Soter, *ib*.1.4.5(485B); τὸν π. ... τὸν Ἰησοῦν λέγουσιν, ὅτι πλήρης τῶν αἰώνων ἐλήλυθεν...καὶ ἐξ εὐδοκίας τῶν αἰώνων Ἰησοῦς προβάλλεται π. τῷ παρελθόντι αἰῶνι. ἐν τύπῳ δὲ παρακλήτου ὁ Παῦλος ἀναστάσεως ἀπόστολος γέγονεν Clem.*exc.Thdot*.23(p.114.16; M.9.669B); Val.Gn. ap.Epiph.*haer*.31.5(p.392.9; M.41.484A); *ib*.31.6(p.393.13; 484D); Didym.*Trin*.2.6(M.39.548C).

E. *called together, assembled* ἐν ταύτῃ τῇ παρακλήτῳ συνελεύσει (Lat. *ad hunc coetum conrogatum*) CCarth.(397)ap.*Cod.Afr*.(H.1.881D).

παρακλήτωρ, ὁ, 1. *comforter, supporter*, ‡Chrys.*poenit*.3(9.768A); of Christ π. γὰρ τῶν τεθλιμμένων ἐστί ‡Chrys.*hom*.13(13.252D); Max. *ambig*.(M.91.1417B); **2.** = παράκλητος as title of H. Ghost *Nomoc*.91.

***παρακλοπή, ἡ,** *fraud*, Max.*opusc*.(M.91.245B).

παρακλύζω, *lap against*, *Orac.Sib*.12.135; *ib*.13.132; Philost.*h.e*. 3.11(M.65.500B).

παρακμή, ἡ, *abatement*; met., of Heraclius π. τῶν παρελθουσῶν νόσων Geo.Pis.*carm*.4.162(p.15).

παρακν-άομαι, *scratch* (as sign of excitement) τὴν παρειὰν ∼ώμενοι ‡Caes.Naz.*dial*.1(M.38.856).

***παρακνίζ-ω, 1.** *irritate*, Chrys.*hom.87.3 in Mt*.(7.821B); id.*hom.49.2 in Jo*.(8.291C); τὰ ∼οντα καὶ διεγείροντα τὴν ψυχήν id.*sac*.6.7 (p.152.10; 1.426B); παρέκνιζεν Ἰουδαίους βασιλέα καλῶν Ephr.3.475E; **2.** *provoke, incite*, Chrys.*hom.29.2 in Jo*.(8.166C); id.*hom.18.2 in Rom*.(9.632C); Isid.Pel.*epp*.4.74(M.78.1133C); Thdt.*Rom*.11:11 (3.120); τὸ παραζηλοῦμεν, ἀντὶ τοῦ ∼ομεν id.*1Cor*.10:22(3.229).

παρακοή, ἡ, I. *disobedience*;

A. def. ἡ γὰρ π. προαιρέσεως, οὐ σώματος ἁμαρτία ἐστίν Gr.Nyss. *Eun*.2(2 p.365.29; M.45.545B); ἴδιον παρακοῆς ἔργον ἐστὶν ἡ ἁμαρτία Max.*cap.theol*.2.7(M.90.1128B); ἡ δὲ π. παράβασις id.*ambig*.(M.91.1041B).

B. opp. ὑπακοή: ὑπακοῆς ἡ χάρις...παρακοῆς ἡ κρίσις Clem.*prot*.10 (p.70.1; M.8.209A); διὰ τοῦτο γὰρ ἡ προφητεία, δι' ὑπακοὴν καὶ π., δι' ἣν μὲν ἵνα σωθῶμεν, δι' ἣν δὲ ἵνα παιδευθῶμεν id.*paed*.1.2(p.93.6; M.8.256A); παιδαγωγὸς ἡμῶν, μόνος [ὁ] τῆς ὑπακοῆς διακρῖναι τὴν π. δυνάμενος *ib*.1.8(p.129.31; 332B); ἡ ὑπακοὴ τῆς θείας προστάξεως ζωὴν...πέφυκεν, ἡ δὲ π. νεκρότητα Nil.*epp*.1.241(M.79.172A); ὥσπερ ἡ ὑπακοὴ ζωὴν κατεργάζεται, οὕτως καὶ ἡ π. θάνατον Ant.Mon.*hom*.38 (M.89.1552B); ref. Adam and Christ, Cyr.*Jo*.11.10(4.991D,E).

C. in gen.; **1.** as an evil that must be punished, Meth.*arbitr*.17 (p.189.15; M.18.264B); *Hom.Clem*.2.31; *ib*.10.13; **2.** in ascetic life ὦ τῆς π., καὶ αὐτὸ τὸ μάννα σκωλήκων καὶ δυσωδίας αἴτιον γέγονεν Ant. Mon.*hom*.38(M.89.1552D); φύγωμεν τὸν ὄλεθρον τῆς π. ἵνα μὴ σὺν τοῖς προλαβοῦσιν κατακριθῶμεν. ποῖον γὰρ ὄφελος ἔσται τῷ τὸ σῶμα παρθένον τηρήσαντι, τὴν δὲ ψυχὴν ὑπὸ τῆς π. μεμοιχευμένῳ δαίμονος; *ib*.(1553B).

D. Adam's disobedience; **1.** ref. Adam's previous state τίμιον τὸ χωρίον πρὸ τῆς π., αὐτὸ τὸ σκεῦος τοῦ Ἀδάμ Mac.Aeg.*hom*.12.1(M.34.557B); πῶς δὲ καὶ πρὸ τῆς π. οὐκ ἐγίνωσκε καλὸν καὶ πονηρὸν ὁ Ἀδάμ; ‡Ath.*Apoll*.1.15(M.26.1120B); ἐνδιδυσκόμενοι τὸν καινὸν ἄνθρωπον, τὸν κατὰ θεὸν κτισθέντα, ἔχουσι τὸ κατ' εἰκόνα. τοιοῦτος γὰρ ἦν ὁ Ἀδὰμ πρὸ τῆς π. ‡Ath.*dial.Trin*.3.16(M.28.1228C); προφητικοῦ χαρίσματος μετέχων πρὸ τῆς π. Chrys.*hom.15.4 in Gen*.(4.120D); **2.** causes of his disobedience ἡ ἀπὸ τοῦ ὄφεως π. τὴν ἀρχὴν ἔλαβε... Εὔα...τὸν λόγον τὸν ἀπὸ τοῦ ὄφεως συλλαβοῦσα, π. καὶ θάνατον ἔτεκε Just.*dial*.100.4(M.6.709D–712A); **3.** its consequences; **a.** corruption of original perfection, Clem.*str*.3.14(p.239.16; M.8.1193C); μήποτε οὖν τέλειος ὢν πως ἀτελὴς διὰ τὴν π. [ὢν] γέγονεν καὶ ἐδεήθη τοῦ τελειώσοντος αὐτὸν ἀπὸ τῆς ἀτελείας Or.*Jo*.13.37(p.262.20; M.14.464B); esp. of divine image ἐγένετο ἐν ἀρχῇ ὁ ἄνθρωπος...κατ' εἰκόνα θεοῦ, ὕστερον δὲ διὰ τὴν αὐτοῦ π. ἀνέλαβε καὶ εἰκόνα χοϊκὴν id.*hom.39 in Lc*.(p.229.9; M.17.369A); πᾶσαν εἰκόνα τοῦ Ἀδὰμ ἠφάνισεν ἐκ τῆς ἐκείνου π. Mac.Aeg.*hom*.11.5(M.34.548C); of the body κατὰ τὴν ἀλλοίωσιν τὴν ἐκ τῆς π. προσγεγενημένην ταῖς ἐνσάρκοις ἡμῶν σκηναῖς Meth.*Porph*.1(p.503.9; M.18.397C); τὴν ἡμετέραν σάρκα, τὴν μετὰ τὴν π. γῆν αὖθις γενομένην Marcell.*fr*.18 ap.Eus.*e.th*.3.2(p.144.27; M.24.981A); **b.** expulsion from paradise τῷ πρωτοπλάστῳ ἡ π. περιεποιήσατο ἐκβληθῆναι αὐτὸν ἐκ τοῦ παραδείσου Thphl.Ant.*Autol*.2.25(M.6.1092C); Ath.*Ar*.2.75(M.26.305C); ‡Just.*coh.Gr*.21(M.6.280B); **c.** subjection to sin and passions, Meth.*res*.2.6(p.339.12; M.18.304B); ‡Ath. *Apoll*.1.15(M.26.1120C); Sophr.H.*mir.Cyr.et Jo*.14(M.87.3465D); Max. *qu.Thal*.61(M.90.636B); **d.** other effects ἡ π. ἐν ἱδρῶτι τοῦ προσώπου ζῆν κατακρίνασα Gr.Naz.*or*.19.14(M.35.1060C); διὰ τῆς π. τοῦ θείου θελήματος ἐγυμνώθημεν Gr.Nyss.*v.Mos*.(M.44.333A); αὐτὸς [sc. Adam] γὰρ ἑαυτῷ πάντων αἴτιος γέγονε τῶν κακῶν...καὶ τῆς ἐκπτώσεως τῶν τοσούτων ἀγαθῶν καὶ τῆς καταδίκης, ἣν διὰ τὴν π. ὑπέμεινεν Chrys. *hom.15.4 in Gen*.(4.120E); death, not an effect of knowledge but of disobedience, ‡*Diogn*.12.2; Thphl.Ant.*Autol*.2.25(M.6.1092A); **4.** God's attitude to man's disobedience ἐμακροθύμησεν ὁ θεὸς... ἐπὶ τῇ π. τῶν ἀνθρώπων Iren.*haer*.1.10.3(M.7.556A); *ib*.4.40.3(1114A); ἠξίωσεν τὸν πεσόντα διὰ τῆς π. ἄνθρωπον τῷ ἑαυτοῦ διὰ τῆς παρθένου συναφθῆναι λόγῳ Marcell.*fr*.96 ap.Eus.*Marcell*.2.3(p.50.32; M.24.809A); θάνατον ἑκούσιον ὑπέστης τὴν π. ἐκριζώσας *Lit.Jac.*(*NBP* 10[2] p.106).

E. of disobedience to Christ, exeg. Heb.2:1–3 εἰ δὲ τῶν γενητῶν εἷς ἦν ὁ υἱός, οὐ κρείττων αὐτῶν ἦν, οὔτε ἐν τῇ π. τὸ μεῖζον τῆς τιμωρίας δι' αὐτὸν ἐπέκειτο Ath.*Ar*.1.59(M.26.136B); and Church, Synes.*ep*.67 (M.66.1413A).

II. *unwillingness to hear*, of God ἔστιν οὖν καιρὸς παρακοῆς, καὶ καιρὸς ἐπακοῆς Nil.*epp*.3.2(M.79.364D).

παρακοιμ-άομαι, *lie* or *keep watch beside*; ὁ ∼ώμενος *chief eunuch of the bedchamber*, Thphn.*chron*.p.240(M.108.604Bf.).

παράκοιτις, ἡ, *mistress*, dist. from παλλακή: παλλακὴ...ἡ νομίμως τινὶ συζῶσα, χωρὶς γάμου· ἡ δὲ ἧττον τιμιωτέρα π. λέγεται Phot. *nomoc*.13.5(M.104.917B).

παρακολουθ-έω, 1. *be a follower, disciple*, Papias *fr*.2.4,15; Just. *dial*.103.8(M.6.717C); **2.** *be in attendance* κατὰ...τὸν ἴδιον ἑαυτῷ λόγον καὶ τὴν...τῶν ∼ούντων δαιμόνων ἐνέργειαν Athenag.*leg*.25.4(M.6.949C); of guardian angels, Clem.*exc.Thdot*.73(p.130.9; M.9.692D); *be a concomitant* ἁμαρτημάτων, ἃ πολλὰ τοῖς ἐν σαρκὶ...∼εῖ id.*ecl*. 11.1(p.139.22; M.9.704A); of one's shadow, Zach.Mit.*opif*.(M.85.1080A); **3.** *be a consequence, product* τῇ τοῦ πάθους αὐτοῦ οἰκονομίᾳ τοσαύτη δύναμις...∼ήσασα καὶ ∼οῦσα Just.*dial*.31.1(M.6.540B); ἐπολολύζοντες [sc. Bacchanals] Εὐάν, Εὐὰν ἐκείνην, δι' ἣν ἡ πλάνη παρηκολούθησεν Clem.*prot*.2(p.11.17; M.8.72A); **4.** *go on and on, be traditional* κατὰ τὸ ∼ῆσαν ἔθος Thdt.*ep*.112(4.1185); **5.** *keep pace with* ἡ σκοτία...διὰ τὴν ἰδίαν βραδυτῆτα τῇ ὀξύτητι τοῦ δρόμου τοῦ φωτὸς οὐδὲ κατὰ τὸ ποσὸν ∼ῆσαι δυναμένη Or.*Jo*.2.27(22; p.84.22; M.14.161C); **6.** *follow example of* γειτόνων καρτερίαν βίου ∼ήσαντες Just.*1apol*.16.4(M.6.352D); **7.** *happen*, Ath.Scholast.*coll*.1.2(p.14); *ib*.4.22(p.64).

παρακολούθημα, τό, 1. *inseparable concomitant* ὡς χρόα σώματι οὗ ἄνευ οὐκ ἔστιν (οὐχ ὡς μέρους ὄντος, ἀλλ' ὡς κατ' ἀνάγκην συνόντος π.), ἐναντίον ἐστὶ τὸ περὶ τὴν ὕλην ἔχον πνεῦμα Athenag.*leg.*24.2(M.6.945B); ἐπακολουθεῖ...τῇ δόσει τοῦ σώματος καὶ τὸ τὴν σκιὰν αὐτοῦ ἡμᾶς λαβεῖν. ... οὕτως...οἰκειότατα ἐροῦμεν π. τῶν μεγάλων καὶ ἐπουρανίων πνευματικῶν χαρισμάτων εἶναι τὰ σωματικά Or.*or.*16.2 (p.337.8; M.11.469A); cf.Zach.Mit.*opif.*(M.85.1077C); *ib.*(1080A); **2.** *tail-end* γέγονεν εἰς οὐράν, τουτέστι, π. Cyr.*Zach.*57(3.736E); id. *glaph.Gen.*4(1.120C).

***παρακολουθησία, ἡ,** Epiph.*haer.*77.18(M.42.668C; cj. ἀπαρακ- p.432.32).

παρακολουθητικός, *as a consequence,* Or.*or.*6.1(p.311.25; M.11.433D); id.*Jo.*20.20(p.357.26; παρακολουθικός M.14.625B).

***παρακολουθία, ἡ,** *following,* sectarian *persuasion,* ref. Maximilla ἡ τῆς π. γνῶσις καὶ διδασκαλία Epiph.*haer.*48.13(p.237.9; παρακολουθίας καὶ διδασκαλίας γνῶσις M.41.876B).

***παρακολουθικός,** v. παρακολουθητικός.

παρακολυμβάω, *swim beside,* ‡Nil.*perist.*11.5(M.79.909D).

παρακομίζω, 1. *adduce* λόγιον ἱερὸν παρεκόμιζε πρὸς πληροφορίαν Cyr.*Abac.*36(3.551D); in retort, id.*ador.*7(1.230A); **2.** *introduce, create* πρῶτος καὶ μόνος υἱὸς λόγος παρακομίσας...ἐκ μὴ ὄντων πᾶσαν προηγουμένην κτίσεως κτίσιν Didym.*Trin.*3.4(M.39.833C); δι' οὗ καὶ παρ' οὗ ἅμα παντὶ τῷ κόσμῳ καὶ οἱ οὐρανοὶ παρεκομίσθησαν *ib.*1.27 (400A); **3.** *lead astray,* Cyr.*ador.*8(1.264D); esp. pass., *be diverted, perverted* παρεκομίσθη τῶν ἐν ἀρχαῖς *ib.*2(68D); id.*Is.*3.3(2.444B); *ib.* 3.4(494D).

παρακομιστής, ὁ, *one who transports* into a new sphere εἰ λαβὼν ἄνθρωπον...ἀνακομίσας δὲ καὶ εἰς οὐρανούς...πῶς...ἂν καὶ αὐτὸς σωτὴρ λέγοιτο γενέσθαι..., καὶ οὐχὶ δὴ μᾶλλον ἀνθρώπου πρόξενος, ἤτοι π. δι' οὗ καὶ σεσώσμεθα; Cyr.*Chr.un.*(5[1].730D).

***παρακομπανιστής, ὁ,** ? *one who has a familiar spirit* μάντεις καὶ μαγιῶτες καὶ π. σταυροπάται *Ep.Chr.dom.*(p.25).

***παρακονδακίζ-ω,** ? *harry* κατέλιπε τοὺς στρατηγοὺς καὶ τὸν λαόν, κελεύσας ~ειν καὶ ὑποσῦραι αὐτοὺς ἐκ τοῦ ὀχυρώματος Thphn.*chron.* p.298(M.108.729A).

παρακόπτ-ω, A. trans.; **1.** *do violence to* text or fact παρακόψας τὸ εἰρημένον ἐν Γενέσει Epiph.*haer.*23.1(p.249.2; M.41.300A); *ib.*42.11 (p.135.7; 741D); παρακέκοπται τὸ περὶ Ἰωνᾶ *ib.*(p.135.4; 741D); **2.** *cut down, restrict, cut out* ἄρχεται ~ειν ἃ μὴ ἤθελε καὶ ἔλεγεν 'ἵνα τί μοι λίβανον ἐκ Σαβᾶ φέρετε;' *ib.*66.71(p.112.22; M.42.141C); οὐ...ἐχρῆν αὐτὸν περικοπῆναι τὸ αὐτεξούσιον Cyr.*Ps.*50 proem.(M.69.1085C); **3.** *make defective* παρακεκόφθαι τὸ οὖς...παρακεκομμένης...ἀκοῆς Cyr.*ador.*12(1.415E); *ib.*14(513C); *castrate,* Epiph.*exp.fid.*10(p.510.20; M.42.800B).

B. intrans., *fall short* in understanding, Meth.*res.*1.25(p.251.2; M.41.1096B); ὁ λογισμὸς ἅμα ταῖς αἰσθήσεσι ~ει Nemes.*nat.hom.*13 (M.40.664B).

παράκουσμα, τό, *disobedience* to, *refusal* of, Bas.*renunt.*4(2.205C; M.31.633B).

παρακουσμάτιον, τό, *scrap of information,* Or.*Cels.*6.12(p.82.11; M.11.1308B).

***παρακουστικός,** *of disobedience,* ‡Nil.*tract.*1(M.79.1281A).

παρακού-ω, 1. *disobey,* ref. Adam's disobedience ἡ τρυφή, ἧς ὁ ~σας ἐκβάλλεται Clem.*str.*2.11(p.140.16; M.8.988B); Meth.*res.*2.2 (p.333.1; M.18.300B); ὁ ἐν ἀρχῇ λόγος οὗ ἐγὼ παρήκουσα Eus.Al.*serm.*11(M.86.376C); οὐδένα τέλειον εἰργάσατο [sc. Law] ~όμενος Chrys.*hom.13.2 in Heb.*(12.131C); contrasted with ἀκούω, Or.*Jo.*20.23(20; p.357.23; M.14.625B); Eus.*d.e.*7.1(p.315.12; M.22.516B); τοὺς ἀεὶ μὲν ἀκούοντας, ἀεὶ δὲ ~οντας Chrys.*hom.32.3 in Jo.*(8.189C); Synes.*ep.*5(M.66.1344B); with ὑπακούω, Clem.*prot.*1(p.9.1; M.8.64C); dist. from παραβαίνω, Ath.*Ar.*1.51(M.26.117B); **2.** *refuse* a person's request μὴ θέλων ~σαι τοῦ γέροντος Jo.Mosch.*prat.*100(M.87.2960A).

***παρακρανίς, ἡ,** *cerebellum* παρεγκεφαλίς, ἣν καὶ π. καλοῦσιν Melet.*nat.hom.*1(M.64.1152C).

παρακρατέω, *support,* Gr.Nyss.*ep.*2(M.46.1012B); †Polyb.*v.Epiph.*52(M.41.88C); Call.*v.Hyp.*(p.105).

***παρακρέκω,** *be discordant;* fig., of tongue as cithara φράζεσθ' ...μή τι παρακρέξῃ ἔκτροπον ἁρμονίης Gr.Naz.*carm.*2.1.4.92(M.37.1314A).

***παράκροαμα (*παρακρόημα), τό,** *something heard by chance* as an omen, *Const.App.*8.32.11; *chance rumour, gossip, Contrad.*2 (-όημα, p.8).

παρακροάομαι, *overhear, eavesdrop, A.Xanthipp.*37(p.83.26); Anast.S.*qu.et resp.*20(M.89.520D).

παρακρόασις, ἡ, *listening to* ἐν τῇ π. τοῦ ἀναγινώσκοντος Thdr.Stud.*epp.*2.178(M.99.1553A).

***παρακροατής, ὁ,** *eavesdropper* τί τὸ ἁμάρτημα αὐτῶν;...οὗτοί εἰσιν οἱ π. *Apoc.Esd.*(p.28); οὐαὶ τοῖς π. †Cyr.*hom.div.*14(5[2].412E); †Jo.Jej.*poenit.*(M.88.1924C).

***παρακρόημα,** v. *παρακρόαμα.

***παρακρότημα, τό,** *clapping, applause,* Cyr.*hom.pasch.*11(5[2].150B).

παρακρού-ω, med.; **1.** *nullify, thwart,* Jo.Mosch.*prat.*171(M.87.3040B); Jo.D.*hom.*8.7(M.96.709C); **2.** *evade, disobey* τὸν θεσμὸν παρεκρούσατο Sophr.H.*mir.Cyr.et Jo.*27(M.87.3500B); of Adam's disobedience, Didym.*Trin.*1.27(M.39.401C); **3.** *hesitate to admit,* ‡Ath.*dial.Trin.*2.16(M.28.1184A); **4.** *put off, parry,* met. τί...~ῃ τὴν εἱμαρμένην; Eus.*Hierocl.*45(543B; ~εις M.22.864B); τοῖς σοῖς με παρεκρούσω λογισμοῖς Thdt.*eran.*2(4.100); *parry;* fig., but also in sense of *divert* from way τοὺς ἀντιπάλους καὶ κατατρέχοντας τῆς γνωστικῆς ὁδοῦ ~σάμενος καὶ καταγωνισάμενος Clem.*ecl.*28(p.145.24; M.9.713A).

παρακρύπτω, *conceal dishonestly,* Epiph.*haer.*42.11(p.145.27; M.41.757B); *ib.*72.4(p.259.15; M.42.388C); *ib.*66.3(p.19.14; 33B).

***παράκτησις, ἡ,** Clem.*ecl.*47(M.9.720B; f.l. for γὰρ κτήσεως p.150.5).

παρακύπτ-ω, 1. *peer inquisitively, interfere,* †Gregent.*leg.Hom.*1 (M.86.583A); **2.** *look* into, *inquire deeply* into μὴ...παρέργως...ἐντυχόντες, ἀλλὰ διασχόντες τὸ γράμμα καὶ εἴσω παρακύψαντες Gr.Naz.*or.*31.21(p.171.6; M.36.156D); **3.** *obtain insight* into εἰς θεοῦ μυστήρια ~οντες *ib.*31.8(p.155.7; 141B); ὅσοι φιλοσόφῳ λόγῳ τῆς τοῦ προπάτορος ἐγείρειν ἑαυτοὺς βούλονται παραπτώσεως, πρῶτον ἀπάρχονται τῆς τῶν παθῶν...ἀφαιρέσεως,...καὶ τέλος τὴν φυσικὴν ὑπερκύψαντες θεωρίαν εἰς τὴν ἄυλον ~ουσι γνῶσιν Max.*ambig.*(M.91.1356B).

παρακωμῳδέω, *poke fun at, make laughable,* Bas.*ep.*135.1(3.226D; M.32.572C).

παραλαλέω, 1. *talk mistakenly,* Epiph.*haer.*66.48(p.85.22; M.42.101C); Chrys.*hom.24.1 in Heb.*(12.219D); **2.** *talk to deceive,* Epiph.*haer.*21.6(p.245.14; M.41.293D).

***παραλάλημα, τό,** *deceptive talk, Exorc.*(p.344).

παραλαμβάν-ω, 1. *take, seize;* fig. λύπη παραληφθήσεται *T.Lev.*17.4; ἐν σκότει παραληφθήσεται *ib.*17.6; *capture* a place, *Chron.Pasch.* p.42(M.92.160C); *ib.*p.273(676A); **2.** *take away, along with one* τρεῖς τῶν μαθητῶν...παραλαβὼν εἰς τὸ ὄρος Just.*dial.*99.2(M.6.708C); Or.*Jo.*19.12(3; p.312.18; M.14.548D); cf. αἱ ψυχαὶ τῶν ἀπαλλαττομένων τοῦ σώματος, ἀπαιτούντων τινῶν αὐτὰς τῶν ἐπὶ τοῦτο τεταγμένων, ~ονται *ib.*19.15(4; p.315.34; 554C); Bas.*hom.*6.2(2.45C; M.31.265B); **3.** *invite* ἀλλήλους ἐπὶ τὸ πίνειν ~οντες *ib.*14.6(2.127B; M.31.456B); **4.** *accept* πείρᾳ ~ων ὁ μάταιος τοῦ θεοῦ τὴν δύναμιν Thdt.*Dan.*3:95(2.1130); **5.** *admit as;* associate, Philost.*h.e.*3.28(M.65.516A); church member, Or.*comm.in 1Cor.*5:3(*JTS* 9 p.364); **6.** *bring in* as worker πρὸς τὴν τοῦ πράγματος διακονίαν παρελήφθησαν Cyr.*Ps.*23:8(M.69.845B); cf. ἕκαστος τῶν ἁγίων προφητῶν ἐπί τινι χρησίμῳ καὶ ἀναγκαίῳ παρελαμβάνετο πράγματι κατὰ καιροὺς τοῖς θείοις ὑπηρετήσων νεύμασι id.*Nah.*proem.(3.474A); *bring into use;* liturg. τὸ...προηγούμενον ἐν τῇ χρίσει τὸ πνεῦμά ἐστι· διὸ καὶ τὸ ἔλαιον ~εται Chrys.*hom.1.1 in Rom.*(9.430B); freq. of usage of words ὁ...τῶν χιλίων ἀριθμὸς ἔχει πρὸς τὴν μονάδα συγγένειαν, διὸ καὶ παρείληπται Cyr.ap.Proc.G.*Cant.*8:11(M.87.1749A); of tetragrammaton ὅπερ ἀνεκφώνητον εἶναι λέγοντες Ἑβραίων παῖδες ἐπὶ μόνου τοῦ θεοῦ ~ειν εἰώθασιν Eus.*d.e.*9.7 (p.420.30; M.22.677C); **7.** *take in, include* τὸ...ὄρος ἐκεῖνο...ὁμώνυμον ὂν τῇ δούλῃ ~ει καὶ τὴν Ἱερουσαλήμ Chrys.*comm.inGal.*4:25(10.710D); οὐδὲ ἀλλότριον τὸ πνεῦμα τοῦ θεοῦ καὶ υἱοῦ...οὐκ αἰῶσι ~όμενα Didym.(‡Bas.)*Eun.*5(1.314B; M.29.753B); Proc.G.*Gen.*17:19(M.87.360A); **8.** *take, interpret* as, Meth.*res.*1.24(p.248.13; M.41.1093C); ταῦτα οὕτως ὡς γέγραπται ~εσθαι *ib.*1.39(p.282.15; M.18.268B); τὴν περικοπὴν οὐκ ἐπὶ συνέρξεως ~εσθαι γυναικός τε καὶ ἀνδρὸς id.*symp.* 3.1(p.27.17; M.18.61B); *ib.*3.12(p.40.17; λαμβάνει 77D); Chrys.*hom.15.5 in Phil.*(11.317C); Nil.*epp.*1.104(M.79.128C); esp. as type ἐν τύπῳ...τῆς παρθενίας τὴν ἰτέαν...~ουσι Meth.*symp.*4.3(p.48.20; 89D); Eus.*d.e.*6.13(p.194.19; M.22.324B); Thdt.*Cant.*1:7(2.44); **9.** *express, refer to* in εὐσπλαγχνίαν ἐλαίας τύπῳ παρέλαβεν ἡ γραφή Meth.*symp.*10.2(p.123.11; M.18.193D); τὰ πράγματα...εἰκότως εἰς πολλὰς εἰκόνας καὶ παραδείγματα παρείληπται Chrys.*hom.8.1 in 2Tim.*(11.707B); **10.** *take, instance* εἰς σύγκρισιν ~έσθωσαν Tat.*orat.*31(p.31.9; M.6.869A); **11.** *quote* from, Didym.*Pss.*proem.(M.39.1156A); **12.** *perceive* ὀφθαλμοῖς παρειλήφαμεν Eus.*d.e.*6.13(p.265.2; M.22.324B); id.*v.C.*1.23(p.19.11; M.20.940A); CSel.*ep.*ap.Epiph.*haer.*73.25(p.298.16; M.42.449B); **13.** *receive* in succession, customs, teaching οὐ...τὴν κατὰ σάρκα παρειλήφαμεν περιτομήν Just.*dial.*43.2(M.6.568A); παρὰ τοῦ παιδαγωγοῦ...αὐτουργίαν καὶ εὐτέλειαν παραλαβόντας Clem.*paed.*3.7(p.259.7; M.8.609B); τῷ τὰ παραδιδόμενα οἵῳ τε ~ειν, δηλωθήσεται τὸ κεκαλυμμένον id.*str.*1.1(p.10.8; M.8.701B); knowledge, *Hom.Clem.*1.

21; *ib.*9.4; divine laws, Herm.*vis.*1.3.4; traditional story *λελιθωμένην ταύτην παρειλήφαμεν τὴν γυναῖκα* Clem.*prot.*10(p.74.25; M.8.220B); pass., *have honourable tradition οἰκεῖον...τοὔνομα Κωνσταντίνου καὶ μετὰ τὴν τοῦ βίου ∼εσθαι τελευτήν* Eus.*v.C.*4.72(p.147.28; M.20.1228B); **14.** *take on, assume,* ref. Inc. *οὐκ ἀνθρωπίνην ὁμοίωσιν ἐνταῦθα τοῦ θεοῦ παρειληφότος* Clem.*fr.*57(p.226.24); *τὸ λογικὸν διέπλαττε ζῷον, ὃ μετὰ πολλὰς ἀνακαινίζειν ἤμελλε γενεάς·...μέλλων δημιουργεῖν τὴν ἐκεῖνα παραληψομένην τὰ μυστήρια φύσιν* Thdt.*qu.19 in Gen.*(1.23).

παραλέγ-ω, 1. *read out* a lesson, pass. *∼εται μετὰ τὴν πρώτην αἴτησιν τὰ προφητικά* ‡Sophr.H.*liturg.*11(M.87.3992C); **2.** *give false reading* in text, pass. *τὸ 'ἐκτήσατο' πάντες...ἐκδεδώκασιν οἱ ἑρμηνευταί· τὸ δὲ 'ἔκτισεν' παραλέλεκται παρ' Ἑβραίοις* Eus.*e.th.*3.2(p.143.12; M.24.980A).

παραλείπω, 1. *leave out* in written accounts *τὰ ὑπ' ἀλλήλων παραλειπόμενα ἀναπληρούντων* Chrys.*hom.26.3 in Mt.*(7.316D); ptcpl. as title of Book of Chronicles: explanation of name *τῆς βίβλου τῶν Παραλειπομένων τὴν ὑπόθεσιν ἡ προσηγορία δηλοῖ. ὅσα γὰρ παρέλιπεν ὁ τὰς Βασιλείας συγγεγραφώς, ταῦτα συντέθεικεν ὁ τόνδε τὸν πόνον ἀναδεξάμενος, ἐκ πολλῶν αὐτὰ προφητικῶν βιβλίων συναγαγών* Thdt.*qu. in 1Par.*proem.(1.554); *Paralipomenon Graece dicitur, quod nos praetermissorum vel reliquorum dicere possumus, quia ea, quae in lege regum libris vel omissa vel non plene relata sunt, in isto summatim ac breviter explicantur,* Isid.H.*etym.*6.2.12; in this sense fem. [sc. *βίβλοι*] *ἡ πρώτη τῶν Π.* Epiph.*mens.*23(M.43.277D); *ταῖς Π. τῶν Βασιλειῶν* Cosm.Ind.*top.*5(M.88.249A); *ib.*(276C); ref. other biblical books *τὰ π. 'Ιερεμίου τοῦ προφήτου Apoc.Bar.rel.*tit.; of literary remains *τότε Ἐλιοὺς ἐμπνευσθεὶς ἐν τῷ σατανᾷ ἐξεῖπεν μοι λόγους θρασεῖς, οἵτινες ἀναγεγραμμένοι εἰσὶν ἐν ταῖς π. τοῦ Ἐλιφὰ T.Job* 41 (p.130.22); **2.** *leave off παραλιπόντας πιστεύειν* Athenag.*leg.*7.2(M.6.904C); **3.** *ignore, neglect, ib.*16.1(920C); **4.** *fail, be wanting ἔλαιον... παρέλειψεν* Gr.Mag.*dial.*(tr.Zach.)1.5(M.*PL.*77.178C).

***παραλελογισμένως,** *by false reasoning,* Max.*ambig.*(M.91.1264C).

[*]**παραλεύκιος,** Epiph.*gemm.*7(M.43.300B, prob. error for *περίλευκος*).

παραληπτέον, 1. *one must receive,* Isid.Pel.*epp.*5.347(M.78.1537B); **2.** *one must assume, indulge in,* e.g. grief, Or.*Jo.*28.4(11; p.393.8; M.14.685C); *take* a bath, Clem.*paed.*3.9(p.263.8; M.8.617A); **3.** *one must take in the sense of,* Clem.*str.*4.8(p.276.15; M.8.1273A); Meth.*res.*1.39 (p.283.2; M.41.1108A).

παράληπτος, *captive,* Jo.Mal.*chron.*16 p.398(M.97.589B).

παραλήπτωρ, ὁ, *reprehender,* Ephr.2.238E,F.

παραλήρημα, τό, *nonsense,* ‡Jo.D.*Artem.*28(p.160.7; M.96.1277A).

παράληψις, ἡ, 1. *acceptance δεῖ...ἐν ταῖς π. τῶν θείων μυστηρίων πίστιν μὲν ἔχειν ἀζήτητον, μηδενὶ δὲ τῶν λεγομένων ἐπιφέρειν τὸ πῶς* Cyr.*Jo.*4.2(4.358E); **2.** *use τῇ π. τῆς κατὰ τὸ μέτρον περιγραφῆς, ἐπὶ τὸ ἄπειρον...χειραγωγεῖ τὸν ἀκούοντα* Gr.Nyss.*v.Mos.*(M.44.405B); *cat. Apoc.*4:2(p.238.15); *τριάδα...ἡ τῶν τριῶν ὀνομάτων π. ἐξαριθμεῖ καὶ παρίστησι* Didym.(‡Bas.)*Eun.*5(1.311C; M.29.748A); of use· for magical purposes of divine name, Or.*Cels.*4.33(p.304.3; M.11.1080A); of materials *ῥιζῶν αἱ ποικιλίαι νευρῶν τε καὶ ὀστέων παραλήψεις* Tat.*orat.*17(p.19.3; M.6.844A); **3.** *taking* of oath *μεθ' ὅρκου παραλήψεως* Eus.*h.e.*1.3.17(M.20.73C).

***παράλιμος,** *dwelling in a seaport,* Thdt.*Is.*23:1(p.94.11).

***παραλιώτης, ὁ,** *one belonging to the sea-coast,* Epiph.*haer.*31.2 (p.384.10; M.41.476A); as adj. *τοῖς π. ἐπισκόποις* Bas.*ep.*203 tit.(3.299C; M.32.737A).

παραλλαγή, ἡ, 1. *deterioration, destruction* of substance, Athenag.*leg.*22.3(M.6.937B); **2.** *discrepancy οὐδ' ἐπίσημος...ἡ τῶν χρόνων π.* Afric.*chron.*(M.10.77B); *differences* of degree *τῇ τοῦ δύνασθαι π.* Const.*or.s.c.*14(p.174.5; M.20.1276A); **3.** *distinction,* Trin. *'παρηλλάχθαι τὰς οὐσίας ἀλλήλων πιστούμεθα.'...τί τοίνυν διὰ τοῦ 'παρηλλαγμένου' σημαίνεται;...λέγεται...ἐν τῇ καταχρήσει τῆς συνηθείας τὸ ῥῆμα τῆς π. ἐπὶ σωμάτων μέν, ὅταν ἐκ παραλύσεως ἤ τινος ἑτέρου πάθους παρατραπῇ τι μέλος τῆς φυσικῆς ἁρμονίας. ... τὴν πρὸς τὸ χεῖρον παρατροπὴν τοῦ παραδεξαμένου τὸ πάθος παραλλαγὴν ὀνομάζομεν· ἐπὶ δὲ τῶν ἐν ἤθει κατ' ἀρετὴν καὶ κακίαν διαφερόντων...πᾶν ὅλως τὸ τῇ παραθέσει τοῦ κρείττονος ἐν κακίᾳ κατηγορουμένων παρηλλάχθαι λέγεται...ἔτι παρηλλάχθαι φαμὲν καὶ τὰς ἐπὶ τῶν στοιχείων θεωρουμένας ποιότητας..., φθαρτικὴν κατ' ἀλλήλων ἔχουσαι δύναμιν, οἷον...εἴ τι τῷ ἑτέρῳ πρὸς τὸ ἐναντίον ἀντικαθέστηκε καὶ τὸ ἐν τούτοις ἀσύμβατον τῷ τῆς π. διερμηνεύομεν ῥήματι, καὶ πᾶν ὅλως τὸ διαφωνοῦν πρὸς τὸ ἕτερον ἐν τοῖς ἐπιθεωρουμένοις γνωρίσμασι τῶν παρηλλαγμένων ἐστὶν* Gr.Nyss.*Eun.*4(2 p.91.27ff.; M.45.668Bf.); *οὐδὲ ...εἶπεν, ἐν δόξῃ οἷα ὁ πατήρ, ἵνα πάλιν π. τινα ὑποπτεύσῃς* Chrys.*hom. 55.4 in Mt.*(7.560B); *ἵνα...μή, ἀκούων ὅτι αἴτιον ἔχει τὸν πατέρα, π. οὐσίας νομίσῃς, καὶ τιμῆς ἐλάττωσιν, αὐτὸς ἔρχεταί σε κρίνων* [Jo. 5:22] id.*hom.39.1 in Jo.*(8.226B); *εἰς π. οὐσίας ἕλκων* [sc. *ὁ Ἄρειος*] *τὴν ἐν τοῖς προσώποις διαφοράν* id.*sac.*4.4(p.115.14; 1.410A).

***παραλλαξία, ἡ, 1.** *discrepancy,* Didym.*Trin.*3.23(M.39.929B); **2.** *aberration π. εἶχεν...εἰς τὰς φρένας* Call.*v.Hyp.*(p.84).

παράλλαξις, ἡ, *change,* in Stoic theory *τὸ πνεῦμα τοῦ θεοῦ διὰ τῆς ὕλης κεχωρηκὸς κατὰ τὰς π. αὐτῆς ἄλλο καὶ ἄλλο ὄνομα μεταλαγχάνειν φατέ* Athenag.*leg.*22.3(M.6.937B); *ib.*6.4(904A).

παραλλάσσω, *alter, make different, vary ὁ δὲ* [sc. *λόγος*] *τῆς ἀϊδίου...φύσεως πάντη κατὰ πάντα τοῦ καθ' ἡμᾶς παρηλλαγμένος οὐδὲν ἀνθρώπειον ἐπάγοιτ' ἄν* Eus.*d.e.*5.5(p.228.21; M.22.377A); Gr. Nyss.*Eun.*4(2 p.91.21ff.; M.45.668Bf.) cit. s. *παραλλαγή*; *οὐκοῦν ταὐτόν ἐστι παρηλλαγμένον τε εἰπεῖν καὶ ἀνάρμοστον. εἰ οὖν παρήλλακται...πρὸς τὴν τοῦ πατρὸς οὐσίαν ἡ τοῦ μονογενοῦς θεοῦ φύσις, οὐδὲ ἁρμόζεται πάντως ib.*(p.93.28; 669C); *παρηλλαγμένων γὰρ τῶν οὐσιῶν, παρηλλαγμένας εἶναι ἔδει καὶ τὰς ἐνεργείας, κατὰ...Εὐνόμιον* Didym.(‡Bas.)*Eun.*5(1.299A; M.29.717B); ref. Eun. *παρηλλάχθαι τὴν τοῦ γεννηθέντος οὐσίαν πρὸς τὴν τοῦ γειναμένου* Philost.*h.e.*4.12(M.65.525C).

παράλληλος, 1. *side by side, alternate,* Gr.Nyss.*v.Mos.*(M.44.320D); neut. plur. as adv., Chrys.*hom.25.1 in Rom.*(9.702A); **2.** of people, *ordinary,* Germ.CP *or.*2(M.98.281A).

παραλλήλως, *similarly,* Didym.*Trin.*3.2(M.39.789A).

παραλογίζομαι, *leave out of reckoning, contemn,* Bas.*Eun.*2.28(1.265B; M.31.637A); Hier.*v.Paul.*B 4(p.9.10); Thphn.*chron.*p.404(M.108.961B).

παραλογισμός, ὁ, *craftiness, Pss.Sal.*4.12; *ib.*4.25; *deceit,* alleged of God *ἀπάτη τις...καὶ π.* Gr.Nyss.*or.catech.*26(p.97.3; M.45.68A); *ἐκ παραλογισμοῦ in order to deceive,* Cyr.*Jo.*proem.(4.2E).

***παραλυμαίνομαι,** *harm,* †Bas.*Chr.generat.*5(2.599E; M.31.1468B).

παραλυπέω, 1. *be troublesome,* Clem.*paed.*3.11(p.270.31; M.8.636B); **2.** trans., *trouble,* Philost.*h.e.*7.7(M.65.545A); pass., *ib.*3.9 (492C).

παράλυσις, ἡ, 1. *loosening, laxness*; of doctrine, Socr.*h.e.*1.37.5 (M.67.176A); of irregularity in calendar, Thphl.Al.*ep.pasch.*proem.3 (M.65.52A); *breaking* of law, Germ.CP *or.*2(M.98.245A); **2.** *paralysis, palsy,* Isid.Pel.*epp.*2.240(M.78.680C); in moral sense *διπλῆ π.* ... *ἡ τῶν ἁμαρτημάτων, καὶ ἡ τοῦ σώματος* Chrys.*hom.8.4 in Eph.*(11.58C); *ib.*(58D).

παράλυτος, *paralysed,* Or.*schol.in Lc.*9:42(M.17.345D); Cyr.H.*hom.*9(M.33.1141A); Amph.*mesopent.*(M.39.121C); Chrys.*hom.36.1 in Jo.*(8.208C); *κυριακὴ τοῦ π. third Sunday after Easter* (when Jo.5 was read), Thdr.Stud.*catech.parv.*4 tit.(M.99.21A).

παραλύ-ω, 1. *loosen,* Chrys.*hom.25.2 in 1Cor.*(10.222D); *relax*; law, id.*hom.16.1 in Mt.*(7.203B); partic. of sabbath *π. τῆς ἀπραξίας τὸν νόμον* Gr.Nyss.*v.Mos.*42(M.44.313B); *λέγετε λύειν με τὸ σάββατον, καὶ π. τὸν νόμον* Chrys.*hom.41.2 in Jo.*(8.245C); of marriage, Thdt.*affect.*9(p.237.21; 4.944); *παραλύσαντα τοὺς κανόνας τοῦ μοναστηρίου* Jo.Mosch.*prat.*192(M.87.3072A); **2.** *weaken ∼ων τὸ μάχιμον* Cyr.*Nah.*22(3.500E); pass. *∼εται...ἡ προθυμία* Clem.*str.*2.18(p.158.2; M.8.1024B); *make ineffectual, thwart,* Cels.ap.Or.*Cels.*5.25(p.26.12; M.11.1220A); *ἤδεν...ὁ...δαίμων οὐδὲν τῶν ἰδίων ∼θησόμενον βούλημα* Or.*Cels.*6.11(p.81.25; 1308A); *τὴν εἰς τοὺς γονέας τιμὴν...παρέλυον ταῖς ἑαυτῶν προσθήκαις* Chrys.*hom.16.1 in Mt.*(7.203C); **3.** *resolve τὰ τῆς φιλοσοφίας ἐγκλήματα π.* Cyr.*Ps.*37:14(M.69.965A); **4.** *cancel, put paid to ∼ω σου τὰ χειρόγραφα. ἐγὼ γὰρ ἀπέδωκα τὰ χρέα τοῦ Ἀδὰμ σταυρωθεὶς καὶ κατελθὼν ἐν τῷ ᾅδῃ* Mac.Aeg.*hom.*11.10(M.34.552C).

παραμελέω, med., *neglect,* Bas.Sel.*or.*21.3(M.85.257C).

παραμέν-ω, 1. *remain constant, persevere, persist* (in) *ἡ μακροθυμία ∼ουσα* Herm.*mand.*5.2.3; *∼ουσιν εἰς ζωὴν αἰώνιον* id.*vis.*2.3.2; Clem.*prot.*10(p.72.11; M.8.213B); *ib.*11(p.82.29; 237A); *τῆς φθορᾶς ∼ούσης κατὰ τῶν ἀνθρώπων* Ath.*inc.*6.1(M.25.105C); *θεωρίᾳ τὰ πολλὰ ∼ουσι* Nil.*exerc.*3(M.79.721A); *Chron.Pasch.*p.112(M.92.296B); **2.** *be concerned with, have care of τοὺς ταῖς ἐκκλησίαις ∼οντας* Leo Mag.*ep.*30.1 (p.46.18; M.*PL.*54.788C); **3.** s.v.l., *await μὴ παραμείνας διωχθῆναι* Vict.*Mc.*1:14(p.274.13).

παραμέρος, for *παρὰ μέρος*; **1.** *at different times, successively οὐσία ἐστὶ τὸ ταὐτόν, καὶ ἓν ἀριθμῷ, τῶν ἐναντίων π. εἶναι δεκτικόν* †Gr.Thaum.*anim.*(M.10.1140D); **2.** *in the neighbourhood* of *π. δὲ τοῦ σπηλαίου αὐτοῦ οἰκοῦντες* Gr.Mag.*dial.*(tr.Zach.)3.16(M.*PL.*77.262B; *παραμέρως* cod.).

***παραμέσως,** *as for the most part, in the ordinary sense* [sc. *ἡ ἁγία θήκη*] *ἔστιν πηγή, πηγὴ οὐχ ἁπλῶς οὐδὲ π., ἀλλ' ἣν ἐγεώργησεν ὁ... βαπτιστὴς Ἰωάννης Mir.Artem.*34(p.54.9).

παραμετρ-έω, 1. *adjust to, adapt to,* Clem.*paed.*2.7(p.192.11; M.8.461B); Isid.Pel.*epp.*5.37(M.78.1349B); **2.** *assess*; pass., of moral judgement *οὐδὲ τῷ τέλει ∼εῖται μόνῳ τὰ πράγματα, ἀλλὰ καὶ τῇ* ἑκάστου κρίνεται προαιρέσει Clem.*str*.2.6(p.127.11; M.8.961B); **3.** *deem sufficient* ὁ ἀρχαῖος ἄνθρωπος...κλάδοις καὶ φύλλοις τὴν σκέπην τῆς αἰσχύνης παρεμέτρει id.*paed*.2.10(p.224.6; M.8.532A); **4.** *draw out* μέχρι θανάτου ~εῖται id.*q.d.s*.25(p.176.18; M.9.629C).

παραμιμνήσκομαι, *remember*, †Apoll.*met.Ps*.73:18(M.33.1417D); *ib*.76:12(1421C).

***παράμιξις, ἡ,** *admixture*, Tit.Bost.*Man*.2.22(M.18.1177B).

παραμίσγ-ω, *use* terms *indifferently* ὁ...Παῦλος ~ει πολλάκις,... τὸν παράκλητόν φημι, καὶ τὸν υἱόν Cyr.*Jo*.9.1(4.812C).

***παραμισ-έω,** *abhor* γίνεται ὁ θεὸς τέλειος ἄνθρωπος, μηδὲν ~ήσας τῆς φύσεως, πλὴν τῆς ἁμαρτίας Gr.Naz.ap.Thdt.*pental*.(5.131).

***παραμοιράζω,** *disinherit*, *Ep.Chr.dom*.1(p.27).

παραμονάριος, ὁ, 1. eccl. official, *administrator, guardian* εἴ τις ἐπίσκοπος...προβάλοιτο ἐπὶ χρήμασιν οἰκονόμον ἢ ἔκδικον ἢ π. CChalc. *can*.2(*ACO* 2.1.2 p.158.14; προσμονάριον Lauchert); ἐν ἀλλοτρίαις παροικίαις προχειριζόμενος ποτὲ μὲν χωρεπισκόπους, ἄλλοτε δὲ π. Epiph.Tyr.*ep*.(p.81.38; H.2.1348E); of individual churches παραμονάρις τοῦ ἁγίου Ἠλία *MAMA* 3.590; Παύλου πρεσβυτέρου π. τῆς ἁγίας Χαριτηνῆς *ib*.3.638; Ταράσις δὶς γενόμενος πρεσβύτερος καὶ π. παροικήσας ἐν τῷ τόπῳ τούτῳ *CIG* 9259 (A.D. 461); τὸν π. τῆς ἁγίας Εὐφημίας τῆς ἐν Χαλκηδόνι Jo.Mal.*chron*.15 p.377(M.97.561A); †Anast.S.*relat*.39(*OC* 2 p.83); **2.** *one who stays by*, as *comforter*, ‡Chrys.*poenit*.1.3(9.768A).

παραμονή, ἡ, 1. *sojourn* τῆς ἀκολουθήσεως, καὶ παρὰ μονῆς Μωϋσέως Or.*adnot.in Dt*.3:27–28(M.17.24C, l. παραμονῆς); in the flesh; of Inc., Epiph.*haer*.42.11(p.134.9; M.41.741B); **2.** *watch, vigil*, Vict.*Mc*.15:40(p.442.16); esp. *eve* of festival τῇ π. τῆς ὑψώσεως τοῦ σταυροῦ Anast.Ap.*a.Max*.2.30(M.90.168A); Anast.*temp*.(p.279); *Catech.Stud*.6,7(M.99.1697A); *Const.Stud*.34(M.99.1717B); **3.** *continuance, lasting quality*, Iren.*haer*.4.38.2,3(M.7.1108A); *Chron. Pasch*.p.72(M.92.217A); *maintenance* τὴν τῶν γενῶν π. Epiph.Gn. ap.Clem.*str*.3.2(p.199.12; M.8.1109A); of virtue, Clem.*str*.7.7(p.35. 17; M.9.468A); **4.** *constancy, patience* διὰ...τὴν π. τῆς πίστεως ἠκολούθει τῷ Ἰησοῦ Epiph.*haer*.66.40(p.78.7; M.42.89C); Chrys.*hom. 82.1 in Jo*.(8.483D); in prayer, Pall.*h.Laus*.70(p.167.1); of patience rewarded, Chrys.*hom.89.2 in Mt*.(7.834E); id.*hom.85.2 in Jo*.(8. 505E).

***παραμονητικός,** *abiding* by, ‡Ath.*comm.essent*.52(M.28.77B).

***παραμορφ-όω,** *take the shape of* ~ῶ τοῖς τεθνεόσι *T.Sal*.17.2(π. ἐμαυτόν M.122.1340D).

παραμύθημα, τό, *sustenance* ἔχων τὰ βρώματα ἐκεῖνα παραμύθημα Pall.*h.Laus*.36(M.34.1179D; παραμυθίαν p.107.15).

παραμυθητικῶς, *comfortingly, without harshness*, Chrys.*hom.15.1 in 1Tim*.(11.635C).

***παραμυθήτωρ, ὁ,** *consoler*, ‡Chrys.*poenit*.3(9.768A).

παραμυθία, ἡ, *comfort, consolation* παραμυθίᾳ παρηγορεῖ τὰ ἁμαρτήματα Clem.*paed*.1.10(p.143.18; M.8.357C); ref. divination παραμυθίαν γνώσεως τῶν μελλόντων Or.*Cels*.1.36(p.87.30; M.11. 729A); Chrys.*hom.1.4 in Phil*.(11.200D); κλαῦσον τοὺς ἐν πλούτῳ τετελευτηκότας, καὶ μηδεμίαν ἀπὸ τοῦ πλούτου π. ταῖς ἑαυτῶν ψυχαῖς ἐπινοήσαντες *ib*.3.4(217C); εἰς ἐπικουρίαν τῶν πενήτων, εἰς π. τῶν ἡμαρτημένων ἡμῖν id.*hom.17.3 in 1Tim*.(11.651A); of material sustenance, v. παραμύθημα; of allowances of money made from eccl. revenues, CChalc.*act*.12(*ACO* 2.1.3 p.55.31; H.2.561E); Hypat.*fr*. (p.126.16).

***παραμύθιος,** *soothing* π. ἴαμα ‡Meth.*Sym.et Ann*.8(M.18.369B).

***παραναγνωστικός,** *for reading out*; as subst.; **1.** masc., *lector* in monastery, Max.*ep*.9(M.91.449A); **2.** neut., *written message* εἰπεῖν ἐφ' ᾧ πάρεισιν. οἱ δὲ λέγουσι· π. ἔχομεν μόνον Pall.*v.Chrys*.8(p.47.20; M.47.28); π. τῆς ἁγίας συνόδου CEph.(431)*act*.1(*ACO* 1.1.2 p.10.4; H.1.1360A); Cyr.*ep*.23(p.67.13; 5².85C).

***παρανακειμένως,** *correspondingly*, Or.*comm.in Mt*.12.7(p.79.2; M.13.992B).

παραναλίσκω (-λόω), pass.; **1.** *be dissipated, spent*, Philost.*h.e*.3.8 (M.65.489D); **2.** s.v.l., *be deprived*, Clem.*str*.1.8(p.28.12, cj. ἁλίσκεται, παραν⟨οίας⟩ ἁλίσκεται; M.8.740A).

παρανάλωμα, τό, *something consumed* or *destroyed, victim* ἑαυτὸν εἰς καταδίκην τῇ μελλούσῃ κρίσει τοῦ πυρὸς παρανάλωμα δέδωκεν Ath. *h.Ar*.70(p.221.20; M.25.776D); θανάτου π. Bas.*renunt*.7(2.208E; M.31. 641B); φθόνου...π. Synes.*ep*.72(M.66.1436C); φθορᾶς τὸ σῶμα...π. ‡Nil.*fr.pasch*.2(M.79.1196B); συκοφαντίας...π. Thdt.*Cant*.8:7(2.157); π. τῆς οἰκείας φρενοβλαβείας id.*haer*.4.12(4.372); χειρὸς ἀδελφικῆς π. Bas.Sel.*or*.8.1(M.85.113A); σκότος ἐπεκράτει τὸ φῶς, καὶ ἦν τῆς ἡμέρας ὁ χρόνος νυκτὸς π. *ib*.9.2(133A); λιμοῦ π. ‡Proc.G.*Pr*.28:31(M. 87.1509C); ἄνθρωποι ἀλλήλων παραναλώματα Max.*ep*.10(M.91.452A); αἰωνίου πυρὸς π. ‡Jo.D.*ep.Thphl*.12(M.95.360C).

***παραναστέλλω,** *turn back, lift up*, Eus.*h.e*.7.15.4(M.20.677A).

παρανατέλλω, 1. *spring up beside*; of plants, Isid.Pel.*epp*.1.181 (M.78.300C); **2.** of day, *come up, dawn*, Synes.*ep*.132(M.66.1516D).

παρανθ-έω, met., *wither, lose attractiveness* σφαλερὰ...ἡ πάροινος ἐλευθερία ~εῖν δυναμένη Clem.*paed*.2.7(p.190.16; M.8.457B).

***παρανόθευμα, τό,** *perversion* ἀδιάβατον...τοῖς σαρκικοῖς π. Thdot. Anc.*hom.BMV et Sym*.6(M.77.1397C).

***παρανοθεύω,** *corrupt, pervert* in faith, Thphn.*chron*.p.425(M.108. 1005A).

παράνοια, ἡ, 1. *eccentricity* ἀνοίᾳ καὶ π. εἰς αὐτὸ ὠθούμενοι τὸ βάραθρον Clem.*prot*.10(p.70.25; M.8.209C); legal t.t. παρανοίας ἡλωκέναι id.*str*.7.16(p.71.10; M.9.540A); τὴν π. τῶν ἀπὸ Φρυγίας Ath. *syn*.4(p.233.23; M.26.688A); τῶν ἐννοιῶν, μᾶλλον δὲ π. Ath.*Ar*.1.52 (M.26.121A); *wandering from the sense* συμβαίνει...ταῖς ἄλλαις παρανοίαις καὶ ὁ περὶ τήνδε τὴν προφητείαν πλάνος Thdt.*Mich*.4:2(2.1494); **2.** *secondary meaning*, opp. ἔννοια (natural meaning), Eun.ap.Gr. Nyss.*Eun*.1(1 p.192.8; M.45.437C).

παρανοίγνυμι (-οίγω), *open*, fig. ἵνα...μικρόν τι παρανοίξω τῆς διαφορᾶς..., καὶ ἀκτῖνά τινα ἀμυδρὰν ἐναφῶ σου τῇ ψυχῇ Chrys.*hom. 34.2 in 1Cor*.(10.311E); *give glimpse, explanation of*, id.*hom.19.1 in Jo*.(8.112A); παρήνοιξεν μικρὰν θυρίδα τῆς θεότητος Eus.Al.*serm*. 11(M.86.377D); of statements, truth, Chrys.*hom.26.5 in Mt*.(7.320B); *ib.39.3*(435A); δόγματα παρανοίγει τὰ σφόδρα ὑψηλά, αἰνιγματωδῶς μέν, παρανοίγει δὲ ὅμως id.*hom.24.1 in Jo*.(8.138D); *partly disclose*; future events, id.*hom.33.3 in Mt*.(380D).

***παρανομητέον,** *one must disobey* οὐδαμῶς π. ... τὰς ἐντολάς Clem.*paed*.2.10(p.211.13; M.8.504B).

παρανομία, ἡ, *lawbreaking, wrongdoing*, ref. demons διὰ τὴν σφῶν π. τάχα μὲν αὐτοῖς διελόντες τοὺς τόπους, ἔνθα ἐρημία ἐστὶ γνώσεως θεοῦ Or.*Cels*.8.33(p.248.29; M.11.1565B); ἀποτάσσομαί σοι [sc. Satan] ...προσποιήσει φιλίας πράξαντι πᾶσαν π. Cyr.H.*catech*.19.4; ἐπὶ τῆς ἁγίας τραπέζης ἡλίκη ἀσέβεια καὶ π. γέγονεν Ath.*ep.encycl*.3(p.172.13; M.25.229A); μιᾶναι δύναται ἀνθρώπου ψυχὴν...μόνη ἀσέβεια ἢ εἰς θεὸν καὶ π. *Const.App*.6.27.8; τοῦτο [sc. ἡ φιλαργυρία] ἐδέσματα παρανομίας ἐνέπλησε Chrys.*hom.65.3 in Jo*.(8.392D); id.*stat*.1.1(2. 1B); ὢ τοῦ διαβόλου· οἵας παροιμίας εἰσήγαγε τῷ βίῳ id.*hom.73.4 in Mt*.(v.l. παρανομίας 7.713D); of Judas' treachery, *ib.28.4*(339D); τὴν ἐσχάτην π. ἐπιδειξάμενος id.*hom.72.2 in Jo*.(424D); of Jewish attitude to Christ, *Const.App*.5.14.20; of Cain's crime, Chrys. *paralyt*.5(3.42C); ref. David's sin παρανομία παρανομίαν διεδέξατο Thdt.*Ps*.3:1(1.625); of heresy, Ath.*ep.encycl*.2(p.171.10; 225D); Thdt.*Ps*.80:11(1183); plur., *acts of lawlessness*, *Pss.Sal*.4.1; *Const. App*.2.12.3.

***παρανοσοκόμος, ὁ,** *assistant nurse*, Thdr.Stud.*poen*.1.68(M.99. 1741B).

***παραντιβάλλω,** *set side by side, compare*, *Chron.Pasch*.p.173(M. 92.425B).

παράξενος, *extraordinary* π. τι...καὶ παρὰ τὸ σύνηθες Eus.*d.e*.10.8 (p.478.15; ξένον M.22.769A); Ephr.2.323B; Jo.Mal.*chron*.7 p.177(M. 97.284C).

παραπαίγνιον, τό, *plaything, sport* μοχθηρῶν πνευμάτων καὶ δαιμόνων γενόμενοι π. Eus.*p.e*.7.2(300A; M.21.509B).

***παραπαιδευτής, ὁ,** Isid.Pel.*epp*.3.259(f.l. for παρὰ τοῦ παιδευτοῦ M.78.937B).

***παραπάλλιον, τό,** ? *actor's change of dress*, hence, met., of inconsistent conduct, Porphyry *Chr*.27 ap.Mac.Mgn.*apocr*.3.30(p.125. 12; A. von Harnack in *Abhandlung der Königlichen Preuss. Akademie der Wissenschaften* 1916 phil.-hist. Klasse 1 p.57.6 conj. παραπαίγνιον, παίγνιον).

***παραπειλέω,** v.l. for ἐπαπειλ-, Ar.*ep.Eus*.(p.2.9)ap.Epiph.*haer*. 69.6(M.42.212A).

παραπέμπ-ω, 1. *conduct, guide*, ὑπὸ μόνου...~όμενοι τοῦ τὸν ὄντως θεὸν καὶ τὸν παρ' αὐτοῦ λόγον εἰδέναι Athenag.*leg*.12.2(M.6.913B); *convey* spiritually, to heaven ~εσθαι τὸν δίκαιον εἰς κληρονομίαν τὴν ἄκραν Clem.*str*.6.12(p.483.26; M.9.324C); παρ' οὗ τὸ εὖ ζῆν ἐκδιδασκόμενοι εἰς ἀΐδιον ζωὴν ~όμεθα id.*prot*.1(p.7.21; M.8.61B); life εἰς ἕξιν ἀϊδιότητος ~εται ὁ διὰ σώματος μελετήσας εὐζωΐαν id.*str*.4.4(p.256. 28; M.8.1232B); *lead up to* source or first principle ὡς ἀνδριάντα θαυμάσας, δι' οὗ κάλλους ἐπὶ τὸν τεχνίτην καὶ τὸ ὄντως καλὸν αὐτὸς αὐτὸν ~ει *ib*.4.18(p.299.17; 1325A); Chrys.*hom.4.3 in Jo*.(8.30B); Manicheans ἀεὶ τὴν δύναμιν τὴν θείαν τῆς ὕλης ἀποχωρίζοντας καὶ πρὸς τὸν θεὸν ~οντας Alex.Lyc.*Man*.3(M.18.416B); **2.** *surrender, give over*, to death ὡς ἀποπομπαῖον αὐτὸν παρεπέμψαντο οἱ πρεσβύτεροι τοῦ λαοῦ ὑμῶν Just.*dial*.40.4(M.6.564A); ἄνθρωπος λιμῷ πιεζόμενος ...~εται τῷ θανάτῳ Thdt.*provid*.3(4.520); θανάτῳ παρέπεμψεν id.*Ps*. 8:3(1.652); *consign* to hell or eternal punishment, Just.*dial*.117.

3(M.6.748A); Chrys.*hom.9.6 in Mt.*(7.139A); τῷ αἰωνίῳ πυρὶ παραπεμφθήσομαι *M.Das.*4.3(p.93.9); Philost.*h.e.*7.13(M.65.552A); **3.** *lay up* in one's mind ἔπρεπε τῇ νύμφῃ...τὸ καὶ σκιᾶς ἐπιθυμεῖν τῆς αὐτοῦ, καὶ παραπέμψαι τῷ βάθει τὴν τούτου ποιότητα Or.*Cant.*3(p.180.30; M.13.151C); **4.** *recall* to memory, *cast back* one's mind, *remind* εἰς ἐκείνην αὐτοὺς ~ων τὴν μνήμην Chrys.*hom.57.1 in Mt.*(7.576C); πρὸς τὴν...μνήμην ἐκείνου ~ομένους *ib.10.4*(7.143E); id.*hom.24.3 in 1Cor.*(10.216B); ἄλλως...~ειν δοκεῖ ἡμᾶς...καὶ ὑπομιμνήσκειν Vict.*Mc.*10:2(p.374.25); **5.** *send back*, Ath.Scholast.*coll.*4.1(p.50); **6.** *refer* to some authority παρέπεμψε τὸν ἀκροατὴν ἐπὶ τὰς οἰκονομίας...τὰς ἐν τῇ παλαιᾷ γενομένας Chrys.*hom.2.6 in Rom.*(9.446A); ἐπὶ τὸν παλαιὸν παρέπεμψε τύπον id.*hom.27.2 in Jo.*(8.155A); *ib.20.1*(8.116A); Gennad.*fr.Gen.*1:26(M.85.1633D); in semi-technical sense, *cross-refer* (cf. παραπομπή) ἐν τέλει ἑκάστου γράμματός εἰσι τίτλοι ~όμενοι Jo.D.*parall.*proem.(M.95.1044A); **7.** *pass by, overlook* ~εσθαι ἀνεξέταστον Or.*fr.hom.39.2 in Jer.*(p.198.5; M.13.544C); ~εσθαι... τὴν...ἀλήθειαν Ath.*Dion.*4(p.49.6; M.25.485B); Proc.G.*Dt.*33:7(M.87.981B); *put up with* ἀνεχόμενοι, φησίν, ἀλλήλων, τουτέστι, ~όμενοι Chrys.*hom.8.2 in Col.*(11.382C); *dismiss* with scorn, *disregard*, *Hom. Clem.*2.31; Or.*princ.*3.1.16(p.224.16; M.11.281B); ~ου τὰς ἀνάγκας τοῦ σώματος Evagr.Pont.*or.*105(M.79.1189C); *reject* ἐπὶ [l. ἐπεὶ] τὴν ἀλήθειαν ~όμενοί τινες ἐπεισάγουσι λόγους ψευδεῖς Iren.*haer.*1 proem.(M.7.437A); *excommunicate* τῷ ἀναθέματι τοῦτον παρεπέμψαντο Philost. *h.e.*2.11(M.65.473A); **8.** *let in* by door ἤνοιξε, καὶ παρέπεμψέ σε ἔνδον Chrys.*hom.10.1 in 1Thess.*(11.496C); **9.** *attract* ἡ τῶν αἰσθήσεων ἐπιθυμία...ἡμᾶς ἐφ' ἑαυτὴν ~ουσα Didym.*Trin.*3.1(M.39.776A).

***παραπεποιημένως**, *distortedly* ὄντα...αὐτοῦ τῇ ἐννοίᾳ π. νοούμενα Epiph.*haer.*71.1(p.250.18; M.42.376B); οὐχ ἃ λέγεις φρονῶν, ἀλλὰ ⟨ἃ⟩ φρονεῖς π. διδάσκων *ib.*73.36(p.311.9; 469C).

παραπέτασμα, τό, *hanging, curtain, veil*; **1.** lit.; **a.** in Temple, = καταπέτασμα: τοῦ π. ⟨δι' οὗ⟩ μόνοις ἐξῆν ἐπιβαίνειν αὐτῶν [sc. τῶν Ἑβραίων] τοῖς ἱερωμένοις Clem.*str.*5.4(p.338.30; M.9.37C); Eus. *v.C.*3.43(M.20.1104A; v.l. for περιπ- p.9.29); v. καταπέτασμα; **b.** in church τῶν κοσμικῶν τούτων π. Chrys.*hom.5.3 in 1Tim.*(11.577F); τὸ ἀμφὶ τὴν ἱερὰν τράπεζαν π. Evagr.*h.e.*5.21(p.216.20; M.86.2836A); cf. οἱ περὶ τὸ θεῖον συμβολικῶς ἀεὶ παρεστηκότες θυσιαστήριον, ὁρῶσι καὶ ἀκούουσι τὰ θεῖα τηλαυγῶς αὐτοῖς ἀνακαλυπτόμενα, καὶ προϊόντες ...ἐπὶ τὰ ἔξω τῶν θείων π., τοῖς ὑπηκόοις θεραπευταῖς...ἐκφαίνουσι κατ' ἀξίαν τὰ ἱερά Dion.Ar.*ep.*8(M.3.1089A); **c.** contrasted with καταπέτασμα: ἄλλο γάρ ἐστι καταπέτασμα, καὶ ἄλλο π., εἰ καὶ ἡ ὁμοιότης τῶν ὀνομάτων τὴν ἐν τοῖς πράγμασιν ἀποκρύπτει διαφοράν. τὸ μὲν γὰρ π. ὡς ἔτυχε σχεδιάζεται...τοῦ μὴ...δημοσιεύεσθαι τὰ συγκαλύψεως δεόμενα...· τὸ δὲ καταπέτασμα ἐξ ὑπερεχόντων δεσμῶν κατεώρηται Nil.*serm.*8(M.79.1276C–D); **d.** in law-court surrounding tribunal, phrase παρὰ τὸ π. ἀγαγών *bringing into the dock*, Chrys. *hom.5.4 in 2Tim.*(11.690D); ὥσπερ οἱ δικασταὶ ὑπὸ παραπετάσματος καθεζόμενοι κρίνουσι, οὕτω καὶ σὺ ἀντὶ παραπετάσματος καιρὸν ζήτησον ἡσυχίας id.*hom.42.4 in Mt.*(7.456B); **2.** met.; **a.** of obscurity in expression, in pagan literature π. ... πρὸς τοὺς πολλοὺς ἡ ποιητικὴ ψυχαγωγία Clem.*str.*5.4(p.340.28; M.9.44A); in OT τῆς...κατὰ τὴν παλαιὰν γραφὴν ἀσαφείας ἡ τῶν παλαιῶν ἀνθρώπων ἀσθένεια δεομένη πρὸς τὴν αὐτῶν ἀξίαν παραπετάσματος Proc.G.*Gen.*proem.(M.87.28C); cf.Dion.Ar. supra 1.b; **b.** of retreat from the world καλῷ τῇ ἐρημίᾳ κεχρημένος π. Diad.*perf.*53(p.60.1) cf. 1.d supra; **c.** of veil between human and divine διὰ...φιλανθρωπίαν ὁ θεὸς π. τῆς οἰκείας θεότητος ἐξέτεινε τὸν οὐρανόν, ἵνα μὴ ἀπολώμεθα Bas.*mor.*15.3(3.555C; M.32. 1309C); ἑκάστῳ...τῶν ἀξίων φαίνεται [sc. ὁ θεός], οὐκ ἄνευ τινὸς π. πρὸς τὸ μέτρον τῆς καθάρσεως τοῦ διακονουμένου ‡Caes.Naz.*dial.*41 (M.38.905–7); **d.** of flesh as covering or garment; **i.** for the soul, †Bas.*Is.*124(2.465C; M.30.320B); Diad.*perf.*71(p.88.11) cit. s. ἀσυνάρπακτος; **ii.** for Godhead in Inc. ἐκ σοῦ..., θεοτόκε, ἐνδυσάμενος τὸ ἐκ πνεύματος ἁγίου τῆς σαρκὸς αὐτοῦ π., προῆλθεν Mod.*dorm.*10(M.86. 3305A).

***παράπεψις, ἡ,** *promotion of digestion*, Clem.*str.*2.20(p.177.20; M. 8.1064A).

παράπηγμα, τό, *mural tablet*, Eus.*h.e.*10.4.41(M.20.865B).

παραπήγνυμι, perf. ptcpl. intrans., *set in opposition*, Clem.*q.d.s.* 1(p.160.4; M. om.); καθαρὰς τῶν κακιῶν τῶν παραπεπηγυιῶν ταῖς ἀρεταῖς Isid.Pel.*epp.*5.518(M.78.1621D).

παραπηδάω, *spring forward*, *A.Pil.*A 6.1(p.237).

παραπιέζω, *weigh down*, pass. παραπεπιεσμένην τῷ πλήθει Bas. *mor.*10.1(3.527C; M.32.1248A) for πεπιεσμένην, Bas.*hom.*1.4(2.3E; M. 31.168C).

παραπικραίν-ω, 1. *provoke, challenge* to παρεπίκραναν ἐπιδείξασθαι τὸν κύριον Clem.*paed.*2.8(p.202.28; M.8.485B); **2.** *provoke, annoy* παρεπικράνθη ὁ ἔνδοξος ἄγγελος Herm.*sim.*7.2; ἐμὲ παρεπικράνατε καὶ ἠθετήσατε ‡Hipp.*consumm.*45(p.307.35; M.10.948B); in interprn. of name Ἀμορραῖοι, Eus.*Ps.*135:19(M.24.36A); Jo.Clim.*scal.*1(M.88. 637C); ~όντων τὸν θεόν Andr.Caes.*Apoc.*55(M.106.388B); ἐπάρατον τὸ πατέρα ~ειν †Jo.D.*B.J.*25(M.96.1092B).

παραπικρασμός, ὁ, *provocation*, Clem.*paed.*1.9(p.140.18; M.8. 352C).

παραπίπτ-ω, A. *go astray, fall into sin*; **1.** in gen., *be delinquent* οἱ εἰς τὰ κυριώτατα ~οντες καὶ ἀθετοῦντες...τὸν κύριον τὸ ὅσον ἐπ' αὐτοῖς Clem.*str.*6.15(p.494.20; M.9.348B); *sin*, *A.Petr.et Paul.*18 (p.187.3); ~οντας ἀσχημόνως ἐκχεῖσθαι περὶ πορνείας Meth.*symp.*3.11 (p.39.14; M.18.77B); *Hom.Clem.*7.7; Rom.Mel.(*AS* 1 p.106); **2.** ref. results for Israel: αὐτίκα τὸ ἁμαρτῆσαι ἀλλότριον παριστᾶσα ἡ γραφὴ τοὺς μὲν παραπεσόντας τοῖς ἀλλοφύλοις πιπράσκει Clem.*str.*7.13(p.58. 27; M.9.513B); αἱ τιμωρίαι τοῖς ~ουσιν Ἰουδαίοις πέμπονται εἰς ἔκπραξιν, ἵνα ἐνταῦθα ἀπολαύοντες τὸ παράπτωμα τῆς ἐκεῖ ἀπαλλαγῶσιν αἰωνίας κολάσεως *Hom.Clem.*11.16; **3.** among Christians; **a.** in gen. μάτην αὐτὸς ὁ Παῦλος αἰτιᾶταί τινας ὡς παραπεπτωκότας Or. *princ.*3.1.19(p.233.11; M.11.292B); *ib.*(p.236.8; 296A); παραπεπτωκότων ἀδελφῶν Dion.Al.ap.Eus.*h.e.*6.42.5(M.20.613B); *Ep.Lugd.*ap. Eus.*h.e.*5.2.8(436C); μίαν ἐπὶ τοῖς παραπεσοῦσιν ὁρίζεσθαι τιμωρίαν, τὴν ἔκπτωσιν τῆς ὑπηρεσίας Bas.*ep.*217 *can.*51(3.325C; M.32.796A); **b.** ref. penitential discipline περὶ τῶν κατηχουμένων καὶ παραπεσόντων ἔδοξε..., ὥστε τριῶν ἐτῶν αὐτοὺς ἀκροωμένους μόνον, μετὰ ταῦτα εὔχεσθαι μετὰ τῶν κατηχουμένων CNic.(325)*can.*14; of post-baptismal sin οἴομαι πάντα τὸν ἅπαξ φωτισθέντα...καὶ παραπεσόντα πάλιν, ἀνακαινίζειν ἑαυτὸν εἰς μετάνοιαν, ἤτοι προσταυροῦντα ἢ ἀνασταυροῦντα τὸν υἱὸν τοῦ θεοῦ καὶ παραδειγματίζοντα Or.*Jo.*20.12(p.341.28; M.14. 600A); dealt with by repetition of baptism βάπτισμα δίδωσιν [sc. Marcion] οὐ μόνον ἕν, ἀλλὰ καὶ δύο καὶ τρία μετὰ τὸ παραπεσεῖν Epiph. *haer.*42 proem.(p.3.10; M.41.580D) ∞ Jo.D.*haer.*42(M.94.704A); of lapse in persecution καὶ διγάμοις κοινωνεῖν καὶ τοῖς ἐν τῷ διωγμῷ παραπεπτωκόσιν CNic.(325)*can.*8; ἀλλὰ Ναυᾶτος, φησίν, οὐκ ἐδέξατο τοὺς ἐν τῷ διωγμῷ παραπεσόντας Gr.Naz.*or.*39.19(M.36.357B); Μελιτιανοί, οἱ ἐν Αἰγύπτῳ, σχίσμα ὄντες ἀλλ' οὐχ αἵρεσις, μὴ συνευξάμενοι τοῖς ἐν τῷ διωγμῷ παραπεπτωκόσι Epiph.*haer.*68 proem.(p.2.4; M.42.12B); **4.** ref. Fall εἰ γὰρ καθ' ὑπόθεσιν ἡ γυνὴ μὴ ἠπάτητο καὶ ὁ Ἀδὰμ μὴ παραπεπτώκει Or.*Jo.*1.20(22; p.25.3; παραπέπτωκε M.14. 57C); Meth.*symp.*8.3(p.84.11; M.18.141C).

B. *be mislaid* ἀληθὲς εἶναι, ὅτι καὶ ἐδέξω τὸν χάρτην, καὶ παρέπεσεν Pall.*v.Chrys.*6(p.36.14; M.47.22).

C. ? f.l. for παραρρίπτ-, Or.*Cels.*1.49(p.100.15; παραπέμπει M.11. 752C, cj. παραρρίπτει); cf. conversely παραρρί- for παραπί-, Mac. Aeg.*hom.*27.13(M.34.704A, perh. παραπίπτουσι).

παραπιστεύω, *believe along with*, *cat.Lc.*11:5(p.91.24).

***παράπλασις, ἡ,** *transformation*, Geo.Pis.*hex.*773(περιπλάσει M. 92.1493A).

παραπλέκ-ω, 1. *weave, plait, entwine*; fig., Epiph.*haer.*45.4(p.201. 18; M.41.836A); ὑπὸ τοῦ...ὄφεως παραπεπλεγμένοι *ib.*48.2(p.222.14; M.41.857C παραπεποιημένοι); παραπέπλεκται τῆς ἀγάπης ὁ στέφανος Cyr.*Lc.*10:36(M.72.684B); **2.** *mingle, introduce*, Clem.*str.*1.1(p.12.1; M.8.705A); Epiph.*haer.*38.3(p.65.12; M.41.657A); *ib.*21.2(p.239.16; 288A); *ib.*26.1(p.275.17; 332B); ~ουσι δὲ τούτοις τὰ εἰς δειλίαν Cyr. *ador.*5(1.151C); *introduce* a notion ~ει...τὸν φόβον Clem.*paed.*1.9 (p.135.3; M.8.341B); σωματικοῦ παρέπλεξεν ἔννοιαν CAnc.(358)*ep.syn.* ap.Epiph.*haer.*73.3(p.272.1; M.42.848C); **3.** *connect, involve* αἵρεσις ...ταύταις παραπεπλεγμένη Epiph.*haer.*19.1(p.217.18; M.41.261A).

παραπλέω, fig., *drift away* from the point ἐλελήθειν παραπλεύσας τῷ πνεύματι τὴν ἀκολουθίαν Clem.*paed.*3.4(p.251.16; M.8.592B); ‡Gr. Nyss.*Ar.et Sab.*14(M.45.1300C).

***παραπληκτίζω,** *go mad* παραπληκτίσωμεν ἄμφω εἰς θεοῦ μυστήρια παρακύπτοντες Gr.Naz.*or.*31.8(p.155.6; -ίσομεν M.36.141B).

παραπληκτικῶς, *severely*, comp. κολάζοιτο π. Thdr.Stud.*epp.*2. 211(M.99.1637B).

παραπλήξ, 1. *speechless*, *A.Andr.*A 4(p.48.1); *A.Paul.et Thecl.*10 (p.243.1); **2.** *crazy*; of heretics, cf. παραπληξία, ‡Gr.Nyss.*hom.6.60 in Jo.*(p.221.2); *ib.*6.67(p.222.31); Nil.*epp.*1.16(M.79.88C).

παραπληξία, ἡ, *madness*, *IG* 12^9.1179 (Euboea); Ephr.1.260A; Isid.Pel.*epp.*3.360(M.78.1016B); esp. of heretics, Thdt.*Heb.*7:18 (3.590); id.*Trin.*15(M.75.1168A).

παραπλήρωμα, τό, *complement*, Clem.*prot.*10(p.77.19; M.8.225A).

***παραπλησιάζ-ω, 1.** intrans., *be like* ἀγγέλοις ~οντες Meth.*res.* 1.51(p.305.9, vv.ll. παραπλησιασθέντας, πλησιασθέντες; πλησιάζοντας M.18.281B); τὴν χροιὰν ταῖς ἡλίου...~ειν φαντάζεται βολαῖς [sc. ὁ χρυσός] id.*symp.*5.8(p.63.5; M.18.112B); **2.** trans., *liken* παρεπλησίασάν με τοῖς κτήνεσιν *A.Andr.et Mt.*2(p.66.17); *ib.*20(p.91.12); παρεπλησίασεν τοὺς Φαρισαίους τῇ ἐχίδνῃ ‡Petr.I Al.*phys.*13.

***παραπλησιαστέον**, *one should compare*, Nil.*epp*.3.153(M.79.457A).

***παραπλ-όω**, *stretch out*, Jo.Mal.*chron*.18 p.452(M.97.664A); met., *extend* εἰς τετάρτην ~οῦν γενεὰν τὴν ὀργήν Cyr.*Jo*.6.1(4.592C).

***παραπόδας (παρὰ πόδας)**, **1.** *in the way, obstructing* παρὰ πόδας κειμένου καὶ ὀπίσω καλεῖν ἰσχύοντος Cyr.*Jo*.11.12(4.1006D); **2.** *obviously* οὐχ ἑώρακέ γε αὐτὸς ἑαυτῷ παρὰ πόδας ἐναντία εἰπών Or.*Cels*.2.23(p.152.14; π. M.11.841B); **3.** *immediately, without delay*, Chrys.*exp.in Ps*.145:8(5.479A) cit. s. πειρασμός; ἐπαπορεῖν...τί δήποτε π. τοῖς παρανομοῦσιν ἡ τιμωρία οὐχ ἕπεται Thdt.*Abac*.proem.(2.1537–8); οὐ κολάζει π. τοὺς ἀσεβεῖς Olymp.*Job* 21:16(M.93.228D).

παραποδίζω, *impede*, Clem.*paed*.2.1(p.163.11; M.8.400A); †Bas.*bapt*.2.2(2.653D; M.31.1581D); †Bas.*Is*.34(1.407D; M.30.188B).

***παραπόδισμα, τό**, *hindrance, obstacle*, Cyr.*ador*.7(1.238D); *ib*.13(474E); ἀμείνων ἔσο τῶν ἐν κόσμῳ π. *ib*.1(26E); θεόν, παραποδισμάτων ἀμείνους ἐργάζεσθαι δυνάμενον id.*Jo*.10.2(4.898E).

παραποίησις, ἡ, *distortion* in exposition φανερὰ...ἡ τῆς ἐξηγήσεως π. Iren.*haer*.1.9.2(M.7.540A); τὰ τῆς π. μέρη τῶν λόγων Epiph.*haer*.76.27(p.375.30; M.42.572B); μύθους οὐ τὸν νόμον φησίν...· ἀλλὰ τὰς π. καὶ τὰ παραχαράγματα καὶ τὰ παράσημα δόγματα Chrys.*hom.1.2 in 1Tim*.(11.551C); μύθους...ἢ διὰ τὰς π., ἢ διὰ τὸ ἄκαιρον *ib.12.2*(611F); cf. διπλῇ μῦθος τὰ Ἰουδαϊκά, καὶ ὅτι π., καὶ ὅτι παρὰ καιρὸν τὸ πρᾶγμα id.*hom.3.2 in Tit*.(11.746D); μὴ ἐκβιάζεσθαι [sc. τοὺς ἑρμηνεύοντας] τὰ μὴ προσήκοντα· ἵνα μὴ καὶ τοῖς προσήκουσιν ὑποψίαν παραποιήσεως τέκωσι Isid.Pel.*epp*.2.63(M.78.508B).

***παραποιητεύ-ομαι**, *support disingenuously* ἑαυτοῖς...ἐπισωρεύουσι λόγους, δι' ὧν ~ονται τὴν ἑαυτῶν πλάνην Epiph.*haer*.48.4(p.225.13; M.41.861B).

παραπολαύ-ω, **1.** *suffer ill consequences* ἀδεεῖς...τοῦ μή τι παραπολαύσωσιν Synes.*provid*.1.2(p.112.20; M.66.1261C); Niceph.Ur.*v.Sym*.207(M.86.3176D); **2.** *catch* a disease, Isid.Pel.*epp*.3.47(M.78.764B); **3.** *possess separately* (ref. Manich. view of God and evil) ἵνα ...μὴ τῶν παρ' ἡμῖν...κακῶν ὑπέχειν δοκῇ τὰς αἰτίας ὁ θεός, αὐτός γε ὅλης τινὸς καὶ ὁλοκλήρου παρ' αὐτῷ κακίας ~ειν Tit.Bost.*Man*.1.1(M.18.1069B).

παραπομπή, ἡ, **1.** *guidance* (towards) ἡ γεωμετρικὴ αὕτη παρέχεται ἀναλογία εἰς π. τῶν ἁγίων ἐκείνων μονῶν Clem.*str*.6.11(p.475.7; M.9.308B); τῇ ἀπὸ τῶν οὐρανῶν εἰς τὰ σώματα καταβάσει καὶ π. τῶν ψυχῶν Meth.*symp*.2.5(p.21.5; καταπ- M.18.53C); **2.** *cross-reference* αἱ π. τῶν τίτλων τῶν ἀπὸ τοῦ αὐτοῦ στοιχείου ἀρχομένων Leont.et Jo.*sacr*.proem.(M.86.2019B); Jo.D.*parall*.proem.(M.95.1044B).

παραπομπός, ὁ, ἡ, **1.** *escort, guide* π. ἀγαθή...τοῖς εἰς οὐρανὸν ἀπαίρουσι Clem.*prot*.11(p.82.30; M.8.237A); π. εἰς ἐκείνην τὴν ὁδὸν δι' ἧς ὀλίγοι πορεύονται *A.Thom*.A 68(p.185.13); **2.** *hander-on, transmitter, middleman* π. τινες...κτημάτων τε καὶ χρημάτων, ἀλλ' οὐ δεσπόται Chrys.*hom.59.7 in Mt*.(7.604E); of goods laid up in heaven οὐκ ἔστιν ἐνταῦθα π. εὑρεῖν τῶν καταβληθέντων *ib.66.5*(659E).

παραπορθμεύ-ω, fig., *convey across* δι' υἱοῦ ~οντος ὥσπερ ἡμῖν τοὺς παρὰ πατρὸς λόγους Cyr.*glaph.Gen*.5(1.152D).

***παραπόρτιον, τό**, (cf. Lat.*porta*) small *side-door*, Thphn.*chron*. p.318(M.108.769C).

***παραπροθεσμέω**, *be late for an appointment*, †Leont.B.*sect*.4.3(M.86.1221D).

παραπροσποι-έομαι, *pretend otherwise* τῆς τῶν...Δονατιστῶν ἐπιβουλῆς...τὴν...ἐκκλησίαν βαρέως πορθούσης, μηδαμῶς ~ησώμεθα *Cod.Afr*.65(tr. Lat. *dissimulemus*).

παραπτύω, *drip* froth from the sides of the mouth, like a mad dog, Eus.*Hierocl*.27(528A; M.22.833B).

παράπτ-ω, **A.** act.; **1.** *kindle* ἐγὼ τὸν νόμον ~ω, αὐτὸς δὲ τὴν χάριν φωταγωγεῖ †Hipp.*theoph*.3(p.259.3; M.10.853D); **2.** *give light* παρῆψε τῷ Σαμαὴλ ὅτε τὸν ὄφιν ἔλαβεν ἔνδυμα *Apoc.Bar*.9(p.91.7).

B. med.; **1.** *touch briefly* ὀλίγα παρήψω τῆς ἀληθείας Epiph.*haer*.33.11(p.463.14); ~εται τῶν τῆς γνώσεως λόγων Chrys.*hom.2.2 in Col*.(11.335D); **2.** *get* insecure *hold of* ~εσθαί τι [sc. τοῦ ἀντιπάλου] Niceph.Ur.*v.Sym*.139(M.86.3115A); **3.** *become contaminated with* ~όμενοι καὶ ἀνθρωπίνων σαρκῶν καὶ ἀκαθαρσιῶν Epiph.*haer*.26.3(p.279.5; M.41.336B); ~όμενοι μυσαρῶν *ib*.63.4(p.402.7; 1068B); **4.** *misappropriate, filch* ἐάν τις...χρήματα πιστευθεὶς τούτων παράψηται ‡Ath.*qu.Ant*.87(M.28.649D); ἐστι κλέμμα καὶ κλέμμα...· ἄλλο γάρ ἐστι τὸ παράψασθαι ἀπὸ τοῦ ἱεροῦ Anast.S.*qu.et resp*.102(M.89.756D).

παράπτωμα, τό, *transgression, sin*; **1.** of Adam, Meth.*symp*.3.3(p.29.20; M.18.64C); οὐ γὰρ πρὸ τῆς ἐνσωματώσεως τὸ π. [i.e. in view of Or.]...ἀλλὰ μετὰ τὴν εἰς τὸ σῶμα σύμφυσιν τῆς ψυχῆς γίγνεται τὸ π. id.*res*.1.55(p.314.15ff.; M.41.1148Df.); id.*symp*.9.2(p.116.16; M.18.181B); **2.** of sin in gen.; to be confessed καλὸν γὰρ ἀνθρώπῳ ἐξομολογεῖσθαι περὶ τῶν π. *1Clem*.51.3; ἐν ἐκκλησίᾳ ἐξομολογήσῃ τὰ π. σου *Did*.4.14; *ib*.14.1; Or.*hom.10.8 in Jer*.(p.78.21; M.13.368B); *Clem.ep*.15(M.2.52A); punished μισθὸν τοῦ π. τὸ ἀπόπτωμα λαμβάνει Clem.*paed*.3.2(p.244.23; M.8.576A); id.*str*.7.16(p.72.17; M.9.541B); Hipp.*Dan*.4.6.4; *Hom.Clem*.11.16; healed by God θεὸς...ἰᾶται τὸ π. Clem.*prot*.10(p.67.24; M.8.204C); *Lit*.ap.*Const.App*.8.9.3; τὸ ὑπὸ πλήθους παραπτωμάτων ἑαυτοῦ ἀπελπίσαν τῆς σωτηρίας μὴ ἐάσῃς [sc. bishop] ἀπολέσθαι *Const.App*.2.20.5; **3.** various kinds of transgression: apostasy ἡ κλῆσις τῶν ἐθνῶν ἀρχὴν ἔσχεν ἐκ τοῦ π. τοῦ Ἰσραὴλ Or.*hom.4.2 in Jer*.(p.24.5; M.13.288A); *ib.12.6*(p.93.13; 388A); τὴν τῶν Ἰουδαίων συναγωγήν...παραπτώματα τοῦ Ἰσραὴλ πεποίηκεν...ἀποθανεῖν id.*fr.15 in Lc*.8:41(p.240; M.17.337D); idolatry, Clem.*prot*.8(p.61.19; M.8.192A); transgressions due to human ignorance and weakness, *A.Thom*.A 38(p.156.7); *ib*.59(p.177.4); of Noah's drunkenness, Clem.*paed*.2.2(p.177.16; M.8.432A); *ib*.2.6(p.188.13; 453B); τῷ θεῷ ἔδοξεν, τὸν ἐν γνώσει τῶν καλῶν παραπίπτοντα, κατὰ λόγον τῶν ἀνθρωπίνων π., μετρίως κολασθέντα σωθῆναι *Hom.Clem*.7.7; οἱ γὰρ ἐν θεοσεβείᾳ πάσχοντες τὰ θλιβερὰ εἰς ἔκπραξιν παραπτωμάτων πάσχουσιν *ib*.12.11; τῶν ἁγίων αἱ ψυχαὶ καὶ ἐν αὐτοῖς τοῖς π. τῆς οἰκείας ἀρετῆς τὰ σύμβολα φέρουσι Chrys.*hom.5.3 in Is.6*:1(6.135A); **4.** exeg.; **a.** Ps.18:13 πολλοὺς οἶδα τὸ τοῦ Δαβὶδ ῥητὸν κακῶς ἐκλαβόντας καὶ λέγοντας εἶναι τὰ τοιαῦτα [sc. sudden deaths] π.· καὶ ἐπειδὴ εἶπεν ὁ προφήτης 'παραπτώματα τίς συνήσει;' εἴδησαν ὅτι 'παραπτώματα' ταῦτα λέγονται, καὶ πλανῶνται μὴ εἰδότες...ἐρῶ σοι τί ἐστιν παράπτωμα· ὅταν ὁ ἄνθρωπος κατορθώσῃ βίον ἐν ἄρτῳ δι' ἀσκήσεως...καὶ ...ἐκπέσῃ εἰς ἁμαρτίαν, τοῦτό ἐστιν π. ... ταῦτά εἰσιν τὰ π. τῶν ἐν ἀρετῇ ὑπαρχόντων...μακάριοι δέ εἰσιν οἱ μὴ πίπτοντες εἰς ταῦτα τὰ π. Eus.Al.*serm*.6(M.86.352D–353A); **b.** Ps.21:2 ἰστέον δέ, ὡς τῶν π., οὐδεὶς τῶν ἄλλων ἑρμηνευτῶν ἐμνημόνευσεν...τῇ τῶν ἑβδομήκοντα ἑρμηνείᾳ χρησόμεθα...πῶς γάρ φησιν οἷόν τε ἦν τὸν οὐχ ἡμαρτηκότα λέγειν, μακρὰν ἀπὸ τῆς σωτηρίας μου οἱ λόγοι τῶν π. μου;...τοῖς ὑπὲρ ἡμῶν ἀνθ' ἡμῶν ἐχρήσατο λόγοις Thdt.*Ps*.21:2(1.734f.).

παράπτωσις, ἡ, *falling away, transgression*, *1Clem*.59.1; Just.*dial*.141.3,4(M.6.800A); of Adam's sin ὅσοι...τῆς τοῦ προπάτορος ἐγείρειν ἑαυτοὺς βούλονται π. Max.*ambig*.(M.91.1356B).

παραπύλιον, τό, *side-gate*, Jo.Mal.*chron*.6 p.159(M.97.261B).

***παραράομαι**, *curse*, Cyr.*Is*.2.3(2.247E).

***παραριπισμός**, v. *παραρρι-.

παραρπάζω, *snatch away* παραρπάσας ἑαυτῷ τὴν ἀξίαν Eus.*h.e*.8.13.15(M.20.780C).

παραρρέ-ω, **1.** *flow past*; **a.** lit., ~ον ὑδάτιον Synes.*ep*.114(M.66.1496B); **b.** met., *be transitory* τὰ τοῦ κόσμου, τὰ πτωχὰ ἀλλότρια καὶ ~οντα Clem.*q.d.s*.37.5(p.184.14; M.9.641D); Cels.ap.Or.*Cels*.7.35(p.185.28; M.11.1469C); *ib*.(p.186.3; 1469C); **2.** *drift away*, met. μὴ παραρρυῶσι τῆς ἀληθείας διὰ χαυνότητα Clem.*paed*.3.11(p.269.19; M.8.632B); τῆς καθόλου μὴ ἐκστῆτε πίστεως...μηδὲ παραρρυῆτε ἀπ' αὐτῆς ἔν τινι δισταγμῷ Ephr.2.243C; **3.** *fail to attain, neglect* ἐὰν ἡ ψυχὴ κατανεύσῃ πρὸς τὸ φαῦλον καὶ πονηρόν, καὶ παραρρυῇ τῶν κρειττόνων ἐνθυμήσεων καὶ διαλογισμῶν †Dion.Al.*fr.Eccl*.4:9f.(p.227.11); **4.** *slip out of mind, be forgotten* πολλὰ...παρερρύηκεν ἡμᾶς χρόνου μήκει Clem.*str*.1.1(p.10.24; M.8.704A); ὁ δὲ πολὺς τῶν πιστεύειν δοκούντων καὶ μὴ τηλικοῦτος δεῖται ὑπομνήσεως χάριν...αἰσθητῶν παραδειγμάτων, ἵνα μὴ παραρρυῇ Or.*Cels*.8.23(p.240.6; M.11.1552B); **5.** *slip in* during discussion, *crop up* καί τινος λόγου παραρυέντος τοῦ οὐρανοῦ πέρι, εἴτε κατὰ σπουδὴν αὐτοῦ, εἴτε τῆς ἀκολουθίας τῶν λεγομένων...ἀπαιτούσης Zach.Mit.*opif*.(M.85.1029A).

***παραρριπισμός, ὁ**, *disturbance* ἐπιθυμίας ἐνθύμησιν...ἐν π. νοὸς ἀνερχομένην Marc.Er.*opusc*.5.7(M.65.1040B); παραριπισμοὶ συνειδήσεως †Sophr.H.*conf*.(M.87.3365B); of a sudden, inexpressible longing ἔστι παρὰ τοῖς ἀκριβεστάτοις τῶν γνωστικῶν πατέρων καὶ ἑτέρα... λεπτοτέρα ἔννοια, ὅπερ παραρριπισμὸν νοός τινες...λέγουσιν, ὅστις χρόνου χωρίς, καὶ λόγου καὶ εἰκόνος ὀξυτέρως τὸ πάθος τῷ πάσχοντι σημαίνειν πέφυκε Jo.Clim.*scal*.15(M.88.897B); of tossing and turning ῥιπισμούς, καὶ παραριπισμούς, καὶ ῥοπάς, καὶ τροπάς *ib*.27(1109B).

παραρριπτ-έω (παραρρίπτ-ω), **1.** *throw aside, reject* τὰ περὶ τοῦ καλουμένου ἀντιχρίστου ~εῖ ὁ Κέλσος Or.*Cels*.6.45(p.115.30; M.11.1368B); ~εῖν ἀτίμως *ib*.8.30(p.246.1; 1561A); ~ούμενος καὶ ἀποξενούμενος Gr.Naz.*or*.22.13(M.35.1145B); Mac.Aeg.*hom*.27.13(M.34.704A) v. παραπίπτω; περιφρονηθεῖσα καὶ παραρριφεῖσα Gr.Naz.*or*.25.8(1209A); παρερρίφθαι ὥσπερ τῶν σκευῶν τὰ ἀτιμότατα Cyr.*Ps*.30:12(M.69.861B); **2.** *abandon, let loose* ταῖς εἰς ἀσέλγειαν ἡδοναῖς ~οῦντες τὸν νοῦν Cyr.*ador*.14(1.484A); **3.** *interject, introduce* a phrase ὡς μὴ εἰκῇ παρερριμμένον Or.*Jo*.32.24(p.468.25; M.14.809C); Jo.D.*Jacob*.52(M.94.1460D).

παράρτημα, τό, **1.** *appendage*, of an expletive κενὸν καὶ ψευδὲς καὶ ἀργὸν καὶ ἄσημον...π., οἷον εἰ καὶ χρέμπτοιτο καὶ πτύοι τό τε πρόσωπον στρέφοι καὶ τὴν χεῖρα κινοίη Dion.Al.ap.Eus.*p.e.*14.27(783B; M.21.1288C); **2.** *subsidiary part* ἡ μὲν ὑπόθεσις ἦν Ἀρειανῶν ἀγὼν καὶ τὸ πρωτότυπον ἐκείνους κατορθοῦν, ὑποβολὴ δὲ καὶ π. τούτων Ἰωάννης καὶ οἱ σὺν αὐτῷ CAlex.*ep.*ap.Ath.*apol.sec.*17(p.99.37; M.25.276B).

παράρτυμα, τό, *seasoning*, Jo.D.*hom.*9.13(M.96.740B).

παρασαλεύ-ω, *shake loose, shake from a position* or *course*; lit., Chrys.*hom.11.2 in Heb.*(12.113D); id.*hom.5.3 in 2Tim.*(11.689B); Isid.Pel.*epp.*4.126(M.78.1204B); met., Or.*adnot.*in *Dt.*27:17(M.17.33C); Eus.*e.th.*1.10(p.68.26; M.24.841C); [sc. πίστει] ~θείσῃ †Ath.*fr.*(M.26.1220C); ὅταν...θεός τι ~σῃ τῆς ἁρμονίας Gr.Naz.*or.*6.16(M.35.741C); ὑπὸ διαβόλου...~όμενοι Epiph.*haer.*68.3(p.142.22; M.42.188A); *ib.*75.5(p.337.34; 512B); τοὺς ἀσθενεστέρους ~ει [sc. ὁ πειράζων] Chrys.*hom.4.1 in 1Thess.*(11.452D); ἵνα...τὴν διάνοιαν...~σῃ id.*hom.1.2 in Philm.*(11.776C); ~όμενοι τὸν λογισμόν id.*hom.65.5 in Gen.*(4.627E); ~ομένους ὑπὸ τῶν πειρασμῶν id.*hom.5.3 in Heb.*(55D); τὴν ἐν Νικαίᾳ πίστιν...~ειν Socr.*h.e.*1.37.4(M.67.176A); ~θῆναι τῆς βεβαιότητος Nil.*Magn.*60(M.79.1049C); *disturb, put into disorder*; a text, Call.*v.Hyp.*(p.4).

***παρασέβ-ομαι,** *belong to a false religion* πάντες οἱ ὄντες Ἰουδαῖοι καὶ ~όμενοι ἐν τῇ πόλει πάντες *A.Phil.*64(p.26.18).

***παρασεσιωπημένως,** *without explicit mention*, Or.*sel.in Ps.*8:13(M.12.1181A).

παρασημαίν-ω, 1. *mis-state* ~ουσι τὸ μυστήριον τῆς μετὰ σαρκὸς οἰκονομίας Cyr.*ep.*1(p.17.6; 5².11A); **2.** *pervert*, id.*ador.*1(1.45E); χρημάτων ἕνεκα τὴν τοῦ δικαίου ~οντας χάριν id.*Zach.*48(3.724D, v.l. προδιδόντας Aubert); fig., *deface*, as a coin ~οντες τῆς ἀληθείας τὸ κάλλος Didym.*Trin.*1.11(M.39.293B); τὸ κάλλος τῆς ἀληθείας ~ων Cyr.*Abac.*5(3.520C); id.*ador.*7(1.228C); id.*apol.Thdt.*10(p.137.29, v.l. κατασημαίνουσι 6¹.232B); id.*hom.pasch.*30(5².347B).

παρασημει-όομαι, 1. *note in passing, mention incidentally, sketch* ἐν ὑπογραφῆς μέρει ~ουμένοις Clem.*paed.*3.8(p.260.22; M.8.612C); id.*str.*6.7(p.459.6; M.9.276C); ἐν βραχεῖ ~ώσασθαι Geo.Laod.*ep.dogm.*ap.Epiph.*haer.*73.17(p.289.20; M.42.433C); ὀλίγα διὰ τὸ μῆκος παρεσημειωσάμεθα Geo.Laod.*ib.*73.21(p.293.17; 440C); Anast.S.*hod.*10(M.89.184D); **2.** *make a note in the margin* τὰς ἀφ᾽ ἑκάστης βίβλου μαρτυρίας ~ωσάμενος Euthal.Diac.*Ac.*(M.85.637D); ‡Jo.D.*icon.*15(M.96.1360D).

παρασημείωσις, ἡ, brief *mention, note*, Eus.*Marcell.*1.1(p.2.25; M.24.713C); Anast.S.*hod.*proem.(M.89.37B); esp. *note* of date ὁ τῆς π. χρόνος Eus.*h.e.*1.9.3(M.20.108B); Epiph.*haer.*51.29(p.300.17; M.41.940A); χρόνος τῆς συνόδου, ὡς ἐν π. εὕρομεν Socr.*h.e.*1.13.13(M.67.109A).

παράσημος, 1. *counterfeit*, Synes.*provid.*1.17(p.105.1; M.66.1253B); λαλοῦσιν...παράσημα...καὶ ψευδῆ Cyr.*Mich.*59(3.451B); *faulty* ὀλίγος εἰς λόγους, καὶ π. ἔχει τὴν γλῶτταν id.*glaph.Ex.*2(1.304E); **2.** *noticeable* οὔτε βίον π. ἀσκοῦσιν *Diogn.*5.2; τὸ λανθάνον τοῦ σχήματος καὶ μὴ π. Clem.*paed.*3.11(p.271.2; M.8.636B); *conspicuous* by being deformed, *Ep.Chr.dom.*(p.28); **3.** neut. as subst., *ornament*, Synes.*ep.*3(M.66.1325A); **4.** neut. as subst., *sign* of things prophesied, Chrys.*hom.6.4 in Mt.*(7.92A); *ib.*57.1(576C); *distinguishing mark*, id.*hom.19.6 in Rom.*(9.651E); Philost.*h.e.*12.8(M.65.616B); *emblem, ensign*, of a ship πλοίῳ π. ἀετῷ ὀνομαζομένῳ Epiph.*anc.*105(p.128.3; M.43.208C); *distinctive name* τί δήποτε λέγουσιν αὐτοῦ τὸ π.; ὅτι ἦν καὶ ἄλλος Ἰούδας [i.e. other than Iscariot] Chrys.*hom.80.2 in Mt.*(7.768D).

παρασιγάω, pass., *be passed over without mention*, Thphl.Ant.*Autol.*2.31(M.6.1104C).

***παρασιτεύω,** *cling to* τριακονταοκτὼ ἔτη τῇ κολυμβήθρᾳ...παρεσίτευσεν Amph.*mesopent.*(M.39.121D).

παρασιωπ-άω, 1. *pass over in silence*; **a.** *overlook* (without idea of silence) τὸ τοῦ θεοῦ ἔλεος παρεσιώπησέν με *A.Xanthipp.*26(p.77.3); δακρύων...οὐ παρεσιώπησας †Jo.D.*B.J.*35(M.96.1196C); **b.** *turn away* from a suppliant μὴ ~ήσῃς ἀπ᾽ ἐμοῦ *Pss.Sal.*5.3; Or.*exc.in Ps.*27:1(M.17.116C); Ephr.3.156C; **2.** *suppress mention* τὸ ὄνομα...ὡς οὐ πρέπον τῷ μεγαλείῳ τῆς δόξης παρεσιώπησε Bas.*Eun.*2.2(1.239D; M.29.576C); in writing, *leave out part* of quotation, Or.*Jo.*10.26(17; p.199.32; M.14.356A); μὴ ~ηθήτω δ᾽ ἡμῖν μηδὲ 'θεοῦ σοφία' *ib.*1.34(39; p.43.16; 89B).

παρασιωπητέον, *one must omit to mention*, Or.*Jo.*28.17(13; p.411.23; M.14.717C).

παρασκευάζω, pass., *go to stool* ποῦ παρεσκευάσθη Μωυσῆς τὴν τεσσαρακονθήμερον; Epiph.*haer.*77.16(p.429.22; M.42.662D).

παρασκευαστής, ὁ, *servant, groom*, Gr.Nyss.*hom.3 in Cant.*(M.44.820B).

παρασκευή, ἡ, *preparation*; hence **1.** *equipment* τεχνίτης καὶ ἡ πρὸς τὴν τέχνην αὐτοῦ π. Athenag.*leg.*15.2(M.6.920A); of arms for spiritual warfare, Mac.Mgn.*apocr.*2.7(p.6.5); of furnishing of table (with food), Gr.Nyss.*infant.*(M.46.185B); **2.** *training, practice* ἡ ...εἰς τὸ εὔχεσθαι π. Or.*or.*9.2(p.318.24; M.11.444C); id.*Jo.*10.10(8; p.179.34; M.14.321C); id.*fr.ep.2* ap.Eus.*h.e.*6.19.13(M.20.568C); οὐδαμοῦ χρείαν ἔχω τῆς ἔξωθεν σοφίας, οὐδὲ λογισμῶν οὐδὲ παρασκευῶν Chrys.*hom.7.4 in 1Cor.*(10.55E); **3.** *day of preparation* for sabbath, *Friday*; **a.** in gen., *M.Polyc.*7.1; ref. relationship of Law to gospel compared with collection of manna on Friday and its consumption on sabbath ἅπερ ἐνταῦθα συλλέξομεν ἐν π. [i.e. by learning from Mosaic types], ταῦτα ἐκεῖσε σαββατίσαντες εὑρήσομεν καὶ τραφησόμεθα Or.*exc.in Ps.*77:31(M.17.144D); **b.** in discussion of chronology of Last Supper and Passion, Eus.*pasch.*9(M.24.704A); Chrys.*Jud.*3.5(1.613C); id.*hom.83.3 in Jo.*(8.494C); v. πάσχα; **c.** as day for reception of Communion κοινωνοῦμεν ἐν τῇ κυριακῇ, ἐν τῇ τετράδι, καὶ ἐν τῇ π., καὶ τῷ σαββάτῳ Bas.*ep.*93(1.186D; M.32.484B); **d.** ref. Friday fast, *Did.*8.1; Clem.*str.*7.12(p.54.5; M.9.504B); Petr.I Al.*ep.can.*15(M.18.508B); *Can.App.*69; *Const.App.*5.13.20; *ib.*5.20.18; *ib.*7.23.2; ‡Pall.*h.mon.*8.58(p.48.22; M.34.1148B); Eus.Al.*serm.*1(M.86.313A); v. νηστεία; **e.** ἁγία or μεγάλη π., *Good Friday*, Chrys.*cruc.*2 tit.(2.411A); Thdr.Lect.*h.e.*2.32(M.86.201A); day for distribution of εὐλογίαι among monks, Jo.Mosch.*prat.*85(M.87.2941D).

παρασοφίζ-ομαι, 1. *produce by trickery* ἔσχε καὶ ἡ μαγγανεία καιρὸν ἐν τῷ παρὰ τοῖς Ἑβραίοις εὑρισκομένῳ ὕδατι, τὸ αἱματῶδες ὕδωρ παρασοφίσασθαι Or.*exc.in Ps.*77:44(M.17.147D) = Gr.Nyss.*v.Mos.*26(M.44.308D); **2.** *change by magic* ὥσπερ ἐκεῖ φησιν ἡ ποιητικὴ τερατεία εἰς διαφόρων θηρίων εἴδη τοὺς φαρμακευθέντας ἀλλάσσεσθαι κατὰ τὸ ἀρέσκον τῇ ~ομένῃ τὴν φύσιν, τὰ αὐτὰ καὶ νῦν γίνεται παρὰ τοῦ Κιρκαίου τούτου κρατῆρος Gr.Nyss.*Eun.*4(2 p.73.7; M.45.645C).

***παρασοφισμός, ὁ,** *trickery* ὁ π. τῆς ἀπάτης Or.*exc.in Ps.*77:44(M.17.147B) = Gr.Nyss.*v.Mos.*(M.44.345A).

***παρασπαίρω,** *pulsate feebly*, Amph.*Seleuc.*144(M.37.1586).

παρασπείρ-ω, 1. *intersperse* ἀνθρωπινώτερον ἐβουλήθη φθέγξασθαι ...ὁ εὐαγγελιστής. ... ἐπειδὴ γὰρ πανταχοῦ ὑψηλὰ λέγει, τούτου ἕνεκεν ταῦτα ~ει Chrys.*hom.50.2 in Jo.*(8.295D); **2.** *introduce insidiously* ~οντες ἃ μηδὲ εἰς νοῦν αὐτῶν ποτε ἀνέβη Ath.*ep.Aeg.Lib.*10(M.25.560B); λόγους περὶ Ἀρείου...παρέσπειρεν, ἠδικῆσθαι φάσκων αὐτὸν ὑπὸ τῆς συνόδου Socr.*h.e.*1.25.2(M.67.148A).

παρασπονδ-έω, 1. *violate* a treaty or covenant, Eus.*h.e.*9.10.2(M.20.829C); εἰς τὰς τῆς σωτηρίας αὐτῶν συνθήκας ~ήσαντες Bas.*Spir.*27(3.22D; M.32.116A); usages, traditions τὰ πάτρια ~ήσας τὴν ἄθεον εἵλετο δόξαν Eus.*v.C.*2.5(p.43.1; M.20.984B); Nil.*exerc.*12(M.79.732C); **2.** in general, *do violence to, outrage*, of images of gods λίθινοι... καὶ ξύλινοι δεσπόται ἀνθρώπων, ὑβρίζοντες καὶ ~οῦντες τὸν βίον διὰ τῆς συνηθείας Clem.*prot.*10(p.74.14; M.8.220A).

παρασπορά, ἡ, *sprinkling, sowing besides*; *interpolation* in scriptures, Jo.Thess.*dorm.BMV* 1.1(p.377.2).

***παραστάσιμον, τό,** penalty of *being made to stand* ἐὰν περίσσευμα ...ῥιφῇ ἀχρειωθέν, π. μετὰ ξηροφαγίας Thdr.Stud.*poen.*1.42(M.99.1737D).

***παραστάσιμος,** *committed for trial*, *M.Scill.*1(p.22.15); Alex.Sal.*cruc.*(M.87.4040A); Jo.Mal.*chron.*10 p.256(M.97.389A); Ath.Scholast.*coll.*1.2(p.7); *ib.*5 paratit.2(p.77).

παράστασις, ἡ, A. (παρίστημι); **1.** *appearance, manifestation*, Chrys.*hom.64.5 in Mt.*(7.643A); **2.** *exhibition, display*, Or.*comm.in Rom.*3:21f.(*JTS* 13 p.221); π. ἀνδρείας παρεσχημένοι Eus.*m.P.*10(p.930.27; M.20.1496D); ὥσπερ ἐπικαλύμματι κεχρημένος τῇ π. τῆς προσευχῆς Evagr.Pont.*or.*40(M.79.1176B); οὐσίαν μίαν ἔλαβε καὶ ὑπόστασιν εἰς δύο ὑποστάσεων π. Chrys.*hom.2.2 in Heb.*(12.16C); **3.** *declaration, announcement* σάλπιγγες...πρὸς παράστασιν τῆς τῶν γινομένων ἐκπλήξεως id.*hom.76.4 in Mt.*(7.737B); Cyr.*Ps.*43:10(M.69.1021C); **4.** *demonstration, proof* εἰς π. τῆς ἀληθείας τῶν λόγων Clem.*str.*7.9(p.40.3; M.9.477A); Or.*Jo.*10.45(29; p.224.7; M.14.396C); Eus.*d.e.*7.2(p.330.18; M.22.540B); Bas.*Eun.*1.11(1.224A; M.29.537C); Anast.S.*hod.*12(M.89.196A); **5.** *assurance* εἰς π. τῶν μὴ διορώντων αὐτοῦ τὸ βέβαιον τῆς ἀποκρίσεως Clem.*str.*7.8(p.38.6; M.9.472B); εἰς π. αὐτοῦ ὅτι...ἐκαθαρίσθη Epiph.*haer.*42.3(p.98.21; M.41.700B); **6.** *retinue, escort of attendants*, Call.*v.Hyp.*(p.56).

B. (παρίσταμαι); **1.** *attendance*, hence *service*, ‡Ath.*Apoll.*2.12(M.26.1152B); Flav.Ant.*anath.*4(M.48.951, v.l. παρουσίᾳ); Mac.Aeg.*hom.*37.10(M.34.757A); π. τε καὶ λειτουργία Cyr.*ador.*13(1.476E); Euthal.Diac.*epp.Paul.*(M.85.768C); **2.** of religious services or attendance at prayer νυκτεριναῖς π. καὶ εὐχαῖς Jo.Clim.*scal.*20(M.88.940C); *ib.*(941A); liturg.; **a.** *assembling of ministers* in sanctuary before enarxis εὐχὴ τῆς π. *Lit.Jac.*(Brightman p.31.16); **b.** *attendance of ministers* at altar π. τοῦ ἁγίου θυσιαστηρίου *ib.*(p.184.26); *ib.*(p.186.4); and of congregation at liturgy, Cyr.*ador.*12(1.445A); **3.** *desire, ardour* ἡ πρὸς τὴν παιδείαν ἡμῶν π. Clem.*str.*2.15(p.146.25;

M.8.1000C); *ib.*4.23(p.316.2; 1361A); τὴν κατὰ τῆς ἀσεβείας π. Ath. *apol.sec.*6(p.92.10; M.25.257C); **4.** *courage*, Cyr.*Ps.*26:5(M.69.853B).

παραστατέον, *one must prove, support*, Clem.*str.*5.14(p.384.17; M. 9.129B); Or.*Jo.*1.3(5; p.7.2; M.14.28C); *ib.*2.3(p.55.15; 109C).

παραστάτης, ὁ, 1. *supporter*, of God τὸν τῷ ὄντι π. καὶ σωτῆρα εἴς τε τὸ παρὸν εἴς τε τὸ μέλλον, στρατηγόν τε καὶ ἡγεμόνα πάσης πράξεως Clem.*str.*4.20(p.304.23; M.8.1337C); **2.** *servant, attendant* θεόν...οὗπερ ἡμεῖς ἠξιώμεθα εἶναι π. καὶ λειτουργοί Gr.Naz.*ep.*208(M.37.345A).

παραστατικός, 1. *indicative* αἱ γὰρ εἰκόνες καὶ τὰ σύμβολα π. ὄντα ἑτέρων πραγμάτων Ptol.*ep.*ap.Epiph.*haer.*33.6(p.456.4; M.41.565B); ταῦτα...π. ἂν εἴη τῆς πρώτης αὐτοῦ ἀφίξεως Eus.*Lc.*19:13(M.24. 592D); ὕδατα...τοῦ μεγέθους τῆς δόξης τῆς περὶ τὸν μονογενῆ παραστατικά †Bas.*hom.in Ps.*28(1.359E; M.30.77A); Chrys.*hom.32.1 in Jo.*(8.183D); τὰ μὲν ἑνικῶς λεγόμενα τῆς ταυτότητος τῆς φύσεως παραστατικά Isid.Pel.*epp.*2.143(M.78.589B); ‡Cyr.*Trin.*3(6³.4C; M. 77.1125A); Max.*ambig.*(M.91.1185C); **2.** *confirmatory, proving*, Anat. Laod.*can.pasch.*ap.Eus.*h.e.*7.32.19(M.10.216A); Eus.*qu.Marin. suppl.*2(M.22.985D); ἄλλα τοῦ προβλήματος π. μυρία id.*p.e.*6.6(254C; M.21.432C); **3.** τὰ π. *genitals*, ‡Caes.Naz.*dial.*139(M.38.1045).

παραστέλλω, 1. *throw aside, dismiss*, Thphn.*chron.*p.85(M.108. 257B); **2.** *remove, cut out* by censorship, Thdr.Stud.*epp.*2.15(M.99. 1164B).

παραστήκω, = παρέστηκα, ‡Ath.*hom.in Mt.21*:9(M.28.1033B); Chrys.*hom.23.3 in Rom.*(9.690A); Thdr.Stud.*poen.*1.8(M.99.1733D).

παράστημα, τό, 1. *thing standing by*, Cyr.*glaph.Ex.*3(1.332A); **2.** *courage*, Clem.*str.*4.8(p.274.12; M.8.1269A); of martyrs, Or.*mart.* 23(p.20.28; M.11.592B); τὸ π. τῆς γνώμης Chrys.*hom.46.3 in Gen.*(4. 470E); ψυχῆς π. id.*hom.12.3 in 2Cor.*(10.524A); Cyr.*ador.*10(1.372E); of inspired courage of martyr μετά τινος θείου π. Eus.*m.P.*4(p.915. 2; M.20.1476B); **3.** *fury*, of Devil τὸ ἄγριον...αὐτοῦ τοῦ π. Chrys. *hom.6.4 in Phil.*(11.240B, v.l. παραστῆσαι); **4.** *disposition* of mind, Cyr.*Mich.*55(3.447E); id.*Zach.*64(3.744B).

***παραστίβω,** *tread upon* ἐπὶ τοῖσι παραστίψει πετεηνά †Apoll.*met. Ps.*103:12(M.33.1465C).

παραστίζω, *show, mark out* οὕτω γὰρ ἂν μᾶλλον τὴν πρὸς τὸν οἰκεῖον δεσπότην παραστίσαιμεν εὔνοιαν Jo.D.*hom.*8.14(M.96.721A), perh. for παραστήσ-.

παραστοχάζ-ομαι, 1. *miss*; the point of an argument, †Bas.*Is.* proem.1(1.378C; M.30.120B); Gr.Nyss.*Eun.*3(2 p.42.20; M.45.609C); the truth, id.*hom.2 in Cant.*(M.44.804C); **2.** *miss* deliberately, *ignore* τοῦ θελήματος τῶν ὁρώντων ~όμενος λέγει τὰ πρὸς ἀπάτην †Bas.*Is.* 219(1.543D; M.30.497B).

***παραστράπτω,** *be manifest*, Sophr.H.*mir.Cyr.et Jo.*36(M.87. 3549B).

***παραστρατίζ-ω,** (cf. Lat. *strata*) *deviate* τῆς ~ούσης ὁδοῦ Leont.N. *v.Sym.*5(M.93.1676B).

***παρασυμβουλευτής, ὁ,** *evil adviser*, Thphn.*chron.*p.422(M.108. 1000A).

***παρασυμβουλεύω,** *give evil counsel*, Isid.Pel.*epp.*3.287(M.78. 961C); *Vaticin.*1(p.48).

***παρασύμβουλος, ὁ,** *evil counsellor*, Thphn.*chron.*p.422(M.108. 1000B).

***παρασύναγμα, τό,** *rival assembly*, in opposition to Church ὁ Αἴλουρος ἐξωρίσθη εἰς Γάγγραν. ἐκεῖ δὲ ἀπελθὼν ἐποίει παραβαπτίσματα καὶ π. Thdr.Lect.*exc.Vat.*44(p.59 n.2); π. ποιοῦντες [sc. Origenist monks] Cyr.S.*v.Sab.*84(p.189.27).

***παρασυνάγ-ω, 1.** *hold rival assembly*, i.e. in separation from Church βασιλέων, οἳ τὴν εὐαγῆ καὶ καθολικὴν συγκροτήσαντες θρησκείαν μεγίστοις ἐπιτιμίοις τοὺς ~ειν τολμῶντας ὑποβάλλεσθαι θεσπίζουσιν Marcian.Imp.*ep.Hier.*(p.127.30; H.2.673A); ἀνεφάνη τις Μανιχαῖος ὀνόματι Κέρδων, δογματίζων καὶ ~ων *Chron.Pasch.*p.273 (M.92.677A); Ath.Scholast.*coll.*2.3(p.35); **2.** *hold assembly in opposition to* παρασυνάξαι τῇ ἐκκλησίᾳ ἐσπούδασε Socr.*h.e.*4.29.3(M.67.541B); of Theophronius' separation from Eunomians, *ib.*5.24.3(648C).

παρασυναγωγή, ἡ, *rival assembly*, i.e. congregation formed in separation from Church by insubordinate individual, opp. heresy and schism, Bas.*ep.*188 *can.*1(3.268D; M.32.665A) cit. s. αἵρεσις, referred to by Thdr.Stud.*epp.*1.33(M.99.1017C); χρὴ...μὴ ἐκβαίνειν τοῦ συστήματος τῆς ἐκκλησίας, καὶ καθ' ἑαυτὸν κατάρχειν παρασυναγωγῆς καὶ σχισμάτων †Bas.*hom.in Ps.*28(1.358A; M.30.73A); Phot. *nomoc.*12.1(p.599; M.104.1157A); Αἴλουρος ἤρξατο παρασυναγωγὰς ποιεῖν Thphn.*chron.*p.96(M.108.284B); ref. establishment of Apollinarian congregations, Bas.*ep.*265.2(3.409C; M.985C); Eunomian, Thphn.*chron.*p.61(205B); ref. CCP(754) σύνοδός ἐστιν ὅτε τὰ πέντε πατριαρχεῖα θεσπίσουσι μίαν πίστιν...εἰ δὲ ἐκ τούτων κἂν εἷς ἀπολείψῃ ...αὕτη σύνοδος οὐκ ἔστιν, ἀλλὰ π. ‡Jo.D.*Const.*16(M.95.332D).

παρασύναξις, ἡ, *rival meeting for worship*, in opposition to church congregation ἔφη γὰρ [sc. Nestorius] ὅτι τίνος ἕνεκεν π. ἐποίησας [sc. Philip] καὶ ἐν τῇ οἰκίᾳ προσφορὰν ἐτέλεσας; Cyr.*ep.* 11a(p.172; M.77.89A); Marcian.Imp.*ep.Hier.*(p.127.27; H.2.673A); Epiph.CP *sent.*(p.111.25; M.86.785D).

παρασύρ-ω, 1. *drag along*, of reins; fig., of reason πάντα παρεσύρη ...καὶ ἀνετράπη, τοῦ ἡνιόχου διαφθαρέντος Chrys.*hom.5.1 in Rom.*(9. 460C); id.*hom.17.4 in 1Cor.*(10.150E); hence **2.** *drag into error* χαλινῶν ...ὥστε μὴ ~ῆναι *ib.23.1*(202B); id.*hom.14.2 in 2Cor.*(10.539D); ~εἰς τῇ ἀπάτῃ Philost.*h.e.*9.15(M.65.580C); **3.** *belittle*, Gr.Naz.*ep.*58(M.37. 116A); pass., *suffer calumny*, *ib.*22(57B); ptcpl. pass., *contemptible* τῆς ἐπαράτου καὶ παρασεσυρμένης κενοδοξίας Nil.*epp.*2.49(M.79.221A).

παρασφάλλω, pass., *suffer a lapse* ὀλίγον τι παρασφαλῆναι τὸν δίκαιον Cyr.*Ps.*36:24(M.69.940C).

***παράσφαλος,** neut. as subst., *lapse*, Chrys.ap.Anast.S.*qu.et resp.*8(M.89.401B).

παρασχεδιάζω, *explain roughly* οὕτω...τὸν σταυρὸν καὶ τὸν κύκλον παρεσχεδίασε Gr.Naz.*or.*4.54(M.35.577B).

παρασχεδόν, *almost, practically*, Thdt.*Ps.*73:14(1.1129).

παρασχηματίζω, 1. *disguise* ὁ γὰρ δαίμων...παρεσχημάτισεν ἑαυτὸν εἰς τὸν σωτῆρα Pall.ap.Anast.S.*qu.et resp.*2(M.89.345C), cf. σχηματίζει ἑαυτόν Pall.*h.Laus.*25(p.79.24; M.34.1090D); **2.** *feign* ἕκαστος καὶ τῶν ἀληθῶν καὶ τῶν παρεσχηματισμένων *cat.Apoc.*16:19(p.423.13); **3.** *treat in unseemly fashion*, Mel.*pass.*97 p.16.18.

***παρασχολ-έω,** *divert* μικρόν τι προσήκει παρασχολῆσαι τὸν λόγον εἰς τὴν φυσιολογίαν τοῦ σώματος Gr.Nyss.*or.catech.*37(p.145.2; M.45. 93D); τὸ ἔργον ~εῖ τὴν διάνοιαν τῶν περισσῶν ἐπιθυμιῶν Chrys. *fr.in Pr.*13:3(M.64.696C).

παρασώζω, Thdr.Stud.*epp.*2.215(M.99.1649A for **παρὰ σεσωσμένου**).

***παράταγμα, τό,** *company* π. τῶν ἀγγέλων Hipp.*haer.*5.26(p.128. 27; M.16.3198A).

παράταξις, ἡ, 1. *company* of people, Herm.*sim.*9.6.1; τῆς τῶν... ἀγγέλων π. ἣν οἱ μὲν ὑπὲρ ἡμῶν, οἱ δὲ καθ' ἡμῶν παρατάσσονται Clem. *exc.Thdot.*72(p.130.3; M.9.692C); π. ἁγίων πνευμάτων Mac.Aeg.*hom.* 16.13(M.34.621D); **2.** *equipment* ὀχήματα, καὶ ὀρεοκόμοι, καὶ ἡμίονοι, καὶ πολλὴ τοιαύτη π. Chrys.*hom.85.3 in Mt.*(7.808E); *resources* τὸν πλοῦτον καὶ τὰς π. πάσας Herm.*sim.*1.8; ἐκ π. *deliberately*, *Const. App.*2.23.2; **3.** *struggle* or *resistance*, against evil ἡμῖν...πρὸς πολλά, ...καὶ ὅλον...τὸν βίον ἡ π. Gr.Naz.*ep.*166(M.37.276C); Chrys.*hom. 6.4 in Mt.*(7.94A); ref. Eph.6:11 εἰς π. τῶν μεθοδειῶν τοῦ ἀντικειμένου †Jo.D.*B.J.*19(M.96.1036B); ἐνίσχυσον πρὸς τὰς ἀοράτους π. *ib.*39 (1232B); **4.** *display, pomp* παρατάξει καὶ δόξῃ βασιλικῆς προόδου *Chron.Pasch.*p.287(M.92.716C); *ib.*p.293(733B).

παραταράσσω, *startle, disturb*, Epiph.*haer.*69.33(p.182.13; M.42. 253D).

παράτασις, ἡ, 1. *duration*; of life, Cyr.*Ps.*119:5(M.69.1273A); of punishment, Gr.Nyss.*ep.can.*5(M.45.232B); Chrys.*hom.9.4 in 2Cor.* (10.504C); of anger, Cyr.*ador.*5(1.162A); id.*Jo.*6.1(4.591E); of a prophet's ministry, id.*Os.*1(3.6B); opp. eternity τὴν ἀνθρωπίνην ἐσχατιάν, ἐξ ἧς ὁ ἁπλοῦς Ἰησοῦς συνετέθη, καὶ π. εἴληφε χρονικὴν ὁ ἀΐδιος Dion.Ar.*d.n.*1.4(M.3.592A); τὴν ὅλην...ἔσθ' ὅτε τοῦ καθ' ἡμᾶς χρόνου π. αἰῶνα προσαγορεύει *ib.*10.3(937C); **2.** *long duration* ἐν...π. τῆς προσευχῆς νομίζοντες δικαιοῦσθαι †Bas.*Is.*36(1.408E; M.30.189C); **3.** *prolongation* of time, *delay*, Gr.Nyss.*tres dii*(M.45.129B) cit. s. βούλημα; **4.** *direction* of prayer towards God, *aspiration*, Evagr. Pont.*or.*44(M.79.1176C).

παρατάσσω, med., *be ready for campaign, stand prepared*; of the Twelve πάσῃ τῇ διαβολικῇ πλάνῃ παρετάξαντο Didym.*Trin.*2.18 (M.39.728A); πρὸς πάντα παραταξάμενοι Chrys.*hom.10.4 in Ac.*(10. 85E); εἰς τὴν οἰκουμένην πᾶσαν παρατάξασθαι id.*hom.4.4 in 1Cor.*(10. 29D).

παρατατικός, 1. *with extension in time*, opp. things eternal ἵνα μή τινι π. νοήματι τῆς ἀρχῆς διαζεύξῃ τὸν λόγον Gr.Nyss.*Eun.*4(2 p.53. 23; M.45.624B); **2.** neut. as subst., *extension* τῷ π. τοῦ προστάγματος id.*hom.8 in Cant.*(M.44.944A).

παρατείνω, 1. *extend*, Gr.Mag.*dial.*(tr.Zach.)4.24(M.*PL.*77.355B); Anast.Ant.*redit.*(p.251); pass., denied of divine οὐσία, Epiph.*haer.* 76.49(p.403.26; M.42.620C) cit. s. πλατύνω; **2.** *apply* oneself to, Gr. Mag.*dial.*(tr.Zach.)3.1(M.*PL.*77.215D); **3.** *continue, go on* doing, Dion.Al.*ep.can.*(p.100.4; M.10.1276C); Cyr.H.*procatech.*10; Thphyl. *exc.gent.*3(p.480.10; M.113.940B).

παρατετηρημένως, 1. *carefully, scrupulously* τὴν ἑβδομάδα τοῦ ἁγίου πάσχα π. φύλασσε ‡Ath.*syntag.*2(p.123; M.28.837C); Nil.*exerc.* 57(M.79.789B); of language, Clem.*str.*3.9(p.225.19; M.8.1165C); Gr. Nyss.*tres dii*(M.45.132D); Bas.*ep.*45(3.134B; M.32.368B); **2.** *deliberately*, Or.*Jo.*13.30(29; p.254.25; M.14.452B); Gr.Nyss.*tres dii*(M.45.

132D); **3.** *with exactitude* πάνυ...π. καὶ οὐχ ὡς Ἑλληνικὴν ἀκριβολογίαν οὐκ ἐπιστάμενος Or.*Jo.*2.2(p.54.12; 108B); Bas.*hex.*6.7(1.56E; M.29.133A); ἐξειλεγμένως καὶ π. id.*reg.fus.*45(2.392D; M.31.1033B); οὐδὲν ...π. καὶ ἀποκεκληρωμένως φθέγγεται ἡ θεία γραφή Chrys.*hom.14.2 in Gen.*(4.108B); **4.** *critically*, opp. ἀδιακρίτως, Didym.(‡Bas.)*Eun.*4 (1.294E; M.29.708B).

παρατήρησις, ἡ, 1. *investigation, examination* π. καὶ ἐξετάσεων Or.*Jo.*13.63(60; p.296.11; M.14.521A); δεῖ τινος ἀκριβεστέρας π. ἡμῖν Eun.*apol.*7(M.30.841D); Thphl.Al.*ep.pasch.proem.*(M.65.52B); *discernment* of good and evil, *Lit.*ap.*Const.App.*8.12.17; **2.** *exactitude, careful expression* μετὰ παρατηρήσεως ἐσήμανεν Ath.*Ar.*2.12(M.26.172B); *ib.*2.44(241B); ὅρα τῆς θείας γραφῆς τὴν π. Chrys.*hom.53.3 in Gen.*(4.517E); *concern, circumspection* ἡ π. ... μὴ περὶ τόπον ἔστω, ἀλλὰ περὶ τὸν τρόπον τῆς εὐχῆς id.*hom.8.1 in 1Tim.*(11.590A); ἄλλο ...κρίμα τοῦ μετὰ π. ἁμαρτάνοντος παρὰ τὸν ἀναισχύντως ἑαυτὸν τῇ ἁμαρτίᾳ ἐκδιδόντα ‡Ath.*qu.Ant.*97(M.28.657A); **3.** superstitious *observation* of portents etc., Gr.Nyss.*fat.*(M.45.164A); π. φυλάττουσι, καὶ κληδονισμοῖς καὶ οἰωνοῖς...κέχρηνται Chrys.*hom.4.6 in 1Cor.*(10.32B); γένεσιν, εἱμαρμένην, π., κληδονισμούς id.*hom.3.3 in 1Tim.*(11.565A); **4.** of Jewish ritual *observance* in gen., *Const.App.* 6.30.7; τὰς τῶν βρωμάτων π. Chrys.*hom.53.3 in Mt.*(7.541E); ref. Mt.15:1ff. ὅτε...ἔδει...αὐτοὺς ἀπαλλαγῆναι τῶν παρατηρήσεων,...τότε αὐτοὺς μᾶλλον πλείοσιν ἔδησαν ταῖς π. *ib.51.1*(520C); **5.** *keeping* of times and seasons, †Bas.*bapt.*1.2.5(2.632D; M.31.1533B); τῆς νομιζομένης ταύτης μικρᾶς π. [sc. τοῦ πάσχα] Chrys.*hom.12.1 in Gen.*(4.91D); **6.** *system of observances* ἀποπηδήσαντες...τῆς τε τῶν ἰδίων θελημάτων συνηθείας, καὶ τῆς τῶν ἀνθρωπίνων παραδόσεων π. Bas.*jud.*8(2.223B; M.31.676B); τῆς π. ... τῆς Ἰουδαϊκῆς Chrys.*paralyt.*6 (3.43C); Euthal.Diac.*epp.Paul.*(M.85.704B); Jo.Philop.*pasch.*(p.210.9); *ib.*(p.210.17); in Christian practice ἡ περὶ τῆς...θρησκείας ἀκριβὴς π. Const.ap.Eus.*v.C.*2.24(p.51.8; M.20.1001B); εἰ δεῖ παρατηρεῖν, ἔστι παρατηρεῖσθαι ὅθεν ὠφέλεια τοῖς παρατηροῦσιν ἔσται. καλὴ π. κακίας ἀποφυγή, καρδίας εὐθύτης, εὐσέβεια εἰς θεόν, πίστις ὀρθή. ... μία ἐστὶ π. τὸ ἁμαρτίας ἀπέχεσθαι Chrys.*hom.33.3 in Heb.*(12.307B).

παρατίθ-ημι, *set beside*; hence **1.** *bring* to, *furnish* μὴ νηπίοις... βλάβην παραθῶ Ign.*Trall.*5.1; **2.** *bring* into, *expose* to εἰς καταφρόνησιν ~έναι τὰ οὕτω μεγάλα Vict.*Mc.*4:34(p.311.17); **3.** *set beside* for comparison, Eus.*d.e.*9.17(p.440.28; M.22.709B); med., Clem.*prot.*8 (p.59.27; M.8.188B); **4.** *adduce, allege* ταῦτα δὲ ἡμῖν...~εται τῶν γραφῶν id.*paed.*3.12(p.284.2; M.8.665B); πολλάκις τὴν αὐτὴν ~εσθαι γραφὴν εἰς ἐντροπὴν Μαρκίωνος id.*str.*4.8(p.278.19; M.8.1277B); *ib.*4.26(p.321.6; 1373B); Or.*princ.*3.1.7(p.204.10; M.11.260A); Eus.*h.e.*2.11.1(M.20.161C); Ath.*Ar.*3.50(M.26.429A); **5.** *commit, entrust* for keeping, Herm.*sim.*9.10.6; Gr.Thaum.*pan.Or.*14(p.33.12; M.10.1093A); τὰ νόμιμα ~εται Gr.Nyss.*v.Mos.*(M.44.321B); Pamph.Mon.*Soter.*2(p.116.3); **6.** *commend, introduce* a person by letter, *Ep.Lugd.* ap.Eus.*h.e.*5.4.2(M.20.440A); βουλόμενοι ὑμῖν ἑαυτοὺς συνιστᾶν καὶ ~εσθαι *cat.2Cor.*3:1(p.364.21); Chrys.*hom.13.3 in Phil.*(11.301B); ταῖς...εὐχαῖς ἑαυτὸν...~έμενος Gr.Mag.*dial.*(tr.Zach.)3.14(M.*PL.*77.247B); παραθέσεις δὲ τὰς ἐπὶ τοῖς κατηχουμένοις εὐχάς, δι' ὧν ~ενται τῷ θεῷ *Schol.* in CCarth.*can.*103(*Mon.*2 p.650).

***παράτιλσις, ἡ,** *plucking out* of hairs, Clem.*paed.*2.10(p.219.22; M.8.521A); *ib.*3.11(p.270.23; 636A).

***παρατιλτέον,** *one must pluck out* hairs, Clem.*paed.*3.3(p.246.26; M.8.594B).

παρατιτρώσκ-ω, 1. *do violence to, hurt* ~ουσι τοῦτο μὲν τὸ θέλημα τοῦ πατρός...τοῦτο δὲ τὴν παράδοσιν τοῦ υἱοῦ Didym.*Trin.*1.34(M.39.436B); Leo Mag.*ep.*45.1(p.47.23; M.*PL.*54.834B); **2.** *violate* decrees etc., Socr.*h.e.*1.37.5(M.67.176A); CCP(449)*act.*(p.151.24; H.2.176D); abs., Didym.*Trin.*2.2(M.39.624B); *ib.*2.11(665A); **3.** *remove violently* from text ἀξιοῦμεν μηδόλως τὴν φωνὴν...ἐκβληθῆναι, ἢ παρατρωθῆναι τῶν ὑπομνημάτων CCP(449)*act.*(p.171.1; H.2.201C).

***παράτοπος,** *amiss* οὐδὲν π. διαπράττεται *A.Thom.*A 85(p.201.27).

***παρατραπέζιον, τό,** *credence-table* μετὰ τὸ ἐκ τῶν π. καὶ τὴν διάδοσιν ἀποτεθῆναι πάντα εἰς τὴν ἁγίαν τράπεζαν *Chron.Pasch.*p.390 (M.92.1001C).

***παρατράπεζον, τό,** = foreg., *Lit.Jac.*(p.234.12).

***παρατραυλίζω,** *lisp feebly*, Mac.Mgn.*apocr.*3.43(p.150.22).

***παρατραχύνω,** *roughen*, Bas.*ep.*14.2(3.94A; M.32.277A); Gr. Nyss.*Eun.*12(1 p.271.19; M.45.977B).

παρατρέπ-ω, 1. trans., *turn aside, off*, or *away, divert*; **a.** from the straight οἴνῳ...ἀμέτρῳ...ὀφθαλμοί...~ονται Clem.*paed.*2.2(p.170.17; M.8.416B); out of course πάντα παρεσύρη...καὶ ἀνετράπη Chrys.*hom.5.1 in Rom.*(9.460C, v.l. καὶ παρετράπη); **b.** from truth, *pervert, distort* ~οντες τὰς ἑρμηνείας Iren.*haer.*1.3.6(M.7.477A); λέγει...τὸν Ἀστέριον παρατρέψαι τὸ φρόνημα Philost.*h.e.*2.15(M.65.477B); **c.** from good, Tat.*orat.*16(p.17.21; M.6.840C); from worship of God, *ib.*17 (p.19.12; 844B); from salvation, Clem.*prot.*10(p.70.20; M.8.209B); justice, Gr.Nyss.*or.catech.*26(p.97.9; M.45.68B); Just.*2apol.*7.9(M.6.456C; παρὰ τρεπόμενα Goodspeed); **d.** in the direction of good τίς δ' ἂν μὴ παρατραπείη ἐκ τῆς...τοῦ Ἰησοῦ μαρτυρίας...ἡκεῖν...καὶ μαθητεύεσθαι αὐτῷ; Or.*fr.78 in Jo.*11:2(p.544.31); **2.** pass. intrans., *turn aside, err*; **a.** from the straight, fig. ὁ τῆς εὐθείας καὶ βασιλικῆς παρατραπεὶς ὁδοῦ Eus.*e.th.*3.13(p.148.3; M.24.985C); οὐ γὰρ τεταγμένα βαδίζουσιν ἐν τῇ φάλαγγι, ἀλλὰ παράφορα, καὶ ~ονται Chrys.*hom.10.2 in 1Thess.*(11.496F, v.l. περιτρέπ-); *be distraught, wander in*, or *be driven out of, one's wits* τὰς φρένας παρατραπέντα Eus.*Hierocl.*35(534D; M.22.848B); **b.** from truth, *be in error, err*, Clem.*prot.*4(p.48.19; M.8.164B); **c.** from good, Iren.*haer.*1.2.2(M.7.453A); Mac.Aeg.*carit.*28(M.34.932A); τὸ κατὰ φύσιν ~όμενον οὐκ ἐκώλυσεν [sc. ὁ νόμος], διὰ τὸ μὴ ἀγαν εἰς τὸ παρὰ φύσιν ἐμπεσεῖν τοὺς ἀνθρώπους Vict.*Mc.*10:3ff.(p.374.5); of fallen human nature, Gr.Nyss.*or.catech.*12(p.59.6; M.45.44D); **3.** theol. οἴεσθαι...γένεσιν μὲν ἀνήνασθαι τὴν διὰ τῆς ἁγίας παρθένου τὸν...λόγον...παρατετράφθαι δὲ μᾶλλον αὐτὸν εἰς τὴν ἀπὸ γῆς σάρκα Cyr.*inc.unigen.*(5^1.682D) = id.*Thds.*(p.48.5; 5^2.8D).

***παρατρεχόντως,** *cursorily*, Didym.*Rom.*7(p.3.2); Cyr.*thes.*15 (5^1.158A).

παρατρέχ-ω, A. intrans.; **1.** *move over* or *across* τοῦτο τὸ ὄρνεον ~ει τῷ ἡλίῳ *Apoc.Bar.*6(p.88.26); **2.** *pass away, be fleeting* οὐ γινώσκετε ~οντας μὲν ὑμᾶς, ἑστῶτα δὲ τὸν αἰῶνα, μέχρις ἂν αὐτὸν ὁ ποιήσας εἶναι θελήσῃ Tat.*orat.*26(p.27.26; M.6.861B); Chrys.*hom.15.5 in Mt.*(7.191A); of time παραδραμόντος...μεταδιώκειν ἀνήνυτον Isid.Pel.*epp.*5.266(M.78.1492C); ~ει...ὁ πλοῦτος Cyr.*Ps.*61:11(M.69.1117D); **3.** *sink into oblivion* μὴ λάθοι...μηδὲ...παραδράμοι διὰ σιωπῆς συγκαλυφθεῖσα Gr.Nyss.*v.Macr.*(p.371.19; M.46.960B); **4.** *be cursory* σύντομον καὶ ~ουσαν τὴν καταγγελίαν πεποίηται [sc. Μάρκος] Iren.*haer.*3.11.8(M.7.888B); ὡς ἄν τις ἐν κεφαλαίῳ καὶ ~ων εἴποι Chrys.*hom.1.1 in 2Cor.*(10.418E); **5.** *be introduced, prevail* ἡ συνήθεια ἐν τῇ ἐκκλησίᾳ παρέδραμεν, ὥστε τοὺς παῖδας ἔμπροσθεν τοῦ ἁγίου ἱερατείου ἵστασθαι ἐν ταῖς ἁγίαις συνάξεσιν, καὶ πρώτους μετὰ τοὺς κληρικοὺς τῶν ἁγίων μεταλαμβάνειν μυστηρίων Jo.Mosch.*prat.*196 (M.87.3081B); cf. ἡ...ἐκκλησία...πανταχοῦ ~ει Chrys.*Eutrop.*3.1(3.382B); **6.** *go the wrong way* ψὶξ παραδραμοῦσα Gr.Naz.*or.*40.14(M.36.376D); **7.** *come from, spring from* χλεύης καὶ ἀπάτης τὰ ἐκείνου παρέδραμε ῥήματα Eulog.*fr.Novat.*(M.104.340A).

B. trans.; **1.** *overlook*; **a.** accidentally τὰ μεγάλα ἀεὶ ~οντες Chrys.*hom.51.1 in Mt.*(7.521A); *miss* παρεδράμετε τὴν ἑαυτῶν σωτηρίαν *M.Thdot.*3(p.140.20); **b.** deliberately, *pass over lightly* ὅπως μὴ παραδράμῃς ἀδακρυτὶ τὸν λόγον Gr.Naz.*ep.*29(M.37.64C); Chrys.*hom.15.1 in 1Cor.*(10.125D); *ib.31.2*(279D); *leave unnoted* μὴ παραδράμῃς...ἀνιστόρητον Gr.Nyss.*v.Macr.*(p.405.1; M.46.989D); Chrys.*hom.13.2 in Mt.*(7.169D); freq. of neglecting the poor, Bas.*hom.*8.2 (2.64A; M.31.309B); Chrys.*hom.13.4 in 2Cor.*(10.536A); id.*hom.11.3 in Heb.*(12.116C); of neglecting or violating an undertaking ἐπαγγελίαν παραδραμών Thdt.*h.rel.*26(3.1277); of indifference to one's own welfare, Chrys.*hom.60.1 in Jo.*(8.351D); of overlooking, condoning sin, id.*Eutrop.*1.5(3.385E); **2.** *put into short form*, Chrys.*hom.14.3 in Mt.*(7.181C); id.*hom.31.2 in 1Cor.*(10.279C); **3.** *spend* time τὸ ἑβδομαδικὸν διάστημα ~οντες ἄσιτοι ‡Nil.*narr.*3(M.79.617A).

παρατριβή, ἡ, 1. *friction*; **a.** of violent jostling ἐκ τῆς π. πολλοὺς ἀποθανεῖν Socr.*h.e.*4.29.6(M.67.541C); **b.** of coition (ref. Ebionite views on birth of Christ) ἐκ π. καὶ σπέρματος ἀνδρός Epiph.*haer.*30.2(p.334.8; M.41.408A); *ib.*51.2(p.250.3; 889C); **2.** *straying from the path, aberration*, of heresies ὑμεῖς ταῖς ὁμοίαις χρώμενοι π., λαλεῖτε τὰ μὴ γεγραμμένα, ἐκτρέποντες τοὺς ἀστηρίκτους ‡Ath.*Apoll.*2.19(M.26.1165A).

παρατρίβω, *rub*, in phrase παρατρῖψαι τὸ μέτωπον *be lost to shame* (cf. Lat. *perfricare frontem*), Epiph.*haer.*51.6(p.255.24; M.41.897C); *ib.*69.59(p.207.3; M.42.296C).

παράτριμμα, τό, *titbit, delicacy*, ‡Nil.*narr.*3(M.79.616A).

παρατροπή, ἡ, 1. act. sense; **a.** *turning away*, hence *alteration*, Eus.*v.C.*3.5(p.79.15; M.20.1060A); **b.** *perversion* of truth αὐτῶν τὰ σοφίσματα καὶ τῆς π. τὰ νοήματα· καὶ οὐκ ἔστιν εἰς ὃ λόγος αὐτῶν· πολλαὶ γὰρ τῆς ἀπιστίας αἱ π. ἀνθρωπίνοις λογισμοῖς ἐπινενοημέναι ‡Ath.*Apoll.*1.3(M.26.1096C); τὴν ἐπὶ τὰ ἐναντία τοῦ λόγου π. οὐχ ὁρῶσιν Gr.Nyss.*Eun.*4(2 p.73.18; M.45.645D); ἀγαλματικὰ εἴδωλα τὰς σεπτὰς εἰκόνας καλέσαντες...ὢ τῆς π. ‡Jo.D.*ep.Thphl.*14(M.95.364A); by a misquotation Νικολάῳ...ἀπομνημόνευμά τι τἀνδρὸς φέροντες ἐκ π. Clem.*str.*2.20(p.177.3; M.8.1061B); of the good ὥστε μηδὲν εἶναι φαῦλον παρὰ τὴν π. τοῦ καλοῦ ‡Just.*qu.et resp.*46(M.6.

1292C); of justice, Cyr.*Soph*.30(3.607E); **c.** *misleading, deception* by the Devil, Chrys.*hom*.4.1 *in 1Thess*.(11.452D); **2.** pass. sense; **a.** s.v.l., = τροπή, *metaphor, simile* ἦν...αἰπόλος, καὶ πεποίηται τὴν π. ὡς ἐκ τοῦ καταφθείρεσθαι πολλάκις τὰς τῶν θρεμμάτων νομὰς Cyr.*Am*. 3(3.252C cj. τροπήν); **b.** *deviation, declension* ἑκουσίου τῆς π. παρὰ τὸ ὀρθόν Clem.*str*.6.15(p.497.12; M.9.353A); τὴν...π. τῶν ἐν ἡμῖν στοιχείων τινός, ἀρχὴν καὶ αἰτίαν τῆς κατὰ τὸ πάθος συστάσεως διωρίζετο Gr.Nyss.*or.dom*.4(p.66.23; M.44.1161A); π. ... καὶ ἁμαρτία τοῦ τοιούτου μέρους ἐστὶν [sc. τοῦ ἐπιθυμητικοῦ] ὅταν τις μεταγάγῃ τὴν ἐπιθυμίαν πρὸς τὴν ἀνυπόστατον κενοδοξίαν id.*ep.can*.(M.45.225A); in moral sphere καὶ τῶν τοῦ σωτῆρος μαθητῶν ἴσμεν τινὰς ἐξ αὐτεξουσίου π. ἀποσφαλέντας Eus.*d.e*.1.9(p.41.36; M.22.80D); τριῶν αἰτιῶν θεωρουμένων ἐξ ὧν πᾶσα ἀποτελεῖται ἐνέργεια· ἡ μὲν γάρ ἐστιν ἐκ φυσικῆς δυνάμεως, ἡ δὲ ἐκ π. τῆς κατὰ φύσιν ἕξεως, ἡ δὲ...ὑπὲρ φύσιν ἐστί Leont.B.*Nest.et Eut*.2(M.86.1333A); ἡ μὲν π. τοῦ ἀγαθοῦ ἀρχὴ γίνεται τοῦ κακοῦ *Disp.Phot*.32f.(M.88.565A); εἴ τις λέγει...τοὺς ἀστέρας...ἐκ π. τῆς ἐπὶ τὸ χεῖρον γεγονέναι τοῦτο ὅπερ ἐστίν, ἀ. ἔ. CCP(543)*anath*.3; **c.** of Fall οὐδὲ...φύσεως ἂν εἴη δημιουργὸς ὁ διάβολος...ἀλλὰ φύσεως (edd. προθέσεως) παρατροπὴν ἐκ παραβάσεως εἰργάσατο ‡Ath.*Apoll*.1.15(M.26.1120C); Cyr.*Ps*.50:12(M.69.1100A); abs. ὥσπερ τὴν π. ἐθεάσατο [sc. God], οὕτω καὶ τὴν ἀνάκλησιν αὐτοῦ πάλιν τὴν πρὸς τὸ ἀγαθὸν κατενόησε Gr.Nyss.*or.catech*.8(p.49.16; M. 45.37C); †Cyr.*Heb*.2:9(p.391.7n.); of demons π. ... ἐστιν αὐτοῖς τὸ κακὸν καὶ τῶν προσηκόντων αὐτοῖς ἔκβασις Dion.Ar.*d.n*.4.23(M.3. 725B); Thdt.*affect*.3(p.97.9; 4.789) cit. s. δαίμων; **d.** state of *perversion, degeneracy* ὡς μήτε...γινώσκειν θεόν...εἰς ἀλόγου...ζῴου σχεδὸν ὅσον παρατροπὴν ἥκοντος Eus.*p.e*.13.3(649A; M.21.1077A); **3.** theol. οὔτ' οὖν τὸ θεῖον ἐν παρατροπαῖς γένοιτ' ἄν ποτε τῆς ἰδίας ἑδραιότητος ἐξωσθὲν ὑπό του τῶν παθῶν Cyr.*inc.unigen*.(5^1.683E); εἴπερ ἐστὶν ἀληθές, ὅτι τὸ εἶναί τι παρατροπῆς οὐκ ἔχει...διαβήσεται που πάντως καὶ εἰς αὐτὸν τὸν πατέρα καὶ εἰς τὸ πνεῦμα τὸ ἅγιον τῆς δυσφημίας ἡ δύναμις id.*synous*.2(p.478.11); σὰρξ...ἐγένετο...καὶ οὐκ εἰς σάρκα μεταχωρήσας ἐκ π. id.*Jo*.4.3(4.375E); id.*inc.unigen*.(5^1.713D); cf. ὁ θεὸς...ἄνθρωπον ἐξ ἡμῶν ἕνα λαβὼν...εἰς οὐρανὸν ἀνήγαγεν ἑαυτῷ συνάψας, ἵνα...φοβερός τε καὶ ἀνεπιβούλευτος ᾖ τοῖς ἐναντίοις ἅτε μηδεμίαν π. ἢ ἀλλοίωσιν ὑπομένειν οἷός τε ὢν Thdr.Mops.ap.Jo. Philop.*opif*.6.10(p.248.2).

***παρατροχάω**, *pass by*, Gr.Naz.*carm*.2.1.1.190(M.37.984A).

παρατρύζ-ω, **1.** *utter an occasional note of* ~ουσιν ἔσθ' ὅτε τὸ ἀληθὲς ἐπιπλέκοντες αὐτῷ τὸ ψεῦδος Cyr.*Juln*.1(6^2.14C); **2.** *chatter in opposition* ~έτωσαν τὸ δοκοῦν *ib*.10(361E).

***παρατρύνω**, Cyr.ap.*cat.Rom*.7:8(p.169.19) for παροτρυνομένους id.*Rom*.7:8(p.198.3).

***παρατρυφάω**, *live luxuriously* amongst, Gr.Naz.*or*.43.60(M.36. 576A).

***παράτρωσις, ἡ**, *misdeed*, Sophr.H.*v.Cyr.et Jo*.38(M.87.3569B).

παρατυπ-όω, *counterfeit, adulterate* τὰς σημαντικὰς τῆς θείας φύσεως λέξεις...εἰς ὀνομάτων σχῆμα ~ούσης Gr.Nyss.*Eun*.3(2 p.38. 7; M.45.605A); ὁ λόγος τῆς πίστεως παρατετυπωμένος ἐστί Cyr.*Ps*. 11:7(M.69.797C); cf.Proc.G.*Is*.1:21–23(M.87.1860A).

***παραϋάλια, τά**, ? *defences* καὶ αὐτὴ [sc. ἡ Κρήτη] ἐκ νοτίου μέρους ἀναφραγήσεται καὶ τὸ ἔθνος περιπατήσει καὶ πρὸ τούτου τὰ παραϋάλια αὐτῆς οὐαί *Apoc.Dan*.C suppl.(p.121.14).

***παραυλακιστής, ὁ**, *one who encroaches, wrongfully extends his boundaries*, †Jo.Jej.*serm*.(M.88.1924C).

***παραυξάνω**, *grow gradually*, *Apoc.Bar*.9(p.91.8); Hipp.*haer*.7.22 (p.197.23; M.16.3306A); of arithmetical progression, *increase*, Anat. Laod.*decad*.(p.35).

παραύξησις, ἡ, **1.** *increase*; of numerical addition of one figure to another, Iren.*haer*.1.16.2(M.7.633A); of progress in spiritual life φόβος...κατὰ π. πίστις γενόμενος Clem.*str*.2.12(p.142.6; M.8.992A); Const.*or.s.c*.20(p.184.27; M.20.1297A); **2.** *preferment, increase of dignity*, Isid.Pel.*epp*.3.152(M.78.844C).

παραυτίκα, ? prepositionally, *after* τὰ π. τῆς...ἐπιβουλῆς Eus.*h.e*. 1.1.2(π., τῆς M.20.49A); τὸ π. τοῦ γενέσθαι οὐρανόν Didym.*Trin*.2.7 (M.39.568B).

παραφαίνω, pass., *be glimpsed*, Gr.Naz.*ep*.51(M.37.105A).

παραφαιρέω, *take away*; pass., Gr.Nyss.*infant*.(M.46.168D).

***παραφανίζω**, *make to disappear, do away with*, Thdr.Mops. *Gal*.4:1(p.61.30; M.66.908A); pass., Ath.*inc*.8.2(M.25.109B); Aët.ap. Epiph.*haer*.76.21(p.368.3; M.42.557C).

***παραφείδομαι**, *spare*, Sophr.H.*v.Anast*.(M.92.1684D).

παραφέρ-ω, **1.** *carry along* ~οντα [sc. ποταμόν] καὶ παρασύροντα Clem.*str*.1.19(p.62.5; M.8.813A); id.*ecl*.5(p.138.17; M.9.701A); *move* δεῖ τὸν πρὸ πάντων ὄντα...μὴ κτίσμα κατὰ σύγκρισιν νοεῖσθαι τῶν παρ' αὐτοῦ παροισθέντων Didym.*Trin*.1.15(M.39.328B); οἶδά σε κύριον καὶ παρενεγκόντα πρὸς σὲ ἥλιον καὶ σελήνην Cyr.*Ps*.8:5(M.69.760B); **2.** *advance, promote*, id.*ador*.13(1.472D); **3.** *induce* παρενεγκούσης εἰς τὸ πείθεσθαι Or.*Ps*.65:3(p.76); **4.** *offer, present*, Cyr.*ador*.16(1.563D); **5.** *introduce* a character, Just.*1apol*.36.2(M.6.385B); **6.** *adduce*, *ib*. 54.10(412A); Chrys.*hom*.3.2 *in Mt*.(7.36A); Cyr.*Jo*.6(4.563D).

***παραφθαρτικός**, *corrupting* τὸ τοῦ θεοειδοῦς π. Dion.Ar.*d.n*.1.3 (M.3.589B).

παράφθεγμα, τό, *mis-statement*, Epiph.*haer*.48.13(p.238.18; M.41. 877A).

παραφθείρ-ω, **1.** *corrupt* or *distort* evidence or text, Epiph.*anc*. 101(p.121.31; M.43.200A); Cyr.*ep*.39(p.20.7,10; 5^2.109A); *lead astray, corrupt* persons ἐπὶ κλοπάς τινας...αὐτὸν παραφθείραντες Anast.S. *Ps*.6(M.89.1108B); ref. 1Cor.15:33 κακαῖς ~ων ὁμιλίαις Cyr.*ador*.5(1. 152B); pass. ptcpl., *insincere* νόθην τινὰ καὶ παρεφθαρμένην νοσοῦντες εὐλάβειαν id.*inc.unigen*.(5^1.679A); **2.** *transgress* ~ειν τὸ δίκαιον Chrys.*hom*.39.4 *in Jo*.(8.233B); id.*hom*.3.4 *in Heb*.(12.31D); of the laws of priesthood, *ib*.8.1(82C); of cheating at games ~ας...ἀγῶνα Epiph.*haer*.61.7(p.387.18; M.41.1049A).

***παραφί-ω**, *be neglectful* οὐδέποτε ~οντες ἢ παραμελοῦντες...τῆς συναγωγῆς *Const.App*.2.60.3.

***παραφλέγ-ω**, **1.** *burn*, Rom.Mel.(*AS* 1 p.161); **2.** pass., *catch fire* ἐν ταῖς παρατρίψεσι...τοῦ μὲν [sc. ἀνίκμου καὶ ξηροῦ] ~ομένου, τοῦ δὲ [sc. διαβρόχου] παρολισθαίνοντος ‡Caes.Naz.*dial*.57(M.38.925).

***παραφλυάρημα, τό**, *nonsense, wild statement*, Nil.*epp*.1.112(M. 79.132A).

παράφορος, **1.** *led astray, wrong-minded, mad*; freq. of heretics, Sophr.H.*ep.syn*.(M.87.3164A); *ib*.(3181B); **2.** *leading astray* π. δαιμόνων Tat.*orat*.12(p.14.7; M.6.833A).

***παραφοσεύω (*-φωσεύω)**, (cf. Lat.*fossa*) *encamp* by, *circumvallate* παρεφόσευσε τῷ κάστρῳ φυλάττων τὴν ἄνοδον αὐτοῦ Jo.Mal.*chron*. 18 p.469(M.98.684B); ἔφυγεν εἰς Κάρρας τὴν πόλιν. καὶ παραφωσεύσαντες οἱ Πέρσαι ἔλαβον αὐτὸν αἰχμάλωτον *Chron.Pasch*.p.274(M.92.680A); παρὰ τὸν...ποταμὸν παραφωσεύει Thphn.*chron*.p.280(M.108.692A).

παραφρον-έω, *suppose wrongly* ὑπόστασιν τοῦ κακοῦ ~οῦσιν εἶναι Ath.*gent*.6(M.25.13A).

***παραφρόνημα, τό**, *aberration* πᾶσα αἵρεσις...μυστήρια ὀνομάζει τὰ π. Nil.*epp*.1.117(M.79.133C).

***παραφυάδιος**, *like an offshoot, adventitious*, *Barn*.4.5 citing Dan.7:8.

***παραφυκισμός, ὁ**, *rouging* the face as a form of ἀπάτη: παραφυκισμῶν καὶ ψιμυθισμοῦ καὶ βαφῆς τριχῶν Clem.*paed*.2.10(p.219.23; M.8.521A).

***παραφύλαγμα, τό**, **1.** *something* (*someone*) *to guard against, to be shunned* ἴσως π. γενόμενος ἐντραπήσεται Bas.*ep*.287(3.426D; M.32. 1024B); **2.** *observance, tradition* ἐν τῇ πρὸς Κολοσσαεῖς...φησὶ...σκιὰν εἶναι τὰ π. Socr.*h.e*.5.22.5(M.67.625C).

παραφυλακή, ἡ, **1.** *guarding against* τοῦ...ἄγους τὴν π. ἐποιήσαντο Gr.Nyss.*ep.can*.(M.45.229D); **2.** *abstinence from* τῶν τοιῶνδε τροφῶν π. Eus.*h.e*.1.4(M.20.77C); Bas.*ascet*.2.2(2.326C; M.31.888A); **3.** *observance* of laws, rules ὁ κύριος διδάσκει ζωῆς κληρονομίαν εἶναι τὴν π. τοῦ νόμου Epiph.*haer*.66.69(p.110.5; M.42.137D); παραφυλακῇ ἐνταλμάτων id.*exp.fid*.21(p.522.4; M.42.824A); of festivals τῇ τοῦ πάσχα...π. Petr.I Al.*fr*.(M.18.516D); **4.** *guardianship*, Clem.*q.d.s*.42 (p.188.17; M.9.648C).

παραφύλαξ, ὁ, *warder*, *A.Pil*.A 12.1(p.252); Thdr.Stud.*epp*.2.38 (M.99.1232B).

***παραφύλαξις, ἡ**, *observance* ἐξουσία...τοῦ ἀκολουθεῖν καὶ αἱρεῖσθαι τὴν τῶν Χριστιανῶν π. ἢ θρησκείαν Const.ap.Eus.*h.e*.10.5.5(M.20. 881B).

παραφυλάσσ-ω, **1.** *guard, preserve* ~έσθωσαν ἄχραντον κοινωνίαν †Jo.Jej.*serm*.(M.88.1929D); *be kept in confinement* ἐξομολογούμενος παραφυλάξεται Bas.*ep*.217 *can*.63(3.327B; M.32.800A); **2.** *guard against, avoid*, Clem.*paed*.1.3(p.95.10; M.8.260A); Isid.Pel.*epp*.2.211 (M.78.652A); **3.** *take care* to τίς...ἂν [τι] παραφυλάξαιτο...μὴ οὐχὶ ἀποκλῖναι τὸν ἴσον κίνδυνον; Clem.*paed*.3.8(p.261.29; ἀντιπαραφυλάξαιτο M.8.613C); **4.** *observe* rules or rites; pass., Eus.*p.e*.10.4 (469C; M.21.781A); abs., *be obedient* παρεφυλαξάμην καὶ οὐχ ἥμαρτον *T.Reub*.4.4; seasons, festivals σελήνης τὴν τεσσαρεσκαιδεκάτην...π. Eus.*h.e*.5.23.1(M.20.492A); Socr.*h.e*.5.22.76(M.67.644C); omens πτήσεις...ὀρνίθων παρεφυλάξαντο πρῶτοι Φρύγες Clem.*str*.1.16(p.48.6; M.8.784B).

παραφυσ-άω, *blow along* ἡμεῖς...οἱ νήπιοι τοὺς ~ῶντας εἰς φυσίωσιν φυλαξάμενοι τῶν αἱρέσεων ἀνέμους Clem.*paed*.1.5(p.101.1; M.8. 269C).

παράφυσις, ἡ, *offshoot*, fig. τὰς π. τῶν ἁμαρτιῶν ἐπικόπτειν Clem. *str*.2.18(p.165.8; M.8.1037B).

παραφύω, intrans., *have common nature with*, Cyr.*thes.*16(5^1.176A).

παραφων-έω, 1. *tell, instruct* τὰ δι' ὧν ἔσται τῷ νυμφίῳ θυμηρεστάτη ~οῦσιν αὐτῇ Cyr.*Ps.*44:11(M.69.1041C); id.*ador.*5(1.143A); *ib.*6 (204A); **2.** *acclaim* ἐπιψηφίζονται λαοὶ τὸ ὡς εἶεν ἄξιοι ~οῦντες *ib.*11 (409E); **3.** *accompany* musically, id.*Os.*19(3.41B).

***παραφωσεύω**, v. *παραφοσεύω.

***παραφώτισμα, τό**, = παραβάπτισμα, *schismatical baptism*, Epiph.Tyr.*ep.*(p.83.3; H.2.1349D).

***παραχάραγμα, τό**, *false coin*, Clem.*str.*6.10(p.472.11; M.9.301B); *ib.*7.15(p.64.18; 525B); Meth.*symp.*2.2(p.17.19; M.18.49C); fig., of false doctrine, Chrys.*hom.1.2 in 1Tim.*(11.551C) cit. s. παραποίησις; of religious practice πονηρόν τι κόμμα θρησκεύματος καὶ π. ἁγιστείας, ὥσπερ νομίσματος Synes.*provid.*1.18(p.108.20; M.66.1257A).

παραχαράκτης, ὁ, *falsifier, counterfeiter* οἱ τῆς ἀληθείας π. Or. *sel.in Ps.*63:7(M.12.1492C); Bas.*ep.*214.3(3.322A; M.32.788B); id.*hex.* 2.2(1.13B; M.29.29C); Thphyl.*exc.Rom.*6(p.226.26; M.113.936A); ref. Christian doctrine παραχαράκται τῆς ἀποστολικῆς...πίστεως Gr. Nyss.*Apoll.*34(M.45.1197A); παρέστωσαν ἐκ πάσης αἱρέσεως, οἱ τῆς θεότητος π. Tim.Ant.*cruc.*(M.86.264D); ref. text of scripture, Andr. Caes.*Apoc.*72(M.106.452C).

***παραχάραξις, ἡ, 1.** *falsification, corruption*; of text, Epiph.*haer.* 42.11(p.124.3; M.41.725C); **2.** *perversion* ἀπάτην...ἐπὶ παραχαράξει τῆς ἀληθείας Pall.*v.Chrys.*4(p.24.9; M.47.16).

παραχειμάζ-ω, *rage like a storm* φόβου ~οντος Cyr.*Is.*4.4(2.669B).

***παραχειμέριος**, *cold, stormy*, Agath.*v.Gr.Ill.*14(p.10).

***παραχορεύω**, *run along beside*, Thdr.Lect.*fr.*(M.86.221B).

παραχορηγέω, *supply*, Gr.Nyss.*v.Macr.*(p.376.15; M.46.965A).

παραχραίν-ω, *defile* ἅγιον...εἶπε τὸ ὄνομα αὐτοῦ, δηλοῦσα ὅτι οὐδὲν ~εται εἰς γυναῖκα συλλαμβανόμενος ὁ τῶν ἁπάντων δημιουργός Tit. Bost.ap.*cat.Lc.*1:49(p.15.5) for ἅγιον γὰρ τὸ ὄνομα αὐτοῦ καὶ οὐ χραίνεται, ὁ συλλαμβανόμενος σωτὴρ ἐν ἐμοί id.*fr.Lc.*1:49(p.145, v.l. καὶ οὐδὲν ~εται).

παραχρ-άομαι, 1. *misuse* χρώμενοι...ἀλλὰ μὴ ~ώμενοι *Const.App.* 2.25.3; Chrys.*hom.9.3 in 2Cor.*(10.501D); Ast.Am.*hom.*1(M.40.165D) cit. s. ἀντινομοθετέω; **2.** *abuse* the flesh μήποτε...παραχρήσῃ αὐτῇ ἐν μιασμῷ τινι Herm.*sim.*5.7.2; Meth.*symp.*3.13(p.43.5; M.18.84A); esp. of Nicolaitans οἱ φάσκοντες ἑαυτοὺς Νικολάῳ ἕπεσθαι, ἀπομνημόνευμά τι τἀνδρὸς φέροντες ἐκ παρατροπῆς τὸ 'δεῖν π. τῇ σαρκί' Clem.*str.*2.20(p.177.4; M.8.1061B); *ib.*3.4(p.207.23; 1129B); ἐκπορνεύειν καὶ ~ᾶσθαι τῇ σαρκὶ ἐδίδασκον *Const.App.*6.10.3; **3.** *pervert* Ἰουδαῖοι...τὰς προφητείας...ἠγνόησαν...καὶ παρεχρήσαντο Just.*1apol.* 49.5(M.6.401A); **4.** reflex., *commit suicide*, Jo.Mal.*chron.*8 p.210(M. 97.328B).

***παραχρηματίζω**, *give false revelation to*, *Exorc.*1(p.333).

παράχρησις, ἡ, *abuse, misuse*, of faculties ὁ κατὰ παράχρησιν τῶν κατὰ φύσιν δυνάμεων τρόπος Max.*opusc.*(M.91.24B); ἡ κατὰ διάνοιαν κακία, ἡ π. ἐστι τῶν νοημάτων Thal.*cent.*3.39(M.91.1452C); as morbid condition οὔτε χρυσός, οὔτε κτήματα παρέχουσι τὴν βλάβην, ἀλλὰ... ἡ ἐμπαθὴς αὐτῶν π. Marc.Er.*opusc.*8.3(M.65.1105A); ἔστιν...ἡ κακία ἡ τῶν φυσικῶν δυνάμεων π. Jo.D.*Man.*1.14(M.94.1517C); cf. Jo.D. *spir.neq.*(M.95.88D); of evil or obscene practices π. ... τοῦ...σώματος Epiph.*haer.*64.2(p.404.6; M.41.1072A); γαστριμαργικὰς π. †Cyr.*hom. div.*14(5^2.405E); of verbal abuse ῥημάτων οὐ καθαρῶν παραχρήσει Philost.*h.e.*6.2(M.65.533B).

***παραχωνεύ-ω**, trans., *melt out of shape* προσβαλεῖν τῷ στερεώματι, ἢ ~σαι αὐτοῦ τι, οὐχ οἷοί τε [sc. ὁ ἥλιος καὶ ἡ σελήνη] καθεστήκασιν ‡Caes.Naz.*dial.*105(M.38.972).

παραχωρ-έω, 1. *make way for*, met., of status αὐτῷ ~εῖν τῆς ὑπεροχῆς Or.*Jo.*32.22(14; p.465.26; M.14.805B); **2.** *omit*, Gr.Mag. *dial.*(tr.Zach.)4.55(M.*PL.*77.422B); **3.** *leave in charge* of, *resign* to, *assign* to πάντα...τὰ νοήματα τῷ ὑπὲρ ἡμᾶς ~ήσωμεν Cyr.*Jo.*10.2(4. 917C); Gel.Cyz.*h.e.*2.19.16(M.85.1277D); **4.** *yield* τὰ νῶτα...~ήσαντες Eus.*theoph.fr.*3(p.8.10; M.24.613B); **5.** *forgo* credit τὰ πρωτεῖα τοῦ πάθους ~ῶν [sc. Ἰσαάκ] τῷ λόγῳ...μὴ σφαγείς Clem.*paed.*1.5(p.104. 2; M.8.277B); ~ήσας τὰ πρωτεῖα Or.*Cels.*4.90(p.362.7; M.11.1168A); ~εῖν πρωτείων id.*mart.*15(p.15.15; M.11.584A); **6.** *be inferior* βόμβος...οὐδεμιᾷ ~ῶν μουσικῇ Synes.*ep.*147(M.66.1545D); **7.** *devote, dedicate* one's life, Pall.*h.Laus.*32(p.93.3; M.34.1100C).

παραχώρησις, ἡ, 1. *cession*; of land, Chrys.*hom.34.2 in Gen.*(4. 342B); **2.** *remission*; of debts, Jo.Mosch.*prat.*193(M.87.3076B); **3.** *permission* οὐχ ὅσον αὐτῷ δοκεῖ ἐκπειράζει [sc. ἡ τῆς παιδείας ῥάβδος]...ἀλλ' ὅσον δὴ τὸ δεσποτικὸν ἐπιτρέψει νεῦμα διὰ τῆς π. Mac. Aeg.*pat.*7(M.34.869D); Diad.*perf.*76(p.96.4); ἡ παιδευτικὴ π. οὐδαμῶς τοῦ θείου φωτὸς τὴν ψυχὴν ἀποστερεῖ *ib.*86(p.118.8); ἡ παιδευτικὴ π. φέρει...λύπην πολλήν *ib.*87(p.120.2); *ib.*99(p.146.17); παραχωρήσεως θεοῦ γινομένης, καὶ ἰσχύουσι [sc. demons], καὶ μεταβάλλονται Jo.D. *f.o.*2.4(M.94.877A).

παραψελλίζω, *speak haltingly*, Mac.Mgn.*apocr.*3.43(p.150.13).

παραψηφίζω, *vote amiss* οὐ ταὐτὸν σημαίνει...τὸ ψηφίσαι καὶ παραψηφίσαι Or.*fr.15 in Mt.*1:18f.(p.22.30).

***παραψιθυρισμός, ὁ**, *deceitful whispering*, Epiph.*haer.*26.18(p.299. 16; M.41.361C).

[*]παρδαλαῖος, = παρδάλειος, *leopard-like*, Tim.Ant.*caec.*11(M. 28.1017B); Leont.B.*mesopent.*1(M.86.1977C).

παρεατέον, *one must pass over, leave unmentioned*, Const.ap.Eus. *v.C.*2.35(p.56.10; M.20.1012B).

παρεάω, 1. *pass over, leave undiscussed*, *Dial.Tim.et Aquil.*98 r°; *ib.*108 r°; Chrys.*hom.29.1 in 1Cor.*(10.260B); †Gregent.*disp.*(M.86. 632C); **2.** c. infin., *allow*, †Gregent.*leg.Hom.*59(M.86.614B); **3.** pass., *be left* or *allowed to remain*, *ib.*54(609B).

παρεγγίζω, *approach* τὸ σάββατον παρέγγισεν *cat.Jo.*9:17(p.290. 31).

παρέγγραπτος, 1. *irregularly put on roll*, ‡Eust.*Laz.*14(p.38.9); τῶν νόθων καὶ π. ἱερέων Gr.Naz.*or.*21.9(M.35.1089C); παρέγγραπτον, τῶν θείων ἀμύητον Eun.ap.Gr.Nyss.*Eun.*1(1 p.44.20; M.45.272D); **2.** *added to list* of gods καθάπερ οὓς Ἕλληνες π. εἰσάγουσιν Gr.Naz.*ep.* 101(M.37.180B); id.*or.*29.18(p.101.8; M.36.97B); **3.** *unfairly cited* οἴει ποθὲν π. ταὐτά σοι κομίζεσθαι τὰ ὑφ' ἡμῶν παρατιθέμενα; Clem.*prot.* 2(p.29.2; πόθεν παραγέγραπταί σοι M.8.117B); **4.** *interpolated, imported* (in books) πολλαὶ...τελέθουσι π. κακότητες Gr.Naz.*carm.*1.1. 12.7(M.37.472A); βιβλίδια, καὶ λογίδρια, καὶ θεομάχα καὶ π. δόγματα Sophr.H.*ep.syn.*(M.87.3189B); **5.** *spurious* ὑποβολιμαίων καὶ π. Synes.*astrolab.*3(p.136.16; M.66.1581B).

παρεγγράφ-ω, 1. *interpolate* τὰ μὲν ἐξαίροι τῶν θείων λογίων, τὰ δὲ παρεγγράφοι Bas.*Eun.*2.8(1.244C; M.29.588B); pass. ptcpl., of writings, *spurious*, Jo.D.*imag.*1.25(M.94.1257A); **2.** *paint in differently* πόσα ἐξαλείφουσι, πόσα ~ουσιν Chrys.*hom.30.5 in Mt.*(7.355A).

παρεγγυ-άω, 1. *commend* θεοδώρητον εἶναι τὸ τῆς παρθενίας ἐπιτήδευμα ~ᾷ Meth.*symp.*3.14(p.44.2; M.18.84C); **2.** *recommend* εἰρήνην ἡμῖν π. *Ep.Lugd.*ap.Eus.*h.e.*5.2.7(M.20.436B); Clem.*paed.*1.1 (p.90.26; M.8.249C); Cyr.*Abac.*4(3.357D); **3.** *give a command, order* ἐνίοις...τῶν...ἀγγέλων...καλῶς ἄρχειν παρηγγύησε Papias *fr.*4; περὶ ἐσθῆτος ~ᾷ Clem.*paed.*2.10(p.218.26; M.8.520B); Meth.*symp.*1.1(p.7. 15; M.18.37A); ἀποστολικὴ ~ᾷ φωνή·...οὐ πάντα συμφέρει Ath.*gent.* 4(M.25.12A); καθὼς ὁ νόμος ~ᾷ Gr.Nyss.*v.Mos.*(M.44.408C); μὴ... βλέπειν ὁ λόγος ~ᾷ id.*or.dom.*5(p.100.29; M.44.1184A); ταῦτα ~ᾷ Chrys.*hom.10.1 in 1Tim.*(11.599B); ὅσα Τιμοθέῳ ~ᾷ...Παῦλος Cyr. *ador.*5(1.168A); ἵπποις χρήσασθαι τοὺς ἐπισκόπους ~ήσας Thdt.*h.e.* 1.7.2(3.754); **4.** *signify* ὁ Παῦλος ~ᾷ, ὅτι...ὁ κύριος...καταβήσεται Meth.*symp.*6.4(p.69.5; M.18.120B); ἡμῶν ἐν τοῖς πρωτοπλάστοις διαγωγὴν ~ᾷ id.*res.*2.1(p.329.14; M.18.297A); Euthal.Diac.*Ac.* proem.(M.85.632A).

***παρεγκεντρίζω**, *graft* into νόθως ἐκ τῆς ἀγριελαίας παρεγκεντρισθέντων εἰς τὴν καλλιέλαιον Max.*ep.*13(M.91.512B).

παρέγκλισις, ἡ, *subsidence*, Philost.*h.e.*12.10(M.65.620A); hence, met., of a reversion to an earlier name Μάζακα τὸ πρῶτον ἐκαλεῖτο Καισάρεια...τοῦ χρόνου δὲ πορευομένου, κατὰ παρέγκλισιν ἤδη Μάζακα προσωνόμασται *ib.*9.12(577A).

***παρεγκοπή, ἡ**, *section* ὡρῶν τε καὶ ἡμερῶν...παρεγκοπαῖς καὶ ἀνακυκλήσεσι Cyr.*ador.*6(1.205B).

παρεγκόπτ-ω, 1. *obstruct* π. τι τῶν κατὰ θεὸν πραγμάτων Chrys. *hom.21.2 in Jo.*(8.122E); **2.** *cut short and turn aside* τῇ τοῦ βίου φαιδρότητι ~οντες ἐπὶ τὸ ῥᾴθυμον καίτοι ζέοντα τὸν θυμόν Cyr.*Am.* 61(3.318B).

***παρεγκρανίς, ἡ**, *cerebellum*, Nemes.*nat.hom.*13(M.40.664A).

***παρεγχάραγμα, τό**, *corruption, debasement*, Jo.D.*imag.*1.2(M. 94.1233B).

***παρεγχαράσσ-ω**, *signify* τῆς ὑμετέρας διαβολῆς, ἐν ᾗ πως τὰς θεοσημείας τοῦ δεσπότου ὡς οὐδὲν ἔχειν δι' οἰκείας ἀποδείξεως ~ειν Leont.H.*Nest.*1.19(M.86.1477B).

***παρεγχείρημα, τό**, *futile attempt* τὰ Ἀρείου παίγνια, καὶ τὰ Εὐνομίου π. Ast.Am.*hom.*8(M.40.281B).

παρεγχείρησις, ἡ, 1. *imposition* δυσβάστακτα φορτία...αὐτοῖς διὰ τῆς ἀνθρωπίνης π. ἐπαναθεμένους Clem.*str.*6.6(p.453.25; M.9.265A); **2.** in argument, *assault, attack* τὰ...ὑπὸ τῶν μακαρίων ἀποστόλων... παραδιδόμενα...σοφίζονται δι' ἑτέρων π. *ib.*7.16(p.73.7; 544A); μηδένα τόπον διδοῦσι παρεγχειρήσεως τοῖς ἐναντίοις Or.*or.*46(p.42.28; M.11. 629A).

***παρεδρευτής, ὁ**, *assiduous person*, hence *devotee* δαιμόνων δὲ μαθητά [sc. Julian], δαιμόνων δὲ π. Libanius ap.Socr.*h.e.*3.23.42(M. 67.445B); Marc.Er.*opusc.*5(M.65.1053B).

παρεδρεύ-ω, **1.** *gaze assiduously* at ∼οντας [sc. Ἰουδαίους]... ἄστροις καὶ σελήνῃ *Diogn.*4.5; **2.** *inhere* in ὁ ἀψάμενος ὀστέων μάρτυρος, λαμβάνει τινὰ μετουσίαν ἁγιασμοῦ ἐκ τῆς τῷ σώματι ∼ούσης χάριτος †Bas.*hom.in Ps.*115(1.375A; M.30.112C); **3.** *sit beside* coffin of a saint in order to obtain healing, Dam.*troph.*4.5(p.273.2).

παρεδρήσσω, *sit by*, Nonn.*par.Jo.*16:5(M.43.877C).

***παρεδρία, ἡ**, *presence, attendance* of familiar spirit, *Hom.Clem.* 2.30.

πάρεδρος, ὁ, *one who sits by*; **1.** esp. in sense of *servant*; **a.** *assessor, administrator* ὡς θεοῦ οἰκονόμοι καὶ π. καὶ ὑπηρέται Ign.*Polyc.* 6.1; ἔφορον...παρεκάλει [sc. ὁ Χριστός] τὸν πατέρα καὶ π., ὡς ἂν δεξιὸν ἀλείπτην, αὐτῷ συμπαρεῖναι Eus.*d.e.*10.8(p.484.33; M.20.780A); οἱονεὶ π. σεαυτῷ τὴν ἐντολὴν ποιησάμενος, δεῖξον τὸ μισοπόνηρον Bas. *hom.*12.10(2.106E; M.31.408B); Thdt.*ep.*72 tit.(4.1122); **b.** *assistant spirit, familiar*, said to be employed by magicians ἀλλὰ καὶ π. τοὺς λεγομένους ἀσκοῦσιν [i.e. followers of Simon Magus] Iren.*haer.* 1.23.3 ap.Hipp.*haer.*6.20(M.16.3226A); among Carpocratians, *ib.*1. 25.2 ap.Hipp.*haer.*7.32(3339A); as adj. εἰκὸς δὲ αὐτὸν [sc. Marcus] καὶ δαίμονά τινα π. ἔχειν, δι' οὗ αὐτός τε προφητεύειν δοκεῖ, καὶ ὅσας ἀξίας ἡγεῖται μετόχους τῆς χάριτος αὐτοῦ, προφητεύειν ποιεῖ *ib.*1.13.2 (M.7.581B); σεμνυνόμενοι [sc. Γνωστικοί]...π. τισὶ δαίμοσιν Eus.*h.e.* 4.7.9(M.20.317B); οὐ μὴν δὲ ἀλλὰ καὶ π. δαίμονας ἑαυτοῖς ἐπισπῶνται [sc. Carpocratians] Epiph.*haer.*27.3(p.303.16; M.41.365D); their existence as argument for survival after death, Just.*1apol.*18.3 (M.6.356A); **2.** of one occupying a place of honour ὦ πάρεδρε θεοῦ [i.e. Sophia] Iren.*haer.*1.13.6(M.7.589A); τῶν τοῦ θεοῦ παρέδρων ὁ ἀποστάτης †Dion.Al.*fr.in Job*(p.202.5); οἱ θεῖοι μάρτυρες...οἱ νῦν τοῦ Χριστοῦ π. καὶ τῆς βασιλείας κοινωνοί id.ap.Eus.*h.e.*6.42.5(M.20.613B); of BMV χαῖρε, πάρεδ[ρε τοῦ ὑψίστου] *Strasbourg Ostraka* 809 (ed. P. Viereck, Berlin 1923).

***παρεζευγμένως**, *implicitly*, Cyr.*Is.*5.6(2.913E).

παρειά, ἡ, plur., *sidewhiskers* ἥρπαξεν...τὰς π. τοῦ πώγωνος αὐτοῦ *T.Abr.*A 11(p.89.13).

***παρείθεα**, ὡς παρείθεα τῆς τῶν ἀοράτων Gr.Nyss.*mart.*2.2(M.46. 764A, error for ὥσπερεὶ θεατής).

παρεικάζ-ω, **1.** *compare*, c. μετά, Gr.Mag.*dial.*(tr.Zach.)3.37(M. *PL.*77.314B); **2.** *make like*, Epiph.*haer.*65.9(p.13.9; M.42.28D); *make in the image of* ὁ νοῦς ὁ ἐν ἀνθρώπῳ, ὁ 'κατ' εἰκόνα' τοῦ θεοῦ καὶ 'καθ' ὁμοίωσιν' διὰ τοῦτο γεγενῆσθαι λεγόμενος, τῇ κατὰ καρδίαν φρονήσει τῷ θείῳ ∼όμενος λόγῳ Clem.*prot.*10(p.71.29; M.8.213A).

***παρεικασμός, ὁ**, *comparison* τὸ...κατὰ χάριν δωρούμενον οὐκέτι ἐν π. τῆς προλαβούσης ἀσθενείας μετρεῖται Mac.Aeg.*hom.*37.7(M.34. 753D); *ib.*(756A).

***παρεικαστέον**, *one must compare*, Cyr.*ador.*9(1.298D); id.*Os.*33(3. 58C); id.*Ps.*47:4(M.69.1061A).

πάρειμι, (εἶμι *ibo*); **1.** *surpass* θεῖος λόγος...πᾶσαν ἔννοιαν παριὼν ἀνθρωπίνην Gr.Nyss.*hex.*12(M.44.76A); **2.** *run through, recite* ὕμνον εἰς τὸν Διόνυσον παρῄει Soz.*h.e.*6.25.9(M.67.1360B).

παρεισάγ-ομαι, *introduce* ἑτέρους προφήτας ∼ονται Jo.D.*haer.*48 (M.94.708A).

παρεισαγωγή, ἡ, *introduction* ὁ κατὰ Μωϋσέα νόμος καὶ ἡ π. τοῦ κρείττονος †Bas.*Is.*26(1.400A; M.30.169B).

***παρεισακούω**, *refuse a hearing to, ignore*, Gr.Mag.*dial.*(tr.Zach.) 3.15(M.*PL.*77.255C).

***παρεισακτέον**, *one must introduce*, Eus.*d.e.*4.3(p.153.33; M.22. 256D).

παρείσακτος, **1.** *novel* ξένον...καὶ π. Gr.Naz.*or.*31.21(p.171.2; M. 36.156C); **2.** *brought in surreptitiously*; of women among certain schismatic monks, Jo.D.*haer.*100(M.94.761B).

παρεισβάλλ-ω, **1.** *introduce* against expectation τιμὰς ἠλπίσαμεν, καὶ ἀτιμίας ∼εις; ‡Bas.*const.*22.4(2.572D; M.31.1408B); at the last moment, Epiph.*haer.*39.3(p.74.11; M.41.669A); **2.** intrans., *occur incidentally, by chance* παρεισβέβληκε μεταξὺ λόγος ἕτερος Cyr. *Is.*4.3(2.635B); παρεισβαλούσης μνήμης id.*Zach.*66(3.745D; παρεμβ- Aubert); *slip in unnoticed* παρεισβέβληκε μὲν γὰρ ἀπειθησάντων αὐτῶν ἡ ἐξ ἐθνῶν ἐκκλησία id.*Is.*4.4(677C).

***παρείσβασις, ἡ**, *entrance, beginning* of a period, Max.*comput.*2 (M.19.1221A); *ib.*18(1236C).

***παρείσδοσις, ἡ**, *entry* ἀποφράττει τὴν ἀκοὴν...ὡς μηδεμίαν τὰς... παραινέσεις εὑρεῖν π. Nil.*exerc.*10(M.79.729C, perh. for -δυσιν).

***παρεισδρομή, ἡ**, *stealthy entry*, Cyr.*ador.*(1.54D).

παρείσδυσις, ἡ, **1.** *slipping in*; of a serpent, Proc.G.*Jos.*6:26(M. 87.1016B); fig., of Devil, *Barn.*2.10; Chrys.*hom.68.5 in Mt.*(7.677D); id.*hom.7.2 in Jo.*(8.47D); ὁ νομοθέτης ἀποκλείων τῆς ἡδονῆς τὴν π., τὴν κεφαλὴν τοῦ ὄφεως τηρεῖν ἐκέλευσεν Nil.*exerc.*39(M.79.768C); of evil spirits, Clem.*str.*2.20(p.175.19; M.8.1160A); of abstract evil, id. *paed.*1.8(p.130.33; M.8.333B); of harmful passions, Nil.*Magn.*22(M. 79.997B); **2.** moral *lapse*, Chrys.*comm.in Gal.*5:1(10.714E).

παρεισέρχ-ομαι, **1.** *enter in* εἰς τὴν βασιλείαν παρέλθοιεν τῶν οὐρανῶν Clem.*paed.*2.3(p.180.20; M.8.437B); *Chron.Pasch.*p.394(M. 92.1009C); of notions, education, etc. ∼εται ἡ ἀναισχυντία *T.Jud.* 16.2; Clem.*str.*1.2(p.14.6; M.8.709B); *ib.*3.2(p.198.31; 1108C); ὅσους ...ἡ συγγνώμη ∼εται *ib.*2.20(p.180.9; 1068C); **2.** *come in adventitiously* σκότος οὐ δεδημιούργηται μέν, ∼εται δέ Tit.Bost.*Man.*2. 19(M.18.1173C).

παρεισκρίν-ω, **1.** pass., of events or time, *be distinguished*, Cyr. *ador.*10(1.357E); id.*glaph.Gen.*6(1.201C); **2.** *interpolate, introduce* τι... ὑδαρεστέρων ἐννοιῶν ∼οντες id.*Is.*1.1(2.25D); τὸ τῆς δόσεως ὄνομα ∼εται id.*Pulch.*28(p.41.9; 5².150C); ἵνα μὴ τομῆς φαντασία ∼ηται διὰ τὸ λέγειν τὸ 'σύν' id.*ep.*4(p.28.4; 5².24B); ἵνα μὴ τομὴ...τῷ μυστηρίῳ τῆς ἐνανθρωπήσεως ∼ηται Max.*ep.*12(M.91.473C); **3.** of faith, *grow up, be instilled* διὰ τῆς εἰλικρινοῦς ἀγάπης ∼εται Cyr.*Jo.*10.2(4. 877D).

παρεισκυκλέω, *bring forward, show up* εἰς μέσον αὐτῶν παρεισκυκλήσωμεν τὰς κατὰ τῆς ἀληθείας ἐπινοίας Leont.B.*Nest.et Eut.*3 proem.(M.86.1360D).

***παρεισπηδ-άω**, *dart in*, of sin ὡς μέλισσα ∼ᾷ Ephr.3.212A.

***παρειστρέχ-ω**, *enter in addition, intervene* τὴν οὐκ ἐν καιρῷ ∼ουσαν σιγήν Cyr.*ador.*1(1.31E); *ib.*13(460D); id.*thes.*6(5¹.46A).

παρεισφέρ-ω, **1.** *bring in beside*, with idea of introducing surreptitiously πλῆθος ἀποκρύφων...γραφῶν...∼ουσιν [sc. Marcosians] Iren.*haer.*1.20.1(M.7.653A); *ib.*3.11.9(890A); Βήρυλλος...ξένα τινὰ τῆς πίστεως ∼ειν ἐπειρᾶτο Eus.*h.e.*6.33.1(M.20.593A); ὡς αἱρετικοὶ ∼ετε ταῦτα Ath.*ep.Epict.*4(p.7.12; M.26.1056C); 'Οφῖται...∼οντες τὰ... νομιζόμενα μυστήρια Epiph.*haer.*37.1(p.53.15; M.41.645A); ὅσα τοῖς ἠπατημένοις ∼ουσιν *ib.*37.5(p.57.1; 648B); **2.** *introduce*, Or.*fr.in 3Reg.*15:23(M.17.56C); Cyr.*Jo.*4.2(4.359C); **3.** *bring to bear* τοῦτο δὲ τέλειον οὐχ ἁπλῶς...εὑρίσκει τις, κἂν πᾶσαν κοσμικὴν σύνεσιν ∼ῃ Marc.Er.*opusc.*4(M.65.1028A).

παρεισφρέω, intrans., *slip in, enter in*; met., Cyr.*Jo.*10.2(4.883B).

παρεκβαίν-ω, **1.** *go beyond, break out of* τὸ κύτος τῆς ἀπείρου θαλάσσης...οὐ ∼ει τὰ περιτεθειμένα αὐτῇ κλεῖθρα *1Clem.*20.6; **2.** *transgress* laws, *ib.*41.1; **3.** *digress*, Or.*Jo.*1.16(p.20.24; M.14.52A); οὐ παρεξέβην...τοῦ προκειμένου id.*engast.*8(p.291.27; M.12.1024D); Meth. *symp.*4.3(p.48.6; M.18.89B); **4.** *desert* to opposite party, Alex.Al.*ep. Alex.*2(p.20.20; M.18.549C); **5.** *step forward*, *A.Pil.*A 12(p.251).

παρεκβάλλ-ω, *reject, repudiate* documents ∼ειν τὰ τοῦ...ἀποστόλου βιβλία Epiph.*haer.*51.34(p.308.24; M.41.949C); Mac.Ant.ap. CCP(678)*act.*8(H.3.1177E); institutions, points of doctrine γάμον Epiph.*haer.*67.2(p.134.25; M.42.173C); ∼ειν τὸν νοῦν ἀπὸ τῆς ἐνσάρκου παρουσίας Χριστοῦ *ib.*77.25(p.438.2; 677A); cf.*ib.*77.26(p.439.6; 680A); people and their practices, *ib.*61.7(p.387.13,15; M.41.1049A); ἐκεῖνοι μὲν ∼έσθωσαν *ib.*77.25(p.438.21; M.42.677B); ? f.l. for παραβάλλω, Didym.*Trin.*2.5(M.39.505A).

παρέκβασις, ἡ, **1.** lit., *going out of the way*, *1Clem.*20.3; Clem. *prot.*10(p.66.12; M.8.201A); **2.** fig., *modification*, in poetry τὴν μυθώδη π. *ib.*7(p.55.19; 180B); *deviation* π. τῆς ἀληθείας *ib.*2(p.20.3; 97A); *irrelevancy*, Or.*Jo.*28.6(5; p.396.14; M.14.692A); **3.** *transgression* ἡ Εὔα ἐν π. παρακοῆς γέγονε Epiph.*ep.Arab.*ap.*haer.*78.18 (p.469.15; M.42.729A).

παρεκβατικός, *digressive*, Or.*Jo.*1.24(23; p.30.10; M.14.65C); Cyr. *Jo.*1.9(4.96ᵇD); *ib.*4.4(385E); μείζονος δεῖται τῆς ἀναπτύξεως καὶ οὐ π. νῦν ζητήσεως Leont.H.*Nest.*2.1(M.86.1532A); comp., μικρόν τι παρεκβατικώτερος Gr.Naz.*or.*41.2(M.36.429C).

***παρέκβρασμα τό**, *hint thrown out* πλέκων κατ' αὐτοῦ ὑπονοίας παρεκβράσματα Gel.Cyz.*h.e.*3.17.10.

παρεκδέχ-ομαι, **1.** *misunderstand*, Or.*hom.14.3 in Jer.*(p.108.11; M.13.408A); Eus.*h.e.*3.39.12(M.20.300A); **2.** *accept without question, be taken in by* μύθους..., οὓς οὐκ ἂν ∼οιτο ὁ φεύγων μὲν μύθους ζητῶν δὲ ἀλήθειαν Or.*Cels.*8.66(p.283.7; M.11.1617A); **3.** deliberately *misinterpret, twist* ἐπὶ τὸ χεῖρον ∼όμενοι id.*Jo.*28.22(17; p.417.10; M.14.728B); εἰς τἀναντία...∼όμενος Eus.*d.e.*3.5(p.124.3; M.22.212A); **4.** *be loth to accept* τῷ πιστεύοντι καὶ μὴ παρεκδεξαμένῳ Or.*Jo.*1.5 (7; p.10.3; M.14.33A).

παρεκδοχή, ἡ, **1.** *variety of interpretation* παρεκδοχαί,...μεταγωγαί,...μετωνυμίαι Leont.H.*Nest.*3.5(M.86.1613A); **2.** *misinterpretation*, Or.*Cels.*3.11(p.211.16; M.11.933B); id.*or.*24.5(p.356.23; M.11. 496B); πολλῶν σφαλμάτων ἀπαλλαττόμεθα καὶ παρεκδοχῶν id.*comm. in Rom.*7:7(*JTS* 14 p.13); of wrong use of scripture, id.*Jo.*13.8 (p.232.30; M.14.409D).

***παρεκδρομή, ἡ**, *digression* ὡς ἐν π. ... εἴρηται Epiph.*haer.*28.7 (p.320.4; M.41.385D); Thdr.Stud.*epp.*1.37(M.99.1040D).

παρεκεῖ, **1.** adv., *near by*, *T.Neph.*5.8; **2.** prep., *near to* τὸν ἔμβολον τὸν παρεκεῖ τοῦ ἁγίου Νικολάου *Chron.Pasch.*p.396(M.92.1013C).

παρεκθέ-ω, **1.** *run aside from*, *leave* the way, fig. εὐλαβείας ~οντες τὴν ὁδόν Cyr.*Abac.*32(3.547B); id.*Is.*3.2(2.417C); in digressing, id. *ador.*16(1.581D); **2.** *run forward* διεκώλυσεν ἀτάκτως ~ειν Thphn. *chron.*p.262 (ἐκθέειν M.108.652B).

***παρέκκλισις**, **ἡ**, *deviation* αἱ π. τῶν ἀρετῶν εἰς κακίαν Isid.Pel. *epp.*4.210(M.78.1305A).

παρεκνεύω, *bend away from*, Cyr.*thes.*11(5^1.96B).

***παρεκνόον**, *without* the *knowledge* of παρεκνόον ἡγεμονῆος Gr. Naz.*carm.*1.2.2.436(M.37.612A).

***παρεκπηδάω**, *jump out*, ‡Ath.*occurs.*11(M.28.988A).

***παρέκπτωσις**, **ἡ**, *falling away*, *lapse*, *Schol.* in Jo.Clim.*scal.*4(M. 88.733A).

***παρέκστασις**, **ἡ**, *spurious ecstasy*, ref. Montanus δόντα πάροδον εἰς ἑαυτὸν τῷ ἀντικειμένῳ πνευματοφορηθῆναί τε καὶ αἰφνιδίως ἐν κατοχῇ τινι καὶ π. γενόμενον ἐνθουσιᾶν ἄρξασθαί τε λαλεῖν καὶ ξενοφωνεῖν Anon.ap.Eus.*h.e.*5.16.7(M.20.465C); ὅ γε ψευδοπροφήτης ἐν π., ᾧ ἕπεται ἄδεια καὶ ἀφοβία, ἀρχομένου μὲν ἐξ ἑκουσίου ἀμαθίας, καταστρέφοντος δὲ εἰς ἀκούσιον μανίαν ψυχῆς...τοῦτον δὲ τὸν τρόπον οὔτε τινὰ τῶν κατὰ τὴν παλαιὰν οὔτε τῶν κατὰ τὴν καινὴν πνευματοφορηθέντα προφήτην δεῖξαι δυνήσονται Anon.*ib.*5.17.2(473A).

***παρέκταμα**, **τό**, *prolongation*, Max.*schol.ep.Dion.Ar.*7.2(M.4. 541B).

παρέκτασις, **ἡ**, **1.** *extent*; of time, *cat.Jo.*4:21(p.219.33); ἔοικε γὰρ οἱονεὶ χρόνων εἶναι π. ταῦτα τὰ ὀνόματα (i.e. expressions of time such as ἦν, ἀεί, πρὸ αἰώνων, opp. eternity) Alex.Al.*ep.Alex.*12(p.27.24; M.18.568A); **2.** *extension*, *continuance* κινδύνου π. Gr.Naz.*or.*15.4(M. 35.917A); of speech, Melet.*nat.hom.*30(M.64.1276B); **3.** *pervasiveness* εἰς ἄπειρα τῶν ἀπείρων ἡ χύσις χυθεῖσα τῇ σῇ τέμνεται π. Geo.Pis. *hex.*1702(M.92.1566B); **4.** *further extension*, Thdt.*haer.*2.10(4.336) cit. s. ἔκτασις; Sophr.H.*v.Anast.*(M.92.1681B).

παρεκτείν-ω, **A.** trans.; **1.** *prolong*, *draw out* prayer, Vict.*Mc.* 12:38(p.406.13); Anast.S.*synax.*(M.89.829B); **2.** *make equal* to, *co-extensive* with τὸ μικρὸν τοῖς εἰρημένοις ~εται Or.*hom.12.10 in Jer.* (p.97.12; M.13.393A); ~εσθαι τῷ μείζονι Epiph.*haer.*76.20(p.366.26; M.42.556B); ref. unacceptable view of relation of soul to body, Chrys.*incomprehens.*5.4(1.485C); **3.** *offer for comparison*, *invite comparison of* οὐ παρεξέτειναν ἑαυτοὺς τοῖς ἀποστόλοις *Const.App.epit.* 2.8; **4.** pass., *pay attention* to, *be affected* by, Epiph.*haer.*76.20(p.366. 14; M.42.556A); *be turned* to, *tend* towards, Gr.Mag.*dial.*(tr.Zach.) 4.6(M.*PL.*77.327C).

B. intrans., with ptcpl., *continue*, Clem.*paed.*2.7(p.191.2; M.8. 460A).

παρεκτίθημι, med., *set aside*, *suppress*, Eus.*h.e.*9.9.13(M.20.824C); ὧν...μηδαμῶς παρεκθέσθαι τὴν μνήμην id.*Hierocl.*22(525C; M.22. 828C).

παρεκτικός, *productive* of θεοῦ...δύναμις...ζωῆς π. Iren.*haer.*5.3.3 (M.7.1131A); τὸν [sc. μονογενῆ] πᾶσι τοῖς οὖσι τοῦ εἶναι παρεκτικόν Bas.*Eun.*2.18(1.253D; M.29.609A); πνεῦμα...ἀγαθῶν πάντων π. Gr. Nyss.*Maced.*22(M.45.1328D).

***παρεκτομή**, **ἡ**, *excision*, *leaving out*, Epiph.*haer.*42.11(p.137.5; M.41.745B).

παρεκτός, **1.** *without* ἥμαρτον...π. ἐννοίας *T.Zab.*1.4; **2.** *except* π. τοῦ ἀπειθεῖν *Hom.Clem.*13.16; **3.** *diverging* from, *so as to lead astray* from π. θεοῦ σε διδάσκει *Did.*6.1 = *Didasc.patr.*1(p.10.18); π. τῆς αὐτῶν διδασκαλίας Const.ap.Eus.*v.C.*3.18(p.85.20; M.20.1076B).

παρεκτρέπ-ω, **1.** *turn aside* from a subject, Epiph.*haer.*28.7(p.320. 7; M.41.388A); from the way, Eus.*e.th.*3.3(p.148.3; M.24.985C); ταῖς παρεκτετραμμέναις τῆς θείας ἐντολῆς πορείαις ‡Proc.G.*Pr.*22:5(M.87. 1440C); from right reason, Epiph.*haer.*27.7(p.311.14; M.41.376A); *ib.*76.10(p.351.6; M.42.533B); *seduce* οὐ παίζει ἡ Αἰγυπτία τὸν σώφρονα Ἰωσήφ, οὐδὲ ~ει *ib.*79.9(p.483.29; 753B); *pervert* ~ειν εἰς τοσαύτην φαυλότητα *ib.*64.8(p.418.5; M.41.1084B); **2.** *set aside*, *impair* τὸν ἐκκλησιαστικὸν κανόνα Eus.*h.e.*6.33.1(M.20.595A); οὔτε...ἡ ἀξία... παρεκτραπήσεται Epiph.*haer.*76.29(p.379.1; M.42.576D).

παρεκτρέχω, *deviate*; abs., Clem.*str.*4.2(p.250.12; M.8.1217C).

***παρεκτρίβιον**, **τό**, *by-way*, Gr.Nyss.*v.Ephr.*(M.46.824D).

παρεκτροπή, **ἡ**, **1.** *bypath*; fig., Clem.*str.*7.12(p.53.3; M.9.501B); οὐ...τοσαῦται π. τῶν λεωφόρων ὅσαι τῆς ἀρετῆς Hipp.*fr.5 in Pr.* (p.158.14); of heresy τὴν εὐθεῖαν καὶ βασιλικὴν ὁδὸν ὀρθοτομοῦσα... παρεκτροπὰς ἀπεδοκίμασεν [sc. ἡ ἐκκλησία] Eus.*e.th.*8.1(p.66.2; M.24. 837A); **2.** *turning aside*, *deviation*; abs., met., of heresy, id.*h.e.*4.27 (M.20.397B); in gen. ἄλλοι ἐσμὲν χαίροντες, ἄλλοι ἀλγοῦντες· ἀμφότερα π. Chrys.*hom.3.4 in 1Thess.*(11.446F); hence *perversion* ὡς κατὰ ἰδίαν ἐξουσίαν καὶ οὐχ ὡς ἐν π. γενομένου [sc. Devil, acc. Encratites] Epiph.*haer.*47.1(p.216.3; M.41.852A).

παρεκφέρω, *utter mistakenly* π. ὑπόνοιαν Epiph.*haer.*74.13(p.331. 24; M.42.500C).

παρελαύν-ω, **A.** trans.; **1.** *pass by* in silence, Cyr.*Jo.*10.1(4.861A); *get past*, *escape*, id.*Is.*4.3(2.627E); **2.** *surpass* ἐπὶ ἀσελγείᾳ πάντας παρελάσασα Chrys.*hom.67.3 in Mt.*(7.665D); id.*hom.18.2 in 1Tim.* (11.657A); id.*hom.3.2 in Philm.*(11.789E); *be more important than* τάχα ~ειν δοκεῖ τὸ στῆθος τοὺς πόδας id.*hom.13.4 in 1Cor.*(10.113D); *overcome* τὸ ψεῦδος ~ει τὴν ἀλήθειαν *ib.*6.2(45C); **3.** *set beside* εἰ... παρὰ τὴν τοῦ πατρὸς ὑπάρχουσαν ~ει μὲν τὴν ἑαυτοῦ [sc. θέλησιν], πληροῖ δὲ ἐκείνην Cyr.*Jo.*4.1(4.339C).

B. intrans.; **1.** of time, *pass by*, Eus.*e.th.*1.13(p.73.29; M.24. 852B); Cyr.*ador.*10(1.358C); *ib.*12(446B); of worldly things, *pass away*, id.*Is.*2.5(2.340A); **2.** *drive on* εἰς τοῦτο...παρήλασαν μανίας Chrys.*hom.5.3 in 1Cor.*(Gaume; ἤλασαν 10.37A).

***παρελεγχής**, *discreditable*, †Apoll.*met.Ps.*106:17(M.33.1477B).

παρέλευσις, **ἡ**, *passing away* προφητεύει...περὶ τῆς π. τῶν σκιῶν Eus.*proph.*(M.22.1268A); συντέλειαν τοῦ ὁρωμένου κόσμου ἤγουν π. Tim.CP *haer.*(M.86.61C); *Vaticin.*2(p.57); of death, †Jo.D.*B.J.*40 (M.96.1236B).

***παρελθετέον**, *one must pass over*, Or.*Jo.*6.35(18; p.144.6; παρελθεῖν ἄξιον M.14.260A).

παρελκυσμός, **ὁ**, *prolongation*, Thdr.Mops.*Ps.*58:12(p.387.17; M. 66.681D).

παρέλκω, **A.** trans.; **1.** *distract* ἐκεῖνον οὐδὲν ἐφάνταζεν, οὐδὲ παρεῖλκεν Chrys.*hom.54.5 in Mt.*(7.553A); **2.** *put off*, *delay* οὐδὲ ἐπὶ πολὺ τοὺς ἀκούσαντας αὐτοῦ...παρείλκυσεν Ath.*inc.*26.5(M.25.141B); Chrys.*hom.32.1 in Mt.*(7.364D); Gel.Cyz.*h.e.*3.18(p.182.16).

B. intrans.; **1.** *continue*, Or.*fr.12 in Jo.*(p.494.14,21); **2.** *be superfluous*, Clem.*str.*5.1(p.327.25; M.9.12C); Or.*Jo.*2.34(28; p.91.23; M. 14.173B); Bas.*hex.*4.2(1.34C; M.29.81B); impers., c. infin., Clem.*str.* 6.16(p.499.13; M.9.357C); Tit.Bost.*Man.*2.26(M.18.1185D); pres. ptcpl. as adj., Evagr.Pont.*cap.pract.*A proem.(M.40.1220C); Chrys. *hom.54.2 in Mt.*(7.547E); id.*hom.2.1 in Jo.*(8.7B).

παρεμβάλλ-ω, **A.** trans.; **1.** *insert*, *interpose* μετὰ σιγῆς ἤκουον, οὐδὲν ~οντες Chrys.*hom.25.1 in Mt.*(7.307B); ref. mediation by Son between human and divine χρῆν...τὸν...πατέρα...ὡς ἂν μὴ παντελῶς ἡ τῶν ἄρτι γενησομένων φύσις ἔρημος οὖσα τῆς αὐτοῦ κοινωνίας τῶν μεγίστων ἀγαθῶν στεροῖτο, μέσην τινὰ ~ειν τὴν τοῦ μονογενοῦς αὐτοῦ καὶ πρωτοτόκου θείαν καὶ παναλκῆ καὶ πανάρετον δύναμιν Eus.*d.e.*4.6 (p.159.1; M.22.265A); **2.** reflex.; **a.** *insinuate* oneself ~ει [sc. ἡ ὀξυχολία] ἑαυτὴν εἰς τὴν καρδίαν Herm.*mand.*5.2.2; **b.** *engage* oneself *in*, Ath.Scholast.*coll.*4.1(p.50); **c.** *intrude* oneself, Phot.*nomoc.* 9.1(p.536; M.104.712D).

B. intrans.; **1.** *encamp*, Clem.*str.*6.3(p.447.16; M.9.252A); †Cyr. *coll.VT*(6^4.35A; M.77.1228B); **2.** *move into position* for battle π. εἰς πόλεμον Eus.*onomast.*(p.128.4); cf. ἀεὶ πρὸς κινδύνους ἦν παρεμβεβλημένος Chrys.*hom.44.1 in 1Cor.*(10.406E); *approach close to*, Leont.H.*Nest.*1.10(M.86.1441B); **3.** *stand on either side*, Niceph.Ur. *v.Sym.*62(M.86.3044B).

παρεμβολή, **ἡ**, **1.** *host*, *army*; **a.** in gen., Eus.*d.e.*7.1(p.321.10; M. 22.525A); **b.** of heavenly host, hosts of God or of Devil δυνάμεις τῶν π. *T.Lev.*3.3; Ἰακὼβ ὁρᾷ π. ἀγγέλων Thdr.Mops.*Gen.*32:1(M.66. 644B); θεωρία...τιτρώσκει τὸν δαίμονα καὶ...τὴν π. φυγαδεύει †Nil. *mal.cog.*20(M.79.1224A); Max.*ambig.*(M.91.1201B); **2.** *company* τῆς ἀποστολικῆς π. *V.Pach.A* 24(p.151.24); **3.** *camp*, *1Clem.*4.11; *ib.*55.4; allegorical interprn. of camp of Israel, Or.*Cels.*6.23(p.93.30; M.11. 1325D); id.*schol.in Lc.*7:22(M.17.333B); *Hom.Clem.*9.21; of Church as typified by camp of Israel, Mac.Aeg.*hom.*44.4(M.34.781B); Cyr. *Jo.*12(4.1047D); τὴν π. τῶν ἁγίων...τὴν...ἐκκλησίαν Areth.*Apoc.*20:8 (M.106.757A); exeg. Heb.13:11, π. representing Judaism, Sever. *Heb.*13:10(p.351.21); Cyr.ap.*cat.Heb.*13:11–12(p.273.8); and the world, Chrys.*hom.33.3–4 in Heb.*(12.307C–308A); **4.** *barracks*, *M. Perp.*7(p.73.29); **5.** *station*, *halting-place for night*; hence, met., of division of a book, *volume*, Or.*Jo.*32.1(p.425.4; M.14.740B); **6.** *dwelling-place* εὐαγγελικαῖς παρεμβάλωμεν λέξεσι· θεοῦ γὰρ ἐκεῖ π. ὀψόμεθα Hesych.H.*serm.*6(M.93.1468B); **7.** *monastery*, Evagr.Pont. *cap.pract.*B 98(M.40.1252A).

***παρεμπεδόω**, *corroborate*, *support*, Hesych.H.*fr.Ps.*40:11(M.93. 1193D); Gr.Agr.*Eccl.*1.17(M.98.796B).

παρεμπίπτ-ω, **1.** *fall into by accident* ὡς εἰς...βράχη παρεμπεσόντες μὴ ἀδικηθῶμεν Epiph.*haer.*28.8(p.320.26; M.41.388B); **2.** *fall in with* or *meet by chance*; of persons, Chrys.*hom.5.4 in Rom.*(9.459A); **3.** *happen*, *occur by chance* διενεγκεῖν ἀνδρείως τὰ ~οντα Cyr.*Lc.*8:22 (M.72.632A); of words ταῦτα παρενέπεσεν ἐκ τῆς ἀκολουθίας τοῦ λόγου

Gr.Nyss.*Eun*.1(1 p.43.27; M.45.272B); cf. μνήμης...παρεμπεσούσης id.*v. Macr*.(p.389.20; M.46.977A); προφέρειν τὰ ὡς ἔτυχε ~οντα opp. τὰ τοῦ θεοῦ ἐντάλματα φθέγγεσθαι ‡Proc.G.*Pr*.31:26(M.87.1541C); hence ptcpl., of food ἡ δὲ πάσης...τῆς ὑφ' ἡλίῳ τροφός [i.e. Egypt], ἄρτου δεῖται τοῦ ~οντος Cyr.*hom.pasch*.7.2(5².89B); neut. as subst., *whatever occurs* ἀπορίαι...τοῦ πρέποντος ἀναγκάζουσι τὸ παρεμπῖπτον ἑλέσθαι Isid.Pel.*epp*.5.370(M.78.1549A); **4.** *coincide with*, Anast.Ant. *serm*.4(M.89.1397C); **5.** of darkness, *fall* ~ων ζόφος ζοφοῖ τὸν λογισμόν Meth.*res*.1.30(p.263.15; M.41.1140D).

παρεμπλαστικός, *formative*, Andr.Cr.*or*.17(M.97.1188A).

παρεμπλέκ-ω, **1.** *intertwine, weave in* τῆς κρόκης...~ομένης Dion. Al.ap.Eus.*p.e*.14.24(774A; M.21.1273A); met., *Hom.Clem*.6.19; **2.** *entangle*, met. τὸ σὸν βόσκημα...εἰς νομὴν ἀκανθώδη παρεμπλέξας Epiph. *haer*.76.15(p.361.21; M.42.548B); hence pass., *be involved* in βιωτικῷ παρεμπεπλεγμένον πράγματι *Clem.ep*.5; **3.** *mix, mingle*; met., Ign. *Trall*.6.2.

παρεμπλοκή, ἡ, *entanglement*; met., *convolution* ἡ τῆς ἀνοίας καὶ ἀγνωσίας π. Epiph.*haer*.59.12(p.377.20, v.l. πάλιν πλοκή M.41.1036C).

παρεμποδίζω, 1. *be a hindrance*; abs., Amph.*hom*.2.3(M.39.40A); c. dat., Proc.G.*Is*.62:1(M.87.2660A); Melet.*nat.hom*.1(M.64.1148D); **2.** *hinder*, c. acc., Tit.Bost.*Man*.2.8(M.18.1148B); †Jo.D.*B.J*.21(M. 96.1049C); pass., Chrys.*scand*.10(3.489A); id.*hom*.7.9 *in 1Cor*.(10. 63D); Eus.Al.*serm*.21.7(M.86.432D).

***παρέμποδος,** *obstructive* τὴν ὑμετέραν μακαριότητα μὴ γενέσθαι παρέμποδον τοῦ θελήματος τοῦ θεοῦ Const.Pogon.*sacr*.1(M.*PL*.87. 1151B).

παρεμποιέω, *introduce secretly*, Epiph.*haer*.21.2(p.239.21; M.41. 288A).

παρεμπόρευμα, τό, *by-product*; met., Tit.Bost.*Man*.1.14(M.18. 1085D); Bas.*ep*.84.1(3.177A; M.32.464A); id.*hom.in Ps*.14(1.107E; M. 29.265C); *incidental activity* οὐκ ἀγεννὲς...π. οἰκονομικὸν γυμνασίου γεωργικοῦ Clem.*paed*.3.10(p.265.17; M.8.624A).

παρέμπτωσις, ἡ, 1. *irruption, assault* τὰς π. τοῦ ἀντικειμένου Clem. *str*.4.18(p.298.2; M.8.1321A); **2.** *intervention* τῇ π. τοῦ σκότους μηδαμοῦ διαιρούμενον [sc. φῶς] Gr.Nyss.*ep*.4(M.46.1028D).

παρεμφέρω, *bring* or *carry up*, Herm.*sim*.9.4.8; met. φύσις... γενητή, καὶ χρόνῳ παρενεχθεῖσα πρὸς ὕπαρξιν Cyr.*inc.unigen*.(5¹.683B).

***παρενδιάω,** *stay* or *stand beside*; c. dat., Nonn.*par.Jo*.1:49(M. 43.760A).

***παρένδοξος,** *greatly glorious*, *M.Thdot*.1 19(p.73.14).

***παρένδυσις, ἡ,** *stealthy entry, intrusion* τὰς κατὰ διαδοχὴν τῶν χρόνων π. [i.e. of heresies] καὶ τῆς πλάνης τὰ βοσκήματα Epiph.*haer*. 13.2(p.207.2; παρεισ- M.41.237C).

***παρενεγγυάω,** s.v.l., *encourage*; c. acc. et infin., Cyr.*Is*.4.2(2. 610B).

παρενείρ-ω, *insert, put into place*; reflex., Gr.Naz.*or*.40.46(M.36. 425C); of taking one's place at table, Niceph.Ur.*v.Sym*.36(M.86. 3020A); trans., *intrude* into a discussion, Gr.Nyss.*ep*.29.7(p.85.24; M.45.240B); *import* elements into one's character παρενείρας αὐτὰ [sc. τὰ πάθη] τοῖς ἐναρέτοις †Cyr.*coll.VT*(6⁴.76A; M.77.1289A); ref. insertion by Eun. of an intermediate term between ἀρχή and λόγος: καὶ εἷς οὗτος, ἀλλὰ καὶ πλείονές τινες...~όμενοι [sc. λόγοι] Gr. Nyss.*Eun*.2(2 p.353.26; M.45.532B); bet. Creator and created μεταξὺ τῆς πάντων ποιητικῆς αἰτίας διαστηματικήν τινα ~ειν ὑπόνοιαν ἐν τῷ λέγειν ποτὲ μὴ εἶναι τὸν πᾶσι δεδωκότα τὸ εἶναι *ib*.1(1 p.132.14; 369C); between Father and Son ἕτερόν τι πάντως ὂν διΐστησιν ἀπ' ἀλλήλων τὸν πατέρα καὶ τὸν υἱὸν μεταξὺ τῶν δύο ~όμενον *ib*.12(1 p.213. 10; 981B); orthodox view καὶ παρ' ἡμῶν ὁμολογεῖται τοῦ υἱοῦ τὸ πρὸς τὸν πατέρα συναφές τε καὶ ἀμεσίτευτον, ὡς μηδὲν εἶναι τὸ διὰ μέσου τούτων ~όμενον *ib*.4(2 p.85.26; 661B); *ib*.9(2 p.208.13; 805C).

παρενεκτέον, 1. *one must lay aside, reject*, Epiph.*haer*.77.35(p.447. 19,20; M.42.693B bis); **2.** *one must add* (*apply*) ἐπὶ τὴν τοῦ σωτῆρος ἐνανθρώπησιν καὶ τοῦτο π. Cyr.*thes*.16(5¹.171C).

παρένθετος, *assumed* ἐν π. προσώπῳ ὑποκρινόμενος λέγει Diod.ap. *cat.Rom*.7:18(p.108.10).

***παρενθέτως,** *by the way* οὐ π., ἀλλ' ἐνσημάντρως ‡Meth.*Sym.et Ann*.11(M.18.376B).

παρενθήκη, ἡ, *something put in beside, addition*, ‡Ath.*dial.Trin*. 2.11(M.28.1176A); Philost.*h.e*.1.1(M.65.625B); Justn.*Sev*.3(p.122.10; M.86.1101A); ref. implications of monothelite doctrine τὸ ἐλλιπὲς τῆς οἰκείας θεότητος δείξαντος, δεομένης π. τινὸς πρὸς τὴν κατ' οὐσίαν ἐντέλειαν Max.*opusc*.(M.91.93A).

παρενθυμέομαι, *disregard*; hence *think of something else*, Nil.*exerc*. 75(M.79.809A); to be avoided in prayer, id.*Magn*.23(M.79.1000A); c. acc., id.*praest*.24(M.79.1089C).

παρενθύμησις, ἡ, *disregard, neglect* ἐπειδὴ...οὐκ ἔστιν ἀσφαλὴς ἡ μακροτέρα π. ..., καὶ τὸν...Νεστόριον...ἀποχωρίζομεν Cael.*ep.Jo. Ant*.2(p.91.3; M.*PL*.50.468B).

παρενσπείρομαι, *be sown alongside* of; met., c. dat., Gr.Nyss. *anim.et res*.(M.46.64C).

***παρεντρίβω,** *rub against in passing*, trans., Epiph.*haer*.30.7(p.342. 23; M.41.417A).

παρεντυγχάνω, *meet with, come across*, Epiph.*haer*.28.8(pp.320. 25,321.6; M.41.388B,C); Jo.D.*haer*.58(M.94.713A).

παρεξάγ-ω, 1. in military metaphor, *lead out*, Cyr.*ador*.5(1.144C); **2.** *take precedence over*, Eus.*d.e*.8.1(p.358.16; M.22.581D); **3.** *draw on, carry further* ἐπὶ θεωρίαν τινὰ τὸν λόγον ~ωμεν Chrysipp.*enc.in Mich*. (p.93.8).

παρεξαγωγή, ἡ, *rejection*, opp. ἀντεισαγωγή, ‡Meth.*Sym.et Ann*. 12(M.18.377C).

παρεξαλλάσσω, *alter* ὁ...υἱὸς οὐκ ἀπαράλλακτος εἰκών, μᾶλλον οὐδὲ ὅλως ἰδιότητα ἢ ὁμοίωσίν τινα τοῦ πατρὸς ἔχων φανήσεται. ποία γὰρ ὁμοίωσις καὶ ἰδιότης τῷ παρεξηλλαγμένῳ παρὰ τὸν πατέρα; Ath.*Ar*. 3.11(M.26.344B).

παρέξειμι, (εἶμι *ibo*), *go beyond, progress*, met. ἐπὶ μήκιστον π. Clem.*str*.5.2(p.335.2; M.9.29A).

παρεξέρχομαι, *transgress*, abs., Anast.S.*qu.et resp*.123(M.89. 773A,B).

παρεξετάζω, *examine, inquire*, Bas.*Eun*.1.5(1.213E; M.29.513C).

***παρεξέτασις, ἡ,** *comparison*, Gr.Naz.*or*.43.75(M.36.597A); Didym.*Trin*.2.8(M.39.613C); for purposes of illustration εἰς π. ... τῶν θεοχρήστων ῥητῶν...κτήνη καὶ οἰκοδομίαν ἄψυχον εἰς μέσον φέρουσιν *ib*.2.10(645B); Thdt.*Ezech*.16:51(2.790).

παρεξευρίσκω, *invent falsely* διδασκαλίαι τῶν τὰς ὀγδοάδας καὶ τετράδας, καὶ δοκήσεις παρεξευρηκότων Iren.*haer*.3.17.4(M.7.931B); Ath.*Ar*.2.11(M.26.168D).

παρεξηγ-έομαι, *misinterpret, give a wrong meaning to* τὰς γραφὰς ...μὴ βλασφημῆτε καὶ ~εῖσθαι σπουδάζητε Just.*dial*.82.4(M.6.672A); μὴ παραγράφειν ἢ ~εῖσθαι τολμᾶτε *ib*.84.4(676A); Cels.ap.Or.*Cels*.4.33 (p.303.22; M.11.1077C); Ath.*Ar*.1.37(M.26.88B); διάνοιαν ὀρθήν...π. *ib*.1.46(105C).

***παρεξήγημα, τό,** *misinterpretation* ἰοβόλα δόγματα, ἢ παρεξηγήματα Olymp.*fr.Lam*.4:3(M.93.752B).

***παρεξήγησις, ἡ,** *misinterpretation, misrepresentation*, Eus. *e.th*.1 proem.(p.62.17; M.24.828D); Gr.Nyss.*Eun*.12(1 p.340.24; M. 45.1060B); Acac.Caes. *fr.Marcell*.ap.Epiph.*haer*.72.6(p.260.6; M.42. 389A); τὰς τῶν αἱρετικῶν π. Leont.B.*arg.Sev*.(M.86.1929B); id.*Nest. et Eut*.3(M.86.1364D); παρακλοπαῖς τισι καὶ π. Max.*opusc*.(M.91.245B).

***παρεξισάζ-ω,** *rank as equal* οὐχὶ τοσοῦτον ἑαυτοὺς ~οντες, ὅσον εἰς φιλοστοργίαν ἐπισπώμενοι καὶ κηδεμονίαν Chrys.*hom*.7.1 *in Ac*.(9. 55E).

παρεξίσταμαι, 1. *be out of* (*one's senses*) τὰς φρένας παρεξεστηκώς Ath.*decr*.13(p.11.31; M.25.'445'(437)C); abs. ἠλίθιον...καὶ παρεξεστηκότα Gr.Nyss.*Eun*.7(2 p.161.5; M.45.749C); **2.** *go into spurious ecstasy* (v. παρέκστασις): εἰς οὐρανὸν παρεκστῆναί τε καὶ καταπιστεῦσαι ἑαυτὸν τῷ τῆς ἀπάτης πνεύματι Anon.ap.Eus.*h.e*.5.16.14(M.20. 469B).

παρέξοδος, ἡ, 1. *digression* ἵνα...μὴ ἐν π. γένωμαι Epiph.*haer*.8.3 (p.188.27; M.41.209A); *ib*.30.17(p.357.8; 433D); *deviation*, Gr.Naz. *carm*.2.1.11.1146(M.37.1107A); **2.** *activity by the way* περιστάσεων..., αἵτινές σε κατά τινας π. καμεῖν πεποιήκασιν Leo Mag.*ep*.139(p.64.3; M.*PL*.54.1104A).

***παρεξοκέλλω,** *come to grief by the way* ἑκάστη αἵρεσις, ὡς συντομίαν τινὰ ἐφευρεῖν διανοηθεῖσα, παρεξώκειλε μὲν διὰ τῆς μακροδίας Epiph.*haer*.59.12(p.377.19; M.41.1036C).

[*]**παρεξουθενέομαι,** *be set at naught*, Const.ap.Eus.*h.e*.10.7.1(M. 20.893A).

παρέξω, *outside*, Cosm.Ind.*top*.1(M.88.100C).

παρεπαίρω, *remove*, Gr.Mag.*dial*.(tr.Zach.)1 proem.(M.*PL*.77. 154B); *ib*.3.15(254C); from text τινὲς ἐπεχείρησαν παρεπᾶραι τοὺς θρόμβους...ἐκ τοῦ κατὰ Λουκᾶν εὐαγγελίου Anast.S.*hod*.22(M.89. 289A); reflex., *keep* oneself *away* ἐπίσχετε...τῆς σωτηρίας...φροντίζοντες καὶ ἐκ τῆς τούτων διδαχῆς ἑαυτοὺς παρεπάρατε *M.Ner.et Ach*. 10(p.10.6).

παρεπιδημ-έω, *sojourn* τῆς ~ούσης τῷ κόσμῳ ἐκκλησίας Or.*Jo*.6.59 (38; p.168.3; M.14.304A).

***παρεπιθύμησις, ἡ,** *lack of attention, neglect* ἡ μακρὰ π. ὥσπερ λοιμικῷ νοσήματι καὶ τοὺς ὑγιαίνοντας χραίνεσθαι ποιεῖ Const.ap. Eus.*v.C*.3.64(p.112.5; M.20.1140D).

παρεπινο-έω, *invent besides, devise* heret. ideas, Iren.*haer*.1.10.3 (M.7.557B); καινοτομίας τινὰς ~οῦσι τῷ ὀρθῷ λόγῳ †Bas.*Is*.232(1. 555C; M.30.525A); Gr.Nyss.*Eun*.2(2 p.298.1; M.45.468C); pass., *be* *thought independently* τι καὶ παρ' ἡμῶν ἐξευρίσκεσθαι διὰ τῶν ἔξωθεν ~ουμένων id.*v.Mos.*(M.44.389C).

***παρεπιστείβ-ω**, *travel about upon* ἰχθυόεντα γένεθλα, ὁππόσα ποντοπόρους ~ουσι κελεύθους †Apoll.*met.Ps.*8:9(M.33.1321A).

***παρέργιον, τό**, *odd job*, Ephr.1.305D; id.1.310F.

***παρερείδομαι**, *be adjacent* to, Cyr.*ador.*10(1.337A).

***παρερμήνευμα, τό**, *perverse interpretation* τὰ π. τῆς κακοδόξου αἱρέσεως Epiph.*haer.*73.38(p.313.2; M.42.473B).

***παρερμηνευταί, οἱ**, a group of heretics defined as οἱ τινὰ κεφάλαια τῶν θείων γραφῶν, τῆς τε παλαιᾶς καὶ νέας διαθήκης, παρερμηνεύοντες, καὶ πρὸς τὸν οἰκεῖον σκοπὸν αὐτὰ μεθοδεύοντες Jo.D.*haer.*97(M.94.760A).

παρερμηνεύ-ω, *misinterpret*; in gen., Or.*Cels.*4.48(p.321.7; M.11.1105C); ὅταν ἀκούωσι γέννημα, καὶ λόγον, καὶ σοφίαν βιάζονται ~ειν Ath.*Ar.*2.4(M.26.153C); περὶ τοῦ πάσχα κακῶς ~ουσιν Epiph.*haer.*70.10(p.242.28; M.42.356C); τό, ἅγιος, ἅγιος, ἅγιος, ~σαι τολμῶντες Isid.Pel.*epp.*2.143(M.78.588B); Anast.S.*hod.*10(M.89.177A); of interprn. of Plato, Eus.*p.e.*11.9(525A; M.21.869C); esp. of scriptural exegesis κατ' ἐξουσίαν ~ειν τὰ ῥήματα Gr.Nyss.*Eun.*6(2 p.146.28; M.45.732D); ὅπερ οἱ αἱρετικοὶ πάντες ποιοῦσι ῥήματά τινα τῶν θείων γραφῶν ~οντες, καὶ πρὸς τὴν διεστραμμένην ἑαυτῶν μεταφέροντες ἔννοιαν Justn.*ep.Thdr.Mops.*(p.48.22; M.86.1045C); Anast.S.*hod.*6(104A).

παρέρπ-ω, *pass by, pass away* ἤματα...σκιῇ ἶσα ~ει †Apoll.*met.Ps.*143:4(M.33.1528D).

***παρερριμμένως, 1.** *at random, wantonly* π. καὶ ὑδαρῶς μετὰ μηδενὸς κατασκευαστικοῦ Or.*Jo.*10.19(14; p.191.2; M.14.341A); **2.** *scattered about*, passim ἰδίωμα Ἑβραϊκόν, π. κείμενον ἐν τῇ Ἑβραϊκῇ φωνῇ Olymp.*Eccl.*3:11(M.93.516C).

παρέρχομαι, 1. *enter into* ἡδονὴ...ὑπουργίας ἕνεκα παρῆλθεν εἰς τὸν βίον Clem.*str.*2.20(p.177.19; M.8.1064A); **2.** *pass away, perish*, met. αἱ γενεαὶ πᾶσαι ἀπὸ Ἀδὰμ...παρῆλθον *1Clem.*50.3; Chrys.*hom.3.4 in Phil.*(11.218A); *V.Dan.*2(p.57.22); **3.** *escape* from illness ἄνοσος π. *T.Zab.*5.2.

πάρεσις, ἡ, 1. in gen., *paralysis*, ref. Jo.5:14 ἡ πηγὴ τῆς π. ἁμαρτήματα ἦν Chrys.*Is.interp.*3.1(6.32D); of suspension of faculties in sleep, Athenag.*res.*16(p.68.4; M.6.1005D); met., of spiritual torpor, Cyr.*Mal.*14(3.832C); **2.** exeg. Rom.3:25, interpreted as; **a.** *paralysis caused by sin* διὰ τὴν π., τουτέστι, τὴν νέκρωσιν. οὐκέτι γὰρ ὑγείας ἐλπὶς ἦν, ἀλλ' ὥσπερ σῶμα παραλυθὲν τῆς ἄνωθεν ἐδεῖτο χειρός Chrys.*hom.7.3 in Rom.*(9.486A); διὰ τὴν π.... τουτέστι τὴν νέκρωσιν· ἐνέκρωσαν γὰρ ἡμᾶς τὰ ἁμαρτήματα Jo.D.*Rom.*3:25(M.95.465B); **b.** *passing over*, Thdt.*Rom.*3:25–26(3.44); cf.Sever.*Rom.*3:25(p.217.5); **c.** *remission*, cf.Or.*comm.in Rom.*3.8(M.14.946B); Cyr.*Rom.*3:27(p.179.22; M.74.780C); id.*Arcad.*(p.99.33; 5[2].98E).

***παρεσκιασμένως**, *surreptitiously, in obscurity* ὁ...τῆς κενοδοξίας πλάνος...π. ἐφίσταται τῇ ψυχῇ Nil.*Eulog.*22(M.79.1121C).

παρετοιμάζ-ω, pass., *get ready* ὡς ἂν ~ομένους ἤδη ἀπονίψασθαι τοὺς πόδας πρὸς τοῦ κυρίου τοὺς μαθητὰς ἀναγράφει [sc. ὁ Ἰωάννης] Clem.*fr.*28(p.216.32, v.l. προετ- M.9.757A).

πάρετος, 1. *paralysed*, esp. ref. Mt.9:2, Mac.Mgn.*apocr.*2.8(p.10.5); Sophr.H.*mir.Cyr.et Jo.*30(M.87.3520C); *weak-limbed* συμβαίνει τὸ τικτόμενον βρέφος ἢ πάρετον...προελθεῖν *M.Ner.et Ach.*4(p.3.21, codd. πάραιτον, παράλυτον); *relaxed*, Gr.Nyss.*hom.10 in Cant.*(M.44.993A); **2.** ref. mental paralysis, *languid*, Bas.*renunt.*5(2.206D; M.31.637A); ref. Christ's healings εὔλογον, εἴπερ πᾶσα νόσος καὶ πᾶσα μαλακία, ἃς ἐθεράπευσεν..., ἀναφέρεται ἐπὶ τὰ ἐν ψυχαῖς διάφορα συμπτώματα, ὡς τοὺς μὲν παρέτους τὴν ψυχὴν καὶ κειμένην αὐτὴν ἔχοντας ἐπὶ τοῦ σώματος παραλελυμένην δηλοῦσθαι διὰ τῶν παραλυτικῶν Or.*comm.in Mt.*13.4(p.188.3; M.13.1101A); **3.** *distraught*, Gr.Nyss.*v.Macr.*(p.399.23; M.46.985C).

παρευδοκιμ-έω, 1. *surpass* ἐρίζει τῷ εὐδοκιμοῦντι, φθονεῖ τῷ ~οῦντι Bas.*reg.br.*289(2.517A; M.31.1285B); θεός ἐστιν ὁ ~ῶν αὐτοὺς Chrys.*hom.29.2 in Jo.*(8.166E); *ib.*79.5(8.471E); **2.** pass.; **a.** *be held inferior, be made null* ~ηθήσεται...ἡ τοῦ ἀγαθοῦ δύναμις Clem.*str.*5.1(p.328.11; M.9.13B); ~εῖται θεὸς οὐρανὸν δεικνὺς ὑπὸ διαβόλου δέρματα δεικνύντος Chrys.*hom.49.5 in Mt.*(7.511B); Dion.Ar.*d.n.*8.8(M.3.896C); **b.** *be slighted*, Thdr.Mops.*Ps.*7:17(M.66.652C); Soz.*h.e.*6.25.3(M.67.1357B).

παρευημερ-έω, *surpass* μὴ...νηστείαν...ἄτιμον ἀποπέμψῃ ~ηθεῖσαν ὑπὸ τῆς ἡδονῆς Bas.*hom.*2.2(2.11D; M.31.188A); φθόνῳ...τῶν βουλομένων αὐτὸν ~ῆσαι βληθεὶς Chrys.*vid.*1.7(1.348D); id.*sac.*5.8(p.138.2; 1.420A); Isid.Pel.*epp.*5.215(M.78.1460C); λέοντες ἀνθρώπους ἐν τῷ τῆς φιλοσοφίας ~ήσαντες μέρει ‡Nil.*perist.*11.10(M.79.917B).

[*]**παρευθύ**, = παρευθύς, Nil.*Eulog.*12(M.1108D); †Jo.D.*B.J.*30(M.96.1149A).

παρευθύνω, *pervert, distort*; justice, Cyr.*Abac.*5(3.520C); id.*Mich.*36(3.422C); truth, id.*Ps.*46:10(M.69.1057B); doctrine, id.*Chr.un.*(5[1].750A); *ib.*(715D).

[*]**παρεύρεμα, τό**, v. παρεύρημα.

παρεύρεσις, ἡ, *invention*, Adam.*dial.*2.20(p.106.30; M.11.1880A); Ath.*Ar.*1.39(M.26.92C); ληρήματα καὶ μισοθέων λογισμῶν ἢ π. Cyr.*Jo.*9.1(4.818D).

παρεύρημα ([*]**παρεύρεμα**), **τό, 1.** *invention*, of heresy χαίρουσιν [sc. Marcosians] ἐπὶ τοῖς π. αὐτῶν Iren.*haer.*1.16.3(M.7.636A); **2.** *irrelevant matter* παρευρέμασιν ὄγκον τινὰ καὶ μέγεθος ἐπιμηχανᾶσθαι τῷ λόγῳ Gr.Nyss.*Eun.*1(1 p.46.26; M.45.276A).

παρεφεδρεύω, *sit at* or *near* τῷ ἀμιάντῳ θυσιαστηρίῳ π. Isid.Pel.*epp.*3.135(M.78.833D).

***παρεφομαρτ-έω**, *be in attendance* τῶν τινι ~ούντων ἰατρῶν Evagr.*h.e.*4.7(p.157.32; M.86.2716A).

παρηβ-άω, fig., of time, *become past* ~ήσαντος τοῦ καιροῦ Cyr.*hom.pasch.*27(5[2].313D).

παρηγόρημα, τό, *soothing remedy*, Bas.*ep.*6.1(3.78E; M.32.241B); *relief* π. τοῦ πονεῖν ποιούμενος Gr.Naz.*carm.*1.1.6.108(M.37.438A); prob. f.l. for κατηγόρημα, ‡Just.*qu.et resp.*1(M.6.1252A).

παρήγορος, ὁ, 1. *consoler*, of Christ ὁ π. ὁ ἐν μέσῳ κατοικῶν *A.Thom.*A 156(p.264.20); Nonn.*par.Jo.*11:31(M.43.844B); **2.** *soother*, fig. ἔχει...τῶν νόσων...τὴν ἐρημίαν π. Diad.*perf.*53(p.58.24).

***παρήκοος**, *disobedient*, Anon.ap.Eus.*h.e.*5.16.9(M.20.468A); Jo.D.*f.o.*4.18(M.94.1188A); id.*hom.*2.2(M.96.580A).

παρῆλιξ, *advanced in age*, comp. παρηλικεστέρων Gr.Nyss.*mort.*(M.46.516A).

παρησυχάζω, *pass over in silence*, Jo.VI CP *ep.*(M.96.1425B).

***παρθεῖα**, fictitious word formed from παρθενία and used to explain that παρθενία is *almost divine*, Meth.*symp.*8.1(p.81.4; M.18.137C) cit. s. παρθενία.

παρθενεύ-ω, *live a virgin life, be celibate*; **1.** in gen. τοὺς μὲν ἀπ' ἀρχῆς ~οντας ὁρῶμεν, τοὺς δὲ ἀπὸ χρόνου †Just.*fr.res.*(p.39; M.6.1577A); Meth.*symp.*3.14(p.44.10; M.18.85A); ἁγνείαν...ἣν...γεωργοῦμεν ἡμεῖς αἱ ~ουσαι καὶ προσφέρομεν κυρίῳ *ib.*9.4(p.119.16; 188A); διαφέρουσιν οἱ μὴ ἐπιθυμοῦντες καὶ ἁγνεύοντες τῶν ἐπιθυμούντων τε καὶ ~όντων *ib.*11(p.138.10; 216B); ref. Mt.19:11 δέδοται γὰρ...τοῖς βουλομένοις...εἰ γὰρ τῆς ἄνωθεν δόσεως μόνης ἐστί, καὶ οὐδὲν αὐτοὶ συνεισφέρουσιν οἱ ~οντες, περιττῶς αὐτοῖς τὴν βασιλείαν τῶν οὐρανῶν ἐπηγγείλατο Chrys.*hom.62.4 in Mt.*(7.624C); as counsel, not precept, id.*hom.21.5 in 1Cor.*(10.186B); ὁ πορνεύων καὶ ὁ ~ων ἀμφότεροι τοῦ νόμου τὰ μέτρα ἐξέβησαν...ἀλλ' ὁ μὲν ἐπὶ τὸ χεῖρον κατενεχθείς, ὁ δὲ ἐπὶ τὸ βέλτιον ἐπαρθεὶς id.*comm.in Gal.*5:13(10.718C); οὐ πᾶς ὁ ποθῶν τὸ πρᾶγμα καὶ ~ει, ἀλλ' ὁ δυνάμενος Pall.*v.Chrys.*1(p.4.15; M.47.5); ref. inferiority of virginity to humility οὐ γὰρ ὁ ~ων γέγραπται, ἀλλ' ὁ ταπεινῶν ἑαυτὸν ὑψωθήσεται Isid.Pel.*epp.*1.286(M.78.352A); τῶν γὰρ...ἀνοήτων φροντίδων ἐλευθέραν ὁ ~ων ἔχει ψυχήν, καὶ τὸν μέλλοντα μιμεῖται βίον ὡς ἔνεστι Thdt.*1Cor.*7:32(3.210); Gr.Mag.*dial.*(tr.Zach.)4.17(M.*PL.*77.349A); motive prescribed εἴ τις ~οι...ὡς ἂν βδελύττων τῶν γάμων ἀναχωρήσας καὶ μὴ δι' αὐτὸ τὸ καλὸν καὶ ἅγιον τῆς παρθενίας, ἀνάθεμα ἔστω CGangr.*can.*9; of BMV πρὶν τόκου ~ουσα, παρθένος μετὰ τόκον Ephr.1.545F; Isid.Pel.*epp.*1.404(M.78.408C); Jo.D.*carm.pasch.*33(p.219; M.96.841A); myst., of birth of Christ in soul ὅπερ...ἐν τῇ...Μαρίᾳ γέγονε σωματικῶς, τοῦ πληρώματος τῆς θεότητος ἐν τῷ Χριστῷ διὰ τῆς παρθενίας ἐκλάμψαντος· τοῦτο καὶ ἐπὶ πάσης ψυχῆς κατὰ λόγον παρθενευούσης γίνεται ...τοῦ κυρίου...πνευματικῶς εἰσοικιζομένου Gr.Nyss.*virg.*2(p.254.27; M.46.324B); **2.** met.; **a.** of purity of life and actions ἅπας ὁ βίος καὶ ἡ ζωὴ καὶ τὸ ἦθος ~ειν ὀφείλει Bas.*ascet.*1.1(2.319B; M.31.872B); πᾶν δὲ μέλος...ὄντως ~ειν Gr.Naz.*or.*43.62(M.36.577A); γλῶσσα ~έτω id.*carm.*1.2.3.51(M.37.636A); Gr.Nyss.*virg.*2(p.254.27; M.46.324B); Nil.*epp.*3.298(M.79.532A); ~ειν οὖν χρὴ τὰς κόρας τῶν ὀφθαλμῶν, ἰσωνυμίαν τῶν παρθένων τετιμημένας ‡Caes.Naz.*dial.*140(M.38.1060); **b.** of freedom from heresy κατὰ τὴν πίστιν π. Thdr.Stud.*epp.*2.19(M.99.1176B); **3.** *be a monk* or *nun* Ἀγαλίασις διάκονος καὶ Εὐτυχία ~σασα καὶ Κλαυδιανὴ ~σασα *ICG As.Min.*209 (Melos, ? saec. iv); ἐπέστη...τινι ~ούσῃ ‡Pall.*h.mon.*11.2(p.54.6; M.65.448D); θυγάτηρ ~ουσα ἐτελεύτησε Jo.Mosch.*prat.*78(M.87.2933C); †Jo.D.*B.J.*30(M.96.1148A); **4.** of Indian ascetics, Clem.*str.*3.7(p.224.8; M.8.1164B).

παρθενία, ἡ, *virginity*;

A. def. and descriptions; etym. παρθεῖα γὰρ ἡ π. κατὰ μίαν ὑπαλλαγὴν καλεῖται στοιχείου, ὡς δὴ μόνη τὸν ἔχοντα καὶ τετελεσμένον αὐτῆς τὰς ἀφθόρους τελετὰς θεῷ παρεικάζουσα Meth.*symp.*8.1(p.81.4; M.18.137C); π. δέ, ὅτι παρὰ τῷ θεῷ τὸ νοούμενον τῆς τοιαύτης σωφροσύνης ἐστί ‡Pion.*v.Polyc.*14; οὐ γὰρ ἐν μόνῳ τῷ φείσασθαι τῆς παιδοποιΐας κατορθοῦται τὸ χάρισμα τῆς π., ἀλλ' ἅπας ὁ βίος...καὶ τὸ ἦθος παρθενεύειν ὀφείλει, διὰ παντὸς ἐπιτηδεύματος τοῦ ἀγάμου τὴν ἀφθορίαν ἐπιδεικνύμενος. ἔστι γὰρ καὶ λόγῳ πορνεῦσαι, καὶ ὀφθαλμῷ μοιχεῦσαι...ὁ γὰρ ἐν τούτοις πᾶσιν ὑπὸ τὸν κανόνα τῆς π. ἑαυτὸν ἐγκρατείᾳ φυλάσσων, ἀληθῶς δείκνυσι τελείαν ἐν ἑαυτῷ...τῆς π. τὴν χάριν Bas.*ascet.*1.1(2.319B; M.31.872B); π. μέν, τὴν ὄντως φημί...τοῦ κατὰ ψυχὴν ἀφθόρου κάλλους...ἐστὶν ἐξαίρετος †Bas.Anc.*virg.*2(M.30.672D); ἀληθὴς π. ἡ παντὸς τοῦ ἐξ ἁμαρτιῶν μολυσμοῦ καθαρεύουσα Gr.Nyss.*virg.*proem.(p.248.14; M.46.317C); νέκρωσις δὲ σώματος ἡ π. ἐστί *ib.* 19(p.323.9; 396B); παρθενίας ὅρος τό, καὶ σώματι καὶ πνεύματι εἶναι ἁγίαν Chrys.*virg.*6(1.272C); οὐκ ἐν τοῖς ἱματίοις, οὐδὲ ἐν τοῖς χρώμασιν ἡ π., ἀλλ' ἐν σώματι καὶ ψυχῇ *ib.*7(272E); ἡ π. διὰ τοῦτο καλόν, ὅτι πᾶσαν ἐκκόπτει φροντίδος ὑπόθεσιν περιττῆς *ib.*77(329D); ἡ ὄντως π. ἐν κυρίῳ, ἁγία ἐστὶν τῷ σώματι καὶ τῷ πνεύματι, ἀπερισπάστως...τῷ κυρίῳ λατρεύουσα ἐν πνεύματι θεοῦ, καθαρῶς...ἀρέσκουσα τῷ κυρίῳ... καὶ ἓν πνεῦμά ἐστιν πρὸς κύριον Ant.Mon.*hom.*21(M.89.1497C).

B. as highest state of human life; **1.** unknown in OT and pagan antiquity μὴ...νομίσῃς τὸ τῆς π. μέγεθος μικρὸν εἶναι. τοσοῦτόν ἐστιν ἡ π., ὅτι οὐδεὶς ἠδυνήθη τῶν ἀρχαίων τοῦτο τηρῆσαι. διὰ τοῦτο γὰρ ἡ χάρις μεγάλη, ὅτι ἃ ἦν φοβερὰ ἐν τοῖς προφήταις...ταῦτα ἐγένετο νῦν εὐκαταφρόνητα...βάρυ γὰρ τὸ τῆς π. κτῆμα οὕτως, ὡς μηδένα ταύτην ἀσκῆσαι. Νῶε...γυναικὶ προσωμίλησεν· ὁμοίως δὲ Ἀβραάμ...βάρυ γὰρ ἦν τὸ ἐπάγγελμα τῆς π. ἐκ τότε ἰσχυρὰ ἡ π. ἐγένετο, ἐξ ὅτε τὸ ἄνθος τὸ τῆς π. ἐβλάστησεν· οὐδεὶς τοίνυν τῶν παλαιῶν ἠδυνήθη π. ἀσκῆσαι· μέγα γὰρ πρᾶγμα, σῶμα χαλινῶσαι Chrys.*poenit.*3.3(2.298A–C); χρημάτων μὲν ἕνεκεν ὀλίγους, εἶχον δὲ ὅμως δεῖξαί τινας Ἕλληνες παρ' αὐτοῖς φιλοσοφήσαντας...π. δὲ ἄνθος οὐδαμοῦ παρ' αὐτοῖς...ὁμολογοῦντες ἀνωτέρω τῆς φύσεως εἶναι τὸ κατόρθωμα id.*fem.reg.*1(1.249A); τὸ τῆς π. καλὸν ἀποστρέφονται μὲν Ἰουδαῖοι...θαυμάζουσι δὲ Ἕλληνες καὶ καταπλήττονται, ζηλοῖ δὲ μόνη ἡ ἐκκλησία τοῦ θεοῦ id.*virg.*1(1.268A); παρὰ δὲ Ἕλλησιν καὶ...φιλοσόφοις, οὐ μόνον δὲ ὅτι οὐδέπω ἐφάνη π., ἀλλ' οὐδὲ πιστεύουσίν τινα ἄνθρωπον...ταύτῃ ἀντοφθαλμῆσαι· καὶ δικαίως· πῶς γὰρ πιστεύσωσιν περὶ παρθενίας, οἱ τὰ αἰσχρὰ πάθη θεοποιήσαντες...; Ἰουδαῖοι δὲ μέχρι τῆς σήμερον, π. μὲν οὔτε ἀσπάζονται, οὔτε μετέρχονται Ant.Mon.*hom.*21(M.89.1496C,D); though practised by some OT saints, Jo.D.*f.o.*4.24(M.94.1209A); **2.** revealed by Christ and present in Church ἐξεταστέον, δι' ἣν αἰτίαν πολλῶν προφητῶν...πολλὰ καὶ καλὰ διδαξάντων...π. οὐδεὶς οὔτε ἐνεκωμίασεν οὔτε εἵλετο. μόνῳ...ἐφυλάσσετο τοῦτο πρεσβεῦσαι τὸ μάθημα τῷ κυρίῳ, ἐπεὶ καὶ μόνος παρελθὼν ἄνθρωπον ἐδίδαξε χωρεῖν εἰς θεόν...τὸ δὲ παλαιὸν οὐδέπω τέλειος ὁ ἄνθρωπος ἦν, καὶ διὰ τοῦτο τὸ τέλειον οὐδέπω χωρῆσαι, τὴν π., ἴσχυεν Meth.*symp.*1.4(p.12.16ff.; M.18.44C); ἡ π. διαδεξαμένη τὸν νόμον Χριστοῦ ταγαῖς τῶν ἀνθρώπων ἐβασίλευσεν *ib.* 10.1(p.122.7; 193A); τίς οὖν ἀνθρώπων μετὰ θάνατον ἢ ὅλως ζῶν περὶ παρθενίας ἐδίδαξε, καὶ οὐκ ἐνόμισεν ἀδύνατον εἶναι τὴν ἀρετὴν ταύτην ἐν ἀνθρώποις; ἀλλ' ὁ ἡμέτερος σωτὴρ...τοσοῦτον ἴσχυσεν ἐν τῇ περὶ ταύτης διδασκαλίᾳ, ὡς καὶ παιδία μήπω τῆς νομίμης ἡλικίας ἐπιβάντα τὴν ὑπὲρ τὸν νόμον ἐπαγγέλλεσθαι π. Ath.*inc.*51.1(M.25.185D–188A); μέγα π. ... καὶ τὸ μετ' ἀγγέλων τετάχθαι...ὀκνῶ γὰρ εἰπεῖν Χριστοῦ, ὅς, καὶ γεννηθῆναι θελήσας διὰ τοὺς γεννητοὺς ἡμᾶς, ἐκ παρθένου γεννᾶται, π. νομοθετῶν Gr.Naz.*or.*43.62(M.36.576C); id.*carm.*1.2.1.193(M. 37.537A); εἶδες...τῆς π. τὸ ἄνθος; τοῦτο τῆς ἐκκλησίας τὸ ἱμάτιον Chrys.*exp.in Ps.*44:15f.(5.180D); foretold in Ps.44:16, †Chrys.*Jud. et gent.*7(1.568A); ἐφ' οὗ γὰρ...Χριστὸς...ηὐδόκησεν ἐκ τῆς...ἀειπαρθένου Μαρίας τῷ κόσμῳ ἐπιφανῆναι...εὐχερῶς ἐξανύεται παντὶ τῷ βουλομένῳ· τοιαύτη τῆς π. ἡ ἀρετή Ant.Mon.*hom.*21(M.89.1497A); highest grade of life in Church, Epiph.*exp.fid.*21(p.521.33f.; M.42. 824A); **3.** even in Church only counselled, not prescribed; **a.** in gen. οὐ νομοθετεῖ...οὔτε διὰ Μωϋσέως π. ὁ κύριος...οὔτε ἐν εὐαγγελίῳ ...οὐδαμοῦ ἐν ταῖς ἐντολαῖς π., οὔτ' ἐν παλαιᾷ, οὔτε ἐν καινῇ διαθήκῃ, νομοθετήσας †Bas.Anc.*virg.*55(M.30.780C); τοσοῦτον γάρ ἐστιν ἡ π. πρᾶγμα...ὅτι κατελθὼν ὁ Χριστὸς ἐξ οὐρανοῦ...οὐδὲ τότε ἐθάρρησεν ἐπιτάξαι τοῦτο...ἀλλ' ἀποθνήσκειν μὲν ἐνομοθέτησεν...καὶ ἐχθροὺς εὐεργετεῖν, παρθενεύειν δὲ οὐκ ἐνομοθέτησεν Chrys.*ep.*2.7(3.542C); Ant. Mon.*hom.*21(M.89.1496B); **b.** exeg. Mt.19:11 μεγάλα περὶ παρθενίας διελέχθη εἰπών· εἰσὶν εὐνοῦχοι...ἔστι φύσει τὸ πρᾶγμα μέγα, καὶ δείκνυται ἐξ ὧν οὔτε ἐν τῇ παλαιᾷ ὑπὸ τῶν...ἁγίων ἀνδρῶν...κατωρθώθη, καὶ ἐν τῇ καινῇ δὲ οὐκ ἦλθεν εἰς ἀνάγκην νόμου Chrys.*hom.78.1 in Mt.* (7.751B); **c.** exeg. 1Cor.7:25ff. θεοδώρητον εἶναι τὸ τῆς π. ἐπιτήδευμα παρεγγυᾷ· ὅθεν τοὺς κατὰ πρόφασιν κενοδοξίας τῶν ἀκρατεστέρων ἐπὶ τοῦτο παρεληλυθότας ἀποβάλλεται, συμβουλεύων γαμεῖν Meth.*symp.* 3.14(p.44.2; M.18.84C); ἐπὶ...τῆς παρθένου γνώμην δίδωσιν, ἐνταῦθα [i.e. for marriage] δὲ συγγνώμην. ἐπιτάττει δὲ οὐδέτερον οὐ διὰ τὴν αὐτὴν αἰτίαν, ἀλλ' ἐνταῦθα μέν, ἵνα μή τις ἀναβῆναι ἀπὸ τῆς ἀκρασίας βουλόμενος κωλύηται, ὡς ἐπιτάγματος ἀνάγκῃ δεδεμένος· ἐκεῖ δέ, ἵνα μή τις ἀναβῆναι πρὸς τὴν π. ἀδυνατῶν κατακρίνηται, ὡς προστάγματος παρακούων Chrys.*virg.*34(1.293E); ἐπειδὴ ὁ κύριος οὐκ ἐπέταξε π., διὰ τοῦτο οὐδὲ ἐγώ· συμβουλεύω δὲ ὑμῖν *ib.*42(1.303A); *ib.*47(1.307D); *ib.* 76(329A); Thdt.*1Cor.*7:26f.(3.208); cf. ὡς οὖν ὁ κύριος τοὺς τρόπους τῆς κατὰ τὴν π. εὐνουχίας ἐρωτηθείς, οὕτως ὁ μαθητὴς τῆς π. τὴν συμβουλὴν εἰσηγήσατο †Bas.Anc.*virg.*56(M.30.781C); **4.** as gift of God needing divine grace τὸ γὰρ μέγιστον...δῶρον, οὗ μηδὲν ἀντάξιον ἄλλο προσενέγκασθαι πάρεστιν ἀνθρώποις θεῷ, τὸν ἄθλον τῆς π. εἶναι πέπεισμαι Meth.*symp.*5.1(p.53.8; M.18.97A); Gr.Nyss.*virg.*1(p.251. 14; M.46.320C); *ib.*19(p.323.20; 396C); τῆς π. τὸ ἀξίωμα...ὑπεραναβαῖνον τὴν φύσιν τὴν ἀνθρωπίνην, καὶ τῆς ἄνωθεν δεόμενον χειρός Chrys. *hom.18.4 in Gen.*(4.155B); **5.** as angelic state of life, Ath.*apol.Const.* 33(M.25.640A); †Bas.Anc.*virg.*68(M.30.808D); Cyr.H.*catech.*6.35; *ib.* 15.23; Gr.Nyss.*virg.*13(p.308.23; M.46.380D) cit. s. ἀνάστασις; π., τὸ τῶν ἀγγέλων πολίτευμα, τὸ πάσης ἀσωμάτου φύσεως ἰδίωμα Jo.D. *f.o.*4.24(M.94.1209B); **6.** as higher state than marriage δύο γὰρ οὐσῶν ὁδῶν ἐν τῷ βίῳ...μιᾶς μὲν μετριωτέρας καὶ βιωτικῆς, τοῦ γάμου λέγω· τῆς δὲ ἑτέρας ἀγγελικῆς καὶ ἀνυπερβλήτου, τῆς π. Ath.*ep.Amun.*(M. 26.1173C); εἰ γάρ τις...ἐξετάζειν ἐθέλοι τοῦ βίου τούτου [sc. marriage] τὸ πρὸς τὴν π. διάφορον, τοσαύτην εὑρήσει τὴν διαφοράν, ὅση σχεδὸν τῶν ἐπιγείων ἐστὶ πρὸς τὰ οὐράνια Gr.Nyss.*virg.*3(p.257.8; M.46.325C); ἔτι οὖν τολμήσει τις,...τῇ π. τὸν γάμον παραβάλλειν;...οὐκ ἀφίησιν ὁ ...Παῦλος, πολὺ τὸ μέσον ἑκατέρου τοῦ πράγματος θείς· ἡ μὲν γὰρ τὰ τοῦ κυρίου, φησίν, ἡ δὲ τὰ τοῦ κόσμου μεριμνᾷ Chrys.*virg.*34(1.293A); ὅσῳ...ἄγγελος ἀνθρώπου ὑπέρτερος, τοσούτῳ π. γάμου τιμιωτέρα Jo.D. *f.o.*4.24(M.94.1209C); superior to widowhood, Chrys.*hom.in 1Tim.* 5:9(3.316B); because surpassing nature, †Bas.Anc.*virg.*55(M.30. 780D); because not, like marriage, followed by death, Chrys.*virg.*14 (1.279E); ref. idea that marriage was consequence of Fall παρὰ τὴν ἀρχήν, εἰ τοῖς προστάγμασιν αὐτοῦ πεισθέντες οἱ περὶ τὸν Ἀδὰμ τῆς ἡδονῆς ἐκράτησαν τοῦ ξύλου, οὐκ ἂν ἠπόρησεν ὁδοῦ δι' ἧς τὸ τῶν ἀνθρώπων γένος αὐξήσει. οὔτε γὰρ ὁ γάμος μὴ βουλομένου θεοῦ δυνήσεται ποιῆσαι πολλοὺς τοὺς ὄντας ἀνθρώπους, οὐδὲ ἡ π., βουλομένου πολλοὺς εἶναι, λυμανεῖται τὸ πλῆθος *ib.*15(280B); as having sanctifying efficacy εἰ καὶ τίμιος ὁ γάμος, ἀλλὰ μέχρι τοσούτου φθάσαι δύναιτ' ἄν, ὥστε μὴ μολῦναι τὸν χρώμενον, τὸ δὲ καὶ ἁγίους ἀποφαίνειν, οὐκέτι τῆς ἐκείνου δυνάμεως, ἀλλὰ τῆς π. ἐστίν *ib.*30(290B); but marriage not therefore to be disparaged, CGangr.*can.*9 cit. s. παρθενεύω; ὁ δὲ τίμιος γάμος ὑπέρκειται παντὸς δώρου γηΐνου, ὡς ἔγκαρπον δένδρον... ὡς ῥίζα τῆς π. ... περίελε...γάμον, καὶ ποῦ εὑρήσεις τὸ τῆς π. ἄνθος; ἔνθεν γὰρ καὶ οὐκ ἄλλοθεν, τὸ τῆς π. ἄνθος ἀναλέγεται. ταῦτα δὲ λέγοντες, οὐ μάχην παρεισβάλλομεν μεταξὺ π. καὶ γάμου...ἄνευ γάρ... θεοσεβοῦς εὐσεβείας οὔτε π. σεμνή, οὔτε γάμος τίμιος Amph.*hom.*2.1 (M.39.45Af.); ὁ...τὸν γάμον κακίζων καὶ τὴν τῆς π. ὑποτέμνεται δόξαν. ὁ δὲ τοῦτον ἐπαινῶν μᾶλλον ἐκείνης ἐπαίρει τὸ θαῦμα...καλὸν ὁ γάμος. καὶ διὰ τοῦτο ἡ π. θαυμαστόν, ὅτι καλοῦ κρεῖττόν ἐστι. καὶ τοσούτῳ κρεῖττον, ὅσῳ τῶν ναυτῶν ὁ κυβερνήτης Chrys.*virg.*10(1.275Bf.); Jo.D. *f.o.*4.24(M.94.1209B).

C. virginity as spiritual rather than physical state; **1.** in gen. πολλοὶ τῷ ὀνόματι τῆς π. μόνῳ προσέχοντες, οὐδέν τι τῆς ἀληθοῦς π. φροντίζουσι· διὰ τοῦτ' ἀναγκαίως οἶμαι τοῖς τὸν ὑπὲρ παρθενίας στέφανον ποθοῦσι λαβεῖν, ὑποφωνῆσαι τὰ ἐνόντα σπουδάσω, ὡς ἂν μὴ δι' ἄγνοιαν ἀμελήσαντες τοῦ προηγουμένου καλοῦ, προσαναλώσωσι μὲν τῇ τῆς θεραπαίνης δουλείᾳ πάντα τὸν βίον, διὰ δὲ τὸ μηδέποτε τὴν δέσποιναν ταύτης θεραπεῦσαι, καὶ τὴν τοῦ σώματος π. οὐ κοσμουμένην τῷ τῆς ἔνδοθεν κάλλει, μετὰ πολλοὺς ἱδρῶτας ζημιωθῶσιν †Bas.Anc.*virg.*2(M. 30.673A); cf.*ib.*13(696D); οὐκ ἀπὸ σωμάτων...ἐπὶ ψυχὰς αὐτὴ ὁδεύει· ἀλλὰ ψυχῆς τῆς ἀσωμάτου οὖσα ἐξαίρετος, τῇ ταύτης θεοφιλεῖ π. ἄφθορα φυλάττει τὰ σώματα. τοῦ γὰρ ὄντως καλοῦ ἡ ψυχὴ φαντασίαν λαβοῦσα...τὴν τοῦ σώματος π., θεράπαιναν εἰς τὴν τοῦ καθ' ἑαυτὴν κάλλους θεραπείαν ἐπάγεται, καὶ πάρεδρον...πρὸς τὴν τοῦ θεοῦ θεωρίαν ταύτην ἔχειν ἀεὶ βουλομένη, τὰς...τοῦ σώματος ἡδονὰς...ἐλαύνει. τὴν μὲν τῶν ὑπὸ γαστέρα ἡδονῶν ἐγκράτειαν, τῆς σωματικῆς π. θεράπαιναν ...ποιουμένη· ὡς τὰ ἄλλα μὲν ἅπαντα, καὶ τροφῶν ἐγκράτειαν...μαχομένην ταῖς ῥεούσαις κατὰ τῆς ἐν σώματι π. διὰ τῶν αἰσθήσεων ἡδοναῖς· ἀλλὰ καὶ αὐτὴν τὴν τοῦ σώματος π. ... δι' ἑαυτὴν...ἀσκεῖσθαι, ἵνα τὴν ἑαυτῆς π. ἄφθορον ἁπάσης μοχθηρᾶς ἐννοίας φυλάξασα, τὴν πρὸς τὸν ἄφθαρτον θεὸν ἐξομοίωσιν...κερδήσῃ *ib.*2(672B,C); οὐχ ἁπλοῦν...τὸ κατόρθωμα τοῦτό ἐστιν, οὐδὲ μέχρι τῶν σωμάτων ἱστάμενον, ἀλλ' ἐπὶ πάντα...διαβαῖνον τῇ ἐπινοίᾳ, ὅσα κατορθώματα ψυχῆς ἐστι...ἡ γὰρ τῷ...νυμφίῳ προσκολληθεῖσα διὰ παρθενίας ψυχή, οὐ μόνον τῶν σωματικῶν μολυσμάτων ἑαυτὴν ἀποστήσει, ἀλλ' ἐντεῦθεν μὲν ἄρξεται τῆς καθαρότητος, ἐπὶ πάντα...μετὰ τῆς ἴσης ἀσφαλείας πορεύσεται Gr. Nyss.*virg.*14(p.310.3; M.46.381C); hence π. not affected by rape, ‡Chrys.*hom.in Ps.95:1*(5.635E); **2.** preservation of true virginity; **a.** in struggle against temptations ἐπειδὴ οὖν θεῖον...τι χρῆμα ἡ π. ἐστί...ἡ δὲ παρθένος οὐδὲν τῆς θήλεος ἡδονῆς ἐπιφερομένη ἐκ σώματος μόλυσμα, πάντα δὲ τὰ σαρκὸς πάθη ἐκδῦσα, καθαρὰν ἑαυτὴν τῷ θεῷ... παραστῆσαι φιλοτιμεῖται· δῆλον ὡς βιαστῶν ἆθλον εἶναι τὴν τῶν οὐρανῶν βασιλείαν γινώσκουσα βιάσασθαι πρὸς τὸν προκείμενον σκοπὸν τὴν ἑαυτῆς φύσιν ὀφείλει †Bas.Anc.*virg*.4(M.30.677B); τοῦ πολέμου τοῦ πρὸς τὴν π. οὐκ ἔστιν ἀποχή· διάβολος γάρ ἐστιν ὁ πολεμῶν...ἕστηκεν ἀεὶ ζητῶν τὴν παρθένον γυμνὴν εὑρεῖν, ἵνα καιρίαν ἐπαγάγῃ τὴν πληγήν Chrys.*poenit*.3.3(2.298C); πολλῶν ἱδρώτων καὶ μεγάλης ἡ π. δεῖται τῆς ἀγωνίας id.*virg*.13(1.277E); cf.*ib*.(278C); *ib*.41(301E); **b.** in practice of virtue ὑποκείσθω...ἀντὶ θεμελίου τινὸς τῷ κατ' ἀρετὴν βίῳ ἡ περὶ τὴν π. σπουδή, ἐποικοδομείσθω δὲ τῷ θεμελίῳ τούτῳ πάντα τὰ ἔργα τῆς ἀρετῆς Gr.Nyss.*virg*.17(p.317.1; M.46.389A); ὁ τῆς π. κόσμος...οὐ γὰρ λίθοι καὶ χρυσός...ἀλλ' ἀντὶ τούτων νηστεῖαι,...πραότης, ἐπιείκεια, πενία...ταπεινοφροσύνη Chrys.*virg*.63(1.320D); *ib*.84(335E); μέγα τὸ τῆς π. ἀξίωμα...π. γὰρ ἀξίωμα οὐκ ἀποσχέσθαι γάμων μόνον, ἀλλὰ τὸ φιλάνθρωπον εἶναι καὶ φιλάδελφον καὶ συμπαθητικόν. τί γὰρ ὄφελος π. μετὰ ὠμότητος id.*hom*.*1.7 in 2Cor.4:13*(3.266B); ref. almsgiving, id.*poenit*.3.3(2.298E); id.*hom.in 1Tim.5:9*(3.316B); ὅτι ἄμωμον...τὴν οἰκείαν π. φυλάξαι σπουδάζουσι...οὐ μόνον τὴν ἐπιθυμίαν κολάσαι ὀφείλουσιν, ἀλλὰ καὶ φιλοχρηματίαν, καὶ κενοδοξίαν, καὶ γαστριμαργίαν ...σὺν πάσῃ κακίᾳ Nil.*epp*.3.298(M.79.532A); v. ἐλεημοσύνη; **c.** in mortified life ἀναγκαῖον τὴν μέλλουσαν τῶν πρὸς τὰς μίξεις ἡδονῶν διὰ παρθενίας κρατεῖν, πολλῷ πλέον πρότερον τῆς κατὰ τὴν γεῦσιν ἡδονῆς, ὡς ἐπαντλούσης ἐκείνῃ τὰς ὕλας, ἄρχουσαν δείκνυσθαι †Bas.Anc.*virg*.7(M.30.681C); οἶδεν ἀρίστη πολιτεία τρέφειν τοὺς τῆς π. καρπούς· μᾶλλον δὲ καὶ ῥίζα καὶ καρπὸς παρθενίας ὁ ἐσταυρωμένος βίος ἐστίν Chrys.*virg*.80(1.332C); **d.** in retirement, ref. Rom.10:6ff. οὕτω καὶ ἐπὶ τῆς π. φησί· μὴ εἴπῃς, πῶς ἀναβῶ εἰς τὸν οὐρανόν, ἐκεῖθεν τὴν τῆς π. μου ἀφθορίαν καταγαγεῖν; ἢ πῶς καταβήσομαι εἰς τὴν ἄβυσσον...; ἐγγύς σου ἐστί...καὶ κατὰ φύσιν σοι συγγεννᾶται ἡ π. ... καὶ εἰ βούλει ταύτην παρά σοι ἄσυλον μένειν, διὰ βίου σαββάτιζε· τουτέστι, μένε ὃ ἐγεννήθης·...οὐκ ἔχεις τοίχους καὶ περιβόλους ὑπεράλλεσθαι, ἵνα τὴν π. θηράσῃς. ἀλλὰ ταῦτα μὲν πράττουσα, καὶ ἀπολέσεις ἴσως τὴν π. ἐπὶ τῆς κοίτης δὲ σαββατίζουσα, καθαρὰν αὐτὴν φυλάξεις, καὶ οὕτω μὲν εὐκόλως...τὴν π. ... ἕξεις †Bas.Anc.*virg*.59(M.30.788B,C); **e.** with help of a guide ἐπειδὴ νέοι ἔτι καὶ ἀτελεῖς τὴν διάνοιαν οἱ πολλοὶ τῆς π. ἀντιλαμβάνονται, τοῦτο πρὸ πάντων αὐτοῖς ἐπιτηδευτέον ἂν εἴη, τὸ ζητῆσαι τῆς ὁδοῦ ταύτης ἀγαθὸν καθηγεμόνα Gr.Nyss.*virg*.23(p.336.19; M.46.408D); **3.** as implying consecration to God ἀνατιθέναι λέγομεν τελείως ἑαυτὸν τῷ θεῷ, ὃς καὶ τὴν σάρκα ἄχραντον ἐκ παίδων φιλοτιμεῖται φυλάττειν, π. ἀσκῶν Meth.*symp*.5.3(p.56.12; M.18.101B); ἡ δὲ παρθένος τὸν ἑαυτῆς νυμφίον...περιέπουσα...τούτῳ μᾶλλον τὰς ἀχράντους νύμφας πρὸς ἀφθορίαν προμνηστευέσθω...ἑπομένη τῷ νυμφίῳ, ἢ τῷ οἰκείῳ φωτὶ τῆς π. καὶ ἑτέρας πρὸς παρθενίαν νυμφεύουσα †Bas.Anc.*virg*.21(M.30.713A); τὴν Χριστῷ διὰ τῆς κατὰ τὴν π. ὑποσχέσεως ἁρμοσθεῖσαν...σοφὴν προσήκει...εἶναι *ib*.50(768C); π. μὲν ὅλην ἀνάθημα θεοῖο Gr.Naz.*carm*.1.2.1.527(M.37.562A); τάχα ὁ τολμήσας εἰπεῖν τὴν σωματικὴν π. τοῦ ἔνδοθεν καὶ πνευματικοῦ γάμου συνεργὸν...γίνεσθαι, οὐ πόρρω τοῦ εἰκότος ἀποτολμήσει Gr.Nyss.*virg*.19(p.325.6; M.46.397A); ‡Chrys.*Thecl*.(2.750E); hence mere fact of physical virginity of no value, ‡Chrys.*hom.in Ps.95:1*(5.635D,E).

D. effects; **1.** natural advantages εἰ βούλει μαθεῖν τὰ δυσχερῆ τοῦ κοινοτέρου βίου, ἄκουσον οἷα λέγουσιν αἱ τῇ πείρᾳ τὸν βίον γνωρίσασαι, ὅπως μακαρίζουσι τὴν ζωὴν τῶν...τὸν ἐν π. βίον προελομένων...ὅτι πάντων τῶν τοιούτων κακῶν ἀνεπίδεκτός ἐστιν ἡ π.· οὐκ ὀρφανίαν θρηνεῖ, οὐ χηρείαν ὀδύρεται Gr.Nyss.*virg*.3(p.264.8; M.46.333C); λυσιτελὲς εἶναι νομίζομεν τοῖς ἀσθενεστέροις εἰς τὴν π. ὡς εἰς ἀσφαλές τι φρούριον καταφεύγειν *ib*.9(p.287.18; 357D); less trouble than in married life, Chrys.*virg*.55–58(1.315A–319A); **2.** union with God τὸ ἐν π. ... μεῖναι μᾶλλον παρίστησι τῷ θεῷ Athenag.*leg*.33.1(M.6.965A); Meth.*symp*.6.2(p.65.14; M.18.116A); Chrys.*virg*.78(1.331C); θυσιαστήρια, καὶ ναός, καὶ κειμήλια θεοῦ διὰ τῆς π. πεφήνατε Nil.*epp*.2.31(M.79.212D); **3.** likeness to angels οἱ τὴν π. ἀσκοῦντες ἄγγελοί εἰσιν, ἐν ἀφθάρτοις σαρξὶ τὸν τῶν ἀνθρώπων βίον περιπολοῦντες· καὶ ἄγγελοι οὐκ ἄσημοί τινες, ἀλλὰ...ἐπιφανέστατοι. ὅτι ἐκείνων ἄνευ σαρκῶν κατὰ τὸν οὐρανὸν τὴν ἀφθαρσίαν καὶ τόπῳ καὶ ἀβιάστῳ φύσει παρὰ τῷ...θεῷ φυλαττόντων, οὗτοι ἐπὶ γῆς σαρκὸς ἡδοναῖς ἐνοχλούμενοι, καὶ τῇ πείρᾳ τοῦ διαβόλου ἐκκείμενοι, τὴν ἀφθαρσίαν ἰσάγγελον δι' ἀρετῆς τῷ ποιητῇ παραδοξότερον διεφύλαξαν †Bas.Anc.*virg*.51(M.30.772B); τῆς ὑψηλῆς ἐπιθυμίας συνεργὸν...τῷ ἀνθρώπῳ τὴν π. δεδόσθαι φαμὲν...δοκεῖ καὶ τὸ τῆς π. ἐπιτήδευμα τέχνη τις εἶναι...τῆς θειοτέρας ζωῆς, πρὸς τὴν ἀσώματον φύσιν τοὺς ἐν σαρκὶ ζῶντας ὁμοιοῦσθαι διδάσκουσα Gr.Nyss.*virg*.5(p.276.24; M.46.348B); εἶδες τῆς π. ἀξίωμα; τοὺς ἐπὶ τῆς γῆς διατρίβοντας τοῖς ἐν οὐρανοῖς διαιτωμένοις ὁμοίως πολιτεύεσθαι ποιεῖ...ἀνθρώπους ὄντας εἰς τὸν αὐτὸν τῶν ἀγγέλων ἄγει ζῆλον Chrys.*virg*.11(1.276A); cf. θεῖον...καὶ τῆς...τῶν ἀσωμάτων τάξεως, τὸ...τῆς π. ἔνδυμα Procl.CP *or*.6.2(M.65.724A); **4.** deification μέγα...π., τῷ ἀφθάρτῳ θεῷ...ἐξομοιοῦσα τὸν ἄνθρωπον †Bas.Anc.*virg*.2(M.30.672B); εἰ γὰρ τὸ κατόρθωμα τῆς...π. ἐστὶ τὸ ἄμωμόν τινα γενέσθαι καὶ ἅγιον (ταῦτα δὲ τὰ ὀνόματα κυρίως...εἰς δόξαν προλαμβάνεται τοῦ ἀφθάρτου θεοῦ), τίς μείζων ἔπαινος παρθενίας, ἢ τὸ ἀποδειχθῆναι διὰ τούτων θεοποιοῦσαν τρόπον τινὰ τοὺς τῶν καθαρῶν αὐτῆς μυστηρίων μετεσχηκότας εἰς τὸ γενέσθαι αὐτοὺς κοινωνοὺς τῆς δόξης τοῦ...ἁγίου...θεοῦ, διὰ καθαρότητος αὐτῷ καὶ ἀφθαρσίας οἰκειουμένους; Gr.Nyss.*virg*.1(p.252.4ff.; M.46.320D); **5.** overcoming of death, *ib*.13(p.305.10ff.; 377A,C,D); **6.** access to heaven π. γὰρ βαίνειν μὲν ἐπὶ γῆς, ἐπιψαύειν δὲ τῶν οὐρανῶν ἡγητέον Meth.*symp*.1.1(p.8.4; M.18.37B); ref. Ps.136 αἱ τὸ...εὐπρεπὲς τῆς π. ὑποδῦσαι...κάλλος, καὶ στεῖραι...τῶν ῥευστῶν...εὑρεθεῖσαι παθῶν, ἐπὶ γῆς ἀλλοτρίας οὐ μελῳδοῦσι τὴν ᾠδήν, ὅτι μὴ φέρονται τὰς ἐλπίδας τῇδε...ἀλλ' εὖ καὶ γενναίως μετὰ φρονήματος ὑψηλοῦ τὰς ἐπαγγελίας ἄνω περιαθροῦσι *ib*.4.5(p.50.21; 93A); *ib*.8.2(p.83.7; 141A); ἡ π. ... τοῦ ἀφθάρτου βίου ...σπέρμα †Bas.Anc.*virg*.51(M.30.772A); ἡ π. κατὰ φύσιν γνωρίσασα, ὅτι ὥσπερ εἰς τὴν τοῦ παρόντος βίου σπορὰν διὰ τῆς τῶν γάμων ἡδονῆς τὰ σπέρματα τῆς ἀνθρωπότητος κατεβάλετο, οὕτω καὶ εἰς τὸν ἐκεῖ βίον τὰ σπέρματα τοῦ βίου ἡμῶν διὰ τῆς ἀφθορίας ἐντεῦθεν ἤδη καταβάλλεσθαι, σπουδάζει δι' ἑαυτῆς καθαρὰ τὰ τῆς ἀφθαρσίας σπέρματα πρὸς τὸν ἄφθαρτον βίον τῷ γεωργῷ εὐτρεπίζειν *ib*.54(776D); ἡ ἀληθινὴ π. ... εἰς τοῦτον τὸν σκοπὸν καταλήγει, τὸ δι' αὐτῆς δυνηθῆναι τὸν θεὸν ἰδεῖν Gr.Nyss.*virg*.11(p.297.4; M.46.368D); hence linking of earth to heaven, *ib*.2(p.255.4; 324B).

E. types of virginity; **1.** willow, exeg. Ps.136 ἐν τύπῳ γὰρ τῆς π. τὴν ἰτέαν πανταχοῦ παραλαμβάνουσιν αἱ θεῖαι γραφαί, ἐπειδήπερ τὸ ἄνθος αὐτῆς εἰς ὕδωρ ἀποτριβέν, ἐὰν ποθῇ, πᾶν ὅσον εἰς ὀχείας ἀναζεῖ καὶ ἐρεθισμοὺς κατασβέννυσιν...εἰς ὕψος γὰρ τότε τὸ τῆς π. ἔρνος μεγεθύνεται...ὁπόταν ὁ δίκαιος καὶ ἐγκεχειρισμένος τηρεῖν αὐτὴν καὶ ἐργάζεσθαι τοῖς ἠπιωτάτοις τοῦ Χριστοῦ νάμασιν ἀρδεύῃ, σοφίᾳ καταψεκάζων, ὃν γὰρ τρόπον τὸ δένδρον τοῦτο χλοηφορεῖν πέφυκεν ὕδατι καὶ βλαστάνειν, οὕτως ἐπανθεῖν ἀεὶ καὶ ἐπακμάζειν πιαινομένη λόγοις πέφυκεν ἡ π. Meth.*symp*.4.3(pp.48.20–49.11; M.18.89D–92A); **2.** altar in Holy of Holies, *ib*.5.8(p.63.2; 112B); **3.** instrument played by Miriam εὐθέως μετὰ τὴν θάλασσαν...εὔηχον μεταχειριζομένη τὸ τύμπανον...τάχα γὰρ διὰ τοῦ τυμπάνου τὴν π. ἔοικεν ὁ λόγος αἰνίττεσθαι ὑπὸ τῆς Μαρίας πρώτης κατορθωθεῖσαν, δι' ἧς οἶμαι καὶ τὴν θεοτόκον προδιατυποῦσθαι Μαρίαν. ὥσπερ γὰρ τὸ τύμπανον πολὺν τὸν ἦχον ἀφίησι, πάσης ἰκμάδος κεχωρισμένον...οὕτω καὶ ἡ π. λαμπρά τε καὶ περιβόητος γίνεται μηδὲν ἐν ἑαυτῇ τῆς ζωτικῆς ἰκμάδος...προσδεχομένη Gr.Nyss.*virg*.19(p.322.27ff.; M.46.396A,B); **4.** lamps of ten virgins οὐ περὶ ἐλαίου ἐνταῦθα καὶ πυρὸς διαλεγομένη ἡ γραφή, ἀλλὰ περὶ π. καὶ φιλανθρωπίας, καὶ τὴν μὲν π. ἐν τάξει πυρός, τὴν δὲ ἐλεημοσύνην ἐν τάξει ἐλαίου τίθησι, δεικνῦσα ὅτι σφόδρα δεῖται φιλανθρωπίας ἡ π. Chrys.*anom*.8.2(1.515E); λαμπάδας...τὸ τῆς π. χάρισμα id.*hom.78.1 in Mt*.(7.751D); **5.** ref. Ps.118:91 ἡμέραν... νοητέον τὴν φωτοειδῆ π. Nil.*epp*.2.118(M.79.252B).

F. reasons why not counselled in pre-Christian times μεγάλη... ὑπερβολὴ τὸ τῆς π. ἀνθρώποις ἀπ' οὐρανῶν κατεπέμφθη φυτόν, καὶ διὰ τοῦτο ταῖς πρώταις οὐκ ἀπεκαλύφθη γενεαῖς. ἔτι γὰρ ὁ ἄνθρωπος ὀλιγοστὸς ἦν, καὶ ἐχρῆν εἰς πλῆθος πρῶτον αὐτὸν αὐξήσαντα τελειωθῆναι Meth.*symp*.1.2(p.9.21; M.18.40C); †Bas.Anc.*virg*.55(M.30.780A); εἶπεν, αὐξάνεσθε καὶ πληθύνεσθε. τοῦτο γὰρ ὁ καιρὸς ἀπῄτει, τῆς φύσεως μαινομένης, καὶ τὸν τῶν παθῶν οἶστρον μὴ δυναμένης ἐνεγκεῖν τί κελεύειν ἐχρῆν; ἐν...π. διάγειν; ἀλλὰ τοῦτο μεῖζον ἂν τὸ πτῶμα εἰργάσατο...διὰ ταῦτα ἐξ ἀρχῆς οὐκ ἐδόθη ἡ π.· μᾶλλον δὲ ἡ π. μὲν ἐξ ἀρχῆς καὶ τοῦ γάμου προτέρα ἡμῖν ἐφάνη· διὰ ταῦτα δὲ ἐπεισῆλθεν ὕστερον ὁ γάμος...ὡς εἴ γε ἔμεινεν ὑπακούων ὁ Ἀδάμ, οὐκ ἂν ἐδέησε τούτου Chrys.*virg*.17(1.282A,B); a later development in Church οὐκ εὐθέως, τῆς ἐκκλησίας συστάσης, τὸ τῆς π. ἤνθησε καλόν, ἀλλ' ὕστερον καὶ μετὰ χρόνον τινὰ id.*exp.in Ps*.44(5.180D).

G. virginity in paradise, ref. Adam and Eve ἐν...τῷ παραδείσῳ διαιτώμενοι...ἐν ἐκείνῳ τῷ χωρίῳ τῇ π. κοσμούμενοι...ἐπειδὴ δὲ παρήκουσαν τοῦ θεοῦ...ἀπώλεσαν μετὰ τῆς μακαρίας ἐκείνης διαγωγῆς καὶ τὸ τῆς π. καλόν...ἕως μὲν γὰρ ἦσαν ἀνάλωτοι τῷ διαβόλῳ... παρέμεινε καὶ ἡ π. Chrys.*virg*.14(1.279B,D); id.*hom.18.4 in Gen*.(4.155B); ἐν παραδείσῳ π. ἐπολιτεύετο Jo.D.*f.o*.4.24(M.94.1208A).

H. in rel. to martyrdom κόρην...καὶ τῇ μὲν τὸν καθ' ἡδονῶν, τῇ δὲ τὸν κατὰ κινδύνων ἀνατείνουσαν στέφανον· καὶ τῇ μὲν τὴν π., τῇ δὲ τὸ μαρτύριον τῷ...δεσπότῃ προσφέρουσαν. ἣν μὲν οὖν αὐτῇ καὶ τὰ τῆς π., ἃ τοῖς ἀκριβῶς σκοπουμένοις μέγα τι πρὸ μαρτυρίου μαρτύριον. αἱ γὰρ ἡδοναὶ δεινοί τινες τοῦ σώματος δήμιοι...ἃ δὴ πάντα τῇ μακαρίᾳ παρθένῳ μακρόν τι μαρτύριον τὴν π. εἰργάζετο· πυκτευούσῃ ταῖς ἡδοναῖς, ὡς ὁ μάρτυς θηρίοις ‡Chrys.*Thecl*.(2.749A–C).

I. vow of virginity and marriage π. γὰρ τῷ κυρίῳ ἐπαγγειλάμεναι, εἶθ' ὑπὸ τῶν σαρκὸς ἡδονῶν νικηθεῖσαι, τὴν τῆς πορνείας ἁμαρτίαν γάμου ὀνόματι περιστέλλειν ἐθέλουσιν· οὐκ ἀγνοοῦσαι...κἂν ἄγνοιαν δὴ προσποιῶνται, ὅτι ἡ παραβᾶσα τὰς πρὸς τὸν νυμφίον ἑαυτῆς δεξιάς, οὔτε τούτου ἐστὶ νύμφη ὃν παρανόμως κατέλιπεν, οὔτ' ἐκείνου, ᾧ διὰ πάθος ἔζευξεν ἑαυτήν, κατὰ νόμους γυνὴ δύναται εὑρεθῆναι †Bas.Anc. *virg.*37(M.30.745C); *ib.*39(748B).

J. as gift made to God *εἶπεν ὁ θεός...σὺ διδούς μοι ἀδιάφθορον τὸν ἀσύλητον θησαυρόν, τὸ κειμήλιον τῆς π. Apoc.Esd.*13(p.25); Or.*Cels.* 7.48(p.199.30; M.11.1492B); *ἐβούλετο* [sc. God] *γὰρ μὴ ἐπίταγμα εἶναι τὸ κατόρθωμα τῆς π., ἀλλὰ πλεονέκτημα φιλαρέτου ψυχῆς, ἀπὸ αὐτεξουσίου αὐθεντίας τὸ ὑπὲρ τὴν ἐντολὴν καὶ ὑπὲρ τὴν φύσιν ἀφ' ἑαυτῆς κατορθούσης* †Bas.Anc.*virg.*55(M.30.780C).

K. as special responsibility *οὐ δεῖ τοῦ ἑαυτῆς ἀβλαβοῦς μόνον φροντίζουσαν, τῆς τῶν βλαβῆναι δυναμένων καταφρονεῖν σωτηρίας, ἀλλὰ πανταχόθεν καὶ ἑαυτῆς ἄσυλον τὸ τῆς π. κάλλος φυλάττειν, καὶ τοῖς ὁρῶσιν αὐτὴν κέρδος ζωῆς, καὶ μὴ τὸν ἐξ ἁμαρτίας θάνατον πραγματεύεσθαι. εἰ γὰρ καὶ αὐτὴ πέποιθε τῷ τῆς π. ἀπτώτῳ, ἀλλ' ὅμως προνοεῖσθαι δεῖ...ὥστε μὴ τιθέναι πρόσκομμα τῷ ἀδελφῷ* †Bas.Anc. *virg.*35(M.30.740C); as guarded by guardian angel, *ib.*29(729A).

L. its loss; irreparable, †Bas.Anc.*virg.*59(M.30.788D); *τρόπον τινὰ mataία...ἡ γνῶσις ἐμοὶ τῶν τῆς π. καλῶν, ὡς τῷ βοῒ τὰ γεννήματα τῷ μετὰ κημῶν ἐπιστρεφομένῳ τὴν ἅλωνα...μακάριοι δὲ οἷς ἐν ἐξουσίᾳ τῶν βελτιόνων ἐστὶν ἡ αἵρεσις, καὶ οὐκ ἀπετειχίσθησαν τῷ κοινῷ προληφθέντες βίῳ, καθάπερ ἡμεῖς οἱόν τινι χάσματι πρὸς τὸ τῆς π. καύχημα διειργόμεθα, πρὸς ἣν οὐκ ἔστιν ἐπανελθεῖν ἔτι τὸν ἅπαξ τῷ κοσμικῷ βίῳ τὸ ἴχνος ἐναπερείσαντα* Gr.Nyss.*virg.*3(p.256.9ff.; M.46. 325A,B).

M. exeg. Mt.19:11f. *οἱ καὶ καλλίονες τῶν ἄλλων ὑπάρχοντες, διότι οὔτε ἐκ τῆς φύσεως πρὸς σωφροσύνην ἐφόδιον ἔχοντες, οὔτε παρὰ ἀνθρώπων κρατούμενοι, αὐτοὶ ἑαυτοὺς διὰ τὴν βασιλείαν τῶν οὐρανῶν πρὸς τὴν π. ἀσκοῦσι...ὁ μὲν γὰρ ἐκ κοιλίας μητρὸς εὐνοῦχος,...οὐδὲν ἴδιον ἔργον ἐν τῷ τῆς π. κάλλει ἐπιδείξασθαι ἔχει· φύσει ὅπερ ἔφην πλεονεκτήματι, καὶ οὐχὶ τῇ πρὸς τὴν π. διαθέσει τὸν γάμον ἀποστραφείς. ὥσπερ οὖν καὶ ὁ παρ' ἀνθρώπων εὐνουχισθεὶς τηρήσει τὴν π. ἀσκεῖν βιαζόμενος, οὐκ ἴδιον κατόρθωμα τὴν ἀφθορίαν τῆς π., ἀλλὰ τῶν τηρούντων δεικνύει, ὁ δὲ ἑαυτὸν εὐνουχίσας, ἐξαίρετον ἔργον διὰ τῆς ἐγκρατείας τε καὶ πρὸς πάντα ἀσκήσεως τὸ τῆς π. κάλλος ποιούμενος, ἰδίοις καὶ οὐκ ἀλλοτρίοις κατορθώμασιν ἐν τῇ βασιλείᾳ σεμνύνεται* †Bas. Anc.*virg.*57(M.30.784D–785A).

N. heret. *τὰς γὰρ τῶν αἱρετικῶν οὐκ ἂν εἴποιμί ποτε παρθένους...αἱ τοίνυν τὸν ἕνα ἄνδρα μὴ στέργουσαι, ἀλλ' ἕτερον αὐτῷ τὸν οὐκ ὄντα ἐπεισάγουσαι θεόν, πῶς ἂν εἶεν ἁγναί; πρῶτον μὲν οὖν κατὰ τὸν λόγον οὐκ ἂν εἶεν παρθένοι· δεύτερον δέ, ὅτι τὸν γάμον ἀτιμάσασαι οὕτως ἦλθον ἐπὶ τὸ ἀποσχέσθαι τοῦ γάμου. τῷ γὰρ νομοθετῆσαι πονηρὸν εἶναι τὸ πρᾶγμα, προλαβοῦσαι τὰ τῆς π. ἑαυτῶν ἀφείλοντο ἔπαθλα* Chrys.*virg.*1(1.269A); hence heretics not to be rewarded, but punished for their virginity *ib.*2(270C); *τῆς ἐκείνου* [sc. *διαβόλου*] *πονηρίας ἐστὶν ἀκριβῶς εὕρημα ἡ τῶν αἱρετικῶν π. ib.*5(272A); true virginity incompatible with false doctrine, *ib.*(272B).

O. feigned virginity *εἰ δὲ ὅτι οὐδεὶς τῶν ἀνθρώπων ὁρᾷ, πρὸς τὸ νεῦμα ἢ τὸν λόγον τολμᾷ, μάλιστα μὲν αὐτόθεν ἑαυτῆς ἐστι κατήγορος... ὅτι τοὺς τῶν ἀνθρώπων ὀφθαλμοὺς ἀπατῶσα, ὡς αὐτῷ ἑαυτὴν διὰ βίου νυμφεύουσα, οὔτ' ἐκείνου νύμφη, οὔτ' ἀνθρώπου καθαρῶς ἐστι γυνή, ἀλλὰ τὴν παρ' ἀνθρώπων δόξαν ἐπὶ τῇ π. διὰ τοῦ παρθενικοῦ σχήματος κλέπτουσα, ἐν ὀφθαλμοῖς τοῦ νυμφίου, παρ' ἀνθρώποις τὴν π. ἑαυτῆς ἐκπομπεύουσα, μοιχεύεται* †Bas.Anc.*virg.*28(M.30.728B).

P. ref. BMV; **1.** perpetual virginity; **a.** *in partu*, Gr.Nyss.*nativ.* (M.46.1136A,B); id.*virg.*19(p.324.14; M.46.396D); *ὁ Χριστὸς ἐκ τῆς ἀλύτου μήτρας προελθὼν οὐκ ἠφάνισε τὴν σφραγῖδα τῆς π.* ‡Chrys. *BMV* 2.3(8.240D); *ὁ Ἐμμανουὴλ φύσεως μὲν πύλας ἀνέῳξεν ὡς ἄνθρωπος, π. δὲ κλεῖθρα οὐ διέρρηξεν ὡς θεός, ἀλλ' οὕτως ἐκ μήτρας ἐξῆλθεν, ὡς δι' ἀκοῆς εἰσῆλθεν* Procl.CP *or.laud.BMV* 9(p.107.18; M. 65.692A); Thdot.Anc.*hom.*1.1(p.81.1; M.77.1349A); Leo Mag.*ep.*35.3 (p.42.3; M.*PL.*54.808B); Abr.Eph.*occurs.*6(p.452.17); **b.** *post partum ἡ παρθένος καὶ μετὰ τὸ τεκεῖν παρθένος ἔμεινεν, ἐκ τοῦ τεκεῖν μὴ ζημιωθεῖσα τὴν π.* ‡Chrys.*BMV* 2.2(8.240B); *παρθένος γὰρ ἡ μήτηρ, καὶ μετὰ τόκον διέμεινε τῆς π. σφραγίς, ἣν ἡ φύσις ἐπέθηκεν ἀπαρασάλευτον φυλάττουσα* Hesych.H.*serm.*4(M.93.1460C); **c.** both *in partu* and *post partum εἴ τις οὐχ ὁμολογεῖ...Μαρίαν...ἀφθόρως γεννήσασαν, ἀλύτου μεινάσης αὐτῆς καὶ μετὰ τόκον τῆς π., εἴη κατάκριτος* CLater. *can.*3; *ὁ τόκος ἄνευ ὠδίνων τὴν τῆς γειναμένης π. οὐκ ἐλυμήνατο, μεμένηκε γὰρ αὐτὴ παρθένος καὶ μετὰ τόκον, ὥσπερ ἦν καὶ πρὸ τόκου* ‡Cyr.*Trin.*14(6³.20D; M.77.1152A); *οὐ γὰρ διήνοιξεν γεννηθεὶς μόνον τὴν μήτραν...ἀλλὰ καὶ κεκλεισμένην τῆς π. τὴν πύλην κατέλιπεν* Leont.N. *serm.*1(M.93.1573A); Germ.CP *or.*3.12(M.98.304C); *ἡ...παρθένος...ἡ τοσοῦτον τὴν π. ποθήσασα, ὡς ὑπ' αὐτῆς οἷά τινος καθαρωτάτου ποιωθῆναι πυρός. παρθένος γὰρ ἅπασα τῷ τόκῳ τὴν π. λυμαίνεται· αὕτη δὲ καὶ πρὸ τόκου, καὶ τίκτουσα μένει παρθένος, καὶ μετὰ γέννησιν* Jo.D.*hom.*9.2(M.96.724C); **d.** as proof of Christ's divinity *ὅτι γὰρ ἐστιν ὁ τεχθεὶς λόγος θεοῦ, δῆλον ἐξ ὧν τὴν π. οὐκ ἔλυσεν. ἡ τίκτουσα σάρκα ψιλὴν τῆς π. παύεται· ἀλλ' ἐπειδὴ ἐτέχθη σαρκὶ λόγος θεοῦ, φυλάττει τὴν π., ἑαυτὸν λόγον δεικνύς* Thdot.Anc.*hom.*1.1(p.81.14ff.; M.77.1349C); *εἰ γὰρ οὐκ ἠλλοιώθη ἡ παρθένος καὶ μήτηρ ἐγένετο· οὐδὲ ἀλλοιωθείσης π. τόκος ἐγένετο, θεοῦ θαυματουργήσαντος παρθένῳ τὸν τόκον· τί θαυμάζεις, εἰ ἐν ἀπαθεῖ φύσει θελήσας θεὸς ὑπεδέξατο πάθος, οὐκ ἀποθέμενος τὴν ἀπάθειαν* id.*exp.symb.*14(M.77.1333A); *οὐ γὰρ ἔτεκον τῷ κόσμῳ ψιλὸν ἄνθρωπον, ἀλλὰ θεὸν σεσαρκωμένον. καὶ μάρτυς ἀξιόπιστος, ἡ σφραγὶς τῆς π. μου* Eulog.*palm.*10(M.86.2933A); Chrysipp.*enc.in BMV* 2(p.340.9); cf.Jo.D.*hom.*8.8(M.96.712A); monophysite *ἢ γὰρ ἂν πάντη...ἔλυεν τὴν π. ἡ ἀνθρώπου φύσις· εἰ γὰρ ἦν ἄνθρωπος κατὰ φύσιν...ὁ μέλλων ἀποτελεῖσθαι ἄνθρωπος ἐν μήτρᾳ τῆς παρθένου, οὐκ ἂν ἐτέχθη ἐξ αὐτῆς, εἰ μὴ πρῶτον τῆς π. λυθείσης* Tim.II Al.*fr.*(M.86.276A); **e.** hence BMV not *ἀνθρωποτόκος*, Thdot. Anc.*exp.symb.*18(M.77.1340C); **f.** in rel. to Assumption *ἔδει τῆς ἐν τῷ τίκτειν φυλαξάσης τὴν π. ἀλώβητον, ἀδιάφθορον τηρηθῆναι τὸ σῶμα, καὶ μετὰ θάνατον. ἔδει...τοῖς θείοις ἐνδιατρίβειν σκηνώμασιν* Jo.D.*hom.*9.14(M.96.741B); **2.** spiritual foundations of her virginity *ἐξ ἄκρας ταπεινώσεως καὶ τῆς πρὸς θεὸν ἀγάπης, τὸν τῆς π. ἄμωμον χιτῶνα ἑαυτῇ κεχαριτωμένη ἐξύφανεν* Ant.Mon.*hom.*21(M.89.1497B); *εὗρε χάριτος ἄβυσσον, ἣ σῶαν τὴν ὁλκάδα τῆς διπλῆς π. τηρήσασα, καὶ τὴν ψυχὴν γὰρ παρθένον ἐτήρησεν, οὐ τοῦ σώματος ἔλαττον. ὅθεν καὶ ἡ τοῦ σώματος π. τετήρατο* Jo.D.*hom.*8.7(M.96.709B); **3.** her virginity a mystery, hidden from the Devil, Ign.*Eph.*19.1; *Ζαχαρίας...τὸ τῆς π. μυστήριον ἐπὶ τοῦ ἀφθάρτου τόκου κατανοήσας* Gr.Nyss.*nativ.*(M. 46.1137A); *πρότερον οὖν γέγονε τὸ κατὰ τὴν π. μυστήριον καὶ ἡ περὶ τὸ πάθος οἰκονομία* id.*Eun.*3(2 p.20.13; M.45.585A); id.*Apoll.*3(M.45. 1128C); **4.** her vow of virginity *Μαριάμ, ἡ τὸ τῆς π. ῥόδον ἀμάραντον φυλάξαι προσευξαμένη* Tim.Ant.*descr.BMV* 6(M.28.952B); **5.** OT types of her virginity *ὁ μέν σε ῥάβδον Ἰεσσαὶ καλεῖ, ἵνα τὸ ἄτρωτον καὶ ἀκαμπὲς τῆς π. αἰνίξηται. ὁ δὲ βάτῳ προβάλλει καιομένῃ, καὶ μὴ κατακαιομένῃ* Hesych.H.*serm.*5(M.93.1461C); **6.** in epithets of BMV *ὁ στέφανος τῆς π.* Cyr.*hom.div.*4(p.102.21; 5².355E); *ἡ στήλη τῆς π.* †Serg.*acath.*228(p.145; M.92.1344D); *τὸ τῆς π. κειμήλιον* ‡Jo.D.*hom.* 6.5(M.96.668C).

Q. ref. Christ *ὁ κύριος...ἄφθορον ἐφύλαξεν ἐν π. τὴν σάρκα κοσμήσας. καὶ ἡμεῖς ἄρα, εἰ μέλλοιμεν καθ' ὁμοίωσιν ἔσεσθαι θεοῦ, τοῦ Χριστοῦ φιλοτιμώμεθα τὴν π. τιμᾶν* Meth.*symp.*1.5(p.13.13ff.; M.18.45B); *ib.* 10.1(p.122.12; 193A); *ὅτι σπέρμα τοῦ ἀφθάρτου βίου τὴν π. ὁ κύριος ἡμῶν ἐκ γῆς εἰς οὐρανὸν παραδόξως πεμπόμενον ἐβουλήθη γενέσθαι, ἐμμελετῆσαι τὰ σώματα ἡμῶν τὸ τῆς ἀφθορίας κάλλος διὰ τῆς τῶν παρθένων ἀφθορίας ἤδη θελήσας, δηλόν ἐστιν ἐξ ὧν πάντα τῷ νόμῳ πεισθεὶς μόνον τὸν γάμον ἀπείπατο* †Bas.Anc.*virg.*54(M.30.777B); *Χριστὸς...τὴν π. τὴν ἀληθῆ...δεικνὺς ἐν ἑαυτῷ* Jo.D.*f.o.*4.24(M.94. 1209C).

R. praise of virginity *μεγάλη τίς ἐστιν...ἔνδοξος ἡ π. ... τὸ οὖθαρ τῆς ἐκκλησίας καὶ τὸ ἄνθος...αὐτῆς τοῦτο τὸ ἄριστον* Meth.*symp.*1.1 (p.7.10; M.18.36B); *ib.*7(p.71.22; 125A); *μεγάλα ἐγκώμια τῆς π. ὦ π., πλοῦτος ἀκατάληπτος· ὦ π., στέφανος ἀμαράντινος· ὦ π., ναὸς θεοῦ καὶ ἁγίου πνεύματος οἰκητήριον· ὦ π., μαργαρῖτα τίμιε* Ath.*virg.*24 (p.59.11ff.; M.28.280C); *παρθενίη...θεόσδοτε, δῶτερ ἐάων, μῆτερ ἀκτημοσύνης, Χριστοῦ λάχος, οὐρανίοισι κάλλεσιν ἀζυγέεσσιν ὁμόζυγε* Gr.Naz.*carm.*1.2.1.11(M.37.523A); *ἔπαινος δὲ μόνος ἱκανὸς τῆς π. ἐστὶ τὸ κρείττονα τῶν ἐπαίνων εἶναι τὴν ἀρετὴν ἀποφήνασθαι, καὶ τῷ βίῳ θαυμάσαι μᾶλλον ἢ τῷ λόγῳ τὴν καθαρότητα* Gr.Nyss.*virg.*1 (p.252.25; M.46.321B); *πολλοὶ τῶν μεγάλων ἀνθρώπων τὴν π. θαυμάζουσιν· καὶ γάρ ἐστι θαυμαστή, ὡς τῶν ἀγγέλων σύμφυτος,...ὡς τῶν ἀσωμάτων φύσεων σύνδρομος, ὡς τῆς ἁγίας ἐκκλησίας λαμπαδοῦχος... θαυμαστή...ἡ π., ὡς ἀδούλωτον κτῆμα...ὡς συνεισελθοῦσα τῷ νυμφίῳ Χριστῷ* Amph.*hom.*2.1(M.39.44C,D); *οἱ καλοὶ τῆς π. λόγοι...αὕτη ὁ λογικὸς τοῦ θεοῦ παράδεισος, ἐν ᾧ πᾶν ξύλον ὡραῖον εἰς ὅρασιν, τουτέστιν πνευματικὴν θεωρίαν· καὶ καλὸν εἰς βρῶσιν, τὴν πνευματικὴν διδασκαλίαν...αὕτη τῆς ἀληθινῆς ἐπαγγελίας ἡ χώρα* Procl.CP *or.*6.3 (M.65.724C); *M.Ner.et Ach.*8(p.7.17ff.).

S. met.; **1.** ref. Church *ἡ ὑπερβάλλουσα νύμφη* [sc. *ἐκκλησία*] *τῷ κάλλει...τῆς π. πάσας* Meth.*symp.*7.7(p.78.5; M.18.133B); *ib.*8.11 (p.94.3; 156A); **2.** Trin. *ὃ...παράδοξον ἐν πατρὶ π. εὑρίσκεσθαι τῷ καὶ υἱὸν ἔχοντι καὶ δίχα πάθους γεννήσαντι· τῷ δὲ μονογενεῖ θεῷ τῷ τῆς ἀφθαρσίας χορηγῷ συγκαταλαμβάνεται ὁμοῦ τῷ καθαρῷ...τῆς γεννήσεως αὐτοῦ συνεκλάμψασα. καὶ πάλιν τὸ ἴσον παράδοξον υἱὸς διὰ παρθενίας νοούμενος. ἐνθεωρεῖται δὲ ὡσαύτως καὶ τῇ τοῦ ἁγίου πνεύματος φυσικῇ...καθαρότητι· τὸ γὰρ καθαρὸν καὶ ἄφθαρτον ὀνομάσας ἄλλῳ ὀνόματι τὴν π. ἐσήμανας* Gr.Nyss.*virg.*2(p.253.11ff.; M.46. 321C).

παρθενικός, 1. *of the Virgin διὰ π. μήτρας...σαρκωθέντα* Just.*dial.* 84.2(M.6.673B); Meth.*symp.*3.5(p.31.19; M.18.68B); Cyr.H.*catech.*

12.28; Gr.Nyss.*Apoll*.54(M.45.1256B); ηὐδόκησε γὰρ ὁ θεὸς...τὸν υἱὸν...κατελθόντα ἐν μήτρᾳ π. συλληφθῆναι Epiph.*inc*.1(p.227.20; M. 41.273C); ref. Valent. Christology μηδὲν δὲ ἀπὸ τῆς π. μήτρας εἰληφέναι, ἀλλὰ ἄνωθεν τὸ σῶμα ἔχειν id.*haer*.31.7(p.396.11; M.41. 488A); Chrys.*hom.12.1 in Mt*.(7.160D); τὸ μὲν γὰρ πνεῦμα αὐτὸν διέπλασεν...οὐ μὴν ἐξ οὐκ ὄντων...ἀλλ' ἐκ τῆς σαρκὸς τῆς π. id.*hom. 26.1 in Jo*.(8.149D); id.*hom.4.1 in 1Cor*.(10.24B); ἐβαστάζετο ἀγκάλαις π. Sophr.H.*ep.syn*.(M.87.3173B); **2.** *virginal, virgin* π. ὠδῖνος Chrys.*hom.26.2 in Jo*.(8.151D); π. ... μήτηρ Nonn.*par.Jo*. 2:2(M.43.760C); *ib*.19:27(904B); ἡ τοῦ σώματος σύμπηξις ἐκ πανάγνων αἱμάτων π. ‡Cyr.*Trin*.14(6³.20D; M.77.1152A); met. παρθενικοῖς δὲ δραμοῦσι καλῶς ἄφθαρτον ἄεθλον δώσει *Orac.Sib*.2.48; ἀνάψυξον ἡ π. μου πίστις *Apoc.Bar.rel*.6.4; in Barbeliote Gnostic system ὑπέθεντο ...αἰῶνα τινὰ ἀνώλεθρον ἐν π. διάγοντα πνεύματι, ὃ Βαρβηλὼθ ὀνομάζουσι Thdt.*haer*.1.13(4.304); **3.** *consisting of maidens* σύλλογος π. Cyr.H.*procatech*.14.

***παρθενικῶς, 1.** *as befitting a virgin* π. ἀποκρίνεται Sophr.H.*or*.2. 45(M.87.3277B); Thdr.Stud.*nativ.BMV* 7(M.96.692B); **2.** *as from a virgin, virginally* ὁ τόκος...θεῖος διὰ τῆς ἀρραγοῦς μήτρας π. ἐδείχθη Leont.H.*Nest*.4.36(M.86.1709D); ἐκυήθη π. Thdr.Stud.*epp*.2. 23(M.99.1188C).

παρθένιος, ἡ, *chalk*, Clem.*str*.1.10(p.8.8; M.8.697A).

***παρθενογενής,** *of virgin birth*, Tim.Ant.*Sym*.(M.86.245B).

***παρθενογέννητος,** *born of a virgin* διὰ τοῦτο ἀληθινὸς θεός, ἐπειδὴ π. Leont.H.*Nest*.4.41(M.86.1716A).

παρθενοκομία, ἡ, *hostel for girls*, Gr.Naz.*or*.43.34(M.36.541C).

***παρθενόλυτος,** *ending virginity* π. ... γάμων Isid.Pel.*epp*.2.92(M. 78.536D).

***παρθενομάρτυς, ἡ,** *virgin martyr*, *Hymn*.(*AS* 1 p.644).

***παρθενομήτηρ, ἡ,** *virgin mother*, as adj. π. κόρη Ephr.3.534C.

***παρθενομήτωρ, ἡ,** = foreg. π. ὡς θεοτόκος ἡ...Μαρία ‡Ath.*Jov*. (M.28.532B); Cyr.*Arcad*.(p.66.33; 5².49E); id.*deip.BMV* 4(p.20.33; M.76.260C); Mod.*dorm*.3(M.86.3288A); Sophr.H.*or*.2.21(M.87.3241A); τῆς ἀχράντου π. CTrull.*can*.79.

***παρθενοποι-έω,** *make virgin*, exeg. parable of ten virgins ἀποστάσας τῆς εἰδωλολατρείας τῷ παραδέξασθαι...τὸν τοῦ θεοῦ καθαρὸν λόγον καὶ ~ηθείσας Or.*comm.ser.63 in Mt*.(p.145.23; *virginificatae* M.13.1699D).

***παρθενοπρεπῶς,** *in a manner becoming virgins* ὁσίως καὶ π. Thdr.Stud.*epp*.2.115(M.99.1384C).

παρθένος, ἡ, *virgin*;

I. of the consecrated virgin also called (π.) κανονική q.v.; **A.** as bride of Christ; **1.** in gen. π. ... Χριστὸν ἔχουσα νυμφίον Gr.Naz. *carm*.1.2.3.67(M.37.638A); *ib*.1.2.29.315(907A); **2.** as calling for renunciation εἰ γὰρ οἱ τῷ κόσμῳ συναπτόμενοι καταλιμπάνουσι τὸν πατέρα καὶ τὴν μητέρα καὶ συνάπτονται ἀνθρώποις θνητοῖς, πόσῳ μᾶλλον ἡ π. ἐγκρατευομένη ὀφείλει καταλιπεῖν τὰ γήϊνα πάντα καὶ τῷ κυρίῳ μόνῳ κολληθῆναι Ath.*virg*.2(p.36.25; M.28.253B); πᾶς μὲν τόπος...ἐν τῇ ψυχῇ τῆς π. τῆς ὄψεως Χριστοῦ πεπληρώσθω...μηδενὸς οὖν...μὴ παρόντος, μὴ ἀπόντος ἀνθρώπου κάτοπτρον ἔστω ἡ τῆς π. ψυχή, ἢ τοῦ ἁγίου αὐτῆς νυμφίου †Bas.Anc.*virg*.49(M.30.768A); ὅλῃ τέτασο πρὸς θεόν, ὦ π., τῇ ψυχῇ...καὶ οὐ μή τί σοι φανῇ τῶν ἄλλων καλόν, ὅσα τοῖς πολλοῖς· οὐ γένος, οὐ πλοῦτος...οὐ...κάλλος...εἰ ὅλην ἐκένωσας πρὸς θεὸν τοῦ φίλτρου τὴν δύναμιν, εἰ μὴ δύο σοι εἴη τὰ ποθούμενα, καὶ τὸ ῥέον, καὶ τὸ ἀόρατον· ἆρα τοσοῦτον ἐτρώθης τῷ ἐκλεκτῷ βέλει, καὶ τοῦ νυμφίου κατέμαθες, ὥστε καὶ δύνασθαι λέγειν... γλυκασμὸς εἶ [cf.Cant.5:16] Gr.Naz.*or*.37.11(M.36.296C); id.*carm*.1. 2.2.658(M.37.630A); **3.** as receiving blessings ἄφθορος οὖν οὐ τῇ πρὸς τὸν ἄφθαρτον λόγον ἑνώσει ἡ π. μένει μόνον, ἀλλὰ καὶ μετὰ τὴν ἕνωσιν γίνεται...ἀλλ' ἐφθαρμένην διὰ τῶν σαρκικῶν ἡδονῶν παρὰ διαβόλου λαβών, καὶ γυναῖκα αὐτοῦ διὰ τῆς φθορᾶς κακῶς γενομένην, τῇ πρὸς αὐτὸν κοινωνίᾳ ἄφθορον ἐκ γυναικὸς παρθένον ποιεῖ †Bas.Anc.*virg*.50 (M.30.769C); ἡ δὲ π. καὶ ποθεῖ τὴν τελευτήν...σπεύδουσα τὸν νυμφίον ἰδεῖν πρόσωπον πρὸς πρόσωπον Chrys.*virg*.59(1.319B).

B. compared with angels οὐ γαμοῦσιν, οὐδὲ γαμίζονται ἄγγελοι; ἀλλ' οὐδὲ ἡ π. παρεστήκασι διαπαντὸς...τῷ θεῷ; τοῦτο καὶ ἡ π. Chrys. *virg*.11(1.275E); ἡ δὲ π. ἐπὶ μείζοσιν ἀπεδύσατο, καὶ τὴν ἀνωτάτω φιλοσοφίαν ἐζήλωσε, καὶ τὴν τῶν ἀγγέλων πολιτείαν δεῖξαι ἐπὶ τῆς γῆς ἐπαγγέλλεται, καὶ μετὰ τῆς σαρκὸς ταύτης τὰ τῶν ἀσωμάτων αὐτῇ δυνάμεων κατορθῶσαι πρόκειται id.*sac*.3.17(p.88.26; 1.398B).

C. conduct; **1.** in gen., Polyc.*ep*.5.3 cit. s. ἁγνός; δεῖν τὴν σώφρονα...π. παντὸς πάθους κατὰ πάντα τρόπον τῆς ψυχῆς ἁπτομένου χωρίζεσθαι Gr.Nyss.*virg*.15(p.313.5; M.46.385A); ἡ π. ... ἔστω ἁγία σώματι καὶ ψυχῇ, ὡς ναὸς θεοῦ, ὡς οἶκος Χριστοῦ, ὡς πνεύματος ἁγίου καταγώγιον. δεῖ γὰρ τὴν ἐπαγγειλαμένην, ἄξια τῆς ἐπαγγελίας ἔργα διαπρασσομένην, δεικνύειν τὸ ἐπάγγελμα αὐτῆς ὅτι ἔστιν ἀληθὲς καὶ διὰ σχολὴν εὐσεβείας, οὐ κατὰ διαβολὴν γάμου γινόμενον *Const.App*.4.14.2; **2.** external appearance; should express sanctity, Gr.Naz.*carm*.1.2. 6.27(M.37.645A); ὅλην σεαυτὴν ἁγνὴν τήρει π. ... ὄμμα σου σωφρονείτω ...μὴ νοῦς πορνεύῃ, μὴ γέλως, μὴ ποῦς ἄτακτα βαίνων. τὴν πιναρὰν στολήν σου, καὶ τὴν αὐχμηρὰν κόμην, μᾶλλον αἰδοῦμαι μαργάρων *ib*.1.2. 3.49(636A); δεῖ...αὐτὴν εἰς ἀγορὰν ἐμβάλλουσαν, ὥσπερ ἄγαλμα φιλοσοφίας ἁπάσης φαίνεσθαι, καὶ πάντας ἐκπλήττειν, ὡς ἄγγελον ἐξ οὐρανοῦ καταβάντα...οὕτω καὶ τὴν π. τοὺς ὁρῶντας ἅπαντας εἰς θαῦμα...τῆς ἁγιωσύνης αὐτῆς ἐμβάλλειν δεῖ Chrys.*fem.reg*.7(1.262E); should conceal beauty, †Bas.Anc.*virg*.16(M.30.704B); *ib*.18(708A); *ib*.(708B); ἡ π. καὶ μόνη οὖσα, τῆς ἀναμαρτησίας ἑαυτῆς προνοήσεται, οὐ τὰς τῶν λοιπῶν ἀνθρώπων ὄψεις μόνον, ἀλλὰ πολλῷ πλέον...τὰς ἑαυτῆς καὶ τῶν ἀπανταχοῦ ὁρώντων ἀγγέλων ἐντρεπομένη...οὐ γὰρ δεῖ, κἂν ἐν οἴκῳ μόνη καθέζηται καθ' ἑαυτὴν ἡ π., διότι μηδεὶς πάρεστι τῶν ἀνθρώπων, ἀδιαφόρως γυμνοῦσθαι...αἰδείσθω οὖν...ἡ π. τοὺς ἀγγέλους ...καὶ ὅταν συμβαίνῃ ἀναγκαίως ἐπιμελεῖσθαι τοῦ σώματος, τά τε κατὰ κεφαλὴν καὶ τὰ καθ' ἕκαστον περιστέλλουσα, ἐπισπευδέτω τὸ ἔργον *ib*. 34(737C–740A); **3.** custody of the senses π. οὖν ἔστω τῆς π. καὶ ἡ ἀκοὴ καὶ τὸ βλέμμα, ἔτι δὲ ἡ ἁφὴ καὶ ὅλον τὸ κίνημα †Bas.Anc.*virg*.15(M. 30.704A); π., π. ἴσθι καὶ οὔασι, καὶ φαεέσσι, καὶ γλώσσῃ Gr.Naz.*carm*. 1.2.2.74(M.37.584A); ἡ π. ὀφείλει ταῖς τῶν αἰσθητηρίων ὀπαῖς τὸν λογισμὸν φρουρὸν ἐπιστήσασα, τήν τε ἐπὶ τὰ ἔξω τούτων φορὰν... ἠρεμαῖον παρέχειν †Bas.Anc.*virg*.4(M.30.677C); ref. individual senses δεῖ μάλιστα τὴν π. τάς τε διὰ τῶν βλεμμάτων καὶ τῆς φωνῆς κολακείας, τῆς φθειροποιοῦ ἡδονῆς φάρμακον οὔσας, τῶν ἰδίων αἰσθήσεων...ἐλαύνειν· τὴν μὲν ἀκοὴν ἔνδοθεν σώφρονι λογισμῷ ἀποφράττουσαν, τοὺς δὲ ὀφθαλμοὺς ἀποστρέφειν κατὰ φύσιν γινώσκουσαν *ib*.15 (700C); δεῖ τὴν π. ... καὶ π. φυλάττειν τὴν γλῶσσαν...ἐκεῖνα γὰρ μόνον τῇ π. ῥητέον, ὅσα τε ἀκουσθέντα τὸν νοῦν ὠφελήσει τῶν ἀκουόντων *ib*.20 (709C); reasons for these precautions ἰστέον οὖν τοῖς τὴν θεράπαιναν τῆς ὄντως παρθενίας, διὰ τῆς ἀποχῆς τῶν τροφῶν...παρθένον φυλάττουσιν, ὅτι δυνατὸν π. ἔχοντα σῶμα, μὴ π. ἔχειν τὴν ψυχήν. ἱκανὸν γὰρ καὶ βλέμμα τύπους ἐμποιῆσαι τῶν αἰσχρῶν τῇ ψυχῇ, καὶ λόγος πεφαρμακωμένος πρὸς ἡδονὴν ἐμπεσὼν τῇ ἀκοῇ φθεῖραι πρὸς ἀκολασίαν τὸν νοῦν. εὐλαβεῖται γοῦν ὁ νυμφαγωγός, μήπως φθαρῇ οὐ τὸ σῶμα, ἀλλὰ τὰ νοήματα τῶν νυμφευομένων Χριστῷ. διὸ δεῖ τὴν π. πρὸ τοῦ σώματος μάλιστα τηρεῖν τὴν ψυχήν...ὡς ἂν μήτε διὰ φωνῆς ταύτης λόγος ῥυείς, πρὸς ἡδονὴν τὸν ἀκουστὴν τοῦ λόγου φαρμάξειε, μήτ' ἔξωθεν αὖθις διὰ τῆς ἀκοῆς λόγος...ἐμπεσών, τὴν καρδίαν αὐτῆς πρὸς ἐπιθυμίαν κυμήνῃ. οὕτω γὰρ καὶ ἐπὶ τοῦ βλέμματος προσήκει ποιεῖν...διὸ δεῖ...μηδενὶ ἀτενὲς τὴν π. ἐπιβάλλειν τὸ ὄμμα *ib*.13(693C–696B); ἐρωτικὸν βλέμμα, ἢ λόγος ἡδονῆς...εἰς τὴν τῆς π. ψυχήν, ὥσπερ εἰς καθαρὸν ὕδωρ... ἐμπεσών, ἄλλας ἐπ' ἄλλας ἐρωτικάς, ὡς ἐν βύθῳ, ἐγείρων ἐννοίας, ὅλην αὐτὴν πρὸς τὴν τοῦ βάλλοντος φαντασίαν πληγεῖσαν κυμαίνει *ib*.14 (700C); **4.** abstinence and other austerities οὕτως γὰρ οὐκ ἐξίσταται ἄνθρωπος ἀπὸ οἴνου καὶ παραπαίει, ὥσπερ ἀπὸ ζήλου καὶ ὀργῆς· οὕτως οὐ μεθύσκεταί τις ἀπὸ οἴνου καὶ παραφρονεῖ, ὡς ἀπὸ λύπης, ὡς ἀπὸ ἔρωτος, ὡς ἀπὸ ἀκρασίας. ἀπὸ ταύτης προστέτακται τῆς ἀμπέλου μὴ γεύσασθαι τὴν π., ἵνα νηφάλιος ὑπάρχουσα καὶ ἄυπνος ἀπὸ μερίμνης βιωτικῆς Meth.*symp*.5.5(p.59.22; M.18.108A); οὐ μόνον δὲ τῶν ἐκ τῆς ἀμπέλου κατεργαζομένων ἐκείνης προστέτακται μηδαμῶς...προσψαύειν τὴν π., ἀλλὰ καὶ τῶν ἀντιμίμων αὐτῆς...σίκερα γὰρ πᾶς ὁ σκευαστὸς οἶνος καλεῖται καὶ νόθος...ὅπως...μὴ μόνον τῶν γενικῶν ἁμαρτημάτων φυλασσομένη τῆς πονηρίας ὑπὸ τῶν ἀντιμίμων αὐτῆς χραίνηται... ἑτέρων μὲν κρατοῦσα, ὑφ' ἑτέρων δὲ κρατουμένη, τουτέστιν ἱματίων διαφερόντων ὑφαῖς ἀβρυνομένη...ἃ δὴ καὶ αὐτὰ μεθύσκει τὴν ψυχήν *ib*. 5.6(p.60.6; 108A); πρώτης οὖν τῆς γεύσεως ἡ π. κρατήσει, τὰς πηγὰς τῶν γαστρὸς ἡδονῶν...παρθένον γὰρ καὶ τὴν γεῦσιν εἶναι δεῖ τῆς π. †Bas. Anc.*virg*.7(M.30.682B); ἡ π. ... διὰ νηστειῶν καὶ ἀσκήσεως τούς τε ἀναδιδομένους...βρασμοὺς καταστείλασα *ib*.47(761C); καλῶς ὁδεύεις, π., εἰς ὄρος...νηστεία σε κενούτω, ἀγρυπνία, προσευχαί, δάκρυα, χαμευνία Gr.Naz.*carm*.1.2.3.33(M.37.635A); **5.** seclusion ἡ ὑπακοὴ τῶν π. ἔστω ἁγία, καὶ μόναι ἡσυχαζέτωσαν· ἐν δὲ ταῖς προόδοις βαδιζέτωσαν δύο δύο *A.Phil*.142(p.82.8); οὐ γὰρ ἁπλῶς ἀγελαίαν δεῖ τὴν π., ἀποστραφεῖσαν τὰ γάμων δεσμά, ἀπανταχοῦ μετὰ αὐθεντίας σοβεῖσθαι †Bas. Anc.*virg*.19(M.30.709A); κάλλιον τὴν π. τὸ ἀσφαλὲς ἑαυτῇ καὶ ἀπρόσκοπον τῶν ὁρώντων πραγματευομένην, πανταχόθεν φρονίμως ἀνεπίμικτον εἶναι *ib*.53(776B); χρὴ τὴν π. πανταχόθεν τειχίζεσθαι, καὶ ὀλιγάκις...προβαίνειν τῆς οἰκίας Chrys.*sac*.3.17(p.91.19; 1.399C); **6.** various virtues οὐκ ἀπὸ τῶν φανερῶν ἁμαρτημάτων μόνον... ἁγνεύειν χρὴ τὴν παρθένον ψυχήν,...ἀλλὰ καὶ πολλῷ πλέον ἀπὸ τῶν κρυφίων Mac.Aeg.*perf*.5(M.34.845A); τὴν π. οὐ τοῦτο ποιεῖ π., τὸ μὴ ὡμιληκέναι γάμῳ, ἀλλὰ πολλῶν καὶ ἑτέρων δεῖ, τοῦ ἀμέμπτου, τοῦ εὐπροσέδρου Chrys.*hom.13.2 in 1Tim*.(11.619D); id.*ep*.2.4(3.539A); ποῖον γὰρ ὄφελος ἔσται τῷ τὸ σῶμα π. τηρήσαντι, εἰ τὴν ψυχὴν ὑπὸ τοῦ τῆς παρακοῆς μεμοίχευται δαίμονος; Diad.*perf*.42(p.48.19); τὸ γὰρ λέγεσθαι π., καὶ τὰς ἀρετὰς μὴ ἔχειν ἀναλόγους, καὶ...ἁρμοζούσας τῇ π., μωρὰν τὴν τοιαύτην π. φησὶν ὁ κύριος Ant.Mon.*hom*.21(M.89.1497B); πρὸ δὲ πάντων χρὴ τὴν π. τῷ ἐλαίῳ τῆς εὐποιΐας κατακοσμῆσαι τὴν ἑαυτῆς λαμπάδα *ib*.(1500C).

D. opp. married women; **1.** separation advocated μεμερισμένη γοῦν πρὸς τὴν ἔγγαμον ἡ π., τόν τε βίον, καὶ ὅλον τὸ ἦθος, τὰ ἐπιβάλλοντα ἔργα τῇ π. ἐν παντὶ ἐπιγνώσεται †Bas.Anc.*virg*.21(M.30.713C); *ib*.(712C); **2.** sorrows of married women and joys of virgins δεσπότην μετὰ προικὸς ἡ γυνὴ ὠνουμένη τὸν ἄνδρα, δούλη μὲν ἀντὶ ἐλευθέρας ἐστί, μικρᾶς τῆς κατὰ τὸν γάμον ἡδονῆς τὴν φυσικὴν ἐλευθερίαν ἀπεμπολήσασα, θύραν δὲ ἀμυθήτων ὠδίνων...ἑαυτῇ τὸν γάμον ἀνοίξασα...ἡ δὲ π. τὸν πρὸς τὸν ἄνδρα ζυγὸν ἀπορρήξασα, καὶ πρὸς τὸν κύριον ὅλη δραμοῦσα, συναπέρρηξε τῷ ζυγῷ καὶ τὴν ἐκ τῆς κατάρας ὀδύνην...τὴν ἐκ τῆς συμπλοκῆς τῶν σαρκῶν συμβαίνουσαν φθορὰν πρώτην φυγοῦσα, ἄφθορος ὅλη ἐν ἀσάρκῳ ψυχῇ, τῷ κυρίῳ νυμφεύεται *ib*.23(717C); ἡ δὲ π. ἀνωτέρω ταύτης ἕστηκε τῆς ὠδῖνος [sc. childbirth] καὶ τῆς ἀρᾶς. ὁ γὰρ τὴν. ἀπὸ τοῦ νόμου κατάραν λύσας καὶ ταύτην ἔλυσε μετ' ἐκείνης Chrys.*virg*.65(1.322A); *ib*.68(323B); **3.** their spiritual state καὶ ἡ ὑπὸ ζυγὸν ἔστω τι Χριστοῦ· καὶ ἡ π. ὅλη Χριστοῦ. ἡ μὲν μὴ παντελῶς ἐνδεσμείσθω τῷ κόσμῳ· ἡ δὲ μηδ' ὅλως γινέσθω τοῦ κόσμου. ὃ γάρ ἐστι τῇ ὑπὸ ζυγὸν τὸ μέρος, τοῦτο παντελὲς τῇ π. Gr.Naz.*or*.37.10(M.36.296A); αἱ ὑπὸ ζυγόν, δότε τι καὶ θεῷ...αἱ π., τὸ πᾶν θεῷ *ib*.44.8(616B); **4.** their mutual harmony ἀλλήλαις συνδεσμεῖσθε, καὶ π., καὶ γυναῖκες, καὶ ἓν ἐστε ἐν κυρίῳ, καὶ ἀλλήλων καλλώπισμα. οὐκ ἂν ἦν ἄγαμος, εἰ μὴ γάμος. πόθεν γὰρ εἰς τοῦτον παρῆλθε τὸν βίον π.; οὐκ ἂν ἦν γάμος σεμνός, εἰ μὴ π. καρποφορῶν *ib*. 37.10(293C).

E. temptations; **1.** to become '*subintroductae*', v. συνείσακτος; **2.** spiritual trials ἡ δὲ π. δι' ὅλου θαλαττεύειν ἀναγκάζεται, καὶ πέλαγος πλεῖν ἀλίμενον· κἂν ὁ χαλεπώτατος διεγερθῇ χειμών, οὐδὲ οὕτως θέμις ὁρμίσαι τὸ σκάφος αὐτῇ καὶ ἀναπαύσασθαι...ὁ...πειρατὴς τῇ π. πολὺν ἐπάγει τὸν χειμῶνα...πάντα ἄνω καὶ κάτω κυκῶν,...ἤκουσε γὰρ ὅτι τὸ Ἐπὶ τὸ αὐτὸ συνέρχεσθαι ἡ π. οὐκ ἔχει, ἀλλ' ἀνάγκη δι' ὅλου παλαίειν αὐτήν Chrys.*virg*.34(1.292B,C); ἡ δὲ π. οὐκ ἔχουσα ὅπως σβέσῃ τὸ πῦρ...ἑνὸς γίνεται μόνου τοῦ μὴ φλεχθῆναι μαχομένην πυρί *ib*.(292E).

F. work and influence ἔστωσαν...πᾶσαι αἱ π. αἱ πιστεύουσαι καθ' ἑκάστην τὴν ἡμέραν ἐπισκέπτουσαι τοὺς νοσοῦντας *A.Phil*.142(p.79.5); ἡ π. σωφροσύνης εἰκών, μᾶλλον δὲ αὐτοαρετῆς ἄγαλμα οὖσα, καὶ μόνον ὀφθεῖσα, τὰς τῶν ὁρώντων ὄψεις πρὸς τὴν τοῦ θείου ἔννοιαν ἐπιστρέφειν ὀφείλει †Bas.Anc.*virg*.22(M.30.716A); μεταρυθμιζέσθω τῶν ἀπαντώντων τῇ π. καὶ βλέμμα καὶ κίνημα πρὸς τὴν τοῦ καλοῦ φαντασίαν· καὶ πάντες μὲν οἱ συντυγχάνοντες ἐπιστυφέσθωσαν τὴν διάνοιαν *ib*.(716B); ἡ π. καὶ γνώμης καὶ κινήσεως καὶ μορφῆς καὶ σχήματος...τοῖς τοῦ νυμφίου φίλοις καθαρῶς ὁμιλήσει. οὐ γὰρ εἰς μισανθρωπίαν φέροντες αὐτὴν ἀπεκλείσαμεν, ἀλλ' ἀκριβέσι τύποις ὅλην ἄνωθεν ἀπὸ κεφαλῆς ἄχρι ποδῶν θεοῦ ἄγαλμα ζωγραφήσαντες, οὕτω πρὸς τοὺς τῆς πίστεως οἰκείους ἐπιδεξίως προάγομεν, ἵνα καὶ σχήματι, καὶ λόγῳ, νύμφη ἀληθῶς τοῦ κυρίου ὀφθεῖσα, ὠφελήσῃ τοὺς ὁμιλοῦντας *ib*.36(740C).

G. reward στέφανος τῶν π. ἐγώ [sc. Christ] *A.Mt*.2(p.219.4); †Bas. Anc.*virg*.24(M.30.720B); τῶν μοναζόντων καὶ τῶν π. τάγμα, τῶν τὸν ἰσάγγελον βίον ἐν κόσμῳ κατορθούντων...μέγας ὑμῖν ἀπόκειται στέφανος Cyr.H.*catech*.4.24; *ib*.13.34; αἱ δὲ π. προσδοκώμεναί εἰσι μετὰ τῶν συνεταιρίδων ἐν οὐρανοῖς Μαρίας ἅμα ἀδελφῆς Ἀαρών, καὶ τῆς Μαρίας καὶ Θέκλης τῆς ἐκτιλάσης τὴν σαρκικὴν ἐπιθυμίαν ἀφ' ἑαυτῆς ‡Ath.*pat*.7(M.26.1305C).

H. in persecutions; gen. sufferings, Ath.*apol.Const*.33(M.25. 640C); id.*ep.encycl*.4(p.173.17f.; M.25.232A,B); Gr.Naz.*or*.33.3(M.36. 217C); *ib*.43.46(556C); rape, †Bas.Anc.*virg*.52(M.30.773B,C).

I. lapsed virgins; their sin λέγει...ὁ κύριος, ὅτι δύο καὶ πονηρὰ ἐποίησεν ἡ π., ἐμὲ ἐγκατέλιπε τὸν ἀληθινὸν...νυμφίον, καὶ ἀπέδρα πρὸς ἀσεβῆ...ψυχῆς ὁμοῦ καὶ σώματος φθορέα Bas.*ep*.46.3(3.137E; M.32. 376B); ἡ π., μετὰ τὴν τῆς παρθενίας ἐπαγγελίαν διαφθαρεῖσα, μοιχείας χεῖρον ἐτόλμησεν Chrys.*vid*.2.3(1.353B); to be judged strictly περὶ τῶν ἐκπεσουσῶν π. τῶν καθομολογησαμένων τὸν ἐν σεμνότητι βίον τῷ κυρίῳ, εἶτα...ἀθετουσῶν τὰς ἑαυτῶν συνθήκας, οἱ μὲν πατέρες ἡμῶν... πρᾴως συμπεριφερόμενοι ταῖς ἀσθενείαις...ἐνομοθέτησαν δεκτὰς εἶναι μετὰ τὸν ἐνιαυτόν...ἐμοὶ δὲ δοκεῖ, ἐπειδὴ...πληθύνεται νῦν τὸ τάγμα τῶν π., προσέχειν ἀκριβῶς τῷ τε κατ' ἔννοιαν φαινομένῳ πράγματι, καὶ τῇ τῆς γραφῆς διανοίᾳ...οὐκοῦν ἡ μὲν χήρα, ὡς δούλη διεφθαρμένη, καταδικάζεται· ἡ δὲ π. τῷ κρίματι τῆς μοιχαλίδος ὑπόκειται Bas.*ep*. 199.*can*.18(3.291B–E; M.32.717A–720A); 1Cor.7:28 not applying to them, Chrys.*virg*.39(1.298C); sin of intercourse with virgins μηδεὶς οὕτως ἔστω ἀνόσιος...αὐτὸν τὸν ναὸν τοῦ κυρίου, τουτέστι, τῆς π. τὸ σῶμα, καὶ αὐτὴν τὴν...ψυχὴν τῆς π., ἱερώτατον ἐν τῷ ναῷ τοῦ κυρίου ἀνάθημα, τοῖς ἀκολασίας πυρσοῖς βαρβαρικῶς καταφλέξαι. ἀλλ' εἰ ἑκοῦσαν ἐπέδωκεν ἑαυτὴν ἡ π. ... μὴ χρήσῃς τοιαύτῃ σαυτὸν εἰς κοινωνίαν τῆς ἁμαρτίας †Bas.Anc.*virg*.41(M.30.749D–752A).

J. ideal of a virgin; **1.** attitude to the world τοιοῦτον δεῖ ἔρωτα τὴν π. ἐρῶσαν, καταφρονεῖν μὲν ἡδυπαθείας, καὶ τοῦ πλούτου καὶ τῆς νομιζομένης ἐν τῷ κόσμῳ τρυφῆς· πατοῦσαν δὲ τὴν πρόσκαιρον δόξαν... καὶ τὰς ἐμπαθεῖς κολακείας, ἀμεταστρεπτὶ τῷ κυρίῳ ἀκολουθεῖν †Bas. Anc.*virg*.26(M.30.724B); **2.** perfect purity, *ib*.27(725B); Gr.Naz.*carm*. 1.2.3.1(M.37.632A); **3.** perfect equilibrium ἡ π. ... οὔτε τοῖς ἐκ σαρκὸς πάθεσι τὸ τῆς ψυχῆς φωτεινὸν συνταράξει, οὔτε τοῖς ἀπὸ ψυχῆς ἔχουσι τὴν ἀρχὴν συγχεῖν τὸ ἑαυτῆς κάλλος ἀνέξεται· ἀλλ' ἑκάτερον ἐν τῇ ἰδίᾳ χώρᾳ...καθ' ἡσυχίαν φυλάττουσα, εἰρήνην μὲν τοῖς μέρεσι μετὰ σοφίας βραβεύσει, ἐν ἠρεμίᾳ δὲ μένειν καὶ ψυχὴν καὶ σῶμα κατὰ φύσιν ἀσκήσασα, τὸ ἐξ ἀμφοῖν ἐναρμόνιον εἶδος καθαρὸν ἐπιδείξει †Bas.Anc. *virg*.47(M.30.760D); *ib*.49(765C); ἡ π. ... μυστικῶς...σαββατιζέτω, μὴ χεῖρα, μὴ πόδα, μὴ ὀφθαλμόν, μήτ' ἄλλο τι τῶν μελῶν, ἀλλὰ μηδὲ νοῦν φθοροποιὸν τοῦ φυσικοῦ κάλλους κινοῦσα· ἀλλ' ἑστηκέτω ὡς ἀγαθὸν γλύμμα θεοῦ ἀκίνητον πρὸς πᾶσαν φαντασίαν *ib*.58(785C); *ib*. 66(804B).

K. eccl. legislation; **1.** requisite age and free choice ἐκεῖνο... προδιομολογεῖσθαι ἡμῖν ἀναγκαῖον, ὅτι π. ὀνομάζεται ἡ ἑκουσίως ἑαυτὴν προσαγαγοῦσα τῷ κυρίῳ, καὶ ἀποταξαμένη τῷ γάμῳ, καὶ τὸν ἐν ἁγιασμῷ βίον προτιμήσασα. τὰς δὲ ὁμολογίας τότε ἐγκρίνομεν, ἀφ' οὗπερ ἂν ἡ ἡλικία τὴν τοῦ λόγου συμπλήρωσιν ἔχῃ. οὐδὲ γὰρ παιδικὰς φωνὰς πάντως κυρίας ἐπὶ τῶν τοιούτων ἡγεῖσθαι προσῆκεν, ἀλλὰ τὴν ὑπὲρ τὰ δέκα ἓξ ἢ δέκα καὶ ἑπτὰ γενομένην ἔτη, κυρίαν οὖσαν τῶν λογισμῶν, ἀνακριθεῖσαν ἐπὶ πλεῖον, εἶτα παραμείνασαν, καὶ λιπαροῦσαν διὰ ἱκεσιῶν πρὸς τὸ παραδεχθῆναι, τότε ἐγκαταλέγεσθαι χρὴ ταῖς π., καὶ τὴν ὁμολογίαν τῆς τοιαύτης κυροῦν Bas.*ep*.199 *can*.18(3.292A,B; M.32.720B); **2.** not ordained π. οὐ χειροτονεῖται...γνώμης γάρ ἐστι τὸ ἔπαθλον οὐκ ἐπὶ διαβολῇ τοῦ γάμου, ἀλλ' ἐπὶ σχολῇ τῆς εὐσεβείας *Const.App*.8.24.2; **3.** under episcopal authority ὥστε τὰς ἱερὰς π., ὅτε τῶν πατέρων χωρίσωνται, ἐξ ὧν ἐφυλάττοντο, τῇ τοῦ ἐπισκόπου, ἤ, αὐτοῦ ἀπόντος, τῇ τοῦ πρεσβυτέρου προνοίᾳ ταῖς τιμιωτέραις γυναιξὶ παρατίθεσθαι, ἢ ἅμα κατοικούσας ἀλλήλας φυλάττειν *Cod.Afr*.44; π. ἑαυτὴν ἀναθεῖσαν τῷ...θεῷ, ὡσαύτως δὲ καὶ μονάζοντα μὴ ἐξεῖναι γάμῳ προσομιλεῖν. εἰ δέ γε εὑρεθεῖεν τοῦτο ποιοῦντες, ἔστωσαν ἀκοινώνητοι. ὡρίσαμεν δὲ ἔχειν τὴν αὐθεντίαν τῆς ἐπ' αὐτοῖς φιλανθρωπίας τὸν κατὰ τόπον ἐπίσκοπον CChalc.*can*.16; **4.** their place in church αἱ π. δὲ καὶ αἱ χῆραι καὶ αἱ πρεσβύτιδες πρῶται πασῶν στηκέτωσαν *Const.App*.2.57.12.

L. widows called virgins ἀσπάζομαι...τὰς π. τὰς λεγομένας χήρας Ign.*Smyrn*.13.1; ἡ χήρα διὰ σωφροσύνης αὖθις π. Clem.*str*.7.12(p.52. 3; M.9.500C); cf. τινὲς καὶ τῆς π. τὴν χήραν εἰς ἐγκράτειαν προτιμῶσι καταμεγαλοφρονήσασαν ἧς πεπείραται ἡδονῆς *ib*.3.16(p.243.6; M.8. 1205A); μή μου τῶν λόγων ἐπιλάβῃ, εἰ καὶ εἰς τὸν χορὸν τῶν π. σε κατελέξαμεν τῶν ἁγίων ἐκείνων, ἐν χηρείᾳ βεβιωκυῖαν. ἤκουσας γάρ μου πολλάκις...διαλεγομένου, τίς ποτέ ἐστι τῆς παρθενίας ὁ ὅρος, καὶ ὡς οὐκ ἂν κωλυθείης ποτὲ εἴς τε τὸν ἐκείνων καταλεγῆναι χορόν, μᾶλλον δὲ καὶ ἐκείνας ὑπερβῆναι...ἡ πολλὴν ἐν τοῖς ἄλλοις ἐπιδειξαμένη φιλοσοφίαν Chrys.*ep*.2.4(3.538E).

M. types and symbols αἵ τε π. εἰς τύπον τοῦ θυμιατηρίου τετιμήσθωσαν καὶ τοῦ θυμιάματος *Const.App*.2.26.8; cf.Meth.*symp*.5.8(p.63. 2; M.18.112B); ἦσαν δέ τινες π. τὸν ἀριθμὸν ἑπτὰ ἐκ νεαρᾶς ἡλικίας ἀσκούμεναι *M.Thdot.1* 13(p.69.4).

N. ref. heretics πῶς οὖν π. ἡ τῆς πίστεως ἀποστᾶσα, ἡ τοῖς πλάνοις προσέχουσα...; πῶς π. ἡ κεκαυτηριασμένη τὴν συνείδησιν; τὴν γὰρ π. οὐ τῷ σώματι μόνον καθαρὰν εἶναι δεῖ, ἀλλὰ καὶ τῇ ψυχῇ Chrys.*virg*.5 (1.272A); οὐχ ὡμίλησας γάμοις; ἀλλ' οὐδέπω τοῦτο π. τὴν γὰρ κυρίαν τοῦ γαμηθῆναι γενομένην, εἶτα οὐχ ἑλομένην, ταύτην ἂν εἴποιμι π. ἐγώ· ὅταν δὲ τῶν κεκωλυμένων τὸ πρᾶγμα εἶναι φῇς, οὐκέτι τῆς σῆς προαιρέσεως τὸ κατόρθωμα γίνεται, ἀλλὰ τῆς ἀνάγκης τοῦ νόμου *ib*.8 (274A); id.*exp.in Ps*.44:15(5.180E).

II. of men παραθέσθαι αὐτὴν [sc. BMV] Ἰωάννῃ τῷ ἁγίῳ π. Epiph. *haer*.28.7(p.319.25; M.41.385C); ‡Chrys.*hom*.12(13.249D); Philost. *h.e*.7.14(M.65.552C); of Jeremiah π. γὰρ ἱστορεῖται εἶναι ὁ προφήτης, ὡς κελευσθεὶς ὑπὸ τοῦ θεοῦ μὴ γῆμαι Olymp.*fr.Jer*.52:1(M.93.724C).

III. exeg. parable of Ten Virgins ὁ τῶν δέκα π. ἀριθμὸς τὰς εἰς τὸν Ἰησοῦν πεπιστευκυίας ἀναμετρεῖσθαι βούλεται ψυχάς,...ἀλλ' αἱ μὲν πέντε ἔμφρονες ἐτύγχανον...αἱ δὲ πέντε μωραί. ... οὐ γὰρ ἐπρομηθεύσαντο ἐλαίου σφῶν τὰ ἀγγεῖα πλήρη παρασκευάσαι, δικαιοσύνης ἀπομείνασαι κεναί. αἰνίσσεται γὰρ διὰ τούτων τὰς ἐπὶ πέρατα παρθενίας ἐπισπερχομένας ἐλθεῖν καὶ πάντα εἰς τὸ συμπληρωθῆναι τὸν ἔρωτα τοῦτον κοσμίως δρώσας Meth.*symp*.6.2(p.65.19; M.18.116A); διὸ... ἰσάριθμοι πρὸς πέντε διαιροῦνται, ἐπειδήπερ τὰς πέντε αἰσθήσεις αἱ μὲν αὐτῶν ἐφυλάξαντο...π. ἁμαρτημάτων, ἃς οἱ πλεῖστοι σοφίας προσηγόρευσαν πύλας, αἱ δὲ τοὐναντίον πλήθεσιν ἀδικημάτων ἐλωβήσαντο *φυράσασαι κακίᾳ...πέντε προσαγορεύεται π., διὰ τὸ τὰς πέντε τῆς αἰσθήσεως ἁγνὰς ἀποκαταστῆσαι τῷ Χριστῷ φαντασίας* ib.6.3(pp.66.17–67.9; 116D–117A); Mac.Aeg.*hom*.4.6,7(M.34.476D–477B); id.*elev*.4 (M.34.893A); interpreted of souls *αἱ γνωστικαὶ ψυχαί, ἃς ἀπείκασεν τὸ εὐαγγέλιον ταῖς ἡγιασμέναις π. ταῖς προσδεχομέναις τὸν κύριον. π. ...ὡς κακῶν ἀπεσχημέναι, προσδεχόμεναι δὲ διὰ τὴν ἀγάπην τὸν κύριον* Clem.*str*.7.12(p.52.11f.; M.9.500C).

IV. of BMV; **A.** her permanent virginity; **1.** no other childbirth *ζητεῖται παρὰ πολλοῖς περὶ τῶν ἀδελφῶν Ἰησοῦ πῶς τούτους, τῆς Μαρίας μέχρι τελευτῆς π. διαμεινάσης, ἀδελφοὺς μὲν οὐκ εἶχεν φύσει οὔτε τῆς π. τεκούσης ἕτερον, οὐδ' αὐτὸς ἐκ τοῦ Ἰωσὴφ τυγχάνων* Or.*fr.31 in Jo.*2:11(p.506.21f.); unorthodox exegesis of Lc.2:7 and Mt.1:25 refuted *δευτέραν σύλληψιν τῆς π. ἐδογμάτισαν,...φάσκοντες...οὐκ ἂν λεχθείη πρωτότοκος, δευτέρου μὴ παρακολουθήσαντος...ταύτας τὰς λέξεις οἱ ἐξ ἐναντίας παρεγγυῶνται, ἐκ δευτέρου τὴν...π. κυοφορῆσαι δογματίζοντες. ἀλλ' ἄπαγε τῆς ἀτοπίας·...πρωτότοκος ὁ κύριος ἤκουσεν ἐκ τῆς π. ... οὐχ ὅτι δεύτερόν τινα ὁμοιογενῆ προσεκαλέσατο· ἀλλ' ὅτι πρωτότοκος ὑπῆρχε, τουτέστιν ἀσύγκριτος* Tim.Ant.*descr. BMV* 8(M.28.956C–957A); *ib*.9(957B,C); *μήπως...μετὰ τὸν θεῖον τόκον νομίζεσθαι, τὴν μὲν π. πεπαῦσθαι τῆς ἁγνείας, τὸν δὲ Ἰωσὴφ ἔχεσθαι τῆς γαμικῆς συναφείας* Procl.CP *or*.6.7(M.65.732D); **2.** virgin *in partu* *ὁ γὰρ ἄνευ σπέρματος ἐν τῇ π. ἐμψυχώσας ἑαυτῷ ναόν, αὐτὸς καὶ ἄλυτον διετήρησε τὴν μήτραν, ὡς θεός* ‡Chrys.*BMV* 2(8.240B); *ἀποροῦσι γὰρ λέγειν τὸ πῶς καὶ π. μένεις καὶ τεκεῖν ἴσχυσας· ἡμεῖς δὲ τὸ μυστήριον θαυμάζοντες* †Serg.*acath*.202(p.145; M.92.1344B); **3.** *post partum* *μέχρι νῦν δοκεῖ ἡ Μαριὰμ λεχὼ εἶναι διὰ τὴν τοῦ παιδίου γέννησιν, οὐκ οὖσα λεχώ (καὶ γὰρ μετὰ τὸ τεκεῖν αὐτὴν μαιωθεῖσάν φασί τινες π. εὑρεθῆναι)* Clem.*str*.7.16(p.66.22; M.9.529B); *μετὰ τὸ γενέσθαι μητέρα, ἔτι π. διαμένουσα* †Bas.*Is*.201(1.529D; M.30.465A); ‡Epiph.*hom*.5(M.43.496C); *π. ... ὑπάρχω μετὰ τὸν τόκον, καθαρωτέρα τοῦ πρώτην* ib.(497A); Hesych.H.*serm*.4(M.93.1456B); †Gregent. *disp*.(M.86.657A); **4.** *pro, in,* and *post* *μεμένηκε γὰρ αὕτη π. καὶ μετὰ τόκον, ὥσπερ ἦν καὶ πρὸ τόκου καὶ πρὸ συλλήψεως, ἡ καὶ διὰ βίου παντὸς ἀειπάρθενος ἄχραντος* ‡Cyr.*Trin*.14(6³.20D; M.77.1152A); *μόνη ἐν παρθένοις π. ἡ καὶ πρὸ τοῦ τόκου, καὶ ἐν τόκῳ, καὶ μετὰ τόκον, π. διαμείνασα* ‡Jo.D.*hom*.5(M.96.656B); *ib*.6.5(668C); **5.** explained by divinity of Christ *αὐτὸς ὁ λόγος ἐν αὐτῇ τῇ μακαρίᾳ π. γενόμενος τὸν ἴδιον ναὸν ἑαυτῷ ἐκ τῆς οὐσίας τῆς π. ἔλαβεν καὶ προῆλθεν ἐξ αὐτῆς ἄνθρωπος μὲν ἔξωθεν θεωρούμενος, ἔνδοθεν δὲ θεὸς ὑπάρχων ἀληθινός, δι' ὃ καὶ μετὰ τὸ τεχθῆναι π. τὴν τεκοῦσαν τετήρηκεν* Cyr.*deip.BMV* 4 (p.20.26ff.; M.76.260B); *ἀληθῶς κεκλεισμένης τῆς παρθενικῆς πύλης, κατὰ φύσιν ἀληθῶς σῶμα οὔσης τῆς θεοδόχου σαρκὸς αὐτοῦ διὰ τῶν ἀρράγων σωμάτων χωρῆσαι τῆς μήτρας τῆς π. τῇ ὑπὲρ φύσιν δυνάμει τοῦ ἐνόντος αὐτῇ πνεύματος τοῦ λόγου πιστεύομεν. πῶς οὖν οὐ παντὸς μᾶλλον...εὐφημήσομεν τὴν π. ταύτην, ἐν ᾗ καὶ ἐξ ἧς ὁ λόγος τὴν σάρκα μνηστευσάμενος προῆλθεν...; καὶ τὸ θαυμαστόν, ὅτι οὐδὲ τῷ τῆς φύσεως ἰδιώματι τοῦ οἰκήματος ἑαυτὴν συνεξήγαγεν* [sc. *σοφία*] *ἐκ τῆς μήτρας τῆς π. ... σὺν αὐτῷ γὰρ πνευματικῶς ἐξιέναι καὶ χωρῆσαι διὰ τῶν ἀρραγῶν σωμάτων τῆς π., τὴν σάρκα ἑαυτοῦ ὁ λόγος ἐδυνάμωσεν* Leont.H. *Nest*.4.9(M.86.1669C,D); **6.** as proof of his divinity *εἰ μὴ π. ἔμεινεν ἡ μήτηρ, ψιλὸς ἄνθρωπος ὁ τεχθεὶς καὶ οὐ παράδοξος ὁ τόκος· εἰ δὲ καὶ μετὰ τόκον ἔμεινεν π., ἐκεῖνος ἀφράστως ἐγεννήθη...ὁ θεός μου* Procl. CP *or.laud.BMV* 2(p.104.3f.; M.65.684A); **7.** compared with Adam's integrity after creation of Eve, ‡Chrys.*BMV* 3(8.240D,E).

B. ref. virgin birth; **1.** in gen. *τὸν κύριον ἡμῶν...γεγεννημένον ἀληθῶς ἐκ π.* Ign.*Smyrn*.1.1; Arist.*apol*.15.1; *λαμβάνει τὸ ἡμέτερον* [sc. *σῶμα*],*...ἐξ...ἀνδρὸς ἀπείρου π. ... αὐτὸς γὰρ δυνατὸς ὢν...ἐν τῇ π. κατασκευάζει ἑαυτῷ ναὸν τὸ σῶμα* Ath.*inc*.8.3(M.25.109C); **2.** discussion of possibility; defended; **a.** by *ad hominem* argument from pagan fables *εἰ...διὰ παρθένου γεγεννῆσθαι φέρομεν, κοινὸν καὶ τοῦτο πρὸς τὸν Περσέα ἔστω ἡμῖν* Just.*1apol*.22.5(M.6.361B); cf.*ib*.54.8(409C); criticized by Trypho *ἐν δὲ τοῖς τῶν...Ἑλλήνων μύθοις λέλεκται ὅτι Περσεὺς ἐκ Δανάης, π. οὔσης...γεγέννηται· καὶ ὑμεῖς τὰ αὐτὰ ἐκείνοις λέγοντες, αἰδεῖσθαι ὀφείλετε* id.*dial*.67.2(M.6.629A); reply: *ὅταν δὲ..., ἔφην, ἐκ π. γεγεννῆσθαι τὸν Περσέα ἀκούσω, καὶ τοῦτο μιμήσασθαι τὸν πλάνον ὄφιν συνίημι* ib.70.5(641B); **b.** by referring to OT theophanies *εἰ οὖν ἐν τοσαύταις μορφαῖς οἴδαμεν πεφανερῶσθαι τὸν θεὸν ἐκεῖνον τῷ Ἀβραὰμ καὶ τῷ Ἰακὼβ καὶ τῷ Μωϋσεῖ, πῶς...ἀπιστοῦμεν...ἄνθρωπον αὐτὸν διὰ παρθένου γεννηθῆναι μὴ δεδυνῆσθαι;* ib.75.4(652C); **c.** defended against both pagan and Jewish objections *διασύρουσιν ἡμᾶς Ἕλληνές τε καὶ Ἰουδαῖοι, καί φασιν, ὅτι ἀδύνατον ἦν τὸν Χριστὸν ἐκ π. γεννηθῆναι. Ἕλληνας μὲν ἐκ τῶν παρ' αὐτοῖς μύθων ἐπιστομίσωμεν. οἱ γὰρ λέγοντες λίθους ῥιπτομένους εἰς ἀνθρώπους μεταβάλλεσθαι, πῶς τὸ π. τεκεῖν λέγετε ἀδύνατον εἶναι;...πρὸς δὲ τοὺς ἐκ περιτομῆς οὕτως ἀπάντησον ἐρωτήσας· ποῖόν ἐστι δύσκολον; στεῖραν πρεσβῦτιν τῶν ἐθίμων ἐκλιπόντων τεκεῖν, ἢ π. νεάζουσαν γεννῆσαι; στεῖρα ἦν Σάρρα, καὶ ἐκλιπόντων τῶν γυναικείων τέτοκε παρὰ φύσιν. οὐκοῦν εἰ τὸ στεῖραν γεννῆσαι παρὰ φύσιν, καὶ τὸ π. γεννῆσαι. ἢ τὰ δύο...ἀθέτησον, ἢ τὰ δύο κατάδεξαι* Cyr.H.*catech*.12.27,28; **3.** brought about by divine action *ib*.12.32; ‡Chrys.*BMV* 1(8.239A); *τὸ πνεῦμα τὸ ἅγιον ...τέλειον ἐδημιούργησεν ἄνθρωπον οὐ νόμῳ φύσεως,...οὐκ ἀνθρωπίνῳ σπέρματι, ἀλλ' ὄψει μόνον, νοερᾷ τε καὶ ἁγίᾳ. δυνάμει πρὸς ὠδῖνας τὴν π. ἐκίνησεν* ib.3(241E); hence not to be explained, Chrys.*hom.4.3 in Mt.*(7.50B); **4.** exeg. Is.7:14 *τὸ οὖν 'ἰδοὺ ἡ π. ἐν γαστρὶ ἕξει' σημαίνει οὐ συνουσιασθεῖσαν τὴν π. συλλαβεῖν· εἰ γὰρ ἐσυνουσιάσθη ὑπὸ ὁτουοῦν, οὐκ ἔτι ἦν π.· ἀλλὰ 'δύναμις θεοῦ ἐπελθοῦσα' τῇ π. 'ἐπεσκίασεν' αὐτήν, καὶ κυοφορῆσαι π. οὖσαν πεποίηκε* Just.*1apol*.33.1–4(M.6.380C–381B); Epiph.*haer*.28.7(p.319.17ff.; M.41.385C); v. *νεᾶνις*; **5.** in rel. to eternal generation of Son *ὁ μονογενὴς υἱὸς τοῦ θεοῦ...ὁ προαιώνιος συνὼν τῷ πατρὶ ἀσώματος ὢν τὴν φύσιν ἀνθρώπου φύσιν οἰκειωσάμενος ὕστερον ἐτέχθη διὰ παρθένου, οὐκ ἀρχὴν λαβὼν τοῦ εἶναι θεός, ἀλλ'...τοῦ φανῆναι ἄνθρωπος...ἐκ τοῦ πατρὸς γεγέννηται τῇ φύσει, ἐκ π. γεγέννηται δι' οἰκονομίαν* Thdot.Anc.*hom*.2.7(p.77.24ff.; M.77.1377B,C); *παρὰ φύσιν γὰρ ἐν ὑστέροις καιροῖς ἐκ τῆς π. ἐτέχθη, κατὰ φύσιν δὲ πρὸ αἰώνων ἐκ τοῦ πατρὸς ἐτέχθη...ὁ πατὴρ ἀρρεύστως ἐγέννησεν, ἡ π. ἀφθόρως ἔτεκεν. οὔτε γὰρ θεὸς ῥεῦσιν ὑπέμεινε γεννήσας· θεοπρεπῶς γὰρ ἐγέννησεν· οὔτε ἡ π. φθορὰν ὑπέστη τεκοῦσα· πνευματικῶς γὰρ ἔτεκεν* ‡Chrys.*BMV* 1(8.238D); **6.** special characteristics *βλέπε τὴν μυστικὴν ἀποκύησιν τῆς π. αὕτη ἔτεκεν, αὕτη ἐσπαργάνωσεν. ἐπὶ τῶν κοσμικῶν γυναικῶν ἄλλη τίκτει, καὶ ἄλλη σπαργανοῖ· ἐπὶ δὲ τῆς π. οὐχ οὕτως· αὕτη ἔτεκεν, καὶ αὕτη ἐσπαργάνωσεν* Tim.Ant.*descr.BMV* 8(M.28.956B); *ἡ π. ἀπόνως τὸν...δεσπότην...κυήσασα* ‡Epiph.*hom*.5(M.43.500A); **7.** belief in it necessary for fullness of faith, Or.*Jo*.32.16(9; p.452.4; M.14.784B); **8.** in rel. to Christ's virginity and celibacy of priests *ἔδει γὰρ ἐξ ἀφθόρου π. ἄφθορον καὶ κατὰ σάρκα τεχθέντα, μηδὲ τῆς κατὰ τὸν γάμον πειραθῆναι φθορᾶς* †Bas.Anc.*virg*.54(M.30.777B); *ἔπρεπε γὰρ τῷ ἁγνοτάτῳ, καὶ διδασκάλῳ τῆς ἁγνείας, ἐξ ἁγνῶν ἐξεληλυθέναι παστάδων. εἰ γὰρ ὁ τῷ Ἰησοῦ καλῶς ἱερατεύων ἀπέχεται γυναικός, αὐτὸς ὁ Ἰησοῦς πῶς ἔμελλεν ἐξ ἀνδρὸς καὶ γυναικὸς ἔρχεσθαι; 'ὅτι σὺ εἶ', φησὶν ἐν ψαλμοῖς, 'ὁ ἐκσπάσας με ἐκ γαστρός.' ... σημαίνοντι τὸ χωρὶς ἀνδρὸς ἐκ π. γαστρὸς καὶ σαρκὸς αὐτὸν ἐκσπασθέντα γεγεννῆσθαι* Cyr.H.*catech*.12.25; **9.** compared with Adam's formation from virgin earth, Iren. *haer*.3.21.10(M.7.954C–955A); *A.Barth*.5(p.137.21) cit. s. *Ἀδάμ*; Meth.*symp*.3.4(p.31.6f.; M.18.68A); Tim.Ant.*descr.BMV* 2(M.28.945C); *διὰ τοῦτο Ἐδὲμ αὐτὴν ἐκάλεσεν, ὅπερ ἐστὶ π. γῆ· αὕτη ἡ π. ἐκείνης τῆς π.* [sc. BMV] *τύπος ἦν* Chrys.*hom.2.3 in Ac.*9:1(3.113A); Jo.D.*f.o*.4.24(M.94.1205D–1208A).

C. BMV and the virgin Eve *διὰ τῆς π. ἄνθρωπος γεγονέναι, ἵνα καὶ δι' ἧς ὁδοῦ ἡ ἀπὸ τοῦ ὄφεως παρακοὴ τὴν ἀρχὴν ἔλαβε, διὰ ταύτης τῆς ὁδοῦ καὶ κατάλυσιν λάβῃ. π. γὰρ οὖσα Εὔα καὶ ἄφθορος, τὸν λόγον τὸν ἀπὸ τοῦ ὄφεως συλλαβοῦσα, παρακοὴν καὶ θάνατον ἔτεκε· πίστιν δὲ καὶ χαρὰν λαβοῦσα Μαρία ἡ π. ... διὰ ταύτης γεγέννηται οὗτος...δι' οὗ ὁ θεὸς τόν τε ὄφιν...καταλύει* Just.*dial*.100.4,5(M.6.709D–712A); *π. καὶ ξύλον καὶ θάνατος τῆς ἡμετέρας ἥττης γέγονε τὰ σύμβολα. καὶ γὰρ π. ἦν ἡ Εὔα...ἀντὶ τῆς Εὔας ἡ Μαρία* Chrys.*pasch*.2(3.752B); *π. ἡμᾶς ἐξέβαλε παραδείσου, διὰ παρθένου ζωὴν εὕραμεν αἰωνίαν* id.*exp.in Ps*.44:5f.(5.171D); *ἀντὶ δὲ τῆς πρὸς θάνατον διακονησαμένης π. Εὔας, θεοχαρίτωτος π., εἰς λειτουργίαν ζωῆς προσεχειρίζετο· π. ἐντὸς γυναικείας φύσεως καὶ ἐκτὸς γυναικείας σκαιότητος, π. ἀνύβριστος...οὐ μαθητευθεῖσα τοῖς τῆς Εὔας κακοῖς* Thdot.Anc.*hom.BMV* 11(p.329.19ff.); *ἐπειδὴ γὰρ ἡ πρώτη π. ταῖς τῆς ἀποφάσεως ἐπὶ τῇ παραβάσει περιεκέκλειστο λύπαις ...ἡ δευτέρα π. διὰ τῆς προσηγορίας, τὸ τοῦ θήλεος πᾶν θλιβερὸν ἀπώσατο* Hesych.H.*serm*.4(M.93.1453B); cf. *οὐδὲ Εὔα φθείρεται, ἀλλὰ π. πιστεύεται* ‡*Diogn*.12.8 (perh., however, to be understood of Church).

D. of BMV in rel. to redemption *διὰ σοῦ γὰρ τὸ μεσότοιχον τοῦ φραγμοῦ τὴν ἔχθραν κατέλυσεν, ὦ ἁγία π. διὰ σοῦ ἡ οὐράνιος εἰρήνη τῷ κόσμῳ ἐδωρήθη...διὰ σοῦ ἄνθρωποι ἄγγελοι γεγόνασι...διὰ σοῦ γνῶσις οὐράνιος...διὰ σοῦ σταυρὸς ἔλλαμψε...ἐν ᾧ τὸ βρέφος σου ἐκρέματο Χριστός* ‡Epiph.*hom*.5(M.43.501B); *πέπαυται γὰρ διὰ σοῦ τὰ τῆς Εὔας στυγνρά· ᾤλοντο διὰ σοῦ τὰ φαῦλα...ἐξήλειπται διὰ σοῦ τὰ τῆς καταδίκης· λελύτρωται Εὔα διὰ σέ· ἅγιον γὰρ τὸ ἐκ τῆς ἁγίας γεννώμενον...χαῖρε τοιγαροῦν, π. κεχαριτωμένη* Thdot.Anc.*hom.BMV* 12 (p.331.29f.); *ἰδοὺ ἡ π. ... ἡ τῶν π. ἐξαίρετος...ἡ τῆς αἰσχύνης τὴν Εὔαν, καὶ τῆς ἀπειλῆς τὸν Ἀδὰμ ἀπαλλάξασα, ἡ τὴν παρρησίαν ἀποτεμοῦσα τοῦ δράκοντος* Hesych.H.*serm*.5(M.93.1465A); *π. ἁγία, σὺ τοῦ Ἀδὰμ τῆς κατάρας ἡ λύσις· σὺ τῆς Εὔας τοῦ ὀφλήματος ἡ πλήρωσις* Taras.*praesent.BMV* 9(M.98.1492A).

E. bodily assumption of BMV *ἤτοι...ἀπέθανεν ἡ ἁγία π. καὶ τέθαπται...ἤτοι ἀνῃρέθη...ἤτοι δὲ ἔμεινε...τὸ τέλος γὰρ αὐτῆς οὐδεὶς ἔγνω* Epiph.*ep.Arab*.ap.*haer*.78.23(p.474.3; M.42.737A); cf.*ib*.78.11

(p.462.4; 716B); ὧν [sc. apostles] ἐκ χειρῶν, πάντων ἀποσκοπούντων τὸ ἄχραντον ἀφηρπάγη τῆς π. σῶμα. καὶ ὁ μὲν ἁρπάσας αὐτό, πᾶσιν ἄβλεπτος· θεὸς γὰρ ἦν ἀθεώρητος...ἴδε ὁ τόπος, ὅπου τέθαπται μὲν ἡ π.· μετετέθη δὲ ἡ ζωοτόκος Μαρία Germ.CP *or*.8(M.98.369C,D); ἡ π. ...οὐκ εἰς γῆν ἀπελήλυθεν, ἀλλ' ἔμψυχος ὄντως οὐρανὸς χρηματίσασα, ταῖς οὐρανίαις σκηναῖς ἐνοικίζεται Jo.D.*hom*.9.2(M.96.725B); σοὶ [sc. Christ] τὸ ἐμὸν σῶμα, καὶ οὐ τῇ γῇ παραδίδωμι. φύλαξον σῶον, ὃ... γεννηθεὶς π. ἐτήρησας *ib*.9.10(736C).

F. her perfect purity κυηθεὶς [sc. Christ] μὲν ἐκ τῆς π., καὶ ψυχὴν καὶ σάρκα προκαθαρθείσης τῷ πνεύματι Gr.Naz.*or*.38.13(M.36.325B); ἡ π. ... ἧς καπνὸς ἐπιθυμίας οὐχ ἥψατο, οὐδὲ σκώληξ αὐτὴν ἡδυπαθείας ἔβλαψεν Hesych.H.*serm*.5(M.93.1465A).

G. her superiority to all other creatures, ‡Epiph.*hom*.5(M.43.492B); *ib*.(497D); Procl.CP *or*.5.2(M.65.717C–718A).

H. types and comparisons; **1.** burning bush τὸ...προδιατυπωθὲν ἐν τῇ φλογὶ καὶ τῇ βάτῳ, διαβάντος τοῦ μέσου χρόνου, σαφῶς ἐν τῷ κατὰ τὴν π. μυστηρίῳ ἀπεκαλύφθη. ὥσπερ γὰρ ἐκεῖ ἡ θάμνος, καὶ ἅπτει τὸ πῦρ καὶ οὐ καίεται, οὕτω καὶ ἐνταῦθα ἡ π., καὶ τίκτει τὸ φῶς, καὶ οὐ φθείρεται. εἰ δὲ βάτος προδιατυποῖ τὸ θεοτόκον σῶμα τῆς π., μὴ αἰσχυνθῇς τῷ αἰνίγματι Gr.Nyss.*nativ*.(M.46.1136B,C); π., ἡ τὸ πῦρ τῆς θεότητος ἀφλέκτως, ὡς νοερὰ βάτος, κατέχουσα ‡Epiph.*hom*.5(M.43.493D); πῶς Μωϋσῆς εἶδε θεόν;...ἐκ τῆς βάτου ἀναπτόμενον πῦρ καὶ τὴν βάτον οὐ φθεῖρον. διὰ τί οὖν ἀπιστεῖς τῷ ἐκ π. γεγεννημένῳ καὶ τὴν παρθενίαν μὴ φθείραντι;...ἆρα ἐν τῇ βάτῳ οὐχ ὁρᾷς τὴν π.; Thdot.Anc.*hom*.2.2(p.74.21; M.77.1372A,B); Procl.CP *or*.6.6(M.65.732B); †Gregent.*disp*.(M.86.657A); **2.** Aaron's rod ὁ οὖν τῇ ῥάβδῳ, διὰ τὸν τυπικὸν ἀρχιερέα, καρπὸν ὑπὲρ φύσιν χαρισάμενος, ἆρα τῇ π., διὰ τὸν ἀληθινὸν ἀρχιερέα, τὸ τεκεῖν οὐκ ἐχαρίζετο; Cyr.H.*catech*.12.28; ‡Chrys.*BMV* 2(8.239B,C); **3.** Eden ὦ γῆς ἀσπόρου καρπὸν βλαστησάσης σωτήριον· ὦ π., αὐτὸν νικήσασα τῆς Ἐδὲμ τὸν παράδεισον. ἐκεῖνος...μοσχευτῶν φυτῶν γένος ἀνέτειλεν, ἐκ π. γῆς ἀνατειλάντων φυτῶν· ἡ δὲ π. αὕτη κρείττων ἐκείνης τῆς γῆς. οὐ γὰρ ὀπώρας ἀνέτειλε δένδρα, ἀλλὰ τὴν ῥάβδον Ἰεσσαὶ καρπὸν σωτήριον τοῖς ἀνθρώποις παρέχουσαν. κἀκείνη ἡ γῆ π. ἦν καὶ αὕτη π. ἀλλ' ἐκεῖ μὲν φῦναι δένδρα προσέταξεν ὁ θεός, ταύτης δὲ τῆς π. αὐτὸς ὁ δημιουργὸς κατὰ σάρκα γέγονε βλάστημα. οὐδὲ ἐκείνη μόσχευμα πρὸ τῶν δένδρων ἐδέξατο οὐδὲ αὕτη ἐκ τοῦ τόκου τὴν παρθενίαν ἠδίκησεν. ἡ π. τοῦ παραδείσου ἐνδοξοτέρα γεγένηται· ὃ μὲν γὰρ θεοῦ γεώργιον γέγονεν, ἡ δὲ κατὰ τὴν σάρκα θεὸν αὐτὸν ἐγεώργησεν Thdot.Anc.*hom*.1.1(p.81.2; M.77.1349A,B); Jo.D.*hom*.8.8(M.96.712B); for comparison with rod of Jesse, mentioned above, v. Thdr.Stud.*nativ.BMV* 2(M.96.681B); **4.** rod of Moses ὥσπερ οὖν ἡ Μωϋσέως ῥάβδος,...κατὰ φύσιν μὲν ἦν ῥάβδος, κατ' οἰκονομίαν δὲ δράκων· οὕτω καὶ ἡ Μαρία κατὰ φύσιν μὲν ἦν π., κατ' οἰκονομίαν δὲ μήτηρ ἐγένετο ‡Chrys.*BMV* 3(8.241B); **5.** ark of covenant, ref. Ps.131:8 κιβωτὸς...ἡ ἀειπάρθενος θεοτόκος... σοὶ γάρ...ἡ π. ἀνάπαυσις· καὶ ἡ μήτρα σὴ ἀνάπαυσις Chrysipp.*enc.in BMV* 2(p.338.15); **6.** the 'shadowy' mount (i.e. Mt. Paran) of Abac. 3:3 ὄρος δὲ κατάσκιον, αὕτη ἡ π. ἐστίν, ἐξ ἧς καὶ προῆλθεν ἀφράστως σαρκωθείς. ὄρος δὲ αὐτὴν λέγει, διὰ τό, ὡς ἐν τῷ Σινᾷ ὄρει, παραπλησίως καταβεβηκέναι ἐν αὐτῇ τὸν θεόν,...εἴτε καὶ διὰ τὸ ἀδιόδευτον τῆς παρθενίας...κατάσκιον δὲ αὐτὴν ἐμφαίνει, διὰ τὸ συσκιάζειν ἐν αὐτῇ τῷ πλήθει τῶν ἀρετῶν τὸ μυστήριον τῆς αὐτῆς παρθενίας †Gregent.*disp*.(M.86.669B); **7.** summaries of various OT types and prophecies, Jo.D.*hom*.8.9(M.96.713B); ‡Meth.*Sym.et Ann*.9(M.18.369A).

I. BMV in rel. to consecrated virgins προσκυνείσθω ὁ ἐκ π. γεννηθεὶς κύριος, γνωριζέτωσαν αἱ π. τῆς οἰκείας πολιτείας τὸν στέφανον Cyr.H.*catech*.12.33; ἡμεῖς δέ φαμεν, τῷ ἐκ π. σαρκωθέντι θεῷ λόγῳ θαρρήσαντες, ὡς ἡ παρθενία ἄνωθεν, καὶ ἐξ ἀρχῆς ἐνεφυτεύθη τῇ φύσει τῶν ἀνθρώπων Jo.D.*f.o*.4.24(M.94.205D).

J. her part in Inc. ἐν τῇ γαστρὶ τῆς π. ὁ ἀποφηνάμενος τὸν κατάδικον ἐνεδύσατο...δοὺς γὰρ πνεῦμα ἔλαβεν σάρκα· ὁ αὐτὸς μετὰ τῆς π. καὶ ἐκ τῆς π.· ᾧ μὲν ἐπεσκίασεν, μετ' αὐτῆς· ᾧ δὲ ἐσαρκώθη, ἐξ αὐτῆς Procl.CP *or.laud.BMV* 8(p.106.20f.; M.65.689A); predestined from beginning of world, Taras.*praesent.BMV* 13(M.98.1497A).

K. as priest and altar ἱερέα καλεῖ τὴν π. ὁμοῦ τε καὶ θυσιαστήριον· ἥτις τραπεζοφοροῦσα τὸν οὐράνιον ἄρτον Χριστὸν ἔδωκεν ἡμῶν εἰς ἄφεσιν ἁμαρτιῶν ‡Epiph.*hom*.5(M.43.497A).

L. her rel. to Church τὸν οἰκίσκον, ἔνθα ἡ π. ἀπεκύησε, τῆς ἐκκλησίας τὸν τύπον δεχόμενον Tim.Ant.*descr.BMV* 7(M.28.953C); εἶδες...πῶς τῆς ἐκκλησίας τὸν τύπον προανεζωγράφησε τὸ εὐτελὲς καταγώγιον, ἔνθα ἡ π. ἔτεκεν, ἡ ἅπαξ κυοφορήσασα, καὶ δεύτερον μὴ γεννήσασα *ib*.8(956C); κύριος...ἔχει γὰρ πολλοὺς ἀδελφούς, οὐ φύσει, ἀλλὰ χάριτι, καὶ ἐν τῇ π., καὶ ἐν τῷ πατρί *ib*.9(957C).

M. called π. βασιλική, ‡Chrys.*BMV* 2(8.239B).

V. met.; **A.** of Trin. πρώτη π. ἐστὶν ἁγνὴ τριάς Gr.Naz.*carm*.1.2.1.20(M.37.523A); interpreted ref. 'virgin' number 7 τριάδα διὰ τοῦ γ' σημαίνεσθαι, καὶ πάλιν τὴν αὐτὴν διὰ τοῦ ζ', τῷ τὸν ζ' ἀριθμὸν π. εἶναι. τῶν γὰρ ἐντὸς δεκάδος ἀριθμῶν μόνος οὗτος οὔτε γεννᾷ, οὔτε γεννᾶται. τοῦτο δὲ σαφῶς ἐνδείκνυται διεξιὼν ἐν τῇ βίβλῳ...Περὶ παρθενίας, οὑτωσὶ λέγων, 'πρώτη π. ...'· ...τῇ ἁγίᾳ τριάδι μυστικῶς ...ἐπιθεωρήσας ἐνέργειαν, φημὶ δὲ τὸ ἀγαθὸν ὅπερ τὰς τέσσαρας ἐμφαίνει γενικὰς ἀρετάς, τὸν ἑπτὰ πληρώσεις ἀριθμόν. τῇ γὰρ...τριάδι μυστικῶς τὴν αὐτῆς ἐπιθεωροῦντες ἐνέργειαν τὸν ἑπτὰ π. ἀπαρτίζομεν ἀριθμόν Max.*ambig*.(M.91.1393D–1396A).

B. of Church, Iren.*haer*.4.33.4(M.7.1075A); Clem.*paed*.3.2(p.244.27; M.8.576B); τροφὴν ἰχθὺν ἀπὸ πηγῆς παμμεγέθη καθαρόν, ὃν ἐδράξατο π. ἁγνή Aberc.*epitaph*.14; ref. Apoc.12:1–6, Meth.*symp*.8.4(p.85.20; M.18.144C); *Ep.Lugd*.ap.Eus.*h.e*.5.1.45(M.20.425B) cit. s. μήτηρ; cf.‡*Diogn*.12.8 cit. s. iv c supra; v. ἐκκλησία.

C. font ἡ κολυμβήθρα...μήτηρ πάντων γίνεται, τῷ ἁγίῳ πνεύματι μένουσα π. Didym.*Trin*.2.13(M.39.692A).

D. of scripture τοιαῦται δ' ἡμῖν αἱ...γραφαί, τὴν ἀλήθειαν ἀποτίκτουσαι καὶ μένουσαι π. Clem.*str*.7.16(p.66.24; M.9.529B).

E. of earth after purgation by fire ἐκλικμήσει κύριος τὴν ἁμαρτίαν ἀπὸ τῆς γῆς...καὶ βοήσει πρός με λέγουσα· π. εἰμὶ ἐνώπιόν σου, κύριε, καὶ οὐκ ἔστιν ἐν ἐμοὶ ἁμαρτία *1Apoc.Jo*.15(p.82) ∾ *Apoc.Dan*.C (p.120).

VI. Manich.; of virgin of light, Hegem.*Arch*.13(p.21.11; M.10.1449A); cf.*ib*.9(pp.13.15–15.1; 1441A,B).

***παρθενοτροφία**, ἡ, *rearing as a virgin*, Clem.*str*.3.12(p.231.21; M.8.1177C).

***παρθενόφυτος**, *giving birth to the Virgin* Ἄννα..., π. ἄνθος θεόβλαστον Andr.Cr.*can.BMV*(M.97.1328D).

***παρθεν-όω**, *make virgin* ~ώσας, καί, ὡς εἰπεῖν, ἐξαγγελώσας, εἰς τὴν ἀνθρωπίνην εἰκόνα σωματικῶς ἐμορφοῦτο ‡Chrys.*pasch*.6(p.167.4; 8.270C).

παρθενών, ὁ, 1. *convent* for women τὴν...ἀδελφὴν παραθέμενος... παρθένοις, δούς τε αὐτὴν εἰς π. ἀνατρέφεσθαι Ath.*v.Anton*.3(M.26.844A); Gr.Naz.*or*.43.62(M.36.577A); ὅσοι...ἀπὸ μοναστηρίων καὶ παρθενώνων Epiph.*haer*.58.4(p.361.15; παρθένων M.41.1016A); Thphn.*chron*.p.373(παρθένων M.108.893A); Thdr.Stud.*epp*.2.177(M.99.1549B); **2.** *retreat of female saint* ἦλθον εἰς Σελεύκειαν φυγάς, τὸν π. ... Θέκλας Gr.Naz.*carm*.2.1.11.548(M.37.1067A).

παρθεσίη, ἡ, *deposit*, *Orac.Sib*.2.65.

***Παρθολέτης, ὁ,** *destroyer of Parthians*, *Orac.Sib*.14.45.

***παριδίως**, *in private*, Dor.*doct*.7.1(M.88.1697B).

παριδρύ-ω, med., *establish, confirm* ~σατο...σύν τινι θείᾳ δυνάμει Gr.Thaum.*pan.Or*.6(p.16.14; M.10.1069D).

παρίημι, 1. *let slide, disobey* μηδὲ μικρὸν...παριέναι τι τῶν διατεταγμένων Bas.*reg.fus*.proem.2(2.328C; M.31.892C); but οὐκ ἐπὶ τοῖς παρεθεῖσι τὴν ὀργὴν ἐκδεχόμεθα, ἀλλ' ἐπὶ τῷ κατορθωθέντι δῆθεν τὰς τιμὰς ἀναμένομεν *ib*.(328D; M.893A); **2.** perf. ptcpl. pass. παρειμένος **a.** *paralysed* in body, Eus.*d.e*.9.13(p.432.6; M.22.696D); Chrys.*hom.26.5 in Mt*.(7.320A); Vict.*Mc*.2:4(p.284.26); **b.** of spiritual state, *sluggish, benumbed* ψυχὴν παρειμένην Chrys.*hom.73.3 in Mt*.(7.711B); τὸ νωθρὸν τῆς ψυχῆς καὶ παρειμένον id.*laud.Paul*.6(2.511D); cf.id.*hom.20.2 in Ac*.(9.164D).

παριππάζω, fig.; **1.** of time, *go by* μικροῦ...παριππάσαντος χρόνου Pall.*v.Chrys*.3(p.17.12; M.47.13); v. sq.; **2.** *live through* ἀμφὶ τὰ ἐνενήκοντα παριππάσας ἔτη Pall.*v.Chrys*.17(p.103.15; M.47.58).

παριππεύ-ω, A. intrans.; **1.** of time, *go past*, Cyr.*glaph.Ex*.2(1.279D); id.*Jo*.3.4(4.284E); Cyr.S.*v.Sab*.11(p.95.2, v.l. παριππάσαντος); Thdr.Stud.*epp*.1.14(M.99.956B); aor. ptcpl., *past, last* ἐν τῷ π. διωγμῷ *ib*.2.113(1377D); τὸ ~σαν ἔτος Gr.Naz.*ep*.57(M.37.112B); Bas.Sel.*v.Thecl*.2.9(M.85.580A); **2.** *be transient* ἐν ἴσῳ σκιᾶς ~οντα Cyr.*Mich*.70(3.469A); Nonn.*par.Jo*.19:28(M.43.904B); **3.** *escape* memory ὃ δὲ δὴ κάλλιστον...μικροῦ ~σαν ᾤχετο Cyr.*hom.pasch*.8 (5².96C); **4.** *deviate* ἔξω τοῦ πρέποντος...~σαι Isid.Pel.*epp*.3.283(M.78.960A).

B. trans.; **1.** *pass, spend* time τρεῖς δεκάδας ~σας Nonn.*par.Jo*.5:5(M.43.785A); **2.** *disregard, gloss over*, Cyr.*Jo*.10.2(4.898B); id.*Jon*.proem.(3.366C); Isid.Pel.*epp*.3.58(M.78.769B); **3.** *escape notice of* πολλὰ τὸν ἰσχνὸν νομοφύλακα ~ει Cyr.*Ps*.18:14(M.69.833A); *transcend* understanding, id.*Jo*.3.2(4.254B).

***παρίππι(ο)ν, τό,** *spare horse* παρίππιν εὑρὼν ἐστρωμένον καὶ ἐπιβὰς αὐτοῦ ἔφυγεν Thphn.*chron*.p.347(M.108.836C).

παρίπταμαι, *fly past, be transitory*, Epiph.*haer*.76.24(p.371.18; M.42.564B).

παρισάζω, *compare*, Bas.*Spir*.36(3.30C; M.32.133A); pass., *be comparable* to, Clem.*str*.6.2(p.431.18; M.9.224A); Bas.*hex*.7.6(1.69A; M.29.161B).

παρισ-όω, 1. *make equal* τῇ ἐνεργείᾳ ~ῶσαιτ ὁ τέλος Bas.*Eun*.1.24

(1.235C; M.29.565B); **2.** pass., *make oneself like*, Cyr.*Jo*.5.1(4.462B); **3.** *compare, regard as comparable* τί τὸ τῆς σαρκώσεως χρῆμα ~οῦν ἀξιοῖς τῇ κατὰ μέθεξιν χάριτι; Cyr.*Nest*.1.5(p.25.20; 6[1].20A); pass., *be comparable to*, Eus.*d.e*.1.7(p.36.24; M.22.72B); Jo.D.*hom*.12.6(M.96.789C); of Father and Son τέλειον εἶναί φαμεν τὸν υἱὸν τὸν τῷ τελείῳ πατρὶ ~ούμενον διὰ τὸ τῆς οὐσίας ἀπαράλλακτον Cyr.*Jo*.1.3(4.23C).

***παρίστασις**, ἡ, prob. f.l. for περί-, Or.*Ps*.37:4(p.16).

παρίστ-ημι (παριστ-άνω), **A.** trans.; **1.** *present, offer*; **a.** in gen. ἕτοιμον ἐμαυτὸν ὑμῖν...π. Tat.*orat*.42(p.43.14; M.6.888B); οὐ γὰρ τὰς ἀκοάς, ἀλλὰ τὴν ψυχὴν ~ησι τοῖς...δηλουμένοις πράγμασιν Clem.*str*.7.11(p.44.8; M.9.485A); id.*ecl*.14(p.140.29; M.9.705A); **b.** to God ἔδει γὰρ τὸν μεσίτην...θεῷ μὲν παραστῆσαι τὸν ἄνθρωπον Iren.*haer*.3.18.7(M.7.937B); Clem.*prot*.3(p.33.25; M.8.129B); τὴν ψυχὴν ~άνειν τῷ δημιουργῷ Or.*Cels*.5.35(p.38.22; M.11.1236A); †Bas.*Is*.24(1.398C; M.30.165B); of Christ παραστήσας ἑαυτὸν...τῷ πατρί Cyr.*Jo*.11.2(4.933A); ἐκκλησίας...ἣν αὐτὸς ἑαυτῷ παρέστη [l. παρέστησεν] ὁ υἱός id.*Ps*.21:23(M.69.840B); **2.** *supply, furnish* οἱ τοὺς ἵππους τοὺς πολεμιστηρίους ~ῶντες...καὶ σὺ τοίνυν παρέστησας τῷ πολέμῳ τῷ κατὰ τοῦ διαβόλου τὰ μέλη Chrys.*hom.20.1 in Rom*.(9.657C); **3.** *set forth, express* παραβολή...λέξις δι' ἑτέρων τὰ κυρίως λεγόμενα μετ' ἐνεργείας ~άνουσα Clem.*str*.6.15(p.496.2; M.9.349C); *ib*.7.14(p.60.19; 517B); τὸ ἀσαφὲς...τῶν...γραφῶν παραστήσειν ὑποσχομένου τοῦ Τατιανοῦ Eus.*h.e*.5.13.8(M.20.461B); τὸ ἀγέννητον τὴν ὑπόστασιν τοῦ θεοῦ ~ησιν Aët.*synt*.12(p.354.20; M.42.537C) Bas.*Eun*.2.5(1.241C; M.29.580C); Didym.(‡Bas.)*Eun*.5(1.306C; M.29.736A); λόγῳ παραστῆσαι τὴν βίαν ...οὐκ ἔχων Chrys.*sac*.1.3(p.11.12; 1.365D); ὄνομα...τὴν σωτηρίαν... ~ησι ‡Hipp.Th.*fr*.17(p.49.19); **4.** *prove, demonstrate*, Tat.*orat*.1(p.2.16; M.6.805B); παραστῆσαι πρεσβυτέραν τὴν ἡμετέραν φιλοσοφίαν τῶν παρ' Ἕλλησιν ἐπιτηδευμάτων *ib*.31(p.31.4; 868C); π. ὅτι τὰ μὲν ἡμέτερα σωφρονεῖ *ib*.33(p.34.2; 873A); Athenag.*leg*.11.3(M.6.912C); λόγους παιδικοὺς εἶναι ~άς Clem.*str*.1.29(p.110.29; M.8.928A); Or.*princ*.3.1.9(p.208.13; M.11.264A); ~άντες τὸν προφητευθέντα id.*Cels*.3.15(p.214.18; M.11.940A); Eus.*p.e*.10.13(502A; M.21.836C); Gr.Nyss.*Eun*.1(1 p.122.5; M.45.357B); **5.** *bring forward, produce*, for trial or punishment τὰ δὲ ὀστᾶ τῶν ἁγίων...δαίμονας...~ησι καὶ βασανίζει Chrys.*hom.26.5 in 2Cor*.(10.626A); πέμπει παραστήσων τὸν προφήτην id.*hom.9.1 in Eph*.(11.69D).

B. intrans. tenses and pass.; **1.** *stand by*; hence *attend, be in attendance*, hence *serve* τῷ θελήματι αὐτοῦ λειτουργοῦσιν [sc. ἄγγελοι] παρεστῶτες *1Clem*.34.5; παρὰ θεῷ...ᾧ παρεστήκαμεν Gr.Naz.*ep*.23(M.37.60A); παρεστάναι γὰρ τοῖς βασιλεῦσιν ἔθος τοὺς δορυφόρους Thdr.Mops.*Rom*.6:12–14(p.122.10; M.66.801C); as monastic penalty ὁ τοῦ μεγαλείου μὴ ὑπακούων, παρεστηκέτω ἐν τῇ τραπέζῃ Thdr.Stud.*poen*.1.8(M.99.1733D); **2.** *support, assist*, Or.*Jo*.2.34(28; p.93.10; M.14.176C); τῷ τῆς ἀληθείας ~αται κανόνι Eus.*h.e*.4.23.4(M.20.385A); id.*d.e*.4.16(p.190.23; M.22.317B); **3.** *come to mind, occur*; *be presented* to one κατὰ τὸ παραστὰν ταῦτα πράττομεν Chrys.*hom.11.2 in 1Cor*.(10.89C); ἂν τὰ παραστάντα μὴ εἴποι id.*hom.11.5 in Eph*.(11.88A); Thdt.*Abac*.1:7(2.1540); **4.** *be expressed* ταραχὴ...λόγῳ παραστῆναι μὴ δυναμένη Chrys.*hom.75.3 in Mt*.(7.726D).

***παριτητός**, *allowing an approach* ἀντινομοθετεῖ μηδὲ π. εἶναι πρὸς τὸν πατέρα τῷ πλουτοῦντι Cels.ap.Or.*Cels*.7.18(p.169.19; M.11.1445D).

παριτός, *accessible*; neut. as subst., *access* οὐ...ἐστι π. ἐπὶ τὸν οἰκίσκον Synes.*ep*.67 (παριτητέον M.66.1420C).

παρό, *seeing that, since*, Athenag.*leg*.8.2 (παρ' ὃ M.6.905A).

παρόδευσις, ἡ, *passage*, Melet.*nat.hom*.synops.(M.64.1085A).

παροδευτικός, *allowing to pass*, Melet.*nat.hom*.22(M.64.1228C); *ib*.23(1236B,C).

***παροδευτικῶς**, *in a cursory way*, Taras.*ep*.4(M.98.1453A); ἀναγινώσκειν ἐρευνητικῶς καὶ οὐ π. ... τὸ ἅγιον εὐαγγέλιον CNic.(787) *can*.2.

παροδεύ-ω, **A.** intrans., **1.** *be a passer-by*, Ign.*Rom*.9.3; of events, *go past* τὰ...~σαντα τοῦ βίου πράγματα Eust.*engast*.12(p.36.7; M.18.640B); fig., *be transitory* οὐδὲν μόνιμον, ἀλλὰ πάντα ~εται Chrys.*hom.23.5 in Mt*.(7.291D); Sev.Ant.ap.*cat.Ac*.2:3(p.17.9); **2.** *wander* (sc. from the Christian way) πάντες εἰς αὐτὴν ἐπιβεβήκαμεν..., εἰ καὶ μὴ πάντες αὐτὴν ὁδεύειν, ἀλλὰ ~ειν ἐκβαίνοντες θέλουσι Ath.*gent*.30(M.25.61A); pass., *be led astray*, Anast.S.*qu.et resp*.8(M.89.405D).

B. trans., **1.** *disregard, turn a deaf ear to* ~ουσι τῶν προφητῶν τὰ μηνύματα ‡Ath.*Apoll*.1.1(M.26.1093B); pass., Clem.*q.d.s*.28(p.178.26; M.9.633C); **2.** *spend* time ~ει...τὸν βίον Ant.Mon.*hom*.83(M.89.1685A).

παροδία, ἡ, *passage*, Capr.*ep.Eph*.(M.*PL*.53.846B; v.l. for παρόδου p.53.2).

παροδικός, **1.** *going past*, esp. of time τὴν π. τοῦ χρόνου κίνησιν Gr.Nyss.*anim.et res*.(M.46.129A); id.*hom.11 in Cant*.(M.44.996B); id.*fat*.(M.45.160D); **2.** *fleeting, transient*, Gr.Nyss.*hom.2 in Cant*.(M.44.804B); Mac.Aeg.*libert.ment*.32(M.34.965A); τὸ φαινόμενον τῆς φύσεως ῥυτὸν καὶ π. ‡Proc.G.*Pr*.9:18(M.87.1309A); esp. of the present life, Gr.Nyss.*anim.et res*.(M.46.149B); ‡Proc.G.*Pr*.9:15(1308B); *Chron.Pasch*.p.112(M.92.293C); of Inc., *temporary* ταχεῖαν, καὶ οἱονεὶ π. ποιεῖται τὴν ἐπιδημίαν †Bas.*Is*.247(1.567E; M.30.553B); τὸ...'διὰ γυναικὸς' παροδικὴν ἔμελλε τὴν ἔννοιαν τῆς γενέσεως ὑποφαίνειν Bas.*Spir*.12(3.9E; M.32.85C); **3.** *passing through* τὸ...τὴν ἐκ παρθένου μὲν γέννησιν ὁμολογεῖν, π. δὲ ταύτην γενέσθαι λέγειν, καὶ μηδὲν ἐκ τῆς παρθένου τὸν θεὸν λόγον λαβεῖν, ἐκ τῆς Βαλεντίνου, καὶ Βαρδησάνου, καὶ τῶν τούτοις ἀγχιθύρων τερατολογίας Thdt.*eran*. proem.(4.3).

παροδικῶς, **1.** *perfunctorily* μηδὲ π. ἀναγινωσκέτω τοῦ αὐτοῦ ἀποστόλου τὰ ῥήματα Leo Mag.*ep*.11(p.18.7; M.*PL*.54.776B); **2.** *transiently* π. ἐπιφοιτῶμεν τῇ παρούσῃ ζωῇ Gr.Nyss.*v.Mos*.(M.44.356D); of Inc. ἐν βραχεῖ τὸ κατὰ τὴν σάρκα μυστήριον π. ἐνδεικνύμενον id.*Eun*.5(2 p.126.15; M.45.708D); **3.** *so as to pass through* (Apollinarian) οὐκ ἐν τῇ παρθένῳ σάρκα γενόμενον, ἀλλὰ π. δι' αὐτῆς διεξελθόντα, οἷος πρὸ τῶν αἰώνων ἦν id.*Apoll*.24(M.45.1173B).

παρόδιος, **1.** *by the wayside*, Gr.Nyss.*hom.2 in Cant*.(M.44.793A); met., in etym. of word παροιμία: ἐπὶ τῶν ἐν ταῖς ὁδοῖς λαλουμένων... οἶμος γὰρ...ἡ ὁδός...' ῥῆμα π. τετριμμένον ἐν τῇ χρήσει τῶν πολλῶν Bas.*hom*.12.2(2.98B; M.31.380B); cf.‡Caes.Naz.*dial*.35(M.38.897); **2.** *common* ἐγείρεται ὁ πνευματικὸς [sc. ναός], οὐχ ὁ σωματικὸς καὶ π. Ephr.2.233D; **3.** *wayfaring*, *Did*.12.2; **4.** as subst. plur., ? *supplies* (s.v.l.) αἱ Ταυρικαὶ πρόσοδοι καὶ παρόδιοι αὐτῷ μὲν ὁρώμεναι, ἐκείνῳ δὲ προσγενόμεναι Gr.Naz.*or*.43.58(M.36.572B).

παροδίτης, ὁ, **1.** *passer-by*, *Orac.Sib*.14.33; fig. ὁδός εἰμί σοι παροδίτῃ *A.Jo*.95(p.198.13); Jo.Mosch.*prat*.167(M.87.3033D); **2.** *bystander*, *A.Jo*.51(p.176.22).

πάροδος, ἡ, **1.** *path, way* τῆς ἐπὶ τὸν σωτήριον λόγον π. Eus.*h.e*.4.7.2(M.20.316B); *wayside* τάχα...σκηνῇ ἀπεικάζει τὸν πρόσκαιρον βίον, καὶ βούλεται ἡμᾶς χρᾶσθαι αὐτῷ ὡς σκηνῇ κατὰ πάροδον Cyr.*Ps*.36:3(M.69.925C); *bypath* (as etym. of παροιμίαι) οἶμος...ὁδός... νοεῖται ὥστε πάροδοι καὶ εἰκόνες τῶν πραγμάτων αἱ παραβολαὶ τυγχάνουσιν ‡Caes.Naz.*dial*.35(M.38.897); *way round, by-pass*; met., of death ἡ μόνη γέφυρα καὶ π. οὐκ ἔχουσα Anast.S.*defunct*.(M.89.1196B); **2.** *coming, arrival* μετὰ τὴν Ἰωάννου π. Cyr.*Jo*.4.2(4.356E); of birth τῆς εἰς κόσμον π. Clem.*q.d.s*.33(p.182.13; M.9.640B); of souls for human lifetime τὸν σύμμετρον τῶν ἀνθρώπων χρόνον κατενόησεν τῇ κατασκευῇ, ὥστε τῇ π. τῶν προορισθεισῶν ψυχῶν συναπαρτηθῆναι αὐτόν ‡Caes.Naz.*dial*.156(M.38.1116); ref. reincarnation πρὸ τῆς ἐς τοῦτο τὸ σῶμα π. τῶν ἐν θαλάττῃ καὶ κύμασι διατριβόντων γεγονέναι σεαυτὸν λέγεις Eus.*Hierocl*.47(543C; M.22.864C); of Inc. as *coming* of Christ, id.*e.th*.1.17(p.78.24; M.24.861A); *ib*.7.2(p.122.7; 941A); id.*v.C*.1.32(p.22.26; M.20.948B); Ammon.*Jo*.8:42(M.85.1452D); heret. ἐκ τοῦ πῶς καὶ ὅπως εἰς ἀπιστίαν ἐχώρησαν, καὶ ἀντὶ γεννήσεως ἐπλάσαντο ποίησιν, καὶ ἀντὶ προόδου κτίσιν καὶ πάροδον κατεσκεύασαν Apoll.*quod un.Chr*.2(p.295.20; M.28.124B); Βαλεντῖνος δέ, καὶ Βασιλείδης, καὶ Βαρδησάνης, καὶ Ἁρμόνιος...δέχονται μὲν τῆς παρθένου τὴν κύησιν, καὶ τὸν τόκον· οὐδὲν δὲ τὸν θεὸν λόγον ἐκ τῆς παρθένου παρειληφέναι φασίν, ἀλλὰ π. τινα δι' αὐτῆς ὥσπερ διὰ σωλῆνος ποιήσασθαι Thdt.*ep*.145(4.1248B); ἐνανθρωπῆσαι...τὸν Ἰησοῦν ἔφη [sc. Valentinus], τὸν ἔξω Χριστὸν ἐνδυσάμενον, καὶ σῶμα ἐκ τῆς ψυχικῆς οὐσίας ἀνειληφότα· π. δὲ μόνην διὰ τῆς παρθένου ποιήσασθαι, οὐδὲν ἐκ τῆς ἀνθρωπείας φύσεως εἰληφότα id.*haer*.5.11(4.420); οὐδὲν...ἔφη [sc. Eutyches] τὸν θεὸν λόγον ἀνθρώπειον ἐκ τῆς παρθένου λαβεῖν, ἀλλ' αὐτὸν ἀτρέπτως τραπέντα καὶ σάρκα γενόμενον· τοῖς γὰρ καταγελάστοις αὐτοῦ κέχρημαι λόγοις· τὴν π. μόνην διὰ τῆς παρθένου ποιήσασθαι *ib*.4.13(4.373); **3.** *addition* of something beyond the normal ἔθος τῇ θείᾳ γραφῇ τὸν ἀριθμὸν τὸν δέκα τέλειον...προσδέχεσθαι...ἐπείπερ ἡ τῶν ἐφεξῆς ἀριθμῶν π. τε καὶ θέσις...πρὸς ὅπερ ἂν ἐθελήσαι βαδίζει Cyr.*Jo*.4.2(4.357A); **4.** met., *loophole, opportunity* π. αὐτοῖς διδόναι τοῦ κρίνειν Chrys.*hom.11.1 in 1Cor*.(10.87C); **5.** *competence* of judge, Heracl.*nov*.25(p.44); Ath.Scholast.*coll*.1.4(p.16); **6.** *admission* ἡ π. μετὰ τῶν ἀγγέλων τῶν ἁγίων Herm.*vis*.2.2.7; τῶν τοιούτων ἡ π. μετὰ τῶν ἀγγέλων ἐστὶν id.*sim*.9.25.2; *means of admission* ὑμεῖς ἐστηριγμένοι, π. ἐστε τῶν εἰς θεὸν ἀναιρουμένων Ign.*Eph*.12.2; **7.** *entry* into being, *creation* τὴν ἐκ τοῦ μὴ ὄντος εἰς τὸ εἶναι π. Eus.*e.th*.3.2(p.143.15; M.24.980A); τὴν εἰς τὸ εἶναι π. Bas.*Eun*.2.3(1.240B; M.29.577B); εἰ...γέννημα παρόδου ἐστὶ δηλωτικόν Aët.ap.Epiph.*haer*.76.12(p.356.11; M.42.540D); τῆς π. τῶν φύσεων Gel.Cyz.*h.e*.2.17.33(M.85.1272D); δοῦναι τοῖς οὐκ οὖσιν τοῦ εἶναι τὴν π. Bas.Sel.*or*.12.1(M.85.157C); **8.** *passing away* or *on* μετὰ τὴν τοῦ βίου π. Chrys.*hom.44.6 in Gen*.(4.454E); τὴν τῶν ὑλικῶν...π. ... καὶ...εἰς τὸν νοητὸν κόσμον εἴσοδον ‡Bas.*h.myst*.56(p.392.12); **9.** *disposal* of, *getting rid* of, Didym.*Gen*.

6:22(M.39.1113A); βάπτισμα...θανάτου π. ὑπισχνούμενον Bas.Sel.*or.* 13.2(M.85.176A).

παροικεσία, ἡ, *sojourn* τῆς π. ἐν γῇ Βαβυλῶνος Thphl.Ant.*Autol.* 3.25(M.6.1160A).

παροικ-έω, 1. *dwell,* Or.*sel.in Ps.*14:1(M.12.1208C); δεῖ...τὸν τοῦ θεοῦ ἄνθρωπον καὶ ~ῆσαι ἐν τῷ σκηνώματι τῷ θεϊκῷ, καὶ κατασκηνῶσαι ἐν τῷ ἁγίῳ ὄρει Mac.Aeg.*ep.*2(M.34.409C); *dwell as a stranger* or *inferior* πάροικος καὶ ἀλλογενὴς οὐ ~ήσει αὐτοῖς ἔτι *Pss.Sal.*17.31; παρῴκησαν εἰς Αἴγυπτον Arist.*apol.*14(p.109.27); τὸ λαμπρὸν καὶ θεσπέσιον Ἰουδαίων γένος...ἔξω που ~εῖν καὶ ποιμαίνειν ἐν τοῖς ἀτίμοις ἐκελεύσθη Cels.ap.Or.*Cels.*4.47(p.320.11; M.11.1105A); **2.** *associate with* τοῖς ἁγίοις μάρτυσι, οἷς ~εῖς Gr.Naz.*ep.*223(M.37.364C); **3.** *be close to* μὴ πόρρωθεν...ἀλλὰ ~οῦντες Thdt.*2Tim.*4:22(3.697); fig., *be akin to* μεγαλοφροσύνης ~οῦσαν τὴν ἀλαζονείαν ἐκφεύγει Synes.*ep.*141(M.66.1536A); **4.** ref. man's temporary sojourn in this life Χριστιανοὶ ~οῦσιν ἐν φθαρτοῖς *Diogn.*6.8; παντὶ δούλῳ θεοῦ πᾶς ὁ κόσμος [sc. πόλις], πατρὶς δὲ ἡ ἐπουράνιος Ἱερουσαλήμ· ἐνταῦθα δὲ ~εῖν, ἀλλ' οὐ κατοικεῖν...τετάγμεθα ‡Pion.*v.Polyc.*6; ἔφη...ὑπερασπιεῖν ὁ τῶν ὅλων θεὸς τῶν κατοικούντων Ἱερουσαλήμ, καὶ οὐχὶ δὴ μᾶλλον τῶν ~ούντων αὐτήν Cyr.*Zach.*92(3.780C); ἔργῳ ἐδείκνυσαν, τί τὸ ~εῖν τοῖς ὧδε, καὶ τί τὸ πολίτευμα ἔχειν ἐν οὐρανῷ [Phil.3:20] Bas. *ep.*223(3.337E; M.32.824C); opp. κατοικέω, Cyr.*Ps.*14:1(M.69.805B); cf.id.*Zach.*92(3.780C); οὐδὲ...κατοικῶ τὴν γῆν, ἀλλὰ ~ῶ Thdt.*Ps.* 38:14(1.855); τὴν παροῦσαν ζωήν, ἐν ᾗ ~οῦμεν, οὐ κατοικοῦμεν *ib.* 54:16(966); **5.** ref. Christ's sojourn among men, Cyr.*glaph.Ex.*1(1. 259C); **6.** ref. the position or location of churches, in gen. αἱ τοῦ θεοῦ Χριστῷ μαθητευθεῖσαι ἐκκλησίαι, συνεξεταζόμεναι ταῖς ὧν ~οῦσι δήμων ἐκκλησίαις, ὡς φωστῆρές εἰσιν ἐν κόσμῳ Or.*Cels.*3.29(p.227.8; M.11.957B); partic. as t.t., *1Clem.*proem.; ἡ ἐκκλησία τοῦ θεοῦ ἡ ~οῦσα Σμύρναν, τῇ ἐκκλησίᾳ τοῦ θεοῦ τῇ ~ούσῃ ἐν Φιλομηλίῳ *M.Polyc.*proem.; Eus.*h.e.*4.23.5(M.20.385A).

παροίκησις, ἡ, 1. *sojourning* ἡ...τῶν Ἑβραίων ἐν Αἰγύπτῳ π. Thphl.Ant.*Autol.*3.24(M.6.1157A); **2.** *living with* as wife, Clem.*str.* 1.5(p.20.5; M.8.724B); **3.** *administrative district, diocese* δεόμεθα... μήτε λοιπὸν ἡμᾶς μοχθεῖν καὶ τῶν ἰδίων π. ἀλλοτρίους ἐπιτρέψειας γίνεσθαι, ἀλλ' ἵνα οἱ ἐπίσκοποι σὺν τοῖς ἰδίοις λαοῖς...εἰς εὐχάς τε καὶ λατρείας σχολὴν ἄγοιεν CArim.*ep.Const.*1(p.238.27; M.26.700B).

παροικία, ἡ, A. *sojourning, temporary period of residence,* esp. in foreign land; **1.** in gen. ἡ π. ἐστὶ διαγωγὴ πρόσκαιρος, οὐχ ἱδρυμένην ζωὴν ἀλλὰ παροδικήν, ἐπ' ἐλπίδι τῆς ἐπὶ τὰ κρείττονα μεταστάσεως, ὑποφαίνουσα Bas.*hom.in Ps.*14(1.352A; M.29.252A); ἑρμηνεύεται δὲ ἡ Γέργεσα π. ἐκβεβληκότων Or.*Jo.*6.41(24; p.150.17; M.14.272A); **2.** of Israel's sojourn in Egypt, *ib.*(p.150.29; 272B); Gr.Nyss.*hom.3 in Cant.*(M.44.812C); Thdt.*qu.4 in Jos.*(1.306); of Babylonian exile, Thphl.Ant.*Autol.*3.28(M.6.1164B); ‡Epiph.*v.proph.Ezech.*(M.43. 401A); **3.** met., of earthly life as temporary abode, *2Clem.*5.1; εὐχαριστήσας μὲν ἐπὶ τῇ π., εὐλογῶν δὲ ἐπὶ τῇ ἐξόδῳ, τὴν μονὴν ἀσπαζόμενος τὴν ἐν οὐρανῷ Clem.*str.*4.26(p.322.7; M.8.1376B); Bas.*hom.in Ps.* 32(1.136E; M.29.336C); κατοικεῖν ἐν σκηναῖς...πάντα τὸν χρόνον τῆς π. ἡμῶν ἀναμένοντας τὴν ἀληθινὴν πατρίδα †Bas.*Is.*27(1.401B; M.30. 172C); τίς διαιρήσει...τὴν κάτω σκηνὴν καὶ τὴν ἄνω πόλιν; τίς π. καὶ κατοικίαν; Gr.Naz.*or.*14.21(M.35.884C); π. ἡγεῖσθαι πρέπειν τὰ ἐν τῷδε τῷ κόσμῳ πράγματα Cyr.*glaph.Gen.*5(1.174B); τὴν τοῦ βίου π. Proc.G. *Is.*16:6–14(M.87.2117B).

B. *place of sojourning, lodging* ἐκκλησίαν μᾶλλον ἢ π. εἶναι τὴν τῆς Τρυφαίνης ἑστίασιν Bas.Sel.*v.Thecl.*1(M.85.548A); δεχόμενος πρὸς παροικίαν...ἄνδρας Gr.Mag.*dial.*(tr.Zach.)4.14(M.*PL.*77.342D); met., of BMV π. αὐτοῦ γέγονα Jo.Thess.*dorm.BMV* 1.6(p.384.11); *ib.*2.13 (p.428.27).

C. *sojourning community*; **1.** of Jewish sojourners in heathen lands, *Pss.Sal.*17.19; **2.** of communities of Christian Church πάσαις ταῖς κατὰ πάντα τόπον τῆς ἁγίας καὶ καθολικῆς ἐκκλησίας π. *M.Polyc.* proem.; Apollon.ap.Eus.*h.e.*5.18.9(M.20.480A); cf. παροικέω; hence

D. community of Christians organized as geographical unit; **1.** *diocese* (i.e. community under pastoral jurisdiction of a bishop), Or.*comm.in 1Cor.*16:10(*JTS* 10 p.50); εἴ τινες ἐπίσκοποι κατασταθέντες καὶ μὴ δεχθέντες ὑπὸ τῆς π. ἐκείνης, εἰς ἣν ὠνομάσθησαν, ἑτέραις βούλοιντο π. ἐπιέναι...τούτους ἀφορίζεσθαι CAnc.(314)*can.*18; μή τις αὐτῶν τολμήσῃ καὶ ταῖς ὑμετέραις π. ἐπιβῆναι Alex.Al.*ep.Alex.*1(p.19. 8; M.18.548A); ἐν ταῖς μάλιστα ἐπισημοτάταις π. Eus.*h.e.*1.1.1(M.20. 48B); τῆς ἐν Ἀλεξανδρείᾳ π. Ἀννιανὸς τὴν λειτουργίαν διαδέχεται *ib.* 2.24(205C); τῆς Ἀσίας ἁπάσης αἱ π. *ib.*5.23.1(492A); Δημητρίῳ τε τῷ τῆς π. ἐπισκόπῳ *ib.*6.19.15(569A); ἀναστρέφειν εἰς τὰς ἑαυτῶν π. CNic. (325)*can.*16; εἴ τις πρεσβύτερος ἢ διάκονος...καταλιπὼν τὴν ἑαυτοῦ π. εἰς ἑτέραν ἀπέλθοι CAnt.(341)*can.*3; Ath.*apol.sec.*36(p.115.11; M.25. 309D); id.*h.Ar.*17(p.191.28; M.25.712D); περὶ τοῦ μὴ τὰ ἅγια εἰς λόγον εὐλογιῶν κατὰ τὴν ἑορτὴν τοῦ πάσχα εἰς ἑτέρας π. διαπέμπεσθαι CLaod.*can.*14; Ἰακώβῳ...ἐπισκόπῳ...πρώτῳ τῆς π. ταύτης Cyr.H. *catech.*14.21; Bas.*ep.*66.1(3.159A; M.32.424C); τοὺς...καθ' ἑκάστην π. προεστῶτας *ib.*70(163E; M.433C); οἱ...ἐμπιστευθέντες τὰς ἐν κυρίῳ π. *Const.App.*7.46.15; εἰ δέ τις ἐκ βασιλικῆς ἐξουσίας ἐκαινίσθη πόλις... τοῖς πολιτικοῖς καὶ δημοσίοις τύποις καὶ τῶν ἐκκλησιαστικῶν π. ἡ τάξις ἀκολουθείτω CChalc.*can.*17; Soz.*h.e.*1.15.7(M.67.905C); Philost. *h.e.*4.3(M.65.520A); *Chron.Pasch.*p.279(M.92.696B); **2.** *province* μὴ παρόντος τοῦ μητροπολίτου καὶ δύο ἄλλων ἐπισκόπων τῆς αὐτοῦ παροικείας, Ath.Scholast.*coll.*1.7(p.18, v.l. παροικίας); **3.** *parish* ἡγεῖτο δὲ Ἀλεξανδρείας καὶ τῆς λοιπῆς Αἰγύπτου Λαῖτος, τῶν δ' αὐτόθι π. τὴν ἐπισκοπὴν...Δημήτριος ὑπειλήφει Eus.*h.e.*6.2.2(M.20.524A); ὑπὲρ τοῦ ἐπισκόπου...καὶ τῶν π. αὐτοῦ δεηθῶμεν *Lit.*ap.*Const.App.*8.10.7; ἐν ὀκτακοσίαις ἐκκλησίαις ἔλαχον ποιμαίνειν· τοσαύτας γὰρ ἡ Κύρρος π. ἔχει Thdt.*ep.*113(4.1190); τὰς καθ' ἑκάστην ἐκκλησίαν ἀγροικικὰς π. ἢ ἐγχωρίους CChalc.*can.*17; τάττονται δὲ αὗται αἱ ἐκκλησίαι [sc. of Mareotis] ὑπὸ τῷ τῆς Ἀλεξανδρείας ἐπισκόπῳ, καὶ εἰσὶν ὑπὸ τὴν αὐτοῦ πόλιν ὡς παροικίαι Socr.*h.e.*1.27.13(M.67.156A).

E. in gen.; *district, neighbourhood,* Geo.Pis.*Pers.*2.212(M.92. 1224A).

***παροικονόμος, ὁ,** *subordinate administrator,* in a monastery τοῦ οἰκονόμου καὶ τοῦ π. Thdr.Stud.*epp.*2.50(M.99.1260C); *ib.*2.61(1277C); *ib.*2.103(1360D).

πάροικος, ὁ, *sojourner* ἕνα καὶ μόνον θεόν, οὐ νόθον καὶ ἐπείσακτον ...καὶ π. Adam.*dial.*5.28(p.240.7; M.11.1884A); π. καὶ προσήλυτον †Bas.*Is.*277(1.591A; M.30.608A); of Abraham, Bas.*hom.in Ps.*14(1. 352B; M.29.252A); and Hebrews, Cyr.*Juln.*6(6^{2}.211D); cf.*Const.App.* 2.53.6; of Jews as homeless race, Gr.Naz.*or.*22.2(M.35.1133A); of Christians as sojourners in this world, *Diogn.*5.5; Ast.Am.*hom.*2 (M.40.181B); Cosm.Ind.*top.*2(M.88.72C).

***παροικτρόω,** *treat with disrespect* or *contempt,* Gr.Mag.*dial.*(tr. Zach.)1.10(M.*PL.*77.206A); Jo.D.*f.o.*4.3(M.94.1105B); Cosm.Mel. *schol.*proem.(M.38.344); med., Gr.Mag.*dial.*(tr.Zach.)3.10(235C).

***παροιμήν,** error for παρ' ἡμῖν, Ephr.3.437E.

παροιμία, ἡ, *proverb, saying*; **1.** def. and supposed etym. τὸ τῶν π. ὄνομα ἐπὶ τῶν δημωδεστέρων λόγων παρὰ τοῖς ἔξωθεν τέτακται, καὶ ἐπὶ τῶν ἐν ταῖς ὁδοῖς λαλουμένων...· ῥῆμα παρόδιον τετριμμένον ἐν τῇ χρήσει τῶν πολλῶν, καὶ ἀπὸ ὀλίγων ἐπὶ πλείονα ὅμοια μεταληφθῆναι δυνάμενον. παρὰ δὲ ἡμῖν π. ἐστὶ λόγος ὠφέλιμος, μετ' ἐπικρύψεως μετρίας ἐκδεδομένος, πολὺ μὲν τὸ αὐτόθεν χρήσιμον περιέχων, πολλὴν δὲ καὶ ἐν τῷ βάθει τὴν διάνοιαν συγκαλύπτων Bas.*hom.*12.2(2.98B,C; M.31.388B,C); π. εἰσὶ λόγοι σοφῶν, ὡς αἰνίγματα, ἅτινα ἕτερον μέν τι αὐτόθεν δηλοῦντά ἐστιν, ἕτερον δὲ ἐν ὑπονοίᾳ ἀπαγγέλλουσι...τῶν π. μὴ ἐκ φανεροῦ ἀλλὰ κεκρυμμένως λεγομένων ‡Ath.*synops.*22(M.28.340C); ref. Proverbs ὠνομάσθη...Παροιμία, ἐπειδὴ παρὰ τὰς ὁδοὺς ἐγράφοντο οἱ τοιοῦτοι λόγοι πρὸς διόρθωσιν καὶ διδασκαλίαν τῶν ἐν ταῖς ὁδοῖς διαπορευομένων. τινὲς γοῦν ὁρίζονται αὐτὰς οὕτως· ῥῆμα παρόδιον ἀπό τινος ἑνὸς εἰς πολλὰ μεταλαμβανόμενον *ib.*(340D); cf. λόγοι...εἰσιν αἱ π. προτρεπτικοὶ παρὰ πᾶσαν τοῦ βίου τὴν ὁδὸν χρησιμεύοντες ‡Hipp.*fr.* *33 in Pr.*(p.169.6; M.10.616B); cf.‡Caes.Naz.*dial.*35(M.38.897) cit. s. πάροδος; **2.** straightforward *moral observation* Δανιὴλ [prob. l. Δαυὶδ]...γὰρ αὐτὸς π. μέμνηται λεγούσης· ἐξῆλθεν ἐξ ἀνόμων πλημμέλεια Chrys.*hom.34.2 in Jo.*(8.198A); τῆς π. λεγούσης, ὅτι δεῖ τοὺς φίλους μετὰ τῶν ἐλαττωμάτων ἔχειν *ib.*79.4(469E); **3.** *popular saying* in cryptic form τῆς κατὰ τὴν π. καλουμένης ὄνου σκιᾶς μάχης Cels. ap.Or.*Cels.*3.1(p.203.13; M.11.921A); Chrys.*hom.34.3 in Jo.*(8.199E); ‡Jo.D.*Artem.*1(p.152.10; M.96.1253A); for use made by Marcellus of pagan proverbs, v. Eus.*Marcell.*1.3(p.14ff.; M.24.744Bff.); **4.** *idiom* π. λέγεται ἐπὶ τῶν σφόδρα λυπουμένων καὶ ἀγωνιώντων αἵματος ἵδρωσις ‡Dion.Al.*fr.in Lc.22:44*(p.241.11; M.10.1592C); Gr.Nyss.*Eun.*6(2 p.145.9; M.45.732A); **5.** with emphasis on its obscurity, *parable, dark saying* οὐ συγχρῶμαι [i.e. with Celsus] ὡς σαφέσι τοῖς ῥητοῖς, ἀκολούθως δὲ τῇ ἐπιγραφῇ (ἐπιγέγραπται γὰρ τὸ βιβλίον Παροιμίαι) ζητῶ ταῦτα ὡς αἰνίγματα Or.*Cels.*4.87(p.358.18; M.11.1161D); ὁμολογεῖται...ἐν τῇ γραφικῇ καταχρήσει τὸ τῆς π. ὄνομα μὴ κατὰ φανεροῦ τετάχθαι νοήματος, ἀλλ' ἐπί τινος κεκρυμμένης λέγεσθαι διανοίας κτλ. Gr.Nyss.*Eun.*3(2 p.9.7ff.); π. εἰκόνες ἑτέρων, οὐκ αὐτὰ τὰ λεγόμενα Didym.(‡Bas.)*Eun.*4(1.293C; M.29.704C); ref. Jo.16:25 τῆς π. οὐκ ἐχούσης τὴν παρρησίαν Cyr.*thes.*15(5^{1}.155D); **6.** OT Book of *Proverbs*; in plur., Clem.*str.*2.2(p.114.25; M.8.933B); Or.*Cels.*7.34(p.185.15; M. 11.1470B) etc.; in sing., Epiph.*anc.*42(M.43.92C; v.l. for παροιμίαι p.52.14); Didym.*Trin.*3.3(M.39.813C); *ib.*(805C); Pall.*v.Chrys.*11 (p.65.9; M.47.37).

παροιμιακός, *of* or *relating to* (*the Book of*) *Proverbs* ὁ π. λόγος Bas.*hom.*5.9(2.43A; M.31.260B); Gr.Nyss.*hom.9 in Cant.*(M.44.957D); π. διδασκαλία id.*Eun.*1(1 p.109.8; M.45.344B); esp. ref. Arian use of

Pr.8:22, Thdr.Mops.*1Cor.*1:24(M.66.877B); Thdt.*h.e.*1.7.18(3.758); ἐν τῇ π. βίβλῳ Σολομῶντος *Dial.Tim.et Aquil.*79 v°.

παροιμιαστής, ὁ, *the author of the Book of Proverbs,* commonly identified with Solomon, ‡Hipp.*fr.38 in Pr.*(p.172.10); Eus.*fr.Lc.*12:39(M.24.564A); Bas.*hom.*18.1(2.142A; M.31.489C); Diod.*Ps.*93:7(M.33.1627B); Epiph.*haer.*69.14(p.163.23; M.42.224B); Isid.Pel.*epp.*3.66(M.78.776A); Cyr.*Ps.*7:15(M.69.756C).

παροιμιώδης, 1. *proverbial,* Clem.*prot.*2(p.31.3; M.8.124B); Marcell.ap.Eus.*Marcell.*1.3(p.15.4; M.24.745B); Chrys.*hom.34.2 in Jo.*(8.197E); **2.** *of the Wisdom literature* τῇ π. διδασκαλίᾳ Bas.*hom.*12.8(2.104E; M.31.404A); Gr.Nyss.*Eun.*2(2 p.297.3; M.45.468A); τῆς π. ἀγωγῆς id.*hom.1 in Cant.*(M.44.769D); ref. OT Book of Proverbs ἡ π. σοφία id.*Eun.*4(2 p.93.7; 669B); ref. use of Pr.8:22 by Arians τινες ἐκ τῆς π. ῥήσεως τὰ ἐν παραβολῇ σκοτεινῶς...εἰρημένα...ἀνερμήνευτα πρὸς ἀνατροπὴν τῆς ἀληθείας...τὴν τοῦ ἐκτίσθαι φωνὴν...προχειρίζωνται *ib.*1(1 p.108.23; 341D); π. παράγγελμα id.*Maced.*1(M.45.1301C); Chrys.*hom.20.1 in Jo.*(8.115A); Nil.*epp.*1.218(M.79.161D).

παροιν-έω, 1. lit., *drink to excess,* Clem.*paed.*2.7(p.191.31; M.8.461A); *Const.App.*8.44.3; **2.** fig., *act as drunk, rave* τοὺς ληναΐζοντας ποιητὰς...~οῦντας Clem.*prot.*1(p.4.5; M.8.53B); *ib.*12(p.84.2; 240B); **3.** *insult* κατὰ τῶν...μαρτύρων ~ήσας Eus.*m.P.*11.31(p.946.17; M.20.1512A); τῷ ~οῦντι Bas.*leg.lib.gent.*5(p.51; M.31.576C); οὐκ ἐπαύετο τοὺς παρεντυγχάνοντας ~ῶν ἐν...καιρῷ τοῦ φωτίσματος *Ep.*ap.CSyr.(*ACO* 3 p.95.31; H.2.1369D); pass. ~ηθεὶς...ἀμείβεται τὴν ὕβριν Clem.*paed.*2.2(p.170.5; M.8.416A); ἧττον Σωκράτους πεπαρῴνησαι Isid.Pel.*epp.*1.11(M.78.185C); perh. with play on sense 1 supra ~ουμένη...ὡς μεθύουσα πράως ἤνεγκε Thdt.*qu.3 in 1Reg.*(1.356); *treat with contempt, defile* ~ουμένην [sc. τὴν ἱερωσύνην] ὑπὸ ἀνδρῶν μιαρῶν Isid.Pel.*epp.*2.52(M.78.493C); God's laws, Cyr.*Ps.*40:5(M.69.993C); of Jews' treatment of Christ, *blaspheme* against, Cyr.*Is.*1.1(2.17B); αὐτὴ γὰρ [sc. ἡ συναγωγή] ἀπέκτεινε, καὶ πεπαρῴνηκεν εἰς αὐτόν id.*Joel.*7(3.205C); id.*Ps.*35:13(924A); ἀκούω δὲ ψάλλοντος τοῦ μακαρίου Δαβὶδ περὶ τῶν εἰς Χριστὸν πεπαρῳνηκότων id.*ador.*4(1.113C); Thdt.*affect.*10(p.260.14; 4.970); in gen., Isid.Pel.*epp.*3.130(M.78.832A); ~ῶν τὸν σταυρωθέντα Χριστὸν *Libell.*ap.CSyr.(*ACO* 3 p.108.9; H.2.1392A); Jo.D.*hom.*4.21(M.96.620A); **4.** *play at when drunk* αἰσχρὸν...~εῖν τὸ ἄνδρα θηλυεύεσθαι καὶ ἐν θηλείας μορφῇ ὑπάρχειν Epiph.*haer.*66.33(p.72.26; M.42.81B).

παροινία, ἡ, 1. *intoxication;* met., of condition of Delphic priestess, Chrys.*hom.29.1 in 1Cor.*(10.260C); **2.** *drunken and disorderly conduct* μέθη μὲν οὖν ἐστιν ἀκράτου χρῆσις σφοδροτέρα, π. δὲ ἡ ἐκ τῆς χρήσεως ἀκοσμία Clem.*paed.*2.2(p.172.9; M.8.420B); **3.** *insulting behaviour* τῆς κατὰ τοῦ Χριστοῦ π. Eus.*h.e.*9.10.15(M.20.837A); ὕβρεων καὶ π. Ath.*apol.sec.*15(p.99.7; M.25.273B); Bas.*hom.*10.5(2.87E; M.31.364C); Isid.Pel.*epp.*1.255(M.78.336C); π. εἰς θεόν Cyr.*Os.*82(3.114D).

***παροινοίας,** f.l. for παροινίας, Thdt.*ep.*145(4.1244).

πάροινος, *enraged,* Chrys.*hom.22.6 in Mt.*(7.282D); cf.id.*hom.2.2 in Tit.*(11.739B).

***παροιστέον,** *one must adduce,* Cyr.*ador.*10(1.347B).

πάροιστρος, *raving, hysterical* τὰ σημεῖα τῆς κολάσεως ἔδειξε καὶ τὰς χεῖρας ὡς ἦσαν πεπερονημέναι, τίς τοῦτο εἶδε; γυνὴ πάροιστρος Cels.ap.Or.*Cels.*2.55(p.178.25; M.11.884C); Cels.*ib.*2.59(p.182.23; 889C); of utterances of self-styled Messiahs ἄγνωστα καὶ π. καὶ πάντῃ ἄδηλα Cels.*ib.*7.9(p.161.15; 1433B) = *ib.*7.10(p.162.12; 1436B).

***παρολίσθησις, ἡ,** *sliding away,* Const.ap.Eus.*v.C.*2.69(p.69.10; M.20.1044A).

***παρόλκιον, τό,** *tow-rope, Apophth.Patr.*(M.65.357C).

παρομαρτ-έω, 1. *accompany,* Cyr.*Mich.*21(3.410D); ref. H. Ghost δύναμιν οὐσιώδη αὐτὴν ἐφ' ἑαυτῆς ἐν ἰδιαζούσῃ ὑποστάσει...οὔτε χωρισθῆναι τοῦ θεοῦ, ἐν ᾧ ἐστιν, ἢ τοῦ λόγου τοῦ θεοῦ, ᾧ ~εῖ Gr.Nyss.*or.catech.*2(p.15.4; M.45.17C); συμπρόεισι γὰρ τῷ λόγῳ τὸ πνεῦμα, οὐ συγγεννώμενον, ἀλλὰ συνὸν καὶ ~οῦν καὶ ἐκπορευόμενον Thdt.*affect.*2(p.65.19; 4.757); **2.** *be equal* to, *reach the standard* of ἄνδρα ~οῦντα τῷ βίῳ τοῖς κρατίστοις Bas.Sel.*v.Thecl.*2.30(M.85.616D).

παρομοιάζω, *give an inaccurate account,* Chrys.*hom.58.1 in Jo.*(8.338A).

[*]**παρομοίιος,** = παρόμοιος, *Orac.Sib.*2.35.

παρομοιόω, pass., *be like, likened* to ὕλῃ παρωμοιωμένον Tat.*orat.*4(p.5.11; M.6.813B); Clem.*paed.*1.13(p.151.8; M.8.373A); Eus.*e.th.*1.12(p.72.34; M.24.849B); of relationship of Son to Father δι' ὅλου σώζειν τοῦ μόνου θεοῦ τὴν ἔμψυχον καὶ ζῶσαν νοερὰν εἰκόνα, κατὰ πάντα τῷ πατρὶ παρωμοιωμένην, [καὶ] τῆς θεότητός τε αὐτῆς τὴν ὁμοίωσιν ἐπιφερομένην Eus.*d.e.*5.4(p.226.1; M.22.373A); *ib.*5.5(p.228.33; 377B).

παρομολογέω, *confess, declare,* Or.*Jo.*20.9(p.336.19; M.14.589C).

παρονομάζω, pass., *be named after,* Or.*fr.22 in Jo.*(p.502.18).

παροξυντής, ὁ, *one who incites* against ἐγενόμην π., ἀθετητὴς τῆς χάριτός σου Ephr.1.144B.

παροξυσμός, ὁ, 1. *fit of temper* τὸ σφοδρότερον ἀπὸ θυμοῦ κίνημα π. ὀνομάζεται Bas.*reg.br.*55(2.434A; M.31.1120B); Diad.*perf.*92(p.132.8); *violent dispute,* Epiph.*haer.*72.1(p.255.12; M.42.381D); Chrys.*hom.34.1 in Ac.*(9.261A,B,D); ὁπόταν π. ἐπιπικράνῃ τοὺς ἐν κοινοβίῳ ἀδελφούς Nil.*Eulog.*5(M.79.1100D); **2.** *incitement* to good ἵνα ὁ θεὸς ὁρῶν τὸν πρὸς ἀλλήλους τῆς ἀγάπης π. ἀνταποδώσει πᾶσι τὰ αἰτήματα Ephr.3.345D; **3.** of illness; **a.** *spasm,* Ign.*Polyc.*2.1; **b.** *disturbance, convulsion* ὁρῶ καθ' ἑκάστην τὸν οὐρανὸν καὶ τὰ δοκοῦντα τῆς γῆς χρηστὰ μειούμενα καὶ ἀπορρέοντα· ταῦτα δὲ γίνονται ἐκ π. ἡμετέρων προδηλούντων, ὡς πάντα τὰ ἐνταῦθα ἀπόλλυνται *Pers.*(p.20.18).

παροξυτονέω, *accent as paroxytone,* Bas.*ep.*236.5(3.363E; M.32.884A).

παροξυτόνως, *with* (circumflex) *accent on penultimate* κᾶτα π. [i.e. not κατά] Max.*schol.e.h.*3.3.2(M.4.137D).

παροπτάω, *roast, burn;* pass., of martyrs, Clem.*str.*2.20(p.181.2; M.8.1069B).

παρόραμα, τό, 1. *thing omitted,* Gr.Nyss.*deit.*(M.46.572A); **2.** *object of contempt* π. καὶ καταπάτημα Mac.Aeg.*pat.*15(M.34.877B); **3.** *error, sin,* Gr.Naz.*or.*44.6(M.36.613B); Cyr.*fr.2Reg.*11:4(M.69.684B); πᾶν ἁμάρτημα ὡς πρὸς τὴν λογικὴν οὐσίαν π. ἐστιν *cat.1Jo.*5:11(p.141.29).

***παροράτεος,** *to be overlooked,* Jo.D.*hom.*8.14(M.96.720D).

παρορ-άω, 1. *neglect* πένητα ~ῶν *Const.App.*2.5.1; Chrys.*hom.44.1 in Ac.*(9.330C); pass., *be slighted,* Bas.*reg.fus.*50(2.395B; M.31.1040B); *abandon,* Clem.*paed.*2.2(p.172.26; M.8.421A); *be remiss* about, Diod.*Ps.*53:3(M.33.1591B); εἴ τι δι' ἀνθρωπίνην ἀσθένειαν παρῶπται *Lit.Jac.*(p.230.20); **2.** *overlook* π. τὰ ἁμαρτήματα τοῦ λαοῦ *Const.App.*2.15.4; π. τὰ παρ' ἑτέρων εἰς αὐτὸν γινόμενα σκάνδαλα ‡Proc.G.*Pr.*17:9(M.87.1396C); *disobey* rules, Bas.*reg.fus.*proem.3(2.330A; M.31.896B); **3.** *allow* to, Ath.*inc.*6.8(M.25.108B); **4.** equivocal use exeg. Cant.1:6a Χριστὸς παρεῖδε διὰ τὴν ἀπιστίαν Or.*Cant.*1:5(p.126.30; M.13.111D); but ὑπὸ τοῦ τῆς δικαιοσύνης ἡλίου παρεωραμένη ὑπῆρχε μεμελανωμένη Ph.Carp.*Cant.*12(M.40.48A).

παροργισμός, ὁ, *provocation, Pss.Sal.*8.9; in interprn. of name Sihon πειρασμὸς καὶ π. Eus.*Ps.*135:10(M.24.36A); ref. Eph.4:26, Ath.*v.Anton.*55(M.26.924A).

παρορισμός, ὁ, *encroachment on land* ὅσοι μετὰ παρορισμοῦ τῶν πλησίον τοὺς ὅρους τῶν οἰκείων κτήσεων ὑπερεξέτειναν...πάντως ἀλλότριοι τῆς θείας ἀπεδείχθησαν εὐλογίας †Bas.*Is.*151(1.486B; M.30.365C).

παροριστής, ὁ, *trespasser, Hom.Clem.*15.7.

***παρορκία, ἡ,** *bad faith, perjury,* Bas.*ep.*45.2(3.134C; M.32.368B); Gr.Naz.*ep.*163(M.37.272A).

***παρορμητικῶς,** *rousingly,* Proc.G.*Is.*2:5ff.(M.87.1880A).

παρουσία, ἡ, A. *presence;* **1.** in gen. οὐκ ἔχει ἐπιθυμίαν ἡ ἄφθαρτος βασιλεία, ἀλλὰ π. πάντων τῶν ἀγαθῶν Clem.*fr.*46(p.223.31); αἱ εὐώνυμοι δυνάμεις...ὑπὸ τῆς τοῦ φωτὸς π. οὐ μορφοῦνται id.*exc.Thdot.*34(p.118.5; M.9.676C); κυριωτέρᾳ γὰρ π. ἀγγέλων αἱ διαθῆκαι ἐνηργήθησαν ἡ ἐπὶ Ἀδάμ, ἡ ἐπὶ Νῶε id.*ecl.*51(p.151.14; M.9.721B); παρουσίᾳ φθορᾶς θνητὸς φανείς [sc. ἄνθρωπος] Meth.*symp.*3.7(p.34.13; M.18.72A); πᾶσιν ἀνθρώποις τὴν π. τῶν ἀνωτάτω...ἀγαθῶν...εὐαγγελίζεται Eus.*p.e.*1.1(2A; M.21.24A); οὐ γὰρ ὄφελός τι τῆς τοῦ σώματος π., τῆς καρδίας...περὶ τὸν γήινον θησαυρὸν πονουμένης Bas.*hex.*3.1(1.22D; M.29.53C); Chrys.*hom.72.3 in Jo.*(8.426C); **2.** of universal presence of Logos, unaffected by Inc., Eus.*d.e.*4.13(p.172.18; M.22.288A); Chrys.*hom.10.2 in Jo.*(8.58D); of Son's presence with Father, Eus.*e.th.*3.3(p.156.24; M.24.1001A); in Creation, Ath.*inc.*4.5(M.25.104B); of presence of Christ's deity in operations of incarnate life, *cat.Lc.*23:43(p.168.5); of Christ's presence in saints, ‡Bas.*h.myst.*62(p.397.23); **3.** of H. Ghost; as present universally, Didym.(‡Bas.)*Eun.*5(1.309C,E; M.29.741B,744A); in inspired prophets, †Bas.*Is.*proem.5(1.381C; M.30.125C); *ib.*254(573D; M.568A).

B. *arrival, appearance, personal visit, advent;* **1.** in gen. ἡ Κάδμου εἰς Θήβας π. Clem.*str.*1.21(p.66.23; M.8.825A); διάδοχον ἀντ' ἐμοῦ καταστῆσαι ἄχρι τῆς ἐμῆς π. *PLond.*1913.8; Chrys.*hom.24.1 in Jo.*(8.138D); Thdt.*Jer.*3:2(2.422); ἀσχολία τὴν πρὸς ὑμᾶς ἐκώλυσε π. id.*Rom.*15:22(3.152); σημαίνει...τὸν τῆς π. καιρόν id.*1Cor.*16:4(3.282); τὴν τοῦ σωτηρίου κηρύγματος π. *Chron.Pasch.*p.164(M.92.404B); ποιεῖται...ἑορτὴν ἐπὶ τῇ π. τοῦ υἱοῦ αὐτοῦ †Jo.D.*B.J.*34(M.96.1188A); of appearance of a demon in response to magic, Eus.*d.e.*3.6(p.138.23; M.22.233C); of appearance of water from rock in wilderness, signifying sudden advent of Christ at Inc., Chrys.*hom.57.1 in Jo.*(8.332D); **2.** of entry into corporeal life of pre-existent souls

(Carpocratian), Hipp.*haer*.7.32(p.220.6; M.16.3339B); Epiph.*haer*. 27.4(p.305.6; M.41.368C); *ib*.27.5(p.307.12; 369D); **3.** of advent of Christ; **a.** in Inc. *τὴν π. τοῦ σωτῆρος..., τὸ πάθος αὐτοῦ καὶ τὴν ἀνάστασιν* Ign.*Philad*.9.2; *πρὸ τῆς τοῦ σωτῆρος π.* Iren.*haer*.1.7.1(M. 7.513A); *τὴν ἔκβασιν τῶν προφητευμένων...ἥτις ἐστὶν ἡ π. τοῦ κυρίου ib*.4.26.1(1052B); *ἡ κατ' ἄνθρωπον αὐτοῦ π. ib*.4.38.1(1106A); *θεοῦ, τοῦ Χριστοῦ π.* Clem.*prot*.1(p.10.5; M.8.65C); *τῆς ἐν σαρκὶ π.* id.*str*. 3.9(p.226.10; M.8.1168B); *Ἰουδαίοις μὲν νόμος, Ἕλλησι δὲ φιλοσοφία μέχρι τῆς π., ἐντεῦθεν δὲ ἡ κλῆσις ἡ καθολικὴ ib*.6.17(p.514.6; M.9. 892C); id.*exc.Thdot*.19(p.112.27; M.9.665C); *Ἰουδαίων τὸν καιρὸν τῆς π. μὴ ἐπιγνόντων* Hipp.*haer*.9.30(p.263.27; M.16.3410C); *πρὸ τῆς π.* Or.*princ*.4.2.9(p.322.12; M.11.376B); *τὰ...κατασκευάζοντα τὴν π. αὐτοῦ* id.*Jo*.1.4(6; p.9.19; M.14.32C); *τὴν π. τοῦ λόγου ib*.13.47 (46; p.273.14; 481C); *μὴ διαφέρειν...τοὺς μετὰ τὴν π. ἁγίους Μωσέως καὶ τῶν πατριαρχῶν ib*.20.12(p.342.13; 600B); *ἁγνείας...ξύλον, ἀπὸ τῆς π. τοῦ ἀρχιπαρθένου Χριστοῦ βασιλεῦσαν* Meth.*symp*.10.3 (p.124.26; M.18.196D); *ἐφυλάττετο γὰρ τῇ αὐτοῦ π. ἡ χάρις τοῦ κηρύγματος τῆς περὶ αὐτοῦ θεολογίας* Eus.*e.th*.1.20(p.96.7; M.24.892C); *τῆς ἐνσάρκου π. αὐτοῦ* Ath.*Ar*.1.8(M.26.28B); ref. Pr.8:22 *οὐ τῆς οὐσίας αὐτοῦ, ἀλλὰ τῆς ἐνσωμάτου π. αὐτοῦ σημαντικόν ἐστι ib*.2.66 (285C); Bas.*Spir*.31(3.26C; M.32.124A); Gr.Nyss.*Eun*.5(2 p.105.16; M.45.684D); *ἐνσάρκου π. τοῦ μονογενοῦς* Epiph.*anc*.1(p.6.16; M.43. 17C); *ἐπειδὴ...ἐν τῷ κόσμῳ ὤν, οὐκ ἐδόκει παρεῖναι, τῷ μήπω γνωρίζεσθαι, ὕστερον δὲ ἑαυτὸν ἐφανέρωσε,...τὴν φανέρωσιν...π. καλεῖ* Chrys.*hom.10.2 in Jo*.(8.58D); *ἐπὶ τέλει τοῦ παρόντος αἰῶνος ἡ μετὰ σαρκὸς τοῦ λόγου γέγονε π.* Cyr.*thes*.15(5[1].172D); *σώσας ἡμᾶς διὰ τῆς ἐκ παρθένου π.* Thdt.*Ps*.66:2(1.1051); *ἐπειδὴ οἱόν τις ὄρθρος ἐστιν ὁ μετὰ τὴν κυριακὴν π. χρόνος, τὴν μέλλουσαν σημαίνων κατάστασιν οἱόν τινος ἡμέρας π.* id.*Cant*.6:9(2.133); *πολλὰ τῆς π. αὐτοῦ τὰ μαρτύρια κἀκ τῶν παρ' ὑμῖν χρησμῶν καὶ τῶν Σιβυλλείων γραμμάτων* ‡Jo.D.*Artem*.27(p.159.16; M.96.1276B); as a coming judgement, Chrys.*hom.28.1 in Jo*.(8.159C); **b.** in Inc. and in future advent *δύο γὰρ αὐτοῦ π. προεκήρυξαν οἱ προφῆται· μίαν μέν, τὴν ἤδη γενομένην, ὡς ἀτίμου...ἀνθρώπου...τὴν δὲ δευτέραν, ὅταν μετὰ δόξης ἐξ οὐρανῶν... παραγενήσεσθαι κεκήρυκται* Just.*1apol*.52.3(M.6.404D); id.*dial*.32.2 (M.6.544A) cit. s. *ἐκκεντέω*; *ib*.40.4(564A); *πολλάκις ἡ γραφὴ ὁμοίως περί τε τῆς ἐν σαρκὶ ἐπιδημίας...καὶ περὶ τῆς ἐν τῇ κρίσει διαλέγεται, καὶ περὶ τῶν δύο π. ἐπιπεπλεγμένως ἀπαγγέλλει ἐνίοτε* †Bas.*Is*.96(1. 445E; M.30.273C); †Jo.D.*B.J*.33(M.96.1176D–1177A); **c.** in future advent *ἡ δὲ ἀποδημία τοῦ δεσπότου, ὁ χρόνος ὁ περισσεύων εἰς τὴν π. αὐτοῦ* Herm.*sim*.5.5.3; *πέμψει γὰρ αὐτὸν κρίνοντα· καὶ τίς αὐτοῦ τὴν π. ὑποστήσεται; Diogn*.7.5; *δεῖν γὰρ εἶναι τὸ προφητικὸν χάρισμα ἐν πάσῃ τῇ ἐκκλησίᾳ μέχρι τῆς τελείας π. ὁ ἀπόστολος ἀξιοῖ* Anon.ap. Eus.*h.e*.5.17.4(M.20.473B); *τὰ ἐν τοῖς εὐαγγελίοις ὑπὸ τοῦ σωτῆρος προφητευθέντα περὶ τῆς π. αὐτοῦ* Or.*Cels*.6.45(p.116.3; M.11.1368B); *ἐδέοντο ἵνα ἄξιοι γένωνται τῆς τοῦ Χριστοῦ π. A.Phil*.138(p.72.6); *ποῖον τῆς π. αὐτοῦ σημεῖόν ἐστι;...σημεῖον δὲ...ἰδικὸν τοῦ Χριστοῦ ἐστιν ὁ σταυρός* Cyr.H.*catech*.15.22; *μνήσθητι τῆς ἐνδόξου τοῦ Χριστοῦ π.* Bas.*hom*.7.6(2.58D; M.31.296D); Gr.Naz.*or*.40.45(M.36.424C); *τοῦ γὰρ υἱοῦ τὴν ἐπιφάνειαν καὶ π. ἐκδεχόμεθα, οὐ τοῦ πατρός* Didym. (‡Bas.)*Eun*.4(1.294E; M.29.708B); *πρὸ τῆς π. οὐ δεῖ κρίνειν* Epiph. *haer*.59.5(p.370.6; M.41.1025D); *μέχρι τῆς τοῦ Χριστοῦ π.* Chrys.*sac*. 4.7(p.122.10, v.l. *τῆς ἐσχάτης τ. Χ. π.*; 1.412E); Jo.D.*hom*.1.7(M.96. 557A); *τὸ κατασφραγίσαι τὸν ἀρχιερέα τὸν λαὸν ὑποδεικνύει τὴν μέλλουσαν...π. ἐν τῷ ἑξακισχιλιοστῷ* ⟨*πεντηκοσιοστῷ*⟩ *ἔτει μέλλειν ἔσεσθαι διὰ τῆς ψηφῖδος τῶν δακτύλων ἐμφαινούσης ἑξακισχιλιοστὸν πεντηκοσιοστόν* ‡Bas.*h.myst*.45(p.389.14); dist. as *ἄλλη*, Iren.*haer*.5. 1.2(M.7.1122B); as *δευτέρα*, Just.*1apol*.52.3(M.6.404D); id.*dial*.32.2(M. 6.544A); *ib*.40.4(564A); *δευτέραν Χριστοῦ π. καὶ θειοτέραν* Or.*Jo*.2.37 (30; p.96.14; M.14.181B); Eus.*d.e*.1.1(p.4.12; M.22.17B); *ib*.6.6(p.256. 34; 421C) cit. s. *δηλωτικός*; id.*e.th*.3.14(p.171.16; M.24.1028A); to take place on 'eighth day' when mysteries of Judgement will be disclosed, ‡Bas.*struct.hom*.2.8(1.342C; M.30.52A); *φοβερὰν καὶ φιλάνθρωπον αὐτοῦ δευτέραν π.* Didym.*Trin*.1.15(M.39.328C); Oecum.*Apoc*. 2:20(p.55); Jo.Eub.*concept.BMV* 18(M.96.1492A); ref. eastward position at prayer *ἐκδεχομένους τὴν ἀνατολὴν τῆς φωτοφανείας τῆς δευτέρας τοῦ Χριστοῦ π.* ‡Bas.*h.myst*.10(p.260.17); **d.** of advent of Christ's kingdom, foretold by prophets, *ib*.39(p.387.3); **4.** of advent of H. Ghost; **a.** at Pentecost, *Const.App*.8.33.5; Chrys.*hom.75.1 in Jo*.(8.439D); *τὴν π. τοῦ παρακλήτου καλεῖ τὰ χαρίσματα τῆς ἀποκαλύψεως τῶν μυστηρίων τοῦ πνεύματος, ὡς εἶναι ἐν τῇ ὑποδοχῇ τοῦ πνεύματος, ἣν οἱ ἀπόστολοι ὑπεδέξαντο ἡ τελείωσις τῆς γνώσεως τῆς πνευματικῆς* Philox.*ep*.27(p.177); **b.** at eucharist in response to *epiclesis ἵνα ἐπιφοιτήσαν τῇ ἁγίᾳ καὶ ἀγαθῇ καὶ ἐνδόξῳ αὐτοῦ π. ἁγιάσῃ καὶ ποιήσῃ τὸν μὲν ἄρτον τοῦτο σῶμα ἅγιον Χριστοῦ Lit.Jac*.(p.206.9); **5.** of advent of antichrist, Oecum.*Apoc*.11:7(p.131).

παρουσιάζω, 1. *be present*; **2.** *approach πρὸς τὸν...ἄρχοντα ἐπαρουσίασε* Gr.Mag.*dial*.(tr.Zach.)4.36(M.*PL*.77.383B).

παροχεύς, ὁ, *provider*; of God, Evagr.Pont.*or*.33(M.79.1173D); †Jo.D.*B.J*.17(M.96.1009B); of Christ, Eus.Al.*serm*.21.2(M.86.424D).

παροχή, ἡ, 1. *act of giving, cat.Apoc*.3:21(p.236.14); *provision* of a festival, Jo.Mal.*chron*.12 tit.(M.97.428B); *bestowal Κονσίλια, ἅπερ ἑρμηνεύεται παροχῆς ἡμέρα ib*.7 p.183(292A); **2.** *contribution*, Chrys. *hom.79.1 in Mt*.(7.759A); ref. 2Cor.4:1 *οὐκ εἶπε π., οὐδὲ χορηγίαν, ἀλλὰ διακονίαν* id.*hom.8.1 in 2Cor*.(10.492C); *alms π. καὶ πολλὰς εὐποιείας MAMA* 1.220; **3.** bodily *endowment*, Marc.Er.*opusc*.1(M. 65.924D); **4.** divine *gift εὐχαὶ πρὸ τῆς τροφῆς ἀξίως γινέσθωσαν τῶν τοῦ θεοῦ π.* Bas.*ep*.2.6(3.75A; M.32.232D); *περὶ τῶν θεϊκῶν ἐνεργειῶν, καὶ παροχῶν τοῦ ἁγίου πνεύματος* Didym.*Trin*.2.7 tit.(M.39.560A); *διὰ τῆς θείας π.* Gr.Mag.*dial*.(tr.Zach.)3.20(M.*PL*.77.271B).

παρόχιον, τό, *ecclesiastical district, parish*, Gr.Mag.*dial*.(tr. Zach.)3.38(M.*PL*.77.315B).

παροχλίζ-ω, *lever up*, met. *μόλις τοῦ φρέατος βραχὺ ~ουσι* Cyr. *glaph.Gen*.4(1.123C).

πάροχος, ὁ, *provider*, in gen., Eus.*v.C*.2.23(p.50.18; M.20.1000D); †Jo.D.*B.J*.10(M.96.944B); of God *ἀρετὴν καὶ τὸν ταύτης π. θεόν* Or. *fr.42 in Jo*.(p.517.5); Eus.*p.e*.11.4(512B; M.21.849C); *δημιουργὸν καὶ π. Hom.Clem*.10.9; of Christ *τὸν ταύτης* [sc. *ἀγαλλιάσεως καὶ εὐφροσύνης*] *π.* Cyr.*Ps*.50:10(M.69.1097B); *ὁ τῆς ἀφθαρσίας π.* †Jo.D. *B.J*.7(916B).

πάροχος, *belonging to a chariot*, Evagr.*h.e*.6.4(p.224.33; M.86. 2849A); *ib*.6.15(p.233.7; 2868C).

παροψ-άομαι, *take as a dainty dish*, ref. 'gnostic' *καὶ τῆς Ἑλληνικῆς ἐφάπτεται φιλοσοφίας, οἷον τρωγάλιόν τι ἐπὶ τῷ δείπνῳ ~ώμενος* Clem.*str*.6.8(p.515.20; M.9.396A).

παρόψημα, τό, *delicacy, titbit*, Bas.*ep*.2.6(3.74D; M.32.232C).

παρρησία, ἡ, I. *freedom of speech*; hence

A. *civic freedom ὁ...Ἰωσὴφ καὶ ἡ...Μαριὰμ ἔφυγον εἰς Αἴγυπτον διὰ τὸ μὴ ἔχειν αὐτοὺς π. ἐν τῷ λαῷ A.Pil*.A 2.3(p.225).

B. in bad sense; *impudence, familiarity*; **1.** in gen. *ἡ π. τὴν ἀκοσμίαν εἰς αἰσχρολογίαν αὔξει* Clem.*paed*.2.5(p.186.28; M.8.452A); *τῶν ἀγαπητῶν ἀσπασμοὶ π. ἀνοήτου γέμοντες ib*.3.11(p.281.20; 661A); *ἔοικεν ἡ π. καύσονι μεγάλῳ...ἀπαυτομολοῦσιν* [sc. *οἱ ἄνθρωποι*] *τοῦ δριμέος καπνοῦ τῆς π.* Ant.Mon.*hom*.16(M.89.1476D) ∞ *Apophth. Patr*.(M.65.109A) ∞ Dor.*doct*.4.5(M.88.1665A); of undesirable friendship *ἐὰν δέ τις βουληθῇ ἔχειν μετά σου φιλίαν δολεράν, καὶ π. θεῷ μὴ ἀρέσκουσαν* Ephr.1.313B; *ib*.1.318C; *τὸ...τῶν χηρῶν γένος...διὰ τὴν φύσιν ἀμέτρῳ τινὶ κέχρηται π.* Chrys.*sac*.3.16(p.85.18; 1.396D); contrast *εἰς τοσοῦτον γὰρ σοφίας ἥκουσιν, ὡς τὴν μὲν π. ἀναισχυντίαν καλεῖν, τὴν δὲ ἀναισχυντίαν π., κατ' ἄμφω ἁμαρτάνοντες. τοῦτο γὰρ δρῶσιν, ἢ ἵνα τὴν π. ἐπιστομίσωσιν, ἢ ἵνα τὴν ἀναισχυντίαν εἰς μείζονα κακίαν παιδοτριβήσωσιν* Isid.Pel.*epp*.5.283(M.78.1501B); *οὔτε τὴν π. ἀναισχυντίαν κλητέον, οὔτε τὴν ἀναισχυντίαν π. ἀλλὰ τὴν μὲν τοὺς πταίοντας κοσμίως ἐλέγχουσαν, π. ib*.5.421(1576B); **2.** of pagans and heretics *οἱ τοῦ Ἀρείου ἤτοι Εὐδοξίου αἱρέσεως...ὥσπερ τινὸς π. ἐπειλημμένοι* Gr.Naz.*ep*.202(M.37.329B); *ἀπιστίας γὰρ...ἡ ἄκαιρος π.* Chrys.*hom.48.1 in Jo*.(8.284C).

II. *confidence, boldness, liberty of approach*;

A. in relationship between God and man; **1.** as condition of man before Fall, by which it was lost, Meth.*res*.2.25(p.381.5; M. 18.328C); Ath.*gent*.2(M.25.8B) cit. s. *ἀνεπαίσχυντος*; *ὁ πρωτόπλαστος ...γυμνὸς μὲν τῆς τῶν νεκρῶν δερμάτων ἐπιβολῆς, ἐν π. δὲ τὸ τοῦ θεοῦ πρόσωπον βλέπων* Gr.Nyss.*virg*.12(p.302.10; M.46.373C); id.*or. catech*.6(p.36.8; M.45.29B); Proc.G.*Gen*.3:7(M.87.194B); **2.** possessed by OT saints *ὅσην ἔσχε π. ὁ Σὴθ πρὸς τὸν θεόν, ὅσην ὁ Ἄβελ, ὅσην ὁ Ἐνὼς κτλ.* Meth.*symp*.7.5(p.76.22; M.18.132B); esp. of Moses *ὁ μὲν π. ἔχων πρὸς τὸν θεὸν ὡς πιστὸς καὶ εὖ βιοὺς...ὁποῖος ἦν Μωσῆς* Or. *princ*.3.1.22(p.239.10; M.11.297C); Chrys.*Jud*.8.6(1.683D); *ἡ Μωσέως καὶ Ἠλίου π.* id.*sac*.6.4(p.146.22; 1.424A); **3.** Christian *τὴν π., τὴν τῇ ἐλευθερίᾳ τῆς ψυχῆς ἐνυπάρχουσαν* Gr.Nyss.*or.dom*.5(p.94.25; M. 44.1180A); **a.** God its ultimate source *ὁ ἀγαθὸς ἐργάτης μετὰ παρρησίας λαμβάνει τὸν ἄρτον τοῦ ἔργου αὐτοῦ...τὸ καύχημα ἡμῶν καὶ ἡ π. ἔστω ἐν αὐτῷ* [sc. *θεῷ*] *1Clem*.34.1,5; *οὔτε ἐν τῷ ὄρει τούτῳ οὔτε ἐν Ἱεροσολύμοις τις προσκυνεῖ, ἐλθούσης τῆς ὥρας προσκυνεῖ μετὰ παρρησίας υἱὸς γεγενημένος τὸν πατέρα* Or.*Jo*.13.16(p.240.24; M.14.424B); given in baptism, hence catechumens still without it, Chrys.*hom. 2.5 in 2Cor*.(10.435C); through Communion *ὥστε γενέσθαι τοῖς μεταλαμβάνουσιν...εἰς π. τὴν πρὸς σέ Lit.Chrys*.(p.330.17); *ib*.(p.338. 22); through priestly ministry, Chrys.*sac*.6.13(p.173.12; 1.436B); founded on the Cross, ‡Chrys.*cruc*.2(3.826D); on divine maternity of BMV, ‡Epiph.*hom*.5(M.43.501B); cf.Jo.Thess.*dorm.BMV* 1.14 (p.402.11); obtained through forgiveness of sins, Chrys.*hom.19.1* *in Heb.*(12.180C); derived from virtues and good works ἐμμείνωμεν οὖν ἐφ' οἷς ἐπιστεύσαμεν δίκαιοι καὶ ὅσιοι, ἵνα μετὰ παρρησίας αἰτῶμεν τὸν θεόν *2Clem.*15.3; τὴν ἐπὶ σωφροσύνῃ φαίνοντι π. Meth.*symp.*6.4 (p.68.4; M.18.117C); cf.Or.*Jo.*28.5(4; p.394.23; M.14.688C); Gr.Nyss. *or.dom.*5(p.92.24; M.44.1177B); Thdr.Pet.*v.Thds.*(p.47.18); *ib.*(p.94. 26); π. μοι δίδωσιν ἡ εὐσέβεια *M.Thdot.*3(p.133.30); from prayer εὐχῶν...τῶν πολλὴν πρὸς τὸν θεὸν π. κεκτημένων Chrys.*ep.*92(3.641E); εἴ τις δίκαιος ἦν καὶ π. πολλὴν ἔχων πρὸς τὸν θεόν id.*stat.*2.7(2.31A); almsgiving, id.*hom.17.2 in 2Cor.*(10.560C); **b.** its relationship to certain virtues; **i.** ἀγάπη, *A.Thom.*A 81(p.196.17); with the growth of which π. is intimately connected ἡ δὲ προσευχὴ εἰς ὠφελείας λόγον ἔχει...θεῷ προσομιλεῖν παρασκευάζουσα...καὶ τηρεῖν πρὸς θεόν, τὸν εἰς ἀγάπην καὶ τοὺς εὐτελεῖς προσιέμενον...ἕως αὐτοῖς π. δίδωσι παραμένων ὁ πόθος· εἰ γὰρ δούλους πρὸς τὴν δεσποτείαν αὐχοῦντας, καὶ τὸ τῆς αὐθεντείας ἀξιόπιστον σοβαρῷ τύφῳ φυλάττειν ἐπιτηδεύοντας θαρρεῖν δίδωσι προλαβόντα εὐνοίας ἐνέχυρα, πόσῳ μᾶλλον τοῖς εὖ βιοῦσιν αὐξήσει τὴν πρὸς θεὸν π. τὸ κατὰ γνώμην αὐτοῦ, καὶ βούλησιν πολιτεύεσθαι, οὐ τοσοῦτον ἀπαιτοῦντα τὸν ἐκ τοῦ φόβου ἐναγώνιον τρόμον, ὅσον χαίροντα τῇ ἐκ τῆς ἀγάπης ἱλαρᾷ π. ‡Nil.*perist.*4.2(M. 79.828A,B); **ii.** σοφία: σὺ [sc. *Χριστέ*] εἶ ὁ δεδωκὼς ἡμῖν τὴν σὴν π. τῆς σοφίας *A.Phil.*144(p.85.2); σοφία γὰρ ἐν ἐξόδοις ὑμνεῖται, ἐν δὲ πλατείαις π. ἄγει Or.*schol.in Cant.*3:1–4(M.17.269A); Chrys.*hom.52. 1 in Jo.*(8.304C); **iii.** ἀλήθεια: ὡς μακάρια...τὰ δῶρα τοῦ θεοῦ...ζωὴ ἐν ἀθανασίᾳ, λαμπρότης ἐν δικαιοσύνῃ, ἀλήθεια ἐν π. *1Clem.*35.2; τῆς ἀληθείας τὴν π. ἀποτέμνουσαν...τὰς ψευδεῖς δόξας Clem.*str.*7.16(p.72. 34; M.9.541C); ἐξουσίαν δὲ αὖθις ὁ τῆς ἀληθείας λόγος λαμβάνει, καὶ π. οἱ βιασθέντες αὐτόνομον Gr.Naz.*or.*21.26(M.35.1112C); and ὀρθοδοξία, Ath.*h.Ar.*78(p.227.11; M.25.788D); **c.** its loss through sin ὁ δὲ ταύτην μὴ κτησάμενος τὴν π., δηλονότι ἡ ἀπολωλεκὼς ἢ περὶ τούτων οὐ κατὰ φιλομάθειαν ἀλλὰ κατὰ φιλονεικίαν ζητῶν Or.*princ.*3.1.22 (p.240.1; M.11.297C); ἡ δὲ ἡμετέρα [sc. *ψυχή*] τοσοῦτον ἔχει περικείμενον αὐτῇ σκότος ἐκ τῆς πονηρᾶς συνειδήσεως, ὡς...μηδέποτε δύνασθαι μετὰ παρρησίας εἰς τὸν αὐτῆς ἀτενίσαι δεσπότην Chrys.*sac.* 6.4(p.148.20; 1.424E); ref. Devil ἔστιν δὲ τὸ κατοικητήριον αὐτοῦ ὁ τάρταρος, καὶ ἐν τῷ σκότει βαδίζει, ἐπειδὴ οὐκ ἔχει π. ἐν οὐδενί *A.Phil.* 110(p.43.7); διάβολος, οὐκ ἔχων μὲν αὐτὸς π. Ath.*ep.Aeg.Lib.*1(M. 25.540C); though sinners possess it if humble, Chrys.*non desp.*8 (3.361A); **d.** as a special quality of certain persons; of Christ in his humanity, Cyr.*Jo.*11.7(4.962A); of martyrs, who, having π. before their persecutors, attain to π. before God, so that their intercession becomes efficacious (the two forms of π. being inseparable) ἀξιῶμεν γενέσθαι προστάτιδας ἡμῶν· πολλὴν γὰρ ἔχουσι π. οὐχὶ ζῶσαι μόνον, ἀλλὰ καὶ τελευτήσασαι· καὶ πολλῷ μᾶλλον τελευτήσασαι Chrys.*pan.Bern.*7(2.645D); πρεσβευτὰς αὐτοὺς τῶν εὐχῶν καὶ αἰτημάτων, διὰ τὸ ὑπερβάλλον τῆς π., ποιοῦμεν Ast.Am.*hom.*10(M. 40.317C); μὴ κλαίετε, ἀδελφοί...ἔσομαι γὰρ ἐν π. ἐν τοῖς οὐρανοῖς *M.Thdot.1* 31(p.80.31); ὁ ἅγιος μάρτυς Θεόδοτος...ἔκπληξιν παρέχων ἐπὶ τῇ π. πολλῶν γὰρ παραινούντων αὐτῷ φυγεῖν τὸν καιρὸν καὶ μὴ τῇ π. κεχρημένον...εἶπεν... *M.Thdot.*3(p.131.21ff.); *ib.*(p.132.13); Procl. CP *or.*17.3(M.65.812C); cf.*A.Andr.*A 8(p.51.9); *M.Ariadn.*(p.124. 17); of other saints and holy people ὁ δὲ ἅγιος οὐ κέκρυπται, ἀλλ' ἔχει καρδίαν μετὰ παρρησίας τῆς κατὰ τὴν ἁγίαν πολιτείαν πρὸς τὸν θεόν Or.*hom.16.4 in Jer.*(p.136.18; M.13.444B); of BMV πάναγνε, π. γὰρ ἔχεις ὡς δέσποινα, δυσωπεῖν τὸν υἱόν σου ἑκάστοτε *Euchol.*(p.459); *ib.*(p.444); of S. Meletius, Chrys.*pan.Melet.*3(2.523A); of an ascetic ἡ πρὸς τὸν θεὸν αὐτῷ π. καθ' ἑκάστην ηὔξετο τὴν ἡμέραν Thdt.*h.rel.*1 (3.1109); π. of saints in heaven more efficacious than while still on earth, *ib.*18(1231); ταῦτα τὴν ψυχὴν ποιεῖ τῆς βασιλίδος [i.e. deceased] ...τῆς εὐδαίμονος...ἔχειν ὑπὲρ σοῦ [sc. Justinian] πρὸς θεὸν π. Paul. Sil.*Soph.*61(M.86.2122A); of freedom of approach between Christ and apostles οὗτοι γὰρ μόνοι τῷ κυρίῳ πάντοτε συσχολάζοντες... ἔχοντες...π., οὐ κατὰ τὴν τῆς ἀνθρωπίνης φιλίας πρόσληψιν, ἀλλὰ κατὰ θεϊκὴν ἀληθείας ἐπίκρισιν Gr.Nyss.*Steph.*2(M.46.732A); **e.** as a special quality of Christian prayer, esp. in possession of right to say Our Father, id.*or.dom.*2(p.30.13; M.44.1137D); εἰπεῖν, πάτερ ...ὅσης τῆς π. *ib.*(p.32.23; 1140C); *ib.*(p.42.10; 1145D); τὴν τοῦ αἰνεῖν τὸν θεὸν π. λῃψόμεθα id.*Pss.titt.*B 2(M.44.496C); πρὸ τῶν ἄλλων ἁπάντων παρρησίαν δεῖ τὸν εὐχόμενον ἔχειν Chrys.*exp.in Ps.*4:2(5.6C); καταξίωσον ἡμᾶς, δέσποτα φιλάνθρωπε, μετὰ παρρησίας, ἀκατακρίτως, ἐν καθαρᾷ καρδίᾳ...λέγειν· πάτερ ἡμῶν κτλ. *Lit.Jac.*(p.224.13); and to assist at eucharistic sacrifice, *ib.*(p.190.21); **f.** strictly given only to souls in higher stages of spiritual life, in contemplation; **i.** its conditions ἡ γνῶσις οἷον ὁ λογικὸς θάνατος, ἀπὸ τῶν παθῶν ἀπάγων καὶ χωρίζων τὴν ψυχὴν καὶ προάγων εἰς τὴν τῆς εὐποιΐας ζωήν, ἵνα τότε εἴπῃ μετὰ παρρησίας πρὸς τὸν θεόν· ὡς θέλεις ζῶ Clem.*str.*7. 12(p.51.21; M.9.500A); sufferings τίς γάρ ἐστιν ἄξιος διὰ τὸν κύριον πεινᾶσαι καὶ γυμνητεῦσαι καὶ ἐν τούτοις χαίρειν; μακάριος ὁ τοιοῦτος, ὄντως μακάριος ὅτι π. μεγάλην ἔμπροσθεν τοῦ θεοῦ κέκτηται Mac. Aeg.*hom.*53.5(p.31); μετὰ πολλῆς π. αἰτεῖν αὐτὸν δυνησόμεθα,...ἀπὸ τῶν ἰδίων θελημάτων ἀναχωροῦντες *ib.*53.18(p.37); κοσμικῶν ἀπηλλαγμένοι πολυπλόκων φροντίδων, ἐθρήσκευον ἀπερισπάστῳ προσεδρίᾳ τὸ θεῖον τῇ πρὸς αὐτὸ π. πρὸς τὸ ἐπιτάττειν αἰδέσιμοι πάσῃ τῇ κτίσει γενόμενοι Nil.*Magn.*20(M.79.996B); ἡ π. νῦν οὐχὶ ὑπεράνω τῶν παθῶν μόνον ἐστίν, ἀλλὰ καὶ ὑπεράνω τῆς καθαρότητος· καὶ οὕτως γίνεται ἡ τάξις τῆς παραδόσεως καθὼς λέγω· ἡ ὑπομονὴ ἡ μετὰ βίας ἀντιπαλαίει τοῖς πάθεσιν ὑπὲρ τῆς καθαρότητος· ἐὰν οὖν νικήσῃ τὰ πάθη προσκτᾶται ἡ ψυχὴ τὴν καθαρότητα· ἡ καθαρότης δὲ ἡ ἀληθὴς ποιεῖ τὸν νοῦν κτᾶσθαι π. ἐν τῇ ὥρᾳ τῆς προσευχῆς Philox.*ep.*(p.168); cf.*ib.*16(p.167); **ii.** its place in spiritual life ἡ νύμφη [i.e. soul]...ἐπικαυχᾶται τῇ τῆς π. προσθήκῃ Gr.Nyss.*hom.12 in Cant.*(M.44.1037A); connected with σοφία and θαυματουργία, Thdt.*h.rel.*3(3.1140); τὴν ἁπλῆν θεωρίαν δέχεται ὁ νοῦς, ἣν οὐδέν τι μυρίζει τὸν φάρυγγα τῆς ψυχῆς καὶ κτήσασθαι αὐτὴν ποιεῖ π. ἐν τῇ ὥρᾳ τῆς προσευχῆς ὥσπερ αὕτη Philox.*ep.*23 (p.174); **iii.** its consummation in heaven πίστευσον εἰς τὸν Ἰησοῦν, ...εἰσάξει δέ σε εἰς τὴν αἰωνίαν ζωήν, παρέχων σοὶ τὴν π. τὴν μὴ παρερχομένην *A.Thom.*A 103(p.216.9); Chrys.*stat.*3.7(2.48C); id.*hom. 8.2 in Jo.*(8.52A); *ib.24.3*(142D); ἀγγελικὴ π. *Euchol.*(p.466).

B. *boldness, liberty of speech*, in relationship of men with one another τοιαύτην ἀναλαβεῖν καθαροῦ συνειδότος παρρησίαν πρὸς πάντας ἀνθρώπους Or.*Jo.*20.31(25; p.368.25; M.14.645A); Marc.Diac.*v.Porph.* 68; of Jo. Bapt. τύραννον εἶδεν ἄνθρωπον γάμων ἀνατρέποντα νόμους, καὶ μετὰ παρρησίας ἐν μέσῳ τῆς ἀγορᾶς φησιν... Chrys.*stat.*1.12(2. 19A); in reprehending others χρὴ τῇ μὴν π. μιγνύναι τὴν προσήνειαν Isid.Pel.*epp.*3.397(M.78.1036C); exeg. 2Cor.3:12 πολλῇ π. χρώμεθα. πρὸς τίνα, εἰπέ μοι; πρὸς τὸν θεόν, ἢ πρὸς τοὺς μαθητάς; πρὸς ὑμᾶς τοὺς μαθητευομένους, φησί Chrys.*hom.7.2 in 2Cor.*(10.482A); of S. Paul σὺ δέδεσαι, καὶ ἄλλους παρακαλεῖς;...μείζονά μοι π. δίδωσι τὰ δεσμά id.*hom.10.3 in Col.*(11.399E).

III. *confidence, trust*;

A. of trust in Christ νῦν καιρὸς ἀναψύξεως καὶ π. τῆς πρὸς σὲ Χριστέ *A.Jo.*22(p.163.7); ἐξέβαλον αὐτὸν οἱ Ἰουδαῖοι ἔξω ἀπ' αὐτῶν διὰ τὴν ἐπὶ τῷ σωτῆρι π. Or.*fr.71 in Jo.*(p.539.9).

B. in prayer οὐκ ἐσομένης ἐν π. τῆς ἐντεύξεως, εἰ μὴ ἐπὶ προληφθείσῃ εὐχῇ τινι καὶ δωροφορίᾳ ἡ πρόσοδος γένοιτο Gr.Nyss.*or.dom.* 2(p.30.33; M.44.1140A).

IV. = ἐξουσία, *authority*, esp. of speech ἀξιόπιστος ὁ θεῖος παιδαγωγὸς τρισὶ τοῖς καλλίστοις κεκοσμημένος, ἐπιστήμῃ, εὐνοίᾳ, π. ...π. δὲ ὅτι θεὸς καὶ δημιουργός Clem.*paed.*1.11(p.148.4f.; M.8.365C); εἷς δέ ἐστιν ἀγαθός, οὗ π. ἡ διὰ τοῦ υἱοῦ φανέρωσις Val.Gn.ap.Clem. *str.*2.20(p.175.1; M.8.1057B); as quality of 'gnostic' ἐμπειρίᾳ πολλῇ χρησάμενος τῇ κατὰ τὴν μάθησίν τε καὶ τὸν βίον, π. ἔχει, οὐ τὴν ἁπλῶς οὕτως ἀθυρόγλωσσον δύναμιν, δύναμιν δὲ ἁπλῷ λόγῳ χρωμένην Clem. *str.*7.7(p.33.29; M.9.464C); Θεόδωρος...παρρησίας ἐν τῷ παλατίῳ τυγχάνων Niceph.Ur.*v.Sym.*235(M.86.3201B); of the natural order violated by Pharaoh's infanticide τόκος ἐδοκιμάζετο, καὶ φύσεως π. σεσύλητο Bas.Sel.*or.*9.1(M.85.129A).

V. phrases μετὰ παρρησίας, παρρησίᾳ, *openly*, Or.*Jo.*28.23(18; p.418.28; M.14.729C); Chrys.*hom.10.2 in Jo.*(8.58C); *clearly, plainly*, ‡*Diogn.*11.2; *A.Phil.*7(p.4.15); μετὰ π. ἀκούειν (though the π. is really of the speaker, not of the hearer): μετὰ π. ἄκουε, Χριστιανός εἰμι *M.Polyc.*10.1; *M.Ign.Rom.*10; Thdt.*Ps.*48:6(1.917).

παρρησιάζ-ομαι, **A.** *speak freely, openly*, of Gnostic Adam μείζονα ἐφθέγξατο τῆς πλάσεως διὰ τὸν ἀοράτως ἐν αὐτῷ σπέρμα δεδωκότα τῆς ἄνωθεν οὐσίας καὶ ~όμενον Val.Gn.ap.Clem.*str.*2.8 (p.132.10; M.8.972B); of a spiritual guide μελέτησον ἀκούειν κἂν ἑνὸς ~ομένου καὶ στύφοντος ἅμα καὶ θεραπεύοντος Clem.*q.d.s.*41(p.187.11; M.9.645C); iron., of pagan philosophers εἰ γοῦν τις ἀφέλοι τὸν φόβον καὶ τὴν τιμήν, οὐκ οἶδ' εἰ ἔτι ὑποστήσονται τὰς θλίψεις οἱ γεννάδαι τῶν ~ομένων φιλοσόφων id.*str.*7.12(p.53.5; M.9.501B); ὁ ἀπόστολος... ~εται πρὸς Ἰουδαίους γράφων Ath.*Ar.*1.55(M.26.128A); Chrys.*hom. 52.2 in Jo.*(8.306B); Euthal.Diac.*Ac.*proem.(M.85.629C); in rebuke καὶ Μωσῆς καὶ Ἠλίας καὶ Ἰωάννης...οὔτε συμβουλεύσαντες, οὔτε παρρησιασάμενοι ὤνησαν ἐκείνους Isid.Pel.*epp.*3.397(M.78.1036C); pass. τὸ πρὸς αὐτὸν [sc. Christ] μῖσος ἐποίει ὁ ἔλεγχος ὁ πεπαρρησιασμένος, οὐχ ἡ τοῦ σαββάτου λύσις Chrys.*hom.48.2 in Jo.*(8.285D); *cry out*, μετὰ τὴν τελευτὴν διὰ τοῦ αἵματος ~εται [sc. Abel] id.*pent.*2.3(2. 473E).

B. *assert boldly, confidently* Σαμουὴλ ἐν ᾅδου ὁ τοιαῦτα παρρησιασάμενος, εἰ ἐπιθύμημά τινος ἔλαβεν; Or.*engast.*(p.285.16; M.12.1016C); πῶς ἂν ἐπιστεύθησαν λέγοντες γεγονέναι πρῶτον θάνατον, εἶτα τὴν ἀνάστασιν, εἰ μὴ παρ' οἷς ἐπαρρησιάζοντο, εἶχον τούτους μάρτυρας τοῦ θανάτου Ath.*inc.*23.3(M.25.136D); Gr.Naz.*or.*21.34(M.35.1124B); pass.

~εται ἡ τριάς *ib.*21.31(1120A); οὐδὲ διὰ τὴν δούλου μετουσίαν [opp. υἱοθεσία] πατέρα τὸν θεὸν ~εται Didym.(‡Bas.)*Eun.*5(1.309B; M.29.741B).

C. *speak* or *act boldly, confidently*; **1.** of man's attitude towards God ~εται θεράπων [sc. Moses] πρὸς κύριον αἰτεῖται ἄφεσιν τῷ πλήθει *1Clem.*53.5; pass., of prayers πεπαρρησιασμένων εὐχῶν ὑμῶν Chrys. *ep.*70(3.631E); of S. Stephen ~ῃ τῇ τοῦ ἁγίου πνεύματος δυναστείᾳ †Bas.Sel.*or.*41(M.85.473B); of disciples towards Christ φαίνονται... ~όμενοι· οἷον, ὅταν ὁ Ἰωάννης ἐπιπίπτῃ αὐτοῦ τῷ στήθει Chrys.*hom.* *33.3 in Jo.*(8.193B); *ib.*(194A); of Nicodemus οὐδὲ ~εσθαι ἠνείχετο ὡς ἐχρῆν *ib.28.3*(163C); in imitation of angelic παρρησία, Jo.Clim. *scal.*4(M.88.704D); **2.** *be bold, courageous*; *make a bold confession* οἱ [sc. ἄρχοντες] τοῖς οἰκείοις...ἐπὶ τῷ θείῳ ~ομένοις λόγῳ τε καὶ βίῳ συνεχώρουν Eus.*h.e.*8.1.3(M.20.740C); of martyrs, Ep.Lugd.*ib.*5.1.18 (416A); ὑπὲρ εὐσεβείας ἀποθνήσκειν καὶ ~εσθαι ἐν αὐτῇ πρὸς ἐσφαλμένους Or.*Cels.*2.40(p.164.16; M.11.861B); of apostles, *ib.*2.45(p.167.25; 868B); of a virgin, Thdr.Stud.*epp.*2.94(M.99.1345B); **3.** *be over-confident, presume*, *Hom.Clem.*4.17; ἐπαρρησιάσατο ἡ τῶν ἀσεβῶν Ἑλλήνων ἀπόνοια *M.Thdot.*3(p.131.5); οὐ δεῖ παρρησίαν διδόναι παιδίῳ ~εσθαι μετ' ἀδελφῶν Ephr.1.318C; πρέπει δὲ τῷ ἐργάτῃ μὴ ~εσθαι, κἂν μόνος ᾖ ἐν τῷ κελλίῳ *Apophth.Patr.*(M.65.109A); κτᾶται ἄνθρωπος τὸν φόβον τοῦ θεοῦ...ἐκ τοῦ μὴ ~εσθαι Dor.*doct.*4.5(M.88.1664D).

D. *have confidence, trust* (in) ~όμεθα ἐν αὐτῷ [sc. Christ] Or.*Cels.* 2.44(p.166.29; M.11.865B); ὡς συνήθης ~ομένη ἐφιλοφρονεῖτο *Hom. Clem.*4.1.

παρρησιαστικός, *enjoying liberty of speech, speaking freely* or *boldly*; superl., Agath.*v.Gr.Ill.*157; Gr.Mag.*dial.*(tr.Zach.)1.2(M.*PL.*77.158B).

παρρησιαστικῶς, *intimately* σφόδρα μοι π. ἐπλησίαζε Gr.Mag.*dial.* (tr.Zach.)3.38(M.*PL.*77.315A).

παρρησιέστερον, *more outspokenly, more freely*, Socr.*h.e.*2.26.9 (M.67.269A); *cat.Ac.*2:13(p.29.17).

***παρρησιοποιός**, ? *given to undue familiarity* μηδεὶς π. [sc. ἔστω]· ὁ γὰρ τοιοῦτος φθορεργάτης Thdr.Stud.*epp.*2.156(M.99.1489B).

παρυβρίζω, *show disrespect to*, Bas.*reg.fus.*3(2.339B; M.31.914C).

παρυπόστασις, ἡ, 1. *dependent existence*, in explanation of evil οὔτε ὑπόστασιν ἔχει τὸ κακόν, ἀλλὰ π., τοῦ ἀγαθοῦ ἕνεκα καὶ οὐχ ἑαυτοῦ γινόμενον Dion.Ar.*d.n.*4.31(M.3.732C)∞Jo.D.*Man.*1.64(M.94.1560C); Max.*qu.Thal.*51(M.90.484C); **2.** *co-existent reality* or *entity* οὐδὲν γάρ ἐστι τὸ συμβεβηκὸς καὶ μὴ καθ' ἑαυτὸ θεωρούμενον χωρὶς τῆς ἐν ὑποκειμένῳ παρυποστάσεως ‡Gr.Nyss.*hom.3.54 in Jo.*(p.149.18).

***παρυφάπτω**, *rekindle*, Leont.H.*Nest.*1.19(M.86.1473A).

παρυφή, ἡ, 1. *web, tissue*, fig. π. κακῶν εἰργάσασθε Juln.Imp.ap. Cyr.*Juln.*7(6^2.238B); **2.** *concealed fabric*, fig. ὅταν...ἄλλα μὲν πράττομεν ἐν π., ἄλλα δὲ ἐπιμορφαζόμεθα πεπλασμένῳ σχήματι σεμνοποιοῦντες τὴν λανθάνουσαν αἰσχύνην Nil.*serm.*9(M.79.1277A).

παρυφιζάν-ω, *lie in ambush for, decoy* πολλάκις δὲ καὶ τὰς σπουδαίας [sc. ψυχάς] ~ει διὰ τούτων ὁ ἐχθρὸς ‡Ath.*v.Syncl.*85(M.28.1540A).

παρυφίστ-ημι, 1. *bring into existence by the side of* or *in antithesis to* τῇ γὰρ ἀληθείᾳ ~ησιν ἀεὶ τὴν ἀπάτην ὁ διάβολος Chrys.*hom.23.6 in Mt.*(7.293B); id.*hom.29.3 in 1Cor.*(10.264A); id.*hom.8.1 in 2Tim.* (11.706C); Max.*opusc.*(M.91.24B); *ib.*(200A); **2.** pass., *subsist co-ordinately with*, Gr.Nyss.*Eun.*9(2 p.223.14; M.45.824A).

[*]**παρφασίη, ἡ**, *comfort, consolation*, †Apoll.*met.Ps.*85:17(M.33.1440D).

παρῳδ-έω, 1. *cite with alteration* εἴπωμεν τὸ τοῦ προφήτου μικρὸν ~ήσαντες Gr.Nyss.*Eun.*11(2 p.270.24; M.45.880C); **2.** *express figuratively*, *cat.Lc.*22:44(p.159.34).

***παρῴδημα, τό**, *laughing-stock*, Olymp.*fr.Job* 30:9(M.93.312C).

παρωνυμία, ἡ, 1. *alternative expression*, Gr.Nyss.*Eun.*12(1 p.227.28; M.45.924B); **2.** *derivative* ἡ ἁμαρτωλὸς φωνή, π. οὖσα ἀπὸ τῆς ἁμαρτίας Didym.*Ps.*9:18(M.39.1197A); **3.** *other name* τῆς τοῦ Χριστοῦ π. [sc. Ἰησοῦς] Eus.*d.e.*7.3(p.345.31; M.22.564B); **4.** *etymological relationship*, Or.*ep.*1.6(M.11.61A); **5.** rhet., *variation in expression* τῆς τεχνικῆς τῶν ὀνομάτων εἴτε παραγωγῆς εἴτε π. Gr.Nyss.*Eun.*4(2 p.52.15; M.45.621C).

παρώνυμος, *formed by a slight change*; neut. as subst., = παρωνύμιον, *name formed from another by a slight change, derivative*, *Doct. Patr.*33(p.264.24); cf. ἀπὸ τοῦ Ἔβερ τὸ π. εἴληφε Eus.*p.e.*11.6(M.21.864A; παρωνύμιον 520B).

***παρώτης**, ? *one-eared*, ? *with side-curls* Ἀμμώνιον τὸν π. Pall.*h. Laus.*46(p.134.18; παρώτιον M.34.1225B).

***πασιπόθητος**, *desired by all*, ‡Jo.D.*hom.*5(M.96.653C).

πασιφαής, *visible to all*, Nonn.*par.Jo.*12:2(M.43.849C).

πάσμα, τό, *remedy*, Geo.Pis.*hex.*1518(M.92.1552A).

πασσαλίσκος, ὁ, *incisor tooth* τοὺς...π. καλουμένους καὶ κυνόδοντας, τάς τε μύλας Epiph.*ep.Arab.*ap.*haer.*78.12(p.463.4; M.42.717A).

***Πασσαλορυγχῖται, οἱ**, in explanation of name of sect of Τασκοδρουγῖται, who prayed with forefinger to nose τασκὸς παρ' αὐτοῖς [sc. Γαλάταις] πάσσαλος καλεῖται, δροῦγγος δὲ μυκτὴρ εἴτ' οὖν ῥύγχος..., καὶ ἀπὸ τοῦ τιθέναι ἑαυτῶν τὸν δάκτυλον τὸν λεγόμενον λιχανὸν ἐπὶ τὸν μυκτῆρα ἐν τῷ εὔχεσθαι, δῆθεν κατηφείας χάριν καὶ ἐθελοδικαιοσύνης, ἐκλήθησαν ὑπό τινων Τασκοδρουγῖται τουτέστιν π. Epiph.*haer.*48.14(p.239.16; M.41.877B); λέγονται Γαλατιστὶ Τασκοδρουγοί, ὅπερ ἑρμηνεύεται π. Tim.CP *haer.*(M.86.16A).

παστάς, ἡ, 1. *portico* (with suggestion of magnificent building and place of delights) δεῦτε, ἴδετε τὸν τόπον, τὸν πάσης βασιλικῆς π. λαμπρότερον Gr.Ant.*mul.ung.*10(M.88.1861B); fig. τὴν ἀρχαίαν τοῦ ἀνθρώπου π., τὸν παράδεισον λέγω *cat.Lc.*23:43(p.170.28); **2.** *place for wedding festivities* or *bridal chamber*; **a.** in gen. βαλλέτωσαν λόγοις μετὰ τῶν ἀνθῶν τὰς π. Gr.Naz.*ep.*231(M.37.373C); τῆς ἐν π. χαρᾶς Gr. Nyss.*hom.1 in Cant.*(M.44.765A); νύμφην..., τοῖς παραπετάσμασι τῆς π. καλυπτομένην Ast.Am.*hom.*6(M.40.241D); as temporary structure λυθεισῶν τῶν π. Chrys.*hom.20.7 in Eph.*(11.153E); id.*hom.12.7 in Col.*(11.423A); ἐπὶ...γάμων ἕως ἑπτὰ ἡμερῶν αἱ π. ἑστήκασι. διὰ τοῦτο καὶ ἡμεῖς ἑπτὰ ἡμέρας ἐνομοθετήσαμεν πρὸς τὰς ἱερὰς ἑστάναι π. ἀλλ' ἐκεῖ μὲν μετὰ τὰς ἑπτὰ ἡμέρας λύονται, ἐνταῦθα δὲ... id.*res.Chr.*5(2.445D); πηγνύναι γαμηλίους π. Bas.Sel.*v.Thecl.*1(M.85.484D); **b.** ref. parable of ten virgins, ‡Nil.*perist.*9.3(M.79.868B); τῆς π. ἀπεστερήθησαν Thdt.*affect.*11(p.292.5; 4.1004); spiritually interpreted ἐν παντὶ καιρῷ ἔστω ὁ χιτὼν τοῦ μοναχοῦ ἄσπιλος· οὐχ ὁ ὑφαντός, ἀλλ' ὁ πνευματικός. ἐν μέσῃ γὰρ νυκτὶ ὁ τοιοῦτος συνεισελεύσεται τῷ νυμφίῳ Χριστῷ εἰς τὴν π. Hyper.*mon.*24(M.79.1476C); **c.** ref. consecrated virgins ἡ ἁρμοσθεῖσα τῷ κυρίῳ παρθένος ἁγνή, πρὸς μετουσίαν τῆς ἀχράντου π. νύμφη κυρίως κατονομάζεται Gr.Nyss.*hom.9 in Cant.*(M.44.953D); τὴν ἁγνὴν κοίτην, τὴν ἄσπιλον π. ‡Chrys.*hom.*13(13.239D); **d.** ref. spiritual marriage of soul with Christ αἱ πνευματικαὶ π., αἱ φαιδραὶ λαμπάδες Chrys.*hom.49.4 in Mt.*(7.509B); αὐτὸς μέν σε ἐπὶ τὰς π. εἵλκυσε τὰς πνευματικάς id.*fem.reg.*2(1.252D); τῷ ᾅδῃ βοῶ, οὐκ ἔξεστί σοι κατέχειν τὴν φύσιν ἣν ὁ θεὸς ἐμνηστεύσατο, ἣν εἰς οὐρανίους π. ἀνακαλεῖται Germ.CP *or.*2(M.98.281B); μὴ εἰσαγάγῃς ἄλλον νυμφίον ἐν τῇ π. τῆς καρδίας σου Jo.D.*hom.*2.7(M.96.588B); **e.** ref. BMV ὁ οὐράνιος νυμφίος μετὰ θεομήτορος π. ‡Cyr.H.*occurs.*2(M.33.1189B); μετῳκίσθη ἐν τῇ ἄνω Ἱερουσαλὴμ ἡ πανάχραντος νοητὴ π. Mod.*dorm.* 3(M.86.3288B); Thdr.Stud.*nativ.BMV* 7(M.96.696B); **3.** *marriage* μνηστείας...καιρὸς ὁ παρών..., ὁ δὲ τῶν π. ἕτερος Chrys.*hom.23.1 in 2Cor.*(10.595E).

[*]**πάστιλ(λ)ος, ὁ (παστίλλιον, τό)**, *lozenge* or *small cake*, in charge made against Chrys. ἐν θρόνῳ ἀποδύεται καὶ ἐνδύεται καὶ π. τρώγει CQuerc.(M.103.109A, v.l. παστῖλον); Pall.*v.Chrys.*8(p.45.9; M.47.27); παστίλλιον *Mir.Artem.*43(p.72.8).

παστός, ὁ, 1. *bridal chamber*, Or.*schol.in Cant.*6:7–8(M.17.277D); *A.Thom.*A 124(p.233.23); Ast.Soph.*hom.2 in Ps.*5(M.40.404C); ref. parable of ten virgins, Cyr.*Joel.*7(3.205D); Eus.Al.*serm.*21.7(M.86.432D); of baptistery, †Anast.S.*relat.*51(*OC* 3 p.74); of heaven as bridal chamber of Christ ἐν τῷ ὑπερκοσμίῳ π. Hipp.*fr.4 in Pr.* (p.158.8; M.10.617A); τὰ ἔθνη...εἰς τὸν οὐράνιον εἰσάξει π., εἰς τὴν τῶν πρωτοτόκων ἐκκλησίαν δηλαδὴ Cyr.*Jo.*2.1(4.140A); of Church π. ... πνευματικὸς ἡ ἐκκλησία τυγχάνει Alex.Sal.*Barn.*19(442A); **2.** *banqueting-couch*, Nonn.*par.Jo.*2:2(M.43.760C); *ib.*2:3,11(761C).

παστοφόριον, τό, 1. in OT; **a.** *priests' quarters*, Thdt.*Ezech.*40:17–21(2.1022); **b.** *treasury*, Olymp.*fr.Jer.*35:4(M.93.696D); **c.** ? *making of tabernacles* εἰς τὸ π., ἢ κατὰ τὸν Σύμμαχον, 'τὸν σκηνοποιοῦντα', ἢ κατὰ τὸν Ἀκύλαν, 'πρὸς τὸν σκηνοῦντα' Eus.*Is.*22:15–19(M.24.249C); **2.** Christian; plur., *sacristy*, *Lit.*ap.*Const.App.*8.13.17 cit. s. περισσεύω; ὁ οἶκος...κατὰ ἀνατολὰς τετραμμένος, ἐξ ἑκατέρων τῶν μερῶν ἔχων τὰ π. πρὸς ἀνατολήν *Const.App.*2.57.3.

παστ-όω, *make a bridal chamber* τὸ δὲ ὅσον καθαρὸν...~ώσας καὶ παρθενώσας, καί, ὡς εἰπεῖν, ἐξαγγελώσας, εἰς τὴν ἀνθρωπίνην εἰκόνα σωματικῶς ἐμορφοῦτο ‡Chrys.*pasch.*6.4(p.167.3; 8.270C).

πάσχα, τό, indecl.; **I.** *Passover*;

A. derivations and interpretations; **1.** = διάβασις, q.v.; **2.** see s.v. διαβατήριος; **3.** = ὑπέρβασις, q.v. **4.** connected with πάσχω: τί ἐστιν τὸ π.; ἀπὸ γὰρ τοῦ συμβεβηκότος τὸ ὄνομα κέκληται· ἐκ γὰρ τοῦ παθεῖν καὶ πάσχειν Mel.*pass.*46 p.7.30; cf.Iren.*haer.*4.10.1(M.7.1000B); τοῦ γὰρ σωτηρίου πάθους ὄνομα τοῦτο εἶναί τινες νομίσαντες, εἶτα ἐξελληνίζοντες τὴν φωνήν, κατὰ τὴν τοῦ φῖ πρὸς τὸ πῖ, καὶ τοῦ κάππα πρὸς τὸ χῖ μεταποίησιν, π. ... προσηγορεύκασιν Gr.Naz.*or.*45.10(M.36.636C); cf.‡Chrys.*pasch.*6.5(p.175.11; 8.271D); ὃ δή τινες ἐξελλήνισαν, διὰ τὸ Χριστοῦ πάθος...καὶ π. τὸ φασὲ πεποιήκασι Proc.G.*Ex.*12:2(M.87.561B); Eutych.*pasch.*2(M.86.2393B); **5.** other interprns. τὸ δὲ π. ὁ μὲν Φίλων ἡρμήνευσε διαβατήρια· ὁ δὲ Ἰώσηπος ὑπέρβασιν· ὁ δὲ Σύμμαχος ὑπερβάσεις· ὁ δὲ Θεοδοτίων φασέχ,... σημαίνει δὲ τὸ ὄνομα τῶν Ἑβραίων πρωτοτόκων τὴν σωτηρίαν Thdt. *qu.*24 *in Ex.*(1.139); καλεῖται γὰρ φασέ, ὅπερ ἐστὶ πλατέσι τοῖς βήμασι χρῆσθαι Proc.G.*Ex.*12:2(M.87.561B); in licentious practices of Barbeliote Gnostics τοῦτό ἐστι τὸ σῶμα τοῦ Χριστοῦ καὶ τοῦτό ἐστι τὸ π., δι' ὃ πάσχει τὰ ἡμέτερα σώματα καὶ ἀναγκάζεται ὁμολογεῖν τὸ πάθος τοῦ Χριστοῦ Epiph.*haer.*26.4(p.281.12; M.41.337D).

B. abolished for Jews after destruction of Temple, Just.*dial.*46.2 (M.6.573B); so proving annulment of Mosaic Law, cf.Or.*hom.*6.3 *in Gen.*(p.69.4; M.12.197B); Chrys.*Jud.*3.3(1.610A) cit. s. ἄζυμος; *Dial. Christ.et Jud.*16(p.79.8).

C. as type; **1.** of sacrifice of Christ, cf.‡*Diogn.*12.9; Just.*dial.*40.1 (M.6.561B) cit. s. αἷμα; ἦν γὰρ τὸ π. ὁ Χριστός, ὁ τυθεὶς ὕστερον *ib.*111. 3(732C); ἐστὶν καινὸν καὶ παλαιόν, ἀΐδιον καὶ πρόσκαιρον, φθαρτὸν καὶ ἄφθαρτον, θνητὸν καὶ ἀθάνατον τὸ τοῦ π. μυστήριον· παλαιὸν μὲν κατὰ τὸν νόμον, καινὸν δὲ κατὰ τὸν λόγον...θνητὸν διὰ τὴν τοῦ κυρίου ταφήν, ἀθάνατον διὰ τὴν ἐκ νεκρῶν ἀνάστασιν Mel.*pass.*3 p.1.8; καθ' ὃ πάσχει πρόβατον, καθ' ὃ θάπτεται ἄνθρωπος, καθ' ὃ ἀνίσταται θεός. οὗτός ἐστιν Ἰησοῦς ὁ Χριστός,...τοῦτό ἐστιν τὸ τοῦ π. μυστήριον *ib.*10 p.2.23; *ib.*16 p.3.12; τὸ τοῦ π. μυστήριον τετέλεσται ἐν τῷ τοῦ κυρίου σώματι *ib.*56 p.9.26; τὸ τοῦ π. μυστήριον, ὅ ἐστιν Χριστός *ib.*65 p.10. 34; τὸ ἀληθινὸν τοῦ κυρίου π., ἡ θυσία ἡ μεγάλη, ὁ ἀντὶ τοῦ ἀμνοῦ παῖς θεοῦ Claud.*fr.pasch.*(M.5.1297A); cf. *figuratim praenuntiavit* [sc. Moses] *eum, pascha nominans: et...passus est dominus adimplens pascha,* Iren.*haer.*4.10.1(M.7.1000B); ref. Jos.2:11ff. *coccini signum... quod erat pascha, ib.*4.20.12(1043B); cf.Heracleon ap.Or.*Jo.*10.19(14; p.190.30; M.14.340D) cit. s. ἀνάπαυσις; περὶ τοῦ νομικοῦ π. ... φησίν· ὡσεί τινος εἰκὼν μὴ παρόντος μὲν τοῦ ἀρχετύπου τὴν ἴσην ἐκείνῳ δόξαν ἀποφέρεται καὶ παρούσης τῆς ἀληθείας καταλάμπεται ἡ εἰκὼν πρὸς αὐτῆς, τῆς ὁμοιώσεως ἐκείνης ἀποδεκτῆς μενούσης διὰ τὸ σημαίνειν τὴν ἀλήθειαν Clem.*fr.*33(p.218.2); Or.*Cels.*8.22(p.239.20; M.11.1552A); cf. *secundo...mense, quinta decima die mensis* [Ex.16:1]...*invenies ...hoc esse tempus, quod statuitur ad secundum pascha faciendum his, qui immundi...fuerunt. ... primum pascha primi populi est; secundum pascha nostrum est. ... non datur manna...in illa die, qua primum pascha fit, sed in illa, qua secundum. ... 'nostrum enim pascha...Christus', qui verus nobis panis de caelo descendit,* id. *hom.*7.4 *in Ex.*(p.209.5ff.; M.12.344A); *agnus immolari jubetur in pascha, non quo vere agni hostiam...requireret deus, sed quod designaret immolari...agnum, qui tollit peccatum mundi,* id.*hom.* 2.5 *in Lev.*(p.299.7; M.12.421A); id.*hom.*5.1 *in Num.*(p.26.4; M.12. 603A); ὁ ἀκούων τῶν περὶ τοῦ π. νενομοθετημένων κεκρυμμένως, ἐσθίει ἀπὸ τοῦ προβάτου Χριστοῦ id.*hom.*12.12 *in Jer.*(p.99.27; M.13.396C); ref. Jos.5:10, Passover celebrated after crossing of Jordan typifies Jesus as heavenly bread, id.*Jo.*6.45(26; p.154.22; M.14.277D); typology fully discussed, *ib.*10.13–15(11f.; pp.183–6; 328B–332D); *ib.*10.18(13; p.189.30; 340A); id.*comm.ser.*79 *in Mt.*(p.189.28; M.13. 1729A); Eus.*pasch.*1,2(M.24.696A,B); passover season was time of Creation, and in all its aspects Passover was fulfilled by Christ, *ib.*3(697A,B); fulfilled in Christ's Passion, *ib.*5(700D); καιρός ἐστιν οὗτος [i.e. spring]...ἐν ᾧ ἡ ἑορτὴ τοῦ π. τοῦ πρότερον τυπικοῦ, νῦν δὲ ἀληθινοῦ Cyr.H.*catech.*14.10; †Bas.*Is.*27(1.401A,B; M.30.172C); Ἰησοῦς μὲν οὖν ἔφαγε τὸ π. τὸ νομικόν...ἡμῖν δὲ καταλέλοιπε τὸ π. τὸ ἐπουράνιον. ἦλθεν ἡ ἀλήθεια καὶ ἔφαγε τὸ π. καὶ κατανάλωσε τὸν τύπον, ἵνα κρατήσῃ ἡ ἀλήθεια. ὁ μὲν γὰρ τύπος προεδήλου, ὁ δὲ δηλούμενος καιρὸν ἐξεδέχετο τὸν προσήκοντα. καὶ ἐπειδὴ ἔδει πληρωθῆναι τὸν τύπον, ἀνῆλθεν...εἰς Ἱερουσαλὴμ...πρὸς τὸ πάθος. ὅπου γὰρ ὁ τύπος, ἐκεῖ καὶ ἡ ἀλήθεια Tit.Bost.*fr.Lc.*22:14(p.241); μυσταγωγεῖ τὸ π. τοὺς μαθητὰς ἐν ὑπερῴῳ Gr.Naz.*or.*40.30(M.36.401B); τοιοῦτόν σοι τὸ τοῦ π. μυστήριον. ταῦτα ὁ νόμος ὑπέγραψε· ταῦτα Χριστὸς ἐτελείωσεν *ib.* 45.21(652D); Didym.*Trin.*2.16(M.39.721A) cit. s. ἄζυμος; Χριστὸς... μετ' αὐτῶν τὸ π. ἐποίησεν,...ἵνα τῇ σκιᾷ τὴν ἀλήθειαν ἐπαγάγῃ Chrys. *Jud.*3.3(1.610D); π. τὸ μυστικόν, τυπικῶς μὲν διὰ νόμου λειτουργούμενον ‡Chrys.*pasch.*6.1(p.117.11; 8.264D); π. κυρίου...ὅτι π. οὐ τύπος, οὐχ ἱστορία, οὐ σκιά, ἀλλὰ π. ἀληθῶς κυρίου. τὸ δὲ αἷμα εἰς σημεῖον, σημεῖον δὲ τῆς μελλούσης ἀληθείας, τοῦ ἀληθινοῦ πνεύματος τὸ πρωτότυπωμα, τὸ μίμημα τοῦ μεγάλου χρίσματος *ib.*6.3(p.159.13ff.; 269D); Procl.CP *or.*14.2(M.65.796C,D); Cyr.*ador.*17(1.606Eff.); typifies Christ; may be eaten within house but not outside, signifying that eucharist may be offered only in Catholic Church, id.*resp.*11(p.595. 9; 6².380B); νομικὸν π. contrasted with τὸ ἀληθινόν, ἐν ᾧ τὸ μυστήριον τῆς ὑπὲρ ἡμῶν ἑαυτοῦ θυσίας παρέδωκε τοῖς μαθηταῖς...οὗ τύπος ἐκεῖνο ἦν Jo.Philop.*pasch.*(p.209.9); Dor.*doct.*22.1(M.88.1821C); hence legal Passover abolished for Christians, cf. *pascha visibile necesse est aeternum non esse, sed temporale, quia quae videntur, temporalia sunt,* Or.*hom.*11.7 *in Num.*(p.89.31; M.12.653B); οὐκέτι γὰρ περιτέμνομαι κατὰ τὸ γράμμα, οὐ π. ποιῶ id.*hom.*20.6 *in Jos.*(p.426.21; cf.M.12.927C); cf. *forsitan aliquis imperitorum requiret cadens in Ebionismum (ex eo quod Jesus celebravit...pascha corporaliter...), dicens quia convenit et nos imitatores Christi similiter facere,* id. *comm.ser.*79 *in Mt.*(p.189.16; M.13.1728C); id.*hom.*5 *in Lc.*(p.32.9; M.13.1812C); ποιεῖν τὸ π. οὐ δυνάμεθα, φασίν. ὑπὲρ ἡμῶν γὰρ ἅπαξ ἐτύθη Χριστός Juln.Imp.ap.Cyr.*Juln.*10(6².354A); Chrys.*hom.*12.3 *in Mt.*(7.164D,E); *Chron.Pasch.*p.5(M.92.79A); **2.** observance of 'second Passover' by those unclean at actual festival typifies calling of 'unclean' gentiles, Thdt.*qu.*14 *in Num.*(1.229); **3.** Passover typifies spiritual life of Christians ὅπερ τοίνυν τῷ αἰσθητῷ φωτὶ κατὰ τὴν τεσσαρεσκαιδεκάτην συμβαίνει, τὸ διὰ πάσης νυκτός τε καὶ ἡμέρας ἀπαράδεκτον εἶναι τῆς ἐπιμιξίας τοῦ σκότους, τοῦτο βούλεται ὁ πνευματικὸς νόμος, σύμβολον γενέσθαι τοῖς πνευματικῶς ἑορτάζουσιν, ὥστε διὰ πάσης τῆς κατὰ τὴν ζωὴν ἑβδομάδος ἐν π. φωτεινὸν...ὅλον τὸν χρόνον αὐτοῖς τῆς ζωῆς ἐργάζεσθαι Gr.Nyss.*res.*1(M.46.621B); ὥσπερ...ἐν τῷ καιρῷ τοῦ π., πάντες τρόπον τινὰ ἱερωσύνῃ ἐτιμῶντο (ἕκαστος γὰρ τὸ πρόβατον ἔθυεν)· οὕτω...ἕκαστος...οἰκείου σώματος ἱερεὺς κεχειροτόνηται...ἵνα...τὸ σῶμα...ἱερὸν τῆς ἁγνείας κατασκευάσῃ Isid.Pel.*epp.*3.75(M.78.781D); cf. ὅτε γὰρ διαβαίνει ἡ ψυχὴ ἀπὸ τῆς ἁμαρτίας πρὸς τὴν ἀρετήν, τότε ποιεῖ τὸ φασὲχ τῷ κυρίῳ Dor.*doct.*22.1 (M.88.1821C); or Christians' sacrifice of praise, cf.Or.*hom.*5.8 *in Lev.* (p.348.14; M.12.458C); **4.** celebration of Passover in one place only (Jerusalem) symbolizes celebration of eucharist in Catholic Church alone, cf.Cyr.*resp.*11(p.595.9; 6².380B), cf. supra I.C.1; Proc.G.*Dt.* 16:5(M.87.913A); **5.** eating with shoes on feet signifies unholy character of Egypt as symbol of wickedness, id.*Is.*11:15–16(M.87. 2060B); **6.** typifying eucharist, v. H infra; hence

D. Christ as Christians' Passover (cf. 1Cor.5:7) οὗτός ἐστιν τὸ π. τῆς σωτηρίας ἡμῶν Mel.*pass.*69 p.11.19; ἐγὼ τὸ π. τῆς σωτηρίας *ib.* 103 p.17.23; Iren.*haer.*4.10.1(M.7.1000B); αὐτὸς ὢν τὸ π. Clem.*fr.*28 (p.216.27; M.9.757A); cf.Or.*hom.*14.1 *in Gen.*(p.122.2; M.12.236B); cf. id.*hom.*7.4 *in Ex.*(p.209.21; M.12.344C); cf.id.*hom.*5.1 *in Num.*(p.26. 4ff.; M.12.603A); id.*hom.*12.12 *in Jer.*(p.99.29; M.13.396C); id.*Jo.* 10.15(12; p.186.6ff.; M.14.332Dff.); τὸ τυθὲν π. Χριστός *ib.*10.18(13; p.189.27; 337D); Eus.*pasch.*1(M.24.696A); Ath.*ep.fest.*42(p.297.5; M. 26.1440B); Didym.*Trin.*2.16(M.39.721A); cf.Cyr.*glaph.Ex.*2(1.270D); cf.Proc.G.*Ex.*12:2(M.87.563); ὦ π. τὸ μέγα καὶ ἱερώτατον Χριστέ Jo.D.*carm.pasch.*122(p.221; M.96.844B); partaken of in eucharist σπουδαῖον...χρὴ τυγχάνειν...τὸν μέλλοντα ἐσθίειν τὸ...ἀληθινὸν π. ἴσασι δὲ οἱ μύσται τὸ λεγόμενον Isid.Pel.*epp.*4.162(M.78.1248C); τὸ γὰρ ἀληθινὸν π. οὐκ Ἰουδαίων, ἀλλὰ Χριστιανῶν τῶν ἐσθιόντων τὴν σάρκα Χριστοῦ Cyr.*Jo.*7(4.693E); cf.Proc.G.*Ex.*12:2(564).

E. question whether Christ ate Jewish Passover at Last Supper; **1.** Last Supper not held on day of Passover but at beginning of day of preparation, Christ then proclaiming himself as true Passover and suffering as such, Clem.*fr.*(p.216.26; M.9.757A); cf. Claud.*fr.pasch.*(M.5.1297A); ὁ πάλαι προειπὼν ὅτι οὐκέτι φάγομεν τὸ π., εἰκότως τὸ μὲν δεῖπνον ἐδείπνησε πρὸ τοῦ π., τὸ δὲ π. οὐκ ἔφαγεν, ἀλλ' ἔπαθεν. οὐδὲ γὰρ καιρὸς ἦν τῆς βρώσεως αὐτοῦ Hipp.*pasch.*5 (p.270.10; M.10.869A); ᾧ καιρῷ ἔπασχεν ὁ Χριστὸς οὐκ ἔφαγε τὸ κατὰ νόμον π., οὗτος γὰρ ἦν τὸ π. τὸ προκεκηρυγμένον καὶ τὸ τελειούμενον τῇ ὡρισμένῃ ἡμέρᾳ id.ap.*Chron.Pasch.*p.6(M.92.80B); ὁ σωτὴρ οὐ μετὰ Ἰουδαίων ἐπετέλεσε τὸ π. κατὰ τὸν καιρὸν τοῦ...πάθους. οὐ γὰρ ὅτε ἔθυον ἐκεῖνοι τὸ πρόβατον, τότε καὶ αὐτὸς μετὰ τῶν...μαθητῶν τὸ ἑαυτοῦ ἤγαγε π. οἱ μὲν γὰρ κατὰ τὴν παρασκευὴν...τοῦτ' ἔπραττον... αὐτὸς δὲ πρὸ ὅλης ἡμέρας τῇ πέμπτῃ...συνεσθίων...ἔλεγεν· ἐπιθυμίᾳ ἐπεθύμησα κτλ. ... οὐ μετὰ τῶν Ἰουδαίων τὸ π. ἤσθιεν. ἐπειδὴ καινὸν ἦν ἐκεῖνο καὶ ξενίζον παρὰ τὰ...Ἰουδαϊκὰ ἔθη. ... τὸ μὲν Μωϋσέως π. ...οὐκ ἦν ἐπιθυμητόν· τὸ δὲ σωτήριον μυστήριον τῆς καινῆς διαθήκης... αὐτῷ ἐπιθυμητὸν ἦν. ἀλλ' αὐτὸς μὲν πρὸ τοῦ παθεῖν...ἔφαγε τὸ π. ... οὐ μετὰ τῶν Ἰουδαίων Eus.*pasch.*9,10(M.24.704A–C); Christ's Passover, at which he mystically offered himself as sacrifice, preceded day of Mosaic Passover which was superseded by it so as to be no longer the true Passover, Eutych.*pasch.*2–3(M.86.2393B–2396B); Last Supper not Jewish Passover which did not happen on same day (nor was lamb eaten at it), but was ἀληθινὸν καὶ μυστικὸν π. Jo. Philop.*pasch.*(p.209.19); no part of passover law observed at it, *ib.* (p.212.7); that it was not Passover is proved by Mc.14:2, Mt. 26:1ff. and by holding of trial at night, *ib.*(p.213.2); cf. οὐχ ὥς τινες ἀμαθίᾳ φερόμενοι διαβεβαιοῦνται ὡς φαγὼν τὸ π. παρεδόθη· ἅπερ οὔτε παρὰ τῶν...εὐαγγελίων μεμαθήκαμεν, οὔτε τις τῶν...ἀποστόλων τι τοιοῦτον παραδέδωκεν. ἐν ᾧ οὖν καιρῷ ἔπαθεν...τὸ κατὰ νόμον οὐκ ἔφαγε π., ἀλλ'...αὐτὸς...ἐτύθη...ἐν τῇ τοῦ σκιώδους π. ἑορτῇ...τῇ ιδ' τοῦ πρώτου μηνός Petr.I Al.*fr.*(M.18.520A); **2.** Jews observed wrong date *τῷ μὲν γὰρ κυρίῳ ἐπιμαρτυρεῖ τὸ π. βεβρωκέναι τῇ πρώτῃ τῶν ἀζύμων· μηδ', ὥς φησιν ὁ Λουκᾶς, ἐν ᾗ ἔδει θύεσθαι τὸ π. ἡμέρᾳ τὸ σύνηθες αὐτοῖς βεβρώκασι π., ἀλλὰ τῇ μετ' ἐκείνην ἑξῆς, ἥτις ἦν τῶν μὲν ἀζύμων δευτέρα, σελήνης δὲ πεντεκαιδεκάτη...οὐκ ἄρα τῇ πρώτῃ τῶν ἀζύμων...βεβρώκασιν αὐτὸ κατὰ τὸν νόμον· ἢ γὰρ ἂν μετὰ τοῦ σωτῆρος καὶ αὐτοὶ τὸ π. πεποιήκεσαν* Eus.*pasch.*11(M.24.705B); Jews postponed Passover from proper date in order to carry out trial and execution of Jesus, Chrys.*hom.84.2 in Mt.*(7.800A); **3.** question discussed, id.*hom.83.3 in Jo.*(8.494C); **4.** Christ ate Passover at Last Supper, cf. *manducans pascha, et sequenti die passus*, Iren. *haer.*2.22.3(M.7.783B); Or.*hom.19.13 in Jer.*(p.169.23; M.13.489B); cf. id.*comm.ser.74 in Mt.*(p.175.10; M.13.1719A); *ib.*79(p.189.9; 1728C); *ἔφαγε τὸ π. τὸ π. τὸ νομικὸν μετὰ τῶν μαθητῶν* Tit.Bost.*fr.Lc.*22:14 (p.241); *Const.App.*5.14.6; cf.Proc.G.*Ex.*12:6(M.87.566); *τὸ παλαιὸν π. μετὰ τῶν μαθητῶν...φαγών* Jo.D.*f.o.*4.13(M.94.1140A); id.*hom.* 9.4(M.96.729B); Last Supper as Passover allegorized, Or.*hom.19.13 in Jer.*(p.169.27; M.13.489C).

F. Passover and date of Crucifixion *ὅτι ἐν ἡμέρᾳ τοῦ π. συνελάβετε αὐτόν, καὶ ὁμοίως ἐν τῷ π. ἐσταυρώσατε, γέγραπται* Just.*dial.*111.3 (M.6.732C); Christ suffered on passover day as true paschal sacrifice, Clem.*fr.*(p.217.2; M.9.757A); *ὁ δὲ ἀληθὴς ἁγνισμὸς οὐ πρὸ τοῦ π. ἦν ἀλλ' ἐν τῷ π., ὅτε Ἰησοῦς ἀπέθανεν...ὡς ἀμνὸς θεοῦ* Or.*Jo.*28.25 (20; p.423.9; M.14.737A); Eus.*pasch.*9(M.24.704A); *ἐν ἀζύμοις γὰρ ἦν τὸ πραχθέν, καὶ τῇ τοῦ π. ἑορτῇ* Cyr.H.*catech.*13.25; cf.Chrys.*Jud.*3.5 (1.613C); id.*hom.83.3 in Jo.*(8.494C); cf. *θύεται μυστικῶς τῆς τεσσαρεσκαιδεκάτης ἐναρχομένης* Eutych.*pasch.*1(M.86.2392D).

G. Christians spiritually celebrate continual Passover, feeding on flesh of Logos and passing over from worldly affairs to God, Or. *Cels.*8.22(p.239.22; M.11.1552A); cf.id.*hom.10.3 in Gen.*(p.97.8; M. 12.218B).

H. eucharist as Christian Passover, (?) ‡*Diogn.*12.9; *ἐφ' ἑκάστης κυριακῆς ἡμέρας τὸ...π. τελοῦντες, ἀεὶ τοῦ σώματος τοῦ σωτηρίου ἐμφορούμεθα, ἀεὶ τοῦ αἵματος τοῦ προβάτου μεταλαμβάνομεν* Eus. *pasch.*7(M.24.701A); *διὰ πάσης δὲ κυριακῆς ἡμέρας τῷ...σώματι τοῦ αὐτοῦ σωτηρίου π. ζωοποιούμενοι* *ib.*12(705D); cf.Gr.Naz.*or.*40.30(M. 36.401B); Didym.*Trin.*3.21(M.39.905C); Chrys.*Jud.*3.2(1.608D); Isid. Pel.*epp.*4.162(M.78.1248C).

I. passover date announced in advance, like that of Easter, Jo. Philop.*pasch.*(p.214.25).

J. Christ's observance of Passovers as evidence for chronology of his life, Iren.*haer.*2.22.3(M.7.783A,B).

II. *Easter*;

A. in gen. *ἀπόδειξις χρόνων τοῦ π.* Hipp.*can.pasch.*tit.(M.10.876); *αἱ κυριακαὶ τοῦ π.* *ib.*(879); Or.*Cels.*8.22(p.239.12; M.11.1549D); *ψαλμοὺς δὲ τοὺς μὲν εἰς...Χριστὸν παύσας* [sc. Paul. Sam.], *εἰς ἑαυτὸν δὲ ἐν μέσῃ τῇ ἐκκλησίᾳ τῇ μεγάλῃ τοῦ π. ἡμέρᾳ ψαλμῳδεῖν γυναῖκας παρασκευάζων* Malch.*ep.*ap.Eus.*h.e.*7.30.10(M.20.713B); *τῇ ἁγίᾳ τεσσαρακοστῇ περὶ τὸ π.* Ath.*ep.encycl.*4(p.173.12; M.25.232A); *ἐν...ἡμέραις τοῦ ἁγιωτάτου π.* id.*h.Ar.*20(p.193.18; M.25.717A); *μετὰ...τὰ ἕβδομα τοῦ π.* id.*fug.*6(p.72.4; M.25.652A); *τὴν ἑβδομάδα τοῦ ἁγίου π. ... φύλαττε* ‡Ath.*syntag.*2.11(p.152; M.28.837C); Cyr.H.*catech.*18. 22; Bas.*ep.*89.2(3.181A; M.32.472B); *μέχρι τῶν ἡμέρων τοῦ π.* *ib.*198. 1(289D; M.713C); *σωτήριον ἡμέραν τοῦ π.* *ib.*322(448B; M.1068D); *π. κυρίου...ἑορτῶν ἡμῖν ἑορτή* Gr.Naz.*or.*45.2(M.36.624B); *Const.App.*5. 13.4; *ib.*5.17.1; *ἑορτὴν τοῦ π., τουτέστι τὴν ἑβδομάδα τὴν ὡρισμένην καὶ ἀπ' αὐτῶν τῶν ἀποστόλων ἐν τῇ Διατάξει* Epiph.*haer.*70.12(p.245. 16; M.42.364C); ‡Chrys.*pasch.*1(8.251A); *Supplicatio* ap.Evagr.*h.e.* 2.8(p.58.28; M.86.2525B); *τὴν σεπτὴν τῆς...ἀναστάσεως...ἑορτὴν π. προσαγορεύει*) *Chron.Pasch.*p.226(M.92.549B); Jo.D.*carm.pasch.*2 (p.218; M.96.840C; Thdr.Stud.*or.*4.8(M.99.720A).

B. ref. Quartodeciman and other controversies; **1.** dispute about Asiatic observance of Easter on Jewish Passover day, 14th day of Nisan *ἐπὶ Σερουιλλίου Παύλου ἀνθυπάτου τῆς Ἀσίας...ἐγένετο ζήτησις πολλὴ ἐν Λαοδικείᾳ περὶ τοῦ π., ἐμπεσόντος κατὰ καιρὸν ἐν ἐκείναις ταῖς ἡμέραις* Mel.*fr.*4(p.309; M.5.1208); hence denial by orthodox that Christ ate Passover on Jewish date, Claud.*fr.pasch.*(M.5. 1297A); v. I.E.1 supra; or insistence that his doing so was history, not precept, Eus.*pasch.*8(M.24.704A); Polycarp and Anicetus dispute the question, each maintaining his own tradition (claimed by Polyc. to be Johannine), without severing communion, Iren.*ep. Vict.*ap.Eus.*h.e.*5.24.16(M.20.508A); *ζητήσεως...οὐ σμικρᾶς ἀνακινηθείσης, ὅτι...τῆς Ἀσίας ἁπάσης αἱ παροικίαι ὡς ἐκ παραδόσεως ἀρχαιοτέρας σελήνης τὴν τεσσαρεσκαιδεκάτην ᾤοντο δεῖν ἐπὶ τῆς τοῦ...π. ἑορτῆς παραφυλάττειν...ὁποίᾳ δ' ἂν ἡμέρᾳ τῆς ἑβδομάδος περιτυγχάνοι, ...οὐκ ἔθους ὄντος τοῦτον ἐπιτελεῖν τὸν τρόπον ταῖς ἀνὰ τὴν λοιπὴν ἅπασαν οἰκουμένην ἐκκλησίαις, ἐξ ἀποστολικῆς παραδόσεως τὸ...ἔθος φυλαττούσαις, ὡς μηδ' ἑτέρᾳ προσήκειν παρὰ τὴν τῆς ἀναστάσεως ...ἡμέρᾳ τὰς νηστείας ἐπιλύεσθαι* Eus.*h.e.*5.23.1(492A); councils convened and decision that feast must be kept on Sunday only, *ib.*5. 23.2(492A); esp. at Caesarea under Theophilus of Caesarea and Narcissus of Jerusalem, Rome under Victor, Pontus, Gaul, and Osrhoene, *ib.*5.23.3(492B); Asiatic tradition defended, Polycr.ap. Eus.*h.e.*5.24.2ff.(493Bff.); action of Victor *τῆς Ἀσίας πάσης ἅμα ταῖς ὁμόροις ἐκκλησίαις τὰς παροικίας ἀποτέμνειν...τῆς κοινῆς ἑνώσεως πειρᾶται* *ib.*5.24.9(497A); protest, Iren.*ep.Vict.*ap.Eus.*h.e.*5.24.12ff. (500Aff.); decision of Palestinian council, Eus.*h.e.*5.25(508Bf.); Quartodeciman view explained and condemned, Hipp.*haer.*8.18 (p.237.16; M.16.3366B); Epiph.*haer.*50.1ff.(p.244.20ff.; M.41.884Aff.); ‡Pion.*v.Polyc.*2; ‡Chrys.*pasch.*7(8.276B); Socr.*h.e.*5.22.17(M.67. 629A); Thdt.*haer.*3.4(4.343); cf.Tim.CP *haer.*(M.86.36A); *Chron. Pasch.*pp.7–8(M.92.84A); *ib.*p.226(549A); Jo.D.*haer.*50(M.94.709A); Jo.Nic.*nativ.*(M.96.1440C); **2.** dispute at Alexandria cf. *θόρυβος ἐκινεῖτο...περὶ τοῦ τῆς ἑορτῆς ταύτης ζητήματος, ἔν τε χρόνοις Πολυκάρπου καὶ Βίκτωρος...ἔν τε χρόνοις Ἀλεξάνδρου ἐπισκόπου Ἀλεξανδρείας καὶ Κρισκεντίου, ὡς πρὸς ἀλλήλους εὑρίσκονται ἕκαστος αὐτῶν γράφοντες καὶ διαμαχόμενοι, ἕως τῶν ἡμετέρων χρόνων* Epiph. *haer.*70.9(p.242.17; M.42.356B); **3.** decision of CNic.(325): Easter to be observed after vernal equinox and so once only in any year; hence to be further removed from Jewish practice (question much confused with Quartodeciman controversy), a rule already laid down by Anat.Laod.*can.pasch.*ap.Eus.*h.e.*7.32.19(M.20.729B) (where based on Jewish rule of Aristobulus) and Dion.Al.ap.Eus.*h.e.*7.20 (M.20.681B); cf. *ἀνάξιον ἔδοξεν εἶναι τὴν ἁγιωτάτην...ἑορτὴν τῇ τῶν Ἰουδαίων ἑπομένους συνηθείᾳ πληροῦν* Const.ap.Eus.*v.C.*3.18(p.85. 8; M.20.1076A); Eus.*pasch.*8(M.24.701C); *οἱ μὲν γὰρ ἀπὸ τῆς Συρίας καὶ Κιλικίας καὶ Μεσοποταμίας ἐχώλευον περὶ τὴν ἑορτὴν καὶ μετὰ τῶν Ἰουδαίων ἐποίουν τὸ π. ... καὶ αὕτη αἰτία γέγονεν...συναχθῆναι σύνοδον, ἵνα πανταχοῦ μία τῆς ἑορτῆς ἡμέρα ἐπιτελῆται...καὶ οἱ μὲν ἀπὸ τῆς Συρίας ἐπείσθησαν* (expression of Council's decision on Easter contrasted with its expression of truths of faith) Ath.*syn.*5(p.234. 1; M.26.688B,C); id.*ep.Afr.*2(M.26.1032C); cf. *dominus illos increpat qui pascha Judaeorum more celebrant*, id.*ep.fest.*6.3(M.26.1384C); CAnt.(341)*can.*1; clergy celebrating Easter before equinox (with Jews) to be deposed, *Can.App.*8; *Const.App.*5.17.1; *κέχρηται γὰρ* [sc. Church] *οὐ μόνον τῇ τεσσαρεσκαιδεκάτῃ ἀλλὰ καὶ τῇ ἑβδομάδι... καὶ κέχρηται οὐ μόνον τῇ τεσσαρεσκαιδεκάτῃ τῆς σελήνης, ἀλλὰ καὶ τῷ δρόμῳ τοῦ ἡλίου, ἵνα μὴ ἐν ἑνὶ ἐνιαυτῷ δύο π. ποιοῦντες ἐν τῷ ἑτέρῳ μηδὲ ἓν π. τελέσωμεν. διὸ παρατηρούμεθα μὲν τὴν τεσσαρεσκαιδεκάτην, ὑπερβαίνομεν δὲ τὴν ἰσημερίαν φερόμεν τε ἐπὶ τὴν...κυριακὴν τὸ τέλος τῆς συμπληρώσεως* Epiph.*haer.*50.3(p.248.8; M.41.888C); *ib.*70.9 (p.242.7; M.42.353C–356A); *ib.*70.11(p.244.27; 364A); schisms about date of Easter thereby healed, *ib.*70.14(p.247.14; 369C); Chrys. *Jud.*3.3(1.609B); ‡Chrys.*pasch.*7(8.276A); *οἱ δὲ μετ' ἰσημερίαν ἐπετέλουν, τὸ συνεορτάζειν Ἰουδαίοις ἐκτρεπόμενοι· φάσκοντες ἀεὶ τοῦ ἡλίου ἐν κριῷ ὄντος καθήκειν τὸ π. ἐπιτελεῖν...καὶ τοῦτο ποιεῖν πειθομένους, μὴ τοῖς νῦν...πεπλανημένοις Ἰουδαίοις, ἀλλὰ τοῖς ἀρχαίοις, καὶ Ἰωσήπῳ...πάντες δὲ οἱ λοιποὶ ἄχρι τῶν ἑσπερίων μερῶν...μετὰ ἰσημερίαν ἐξ ἀρχαίας τινὸς παραδόσεως τὸ π. ποιήσαντες εὑρίσκονται* Socr.*h.e.*5.22.19(M.67.629A); cf. *οὐχ ὥς τινες ἐπεθρύλησαν, ἡ ἐπὶ Κωνσταντίνου σύνοδος τὴν ἑορτὴν...παρέτρεψεν* *ib.*(629B); *ib.*5.22.64 (641B); Church following in this respect passover practice of Samaritans, *ib.*5.22.72(644B); Eutych.*pasch.*6(M.86.2397C); *ib.* (2400A); *Chron.Pasch.*p.8(M.92.84B,C); Jo.Nic.*nativ.*(M.96.1440C); *ib.*(1449A); **4.** Montanist practice; **a.** quartodeciman *οὔτε παρὰ τὸν καιρὸν τῶν ἀζύμων δεῖ ποιεῖν, ὥσπερ οἱ αἱρετικοὶ ποιοῦσι, μάλιστα οἱ Φρύγες* ‡Pion.*v.Polyc.*2; Epiph.*haer.*50.1(p.244.14ff.; M.41.884A); **b.** observing solar calendar only *ἕτεροι δὲ...τὴν αὐτὴν μίαν ἡμέραν ἄγοντες καὶ τὴν αὐτὴν μίαν ἡμέραν νηστεύοντες καὶ τὰ μυστήρια ἐπιτελοῦντες, ἀπὸ τῶν Ἄκτων δῆθεν Πιλάτου αὐχοῦσι τὴν ἀκρίβειαν εὑρηκέναι, ἐν οἷς ἐμφέρεται τῇ πρὸ ὀκτὼ καλανδῶν Ἀπριλλίων τὸν σωτῆρα πεπονθέναι· καὶ ἐν ἐκείνῃ τῇ ἡμέρᾳ βούλονται ἄγειν τὸ π. ὁποίᾳ δ' ἂν ἐμπέσῃ ἡ τεσσαρεσκαιδεκάτη τῆς σελήνης* *ib.*(p.245.5; M.41.885A); similar practice in Cappadocia, *ib.*(p.245.11; 885A); cf. *αἵρεσις ἡ τῶν Μοντανιστῶν, ἥτις δῆθεν μὲν ἀποδύεται τὸ μετὰ Ἰουδαίων ποιεῖν, ἀφέστηκε δὲ σὺν τούτῳ καὶ τῆς ἐκκλησίας εἰς ἴδιον κίνδυνον. τεσσαρεσκαιδεκάτην γὰρ μηνὸς τοῦ πρώτου φυλάττει, τουτέστι μηνὸς ἑβδόμου κατ' Ἀσιανούς, οὐ τεσσαρεσκαιδεκάτην δὲ σελήνης· οὐκ οἶδα πόθεν λαβοῦσα τὸν θεσμόν* ‡Chrys.*pasch.*7(8.276C); *Μοντανισταὶ...ξένην τινὰ μέθοδον εἰσαγαγόντες, κατὰ ταύτην τὸ π. ἄγουσι. τοῖς μὲν γὰρ ἐπὶ τούτῳ τὸν τῆς σελήνης δρόμον πολυπραγμονοῦσι* καταμέμφονται· φασὶ δὲ χρῆναι μόνοις τοῖς ἡλιακοῖς ἕπεσθαι κύκλοις τοὺς ὀρθῶς ταῦτα κανονίζοντας· καὶ μῆνα μὲν ἕκαστον εἶναι ἡμερῶν τριάκοντα ὁρίζουσιν· ἄρχεσθαι δὲ τὴν πρώτην ἀπὸ τῆς ἐαρινῆς ἰσημερίας, ἣ ῥηθείη ἂν κατὰ Ῥωμαίους πρὸ ἐννέα καλανδῶν Ἀπριλλίων ...ἀπὸ γὰρ τῆς πρὸ ἐννέα καλανδῶν Ἀπριλλίων, ὡς ἀρχῆς οὔσης κτίσεως ἡλίου καὶ πρώτου μηνός, ἀναλογίζονται τὴν εἰρημένην ταῖς ἱεραῖς γραφαῖς τεσσαρεσκαιδεκαταίαν· καὶ ταύτην εἶναι λέγουσι τὴν πρὸ ὀκτὼ εἰδῶν Ἀπριλλίων· καθ' ἣν ἀεὶ τὸ π. ἄγουσιν, εἰ συμβαίη καὶ τὴν ἀναστάσιμον αὐτῇ συνδραμεῖν ἡμέραν, ⟨εἰ δὲ μὴ⟩ ἐπὶ τῇ ἐχομένῃ κυριακῇ ἑορτάζουσι Soz.*h.e.*7.18.12ff.(M.67.1472Bff.); **5.** Novatianist; Phrygian Novatianists adopt quartodeciman practice in later 4th cent., contrary to earlier custom of sect, and cause schism, Socr. *h.e.*4.28.17(M.67.540B); *ib.*5.22.82(645A); Soz.*h.e.*6.24.7(M.67.1356B); schism created by reversion to Jewish practice of presbyter Sabbatius, Socr.*h.e.*7.5.2(M.67.745C); **6.** Audian quartodecimanism; refutation of Audian view that traditional and apostolic observance was changed under Constantine in deference to his wish or to be accommodated to emperor's birthday, Epiph.*haer.*70.9(p.241.17ff.; M.42.353B); *ib.*70.14(p.247.3ff.; 369B); **7.** varieties of practice discussed; no rules laid down by NT about Easter or other feasts, Socr.*h.e.*5.22.7ff.(M.67.628Aff.).

C. canons for settling date of Easter Ἱππόλυτος...κανόνα ἑκκαιδεκαετηρίδος περὶ τοῦ π. προθείς, ἐπὶ τὸ πρῶτον ἔτος αὐτοκράτορος Ἀλεξάνδρου τοὺς χρόνους περιγράφει Eus.*h.e.*6.22(M.20.573C); cf. Hipp.*can.pasch.*(M.10.879); of Anat. Laod., Eus.*h.e.*7.32.13ff.(728Aff.); rules of Dion. Al., *ib.*7.20(681B); Epiph.*haer.*70.12–13 (p.245.8ff.; M.42.364Bff.); ‡Chrys.*pasch.*7(8.276A); *Chron.Pasch.* pp.10–17(M.92.88B–100C); *ib.*225f.(548Cff.).

D. announcement of date by annual festal letters of bishop of Alexandria (Dion. Al.), Eus.*h.e.*7.20(M.20.681B); v. ἑορταστικός; ? and by other bishops to congregations, Ath.*ep.Drac.*10(M.25.533B).

E. fasting before Easter, v. νηστεία.

F. standing for prayer during Easter season, Eus.*pasch.*4(M.24.700B); ‡Just.*qu.et resp.*115(M.6.1364A); v. εὐχή, γόνυ, γονυκλισία.

G. administration of baptism at Easter, (?) cf.Hipp.*trad.ap.*20.7ff.; Cyr.H.*catech.*18.32; cf.Synes.*hom.*2(p.281; M.66.1564A); Pall. *v.Chrys.*9(p.56.22; M.47.33); ἐν Θεσσαλίᾳ...ἐν ταῖς ἡμέραις τοῦ π. μόνον βαπτίζουσι· διὸ σφόδρα...οἱ λοιποὶ μὴ βαπτισθέντες ἀποθνήσκουσι Socr.*h.e.*5.22.52(M.67.640A); *Supplicatio* ap.CBeryt.*act.*(*ACO* 2.1.3 p.35.19; H.2.533A).

H. delivery of catecheses by bishop to newly baptized in Easter week, Cyr.H.*catech.*18.33; *Supplicatio* ap.CBeryt., v. II.G supra.

I. preaching each day in Easter week by bishop, cf.Chrys.*res. Chr.*5(2.445B).

J. Easter vigil, (?) cf.Hipp.*trad.ap.*20.9; in time of Narcissus of Jerusalem, Eus.*h.e.*6.9.2(M.20.537C); in reign of Philip, *ib.*6.34 (596A); Gr.Naz.*or.*45.2(M.36.624C).

K. prohibition of distribution of bishop's eucharist at Easter to other dioceses by way of εὐλογίαι, CLaod.*can.*14, cit. s. εὐλογία; cf.Iren.*ep.Vict.*ap.Eus.*h.e.*5.24.15(M.20.505A).

L. Easter as fulfilled for believer after death, Gr.Naz.*ep.*120(M.37.216A).

III. 'Gnostic' cannibalistic rite as τὸ τέλειον π. Epiph.*haer.*26.5 (p.282.13; M.41.340C).

***πασχάζ-ω**, *celebrate Easter* τινὲς τῶν Ναυατιανῶν ἐν Φρυγίᾳ... νόμον ἐξέθεντο μετὰ Ἰουδαίων ~ειν Thphn.*chron.*p.53(M.108.188B).

***πασχαλία, ἡ**, *Eastertide*, Marc.Diac.*v.Porph.*52; *ib.*94; *ib.*102; Leont.N.*v.Sym.*49(M.93.1729C); †Anast.S.*relat.*51(*OC* 3 p.71).

***πασχάλι(ο)ν, τό, 1.** *paschal canon* π. τῶν γεγραμμένων ἐπὶ τῆς βασιλείας Κωνσταντίνου †Hipp.Th.*fr.*8c.6(p.40.1; M.117.1048A); hence *Eastertide* ἐκοινώνησα...ἔξω τοῦ π. †Jo.Jej.*serm.*(M.88.1929B); **2.** *annals* drawn up acc. date of Easter, *Chron.Pasch.*p.274 (M.92.681A); τῷ π. καὶ τοῖς ὑπαταρίοις ἐντυχών *ib.*p.381(977A); ἀπὸ τούτων τῶν ὑπάτων ψηφίζονται τὰ ἔτη τῶν Συρομακεδόνων, ἤγουν καὶ Ἀπαμέων εἰς τὸ πασχάλιν *ib.*p.171(421C).

***πασχάλιος**, *of Easter* ταῖς π. ἡμέραις Isch.*libell.*(p.215.1; H.2.328E); ἐν Ῥώμῃ τὸ Ἀλληλούϊα ψάλλουσι, κατὰ τὴν πρώτην ἡμέραν τῆς πασχαλίας ἑορτῆς Soz.*h.e.*7.19.4(M.67.1476B); τῇ π. ἑορτῇ τῆς ἀναστάσεως Jo.Mosch.*prat.*25(M.87.3108A); ref. computation and prediction of Easter, Cosm.Ind.*top.*3(M.88.172A).

πασχητιασμός, ὁ, *lechery*, Clem.*paed.*2.10(p.209.35; M.8.501A); id.*prot.*4(p.46.26; M.8.160A).

πασχητιάω, *incite to lust*, Clem.*paed.*2.1(p.164.4; M.8.400C); id. *str.*2.20(p.181.17; M.8.1069C).

πάσχ-ω, A. *suffer*; **1.** in particular of martyrs βασάνους διὰ ζῆλος παθόντες ὑπόδειγμα κάλλιστον ἐγένοντο *1Clem.*6.1; esp. of suffering death ἐάνπερ διὰ τοῦ παθεῖν θεοῦ ἐπιτύχω Ign.*Polyc.*7.1; ἐὰν ~ομεν διὰ τὸ ὄνομα αὐτοῦ, δοξάζωμεν αὐτόν Polyc.*ep.*8.2; οἱ ὑπὲρ τοῦ νόμου παθόντες Herm.*sim.*8.3.6; οἱ παθόντες ὑπὲρ τοῦ ὀνόματος...οἳ καὶ προθύμως ἔπαθον ἐξ ὅλης τῆς καρδίας *ib.*9.28.2; **2.** of Christ; **a.** in gen. ὅσα ὑπέμεινεν Ἰησοῦς Χριστὸς παθεῖν ἕνεκα ἡμῶν *2Clem.*1.2; ταῦτα γὰρ πάντα ἔπαθεν δι' ἡμᾶς, ἵνα σωθῶμεν Ign.*Smyrn.*2.1; αὐτὸς δὲ ἠθέλησεν οὕτω παθεῖν· ἔδει γάρ, ἵνα ἐπὶ ξύλου πάθῃ *Barn.*5.13; ἐν σαρκὶ οὖν αὐτοῦ μέλλοντος φανεροῦσθαι καὶ π., προεφανερώθη τὸ πάθος *ib.*6.7; εἰ οὖν ὁ υἱὸς τοῦ θεοῦ, ὢν κύριος...ἔπαθεν...πιστεύσωμεν, ὅτι ὁ υἱὸς τοῦ θεοῦ οὐκ ἠδύνατο παθεῖν εἰ μὴ δι' ἡμᾶς *ib.*7.2; ὑπὲρ ἡμῶν γενόμενος ἄνθρωπος παθεῖν...ὑπέμεινε Just.*1apol.*50.1(M.6.401B); ἄρτου τῆς εὐχαριστίας, ὃν εἰς ἀνάμνησιν τοῦ πάθους, οὗ ἔπαθεν ὑπὲρ τῶν καθαιρομένων τὰς ψυχὰς ἀπὸ...πονηρίας ἀνθρώπων,...Χριστὸς... παρέδωκε ποιεῖν id.*dial.*41.1(M.6.564B); ἡ αὐτοῦ τοῦ κυρίου μαρτυρία, καθ' ἣν παθὼν ἀνέστη Clem.*ecl.*59(p.154.20; M.9.728B); **b.** Christol., ref. problem of divine impassibility εἰ δέ, ὥσπερ τινὲς ἄθεοι ὄντες... λέγουσιν, τὸ δοκεῖν πεπονθέναι αὐτόν...ἐγὼ τί δέδεμαι; Ign.*Trall.*10.1; ἀληθῶς ἔπαθεν...οὐχ ὥσπερ ἄπιστοί τινες λέγουσιν, τὸ δοκεῖν αὐτὸν πεπονθέναι id.*Smyrn.*2.1; ὁ λόγος τῇ οὐσίᾳ μένων λόγος οὐδὲν μὲν ~ει ὢν ~ει τὸ σῶμα ἢ ἡ ψυχή, συγκαταβαίνων δ' ἔσθ' ὅτε...οἱονεὶ σὰρξ γίνεται Or.*Cels.*4.15(p.285.17; M.11.1048A); πέπονθεν ὁ ἀπαθὴς τῷ σπλαγχνισθῆναι id.*comm.in Mt.*10.23(p.33.3; M.13.900C); reality of suffering denied, *A.Jo.*96(p.198.18ff.); *ib.*101(p.201.13ff.); δυνάμει καὶ ἔπαθεν ἀπαθὴς μένων Meth.*Porph.*2(p.505.21; M.18.404A); ὡς ἄνθρωπος ἐπολιτεύετο, καὶ...ὡς υἱὸς τῷ πατρὶ συνῆν. ὅθεν οὐδὲ τῆς παρθένου τικτούσης ἔπασχεν αὐτός Ath.*inc.*17.5(M.25.125C); δύναμις δέ ἐστι θεοῦ ὁ υἱός, παθὼν ἐξ ἀσθενείας, τουτέστιν, ἐκ τῆς σαρκικῆς συμπλοκῆς id.*inc.et c.Ar.*21(M.26.1024A); ἃ γὰρ τὸ ἀνθρώπινον ἔπασχε σῶμα τοῦ λόγου, ταῦτα, συνὼν αὐτῷ ὁ λόγος, εἰς ἑαυτὸν ἀνέφερεν...καὶ ἦν παράδοξον, ὅτι αὐτὸς ἦν ὁ ~ων καὶ μὴ ~ων· ~ων μέν, ὅτι τὸ ἴδιον αὐτοῦ ἔπασχε σῶμα, καὶ ἐν αὐτῷ τῷ ~οντι ἦν· μὴ ~ων δέ, ὅτι τῇ φύσει θεὸς ὢν ὁ λόγος, ἀπαθής ἐστι...τὸ δὲ σῶμα εἶχεν ἐν ἑαυτῷ τὸν ἀπαθῆ λόγον id.*ep.Epict.*6(p.10.16; M.26.1060C); αὐτὸν δὲ τὸν λόγον, ἄτρεπτον καὶ ἀναλλοίωτον πιστεύωμεν. διὸ αὐτός ἐστιν ὁ παθὼν καὶ μὴ παθών· τῇ μὲν θεϊκῇ φύσει ἀπαθὴς καὶ ἄτρεπτος καὶ ἀναλλοίωτος ὤν, τῇ δὲ σαρκὶ παθών ‡Ath.*Apoll.*1.11(M.26.1112C); εἰ δέ τινες...παραχαράττουσι τὴν...πίστιν...τῆς θεότητος διϊστῶντες τὸ...~ον σῶμα ὡς ἰδιαζόντως ὑφεστός, καὶ οὗτοι τῆς...σωζούσης ὁμολογίας ἐκτός Apoll.*fid.sec. pt.*3(p.168.20; M.10.1105D); ~ει τὸ ἀπαράδεκτον πάθους οὐκ ἀνάγκῃ φύσεως ἀβουλήτου, καθάπερ ἄνθρωπος, ἀλλ' ἀκολουθίᾳ φύσεως id.*fr.* 102(p.231.10); id.*anac.*29(p.246.1; M.28.1284A); παθὼν μὲν τὰ ἡμέτερα πάθη κατὰ σάρκα,...ἀπαθὴς δὲ διαμείνας...κατὰ τὴν θεότητα id.*ep. Jov.*2(p.251.15; M.28.28B); εἴ τις τολμᾷ λέγειν τὸν Χριστὸν θεότητι πεπονθέναι καὶ μὴ σαρκί,...ἔστω ἀνάθεμα Vital.*fr.*(p.273.21); περὶ τὸ ~ον τὰ τοιαῦτα τῶν ὀνομάτων [sc. θάνατος, ἀγωνία κτλ.], οὐ τὴν ἄτρεπτον φύσιν καὶ τοῦ ~ειν ὑψηλοτέραν Gr.Naz.*or.*30.16(p.134.10; M.36.125A); Gr.Nyss.*Apoll.*54(M.45.1256C); ὁ σωτήρ, φησί [sc. Apoll.], πέπονθε...τίς ὢν ὁ σωτήρ; ὁ θεός, φησὶν ἐν τοῖς πρὸ τούτου...οὐκοῦν ὁ θεὸς πέπονθεν, ἅπερ παθεῖν αὐτὸν εἴρηκε *ib.*58(1265C); οὔτε τὸ παθεῖν τὸν μονογενῆ ἐν σαρκὶ πάθος περιποιεῖται τῇ αὐτοῦ θεότητι, καίτοι γε ἐξ ἀληθινῆς ὁμολογίας πιστευόμενον ἀπὸ τῆς ἀληθινῆς πίστεως, ὅτι πέπονθεν ὁ ἀπαθὴς θεὸς ὢν λόγος Epiph.*haer.*76.39(p.392.30; M.42.601A); ἑνωθεὶς δὲ μᾶλλον τῇ καθ' ἡμᾶς ἀνθρωπότητι, πάθοι ἂν ἀπαθῶς σαρκὶ τῇ ἰδίᾳ τὰ ἀνθρώπινα Cyr.*Pulch.*42(p.50.9; 5².163E); οὐχ ὡς τοῦ θεοῦ λόγου παθόντος εἰς ἰδίαν φύσιν...ἀπαθὲς γὰρ τὸ θεῖον...ἐπειδὴ δὲ τὸ γεγονὸς αὐτοῦ ἴδιον σῶμα πέπονθεν ταῦτα, πάλιν αὐτὸς λέγεται παθεῖν...ἦν γὰρ ὁ ἀπαθὴς ἐν τῷ ~οντι σώματι id.*ep.*4(p.27.15; 5².23E); εἴ τις οὐχ ὁμολογεῖ τὸν τοῦ θεοῦ λόγον παθόντα σαρκί,...ἀνάθεμα ἔστω id.*ep.*17 *anath.*12(p.42.3; 5².77D); Thdot.Anc.*hom.*3.2(M.77.1385D); ἀπαθῶς αὐτὸν πεπονθέναι φαμέν [sc. monophysites]. καὶ τίς σωφρονῶν τῶν καταγελάστων τούτων ἀνάσχοιτ' ἂν γρίφων; ἀπαθὲς γὰρ πάθος οὐδεὶς ἀκήκοέ ποτε...τὸ γὰρ ἀπαθὲς οὐ πέπονθε καὶ τὸ πεπονθὸς οὐκ ἀπαθὲς μένοι ἄν Thdt.*eran.*3(4.216); Procl.CP *or.*11(M.65.784C); Leont.H.*Nest.*3.6(M.86.1617B); *ib.*7.2(1761Aff.); ὑποστάσει καὶ ὁ λόγος λέγεται παθεῖν· προσελάβετο γὰρ παθητὴν οὐσίαν εἰς τὴν ἑαυτοῦ ὑπόστασιν σὺν τῇ οἰκείᾳ τῇ ἀπαθεῖ· καὶ τὰ τῆς οὐσίας κατηγορήματα εἰώθει τῆς ὑποστάσεως κατηγορεῖσθαι ὀρθῶς *ib.*7.9(1768hA); ‡Hipp. *Ber.Hel.*1(p.321.24; M.10.832A); **c.** of Christ as God τοῦ πεπονθότος θεοῦ Tat.*orat.*13(p.15.5; M.6.836A); πίστευσον...τῷ παθόντι καὶ προσκυνουμένῳ, θεῷ ζῶντι πιστεύσατε οἱ δοῦλοι τῷ νεκρῷ Clem.*prot.*10 (p.76.15; M.8.224A; punctuation uncertain); **3.** of God; **a.** heret., Valent. παθεῖν αὐτὸν λέγουσιν ἀθέως. ὃ γὰρ συνεπάθησεν ὁ πατήρ, στερεὸς ὢν τῇ φύσει..., ἐνδόσιμον ἑαυτὸν παρασχών, ἵνα ἡ σιγὴ τοῦτο καταλάβῃ, πάθος ἐστίν. ἡ γὰρ συμπάθεια πάθος τινὸς διὰ πάθος ἑτέρου. ναὶ μὴν καὶ τοῦ πάθους γενομένου τὸ ὅλον συνεπάθησεν καὶ αὐτὸ εἰς διόρθωσιν τοῦ παθόντος Clem.*exc.Thdot.*30(p.116.26; M.9.673C);

Noëtus ἔπαθεν δὲ Χριστός, αὐτὸς ὢν θεός· ἄρα οὖν ἔπαθεν πατήρ, ⟨πατὴρ⟩ γὰρ αὐτὸς ἦν. ... ἀνάγκην...ἔχω, ἑνὸς ⟨θεοῦ⟩ ὁμολογουμένου, τοῦτον ὑπὸ πάθος φέρειν. Χριστὸς γὰρ ἦν θεὸς καὶ ἔπασχεν δι' ἡμᾶς αὐτὸς ὢν πατήρ Noëtus ap.Hipp.*Noët*.2(p.237.9,28; M.10.805B,C); Sabellian, Eus.*e.th*.1.4(p.64.17; M.24.833A); ἔσται οὖν ὁ πατὴρ... παθών *ib*.2.12(p.114.4; 925C); **b.** denied in generation of Son, ‡Ath. *dial.Trin*.1.10(M.28.1132C) (v. πάθος); Didym.(‡Bas.)*Eun*.5(1.316E; M.29.760B); **4.** of pagan gods; in argument against idolatry, Arist. *apol*.13.7.

B. *experience*; hence *receive, obtain* ὁ...ἀδικηθεὶς...εἰ προσελθὼν τῷ ἄρχοντι μὴ πάθῃ ἀπόκρισιν, προσίτω τῷ ἐπισκόπῳ Ath.Scholast. *coll*.1.3(p.15); *ib*.4.3(p.52).

***παταγητικός**, *chattering*, Clem.*paed*.2.10(p.209.6; M.8.500A).

***παταγίζω**, *be noisy*, Epiph.*exp.fid*.11(p.511.13, cj. for παταλιζόντων; καταλι- M.42.801B).

***παταγμός, ὁ**, *beating*, Cyr.*Ps*.68:27(M.69.1173A).

***πάταχρον, τό**, *idol* τὸν ἄρχοντα, καὶ τὰ πάτρια. ἔνια δὲ τῶν ἀντιγράφων πάταχρα ἔχει. ... τὸ...παταχρ(ὴ) (sic) Σύρων μέν ἐστιν ὄνομα· σημαίνει δὲ τῇ Ἑλλάδι φωνῇ τὰ εἴδωλα Thdt.*Is*.8:21(p.46.25; 2.230).

πατερεύω, *be a* pater civitatis, *IGC As.Min*.219.

***πατερικός**, *of the church fathers* πολλὰ π. ἀνέγνων Leont.N.*v.Jo. Eleem*.38(p.77.15); κηρύξας ἐκ π. μαρτυριῶν Anast.S.*serm.imag*.3(M. 89.1156B); Thphn.*chron*.p.375(M.108.900B).

πατ-έω, *tread*; *make to tread* ~ησον τοὺς πόδας σου εἰς τὸν τράχηλον αὐτοῦ *Ev.Barth*.(Vassiliev p.16); met., *treat with contempt* ὡς οὐδὲν ...ὄντα ~οῦσι Ath.*inc*.27.2(M.25.141D); τὸν διορισθέντα διὰ Μωσέως πεπάτηκε νόμον Cyr.*Jo*.12.1(4.1115A); id.*Lc*.20:20(M.72.889C); *rebut, confute* πᾶσαν αὐτοῦ ~εῖ τὴν αἵρεσιν τοῖς...λογισμοῖς Ath.*Dion*.19 (p.60.12; M.25.508B); τὴν...τερθρείαν πεπατηκὼς ‡Jo.D.*Artem*.34 (p.162.15; M.96.1281D); *do away with* τὴν ἀρχαίαν ~οῦντες διαφοράν Cyr.*Am*.6(3.259C); perf. ptcpl. pass., *humble, contemptible*, Chrys. *hom.11.2 in Col*.(11.407F); Cyr.*Os*.129(3.162C).

πατήρ, ὁ, *father*;

A. of men; **1.** in respectful address to seniors and persons of dignity: a philosopher, Just.*dial*.3.7(M.6.481D); an apostle, *A.Jo*. 81(p.191.4); *A.Xanthipp*.11(p.65.11); *A.Petr.et Andr*.1(p.117.9); a bishop, *M.Niceph*.2(p.284); Jo.Disc.*v.Epiph*.34(M.41.68C); any person of dignity, *ib*.; esp. a priest, *PLond*.1914.57(p.61) et freq.; monks, *V.Dan*.(p.388.13); **2.** as designation of apostles οἱ...π. ἡμῶν *1Clem*.62.2 (or perh. of patriarchs, v. A.6 infra); ἡμῶν Ἀνδρέας ὁ... π. καὶ διδάσκαλος καὶ ἰατρός *A.Andr*.A 9(p.52.3); of bishops ὁ τῆς Ἀσίας διδάσκαλος καὶ π. τῶν Χριστιανῶν *M.Polyc*.12.2; οὗτος κατὰ θεὸν π. ὑμῶν, δι' ὕδατος καὶ πνεύματος ἀναγεννήσας ὑμᾶς *Const.App*. 2.26.4; εἰσιὼν ὁ π. Chrys.*Jud*.6(1.614C); κοινός τίς ἐστι π. τῆς οἰκουμένης...ὁ ἱερεύς id.*hom.6.1 in 1Tim*.(11.578D); of abbots and ascetics, *PLond*.1918.1(p.86); Pall.*h.Laus*.17(M.34.1043A); of priests, Chrys.*hom.4.1 in Ac.9*:1(3.129D); of OT priests, Cyr.*hom.pasch*.7 (5^2.90A); of pagan high priest σε καταστήσας...ἀρχιερέα τῶν μεγάλων θεῶν, π. ἐμὸν ὀνομάσω ‡Jo.D.*Artem*.40(M.96.1288D); **3.** of fathers of Church τοὺς ἐκκλησιαστικοὺς π. ἀθετεῖ Eus.*Marcell*.1.4 (p.18.11; M.24.752B); τὸ ὄνομα τῆς οὐσίας διὰ τὸ ἁπλούστερον παρὰ τῶν π. τεθεῖσθαι *Symb.Sirm*.3(p.236.10; M.26.693B); π. ... τῶν κατὰ Νικαίαν ποτὲ τὸ μέγα τῆς εὐσεβείας ἐξαγγειλάντων κήρυγμα Bas.*ep*.52. 1(3.145A; M.32.392C); καταπεφρόνηται τὰ τῶν π. δόγματα· ἀποστολικαὶ παραδόσεις ἐξουδένωνται *ib*.90.2(182A; M.473B); Gr.Nyss.*ep.can*.(M. 45.225C); τὴν πίστιν τῶν π. τῶν τριακοσίων δεκαοκτὼ CCP(381)*can*.1; τῶν π. ὁ νόμος κελεύει μετὰ τὴν πεντηκοστὴν ἀποτίθεσθαι τὸ βιβλίον [sc. Acts] Chrys.*hom.1.3 in Ac.9*:1(3.102B); ἀναγίνωσκε δὲ τὴν νέαν διαθήκην, μαρτυρικὰ δέ, καὶ τοὺς βίους τῶν π. Nil.*epp*.4.1(M.79.545A); *Symb.Chalc*.(p.129.23; H.2.456B); in curses ἔχ(ο)ι τὴν ἀρὰν τῶ(ν) ἁγίω(ν) π(ατέ)ρ(ων) *Hesp*.16 p.29 (post saec. v); cf.*CG–CI* 1 p.41; **4.** of a spiritual father μαθητευομένους ἀπὸ τῶν π. κρύπτειν τοὺς ἰδίους λογισμούς ‡Ath.*ep.Cast*.1.4(M.28.856B); **5.** θεῖος π. *godfather*, Dion.Ar.*e.h*.7.3.11(M.3.568B); **6.** of Hebrew patriarchs ὁ π. ἡμῶν Ἰακὼβ *1Clem*.4.8; τοῖς π. ἡμῶν τοῖς δικαίοις *ib*.30.7; ἄνω μετὰ τῶν π. ἀναβιώσας *2Clem*.19.4; *Barn*.14.1; ‡*Diogn*.11.5; Eus.*e.th*.1.20(p.83. 32; M.24.869C); Proc.G.*Dt*.33:24(M.87.989A); ὀλίγοι τινὲς...οἱ π. ἐκ τοῦ φυσικοῦ νόμου κινούμενοι ἐγίνωσκον τὸν θεόν. οἷος ἦν ὁ Ἀβραάμ, καὶ οἱ λοιποὶ πατριάρχαι, καὶ Νῶε, καὶ Ἰακὼβ Dor.*doct*.1.1(M.88. 1620A); ἐκκλησία, ὅτε φθάσῃ ἡ ια' τοῦ Δεκεμβρίου μηνός, καὶ μετὰ τὴν γενέσθαι κυριακὴν ἑορτὴν ἑορτάζει τὴν μνήμην τῶν ἁγίων π. τῶν πρὸ τοῦ νόμου Jo.Nic.*nativ*.(M.96.1448C); exeg. Gen.15:15 with Mt. 19:27–29 εἴπερ δέ εἰσι π., περὶ ὧν εἴρηται τῷ Ἀβραάμ· σὺ δὲ ἀπελεύσῃ πρὸς τοὺς π. σου..., εἴποι ἄν τις...τάχα ἐκεῖνοι π. εἰσὶ μαρτυρήσαντές ποτε καὶ ἀφέντες τέκνα, ἀνθ' ὧν π. γεγόνασι πατέρων τοῦ πατριάρχου Ἀβραὰμ καὶ ἄλλων τοιούτων πατριαρχῶν Or.*mart*.14(p.14.27); **7.** π. πατέρων, title of pope, Thdr.Stud.*epp*.1.33(M.99.1017B); **8.** π. πατρίδος, pater patriae, *Chron.Pasch*.p.254(M.92.616C); **9.** π. πόλεως, pater civitatis, *M.Con*.2.1; **10.** *patrician* βασιλέως πατήρ Men.*exc. gent*.25(p.469.8; M.113.836B); ἐν τοῖς βασιλείοις π. τελῶν id.*exc.Rom*. 11(p.198.27; M.113.893B); **11.** *author*, Clem.*str*.1.19(p.60.18; M.8. 809B); δογμάτων π. Or.*Cels*.1.25(p.76.2; M.11.705C); π. τῆς πλάνης Meth.*res*.1.38(p.281.9; M.41.1105B); π. τοῦ λόγου Bas.*ep*.2.5(3.74A; M.32.229C); Nil.*sent*.50(M.79.1244D); Ἄρειος ὁ...βλασφημίας π. καὶ δημιουργός Thdt.*h.rel*.1(3.1113); ὁ π. τοῦ βιβλίου τούτου Jo.Philop. *arith*.(p.392); of Christ as π. ἀληθείας, *A.Thom*.A 26(p.142.3); of Devil as π. ἁμαρτίας, Gr.Nyss.*Eun*.12(2 p.278.3; M.45.889A); met., of a debtor φοβεῖται τοὺς μῆνας ὡς τόκων πατέρας Bas.*hom.in Ps*.14 (1.108E; M.29.268E).

B. theol.; of God the Father; **1.** def. π. μὲν οὖν κυρίως εἴρηται ἀναίτιος ὑπόστασις, γενητική, ἀγένητος. εἴρηται δὲ π., ἢ ὡς τὰ πάντα τηρῶν, ἢ ὡς τοὺς οἰκείους παῖδας τηρῶν, οἷον π. διττῶς δὲ λέγεται π. ὁ θεός, φύσει, καὶ χάριτι. φύσει μέν, τοῦ...θεοῦ λόγου· χάριτι δὲ καὶ ἡμῶν Anast.S.*hod*.2(M.89.53D); **2.** of God as universal father of all creation ὁ δημιουργὸς καὶ π. τῶν αἰώνων *1Clem*.35.3; δόξαν τῷ π. τῶν ὅλων Just.*1apol*.65.3(M.6.428A); ἁπάντων πατὴρ κατὰ τὴν δημιουργίαν Clem.*str*.3.12(p.236.22; M.8.1188C); Meth.*symp*.1.2(p.10.11; M. 18.41A); †Gregent.*disp*.1(M.86.625B); but fatherhood not dependent on Creation ἦν ἄρα καὶ πρὸ κόσμου...π. καὶ παντοκράτωρ καὶ δημιουργός Meth.*creat*.3(p.496.1; M.18.336B); **3.** as father of Christians, *1Clem*.23.1; Iren.*haer*.5.1.3(M.7.1123A); π. φιλόστοργος Clem.*paed*. 1.11(p.147.26; M.8.365B); θεοῦ τοῦ τροφέως καὶ π. τῶν γεννωμένων καὶ ἀναγεννωμένων *ib*.1.6(p.114.28; 300A); ἡμῶν ἐθέλει μόνων κεκλῆσθαι π., οὐ τῶν ἀπειθούντων id.*prot*.12(p.86.20; M.8.245A); αὐτὸς [sc. Christ] υἱοποίησεν ἡμᾶς τῷ π. Ath.*Ar*.1.38(M.26.92B); π. μὲν γὰρ τῶν δικαίων ὁ θεὸς οὐ κατὰ φύσιν, ἀλλὰ κατὰ χάριν· θεὸς δέ, ὡς ...δημιουργήσας αὐτούς †Gregent.*disp*.4(M.86.768B); ὁ Χριστὸς... μητέρα μόνον ἔχει ἐπὶ τῆς γῆς, καὶ ἡμεῖς π. μόνον ἔχομεν ἐν οὐρανῷ. λαβὼν γὰρ τὸν θνητὸν π. τῶν ἀνθρώπων, τὸν Ἀδάμ, ἔδωκε τοῖς ἀνθρώποις τὸν ἑαυτοῦ π. ἀθάνατον Justn.*conf*.(p.76.19; M.86.999A); in rel. to fatherhood of God in OT ἐπιτηρῆσαι τὴν...παλαιὰν διαθήκην, εἰ ἔστι που εὑρεῖν ἐν αὐτῇ εὐχήν τινος λέγοντος τὸν θεὸν π.·...ἐξετάσαντες οὐχ εὕρομεν, οὐ τοῦτο δέ φαμεν, ὅτι ὁ θεὸς π. οὐκ εἴρηται...ἀλλ' ὅτι ἐν προσευχῇ τὴν ἀπὸ τοῦ σωτῆρος κατηγγελμένην παρρησίαν περὶ τοῦ ὀνομάσαι τὸν θεὸν π. οὐχ εὕρομέν πω. ... καὶ εἰ λέγεται τοίνυν π. ὁ θεὸς...τὸ βέβαιόν γε καὶ τὸ ἀμετάπτωτον τῆς υἱότητος οὐκ ἔστιν ἰδεῖν παρὰ τοῖς ἀρχαίοις Or.*or*.22.1(p.346.14; M.11.481C); on Sabellian view that Logos became Son at Inc. μήπω δὲ ὄντος τοῦ λόγου υἱοῦ, οὐδέπω τις ἐγίνωσκε τὸν π.· πῶς οὖν Μωσεῖ, πῶς τοῖς π. ὤφθη; ‡Ath. *Ar*.4.23(p.70.8f.; M.26.501D); Basileidean αὐτοὺς εἶναι υἱούς φασιν, οἱ...εἰσιν ἐν κόσμῳ, ἵνα...ἀνέλθωσι πρὸς τὸν ἄνω π. Hipp.*haer*.10.14 (p.276.6; M.16.3430D); **4.** Trin., of first Person in rel. to second; **a.** in gen., Just.*1apol*.65.3(M.6.428A); cf. *per manus...patris, id est, per filium et spiritum*, Iren.*haer*.5.6.1(M.7.1137A); υἱὸς ἐν π., καὶ π. ἐν υἱῷ Clem.*paed*.1.5(p.104.14; M.8.277C); υἱὲ καὶ π., ἓν ἄμφω, κύριε *ib*. 3.12(p.291.1; 680B); οὐδὲ ὁ π. ἄνευ υἱοῦ· ἅμα γὰρ τῷ πατὴρ υἱοῦ πατήρ, υἱὸς δὲ περὶ πατρὸς ἀληθὴς διδάσκαλος id.*str*.5.1(p.326.10; M. 9.9A); δι' υἱοῦ ὁ π. γνωρίζεται *ib*.(p.334.8; 28A); πρόσωπον δὲ πατρὸς ὁ υἱὸς id.*exc.Thdot*.10(p.110.5; M.9.661A); τὸ δὲ πᾶν π., ἐξ οὗ δύναμις λόγος· οὗτος δὲ νοῦς, ὃς προβὰς ἐν κόσμῳ ἐδείκνυτο παῖς θεοῦ· πάντα τοίνυν δι' αὐτοῦ, αὐτὸς δὲ μόνος ἐκ π. Hipp.*Noët*.11(p.253.11; M.10. 817C); ὁ μὲν...π. συνέχων τὰ πάντα φθάνει εἰς ἕκαστον τῶν ὄντων... ἐλαττόνως δὲ παρὰ τὸν π. ὁ υἱὸς φθάνων ἐπὶ μόνα τὰ λογικά (δεύτερος γάρ ἐστι τοῦ π.) ... ὥστε κατὰ τοῦτο μείζων ἡ δύναμις τοῦ π. παρὰ τὸν υἱόν Or.*princ*.1.3.5(p.56.1; M.11.150B); οὗτος δὲ ὁ υἱὸς ἐκ θελήματος τοῦ π. ἐγενήθη...κτίσμα, σοφία *ib*.4.4.1(p.349.11); id.*Cels*.6.47(p.119. 3; M.11.1372C); φαμὲν τὸν υἱὸν οὐκ ἰσχυρότερον τοῦ π. ἀλλ' ὑποδεέστερον *ib*.8.15(p.233.7; 1537D); Dion.Al.ap.Ath.*Dion*.17(p.58.16; M.25.504D) cit. s. ἀδιαίρετος; λόγον δὲ ἐνεργῇ ἐξ οὐρανοῦ καὶ φύσιν ἐν αὐτῷ [sc. τῷ ἐκ τῆς παρθένου] ὁμολογεῖ, ἵνα εἷς εἴη...ὁ ἐπὶ πάντων θεός, ὁ π. Paul.Sam.*fr*.D 2(p.338.5); ὁ π. γὰρ ἅμα τῷ υἱῷ εἷς θεός, ὁ δὲ ἄνθρωπος κάτωθεν τὸ ἴδιον πρόσωπον ὑφαίνει *ib*.E 5 (p.338.27)ap.Epiph.*haer*.65.7(M.42.24B); τὸν ἁπάντων μείζονα τῶν ἄλλων μετὰ τὸν π. μόνῳ τῷ ἑαυτοῦ μείζονι π. χρήσασθαι μάρτυρι Meth. *symp*.7.1(p.71.16; M.18.124B); ὁ θεὸς ὁ παντοκράτωρ,...ὁ π. τοῦ Χριστοῦ id.*res*.1.56(p.317.7; M.41.1152B); ὁ υἱός, ἡ...κραταιὰ χεὶρ τοῦ π. id.*creat*.9(p.498.29; M.18.341A); ὁ μὲν γὰρ υἱὸς...εἰκών ἐστι τοῦ π. Eust.*fr.in Pr.8*:22(M.18.677D); for Marcellus' view of relation of Father to Son, v. υἱός; ὁ υἱὸς ἐκ τοῦ π. ἐκπορεύεσθαι λέγεται καὶ τὸ ἅγιον πνεῦμα ὁμοίως Eus.*e.th*.3.4(p.159.4; M.24.1005A); ἕν εἰσιν ὁ π. καὶ ὁ υἱὸς κατὰ τὴν κοινωνίαν τῆς δόξης *ib*.3.19(p.180.30; 1044C); τὸ γὰρ ἀτρέπτως π. ἰδεῖν υἱοῦ μόνου ἐστίν *Hom.Clem*.17.16; κἀμοὶ ἀπὸ τοῦ π. ἀπεκαλύφθη ὁ υἱός *ib.*17.18; ὁ...υἱός...γέννημα ἐκ τῆς οὐσίας τοῦ π. Ath.*decr.*3(p.3.11; M.25.'428'(420)D); id.*Ar.*1.28(M.26.69A) cit. s. ἁπλοῦς; ὁ μὲν υἱὸς ἐν τῷ π. ἐστιν, ὡς λόγος ἴδιος *ib.*3.24(373B); θελόμενός ἐστιν ὁ υἱὸς παρὰ τοῦ πατρός *ib.*3.66(461C); τὸ π. ἀεὶ π., καὶ τὸ υἱὸς ἀεὶ υἱός id.*ep.Serap.*1.16(M.26.569B); denial that, since Son is image of Father and Spirit is image of Son, οὐκοῦν κατὰ τοῦτο πάππος ὁ π. *ib.*4.3(641A); distn. bet. father and creator, id.*decr.*13 (p.11.30; '445'(437)C); κἂν π. ὀνομάζωμεν, ἔχομεν τῷ ὀνόματι τοῦ π. συνυπακουομένην τὴν ἔννοιαν τοῦ υἱοῦ (π. γὰρ υἱοῦ π. λέγεται) Geo. Laod.*ep.dogm.*ap.Epiph.*haer.*73.19(p.292.7; M.42.437C); πάντα ἐστὶν [sc. ὁ υἱός] ὅσα ἐστὶν ὁ π. Bas.*hom.*15.2(2.132A; M.31.468A); ὁ θεὸς καὶ π. τοῦ κυρίου ἡμῶν. ... πάλιν τὸ θεὸς διέλωμεν τοῦ π.· ἡμῶν γὰρ θεός, τοῦ δὲ κυρίου πατήρ Thdt.*2Cor.*11:31(3.347); **b.** in rel. to Christ's descent from David υἱὸς...Δαβὶδ ἐπὶ συντελείᾳ τῶν αἰώνων· ...δύο ἔχει πατέρας· ἕνα τὸν Δαβὶδ κατὰ σάρκα, καὶ ἕνα τὸν θεὸν πατέρα θεϊκῶς Cyr.H.*catech.*11.5; **c.** God's fatherhood of men by grace dist. from his natural fatherhood of Son, Justn.*conf.*(p.76.25; M. 86.999B); Anast.S.*hod.*2(M.89.53D); **d.** Sabellian οὐκ ἄλλο εἶναι π., ἄλλο δὲ υἱόν, ἓν δὲ καὶ τὸ αὐτὸ ὑπάρχειν Hipp.*haer.*9.12(p.248.27; M. 16.3383C); τὸν υἱὸν εἶναι τὸν π. Dion.R.ap.Ath.*decr.*26(p.22.7; M.25. 464A); as ascribed by Eus. to Marcell. θεὸν...ἑαυτοῦ π. καὶ αὖ πάλιν υἱὸν ἀποκαλεῖν ἑαυτοῦ Eus.*e.th.*1.1(p.63.2; M.24.829C); τὸν αὐτὸν εἶναι π. καὶ υἱόν *ib.*1.3(p.64.1; 832D); Σαβέλλιος...τὸν π. ... υἱὸν λέγειν ἐτόλμα *ib.*1.14(p.74.23; 853B); τὸν ἀχώρητον καὶ ἀπαθῆ π. χωρητὸν ἅμα καὶ παθητὸν διὰ τῆς ἐνανθρωπήσεως ὑποτίθενται· τοιοῦτοι γάρ εἰσιν οἱ Πατροπασσιανοὶ μὲν παρὰ Ῥωμαίοις, Σαβελλιανοὶ δὲ καλούμενοι παρ' ἡμῖν *Symb.Ant.*(345)7(p.253.16; M.26.732C); ὁ μὲν γὰρ Σαβέλλιος τὸν αὐτὸν ἔλεγε π. καὶ υἱὸν καὶ ἅγιον πνεῦμα, καὶ τριώνυμον πρᾶγμα ἔλεγε τὸν θεόν...ὁ δὲ Παῦλος, οὐ τὸν αὐτὸν ἔλεγε π. καὶ υἱὸν καὶ ἅγιον πνεῦμα· ἀλλὰ π. μὲν ἔλεγε τὸν θεὸν...υἱὸν δὲ τὸν ἄνθρωπον, πνεῦμα δὲ τὴν ἐπιφοιτήσασαν χάριν τοῖς ἀποστόλοις †Leont.B.*sect.*4.3 (M.86.1216A); **e.** Arian ξένος τοῦ υἱοῦ κατ' οὐσίαν ὁ π., ὅτι ἄναρχος ὑπάρχει Ar.*Thal.fr.*2.19 ap.Ath.*syn.*15(p.242.27; M.26.708A); οὐκ ἀεὶ ὁ θεὸς π. ἦν id.ap.Ath.*Ar.*1.9(M.26.29B); τὸ μὲν ἐν τῷ υἱῷ φῶς ἓν πρὸς τὸν π., αὐτὸς δὲ ξένος...ὡς κτίσμα id.ap.eund.*decr.*24(p.20.19; M.25. 460A); ὑπέστη δὲ βουλήσει τοῦ π. ὁ μονογενής, οὐ πρὸς τὴν οὐσίαν...εἰ δέ τις...ἐκβιάζοιτο...τὴν τοῦ π. προσηγορίαν οὐσίας εἶναι σημαντικήν, μεταδιδότω καὶ τῷ υἱῷ καὶ τῆς ὁμοίας φωνῆς, ᾧ προλαβὼν μετέδωκε καὶ τῆς ὁμοίας οὐσίας· μᾶλλον δὲ ἀμφοῖν ἑκατέρῳ, τῷ τε π. τῆς υἱοῦ, καὶ τῷ υἱῷ τῆς πατρός· ἡ γὰρ τῆς οὐσίας ὁμοιότης ταῖς αὐταῖς ὀνομάζειν προσηγορίαις ἀναγκάζει τοὺς ταύτην περὶ αὐτῶν ἔχοντας τὴν δόξαν Eun.*apol.*24(M.30.860B); id.ap.Gr.Nyss.*Eun.*12(2 p.276.28; M.45. 888B); μείζονα γὰρ εἰπὼν τὸν...π. τοῦ μονογενοῦς, καὶ τοῖς τὸ ἴσον λέγουσι μανίαν ἐπικαλέσας Bas.*Eun.*1.26(1.236C; M.29.569A); **f.** in implications of Nestorian teaching εἰ οὖν ἀδιάφορον αὐτῶν τὸ τῆς υἱότητος εἶδος...δύνανται δύο νοεῖσθαι διὰ τὴν ὁμοιότητα πρὸς ἄλληλα ὡς τὰ ὁμοειδῆ, καὶ ἡ σὰρξ φύσει υἱὸς τοῦ θεοῦ, ἢ καὶ ὁ λόγος χάριτι υἱὸς θεοῦ· ἔσται δὲ καὶ ὁ π. σάρξ· ὅμοια γὰρ τίκτει ἑαυτῷ κατ' οὐσίαν ὁ φύσει π.· εἰ οὖν σάρκα τέτοκε φύσει, καὶ σάρξ ἐστι φύσει· καὶ ὁ λόγος δὲ θεὸς ὢν φύσει, οὐ φύσει υἱός ἐστι τοῦ π., ἀλλὰ χάριτι σὺν τῇ σαρκί· οὐ θεὸς ἄρα ὁ π. ἐστιν, εἴτε οὖν ὅμοιοι εἴτε ἀνόμοιοί εἰσιν οἱ υἱοί Leont.H. *Nest.*4.13(M.86.1648D); **g.** in implications of monophysitism ἡ μία φύσις τοῦ...λόγου σεσαρκωμένη διαφέρει τῆς μιᾶς τοῦ...π. φύσεως τῆς μὴ σεσαρκωμένης, ἢ οὐχί;...εἰ μὲν οὖν φασι διαφέρειν, οὐχ ὁμοούσιος ἀληθῶς ἔσται τῷ π. υἱὸς διαφέρων αὐτοῦ κατὰ φύσιν...εἰ δὲ μὴ διαφέρειν ἐροῦσιν, ἄρα καὶ ἡ τοῦ π. μία φύσις σεσαρκωμένη id.*monoph.* 37(M.86.1792C); **5.** Valent., Iren.*haer.*1.5.1(M.7.492A,B); υἱὸν μονογενῆ...ἐν ᾧ τὰ πάντα ὁ π. προέβαλε σπερματικῶς *ib.*1.8.5(532B); *ib.*1. 14.5(604B); ἐκλαθόμενοι τῆς δόξης τοῦ θεοῦ παθεῖν αὐτὸν λέγουσιν ἀθέως. ὁ γὰρ συνεπάθησεν ὁ π., στερεὸς ὢν τῇ φύσει, φησὶν ὁ Θεόδοτος ..., ἐνδόσιμον ἑαυτὸν παρασχών, ἵνα ἡ σιγὴ τοῦτο καταλάβῃ, πάθος ἐστίν Clem.*exc.Thdot.*30(p.116.27; M.9.673C); Val.Gn.ap.Epiph.*haer.*31.5 (p.392.5; M.41.484A); **6.** Manich. τὸν υἱὸν αὐτοῦ ἀπέστειλεν ὁ ἀγαθὸς π. ἐκ τῶν κόλπων εἰς τὴν καρδίαν τῆς γῆς Hegem.*Arch.*8(p.11.12; M. 10.1437C); ὁ π. ὁ ζῶν *ib.*(p.12.7; 1440A); **7.** Montanist οὔτε ἄγγελος, οὔτε πρέσβυς, ἀλλ' ἐγὼ κύριος ὁ θεὸς πατὴρ ἦλθον Mont.*fr.*ap.Epiph. *haer.*48.11(p.235.2; M.41.872D).

C. of Christ π. ἐλεήμων, σωτὴρ Χριστέ *A.Thom.*A 97(p.210.8, v.l. καὶ σωτὴρ Χριστέ); τῶν αἰώνων τούτων πάντων π. ἐγώ εἰμι *A.Mt.*3 (p.220.4); π. τοῦ μέλλοντος αἰῶνος. ὥσπερ γὰρ ὁ Ἀδὰμ τοῦ παρόντος αἰῶνος π. ὀνομάζεται· οὕτως αὐτὸς τοῦ μέλλοντος Thdt.*Is.*9:5(p.50.1; 2.236).

D. of Devil as father of the wicked, *M.Tar.*3(p.455); and of demons, *A.Thom.*A 32(p.149.5).

***πατήτιον, τό,** *footmark*; constituting desecration, CSyr.*act.* (p.103.10; H.2.1381E).

πάτος, ὁ, upper *floor* of house, Philost.*h.e.*12.9(πάλων M.65.617C).

***πατρακού-ομαι,** *be heard as from the Father* μνήμην ὁ Χριστὸς τῶν βροτοσσόων ἐπῶν, ἃ ~σθεὶς τοῖς ἀποστόλοις ἔφη, τὸ πνεῦμα τεύχει γλωσσοπυρσεύτῳ θεῷ ἐφίζον Jo.D.*carm.pent.*107(p.217; M.96. 837B).

πατραλοίας, ὁ, *parricide*; of a sinner in that he despises the Father, Ast.Am.*prod.*(p.110.9).

πάτραρχος, ὁ, 1. *ancestor*, ref. Is.37:38 π. ..., ἕνα δηλονότι τῶν κατὰ σάρκα πατέρων ἢ πάππων αὐτοῦ Cyr.*Is.*3.4(2.493A); *ib.*3.5(514E); *Chron.Pasch.*p.116(M.92.304A); **2.** *patriarch*, Gr.Naz.*carm.*1.1.13.1 (M.37.475A); *ib.*1.2.1.301(545A); *ib.*2.1.11.53(1033A).

πατριά, ἡ, 1. *fatherhood*, Cyr.*Jo.*1.3(4.24B); θεία π. καὶ υἱότης Dion.Ar.*d.n.*2.8(M.3.645B); **2.** *kinship* μηδενὶ καταδεθέντα...πατριᾶς δεσμῷ πρὸς τοῦτον τὸν πλάνον κόσμον Max.*ep.*44(M.91.644C); **3.** *lineage* ἐπὶ τὸν ποιητὴν τὸν θεὸν πᾶσα ἀνατρέχει π. Clem.*str.*6.7 (p.461.20; M.9.280C); πᾶσα γὰρ ἀρχὴ πατριῶν τῶν ὡς πρὸς τὸν τῶν ὅλων θεὸν κατωτέρω ἀπὸ Χριστοῦ ἤρξατο τοῦ μετὰ τὸν τῶν ὅλων θεὸν καὶ πατέρα οὕτω πατρὸς ὄντος πάσης ψυχῆς Or.*princ.*4.3.7(p.333.21; M.11.388A); **4.** *family*, hence *group*, *class* πᾶσαι αἱ π. τῶν ἐθνῶν †Hipp.*theoph.*8(p.262.13; M.10.860B); μὴ τάγμα ἓν καὶ μία σύστασις καὶ φυλὴ καὶ π. τῶν ἀθανάτων Meth.*res.*1.49(p.302.15; M.18.277B); id.*symp.*7.3(p.73.21; M.18.128C); π. δὲ ὀνομάζει, τὸ σύστημα τῶν εἰς τὸν θεῖον κατάλογον συντελούντων Gr.Nyss.*Pss.titt.*A 8(M.44.480C); πατριὰς νοητέον τὰς τάξεις...χερουβίμ, σεραφίμ, κτλ. Max.*schol.d.n.* 19.3(M.4.196B).

πατριάζω, = πατρῴζω, *take after one's father*, Cyr.*Am.*56(3.311A).

***πατριαρχεῖον, τό, 1.** *residence of patriarch*, Jo.Mal.*chron.*18 p.468(M.97.681C); Tim.CP *haer.*(M.86.45B); *V.Dan.*(p.381.10); **2.** *patriarchal see* σύνοδός ἐστιν ὅτε τὰ πέντε π. θεσπίσουσι μίαν πίστιν ‡Jo.D.*Const.*16(M.95.332D).

***πατριαρχ-έω,** *be patriarch* (of) πατριαρχῆσαι Κωνσταντινουπόλεως Thphn.*chron.*p.302(M.108.737A); πατριάρχην...ἀνάξιον τοῦ ~εῖν ‡Jo.D.*Const.*16(M.95.333A).

πατριάρχης, ὁ, *patriarch*;

A. of Hebrew patriarchs; as recipients of revelation of Logos, Iren.*haer.*3.11.8(M.7.888B); Thdt.*Trin.*7(M.75.1153D); ass. Church in reception of divine promises, Clem.*str.*2.6(p.128.18; M.8.964C); ass. prophets as being saints of pre-Christian era and as knowing and foretelling Christ, Just.*dial.*26.1(M.6.532A); *ib.*80.2(664B); cf. *per patriarchas suos et prophetas praefigurans* [sc. *Christus*]...*futura*, Iren.*haer.*4.21.3(M.7.1046A); *ib.*4.23.1(1047D); Clem.*str.*7.11(p.45.19; M.9.488B); id.*ecl.*52(p.151.21; M.9.721B); Or.*Jo*6.19(11; p.128.12; M. 14.233B); Eus.*e.th.*2.9(p.109.34; M.24.917D); Ath.*inc.*36.4(M.25.157C); their virtues, Gr.Nyss.*v.Mos.*(M.44.392C); as recipients of divine Spirit, like bishops, Serap.*euch.*28.1; Gr.Nyss.*Eun.*2(1 p.245.6; M.45.944D); *Const.App.*2.55.1; *Lit.*ap.*Const.App.*8.12.43; *Lit.Jac.* (p.212.17); their πολιτεία contrasted with that of priests, Scribes, and Pharisees, and represented at Inc. by the shepherds, Or.*schol. in Lc.*1:46(M.17.324B); their number discussed in rel. to that of twelve apostles and twelve wells of Elim, Eus.*e.th.*3.3(p.149.17; M.24.988D); raised from dead by Christ, *A.Andr.et Mt.*15(p.83.3); contrasted with spiritual ancestry of Christians, Or.*princ.*4.3.7 (p.333.15; M.11.388B).

B. of head of Jewish community, Epiph.*haer.*30.4(p.338.21; M. 41.409D); office hereditary, *ib.*30.6(p.341.15; 413D); cf.*ib.*30.7(p.342. 1; 416B); cf.*Cod.Thds.*16.8.1,2,8; Pall.*v.Chrys.*15(p.90.23; M.47.51).

C. in Church; **1.** of senior bishops in gen. πρεσβυτέρων ἐπισκόπων ...οἰκειότερον δὲ πατριαρχῶν εἰπεῖν, σφαγάς Gr.Naz.*or.*42.23(M.36. 485B); of Basil νέον Ἀβραὰμ καὶ π. ἡμέτερον *ib.*43.37(545C); of fathers of Church, *M.Thdot.1* 15(p.70.29); *ib.1* 19(p.73.20); **2.** of patriarchs, chief bishops of imperial dioceses πατριάρχας κατέστησαν [sc. bishops at CCP(381)] διανειμάμενοι τὰς ἐπαρχίας...καὶ κληροῦται Νεκτάριος μὲν τὴν Μεγαλόπολιν καὶ τὴν Θρᾴκην· τῆς δὲ Ποντικῆς διοικήσεως Ἑλλάδιος...Γρηγόριος ὁ Νύσσης...καὶ Ὀτήριος...τὴν πατριαρχίαν ἐκληρώσατο Socr.*h.e.*5.8.14(M.67.577C) where Socr. prob. confuses action of CCP with law of 30th July, 381 (cf.*Cod. Thds.*16.1.3) and perh. confuses π. in sense C.1 with π. in sense C.2; οἱ ὁσιώτατοι π. διοικήσεως ἑκάστης CChalc.*act.*2(p.78.26; H.2. 285B); CTrull.*can.*7; of Rome τῷ ἁγιωτάτῳ καὶ μακαριωτάτῳ οἰκουμενικῷ ἀρχιεπισκόπῳ καὶ π. τῆς μεγάλης Ῥώμης Λέοντι Isch.*libell.* (p.17.11; H.2.325B); Λέοντα τὸν π. Ῥώμης Leont.H.*monoph.*(M. 86.1876D); Jo.Nic.*nativ.*(M.96.1445B); ‡Jo.D.*Const.*15(M.95.332B); patriarch of CP as οἰκουμενικὸς π. Justn.*nov.*7 proem.(p.48.16); *ib.* 16 proem.(p.115.27); cf. ἐκκλησίας...ὑπὸ τὸν πατριαρχικὸν θρόνον τῆς ...πόλεως [sc. CP] καθεστώσας, ὧν τοὺς μητροπολίτας αὐτὸς χειροτονεῖ *ib.*7.1(p.52.2); Cyr.S.*v.Sab.*71(p.173.15); CTrull.*can.*2; of Jerusalem,

Cyr.S.*v.Sab.*71(p.173.12); *ib.*30(p.115.16); Jo.Mosch.*prat.*149(M.87.3013B); ref. S. James, *Chron.Pasch.*p.246(M.92.592A); of Antioch, Cyr.S.*v.Sab.*85(p.191.1); of Alexandria, Leont.N.*v.Jo.Eleem.*1(p.5.17); *ib.*27(p.59.3); of old and new Rome, Alexandria, and Antioch, Eustrat.*v.Eutych.*29(M.86.2308C); in liturg. commemoration, *Lit. Jac.*(p.220.20); **3.** of highest officers of Montanist church, cf.Hier. *ep.*41.3(M.*PL.*22.476); *Inscr.* in *Byzantion* 8, 1933 (p.70).

***πατριαρχία, ἡ, 1.** *paternity, fatherhood,* Epiph.*haer.*55.3(p.328.4; M.41.976B); ref. Adam, id.*exp.fid.*4(p.499.22; M.42.780A); divine πᾶσα θεία πατριὰ...ἐκ τῆς πάντων ἐξῃρημένης π.... δεδώρηται...ἡμῖν Dion.Ar.*d.n.*2.8(M.3.645C); **2.** *lineage* φυλήν τε καὶ π. Epiph.*haer.*8.9 (p.196.23; M.41.221D); *descent from father to son, generation* ἑξήκοντα καὶ δύο γενεαί τε καὶ π. id.*exp.fid.*4(p.499.29; M.42.780B); id. *haer.*39.2(p.72.24; M.41.668B); **3.** *position of authority,* Bas.*ep.*149(3.258C; M.32.641D); Gr.Naz.*carm.*2.1.12.799(M.37.1224A); Socr.*h.e.*5.8.15(M.67.580A); **4.** *patriarchate, office of patriarch;* **a.** of headship of Jewish community, Epiph.*haer.*30.7(p.341.30; M.41.416B); **b.** Christian, Jo.Mosch.*prat.*149(M.87.3013B); Thphn.*chron.*p.302 (M.108.736B).

πατριαρχικός, *patriarchal;* **1.** ref. OT patriarchs Ῥαχὴλ...ψυχὴ π. Gr.Naz.*or.*45.21(M.36.652B); τὸν π. λόγον Mac.Mgn.*apocr.*3.13(p.89.13); τὴν π. δόξαν ἀπώλεσε [sc. Esau] Ast.Am.*hom.*14(M.40.376C); Isid.Pel.*epp.*2.47(M.78.489A); Ἰακὼβ ὁ πατριαρχικώτατος Thdr. Stud.*nativ.BMV* 3(M.96.681C); **2.** ref. Christian patriarchs ἡ τάξις ἡ π. Eustrat.*v.Eutych.*39(M.86.2320C); τὸ π. δίκαιον *patriarchal status,* taken from Ephesus by CChalc. and restored by Basiliscus, Evagr.*h.e.*3.6(p.106.13; M.86.2609A); π. θρόνος [i.e. of Antioch] Alex.Sal.*Barn.*37(p.449D); of a monastery directly dependent on patriarchate of CP μονὴ...π. *IGC As.Min.*232 (Myndos, ? saec. vii).

πατρίκιος, ὁ, *patrician* (i.e. one possessing rank created by Constantine in imitation of ancient patrician order and granted to highest dignitaries), Ath.*apol.sec.*76(p.156.17; M.25.385C); Philost. *h.e.*8.8(M.65.361C); Thphn.*chron.*p.170(M.108.452B).

πατρικός, A. *of one's father;* hence **1.** *ancestral* π. καὶ ὑλικοὶ θεοί Just.*dial.*134.5(M.6.788B); of eccl. tradition, Bas.*ep.*243.2(3.373C; M.32.904C); **2.** *of* God *the Father;* **a.** in gen. τὰ ἀποστάντα τοῦ π. φωτός Iren.*haer.*4.39.3(M.7.1111B); Clem.*paed.*1.6(p.117.22; M.8.304C); π. θεότητι ἕλκει πρὸς ἑαυτὸν τὰ πρόβατα Apoll.*fr.*99(p.230.25) ap.Gr.Nyss.*Apoll.*58(M.45.1265B); Chrys.*hom.79.2 in Mt.*(7.760E); **b.** Trin., in respect of various divine attributes and activities, e.g. will ἔχει [sc. ὁ υἱός] πάντα προσονομάζεσθαι ἔκ τε τοῦ ὑπηρετεῖν τῷ π. βουλήματι Just.*dial.*61.1(M.6.613C); Χριστῷ ἡ τροφὴ τῆς π. βουλῆς ἡ τελείωσις ἦν Clem.*paed.*1.6(p.117.19; M.8.304C); Or.*Jo.*13.36(p.261.17; M.14.461C); Eus.*e.th.*1.13(p.73.34; M.24.852C); υἱόν, νεύματι π. παραγενόμενον ἐκ τῶν οὐρανῶν *Symb.Sirm.*3(p.235.31; M.26.693A); γεννητῇ [sc. οὐσίᾳ] καὶ νόμοις π. δουλευούσῃ Eun. *apol.*20(M.30.856A); τὴν τοῦ υἱοῦ κρίσιν τοῦ π. μὴ ἀπηλλοτριῶσθαι βουλήματος Gr.Nyss.*tres dii*(M.45.128B); power διὰ τῆς π. δυνάμεως γνωρίζειν τὸν υἱόν Clem.*str.*6.15(p.499.4; M.9.357A); ὅλης τῆς π. δυνάμεως ἐναποκειμένης αὐτῷ Bas.*Eun.*1.23(1.234D; M.29.564B); glory, Didym.*Trin.*1.32(M.39.429A) cit. s. δόξα; π. δόξης ἀπαύγασμα Procl. CP *annunt.*2(M.85.429A); goodness ἐκ τῆς πηγῆς τῆς π. ἀγαθότητος προελθόντα Bas.*Eun.*2.25(1.261E; M.29.629B); wisdom; of Christ as σοφία π., Clem.*paed.*1.11(p.148.4; M.8.365C); throne αὐτὸς...ἔμελλε καθιεῖσθαι ἐπὶ τοῦ θρόνου τοῦ π. Chrys.*hom.86.2 in Jo.*(8.515C); bosom ἐκεῖνος ὃν οὐδεὶς...βαστάσαι ἰσχύει εἰ μὴ ὁ κόλπος ὁ π. *A.Xanthipp.*15(p.69.9); τέλειος ἐκ τῶν π. προελθὼν κόλπων Chrys. *hom.30.1 in Jo.*(8.171A); light υἱὸν ἀπαύγασμα τοῦ π. φωτός Eus. *e.th.*1.20(p.92.23; M.24.885B); grace μόνῳ...ἔπρεπεν τῷ υἱῷ...τὴν π. ...εὐαγγελίσασθαι χάριν id.*Marcell.*1.1(p.3.13; M.24.716B); loving kindness ἡ π. φιλανθρωπία τὸν...μονογενῆ παῖδα ἐπὶ πᾶσιν καθίστη id.*e.th.*1.13(p.73.7; 849D); thought οὐδὲν ἐκτὸς τῶν π. νοημάτων φθέγγεσθαι [sc. τὸν υἱόν] Chrys.*hom.53.2 in Jo.*(8.311E); voice ἡ π. φωνὴ ...μαρτυροῦσα, οὗτος ἐστὶν ὁ υἱός Eus.*e.th.*1.9(p.67.26; 840B); unction (with H. Ghost) ὁ διὰ τὸ χρῖσμα τὸ π. Χριστὸς ἀνηγορευμένος *ib.*1.20(p.95.22; 892B); in respect of essence αὐτὸ τὸ εἶναι τοῦ υἱοῦ ἴδιον τῆς π. οὐσίας ἐστὶ γέννημα Ath.*Ar.*3.6(M.26.333A); ‡Gr.Nyss.*Ar.et Sab.*6(M.45.1289A); nature ἡ ἀναλλοίωτος αὐτοῦ π. φύσις Ath.*Ar.*1.40(M.26.93B); θεὸς ὁ υἱὸς π. φύσει Didym.(‡Bas.)*Eun.*5(1.310C; M.29.744C); form τὸ ἐν αὐτῷ π. εἶδος δείκνυσιν ἐν αὐτῷ τὸν πατέρα Ath. *Ar.*3.6(M.26.332C); Godhead αὐτὸν ὄψονται ἐρχόμενον μετὰ δόξης... τῆς π. δηλαδὴ θεότητος Eus.*fr.Lc.*21:28(M.24.600A); τὸ πλήρωμα τῆς π. θεότητος καὶ...υἱὸν θεοῦ ὑπεστήσατο id.*e.th.*1.2(p.63.21; M.24.832B); π. πληρώσεως Sophr.H.*ep.syn.*(M.87.3196C); property ἦν...πρὶν ἄνθρωπος γένηται, προσκυνούμενος...κατὰ τὴν π. ἰδιότητα Ath.*Ar.*1.42(M.26.97C); Cyr.*Jo.*1.9(4.100A); of Logos as π., Ath.*inc.*1.3(M.25.97B); Epiph.*haer.*51.28(p.299.18; M.41.937A); of H. Ghost as πνεῦμα π., *Ep.Lugd.*ap.Eus.*h.e.*5.1.34(M.20.421A, v.l. παράκλητον); **3.** *of a* spiritual *father* σπλάγχνοις π. κινουμένων Gr.Naz.*or.*27.2(p.3.14; M.36.13B); Chrys.*hom.29.5 in 2Cor.*(10.646E); id.*comm.in Gal.*4:19(10.708B); id.*hom.4.3 in 2Thess.*(11.434E); ref. a religious superior π. νουθεσίας Nil.*Eulog.*15(M.79.1113B); of a bishop, Euthal.*Ac.*proem. (M.85.629C); complimentary, of bishops τὴν ὑμετέραν...π. ἁγιότητα Sophr.H.*ep.syn.*(M.87.3196B); π. ἁγιωσύνης Max.*ep.*7(M.91.433A); **4.** *of the fathers of the Church, patristic* διδασκαλίαν π. Leont.H. *monoph.*(M.86.1804D); *ib.*(1817A); π. ἀληθείας Leont.B.*Nest.et Eut.*2(M.86.1356A); Max.*opusc.*(M.91.32C); Anast.S.*hod.*3(M.89.92A); εὐαγγελικῶν καὶ π. διδαγμάτων *Chron.Pasch.*p.5(M.92.80A); **5.** as subst., as name of Valent. aeon Π. καὶ Ἔλπις Iren.*haer.*1.1.2(M.7.449B); Epiph.*haer.*31.2(p.386.10; M.41.477A); one of male aeons, Val.Gn.ap.Epiph.*haer.*31.5(p.392.9; M.41.484A).

B. *with a father, concerned with* or *respecting a father,* Christol. πατρικῆς ἐστιν ἰσότητος Proc.G.*Gen.*1:9(M.87.77C); in gen., Thdt. *serm.Chrys.*(5.103); τιμὴν...π. Dor.*doct.*4.2(M.88.1660B).

πατρικῶς, 1. *like a father, in a fatherly manner;* in gen., Chrys. *hom.9.1 in Phil.*(11.264F); of God towards man, Gr.Naz.*carm.*1.2.8.77(M.37.654A); Trin. τῶν αὐτῶν πραγμάτων τοὺς τύπους ἐνσημαίνεται μὲν ὁ πατήρ, ἐπιτελεῖ δὲ ὁ λόγος, οὐ δουλικῶς ἀλλὰ...δεσποτικῶς, καὶ οἰκειότερον εἰπεῖν, π. id.*or.*30.11(p.124.17; M.36.117B); in anonymous accusation against Basil of following Apollinarius περιφέρουσι σύνταγμα ἐξ οὗ...ἡμᾶς καταδικάζουσιν...ἔχον ῥήσεις τοιαύτας·...ὡς βιαιότερον σημᾶναι τὸ ἄρρητον, τὸν πατέρα π. υἱὸν εἶναι· τὸν δὲ υἱὸν υἱϊκῶς πατέρα Bas.*ep.*129.1(3.220D; M.32.557C); reproduced as teaching of Apoll., Tim.CP *haer.*(M.86.40A); ref. Inc., Jo.D.*hom.*1.18(M.96.573B) cit. s. δεσποτικῶς; **2.** *from the fathers, patristically* γραφικῶς καὶ π. δέδεικται Max.*ambig.*(M.91.1089A); Anast.Ant.*fr.*3 (M.89.1284C); Anast.S.*hod.*22(M.89.292C); Thdr.Stud.*epp.*1.48(M.99.1080C); *by the fathers, ib.*1.10(944B).

***πατριμόνιον, τό,** (Lat. *patrimonium*) *patrimony,* Ath.Scholast. *coll.*4.13(p.58).

πάτριος, 1. *ancestral* οὐδεὶς...νόμῳ καὶ φόβῳ δίκης, κἂν γελοῖα ᾖ, μὴ στέργειν τὰ π. εἴργεται Athenag.*leg.*1.1(M.6.889A); of paganism τὰ π. ... ἔθη Clem.*prot.*10(p.70.17; M.8.209B); Χριστιανοὺς δὲ τὰ π. καταλιπόντας καὶ οὐχ ἕν τι τυγχάνοντας ἔθνος ὡς Ἰουδαῖοι ἐγκλήτως προστίθεσθαι τῇ τοῦ Ἰησοῦ διδασκαλίᾳ Cels.ap.Or.*Cels.*5.35(p.38.11; M.11.1233D); Or.*Cels.*8.47(p.262.14; 1588A); Gr.Thaum.*pan.Or.*5 (p.10.27; M.10.1064B); καταλιπὼν μὲν τὰ π., ἀποκλίνας δὲ εἰς ἔθη βάρβαρα *Hom.Clem.*4.7; οὐκ ἔστι ῥᾳδίως ἀποδύσασθαι τὴν π. διδασκαλίαν *ib.*4.11; Eus.*p.e.*1.5(16C; M.21.48A); Juln.Imp.ap.Cyr.*Juln.*7(6^2.238A); π. εἴδωλον Petr.II Al.*encycl.*ap.Thdt.*h.e.*4.22.13(M.33.1281A); **2.** theol., *of the Father* τὴν π. τοῦ θεοῦ βούλησιν Clem.*prot.*1(p.6.10; M.8.57D).

***πατριότης, ἡ,** *fatherliness,* as courtesy title of address to clergy, *PLond.*1916.31.

***πατριπροβλήτως,** v. *πατροπροβλήτως.

πατρίς, ἡ, *fatherland, native country;* **1.** in gen. π. οἰκοῦσιν [sc. Christians] ἰδίας, ἀλλ' ὡς πάροικοι...πᾶσα ξένη π. ἐστιν αὐτῶν, καὶ πᾶσα π. ξένη *Diogn.*5.5; γαμητέον οὖν πάντως καὶ τῆς π. ἕνεκα Clem. *str.*2.23(p.190.15; M.8.1089B); εἰ δὲ βούλεται ἡμᾶς ὁ Κέλσος καὶ στρατηγεῖν ⟨ὑπὲρ⟩ πατρίδος, ἴστω ὅτι καὶ ταῦτα ποιοῦμεν...ἐν γὰρ τῷ κρυπτῷ ἡμῶν...εὐχαί εἰσιν, ἀναπεμπόμεναι ὡς ἀπὸ ἱερέων ὑπὲρ τῶν ἐν τῇ π. ἡμῶν. Χριστιανοὶ δὲ μᾶλλον εὐεργετοῦσι τὰς π. ἢ οἱ λοιποὶ τῶν ἀνθρώπων, παιδεύοντες τοὺς πολίτας καὶ εὐσεβεῖν διδάσκοντες εἰς τὸν πολιέα θεόν Or.*Cels.*8.74(p.291.18; M.11.1629A); **2.** of Christians' spiritual fatherland οὐρανὸς μέν σοι ἡ π. Clem.*prot.*10(p.77.16; M.8.225A); προτρέπει δὲ ἡμᾶς Κέλσος καὶ ἐπὶ τὸ ἄρχειν τῆς π. ... ἡμεῖς δὲ ἐν ἑκάστῃ πόλει ἄλλο σύστημα πατρίδος κτισθὲν λόγῳ θεοῦ ἐπιστάμενοι τοὺς δυνατοὺς...ἐπὶ τὸ ἄρχειν ἐκκλησιῶν παρακαλοῦμεν...καὶ...ἄρχουσιν οἱ καλῶς ἄρχοντες ἐν τῇ ἐκκλησίᾳ τῆς κατὰ θεὸν π. Or.*Cels.*8.75(p.292.2; M.11.1629B); γῆν τὴν ἀγαθὴν ἔνθα μοι οὖσα ἡ ἀγαθὴ π. ἠγνοεῖτο πάλαι Gr.Thaum.*pan.Or.*16(p.36.8; M.10.1097A); ἔστι γάρ μοι π. ... ᾧ πᾶσα π., καὶ οὐδεμία; οὐκ ἐπαινῶ σου τὴν κατοικίαν, ἂν οὕτως ἔχῃς, μὴ τῆς ἀληθινῆς π. ἐκπέσῃς Gr.Naz.*or.*26.14(M.35.1248A); εἰς γὰρ τὸν οὐρανόν τις ἰδὼν καὶ τὰ ἐν αὐτῷ κάλλη...ταῦτα τῆς ἡμετέρας π. εὑρήσει τὰ διηγήματα Gr.Nyss.*v.Gr.Thaum.*(M.46.896C); ἔχομεν π., ἀλλ' οὐ τὴν ὄντως π. Chrys.*hom.24.2 in Heb.*(12.223A); **3.** of Christ's π. (Mt.13:53 etc.): ζητητέον...πότερον Νάζαρα λέγει τὴν π. αὐτοῦ ἢ Βηθλεέμ· Νάζαρα μὲν διὰ τὸ Ναζωραῖος κληθήσεται, Βηθλεὲμ δὲ ἐπεὶ ἐν αὐτῇ γεγέννηται...π. δὲ ὠνομάκασι διά τι μυστικῶς ἐν τῷ τόπῳ περὶ τῆς π. αὐτοῦ δηλούμενον ὅλης οὔσης τῆς Ἰουδαίας, ἐν ᾗ ἠτίμωται...καὶ ἐάν τις κατανοήσῃ Ἰησοῦν...Ἰουδαίοις μὲν σκάνδαλον...ἐν δὲ τοῖς ἔθνεσι...πεπιστευμένον...ὄψεται ὅτι Ἰησοῦς ἐν μὲν τῇ ἰδίᾳ π. τιμὴν οὐκ εἶχε, παρὰ δὲ τοῖς ξένοις τῶν διαθηκῶν τιμᾶται, τοῖς ἔθνεσι Or.*comm. in Mt.*10.16(p.21.1; M.13.873D); χρὴ γὰρ π. νομίζειν αὐτῶν [sc. προφητῶν] τὴν Ἰουδαίαν καὶ συγγενεῖς τὸν Ἰσραὴλ ἐκεῖνον, οἰκίαν δὲ τάχα τὸ σῶμα *ib.*10.18(p.23.10; 880B); π. μὲν γὰρ τῶν προφητῶν ὁ ἐκ περιτομῆς λαός, παρ' οἷς οὐκ εἰσι δεκτοί id.*hom.33 in Lc.*(p.197.5; M.13.1884D); ref. Jo.4:44 εἰ μὲν γὰρ ἦν π. αὐτοῦ ἡ Σαμάρεια...ἀκολούθως ἂν εἴρητο τό αὐτὸς γὰρ Ἰησοῦς ἐμαρτύρησεν ὅτι προφήτης...τιμὴν οὐκ ἔχει. ἀλλὰ καὶ εἰ ἐγέγραπτο...ἐξῆλθεν εἰς τὴν Γαλιλαίαν, ἀλλ' οὐκ ἐγένετο ἐν τῇ ἰδίᾳ π. ... καὶ οὕτως χώραν τὸ λεγόμενον εἶχεν ἄν. καὶ τάχα τὸ μὲν βούλημα τοῦ ῥητοῦ τοῦτ' ἔστιν, ὡς ἰδιώτης δὲ τῷ λόγῳ ὁ Ἰωάννης δυσπαραστάτως ἔφρασεν ὃ νενόηκεν...π. δὲ τῶν προφητῶν ἐν τῇ Ἰουδαίᾳ ἦν id.*Jo.*13.54(53; p.284.3; M.14.500C); Judaea as π. of Christ and prophets; rejected by Jews, id.*fr.60 in Jo.*(p.532.12); π. αὐτὸν ἐνταῦθα ἡγοῦμαι λέγειν τὴν Καπερναούμ...π. δὲ ἰδίαν καλεῖ, τὸν τῆς οἰκονομίας δηλῶν λόγον, καὶ τούτῳ τὸ πλέον ἐνδιατρίβων Chrys.*hom.35.2 in Jo.*(8.203B); ref. Ac.2:22 τὴν π. λέγει, ἥπερ ἐδόκει εὐτελὴς εἶναι id.*hom.6.1 in Ac.*(9.47D); **4.** *land* in gen., Mac.Aeg. *hom.*12.12(M.34.564D); Euthal.Diac.*epp.Paul.*(M.85.724C); Agath. *v.Gr.Ill.*157(p.80).

***πατρογέννητος**, *begotten of the Father* γνώρισμα, πνεῦμα πατρογεννήτου λόγου Jo.D.*carm.pent.*78(p.216; -γένη- M.96.836C).

***πατρόδοτος**, *given by one's father, ancestral*, Vergil *ecl.*4.18 ap. Const.*or.s.c.*20(p.183.5; M.20.1293B).

***πατροδότωρ, ὁ**, *giver of fatherhood* (ref. Marcosian heresy) τὸν αὐτογεννήτορα καὶ π. λόγον ἀπὸ στομάτων Ἀληθείας ἄκουε Iren.*haer.* 1.14.3(M.7.601B) = Hipp.*haer.*6.44(M.16.3267B; προπάτορα p.177.9).

***πατροείκελος**, *like one's father*, Thdr.Stud.*or.*11.4(M.99.824D).

***πατρόθεος**, *who is ancestor of God*; of David, ‡Jo.D.*hom.*5(M.96. 649D).

***πατροθετ-έομαι**, *become father by adoption*, ref. Ps.26:10 ὁ δὲ κύριος προσλαμβάνεται...υἱοθετῶν τοὺς ἀξίους, καὶ τοῖς ἀξίοις ~ούμενος Max.*ambig.*(M.91.1121B).

***πατροκελεύστως**, *by paternal order*, *Hymn.*(*AS* 1 p.611).

***πατροκίνητος**, *moved by the Father*, Dion.Ar.*c.h.*1.1(M.3.120B).

***πατρολύμας, ὁ**, *one who wrongs one's father, unfilial person* ἵνα μὴ ἀντίθεον αὐτὸν ἢ π. οἰηθῶσι..., φησίν· οὐδὲν δύναται ὁ υἱὸς ποιεῖν ἀφ' ἑαυτοῦ ‡Caes.Naz.*dial.*130(M.38.1032).

***πατρομαχία, ἡ**, *disagreement with the fathers*, Thdr.Stud.*epp.*2. 155(M.99.1484D).

***πατρομιμήτως**, *after the manner of the fathers*, Thdr.Stud.*test.*19 (M.99.1821A); id.*epp.*1.10(M.99.941D).

πατροπαράδοτος, 1. *ancestral, handed down from ancestors*; **a.** of tradition; of pagan belief π. γνώμης Thphl.Ant.*Autol.*2.34(M.6. 1108A); *A.Jo.*3(p.152.27); Eus.*l.C.*10(p.222.13; M.20.1372C); Ammon. *Ac.*13:48(M.85.1544B); of Egyptian worship of infant, handed down by tradition from Jeremiah, ‡Epiph.*v.proph.Jer.*8(p.21.10; M.43. 400B); of eccl. custom, Dion.Al.ap.Eus.*h.e.*4.23.10(M.20.388B); of Pharisaic tradition, Ant.Mon.*hom.*28(M.89.1529A); **b.** of original sin, Olymp.*Job* 41:6–7(M.93.441B); **2.** *given by the Father*, ‡Hipp. *fr.17 in Pss.*(p.145.17).

***πατροπαραδότως**, *as handed down from one's forefathers* in the faith κελευσάτω παρὰ τῆς πρεσβυτέρας Ῥώμης δέξασθαι τὴν διασάφησιν, ὡς ἄνωθέν τε καὶ ἐξ ἀρχῆς π. ἐξεδόθη Thdr.Stud.*epp.*2.87(M. 99.1332B); π. ἤτοι θεοκηρύκτως *ib.*2.121(1397C); id.*test.*(M.99.1816B); *by patristic tradition*, Areth.*Apoc.*1:4f.(M.106.508B).

***Πατροπασσιανοί, οἱ**, *Patripassians* οἱ Π. μὲν παρὰ Ῥωμαίοις, Σαβελλιανοὶ δὲ καλούμενοι παρ' ἡμῖν *Symb.Ant.*(345)7(p.253.18; M. 26.732C).

πατροπάτωρ, ὁ, *father of the fathers* π. Ἀντώνιε Thdr.Stud.*cant.* 18.1(p.377).

***πατροποιέω**, *make father by adoption*, ‡Chrys.*caec.Zacch.*4(8. 126C).

***πατροπρεπής**, *suitable for a father* εἰπὲ αὐτῷ πατροπρεπεῖ διαλέξει Thdr.Stud.*epp.*2.160(M.99.1500C).

***πατροπροβλήτως**, *as sent forth from the Father*; of H. Ghost, Jo. D.*carm.pent.*73(p.215; πατριπ- M.96.836C).

***πατροσθενής**, *having the power of the Father*, Jo.D.*carm.pent.*60 (p.215, conj. for πατρόθεν M.96.836B).

πατροσύνη, ἡ, v. *πατρωσύνη.

***πατρότης, ἡ**, *fatherhood*; **1.** in gen. ὁ φύσει πατὴρ ὁρίζει τοὔνομα [sc. υἱόν] τοῖς τῆς π. ... ἑπομένοις νόμοις Cyr.*inc.unigen.*(5^{1}.699E); υἱοθεσίαι τε καὶ π. τοῖς αὐτοῖς ὑποκειμένοις...ἐμφέρονται Leont.H. *Nest.*2.1(M.86.1536C); ὁ Πλάτων φησὶν ὅτι π. ἐστὶ προΰπαρξις υἱότητος, ἡ δὲ ἐκκλησία...συνάναρχον λέγει τὸν υἱὸν τῷ πατρί Anast.S.*hod.*1(M. 89.49D); **2.** as complimentary title of bishops, *Ep.*ap.CSyr.(*ACO* 3 p.97.21; H.2.1373A); and of abbots, Thdr.Stud.*epp.*1.26(M.99. 992B); *ib.*2.16(1165A); **3.** theol. τῇ...ἀϊδιότητι συμπαρεκτεινομένην ἔχει τὴν...π. Bas.*Eun.*2.12(1.247B; M.29.593B); κοινὴ μὲν ἡ θεότης· ἰδιώματα δέ τινα π. καὶ υἱότης *ib.*2.28(265C; M.637B); τῆς οὐσίας λόγος κοινός...ἡ δὲ ὑπόστασις ἐν τῷ ἰδιώματι τῆς π. id.*ep.*214.4(3.322E; M. 32.789B); αἱ περὶ τοῦ θεοῦ ὑπολήψεις...ἡ π., ἡ ἀγεννησία Gr.Nyss. *Eun.*1(1 p.187.16; M.45.432D); ὁμοούσιον ὄντα τὸν πατέρα τῷ υἱῷ, οὐκ εἰς τὸν τῆς υἱότητος τόπον...καταφέρει λόγος, οὔτε μὴν ἀνατίθησι τὸν υἱὸν εἰς τὴν τῆς π. θέσιν Cyr.*Jo.*1.4(4.35C); ἀπὸ γὰρ τῆς υἱότητος ἡ π. νοεῖται· καὶ τὸ ἀντίστροφον id.*thes.*7(5^{1}.59B); πάντα εἶχεν ὅσα ὁ πατήρ, πλὴν αὐτῆς τῆς π. Thdt.*Trin.*16(M.75.1173B); ἕνα γὰρ θεὸν... ἐν μόναις δὲ ταῖς ἰδιότησι τῆς τε π. καὶ τῆς υἱότητος ‡Cyr.*Trin.*10(6^{3}. 15D; M.77.1144A); Dion.Ar.*d.n.*2.8(M.3.645C); Max.*schol.myst.*3(M. 4.424D); υἱῷ...ἴσῳ τῷ πατρὶ χωρὶς τῆς π. ‡Ath.*Lat.*1(M.28.825C); of God's fatherhood towards man οὐκ ἀρχὴ μόνον ἐστίν, ἀλλὰ καὶ π. Chrys.*hom.15.4 in 2Cor.*(10.549E); exeg. Eph.3:15 τὸ τῆς...π. ὄνομα οὐκ ἐξ ἡμῶν κυρίως ἔχει θεός, ἀλλ' ἡμεῖς μᾶλλον ἐξ αὐτοῦ λαβόντες ὁρώμεθα. ... πῶς δ' ἄν...τὸ τῆς...π. ὄνομα καὶ εἰς τοὺς ἄλλους ἐκβῆναι παρὰ θεοῦ δοίη τις ἄν, εἴ γε ὄντως οὐκ ἔστι πατήρ; Cyr.*Jo.*1.3(4.24B).

***πατροτροφέω**, *provide for parents*, Phot.*nomoc.*11.15(p.599; M. 104.1156C).

***πατροφαής**, *deriving light from the Father*, Gr.Naz.*carm.*2.1.38. 5(M.37.1325A).

***πατροφεγγής**, *with the Father's splendour*, Geo.Pis.*hex.*1783(M. 92.1572A).

***πατροφονία, ἡ**, *parricide*, *Hom.Clem.*6.18; Bas.*hom.*12.8(2.104D; M.31.401D).

πάτρων, ὁ, (Lat. *patronus*) *patron*, Thphl.Ant.*Autol.*3.27(M.6. 1161C); Nil.ap.Jo.D.*parall.*5(M.95.1429D); of martyred apostles as patron saints, *A.Petr.et Paul.*85(p.219.12).

πατρωνεύ-ω, *be a patron, further* someone's *interests* ἑαυτῷ ~εις Ephr.3.168C.

πατρωνυμία, ἡ, *name from one's father, patronymic* ὡς γὰρ ἔοικε, π. ἦν τοῦ λῃστοῦ ὁ Βαραββᾶς, ὅπερ ἑρμηνεύεται διδασκάλου υἱός Or. *schol.in Mt.*27:12ff.(M.17.308A).

***πατρωνυμικῶς**, *after one's father's name* (Valent.) τελειότατον κάλλος...τοῦ πληρώματος...τὸν Ἰησοῦν ὃν καὶ σωτῆρα προσαγορευθῆναι καὶ Χριστὸν καὶ λόγον π. Iren.*haer.*1.2.6(M.7.465A); σοφίαν τε π. (ὁ γὰρ πατὴρ αὐτῆς σοφία κληΐζεται) καὶ πνεῦμα ἅγιον *ib.*1.4.1(480B); Ἰησοῦν...π. καλεῖσθαι φῶς διὰ τὸ ἄνω φῶς Epiph.*haer.*31.4(p.389.1; M.41.480B).

πατρῷος, 1. *of* God *the Father* εἰς τὴν π. ἀποθήκην σωρευθῶμεν Clem.*paed.*1.9(p.139.9; M.8.349C); φιλαργύρους...τῆς π. ἐξέβαλεν αὐλῆς ὁ κύριος *ib.*3.11(p.280.1; 657A); π. νουθεσίας id.*str.*7.16(p.72. 13; M.9.541B); π. κληρονομίαν Or.*Jo.*6.45(26; p.155.2; M.14.280B); πνεῦμα...ἀπὸ τῶν π. ἄνωθεν...καταπνεόμενον θησαυρῶν Meth.*symp.* 7.1(p.71.4; M.18.121C); theol., of Father in rel. to Son ὁ π. λόγος Clem.*fr.*23(p.202.20; M.103.383A); Eus.*e.th.*3.2(p.143.20; M.24.980A); μόνου τοῖς π. κόλποις ἀναπαυομένου *Symb.Ant.*(345)9(p.253.39; M.26. 733A); ἐν γὰρ τῇ π. θεότητί ἐστι...ὁ υἱός Ath.*Ar.*3.6(M.26.332C); δηλοῖ μετὰ τοῦ π. ὀνόματος καὶ τὸν γεγεννημένον Didym.(‡Bas.)*Eun.*5 (1.311A; M.29.745B); **2.** *of a* spiritual *father*; a monastic superior, Nil.*Eulog.*16(M.79.1113B); of a patriarch, Sophr.H.*ep.syn.*(M.87.3196B).

***πατρωσύνη (πατροσύνη), ἡ**, *fatherhood*; of bishop's office εὐφρανθῶμεν ἐπὶ σῇ π. Jo.Disc.*v.Epiph.*34(M.41.68D); as complimentary title ἱκετεύω τὴν σὴν π. *ib.*46(84A); *ib.*62(104D); of office of monastic superior θίγε...τὸ οὖς σου τοῖς τῆς πατροσύνης λόγοις Nil. *Eulog.*15(M.79.1113A); *ib.*28(1129C); as complimentary title, Thdr. Stud.*epp.*1.39(M.99.1048D); of others regarded as fathers in God τοῖς ἁγίοις μου πατράσι καὶ ὁμολογηταῖς...συγχαίρων ὑμῶν τῇ π. *ib.*2. 83(1325A).

***Παυλιανίζω**, *be a follower of Paul of Samosata*; such to be baptized on submission to the Church, CNic.(325)*can.*19; Steph.Hier. *agn.*(p.156.17) cit. s. Νεστοριανίζω; Leont.B.*Apoll.*(M.86.1949B); Thdr.Stud.*epp.*2.169(M.99.1533C).

***Παυλιανικός**, *of Paul of Samosata*, Apoll.*ep.Dion.*4(p.258.10; M.*PL*.8.931A).

***Παυλιανιστής, ὁ**, *follower of Paul of Samosata* Π.· οἱ ἀπὸ Παύλου Σαμωσατέως· ταπεινὰ καὶ χαμαιπετῆ περὶ τοῦ Χριστοῦ φρονήσαντες, ὡς κοινοῦ τὴν φύσιν ἀνθρώπου γενομένου, καὶ τὴν ἀρχὴν ἀπὸ Μαρίας ἐσχηκότος Tim.CP *haer.*(M.86.24C); *ib.*(41B).

***Παυλιανός, ὁ, 1.** *follower of Paul of Samosata*, Const.ap.Eus.*v.C.* 3.64(p.111.18; M.20.1140B); Eus.*e.th.*1.20(p.88.8; M.24.877C); πάντες ἅμα ἐκκλησίαζον καὶ ἐκοινώνουν, πλὴν Ναυατιανῶν...Οὐαλεντιανῶν τε καὶ Μαρκιωνιστῶν καὶ Π. Soz.*h.e.*2.32.1(M.67.1025C); **2.** *'Paulian'*, i.e. follower of S. Paul, word coined by Gr. Naz. to parallel Χριστιανός, Gr.Naz.*or.*37.17(M.36.301C).

***Παυλικιανός, ὁ,** *member of Paulician sect,* derived from Paul and John of Samosata (cf. Euthymius Zigabenus *panoplia* 24(M. 130.1189Cff.)); holding a form of Manichean doctrine, ‡Jo.D.*ep. Thphl.*22(M.95.373B); flourishing in Thrace as result of settlement there by Const. Copronymus of Syrians and Armenians, Thphn. *chron.*p.360(M.108.865A); *Μανιχαίων, τῶν νῦν Π. καλουμένων ib.*p.413 (980D); *ib.*p.420(996A); measures taken for their suppression in Asia Minor by emperor Michael, *ib.*p.419(993B).

***Παῦλος,** *Paul,* ref. fanciful etymology of name *Σαῦλος...ἐσάλευε ...τὴν ἐκκλησίαν, Π. δέ τοι πέπαυται τοῦ διώκειν* Euthal.Diac.*epp. Paul.*proem.(M.85.697B).

***παῦνι,** Coptic month corresponding to June, *A.Barn.*24(p.301. 15n.); Cyr.*ep.*23(p.67.10; 5².85C).

[*]παυράκι, *rarely, occasionally,* Gr.Naz.*carm.*1.2.1.709(M.37. 576A).

***παῦσα, ἡ,** *cessation,* Plato *Phaedr.*245C ap.Gr.Nyss.*Eun.*9(M.45. 813C; v.l. for *παῦλαν* 2 p.215.16); Gr.Nyss.*v.Mos.*(M.44.325C; prob. for *παῦλαν* or *παῦσιν*).

παυσίκακος, *ending evil,* Sophr.H.*mir.Cyr.et Jo.*15(M.87.3469B); ‡Gr.Naz.*Chr.pat.*2262(M.38.314A).

***παυσιμέριμνος,** *ending care,* an 'aeon' in Hesiod's cosmology as compared with Valent. system, Epiph.*haer.*31.3(p.387.6; M.41. 477C).

παῦσις, ἡ, *cessation,* ref. Arian exegesis of 1Cor.15:24 *φασι, παύσεως καὶ καταλύσεως τοῦ βασιλεύοντός ἐστι ταῦτα δηλωτικά* Epiph. *haer.*69.74(p.222.8; M.42.321C).

παυσώδυνος, *ending pain,* Sophr.H.*mir.Cyr.et Jo.*26(M.87.3497A).

παχνήεις, *frosty,* Nonn.*par.Jo.*10:22(M.43.836B).

πάχος, τό, *grossness, materiality, unspirituality σώματος ὑλικοῦ καὶ δεσμίου νοῦ π.* Gr.Naz.*or.*45.11(M.36.637B); *νοῦ πρὸς ὕψος ἐκ π. ἐκδημίαις* id.*carm.*2.1.12.579(M.37.1208A); *ὅπερ...ἐν Ἀδὰμ ὡς ἐν π. πραγμάτων...ὁρᾶται συμβεβηκός, τοῦτο καὶ ἐν ἑκάστῳ τῶν καθ' ἡμᾶς νοητῶς...κατίδοι τις ἂν πληρούμενον* Cyr.*ador.*1(1.10D); *τυπικῶς...καὶ ὡς ἐν π. λατρείας Ἰουδαϊκῆς* id.*Juln.*10(6².357B); ref. lit. sense of scripture *τῆς ἱστορίας τὸ π.* id.*ador.*5(1.157C); id.*Ps.*35:6(M.69. 917B).

παχόω, *freeze stiff,* Nil.*praest.*24(M.79.1089A).

***παχυβάτωρ,** *thick-flowing, sluggish, Chron.Pasch.*p.30(M.92. 129A).

παχυκάρδιος, *dull in understanding, dense,* Ast.Am.*hom.*7(M.40. 257C).

παχυμέρεια, ἡ, *density, coarseness,* hence *grossness τί γὰρ κοινὸν τῇ ἀΰλῳ τῆς ψυχῆς φύσει πρὸς τὴν ὑλικὴν π.;* Gr.Nyss.*hom.9 in Cant.* (M.44.965B); id.*anim.et res.*(M.46.28C).

παχυμερής, 1. *gross τὸ λεπτομερέστερον, ἡ ψυχή, οὐκ ἄν ποτε πρὸς τοῦ παχυμερεστέρου ὕδατος* [i.e. of Flood] *πάθοι τι δεινόν. ... ὃ δ' ἂν π. ἐκ τῆς ἁμαρτίας πεπαχυμμένον τύχῃ, τοῦτο ἀπορρίπτεται σὺν τῷ σαρκικῷ πνεύματι* Clem.*str.*6.6(p.458.7; M.9.273C); **2.** *unspiritual, material, earthly τὸν νόμον...π. σῶμα λαβὼν λεπτύνει διὰ τῆς θεωρίας* Gr.Nyss.*hom.7 in Cant.*(M.44.925D); Leont.H.*Nest.*7.5(M.86. 1768ᵈA); **3.** *bodily,* of Inc. *τῇ δὲ θεότητι συνηνωμένος τὸ π. λεπτομερὲς ἐτελείου* Epiph.*haer.*77.29(p.441.28; M.42.684B); *εἰσῆλθε... θυρῶν κεκλεισμένων ἵνα δείξῃ τὸ π. λεπτομερές* id.*anc.*91(p.112.11; M. 43.184C); **4.** *rough, cursory,* of bipartite opp. tripartite division of man *κατὰ τὴν παχυμερεστέραν...τομήν* Gr.Nyss.*Apoll.*35(M.45. 1200C).

παχυμερῶς, 1. *crassly, unspiritually;* of lit. exegesis, Gennad.*fr. Gen.*49:11(M.85.1660B); **2.** *dull-wittedly, without understanding,* Socr. *h.e.*5.24.2(M.67.648C).

παχύνους, *dull-witted, weak-minded,* Didym.*Trin.*1.15(M.39. 316A); Cyr.*ador.*1(1.7A).

παχύν-ω, *make thick* or *gross;* theol., *make corporeal,* pass., ref. Inc. *ὁ τοῦ θεοῦ λόγος, μένων θεός..., ~εται* Sophr.H.*or.*2.15(M.87. 3233C); Jo.D.*carm.theog.*29(p.206; M.96.820C).

παχύς, 1. *earthly, of this world,* opp. spiritual *παχυτέρᾳ κέχρηται τῇ λέξει* Chrys.*scand.*4(3.472B); *ib.*6(475B); id.*hom.25.2 in Jo.*(8. 145A); *ib.39.2*(228C); *οὐχ ὁρᾶτος ἢ π. ὁ πόλεμος* Cyr.*ador.*11(1.389D); *ἀναγκαῖα πρὸς θεωρίαν...πνευματικὴν...λέγωμεν, τὸ τῆς ἱστορίας ὑποτρέχοντες π. ib.*12(414B); *ib.*16(562A); of the five loaves as symbol of the *παχυτέρα τῆς πεντατεύχου διδασκαλία* Ammon.*Jo.*6:13(M.85. 1433A); *τύπος π.* [sc. of angels] *τὰ καθ' ἡμᾶς* Max.*schol.c.h.*15.3(M. 4.105C); **2.** *carnal σάρκα τοὺς παχυτέρους...ἀνθρώπους λέγει* Thdt.*Ps.* 55:5(1.973); *παχυτέρους καὶ σαρκικούς* id.*Dan.*7:11(2.1200); **3.** *dense, insensitive π. ποιεῖ* [sc. *γαστριμαργία*] *διάνοιαν* Chrys.*hom.45.1 in Jo.* (8.261D); *τὰ σημεῖα γὰρ...τοῖς ἀπίστοις καὶ παχυτέροις ib.35.2*(8.205A).

παχύσαρκος, *gross, materialistic, cat.Apoc.*8:2(p.298.27).

παχύτης, ἡ, 1. *grossness, materiality τῆς καθαρωτέρας...χώρας... ἔνθα μὴ φθάνουσιν αἱ ἀπὸ τῆς γῆς...παχύτητες* Or.*Cels.*3.35(p.232. 2; M.11.965A); *τὴν ἀπερίγραφον...ἐξουσίαν...μὴ περικλείεσθαι...παχύτητι σώματος* Mac.Mgn.*apocr.*3.14(p.90.15); Chrys.*hom.25.2 in Jo.* (8.145A); *θεϊκῶς συναπτόμεθα, καὶ τρόπον ἄλλον ἢ ὃν αἱ π.* Gr.Naz. *or.*34.6(M.36.245C); ref. Christ at parousia *οὐκ ἔτι μὲν σάρκα, οὐκ ἀσώματον δέ,...θεοειδεστέρου σώματος, ἵνα καὶ ὀφθῇ...καὶ μείνῃ θεὸς ἔξω παχύτητος ib.*40.45(424C); ‡Thdt.*nativ.Jo.Bapt.*(5.90); **2.** *dullness, insensibility,* Thdt.*Heb.*12:25(3.631); opp. spirituality *τὴν ἐκ τοῦ γράμματος π.* Cyr.*Mich.*70(3.470C); Diad.*perf.*16(p.18.24) cit. s. *γεώδης;* **3.** *earthliness ὁ...δεσπότης τοσαύτῃ π. λέξεως ἐχρήσατο πρὸς ὠφέλειαν τῶν ἡμετέρων ψυχῶν* Chrys.*hom.42.4 in Gen.*(4.428C).

***πάχωμα, τό,** disease of the eye producing a thick film, *Exorc.* 15(p.338).

***παχών,** Coptic month corresponding to May, Epiph.*mens.*20 (M.43.272A); acc. some the month of Christ's birth *ἔτους κη' Αὐγούστου ἐν πέμπτῃ π. καὶ εἰκάδι* Clem.*str.*1.21(p.90.20; M.8.885A).

***πεδατοῦρα, ἡ,** (Lat. *pedatura*) *space measured in feet,* hence *station* of troops on guard *τοὺς τῆς π. στρατιώτας* Jo.Mal.*chron.*14 p.351(M.97.524B).

πεδάω, 1. *bind with fetters,* met., *ἐσωφρονίσθη πεδηθεῖσα ἡ κακία* Tit.Bost.*Man.*1.25(M.18.1104A); *ταῖς τοῦ κόσμου πεπεδημένος ἐπιθυμίαις* Chrys.*sac.*1.1(p.3.10; 1.363A); **2.** perf. ptcpl. pass., *crippled, paralysed,* Thdt.*h.e.*1.7.5(3.755).

***πέδησις, ἡ,** *fettering, restriction,* Ephr.Chers.*mir.Clem.*16(M.2. 644B).

[*]πεδιάσιμος, *consisting in plains,* Bas.*hom.*5.6(2.40B; M.31. 253B); Pamph.Mon.*Soter.*3(p.118.12).

πέδιλον, τό, plur., *sandals; boots,* Epiph.*haer.*59.11(p.376.14; M. 41.1033C *πέδια*) cit. s. *ὀδώνιον.*

πεδοσκαφής, *dug in the earth,* Nonn.*par.Jo.*4:6(M.43.773B).

πεδοστιβής, *trodden under foot,* Gr.Naz.*carm.*1.2.8.136(M.37. 659A).

***πεδοτρεφής,** *fed from the earth,* Nonn.*par.Jo.*4:12(M.43.776B).

***πεδουκλόω,** *fetter,* Barth.Edess.*Agar.*(M.104.1424B).

***πεδ-όω,** *fetter οἷα ἀνθρώπου ψυχὴ τῷ σώματι ~ούμενος* Eus.*d.e.*7.1 (p.302.9; M. om.).

πέζα, ἡ, *region,* Nonn.*par.Jo.*3:14(M.43.768C); *ib.*4:4(773B); *ib.* 12:1(840B).

***πεζαίτεροι, οἱ,** v. *πεζέταιροι.*

***πεζέρως, ὁ,** *carbuncle τὸν π. λίθον, αὐτὸν γὰρ καλεῖ ἄνθρακα* Cosm.Ind.*top.*11(M.88.452B).

πεζέταιροι, οἱ, *foot-guards,* Thdt.*h.e.*3.15.4 (v.l. *πεζαίτεροι* 3.930); id.*qu.40 in 2Reg.* (*πεζαιτέρων* 1.443); id.*Dan.*4:9 (*πεζαιτέροις* 2. 1144).

πεζεύ-ω, 1. *go on foot upon κύματα ~σει Orac.Sib.*6.13; Mac.Mgn. *apocr.*2.8(p.9.21); **2.** *dismount ἐκυνήγησεν...πρόβατον, καὶ ἐπέζευσεν τοῦ σφάξαι αὐτό* Barth.Edess.*Agar.*(M.104.1425C); **3.** *make pedestrian ~έ μοι τὴν λέξιν, ἀγροικοστόμει* Gr.Naz.*carm.*2.1.12.295(M.37.1187A); **4.** *make passable on foot ἔσχισε τὴν θάλασσαν καὶ ἐπέζευσε τῷ λαῷ αὐτοῦ* Barth.Edess.*Agar.*(M.104.1444D).

***πεζινός,** *on foot,* Jo.Mal.*chron.*18 p.464(M.97.677C).

πεζοβατέω, *go on foot, A.Thom.*A 137(p.243.21n.).

πεζοπορέω, *go on foot; walk,* fig., Nil.*epp.*1.331(M.79.201C).

πεζοπορία, ἡ, *travelling on foot ἡ ἐπὶ γῆς τοῦ Χριστοῦ διατριβὴ ἐν πτωχείᾳ καὶ π. γέγονεν* Anast.S.*hod.*13(M.89.237C); †Jo.D.*B.J.*25(M. 96.1089B); of the walking on the water, Ath.*v.Anton.*75(M.26. 949A).

[*]πειθανολογία, ἡ, v. *πιθ-.*

[*]πειθανός, = *πιθανός, persuasive,* †Thdt.*Pss.proem.*(5.74).

[*]πειθανότης, ἡ, *persuasiveness,* Didym.*Trin.*3.11(M.39.860B).

[*]πειθανουργία, ἡ, *plausible argumentation,* Didym.*Trin.*2.6(M. 39.516C); *ib.*2.7(585A).

[*]πειθανῶς, = *πιθανῶς, persuasively,* Gr.Naz.*carm.*1.1.10.29(M. 37.467A).

πειθαρχ-έω, *obey πάντας...~εῖν τῷ λόγῳ τῆς δικαιοσύνης* Polyc.*ep.* 9.1; *θεὸς...ᾧ ~εῖ σελήνη Diogn.*7.2; *~εῖν ταῖς ἐντολαῖς* Meth.*symp.* 10.4(p.126.11; M.18.200A); Eus.*h.e.*6.34(M.20.596A); CNic.(325)*can.* 18; *~εῖν...τῷ ψευδεῖ* Ephr.3.142A.

***πειθάρχημα, τό,** *act of obedience,* ‡Chrys.*hom.*13(13.254B).

πειθήνιος, 1. *persuasive οὓς ὁ λόγος ὁ π. οὐκ ἰᾶται, ἀπειλὴ ἰάσεται* Clem.*paed.*1.7(p.126.6; M.8.324A); *Hom.Clem.*12.12; **2.** *obedient,* in gen. *π. οἱ ἀρχόμενοι τοῖς ἄρχουσιν* Clem.*str.*1.25(p.103.23; M.8. 913A); *τὸν ταῖς ἐντολαῖς π. ib.*2.16(p.151.19; 1012B); *κρείττονι γνώμῃ π.* Eus.*v.C.*1.44(p.28.27; M.20.960A); *πόλις...π. ἑαυτὴν...παρέσχηκεν* Constantius ap.Ath.*apol.Const.*30(M.25.632D); Chrys.*hom.34.1 in*

Heb.(12.312C); to God ψυχὰς π. πάρεσχον τῷ θεῷ *A.Thom.*A 59 (p.175.19); †Apoll.*met.Ps.*50 tit.(M.33.1381D); Nonn.*par.Jo.*3:1(M. 43.765B); Nil.*epp.*3.33(M.79.400D); Cyr.*Ps.*49:4(M.69.1077D); abs. ἐκ μεταβολῆς π., ἀλλ' οὐκ ἐκ φύσεως τὴν σωτηρίαν Clem.*str.*2.20(p.175. 22; M.8.1060A); Chrys.*hom.15.2 in Ac.*(9.121A); Cyr.*Jo.*5.2(4.486B); neut. as subst., Chrys.*hom.54.3 in Jo.*(8.319E); Cyr.*Jo.*4.1(4.335C).

πειθηνίως, *obediently*, Clem.*str.*7.7(p.32.12; M.9.460A); Chrys. *hom.84.1 in Mt.*(7.798A).

***πειθικός**, *persuasive*, Thphn.*chron.*p.166(v.l. ἠθικῷ M.108.444B).

πείθ-ω, **A.** trans., *persuade*; ref. God sending Son to earth ὡς βασιλεὺς πέμπων υἱὸν βασιλέα ἔπεμψεν...ὡς ~ων, οὐ βιαζόμενος *Diogn.*7.4; of prevailing over, persuading, God in prayer ἔχων γὰρ τὴν ἐκ τῆς καθαρᾶς βιοτῆς παρρησίαν ῥᾷστα πείσεις τὸν εὐεργετεῖν ἐπειγόμενον Thdt.*ep.*143(4.1239); id.*Jer.*15:1(2.488); opp. ἀναγκάζω, Ath.*h.Ar.*67(p.220.1; M.25.773A).

B. intrans.; **1.** *trust* πεποιθότες ἐπὶ τὸ ὁσιώτατον τῆς μεγαλωσύνης αὐτοῦ ὄνομα *1Clem.*58.1; ἡ περιτομὴ ἐφ' ᾗ πεποίθασιν *Barn.*9.4; Just. *dial.*8.2(M.6.492D); πεποιθότα ἐπὶ κύριον Clem.*str.*7.11(p.48.21; M.9. 493B); τὸ ἐπὶ τῇ ἀληθείᾳ πεποιθέναι *ib.*7.16(p.74.7; 545A); Const.ap. Eus.*v.C.*4.12(p.122.26; M.20.1161A); **2.** *be convinced* π. περὶ τῆς σωφροσύνης σου *T.Jos.*4.2; π. ὅτι...οὐκ...ἔδραμον Polyc.*ep.*9.2; πιστεύοντες, μᾶλλον δὲ καὶ πεπεισμένοι Just.*1apol.*17.4(M.6.353D); πεισθῆναί τε καὶ πιστεῦσαι ὅτι ἀληθῆ ταῦτά ἐστι *ib.*18.2(356A); Clem. *str.*4.22(p.312.29; M.8.1356B); Ath.*ep.Aeg.Lib.*23(M.25.592D); **3.** *be resolved* ὁ ὑπακούειν ταῖς ἐντολαῖς πεπεισμένος Clem.*str.*2.2(p.116.19; M.8.937B); ὁ τεύξεσθαι πεπεισμένος τῶν ὄντως ἀγαθῶν *ib.*6.9(p.470.6; M.9.297B); **4.** abs., *be a believer, be converted,* Clem.*ecl.*36(p.148.3; M.9.717A); Philost.*h.e.*2.5(M.65.469A); **5.** *obey* ~όμενος τῷ Ἰησοῦ Or. *hom.16.4 in Jer.*(p.136.4; M.13 om.); Meth.*symp.*10.4(p.126.14; M. 18.200A om.); Jo.D.*f.o.*1.5(M.94.800C).

πειθώ, ἡ, **1.** *persuasiveness, persuasion*; hence *conviction, assurance* π. καὶ πίστιν...ἐμφορῆσαι Just.*1apol.*53.12(M.6.408B); ἀπὸ τῶν...θεοσεβῶν τὴν π. ἔχομεν id.*dial.*53.6(M.6.593C); Clem.*prot.*10 (p.70.16; M.8.209B); π. δὲ ἡ βεβαίωσις τῆς πίστεως id.*str.*1.11(p.34.2; M.8.749B); Meth.*res.*1.33(p.270.3; M.41.1145A); **2.** *obedience* ἔνθεον πρὸς τὴν διδασκαλίαν π. Clem.*str.*4.4(p.254.14; M.8.1228A); Or.*princ.* 3.1.11(p.212.6; M.11.268A); τὴν πρὸς τὸν ὄφιν π. Meth.*res.*1.29(p.260. 11; M.41.1137C).

***πειναλέως**, *hungrily*, Nil.*epp.*4.51(M.79.573C).

πειν-άω, **1.** lit., *hunger (for)*, Christol. ἐπείνασε διὰ τὸ ἴδιον τοῦ σώματος Ath.*inc.*21.7(M.25.133C); Leo Mag.*ep.*28(p.15.18; M.*PL.*54. 768); **2.** met. τοὺς ~ῶντας τὸν λόγον Clem.*paed.*1.6(p.118.17; M.8. 305C).

πεῖρα, ἡ, **1.** *attempt* π. προσαγαγόντες τῇ γυναικὶ Or.*Jo.*28.5(p.394. 27; M.14.688D); κἂν τις δι' ἔργων ταύτης [sc. εὐεργεσίας] τυχεῖν πειρασθείη, εἰς μάτην ἔσται ἡ π. Gennad.*fr.Rom.*11:6(M.85.1716C); **2.** *enterprise*; of an athletic contest, met. θεοῦ ζῶντος πεῖραν ἀθλοῦμεν *2Clem.*20.2; **3.** *trial, test,* Just.*dial.*132.2(M.6.784A); π. ὑμῶν ἐποιούμην πῶς διάκεισθε ἤδη τὴν γνώμην *ib.*137.3(792B); βίβλους μηδενὶ...μεταδοῦναι...πρὸ πείρας *Clem.ep.Petr.*1(M.2.25A); of candidates for monastic life χρόνῳ καὶ...ἀγωνίσμασι π. τῆς κρίσεως αὐτῶν λαμβάνοντας...ὥστε ἀζήμιον τὴν π. τῇ ἀδελφότητι γίνεσθαι Bas.*reg. fus.*10.2(2.352E; M.31.945B); of Christ's temptations, Gr.Naz.*or.*40. 30(M.36.401B); **4.** *experience* ἡ πίστις εἰσάξει, ἡ π. διδάξει Clem.*prot.* 9(p.65.20; M.8.200B); ἐκ τῆς π. ἑαυτὸν ἐπανορθούμενος id.*fr.*(p.228. 2); τοῦ δυνατοῦ τὴν π. λαβόντες *Hom.Clem.*7.11; πάντες ἀπέθανον, εἰ καὶ μὴ τῇ π., ἀλλὰ τῇ ἀποφάσει Chrys.*comm.in Gal.*2:20(10.693C); εἰ καὶ μὴ ἔσφαξαν τῇ π., ἀλλ' ἔσφαξαν τῇ γνώμῃ id.*dimiss.Chan.*1(3. 433D); π. ἔχων αὐτοῦ Jo.Mosch.*prat.*83(M.87.2940C); ref. Inc. μιᾶς γὰρ οὔσης τῆς κατὰ θεὸν ζωῆς καὶ θατέρας τῆς κατὰ ἄνθρωπον... ἀμφοτέρων εἰκότως ὁ κύριος διὰ πείρας ἐλθών, ἐν μέσῳ δύο ζωῶν γνωσθῆναι λέγεται Eus.*d.e.*6.15(p.270.11; M.22.444D); ἑκατέρων π. ἔσχε Eust.*fr.in Ps.15*(p.68; M.18.685D); τίς ὁ πείρᾳ μαθὼν τὴν ὑπακοὴν καὶ ταύτην ἀγνοῶν πρὸ τῆς π.; οὐχ ὁ λόγος ὁ ἀθάνατος ὁ ἀπαθὴς...ἀλλὰ τὸ ἐκ σπέρματος Δαυὶδ ληφθὲν ὑπ' αὐτοῦ...ἐν π. δὲ γέγονε τῶν ἡμετέρων παθημάτων...ἡ ἐξ ἡμῶν...ληφθεῖσα φύσις Thdt. ap.Cyr.*apol.Thdt.*10(p.136.22; 6^{1}.230E); τῇ π. ... μεμαθηκὼς τῆς ἀνθρωπείας φύσεως τὴν ἀσθένειαν...οὔτε ὡς θεὸς διὰ τῆς π. μεμάθηκε τὰ ἡμέτερα id.*Heb.*2:18(3.561); οὐ μόνον ὡς θεὸς οἶδε τῆς ἡμετέρας φύσεως τὴν ἀσθένειαν, ἀλλὰ καὶ ὡς ἄνθρωπος π. τῶν ἡμετέρων ἔλαβε παθημάτων *ib.*4:15(571).

πειράζ-ω, **1.** *test, put to trial*; **a.** of God δεῖ σε...θλιβῆναι· οὕτω γὰρ προσέταξεν ὁ ἔνδοξος ἄγγελος τὰ περὶ σοῦ· θέλει γάρ σε πειρασθῆναι Herm.*sim.*7.1; ~ει σε ὁ κύριος ἐκλέξασθαι τὴν ζωήν Clem.*prot.*10 (p.69.26; M.8.208C); εὐλογήσει ~όμενος ὡς ὁ γενναῖος Ἰὼβ id.*str.*2. 20(p.170.6; M.8.1048C); Or.*or.*29(p.382.24; M.11.532C); contrasted with tempting by Devil, ‡Dion.Al.*fr.Lc.22:46*(p.247.19; M.10. 1596A); ἀπείη πιστεύειν, ὅτι...~ει ὡς ἀγνοῶν, καὶ τίς προγινώσκει; *Hom.Clem.*2.43; οὐ γὰρ ἂν ὁ τὰ πάντα γινώσκων...ἐπείρασεν, ἵνα γνῷ αὐτὸς ὁ τὰ πάντα προγινώσκων *ib.*16.13; ref. Gen.22:1 ἐπείρασεν· οὐχ ὡς αὐτὸς ἀγνοῶν, ἀλλὰ προσῆγεν αὐτῷ τὴν πεῖραν, ἵνα καὶ οἱ τότε παρόντες...παιδεύωνται...τὴν ὑπακοὴν ἐπιδείκνυσθαι Chrys.*hom.47.1 in Gen.*(4.474A); Thdt.*qu.73 in Gen.*(1.85); **b.** of Devil, ref. temptations of Christ ἐπείρασεν αὐτόν, ἵνα γνῷ...καὶ ἀπέστη ἀπ' αὐτοῦ εἰς καιρόν, τουτέστιν ἀνεβάλλετο τὴν εὕρεσιν εἰς τὴν ἀνάστασιν. ᾔδει γὰρ τοῦτον εἶναι τὸν κύριον τὸν ἀναστησόμενον Clem.*ecl.*53(p.152.2; M.9. 721D); **c.** of men tempting God, Meth.*lepr.*10(p.464.12); Chrys. *hom.13.3 in Mt.*(7.171C); Cyr.*Jo.*2.1(4.141C); ref. temptations of Christ, Iren.*haer.*5.22.2(M.7.1183C); οὐχ ὁ σωτήρ γε ἐπείρασεν· εὖ γὰρ ᾔδει...περὶ τῆς τοῦ πατρὸς δυνάμεως τῆς συνεργούσης αὐτῷ Eus.*Ps.* 90:10–12(M.23.1161C); **2.** *tempt, seduce* to evil; **a.** of Christ's temptations, Just.*dial.*125.4(M.6.768A); as recapitulation of temptation of Adam, Iren.*haer.*5.21.2(M.7.1180A–1181B); cf. *quadraginta diebus tentatur..., et quae fuerint tentamenta, nescimus; quae ideo forsitan praetermissa sunt, quia majora erant, quam ut litteris crederentur...* πάντα πειρασμόν, ὃν ἤμελλον οἱ ἄνθρωποι ~εσθαι, πρῶτον ἐπειράσθη κατὰ τὸ ἀνθρώπινον ὁ σωτήρ...ἄνθρωπός ἐστι ~όμενος...ἐπειδὴ γὰρ Ἰωάννης ἀπὸ θεοῦ ἤρξατο, οὐκ ἐγενεαλόγησεν αὐτὸν ὡς θεόν...διὰ τοῦτο, ἐπειδὴ θεός, οὐκ ἐπειράζετο· οἱ δὲ ἄλλοι, ὡς τὰ ἀνθρώπινα διηγούμενοι τοῦ σωτῆρος, εἰσάγουσιν αὐτὸν καὶ ~όμενον Or.*hom.29 in Lc.*(pp.178.15–181.14; M.13.1874D–1876B); as example in human temptations, *ib.*(p.181.26; 1876C); Eus.*Ps.*90:9(M.23.1153Aff.); purpose discussed: to demonstrate completeness of Christ's power over demons and Devil and to compel their recognition of himself (Mt.8:29), id.*d.e.*9.7(p.419.9; M.22.676B); to demonstrate his humanity, cf.Hegem.*Arch.*60(p.88.27; M.10.1516A); give example to newly baptized Christians when tempted, Chrys.*hom.13.1 in Mt.* (7.168Aff.); show his sympathy with human sinners, id.*hom.5.2 in Heb.*(12.53B); τὸ δέ, πειρασθεὶς δύναται βοηθεῖν, ταπεινὸν σφόδρα, πλὴν οὐκ ἔξω τῶν τῆς ἑνώσεως μέτρων...ἑαυτὸν...ὡς ἄμωμον ἱερεῖον προσεκόμισε τῷ πατρί, ἵνα διὰ τῆς ἑαυτοῦ σαρκὸς βοηθήσῃ τοῖς... ~ομένοις Cyr.*Heb.*2:18(M.74.968D); reality dependent on fact of Inc., id.*inc.unigen.*(5^{1}.681C); **b.** in gen., Clem.*str.*4.5(p.257.2; M.8. 1232C); ~ει γὰρ ὁ διάβολος εἰδὼς μὲν ὅ ἐσμεν, οὐκ εἰδὼς δὲ εἰ ὑπομενοῦμεν· ἀλλὰ ἀποσεῖσαι τῆς πίστεως ἡμᾶς βουλόμενος καὶ ὑπάγεσθαι ἑαυτῷ ~ει *ib.*4.12(p.285.20; 1293B); ὁ γνωστικὸς...~εται ὑπ' οὐδενός, πλὴν εἰ μὴ ἐπιτρέψαι ὁ θεὸς καὶ τοῦτο διὰ τὴν τῶν συνόντων ὠφέλειαν *ib.*7. 12(p.53.13; M.9.501C); ‡Dion.Al.*fr.Lc.22:46*(p.247.18; M.10.1596A); Meth.*symp.*3.11(p.39.20; M.18.77B); **3.** *try, afflict* πεπειρασμένον δὲ κατὰ πάντα καθ' ὁμοιότητα...τουτέστιν, ἐδιώχθη, ἐνεπτύσθη... ἐσταυρώθη Chrys.*hom.7.2 in Heb.*(12.74D); *cat.Jo.*3:19(p.208.27); **4.** *make an attempt* ἵνα μὴ...ὁ θάνατος ἀπόσχηται τοῦ κυρίου, ὡς μάτην ~ων ἐπὶ ἀνηνύτῳ Clem.*exc.Thdot.*5(p.209.12; M.9.656C).

***πειρασία, ἡ**, *temptation*, *A.Barth.*5(p.139.17).

πειρασμός, ὁ, *temptation, trial*;

A. two kinds distinguished διπλοῦν τὸ εἶδος τῶν π.· ἢ γὰρ αἱ θλίψεις βασανίζουσι τὰς καρδίας, ὥσπερ χρυσὸν ἐν καμίνῳ, διὰ τῆς ὑπομονῆς τὸ δοκίμιον αὐτῶν ἀπελέγχουσαι· ἢ καὶ πολλάκις αὐταὶ αἱ εὐθηνίαι τοῦ βίου ἀντὶ πειρατηρίου γίνονται τοῖς πολλοῖς...παράδειγμα δὲ τοῦ μὲν προτέρου εἴδους τῶν π., ὁ μέγας Ἰώβ...ὃς πᾶσαν τοῦ διαβόλου τὴν βίαν ...ἀσείστῳ καρδίᾳ ὑποδεξάμενος, τοσούτῳ μείζων τῶν π. ἀνεφάνη, ὅσῳ μεγάλα αὐτῷ καὶ δυσέκλυτα ἐδόκει παρὰ τοῦ ἐχθροῦ προβεβλῆσθαι τὰ παλαίσματα. τῶν δὲ κατὰ τὴν εὐημερίαν τοῦ βίου π. ὑποδείγματα ἄλλα τέ τινα, καὶ οὗτος ὁ νῦν ἡμῖν ἀναγνωσθεὶς πλούσιος [sc. Lc.12:16ff.] Bas.*hom.*6.1(2.43D,E; M.31.261A,B); ref. Mt.6:13, Jac.1:2ff. τῶν π. διττὸν ἐπίσταται τὸν τρόπον· τὸν μέν, κατὰ γνώμην, τὸν δέ, παρὰ γνώμην· καὶ τὸν μέν, ἑκουσίων ἡδονῶν δημιουργόν· τὸν δέ, ἀκουσίων ὀδυνῶν ἐπακτικόν. ὁ γὰρ κατὰ γνώμην π., τὰς κατὰ προαίρεσιν ἑκουσίους σαφῶς συνίστησι ἡδονάς· ὁ δὲ παρὰ γνώμην, προδήλως τοὺς ἀκουσίους παρὰ προαίρεσιν ἐφίστησι πόνους...οἶμαι τὸν κύριον...πῶς δεῖ προσεύχεσθαι τοὺς...διδάσκοντα μαθητάς, πρὸς τό, τὸ κατὰ γνώμην εἶδος τῶν π. ἀπεύχεσθαι...τῶν ἡδονικῶν...καὶ ἑκουσίων π., μὴ ἐγκαταλειφθῆναι πεῖραν λαβεῖν...τὸν δὲ μέγαν Ἰάκωβον...πρὸς τὸ τῶν ἀκουσίων π. εἶδος διδάσκοντα μὴ συστέλλεσθαι...δηλονότι τοῖς ἀκουσίοις...καὶ πόνων ποιητικοῖς π. ... τέλειός ἐστιν, ὁ τοῖς ἑκουσίοις δι' ἐγκρατείας μαχόμενος, καὶ τοῖς ἀκουσίοις δι' ὑπομονῆς ἐγκαρτερῶν π. Max.*qu. Thal.*58(M.90.593B–D); id.*or.dom.*(M.90.908B).

B. ref. God's permission κύριος, καὶ τοὺς π. ἐπάγων μὴ ὑπερβαίνοντας ἡμῶν τὴν δύναμιν, ἀλλὰ δοκιμάζων μὲν διὰ τῆς περιστάσεως τοὺς ἀγωνιστὰς τῆς εὐσεβείας, οὐκ ἐῶν δὲ πειρασθῆναι ὑπὲρ ὃ δύνανται ὑπενεγκεῖν Bas.*ep.*219.1(3.332A; M.32.812A); σὺ δὲ τὸν εὐεργέτην [sc. God]...λέγεις κακῶς μηδὲν ἠδικημένος; μὴ γὰρ οὐκ ἠδύνατο λῦσαι τὸν π.; ἀλλὰ συνεχώρησεν, ἵνα γένῃ δοκιμώτερος. ἀλλ' ἰδού, φησί, καταπίπτω καὶ ἀπόλλυμαι· οὐ παρὰ τὴν τοῦ π. φύσιν, ἀλλὰ παρὰ τὴν ῥᾳθυμίαν τὴν σήν Chrys.*Laz*.3.7(1.747A); διὰ τοῦτο οὐδὲ ἐπιόντας κωλύει τοὺς π. ὁ θεός· πρῶτον μὲν ἵνα μάθῃς ὅτι πολλῷ γέγονας ἰσχυρότερος· ἔπειτα ἵνα μένῃς μετριάζων, μηδὲ τῷ μεγέθει τῶν δωρεῶν ἐπαρθῇς, τῶν π. συστέλλειν σε δυναμένων· πρὸς τούτοις, ἵνα ὁ πονηρὸς δαίμων ἐκεῖνος, ὁ τέως ἀμφιβάλλων περὶ τῆς σῆς ἀποστάσεως, ἀπὸ τῆς βασάνου τῶν π. πληροφορηθῇ, ὅτι τέλεον αὐτὸν ἐγκαταλιπὼν ἀπέστης· τέταρτον, ἵνα ἰσχυρότερος...κατασκευασθῇς· πέμπτον, ἵνα ἀπόδειξιν λάβῃς σαφῆ τῶν πιστευθέντων σοι θησαυρῶν id.*hom.13.1 in Mt*.(7.168A); id.*Dan*.6:4(6.233B); Max.*carit*.2.44(M.90.1000A); οἱ κατὰ τὸν βίον τοῦτον ὑπὸ τῆς θείας προνοίας εἰς εὐσέβειαν ἐγγυμναζόμενοι, διὰ τῶν τριῶν τούτων π. δοκιμάζονται· οἷον, ἢ διὰ τῆς τῶν ἡδέων δόσεως, ὡς ἐπὶ ὑγείας καὶ κάλλους...ἢ διὰ τῆς τῶν λυπηρῶν ἐπιφορᾶς· οἷον, στερήσεως τέκνων...ἢ διὰ τῶν ὀδύνας ἐμποιούντων τῷ σώματι· οἷον νοσημάτων *ib*.2.92(1013C); in life of 'gnostic' οἱ π. προσάγονται οὐκ εἰς τὴν ἀποκάθαρσιν, ἀλλ' εἰς τὴν τῶν πέλας...ὠφέλειαν, εἰ πεῖραν λαβὼν πόνων...κατεφρόνησεν Clem.*str*.7.12(p.54.13; M.9.504B).

C. caused by demons, esp. in case of monks and hermits δαίμονες διὰ ποικίλων π. σπουδάζουσι κλεῖσαι τὸ ἡμέτερον στόμα, ὅπως μὴ ὑμνῶμεν Nil.*epp*.1.137(M.79.140D); εἰσί τινες ἐν κόσμῳ βιωτικοί...καὶ πλείστῃ προσανεχόμενοι ἀγρυπνίᾳ, καὶ προσευχῇ...μηδέποτε δὲ λαβόντες δαιμόνων πεῖραν τὸ σύνολον· διότι οὐδὲ πάνυ περὶ αὐτῶν τῷ διαβόλῳ μέλει, μᾶλλον δὲ κατὰ τῶν τὸν μονήρη καὶ ἡσύχιον ἑλομένων βίον, τὴν ἀμφήκη τῶν μυρίων π. καθεκάστην...ὥραν...ὀξύνει μάχαιραν *ib*.3.153(456A); ἠξίου δέ τις αὐτὸν τῶν ἀδελφῶν συνδιάγειν αὐτῷ ἐν τῇ ἐρήμῳ βουλόμενος. λέγοντος δὲ αὐτοῦ, μὴ δύνασθαι ὑπενεγκεῖν τοὺς π. τῶν δαιμόνων ‡Pall.*h.mon*.13.12(p.67.17; M.34.1162B); ἀμφοτέρους δὲ τοὺς π., τὸν ἑκούσιόν τε καὶ τὸν ἀκούσιον, περιέπει...ὁ πονηρός· τὸν μέν, σπείρων καὶ διερεθίζων τὴν ψυχὴν ἡδοναῖς σώματος, ἀποστῆσαι τῆς θείας ἀγάπης τὴν ἔφεσιν μηχανώμενος· τὸν δὲ σοφιστικῶς ἐξαιτεῖται, δι' ὀδύνης φθεῖραι τὴν φύσιν βουλόμενος Max.*or.dom*.(M.90.908C).

D. conduct in temptations; **1.** patience and courage παρ' ὅλον τὸν...τοῦ π. χρόνον μὴ διδοίημεν τόπον τῷ διαβόλῳ...μολύνειν ἡμᾶς διαλογισμοῖς πονηροῖς θέλοντι ἀρνήσεως ἢ διψυχίας...προκαλουμένης ἐπὶ τὰ ἐχθρὰ τῷ μαρτυρίῳ Or.*mart*.11(p.11.5; M.11.577A); τούς...βαπτισθέντας, εὐθὺς παρασκευάζεσθαι δεῖ πρὸς τοὺς π., καὶ παρ' αὐτῶν τῶν οἰκείων, μέχρι θανάτου Bas.*moral*.62.1(2.281E; M.31.796C); †Bas.*ep*.42.4(3.128B; M.32.353C); μὴ...ἐν π. θορυβώμεθα...ἂν μὴ παρὰ πόδας ἡ λύσις γένηται, ἀλλ' αὐτῷ παραχωρῶμεν τὸν καιρὸν τῷ κυρίῳ τῆς λύσεως Chrys.*exp.in Ps*.145:8(5.479A); μὴ δὴ καταπίπτωμεν ἐν τοῖς π. οὐδεὶς γὰρ κοινωνεῖ τῷ Χριστῷ τρυφῶν...ἀλλ' ὁ ἐν θλίψει καὶ π., οὗτος ἐγγὺς ἕστηκεν ἐκείνου id.*hom.1.4 in 2Cor*.(10.423B); εὐχώμεθα μὲν μὴ εἰσελθεῖν εἰς π.· εἰ δὲ παραγένοιτο, μετὰ πολλῆς ἱστάμενοι τῆς ἀνδρείας, τὴν προσήκουσαν ἐπιδειξώμεθα προθυμίαν *ib.28.4*(639A); τί...προσεδόκησας προαιρούμενος...τὴν ἀναχώρησιν; πάντως θλίψεις καὶ π. ... πῶς οὖν νῦν δυσανασχετεῖς...κεντούμενος...ταῖς τῶν π. λόγχαις...ἀλλ' ὑπόμεινον εὐχαρίστως...καὶ θεάσῃ τὸ τέλος Nil.*epp*.2.137(M.79.257A,B); μή σου τὴν προθυμίαν οἱ ἐχθροὶ ἀμβλυνέτωσαν, τοῖς ποικίλοις...π. τὴν ψυχὴν κολαφίζοντες. ἐκ γὰρ δὴ τῶν θλίψεών σοι...ὁ στέφανος πλέκεται *ib*.3.154(457B); φύγε π. δι' ὑπομονῆς καὶ δεήσεως· εἰ δὲ ἐκτὸς τούτων ἀντιτάσσει, περισσοτέρως ἐπέρχεται Marc.Er.*opusc*.2.98(M.65.944D); **2.** prayer and fasting, ref. Ac.1:14 μέγα γὰρ τοῦτο ὅπλον ἐν τοῖς π. Chrys.*hom.3.1 in Ac*.(9.23A); νηστεύειν ἐδίδασκον ἐν τοῖς π. *ib.31.2*(243E); **3.** obedience διὰ τὴν πρὸς τὸν θεὸν ὑπακοὴν νικῶντες τοὺς ἐπαγομένους ὑπὸ τῶν ἐχθρῶν π. †Bas.*bapt*.2.13.1(2.673A; M.31.1625D); **4.** temptations not to be sought οὐ δεῖ ἑαυτὸν ἐπιρρίπτειν ~οῖς πρὸ καιροῦ τῆς τοῦ θεοῦ συγχωρήσεως, ἀλλὰ καὶ προσεύχεσθαι μὴ ἐμπεσεῖν εἰς π. Bas.*moral*.62.2(2.282D; M.31.797C); ref. Mt.26:41 πῶς οὖν φησιν, εὔχεσθαι μὴ εἰσελθεῖν εἰς π.; διὰ τοῦτο οὐκ ἀνιόντα αὐτὸν ἁπλῶς δείκνυσί σοι τὸν Ἰησοῦν, ἀλλὰ ἀναγόμενον κατὰ τὸν τῆς οἰκονομίας λόγον, αἰνιττόμενος διὰ τούτων, ὅτι οὐκ αὐτοὺς ἐπιπηδᾶν χρή, ἀλλ' ἑλκομένους ἑστάναι γενναίως Chrys.*hom.13.1 in Mt*.(7.168C).

E. effects; **1.** testing of love of God ἐξεταστήριον τῆς πρὸς τὸ θεῖον ἀγάπης νομιστέον ἡμῖν γεγονέναι τὸν ἐστηκότα π. Or.*mart*.6(p.8.2; M.11.572A); **2.** humility, Nil.*epp*.2.58(M.79.225B); **3.** improvement of soul's condition τίνα οὖν ἂν ἔχοιμεν ἀπολογίαν...οὕτως ἀνθρώπινον π. οὐ φέροντες...ὑμεῖς μάρτυρες...ὅσον ἀπὸ τοῦ π. τούτου τὸ κέρδος ἐσχήκαμεν. ὁ ἀκόλαστος σώφρων ἐγένετο νῦν, ὁ θρασὺς ἐπιεικέστερος Chrys.*stat*.4.2(2.52B); καθάπερ γὰρ τὸ χρυσίον τῷ πυρὶ παραδιδόμενον πᾶσαν ἀποτίθεται κηλῖδα, οὕτω καὶ οἱ σπουδαῖοι σπουδαιότεροι καθίστανται ἐν τοῖς π. id.*Is.interp*.4:3(6.49D); οὐ...αἱ θλίψεις μόνον, ἀλλὰ καὶ αὐτοὶ οἱ π. λαμπροτέρους ἡμᾶς ἐργάζονται id.*hom.33.3 in Ac*.(9.258B); ἀκηδία ἐστὶν ἀτονία ψυχῆς...οὐκ ἔχουσα τὸ κατὰ φύσιν, οὐδὲ πρὸς πειρασμοὺς ἵσταται γενναίως. ὅπερ γάρ ἐστι τροφὴ εὐεκτοῦντι σώματι, τοῦτό ἐστι π. γενναίᾳ ψυχῇ...π. βεβαιοῦσι καρτερίαν ψυχῆς Nil.*spir.mal*.13(M.79.1157D).

F. exeg. Lord's Prayer ᾗ γάρ ἐσμεν ἐπὶ γῆς περικείμενοι τὴν στρατευομένην σάρκα κατὰ τοῦ πνεύματος...ἐν π. ἐσμεν Or.*or*.29.1(p.382.4; M.11.532A); πῶς οὖν κελεύει ἡμᾶς ὁ σωτὴρ εὔχεσθαι μὴ εἰσελθεῖν εἰς π., πειράζοντός πως πάντας τοῦ θεοῦ; *ib*.29.3(p.382.24; 532C); χρὴ τοίνυν εὔχεσθαι οὐχ ἵνα μὴ πειρασθῶμεν (τοῦτο γὰρ ἀδύνατον) ἀλλ' ἵνα μὴ ὑπὸ τοῦ π. περιβληθῶμεν, ὅπερ πάσχουσιν οἱ ἐνεχόμενοι αὐτῷ καὶ νενικημένοι *ib*.29.11(p.386.13; 537A); τοῦ κυρίου διδάσκοντος προσεύχεσθαι μὴ εἰσελθεῖν εἰς π., εἰ δεῖ προσεύχεσθαι μὴ περιπεσεῖν ὀδύναις σωματικαῖς· ἐὰν δὲ περιπέσῃ τις, πῶς παρέλθῃ. οὐ διέκρινε π. ποιότητα, καθολικῶς δὲ προσέταξε 'προσεύχεσθε μὴ εἰσελθεῖν εἰς π.' εἰσαχθέντα δὲ σὺν τῷ π. τὴν ἔκβασιν τοῦ δύνασθαι ὑπενεγκεῖν παρὰ τοῦ κυρίου αἰτεῖν δεῖ Bas.*reg.br*.221(2.489B; M.31.1229A); δοκεῖ μοι πολυτρόπως ὁ κύριος τὸν κακὸν ὀνομάζειν...διάβολον, Βεελζεβούλ...καὶ ἄλλα τοιαῦτα. τάχα τοίνυν ἓν τῶν περὶ αὐτὸν νοουμένων ὄνομά τί ἐστι ὁ π., καὶ βεβαιοῖ τὴν τοιαύτην ἡμῖν ὑπόνοιαν ἡ τῶν εἰρημένων σύστασις. εἰπὼν γάρ, μὴ εἰσενέγκῃς ἡμᾶς εἰς π. ἐπήγαγεν τὸ ῥυσθῆναι ἀπὸ τοῦ πονηροῦ. ὡς τοῦ αὐτοῦ δι' ἑκατέρων τῶν ὀνομάτων σημαινομένου. εἰ γὰρ ὁ μὴ εἰσελθὼν εἰς π., ἔξω πάντως ἐστὶ τοῦ πονηροῦ· καὶ ὁ ἐν τῷ π. γενόμενος, ἐν τῷ πονηρῷ κατ' ἀνάγκην γίνεται· ἄρα ὁ π. τε καὶ ὁ πονηρὸς ἕν τι κατὰ τὴν σημασίαν ἐστὶ Gr. Nyss.*or.dom*.5(p.114.4; M.44.1192B,C); cf. π. μὲν λέγεται καὶ αὐτὸς ὁ διάβολος· π. δὲ καὶ ὁ τρόπος, καθ' ὃν πειράζειν εἴωθεν ὁ ἐχθρὸς τοὺς ἀνθρώπους Nil.*epp*.4.50(M.79.573B); Pall.*h.Laus*.16(p.41.13; M.34.1042A).

G. of temptation of Christ λεγέτωσαν...οἱ παραδεχόμενοι τὰ τέσσαρα εὐαγγέλια, καὶ τὴν δοκοῦσαν διαφωνίαν οἰόμενοι μὴ λύεσθαι διὰ τῆς ἀναγωγῆς...περὶ τῶν τεσσαράκοντα τοῦ π. ἡμερῶν οὐδαμῶς δυναμένων χώραν ἔχειν παρὰ τῷ Ἰωάννῃ Or.*Jo*.10.3(2; p.172.26; M.14.309B); πάντα τὸν π. συνετέλεσεν ὁ Ἰησοῦς, ὅτι πάντα ἔλαβε τὰ πειρασμοῦ πεῖραν ἐσχηκότα, δι' ὧν τὴν ὑπὲρ ἀνθρώπων νίκην πεποίηται ‡Ath.*Apoll*.2.9(M.26.1148A); ἐπειδὴ γὰρ πάντα πρὸς διδασκαλίαν ἡμῶν ἔπραττέ τε καὶ ὑπέμενεν, ἀνέχεται καὶ τῆς ἐκεῖσε ἀναγωγῆς, καὶ τῆς πρὸς τὸν διάβολον πάλης· ἵνα ἕκαστος τῶν βαπτιζομένων, εἰ μετὰ τὸ βάπτισμα μείζονας ὑπομείνειε π., μὴ ταράττηται, ὡς παρὰ προσδοκίαν τοῦ πράγματος γινομένου, ἀλλὰ μένῃ γενναίως πάντα φέρων, ὡς κατὰ ἀκολουθίαν τούτου συμβαίνοντος Chrys.*hom.13.1 in Mt*.(7.168A).

H. other aspects of temptation; **1.** ubiquity εἴτε γὰρ ἡ πάλη ἐστὶ πρὸς τὴν ἐπιθυμοῦσαν...κατὰ τοῦ πνεύματος σάρκα ἢ πρὸς τὴν ψυχὴν πάσης σαρκὸς...ὁποία ἐστὶν ἡ πάλη τοῖς τοὺς ἀνθρωπίνους πειραζομένοις π., εἴτε ὡς διαβεβηκόσι καὶ τελεωτέροις ἀθληταῖς, οὐκέτι πρὸς αἷμα καὶ σάρκα παλαίουσιν οὐδὲ ἐν τοῖς ἀνθρωπίνοις π. ἐξεταζομένοις, ...ἐστὶν ἡμῖν τὰ ἀγωνίσματα, τοῦ πειράζεσθαι οὐκ ἀπηλλάγμεθα Or.*or*.29.2(p.382.17ff.; M.11.532B); ὅπου ἐντολὴ θεοῦ, ἐκεῖ πάντως καὶ π. Nil.*epp*.2.193(M.79.301A); **2.** ref. baptism μόνον δός μοι τὴν ἐν Χριστῷ σφραγῖδα, καὶ οὐχ ἅψεταί μοι π. *A.Paul.et Thecl*.25(p.253.5ff.); **3.** hour of temptations κατὰ τὴν τοῦ πάθους ὥραν, ὅτε ἀπὸ ὥρας ἕκτος ἕως ἐννάτης σκότος ἐγένετο,...ἐν ᾗ καὶ ἀκμὴ τοῦ καύσωνος τῶν π. Ph.Carp.*Cant*.15(M.40.49B); **4.** spiritual trials and consolations τοῦτο καὶ ἡμεῖς ἐν τοῖς π. στρέφωμεν, ὅταν παρὰ πονηρῶν τι πάσχωμεν ἀνθρώπων, εἰς τὸν ἀρχηγὸν ἡμῶν ὁρῶντες καὶ τελειωτὴν τῆς πίστεως, καὶ ὅτι παρὰ φαύλων ἀνθρώπων, καὶ ὅτι δι' ἀρετὴν καὶ ὅτι δι' αὐτὸν Chrys.*hom.77.4 in Jo*.(8.455B); κἂν τῷ πλήθει τῶν π. τὴν ψυχὴν ἀπενάρκησας, οὐδὲν ἧττον...παρακαλεῖ ὁ...λόγος φάσκων· γενέσθω παράκλησις τοῖς ὀλιγοψύχοις Nil.*epp*.3.216(M.79.481C); ἔστιν ὅτε μέλλοντος τοῦ ἀνθρώπου π. ψυχικῷ...περιπίπτειν, προλαβοῦσα ἡ χάρις τοῦ ἁγίου πνεύματος παρηγορεῖ τὴν ψυχὴν ὑπερβαλλόντως *ib*.3.40(405C); consolation by angels, *ib*.3.33(389A); ἀμήχανον χωρὶς λύπης παρελθεῖν τὸν ἐμπαιδευόμενον τοῖς π. πλὴν ὅμως μετὰ τὴν παραδρομὴν τῶν π. ... πολλῆς χαρᾶς πληροῦνται οἱ τοιοῦτοι *ib*.3.147(452C); ἡ πρώτη τοῦ π. προσβολή, ὅθεν τὰ πάθη λαμβάνει τὴν ἀρχήν, τοῦτο τῆς ἡμετέρας δυνάμεως κατάσκοπος γίνεται *ib*.1.275(184B); **5.** succumbing to temptation οὐ γὰρ ἡ τῶν π. φύσις, ἀλλ' ἡ τῶν πειραζομένων ῥᾳθυμία τὰ πτώματα ἐργάζεσθαι πέφυκεν. ὥστε εἰ βούλει...ἀνέσεως ἀπολαύειν καὶ ἡδονῆς, μὴ ζήτει ἡδονὴν μήτε ἄνεσιν, ἀλλὰ ζήτει ψυχὴν ὑπομονῆς γέμουσαν...ὡς ἐὰν μὴ τοῦτο ἔχῃς, οὐχὶ π. σε ἐλέγξει μόνον, ἀλλὰ καὶ ἄνεσίς σε ἀπολεῖ Chrys.*stat*.4.2(2.51A); *ib*.(51B); **6.** ref. thanksgiving τὸ εὑρεῖν τὴν εὐχαριστίαν ἐν καιρῷ π. ἀποστρέφει εἰς τὰ ὀπίσω τοὺς ἐπερχομένους π. Esaias *or*.23; **7.** heret. view that scripture contains occasions of temptations τὰς κατὰ τοῦ θεοῦ ἐν ταῖς γραφαῖς πειρασμοῦ χάριν προκειμένας περικοπὰς *Hom.Clem*.2.39; εἴτε αἱ γραφαὶ εἴτε προφῆται θεοὺς λέγουσιν, εἰς π. τῶν ἀκουόντων λέγουσιν *ib*.16.13; ref. Mt.11:27 εἰ γὰρ ἠπίσταντο, οὐκ ἂν ταῖς ὄντως πρὸς πειρασμὸν κατὰ τοῦ θεοῦ γραφείσαις βίβλοις πιστεύοντες ἡμάρτανον *ib*.19.20.

πειραστής, ὁ, 1. *one who makes trial, experimenter* π. διὰ βίου, κατάσκοπος μέχρι γήρως, πότε γενήσῃ Χριστιανός; Bas.*hom.*13.1(2.114C; M.31.425B); **2.** *tempter* ὁ μὲν γὰρ πειράζων εἰς τοὺς πειρασμοὺς καθέλκει, οἷα π. κακῶν, ὁ δὲ θεὸς πειράζων τοὺς πειρασμοὺς παραφέρει ὡς ἀπείραστος κακῶν ‡Dion.Al.*fr.Lc.22:46*(p.247.19; M.10.1596A); ὁ τοῦ φωτὸς διώκτης καὶ π. Gr.Naz.*or.*40.10(M.36.369B); id.*carm.*1.1.2.68(M.37.407A).

πειρατεύω, *be a pirate*, Gr.Nyss.*fat.*(M.45.149A).

πειρατήριον, τό, 1. *place of trial* or *testing*; of earthly life, ref. Job 7:1, Or.*or.*29(p.382.5; M.11.532A); Isid.Pel.*epp.*2.76(M.78.517D); *ib.*5.226(1469B); Olymp.*Job* 6 proem.(M.93.88A); *ib.*38 proem.(393A); of an ascetic's cell ἔσται γὰρ τὸ σπήλαιόν σου μαρτύριον τῆς ἐρήμου,...π. καὶ βάσανος τῶν δαιμόνων *V.Zos.*18(p.107.3); **2.** *temptation, testing, Narr.Jos.*1.2(p.460); ῥύσεται ἡμᾶς ἀπὸ παντὸς π. *A.Mt.* 11(p.229.16); ἐγγυμνασάμενοι τοῖς π. Eus.*d.e.*3.7(p.147.1; M.22.248A); Mac.Aeg.*cust.cor.*12(M.34.833A); τὰ π. τὰ συμβεβηκότα σοι καὶ τὰς θλίψεις Nil.*epp.*2.196(M.79.301C); Thdt.*Ps.*17:30(1.710); σαρκικῶν π. Jo.Eub.*concept.BMV* 14(M.96.1481C); **3.** *gang of robbers, T.Isach.*5.8; γαδδοὺρ...ὃ ἑτέρωθι ἑρμηνεύεται π. Thdt.*qu.65 in 1Reg.*(1.403).

πειρατής, ὁ, *pirate*; met., of demons τοὺς π. ἀφῆκεν πειράζειν ἡμᾶς Meth.*fr.Job* 7(p.512.14; perh. l. πειραστὰς); Chrys.*sac.*4.4 (p.112.5; 1.408E); of Devil, id.*virg.*34(1.292C).

πειράω, 1. c. acc. pers., *test, try, T.Jos.*16.3; *Did.*11.7; **2.** *learn by experience*, folld. by ὅτι, *T.Dan* 1.3.

***πείρημα, τό,** *end, limit*, of Christ αἰῶνος πείρημα Gr.Naz.*carm.*2.1.38.9(M.37.1326A).

πειρητίζω, *test, try*; c. acc. pers., Nonn.*par.Jo.*4:16(M.43.776C); *ib.*6:6(793B).

πεῖσις, ἡ, = πάθος, of 'passion' of Sophia, Clem.*exc.Thdot.*31 (p.117.7; M.9.673D).

πεῖσμα, τό, (A) *cable, rope*; met., ref. Ps.136:2 ὄργανα καλοῦσαι τὰ σκηνώματα...ἑαυτῶν, ἃ ἀνεκρέμασαν ἀπὸ τῶν π. τῆς ἁγνείας ἐξάψασαι τοῦ ξύλου Meth.*symp.*4.3(p.48.12; M.18.89C); ἀπὸ τῆς κεφαλῆς ἐξῆφθαι τῷ παντὶ σώματι τά τε τῶν νόσων καὶ τὰ τῆς ὑγιείας π. Synes.*calv.*12(p.212.20; M.66.488D).

πεῖσμα, τό, (B) *fixed intention*, of will of God for man's salvation εὐδοκίαν οὖν τὸ πρῶτον θέλημά φησι, τὸ σφοδρὸν θέλημα, τὸ μετὰ ἐπιθυμίας θέλημα,...ὃ λέγομεν ἡμεῖς π. Chrys.*hom.1.2 in Eph.*(11.5E); id.*hom.2.1 in 2Thess.*(11.523F).

πεισμονή, ἡ, 1. *persuasion*, Ign.*Rom.*3.3; Epiph.*haer.*30.21(p.361.19; M.41.440D); Chrys.*hom.1.2 in 1Thess.*(11.427D); **2.** *conviction, assurance*, Just.*1apol.*53.1(M.6.405C); Iren.*haer.*4.33.7(M.7.1077A); ἵνα τὸ διπλοῦν κήρυγμα...ἔχῃ τὴν π. τοῦ τε πάθους καὶ τῆς ἀπαθείας ‡Ath.*Apoll.*1.10(M.26.1112A); **3.** *reliability, trustworthiness*, Pall.*v.Chrys.*20(p.125.15; M.47.70).

***πεισμοσύνη, ἡ,** = foreg., Petr.Full.*ep.Acac.*(p.116.15; M.86.2632A).

πεκούλιον ([*]πεκουλλίον), τό, (Lat. *peculium*) *personal property*, Gr.Naz.*test.*(M.37.392A); σὺ δοῦλος καὶ τὰ σὰ τοῦ κυρίου. δοῦλος γὰρ ἐλεύθερον π. οὐκ ἔχει Ast.Am.*hom.*2(M.40.188B); μοναχὸς ὁ ἔχων πεκουλλία, ἀφοριζέσθω τῆς μονῆς †Pach.*poen.*(p.60).

πελαγίζ-ω, 1. *form a sea, be like a sea*, met. Παῦλος ἦν ποταμὸς διὰ μεγαληγορίας ~ων Gr.Nyss.*hom.11 in Cant.*(M.44.1004B); **2.** *make like a sea, make very abundant* ἐκκλησία ἣν ἐπελάγισε Procl.CP *or.*18 (M.65.817D); pass., Chrys.*pan.Phoc.*1(2.705B); **3.** pass.; **a.** *be flooded*, Bas.Sel.*or.*35.1(M.85.376A); **b.** *be swamped*; met., by sin, *Schol.* in CAnc.*can.*17(*Mon.*2 p.659).

πελάγιος, *out at sea*, met., π. διὰ τῆς θεωρίας γενόμενοι Gr.Nyss.*hom.12 in Cant.*(M.44.1016B).

πελάζω, 1. *draw near*; abs., Thdt.*Ps.*18:7(1.721); *ib.*103:2(1331); met., *enter upon* π. τῇ τῆς διηγήσεως ἱστορίᾳ id.*h.rel.*9(3.1186); **2.** *be near*, id.*Col.*4:13(3.500); **3.** med., *sojourn, spend time* ἐν ἐρημίαις π. Mac.Aeg.*hom.*9.3(M.34.533B).

[*]πελεκᾶνος, ὁ, *pelican*; typifying aggressive people, Or.*adnot. in Dt.*14:19(M.17.28A).

πελέκησις, ἡ, *hewing*, Or.*Jo.*10.40(24; p.217.21; M.14.385A).

πελεκητός, *capable of being hewn*; neut. as subst., Leont.H.*Nest.*1.14(M.86.1453C).

***πελεκοειδής,** *hatchet-shaped*, Or.*Cels.*6.38(p.107.10; M.11.1353C).

πελιδνήεις, *livid*, Paul.Sil.*ambo.*96(M.86.2255B).

πελιδνόομαι, *be livid*, Thdt.*Nah.*2:10(2.1528); Paul.Sil.*Soph.*631 (M.86.2143B); Jo.Clim.*scal.*4(M.88.720B).

***πελίη, ἡ,** *dove, Orac.Sib.*1.242.

πέλμα, 1. *floor* of theatre, Leont.N.*v.Sym.*37(M.93.1716B); *arena* of circus, Jo.Mal.*chron.*7 p.175(M.97.280D); **2.** *ground*, Barth.Edess.*Agar.*(M.104.1412D).

[*]πελτόν, τό, = παλτόν, *spear*, Thdt.*h.e.*3.3.7(3.914); *ib.*5.24.12 (1065).

πέλυξ, ὁ, *axe*, met. πνευματικοὶ λόγοι π. κόπτων πέτραν εἴρηνται Nil.*epp.*2.237(M.79.321B); Εἰρηναῖος ὁ τῶν αἱρέσεων π. Anast.S.*hod.*7 (M.89.113C); of Jo. Bapt. λαγνείας π. Geo.Pis.*carm.*5.2.

πεμπταῖος, *of five days* π. ἄγγελον [i.e. dispatched after five days] Thphyl.*exc.gent.*6(p.484.1; M.113.945A).

***πεμπτήριος,** *in dismissal*; hence *as parting gift*, Gr.Naz.*carm.*1.1.9.71(M.37.462A); *ib.*2.2(poem.)5.264(1540A); *ib.*2.2(poem.)6.1 (1542A).

πέμπτος, *fifth*; **1.** τὸ π. *the fifth* or celestial *element* acc. pagan thought, Gr.Naz.*or.*28.8(p.33.6; M.36.36A); **2.** of fifth commandment as enjoining reverence to God and θεία γνῶσις, Clem.*str.*6.16 (p.506.28; M.9.377A); **3.** ὁ π. *the fifth* (male) *aeon* in Valent. system, Val.Gn.ap.Epiph.*haer.*31.6(p.394.6; M.41.484C); id.*ib.*(p.395.4; 485B); **4.** π. καιρός, of the time of Christ's manifestation on earth, corresponding to 'eleventh hour' of Parable of Vineyard, Cyr.*ador.*6(1.208A); **5.** ἡ π., *Thursday*, esp. of Maundy Thursday; **a.** in gen., Socr.*h.e.*7.40.2(M.67.829A); **b.** as day of betrayal, Isid.Pel.ap.*cat. Mt.*suppl.(p.256.18); καταμυσάττεσθαι...δοκεῖ τήν τε π. καὶ ὀγδόην ἡμέραν ὁ σατανᾶς...τῇ π. ... παραδεδόσθαι φαμὲν αὐτόν, καὶ εἰς ἀρχὰς...ἥκειν τῆς ὅλης οἰκονομίας Cyr.*ador.*6(1.207E); **c.** as day of Last Supper; Christ did not eat Passover on day observed by Jews, but with his disciples on previous day (Thursday), Eus.*pasch.*9(M.24.704B); Jo.Philop.*pasch.*(p.211.16); **d.** as end of forty days fast of Lent, Leont.N.*v.Sym.*47(M.93.1728A); but ἐν τῇ π. τῇ μεγάλῃ μεταλαμβάνειν οἴνου καὶ ἐλαίου τοὺς ἐν ταῖς προτέραις τρισὶν ἡμέραις μὴ μετειληφότας, οὐ καλόν Eutych.*pasch.*3(M.86.2396A); Jo.Jej.*canonar.*1(p.113A); Anast.*temp.*(p.280); **e.** Communion on that day, Epiph.*exp.fid.*22(p.524.1; M.42.828C); Eutych.*pasch.*3(M.86.2396A); τῇ π. ἡ ἐκκλησία ἐπιτελεῖ τὴν ἑορτὴν τοῦ πάσχα τοῦ μυστικοῦ· καθ' ἣν καὶ ὁ κύριος ἑαυτὸν μυστικῶς ἔθυσε τότε *ib.*5(2397B); †Jo.Jej.*poenit.*(M.88.1913A); Jo.Mosch.*prat.*79(M.87.2936D); and distribution of food and εὐλογίαι to poor, *ib.*85(2941B); **f.** Friday fast beginning μετὰ τὴν π. Epiph.*exp.fid.*22(p.523.25; 828C); ref. a hermit who fasted except on Sunday and Thursday, ‡Pall.*h.mon.*17.4 (p.77.18; M.34.1178D); private fasting on Thursday to be broken for entertainment of strangers, ‡Ath.*syntag.*2.12(p.123; M.28.840A).

πέμπ-ω, 1. *send*, of divine sending ὁ ἄγγελος τοῦ θεοῦ, τοῦτ' ἔστιν ἡ δύναμις τοῦ θεοῦ ἡ πεμφθεῖσα ἡμῖν διὰ Ἰησοῦ Χριστοῦ Just.*dial.*116.1(M.6.744C); οὐ γὰρ αὐτοποίητον...τὸ κάλλος, ἀλλὰ ὑπὸ χειρὸς...~όμενον τοῦ θεοῦ Athenag.*leg.*34.1(M.6.968B); ref. Moses, Cyr.H.*catech.*19.3; ref. sending out of a Christian minister, Chrys.*hom. in 1Tim.*proem.(11.548B); ref. Christ, *Diogn.*7.4; Cyr.*Jo.*2.9(4.242B); cf. ἀποστέλλω; Manich., ref. light particle sent into matter, Thdt.*haer.*26(4.319); of sending up prayers etc., to God ὕμνους ~ειν Just.*1apol.*13.2(M.6.345B); Petr.II Al.*encycl.*(M.33.1281A)ap.Thdt.*h.e.*4.22.12; of soul's ascent after death μηκέτι μὲν εἰς ᾅδου τρέχειν τὰς...ψυχὰς...~εσθαι δὲ μᾶλλον εἰς χεῖρας θεοῦ Cyr.*Lc.*23:46(Pusey, p.475.3; M.72.940A n.); **2.** *send forth, send on one's way*, Gr.Thaum.*pan.Or.*19(p.39.13; M.10.1101B).

***πενακάς, ὁ,** ? for ⟨πινακάς⟩ one who makes tablets, *IG* 3.3459 (Attica).

***πενηθεία, ἡ,** *poverty of divinity*; of Jewish monotheism contrasted with Trinitarian belief and with pagan polytheism, †Gregent.*disp.*(M.86.628C).

πένης, *poor, needy* (dist. from πτωχός); **1.** ref. attitude to poverty; **a.** of one's own ἐὰν π. σε προείπῃ, εἰ μὲν ἀληθῆ λέγει, κατάδεξαι τὴν ἀλήθειαν· εἰ δὲ ψεύδεται, τί πρὸς σὲ τὸ λεγόμενον;...τί δέ σε ταράσσει ἡ προσηγορία τοῦ π.;...τίς ποτε ἀπήχθη διὰ πενίαν εἰς δεσμωτήριον; οὐ τὸ πένεσθαι ἐπονείδιστον, ἀλλὰ τὸ μὴ φέρειν εὐγενῶς τὴν πενίαν Bas.*hom.*10.4(2.87A,B; M.31.361C,D); ἐρεῖς π. κἀγώ. ἔστω...δὸς ὃ ἔχεις Gr.Nyss.*paup.*1(M.46.460B); βούλει γενέσθαι πλούσιος σὺ ὁ π.; ἔξεστί σοι βουλομένῳ...καταφρόνησον τῶν τοῦ κόσμου χρημάτων...ἔκβαλε τὴν ἐπιθυμίαν τοῦ πλούτου, καὶ ἐπλούτησας Chrys.*hom.2.5 in Phil.*(11.210A); **b.** of others καθάπερ εὐεργέτας, καὶ τῆς σωτηρίας ἡμῖν τὰς ἀφορμὰς παρέχειν δυναμένους, οὕτως ὁρῶμεν τοὺς π., καὶ μετὰ δαψιλείας καὶ ἱλαρᾶς τῆς προθυμίας παρέχωμεν id.*hom.34.3 in Gen.*(4.343A); ὅταν οὖν ἴδῃς π. πιστόν, θυσιαστήριον ὁρᾶν νόμιζε id.*hom.20.3 in 2Cor.*(10.582B); ref. Manicheans despising poor, Ath.*h.Ar.*61(p.217.24ff.; M.25.768B) cit. s. ἐλεέω; **c.** oppression of poor condemned μὴ βουληθῇς ἐπᾶραι χεῖρα θεὸν κατὰ τῶν...παρατρεχόντων τοὺς π. Gr.Naz.*or.*14.28(M.35.896B); ὢ ὠμότητος· ὅτι καὶ ζῶσιν οἱ π., μικροῦ δυσχεραίνομεν...μὴ φθονήσωμεν συμμεριστὰς κἂν τῶν περιττῶν προσλαβέσθαι τοὺς π., ὡς ἂν μὴ ἀκούσωμεν 'ἀπελάβετε τὰ ἀγαθὰ ὑμῶν ἐν τῇ ζωῇ ὑμῶν' Nect.*Thdr.*20(M.39.1837A); οὐδὲν γὰρ οὕτω τὸν θεὸν παροξύνειν εἴωθεν, ὡς ἡ κατὰ τῶν π. ἀδικία κατ' αὐτοὺς γινομένη Chrys.*Is.interp.*1:24(6.16A); οὐδὲν ἀναιδέστερον, φησί, πένητος. διατί; ...ὅτι ἐπιτρέχων καταβοᾷ; βούλει οὖν δείξω, ὅτι ἐκείνων ἡμεῖς ἐσμεν ἀναισχυντότεροι, καὶ σφόδρα ἀναιδεῖς; id.*hom.35.5 in Mt.*(7.404D); ref. three holy children μὴ τοίνυν ἔξω τῆς καμίνου καθεζώμεθα, ἀνηλεῶς πρὸς τοὺς π. ἔχοντες, ἵνα μὴ πάθωμεν ὅπερ ἔπαθον τότε ἐκεῖνοι [sc. their persecutors] *ib.4.12*(70B); **2.** beneficial influence of poor in Christian life ὁ πολλοὺς εὐποιῶν π.· πολλοὺς γὰρ εὑρήσει συνηγόρους κρινόμενος Ephr.1.38E; ἰατροὶ τῶν ψυχῶν ἡμῶν εἰσιν οἱ π. ... οὐ γὰρ τοσοῦτον δίδως, ὅσον λαμβάνεις· δίδως ἀργύριον, καὶ λαμβάνεις βασιλείαν οὐρανῶν· λύεις πενίαν, καὶ καταλλάττεις σεαυτῷ τὸν δεσπότην Chrys.*hom.3.11 in 2Cor.4:13*(3.289B); π., δεξιὰν ἐκτείνων καὶ ἐλεημοσύνην λαμβάνων, περιαιρεῖ τῶν τραυμάτων τοὺς μώλωπας id.*hom.30.4 in 1Cor.*(10.275B); κοινοὺς διδασκάλους ἡμῖν τῶν συμφορῶν καὶ παραμυθίαν ἀφῆκε διὰ τῆς οἰκουμένης ὁ θεὸς τοὺς π. id.*hom.11.3 in 1Thess.*(11.507A); χάριν ὀφείλεις μᾶλλον τῷ π. ἔχειν τοῦ λαβεῖν. εἰ μὴ π. ἦσαν, οὐκ ἂν τὸ πολὺ τῶν ἁμαρτημάτων ὑπετέμου id.*hom.14.2 in 1Tim.*(11.627E); v. δωροδοκέω; **3.** rich and poor; **a.** their need of each other ὅταν οὖν ἀναβῇ ὁ πλούσιος ἐπὶ τὸν π. καὶ χορηγήσῃ αὐτῷ τὰ δέοντα...ἀμφότεροι οὖν τὸ ἔργον τελοῦσιν· ὁ μὲν π. ἐργάζεται τὴν ἔντευξιν ἐν ᾗ πλουτεῖ...καὶ ὁ πλούσιος τὸν πλοῦτον...παρέχει τῷ π. ... οὕτω καὶ οἱ π. ἐντυγχάνοντες πρὸς τὸν κύριον ὑπὲρ τῶν πλουσίων πληροφοροῦσι τὸν πλοῦτον αὐτῶν, καὶ πάλιν οἱ πλούσιοι χορηγοῦντες τοῖς π. τὰ δέοντα πληροφοροῦσι τὰς ψυχὰς αὐτῶν Herm.*sim.*2.5.8; **b.** advantages of poor over rich in natural sphere πλειόνων χρῄζουσιν οἱ πλουτοῦντες καὶ δι' ἀξιοπιστίας μετὰ τῆς δόξης γίνονται, π. δὲ...τῶν καθ' ἑαυτὸν ἐφιέμενος εὐμαρέστερον περιγίνεται Tat.*orat.*11(p.12.7; M.6.829B); ἑνὶ τούτῳ διαφέρωμεν τῶν πλουτούντων οἱ π., τῇ ἀμεριμνίᾳ. καὶ καταγελῶμεν αὐτῶν ἀγρυπνούντων, αὐτοὶ καθεύδοντες Bas.*hom.2 in Ps.*14(1.110C; M.29.273A); τί δὲ ὁ ἥλιος...τὰς ὄψεις ἡμῶν εὐφραῖνον,...πάντες ἀπολαύουσιν ἐξ ἴσης αὐτοῦ, καὶ π. καὶ πλούσιοι;...μᾶλλον δέ...πλέον ἡμεῖς οἱ π. ἀπολαύομεν, ἢ ἐκεῖνοι. ἐκεῖνοι μὲν γὰρ τὰ πολλὰ μέθῃ βαπτιζόμενοι...οὐδὲ ἐπαισθάνονται τούτων, ὑπωρόφιοι ὄντες καὶ σκιατραφούμενοι· οἱ δὲ π. μάλιστα πάντων εἰσὶν οἱ τοῖς στοιχείοις ἐντρυφῶντες τούτοις Chrys.*hom.12.5 in 2Cor.*(10.527E–528A); ποιήσωμεν, εἰ δοκεῖ, δύο πόλεις, τὴν μὲν πλουσίων μόνον, τὴν δὲ π.· καὶ μήτε ἐν τῇ τῶν πλουτούντων ἔστω τις π., μήτε ἐν τῇ τῶν π. ἔστω τις πλούσιος ἀνήρ...ἐν μὲν ἐκείνῃ τῇ τῶν εὐπόρων οὐδεὶς ἔσται δημιουργός, οὐκ οἰκοδόμος...πῶς οὖν ἡ πόλις ἡμῖν στήσεται αὕτη; δόντες, φησίν, ἀργύριον οἱ πλουτοῦντες, ταῦτα ὠνήσονται παρὰ τῶν π. οὐκοῦν οὐκ ἀρκέσουσιν ἑαυτοῖς, εἴ γε ἐκείνων δέονται...ὅθεν δῆλον, ὡς ἀδύνατον χωρὶς π. συστῆναι πόλιν. ἴδωμεν οὖν καὶ τὴν τῶν π. πόλιν, εἰ καὶ αὕτη ὁμοίως ἐνδεῶς διακείσεται τῶν πλουτούντων ἐστερημένη...ἐνδεῶς σχήσει τὰ τῆς πόλεως ταύτης ...; οὐδέν. ἄν τε γὰρ οἰκοδομεῖν δέῃ, οὐ χρυσοῦ καὶ ἀργύρου δεῖ...ἀλλὰ τέχνης καὶ χειρῶν...ἐὰν γεωργεῖν δέῃ...πλουτούντων ἢ πενομένων χρεία;...δῆλον, ὅτι π. id.*hom.34.5 in 1Cor.*(10.316C–317C); ὁ...π. οὐδένα δεδοικὼς διάγει, ἐπειδὴ πλουτεῖ μόνον τῇ φιλοσοφίᾳ καὶ ὑπομονῇ· ὁ δὲ πλούσιος, ἐπειδὴ πλεονεξίᾳ συζῇ, μισεῖται παρὰ πάντων id. *hom.1.3 in Ps.48:17*(5.508C); **c.** in spiritual sphere καὶ ὁ πλούσιος καὶ ὁ π. τῆς ὠφελείας [sc. of scripture] κοινωνοῦσιν ὁμοίως· μᾶλλον δὲ οὐχ ὁμοίως κοινωνοῦσι τῆς ὠφελείας, ἀλλὰ πολλάκις πλείονος ἀπολαύσας ὁ π. ἀπέρχεται. τί δήποτε; ὅτι ὁ μὲν πλούσιος πολλαῖς προκατειλημμένος φροντίσιν, ἔχων τὴν ἀπόνοιαν καὶ τὸ φύσημα τῆς εὐπορίας...οὐ μετὰ πολλῆς τῆς ἀκριβείας...τὸ φάρμακον τῆς ἀκροάσεως τῶν γραφῶν δέχεται· ὁ δὲ π. τρυφῆς...ἀπηλλαγμένος...μετὰ πλείονος προσέχει ἀκριβείας τοῖς λεγομένοις id.*pecc.*1(3.345A,B); πόσοι τῶν π. τῶν πλουτούντων εἰσὶ συνετώτεροί τε καὶ φιλοσοφώτεροι, καὶ τὰ σώματα ὑγιεινότερα, πενίας αὐτοῖς καὶ τὴν σάρκα καὶ τὴν ψυχὴν διορθουμένης id.*exp.in Ps.*4:8(5.25B); πλουσίους μὲν ὀλίγους, τῶν δὲ π. πολλῷ πλείους σωζομένους id.*hom.13.4 in 2Cor.*(10.536B); both enjoy Christian teaching φιλοσοφοῦσί τε οὐ μόνον οἱ πλουτοῦντες, ἀλλὰ καὶ οἱ π. προῖκα τῆς διδασκαλίας ἀπολαύουσιν Tat.*orat.*32(p.33.6; M.6.872B); **d.** poverty of rich οὐδ' ἂν Μίδας τις αὐτῶν γένηται, πεπλήρωται, ἀλλὰ ἔτι π. ἐστὶ πλοῦτον ἄλλον ποθῶν Clem.*paed.*3.2 (p.242.5; M.8.569C); **e.** wrong attitude to rich and poor ὁ τιμῶν τὸ ἀργύριον...καὶ ἀποδεχόμενος τοὺς πλουσίους ὡς θεούς, τοὺς δὲ π. ὡς μὴ ἔχοντας τὸν θεὸν αὐτῶν ἐξουθενῶν, οὗτος θεοποιεῖ τὸ ἀργύριον Or.*hom.7.3 in Jer.*(p.53.32; M.13.333A); **f.** question whether rich martyrs have more glory than poor, answered in affirmative, Or. *mart.*15(p.15.4ff.; M.11.581D–584B) cit. s. μάρτυς; **4.** spiritually π. γὰρ καὶ γυμνὸς ἀπὸ κοινωνίας πνεύματος ὑπάρχων Mac.Aeg.*hom.*18.3 (M.34.636C); ὁ δὲ π. καὶ μὴ κεκτημένος ἐκ τοῦ πλούτου τοῦ Χριστοῦ ...εἰ καὶ βούλεται οὗτος λόγον ἀληθείας λαλεῖν...ἀλλ' ἐν δυνάμει καὶ ἀληθείᾳ τὸν λόγον τοῦ θεοῦ μὴ κεκτημένος ἐν ἑαυτῷ, ἀλλὰ μόνον ἀπομνημονεύων καὶ κιχρώμενος λόγους ἐξ ἑκάστης γραφῆς, ἢ παρὰ πνευματικῶν ἀνδρῶν ἀκούσας...ἰδοὺ ἄλλους μὲν δοκεῖ εὐφραίνειν,... μετὰ δὲ τὸ διηγήσασθαι αὐτόν, ἕκαστος λόγος πρὸς τὰ ἴδια ἀφ' ὧν ἤρθη, ἀπέρχεται, καὶ αὐτὸς πάλιν γυμνὸς ἀπομένει καὶ π., μὴ ἔχων ἴδιον θησαυρὸν πνεύματος *ib.*18.5(637B,C); οὐκ ἔστι π. ὁ μηδὲν ἔχων, ἀλλ' ὁ πολλῶν ἐπιθυμῶν Chrys.*hom.2.5 in Phil.*(11.209E).

***πενητοκόμος**, *ministering to the poor*, Gr.Naz.*carm.*2.2(epitaph.) 13.4(M.38.49A); *ib.*2.1.50.47(M.37.1388A).

***πενηχρός**, = πενιχρός, *humble, poor*, *Mir.Geo.*6(p.75.20).

***πενηχρόφρων**, *small-minded, of narrow understanding*, Ph.Carp. *Cant.*proem.(M.40.28A).

πενθαλέος, *sorrowful*, Gr.Naz.*carm.*1.2.17.26(M.37.783A); Nonn. *par.Jo.*11:32(M.43.844C); *ib.*20:1(908B).

πενθερίδης, ὁ, *brother-in-law*; of Aquila as brother-in-law of Hadrian, Epiph.*mens.*14(M.43.261A); *Dial.Tim.et Aquil.*117 v° (p.91); in gen. πενθερὸν δὲ αὐτὸν κέκληκεν, ὡς τῆς γαμετῆς ἀδελφόν. καὶ γὰρ νῦν πολλοὶ τοὺς τοιούτους π. καλοῦσι Thdt.*qu.4 in Jud.*(1. 322).

πενία, ἡ, **A.** *poverty* (dist. from πτωχεία); **1.** not a good in itself οὔτε τοὺς πένητας ἡ π. ῥύσεται ἀπὸ τῆς δίκης *A.Thom.*A 83 (p.199.10); οὔτε ἡ π. καλόν, ἀλλὰ τὸ καλῶς κεχρῆσθαι τῇ π. Chrys.*pecc.* 2(3.345B); ἀκόρεστόν πως κακὸν ἡ ἀκούσιος π., καὶ μεμψίμοιρον, καὶ ἀχάριστον...τῆς π. τὴν φύσιν καταμαθών, δεινὴν οὖσαν καὶ τὴν γενναιοτάτην ψυχὴν καταβαλεῖν id.*sac.*3.16(pp.85.3,86.2; 1.396C,E); πονηρὰ ἡ π., ἀλλ' οὐχ ἁπλῶς, ἀλλ' ἐν στόματι ἀσεβοῦς id.*pecc.*2(3. 346A); δεινὸν...ἡ π., καὶ ἴσασιν ὅσοι πεῖραν ταύτης εἰλήφασι id.*Laz.*1.9 (1.720C); π. γὰρ ἀκούσιος καὶ καμίνου καὶ θηρίων χαλεπώτερον id.*hom. 81.3 in Mt.*(7.778B); **2.** its possibilities for good or evil περὶ τῆς π. ἐστὶν εἰπεῖν· ἂν μὲν γὰρ γενναίως αὐτὴν ἐνέγκῃς εὐχαριστῶν τῷ δεσπότῃ, γέγονέ σοι στεφάνων τὸ πρᾶγμα ἀφορμή...ἂν δὲ βλασφημῇς διὰ τοῦτο τὸν πεποιηκότα...ἐπὶ κακῷ πάλιν ἐχρήσω τῷ πράγματι Chrys.*pecc.*2(3.345D); ἐπῃνεῖτο ὁ πένης ἐκεῖνος [sc. Lazarus] ὁ ἐν τοῖς κόλποις τοῦ Ἀβραάμ, οὐκ ἐπειδὴ πένης ἦν, ἀλλ' ἐπειδὴ μετ' εὐχαριστίας τὴν π. ἤνεγκε *ib.*(345C); **3.** of scriptural attitude to poverty, ref. Eccl.9:16, Pr.30:8 etc. ταῦτα ἐλέγετο ἐν τῇ παλαιᾷ, ἔνθα πολὺς ὁ λόγος τοῦ πλούτου, ἔνθα τῆς π. πολλὴ ἦν ὑπεροψία, ἔνθα τὸ μὲν κατάρα ἦν, τὸ δὲ εὐλογία...ἀλλὰ θέλεις ἀκοῦσαι τῆς π. ἐγκώμια; αὐτὴν μετῆλθεν ὁ Χριστός...ἐν αὐτῇ δὲ τῇ παλαιᾷ...τίνες ἦσαν οἱ θαυμαστοί; οὐχὶ Ἠλίας...; οὐχὶ Ἐλισσαῖος, οὐχὶ Ἰωάννης; μηδεὶς τοίνυν ἔστω ταπεινὸς διὰ πενίαν· οὐκ ἔστι π. ἡ ποιοῦσα ταπεινόν, ἀλλὰ πλοῦτος, ὁ πολλῶν δεῖσθαι καταναγκάζων...ἆρα ἀπαρρησίαστοι ἦσαν οἱ περὶ Ἠλίαν καὶ Ἰωάννην; οὐχ ὁ μὲν τὸν Ἀχαὰβ ἤλεγχεν, ὁ δὲ τὸν Ἡρώδην;...ὁρᾷς ὅτι τοῦτο μάλιστα ποιεῖ τὴν παρρησίαν, ἡ π.;...οὐκ ἂν οὖν, εἰ ἡ π. ἐποίει ἀπαρρησιάστους, ὁ Χριστὸς μετὰ πενίας ἔπεμπε τοὺς μαθητὰς εἰς πρᾶγμα παρρησίας πολλῆς δεόμενον Chrys.*hom.18.2 in Heb.*(12. 176C–177B); **4.** poverty and riches; **a.** as morally indifferent οὐδὲν ὁ πλοῦτος ἀγαθόν, οὐδὲν ἡ π. κακόν, ἀλλ' ἀδιάφορά ἐστι πράγματα Chrys.*hom.2.4 in 2Thess.*(11.521D); id.*Laz.*2.1(1.727A); id.*exp.in Ps.* 48:3(5.205A); **b.** virtue can be practised in either state ὡς ἐν π. βίου ὀρθῶς ἔστι βιοῦν, οὕτω δὲ καὶ ἐν περιουσίᾳ ἔξεστιν Clem.*str.*1.6(p.23.12; M.8.729B); Chrys.*stat.*15.3(2.156C) cit. s. πλοῦτος; **c.** but poverty more conducive to it πρὸς ἀρετὴν ἐπιτηδειότερον π. πλούτου id. *eleem.*5(3.256E); εἰ δέ τις εἴποι, καὶ πῶς π. ἡ ταπεινοφροσύνη; ἐκεῖνο ἐροῦμεν, ὅτι αὕτη ἐπιτηδειοτέρα πρὸς ἀρετήν. ὁ μὲν γὰρ πλουτῶν ἀλύει, καὶ θορυβεῖται· ὁ δὲ πένης πάντα ῥᾳδίως φέρει, καθάπερ ἐν παλαίστρᾳ τῇ π. πολλάκις γυμναζόμενος id.*exp.in Ps.*9:19(5.106C); **d.** true poverty and true riches πλοῦτος δὲ ἄριστος ἡ τῶν ἐπιθυμιῶν π. Clem.*paed.*2.3 (p.181.7; M.8.440A); πλοῦτος...ἀληθὴς ὁ ἐν ταῖς κατὰ τὴν ἀρετὴν πράξεσι πλεονασμός, π. δὲ ἡ κατὰ τὰς κοσμικὰς ἐπιθυμίας ἀπορία id. *str.*6.12(p.481.32; M.9.321A); πλοῦτος, ἡ τῆς ἐντολῆς μόνη τήρησις ἦν· π. δὲ ἀληθής...ἡ ταύτης παράβασις Gr.Naz.*or.*14.25(M.35.892B); οὐδὲ βλάβος πενίας, ψυχῆς οὔσης πλουσίας. καὶ πῶς ἂν γένοιτο πλουσία, φησί, ψυχή, ἐν π. χρημάτων οὖσα; μάλιστα ἂν τότε γένοιτο·...εἰ γάρ...τοῦτο πλουτοῦντος τεκμήριον, τὸ καταφρονεῖν χρημάτων...εὐκολώτερον δ' ἄν τις ἐν π. ἢ ἐν πλούτῳ καταφρονήσειε χρημάτων· εὔδηλον ὅτι μάλιστα τὸ ἐν π. εἶναι μᾶλλον ποιεῖ πλουτεῖν...εἰ τοίνυν τὸ πλειόνων ἐφίεσθαι, πενίας, ὁ δὲ ἐν πλούτῳ τοιοῦτος, οὗτος μάλιστα ἐν π. ὁρᾷς ὅτι τότε μάλιστα πένεται ἡ ψυχή, ὅταν πλουτῇ, καὶ τότε πλουτεῖ, ὅταν ἐν π. ᾖ; Chrys.*hom.80.4 in Mt.*(7.771E,772B); **e.** spiritual poverty of world opp. true riches ὁ εἰς τὴν τοῦ κόσμου π. ἀγαγών με καὶ εἰς πλοῦτον ἀληθινὸν παρακαλέσας με *A.Thom.*A 144(p.251.6); ἐν τῇ τοῦ κόσμου π. παρέμεινον, ἕως οὗ ὁ ἀληθινὸς πλοῦτος ὀφθεὶς κἀμὲ...ἐπλήρωσας πλούτου *ib.*145(p.252.5); μήτε ἐπὶ πενίᾳ καταπίπτωμεν· ἀλλ' ἐκεῖνον ζητῶμεν τὸν πλοῦτον, τὸν ἐν ἔργοις ἀγαθοῖς· ἐκείνην φεύγωμεν τὴν π., τὴν ἐν κακίᾳ...δι' ἣν καὶ ὁ πλούσιος ἐκεῖνος πένης ἦν...ὅτι οὐδὲ παραμυθήσασθαί ποθεν τὴν π. ἠδύνατο Chrys.*hom.9.5 in Mt.*(7.137B); **f.** in gen. ἐπὶ τοῦ παρόντος βίου καὶ π. καὶ πλοῦτος προσωπεῖα μόνον εἰσίν id.*Laz.*2.3(1.731B); οὐ γὰρ τῷ μέτρῳ τῆς οὐσίας, ἀλλὰ τῇ διαθέσει τῆς γνώμης ὁ πλοῦτος καὶ ἡ π. κρίνονται· καὶ ἐκεῖνος μάλιστά ἐστιν ὁ πάντων πτωχότατος, ὁ ἀεὶ τοῦ πλείονος ἐπιθυμῶν id.*hom.*23.6 *in 1Cor.*(10.211A); ἐμοὶ γὰρ ἡ π. κόρῃ τινὶ κοσμίᾳ, καὶ καλῇ...προσεοικέναι δοκεῖ· ἡ δὲ φιλαργυρία θηριομόρφῳ γυναικὶ id.*hom.*90.4 *in Mt.*(7.843D); ἃ μὲν τῆς π. δοκεῖ εἶναι κακά, κοινὰ ἑκατέρων ἐστίν· ἃ δὲ τοῦ πλούτου, μόνα ἐκείνου id.*hom.*13.4 *in 2Cor.*(10.536C); πλουτεῖς; ἔλπιζε π. καθ' ἑκάστην ἡμέραν. τίνος ἕνεκεν...; ὅτι τὰ μάλιστά σε ὠφελῆσαι δυνήσεται ἡ προσδοκία αὕτη. ὁ γὰρ ἐλπίζων π., ἐν πλούτῳ ὢν οὐ τυφοῦται id.*Saturn.*3(3.407E); ref. Pr.10:4 τὴν φειδωλίαν π. λέγει, καθ' ἣν οἱ πλούσιοι πένονται μεταδόσεως, ὡς οὐκ ἔχοντες Clem. *paed.*3.4(p.254.9; M.8.600A); **5.** advantages of poverty rightly borne; **a.** natural εἰ καὶ μηδὲν ἕτερον ἦν τὸ συνιστῶν τὴν τοῦ θεοῦ πρόνοιαν, ὁ πλοῦτος καὶ ἡ π. ταύτην ἂν...ἀπέδειξεν. ἂν γὰρ ἀνέλῃς τὴν π., τοῦ βίου τὴν σύστασιν ἀνεῖλες ἅπασαν...καὶ οὔτε ναύτης, οὔτε κυβερνήτης...οὐκ ἄλλος τις τῶν δημιουργῶν ἔσται τούτων...νῦν μὲν γάρ, καθάπερ διδάσκαλός τις ἀρίστη, ἑκάστῳ τούτων ἐπικαθημένη ἡ τῆς π. ἀνάγκη, πρὸς τὰ ἔργα καὶ ἄκοντας συνωθεῖ Chrys.*Anna* 5.3(4.744A,B); id.*hom.*2.3 *in Eph.*(11.13C); **b.** spiritual and moral π. ... καὶ νόσος καὶ τοιαῦται πεῖραι ἐπὶ νουθεσίᾳ προσφέρονται καὶ πρὸς διόρθωσιν τῶν παρεληλυθότων καὶ πρὸς ἐπιστροφὴν τῶν μελλόντων Clem.*str.*7.13(p.58.14; M.9.513A); π. πολλοὺς ἐσωφρόνισε τῶν ὡρμημένων κακῶς Bas. *hom.in Ps.*45(1.171A; M.29.417B); τὴν φίλην ἡμῖν π., καὶ φιλοσοφίας τροφὸν id.*ep.*4(3.76C; M.32.236C); βούλει τῆς π. τὸν πλοῦτον καταμαθεῖν; οὐκ ἐπιτάττει ἀνδράσιν, ἀλλὰ δαίμοσιν ἐπιτάττει· οὐ παρίσταται βασιλεῖ, ἀλλὰ παρέστηκε θεῷ· οὐ στρατεύεται μετὰ ἀνθρώπων, ἀλλὰ στρατεύεται μετὰ ἀγγέλων Chrys.*hom.*47.4 *in Mt.*(7.492C); τοῖς παισὶν ἐκείνοις [sc. three holy children] ἴσοι γίνονται οἱ πενίαν μετ' εὐχαριστίας φέροντες. καὶ γὰρ πυρὸς φοβερώτερον ἡ πτωχεία...ἀλλὰ τοὺς παῖδας οὐκ ἐνέπρησεν ἐκείνους...οὕτω καὶ νῦν, ἂν ἐμπεσὼν εἰς π. εὐχαριστήσῃς, καὶ τὰ δεσμὰ λύεται, καὶ ἡ φλὸξ σβέννυται *ib.*4.12(70A); ἡ δὲ π. φρούριον ἀσφαλές, χαλκῷ περιβεβλημένον πολλῷ, καὶ δύσκολον ἔχον τὴν ἄνοδον id.*hom.*13.4 *in Ac.*(9.108D); ἡ π. προσθήκη γίνεται καὶ τρυφῆς καὶ ἀναπαύσεως ἡμῖν. ... ἁμαρτήματα ἀποτιθέμεθα, ἂν εὐχαρίστως ταύτην φέρωμεν, καὶ πολλὴν παρὰ τῷ θεῷ κτώμεθα τὴν παρρησίαν id.*hom.*77.4 *in Jo.*(8.456E); esp. of voluntary poverty εἰ γὰρ βούλει μηδενὸς σφόδρα δεῖσθαι, εὔχου πενίαν· κἂν τινος δεηθῇς, ὑπὲρ ἄρτου δεήσῃ μόνον ἢ ἱματίου...εἰ δὲ θέλεις τὸν ὄχλον φυγεῖν· ἔξεστι γὰρ ἐπὶ τὸν ἀκύμαντον τῆς π. καταφυγεῖν λιμένα id.*hom.*17.3 *in 2Cor.*(10.562A,B); τὴν τελειότητα μὲν ὁ δεσπότης ὁρίζεται...τῇ αὐθαιρέτῳ π. Thdt.*2Cor.*8:13ff.(3.330); **6.** illustrious representatives of poverty τίς πένης...βλέπων αὐτόν [sc. S. Antony], οὐ κατεφρόνει τοῦ πλούτου, καὶ παρεμυθεῖτο τὴν π.; Ath.*v.Anton.*87(M.26.965A); φιλοσοφῶμεν ...καὶ οὐδὲν ἡμᾶς π. παραβλάψαι δυνήσεται, ἀλλὰ καὶ ὠφελήσει τὰ μέγιστα...τί γὰρ...τοῦ Ἠλία πενέστερον ἦν; ἀλλὰ διὰ τοῦτο πάντας ἐνίκα τοὺς πλουτοῦντας, ἐπειδὴ οὕτω πένης ἦν, καὶ αὐτὴν τὴν π. ἀπὸ πλουσίας εἵλετο διανοίας. ἐπειδὴ γὰρ ἅπαντα τῶν χρημάτων τὸν πλοῦτον ἐλάττονα τῆς ἑαυτοῦ μεγαλοψυχίας ἐνόμιζεν εἶναι, καὶ οὐκ ἄξιον αὐτοῦ τῆς φιλοσοφίας, διὰ τοῦτο π. τοσαύτην ἠσπάσατο Chrys.*stat.* 2.9(2.33E–34A); μὴ γάρ μοι τοὺς κατηγοροῦντας τῆς π. ἐνέγκῃς εἰς μέσον, ἀλλὰ τοὺς δι' αὐτῆς λάμψαντας. μετὰ ταύτης Ἠλίας τραφείς, ἡρπάγη τὴν μακαρίαν ἐκείνην ἁρπαγήν· μετὰ ταύτης Ἐλισσαῖος ἔλαμψε· μετὰ ταύτης Ἰωάννης, μετὰ ταύτης οἱ ἀπόστολοι πάντες id.*hom.*90.4 *in Mt.*(7.843D); ὁ Λάζαρος π. συνέζη, καὶ ἐστεφανοῦτο· καὶ ὁ Ἰακὼβ ἄρτου μόνου ἐπιτυχεῖν ἐπεθύμει· καὶ ὁ Ἰωσὴφ ἐν ἐσχάτῃ π. ἐγεγόνει id.*hom.*76.3 *in Jo.*(8.450C); **7.** praises of poverty ἐγὼ δὲ καυχῶμαι ἐπὶ πενίᾳ *A.Thom.*A 139(p.246.11); π. μετὰ αὐταρκείας ἀληθοῦς, πάσης ἀπολαύσεως τοῖς σωφρονοῦσι προτιμοτέρα Bas.*hex.*7.3(1.65D; M.29.153B); μέγα κτῆμα π. τοῖς φιλοσόφως αὐτὴν φέρουσι, θησαυρὸς ἄσυλος, βακτηρία ἰσχυροτάτη Chrys.*stat.*2.8(2.33A); π. γὰρ μυρία εἰς τὸν βίον ἡμῶν εἰσήγαγεν ἀγαθά, καὶ χωρὶς π. ὁ πλοῦτος ἄχρηστος *ib.*13.3(156C); π. ... χωρίον ἄσυλόν ἐστι καὶ ἀσφαλές...γυμνάσιον φιλοσοφίας, ἀγγελικοῦ βίου μίμημα...οὐ τὸ πένεσθαι δεινόν, ἀλλὰ τὸ μὴ βούλεσθαι πένεσθαι. μηδὲν δεινὸν νόμιζε εἶναι π., καὶ οὐκ ἔσται σοι δεινόν. οὐδὲ γὰρ ἐν τῇ φύσει τοῦ πράγματος, ἀλλ' ἐν τῇ κρίσει τῶν μαλακοψύχων ἀνδρῶν τοῦτό ἐστι τὸ δέος. μᾶλλον δὲ καὶ αἰσχύνομαι, εἰ τοσοῦτον ὑπὲρ πενίας ἔχοιμι λέγειν, ὅτι οὐδέν ἐστι δεινόν· ἐὰν γὰρ φιλοσοφῇς, καὶ μυρίων ἀγαθῶν ἔσται σοι πηγή. καὶ εἴ τίς σοι ἀρχὴν...καὶ πλοῦτον καὶ τρυφὴν προετίθει, εἶτα τὴν π. ἀντιτιθείς, αἵρεσιν ἐδίδου λαβεῖν ὅπερ ἤθελες, ταύτην ἂν εὐθέως ἥρπασας, εἴ γε αὐτῆς ἔγνως τὸ κάλλος id. *hom.*90.3 *in Mt.*(7.843B,C); id.*Saturn.*3(3.406D); id.*hom.*18.3 *in Heb.*(12.177D); **8.** poverty and spiritual life μηδεὶς πενίαν ὀδυρέσθω· μηδὲ ἀπογινωσκέτω ἑαυτοῦ τὴν ζωήν, ὁ μηδεμίαν οἴκοι περιουσίαν καταλιπών...μὴ διὰ πενίαν πρὸς κακουργίαν τρέπεσθαι· μηδὲ ἐν χαλεπωτάτοις πάθεσι πᾶσαν ἐλπίδα ῥίψαντα...ἀλλ' ἐπὶ θεὸν καταφεύγειν Bas. *hex.*8.5(1.75C,E; M.29.176D–177A); ταύτης τῆς λειτουργίας οὐκ ἄν ποτε γένοιτο κώλυμα, ἀλλὰ δυνατὸν καὶ τὸν πένητα, ἅτε πάσης ἀπηλλαγμένον φαντασίας βιωτικῆς...ὥσπερ οὖν οὐδὲ βλάβος ἔσται π., ἐὰν τὸν ἔνδοθεν ἔχῃ πλοῦτον ἐναποκείμενον Chrys.*Anna* 3.5(4.728E–729A); **9.** poverty of Christ ἠπάτησεν δὲ ἡμᾶς [sc. demons] τῇ μορφῇ αὐτοῦ ...καὶ τῇ π. αὐτοῦ *A.Thom.*A 45(p.162.19); ἀποβλέψατε γὰρ εἰς τὸν τῶν ὅλων ποιητὴν...ὃς τῆς ὑμετέρας ἕνεκα σωτηρίας τὴν ἐσχάτην μετελήλυθε π., ἡμῖν τὸν ἐκ τῆς π. φυόμενον πραγματευόμενος πλοῦτον Thdt.*2Cor.*8:9(3.329).

B. *lack, deficiency* ὀνομάτων...π. Clem.*prot.*2(p.31.14; M.8.124C); Παῦλος...οὐδὲ ἐγκαλύπτεται ἐπὶ τῇ τοῦ λόγου π. Chrys.*sac.*4.5(p.117.10; 1.410D).

***πενίχρομαι**, *be poor*, *Orac.Sib.*3.245.

***πενόλιον, τό,** (Lat. *paenula*) *cloak*, *Chron.Pasch.*p.310(M.92.792A).

***πεντάβολος**, *with five projections*, Max.*qu.dub.*79(M.90.853B).

***πενταδικός**, *containing* or *consisting in five*, †Cyr.*coll.VT*(6⁴.73B; M.77.1285A); ‡Proc.G.*Pr.*2:10(M.87.1237A); Max.*ambig.*(M.91.1397A).

***πενταδικῶς**, *in five ways*, *in a five-fold manner*, ‡Proc.G.*Pr.*2:3 (M.87.1236A).

***πεντάζω**, *be fifth*, Thdr.Stud.*epp.*2.15(M.99.1161A).

πένταθλος, ὁ, 1. *victor in pentathlon*; hence *great athlete*; of Job, Sophr.H.*ep.syn.*(M.87.3149A); as adj., of Athanasius ὁ π. τῆς ἀληθείας ἀγωνιστής Thdt.*h.e.*3.9.1(3.921); of Symeon Stylites, id. *h.rel.*26.4(p.3.25; 3.1267); and other ascetics, *ib.*21(1239); **2.** as adj., *operating in five ways* τὴν π. ... αἴσθησιν *Lit.*ap.*Const.App.*8.12.17.

***πεντακισχιλιοστός**, *five-thousandth*, Dam.*troph.*4.3(p.266.9); *Chron.Pasch.*p.205(M.92.501C); †Hipp.Th.*fr.*8c.5(p.38.22; M.117.1045A).

***πεντακόρυφος**, *having five heads, five-headed*; met. of Church, ref. five patriarchates, Thdr.Stud.*epp.*2.62(M.99.1280B); *ib.*2.129 (1417C).

πενταμηνιαῖος, *of five months*, ref. period of gestation ὁ π. ... χρόνος...ὁ τὸν αἰσθητὸν ἡμῖν νόμον παραδηλῶν διὰ τὴν σύστοιχον αὐτῷ πεντάδα καὶ προσφιλῆ τῶν σωματικῶν...αἰσθήσεων Sophr.H.*or.*7.12 (M.87.3341B).

***πενταμόδιον, τό,** *measure containing five modii*, Jo.Mal.*chron.* 11 p.278(M.97.420C).

πενταπλασιάζω, *multiply by five*, Or.*comm.in Mt.*14.9(p.296.15; M.13.1205A).

πενταπλοῦς, *five-fold*, Chrys.*hom.*39.1 *in 1Cor.*(10.363A).

***πενταπλόω**, *multiply by five*, Max.*comput.*16(M.19.1233A).

***πεντάπλωσις, ἡ,** *five-fold increase*, Max.*comput.*1.11(M.19.1228B).

***πεντάριθμος**, *five in number*, Geo.Pis.*Pers.*3.14(M.92.1237A); id. *hex.*1794(M.92.1573A).

πεντάς, ἡ, *group of five*, *the number five*, hence *fifth day* of week, *Thursday* τῇ ἁγίᾳ καὶ μεγάλῃ π. Chrys.*prod.Jud.*2 tit.(2.386A).

πεντάτευχος, ἡ, *Pentateuch*, Ptol.*ep.*ap.Epiph.*haer.*33.4(p.452.11; M.41.560A); Or.*comm.in Mt.*11.10(p.50.7; M.13.933B); Epiph. *haer.*9.2(p.198.11; 225A).

***πεντάτροπος**, *of five kinds*, Dion.Ar.*ep.*7.2(M.3.1080D); Melet. *nat.hom.*30(M.64.1304D).

***πεντάφωτος**, *with five lights*; met., of body with five senses, Meth.*symp.*6.3(p.67.11; M.18.117B) cit. s. αἴσθησις; *ib.*9.2(p.116.22; 181B); ἀναγνοὺς τὴν Πεντάλογον, ἀπέφηνας αὐτὴν π. εἶναι Thdr.Stud. *epp.*1.48(M.99.1069C).

πένταχα, *in five divisions*, Paul.Sil.*Soph.*408(M.86.2135A).

πεντάχορδος, *like a five-stringed lyre* π. ... δακτύλους Geo.Pis. *hex.*1448(M.92.1545A).

πεντάχρονος, *of five units of time* φοίνικος...π. [i.e. centuries] *Orac.Sib.*8.139.

***πεντάχροος**, *of five colours*, Max.*ep.*12(M.91.476A).

πεντεκαιδεκαετηρίς, ἡ, *period of fifteen years*, Max.*comput.*3.9(M.19.1272A); *Chron.Pasch.*p.187(M.92.460A).

***πεντηκονταετηρίς, ἡ,** *period of fifty years*, Or.*sel.in Pss.*proem. (M.12.1075B); *Chron.Pasch.*p.209(M.92.512D).

πεντηκονταετία, ἡ, *period of fifty years*; as span of human life, Or.*princ.*3.1.13(p.218.10; M.11.273A).

***πεντηκοντάκις**, *fifty times*, Thdr.Stud.*epp.*2.202(M.99.1617A).

πεντηκόνταρχος, ὁ, *captain of fifty*, in analogy between eccl. order and military ranks οὐ πάντες εἰσὶν...χιλίαρχοι οὐδὲ...π. *1Clem.* 37.3; of the third captain of fifty (4Reg.1:13), identified with prophet Obadiah (perh. by confusion with 3Reg.18:13), ‡Epiph.*v.proph.Abd.*3(p.27; M.43.416A).

πεντηκοντάς, ἡ, *the fiftieth part*, Epiph.*haer.*15.1(p.211.3; M.41.249A).

***πεντηκοντάωρος**, *consisting of fifty hours*, Evagr.Pont.*vit.cog.* 7(M.40.1273B) cit. s. ἀκηδία.

πεντηκοστή, ἡ, *Pentecost*;

A. Jewish *Feast of Weeks*, Epiph.*haer.*51.31(p.304.23; M.41.945A).

B. festival period of fifty days after Easter; **1.** in gen., cf.Tert. *de idololatria* 14(M.*PL*.1.682C); id.*de baptismo* 19(M.*PL*.1.1222A); Or.*Cels*.8.22(p.239.12; M.11.1549D); ὁ δυνάμενος μετ' ἀληθείας λέγειν· συνανέστημεν τῷ Χριστῷ...ἀεί ἐστιν ἐν ταῖς τῆς π. ἡμέραις *ib.*(p.239. 27; 1552A); μεγίστης...ἑορτῆς, τῆς...σεβασμίας π. ἑβδομάσι μὲν ἑπτὰ τετιμημένης μονάδι δ' ἐπισφραγιζομένης, καθ' ἣν τὴν εἰς οὐρανοὺς ἀνάληψιν τοῦ...σωτῆρος τήν τε τοῦ ἁγίου πνεύματος...κάθοδον γεγενῆσθαι λόγοι περιέχουσι θεῖοι. ... ἐπὶ τῆς ὑστάτης ἁπασῶν ἡμέρας, ἣν δὴ ἑορτὴν ἑορτῶν οὐκ ἄν τις διαμάρτοι καλῶν Eus.*v.C*.4.64(p.144.11; M.20.1220B); Ath.*ep.Ors*.2(M.26.980B); ἐν...ταῖς ἁγίαις ταύταις ἡμέραις τῆς ἁγίας π. Cyr.H.*ep.Const*.4(M.33.1169A); πᾶσα δὲ ἡ π. τῆς ἐν τῷ αἰῶνι προσδοκωμένης ἀναστάσεώς ἐστιν ὑπόμνημα· ἡ γὰρ μία ἐκείνη καὶ πρώτη ἡμέρα, ἑπτάκις ἑπταπλασιασθεῖσα, τὰς ἑπτὰ τῆς ἱερᾶς π. ἑβδομάδας ἀποτελεῖ. ἐκ πρώτης γὰρ ἀρχομένη, εἰς τὴν αὐτὴν καταλήγει...διὸ καὶ αἰῶνα μιμεῖται τῇ ὁμοιότητι Bas.*Spir*.66(3.56C; M.32.192B); in comparison of Christ's body with first-fruits offered at Feast of Weeks ἐπὶ τῷ τέλει τῆς π. εἰσφέροντος αὐτὸ εἰς τὰ ἐπουράνια τῷ πατρί Epiph. *haer*.51.31(p.305.2; M.41.945A); Cyr.*hom.pasch*.1(5^2.16D); *Chron. Pasch*.p.223(M.92.544A); **2.** as period when liturgical prayer is made standing, v. γόνυ, γονυκλισία, γονυπετέω; **3.** and no fasting is practised, Epiph.*exp.fid*.22(p.523.6; M.42.828A); ‡Ath.*syntag*.2. 10(p.123; M.28.840A); **4.** as a season for administration of baptism, Gr.Naz.*or*.40.24(M.36.392A); v. βάπτισμα; **5.** when Acts is read liturgically, cf.Chrys.*hom.33.1 in Gen*.(4.331C); question discussed why reading takes place *before* actual day of Pentecost; reason given that miracles of apostles are proof of reality of Christ's Resurrection, id.*hom.4.3–6 in Ac.princ*.(3.85B–89E); **6.** when episcopal synods regularly assemble δεύτερον τοῦ ἔτους σύνοδος γινέσθω ...ἅπαξ μὲν τῇ τετάρτῃ ἑβδομάδι τῆς π. *Can.App*.38; ἅπαξ μὲν μετὰ τὴν τρίτην ἑβδομάδα τῆς ἑορτῆς τοῦ πάσχα, ὥστε τῇ τετάρτῃ ἑβδομάδι τῆς π. ἐπιτελεῖσθαι τὴν σύνοδον CAnt.(341)*can*.20; **7.** origin of feast ascribed to apostolic times, Epiph.*haer*.75.6(p.338.4; M.42.512C).

C. *day of Pentecost*, Ath.*fug*.6(p.72.9; M.25.652B) (or perh. under B.1 supra); τιμῶσι μὲν Ἑβραῖοι τὴν π. ἡμέραν, τιμῶμεν δὲ καὶ ἡμεῖς... π. ἑορτάζομεν, καὶ πνεύματος ἐπιδημίαν καὶ προθεσμίαν ἐπαγγελίας καὶ ἐλπίδος συμπλήρωσιν Gr.Naz.*or*.41.4–5(M.36.436A); μετὰ δὲ δέκα ἡμέρας τῆς ἀναλήψεως, ἥτις ἀπὸ τῆς πρώτης κυριακῆς π. γίνεται, ἑορτὴ μεγάλη...ἔστω· ἐν αὐτῇ γὰρ...ἀπέστειλεν...ὁ κύριος...τὴν δωρεὰν τοῦ...πνεύματος *Const.App*.5.20.8; Didym.ap.*cat.Ac*.2:3(p.21.23); as day when sickle is to be applied to harvest, hence beginning of apostles' mission, Chrys.*hom.4.1 in Ac*.(9.32D); id.*Philogon*.3(1. 497C); as μητρόπολις τῶν ἑορτῶν, id.*pent*.2.1(2.469A); ἐν τοίνυν ἡμέρᾳ τῆς π. ἐδόθη νόμος...ἔδει οὖν καθ' ἣν ἡμέραν ἐδόθη ὁ παλαιὸς νόμος, κατ' αὐτὴν δοθῆναι καὶ τὴν τοῦ πνεύματος χάριν Sever.ap.*cat.Ac*.2:1 (p.16.15); Socr.*h.e*.7.34.3(M.67.813C); *Chron.Pasch*.p.286(M.92.716B).

πεπανός, *mature* φρόνημα π. Clem.*q.d.s*.8(p.165.7; M.9.612D).

***πεπαρρησιασμένως**, *with freedom of speech, openly, boldly*, Eus.*v.C*.4.75(p.148.13; M.20.1229B); Epiph.*haer*.63.2(p.399.27; M.41. 1064C); *Mir.Artem*.10(p.10.19); ref. actions, *boldly, publicly*, Eus.*Is*. 57:7(M.24.473D).

***πεπερασμένως**, *completely, thoroughly*, *cat.Apoc*.19:16(p.462.14).

***πεπηγότως**, *firmly*, Cyr.*Jo*.10.1(4.853A).

***πεπληροφορημένως**, *with full assurance*, Pall.*v.Chrys*.20(p.125. 14; M.47.70).

πέπλος, ὁ, *woven work*; **1.** *veil, curtain*, screening sanctuary in Egyptian temples, Clem.*paed*.3.2(p.238.5; M.8.560B); of veil of Temple, *Ev.Barth*.(Vassiliev, p.13); **2.** *chalice veil*; of the ἀνώτατος π. covering chalice and paten, *Lit.Praesanct*.(p.348.24); **3.** *robe* of Athena carried in Panathenaic procession τῶν τοιούτων...ἔχεσθαι νοημάτων καὶ τὸν περὶ τῆς Ἀθηνᾶς π. ... δηλοῦται γὰρ...ἀπ' αὐτοῦ ὅτι ἀμήτωρ τις καὶ ἄχραντος δαίμων ἐπικρατεῖ θρασυνομένων τῶν γηγενῶν Cels.ap.Or.*Cels*.6.42(p.113.2; M.11.1364A); cf. Suidas s.v.; **4.** met., *patchwork of writings, anthology*, Clem.*str*.6.1(p.423.2; M.9.209A); title of work attributed to Orpheus but ascribed by Epigenes to Brontinus, *ib*.1.21(p.81.13; M.8.864B); cf. Suidas s.v. Ὀρφεύς.

***πεποιθέω**, *put one's trust in* οὐδενὶ τῶν ματαίων...ἐπεποίθησα Cyr.*Ps*.51:10(M.69.1105D).

πεποίθησις, ἡ, 1. *assurance, confidence* μετ' εὐσεβοῦς π. ἐξετείνετε τὰς χεῖρας...πρὸς...θεόν *1Clem*.2.3; ποίᾳ π. εἰσελευσόμεθα εἰς τὸ βασίλειον τοῦ θεοῦ; *2Clem*.6.9; ἡ εἰς τὸν κύριον π. αὔξει τὴν πίστιν Clem.*str*.5.13(p.382.24; M.9.128A); *ib*.7.2(p.5.16; 408B); Eus.*Ps*.143 proem.(M.24.52C); π. ἔχων διὰ τοῦ Χριστοῦ πρὸς τὸν θεόν Bas.*fid*.1 (2.223D; M.31.676D); τῆς ἐν θεῷ π. id.*moral*.63 tit.(2.284A; M.31. 800D); τὸ εἰπεῖν πεποιθήσει πατέρα τὸν θεόν Didym.*Trin*.3.18(M.39. 885A); ὦ μάρτυς...πολλή σοι π. ὑπὲρ Χριστοῦ †Bas.Sel.*or*.41(M.85. 472C); of false confidence in pagan gods, Eus.*l.C*.9(p.218.33; M.20. 1364C); **2.** *self-confidence* τίς ἂν εἰς τοσοῦτον πεποιθήσεως ἦλθεν, ὥστε ...τολμῆσαι Gr.Nyss.*Eun*.1(1 p.22.23; M.45.249D); Nil.*Magn*.17(M. 79.992B); **3.** *assurance* given ἡ ἡμετέρα δῆλον π. τῇ τούτων τάξει ἕπηται (tr. Lat. *nostrae erit fiduciae istorum ordinem sequi*) *Cod.Afr*.64.

πεποιθότως, *with confidence*, Clem.*str*.7.11 (conj. p.46.18 for πεποιθὼς M.9.489A).

πεπονημένως, *diligently, with toil*, Hipp.*haer*.5.6(p.77.16; M.16. 3123B); Pall.*v.Chrys*.18(p.111.18; M.47.62); Gr.Mag.*dial*.(tr.Zach.) 3.1(M.*PL*.77.219C).

πεπονθέω, *be affected*, Mac.Mgn.*apocr*.3.11(p.76.8).

***Πεπουζιανοί (*Πεπουζηνοί), οἱ**, *Pepuzans*, name given to Montanist sect from its belief, based on prophetic revelation, that Pepuza in Phrygia was sacred spot where heavenly Jerusalem would descend, Epiph.*haer*.49.1(p.241.20; M.41.880C); *ib*.48.14(p.240. 1; 877C); τὸ δὲ [sc. βάπτισμα] τῶν Π., οὐδένα μοι λόγον ἔχειν δοκεῖ· καὶ ἐθαύμασα πῶς κανονικὸν ὄντα τὸν Διονύσιον παρῆλθεν Bas.*ep*.188 *can*.1(3.268C; M.32.664C); οἱ τοίνυν Πεπουζηνοὶ προδήλως εἰσὶν αἱρετικοί· εἰς γὰρ τὸ πνεῦμα...ἐβλασφήμησαν *ib*.(269C; M.668A); Thdt.*haer*.3.2(4.341); rebaptized on admission to Church, Thdr. Stud.*epp*.1.53(Πεπουζηνοί M.99.1104A).

***Πεπουζῖται, οἱ**, = foreg. Μοντανισταὶ δέ, οὓς Π. ... ὀνομάζουσι, ξένην τινὰ μέθοδον εἰσαγαγόντες, κατὰ ταύτην τὸ πάσχα ἄγουσι Soz. *h.e*.7.18.12(M.67.1472B).

***πεπωπασμένος**, v. πυκάζω.

περαίνω, 1. *fulfil* prophecy, Eus.*h.e*.1.6.11(M.20.89A); **2.** *limit*, Tat.*orat*.20(p.22.20; M.6.852A); ref. Or's. theory of limitation of God's power, Justn.*Or*.(p.190.9; M.86.947C) cit. s. περιγραφή; in refutation of Manich. doctrine of two ultimate principles εἰ δὲ χωρὶς ἀλλήλων ἐστί, πάντως ἕκαστον τούτων πεπέρασται· πᾶν δὲ τὸ πεπερασμένον οὐ τέλειον. ὁρίζεται γὰρ διὰ τοῦ πεπεράσθαι Epiph.*haer*.66.14 (p.37.4; M.42.49C); ὁ θεὸς οὔτε κινεῖται παντελῶς οὔτε ἵσταται (τοῦτο γὰρ τῶν κατὰ φύσιν πεπερασμένων...ἴδιον) Max.*ambig*.(M.91.1221A).

περαίτερος, *further*, neut. as subst. εἰ δὲ περαιτέρω χρήσηται, γνώσεται οἷα ἰσχύει κράτος βασιλείας [i.e. *if he goes too far, exceeds his commission*] *Pers*.(p.23.2).

περαίωσις, ἡ, *accomplishment*, ‡Meth.*Sym.et Ann*.3(M.18.353B).

πέραμα, τό, 1. *crossing* of river, Ath.*v.Anton*.60(M.26.929B); met., of death χαλεπὸν τὸ π. Anast.S.*defunct*.(M.89.1196B); **2.** *means of crossing* ἔκοψαν τὰς γεφύρας, καὶ οὐκ ἔχει π. ὁ Ναρβᾶς Thphn.*chron*. p.270(M.108.669B); **3.** *ferry*, Ath.Scholast.*coll*.4.14(p.58).

***περαματίζω**, *cross over*, Thphn.*chron*.p.320(M.108.776A).

***περαματικός**, *overseas* οἱ δὲ πρὸς π. δικαστήρια διεκκαλούμενοι παρ' οὐδενὸς ἐν τῇ Ἀφρικῇ δεχθῶσιν κοινωνίαν (tr. Lat. *transmarina*) *Cod.Afr*.28.

πέραν, *beyond* τὸ π. ref. Mt.14:22 mystically interpreted, Or. *comm.in Mt*.11.5(p.41.2; M.13.913C) cit. s. περατικός.

***πέραντος**, f.l. in ‡Jo.D.*Artem*.16(M.96.1265C for πέραν p.59.26).

πέρας, τό, 1. temporal *end*; of world, Tat.*orat*.12(p.13.24; M.6. 832C); Gr.Naz.*or*.30.15(p.132.1; M.36.124A); Thdr.Mops.*Gen*.2:2(M. 66.636C); **2.** *end, object, goal*, Clem.*str*.8.3(p.83.11; M.9.565B); Meth. *res*.1.37(p.279.7; M.41.1104C); Cyr.*Is*.5.2(2.775B); π. τὸ καλὸν καὶ ἀγαθόν Dion.Ar.*d.n*.4.10(M.3.705C); Max.*myst*.(M.91.677C); **3.** *completion, perfection, consummation* π. τῆς γνώσεως ἡ ἀνάπαυσις Clem. *paed*.1.6(p.107.25; M.8.285B); π. παρθενίας Meth.*symp*.6.2(p.65.25; M.18.116B); of a person ὦ τῶν ἀγγέλων...π. Chrysipp.*enc.in Mich*. (p.93.31); **4.** *fulfilment* of prophecy, Eus.*d.e*.6.15(p.272.6; M.22. 448A); Thdt.*qu.13 in Jos*.(1.311); ‡Bas.*inc*.54(p.247.7); Χριστὸς τὸ π. πάσης προφητείας Cosm.Ind.*top*.5(M.88.280B); **5.** local *limit, end* τὰ π. *the ends of the earth*, Thdr.Stud.*epp*.1.48(M.99.1076C).

***περαστυφόω**, v. περιστύφω.

περάτης, ὁ, *one who crosses over*, hence *emigrant, foreigner*; **1.** in explanation of Ἑβραῖος: Ἑβραῖοι γὰρ οἱ π. ἑρμηνεύονται, οἱ διεπεράσαντο Εὐφράτην μετὰ Ἀβραάμ· καὶ οὐχ...ἀπὸ Ἑβέρ Afric.*chron*.8(M. 10.69A); π. καλεῖται ὁ Ἀβραάμ, ἐπειδὴ...διαπεράσας τὴν Μεσοποταμίαν ἦλθεν εἰς τὰ μέρη τῶν Χαναναίων. ἑρμηνεύεται δὲ καὶ τοῖς περὶ Ἀκύλαν Ἑβραῖος Or.*sel.in Gen*.14:13(M.12.113A); ἐπειδὴ γὰρ πέραν τοῦ Εὐφράτου τὴν κατοίκησιν εἶχε, διὰ τοῦτο καὶ π. ἐλέγετο Chrys.*hom*. *35.3 in Gen*.(4.354D); id.*serm.9.3 in Gen*.(4.692C); Thdt.*qu.61 in Gen*.(1.74); **2.** as name of adherent of Gnost. sect, *one who transcends the bounds of fate* καλοῦσι δὲ αὐτοὺς π., μηδὲν δύνασθαι νομίζοντες τῶν ἐν γενέσει καθεστηκότων διαφυγεῖν τὴν ἀπὸ τῆς γενέσεως τοῖς γεγενημένοις ὡρισμένην μοῖραν. ... μόνοι δὲ...ἡμεῖς..

περᾶσαι τὴν φθορὰν μόνοι δυνάμεθα Hipp.*haer*.5.16(p.111.6; M.16.3170D); but ὁ περατικὸς Εὐφράτης, ἀφ' οὗ π. προσηγορεύθησαν Thdt. *haer*.1.17(4.310).

περατικός, 1. *from the other side*, hence *foreign*; **a.** in interpretation of Ἑβραῖος: οὐ γὰρ ἠδύναντο οἱ ὄχλοι εἰς τὸ πέραν ἀπελθεῖν, ὡς οὐ μυστικῶς Ἑβραῖοι (οἵτινες ἑρμηνεύονται π.)· ἀλλὰ τοῦτο ἔργον ἦν τῶν Ἰησοῦ μαθητῶν,...εἰς τὸ πέραν ἀπελθεῖν καὶ ὑπερβῆναι τὰ βλεπόμενα Or.*comm.in Mt*.11.5(p.41.3; M.13.913C); cf.id.*hom.19.4 in Num*.(p.183.26; M.12.725B); π. γάρ τινες ἑρμηνεύονται, τὴν ἀπὸ τῶν τῇδε ἐπὶ τὴν τοῦ τῶν ὅλων θεοῦ διάβασίν τε καὶ θεωρίαν στειλάμενοι Eus.*p.e*.7.8(309B; M.21.524B); *ib*.11.7(520C; M.864A); **b.** as name of Gnost. sect τῶν δ' αἱρέσεων αἱ μὲν ἀπὸ ὀνόματος προσαγορεύονται...αἱ δὲ ἀπὸ τόπου, ὡς οἱ π. Clem.*str*.7.17(p.76.24; M.9.552C); Hipp.*haer*.5.12(p.104.13; M.16.3159C); name derived from ὁ π. Εὐφράτης, Thdt. *haer*.1.17(4.310); cf.Hipp.*haer*.5.13(p.107.9; M.16.3166A); v. περάτης; **2.** *on the other side*, of district opp. CP τὰ π. μέρη Thphn.*chron*.p.264 (M.108.657A).

***περατιόω,** for περατόω, Gr.Nyss.*anim.et res*.(M.46.97A).

πέρατος, *limited*, Gr.Nyss.*hom.opif*.30(M.44.241D).

περατ-όω, 1. *bring to an end*, *A*.(*Pass*.)*Andr*.7(p.17.25); Bas.*Spir*.35(3.29A; M.32.129B); ὃ δὴ καὶ τοῦ αἰῶνος ἴδιον, εἰς ἑαυτὸν ἀναστρέφειν, καὶ μηδαμοῦ ~οῦσθαι id.*hex*.2.8(1.21B; M.29.49C); τὸ 'ἦν', περὶ μὲν τῆς ἡμετέρας λεγόμενον φύσεως, τὸν παρελθόντα σημαίνει χρόνον ἡμῖν, καὶ αὐτὸν...πεπερατωμένον· ὅταν δὲ περὶ θεοῦ, τὸ ἀΐδιον ἐμφαίνει Chrys.*hom.3.2 in Jo*.(8.19A); of spiritual life ζωὴν...μηδενὶ θανάτῳ ~ουμένην Max.*ambig*.(M.91.1144C); **2.** *limit*, Clem.*ecl*.6(p.138.21; M.9.701A); ποῦ δὲ μετρεῖται τὸ ἄπειρον, ἵν' ὃ τῶν ~ουμένων ἐστί, τοῦτο πάθῃ θεότης; Gr.Naz.*or*.18.16(M.35.1005A); id.*hom.6 in Cant*.(M.44.885D); πνεῦμα...οὔποτε...~ούμενον Didym.*Trin*.2.6(M.39.516B); Chrys.*hom.4.1 in Jo*.(8.28A); view that incarnate Son was not with Father κατὰ τὸν τῆς ὑποστάσεως λόγον means that οὐσία of God would be καταληπτή and πεπερατωμένη, Cyr.*resp*.2(p.577.15; 6^2.385E); **3.** *bring to completion*, CSard.*can*.5 ap.*Cod.Afr*.134(H.1.941E); Max.*myst*.(M.91.677C); **4.** *accomplish, fulfil*; of a prophecy, Thdt.*affect*.11(p.296.17; 4.1009); **5.** *bring to perfection*, Ant.Mon.*hom*.111(M.89.1776A).

περάτωσις, ἡ, *consummation*, Dion.Ar.*c.h*.10.1(M.3.273A).

περατωτικός, *limiting* πνεῦμα...οὔποτε...περατούμενον, τῶν δ' ὑπ' αὐτοῦ γενομένων δυνάμενον εἶναι π. Didym.*Trin*.2.6(M.39.516B).

περ-άω, 1. *cross*; *pass over* οἱ ~άσαντες ἀπὸ τῆς γῆς, τῷ ἔχειν ἐν οὐρανῷ τὸ πολίτευμα Didym.*Ps*.21:28(M.39.1288B); in Peratic doctrine, v. περάτης; **2.** *transport* ~άσας τὰ καβαλλαρικὰ θέματα εἰς τὴν Θρᾴκην Thphn.*chron*.p.314(M.108.761B).

***περδικοφασιανός, ὁ,** *cross between a partridge and a pheasant*, Leont.H.*Nest*.4.8(M.86.1665D).

***περεηφικόλα, ἡ,** word inscribed on a παστάς in Phlius, interpreted by Sethian Gnostics allegorically ἐπιγέγραπται δὲ ἐπὶ τοῦ πρεσβύτου· φάος ῥυέντης, ἐπὶ δὲ τῆς γυναικός· π. ἔοικε δὲ εἶναι...ὁ φάος ῥυέντης τὸ φῶς, τὸ σκοτεινὸν ὕδωρ δὲ ἡ φικόλα Hipp.*haer*.5.20(p.122.9, conj. Περσεφόνη Φλυᾶ; M.16.3187A).

***περιαγερμός, ὁ,** *gathering together*, Clem.*paed*.2.8(p.201.14; ἐπεγερμός M.8.481B).

περιάγ-ω, 1. intrans., *go about, live, exist* ὁ ἅγιος...~ων ἐν σαρκί Call.*v.Hyp*.(p.109); **2.** med., *bear about* Σκύθης ἀνὴρ Βολοκαλάβρα τὴν ἐπωνυμίαν ~όμενος Thphyl.*exc.Rom*.3(p.222.26; M.113.929B).

περιαγωγή, ἡ, 1. ? *outline*, Chrys.*hom.19.4 in Eph*.(11.139E); **2.** *distraction* ἡδονῶν περιαγωγαῖς Meth.*res*.2.1(p.330.2; M.41.1161D).

***περιαγωγικός,** *prolix* π. βίβλος *Pers*.(p.5.5).

περιαγωγός, ὁ, *one who leads astray*, †Nil.*vit*.4(M.79.1144B).

περιαθρητέον, *one must consider thoroughly*, Cyr.*Zach*.16(3.671E).

περιαίρεσις, ἡ, *opening* ἡ π. τῆς θύρας Andr.Caes.*Apoc*.4(M.106.253A).

περιαιρετέον, *one must do away with*, Justn.*Or*.(p.190.11; M.86.947C) cit. s. περιγραφή.

περιαίρω, *remove*, *A.Barth*.6(p.142.34); Epiph.*haer*.76.54(p.410.30; M.42.632C).

περίακτος, *unstable, wavering*, Max.*ascet*.32(M.90.937B).

περίαλλα, adv., *before all*, as prep. c. genit. βροτέης π. γενέθλης †Apoll.*met.Ps*.44:3 (περὶ ἄλλα M.33.1373C).

περίαμμα, τό, *amulet* μηδὲ...πετάλων ἐπιγραφαῖς καὶ π. χρῆσθαι Eus.*d.e*.3.6(p.133.29; M.22.225C); μαντεῖα...ἢ π., ἢ ἐν πετάλοις ἐπιγραφαὶ...λατρεῖαί εἰσι διαβόλου Cyr.H.*catech*.19.8; those using them to be excommunicated, *Const.App*.8.32.11; used by Jews in effecting magical cures, Chrys.*Jud*.8.5(1.681C); and by superstitious people in gen., id.*hom.3.5 in 1Thess*.(11.447D); id.*hom.10.3 in 1Tim*.(11.603B).

[*]**περιαμφιάζω,** = περιαμφιέννυμι, *clothe completely*, of God in baptism περιαμφιάσας ἡμᾶς ἀφθάρτῳ πανοπλίᾳ †Hipp.*theoph*.8(p.262.9; M.10.860A).

περιανθ-έω, *bloom*; hence met., *be rich in colour* ~ούσης πορφυρίδος ‡Meth.*Sym.et Ann*.6(M.18.361C).

***περιανθίζ-ω,** *deck out with colours, adorn* βαφαῖς...τὴν εἰκόνα περιανθίσαντα Gr.Nyss.*hom.opif*.5.1(M.44.137A); ἀρετῶν χάρισι ~ων id.*or.dom*.3(p.46.23; M.44.1149A); id.*Eun*.1(1 p.158.19; M.45.400B); περιηνθισμένην ἔχουσα τὴν καρδίαν Cyr.*Joel*.6(3.204E); id.*Nah*.22(3.501A); id.*Jo*.2.1(4.149A); Jo.Clim.*scal*.7(M.88.812B).

περιαντλ-έω, 1. *overwhelm, exhaust* ψυχὴν...~ουμένην ταῖς τρικυμίαις τῶν παθημάτων Meth.*symp*.11.3(p.139.7; M.18.217B); αἱ τοῦ βίου περιστάσεις ~οῦσι τοὺς τῆς ἀρετῆς ἐμπορίαν ἀνύοντας Bas. Sel.*or*.8.1(M.85.113A); τὴν ὁδὸν ἀχθόμενοι ~ούμενοι διεπεράναμεν Thdr.Stud.*epp*.1.3(M.99.916C); **2.** *pour out upon*, c. dupl. acc., met. τοσαύτας αὐτοὺς θαυματουργίας ὁ Χριστὸς περιήντλησε Hesych.H. *serm*.4(M.93.1457D).

περιαπλόω, *enfold all round*, Bas.Sel.*or*.12.3(M.85.168C).

περιαπτέον, *one must attribute*, *cat.Rom*.7:18(p.112.21).

περίαπτον, τό, *amulet*, Clem.*prot*.11(p.81.14; M.8.233B) cit. s. περιάπτω; τὰ γὰρ π. ... μάταια βοηθήματα ὑπάρχουσιν †Ath.*fr*.(M.26.1320A); ref. Job οὐκ ἐπέδησε περίαπτα, ἀλλ' ἀνέμενε τὴν παρὰ τοῦ θεοῦ βοήθειαν Chrys.*Jud*.8.6(1.682D); used by nominal Christians, id. *hom.4.6 in 1Cor*.(10.32B); id.*hom.13.1 in 1Tim*.(11.617D); a snare of the Devil, Thdt.*Eph*.4:14(3.425); Leont.B.*mesopent*.(M.86.1989D); penance for women who make them, ‡Jo.Jej.*exc.poenit*.(M.88.1933B).

περιάπτ-ω, 1. *fasten, tie round*, of fastening amulets upon oneself; hence **i.** of making sign of cross σφραγῖδα τοῦ σταυροῦ ~ειν ἑαυτοῖς Arc.C.*v.Sym*.ap.Jo.D.*imag*.3(M.94.1396B); **ii.** met. οἱ μὲν τοῖς γόησι πεπιστευκότες τὰ περίαπτα...ἀποδέχονται, ὑμεῖς δὲ οὐ βούλεσθε τὸν οὐράνιον αὐτὸν περιάψασθαι, τὸν σωτῆρα λόγον Clem. *prot*.11(p.81.16; M.8.233B); **2.** *attribute* τὴν ὕδατος ἀξίαν τῷ πνεύματι ...~εις Didym.(‡Bas.)*Eun*.5(1.308B; M.29.740A); Chrys.*hom.4.2 in 2Tim*.(11.680E); Cyr.*Nest*.2.8(p.44.17; 6^1.48A).

***περιαργ-έω,** *be amazed, be left entirely at a loss* ~ήσας τοῖς ῥήμασι Bas.Sel.*or*.31.3(M.85.345B).

περιάργυρος, *covered with silver*, Cyr.*Is*.4.3(2.627B).

περιαργυρόω, *ornament as with silver* γυνὴ...ὀρθοδοξίᾳ περιηργυρωμένη Thdr.Stud.*epp*.2.149(M.99.1465A).

***περιάρπαστος,** *eagerly grasped at*, Eus.*theoph*.(M.24.673C).

***περιασπασμός, ὁ,** *embrace*, Cyr.*Lc*.16:1(M.72.812B).

περιαστράπτ-ω, 1. *shine round*, *M.Thdot*.1 32(p.80.35); pass., *be surrounded with light*, Or.*hom.13 in Lc*.(p.92.22); Gr.Naz.*or*.19.12 (M.35.1057B); **2.** *dazzle*, Gr.Nyss.*v.Mos*.20(M.44.305C); Ast.Am. *hom*.3(M.40.209D); **3.** *illuminate*, Cyr.*Ps*.91:2(M.69.1225B); met. ἡ γνῶσις...~ουσα τὸν νοῦν Clem.*paed*.1.6(p.108.6; M.8.285C); θεοῦ δὲ ὅταν εἴπω, ἑνὶ φωτὶ περιαστράφθητε καὶ τρισί Gr.Naz.*or*.39.11(M.36.345C); Isid.Pel.*epp*.3.142(M.78.840A); **4.** med., *glitter*, Bas.*hom*.7.4 (2.56C; M.31.292A); Eus.Al.*serm*.21.17(M.86.444B); **5.** intrans., *shine, be brilliant* βασίλεια...~οντα τῇ τῶν λίθων αἴγλῃ Chrys.*hom.10.1 in 1Thess*.(11.496C).

***περιασφαλίζομαι,** *be secured on every side*, Ephr.3.211F.

***περιάσχολος,** *very busy*, Pall.*v.Chrys*.6(p.36.9; M.47.22).

περιαυγάζ-ω, 1. *illuminate*, Gr.Nyss.*hex*.10(M.44.73A); of mental and spiritual illumination, Clem.*str*.6.2(p.424.8; M.9.212B); Gr. Nyss.*v.Mos*.20(M.44.305C); Dion.Ar.*d.n*.1.4(M.3.592C); Sophr.H.*or*.2.25(M.87.3248A); **2.** *dazzle*, met. περιαυγασθέντας ὑπὸ τῆς τῶν ἐνθάδε δοκούντων ἀγαθῶν τιμίων λαμπρότητος Nil.*exerc*.63(M.79.796D); **3.** med., *shine round about* ἡ δόξα...τῷ ἀληθινῷ φωτὶ πανταχόθεν ~εται Gr.Nyss.*Eun*.8(2 p.180.17; M.45.773B).

περιαυγασμός, ὁ, *illumination*, Or.*comm.in Pr*.1:9(M.13.28A).

***περιαυλίζ-ω, 1.** *pitch* tent, Tim.Ant.*cruc*.(M.86.264A); **2.** med., *stay round about* ἄλλην περίβλεψαί τινα σκάφην, εἴ γε βούλει τὴν λίμνην ~εσθαι ‡Chrys.*hom*.13(13.252E).

***περιαυτία, ἡ,** *boastfulness*, ‡Nil.*narr*.3(M.79.624B).

περιαυτίζ-ομαι, 1. *be selfish, concerned with oneself* ~εται γὰρ ἀεὶ τὰ τῶν γυναίων ἑταιριζόμενα Cyr.*Am*.34(3.288E; περιανδρίζεται Aubert); **2.** *boast*, Gr.Nyss.*ep*.17(M.46.1067C); Cyr.*Is*.1.4(2.94C); ~εται...ὅτι καταδράξηται *ib*.1.6(175E); id.*Juln*.3(6^2.100D).

περιαυτολογία, ἡ, *egotistical speech*, Or.*Cels*.1.48(p.99.29; M.11.752B); Chrys.*hom.38.4 in 1Cor*.(10.356E, v.l. περιτautολογία); id. *hom.22.1 in 2Cor*.(10.588C).

***περιαυτόλογος,** *speaking of oneself, boastful*, neut. as subst. τὸ τῶν φαρισαίων π. Or.*Jo*.6.23(13; p.133.3; τὸν...περὶ αὐτῶν λόγον M. 14.241A); Eus.*fr.Lc*.20:3(M.24.596A).

***περιαφίημι**, *leave over*, Bas.*hom*.13.6(2.119E; M.31.437C); †Bas. *Is*.247(1.568A; M.30.553C).

***περιαφρίζω**, *foam violently*, Gr.Nyss.*anim.et res*.(M.46.37A).

περιβάδην, *astride*, Evagr.*h.e*.3.25(p.122.22; M.86.2649A).

περιβάλλ-ω, *surround*;

A. *charge with, accuse of* σφάλμασί τε εὐηθείας αὐτὸν π. Thphyl. *exc.Rom*.5(p.226.5; M.113.933C).

B. med., *put on* garment, *clothe with*; **1.** ref. relationship of body and soul σάρκα περιβεβλημένη ψυχή Eus.*d.e*.5.20(p.243.26; M. 22.401B); of soul putting on resurrection body, Cyr.H.*catech*.15. 20; **2.** man's mortal nature, Meth.*res*.1.38(p.281.14; M.18.293B) cit. s. νεκρότης; garment of immortality, Thdt.*2Cor*.5:3(3.313) cit. s. ἔνδυμα; cf.Gr.Nyss.*hom.1 in Cant*.(M.44.764D) cit. s. περιβόλαιον; **3.** Christol., ref. Inc. κατοικεῖ δὲ ἐπὶ τῆς γῆς, σάρκα ~όμενος Clem.*fr*. 36(p.218.31; M.9.769A); σώματι, ὃ...ἐνανθρωπήσας περιβέβληται Eus. *d.e*.5.21(p.244.24; M.22.404B); ἐθεμελίωσέ με· ἴσον τῷ εἰπεῖν· λόγον ὄντα με περιέβαλε γηΐνῳ σώματι Ath.*Ar*.2.74(M.26.305A); ἀνθρώπινόν με περιβεβλημένον σῶμα *ib*.3.56(440A); σῶμα γὰρ περιβέβλημαι *cat. Jo*.14:9(p.346.29); τὴν ἡμῶν σάρκα περιεβάλετο Cyr.*thes*.10(5^{1}.72C); *ib*.15(166A); τὴν αὐτὴν ἡμῖν περιεβάλετο φύσιν Thdt.*haer*.5.12(4.428); ~όμενος ἄνθρωπον Bas.Sel.*or*.19.1(M.85.237C); Marcosian ἐφανερώθη τὸ ἐξαγράμματον ὄνομα, ὃς σάρκα περιεβάλλετο, ἵνα εἰς αἴσθησιν τοῦ ἀνθρώπου κατέλθῃ Iren.*haer*.1.15.2(M.7.620A).

C. med., *acquire*, Chrys.*hom.13.10 in Rom*.(9.573B); Thdt.*affect*. 6(p.162.24; 4.861); *win* victory νίκας περιεβάλετο Men.*exc.Rom*.3 (p.177.4; M.113.860D).

D. med., *appropriate*, of Arian heresy ~ομένη τὰς τῶν γραφῶν λέξεις Ath.*Ar*.1.1(M.26.13A).

E. pass., *revert* property ἐὰν...περιβληθῇ εἰς τὸν πατέρα ἢ...προῖξ Ath.Scholast.*coll*.10.6(p.124).

***περιβλάπτω**, Hipp.*antichr*.52(M.10.772C; περιλειπομένων p.35.8).

περίβλεψις, ἡ, **1.** *looking about, idle glance*, Mac.Aeg.*pat*.1(M.34. 865C); **2.** *circumspection* ἐν τῇ π. τοῦ φόβου τοῦ θεοῦ Philox.*ep*.20 (p.172).

περίβλημα, τό, *garment, covering*; of the body, as garment of soul, Meth.*res*.3.18(p.416.1; M.18.328A); σῶμα...γεῶδες...π. ψυχῆς Eus.*p.e*.7.10(316A; M.21.533D); id.*v.C*.1.2(p.8.1; M.20.912C); Gr. Naz.*or*.18.38(M.35.1036B); of Christ's flesh, Cyr.*Jo*.12(4.1063B); of sinful human nature ἔνδυμα...εἰ βούλεσθε γενέσθαι θείου πνεύματος, σπουδάσατε πρῶτον ἐκδύσασθαι τὸ ῥυπαρὸν ὑμῶν πρόλημμα, ὅπερ ἐστὶν ἀκάθαρτον πνεῦμα, καὶ μιαρὸν π. *Hom.Clem*.8.23.

***περίβλητος**, **1.** *to be acquired*, Clem.*q.d.s*.17(p.170.31; M.9. 621B); **2.** *surrounding, covering*, Areth.*Apoc*.2:9(M.106.533A).

περιβόλαιον, τό, **A.** *envelope, covering*, Gr.Nyss.*v.Mos*.(M.44. 417C); of the hair τῷ ἐκ φύσεως π. ἐκμάσσουσα [sc. Μαρία] τὸ ἁγίασμα Eust.*Laz*.22(p.44.12).

B. *cloak*, as monastic habit εἴ τις...διὰ νομιζομένην ἄσκησιν περιβολαίῳ χρῆται CGangr.*can*.12; τὸ δὲ π., ἐπειδὴ τετράγωνόν ἐστιν, ἐκ τεσσάρων δὲ στοιχείων καὶ ὁ κόσμος, σημαίνει ὅτι χρὴ περιβεβλῆσθαι ἡμᾶς τὴν φυσικὴν θεωρίαν, ὥστε μὴ πρὸς αἴσθησιν καὶ πάθη τὰ ὁρώμενα βλέπειν Max.*qu.dub*.67(M.90.841B); as robe of bishop ἁρπάσαντες τὸ π. τῆς ἐμῆς ἱερωσύνης Bassn.*supplic*.(p.45.15; H.2.548B); π. of Alex. Al. borne by Ath. as young deacon, and equated with ephod of child Samuel, Jo.Mosch.*prat*.197(M.87.3085A); as typical garment of town-dweller, Thdr.Stud.*epp*.2.137(M.99.1437C); met.; **1.** exeg. Gen.49:11 τὰ ἔθνη ἀπολουόμενα καθαίρονται, ἅτινα ὡς π. λελόγισται Χριστῷ Hipp.*antichr*.11(p.10.20; M.10.737A); interpreted of man's sinful nature cleansed by blood of Christ, Eus.*d.e*.8.1(p.366.3; M. 22.593D); **2.** of carnal nature τὸν παλαιὸν ἄνθρωπον, ὥσπερ τι π. ῥυπαρὸν ἀπεδύσασθε...καὶ τὰ φωτεινὰ τοῦ κυρίου ἱμάτια...διὰ τῆς καθαρότητος τοῦ βίου περιεβάλεσθε Gr.Nyss.*hom.1 in Cant*.(M.44. 764D); **3.** of the body τὸ μὲν π., τουτέστι, τὸ σῶμα λιπαίνοντες Chrys. *hom.13.1 in Phil*.(11.298C); **4.** of garment of virtue, *cat.Lc*.10:30 (p.87.28); **5.** Christol., of Christ's body ἐν τάφῳ παρὴν [sc. ἡ θεότης] ἀπαθῶς, ἄφθαρτον φυλάττουσα τὸ ἑαυτῆς π. Gr.Ant.*mul.ung*.2(M.88. 1849B); human nature οὐχ ἡ θεότης ἐσταυρώθη, ἀλλὰ τὸ π. τῆς θεότητος ‡Chrys.*serm.pasch*.(p.110).

C. *surrounding country* κάτελθε ἐπὶ τὰ π. καὶ τὰς νήσους *Apoc. Dan*.C(p.115).

περιβολή, ἡ, **A.** *covering, wrapping, envelope*; **1.** *dress, vesture*; of the body, ref. Platonic conception of immortality τῷ γὰρ καὶ μετὰ τὴν ἀπὸ τοῦ κόσμου ἀποφοίτησιν ὀχήματος αὐτὴν δέεσθαι καὶ περιβολῆς λέγειν...πῶς οὐκ ἂν καθ' ἑαυτὴν ἀσώματος εἴη; Meth.*res*.3.18(p.415. 2; M.18.325B); of Christ's flesh τὸν...λόγον ἥξειν...οὐκ ἀφανῶς...οὐδ' ἄνευ τινὸς σωματικῆς π. Eus.*d.e*.6.22(p.285.20; M.22.469A); οὐδὲν ἧττον ἦν θεός· οὐ γὰρ ἠλαττοῦτο τῇ π. τοῦ σώματος Ath.*decr*.14(p.12. 30; M.25.'448'(440)D); id.*Ar*.3.67(M.26.465C); σάρκωσις κένωσις οὐκ ἄνθρωπον, ἀλλὰ υἱὸν ἀνθρώπου τὸν κενώσαντα ἑαυτὸν ἀπέφηνε κατὰ τὴν π., οὐ κατὰ μεταβολήν Apoll.*fr*.124(p.237.31)ap.Thdt.*eran*.1(4.70); ἄκτιστος θεὸς κτιστῇ π. φανερούμενος id.*corp.et div*.6(p.187.21; M.*PL*. 8.874A); διὰ τῆς τοῦ σώματος π. χωρητὴν τὴν θείαν δύναμιν...γενέσθαι, ὡς ἂν ἡ ὑπὲρ ἡμῶν οἰκονομία μὴ παραποδισθείη τῷ φόβῳ τῆς ὑψηλῆς ἐμφανείας Gr.Nyss.*or.catech*.23(p.90.8; M.45.64A); σχέσει καὶ οἰκονομίᾳ...ἐγγύτερος ἡμῖν γενόμενος διὰ τῆς κατὰ σάρκα π. Chrys.*hom. 44.3 in Mt*.(7.470C); ἀγνοούμενος...διὰ τὴν ἐκ τῆς σαρκὸς π. Cyr.*Jo*. 1.10(4.111A); ἰδού σοι καὶ τὸ τῆς π. ὄνομα προσενήνοχεν ὁ τῶν σῶν δογμάτων διδάσκαλος Thdt.*eran*.1(4.70) commenting on Apoll.*fr*. 124 (cit. supra); οὐκ ἠμαύρωσε γὰρ αὐτοῦ τὰς τῆς θεότητος ἀκτῖνας ἡ π. τῆς σαρκός id.*affect*.2(p.60.20; 4.752); **2.** *habit* ἀποδύσασθαι τὴν πάτριον π. *Hom.Clem*.4.11; **3.** in oratory; **a.** *ornament*, Clem.*str*.1.2 (p.14.2; M.8.709B); κάλλος καὶ π. φράσεως Or.*Jo*.4.2(p.99.11; M.14. 185B); id.*Cels*.3.39(p.236.7; M.11.972B); **b.** of involved or obscure style as wrapping up meaning μήποτε τῇ π. τῶν γραμμάτων ἀπάτη τις γένηται Ath.*ep.Aeg.Lib*.20(M.25.585A); αἰνιγματώδη τῶν λόγων... π. Cyr.*Jo*.2.5(4.200D).

B. *protection, defence* περισκεπτόμενοι τῇ π. ... τοῦ κυρίου *A.Andr. fr*.2(p.39.4); ψυχῆς ἄρρηκτον π. *Hom.Clem*.3.20; Gr.Nyss.*hom.9 in Cant*.(M.44.969C).

C. *endowment, wealth* ἐπίγειον...περιβεβλημένος π. Clem.*q.d.s*.3 (p.161.28; M.9.608B); Ephr.2.171C; Bas.*hom.in Ps*.48(1.187B; M.29. 456B); Thphyl.*exc.gent*.8(p.485.27; M.113.948B).

D. *enclosure, precinct*, Cyr.*Jo*.2.1(4.140B).

περίβολος, ὁ, **1.** *covering, vesture* τὸν π. τὸν σαρκικόν Clem.*paed*. 3.2(p.238.18; M.8.560C); **2.** *surrounding wall*, Chrys.*sac*.4.4(p.112. 13; 1.408E); Thdt.*Ps*.16:8(1.697); met. εἰρήνη...τῶν οὐρανῶν π. Serap.*ep.mon*.3(M.40.929A); **3.** *enclosed precinct, sacred court, temple*; **a.** pagan, Tat.*orat*.21(p.24.8; M.6.853B); Clem.*prot*.3(p.34. 13; M.8.132A); Or.*Cels*.6.80(p.151.27; M.11.1420B); **b.** in Jewish Temple κάλυμμα...εἶργον τοὺς ἐν τῷ π. Clem.*str*.5.6(p.348.1; M.9. 57A); symbolism of its courts, *ib*.(p.347.4; 56B); Eus.*h.e*.10.4.40(M. 20.865A); **c.** of Christian Church, id.*l.C*.proem.(p.195.19; M.20. 1317B); Chrys.*nativ*.1(2.355B); Thdt.*eran*.3(4.230); Gel.Cyz.*h.e*.3.10. 14; **d.** of heaven θείων...περιβόλων Meth.*symp*.6.3(p.67.2; M.18. 117A); Const.ap.Gel.Cyz.*h.e*.2.7.5(M.85.1233A); **e.** met., of widows as a temple court where offerings are sacrificed, Meth.*symp*.5.8 (p.62.21; M.18.112A); of order of priesthood τοιούτους...τῶν τῆς ἱερωσύνης ἀπείρξομεν π. Chrys.*sac*.3.13(p.70.2; 1.389E).

περιβομβ-έω, **1.** *buzz round*, Cels.ap.Or.*Cels*.3.16(p.215.8; M.11. 940B); Ath.*Ar*.3.59(M.26.445C); v. περικομπέω; **2.** *make a noise about* something *round about, bruit abroad* τοῦτο...~οῦσιν ὡς ἀγέλη κωνώπων Ath.*decr*.14(p.12.4; M.25.'448'(440)A); id.*fug*.2(p.69.19; M. 25.648A); **3.** pass., *be surrounded with noise* of, *resound* with δεῖ ...ἀγορὰν ~εῖσθαι τοῖς τούτων λόγοις Gr.Naz.*or*.27.2(p.3.5; M.36. 13A).

***περιβουκολ-έω**, *pasture round about, lead about to feed*, met., αὐτὸν ταύταις ~ήσας ταῖς ἐννοίαις Nil.*exerc*.40(M.79.769A).

***περιβράσσω**, *surge round*, ‡Nil.*fr.pasch*.1(M.79.1496C).

***περιβρέχω**, *bedew all round*, Geo.Pis.*carm*.1.53.

***περιβρύχομαι**, *roar round*; c. dat., Bas.*hex*.9.6(1.87E; M.29. 205B).

***περιβυθίζω**, *immerse*, met. τῷ τῆς εὐσεβείας κάλλει περιβυθισμέναις Cyr.*Abac*.30(3.545B).

***περιβωμβέω**, s.v.l., *lead round in procession* περιεβωμβήθησαν ἐν καμήλοις Jo.Mal.*chron*.18 p.451(M.97.661D; perh. for περιεπομπεύθησαν or περιεβωμίσθησαν).

***περιβωμίζομαι**, *be led round in procession*; of criminals, Jo. Mal.*chron*.18 p.473(M.97.688C); *ib*.p.491(712A); *Mir.Artem*.18(p.23. 15).

περίβωτος, poet. for περιβόητος, *famous*, Gr.Naz.*carm*.2.1.50.65 (M.37.1390A).

περιγανόω, *make smooth all round*, Melet.*nat.hom*.22(M.64. 1229D); *ib*.(1232A).

***περιγάνυμαι**, *be very glad*, Thphyl.*exc.gent*.5(p.482.1; M.113. 941C).

περιγεγονότως, *successfully*, Didym.*Trin*.2.8(M.39.616A); Chrys. *hom.12.2 in Heb*.(12.124A).

περίγειος, *of the earth, earthly*; **1.** in gen. ἡ...τῶν π. διοίκησις Athenag.*leg*.25.2(M.6.949A); Clem.*str*.6.16(p.504.20; M.9.369C); Thdr. Stud.*epp*.2.29(M.99.1197D); τὸ π. *the whole world*, Jo.VI H.*v.Jo.D*. 1(M.94.432A); *ib*.14(453A); **2.** opp. heavenly, Or.*princ*.4.3.10(p.337. 6; M.11.393A); id.*Cels*.1.60(p.111.6; M.11.769C); τοὺς π. δαίμονας *ib*.8.54(p.271.7; 1600A); id.*Cant*.3(p.178.25; M.13.149D); of Christ καταλείπει...τὴν ἄνω Ἱερουσαλήμ, καὶ ἔρχεται εἰς τὸν π. τόπον id.*hom.* 10.7 *in Jer.*(p.77.14; M.13.365C); id.*Jo.*1.15(p.19.21; M.14.49A); π.... πνεύματα Eus.*d.e.*6.2(p.254.6; M.22.417B); τῆς νοητῆς Αἰγύπτου, εἰς ἣν ἐνανθρωπήσας κατελήλυθεν, οὕτω δηλουμένου τοῦ π. τόπου *ib.*9. 4(p.413.9; 665C); Ath.*inc.*11.2(M.25.116A); Didym.*Ps.*30:8(M.39. 1313C); ἐν τῷ π. βίῳ τούτῳ Pall.*v.Chrys.*18(p.116.26; M.47.65); **3.** opp. divine, Thdt.*Cant.*1:1(2.25); id.*Os.*2:21(2.1324).

***περιγέλαστος,** *very ridiculous,* Epiph.*haer.*52.1(p.312.13; M.41. 956B); of Montanist prophetesses' utterances, *ib.*79.1(p.476.15; M. 42.741A); *ib.*80.3(p.487.4; 760C).

***περιγέλως, ὁ,** *laughing-stock* μήπως π. γένωμαι τοῖς υἱοῖς Ἰσραήλ *Protev.*9.2(p.18).

περιγί(γ)ν-ομαι, 1. *prevail over, overcome,* c. genit. pers.; c. dat. ὁ ὕπνος μοι περιεγένετο *T.Isach.*3.5(vv.ll. μου, με, π.); **2.** *secure, win* τὸ ἔργον...~εται τοῦ πράγματος οὗ θέλει Herm.*vis.*1.3.2; Tat.*orat.*11 (p.12.8; M.6.829B); νίκης ~εσθαι Const.ap.Eus.*v.C.*3.60(p.107.18; M. 20.1129B); ἵνα...τὸ σπουδαζόμενον περιγένηται Bas.*Eun.*2.12(1.247B; M.29.593B).

περιγλύφω, 1. *peel away,* Geo.Pis.*hex.*1584(M.92.1558A); **2.** *hatch out,* ‡Eust.*hex.*(M.18.733B); **3.** *efface* an impression, Gr.Nyss.*Eun.*4 (2 p.94.13; M.45.672A).

περιγνάμπτω, *bend* περιγναμφθέντας ἀγοστούς Paul.Sil.*Soph.*374 (M.86.2134A).

***περίγοργος,** *very quick,* Jo.Mal.*chron.*2 p.35(M.97.105A); *ib.*5 p.103(192B); τὸ σπουδαῖον καὶ π. τῆς φρονήσεως *ib.*8 p.195(308A); *Chron.Pasch.*p.38(M.92.152A).

***περιγραμμός, ὁ,** *thing circumscribed*; of man, Thdr.Stud.*epp.*2. 84(M.99.1328B).

***περιγραπτικός,** *limiting* οὐδὲν γάρ ἐστι περὶ αὐτὴν [sc. divine nature] θεωρούμενον, οὐ χρόνος, οὐ τόπος,...οὐδὲ ἄλλο τι τῶν π. ὄνομα Gr.Nyss.*hom.*5 *in Cant.*(M.44.873C).

περιγραπτός, *circumscribed, limited*; **1.** in gen., of the mind πῶς ὁ νοῦς καὶ π. καὶ ἀόριστος, ἐν ἡμῖν μένων, καὶ πάντα ἐφοδεύων; Gr. Naz.*or.*28.22(p.54.13; M.36.56A) = Melet.*nat.hom.*30(M.64.1284A); **2.** ref. God, against theory that God is σῶμα: πῶς γὰρ σεπτόν, εἰ π.; Gr.Naz.*or.*28.7(p.31.14; M.36.33B); θεός,...οὐ π. id.*carm.*1.1.1.25(M. 37.400A); οὐκ ἐν τόπῳ ἐστὶ π. Didym.ap.*cat.Ac.*17:23(p.292.8); Cyr. *Jo.*1.9(4.77A); οὐ γὰρ πεποσῶσθαι τὸ θεῖον, ἢ καὶ σχήματι π. *ib.*2.8 (230E); εἰ ἐν τόπῳ τῆς οὐσίας ὁ θεός, πῶς οὐ π. τὴν οὐσίαν ὁ θεός; εἰ δὲ π. τὴν οὐσίαν ὁ θεός, πῶς πανγνώστης τῆς οὐσίας ὁ θεός; πῶς θεὸς τὴν οὐσίαν ὁ θεός; εἰ ἐν τῷ τί ἐστι π. ὁ θεός, ἐν δὲ τῷ ποσῷ ἐστιν ἀπερίγραπτος, πῶς ταὐτόν ἐστι τὸ ποσὸν τοῦ θεοῦ καὶ τὸ τί αὐτό; *Disp.Phot.* 45(M.88.569D); Jo.D.*f.o.*1.4(M.94.797B); ref. problem of locality of Devil εἰ...ἴδιον τόπον ἔχειν τὸν σατανᾶν, καὶ ἴδιον τὸν θεόν, ποιεῖ αὐτὸν καὶ π. εἰς ἐκεῖνον τὸν τόπον ἔνθα κατοικεῖ ὁ πονηρός Mac.Aeg. *hom.*7.2(M.34.524D); **3.** ref. Son ὁ τοίνυν ἀριθμὸν ἢ κτίσμα ὁμολογῶν τὸν υἱόν...ἢ τὸ πνεῦμα...λανθάνει ἔνυλον καὶ π. φύσιν εἰσάγων. π. δὲ λέγω, οὐ μόνον τὴν περιεχομένην ὑπὸ τόπου, ἀλλ' ἥνπερ καὶ τῇ προγνώσει ἐμπεριείληφεν ὁ μέλλων αὐτὴν ἀπὸ τοῦ μὴ ὄντος εἰς τὸ εἶναι παράγειν...πᾶν οὖν ἅγιον, ὃ π. ἔχει τὴν φύσιν...οὐκ ἀνεπίδεκτόν ἐστι κακίας Evagr.Pont.*ep.*2(M.32.249B); ἀεὶ συνυπάρχει τῷ πατρὶ ὁ υἱός,...οὐ π. τόπῳ Gel.Cyz.*h.e.*2.15.3(M.85.1257C); **4.** ref. Inc., Gr. Naz.*ep.*101(M.37.177B) cit. s. ἀπερίγραπτος; ἐν τῷ π. νοεῖται τὸ ἀπερίγραπτον Isid.Pel.*epp.*2.192(M.78.640D); ref. Nestorian division of Christ πῶς οὐ θατέρα μὲν ὁρατὴ καὶ π. ὑπόστασις, θατέρα δὲ ἀόρατος καὶ ἀπερίγραπτός ἐστιν; Leont.H.*Nest.*2.17(M.86.1576A); Leont.B.*Nest.et Eut.*1(M.86.1284B); θεὸν ἄπειρον ὁμοῦ καὶ π. ἄνθρωπον ὄντα τε καὶ νοούμενον ‡Hipp.*Ber.Hel.*1(p.321.31; M.10.832B); definition of π. φύσις which is implied when Son or H. Ghost is regarded as creature, Evagr.Pont.*ep.*2(M.32.249B) cit. s. 3 supra.

περιγραφή, ἡ, A. *circumscription, limitation*; **1.** denied of God, Or.*Jo.*10.4(3; p.174.29; M.14.313A); οὐ γὰρ ἐν τόπῳ καὶ π. τὸ θεῖον εἶναι φαμέν, ὅτι καὶ ἁπλοῦν ἐστι καὶ ἀσώματον Cyr.*Is.*5(2.883D); π. πάσης ἐλεύθερον Zach.Mit.*opif.*(M.85.1048A); of Logos φύσεως περιγραφῆς οὐδαμῶς ἀνεχόμενος Sophr.H.*ep.syn.*(M.87.3160C); **2.** but asserted by Or. in respect of limitation set on creation of rational beings ἐν τῇ...ἀρχῇ τοσοῦτον ἀριθμὸν τῷ βουλήματι αὐτοῦ ὑποστῆσαι τὸν θεὸν νοερῶν οὐσιῶν ὅσον ἠδύνατο διαρκέσαι· πεπερασμένην γὰρ εἶναι καὶ τὴν δύναμιν τοῦ θεοῦ λεκτέον, καὶ μὴ προφάσει εὐφημίας τὴν π. αὐτῆς περιαιρετέον. ἐὰν γὰρ ἄπειρος ᾖ ἡ θεία δύναμις, ἀνάγκη αὐτὴν μηδὲ ἑαυτὴν νοεῖν Justn.*Or.*(p.190.10; M.86.947C); **3.** of Son, ref. Inc. σώματος, ὃ κατὰ περιγραφὴν τόπον ἔνθεον ἑαυτῷ καθιέρωσεν ἐπὶ γῆς Clem.*fr.*36(p.219.6; M.9.769A); τῇ π. τῆς σαρκὸς καθάπερ ἀγγείῳ τινὶ ἡ ἀπειρία τῆς θεότητος περιελήφθη; Gr.Nyss.*or.catech.*10(p.54.10; M.45.41B); Leont.H.*Nest.*2.17(M.86.1576A); Leont.B.*Nest.et Eut.*1 (M.86.1284B); ‡Hipp.*Ber.Hel.*1(p.321.28; M.10.832B); περιγραφῆς ἠνέσχετο σώματος Sophr.H.*ep.syn.*(M.87.3173A); of BMV ἡ π. ... τοῦ ἀπεριγράπτου ‡Meth.*Sym.et Ann.*10(M.18.372C).

B. *delimitation as an individual, individuality*; **1.** in gen. εἰς μορφὴν καὶ...π. ἰδίαν ἀγαγών Heracleon ap.Or.*Jo.*2.21(15; p.77.29; παραγραφήν M.14.149D); Const.*or.s.c.*21(p.187.11; M.20.1301A); Gr. Nyss.*tres dii*(M.45.125C); *ib.*(132A); **2.** of Son ὁ ἐν ταὐτότητι λόγος, κατὰ π. καὶ οὐ κατ' οὐσίαν γενόμενος [ὁ] υἱός Clem.*exc.Thdot.*19(p.112. 29; M.9.665D); ref. heretics ἤτοι ἀρνουμένους ἰδιότητα υἱοῦ ἑτέραν παρὰ τὴν τοῦ πατρός...ἢ ἀρνουμένους τὴν θεότητα τοῦ υἱοῦ τιθέντας δὲ αὐτοῦ τὴν ἰδιότητα καὶ τὴν οὐσίαν κατὰ περιγραφὴν τυγχάνουσαν ἑτέραν τοῦ πατρός Or.*Jo.*2.2(p.54.28; M.14.109A); τὸν λόγον ἰδίαν π. ἔχοντα *ib.*1.39(42; p.51.17; 104A); ref. heresy of Beryllus τὸν... κύριον...μὴ προϋφεστάναι κατ' ἰδίαν οὐσίας π. πρὸ τῆς εἰς ἀνθρώπους ἐπιδημίας Eus.*h.e.*6.33.1(M.20.593A).

περίγραφος, *limited, circumscribed,* of Christ incarnate π. ἀλλ' ἀμέτρητος Gr.Naz.*carm.*1.1.2.64(M.37.406A); *ib.*1.1.4.42(419A); *ib.*1. 2.10.423(710A).

περιγράφ-ω, A. *circumscribe, limit*; **1.** denied of God οὐ ~εται τόπῳ θεός Clem.*str.*7.6(p.22.6; M.9.440B); ἐὰν τόπον τοῦ θεοῦ τὴν ὕλην εἴπωμεν, ἐξ ἀνάγκης αὐτὸν καὶ χωρητὸν λέγειν δεῖ καὶ πρὸς τῆς ὕλης ~όμενον Meth.*arbitr.*6(p.159.10; M.18.252A); ἀσώματον νόει τὸν θεὸν ἐκ τῆς ἐνυπαρχούσης σοι ψυχῆς ἀσωμάτου, μὴ ~όμενον τόπῳ Bas. *hom.*3.7(2.23D; M.31.216A); εἰ μὲν ἔν τινι, ὑπ' ἐλάττονος περιγραφήσεται τοῦ τινος, εἰ δὲ πανταχοῦ, ὑπὸ πλείονος καὶ ἄλλου πολλοῦ, λέγω δέ, τὸ περιεχόμενον τοῦ περιέχοντος Gr.Naz.*or.*28.10(p.37.8; M.36. 37C); θεὸς...ὁ τόποις μὴ ~όμενος *Lit.*ap.*Const.App.*8.15.7; ref. purpose of Tabernacle, Thdt.*qu.60 in Ex.*(1.161); **2.** ref. generation of Son ἔχθιστοι...οἱ τὴν γέννησιν τοῦ υἱοῦ τὴν ἐκ πατρὸς ἀνθρωπίνως ~οντες διαστήματι μετρουμένῳ Apoll.*fid.sec.pt.*1(p.167.12; M.10. 1105A); **3.** ref. Inc. τὸν ἐν τῷ Ἰησοῦ λέγοντα τὸ 'ἐγώ εἰμι ἡ ὁδός...' οὐδὲ τὰ εὐαγγέλια οἶδε περιγεγραμμένον τινὰ γεγονέναι, ὡς οὐδαμοῦ ἔξω τῆς ψυχῆς καὶ τοῦ σώματος τοῦ Ἰησοῦ τυγχάνοντα Or.*Cels.*2.9 (p.136.15; M.11.809B); πῶς δὲ ἡ ἀπερίληπτος θεότης εἰς μικροῦ σώματος ὄγκον περιεγράφη, εἴπερ ἐτράπη πᾶσα ἡ τοῦ μονογενοῦς φύσις; Bas.*ep.*262.2(3.404C; M.32.973C); οὐδέπω φαμὲν ἐν τῷ ἀνθρωπίνῳ σώματι τὴν τοῦ θεοῦ λόγου περιγεγράφθαι φύσιν· ἄποσον γὰρ τὸ θεῖον Cyr.*Heb.*(p.421.9; M.74.1004B); ἡ γὰρ εἰς θεὸν ἕνωσις οὐκ ἀφίησιν εἰς ἄνθρωπον μόνον ~εσθαι τὰ παθήματα. διὰ τοῦτο δὲ τὸν... υἱὸν τοῦ θεοῦ καλεῖ Ἰησοῦν...τὸν αὐτὸν ποιητὴν...ἁπάντων δεικνύς, καὶ ἄνθρωπον θάνατον γευσάμενον Thdot.Anc.*exp.symb.*3(M.77.1317C); ἀλλ' ἡ ψυχή, φασὶν οἱ τῆς διαιρέσεως πρόμαχοι, περιγέγραπται ἐν τῷ σώματι...καὶ εἰ οὕτως ἥνωται ὁ λόγος, ὥρα σοι...ποιεῖν αὐτόν... περιγραπτόν. ... εἴποιμ' ἂν ἅπερ ἡμῖν ἐγκαλεῖτε. δεδοίκατε γὰρ αὐτὸν σαρκὶ συνάπτειν...ὡς ἐξ ἀνάγκης περιγραφησόμενον. ... εἰ μὲν οὖν φύσει...δέχεται περιγραφήν, ἔσται...περιγραπτός, κἂν μὴ πέπονθε μηδὲ περιγέγραπται Leont.B.*Nest.et Eut.*1(M.86.1284B); Tim.Ant. *cruc.*(M.86.264A); ref. Christ's eternal humanity τὸ ἀναβῆναι...εἰς οὐρανόν, καὶ τὸ καταβῆναι δὲ πάλιν, ἐνέργειαί εἰσι ~ομένου σώματος Jo.D.*f.o.*4.1(M.94.1104B); **4.** ref. angels οἱ δὲ πρωτόκτιστοι, εἰ καὶ ...ὁ καθ' ἕκαστον...περιγέγραπται Clem.*exc.Thdot.*10(p.109.27; M.9. 660C); **5.** of the soul πῶς ψυχὴ ~εται; Gr.Naz.*or.*28.22(p.54.12; M.36. 56A); **6.** ref. Manich. principles of light and darkness ἢ ἐν ἀλλήλοις ἔσονται, ἢ τόπῳ ~ήσονται καὶ οὐκ ἄναρχά εἰσι Jo.D.*Man.*1.22(M.94. 1525C); **7.** of Law as limited in scope and time, Juln.Imp.ap.Cyr. *Juln.*9(6^2.319D).

B. *remove from a text, excise,* ref. Marcion's excision of gospel passages about Christ's birth, Or.*Jo.*10.6(4; p.176.11; M.14.316B); τὰ μὲν πλείονα ~ει [sc. Manes], βραχέα καὶ καταλιπών Tit.Bost.*Man.* 3 proem.(M.18.1209A).

C. *defraud, circumvent,* Dion.Com.(A)ap.Ath.*apol.sec.*81(p.161.8; M.25.393D).

περιγυρεύω, *go around,* Gr.Mag.*dial.*(tr.Zach.)3.37(M.*PL.*77. 307B, v.l. περιέτρεχεν).

***περιγυρόομαι,** *be encircled,* Gr.Naz.*carm.*2.2(poem.).4.174(M.37. 1518A).

***περιγύρου,** *round about* ἐστάθησαν π. †Anast.S.*relat.*51(*OC* 3 p.72).

περίδακρυς, *weeping bitterly, very sorrowful, Protev.*16.1(p.30); *Hom.Clem.*12.23; Bas.Sel.*v.Thecl.*1(M.85.489A).

περιδέεια, ἡ, *excessive fear, V.Const.*17(p.555.15).

περιδεής, *frightening*; hence *dangerous,* Gr.Naz.*carm.*2.1.11.1247 (M.37.1115A).

***περίδεμα, τό,** *head-band, M.Thdot.*1 13(p.69.28).

περιδέξιος, 1. *ambidexterous*; met.; **a.** *expert,* Clem.*str.*1.10(p.30. 28; M.8.744A); ὁ π. ... καὶ γνωστικός *ib.*6.12(p.484.3; M.9.325A);

περιδέξιοι τὴν ἀρετήν Gr.Naz.*or*.36.10(M.36.277C); Nonn.*par.Jo.* 13:14(M.43.861C); Zach.Mit.*opif.*(M.85.1072B); **b.** *adaptable* πρὸς τοὺς γνωρίμους ἐν πᾶσι περιδέξιοι Max.*ep*.4(M.91.420A); **2.** *for the right hand,* Gr.Nyss.*hom.1 in Cant.*(M.44.768C); π. ψέλλια ‡Jo.D. *hom*.5(M.96.657D).

[*]**περιδέρρεον, τό,** *necklace,* Thdt.*affect*.3(4.764; περιδέραιον p.73. 20).

περιδεσμέω, *bind round;* in practices designed to procure abortion, Hipp.*haer*.9.12(p.250.18; M.16.3387A).

περιδόμημα, τό, *surrounding edifice* σῶμα...ψυχῆς...π. ... καὶ οἰκητήριον Melet.*nat.hom*.30(M.64.1269A).

περιδον-έω, A. pass.; **1.** *be whirled about,* Bas.*hom.in Ps*.61(1. 194D; M.29.473A); Evagr.*h.e*.3.25(p.122.27; M.86.2649A); fig. κλύδωνι παθῶν...~ούμενος Max.*myst.*(M.91.717C); **2.** *be shaken all round* τεῖχος τῆς πίστεως τοῖς μηχανήμασι τῆς αἱρέσεως...~ούμενον Gr.Nyss.*Eun*.12(1 p.218.18; M.45.912C).

B. ? med., *shake all round* κώδωνες...τοῖς ῥοΐσκοις ~ούμενοι Gr. Nyss.*v.Mos.*(M.44.389A).

***περιδόνησις, ἡ,** *gyration,* Chrys.*pan.Barl*.4(2.687A).

***περίδοξος,** *illustrious,* Thphn.*chron*.p.221(M.108.564B); Thdr. Stud.*epp*.2.29(M.99.1197D).

***περιδρακτικός,** *able to grasp* or *comprehend,* of BMV πλάσμα καὶ περιδρακτικὸν τοῦ πλαστουργοῦ Thdot.Anc.*hom.BMV et Sym*.3(M. 77.1393C).

περίδραξις, ἡ, *grasping* π. τῆς παιδείας Or.*sel.in Ps*.2:12(M.12. 1116C); εὐσεβῶν δογμάτων π. CLater.*act*.4(H.3.821E).

περιδράσσ-ω, A. *lay hold* of ἡμεῖς δὲ τοῦ λόγου ~ωμεν Gr.Naz.*ep.* 178(M.37.293A).

B. med.; **1.** *grasp, take hold* of; **a.** lit., Meth.*res*.1.24(p.250.2; M. 41.1096A); σπέρμα...γῆς ~όμενον Bas.*hex*.5.3(1.42C; M.29.100C); id. *renunt*.4(2.205C; M.31.633B); ὅταν...τὸ πονηρὸν...πνεῦμα περιδράξηται τῆς ψυχῆς Ant.Mon.*hom*.25(M.89.1509B); **b.** met. Χριστοῖο ~εσθαι Gr.Naz.*carm*.1.2.2.253(M.37.598A); Gr.Nyss.*hom.13 in Cant.*(M.44. 1052B); ὁ θείῳ ἔρωτι περιδεδραγμένος ὅλος ἐστὶν αὐτοῦ Max.*schol. c.h*.2.4(M.3.44B); **2.** *grasp, understand* τοὺς χρόνους καθ' οὓς ἧξειν ἀνείρηται...~όμενοι Eus.*d.e*.4.1(p.150.12; M.22.252A); Eust.*Laz*.9 (p.34.5); Chrys.*hom.2.4 in Jo.*(8.12E); Cyr.*Jo*.3.4(4.279D); **3.** *hold under one's sway, control,* of God τῆς τῶν ὅλων δημιουργίας τοὺς οἴακας περιδεδραγμένον Eus.*d.e*.4.2(p.152.7; M.22.253B); ἁπάντων μία τοῦ...υἱοῦ...χεὶρ ~ομένη id.*e.th*.1.20(p.85.25; M.24.873B); Gr.Nyss. *Apoll*.9(M.45.1141B); πάντα τὰ ὄντα...περιδέδρακται ἡ θεία φύσις Zach.Mit.*opif.*(M.85.1137B); acc. Or. πεποίηκε...τοσαῦτα ὧν ἠδύνατο περιδράξασθαι Justn.*Or.*(p.190.13; M.86.947C); εἴ τις λέγει...τοσαῦτα αὐτὸν δημιουργῆσαι, ὅσον περιδράξασθαι...ἀ. ἔ. *ib.*(p.214.2; 989C); **4.** *grapple with,* Or.*comm.in 1Cor*.3:16–20(*JTS* 9 p.247).

περιδρομή, ἡ, 1. *going round,* Gr.Nyss.*hex*.24(M.44.85B); **2.** *going round to canvass,* hence *courting favour, cajolery,* Alex.Al.*ep.Alex*.2 (p.20.20; M.18.549C); Ἀρειομανῖται...προεδριῶν διὰ πλείστης ὅσης π. κρατήσαντες Eust.*fr.in Pr.8:22*(M.18.676D)ap.Thdt.*h.e*.1.8.4; τοῖς ...διὰ περιδρομήν τινων κοινωνήσασι Γρηγορίῳ CSard.*ep.Alex*.ap.Ath. *apol.sec*.39(p.118.5; M.25.316C); Petr.II Al.*encycl.*(M.33.1280C)ap. Thdt.*h.e*.4.22.10; Chrys.*hom.3.5 in Ac.*(9.31C); ἱερωσύνην περιδρομῇ ...ἥρπασας Isid.Pel.*epp*.1.145(M.78.280B).

περιεγείρω, *arouse;* pass., Hipp.*haer*.5.25(p.126.12; M.16.3194A).

περίειμι, (εἰμί *sum*); **1.** *survive* ὑπόμνησιν τῶν περιόντων καὶ τῶν κεκοιμημένων *Const.App*.8.42.2; *ib*.8.43.2; **2.** *gain the mastery* of, *gain possession* of περιέσῃ τῆς ἀρετῆς Chrys.*hom.43.5 in Mt.*(7. 466C).

περίειμι, (εἶμι *ibo*) *go about;* of evangelists in NT ministry, opp. pastors and teachers τί οὖν; οἱ ποιμένες καὶ οἱ διδάσκαλοι ἐλάττους; καὶ πάνυ, τῶν περιϊόντων καὶ εὐαγγελιζομένων οἱ καθήμενοι καὶ περὶ ἕνα τόπον ἠσχολημένοι Chrys.*hom.11.2 in Eph.*(11.83C); ποιμένας δὲ καὶ διδασκάλους τοὺς κατὰ πόλιν καὶ κώμην ἀφωρισμένους λέγει. οὗ δὴ χάριν μετὰ τοὺς εὐαγγελιστὰς τέθεικεν, ἐπειδὴ ἐκεῖνοι περιϊόντες ἐκήρυττον Thdt.*Eph*.4:11(3.424).

***περιεκτέον,** *one must embrace,* Niceph.Ur.*v.Sym*.36(M.86.3017D).

***περιεκτίζω,** *constrain,* Didym.*Ps*.115:2(M.39.1553C).

περιεκτικός, *embracing, comprehensive* τὸν π. αὐτῶν [sc. τῶν οὐρανῶν] κύκλον, ὃν καὶ ὄγδοον οὐρανὸν ὀνομάζουσι Iren.*haer*.1.17.1 (M.7.637A); Meth.*symp*.8.11(p.94.16; M.18.156B); ref. love of God πάσης...π. ἐστιν ἐντολῆς Bas.*reg.fus*.2.1(2.336D; M.31.908D); Gr. Nyss.*hex*.8(M.44.69D); ref. 1Cor.14:19 πέντε δὲ λόγοι εἰσὶν αἱ π. ἀρεταί Mac.Aeg.*hom*.37.8(M.34.756B); ἀποστολὴν...πρᾶγμα...χαρισμάτων ἁπάντων...π. Chrys.*hom.1.1 in Rom.*(9.430C); τῶν π. στοιχείων Thdt.*Ps*.101:27(1.1322); π. δὲ πασῶν ἐντολῶν, ἡ τῆς ψυχῆς ἄρνησις Marc.Er.*opusc*.4(M.65.1005B); Max.*opusc.*(M.91.1136C); of God, Clem.*str*.5.6(p.350.18; M.9.61B); τῶν ἁπάντων καὶ τῶν ὅλων π. *ib*.5.11 (p.375.20; 112A); *ib*.7.5(p.20.20; 436C); κἂν δεύτερον...λέγωμεν θεόν, ἴστωσαν ὅτι τὸν δεύτερον θεὸν οὐκ ἄλλο τι λέγομεν ἢ τὴν π. πασῶν ἀρετῶν ἀρετὴν καὶ τὸν π. παντὸς...λόγου...λόγον Or.*Cels*.5.39(p.43. 23; M.11.1244B); *ib*.7.34(p.184.16; 1468C); Gr.Nyss.*or.catech*.4(p.18. 5; M.45.20B); of divine attributes or descriptions εἰ ἀσώματον... οὐδὲ τοῦτο τῆς οὐσίας...περιεκτικόν Gr.Naz.*or*.28.9(p.35.5; M.36.36C); ἡ π. τῶν ὄντων...δύναμις Gr.Nyss.*hom.15 in Cant.*(M.44.1093A); ἡ γὰρ πρόνοια τοῦ θεοῦ τῶν οἰκείων ποιημάτων ἐστὶν π. Ast.Am.*hom*.3 (M.40.213A).

περιεκτικῶς, *comprehensively* οἶκον γὰρ θεοῦ π. τὴν καθόλου ἐκκλησίαν προσηγόρευσεν Cyr.*Ps*.91:16(M.69.1229B); Marc.Er.*opusc*. 1.173(M.65.925C); π. πάσας τὰς ἐντολὰς ἐργάσασθαι *ib*.4(1005B); Dor. *doct*.4.3(M.88.1661D).

[*]**περιεκχύν-ω, 1.** *overflow all round,* Jo.Mosch.*prat*.16(M.87. 2864B); **2.** pass., *be shed all round* τὸ βάπτισμα...ἀναγεννᾷ φῶς ~όμενον *A.Thom.*A 132(p.239.10).

περιέλιξις, ἡ, *revolution,* Dion.Ar.*d.n*.8.5(M.3.892D).

περιελίσσ-ω, 1. *make to go round, pass round* ἐν μέρει ~όντων τὰς προπόσεις τῆς ᾠδῆς Clem.*paed*.2.4(p.184.13; M.8.445A); **2.** pass., *wind round, ib*.2.9(p.205.23; v.l. ἐφελισσομένων M.8.492C); κύκλῳ γε αὐτὴν περιελιχθεὶς Philost.*h.e*.3.10(M.65.493C); **3.** *surround* ἴριδος... αὐτὸν ~ούσης *ib*.3.26(513A); **4.** *cast* the eye *round* τῆς διανοίας τὸν ὀφθαλμὸν ἐν κύκλῳ ~οντες Cyr.*ador*.6(1.172B).

περιελκυσμός, ὁ, *hesitation,* Or.*mart*.3(p.4.22; M.11.565C); Didym.*Ac*.2:31(M.39.1660B).

περιέλκ-ω, 1. *drag about,* Clem.*str*.4.8(p.278.27; M.8.1277C); **2.** *draw to and fro,* met. τῆς δ' Ἀποκαλύψεως εἰς ἑκάτερον ἔτι νῦν παρὰ τοῖς πολλοῖς ~εται ἡ δόξα Eus.*h.e*.3.24.18(M.20.268C); **3.** *draw to, attract* ἵππον ἀροῦν οὐ βιαζόμεθα...πρὸς ὃ πέφυκε δὲ ἕκαστον τῶν ζώων ~ομεν Clem.*prot*.10(p.72.27; M.8.216A); **4.** *divert, draw aside,* id.*paed*.2.1(p.163.29; M.8.400B); met., *draw aside, distract, ib*.2.10 (p.214.7; 509B); Or.*mart*.11(p.11.12; M.11.577B); Chrys.*hom.54.5 in Mt.*(7.553A, v.l. παρ-); id.*hom.5.4 in 2Cor.*(10.471C); **5.** *pervert* from truth to heresy, Eus.*h.e*.5.15(M.20.464A); **6.** *turn* an argument ἐκεῖνον μὲν ἀπαλλάττων τῆς κατηγορίας, εἰς δὲ τούτους τὸ πᾶν ~ων Chrys.*hom.51.4 in Mt.*(7.525A); **7.** *draw out, prolong,* ‡Ath.*dial. Trin*.3.25(M.28.1241A).

***περιένεξις, ἡ,** *comprehension,* Jo.D.*f.o*.3.15(M.94.1049A).

***περιενοχλέομαι,** *be troubled on every side,* Eustrat.*v.Eutych*.54 (M.86.2336D).

***περιεξέρχ-ομαι,** *go round* so as to assault from another side τῷ Ἀδὰμ...ἀφεὶς [sc. ὁ διάβολος] τὸ τῆς συζυγίας εὐχείρωτον, ἕτερον ~εται μέρος Bas.Sel.*or*.3.3(M.85.53D).

περιεργάζ-ω, A. *seek diligently* τὰς ὁδοὺς τοῦ κυρίου ~οντες Cyr.*Ps*. 24:4(M.69.848A).

B. med.; **1.** *take much trouble* περιεργασάμενοι τροπολογεῖν Or. *comm.in Mt*.12.41(p.163.4; M.13.1077C); **2.** *exercise oneself about, be much concerned with,* Chrys.*hom.22.3 in Heb.*(12.207B); Cyr.*Is*.2.4 (2.313D); Euthal.Diac.*Ac.*(M.85.633B); Εὐσέβιος...χρόνους ἀκριβῶς περιεργασάμενος id.*epp.Paul.*(M.85.709B); **3.** *inquire diligently about, investigate* πῶς ἂν περιεργάσαιτό τις τὴν τοῦ θεοῦ λόγου ὑπόστασιν; Alex.Al.*ep.Alex*.5(p.23.4; M.18.556A); τὰς πράξεις αὐτοῦ π. †Ath. *fr.Mt.*(M.27.1381A); Chrys.*fr.Job* 29:16(M.64.632C); Cyr.*ador*.4(1. 122B); **4.** *be inquisitive about, inquire into out of curiosity* μήτε ~εσθε πρᾶξιν γυναικῶν *T.Reub*.3.10; περὶ τῶν λοιπῶν μὴ ~ου Herm. *sim*.9.2.7; πιστεῦσαι· μὴ γὰρ ἀπίστως ~εσθαι ὅ τι ἐστὶν Didym. (‡Bas.)*Eun*.5(1.313D; M.29.752B); τὰ ὑπὲρ ἄνθρωπον μὴ ~εσθαι τοὺς εὖ διακειμένους Acac.B.*ep.Cyr.*(p.99.16; M.77.100C); ~εσθαι τὸ πίστει παραδεκτὸν...οὐκ ἀσφαλὲς Cyr.*Jo*.2.8(4.227C); οὐ δεῖ ~εσθαι τὰ σεσιωπημένα τῇ γραφῇ Anast.S.*hod*.4(M.89.93C); ref. persons, *make censorious inquiries about* ἐκείνους δὲ πάλιν ~όμενος, καὶ λέγων, ἐὰν μὴ ᾖ ἄξιος...ἐὰν μὴ σημεῖα ποιῇ, οὐκ ὀρέγω χεῖρα Chrys.*hom.10.4 in Heb.*(12.108D); **5.** *meddle with, be a busybody about* παῦσαι...τὰ τοῦ δεῖνος κακὰ ~όμενος Bas.*hom*.3.5(2.21B; M.31.209A); Gr.Naz.*ep*.183 (M.37.300A); Nil.*epp*.2.65(M.79.229B); **6.** *give trouble to* δολοφωνεῖ σε ἢ ~εταί σε ἐν κακοῖς *T.Gad* 6.5; Eus.*h.e*.8.12.3(M.20.769C); id.*v.C*.1. 51(p.31.18; M.20.965B); **7.** *pay attention to* (lasciviously) κάλλη γυναικῶν ~ῃ; Chrys.*hom.73.3 in Mt.*(7.712A); id.*fr.Job* 31:1(M.64. 633D); Thdt.*provid*.9(4.643); **8.** *practise, be concerned with,* superstitious observances μὴ μαντεία ~εσθαι Eus.*v.C*.4.25(p.126.15; M.20. 1172B); Φρυγῶν, τῶν πρώτων ~ομένων ὀρνίθων πτῆσιν Gr.Naz.*or*.4. 109(M.35.645A); c. dat., Cyr.*Is*.1.4(2.120E); abs., *practise magic,* Chrys.*hom.6.4 in Mt.*(7.93B).

περιεργασία, ἡ, 1. *idle curiosity,* Clem.*prot*.10(p.72.3; M.8.213A); Marc.Er.*opusc*.4(M.65.985B); **2.** *unnecessary labour,* Chrys.*hom.14.3* *in 1Tim.*(11.628B, v.l. ἐργασίας); 3. *magical practice*, Eus.*v.C.*3.57 (p.104.19, v.l. περιεργίαις M.20.1124B).

περιεργαστέον, *one must interfere* with, Alex.Lyc.*Man.*25(p.36.16).

***περιεργαστικός,** *contrived*, Sever.*1Cor.*5:7f.(p.244.25).

περιεργία (-εία), ἡ, 1. *idle curiosity*, Clem.*str.*1.1(p.6.4; M.8.692D); *M.Perp.*17(p.87.14); Meth.*res.*2.3(p.334.13; M.41.1168A); ref. unworthy candidates for baptism who wish to learn secrets reserved for the initiated, Cyr.H.*procatech.*4; Chrys.*hom.16.2 in Jo.*(8.92E); 2. *excess, superfluity* μύρων ποικίλων περιεργίαις χρώμενοι Eus.*d.e.*4.15(p.174.28; M.22.292B); βρωμάτων...περιεργίᾳ πρὸς ἡδονὴν μετασκευάζων...τὴν τράπεζαν Bas.*reg.fus.*20.3(2.365A; M.31.973A); 3. *over-elaboration*, Gr.Nyss.*or.dom.*3(p.46.20; περιεργασίας M.44.1149A); Chrys.*hom.2.3 in Jo.*(8.11A); 4. *unnecessary labour, vain effort* πολλῇ γὰρ οἱ...σοφισταὶ κεχρημένοι π. τὰ ὅσα παρὰ τῶν κατὰ Μωσέα...φιλοσοφούντων ἔγνωσαν, παραχαράττειν ἐπειράθησαν Tat.*orat.*40(p.41.5; M.6.884B); ἡ τῆς ἁπλότητος πίστις βελτίων ἐστὶ τῆς ἐκ π. πιθανολογίας Ath.*Ar.*3.1(M.26.324A); Sophr.H.*mir.Cyr.et Jo.*23 (M.87.3488B); 5. *meddlesomeness, officiousness*, Gr.Naz.*ep.*14(M.37.48A); πράγματα ἔχειν ἀπό τινος σοφιστικῆς τῶν κρατούντων καὶ συνήθους π. *ib.*47(96C); ἀπὸ γὰρ ἀργίας π., καὶ ἀπὸ π. ἀταξία Leont.et Jo.*sacr.*2(M.86.2068D); Esaias *or.*5(p.37); Dor.*doct.*9.1(M.88.1716C); 6. *superstition*, esp. *practice of magic* σεμνυνόμενοι [sc. Carpocratians] τοῖς κατὰ περιεργίαν πρὸς αὐτῶν ἐπιτελουμένοις φίλτροις ὀνειροπομποῖς τε καὶ παρέδροις...δαίμοσιν Eus.*h.e.*4.7.9(M.20.317B); τὴν τῶν ἀφανῶν πνευμάτων π. id.*d.e.*4.9(p.164.14; M.22.273C); *ib.*9.2(p.407.22; 657A); δύο...ἐπέμποντο νόμοι, ὁ μὲν εἴργων...ὡς μήτε ἐγέρσεις ξοάνων ποιεῖσθαι τολμᾶν, μήτε μαντείαις καὶ ταῖς ἄλλαις π. ἐπιχειρεῖν id.*v.C.*2.45(p.60.9; M.20.1021B); οἰωνιστικῆς π. Gr.Nyss.*Trin.*5(p.76.21; M.32.692A); δεισιδαιμονίας...καὶ π. Didym.*Trin.*3.24(M.39.937A); ἐπῳδαῖς καὶ π. χρησάμενοι Soz.*h.e.*5.15.15(M.67.1260B); Call.*v.Hyp.*(p.38); Καρποκράτης...τὰς π. τὰς ἐπὶ φίλτρων γινομένας δημοσίᾳ ἐξαγγέλλει Tim.CP *haer.*(M.86.29A).

***περιεργολογία, ἡ,** *excessive subtlety in speech, quibbling*, Eust.Mon.*ep.*(M.86.916B).

περίεργος, 1. *of inquiring mind, curious* τὸ μὲν γὰρ σαφῶς λεχθέν, ...παρατρέχει τὸν ἀκροατήν· τὸ δὲ ἀσαφὲς περιεργότερον αὐτὸν ποιεῖ Chrys.*hom.24.2 in Jo.*(8.140C); Antip.Bost.*Jo.Bapt.*7(M.85.1769B); 2. *inquisitive, meddling*, Herm.*vis.*4.3.1; Clem.*paed.*1.5(p.102.24; M.8.276A); Ath.*ep.Serap.*2.3(M.26.612B); 3. *over-elaborate* τῷ π. τῆς ἑρμηνείας Clem.*paed.*3.2(p.240.15; M.8.565A); τοῖς ἀρτίον ἐπὶ τὸ πιστεύειν ἰοῦσιν ἀμείνων ἡ πίστις ἐν ἁπλοῖς λογισμοῖς, ἢ...περιεργοτέρα ...ἐξήγησις Cyr.*Jo.*2.1(4.149E); ref. δερμάτινοι χιτῶνες: οἱ μὲν ἀλληγορηταὶ τὴν θνητὴν σάρκα φασὶ τὰ δέρματα· ἄλλοι δέ τινες ἀπὸ φλοιῶν δένδρων τούτους κατεσκευάσθαι εἰρήκασιν· ἐγὼ...οὐδέτερον τούτων προσίεμαι. τὸ μὲν γὰρ π., τὸ δὲ ἄγαν μυθῶδες Thdt.*qu.39 in Gen.*(1.52); 4. *ingenious, well devised*, Gr.Naz.*or.*15.6(M.35.921B); 5. persons, *vain, flashy*, Chrys.*hom.49.5 in Mt.*(7.511A); 6. *superstitious, magical*, Iren.*haer.*1.23.4(M.7.673A); δαιμόνων κατακλήσεσι π. θελγομένων Or.*Cels.*2.51(p.174.13; M.11.877B); Eus.*Hierocl.*29 (529C; M.22.836D); *ib.*35(534B; M.848A); π. φάρμακον Bas.*ep.*88 *can.*8(3.273C; M.32.677A); Chrys.*hom.41.4 in Ac.*(9.309B); εἰ βούλει Χριστιανὸς γενέσθαι, φέρε μοι...πάντα τὰ π. σου Call.*v.Hyp.*(p.90); ὁ π. *magician*, Or.*comm.in Eph.*6:2(p.572).

***περιερευνάομαι,** *make inquisitive investigation into*, Bas.*hom.*3.5 ap.Jo.D.*parall.*(M.95.1300A) for περιεργαζόμενος *ib.*(2.21B; M.31.209B).

***περιερμηνεία, ἡ,** *interpretation*, cf. *Aristoteles...perihermeniam nominat, quam interpretationem nos appellamus*, Isid.H.*etym.*2.27.3.

περιέρχ-ομαι, 1. *go round*, of wandering monks μοναστήρια ~εσθαι Cassianus ap.Leont.et Jo.*sacr.*2(M.86.2068A); 2. *scrutinize, survey*, met. κακοδοξίαν...περιελθόντας Eus.*Marcell.*2.1(p.31.25; M.24.776B); 3. *circumvent, overreach* ~εται δι' ἀπάτης τὸν ἄνθρωπον Gr.Nyss.*or.catech.*6(p.36.1, v.l. διέρχεται M.45.29B); Philost.*h.e.*1.3 (M.65.461C); 4. *go, run* into μὴ...ἐν πταίσματι...περιέλθῃ Gr.Mag.*dial.*(tr.Zach.)4.11(M.*PL*.77.335C); 5. *pass* to; of property, Ath.Scholast.*coll.*2.9(p.40).

***περιευρίσκω,** *discover*, Gr.Mag.*dial.*(tr.Zach.)3.1(M.*PL*.77.218A).

περιέχ-ω, 1. *surround, embrace*; hence *include, comprehend* ὁ πάντα ~ων...κόσμος *Hom.Clem.*10.19; τὸ ἀγέννητον...ἐν τῷ τῆς οὐσίας λόγῳ ~όμενον Bas.*Eun.*1.6(1.215E; M.29.520A); καὶ εἰ μὲν ἔν τινι, ὑπ' ἐλάττονος περιγραφήσεται τοῦ τινος, εἰ δὲ πανταχοῦ, ὑπὸ πλείονος καὶ ἄλλου πολλοῦ, λέγω δέ, τὸ ~όμενον τοῦ ~οντος, εἰ τὸ πᾶν ὑπὸ τοῦ παντὸς μέλλοι περισχεθήσεσθαι, καὶ μηδένα τόπον εἶναι περιγραφῆς ἐλεύθερον Gr.Naz.*or.*28.10(p.37.9; M.36.37C); ἡ φύσις, πάντα τὰ ὄντα ἐν ἑαυτῇ ~ουσα, ὑπ' οὐδενὸς ~εται ὅρου Gr.Nyss.*hom.5 in Cant.*(M.44.873C); Gel.Cyz.*h.e.*2.22.3(M.85.1292A); ‡Cyr.*Trin.*7(6³.8B; M.77.1132A) = Jo.D.*f.o.*1.8(M.94.808C); Jo.D.*Man.*2(M.96.1321C); 2. *contain provision* that ἡ ψῆφος...~έτω μὴ ἄλλως προσάγεσθαι τὴν ὑπόμνησιν Ath.Scholast.*coll.*5.2(p.71); 3. pass., *be involved* οὔτε γὰρ εἴσω παθῶν ~εται Epiph.*haer.*76.35(p.384.29; M.42.588A); med., *be wrapped up in, be taken up with* τοῦ πολυχρημάτου καὶ δεινῶς τῆς κτήσεως ~ομένου Clem.*q.d.s.*20(p.173.9; M.9.625B); οὐ δεῖ ~εσθαι τοῦ γράμματος τῆς γραφῆς Or.*sel.in Gen.*2:16–17(M.12.101B); παθημάτων τῆς σαρκὸς ~εσθαι Didym.*Man.*9(M.39.1097B).

***περιέψω,** *boil thoroughly*, ref. spiritual interprn. of passover law, Or.*Jo.*10.18(13; p.189.24; M.14.337D).

***περιζήτησις, ἡ,** *inquiry*, Chrys.*hom.3.3 in Heb.*(12.30A, v.l. ἐπιζητήσει).

περίζωμα, τό, *loin-cloth, girdle*, *T.Benj.*2.3; as monastic dress τὰ τῶν μηλωτῶν π. μόνοις τοῖς τὴν σάρκα νεκρώσασιν ἀνδρείως περίκειται, σημεῖα ὄντα νεκρώσεως Isid.Pel.*epp.*1.427(M.78.420A); worn by those being baptized, *A.Thom.*A 157(p.266.9); by criminals on trial, *ib.*163(p.275.3); ref. Jer.13:1 as illustration of poverty of prophets, Clem.*paed.*2.10(p.224.23; M.8.532B); κολλᾷ οὖν περὶ τὴν ὀσφὺν αὐτοῦ τὸ π. ... ἵνα δηλωθῇ ὅτι ὁ λαὸς οἱονεὶ σκέπη ἐστὶ τοῦ θεοῦ ...καὶ οὐκ ἐᾷ τι ἄτοπον λέγεσθαι ἐν τοῖς περὶ τοῦ θεοῦ· ἐπὰν δὲ ἁμαρτήσωμεν, τὸ π. τοῦτο ὡς ἀποτίθεται ὁ προφήτης...οὕτως ὁ ἁμαρτάνων ἀποβάλλεται ἀπὸ τῆς ὀσφύος τοῦ θεοῦ Or.*hom.11.6 in Jer.*(p.84.1; M.13.376A); figure of Church of gentiles, *ib.*(p.85.8; 376D).

περιζωμάτιον, *loin-cloth*, Or.*hom.11.6 in Jer.*(p.84.12; M.13.376B).

περίζωσις, ἡ, *cincture*, *T.Job* 52(p.136.19); *Pers.capt.*(M.86.3245A).

περιηγέομαι, *expound*, Thdt.*Ps.*81:8(1.1189).

περιηγής, *circular*, hence ? *rolled*; of a book, †Apoll.*met.Ps.* epilog.(M.33.1537C; *Teub.* om.).

περιήλυσις, ἡ, *cycle, revolution*, Clem.*str.*7.14(p.61.5; M.9.520A).

περιηχ-έω, 1. *sound all round* ~οῦσιν οἰμωγαὶ τὴν πόλιν Dion.Al.ap.Eus.*h.e.*7.22.2(M.20.688A); Gr.Nyss.*v.Macr.*(p.406.23; M.46.992D); 2. pass.; *be surrounded with noise*, Clem.*paed.*2.1(p.155.20; M.8.381B); Cyr.H.*procatech.*6 cit. s. ἐνηχέω; 3. *clamour about, reiterate* ~οῦσιν...τὰ περὶ πολλῶν θεῶν Or.*Cels.*3.75(p.266.17; M.11.1017B); 4. pass., *resound*, Gr.Nyss.*ep.*19(M.46.1073D); 5. pass., *be informed* ~ητο περὶ τῶν...'Οφιανῶν Or.*Cels.*3.13(p.213.9; M.11.936C); *ib.*6.15(p.85.6; 1312C); Cyr.*deip.BMV*(p.28.12; M.76.280B); CChalc.*can.*25.

περιήχημα, τό, *that which resounds, which is full of talk* about, of BMV πόλις, τὸ τοῦ...βασιλέως...π. Thdr.Stud.*nativ.BMV* 7(M.96.697A).

περιήχησις, ἡ, *instruction* (in evil, opp. κατήχησις) γεγονέναι δὲ πολλοὺς κακοὺς παρὰ τὰς ἀνατροφάς, καὶ τὰς διαστροφάς, καὶ τὰς π. Or.*Cels.*3.69(p.261.15; M.11.1009D).

περιθαλπής, *very hot*, †Apoll.*met.Ps.*25:2(M.33.1344D).

περιθάλπ-ω, *cherish*, Bas.*ep.*45.1(3.134A; M.32.368A); of BMV ἡ περιθαλψαμένη τὸν ἐπιβλέποντα ἐπὶ τὴν γῆν Mod.*dorm.*8(M.86.3300A); met. ἱερὸν συγκρότημα...~οντες Ephr.3.338F; ἐξ αὐτῆς [sc. αὐτοζωῆς] ...~εται...ζῷα πάντα Dion.Ar.*d.n.*6.3(M.3.857B); ἀληθὴς φιλοσοφία τοὺς αὐτῆς ἐραστὰς...~ει †Jo.D.*B.J.*15(M.96.996A).

περιθαρσής, *very confident*, †Apoll.*met.Ps.*24:1(M.33.1344A); *ib.*70:6(1412A); *ib.*75:6(1420D).

***περιθάρσυνος,** = foreg., †Apoll.*met.Ps.*22:4(M.33.1341B).

περίθεμα, τό, *thing placed round*; 1. *covering* of altar, ref. Num.16:38 πυρεῖα τῶν περὶ Κορὲ...π. ὄντα τῷ θυσιαστηρίῳ Or.*sel.in Num.*16:37(M.12.577A); 2. *head-band, crown*, Ephr.1.31F; Στέφανος, τὸ αὐτοχάλκευτον π. Procl.CP *or.*17.2(M.65.809D).

***περιθεμελιόω,** *establish on a firm foundation all round*, ‡Bas.*struct.hom.*1.18(1.331D; M.30.28A).

***περιθεραπεύω,** *cure completely*, Hipp.*antichr.*49(p.32.8, v.l. ὥσπερ θεραπεύσει M.10.768B).

***περιθερμαίν-ω,** *heat all round* οὕτως ἐστὶν ἓν πρὸς τὸν...πατέρα, οὐ καθάπερ ἡμεῖς...μετοχικῶς..., ὥσπερ ἂν εἰ καὶ σίδηρος πυρὶ ὁμιλήσας ~οιτο παρ' αὐτοῦ Cyr.*thes.*12(5¹.119E); ~ομένης τῆς καρδίας Dor.*doct.*8.2(M.88.1709A).

περιθέ-ω, 1. *flow round* ὕδωρ ~ον...τὴν γῆν ‡Eust.*hex.*(M.18.749A); 2. pass., *be encircled* with flowing water ~όμενα πέδια Men.*exc.Rom.*14(p.204.13; M.113.901B).

περιθεωρέω, *interpret with reference to*, c. dat., Gr.Nyss.*Eun.*1(1 p.201.29; M.45.449A).

***περιθλιβής,** *greatly distressed*, Bas.*renunt.*2(2.204C; M.31.632A).

περιθριγκόω, *fence round* from, Clem.*paed.*3.12(p.283.8; M.8.664B) cit. s. περισταυρόω.

περιθρυλ(λ)-έομαι, 1. *be noised abroad*, Bas.*ep.*9.2(3.90C; M.32.268C); τὰ ~ούμενα Gr.Nyss.*ep.*5(M.46.1029B); 2. *resound* ὦτα

~ούμενα Bas.*Eun*.2.5(1.241D; M.29.581A); id.*ep*.26.2(3.104C; M.32.300C).

περιθρύπτω, *smash*, Gr.Nyss.*or.catech*.8(p.45.3; M.45.36A); *ib*.16 (p.71.8; 52C).

[*]**περιθύω**, v.l. for θύω, Chrys.*comm.in Gal*.2:17(10.691B).

***περιθωρακίζ-ω**, **1.** *arm, equip* ὁ Παῦλος ~ων τοῖς ὅπλοις τοῦ πνεύματος †Jo.Jej.*serm*.(M.88.1952A); περιθωρακίσωμεν ἑαυτούς Dor.*doct*. 10.7(M.88.1733D); **2.** med., *arm* or *equip oneself* with περιτεθωρακισμένος τὸν φόβον τοῦ κυρίου Bas.*renunt*.5(2.206E; M.31.637A).

***περιϊζάνω**, *settle round about*, Isid.Pel.*epp*.3.245(M.78.924B).

περιΐστ-ημι, **A.** trans. tenses; **1.** *bring* upon oneself εἰς σεαυτὸν π. τὴν πραγματείαν Gr.Naz.*ep*.14(M.37.48A); Chrys.*hom.76.2 in Jo*. (8.449A); id.*hom.31.3 in 1Cor*.(10.283B); **2.** *refer, attribute* οὐκ εἰς ἐκείνους δὲ ~ησι τὰ λεγόμενα id.*hom.15.1 in Mt*.(7.185C); *ib.55.1* (556C); Cyr.*ep*.55(p.59.33; 5².188E); **3.** *suggest, bring to mind* τὸ συλλήβδην τὰ πάντα γεγενῆσθαι ~ησι Gr.Nyss.*hex*.8(M.44.72A).

B. intrans. tenses; **1.** *turn* δι' ἐκτόπων ἐννοιῶν περιστάντες ἀνοσίως εἰς τὸ ἀκαλλές Cyr.*Is*.3.4(2.511A); **2.** *be reduced* to εἰς ἕνα ἄρτον περιστῇ ἡ τροφή Bas.*hom*.8.6(2.68E; M.31.320C); Thdr.Mops. *Mal*.3:13–16(M.66.628C); **3.** med., *come to, be presented* to, ‡Pion.*v. Polyc*.18.

περικαθαίρ-ω, **1.** *purify* by means of application of an object calculated to absorb defilement or contagion μὴ γίνου οἰωνοσκόπος ...μηδὲ μαθηματικὸς μηδὲ ~ων *Did*.3.4 = *Ordo Eccl.App*.10(p.229.8); cf. οὐκ ἔσῃ ἐπᾴδων ἢ ~ων τὸν υἱόν σου (cf. Dt.18:10) *Const.App*.7.6.2; ᾠὰ τὰ ἀπὸ τῶν περικαθαρθέντων Clem.*str*.7.4(p.19.9; ᾦτα M.9.433B); μὴ ἀπέρχεσθαι πρὸς ἐπαοιδὸν...μήτε ~ειν ‡Ath.*syntag*.2.5(p.123; M.28.837B); οὐ φοιβήσετε. ... δηλοῖ οὖν ἡ λέξις τὸ μὴ ~εσθαι. οὐ γὰρ οἶδε σώματος καθαρμὸς μολυσμοὺς ἀπονίψαι ψυχῆς Proc.G.*Dt*.14:1(M.87.909D); **2.** *purge, purify* θεοῦ δὲ μόνου περικαθᾶραι ψυχὴν *ib*.; **3.** *purge away* ἁμαρτίας σου περικαθαρεῖ ‡Meth.*Sym.et Ann*.7(M.18.365A).

περικαθαρίζω, *thoroughly cleanse*, Jo.Mosch.*prat*.107(M.87.2968A).

περικάθαρμα, τό, *means of purification* or *expiation, scapegoat* μαρτύρων...περικαθαρμάτων τοῦ κόσμου γινομένων Or.*Jo*.6.55(37; p.164.2; M.14.296B).

περικαθεζ-ομαι, *sit over* ~ομένη τὸ τῆς Κασταλίας στόμιον ἡ τοῦ Ἀπόλλωνος προφῆτις Or.*Cels*.7.3(p.155.13; M.11.1424D).

περικαίω, **1.** med., *scorch*, *A.Paul.et Thecl*.35(p.262.4); **2.** med., *be inflamed, be on fire with desire for* π. τοῦ Χριστοῦ Chrys.*hom.56.3 in Mt*.(7.568E); id.*hom.23.5 in Rom*.(9.693D); id.*hom.23.1 in 2Cor*. (10.595C); *ib.26.4*(623D); **3.** pass., *be burnt* ἀποφάσει περιεκαύθησαν *M.Agap*.5.8 (conj. πυρὶ ἐκαύθησαν).

περικακ-έω, **1.** *be depressed*, Mac.Aeg.*hom*.29.2(M.34.716D); Chrys. *hom.72.3 in Jo*.(8.421A); πρὸς τούτους ~εῖν id.*hom.6.2 in 2Tim*. (11.695A); Jo.Clim.*scal*.5(M.88.780B); **2.** *find difficulty in* ~ῶ τοσούτων αἱρέσεων ὀνόματα εἰς ἀριθμὸν φέρειν Epiph.*anc*.14(p.22.13; M.43.41A); ~ῶ...ἐξειπεῖν id.*haer*.26.14(p.294.3; M.41.353C); *ib*.26.2(p.276.23; 333B); ~οῦμεν λέγοντες Chrys.*hom.6.3 in 1Tim*.(11.582D).

περικαλύπτ-ω, *veil, conceal*, ref. Inc. ~εται τῇ σαρκὶ ἡ θεότης Gr. Nyss.*or.catech*.23(p.89.6; M.45.64A).

***περικάμμορος**, *most wretched*, †Apoll.*met.Ps*.136:8(M.33.1520B).

***περικαρτέον**, *one must shave round*, Clem.*paed*.3.11(p.270.30; M. 8.636B).

περικαταρρέω, *collapse, fall into ruin*, Clem.*prot*.11(p.81.20; M. 8.233B); id.*str*.7.2(p.8.27; M.9.413B).

περικατατίθεμαι, *conceal*, †Apoll.*met.Ps*.73:11(M.33.1417C).

***περικαῶς**, *very ardently*, *cat.2Cor*.11:2(p.419.22).

περίκει-μαι, **1.** *be set around, enclose*, *2Clem*.1.6; ὁ...τοῦ κυρίου στέφανος ἡμᾶς ἠνίττετο...τοὺς ~μένους αὐτῷ διὰ τῆς ἐκκλησίας Clem. *paed*.2.8(p.202.12; M.8.485A); τὸν ~μενον...ἀέρα *Hom.Clem*.2.26; ~μένης αὐταῖς [sc. ψυχαῖς] ἐκ τῆς ἀγνοίας ἀχλύος Dion.Ar.*d.n*.4.5(M.3.700D); **2.** *be clothed with, wear*; **a.** in gen., Herm.*vis*.5.1; Just.*dial*. 1.2(M.6.473A); ref. idols πῶς...γνωρίζεται θεὸς διὰ τούτων; πότερον διὰ τὴν ~μένην αὐτοῖς ὕλην, ἢ διὰ τὴν ἐν αὐτοῖς μορφήν; Ath.*gent*. 20(M.25.40D); Nil.*epp*.2.156(M.79.273B); **b.** of the body σωμάτων ὧν νῦν ~μεθα Meth.*res*.1.20(p.242.7; M.41.1088C); Σαμουὴλ...δῆλόν ἐστιν...ὁρατὸς ὢν παρίστησιν ὅτι σῶμα περιέκειτο *ib*.3.17(p.414.11; M. 18.325A); οὐχ ὡς σάρκα ~μένῳ...ἀλλ' ὡς ἀγγέλῳ...δικάζειν ἅπαντες ἐθέλουσι τῷ ἱερεῖ Chrys.*sac*.3.14(p.74.14; 1.391E); μὴ...φοβηθῇς...ὅτι νεκρὸν περίκεισαι σῶμα· ἐχέτω πνεῦμα, καὶ ἀναστήσεται id.*hom. 13.8 in Rom*.(9.570C); πνεῦμα...γίνεται λοιπὸν...κἂν σῶμα ~ται id. *hom.18.3 in 1Cor*.(10.155B); θνητὸν ~μενος σκῆνος Nil.*epp*.2.87(M. 79.241A); Cyr.*Jo*.1.9(4.80C); Gennad.*fr.Rom*.7:14(p.372.5; M.85. 1684C); **c.** ref. Inc. τὴν τοῦ δούλου μορφὴν ~μενος Cyr.*Jo*.2.6(4.220A); τὸ ἴδιον φόρημα ~μενος...τὸ ἀνθρώπινον σῶμα *ib*.3.5(301B); σάρκα ~μενος ἐδείκνυ τὴν πατρῴαν εὐγένειαν Thdt.*haer*.5.2(4.383); id. *affect*.2(p.60.16; 4.752); **d.** met. κακὰς ~μενε κῆρας *Orac.Sib*.5.228; Clem.*paed*.2.12(p.231.14; M.8.548A); προσηγορίας...ἦν ὥσπερ διάδημα ~νται id.*q.d.s*.36(p.183.17; M.9.641A); εὐλαβείας δόκησιν ~μενοι Cyr.*Is*.5.3(2.812D); Thdt.*Ps*.111:1(1.1403); **3.** *be invested with* τὸ τῆς ἱερωσύνης ~μενος ἀξίωμα †Jo.Jej.*poenit*.(M.88.1889C); **4.** *be afflicted with* disease; c. dat., *PLond*.1926.12 (saec. iv); **5.** *be shed round* ἱερατικὸν δὲ χρῖσμα ~μενον κέκτημαι Jo.VI H.*v.Jo.D*.8(M.94.441A).

περικείρω, *shave all round*; med., *A.Paul.et Thecl*.25(p.253.3).

περικεκαλυμμένως, *secretly, covertly*, Bas.*Eun*.2.27(1.264A; M.29. 636A); Nil.*epp*.4.6(M.79.553A).

***περικεκομμένως**, *concisely*, Just.*dial*.118.4(M.6.752A).

περικεντέω, **1.** *pierce all round*, Bas.*hom*.5.4(2.36C; M.31.245A); **2.** *pin round, fasten together*, Gr.Nyss.*bapt.diff*.(M.46.420C); id.*Eun*. 2(p.252.2; M.45.953A).

περικεφάλαιος, *round the head*; hence **1.** fem. as subst., *helmet*, met. ἡ πίστις ὡς π. Ign.*Polyc*.6.2; π. ἐλπίδος Chrys.*hom.suppl*.2(M. 64.428B); ὁ γὰρ ἀποκειράμενος τὰ τοῦ κόσμου νοήματα, τὴν π. δέχεται τοῦ σωτηρίου Max.*qu.dub*.67(M.90.841B); **2.** neut. as subst., *headdress* τὰ καισαρίκια π. Thphn.*chron*.p.374(M.108.896B).

περικήδομαι, *be sorely troubled*, †Apoll.*met.Ps*.30:10(M.33.1352A).

περικλάω, pass.; **1.** *be broken off*; of heresies from Church, Epiph. *rescr*.4(p.157.24; M.41.161B); **2.** *be dissolute*, Bas.Sel.*or*.18.2(M.85. 232C).

περίκλεισις, ἡ, *sheep-fold*, Cael.*ep.Cyr*.(p.76.18; M.77.92C).

***περικλεισμός, ὁ**, *limitation*, ref. Inc. οὔτε γὰρ ἄλλαξις οὔτε μετακίνησις οὔτε π. ἐν πνεύματι γέγονεν περὶ τὴν ἁγίαν τοῦ θεοῦ δύναμιν Apoll.*fid.sec.pt*.11(p.171.4; M.10.1109A).

περικλίνω, med., *incline*, Gr.Nyss.*Eun*.10(2 p.238.5; M.45.840C).

περίκλισις, ἡ, *declination* of stars, Gr.Nyss.*fat*.(M.45.169B).

περικλονέω, pass., *be stirred up*, Pall.*v.Chrys*.10(p.60.22; M.47.35).

περικλύζ-ω, **1.** *wash all round*, Chrys.*hom.51.4 in Mt*.(7.526C); *ib.88.3*(829B); id.*hom.44.4 in 1Cor*.(10.413B); ref. baptism ὕδατος τοῦ περικλύσαντός σου τὴν ὄψιν id.*hom.30.6 in Mt*.(7.355D); **2.** *overwhelm, swamp*, id.*sac*.6.12(p.169.5; 1.434A); met. ~εται ἡ καρδία πολυποσίᾳ Clem.*paed*.2.2(p.173.14; M.8.424A); Meth.*symp*.3.6(p.33. 6; M.18.69B); *ib*.4.3(p.48.15; 89C); Thdt.*qu.77 in Gen*.(1.89); δωρεαῖς ~ειν ὑμᾶς id.*ep*.57(4.1111); Euthal.Diac.*epp.Paul*.(M.85.696C).

περικομίζω, *take round*, Clem.*str*.3.6(p.220.17; M.8.1157A).

περικομπ-έω, *make a sound round about*, met. τοὺς ἀπείρους τούτων ταῖς Πλατωνικαῖς καλλιφωνίαις ~ήσειε Gr.Nyss.*Eun*.9(2 p.215.19, v.l. περιβομβήσειεν M.45.813C); τοὺς ~οῦντας τὴν ἀκοὴν λόγους Max. *ambig*.(M.91.1064D); med., *make a noise about, boast of* Φαρισαῖος ἀρετῶν μνήμην ~ούμενος Bas.Sel.*or*.35.2(M.85.380B).

***περικονδυλίζομαι**, *be much buffeted*; met., Ephr.2.393E.

περικοπή, ἡ, **1.** *section* τόμους κεφαλαίων ἔχοντας περικοπάς Cyr. *ep*.11(p.12.21; 5².39E); Nil.ap.Proc.G.*Cant*.4:4(M.87.1649B); perh. error for προκοπή); **2.** *passage* of scripture, Just.*dial*.65.3(M.6. 625D); *ib*.110.1(729A); Clem.*str*.2.18(p.154.9; M.8.1017A); ἔκ τινων προφητικῶν π. *ib*.3.4(p.213.12; 1141B); Afric.*chron*.16(M.10.80B)ap. Eus.*d.e*.8.2(p.374.28); τοῦτό τινες τοῖς προλαβοῦσιν ἀπέδωκαν, τὸ δὲ Ἑβραϊκὸν ἐξ ἰδίας τάττει π. Or.*Cant*.3(p.199.28; M.13.165C); Eus.*d.e*. 2.3(p.72.14; M.22.132A); Ath.*Ar*.2.9(M.26.164C); ἐν τῇ π. τοῦ τοιούτου βαπτίσματος †Bas.*bapt*.1.2.26(2.648C; M.31.1569D); προλαμβάνειν τὴν π. τῆς γραφῆς, ἣν ἂν μέλλωμεν ἐξηγεῖσθαι Chrys.*hom.1.6 in Mt*. (7.13B); τοῦτο δὲ ἐκ π. ἐρωτῶσι, τὰ πλείονα τοῦ κεφαλαίου παρατρέχοντες Marc.Er.*opusc*.10.3(M.65.1120C); of entire lection appointed for liturgical Gospel, Anast.S.*synax*.(M.89.829A).

περικοπτέον, *one must cut out, eschew* τὸ χρυσοφορεῖν...οὐ τέλεον π. Clem.*paed*.3.11(p.266.27; M.8.625C); *ib*.(p.269.15; 632B).

περικόπτ-ω, **1.** *cut round, trim*, Herm.*vis*.3.6.6; id.*sim*.9.7.5; **2.** *cut off* ~ειν ἀπὸ τῆς Ἀντιοχείας ἐξόδους Philost.*h.e*.3.28(M.65. 513D); **3.** *cut short, curtail*, Just.*dial*.72.2(M.6.645A); Eus.*h.e*.4.18. 8(M.20.376B); Ath.*Dion*.14(p.56.19; M.25.501A); ref. circumcision οὐ γὰρ σάρκα, ἀλλὰ πονηροὺς δεῖ ~ειν λογισμοὺς Chrys.*hom.33.2 in Jo*.(8.192A); ~ειν...τὰ περιττὰ...τῶν λογισμῶν *ib.61.3*(366A); Isid. Pel.*epp*.2.40(M.78.484A); Cyr.*Ps*.50 proem.(M.69.1085C); id.*Nah*.22 (3.501B); Thdt.*qu.42 in Num*.(1.247); **4.** *circumscribe*, Gr.Naz.*or*. 30.18(p.137.2; M.36.128A); **5.** *rule out, exclude*, Clem.*paed*.2.2(p.176. 28; M.8.429B); τὰ μὲν οἰκειότητος τῆς πρὸς θεὸν σύμβολα...~εις Didym.(‡Bas.)*Eun*.5(1.307D; M.29.737A); **6.** *lay waste, plunder*, Afric.*ep.Arist*.4(p.61.3; M.10.60B); **7.** med., *bewail, lament* τὴν συμφορὰν ~ομαι *A.Thom*.B 54(p.41.12); **8.** ? *reproach* ἐμέμφοντο ἀλλήλους...πάντων ἐπ' ἐξουσίας ~όντων ἃ βούλοιντο Malchus *exc.gent*. 6(p.574.33; M.113.789D); **9.** ? *come to an end, terminate* βασιλείας ἔρως εἰς τοῦτο περιέκοψεν Philost.*h.e*.11.3 (conj. προέκοψεν; M.65. 597B).

περικοσμ-έω, *deck out, ornament fully,* Ath.*gent.*22(M.25.45A); of vesting a corpse, Gr.Nyss.*v.Macr.*(p.406.11; M.46.992C); met. ∼εῖ τὸ ἀποκτεῖνον γράμμα Or.*Jo.*13.55(54; p.285.29; M.14.504B).

περικόσμιος, *surrounding the world* ὃς ἔδωκεν ἄστρα νυκτί, περικοσμίαν χορείαν Synes.*hymn.*2.8(p.43; M.66.1592); οὐδὲ κόσμον κτίζων, καὶ εἰς τόδε τὸ σχῆμα ἄγων αὐτὸν οὐκ ὄντα πρότερον, ἐκ τοῦ ὑπερκοσμίου εἰς τὸ π. τοῦτο ἢ ἐγκόσμιον ἐκπεπτωκὼς φαίνεται Leont.B.*Nest.et Eut.*1(M.86.1284C); ἱεραρχία...περικόσμιος Dion.Ar.*c.h.*9.2(M.3.260A); of God ἐγκόσμιον, π., ὑπερκόσμιον id.*d.n.*1.6(M.3.596C); ἐσχάτη τάξις ἀγγέλων, καὶ π. Max.*schol.c.h.*9.2(M.4.84B).

***περικουρεῖον, τό,** *clipping round*; of the hair, ‡Ath.*syntag.*4.9(p.125; M.28.841A) = *Didasc.patr.*4(p.14.14).

περικρατ-έω, 1. *control, A.Barth.*8(p.147.22); Gr.Nyss.*or.dom.*3(p.52.1; M.44.1152C); δύναμις ἡ τὸν περίγειον τόπον...∼εῖν τεταγμένη id.*or.catech.*6(p.32.4; M.45.28A); **2.** *prevail over* ∼εῖν ἡμῶν ἐν ταῖς ζητήσεσι Just.*dial.*80.1(M.6.664B); ‡Just.*monarch.*1(M.6.313A); *Chron.Pasch.*p.77(M.92.229A); **3.** *maintain, support* εἰ μυῶν περιβολαῖς καὶ ἀδένων ἡ τῶν νεύρων ∼εῖται θέσις Gr.Nyss.*Eun.*10(2 p.227.10; M.45.828B); βρώσει καὶ πόσει ∼ῶν τὴν ὑπόστασιν Gr.Nyss.*or.catech.*37(p.148.8; M.45.96C).

περικρατής, 1. *having full possession* of, *being in control* of, Gr.Nyss.*or.dom.*4(p.90.13; M.44.1176D); Nil.*epp.*3.134(M.79.445A); **2.** ? *controlled by, obedient to* ἐὰν δὲ π. γένηται ὁ ἀδελφὸς τῷ εὐσεβεῖ λογισμῷ, εἰς...ἔρημον προβάλλει Ephr.2.104A.

***περικρατητικός,** *controlling,* of H. Ghost τὸ πάσης τῆς κτίσεως π. Gr.Nyss.*Eun.*2(2 p.301.1; M.45.472B); *ib.*6(2 p.138.3; 724A).

***περικρατῶς,** *so as to have full control,* Bas.*reg.fus.*17.1(2.360A; M.31.961B).

περικροτέω, *be eminent, cat.Apoc.*7:13(p.294.25).

περικρούω, pass., *be overcome in a struggle,* Marc.Er.*opusc.*1.6(M.65.905B).

περικτάομαι, pass., *be acquired,* Clem.*paed.*2.1(p.164.3; M.8.400C); id.*str.*4.6(p.263.7; M.8.1245A).

περικτυπέω, *make a noise round,* Cyr.*Jo.*3.5(4.301D).

***περικυδαίνω,** *honour exceedingly, Orac.Sib.*3.575.

περικυκλέω, *embrace,* Thdr.Stud.*epp.*2.144(M.99.1453A).

περικυκλόω, 1. *go round, encircle,* Rom.Mel.(*SBBAW* 1898[2] p.125); **2.** *encompass* for protection, id.(*AS* 1 p.152).

περικυμαίνω, *surge around*; met., of afflictions, ‡Nil.*perist.*11.3(M.79.905C).

περικυρτόομαι, *be curved, bent,* Gr.Nyss.*Eun.*5(2 p.125.4; M.45.708A); Bas.Sel.*v.Thecl.*1(M.85.513C).

***περιλακτίζω,** *kick round about,* Clem.*str.*2.18(p.163.21; M.8.1036A).

περιλαλ-έω, 1. *prate about,* Bas.*Eun.*1.9(1.221B; M.29.352A); **2.** *utter* a sound σύριγγα...ποιμενικὸν ∼οῦσαν τερέτισμα Thphyl.*exc.gent.*3(p.479.18; M.113.937B).

περιλαμβάν-ω, 1. *embrace, grasp,* ref. crowning with thorns δηλῶν ὡς τοῦ κύκλου τοῦ κόσμου τὰς ἁμαρτίας περιλαβών Sev.Ant.ap.*cat.Mt.*27:27(p.235.10); met. ὡς μηδενὶ περιληφθῆναι φιλαργυρίας πρόφασιν *IGC As.Min.*108; *hold firmly to* ∼ομεν τὸν παράκλητον CSard.*ep.cath.*ap.Thdt.*h.e.*2.8.48(3.847); **2.** *hold in check, restrain, withdraw* ὁ...θεὸς...ἐσμίκρυνεν αὐτὸν...καὶ περιέλαβεν ἑαυτὸν ἀπὸ τῆς ἀπροσίτου δόξης Mac.Aeg.*hom.*4.10(M.34.480B).

***περιλάμπρως,** *splendidly,* Gr.Naz.*or.*42.40(M.36.488A).

περιλάμπω, *shine round,* fig. ἀλήθεια τὴν κτίσιν πᾶσαν περιέλαμψεν Chrysipp.*enc.in Jo.Bapt.*16(p.48.12).

περίλαμψις, ἡ, *illumination,* Thdr.Stud.*epp.*2.13(M.99.1153D).

περίλευκος, *edged with white,* name of gem ἀχάτης...π. καλούμενος, ὃς ὑπὸ τὸν ὑάκινθον εὑρίσκεται...τῷ εἴδει ὑποκυανίζων, ἔξωθεν περιφέρειαν λευκὴν ἔχων Epiph.*gemm.*8(M.43.300B).

***περιληπτέον,** *one must comprehend,* Epiph.*haer.*66.14(p.36.8; M.42.49A).

περιληπτικός, 1. *comprehensive* ἐμπειρία ἐπιστήμη π. Clem.*str.*2.17(p.153.3; M.8.1013C); πάντων περιληπτικὸν τὸν τῷ ὄντι γνωστικόν *ib.*6.8(p.466.7; M.9.289B); ἡ...θεοῦ δύναμις...πλείστων ἐπινοιῶν...περιληπτικὴ τυγχάνει...μύρῳ πάλιν ἡ τῶν πολλῶν καὶ ἀγαθῶν π. δύναμις ἀπείκασται, ᾧ κεχρῖσθαι τὸν ἀληθῆ...ἀρχιερέα τοῦ θεοῦ θεῖοι λόγοι παιδεύουσιν Eus.*d.e.*4.15(p.176.8; M.22.293A); ἡ...ἀσύνθετος φύσις, ἡ π. τῶν ὅλων Thdt.*eran.*2(4.114); τῆς ὑπὲρ πάντα καὶ πάντων π. ἀπειρίας Dion.Ar.*d.n.*3.1(M.3.680B); **2.** *inclusive* προσεκτέον τῷ 'πάντα', τῆς τῶν γενητῶν ἁπάντων ὑπάρξεως περιληπτικῷ ὄντι Eus.*e.th.*1.20(p.85.17; M.24.873A); †Bas.*bapt.*2.5.1(2.657D; M.31.1592B); ref. Jo.1:3 πάντα γὰρ ὅσα γέγονεν, εἴρηται, οὐχ ἁπλῶς ἅπαντα. ... δείξας οὖν ὅτι γέγονε [sc. τὸ πνεῦμα] τότε...τοῖς κτίσμασι συναρίθμησον. ἕως δ' ἂν μὴ τοῦτο δεικνύεις, οὐδὲν τῷ π. βοηθῇ Gr.Naz.*or.*31.12(p.160.13; M.36.148A); Gr.Nyss.*or.catech.*5(p.24.2; M.45.21D); Chrys.*hom.*3.2 *in Col.*(11.344D); **3.** *general* περιληπτικώτερα πάθη, σεισμοὺς καὶ ναυάγια Gr.Nyss.*fat.*(M.45.148D); **4.** *able to contain,* of S. Paul οἶκος π. τῆς ἀπεριλήπτου γενόμενος φύσεως id.*hom.*3 *in Cant.*(M.44.821C); **5.** *able to embrace* or *lay hold on* πῦρ...π., ἀπερίληπτον Dion.Ar.*c.h.*15.2(M.3.329B).

περιληπτικῶς, *comprehensively,* Clem.*str.*6.15(p.494.2; M.9.345D); Eus.*e.th.*3.3(p.155.9; M.24.997C); περιληπτικώτερον...εἰπεῖν Vict.*Mc.*3:12(p.295.26).

περιληπτός, *comprehensible,* Tat.*orat.*4(p.4.27; M.6.813A).

περίληψις, ἡ, 1. *embrace,* Thdt.*Cant.*1:1(2.25); **2.** *comprehension* ποῦ...ἔσται ὁ κατ' αὐτοὺς θεός, τὰ πάντα τοῦ μόνου καὶ ἀληθινοῦ πληροῦντος κατὰ τὴν τοῦ οὐρανοῦ καὶ γῆς π.; Ath.*gent.*6(M.25.13B); **3.** *understanding, grasp,* Clem.*str.*6.15(p.494.7; M.9.348A); Thdt.*pental.*(5.131); Max.*ambig.*(M.91.1237A); ἐπιστημονικὴ...π. *ib.*(1240B); τὸν ἐν π. ἀπερίληπτον ‡Meth.*Sym.et Ann.*6(M.18.360C).

περιλιμνάζ-ω, 1. *be a lake, form inundations*; of Nile, Zach.Mit.*opif.*(M.85.1028B); **2.** *insulate, surround as with a flood* ∼ούσης τὸν οἶκον πυρκαϊᾶς Chrysipp.*enc.in Thdr.*(p.75.15).

***περιλιμνάω,** *insulate, form a moat round,* Const.Diac.*laud.*28(M.88.509D).

***περιλογή, ἡ,** *colloquy, conference*; in preparation for treaty, Thphn.*chron.*p.317(M.108.768A).

***περίλοξος,** *crooked,* Germ.CP *or.*1(M.98.233D).

περίλυσις, ἡ, *breaking off, termination* ἀπονηστίζεσθαι...τῇ τοῦ πάσχα π. Dion.Al.*ep.can.*1(p.94.5, v.l. ἡμέρᾳ M.10.1273A).

περιλύ-ω, 1. *set free* ψυχὴ...περιλυθεῖσα τῶν...κακῶν ‡Just.*or.Gr.*5(M.6.240A); εἰ μὴ περιλυθείη τῶν τῆς ψυχῆς βάσεων ἡ νεκρὰ...περιβολή Gr.Nyss.*v.Mos.*(M.44.333A); **2.** *break off, terminate* ∼οντες τὰς νηστείας Cyr.*hom.pasch.*1(5[1].16C).

περιμέν-ω, 1. *wait* περιέμενεν γάρ, ἵνα παραδοθῇ *M.Polyc.*1.2; **2.** *await, wait for,* Herm.*sim.*9.11.1; χρὴ...τὴν ἀφ' ἑτέρων ∼ειν μαρτυρίαν Tat.*orat.*1(p.2.1; M.6.805A); ὁ λόγος...μηδὲ αἰτεῖσθαι ∼ειν ἀλλ' αὐτὸν ἀναζητεῖν, ὅστις ἄξιος εὖ παθεῖν Clem.*q.d.s.*31(p.181.4; M.9.637B); ∼ειν δὲ τὴν τῆς ποθούσης ἀνάστασιν ὁ ποθούμενος Or.*schol.in Cant.*3:1–4(M.17.268D); μετὰ τὸ ἁμαρτάνειν...τί ἡμᾶς ∼ει, κατανοητέον id.*hom.*16.5 *in Jer.*(p.137.27; M.13.445B); **3.** *expect, hope for,* Thdr.Mops.*Gal.*3:16(p.45.27; M.66.904B); ψυχαὶ...οὐ...τὰς ἐπιτυμβίους ∼ουσαι χοάς Cyr.*Jo.*12(4.1069C); Thdt.*ep.*14(4.1074).

***περιμέριμνος,** *very careful,* Leo Mag.*ep.*28.2(p.11.18; M.*PL.*54.758B).

***περιμερίμνως,** *with great care,* Sophr.H.*or.*7.17(M.87.3349A); Thdr.Stud.*epp.*2.150(M.99.1468D).

περίμετρος, 1. *very far,* Nonn.*par.Jo.*21:8(M.43.916C); **2.** fem. as subst., *surrounding district, environs,* ref. Egyptian nome τὴν π. τῆς πόλεως Epiph.*haer.*24.1(p.256.18; περίχωρον M.41.308C).

***περίμηρος,** *round the thighs* τοῖς π. τοῦ σώματος μέρεσιν Cyr.*ador.*11(1.390B).

***περιμονία, ἡ,** *solitude* βέλτιόν σοι...ὁ κόπος τῆς τοῦ θεοῦ ἐργασίας ἢ π. τῆς ἐν ἐρήμῳ κατοικίας Agath.*v.Gr.Ill.*159(p.81).

***περιμορφόομαι,** *be formed by, take one's form from*; c. dat., Gr.Nyss.*hex.*25(M.44.88A).

περιναίω, *dwell around,* †Apoll.*met.Ps.*83:3(M.33.1437A).

***περινείσσομαι,** *go round,* Paul.Sil.*Soph.*657(M.86.2144B).

[*]**περινίπτω,** *wash thoroughly,* Pall.*h.Laus.*63(p.159.8; M.34.1235C).

περινο-έω, 1. *consider* ∼οῦντι...μοι τὰ σπουδαῖα Tat.*orat.*29(p.30.4; M.6.868A); Clem.*str.*5.11(p.374.3; M.9.108B); Cyr.*Ps.*49:3(M.69.1076C); **2.** *conceive, form idea of* ἀνδρός, ἐν ἰδιωτικῇ λέξει μεγάλα ∼οῦντος Or.*Cels.*3.20(p.217.16; M.11.944A); Val.Gn.ap.Epiph.*haer.*31.5(p.390.9; M.41.481A); **3.** *devise* ἀνεξίτητον ἑαυτῷ ∼ήσας ὁδόν Eus.*e.th.*3.2(p.144.30; M.24.981A); Bas.*Eun.*2.13(1.248B; M.29.596C).

περίνοια, ἡ, 1. *comprehension* ὀλίγην τούτων π. εἰληφὼς Or.*Cels.*1.24(p.75.13; M.11.705B); ἐν π. κατανοήσωμεν id.*hom.*18.1 *in Jer.*(p.151.6; M.13.464B); ἐν βραχείᾳ π. γενέσθαι ἡμᾶς id.*Jo.*10.42(26; p.220.35; 392A); οὐκ ἐκ τῶν ἔργων τοῦ τεχνίτου, ἐν π. τῆς οὐσίας αὐτοῦ γινομένους ἡμᾶς Bas.*Eun.*2.32(1.269E; M.29.648C); οὐ γὰρ οἷόν τε ἄλλως ἐν π. θεοῦ γενέσθαι σώματος ὑλικοῦ καὶ δεσμίου νοῦ πάχος μὴ βοηθούμενον Gr.Naz.*or.*45.11(M.36.637B); ἐπειδὴ γὰρ ἐπέγνωμεν τὸν υἱόν, ἐπέγνωμεν ἐξ αὐτοῦ τὸν γεννήσαντα. εἰσφέρεται...δι' ἀμφοῖν ἢ θατέρου π. Cyr.*Jo.*5.2(4.495D); Thdt.*Ps.*103:2(1.1331); Leont.H.*monoph.*(M.86.1808B); **2.** *subtlety, over-cleverness* π. τινὶ λόγων...τὸ δόγμα...ἐκβάλλοντας Gr.Nyss.*Eun.*12(2 p.285.30; M.45.897C); id.*ep.*24(M.46.1088D); **3.** *devising,* Soz.*h.e.*5.5.6(M.67.1228B); †Leont.B.*sect.*4.2(M.86.1220C); **4.** *deceit, craftiness,* Gr.Nyss.*virg.*1(p.252.22; M.46.321A).

[*]**περινοστεύ-ω**, *go about, wander through, traverse* οὐκ ὀρθῶς βαδίζων, ἀλλὰ ἐρρᾳδιουργημένως πάντα ∼ων Epiph.*haer*.42.11(p.108.4; M.41.712A).

περινοστ-έω, **1.** = foreg., Just.*dial*.69.3(M.6.637A); οἱ...∼ήσαντες τὴν οἰκουμένην ἀπόστολοι Clem.*paed*.2.8(p.194.15; M.8.465C); Cyr.*glaph.Dt*.(1.426E); τὴν καθ' ἡμᾶς οἰκουμένην ∼εῖ [sc. σατανᾶς] id.*Ps*.103:26(M.69.1265C); abs. Ἑλένην τινά, τὴν ∼ήσασαν αὐτῷ Just.*1apol*.26.3 (v.l. συμπερινοστήσασαν M.6.368B); οἱ ἦσαν σὺν αὐτῷ ∼οῦντες Ammon.*Ac*.18:18(M.85.1572A); παρὰ πᾶσιν ἀνθρώποις τὴν κακηγορίαν ∼εῖν Men.*exc.Rom*.14(p.206.24; M.113.904D); **2.** *visit*; of a bishop, Chrys.*sac*.3.18(p.93.10; 1.400B); **3.** *examine, consider carefully*, Clem.*prot*.4(p.44.26; M.8.156A); Cyr.*Jo*.4.2(4.357E); τὴν θείαν ∼οῦντες γραφήν *ib*.5.5(544B); Thdt.*provid*.1(4.490).

περινόστησις, ἡ, *circuit* τῆς τοῦ ὠκεανοῦ π. Const.*or.s.c*.5(p.158.24; M.20.1244B).

περίξηρος, *very dry*; of profitless arguments, Gr.Thaum.*fid. cap*.12(p.150.19; M.10.1136B).

περιοδ(ε)ία ([*]**περιωδία**), **ἡ**, **1.** *periodical return* of heavenly bodies, Dion.Al.ap.Eus.*p.e*.14.25(778A; M.21.1280B); **2.** *medical treatment* or *attention*, Didym.*Trin*.2.14(M.39.700C); Nil.*epp*.2.110 (-ωδία M.79.248D); Tim.Ant.*caec*.4(M.28.1008B); Sophr.H.*mir.Cyr. et Jo*.10(M.87.3449C); met., Chrys.*Jud*.3(2.722D); **3.** *visitation* of bishop, CAlex.*ep*.ap.Ath.*apol.sec*.17(p.99.22; M.25.273D); Ath.*ib*.74 (p.153.27; 381A).

περιοδευτής, ὁ, **1.** *medical practitioner*, Tim.Ant.*caec*.12(M.28.1020C); **2.** *priest entrusted with visiting and supervising of country districts*, ref. ordinations performed outside his own diocese by Meletius, cf. *forsitan dices: egentibus gregibus...pastore non subsistente...ad hoc perveni. sed...illos non egere: primum quia multi sunt circumeuntes*, Phil.Thm.*ep*.(M.10.1566B); οὐ δεῖ ἐν ταῖς κώμαις καὶ ἐν ταῖς χώραις καθίστασθαι ἐπισκόπους, ἢ ἀλλὰ π. CLaod.*can*.57; Soz.*h.e*.4.24.7(M.67.1192A); ἐχειροτόνησεν πρεσβύτερον καὶ π. *Cap*.5 ap.CBeryt.*act*.(*ACO* 2.1.3,p.25.1; H.2.517E); παρ' ἐπισκόποις ἢ π. δεχθῆναι Marc.Er.*opusc*.10.10(M.65.1137A); τοῖς ὑπὸ σὲ...ἐπισκόποις καὶ π. Gennad.*encycl*.(M.85.1617C); πρεσβύτερος π. τῶν ἁγίων ἐκκλησιῶν ἐπιχωρίων τῆς πρώτης Σύρων ἐπαρχίας CCP(536)*act*.1(*ACO* 3 p.146.32; H.2.1216E); Jo.Mal.*chron*.18 p.452(M.97.664A).

περιοδεύ-ω, **1.** *go about, traverse* οὓς ἐξαπέστειλε κύριος ∼σαι τὴν γῆν Or.*schol.in Cant*.3:1–4(M.17.269B); Gr.Nyss.*hom.3 in Cant*.(M.44.812B); abs. ἣν ∼ων ὁ Φίλιππος *A.Phil*.6(p.4.7); **2.** *visit*, Rom.Mel.(*SBBAW* 1903 p.668); of a bishop, *carry out a visitation of*, *Ep.Mareot*.1 ap.Ath.*apol.sec*.74(p.154.12; M.25.381D); **3.** medic., *treat*, *A.Xanthipp*.1(p.58.24); Epiph.*mens*.16(M.43.264C); Tim.Ant.*caec*.9(M.28.1013D); Jo.Mosch.*prat*.77(M.87.2932A); met. πάθει γὰρ κακῷ τὸ κακὸν περιώδευσεν Bas.Sel.*or*.17.3(M.85.220D); *treat with, apply to as remedy* ἔμπλαστρα αὐτὴν π. ‡Chrys.*Bass*.2(2.726E).

περιοδικός, **1.** *circuitous*, Gr.Nyss.*hom.6.1 in Eccl*.(M.44.701C); **2.** *full, prolix*, Max.*ambig*.(M.91.1245C); *ib*.(1245D).

περίοδος, ἡ, **1.** *round-about way, circuitous route*, met. τί οὐχὶ θελήματι μόνῳ τὸ κατὰ γνώμην ποιεῖ, ἀλλ' ἐκ π. τὴν σωτηρίαν ἡμῶν κατεργάζεται; Gr.Nyss.*or.catech*.17(p.73.6; M.45.53A); **2.** *circuit*, Clem.*ecl*.51(p.151.12; M.9.721B); **3.** *orbit* of star, Philost.*h.e*.10.9(M.65.592A); **4.** *sphere* προελθεῖν ἐπὶ τὴν τῶν ἐθνῶν ἁπάντων π. Eus.*d.e*.3.5 (p.123.5; M.22.209B); **5.** *cycle, period* of time ψυχῶν...αἰωνίαν κόλασιν κολασθησομένων, ἀλλ' οὐχὶ χιλιονταετῆ π., ὡς ἐκεῖνος [sc. Πλάτων] ἔφη, μόνον Just.*1apol*.8.4(M.6.337C); ἀνάστασιν ἔσεσθαι...μετὰ τὴν τῶν ὅλων συντέλειαν, οὐχ ὡς οἱ Στωϊκοὶ δογματίζουσι κατά τινας κύκλων περιόδους Tat.*orat*.6(p.6.17; M.6.817B); ὁ χρόνος εἴη ὁ διὰ τῶν ἑπτὰ π. τῶν ἀριθμουμένων εἰς τὴν ἀκροτάτην ἀνάπαυσιν ἀποκαθιστάς Clem.*str*.4.25(p.318.29; M.8.1368B); ἑπτὰ πλανωμένων...δι' ὧν ὁ μέγας ἐνιαυτὸς γίνεται οἷον π. τις τῆς τῶν ἐπηγγελμένων ἀνταποδόσεως *ib*.6.16(p.503.9; M.9.368A); ἀπ' ἀρχῆς εἰς τέλος ἡ τῶν θνητῶν π. Cels.ap.Or.*Cels*.4.65(p.335.20; M.11.1133A); ὁ μὲν οὖν Κέλσος μόνην τὴν θνητῶν π. κατὰ τὰς τεταγμένας ἀνακυκλήσεις ἐξ ἀνάγκης φησὶν ἀεὶ γεγονέναι...τῶν δὲ Στωϊκῶν οἱ πλείους οὐ μόνον τὴν τῶν θνητῶν π. τοιαύτην εἶναί φασιν ἀλλὰ καὶ τὴν τῶν ἀθανάτων καὶ τῶν κατ' αὐτοὺς θεῶν *ib*.4.68(p.338.1; 1136C); Meth.*symp*.2.4(p.20.15; M.18.53A); ἥλιος...ἐπιπορευόμενος ἐτησίοις τὰ ζῴδια περιόδοις τὰς μεταβολὰς ἀποτελεῖ *ib*.8.15(p.103.13; 165D); βασιλέα ἀεὶ εἰς πολλὰς ἐτῶν π. νικῶντα *Ep.Dion*.2(p.160.15; M.25.393B); **6.** *prolixity* of speech, Meth.*res*.2.5(p.339.8; M.41.1172B); Chrys.*hom.77.6 in Mt*.(7.749A); Thdt.*Rom*.9:28(3.109); met. κήρυγμα, ἐν ᾧ, πάσης τῆς κατὰ Μωσέα π. ἐν εἰκόσι...περιαιρεθείσης, ὁ σύντομος τοῦ εὐαγγελίου λόγος ...ἐπιστώσατο Eus.*d.e*.2.3(p.80.7; M.22.144B); **7.** plur., *travels, journeyings*, title of work Κλήμης δὲ ὁ Ῥωμαῖος, Πέτρου ἀποστόλου μαθητὴς...πρὸς τὸν πατέρα ἐν Λαοδικείᾳ εἰπὼν ἐν ταῖς Π. Or.*comm. in Gen*.ap.*philoc*.23.22(p.210.24; M.12.85A); Π. Πέτρου, Π. Ἰωάννου, Π. Θωμᾶ ‡Ath.*synops*.76(M.28.432B); χρῶνται [sc. Ebionites]...ταῖς Π. καλουμέναις Πέτρου ταῖς διὰ Κλήμεντος γραφείσαις, νοθεύσαντες μὲν τὰ ἐν αὐταῖς Epiph.*haer*.30.15(p.352.4; M.41.429D); κέχρηνται [sc. Quartodecimans] νόθοις βιβλίοις, Π. τινὰς ἀποστόλων προφέροντες Tim.CP *haer*.(M.86.36A).

***περιοιδαίν-ω**, *swell all round*, met. καρδίαν τῇ τῶν κακῶν μνήμῃ ∼ουσαν Gr.Naz.*or*.35.3(M.36.260B); νεότης...ἐλπίδι...∼ουσα Gr.Nyss.*v.Gr.Thaum*.(M.46.925D).

περιοικία, ἡ, *country round a city*, Acac.et Paul.*ep*.tit.(p.153.5; M.41.156A).

περιοικίς, ἡ, *district* κώμην τῆς Κασχάρων π. Epiph.*mens*.20(M.43.269B).

***περιοικιώδης, ἡ**, s.v.l., *district* ἐν τῇ π. τῆς πόλεως...κατῴκει Gr.Mag.*dial*.(tr.Zach.)4.55(M.*PL*.77.418A, v.l. περιοικήσει).

περιολισθαίνω, *slip*, Bas.*hex*.3.4(1.25A; M.29.60B); *ib*.5.3(42C; M.100C); Cyr.*Ps*.34:6(M.69.897C).

περιοπτέος, *to be despised*, Gr.Naz.*or*.15.2(M.35.913A).

***περιόρασις, ἡ**, *looking all round, all-round view*, Clem.*str*.6.17 (p.512.23; M.9.388C).

περιορατέον, *one must overlook*, Clem.*paed*.2.1(p.165.4; M.8.401B).

***περιόρθριον, τό**, *dawn*, Sophr.H.*v.Anast*.(M.92.1728B).

περιορίζ-ω, **1.** *limit, confine* ἐν...περιωρισμένῳ τόπῳ Athenag.*leg*.8.3(M.6.905B); ὀρέξεις αὐταρκείᾳ ∼ονται Clem.*paed*.2.1(p.166.6; M.8.405A); θεοῦ...εὐεργεσία...οὐδὲ ∼εται τόποις ἢ ἀνθρώποις τισίν id.*str*.6.8(p.463.32; M.9.285B); ἀδύνατον γὰρ τὸ γενέσεως ἀρχῇ περιορισθὲν συναπέραντον εἶναι τῷ ἀπεράντῳ Meth.*creat*.5(p.497.5; M.18.337A); σκηνῆς γενομένης περιώριστο λοιπὸν τῆς εὐχῆς ὁ τόπος Ath.*apol.Const*.17(M.25.616C); Bas.*ep*.101(3.197C; M.32.508A); Gr.Nyss.*castig*.(M.46.312C); οὐ τοίνυν εἰς τόπον περιώρισε τὴν εὐχήν Chrys.*hom.8.1 in 1Tim*.(11.589E); μεμήνασι, νομίζοντες τὸ φῶς τοῦ εὐαγγελίου σου ∼ειν σὺν σοὶ ἐν Πάτμῳ τῇ νήσῳ Max.*schol.epp.Dion.Ar*.10 (M.4.576A); **2.** *bring to an end* μονάδες...τοῖς δέκα ∼ονται Eus.*l.C*.6(p.210.23; M.20.1348C); **3.** *contain* ἐν ἀριθμῷ τοσούτῳ...τὸ πλῆθος περιώριστο Meth.*symp*.1.5(p.14.16; M.18.45D); **4.** *comprise* χιλίων γὰρ ἐτῶν ∼ομένων εἰς μίαν ἡμέραν ἐν ὀφθαλμοῖς θεοῦ id.*creat*.12(p.499.26; διοριζομένων M.18.344B); ταῦτα γὰρ πάντα ἐκ μιᾶς φωνῆς, τῆς Παῦλος, ∼εται Bas.*Eun*.2.4(1.241A; M.29.580A); **5.** *define, define as consisting in* τῇ εὐπορίᾳ τοῦ ἄρτου τὴν ζωὴν ∼εται Gr.Nyss.*or.dom*.4 (p.84.28; M.44.1173A); νηστείαν...οὐκ ἐν μόνῃ τῇ τῶν κρεῶν ἀποχῇ ∼εσθαι Philost.*h.e*.10.12(M.65.592C); **6.** theol., *circumscribe* τούτοις [sc. Sethians] δοκεῖ τῶν ὅλων εἶναι τρεῖς ἀρχὰς περιωρισμένας, ἑκάστην δὲ τῶν ἀρχῶν ἀπείρους ἔχειν δυνάμεις Hipp.*haer*.5.19(p.116.18; M.16.3179A); τὸν...λόγον οὐχ ὡς ἐν βραχεῖ περιορισθέντα σώματι, πανταχῇ γὰρ...ὁ υἱός Cyr.*ador*.10(1.334B); id.*Jo*.1.3(4.25D); **7.** *banish, deport* εἰς Πάτμον νῆσον περιορισθείς Hier.*vir.ill*.(tr.Sophr.Pal.)9 (p.6.32; M.*PL*.23.624C); Pall.*v.Chrys*.20(p.127.1; M.47.71); Socr.*h.e*.4.15.3(M.67.500A); Thdt.*ep*.80(4.1137); τίς τῶν πατέρων περιώρισεν ἑαυτὸν...ἔν τινι σπηλαίῳ; †Anast.S.*relat*.26(*OC* 2 p.76).

***περιόρισις, ἡ**, **1.** *seclusion, confinement*, Thdr.Stud.*epp*.2.137 (M.99.1437B); **2.** *exile*, *ib*.2.9(1140B).

περιορισμός, ὁ, **1.** *banishment* εἰς π. ἢ νῆσον καταδικασθέντας CSard.*can*.7; Pall.*v.Chrys*.20(p.144.25; M.47.80); Thdt.*ep*.111(4.1183); **2.** *limitation* τὸ δὲ 'ἕως ἂν θῶ' οὐ κατὰ περιορισμόν, ἀλλὰ κατὰ περιουσίαν λέγει Or.*Ps*.109:1(p.228); θείαν...φύσιν...ἀσώματον καὶ περιορισμῶν ἐπέκεινα Cyr.*Pulch*.13(p.32.13; 5^{2}.137B); id.*inc.unigen*.(5^{1}.693A); θείας δυνάμεως...περιορισμὸν οὐκ ἀνεχομένης Zach.Mit.*opif*.(M.85.1137B); Max.*ambig*.(M.91.1304B).

***περιοριστέος**, *to be banished* from κενοδοξία...περιοριστέα τῆς εὐνομίας ἡμῶν Clem.*paed*.2.3(p.178.5; M.8.433A).

περιοριστικός, **1.** *definitive* τὸ 'μέχρι' ῥητὸν οὐ χρόνου ἐστὶ π. Cyr.H.*catech*.15.31; Max.*ambig*.(M.91.1220A); **2.** *defined* οὐ χρόνων... περιοριστικῶν ὑπάρχει τὸ...τῆς θείας πεφρᾶσθαι γραφῆς, τὸ 'ἄχρις οὗ', ἢ 'τήμερον' ‡Caes.Naz.*dial*.129(M.38.1029).

περιόριστος, *circumscribed*, *Hom.Clem*.17.3; Thdr.Stud.*antirrh*.3.1.47(M.99.412B).

περιορύττω, *chisel round*, Cyr.*Ag*.4(3.630B).

περιουσία, ἡ, **1.** *superfluity, superabundance* ἡ δὲ πρὸς ταπεινὸν κάθοδος, π. τίς ἐστι τῆς δυνάμεως Gr.Nyss.*or.catech*.24(p.91.15; M.45.64C); *ib*.34(p.128.1; 85B); **2.** *extraneous addition* ἔστι γὰρ κύριος ἐν τῇ ὑποστάσει αὐτοῦ...'χαρακτὴρ τῆς ὑποστάσεως αὐτοῦ'. οὐσία οὖν ἐστιν, οὐχὶ π. Epiph.*haer*.69.72(p.220.13; M.42.317D); **3.** *wealth, possessions* πτωχοὶ εἴτε πνεύματι εἴτε περιουσίᾳ Clem.*str*.4.6(p.259.23; M.8.1237C); Eus.*h.e*.5 proem.3(M.20.408B); Cyr.*ador*.10(1.341A); **4.** *supply* ἀπίστοις...πολλὴν παρέχειν...δυσφημίας π. Eus.*h.e*.4.7.10(M.20.

320A); 5. *power, authority* τοσαύτη ἦν ἡ π. τοῦ δικαστηρίου Chrys.*hom.5.2 in Rom.*(9.462C); 6. *survival* Νῶε...διασωθεὶς εἰς δευτέραν π. ... ἀποδοθῇ *Hom.Clem.*8.17 ap.*Chron.Pasch.*p.23(M.92.109C; εἰς δευτέραν βίου ἀρχήν M.2.236B); 7. phrases, ἐκ π. *superabundantly, more than is necessary,* Clem.*prot.*1(p.6.32; M.8.60B); Or.*Cels.*4.90 (p.362.24; M.11.1168B); Eus.*d.e.*2.1(p.53.6; M.22.97C); of a work undertaken outside one's necessary sphere of duty διά τε τὸ ἐκ π. καὶ τοῖς Ἑβραίοις ἐπιστέλλειν, ἐθνῶν...ὄντα...ἀπόστολον Clem.*fr.*22 (p.202.4; M.9.749B); ἐν π. *with abundance* ὀλιγοδεὴς ὢν καὶ ἐν π. παντὸς ἀγαθοῦ id.*str.*7.3(p.14.1; M.9.424A); *Hom.Clem.*2.20; Chrys. *sac.*3.16(p.87.3; 1.397C); μετὰ περιουσίας *vigorously, powerfully* τρυφὴν ἀτιμάζων μετὰ πολλῆς τῆς π. id.*hom.10.5 in Mt.*(7.145B); id.*hom.5.5 in Rom.*(9.467C); also σὺν π. Gr.Thaum.*pan.Or.*15(p.34.27; παρρησίᾳ M.10.1096A).

περιουσιασμός, ὁ, *peculiar possession,* Eus.*Ps.*134:3(M.24.29D); derivation discussed, Thdr.Raith.*praep.*(p.201.6).

περιούσιος, 1. *redundant,* Evagr.*h.e.*2.5(p.53.14; M.86.2516A); 2. *peculiar,* of Israel as belonging especially to God (Ex.19:5 etc.), hence also of Church ἐκλεξάμενος...ἡμᾶς δι' αὐτοῦ εἰς λαὸν π. *1Clem.* 64; Clem.*str.*6.13(p.485.22; M.9.328B); ἡ κλῆσις ἡ καθολική, εἰς π. δικαιοσύνης λαὸν κατὰ τὴν ἐκ πίστεως διδασκαλίαν συνάγοντος τοῦ... ἀμφοῖν θεοῦ, Ἑλλήνων τε καὶ βαρβάρων *ib.*6.17(p.514.7; 392C); λαὸς π. ... λέξις...ἡ...τὸν περὶ τὴν οὐσίαν καταγινόμενον λαὸν καὶ κοινωνοῦντα αὐτῇ σημαίνουσα Or.*or.*27(p.367.9; M.11.509D); 'λαὸν π.', ἐξηλλαγμένον, οὐδὲν ἔχοντα κοινὸν πρὸς τοὺς λοιπούς Chrys.*hom.5.2 in Tit.*(11.759D); Thdr.Raith.*praep.*(p.201.6); ref. Ex.19:5 τὸ...π., ἐξαίρετος ὁ Σύμμαχος ἡρμήνευσεν Thdt.*qu.35 in Ex.*(1.147); Jo.D. *hom.*2.5(M.96.585B); of Slavonic troops of Justinian II ἐπωνόμασεν αὐτοὺς λαὸν π. Thphn.*chron.*p.305(M.108.741D).

***περιουσιωδῶς,** διότι π. Max.*qu.Thal.*10 ap.*cat.1Jo.*4:18(p.136. 22), error for διόπερ οὐσιωδῶς (M.90.289B).

***περιοχετεύω,** *conduct water all round*; fig., *provide a plentiful supply* π. ... περιουσίαν λόγων ἡμῖν Bas.Sel.*or.*37.1(M.85.389A).

περιοχή, ἡ, 1. *comprehension, embracing* ἐπιστήμη ἡ π. τῶν ὡσαύτως ἐχόντων θεωρία· σύνεσις δὲ ἡ διάκρισις Or.*enarr.in Job* 28:12(M.17.89C); 2. *circumference*; hence *that which bounds* or *contains,* of God π. τῶν ὄντων Dion.Ar.*d.n.*4.34(M.3.736B); κατὰ μίαν τῆς αἰτίας π. τὰ πάντα...συνέχων *ib.*7.2(869B); οὐδὲν...τῶν ὄντων τὴν... π. τῆς θείας δυνάμεως ἀφῃρημένον *ib.*8.5(893A); *ib.*9.9(917C); of BMV ἡ π. τοῦ περιέχοντος ‡Meth.*Sym.et Ann.*10(M.18.372C); 3. *fence, fortification* Ἰάκωβος...ἐκαλεῖτο...ὠβλίας, ὅ ἐστιν Ἑλληνιστὶ π. τοῦ λαοῦ Heges.ap.Eus.*h.e.*2.23.7(M.20.197B); of Christ θύρα περιοχῆς Gr.Nyss.*Eun.*10(2 p.229.26; M.45.829D); ref. Abd.1 ὥσπερ π. τὸ πρόσταγμα ἐξαπέστειλε τὸ οἰκεῖον εἰς τὰ ἔθνη ὁ θεός, ἅπαντας αὐτοὺς ἐν κύκλῳ κατὰ τῆς Ἰδουμαίας συλλέγων Thdr.Mops.*Abd.*1:1(M.66. 309B); ἀντὶ τοῦ περιοχήν, ἀγγελίαν ὁ Σύμμαχος εἴρηκε Thdt.*Abd.* 1:1(2.1451); ἐγένετο...ἡ σκέπη τοῦ θεοῦ ὡς πόλις περιοχῆς Esaias *or.*4.12(p.31); ἐκκλησία...ὀνομάζεται...π., ὥσπερ ἔχουσα τὰ τοῦ θεοῦ τεράστεια ‡Sophr.H.*liturg.*2(M.87.3984A); 4. *country surrounding a place, suburban district,* Ephr.2.3C; *Chron.Pasch.*p.283(M.92.708A); 5. *extent*; *space contained,* Dion.Ar.*e.h.*3.2(M.3.425B); 6. *whole content* π. τῆς Μωσέως γραφῆς Eus.*d.e.*5 proem.(p.206.35; M.22.344B); ‡Barth.Edess.*Muham.*(M.104.1453D); 7. *part marked off* or *circumscribed, passage* of book, Didym.*Trin.*3.36(M.39.965B); †Gregent. *disp.*(M.86.641B); Jo.Mosch.*prat.*32(M.87.2880C); 8. *summary,* Cyr. *Ps.*39:8(M.69.988D).

***περιοχικῶς,** *comprehensively,* Jo.D.*inst.el.*7(M.95.105C).

***περιοχυρόω,** *fence round,* ‡Caes.Naz.*dial.*191(M.38.1169).

περιπάθεια, ἡ, *strong emotion,* Chrys.*hom.28.4 in 1Cor.*(10.256B; προσπάθειαν Gaume).

περιπαθής, 1. *emotional, expressing emotion* περιπαθεῖς ἡ γραφὴ τοὺς λόγους ποιεῖ καὶ τοῖς ἀναισθήτοις δίδωσιν αἴσθησιν Or.*fr.59 in Lam.*(p.260.6; M.13.640A); of words of Christ expressive of emotion οὐκ ἀνθρώπου τοῦ ἐκ γῆς εἰσιν αἱ π. ἐκεῖναι φωναί, ἀλλὰ θεοῦ τοῦ καταβάντος Apoll.*fr.*63(p.219.8)ap.Gr.Nyss.*Apoll.*33(M.45.1196B); ἐμοῦ τοῦ ἀμαθοῦς καὶ π. Thdr.Stud.*epp.*1.11(M.99.944B); neut. as subst., τὸ ἄγαν π. καὶ ταπεινόν Bas.*hom.*4.5(2.29A; M.31.228B); Gr.Naz.*ep.* 165(M.37.273B); Thdr.Stud.*epp.*1.18(965C); 2. *pathetic,* Chrys.*hom. 37.1 in Jo.*(8.211C); Soz.*h.e.*6.37.14(M.67.1408A); Bas.Sel.*v.Thecl.*1 (M.85.524B); neut. as subst., ‡Dion.Al.*fr.in Lc.22:46*(p.246.8; M. 10.1600D).

***περιπάρειμι,** *be close* upon, *be very near* to; c. dat., Thdr.Stud. *epp.*2.22(M.99.1185C).

***περιπαρίημι,** ? *pass over* ταῖς ἄλλαις δυσὶ προτάσεσι περιπαρείς, ...ἑτέρα πάλιν ἔγκλησις Thdr.Stud.*epp.*2.162(M.99.1513A).

περιπατ-έω, 1. *walk* ὁ γὰρ ἄρρητος πατὴρ...οὔτε ποι ἀφίκται οὔτε ~εῖ Just.*dial.*127.2(M.6.772B); 2. *go about,* ref. Heb. 11:37, *1Clem.* 17.1; 3. of things, *go,* Jo.Mosch.*prat.*76(M.87.2929C); 4. *conduct oneself, live* ἐν ἀλλοτρίᾳ γνώμῃ ~εῖ Ign.*Philad.*3.3; Polyc.*ep.*5.1; Herm.*mand.*6.1.4; 5. *beat about the bush* οὐ κατοκνήσω, οὐ ~ήσομαι βεβαίαν δὲ ἕξω τὴν αἴτησιν Cyr.*Ps.*25:1(M.69.852C).

περιπατητικός, *Peripatetic, belonging to Aristotelian school of philosophy*; also of Pythagoreans ἕκτη Πυθαγόρειοι εἴτ' οὖν π., διὰ τῶν περὶ τὸν Ἀριστοτέλην διαιρεθεῖσα Epiph.*rescr.*3(p.157.6; M.41. 160D); id.*haer.*7(p.186.2; M.41.205A); Jo.D.*haer.*5(M.94.681C).

περίπατος, ὁ, 1. *walk,* of God with man ὁποῖος γὰρ αὐτοῦ ὁ π. ἐν τοῖς ἁγίοις, τοιοῦτός τις καὶ ὁ ἐν τῷ παραδείσῳ Or.*or.*23(p.352.11; M. 11.489C); ref. Jo.20:14 ὁ Χριστὸς ἐν τῷ ᾄσματι τῶν ᾀσμάτων διαμέμνηται πως τῶν ἐν τῇδε τῇ νυκτὶ περιπάτων...ὅτι ἡ κεφαλή μου ἐπλήσθη δρόσου Cyr.*Jo.*12(4.1082C); 2. met., *conduct, way of life* π. τὸν κατὰ θεόν Chrys.*hom.12.1 in Eph.*(11.90B); *cat.Col.*1:9(p.299. 22).

***περιπαφλάζ-ω,** *rage around* κυμάτων δίκην...τοῦ κόσμου ~οντος Cyr.*Jo.*11.8(4.969B; περιπαμφ- Aubert).

περιπέζιος, *earthly,* Dion.Ar.*c.h.*7.1(M.3.205D); ‡Max.*cap.al.*209 (M.90.1449D); neut. plur. as subst., Areth.*Apoc.*4:1(M.106.565D).

περιπείρ-ω, 1. *pierce through,* of holing ships καθάπερ πειραταί [sc. αἱρέσεις]...ναῦς ἐπὶ τοὺς προειρημένους τόπους ~ουσιν Thphl.Ant. *Autol.*2.14(M.6.1076C); met. ἀγκίστροις τῶν τόκων ἑαυτοὺς ~οντας Gr.Nyss.*usur.*(M.46.452D); Jo.VI H.*v.Jo.D.*27(M.94.468C); 2. *entangle*; met., Hipp.*haer.*4.7(p.39.19; M.16.3070A); Or.*enarr.in Job* 2:10(M.17.64B); ~η δεσμοῖς Ath.*ep.Aeg.Lib.*1(M.25.540C); Bas.*hom.* 12.6(2.103A; M.31.400A); εἰς τὰς ἀκάνθας...τοῦ κόσμου ~εται Mac.Aeg. *hom.*4.5(M.34.476B); Chrys.*hom.7.7 in 2Cor.*(10.490C); Isid.Pel.*epp.* 5.316(M.78.1520B); reflex. τοῦ κόσμου τὴν ψυχὴν θεὸν ὑπολαμβάνων αὐτὸς αὑτῷ ~εται Clem.*prot.*5(p.51.2; M.8.172A); id.*paed.*1.6(p.116. 15; M.8.301C); ἑαυτῇ ~εται Chrys.*hom.38.2 in 1Cor.*(10.352E).

περιπέτασμα, τό, *hanging, curtain,* Eus.*v.C.*3.43(p.9.29, v.l. παραπετάσμασι M.20.1104A); id.*l.C.*1(p.197.1; M.20.1320B).

περιπέτ-ομαι, *fly around,* met. Ἰουδαῖοι ψιλῷ τῆς γραφῆς τῷ γράμματι ~όμενοι, ὥσπερ...ψυχία...τοῖς φύλλοις Meth.*symp.*9.1(p.113.24; M.18.177A).

περιπήγνυμι, 1. *fix round* as frame or tabernacle ἐν ἀνθρώπῳ...ὃν ἑαυτῷ περιέπηξεν Gr.Naz.*ep.*102(M.37.197B); ἐν μήτρᾳ παρθενικῇ τὴν ἀνθρωπείαν ἑαυτῷ περιπήξας σκηνήν Thdt.*affect.*6(p.176.12; 4.877); τὸν ἄνθρωπον ἑαυτῷ περιέπηξεν Leont.B.*Nest.et Eut.*1(M.86.1284C); 2. *establish* ἐπὶ πάντας τὸ ἔλεος αὐτοῦ περιεπήξατο Hesych.H.*Ps.tit.* 116(M.27.1168C).

***περιπίλναμαι,** *approach,* c. dat., †Apoll.*met.Ps.*43:26(M.33. 1373C).

περιπίπτ-ω, 1. *fall into, meet with* something evil καχεξίᾳ π. Clem.*str.*7.2(p.8.26; M.9.413A); μηδενὶ τῶν παθῶν...~οντι *ib.*7.14 (p.62.8; 521A); κολάσεις...εἰς ἃς...~ουσιν *ib.*7.16(p.72.18; 541B); π. κρίσει id.*ecl.*40(p.148.28; M.9.717C); Or.*princ.*3.1.17(p.225.16; M.11. 284A); ~οντας ψευδέσι...δόγμασιν id.*Jo.*2.2(p.54.24; M.14.108C); ναυαγίῳ περιέπεσα *Hom.Clem.*12.16; Eus.*e.th.*2.8(p.108.6; M.24. 916B); τῷ ἀντιχρίστῳ π. Chrys.*hom.33.2 in Heb.*(12.303D); 2. *come to grief over* ὅτε μὲν καὶ ἑκουσίοις, πολλάκις δὲ καὶ ἀκουσίοις ~ομεν Didym.*Job* 4:17(M.39.1132C); of self-contradiction ἑαυτῷ ~ει Eus. *Marcell.*2.3(p.47.11; M.24.804B); πονηρία ἑαυτῇ ~ει Chrys.*hom.7.3 in Mt.*(7.107A); φθόνος...ἑαυτῷ ~ει *ib.48.1*(494A); 3. *have sexual intercourse with* εἰς δύο π. ἀδελφάς †Jo.Jej.*poenit.*(M.88.1893D); 4. in gen., *fall* ὑπὸ πάθη...τῆς σαρκὸς π. Ephr.2.338B.

περιπλανάω, 1. *lead astray, make to wander from one's course,* Cyr.*Jo.*3.4(4.271A); Jo.D.*hom.*3.7(M.96.597C); 2. med., *wander about,* Thdt.*eran.*1(4.31).

περίπλασις, ἡ, *overlaying, covering,* Gr.Nyss.*res.*3(M.46.660D); v. παράπλασις.

***περίπλασμα, τό,** *plaster, poultice,* Bas.*hom.in Ps.*32(1.135A; M. 29.332B).

περιπλάσσ-ω, *smear over,* Tat.*orat.*3(p.3.20; M.6.809B); Eus.*p.e.* 7.18(332A; M.21.560D); Chrys.*hom.88.3 in Mt.*(7.829B); met. δελέατος δίκην τῷ τῆς κακίας ἀγκίστρῳ τῆς τοῦ καλοῦ φαντασίας περιπλασθείσης Gr.Nyss.*or.catech.*22(p.84.6; M.45.60C); λαβὼν τὸν ἐκ τῆς παρθενίας χοῦν οὐχ ἁπλῶς τὸν ἄνθρωπον ἔπλασεν, ἀλλ' ἑαυτῷ περιέπλασε id.*Eun.*4(2 p.65.19; M.45.637B); id.*Apoll.*24(M.45.1173B); προσωπεῖον ἑαυτοῖς ~οντες Cyr.*Os.*29(3.53D); οὐκ ἀγαθὸς...ἀνὴρ... χρηστότητος ὄνομα ~εται id.*Soph.*5(3.583E).

περιπλέκ-ω, *twine* or *fold round*; 1. *weave,* Nonn.*par.Jo.*19:2(M. 43.897B); met. ἔγκλημα ~οντες Cyr.*Jo.*10.2(4.913E); 2. *clasp* the hands *round,* *A.Xanthipp.*8(p.63.3); 3. pass., *be coiled up*; of a snake, Clem.*paed.*3.6(p.256.22; M.8.605A); 4. pass., *be enfolded* πῶς ἐπιζητεῖ τις ἐκεῖθεν τῷ θεῷ περιπλακῆναι τὸν ἄνθρωπον; Gr.Nyss.*or. catech.*27(p.103.1; M.45.72A).

περιπλοκή, ἡ, 1. *braiding, plaiting*; of hair, Clem.*paed.*3.11(p.271.13; M.8.637A); **2.** met., *intricacy, complication*, id.*str.*1.3(p.15.3; M.8.712C); Eus.*p.e.*3.13(122A; M.21.217C); **3.** *embrace*, Clem.*prot.*4(p.46.30; M.8.160A); Gr.Naz.*or.*43.24(M.36.529A); **4.** *union, coming together* ψυχὴ δέ, διὰ περιπλοκῆς σοφίᾳ ἑνωθεῖσα, ἁγιασμοῦ πληροῦται Or.*fr.in Pr.*4:25(M.17.157B); ἕλιξ δὲ τοῦ ἀμπελῶνος, ἡ πρὸς τὴν ἀΐδιον ζωὴν π. τε καὶ συμφυΐα Gr.Nyss.*hom.2 in Cant.*(M.44.800C).

περίπλοκος, *entangled*; of involved sexual unions within forbidden degrees, †Jo.Jej.*poenit.*(M.88.1893D).

[*]**περιπνείω,** *blow*, Nonn.*par.Jo.*3:8(M.43.768A).

περιπνοία, ἡ, *blowing round*, Bas.*hex.*9.5(1.86C; M.29.201C).

περιπόθητος, 1. *much desired*, Or.*schol.in Cant.*7:6(M.17.284A); Bas.*ep.*154(3.243D; M.32.609D); τὸν μακάριον καὶ π. βίον Epiph.*anc.* proem.(p.5.12; M.43.17A); Nil.*epp.*3.119(M.79.437C); **2.** *much beloved*, *Hom.Clem.*12.3; τινὲς δὲ τῆς ἀληθείας ἀλλότριοι...ἀσχημάτιστον αὐτὸν λέγουσιν ἵνα ἄμορφος...ὢν μηδενὶ ὁρατὸς ᾖ, ὅπως μὴ π. γένηται *ib.*17.11(393C); Cyr.H.*catech.*19.1.

περιποι-έω, 1. *preserve, keep safe* ὡς φιλάνθρωπος ~ησον...ἡμᾶς Gr.Ant.*mul.ung.*12(M.88.1865A); **2.** *acquire, make one's own* συναγωγῆς...ἣν ~ήσω τοῖς τοῦ...λόγου πάθεσιν Gr.Naz.*or.*5.27(M.35.697B); Χριστὸς...τῇ ἑαυτοῦ θεότητι ~εῖ τὸν λαόν Didym.*Trin.*1.27(M.39.396A); τὸν λόγον...τὰς τῶν προτετελευτηκότων ψυχὰς διὰ μόνης ~εῖσθαι τῆς πίστεως δύνασθαι Max.*ambig.*(M.91.1384C); ἐκκλησίᾳ, ἣν ~ήσω τῷ τιμίῳ αἵματι τοῦ μονογενοῦς *Lit.Jac.*(p.162.22); **3.** *bring about, effect* εἰ...τὴν μὲν μονάδα ἡ φύσις περιεποίησεν, τὴν δὲ τριάδα ἡ χρεία, πῶς οὐκ ἠνάγκαζε τὴν φύσιν ἡ χρεία;...εἰ δ' οὐκ ἠνάγκαζε, πῶς τὴν τριάδα τῶν ὀνομάτων ἡ χρεία περιεποίησεν; *Disp.Phot.*(M.88.572A).

περιποίησις, ἡ, 1. *preservation, saving* ἵνα γένηται π. τῷ Ἰωσήφ *T.Zab.*2.8; εἰς εὐφρασίαν καὶ π. καὶ πληροφορίαν τῶν πιστῶν Epiph.*anc.*64(p.76.29; M.43.132A); **2.** *acquiring, securing* φυλακὴ δὲ τῶν ἐντολῶν...π. ἐστιν ἀσφαλείας βίου Clem.*str.*2.18(p.154.24; M.8.1017B); *ib.*6.12(p.482.4; M.9.321A); †Bas.*bapt.*2.10.1(2.669D; M.31.1620A); *Const.App.*2.20.2.

***περιποιητέον,** *one must acquire*, Or.*Jo.*20.20(18; p.352.1; M.14.616B).

περιποιητικός, 1. *preservative, capable of saving* ἐπινοίαις τῶν π. τῆς σαρκὸς τρόπων λιπαινόμενος Max.*qu.Thal.*58(M.90.597A); id. *ambig.*(M.91.1317A); neut. as subst., *protection*, Thdr.Stud.*epp.*2.144(M.99.1452C); **2.** *productive, capable of securing* ὅρασις δὲ θεοῦ π. ἀφθαρσίας Iren.*haer.*4.38.3(M.7.1108C); Clem.*paed.*1.10(p.146.7; M.8.364A); ἁγιασμὸν τὸν π. τοῦ ἁγίους γενέσθαι τοὺς πιστεύοντας Or. *hom.8.2 in Jer.*(p.57.13; M.13.337C); διδασκαλίαν τῶν ἐντολῶν...ζωῆς αἰωνίου καὶ βασιλείας οὐρανῶν π. Bas.*moral.*72.4(2.307B; M.31.849A); Thdot.Anc.*hom.*4.8(M.77.1401A).

περιποικίλλομαι, v. ποικίλλω.

***περιπόλευσις, ἡ,** *revolution* of stars, Eus.*d.e.*4.5(p.158.7; M.22.264B).

περιπολεύω, *wander round*, Thphn.*chron.*p.405(M.108.964B); v. περισκοπεύω.

περιπόλησις, ἡ, *revolution* of stars, Clem.*str.*5.6(p.349.5; M.9.60A); Ath.*gent.*35(M.25.72A).

περιπολίζω, *wander about*, Iren.*haer.*1.13.6(M.7.588B).

περιπόλι(ο)ν, τό, *suburb*, Leont.Abb.*v.Gr.Agr.*48(M.98.629C).

περιπομπεύω, *parade about*, *Apophth.Patr.*(M.65.257C).

περιπον-έω, med., *be solicitous about* ~ουμένη ἐστὶ τὰ καθ' ἡμᾶς ἡ μεγίστη σου ὑπεροχή Thdr.Stud.*epp.*1.24(M.99.981D).

***περιπόνησις, ἡ,** *grief, trouble*, Thdr.Stud.*epp.*1.56(M.99.1109B).

***περιποππύζομαι,** *be applauded from all sides*, Gr.Naz.*or.*42.24(M.36.488A).

περιπόρφυρος, *clothed in purple*, Iren.*haer.*1.13.3(M.7.581B).

περιποτάομαι, *hover about*, Clem.*prot.*4(p.46.31; M.8.160B); Meth.*res.*2.2(p.333.6)ap.Epiph.*haer.*64.56(p.489.20; περιϊπτάμενος M.41.1165B); Thdt.*eran.*3(4.262).

περίπους, ὁ, *shoe* πεσόντες ἐπὶ τὸν χρυσόστρωτον αὐτοῦ π. εἶπον· δέσποτα *Pers.*(p.2.14).

***περιπρέπω,** *match, harmonize with* ἀρνειὸς Τυρίῃσι περιπρέψει λιβάδεσσι Vergil *ecl.*4 ap.Const.*or.s.c.*20(p.186.6; παρὰ πρέψει M.20.1300A).

***περιπρόσωπος,** *all round the face*, Cosm.Mel.*schol.*(M.38.489) in Gr.Naz.*carm.*2.2(poem.)7.136.

***περιπτοέω,** *alarm on every side*, Ephr.1.196E.

περιπτύσσ-ω, 1. *enfold*, hence *overlay* edge of a garment with gold leaf, Clem.*paed.*3.3(p.246.31; M.8.580C); **2.** *fold up* a letter, *A.Pil.*A 15.3(p.268); **3.** med., *embrace*, *T.Jos.*3.8; Or.*schol.in Cant.*8:1(M.17.285A); Meth.*symp.*proem.(p.5.13; M.18.32B); Bas.*ep.*45.1(3.134A; M.32.368A); ἐπὶ τὸ π. τοὺς ἁγίους...μάρτυρας Κῦρον καὶ Ἰωάννην Leont.N.*v.Jo.Eleem.*1(p.4.2); met., *embrace, hold fast to*, Ath.*tom.*2(M.26.797A) cit. s. διάθεσις; σωτηρίαν π. Chrys.*hom.54.5 in Mt.*(7.552B); Isid.Pel.*epp.*3.322(M.78.985C); ~όμεθα...τὴν ἐν Νικαίᾳ συνελθοῦσαν...σύνοδον Epiph.Tyr.*ep.*(p.83.26; H.2.1352B); τὰς...τέτταρας συνόδους...~ομαι Sophr.H.*ep.syn.*(M.87.3188A); Max.*ep.*2(M.91.396C).

περίπτωσις, ἡ, *accident, fortuitous circumstance*, Clem.*str.*1.16(p.52.15; M.8.796A); εἴτ' οὖν κατὰ περίπτωσίν φασιν ἀποφθέγξασθαί τινα τῆς ἀληθοῦς φιλοσοφίας τοὺς Ἕλληνας, θείας οἰκονομίας ἢ π. *ib.*1.19(p.60.12; 809B); φοραὶ καὶ ἀφορίαι τοιῶνδε ψυχῶν καὶ σωμάτων, κατά τινα π. οἰκείως τῇ τοῦ παντὸς διοικήσει συντελούμεναι Eus.*p.e.*6.6(249B; M.21.424B); Bas.*hex.*2.5(1.16D; M.29.40A).

***περιράντρος,** v. *περιρραντήριος.

***περιρραγή, ἡ,** *bursting*; of a bladder used by children at play, ‡Caes.Naz.*dial.*7(M.38.865).

περιρραγής, *opened wide, gaping* μὴ...τὰ χείλη περιρραγεῖς γένωνται [sc. γυναῖκες] Clem.*paed.*2.2(p.176.15; M.8.429A); π. ἕλκος Paul.Sil.*Soph.*223(M.86.2128A).

περιρραίν-ω, *sprinkle*, Nonn.*par.Jo.*11:33(M.43.844C); *ib.*21:8(916C); Jo.D.*hom.*4.21(M.96.620A); in ritual purification π. αὐτοὺς ἀπὸ τῆς συνηθείας ταῖς ἀληθιναῖς σταγόσιν Clem.*prot.*10(p.72.7; M.8.213B); ὁ λόγος ἀντὶ ὑσσώπου τῷ αἵματι ἐμβαφείς, πάντας ~ει Chrys.*hom.16.2 in Heb.*(12.160A); *ib.19.1*(182D) cit. s. sq.

περιρραντήριον, τό, *sprinkling, ritual washing*, Clem.*str.*1.23(p.94.11; M.8.897A); Gr.Nyss.*anim.et res.*(M.46.133B); of Mosaic lustrations, Eus.*d.e.*4.16(p.195.2; M.22.324D); Gr.Nyss.*v.Mos.*45(M.44.316A); signifying spiritual purification, *ib.*(373B); superseded for Christians, *Const.App.*2.35.1; Isid.Pel.*epp.*4.20(M.78.1288C); Cyr.*Jo.*5.5(4.536B); as type of sacraments, Thdt.*haer.*5.28(4.476); of baptism π. τῶν διὰ ὕδατος καὶ ἁγίου πνεύματος Eus.*h.e.*10.4.45(M.20.868A); ref. Heb.10:22 διὰ τί μὴ εἶπε, κεκαθαρμένοι; τὴν διαφορὰν τῶν π. δεῖξαι βουλόμενος. ... τὸ μὲν...περιρρᾶναι τὴν συνείδησιν, τοῦ θεοῦ· τὸ δὲ μετὰ ἀληθείας προσελθεῖν...ἡμέτερον Chrys.*hom.19.1 in Heb.*(12.182D); met. τοῖς καθήκουσι τῶν λογισμῶν π. τὰς ψυχὰς ἀφαγνίσασθαι Gr.Nyss.*hom.1 in Cant.*(M.44.773A); of soul's initial purification, *ib.3*(808D).

***περιρραντήριος** (*περιράντρος), **1.** *of* or *concerned with ritual sprinkling* τὸ...ἀνθρώπων γένος...τῷ περιράντρῳ λουτρῷ [i.e. baptism] καθηράμενον Gr.Nyss.*anim.et res.*(M.46.133C; v.l. περιρραντηρίῳ); τῷ π. ὕδατι κατὰ τὸν Ἰορδάνην ἐκπλύνων [sc. Ἰωάννης] id.*laud.Bas.*(M.46.793C); **2.** *sprinkled* οὐ μὴ προσεγγίσῃ π. βωμούς Nil.*spir.mal.*10(M.79.1156B).

περιρραντίζ-ω, 1. *sprinkle*, met. ἐκεῖνοι τὸ σῶμα ἐρραντίζοντο, ἡμεῖς τὴν συνείδησιν· ὥστε ἔστι καὶ νῦν ~εσθαι αὐτῇ τῇ ἀρετῇ Chrys.*hom.19.1 in Heb.*(12.181D); **2.** pass., *be splashed, be dashed with water* ναῦς πανταχόθεν ~εται id.*res.Chr.*3(2.442C).

περιρραντισμός, ὁ, *sprinkling*; of purificatory lustration, Gr.Nyss.*or.dom.*2(p.26.32; M.44.1136D).

***περίρρεθος, τό,** ἁπαλοῖσι περιρρεθέεσσι χιτῶνας Gr.Naz.*carm.*1.2.1.218(M.37.539A, error for περὶ ῥεθέεσσι).

***περιρρεμβάζομαι,** *wander about*; met., *hold erroneous opinion*, †Gregent.*disp.*2(M.86.705C).

περιρρέμβω, act., *cause to wander round*, Thphn.*chron.*p.227(M.108.576C).

περιρρεπής, *falling to one side, unstable*, Bas.*hex.*4.2(1.34D; M.29.81C; v.l. διερρεπής); ‡Nil.*fr.pasch.*2(M.79.1496C).

περιρρέω, 1. *flow round*; pass., *be surrounded*; by water, Clem.*str.*6.11(p.475.26; M.9.309A); by a crowd, Bas.Sel.*v.Thecl.*1(M.85.485C); **2.** *crowd round, surround in abundance*, Chrys.*hom.31.2 in Mt.*(7.359C; ὑπέρρει Gaume); αὐτοὺς περιέρρει τῆς διδασκαλίας ἡ δόξα id.*hom.35.5 in 1Cor.*(10.329A); πολλά με περιρρεῖ. οὐκ οἶδα ποῖον εἴπω πρῶτον id.*hom.8.8 in Eph.*(11.65B); πλοῦτος ἡμᾶς περιρρεῖ Constantius Ant.*ep.*1(M.52.743); pass., *be crowded* περιρρεῖσθαι δὲ τὸν στενωπὸν...ὑπ' ἀνδρῶν Bas.Sel.*v.Thecl.*1(M.85.485C); **3.** pass., *be dripping* with blood, Chrys.*hom.13.3 in Mt.*(7.172A); with sweat, id.*terr.mot.*(2.717A); **4.** *make to flow round*, c. dat. et acc., met. τοῖς ὑψηλοῖς καὶ εὐτελῆ πολλὰ καὶ ταπεινὰ περιρρεῖ [sc. ὁ κύριος] Vict.*Mc.*7:32(p.338.25).

περιρρήσσω, *break in pieces, shatter all round*, *T.Neph.*6.5.

περίρρυτος, 1. *surrounded by water*; hence met., *stormy* τὸν π. βίον Meth.*symp.*4.3(p.48.14; M.18.89C); **2.** *encircling, flowing round* π. ... θαλάσσῃ Const.ap.Eus.*v.C.*2.31(p.54.19; M.20.1009A).

***περισαίρω,** perf. περισέσηρα in present sense, *grin widely*, Gennad.*fr.Gen.*49:11(M.85.1661A).

περισαλπίζω, *sound trumpets round*; pass., *be surrounded with sound of trumpets*, i.e. by din of war, Clem.*ecl*.29(p.146.9; M.9.713C).

περισαρκόω, *cover all round with flesh*, Bas.*hom.in Ps*.29(1.130B; M.29.320C).

περισάρκωσις, ἡ, *covering of flesh*, Olymp.*Job* 15:27(M.93.180A).

περισείω, *shake all round*, Thdr.Lect.*fr*.(M.86.225A); pass., Chrys. *hom.14.10 in Rom*.(9.591A).

περισκαίρω, *frisk about*; c. acc., Nonn.*par.Jo*.10:3(M.43.832C); abs., Cyr.*hom.pasch*.16(5^{2}.212E).

περισκάλλω, *hoe*, Thdr.Mops.*Am*.7:14–17(M.66.292B).

***περισκεδάννυμι**, *scatter, spread around*, Clem.*paed*.2.10(p.214.4; M.8.509A).

περισκελία, ἡ, *difficulty*, Cyr.*Ps*.44:3(M.69.1029D).

περισκελίς, ἡ, *leg-band*; of high priest, Gr.Nyss.*v.Mos*.(M.44. 388B); τὸ τῆς σωφροσύνης περιβόλαιόν ἐστιν [sc. ἡ π.] id.*or.dom*.3 (p.46.28; M.44.1149B).

περισκέλλω, perf. ptcpl. περιεσκληκώς *dried up, shrivelled*, Gr. Nyss.*fat*.(M.45.164B).

περισκεπής, *obscure* π. ὁ λόγος Cyr.*Mich*.11(3.400B).

[*]**περισκέπτομαι**, *consider well*, Clem.*str*.4.22(p.312.23; M.8. 1356A); Cyr.*ador*.8(1.265E).

περισκέπ-ω, **1.** *screen*, *A.Jo*.76(p.188.21); †Bas.*Is*.138(1.476C; M. 30.344B); **2.** *obscure* ὁ τῆς ἀιδιότητος λόγος καθ' ἑκάτερον μέρος ὁμοίως τῷ ἀνυπάρκτῳ ~όμενος Gr.Nyss.*Eun*.8(2 p.176.22; M.45. 769A); **3.** *shield, protect* εἰρήνη ~ει Thphl.Ant.*Autol*.3.15(M.6. 1141B); *A.Jo*.82(p.191.29).

περισκήνιον, τό, plur., *tents*; met., ‡Max.*cap.al*.80(M.90.1417C).

[*]**περισκοπεύω**, *keep watch around*, *A.Phil*.139(p.73.2, v.l. περιπολεύειν).

περισκυθίζω, *scalp*, Hipp.*Dan*.2.20.4; Or.*mart*.23(p.21.5; περισκυτ- M.11.592B).

περισκυθισμός, ὁ, *scalping*, Or.*mart*.23(p.21.6; περισκυτ- M.11. 592B).

περισμήχω, *make clean*, Gennad.*fr.Gen*.49:11(M.85.1661A).

***περισπαράσσ-ω**, *rend round about* one's person αὐτῷ τὴν ἐσθῆτα ~οντα Gr.Nyss.*res*.3(M.46.656B).

περίσπασις, ἡ, *drawing away, diversion* σπουδάζει ὁ σατανᾶς τὴν ψυχὴν ἐν π. τῶν κρειττόνων ποιῆσαι Nil.*epp*.3.283(M.79.524B).

περισπασμός, ὁ, **A.** *wheeling round*, hence, met., *assiduous attention* or *service* of servants, Eus.Al.*serm*.21.17(M.86.444C).

B. *distraction*; **1.** spiritual οὐδὲ π. ἐν ἀπληστείᾳ ἐν νοΐ *T.Isach*. 4.5; πένης...οὐκ ἔχει τὸν π. τῶν ματαίων ἀνθρώπων *T.Gad* 7.6; τοῖς εἰς τὸν π. τοῦ βίου τὴν ψυχὴν ἀσχολοῦσιν ἐπαλγὴς μὲν ἡ ζωή †Dion.Al. *fr.Eccl*.2:22(p.223.5; M.10.1585B); ἡ ἄσκησις...ἐν τῇ παντελεῖ ἀλλοτριώσει τῶν π. ἡμῖν κατορθοῦται Bas.*reg.fus*.5.1(2.341E; M.31. 920C); πολὺν παρέχει π. τῇ ψυχῇ ἡ τῶν ὑλικῶν πραγμάτων φροντίς τε καὶ ἐπιμέλεια id.*ascet*.2.1(2.324A; M.31.881C); ἡ μέριμνα τῶν ἐκκλησιῶν καὶ σοὶ τὸν αὐτὸν ἐμβάλλει π. id.*ep*.200(3.298A; M.32.733A); πολλῶν δὲ τῷ κοινοτέρῳ βίῳ...τῶν π. ἐγκειμένων, ἀναγκαίως ὁ λόγος... τὸν τῆς παρθενίας ὑποτίθεται βίον Gr.Nyss.*virg*.proem.(p.247.4; M.46. 317A); Mac.Aeg.*hom*.4.3(M.34.473D); οὐ δύναται ἡ ψυχὴ...τὸν θεὸν ἐπιγνῶναι, ἐὰν μὴ συστείλῃ ἑαυτὴν ἀπὸ...παντὸς π. Ammonas *ep*.1 (p.432.7); παρ' οὐδὲν μὲν ποιεῖσθαι τὸν ἐν τῷδε τῷ βίῳ π. Cyr.*Is*.3.4 (2.507E); ὁ π. τῆς καρδίας μου Esaias *or*.14.3(p.80; cf.M.40.1140C); **2.** intellectual, Or.*or*.23(p.351.12; M.11.489A); διψυχίαν πᾶσαν καὶ π. ἀποθέμενος id.*princ*.4.1.7(p.302.13; M.11.353B); id.*Apoc*.11(p.26).

περισπ-άω, **1.** *draw away, remove* τὸν τῦφον ~ᾷ...ἡ θλῖψις Chrys. *hom.26.3 in 2Cor*.(10.622D); Bas.Sel.*or*.3.2(M.85.52B); **2.** *draw aside, divert*, Just.*dial*.2.4(M.6.477B); Or.*princ*.3.1.7(p.204.9; M.11.260A); πρὸς τὸ μὴ ἡμᾶς εἶναι αὐτεξουσίους δόξει τὸ ἀποστολικὸν ῥητὸν ~ᾶν *ib*.3.1.20(p.235.10; 293B); id.*Jo*.2.11(6; p.27.18; M.14.132C); ἀνθέλκει σε καὶ ~ᾷ ἀπὸ τῆς κακίας ὀδύναις καὶ λύπαις Chrys.*hom.17.4 in 1Cor*.(10.150D); Nil.*epp*.2.12(M.79.225C); **3.** *distract*, Herm.*sim*.2.5; Clem.*str*.2.18(p.156.4; M.8.1021A); Meth.*symp*.5.2(p.54.1; M.18.97C); Chrys.*hom.5.4 in 2Cor*.(10.471C); hence *occupy* ἡμέρας ~ῶσιν ἐν ἔργοις Pall.*h.Laus*.7(p.25.24; M.34.1020C); **4.** pass., *be troubled, disquieted*, Thphn.*chron*.p.324(M.108.784D).

περισπείρω, *scatter about*, Serap.*Man*.43(p.61; M.18.1228D).

περισπέρχ-ω, *send round about* αἰνὰ ~οντες ἐς ὕλην Eudoc.*Cypr*. 2.109(M.85.849B).

***περισπουδαῖος**, *much desired*, Jo.Mosch.*prat*.130(M.87.2996A).

περισπούδαστος, **1.** *much desired* ἐγκράτεια τῶν π. ἡδονῶν Clem. *str*.3.4(p.208.4; M.8.1132A); εἰρήνην π. Eus.*v.C*.3.21(p.87.28; M.20. 1081A); μὴ π. σοι ἔστω ἡ θεατρομανία Cyr.H.*catech*.19.6; Bas.*hex*.9.4 (1.83E; M.29.196C); Chrys.*hom.73.2 in Mt*.(7.709C); οἱ...τῷ θεῷ π. id.*hom.28.2 in 1Cor*.(10.252A); περισπουδάστου πολλοῖς γενομένης τῆς ἐπισκοπῆς Socr.*h.e*.6.20.2(M.67.725A); Jo.D.*hom*.8.14(M.96. 720D); **2.** *much to be admired, very admirable*, Tat.*orat*.34(p.36.9; M.6.877A); Chrys.*hom.79.1 in Mt*.(7.758D); Cyr.*Am*.74(3.332D); id.*Ag*.8(3.635E); **3.** *zealously performed* ἀμοιβὴν...τῆς πιστῆς καὶ π. ἐλεημοσύνης †Ath.*fr.Mt*.6:1(M.27.1372A); **4.** neut. as subst.; **a.** *zeal*, Bas.*Spir*.66(3.55D; M.32.189B); τὸ περὶ τὴν εὐποιΐαν π. Olymp.*Job* 31:20(M.93.328C); **b.** *object of zealous attention*, Chrys.*hom.5.1 in Heb*.(12.51D).

περισσεία, ἡ, **1.** *superabundance, surplus*, Clem.*paed*.3.11(p.272. 33; M.8.640C); Hipp.*fr.2 in Gen*.(p.51.7; M.10.585B); τὴν π. ὑμῶν τῆς νηστείας πένησιν ἐπιχορηγεῖν *Const.App*.5.20.18; τῆς κατὰ τὸν νόμον δικαιοσύνης τὴν π. φυλάσσειν...διδασκόμεθα †Bas.*bapt*.1.2.12(2. 637E; M.31.1545B); **2.** *superfluity, redundance*, Hadr.*introd*.104(M. 98.1300A).

περίσσευμα, τό, **1.** *that which is left over*, Firm.*ep*.35(M.77.1505B); of remains of offerings at eucharist, *Const.App*.8.31.1; **2.** *excretion, excrement*, Clem.*paed*.2.8(p.201.8; M.8.481A); Pall.*h.Laus*.63(p.159. 8, v.l. περισσώματα M.34.1235C).

***περισσευόντως**, *more abundantly, more frequently*, Or.*comm.in Rom*.ap.*philoc*.25.4(p.230.31; M.14.843C).

περίσσευσις, ἡ, *abundance*, Or.*comm.in Mt*.11.14(p.57.31; M.13. 949A).

περισσεύ-ω, **A.** trans.; **1.** *cause to abound, cause to have more than enough*, ref. Mt.14:21 κοφίνους κλασμάτων ~η Eust.Mon.*ep*.(M.86. 925A); **2.** *exceed* ~εις...τὸν τῆς ἀγάπης θεσμόν Cyr.*hom.pasch*.8(5^{2}. 97B); **3.** pass., *be left over*, Nonn.*par.Jo*.6:13(M.43.796A).

B. intrans.; **1.** *abound, have abundance*, of Christians πάντων ὑστεροῦνται, καὶ ἐν πᾶσι ~ουσιν *Diogn*.5.13; of things πάντα...ὑμῖν ~έτω Ign.*Smyrn*.9.2; **2.** *abound in* παντὸς χαρίσματος ~ῃς id.*Polyc*. 2.2; **3.** *remain over*, Herm.*sim*.9.8.7; Max.*ambig*.(M.91.1401C); of surplus of offerings at eucharist τὰς ~ούσας ἐν τοῖς μυστικοῖς εὐλογίας...οἱ διάκονοι διανεμέτωσαν τῷ κλήρῳ *Const.App*.8.31.2; of consecrated remains οἱ διάκονοι τὰ ~σαντα εἰσφερέτωσαν εἰς τὰ παστοφόρια *Lit*.ap.*Const.App*.8.13.17; **4.** *be superfluous*, Dion.Al. ap.Eus.*p.e*.14.26(780A; M.21.1284A); **5.** *be immoderate* ~οντας εἰς ὕβριν Clem.*paed*.2.10(p.213.14; M.8.508B); **6.** *be superior*, of God ὑπὲρ τὸ πᾶν ~ει ‡Gr.Nyss.*or.1 in Gen.1*:26(M.44.261B).

***περισσόβοτος**, *with more than enough food* π. τραπέζης Nonn. *par.Jo*.6:12(M.43.796A).

***περισσοέπεια, ἡ**, *extravagant speech*, Cyr.*Nah*.10(3.487D).

περισσοεπέω, *talk superfluously, waste words*, Cyr.*ador*.9(1.292E); id.*Nest*.2.8(p.46.18; 6^{1}.51A).

***περισσοεπής, ὁ**, *one who says too much, prater*, Cyr.*Chr.un*.(5^{1}. 737A).

***περισσοθρησκεία, ἡ**, *excessive religious ritual*; of Pharisees, ‡Epiph.*epit.haer*.16(p.351.27).

περισσολογ-έω, *say what is superfluous, waste words*, Just.*dial*. 128.2(M.6.773C); ὁ δὲ λέγων αὐτὸν ἀγένητον, ὃ οὐκ εἶπεν ἡ γραφή, ~εῖ ‡Ath.*dial.Trin*.2.5(M.28.1164B); Chrys.*hom.1.3 in Rom*.(9.434B); ἡ μὲν θεία γραφὴ οὐ ~εῖ Marc.Er.*opusc*.10.9(M.65.1133B).

περισσολογία, ἡ, *verbosity, waste of words*, Meth.*res*.1.29(p.260. 15; M.41.1137C); Eus.*Marcell*.1.3(p.16.3; M.24.748B); Chrys.*hom. 19.6 in 1Cor*.(10.168A); cf. *perissologia adiectio plurimorum verborum supervacua, ut 'vivat Ruben et non moriatur'*, Isid.H.*etym*. 1.34.7.

περισσολόγος, *garrulous*, Epiph.*haer*.71.5(p.254.17; M.42.381B).

***περισσολόγως**, *superfluously*, Thdr.Stud.*epp*.1.48(M.99.1076C).

***περισσοπρακτέω**, *exact too much taxation*, Ath.Scholast.*coll*.20. 1(p.172).

***περισσοπρακτία, ἡ**, *excessive taxation* δυσωποῦμεν ὑμᾶς κουφίσαι τὴν ἐπιτεθεῖσαν π. τῇ...ἁγίᾳ Ἀναστάσει...τῶν τοίνυν ἑκατὸν τοῦ χρυσίου λιτρῶν καθ' ὃν εἴρηται τρόπον διανεμηθεισῶν περισσοπρακτίᾳ ἀπεγράφησαν ἥ τε ἁγία Ἀνάστασις καὶ οἱ λοιποὶ σεβάσμιοι τόποι καὶ οἱ κτήτορες Cyr.S.*v.Sab*.54(p.145.19ff.).

περισσός, **1.** *superfluous, unnecessary*, *Diogn*.2.10; π. ἡ περὶ αὐτοὺς [sc. τοὺς θεούς] εὐσέβεια Athenag.*leg*.30.3(M.6.960C); Gr. Thaum.*pan.Or*.7(M.10.1076B); ὅτε τοίνυν οὐδ' οὕτως ἀναίτιον τῶν κακῶν δυνατὸν εἰπεῖν τὸν θεόν, ὕλην αὐτῷ προσάπτειν π. εἶναί μοι δοκεῖ Meth.*arbitr*.8(p.165.8); περισσὸν μαντείας πολυπραγμονεῖν Eus.*d.e*.9. 14(p.435.25; M.22.701C); θυσιῶν...τὸ π. Thdt.*affect*.proem.(p.3.6; 4. 692); Ἰουδαῖοι περὶ...τὰ π. τοῦ νόμου κεχηνότες id.*Rom*.9:33(3.110); σωματικὰ ἦν τοῦ νόμου τὰ π. id.*Gal*.3:3(3.373); theol. κτίσμα γὰρ καθ' ὑμᾶς κἀκεῖνος...καὶ π. λοιπὸν τοῦ λόγου ἡ γένεσις κατὰ τὴν...ὑμῶν ἐπίνοιαν, αὐτάρκους ὄντος τοῦ θεοῦ τὰ πάντα αὐτουργεῖν Ath.*decr*.8 (p.8.5; M.25.'457'(429)B); εἰ δὲ οὐκ ἐγέννησε, π. καὶ ἡ τοῦ πατρὸς προσηγορία ‡Ath.*dial.Trin*.2.13(M.28.1180A); **2.** *left outside, outside* *scope of* ἡμᾶς δὲ π. τούτων ὑπάρχειν, οἷα τὸ γένος ἀλλοφύλους ὄντας Eus.*d.e.*2 proem.(p.52.12; M.22.97A); *ib.*2.3(p.68.26; M.22.124D); **3.** *superior*, Tat.*orat.*14(p.15.17; M.6.836B); Eus.*d.e.*3.5(p.131.6; M.22.221B); **4.** κατὰ περιττὸν *most abundantly*, Ath.*inc.*26.1(M.25.140D); id.*decr.*3(p.3.23; M.25.'429'(421)A); ἐκ π. *Hom.Clem.*1.4; **5.** comp.; **a.** *more abundant*, Gr.Nyss.*Eun.*1(1 p.106.23; M.45.340D); **b.** *more excessive* π. ἐκδίκησιν *Ep.Lugd.*ap.Eus.*h.e.*5.1.60(M.20.243A); **c.** *higher*; of price, *V.Pach.A* 23(p.150.13).

περισσότης, ἡ, *superfluity* ἑρμηνεύεται δὲ ὁ Ἰεθὸρ π. ἢ περισσός. τοιοῦτος δὲ καὶ ὁ κόσμος, π. ὧν ὅλος Cyr.*glaph.Ex.*1(1.257A).

***περισσόψυχος,** *exceedingly high-souled, most noble*, Pall.*v.Chrys.*9(p.56.4; M.47.32).

περίσσωμα, τό, 1. *excretion*, theol. μήποτε ἀκούσιον τὴν γέννησιν εἰσαγάγωμεν καὶ οἷον π. τι φυσικὸν καὶ δυσκάθεκτον, ἥκιστα ταῖς περὶ θεότητος ὑπονοίαις πρέπον Gr.Naz.*or.*29.2(p.76.6; M.36.76C); ref. creation οὐδ' αὖ παρυποστῆναι τὸν κόσμον αὐτῷ φαμεν...ἵνα μὴ τοῦτον ἀπροαίρετον αἴτιον εἰσάγωμεν τοῦ παντός· οἷον π. τι φυσικὸν ἢ ἐφόλκιον ἐπαγόμενοι Zach.Mit.*opif.*(M.85.1129A); **2.** *excrescence*, met. ψυχαῖς...ὑλώδη περισσώματα ἐπιπωροῦται Gr.Nyss.*or.catech.*8(p.48.1; M.45.36D).

περισσωματικός, *superfluous, unnecessary*, Gr.Nyss.*anim.et res.*(M.46.105B).

περισσῶς, 1. *superfluously, unnecessarily*, Meth.*arbitr.*7(p.163.10; M.18.253C); id.*res.*2.18(p.370.4; M.18.284C); hence *uselessly* εἰ μὲν οὖν ὅλως ἀρνοῦνται λόγον εἶναι θεοῦ, π. ποιοῦσι, περὶ οὗ μὴ ἴσασι χλευάζοντες Ath.*inc.*41.3(M.25.168C); **2.** comp., *exceedingly*, *T.Jos.*17.5; Bas.*reg.fus.*2.4(2.340A; M.31.916C).

περιστάζω, pass., *drip all over* ἱδρῶσι περιεστάζετο ‡Dion.Al.*fr. in Lc.*22:44(p.242.7).

περίστασις, ἡ, 1. *fortuitous circumstance, accident, contingency*, Clem.*exc.Thdot.*71(p.129.28; M.9.692C); τὴν καταβᾶσαν εἰς ἀνθρωπίνην φύσιν καὶ εἰς ἀνθρωπίνας π. δύναμιν Or.*Cels.*3.28(p.226.11; M.11.956C); π. αἰτία ποτὲ γίνεται τοῦ προφητεύειν, ὥσπερ καὶ νῦν τῷ Καιάφᾳ τὸ εἶναι αὐτὸν ἀρχιερέα τοῦ ἐνιαυτοῦ ἐκείνου id.*Jo.*28.20(15; p.414.32; M.14.724B); οὐ γνώμης ἦν, ἀλλὰ περιστάσεως τὸ πλημμέλημα Thdt.*qu.23 in 2Reg.*(1.421); κατὰ περίστασιν *by chance, haphazardly*, Clem.*str.*1.1(p.12.23; M.8.708A); Or.*Cels.*1.13(p.66.10; M.11.680B); so also ἐκ π. *ib.*4.19(p.289.1; 1052C); μετὰ περιστάσεως: ταῦτα δὲ λέγομεν χωρὶς πάσης π. δεῖν γενέσθαι προηγουμένως· μετὰ γὰρ π. δέδοται καθηκόντως ποτὲ καθεζόμενον εὔξασθαι διά τινα νόσον τῶν ποδῶν id.*or.*31(p.396.15; M.11.552A); **2.** *misfortune, adverse circumstance*, Clem.*str.*4.7(p.273.21; M.8.1268A); τὸ ἐν τῷ ὀνόματι τοῦ Ἰησοῦ ...καλούμενον οὐκ ὀλίγους ἀπὸ νόσων...καὶ ἄλλων π. ἰάσατο Or.*Cels.*8.58(p.275.17; M.11.1605B); δεδεμένον μὲν εἶπεν τὸν ἄνδρα τὸν γεγαμηκότα· εἰ δὲ π. ἐστι τὸ δεδέσθαι, καὶ δεῖ φεύγειν τὰς π. ὅση δύναμις. καὶ τὸ δεδέσθαι γυναικὶ μὴ ζήτει λύειν, ὁ δὲ μὴ δεδεμένος ὀφείλει φυλάττεσθαι ἵνα μὴ δεθῇ id.*comm.in 1Cor.*7:27(*JTS* 9 p.509); Chrys.*hom.11.4 in Heb.*(12.117C); ἐν πολλῇ π. ἐγένετο Pall.*h.Laus.*18(p.50.11; M.34.1057A); φάσκοντες [sc. Euchites]...οὐδὲ τοῖς π. χρησαμένοις ...ἀπαρκεῖν ἁρμόττον τοῖς ἀποταττομένοις Jo.D.*haer.*80(M.94.732C); **3.** *assault, siege* ἀπὸ...πάσης π. τοῦ ἀντικειμένου Chrys.*hom.2.7 in 2Cor.*(10.438C); id.*hom.3.4 in 1Thess.*(11.446E); διὰ...π. καὶ ἐνεδρῶν τῆς κακίας Mac.Aeg.*hom.*50.4(M.34.820A); **4.** *pressure, besieging with importunate requests* γίνεταί τις αὐτῷ π. ... ἐπὶ τὸ γενέσθαι αὐτὸν ἐπίσκοπον Eustrat.*v.Eutych.*12(M.86.2288C).

***περιστατ-έομαι,** med.; **1.** sens. dub., perh. *stand about*, of a bored congregation ἀγανακτοῦμεν καὶ ~ούμεθα Anast.S.*synax.*(M.89.829A); **2.** *beset* τὰ ~ούμενα Areth.*Apoc.*8:11(M.106.617D); pass. ὑπὸ λεόντων ~ούμενος Chrys.*hom.57.4 in Gen.*(4.555B, vv.ll. περιτειχιζόμενος, περιστοιχιζόμενος); Thphn.*chron.*p.325(M.108.785A).

περιστατικός, 1. *accidental, contingent, occurring by force of circumstances*, Clem.*str.*6.10(p.473.12; M.9.304B); *ib.*7.3(p.13.10; 421C); τοῦ ἀπροαιρέτως συμβαίνοντος π. Or.*or.*30(p.393.19; M.11.545D); id.*Jo.*10.12(10; p.183.3; M.14.328A); Gr.Nyss.*hom.12 in Cant.*(M.44.1016D); Pall.*h.Laus.*12(p.36.8; M.34.1035B); εἰσὶ καὶ π. ἀρεταί, ὅταν μὴ ἑκουσίως τις τῷ ἀγαθῷ προσέλθῃ *ib.*15(p.40.9; 1041B); εἰσὶν καὶ π. ἀρεταὶ συμβαίνουσαι τοῖς ἀνθρώποις Marc.Diac.*v.Porph.*73; **2.** *besetting* μή...ὁ πόλεμος πρὸς τὸν νοῦν π. γένηται *Apophth.Patr.*(M.65.161C).

περιστατικῶς, 1. *with regard to circumstances*, Or.*Jo.*32.3(p.431.14; M.14.749B); **2.** *with misfortune, adversely, unhappily* ζῆν π. id.*Cels.*3.27(p.224.24; M.11.953C); τῶν...π. συμβαινόντων Bas.*hex.*18(1.389E; M.30.145C).

περισταυρ-όω, *protect with a palisade, fence round* ὅρον ἔχωμεν τὸν σταυρὸν τοῦ κυρίου, ᾧ ~ούμεθα καὶ περιθριγκούμεθα τῶν προτέρων ἁμαρτιῶν Clem.*paed.*3.12(p.283.8; M.8.664B).

***περιστεγάζομαι,** *be contained*, Gr.Nyss.*virg.*7(p.281.3; M.46.352C).

περιστέγω, *enclose, encase*, Clem.*paed.*2.12(p.228.9; M.8.540C); Gr.Nyss.*or.catech.*16(p.71.10; M.45.52C).

περιστέλλ-ω, 1. *keep in check, restrain, straiten*, Clem.*str.*5.5(p.346.6; M.9.53B); οὐχ ἵνα μέλλωμεν ~εσθαι τοὺς ἀδελφοὺς ἐν τῷ εὖ ποιεῖν †Ath.*fr.Mt.*(M.27.1372A); περιστεῖλαι ταπεινοφροσύνῃ τὸν τῶν χρημάτων θησαυρόν ‡Nil.*perist.*12.13(M.79.965B); Thphyl.*exc.gent.*3(p.480.8; M.113.940A); **2.** *withdraw from, avoid*; med., Clem.*str.*4.10(p.282.24; M.8.1285B); *ib.*7.11(p.48.2; M.9.492C); Chrys.*hom.14.3 in 2Cor.*(10.541B); pass., *withdraw*, Call.*v.Hyp.*(p.90).

περιστένω, *straiten*, *Pers.*(p.26.19).

περιστερά, ἡ, *dove*;

A. in pagan worship τὰς π. διὰ τὴν Σεμίραμιν σέβουσι Σύροι· τὸ γὰρ ἀδύνατον, εἰς π. μετέβαλεν ἡ γυνή Athenag.*leg.*30.1(M.6.960A).

B. at Christ's baptism; **1.** interpreted of heavenly Christ's descent upon man Jesus; **a.** by Valentinians, Iren.*haer.*1.7.2(M.7.513B); Ἡρακλέων καὶ Πτολεμαῖος ψυχικόν φασι τὸ σῶμα τοῦ Ἰησοῦ γεγονέναι, καὶ διὰ τοῦτο ἐπὶ τοῦ βαπτίσματος τὸ πνεῦμα ὡς π. κατελήλυθε, τουτέστιν ὁ λόγος ὁ τῆς μητρὸς ἄνωθεν τῆς σοφίας Hipp.*haer.*6.35(p.165.8; M.16.3250A); cf. ἡ π. δὲ σῶμα ὤφθη, ἣν οἱ μὲν τὸ ἅγιον πνεῦμά φασιν, οἱ δὲ ἀπὸ Βασιλείδου τὸν διάκονον, οἱ δὲ ἀπὸ Οὐαλεντίνου τὸ πνεῦμα τῆς ἐνθυμήσεως τοῦ πατρός, τὸ τὴν κατέλευσιν πεποιημένον ἐπὶ τὴν τοῦ λόγου σάρκα Clem.*exc.Thdot.*16(p.112.4; M.9.665A); **b.** Marcosians κατελθεῖν εἰς αὐτὸν ὡς π. τὸν ἀναδραμόντα ἄνω καὶ πληρώσαντα τὸν δωδέκατον ἀριθμόν...αὐτὴν δὲ τὴν δύναμιν κατελθοῦσαν σπέρμα...εἶναι τοῦ πατρός Iren.*haer.*1.15.3(M.7.620B); **c.** 'Gnostics', cf. *Christum...non natum esse, sed et post baptisma...Jesu, ipsum sicut columbam in eum descendisse*, *ib.*3.10.4(M.7.875B); *Jesum ...receptaculum Christi fuisse, in quem desuper quasi columbam descendisse Christum*, *ib.*3.16.1(919C); **d.** Cerinthus μετὰ τὸ βάπτισμα κατελθεῖν εἰς αὐτὸν...τὸν Χριστὸν ἐν εἴδει περιστερᾶς *ib.*1.26.1 ap.Hipp.*haer.*7.33(M.16.3342A); *ib.*10.21(p.281.12; 3438C); κατεληλυθέναι τὸν Χριστὸν εἰς αὐτὸν τουτέστι τὸ πνεῦμα τὸ ἅγιον ἐν εἴδει περιστερᾶς Epiph.*haer.*28.1(p.314.6; M.41.380A); **e.** Ebionites, *ib.*30.14(p.351.19; 429C); **2.** interpreted of H. Ghost ἀναδύντος αὐτοῦ ἀπὸ τοῦ ὕδατος, ὡς π. τὸ ἅγιον πνεῦμα ἐπιπτῆναι ἐπ' αὐτόν Just.*dial.*88.3(M.6.685B); form of dove indicating gentleness of H. Ghost's new manifestation, Clem.*fr.*57(p.226.25; M.9.765C); ὥσπερ γὰρ ἐν τῇ κιβωτῷ τοῦ Νῶε διὰ περιστερᾶς μηνύεται ἡ φιλανθρωπία τοῦ θεοῦ, οὕτω καὶ νῦν τὸ ἐν εἴδει περιστερᾶς κατελθὸν πνεῦμα ὡς καρπὸν ἐλαίας βαστάσαν ἐπὶ τὸν μαρτυρούμενον κατέστη †Hipp.*theoph.*7(p.261.13; M.10.857C); genuineness of H. Ghost's appearance as dove defended against Celsus' objection that it was not seen by the bystanders, Or.*Cels.*1.41(p.91.31ff.; M.11.736ff.); cf. *descendit autem spiritus sanctus super salvatorem in specie columbae, avis mansuetae, innocentis et simplicis* [ἤτοι] διὰ τὸ πρᾶον καὶ ἀκέραιον, ἵνα καὶ ἡμεῖς τὸ πρᾶον καὶ ἀκέραιον τῆς π. μιμησώμεθα, καὶ τὸ πέτασθαι τῷ νῷ ὑπὲρ τὰ γήϊνα id.*hom.27 in Lc.*(p.171.7; M.13.1871B); χωρεῖ τὴν ἀκέραιον καὶ ἄδολον π. τοῦ πνεύματος, συνδεδεμένην αὐτῷ καὶ μηκέτι ἀποπτῆναι δυναμένην id.*Jo.*6.42(25; p.152.1; M.14.273C); πνεύματος...εἶδος οὐχ ἔχοντος, ὡς περιστερᾶς νόησιν δέχεται id.*fr.20 in Jo.*(p.500.17); cf. '*habitu repertus est ut homo*' [Phil.2:7]...*necesse est ergo et spiritum, qui sicut columba adparuit, non aliud esse quam naturalem columbam; 'sicut homo' enim dictum est et 'sicut columba'*, Hegem.*Arch.*59(p.86.21; M.10.1514A); cf. *quomodo poterit vera columba verum hominem ingredi atque in eo permanere?* *ib.*(p.87.8; 1514B); typified by Noah's dove which, at time of salvation through wood and water, returned at evening bearing olive branch; so at Christ's baptism dove appeared to signify salvation through Cross, bestowed by Christ at evening (i.e. by death), Cyr.H.*catech.*17.10; διὸ καὶ τὸ πνεῦμα ἐν εἴδει περιστερᾶς κάτεισιν· ὅπου γὰρ καταλλαγὴ θεοῦ, π. καὶ γὰρ ἐπὶ τῆς κιβωτοῦ τῆς ἐπὶ Νῶε φέρουσα κλάδον ἐλαίας ἦλθεν ἡ π., σύμβολον τῆς τοῦ θεοῦ φιλανθρωπίας...καὶ νῦν ἐν εἴδει περιστερᾶς, οὐκ ἐν σώματι...τὸ πνεῦμα ἔρχεται, τὸν ἔλεον τοῦ θεοῦ καταγγέλλον τῇ οἰκουμένῃ, ἅμα καὶ δηλοῦν, ὅτι τὸν πνευματικὸν ἄνδρα ἀπόνηρόν τινα εἶναι χρή Chrys.*bapt.Chr.*4(2.373C); τὸ δὲ πνεῦμα οὐ φύσιν ἀνέλαβε περιστερᾶς. διὰ τοῦτο ὁ εὐαγγελιστὴς οὐκ εἶπεν, ὅτι ἐν φύσει περιστερᾶς, ἀλλ' ἐν εἴδει id.*hom.12.3 in Mt.*(7.164C).

C. of H. Ghost in gen.; **1.** exeg.; **a.** Ps.67:13, cf. *quia autem dedit et ei pennas columbae, posteaquam dormivit in medio sortium: media autem inter duas vocationes Israelis ecclesia vocata est quia primo Israel vocatus est, post haec...vocata est ecclesia gentium...tum iterum...Israel...salvabitur;...et propter hoc dedit ei pennas columbae...quod significat rationabiles pennas in sancti spiritus donis*, Or.

*Cant.*3(p.233.19; M.13.192A); τοῦ γὰρ ἁγίου πνεύματος περιστερᾶς νοουμένου, οἱ ἐν τῇ παλαιᾷ καὶ καινῇ λελαλημένοι λόγοι, κατὰ τὴν ἐπιπόλαιον ἀνάγνωσιν, πτέρυξιν ὥσπερ ἐγκεκαλυμμένοι τυγχάνουσιν ...τὰ δὲ κατὰ βάθους ἐγκεκρυμμένα νοήματα, ἅπερ ἔοικε μεταφρένοις τῆς ἀποδοθείσης π. ... ἐν χλωρότητι λέγεται εἶναι Eus.*Ps.*67:10–11(M. 23.700A); κλήρους δὲ τοὺς...πιστεύσαντας ἔφη...λέγει δὲ ὡς πνεύματος ἁγίου ἀξιωθήσονται οἱ τοὺς ἁγίους ἀποστόλους δεξάμενοι. μετάφρενα δὲ τῆς π. κεχρυσωμένα φησί, διότι τιμίας...τὰς φρένας τῶν δεξαμένων ποιεῖ Ath.*exp.Ps.*67:14(M.27.296D); cf.Didym.*Ps.*67:14(M.39. 1444D); πτέρυγας δὲ καλεῖ περιστερᾶς, τὴν χάριν τοῦ πνεύματος...τὰς μὲν πτέρυγας περιηργυρῶσθαί φησι· τὰ δὲ μετάφρενα κεκοσμῆσθαι χρυσίῳ. τὰ μὲν γὰρ ἁπλούστερα...τοῖς ἁπλουστέροις προσφέρει· τοῖς δὲ τελειοτέροις, τὰ βαθύτερα Thdt.*Ps.*67:14(1.1062); **b.** Cant.1:14, cf. *quod autem oculi ejus comparantur columbis, ob hoc...contingit quia divinas scripturas non iam secundum litteram, sed secundum spiritum intelligat...columba enim indicium est spiritus sancti*, Or. *Cant.*3(p.173.13; M.13.145D); οἱ ὀφθαλμοί σου π., τουτέστι πνευματικοί· ἐν εἴδει γὰρ περιστερᾶς ἐπεφοίτησε τὸ πνεῦμα...καὶ ἐνῴκησε τῷ νυμφίῳ Thdt.*Cant.*1:15(2.51); *ib.*2:10(68); **c.** Cant.2:10, cf. *hi qui virtutem spiritus sancti recipiunt, et sanctificantur ex eo, et donis ejus replentur, quia ipse in specie columbae apparuit, etiam ipsi columbae fiant*, Or.*Cant.*3(4; p.224.4; M.13.184C); τῷ δὲ φωτὶ τὸ καλὸν τῆς π. εἶδος ἐνεικονίζεται, ἐκείνης λέγω τῆς π., ἧς τὸ εἶδος τὴν τοῦ ἁγίου πνεύματος παρουσίαν ἐγνώρισεν Gr.Nyss.*hom.5 in Cant.*(M. 44.869A); π. καλῶν διὰ τὴν δωρεὰν τοῦ ἁγίου πνεύματος Ph.Carp. *Cant.*52(M.40.68B); Thdt.*Cant.*2:10(2.68); **d.** Cant.2:14, Or.*Cant.*3 (4; p.234.12; M.13.192B); cf.id.*hom.2.12 in Cant.*(p.59.7; M.13.58A); **2.** indwelling a martyr, *M.Polyc.*16.1; **3.** typified by Noah's dove ἡ π., κλάδον ἐλαίας κομίσασα ἐν τῇ κιβωτῷ, καὶ τῆς γῆς τὴν ἀνάδειξιν μηνύσασα, ἐσήμαινε τοῦ ἁγίου πνεύματος τὴν ἐπιφοίτησιν καὶ τὴν ἄνωθεν διαλλαγήν Didym.*Trin.*2.14(M.39.696A); **4.** appearing at a consecration, ‡Pion.*v.Polyc.*21.

D. exeg. Ps.54:7 πτέρυγές εἰσι τῆς ἁγίας π. ἡ θεωρία σωμάτων καὶ ἀσωμάτων, δι' ἧς ὑψωθεὶς ὁ νοῦς καταπαύει εἰς γνῶσιν τῆς ἁγίας τριάδος Or.*sel.in Ps.*54:7(M.12.1465C); Thdt.*Ps.*54:7–8(1.962A); 'wings of dove' represent soul's flight from evil, Eus.*Ps.*54:7–12 (M.23.477B,C); τὰς τοῦ πνεύματος νοήσεις...ἐπαιρούσας, πτέρυγας π. ...ὀναμοζομένας Diod.*Ps.*54:6(M.33.1592C).

E. Cant.1:15 interpreted of spiritual purity enabling soul to perceive Christ ἡ τῆς σωματικῆς προσπαθείας ἀπηλλαγμένη ψυχή, τὸ τῆς π. εἶδος ἐν τοῖς ὄμμασιν ἔχειν, τουτέστι τὸν χαρακτῆρα τῆς πνευματικῆς ζωῆς τῷ διορατικῷ τῆς ψυχῆς ἐναυγάζεσθαι· ἐπεὶ οὖν γέγονε καθαρὸς ὁ αὐτῆς ὀφθαλμὸς δεκτικὸς τοῦ τῆς π. χαρακτῆρος, διὰ τοῦτο χωρεῖ καὶ τοῦ νυμφίου τὸ κάλλος θεάσασθαι. νῦν γὰρ πρῶτον ἡ παρθένος ἀτενίζει τῇ τοῦ νυμφίου μορφῇ, ὅτε ἔσχε τὴν π. ἐν τοῖς ὄμμασιν Gr.Nyss.*hom.4 in Cant.*(M.44.836A); of steadfast faith within soul, Nil.ap.Proc.G.*Cant.*1:14(M.87.1572A); of virgin soul, Gr.Nyss.*hom. 5 in Cant.*(880A); ref. Ps.67:13, Chrys.*hom.32.3 in Heb.*(12.299B,C).

F. of BMV π. λελευκασμένη καὶ ἀκέραιε Thdot.Anc.*hom.*4.13(M.77. 1409A); Jo.Thess.*dorm.BMV* 2.13(p.430.21); ἡ πάναγνος π. Thdr. Stud.*or.*5.2(M.99.721B).

G. images of doves in gold and silver, representing Holy Spirit, hung above fonts and altars, CCP(536)*ep.*(H.2.1320A).

H. sum of letters of περιστερά (801) denotes *A* and *Ω*, hence π. interpreted as *A* and *Ω* = heavenly Christ (Marcosian), Iren.*haer.* 1.14.6(M.7.608A); = H. Ghost, Didym.*Trin.*2.14(M.39.696A).

περιστερίδιον, τό, *young dove*, AQ ap.Proc.G.*Gen.*15:8(M.87. 348A).

***περιστεφάνωσις, ἡ,** *parapet round a roof* ἡ δὲ στέγη ἐστὶν ἡ ἀγάπη...εἶτα μετὰ τὴν στέγην ἡ π. τοῦ δώματος· τί ἐστιν ἡ π. τοῦ δώματος;...ἡ ταπείνωσις...στεφανοῦσα...πάσας τὰς ἀρετάς Dor.*doct.* 14(M.88.1776B).

περιστέφ-ω, *surround, encircle* ἀέρα...τὰ σώματα...~οντα *Pers.* (p.19.12, cj. for περιστύφοντα); met., *enwreathe* αἱ λοιπαὶ τῶν ἀρετῶν...~ουσι τὴν...κορυφήν Jo.Mal.*chron.*10 p.237(M.97.365A).

***περιστηγματίζομαι,** for ⟨περιστιγ-⟩, *be marked all over*, Ephr.2. 351E.

περιστήθιος, *worn round the breast*, Gr.Nyss.*or.dom.*3(p.46.5; M. 44.1148D); neut. as subst., *breastband*, Clem.*str.*5.6(p.352.1; M.9.64B).

***περιστηθίς, ἡ,** *breast-band*, Chrys.*hom.8.2 in 1Tim.*(11.592A).

***περιστήρα, ἡ,** an instrument of torture, Ephr.3.249F,250B.

***περιστήριγμα, τό,** plur., *bodies fixed round* the heavens; of signs of zodiac, *Hom.Clem.*6.14.

περιστίζω, gram., *mark with dots*, Isid.H.*etym.*1.21.15.

***περιστοιχείομαι,** *be surrounded with defences*; met., *be protected*, Or.*exp.in Pr.*3:23(M.17.169A).

περιστοιχέω, *range round*, Areth.*Apoc.*14:4(M.106.685A).

περιστοιχίζ-ω, **1.** *range, post round*; med., Gr.Nyss.*hom.6 in Cant.*(M.44.901A); pass., †Bas.*Is.*110(1.455B; M.30.296B); Gr.Nyss. *v.Gr.Thaum.*(M.46.948C); **2.** *beset*, Chrys.*sac.*6.3(p.144.10; 1.423A); med. ναῦν...~ονται χειμῶνες *ib.*6.4(p.149.17; 425C); Bas.Sel.*or.*16.2 (M.85.205C); met. ἡ...βασκανίας ~εται φλόξ Chrys.*sac.*3.14(p.73.23; 391D); Thdt.*Rom.*5:4–5(3.54); Bas.Sel.*or.*36.1(384B); **3.** *surround*, Eus.*v.C.*1.44(p.28.26; M.20.960A); *ib.*3.50(p.99.4; 1112A); Gr.Nyss. *hex.*26(M.44.89A); Chrys.*hom.32.3 in Heb.*(12.299C); med., Eus.*v.C.* 4.66(p.145.10; 1221B); Chrys.*paralyt.*4(3.39B); **4.** med., *range round oneself, surround oneself with* τοὺς ὑπ' αὐτοῦ πάντας χοροῦ δίκην περιστοιχισάμενος τῷ θεῷ...προσάξει Eus.*e.th.*3.15(p.174.3; M.24. 1032B); **5.** *clothe* αἰθερίῳ σώματι ~εται Aen.*dial.*(M.85.973C).

περιστολή, ἡ, **1.** *robe*, met. χάριτος τὴν π. ἀποβαλοῦσα ψυχή Cyr. *Os.*12(3.34C); τῆς ἄνωθεν π. ἀμοιροῦσαν [sc. συναγωγήν] id.*Nah.*29(3. 507C); **2.** *shroud*, Dion.Al.ap.Eus.*h.e.*7.11.24(M.20.672B); Dion.Al. *ib.*7.22.9(689B); Cyr.*Jo.*12(4.1075D); **3.** *covering*, id.*1Cor.*15:42(p.310. 21; M.74.905C); **4.** *concealment* ἐν π. παιδεύεται δίκαιος *Pss.Sal.*13. 7; Cyr.*Jo.*11.2(4.941E).

περιστολίζω, **1.** *clothe, array* αὐτὸν...ἀμφιθέμασι περιστολίσαι Cosm.Mel.*schol.*(M.38.482) in Gr.Naz.*carm.*2.2(poem.)5.213; reflex., Nil.*Eulog.*24(M.79.1125A); **2.** med., *put on*, met. τὴν νυμφικὴν περιστολισάμενοι ἀκήρατον πίστιν †Cyr.*hom.div.*10(5².371A).

περιστόμιον, τό, *collar, neck* of garment, Hesych.H.*Ps.tit.*32 (M.27.1256C); Cosm.Ind.*top.*5(M.88.213B); of a band of flesh οἱ εὐτραφεῖς ὑπὸ τῆς ἄγαν τρυφῆς...περισαρκώσεις ποιοῦσιν ἐπὶ τῶν μηρῶν, ἃ δὲ π. καλεῖ, ὡς συνέχοντα τοὺς μηρούς, καὶ οἷον θλίβοντα, καθάπερ τὸ π. τὸν τράχηλον Olymp.*Job* 15:27(M.93.180A).

περιστρέφ-ω, **1.** *turn round, make to revolve* θεοῦ δύναμις...ὧν [sc. ὁ λόγος] οὐρανὸν...~ει Ath.*gent.*40(M.25.81B); **2.** *turn about* in the mouth, *chew over*, Gr.Ant.*mul.ung.*5(M.88.1853A); **3.** *turn over, revolve* in the mind, Chrys.*hom.30.1 in Jo.*(8.170B); Socr.*h.e.*4.7.6(M. 67.473A); **4.** *dwell upon, mention frequently* οἱ ἀνακαλοῦντες τοὺς τετελευτηκότας...συνεχῶς τὰ ὀνόματα αὐτῶν ~οντες Chrys.*stat.*7.3 (2.88E); id.*hom.3.5 in Mt.*(7.41B); τοῦτο τῆς ἀποδείξεως τὸ εἶδος ~ουσιν οἱ προφῆται id.*hom.4.3 in Jo.*(8.30E); id.*hom.7.2 in 2Cor.* (10.482B); Ammon.*Jo.*16:25(M.85.1500B); **5.** *consider, explore* κἂν πάντα ~ωμεν [i.e. *leave no stone unturned*] Chrys.*hom.22.3 in Heb.* (12.207C); **6.** *pervert*, Bas.*hom.*7.7(2.59B; M.31.297C); **7.** *transfer* ὡς ἂν μὴ ~οιτο τοῦ γένους ὁ κλῆρος ἀπὸ φυλῆς ἐπὶ φυλήν Eus.*h.e.*1.7.17 (M.20.100A); Eustrat.*stat.anim.*14(p.429); **8.** med., *turn and toss*, on sick-bed, Chrys.*hom.2.4 in Phil.*(11.208A); πολλοὶ...τῶν πλουσίων δι' ὅλης ~ονται τῆς νυκτός id.*hom.5.4 in 1Thess.*(11.465D); id.*hom. 15.3 in Heb.*(12.153C); *fidget*, id.*exp.in Ps.*4:2(5.8B).

περιστροβέω, *alter, correct* τῆς δὲ ψυχῆς τὸ κενόδοξον καταλλήλῳ φαρμάκῳ περιστροβοῦσιν οἱ μάρτυρες Sophr.H.*mir.Cyr.et Jo.*1(M.87. 3428C).

περιστροφή, ἡ, **1.** *turning* this way and that, Chrys.*hom.8.2 in 1Tim.*(11.592A); **2.** *vicissitude*, Bas.*hom.*12.15(2.111B; M.31.417C); **3.** *turn* of speech, Cyr.*Jo.*3.6(4.322A).

***περιστυγνάζω,** *be vexed*, Cyr.*hom.pasch.*5(5².49A).

περιστύφω, *dry up* by astringents, f.l. περασ-, Nil.*epp.*2.111(M. 79.249A); v. περιστέφω.

περίστῳον, τό, *atrium, peristyle*, Gr.Nyss.*ep.*25(M.46.1100A).

περισυλλέγω, *collect together*, Gr.Nyss.*Eun.*12(1 p.251.31; M.45. 953A); περισυνελέξαντο καὶ κακούργημα Geo.Laod.*ep.dogm.*ap.Epiph. *haer.*73.14(M.42.432A; p.287.10 πέρυσιν ἤλεγξαν τὸ).

***περισυλληπτικός,** *able to hold fast*, Epiph.*anc.*tit.(p.1.6; M.43. 12A).

περισυνάγω, *gather together*, Epiph.*haer.*69.57(p.204.27; M.42. 292C); Cyr.S.*v.Sab.*31(p.116.6).

περισύρ-ω, **1.** *drag about* τὸ μὲν σῶμα ὡς σκιὰν ~οντες ἐπὶ τῆς γῆς, τὴν δὲ ψυχὴν συμπολιτευομένην τοῖς ἐπουρανίοις φυλάσσοντες †Bas. *bapt.*1.2.21(2.644E; M.31.1561C); **2.** *drag away, distract* μυρία τὰ ἐκτὸς...εἰς ἀλλοκότους φροντίδας ~οντα Eus.*d.e.*1.9(p.40.31; M.22. 77D); hence pass., *be dissolute*, Cyr.H.*catech.*12.34; **3.** *collect, sweep in together*, Pall.*v.Chrys.*7(p.41.24; M.47.25); **4.** *tear off*, Cyr.*glaph. Gen.*5(1.147C).

***περισφαιρόω,** *encircle*, Gnost.ap.Hipp.*haer.*5.14(p.109.6; M.16. 3167B); Hipp.*ib.*5.16(p.111.14; 3171A).

περισφαλής, *unstable*, Gr.Nyss.*v.Mos.*(M.44.405C).

περισφίγγ-ω, **1.** *bind together* ὁ πᾶσαν τῇ παλάμῃ ~ων [sc. God] τὴν κτίσιν Gr.Nyss.*hom.2 in Cant.*(M.44.805D); *Lit.*ap.*Const.App.*8. 12.14; Chrys.*hom.34.1 in 1Cor.*(10.310B); **2.** *bind*, *Orac.Sib.*2.289; ἔθνη ...ἁμαρτήμασι ~εται Or.*Ps.*2:3(p.448); **3.** *gird*, Nonn.*par.Jo.*21:18 (M.43.920A); met. τὴν ὀσφύν μου ἐν ἀληθείᾳ περιέσφιγξα *A.Thom.*A

147(p.255.16); Chrys.*hom.82.3 in Mt.*(7.786A); ‡Chrys.*pasch.*4(8.260C); **4.** *embrace*, Bas.*hom.*21.3(2.165E; M.31.545C); Gr.Naz.*or.*44.8 (M.36.616B); Chrys.*hom.88.3 in Jo.*(8.529B); **5.** *confine, bound*, Bas.*hex.*4.7(1.39C; M.29.93B); †Bas.*Is.*proem.1(1.378B; M.30.120A); θεὸς ...οὔτε χρόνοις ~εται ‡Gr.Nyss.*or.1 in Gen.1:26*(M.44.261B); **6.** *restrict* διὰ δὲ τοῦ 'ἐσμὲν' εἰς δυάδα τέμνει τὸ νοούμενον, καὶ πάλιν εἰς μίαν ~ει θεότητα Cyr.*Jo.*7(4.667A); **7.** *restrain* γυναῖκας...~ειν αἰδοῖ Clem.*paed.*3.11(p.269.18; M.8.632B); ἡ γραφὴ...~ουσα...τὴν διάνοιαν Epiph.*anc.*77(p.97.9; M.43.161C); Mac.Aeg.*elev.*3(M.34.892C); **8.** *sustain*, Ath.*exp.Ps.*58:10(M.27.265C); Cyr.*Jo.*1.9(4.76D); Zach.Mit.*opif.*(M.85.1077A); **9.** *contain* τὴν κτίσιν ἐν ἑαυτῷ ~οντα Bas.Sel.*or.*1.3(M.85.33B).

***περισφραγίζω**, *mark with sign of cross*, Gr.Nyss.*v.Macr.*(p.406.4; M.46.992B).

περισφύριος, *worn round the ankle*, Clem.*paed.*2.12(p.231.3; M.8.545B).

περίσχετος, *hemmed in, surrounded*, Cyr.*Mich.*45(3.434A); id.*Jon.*15(3.378D).

περισχίζω, **1.** *tear, rend*, Agath.*v.Gr.Ill.*153(p.77); pass., of garments ἄγγελος...Φαραὼ...ἐνδύσας...οὐ πέπλον περιεσχισμένον, ἀλλ' ὅλην Αἴγυπτον περιεσχ[ι]σμένην Mel.*pass.*17 p.3.21,22; **2.** med., *rend* garments, *T.Zab.*4.5; abs. *rend one's garments* τοῦ λαοῦ μὴ περιεσχισμένου περιεσχίσατο ὁ ἄγγελος Mel.*pass.*98 p.16.28; ref. rending of veil at Crucifixion, *Protev.*24.3(p.48); ἐνήστευσεν; ἐδάκρυσεν; περιεσχίσατο; Chrys.*serm.7.4 in Gen.*(4.679D); **3.** *strip*, Pall.*v.Chrys.*8 (p.50.12; M.47.29); *ib.*9(p.58.1; M.47.33); **4.** *divide, put asunder*, Gr.Naz.*or.*42.24(M.36.488A); Gr.Nyss.*hex.*25(M.44.88B); Gr.Ant.*bapt.*2.4(M.88.1873D); **5.** *divide, distract* the mind, Clem.*paed.*2.10(p.223.2; M.8.528B); **6.** *pull, drag about*; of those dragged by force to touch pagan sacrifices in persecution, CAnc.(314)*can.*3(prob. l. περισχεθέντας); **7.** *break* peace, Thphyl.*exc.gent.*14(p.487.31; M.113.949D).

περισχοινίζ-ω, **1.** *part off by a rope*; met.; **a.** *confine* οἱονεὶ μέτρῳ τινὶ τῇ ποσότητι τῆς ὑποστησαμένης αὐτὸν [sc. Χριστόν] ἐνεργείας ~οντες Gr.Nyss.*Eun.*1(1 p.99.6; M.45.332C); Cyr.*Zach.*30(3.698C); id.*Jo.*9.1(4.786C); **b.** *include* ὁ σύμπας λόγος ἐν τῷ τῆς ἀγάπης ὅρῳ ~εται id.*hom.pasch.*8(5².95B); id.*Jo.*2.2(4.164A); **2.** *tie round*; pass., Clem.*str.*6.15(p.492.2; M.9.344A).

περισχοίνισμα, τό, *enclosure*, in Temple, Isid.Pel.*epp.*4.40(M.78.1092A).

***περισχύτης, ὁ**, v. περιχύτης.

***περιτάνυσμα, τό**, *something stretched over*; of veil stretched over entrance to Holy of Holies, Cyr.*ador.*10(1.336D); id.*Am.*19(3.269B; τανύσματα Aubert).

***περιτανύω**, *stretch over*, Cyr.*ador.*10(1.337E); id.*Jo.*12(4.1070B).

***περιτάσσω**, *arrange in order*, Dion.Al.ap.Eus.*p.e.*14.25(776D; M.21.1277B).

***περιταυτολογία, ἡ**, v. περιαυτολογία.

περιτείνω, **1.** *stretch over*, Clem.*prot.*10(p.71.19; M.8.212B); **2.** medic., *distend*, Bas.Sel.*v.Thecl.*2.27(M.85.612C).

περιτειχίζω, **1.** *surround with a wall*, met. τὸ...πῦρ...κύκλῳ περιετείχισεν τὸ σῶμα τοῦ μάρτυρος *M.Polyc.*15.2; **2.** *fortify, protect* τούτοις [sc. angels]...περιτετείχισται ὁ κύριος Herm.*sim.*9.12.6; δρόσῳ πνεύματος ἁγίου περιτετειχισμένον Clem.*q.d.s.*34(p.182.22; M.9.640C); Esaias *or.*16.1(cf.M.40.1142C).

περιτείχισμα, τό, *enclosure*, Thdr.Lect.*fr.*(M.86.221B).

***περίτειχος**, *walled round*, Afric.*chron.*16.2(M.10.81B).

περίτειχος, τό, *surrounding wall*; ref. Is.26:1, of God, Cyr.*Is.*3.1 (2.358A).

περιτέμν-ω, **1.** med., *cut off*, Philost.*h.e.*3.7(M.65.489B); **2.** *cut short, bring to an end*, Cyr.*ador.*1(1.37B); **3.** *abbreviate* ~ειν τὰ εὐαγγέλια Serap.*Man.*36(p.53; M.18.1213A); **4.** *circumcise*; **a.** of Jewish circumcision, *Barn.*9.6 cit. s. περιτομή; οἱ τὴν σάρκα περιτετμημένοι Just.*dial.*19.3(M.6.516C); Afric.*chron.*13.6(M.10.77B); ὁ... Ἀβραὰμ πρῶτος ἐν διαθήκῃ τὴν περιτομὴν λαβὼν οὐδὲν ἕτερον αἰνίσσεσθαι δοκεῖ, τὸ οἰκεῖον ~όμενος τῆς σαρκὸς αὐτοῦ μέλος, ἢ τοῦτο, τὸ μηκέτι εἰς τὴν ἐκ τοῦ αὐτοῦ αἵματος σάρκα δημιουργηθεῖσαν παιδοσπορεῖν, ἀπὸ τῆς ἰδίας ἕκαστον διδάσκων ἀδελφῆς οἷα σαρκὸς ἀποτέμνειν τὴν κατὰ συνουσίαν ἡδονὴν Meth.*symp.*1.3(p.11.5; M.18.41C); οἱ ~οντες αὐτὸ τὸ γεννηθὲν ἐν σαββάτῳ, ἐὰν θελήσωσιν ἀκριβολογήσασθαι τὴν ὀγδόην ἡμέραν, εὑρίσκοντες ἐμπίπτουσαν ἐν σαββάτῳ καὶ ~οντες ἔργον εἰργάσαντο καὶ τὸ σάββατον ἔλυσαν· ἐὰν δὲ ὑπερθῶνται διὰ τὸ μὴ λῦσαι τὸ σάββατον, ἐνάτῃ λοιπὸν ~ουσι τὴν περιτομὴν καὶ ἔλυσαν αὐτὴν τὴν περιτομὴν καὶ τὸν...τῶν ὀκτὼ ἡμερῶν ὅρον Epiph.*haer.*30.32(p.379.6; M.41.468C); **b.** of spiritual circumcision κἂν Σκύθης ᾖ τις...ἔχει δὲ τὴν τοῦ θεοῦ γνῶσιν...περιτέτμηται τὴν καλὴν καὶ ὠφέλιμον περιτομὴν Just.*dial.*28.4(M.6.536C); ἡ δὲ ἐντολὴ τῆς περιτομῆς... τύπος ἦν τῆς ἀληθινῆς περιτομῆς ἣν περιετμήθημεν ἀπὸ τῆς πλάνης... διὰ...Χριστοῦ *ib.*41.4(564D); περιτέτμηται τὸν λογισμὸν Clem.*paed.*2.8 (p.202.22; M.8.485B); id.*ecl.*31(p.146.21; M.9.716A) cit. s. ἐλευθερόω; ~ονται τὰ ἤθη καὶ τὴν καρδίαν...οἱ φιλοσοφοῦντες...οὐ τῷ θεῷ δέ... ὅταν δὲ κατὰ τὸν ἐκκλησιαστικὸν κανόνα, κατὰ τὴν πρόθεσιν τῆς ὑγιοῦς διδασκαλίας κοινωνικὸς ᾖς, οὐ περιτέτμησαι μόνον, ἀλλὰ περιτέτμησαι τῷ θεῷ Or.*hom.5.14 in Jer.*(p.43.30ff.; M.13.317A); Meth.*symp.*7.6 (p.77.14; M.18.133A); τὰς καρδίας, φασί, ~όμεθα...οὐδεὶς γὰρ παρ' ὑμῖν κακοῦργος, οὐδεὶς μοχθηρός. οὕτω ~εσθε τὰς καρδίας Juln.Imp. ap.Cyr.*Juln.*10(6².354A); Esaias *or.*22.1(p.133; cf.M.40.1166B); effected in baptism, †Bas.*bapt.*2.1.2(2.652E; M.31.1580C); Jo.D.*f.o.*4.25 (M.94.1213C); **c.** of Mohammedan circumcision τούτους ~εσθαι σὺν γυναιξὶ νομοθετήσας id.*haer.*101(M.94.773A).

***περιτεύχομαι**, *equip oneself against*; c. dat., Cyr.*Jo.*3.4(4.271B).

περιτίθημι, **1.** *put upon*, met. περίβλημα πονηρὸν...περιτεθειμένον ...τοῖς Χριστιανῶν...διδάγμασι Just.*2apol.*13.1(M.6.465B); id.*dial.* 117.3(M.6.748A) cit. s. ἔνδυμα; εἶδος...ὃ ἐν τῇ ἀναστάσει περιτίθεται πάλιν τῇ ψυχῇ Meth.*res.*3.4(p.245.11; M.41.1092A); Gr.Nyss.*v.Mos.* (M.44.333A); Christol., Thdt.*eran.*1 suppl.10(4.267); med., *put on*; Christol., ‡Ath.*Ar.*4.33(p.82.6; M.26.517C) cit. s. ἀνακεράννυμι; λόγος τὴν ἀνθρωπείαν περιθέμενος φύσιν Thdt.*qu.25 in Num.*(1.238); ὁ πᾶσαν τὴν ἀνθρωπίνην φύσιν...περιθέμενος *cat.Lc.*10:35(p.88.12); **2.** *attribute*, Just.*2apol.*11.7(M.6.464A); Ath.*gent.*16(M.25.33C); ἀσθένειαν περιτιθέασι τῷ θεῷ id.*inc.*2.4(M.25.100B); **3.** *apply*, Cyr.*Ps.*16:12(M.69.817D); id.*Jo.*5.1(4.459D); **4.** *charge to* someone's *account* ὁ ἐλεῶν πένητα δανείζει θεῷ. θεῷ ἐδάνεισας· αὐτῷ περίθες Chrys.*hom.15.8 in Mt.*(7.199C; ἀπαίτει Gaume); **5.** *bring charge* against, Pall.*v.Chrys.*20(p.138.17; M.47.77); **6.** *propose* for consideration δύο σοι π. πρόσωπα Gr.Mag.*dial.*(tr.Zach.)3.17(M.*PL.*77.266A).

***περιτιμάω**, *honour exceedingly*, *Orac.Sib.*5.266.

περίτιμος, *very precious*, *Orac.Sib.*4.170.

Περίτ(τ)ιος, a Macedonian month Π. μηνὸς ἑξκαιδεκάτῃ, κατὰ Ῥωμαίους δὲ τῇ πρὸ δεκατεσσάρων Καλανδῶν Μαρτίων Eus.*m.P.* (p.936.7; M.20.1449A); Chrys.*nativ.*5(2.362B); corresponding to Hebr. eleventh month Shabat, Thdt.*Zach.*1:7(3.1597).

***περιτιτρώσκω**, *wound sorely*, Const.ap.Gel.Cyz.*h.e.*3.19.3(M.85.1345B).

περίτμημα, τό, *part cut off*, Valent. τὴν περιτομήν, ὀκταήμερον γινομένην, τὸ π. τῆς ἄνω ὀγδοάδος δηλοῦν Iren.*haer.*1.18.3(M.7.645B).

περιτομεύς, ὁ, *shoemaker's knife*, Thdt.*affect.*1(p.28.21; 4.719).

περιτομή, ἡ, **I.** *cutting off* τῶν τοῦ σώματος ἀκρωτηρίων τῇ π. τὴν τοῦ ὅλου σωτηρίαν ὠνήσασθαι Philost.*h.e.*12.3(M.65.608C).

II. *circumcision*;

A. practised by various peoples ἐρεῖς· καὶ μὴν περιτέτμηται ὁ λαὸς εἰς σφραγῖδα. ἀλλὰ καὶ πᾶς Σύρος καὶ Ἄραψ καὶ πάντες οἱ ἱερεῖς τῶν εἰδώλων. ἄρα οὖν κἀκεῖνοι ἐκ τῆς διαθήκης αὐτῶν εἰσιν. ἀλλὰ καὶ οἱ Αἰγύπτιοι ἐν π. εἰσιν *Barn.*9.6; τὸ δ' αἴτιον τῆς Ἰουδαίων π. οὐ ταὐτόν ἐστι τῷ αἰτίῳ τῆς Αἰγυπτίων π. ἢ Κόλχων· διὸ οὐχ ἡ αὐτὴ νομισθείη ἂν π. ... οὕτως δ' εἴη ἂν κατὰ τὰ διάφορα τῶν περιτεμνομένων δόγματα διάφορος ἡ π. Or.*Cels.*5.47(p.51.10; M.11.1253C); τῶν Αἰγυπτίων οἱ ἱερεῖς περιτέμνονται, ἀλλ' ἐκείνη ἡ π. εἰδώλοις π. ἐστιν καὶ οὐκ ἔστιν τῷ θεῷ γινομένη π. id.*hom.5.14 in Jer.*(p.43.22; M.13.316A); οἱ εἰδωλολάτραι καὶ ἱερεῖς τῶν Αἰγυπτίων π. ἔχουσιν· ἀλλὰ καὶ οἱ Σαρακηνοὶ οἱ καὶ Ἰσμαηλῖται π. ἔχουσι, καὶ Σαμαρεῖται [καὶ Ἰουδαῖοι] καὶ Ἰουμαῖοι καὶ Ὁμηρῖται. τούτων δὲ οἱ πλείους οὐ διὰ νόμον τοῦτο ποιοῦσιν, ἀλλὰ ἀλόγῳ τινὶ συνηθείᾳ Epiph.*haer.*30.33 (p.379.26; M.41.469A); παρὰ μὲν γὰρ τοῖς Ἰουδαίοις ἄριστον ἡ π.· Αἰγυπτίων δέ, τοὺς ἱερωτέρους τῶν τεμενιτῶν, καὶ...Χαλδαίους καὶ Σαρακηνούς, οὐκ ἀπαράδεκτον ποιεῖσθαί φησιν αὐτήν Cyr.*Juln.*9(6².298B); Moses' circumcision explains his recognition as a Hebrew by Pharaoh's daughter; Egyptians therefore did not then practise it, but imitated Mosaic practice later, Thdt.*qu.68 in Gen.*(1.82); id.*qu.3 in Ex.*(1.120); second circumcision of Samaritan convert to Judaism, *Chron.Pasch.*p.266(M.92.652B).

B. Jewish; **1.** in gen., Ign.*Philad.*6.1; οἱ Σικάριοι διὰ τὴν π. ἀκρωτηριάζοντες παρὰ τοὺς καθεστῶτας νόμους καὶ τὰ Ἰουδαίοις συγκεχωρημένα μόνοις ἀναιροῦνται...ἀρκεῖ δειχθεῖσα ἡ π. πρὸς ἀναίρεσιν τοῦ πεπονθότος αὐτήν Or.*Cels.*2.13(p.142.11; M.11.821A); κατὰ διαδοχὴν τὴν π. φυλάξαντας *ib.*2.52(p.175.17; 880B); **2.** as sign or seal of covenant-relationship to God π. μὲν τοῦ Ἀβραὰμ ἔχουσιν ...ἐπὶ σώματος...σφραγῖδα...ὑπομνήσεως χάριν καὶ ἐλέγχου, εἰς τὸ ἐμμένειν τῇ τοῦ πατρὸς αὐτῶν θεοσεβείᾳ Epiph.*haer.*8.4(p.189.8; M.41.209B); ἐγένετο γὰρ ἡ φαινομένη π. ἕνεκεν δισταγμοῦ τοῦ Ἀβραάμ... δι' ὃν εἶπεν, εἰ τῷ ἑκατονταετεῖ υἱὸς γεννηθήσεται, ἵνα μὴ...τὸ σπέρμα ...ἐπιλάθηται θεοῦ τῶν πατέρων αὐτοῦ, ἐπέθηκεν αὐτῷ καὶ αὐτοῖς τὴν ἔνσαρκον π., ἵνα ὁρῶντες...μὴ ἀρνῶνται αὐτόν *ib.*30.28(p.371.22;

453C); π. ... οὐχ ὡς πρὸς τὴν τῆς ψυχῆς σωτηρίαν συντελέσαι τι ταύτης δυναμένης, ἀλλ' ἵνα ὥσπερ σημεῖόν τι καὶ σφραγῖδα περιφέρωσι, δεῖγμα τῆς οἰκείας εὐγνωμοσύνης Chrys.*hom.27.2 in Gen.*(4.258C); σημείου χάριν τὴν π. ... διατάττεται...οὐδενὸς ἑτέρου χάριν...ἢ ὥστε ἐπίσημον εἶναι τὸν λαὸν τὸν αὐτῷ ἀνακείμενον *ib.39.4*(400D); Isid.Pel. *epp.*2.115(M.78.556D); Thdt.*qu.68 in Gen.*(1.81); οὐκ ἄρα διαθήκη ἡ π., ἀλλὰ σημεῖον καὶ σφραγὶς τῆς διαθήκης Proc.G.*Gen.*17:8(M.87.356C); τὴν θείαν σφραγῖδα, τουτέστιν ἡ π. Cosm.Ind.*top.*2(p.55.25; M.88.76C); Jo.D.*f.o.*4.25(M.94.1212B); **3.** as sign of separation from other peoples, Just.*dial.*16.2(M.6.509A); cf.Iren.*haer.*3.12.11(M.7.905A); Isid.Pel.*epp.*2.115(M.78.556D); Thdt.*qu.68 in Gen.*(1.81); Jo.D.*f.o.*4.25(M.94.1213A); **4.** as sign of Abraham's faith, hence not a means of justification, cf.Iren.*haer.*4.16.1,2(M.7.1015A,1016A); cf.*ib.*4.25.1(1051A); Chrys.*hom.8.2 in Rom.*(9.500C); ἡ π. ἐδόθη διὰ τρεῖς αἰτίας ταύτας, ὥστε σημεῖον εἶναι πίστεως καὶ τοῦ Ἀβραμιαίου γένους δηλωτικὸν καὶ σύμβολον καὶ αἴνιγμα πολιτείας καθαρᾶς ...ὥστε οὐχ ὡς δικαιοσύνης ποιητικὴ ἐδόθη, ἀλλὰ σφραγὶς καὶ σημεῖον τῆς ἐκ πίστεως δικαιοσύνης Sever.*Rom.*4:11(p.217.11); Cyr.*Juln.*10(6^2.351E); οὐ δικαιοσύνη...ἐστιν ἡ π., ἀλλὰ μαρτυρία δικαιοσύνης, καὶ σφραγὶς καὶ σημεῖον τῆς πίστεως Thdt.*Rom.*4:11 (3.48); **5.** as scriptural warrant for importance of chastity Meth.*symp.*1.3(p.11.4; M.18.41B) cit. s. περιτέμνω; **6.** its practice due to misunderstanding of nature of spiritual circumcision π. γὰρ εἴρηκεν οὐ σαρκὸς γενηθῆναι· ἀλλὰ παρέβησαν, ὅτι ἄγγελος πονηρὸς ἐσόφιζεν αὐτούς *Barn.*9.4; Or.*hom.12.12 in Jer.*(p.99.26; M.13.396B); **7.** Abraham's circumcision as type of Christ Ἀβραὰμ πρῶτος περιτομὴν δοὺς ἐν πνεύματι προβλέψας εἰς τὸν Ἰησοῦν περιέτεμεν, λαβὼν τριῶν γραμμάτων δόγματα [i.e. the 318 men circumcised by him signifying Jesus (ιη) and the Cross (τ)] *Barn.*9.7; **8.** as sign or type of spiritual circumcision, Just.*dial.*41.4(M.6.564D); cf. *secundum carnem circumcisio circumcisionem significabat spiritalem*, Iren.*haer.*4.16.1(M.7.1015B); Or.*princ.*2.6.7(p.147.5; M.11.215B); ἡ π. λεγομένη σημεῖον τῆς παρὰ τῷ Παύλῳ δηλουμένης ἐν τῷ 'ἡμεῖς γάρ ἐσμεν ἡ π.' id.*comm.in Mt.*12.4(p.73.15; M.13.980D); ἔφθασεν ἡ δόξα τοῦ θεοῦ, ἵνα δείξῃ π. μὲν παρερχομένην τὴν ἔνσαρκον καὶ τύπῳ ὑπηρετήσασαν ἄχρι χρόνου, τὴν δὲ ἐν σαρκὶ ἀκροβυστίαν ἐν πνεύματι ἔχουσαν μείζονα π., θεωροῦσαν Χριστόν Epiph.*haer.*30.27(p.371.5; M.41.453B); *ib.*30.33(p.379.13; 468D); Chrys.*hom.33.2 in Jo.*(8.192A); ἐθεσμοθέτει γὰρ ὁ θεὸς τὸ χρῆναι πληροῦν τὴν π., διὰ σαρκικῶν... παραδειγμάτων προαναφαίνων τὰ νοητά Cyr.*glaph.Gen.*3(1.80B); τί τὸ χρῆμα τῆς π.;...καλὸν γε...καὶ ὀνησιφόρον, εἰ τύπος εἶναι πιστεύοιτο πράγματος νοητοῦ id.*Juln.*10(6^2.353A); προανεκηρύττετο δὲ καὶ διὰ τῆς σαρκίνης π. ἡ ἐν πνεύματι· κατὰ γὰρ τὴν ὀγδόην ἐπράττετο καθ' ἣν ἀνέστη Χριστός...καὶ τοῦ πνεύματος ὥσπερ ἀπαρχὴν τοῖς ἰδίοις ἐνεφύσησε μαθηταῖς Proc.G.*Gen.*17:16(M.87.361C); Gnost. ἐκκλησίας ...ἐπουρανίου...ἀπόρροιαν εἶναι τὴν ἐπὶ γῆς ἐκκλησίαν, καὶ περιτομῆς τινος ἐν καθαρσίῳ τινὶ ἐκεῖ γεγενημένης σύμβολον εἶναι τὴν ἐν τῷ νόμῳ γεγραμμένην Or.*Cels.*6.35(p.104.22; M.11.1349B); **9.** useless except as sign of obedience, Cyr.*hom.pasch.*6(5^2.73C); cf.Thdt.*Rom.* 2:24(3.34); **10.** its inefficacy to justify indicated by uncircumcision of the righteous before Abraham, Just.*dial.*23.1(M.6.525C); ἡ π. οὐ δικαιοῖ· Νῶε ἄνθρωπος δίκαιος...ἦν ἄνευ τῆς π., Ἐνὼχ μετετέθη ...ἀπερίτμητος ὢν *Dial.Ath.et Zacch.*126(p.62); Chrys.*hom.27.3 in Gen.*(4.258D); εἰ γὰρ καὶ Ἄβελ καὶ Ἐνὼχ...πρὸ τοῦ ὀφθῆναι ἢ λεχθῆναι π. ηὐδοκίμησαν, οὐκ εὐδοκιμήσεώς ἐστιν ὑπόθεσις, ἀλλ' ἢ ἄρα εὐδοκιμήσεως σφραγίς Isid.Pel.*epp.*2.115(M.78.556D); **11.** as part of old dispensation superseded by gospel π. ... κατήργηται *Barn.*9.4; τὴν τῆς π. ἀλαζονείαν, τὸ...περὶ τὰς βρώσεις...ψοφοδεές...οὐδενὸς ἄξια λόγου *Diogn.*4.1; ἡ ἀνόσιον μὲν τὸ ἀφιστάνειν σωματικῆς π. ... μετατιθέναι δὲ τὸν νοῦν ἐπὶ νόμον θεοῦ...πνευματικόν; Or.*Cels.*2.7(p.133.13; M.11.805A); αὐτοῖς...ἐπιτελεῖν ἐνομοθέτει...σώματος περιτομὴν...ἀλλ' οὐ βασιλείας οὐρανῶν ἐπαγγελίας Eus.*e.th.*2.20(p.127.13; M.24.949C); Chrys.*comm.in Gal.*1:7(10.668B); cf.*ib.*5:1,2(713A,B); **12.** as type of baptism, or as replaced (as an ordinance) by baptism τίς οὖν ἔτι μοι περιτομῆς λόγος...ἁγίῳ πνεύματι βεβαπτισμένῳ; Just.*dial.*29.1 (M.6.537A); οὐ ταύτην τὴν κατὰ σάρκα παρελάβομεν π., ἀλλὰ πνευματικήν, ἣν Ἐνὼχ καὶ οἱ ὅμοιοι ἐφύλαξαν· ἡμεῖς δὲ διὰ τοῦ βαπτίσματος αὐτὴν...ἐλάβομεν *ib.*43.2(568A); baptism being typified by the second circumcision under Joshua, cf.Or.*hom.5.6 in Jos.*(p.320.15; M.12.851D); Cyr.H.*catech.*5.6; τὴν ἀχειροποίητον π. ἀναβάλλῃ ἐν τῇ ἀπεκδύσει τῆς σαρκός, ἐν τῷ βαπτίσματι τελειουμένην Bas.*hom.*13.2 (2.115A; M.31.428A); Gr.Nyss.*Ps.*6(M.44.609A); ἐκεῖ γὰρ π. σαρκική, ὑπηρετήσασα χρόνῳ ἕως τῆς μεγάλης π., τουτέστι τοῦ βαπτίσματος τοῦ περιτέμνοντος ἡμᾶς ἀπὸ ἁμαρτημάτων καὶ σφραγίσαντος ἡμᾶς εἰς ὄνομα θεοῦ Epiph.*haer.*8.6(p.192.18; M.41.213C); ἡ διὰ τοῦ βαπτίσματος π. τὸν χωρισμὸν ἀκριβέστερον καθίστησι, καὶ τὴν διαίρεσιν τῶν πιστῶν καὶ τῶν οὐ τοιούτων...ὅπερ γὰρ ἐκεῖ ἐργάζεται ἡ π. εἰς τὴν τῆς σαρκὸς ἀπόθεσιν, τοῦτο ἐνταῦθα τὸ βάπτισμα εἰς τὴν τῶν ἁμαρτημάτων ἀπόθεσιν Chrys.*hom.39.5 in Gen.*(4.403C); ἡ δὲ ἡμετέρα π., ἡ τοῦ βαπτίσματος λέγω χάρις *ib.40.4*(409D); Ἰουδαῖοι μὲν γὰρ εἶχον σφραγῖδα τὴν π., ἡμεῖς δὲ τὸν ἀρραβῶνα τοῦ πνεύματος id.*hom.3.7 in 2Cor.*(10.454B); cf.id.*hom.2.2 in Eph.*(11.11A); id.*hom.6.2 in Col.* (11.367C); circumcision on eighth day prefigured Resurrection, and baptism is figure of Resurrection, ‡Chrys.*occurs.*(2.812C); ἀντὶ βαπτίσματος γὰρ τῇ π. Ἰουδαῖοι ἐκέχρηντο Isid.Pel.*epp.*1.125(M.78.265D); Jo.D.*f.o.*4.25(M.94.1213C).

C. spiritual ἡ δὲ ἐντολὴ τῆς π. ... τύπος ἦν τῆς ἀληθινῆς π., ἣν περιετμήθημεν ἀπὸ τῆς πλάνης...διὰ τοῦ ἀπὸ νεκρῶν ἀναστάντος... Χριστοῦ Just.*dial.*41.4(M.6.364D); represented in Jos.5:2 ἡμεῖς οἱ περιτμηθέντες πετρίναις μαχαίραις τὴν δευτέραν π. ὑμῶν μὲν γὰρ ἡ πρώτη διὰ σιδήρου γέγονε...ἡμῶν δὲ ἡ π. ... διὰ λίθων ἀκροτόμων, τοῦτ' ἔστι διὰ τῶν λόγων τῶν διὰ τῶν ἀποστόλων τοῦ ἀκρογωνιαίου λίθου *ib.*114.4(740B); τὴν ἐκ πίστεως τῆς καρδίας π. Clem.*str.*7.9 (p.39.19; M.9.476A); cf.Or.*hom.3.4 in Gen.*(p.43.20; M.12.178B); cf. *dignam circumcisionem verbi dei in auribus...et in labiis et in corde*, *ib.3.5*(p.45.24; 180A); cf. *circumcisio, qua ecclesia...aures suorum circumcidit infantum*, *ib.*(p.46.6; 180A); cf.id.*hom.8.3 in Lev.*(p.398.25; M.12.496C); exeg. Jos.5:2, cf. *si ergo secundam hanc circumcisionem acceperis vitiorum et absciderís abs te omne vitium...tunc a te Aegypti abstergentur opprobria et...hereditatem regni coelestis accipies*, id.*hom.1.7 in Jos.*(p.296.2; M.12.833A); cf. *abjecit idololatriae errores...haec est circumcisio prima per legem. si vero is veniat a lege et prophetis ad evangelicam fidem, tunc accipit etiam secundam circumcisionem per petram qui est Christus*, *ib.5.5*(p.318.6; 850A); cf. *nemo...si fideliter Jordanis fluenta digressus est, si secunda per evangelium circumcisione purgatus est, praeteritorum metuat opprobria delictorum*, *ib.5.6*(p.319.6; 850C); cf. *misit enim Jesum qui omnes...circumcideret...non filium Nave...non enim vera...circumcisione ille populum circumcidit, sed...dominum...hic enim est, qui vere a nobis pollutionem carnis abscidit*, *ib.6.1*(p.321.14; 852C); ὁ δὲ Κάρμηλος ἐπίγνωσις περιτομῆς ἑρμηνεύεται· γινώσκει δὲ π. ὁ μετὰ παρρησίας λέγειν δυνάμενος 'ἡμεῖς ἐσμεν ἡ π.'· ἀπὸ δὲ τῆς κεφαλῆς, τουτέστι Χριστοῦ, ἐπίγνωσις πνευματικῆς ἐγεννήθη π. id.*schol.in Cant.* 7:4–5(M.17.281D); id.*hom.5.14 in Jer.*(p.44.7; M.13.317B); *Dial. Ath.et Zacch.*125(p.62); μήτε δὲ περιτέμνεσθαι τὴν σάρκα, ἀρκεῖσθαι δὲ πιστοῖς τὴν τῆς καρδίας π. ἐν πνεύματι *Const.App.*6.14.5; π. ἐν τῷ τοίχῳ, καὶ π. ἐν τῇ πέτρᾳ...πλὴν ὅσον πνευματικὴ ἡ πέτρα, χοϊκὸς δ' ὁ τοῖχος. ἡ δ' εὐαγγελικὴ πέτρα τὸν σαρκώδη τῶν νοημάτων πηλὸν οὐκ ἔχει. ἀλλὰ καὶ π. λαμβάνει ὁ ἄνθρωπος, καὶ ὅλος ὑγιὴς μένει Gr.Nyss. *hom.5 in Cant.*(M.44.877C); Epiph.*haer.*30.27(p.371.7; M.41.453B); ἡ π. μέγα...ὅταν ἔχῃ τὴν ἔνδον π. Chrys.*hom.6.2 in Rom.*(9.474C); π. μία μὲν ἡ ἐν τῇ σαρκί, δευτέρα δὲ ἡ ἀπὸ προαιρέσεως...περιετμήθη τις ὀκταήμερος· αὕτη σαρκὸς π. ... αὕτη διανοίας π., ἣν μάλιστα ὁ Παῦλος ζητεῖ, μᾶλλον δὲ καὶ ὁ νόμος *ib.*(475Cf.); prefigured by Jos.5:2, Cyr. *ador.*2(1.78E); οὐ γὰρ διὰ τῆς κατὰ νόμον π., τουτέστι τῆς κατὰ σάρκα καὶ αἰσθητῆς ἀπελήλαται θάνατος, ἀλλὰ διὰ τῆς ἐν Χριστῷ, διὰ πνεύματος, ἣν ἐνήργηκεν ἐν τῷ πρωτοτόκῳ καὶ νέῳ λαῷ...ἣν ἡ νοητὴ Σεπφώρα, τουτέστιν ἡ ἐκκλησία...περιτέτμηκε ψήφῳ id.*glaph.Ex.*2 (1.307D); ref. Jos.5:2, id.*Jo.*4.7(4.436D); ὁ...τὴν ἐν πνεύματι π. διὰ τοῦ εὐαγγελικοῦ δεχόμενος κηρύγματος, αὐτῷ...τῷ πάντων δεσπότῃ, οὐ τῷ νομικῷ γράμματι περιτέμνεται id.*hom.pasch.*6(5^2.73B); ref. Jos.5:2, cf.id.*hom.div.*12(5^2.387C); Thdt.*qu.3 in Jos.*(1.306); id. *Rom.*2:25(3.35); ref. Jos.5:2, Proc.G.*Num.*14:21(M.87.832B); Max. *cap.theol.*1.36(M.90.1097A,B); π. ἐστιν ἡ περὶ γένεσιν τῆς κατὰ ψυχὴν ἐμπαθοῦς ἀπόθεσις διαθέσεως. περιτομὴ περιτομῆς ἐστιν ἡ καὶ αὐτῶν τῶν κατὰ ψυχὴν περὶ τὴν γένεσιν φυσικῶν κινημάτων παντελὴς ἀποβολὴ καὶ περιαίρεσις *ib.*1.40,41(1097C,D); πνευματικὴν δὲ π. ὁ λόγος οἶδε καλεῖν, τὴν τῆς ἐμπαθοῦς σχέσεως πρὸς σῶμα τῆς ψυχῆς ἐκτομὴν *ib.*1.85 (1216A); *ib.*5.41(1365A); π. μὲν γάρ ἐστιν ἡ τῆς σωματικῆς ἡδονῆς, καὶ τῶν περιττῶν καὶ οὐκ ἀναγκαίων ἀπόθεσις Jo.D.*f.o.*4.23(M.94.1205B).

D. Christ's circumcision ὥσπερ οὖν συναπεθάνομεν αὐτῷ ἀποθνήσκοντι τότε, οὕτω περιετμήθημεν αὐτῷ περιτμηθέντι τότε· καὶ μετὰ τὴν π. αὐτὴν γέγονεν οἰκονομία ἡ διὰ τοῦ προτέρου καθαρισμοῦ. διὰ τοῦτο ἡμεῖς οὐκέτι περιτεμνόμεθα, ὅτε ἡ π. αὐτοῦ δι' ἡμᾶς γεγένηται Or.*hom. 14 in Lc.*(p.95.2); cf. *ejus circumcisio satis coangustabit eos qui ex diverso sunt. spiritale enim corpus quomodo poterat circumcidi ferro terreno?* id.*fr.in Gal.*(M.14.1296C); as proof of reality of his humanity, ‡Ath.*Apoll.*1.4(M.26.1100A); τὴν π. ἔπαυσεν, εἰς ἑαυτὸν πληρώσας· αὐτὸς γὰρ ἦν ᾧ ἀπέκειτο *Const.App.*6.23.4; cf. περιετμήθη ἀληθινῶς, καὶ οὐ δοκήσει...ἦλθε γὰρ πληρῶσαι τὸν νόμον Epiph.*haer.* 30.27(p.370.8; M.41.452C); περιετμήθη...ἵνα δείξῃ ἐν ἀληθείᾳ σάρκα ἑαυτὸν ἀνειληφέναι...ἵνα δείξῃ, ὡς οὐκ ἦν ὁμοούσιον τὸ σῶμα τῇ θεότητι...ἵνα βεβαιώσῃ ἣν πάλαι ἔδωκε π. δικαίως ὑπηρετήσασαν ἕως τῆς αὐτοῦ παρουσίας *ib.*30.28(p.371.16; 453C); μὴ ἐν τῇ π. αὐτοῦ ὁμοιοῦ...παρήνεγκε γὰρ ὁ κύριος τὸν ταύτης χρόνον...καὶ ἐπλήρωσε δοὺς τὴν τελείαν π. ... ὅλον σῶμα σφραγίσας, καὶ περιτεμὼν ἀπὸ ἁμαρτίας *ib.*30.34(p.380.28; 469D); ἐδεξάμην ἐν τῇ σαρκί μου π., ἣν ἐγὼ πρῴην ἐνομοθέτησα, ἵνα τὴν ἀχειροποίητον ἐπεισάγω π. ‡Chrys.*praecurs.*1.2(2.807D); Andr.Cr.*or.*6(M.97.913B).

E. Timothy's circumcision προσδοποιῶν...τῇ ἀναιρέσει τῆς π. καὶ ἀνοίγων ὁδὸν τῇ διδασκαλίᾳ τοῦ Τιμοθέου, περιέθηκεν αὐτῷ π., ἵνα ἀνέλῃ π. Chrys.*hom.4.4 in Ac.princ.*(3.86C); id.*hom.34.4 in Ac.*(9.265B); cf.Isid.Pel.*epp.*4.68(M.78.1125B).

F. practised by Ebionites and Cerinthians αὐχοῦσι δὲ πάλιν π. ἔχοντες, καὶ σεμνύονται δῆθεν εἶναι ταύτην σφραγῖδα ἡγούμενοι, καὶ χαρακτῆρα τῶν τε πατριαρχῶν καὶ δικαίων τῶν κατὰ τὸν νόμον πεπολιτευμένων, δι' οὓς ἐξισοῦσθαι ἐκείνοις νομίζουσι, καὶ δῆτα ἀπ' αὐτοῦ τοῦ Χριστοῦ τὴν σύστασιν ταύτης βούλονται φέρειν Epiph.*haer.*30.26(p.368.8; M.41.449B); *ib.*30.33(p.379.25; 469A); *ib.*30.34(p.380.27; 469D).

***περιτόμιος**, *circumcised* π. σάρκα Anast.S.*hod.*14(M.89.245C).

περιτόναιον, τό, plur., *projecting beams at stern of ship*, Epiph.*haer.*61.3(p.383.8; M.41.1041D).

περιτορνεύω, *smooth away*, Nil.*exerc.*28(M.79.756C).

***περιτραπέζιος,** *being round a table*, Cyr.*Jo.*11.12(4.1012B).

περιτραχήλιος, 1. *round the neck* ὁ δὲ ἐποχὴν ποιῶν τοῦ νοῦ μὴ παραρίπτεσθαι ἐν τῇ...κακίᾳ, ὡς π. κόσμον προξενεῖ λαβεῖν τῇ...ψυχῇ ἄφθαρτον Or.*exp.in Pr.*28:17(M.17.244D); †Bas.*Is.*126(1.467A; M.30.321C); Gr.Nyss.*hom.3 in Cant.*(M.44.816B); Socr.*h.e.*3.1.35(M.67.373C); οἷά τινα κόσμον π. τὸν λαμπρὸν κατ' ἀρετὴν βίον Proc.G.*Pr.*1:8(M.87.1228C); **2.** neut. as subst.; **a.** *necklace*, Or.*schol.in Cant.*7:1(M.17.281B); **b.** *stole* τὸ π. ἐστι τὸ φακεώλιον, μεθ' οὗ ἐπεφέρετο ὑπὸ τοῦ ἀρχιερέως δεδεμένος, καὶ συρόμενος ἐπὶ τὸ πρόσθεν ἐπὶ τῷ τραχήλῳ ὁ Χριστός ‡Germ.CP *contempl.*(M.98.393C).

***περιτραχύνω,** *make rough*; pass., Gr.Nyss.*virg.*14(p.310.27; M.46.384A); id.*nativ.*(M.46.1133B).

περιτρέμω, 1. *quiver*, Gr.Naz.*or.*31.32(p.188.9; M.36.169C); **2.** *tremble*, Chrys.*comm.in Gal.*4:18(10.708B).

***περίτρεπτος,** *liable to be overthrown*, Eus.*Ps.*127 proem.(M.24.21A).

περιτρέπ-ω, 1. *turn round* upon; **a.** trans. ~ουσιν ἡμῖν...τὸ ὄνειδος Bas.*ep.*135.2(3.359B; M.32.872C); Chrys.*hom.27.1 in 2Cor.*(10.627A); εἰς αὐτοὺς...περιτραπήσεται λόγος Cyr.*Jo.*10.2(4.915A); **b.** intrans. ἡμῖν περιτρέψαντες λέγουσιν Bas.*ep.*134.1(3.357B; M.868C); **2.** *turn* to; **a.** trans. εἰς χαρὰν περιτρέψει τὴν κατήφειαν *cat.Lc.*2:36(p.25.13); **b.** intrans. οὐ γὰρ ἔγνω τὸν φύσει βασιλέα, ἀλλ' εἰς ἕτερον τὸν μὴ φύσει...~ει ‡Chrys.*pasch.*1(8.253D); **3.** *turn* into πάντα εἰς ἄλληλα περιχωρεῖ τε καὶ ~εται Gr.Naz.*or.*22.4(M.35.1136B); **4.** *convert* ~ει δὲ [sc. θεός] τοὺς τοιούτους, μονονουχὶ καὶ ἀνασειράζων...εἰς τὸ...τελοῦν εἰς ὄνησιν αὐτοῖς Cyr.*Is.*1.6(2.172A); **5.** *pervert* εἰς ἀδοξίαν τοὺς ἀνθρώπους ~ουσιν [sc. πανηγύρεις] Tat.*orat.*22(p.24.20; M.6.856A); Clem.*prot.*5(p.51.4; M.8.172A); Or.*enarr.in Job* 2:9(M.17.61A); **6. a.** trans., *upset, overthrow*, Clem.*prot.*2(p.20.4; M.8.97A); Ἱερουσαλὴμ...ἐρημίας ἐπ' ἔσχατα περιτραπεῖσα Eus.*v.C.*3.33(p.93.11; M.20.1093B); Jo.D.*hom.*1.6(M.96.556B); met. τῷ Χριστῷ διαλεγόμενος [sc. διάβολος] ~εται Chrys.*hom.13.3 in Mt.*(7.171E); id.*hom.17.2 in 1Tim.*(11.650C); **b.** intrans., *stagger and fall*, Niceph.Ur.*v.Sym.*180(M.86.3153A).

περιτρίβω, *break in pieces*, Gr.Nyss.*v.Mos.*(M.44.393A).

περίτριμμα, τό, *street idler*; of wandering monk, Pall.*v.Chrys.*6(p.34.6; M.47.21).

***περιτριχόομαι,** *be covered over* ἐν τῷ κρυπτῷ δὲ περιτετρίχωται καὶ περιπέφρακται, καὶ περιτετείχισται...ἡ ψυχή Mac.Aeg.*hom.*21.2(M.34.656D).

περίτρομος, *quivering*, Gr.Naz.*carm.*1.1.3.66(M.37.413A).

περιτροπή, ἡ, *turning round, revolution, change*; hence *interchange* μηδαμῶς συμφύραντες τῶν λεγομένων [sc. οὐσία, φύσις, πρόσωπον] τὴν ἔννοιαν, διὰ τῆς τούτων εἰς ἀλλήλας π. καὶ συγχύσεως Max.*ep.*15(M.91.549A); *ib.*(553A).

περιτροχάζω, *gad about in*, c. acc., Alex.Al.*ep.Alex.*1(p.20.15; M.18.549B); Nil.*epp.*1.292(M.79.189B).

***περιτροχάς, ἡ,** *gad-about woman* ἡ χήρα μὴ π. ἢ ῥεμβομένη *Const.App.*3.6.4; ‡Ign.*Philad.*4.

περίτροχος, *spherical*, Nonn.*par.Jo.*9:11(M.43.825B).

περιτρύζω, *twitter round about*, Gr.Naz.*or.*15.8(M.35.925A).

***περιτρυχόω,** *wear out, debilitate*, ‡Jo.D.*ep.Thphl.*20(M.95.372B).

περιτρύχω, *gnaw*, Pall.*h.Laus.*19(22; M.34.1066D).

περιτρώγ-ω, *nibble at*, met. ποιηταὶ τοὺς ἐκλεκτοὺς παρὰ σφίσι θεοειδέας προσαγορεύειν δοκοῦσι...τὸ κατ' εἰκόνα καὶ ὁμοίωσιν ~οντες Clem.*str.*4.26(p.324.18; M.8.1380C).

περιτυγχάνω, 1. *light upon, encounter*; c. acc., Thphn.*chron.*p.286(M.108.704A); **2.** *discover, find to be* μαλθακωτέρῳ...περιτεύξεται τῷ φόβῳ Cyr.*Jo.*10.2(4.915D).

περιτυλίσσω, *wrap up*, Thdr.Lect.*fr.*4(M.86.224A).

περιτυπ-όω, *impress in outline* κηρῷ τὸ...εἶδος ~οῦται Gr.Nyss.*fat.*(M.45.153B); id.*Apoll.*20(M.45.1164C).

***περιύμνητος,** *far-famed*, Eus.*d.e.*1.6(p.27.9; M.22.56A).

περιυπνίζω, *be fulfilled in waking reality*; of a dream, Rom.Mel.(*SBBAW* 1898² p.147).

περιυφαίν-ω, pass., *be composed* συμμέτρως ταῖς οἰκείαις ἀρχαῖς ~ομένου τοῦ σώματος Bas.*hom.in Ps.*1(1.91E; M.29.213D); Melet.*nat.hom.*synops.(M.64.1085C).

***περιφαιδρύνω,** *make illustrious*, Bas.Sel.*enc.in Andr.*1(M.28.1101B).

περιφάνεια, ἡ, 1. *conspicuousness, openness to view, publicity* ἐπέβη...πρότερον, ἀλλ' οὐδέποτε μετὰ τοσαύτης π. Chrys.*hom.66.1 in Mt.*(7.654C); Cyr.*Jo.*3.4(4.286A); Bas.Sel.*or.*21.4(M.85.264A); **2.** *notoriety*, Chrys.*hom.15.1 in 1Cor.*(10.126C); id.*hom.1.2 in 1Tim.*(11.551B); **3.** *splendour, pomp* πλοῦτον...π. βίου Bas.*hom.in Ps.*1(1.92C; M.29.216C); δυναστεία καὶ π. id.*hom.*21.5(2.167C; M.31.349B); τὰς ἐν τῷ κόσμῳ π. Gr.Nyss.*hom.2 in Cant.*(M.44.804D); ‡Nil.*perist.*4.16(M.79.848A); **4.** *glory, honour*, Hipp.*fr.49 in Gen.*(p.70.1); ref. second advent in contrast with Inc., Chrys.*hom.76.2 in Mt.*(7.735A); id.*hom.88.3 in Jo.*(8.525B); τὴν ἀπὸ τῶν δεσμῶν π. id.*hom.33.6 in 1Cor.*(10.307E); Thdt.*Rom.*10:19(3.116); Zach.Mit.*opif.*(M.85.1073A); **5.** *eminence, distinction*, Bas.*ep.*75(3.170D; M.32.449A); Cyr.*Jo.*1.7(4.61A).

περιφανής, 1. *bright, splendid* ἱμάτια π. Chrys.*hom.52.4 in Jo.*(8.309C); id.*hom.10.5 in Phil.*(11.282A); π. ... ἥλιος *M.Ner.et Ach.*8(p.7.26); **2.** *eminent, distinguished*, Dion.Al.ap.Eus.*h.e.*6.41.11(M.20.608B); γένει τε καὶ πλούτῳ π. ἀνήρ Eus.*h.e.*7.15.1(676C); Chrys.*hom.13.2 in Jo.*(8.74C); ἀνδραγαθία περιφανεστέρα *ib.88.1*(526E); Nil.*epp.*1.243(M.79.172D); Bas.Sel.*v.Thecl.*1(M.85.540D); **3.** *conspicuous, apparent* σημεῖον...π. ἐν τῷ προσώπῳ μαλακίας Clem.*paed.*3.11(p.276.27; M.8.649B).

περιφέρεια, ἡ, 1. *circumference*, Meth.*symp.*8.14(p.100.8; M.18.164A); Isid.Pel.*epp.*2.228(M.78.665C); **2.** *rounded shape, sphere*, *Hom.Clem.*6.4; in pagan cosmology ἔνδοθεν γὰρ τῆς π. ζῷόν τι ἀρρενόθηλυ εἰδοποιεῖται προνοίᾳ τοῦ ἐνόντος ἐν αὐτῷ θείου πνεύματος *ib.*6.5; **3.** *outline* οὐχ ὅσιον οἴεσθε μείζονα ὑπάρχειν τοῦ υἱοῦ τὸν πατέρα ἢ π. ἢ ὄγκῳ ‡Caes.Naz.*dial.*18(M.38.873); **4.** *curved line*, Philost.*h.e.*3.11(M.65.497D); **5.** *encircling, encompassing* τὰ δὲ ῥιπίδια καὶ οἱ διάκονοι ἐμφαίνουσι...τὴν τῶν...χερουβὶμ π. ‡Bas.*h.myst.*60(p.394.12).

περιφέρ-ω, 1. *bear, carry about*; of believer bearing God in his heart, Chrys.*hom.26.3 in Heb.*(12.241A); ‡Proc.G.*Pr.*10:23(M.87.1320B); of man bearing about divine image, *Hom.Clem.*10.7; faithful bearing seal ἡ ψυχή...λαβοῦσα σφράγισμα τὰ στίγματα τοῦ Χριστοῦ ~ει Clem.*exc.Thdot.*86(p.133.7; M.9.697B); in internal disposition of Persons of Trin. ἡ...τριὰς...τὴν αὐτὴν καὶ μίαν μόνην θεότητα πανταχοῦ ~ουσα Didym.(‡Bas.)*Eun.*5(1.317C; M.29.760D); **2.** *wear*; med., *Mir.Geo.*11(p.111.9); **3.** *boast of, vaunt* Μανιχαίους τὸ ὄνομα τοῦ Χριστοῦ ~οντας Gr.Nyss.*Maced.*15(M.45.1320B); ἐπὶ τῆς γλώττης αὐτὰ ~ων Chrys.*hom.3.5 in Mt.*(7.41B); ὁ...~όμενος Πλάτων id.*hom.2.5 in Rom.*(9.443B) = Nil.*epp.*2.145(M.79.268A); **4.** pass., *be carried to and fro, be unstable*; cf.Eph.4:14, Or.*Jo.*32.5(p.433.29; M.14.753B); Ath.*Ar.*1.34(M.26.81B); Chrys.*hom.37.1 in Mt.*(7.415A); **5.** pass., *stagger* in drunkenness, *ib.*57.4(582B); id.*hom.13.10 in Rom.*(9.573D); of a punch-drunk boxer, id.*hom.13.3 in Mt.*(7.172A); met. ~ομένην...τὴν Καππαδοκίαν Bas.*ep.*98.2(3.192E; M.32.497A); **6.** *refer, attribute* εἰς αὐτὸν ἐκεῖνο τὸ λόγιον ~εται Eus.*p.e.*11.10(527A; M.21.873B).

περιφθείρομαι, *wander about in destitution*; of Christ, ref. flight into Egypt, Cels.ap.Or.*Cels.*1.61(p.112.28; M.11.773A).

περιφλέγ-ω, pass., *be burnt*; met., *be consumed* ζήλῳ ~εσθαι Nil.*epp.*2.190(M.79.297D); *be worn away* βλέφαρα περιπεφλεγμένα... ταῖς ῥοαῖς τῶν δακρύων †Jo.D.*B.J.*38(M.96.1217D).

***περίφλεκτος,** *burning passionately* π. ὁρμάς *Hymn.*(*AS* I p.595).

περιφλύω, *make to bud*; of Word causing Aaron's rod to bud, ‡Caes.Naz.*dial.*183(M.38.1160).

***περιφοινίσσω,** *turn red*, Gr.Nyss.*v Mos.*(M.44.345A).

***περιφοίτης, ὁ,** s.v.l., *wanderer*; as adj., Eudoc.*Cypr.*2.108(M.85.849B).

περιφορά, ἡ, 1. *passing round* of cup, Synes.*ep.*32(M.66.1361A); **2.** *revolution* of heavenly bodies, Hipp.*haer.*1.8(p.14.2; M.16.3033B); Meth.*symp.*8.14(p.100.4; M.18.161C); Gr.Naz.*or.*20.11(M.35.1077C);

3. *sphere*; of heavenly spheres in Gnost. systems, Iren.*haer*.1.25.1 ap.Hipp.*haer*.7.32(p.218.6; M.16.3338A); Epiph.*haer*.27.2(p.301.15; M.41.364D); of earth, *Hom.Clem*.6.24; 4. *cycle* of time, Chrys.*hom.* 75.4 *in Mt*.(7.728C); of an indiction period, Men.*exc.Rom*.7(p.192. 21; M.113.884D); 5. *chance, accident*, Bas.*hom*.8.5(2.67A; M.31. 316C); εἴτε θεήλατος ἦν ἡ πληγή, εἴτε ἐκ π. τινος Chrys.*hom.6.3 in Mt.* (7.91A); Philost.*h.e*.8.1(M.65.556A); 6. *distraction*, Gr.Naz.*or*.7.17 (M.35.776C); *Apophth.Patr*.(M.65.144A); Cyr.*ador*.15(1.520C); 7. *turbulence*, Gr.Naz.*or*.28.1(p.21.6; M.36.25C); exeg. Eccl.2:2 διπλῆν ὁ γέλως ἔχει π.· ὅτι δὴ π. γεννᾷ γέλωτας, καὶ πενθεῖν οὐ συγχωρεῖ τὰς ἁμαρτίας, καὶ ὅτι οὗτος περιφέρεται, καιροὺς καὶ τόπους ἐναλλάττων †Dion.Al.*fr.Eccl*.2:2(p.214.8; M.10.1580B); Olymp.*Eccl*.2:2(M.93. 493B); ἀφροσύνην ἦν...π. καλεῖ *ib*.2:12(497D); π. ἤγουν κίνησιν ἀνώμαλον καὶ μεταβολὴν ἄτακτον Gr.Agr.*Eccl*.1.20(M.98.800B).

***περιφραγμός, ὁ,** *enclosing fence*, *Orac.Sib*.2.319; *ib*.8.209.

περιφράσσω, 1. *fence, fortify, all round*, met. ἑαυτὸν περιφράξας σκληροκαρδίᾳ Eus.*e.th*.2.18(p.123.4; M.24.941D); Chrys.*hom.24.1 in Eph*.(11.180C); Cyr.*Jo*.11.2(4.943E); 2. *block up* περιεφράξαμεν τὰ ὦτα Thdr.Stud.*epp*.1.48(M.99.1073A).

περιφραστικῶς, *periphrastically* τὸ υἱοὶ ἀνθρώπων...π. εἰρῆσθαι ὡς καὶ Ἕλλησιν ἔθος· υἷες Ἀχαιῶν Or.*Ps*.4:3(p.452) = id.*sel.in Ps*.4:3 (M.12.1137C) = Gennad.*fr.Ps*.1:3(M.85.1668C); Meth.*symp*.8.6(p.88. 21; παραφ- M.18.148C); Max.*Pyrr*.(M.91.348A).

περιφρίσσω, *bristle with*; c. dat., Nonn.*par.Jo*.4:35(M.43.780C).

περιφρονέω, 1. *despise* τὰ γήϊνα περιφρονήσας Isid.Pel.*epp*.1.227 (M.78.324C); *ib*.1.274(344C); τῶν γηΐνων περιφρονήσωμεν Jo.D.*hom*. 1.1(M.96.545B); 2. *neglect, ignore*, Gr.Thaum.*pan.Or*.2(p.3.23; M.10. 1053B); Cyr.*Jo*.6.1(4.636E).

περιφρόνησις, ἡ, 1. *contempt*, Clem.*q.d.s*.12(p.167.20; M.9.616C); Bas.Sel.*or*.3.2(M.85.53A); 2. *neglect*, (Lat. *negligentia*) *Cod.Afr*.123.

***περιφρονητέος,** *to be despised*, Gr.Naz.*carm*.2.1.12.780(M.37. 1223A).

περίφρων, 1. *haughty*, †Apoll.*met.Ps*.151:7(M.33.1537C); 2. *despising* κόσμοιο π. Gr.Naz.*carm*.1.2.1.211(M.37.538A).

***περιφύλαγμα, τό,** *safeguard*, of BMV νηπίων...π. Taras.*praesent. BMV*(M.98.1500B).

***περιφυλακή, ἡ,** *care, circumspection*, Gennad.*encycl*.(M.85. 1617C; φυλακῆς p.81.14).

περιφυλάσσω, 1. *guard, protect*, ‡Proc.G.*Pr*.2:11(M.87.1237A); Melet.*nat.hom*.1(M.64.1153A); 2. *keep, observe completely* περιφυλάξασθαι τὸν νόμον Vict.*Mc*.10:24(p.380.9).

***περιφύσησις, ἡ,** *blowing round, blast* coming from all sides, Oecum.*Apoc*.11:7(p.131).

περιφύω, 1. *cling to, embrace*; persons, Cyr.*glaph.Gen*.5(1.160D); 2. *adhere to, be wedded to* περιπεφυκότες τῷ κόσμῳ Clem.*prot*.9(p.64. 27; M.8.197B); id.*ecl*.25(p.144.2; διαπεφυκός M.9.709C).

περίφωρος, *detected*, *Hom.Clem*.14.10.

περιχαλκόω, *gild*, Meth.*symp*.5.8(p.62.20; M.18.112A).

***περιχαρακτηρίζω,** *sketch*, Ephr.1.263A.

περιχάραξις, ἡ, *digging round*; of making a well, Proc.G.*Num*. 21:16(M.87.860A).

περιχαράσσω, *mark round, trace round in outline*, Jo.Mal.*chron*.8 p.203(M.97.317C); *mark round* with sign of cross περιεχάραξεν τὴν ...θύραν τῷ σημείῳ τοῦ σταυροῦ *A.Andr.et Mt*.19(p.90.4); περιχαράξας...τὸν τόπον ‡Pall.*h.mon*.13.13(p.67.22; M.34.1162C).

περιχαρής, *full of joy*; neut. as subst., *happiness*, Diod.*proem. Pss*.(p.82.15).

***περίχαρις,** *full of grace*, of BMV χαῖρε, τὸ π. πρόσωπον Thdot. Anc.*hom.BMV et Sym*.3(M.77.1393B).

***περιχαρῶς,** *with great joy*, Bas.*hex*.3.2(1.23C; M.29.56B); id. *hom*.2.1(2.11C; M.31.185D); Isid.Pel.*epp*.1.394(M.78.404C); Thphyl. *exc.gent*.15(p.488.25; M.113.952B).

περιχέ-ω, 1. *pour water over*; pass., *be baptized* (clinically by affusion), Corn.ap.Eus.*h.e*.6.43.14(M.20.621B); *ib*.6.43.17(624B); 2. pass., *be poured round, surround, envelop* περικέχυται γὰρ αὐταῖς ἀὴρ καθαρός Meth.*symp*.8.3(p.84.25; M.18.144A); Bas.*hex*.9.5(1.86A; M.29.201A); ὁπόση τῷ Χοσρόῃ ὑπὸ τοῦ αὐτοκράτορος ῥώμη περικέχυτο Thphyl.*exc.gent*.9(p.486.15; M.113.948D); *come flooding in upon*, met. Τιβερίῳ ἤδη τὰ τῆς πολιτείας περιεκέχυτο πράγματα Men.*exc. Rom*.12(p.199.17; M.113.893C); of having in abundance νεανίας... κτημάτων περιουσίᾳ ∼όμενος Cyr.*Jo*.3.5(4.307E); id.*hom.pasch*.8(5^{2}. 99C); *ib*.9(119A); *ib*.18(238D); 3. pass., *embrace* περιεχύθη καὶ κατεφίλησε Chrys.*hom.10.5 in Rom*.(9.528A); *ib.32.3*(757D); Gr.Ant. *mul.ung*.3(M.88.1852A).

περιχορεύ-ω, 1. *dance round*, met., *circle round* οἱ θεῖοι...νόες... ἀνεκφοιτήτως μένουσιν ἐν ταὐτότητι περὶ τὸ τῆς ταὐτότητος αἴτιον καλὸν καὶ ἀγαθὸν ἀκαταλήκτως ∼οντες Dion.Ar.*d.n*.4.8(M.3.705A); ἡ πρώτη τῶν οὐρανίων οὐσιῶν διακόσμησις, ἡ κύκλῳ θεοῦ...ἑστηκυῖα, καὶ ...ἀκαταλήκτως ∼ουσα τὴν αἰώνιον αὐτοῦ γνῶσιν id.*c.h*.7.4(M.3.212A); 2. pass., *be danced round*, Mod.*dorm*.12(M.86.3308A).

περίχροος, *coloured over*, Gr.Naz.*carm*.2.1.11.1883(M.37.1161A).

***περιχρόω,** *colour over*, Gr.Nyss.*hom.opif*.19(M.44.197B).

περίχρυσος, *overlaid with gold*, Meth.*symp*.5.8(p.62.23; M.18. 112B); Cyr.*Is*.4.3(2.627B).

περιχύτης, ὁ, *attendant at baths*, Isch.*libell*.(p.19.24; περισχύτην H.2.329C).

περιχωρ-έω, A. in gen.; 1. *encompass* κύκλῳ γὰρ τῆς καρδίας τὸ κάλυμμα τοῦ σκότους ∼εῖ Mac.Aeg.*pat*.5(M.34.869A); 2. *alternate* by revolution, *pass* into *reciprocally* ζωὴ...καὶ θάνατος...εἰς ἄλληλα ∼εῖ πως καὶ ἀντικαθίσταται Gr.Naz.*or*.18.42(M.35.1041A); id.*or*.22.4 (1136B) cit. s. περιτρέπω.

B. Christol.; 1. *interchange* with, *pass* into reciprocally κιρναμένων ὥσπερ τῶν φύσεων, οὕτω δὴ καὶ τῶν κλήσεων, καὶ ∼ουσῶν εἰς ἀλλήλας τῷ λόγῳ τῆς συμφυΐας Gr.Naz.*ep*.101(M.37.181C) cit. Pamph. H.*panopl*.4.1(p.610) and Max.*schol.ep.Dion.Ar*.4(M.4.533C); ἡ φύσις ἀσυγχύτως ἑνωθεῖσα τῇ φύσει δι' ὅλου περικεχώρηκε, μηδὲν ἀπόλυτον παντάπασιν ἔχουσα καὶ τῆς ἡνωμένης αὐτῇ καθ' ὑπόστασιν κεχωρισμένον θεότητος Max.*ambig*.(M.91.1053B); πᾶσαν [sc. τὴν ἡμετέραν οὐσίαν] θεουργὸν ἀποφήνας, ὡς διόλου κατ' ἄκρον αὐτῇ ∼ήσας διὰ τὴν ἕνωσιν id.*opusc*.(M.91.60B); ἴδιον τῆς προσλαβομένης θεοῦ λόγου φύσεως τὸ εἶναι υἱὸν θεοῦ· ἴδιον τῆς προσληφθείσης ἀνθρώπου φύσεως τὸ εἶναι υἱὸν ἀνθρώπου. κιρναμένων οὖν τῶν τοιούτων φύσεων καὶ ∼ουσῶν εἰς ἀλλήλας τῷ λόγῳ τῆς συμφυΐας καὶ τῆς ἑνώσεως, κιρνῶνται καὶ ∼οῦσιν εἰς ἀλλήλας ὡσαύτως καὶ αἱ κλήσεις καὶ γίνεται ἀμφότερα εἷς υἱὸς θεοῦ τε ὁμοῦ καὶ ἀνθρώπου Thdr.Raith.*praep*.(p.194.14; M.91.1496A); 2. *interpenetrate* (it is often difficult to distinguish whether π. is used in sense 1 or 2) ἀδύνατον γὰρ τὴν σάρκα ∼ῆσαι διὰ τῆς θεότητος· ἀλλ' ἡ θεία φύσις ἅπαξ ∼ήσασα διὰ τῆς σαρκὸς ἔδωκε καὶ τῇ σαρκὶ τὴν πρὸς αὐτὴν ἄρρητον περιχώρησιν ‡Cyr.*Trin*.24(6^{3}.30A; M.77.1165C); μία τῶν δύο φύσεων χρηματίζει ὑπόστασις σύνθετος· καὶ ἐν αὐτῇ διὰ τῆς σαρκώσεως ἑνοῦνται αἱ δύο φύσεις...καὶ ∼οῦσιν ἐν ἀλλήλαις, ἡ δὲ περιχώρησις ἐκ τῆς θεότητος γίνεται Jo.D.*Jacob*.52(M.94.1461C); αἱ τοῦ Χριστοῦ φύσεις, εἰ καὶ ἥνωνται, ἀλλ' ἀσυγχύτως ἥνωνται· καὶ εἰ ἐν ἀλλήλαις ∼οῦσιν, ἀλλὰ τὴν εἰς ἀλλήλας τροπήν τε καὶ μεταβολὴν οὐ προσίενται id.*f.o*.3.5(M.94.1001A); εἰ καὶ ∼εῖν ἐν ἀλλήλαις τὰς...φύσεις φαμέν, ἀλλ' οἴδαμεν, ὡς ἐκ τῆς θείας φύσεως ἡ περιχώρησις γέγονεν. αὕτη μὲν γὰρ διὰ πάντων διήκει...καὶ ∼εῖ, δι' αὐτῆς δὲ οὐδέν *ib*.3.7 (1012C); ἡνωμέναι γὰρ καθ' ὑπόστασιν, καὶ ἐν ἀλλήλαις ∼οῦσαι, ἀσυγχύτως ἥνωνται *ib*.3.8(1016B).

C. Trin., *interpenetrate* τρεῖς δὲ ὑποστάσεις...ἐν ἀλλήλαις ἀσυγχύτως ∼ούσας ἐπιστάμεθα Jo.D.*f.o*.3.5(M.94.1000B); cf. θεαρχικῶν ὑποστάσεων...∼ουσῶν εἰς ἀλλήλας, ἀλλ' ἐφ' ἑκάστης τούτων...ἀσυγχύτου φυλαττομένης τῆς ἀϊδιότητος, πόρρω γὰρ ἀποπεμπέσθω...ἡ τοῦ... Σαβελλίου...σύγχυσις Nicephorus Constantinopolitanus *epistula ad Leonem*(M.100.184D).

περιχώρησις, ἡ, A. in gen., *cyclical movement, recurrence* τὴν πρὸς τὸ μὴ ὂν...δέχεται π. Gr.Agr.*Eccl*.2.1(M.98.808B); τέλος δὲ πίστεώς ἐστιν, ἡ τοῦ πιστευθέντος ἀληθὴς ἀποκάλυψις. ἀληθὴς δὲ τοῦ πιστευθέντος...ἀποκάλυψις, ἡ κατὰ ἀναλογίαν τῆς ἐν ἑκάστῳ πίστεως ἄρρητος τοῦ πεπιστευμένου π.· π. δὲ τοῦ πεπιστευμένου καθέστηκεν, ἡ πρὸς τὴν οἰκείαν ἀρχὴν κατὰ τὸ τέλος τῶν πεπιστευκότων ἐπάνοδος Max.*qu.Thal*.59(M.90.608D).

B. Christol.; 1. *reciprocity*, in analogy of human speech ἐπὶ τοῦ κατὰ προφορὰν δὲ λόγου ὡσαύτως, καὶ τὴν ἐγκειμένην τῷ λόγῳ ὁρῶμεν ἔννοιαν, καὶ τὸν ὑποκείμενον τῇ ἐννοίᾳ λόγον, καὶ τὴν αὐτῶν δι' ὅλου εἰς ἄλληλα π. Max.*Pyrr*.(M.91.337C); τῷ ἀπορρήτῳ τρόπῳ τῆς εἰς ἀλλήλας τῶν Χριστοῦ φύσεων π. *ib*.(345D); ἡνωμένας διόλου τῇ πρὸς ἀλλήλας συμφυΐᾳ καὶ π. id.*opusc*.(M.91.88A); τὴν ἄκραν τούτων εἰς ἄλληλα π. καὶ ἀντίδοσιν *ib*.(189D); μίαν...ἐνέργειαν, διὰ τὸ μηδὲν θεῖον ἢ ἀνθρώπινον κεχωρισμένως ἐπιτελεῖσθαι, ἀλλ' ἐξ ἑνὸς καὶ τοῦ αὐτοῦ συμφυῶς ἅμα καὶ ἡνωμένως προάγεσθαι, κατὰ τὴν ἐν τούτοις ἑνιαίαν π. *ib*.(232A); 2. *interpenetration* χρῖσιν δὲ νοητέον, τὴν ὅλου τοῦ χρίσματος εἰς ὅλον τὸ χριωθὲν π. ‡Cyr.*Trin*.22(6^{3}.28A; M.77.1164A); *ib*.27(34A; M. 1172D); μεταδίδωσι τῇ σαρκὶ τῶν ἰδίων, κατὰ τὸν ἀντιδόσεως τρόπον, διὰ τὴν εἰς ἄλληλα τῶν μερῶν π., καὶ τὴν καθ' ὑπόστασιν ἕνωσιν Jo.D. *f.o*.3.3(M.94.993D); ἀντιδιδούσης τῇ ἑτέρᾳ τὰ ἴδια διὰ τὴν τῆς ὑποστάσεως ταυτότητα, καὶ τὴν εἰς ἄλληλα αὐτῶν π. *ib*.3.4(1000A); *ib*.3.7 (1012C) cit. s. περιχωρέω; ἡνωμέναι γὰρ καθ' ὑπόστασιν, καὶ τὴν ἐν ἀλλήλαις π. ἔχουσαι, ἀσυγχύτως ἥνωνται *ib*.3.8(1013B); οὐ κατὰ μεταβολὴν φύσεως, ἀλλὰ κατὰ τὴν οἰκονομικὴν ἕνωσιν, τὴν καθ' ὑπόστασιν ..., καὶ τὴν ἐν ἀλλήλαις τῶν φύσεων π., ὡς φαμεν καὶ τὴν τοῦ σιδήρου πύρωσιν *ib*.3.17(1069A); ἡ δὲ π. οὐκ ἐκ τῆς σαρκός, ἀλλ' ἐκ τῆς θεότητος γέγονεν...ἀλλ' ἡ θεία φύσις ἅπαξ περιχωροῦσα διὰ τῆς σαρκός, ἔδωκε καὶ τῇ σαρκὶ τὴν πρὸς ταύτην ἄρρητον π., ἣν δὴ ἕνωσιν λέγομεν *ib.*4.18(1184C); ἀμεταβλήτως τὴν σάρκα ἐθέωσε, διὰ τῆς ἐν ἀλλήλαις τῆς αὐτοῦ θεότητος, καὶ τῆς αὐτοῦ σαρκὸς ἀσυγχύτου παραχωρήσεως id.*imag.*1.21(M.94.1253B, conj. περιχωρήσεως); id.*Jacob.*52(M.94.1461C) cit. s. περιχωρέω; *ib.*81(1480B); θεοῦ μὲν τὰ ἀνθρώπινα γίνεται, ἀνθρώπου δὲ τὰ θεῖα, τῷ τρόπῳ τῆς ἀντιδόσεως, καὶ τῆς ἐν ἀλλήλοις ἀσυγχύτου π. id.*hom.*1.2(M.96.549A).

C. Trin., *interpenetration* ἑνοῦνται γάρ,...οὐχ ὥστε συγχεῖσθαι, ἀλλ' ὥστε ἔχεσθαι ἀλλήλων· καὶ τὴν ἐν ἀλλήλαις π. ἔχουσι δίχα πάσης συναλοιφῆς καὶ συμφύρσεως ‡Cyr.*Trin.*10(6^3.16A; M.77.1144B) = Jo.D.*f.o.*1.8(M.94.829A); ἡ ἐν ἀλλήλαις τῶν ὑποστάσεων μονή τε καὶ ἵδρυσις· ἀδιάστατοι γὰρ αὗται, καὶ ἀνεκφοίτητοι ἀλλήλων εἰσίν, ἀσύγχυτον ἔχουσαι τὴν ἐν ἀλλήλαις π. Jo.D.*f.o.*1.14(M.94.860B); *ib.*4.18(1181B); id.*rect.sent.*1(M.94.1424A); οὐδὲ γὰρ οὐσίᾳ τέμνονται, οὐ δυνάμει χωρίζονται, οὐ τόπῳ, οὐκ ἐνεργείᾳ, οὐ βουλήσει μερίζονται, ἀνεκφοίτητον ἔχοντες τὴν ἐν ἀλλήλοις ἵδρυσίν τε καὶ π. id.*Jacob.*78(M.94.1476B); αἱ τρεῖς ὑποστάσεις ἀδιαιρέτως ἅμα καὶ ἀσυγχύτως ἥνωνται· ἀδιαιρέτως μέν, διὰ τὸ μοναδικὸν τῆς φύσεως, καὶ τὴν ἐν ἀλλήλαις ἀσύγχυτον π. id.*nat.*4(M.95.117D); ὥσπερ ἐπὶ τῆς...τριάδος αἱ τρεῖς ὑποστάσεις διὰ τὴν φυσικὴν ταυτότητα καὶ τὴν ἐν ἀλλήλαις π. εἷς θεός εἰσί τε καὶ λέγονται, οὕτως ἐπὶ τοῦ...Χριστοῦ αἱ δύο φύσεις διὰ τὴν ὑποστατικὴν ταυτότητα καὶ τὴν ἐν ἀλλήλαις π. εἷς υἱός εἰσι id.*fid.Nest.*36(p.576).

***περιψάλλομαι**, *make music round, serenade*, Mac.Mgn.*apocr.*4.11(p.171.2).

περίψημα, τό, *offscouring, contemptible thing*; also in polite address, *devoted servant*, Ign.*Eph.*8.1; π. τὸ ἐμὸν πνεῦμα τοῦ σταυροῦ *ib.*18.1; γράφειν ἐσπούδασα, π. ὑμῶν *Barn.*4.9; ἐγὼ π. τῆς ἀγάπης ὑμῶν *ib.*6.5; of Christians who voluntarily incurred plague through tending sick τὸ δημῶδες ῥῆμα, μόνης ἀεὶ δοκοῦν φιλοφροσύνης ἔχεσθαι, ἔργῳ δὴ τότε πληροῦντες, 'ἀπιόντες αὐτῶν π.' Dion.Al.ap.Eus.*h.e.*7.22.7(M.20.689A); ὁ ἔχων ἀγάπην,...πάντων π. γίνεται Ephr.1.3F; μακάριος...ὁ μοναχὸς ὁ πάντων π. ἑαυτὸν ἔχων Ant.Mon.*hom.*68(M.89.1633A).

***περίψιμος, ὁ**, (cf. foreg.), *contemptible person*; plur., *riff-raff* βάναυσοί τινες οὐδὲ π. †Cyr.*hom.div.*10(5^2.371C).

περίψυξις, ἡ, *cooling, condensation*, acc. Stoics ψυχὴν...εἶναι...σῶμα καὶ γενέσθαι ἐκ τῆς π. τοῦ ἀέρος...διὸ καὶ καλεῖσθαι ψυχήν Hipp.*haer.*1.21(p.26.1; M.16.3049A).

***περιωγή, ἡ**, *revolving movement*, Gr.Naz.*carm.*1.1.5.49(M.37.428A); *ib.*1.1.7.2(439A).

[*]περιωδία, ἡ, v. περιοδεία.

περιωδυν-άω, *afflict with pain* ∼ησε τὴν καρδίαν Thdr.Stud.*epp.*2.214(M.99.1644C).

περιώνυμος, *far-famed, renowned*, Ath.Presb.*libell.*(p.20.33; H.2.332C); Philost.*h.e.*3.2(M.65.481A); Sophr.H.*ep.syn.*(M.87.3173B); Jo.D.*f.o.*4.12(M.94.1136A); neut. as subst. τὸ τῆς δυνάμεως π. Philost.*h.e.*12.3(609A).

περιωπή, ἡ, **1.** *vantage-point*; met., Chrys.*sac.*2.2(p.30.14; 1.373C); **2.** *summit, height*; **a.** of God's dwelling, divine sphere of existence θεὸν...περὶ τὰ νῶτα τοῦ οὐρανοῦ ἐν τῇ ἰδίᾳ καὶ οἰκείᾳ π. ὄντως ὄντα Clem.*prot.*6(p.52.6; M.8.173A); οὐ γὰρ ἐξίσταταί ποτε τῆς αὐτοῦ π. ὁ υἱὸς τοῦ θεοῦ id.*str.*7.2(p.5.26; M.9.408B); ref. Gen.2:2–3 κατέπαυσεν...ὁ θεὸς ἀναχωρῶν εἰς τὴν ἑαυτοῦ π. Cels.ap.Or.*Cels.*5.59(p.62.28; M.11.1276A); Or.*schol.in Cant.*8:1(M.17.285A); of Christ εἰ ἐπὶ τῆς ἰδίας ἔμεινε π. ... ὀλίγοι ἂν ἠκολούθησαν τυχόν Gr.Naz.*or.*37.3(M.36.285B); of the two natures τὸ μὲν περιωπῆς, τὸ δὲ ταπεινώσεως *ib.*41.12(445B); *ib.*45.11(637B); οὐρανὸν...σημαίνεσθαι τὴν...π. καὶ κατάστασιν τοῦ θεοῦ Didym.ap.*cat.Jo.*6:58(p.255.33); ἑαυτὸν ἐταπείνωσεν ἐν π. θεότητος ὤν Thdot.Anc.*exp.symb.*7(M.77.1324B); Olymp.*Eccl.*5:1(M.93.537D); Max.*myst.*5(M.91.680C); **b.** of heights of spiritual life τὸν γὰρ μὴ δυνηθέντα ἀναπτῆναι...μηδὲ ἐν ταύτῃ καθίσαι τῇ π., οὐκ ἔνι τὴν γῆν ἰδεῖν...ὡς ἰδεῖν ἄξιον Chrys.*compunct.*2.1(1.141B); τὴν τῆς ἀρετῆς...π. Isid.Pel.*epp.*5.109(M.78.1389A); of original state of Adam, Gr.Agr.*Eccl.*4.3(M.98.925B); **c.** *head, capital* πόλις...τῆς οἰκουμένης π. CCP(681)*or.imp.*(H.3.1424D); **3.** *contemplation* μειζόνως αὐτὸν ἐν ἑαυτῷ δοξαζόμενον, ὅτε ἐν τῇ ἑαυτοῦ γινόμενος π., ἐπὶ τῇ ἑαυτοῦ γνώσει καὶ τῇ ἑαυτοῦ θεωρίᾳ Or.*Jo.*32.28(18; p.473.30; M.14.817D).

***περιωρισμένως**, *definitely*, Thdt.*Is.*13:20(p.68.25; 2.264).

***περιωχείμας**, vox nihili, *A.Thom.*A 157(p.267.5).

***περκασμός, ὁ**, *dark colour* of grapes ripening, Jo.Eleem.*v.Tych.*(p.127).

§περνάω, = περάω, *Apophth.Patr.*(M.65.440A).

***περνέω**, = περάω, Thphn.*chron.*p.198(M.108.512) prob. error for foreg.

***περπερεία, ἡ**, *vainglory, boastfulness, ostentation* π. γὰρ ὁ καλλωπισμὸς περιττότητος καὶ ἀχρειότητος ἔχων ἔμφασιν Clem.*paed.*3.1(p.237.13; M.8.557B); πᾶν ὃ μὴ διὰ χρείαν, ἀλλὰ διὰ καλλωπισμὸν παραλαμβάνεται, περπερείας ἔχει κατηγορίαν Bas.*reg.br.*49(2.432A; M.31.1116C); πραότητα, ἥπερ πᾶσαν ἐκκλίνει π. Isid.Pel.*epp.*1.162(M.78.292A); Nil.*Magn.*14(M.79.988D); Dor.*doct.*3.3(M.88.1657A); one of σωματικὰ πάθη, Jo.D.*virt.*(M.95.88D).

περπερεύ-ομαι, *vaunt oneself, put oneself forward*, Clem.*paed.*3.11(p.278.27; M.8.656A); ὅταν τις προπετὴς ᾖ ἐπαγγελλόμενος εἰδέναι ἢ περὶ τέχνης ἢ περὶ ἐπιστήμης ἢ περὶ γνώσεως οὗτός ἐστιν ὁ ∼όμενος παρὰ τὸ μὴ ἔχειν τὴν ἀγάπην Or.*comm.in 1Cor.*13:4(*JTS* 10 p.34); ὅτε δὲ ἔπταισαν [sc. clerics], ὡς ἂν ∼σάμενοι καὶ ἑαυτοὺς μωμησάμενοι, οὐκέτι δύνανται λειτουργεῖν Petr.I Al.*ep.can.*10(M.18.488C); οὐ ∼εται· τουτέστιν, οὐ προπετεύεται Chrys.*hom.33.1 in 1Cor.*(10.300B); οὐ πολυπραγμονεῖ τὰ μὴ ἀνήκοντα· τοῦτο γάρ ἐστι τὸ ∼εσθαι Thdt.*1Cor.*13:4(3.253); τὸ ἐπιχαίρειν οἱῳδήποτε ἀνθρώπῳ ἐν θλίψει...ἀνθρώπου ἐστὶ ∼ομένου Ant.Mon.*hom.*58(M.89.1608D).

***περπερότης, ἡ**, *vaingloriousness, boastfulness*, Ephr.3.102F; ‡Chrys.*hom.*10(13.242C).

§περσίς, ἡ, ? = περσέα; name of an Egyptian tree with healing properties, shown at Hermopolis, said to have bowed down in adoration of Christ at flight into Egypt, or, as object of pagan worship, to have been shaken down by Christ's approach, Soz.*h.e.*5.21.8(M.67.1281A).

***Περσοκράτης, ὁ**, *ruler of Persia*, Geo.Pis.*Heracl.*1.13(M.92.1298A).

Περσολέτης, ὁ, *destroyer of Persians*, Bas.Sel.*v.Thecl.*2.4(M.85.572C).

***περσονάλιος**, (Lat. *personalis*) *personal*, Ath.Scholast.*coll.*5 paratit.17(p.79).

***Περσόφρων**, *Persian-minded* ὦ τοῦ νέου Μανιχαίου καὶ Π. ‡Jo.D.*ep.Thphl.*21(M.95.373A).

πέσκος, τό, *rind* of fruit, Eudoc.*Cypr.*2.255(M.85.856B).

πετάζ-ω, = πετάννυμι, *spread out*, of monks moving from place to place μὴ ∼ωμεν ἑαυτοὺς ἀπὸ τόπων εἰς τόπους Nil.*Eulog.*12(M.79.1109A).

***πεταλογραφία, ἡ**, *writing on* magical *tablets*, Ephr.2.196A.

***πεταλογράφος, ὁ**, *writer on* magical *tablet, maker of charms*, Ephr.3.111F.

πέταλον, τό, **1.** *leaf*, met. τῆς ἐγκρατείας τὰ π. Clem.*prot.*1(p.10.12; M.8.68A); **2.** *leaf, plate, tablet*, of metal etc.; **a.** used for sacred and magical writings πετάλων ἐπιγραφαῖς καὶ περιάμμασιν χρῆσθαι Eus.*d.e.*3.6(p.133.29; M.22.225C); ἐν πετάλοις ἐπιγραφαί, μαγεῖαι, ἢ ἄλλαι κακοτεχνίαι Cyr.H.*catech.*19.8; Chrys.*Jud.*8.6(1.682E); *Pers.*(p.15.24); **b.** *gold leaf* used in decoration, met. γένηται π. χρυσοῦν καὶ δέξηται τοὺς τύπους τῶν γραμμάτων τοῦ θεοῦ Or.*enarr.in Job* 41:15(M.17.105A); **c.** *gold plate on mitre of high priest* inscribed with divine name, Clem.*str.*5.6(p.352.14; M.9.65A); ὁ ἱερεὺς εἰσιὼν ἐντὸς τοῦ καταπετάσματος τοῦ δευτέρου τό τε π. ἀπετίθει παρὰ τῷ θυσιαστηρίῳ...αὐτὸς δὲ...τὸ ἐν τῇ καρδίᾳ ἐγκεχαραγμένον ὄνομα ἔχων εἰσῄει, δεικνὺς τὴν ἀπόθεσιν τοῦ καθάπερ π. χρυσοῦ καθαροῦ γενομένου ...τοῦ ὥσπερ σώματος τῆς ψυχῆς [ἀπόθεσιν], ἐν ᾧ ἐγκεχάρακτο τὸ γάνωμα τῆς θεοσεβείας id.*exc.Thdot.*27(p.115.23; M.9.672C); κεφαλὴ δὲ κοσμουμένη τῷ διαδήματι, τὸν ἀποκείμενον τοῖς εὖ βεβιωκόσι στέφανον ἀποσημαίνει, ὃν κοσμεῖ ὁ ἐσφραγισμένος τῷ χρυσῷ π. τοῖς ἀρρήτοις χαράγμασιν Gr.Nyss.*v.Mos.*(M.44.392D); Epiph.*gemm.*12(M.43.301D); Chrys.*sac.*3.4(p.51.11; 1.382C); worn by John at Ephesus ὃς ἐγενήθη ἱερεὺς τὸ π. πεφορεκώς Polycr.ap.Eus.*h.e.*5.24.3(M.20.493C); by James of Jerusalem π. ἐπὶ τῆς κεφαλῆς ἐφόρεσε Epiph.*ep.Arab.*ap.*haer.*78.14(p.464.24; M.42.721B); met. τὸ π. τῆς πίστεως *T.Lev.*8.2; **3.** *plate* of a beetle's wing, Bas.*hex.*8.8(1.79A; M.29.184D); **4.** heavenly *sphere* τὰ ἐννέα π. τοῦ οὐρανοῦ *Apoc.Jo.*17(p.85); ἔξωθεν δὲ τῶν ἑπτὰ οὐρανῶν τὸ π. ἐστιν τὸ πρῶτον, ὅπου εἰσὶν αἱ ἐξουσίαι ἐνεργοῦσαι τοῖς ἀνθρώποις *Ev.Barth.*4.30(*RB* 10 p.332, v.l. πέταλος Vassiliev p. 17).

πεταλώδης, *leaf-like*, Melet.*nat.hom.*1(M.64.1152D).

πετάλωσις, ἡ, *foliage*, Mac.Mgn.*apocr.*4.11(p.171.11); *ib.*4.16(p.188.7).

πετάννυμι, *open, spread out* ὁ ἄνθρωπος τὰς χεῖρας πετάσας οὐδὲν ἄλλο ὑπάρχων φαίνεται ἢ τοῦτο [sc. the Cross] Meth.*Porph.*1(p.505.1; M.18.400D); Ast.Am.*phar.*(p.117.18); liturg., at beginning of anaphora, of attitude of congregation at prayer ὁ διάκονος· πετάσατε *Lit.Marc.*(Brightman, p.125.19); εἰς τὸν οὐρανόν τε πετάσας τὸ ὄμμα καὶ τὰς παλάμας Jo.Eleem.*v.Tych.*(p.153).

πέτασμα, τό, **1.** *veil* of Temple, *Orac.Sib.*8.305; **2.** *flight* of a bird, Didym.*Pr.*30:19(M.39.1641C); Geo.Pis.*hex.*45(M.92.1430A).

πέταυρον, τό, *trap*, ref. Pr.9:18 ἐπὶ π. ᾅδου συναντᾷ Ath.*Ar*.1.10 (M.26.32B); Cyr.*ador*.6(1.186A); id.*Is*.4.4(2.686E); id.*Os*.3(3.16C); π. ἀπωλείας Gr.Agr.*Eccl*.2.2(M.98.809C).

πέτ-ομαι (πέτ-αμαι), 1. *fly* οἱ ἀετοὶ Ἰσραὴλ ~ασθήσονται ἐν χαρᾷ *T.Jud*.25.5; οὐδὲν οὕτως ἀνέχει, καὶ μικροῦ ~εσθαι ποιεῖ, ὡς συνειδὸς ἀγαθόν Chrys.*hom.12.7 in Rom*.(9.552D, v.l. ~ασθῆναι); ἄνω ~ασθαι διηνεκῶς, καὶ πρὸς τὸν ἥλιον τῆς δικαιοσύνης ἐνορᾶν id.*hom.24.3 in 1Cor*.(10.216D); δεῖ ~ασθῆναι τοῖς τοῦ πνεύματος πτεροῖς id.*hom.12.2 in Phil*.(11.292A); **2.** *flit, gad about* οὐκ ἔσῃ ὡς ~όμενος...ἐν ταῖς ῥύμαις *Const.App*.1.4.1.

πέτρα, ἡ, *rock*; **1.** in gen.; ref. 1Cor.10:4 ἀπανταχοῦ παρεπομένης αὐτοὺς π., καὶ κατὰ σταθμοὺς καὶ κατὰ μονὰς...παρούσης [explained by reference to Ex.17:1ff., Num.20:1ff.] Eus.*Ps*.77:15(M.23.913C); met. σου τὴν ἐν θεῷ γνώμην, ἡδρασμένην ὡς ἐπὶ πέτραν ἀκίνητον Ign.*Polyc*.1.1; **2.** of Christ; **a.** in gen., ref. Jos.5:2–3, Just.*dial*.113.6(M.6.737B) cit. s. λίθος; ref. Ex.17:6 τὸ ὄνομα τὸ τῆς καλῆς π., καὶ ζῶν ὕδωρ...βρυούσης *ib*.114.4(740C); Pauline exegesis of π. ἀκολουθοῦσα taken as example of spiritual exegesis, Or.*hom.5.1 in Ex*.(p.184.20; M.12.326C); πέτρᾳ παρεικονίζεται [sc. ὁ Χριστός] διὰ τὸ ἄθραυστον καὶ ἀκλόνητον. ἐρήρεισται γὰρ ἐν ἰδίοις ἀγαθοῖς ἡ θεία...φύσις Cyr.*glaph.Ex*.3(1.314D); Proc.G.*Ex*.33:21(M.87.680A); exeg. Cant.2:14, Ph.Carp.*Cant*.62(M.40.72B); Nil.ap.Proc.G.*Cant*.2:14(M.87.1608A); Cyr.*fr.Cant*.2:14(M.69.1285B); **b.** as foundation of Church; **i.** in gen., Herm.*sim*.9.2.1; *ib*.9.4.2; ἡ π. ... καὶ ἡ πύλη ὁ υἱὸς τοῦ θεοῦ ἐστι *ib*.9.12.1; **ii.** exeg. Mt.16:18 ἐκκλησίαν...ἑστάναι...ὡς ἂν ἐπ' ἀσείστῳ καὶ ἀρραγεῖ π. τῇ αὐτοῦ δυνάμει βεβηκυῖαν Eus.*p.e*.1.3(8A; M.21.33A); θεμέλιον δὲ αὐτῆς...τὴν ἀρραγῆ...π., ἐφ' ᾗ ᾠκοδόμηται κατὰ τὸ 'ἐπὶ τὴν π. οἰκοδομήσω μου τὴν ἐκκλησίαν...' ἡ π. δὲ ἦν ὁ Χριστός id.*Ps*.17:15(M.23.173D); id.*Is*.28:16–17(M.24.292B,C); ἡ ἀπαρχὴ τῶν ἀποστόλων Πέτρος ὠνομάσθη διὰ τὴν ἀσάλευτον πίστιν, ἣν εἶχεν ἐπὶ Χριστὸν τὴν π. Mod.*mul.ung*.(M.86.3276A); **3.** other exegeses of Mt.16:18; **a.** S. Peter's confession of faith, made through H. Ghost, †Hipp.*theoph*.9(p.262.32; M.10.860C); cf.Thdt.*Cant*.2:14(2.71); τόπος, π. καλούμενος, ἐν τοῖς ἀγαθοῖς ἡ θεία...φύσις Or.*sel.in Ex*.17:6(M.12.289B); ref. Ex.33:22–23 ἐὰν νοήσῃς ἐκεῖ τὴν π. καὶ ἴδῃς ἐκεῖ τὴν ὀπὴν τῆς π., τίνα τρόπον ὁ ἐπὶ τῆς π. στὰς καὶ τὴν ὀπὴν τὴν ἐν τῇ π. ἰδὼν βλέπει τὸν θεὸν διὰ τῆς ὀπῆς τῆς π., ὄψει καὶ τὰς πολλὰς π. καὶ τὰς τρυμαλιὰς αὐτῶν. τίς οὖν ἐκείνη ἡ μία; ἡ π. δὲ ἦν ὁ Χριστός·...τίς ἡ ὀπὴ ἐν τῇ π.; ἐὰν ἴδῃς τὴν Ἰησοῦ ἐπιδημίαν, ὅλον αὐτὸν νοήσας πέτραν, ὄψει τὴν ὀπὴν κατὰ τὴν ἐπιδημίαν αὐτοῦ, δι' ἧς ὀπῆς θεωρεῖται τὰ μετὰ τὸν θεόν id.*hom.16.2 in Jer*.(p.134.11; M.13.441A); id.*comm.in Mt*.12.11(p.88.17; M.13.1004A); π. ὁ Χριστός, καὶ οἱ μιμηταὶ αὐτοῦ ἀπόστολοι καὶ προφῆται πέτραι ὀνομάζονται id.*comm.ser.139 in Mt*.(p.287.8); id.*Jo*.1.27(26; p.34.18; M.14.73B); ἐπήρας με...στήσας ἐν τῇ παρὰ σοὶ π., ἥτις ἐστὶν ὁ προιών σου λόγος· ἡ π. γὰρ ἦν ὁ Χριστός Eus.*Ps*.60:2–3(M.23.577C); id.*e.th*.1.20(p.90.22; M.24.881C); Bas.*Spir*.31(3.26A; M.32.121C); Gr.Naz.*or*.26.9(M.35.1240A); πέτρᾳ δὲ παρεικάζεται, ἡ περὶ θεολογίας διάληψις. οὕτω γὰρ καὶ τὴν ὁμολογίαν Πέτρου κέκληκεν ὁ σωτήρ. τούτῳ σύμφωνον καὶ τὸ 'ἔστησας ἐπὶ π. τοὺς πόδας μου.' δηλαδὴ ἐπὶ τὸν ἀρραγῆ τοῦ θεοῦ λόγον, ὄντα π. πνευματικήν Proc.G.*Ex*.33:21(M.87.680A); **b.** the faith ἐκκλησίας ἣν ἐθεμελίωσας ἐπὶ τὴν π. τῆς πίστεως *Lit.Jac*.(p.206.18); **c.** truth of doctrine maintained by fathers, Jo.V H.*icon*.16(M.96.1361B); **d.** all disciples of Christ, represented by S. Peter φήσαντες καὶ ἡμεῖς ὡς ὁ Πέτρος...γινόμεθα Πέτρος, καὶ ἡμῖν ἂν λέγοιτο...τὸ 'σὺ εἶ Πέτρος κτλ.' π. γὰρ πᾶς ὁ Χριστοῦ μιμητής, ἀφ' οὗ ἔπινον οἱ 'ἔπινον ἐκ πνευματικῆς...π.' καὶ ἐπὶ πᾶσαν τὴν τοιαύτην π. οἰκοδομεῖται ὁ ἐκκλησιαστικὸς πᾶς λόγος καὶ...πολιτεία...εἰ δὲ ἐπὶ τὸν ἕνα ἐκεῖνον Πέτρον νομίζεις ὑπὸ τοῦ θεοῦ οἰκοδομεῖσθαι τὴν...ἐκκλησίαν μόνον, τί ἂν φήσαις περὶ Ἰωάννου...ἢ ἑκάστου τῶν ἀποστόλων;...οὐχὶ δὲ καὶ ἐπὶ πάντων...τὸ προειρημένον...γίνεται...ἐπὶ ταύτῃ τῇ π. οἰκοδομήσω κτλ.; Or.*comm.in Mt*.12.10(p.86.1; M.13.997B); παρώνυμοι γὰρ πέτρας πάντες οἱ μιμηταὶ Χριστοῦ...οὗτοι δὲ παρώνυμοί εἰσι τῆς π. ὡς Χριστός *ib*.12.11(p.88.15; 1004A); ἡ ἔχουσα σπίλον...ψυχὴ οὔτε π. ἐστίν, ἐφ' ἣν ὁ Χριστὸς οἰκοδομεῖ *ib*.12.12(p.90.7; 1005A); cf.id.*comm.ser.139 in Mt*.(p.287.8); cf.id.*Cels*.6.77(p.147.18; M.11.1416B); **e.** S. Peter, cf.Or.*hom.5.4 in Ex*.(p.188.29; M.12.329D); cf. *Petrus, adversus quem portae inferi non praevalent*, id.*princ*.3.2.5(p.253.6; M.11.311A); Πέτρος, ἐφ' ᾧ οἰκοδομεῖται ἡ ἐκκλησία id.*Jo*.5.3(p.101.25; M.14.188D); πρὸς γὰρ στερεὰν π. ὄντα με, θεμέλιον ἐκκλησίας, ἐναντίος ἀνθέστηκάς μοι *Hom.Clem*.17.19; Πέτρος θεόθεν ἐμπνευσθεὶς καὶ διὰ τῆς οἰκείας ὁμολογίας πᾶσιν μέλλων γίνεσθαι σωτηρία τοῖς ἔθνεσι...μακάριος ἀπεφάνθη...καὶ ἀπὸ τῆς πρωτοτύπου π. τὸ στερεὸν ἐπεσπάσατο τῆς τε ἀρετῆς καὶ τῆς προσηγορίας Leo Mag.*ep*.28(p.16.23; M.*PL*.54.772D); Πέτρου...ὅς ἐστι π. καὶ κρηπὶς τῆς καθολικῆς ἐκκλησίας CChalc.*act*.3 (*ACO* 2.1.2 p.29.16; H.2.345C); Ῥώμης ὁ πολιοῦχος...ἡ π. τῆς πίστεως Jo.Mon.*hymn.Petr*.5(M.96.1393A); **4.** the gospel; ref. Cant.2:14, Gr.Nyss.*hom.5 in Cant*.(M.44.877B); **5.** of BMV as precious stone μαργαρίτου πέτρα Chrysipp.*enc.in BMV* 1(p.337.5, conj. for πεῖρα; perh. l. πήρα).

***πετραρία, ἡ,** *catapult*, *Chron.Pasch*.p.394(M.92.1009A).

πετρήεις, *stony, like stone*, Paul.Sil.*ambo*.280(M.86.2262A).

***Πετριανός, ὁ, 1.** *follower of S. Peter* Πέτρον τιμῶ, ἀλλ' οὐκ ἀκούω Π. Gr.Naz.*or*.37.17(M.36.301C); **2.** member of a monophysite sect Πετριανοί· οἱ διαβεβαιούμενοι τὴν ὑπόστασιν μόνα εἶναι ἰδιώματα χωρὶς οὐσίας Tim.CP *haer*.(M.86.45B).

πέτρινος, *of stone*; of stone knives used in second circumcision of Israel by Joshua, as type of spiritual circumcision by Christ the Rock Χριστὸς πάντας...περιτέμνει...π. μαχαίραις, ἵνα γένηται ἔθνος δίκαιον Just.*dial*.24.2(M.6.528C); *ib*.114.4(740B); Gr.Nyss.*Ps.6*(M.44.609A); cf.Or.*hom.5.5 in Jos*.(p.318.6; M.12.850A) cit. s. περιτομή; Cyr.*ador*.2(1.78D); id.*hom.div*.12(5².387C).

***πετροκίσσηρος, ὁ,** ? *piece of pumice*, Thphn.*chron*.p.338(M.108.816C).

***πετροπομπός, ὁ,** *slinger*, Geo.Pis.*bell.Avar*.243(M.92.1279A); as adj., id.*Heracl*.2.209(M.92.1331A).

***πετρόστεγος,** *living under rocks*, Geo.Pis.*hex*.1541(M.92.1554A).

πετροφυής, *clinging to rock*, *Orac.Sib*.2.121; *ib*.5.321.

πετρόω, 1. *petrify*; met., of Joseph ὁ στερρός, ὁ πεπετρωμένος Chrys.*hom.4.5 in 1Thess*.(11.458A); **2.** *stone*, Thphn.*chron*.p.416(M.108.985C).

πεῦσις, ἡ, 1. *question, inquiry*; hence *interrogation, judicial inquiry*, Chrys.*pan.Lucn*.3(2.528A); Sophr.H.*v.Anast*.(M.92.1700A); **2.** a rhetorical figure, *interrogation* of oneself in course of a speech, Isid.H.*etym*.2.21.43.

πευστέον, *one must inquire*, Or.*Jo*.10.32(18; p.206.21; M.14.305B); id.*princ*.3.1.18(p.229.13; M.11.288A).

***πεφαντασμένως,** *in dreams*, Diad.*perf*.37(p.42.24).

πεφασμένως, *in appearance, in seeming*, Olymp.*Job* 2:6(M.93.41B).

πεφεισμένως, *indulgently* π. ... ἠρέμα καὶ μετρίως Eus.*h.e*.8.1.7(M.20.741B); ‡Just.*qu.et resp*.108(M.6.1357A); Jo.Ant.*relat.imp*.3(p.130.34; M.83.1453B).

***πεφορτισμένως,** *as though weighed down*, Nil.*exerc*.16(M.79.740A).

πέψις, ἡ, 1. *mellowing*, met. πέψιν δὲ λύπης οἶδα μακροθυμίαν Gr.Naz.*carm*.1.2.34.46(M.37.949A); **2.** *digestion*, met. διὰ τῆς...μελέτης, οἷον διά τινος π. Bas.*hex*.3.10(1.32C; M.29.77B); Cyr.*Am*.37(3.292D).

πῇ μὲν . . . πῇ δέ, 1. *in one place . . . in another place*, Didym.*Trin*.1.7(M.39.272A); **2.** *at one time . . . at another time*, Thdr.Stud.*epp*.2.180(M.99.1557B).

***πηγάδιον, τό,** *little spring*, Jo.Mosch.*prat*.170(M.87.3037A); †Anast.S.*relat*.24(*OC* 2 p.74); εἰς τὸ βασιλικὸν πηγάδι Barth.Edess.*Agar*.(M.104.1429C; l. πηγάδιν).

πηγάζ-ω, I. intrans., *flow abundantly, well up*;

A. lit., Clem.*paed*.1.6(p.111.7; M.8.292C); Eus.*l.C*.1(p.197.22; M.20.1321B); πολυομβρίας γενομένης, λέγειν εἰώθαμεν, ὅτι ~ει ἡ γῆ, οὐχ ὡς ἐκδιδούσης, ἀλλὰ τὸ πλῆθος ἐμφαίνοντες Proc.G.*Gen*.2:5(M.87.149B).

B. met., *issue, spring forth*; **1.** in gen. ὁ σταυρὸς...εἰς πάντα πηγάσας [? as source of life] *A.Jo*.99(p.200.19, conj. πήξας); ζωὴν...ἐν ἑαυτῷ ~ουσαν Eus.*e.th*.1.20(p.86.29; M.24.876B); πνεῦμα, ἀφ' οὗ πᾶσα...ἡ τῶν ἀγαθῶν χορηγία ~ει Gr.Nyss.*diff.ess*.4(M.32.329C); ref. apostles as twelve springs of Elim κυρίου...~ειν δι' αὐτῶν τὸν λόγον ποιήσαντος id.*v.Mos*.(M.44.365C); Chrys.*hom.22.6 in Mt*.(7.283B); καθαρισμὸς...~ων ἐν ταῖς...ψυχαῖς id.*hom.16.2 in Heb*.(12.160A); οἴνῳ τὸ...κήρυγμα ὁ θεῖος...χρησμὸς ὁμοιοῖ, ποτὲ μὲν ἐκ τῆς δεσποτικῆς ~οντι πλευρᾶς Isid.Pel.*epp*.1.293(M.78.353C); τὰς πρεσβείας τῆς...παρθένου...δι' ὧν ἡμῖν ~ει βοήθεια Thphn.*chron*.p.370(M.108.885B); med., Sophr.H.*ep.syn*.(M.87.3172D); Jo.D.*Man*.1.74(M.94.1573A); **2.** theol. ταύτης γε τῆς ἐνθέου πνοῆς τὴν ἀντίληψιν τοῖς τὰς λογικὰς αἰσθήσεις μὴ πεπηρωμένοις ὁ σύμπας ἀποδίδωσι κόσμος, ὡς τὰ τῇ φύσει γεώδη...σώματα τῆς ἀΰλου...εὐωδίας ἀποπνεῖν, ~οντος μὲν ἄνωθεν τοῦ τῶν ὅλων θεοῦ Eus.*d.e*.5.1(p.214.14; M.22.356B); πνεῦμα τὸ ἅγιον τὸ ~ον ἐν τῇ ἐκκλησίᾳ id.*Is*.41:17(M.24.381A); ζωὴ...ἐκ μὲν τοῦ θεοῦ...~ουσα, διὰ δὲ τοῦ υἱοῦ προϊοῦσα, ἐν δὲ τῷ... πνεύματι ἐνεργουμένη Gr.Nyss.*ep*.5(M.46.1032C); πνεῦμα...αἴτιον αὐτὸν ἔχον ὡς πηγὴν ἑαυτοῦ, κἀκεῖθεν ~ον. ... ἀλλὰ τὸ μὲν ἐκ θεοῦ ~ον ἐνυπόστατόν ἐστι· τὰ δὲ ἐξ αὐτοῦ ~οντα ἐνέργειαι αὐτοῦ εἰσι Didym.(‡Bas.)*Eun*.5(1.322C; M.29.772C).

C. *give water* πέτρα δὲ διψῶσιν ἐπήγαζε Gr.Naz.*or*.6.17(M.35.744B).

II. trans.; **A.** *make to flow, cause to well up*, Clem.*paed*.1.6(p.115.5; M.8.300A).

B. met., *produce in abundance*; **1.** in gen. προφήτας...~οντας τὴν γλυκύτητα Thphl.Ant.*Autol*.2.14(M.6.1076A); Meth.*symp*.1.1(p.8.4; M.18.37B); Χριστὸς...~ων τὸ θεῖον νᾶμα τοῖς διψῶσι Or.*exc.in Ps*.77:31(M.17.141D); Gr.Nyss.*hom.1 in Cant*.(M.44.780A); *ib.2*(801B) cit. s. πηγή; id.*ep.can*.1(M.45.225A); ~ει ἡμῖν...ἑορτάς ‡Tit.Bost.*palm*.1(M.18.1264B); ἔρημος ἄρτους ἐπήγαζεν Bas.Sel.*or*.36.1(M.85.384D); Max.*ambig*.(M.91.1125C) cit. s. καμψάκης; of BMV σῶμα αὐτῆς τὸ πηγάσαν τὴν ἔμφυτον ἀθανασίαν ἐν τῇ θνητῇ...ἡμῶν φύσει Mod.*dorm*.12(M.86.3308C); **2.** theol., ‡Ath.*dial.Trin*.2.28(M.28.1200B) cit. s. πηγή; τῶν γενητῶν ἡ φύσις, οὐδὲν...ἐξ ἑαυτῆς ~ουσα, σύμπαν δὲ τὸ εἶναι...δεχομένη παρὰ τοῦ δημιουργοῦ Cyr.*Jo*.1.7(4.59C).

C. *water* ποίμνην...τοῖς λόγοις ἐπήγασα Gr.Naz.*carm*.2.1.12.116(M.37.1174A); Gr.Nyss.*hom.9 in Cant*.(M.44.977A).

***πηγαστικός**, *providing a source* νοῦς δὲ ὢν ὁ ἄναρχος φύσει θεός, ὁμοφυοῦς ὑπάρχει λόγου π.‡Cyr.*Trin*.13(6^{3}.20A; M.77.1149C); of Christ ζωῆς καὶ ἀθανασίας π. Germ.CP *or*.1(M.98.229D).

πηγή, ἡ, *source, fount*;

I. lit.; **A.** in pagan worship ἀνεγείρειν...τὸ εἴδωλον τῆς...κόρης ἐπὶ ταῖς τῶν ὑδάτων π. ἐνεργῆσαι τοὺς δαίμονας Just.*1apol*.64.1(M.6.425C); περὶ...τὰς π. τὰς Ναΐδας Clem.*prot*.4(p.45.30; M.8.157B); λατρεία δέ ἐστι διαβόλου...τὸ...θυμιᾶν παρὰ πηγάς Cyr.H.*catech*.19.8.

B. of πηγαὶ τοῦ πυρός above firmament, Meth.*res*.1.54(p.313.3; M.41.1148A).

C. of baptismal water παρέθηκε τροφὴν...ἰχθὺν [sc. Christ] ἀπὸ πηγῆς Aberc.*epitaph*.13; ἀεννάῳ ποταμῷ ἢ π. ... ἀπολουσάμενοι *Hom.Clem*.9.19.

D. of well of Samaria (Jo.4:6ff.), ref. literal and spiritual exegesis ἕκαστος...νοεῖ τὰ γεγραμμένα, ὁ μὲν ἐπιπολαιότερον οἷον ὡς ἐξ ἐπιπέδου π. λαμβάνων τὸν νοῦν ἀπ' αὐτῶν, ὁ δὲ βαθύτερον ὡς ἀπὸ φρέατος ἀνιμῶν. καὶ δύνανται ἀμφότεροι ὠφελεῖσθαι, ἐπεὶ τὸ αὐτὸ τῷ μέν ἐστι π., τῷ δὲ φρέαρ· μαρτυρεῖ τὸ εὐαγγέλιον, ἡνίκα διηγεῖται τὰ περὶ τῆς Σαμαρίτιδος· ἐκεῖ γὰρ ὀνομάζεται τὸ αὐτὸ π. καὶ φρέαρ, καὶ ἀνὰ μέρος ποτὲ λέγεται π. καὶ ποτὲ φρέαρ...τὸ αὐτὸ τῇ ὑποστάσει τῷ μὲν ἐπιπολαίῳ π. ἐστι, τῷ δὲ βαθυτέρῳ φρέαρ ἐστί Or.*hom.18.4 in Jer*.(p.154.15; M.13.468C).

E. of springs of Elim, typifying apostles, Marcell.*fr*.20 ap.Eus.*e.th*.3.3(p.149.14; M.24.988C); v. ἀπόστολος.

II. met., *source, origin*;

A. in gen. δεισιδαιμονία...κακίας ἀνοήτου γέγονε π. Clem.*prot*.3(p.34.2; M.8.129C); Meth.*lepr*.5(p.455.17); of source of instruction ὅπως κορεσθῶμεν τῆς σῆς π. *A.Andr.et Mt*.32(p.114.14); Thdt.*qu.53 in 3Reg*.(1.499); παρά σου...ἐδεξάμην τὰς τοῦ ἐλέους π. id.*Ps*.143:2(1.1554); ἐλέους πολλαὶ παρ' αὐτῷ π. id.*Joel* 2:13(2.1392); of copious speech, *Didasc.Jac*.3.2(p.52.24); for various other met. uses v. ἀναβλύζω.

B. of persons as fountain-heads; **1.** exeg. Pr.8:24 προφῆται, καθ' ὃ τοῦ αὐτοῦ μετέσχον πνεύματος ἁγίου, οὐκ ἦσαν ἀλλότριοι τῶν π. διὸ λέλεκται περὶ αὐτῶν...εὐλογεῖτε τὸν...κύριον ἐκ πηγῶν Ἰσραήλ. ὥστε καὶ πρὸ ἐκείνων τῶν π. ἀναγκαῖον ὁμολογεῖν τὸν υἱὸν εἶναι Eus.*e.th*.3.3(p.149.23; M.24.989A); τοὺς μὲν ἀποστόλους τὰς π. εἶναι βούλεται [sc. Marcellus], οὐκ ἀρέσκουσιν δὲ αὐτῷ οἱ προφῆται· διατί, ἀλλ' ἢ ὅτι μὴ ἐδύνατο τὴν σάρκα τοῦ σωτῆρος πρὸ ἐκείνων διδόναι; καίτοι καὶ πρὸ τῶν κατὰ φύσιν αἰσθητῶν π. ... προϋπῆρχεν ὁ...υἱός *ib*.(p.150.1; 989B); **2.** of Isaac as ἐθνῶν...μεγάλη π. Thdt.*carit*.(3.1314); **3.** of God in external relations; **a.** in gen. τῆς τοῦ θεοῦ ζώσης π. Just.*dial*.140.1(M.6.796D); ref. Jer.18:14 ταῦτα τὰ τρία εἴδη τῶν ὑδάτων αἱ π. εἰσι τῶν ὑδάτων ἃς ἐπιποθεῖ ἡ ὡμοιωμένη τῇ ἐλάφῳ ψυχή. ... ἐὰν μὴ τὰς τρεῖς π. τῶν ὑδάτων διψήσωμεν, οὐδὲ μίαν π. ... εὑρήσομεν. ἔδοξαν δεδιψηκέναι μιᾶς π. τῶν ὑδάτων, τοῦ θεοῦ, Ἰουδαῖοι Or.*hom.18.9 in Jer*.(p.162.30; M.13.481A); θεὸς...ἀγαθοῦ...π. Eus.*d.e*.4.1(p.150.19; M.22.252A); σὺ εἶ ἡ π. τῆς ζωῆς, ἡ π. τοῦ φωτός, ἡ π. πάσης χάριτος καὶ...ἀληθείας Serap.*euch*.13.5; Ath.*exp.Ps*.58:17(M.27.268C); Nil.*exerc*.20(M.79.745C); Cyr.*thes*.4(5^{1}.27C); θεὸς ἢ τοῦ εἶναι π. Bas.Sel.*or*.12.1(M.85.157C); ‡Cyr.*Trin*.7(6^{3}.8A; M.77.1132A); *Lit.Jac*.(p.198.22); **b.** of Father specifically πάντων...π. ... τῶν ἀγαθῶν Eus.*e.th*.2.7(p.106.23; M.24.913A); τὸ θεῖον βούλημα, οἷον πηγῆς τινος τῆς πρώτης αἰτίας ἀφορμηθέν, διὰ τῆς...εἰκόνος τοῦ...λόγου πρόεισιν εἰς ἐνέργειαν Bas.*Eun*.2.21(1.257B; M.29.617C); **c.** of Son π. ζωοποιός Clem.*prot*.10(p.78.22; M.8.228B); Eus.*e.th*.1.8(p.66.30; M.24.837C) cit. s. ἀκτίς; *ib*.1.20(p.94.5; 888D); τῶν ἀγαθῶν ἡ π. Gr.Nyss.*hom.1 in Cant*.(M.44.765C); τὰ ῥήματα τοῦ νυμφίου πνεῦμα καὶ ζωή ἐστι...διὰ τοῦτο ποθεῖ προσεγγίσαι τὴν ψυχὴν τῇ π. τῆς πνευματικῆς ζωῆς ἡ παρθένος ψυχή· ἡ δὲ π. ἐστι τοῦ νυμφίου τὸ στόμα...π. δὲ ὁ κύριος *ib*.(777D); ἠγάπησε τοὺς μαζοὺς τοῦ λόγου, ὁ ἐπὶ τὸ στῆθος τοῦ κυρίου ἀναπεσὼν Ἰωάννης, καὶ οἷόν τινα σπογγιὰν τὴν ἑαυτοῦ καρδίαν παραθεὶς τῇ π. τῆς ζωῆς *ib*.(785C); δραμοῦσα πρὸς σὲ τὴν π., σπάσω τοῦ θείου πόματος, ὃ σὺ τοῖς διψῶσι πηγάζεις, προσχέων τὸ ὕδωρ ἐκ τῆς πλευρᾶς *ib.2*(801B); id.*tres dii*(M.45.129A); ἁγιότητος ὑπάρχων π. τοὺς μαθητὰς ἁγιάζει Cyr.*thes*.13(5^{1}.139A); π. τοῦ ἐλέους Χριστόν Mod.*dorm*.2(M.86.3285A); Max.*opusc*.(M.91.33A); **d.** of Son and H. Ghost π. ἁγιασμοῦ Evagr.Pont.*ep.2*(3.82C; M.32.249B); **e.** of H. Ghost π. ἁγιασμοῦ Bas.*Eun*.3.2(1.274C; M.29.660C); π. τῆς ἁγιότητος id.*ep*.105(3.200B; M.32.513B); Didym.(‡Bas.)*Eun*.5(1.303A; M.29.725C); π. ὃν τῆς ἀιδίου ζωῆς *ib*.(320E; M.769A); *ib*.(322C; M.772C); ‡Thdt.*fr*.(4.1313); ‡Cyr.*Trin*.9(6^{3}.13C; M.77.1140B); **4.** of BMV ἀνθρώποις π. πνεύματος αἰωνίου Ephr.2.275D; π. ἐσφραγισμένη id.3.529F; π. τῆς χάριτος καὶ τῆς ἀθανασίας...ἁγίου πνεύματος π. ἐσφραγισμένη id.3.547F; as identified with Hera or Urania, *Pers*.(p.12.9ff.; M.10.100B); *ib*.(p.13.13; 101B); ἔμεινε δ' ὁ ἀστὴρ ἐπάνω τῆς π. τῆς κεκλημένης Οὐρανίας, ἄχρις ἂν ἐξῆλθον οἱ μάγοι *ib*.(p.14.13; 104A); π. ἀένναος, ἐν ᾗ τὸ ζῶν ὕδωρ ἔβλυσε τὴν ἔνσαρκον τοῦ κυρίου παρουσίαν ‡Gr.Thaum.*annunt*.2(M.10.1160B); ἡ τῶν θείων χαρισμάτων ἐσφραγισμένη π. τοῦ κυρίου ἀειπάρθενος Mod.*dorm*.6(M.86.3292C); of girdle of BMV, Germ.CP *or*.9(M.98.376D); **5.** of divine wisdom μόνη...ἡ παρ' ἡμῖν θεοδίδακτός ἐστι σοφία, ἀφ' ἧς αἱ πᾶσαι π. τῆς σοφίας ἤρτηνται Clem.*str*.6.18(p.517.28; M.9.400A); **6.** Trin.; **a.** of Father οὕτως αὐτῷ παρίστατο ἕτερος, ἕτερον δὲ λέγων οὐ δύο θεοὺς λέγω, ἀλλ' ὡς φῶς ἐκ φωτὸς ἢ ὡς ὕδωρ ἐκ π. Hipp.*Noët*.11(p.253.10; M.10.817C); Ar.*ep.Alex*.(p.13.7; M.26.709B); ποταμὸν ἀπὸ π. ῥέοντα ἕτερον σχῆμα καὶ ὄνομα μετειληφέναι· μήτε γὰρ τὴν π. ποταμὸν μήτε τὸν ποταμὸν π. λέγεσθαι καὶ ἀμφότερα ὑπάρχειν καὶ τὴν μὲν π. οἱονεὶ πατέρα εἶναι, τὸν δὲ ποταμὸν εἶναι τὸ ἐκ τῆς π. ὕδωρ...ζωὴ ἐκ ζωῆς ἐγεννήθη καὶ ὥσπερ ποταμὸς ἀπὸ π. ἔρρευσε καὶ ἀπὸ φωτὸς ἀσβέστου λαμπρὸν φῶς ἀνήφθη Dion.Al.ap.Ath.*Dion*.18(p.60.2; M.25.505C); τὴν ζωὴν καὶ τὴν σοφίαν μήτε ξένα τῆς οὐσίας τῆς π. εἶναι, ἀλλ' ἴδια...πῶς τοίνυν οὐκ ἀσεβεῖ ὁ λέγων, ἦν ποτε ὅτε οὐκ ἦν ὁ υἱός; ἴσον γάρ ἐστιν εἰπεῖν ἦν ποτε ὅτε ἡ π. ξηρὰ ἦν χωρὶς τῆς ζωῆς...ἡ δὲ τοιαύτη οὐκ ἂν εἴη π.· τὸ γὰρ μὴ ἐξ ἑαυτοῦ γεννῶν οὐκ ἔστι π. ... ἡ δὲ ἀλήθεια μαρτυρεῖ π. ἀΐδιον εἶναι τὸν θεὸν τῆς ἰδίας σοφίας. ἀϊδίου δὲ τῆς π. οὔσης, ἐξ ἀνάγκης καὶ τὴν σοφίαν ἀΐδιον εἶναι δεῖ Ath.*Ar*.1.19(M.26.52A); αὐτὸς γὰρ ὡς ἐκ π. τοῦ πατρός ἐστιν ἡ ζωή *ib*.3.1(324C); ἔστι μὲν ὁ πατὴρ...ῥίζα καὶ π. τοῦ υἱοῦ καὶ τοῦ πνεύματος ‡Ath.*Sabell*.11(M.28.116B); τὸ πνεῦμα...ἔχει...αἴτιον τὸν θεόν, οὐχ ὡς γενεσιουργόν, ἀλλ' ὡς π. ἑαυτοῦ· καθάπερ γὰρ ἡ π. οὐ γενεσιουργεῖ ἔξωθεν ὃ χορηγεῖ ὕδωρ, ἀλλ' ἐξ ἑαυτῆς πηγάζουσα ἔχει· οὕτως καὶ ὁ θεὸς π. τοῦ πνεύματός ἐστιν...ἐξ ἑαυτοῦ πηγάζων ‡Ath.*dial.Trin*.2.28(M.28.1200B); αὐτοάγαθον ἐκ τῆς ζωοποιοῦ π. τῆς πατρικῆς ἀγαθότητος προελθόντα Bas.*Eun*.2.25(1.261E; M.29.629B); Gr.Nyss.*tres dii*(M.45.128C); π. μὲν δυνάμεώς ἐστιν ὁ πατήρ, δύναμις δὲ τοῦ πατρὸς ὁ υἱός id.*Maced*.13(M.45.1317A); μία π. ἐκ π., ὁ υἱὸς προελθὼν Epiph.*haer*.69.54(p.201.14; M.42.285D); ἦν δὲ καὶ διὰ παντὸς ὡς ἐν π. τῷ πατρί...πηγῆς τοιγαροῦν νοουμένου τοῦ πατρός, ἦν ὁ λόγος ἐν αὐτῷ...ἀδικήσει δὲ ὅλως οὐδὲν τὸ ὡς ἐν π. τῷ πατρὶ τὸν υἱὸν ὑπάρχειν ἐννοεῖν· μόνον γὰρ τὸ ἐξ οὗ τὸ τῆς π. ἐν τούτοις ὄνομα σημαίνει Cyr.*Jo*.1.1(4.11E); πατὴρ...π. τοῦ δημιουργοῦντος λόγου *ib*.1.5(4.47B); id.*thes*.4(5^{1}.27D); πότε δὲ ἦν δίχα τῆς ἑαυτοῦ σοφίας ἡ τῆς σοφίας π.; id.*Heb*.1:8(p.375.18; M.74.960D); εἰ προχεῖται μὲν οἷά περ ἀπὸ π. τοῦ πατρὸς τὸ πνεῦμα, ἔστι γε μὴν οὐκ ἀλλότριον τοῦ υἱοῦ id.ap.*cat.Heb*.suppl.2:11(p.403.6); π. ὄντα τοῦ πνεύματος τὸν πατέρα Thdt.*haer*.5.3(4.389); **b.** of Son, Epiph.*haer*.69.54(p.201.14; M.42.285D); ὁ ἐκ τῆς θείας κρήνης π. ἀένναος ‡Caes.Naz.*dial*.20(M.38.876).

III. met., *stream, copious supply* ἄφθονοι μαρτύρων πηγαὶ Clem.*str*.2.20(p.181.1; M.8.1069A); μεμαρτυρήκασιν αἱ ἅγιαι παρθένοι, ὧν τὴν θείαν π. ἔχομεν ἐν τοῖς τοῦ ἁγίου...Μάρκου Cyr.*hom.div*.18.2(M.77.1101B) or perh. in lit. sense of place where martyr's blood flowed or bodies were cast, Thdt.*Is*.arg.(p.2.8; 2.166).

πῆγμα, τό, **1.** *outline, mark* left by an object οὐκ ὀδόντων τὰ π. τοῦ θηρίου ὑπάρχουσιν ἐν τῷ χιτῶνι Ephr.2.29B; **2.** *congealed state, coagulation*, ref. Jos.3:16 τὸ μέντοι π., ἄσκωμα ὁ Σύμμαχος ἡρμήνευσεν· ἐπεχομένη γὰρ τῶν ὑδάτων ἡ ῥύμη οἷον ἠσκοῦτο, καὶ ἐκορυφοῦτο Thdt.*qu.2 in Jos*.(1.305); of collocation of atoms, Dion.Al.ap.Eus.*p.e*.14.25(778A; M.21.1280B).

[*]**πηγμεντάριος**, ὁ, v. [*]πημεντάριος.

πήγνυμι, **1.** *fix*, exeg. Ps.21:17 τὸ δὲ 'ὤρυξάν μου χεῖρας...' ἐξήγησις τῶν ἐν τῷ σταυρῷ παγέντων...ἥλων ἦν Just.*1apol*.35.7(M.6.384C); **2.** *set in place, set up*, of Creation ῥήματι πήξας τὸν οὐρανόν Herm.*vis*.1.3.4; Clem.*paed*.3.12(p.290.19; M.8.680A); ὁ ἐν ἀπείρῳ τὸν μέγαν αἰῶνα ὡς κέντρον πήξας *Hom.Clem*.2.45; of formation of Christ's human nature in womb of BMV, Eust.*fr.in Pr.8:22*(M.18.677B) cit. s. ἄνθρωπος; of setting up Cross, Cyr.*Jo*.12(4.1046E); Oecum.*Apoc*.4(p.95); **3.** *pitch* a tent, ref. resurrection life αἱ σκηναὶ πήγνυνται πάντων ἡμῶν, ὁπότε...ἀνίσταται σῶμα Meth.*symp*.9.2 (p.116.7; M.18.181A); **4.** *establish*, a church ἀπόστολοι...ὑπὲρ τῶν ἐκκλησιῶν ἃς ἔπηξαν ἔπαθον Clem.*str*.4.9(p.282.2; M.8.1284D); Or. *Cels*.1.63(p.116.6; M.11.777C); id.*hom.12.8 in Jer*.(p.95.10; M.13. 389C); teaching, laws, etc., id.*Cels*.proem.5(p.54.22; 648C); Eus. *l.C*.11(p.224.28; M.20.1377A); Jo.D.*Gal*.6:17(M.95.821A); **5.** pass., *grow firm, strong* ἕως ἂν...παγῇ τὰ πτερά Chrys.*hom.4.2 in Phil*.(11. 221D); **6.** perf. intrans., *be firmly grounded* πέπηγεν...τῇ πίστει ὁ γνωστικός Clem.*str*.2.11(p.140.11; M.8.988A); πεπηγυῖα ἡ γνώμη Bas.*ep*.293(3.431E; M.32.1036A); οἱ γὰρ πεπηγότες...οὐδὲν πάσχουσιν Chrys.*hom.5.3 in 2Tim*.(11.688D).

πηδάλιον, τό, *rudder*; met., of Christ π. τῶν ψυχῶν Jo.Thess. *dorm.BMV* A 9(p.391.1).

πηδαλιουχ-έω, *steer*, hence *direct, govern*, of emperor τοῦ Ῥωμαίων κράτους τὸν σύμπαντα ~ῶν βίον Eus.*v.C*.2.19(p.48.28; M.20. 997A); of God πάντα ~οῦντα Didym.*Trin*.2.8(M.39.608D); αὐτοῦ νεύμασι ~εῖται τὰ σύμπαντα Cyr.*Am*.46(3.299E); id.*Nah*.11(3.488C); of Son, Eus.*e.th*.1.13(p.73.18; M.24.852A); πατρικῷ νεύματι τὸ μέγα τοῦ...κόσμου ~ῶν σκάφος id.*l.C*.12(p.231.27; M.20.1389B); of man as lord of creation, Cyr.*hom.pasch*.7(5².86C); of νοῦς as ruler of body, Melet.*nat.hom*.1(M.64.1161B); of law of conscience, Cyr.*Is*.2.5(2. 338C); of reason, id.*hom.pasch*.22(277A); of virtue, Procl.CP *Arm*.3 (p.188.15; M.65.857B); of fortune, fate, and genesis as controllers of destiny of pagans, Cyr.*Is*.1.1(2.22E).

πηδάω, *leap*; s.v.l., *leap over* ὁ ποταμὸν πηδήσας ‡Just.*or.Gr*.1(M. 6.232A).

πήληξ, ἡ, *crown of a building*, Paul.Sil.*Soph*.489(M.86.2138A).

πηλικότης, ἡ, *magnitude, size*; **1.** in gen. μόνα γὰρ τὰ πηλικότητι περιγεγραμμένα τινὶ καὶ ἄρχεται γινόμενα καὶ εἰς πέρας λήγει Gr.Nyss. *Eun*.9(2 p.215.1; M.45.813B); id.*anim.et res*.(M.46.40C); Isid.Pel. *epp*.2.172(M.78.624B); **2.** ref. Father and Son in divine nature τὸν μὴ ἔχοντα π. Bas.*Eun*.1.23(1.234C; M.29.561C); *ib*.1.25(236D; M. 568C); πῶς...ἐκ τοῦ ἀμεγέθους...τὸ...πηλικότητι ὁριζόμενον; Gr.Nyss. *hex*.7(M.44.69B); id.*hom.5 in Cant*.(M.44.873C); id.*Eun*.1(1 p.87.1; M.45.317D); Marc.Er.*opusc*.10.6(M.65.1125C).

***πηλινόγλωσσος,** *with earth-bound tongue*, ‡Jo.D.*hom*.5(M.96. 649A).

πήλινος, *of clay*; **1.** in gen., esp. of idols, Tat.*orat*.22(p.24.25; M.6.856A); Clem.*prot*.4(p.45.22; M.8.157A); *Hom.Clem*.16.19; **2.** of human body and organs, Hipp.*haer*.5.7(p.86.9; M.16.3135B); Mac. Mgn.*apocr*.2.7(p.5.15); γλώττῃ π. Thdt.*haer*.5.1(4.380); id.*provid*.1 (4.484); Eus.Al.*serm*.3(M.86.332A); of men, Rom.Mel.1.13(*AS* 1 p.46); **3.** *earthly, worldly*; of persons, Chrys.*hom.68.4 in Mt*.(7. 675C); id.*hom.4.3 in Ac*.(9.37B); of things, id.*hom.67.5 in Mt*. (668B); ‡Nil.*perist*.12.13(M.79.965C).

***πηλογενής,** *born of clay*, Geo.Pis.*carm.vit*.21; ‡Jo.D.*hom*.5(M. 96.660A).

***πηλόδετος,** *bound in clay, earth-bound*, Gr.Naz.*carm*.2.1.28.6 (M.37.1288A).

***πηλοειδῶς,** *like mud*, Gr.Nyss.*hex*.26(M.44.89A).

***πηλόν, τό,** *mud* τὰ π. τοῦ χειμῶνος Call.*v.Hyp*.(p.18.27).

πηλόομαι, 1. *be made into mud*, Hipp.*haer*.1.14(p.18.2; M.16. 3040B); **2.** *be defiled*, Eus.*d.e*.4.13(p.173.1; M.22.288C).

***πηλοπλαστέω,** *form from clay*; Adam, Meth.*symp*.3.3(p.29.22; M.18.64C); *ib*.3.5(p.31.18; 68B); Leont.B.*mesopent*.(M.86.1984B).

πηλοποι-έω, 1. *make muddy*; in gen., Ephr.2.273D; ref. Pharaoh's oppression of Hebrews τῷ πηλῷ καὶ τῇ πλινθείᾳ· πηλῷ φίλος τυγχάνων βούλεται καὶ τοὺς Ἑβραίους ~εῖν Or.*Cant*.2(p.128.30; M.13. 113B); **2.** ? *work with clay*; of monks, Pach.*reg*.A 59(p.21.5, v.l. πελο-; πληρο- M.40.952D); *ib*.B 134(p.21.5).

***πηλουργέω, 1.** *make clay*, Gr.Nyss.*Apoll*.18(M.45.1157D); **2.** *make from clay*, Meth.*symp*.3.5(p.31.14; M.18.68B); ‡Nil.*fr.pasch*. 2(M.79.1496B); Bas.Sel.*or*.2.1(M.85.37C).

πηλουργία, ἡ, *working in clay*, Epiph.*haer*.3(p.177.20; M.41. 189A); *ib*.66.19(p.43.2; M.42.57A).

πηλοφόρος, *bearing clay*, Tim.Ant.*caec*.5(M.28.1008C).

[*]πημεντάριος ([*]πηγμ-, [*]πιγμ-), ὁ, = πιμεντάριος, *apothecary*, Ephr.2.75F; Phot.*nomoc*.9.25(πηγμ- p.556; M.104.768C); πιγμ-, Gr. Mag.*dial*.(tr.Zach.)4.36(M.*PL*.77.383A).

πῆξις, ἡ 1. *fixing, stabilization* τὸν Μονογενῆ...ἑτέραν προβαλέσθαι συζυγίαν...Χριστὸν καὶ πνεῦμα ἅγιον, εἰς π. ... τοῦ πληρώματος Iren. *haer*.1.2.5(M.7.461A); εἰς π. καὶ βεβαίωσιν τῶν ἐκκλησιῶν Clem.*str*.7. 12(p.53.16; M.9.501C); **2.** *solidity, making solid, materialization* ἀέρα τε κατὰ τὴν λύπης [sc. of Achamoth] πῆξιν Iren.*haer*.1.5.4(M.7. 500A); **3.** *fixity, stability* ἐν τῷ τρεπομένῳ τὸ ἄτρεπτον ἀδύνατον λαβεῖν π. Clem.*str*.6.9(p.470.16; M.9.297B); Hipp.*haer*.8.9(p.228.13; M.16. 3351B); **4.** *fastening* to Cross, *A.Jo*.101(p.201.26); Gr.Naz.*carm*.1.2. 34.207(M.37.960A).

πήρα, ἡ, *wallet, pouch*; met., of BMV π., ἧς ὁ μαργαρίτης τοῦ ἡλίου λαμπρότερος Hesych.H.*serm*.5(M.93.1461A); cf. πέτρα.

***πήριον, τό,** *little wallet*, Jo.Mosch.*prat*.31(M.87.2880B); *V.Dan*.9 (p.258.4).

πηρός, 1. *disabled*, *Orac.Sib*.3.793; **2.** *blind*, of mental and spiritual blindness π. ... τῇ διανοίᾳ *2Clem*.1.6; Meth.*symp*.3.13(p.43.18; M.18. 84B); ἔστω σου π. ὁ νοῦς περὶ τὰ αἴσχιστα Nil.*Eulog*.19(M.79.1117B).

πηρ-όω, A. *maim, disable*; **1.** in gen. πηρωθεὶς τὼ πόδε Clem.*prot*. 2(p.22.4; M.8.101B); Chrys.*hom.53.1 in Mt*.(7.537D); Thdt.*h.rel*.8(3. 1182); met. μὴ τὴν βλαστήσασαν...πίστιν πηρώσωσιν Chrys.*hom.80.2 in Mt*.(767D); **2.** of sterility ἀτοκίαν...ὠνήσαντο, καὶ τὴν φύσιν ἐπήρωσαν *ib*.28.5(340E); πεπηρωμένην...μήτραν Thdt.*qu.3 in 1Reg*. (1.356); met. ~ῶ τὴν γαστέρα τῆς γῆς Chrys.*hom.35.3 in Mt*.(402C); *ib*.56.6(575A); **3.** esp. of infirmity of the eyes, Just.*dial*.12.2(M.6. 500B); Cels.ap.Or.*Cels*.6.66(p.136.18; M.11.1397D); Chrys.*hom.20.5 in Mt*.(7.266C); met., of spiritual blindness, Meth.*symp*.8.3(p.84.11; M.18.141C); ~οῦται τὸ τῆς διανοίας ὄμμα Chrys.*hom.2.1 in 1Tim*. (11.556B); hence

B. *blind*, *A.Jo*.113(p.212.12); Cels.ap.Or.*Cels*.3.77(p.268.23; M.11. 1020D); Chrys.*hom.14.2 in 1Cor*.(10.119D); met., of spiritual blindness, cf. καρδίαι πεπώρωνται Just.*dial*.33.1 (v.l. πεπήρωνται M.6. 545B); πεπηρωμένοις...τὴν διάνοιαν Hipp.*haer*.8.14(p.234.13, cj. for πεπληρωμένοις M.16.3362A); Eus.*d.e*.9.15(p.437.19; M.22.705A); Ath. *gent*.47(M.25.96A); Cyr.*ador*.8(1.270E).

πήρωμα, τό, *disablement, disability*, Bas.*hom.1 in Ps*.14(1.357C; M.29.264B); Chrys.*hom.56.2 in Jo*.(8.328B).

πήρωσις, ἡ, 1. *mutilation, disablement, disability*, in gen., Cels.ap. Or.*Cels*.8.45(p.260.6; M.11.1584B); Gr.Nyss.*ep*.3(M.46.1021A); Chrys. *hom.38.6 in 1Cor*.(10.359C); met. νοητῆς ἀκοῆς...π. Cyr.*ador*.12(1. 416A); esp. of the eyes, Clem.*prot*.10(p.75.8; M.8.220C); *M.Ner.et Ach*.22(p.21.14); hence **2.** *blindness*, Const.*or.s.c*.11 (cj. for ῥώσεως p.169.11; πωρ- M.20.1265); Gr.Nyss.*or.catech*.5(p.27.11; M.45.24D); Chrys.*hom.45.1 in Mt*.(7.476D); of mental and spiritual blindness, Eus.*v.C*.3.57(p.104.31; M.20.1124C); Ath.*ep.Serap*.4.15(M.26.660A); ἡ πλεονεξία πήρωσιν ἐπάγει τῷ διορατικῷ τῆς καρδίας Gr.Nyss.*or. dom*.3(p.50.19; M.44.1152B); Chrys.*hom.81.3 in Mt*.(7.776C); id.*hom. 8.1 in Jo*.(8.48C).

[*]πήχη, ἡ, = πῆχυς, *cubit* ὡς ἐπὶ πήχην μίαν *V.Mac*.A(p.149 where *V.Mac*.B has πῆχυν ἕνα); *Contrad*.1(p.7).

πηχισμός, ὁ, *measurement by cubits*, Iren.*haer*.5.29.2(M.7.1202C); Cosm.Ind.*top*.11(M.88.449C).

πῆχυς, ὁ, *cubit, cubit rule*; hence *cubit measure of Nile inundation, Nilometer*, transferred by Const. from Serapeum to church, Socr.*h.e*.1.18.47(M.67.121B); Thphn.*chron*.p.13(M.108.88A).

[*]πηχυσμός, ὁ, *measurement by cubits* of inundation of Nile, Anast.S.*qu.et resp*.20(M.89.521C, perh. for πηχισμός).

[*]πιθύχιον, τό, = πτύχιον, *folding tablet*, Alex.Sal.*Barn*.44(451B).

[*]πιγμεντάριος, ὁ, v. [*]πημεντάριος.

πιεστήριον, τό, *press*; for torture, Synes.*ep*.58(M.66.1400B).

[*]πιθανάομαι, = sq., ‡Just.*monarch*.6(M.6.325B).

πιθανεύομαι, *be persuasive, use plausible arguments*, Clem.*str*.1.19 (p.61.19; M.8.812B).

πιθανολογ-έω, 1. *use plausible language about*, Hipp.*Dan*.2.20.1; abs., *play the sophist*, Meth.*symp*.2.7(p.24.8; M.18.57B); **2.** *make plausible* τὰ...οὐκ ὄντα ~εῖν ἔοικεν ὡς ὄντα Eust.*engast*.27(p.59.6; M.18.669D).

πιθανολογία ([*]πειθανολ-), ἡ, 1. *plausibility in argument*, Clem.*str*.6.10(p.472.4; M.9.301B); σοφιστικὴν π. *ib*.(p.473.17; 304B); Ath.*syn*.20(p.247.5; M.26.716D); Bas.*Eun*.1.1(1.207B; M.29.500A); Gennad.*fr.Rom*.9:1(p.386.31; M.85.1708A); πειθ-, Max.*ep*.12(M.91. 508D); **2.** plur., *plausible arguments* πιθανολογίαις παρατραπεὶς Bas. *Spir*.26(3.22B; M.32.113B).

πιθανοποιέω, *make plausible*, Nil.*Eulog*.22(M.79.1124A).

πιθανότης, ἡ, 1. *plausible argument* συλλογισμῶν πιθανότητες Tat. *orat*.27(p.29.14; M.6.865B); Or.*hom.4.4 in Jer*.(p.27.11; M.13.292A); Ath.*syn*.45(p.271.9; M.26.776A); Isid.Pel.*epp*.3.6(M.78.732A); **2.** *persuasion, conviction* ἀπόστητε ἀπὸ τῆς...ταύτης π. *M.Scill*.7; *ib*.8; ἆρα γὰρ ὡς ἔτυχε...ἔλεγον οἱ προφῆται σὺν οὐδεμιᾷ π., τῇ κινούσῃ αὐτούς; Or.*Cels*.3.2(p.204.16; M.11.921C); Ath.*syn*.39(p.265.22; M.26. 761C).

πιθανουργία, ἡ, *plausible argumentation*, Didym.*Trin*.2.6(M.39. 516C).

***πιθανώδης,** *persuasive, seductive*, *A.Phil*.142(p.80.16).

πιθάριον, τό, *jar*, ‡Pion.*v.Polyc*.25,26; Dor.*doct*.7(M.88.1693C).

πιθήκειος, *ape-like, simian*, Gr.Naz.*or*.43.64(M.36.581C); Isid. Pel.*epp*.3.99(M.78.805D); Philost.*h.e*.3.11(M.65.496C).

πιθηκισμός, ὁ, *travesty, aping, spurious imitation*; of baptism administered outside Church, CCarth.*act*.(H.1.176E).

πικράζω, 1. *make bitter*, Or.*Cels*.3.70(p.262.30; M 11.1012D); pass., *be grieved, embittered*, Didym.*exp.in Ps*.5:11(M.39.1173B); **2.** *taste bitter to* τὸ μέλι γλυκάζει μὲν τοὺς ὑγιαίνοντας, πικράζει δὲ τοὺς πυρέσσοντας Clem.*str*.8.9(p.101.1; M.9.600B).

πικραίνω, *make bitter*; pass., *be embittered, exasperated*, ‡Chrys. *pasch*.1(8.250C).

***πικραλίς, ἡ,** *bitter herb*, as one of three ὕλαι of Passover, ‡Ath. *azym*.(M.26.1328A).

πικρία, ἡ, *bitterness*; **1.** lit., in simile of Israel as vine λέγει...τῇ στραφείσῃ εἰς π. ἀμπέλῳ Or.*hom.2.2 in Jer*.(p.18.6; M.13.280A); Eus.*Is*.1:8(M.24.93A); **2.** met. οὐκ ἐπιτάξεις δούλῳ...ἐν π. σου *Did*. 4.10; ἐκ τῆς ἀφροσύνης γίνεται π., ἐκ δὲ π. θυμός Herm.*mand*.5.2.4; defined as ὀργὴ δυσπαράδεκτος ἢ παραχρῆμα ἐκρηγνυμένη Or.*comm. in Eph*.4:31(p.556); ἔοικεν δὲ...τὴν ἐναντίαν τάξιν τῇ π. χρηστότητα νῦν λέγειν, ἀπὸ τῶν βρωμάτων μεταφορικῶς *ib*.4:32(p.558); of sin πικρίας μὲν διδάγματα καὶ ἀθεότητος συμπίνοντες Just.*dial*.120.2(M.6.753C); *Clem.ep*.15(M.2.52A); of heresy, Gr.Nyss.*Eun*.10(2 p.238.13; M.45. 840D); of distress δεῖ σε πικρίας ἐμπλησθῆναι ἐν τῷ βίῳ τούτῳ Or. *hom.14.16 in Jer*.(p.122.23; M.13.425A); π. ἢ μᾶλλον συμπάθειαν τοῦ πατρός Max.*schol.ep.Dion.Ar*.8.4(M.4.552A).

[*]**πικριασμός, ὁ,** = πικρασμός, *bitterness*, *T.Lev*.11.7 (v.l. πικρία μου).

πικρίς, ἡ, *bitter herb, ox-tongue*, Mac.Aeg.*hom*.7.3(M.34.525B); in monastic diet πολλοὶ...οὔτε ἄρτον ἤσθιον οὔτε ὀπώρας, ἀλλὰ π. μόνον ‡Pall.*h.mon*.24.4(p.85.11; M.34.1177C); ref. Ex.12:8 ἔχε δὲ εἰλικρίνειαν καὶ ἀλήθειαν, καὶ π. ἔσονταί σοι, καὶ ἐσθίεις μετὰ πικρίδων τὰ ἄζυμα τῆς εἰλικρινείας καὶ ἀληθείας. οἷον Παῦλος, ἐπειδήπερ ἤσθιε τὰ ἄζυμα εἰλικρινείας...καὶ π. ἤσθιε. πῶς π. ἤσθιε; λέγων, ἐχθρὸς ὑμῶν γέγονα ἀληθεύων ὑμῖν. πῶς π. ἤσθιεν; ἐν κόπῳ καὶ μόχθῳ Or.*hom. 14.16 in Jer*.(p.123.6; M.13.425B); τῷ δὲ τὴν τελειοτέραν ἐπιζητοῦντι τροφήν, ἄρτος γίνεται, οὐκέτι ἐπὶ πικρίδων ἐσθιόμενος...πρὸς γὰρ τὸ παρόν ἐστιν ἡ π. Gr.Nyss.*hom.10 in Cant*.(M.44.988D); πικρίδας συνεσθίεσθαι τοῖς ἄρτοις τοῖς οὐκ ἐζυμωμένοις, τὴν ἄδολον...ἐν Χριστῷ ζωὴν οὐ δίχα πικρίας ἐσομένην ὑποδηλοῖ Cyr.*ador*.2(1.80B); τοῦ...ἐπ' ἀζύμων ἐσθίεσθαι καὶ π. ... ὑπογράφοντος, ὅτι δεήσει καὶ ἡμᾶς...ζύμης ἀπηλλάχθαι τῆς νοητῆς, τουτέστι κακίας...καὶ πικρῶν ἀνέχεσθαι πόνων *ib*.17(595D).

***πικρογόνος**, *producing bitterness*, Cosm.Mel.*hymn*.12(1.48 p.162; M.98.504C).

***πικροθάνατος**, *subject to a cruel death*, Thphn.*chron*.p.313(M.108. 760D).

***πικρόνους**, *of venomous mind*, Cyr.*Jo*.9(4.743C).

πικρός, 1. *sharp* κέρας αὐτοῦ...πικρὸν τὴν πορνείαν Meth.*symp*.8.13 (p.98.11; M.18.160C); met. τοὺς π. εἰς σύνεσιν Cyr.*Is*.4.2(2.597A); **2.** *accurate, exact*, Cyr.*ador*.1(1.45A).

***πικροφόρος**, *bearing bitter fruit*; of withered fig-tree, Meth. *symp*.10.5(p.127.29; M.18.201A); Chrys.ap.*cat.Lc*.12:49(p.105.19).

***πικρόφυλλος**, *with bitter leaves*, Geo.Pis.*hex*.933(M.92.1506A).

[*]**πικρόχυλος**, *bilious*, Melet.*nat.hom*.31(M.64.1293C).

πικρῶς, 1. *bitterly, in misery*, Arist.*apol*.12.2; Meth.*symp*.11.11 (p.133.18; M.18.209B); **2.** s.v.l., *with difficulty*, id.*creat*.7(p.498.2; M. 18.340A); **3.** *accurately, exactly*, Cyr.*Jo*.10.2(4.885A).

πίλα, ἡ, (Lat. *pila*) *mole, pier*, Jo.Mal.*chron*.11 p.278(M.97.420B).

***πιλλός**, *blear-eyed, dim-sighted* π. δὲ τοὺς ὀφθαλμοὺς ὁ βλέπων μέν, οὐχ ὑγιῶς δέ, ὡς οἱ αἱρετικοί, θεὸν μὲν εἶναι πιστεύοντες, οὐχ ὑγιῶς δὲ περὶ αὐτοῦ δογματίζοντες †Cyr.*coll.VT*(6[4].27D; M.77.1216C).

πῖλος, ὁ, *mitre* of high priest ὁ π. ... τὴν ἐξουσίαν μηνύει τὴν βασιλικὴν τοῦ κυρίου Clem.*str*.5.6(p.351.22; M.9.64B).

πιλ-όω, 1. *make firm* or *compact* κύριος...γῆν ~ώσας *Hom.Clem*.2. 45; *ib*.3.32; **2.** med., *contract, shrink* ἐρίων ⟨τὰ⟩ ὑγραινόμενα ~οῦται Adam.*dial*.5.16(p.206.12; codd. πιλῇ M.11.1856A).

πίμπλημι, pass., *reach full measure, be complete* ἐπλήσθησαν αἱ ἀνομίαι αὐτῶν Herm.*vis*.2.2.2.

πινακίδιον, τό, *tablet* for writing, Dor.*doct*.1.17(M.88.1640C).

πινάκιον, τό, 1. = foreg., Synes.*provid*.15(p.98.20; πινακίδιον M. 66.1248B); **2.** *plate, dish*, Chrys.*hom.7.4 in Col*.(11.377E).

πινακίς, ἡ, *tablet*, on which sentence of court was recorded, *M.Pion*.20.7(p.56.10); of a child's slate, Chrys.*hom.4.3 in Col*.(11. 355B,E).

***πιναροποιός, ὁ,** *worker in mother-of-pearl*, Epiph.*gemm*.3(M.43. 296C).

πίννη (πίννα), ἡ, = πίνη, πῖνα, a kind of shell-fish, Clem.*paed*.2. 12(p.228.2; M.8.540C) citing Theophrastus *lapid*.36; ‡Ath.*qu.al*.19 (M.28.789D); Nemes.*nat.hom*.1(M.40.509A).

***πίξος, ὁ,** ? *harness* οἱ π. τῶν ἵππων *Vaticin*.1(p.49).

***πιπι**, Hebr. יהוה transcribed as divine name π. ὁ θεός Evagr. Pont.*schol*.(p.206).

***πιπτεγείρω**, *fall so as to rise*, Ephr.1.205D.

πίπτ-ω, A. *fall*; hence *die*, in rel. to B infra, of Christ's death ἑορτή...ἐπὶ τῇ ἀναστάσει τοῦ πεπτωκότος ἐπιτελεῖται· πτῶσις δέ ἐστιν ἡ ἁμαρτία· ἀνάστασις δὲ ἡ ἐκ τοῦ πτώματος...ἀνόρθωσις Gr.Nyss.*ep. can*.1(M.45.221B).

B. met., *fall* into sin, from blessedness; **1.** in gen. τοὺς πεπτωκότας ἔγειρον *1Clem*.59.4; *2Clem*.2.6; ~οντος τοῦ Ἰσραὴλ *Barn*.12. 5; ὡς εἷς τῶν ἀρχόντων πίπτετε. πλειόνων γὰρ ἀρχόντων γενομένων, εἷς πέπτωκεν, ᾧ παραπλησίως μιμούμενοι τὴν ἐκείνου πτῶσιν ~ουσιν οἱ ἁμαρτάνοντες...καὶ πρὸς οὓς ὁ λόγος φησὶ τό...θεοί ἐστε...ἀποπεσόντες τῆς μακαριότητος...ὡς ἄνθρωποι ἀποθνήσκουσιν καὶ ὡς εἷς τῶν ἀρχόντων ~ουσιν Or.*Jo*.32.18(11; p.457.6; M.14.792B); πεσόντες εἰς τὰς ἡδονάς Meth.*symp*.8.2(p.82.7; M.18.140B); πεπτωκότα φρονήματα Chrys.*stat*.1.1(2.1A); **2.** of heretics ~ουσι καὶ οἱ λέγοντες αὐτὸν μηδὲν εἰληφέναι ἐκ τῆς παρθένου Iren.*haer*.3.22.1(M.7. 955C); **3.** of 'lapsed' in persecution οὐ γὰρ ἔλαβον καύχημα κατὰ τῶν πεπτωκότων *Ep.Lugd*.ap.Eus.*h.e*.5.2.6(M.20.436B); ἐν...τῷ πειρασμῷ πεσών Dion.Al.ap.Eus.*h.e*.6.44.2(M.20.629B); ὁ Ναυᾶτος...ἀντέλεγεν ...μὴ δεῖν τοῖς πεπτωκόσι δοῦναι χεῖρα Tim.CP *haer*.(M.86.37A); **4.** of sexual immorality ἔπεσε μετ' αὐτῆς *Apophth.Patr*.(M.65. 309B); Jo.Mosch.*prat*.39(M.87.2892B); περὶ ~οντος εἰς ἀβάπτιστον †Jo.Jej.*poenit*.(M.88.1921D); **5.** of Fall ἐκεῖνος ἐν θεότητι τυγχάνων πέπτωκεν Or.*Jo*.32.18(11; p.457.9; M.14.792B); συνέβη παρεληλυθότα τὴν ἐντολὴν ὀλέθριον πτῶμα καὶ δεινὸν πεσεῖν Meth.*symp*.3.6(p.32.18; M.18.69A); *ib*.10.3(p.125.6; 197A); id.*res*.1.37(p.279.15; M.41.1104C); Chrys.*hom.18.1 in Gen*.(4.151B); hence of human nature assumed by Christ ἑνωθέντος...τοῦ πεσόντος σώματος τῷ τὰ πάντα ζωογονοῦντι λόγῳ Cyr.*Jo*.1.9(4.95B).

C. *enter*, of prayer εἰς ὦτα θεοῦ μάλιστα ~ουσα ‡Thdt.*nativ.Jo. Bapt*.(5.97).

D. *fall, come under* τῶν ὑπὸ τὴν ἐπίσκεψιν ~όντων Hipp.*haer*.4.3 (p.34.10; M.16.3062A); CAnc.(314)*can*.24.

E. *be applied to, relate to* τὸ γὰρ ἐπιθυμῆσαι οὐχὶ ἐπὶ τῶν παρόντων καὶ ὑποκειμένων ἐν ἐξουσίᾳ ~ει Meth.*res*.2.1(p.330.8; M.18.297A); μετάνοια...οὐ ~ει πρὸς τὸν κατ' οὐσίαν κακόν Didym.*Man*.15(M.39. 1105A).

[*]**πισάριον, τό,** = πιθάριον, *jar* used as dry measure, Cyr.S. *v.Sab*.40(p.130.32).

***πισκινή, ἡ,** (Lat. piscina) *bath*, of π. πουπλική in Rome, Hipp. *haer*.9.12(p.246.18; M.16.3379C).

πισσηρός, *pitched*, ‡Ath.*v.Syncl*.71(M.28.129B).

***πιστακοκενός**, *consisting of empty nuts* καρπὸς...π. Ant.Mon. *hom*.45(M.89.1573D).

πιστευτός, *reliable, trustworthy*, Or.*Jo*.2.6(4; p.60.14; M.14.120A).

πιστεύ-ω, A. *trust* in, *have confidence* in, in gen. ἐπὶ ὄφιν...~ειν Just.*dial*.91.4(M.6.693B); ~ειν τῷ παρὰ τοῦ θεοῦ πνεύματι Athenag. *leg*.7.2(M.6.904C); ὅταν ἀνδριᾶσι πιστεύσωσιν Clem.*prot*.10(p.71.15; M.8.212B); τοὺς ἄνευ νοῦ καὶ ἐπιστήμης δόξαις ~οντας id.*str*.1.8(p.28. 7; M.8.740A); ὑπονοίᾳ γὰρ μᾶλλον ἢ τῷ φρονεῖν πεπιστευκότες Meth. *symp*.8.13(p.99.6; M.18.161B); τοῖς ἀτόμοις ~ων Thdt.*affect*.11(p.276. 18; 4.988); pass., *be object of trust*, Clem.*str*.7.12(p.56.10; M.9.508C).

B. *have faith* in, *believe* in; **1.** God ~ω τῷ θεῷ ὅτι ζῇ Ἰωσήφ *T.Neph*.7.2; πρὸ τοῦ ἡμᾶς πιστεῦσαι τῷ θεῷ ἦν...τὸ κατοικητήριον τῆς καρδίας φθαρτόν *Barn*.16.7; ἐπὶ τὸν παντοκράτορα θεὸν δι' αὐτοῦ ~ειν Just.*dial*.83.4(M.6.673A); Or.*hom.1.4 in Jer*.(p.3.22; M.13.260A); ~ειν βεβαίως τῷ θεῷ Meth.*symp*.10.4(p.126.18; M.18.200B); βέβαιον γὰρ τῶν εἰς τὸν θεὸν πεπιστευκότων τὸ φρόνημα Thdt.*Is*.32:17(p.130. 20; 3.311); **2.** Christ ~σωσιν ἐπὶ...τὸν σταυρωθέντα Ἰησοῦν Just. *dial*.46.1(M.6.573A); τοὺς ~οντας εἰς αὐτόν *ib*.70.4(641A); Or.*princ*. 4.2.1(p.306.3; M.11.357A); id.*hom.9.1 in Jer*.(p.65.18; M.13.349C); ~οντες εἰς Χριστὸν...καὶ ~οντες ἀνάστασιν σωμάτων, ~οντες δὲ ὅτι ζησόμεθα id.*comm.in 1Cor*.1:19–21(*JTS* 9 p.236); Meth.*symp*.6.2 (p.65.20; M.18.116A); μὴ ~ειν εἰς τὸν υἱὸν τοῦ θεοῦ Eus.*e.th*.1.20(p.97. 3; M.24.893C); Didym.*Trin*.1.7(M.39.269A); κἂν γὰρ εἰς τὸν πατέρα τις καὶ τὸν υἱὸν ὀρθῶς ~σῃ καὶ εἰς τὸ πνεῦμα τὸ ἅγιον, βίον δὲ μὴ ἔχῃ ὀρθόν, οὐδὲν αὐτῷ κέρδος τῆς πίστεως Chrys.*hom.31.1 in Jo*.(8. 175C); τῷ ἐν Βηθλεὲμ γεννηθέντι...πεπιστευκότες Thdt.*Mich*.5:6(2. 1503); ἐπίστευσαν ὑπὸ τὸν κύριον *Mir.Geo*.12(p.129.4); in rel. to knowledge, v. γινώσκω; **3.** H. Ghost, Chrys.*hom.31.1 in Jo*.(8. 175C); **4.** in credal profession of faith in three Persons ~ω εἰς θεόν *Lit.Marc*.(*PDêr-Baliz*.p.3 v° 3); ~ω εἰς θεὸν παντοκράτορα...καὶ εἰς Χριστὸν...καὶ εἰς τὸ ἅγιον πνεῦμα Marcell.*ep*.ap.Epiph.*haer*.72.3 (p.258.6; M.42.385D); *Symb.App*.(pp.23,30,31); ~ω εἰς ἕνα θεόν Cyr.H. *catech*.6 tit.(M.33.538); ~ω καὶ βαπτίζομαι εἰς ἕνα...θεόν *Symb*.ap. *Const.App*.7.41.4; ~ομεν εἰς ἕνα θεόν *Symb.Nic*.(325)(p.51; M.20. 1540B); *Symb.Ant*.(341)2(p.249.11; M.26.721B); *Symb.Ant*.(341)4 (p.251.1; M.26.725B); *Symb.Ant*.(345)1(p.251.22; M.26.728A) etc.

C. *hold a belief, hold the faith* πεπιστεύκαμεν ἕνα θεὸν εἶναι Athenag.*leg*.7.1(M.6.904B); οὔτε...ἄλλως πεπιστεύκασιν ἢ ἄλλως παραδιδόασιν Iren.*haer*.1.10.2(M.7.552B); Apollon.ap.Eus.*h.e*.5.18.5 (M.20.477A); ἀνάγκη...οὕτω ~ειν ὡς ἐβαπτίσθημεν Amph.*ep.syn*.(M. 39.96D); ~εσθαι κατὰ τὰς ἀποστολικὰς ἐξηγήσεις ‡Chrys.*pasch*.1(8. 251C); hence

D. *believe, hold Christian faith, be a Christian*, Clem.*paed*.1.6 (p.107.20; M.8.285A); id.*str*.2.13(p.144.1; M.8.996B); ἁγίους γενέσθαι τοὺς ~οντας Or.*hom.8.2 in Jer*.(p.57.14; M.13.337C); Gr.Thaum. *pan.Or*.15(p.34.11; M.10.1093D); συλλαβεῖν τοὺς ~οντας καὶ ἀναγεννῆσαι διὰ τοῦ λουτροῦ Meth.*symp*.3.8(p.35.23; M.18.73B); *ib*.3. 11(p.39.7; 77A); Serap.*euch*.5.4; Gr.Nyss.*Eun*.10(2 p.231.18; M.45. 832D); τὸ μὴ ~ειν ἀπὸ πονηρᾶς γίνεσθαι συνειδήσεως Chrys.*hom.28.3 in Jo*.(8.163B); Thdt.*qu.12 in Ex*.(1.129); id.*qu.16 in Jos*.(1.313); esp. in aor., of acceptance of Christian faith in connexion with baptism, Clem.*paed*.1.6(p.107.16; M.8.285A); τὸν δὲ μετὰ τὸ ~σαι ...πάλιν ἡμαρτηκότα Or.*hom.2.3 in Jer*.(p.19.12; M.13.281A); μετὰ τὸ π. καὶ ἐπὶ τὸ ὕδωρ ἐλθεῖν Meth.*res*.1.41(p.287.1; M.18.269B); Chrys. *hom.28.1 in Jo*.(8.160C).

E. *have faith, Barn*.11.11; μόνος ~σας ἐτέθη εἰς δικαιοσύνην *ib*. 13.7; πῶς...εἰ τὸ ~ειν ὑπολαμβάνειν ἐστί, βέβαια τὰ παρ' αὐτῶν οἱ φιλόσοφοι νομίζουσιν; Clem.*str*.2.6(p.127.28; M.8.964A); opp. have knowledge τῷ μὲν γνωστικῷ...τῷ δὲ ἁπλῶς πεπιστευκότι *ib*.4.18 (p.298.20; 1321C); πλέον δέ ἐστι τοῦ πιστεῦσαι τὸ γνῶναι *ib*.6.14(p.486. 21; M.9.332A); πάντες μὲν οὖν κέκληνται ἐπ' ἴσης...ἐκλέγονται δὲ οἱ μᾶλλον ~σαντες id.*exc.Thdot*.9(p.109.13; M.9.660B); ὁ μὲν ~σας ἄφεσιν ἁμαρτημάτων ἔλαβεν παρὰ τοῦ κυρίου, ὁ δ' ἐν γνώσει γενόμενος ἅτε μηκέτι ἁμαρτάνων παρ' ἑαυτοῦ τὴν ἄφεσιν τῶν λοιπῶν κομίζεται id.*ecl*.15(p.141.5; M.9.705A); Or.*Cels*.1.10(p.62.25; M.11.673C); πίστευσον πρῶτον, καὶ εὑρήσεις ὑπὸ τὸ νομιζόμενον σκάνδαλον πολλὴν ὠφέλειαν ἁγίαν id.*fr.hom.39 in Jer*.(p.197.2; M.13.541D); ἐξαλείφονται αἱ ἁμαρτίαι...τῷ θέλειν, τῷ ~ειν Cyr.H.*procatech*.8; ~ω, οὐκ ἐρευνῶ· ~ω, οὐ διώκω τὸ ἀκατάληπτον· ~ω, οὐ μετρῶ τὸ ἀμέτρητον. ἐὰν ~σω, φωτίζομαι τὴν ψυχήν· ἐὰν περιεργάζωμαι, σκοτίζω μου τοὺς λογισμούς· ἐὰν ~σω καλῶς, ἀνυψοῦμαι πρὸς οὐρανόν· ἐὰν ζητήσω περιέργως, καταφέρομαι πρὸς βυθόν ‡Chrys.*Mt.20:1*(8.104A).

F. *believe* in, *give credence* to ἐν τοῖς εἰρημένοις ἐν εὐαγγελίοις... ~ουσιν Hegem.*Arch*.5(p.7.4; M.10.1436A); ὁ μὴ τούτῳ ~ων, οὐκ αὐτῷ μόνον, ἀλλὰ καὶ τῷ πατρὶ ἀπιστεῖ Chrys.*hom.30.2 in Jo*.(8. 172B); Thdt.*eran*.3(4.211); pass., *be believed*; of a person, Meth. *symp*.2.7(p.24.12; M.18.57C).

G. *be faithful* to οὕτω τοῖς θείοις πεπίστευκε νόμοις Thdt.*h.e*.5.37.2 (3.1079).

H. *believe* a fact ~σωμεν ὅτι ὁ υἱὸς...οὐκ ἠδύνατο παθεῖν εἰ μὴ δι' ἡμᾶς *Barn*.7.2; ~ειν...τὰ τῇ ἑαυτῶν φύσει...ἀδύνατα Just.*1apol*.19.6 (M.6.357B); μὴ ~όντων εἰ ἀληθῶς...ἀνέστη †Just.*fr.res*.(p.47; M.6. 1588C); πεπιστεύκαμεν ἕνα θεὸν εἶναι Athenag.*leg*.7.2(M.6.904B); ἀνάστασιν πεπιστευκὼς *ib*.36.1(969B); ~οντα ὅτι ἀληθεῖς αἱ γραφαί Or. *princ*.3.1.9(p.209.8; M.11.264A); id.*hom.19.15 in Jer*.(p.175.21; M. 13.497D); τὸν...ἄρτον εἰς σῶμα τοῦ θεοῦ λόγου μεταποιεῖσθαι ~ομεν Gr.Nyss.*or.catech*.37(p.149.4; -ομαι M.45.96D).

I. pass., *be persuaded, be convinced* ἀλλοτρίους τῆς...ἐκκλησίας εἶναι πεπίστευμαι Marcell.*ep*.ap.Epiph.*haer*.72.2(p.257.20; M.42.385B); δεῖ ...ἀπὸ τῶν γραφῶν ~εσθαι Chrys.*hom.51.1 in Jo*.(8.299E).

J. pass., *be believed, credited* εἰς τὸν οὐρανὸν ἀνεληλυθέναι φήσας πεπίστευται Tat.*orat*.10(p.11.12; M.6.828B); Athenag.*leg*.18.2(M.6. 928A); ~θεὶς εἶναι ἀληθής Or.*princ*.3.1.1(p.195.5; M.11.249A); Gr. Nyss.*ep*.3(M.46.1017D).

K. *have confidence* to, *venture* to κατηγορεῖν οὐ ~ουσιν Cyr.*Jo*.9.1 4.790E).

L. *entrust* ἐπίστευσέ μοι τὸν οἶκον *T.Jos*.2.1; Hipp.*haer*.9.12(p.247. 8; M.16.3382B); pass.; **1.** *be entrusted with* οἰκονομίαν μυστηρίων πεπίστευνται *Diogn*.7.1; Athenag.*leg*.24.3(M.6.948A); Clem.*str*.5.10 (p.368.8; M.9.96B); **2.** *be entrusted with function of, be given task of* τινι τῶν...διδασκάλων...τὴν Ῥωμαίων φωνὴν ἐκπαιδεύειν με πεπιστευμένῳ Gr.Thaum.*pan.Or*.5(p.12.15; M.10.1065B); Meth.*symp*.8.3(p.84. 14; M.18.141C); Cyr.*Jo*.2.1(4.129A).

πιστικός, 1. *trustworthy, reliable*, Or.*Jo*.2.31(25; p.89.18; M.14. 169C); Epiph.*haer*.66.3(p.20.2; M.42.33C); Gr.Agr.*Eccl*.1.13(M.98. 785C); **2.** *genuine, of pure quality* (cf. Mc.14:3, Jo.12:3) νοερὰν... εὐφροσύνην τοῦ π. τῆς καινῆς διαθήκης κράματος Eus.*d.e*.9.8(p.424. 20; M.22.684D); νάρδος ἡ π. spiritually interpreted, Gr.Nyss.*hom.3 in Cant*.(M.44.825B); **3.** as subst.; **a.** *confidential servant, agent* οἱ... τοῦ βασιλέως ἄρχοντες καὶ π. *M.Pers*.4.3(p.449.7); Sophr.H.*mir.Cyr. et Jo*.46(M.87.3597B); Jo.Mosch.*prat*.79(M.87.2936D); **b.** *master* of a ship, Ephr.1.331C.

πίστις, ἡ, *trust, belief, faith*; fanciful etym. τὴν π. ἐτυμολογητέον τὴν περὶ τὸ ὂν στάσιν τῆς ψυχῆς ἡμῶν Clem.*str*.4.22(p.311.20; M.8. 1353A).

I. *faith, belief* in rel. to the individual;

A. def. and descriptions; **1.** gen., pagan: Aristotelian τὸ ἑπόμενον τῇ ἐπιστήμῃ κρῖμα, ὡς ἀληθὲς τόδε τι, π. εἶναί φησι. κυριώτερον οὖν τῆς ἐπιστήμης ἡ π. καὶ ἔστιν αὐτῆς κριτήριον Clem.*str*.2.4(p.120.26f.; M.8.948A); Epicurean πρόληψιν εἶναι διανοίας τὴν π. *ib*.(p.121.10; 948B); **2.** gen. Christian, *ib*.2.6(p.128.1; M.8.964A) cit. s. προσδοκία; π. ... ἐνδιάθετόν τι ἐστιν ἀγαθόν, καὶ ἄνευ τοῦ ζητεῖν τὸν θεὸν ὁμολογοῦσα εἶναι τοῦτον καὶ δοξάζουσα ὡς ὄντα *ib*.7.10(p.40.25; M.9. 477C); ἡ τοῦ λόγου ὑπακοή, ἣν δὴ π. φαμέν id.*paed*.1.13(p.150.26; M.8.372B); π. ... ἐστι συγκατάθεσις ἀδιάκριτος τῶν ἀκουσθέντων ἐν πληροφορίᾳ τῆς ἀληθείας τῶν κηρυχθέντων θεοῦ χάριτι Bas.*fid*.1(2. 224C; M.31.677C); π. γάρ ἐστιν ἀπράγμων συναίνεσις Gr.Naz.*carm*. 1.1.6.40(M.37.432A); π. ἐστιν ἑκούσιος τῆς ψυχῆς συγκατάθεσις, ἤ, ἀφανοῦς πράγματος θεωρία, ἤ, περὶ τὸ ὂν ἔνστασις, καὶ κατάληψις τῶν ἀοράτων τῇ φύσει σύμμετρος Thdt.*affect*.1(p.26.13; 4.717); π. γάρ ἐστι, γνῶσις ἀληθὴς ἀναποδείκτους ἔχουσα τὰς ἀρχάς, ὡς τῶν ὑπὲρ νοῦν ...ὑπάρχουσα πραγμάτων ὑπόστασις Max.*cap.theol*.1.9(M.90.1085D); **3.** defined ref. pagan opinions π. δέ, ἣν διαβάλλουσι κενὴν καὶ βάρβαρον νομίζοντες Ἕλληνες, πρόληψις ἑκούσιός ἐστι, θεοσεβείας συγκατάθεσις Clem.*str*.2.2(p.117.8; M.8.940A); οὔκουν...πρόχειρον τὴν π. διαβλητέον ὡς εὔκολόν τε καὶ πάνδημον...εἰ γὰρ ἀνθρώπινον ἦν... ὡς Ἕλληνες ὑπέλαβον, κἂν ἀπέσβη...φημὶ τοίνυν τὴν π., εἴτε ὑπὸ ἀγάπης ἐθεμελιώθη εἴτε καὶ ὑπὸ φόβου, ᾗ φασιν οἱ κατήγοροι, θεῖόν τι εἶναι *ib*.2.6(p.129.2ff.; 965A); **4.** dist. from other terms ἡ...ἐπιστήμη ἕξις ἀποδεικτική, ἡ π. δὲ χάρις ἐξ ἀναποδείκτων εἰς τὸ καθόλου ἀναβιβάζουσα τὸ ἁπλοῦν *ib*.2.4(p.120.6; 945A); πολυμερὴς δὲ οὖσα ἡ φρόνησις,...ἐπειδὰν μὲν ἐπιβάλλῃ τοῖς πρώτοις αἰτίοις, νόησις καλεῖται ...ἐν δὲ τοῖς εἰς εὐλάβειαν συντείνουσι γινομένη καὶ ἄνευ θεωρίας παραδεξαμένη τὸν ἀρχικὸν λόγον κατὰ τὴν ἐν αὐτῇ ἐξεργασίας τήρησιν π. λέγεται *ib*.6.17(p.511.32; M.9.388A); *ib*.8.3(p.82.17; 564C); **5.** as principle of action ἡ δὲ π. ὑμῶν ἀναγωγεὺς ὑμῶν Ign.Eph.9.1; Clem.*str*.2.11(p.223.13; M.8.929A); ἄλλοι δ' ἀφανοῦς πράγματος ἐννοητικὴν συγκατάθεσιν ἀπέδωκαν εἶναι τὴν π. ... εἰ μὲν οὖν προαίρεσίς ἐστιν, ὀρεκτική τινος οὖσα, ἡ ὄρεξις νῦν διανοητική, ἐπεὶ δὲ πράξεως ἀρχὴ ἡ προαίρεσις, π. εὑρίσκεται ἀρχὴ [γὰρ] πράξεως, θεμέλιος ἔμφρονος προαιρέσεως, προαποδεικνύντος τινὸς αὐτῷ διὰ τῆς π. τὴν ἀπόδειξιν *ib*.2.2(p.117.14ff.; 940A,B); ἡ π. ... ἐργάτις ἀγαθῶν καὶ δικαιοπραγίας θεμέλιος *ib*.5.13(p.383.1; M.9.128A); ἡ δὲ π. ἀνθρώπου ἀγωγεύς ἐστι Ant.Mon.*hom*.1(M.89.1432B); **6.** varieties of faith; **a.** philos. π. δ' οὔσης διττῆς, τῆς μὲν ἐπιστημονικῆς, τῆς δὲ δοξαστικῆς Clem.*str*.2.11(p.138.20; M.8.984C); *ib*.2.12(p.142. 18; 992B); π. δὲ διττή. ἡ μὲν ἐκ λόγου βίας, ἣ καὶ δικαία. ἡ δ' ἕτοιμος συνδρομή Gr.Naz.*carm*.1.2.34.155(M.37.956A); **b.** theol., cf. Mt.17:19; 1Cor.12:9, Eph.2:8; as a theol. virtue and as a charism τὸ γὰρ τῆς π. ὄνομα ἓν μέν ἐστι κατὰ τὴν προσηγορίαν, διχῇ δὲ διαιρεῖται. ἔστι μὲν γὰρ ἓν εἶδος τῆς π., τὸ δογματικὸν συγκατάθεσιν τῆς ψυχῆς ἔχον...καὶ ὠφελεῖ τὴν ψυχὴν...δεύτερον δέ ἐστιν εἶδος πίστεως, τὸ ἐν χάριτος μέρει παρὰ τοῦ Χριστοῦ δωρούμενον...αὕτη τοίνυν, ἡ κατὰ χάριν δωρουμένη π. ἐκ τοῦ πνεύματος, οὐ δογματικὴ μόνον ἐστίν, ἀλλὰ καὶ τῶν ὑπὲρ ἄνθρωπον ἐνεργητική. ὃς γὰρ ἂν ἔχῃ τὴν π. ταύτην, ἐρεῖ τῷ ὄρει τούτῳ 'μετάβα ἐντεῦθεν' κτλ. ... ἔχε τοίνυν τὴν παρὰ σεαυτοῦ π. τὴν εἰς αὐτὸν ἵνα λάβῃς καὶ παρ' ἐκείνου [sc. θεοῦ] τὴν τῶν ὑπὲρ ἄνθρωπον ἐνεργητικήν Cyr.H.*catech*.5.10,11; τὸ γὰρ τῆς π. ὄνομα διπλῆν ἔχει τὴν σημασίαν...λέγεται τοίνυν π. ἡ τῶν σημείων...ποιητική. λέγεται δὲ π. καὶ ἡ τῆς εἰς τὸν θεὸν γνώσεως παρασκευαστική, καθ' ἣν ἕκαστος ἡμῶν ἐστι πιστός Chrys.*hom.1.4 in 2Cor.4:13*(3.263C,D); id.*hom.29.3 in 1Cor*.(10.263D,E); Cyr.*Lc*.17:5(M.72.832B,C); exeg. 1Cor.12:9, id. *1Cor*.12:9(p.288.7ff.; M.74.888A); ἡ...π. διπλῆ ἐστιν· ἔστι γὰρ π. ἐξ ἀκοῆς. ἀκούοντες γὰρ τῶν θείων γραφῶν, πιστεύομεν τῇ διδασκαλίᾳ... ἔστι δὲ πάλιν π. ἐλπιζομένων ὑπόστασις...ἀδιάκριτος ἐλπὶς τῶν τε ὑπὸ θεοῦ ἡμῖν ἐπηγγελμένων, καὶ τῆς τῶν αἰτήσεων ἡμῶν ἐπιτυχίας. ἡ μὲν οὖν πρώτη, τῆς ἡμετέρας γνώμης ἐστί, ἡ δὲ δευτέρα, τῶν χαρισμάτων τοῦ πνεύματος Jo.D.*f.o*.4.10(M.94.1125C–1128A); cf. τί π.; καὶ κατὰ τί εἴρηται π.; καὶ ὁσαχῶς ἡ ὀρθὴ π.; π. ἐστὶν ἐνδιάθετος ὕπαρξις, π. δὲ εἴρηται κατὰ τὸ πείθεσθαι εἴς τι. διττῶς δὲ νοεῖται ἡ π. ἡ ὀρθή. ἔστι γὰρ π. ἐξ ἀκοῆς τοῦ κηρύγματος. καὶ ἔστι βεβαιοτέρα π., ἡ τῶν ἐλπιζομένων ἀγαθῶν ὑπόστασις. καὶ τὴν μὲν ἐξ ἀκοῆς πάντες ἄνθρωποι ἔχειν δύνανται· τὴν δὲ δευτέραν μόνοι οἱ δίκαιοι κέκτηνται Anast.S.*hod*.2(M.89.76C,D); **7.** met. descriptions π. δὲ ὦτα ψυχῆς, καὶ ταύτην αἰνίσσεται Clem.*str*.5.1(p.326.21f.; M.9.9B); τῆς ζωοποιοῦ ῥίζης, τῆς εἰς Χριστὸν π. †Bas.*Is*.19(1.391E; M.30.149C); ἱμάτιον δὲ Χριστιανῶν...ἡ εἰς Χριστὸν π. *ib*.225(1.549D; M.512A); ὀφθαλμὸς πάσης συνειδήσεώς ἐστι φωτιστικὸς ἡ π., καὶ συνέσεως ἐμποιητικός Cyr.H.*catech*.5.4; πραγματεία πλατεῖα ἡ π. *ib*.17.37; ἡ π. ἱερά τίς ἐστιν ἄγκυρα, πάντοθεν ἀνέχουσα τὴν ἔχουσαν αὐτὴν διάνοιαν Chrys.*exp.in Ps*.115:2(5.312B); id.*hom*.12.1 *in* 1*Tim*.(11.609E); εἷς γάρ ἐστι πλοῦς, μία ὁδός, εἷς λιμήν, ἡ π. ‡Chrys.*mart*.4(3.817C); ἡ δὲ βεβαία π., πύργος ἐστὶν ἰσχυρός Marc.Er.*opusc*.1.2(M.65.905A); π. πτερὸν προσευχῆς...π. ἐστὶν ἀνενδοίαστος ψυχῆς στάσις...π. ἐστὶ ἀνελπίστων πρόξενος... ἡσυχαστῶν μήτηρ π.· εἰ μὴ γὰρ πιστεύσει, πῶς ἡσυχάσει; Jo.Clim.*scal*.27(M.88.1113B); as kingdom of God within men, Max.*qu.Thal*.33(M.90.373B,C); **8.** Gnost. φυσικὴν ἡγοῦνται τὴν π. οἱ ἀμφὶ τὸν Βασιλείδην, καθὸ καὶ ἐπὶ τῆς ἐκλογῆς τάττουσιν αὐτήν, τὰ μαθήματα ἀναποδείκτως εὑρίσκουσαν καταλήψει νοητικῇ Clem.*str*.2.3(p.118.11; M.8.941B); *ib*.(p.118.18ff.; 941B); ὁρίζονται γοῦν οἱ ἀπὸ Βασιλείδου τὴν π. ψυχῆς συγκατάθεσιν πρός τι τῶν μὴ κινούντων αἴσθησιν διὰ τὸ μὴ παρεῖναι *ib*.2.6(p.127.19; 961C); refuted εἰ γὰρ φύσει τις τὸν θεὸν ἐπίσταται, ὡς Βασιλείδης οἴεται, [τὴν] νόησιν τὴν ἐξαίρετον π. ἅμα καὶ βασιλείαν...οὐσίας ἀξίαν τοῦ ποιήσαντος πλησίον ὑπάρχειν αὐτήν, ἑρμηνεύων, οὐσίαν, ἀλλ' οὐκ ἐξουσίαν...κτίσεως ἀνυπερθέτου κάλλος ἀδιόριστον, οὐχὶ δὲ ψυχῆς αὐτεξουσίου λογικὴν συγκατάθεσιν λέγει τὴν π. *ib*.5.1(p.327.21ff.; M.9.12B,C).

B. source; **1.** as God's gift, *Orac.Sib*.3.585; 1*Clem*.35.2; ἡ π. ἄνωθέν ἐστι παρὰ τοῦ θεοῦ Herm.*mand*.9.11; *A.Jo*.113(p.213.11); χάρις δὲ ἡ π. Clem.*str*.1.8(p.25.16; M.8.733A); *ib*.2.6(p.129.13; 965B); Or.*fr*.11 *in Jo*.(p.493.24); Eus.*h.e*.4.18.6(M.20.376A); π., ἣν ἡ τοῦ θεοῦ χάρις ἐν ὑμῖν ἐργάζεται Ath.*ep.mon*.(M.26.1188A); Mac.Aeg. *hom*.15.22(M.34.589C); Nil.*epp*.2.228(M.79.317C); exeg. Eph.2:8, Chrys.*exp.in Ps*.115:1(5.310E); **2.** faith in and through Christ; **a.** in gen., Clem.*str*.3.18(p.246.10; M.8.1212A); Or.*Cels*.1.52(p.103.29; M.11.757C); *A.Thom*.A 160(p.271.21); Meth.*creat*.(p.493.11; M.18.332B); Eus.*h.e*.8.9.6(M.20.761A); Ath.*inc*.28.5(M.25.145A); **b.** Christ as source of faith ἐμοὶ δὲ ἀρχεῖά ἐστιν Ἰησοῦς Χριστός...καὶ ἡ π. ἡ δι' αὐτοῦ Ign.*Philad*.8.2; ὁ μονογενὴς ἐκ κόλπων πατρὸς καταπέμπεται λόγος τῆς π. [ἡ] π. ἐκ περιουσίας αὐτὸς σαφῶς ὁ κύριος ὁμολογῶν Clem.*paed*.1.3(p.94.30; M.8.257C); π. ἐπιχορηγουμένης ἡμῖν διὰ... Χριστοῦ παρὰ θεοῦ Ath.*v.Anton*.78(M.26.952B); **c.** Christ as π. ἐνυπόστατος, Max.*qu.Thal*.25(M.90.332A); ἐνυπόστατος π. ἐστίν, ἡ ἐνεργὴς καὶ ἔμπρακτος, καθ' ἣν ὁ τοῦ θεοῦ λόγος ἐν τοῖς πρακτικοῖς δείκνυται ταῖς ἐντολαῖς σωματούμενος id.*cap*.1.84(M.90.1213D); **3.** obtained through instruction, Clem.*paed*.1.6(p.108.9; M.8.285C); cf. *ib*.(p.107.14; 285A); Ath.*Ar*.2.42(M.26.237B); **4.** esp. in scriptures, cf.Iren.*haer*.3.21.3(M.7.949A); Clem.*str*.2.11(p.139.6; M.8.985A); Or. *Jo*.1.4(6; p.7.29; M.14.29B); *ib*.10.3(2; p.172.21; 309A); Ath.*ep.Jov*. 1(M.26.816A); Cyr.H.*catech*.4.17; **5.** ref. man's responsibility π. ποιεῖν προκαταλαβοῦσαν ἡμῶν τὴν ψυχὴν τὴν περὶ τοῦ Ἰησοῦ τοιάνδε συγκατάθεσιν. ἀληθῶς ⟨μὲν⟩ γὰρ π. ἡμῖν ποιεῖ τὴν τοιάνδε συγκατάθεσιν. ὅρα δὲ εἰ μὴ αὐτόθεν ἡ π. αὐτὴ τὸ ἐπαινετὸν παρίστησιν, ὅτε πιστεύομεν ἑαυτοὺς τῷ ἐπὶ πᾶσι θεῷ, χάριν ὁμολογοῦντες τῷ εἰς τοιαύτην π. ὁδηγῷ Cels.ap.Or.*Cels*.3.39(p.235.15ff.; M.11.969C,D); ἵνα τοῦ διδόντος ῥῆμα τοῖς εὐαγγελιζομένοις δυνάμει πολλῇ καὶ ἡμῖν τοῦτ' ἐπιχορηγοῦντος...ἐγγένηται π. τοῖς ἐντευξομένοις ἐν λόγῳ καὶ δυνάμει τοῦ θεοῦ Or.*ib*.5.4(p.2.17; 1181C); Chrys.*hom*.1.4,5 *in* 2*Cor*.4:13(3.263E–264C); cf. *etiam in fide liberum et suae potestatis arbitrium servavit dominus*, Iren.*haer*.4.37.5(M.7.1102B).

C. ref. baptism, v. βάπτισμα: Χριστός...ἀρχὴ...ἄλλου γένους γέγονε, τοῦ ἀναγεννηθέντος ὑπ' αὐτοῦ δι' ὕδατος καὶ π. καὶ ξύλου Just. *dial*.138.2(M.6.793B); *ib*.138.3(793C); π. δὲ ἅμα βαπτίσματι ἁγίῳ παιδεύεται πνεύματι Clem.*paed*.1.6(p.108.9; M.8.285C); κυρίως γὰρ π. ἐστὶν κατὰ τὸ βάπτισμα τοῦ ὅλῃ ψυχῇ παραδεχομένου τὸ πιστευόμενον Or.*Jo*.10.43(27; p.221.15; M.14.392B); τῆς...μυστικῆς π. τὴν ἐν Χριστῷ παρεχούσης ἀναγέννησιν τοῖς δι' αὐτῆς φωτιζομένοις Eus.*e.th*. 2.6(p.103.17; M.24.905D); μετὰ πίστεως ἡ τοῦ βαπτίσματος τελείωσις Ath.*Ar*.2.42(M.26.237B); ἔστι γὰρ τὸ βάπτισμα σφραγὶς τῆς π., ἡ δὲ π., θεότητος συγκατάθεσις Bas.*Eun*.3.5(1.276E; M.29.665C); τὸ ῥῆμα τῆς π., καὶ προσέτι τούτῳ τὸ...βάπτισμα Cyr.*Os*.55(3.85B).

D. development of faith; **1.** growth in faith both possible and necessary, Clem.*str*.4.16(p.293.2; M.8.1308B); *ib*.7.11(p.44.5; M.9.485A); ἔνιοι δὲ εὐφυεῖς οἰόμενοι εἶναι ἀξιοῦσι μήτε φιλοσοφίας μήτε διαλεκτικῆς...μόνην δὲ καὶ ψιλὴν τὴν π. ἀπαιτοῦσιν, ὥσπερ εἰ μηδεμίαν ἠξίουν ἐπιμέλειαν ποιησάμενοι τῆς ἀμπέλου εὐθὺς ἐξ ἀρχῆς τοὺς βότρυας λαμβάνειν *ib*.1.9(p.28.20; M.8.740B); id.*exc.Thdot*.9(p.109.3; M.9.660A); ἐνδέχεται τὸν ἤδη πιστεύοντα μανθάνειν τινά, ἵνα πάλιν πιστεύῃ, καὶ διὰ τῆς προσθήκης τῶν μαθημάτων προστιθέναι τῇ π. Or. *Jo*.32.15(9; p.450.31; M.14.781A); *ib*.32.16(9; p.451.23ff.; 781D); εἰ δὲ καὶ πιστὸς εἶναι νομίζεις, ἀλλ' οὔπω τὸ τέλειον τῆς π. ἔχεις. χρεία καὶ σοὶ...εἰπεῖν· κύριε, πρόσθες ἡμῖν π. Cyr.H.*catech*.5.9; *Const.App*.6.7.12; Cyr.*Lc*.17:5(M.72.833C); ἀπαιτεῖ τὴν ἐπὶ τῇ π. συναίνεσιν...χρὴ γὰρ οὐ διάκενον ἡμᾶς εἰς ἀέρα ῥιπτοῦντας φωνήν,...ἀλλ' ἐν καρδίᾳ καὶ νῷ τὴν π. ῥιζώσαντας, καρπὸν τοῦ πράγματος ποιεῖσθαι τὴν ὁμολογίαν id.*Jo*.7(4.683C); **2.** development through increase of knowledge καθάπερ καὶ ἄνευ γραμμάτων πιστὸν εἶναι δυνατόν φαμεν, οὕτως συνιέναι τὰ ἐν τῇ π. λεγόμενα οὐχ οἷόν τε μὴ μαθόντα ὁμολογοῦμεν. τὰ μὲν γὰρ εὖ λεγόμενα προσίεσθαι, τὰ δὲ ἀλλότρια μὴ προσίεσθαι οὐχ ἁπλῶς ἡ π., ἀλλ' ἡ περὶ τὴν μάθησιν π. ἐμποιεῖ Clem.*str*.1.6(p.23.7; M.8.729B); *ib*.5.1(p.332.27; M.9.24B); and angelic agency, Herm. *mand*.12.6.1; id.*sim*.6.3.6; **3.** faith as foundation of perfection φαίνεται οὖν ὁ ἀπόστολος διττὴν καταγγέλλων π., μᾶλλον δὲ μίαν, αὔξησιν καὶ τελείωσιν ἐπιδεχομένην. ἡ μὲν γὰρ κοινὴ π. καθάπερ θεμέλιος ὑπόκειται...ἡ δὲ ἐξαίρετος ἐποικοδομουμένη συντελειοῦται τῷ πιστῷ καὶ συναπαρτίζεται αὖ τῇ ἐκ μαθήσεως περιγινομένῃ καὶ τοῦ λόγου τὰς ἐντολὰς ἐπιτελεῖν, ὁποῖοι ἦσαν οἱ ἀπόστολοι, ἐφ' ὧν τὴν π. ὄρη μετατιθέναι...δύνασθαι εἴρηται. ὅθεν αἰσθόμενοι τοῦ μεγαλείου τῆς δυνάμεως ἠξίουν προστιθέναι αὐτοῖς π. τὴν ὡς κόκκον σινάπεως ἐπιδάκνουσαν ὠφελίμως τὴν ψυχὴν καὶ ἐν αὐτῇ αὔξουσαν...ὡς ἐπαναπαύεσθαι αὐτῇ τοὺς περὶ τῶν μεταρσίων λόγους Clem.*str*.5.1(p.327.9ff.; M.9.12A,B); *ib*.5.4(p.342.3; 45A); **4.** ref. interprn. of scripture τὴν μὲν γραφὴν πρόδηλον εἶναι πᾶσι κατὰ τὴν ψιλὴν ἀνάγνωσιν ἐκλαμβανομένην, καὶ ταύτην εἶναι τὴν π. στοιχείων τάξιν ἔχουσαν, διὸ καὶ ἡ πρὸς τὸ γράμμα ἀνάγνωσις ἀλληγορεῖται· τὴν διάπτυξιν δὲ τὴν γνωστικὴν τῶν γραφῶν, προκοπτούσης ἤδη τῆς π., εἰκάζεσθαι τῇ κατὰ τὰς συλλαβὰς ἀναγνώσει ἐκδεχόμεθα *ib*.6.15(p.498.7ff.; 356A,B).

E. objects of faith; **1.** existence of God, Clem.*str*.2.4(p.119.30; M.8.944C); cf.*ib*.2.5(p.125.25; 957B); *ib*.7.16(p.67.25; M.9.532C); *ib*.8.3(p.83.23; 568A); π. δὲ αὐτάρκης εἰδέναι ὅτι ἔστι θεός, οὐχὶ τί ἐστι Bas. *ep*.234.2(3.358A; M.32.869B); and of Logos as creator, Ath.*ep. Adelph*.8(M.26.1084A); **2.** the Trinity ζῇ γὰρ ὁ θεὸς καὶ ζῇ ὁ κύριος Ἰησοῦς Χριστὸς καὶ τὸ πνεῦμα τὸ ἅγιον, ἥ τε π. καὶ ἡ ἐλπὶς τῶν ἐκλεκτῶν 1*Clem*.58.2; Ath.*Ar*.1.18(M.26.49B); Gr.Nyss.*Maced*.15(M.45.1320C); Ant.Mon.*hom*.1(M.89.1433C); and eternal generation of Son, Didym.(‡Bas.)*Eun*.4(1.288B; M.29.692D); ‡Ath.*Apoll*.1.21(M.26.1124B); **3.** Christ and his work; **a.** in gen. ἡ...ἡμετέρα π. ἐπὶ σωτηρίᾳ τῶν ἀνθρώπων τὴν τοῦ Χριστοῦ παρουσίαν λέγει Ath.*v.Anton*. 74(M.26.948A); τῇ περὶ τῆς εὐσεβείας π. καὶ τὰ περὶ τῆς ἐνανθρωπήσεως τοῦ λόγου διηγησώμεθα, καὶ περὶ τῆς θείας...ἐπιφανείας id.*inc*. 1.1(M.25.97A); Cyr.*Jo*.3.5(4.309B); ἰλιγγιᾷς ἐπὶ ταῖς ἀπορίαις, καὶ ...δέδιας μήπου τι τῶν εἰρημένων τὸν τῆς π. ἡμῶν παραλύσῃ λόγον. ἀλλ' ὅταν ἐγὼ ζητῶν ἐπαπορήσω, τότε τοῦ μυστηρίου τῶν Χριστιανῶν ἀνακράζω τὸ θαῦμα, ὅτι ὑπὲρ νοῦν...τὰ ἡμέτερα. ὅταν...τὰ τοιαῦτα ζητοῦντι ἀπορία τις ἐπείη, πρόσφερε τοῖς ζητουμένοις...λύσιν τὴν π. λογιζόμενος Thdt.*rect.conf*.16(M.6.1236B,C); **b.** his divinity, Ath. *Dion*.8(p.51.16; M.25.492A); Cyr.*Jo*.6.1(4.630D); **c.** manner of Inc. τὰ γὰρ ὑπερβαίνοντα λογισμὸν π. δεῖται μόνης. καὶ γάρ, ἂν θέλωμεν πείθειν διὰ λογισμῶν, πῶς ἄνθρωπος ἐγένετο ὁ θεός, καὶ εἰς μήτραν εἰσῆλθε παρθενικήν, καὶ μὴ τῇ π. τὸ πρᾶγμα ἐπιτρέψωμεν, μᾶλλον ἐκεῖνοι [sc. pagans] καταγελάσονται Chrys.*hom*.4.1 *in* 1*Cor*.(10.24B); **d.** Cross σοφίαν...ὑπομεῖναι σταυροῦ, ἵνα διὰ τῆς ἐν τούτῳ π. πάντες ...οἱ πιστεύοντες σώζεσθαι δύνωνται Ath.*Ar*.2.81(M.26.320A); id.*inc*. 28.2(M.25.144C); cf. ἐνόησα γὰρ ὑμᾶς κατηρτισμένους ἐν ἀκινήτῳ π., ὥσπερ καθηλωμένους ἐν τῷ σταυρῷ τοῦ...Χριστοῦ Ign.*Smyrn*.1.1; **e.** Resurrection, v. ἀνάστασις; **4.** divine promises and eschatological expectations τοῖς μέλλουσιν, ὡς ἤδη διὰ τὴν π. παροῦσιν Clem. *str*.7.12(p.56.19; M.9.509A); οἷς [sc. Χριστιανοῖς] ἡ πᾶσα ὑπόθεσίς ἐστι τῆς π. ὁ θεὸς καὶ αἱ διὰ τοῦ Χριστοῦ περὶ τῶν δικαίων ἐπαγγελίαι καὶ περὶ τῶν ἀδίκων αἱ περὶ κολάσεως διδασκαλίαι Or.*Cels*.8.51(p.266.12; M.11.1592B); resurrection of flesh, Meth.*res*.1.62(p.329.8; M.41.1161D); φανερόν ἐστιν, ὅτι πιστεύει περὶ τῶν ἀφθάρτων, καὶ ὄντως ζητεῖ τὰ αἰώνια ἀγαθά, εἰ...ὑγιῆ τὴν π. ἀποσῴζει Mac.Aeg.*hom*.48.2(M.34.809A); immortality, Ath.*inc*.48.2(M.25.181B); περὶ ἀναστάσεως, καὶ τῆς τῶν μελλόντων ἀγαθῶν ἀπολαύσεως, ἃ καὶ λόγον ὑπερβαίνει πάντα...πίστεως δὲ πρὸς τὸ παραδέχεσθαι χρεία Chrys.*exp.in Ps*.115:1(5.308C).

F. effects of faith; **1.** salvation, v. ἀθανασία; ἡ μὲν πρώτη αὐτῶν [sc. γυναικῶν]...π. καλεῖται· διὰ ταύτης σῴζονται οἱ ἐκλεκτοὶ τοῦ θεοῦ Herm.*vis*.3.8.3; Tat.*orat*.15(p.17.6; M.6.840A); ἡ πρώτη πρὸς σωτηρίαν νεῦσις ἡ π. ὑμῖν ἀναφαίνεται Clem.*str*.2.6(p.129.17; M.8.965B); π. δὲ ἰσχὺς εἰς σωτηρίαν καὶ δύναμις εἰς ζωὴν αἰώνιον *ib*.2.12(p.142.12; 992B); Eus.*Marcell*.1.1(p.8.21; M.24.728C); Cyr.H.*hom*.4(M.33.1136A); Max.*cap*.4.19(M.90.1312A); which cannot be attained without faith, Clem.*paed*.1.6(p.108.11; M.8.285C); Or.*Jo*.2.16(10; p.73.16; M.14.144A); Bas.*Spir*.44(3.37D; M.32.148D); *οὐκ ἔνι σωθῆναι ἑτέρως, ἀλλ' ἢ διὰ πίστεως* Chrys.*hom.8.1 in Rom*.(9.497A); id.*exp. in Ps*.115:1(5.309C,D); id.*hom.7.1 in Heb*.(12.70D); ‡Chrys.*fid*.1(3.826D); *ἐν π., καὶ οὐχ ἑτέρως εὑρεῖν ἣν δύνασθαι τῆς σωτηρίας τὴν ὁδόν* Cyr.*glaph.Ex*.2(1.282D); faith sufficient for salvation, Clem.*str*.5.1(p.331.19; M.9.20B); *ib*.5.3(p.337.27; 36B); ‡Chrys.*fid*.1(3.826D); of oneself and others *τοσοῦτον δὲ ἔχει δυνάμεως ἡ π., ὥστε οὐ μόνος ὁ πιστεύων σώζεται ἀλλὰ γὰρ καὶ οἱ ἄλλοι ἄλλων πιστευσάντων ἐσώθησαν* Cyr.H.*catech*.5.8; hence compared with anchor, Chrys.*hom.1.3 in 2Cor.4:13*(3.262D); **2.** freedom from power of Devil, Ign.*Eph*.13.1; Herm.*mand*.11.4; *ib*.12.5.4; *ἔστι τι τοῦ διαβόλου δεινότερον; ἀλλὰ καὶ πρὸς τοῦτον οὐδὲν ἕτερον ὅπλον ἔχομεν ἢ τὴν π.* Cyr.H.*catech*.5.4; Cyr.*Nah*.13(3.491C); **3.** conversion *μεταβαλόντες...ἐκ τοῦ εἶναι θηρία διὰ τῆς κυριακῆς π. ἄνθρωποι γίνονται θεοῦ* Clem.*str*.6.6(p.457.21; M.9.273A); Or.*Cels*.3.40(p.236.9; M.11.972B); **4.** virtues: repentance, Clem.*str*.2.6(p.127.15; M.8.961B); hence rewarded by remission of sins, Cyr.*glaph.Gen*.4.11(1.136D); *μεγίστη δὲ ἀρετῶν μήτηρ ἡ π.* Clem.*str*.2.5(p.125.19; M.8.957A); which fact is used in apologetics *πυνθανόμεθά γε περὶ τοῦ πλήθους τῶν πιστευόντων, τὴν πολλὴν χύσιν τῆς κακίας ἀποθεμένων...πότερον βέλτιόν ἐστιν αὐτοῖς ἀλόγως πιστεύουσι κατεστάλθαι πως τὰ ἤθη καὶ ὠφελῆσθαι διὰ τὴν περὶ τῶν κολαζομένων ἐπὶ ἁμαρτίαις καὶ τιμωμένων ἐπὶ ἔργοις χρηστοῖς πίστιν, ἢ μὴ προσίεσθαι αὐτῶν τὴν ἐπιστροφὴν μετὰ ψιλῆς π., ἕως ἂν ἐπιδῶσιν ἑαυτοὺς ἐξετάσει λόγων; φανερῶς γὰρ οἱ πάντες παρ' ἐλαχίστους οὐδὲ τοῦτο λήψονται* Or.*Cels*.1.9(p.62.8f.; M.11.673B); prudence, †Bas.*hom.in Ps*.115(1.372C; M.30.105C); *ἐὰν τηρήσωμεν τὴν π., ἀκατάγνωστοι ἐσόμεθα καὶ παντοίοις ἀρετῶν εἴδεσι κοσμηθησόμεθα* Cyr.H.*catech*.5.7; *παρρησία*, Chrys.*hom.16.10 in Rom*.(9.620B); *ἀπάθεια*, Clem.*str*.7.3(p.11.6; M.9.417B); renunciation, Jo.Clim.*scal*.26(M.88.1084C); long-suffering, Herm.*mand*.5.2.3; **5.** progress to perfection, Clem.*str*.7.2(p.8.3; 412C); *ib*.(p.9.17; 413C); **6.** union with God; **a.** in gen. *αὐτὸς* [sc. *θεός*] *δὲ ἑαυτὸν ἐπέδειξεν...διὰ πίστεως, ᾗ μόνῃ θεὸν ἰδεῖν συγκεχώρηται* *Diogn*.8.6; cf. *dominus dicebat 'qui credit in me, non judicatur', id est, non separatur a deo: adunitus est enim per fidem deo*, Iren.*haer*.5.27.2(M.7.1197B); *διὰ τῆς π. ἑνοῦσιν ἑαυτοὺς τῷ θεῷ* *ib*.5.28.1(1197C); *τῷ πίστεως ἀλείμματι...δι' οὗ πρὸς τὸν θεὸν ἀναβαίνετε* Clem.*prot*.12(p.85.10; M.8.241C); by making men sons of God, Or.*or*.22.2(p.346.30; M.11.484A); Cyr.H.*catech*.7.13; *ἡ π. τὸν ἀπὸ γῆς ἄνθρωπον θεοῦ συνόμιλον ἀπεργάζεται* ‡Chrys.*fid*.1(3.826B); by producing indwelling of Son, Cyr.*Jo*.2.4(4.173C); *ib*.4.4(393B); *ib*.6.1(639E); of H. Ghost, *ib*.5.2(474E); and conformation to Christ, id.*thes*.32(5¹.288B); *ἐὰν ἔχωμεν π., ἐσμὲν ἐν τῇ π., καὶ στήκομεν ἐν αὐτῇ ἑδραῖοι, καὶ ἐν κυρίῳ κατοικοῦμεν* Ant.Mon.*hom*.1(M.89.1432C); **b.** myst. *τὸ διὰ τῆς π. προσγινόμενον ἁγίου πνεύματος χαρακτηριστικόν* Clem.*str*.6.16(p.500.4; M.9.360A); *ὦ ψυχή...ὑποζύγιόν τε καὶ οἰκητήριον γενήσῃ διὰ πίστεως τοῦ σοι ἐνανακλίνεσθαι μέλλοντος* Gr.Nyss.*hom..3 in Cant*.(M.44.821B); *πρὸς τὴν ἀδίδακτον...καὶ μυστικὴν ἀποτελεσθεὶς ἕνωσιν καὶ π.* Dion.Ar.*d.n*.2.9(M.3.648B); *π. προσευχὴν ἐπτέρωσε· χωρὶς γὰρ ταύτης εἰς οὐρανὸν τετασθῆναι οὐ δύναται* Jo.Clim.*scal*.28(M.88.1133C); *ἡ π. ἀπεδείχθη...ὑπάρχουσα δύναμις σχετικὴ τῆς ὑπὲρ φύσιν ἀμέσου τοῦ πιστεύοντος πρὸς τὸν πιστευόμενον θεὸν τελείας ἑνώσεως* Max.*qu.Thal*.33(M.90.373C); *ib*.(373D); *διὰ...τὴν π., ἤγουν τὴν πρὸς θεὸν ἄμεσον ἕνωσιν* *ib*.34(377B); *ὁ τῆς μυστικῆς θεολογίας ἐντὸς γενόμενος νοῦς, κεφαλὴν ἔχων ἀκατακάλυπτον τὸν Χριστόν· τουτέστι...ἀνοήτως γινωσκόμενον λόγον τῆς π.* *ib*.25(332C); various effects: assurance in prayer, Herm.*mand*.9.6–12; growth of grace, Cyr.*Jo*.6.1(4.603C); overcoming of nature, Chrys.*virg*.64(1.321C); freedom from fear, Clem.*paed*.3.12(p.284.6; M.8.665B); esp. from fear of death, Chrys.*hom.27.1 in Heb*.(12.246B); leading to adoration, Bas.*ep*.234.3(1.358C; M.32.869D); and vision of God, Chrys.*hom.4.8 in Ac.princ*.(3.93A); *μέγα...ἀγαθὸν ἡ π.· πλουτεῖ γὰρ ἁμαρτιῶν ἀπόθεσιν, ῥύπου παντὸς ἀποκάθαρσιν· ἔστι δὲ καὶ μνηστείας πρόξενος τῆς παρὰ θεοῦ, καὶ ὁδὸς εἰς ἁγιασμὸν καὶ υἱοθεσίαν, καὶ... παντὸς ἀγαθοῦ προμνήστρια* Cyr.*Heb*.11:3(p.411.15; M.74.989D).

G. faith and miracles; **1.** miracles as a confirmation of faith *σημεῖον ἢ τεράστιον, τὸ συνεργοῦν καὶ βεβαιοῦν αὐτῶν τὴν εἰς τὸν κτίσαντα τὰ ὅλα π.* Or.*Cels*.3.3(p.205.15; M.11.924B); *θαύμασιν ἡ τῆς ἀληθείας π. ἐπιδείκνυσιν* Const.ap.Eus.*v.C*.3.30(p.92.3; M.20.1089D); *διὰ τῶν...ἑκάστοτε γενομένων θαυμάτων, ὁ κύριος τοὺς μὲν ὀλιγοπίστους καὶ τοὺς ἀπίστους πρὸς π. βεβαίαν ἐκκαλεῖται, τῶν δὲ πιστῶν τὴν π. ... αὔξει* Nil.*epp*.4.62(M.79.580B); **2.** miracles as outcome of faith *τοσοῦτον γὰρ ἰσχύει ἡ π., ὡς καὶ ἀνθρώπους ἐπὶ θαλάσσης κουφίζειν περιπατοῦντας* Cyr.H.*catech*.5.7; *πολλοὶ γὰρ τῶν ἀρρωστούντων...τὴν ὑγείαν διὰ τῆς π. δρέπονται* Thdt.*h.e*.4.16.3(3.975); Thdot.Anc.*hom*.1.5(p.83.21; M.77.1356A); **3.** but no useless miracles are to be expected *ὅτι δὲ μέγα...τὸ ἀραρὸς ἐν π., διαδείκνυσι λέγων ὁ κύριος· εἰ ἔχετε π. ὡς κόκκον σινάπεως...δεῖ δὲ ὅμως ἑαυτοὺς παρασκευάσαι, δεκτικοὺς γίνεσθαι τῆς τοιαύτης χάριτος· εἰ γὰρ τὸ πεπηγὸς αὐτῷ... μετακινεῖ ἡ τῆς π. δύναμις, καθ' ὅλου φαίη τις ἄν, μηδὲν ἀκίνητον εἶναι οὕτως ὃ μὴ σαλεύσειεν ἡ π. ... ἐκείνῳ μέντοι προσεκτέον ἀσφαλῶς, ὡς οὐ κενὴν ἔκπληξιν...κινεῖ ὁ θεός...μηδ' αὖ περὶ τὴν π. ἀσθένειαν νομίζειν εἰ μὴ ταῦτα ἰσχύει· ἀλλ' ἔστω τὸ χρήσιμον τὸ πρὸς ὠφέλειαν ἀληθινήν, καὶ ἡ δύναμις οὐκ ἀπολείψεται* Cyr.*Lc*.17:5(M.72.833C–836A).

H. faith and works; **1.** works without faith futile *οὐδὲν οὖν ὄφελος αὐτοῖς μετὰ τὴν τελευτὴν τοῦ βίου, κἂν εὐεργεῖς ὦσι νῦν, εἰ μὴ π. ἔχοιεν* Clem.*str*.1.7(p.25.9; M.8.733A); **2.** faith can justify without works *ἡ π. καθ' ἑαυτὴν ἔσωσεν, ἔργα δὲ καθ' ἑαυτὰ οὐδαμοῦ τοὺς ἐργάτας ἐδικαίωσε* ‡Chrys.*fid*.1(3.826D); and takes precedence *τοῖς γὰρ ἐθέλουσιν ἐλθεῖν* [sc. to eternal life], *δεῖ δὴ πάντως πίστεως μέν, καὶ πρό γε τῶν ἄλλων, ὀρθῆς· εἶτα, βίου ἀλήπτου* Cyr.*Lc*.13:23(M.72.776D); **3.** but usu. both held to be necessary; **a.** faith insufficient without works, *Barn*.4.9; Bas.*ep*.295(3.433D; M.32.1040A); *τί τῆς π. ὄφελος...βίου μὴ ὄντος καθαροῦ;* Chrys.*oppugn*.1.6(1.52D); *οὐ γάρ ἐστιν ἡ π. ἱκανὴ εἰς τὴν βασιλείαν εἰσαγαγεῖν, ἀλλὰ καὶ ταύτῃ μάλιστα κατακρίναι τοὺς βίον φαῦλον ἐπιδεικνυμένους ἔχει* id.*hom.84.3 in Jo*.(8.502B); *κἂν...ὀρθῶς πιστεύσῃ,...βίον δὲ μὴ ἔχῃ ὀρθόν, οὐδὲν αὐτῷ κέρδος τῆς π. εἰς σωτηρίαν* *ib.31.1*(175C); proved from Mt.7:21ff. and Heb.12:14, *ib.63.4*(379D–380A); *ib.10.3*(61A); id.*hom.11.2 in Phil*.(11.286B); id.*hom.8.1 in 2Tim*.(11.707C); *οὐ...μόνον...ὁ π. ἔχων, τοῦ βίου ἠμελημένου, τῶν οὐρανῶν ἐκβάλλεται, ἀλλὰ κἂν μετὰ τῆς π. σημεῖα πολλὰ πεποιηκὼς ᾖ, καὶ οὐδὲν ἀγαθὸν ἐργασάμενος* id.*hom.24.1 in Mt*.(7.299C); *οὐ ῥύσεται π. καὶ βάπτισμα τοῦ αἰωνίου πυρός, χωρὶς ἔργων δικαιοσύνης* Nil.*inst*.(M.79.1240A); *καίτοι τὸ εἰδέναι θεὸν τὸν ἕνα καὶ φύσει, καὶ ὁμολογεῖν ἀδόλως...τουτό ἐστιν ἡ π., ἀλλὰ καὶ τοῦτο νεκρόν, μὴ παρεπομένης αὐτῷ τῆς ἐξ ἔργων φαιδρότητος* Cyr.*Jo*.9(4.729A); Ant.Mon.*hom*.1(M.89.1432B); *μὴ...τυφλὴν ἡμῶν τὴν π. καταστήσωμεν, οὐκ ἔχουσαν τοὺς διὰ τῶν ἀρετῶν τοῦ πνεύματος φωτισμούς· καὶ κολασθῶμεν δικαίως εἰς ἀπείρους αἰῶνας, ὡς ἐν ἑαυτοῖς κατὰ τὴν π. ... τοὺς θείους ἐκτυφλώσαντες ὀφθαλμούς. πᾶς γὰρ ὁ τῆς π. ἐν ἑαυτῷ διὰ τῆς ἀργίας τῶν ἐντολῶν τοὺς τοιούτους ἀνορύξας ὀφθαλμούς, πάντως κατάκριτος* Max.*qu.Thal*.54(M.90.524C); id.*ep*.12(M.91.504B); **b.** their interrelation *ἡ βεβαία τῆς π. ὑμῶν ῥίζα...μέχρι νῦν διαμένει καὶ καρποφορεῖ εἰς τὸν κύριον ἡμῶν* Polyc.*ep*.1.2; *τὰ μὲν περὶ τῆς π. αὐτὴ ἡ ἐντολὴ δηλοῖ, ἵνα τοῖς ἔργοις τοῦ ἀγγέλου τῆς δικαιοσύνης πιστεύσῃς, καὶ ἐργασάμενος αὐτὰ ζήσῃ τῷ θεῷ* Herm.*mand*.6.2.10; *ἀνοίγει...δι' ἑκατέρων...τῆς βασιλείας τὴν θύραν, διά τε τῶν χειρῶν, δι' ὧν τὰ ἔργα δηλοῦται· καὶ διὰ τοῦ κλεῖθρου τῆς π. δι' ἀμφοτέρων... ἔργων τε καὶ π. λέγω, ἡ κλεὶς τῆς βασιλείας ἐν ἡμῖν ὑπὸ τοῦ λόγου κατασκευάζεται* Gr.Nyss.*hom.12 in Cant*.(M.44.1024C); *τὴν π. ἔργον ἐκάλεσεν. οὐκοῦν ἅμα ἐπίστευσας, ἅμα καὶ τοῖς ἔργοις ἐκόμησας, οὐχ ὅτι ἐλλείπῃ πρὸς τὰ ἔργα, ἀλλ' ὅτι καθ' ἑαυτὴν π. πλήρης ἐστὶν ἀγαθῶν ἔργων. τὰ...ἔργα εἰς ἀνθρώπους καὶ ἐξ ἀνθρώπων, ἡ δὲ π. ἐξ ἀνθρώπων πρὸς θεόν...οὐ δεῖ μὲν τὴν π. γυμνὴν εἶναι τῶν ἔργων, ἵνα μὴ ὑβρίζηται, πλὴν ἀνωτέρα τῶν ἔργων ἡ π. ... δεῖ μὲν τοῖς ἔργοις τρέφεσθαι, δεῖ δὲ πρὸ τῶν ἔργων τὴν π. ἐνδύεσθαι* ‡Chrys.*fid*.1(3.826B–D); *ib*.(827B); Cyr.*Jo*.10(4.827E); *συμπαραζευγνύσθω...τῇ τῆς π. ὁμολογίᾳ καὶ ἡ διὰ τῶν ἔργων θερμότης* *ib*.10.2(869D); Diad.*perf*.20(p.22.25) cit. s. *ἀεργός*; *ὁ π. μὲν ὀρθὴν κεκτῆσθαι λέγων, ἁμαρτίας δὲ διαπραττόμενος ὅμοιός ἐστι προσώπῳ ὀφθαλμοὺς μὴ ἔχοντι. ὁ π. μὴ ἔχων, καλὰ δὲ ἴσως τινὰ ἐργαζόμενος, ὅμοιός ἐστι τῷ ὕδωρ ἀντλοῦντι, καὶ εἰς πίθον τετρημένον βάλλοντι* Jo.Clim.*scal*.26(M.88.1089A); cf.*Schol*.9 *ib*.(M.88.1093D); **c.** views of S. Paul and S. James reconciled *κἂν εἰ λέγοιτο* [sc. *ὁ Ἀβραάμ*] *τυχὸν ἐξ ἔργων δεδικαιῶσθαι διά τοι τὸ προσενεγκεῖν τὸν Ἰσαὰκ πειραζόμενον, ἀλλ' ἦν καὶ τοῦτο αὐτῷ πίστεως τῆς ἑδραιοτάτης ἀπόδειξις ἐναργής* Cyr.*Rom*.4:2(p.181.18; M.74.781C); *Ἀβραὰμ καὶ τῆς ἀπράκτου καὶ τῆς μετὰ τῶν ἔργων π. ἐστιν εἰκών...καὶ τῆς πρὸ τοῦ βαπτίσματος, τῆς μὴ ἐπιζητούσης ἔργα, μόνον δὲ τὴν ὁμολογίαν... τῆς σωτηρίας, ᾧ δικαιούμεθα πιστεύοντες εἰς Χριστόν, καὶ τῆς μετὰ τὸ βάπτισμα, τῆς συνεζευγμένης τοῖς ἔργοις* *cat.Jac*.2:20f.(p.16.25).

I. faith, reason, and wisdom; **1.** divine mysteries to be accepted by faith *οὐκέτ' οὖν π. γίνεται δι' ἀποδείξεως ὠχυρωμένη* Clem.*str*.2.2(p.118.6; M.8.941A); *εἴπατε...τὰ πράγματα, καὶ μάλιστα ἡ περὶ τοῦ θεοῦ γνῶσις, πῶς ἀκριβῶς διαγινώσκεται, δι' ἀποδείξεως λόγων, ἢ δι' ἐνεργείας πίστεως; καὶ τί πρεσβύτερόν ἐστιν, ἡ δι' ἐνεργείας π., ἢ ἡ διὰ λόγων ἀπόδειξις; τῶν δὲ ἀποκριναμένων, πρεσβυτέραν εἶναι τὴν δι' ἐνεργείας π., καὶ ταύτην εἶναι τὴν ἀκριβῆ γνῶσιν· ἔφη ὁ Ἀντώνιος· καλῶς εἴπατε· ἡ μὲν γὰρ π. ἀπὸ διαθέσεως ψυχῆς γίνεται· ἡ δὲ διαλεκτικὴ ἀπὸ τέχνης τῶν συντιθέντων ἐστίν. οὐκοῦν οἷς πάρεστιν ἡ διὰ πίστεως ἐνέργεια, τούτοις...περιττὴ ἡ διὰ λόγων ἀπόδειξις...ὅπερ ἡμεῖς ἐκ π. νοοῦμεν, τοῦτο ὑμεῖς διὰ λόγων κατασκευάζειν πειρᾶσθε· καὶ πολλάκις οὐδὲ φράσαι ἃ νοοῦμεν δύνασθε· ὥστε...ὀχυρωτέρα ἡ διὰ π. ἐνέργεια τῶν σοφιστικῶν ὑμῶν συλλογισμῶν Ath.v.Anton.77(M.26.952A); τῶν ὑπεραναβεβηκότων δογμάτων, κρείττων ἐστὶ τῆς διὰ λογισμῶν καταλήψεως ἡ π. Gr.Nyss.diff.ess.(M.32.336B); π. ἡγείσθω τῶν περὶ θεοῦ λόγων· π., καὶ μὴ ἀπόδειξις. π., ἡ ὑπὲρ τὰς λογικὰς μεθόδους τὴν ψυχὴν εἰς συγκατάθεσιν ἕλκουσα· π., οὐχ ἡ γεωμετρικαῖς ἀνάγκαις, ἀλλ' ἡ ταῖς τοῦ πνεύματος ἐνεργείαις ἐγγινομένη †Bas.hom.in Ps.115(1.371B,C; M.30.104B); ἔνθα γὰρ π., οὐ χρεία ζητήσεως· ἔνθα μηδὲν δεῖ περιεργάζεσθαι, τί δεῖ ζητήσεως; ἡ ζήτησις τῆς π. ἐστιν ἀναιρετική... ἐπεὶ εἰ ζητοῦμεν, οὐκ ἔστι τοῦτο π.· ἡ γὰρ π. ἀναπαύει τὸν λογισμόν Chrys.hom.1.2 in 1Tim.(11.551D); ἡ π. τοὺς λογισμοὺς ὑπερβαίνει τοὺς ἀνθρωπίνους id.hom.27.1 in Heb.(12.246A); id.hom.27.1 in Rom.(9.719C); id.incomprehens.2.2(1.454A); ib.2.6(460D); ὅσα δὲ ὑπὲρ τὸν ἡμέτερον λόγον καὶ τὴν φύσιν θαυματουργεῖ, πίστει κρατεῖν ὀφείλομεν, οὐ ζητεῖν λόγοις Thdot.Anc.exp.symb.4(M.77.1320B); π. ... τὰ ὑπὲρ ἡμᾶς, καὶ οὐ ζητήσει λαμβάνεται Cyr.Jo.3.4(4.279D); **2.** but faith to be followed by understanding and wisdom (v. γνῶσις); πολλῷ διαφέρει μετὰ λόγου καὶ σοφίας συγκατατίθεσθαι τοῖς δόγμασιν ἤπερ μετὰ ψιλῆς τῆς π. Or.Cels.1.13(p.66.10; M.11.680B); ib.6.13(p.83.29ff.; 1309C); ‡Ath.confut.16(M.28.1388A); ref. Abraham τῆς μὲν γνώσεως αὐτοῦ προώδευσεν ἡ π., τῆς δὲ π. ἀκόλουθος ἦν ἡ συνθήκη Const.App.7.33.4; ὧν τὰς ἀποδείξεις ὁ τῆς ἀληθείας ἀκριβῶς παραστήσει λόγος, οὐ πίστεως ἀναποδείκτου φαντασίαν ἀπορίᾳ τῆς ἀποδείξεως ἀλόγως προϊσχόμενος...ἀλλὰ ζητήσεως ἀκριβοῦς κατανοήσει...τὴν τοῦ θεωρήματος πίστωσιν...προτιθέμενος †Gr.Thaum.ep.Philagr.(M.46.1101B); οὐκ ἐπείπερ ἐστὶ πίστει παραδεκτὰ τὰ θειότερα, διὰ τοῦτο χρὴ πάντως τῆς ἐπ' αὐτοῖς ἐρεύνης ὁλοκλήρως ἀποφοιτᾶν, πειρᾶσθαι δὲ μᾶλλον καὶ γοῦν εἰς μετρίαν ἀναβαίνειν γνῶσιν...εὖ δὲ δὴ πάλιν οὐ πρότερον ἐγνωκέναι φασίν, εἶτα πιστεύειν, ἀλλὰ προθέντες τὴν π., δευτέραν τὴν γνῶσιν ἐπάγουσι. μετὰ γὰρ τὴν π. ἡ γνῶσις, καὶ οὐ πρὸ τῆς π. Cyr.Jo.4.4(4.393A); ib.4.2(360D); διὰ γὰρ γνώσεως ἡ π., διὰ δὲ τῆς π. ἡ σύνεσις id.Is.4.1(2.566B); ῥίζα γὰρ συνέσεως καὶ τρόφος ἡ π. ib.5.1(740A); id.Lc.20:40(M.72.892D); δεῖται...ἡ π. τῆς γνώσεως, καθάπερ αὖ ἡ γνῶσις τῆς π. οὔτε γὰρ π. ἄνευ γνώσεως, οὔτε γνῶσις δίχα π. γένοιτο ἄν. ἡγεῖται...τῆς γνώσεως ἡ π., ἕπεται δὲ τῇ π. ἡ γνῶσις Thdt.affect.1(p.26.17; 4.717); λαβόντες οὖν θεοῦ γνῶσιν διὰ τῆς π. Ant.Mon.hom.1(M.89.1436D); **3.** ref. vain reasonings τὰ γὰρ τῇ π. παραδιδόμενα ἀπεριέργαστον ἔχει τὴν γνῶσιν Ath.ep.Serap.4.5(M.26.644B); ἅπερ γὰρ ἡ π. ... ᾠκοδόμησε, ταῦτα αὕτη [sc. ζήτησις] καταστρέφει...τὴν π. ἐκβάλλουσα Chrys.hom.1.2 in 1Tim.(11.552A); ib.5.1(575E); ἄρα π. βεβαιοῖ· οὐκοῦν λογισμοὶ σαλεύουσιν· ἐναντίον γὰρ ἡ π. λογισμῷ id.hom.33.3 in Heb.(12.307A); **4.** faith preceded by rational choice to obey God τὸ δ' ἐξακολουθῆσαι οἷς φίλον αὐτῷ [sc. θεῷ] αἱρουμένους δι' ὧν αὐτὸς ἐδωρήσατο λογικῶν δυνάμεων πείθει τε καὶ εἰς π. ἄγει ἡμᾶς Just.1apol.10.4(M.6.341A); **5.** a right balance necessary δεῖ...σοφοὺς εἶναι τοὺς τῶν θείων μυστηρίων ἀκροατάς...καὶ μήτε τοῖς πίστει παραδεκτοῖς ἀκαίρως ἐπάγειν τὴν ἀνεξίτητον ζήτησιν, μήτε τοῖς τῆς ζητήσεως δεομένοις ἐπασωτεύεσθαι π. ἔσθ' ὅτε τὴν ἐπιζήμιον, ἀποδιδόναι δὲ τὸ ἑκάστῳ πρέπον τῶν λαλουμένων, καὶ δι' εὐθείας ὥσπερ ἰέναι τρίβου, τὸ ἐκκλίνειν ἐπ' ἄμφω παραιτουμένους Cyr.Jo.4.3(4.374C); **6.** π. as 'confidence' in daily life an argument for reasonableness of faith οὐ παρ' ἡμῖν γε μόνοις, τοῖς τὴν τοῦ Χριστοῦ προσηγορίαν ἔχουσιν, μέγα τὸ τῆς π. ἐστιν ἀξίωμα· ἀλλὰ γὰρ καὶ πάντα τὰ ἐν τῷ κόσμῳ τελούμενα...τῇ π. τελεῖται. πίστει γαμικοὶ νόμοι τοὺς ἀπεξενωμένους συνάπτουσιν εἰς ταὐτόν...π. καὶ γεωργία συνίσταται· ὁ γὰρ μὴ πιστεύων λήψεσθαι καρποφορίαν, οὐχ ὑπομένει τοὺς καμάτους...κατὰ πίστιν τοίνυν συνέστηκε τὰ πλεῖστα τῶν ἀνθρώπων πράγματα· καὶ οὐ παρ' ἡμῖν μόνοις τοῦτο πεπίστευται, ἀλλὰ καὶ παρὰ τοῖς ἔξωθεν Cyr.H.catech.5.3; Jo.D.f.o.4.11(M.94.1128C).

J. faith and sense-perception, cf. αἴσθησις: τοῦτο γὰρ π., ὅταν μὴ τοῖς σωματικοῖς ὀφθαλμοῖς ἀρκώμεθα μόνον, ἀλλὰ τοῖς τῆς διανοίας ὄμμασι φανταζώμεθα τὰ μὴ ὁρώμενα Chrys.hom.63.5 in Gen.(4.607A); id.hom.in 2Tim.3:1(6.279B,C); ἡμῖν αἰσθητῆς οὐ χρεία ὄψεως, τῆς π. ἀντὶ πάντων ἀρκούσης· τὰ γὰρ σημεῖα οὐ τοῖς πιστεύουσιν, ἀλλὰ τοῖς ἀπίστοισι id.hom.12.3 in Mt.(7.163D); cf.id.hom.57.2 in Jo.(8.333D); τοῖς...ἐν ὄψει κειμένοις οὐδαμόθεν ἀμφίλογος ὀφείλεται π. ... ὃ δὲ μὴ τεθέαταί τις εἰ παραδέξαιτο, καὶ ἀληθὲς εἶναι πιστεύσειεν ὅπερ ἂν εἰς ὦτα διακομίσειαν τοῦ μυσταγωγοῦντος οἱ λόγοι, ἀξιολογωτάτη τετίμηκε π. τὸν κηρυττόμενον Cyr.Jo.12.1(4.1111A).

K. obstacles in way of faith: lack of resolution βλέπε τὴν διψυχίαν...πολλοὺς ἐκριζοῖ ἀπὸ τῆς π. Herm.mand.9.9; Bas.moral.8(2.240D; M.31.712C); wavering under persecution, when faith must be strengthened by prayer and vigilance, Max.ep.14(M.91.541Cff.); absence of proof οὔτε γὰρ π. κατὰ δήλου φαινομένη π. ἂν λέγοιτο· ἀλλ' ἔστι π. ἡ τὸ ἀδύνατον ἐν δυνάμει πιστεύουσα...καὶ τὸ φθαρτὸν ἐν ἀφθαρσίᾳ, καὶ τὸ θνητὸν ἐν ἀθανασίᾳ ‡Ath.Apoll.2.11(M.26.1149C); its acceptance depending on free will, Gr.Nyss.or.catech.30(p.110.11ff.; M.45.76D–77A).

L. faith and sin: coexisting, Herm.sim.8.9.1; πολλοὶ γὰρ π. ἔχοντες ἀκριβῆ, βίον δὲ διεφθαρμένον, ἀθλιώτεροι πάντων γεγόνασιν Chrys.exp.in Ps.127:1(5.360B); but οὐδεὶς π. ἐπαγγελλόμενος ἁμαρτάνει Ign.Eph.14.2; faith weakens sin, Meth.res.1.41(p.287.5; M.18.269C).

M. metaphors and types; **1.** as light of the world, Clem.str.4.11(p.283.30; M.8.1289A); Meth.symp.5.3(p.55.17; M.18.100C); νικάτω γὰρ ἡ π. πάντῃ, καὶ ἀπωθείσθω τὸ φῶς αὐτῆς τὰ φερόμενα τοῦ πονηροῦ ib.8.4(p.85.10; 144B); ref. Apoc.12:1 σελήνην...τροπικῶς τὴν π. τῶν ἀποκαθαιρομένων τὴν φθορὰν τῷ λουτρῷ λέγων, διὰ τὸ προσεοικέναι τὸ φῶς αὐτῆς μᾶλλον ὕδατι χλιαρῷ ib.8.6(p.88.6; 148A); **2.** as a mother π. ἥτις ἐστὶν μήτηρ πάντων ἡμῶν Polyc.ep.3.2; Chrys.hom 33.1 in Jo.(8.189D); id.hom.2.6 in Rom.(9.447C); μητέρα τῆς αἰωνίου ζωῆς τὴν π. ὡρίσατο Cyr.Jo.11.5(4.952B); and teacher, Chrys.exp.in Ps.115:1(5.310A); **3.** as flesh or body, with eucharistic reference; of Christ π., ὅ ἐστιν σὰρξ τοῦ κυρίου Ign.Trall.8.1; of Church φάγεσθέ μου τὰς σάρκας εἰπὼν καὶ πίεσθέ μου τὸ αἷμα, τὸ ἐναργὲς τῆς π. καὶ τῆς ἐπαγγελίας ⟨τὸ βρώσιμον καὶ⟩ τὸ πότιμον ἀλληγορῶν· δι' ὧν ἡ ἐκκλησία ...συμπήγνυται ἐξ ἀμφοῖν, σώματος μὲν τῆς π., ψυχῆς δὲ τῆς ἐλπίδος Clem.paed.1.6(p.113.1ff.; M.8.296B); **4.** as food: meat opp. γάλα, ib.(p.112.26; 296A); honey, ref. milk and honey of promised land, Barn.6.17; typified by meal desired by Isaac, Cyr.glaph.Gen.3(1.103B); **5.** as garment of Church, Clem.paed.2.10(p.223.23; M.8.529B); **6.** typified by crown of thorns, ib.2.8(p.202.13; 485A).

N. scriptural examples of faith; **1.** Abraham τίνος χάριν ηὐλογήθη ὁ πατὴρ ἡμῶν Ἀβραάμ, οὐχὶ δικαιοσύνην καὶ ἀλήθειαν διὰ πίστεως ποιήσας; 1Clem.31.2; ib.10.7; οὐδεὶς γὰρ οὐδὲν ἐκείνων [sc. good things promised]...λαβεῖν ἔχει πλὴν οἱ τῇ γνώμῃ ἐξομοιωθέντες τῇ π. τοῦ Ἀβραάμ Just.dial.44.2(M.6.569B); ref. Gal.3:7, cf. *ob quae non solum prophetam eum dixit fidei, sed et patrem eorum qui ex gentibus credunt in Christum Jesum, eo quod una et eadem illius et nostra sit fides*, Iren.haer.4.21.1(M.7.1044A); Cyr.H.catech.5.5; ib.5.6; Chrys.hom.9.1 in Rom.(9.511C); οὔτι γὰρ τῷ πατρὶ ἡμῶν Ἀβραὰμ εἰς δικαιοσύνην λελόγιστο ἡ π., εἰ μὴ καρπὸν αὐτῆς τὸν παῖδα προσήγαγεν Schol.9 in Jo.Clim.scal.26(M.88.1093D); **2.** Moses, Orac.Sib.8.252; **3.** Daniel, Clem.str.2.20(p.170.1; M.8.1048C); **4.** stone of Zach.4:10 Ζοροβάβελ ἐστί...ὁ κύριος...τούτου δὲ λίθος ἐστὶν ἡ π. ἡ εἰς αὐτόν· ἐν τῇ χειρὶ δέ, ὅτι τῇ πράξει τῶν ἐντολῶν π. τοῦ Χριστοῦ διαφαίνεται. π. γὰρ χωρὶς ἔργων, νεκρά· ὥσπερ καὶ ἔργα δίχα π. πράξεως δὲ σύμβολόν ἐστι...ἡ χείρ. φέρων οὖν ἐν τῇ χειρὶ τὸν λίθον ὁ κύριος, ἔμπρακτον ἡμᾶς διδάσκει τὴν εἰς αὐτὸν π. ἔχειν, τοῖς ἑπτὰ τοῦ κυρίου κοσμουμένον ὀφθαλμοῖς· τουτέστι, ταῖς ἑπτὰ τοῦ ἁγίου πνεύματος ἐνεργείαις Max.qu.Thal.54(M.90.521A,B); τυχὸν δὲ καὶ διὰ τοῦτο κασσιτερίνῳ λίθῳ κατὰ τὴν γραφὴν παρεικάζεται ἡ π., τῶν ἐν τοῖς μελαίνουσιν αὐτῆς τὴν ἀρετὴν...δυναμένων πάλιν διὰ μετανοίας...λαμπρύνεσθαι ib.(525C); λίθος ἡ π. ἐκλήθη, διὰ τὸ στερρὸν...τῆς κατ' αὐτὴν ἀληθείας Schol.24 ib.(M.90.532D); **5.** patriarchs, prophets, and apostles, Clem.str.1.9(p.30.7; M.8.741C); Rahab, 1Clem.12.1; Esther, ib.55.6; **6.** BMV θεοτόκος...ἡ νοερὰ τῆς π. τράπεζα, ἡ τὸν ἄρτον τῆς ζωῆς τῷ κόσμῳ χορηγήσασα ‡Epiph.hom.5(M.43.493B); her faith opp. Eve's credulity Εὔα...τὸν λόγον τὸν ἀπὸ τοῦ ὄφεως συλλαβοῦσα...π. δὲ καὶ χάριν λαβοῦσα Μαρία Just.dial.100.5(M.6.712A); and lack of faith, cf.Iren.haer.3.22.4(M.7.960A).

O. opp. Law τὸ ἀληθινὸν πάσχα...τὸ...πίστει νοούμενον, οὐ γράμματι νῦν τηρούμενον Hipp.haer.8.18(p.237.21; M.16.3366B); ἀπὸ τῆς εἰς Χριστὸν π. ἐπὶ τὴν Ἰουδαϊκὴν ἐθελοθρησκείαν Eus.h.e.6.12.1(M.20.545A); faith superior to Law, Chrys.hom.8.4 in Rom.(9.502E); but does not contradict it, ib.7.4(488E–489A); πολλῷ γὰρ μᾶλλον ἐνταῦθα [sc. NT] πίστεως χρεία, ἢ ἐκεῖ [OT], διά τε τὴν φύσιν τῶν ἐπαγγελιῶν ἀόρατόν τε οὖσαν καὶ νοεράν, διά τε τὴν τάξιν τῶν καιρῶν. οὐ γὰρ ἐν τῷ παρόντι βίῳ, ἀλλ' ἐν τῷ μέλλοντι ἦν τὰ ἔπαθλα id.exp.in Ps.115:1(5.311A); Cyr.Jo.12(4.1070D); Thdt.Rom.9:32(3.40).

II. as t.t., the *faith* as equivalent of Christian religion (freq. merging into sense I supra);

A. in gen. ὁ ἀπόστολος δεικνὺς τὸν καταισχυμμὸν τῆς π. Clem.str.4.7(p.272.4; M.8.1264B); ib.2.13(p.143.26; 996A); ἐν καιρῷ βασάνου... τῆς π. Or.mart.10(p.10.20; M.11.576C); ὑπὲρ τῆς π. ... ἀπολογίας προσεφώνησαν Eus.h.e.4.26.1(M.20.392A); ib.6.36.1(596B); ἀνθρώπους ἀπὸ ἐθνικοῦ βίου ἄρτι προσελθόντας τῇ π. CNic.(325)can.2.

B. its spread ἡ παρ' ἡμῖν δὲ τῆς ἀληθείας ἐπίγνωσις ἐκ τῶν ἤδη πιστῶν τοῖς οὔπω πιστοῖς ἐκπορίζεται τὴν π. Clem.str.7.16(p.69.24; M.9.536C); through apostolate, Eus.h.e.6.3.13(M.20.529D); Cyr.Jo.2.5(4.202B); ib.5.2(482C); as proof of its truth, agst. pagan objections ὅτι ἐνεργής ἐστιν ἡ π. ἡμῶν, ἰδοὺ νῦν ἡμεῖς ἐπερειδόμεθα τῇ π. τῇ εἰς τὸν Χριστόν...τὰ μὲν παρ' ὑμῖν τῶν εἰδώλων φάσματα καταργεῖται, ἡ δὲ παρ' ἡμῖν π. ἐπεκτείνεται πανταχοῦ Ath.*v.Anton*.78(M.26.952B).

C. apostasy from faith; a sin of pride, Bas.*fid*.1(2.224D; M.31.680A); eccl. legislation ἐπειδὴ δὲ πολλοὶ ἐν τῇ τῶν βαρβάρων καταδρομῇ παρέβησαν τὴν εἰς θεὸν π., ὅρκους ἐθνικοὺς ἐπιτελέσαντες...οὗτοι κατὰ τοὺς ἤδη παρὰ τῶν πατέρων ἡμῶν ἐξενεχθέντας κανόνας οἰκονομείσθωσαν. οἱ...μὴ φέροντες τοὺς πόνους, καὶ ἑλκυσθέντες πρὸς τὴν ἄρνησιν, ἐν τρισὶν ἔτεσιν ἀδέκτους εἶναι, καὶ ἐν δυσὶν ἀκροᾶσθαι· καὶ ἐν τρισὶν ὑποπεσόντας, οὕτω δεκτοὺς γενέσθαι εἰς τὴν κοινωνίαν Bas.*ep*.217 *can*.81(3.329C; M.32.805B); final apostasy οὐ γὰρ ὀνήσει ὑμᾶς τὰ πρότερα κατορθώματα, ἐὰν εἰς τὰ ἔσχατα ὑμῶν ἀποπλανηθῆτε τῆς π. τῆς ἀληθοῦς *Const.App*.7.31.6.

D. in various phrases; **1.** οἱ κατὰ πίστιν *the faithful*, Clem.*str*.7.14(p.61.9; M.9.520B); **2.** οἱ ἔξω τῆς π. *unbelievers*, Or.*Cels*.7.46(p.197.15; M.11.1488B); also οἱ ἀλλότριοι τῆς π. *ib*.8.73(p.290.27; 1628A); **3.** οἱ ἐν π. ἀναπαυσάμενοι *the faithful departed*, *Lit*.ap.*Const.App*.8.13.6; also οἱ ἐν π. παρελθόντες Chrys.*hom*.3.4 *in Phil*.(11.218A); **4.** ὁ λόγος τῆς π. *the doctrine of the faith*, Cels.ap.Or.*Cels*.3.18(p.216.15; M.11.941B); plur., Or.*ib*.2.1(p.127.19; 796B).

III. the sum of what is to be believed; system of orthodox belief;

A. based on scripture and transmitted from apostles ἡ...ἐκκλησία...παρὰ δὲ τῶν ἀποστόλων, καὶ τῶν ἐκείνων μαθητῶν παραλαβοῦσα τὴν εἰς ἕνα θεὸν...π. Iren.*haer*.1.10.1(M.7.549A); cf. *in fide nostra; quam perceptam ab ecclesia custodimus*, *ib*.3.24.1(966B); πίστιν δὲ ἡμεῖς οὔτε παρ' ἄλλων γραφομένην ἡμῖν νεωτέραν παραδεχόμεθα, οὔτε αὐτοὶ τὰ τῆς ἡμετέρας διανοίας γεννήματα παραδιδόναι τολμῶμεν, ἵνα μὴ ἀνθρώπινα ποιήσωμεν τὰ τῆς εὐσεβείας ῥήματα· ἀλλ' ἅπερ παρὰ τῶν ἁγίων πατέρων δεδιδάγμεθα, ταῦτα τοῖς ἐρωτῶσιν ἡμᾶς διαγγέλλομεν Bas.*ep*.140.2(3.233B; M.32.588B); οὐδὲ νῦν ἡ π. ἤρξατο, ἀλλ' ἐκ τοῦ κυρίου διὰ τῶν μαθητῶν εἰς ἡμᾶς διαβέβηκεν Ath.*ep.encycl*.1(p.170.14; M.25.225A); id.*decr*.3(p.3.14; M.25.'429'(421)A); π. δὲ ἐν μαθήσει καὶ ἐπαγγελίᾳ κτῆσαι καὶ τήρησον μόνην, τὴν ὑπὸ τῆς ἐκκλησίας νυνί σοι παραδιδομένην, τὴν ἐκ πάσης γραφῆς ὠχυρωμένην Cyr.H.*catech*.5.12; οὐ γὰρ ὡς ἔδοξεν ἀνθρώποις συνετέθη τὰ τῆς π.· ἀλλ' ἐκ πάσης γραφῆς τὰ καιριώτατα συλλεχθέντα, μίαν ἀναπληροῖ τὴν τῆς π. διδασκαλίαν *ib*.; καθολικὴ ἐκκλησία...τὴν π. κεκρατηκυῖα *Const.App*.2.26.2; Cyr.*ep*.55(p.60.28f.; 5².190B); τῆς...καθολικῆς...ἐκκλησίας, ἣν ἐθεμελίωσας ἐπὶ τὴν πέτραν τῆς π. *Lit.Jac*.(p.206.18).

B. transmitted by bishops, cf. *Romae fundatae...ecclesiae, eam quam habet ab apostolis traditionem, et annuntiatam hominibus fidem, per successiones episcoporum pervenientem usque ad nos*, Iren.*haer*.3.3.2(M.7.848B); *ubi...charismata domini posita sunt, ibi discere oportet veritatem, apud quos est ea quae est ab apostolis ecclesiae successio...hi enim et eam quae est in unum deum qui omnia fecit fidem nostram custodiunt*, *ib*.4.26.5(1056A).

C. maintenance of its purity the responsibility of Church, CSard.*ep.Alex*.ap.Ath.*apol.sec*.38(p.117.12; M.25.316A); Ath.*h.Ar*.36(p.203.26; M.25.736B); id.*Ar*.3.58(M.26.445A).

D. its unity, cf.Eph.4:5 συνέρχεσθε ἐν μιᾷ π. Ign.*Eph*.20.2; μιᾶς ...τῆς αὐτῆς π. οὔσης, οὔτε ὁ πολὺ περὶ αὐτῆς δυνάμενος εἰπεῖν, ἐπλεόνασεν, οὔτε ὁ τὸ ὀλίγον, ἠλαττόνησε Iren.*haer*.1.10.2(M.7.553A); *ib*.5.20.1(1177B); Clem.*str*.7.2(p.7.25; M.9.412B); τῆς ἁγίας τριάδος μία ἡ θεότης καὶ π. ἐστίν Ath.*ep.Serap*.1.16(M.26.569B); *ib*.3.6(636A); id.*ep.Jov*.4(M.26.820A)ap.Thdt.*h.e*.4.3.14(3.951); οὐ τὸ διαιρεῖσθαι τὰς κατηχήσεις, διαίρεσιν εἶχε τῆς π.·...εἰς πολλὰς μὲν διαλέξεις τοὺς περὶ τοῦ...Χριστοῦ λόγους διαιροῦντες, ἀδιαίρετον δὲ τὴν εἰς αὐτὸν π. καταγγέλλοντες· οὕτως καὶ νῦν τῶν περὶ τοῦ ἁγίου πνεύματος κατηχήσεων διαιρουμένων, ἀδιαίρετον καταγγέλλομεν τὴν εἰς αὐτὸ π. Cyr.H.*catech*.17.2; τοῦτο γάρ ἐστιν ἑνότης πίστεως, ὅταν πάντες ἓν ὦμεν, ὅταν πάντες ὁμοίως τὸν σύνδεσμον ἐπιγινώσκωμεν Chrys.*hom*.11.3 *in Eph*.(11.83E); Cyr.*Jo*.9(4.762B,C); id.*Nah*.13(3.491D); id.*hom.pasch*.30(5².347B); ἐκκλησία...κατὰ μίαν τὴν π. ... τοὺς πιστοὺς ἀλλήλοις ἑνοειδῶς συνάπτουσα Max.*myst*.2.4(M.91.705B).

E. founded on truth πρὸς τὴν πλάνην...ἑδραῖοι τῇ π. Ign.*Eph*.10.2; ἀμεταπτώτῳ κριτηρίῳ τῇ π. ἐπαναπαυώμεθα Clem.*str*.2.4(p.119.6; M.8.944A); *ib*.2.12(p.142.33; 992C); *ib*.6.8(p.467.2; M.9.292A); Ath.*ep.Aeg.Lib*.20(M.25.585C); id.*Dion*.5(p.49.26; M.25.488A); ἡ ἁπλῆ... ἀλήθεια, περὶ ἣν...ἡ θεία π. ἐστίν, ἡ μόνιμος τῶν πεπιστευμένων ἵδρυσις Dion.Ar.*d.n*.7.4(M.3.872C); *Schol*.21 in Max.*qu.Thal*.54(M.90.532C); opp. spurious 'faith' of heretics with its instability ποία π. παρὰ τούτοις, παρ' οἷς οὐ λόγος, οὐ γράμμα βέβαιον, ἀλλὰ πάντα κατὰ καιρὸν ἀλλάσσεται; Ath.*syn*.38(p.264.21; M.26.760B); τοῖς ῥήμασι τῆς π. ὡς ἰατροὶ κέχρηνται κατὰ καιρόν, ἄλλοτε ἄλλως πρὸς τὰ ὑποκείμενα πάθη μεθαρμοζόμενοι...εἰ γὰρ ἄλλοτε ἄλλας δεῖ π. συγγράφειν, καὶ μετὰ τῶν καιρῶν ἀλλοιοῦσθαι, ψευδὴς ἡ ἀπόφασις τοῦ εἰπόντος· εἷς κύριος, μία π. Bas.*ep*.226.3(3.348B; M.32.848C); its novelty τί γὰρ ἔλειπε διδασκαλίας εἰς εὐσέβειαν τῇ καθολικῇ ἐκκλησίᾳ, ἵνα νῦν περὶ πίστεως ζητῶσι καὶ τὴν ὑπατείαν τῶν παρόντων χρόνων προστάσσωσι τῶν παρ' αὐτῶν ἐκτιθεμένων ῥημάτων δῆθεν περὶ π.;...γράψαντες γὰρ ὡς ἤθελον αὐτοὶ πιστεύειν προέταξαν τὴν ὑπατείαν...ἵνα δείξωσι πᾶσι φρονίμοις ὅτι μὴ πρότερον, ἀλλὰ νῦν ἐπὶ Κωνσταντίου ἀρχὴν ἔχει τούτων ἡ π. Ath.*syn*.3.3(p.232.23ff.; M.26.684C–685A); *ib*.4(p.233.21ff.; 688A,B); its rationalist tendencies ἡ τῆς ἁπλότητος π. βελτίων ἐστὶ τῆς ἐκ περιεργίας πιθανολογίας id.*Ar*.3.1(M.26.324A); μόνον, φησί, [sc. Apoll.] τὴν εὐσεβῆ π. ἀγαθὸν ἦν νομίζεσθαι· μηδὲ γὰρ τῇ Εὐᾳ συνενεγκεῖν τὴν ἀνεξέταστον π.· ὥστε προσῆκε καὶ τὴν Χριστιανῶν ἐξητασμένην εἶναι, μή που λάθῃ ταῖς τῶν Ἑλλήνων ἢ τῶν Ἰουδαίων συνεμπεσοῦσα δόξαις Gr.Nyss.*Apoll*.4(M.45.1129C); τὴν δὲ π. οὐ βλέπουσι τῷ τῆς ψυχῆς ὀφθαλμῷ, ὅπερ δὴ μόνον σύμμετρόν ἐστι τῇ ἡμετέρᾳ κατανοήσει, τὴν ἐκ τῶν λογισμῶν ἐπίγνωσιν ἐπίπροσθεν ταύτης ποιούμενοι id.*Eun*.10(2 p.230.20; M.45.832B); objection to heretics defining or usurping 'the faith', Ath.*ep.Aeg.Lib*.7(M.25.553A); εἴθε περὶ τῆς πίστεως ἑαυτῶν ἔγραφον 'νῦν γὰρ ἤρξατο' καὶ μὴ ὡς περὶ τῆς καθολικῆς ἐπεχείρουν· οὐ γὰρ ἔγραψαν 'οὕτω πιστεύομεν' ἀλλ' ὅτι 'ἐξετέθη ἡ καθολικὴ π.' id.*syn*.3.3(p.233.15; M.26.685C).

F. as embodied in a creed; **1.** *faith, creed*, of Nicaea as pre-eminently orthodox faith κατέχων ἕκαστος τὴν ἐκ πατέρων π., ἣν καὶ οἱ ἐν Νικαίᾳ συνελθόντες ὑπέμνησαν γράψαντες Ath.*ep.Aeg.Lib*.8(M.25.556A); *ib*.21(588A); id.*ep.Adelph*.6(M.26.1080A); Bas.*ep*.226.3(3.348A; M.32.848B); μὴ ἀθετεῖσθαι τὴν π. τῶν πατέρων...τῶν ἐν Νικαίᾳ...συνελθόντων CCP(381)*can*.1; Thdt.*h.e*.2.21.1(3.879); to which no additions are to be made, Ath.*tom*.5(M.26.800C,D); οὐδὲν δυνάμεθα τῇ κατὰ Νίκαιαν π. προστιθέναι ἡμεῖς, οὐδὲ τὸ βραχύτατον, πλὴν τῆς εἰς τὸ πνεῦμα τὸ ἅγιον δοξολογίας...τὰ δὲ προσυφαινόμενα τῇ π. ἐκείνῃ δόγματα, περὶ τῆς τοῦ κυρίου ἐνανθρωπήσεως, ὡς βαθύτερα τῆς ἡμετέρας καταλήψεως, οὔτε ἐβασανίσαμεν, οὔτε παρεδεξάμεθα· εἰδότες ὅτι ἐπειδὰν τὴν ἁπλότητα τῆς π. ἅπαξ παρακινήσωμεν, οὔτε τι πέρας τῶν λόγων εὑρήσομεν Bas.*ep*.258.2(3.393D; M.32.949B,C); **2.** of other creeds ἡ γραφεῖσα παρὰ τῶν ἁγίων πατέρων π. τῶν κατὰ τὴν Νίκαιαν συνελθόντων *ib*.140.2(3.233B; M.32.588B); *ib*.51.2(3.144B; M.389C); δεῖ τοὺς φωτιζομένους τὴν π. ἐκμανθάνειν, καὶ...ἀπαγγέλλειν CLaod.*can*.46,47 = CTrull.*can*.78; Philost.*h.e*.5.1(M.65.528C); ref. *traditio symboli* to catechumens π. ... ἐστι τὸ βαλεῖν τὸ ἀργύριον ἐπὶ τὴν τράπεζαν, ὅπερ ἡμεῖς νῦν πεποιήκαμεν· θεὸς δὲ παρ' ὑμῶν ἀπαιτεῖ τῆς παρακαταθήκης τοὺς λόγους...τηρῆσαι ταύτην ὑμᾶς τὴν παραδεδομένην π. ἄσπιλον Cyr.H.*catech*.5.13.

G. various epithets of orthodox faith ὑγιαίνουσα, Ath.*syn*.6(p.234.22; M.26.689A); id.*ep.Afr*.1(M.26.1029A); Bas.*ep*.243.4(3.375A; M.32.908C); Chrys.*hom*.47.4 *in Ac*.(9.357A); ἐκκλησιαστική, Ath.*ep.Aeg.Lib*.13(M.25.568A); id.*h.Ar*.66(p.219.19; M.25.772B); Symb.*Ant*.(345)8(p.253.30; M.26.733A); ὀρθόδοξος, Jov.*ep*.(M.26.813A); Gel.Cyz.*h.e*.proem.12(M.85.1196A); ὀρθή, Eus.*e.th*.2.25(p.136.33; M.24.968A); Ath.*Ar*.3.18(M.26.360C); ἀποστολική, id.*ep.Serap*.1(M.26.565A); Gel.Cyz.*h.e*.proem.1(1192D); καθολική, Ath.*ep.Serap*.3.7(636B); CArim.*decr*.(p.239.6; M.26.701A).

IV. as Gnost. aeon, Iren.*haer*.1.1.2(M.7.449A); Hipp.*haer*.6.30(p.157.20; M.16.3239A); Epiph.*haer*.31.2(p.386.2; M.41.477A).

V. *sect, body of believers* ἐν ἄλλῃ π. ἢ συναγωγῇ Ἰουδαίων ἢ Ἀράβων †Anast.S.*relat*.38(*OC* 2 p.82).

***πιστολέτης**, ὁ, *faith-destroyer*, *Orac.Sib*.2.262; *ib*.8.187 (codd. πιστοπορθεῖς).

***πιστολογία**, ἡ, *assurance in speaking*, Marc.Er.*opusc*.1.150(M.65.924B).

πιστοποι-έω, **1.** *convince, assure*, Or.*comm.in Ex*.ap.*philoc*.27.5(p.247.17; M.12.272B); π. τοὺς ἀκροωμένους id.*Jo*.28.17(13; p.411.34; M.14.717D); c. ὅτι, ‡Eust.*Laz*.10(p.35.8); Bas.*hom.in Ps*.14(1.356B; M.29.261A); *Const.App*.5.6.4; Epiph.*haer*.70.6(p.238.17; M.42.348C); Mac.Mgn.*apocr*.3.13(p.85.15); πιστοῦ μὲν γὰρ τὸ ~εῖν Cyr.*thes*.32(5¹.289D); Eus.Al.*serm*.12(M.86.381A); **2.** *give assurance of, establish faith in* τὰ...ἐσόμενα διὰ τῶν οὔπω μελλόντων πληροῦσθαι ~εῖ Proc.G.*Is*.20:1–6(M.87.2157A); ‡Caes.Naz.*dial*.178(M.38.1149); **3.** pass., *be believed in, accepted* σταυρὸν...ὑπὸ...τοῦ κόσμου ~ούμενον Eus.Al.*serm*.10(M.86.369C); **4.** *make one of the faithful, make a baptized Christian*, Cyr.H.*catech*.3.15.

***πιστοποίησις**, ἡ, *assurance*, *T.Benj*.10.3 margin; Or.*Jo*.1.3(5; p.7.13; M.14.29A); *Dial.Tim.et Aquil*.107 r°.

***πιστοποιητικός**, *giving assurance*, Or.*Jo*.32.15(9; p.450.8; M.14.780C).

***πιστοποιός**, *producing faith*, Cyr.*Is*.5.2(2.776B).

πιστός, **A.** used in two senses, *reliable, faithful* διπλοῦν εἶναι τὸν νοῦν ἐν τῇ γραφῇ περὶ τοῦ π.· τὸ μὲν ὡς πιστεῦον, τὸ δὲ ὡς ἀξιόπιστον·

καὶ τὸ μὲν ἐπ' ἀνθρώπων, τὸ δὲ ἐπὶ θεοῦ ἁρμόζειν. π. γοῦν ὁ Ἀβραάμ, ὅτι...πεπίστευκε θεῷ, π. δὲ ὁ θεός, ὅτι...ἀδύνατόν ἐστιν αὐτὸν ψεύσασθαι Ath.*Ar*.2.6(M.26.160A); τὸ δὲ π. διττὸν κατὰ τὴν...γραφήν, ἢ τὸ ἀξιόπιστον, ὅπερ κυρίως ἐπὶ μόνου θεοῦ...π. δὲ καὶ ὁ πιστεύων Proc.G. *Dt*.22:4(M.87.953D).

B. *reliable, trustworthy*; **1.** of God τῷ π. ἐν ταῖς ἐπαγγελίαις *1Clem*. 27.1; ὁ π. ἐν πάσαις ταῖς γενεαῖς *ib*.60.1; π. ὁ πατὴρ...πληρῶσαι...τὴν αἴτησιν Ign.*Trall*.13.3; Clem.*str*.2.6(p.127.26; M.8.964A); Thdt.*Ps*. 1:1(1.610); **2.** of Christ ὁ π. ... ὁ σωτὴρ ὑπάρχει οὐ διὰ τὸ πίστεως... μετέχειν, ἀλλὰ διὰ τὸ βέβαιον κατ' οὐσίαν εἶναι...τὸ πιστὸς ἀντὶ βεβαίου καὶ ἀτρέπτου κεῖται...εἴρηται δὲ ὁ μάρτυς ὁ π. ... πρὸς παράστασιν βεβαιότητος ὡς αὐτός ἐστι τὸ ἀμήν Or.*Apoc*.22(p.30); Ath.*Ar*.2.6(M.26.160B); of Christ as διαθήκη π., Just.*dial*.11.2(M.6. 497B); in comparison with Moses, Ath.ap.*cat.Heb*.3:2(p.172.31); **3.** of prophecies, divine promises, words of scripture etc., Just. *dial*.84.2(M.6.673B); Ath.ap.*cat.Heb*.3:2(p.172.25); Gr.Nyss.*v.Mos*. (M.44.337D); of hope, Or.*Cels*.3.80(p.271.13; M.11.1025B); ὄψιν ἀκοῆς ...πιστοτέραν Cyr.H.*catech*.19.1; οὐδὲν...παρ' οὐδενὶ π. Bas.*epp*.223.3 (3.338C; M.32.825B).

C. *loyal, faithful*; **1.** in gen. δοῦλον...π. Herm.*sim*.5.2.2; π. δὲ ὁ ἀπαραβάτως τηρητικὸς τῶν ἐγχειρισθέντων Clem.*str*.2.6(p.127.22; M. 8.961C); Or.*hom.8.5 in Jer*.(p.60.28; M.13.344A); *Πλακίλλα...πιστοτάτη...φύλαξ τοῦ δόγματος τῆς ἐν Νικαίᾳ συνόδου* Soz.*h.e*.7.6.3(M.67. 1428B); **2.** towards God δύναμαι...π. εἶναι, ὅταν κόσμῳ μὴ φαίνωμαι Ign.*Rom*.3.2; Just.*dial*.56.1(M.6.596C); Ath.ap.*cat.Heb*.3:2(p.172. 34); π. τοὺς ἀναμφιβόλως δεχομένους αὐτοῦ τοὺς λόγους Thdt.*Ps*.1:1 (1.610); *Χριστιανὸς π. IG* 3.3435 (Athens, saec. iv–v).

D. *having faith, believing* γυναῖκα...π. ἐν κυρίῳ Herm.*mand*.4.1.4; οἱ ἀπὸ τῶν ἐθνῶν...πιστότεροι προεγινώσκοντο Just.*1apol*.53.10(M.6. 408B); π. ... διὰ τοῦ ὀνόματος τοῦ Ἰησοῦ γίνονται id.*dial*.110.4(M.6. 729C); Iren.*haer*.4.20.5(M.7.1035C); ἄνευ γραμμάτων πιστὸν εἶναι δυνατόν Clem.*str*.1.6(p.23.6; M.8.729B); τὸν δι' ἀγάπης π. *ib*.4.4(p.254. 13; 1228A); *ib*.7.14(p.60.6; M.9.517A); id.*exc.Thdot*.86(p.133.3; M.9. 697B); Hipp.*haer*.9.13(p.252.3; M.16.3387C); τὸν Χριστιανισμόν τινες οὐδένα λόγον ἀποσώζειν, ἀλόγῳ δὲ πίστει...τὸ δόξαν κυροῦν ὑπειλήφασιν, μηδὲν φάσκοντες δύνασθαι δι' ἀποδείξεως ἐναργοῦς παρέχειν τεκμήριον τῆς...ἀληθείας, πίστει δὲ μόνῃ προσέχειν ἀξιοῦν τοὺς προσιόντας, παρ' ὃ καὶ πιστοὺς χρηματίζειν τῆς ἀκρίτου χάριν... πίστεως Eus.*p.e*.1.1(4A; M.21.25D); Ath.*Ar*.2.6(M.26.160A); Gel. Cyz.*h.e*.2.23.5(M.85.1296C); Cosm.Ind.*top*.2(M.88.128C); Proc.G.*Dt*. 22:4(M.87.956A); *Lit.Jac*.(p.176.22).

E. *believing, faithful* (freq. as subst.); hence = *Christian*; **1.** in gen., Clem.*str*.6.7(p.462.11; M.9.281B); Or.*Cels*.proem.6(p.55.15; M. 11.649C); Chrys.*hom.76.1 in Mt*.(7.732E); plur. οἱ π. *members of the Church, the Church* τῶν ἐκεῖ π. Ign.*Eph*.21.2; *M.Polyc*.12.3; τῷ...π. λαῷ Just.*dial*.138.2(M.6.793B); τότε ἦσαν π. ὀλίγοι μέν, π. δὲ ἀληθῶς ...νῦν δὲ ὅτε...γεγόναμεν πολλοὶ...εἰσὶν ὀλίγοι οἱ καταντῶντες ἐπὶ τὴν ἐκλογὴν τοῦ θεοῦ Or.*hom.4.3 in Jer*.(p.25.25; M.13.289A); Meth.*res*. 2.8(p.343.17; M.41.1176A); Bas.*jud*.8(2.221E; M.31.672C); Chrys. *hom.27.2 in Jo*.(8.156A); imperial epithet of Theodosius I ὁ πιστότατος βασιλεύς Thdt.*h.e*.5.18.22(3.1050); Καῖσαρ...Ἡράκλειος π. ἐν Χριστῷ Heracl.*nov*.22(p.33); cf. ἐν Ἰησοῦ Χριστοῦ π. δεσποτῶν ὀρθοδόξων *CG–CI* 1.9 (Corinth, 574–8); πιστοτάτων καὶ φιλοχρίστων ἡμῶν βασιλέων *Lit.Chrys*.(p.389.9); **2.** as subst., *baptized Christian* opp. catechumen, Or.*hom.18.8 in Jer*.(p.162.3; M.13.480C); ref. penitential discipline ἡ σύστασις, ἵνα συνιστῆται τοῖς π., καὶ μὴ ἐξέρχηται μετὰ τῶν κατηχουμένων Gr.Thaum.*ep.can*.11(M.10.1048B); CLaod.*can*.7; *ib*.19; ἴδωμεν τί ποιοῦσιν οἱ π. Cyr.H.*procatech*.2; πρὸ τούτου κατηχούμενος ἦς, νῦν δὲ π. κληθήσῃ id.*catech*.1.4; such status not guaranteeing freedom from sin, *ib*.2.3; ἀπὸ τοῦ κατηχουμένων τάγματος εἰς τὸ τῶν π. μετατιθέμενος...π. ὁ θεὸς...θεοῦ γὰρ π. καλουμένου, καὶ σὺ ταύτην τὴν προσηγορίαν λαμβάνεις, μέγα λαμβάνων ἀξίωμα *ib*.5.1; οἱ μὲν ἐν τῷ λαϊκῷ ὄντες τάγματι, ἐκβεβλημένοι τοῦ τόπου τῶν π., πάλιν εἰς τὸν ἀφ' οὗ ἐξέπεσον τόπον ἀναλαμβάνονται Bas. *ep*.188 *can*.3(3.271B; M.32.762B); *Lit*.ap.*Const.App*.8.9.7; †CCP(381) *can*.2(p.164); *ib*.3(p.164); Chrys.*hom.4.8 in Mt*.(7.61B); τὰς εὐχὰς οὕτω γίνεσθαι κελεύουσιν οἱ τῆς ἐκκλησίας νόμοι, οὐ τὰς ὑπὲρ τῶν π. μόνον, ἀλλὰ καὶ τὰς ὑπὲρ τῶν κατηχουμένων. τοὺς γὰρ π. ὁ νόμος διεγείρει πρὸς τὴν τῶν ἀμυήτων ἱκετηρίαν. ὅταν γὰρ ὁ διάκονος λέγῃ, 'ὑπὲρ τῶν κατηχουμένων ἐκτενῶς δεηθῶμεν', οὐδὲν ἄλλο ἢ τὸν δῆμον ἅπαντα τῶν π. διανίστησιν εἰς τὰς ὑπὲρ ἐκείνων εὐχάς id.*hom.2.5 in 2Cor*.(10.435B); ἐν τοῖς π., ἐν τοῖς ὑπακούουσιν, ἐν τοῖς κατηχουμένοις id.*hom.22.4 in Eph*.(11.171D); ‡Chrys.*pasch*.1(8.251C); ‡Pall.*h.mon*. 5.4(p.29.15; M.65.448A); ὥσπερ ἡμεῖς π. ὀνομάζομεν τοὺς τῶν θείων μυστηρίων μετέχοντας, οὕτως τετελεσμένους ἐκάλει τὰ ἔθη τοὺς δαιμόνων τινῶν διδασκομένους μυστήρια Thdt.*qu.28 in Dt*.(1.278); id. *Os*.4:14(2.1330); τὰς τῶν π. ψυχὰς σημειουμένων καὶ ἀπογραφομένων Anast.S.*synax*.(M.89.840B).

***πιστοτερ-έω**, *be more worthy of credence* πράγματα ~οῦσι τῶν ῥημάτων Anast.S.*hod*.23(M.89.297A).

***πιστοφόρος**, *bearing the faithful* π. βήμασι σκιρτῶντες †Cyr.*hom. div*.11(5^2.379D).

***πίστρινον, τό,** (Lat. *pistrinum*) *mill*, operated by slaves, to which recaptured fugitive slave might be assigned as punishment, Hipp.*haer*.9.12(p.247.2; M.16.3382A).

πιστῶς, 1. *faithfully, loyally, reliably*, *Diogn*.7.2; Or.*Cels*.5.1(p.2. 5; M.11.1181B); Meth.*symp*.8.2(p.83.10; M.18.141A); **2.** *with faith, as a believer*, Clem.*str*.4.23(p.313.18; M.8.1357A); *ib*.5.1(p.327.11; M. 9.12A); Gel.Cyz.*h.e*.2.19.21(M.85.1280C); **3.** *confidently, with trust* π. τὴν ἐπαγγελίαν δεξώμεθα Thdt.*Heb*.13:5(3.633).

πίστωσις, ἡ, *assurance, confirmation*, Or.*Apoc*.25(p.32); ταῖς δι' ὅρκων π. id.*mart*.26(p.23.4; M.11.596A); Eus.*p.e*.10.6(477A; M.21. 793A); id.*e.th*.proem.(p.62.11; M.24.828C); πρὸς πίστωσιν τῆς ἀληθείας Eun.*apol*.6(M.30.841A); Gr.Naz.*carm*.1.2.34.149(M.37.956A); τῶν ἐπηγγελμένων βεβαία...π. Max.*ambig*.(M.91.1124B).

πιττάκιον (πιτάκιον), τό, 1. *written note, short document*; of creed falsely alleged to have been approved at Sardica, Ath.*tom*.5(M.26. 800C); of manifesto of Arians at Nicaea, Gel.Cyz.*h.e*.2.26.3(M.85. 1308A); †Gregent.*leg.Hom*.proem.(M.86.577A); Leont.N.*v.Jo.Eleem*. 46(p.97.3); ‡Jo.D.*ep.Thphl*.20(M.95.372B); **2.** *pocket tablet, notebook*, Jo.Mosch.*prat*.192(M.87.3072B); **3.** *promissory note, bond*, Jo.Mosch.*prat*.195(M.87.3080C); Leont.N.*v.Jo.Eleem*.11(p.22.17); **4.** *label* on a jar, *ib*.12(p.24.6).

πλαγιάζ-ω, 1. *turn aside*; intrans., met.; **a.** abs. π. τῷ νῷ Cosm. Ind.*top*.2(M.88.128D); from righteousness, Clem.*fr*.58(p.227.9; M. 9.768A); **b.** c. prep. π. ἐκ τῆς ὁδοῦ Nil.*epp*.4.1(M.79.545B); εἰς τὰ... πάθη...π. Proc.G.*Cant*.7:9(M.87.1765B); **2.** *lead astray*; met., *deprave* π. τὸν ἴδιον νοῦν id.*Is*.33:13–19(M.87.2308A); **3.** *make to wander* ~ειν τὸν ὀφθαλμόν Or.*Jo*.32:21(13; p.463.20; M.14.801C).

πλάγιος, 1. *lying athwart* Συμεών, π. τόπον λαβών, διὰ πασῶν τῶν φυλῶν...διατρέχοντα Proc.G.*Dt*.33:7(M.87.981C); **2.** *at the side* ἔμεινεν...ἐν κελλίῳ π. Pall.*h.Laus*.29(p.85.20; M.34.1098B); neut. as subst., *the side*, Gr.Nyss.*v.Mos*.17(M.44.304D); Anton.Hag.*v.Sym. Styl*.9(p.32.6); **3.** *transverse, horizontal*; of cross-bar of cross, Gr. Nyss.*or.catech*.32(p.121.2; M.45.81A); τί γάρ ἐστιν Χριστὸς ἀλλ' ὁ... ἦχος τοῦ θεοῦ;...ἦχος δὲ τὸ π. ἐστιν, ἀνθρώπου φύσις· ὁ δὲ ἧλος ὁ συνέχων ἐπὶ τῷ ὀρθῷ ξύλῳ τὸ π. κατὰ μέσου, ἡ...μετάνοια τοῦ ἀνθρώπου *A.Petr.c.Sim*.9(p.96.9); **4.** *crooked, bent*; met., Clem.*fr*.58(p.227. 4; M.9.765D); **5.** π. ὀφθαλμῷ *with a sidelong glance*, ‡Nil.*perist*.4. 14(M.79.844A); **6.** *indirect, obscure* π. ... αἰνίγμασι *Hom.Clem*.6.17; Gr.Nyss.*Eun*.1(1 p.109.9; M.45.344B).

***πλαγιότης, ἡ,** *perversity*, Gr.Naz.*or*.16.12(M.35.949A).

πλαγίως, 1. *indirectly, figuratively*, of rationalistic interpretations of mythology οἱ π. φυσιολογήσαντες περὶ θεῶν καὶ τὸ εἶναι θεοὺς ἀνῃρήκασιν *Hom.Clem*.6.20; of types and allegories, Cyr.*ador*.8(1. 275A); id.*Is*.1.5(2.133A); id.*Os*.27(3.50D); id.*Jo*.4.5(4.414E); **2.** *perversely* ἐξ ὀρθότητος...ἐπὶ τὸ π. ἔχον id.*ador*.8(1.263B).

***πλάγκτης, ὁ,** *deceiver*, Gr.Naz.*carm*.1.1.7.77(M.37.444A); *ib*.1.2.2. 318(603A).

πλαδαρόομαι, *be enfeebled*, AQ ap.Proc.G.*Is*.19:1–15(M.87. 2148A).

πλαδαρός, 1. *flabby*; *watery* τὸ π. ... τῆς τρυφῆς Germ.CP *or*.2(M. 98.289A); **2.** *inert, feeble*, Philost.*h.e*.8.12(M.65.565A); **3.** *weak, inept*, Or.*Jo*.10.18(13; p.188.20; M.14.336D).

πλακίον, τό, *small tablet*; on which money was reckoned, Zos. *alloquia* 14(M.78.1700C).

πλακουντάριος, ὁ, *pastry-cook, confectioner*, Pall.*h.Laus*.7(p.26.3; M.34.1020C); Leont.N.*v.Sym*.31(M.93.1709A).

πλακόω, 1. *overlay, face*, Eus.*v.C*.4.58(p.141.12; M.20.1209A); **2.** *pave*; met., of path of virtue πεπλακωμένης ὁδοῦ Gr.Nyss.*hom.11 in Cant*.(M.44.1008B); **3.** *use as paving* τὰ...σκύβαλα τῆς μαρμαρώσεως...ἐκέλευσεν...εἰς τὴν πλατεῖαν πλακωθῆναι Marc.Diac.*v. Porph*.76.

πλάκωσις, ἡ, *paving, incrustation, overlay*, Eus.*v.C*.3.36(p.94.2; M.20.1096B); Jo.Mal.*chron*.11 p.280(M.97.424B).

πλαν-άω, A. trans.; **1.** *lead astray*, esp. in morals and belief ἀσεβείας...ἣν ποιήσετε...~ῶντες τὸν Ἰσραήλ *T.Lev*.10.2; οὐκ ἐπλανήθην ἀλλ' ἔμεινα ἐν τῇ ἀληθείᾳ *T.Jos*.1.3; *Did*.6.1; Arist.*apol*.3.2; ref. Jews ἑαυτοὺς ~ᾶτε Just.*dial*.117.4(M.6.748A); ἄνθρωπον τὸν ἡδονῇ πεπλανημένον Clem.*prot*.11(p.79.3; M.8.228C); Or.*hom.14.8 in Jer*. (p.113.15; M.13.413B); hence esp. **2.** *deceive*, Ign.*Magn*.3.2; id. *Philad*.7.1; ‡*Diogn*.12.6; Clem.*exc.Thdot*.9(p.109.5; M.9.660A);

3. pass., *go astray* ἐπλανήθημεν τὴν ὁδόν Jo.Mosch.*prat*.16(M.87.2864A); *be at a loss* ἐπλανήθη ποῦ τέθηκεν αὐτό *ib*.116(2980C).

B. intrans.; 1. *lead in wrong direction* ὁδὸν...τὴν ~ῶσαν Thdt.*qu*. *38 in Dt*.(1.286); 2. med.; a. *wander*; i. of planets, Clem.*paed*.2.2 (p.177.4; M.8.429C); id.*str*.1.25(p.103.28; M.8.913A); τὰς ἑπτὰ [sc. μοίρας] τὰς ~ωμένας *ib*.2.11(p.140.5; 988A); id.*exc.Thdot*.70(p.129.20; M.9.692B); ii. of demons οἱ περὶ τὸν κόσμον...~ώμενοι δαίμονες Athenag.*leg*.25.1(M.6.948C); b. *go astray* in error or sin, *1Clem*.59.4; Ign.*Philad*.3.3; of pagans, Clem.*prot*.3(p.33.22; M.8.129B); id.*paed*.2.2(p.167.23, v.l. ἐπιπλανωμένους M.8.409A); τοὺς ~ωμένους τὰ νοήματα id.*str*.3.14(p.239.14; M.8.1193C); ~ᾶται καὶ ἐν τῇ περὶ ἀγαθῶν κρίσει Or.*hom.16.3 in Jer*.(p.135.27; M.13.444A); Epiph.*haer*.16.2(p.211.14; M.41.249B); of heretics, *ib*.19.2(p.219.19; 264B); *ib*.42.12(p.158.20; 777B); c. *be erroneous*; of opinions, etc., Clem.*str*.5.12(p.380.28; M.9.121B); Chrys.*hom.28.1 in Mt*.(7.335A); *ib.57.3* (580A); d. *be false* or *fictitious*, id.*comm.in Gal*.1:7(10.669C); κέχρηνται δὲ [sc. Quartodecimans]...ταῖς πεπλανημέναις τῶν ἀποστόλων πράξεσι Thdt.*haer*.3.4(4.343); τὸ πεπλανημένον *falsehood*, Epiph.*haer*.19.2(p.219.20; M.41.264B); Philost.*h.e*.7.12(M.65.549C); e. *wander in mind, be mad*, Call.*v.Hyp*.(p.86); *ib*.(p.87).

πλάνη, ἡ, A. *error*; 1. moral, Polyc.*ep*.2.1; π. τῶν ἁμαρτωλῶν *Barn*.12.10; Gr.Thaum.*pan.Or*.5(p.11.13; M.10.1064C); ἡδοναῖς τῆς π. Meth.*symp*.8.1(p.81.17; M.18.140A); 2. esp. of paganism, Ign.*Eph*.10.2; opp. ἀλήθεια of Christianity, Arist.*apol*.2.1; ἀπολείποντας τὴν ὁδὸν τῆς π. Just.*dial*.39.2(M.6.560B); Eus.*Marcell*.1.1(p.3.18; M.24.716B); Ath.*gent*.45(M.25.89D); Cyr.*glaph.Gen*.2(1.35D); *V.Aberc*.1; 3. of heresy, Iren.*haer*.1.1.3(M.7.449B); Meth.*symp*.2.3(p.19.1; M.18.52B); *Hom.Clem*.2.37; Cyr.H.*catech*.4.6.

B. *falsehood, fraud, deceit*, Athenag.*leg*.22.1(M.6.936C); Chrys.*hom.84.3 in Mt*.(7.801E); *ib.89.1*(831C); esp. of deceit of Devil and as evil spirit πνεύμασι τῆς π. *T.Lev*.3.3; ὁ ἄρχων τῆς π. *T.Jud*.19.4; *Barn*.2.10; π. τοῦ ὄφεως ‡*Diogn*.12.3; Just.*dial*.35.2(M.6.549B); of spirit inspiring Montanist prophets, Anon.ap.Eus.*h.e*.5.16.8(M.20.468A); πατὴρ τῆς π. Meth.*res*.1.38(p.281.10; M.41.1105B); Epiph.*haer*.8.9(p.197.8; M.41.224A).

πλάνης, ὁ, *wanderer*; met., of one in error, Gr.Naz.*ep*.225(M.37.369A).

πλάνησις, ἡ, *error*, esp. of falsehood and moral error, *Pss.Sal*.8.15; Cyr.*Os*.21(3.44B); id.*Nah*.3(3.476D); id.*inc.unigen*.(5[1].694E).

πλανήτης, ὁ, *wandering star, planet* εὐαρεστοῦσι δὲ αὐτοῖς [sc. demons] οἱ ἑπτὰ π. Tat.*orat*.9(p.10.6; M.6.825B); ἐχέτωσαν...τὴν εἱμαρμένην· τοὺς π. προσκυνεῖν οὐ βούλομαι *ib*.10(p.11.6; 828B); Athenag.*leg*.23.2(M.6.941C); Ξενοκράτης...ἑπτὰ μὲν θεοὺς τοὺς π. ... αἰνίττεται Clem.*prot*.5(p.50.23; M.8.169A); symbolized by five stones and two carbuncles on high-priestly robe, id.*str*.5.6(p.351.10; M.9.64A); Pythagorean Φερσεφόνης μὲν κύνας τοὺς π. *ib*.5.8(p.360.21; 80B); relation of number of planets to other groups of seven, *ib*.6.16(p.504.20; M.9.369C); in Peratic system, Gnost.ap.Hipp.*haer*.5.14(p.109.12; M.16.3167C); Meth.*symp*.8.14(p.101.8; M.18.164B); as governors of world corresponding to chief gods of paganism, ‡Jo.D.*Artem*.42(p.163.8; M.96.1289C).

***πλανόλογος,** *leading astray by words*, *Schol*.40 in Jo.Clim.*scal*.27 (M.88.1228A).

πλάνος, ὁ, 1. *wanderer*, Chrys.*hom.7.7 in 2Cor*.(10.490C); of Ishmael, id.*comm.in Gal*.4:30(10.711E); Thdt.*Is*.10:28(p.58.21; 2.248); 2. *misleader, deceiver* π. καὶ γόητες Cels.ap.Or.*Cels*.7.36(p.186.22; M.11.1472A); π. καὶ...ψευδοπροφητῶν *Clem.ep*.14(M.2.49B); Cyr.*Ps*.9:23(M.69.780A); of Christ acc. Jews and heathen, *T.Lev*.16.3; Eus.*d.e*.3.2(p.108.24; M.22.188A); Chrys.*laud.Paul*.4(2.494B); of Devil, Meth.*res*.1.38(p.281.13; M.41.1105B); of antichrist, Hipp.*Dan*.4.7.1; 3. *error*, *Pers*.(p.34.19); ὁ περὶ τήνδε τὴν προφητείαν π. Thdt.*Mich*.4:3(2.1494); id.*provid*.9(4.643); 4. as adj., *misleading, deceiving*, Cels.ap.Or.*Cels*.4.33(p.303.20; M.11.1077C); *Hom.Clem*.3.24; Eus.*d.e*.3.4(p.115.25; M.22.197B).

πλάξ, ἡ, 1. *flat stone, slab*; of tombstone, Ast.Am.*hom*.3(M.40.204D); Jo.Mosch.*prat*.87(M.87.2944C); 2. *tablet*; a. of tables of Law, *T.Lev*.5.4; *T.Aser* 2.10; contrasted with writing of Law in heart (cf. 2Cor.3:3), Clem.*paed*.3.12(p.287.24; M.8.673A); symbolizing heaven and earth, God's finger representing his creative power, id.*str*.6.16(p.499.14; M.9.357C); related to writing on Belshazzar's wall, Hipp.*Dan*.3.14.7; Gr.Nyss.*v.Mos*.(M.44.321A); id.*Eun*.5(2 p.101.15; M.45.680A); Ast.Am.*hom*.14(M.40.376D); as object of προσκύνησις to Jews, *Dial.Christ.et Jud*.1(p.51.17); destruction as proof of Israel's rejection, *ib*.9(p.59.13); as type of human nature assumed by Logos, Gr.Nyss.ap.Thdt.*eran*.1(4.64); b. of heavens as 'book' ἀνέγνων...ἐν ταῖς π. τοῦ οὐρανοῦ ὅσα συμβήσεται *Prec. Josephi* ap.Or.*comm.in Gen*.ap.Eus.*p.e*.6.11(292B; M.12.73B); c. of heavenly 'books' for divine judgement, *Apoc.Paul*.19(p.49); Eus.*v.C*.1.9(p.11.23; M.20.921B); d. met., of BMV ζωηφόρον τοῦ λόγου π. Germ.CP *hymn.BMV*(M.98.453C).

πλάσμα, τό, A. *thing moulded* or *fashioned*; 1. of Adam, Just.*dial*.40.1(M.6.561B); Gr.Naz.*or*.24.9(M.35.1180B); ὁ Ἀδὰμ τί ποτε ἦν; π. θεοῦ. τί δὲ ἡ Εὔα; τμῆμα τοῦ π. *ib*.31.11(p.158.7,8; M.36.144D); of Valent. primal man as creature of angels, Val.Gn.ap.Clem.*str*.2.8 (p.132.8; M.8.972B); 2. of human race τοῦ θεοῦ λόγου τὰ λογικὰ π. ἡμεῖς Clem.*prot*.1(p.7.13; M.8.61A); Heracleon ap.Or.*Jo*.2.38(22; p.214.33; M.14.380B); δούλου μορφὴν φέρων, ἵνα σώσω τὸ π. τὸ ἠλεώτερον Or.*Ps*.54:4(p.56); ὁ λυτρωσάμενος τὸ π. Serap.*euch*.19.1; Gr.Naz.*or*.40.2(M.36.361A); τὸ φώτισμα...πλάσματος ἐπανόρθωσις *ib*.40.3 (361B); διὰ τὸ π. τῶν ἰδίων χειρῶν, ὑπὸ τῶν χειρῶν τοῦ πλάσματος παθεῖν Didym.*Trin*.3.15(M.39.864B); id.*2Reg*.22:14(M.39.1117D); Nil.*epp*.1.20(M.79.89B); Cyr.*Ps*.17:9(M.69.821B); Dor.*doct*.1.1(M.88.1620A); 3. of individual human beings, Dion.Al.ap.Eus.*h.e*.7.10.4 (M.20.660A); ἄνθρωπός εἰμι, π. καὶ εἰκὼν θεοῦ Gr.Naz.*carm*.1.2.34.20 (M.37.947A); of BMV π. καὶ περιδρακτικὸν τοῦ πλαστουργοῦ Thdot.Anc.*hom.BMV et Sym*.3(M.77.1393C); μὴ...διώξῃς ἡμᾶς [sc. evil spirits] ἀπὸ τῶν πλασμάτων ἔνθα ἐδόθη ἡμῖν κατοικεῖν *V.Aberc*.9; 4. of human nature, *Barn*.6.12; δημιουργοῦ...εἰδότος τὸ π. ἡμῶν Cyr.*Ps*.50:12(M.69.1100A); esp. in physical aspect, *Did*.5.2; Or.*Jo*.20.22(20; p.355.11; M.14.621B); Cyr.*Ps*.32:9(M.69.876C); Gnost., of physical nature of primal man, Hipp.*haer*.5.7(p.80.13; M.16.3130A); *ib*.7.28(p.208.18; 3322B); of physical nature into which fallen souls descend, *ib*.5.7(p.86.9; 3135B); of flesh assumed by Christ, Iren.*haer*.3.22.2(M.7.958A); ἕνωσιν τοῦ λόγου...πρὸς τὸ π. αὐτοῦ *ib*.4.33.11 (1080B); Gr.Nyss.*Eun*.2(2 p.355.5; M.45.533A); Chrys.*nativ*.1.6(2.363C).

B. *thing imagined*, *T.Neph*.2.5; κενταύρῳ, Θετταλικῷ π. Clem.*str*.4.3(p.252.13; M.8.1221B).

C. *invention, something fictitious*; of Valent. system, Iren.*haer*.1.8.1(M.7.521A); Clem.*prot*.4(p.43.12; M.8.152B); ψεύσματα καὶ π. id.*str*.7.16(p.70.7; M.9.537A); ref. Christ's miracles οὐκ ἔστι π. τῶν τὰ εὐαγγέλια γραψάντων Or.*Cels*.2.48(p.169.23; M.11.869D); id.*Jo*.13.17 (p.241.9; M.14.424C); of Apoc. as work of Cerinthus, Dion.Al.ap.Eus.*h.e*.3.28.4(M.20.276A); of pagan myths, Ath.*gent*.16(M.25.33A); of Christian doctrine, Juln.Imp.ap.Cyr.*Juln*.2(6[2].39A); Chrys.*hom.70.2 in Mt*.(7.689C).

D. *appearance, guise* συνέγραφε τοῦ μοναδικοῦ βίου νομοθεσίαν, ἐν π. διηγήσεως Gr.Naz.*or*.21.5(M.35.1088A); *false appearance, show* π. ὀρθότητος Bas.*ep*.48(3.141E; M.32.385A); *ib*.238(366E; M.889B).

E. *formulation, form of words* ὅλῳ τῷ π. τῷ τῆς ἑρμηνείας προσίασιν Clem.*str*.1.29(p.110.21; M.8.925C).

***πλασμός, ὁ,** ? *plain*, Geo.Pis.*Pers*.2.284(M.92.1229A).

πλάσσ-ω, A. *form, mould, fashion*; 1. ref. man's creation; a. by God ἄνθρωπον...ἔπλασεν τῆς ἑαυτοῦ εἰκόνος χαρακτῆρα *1Clem*.33.4; ὁ πλάσας ἡμᾶς καὶ δημιουργήσας *ib*.38.3; ἀγαπήσεις τὸν ποιήσαντά σε, φοβηθήσῃ τόν σε πλάσαντα *Barn*.19.2; τῷ πρώτῳ πλασθέντι ἀνθρώπῳ Just.*1apol*.44.1(M.6.393C); ἐποίησεν ζῷα καὶ ἄνθρωπον ἔπλασεν Athenag.*leg*.13.2(M.6.916B); Iren.*haer*.3.18.7(M.7.938A); Clem.*fr*.42 (p.220.28; M.9.768B); ὅτε μὲν γὰρ ὁ κατ' εἰκόνα ἐκτίζετο, εἶπεν ὁ θεός· 'ποιήσωμεν...' οὐκ εἶπεν· 'πλάσωμεν'. ὅτε δὲ ἔλαβε χοῦν ἀπὸ τῆς γῆς, οὐ πεποίηκε τὸν ἄνθρωπον, ἀλλ' ἔπλασε τὸν ἄνθρωπον...ὁ λέγων κύριος εἴτε πρὸς τὸν 'Ιερεμίαν εἴτε πρὸς τὸν σωτῆρα οὐκ εἶπεν 'πρὸ τοῦ με ποιῆσαί σε ἐν κοιλίᾳ ἐπίσταμαί σε', τὸ γὰρ ποιούμενον οὐκ ἐν κοιλίᾳ γίνεται, ἀλλὰ τὸ ~όμενον ἀπὸ τοῦ χοῦ τῆς γῆς τοῦτο ἐν κοιλίᾳ κτίζεται Or.*hom.1.10 in Jer*.(p.9.2; M.13.265D); Meth.*symp*.3.4(p.31.8; M.18.68A); Ath.*gent*.3(M.25.8D); Ἀδὰμ μὴ γεννηθέντος ἀλλὰ πλασθέντος Didym.(‡Bas.)*Eun*.4(1.282D; M.29.680A); ἔπλασέ σε κατ' εἰκόνα Chrys.*hom.59.4 in Jo*.(8.350B); Cosm.Ind.*top*.2(M.88.124D); Sophr.H.*mir.Cyr.et Jo*.50(M.87.3609A); b. by Logos, ref. birth of Isaac οὐδὲ τὸ σπέρμα τὸν τόκον εἰργάσατο, ἀλλ' ὁ τοῦ θεοῦ λόγος αὐτὸν ἔπλασεν Chrys.*comm.in Gal*.4:23(10.710A); c. by demiurge (Valent.) ἄνθρωπον πεπλακέναι, μὴ εἰδότα τὸν ἄνθρωπον Iren.*haer*.1.5.3(M.7.496A); 2. ref. spiritual re-creation ἄνθρωπος...ᾧ σύνοικος ὁ λόγος, οὐ ποικίλλεται, οὐ ~εται, μορφὴν ἔχει τὴν τοῦ λόγου Clem.*paed*.3.1(p.236.22; M.8.556C); in teaching of Cassian (Gnost.) ὅταν οὖν ὁ ἀπόστολος εἴπῃ 'ἐνδύσασθε τὸν καινὸν ἄνθρωπον...' ἡμῖν λέγει τοῖς πεπλασμένοις ὑπὸ τῆς τοῦ παντοκράτορος βουλήσεως ὡς πεπλάσμεθα, παλαιὸν δὲ καὶ καινὸν οὐ πρὸς γένεσιν...φησιν, ἀλλὰ πρὸς τὸν βίον τόν τε ἐν παρακοῇ τόν τε ἐν ὑπακοῇ id.*str*.3.14(p.239.23; M.8.1196A).

B. *devise, invent*; perf. ptcpl. pass., *feigned, counterfeit*; of false Christians (i.e. disbelievers in flat earth), Cosm.Ind.*top*.2(M.88.76B).

***πλαστεῖον** (*-ίον), τό, *fashioning*; of creation of man, Epiph. *haer*.23.3(p.251.26; M.41.301C); *ib*.69.25(p.175.18; M.42.244A).

***πλαστήριον**, τό, *sculptor's workshop*; met., of BMV νεογενίας τὸ π. Thdot.Anc.*hom.BMV et Sym*.3(M.77.1393B).

πλάστης, ὁ, *modeller, shaper*, of God in Creation Ἀδὰμ...ἐκ γῆς ἐλήφθη, π. δὲ αὐτοῦ ὁ θεός Iren.*haer*.3.21.10(M.7.955B); π. τοῦ σώματος καὶ ποιητὴν τῆς ψυχῆς Serap.*euch*.7.1; Bas.*hom*.21.10(2.171D; M.31.560B); Gr.Naz.*carm*.1.2.26.27(M.37.853A); Gr.Nyss.*hom.5 in Cant*.(M.44.865A); ἵνα μὴ ὁ π. αἴτιος νομισθῇ ἁμαρτίας Epiph. *haer*.42.12(p.157.27; M.41.776D); Chrys.*hom.in Mt*.7:14(3.25D); of Logos in Creation, Epiph.*haer*.77.26(p.438.28; M.42.677C); in Inc. ὡς π. καὶ ἐξουσιαστὴς τοῦ πράγματος ἑαυτὸν ἀπὸ παρθένου ὥσπερ ἀπὸ τῆς γῆς ἀνεπλάσατο *ib*.79.7(p.481.29; 749D); of the echo of the aeons' doxology to Father (Marcosian) πᾶσαι...δοξάζουσιν ἐκεῖνον, ὑφ' οὗ προεβλήθησαν...ταύτης μέντοι τῆς δοξολογίας τὸν ἦχον εἰς τὴν γῆν φερόμενον...π. γίνεσθαι...τῶν ἐπὶ τῆς γῆς Hipp.*haer*.6.48(p.180.14; M.16.3275A).

πλάστιγξ, ἡ, *beam of scale*, met. καθάπερ ἐπὶ ζυγοῦ τὰς ἰσοστασίους ἀντισηκώσωμεν τοῦ δικαίου πλάστιγγας Clem.*paed*.1.10(p.142.27; M.8.356C); *Hom.Clem*.9.15; ref. final judgement, Diad.*perf*.42(p.48.24); τῇ τῶν ἀνταποδόσεων...π. *ib*.62(p.72.16).

πλαστογραφέω, *forge*, Eut.*conf*.(p.92.20; H.2.100C).

πλαστογραφία, ἡ, *forgery*, Bas.*hom*.7.7(2.59B; M.31.297C); of falsification of scripture by Sabattius, Socr.*h.e*.7.5.6(M.67.748A).

πλαστογράφος, ὁ, *forger*, Ath.*apol.Const*.11(M.25.608C); †Cyr. *hom.div*.14(5².411D); met., of Devil, ref. Col.2:14, Procl.CP *or.laud. BMV* 5(p.105.4; M.65.685B).

πλαστολογέω, *tell a fictitious tale about*, Hipp.*haer*.6.19(p.145.10; M.16.3222C).

πλαστουργ-έω, **A.** *fashion, form*; **1.** in gen.; pass., of sculpture, Didym.*Trin*.1.16(M.39.336B); Cyr.*Os*.26(3.49E); *ib*.101(133A); **2.** of God in Creation, id.*ador*.1(1.9E); Nil.*epp*.4.44(M.79.572A); Bas.Sel. *or*.25.1(M.85.288D); **3.** of Son in Creation, ref. significance of miracle of man born blind τὸ μὲν γὰρ εἰπεῖν, ὅτι ἐγώ εἰμι ὁ καὶ τότε ~ήσας τὸν ἄνθρωπον πρόσαντες ἐδόκει τοῖς ἀκούουσι Thdr.Mops. *fr.in Jo*.9:3(M.66.753B); Nil.*epp*.1.250(M.79.176A); Jo.D.*hom*.4.21(M.96.620A); **4.** of formation of Christ's human body τὸ θεῖον... σῶμα ~ούμενον ἀρρήτως ἐν τῇ...παρθένῳ Cyr.*ador*.15(1.554A); id. *Nest*.1(p.17.13; 6¹.8A); οὐκ ἐκ τῆς θείας ἑαυτοῦ φύσεως τὸ ἱερὸν... πεπλαστουργηκε σῶμα, ἀλλ' ἐκ παρθένου μᾶλλον ἔλαβεν αὐτό id.*ep*.45(p.153.15; 5².137C); id.*Juln*.8(6².279D); ἡ...σὰρξ...ἤρξατο ~εῖσθαι ἐν τῇ ἐμψύχῳ γῇ τῇ θεοτόκῳ *Chron.Pasch*.p.198(M.92.489A).

B. *represent, typify* διὰ τῆς ἀρχαίας ἐντολῆς...τὸ σωτήριον ἡμῖν οἱονεὶ ~εῖται πάθος Cyr.*ador*.8(1.277A).

C. *invent, devise* εἱμαρμένην...τινα ~οῦντες καὶ τύχην Cyr.*Rom*.7:15(p.203.1; M.74.808C).

***πλαστούργημα**, τό, *thing fashioned*; of Adam, Bas.Sel.*or*.3.3(M.85.60B); of man in gen., Jo.VI CP *ep*.(M.96.1416A); Jo.D.*f.o*.2.11(M.94.913A); of humanity assumed by Christ συναναψώσας αὐτοῦ τῇ θεότητι ὁ πλαστουργὸς τὸ π. ‡Nil.*fr.ascens*.3(M.79.1501C); Jo.D.*hom*.4.23(M.96.621B).

πλαστουργία, ἡ, **1.** *formation, moulding*; of Creation, Jo.Mal. *chron*.4 p.72(M.97.152B); **2.** *invention, devising*; of fictions, Eust. *engast*.27(p.59.9; M.18.669B); Geo.Pis.*Pers*.2.262(M.92.1227B).

***πλαστουργός**, ὁ, **A.** *modeller, fashioner*; **1.** of sculptors, Epiph. *haer*.73.24(p.297.16; M.42.448C); Cyr.*Os*.143(3.176A); **2.** of Creator; **a.** of Father, Bas.Sel.*or*.4.2(M.85.68B); ‡Proc.G.*Pr*.17:5(M.87.1393C); Ant.Mon.*hom*.101(M.89.1737D); Jo.D.*f.o*.2.12(M.94.920A); **b.** of Son, ‡Eust.*Laz*.8(p.33.11); Antip.Bost.*Jo.Bapt*.2(M.85.1764B); ‡Nil.*fr.ascens*.3(M.79.1501C); **c.** of pagan gods προσκυνοῦσιν ἃ ἐποίησαν...λέγοντες· οὗτοι οἱ π. ἡμῶν. πῶς οὖν π. τοὺς ὑπ' αὐτῶν δημιουργηθέντας...νομίζουσιν; †Jo.D.*B.J*.10(M.96.944B).

B. *inventor, maker of fictions*, Epiph.*haer*.66.33(p.73.2; M.42.81B); id.*ep.Arab*.ap.*haer*.78.9(p.459.15; 712B).

πλάτος, τό, **1.** *breadth, width*; in phrase διὰ πλάτους *widely*, Gr. Mag.*dial*.(tr.Zach.)3.38(M.*PL*.77.315A); **2.** *space* of time; of *inside* of week opp. Sunday ἐὰν μὲν εἰς τὸ π. τῆς ἑβδομάδος συμπέσῃ [sc. ἡ τεσσαρεσκαιδεκάτη] ‡Chrys.*pasch*.7.5(8.284C).

***πλατόψις**, *broad-faced*, Jo.Mal.*chron*.4 p.88(M.97.172C); *ib*.5 p.103(192B).

πλατυαύχην, *broad-necked*, ‡Nil.*perist*.10.7(M.79.897D).

***πλατυλογέω**, *talk diffusely, be long-winded*, Nil.*epp*.3.229(M.79.489C); Marc.Er.*opusc*.1.87(M.65.916C).

***πλατύνευρον**, τό, *broad tendon*, ‡Caes.Naz.*dial*.125(M.38.1020).

πλατύν-ω, **1.** *broaden, expand*; Trin.; **a.** orthodox ἡμεῖς εἴς τε τὴν τριάδα τὴν μονάδα ~ομεν ἀδιαίρετον, καὶ τὴν τριάδα ἀμείωτον εἰς τὴν μονάδα συγκεφαλαιούμεθα Dion.Al.ap.Ath.*Dion*.17(p.58.24; M.25.505A); τὸ δὲ ~οντα εἰς τὴν ἁγίαν τριάδα τὰς ὑποστάσεις εἰς μίαν οὐσίαν συνάγειν, ὀρθότατόν ἐστι...δόγμα Isid.Pel.*epp*.2.143(M.78.589B); **b.** Sabellian and Marcellan τοῦτο δὲ ἴσως ἀπὸ τῶν Στωϊκῶν ὑπέλαβε διαβεβαιουμένων συστέλλεσθαι καὶ πάλιν ἐκτείνεσθαι τὸν θεόν...τὸ γὰρ ~όμενον ἀπὸ στενότητος ~εται,...καὶ αὐτὸ μὲν ἔστιν...εἰ τοίνυν ἡ μονὰς ~θεῖσα γέγονε τριάς, ἡ δὲ μονάς ἐστιν ὁ πατήρ, τριὰς δὲ πατήρ, υἱός, ἅγιον πνεῦμα, πρῶτον μὲν ~θεῖσα ἡ μονὰς πάθος ὑπέμεινε καὶ γέγονεν, ὅπερ οὐκ ἦν (ἐπλατύνθη γὰρ οὐκ οὖσα πλατεῖα), ἔπειτα εἰ αὐτὴ ἡ μονὰς ἐπλατύνθη εἰς τριάδα, τριὰς δέ ἐστι πατὴρ καὶ υἱὸς καὶ... πνεῦμα, ὁ αὐτὸς ἄρα πατὴρ γέγονε καὶ υἱὸς καὶ πνεῦμα κατὰ Σαβέλλιον ...οὐκ ἔτι οὖν ~εσθαι ἔδει λέγειν, ἀλλ' ἡ μονὰς τριῶν ποιητική ‡Ath.*Ar*.4.13(p.57.5ff.; M.26.484C); τίς ἡ ἐνέργεια τοῦ τοιούτου πλατυσμοῦ;... τὸ γὰρ μὴ μένον τὸ αὐτό, ἀλλ' ὕστερον ~όμενον, ἔχειν ἀνάγκη δεῖ τὴν αἰτίαν, δι' ἣν καὶ ἐπλατύνθη. ... εἰ δὲ διὰ τὴν ἐνανθρώπησιν ἐπλατύνθη... ἄρα πρὸ τῆς ἐνανθρωπήσεως οὔπω ἦν τριάς. ... εἰ δὲ διὰ τὸ κτίσαι ἐπλατύνθη, ἄτοπον. ... οὐ γὰρ ἐνδεὴς ἦν πλατυσμοῦ ἡ μονὰς οὐδὲ ἀσθενὴς ἦν πρὸ τοῦ ~θῆναι. ... εἰ γὰρ διὰ τὴν κτίσιν ἐπλατύνθη, ἕως δὲ μονὰς ἦν, οὐκ ἦν ἡ κτίσις· πάλιν δὲ ἔσται...μονὰς ἀπὸ πλατυσμοῦ· ἀναιρεθήσεται καὶ ἡ κτίσις...παυομένου τοῦ πλατυσμοῦ παύσεται καὶ ἡ κτίσις *ib*.4.14(p.58.14ff.; 485C–488B); ὁ πατὴρ ὁ αὐτὸς μέν ἐστιν, ~εται δὲ εἰς υἱὸν καὶ πνεῦμα. ἔστι δὲ τοῦτο μεστὸν ἀτοπίας. ... ἔσται ὁ πατὴρ λόγος καὶ πνεῦμα ἅγιον, ᾧ μὲν γινόμενος πατήρ, ᾧ δὲ λόγος, ᾧ δὲ πνεῦμα πρὸς τὴν χρείαν ἑκάστου ἁρμοζόμενος *ib*.4.25(p.73.2; 505C); ἡ μονὰς...~ομένη μὲν εἰς τριάδα, διαιρεῖσθαι δὲ μηδαμῶς ὑπομένουσα Marcell.*fr*.60 ap.Eus.*e.th*.3.4(p.158.9; M.24.1004B); πῶς γάρ, εἰ μὴ ἡ μονὰς ἀδιαίρετος οὖσα εἰς τριάδα ~οιτο, ἐγχωρεῖ αὐτὸν περὶ τοῦ πνεύματος ποτὲ μὲν λέγειν ὅτι ἐκ τοῦ πατρὸς ἐκπορεύεται, ποτὲ δὲ λέγειν, ἐκεῖνος ἐκ τοῦ ἐμοῦ λήψεται κτλ. *ib*.(p.158.15; 1004B); ἐνεργείᾳ ὁ θεότης μόνῃ ~εσθαι δοκεῖ id.*fr*.62 ap.Eus.*Marcell*.2.2(p.35.36; M.24.784C); τὴν μονάδα φησὶν Μάρκελλος ἐνεργείᾳ ~εσθαι, ὃ ἐπὶ μὲν σωμάτων χώραν ἔχει, ἐπὶ δὲ τῆς ἀσωμάτου καὶ...ἀνεκφράστου οὐσίας οὐκέτι. οὐδὲ γὰρ ἐν τῷ ἐνεργεῖν ~εται οὐδ' ἐν τῷ μὴ ἐνεργεῖν συστέλλεται, οὐδ' ὅλως ὁμοίως ἀνθρώποις ἐνεργεῖ οὐδ' ὁμοίως ἀνθρώποις κινεῖται· μονὰς δὲ ὢν ἀδιαίρετος ὁ θεὸς τὸν...υἱὸν ἐξ ἑαυτοῦ ἐγέννα, οὐ διαιρούμενος Eus.*e.th*.2.6(p.103.19; 908A); εἴ τις τὴν οὐσίαν τοῦ θεοῦ ~εσθαι ἢ συστέλλεσθαι φάσκοι, ἀ. ἔ. εἴ τις ~ομένην τὴν οὐσιαν τοῦ θεοῦ τὸν υἱὸν λέγοι ποιεῖν ἢ τὸν πλατυσμὸν τῆς οὐσίας αὐτοῦ υἱὸν ὀνομάζοι, ἀ. ἔ. *Symb.Sirm*.1 *anath*.6,7; οὔτε παρατεινομένης τῆς οὐσίας οὔτε συστελλομένης, ἀλλὰ πνεῦμα ὢν ὁ πατὴρ πνεῦμα...τὸν υἱὸν ἐγέννησεν...οὔτε τὴν ἑαυτοῦ οὐσίαν συστελλομένην ἢ ~ομένην οἶδεν Epiph.*haer*.76.49(p.403.29; M.42.620D); **c.** ref. Arian teaching ποῦ μονάς,...εἰ...πρὸς φύσεις τρεῖς ~θήσεται καὶ εἰς τρεῖς θεότητας πληθυνθήσεται; Sophr.H. *ep.syn*.(M.87.3153C); **2.** *spread, extend* ὁ Χριστιανισμὸς ἐπλατύνετο Socr.*h.e*.1.19.1(M.67.125A); *ib*.7.8.1(752A); Thphn.*chron*.p.69(M.108.221C); **3.** *increase* ὑμᾶς δὲ ὁ κύριος...~εῖ ἐν αὐτῷ *A.Petr.c.Sim*.7(p.88.19); **4.** *enlarge, prosper*, Just.*dial*.80.5(M.6.668A); Didym.*Ps*.4:2(M.39.1165C); τῷ μὲν ~ομένῳ συνεστάλη τὰ δάκρυα ‡Max.*cap.al*.58(M.90.1413C); **5.** *draw out, treat at length*, Chrys.*hom*.20.5 *in Eph*.(11.149B); Thdt.*haer*.3 proem.(4.339); Jo.Carp.*cap*.(M.85.1860); **6.** *open wide* the mouth, Thphn.*chron*.p.257(M.108.641C).

πλατύνωτος, *broad-backed*, *Orac.Sib*.8.21.

[*]**πλατυόνυχος**, v. πλατυώνυχος.

πλατυπόρφυρος, *with broad purple stripe*, *Orac.Sib*.8.72.

πλατύπους, *flat-footed*, *A.Paul*.(LB p.108.13).

πλατύς, *broad, wide*; **1.** *of wide scope, encompassing* π. χάριν Mel. *pass*.32 p.7.21; **2.** *far-reaching* ἡ ὄψις τῆς ἀκοῆς πλατυτέρα Jo.D.*creat*.2(p.64.2); met., of divine law, Thdt.*Ps*.118:96(1.1462); **3.** *extended*, ref. Sabellian doctrine of divine monad γέγονεν, ὅπερ οὐκ ἦν· (ἐπλατύνθη γὰρ οὐκ οὖσα π.) ‡Ath.*Ar*.4.13(p.57.11; M.26.485A); **4.** *broadly-based, well established* π. εἰρήνην Thphn.*chron*.p.296(M.108.724A); **5.** ? *far-famed* ὁ ἅγιος καὶ π. Γρηγόριος Eustrat.*stat.anim*.13(p.411).

πλατύσημος, *with broad border*; of Scribes' dress, Epiph.*haer*.15.1(p.209.16; M.41.245A).

πλατυσμός, ὁ, **1.** *extension, expansion*; **a.** in gen. π. ... τῶν μοναστηρίων *V.Pach.Λ* 17(p.140.21); **b.** Trin., of temporary extension of Godhead (Sabellian and Marcellan), *Symb.Sirm*.1 *anath*.7, ‡Ath.*Ar*.4.14(p.58.13ff.; M.26.485C,488B) citt. s. πλατύνω; ὁ...θεὸς... μόνος μονογενῆ γεγέννηκε, καὶ οὐ κατά τινα ῥύσιν οὐδὲ συστολὴν οὐδὲ π. Epiph.*haer*.76.6(p.346.33; M.42.525C); ἀναθεματίζοντες [sc. ἡμεῖς, i.e. Ancyran clergy, followers of Marcellus]...τοὺς π. ἢ συστολὴν ἢ ἐνέργειαν τοῦ πατρὸς τὸν υἱὸν λέγοντας Photinus et al.*ep*.ap.Epiph. *haer*.72.11(p.266.6; M.42.397C); **2.** *enlargement* of soul (opp. straitening) πᾶσα δόξα καὶ π. ἐδόθη ὑμῖν *1Clem*.3.1; Herm.*mand*.5.2.3; τὸ τῆς διανοίας ἡμῶν ἱλαρὸν καὶ εὔθυμον...π. ὠνόμασται Or.*or*.30(p.393.26; M.11.548A); **3.** *boasting*, Esaias *or*.1(p.3; cf.M.40.1106C).

πλατύτης, ὁ, *breadth, range, scope* τὴν π. τῆς τοῦ πατρὸς προσηγορίας Dion.Al.ap.Ath.*Dion*.20(p.61.23; M.25.509C); Gr.Nyss.*v. Mos*.(M.44.357B); id.*hom.4 in Cant*.(M.44.840D).

πλατυώνυχος, *with broad nails* (opp. claws); characteristic of man, Gr.Nyss.*Maced*.15(M.45.1320B); Anast.S.*hod*.2(M.89.76C); πλατυόνυχος, ‡Ath.*def*.3(M.28.541C); Jo.D.*dialect*.8(M.94.553C).

***Πλατωνίζ-ω,** *be a follower of Plato*; of Celsus, Or.*Cels*.4.83(p.354.11; M.11.1157B); ἐρρέθη...ἢ Πλάτων ἐφιλώνισεν, ἢ Φίλων ἐπλατώνισεν Isid.Pel.*epp*.3.81(M.78.788C); οὐ χαίρω τοῖς ~ουσι Rom.Mel.(*AS* 1 p.175).

πλέγμα, τό, 1. *wreath,* Clem.*paed*.2.8(p.202.17; M.8.485B); **2.** *complex* σύνθετον γὰρ ζῷον οἷα π. ... ὁ ἄνθρωπος Meth.*lepr*.9(p.463.10); Chrys.*sac*.6.2(p.143.7; 1.422C); **3.** *wicker-work cage,* Philost.*h.e*.3.11 (M.65.497A); **4.** *net,* Or.*hom.16.1 in Jer*.(p.132.8; M.13.437D).

***πλειοτέρως,** *more,* Gr.Mag.*dial*.(tr.Zach.)1.6(M.*PL*.77.182A).

***πλεισταρχία, ἡ,** *rule of the masses* ἀναρχία γάρ ἐστιν ἡ π. Gr.Naz. *carm*.2.1.11.1744(M.37.1151A).

***πλεισταχοῦ,** *in very many places,* Cyr.*Ps*.34:6(M.69.897B).

πλειστηριάζω, pass., *be multiplied,* Nemes.*nat.hom*.2(M.40.573B) = ‡Gr.Nyss.*anim*. (πληστ- M.45.205B).

πλειστονίκης, ὁ, *victor in many contests, champion*; of Apion the *grammaticus,* Clem.*str*.1.21(p.65.1; M.8.820A); *Hom.Clem*.4.6.

πλεκτάνη, ἡ, 1. *intertwining* ἀτόμων πλεκτάναι Dion.Al.ap.Eus. *p.e*.14.25(776A; M.21.1276D); **2.** *coil*; met., *entanglement* τῶν συλλογισμῶν αἱ π. Gr.Nyss.*Apoll*.45(M.45.1232B); Chrys.*hom.25.3 in Heb*.(12.232A); π. σοφιστικῆς Leont.B.*mesopent*.(M.86.1984C).

πλεκτός, *plaited, twisted,* hence met., *composite* ἐγὼ πλεκτὴ φύσις ἀμφοτέρωθεν Gr.Naz.*carm*.1.1.4.36(M.37.418A); *ib*.2.2(poem.)7.196 (1566A).

πλέκ-ω, 1. *plait, twine* ἐξ ἄμμου σχοινία ~ειν Iren.*haer*.1.8.1(M.7.520B); ~ουσαι τῇ βασιλίσσῃ τὸν...στέφανον...τῆς παρθενίας Meth. *symp*.8.11(p.94.2; M.18.156A); met. ~όμεθα ἐπὶ τὸ περίζωμα τοῦ θεοῦ Or.*hom.11.6 in Jer*.(p.85.2; M.13.376C); Meth.*arbitr*.8(p.167.2; M.18.256B); Jo.D.*f.o*.1.4(M.94.797C); **2.** *devise, compose*; πράγματα π. τινί *involve one in dispute,* Didym.*Trin*.2.6(M.39.549C); **3.** *plot, fabricate charge* against ἥρπασεν οὐσίαν ἀπὸ...χήρας...πλέξας αὐτῇ Jo.Mal.*chron*.13 p.340(M.97.508A); c. acc., Thphn.*chron*.p.156(M.108.421C); pass., *incur a charge* ἐπλάκη ὡς Ἕλλην Jo.Mal.*chron*.14 p.362(537C).

πλεομακάριστος, *most blessed,* Thdr.Stud.*epp*.2.62(M.99.1280C).

πλεονάζω, trans., *cause to increase* or *abound, M.Tar*.7(p.464); Bas.*Eun*.1.1(1.207A; M.29.500A); Gr.quidam *ep*.(p.90.1).

πλεονασμός, ὁ, 1. *increase, multiplication,* Chrys.*hom.5.5 in Mt*. (7.81C); ἐν π. δυνάμεως Cyr.*Os*.167(3.194A); π. τῶν πέντε ἄρτων *cat.Mt*.16:6(p.129.32); **2.** *profit, gain,* Bas.*hom*.12.10(2.106C; M.31.408A); μὴ διδόναι τὸ ἀργύριον ἐπὶ τόκῳ, μὴ σῖτον καὶ οἶνον καὶ ἔλαιον ἐπὶ πλεονασμῷ id.*ascet.disc*.1(2.212D; M.31.649C); Cyr.*Ag*.5(3.631C); *usury,* id.*ador*.8(1.272E); *ib*.(273C); met. πλεονασμὸν ποιῆσαι τῶν μαθημάτων ὧν λαμβάνω Or.*hom.20.3 in Jer*.(p.180.1; M.13.504D); Chrysipp.*enc.in Jo.Bapt*.15(p.47.10); **3.** *excess,* Clem.*str*.2.20(p.178.4; M.8.1064B); Nil.*praest*.2(M.79.1064B); **4.** *superabundance,* Chrys. *hom.26.3 in Gen*.(4.248D); **5.** *superfluous addition*; of scribal additions to Law, id.*hom.16.1 in Mt*.(7.203C).

πλεονεκτ-έω, 1. *covet, T.Isach*.4.2; Hipp.*haer*.7.29(p.214.25; M.16.3331A); Chrys.*hom.43.2 in Jo*.(8.257D); **2.** *be covetous, rapacious,* Clem.*paed*.3.9(p.263.29; M.8.620A); id.*str*.7.14(p.61.10; M.9.520A); *Hom.Clem*.19.18; **3.** *do violence to, treat aggressively, tyrannize over,* χήρας ~οῦντες *A.Thom*.A 12(p.117.6); Ath.*fug*.27(p.86.9; M.25.677C); Chrys.*hom.27.3 in 1Cor*.(10.245D); ἄσκησις γὰρ οὐ ~εῖ φύσιν ποτέ Nil.*Magn*.46(M.79.1028B); ἐδίκασε...ἡμῖν τε καὶ τῷ σατανᾷ· καὶ τὸν μὲν ὡς ~ήσαντα τὴν ὑπ' οὐρανόν, τῆς...τυραννίδος ἀπώσατο Cyr. *Ps*.7:9(M.69.752A); id.*ador*.14(1.488E); Christol. ὑποβιβάζει δέ πως ἡ κένωσις εἰς τὸ καθ' ἡμᾶς οὐχ ὥσπερ ἐκ βίας ~εῖν ἰσχύσασα τὸν τῶν ὅλων βασιλέα id.*Jo*.11.19(4.970B); **4.** *overcome, vanquish, get the better of* θεὸς...Αἰγυπτίους ~ήσας Epiph.*anc*.110(p.133.30; M.43.216A); τὴν τοῦ διαβόλου χεῖρα ~εῖν Cyr.*Jo*.11.9(4.976D); Thdt.*provid*.4(4.530); **5.** *be superior, excel* ὁ δὲ πειθόμενος αὐτῷ κατὰ πάντα δὴ ~εῖ Clem.*prot*.11(p.81.29; M.8.236A); id.*paed*.2.10(p.221.9; M.8.524B); τὸ γράμμα ὑποχωρεῖ, τὸ πνεῦμα ~εῖ Gr.Naz.*or*.38.2(M.36.313A); **6.** *surpass* τῶν ἀλόγων ζῴων ~εῖτε τῷ λόγῳ Clem.*prot*.12(p.84.35; M.8.241B); Eus.*v.C*.1.19(p.17.26; M.20.936B); ~ήσω σε κἀγώ Chrys.*hom. 34.3 in Mt*.(7.393B); theol. εἰ ἐν ψιλῷ...τῷ ὀνόματι διακέκριται θεὸς ὁ υἱός, ~εῖ τὴν κτίσιν οὐδέν Didym.*Trin*.3.10(M.39.856B); πατὴρ... ~ήσει μὲν οὐδαμῶς κατὰ τοῦτο τὸν υἱόν, γνήσιον δὲ μᾶλλον ἀποδείξει Cyr.*Jo*.1.4(4.37E).

πλεονέκτημα, τό, 1. *act of greediness, rapacious conduct,* Clem. *str*.5.4(p.340.19; M.9.41B); *ib*.7.16(p.68.22; 533C); Chrys.*ep*.130(3.675B); **2.** *excess, extravagance* ἀπιστία καὶ...ἄνοια καὶ τὰ ἄλλα ὡσαύτως τῆς πονηρίας π. Meth.*symp*.8.13(p.98.3; M.18.160B); **3** *excellence, pre-eminence, advantage* π. ... τοῦ κατ' ἀλήθειαν γνωστικοῦ Clem.*str*.7.11(p.45.16; M.9.488A); Meth.*symp*.8.1(p.81.3; M.18.137C); Chrys.*hom.44.4 in 1Cor*.(10.413B); θείοις π. πλουτείτωσαν Isid.Pel. *epp*.2.1(M.78.456A); ἀκτημοσύνης τὰ π. Nil.*Magn*.18(M.79.992D); Jo.Mosch.*prat*.103(M.87.2961A); of divine prerogatives, Cyr.*Is*.5.2 (2.780D); ὁ [sc. υἱός] κοινὰ πρὸς τὸν πατέρα τὰ τῆς οὐσίας ἔχων π. id. *Jo*.1.3(4.27D); ἐν τοῖς ἰδίοις ἑστάναι φυσικοῖς π. *ib*.1.4(33B).

πλεονεξία, ἡ, 1. *covetousness, 1Clem*.35.5; ἀπεχόμενοι πάσης...π. Polyc.*ep*.2.2; βαπτίσθητε τὴν ψυχὴν ἀπὸ ὀργῆς καὶ ἀπὸ π. Just.*dial*. 14.2(M.6.504D); εἰδωλολατρία λέγεται ἡ π., οἱονεὶ λατρευόντων τοῖς ἐγγεγραμμένοις εἰδώλοις ἐν τοῖς ἀργυρίοις τῶν ἀγαπώντων τὸ ἀργύριον Or.*comm.in Eph*.5:5(p.560); **2.** *gain, profit* ἡ διὰ τῶν ἀστραγάλων μελέτη πλεονεξίας Clem.*paed*.3.11(p.277.24; M.8.652B); οὐδὲν γὰρ οὕτως ὑποπίπτειν τῷ διαβόλῳ ποιεῖ, ὡς τὸ τοῦ πλείονος ἐφίεσθαι, καὶ πλεονεξίας ἐρᾶν Chrys.*hom.13.4 in Mt*.(7.172D); **3.** *extortion, oppression, T.Lev*.14.6; μαντική...τῶν ἐν κόσμῳ π. ... διάκονος Tat.*orat*. 19(p.21.15; M.6.849A); τοῖς ἀδικήσασιν ἀνταποδοθῆναι τὴν π. Clem. *str*.7.14(p.60.28; M.9.517C); CSard.*ep.Alex*.ap.Ath.*apol.sec*.38(p.117.10; M.25.313D); Chrys.*hom.50.3 in Jo*.(8.298C); οὐδὲν...μιαρώτερον ἁρπαγῆς καὶ π. *ib.52.4*(309D); Cyr.*ador*.8(1.281D); esp. of oppression by Devil, id.*Is*.3.3(2.475D); id.*Abac*.22(3.536C); ὑπὸ χεῖρα καὶ π. γενομένους διαβολικήν id.*Jo*.1.2(4.18D); π. ... τὴν μοιχείαν ἐκάλεσε. τοῦ γὰρ μὴ προσήκοντος ἅπτεται ὁ γάμον διορύττων ἀλλότριον Thdt. *1Thess*.4:6(3.516); Christol. φυσική...ἕνωσις...οὐχ ὑποτίθησιν ἀνάγκαις καὶ π. φυσικαῖς τὸν ἀπαθῆ...θεοῦ λόγον Cyr.*apol.Thdt*.3(p.120.5; 6^1.213D); οὐκ ἐξ ἀνθρωπίνης ἀνάγκης, ἤγουν ἐξ ἑτέρας π. ἀβουλήτως... τὸν θάνατον τὸν Ἰησοῦν παθόντα id.*Jo*.5.3(496E); **4.** *unfair, harsh, treatment* ἣν δ' ἂν πλεονεξίας οὐ τῆς τυχούσης ἔργον τοὺς προεξεληλυθότας τῆς παρουσίας τοῦ κυρίου, μὴ εὐηγγελισμένους...κολάσεως μετασχεῖν Clem.*str*.6.6(p.456.15; M.9.272A); **5.** *arrogance,* Apollon.ap. Eus.*h.e*.5.18.7(M.20.477B); **6.** *superiority, advantage* τὴν μὲν πίστιν τοῖς ἁπλοῖς ἀπονείμαντες [sc. Valentinians] ἡμῖν, αὐτοῖς δὲ τὴν γνῶσιν, τοῖς φύσει σῳζομένοις κατὰ τὴν τοῦ διαφέροντος πλεονεξίαν σπέρματος ἐνυπάρχειν βούλονται Clem.*str*.2.3(p.118.15; M.8.941B); Θεμίσων, ὁ τὴν ἀξιόπιστον π. ἠμφιεσμένος Apollon.ap.Eus.*h.e*.5.18.5(M.20.477A); **7.** *abundance, T.Benj*.5.1; Chrys.*hom.22.4 in Mt*.(7.280B); Thdr. Mops.*Os*.2:6–8(M.66.137A); **8.** *possession of excess* τῇ δὲ δικαιοσύνῃ μειονεξίαν κατὰ μείωσιν, π. καθ' ὑπερβολήν Hipp.*haer*.1.19(p.22.17; M.16.3044D); Or.*hom.1.14 in Jer*.(p.12.21; M.13.272B); *Hom.Clem*.12.6.

πλευρά, ἡ, *rib, side*;

A. of side of Adam and side of Christ; **1.** in gen. ἐνύγη...τῇ λόγχῃ τὴν π., διὰ τὴν ἐκ τῆς π. τοῦ Ἀδὰμ ληφθεῖσαν γυναῖκα ‡Chrys.*trid*.(2.825E); **2.** ref. corruption and redemption λόγχῃ νυγεὶς τὴν π., ἵνα τὴν ἐκ τῆς π. γενομένην πληγὴν τῷ Ἀδὰμ ἀποθεραπεύσῃς· π. γὰρ οὖσα ἡ Εὕα πληγὴν εἰργάσατο τῷ Ἀδὰμ *A.Xanthipp*.12(p.65.34ff.); ἐσφάγη γὰρ οὐκ εἰς ἄλλο μέρος, ἀλλ' εἰς τὴν π., ἀφ' ἧς ἔρρευσεν ὕδωρ καὶ αἷμα· ἵνα, ἐπειδὴ πρότερον διὰ τῆς ἐκ π. πλασθείσης γυναικὸς ἦλθεν ἀπάτη, οὕτως διὰ τῆς π. τοῦ δευτέρου Ἀδὰμ λύτρον καὶ καθάρσιον τῆς προτέρας γένηται· λύτρον μὲν διὰ τοῦ αἵματος, καθάρσιον δὲ διὰ τοῦ ὕδατος ‡Ath. *pass*.25(M.28.228D); ἐκ τῆς π. τοῦ Ἀδὰμ εἰσῆλθε φθορά, ἐκ τῆς π. τοῦ Χριστοῦ ἐπήγασεν ἡ ζωή Chrys.*hom.20.3 in Eph*.(11.147D not.*t*); **3.** ref. typology of Eve and Church καθάπερ, τοῦ Ἀδὰμ καθεύδοντος, ἡ γυνὴ κατεσκευάζετο, οὕτω, τοῦ Χριστοῦ ἀποθανόντος, ἡ ἐκκλησία διεπλάττετο ἐκ τῆς π. αὐτοῦ Chrys.*laud.Max*.3(3.215D); μῆτερ Χριστοῦ ἐκκλησία, ἡ σύζυγος τοῦ πνευματικοῦ Ἀδὰμ τοῦ θεοῦ...σὺ π., καὶ μέρος τοῦ Ἀδὰμ θεοῦ Anast.S.*hex*.12(M.89.1072B); **4.** various aspects of parallel summarized ἐνύγη καὶ λόγχῃ τὴν π., διὰ τὴν ἐκ τῆς π. τοῦ Ἀδὰμ ληφθεῖσαν γυναῖκα·...διὰ τοῦτο τιτρώσκεται ἡ π., ἵνα μάθωμεν ὅτι οὐ μόνον ἀνδράσιν ἤνεγκε σωτηρίαν τὸ πάθος τοῦ Χριστοῦ, ἀλλὰ καὶ γυναιξί...καὶ ἡ π. πλήσσεται τοῦ Χριστοῦ, ἵνα...τὸ μυστήριον τοῦ βαπτίσματος κηρυχθῇ, καὶ ἡ χάρις ἡ μέλλουσα λάμψῃ· πηγάζει γὰρ αἷμα καὶ ὕδωρ ἐκ τῆς π. τοῦ Χριστοῦ, ἵνα καὶ τὸ καθ' ἡμῶν χειρόγραφον τῆς ἁμαρτίας ἀπαλείψῃ, καὶ τῷ αἵματι αὐτοῦ καθαρισθῶμεν Thdr.Stud. *or*.4.5(M.99.716B,C).

B. of side of Christ; **1.** exeg. Is.53:7 τὸ τῇ λόγχῃ δὲ τρωθῆναι τὴν π., πληροῖ τὸ 'ὡς πρόβατον κτλ.' Ath.*Ar*.2.16(M.26.180C); **2.** as source of redemption and sacraments, Cyr.H.*catech*.13.21 cit. s. αἷμα; προσχέων τὸ ὕδωρ ἐκ τῆς π., τοῦ σιδήρου τὴν φλέβα ταύτην ἀναστομώσαντος· οὗ ὁ γευσάμενος πηγὴ γίνεται ὕδατος ἀλλομένου εἰς ζωὴν αἰώνιον Gr.Nyss.*hom.2 in Cant*.(M.44.801B); οἴνῳ τὸ εὐαγγελικὸν κήρυγμα ὁ θεῖος αἰνίγματι χρησμὸς ὁμοιοῖ, ποτὲ μὲν ἐκ τῆς δεσποτικῆς πηγάζοντι π. Isid.Pel.*epp*.1.293(M.78.353C); ἐπειδὴ γὰρ οὐχ οἷόν τε ἦν εἰσελθεῖν εἰς τὴν βασιλείαν τὸν λῃστὴν δίχα βαπτίσματος, *αἷμα καὶ ὕδωρ προσήκατο τῆς νυγείσης αὐτοῦ π. ὁ σωτήρ, ἵνα αὐτὸν ληστὴν ἐλευθερώσῃ* Thdr.Stud.*or*.4.6(M.99.716D); **3.** ref. origin of Church *ἀπ' αὐτῆς δὲ τῆς π. οἰκοδομηθῆναι ἐκκλησίαν, ἐν τῷ νυχθῆναι αὐτοῦ τὴν π. καὶ τὰ μυστήρια τοῦ αἵματος καὶ ὕδατος ἐν ἡμῖν λύτρα γενέσθαι* Epiph.*ep.Arab*.ap.*haer*.78.19(p.470.12; M.42.729D); *Χριστόν, μέλλειν ὑπνοῦν τὸν ἀνθρώπινον θάνατον ἐν τῷ σταυρῷ, ὅπως ἐκ τῆς ἁγίας αὐτοῦ π. λόγχῃ νυγείσης, καὶ ῥευσάσης αἷμα καὶ ὕδωρ οἰκοδομηθῇ ἡ νοητὴ νύμφη αὐτοῦ, τουτέστιν ἡ καθολικὴ ἐκκλησία* Nil.*epp*.1.26(M.79.92C); *ib*.1.268(181A); v. *ἐκκλησία*; **4.** ref. soul, compared with side of Christ *σοφὴ* [sc. soul] *ὡς π. τοῦ λόγου ᾧ ἐκολλήθη* †Bas.Anc.*virg*.50 (M.30.769A); **5.** ref. sufferings of Christ in his members *Ἀρειανοί... ταύτας* [sc. virgins] *γυμνώσαντες...αὐτῶν...ἔξεσαν τὰς π. ... Πιλᾶτος μὲν...λόγχῃ μίαν π. τοῦ σωτῆρος ἔνυξεν· οὗτοι δὲ μὴ μίαν, ἀλλ' ἀμφοτέρας ἔξεσαν· τὰ γὰρ μέλη τῶν παρθένων ἐξαιρέτως ἴδια τοῦ σωτῆρός ἐστι* Ath.*apol.Const*.33(M.25.640B,C).

C. met.; **1.** of H. Ghost as rib of Christ from which souls wedded to him are formed, Meth.*symp*.3.8(p.36.15; M.18.73C); **2.** of Eve *ἐσφράγισε τὸ μνημεῖον* [sc. of Adam]...*ἕως οὗ ἀποστραφῇ ἡ π. αὐτοῦ πρὸς αὐτόν Apoc.Mos*.42(p.22); hence *wife*, Gr.Naz.*carm*.1.2.1.215 (M.37.538A); *τὴν τούτου* [sc. *Πιλάτου*] *π. ὄναρ βασανίζων* Rom.Mel. (*AS* 1 p.120); Thdr.Stud.*epp*.2.120(M.99.1396A).

πλευριτικός, *of* or *belonging to the side*, Bas.*ep*.45.1(3.133E; M.32.368A).

***πλευρογέννητος**, *born from side*, neut as subst. *τὸ π. τῆς Εὔας* Anast.S.*hod*.17(M.89.264D).

***πλευρόμητρος**, *with reproductive organs in the side π. ... θαλάττια* Geo.Pis.*hex*.1023(M.92.1513A).

πλευρόν, τό, *side, flank*; met., *person, presence*, ref. appeals to bishop of Rome *εἰ...τῇ δεήσει τῇ ἑαυτοῦ τὸν Ῥωμαίων ἐπίσκοπον δόξειεν ἀπὸ τοῦ ἰδίου π. πρεσβυτέρους ἀποστείλοι* CSard.*can*.5 [Latin version *de latere suo* (earliest instance of phrase)]; *side* of family *ἐξ ἑνὸς π. συνάπτονται τῷ τελευτήσαντι* Ath.Scholast.*coll*.9.10 (p.105).

πλεύστης, ὁ, *sailor*, Pall.*v.Chrys*.7(p.36.16; M.47.22).

[*]**πλεύτης, ὁ,** = foreg., Nil.*epp*.4.35(M.79.565C).

***πλευτρικός**, perh. for *παλαιστρικός*, *T.Job* 27(p.120.12).

πληγάς, ἡ, *sickle*, *Orac.Sib*.5.222 (v.l. *πλαγάς*).

***πλήγατος**, (Lat. *plagatus*) *wounded*, Jo.Mal.*chron*.12 p.305(M.97.460C); Call.*v.Hyp*.(p.16).

πληγή, ἡ, A. *blow, stroke*, met. *ἔλεγχος γὰρ καὶ ἐπίπληξις...π. ψυχῆς εἰσι, σωφρονίζουσαι τὰς ἁμαρτίας* Clem.*paed*.1.9(p.138.9; M.8.348C); exeg. Lev.26:21 *τὸ γὰρ 'προσθήσω π. ἑπτά' ὁτίποτε μυστήριον δηλοῖ μιᾶς π. γινομένης καὶ δευτέρας καὶ τρίτης μέχρι τῶν εἰρημένων ἑπτὰ ἐπί τινας. οὐ πάντες δὲ ἑπτὰ π. πλήσσονται· ἀλλ' οἶμαί τινας πληγήσεσθαι π. ἕξ, ἄλλους πέντε...τοὺς δὲ πάντων ὑποδεεστέρους ἐν κολάσεσιν π. νομίζω πληγήσεσθαι μίαν. οἶδεν οὖν ὁ θεὸς καὶ τὰ περὶ τῶν π.* Or.*hom.7.2 in Jer*.(p.53.1ff.; M.13.332B).

B. *wound*; **1.** ref. Christ *ἵνα π. αὐτοῦ ζωοποιήσῃ ἡμᾶς Barn*.7.2; exeg. Zach.13:6 *λέγει γὰρ ὁ θεὸς τὴν π. τῆς σαρκὸς αὐτοῦ ὅτι ἐξ αὐτῶν ib*.5.12; *αὗται αἱ π. ἃς ἑκὼν ἐπλήγην ἐν τῷ οἴκῳ τοῦ ἀγαπητοῦ μου* Procl.CP *or*.11.3(M.65.785B); exeg. Jer.15:18, of Christ and others *'ἡ π. μου στερεά, πόθεν ἰαθήσομαι;' οἱ κατισχύοντές με πλήσσουσί με, καὶ ἡ π. μου ἐστὶ στερεά. εἴτε προφητεύει τὸν σταυρὸν τοῦ κυρίου (στερεὰ γὰρ π. ἐστιν ὁ σταυρός...) ⟨εἴτε περὶ⟩ πάντων τῶν δικαίων λέγεται ἐν οἷς π. στερεὰν λαμβάνει, εἴτε καὶ ἐπὶ τοῦ προφήτου ἀκούεις τοῦτο...τὸν αὐτὸν ἐπιδέχεται [τὸν] νοῦν κατὰ τὴν λέγουσαν λέξιν· 'ἡ π. μου στερεά, πόθεν ἰαθήσομαι;' κἂν ὁ σωτὴρ λέγῃ...τὴν ἀνάστασιν τὴν ἐκ νεκρῶν προφητεύει μετὰ τὴν στερεὰν π., κἂν ἐπὶ τοῦ δικαίου δὲ λαμβάνηται, μετὰ τὰς π. γίνεται πάλιν ἴασις* Or.*hom.14.18 in Jer*. (p.124.5ff.; M.13.428A,B); **2.** met., ref. wound received by soul from sin *π. ψυχῆς, ἁμαρτία· γύμνωσις ψυχῆς, ἀπόθεσις τοῦ ἐνδύματος τῆς ἀφθαρσίας. ἡ δὲ ἁμαρτία, ἀφανιστικὴ τῆς χάριτος τῆς δεδομένης ἡμῖν διὰ τοῦ λουτροῦ τῆς παλιγγενεσίας. πορνεία, π., μοιχεία, ἄλλη π., π. ὁ φθόνος, π. ἕκαστον τούτων, π. αὐτὰ τὰ καίρια τύπτουσα, π. παρὰ λῃστῶν ἐμβαλλομένη, παρὰ δαιμόνων τῶν συνεργούντων ἡμῖν πρὸς τὰς ἁμαρτίας* ‡Bas.*Lac*.9(2.595C,D; M.31.1457A,B); **3.** myst., ref. wound received by soul from Christ *τὸ ἐκλεκτὸν βέλος ἐν τῇ καρδίᾳ δεξαμένη διὰ τῆς γλυκείας π.* Gr.Nyss.*hom.6 in Cant*.(M.44.889A); *ib*.4(852B); *Δαβὶδ οὐχὶ π. εἶπεν, ἀλλὰ παράκλησιν ἐκ τῆς τοιαύτης γίνεσθαι ῥάβδου* ...[Ps.22:4] *δι' ὧν γίνεται καὶ θείας τραπέζης ἑτοιμασία...εἰ οὖν ταῦτα παρέχει ἡ γλυκεῖα ἐκείνη π. ... ἀγαθὸν ἄρα ἐστὶ τὸ παταχθῆναι τῇ ῥάβδῳ ib*.12(1032B,C); *ἡ π. ᾗ ἐγκαυχᾶται ἡ νύμφη...οὕτω γὰρ καὶ Παῦλος ὁ τῶν τοιούτων στιγματίας...ἐπαγαλλόμενος ib*.(1033C); *ἡ νύμφη, οὐκ ὀδύνην ἐκ τῆς π. αἰτιᾶται, ἀλλ' ἐπικαυχᾶται τῇ τῆς παρρησίας προσθήκῃ ib*.(1037A).

πληγόω, *wound*, Thphn.*chron*.p.200(M.108.516A).

πλῆθος, τό, 1. *multitude*; of congregation or whole body of faithful: Israel, *1Clem*.53.5; Church, *ib*.54.2; Ign.*Magn*.6.1; *τὸ ἐν θεῷ π.* id.*Trall*.8.2; Cels.ap.Or.*Cels*.5.61(p.65.10; M.11.1277C); *τὸ π. τῶν ἀδελφῶν A.Mt*.25(p.253.6); *π. τῶν πιστῶν Hom.Clem*.3.61; *ἁγίου Χριστιανικοῦ* [*π*]*λήθους PLond*.1913.7; **2.** *plurality Ἐμπεδοκλῆς...εἰς π. ἐμπεσών* Clem.*prot*.4(p.49.5; M.8.165A); *τὸ εἰπεῖν υἱὸν ἐξ υἱοῦ, τὴν τριάδα τῆς θεότητος εἰς πλήθους ὑποψίαν προσῆγεν* Didym.(‡Bas.) *Eun*.5(1.305D; M.29.733A); Dion.Ar.*d.n*.2.11(M.3.649C).

πληθυντικός, 1. *plural*, ref. Jo.14:23 *π. κέχρηται τρόπῳ τὸ ἐλευσόμεθα* Eus.*e.th*.3.5(p.160.26; M.24.1008C); ref. Gen.1:26 *οὐκ εἶπε, 'καὶ ἐποίησαν...'. εἰ γὰρ πληθυντικὸν παρεισήχθη τὸ πρόσωπον, ἀφειδεῖς ἂν ἐγένοντο οἱ ἄνθρωποι...πλήθη θεῶν ἑαυτοῖς ἐπισωρεύοντες* ‡Gr.Nyss. *or.1 in Gen.1:26*(M.44.260C); Cosm.Ind.*top*.5(M.88.312A); *οὐσία... οὔτε ἀριθμὸν π. ἐπιδέχεται...τὸ δὲ ἀριθμὸν π. ἐπιδεχόμενον...ἰδιότητα ἔχει* ‡Ath.*dial.Trin*.1.13(M.28.1137B); **2.** *manifold*, Gr.Nyss.*or.catech*. 3(p.17.6; M.45.20A).

πληθυντικῶς, *in the plural*; theol., ref. *τῷ δυναμένῳ* (Ac.20:32): *οὐ γὰρ εἶπε 'τοῖς δυναμένοις' π., ἀλλ' ἑνικῷ ὀνόματι τὴν μοναδικὴν οὐσίαν ἀμφοτέρων ἐσήμανεν* Ammon.*Ac*.20:32(M.85.1584A); *τὸν ἀσώματον θεόν, καὶ τὸν αὐτοῦ λόγον θεὸν ὄντα, οὐκ ἂν π. ἐκάλεσεν Dial.Ath.et Zacch*.20(p.17).

πληθύνω, intrans., = *πληθύω LS*; *increase in number, multiply*, Clem.*str*.5.6(p.348.2; M.9.57A); Hipp.*haer*.10.33(p.289.12; M.16.3447C); *Hom.Clem*.9.3.

πληθυσμός, ὁ, *increase, multiplication*; of growth of Church, Or.*Jo*.13.52(51; p.281.4; M.14.496B); id.*or*.11(p.323.9; M.11.449C); Cosm.Ind.*top*.9(M.88.409B); of God *μένοντος...ἑνὸς ἐν τῷ π.* Dion. Ar.*d.n*.2.11(M.3.649B); in refutation of Eunomian teaching *ἐποίησεν ὁ θεὸς τὸν ἄνθρωπον. οὐχὶ ἐποίησαν. ἔφυγεν ἐνταῦθα τὸν π. τῶν προσώπων* Bas.*hex*.9.6(1.88B; M.29.208A); *θεότης...πρὸς θεοτήτων π. οὐκ ἐκτρέχουσα, καὶ εἰ ἐν τρισίν ἐστιν ὑποστάσεσιν* Sophr.H.*ep.syn*. (M.87.3157C).

πληθύ-ω, trans., = *πληθύνω LS*; *make multiple ἑνώσεως τῆς θείας...ἑαυτὴν ἀγαθότητι ~ούσης* Dion.Ar.*d.n*.2.5(M.3.644A).

***πληθωρία, ἡ,** *satiety, biliousness*, Sophr.H.*mir.Cyr.et Jo*.35(M.87.3544A).

πληθωρικός, *plethoric*, Gr.Nyss.*ep.can*.6(M.45.233A).

πληκτικός, 1. *wounding, offensive ῥῆμα τῆς ὕβρεως πληκτικώτερον* Chrys.*hom.16.8 in Mt*.(7.215C); Nil.*Alb*.(M.79.708A); *τὸ τῶν ἁμαρτιῶν...π.* Sev.Ant.ap.*cat.Mt*.27:27(p.235.17); **2.** *causing compunction ψόγος π.* Clem.*paed*.1.9(p.135.21; M.8.341B); †Bas.*Is*.73(1.431C; M.30.241C); Gr.Naz.*ep*.166(M.37.276B); Chrys.*hom.18.1 in 1Cor*. (10.159A); **3.** *striking in appearance, conspicuous*, Clem.*paed*.2.12 (p.227.21; M.8.540B); **4.** *startling, impressive*, Or.*princ*.4.3.8(p.333.29; M.11.388B); id.*Cels*.2.55(p.179.26; M.11.885C); **5.** neut. as subst., *pungency* of speech, Men.*exc.gent*.6(p.448.24; M.113.804A).

πληκτικῶς, *severely, sharply*, Max.*ambig*.(M.91.1132C); comp., Eus.*h.e*.5.24.10(M.20.497B); Chrys.*hom.30.9 in Mt*.(7.350A).

πληκτισμός, ὁ, *striking*, Meth.*symp*.5.4(p.57.24; M.18.104B); met., of eccl. censure, *Const.App*.2.20.2.

πλῆκτρον, τό, 1. *striker, plectrum*; **a.** in interpretation of pagan mystery-formula *βέδυ, ζάψ, χθώμ, π., σφίγξ κτλ.*: *π. οἱ μὲν τὸν πόλον, οἱ δὲ τὸν ἀέρα τὸν πάντα πλήσσοντα καὶ κινοῦντα εἰς φύσιν... ἄντικρυς π. τὸν ἥλιον καλεῖ* [sc. Cleanthes]...*οἷον πλήσσων τὸν κόσμον* Clem.*str*.5.8(p.358.12; M.9.76B); **b.** of Logos as plectrum evoking response of prophecy *ὀργάνων δίκην ἑαυτοῖς ἡνωμένοι ἔχοντες ἐν ἑαυτοῖς ἀεὶ τὸν λόγον ὡς π., δι' οὗ κινούμενοι ἀπήγγελλον ταῦτα ἅπερ ἤθελεν ὁ θεός* Hipp.*antichr*.2(p.4.24; M.10.729A); of H. Ghost evoking praise [Ps.150:3] *κιθάρα νοείσθω τὸ στόμα, οἱονεὶ πλήκτρῳ κρουόμενον τῷ πνεύματι* Clem.*paed*.2.4(p.182.23; M.8.441B); in prophetic inspiration *οἷς...ἐδέησε...καθαροὺς ἑαυτοὺς τῇ τοῦ θείου πνεύματος παρασχεῖν ἐνεργείᾳ, ἵνα...τὸ...θεῖον ἐξ οὐρανοῦ κατιὸν π. ὥσπερ ὀργάνῳ κιθάρας ἢ λύρας τοῖς δικαίοις ἀνδράσι χρώμενον τὴν τῶν θείων ἡμῖν...ἀποκαλύψῃ γνῶσιν* ‡Just.*coh.Gr*.8(M.6.257A); Montanist *ὁ ἄνθρωπος ὡσεὶ λύρα· κἀγὼ ἐφίπταμαι ὡσεὶ π. ὁ ἄνθρωπος κοιμᾶται κἀγὼ γρηγορῶ. ἰδοὺ κύριός ἐστιν ὁ ἐξιστάνων καρδίας ἀνθρώπων καὶ διδοὺς καρδίαν ἀνθρώποις* Mont.*fr*.ap.Epiph.*haer*.48.4(p.224.23; M.41.861A); **c.** of H. Ghost as *π.* evoking harmony of virtues in good life, *cat.Apoc*.15:4(p.405.24); **d.** of S. Barnabas as *τῆς χάριτος τὸ π.* Alex.Sal.*Barn*.proem.5(437C); **2.** *hammer*; met., of force of conscience, Chrys.*hom.64.5 in Mt*.(7.643A).

***πληκτρωτής, ὁ,** *striker* of strings of musical instrument *ζωὴν ἐν συμφωνίᾳ τῶν ἀρετῶν κρουομένην τοῦ π. θείου πνεύματος cat.Apoc*. 15:4(p.548.6).

πλημμέλεια, ἡ, 1. *trespass, sin ἄφες ἡμῖν τὰς ἀνομίας ἡμῶν...καὶ πλημμελείας 1Clem*.60.1; Eus.*h.e*.4.23.6(M.20.385B); Chrys.*hom.74.3* *in Jo.*(8.434A); **2.** *offence, trouble, difficulty,* Marc.Er.*opusc.*1.157(M. 65.924D).

πλημμέλημα, τό, A. *sin, offence*; **1.** in gen. (often in conjunction with ἁμαρτία, ἁμάρτημα with which it is virtually synonymous) οὐ γὰρ ἐντίθησι τὰ π., τὰ δὲ προσόντα ἐπιδείκνυσιν ἁμαρτήματα εἰς τὴν τῶν ὁμοίων ἐπιτηδευμάτων ἀποτροπήν Clem.*paed.*1.9(p.141.23; M.8.356A); μοιχεύειν καὶ φονεύειν καὶ τὰ συγγενῆ τούτοις ἀθέμιτα π. Eus.*h.e.*3.33.1(M.20.285B) based on Pliny *epp.*10.96.7; τὸ γὰρ μετὰ θυμοῦ...ἐλέγχειν τὸν ἀδελφὸν οὐχὶ ἐκεῖνόν ἐστιν ἁμαρτίας ἐλευθερῶσαι, ἀλλ' ἑαυτὸν περιβαλεῖν πλημμελήμασιν id.*reg.fus.*50(2.395B; M.31. 1040B); τὴν ἁμαρτίαν ἐξηφάνισεν, ἔλυσε τὸ π. Chrys.*stat.*5.4(2.65D); τὸ βούλημα τοῦ θεοῦ τὰ π. ἡμῶν δαπανᾷ καὶ πρόρριζα ἀνασπᾷ id. *dimiss.Chan.*3(3.435B); ὅτε...πληθυνθῶσι τῶν ἀνθρώπων τὰ π., Ἰησοῦς ἐνανθρωπήσας κληθήσομαι Isid.Pel.*epp.*1.453(M.78.432B); of S. Peter's denial, Cyr.*Lc.*22:57(M.72.928D); **2.** of paganism and life as lived before conversion τῆς παλαιᾶς ἀπάτης...πλημμελήματα Gr. Thaum.*pan.Or.*16(p.35.22; M.10.1096C); τοῖς...π. τοὺς ἑαυτῶν θεοὺς ἐμιμήσαντο Ath.*gent.*25(M.25.49C); οὔτε γὰρ ἴσα πάντων τὰ π., οὐδὲ εἷς τῆς ἀσεβείας ὁ τρόπος· ἀλλὰ γὰρ τὰ Αἰγυπτίων εἴδωλα, καὶ ἄλλα τὰ Φοινίκων Thdt.*Is.*53:6(p.211.37; 2.359); **3.** of heresy, Jul.Papa *ep. Dian.*ap.Ath.*apol.sec.*23(p.104.26; M.25.285D); **4.** of Adam's sin εἰ μὲν οὖν μόνον ἦν π. καὶ μὴ φθορᾶς ἐπακολούθησις, καλῶς ἂν ἦν ἡ μετάνοια Ath.*inc.*7.4(M.25.108D); **5.** ref. punishment of sins φόβῳ τῆς ἀπειλῆς τοῦ μὴ τὰ ὅμοια παθεῖν ἀποσχώμεθα τῶν ἴσων π. Clem. *paed.*1.7(p.124.25; M.8.321A); τῶν οἰκείων π. εὐθύνας ὑπέχοντες φρίττομεν, ὡς οὐ δυνησόμενοι τὸ πῦρ ἐκφυγεῖν ἐκεῖνο Chrys.*sac.*3.18 (p.95.7; 1.401B); ἵνα...ἴδωσι τῷ θεῷ χάριτας, οὐ τὴν ἀξίαν τῶν π., ἀλλὰ ἐλάττονα πολλῷ τὴν δίκην τίνοντες id.*Is.interp.*1:9(6.8C); **6.** of offences against eccl. discipline, Jul.Papa *ep.Dian.*ap.Ath.*apol.sec.* 31(p.110.15; M.25.300D); *Const.App.*3.14.3; **7.** ref. forgiveness of sins in baptism ἀφιεμένων τῶν π. ἑνὶ παιωνίῳ φαρμάκῳ, λογικῷ βαπτίσματι Clem.*paed.*1.6(p.108.2; M.8.285B); and through repentance for post-baptismal sins, id.*str.*2.13(p.143.19; M.8.993C); ἄχρις ἂν τοῖς ἀξίοις τῆς μετανοίας καρποῖς διορθώσηται τὸ π. Bas.*jud.*7(2.220E; M. 31.669C); which are to be confessed in detail οὐ γὰρ ἀρκεῖ τὸ εἰπεῖν, ὅτι ἁμαρτωλός εἰμι, ἀλλὰ δεῖ καὶ κατ' εἶδος αὐτῶν μεμνῆσθαι τῶν π. Chrys.*grat.*5(2.667B); ὑπὲρ ποίων παρακαλέσεις τὸν θεὸν π.; ὑπὲρ ὧν οὐκ οἶδας;...εἰπὲ τοίνυν σοῦ τὰ π. κατ' εἶδος, ἵνα μάθῃς τίνων λαμβάνεις συγχώρησιν id.*hom.14.4 in Mt.*(7.182D).

B. *excess* (in good sense), *excellence* τοῖς κατ' ἀρετὴν π. Gr.Nyss. ap.Proc.G.*Cant.*4:1(M.87.1640C) for προτερήμασιν Gr.Nyss.*hom.7 in Cant.*(M.44.924B).

πλημμελῶς, *irregularly, discordantly,* Meth.*creat.*6(p.497.13; M. 18.337B); Zach.Mit.*opif.*(M.85.1104A).

***πλημμυρίζω,** *be in spate,* met. πλημμυρίσαντος τοῦ πονηροῦ Meth. *lepr.*5(p.455.17).

***πληρεστάτως,** *most fully,* Gr.Mag.*dial.*(tr.Zach.)2.38(M.*PL*.66. 203A).

πλήρης, [indecl., *Asen.*16(p.63.10); *Apoc.Bar.rel.*9.22; *A.Thom.* A 12(p.118.10); *A.Petr.et Andr.*5(p.119.20); ‡Chrys.*hom.*10(13.240F); *Chron.Pasch.*p.215(M.92.524C)]; **1.** *full* of π. ... τῆς χάριτος τοῦ θεοῦ *M.Polyc.*7.3; τὸν παράκλητον οἱ ἀπὸ Οὐαλεντίνου τὸν Ἰησοῦν λέγουσιν, ὅτι π. τῶν αἰώνων ἐλήλυθεν Clem.*exc.Thdot.*23(p.114.17; M.9.669B); Naassene ὁ π. τῶν πληρῶν ὄφις Hipp.*haer.*5.16(p.112.12; M.16.3174A); **2.** *in full measure* πλήρης πνεύματος ἁγίου ἔκχυσις *1Clem.*2.2; Or. *princ.*3.1.19(p.232.9; M.11.289C); τὰ δὲ θεῖα τῆς εὐαγγελικῆς διδασκαλίας παιδεύματα πληρεστάτην εἰσφέρει τὴν εὐλογίαν Cyr.*Jo.*2.1(4. 138A); **3.** *complete, perfect* ἡ ἱερωσύνη αὐτοῦ π. μετὰ κυρίου *T.Lev.*17. 2; μακάριος...ὁ...ἐν τούτοις π. *2Clem.*16.4; π. ὄντας ἐν τῇ πίστει Herm.*mand.*5.2.1; νηστεία π. καὶ δεκτὴ τῷ κυρίῳ id.*sim.*5.1.3; γέγονεν ὁ Χριστὸς τοῦτο πλῆρες Clem.*paed.*1.12(p.148.24; M.8.368B); τὸ τελειότατον ἀγαθὸν καὶ πληρέστατον id.*str.*2.22(p.185.21; M.8. 1080B); Βραχμᾶνες ζῶσι...πληρέστατον χρόνον τῆς ζωῆς τῶν ἀνθρώπων id.*fr.*43(p.221.8); εἰς...δόξαν τοῦ πλήρους Gr.Naz.*or.*28.11(p.39. 14; M.36.40B).

***πληρηφαής,** = πληροφαής, ‡Caes.Naz.*dial.*97(M.38.961); *ib.*112 (992).

***πληροποιέω,** v. πηλοποιέω.

πληροσέληνος, *full*; of the moon Σευῆρος ὑποβάλλων τὸν Χριστόν, ποτὲ μὲν αὐτὸν λειψοφωτοῦντα, ποτὲ δὲ πάλιν π. ὄντα φανταζόμενος Anast.S.*hod.*7(M.89.116A); fem. as subst., *full moon,* met. ἐκκλησία ...νικήσασα τὸν ὄφιν καὶ τῆς π. τῆς ἑαυτῆς τὰς νεφέλας...ἀπωσαμένη Meth.*symp.*8.12(p.96.16; M.18.157C).

πληρότης, ἡ, 1. *consummation* υἱὸν...μετὰ τὴν τοῦδε τοῦ παντὸς π. εἰς ἀεὶ...διαμένειν Didym.*Trin.*3.5(M.39.841A); **2.** *fullness, perfection,* Or.*fr.45 in Jo.*(p.521.9); of God πηγή εἰμι πληρότητος †Bas.*Is.*25 (1.399A; M.30.168A); Chrys.*hom.14.1 in Jo.*(8.78D); *cat.1Jo.*2:3–6 (p.111.28).

***πληροφαής,** *shining in full orb,* ref. paschal moon ἦν δὲ ἡ σελήνη ...π.· ἵνα νοήσῃς ὡς τοῦ σκότους ἄρχων διάβολος πλήρη...εἶχε δόξαν †Cyr.*coll.VT*(6[4].20A; M.77.1204D).

πληροφορ-έω, 1. *fulfil,* Ephr.2.113F; ref. 2Tim.4:5 τὴν διακονίαν σου ~ησον τουτέστι πλήρωσον Chrys.*hom.9.2 in 2Tim.*(11.716C); **2.** *fulfil a demand, satisfy* τὸ αἴτημα τῆς ψυχῆς σου ~ήσει Herm. *mand.*9.2; *Hom.Clem.*5.25; Nil.*Magn.*15(M.79.989A); μανίαν ~εῖν Jo.Carp.*cap.*16(M.85.1841); Anast.S.*synax.*(M.89.836B); **3.** reflex., *satisfy one's wish* με ἔασον ἑαυτὴν ~ῆσαι ὡς βούλομαι *A.Xanthipp.*5 (p.61.17); **4.** *give assurance to* λέγε μοι...Δανιήλ, ~ησόν με Hipp. *antichr.*32(p.21.4; M.10.752B); ~ήσω σε, ὅτι...ζῶσιν αἱ ψυχαὶ *Hom. Clem.*12.14; Jul.Papa *ep.Dian.*ap.Ath.*apol.sec.*35(p.113.8; M.25. 308A); ~εῖ τούτους, ὅστις ἐστί Ath.*Ar.*2.23(M.26.197A); τὸν μὲν ~ήσας ὅτι ὁ ζυγὸς τῆς δουλείας...βασιλείας...ἄξιον συνίστησι Bas.*reg. fus.*11(2.353D; M.31.948A); ἑαυτὸν τῇ πίστει ~ήσας Mac.Aeg.*hom.*9. 5(M.34.536A); Chrys.*hom.31.3 in Mt.*(7.360C); ὑπὲρ...τούτων...~ῶν αὐτοὺς id.*hom.10.1 in Phil.*(11.274F); Cyr.*Os.*131(3.164A); ἵνα ἔργῳ με ~ήσῃ τὸ ποία ἐστὶν ἀληθινὴ πίστις Jo.Mosch.*prat.*26(M.87.2872C); ἕνα ~ῶν εἶναι θεόν Max.*qu.Thal.*64(M.90.704B); abs. οὐδὲν γὰρ οὕτω ~εῖ ὡς νοῦς καὶ λόγος Or.*schol.in Lc.*1:1(M.17.313C); ‡Ath.*Ar.*4.35 (p.85.5; M.26.521C); Cyr.*Os.*8(3.27E); **5.** pass., *be convinced, fully assured* ~ηθέντες διὰ τῆς ἀναστάσεως τοῦ...Χριστοῦ *1Clem.*42.3; Ign. *Magn.*8.2; πεπληροφορημένους εἰς τὸν κύριον...ἀληθῶς ὄντα ἐκ γένους Δαυίδ id.*Smyrn.*1.1; id.*Philad.*proem.; πολλῶν ~ηθέντων...ἐπὶ τῇ μαρτυρίᾳ τοῦ Ἰακώβου Heges.ap.Eus.*h.e.*2.23.14(M.20.200B); περὶ ἀληθείας...~ηθῆναι θέλω *Hom.Clem.*1.17; πεπληροφόρηται ἀθάνατον εἶναι τὴν ψυχήν *ib.*2.29; ~εῖται ἐπὶ τοῖς λεγομένοις *ib.*17.13; ~ηθέντες ...ὑπὲρ τῆς συκοφαντίας...τῶν αἱρετικῶν Ath.*h.Ar.*79(p.228.5; M.25. 789D); προπέμπειν αὐτά...~ούμενος Bas.*renunt.*2(2.204B; M.31. 632A); Mac.Mgn.*apocr.*3.13(p.87.30); ~οῖτο καὶ δι' αὐτοῦ ὡς οὐκ ἂν γένοιτο...ἁλώσιμος ὁ Ἰσραήλ Cyr.*ador.*6(1.192C); κύριον...ὄντα τὸν λόγον ~ούμενοι Max.*ambig.*(M.91.1161D); ~ηθεὶς τὸ ἀληθές Thphn. *chron.*p.269(M.108.668C); **6.** *give* someone *assurance* or *confidence for* the doing of something ὑπάγω εἰς τοὺς μαθητάς μου, ἵνα ~ήσω αὐτοὺς κηρύττειν τὴν ἐμὴν ἀνάστασιν *A.Pil.*B 15.5(p.321); Nil.*epp.*3.7 (M.79.369B); pass., *have confidence to* do something οὐ ~εῖται ὁ γέρων λαλῆσαι ἡμῖν *Apophth.Patr.*(M.65.140B); **7.** pass., ? *be determined on* ἐπληροφορήθημεν τῆς ἀναιρέσεως αὐτοῦ *T.Gad* 2.4.

***πληροφορητικῶς,** *fully, completely,* Diad.*perf.*85(p.116.5).

πληροφορία, ἡ, 1. *fullness, full reality* ἵνα ἐν π. τῆς...ἀρετῆς... ἡμᾶς συντηρήσῃ *Lit.*ap.*Const.App.*8.10.3; ἁγιασμὸς...ἐν π. γενόμενος Mac.Aeg.*perf.*2(M.34.844B); **2.** *satisfaction* ὠκυμόρους τῆς σαρκὸς π. Gr.Nyss.*or.dom.*5(p.102.3; M.44.1184B); Chrys.*hom.3.1 in 2Thess.* (11.523F); Nil.*epp.*2.167(M.79.281B); πρὸς πληροφορίαν Σεβηριανοῦ ἀφορίζει τὸν Σαραπίωνα Socr.*h.e.*6.23.12(M.67.733C); **3.** *assurance, conviction* ἀπόστολοι...μετὰ πληροφορίας πνεύματος ἁγίου ἐξῆλθον εὐαγγελιζόμενοι *1Clem.*42.3; τὴν τῆς ἀναστάσεως π. Or.*schol.in Cant.* 5:2(M.17.273B); ἡ περὶ τὴν πίστιν π. †Ath.*fr.*(M.26.1220B); ref. Resurrection σὺν τῷ σώματι παρεστώς, καὶ τὴν π. παρέχων ‡Ath. *Ar.*4.35(p.85.19; M.26.524A); πίστις μὲν οὖν ἐστι συγκατάθεσις ἀδιάκριτος τῶν ἀκουσθέντων ἐν π. ἀληθείας τῶν κηρυχθέντων θεοῦ χάριτι Bas.*fid.*1(2.224D; M.31.680A); ἀξιοπιστότερα...τῆς ἰδίας π. τὰ τοῦ κυρίου ῥήματα id.*moral.*8.2(2.241D; M.31.713C); πολλοί...π. ζητοῦσι περὶ πίστεως Gr.Naz.*ep.*102(M.37.193B); κατηξίωσας ἡμᾶς μεταλαβεῖν τῶν ἁγίων σου μυστηρίων, ἃ παρέσχου ἡμῖν εἰς π. τῶν καλῶς ἐγνωσμένων *Lit.*ap.*Const.App.*8.15.2; οὐ πάντως ἀρέσκει τῷ κυρίῳ ἡ σὴ π. Nil.*epp.*2.331(M.79.361D); π. περὶ τῶν ἐπαγγελιῶν...λαβὼν Gennad.*fr. Gen.*47:31(M.85.1656C); πίστιν, τὴν ὄντως βεβαίαν καὶ ἄπτωτον τῶν θείων π. Max.*myst.*5(M.91.677B); **4.** *confidence* in πολλὴν π. εἰς τὸν Χριστιανισμὸν προσελάβετο Thphn.*chron.*p.73(M.108.232A); **5.** religious *persuasion* εἰς πεισμονὴν τῆς ἑαυτῶν π. τῷ ὕδατι δαψιλῶς χρῶνται Epiph.*haer.*30.21(p.361.20; M.41.440D); **6.** *assurance* given π. γενομένη παρὰ Κύρου Cyrus Al.*cap.*proem.(H.3.1340D).

πληρ-όω, A. *fill*; **1.** with spiritual gifts, power, etc. πρόσωπον... χάριτος ἐπληροῦτο *M.Polyc.*12.1; ὁ ἄγγελος τοῦ προφητικοῦ πνεύματος...~οῖ τὸν ἄνθρωπον, καὶ ~ωθεὶς ὁ ἄνθρωπος τῷ πνεύματι τῷ ἁγίῳ λαλεῖ Herm.*mand.*11.9; ~ωθήσεσθαι χαρᾶς *Diogn.*10.3; ~ωθέντας χαρᾶς καὶ πίστεως Just.*1apol.*49.5(M.6.401A); δικαιοσύνης ~οῖ Clem.*prot.*10(p.76.14; M.8.224A); πεπλήρωκεν τὸ πάθος τοῦ κυρίου ἡμᾶς μὲν εὐωδίας, Ἑβραίους δὲ ἁμαρτίας id.*paed.*2.8(p.195.17; M.8. 468C); οὐ χρὴ οὖν μόνον κενῶσαι τὴν ψυχήν, ἀλλὰ καὶ ~ῶσαι θεοῦ...διὸ κενώσαντας τῶν κακῶν δεῖ ~ῶσαι τὴν ψυχὴν τοῦ ἀγαθοῦ θεοῦ, ὅπερ ἐστὶν οἰκητήριον ἐπιλελεγμένον, ~ωθέντων γὰρ τῶν κενῶν, τότε ἡ σφραγὶς ἐπακολουθεῖ ἵνα φυλάσσηται τῷ θεῷ τὸ ἅγιον id.*ecl.*12(p.140.

12; M.9.704C); in Marcosian administration of Communion ἡ... χάρις ~ῶσαι σου τὸν ἔσω ἄνθρωπον Iren.*haer*.1.13.2(M.7.581A); χωρίον...πολλῆς ἀναπαύσεως πεπληρωμένον Meth.*symp*.proem.(p.6.2; M.18.33A); in consecration prayer ~ωσον καὶ τὴν θυσίαν ταύτην τῆς σῆς δυνάμεως καὶ τῆς σῆς μεταλήψεως Serap.*euch*.13.11; at commixture ~ωσον...τὸ...ποτήριον. ὁ δὲ ἱερεὺς...λέγων πλήρωμα ποτηρίου πίστεως, πνεύματος ἁγίου *Lit.Chrys*.(p.394.3); **2.** of God πάντα γὰρ ὑπὸ τούτου πεπλήρωται Athenag.*leg*.8.3(M.6.905B); τὸ μὲν γὰρ πεπληρῶσθαι τῆς ἰδίας μακαριότητος...πρεπωδέστατον τῷ θεῷ †Bas.*Is*.25(1.398A; M.30.165C); αὐτοὺς δύνασθαι εἶναί τε καὶ καλεῖσθαι...κατὰ τὴν χάριν θεούς, διὰ τὸν αὐτοὺς ὅλως ~ώσαντα ὅλον θεόν ‡Bas.*h.myst*.62(p.397.23); διὰ πάντων ἥκειν καὶ ~οῦν τὰ πάντα θεόν Jo.D.*f.o*.1.4(M.94.797C); **3.** of Christ ὁ διδάσκαλος...~ώσας τὰ πάντα δυνάμεσιν ἁγίαις Clem.*prot*.11(p.79.10; M.8.229A); Ath.*gent*.1(M.25.4B); τῇ γὰρ θεότητι αὐτοῦ τὰ πάντα σὺν τῷ πατρὶ ~οῖ ἀεί Gel.Cyz.*h.e*.2.24.21(M.85.1304A); ref. Eph.1:23 (sts. in sense B.1 infra) ~οῦται ἐν πᾶσι τοῖς προσιοῦσιν ὁ Χριστός, λείπων τούτοις πρὶν προσέλθωσι...ἐννόει βασιλέας ~ούμενον τῆς βασιλείας καθ' ἕκαστον τῶν αὐξόντων τὴν βασιλείαν, κενούμενον δὲ ταύτης ἐν τοῖς ἀφισταμένοις Or.*comm.in Eph*.1:23 (p.402); πλήρωμα, φησίν· οἷον κεφαλὴ ~οῦται παρὰ τοῦ σώματος· τουτέστι, διὰ πάντων τὸ σῶμα συνέστηκε, καὶ ἑνὸς ἑκάστου, οὐχὶ κοινῇ μόνον αὐτὸν χρήζοντα εἰσάγει. ἂν γὰρ μὴ ὦμεν πολλοί,...οὐ ~οῦται ὅλον τὸ σῶμα. διὰ πάντων οὖν ~οῦται τὸ σῶμα αὐτοῦ. τότε ~οῦται ἡ κεφαλή, τότε τέλειον σῶμα γίνεται, ὅταν ὁμοῦ πάντες ὦμεν συνημμένοι Chrys.*hom.3.2 in Eph*.(11.20A,B); πλήρωμα τοῦ θεοῦ λέγει τὸ σῶμα τοῦ Χριστοῦ, τοῦτ' ἔστι τὴν ἐκκλησίαν. διὰ τί δὲ πλήρωμα; ἐπειδὴ πεπλήρωται θεοῦ· ὥσπερ γὰρ...ἐν πᾶσι τὰ πάντα ~οῖ, οὕτως καὶ ἐν τῇ ἐκκλησίᾳ ~οῦται κατὰ τὸ εἶναι αὐτὴν σῶμα τοῦ Χριστοῦ...τοῦ τὰ πάντα ἐν πᾶσι ~ουμένου. ἔστι γὰρ ἐν οὐρανῷ...ἐνεργῶν οὐχ ὡς ἐν γῇ, καὶ ἔστιν ἐν γῇ, οὐχ ὡς ἐν οὐρανῷ ἐνεργῶν, ἀλλ' ἐν ἑκάστῳ κατὰ τὴν αὐτοῦ φύσιν Sever.*Eph*.1:22–23(p.307.18ff.); 'τὸ πλήρωμα τοῦ τὰ πάντα ἐν πᾶσι ~ουμένου'. ἐκκλησίαν...προσηγόρευσε τοῦ...Χριστοῦ σῶμα...ἐπλήρωσε γὰρ αὐτὴν παντοδαπῶν χαρισμάτων, καὶ οἰκεῖ ἐν αὐτῇ Thdt.*Eph*.1:23(3.409); ref. Is.11:1–3 πῶς δύναται ἀποδειχθῆναι προϋπάρχων, ὅστις διὰ τῶν δυνάμεων τοῦ πνεύματος τοῦ ἁγίου...~οῦται ὡς ἐνδεὴς τούτων ὑπάρχων; Just.*dial*.87.2(M.6.684A); **4.** Trin. οὐ γὰρ...ἀντεμβιβαζόμενοι εἰς ἀλλήλους εἰσίν, ἐν τῷ λέγεσθαι [Jo.14:10], ὥσπερ ἐν ἀγγείοις κενοῖς ἐξ ἀλλήλων ~ούμενοι· ὥστε τὸν υἱὸν ~οῦν τὸ κενὸν τοῦ πατρός, τὸν δὲ πατέρα ~οῦν τὸ κενὸν τοῦ υἱοῦ...πλήρης γὰρ...ἐστιν ὁ πατήρ, καὶ πλήρωμα θεότητος ὁ υἱός Ath.*Ar*.3.1 (M.26.324B).

B. *make complete*; **1.** in gen., Clem.*paed*.3.12(p.290.4; M.8.677B); id.*str*.4.13(p.287.26; M.8.1297B); ἕκαστος ἴδιον ἔχει χάρισμα...οἱ ἀπόστολοι δὲ ἐν πᾶσι πεπληρωμένοι *ib*.4.21(p.307.27; 1345A); ~ωθείσης...τῆς...περιόδου ὁ κύριος ἐλεύσεται id.*ecl*.56(p.153.5; M.9.725A); Σίμων, ὃς ἐβαπτίσθη μέν,...μὴ γενόμενος πεπληρωμένος, ἀλλ' ἐλλείπων Thdt.*Cant*.5:12(2.118); **2.** *set out fully* π. καὶ κηρῦξαι τὴν γνῶσιν πᾶσιν Eus.*d.e*.3.6(p.136.11; M.22.229C); **3.** pass., of the moon, *wax*, Thdt.*Cant*.6:9(2.132); Manichean τὰς ψυχὰς...ὁ μέγας φωστὴρ ταῖς ἀκτῖσι λαβὼν καθαρίζει καὶ μεταδίδωσι τῇ σελήνῃ, καὶ οὕτως ~οῦται τῆς σελήνης ὁ δίσκος Hegem.*Arch*.8(p.13.2; M.10.1440B); **4.** *fill in, complete* an outline sketch, Clem.*str*.4.1(p.248.15; M.8.1216A); **5.** *pay in full*, *A.Thom*.B 11(p.30.23); ἔλαβον τὸ...γεγραμμένον καὶ ἐπληρώθην, καὶ οὐδένα λόγον ἔχω πρὸς σέ Jo.Mosch.*prat*.195(M.87.3080C); **6.** *grow up, come of age*, Jo.Mal.*chron*.14 p.361(M.97.537A); **7.** *finish* ~ώσαντος τὴν εὐχήν *M.Polyc*.15.1; Thdt.*Heb*.proem.(3.544); Jo.Mal.*chron*.6 p.152(M.97.252C); abs. ἐπλήρωσας διάβολε; *Contrad*.1(p.7).

C. *fulfil*; **1.** *carry out fully* ~οῦσθαι...τὴν ἀνάστασιν Meth.*res*.3.5(p.394.18; M.18.317D); ὁ πάντων θάνατος ἐν τῷ κυριακῷ σώματι ἐπληροῦτο Ath.*inc*.20.5(M.25.132B); εἰ ἐν τοῖς ἀποστόλοις καὶ ἐν ἡμῖν τὸ δικαίωμα τοῦ νόμου πεπλήρωται, πῶς σύ, ὦ Μαρκίων, τολμᾷς λέγειν τὸν νόμον ἀλλότριον τῶν κατὰ τὸ πλήρωμα τοῦ νόμου δικαιουμένων ἀποστόλων; Epiph.*haer*.42.12(p.177.29; M.41.805C); τὸν υἱὸν...πέπομφεν, ὥστε τὸ τῆς ἐνανθρωπήσεως ~ῶσαι μυστήριον Thdt.*Gal*.4:5(3.382); **2.** *execute, perform*, Meth.*res*.1.60(p.324.14; M.41.1157A); Const.ap.Eus.*v.C*.2.32(p.55.6; M.20.1009B); μὴ χειρὸς ἐνέργειαν ἀλλὰ ποδὸς ~οῖς Thdt.*1Cor*.12:16(3.247); διακόνου...~οῦντος τὰς ἀποκρίσεις...τοῦ...πατριάρχου CCP(536)*act*.1(*ACO* 3 p.127.33; H.2.1189B); hence *celebrate* a festival, Const.ap.Thdt.*h.e*.1.10.3(3.770); **3.** *fulfil* a rule τάξιν Ἀβραμιαίαν ~ῶν Cosm.Ind.*top*.2(M.88.73A); **4.** *fulfil* a prophecy or type, *T.Neph*.7.1; Clem.*prot*.12(p.85.21; M.8.244A); id.*exc.Thdot*.4(p.106.22; M.9.656B); Meth.*symp*.8.8(p.90.6; M.18.149B); Eus.*d.e*.9.1(p.407.13; M.22.656D); Thdt.*Ezech*.24:18(2.881).

D. phrase π. τὰς χεῖρας; **1.** *fill the hands* (Hebr. מִלֵּא אֶת־יַד) of a priest so as to consecrate him, *T.Lev*.8.9–10; **2.** *bribe*, Pall.*v.Chrys*.16(p.96.26; M.47.55).

πλήρωμα, τό, A. in gen.; **1.** *that which fills, filling* τὸ ἄλογον τῆς τροφῆς πλήρωμα χόρτασμα, οὐ βρῶμα εἰπών Clem.*paed*.1.11(p.147.17; M.8.365B); τὸ π. ... τῆς ἐνδείας *ib*.2.10(p.219.4; 520C); π. ποτηρίου πίστεως, πνεύματος ἁγίου *Lit.Chrys*.(p.394.3); **2.** *totality, sum* σύστημα καὶ...π. τῶν ἀρετῶν †Dion.Al.*fr.4 in Job*(p.206.18); τὸ π. πατρὸς καὶ υἱοῦ οὐσίαν μίαν εἶναι Const.ap.Gel.Cyz.*h.e*.3.19.14; Gr.Naz.*carm*.1.2.25.529(M.37.849A); Gr.Nyss.*anim.et res*.(M.46.85A); θεὸς...ὅς ἀγαθῶν ἐστι τὸ π. Proc.G.*Gen*.1:27(M.87.128D); πνεῦμα τὸ ἅγιον...ἐν ᾧ τὸ π. ὑπάρχει τῶν ἀγαθῶν Max.*myst*.7(M.91.688A); τὸ π. τῆς ὀργῆς Olymp.*Job* 20:29(M.93.220D); π. τῶν δέκα ἑορτῶν Jo.Eub.*concept.BMV* 22(M.96.1497B); **3.** *completion* of a number or series, Gr.Nyss.*hom.6 in Cant*.(M.44.904D); ‡Ath.*qu.Ant*.52(M.28.629C); **4.** *completion, perfection* π. δὲ νόμου Χριστὸς εἰς δικαιοσύνην παντὶ τῷ πιστεύοντι Clem.*q.d.s*.9(p.165.21; M.9.613A); ἀγάπη δὲ εἰς π. συνέρχεται *ib*.38(p.185.2; 644B); Gr.Nyss.*ep*.12(M.46.1045C); ref. title Χριστός: τὸ δὲ τοῦ κυρίου χρῖσμα, πάσης ἐστὶν ἁγιωσύνης π. Hesych.H.*fr.Ps*.110:9(M.93.1328A); Olymp.*fr.Jer*.51:5(M.93.717C); of Pentecost ἐσχάτην καὶ μεγάλην...ἑορτήν, π. τῆς...τοῦ κυρίου...οἰκονομίας Jo.Eub.*concept.BMV* 22(M.96.1497B); **5.** *fulfilment*; **a.** of time ὥσπερ ὁ καιρὸς τοῦ παραλαβεῖν τὴν πατρῴαν κτῆσιν τὸν κληρονόμον ἐν ἡλικίᾳ ἀνδρὸς π. ἄν πως ὀνομάζοιτο...οὕτως ἐν π. τῶν καιρῶν γένοιτ' ἂν ὁ διὰ...προκοπῶν καταντήσας ἐπὶ τὸ δύνασθαι τὰ προωρισμένα...τοῖς ἁγίοις λαβεῖν Or.*comm.in Eph*.1:9(p.241); τὴν ἐκ τοῦ νόμου σκιάν, ἣν ἀπέβαλεν ἀφ' ἑαυτοῦ ἐν τῷ π. τῶν καιρῶν †Bas.*Is*.63 (1.425C; M.30.228D); ref. time of Last Supper ἡ δὲ ἑσπέρα τοῦ π. τῶν καιρῶν τεκμήριον ἦν Chrys.*hom.82.1 in Mt*.(7.782B); ὅτε ἦλθε τὸ π., τίκτει id.*comm.in Gal*.4:29,30(10.712B); **b.** of prophecy, types, etc. ἀπὸ νόμου καὶ προφητῶν τοῦ τε εὐαγγελικοῦ π. Or.*or*.2(p.300.31; M.11.420B); Manichean τὸ καινὸν οὐκ ἔστι π. τοῦ παλαιοῦ...οὐκ ἔστι π. νόμου οὐδ' ὁ Χριστὸς οὐδ' ὁ ἀπόστολος Adam.*dial*.2.16(p.90.7; M.11.1784C); Epiph.*haer*.30.27(p.370.17; M.41.452D); Cyr.*Jo*.1.7(4.61A); ὅτε δὲ ἦλθεν τὸ π. τοῦ νόμου, ἐξαπέστειλεν ὁ θεὸς τὸν υἱὸν αὐτοῦ [cf. Gal.4:4] Procl.CP *hom*.2.2(M.65.840A); τὸ π. τοῦ νόμου καὶ τῶν προφητῶν αὐτὸς ὑπάρχων Χριστέ *Lit.Chrys*.(p.398.12); **6.** *satiety* π. τῆς γαστρός Niceph.Ur.*v.Sym*.34(M.86.3017A); **7.** ἐν π. *fully, completely*, Epiph.*haer*.26.8(p.285.8; M.41.344B); *ib*.26.10(p.288.6; 345D); **8.** *complement, crew* ναυτῶν π. Chrys.*kal*.1(1.697A); **9.** *whole body* or *company, total number of persons*; **a.** in gen., of citizens τὸ π. τῆς οὐρανοπόλεως Meth.*lepr*.10(p.464.15); τὸ π. τῆς συνόδου Eus.*v.C*.4.43(p.135.23; M.20.1193B); Bas.*ep*.92.3(3.185D; M.32.481B); Cyr.*ep*.49(p.34.21; 5².158C); πεντήκοντα δὲ καὶ διακοσίους φησὶν εἶναι τὸ π. τοῦ...συνεδρίου Philost.*h.e*.2.7(M.65.472A); in derogatory sense, *crew, gang*, Epiph.*haer*.76.15(M.42.548A; conj. συστήματος p.361.10); **b.** of angels ἅπαν τῶν ἀγγέλων τὸ π. Gr.Nyss.*Eun*.4(2 p.63.23; M.45.636A); **c.** of Christian congregation μήθ' ὅλως εἰς ἐκκλησίας π. παραδέχεσθαι Bas.*ep*.160.2(3.249D; M.32.624B); τῶν πιστῶν τὸ π. Chrys.*pan.Barl*.1(2.681C); Thphn.*chron*.p.275(M.108.681B); **d.** of clergy τοῦ ἱεροῦ π. τοῦ ὑπὸ σὲ κλήρου Bas.*ep*.69.1(3.162A; M.32.429B); τῷ ἱερατικῷ π. *ib*.240.3(370D; M.897B); Chrys.*hom.3.4 in Phil*.(11.217F); Philost.*h.e*.10.1(M.65.584B); **e.** of members of universal Church, Gr.Naz.*or*.4.12(M.35.541B); ὑπὲρ...παντὸς τοῦ π. τῆς ἐκκλησίας δεηθῶμεν *Lit*.ap.*Const.App*.8.13.4; τὸ κοινὸν τῆς ἀδελφότητος π. Gr.Nyss.*instit*.(p.67.6; M.34.424A); Chrys.*hom.2.2 in Rom*.(9.437E); id.*hom.3.3 in Col*.(11.348B); cf.Thdr.Mops.*Col*.1:19(p.275.11); π. τὴν ἐκκλησίαν...ὡς τῶν θείων χαρισμάτων πεπληρωμένην Thdt.*Col*.1:19(3.479); CCP(448)*act*.2(*ACO* 2.1.1 p.214.12; H.2.128E); of all orders in Church ὕμνον...ἅμα πᾶσι τοῖς τῆς ἐκκλησίας π. ἱερολογεῖ Dion.Ar.*e.h*.2.2.4(M.3.393C).

B. theol., *plenitude, fullness, divine perfection*; **1.** of God Ἰγνάτιος ...τῇ εὐλογημένῃ ἐν μεγέθει θεοῦ πατρὸς πληρώματι...ἐκκλησίᾳ Ign.*Eph*.proem.; cf. ἣν καὶ ἀσπάζομαι ἐν τῷ π. id.*Trall*.proem.(where perh. = *fullness* of blessing); τάχα γὰρ ἡ μὲν τοῦ Ἰησοῦ ψυχὴ ἐν τῇ ἑαυτῆς τυγχάνουσα τελειότητι ἐν θεῷ καὶ τῷ π. ἦν, καὶ ἐκεῖθεν ἐξεληλυθυῖα...ἀνέλαβεν τὸ...σῶμα Or.*Jo*.20.19(17; p.351.26; M.14.616A); τὸ ...αὐτὸ δι' ἑαυτοῦ π. ὂν καὶ αὐτὸ ἐν ἑαυτῷ μένον Meth.*creat*.3(p.495.7; M.18.333D); of Father τὸ π. τοῦ αἰῶνο[ς] *Pap.Chr*.(p.405); οὐδὲν ἐν ἑαυτῷ κτιστὸν...ἔχει θεός...οὐκ ἀλήθειαν οὐδὲ ὅλως τι τῶν ἐν τῷ π. τοῦ θείου κόλπου θεωρουμένων Gr.Nyss.*Eun*.3(2 p.17.21; M.45.581B); Nonn.*par.Jo*.1:16(M.43.752C); **2.** of Son, ref. inspiration of scripture ἐκ γὰρ τοῦ π. αὐτοῦ λαβόντες οἱ προφῆται λέγουσι· διὸ πάντα πνεῖ ⟨αὐ⟩τῶν ἀπὸ π.· καὶ οὐδέν ἐστιν ἐν προφητείᾳ ἢ νόμῳ ἢ εὐαγγελίῳ ἢ ἀποστόλῳ, ὃ οὐκ ἔστιν ἀπὸ π. διὰ τοῦτο ἐπεὶ ἐστιν ἀπὸ π., πνεῖ τοῦ π. τοῖς ἔχουσιν ὀφθαλμοὺς βλέποντας τὰ τοῦ π., καὶ ὦτα ἀκούοντα τῶν ἀπὸ π., καὶ αἰσθητήριον τῆς εὐωδίας τῶν ἀπὸ π. πνεόν⟨των⟩ Or.*fr.hom.21* *in Jer.*(p.196.1ff.; M.14.1310C); οὐ μόνον νόμου ἐστὶ π., ἀλλὰ καὶ πάντων τῶν π. ἐστὶ π., οὐκ ἂν χωρὶς αὐτοῦ τινὸς πλήρους γινομένου... καθάπερ διὰ τὴν πολλὴν...κοινωνίαν τοῦ υἱοῦ πρὸς τὰ λογικὰ ὥσπερ π. ἐστι πάντων τῶν λογικῶν ὁ υἱός...οὕτως καὶ αὐτὸς ὡσπερεὶ π. εἰς ἑαυτὸν ἀναλαμβάνει, πληρέστατος ἀποδεικνύμενος καθ' ἕκαστον τῶν μακαρίων id.*comm.in Eph.*1:20–23(p.402); ref. Inc. ἀπὸ τοῦ π. τῆς θεότητος εἰς τὸν βίον ἐληλυθότος Meth.*symp.*8.11(p.95.16; M.18.156A); τὸ π. τῆς πατρικῆς θεότητος καὶ αὐτὸν υἱὸν θεὸν ὑπεστήσατο Eus.*e.th.*1.2(p.63.21; M.24.832B); λόγον ὄντα...παντός τε καλοῦ καὶ ἀγαθοῦ π. *ib.*3.2(p.142.14; 977A); πλήρης γὰρ...ὁ πατήρ, καὶ π. θεότητός ἐστιν ὁ υἱός Ath.*Ar.*3.1(M.26.324B); π. τῆς τοῦ πρώτου καὶ μόνου θεότητος, ὅλος καὶ πλήρης ὢν θεός *ib.*3.6(333C); ἀγαθοῦ παντὸς π. ὁ υἱός Gr.Nyss.*Eun.*9(2 p.210.31; M.45.808D); περὶ...πάντων, ὅσα τὸν πατρικὸν πληροῖ κόλπον, ὁ μονογενὴς θεὸς ἐν τῷ ἰδίῳ π. τὰ πάντα ὢν *ib.*3(2 p.28.29; 593D); ἐκεῖνος φύσει π. ἐστιν,...θεότης ὑπάρχων τῇ οὐσίᾳ...ἡμεῖς δὲ ἐκ τοῦ π. ... χάριν ἐλάβομεν, ἥνπερ φύσει...οὐκ εἴχομεν Didym.*Trin.*1.27(M.39.401B); ref. Col.2:9 περὶ τοῦ πατρός τινές φασι λέγειν, ὅτι τῆς θεότητος τὸ π. ἐν αὐτῷ οἰκεῖ· πρῶτον μέν, ὅτι τὸ οἰκεῖν οὐ κυρίως λέγεται ἐπὶ θεοῦ· δεύτερον, ὅτι τὸ π. οὐ τὸ δεχόμενόν ἐστι· 'τοῦ γὰρ κυρίου ἡ γῆ, καὶ τὸ π. αὐτῆς'...τὸ ὅλον λέγεται π. Chrys.*hom.6.2 in Col.*(11.366E); cf. *omnem plenitudinem divinitatis hoc in loco iterum dicit universam creaturam repletam ab eo*, Thdr.Mops.*Col.*2:9(p.286.3); cf.Thdt.*Col.*1:19(3.479); π. τῆς θεότητος, τὸ ὡς ἐν ἰδίῳ ναῷ τῇ ἰδίᾳ σαρκὶ καταλῦον Cyr.*Is.*2.1(2.194B); τὸ π. τοῦ δι' ἡμᾶς ἑαυτὸν κενώσαντος id.*Heb.*1:2(p.365.1); in rel. to H. Ghost ἡμεῖς...ἔχομεν τὴν τοῦ πνεύματος χάριν, ἐκ τοῦ π. αὐτοῦ λαμβάνοντες Ath.*Ar.*1.50(M.26.117B); 'abiding' of Spirit upon Christ at baptism signifies his possession of divine π., Cyr.*Is.*2.1(2.194B); **3.** of Trin., Ath.*Ar.*1.18(M.26.49A); Cyr.*Jo.*1.2(4.16B); ὁμοουσίου τριάδος τὸ π. *ib.*3.2(262E); id.*thes.*4(5^1.27A); **4.** Gnost., of totality of aeons, whole of divine sphere, Iren.*haer.*1.1.3(M.7.449B) cit. s. αἰών; from which Sophia fell, *ib.*1.2.4(460A); ὅρους τε δύο ὑπέθετο, ἕνα μὲν μεταξὺ τοῦ βυθοῦ καὶ τοῦ λοιποῦ π., διορίζοντα τοὺς γεννητοὺς αἰῶνας ἀπὸ τοῦ ἀγεννήτου πατρός· ἕτερον δὲ τὸν ἀφορίζοντα αὐτῶν τὴν μητέρα ἀπὸ τοῦ π. καὶ τὸν Χριστὸν δὲ οὐκ ἀπὸ τῶν ἐν τῷ π. αἰώνων προβεβλῆσθαι, ἀλλὰ ὑπὸ τῆς μητρὸς ἔξω γενομένης...καὶ...ἀναδραμεῖν εἰς τὸ π. *ib.*1.11.1(561B); π. τῆς πρώτης ὀγδοάδος *ib.*1.11.5(569A); in Ptolemaean doctrine of Σωτήρ: οἱ μὲν γὰρ αὐτὸν ἐκ πάντων γεγονέναι λέγουσιν· διὸ καὶ εὐδοκητὸν καλεῖσθαι, ὅτι πᾶν τὸ π. ηὐδόκησεν *ib.*1.12.4(576A); Clem.*str.*2.8(p.133.22; M.8.973C); also of syzygies of aeons ὅσα ἐκ συζυγίας προέρχεται, π. ἐστιν, ὅσα δὲ ἀπὸ ἑνός, εἰκόνες *ib.*4.13(p.288.1; 1297B); ἐν π. οὖν ἑνότητος οὔσης ἕκαστος τῶν αἰώνων ἴδιον ἔχει π., τὴν συζυγίαν...ὅθεν ὁ Θεόδοτος τὸν Χριστὸν ἐξ ἐννοίας προελθόντα τῆς σοφίας εἰκόνα τοῦ π. ἐκάλεσεν. οὗτος δὲ καταλείψας τὴν μητέρα ἀνελθὼν εἰς τὸ π. ἐκράθη, ὥσπερ τοῖς ὅλοις, οὕτω δὲ καὶ τῷ παρακλήτῳ· υἱόθετος...γέγονεν ὁ Χριστὸς ὡς πρὸς τὸ π. ἐκλεκτὸς γενόμενος καὶ πρωτότοκος τῶν ἐνθάδε πραγμάτων id.*exc.Thdot.*32–33(p.117.15; M.9.676A); τὰ δὲ τοῦ προνάου, ὅπου καὶ οἱ Λευῖται, σύμβολον εἶναι τῶν ἔξω τοῦ π. ψυχικῶν εὑρισκομένων ἐν σωτηρίᾳ Heracleon ap.Or.*Jo.*10.33(19; p.206.34; M.14.365C); τῆς Σαμαρείτιδος τὸν...ἄνδρα τὸ π. εἶναι αὐτῆς, ἵνα σὺν ἐκείνῳ γενομένη πρὸς τὸν σωτῆρα κομίσασθαι παρ' αὐτοῦ τὴν δύναμιν καὶ τὴν ἕνωσιν...τὴν πρὸς τὸ π. αὐτῆς δυνηθῇ. ... αὐτῇ τὸν σωτῆρα εἰρηκέναι· φώνησόν σου τὸν ἄνδρα...δηλοῦντα τὸν ἀπὸ τοῦ π. σύζυγον Heracleon *ib.*13.11(p.235.20; 416A); Heracleon *ib.*13.19(p.243.21; 432A); Naassene τοῦτο...ἐστὶ τὸ μέλι καὶ τὸ γάλα, οὗ γευσαμένους τοὺς τελείους ἀβασιλεύτους γενέσθαι καὶ μετασχεῖν τοῦ π. τοῦτο...ἐστὶ τὸ π., δι' οὗ πάντα ⟨τὰ⟩ γινόμενα γεννητὰ ἀπὸ τοῦ ἀγεννήτου γέγονέ τε καὶ πεπλήρωται Hipp.*haer.*5.8(p.94.28; M.16.3147C); νοῦν καὶ ἀλήθειαν, τουτέστι δυάδα, ἥτις...ἀρχὴ γέγονε...πάντων τῶν ἐντὸς π. καταριθμουμένων αἰώνων *ib.*6.29(p.156.18; 3238A); γενομένης οὖν ἐντὸς π. ἀγνοίας κατὰ τὴν σοφίαν καὶ ἀμορφίας κατὰ τὸ γέννημα τῆς σοφίας, θόρυβος ἐγένετο ἐν τῷ π. *ib.*6.31(p.158.15; 3239B); σταυρὸν ὅς...ὅρος γίνεται τοῦ π., ἔχων ἐντὸς ἑαυτοῦ πάντας...τοὺς...αἰῶνας *ib.*(p.159.10; 3242A); *ib.*6.37(p.168.1; 3254A); *ib.*8.10(p.229.24; 3354C); τάς τε ἐντὸς τοῦ ὅρου προβολὰς γεγενημένας πάλιν καλεῖσθαι ἐντὸς π., δεύτερα δὲ τὰ ἐκτὸς π., καὶ τρίτα τὰ ἐκτὸς τοῦ ὅρου, ὧν ἡ γέννησις τὸ ὑστέρημα ὑπάρχει *ib.*10.13(p.274.6; 3427B); Χριστὸν ἐκ τοῦ ἐντὸς π., κατεληλυθέναι ἐπὶ σωτηρίᾳ τοῦ ἀποπλανηθέντος πνεύματος *ib.*(p.274.11; 3427B); Epiph.*haer.*21.4(p.243.20; M.41.292B); *ib.*23.4(p.252.16; 304A); ἡ κατὰ συζυγίαν πνευματικοῦ...π. κενοφωνία *ib.*31.3(p.386.15; 477B).

***πληρωματικός**, *perfecting* π. ἐστι καὶ τέλειος ὁ ἀριθμὸς ὁ ἑπτά Didym.*Trin.*2.14(M.39.700C); id.ap.*cat.Rom.*8:10(p.229.30) for πληρωτικόν id.(‡Bas.)*Eun.*5(1.305B; M.29.732B); Eutych.*pasch.*5(M.86.2397B).

πλήρωσις, ἡ, 1. *filling, making full* τὸ γὰρ κενὸν πᾶν ἐπιθυμεῖ πληρώσεως Clem.*paed.*2.10(p.211.4; M.8.504A); of fullness of Logos replacing former emptiness of things when they receive him, Eus.*d.e.*4.13(p.173.8; M.22.288C); of fullness of God ἀπ' ἐμοῦ πληροῦνται οἱ ἅγιοι. Στέφανος πλήρης χάριτος...Παῦλος...πλήρης πνεύματος ἁγίου...ἐκ ταύτης τῆς π. καὶ Ἀβραὰμ ἦν...πλήρης ἡμερῶν †Bas.*Is.*25(1.399B; M.30.168B); τὴν διὰ τοῦ θείου πνεύματος π. Didym.(‡Bas.)*Eun.*5(1.309D; M.29.741C); εἰ κτίσμα ἐτύγχανεν ὂν τὸ ἅγιον πνεῦμα, ἢ ὁ υἱός· ποῦ ἦν χρεία τὸ κτίσμα ἁγιάζειν, καὶ ποιεῖν τὴν π.; id.*Trin.*2.6(M.39.525A); κατὰ τὸν τρόπον τῆς μυστικῆς π. ... ἡ ὑπόσχεσις· δέδοται γὰρ ἡμῖν...τὸ ὕδωρ τὸ ζῶν τοῦ...βαπτίσματος Cyr.*Joel.*32(3.224E); Vict.*Mc.*10:13(p.375.3); **2.** *fulfilment*; **a.** of divine law ἡ εἰς Χριστὸν πίστις...νόμου...π. Clem.*str.*4.21(p.307.34; M.8.1345A); δικαιοσύνη ἐστὶν ἡ πασῶν τῶν ἐντολῶν π. Meth.*fr.*(p.520.8); Vict.*Mc.*10:24(p.379.34); **b.** of hope or expectation, Epiph.*haer.*33.9(p.461.5; M.41.573A); Cyr.*Jo.*2.5(4.204C); **3.** *completeness, totality* κεφαλὴν γωνίας τῆς π. τοῦ ναοῦ *T.Sal.*22.7 (v.l. συμπληρώσεως M.122.1352C); **4.** *payment in full, full discharge* of debt, met. θάνατος...χρεωστούντων π. ‡Chrys.*pat.*1(9.808C).

πληρωτέον, *one must fill up the meaning of, one must interpret the significance of* οὔτε τὸ 'θεόν μου καὶ θεὸν ὑμῶν' κατὰ τὴν τοῦ υἱοῦ θεότητα καὶ κατὰ τὴν μαθητῶν υἱοθεσίαν π. Epiph.*haer.*76.34(p.383.14; M.42.585A).

πληρωτής, ὁ, 1. *one who completes*, of Logos ἐκ σαρκὸς γεγεννημένος καὶ τελείως τὰ πάντα πληρώσας, ὡς π. ὢν ὅλου τοῦ σκεύους Epiph.*haer.*77.27(p.440.1; M.42.680D); τοῦ νοῦ καὶ παντὸς τοῦ σώματος π. ἐγένετο *ib.*77.35(p.447.17; 693B); **2.** *one who fills up, supplies* π. τῶν ἐμῶν ὑστερημάτων *A.Thom.*A 149(p.258.11); **3.** *one who fulfils*; **a.** Law, Eus.*d.e.*1.7(p.35.9; M.22.69A); Bas.*hom.*5.8(2.41C; M.31.256C); **b.** OT types, †Cyr.*hom.div.*10(5^2.375A); **4.** *one who fulfils a debt* for another, Eus.Al.*serm.*21.3(M.86.425D); of Christ μετὰ τῶν χρεωφειλετῶν ὁ π. Eulog.*palm.*1(M.86.2916A).

πληρωτικός, 1. *filling* ἀέρα...πάντων πληρωτικόν Clem.*str.*5.8(p.358.11; M.9.76B); Gr.Naz.*or.*31.29(p.183.7; M.36.165C); εἰ...τὸ θεῖον ἀκίνητον, ὡς πάντων πληρωτικόν Max.*ambig.*(M.91.1069B); **2.** *fulfilling* πνεῦμα...τὸ τῶν θείων ἐνεργειῶν π. Didym.(‡Bas.)*Eun.*5(1.305B; M.29.732B); τὸ π. τοῦ νόμου διὰ τῆς ἀγάπης Epiph.*haer.*42.12(p.157.14; M.41.776C); **3.** *completing* Χριστὸς οὐκ ἄλλο πρόσωπόν ἐστι παρὰ τὸν υἱόν, ἀλλὰ τῆς τριάδος πληρωτικόν Thdt.*ep.*146(4.1261).

***πληρωτικῶς**, *fully, completely*, Sophr.H.*ep.syn.*(M.87.3157C).

πλησίος, *near*; **1.** masc. as subst., *neighbour* φοβεῖσθε κύριον καὶ ἀγαπᾶτε τὸν π. *T.Benj.*3.3; μηδεὶς κατὰ σάρκα βλεπέτω τὸν π. Ign.*Magn.*6.2; Polyc.*ep.*3.3; ἀγαπήσεις τὸν π. σου ὑπὲρ τὴν ψυχήν σου *Barn.*19.5; ref. Lc.10:30–37 τὰ πρωτεῖα τῆς ἀγάπης ἀνάπτει τῷ θεῷ... τὰ δευτερεῖα νέμει τῷ π. τίς δ' ἂν ἄλλος οὗτος εἴη πλὴν αὐτὸς ὁ σωτήρ; Clem.*q.d.s.*29(p.179.3; M.9.633C); cf. *salvator noster factus est proximus nobis*, Or.*Cant.*proem.(p.70.28; M.13.70A); Epiph.*haer.*42.12(p.157.14; M.41.776C); **2.** neut. as adv.; **a.** *near* π. ... τοῦ πείθεσθαι Men.*exc.Rom.*3(p.185.24; M.113.873B); **b.** *just after*, ‡Hipp.Th.*fr.*14(p.46.10).

πλησισέληνος, *nearly full*; of the moon, Jo.D.*f.o.*2.7(M.94.897D).

***πλησιστίως**, *in full sail* π. ἔφθασεν ἐνορμισθεῖσα ταῖς θείαις ἀκοαῖς ἡ προσευχή ‡Nil.*perist.*4.6(M.79.829D).

πλήσμιος, *sated*, Nil.*praest.*13(M.79.1076D).

πλησμονικός, *for filling* with food περὶ κοινωνίας θεοπρεποῦς, οὐ πλησμονικῆς Euthal.Diac.*epp.Paul.*(M.85.756B).

[*]**πληστηριάζω**, v. πλειστηριάζω.

πλινθάριον, τό, *brick*, Dor.*doct.*13.8(M.88.1769C).

***πλινθάριος, ὁ**, s.v.l., *brick-maker* οἱ...π. ἐργαζόμενοι Dor.*doct.*13.8(M.88.1769B, perh. l. πλινθαρίῳ from πλινθάριον).

πλινθεία, ἡ, *brick-making*, ref. Israelites' bondage as symbolizing man's sinful state οὗτοι...τῇ γαστρὶ ζῶντες...μέγα...οὐδὲν...ἐπὶ τῶν ἔργων ἐνδείκνυνται, τῷ...τῇ π. καὶ τῷ πηλῷ προσηλοῦν ἑαυτούς Chrys.*hom.1.1 in Jo.*(8.3A); *ib.*8.2(51C); Cyr.*Is.*4.1(2.542E); id.*Jo.*4.7(4.437A); Nil.*Magn.*33(M.79.1009A); from which baptism liberates, Proc.G.*Is.*42:10–25(M.87.2369B); Dor.*doct.*13.8(M.88.1769B); †Jo.D.*B.J.*1(M.96.872B); symbolizing life of good works, Isid.Pel.*epp.*1.196(M.78.309A).

πλινθοποιΐα, ἡ, *brick-making*, ref. Egyptian bondage as typical of man's unredeemed state, Leont.B.*mesopent.*(M.86.1976C); Dor.*doct.*13.8(M.88.1769B).

***πλινθότης, ἡ**, *brick-like nature*, Gr.Nyss.*infant.*(M.46.164C).

πλινθουργία, ἡ, *brick-making*; met., of evil thoughts καλάμην συνάγουσιν εἰς τὴν παράνομον π. Evagr.Pont.*cap.pract.*A 68(M.40.1241C) = †Nil.*mal.cog.*26(M.79.1232A); Μωϋσῆς...εἰς Αἴγυπτον, ἤγουν σκοτασμόν, πρὸς τὴν π. τοῦ νοητοῦ ἴσως Φαραὼ ὑπέστρεψεν Jo.Clim.*scal.*5(M.88.780C).

πλοιάριον, τό, *skiff, boat*; met., Thdr.Stud.*epp*.1.11(M.99.944D).

***πλοιέκδικος, ὁ,** *maritime lawyer* Ἀναστάσιος ὁ...διάκονος καὶ νοτάριος ὁ π. CCP(681)*act*.10(H.3.1201B).

πλοῖον, τό, 1. *boat*; met., ref. transference of souls to moon (Manich.) π. γὰρ ἤτοι πορθμεῖα εἶναι λέγει τοὺς δύο φωστῆρας Hegem. *Arch*.8(p.13.3; M.10.1440B); **2.** *vessel, receptacle* ποιῆσαι π. μεγάλα εἰς τὴν ἐργασίαν τοῦ τέκτονος, καὶ μόδια *A.Thom*.B 14(p.31.7); *ib*.36 (p.36.14).

***πλοιοποιΐα, ἡ,** *shipbuilding*, Thphn.*chron*.p.287 (v.l. ναυπλοΐας M.108.704C).

πλοκή, ἡ, 1. *wreath*; pagan use in garlanding statues of gods eschewed by Christians, Just.*1apol*.9.1(M.6.340A); worn at banquets, a sign of pagan effeminacy, Clem.*str*.7.7(p.28.16; M.9.452C); met. ὁ τὸν στέφανον τοῦτον πλέξας τῇ σῇ π. Ἰησοῦ *A.Jo*.108(p.206.7); **2.** *woven work*; in embroidery of garments, Clem.*paed*.2.10(p.221.15; M.8.525A); Gr.Nyss.*v.Mos*.(M.44.320C); **3.** *coils* of serpent, Meth.*symp*.8.10(p.92.23; M.18.153B) cit. s. ἐκσείω; **4.** *marking* of zebra, Philost.*h.e*.3.11(M.65.497D); **5.** *complication* of thought or speech, Gr.Thaum.*pan.Or*.7(p.20.20; M.10.1076B); Gr.Naz.*carm*.1.2.10.207(M.37.695A); Chrys.*hom.1.2 in Rom*.(9.432B); **6.** *concoction* ὀψοποιῶν καὶ κερασμάτων π. Gr.Naz.*carm*.2.1.12.615(M.37.1210A); **7.** *conjunction, union* οὐ...κατὰ...πλοκὴν ἄστρων...ζῶμεν Cyr.H. *catech*.2.15; of union of Persons of Trin., Didym.(‡Bas.)*Eun*.5(1.317D; M.29.761A); of *bond* of faith, hope, charity, Sophr.H.*ep.syn*.(M.87.3149D); **8.** *embrace*, Tat.*orat*.8(p.8.24; M.6.824A); *Hom.Clem*. 6.23.

***πλοκολογία, ἡ,** *tangled story, web of deceitful speech*, Esaias *or*. 22.8(p.141; cf.M.40.1170B); Ant.Mon.*hom*.13(M.89.1841C).

***πλοτήρ, ὁ,** *sailor*, in comparison of Church with ship πλοτῆρας... τοὺς ἡγιασμένους Cyr.*Ps*.103:25(M.69.1265A).

πλουμαρικός, (Lat. *plumarius*) *embroidered*; neut. as subst., *embroidered robe*, Thdt.*qu.28 in 2Reg*.(1.429) cit. s. ἀστραγαλωτός; Proc.G.*2Reg*.13:18(M.87.1136A).

πλουμίον ([*]**πλουμμίον**), **τό,** *embroidery*, Jo.Mal.*chron*.17 p.413 (M.97.612B) = πλουμμία Chron.*Pasch*.p.332(M.92.861B).

[*]**πλουσιόδωρος,** *giving rich gifts, generous*; of God, Cyr.*fr.3Reg*. 3:10(M.69.688D); id.*Zach*.59(3.739E); id.*Jo*.2.1(4.137E); of Christ, id. *Is*.5.1(2.732A); id.*Abac*.51(3.566B); of Joasaph π. γὰρ ὢν τὴν ψυχὴν †Jo.D.*B.J*.33(M.96.1181C).

***πλουσιολόγος,** *rich in words*, hence *speaking in many ways*; of Son, Didym.*Trin*.3.5(M.39.840B).

***πλουσιοπάροχος,** *munificent*, †Gregent.*leg.Hom*.proem.(M.86.580C).

***πλουσιοπαρόχως,** *munificently*, †Gregent.*leg.Hom*.proem.(M.86.580B).

***πλουσιοποιός,** *enriching*, Pall.*h.Laus*.(M.34.1220B).

πλούσιος, fanciful etym. πλούσιον καλοῦμεν ἀντὶ τοῦ πολυούσιον Thdr.Raith.*praep*.(p.201.5).

A. *wealthy*; **1.** in gen. τὴν φειδωλίαν πενίαν λέγει, καθ' ἣν οἱ π. πένονται μεταδόσεως, ὡς οὐκ ἔχοντες Clem.*paed*.3.4(p.254.9; M.8.600A); τοὺς π. μαθηματικῶς ἀκουστέον, τοὺς δυσκόλως εἰσελευσομένους εἰς τὴν βασιλείαν, μὴ...σαρκίνως...οὕτως καὶ ἄπορός τις ὢν...εὑρεθείη ποτ' ἂν μεθύων ταῖς ἐπιθυμίαις, καὶ χρήμασι πλούσιος νήφων καὶ πτωχεύων ἡδονῶν id.*q.d.s*.18(p.171.4; M.9.621C); ὁ...ἀποδεχόμενος τοὺς π. ὡς θεούς, τοὺς δὲ πένητας...ἐξουθενῶν, οὗτος θεοποιεῖ τὸ ἀργύριον Or.*hom.7.3 in Jer*.(p.53.32; M.13.333A); π. εἶ; μὴ δανείζου. πένης εἶ; μὴ δανείζου Bas.*hom.in Ps*.14(1.110C; M.29.272C); ἀκούετε, οἱ π., ὁποῖα συμβουλεύομεν τοῖς πτωχοῖς διὰ τὴν ὑμετέραν ἀπανθρωπίαν· ἐγκαρτερεῖν μᾶλλον τοῖς δεινοῖς, ἢ τὰς ἐκ τῶν τόκων συμφορὰς ὑποδέχεσθαι *ib*.(112D; M.277B); π. ἐστι; φιλοσοφήσει τὸ ἀποπλουτεῖν Gr.Naz.*or*.26.11(M.35.1244A); πάντες ἀπολαύουσιν ἐξ ἴσης αὐτοῦ [sc. τοῦ ἡλίου], καὶ πένητες καὶ π. Chrys.*hom.12.5 in 2Cor*.(10.527E); π., ἵνα μὴ μέγα εἶναι νομίζητε τὸν πλοῦτον χωρὶς ἀρετῆς id.*Laz*.2.1(1.727A); **2.** ref. disadvantages of wealth, Herm.*sim*.2.5; δύσκολον εἶναι π. εἰσέρχεσθαι εἰς τὴν τοῦ θεοῦ βασιλείαν· εἴτε πλούσιόν τις λαμβάνει ἁπλούστερον τὸν ὑπὸ πλούτου περισπώμενον καὶ...ἐμποδιζόμενον φέρειν τοὺς τοῦ λόγου καρποὺς εἴτε καὶ τὸν ἐν τοῖς ψευδέσι δόγμασι πλουτοῦντα Or.*Cels*.7.23(p.174.26; M.11.1453B); ὁ μὲν π. πολλαῖς προκατειλημμένος φροντίσιν...οὐδὲ μετὰ πολλῆς τῆς σπουδῆς τὸ φάρμακον ...τῶν γραφῶν δέχεται Chrys.*pecc*.1(3.345A); ὁ π. ἔχει Θάσιον...ἀλλ' αἱ τῶν ὑδάτων πηγαὶ κοινῇ πᾶσι πρόκεινται id.*Anna* 5.3(4.744D); ὁ δὲ π., ἐπειδὴ πλεονεξίᾳ συζῇ, μισεῖται παρὰ πάντων id.*hom.1 in Ps.48*:17(5.508C); π. μὲν ὀλίγους, τῶν δὲ πενήτων πολλῷ πλείους σωζομένους id.*hom.13.4 in 2Cor*.(10.536B); id.*hom.34.7 in 1Cor*.(10.320Aff.); **3.** ref. mutual service of rich and poor in almsgiving and prayer, Herm.*sim*.2.5–8; Chrys.*hom.34.4 in 1Cor*.(10.316C); **4.** ref. spiritual wealth ὁ πένης π. ἐστιν ἐν τῇ ἐντεύξει Herm.*sim*.2.5; ὁ μὲν ἄρα ἀληθῶς...π. ἐστιν ὁ τῶν ἀρετῶν π. ... ὁ δὲ νόθος π. ὁ κατὰ σάρκα πλουτῶν Clem.*q.d.s*.19(p.171.29; M.9.624A); πῶς ἂν γένοιτο π. ... ψυχή, ἐν πενίᾳ χρημάτων οὖσα; μάλιστα ἂν τότε γένοιτο Chrys.*hom.80.4 in Mt*.(7.772A); βούλει γενέσθαι π. ...; ἔξεστί σοι. ... καταφρόνησον τῶν τοῦ κόσμου χρημάτων id.*hom.2.5 in Phil*.(11.210A); εἰσὶ γὰρ π. καὶ τοῦ μέλλοντος αἰῶνος Thdt.*1Tim*.6:17(3.672).

B. *abundant, rich* π. τῶν τοῦ θεοῦ δικαιωμάτων *Barn*.1.2; πλουσιότερος ὁ ἁγιασμός Cyr.*Jo*.12(4.1070E).

πλουτ-έω, 1. abs., *be rich*; **a.** in gen., Tat.*orat*.32(p.33.6; M.6.872B) cit. s. πένης; Clem.*q.d.s*.2(p.160.19; M.9.605B); ἑνὶ τούτῳ διαφέρωμεν τῶν ~ούντων οἱ πένητες, τῇ ἀμεριμνίᾳ Bas.*hom.in Ps*.14(1.110C; M.29.273A); πόσοι τῶν πενήτων τῶν ~ούντων εἰσὶ συνετώτεροί τε καὶ φιλοσοφώτεροι Chrys.*exp.in Ps*.4:8(5.25B); ὁ μὲν γὰρ ~ῶν ἀλύει, καὶ θορυβεῖται *ib*.9:19(106C); ὁ δὲ μὴ βουλόμενος ~εῖν, ἀεί ἐστιν ἐν εὐπορίᾳ id.*hom.1 in Ps.48*:17(5.508B); **b.** met. ἡ ~οῦσα τῶν ἐπιθυμιῶν Clem.*q.d.s*.16(p.170.1; M.9.620C); τὸν ἐν τοῖς ψευδέσι δόγμασι ~οῦντα Or.*Cels*.7.23(p.174.30; M.11.1453C); in spiritual wealth, Herm.*sim*.2.5.8; Chrys.*hom.15.4 in Mt*.(7.190A); *ib*.80.4(772A); ἔκβαλε τὴν ἐπιθυμίαν τοῦ πλούτου, καὶ ἐπλούτησας id.*hom.2.5 in Phil*. (11.210A); ~εῖ μόνον τῇ φιλοσοφίᾳ id.*hom.1 in Ps.48*:17(5.508C); τῶν ἐν εὐσεβείᾳ καὶ ἀγχινοίᾳ ~ούντων Gel.Cyz.*h.e*.2.16.15(M.85.1264B); **2.** *be rich in, enriched by* ὅσῳ ~εῖ τις...τὸν πλοῦτον, πένητα ἑαυτὸν εἶναι κατανοεῖ Mac.Aeg.*carit*.3(M.34.909B); ref. spiritual riches, Gr.Naz.*or*.26.11(M.35.1244B); *ib*.14.26(892C); τὴν θείαν...εἰκόνα... ~εῖν Cyr.*ador*.1(1.10A); διὰ τοῦ βαπτίσματος τὴν ἐξ οὐρανοῦ...ἰσχὺν πεπλουτήκαμεν *ib*.4(114D); τὴν εἰς θεὸν οἰκειότητα πεπλουτηκότας *ib*. 11(375B); τὴν διὰ τοῦ...βαπτίσματος ~οῦντες ἄφεσιν *ib*.14(508C); τὴν πρὸς αὐτὸν πεπλουτήκασι συμμορφίαν id.*glaph.Gen*.3(1.68B); συμμορφίαν...πεπλουτηκότων δι' ἁγιασμοῦ ἐν πνεύματι id.*glaph.Ex*.2(1.276D); τὴν γνῶσιν διὰ τῆς ἄνωθεν δᾳδουχίας πεπλουτηκὼς id.*Is*.2.1(2.204C); ἐλπίδα ~ήσαντες *ib*.4.4(673A); id.*Os*.6(3.26D); διὰ Χριστοῦ τὸ θεῖον πεπλουτήκαμεν πνεῦμα id.*Abac*.37(3.553A); βοηθὸν ~ήσας τὸν παντοκράτορα Jo.Mon.*hymn.Nic*.9(M.96.1389C); παρρησίαν πρὸς τὸν σωτῆρα ~ῶν id.*hymn.Geo*.7(M.96.1397D).

πλουτισμός, ὁ, *enriching*, †Max.*hymn*.2(M.91.1422A).

πλουτοδότειρα, ἡ, fem. of πλουτοδότηρ, *giver of riches*; of BMV, Jo.D.*hom*.8.3(M.96.701C).

πλουτοδότης, ὁ, = foreg.; of God, *A.Xanthipp*.14(p.67.24); ‡Chrys.*hom*.5(13.213C).

***πλουτοποιός,** *making rich* π. χαρίσμασι Ephr.3.499A; πλούσιος γὰρ ὢν ἐν θεότητι, πτωχεύει τὴν π. πτωχείαν Max.*schol.d.n*.3.1(M.4.236C).

***πλουτοπράτης, ὁ,** *dealer in wealth*, Geo.Pis.*hex*.474(M.92.1472A).

πλοῦτος, ὁ, *wealth*; **1.** in gen., ref. mutual obligations of rich and poor ὁ πλούσιος ὡσαύτως τὸν π. ὃν ἔλαβεν ἀπὸ τοῦ κυρίου ἀδιστάκτως παρέχει τῷ πένητι. καὶ τοῦτο ἔργον...δεκτὸν παρὰ τῷ θεῷ, ὅτι συνῆκεν ἐπὶ τῷ π. αὐτοῦ...καὶ ἐτέλεσε τὴν διακονίαν τοῦ κυρίου ὀρθῶς Herm. *sim*.2.7; ὁ...θαυμάζων τὸν π. ... θεοποιεῖ τὸ ἀργύριον Or.*hom.7.3 in Jer*.(p.53.31; M.13.333A); id.*or*.29(p.384.13; M.11.533C); its uselessness διάβλεψον...πρὸς τὴν φύσιν τοῦ π. ... λίθος ἐστὶν ὁ χρυσός,...τίνος ἐφείσατο θάνατος διὰ τὸν π.; Bas.*hom*.7.7(2.58E; M.31.297A); Chrys. *hom.2.5 in Phil*.(11.210A) cit. s. πλουτέω; **2.** responsibility for its right use ὁ π. ὀργανόν ἐστι. δύνασαι χρῆσθαι δικαίως αὐτῷ· πρὸς δικαιοσύνην καθυπηρετεῖ Clem.*q.d.s*.14(p.168.29; M.9.617C); **3.** as morally indifferent π. καὶ...δόξα καθὸ μὲν οὐ ποιεῖ τοὺς ἔχοντας ἀγαθούς, οὐκ ἔστι τῶν κατὰ φύσιν ἀγαθῶν· καθὸ δὲ εὔροιάν τινα παρέχεται ἡμῶν τῷ βίῳ,...ἔχει τινὰ ἀξίαν Bas.*ep*.236.7(3.364C; M.32.884C); ὁ γὰρ π. τῷ ἰδίῳ λόγῳ οὐδὲ ἀγαθὸς οὐδὲ φαῦλος τυγχάνει, ἀλλὰ τῇ προαιρέσει τοῦ χρωμένου εἰς ἑκάτερα κρίνεται...οὔτε ἡ πενία κακόν, οὔτε ὁ π. φαῦλος ‡Ath.*hom.in Lc.19*:36(M.28.1037A); πενία γὰρ καὶ π. ὅπλα ἐστὶ πρὸς ἀρετὴν ἑκάτερα φέροντα, ἂν ἐθέλωμεν...οὔτε γὰρ π. κακόν, οὔτε πενία ἁπλῶς· ἀλλὰ παρὰ τὴν προαίρεσιν τῶν χρωμένων ἑκάτερα ταῦτα γίνεται Chrys.*stat*.15.3(2.156C); οὐδὲν ὁ π. ἀγαθόν, οὐδὲν ἡ πενία κακόν, ἀλλ' ἀδιάφορά ἐστι πράγματα id.*hom.2.4 in 2Thess*.(11.521D); id.*Laz*.2.3(1.731B) cit. s. πενία; **4.** its moral dangers ἐοικέναι γοῦν μοι δοκεῖ ὁ π. ἑρπετῷ, οὗ εἰ μή τις ἐπίσταιτο λαβέσθαι ἀβλαβῶς,...περιπλέξεται τῇ χειρὶ καὶ δήξεται· δεινὸς δὲ καὶ ὁ π. ἰλυσπώμενος παρὰ τὴν ἔμπειρον ἢ ἄπειρον αὐτοῦ λαβὴν προσφῦναι καὶ δάκνειν, εἰ μή τις αὐτῷ...ἐπιστημόνως χρῷτο Clem.*paed*.3.6(p.256.20; M.8.604C); wealth which debars from Kingdom of God identified with spiritual infirmities, id.*q.d.s*.16(p.169.30; M.9.620C); pursuit of it as idolatry, Or.*hom.7.3 in Jer*.(p.53.27; M.13.333A); π., ἡ τοῦ πολέμου ὑπόθεσις...διὰ τὸν π. αἱ ἐρημίαι τοὺς φονευτὰς τρέφουσιν ...τίς ἐστιν ὁ ψεύδους πατήρ...οὐχ ὁ π.;...ἀλλ' ἀναγκαῖος ὁ π. διὰ τοὺς παῖδας. εὐπρόσωπος ἀφορμὴ πλεονεξίας αὕτη Bas.*hom*.7.7(2.59A; M.

31.297B); πρὸς ἀρετὴν ἐπιτηδειότερον πενία πλούτου Chrys.*eleem*.5(5.256E); π. τοῖς μὴ προσέχουσι πονηρίας ἐστὶν ὑπηρέτης id.*exp.in Ps.*4:8(5.25A); οὐ πᾶς π. παρὰ θεοῦ id.*hom.34.6 in 1Cor.*(10.318E); wealth regarded as blessing under Old Covenant, poverty under New, but even in OT chief heroes were poor, id.*hom.18.2 in Heb.*(12.176C) cit. s. πενία; wealth despised by those influenced by monastic example, Ath.*v.Anton*.87(M.26.965A); **5.** not to be personified as a god, as pagan art suggests, Clem.*prot*.10(p.73.25; M.8.217B); **6.** spiritual π. γὰρ ἀληθινὸς ἡ δικαιοσύνη...π. ἀναφαίρετος id.*paed*.3.6(p.257.23; M.8.605C); π. δὲ ἄριστος ἡ τῶν ἐπιθυμιῶν πενία *ib*.2.3(p.181.7; 440A); εἰς τὴν τοῦ κόσμου πενίαν ἀγαγών με καὶ εἰς π. ἀληθινὸν παρακαλέσας με *A.Thom*.A 144(p.251.6); οἱ πλούσιοι τῷ πνεύματι τῷ ἁγίῳ, ἔχοντες τὸν π. τὸν ἐπουράνιον ἐν ἀληθείᾳ Mac.Aeg.*hom*.18.5(M.34.637B); ζητῶμεν τὸν π., τὸν ἐν ἔργοις ἀγαθοῖς Chrys.*hom.9.5 in Mt.*(7.137B); of wealth of divine grace, Thdt.*1Cor*.15:10(3.267); Jo.Clim.*scal*.30(M.88.1157D) cit. s. ἐλπίς.

***πλουτοταπείνωσις, ἡ,** *riches of humility,* Jo.Clim.*scal*.5(M.88.777C).

***πλυνόκωλος,** *with limbs washed,* Barth.Edess.*Agar*.(M.104.1413B).

***πλυντήρ, ὁ,** *wash-tub,* Mac.Mgn.*apocr*.4.16(p.189.21).

πλύσις, ἡ, 1. *washing,* ref. Ps.50:9 ὁ ὕσσωπος σύμβολόν ἐστιν ἀπαθείας, καὶ ἡ π. γνῶσιν σημαίνει Or.*Ps*.50:9(p.51); **2.** *washing away* τῶν ἀκαθάρτων π. Arist.*apol*.5(*TS*[1] p.102.22).

***πλύτρα, ἡ,** *laundry,* Pall.*h.Laus*.43(p.130.20; λουτροῦ M.34.1210D).

***πλυτρίς, ἡ,** *washerwoman*; met., of a servile labour χρῆσις ῥυπώδης, ἀλλὰ π. πταισμάτων Thdr.Stud.*iamb*.14(M.99.1785A).

Πλωάς, ἡ, the constellation *Ursa Major,* Eus.Al.*serm*.22.1(M.86.453B).

πλωΐζω, *put aboard, carry on board ship,* Marc.Diac.*v.Porph*.26; Thphn.*chron*.p.91(M.108.273A).

***πλώϊμα, τό,** *man-of-war* μετὰ πάντων τῶν Ῥωμαϊκῶν π. Thphn.*chron*.p.309(M.108.752B, vv.ll. πλοϊμάτων, πλοημάτων); *ib*.p.392 (πλώϊμα M.108.936B, vv.ll. πλοΐματα, πλοήματα).

πλώϊμον, τό, *fleet,* Thphn.*chron*.p.314(M.108.761B); *ib*.p.317(768B); v. foreg.

πλωτεύω, *sail, Orac.Sib*.5.448.

***πλωτής, ὁ,** *sailor,* Geo.Pis.*Pers*.1.187(M.92.1210A).

***πλωτόρσιος,** *swift-sailing,* ‡Jo.D.*ep.Thphl*.11(M.95.357C).

πλωτός, *prostrate* ἔπεσεν εἰς τοὺς πόδας αὐτοῦ π. ἱκετεύων Jo.Mal.*chron*.5 p.124(M.97.217D).

πνεῦμα, τό, I. *spirit*; def. καλεῖται γὰρ πνεύματα πολλά. καὶ γὰρ καὶ ἄγγελος καλεῖται π.· ἡ ψυχὴ ἡμῶν καλεῖται π.· καὶ ὁ ἄνεμος οὗτος ὁ πνέων...καὶ ἀρετὴ μεγάλη...καὶ ἀκάθαρτος πρᾶξις...καὶ δαίμων ἀντικείμενος καλεῖται π. Cyr.H.*catech*.16.13; π. μέν ἐστι λεπτὴ καὶ ἄϋλος καὶ ἀσχημάτιστος ἐκπορευτὴ ὕπαρξις. ... εἴρηται δὲ τὸ π. ἐν τῇ γραφῇ τετραχῶς· τὸ π. τὸ ἅγιον· π. ὁ ἄγγελος· π. ἡ ψυχή· π. καὶ ὁ ἄνεμος. ἔστι δὲ ὅτε καὶ ὁ νοῦς εἴρηται π. Anast.S.*hod*.2(M.89.56B); τὸ π. νοεῖται πολλαχῶς. τὸ ἅγιον π. λέγονται δὲ καὶ αἱ δυνάμεις τοῦ π. τοῦ ἁγίου πνεύματα. π. καὶ ὁ ἄγγελος...π. καὶ ὁ δαίμων· π. καὶ ἡ ψυχή· ἔστι δὲ ὅτε καὶ νοῦς π. λέγεται· π. καὶ ὁ ἄνεμος· π. καὶ ὁ ἀὴρ Jo.D.*f.o*.1.13(M.94.857Bf.).

II. *wind, air; breath* in rel. to spoken word as analogy of H. Ghost in rel. to Logos, Gr.Nyss.*or.catech*.2(p.13.9; M.45.17A).

III. *life-force, life*;

A. in plants, Max.*schol.d.n*.1.5(M.4.205D).

B. in man τὸ π. τὸ ἀπὸ τοῦ ἐγκεφάλου καταβαῖνον, τὸ διὰ τῶν νεύρων, τὸ αἰσθητικὸν...δίδωσι Chrys.*hom.11.3 in Eph.*(11.84E); τοῦ συνέχοντος τὸ ζῷον ζωτικοῦ καὶ ὀργανικοῦ π. Leont.B.*Nest.et Eut*.1(M.86.1296D).

IV. *soul*;

A. *living soul, self,* Ign.*Rom*.9.3; ὑπερευφραίνομαι ἐπὶ τοῖς μακαρίοις καὶ ἐνδόξοις ὑμῶν π. *Barn*.1.2; hence *person* τὸν παντὸς π. κτίστην *1Clem*.59.3; *Barn*.1.5; ὁ ἄνθρωπος ὁ δίκαιος καὶ ὁ Χριστὸς π. ἐν Or.*dial*.3(p.126.8).

B. *rational and spiritual element* in man (opp. σάρξ), Ign.*Polyc*.5.1; Just.*dial*.135.6(M.6.789B); = νοῦς, Anast.S.*hod*.2(M.89.56B), Jo.D.*f.o*.1.13(M.94.860A) citt. s. I supra.

C. opp. ψυχή (when latter is regarded as principle of animal life); **1.** two π. dist. δύο πνευμάτων διαφορὰς ἴσμεν ἡμεῖς, ὧν τὸ μὲν καλεῖται ψυχή, τὸ δὲ μεῖζον μὲν τῆς ψυχῆς, θεοῦ δὲ εἰκὼν καὶ ὁμοίωσις Tat.*orat*.12(p.12.18; M.6.829C); τῷ τε ἡγεμονικῷ τῷ τε ὑποκειμένῳ Clem.*str*.6.16(p.499.29; M.9.360A); *ib*.(p.501.2; 361A); compared with H. Ghost in rel. to Father, Ath.*ep.Serap*.1.22(M.26.581C); Gr.Nyss.*Eun*.2(2 p.383.7; M.45.564D); ref. ψυχή illuminated by divine fire ὅλη π. γίνεται Mac.Aeg.*hom*.1.2(M.34.452B); **2.** in tripartite division of personality, Ign.*Philad*.11.2; cf.Iren.*haer*.5.9.1(M.7.1144B); v. ψυχή; Or.*princ*.4.2.4(p.313.2; M.11.365A); id.*dial*.3(p.126.2); Apoll.*fr*.89(p.227.22)ap.Gr.Nyss.*Apoll*.48(M.45.1240C); id.*anac*.23(p.245.1; M.28.1276D); ἁγίασον ἡμῶν τὰς ψυχὰς καὶ τὰ σώματα καὶ τὰ π. *Lit.Jac*.(p.166.1); ἑτέρου ὄντος τοῦ π. παρὰ τὴν ψυχὴν κατ' οὐσίαν...τὸ εὐκινητότερον καὶ ἀνώτερον τῆς ψυχῆς πνεῦμα καλοῦντες Olymp.*Eccl*.4:12(M.93.532C).

D. *soul* of departed τὴν ψυχήν, τὸ π. αὐτοῦ ἀνάπαυσον Serap.*euch*.30.2; π. and δύναμις dist. from ψυχή, Or.*comm.in Mt*.13.2(p.178.9ff.; M.13.1092C).

E. in rel. to God; **1.** dist. from H. Ghost since human spirit is not a part of God in each man, Clem.*str*.5.13(p.384.11; M.9.129A); ref. 1Thess.5:23 τοῦτο τὸ π. οὐκ ἔστι τὸ ἅγιον π., ἀλλὰ μέρος τῆς τοῦ ἀνθρώπου συστάσεως Or.*dial*.6(p.136.10); Gr.Nyss.*or.catech*.2(p.14.5ff.; M.45.17B); Jo.D.*f.o*.1.7(M.94.804A); **2.** but deriving its true life from H. Ghost, Just.*dial*.6.1,2(M.6.489B,492A); Tat.*orat*.13(p.14.19; M.6.833B); cf.Cyr.*ador*.1(1.9D).

F. Christol. οὕτως ἠθέλησεν σῶσαι σῶμα, ὡς ἠθέλησεν ὁμοίως σῶσαι καὶ ψυχήν, ἠθέλησεν καὶ τὸ λεῖπον ἀνθρώπου σῶσαι, τὸ π. ... οὐκ ἂν δὲ ὅλος ἄνθρωπος ἐσώθη, εἰ μὴ ὅλον τὸν ἄνθρωπον ἀνειλήφει Or.*dial*.7(p.136.16); θέλων σῶσαι τὸ π. τοῦ ἀνθρώπου...ἀνέλαβεν καὶ ἀνθρώπου π. *ib*.(p.138.1); τὸ δὴ π. τουτέστι τὸν νοῦν θεὸν ἔχων ὁ Χριστὸς μετὰ ψυχῆς καὶ σώματος εἰκότως ἄνθρωπος ἐξ οὐρανοῦ λέγεται Apoll.*fr*.25(p.210.23)ap.Gr.Nyss.*Apoll*.9(M.45.1140D); εἰ οὖν ἐκ τριῶν ὁ ἄνθρωπος, ἄνθρωπος δὲ καὶ ὁ κύριος, ἐκ τριῶν πάντως ἐστὶ καὶ ὁ κύριος, πνεύματος καὶ ψυχῆς καὶ σώματος. ἀλλὰ καὶ ἐπουράνιος ἄνθρωπος καὶ π. ζωοποιοῦν Apoll.*fr*.89(p.227.22)*ib*.48(1240C); εἰ ἐκ πάντων...τῶν ἴσων ἡμῖν ἐστι τοῖς χοϊκοῖς ὁ ἐπουράνιος ἄνθρωπος, ὥστε καὶ τὸ π. ἴσον ἔχειν τοῖς χοϊκοῖς, οὐκ ἐπουράνιος ἀλλ' ἐπουρανίου θεοῦ δοχεῖον Apoll.*fr*.90(p.228.1)*ib*.(M.45.1240D).

V. ref. world-soul, as in Stoic thought π. γὰρ τὸ διὰ τῆς ὕλης διῆκον, ἔλαττον ὑπάρχον τοῦ θειοτέρου π. Tat.*orat*.4(p.5.10; M.6.813A); τὸ π. τοῦ θεοῦ διὰ τῆς ὕλης κεχωρηκὸς...φθειρομένων δὲ τῶν στοιχείων κατὰ τὴν ἐκπύρωσιν ἀνάγκη συμφθαρῆναι ὁμοῦ τοῖς εἴδεσι τὰ ὀνόματα, μόνου μένοντος τοῦ π. τοῦ θεοῦ Athenag.*leg*.22.3(M.6.937B); Thphl.Ant.*Autol*.2.4(M.6.1052A); ὃν τρόπον γὰρ ῥόα...πολλοὺς κόκκους ἔχει τοὺς ἐν αὐτῇ κατοικοῦντας· οὕτως ἡ πᾶσα κτίσις περιέχεται ὑπὸ π. θεοῦ *ib*.1.5(1032B); tenuous in substance and joined with water at Creation, *ib*.2.13(1073A).

VI. *influence, spiritual force*;

A. of physical or psychical attraction, ref. attraction by magnetic stone, amber, etc. πείθεται δὲ αὐτοῖς τὰ ἑλκόμενα ἀρρήτῳ ἑλκόμενα π. Clem.*str*.2.6(p.126.29; M.8.961A); συγκινεῖται...σιδήρου μοῖρα τῷ τῆς Ἡρακλείας λίθου π. *ib*.7.2(p.8.22; M.9.413A); ὄφεις τοῖς αὐτῶν π. τοὺς στρούθους ἐπισπῶνται *Hom.Clem*.9.15.

B. of spiritual influence; **1.** of intellectual or moral disposition π. σοφίας Or.*Jo*.10.39(23; p.215.28; M.14.381B); *ib*.32.19(12; p.460.1; 796C); λέγεται δὲ π. κατανύξεως εἶναι καὶ π. δειλίας καὶ π. Πύθωνος καὶ π. πορνείας...καὶ π. ἀσθενείας Epiph.*anc*.72(p.90.12; M.43.152A); this meaning often allied with that of evil *spirit* (evil quality being personified) ἀπέχου οὖν ἀπὸ τῆς ὀξυχολίας, τοῦ πονηροτάτου π. Herm.*mand*.5.2.8; **2.** of 'spirit' of a person τοῦ ἐν Μωϋσεῖ π. Just.*dial*.49.7(M.6.585A); Serap.*euch*.27.2; τὸ τοῦ προφήτου Ἠλία π. ‡Pall.*h.mon*.7.1(p.31.7; M.34.1132D); cf.Or.*comm.in Mt*.13.2(p.178.9ff.; M.13.1092Cf.); **3.** of supernatural power or 'soul' in rel. to pagan idol ξόανον οὔτε ζῷόν ἐστιν οὔτε θεῖον ἔχει π. *Hom.Clem*.9.15; **4.** of 'sense' of a passage of scripture δηλοῖ τὸ πνευματικὸν π. Or.*schol.in Cant*.7:2(M.17.281B); of spiritual opp. literal sense, v. γραφή.

VII. a kind of *immaterial substance* proper to spiritual beings, Hipp.*haer*.1.20(p.24.19; M.16.3048A); of angels' substance ἀέριον π. ...ἢ πῦρ ἄϋλον Bas.*Spir*.38(3.32C; M.32.137A); οὐ μετεβλήθη οὖν εἰς πνεῦμα τὸ σῶμα [i.e. of Christ] Thdt.*eran*.(4.272).

VIII. of God as π. (i.e. π. as describing nature or power of God);

A. in gen., of Father φῶς ἀπρόσιτον...π., δύναμις, λόγος Athenag.*leg*.16.2(M.6.920D); Father is π., Son is π., H. Ghost is π., Eus.*e.th*.3.5(p.163.6ff.; M.24.1012C); Geo.Laod.*ep.dogm*.ap.Epiph.*haer*.73.16(p.288.22; M.42.433A); τῷ πατρὶ καὶ τῷ υἱῷ, κατὰ τὸ ἴσον ἥ τε τοῦ π. καὶ ἡ τοῦ ἁγίου κλῆσις παρὰ τῆς γραφῆς ἐφαρμόζεται (π. γὰρ ὁ θεὸς καὶ π. πρὸ προσώπου ἡμῶν Χριστὸς κύριος...) Gr.Nyss.*Eun*.2(2 p.369.24ff.; M.45.549C).

B. God as π. dist. from spirit permeating material universe as in Stoic theory, Tat.*orat*.4(p.5.2; M.6.813A); and from physical world itself εἰ δὲ π., δῆλον ὅτι θεῖον, κρεῖττον παντὸς αἰσθητοῦ καὶ συνθέτου σώματος Eus.*Marcell*.1.1(p.5.14; M.24.721A); hence cannot be corporeal, Cyr.*ep.Calos*.(p.604.5; 6^2.364A).

C. Father as π. dist. from H. Ghost ὁ γὰρ πατὴρ οὐκ ἔστι π.

ἅγιον; καὶ ὁ πατὴρ π. ἅγιόν ἐστιν, ἀλλ' οὐ π. θεοῦ ‡Ath.*dial.Trin.*1.14 (M.28.1140A).

D. but category of spirit is inadequate for description of God, Thphl.Ant.*Autol.*1.3(M.6.1028C); οὐδὲ π. ἐστιν ὡς ἡμᾶς εἰδέναι Dion. Ar.*myst.*5(M.3.1048A).

E. exeg. Jo.4:24, v. ἀσώματος and IX.A.3.c.vi infra.

F. of Son as spirit (i.e. a being of divine nature) Χριστὸς...ὢν μὲν τὸ πρῶτον π. ἐγένετο σάρξ *2Clem.*9.5; λόγος γὰρ ὁ ἐπουράνιος, π. γεγονὼς ἀπὸ τοῦ π., καὶ λόγος ἐκ λογικῆς δυνάμεως...εἰκόνα τῆς ἀθανασίας τὸν ἄνθρωπον ἐποίησεν Tat.*orat.*7(p.7.6; M.6.820A,B); esp. ref. Lam.4:20, cf. *salutare autem quoniam spiritus, spiritus enim, inquit, faciei nostrae, Christus dominus,* Iren.*haer.*3.10.3(M.7.875A); εἰ δὲ μὴ ὢν ἄνθρωπος, ἐφαίνετο ἄνθρωπος, οὔτε ὃ ἦν ἐπ' ἀληθείας ἔμεινε, π. θεοῦ, ἐπεὶ ἀόρατον τὸ π. *ib.*5.1.2(1122A); τὸ ἐν τῇ παρθένῳ σαρκωθὲν π. Hipp.*haer.*9.12(p.248.29; M.16.3383C); ὁ κύριος π. καὶ λόγος Clem. *paed.*1.6(p.116.2; M.8.301B); ἐπειδὴ θεῖον π. ἦν ἐν σώματι Cels.ap.Or. *Cels.*6.77(p.146.14; M.11.1413C); λόγον...θεὸν μὲν κατὰ π., ἄνθρωπον δὲ καθ' ὃ γεγέννηται ἐκ τῆς Μαρίας Heraclides ap.Or.*dial.*2(p.122. 14); ὁ υἱὸς τοῦ θεοῦ π. ὢν τυγχάνει, καὶ π. καὶ αὐτὸς ἁγίων ἅγιον Eus. *e.th.*3.5(p.163.9; M.24.1012C); Ath.*inc.et c.Ar.*11(M.26.1004A); Geo. Laod.*ep.dogm.*ap.Epiph.*haer.*73.16(p.288.23; M.42.433A); προύχων τῆς γεννήσεως, εἰ καὶ γεγέννηται ἀπὸ γυναικός, κύριος ὤν, εἰ καὶ μεμόρφωται κατὰ τοὺς δούλους, π. ὤν, εἰ καὶ σὰρξ κατὰ τὴν ἕνωσιν τῆς σαρκὸς ἀποδέδεικται Apoll.*corp.et div.*6(p.187.17; M.*PL.*8.873D); id.*fr.*19(p.209.26)ap.Gr.Nyss.*Apoll.*7(M.45.1136D); τοῦ κυρίου ἐν τῇ τοῦ θεοῦ ἀνθρώπου φύσει θείου π. ὄντος Apoll.*fr.*32(p.211.28)*ib.*12 (1145D); εἶναι τὸν αὐτὸν υἱὸν θεοῦ καὶ θεὸν κατὰ πνεῦμα, υἱὸν δὲ ἀνθρώπου κατὰ σάρκα Apoll.*ep.Jov.*1(p.250.6; M.28.25A); Gr.Nyss.*Eun.*2 (2 p.369.24; M.45.549C); λόγος...π. ἐκ π. Epiph.*haer.*76.35(p.385.22; M.42.588D); δεδόξασται δὲ οὐδαμῶς, μὴ οὐχὶ τοῦτο λαβὼν κατὰ σάρκα, ὅπερ ἀεὶ ἔχων ἦν κατὰ π. Leont.B.*Nest.et Eut.*2(M.86.1321D); hence π. Χριστοῦ = Christ's divinity αὐτὸς ὑπὲρ τῶν ἡμετέρων ἁμαρτιῶν ἔμελλεν τὸ σκεῦος τοῦ π. προσφέρειν θυσίαν *Barn.*7.3; this being Spirit, blasphemy against whom is unforgivable, Ath.*ep.Serap.*4. 19(M.26.665B); ἀπαθὲς δέδεικται τὸ θεῖον τοῦ Χριστοῦ π. Thdt.*eran.*3 (4.235); ζῇ γὰρ ἐκ δυνάμεως θεοῦ, τῷ θείῳ πνεύματι δηλονότι συνδιαιτώμενος ὁ ἄνθρωπος...τὸ μὲν γὰρ σῶμα μετάρσιον ἐσταυροῦτο, τὸ δὲ θεῖον τῆς σοφίας π. καὶ τοῦ σώματος εἴσω διῃτᾶτο, καὶ τοῖς οὐρανίοις ἐπεβάτευε *ib.*(4.236).

G. hence some confusion between π. (= Christ's divine nature) and π. (= H. Ghost) τὸ π. τὸ ἅγιον τὸ λαλῆσαν μετὰ σοῦ ἐν μορφῇ τῆς ἐκκλησίας· ἐκεῖνο...τὸ π. ὁ υἱὸς τοῦ θεοῦ ἐστιν Herm.*sim.*9.1.1; οὗτος..., ὢν π. θεοῦ καὶ ἀρχὴ καὶ σοφία καὶ δύναμις ὑψίστου, κατήρχετο εἰς τοὺς προφήτας καὶ δι' αὐτῶν ἐλάλει Thphl.Ant.*Autol.*2.10(M.6.1064C); Hipp.*haer.*9.12(p.248.29; M.16.3383C); v. infra IX.E.

IX. τὸ πνεῦμα, ἅγιον πνεῦμα etc., *Holy Ghost;*

A. ref. deity; **1.** associated with Father and Son, *1Clem.*46.6 (where π. is treated somewhat impersonally); Ign.*Eph.*9.1; Just. *1apol.*13.3(M.6.348A); **2.** as distinct Person of Godhead πατέρα θεὸν παντοκράτορα, καὶ Χριστὸν Ἰησοῦν υἱὸν θεοῦ...καὶ π. ἅγιον, καὶ ταῦτ' εἶναι ὄντως τρία Hipp.*Noët.*8(p.249.19, conj. for π. ἁγίου M.10. 816A); πρόσωπα δὲ δύο, ὅτι καὶ ὁ υἱός, τὸ δὲ τρίτον τὸ ἅγιον π. *ib.*14 (p.257.3; 821A); as exercising will and purpose (Jo.3:8, Ac.15:28) he is not an ἐνέργεια θεοῦ but οὐσία ἐνεργετική, Or.*fr.37 in Jo.*(p.513. 17); but cf. ζῶσαν ἐνέργειαν...καὶ δωρεάν Ath.*ep.Serap.*1.20(M.26. 580A); scriptural proofs of distinctness of H. Ghost from Son, Eus. *e.th.*3.5(p.159.34ff.; M.24.1005D); οὔτε τὸ π. λέγειν ἔξεστιν αὐτὸ εἶναι τὸν υἱόν, οὔτε τὸν υἱὸν αὐτὸν εἶναι τὸ π. τὸ ἅγιον Ath.*ep.Serap.*4.7(M.26. 648B); *ib.*4.3(640C); εἴ τις τὸ π. τὸ ἅγιον μέρος λέγοι τοῦ πατρὸς ἢ τοῦ υἱοῦ, ἀ. ἔ. *Symb.Sirm.*1 *anath.*22; Geo.Laod.*ep.dogm.*ap.Epiph.*haer.* 73.16(p.288.24; M.42.433A); τοὺς γάρ τοι πεπιστευκότας ἐνέργειαν εἶναί τινα τοῦ θεοῦ τὸν παράκλητον...λίαν εὐήθεις Eun.*apol.*25(M.30. 861D); π. μεμαθηκότες θεοῦ...οὐ πνοὴν ἄσθματος ἐννοοῦμεν...ἀλλὰ δύναμιν οὐσιώδη αὐτὴν ἐφ' ἑαυτῆς ἐν ἰδιαζούσῃ ὑποστάσει θεωρουμένην Gr.Nyss.*or.catech.*2(p.14.15; M.45.17C); ἐν ὑποστάσει δὲ τελειότητος ...τέλειον τὸ π. τὸ ἅγιον· πατὴρ καὶ υἱὸς καὶ ἅγιον π. Epiph.*anc.* 7(p.14.2; M.43.28B); *ib.*8(p.15.7; 29A); ἐνυπόστατον ἅγιον π. Didym. *Trin.*2.1(M.39.452B); π. ... ἰδιοσύστατον Cyr.*thes.*33(5^1.334E); οὔτε τοῦ π. ἢ εἰς πατέρα μεταπίπτοντος ἢ εἰς υἱόν, ὅτι ἐκπορεύεται, καὶ ὅτι θεός. ἡ γὰρ ἰδιότης ἀκίνητος ‡Cyr.*Trin.*10(6^3.16D; M.77.1144D); Dion.Ar.*d.n.*2.3(M.3.640C); ἐνυπόστατον ἐν ἰδίᾳ ὑποστάσει ὑπάρχον Jo.D.*f.o.*1.8(M.94.821C); heret. identification of H. Ghost with Father and Son by Sabellius, †Leont.B.*sect.*3.3(M.86.1216A); and Marcell., Eus.*e.th.*3.6(p.164.28; M.24.1016A); Thdt.*haer.*2.10(4.336); **3.** ref. coequality with Father and Son; **a.** as subordinate to Father and Son, cf. εἷς γάρ ἐστιν ὁ θεός· ὁ γὰρ κελεύων πατήρ, ὁ δὲ ὑπακούων υἱός, τὸ δὲ συνετίζον ἅγιον π. Hipp.*Noët.*14(p.257.6; M.10. 821A); ὑπερβαλλούσῃ ὑπεροχῇ φαμὲν τὸν σωτῆρα καὶ τὸ π. τὸ ἅγιον, ὑπερεχόμενον τοσοῦτον ἢ καὶ πλέον ὑπὸ τοῦ πατρός, ὅσῳ ὑπερέχει αὐτὸς καὶ τὸ ἅγιον π. τῶν λοιπῶν, οὐ τῶν τυχόντων ὄντων Or.*Jo.*13.25 (p.249.20; M.14.441B); ἡττόνως τὸ π. τὸ ἅγιον ἐπὶ μόνους τοὺς ἁγίους διϊκνούμενον· ὥστε κατὰ τοῦτο μείζων ἡ δύναμις τοῦ πατρὸς παρὰ τὸν υἱὸν καὶ τὸ π. τὸ ἅγιον, πλείων δὲ ἡ τοῦ υἱοῦ παρὰ τὸ π. τὸ ἅγιον, καὶ πάλιν διαφέρουσα μᾶλλον τοῦ ἁγίου π. ἡ δύναμις παρὰ τὰ ἄλλα ἅγια id. *princ.*1.3.5(p.56.6; M.11.150B,C); but cf. *origo et fons filii vel spiritus sancti pater est, et nihil in his anterius posteriusve intellegi potest, ib.* 2.2.1(p.111.30; 186C); *nihil in trinitate majus minusve dicendum est, ib.*1.3.7(p.60.1; 153C); ἀλλότριοι καὶ ἀμέτοχοί εἰσιν ἀλλήλων αἱ οὐσίαι τοῦ πατρὸς καὶ τοῦ υἱοῦ καὶ τοῦ ἁγίου π. Ar.*Thal.fr.*13–15 ap.Ath.*Ar.*1. 6(M.26.24B); τοῦτο μέν [sc. π.], τρίτην ἐπέχον τὴν τάξιν...οὐ...ἀντιλαμβάνει παρ' ἑτέρου του ἢ παρὰ θεοῦ λόγου, τοῦ δὴ καὶ ἀνωτέρω καὶ κρείττονος Eus.*p.e.*7.15(325C; M.21.549C); ὁ σωτὴρ τὸ π. τὸ ἅγιον ἕτερον ὑπάρχειν παρ' ἑαυτὸν ἐδίδαξεν...ὑπερέχον...πάσης τῆς νοερᾶς καὶ λογικῆς...οὐσίας...ὑποβεβηκός γε μὴν εἶναι αὐτοῦ id.*e.th.*3.5(p.162. 28; M.24.1012B); dist. from ἀγέννητος θεός, *Symb.Sirm.*1 *anath.*20; acc. Eust. Seb., H. Ghost is neither θεός nor κτίσμα, Socr.*h.e.*2.45.6 (M.67.360B); inferior in ἀξίωμα and τάξις (as baptismal formula implies) but not (as Eun. held) in φύσις, Bas.*Eun.*3.2(1.273C; M.29. 657C); cf. τρίτον...ἀξιώματι καὶ τάξει...τρίτον...καὶ τῇ φύσει Eun. *apol.*25(M.30.861B); **b.** as creature: discussion whether H. Ghost δι' αὐτοῦ [sc. τοῦ λόγου] ἐγένετο (Jo.1:3) or is ἀγέννητον in sense that he has no ἰδία οὐσία apart from Father and Son; conclusion that there are three hypostases, that none but Father is ἀγέννητος and H. Ghost is πάντων τιμιώτερον, καὶ τάξει πρῶτον πάντων τῶν ὑπὸ τοῦ πατρὸς διὰ Χριστοῦ γεγενημένων Or.*Jo.*2.10(6; p.64.33ff.; M.14. 125Cff.); cf. πατέρα μὲν ἔλεγε [sc. Paul. Sam.] τὸν θεὸν...υἱὸν δὲ τὸν ἄνθρωπον τὸν ψιλόν. π. δέ, τὴν ἐπιφοιτήσασαν χάριν τοῖς ἀποστόλοις †Leont.B.*sect.*3.3(M.86.1216B); full statement of theory that H. Ghost is among things created through Son (Jo.1:3), Eus.*e.th.*3.6 (p.164.5ff.; M.24.1013B); cf. τὸ ἅγιον π. συναναλαβεῖν εἰς τὴν θεολογίαν τῆς τριάδος ἐξέκλινε [sc. Macedonius] Socr.*h.e.*2.45.6(M.67.360A); Soz.*h.e.*4.27.1(M.67.1200B); cf.Eun.*apol.*25(M.30.861D); πρῶτον μὲν πάντων καὶ μεῖζον τὸ π. τὸ ἅγιον ἐποίησεν *ib.*28(868B); **c.** as fully divine; **i.** deity asserted in scripture, Gr.Nyss.*Eun.*2(2 p.373.1ff.; M.45.553Bff.); but ἐκήρυσσε φανερῶς ἡ παλαιὰ τὸν πατέρα, τὸν υἱὸν ἀμυδρότερον. ἐφανέρωσεν ἡ καινὴ τὸν υἱόν, ὑπέδειξε τοῦ π. τὴν θεότητα. ἐμπολιτεύεται νῦν τὸ π., σαφεστέραν ἡμῖν παρέχον τὴν ἑαυτοῦ δήλωσιν Gr.Naz.*or.*31.26(p.178.6ff.; M.36.161C); not fully determined by apostolic preaching, Or.*princ.*1 proem.4(p.11.4; M.11. 117C); **ii.** H. Ghost is uncreated, Ath.*ep.Serap.*1.21(M.26.580C); argument developed at length with scriptural proofs, *ib.*3.5(632B); hence not to be numbered among things created, Bas.*Eun.*3.2(1. 273D; M.29.660A); not subject (like creatures) to change, id.*Spir.*22 (3.19B; M.32.108B); οὐδὲ ἐκεῖνο φοβηθήσομαι τὸ πάντα διὰ τοῦ υἱοῦ γεγονέναι λέγεσθαι, ὡς ἑνὸς τῶν πάντων ὄντος καὶ τοῦ ἁγίου π. πάντα γὰρ ὅσα γέγονεν εἴρηται, οὐχ ἁπλῶς ἅπαντα. ... δείξας οὖν ὅτι γέγονε, τότε τῷ υἱῷ δός, καὶ τοῖς κτίσμασι συναρίθμησον Gr.Naz.*or.*31.12 (p.160.9; M.36.145Dff.); εἰ κτίσμα τὸ π. ... μάτην ἐβαπτίσθης *ib.*37.18 (304A); τὸ δὲ π. τὸ ἅγιον, ὡς ὑπὲρ τὴν φύσιν τῶν γεγονότων, ἐν τῇ ἀπαριθμήσει τῶν ὄντων ὁ Παῦλος ἀπεσιώπησεν, οὔτε τὸ γενέσθαι, οὔτε τὸ ὑποτετάχθαι διὰ τῶν ἑαυτοῦ λόγων ἡμῖν ἐνδειξάμενος Gr.Nyss.*Eun.*2 (2 p.375.11; M.45.556C); π. ἅγιον...ἄκτιστον *Symb.*ap.Epiph.*anc.*119 (p.148.29; M.43.236B); π. ἅγιον ἀεί, οὐ γεννητόν, οὐ κτιστόν, οὐ συνάδελφον οὐ πατράδελφον, οὐ προπάτορον οὐκ ἔκγονον Epiph.*anc.*7(p.14. 19; 29A); Didym.*Trin.*2.2(M.39.464C); Thdr.Mops.*symb.*(p.97.22; M. 66.1016–1020); πῶς οὖν ἐν ποιήμασι τὸ π. τὸ ἅγιον καταριθμηθήσεται, εἴπερ ἐστὶν εἰκὼν...τοῦ υἱοῦ τοῦ θεοῦ; Cyr.*thes.*33(5^1.336D); exeg. Am.4:13, Ath.*ep.Serap.*1.3(M.26.536Aff.); ‡Ath.*disp.*40(M.28.492C); ‡Ath.*dial.Trin.*3.26(M.28.1244A); Bas.*Eun.*3.7(1.278A; M.29.669A); Gr.Nyss.*fid.*(M.45.144C); Didym.*Trin.*3.31(M.39.951A,B,956A); Epiph.*haer.*74.8(p.324.22; M.42.489B); **iii.** equality of adoration accorded to H. Ghost and other Persons of Godhead, cf. π. γὰρ τὸ διὰ ὕλης διῆκον, ἔλαττον ὑπάρχον τοῦ θειοτέρου π. ... οὐ τιμητέον ἐπ' ἴσης τῷ τελείῳ θεῷ Tat.*orat.*4(p.5.10; M.6.813B), but θειοτέρου π. perh. = *God,* cf.Or.*princ.*1.3.2(p.50.10; M.11.147C); π., ὃ καὶ αὐτὸ ἐν τῇ πρώτῃ καὶ βασιλικῇ τῆς τῶν ὅλων ἀρχῆς ἀξίᾳ καὶ τιμῇ καταλέγουσιν Eus.*p.e.*7.15(325B; M.21.549B); ὅπερ σὺν πατρὶ καὶ υἱῷ τῇ τῆς θεότητος δόξῃ τετίμηται Cyr.H.*catech.*4.16; *ib.*16.4; Gr.Naz.*or.*37.24(M. 36.308C); πότε οὖν τοῦ υἱοῦ τὸ π. χωρίζεται, ὥστε τοῦ πατρὸς προσκυνουμένου, μὴ συμπεριλαμβάνεσθαι μετὰ τοῦ υἱοῦ καὶ τοῦ π. προσκύνησιν; Gr.Nyss.*Maced.*24(M.45.1332B); v. συνδοξάζω; **iv.** united with Father and Son in Trin., Athenag.*leg.*12.2(M.6.913B,C); as ἀπόρροια of God, *ib.*10.3(909B); like light from fire, *ib.*24.2(945B); *ὡς γὰρ θεόν φαμεν καὶ υἱὸν τὸν λόγον αὐτοῦ καὶ π. ἅγιον, ἑνούμενα μὲν κατὰ δύναμιν ...τὸν πατέρα, τὸν υἱόν, τὸ π.* *ib.*24.1(945B); sharing divine unity, Clem.*paed.*1.6(p.115.11; M.8.300B); *ἐμφιλοχωρεῖν δὲ τῷ θεῷ καὶ ἐνδιαιτᾶσθαι δεῖ τὸ ἅγιον π.* Dion.R.ap.Ath.*decr.*26(p.22.10; M.25.464A); Ath.*ep.Serap.*1.20(M.26.577A); *τὸ τῇ...τριάδι συναριθμούμενον* Bas.*Eun.*3.2(1.273E; M.29.660A); *ἀχώριστόν ἐστι καὶ ἀδιάστατον παντελῶς πατρὸς καὶ υἱοῦ τὸ ἅγιον π.* id.*Spir.*37(3.30D; M.32.133A); *τὸ π. πατρὶ δὲ καὶ υἱῷ οὐχὶ ἐνεῖναι μᾶλλον, ἀλλὰ συνεῖναι εἰπεῖν εὐσεβέστερον* *ib.*63(53A; M.184B); coexistence illustrated, Gr.Nyss. *diff.ess.*4(M.32.332C); id.*or.dom.*3(p.62.37ff.; M.44.1160B); id.*Maced.* 2(M.45.1304A); in simile of torches kindled from each other, *ib.*6 (1308B); *ὁ πατὴρ καὶ ὁ υἱὸς καὶ τὸ π. ... ἀεὶ μετ' ἀλλήλων ἐν τελείᾳ τῇ τριάδι γνωρίζονται* *ib.*12(1316B); **v.** sharing in operation of Trin. *διὰ γὰρ τῆς τριάδος ταύτης πατὴρ δοξάζεται· πατὴρ γὰρ ἠθέλησεν, υἱὸς ἐποίησεν, π. ἐφανέρωσεν* Hipp.*Noët.*14(p.257.18; M.10.821C); *ὁ γὰρ πατὴρ διὰ τοῦ λόγου ἐν π. ἁγίῳ τὰ πάντα ποιεῖ* Ath.*ep.Serap.*1.28(M.26.596A); *ἡ τοῦ ἁγίου π. ἐνέργεια συντεταγμένη ἐστὶ τῇ πατρὸς καὶ υἱοῦ ἐνεργείᾳ* Bas.*Eun.*3.4(1.275E; M.29.664B); *τὰ αὐτὰ εἰς τὸ π. τὸ ἅγιον καὶ εἰς θεόν ἐστιν τὰ ἁμαρτήματα. καὶ οὕτω δ' ἂν τὸ συναφὲς καὶ ἀδιαίρετον κατὰ πᾶσαν ἐνέργειαν, ἀπὸ πατρὸς καὶ υἱοῦ, τοῦ π. διδαχθείης* id.*Spir.*37(3.31A; M.32.133B); *ib.*38(31E,32A; M.136B,C); *μίαν εἶναι θεότητα, ἐμπεριέχουσαν δι' υἱοῦ ἐν π. ἁγίῳ τὰ πάντα* Geo. Laod.*ep.dogm.*ap.Epiph.*haer.*73.16(p.289.1; M.42.433A); *πᾶσα ἐνέργεια ἡ θεόθεν ἐπὶ τὴν κτίσιν διήκουσα,...ἐκ πατρὸς ἀφορμᾶται καὶ διὰ τοῦ υἱοῦ πρόεισι, καὶ ἐν τῷ π. ... τελειοῦται...ἡ αὐτὴ ζωὴ καὶ παρὰ τοῦ πατρὸς ἐνεργεῖται καὶ παρὰ τοῦ υἱοῦ ἑτοιμάζεται, καὶ τῆς τοῦ π. ἐξῆπται βουλήσεως* Gr.Nyss.*tres dii*(M.45.125C,D); *συνεργεῖ...τῷ πατρὶ ὁ υἱὸς καὶ τὸ π.* Epiph.*anc.*70(p.87.8; M.43.145B); as *σύνδεσμος τῆς τριάδος* *ib.*7(p.13.20; 28B); **vi.** fully and substantially God, cf. *τοῦ θεοῦ ἑνὸς ὄντος ἴδιον καὶ ὁμοούσιόν ἐστι* Ath.*ep.Serap.*1.27(M.26.593C); *ἐν πατρὶ καὶ ἐν υἱῷ καὶ ἐν αὐτῷ τῷ π. μία θεότης ἐστὶ* *ib.*4.3 (641B); not by participation, Bas.*Eun.*3.5(1.276E; M.29.665C); Jo. 4:24 interpreted to mean H. Ghost is God, id.*Spir.*22(3.19B; M.32.108B); as *θεός* and *ὁμοούσιον*: not nullifying personal distn. bet. Son and H. Ghost as generated and proceeding, Gr.Naz.*or.*31.10 (p.156.11ff.; M.36.144A,B); doctrine of H. Ghost's divinity as starting point for theology of Trinity, *ib.*31.3(p.147.12; 136B); *π. ἅγιον ...ἐκ τῆς οὐσίας τοῦ θεοῦ ὑπάρχον* Apoll.*fid.sec.pt.*27(p.176.22; M.10.1116B); *ὁμογενές* with Son, Gr.Nyss.*Eun.*2(2 p.379.13; M.45.560D); *εἰ δὲ μὴ κτίσμα, ὁμοούσιόν ἐστι τῷ θεῷ* Evagr.Pont.*ep.*10(M.32.261C); Didym.*Trin.*2.3(M.39.477B); Susanna 45 THDN interpreted as showing him to be God, *ib.*2.11(653A) but cf. Ath.*ep.Serap.*1.5(M.26.541A); *παναρκὴς θεός* Didym.*Trin.*3.46(804B); *ἐκ τῆς αὐτῆς οὐσίας πατρὸς καὶ υἱοῦ π. ἅγιον. π. γὰρ ὁ θεός* Epiph.*anc.*7(p.14.19; M.43.29A); *τῆς αὐτῆς οὐσίας, τῆς αὐτῆς θεότητος, π. θεῖον* *ib.*8(p.15.6; 29B); proof of deity given in baptismal formula, *ib.*(p.15.16; 32A); *φυσικῶς ἐν θεῷ* Cyr.*thes.*33(5[1].334A); id.*Jo.*12.1(4.1098B); Thdot.Anc. *exp.symb.*24(M.77.1348B,C); Dion.Ar.*d.n.*2.1(M.3.637C); *φύσει κατ' οὐσίαν ὑπάρχει τοῦ θεοῦ καὶ πατρός, οὕτως καὶ τοῦ υἱοῦ φύσει κατ' οὐσίαν ἐστίν* Max.*qu.Thal.*63(M.90.672C); Jo.D.*f.o.*1.13(M.94.856B); **vii.** relation to Father and Son implied in formulae and doxologies *θεὸς...ὁ ἐπὶ πάντων καὶ διὰ πάντων καὶ ἐν πᾶσιν· ἐπὶ πάντων μὲν ὡς πατήρ, ὡς ἀρχὴ καὶ πηγή· διὰ πάντων δὲ διὰ τοῦ λόγου· ἐν πᾶσι δὲ ἐν τῷ π. τῷ ἁγίῳ* Ath.*ep.Serap.*1.28(M.26.596A); *σὺν ἁγίῳ π., δι' ἑνὸς υἱοῦ, ἕνα θεὸν καταγγέλλομεν* Cyr.H.*catech.*16.4; v. *διά, ἐν, μετά, σύν*; ref. 2Cor.13:13, Cyr.*thes.*34(5[1].358E); **viii.** analogies and metaphors of relationship of H. Ghost to Godhead *τρίτον περὶ τὰ τρίτα οὐκ ἄλλως ἔγωγε ἐξακούω ἢ...τρίτον...εἶναι τὸ ἅγιον π.* Clem.*str.*5.14(p.395.16; M.9.156B); moon in rel. to sun of righteousness, Eus.*p.e.*7.15 (325B; M.21.549B); compared with human *π.*, Ath.*ep.Serap.*1.22 (M.26.581C); as *ψυχή* of Godhead, Eulog.Al.*fr.Trin.*2.5(p.365); as *βλαστός* and *ἄνθος* of Godhead, Dion.Ar.*d.n.*2.7(M.3.645B); as light from light, Athenag.*leg.*24.2(M.6.945B); Gr.Nyss.*Maced.*2(M.45.1304A); Jo.D.*f.o.*1.8(M.94.833A); **4.** procession of H. Ghost, v. *ἐκπορεύω, ἐκπόρευσις, ἐκπορευτικός*; cf. *in eo fonte, de quo natus est filius, vel procedit spiritus sanctus*, Or.*princ.*1.2.13(p.48.4; M.11.144C); *filium generat pater et sanctum spiritum profert*, *ib.*2.2.1(p.111.29; 186C); *ἅγιον π. προσέθηκα· ἀλλ' ἅμα καὶ πόθεν καὶ διὰ τίνος ἧκεν ἐφήρμοσα* Dion.Al.ap.Ath.*Dion.*17(p.58.18; M.25.504C); Eus.*e.th.*3.5 (p.161.21; M.24.1009B); †Ath.*exp.fid.*4(M.25.208A) cit. s. *ἀεί*; of God, but not by filiation, id.*ep.Serap.*1.25(M.26.588C); heret. *προστάγματι τοῦ πατρός, ἐνεργείᾳ δὲ τοῦ υἱοῦ γενόμενον* Eun.*apol.*25(M.30.861D); *ib.*28(868B); Gr.Naz.*or.*20.11(M.35.1077C), *ib.*30.19(p.138.11; M.36.128C) citt. s. *πρόειμι* (*ibo*); *ib.*39.12(348B) cit. s. *ἐκπορευτῶς*; *ἐκ τοῦ θεοῦ ἐστι, καὶ τοῦ Χριστοῦ ἐστι* Gr.Nyss.*Maced.*2(M.45.1304A); *Symb. Nic.–CP*(p.80.12; H.2.288B); Diod.*Rom.*8:11(p.92.4); Cyr.*Jo.*9.1(4.824B) cit. s. *πρόειμι* (*ibo*); *ἐν δὲ τῷ υἱῷ φυσικῶς τε καὶ οὐσιωδῶς διῆκον παρὰ πατρὸς τὸ π.* id.*thes.*34(5[1].340A); typified by formation of Eve acc. Meth., ‡Gr.Nyss.*imag.*(M.44.1329D); double procession (Latin doctrine) interpreted as meaning *οὐκ αἰτίαν τὸν υἱὸν...τοῦ π. ... μίαν γὰρ ἴσασιν υἱοῦ καὶ π. τὸν πατέρα αἰτίαν· τοῦ μὲν κατὰ τὴν γέννησιν· τοῦ δέ, κατὰ τὴν ἐκπόρευσιν· ἀλλ' ἵνα τὸ δι' αὐτοῦ προϊέναι δηλώσωσι* Max.*opusc.*(M.91.136A); denied *ἐκ τοῦ υἱοῦ δὲ τὸ π. οὐ λέγομεν* Jo.D.*f.o.*1.8(M.94.832B).

B. attributes; **1.** lists of attributes, Bas.*Spir.*22(3.19Bff.; M.32.108ff.); Gr.Nyss.*Maced.*10(M.45.1313B); Epiph.*anc.*70(p.87.22; M.43.148A); Didym.*Trin.*2.1(M.39.452C); Jo.D.*f.o.*1.8(M.94.821B); **2.** unity, *1Clem.*46.6; Clem.*paed.*1.6(p.115.11; M.8.300B); id.*str.*5.6 (p.352.12; M.9.65A); Ath.*ep.Serap.*1.20(M.26.580A); *ἕν ἐστι τοῦτο τὸ ...π., ἀδιαίρετον, πολυδύναμον* Cyr.H.*catech.*4.16; ‡Cyr.*Trin.*10(6[3].16D; M.77.1144D); **3.** unchanging continuance, Ath.*ep.Serap.*1.27 (M.26.593A); **4.** sharing other attributes of God *ἄτρεπτον καὶ ἀναλλοίωτον* *ib.*1.26(589C); Cyr.*ador.*1(1.9E); *μεθεκτόν ἐστι καὶ οὐ μετέχον* Ath.*ep.Serap.*1.27(593A); *φύσει ἅγιον* Bas.*Eun.*3.2(1.274C; M.29.660C); *φύσει ἀγαθόν* *ib.*(1.273E; M.660A); as *δόξα*, Didym.*Trin.*2.1(M.39.452C); as incorporeal, Bas.*Spir.*22(3.19B; M.32.108A); Anast.S. *hod.*2(M.89.56B) cit. s. I supra; **5.** lordship *κύριον καὶ ἡγεμονικόν... π.* Clem.*str.*6.17(p.512.4; M.9.388B); *κύριον καὶ ζωοποιόν* *Symb.*ap. Epiph.*anc.*118(p.147.12; M.43.232D); *Symb.Nic.–CP*(p.80.12; H.2.288B); *αὐτοκύριος* Jo.D.*f.o.*1.13(M.94.856B); **6.** as life-giver (creative and redemptive) *προσλαβόμενος* [sc. Adam recapitulated in Christ] *τὸ ζωοποιοῦν π., εὑρήσει τὴν ζωήν* Iren.*haer.*5.12.2(M.7.1153B); *π. ζωοποιὸν λέγεται· ὁ ἐγείρας γάρ, φησίν, Ἰησοῦν...ζωοποιήσει καὶ τὰ θνητὰ ὑμῶν σώματα* Ath.*ep.Serap.*1.23(M.26.584B); Bas.*Eun.*3.4(1.276B; M.29.665A); *τὸ ζωοποιοῦν τὰ πάντα* Gr.Nyss.*Eun.*2(2 p.376.31; M.45.557C); *Symb.*ap.Epiph.*anc.*118 cit. s. 5 supra; *Symb.Nic.–CP* (p.80.12; H.2.288B); Didym.*Trin.*2.1(M.39.452B); **7.** as power of Father, Jo.D.*f.o.*1.11(M.94.849A); **8.** as image of God, Eus.*e.th.*3.5 (p.163.10; M.24.1012C); as image of Son, Gr.Thaum.*symb.*(p.3.8; M.10.985A); Ath.*ep.Serap.*1.24(M.26.588B); *εἰκὼν μὲν θεοῦ Χριστός, ...εἰκὼν δὲ υἱοῦ τὸ π.* Didym.(‡Bas.)*Eun.*5(1.302A; M.29.724C); *ὁμοίωσις...φυσικὴ τοῦ υἱοῦ τὸ π. ἐστι* Cyr.*dial.Trin.*7(5[1].639B); *εἰκὼν ...τοῦ υἱοῦ τὸ π., δι' οὗ ὁ Χριστὸς ἐνοικῶν ἀνθρώπῳ δίδωσιν αὐτῷ τὸ κατ' εἰκόνα* Jo.D.*f.o.*1.13(M.94.856B); **9.** perfection, Bas.*Eun.*3.5(1.276D; M.29.665B); Gr.Nyss.*Eun.*2(2 p.378.10; M.45.560B); **10.** derivation of *π.* from *πᾶν νεῦμα*: *δι' αὐτὸ ὡς νεῦμα ὀξέως παντὶ νεῦον καὶ κινούμενον* Anast.S.*hod.*2(M.89.56B).

C. credal *πιστεύομεν...καὶ εἰς τὸ ἅγιον π.* *Symb.Nic.*(325)(p.45.1; M.20.1540C); *Symb.Ant.*(341)1(p.249.6; M.26.721A); *τὸ π. τὸ ἅγιον τὸ εἰς παράκλησιν καὶ ἁγιασμὸν καὶ τελείωσιν τοῖς πιστεύουσι διδόμενον* *ib.*2(p.249.26; 724A); *τὸν παράκλητον, τὸ π. τῆς ἀληθείας* *ib.*3(p.250.17; 725A); *ib.*4(p.251.12; 725C); *Symb.Ant.*(345)1(p.252.1; M.26.728C); *Symb.Sirm.*1(p.254.28; M.26.736B); *ὁ δὲ παράκλητος τὸ π. τὸ ἅγιον δι' υἱοῦ ἀποσταλὲν ἦλθε κατὰ τὴν ἐπαγγελίαν* *Symb.Sirm.*2 (p.257.26; 744A); *εἰς ἓν ἅγιον π., τὸν παράκλητον, τὸ λαλῆσαν ἐν τοῖς προφήταις* *Symb.Hier.*(M.33.533B); *τὸ π. τὸ ἅγιον, τὸ κύριον καὶ ζωοποιόν, τὸ ἐκ τοῦ πατρὸς ἐκπορευόμενον, τὸ σὺν πατρὶ καὶ υἱῷ συμπροσκυνούμενον καὶ συνδοξαζόμενον, τὸ λαλῆσαν διὰ τῶν προφητῶν* *Symb.*ap.Epiph.*anc.*118(p.147.11; M.43.232D); *Symb.Nic.–CP*(p.80.12; H.2.288B).

D. in OT teaching *οἱ πάντες Ἑβραίων θεολόγοι, μετὰ τὸν ἐπὶ πάντων θεόν, καὶ μετὰ τὴν πρωτότοκον αὐτοῦ σοφίαν, τὴν τρίτην καὶ ἁγίαν δύναμιν, ἅγιον π. προσειπόντες, ἀποθειάζουσιν, ὑφ' οὗ καὶ ἐφωτίζοντο θεοφορούμενοι* Eus.*p.e.*7.15(326A; M.21.552A); *ἡ παλαιὰ... π. ἅγιον ἐν ἰδίῳ προσώπῳ καὶ ὑποστάσει ἰδίᾳ, κεχωρισμένως τοῦ θεοῦ οὐκ ἠπίστατο· π. δὲ ἅγιον ἐκάλει, ἤτοι π. θεοῦ, τὴν χάριν αὐτοῦ, ἢ τὴν ἐπιστασίαν...ἢ τὴν περί τι διάθεσιν* Thdr.Mops.*Ag.*2:1–5(M.66.485A).

E. H. Ghost in rel. to Son; **1.** identified with Wisdom *ὁ θεὸς διὰ τοῦ λόγου αὐτοῦ καὶ τῆς σοφίας ἐποίησε τὰ πάντα. τῷ γὰρ λόγῳ αὐτοῦ ἐστερεώθησαν οἱ οὐρανοὶ καὶ τῷ π. αὐτοῦ πᾶσα ἡ δύναμις αὐτῶν* Thphl. Ant.*Autol.*1.7(M.6.1036A); cf. *sapientia quae est spiritus*, Iren.*haer.*4.20.3(M.7.1033C); **2.** identified with Logos and Wisdom, Thphl. Ant.*Autol.*2.10(M.6.1064C); Ar.*Thal.fr.*2.25 ap.Ath.*syn.*15(p.243.6; M.26.708B); **3.** not among things created through Logos (Jo.1:3), v. supra A.3.b; **4.** to be subordinated to Son at parousia, Eun. *apol.*27(M.30.865A); **5.** operations point to, and depend upon, Son, Clem.*prot.*1(p.6.14; M.8.60A); *πᾶσαι δὲ αἱ δυνάμεις τοῦ π. ... συντελοῦσιν εἰς τὸ αὐτό, τὸν υἱόν* id.*str.*4.25(p.317.24; M.8.1365A); *ἔνθα ὁ λόγος, ἐκεῖ καὶ τὸ π.* Ath.*ep.Serap.*3.5(M.26.632B); *ἡ αὐτὴ δὲ ἡ διακονία τοῦ π. καὶ τοῦ λόγου* Epiph.*anc.*69(p.87.2; M.43.145B); *λαλεῖ ἐν ἁγίοις Χριστός, λαλεῖ τὸ π. ... ἰᾶται Χριστός, ἰᾶται τὸ π. ... ἁγιάζει*

Χριστός, ἁγιάζει τὸ π. *ib.*68(p.83.2; 140C); sharing ἐνέργεια of Son, Bas.*Eun.*3.4(1.275A,B; M.29.660B,C); Gr.Nyss.*Eun.*2(2 p.381.23; M. 45.564A); Cyr.*thes.*34(5^{1}.344C); **6.** related to Son in φύσις and τάξις as Son to Father, Ath.*ep.Serap.*1.21(M.26.580B); **7.** image of Christ, v. supra B.8; **8.** sharing Son's attributes, Ath.*ep.Serap.*1.25(M.26. 589A); **9.** possessing identity of will with Son, Gr.Nyss.*Eun.*2(2 p.382.12; M.45.564C); Cyr.*thes.*34(5^{1}.344C); **10.** mutual relationship of Son and H. Ghost, ref. Rom.8:9–10 *Χριστὸν δὲ πάλιν εὐθὺς τὸ π. καλεῖ λέγων 'εἰ δὲ Χριστὸς ἐν ὑμῖν', οὐκ ἀλλότριον αὐτὸ δεικνύων τῆς τοῦ λόγου φύσεως. ἀλλ' οὕτως ἡνωμένον, εἰ καὶ ἔστιν ἰδιοσύστατον, ὡς αὐτό τε ὑπάρχειν ἐν υἱῷ, καὶ υἱὸν ἐν αὐτῷ διὰ τὴν τῆς οὐσίας ταυτότητα* Cyr.*thes.*33(5^{1}.334E); *φῶς τὸ ὁμοούσιον τοῦ θεοῦ καὶ πατρός, φῶς τὸ ἐν τῷ π. καὶ ἐν ᾧ ὁ πατήρ· Χριστὸς ἀληθινὸς ἡμῶν θεός* ‡Meth.*Sym.et Ann.*13(M.18.380A); **11.** as Spirit of Christ *τὸ π. τοῦ σωτῆρος* Clem. *q.d.s.*5(p.163.30; M.9.609D); Ath.*Ar.*1.48(M.26.112B); *σοῦ γάρ ἐστι καὶ τὸ π. ib.*1.49(113B); *ἴδιον εἶναι τοῦ υἱοῦ, καὶ οὐ ξένον τοῦ θεοῦ* id. *ep.Serap.*1.25(M.26.588C); *ἐστὶ τὸ π. ἀδιαίρετον πρὸς τὸν υἱόν ib.*3.5 (632C); *υἱός, δι' οὗ τὰ πάντα, ᾧ πάντοτε τὸ π. τὸ ἅγιον ἀχωρίστως συνεπινοεῖται* Gr.Nyss.*diff.ess.*4(M.32.329C); *ἀδιαίρετον γὰρ τοῦ υἱοῦ τὸ π. αὐτοῦ* Cyr.*Jo.*4.3(4.378B); equally Spirit of God and Spirit of Christ, id.*thes.*33(5^{1}.334D); as *ἴδιον φυσικῶς* of Christ, id.*Jo.*10.2(4. 910B); *ἴδιον...τὸ π. τοῦ υἱοῦ, εἰ μὲν ὡς ὁμοφυὲς καὶ ἐκ πατρὸς ἐκπορευόμενον ἔφη* Thdt.ap.Cyr.*apol.Thdt.*9(p.134.9; 6^{1}.228C); being in Christ as human spirit is in man, Cyr.*Jo.*2.1(4.125E); Logos has Spirit as human word requires breath (π.) but human π. is *ἀλλότριον* from *οὐσία* of man, Jo.D.*f.o.*1.7(M.94.804C); as *νοῦς Χριστοῦ*, Cyr.*thes.*34 (5^{1}.344C); but not to be identified with Son, despite apparent arguments to contrary, Ath.*ep.Serap.*4.3(M.26.640Cff.); as 'rib' of Christ from which souls wedded to him are formed, Meth.*symp.*3.8 (p.36.16; M.18.73C); **12.** H. Ghost's knowledge of Father not mediated through Son, Or.*princ.*1.3.4(p.54.4; M.11.149B); **13.** ref. Inc.; **a.** Son alone incarnate, but Father and H. Ghost share in Inc. *κατὰ τὴν ἀγαθοπρεπῆ καὶ φιλάνθρωπον βούλησιν* Dion.Ar.*d.n.*2.6 (M.3.644C); **b.** passages suggesting incarnation of H. Ghost, Herm. *sim.*9.1.1, Thphl.Ant.*Autol.*2.10(M.6.1064C), citt. s. VIII.G supra; Hipp.*haer.*9.12(p.248.29; M.16.3383C); cf.id.*Noët.*4(p.243.4; M.10. 809B); *τὸ ἐνεργῆσαν ἐν τοῖς προφήταις π. ἦν ὁ Χριστός, ὃς καὶ ἐνανθρωπήσας φησίν· αὐτὸς ὁ λαλῶν πάρειμι, αὐτὸς ὢν π. καὶ κύριος καὶ Χριστός* Or.*fr.116 in Lam.*(p.276.18; M.13.657D); but v. VIII.F, G supra; Apollinarian *τοῦτον* [sc. second Adam]...*ἐξ οὐρανοῦ διὰ τοῦτο καλεῖσθαι, διότι τὸ π. τὸ οὐράνιον ἐσαρκώθη* Gr.Nyss.*Apoll.*12 (M.45.1145C); **c.** in rel. to Christ's birth *Χριστὸς ἐκυοφορήθη ὑπὸ Μαρίας κατ' οἰκονομίαν θεοῦ, ἐκ σπέρματος μὲν Δαυείδ, πνεύματος δὲ ἁγίου* Ign.*Eph.*18.2; cf. *ex spiritu sancto et virgine natus*, Hipp. *trad.ap.*4.6; *μυστήριον οἰκονομίας ἦν αὐτὸς ὁ λόγος, ἐκ π. ἁγίου καὶ παρθένου. ... ὁ ἐκ π. καὶ παρθένου τέλειος υἱὸς θεοῦ ἀποδεδειγμένος* id. *Noët.*4(p.241.27,p.243.4; M.10.809A,B); cf. *corpus...natum ex virgine et spiritu sancto*, Or.*princ.*1 proem.4(p.10.10; M.11.117B); *τὸν γεννηθέντα ἐκ π. ἁγίου καὶ Μαρίας τῆς παρθένου* Marcell.*ep.*ap.Epiph. *haer.*72.3(p.258.8; M.42.385D); *τὸ π. τὸ ἅγιον...τὸ ἐλθὸν ἐπὶ τὴν... Μαρίαν* Cyr.H.*catech.*17.6; *πῶς γὰρ ὁ καθ' ὑμᾶς οὐκ ἐξ 'Ιωσήφ, ἀλλ' ἐξ ἁγίου π. γεγονώς*; Juln.Imp.ap.Cyr.*Juln.*8(6^{2}.253E); not divine nature but human was formed by H. Ghost, Thdt.ap.Cyr.*apol. Thdt.*9(p.134.7; 6^{1}.228B); but π. and *δύναμις* which overshadowed BMV identified with Logos, Just.*1apol.*33.6(M.6.381B,C); **d.** in Christ's baptism: H. Ghost revealed Christ, Cyr.H.*catech.*16.3; Christ as man received his own Spirit, Cyr.*Joel.*2(3.228B); *ἔχων οὐσιωδῶς ἐν ἑαυτῷ τὸ ἴδιον π., λαμβάνειν ὡς ἄνθρωπος λέγεται* id.*Jo.*2.1 (4.125D); rested on Christ, but not on Adam, Moses, or prophets, cf. Or.*hom.3.1 in Is.*(p.254.19ff.; M.13.228D); Cyr.*Is.*2.1(2.193E–194A); id.*Joel.*2(3.228B); Proc.G.*Is.*11:2(M.87.2041B); Valent. *ἀπέθανεν δὲ* [sc. *Χριστός*] *ἀποστάντος τοῦ καταβάντος ἐπ' αὐτῷ ἐπὶ τῷ 'Ιορδάνῃ π., οὐκ ἰδίᾳ γενομένου, ἀλλὰ συσταλέντος* Clem.*exc.Thdot.*61(p.127.16; M.9.688C); Adoptionist *κατελθὸν ἀνεδείχθη ἐν αὐτῷ τὸ π., ὃ εἶναι τὸν Χριστὸν προσαγορεύει* Hipp.*haer.*7.35(p.222.11; M.16.3343A); cf. *τῷ ἁγίῳ π. χρισθεὶς προσηγορεύθη Χριστός* ‡Paul.Sam.*fr.*1(p.339.1); **e.** in rel. to whole incarnate life *τὰ περὶ τὴν ἔνσαρκον τοῦ κυρίου παρουσίαν οἰκονομηθέντα, διὰ τοῦ π.* Bas.*Spir.*39(3.33D; M.32.140C); *ἐνεργῆσαι...ὡς δι' ἰδίου π. τὰς θεοσημίας* Cyr.*Nest.*4.1(p.78.4; 6^{1}.99A); Christ's works performed *εὐδοκίᾳ τοῦ...πατρὸς ἐν π. ἁγίῳ* Dion.Ar. *e.h.*3.3.12(M.3.441C); **14.** H. Ghost as sent or mediated by Christ, cf. *donum spiritus...ministratur per filium et inoperatur per deum patrem*, Or.*princ.*1.3.7(p.60.19; M.11.154B); purpose of Ascension being to receive again Spirit yielded up at death, id.*dial.*7(p.138. 6ff.); *ib.*8(p.138.15,p.140.4); *π. ἅγιον...διὰ υἱοῦ πεφηνὸς...τοῖς ἀνθρώποις* Gr.Thaum.*symb.*(p.3.7; M.10.985A); *ὁ μὲν παρέχων ἦν ὁ σωτήρ, τὸ δὲ διδόμενον τὸ ἅγιον π.* Eus.*e.th.*3.5(p.160.15; M.24.1008B); given *ἐκ μέρους* in 'insufflation' (Jo.20:27) for remission of sins, and in fuller measure for more perfect power after Ascension, *ib.*(p.162. 3ff.; 1009C); given through Christ to saints, *ib.*3.6(p.163.30; 1013B); *πρὸ τῆς ἐνανθρωπήσεως λόγος ὢν ἐχορήγει τοῖς ἁγίοις ὡς ἴδιον τὸ π. οὕτως καὶ ἄνθρωπος γενόμενος, ἁγιάζει τοὺς πάντας τῷ π.* Ath.*Ar.*1.48 (M.26.112B); given through Christ to faithful, *ib.*3.25(376A); id.*ep. Serap.*1.20(M.26.580A); *Symb.Ant.*(345)1(p.252.1; M.26.728C); *Symb. Sirm.*1(p.254.28; M.26.736B); *Symb.Sirm.*2(p.257.26; 744A); *Symb. Sirm.*3(p.236.6; 693B); *Symb.Nic.*(359)ap.Thdt.*h.e.*2.21.6(3.880); *Symb.Sel.*(359)(p.258.14; M.26.745B); *Symb.CP*(360)(p.259.10; M. 26.748B); 'sending' and 'coming' discussed, Gr.Naz.*or.*31.26(p.179.9; M.36.164A); Gr.Nyss.*diff.ess.*4(M.32.329C); *ἐστι χορηγὸς καὶ δοτήρ* [sc. *Χριστός*] Cyr.*Jo.*12.1(4.1098B); given through Christ, as its head, to Church, Max.*qu.Thal.*63(M.90.672B); hence through H. Ghost faithful partake of Christ, Ath.*ep.Serap.*1.27(593B); and have knowledge of him, Gr.Nyss.*diff.ess.*4(329C); **15.** images of Christ and H. Ghost: two seraphim of Is.6:3, and two animals of Abac. 3:3, Or.*princ.*1.3.4(p.53.2; M.11.148C); view refuted, Antip.Bost. *fr.*ap.Jo.D.*parall.*(M.96.505B); sun and moon, Eus.*p.e.*7.16(328B; M.21.553C); cf.*ib.*7.15(327B; M.552D).

F. work of H. Ghost in Creation and ordering of universe; **1.** in rel. to other Persons of Trin., esp. Logos *ὁ γὰρ πατὴρ διὰ τοῦ λόγου ἐν τῷ π. κτίζει τὰ πάντα, ἐπεὶ ἔνθα ὁ λόγος, ἐκεῖ καὶ τὸ π. καὶ τὰ διὰ τοῦ λόγου κτιζόμενα ἔχει ἐκ τοῦ π. παρὰ τοῦ λόγου τὴν τοῦ εἶναι ἰσχύν* Ath.*ep.Serap.*3.5(M.26.632B,C); *ἐν δὲ τῇ τούτων κτίσει ἐννόησόν μοι τὴν προκαταρκτικὴν αἰτίαν τῶν γινομένων, τὸν πατέρα, τὴν δημιουργικήν, τὸν υἱόν, τὴν τελειωτικήν, τὸ π.· ὥστε βουλήματι μὲν τοῦ πατρὸς τὰ λειτουργικὰ πνεύματα ὑπάρχειν, ἐνεργείᾳ δὲ υἱοῦ εἰς τὸ εἶναι παράγεσθαι, παρουσίᾳ δὲ τοῦ π. τελειοῦσθαι* Bas.*Spir.*38(3.31D; M. 32.136B); *τὸν προστάσσοντα κύριον, τὸν δημιουργοῦντα λόγον, τὸ στερεοῦν τὸ π. ib.*(32B; M.136C); *πνεῦμα γὰρ τῷ ζῶντι λόγῳ συντεταγμένον εἰς τὸ δημιουργεῖν, ζῶσα δύναμις, καὶ θεία φύσις, ἄρρητος ἐξ ἀρρήτου στόματος πεφυκυῖα* Didym.(‡Bas.)*Eun.*5(1.303E; M.29. 728D); *τὰ δὲ τῆς ἐνεργείας ἔργα καὶ ποιήματα, δι' υἱοῦ ἐν π. γεγονότα καὶ οὕτως ἐκ θεοῦ νοούμενα* Cyr.*thes.*33(5^{1}.333D); hence relation of creatures to God is altogether different from that of H. Ghost, *ib.*; in simile of musician with instrument *ὁ...λόγος...κόσμον...τόνδε καὶ δὴ καὶ τὸν σμικρὸν κόσμον, τὸν ἄνθρωπον...ἁγίῳ π. ἁρμοσάμενος, ψάλλει τῷ θεῷ* Clem.*prot.*1(p.6.14; M.8.60A); **2.** function in Creation; **a.** holding universe together (cf. Stoic theories of π.), Athenag.*leg.* 6.3(M.6.901C); **b.** strengthening, stabilizing, and perfecting, Bas. *Spir.*38(3.31D; M.32.136B); *πᾶσα γὰρ ἡ τελειότης τοῖς πεποιημένοις διὰ τοῦ π.* Cyr.*thes.*34(5^{1}.344E); id.*dial.Trin.*7(5^{1}.652D); **c.** generative activity in Creation (Gen.1:2) compared with regenerative activity in water of baptism, Clem.*ecl.*7(p.138.27; M.9.701A); **3.** universally diffused in living things, cf. *sine dubio enim omnis qui calcat terram, id est terrena et corporalia, particeps est spiritus sancti, a deo eum accipiens*, Or.*princ.*1.3.4(p.52.16; M.11.148C); but cf. *quod omnes homines non sunt extra communionem dei, hoc modo evangelium docet ...*[Lc.17:20–21] *sed et illud videndum est ne forte eadem significet quod in Genesi scriptum est, cum ait 'et insufflavit in faciem ejus spiramentum vitae...' quod si generaliter in omnes homines datum esse intelligitur, omnes homines habent participium dei; si vero hoc de spiritu dei dictum intellegendum est, quoniam et Adam prophetasse de nonnullis invenitur, ergo jam non generaliter, sed sanctis quibusque datum accipi potest, ib.*1.3.6–7(p.57.25ff.; 152A,B); **4.** inbreathed Spirit (Gen.2:7) is H. Ghost and is cause of man being made in image of God, Didym.(‡Bas.)*Eun.*5(1.303E; M.29.729A); Cyr.*thes.*34(5^{1}.344E); id.*ador.*1(1.9D).

G. work in rel. to men; **1.** in gen. *ἔρχεται γὰρ σῶσαι, καὶ ἰάσασθαι, διδάξαι, νουθετῆσαι, ἐνισχῦσαι, παρακαλέσαι, φωτίσαι τὴν διάνοιαν, πρώτου αὐτοῦ τοῦ δεχομένου, εἶτα δι' αὐτοῦ καὶ τῶν ἄλλων* Cyr.H. *catech.*16.16; *ἁγιασμοῦ γένεσις, φῶς νοητόν, πάσῃ δυνάμει λογικῇ πρὸς τὴν τῆς ἀληθείας εὕρεσιν οἷόν τινα καταφάνειαν δι' ἑαυτοῦ παρεχόμενον, ἀπρόσιτον τῇ φύσει, χωρητὸν δι' ἀγαθότητα, πάντα μὲν πληροῦν τῇ δυνάμει, μόνοις δὲ ὂν μεθεκτὸν τοῖς ἀξίοις, οὐχ ἑνὶ μέτρῳ μετεχόμενον, ἀλλὰ κατ' ἀναλογίαν τῆς πίστεως διαιροῦν τὴν ἐνέργειαν. ἁπλοῦν τῇ οὐσίᾳ, ποικίλον ταῖς δυνάμεσιν, ὅλον ἑκάστῳ παρὸν καὶ ὅλον ἁπανταχοῦ ὄν, ἀπαθῶς μεριζόμενον καὶ ὁλοσχερῶς μετεχόμενον, κατὰ τὴν εἰκόνα τῆς ἡλιακῆς ἀκτῖνος, ἧς ἡ χάρις τῷ ἀπολαύοντι ὡς μόνῳ παροῦσα καὶ γῆν ἐπιλάμπει καὶ θάλασσαν καὶ τῷ ἀέρι ἐγκέκραται, οὕτω δὴ καὶ τὸ π. ἑκάστῳ τῶν δεκτικῶν, ὡς μόνῳ παρόν, διαρκῆ τοῖς πᾶσι τὴν χάριν ὁλόκληρον ἐπαφίησιν, οὗ ἀπολαύει τὰ μετέχοντα, ὅσον αὐτὰ πέφυκεν, οὐχ ὅσον ἐκεῖνο δύναται* Bas.*Spir.*22(3.19D; M.32.108C); *τὸ ἁγιαστικὸν καὶ ζωοποιόν, καὶ φωτὸς οὐρανίου μεταδοτικόν· τὸ φρουρητικὸν* ἑκάστων τῆς ἐν ταυτότητι διαμονῆς· τὸ προφήταις καὶ ἀποστόλοις ἐνηχῆσαν καὶ μάρτυρας ἀντιστῆναι...ἐνισχύσαν· τὸ ἀνακαινίζον καὶ ἐλευθεροῦν ὡς κύριος, καὶ υἱοὺς θεοῦ ἡμᾶς ποιοῦν ὡς π. υἱοθεσίας· τὸ ἀπελαῦνον τῷ φωτίσματι δαιμόνων στίφη...τὸ ἀναπετάζον ἡμῖν τὰς οὐρανῶν πύλας, καὶ ἄγον ἐπὶ τὴν εἴσοδον τῆς σωτηρίας...ἡ θεία χάρις, ἡ τὰ λείποντα ἀναπληροῦσα, καὶ τὰ ἀσθενῆ ἰωμένη·...ἡ πηγὴ τῶν ἀνεκλείπτων χαρισμάτων, καὶ παντὸς ἀγαθοῦ νοῦ πρόοδος. ἡ μελλόντων ...ἀληθὴς φανέρωσις· ἡ σωτήριος σφραγίς, καὶ τὸ θεῖον χρῖσμα· ὁ ἀρραβὼν τῶν ἀϊδίων ἀγαθῶν· παρ' οὗ πᾶσα κτίσις, ὁρατὴ καὶ ἀόρατος, λογικὴ καὶ μὴ λογική, ἐνδυναμοῦται· παρ' οὗ ἡμῖν ἡ θεία ἀναγέννησις, καὶ τῶν ἀνομιῶν ἡ ἄφεσις, καὶ τῶν ἁμαρτιῶν ἡ ἐπικάλυψις, καὶ ἡ πρὸς τὸν θεὸν οἰκείωσις· στέφανός τε δικαίοις, καὶ ἀγαθῶν ἀπόληψις· οὐράνιόν τε ἐνδιαίτημα, καὶ ζωὴ ἀτελεύτητος, καὶ βασιλείας θεοῦ κληρονομία αἰώνιος· οὗτινος τῆς κοινωνίας διὰ τῆς παλιγγενεσίας ὁ μετέχων, τυγχάνει τῶν μνημονευθέντων ἀγαθῶν καὶ...θείας ἐστὶ κοινωνὸς φύσεως Didym.*Trin*.2.1(M.39.452Bff.); **2.** H. Ghost's approach, and gifts, to men are manifold and adapted to their needs, cf.Or.*princ*.2.7.3(p.150.6; M.11.217B); Cyr.H.*catech*.16.12; Max.*qu. Thal*.29(M.90.365C); **3.** operations and gifts; **a.** ass. Christ in justification, Epiph.*anc*.69(p.85.3; M.43.144A); **b.** bestowal of life, from which life of human spirit is derived, Tat.*orat*.13(p.14.24; M.6.833B); this life dist. from πνοὴ ζωῆς, Iren.*haer*.5.12.3(M.7.1152B–1153B); ἡ ζωὴ ἡμῖν ἀπὸ τοῦ θεοῦ διὰ Χριστοῦ ἐν ἁγίῳ π. χορηγεῖται Bas.*Eun*.3.4(1.276A; M.29.664C); cf. ἐκ τῆς γαστρὸς τοῦ π. τῆς θεότητος γεννηθῆναι Mac.Aeg.*hom*.30.2(M.34.721D); **c.** activity confined to ἅγιοι, hence argument that he is inferior in power to Father whose activity extends to all things that are, and Son whose dealings are with all τὰ λογικά, Or.*princ*.1.3.5(p.56.4; M.11.150B); **d.** Christians participating in H. Ghost, Clem.*str*.2.8(p.135.8; M.8.977A); *ib*.3.2(p.199.22; 1109B); flowing into them from heaven, id. *paed*.1.6(p.106.25; M.8.284A); to partake of H. Ghost is to participate in Father and Son, cf.Or.*princ*.4.4.5(p.356.8; M.11.406D); Euchite δυνατὸν...δέξασθαι αἰσθητῶς τὴν ὑπόστασιν τοῦ ἁγίου π., τὸν ἄνθρωπον ἐν πάσῃ πληροφορίᾳ καὶ πάσῃ ἐνεργείᾳ Jo.D.*haer*.80(M.94.732B); **e.** indwelling the soul; **i.** in gen. ἐὰν γὰρ μακρόθυμος ἔσῃ, τὸ π. τὸ ἅγιον τὸ κατοικοῦν ἐν σοὶ καθαρὸν ἔσται, μὴ ἐπισκοτούμενον ὑπὸ ἑτέρου πονηροῦ π. Herm.*mand*.5.1.2; π. δὲ τὸ τοῦ θεοῦ παρὰ πᾶσιν μὲν οὐκ ἔστι, παρὰ δέ τισι τοῖς δικαίως πολιτευομένοις καταγινόμενον καὶ συμπεριπλεκόμενον τῇ ψυχῇ Tat.*orat*.13(p.14.31; M.6.836A); Clem.*paed*.2.2(p.168.4; M.8.409B); κεκοσμημένη ψυχὴ ἁγίῳ π. *ib*.3.11 (p.272.4; 640A); id.*str*.4.26(p.320.26; M.8.1373A); τὸ ἅγιον π. ταύτῃ πως μεταφυτεύεται διανενεμημένον κατὰ τὴν ἑκάστου περιγραφὴν ἀπεριγράφως *ib*.6.15(p.492.10; M.9.344B); ἀντὶ θεοῦ π. ἐν τῇ καρδίᾳ χρυσὸν φέρων id.*q.d.s*.17(p.170.14; M.9.621A); uniting men to God χωρὶς μὲν τοῦ π. ξένοι...ἐσμεν τοῦ θεοῦ· τῇ δὲ τοῦ π. μετοχῇ συναπτόμεθα τῇ θεότητι· ὥστε τὸ εἶναι ἡμᾶς ἐν τῷ πατρὶ μὴ ἡμέτερον εἶναι ἀλλὰ τοῦ π. τοῦ ἐν ἡμῖν ὄντος καὶ ἐν ἡμῖν μένοντος Ath.*Ar*.3.24(M.26.373C); ἐν ἡμῖν ὁ θεὸς ἐνοικεῖν λέγεται διὰ τοῦ π. Bas.*Eun*.3.5(1.276D; M.29.665B); dist. from coexistence of H. Ghost with Father and Son, id.*Spir*.63(3.53B; M.32.184B); οἱ σπουδάζοντες εἶναι ναὸς κἂν ποσῶς ἄξιος τοῦ οἰκοῦντος ἐν τοῖς πιστοῖς ἁγίου π. Didym.*Trin*.2.1 (M.39.448C); result of progress in spiritual life ὅταν...πλείονα τὴν πρὸς αὐτὸν πίστιν καὶ ἀγάπην προσλαμβάνῃς, π. ἅγιον ἀοράτως ἐν τῇ ψυχῇ σου ἐνῴκησε, καὶ δύναμις ὑψίστου ἐπεσκίασέ σοι, γίνωσκε Jo.Clim.*scal*.4(M.88.725D); associated by Euchites with attainment of ἀπάθεια, Jo.D.*haer*.80(M.94.729B); **ii.** participation in H. Ghost as means whereby soul attains immortality, Tat.*orat*.13(p.14.19; M.6.833B); his departure from Adam at Fall resulting in mortality, *ib*.7(p.7.30; 821A); **iii.** indwelling presence is sign by which angels recognize the elect, Clem.*str*.4.18(p.299.21; M.8.1325A); **iv.** through his indwelling Christians are in God, Ath.*Ar*.3.24(M.26.373C); and Trin. dwells in them, id.*ep.Serap*.1.19(M.26.576B); cf.Bas.*Spir*.37 (3.30E; M.32.133B); **v.** in relation to work of other Persons τοῦ μὲν πατρὸς αὐθεντοῦντος καὶ δωρουμένου τὴν χάριν, τοῦ δὲ υἱοῦ ταύτῃ διακονουμένου...τοῦ δὲ ἁγίου π. ... αὐτοῦ ὄντος τοῦ χορηγουμένου Eus. *e.th*.3.5(p.163.23; M.24.1013A); Father is source, Son river, hence men 'drink the Spirit', Ath.*ep.Serap*.1.19(573D); esp. in rel. to work of Son; H. Ghost's work confined to the converted, cf.Or. *princ*.1.3.5(p.56.16; M.11.151A); possession of H. Ghost the result of belief in Christ, hence Nicodemus did not possess him but could only hear his voice (Jo.3:8), since he did not rightly believe in Jesus, id.*fr.37 in Jo*.(p.513.27); possession unites men in Christ, and so in Father, Ath.*Ar*.3.25(M.26.376B); Christ illuminates men in the Spirit, id.*ep.Serap*.1.19(M.26.573C); Christ lives in men through quickening of Spirit, *ib*.(576C); in respect of activity towards men Χριστός and π. are equivalent terms, Epiph.*anc*.68(p.84.11; M.43.141C); Christ being within men through Spirit, Cyr.*Jo*.9.1(4.824B); hence through indwelling of Spirit Christ is formed in men, id.*dial. Trin*.7(5^1.639B,C); **f.** through H. Ghost man receives image of God; **i.** in Creation, differentiating him from animals, Tat.*orat*.15(p.16.5ff.; M.6.837Aff.); Didym.(‡Bas.)*Eun*.5(1.304A; M.29.729A); κατ' εἰκόνα θεοῦ τὸ τεχνηθὲν ἐποιήθη ζῷον, ὡς διὰ τῆς μετουσίας τοῦ π. πρὸς αὐτὸν μεταμορφούμενον Cyr.*thes*.34(5^1.344E); id.*ador*.1(1.9D); **ii.** in redemption τὸ π. χρῖσμα καὶ σφραγίς ἐστιν, ἐν ᾧ χρίει καὶ σφραγίζει πάντα ὁ λόγος...ἡ δὲ σφραγὶς τὴν μορφὴν Χριστοῦ τοῦ σφραγίζοντος ἔχει, καὶ ταύτης οἱ σφραγιζόμενοι μετέχουσι, μορφούμενοι κατ' αὐτήν Ath.*ep.Serap*.1.23(M.26.585A); παρὰ τοῦ π. ... ἡ πρὸς θεὸν ὁμοίωσις Bas.*Spir*.23(3.20C; M.32.109C); ἀνανεοῦσθαι τοιγαροῦν καὶ ἀναπλάττεσθαί πως εἰς εἰκόνα τὴν πρώτην τὴν ἀνθρώπου φύσιν ἐρωτᾷ διὰ μετουσίας τοῦ π. Cyr.*Jo*.11.10(4.988B); **g.** man's transformation by H. Ghost οὔτε βάρβαρός ἐστιν οὔτε Ἰουδαῖος οὔτε Ἕλλην, οὐκ ἄρρεν, οὐ θῆλυ· καινὸς δὲ ἄνθρωπος θεοῦ π. ἁγίῳ μεταπεπλασμένος Clem.*prot*.11(p.79.19; M.8.229B); like iron permeated by fire, Cyr.H.*catech*.17.14; cf.Bas.*Eun*.2.3(1.274A; M.29.660B); **h.** H. Ghost makes men sons of God in Christ, Ath.*ep.Serap*.1.19 (M.26.576A); Bas.*Eun*.3.4(1.275C; M.29.664A); Didym.*Trin*.2.1(M.39.452B); **i.** and gives liberty, Bas.*Spir*.55(3.47E; M.32.172B); Didym.*Trin*.2.1(M.39.452B); **j.** sanctifies, when faith is present, v. ἁγιάζω, ἁγιασμός, ἁγιαστικός etc., Clem.*str*.6.16(p.502.5; M.9.364B); cf. *adest etiam gratia spiritus sancti, ut ea quae substantialiter sancta non sunt, participatione ipsius sancta efficiantur. cum ergo primo ut sint habeant ex deo patre, secundo ut rationabilia sint habeant ex verbo, tertio ut sancta sint habeant ex spiritu sancto: rursum Christi secundum hoc, quod justitia dei est, capacia efficiuntur ea, quae jam sanctificata ante fuerint per spiritum sanctum; et qui in hunc gradum proficere meruerint per sanctificationem spiritus sancti, consequuntur nihilominus domum sapientiae secundum virtutem inoperationis spiritus dei*, Or.*princ*.1.3.8(p.61.7; M.11.154B); Eus. *e.th*.3.6(p.163.32; M.24.1013B); for Eunomian view v. ἁγιαστικός; παρὰ τοῦ π. ... τὸ ἀκρότατον τῶν ὀρεκτῶν, θεὸν γενέσθαι Bas.*Spir*.23 (3.20C; M.32.109C); Apoll.*fid.sec.pt*.27(p.176.22; M.10.1116B); Didym. *Trin*.2.4(M.39.481C); *ib*.2.25(748C); making men partake of divine nature, Cyr.*thes*.34(5^1.353A); **k.** as light, H. Ghost illuminates soul; in proportion to man's moral advance, Clem.*str*.4.16(p.295.23; M.8.1316A); τὸ γὰρ φῶς τῆς ἀληθείας φῶς ἀληθές...π. κυρίου *ib*.6.16(p.502.5; M.9.364B); Eus.*p.e*.7.15(326A; M.21.552A) cit. s. D supra; τοῦτο φωτίζει τὰς ψυχὰς τῶν δικαίων Cyr.H.*catech*.16.3; ὁ τοῦ ἁγίου π. καταξιωθεὶς φωτίζεται τὴν ψυχήν, καὶ ὑπὲρ ἄνθρωπον βλέπει ἃ μὴ ᾔδει...πάρεστι γὰρ ὁ ἀληθινὸς φωταγωγός *ib*.16.16; ὥσπερ τὸ φῶς μιᾷ τῆς ἀκτῖνος προσβολῇ καταυγάζει τὰ πάντα· οὕτω καὶ τὸ π. τὸ ἅγιον, φωτίζει τοὺς ἔχοντας ὀφθαλμοὺς *ib*.16.22; Ath.*ep.Serap*.1.19(M.26.573C); *ib*.1.20(580A); φῶς νοητόν Bas.*Spir*.22(3.19D; M.32.108C); αἱ πνευματοφόροι ψυχαὶ ἐλλαμφθεῖσαι παρὰ τοῦ π. αὐταί τε ἀποτελοῦνται πνευματικαί *ib*.23(20B; M.109B); leading men to contemplate beauty of image of invisible God, *ib*.47(39C; M.153A); as light, is identical in function with Son, cf.Gr.Naz.*or*.31.3(p.148.5; M.36.136B); Didym.*Trin*.2.1(M.39.448C); π. ... φωτὸς οὐρανίου μεταδοτικόν *ib*.(452B); Diad.*perf*.29(p.32.21); **l.** action of H. Ghost, like fire, burns up sin, Cyr.H.*catech*.17.15; **m.** renews man (Tit.3:5), Ath.*ep.Serap*.1.22(M.26.581C); τὸ ἀνακαινίζον...ὡς κύριος Didym. *Trin*.2.1(M.39.452B); **n.** establishes new covenant and releases from Law, Cyr.H.*catech*.17.29; **o.** reveals to man the things of God, cf.Or.*princ*.1.3.4(p.54.2; M.11.149B); Bas.*Spir*.23(3.20B; M.32.109B); ἐν ἑαυτῷ δείκνυσι τὴν δόξαν τοῦ μονογενοῦς, καὶ τοῖς ἀληθινοῖς προσκυνηταῖς ἐν ἑαυτῷ τὴν τοῦ θεοῦ γνῶσιν παρέχεται. ἡ τοίνυν ὁδὸς τῆς θεογνωσίας ἐστὶν ἀπὸ ἑνὸς π. διὰ τοῦ ἑνὸς υἱοῦ ἐπὶ τὸν ἕνα πατέρα, καὶ ἀνάπαλιν ἡ φυσικὴ ἀγαθότης καὶ ὁ κατὰ φύσιν ἁγιασμὸς καὶ τὸ βασιλικὸν ἀξίωμα ἐκ πατρὸς διὰ τοῦ μονογενοῦς ἐπὶ τὸ πνεῦμα διήκει *ib*.47 (39E; M.153B,C); hence is τόπος (Ex.33:21, Dt.12:13), as sphere in which contemplation and worship can alone take place, *ib*.62 (52C,D; M.181C); hence mentioned third among Persons of Trin., cf. ἀπὸ γὰρ τῆς ἡμετέρας σχέσεως τὴν ἀρχὴν ἔλαβεν, ἐπειδὴ ὑποδεχόμενοι τὰ δῶρα, πρώτον ἐντυγχάνομεν τῷ διανέμοντι, εἶτα ἐννοοῦμεν τὸν ἀποστείλαντα, εἶτα ἀνάγομεν τὴν ἐνθύμησιν ἐπὶ τὴν πηγὴν καὶ αἰτίαν τῶν ἀγαθῶν *ib*.37(3.31C; M.133D); οὔτε πατὴρ χωρὶς υἱοῦ ποτε ἐννοεῖται, οὔτε υἱὸς δίχα τοῦ ἁγίου π. καταλαμβάνεται Gr.Nyss. *Maced*.12(M.45.1316B); leads contemplative to perceive mysteries, Dion.Ar.*e.h*.2.2.8(M.3.397A); hence confession of Jesus as Lord is rendered possible by his activity (1Cor.12:3), Gr.Nyss.*Maced*.12 (1316B); Chrys.*pent*.1.4(2.462E); revelation being through H. Ghost because to him alone is it immediate, Cyr.*thes*.33(5^1.333D); Jo.D. *f.o*.1.12(M.94.849A); **p.** Christian faith given by H. Ghost, Clem.

*paed.*1.6(p.111.21; M.8.293A); id.*str.*5.13(p.384.6; M.9.129A); *ib.*6.17 (p.512.5; 388B); διὰ τί π. πίστεως αὐτὴν καλεῖ, καὶ εἰς τὴν τῶν χαρισμάτων καταλέγει τάξιν; εἰ γὰρ χάρισμά ἐστιν ἡ πίστις καὶ τῆς τοῦ π. δωρεᾶς μόνον, ἀλλ' οὐχ ἡμέτερον κατόρθωμα, οὔτε οἱ ἀπιστοῦντες κολασθήσονται, οὔτε οἱ πιστεύοντες ἐπαινεθήσονται· τοιαύτη γὰρ τῶν χαρισμάτων ἡ φύσις, οὐκ ἔχει στεφάνους, οὔτε ἀμοιβάς...εἰ τοίνυν καὶ ἡ πίστις τοιοῦτόν ἐστι, καὶ οὐδὲν ἡμεῖς εἰσηνέγκαμεν, ἀλλὰ τὸ πᾶν τῆς τοῦ π. ἐστι χάριτος...καὶ οὐδένα ἀντὶ τούτων ληψόμεθα μισθόν, πῶς οὖν ἔλεγε 'καρδίᾳ γὰρ πιστεύεται εἰς δικαιοσύνην...' ὅτι καὶ τῆς τοῦ πεπιστευκότος ἀρετῆς ἐστι κατόρθωμα ἡ πίστις...τίνος οὖν ἕνεκα π. πίστεως αὐτὴν καλεῖ; ἐκεῖνο δεῖξαι βουλόμενος, ὅτι τὸ μὲν παρὰ τὴν ἀρχὴν πιστεῦσαι, τῆς ἡμετέρας εὐγνωμοσύνης ἐστί, καὶ τὸ ὑπακοῦσαι κληθέντας· μετὰ δὲ τὸ καταβληθῆναι τὴν πίστιν, τῆς τοῦ π. δεόμεθα βοηθείας, ὥστε μένειν αὐτὴν διηνεκῶς ἄσειστον καὶ ἀπερίτρεπτον Chrys. *hom.1.5 in 2Cor.4:13*(3.263E–264C); ἡ μὲν γὰρ πίστις τῆς τοῦ π. δεῖται βοηθείας καὶ τῆς παραμονῆς ἵνα ἄσειστος μένῃ· ἡ δὲ τοῦ π. βοήθεια διὰ βίου καθαροῦ καὶ πολιτείας ἀρίστης ἡμῖν εἴωθε παραμένειν *ib.1.9*(268C); but πρὸς τοῖς ἄλλοις ἀγαθοῖς καὶ πίστεως φαίνεται τὸ π. παρεκτικόν, καὶ τὸ ἀρκοῦν ἑκάστῳ μέτρον ὁρίζον ὡς θεός Cyr. *thes.*34(5^1.355C); though dwelling of H. Ghost in soul is said to follow on increase of faith and love on part of believer, Jo.Clim. *scal.*4(M.88.725D); **q.** H. Ghost and love: love unites true 'gnostic' with him, Clem.*str.*7.7(p.33.20; M.9.464B); φιλανθρωπία being means whereby men maintain fire of Spirit, Chrys.*hom.1.5 in 2Cor.4:13* (3.268C); Jo.Clim.*scal.*4(M.88.725D); supreme gift of H. Ghost is perfect and immediate love of God; another gift, according to proportion of faith, is perfect love of one's neighbour, Max.*qu. Thal.*29(M.90.365B); **r.** H. Ghost and truth, v. ἀλήθεια; **s.** H. Ghost and wisdom πάρασχε...γαληνιῶντας ἁγίῳ συμφέρεσθαι π., σοφίᾳ τῇ ἀνεκφράστῳ Clem.*paed.*3.12(p.291.6; M.8.680C); cf. *quod participatione spiritus sancti sanctificatus est quis, purior ac sincerior effectus, dignius recipit sapientiae ac scientiae gratiam*, Or.*princ.* 1.3.8(p.62.1; M.11.155A); τοῦ δὲ υἱοῦ ὄντος τῆς σοφίας, ἡμεῖς π. σοφίας λαμβάνοντες, τὸν υἱὸν ἔχομεν Ath.*ep.Serap.*1.19(M.26.576A); as all men partake of wisdom, so all partake of H. Ghost, Or.*princ.*2.7.2 (p.149.2; 216B); **t.** instructing men, Clem.*paed.*1.6(p.112.8; M.8. 293C); εἰ δὲ οἱ προφῆται καὶ οἱ ἀπόστολοι οὐ τὰς τέχνας ἐγνώκεσαν, δι' ὧν τὰ κατὰ φιλοσοφίαν ἐμφαίνεται γυμνάσματα, ἀλλ' ὁ νοῦς γε τοῦ προφητικοῦ καὶ τοῦ διδασκαλικοῦ π. ἐπικεκρυμμένως λαλούμενος διὰ τὸ μὴ πάντων εἶναι τὴν συνιεῖσαν ἀκοήν, τὰς ἐντέχνους ἀπαιτεῖ πρὸς σαφήνειαν διδασκαλίας· ἀσφαλῶς γὰρ ἐγνώκεσαν τὸν νοῦν ἐκεῖνον οἱ προφῆται καὶ οἱ τοῦ π. μαθηταί id.*str.*1.9(p.30.1; M.8.741B); *ib.*6.16 (p.502.5; M.9.364B); *ib.*5.4(p.341.27; 44C); teaching men full implications of Christian revelation which could not be expounded by Christ during earthly life, Eus.*e.th.*3.5(p.161.29; M.24.1009B,C); π. ...δημιουργικῆς δυνάμεως ἀπολειπόμενον, ἁγιαστικῆς δὲ καὶ διδασκαλικῆς πεπληρωμένον Eun.*apol.*25(M.30.861D); *ib.*27(864D); τὸ π. τὸ ἅγιον διδάσκειν πάντας τοὺς εἰς τὸ ὄνομα τοῦ κυρίου πεπιστευκότας Bas. *Eun.*3.4(1.275C; M.29.664A); Chrys.*pent.*1.4(2.463A); **u.** instructing the conscience and bestowing various virtues, Cyr.H.*catech.*16.12; οὐχὶ πολλάκις ἄνθρωπος ἐν παλατίοις διαπρέπων, κατέπτυσε πλούτου καὶ ἀξίας, διδαχθεὶς ὑπὸ τοῦ π. τοῦ ἁγίου...τοσαῦται πλεονεξίαι ἐν κόσμῳ καὶ ἀκτημονοῦσι Χριστιανοί. διὰ τί; διὰ τὴν τοῦ π. ἐπαγγελίαν *ib.*16.19; *ib.*16.22; Bas.*Spir.*23(3.20C; M.32.109C); cheering on Christian athlete, Gr.Nyss.*Eun.*2(2 p.387.18ff.; M.45.569A); **v.** in rel. to martyrs, v. μάρτυς; **w.** various functions of H. Ghost in rel. to Christian life; **i.** as guide, Clem.*prot.*12(p.83.27; M.8.240A); cf.id.*paed.*3.12(p.291.6; M.8.680C); Gr.Nyss.*Eun.*2(2 p.385.1; M.45. 565D); **ii.** as strengthener and helper, cf.Or.*princ.*1.3.8(p.62.11; M. 11.155B); Eun.*apol.*27(M.30.864D); his help being proportionate to human works, Chrys.*hom.1.6 in 2Cor.4:13*(3.264E); **iii.** watching over men, Clem.*fr.*24(p.205.6; M.9.731A); cf.id.*str.*6.17(p.512.5; M. 9.388B); **iv.** protecting men, esp. against demons, Tat.*orat.*16(p.18. 5; M.6.841A); and enabling men to see spiritual beings ordinarily invisible, *ib.*15(p.16.29; 840A); as ὑπεραγωνιστής against Devil, Cyr.H.*catech.*16.19; *ib.*17.37; τὸ δὲ ἀπείργειν τοὺς δαίμονας ὅ τοῦ π. ἴδιόν φησιν ὁ Εὐνόμιος Gr.Nyss.*Eun.*2(2 p.385.19; M.45.568A); π. ...παρ' οὗ ἁγιασθέντες ἐνεδυναμώθησαν Didym.*Trin.*2.1(M.39.452B); **v.** as comforter, or advocate, v. παράκλητος; **x.** sevenfold gifts, Clem.*paed.*3.12(p.284.18; M.8.665C); likened to seven-branched candlestick, Max.*qu.Thal.*63(M.90.672B); **y.** miraculous gifts of H. Ghost bestowed on primitive Church by special providence in order to further progress of gospel, but have now ceased because no longer necessary, Chrys.*pent.*1.4(2.463Dff.); **z.** gift of H. Ghost sometimes approximates closely to grace οὐχὶ ἕνα θεὸν ἔχομεν καὶ ἕνα Χριστὸν καὶ ἓν π. τῆς χάριτος τὸ ἐκχυθὲν ἐφ' ἡμᾶς; *1Clem.*46.6; αὐτὴν γὰρ ἐκείνην...δύναμιν ἁγιαστικὴν τὴν τοῖς ἀτελέσι τὸ τέλειον παρεχομένην, φαμὲν εἶναι τὸ π. τὸ ἅγιον Cyr.*thes.*34(5^1. 352C); **aa.** H. Ghost leads soul to heaven, cf.Iren.*haer.*3.24.1(M.7. 966B); cf. τὸ δὲ εἰς ἀφθαρσίαν ὁδηγεῖ, τὸ π. Clem.*paed.*2.2(p.168.5; M. 8.412A); ἐγὼ δὲ ἂν εὐξαίμην τὸ π. τοῦ Χριστοῦ πτερῶσαί με εἰς τὴν Ἱερουσαλὴμ τὴν ἐμήν id.*str.*4.26(p.324.24; M.8.1381A); π. ... τὸ ἀναπετάζον ἡμῖν τὰς οὐρανῶν πύλας Didym.*Trin.*2.1(M.39.452C); hence, 'earnest of Spirit' is pledge of immortality, cf.Iren.*haer.*3.24. 1(M.7.966B); proving that H. Ghost will be reward of righteous, Bas.*Spir.*40(3.35A; M.32.144A); **bb.** H. Ghost and final judgement; **i.** to be associated with Christ at parousia, *ib.*(34B; M.141A); **ii.** those sealed with H. Ghost who have preserved first-fruits of Spirit unsullied, will be rewarded as faithful servants, *ib.*(34C; M. 141B); **iii.** grace of Spirit is crown of righteous, *ib.*(34B; M.141B); **iv.** those who have grieved Spirit will be 'cut asunder' (Mt.24:25), i.e. separated from him entirely, *ib.*(34C,D; M.141B,C); **4.** conditions for reception of H. Ghost; **a.** universal bestowal of H. Ghost rendered possible by work of Christ, hence given to few before Ascension, but to all believers thereafter, cf.Or.*princ.*2.7.2(p.149.3; M.11.216C); disciples were not previously given H. Ghost, hence possible for them to deny Christ, Hipp.*Noët.*14(p.257.10; M.10. 821B); **b.** purification necessary, Bas.*Spir.*23(3.20A; M.32.109A); **c.** active co-operation required from man τὸ ἅγιον π. μόνοις σπουδαίοις ἐπιφοιτᾷ, τῶν φαύλων μακρὰν ὑπάρχον· οὐ τοπικῶς δὲ τοῦ μακρὰν καὶ τοῦ ἐγγὺς ἀκούειν δεῖ, ἀλλ' ὡς ἐνδέχεται περὶ ἀσωμάτων αὐτὰ νοεῖν Or.*fr.37 in Jo.*(p.513.5); οὔτε ἡ τοῦ π. χάρις τὴν ἡμετέραν προφθάνει προαίρεσιν· ἀλλὰ καλεῖ μέν, ἀναμένει δὲ ὥστε ἑκόντας καὶ βουληθέντας οἴκοθεν προσελθεῖν Chrys.*hom.1.5 in 2Cor.4:13*(3. 264C); **d.** H. Ghost departs from sinners, Herm.*mand.*5.1.3; cf. Or.*princ.*1.3.7(p.58.11; M.11.152C); to lose H. Ghost through sin is the 'blasphemy against H. Ghost', cf.*ib.*(p.59.15; 153C); ὅτε γοῦν ἐκπίπτει τις ἀπὸ τοῦ π. διά τινα κακίαν, ἡ μὲν χάρις ἀμεταμέλητος διαμένει τοῖς βουλομένοις, κἄν τις ἐκπεσὼν μετανοῇ· οὐκέτι δὲ ἐν τῷ θεῷ ἐστιν ἐκεῖνος ὁ πεσών, διὰ τὸ ἀποστῆναι ἀπ' αὐτοῦ τὸ ἐν τῷ θεῷ ἅγιον καὶ παράκλητον π., ἀλλ' ἐν ἐκείνῳ ἔσται ᾧ ἑαυτὸν ὑπέταξεν ὁ ἁμαρτάνων, ὡς ἐπὶ τοῦ Σαοὺλ γέγονεν Ath.*Ar.*3.25(M.26.376C); hence Novatian put H. Ghost to flight by denying possibility of post-baptismal penance, Dion.Al.ap.Eus.*h.e.*7.8(M.20.653A); Euchite συνοικοῦσιν ὁ σατανᾶς καὶ τὸ π. τὸ ἅγιον ἐν τῷ ἀνθρώπῳ Jo.D.*haer.*80 (M.94.729A); **5.** operation of H. Ghost in Church; **a.** Church as sphere of his activity, cf. *ubi enim ecclesia, ibi et spiritus dei; et ubi spiritus dei, illic ecclesia, et omnis gratia; spiritus autem veritas*, Iren.*haer.*3.24.1(M.7.966C); τὸ ἐν ἐκκλησίᾳ παραδοθὲν ἅγιον π. Hipp. *haer.*1 proem.(p.3.2; M.16.3020C); Church would not exist without H. Ghost, and where Church is he is also, Chrys.*pent.*1.4(2.463C); he is Church's ruler and provides universal Church with charismata, Cyr.H.*catech.*16.22; bestowed on Church by Christ as its head, Max.*qu.Thal.*63(M.90.672B); **b.** Church's ministry as instrument of H. Ghost, cf. *in ecclesia enim, inquit, posuit deus apostolos, prophetas, doctores, et universam reliquam operationem spiritus*, Iren.*haer.*3.24.1(M.7.966B); H. Ghost, manifested in teaching and refutation of heresy, handed down in Church from apostles, through their converts, to bishops, Hipp.*haer.*1 proem.(p.3.2; M. 16.3020C); εἰ μὴ π. ἅγιον ἦν, ποιμένες καὶ διδάσκαλοι ἐν τῇ ἐκκλησίᾳ οὐκ ἂν ἦσαν· καὶ γὰρ οὗτοι διὰ τοῦ π. γίνονται, καθὼς καὶ ὁ Παῦλός φησιν· ἐν ᾧ ἔθετο ὑμᾶς τὸ π. τὸ ἅγιον ποιμένας καὶ ἐπισκόπους...εἰ μὴ π. ἅγιον ἦν ἐν τῷ κοινῷ τούτῳ πατρὶ καὶ διδασκάλῳ, οὐκ ἂν ὅτε πρὸ μικροῦ ἀνέβη ἐπὶ τὸ ἱερὸν βῆμα τοῦτο, καὶ πᾶσιν ὑμῖν ἔδωκεν εἰρήνην, καὶ ἐπεφθέγξασθε αὐτῷ κοινῇ πάντες 'καὶ τῷ π. σου' Chrys.*pent.*1.4(2. 463B,C); cf. in consecration prayer for bishops, *effunde eam virtutem quae a te est, principalis spiritus quem dedisti dilecto filio tuo... quod donavit sanctis apostolis qui constituerunt ecclesiam*, Hipp. *trad.ap.*3.3; connected esp. with power of absolution, cf.*ib.*3.5; δὸς αὐτῷ χάριν καὶ π. θεῖον, ὃ ἐχαρίσω πᾶσιν τοῖς γνησίοις σου δούλοις καὶ προφήταις καὶ πατριάρχαις Serap.*euch.*28.1; *Lit.*ap.*Const.App.*8.5.7; τῇ ἐπιφοιτήσει καὶ δυνάμει καὶ χάριτι τοῦ ἁγίου σου π. ἐνίσχυσον, ὡς ἐνίσχυσας τοὺς...ἀποστόλους καὶ προφήτας *Euchol.*(p.250); cf. in ordination of presbyters, *respice super servum tuum istum et impartire spiritum gratiae et consilii*, Hipp.*trad.ap.*8.2; τὴν χεῖρα ἐκτείνομεν...ἵνα τὸ πνεῦμα τῆς ἀληθείας ἐπιδημήσῃ αὐτῷ...ὁ χαρισάμενος ἀπὸ τοῦ π. τοῦ Μωσέως ἐπὶ τοὺς ἐκλελεγμένους πνεῦμα ἅγιον· μέρισον καὶ τῷδε π. ἅγιον ἐκ τοῦ π. τοῦ μονογενοῦς εἰς χάριν σοφίας καὶ γνώσεως καὶ πίστεως ὀρθῆς Serap.*euch.*27.1–2; *Const.App.*8.16.4; πλήρωσον τῆς τοῦ ἁγίου σου π. δωρεᾶς *Euchol.*(p.243); of deacon, cf. *non accipiens communem presbyterii spiritum eum cujus participes presbyteri sunt*, Hipp.*trad.ap.*9.4; cf. *da spiritum sanctum gratiae et* *sollicitudinis et industriae in hunc servum tuum*, ib.9.11; δὸς ἐν αὐτῷ πνεῦμα γνώσεως καὶ διακρίσεως Serap.euch.26.2; πλῆσον αὐτὸν π. καὶ δυνάμεως Const.App.8.18.2; Euchol.(p.209); of deaconess ὁ πληρώσας πνεύματος Μαριὰμ καὶ Δεββῶραν...δὸς αὐτῇ π. ἅγιον Const. App.8.20.1; **6.** H. Ghost and worship; **a.** worship is in him, hence he is τόπος of Dt.12:13, Gen.28:16, Bas.Spir.62(3.52D,E; M.32.184A); **b.** his assistance necessary πῶς μὲν γὰρ εἴπωσιν ἄγγελοι, δόξα ἐν ὑψίστοις θεῷ, μὴ δυναμωθέντες ὑπὸ τοῦ π.;...τὰς ἀοράτους δυνάμεις... δεομένας τῆς βοηθείας τοῦ π. ib.38(32D,E; M.137B); **c.** hence offers worship to himself through men τὸ π. ἐστιν, ἐν ᾧ προσκυνοῦμεν, καὶ δι' οὗ προσευχόμεθα...τὸ οὖν προσκυνεῖν τῷ π., ἢ προσεύχεσθαι, οὐδὲν ἄλλο εἶναί μοι φαίνεται, ἢ αὐτὸ ἑαυτῷ τὴν εὐχὴν προσάγειν καὶ τὴν προσκύνησιν Gr.Naz.or.31.12(p.159.13ff.; M.36.145C); **d.** intercedes for men, Gr.Nyss.Eun.2(2 p.384.15ff.; M.45.565C); **e.** leads believer to understand sacramental mysteries, Dion.Ar.e.h.3.2(M.3.428A); **f.** cult of H. Ghost not traditional or familiar, because worship is *in* him, Gr.Naz.or.31.12(p.159.13; M.36.145B); **g.** Heracleon's teaching on worship 'in spirit and truth' (Jo.4:24) αὐτοὶ τῆς αὐτῆς φύσεως ὄντες τῷ πατρὶ πνεῦμά εἰσιν, οἵτινες κατὰ ἀλήθειαν καὶ οὐ κατὰ πλάνην προσκυνοῦσιν Heracleon ap.Or.Jo.13.25(p.249.2; M.14.441A); refuted by teaching that to suppose those who worship in Spirit to be ὁμοούσιοι with divine nature is impious, Or.ib.(p.249.5; M.14. 441A); **7.** H. Ghost and sacraments; **a.** baptism, v. βάπτισμα; **i.** not present in John's baptism, Ammon.Ac.18:25(M.85.1572C); **ii.** in Christ's baptism, Clem.paed.1.6(p.105.17; M.8.280D) cit. s. λουτρόν; ἐχρίσθη τὴν σάρκα τῷ τοῦ πατρὸς αὐτοῦ π. id.str.1.21(p.78.32; M.8. 856B); purpose of appearance as dove τὸ πρᾶον τῆς νέας ἐπιφανείας τοῦ π. ἐβούλετο δεῖξαι τῷ τῆς περιστερᾶς ὁμοιώματι id.fr.57(p.226.26; M.9.765C); Christ as God sent forth H. Ghost and received him as man, Nil.epp.2.293(M.79.345B); **iii.** in Christian baptism; ref. Trinitarian formula, v. βαπτίζω, βάπτισμα, λουτρόν; ref. gift of Spirit in baptism as distinctive of Christian sacrament, v. βάπτισμα; associated particularly with water of baptism, v. ὕδωρ, λουτρόν; regarded as bestowed after baptism, and associated esp. with chrismation, v. χρῖσμα, χρίω; cf.Thdt.Ps.22:5(1.749) cit. s. ἔλαιον; ass. imposition of hands (ref. Ac.8:18, Heb.6:2), cf.Or. princ.1.3.2(p.50.4; M.11.147B); cf.ib.1.3.7(p.58.20; 153A); Chrys.hom. 9.2 in Heb.(12.95C); Thdt.Heb.6:2(3.577); Anast.S.qu.et resp.86(M. 89.712C); effects of his operation in baptism: sealing of baptized, cf. ἐσφράγισεν ἡμῶν τὰς ψυχὰς τῷ ἰδίῳ π. καὶ τὰ μέλη τοῦ σώματος τῷ ἰδίῳ αἵματι Mel.pass.67 p.11.8; Cyr.H.catech.4.16; τοῦτο [sc. π.] γὰρ ἕτοιμον πάρεστι σφραγίσαι σου τὴν ψυχήν, καὶ δίδωσι σφραγῖδα, ἣν τρέμουσι δαίμονες ib.17.35; παρεῖναι δοκεῖ πως τοῖς ἅπαξ ἐσφραγισμένοις, τὴν ἐκ τῆς ἐπιστροφῆς σωτηρίαν αὐτῶν ἀναμένον Bas.Spir.40(3.34D; M.32.141C); sts. connected with external σφραγίς of consignation, CCP(381)‡can.7; Rit.Bapt.(p.405); Euchol.(p.291); connected with invocation of Trin., Clem.exc. Thdot.80(p.131.27; M.9.696B); remitting sins, id.paed.1.6(p.106.23; M.8.284A); Chrys.pent.1.4(2.462E); regenerating and re-creating τὸν οὐκ ἐξ αἱμάτων...ἐν π. δὲ ἀναγεννώμενον Clem.str.2.13(p.144.17; M.8.996C); cf. *lavacrum regenerationis spiritus sancti*, Hipp.trad. ap.22.1; παλιγγενεσίας ὀνομαζόμενον λουτρὸν μετὰ ἀνακαινώσεως γινόμενον πνεύματος Or.Jo.6.33(17; p.143.14; M.14.257B); π. ... τὸ ἀνακτίζον διὰ βαπτίσματος Gr.Naz.or.31.29(p.184.1; M.36.165C); Didym. (‡Bas.)Eun.5(1.303A; M.29.725D); ἐνοικεῖ τοῦ...π. ἡ χάρις τῇ τοῦ βαπτισθέντος ψυχῇ...τὸ κατ' εἰκόνα καὶ καθ' ὁμοίωσιν αὐτῇ ἀνακαινίζουσα †Jo.D.B.J.8(M.96.920A); mediating divine sonship, Clem. paed.1.5(p.102.20; M.8.276A); giving spiritual growth ἀναγεννῆσαι ὕδατι, αὐξῆσαι πνεύματι ib.1.12(p.148.19; M.8.368A); and sanctification, Symb.Sel.(p.258.14; M.26.745B); faith the necessary condition of reception of H. Ghost in baptism, Cyr.H.catech.17. 36; Jo.D.f.o.4.9(M.94.1121C); baptism the means of union with H. Ghost, Dion.Ar.e.h.2.3.8(M.3.404C); his operation in baptism compared with winnowing of corn, Clem.ecl.25(p.143.26; M.9.709B); **b.** eucharist; **i.** ref. reception of H. Ghost in eucharist, cf. σάρκα ἡμῖν τὸ π. τὸ ἅγιον ἀλληγορεῖ, καὶ γὰρ ὑπ' αὐτοῦ δεδημιούργηται ἡ σάρξ· αἷμα ἡμῖν τὸν λόγον αἰνίττεται, καὶ γὰρ ὡς αἷμα πλούσιον ὁ λόγος ἐπικέχυται τῷ βίῳ· ἡ κρᾶσις δὲ ἡ ἀμφοῖν ὁ κύριος, ἡ τροφὴ τῶν νηπίων· ὁ κύριος πνεῦμα καὶ λόγος Clem.paed.1.6(p.115.30; M.8.301A); ἰσχὺς δὲ τοῦ λόγου τὸ π., ὡς αἷμα σαρκός. ἀναλόγως τοίνυν κίρναται ὁ μὲν οἶνος τῷ ὕδατι, τῷ δὲ ἀνθρώπῳ τὸ π., καὶ τὸ μὲν εἰς πίστιν εὐωχεῖ, τὸ κρᾶμα, τὸ δὲ εἰς ἀφθαρσίαν ὁδηγεῖ, τὸ π., ἡ δὲ ἀμφοῖν αὖθις κρᾶσις... εὐχαριστία κέκληται ib.2.2(p.168.2; M.8.409B); cf. *des omnibus qui percipiunt sanctis in repletionem spiritus sancti ad confirmationem fidei in veritate*, Hipp.trad.ap.4.12; ἵνα οἱ μεταλαβόντες αὐτοῦ...π. ἁγίου πληρωθῶσιν Lit.ap.Const.App.8.12.39; **ii.** ref. operation in consecration of elements, cf. *ut mittas spiritum tuum sanctum in oblationem sanctae ecclesiae*, Hipp.trad.ap.4.12; Cyr.H.catech.23.7 cit. s. σῶμα; ὅταν ἑστήκῃ πρὸ τῆς τραπέζης ὁ ἱερεὺς...καλῶν τὸ π. τὸ ἅγιον, τοῦ παραγενέσθαι καὶ ἅψασθαι τῶν προκειμένων...ὅταν διδῷ τὴν χάριν τὸ π., ὅταν κατέλθῃ, ὅταν ἅψηται τῶν προκειμένων Chrys. coemet.3(2.401D); καταπέμψῃς τὸ ἅγιόν σου π. ἐπὶ τὴν θυσίαν ταύτην Lit.ap.Const.App.8.12.39; αὐτὸ τὸ π. σου τὸ πανάγιον κατάπεμψον... ἐφ' ἡμᾶς καὶ ἐπὶ τὰ προκείμενα ἅγια δῶρα ταῦτα Lit.Jac.(p.206.6); Lit.Chrys.(p.329.16); cf. ἐξαπόστειλον ἐπὶ τοὺς ἄρτους τούτους καὶ ἐπὶ τὰ ποτήρια ταῦτα τὸ π. σου τὸ ἅγιον ἵνα αὐτὰ ἁγιάσῃ καὶ τελειώσῃ Lit. Marc.(p.134.10); Lit.Bas.(p.329.29); **8.** H. Ghost and revelation; **a.** as spirit of prophecy; **i.** freq. described as π. προφητικόν Just. 1apol.13.3(M.6.348A); Athenag.leg.10.3(M.6.909A); ib.18.2(925B); revealing God, cf.Iren.haer.4.20.5(M.7.1035A); as 'mouth of the Lord', Clem.prot.9(p.62.9; M.8.192D); πλησθεὶς ὁ ἄνθρωπος...τῷ π. λαλεῖ καθὼς ὁ κύριος βούλετε, οὕτως φανερὸν ἔστε τὸ π. τῆς θειότητος. τὸ γὰρ προφητικὸν π. τὸ σωματεῖόν ἐστιν τῆς προφητικῆς τάξεως ὅ ἐστιν τὸ σῶμα τῆς σαρκὸς...Χριστοῦ τὸ μιγὲν τῇ ἀνθρωπότητι διὰ Μαρίας POxy.5.9 (saec. iii–iv); **ii.** esp. as inspiring OT prophets, and enabling them to testify to Christ, Athenag.leg.10.3(909A) v. προφήτης; in credal formularies, Symb.Hier.(M.33.533B); Symb. ap.Epiph.anc.118(p.147.11; M.43.232D) cit. s. C supra; Symb.ap. Epiph.anc.119(p.148.26; 236A) cit. s. c.iii infra; Symb.Nic.–CP(p.80. 12; H.2.288B); enabling Gabriel to predict future, Bas.Spir.38(3. 32E; M.32.137C); in prophetic inspiration H. Ghost mediates presence of God, ib.37(30E; M.133B); Cyr.thes.33(5^1.337A); his operation in ecstatic prophecy does not necessitate suspension of human faculties, †Bas.Is.5(1.381A; M.30.125B); **iii.** prophetic Spirit subject to Christ, Clem.q.d.s.6(p.164.9; M.9.612A); cf.id.fr.24(p.204.1; M.9.729B); **iv.** prophetic Spirit held by orthodox to operate normally through inspiration and interpretation of scripture, cf. Clem.str.1.9(p.30.3; M.8.741B); but direct gift of prophecy may be expected by the baptized, if they are worthy to receive it, Cyr.H. catech.17.37; **v.** Montanist πολλοὺς ἔχειν μάρτυρας, καὶ τοῦτ' εἶναι τεκμήριον...τῆς δυνάμεως τοῦ παρ' αὐτοῖς λεγομένου προφητικοῦ π. Anon.ap.Eus.h.e.5.16.20(M.20.472B); Apollon.ib.5.18.3(M.20.476C); **b.** direct revelation is granted by H. Ghost in visions, Cyr.H.catech. 23.6; Bas.Spir.38(3.32E; M.32.137C); **c.** in scripture; **i.** H. Ghost as speaker, inspirer, or author of scriptures, v. γραφή, ἐπίπνοια; **ii.** in OT ὁ νόμος πνευματικὸς...ὁ γὰρ π. ἁγίῳ γενόμενος πνευματικός. οὗτος δὲ τῷ ὄντι νομοθέτης Clem.str.1.26(p.105.19; M.8. 917A); Cyr.H.catech.4.16; Symb.ap.Epiph.anc.119(p.148.26; M.43. 236A) cit. s. iii infra; **iii.** in both Testaments, esp. in prophets and apostles, Clem.str.5.6(p.352.11; M.9.65A); cf. *quod iste spiritus sanctus unumquemque sanctorum vel prophetarum vel apostolorum inspiraverit, et non alius spiritus in veteribus, alius vero in his, qui in adventu Christi inspirati sunt, fuerit...praedicatur*, Or.princ.1 proem.4(p.11.8; M.11.118A); cf. *idem...spiritus sanctus est, qui et in prophetis et in apostolis fuit...et duos quidem deos ausos esse haereticos dicere...audivimus...duos autem spiritus sanctos numquam cognovimus ab aliquo praedicari. quomodo enim hoc de scripturis poterunt affirmare, aut quam differentiam dare poterunt inter spiritum sanctum et spiritum sanctum?* ib.2.7.1(p.148.10; 216A); Cyr.H. catech.4.16; ἓν π. ἅγιον, διὰ προφητῶν μὲν περὶ τοῦ Χριστοῦ κηρῦξαν· ἐλθόντος δὲ τοῦ Χριστοῦ καταβάν, καὶ ἐπιδεῖξαν αὐτόν. μηδεὶς οὖν χωριζέτω τὴν παλαιὰν ἀπὸ τῆς καινῆς διαθήκης· μηδεὶς λεγέτω, ὅτι ἄλλο τὸ π. ἐκεῖ, καὶ ἄλλο ὧδε ib.16.3–4; εἰς τὸ ἅγιον π. πιστεύομεν, τὸ λαλῆσαν ἐν τῷ νόμῳ καὶ κηρῦξαν ἐν τοῖς προφήταις...λαλοῦν ἐν ἀποστόλοις Symb.ap.Epiph.anc.119(p.148.26; M.43.236A); τὸ αὐτὸ π. καὶ ἐν τῇ παλαιᾷ, καὶ ἐν τῇ καινῇ Chrys.hom.2.2 in 2Cor.4:13(3. 270E); ib.2.7(275D); **iv.** his revelations obscure, needing faith for their understanding, Clem.str.1.9(p.30.7; M.8.741B,C); 'gnostic' alone can interpret what is said by him in scripture, ib.6.15(p.490. 10; M.9.340B); which is purposely concealed except from faithful, ib.(p.495.21; 349B); and needs interpretation by H. Ghost himself, id.q.d.s.5(p.163.30; M.9.609D); Or.fr.37 in Jo.(p.513.30); **9.** images and metaphors of his work in rel. to man ἀναφερόμενοι εἰς τὰ ὕψη διὰ τῆς μηχανῆς Ἰησοῦ Χριστοῦ, ὅς ἐστιν σταυρός, σχοινίῳ χρώμενοι τῷ π. τῷ ἁγίῳ Ign.Eph.9.1; compared with a magnet, Clem.str.7.2(p.8.24; M.9.413A); gold, ib.5.14(p.391.5; 148A); dew, id.q.d.s.34(p.182.22; M.9.640C); ib.40(p.186.11; 645A); cf. θηλῆς λογικῆς πνεύματι δροσερῷ ἐμπιμπλάμενοι id.paed.hymn.51(p.292; M. 8.684B); water, id.ecl.8(p.139.5; M.9.701B); simile explained at length, Cyr.H.catech.16.12; hence drinking of Spirit, Ath.ep. Serap.1.19(M.26.576A); 'new wine' (Mt.9:17), Or.princ.1.3.7(p.59.2; M.11.153A); fig-tree (as healer and provider of shelter), Meth.

*symp.*10.5(p.127.31; M.18.201B); oil, Hipp.*Dan.*1.16.3(M.10.693A); fire, Cyr.H.*catech.*17.14; robe, *ib.*17.15; **10.** claims of enthusiasts to be identified with H. Ghost: Maximilla *ῥῆμά εἰμι καὶ π. καὶ δύναμις* Anon.ap.Eus.*h.e.*5.16.17(M.20.472A); Manes, *ib.*7.31.1(720C); Thdt. *haer.*1.26(4.321); v. *παράκλητος*; **11.** work of H. Ghost acc. non-orthodox theology: **a.** Gnost.; **i.** operation of Christ and H. Ghost as syzygy in Valentinian system *τὸν Μονογενῆ πάλιν ἑτέραν προβαλέσθαι συζυγίαν...Χριστὸν καὶ π. ἅγιον, εἰς πῆξιν καὶ στηριγμὸν τοῦ πληρώματος, ὑφ' ὧν καταρτισθῆναι τοὺς αἰῶνας...τὸ δὲ ἐν π. τὸ ἅγιον ἐξισωθέντας αὐτοὺς πάντας εὐχαριστεῖν ἐδίδαξε, καὶ τὴν ἀληθινὴν ἀνάπαυσιν ἡγήσατο. οὕτως τε μορφῇ καὶ γνώμῃ ἴσους κατασταθῆναι τοὺς αἰῶνας λέγουσι, πάντας γενομένους Νόας καὶ πάντας Λόγους κτλ.* Iren.*haer.*1.2.5–6(M.7.461A,464A); **ii.** Basilidean, H. Ghost (corresponding to *πτερόν* of Plato *Phaedr.*246Aff.) assists *υἱότης* in *σπέρμα* to rise *κάτωθεν ἄνω*, Hipp.*haer.*7.22(p.199.9; M.16.3307A); **iii.** Naassene (related to Attis cult) *συρικτὰν δέ φασιν εἶναι Φρύγες τὸ ἐκεῖθεν γεγεννημένον, ὅτι π. ἐναρμόνιόν ἐστι τὸ γεγεννημένον...τὸ δὲ π., φησίν, ἐκεῖ ὅπου καὶ ὁ πατὴρ ὀνομάζεται καὶ ὁ υἱός* Hipp.*haer.*5.9 (p.98.9; M.16.3154A); **b.** Manich., *ζῶν π.* as emanation from Father, created stars, Hegem.*Arch.*8(p.11.4ff.; M.10.1437C); sent to rescue primal man from power of darkness, *ib.*7(p.10.13; 1437B); **c.** as female principle, (cf. Hebr. רוּחַ); in Gospel acc. Hebrews *ἔλαβέ με ἡ μήτηρ μου, τὸ ἅγιον π.* Or.*Jo.*2.12(p.67.20; M.14.132C) where interpreted in light of Mt.12:50, cf.Or.*hom.15.4 in Jer.*(p.128.27; M.13. 433B); as female aeon (Valent.), Iren.*haer.*1.2.5–6(M.7.461A–464A); cf. Naassene, Hipp.*haer.*5.8(p.97.17; M.16.3151B); Elchezaite, *ib.*9. 13(p.251.20; 3387C); *εἶναι δὲ καὶ τὸ ἅγιον π. ... θήλειαν, ὅμοιον τῷ Χριστῷ* Epiph.*haer.*19.4(p.221.10; M.41.265B) (Ossaean).

H. site of pentecostal descent marked by upper church at Jerusalem where catechetical lecture on H. Ghost is delivered, Cyr.H.*catech.*16.4.

I. work of H. Ghost in rel. to angels: angels partake of H. Ghost along with rest of creation, Ath.*ep.Serap.*1.27(M.26.593A); are thereby sanctified and perfected, Bas.*Spir.*38(3.31Cff.; M.32.136A); their service is accomplished in him, *ib.*(33B; M.140A); they praise God in him, *ib.*(32D; M.137B).

X. angels as *πνεύματα*; **1.** dist. from *ἅγιον π.*, Eus.*e.th.*3.5(p.163. 16; M.24.1013A); Cyr.H.*catech.*16.23; Bas.*Eun.*3.2(1.273E; M.29. 660A); Didym.*Trin.*2.4(M.39.489A); **2.** as *λειτουργικὰ πνεύματα*, v. *λειτουργικός*.

XI. evil *πνεύματα*; **1.** composed of spirit derived from matter, Tat.*orat.*12(p.13.11; M.6.832B); cf. *ὑλικῶν πνευμάτων* Meth.*Porph.*1 (p.504.23; M.18.400C); **2.** dwell in soul and war against H. Ghost, Herm.*mand.*5.1.2–4; *Const.App.*6.27.4; as familiar spirits, Or. *princ.*3.3.5(pp.261.19–262.1; M.11.318B,C); entering human bodies in order to enjoy sensual pleasures inaccessible to mere spirits, *Hom. Clem.*9.10; **3.** cause disease and madness, Or.*comm.in Mt.*13.6 (p.193.13; M.13.1105C); **4.** liturg., ref. those possessed by evil spirits *εὔξασθε, οἱ ἐνεργούμενοι ὑπὸ π. ἀκαθάρτων...δεηθῶμεν, ὅπως...θεὸς... ἐπιτιμήσῃ τοῖς ἀκαθάρτοις...π.* *Lit.*ap.*Const.App.*8.7.2; **5.** incite to sin, cf.Or.*hom.20.3 in Num.*(p.193.13ff.; M.12.732C); **6.** cause men to anathematize Christ, Bas.*Spir.*38(3.32E; M.32.137B); and inspire heresy, Rhod.ap.Eus.*h.e.*5.13.2(M.20.460B); Anon.*ib.*5.16.8 (468A); confused by Montanists with Paraclete, cf.Or.*princ.*2.7.3 (p.150.13; M.11.217B); id.*comm.in Mt.*15.30(p.441.16; M.13.1344A); **7.** subject to Christian exorcists, Just.*dial.*76.6(M.6.653C); **8.** identified with pagan gods, *Const.App.*2.28.8; Chrys.*pan.Bab.*1.2(2.533B).

XII. of inspiration of Delphic priestess *διὰ τοῦ Πυθίου στομίου περικαθεζομένῃ τῇ...προφήτιδι π. διὰ τῶν γυναικείων ὑπεισέρχεται τὸ μαντικόν* Or.*Cels.*3.25(p.221.28; M.11.949B); *ib.*7.3(p.155.15; 1424D).

πνευματέμφορος, *inspired*, of prophets *π. στόμα* Jo.D.*carm.pent.* 116(p.217; M.96.837C).

πνευματιάω, *be possessed by an evil spirit*, ref. question whether husband may divorce demoniac wife, Tim.I Al.*resp.*(M.33.1305D); in gen., *Apophth.Patr.*(M.65.304A).

πνευματικός, **A.** *of the breathing* *ἀσχολία καὶ ἀρρωστία π. τὸ κωλῦσαν ἣν ἡμᾶς γενέσθαι μέχρι Ναυτίλων* Gr.Naz.*ep.*205(M.37.340B).

B. *spirited, fierce* *πάντων δὲ τῶν θηρίων πνευματικώτατον τυγχάνει καὶ πυρωδέστατον* ‡Eust.*hex.*(M.18.745C).

C. *spiritual*; **1.** opp. physical *σαρκικὸς εἶ καὶ π.* Ign.*Polyc.*2.2; cf. *σωματικός*; **2.** *partaking of substance proper to spirits*, i.e. of refined and impalpable substance *δαίμονες δὲ πάντες σαρκίον μὲν οὐ κέκτηνται, π. δέ ἐστιν αὐτοῖς ἡ σύμπηξις ὡς πυρὸς καὶ ἀέρος* Tat.*orat.* 15(p.16.27; M.6.840A); *οἱ ἀστέρες, σώματα π.* Clem.*ecl.*55(p.152.14; M. 9.724B); of body ascribed to God by anthropomorphites *σῶμα...π. καὶ αἰθερῶδες* Or.*Jo.*13.21(p.245.10; M.14.433B); esp. of resurrection body of Christ and of faithful, cf. *ἀνάστασις*: *μεταβαλοῦντες δὲ τὸ σῶμα ἐπὶ τὸ πνευματικώτερον* id.*dial.*24(p.166.20); cf. *quantum ergo sensus noster capere potest, qualitatem spiritalis corporis talem quondam esse sentimus, in quo inhabitare deceat non solum sanctas quasque perfectasque animas, verum etiam omnem illam creaturam quae liberabitur a servitute corruptionis*, id.*princ.*3.6.4(p.285.10; M. 11.337B); defined as *non nova aliqua corpora...sed haec ipsa, quae viventes habuerant, ex deterioribus in melius transformata...* it being necessary that when *animalis homo* is rendered *spiritalis, tum corpus quasi spiritui ministrans in statum qualitatemque proficiat spiritalem*, *ib.*3.6.6(p.288.27; 339C); cf. *πᾶν γὰρ τὸ ἐκ καθαροῦ ἀέρος καὶ καθαροῦ πυρὸς συνιστάμενον σύγκριμα, καὶ τοῖς ἀγγελικοῖς ὁμοούσιον ὑπάρχον, οὐ δύναται γῆς ἔχειν ποιότητα καὶ ὕδατος, ἐπεὶ συμβήσεται ἔσεσθαι αὐτὸ γεῶδες. τοιοῦτον καὶ ἐκ τούτων τὸ ἀναστῆναι μέλλον σῶμα ἀνθρώπου ὁ Ὠριγένης ἐφαντάζετο, ὃ καὶ π. ἔφησεν* Meth.*res.*2.30(p.388.15; M.18.316C); *βούλεται τοίνυν ὁ Ὠριγένης τὴν μὲν αὐτὴν σάρκα μὴ ἀποκαθίστασθαι τῇ ψυχῇ...τὴν δὲ ποιὰν ἑκάστου μορφήν, κατὰ τὸ εἶδος τὸ τὴν σάρκα καὶ νῦν χαρακτηρίζον, ἐν ἑτέρῳ π. τετυπωμένην ἀναστήσεσθαι σώματι* *ib.*3.3(p.391.3; M.18. 317B); *ὅτι δὲ ἔστι σῶμα ψυχικὸν καὶ ἔστι σῶμα π., οὐκ ἄλλο σῶμα π. καὶ ἄλλο ψυχικόν, ἀλλ' αὐτὸ ψυχικὸν αὐτὸ π.,...ὅτε δὲ ἐγειρόμεθα, οὐκέτι τῆς ψυχῆς ἡ δουλεία, ἀλλὰ πνεύματος ἡ ἀκολουθία. ... Ἐνὼχ...ἐν σώματι γὰρ ζῶντι ὑπάρχει, πνευματικῶς φερόμενος καὶ οὐ ψυχικῶς διὰ τὴν μετάθεσιν, καίτοι γε ἐν σώματι ὢν π. ἀλλὰ καὶ περὶ τοῦ Ἠλία...ὅτι ἀνελήφθη...καὶ ἔστιν ἔτι ἐν σαρκί, σαρκὶ δὲ π.* Epiph.*haer.*64.63–64 (p.502.20ff.; M.41.1180Bff.); *ἐν τῇ...μελλούσῃ καταστάσει ὡς π. ἀνιστάμενοι πάλιν, ἀκριβέστερον γνωσόμεθα περὶ θεοῦ* Cosm.Ind.*top.*5 (M.88.312A); *πνευματικόν, οἷον τὸ τοῦ κυρίου σῶμα μετὰ τὴν ἀνάστασιν κεκλεισμένων τῶν θυρῶν διερχόμενον* Jo.D.*f.o.*4.27(M.94.1225A); Origen's views attacked *εἰ δέ τις εἰκόνα μὲν χοϊκὴν τὴν σάρκα αὐτὴν οἴοιτο λέγεσθαι, εἰκόνα δὲ ἐπουράνιον ἄλλο παρὰ τὴν σάρκα σῶμα π., ἐνθυμηθήτω...ὅτι Χριστός, ὁ οὐράνιος ἄνθρωπος, τὸ αὐτὸ σχῆμα τοῦ σώματος...καὶ σάρκα τὴν αὐτὴν τῇ ἡμετέρᾳ φορέσας ἐφάνη, δι' ἣν καὶ...ἄνθρωπος ἐγένετο, ἵνα...οὕτως...πάντες ζωοποιηθήσονται* Meth. *res.*2.18(p.369.15; M.18.284C); *ib.*3.16(p.413.6; M.118.888A) cit. s. *ἀνάστασις*; or modified *τοῦτο δὲ* [sc. *σῶμα*] *οὐ π.; π. μέν, ἀλλ' ἐκεῖνο πολλῷ πλέον. νῦν μὲν γὰρ καὶ ἀφίπταται τοῦ πνεύματος...ἡ...χάρις... τότε δὲ οὐχ οὕτως...ἢ γάρ τι τοιοῦτον ἠνίξατο, εἰπὼν π., ἢ ὅτι κουφότερον ἔσται καὶ λεπτότερον, καὶ οἷον καὶ ἐπ' ἀέρος ὀχεῖσθαι, μᾶλλον δὲ ἀμφότερα* Chrys.*hom.41.3 in 1Cor.*(10.390D,E); *δέον πιστεύειν, αὐτὸ μὲν ἀνίστασθαι κατ' οὐσίαν καὶ εἶδος τὸ σῶμα, ἄφθαρτον δὲ καὶ ἀθάνατον, καὶ ἀποστολικῶς εἰπεῖν...π.* Max.*ep.*7(M.91.440A); risen body as *π. ναός*, Ephr.2.233D; of Christ's earthly body (Gnost.) *οἱ δ' αὖ ἀπὸ τῆς ἀνατολῆς λέγουσιν...ὅτι π. ἦν τὸ σῶμα τοῦ σωτῆρος* Hipp. *haer.*6.35(p.165.14; M.16.3250A); *ταῦτα* [sc. burial etc.] *δὲ σῶμα π. παθεῖν οὐ δύναται* Or.*dial.*5(p.132.9); **3.** as subst., *spiritual being, spirit* *δαίμονας ἢ πνευματικὰ τῆς πονηρίας εἶναι* CCP(543)*anath.*4; **4.** *pertaining to unseen world*, Cyr.H.*procatech.*6; *καπηλείαν γὰρ ἐπεισάγεις τοῖς π.* Bas.*ep.*53.1(3.147C; M.32.397B); Chrys.*stat.*1.9(2. 14E); *π. θεωρίας* Evagr.Pont.*cap.pract.*A 21(M.40.1228A); **5.** *pertaining to the soul*, *Did.*10.3; *π. ὀφθαλμοῖς ὑμᾶς θεωρῶν* Eustrat.*stat. anim.*14(p.431); *ἡλικίας π.* Proc.G.*Is.*22:15ff.(M.87.2181A).

D. *supra-natural, heavenly, spiritual*; **1.** *heavenly, divine*; of Christ, Ign.*Eph.*7.2 cit. s. *ἰατρός*; cf.id.*Smyrn.*3.3; of gifts of H. Ghost, Mac.Aeg.*hom.*16.11(M.34.621B); of baptism with H. Ghost, *Const.App.*3.16.4; **2.** of pleroma (Valent.), Iren.*haer.*1.1.3(M.7. 449B); **3.** of Church *ἡ ἐκκλησία δὲ π. οὖσα ἐφανερώθη ἐν τῇ σαρκὶ Χριστοῦ* *2Clem.*14.3; *συνάφθητε τοίνυν τῇ π. μητρὶ ἐκκλησίᾳ* Zeno *henot.*(p.54.15; M.86.2624C); **4.** of Bible, prophets, scriptural writers, *inspired* *ὅλων τῶν γραφῶν π. οὐσῶν...καὶ πᾶσα γραφὴ δεδομένη ἡμῖν ἀπὸ θεοῦ* Iren.*haer.*2.28.3(M.7.806A); *τὸ τῶν προφητικῶν λόγων ἔνθεον καὶ τὸ π. τοῦ Μωσέως νόμου* Or.*princ.*4.1.6(p.301. 14; M.11.352B); *ἡ π. ἀνάγνωσις* Chrys.*hom.32.3 in Jo.*(8.188C); Thdt. *1Cor.*2:13(3.178); *ὁ προφήτης...π. ὢν* id.*Cant.*2:2(2.54); '*νόμος π. ἐστι*'...*θείῳ γάρ, φησίν, ἐγράφη πνεύματι* id.*Rom.*7:14(3.75); **5.** of virtues and spiritual states *συνήθειαν...οὐκ ἀνθρωπίνην οὖσαν ἀλλὰ π.* Ign.*Eph.*5.1; *ὁ ἔρως ὁ πνευματικώτατος* ‡Chrys.*pasch.*6.5(p.175. 15; 8.271E); of contemplation of eternal truths as spiritual food, Cyr.H.*catech.*4.27; of weapons of soul's warfare, Chrys.*stat.*3.3(2. 39C); of spiritual *γνῶσις* (i.e. monastic 'philosophy'), Pall.*h.Laus.* proem.(p.4.7; M.34.995); *διδασκάλων ὁμόνοια π.* Cosm.Ind.*top.*10(M. 88.433A); **6.** opp. natural, literal, superficial: of spiritual realities shadowed forth in symbols, types, and allegories; **a.** in sacraments; **i.** of baptism *τοῦ π. λουτροῦ τῆς παλιγγενεσίας* Hipp.*Dan.* 4.59.5; *ψυχῆς τὴν π. ἀναγέννησιν* Cyr.H.*catech.*1.2; *ἐν τούτοις* [sc. *ὕδασι*] *κατερχέσθω καὶ ἅγια καὶ π. ποιησάτω* Serap.*euch.*19.4; **ii.** of eucharist, cf.*Did.*10.3; Cyr.H.*catech.*1.6; μεταλαμβάνων αὐτοῦ [sc. ἄρτου] ὡς π. *ib.*22.9; τῶν ἱερῶν...καὶ π. ... μυστηρίων *ib.*23.23; ‡Pall. *h.mon.*2.8(p.26.5; M.34.1027D); cf.Cyr.*1Cor.*10:1(p.279.27; M.74.880B); **iii.** in gen. π. ... μυστηρίων Cyr.H.*catech.*19.1; **b.** of mystical sense of scripture, Or.*princ.*4.3.5(p.331.14; M.11.385B) cit. s. γραφή; π. δὲ διήγησις τῷ δυναμένῳ ἀποδεῖξαι, ποίων 'ἐπουρανίων ὑποδείγματι καὶ σκιᾷ' οἱ κατὰ σάρκα Ἰουδαῖοι ἐλάτρευον, καὶ...ἐπὶ πάντων... ζητητέον 'σοφίαν ἐν μυστηρίῳ τὴν ἀποκεκρυμμένην...' *ib.*4.2.6(p.315.15; 368B); τοῦ προηγουμένου σκοποῦ τυγχάνοντος τὸν ἐν τοῖς π. εἱρμὸν ἀπαγγεῖλαι γεγενημένοις καὶ πρακτέοις, ὅπου μὲν εὗρε γενόμενα κατὰ τὴν ἱστορίαν ὁ λόγος ἐφαρμόσαι δυνάμενα τοῖς μυστικοῖς τούτοις, ἐχρήσατο ἀποκρύπτων ἀπὸ πολλῶν τὸν βαθύτερον νοῦν· ὅπου δὲ ἐν τῇ διηγήσει τῆς περὶ τῶν νοητῶν ἀκολουθίας οὐχ εἵπετο ἡ τῶνδέ τινων πρᾶξις ἡ προαναγεγραμμένη διὰ τὰ μυστικώτερα, συνύφηνεν ἡ γραφὴ τῇ ἱστορίᾳ τὸ μὴ γενόμενον, πῇ μὲν μηδὲ δυνατὸν γενέσθαι, πῇ δὲ δυνατὸν μὲν γενέσθαι, οὐ μὴν γεγενημένον *ib.*4.2.9(p.321.12; 376A); hence opp. σωματικός; of truth in scripture, id.*Jo.*10.5(4; p.175.19; M.14.313C); ἡ μυστικὴ καὶ π. τῶν γραφῶν διάνοια Didym.*Ps.*1:3(M.39.1160A); π. θεωρία Cyr.*ador.*1(1.3E); hence of fourth gospel 'Ἰωάννην ἔσχατον, συνιδόντα ὅτι τὰ σωματικὰ ἐν τοῖς εὐαγγελίοις δεδήλωται...π. ποιῆσαι εὐαγγέλιον Clem.*fr.*8(p.197.29; M.9.749C); **c.** of antitypes of OT types: Church as 'Ἰσραηλιτικὸν...π. γένος Just.*dial.*11.3(M.6.500A); Clem.*exc.Thdot.*56(p.126.3; M.9.685C); Eleazar as 'spiritual father' of priests, Gr.Naz.*or.*15.12(M.35.932C); Christ as 'spiritual Moses', Mac.Aeg.*hom.*47.7(M.34.800D); Devil as π. Φαραώ, *ib.*47.12(804B); and π. ὄφις, Mac.Mgn.*apocr.*3.9(p.72.20); **7.** of things, *sacred, holy*; altar as π. τράπεζα, *Lit.Jac.*(p.160.14); of clergy as bishop's π. στέφανος, Ign.*Magn.*13.1; unity of Church, Cyr.*fr.1Petr.*2:6(p.447; M.74.1013A); Law (Rom.7:14) π. γὰρ εἰπών, διδάσκαλον αὐτὸν ἀρετῆς δείκνυσιν ὄντα...τοῦτο γάρ ἐστιν εἶναι π., τὸ πάντων ἁμαρτημάτων ἀπάγειν Chrys.*hom.13.1 in Rom.*(9.557C,D); id.*hom.29.5 in 1Cor.*(10.265D); π. ... τὸν νόμον, ὡς πνευματικοὺς ἀποφαίνοντα τοὺς ἑπομένους αὐτῷ Cyr.*Rom.*7:14(p.202.9,10; M.74.808B); worship, Cosm.Ind.*top.*5(M.88.208D); kiss of peace ὁ π. ἀσπασμός ‡Bas.*h.myst.*55(p.392.4); ref. 1Petr.2:4, cf. *spirituales hostiae...haec vero sunt sanctorum orationes, contemplatio, et actus egregii oblati*, Didym.*1Petr.*2:4(M.39.1762B); **8.** of persons, *spiritual, holy*, opp. σωματικός, ψυχικός, σαρκικός; **a.** in gen., Ign.*Eph.*8.21 cit. s. σαρκικός; γενώμεθα π. *Barn.*4.11; Iren.*haer.*5.5.1(M.7.1134B); οὐκ ἄρα οἱ μὲν γνωστικοί, οἱ δὲ ψυχικοὶ ἐν αὐτῷ τῷ λόγῳ, ἀλλ' οἱ πάντες ἀποθέμενοι τὰς σαρκικὰς ἐπιθυμίας ἴσοι καὶ π. παρὰ τῷ κυρίῳ Clem. *paed.*1.6(p.108.25; M.8.288B); ἀνακέκραται τῷ ἁγίῳ πνεύματι ἡ ἑκάστου ψυχὴ καὶ γέγονεν ἕκαστος τῶν σωζομένων π. Or.*Jo.*1.28(30; p.36.14; M.14.77A); λογιώτερος ἢ ὁ πνευματικώτερος Gr.Naz.*or.*42.21(M.36.484A); νοεῖται δὲ π. ὁ μὴ κατὰ σάρκα ζῶν, ἀπονενευκὼς δὲ μᾶλλον ἐπὶ τὸ θέλειν ἕπεσθαι τῇ θελήσει τοῦ πνεύματος Cyr.*Rom.*7:14(p.202.1; M.74.808A); σαρκικός, ἢ ψυχικός, ἢ π. Max.*ep.*9(M.91.448A); **b.** Gnost., opp. ὑλικός, ψυχικός: ἀνθρώπων δὲ τρία γένη ὑφίστανται, π., χοϊκόν, ψυχικόν Iren.*haer.*1.7.5(M.7.517B); οἱ π. ἄνθρωποι οἱ τὴν τελείαν γνῶσιν ἔχοντες περὶ θεοῦ καὶ τῆς Ἀχαμώθ *ib.*1.6.1(505A); αὐτοὺς δὲ μὴ διὰ πράξεως ἀλλὰ διὰ τὸ φύσει π. εἶναι πάντῃ τε καὶ πάντως σωθήσεσθαι δογματίζουσιν *ib.*1.6.2(505B); exeg. Rom.11:16 ἀπαρχὴν μὲν τὸ π. εἰρῆσθαι διδάσκοντες, φύραμα δὲ ἡμᾶς, τουτέστι τὴν ψυχικὴν ἐκκλησίαν *ib.*1.8.3(529A); πολλοὶ μὲν οἱ ὑλικοί, οὐ πολλοὶ δὲ οἱ ψυχικοί· σπάνιοι δὲ οἱ π. τὸ μὲν οὖν π. φύσει σωζόμενον, τὸ δὲ ψυχικὸν αὐτεξούσιον ὂν ἐπιτηδειότητα ἔχει...κατὰ τὴν οἰκείαν αἵρεσιν, τὸ δὲ ὑλικὸν φύσει ἀπόλλυται Clem.*exc.Thdot.*56(p.125.17; M.9.685C); Cels.ap.Or.*Cels.*5.61(p.64.23; M.11.1277B); **c.** of the body as 'spiritualized' by union with H. Ghost, ref. 'second Adam' Christology προγενέστερον δείκνυσι τὸν πρωτόπλαστον ὁ ἀπόστολος, πρῶτον τὸ ψυχικὸν δεικνύς, ἔπειτα τὸ π. ψυχικὸν δὲ καὶ π. λέγων, οὐχ ἕτερον καὶ ἕτερον δείκνυσι σῶμα, ἀλλὰ τὸ αὐτὸ σῶμα· τὸ μὲν πρῶτον ἐν ἐξουσίᾳ καὶ φύσει ψυχῆς, διὸ ψυχικόν· τὸ δὲ δεύτερον...τοῦ πνεύματος· διὸ π. ... ἑνὸς ὄντος ἑκατέρων τοῦ σώματος, τὸ μὲν τοῦ πνεύματος μέτοχον νοεῖσθαι π. δείκνυσι, τὸ δὲ τῇ ἐξουσίᾳ τῆς ψυχῆς μόνῃ ἐμμείναντα δείκνυσθαι ψυχικόν ‡Ath.*Apoll.*1.8(M.26.1105B); Χριστὸς...τὴν σάρκα...πνευματικωτέραν ἐποίησεν, οὐ τῷ τὴν φύσιν μεταβαλεῖν, ἀλλὰ τῷ πτερῶσαι μᾶλλον αὐτήν. καθάπερ γὰρ πυρὸς ὁμιλοῦντος σιδήρῳ, καὶ ὁ σίδηρος γίνεται πῦρ ἐν τῇ οἰκείᾳ μένων φύσει· οὕτω καὶ τῶν πιστῶν καὶ πνεῦμα ἐχόντων καὶ ἡ σὰρξ ...πρὸς ἐκείνην μεθίσταται τὴν ἐνέργειαν, ὅλη π. γινομένη Chrys.*hom.13.8 in Rom.*(9.569B); ἀποδυσάμενοι τὴν φθοράν, καὶ π. ἔχοντες τὸ σῶμα, τουτέστιν εἰς μόνα βλέπον τὰ τοῦ πνεύματος Cyr.*dogm.*5(p.559.19; 6^2.375B); φαντάζονται τὸν ἐρώμενον, καὶ πρὸ τῆς ἐλπιζομένης ἀφθαρσίας τὸ σῶμα π. ἀπετέλεσαν Thdt.*carit.*(3.1318); **d.** esp. of **i.** the baptized π. μὲν γὰρ τοὺς πεπιστευκότας ἤδη τῷ ἁγίῳ πνεύματι προσείπεν, σαρκικοὺς δὲ τοὺς νεοκατηχήτους καὶ μηδέπω κεκαθαρμένους Clem.*paed.*1.6(p.111.20; M.8.293A); πνευματικὰ ποιησάτω [sc. ὕδατα] πρὸς τὸ μηκέτι σάρκα καὶ αἷμα εἶναι τοὺς βαπτιζομένους, ἀλλὰ π. καὶ δυναμένους προσκυνεῖν σοὶ ...ἐν ἁγίῳ πνεύματι Serap.*euch.*19.4; **ii.** advanced ('gnostic') Christians ἡ γνωστικὴ ψυχὴ...π. ... ὅλη γενομένη πρὸς τὸ συγγενὲς χωρήσασα ἐν π. τῇ ἐκκλησίᾳ μένει εἰς τὴν ἀνάπαυσιν τοῦ θεοῦ Clem.*str.*7.12(p.49.18; M.9.496A); cf. τὸ μὲν γὰρ Ἰακὼβ ἐπὶ τοῦ ἔτι στοιχειουμένου καὶ σωματικοῦ λαμβάνεται, τὸ δὲ Ἰσραὴλ ἐπὶ τοῦ κρείττονος καὶ π. †Bas.*Is.*277(1.590E; M.30.605C); **iii.** of monks ὁσίων καὶ ἀθανάτων π. ἡμῶν πατέρων ‡Pall.*proem.*(p.4.1; M.34.995); cf. τῶν ἁγίων πατέρων πνευματικοῦ βίου ἀνάξιος *ib.*(p.4.8); μόνων τῶν π. εἰδότων τὰ σημαινόμενα Pall.*h.Laus.*32(p.91.5; 1100B); ἐμπείροις π. πατέρων συναναστρέφεσθαι Marc.Er.*opusc.*5.11(M.65.1048A); hence of monastery, Pach.*reg.*A,B(M.40.949B; πατρικῷ p.15.1); of monastic system ὁ τῆς π. καθηγούμενος πολιτείας ‡Bas.*const.*20.1(2.565A; M.31.1389D); **iv.** of spiritual counsellors, leaders, and teachers, and their pupils τέκνον ἐστὶ π. τοῦ διδασκάλου ὁ μαθητής...τί ποτε ἄρα διδάσκειν μέλλει ὁ π. ἡμῶν πατήρ; Bas.*hom.in Ps.*33(1.150E; M.29.369A); of Ath. τὸν π. πατέρα id.*ep.*82(3.175E; M.32.460C); ἔδωκεν ἡμῖν εὐφρανθῆναι ὡς ἐπὶ τέκνῳ π. *ib.*73.1(167A; M.441A); esp. of bishops, *ib.*227.1(349E; M.852B); *Const.App.*2.33.2; **v.** of spiritual guides and confessors οὐ γὰρ εἴδομεν αὐτοὺς εἰσελθεῖν ἐν ἐκκλησίᾳ ποτέ, οὐδὲ εἰς π. πατέρας οὐδὲ εἰς ἀγαθὸν ἕν *Apoc.Bar.*13(p.93.15); cf. πνευματικῶν [sc. γάμων] ὀρέγεσθαι, ἄρχειν ψυχῶν, καὶ παιδογονεῖν πνευματικῶς Bas. *inst.ascet.*2(2.200B; M.31.621B) ὦ σὺ πάτερ ἐκείνης πνευματικέ Gr. Naz.*or.*8.22(M.35.813C); ὅταν λυπηρόν τι ἢ τραχὺ πρὸς σὲ εἴπῃ ὁ π. πατήρ, δέξαι Nil.*epp.*3.333(M.79.364B); τῷ π. πατρὶ καὶ διδασκάλῳ τοῦ νοσοῦντος Sophr.H.*mir.Cyr.et Jo.*(M.87.3668B); ὥσπερ σπόρος οὐκ αὐξηθήσεται δίχα τῆς γῆς καὶ ὕδατος· οὕτως οὐδὲ ὁ ἄνθρωπος σωθήσεται, ἑκούσιος ποιῶν, ἐκτὸς πατρὸς π. *Nomoc.*262; esp. in monasteries ἐὰν καθίζεις ἐν ὑποταγῇ π. πατέρων Ephr.1.217D; ἀδελφός τις...ἑτέρῳ ἀδελφῷ...εἶπε· βούλομαι ἐξελθεῖν τῶν π. μου πατέρων id.1.220A; id. 2.154D; esp. of confessor γενόμενος π. τῷ ὑπὸ τοῦ πνεύματος ἄγεσθαι τρόπον υἱοῦ θεοῦ Or.*or.*28.8(p.380.10; M.11.528C); οὐκ ἐγώ σου, τέκνον π., τὴν ἐξομολόγησιν προηγουμένως δέχομαι, καὶ τὴν συγχώρησίν σοι παρέχομαι, δι' ἐμοῦ δὲ ὁ θεός †Jo.Jej.*poenit.*(M.88.1892A); ἐὰν οὖν εὕρῃς ἄνδρα π., ἔμπειρον, δυνάμενόν σε ἰατρεῦσαι,...ἐξομολόγησαι αὐτῷ, ὡς τῷ κυρίῳ καὶ οὐκ ἀνθρώπῳ Anast.S.*qu.et resp.*6(M.89.372A); as competent to debar penitent from Communion, *Nomoc.*411; dist. from priest, †Jo.Jej.*serm.*(M.88.1924A); abs., *confessor* παρηγγέλθη ὑπὸ τοῦ π. Sophr.H.*conf.*(M.87.3369C); of a priest, *Nomoc.*79; *ib.*477; **9.** ref. spiritual affinity, cf. μείζων ἐστὶν ἡ κατὰ τὸ πνεῦμα οἰκειότης τῆς τῶν σωμάτων συναφείας CTrull.*can.*53; **a.** established by baptism, cf. τῶν...κατὰ σάρκα καὶ κατὰ πνεῦμα πατέρων Gr.Naz.*or.*8.11(M.35.801A); τῷ ἐμῷ γνησίῳ ἐκγόνῳ καὶ π. υἱῷ *CIG* 8855 (Smyrna); hence ἀδελφὸς π. of one having same godparent, *Nomoc.*185,187,188; *ib.*190; **b.** by adoption εἰς υἱὸν ἐποιησάμην π. Jo.VI H.*v.Jo.D.*10(M.94.445A); cf.*Euchol.*(p.561); **c.** in gen., *Nomoc.*159; esp. of inhabitants of monasteries as spiritually related to each other, Thdr. Stud.*test.*(M.99.1817D); id.*ep.*2.60(M.99.1276A); cf. πνευματικῶς, id. *epp.*1.10(M.99.940C).

πνευματικῶς, *spiritually*; **1.** *in respect of the spirit* σωματικῶς μένετε ἐν Χριστῷ...σαρκικῶς καὶ π. Ign.*Eph.*10.3; π. καὶ σωματικῶς Χριστιανίζειν Or.*Jo.*1.7(9; p.13.2; M.14.37A); ref. Christ in respect of divinity συνέφαγεν...ὡς σαρκικός, καίπερ π. ἡνωμένος τῷ πατρί Ign.*Smyrn.*3.3; Cyr.*Jo.*11.12(4.1001E) cit. s. ἐν; **2.** *after a spiritual or supernatural manner* θεὸν ὑπὸ μὲν Ἑλλήνων ἐθνικῶς, ὑπὸ δὲ Ἰουδαίων Ἰουδαϊκῶς...ὑφ' ἡμῶν καὶ π. γινωσκόμενον Clem.*str.*6.5(p.452.20; M.9.261B); ref. inspiration, *ib.*2.4(p.120.18; M.8.945B); *ib.*5.1(p.330.6; M.9.17A); iron. σαρκικὲ Ἀέτιε καὶ ψυχικὲ π. ἀνακρινόμενε Epiph.*haer.*76.24(p.371.14; M.42.564B); ref. non-literal interpretation of scripture διηγούμενοι...π. Or.*Cels.*2.3(p.130.10; M.11.800C); cf. *illius Tyri, quae spiritaliter intellegitur*, id.*princ.*1.5.4(p.75.25; M.11.163A); ἡ π. καλουμένη Αἴγυπτος id.*hom.9.2 in Jer.*(p.66.23; M.13.352B); σαρκικῶς...ἀνεκρίθησαν, π. μὴ νενοηκότες τὰ...εἰρημένα Epiph.*haer.*55.5(p.330.10; M.41.980C); ref. actions of biblical characters which typify spiritual realities π. ἔπινεν Or.*fr.55 in Jo.*(p.528.32); ref. spiritual feeding on Christ, Clem.*str.*5.10(p.370.18; M.9.101A); ref. spiritual guidance and leadership, *1Clem.*47.3; παιδογονεῖν π. Bas.*inst.ascet.*2(2.200B; M.31.621B); id.*hom.*20.7(2.162C; M.31.537D); π. οὐ δικαστικῶς ἐπιμέμφεται Thdt.*1Cor.*11:22(3.237).

***πνευματῖται, οἱ**, *adherents of* party usually known as πνευματομάχοι, Epiph.*anc.*63(p.76.14; M.43.129C).

***πνευματογράφος, ὁ**, *inspired writer* (i.e. author of scripture), Cyr.*Is.*1.5(2.132D).

***πνευματοδόχος**, **1.** *breath-receiving*, of lungs π. ἀγγείων Gr.

Nyss.*hom.opif.*9(M.44.149C); **2.** *Spirit-receiving, inspired*; of Psalmist, Jo.Clim.*scal.*4(M.88.677C).

***πνευματοεργός, ὁ,** *creator of spirits*, Synes.*hymn.*3.169(p.12; M. 66.1596).

***πνευματοκίνητος,** *moved by the Spirit, inspired*, Dion.Ar.*d.n.*1.1 (M.3.585B); Leont.B.*Nest.et Eut.*3(M.86.1357B); Thdr.Stud.*epp.*2. 121(M.99.1397A).

***πνευματοκινήτως,** *under the inspiration of the Spirit*, Thdr. Stud.*epp.*2.79(M.99.1317D); *ib.*2.129(1416C); *ib.*2.158(1496D).

***πνευματοκλήτωρ, ὁ,** *summoner of the Spirit*, of apostles *π. γὰρ ἤπερ ὄντως τοῦ πνεύματος χορηγοὺς...εἶναι πιστεύομεν* Cyr.*Jo.*2.3 (4.169E).

***πνευματομαχέω,** *fight against the Spirit*; of those who deny full divinity of H. Ghost, Ath.*ep.Serap.*1.32(M.26.605B); *ib.*4.1(637B); hence of Macedonians, Gr.Nyss.*or.dom.*3(p.64.32; M.44.1160C); Didym.(‡Bas.)*Eun.*5(1.314B; M.29.753A).

***πνευματομαχία, ἡ,** *fight against the Spirit*, of denial of divinity of H. Ghost *ἔνδυμα...μὴ Μακεδονικῇ π. φορέσῃς* Chrys.ap.Anast.S. *qu.et resp.*8(M.89.401B).

***πνευματομάχος,** *fighting against the Spirit*, Pall.*h.Laus.*46(p.136. 9; M.34.1226B); masc. as subst., of Macedonians, ‡Ath.*Maced.*(M. 26.1313B); *παραγωγαῖς τῶν π. παρακρουσθέντας* Bas.*Spir.*27(3.22E; M. 32.116A); *ἀδιόριστός ἐστιν ὁ περὶ τοῦ ἁγίου πνεύματος λόγος* [sc. in Nicene creed] *οὔπω τότε τῶν π. ἀναφανέντων* id.*ep.*140.2(3.233E; M. 32.589A); *πρωτοστάτης* [sc. Eust. Seb.]...*τῶν π. αἱρέσεως ib.*263.3 (406C; M.980B); of Bas. Anc., Geo. Laod., and Semi-Arians *αὐτοὶ καὶ περὶ τοῦ ἁγίου πνεύματος ἴσως τοῖς π. εἰσὶν ἔχοντες* Epiph.*haer.*73. 1(p.268.19; M.42.401B); *ἡμιαρείων ἤγουν π.* CCP(381)*can.*1; ‡Gr. Nyss.*hom.9.24 in Jo.*(p.289.15); *Διόδωρός τις, π. ὤν* Cyr.*ep.*45(p.151. 15; 5^{2}.135D); Jo.D.*haer.*74(M.94.724A); *Μακεδονίου τοῦ π. CIG* 8960 (Bethlehem); identified with *τροπικοί*, ‡Ath.*haer.*5(M.28.509D).

πνευματοποιός, *producing flatulence*, Clem.*str.*3.3(p.206.23; M.8. 1128A).

***πνευματοτόκος,** *bearing the Spirit, who is mother of the Spirit*, of S. Elisabeth in iron. attack on orthodox use of *θεοτόκος*: *πνεῦμα ἅγιον ἔχων οὗτος ὁ μακάριος βαπτιστὴς ἀπετίκτετο. τί οὖν; καλεῖς τὴν Ἐλισάβετ π.;* Nest.*fr.*D 1(p.352.19)ap.Cyr.*Nest.*1.4(p.25.5; 6^{1}. 19D).

πνευματοφορ-έομαι, 1. med., *bear the Spirit, be inspired*; of OT prophets, Eus.*d.e.*8.2(p.372.29; M.22.605B); Cyr.*Jo.*5.2(4.471B); **2.** pass.; **a.** *be carried away, as though on the wind*, cf.Jer.2:24 *ἐν ἐπιθυμίαις ψυχῆς αὐτῆς ἐπνευματοφορεῖτο. ~ουμένη δὲ ψυχὴ πάντως που καὶ ἀκατάστατος* Cyr.*Is.*5.2(2.765D); **b.** of false prophets, *be carried away with enthusiasm*, ref. Jer.2:24 *τὸ γὰρ ἐπνευματοφορεῖτο περὶ τῶν ψευδοπροφητῶν τέθεικε* Thdt.*Jer.*2:24(2.418); of Montanus *~ηθῆναί τε καὶ αἰφνιδίως ἐν κατοχῇ τινι καὶ παρεκστάσει γενόμενον ἐνθουσιᾶν* Anon.ap.Eus.*h.e.*5.16.7(M.20.465C); *τοῦτον δὲ τρόπον οὔτε τινὰ τῶν κατὰ τὴν παλαιὰν οὔτε τῶν κατὰ τὴν καινὴν ~ηθέντα προφήτην δεῖξαι δυνήσονται* Anon.*ib.*5.17.3(473B).

πνευματοφόρος, A. *spirit-bearing, inspired*; **1.** of prophets *δοκίμαζε...ἀπὸ τῆς ζωῆς...τὸν λέγοντα ἑαυτὸν π. εἶναι* Herm.*mand.*11.16; *οἱ...τοῦ θεοῦ ἄνθρωποι, π. πνεύματος ἁγίου καὶ προφῆται γενόμενοι* Thphl.Ant.*Autol.*2.9(M.6.1064A); Eus.*d.e.*6.18(p.275.9; M.22.452D); Cyr.H.*catech.*16.28; of Jo. Bapt., Antip.Bost.*Jo.Bapt.*13(M.85. 1776B); of a monk (S. Antony) as prophet *γέγονε π., ἀλλ' οὐκ ἤθελε λαλεῖν διὰ τοὺς ἀνθρώπους Apophth.Patr.*(M.65.85B); **2.** of scriptural writers, Thphl.Ant.*Autol.*2.22(M.6.1088B); *τῶν ἁγίων εὐαγγελιστῶν καὶ π. τῶν τὸν λόγον παρὰ πατρὸς ἀπεσταλμένον φησάντων* Epiph.*haer.*65.5(p.8.11; M.42.20D); Pall.*v.Chrys.*12(p.72. 25; M.47.41); of S. Paul, *ib.*18(p.119.16; M.47.66); of Psalmist, Cyr. *Ps.*36:25(M.69.941A); *ὁ π. εὐαγγελιστής* Oecum.*Apoc.*13:3(p.151); **3.** of doctors of Church *τὴν ἐξ ἀρχῆς παραδοθεῖσαν ἡμῖν ἐκ τῶν ἁγίων καὶ π. ἡμῶν πατέρων ὀρθόδοξον πίστιν* Cyr.*ep.*39(*ACO* 1.1.4 p.19.25; H.2.416A); of Nicene fathers, Anast.S.*hod.*9(M.91.141C); of S. Basil, Eustrat.*stat.anim.*15(p.445); **4.** of monks, *V.Pach.A* 26(p.153.19); **5.** of false prophets, *enthusiastic* (cf. Os.9:7); Chrys.*hom.43.3 in Mt.* (7.462A); Thdt.*Os.*9:7(2.1352).

B. *united to the Spirit αὐτὸς οὖν ἐστι θεὸς σαρκοφόρος, καὶ ἡμεῖς ἄνθρωποι π.* Ath.*inc.et c.Ar.*8(M.26.996C); *αἱ π. ψυχαὶ ἐλλαμφθεῖσαι παρὰ τοῦ πνεύματος* Bas.*Spir.*23(3.20B; M.32.109B); hence *holy, saintly*, Iren.*haer.*5.5.1(M.7.1135B); Mac.Aeg.*hom.*47.14(M.34.805B); Pall.*h.Laus.*11(p.34.11; M.34.1034C); Isid.Pel.*epp.*5.144(M.78.1409D); *Apophth.Patr.*(M.65.280A); ref. baptism *ψυχὰς λογικὰς καὶ π. τὸ ὕδωρ ἀναδίδωσι* Chrys.*hom.26.1 in Jo.*(8.149A); esp. ref. Christ, in adoptionist view *ἄνθρωπον...γεγονότα π.* Cyr.*Is.*2.1(2.193B); Proc.G.*Is.*11:1–10(M.87.2041B).

πνευματόω, 1. *inflate, blow out εἰσῆλθεν εἰς τὸν ἀσκὸν* [sc. *τὸ πνεῦμα*] *καὶ ἐπνευμάτωσεν αὐτόν T.Sal.*22.13(M.122.1353B); **2.** of God, *inbreathe ὁ χοῦς ὁ θείᾳ πνευματωθεὶς εἰκόνι* Gr.Naz.*carm.*1.2.18.14(M. 37.787A); Geo.Pis.*hex.*1764(M.92.1570A); **3.** pass., *be possessed by a spirit, Mir.Artem.*6(p.7.5).

***πνευστός,** *breathed*, Gr.Naz.*carm.*1.1.8.9(M.37.447A); *ib.*2.2 (poem.)5.72(1526A).

πνέ-ω, 1. *breathe out μύρον ἔλαβεν...ὁ κύριος, ἵνα πνέῃ τῇ ἐκκλησίᾳ ἀφθαρσίαν* Ign.*Eph.*17.1; met. *ἔπνει...οὐκ ἀμπέλων ὀσμὴν...ἀλλ' ἀγάπης, χαρᾶς* Or.*fr.62 in Jer.*(p.229.5); *Hom.Clem.*4.19; *ib.*10.18; **2.** abs. *breathe out odour, smell*, of resurrection garden *εἰσελθόντος τοῦ Ἰησοῦ, ἔπνευσεν ὁ κῆπος* Ath.*fr.4 in Cant.*(M.27.1356A); **3.** *be redolent of π. στακτῆς* Or.*Cant.*2(p.168.27; M.13.141D); met. *π. τοῦ πληρώματος* id.*fr.hom.21 in Jer.*(p.196.4; M.13.1310C); *τῆς τοῦ πεποιηκότος αὐτὸν ~ων* [sc. *ἄνθρωπος*] *θειότητος Hom.Clem.*8.10; Eus.*v.C.*2.20(p.49.10; M.20.997B); *θυμοῦ...~ων ib.*2.1(p.40.7; 980A); *μέχρι τίνος ἀπὸ γῆς ~ομεν;* Chrys.*hom.14.4 in Ac.*(9.117D); Zach. Mit.*opif.*(M.85.1060A); **4.** *rage ὁρᾷς ποῦ ἔπνει;* Chrys.*hom.20.4 in Heb.*(12.192A); *κατ' αὐτῶν ἔπνευσεν ὁ διάβολος* id.*hom.6.1 in Mt.* (7.84B); ‡Nil.*perist.*10.2(M.79.889A); **5.** *inspire εἰ αἱ πνευσθεῖσαι γραφαὶ...θεόπνευστοί εἰσιν* ‡Ath.*dial.Trin.*3.21(M.28.1236A).

***πνηγηδόν,** s.v.l., *in a crowd*, Ph.Carp.*Cant.*197(M.40.124B).

πνικτός, *strangled*, ref. Ac.15:29; Or.*Cels.*8.30(p.245.5; M.11. 1560B) cit. s. *αἷμα*; 'what is strangled' renounced by Christian at baptism, Ephr.2.196A.

πνοή, ἡ, 1. *wind νομίζοντες τὴν τῶν ἀνέμων π. εἶναι θεάν* Arist. *apol.*5.4; **2.** *breath*; **a.** of man's breath, compared with H. Ghost *πνεῦμα...οὐχ ὡς ὑπ' ἀνθρώπου π. ἐμπνευσθεῖσαν ἀνυπόστατον* Apoll. *fid.sec.pt.*37(p.181.21; M.10.1120B); of name of Jesus united to breath of hesychast *ἡ Ἰησοῦ μνήμη ἑνωθήτω τῇ π. σου, καὶ τότε γνώσῃ ἡσυχίας ὠφέλειαν* Jo.Clim.*scal.*27(M.88.1112C); **b.** of breath of life, bestowed on man by God, *1Clem.*21.9; Athenag.*leg.*7.1(M.6. 904B); **3.** hence of human *spirit* as immortal principle, Iren.*haer.* 1.6.1(M.7.504A); *ὁ κύριος...πάσης π. καὶ σαρκός A.Jo.*8(p.156.6); *πιστὸς πνοῇ κρύπτει πράγματα* Or.*schol.in Cant.*4:3(M.17.272A); **4.** *soul, person*, Polyc.*ep.*2.1; *ὅταν ἴδωμεν φύσιν καὶ πᾶσαν π. ἀνθρώπων...ἀνισταμένην* Ephr.3.145B; **5.** of *Holy Ghost* indwelling soul, *Hom.Clem.*13.19; *ψυχὰς...τὴν τοῦ θεοῦ π. ἠμφιεσμένας ib.*16. 16; *αἰτία ἐστὶν ἡ τοῦ θεοῦ φύσις...τοῦ...πνεύματος ὡς πνοῆς· π. γὰρ παντοκράτορος ἡ διδάξασά με* ‡Ath.*dial.Trin.*2.23(M.28.1193A).

***πνοϊκός,** *respiratory*; neut. plur. as subst., *respiratory organs*, Arc.C.*v.Sym.*(M.94.1393C).

ποάζ-ω, *produce grass τὸ...χλοερὸν καὶ ~ον* Bas.*hex.*5.1(1.40B; M. 29.96A).

***ποδάλγη, ἡ,** = *ποδάγρα, gout*, Gr.Mag.*dial.*(tr.Zach.)4.27(M.*PL.* 77.363D).

ποδαλγός, *gouty*, Ephr.1.214F; Gr.Naz.*ep.*193(M.37.316C); *ποδαλγὸς ποδαλγὸν τίκτει* Isid.Pel.*epp.*4.141(M.78.1220D).

***ποδηγεσία, ἡ,** *leading*, Gr.Naz.*carm.*1.1.9.27(M.37.459A).

ποδηγία, ἡ, *guidance*, Gr.Naz.*carm.*2.1.72.12(M.37.1420A); *λαὸς...τὴν διὰ νόμου πεπλουτηκὼς π.* Cyr.*Os.*38(3.69D); *τῇ τῆς πίστεως π.* Thdt.*Rom.*4:12(3.49); Sophr.H.*ep.syn.*(M.87.3149C).

ποδήρης, *down to the feet*, of a robe; masc. as subst., of high priest's robe, Just.*dial.*42.1(M.6.565A); Chrys.*sac.*3.4(p.51.11; 1. 382C); of robe worn by angel of Ezech.9:2, Cyr.*Os.*58(3.89D); of Christ as high priest *οἱ δὲ ἐργαζόμενοι πατριάρχαι τε καὶ προφῆται οἱ τὸν καλὸν π. καὶ τέλειον χιτῶνα ὑφαίνοντες Χριστοῦ* Hipp.*antichr.*4 (p.7.7; M.10.732C); *ἐν μέσῳ καὶ ὁ τὸν μέγαν π. περικείμενος ἀρχιερεύς* ‡Pion.*v.Polyc.*22; met. *τὸν π. τῆς ἀληθείας T.Lev.*8.2; *κἂν τὸν π. τις παραφέρῃ τὸν κυρίου* Clem.*paed.*2.10(p.225.4; M.8.533A); Eus.*h.e.*10. 4.2(M.20.849A).

***ποδήριον, τό,** = *ποδήρης, robe π. δόξης* Ephr.1.83A.

***ποδηροφορέω,** *wear a long robe*, Clem.*paed.*3.1(p.235.22; M.8. 556A).

πόδιον, τό, *sheet* (nautical), Mac.Aeg.*hom.*57.3(p.47).

ποδιστήρ, ὁ, *foot-bath*, Thdt.*Jer.*52:17(2.628).

ποδοκέφαλα, τά, *feet and head*, i.e. *offal*; not to be eaten in month of May, Jo.D.*fr.*(M.95.236D).

***ποδοκοπέω,** *cut off the feet of*, Thphn.*chron.*p.353(M.108.848A).

***ποδονίπτα, ἡ,** *foot-bath, pan*; worshipped by Egyptians, *M.Apollon.*17.

ποδόνιπτρον, τό, *foot-pan*: Amasis, raised from the ranks to be king, ordered worship of a pan, thus raised to be a god, cf.Thphl. Ant.*Autol.*1.10(M.6.1040A).

ποδοστράβη, ἡ, *snare*, Gr.Naz.*carm.*1.2.10.45(M.37.684A); Thdt. *provid.*5(4.552).

***ποδοφιλ-έω**, *kiss the feet of* τοὺς ἐπισκόπους ~ήσαντες *Pers.*(p.43.18).

***ποδοφορία**, ἡ, *journey on foot*, Steph.Diac.*v.Steph.*(M.100.1105A).

***ποδωτός**, *having feet*, Or.*Ps.*35:12(p.8).

[*]**ποηφαγής**, *grass-eating*, Cyr.*Is.*2.1(2.200C).

***ποθεινότης**, ἡ, *dearness*; as complimentary title, Thds.Imp.*ep. Licin.*(p.8.7; M.*PL.*54.878C); Max.*ep.*3(M.91.408C).

ποθ-έω, *long for, desire*; of spiritual desire, for virtues τῇ ἀγαθότητι κολλήθητε, ὅτι...ἄνθρωποι αὐτὴν ~οῦσιν *T.Aser* 3.1; Just.*1apol.*5.4(M.6.336C); Bas.*hom.*17.2(3.139E; M.31.485B); for God τὸν θεὸν ~εῖν ἑλομένας ψυχάς Meth.*symp.*7.5(p.76.17; M.18.132B); ἡ σώφρων τὸν θεὸν ~εῖ *Hom.Clem.*13.15; pass., of object of prayer, Clem.*str.*7.7(p.32.20; M.9.460B); of Christian hope, Just.*1apol.*39.4(388C).

πόθησις, ἡ, *affection* ἑλκομένου τῇ π. τῆς σῆς θεοσεβείας Acac.et Paul.*ep.*(p.154.13; M.41.156D).

ποθητός, **1.** *beloved*; **a.** of persons ποθητός σου ἀεὶ ἐγενόμην *A.(Pass.)Andr.*10(p.24.26; πιστός M.2.1237A); ἠρξάμην θεάσασθαι τὸν π. μου Χριστόν *M.Ner.et Ach.*16(p.15.28); of BMV πᾶσι ποθητέ ‡Meth.*Sym.et Ann.*10(M.18.372C); **b.** of things, *pleasant, agreeable* ἐμοὶ γὰρ πάνυ π. πρᾶγμα πράξεις Just.*dial.*57.4(M.6.605D); παρθενεία ...ποθητή...ἐστιν θεῷ *M.Ner.et Ach.*5(p.4.2); ἡ ποθητὴ σκηνὴ τῆς ψυχῆς Meth.*res.*1.51(p.307.1; M.18.281D); Chrys.*hom.2.1 in Mt.*(7.20A); **2.** *lovable*, opp. μισητός, Chrys.*hom.19.8 in Rom.*(9.655C, v.l. ποθεινός).

ποθόβλητος, *raising desire*, Nonn.*par.Jo.*8.44(M.43.820B).

πόθος, ὁ, *longing, desire*; **1.** spiritual, Clem.*str.*7.7(p.30.23; M.9.456B); πόθῳ...ἀγόμενος πρὸς τὴν εὕρεσιν τοῦ καλοῦ *ib.*8.1(p.80.23; 561A); τῷ π. τὴν πίστιν ἐγκαταμίξαντα id.*ecl.*36(p.148.4; M.9.717A); **2.** *affection* τοιοῦτον π. εἶχεν ὁ γέρων εἰς τοὺς ἁγίους πατέρας ἡμῶν Jo.Mosch.*prat.*40(M.87.2896A).

ποι-έω, **I.** *make, produce*;

A. of Creation; **1.** by God; **a.** dist. from other words of kindred meaning; πράσσω: κἂν ὁ Ἀριστοτέλης τεχνολογῇ, τὸ μὲν ~εῖν καὶ ἐπὶ τῶν ἀλόγων ζῴων τάσσεσθαι ἐπὶ ἀψύχων διδάσκων, τὸ δὲ πράττειν ἀνθρώπων εἶναι μόνων, εὐθυνέτω τοὺς λέγοντας ποιητὴν τῶν ὅλων εἶναι τὸν θεόν Clem.*str.*5.13(p.383.3; M.9.128A); κτίζω: Dion.R.ap.Ath.*decr.*26(p.23.3; M.25.464C) cit. infra, 3.b.ii; but τὸ γὰρ ~ῆσαι τῷ κτίσαι ταὐτόν ἐστιν Gr.Nyss.*Eun.*4(2 p.82.1; M.45.656D); γεννάω: Didym.(‡Bas.)*Eun.*4(1.280A; M.29.673B) cit. infra, 3.b.i; εἰ τὸ γεννᾶν καὶ τὸ ~εῖν ταὐτόν ἐστι παρὰ θεῷ, γεννᾷ δὲ τὸν υἱὸν ἀμεσιτεύτως, δῆλον ὅτι καὶ πάντα γεννᾷ ἢ ~εῖ ἀμεσιτεύτως. ... πῶς τὸ γεννᾶν ταὐτόν ἐστι τῷ ~εῖν παρὰ θεῷ; ~εῖ δὲ σεισμόν, λοιμόν..., ταῦτα ἔσται γεννῶν ἃ ~εῖ, εἴπερ τῷ ~εῖν τὸ γεννᾶν ταὐτόν ἐστι παρ' αὐτῷ Cyr.*thes.*18(5^1.183E); πλάσσω: τὸ γὰρ ~ούμενον οὐκ ἐν κοιλίᾳ γίνεται, ἀλλὰ τὸ πλασσόμενον ἀπὸ τοῦ χοῦ τῆς γῆς τοῦτο ἐν κοιλίᾳ κτίζεται Or.*hom.1.10 in Jer.*(p.9.8; M.13.268A); **b.** in gen. θεὸν τὸν ~ήσαντά σε *Did.*1.2; *Diogn.*10.8; Or.*Apoc.*26(p.32); Bas.*Eun.*2.2(1.239B; M.29.576A); Gr.Nyss.*Eun.*3(2 p.13.3; M.45.577A); οὐχ ὁμοίως ~εῖ ἄνθρωπος καὶ θεός· ὁ μὲν γὰρ ἄνθρωπος...ἐκ προϋποκειμένης ὕλης ~εῖ...ὁ δὲ θεὸς θελήσας μόνον ‡Cyr.*Trin.*7(6^3.10B; M.77.1133C); exeg. Is.45:7 ἁρμοδίως δὲ ἄγαν ἑκάτερα τέθεικεν, τὸ μὲν ~ήσας ἐπὶ τοῦ φωτός, τὸ δὲ κατασκευάσας ἐπὶ τοῦ σκότους· συμβεβηκὸς γάρ ἐστι, συνιστάμενον, καὶ διαλυόμενον Thdt.*qu.7 in Gen.*(1.12); **c.** hence ὁ πεποιηκώς *the Creator*, Gr.Nyss.*hom.opif.*2.1(M.44.133A); Thdt.*Dan.*3:15(2.1109); ὁ ποιήσας, Athenag.*res.*18(p.70.13; M.6.1009B); Nil.*Magn.*61(M.79.1052B); τὸ ποιῆσαν, *Disp.Phot.*(M.88.564B); **d.** of Creation effected through Son, cf. φάσκει 'ποιήσωμεν ἄνθρωπον...' καὶ οὐκ εἶπε, 'δεῦρο ~ήσω καὶ ὑποδείξω πῶς ἐργάσῃ'... 'καὶ ἐποίησεν ὁ θεὸς τὸν ἄνθρωπον', καὶ οὐκ εἶπεν, 'ἐποίησε καὶ ἔδειξε τῷ υἱῷ πῶς δεῖ ~εῖν τὸν ἄνθρωπον' Epiph.*haer.*69.78(p.226.21; M.42.329A); δι' οὗ τὰ πάντα ἐποίησας *Lit.Jac.*(p.200.9); cf. φησὶν ὁ ἅγιος... ὁ υἱός, ἡ...χεὶρ τοῦ πατρός, ἐν ᾗ μετὰ τὸ ~ῆσαι τὴν ὕλην ἐξ οὐκ ὄντων κατακοσμεῖ Meth.*creat.*9(p.498.29; M.18.341A); **e.** exeg. ποιήσωμεν Gen.1:26; **i.** not said by God to himself, to elements, or to angels, as some Jews asserted, Just.*dial.*62.2–3(M.6.617A,B); **ii.** nor by angels to each other, as some Gnostics held, Iren.*haer.*1.24.1(M.7.674A); Epiph.*haer.*23.1(p.249.1; M.41.300A); **iii.** said by God to his immanent λόγος, hence πρὸς ἑαυτὸν ὡς πρὸς ἕτερον παρακελεύεται λέγων, ἄγε ~ήσωμεν Marcell.*fr.*52(p.42.9; M.24.860C); **iv.** Marcellus' theory refuted by Trinitarian argument, Eus.*e.th.*2.18(p.122.30; M.24.941C); as Sabellian, *ib.*3.3(p.157.28; 1001C); *Symb.Ant.*(345)6(p.253.8; M.26.732B); Trinitarian argument also refutes Arian inference from this text that Son is ἐργαλεῖον εἰς ποίησιν Gel.Cyz.*h.e.*2.16.10(M.85.1261C); **v.** referred to first Creation of man κατ' εἰκόνα, dist. from πλάσις, Or.*hom.1.10 in Jer.*(p.9.3; M.13.265D); **2.** of Son as creator, Or.*fr.1 in Jo.*(p.483.8); Ath.*Ar.*2.10(M.26.168C); id.*inc.*10.3(M.25.113B); Gr.Nyss.*Eun.*7(2; p.161.25; M.45.752A); power of Christ is 'hand of God' in Creation, *ib.*(p.161.11; 749D); **3.** question whether Son is included in things made by God; **a.** Arian οἱ μὲν περὶ Εὐσέβιον καὶ Ἄρειον...τὸν υἱὸν ἔλεγον πεποιῆσθαι Ath.*syn.*45(p.270.27; M.26.773C); τὸν...υἱὸν...ἐγέννησέ τε καὶ ἔκτισε καὶ ἐποίησεν Eun.*apol.*28(M.30.868A); **b.** orthodox; **i.** generation dist. from Creation, Gr.Nyss.*Eun.*4(2 p.82.1; M.45.656D); τὸ ~ούμενον οὐκ ἐκ τῆς οὐσίας τοῦ ~οῦντος, τὸ δὲ γεννώμενον ἐκ τῆς αὐτῆς οὐσίας τοῦ γεννῶντος· οὐ ταὐτὸν ἄρα τὸ ~εῖν καὶ τὸ γεννᾶν Didym.(‡Bas.)*Eun.*4(1.280A; M.29.673B); Cyr.*thes.*18(5^1.183E); credal γεννηθέντα, οὐ ~ηθέντα *Symb.Nic.*(p.44.14; M.20.1540B); *Symb.*ap.Epiph.*anc.*118(p.147.3; M.43.232C); *Symb.*ap.Epiph.*anc.*119(p.148.8; 233B); *Symb.Nic.–CP*(p.80.6; H.2.288B); **ii.** ref. Pr.8:22 οὐχὶ δέ γε τὸ ἔκτισε λέγοιτ' ἂν ἐπὶ τοῦ ἐποίησε· διαφέρει γὰρ τοῦ ~ῆσαι τὸ κτίσαι Dion.R.ap.Ath.*decr.*26(p.23.3; M.25.464C); **iii.** ref. Ac.2:36, Ath.*Ar.*2.17(M.26.181C); Bas.*Eun.*2.2(1.239C; M.29.576B); **iv.** ref. Heb.3:2 οὐ τὴν οὐσίαν ἄρα τοῦ λόγου, οὐδὲ τὴν ἐκ τοῦ πατρὸς φυσικὴν γέννησιν σημαίνειν θέλων...μὴ γένοιτο· ~ῶν γάρ ἐστιν ὁ λόγος, οὐ ~ούμενος αὐτός Ath.*Ar.*2.7(M.26.161A); κἂν ἐπ' αὐτοῦ τοῦ λόγου τις λέγῃ τὸ 'ἐποίησεν' ἀντὶ τοῦ ἐγέννησε λέγει· ποίαν ἄρα παρεξευρεῖν ἐπίνοιαν ἔτι μᾶλλον κακονοίας εἰς τοῦτο δυνήσονται, ὅπου...ἔδειξε μὴ εἶναι ποίημα τὸν υἱὸν ἀλλὰ τῇ μὲν οὐσίᾳ γέννημα τοῦ πατρός, τῇ δ' οἰκονομίᾳ κατ' εὐδοκίαν τοῦ πατρὸς ἐποιήθη...ἄνθρωπος *ib.*2.11(169A); τὸ 'ἐποίησεν' ἀντὶ τοῦ, ἀπέδειξεν, νοητέον Cyr.*thes.*21(5^1.216A); ποίησιν...οὐ τὴν δημιουργίαν, ἀλλὰ τὴν χειροτονίαν κέκληκεν. πιστὸν γὰρ ὄντα, φησίν, τῷ ~ήσαντι αὐτόν, τουτέστιν ἀπόστολον καὶ ἀρχιερέα Thdt.*Heb.*3:2(3.562); **v.** ref. Rom.6:10 τὴν...φωνὴν...ἁμαρτίαν αὐτὸν ὁ θεὸς ἐποίησεν, εἰς τὴν πρώτην τῆς οὐσίας ἀνάγειν ὑπόστασιν, καὶ διὰ τοῦτο πεποιῆσθαι αὐτὸν...ἀποδεικνύειν πειρᾶσθαι [sc. Eun.] ἵνα τὴν 'ἐποίησεν' λέξιν εἰς τὴν οὐσίαν ἀνενέγκοι, ἀκολούθως ἑαυτῷ ~ῶν, καὶ τὴν ἁμαρτίαν ἐν τῇ οὐσίᾳ βλέποι...πεισάτω ἑαυτὸν διὰ τῆς αὐτῆς ἀκολουθίας κἀκεῖ τὸ 'ἐποίησε' πρὸς τὴν οἰκονομίαν βλέπειν Gr.Nyss.*Eun.*6(2 p.130.28; M.45.713D); **vi.** ref. Christ as ἀδελφὸς τῶν πεποιημένων Cyr.*dial.Trin.*6(5^1.597A); **4.** ref. H. Ghost as created (Eunomian), Eun.*apol.*28(M.30.868B) cit. s. πνεῦμα.

B. *make one's own*; pass., *be conformed to, instructed in* ἡ ψυχὴ... οὐ θνήσκει...τὴν ἐπίγνωσιν τοῦ θεοῦ πεποιημένη Tat.*orat.*13(p.14.16; M.6.833B); Δημόκριτος...Βαβυλωνίων λόγους ἠθικοὺς πεποιῆσθαι λέγεται Eus.*p.e.*10.4(472A; M.22.785A); c. dat. ~ηθέντα τοῖς Ἀράβων δόγμασιν Thphn.*chron.*p.336(M.108.812B).

C. *make* (i.e. *become* cf. Lat.*facio*) ἐὰν ~ῶ μοναχόν Jo.Clim.*scal.*4(M.88.693D); οὐδεὶς ~εῖ βασιλέα Ῥωμαίων ὡς οὗτος Jo.Mal.*chron.*13 p.338(M.97.504B).

D. *pass* time ἐποίησεν τρεῖς μῆνας πρὸς τὴν Ἐλισάβετ *Protev.*12.3(p.24); ~ῆσαι τὸν χειμῶνα *A.Barn.*7(p.294.26); *M.Ner.et Ach.*19(p.18.8); ref. penitents τρία ἔτη ~ήσουσιν ἐν ἀκροωμένοις CNic.(325)*can.*11; Chrys.*hom.10.1 in Phil.*(11.263E); Jo.Mosch.*prat.*59(M.87.2912C); abs., *stay* ~ήσεις ἐκεῖ ἕως τῆς συντελείας τοῦ αἰῶνος *Contrad.*2(p.9).

E. *make a difference* (cf. French, *cela ne fait rien*), in phrase οὐδὲν ~εῖ Chrys.*hom.8.3 in Phil.*(11.248E); id.*hom.11.2 in Eph.*(11.81F).

F. *make to be* εἰ γὰρ ἀθάνατον αὐτὸν [sc. τὸν ἄνθρωπον] ἀπ' ἀρχῆς ἐπεποιήκει θεὸν αὐτὸν ἐπεποιήκει Thphl.Ant.*Autol.*2.27(M.6.1093B); τούς...ἐξ Ἰουδαίων...ὑφ' ἑαυτὸν ~ήσεται Thdt.*Cant.*7:5(2.146); of reception of catechumens τὴν πρώτην ἡμέραν ~οῦμεν αὐτοὺς Χριστιανούς CCP(381)‡*can.*7; in eucharistic epiclesis κατ[απ]έμψαι τὸ πνεῦμα τὸ [ἅ]γιον...[καὶ ποιῆσ]ον τὸν μὲν ἄρτον σῶμα...Χριστοῦ, τὸ δὲ π[οτήριον α]ἷμα *Lit.Marc.*(*PDêr-Baliz.*2 r° 28); *Lit.Jac.*(p.206.9).

G. *set* oneself, *betake* oneself ἐν τῷ ἰδιάζοντι μέρει τοῦ κελλίου ἑαυτὸν ἐποίησεν Gr.Mag.*dial.*(tr.Zach.)3.16(M.*PL.*77.259D).

H. *appoint, ordain* Ἀαρὼν...πεποίηται ἀρχιερεύς Ath.*Ar.*2.8(M.26.161C); οὕτινα τῶν...γυναικῶν τοῦτο ποιεῖν προσέταξε τὸ ἀξίωμα Epiph.*haer.*79.7(p.482.13; M.42.752A); ref. Ac.2:35 ἐποίησε, τουτέστι, κατέστησεν Chrys.*hom.6.3 in Ac.*(9.51E); χειροτονεῖ αὐτὸν διάκονον...καὶ...~εῖ αὐτὸν πρεσβύτερον *Dial.Tim.et Aquil.*(138 v°; M.86.253B); ref. Christ as appointed high priest (Heb.3:2), Thdt.*Heb.*3:2(3.562).

I. *arrange, make*, marriages, CLaod.*can.*31.

J. ? *settle, make comfortable* ~ήσαντες τὸν πατέρα ἀνέπλευσαν *Mir.Artem.*35(p.55.20).

II. *do*;

A. *perform* religious rites; **1.** in gen., *1Clem.*40.1; χωρὶς τοῦ ἐπισκόπου μηδὲν ~εῖτε Ign.*Philad.*7.2; abs. νῦν οὖν καιρὸς τοῦ ποιῆσαι τῷ κυρίῳ *Apophth.Patr.*(M.65.221C); **2.** prayer ἔντευξιν...ἐποιησάμεθα *1Clem.*63.2; εὐχαὶ καὶ εὐχαριστίαι...τέλειαι μόναι...εἰσὶ τῷ θεῷ θυσίαι

...ταῦτα γὰρ μόνα καὶ Χριστιανοὶ παρέλαβον ~εῖν Just.*dial.*117.2–3(M. 6.745C); id.*1apol.*65.1(M.6.428A); Chrys.*hom.6.1 in Phil.*(11.578E); Pall.*v.Chrys.*11(p.68.9; M.47.38); **3.** *agape* οὐκ ἐξόν ἐστι χωρὶς τοῦ ἐπισκόπου...ἀγάπην ~εῖν Ign.*Smyrn.*8.2; CLaod.*can.*28; and eucharist, Just.*dial.*117.2(M.6.745C), (if εὐχαριστίαι means more here than *thanksgivings*, cf.*ib.*41.1(564B); *ib.*70.4(641A); but v. infra 6); τὸ ὁμοίωμα τοῦ θανάτου ~οῦντες τὸν ἄρτον προσηνέγκαμεν Serap.*euch.*13.13; ‡Bas.*h.myst.*60(p.395.28); ref. celebration on martyrs' anniversaries μαρτύρων μνείαν ~εῖν CLaod.*can.*51; **4.** repentance ἀπὸ παντὸς μετάνοιαν πεποιῆσθαι ἀπὸ τῆς...κακῆς...πολιτείας Just.*dial.*121.2(M.6.757B); **5.** ordinations; med., CChalc.*can.* 2; **6.** *perform, offer* sacrifice αὐτούς [sc. Christ's disciples] σοι ἀνατίθημι καὶ ~ῶ προσφοράν Chrys.*hom.82.1 in Jo.*(8.484B); of offering of bread and wine at eucharist ποιήσας γὰρ τὰς προσφορὰς καὶ διανέμων ἑκάστῳ τὸ μέρος Corn.ap.Eus.*h.e.*6.43.18(M.20.625A); **7.** *observe* festival παρατήρησιν τῶν μηνῶν...~εῖσθαι *Diogn.*4.5; τὸ πάσχα ἐκήρυξε, καὶ ἐποίησεν αὐτό ‡Ath.*synops.*(M.28.324D); οἱ... Ἱεροσολυμῖται...τοῖς Ἐπιφανίοις ~οῦσι τὴν γένναν Cosm.Ind.*top.*5 (M.88.197B); **8.** π. εἰς ἀνάμνησιν *make a memorial* or *commemoration* with τοῦ ἄρτου τῆς εὐχαριστίας, ὃν εἰς ἀνάμνησιν τοῦ πάθους... ὁ κύριος...παρέδωκε ~εῖν Just.*dial.*41.1(M.6.564B); *ib.*70.4(641A) cit. s. ἀνάμνησις.

B. c. ptcpl., *continue* ἐποίησεν δὲ βρέχων ὁ κύριος Marc.Diac. *v.Porph.*21.

C. ~ῶ ἀγάπην, *be so good as to* ποιήσατε ἀγάπην, μὴ λαλεῖτε *Apophth.Patr.*(M.65.117B); ποίησον ἀγάπην ὑποδέξαι ἡμᾶς Ephr.2. 155A; Jo.Mosch.*prat.*93(M.87.2952C); *ib.*16(2864B).

***ποιηβορέω**, *eat grass*, ‡Caes.Naz.*dial.*145(M.38.1096).

ποίημα, τό, *thing made*;

A. dist. by implication from κτίσμα: τὰ λογικὰ δὲ μετὰ τὸ οὐσιωθῆναι καὶ εἶναι δέχονται τὸ κτισθῆναι...κτίζεται γάρ τις ἐπὶ ἔργοις ἀγαθοῖς, πρὸ τούτου ὢν θεοῦ π., εἰς καρδίαν καθαράν Or.*Apoc.*26 (p.32).

B. of created things; **1.** in gen. οὗ οὖν τὰ π. ... τοῦτον κατελαμβάνετο εἶναι θεόν Athenag.*leg.*5.2(M.6.900B); ἡ σὰρξ...π. τῆς ἀφθαρσίας...ὑπάρχουσα Meth.*res.*2.18(p.368.15; M.18.312C); of man φεῖσαι τοῦ σοῦ π. Serap.*euch.*19.3; Cyr.*Ps.*48:1(M.69.1068B); Jo. Thess.*dorm.BMV* A 12(p.426.34); **2.** as means by which creator is known (cf. Rom.1:20), Tat.*orat.*4(p.5.6; M.6.813B); τὰ ἀόρατα...τοῖς π. νοούμενα καθορᾶται Proc.G.*Is.*5:8–17(M.87.1913A); **3.** ref. coeternity of creation with God Ὠριγένης...ἔφασκε...εἰ οὐκ ἔστι... ποιητὴς ἄνευ ποιημάτων...(τὸν γὰρ δημιουργὸν διὰ τὰ δημιουργήματα ἀνάγκη καὶ τὸν ποιητὴν διὰ τὰ π. ... λέγεσθαι), ἀνάγκη μὴ εἶναι χρόνον ὅτε οὐκ ἦν ταῦτα Meth.*creat.*1.2(p.494.18; M.18.333B); cf. *si quis est qui velit vel saecula aliqua transisse vel spatia...cum nondum facta essent quae facta sunt, sine dubio hoc ostendet, quod in illis vel saeculis vel spatiis omnipotens non erat deus*, Or.*princ.*1.2.10(p.42. 5; M.11.139A); εἰ γὰρ ἦν χρόνος ὅτε οὐκ ἦν τὰ π., ἐπεὶ τῶν ποιημάτων μὴ ὄντων οὐδὲ ποιητής ἐστιν, ὅρα οἷον ἀσεβὲς ἀκολουθεῖ Meth.*creat.*1.2 (p.494.23; 333C); **4.** of eucharistic elements as God's creatures, Clem.*paed.*2.2(p.170.13; M.8.416B); **5.** of wine as God's creature, yet to be used for certain purposes only, ‡Just.*ep.Zen.et Ser.*12(M. 6.1197B); **6.** theory that man is creature of angels; **a.** suggested by Jews, exeg. Gen.1:26 οὐ γὰρ ὅπερ ἡ παρ' ὑμῖν λεγομένη αἵρεσις δογματίζει φαίην ἂν ἐγὼ ἀληθὲς εἶναι, ἢ οἱ ἐκείνης διδάσκαλοι ἀποδεῖξαι δύνανται ὅτι ἀγγέλοις ἔλεγεν ἢ ὅτι ἀγγέλων π. ἦν τὸ σῶμα τὸ ἀνθρώπειον Just.*dial.*62.3(M.6.617C); **b.** Gnost. τὸν δὲ ἄνθρωπον ἀγγέλων εἶναι π. Iren.*haer.*1.24.1 ap.Hipp.*haer.*7.28(p.208.13; M.16.3322A); **7.** of Son; view that Son is ποίημα; **a.** ascribed to Dion. Al. ὡς π. ὤν, οὐκ ἦν πρὶν γένηται Ath.*Dion.*4(p.48.22; M.25.485A); but ὡς γὰρ οὐ π. φρονῶ τὸν λόγον, καὶ οὐ ποιητὴν ἀλλὰ πατέρα τὸν θεὸν αὐτοῦ λέγω id.ap.Ath.*Dion.*21(p.62.8; M.25.512A); ὥστε πανταχόθεν τὸν μὲν υἱὸν μὴ εἶναι κτίσμα, μηδὲ π., ἑαυτὸν δ' ἀλλότριον τῆς Ἀρειανῆς κακοδοξίας ἀποδείκνυσιν Ath.*ib.*(p.62.13; M.25.512B); held by Ar. π. ἐστιν, ἀλλ' οὐχ ὡς ἓν τῶν π. Ath.*Ar.*2.19(M.26.185C); ὁ υἱὸς...πολὺ λείπεται τῆς τοῦ θεοῦ δόξης, ὡς π. ‡Ath.*disp.*6(M.26.444A); Cyr.*thes.* 15(5^1.146D); by Eun. μήτε τὸν υἱὸν ἀκούοντας π. δυσχεραίνειν...οὐρανὸς δὲ καὶ ἄγγελοι, πᾶν ὅπερ ἐστὶν ἄλλο π., τούτου τοῦ π. ἐστι ποιήματα... οὕτω γὰρ ἂν ταῖς γραφαῖς τὸ ἀψευδεῖν φυλάττοιτο, π. καὶ γέννημα λεγούσαις τὸν υἱόν Eun.*apol.*17(1.624B,C; M.30.852C,D); τὰς τῶν ἁγίων φωνὰς...δι' ὧν υἱὸν καὶ γέννημα καὶ π. καταγγέλλουσι Bas.*Eun.* 2.1(1.238B; M.29.573A); τὸν κτίστην πάντων...ποίημα διορίζεται Gr. Nyss.*Eun.*1(1 p.56.2; M.45.284D); **b.** refuted by orthodox, cf. ἀπὸ τοῦ πατρὸς προβληθὲν γέννημα πρὸ πάντων τῶν π. συνῆν τῷ πατρί Just. *dial.*62.4(M.6.617C); ὦ ῥιψοκίνδυνοι ἄνθρωποι, π. ὁ πρωτότοκος πάσης κτίσεως, ὁ...πρὸ ἑωσφόρου γεννηθείς; Dion.R.ap.Ath.*decr.*26(p.23.6; M.25.464D); Ἰγνάτιος ὀρθῶς ἔγραψε...λέγων...ἀγένητον...ὅτι μὴ τῶν π. ... ἐστιν...εἰ μὲν π. ἐστιν ὁ λόγος...οὐκ ἂν εἴη ὁμοούσιος τῷ πατρί, ἀλλὰ μᾶλλον ὁμογενὴς τῇ φύσει τοῖς π. ... εἰ δὲ ὁμολογοῦμεν μὴ εἶναι αὐτὸν π., ἀλλὰ γνήσιον ἐκ τῆς οὐσίας τοῦ πατρὸς γέννημα, ἀκόλουθον ἂν εἴη...ὁμοφυῆ ὄντα διὰ τὸ ἐξ αὐτοῦ γεγεννῆσθαι Ath.*syn.*47,48(p.272. 4,22; M.26.777A,C); ref. Ac.2:36 τὸ λεγόμενον...'κύριον αὐτὸν ἐποίησε', ...οὐ π. εἶναι τὸν υἱὸν σημαίνει...οὐ π. τὴν οὐσίαν τοῦ λόγου σημαίνων ...ἔλεγεν...ἀλλὰ τὴν κατὰ χάριν ποιηθεῖσαν...βασιλείαν καὶ κυριότητα id.*Ar.*2.17,18(M.26.181C,184B); εἴ τις βουλήσει τοῦ θεοῦ ὡς ἓν τῶν π. γεγονέναι λέγοι τὸν υἱὸν τοῦ θεοῦ, ἀ. ἔ. *Symb.Sirm.*1 *anath.*24; ref. Ac.2:36, Bas.*Eun.*2.2(1.239C; M.29.576B); τῶν σωματικὴν τὴν γέννησιν ὑπολαμβανόντων ἐπιμελούμενος [sc. Eun.], τοὺς τῇ προσηγορίᾳ τοῦ π. περιπταίοντας παρορᾷ *ib.*2.6(242B; M.581C); τὸν οἱονεὶ χαρακτῆρα τῆς λατρείας ἡμῶν ἀρνούμενος· οὐ γὰρ εἰς δημιουργὸν καὶ π. ἐπιστεύσαμεν· ἀλλ' εἰς πατέρα καὶ υἱὸν διὰ τῆς ἐν τῷ βαπτίσματι χάριτος ἐσφραγίσθημεν *ib.*2.22(258B; M.620C); δυνάμεως γάρ, καὶ σοφίας, καὶ τέχνης, οὐχὶ δὲ τῆς οὐσίας αὐτῆς ἐνδεικτικά ἐστι ποιήματα *ib.*2.32(269B; M.648A); γεννήματος καὶ π. κατὰ ταὐτὸν μνημονευθέντων, ἐκ τῶν φωνῶν ἐπὶ τὰ σημαινόμενα μεταβάντες οὐ τὴν αὐτὴν ἑκάστῳ τῶν ὀνομάτων ἐθεωροῦμεν διάνοιαν· ἄλλο γάρ τι τὸ κτίσμα καὶ ἕτερον σημαίνει τὸ γέννημα Gr.Nyss.*Eun.*4(2 p.80.27; M.45.656A); εἰ ...πρῶτον θεοῦ π. ὁ Χριστός, καὶ οὕτω πιστεύοντες αὐτῷ λατρεύουσιν Ἀρειανοί· Ἰὼβ δὲ πρῶτον π. θεοῦ τὸν διάβολον λέγει [Job 40:14] λανθάνουσι τῷ διαβόλῳ λατρεύοντες Didym.(‡Bas.)*Eun.*4(1.288C; M.29.693A); id.*Trin.*1.7(M.39.272A); ref. Heb.3:5–6 π. καὶ ποιητὴν διΐστησι Chrys.*hom.5.3 in Heb.*(12.55C); οὐδεὶς γὰρ πώποτε τὸ ἑαυτοῦ π. γέννημα καὶ υἱὸν ἀποκαλεῖ Cyr.*thes.*15(5^1.158D); οὐκ ἄρα π. ἐστιν, οὐδὲ κτίσμα...τῆς τοῦ πατρὸς οὐσίας ἴδιον ὑπάρχων γέννημα *ib.* (147E); Gel.Cyz.*h.e.*2.16.15(M.85.1264B); **c.** of Christ's body π. ἀτρέπτως ἐν σοὶ τῇ παρθένῳ γενόμενον Sophr.H.*or.*2.20(M.87.3240C); **8.** of H. Ghost, cf. πνεῦμα; **a.** as created by Son, Eun.*apol.*25(M. 30.861D); **b.** as created by Father, Didym.(‡Bas.)*Eun.*4(1.288D; M. 29.693A); **c.** doctrines refuted, Cyr.*thes.*33(5^1.336D).

ποίησις, ἡ, A. in gen., *making* χρίσματος π. ... ἀπὸ πρεσβυτέρων μὴ γένηται *Cod.Afr.*6 (Lat. *confectio*).

B. *creating, act of creation*; **1.** in gen., Just.*dial.*62.1(M.6.617A); δύο π. ἔχει ὁ ἥλιος, μίαν μὲν τῆς οὐσίας, ἑτέραν δὲ τῆς κινήσεως ‡Just. *qu.Chr.*2.5(M.6.1421D); cf.*ib.*3.5(1441B) cit. s. ἀδιάβλητος; dist. from πλάσις, Or.*hom.1.10 in Jer.*(p.9.5; M.13.265D); **2.** ref. work of Son εἰ οὖν...ἐργαλεῖον ὁ υἱὸς εἰς π. τῶν κτιστῶν φύσεων...ἐκτίσθη, ἐκ τῶν σεαυτοῦ καταπίπτεις λόγων Gel.Cyz.*h.e.*2.16.5(M.85.1261A); **3.** ref. question whether Son is created γέννησις...ἐστι, τὸ ἐκ τῆς οὐσίας τοῦ γεννῶντος προάγεσθαι τὸ γεννώμενον, ὅμοιον κατ' οὐσίαν· κτίσις δὲ καὶ π. τὸ ἔξωθεν ‡Cyr.*Trin.*7(6^3.9E; M.77.1133B); exeg. Heb.3:2 π. δέ, οὐ τὴν δημιουργίαν ἀλλὰ τὴν χειροτονίαν κέκληκεν Thdt.*Heb.* 3:2(3.562); orthodox use ὁ ἡμέτερος λόγος, οὐκ ἀριθμὸν Χριστῶν,... ἀλλὰ ἕνωσιν τοῦ ἀνθρώπου πρὸς τὸ θεῖον πρεσβεύων...καὶ τὴν τοῦ ἀνθρώπου πρὸς τὸν Χριστὸν μεταστοιχείωσιν ποίησιν ὀνομάζων Gr. Nyss.*Eun.*5(2 p.126.9; M.45.708D); **4.** exeg. Ps.18:2 π. ... τῶν χειρῶν αὐτοῦ αὐτὸ τὸ στερέωμα ἀναγγέλλει, τοῦτ' ἔστιν δείκνυσι καὶ φαίνει τὴν π. τῶν ἀγγέλων αὐτοῦ· ἀναγγέλλει γὰρ...οὓς ἐποίησεν Clem.*ecl.*51 (p.151.26; M.9.721C).

C. *creation, that which is created* σπλαγχνίζεται ἐπὶ τὴν π. αὐτοῦ Herm.*mand.*9.3; τοῦτον [sc. θεόν] διὰ τῆς π. αὐτοῦ ἴσμεν Tat.*orat.*4 (p.5.5; M.6.813B); θεὸν κρείττονα τῆς π. Clem.*str.*5.1(p.331.6; M.9. 20A); κακίζει [sc. Apelles] τὴν πᾶσαν π. Epiph.*anac.*44(p.3.17; M.41. 581A).

D. *poetry*, Athenag.*leg.*29.1(M.6.957A); ‡Just.*coh.Gr.*17(M.6. 273A); πᾶσα μὲν ἡ π. τῷ Ὁμήρῳ ἀρετῆς ἐστιν ἔπαινος Bas.*leg.lib. gent.*4(p.47; M.31.572B).

***ποιήτευμα, τό, 1.** *poetical composition*, as derogatory word for heathen poem, Epiph.*haer.*26.2(p.277.12; M.41.333C); Ἡσίοδος...τὰ περὶ τῆς θεογονίας π. διηγησάμενος *ib.*66.46(p.84.23; M.42.100D); **2.** *fiction*, of Marcion's teaching ἡ...ἀποστόλου ὑπόστασις καὶ... κήρυγμα,...τὸ σὸν π. *ib.*42.12(p.182.22; M.41.812C).

***ποιητεύω**, *make up* fables and falsehoods; of Gnost. cosmologies, Epiph.*haer.*24.2(p.258.7; M.41.309C); books, *ib.*25.3(p.270.12; 324C); systems of aeons, *ib.*31.4(p.389.23; 480D); *ib.*35.2(p.41.21; 629B); heathen mythology, *ib.*36.1(p.44.22; 633B); Marcion's interpolations in scripture, *ib.*42.12(p.170.9; 796A).

ποιητής, ὁ, I. *maker*;

A. in gen.; of makers of idols, Clem.*prot.*4(p.45.27; M.8.157A); of man as responsible for evil τῶν κακῶν...οἱ ἄνθρωποι...π. Meth. *arbitr.*16(p.186.3).

B. of God as creator; **1.** in pagan thought, Athenag.*leg.*23.5 (M.6.944C); **2.** Christian; **a.** in gen. κρεῖττόν τι τῶν μεταβαλλομένων νοοῦμεν τὸν πάντων π. θεόν Just.*1apol*.20.2(M.6.357C); Athenag.*leg*. 8.1(M.6.904C); Meth.*arbitr*.3(p.152.9; M.18.245C); *Hom.Clem*.10.5; Serap.*euch*.21; abs., *the creator* τοῖς...ἐν ἑαυτοῖς ἀγαλματοφοροῦσι τὸν π. Athenag.*res*.12(p.62.16; M.6.997B); μηδεὶς ἐγκαλείτω...τῷ π. ὅτι ἰοβόλα ζῷα...ἐπεισήγαγεν Bas.*hex*.9.5(1.86D; M.29.201D); Bas.Sel. *or*.1.2(M.85.32B); Cosm.Ind.*top*.1(M.88.64C); **b.** ass. κτίστης, Eus. *e.th*.1.10(p.68.22; M.24.841B); Ath.*Ar*.1.21(M.26.56A); with πατήρ: π. τε καὶ πατὴρ πάντων Clem.*str*.3.2(p.198.22; M.8.1108B); Zach.Mit. *opif*.(M.85.1029A); cf. credal forms infra, but dist. from πατήρ for purpose of Trin. theology οὐ ποίημα φρονῶ τὸν λόγον, καὶ οὐ π. ἀλλὰ πατέρα τὸν θεὸν αὐτοῦ λέγω Dion.Al.ap.Ath.*Dion*.21(p.62.8; M.25. 512A); τοῦ μὲν υἱοῦ πατήρ, τοῦ δὲ κόσμου...π. Eus.*e.th*.1.10(p.68.22; M.24.841B); πάντων μὲν π., ἑνὸς δὲ μόνου πατέρα φύσει τοῦ...υἱοῦ αὐτοῦ ‡Cyr.*Trin*.7(6[3].8E; M.77.1132C); **c.** dist. from δημιουργός: ὁ μὲν γὰρ π., οὐδενὸς ἑτέρου προσδεόμενος, ἐκ τῆς ἑαυτοῦ δυνάμεως καὶ ἐξουσίας ποιεῖ τὸ ποιούμενον· ὁ δὲ δημιουργός...κατασκευάζει τὸ γινόμενον ‡Just.*coh.Gr*.22(M.6.281B); but also equated with δημιουργός, Meth.*arbitr*.22(p.206.12); *Const.App*.6.11.2; cf.*Symb.Ant*.(341) 2, v. infra f.; **d.** dist. from πλάστης: πλάστην τοῦ σώματος καὶ π. τῆς ψυχῆς Serap.*euch*.7.1; **e.** title vindicated agst. Aristotelian view of relationship of ποιέω to πράττω, Clem.*str*.5.13(p.383.5; M.9.128A) cit. s. ποιέω; **f.** in creeds θεὸν...ἁπάντων ὁρατῶν τε καὶ ἀοράτων π. *Symb.Caes*.ap.Eus.*ep.Caes*.3(p.43.10; M.20.1537B); *Symb.Nic*.(325) (p.44.12; M.20.1540B); τὸν τῶν ὅλων δημιουργόν τε καὶ π. *Symb. Ant*.(341)2(p.249.12; M.26.721B); *ib*.3(p.250.9; 724C); *ib*.4(p.251.1; 725B); *Symb.Ant*.(345)1(p.251.22; M.26.728A); π. οὐρανοῦ καὶ γῆς, ὁρατῶν τε πάντων καὶ ἀοράτων *Symb.Hier*.(M.33.533A); τὸν κτίστην καὶ π. τῶν πάντων *Symb.Sirm*.1(p.254.17; M.26.736A); π. οὐρανοῦ τε καὶ γῆς, ὁρατῶν τε πάντων καὶ ἀοράτων *Symb*.ap.Epiph.*anc*.118(p.146. 22; M.43.232B); *Symb*.ap.Epiph.*anc*.119(p.148.5; 233B); π. οὐρανοῦ καὶ γῆς ὁρατῶν τε πάντων καὶ ἀοράτων *Symb.Nic.–CP*(p.80.3; H.2. 288B); **g.** God as maker of evil things; **i.** view ascribed to Christians by Celsus, Or.*Cels*.6.53(p.124.26; M.11.1381A); and by Manicheans, *Ep*.ap.Hegem.*Arch*.5(p.7.7; M.10.1436A); **ii.** implied in astrological determinism, Meth.*symp*.8.16(p.105.9; M.18.168D); **h.** God acts as π. through Son, *Const.App*.8.37.2; **i.** God as π. of Son (Eunomian), Thdt.*Eph*.3:8(3.418).

C. of Son; **1.** in gen. τὸν ἐσταυρωμένον, τὸν οὐρανοῦ καὶ γῆς π. *A.Phil*.73(p.29.9); ὁ δὲ υἱὸς καὶ τῶν αἰώνων πάντων ἐστὶ π. Chrys. *hom.7.1 in Jo*.(8.46B); αὐτὸς μόνος καλεῖται π. Cyr.*thes*.12(5[1].119C); Max.*ep*.13(M.91.517B); **2.** as maker of angels, Gel.Cyz.*h.e*.2.19.14 (M.85.1277D); **3.** against Eunomian teaching πῶς π. χρόνων ὁ ὑπὸ χρόνον; Gr.Naz.*or*.20.7(M.35.1073B); οἱ ἐχθροὶ κυρίου...λέγουσιν...τὸν π. ποίημα Didym.(‡Bas.)*Eun*.5(1.314A; M.29.753A); θεὸς...ὁ Χριστὸς ...π. καὶ οὐ ποίημα Cyr.*thes*.32(5[1].288C); **4.** as creator of H. Ghost (Eunomian), Eun.*apol*.26(M.30.864B); Bas.*Eun*.2.33(1.270D; M.29. 649C).

II. *poet*; poets and philosophers as inventors of false mythology, Arist.*apol*.13.5; Just.*1apol*.20.3(M.6.357C); *ib*.44.9(396A); Athenag. *leg*.24.1(M.6.945A); Thphl.Ant.*Autol*.3.7(M.6.1133A); πᾶς δὲ π. ἄκρος εἶναι δοκῶν ποτήριον χρυσοῦν κατεσκεύασε, δηλητήριον ἐμβαλὼν εἰδωλολατρείας, αἰσχρολογίας Or.*fr.36 in Jer*.(p.217.2; M.13.600D); τὰ ἀνθρώπινα δόγματα κρατυνόντων π. καὶ λογογράφων Meth.*symp*.5.4 (p.57.18; M.18.104A); expelled from Plato's republic as false teachers, Just.*2apol*.10.6(M.6.461A); to be read by Christians with discrimination οὐ...ἐπαινεσόμεθα τοὺς π., οὐ λοιδορουμένους, οὐ σκώπτοντας...πάντων δὲ ἥκιστα περὶ θεῶν τι διαλεγομένοις προσέξομεν ...ἐπειδήπερ δι' ἀρετῆς ἡμᾶς ἐπὶ τὸν βίον κα⟨τα⟩θεῖναι δεῖ τὸν ἕτερον, εἰς ταύτην δὲ πολλὰ μὲν ποιηταῖς...ὕμνηται, τοῖς τοιούτοις τῶν λόγων μάλιστα προσεκτέον Bas.*leg.lib.gent*.2,3(pp.45–46; M.31.569A,572A); cf. defence of reading Greek poets, Socr.*h.e*.3.16.25ff.(M.67.421Dff.); poets lived later than Moses, Tat.*orat*.31(p.31.7; M.6.869A); cf. Just.*1apol*.54.5(M.6.409A); and stole material from scriptures, Thphl.Ant.*Autol*.1.14(M.6.1045A); but expressed sacred truths allegorically, Clem.*str*.5.8(p.360.22; M.9.80B).

III. *doer* οἱ...τούτων [sc. φόνων] π. *Const.App*.7.18.2.

ποιητικός, A. *creative, productive*; **1.** in gen. φῶς π. τοῦ ἀπαυγάσματος Or.*hom.9.4 in Jer*.(p.70.19; M.13.357A); οὐκ ἔστι τελικὰ ἰατρικῆς ἀγαθά, ἀλλὰ π. ... οὕτω...αἱ ἀγαθαὶ πράξεις ἔσονται οὐκ ἀγαθαὶ ὡς τελικαί, ἀλλ' ἢ ἄρα ὡς ποιητικαὶ ἀγαθῶν id.*sel.in Ps*.4:6(M.12. 1160B)ap.*philoc*.26.6(p.238.24ff.); ἐχρῆν δὲ τὸ π. τοῦ καὶ ἐν τῇ παλαιᾷ διαθήκῃ νομιζομένου εὐαγγελίου εὐαγγέλιον ἐξαιρέτως καλεῖσθαι εὐαγγέλιον id.*Jo*.1.6(8; p.11.24; M.14.36B); ὑπὲρ τοῦ ἁμαρτίας π. λέγειν τὸν νόμον, ἔδειξε...αὐτοῦ τὸ χρήσιμον Thdr.Mops.*Rom*.8:3(M. 66.820D); οὐκ ἔφη δεδωκέναι αὐτοῖς προστάγματα κακά, ἀλλ' οὐ καλά· οὔτε γὰρ κακίαν ἐδίδασκεν, οὔτε ἀρετῆς αὐτὰ καθ' ἑαυτὰ π. ὄντα ἐτύγχανεν Thdt.*Ezech*.20:25(2.829); **2.** of causes, *efficient* τὸ γὰρ π. αἴτιον προκατάρχειν τῶν γιγνομένων ἀνάγκη Athenag.*leg*.19.3(M.6. 929B); Clem.*str*.8.7(p.93.19; M.9.588B); **3.** ref. pagan astrological beliefs ἴδωμεν...πῶς οὐ δύνανται οἱ ἀστέρες εἶναι π., ἀλλ' εἰ ἄρα, σημαντικοί Or.*comm.in Gen*.ap.Eus.*p.e*.6.11(292D; M.12.73C); **4.** ref. God διὰ πάντων ἡ π. δύναμις διοικοῦσα τοῦ θεοῦ Meth.*symp*.2.4(p.19. 8; M.18.52C); ὅτι φησὶν ὁ ἅγιος, δύο δὲ δυνάμεις...ἔφαμεν εἶναι π., τὴν ἐξ οὐκ ὄντων...αὐτουργοῦσαν ὃ βούλεται ποιεῖν· τυγχάνει δὲ πατήρ· θατέραν δὲ κατακοσμοῦσαν καὶ ποικίλλουσαν κατὰ μίμησιν τῆς προτέρας τὰ ἤδη γεγονότα· ἔστι δὲ ὁ υἱός Meth.*creat*.9(p.498.25; M.18.341A); Eus.*e.th*.1.20(p.81.21; M.24.865C); ἔρροιεν οἱ τὸ θεῖον ἐξηρνημένοι, καὶ μηδὲ τὴν...εὐαρμοστίαν τοῦ παντὸς εἴς τιν' ἀναφέροντες αἰτίαν π. τε καὶ συνεκτικὴν ὅλων Gr.Naz.*carm*.1.1.6.4(M.37.430A); δύναμιν...πάντων κτισμάτων...ποιητικήν ‡Cyr.*Trin*.7(6[3].8B; M.77.1132A); neut. as subst. χεῖρας ἀκούων θεοῦ, τὸ π. αὐτοῦ γνώριζε Didym.(‡Bas.)*Eun*. 5(1.316C; M.29.757C); **5.** of Son, Meth.*creat*.9(p.498.27; M.18.341A); θεὸς ἦν ὁ λόγος...ἔφη, ἵνα μὴ τοῦ θεοῦ ἐνέργειάν τινα σημαντικήν τινος ἢ π. εἶναι αὐτὸν ὑπολάβωμεν Eus.*e.th*.2.12(p.113.31; M.24.925B); ἔστι γὰρ ὁ λόγος...π., καὶ αὐτός ἐστιν ἡ τοῦ πατρὸς βουλή Ath.*Ar*.2.31(M. 26.213A).

B. *poetical*; **1.** in gen. κατὰ τὴν π. χάριν Clem.*str*.7.6(p.26.25; M.9. 449A); π. ἀλληγορίαν *Hom.Clem*.6.19; neut. as subst., *poetical saying*, Meth.*res*.1.27(p.254.14; M.41.1132C); ἡ π. *poetry*, Clem.*str*.5.14 (p.409.13; 184A); **2.** with connotation of falsehood (ref. pagan mythology) ἡμῶν τὰ διδάγματα...τοῖς...π. διδάγμασιν οὐχ ὅμοια Just. *2apol*.15.3(M.6.469A); Tat.*orat*.1(p.2.16; M.6.805B); πλάνη π. Athenag.*leg*.22.1(M.6.936C); Thdt.*Is*.42:15(p.167.35; 2.335).

ποιητικῶς, 1. *so as to effect something*, Or.*ep*.2(p.64.21; M.11.88A) cit. s. τελικῶς; **2.** *poetically*, Clem.*prot*.2(p.22.25; M.8.104B); id.*str*. 4.4(p.254.30; M.8.1228B).

ποιητός, *made*, of the body τὸ π. τοῦ θεοῦ καλόν Athenag.*leg*.34.1 (M.6.968B); of Christ's body as created, Ath.*Ar*.2.8(M.26.164A); ref. Origen's Christology πῶς δέ ἐστι προσκυνητός, εἰ ἔστι π.; Epiph. *haer*.64.8(p.417.22; M.41.1084A).

***ποικιλανθής,** *of variegated colours*, Clem.*paed*.2.10(p.225.5; M.8. 533A).

[*]**ποικιλλεύομαι,** *make ornamentation*, *Chron.Pasch*.p.48(M.92. 173A).

ποικίλλ-ω, 1. *embellish, adorn*; **a.** in gen. ἡ τῶν Στρωματέων ὑποτύπωσις λειμῶνος δίκην πεποίκιλται Clem.*str*.6.1(p.423.5; M.9. 209A); κροσσωτοῖς χρυσοῖς πεποικιλμένοις *Ep.Lugd*.ap.Eus.*h.e*.5.1.35 (v.l. περιπεποικιλμένοις M.20.421B); ~ειν τῶν νοημάτων τὴν ἀκολουθίαν Chrys.*Is.interp*.2:2(6.21A); τὸ σύστημα Χριστιανῶν...πεποικιλμένον τοῖς μυρίοις τῶν ἀρετῶν εἴδεσιν Nil.*epp*.1.267(M.79.181A); **b.** of function of Logos in Creation ~ουσαν [sc. δύναμιν] κατὰ μίμησιν... τὰ ἤδη γεγονότα Meth.*creat*.9(p.498.27; M.18.341A); **2.** *equivocate* ~ονται καὶ προφάσεις πλάττονται Cyr.*ep*.10(p.110.31; 5[2].33D); Jo. Clim.*past*.14(M.88.1200D); **3.** med., *use deceits*, of demons ~όμενοι ταῖς φαντασίαις Ath.*v.Anton*.35(M.26.893C); *try a trick*, Synes.*ep*.121 (M.66.1500D).

***ποικιλόδωρος,** *making various gifts*, Nonn.*par.Jo*.12:15(M.43. 853A).

***ποικιλοειδής,** *of varied forms*, ‡Ath.*pat*.5(M.26.1301C).

***ποικιλοεργός,** *working with many devices*, Paul.Sil.*ambo*.291(M. 86.2262B).

ποικιλόμητις, *full of various wiles*, *Orac.Sib*.3.217; *ib*.12.257.

***ποικιλομορφία, ἡ,** *manifold variety*, Dion.Ar.*ep*.9(M.3.1105A).

***ποικιλοπράγμων,** *cunning, subtle*, Synes.*provid*.13(p.92.21; M. 66.1241B).

ποικίλος, 1. *manifold* θεῷ σωτηρίαν κατηγγελκότι ποικίλην Clem. *str*.7.3(p.15.14; M.9.425B); π. ... δημιουργίᾳ τῇ τοῦ κόσμου Gr.Thaum. *pan.Or*.8(p.22.3; M.10.1077B); τὸ π. τῆς ἐνεργείας Thdt.*provid*.6(4. 573); **2.** *complex* οὐκ ἂν αὐτὸ οἶμαι τοῦτο εἰπεῖν· ὥστε π. τι χρῆμα καὶ σύνθετον νομίζειν τοῦ θεοῦ τὴν οὐσίαν Gr.Nyss.*Eun*.1(1 p.82.12; M. 45.313B).

***ποικιλότης, ἡ,** *varied abundance*, Or.*or*.2.3(p.301.1; M.11.420B).

***ποικιλότροπος,** *manifold*; of Christ's glory, as antitype of Joseph's coat, Cyr.*glaph.Gen*.6(1.189C); of snares of Devil, ‡Proc.G. *Pr*.6:5(M.87.1269B).

***ποικιλουργία, ἡ,** *ornamental work*; of making of high priest's robe, Cyr.*ador*.11(1.378E).

***ποικιλτικός,** *variegated*; met., Thdr.Stud.*cant*.6.2(p.346).

***ποιμαινεύω,** *act as a shepherd*, *T.Abr*.10(p.87.22).

ποιμαίν-ω, A. intrans., *act as a shepherd*; **1.** lit. ὡς δὲ ἐποίμαινον... πνεῦμα συνέσεως κυρίου ἦλθεν ἐπ' ἐμέ *T.Lev*.2.3; *T.Zab*.6.8; ὅτι δὲ πνευματικὸς ὁ Σήθ, οὔτε ~ει οὔτε γεωργεῖ Clem.*exc.Thdot*.54(p.125.4;

M.9.685A); **2.** met., of clergy ~ε ἡμᾶς ~οντας Gr.Naz.*or*.9.5(M.35.825A).

B. trans., *tend, shepherd*; **1.** lit., in proverbial phrase ᾑρεῖτο γὰρ...σκορπίους ποιμᾶναι ἢ μοιχαλίδι γυναικὶ συζῆσαι Pall.*h.Laus*.22(p.72.9; M.34.1082A); **2.** met.; **a.** in gen. ὁ τὴν ψυχὴν ~ων λογισμός *Hom. Clem*.6.15; οἱ ~όμενοι τῷ λόγῳ τῆς παιδείας Mac.Mgn.*apocr*.3.39 (p.136.15); **b.** of God, Gr.Naz.*or*.9.5(M.35.825A); **c.** of Christ παιδαγωγέ, ποίμανον ἡμᾶς εἰς τὸ ἅγιόν σου ὄρος, πρὸς τὴν ἐκκλησίαν Clem.*paed*.1.9(p.139.21; M.8.352A); ~ων τὰ πλήθη τῶν...ἀγγέλων Meth.*symp*.3.6(p.32.12; M.18.68D); τὴν μυστικὴν ἐξηγοῦνται εὐωχίαν ἣν παρέθηκεν αὐτοῖς ὁ ~ων αὐτούς Thdt.*Ps*.22:1(1.747); **d.** of clergy, esp. bishops, cf.Hipp.*trad.ap*.3.4; ποίησον αὐτὸν ἄξιον εἶναι ~ειν σου τὴν ποίμνην Serap.*euch*.28.2; *Lit*.ap.*Const.App*.8.5.6; Thdt.*h.rel*.5(3.1165); Gr.Mag.*dial*.(tr.Zach.)2 proem.(M.*PL*.66.125B).

***ποιμαντέον**, *one must tend* or *shepherd*; of pastoral care of clergy, Gr.Naz.*or*.9.6(M.35.825B).

ποιμαντικός (ποιμενικός, ποιμένιος), *of* or *belonging to a shepherd, pastoral*;

A. lit.; **1.** in gen. ἀνὴρ...σχήματι ποιμενικῷ Herm.*vis*.5.1; ποιμενίην σύριγγα Gr.Naz.*carm*.2.2(epitaph.)64.1(M.38.43A; v.l. ποιμενικὴν); id.*or*.45.19(M.36.649C); neut. as subst., *flock*, Ac.20:28 cit.ap.‡Ath.*comm.essent*.3(M.28.32B); **2.** esp. of work of a shepherd ἡ ποιμενικὴ...καὶ βουκολικὴ...τέχναι Clem.*str*.1.7(p.24.26; M.8.732C); Mac.Aeg.*hom*.9.4(M.34.533D); Chrys.*hom.15.3 in 2Cor*.(10.547A).

B. met., *pastoral* τὸν ποιμαντικὸν...λόγον Mac.Mgn.*apocr*.3.39 (p.136.18); ποιμαντικῆς ψυχῆς Gr.Naz.*or*.9.5(M.35.825A); πάθος...ὁμολογῶ πάσχων ποιμαντικόν Gr.Nyss.*bapt.Chr*.(M.46.577A); παραίνεσις...ποιμαντική Euthal.Diac.*Ac*.(M.85.660B); of Christ's pastoral office ποιμανεῖς...ποιμαντικῇ ῥάβδῳ Eus.*Ps*.2:9(M.23.88D); of pastoral care and duty of clergy, Cyr.*Lc*.9:12(M.72.644D); Sophr. H.*ep.syn*.(M.87.3200C); of office of head of monastery, Gr.Mag.*dial*.(tr.Zach.)2 proem.(M.*PL*.66.125B).

C. as subst. ἡ ποιμαντική, ἡ ποιμενική; **1.** lit., *work of a shepherd* τὴν ποιμενικὴν τὸ τῶν προβάτων προνοεῖν φαμεν Clem.*str*.1.26(p.105.9; M.8.916C); ref. David, Gr.Naz.*ep*.139(M.37.236B); Isid.Pel.*epp*.1.133 (M.78.272A); his work as shepherd allegorized as 'practical philosophy', and his kingdom as contemplation, Max.*ambig*.(M.91.1297B); **2.** met., *pastoral office*; **a.** of Christ, Chrys.*hom.59.2 in Jo*.(8.347E); **b.** of clergy πρόσεχε μή τι παρέλθῃ τῶν ἐπιβαλλόντων τῇ ποιμαντικῇ Bas.*hom*.3.4(2.20A; M.31.208A); Gr.Naz.*or*.9.4(M.35.824A); ἀναλαβὼν...τὴν...σὴν εὐλάβειαν εἰς ποιμαντικὴν ἀπὸ ποίμνης [i.e. to a bishopric] id.*ep*.139(M.37.236B); τὸν κύριον, τὸν τῆς ποιμαντικῆς ἡγεμόνα Isid.Pel.*epp*.1.136(M.78.272D); Jo.VI H.*v.Jo.D*.23(M.94.464A).

***ποιμενάρχης, ὁ,** *chief shepherd*; of abbot, Jo.VI H.*v.Jo.D*.23 (M.94.464A); of pope, *Proem*.ad Gr.Mag.*dial*.(tr.Zach.)(M.*PL*.77.147C); of bishop, Thdr.Stud.*cant*.11.4(p.359).

ποιμενικός, = ποιμαντικός.

ποιμένιος, = ποιμαντικός.

ποιμήν, ὁ, *shepherd*;

A. lit. ὁ π. Πάρις ἡ ἀλόγιστος ὁρμὴ καὶ βάρβαρος. ἐὰν...ὁ τὴν ψυχὴν ποιμαίνων λογισμὸς τύχῃ ὢν βάρβαρος...μόνας ἕληται τὰς ἡδονάς *Hom.Clem*.6.15.

B. met.; **1.** of God ἐκκλησίας, ἥτις ἀντὶ ἐμοῦ ποιμένι τῷ θεῷ χρῆται Ign.*Rom*.9.1; **2.** of Christ π. τῆς...καθολικῆς ἐκκλησίας *M. Polyc*.19.2; Aberc.*epitaph*.3; ὁ τῶν νηπίων κηδεμονικὸς π. Clem.*paed*.1.7(p.121.31; M.8.313A); π. ... ἀγαθὸς μιᾶς τῆς ἀγέλης τῶν αὐτοῦ ἐπαΐοντων προβάτων id.*str*.1.26(p.105.15; M.8.916C); 'ὁ π. ὁ καλός' οὐκ ἀκούω μόνον καθολικῶς,...ὅτι π. ἐστι τῶν πιστευόντων...ἀλλὰ καὶ ἐν τῇ ἐμῇ ψυχῇ ὀφείλω ἔχειν ἔνδον μου τὸν Χριστόν, ἔνδον μου τὸν καλὸν π., ποιμαίνοντα τὰ ἐν ἐμοὶ ἄλογα κινήματα...ἐὰν π. ᾖ ἐν ἐμοί, ἄρχει μου τῶν αἰσθήσεων· οὐκέτι εἰσὶν ὑπὸ νοῦν ἀλλότριον...ἀλλὰ ὑπὸ τὸν καλὸν π. Or.*hom.5.6 in Jer*.(p.36.19; M.13.304C); *A.Thom*.A 25(p.141.3); *A.Barn*.1(p.292.4); ἐπεσκέψατο ὑμᾶς ὁ ἀληθινὸς π. ... ὁ τῶν ἰδίων προβάτων κηδόμενος CHier.(350)*ep*.(p.137.6; M.25.352B); *Const.App*.2.20.8; ὁ π. τοὺς ἔχοντας τὴν ἰδίαν σφραγῖδα γνωρίζει, καὶ ἐπισυνάγει ἀπὸ πάντων τῶν ἐθνῶν Mac.Aeg.*hom*.12.13(M.34.565A); appearance in vision of Christ as shepherd, *M.Perp*.4; **3.** of 'angel of repentance', and 'angel of luxury and deceit' in visions of Hermas ὁ π. ... ὁ ἄγγελος τῆς μετανοίας Herm.*vis*.5.7; βλέπεις τὸν π. τοῦτον;...οὗτος...ἄγγελος τρυφῆς καὶ ἀπάτης ἐστίν id.*sim*.6.2.1; of angels in gen., Eus.*d.e*.4.6(p.160.18; M.22.268A); guardian angel, Bas.*Eun*.3.1(1.272D; M.29.656B); **4.** of rulers, esp. eccl. ministers; **a.** Jewish πρεσβύτεροι ἄνομοι καὶ π. ἄδικοι *Ascens.Is*.A 3.24; *A.Thom*.A 66 (p.183.6); of kings, priests, and prophets, Eus.*d.e*.10.4(p.465.10; M.22.748D); **b.** Christian; **i.** of apostles; S. Peter πατὴρ καὶ π. πάντων *A.Petr.et Andr*.4(p.119.10); **ii.** of Christian ministers in gen. π. ἐσμὲν οἱ τῶν ἐκκλησιῶν προηγούμενοι κατ' εἰκόνα τοῦ ἀγαθοῦ π. Clem.*paed*.1.6(p.112.17; M.8.293C); πολλοὶ γὰρ τοῖς τῶν ἁγίων ἀποστόλων συνήραντο καὶ συναίρονται πόνοις...οἱ...ἀνερευνῶντες γραφάς, καὶ μετ' ἐκείνους ἕτεροι π. τε καὶ διδάσκαλοι Cyr.*Lc*.5:4(M.72.553D); ref. Eph.4:11, Thdt.*Eph*.4:11(3.424) cit. s. περίειμι (εἶμι *ibo*); **iii.** esp. of bishops ὅπου δὲ ὁ π. ἐστιν, ἐκεῖ ὡς πρόβατα ἀκολουθεῖτε Ign.*Philad*.2.1; τὸν μέντοι π. τὸν ἀγαθὸν ὁ λαϊκὸς τιμάτω...φοβείσθω ὡς πατέρα *Const.App*.2.20.1; *ib*.2.1.1; *ib*.2.42.1; Philost.*h.e*.8.2(M.65.556C); τοὺς τῶν ἐκκλησιῶν καλῶς ἡγησαμένους π. Oecum.*Apoc*.20:6 (p.223); **iv.** of Const. οἷα ἐν ἀγέλαις τὸν ἀγαθὸν ἐπόθουν π. Eus.*v.C*.4.65(p.144.28; M.20.1220C); θύει δ' ἅτε π. ἀγαθός...τῶν ὑπ' αὐτῷ ποιμαινομένων λογικῶν θρεμμάτων τὰς ψυχὰς τῇ αὐτοῦ γνώσει...προσάγων id.*l.C*.2(p.200.15; M.20.1328B); **5.** ref. Jo.10:1ff. π. δὲ ἔστω τῶν προβάτων πᾶς ὁ τὸ διδασκαλικὸν ἐκ τῶν πραγμάτων ἐγκεχειρισμένος ἀξίωμα, ὃς τῇ νομίμῳ χρησάμενος εἰσόδῳ· τουτέστιν, ὃς κατὰ πᾶσαν ἀκρίβειαν τοῦ νόμου πολιτευσάμενος Thdr.Mops.*Jo*.10:1(p.348.5; M.66.757B); **6.** title of work, the *Shepherd* of Hermas, Clem.*str*.2.9(p.136.5; M.8.980A); Or.*comm.in Mt*.14.21(p.335.29; M.13.1240C); cf. *puto tamen quod Hermas iste* [Rom.16:14] *sit scriptor libelli illius qui Pastor appellatur, quae scriptura valde mihi utilis videtur, et ut puto divinitus inspirata*, id.*comm.in Rom*.10(M.14.1282B); τῆς ὠφελιμωτάτης βίβλου τοῦ π. Ath.*inc*.3.1(M.25.101A); id.*ep.Afr*.5(M.26.1037B); βιβλία...οὐ κανονιζόμενα μέν, τετυπωμένα δὲ παρὰ τῶν πατέρων ἀναγινώσκεσθαι τοῖς...προσερχομένοις...κατηχεῖσθαι τὸν τῆς εὐσεβείας λόγον· Σοφία...καὶ Διδαχὴ...καὶ ὁ Π. id.*ep.fest*.39.11(M.26.1437C).

ποίμνη, ἡ, *flock*, met.; **1.** of Christ's flock, the Church ἡ π. ἡ ἀλληγορουμένη πρὸς τοῦ κυρίου οὐδὲν ἄλλο ἢ ἀγέλη τις ἀνθρώπων ἐστίν Clem.*str*.1.26(p.105.14; M.8.916C); Meth.*symp*.2.3(p.18.12; M.18.52B); ref. those about to be baptized οὕτως συνδεθῆναι καὶ συνενωθῆναι τῇ π. τοῦ κυρίου Serap.*euch*.22.2; *Const.App*.2.20.5; *ib*.6.18.10; ἐν τῷ καιρῷ τῆς κρίσεως...ὅταν καλέσῃ ὁ ποιμὴν τὴν ἰδίαν π., ὅσοι ἔχουσι τὸν καυτῆρα ἐπιγινώσκουσι τὸν ἴδιον ποιμένα...εἰς δύο γὰρ μέρη ἵσταται ὁ κόσμος, καὶ γίγνεται μία π. σκοτεινὴ...καὶ μία πλήρης φωτός Mac.Aeg.*hom*.12.13(M.34.565A); **2.** of church presided over by an apostle or bishop, *congregation*, cf.Hipp.*trad.ap*.3.4; *A.Petr. et Paul*.83(p.216.7); π. πνευματικῆς ἄξιον ἡνίοχον *MAMA* 1.171 (Phrygia, saec. iv); Serap.*euch*.28.2; *Lit*.ap.*Const.App*.8.5.6; **3.** in gen. τυγχάνει οὗτος ἐκ τῆς π. τῶν κηρύκων *A.Xanthipp*.7(p.62.24).

***ποιμνιαρχία, ἡ,** *ruling of the flock*, Thdr.Stud.*epp*.2.103(M.99.1360C); *ib*.1.33(1017B).

ποίμνιον, τό, = ποίμνη, met.; **1.** of Christ's Church ταπεινοφρονούντων...ἐστιν ὁ Χριστός, οὐκ ἐπαιρομένων ἐπὶ τὸ π. αὐτοῦ *1Clem*.16.1; *ib*.54.2; *Const.App*.2.17.3; **2.** of local congregation, esp. as bishop's flock εἰμί...π. μικροῦ προεστηκώς Gr.Naz.*ep*.41(M.37.84B); *Const.App*.2.10.4; τοῦ θεοῦ προεστῶσι τοῦ λογικοῦ π. Eustrat.*stat.anim*.11(p.399); **3.** of Jews as chosen people, Or.*hom.12.13 in Jer*.(p.102.5; M.13.397C).

***ποιναλίζω**, *exact punishment*, Or.*exp.in Pr*.24:17(M.17.229D).

ποινήτωρ, *avenging*, Nonn.*par.Jo*.15:24(M.43.877A); *ib*.16:11 (880A).

***ποιορρω-έω**, s.v.l., *decay*, of Devil as 'lord of flies' (cf. 4Reg.1:2) ἐφιζάνει γὰρ ἐπὶ τὰς ψυχὰς τῶν ἀσεβῶν, ὡς ἐπὶ ~ούσαις νομαῖς Ephr.3.212D, perh. for προσοζούσαις.

ποιότης, ἡ, *quality*; **1.** in gen. ὄνομα...ἐστι...προσηγορία τῆς ἰδίας π. τοῦ ὀνομαζομένου παραστατική· οἷόν ἐστί τις ἰδία π. Παύλου...ἡ μέν τις τῆς ψυχῆς, καθ' ἣν τοιάδε ἐστίν, ἡ δέ τις τοῦ νοῦ, καθ' ἣν τοιῶνδέ ἐστι θεωρητικός, ἡ δέ τις τοῦ σώματος αὐτοῦ, καθ' ἣν τοιόνδε ἐστί Or.*or*.24.2(p.353.22; M.11.492B); ἐν ᾧ ἄποιον εἶναι λέγει [sc. τὴν ὕλην] τὴν π. αὐτῆς μηνύει, ὁποία ἐστὶν ἡ ὕλη διαγραφόμενος, ὅπερ ἐστὶ ποιότητος εἶδος Meth.*arbitr*.9(p.169.8; M.18.257A); πᾶσα...κίνησις περὶ τὸ ποσόν, κακίας δὲ καὶ ἀρετῆς ἡγεμών ἐστιν ἡ π. Alex.Lyc.*Man*.8(p.13.1; M.18.421C); Isid.Pel.*epp*.1.16(M.78.189C); Thdt.*h.rel*. proem.(3.1100); τῶν ὄντων τὰ μὲν ἔστιν οὐσία, τὰ δὲ π., τὰ δὲ ἐνέργεια· καὶ οὐσία μέν ἐστιν ἐγώ, σύ· π., λευκόν, μέλαν, γλυκύ,...καὶ ὅσα τοιαῦτα ἐν ὑποκειμένοις σώμασι θεωρούμενα Jo.D.*Man*.1.2(M.96.1325D); **2.** opp. substance: ref. transmigration of souls εἰ ἐνδέχεται αὐτὴν εἰσκριθῆναι δεύτερον ἐν σώματι ἢ μή,...καὶ τῷ αὐτῷ σώματι ἢ ἑτέρῳ, καὶ εἰ τῷ αὐτῷ, πότερον καθ' ὑποκείμενον μένοντι τῷ αὐτῷ κατὰ δὲ ποιότητα μεταβαλομένῳ, ἢ καὶ καθ' ὑποκείμενον καὶ ποιότητα ἐσομένῳ τῷ αὐτῷ Or.*Jo*.6.14(7; p.124.3; M.14.225C); in gen., Meth.*arbitr*.7 (p.163.5; M.18.253B); Gr.Naz.*or*.9.2(M.35.821A); οὔτε γὰρ ἀκτίς, οὔτε φῶς, ἄλλος ἥλιος, ἀλλ' ἡλιακαί τινες ἀπόρροιαι καὶ π. οὐσιώδεις *ib*.3.32(M.36.169B); ἐάν τις αὐτὴν [sc. τὴν οὐσίαν] ἀπογυμνώσας τῶν ἐπιθεωρουμένων π. τε καὶ ἰδιωμάτων αὐτὴν ἐφ' ἑαυτῆς ἐξετάζῃ κατὰ τὸν τοῦ εἶναι λόγον Gr.Nyss.*Eun*.1(1 p.104.7; M.45.337B); τὰς τῶν αἰσθητῶν οὐσίας καὶ π. Dion.Ar.*d.n.*5.8(M.3.824B); ποιότητες, αἵ τε οὐσιώδεις καὶ ἐπουσιώδεις καλούμεναι, ὧν οὐδετέρα ἐστὶν οὐσία, τουτέστι πρᾶγμα ὑφεστώς, ἀλλ' ὃ ἀεὶ περὶ τὴν οὐσίαν θεωρεῖται... ὡς ἐπιστήμη ἐν ψυχῇ Leont.B.*Nest.et Eut.*1(M.86.1277D); id.*Nest.* 1.6(M.86.1425B); **3.** of men, Just.*1apol.*13.2(M.6.345B); Ἀβραὰμ γεγεωργηκέναι οὓς εἶχεν ἐν ἑαυτῷ σπερματικοὺς λόγους,...καὶ τούτοις προστεθεικέναι ἁγίαν ἰδίαν π. Or.*Jo.*20.3(p.330.8; M.14.580A); Nil. *Magn.*53(M.79.1040A); τρεῖς εἶναι τὰς γυναῖκας [sc. Μαρίας] λογίζομαι ...ἐκ τῆς τῶν προσώπων π. *cat.Lc.*7:36(p.60.24); **4.** of things: foods αἱ...πολυειδεῖς π. ἀποπτυστέαι Clem.*paed.*2.1(p.154.22; M.8.380A); in gen. μεταδίδωσι τῆς π. ἡ ὕλη λυμαινομένη τὸ κρᾶμα *ib.*2.3(p.177.26; 432B); *ib.*2.10(p.208.18; 497B); *Hom.Clem.*3.34; ref. a miracle μεταβαλεῖν ἐξ ὕδατος εἰς ἐλαίου π. τὴν φύσιν Eus.*h.e.*6.9.3(M.20.540A); πᾶσαν...σωματικὴν οὐσίαν ἐν μόναις...ταῖς π. διακεκριμένην id.*d.e.*4.15 (p.174.21; M.22.292A); γεωργία μὲν τὰς τῶν φυτῶν π. μεταβάλλει Bas. *hex.*5.7(1.47A; M.29.109D); ποιότητα πραγμάτων πνευματικήν Cyr.*Jo.* 1.9(4.98C); of water at Marah πικρὸν ὕδωρ εἰς γλυκεῖαν μετεβλήθη π. Thdt.*qu.26 in Ex.*(1.143); of tree in Eden οὐ γὰρ ἡ π. τοῦ ξύλου τὴν παράβασιν εἶχεν, ἀλλ' ἡ δόσις τῆς ἐντολῆς Proc.G.*Gen.*1:7(M.87.197A); **5.** of actions ἡ τῶν ἔργων π. Cyr.*Os.*140(3.174A); and abstracts κατ' οὐσίαν καὶ κατὰ π. καὶ κατὰ τὸ συμβεβηκός· κατ' οὐσίαν μὲν σκότος ἀντίκειται φωτί, κατὰ π. δὲ κακὸν ἀγαθῷ Adam.*dial.*3.6(p.122.14; M.11.1797A); Thdt.*eran.*2(4.95); διὰ Χριστοῦ ἀναμορφούμεθα, τῆς διανοίας ἡμῶν εἰς πνευματικὴν π. διαπλαττομένης Ammon.*Jo.*3:8(M. 85.1409B); **6.** as created by God δοκεῖ σοι τὰς τοῦ κόσμου π. μὴ ἐξ ὑποκειμένων π. γεγονέναι;...οὐκοῦν εἰ μήτε ἐξ ὑποκειμένων π. τὰς π. ἐδημιούργησεν ὁ θεός, μήτε ἐκ τῶν οὐσιῶν ὑπάρχουσιν, τῷ μηδὲ οὐσίας αὐτὰς εἶναι, ἐκ μὴ ὄντων αὐτὰς ὑπὸ τοῦ θεοῦ γεγονέναι ἀνάγκη εἰπεῖν Meth.*arbitr.*7(p.163.2; M.18.253B); problem discussed, *ib.*10(p.170. 11ff.; 257Bff.); **7.** ref. God; **a.** quality of God ἐμπεφυκυῖα καὶ οὐσιώδης π. εἴρηται τοῦ θεοῦ CCP(681)cit.ap.Manuel Calecas *de essentia et operatione* (M.152.421D); predication improper in case of God οὔτε ὅμοιον οὔτε ἀνόμοιον λέγομεν τὸν υἱὸν τῷ πατρί. ἑκάτερον γὰρ αὐτῶν ἐπίσης ἀδύνατον· ὅμοιον γὰρ καὶ ἀνόμοιον κατὰ τὰς π. λέγεται· ποιότητος δὲ τὸ θεῖον ἐλεύθερον Evagr.Pont.*ep.*3(M.32.249B); **b.** Trin. τὸ ὅμοιον οὐκ ἐπὶ τῶν οὐσιῶν, ἀλλ' ἐπὶ σχημάτων καὶ π. λέγεται ὅμοιον· ἐπὶ γὰρ τῶν οὐσιῶν οὐχ ὁμοιότης, ἀλλὰ ταυτότης ἂν λεχθείη. ... τὸ γὰρ ὅμοιον π. ἐστίν, ἥτις τῇ οὐσίᾳ προσγένοιτ' ἄν. τοῦτο δὲ τῶν ποιημάτων ἴδιον ἂν εἴη Ath.*syn.*53(p.276.25ff.; M.26.788B,C); of Persons, id.*ep.Afr.*8(M.26.1044B) cit. s. βελτίωσις; εἰ μὴ οὐσιώδης σοφία...καὶ ὢν υἱός...ὄνομα μόνον ἐστὶ λόγος, καὶ σοφία...ἀλλ' εἰ τοῦτο, εἴη ἂν αὐτὸς ἑαυτοῦ πατὴρ καὶ υἱός· πατὴρ μέν, ὅτι σοφός, υἱὸς δέ, ὅτι σοφία· ἀλλὰ μὴ ὡς π. τις ταῦτα ἐν τῷ θεῷ...εὑρεθήσεται γὰρ σύνθετος ὁ θεὸς ἐξ οὐσίας καὶ π. ‡Ath.*Ar.*4.2(p.45.15,16; M.26.469A,B); ἐγεννήθη [sc. Χριστός]...ἀμερίστῳ προελεύσει· ἡ γὰρ βούλησις ὁμοῦ καὶ τῷ οἰκητηρίῳ αὐτῆς ἐμπέπηγε καὶ ταῦθ', ἅπερ διαφόρου δέεται τημελείας κατὰ τὴν ἑκάστου π. πράττει τε καὶ διοικεῖ Const.*ep.*(Opitz 3 p.58.12); of H. Ghost οὐκοῦν ἐκ τῆς οὐσίας τοῦ υἱοῦ τὸ πνεῦμα, π. τις, ἵν' οὕτως εἴπωμεν, ὑπάρχων τοῦ κυριεύοντος ἁπάντων θεοῦ Cyr.*thes.*34(5^1. 346C); **c.** Christol. δύο φύσεις, δύο οὐσίαι ἡνωμέναι καθ' ὑπόστασιν· καὶ διῃρημέναι ὅσον ἐπινοίᾳ μόνῃ, ταῖς τε π. καὶ ἐνεργείαις *Lit.Jac.* proem.(*NBP* 10^2 p.37); ἀντικίρνανται τὰς φυσικὰς π., καὶ διεστῶτά τε καὶ διωρισμένα τὰς ὑποστάσεις Leont.H.*monoph.*(M.86.1816D); Σευῆρος...ταυτὸν εἶναι φάσκων...τὴν ἐν π. φυσικὴ διαφορὰν τῇ πραγματικῇ καὶ κατὰ φύσιν· διὰ τὸ καὶ φυσικὴν εἶναι πᾶσαν π. ... εἰ δὲ πάλιν ἐγκληθῇ δικαίως...εὕροι πρὸς ἀπολογίαν καταφυγὴν τὴν ὡς ἐν π. φυσικῇ διαφοράν· π. λέγων φυσικῶν, ἀλλ' οὐ φύσεων, ἤγουν οὐσιῶν ἐπὶ Χριστοῦ διαφορὰν μετὰ τὴν ἕνωσιν...ἐπικάλυμμα ποιεῖται τῆς τῶν φύσεων συγχύσεως τὴν ψιλὴν ἐν π. φυσικῇ διαφοράν Max.*opusc.*(M.91. 40B–41C); ὑπευθύνους ἑαυτοὺς ἐλέγχοις πεποίηνται...μόνῃ π. λέγοντες τὴν διαφορὰν σώζεσθαι, τῶν πραγμάτων χωρίς ... κενούντων τὸ εὐαγγέλιον, ἄνευ οὐσιῶν ὑποκειμένων, εἶναι ποιότητας δύνασθαι νομοθετούντων id.*ep.*12(M.91.485B).

ποι-όω, **1.** *give quality to,* of God in Creation εἰ δὲ οἵαν αὐτὸς ἐβούλετο...ἐποίωσε τὴν ὕλην...σχῆμα καὶ τύπον ἐνσφραγιζόμενος αὐτῇ Dion.Al.*fr.*ap.Eus.*p.e.*7.19(334B, v.l. ἐποίησε M.21.564C); ὕλη...ὑπὸ τῆς τοῦ θεοῦ δυνάμεως μετεβλήθη εἰς ταῦτα πάντα καὶ γέγονεν οὐσία πεποιωμένη καὶ πεποσωμένη ‡Just.*confut.*50(M.6.1544B); τί δεῖ ζωγραφίας ἡμῖν, δέον τοὺς κατ' αὐτὴν πεποιωμένους εἰς μέσον ἀγαγεῖν; Chrys.*hom.*9.4 *in 1Cor.*(10.78D); τὸ ὕδωρ καθ' ἑαυτὸ μὲν τὸ στοιχεῖον ἄποιον λέγεται εἶναι, διὰ δὲ γῆς παριόν, ἐκεῖθεν ~οῦται Max.*schol.d.n.* 4.20(M.4.280C); ref. delineation by means of images πῶς ~ωθήσεται τὸ ἀνείδεον; Jo.D.*imag.*1.8(M.94.1237D); **2.** *make to be of a certain quality, affect in character, in form*; **a.** of body of Christ partaken of by faithful σῶμα...ὅλην ἔχον ἐν ἑαυτῷ τὴν τοῦ ἑνωθέντος λόγου δύναμιν, καὶ πεποιωμένον ὥσπερ, μᾶλλον δὲ ἤδη καὶ ἀναπεπλησμένον τῆς ἐνεργείας αὐτοῦ Cyr.*Jo.*3.6(4.324E); **b.** Christol. ὡς εἴ τις λέγοι ὅτι τὴν σταγόνα τοῦ ὄξους ἐμμειχθεῖσαν τῷ πελάγει θάλασσαν ἡ μεῖξις ἐποίωσε Gr.Nyss.*Eun.*5(M.45.708C; ἐποίησε 2 p.126.2); **c.** ref. moral character δόγματα...ποιώσαντα αὐτῶν τὴν ψυχήν Or.*Cels.*1.52(p.103. 7; M.11.757A); τὸ...λογικὸν τετελείωται καὶ κατὰ πᾶσαν ἀρετὴν πεποίωται *ib.*4.24(p.293.30; 1061B); δικαιοσύνην ἀγαπῶν ὁ θεὸς οὐχ οὕτως αὐτὴν ἀγαπᾷ ὡς ὁ δίκαιος ἄνθρωπος, ἐπὶ τῷ ἔχειν αὐτὴν ἐν ἑαυτῷ καὶ πεποιῶσθαι κατ' αὐτήν id.*fr.*50 *in Jo.*(p.524.29); υἱὸς δὲ ἀρετῶν ὁ κατ' αὐτὰς πεποιωμένος id.*exp.in Pr.*4:1(M.17.169D); οὕτω τάχιστα τοῖς πέλας ~ούμεθα, καλοῖς μὲν ἧττον, τοῖς κακοῖς δὲ καὶ λίαν Gr.Naz. *carm.*2.1.12.718(M.37.1218A); πρὸς γὰρ τὰς διαλέξεις καὶ ἡ ψυχὴ ~οῦται Chrys.*hom.*2.4 *in 2Thess.*(11.520D); μόνῳ θεῷ πεποιωμένην τῆς ψυχῆς διατηρήσας τὴν ἔφεσιν *Schol.*5 in Max.*qu.Thal.*40(M.90. 401B); εἰς αὐτὸν εἰσδὺς τὸν θεόν, καὶ ὅλῳ ποιωθεὶς τε καὶ μεταποιωθείς Max.*ambig.*(M.91.1141B); μοναχός ἐστιν ὁ ποιωθεὶς ταῖς ἀρεταῖς, ὡς ἄλλος ταῖς ἡδοναῖς Jo.Clim.*scal.*23(M.88.969A); ἀδύνατον τὸν νοῦν τῇ γνώσει ποιωθῆναι εἰ μὴ...τὸ παθητικὸν...ἐξ αὐτοῦ πελάσει Thal. *cent.*2.50(M.91.1441D); τέλειός ἐστιν ὁ νοῦς ὁ ποιωθεὶς τῇ γνώσει *ib.*2.54 (1444A); **d.** in gen. οὐ γὰρ πῦρ αὐτὸν <σίδηρον> ἢ κρύσταλλον ὀνομάζομεν τὸν ἐνὶ τούτων πεποιωμένον Gr.Nyss.*Eun.*1(1 p.104.23; M.45. 337C); ἐστὶν οἶνος...ὕδωρ ὑπ' ἀμπέλου πεποιωμένον Nemes.*nat.hom.* 1(M.40.517B); **3.** *make a quality of*, hence pass., *become habitual* ἀναλγησία ἐστὶ πεποιωμένη ἀμέλεια Jo.Clim.*scal.*18(M.88.932B); ἡ γὰρ ἕξις τῆς ἀρετῆς τῇ ψυχῇ ποιωθεῖσα, ὡς ἅτε φυσικὴν συγγένειαν πρὸς αὐτὴν ἔχουσα †Jo.D.*B.J.*19(M.96.1037D).

πόκος, ὁ, *fleece*; **1.** in Dionysiac worship τὰ...σύμβολα...ἔσοπτρον, π. Clem.*prot.*2(p.14.16; M.8.80A); **2.** exeg. Jud.6:38ff., Ps.71:6, cf. *vellus lanae populum...Israel, reliquam autem terram reliquas gentes...et ros...verbum esse dei, quod illi soli populo caelitus fuisset indultum,* Or.*hom.*8.4 *in Jud.*(p.512.1; M.12.983C); of Israel as recipients of grace, Thdt.*qu.*15 *in Jud.*(1.333); Proc.G.*Jud.*6:38ff.(M. 87.1068A); of Inc., cf. *descendit in illud vellus populi circumcisionis, et sicut stillicidia stillantia super terram: hoc est super reliquam terram descendit dominus,* Or.*hom.*8.4 *in Jud.*(p.513.4; 984B); id. *sel.in Ps.*71:6(M.12.1524B); ὡς ὑετὸς ἐπὶ πόκον ἀψοφητί, φησί·...διὰ τὴν λαθραίαν αὐτοῦ παρουσίαν Ath.*exp.Ps.*71:6(M.27.324D); σημαίνοι δ' ἂν ὁ μὲν π. τὸν Ἰσραήλ, ἡ δὲ γῆ τὰ ἔθνη, ἐπεὶ πρότερον ἐπὶ πόκον κατῆλθεν, εἶτ' ἐκεῖθεν ἐπὶ τὴν γῆν ἐξ ἀπειθείας τοῦ Ἰσραὴλ Didym. *Ps.*71:6(M.39.1465D); καθάπερ...π. δεχόμενος ὑετόν, οὐδένα κτύπον ἀποτελεῖ...οὕτως ἡ δεσποτικὴ γεγένηται σύλληψις· οὐδὲ τοῦ συνοικοῦντος αἰσθομένου μνηστῆρος Thdt.*Ps.*71:6(1.1104); τὴν κένωσιν τοῦ μονογενοῦς τὴν εἰς τὴν θεοτόκον...λέγει· π. δὲ αὐτῆς τὴν γαστέρα...ἐκάλεσεν Hesych.H.*fr.Ps.*71:6(M.93.1236D); **3.** hence as title of BMV, Procl.CP *or.*6.17(M.65.756D); Thdr.Stud.*nativ.BMV* 7(M.96.696A).

πολεμάρχης, *leader in war, general,* Cyr.*Is.*5.4(2.837D); *Chron. Pasch.*p.261(M.92.636B).

πολεμ-έω, A. *fight, go to war* against; **1.** ref. Christian attitude to war οἱ πάλαι ἀλληλοφόνται οὐ μόνον οὐ ~οῦμεν τοὺς ἐχθρούς, ἀλλ' ὑπὲρ τοῦ μηδὲ ψεύδεσθαι μηδ' ἐξαπατῆσαι τοὺς ἐξετάζοντας, ἡδέως... ἀποθνήσκομεν Just.*1apol.*39.3(M.6.388B); war admissible at proper time (Eccl.3:8), but one must always strive for peace, Gr.Naz.*or.* 22.15(M.35.1148C); **2.** of war against Church (persecution) τύραννοι ...τὸν...θεὸν ~εῖν ὡρμημένοι τὴν αὐτοῦ κατεπόνουν ἐκκλησίαν Eus. *v.C.*1.12(p.13.24; M.20.925C); ταῖς ὑπ' αὐτὸν ἐκκλησίαις...~εῖν ἐτόλμα [sc. Licinius] *ib.*2.1(p.40.9; 980A); id.*h.e.*1.1.2(M.20.49A); βασιλεῖ...~οῦντι τὴν ἐκκλησίαν *M.Thdot.*1 4(p.63.18); **3.** met., of fighting against heresy, Eus.*h.e.*4.23.4(M.20.385A); of strife within Church, Gr.Naz.*ep.*100(M.37.173A); **4.** of spiritual warfare; esp. of struggle of flesh against spirit, *Diogn.*6.4; and of demons against mankind, Ign.*Trall.*4.2; Tat.*orat.*16(p.18.3; M.6.841A); Or.*Cels.*3.36 (p.233.11; M.11.968A); Max.*carit.*2.67(M.90.1005B) cit. s. δαίμων.

B. *attack, ravage, destroy,* Just.*dial.*24.3(M.6.528C); ἀπήχθη ὁ λαὸς...πολεμηθείσης τῆς γῆς καὶ τῶν ἱερῶν σκευῶν ἀρθέντων *ib.*52.3 (592A); Thdt.*h.e.*5.24.13(3.1066).

C. *constrain, urge, tempt* ἐπολεμήθης ἐξελθεῖν τῆς ἐρήμου Pall.*h. Laus.*35(p.103.15; M.34.1114B); ἐπολεμήθη δὲ εἰς πορνείαν Jo.Mosch. *prat.*14(M.87.2861C); *ib.*19(2865C); *ib.*205(3096B).

D. *strive* ἐπολέμει πορευθῆναι *M.Sab.*4.2.

E. *conflict with* οὕτω γὰρ ἂν ἦν ἀντικρὺς ~οῦσα τῆς οἰκουμενικῆς συνόδου ἡ ἐν Σαρδικῇ *Schol.* in CSard.*can.*5(*Mon.*2 p.648).

πολεμήτωρ, ὁ, *enemy*; of Devil, ‡Meth.*palm.*6(M.18.393D); Sophr.H.*triod.*(M.87.3865B); Gr.Mag.*dial.*(tr.Zach.)3.26(M.*PL.*77. 283A).

πολέμιος, *hostile, enemy*; **1.** in gen., of fallen human nature δόγματος οὐρανίου ὀθνεία καὶ π. Mac.Mgn.*apocr.*4.18(p.195.5); of heretics and theological opponents, †Apoll.*ep.Bas.*2(M.32.1105C);

Enther.*confut*.3(M.28.1345B); **2.** esp. of Satan and powers of evil π. ... ἄγγελον Or.*Cels*.5.48(p.52.17; M.11.1256B); πολεμιωτάτου ἀνθρώποις ὄφεως *ib*.6.28(p.98.29; 1337A); τὸν π. τὸν ἐνεστηκότα id.*hom*.5.17 *in Jer*.(p.47.14; M.13.321D); ἑκὼν [sc. Judas]...ἐδέξατο τὸν π. Thdt. *Ps*.108:6(1.1383); id.*h.e*.5.39.11(3.1084).

πολεμιστής, ὁ, *enemy*, Clem.*str*.3.18(p.245.7; M.8.1239B); *A.Andr. et Mt*.24(p.100.13); Gel.Cyz.*h.e*.1.9.3(M.85.1209C).

πολεμοποιέω, *make war on*; c. acc., Leont.et Jo.*sacr*.2(M.86.2093A).

πόλεμος, ὁ, *war*; **1.** classification: τῶν π. γάρ ἐστιν εἴδη τρία τὰ χαλεπώτερα· εἷς μὲν...ὁ κοινός, ὅταν οἱ παρ' ἡμῖν στρατιῶται πολεμῶνται παρὰ βαρβάρων· δεύτερος, ὅταν...πρὸς ἀλλήλους πολεμῶμεν· τρίτος, ὅταν ἕκαστος πρὸς ἑαυτὸν πολεμῇ Chrys.*hom*.7.1 *in 1Tim*.(11.583E); **2.** Christian attitude: war results from original sin and immediately from πλεονεξία, Gr.Naz.*or*.19.14(M.35.1061A); οὐδὲν γὰρ οὕτω ποιεῖ μάχην καὶ π., ὡς ὁ τῶν παρόντων ἔρως, ὡς ἢ δόξης ἢ χρημάτων ἢ τρυφῆς ἐπιθυμία Chrys.*exp.in Ps*.119:7(5.333C); Christianity changes warlike dispositions οἱ πολέμου...μεμεστωμένοι...τὰ πολεμικὰ ὄργανα ἕκαστος, τὰς μαχαίρας εἰς ἄροτρα,...μετεβάλομεν Just.*dial*.110.3(M.6.729B); wars are sign of approaching end of world, Cyr.H.*catech*.15.6; peace promoted by prayer for civil authorities, Chrys.*hom*.7.1 *in 1Tim*.(11.583D); war sometimes right (cf. Eccl.3:8), but peace to be pursued, Gr.Naz.*or*.22.15(M.35.1148C); killing in war dist. from murder φονεύειν οὐκ ἔξεστιν, ἀλλ' ἐν πολέμοις ἀναιρεῖν τοὺς ἀντιπάλους καὶ ἔννομον καὶ ἐπαίνου ἄξιον Ath.*ep.Amun*.(M.26.1173B); τοὺς ἐν πολέμοις φόνους οἱ πατέρες ἡμῶν ἐν τοῖς φόνοις οὐκ ἐλογίσαντο ...συγγνώμην δόντες τοῖς ὑπὲρ σωφροσύνης καὶ εὐσεβείας ἀμυνομένοις. τάχα δὲ καλῶς ἔχει συμβουλεύειν ὡς τὰς χεῖρας μὴ καθαροὺς τριῶν ἐτῶν τῆς κοινωνίας μόνης ἀπέχεσθαι Bas.*ep*.188 *can*.13(3.275C; M.32.681B); **3.** of war against Church (i.e. persecution) τὸν μὲν ἔξωθεν οὐ δέδοικα π., οὐδὲ τὸν νῦν ἐπαναστάντα θῆρα ταῖς ἐκκλησίαις Gr.Naz.*or*.2.87(M.35.492A); κρείττων γὰρ ἐπαινετὸς π. εἰρήνης χωριζούσης θεοῦ *ib*.2.82(488C); π. ἀνερριπίσθη ποτὲ κατὰ τῆς ἐκκλησίας χαλεπός, π. ἁπάντων βαρύτατος Chrys.*pan.Bern*.4(2.639B); πλείονα ἡμῖν τῆς εἰρήνης ὁ π. πορίζει τὴν ὠφέλειαν...ὁ δὲ π. τά τε φρονήματα παραθήγει καὶ τῶν παρόντων ὡς ῥεόντων παρασκευάζει καταφρονεῖν Thdt.*h.e*.5.39.26(3.1087); **4.** of war waged against Church by heretics, †Apoll. *ep.Bas*.2(M.32.1105C); and by orthodox for reconciliation of dissidents λεγέσθω γάρ τις καὶ π. ἱερός Gr.Naz.*or*.42.21(M.36.481D); **5.** of schism, *1Clem*.46.5; Ign.*Eph*.13.2; **6.** of spiritual warfare ἀνατελεῖ ὑμῖν...τὸ σωτήριον κυρίου, αὐτὸς γὰρ ποιήσει πρὸς τὸν Βελίαρ π. *T.Dan* 5.10; δεῖ...δεξιὰς τείνειν...ἵνα π. κυρίου πολεμήσῃς Cyr.H.*procatech*.10; τὸν ἔνδον καὶ ἐν ἡμῖν αὐτοῖς, τὸν ἐν τοῖς πάθεσι π. Gr.Naz.*or*.2.91(M.35.493A); θεῷ, τῷ παθόντι δι' ἡμᾶς, ἵνα...καταλύσῃ τὸν ἐν ἡμῖν π. *ib*.22.15(1149A); μέγας π. ὄντως, καὶ πολὺ μέγας, ἂν ἐθέλωμεν νήφειν· ἔχει στεφάνους καὶ ὁ παρὼν καιρός Chrys.*hom*.3.5 *in 1Thess*.(11.447C); **7.** of any pain or torment τὸν ἕλκων π. Constantius Ant.*ep*.2(M.52.744).

***πολεμοτρόφος,** *fomenting war*; of antichrist, Hipp.*Dan*.4.49.1 (M.10.665A).

***πολεμοχαρής,** *rejoicing in strife*, Leont.B.*Nest.et Eut*.2(M.86.1317B).

πολ-έω, *turn, cause to revolve*, in Phrygian mysteries as interpreted by Peratae τοῦτον [i.e. the Deity]...καλοῦσιν αἰπόλον...ὅτι ἐστὶν ἀείπολος, τουτέστιν ὁ ἀεὶ ~ῶν καὶ στρέφων καὶ περιελαύνων τὸν κόσμον ὅλον στροφῇ. ~εῖν γάρ ἐστι τὸ στρέφειν καὶ μεταβάλλειν τὰ πράγματα. ... καὶ πόλεις, ἐν αἷς οἰκοῦμεν, ὅτι στρεφόμεθα καὶ ~οῦμεν ἐν αὐταῖς, καὶ καλοῦνται πόλεις Hipp.*haer*.5.8(p.95.12; M.16.3150).

***πολήν,** *strongly*, ‡Nil.*perist*.10.2(M.79.889A).

πολιά, ἡ, 1. *greyness of hair, grey hair* τοῦ προσώπου αὐτῶν [sc. γερόντων] ἡ π. ἄνθος πολυπειρίας Clem.*paed*.3.3(p.246.16; M.8.580A); γυναῖκες βάπτουσαι μὲν τὰς π., ... πολιώτεραι θᾶττον γίνονται διὰ τὰ ἀρώματα ξηραντικὰ ὄντα *ib*.2.8(p.199.4; 277A); ἡ αἵρεσις [sc. Arianism] οὐκ οἶδεν οὐδὲ γερόντων τιμᾶν π. [ref. case of Hosius] Ath. *h.Ar*.42(p.207.2; M.25.744A); hence **2.** *old age*, Bas.*hom.in Ps*.1(1.96B; M.29.225A); esp. of honourable old age λέγοντά τινα μειρακιωδῶς καὶ οὐδὲν φιλοσόφου πολιᾶς ἄξιον Or.*Cels*.1.28(p.79.17; M.11.713A); ἀνδρὶ...ἐν π. ζῶντι καὶ πρὸς ἀλήθειαν βλέποντι Gr.Nyss.*Eun*.12 (1 p.385.20; M.45.1113D); Chrys.*hom*.49.6 *in Mt*.(7.512E); **3.** *antiquity* δυσωπήθητι τὴν π. τῆς νηστείας Bas.*hom*.1.3(2.3A; M.31.165D).

πολιαρχία, ἡ, *city government, local administration*, ref. fulfilment of Is.7:16 at birth of Christ τῆς Ῥωμαίων μοναρχίας τῶν ἐθνῶν ἐπικρατησάσης, λέλυτο μὲν καὶ πᾶσα ἡ κατὰ τοὺς τόπους ἐθναρχία τε καὶ π. Eus.*d.e*.7.1(p.307.16; M.22.501D); *ib*.8 proem.(p.349.21; 569A).

πολίζω, 1. *inhabit as a city* πτηνοῖς δὲ ἀὴρ ἐπολίζετο Bas.Sel.*or*.1.2 (M.85.33A); of peopling of desert with monks, Ath.*v.Anton*.14(M.26.865B); Isid.Pel.*epp*.1.191(M.78.305A); Procl.CP *or*.2.1(M.65.692C); **2.** *establish as a city* τὴν ἐπουράνιον Ἱερουσαλὴμ ἐπὶ γῆς πολισθῆναι Thdt.*Ps*.50:21(1.944).

***πολιήτωρ, ὁ,** *citizen*, *Orac.Sib*.11.68.

πολιοπλόκαμος, *grey-haired*, *Orac.Sib*.11.68.

πολιορκ-έω, 1. *besiege*; met., *pester* μὴ δέξῃ ~οῦντά σε δανειστήν Bas.*hom.in Ps*.14(1.109B; M.29.269B); **2.** *attack*, *Chron.Pasch*.p.116 (M.92.304A); *ib*.p.188(464B); ναοὺς καὶ βωμοὺς...ἐπολιόρκει †Jo.D. *B.J*.33(M.96.1176C); esp. of persecution of Christians τὸν...πολέμιον θῆρα τὸν τὴν ἐκκλησίαν...πολιορκήσαντα Eus.*v.C*.3.3(p.78.11; M.20.1057A); id.*h.e*.10.4.27(M.20.860C); εὐαγγελίων οἱ κήρυκες...ὑπὸ Ἑλλήνων καὶ βαρβάρων ~ούμενοι Thdt.*Ps*.109:2(1.1394); τὸ Χριστιανῶν ~ούμενον ἐπερρώννυτο φρόνημα Philost.*h.e*.7.4(M.65.541B); ref. spiritual warfare ~ῆσάν με τὸ κακόν Meth.*res*.2.2(p.333.4; M.18.300B); Eus.*l.C*.7(p.212.15; M.20.1352B); **3.** met., *oppress* ὑπὸ δύο... λογισμῶν ἐναντίων ὁ πατριάρχης ~ούμενος Thdt.*Heb*.11:18(3.618); **4.** fig., *invest*, Jo.Eleem.*v.Tych*.(p.128).

πολιορκία, ἡ, *oppression, hostile treatment*; of persecution of Church, Eus.*v.C*.1.13(p.14.4; M.20.928A); πρῶτον ἔτος τῆς τῶν ἐκκλησιῶν π. *ib*.1.18(p.17.5; 933B); in gen. αἱ π. τῶν δήμων Chrys.*hom*. 25.2 *in 2Cor*.(10.614A); Thdt.*Ps*.24:18(1.762).

πολιοῦχος, *protecting a city*; masc. as subst., *guardian of city*; **1.** lit., of James of Nisibis ἐπίσκοπος ἦν καὶ π. καὶ στρατηγός Thdt. *h.e*.2.30.2(3.905); of martyrs' relics ὡς πολιούχους τιμῶσι id.*affect*.8 (p.199.9; 4.902); προνοοῦσιν οἱ π. μάρτυρες τῆς ταλαίνης [sc. Πηλουσίου] Isid.Pel.*epp*.1.226(M.78.324B); **2.** of Adam as keeper of paradise, Jo.D.*hom*.4.7(M.96.609A).

***πολιόφαγος, ὁ,** *old eater*, Pall.*h.Laus*.21(p.56.18, v.l. πολυφ- M. 34.1065C).

***πολιοφανής,** *of venerable aspect*, ‡Jo.D.*hom*.5(M.96.652C).

πολιόω, *make grey, make aged*; **1.** lit., Clem.*paed*.3.3(p.246.14; M. 8.580A); Nil.*epp*.3.236(M.79.493A); ‡Caes.Naz.*dial*.170(M.38.1133); **2.** met., *make venerable* πρεσβυτέροις πεπολιωμένοις ὑπὸ φρονήσεως Or.*princ*.4.2.4(p.314.5; M.11.365B); τὴν πολιώσασαν αὐτοῦ τὴν ψυχὴν ἀρετήν †Bas.*Is*.104(1.451E; M.30.288B); Pall.*v.Chrys*.4(p.27.5; M.47.17); τὸν νοῦν πεπολιωμένον ἔχοντας Cyr.*Is*.2.5(2.348C); id.*Joel*.35(3.229C).

πόλις, ἡ, *city*; **1.** earthly; **a.** descriptions and def. σπουδαῖον γὰρ ἡ π. καὶ ὁ δῆμος ἀστεῖόν τι σύστημα καὶ πλῆθος ἀνθρώπων ὑπὸ νόμου διοικούμενον Clem.*str*.4.26(p.324.27; M.8.1381A); ὁρίζονται γάρ τινες π. εἶναι σύστημα ἱδρυμένον, κατὰ νόμον διοικούμενον Bas.*hom.in Ps*. 45(1.173B; M.29.421C); π. ἐστὶ σύστημα ἀνθρώπων ἐκ διαφόρων ἐπιτηδευμάτων ἐπὶ κοινωνίᾳ βίου συγκεκροτημένον †Bas.*Is*.19(1.391C; M.30.149B); π. πολλάκις ἡ θεία γραφή, οὐ τὴν οἰκοδομίαν, ἀλλὰ τὴν πολιτείαν καλεῖ Thdt.*Ps*.47:2(1.908); purpose αἱ π. οἰκιζόμεναι πρὸς τὰ ἀναγκαῖα μόνα ὁρῶσιν, ὅπως ἂν σῴζοιντο καὶ ὅπως ἂν διαγίνοιντο· ἐπιδιδοῦσαι δὲ οὐκέτ' ἀγαπῶσι τὸ ἀναγκαῖον...ἡ μὲν πρόοδος ἐν τοῖς ἀναγκαίοις, ἡ δὲ αὔξησις ἐν τοῖς περιττοῖς Synes.*astrolab*.5(p.139.12; M.66.1584C); **b.** Christians in rel. to city Χριστιανοὶ...οὔτε...π. ἰδίας κατοικοῦσιν...κατοικοῦντες δὲ π. Ἑλληνίδας τε καὶ βαρβάρους...παράδοξον ἐνδείκνυνται τὴν κατάστασιν τῆς ἑαυτῶν πολιτείας *Diogn*.5.1–4; ἀτεχνῶς 'ξένος γὰρ καὶ παρεπίδημος' ἐν τῷ βίῳ παντὶ πᾶς οὗτος, ὃς π. οἰκῶν τῶν κατὰ τὴν π. κατεφρόνησεν παρ' ἄλλοις θαυμαζομένων, καὶ καθάπερ ἐν ἐρημίᾳ τῇ π. βιοῖ, ἵνα μὴ ὁ τόπος αὐτὸν ἀναγκάζῃ Clem.*str*.7.12(p.55.5; M.9.505B); ἐγκώμιον τῆς π. ... οὐχ ὅτι σύγκλητον ἔχει... ἀλλ' ὅτι δῆμον ἔχει φιλήκοον, καὶ ναοὺς θεοῦ πεπληρωμένους...ἡ γὰρ π. οὐκ ἀπὸ τῶν οἰκοδομῶν ἀλλὰ ἀπὸ τῶν ἐνοίκων θαυμάζεται...ἄλλως...ἡ ἔρημος πόλεως εὐγνωμονεστέρα Chrys.*hom*.4.1 *in Is*.6:1(6.120Eff.); οὐ τὸ μητρόπολιν εἶναι, οὐδὲ τὸ μέγεθος ἔχειν καὶ κάλλος οἰκοδομημάτων...ἀλλ' ἡ τῶν ἐνοικούντων ἀρετὴ καὶ εὐσέβεια, τοῦτο καὶ ἀξίωμα, καὶ κόσμος, καὶ ἀσφάλεια πόλεως...ἐμοὶ π. μὴ ἔχουσα πολίτας θεοφιλεῖς πάσης κώμης ἐστὶν εὐτελεστέρα, καὶ σπηλαίου παντὸς ἀτιμοτέρα id.*stat*.17.2(2.176A,E); τῶν δὲ ἁγίων λεγόντων, οὐκ ἔχομεν ὧδε μένουσαν π. ... οἱ ἁμαρτωλοὶ γήινοι ὄντες προσεδρεύουσι τῇ γῇ καὶ πόλεις οἰκοδομοῦσιν Proc.G.*Gen*.4:17(M.87.253C); **c.** partic. ἡ π. *Jerusalem*, *Barn*.16.5; ἡ μεγάλη πόλις *Rome*, Tat.*orat*.19(p.21.1; M.6.848B); Eus.*l.C*.13(p.239.6; M.20.1404A); **d.** exeg. Gen.4:17 ποία π. ὑπ' ὀλίγων οὕτω συνίσταται;...μή ποτε οὖν τὴν ἐν οἴκῳ ἑνὶ μετ' ἀλλήλων ἀναστροφὴν οὕτως ἐκάλεσεν...ὡς καὶ οἶκος μέγας ἡ π. ἀφ' οὗ καὶ τῶν πόλεων ἦλθον εἰς ἔννοιαν Proc.G.*Gen*.4:17(M.87.253C); **2.** spiritual or heavenly; **a.** of Church τῶν ἁγίων ἡ π. πνευματικῶς οἰκοδομουμένη Clem.*paed*.2.12(p.228.15; M.8.541A); ἡ ἐκκλησία...ἀπολιόρκητος ἀτυράννητος π. ἐπὶ γῆς, θέλημα θεῖον ἐπὶ γῆς ὡς ἐν οὐρανῷ id.*str*.4.26 (p.325.1; M.8.1381A); cf. ἐκλεκτῆς π. ὁ πολίτης Aberc.*epitaph*.1; ἔστιν γὰρ ἡ π. τοῦ θεοῦ ἡ ἐκκλησία Or.*hom*.9.2 *in Jer*.(p.65.21; M.13.349D); παράδειγμα π. οὐρανίας, ἣν ἐζήτησε μὲν διαγράψαι καὶ Πλάτων...γένος τι ἐκλεκτόν, καὶ ἔθνος ἅγιον, καὶ θεῷ ἀνακείμενον id.*Cels*.5.43(p.47.8;

M.11.1249A); τὴν π. τοῦ θεοῦ, ἤτοι τὴν ἐκκλησίαν τῶν τὸ πολίτευμα ἐχόντων ἐν οὐρανοῖς, ἢ πᾶσαν τὴν νοητὴν κτίσιν, ἀπὸ τῶν ὑπερκοσμίων δυνάμεων, μέχρι τῶν ἀνθρωπίνων ψυχῶν, πόλιν χρὴ νοεῖν εὐφραινομένην ὑπὸ τῆς ἐπιρροῆς τοῦ ἁγίου πνεύματος Bas.*hom.in Ps.*45(1.173B; M.29.421C); **b.** of heavenly Jerusalem (often very closely ass. with foreg.) dist. from heaven and paradise, Iren.*haer.*5.36.1(M.7.1221B); τὴν Ἱερουσαλὴμ τὴν ἐμήν· λέγουσι γὰρ καὶ οἱ Στωϊκοὶ τὸν μὲν οὐρανὸν κυρίως π., τὰ δὲ ἐπὶ γῆς ἐνταῦθα οὐκέτι πόλεις...ἴσμεν δὲ καὶ τὴν Πλάτωνος π. παράδειγμα ἐν οὐρανῷ κειμένην Clem.*str.*4.26(p.324.26; M.8.1381A); τὰ περὶ τῆς π. τοῦ θεοῦ Ἱερουσαλὴμ ἐπουρανίου Or.*Cels.*6.23(p.93.25; M.11.1325C); Χριστιανοὶ δὲ μᾶλλον εὐεργετοῦσι τὰς πατρίδας ἢ οἱ λοιποὶ τῶν ἀνθρώπων, παιδεύοντες τοὺς πολίτας... ἀναλαμβάνοντες εἰς θείαν τινὰ καὶ ἐπουράνιον π. τοὺς ἐν ταῖς ἐλαχίσταις π. καλῶς βιώσαντας *ib.*8.74(p.291.25; 1629A); *Apoc.Paul.*19(p.49); εἰσάξω σε εἰς τὴν π. τοῦ θεοῦ καὶ εἰς τὸ φῶς αὐτῆς *ib.*23(p.52); ὑμεῖς ἐστε τοῦ γένους μου κατὰ Χριστόν, ὕπαρξις τῆς ἐμῆς π. τῆς ἄνω Ἱερουσαλὴμ *A.Phil.*109(p.42.16); Bas.*hom.in Ps.*45(1.173B; M.29.421D); τῷ δὲ καθ' ἡμᾶς λόγῳ μία τετίμηται πατρίς, ὁ παράδεισος,...μία π., ἡ ἐπουράνιος Gr.Nyss.*v.Gr.Thaum.*(M.46.896B); Cosm.Ind.*top.*5(M.88.244A); **c.** of πολίτεια of Christians πόλιν λέγων, τὴν ὑπὸ τῆς ἀρετῆς συνῳκισμένην εὐπρεπῆ τε καὶ εὐδιάθετον πολιτείαν Gr.Nyss.*Pss.titt.*B 16(M.44.605A); ἀχειροποίητον δὲ π., τὴν ἐν οὐρανοῖς πολιτείαν ἐκάλεσε Thdt.*Heb.*11:10(3.616); **3.** *country* ἐν ὅλῃ τῇ π. τῆς Ἱσπανίας *A.Xanthipp.*42(p.85.31); **4.** met., *throng* δριμυτάτην τῶν μεριμνῶν π. ἔχοντα συμπεπλεγμένην ‡Chrys.*pasch.*5.1(8.262A).

πολισμός, ὁ, *building of a city,* exeg. Gen.4:17 οἶκος μέγας ἡ πόλις, ἀφ' οὗ καὶ τῶν πόλεων ἦλθον εἰς ἔννοιαν, ἴσως δὲ καὶ πολισμοῦ μεθόδους Proc.G.*Gen.*4:17(M.87.253C).

πολιστής, ὁ, *founder of a city, A.Thadd.*5(p.275n.); Chrys.*hom.* 7.7 *in 1Cor.*(10.60B, v.l. πολῖται); of Christ as founder of heavenly Jerusalem, Gr.Naz.*or.*8.6(M.35.796B); *ib.*36.12(M.36.280B); of founder of monastery Σάβαν τὸν π. καὶ πολιοῦχον τῆς καθ' ἡμᾶς ἐρήμου Cyr.S.*v.Sab.*50(p.141.9).

πολιτάρχης, ὁ, *civic magistrate* (cf. Ac.17:6), Sophr.H.*v.Cyr.et Jo.*20(M.87.3401D).

πολιτεία, ἡ, A. *citizenship, citizen rights*; **1.** lit., *Ep.Lugd.*ap.Eus. *h.e.*5.1.47(M.20.425C); **2.** of heavenly citizenship, Clem.*str.*1.1(p.7.34; M.8.696C).

B. *polity, constitution* οὔτε πόλιν οὔτε π. ... ἐπὶ νοῦν ἐβάλλοντο [sc. fallen men] Eus.*h.e.*1.2.19(M.20.61C); μετὰ δὲ τὴν ἀπὸ Βαβυλῶνος ἐπάνοδον, οὐ διέλιπον π. χρώμενοι ἀριστοκρατικῇ *ib.*1.6.6(88B); hence *religious system*; of Judaism, id.*p.e.*7.8(312D; M.21.528D); of Christianity, Gr.Nyss.*ep.*24(M.46.1089A); Chrys.*hom.26.3 in Mt.*(7.411B); Cyr.*Jo.*4.5(4.414E).

C. *regulation, order,* for conduct of civil affairs ἐπάρχου π. ἐν τῷ θεάτρῳ ποιοῦντος, οὕτω δὲ ὀνομάζειν εἰώθασιν τὰς δημοτικὰς διατυπώσεις Socr.*h.e.*7.13.6(M.67.761B).

D. *organized society, commonwealth, state* ἐκβαλὼν [sc. Plato]·τῆς π. ... Ὅμηρον Just.*2apol.*10.6(M.6.461A); of republics of Plato and Zeno, Chrys.*hom.1.4 in Mt.*(7.9C); Clem.*prot.*10(p.73.25; M.8.217B); Gr.Naz.*ep.*242(M.37.384C); of commonwealth of Israel ἀπηλλοτριωμένοι τῆς π., οὐκ εἶπεν, οὐ προσέχοντες, ἀλλ', οὐδὲ μετέχοντες, καὶ ξένοι...τῆς π. ἦσαν ἐκτός, ἀλλ' οὐχ ὡς ἀλλότριοι, ἀλλ' ὡς ῥάθυμοι, καὶ τῶν διαθηκῶν ἐξέπεσον, ἀλλ' οὐχ ὡς ξένοι Chrys.*hom.5.1 in Eph.*(11.33C); of angelic order, Bas.Sel.*or.*1.3(M.85.33B); of five orders in Church, i.e. bishops, presbyters, deacons, baptized laity, and catechumens, Eus.*Is.*19:18(M.24.232C).

E. plur., *civil affairs,* Eus.*h.e.*8.9.7(M.20.761A).

F. *way of life*; **1.** of a community or society; in gen., Tat.*orat.*4(p.4.21; M.6.812B); ἑτέραν ἡμῖν ζωὴν εἰσάγοντες...καὶ κόσμον, καὶ π. Chrys.*hom.1.4 in Mt.*(7.9C); **2.** of Jewish manner of life τὴν ἔννομον π. Just.*dial.*47.4(M.6.577B); Ἰουδαϊσμὸς οὐδὲν ἦν ἕτερον ἢ ἡ κατὰ Μωσέα π. Eus.*d.e.*1.2(p.8.9; M.22.24C); *Hom.Clem.*2.20; τὴν κατὰ τὸν...νόμον αἰσθητὴν π. †Bas.*Is.*38(1.409D; M.30.192C); Chrys.*Jud.*4.5(1.623B); Thdr.Mops.*Gal.*4:24(p.78.25; M.66.908D); Cyr.*thes.*15(5^1.157A); **3.** hence *conduct, behaviour,* social or individual; **a.** def. π. γάρ ἐστι βίος κατὰ νόμον φύσεως διεξαγόμενος Max.*ambig.*(M.91.1057C); **b.** in gen. τὴν...ἀνεπίληπτον π. *M.Polyc.*17.1; μηδὲν...διὰ τὴν π. εὑρισκόμεθα ἀδικοῦντες Just.*1apol.*4.2(M.6.332C); χάριν ὁμολογεῖ τῆς γνώσεως καὶ τῆς π. Clem.*str.*7.7(p.27.18; M.9.449C); Epiph.*exp.fid.*13(p.513.5; M.42.804D); Chrys.*hom.36.3 in Mt.*(7.410D); Euthal.Diac.*epp.Paul.*(M.85.708A); ἡ π. τοῦ ὁσίου ἀββᾶ Ἰσαὰκ *Apophth.Patr.*(M.65.241B); **c.** of specifically Christian life and conduct; **i.** in gen. τῇ παναρέτῳ καὶ σεβασμίῳ π. κεκοσμημένοι πάντα ἐν τῷ φόβῳ αὐτοῦ ἐπετελεῖτε *1Clem.*2.8; οἱ πολιτευόμενοι τὴν ἀμεταμέλητον π. τοῦ θεοῦ *ib.*54.4; παράδοξον ἐνδείκνυνται τὴν κατάστασιν τῆς ἑαυτῶν π. *Diogn.*5.4; οὐ καὶ ἐπὶ τοσοῦτον ἠκρίβωτο ἡ π. *Ep.Lugd.*ap.Eus.*h.e.*5.1.9(M.20.412A); Rhod.*ib.*5.13.2(460B); τὰ γὰρ τῆς π. ἐλέγχει σαφῶς τοὺς ἐγνωκότας τὰς ἐντολάς, ἐπεὶ οἷος ὁ λόγος, τοῖος ὁ βίος...ἡ γνῶσις οὖν ἐκ τοῦ καρποῦ καὶ τῆς π., οὐκ ἐκ τοῦ λόγου καὶ τοῦ ἄνθους Clem.*str.*3.5(p.216.14; M.8.1148B); εἰλικρινείας, κατὰ τὴν π.· ἀληθείας, κατὰ τὴν γνῶσιν Or.*comm.in 1Cor.*5:8(*JTS* 9 p.365); διὰ τῆς ἀγαθῆς π., τῆς τοῦ θανάτου κοινωνίας ἀλλοτρίους ἑαυτοὺς καταστήσετε Gr.Naz.*ep.*238(M.37.381B); Gr.Nyss.*Cant.*proem.(M.44.757B); ὁ Χριστιανισμὸς καὶ τὸ τῆς τῶν δογμάτων ὀρθότητος καὶ π. ὑγιαίνουσαν ἀπαιτεῖ Chrys.*hom.28.2 in Jo.*(8.161B); ἐνηνθρώπησε...ἵνα...διδάξῃ ...ἡμᾶς τὴν ἐνάρετον π. ‡Cyr.*Trin.*28(6^3.34A; M.77.1173A); ταῦτα ἀκμὴ π. ἐστιν ἀγαθῆς. ... ἵνα ὧν καλῆς π. ... μὴ ἡγήσαιτο τὴν ψυχὴν αὐτοῦ τιμίαν †Marc.Er.*temp.*28(M.65.1069A,C); Παῦλος...τὴν ὅλην ἀνθρώποις διέγραψε π. Euthal.Diac.*epp.Paul.*(M.85.701A); **ii.** described: as ἐν Χριστῷ, Mac.Aeg.*ep.*2(M.34.416C); Cyr.*Is.*1.1(2.20D); as κατὰ θεόν or Χριστόν, Clem.*str.*4.18(p.298.14; M.8.1321B); Ath.*ep.encycl.*2(p.170.25; M.25.225B); Cyr.*Ps.*9:35(M.69.785D); Olymp.*Eccl.*7:2(M.93.560B); as evangelical ἔννομός εἰμι τοῦ Χριστοῦ τηρῶν τὴν π. τὴν κατὰ τὸ εὐαγγέλιον Or.*comm.in 1Cor.*9:19–23(p.513); τῆς κατὰ Χριστιανοὺς εὐαγγελικῆς π. Eus.*h.e.*2 proem.1(M.20.133A); τῶν εἰς Χριστὸν πεπιστευκότων καὶ τὴν κατὰ τὸ εὐαγγέλιον π. ἀσπαζομένων †Bas.*Is.*42(1.412C; M.30.197C); Chrys.*scand.*13(3.497D); freq. contrasted with Mosaic π., e.g., ἤρξατο ὁ κύριος τῆς εὐαγγελικῆς π., οὔσης ἔξωθεν τῆς τοῦ νόμου φυλακῆς ‡Just.*qu.et resp.*28(M.6.1277A); Cyr.*Is.*2.1(2.192E); ἐξ Αἰγύπτου μετακεχωρήκαμεν εἰς τὴν ἔρημον, τουτέστιν, εἰς καθαρωτάτην, καὶ πλατεῖαν ἀληθῶς, καὶ ἀσυμμιγῆ τοῦ χείρονος π., φημὶ δὴ τὴν εὐαγγελικήν id.*Am.*21(3.271D); Proc.G.*Dt.*21:16(M.87.925A); as holy, Or.*hom.16.4 in Jer.*(p.136.19; M.13.444B); σεμνὴ π. Gr.Nyss.*ep.*2(M.46.1012A); esp. ref. monastic life ὁ ...τῆς ἱερᾶς π. διδάσκαλος...Χριστός Diad.*perf.*51(p.56.11); as spiritual, Gr.Nyss.*Eun.*3(2 p.22.5; M.45.385D); ἡ δὲ τῆς πνευματικῆς π. ὁδὸς πράξει μᾶλλον ἢ φράσει εὐοδοῦται [esp. ref. monastic life] Isid.Pel.*epp.*1.14(M.78.189A); Euthal.Diac.*epp.Paul.*(M.85.749C); as ἔνθεος, Bas.Sel.*or.*8.1(M.85.112C); ‡Proc.G.*Pr.*9:18(M.87.1309B); as heavenly, Or.*fr.102 in Lam.*(p.272.6; M.13.653B); οὐρανίου π. ἐπιθυμία Cyr.H.*procatech.*1; ἀναβὰς δὲ διὰ τῆς ὑψηλῆς ἐπιθυμίας εἰς τὴν ἐπουράνιον π. καὶ τὰ ἄνω φρονῶν Gr.Nyss.*ep.*3(M.46.1016C); of divine life manifested in incarnate Christ, Chrys.*nativ.*1.6(2.363E); as angelic, Gr.Naz.*carm.*1.2.3.6(M.37.633A); Chrys.*Jud.*4.5(1.623C); ἡ ἀνθρωπίνη φύσις πρὸς τὴν ἀγγελικὴν π. ἁμιλλᾶται id.*cruc.*2.1(2.411D); Leont.N.*v.Sym.*3(M.93.1672C); as apostolic οὗτος ἡμῶν ὁ βίος, αὕτη τῆς ἀποστολικῆς π. ἡ ἀκολουθία, τὸ μυρία πάσχειν κακά Nil.*epp.*3.26(M.79.384B); as conferring freedom, in contrast to Jewish π., Chrys.*hom.3.3 in Mt.*(7.38A); and involving new worship, Thdt.*Ps.*50:21(1.944); Christians' πνευματικὴ π. contrasted with Law, Jo.Philop.*pasch.*(p.210.8); as consisting in fulfilment of Christ's command to 'watch' ὥστε...καὶ τῆς νυκτὸς τὴν π. ὡς ἐν ἡμέρᾳ ἐνεργουμένην καθαρὰν...διαφυλάττειν Clem.*str.*4.22(p.310.6; M.8.1349A); **iii.** associated with faith συμβάλλεται γοῦν τὰ μέγιστα τῷ περιτυχόντι κατὰ τὴν θείαν πρόνοιαν, ἀρχὴν πίστεως, πολιτείας προθυμίαν *ib.*1.1(p.5.5; M.8.692A); ἀεὶ τῇ πίστει συζεύγνυσι τὴν π. Chrys.*hom.1.1 in Col.*(11.334A); μέγα μὲν πίστις καὶ σωτήριον...ἀλλ' οὐκ ἀρκεῖ καθ' ἑαυτὴν τοῦτο ἐργάσασθαι, ἀλλὰ δεῖ καὶ π. ὀρθῆς id.*hom.7.1 in Heb.*(12.70D); relationship to H. Ghost οὐδέπω τὸ πνεῦμα τοῦ πατρὸς ἦν σὺν αὐτοῖς, διὰ ἀκατάρτιστον αὐτῶν καὶ ἀσθενὲς τῆς π. Iren.*haer.*4.38.2(M.7.1106C); οὗτος ὑμῖν δοθείη τῆς π. μισθός, ὁμολογῆσαι τὸ πνεῦμα τελείως Gr.Naz.*or.*41.8(M.36.440C); to baptism συνθήκας πρὸς θεὸν δευτέρου βίου καὶ π. καθαρωτέρας ὑποληπτέον τὴν τοῦ βαπτίσματος δύναμιν *ib.*40.8(368B); τὴν ἐν τῇ χάριτι μετιὼν π. μετὰ τὸ βάπτισμα Thdr.Mops.*fr.inc.*(p.297.1; M.66.977B); associated with truth, *Hom.Clem.*2.6; οὐδὲν γὰρ οὕτως ἐνάγει πρὸς τὴν τῆς ἀληθείας ὁδόν, ὡς πολιτείας ἀκρίβεια Chrys.*hom.8.5 in Gen.*(4.62C); with knowledge, Clem.*str.*7.3(p.10.8; M.9.416C); Or.*sel.in Ps.*17:36(M.12.1237B); with orthodox doctrine, †Jo.D.*B.J.*11(M.96.956B); **d.** of ascetic and monastic discipline (often included under gen. Christian way of life) φιλοσόφῳ π. καὶ ἀσκήσει Eus.*m.P.*11.2(M.20.1500A); π. καὶ παρθενία τε καὶ ἄσκησις Epiph.*haer.*70.14(p.247.30; M.42.372B); id.*exp.fid.*23(p.524.12; M.42.829A); ἀγαπῶ γὰρ τὴν παρθενίαν ...ἐραστὴς εἰμι τῆς π. ταύτης Chrys.*hom.57.3 in Jo.*(8.336B); Pall.*h.Laus.*proem.(p.8.10; M.34.1002); *ib.*33(p.96.7; M.34.1105B) cit. s. διατύπωσις; Nil.*Magn.*32(M.79.1008B); Thdt.*h.rel.*1(3.1112); †Marc.Er.*temp.*6(M.65.1069A); **4.** of incarnate life of Christ τοὺς τῆς ἐνσάρκου π. αὐτοῦ χρόνους Eus.*h.e.*1.4.1(M.20.76C); cf.Cyr.*resp.*(6^2.392E); τῆς ἐπὶ γῆς αὐτοῦ π. †Jo.D.*B.J.*8(M.96.924A); **5.** *course of activity* τοῦ πνεύματός ἐστι π. τὸ βιβλίον τοῦτο Chrys.*hom.3.1 in Ac.*(9.24A); αὐξάνει ὁ νοῦς ἐν τῇ π. τῆς διανοίας Philox.*ep.*31(p.179); **6.** *state of life*; of present opp. future state, Tit.Bost.*Man*.suppl.1(M.18.1260C); of married state, Or.*comm.in 1Cor*.7:18–20(*JTS* 9 p.507).

G. *ascetic practice, act of religious behaviour* πολλὰς π. ἐποίησεν ἐν τῇ νεότητι αὐτοῦ *Apophth.Patr*.(M.65.136C); Philox.*ep*.19(p.170); Dor.*doct*.7.2(M.88.1697D); δεῖ ὑπάρχειν ἡμᾶς ἐν ἁγίαις ἀναστροφαῖς καὶ εὐσεβέσι π. †Jo.D.*B.J*.8(M.96.928B).

πολίτευμα, τό, 1. *government*, of civic *ordo* οἴχεται μὲν γὰρ τὸ π.· πᾶν δὲ τὸ πολιτικὸν σύνταγμα...διὰ τῆς ἀγροικίας πλανᾶται Bas.*ep*.76 (3.171C; M.32.452A); Evagr.*h.e*.5.11(p.207.31; M.86.2813C); διώκει δὲ τὸ π. Τιβέριος *ib*.(p.207.24; 2813C); **2.** *organization, system*; of Jewish state, Eus.*p.e*.7.8(312D; M.21.528D); of Christianity οὔτε Ἑλληνισμός τις ὢν οὔτε Ἰουδαϊσμός, ἀλλὰ τὸ μεταξὺ τούτων παλαιότατον εὐσεβείας π. id.*d.e*.1.2(p.8.35; M.22.25A); *ib*.4.17(p.199.19; 332C); **3.** *principle* ἐγκράτεια...ἁγιασμοῦ πολίτευμα †Nil.*vit*.2(M.79. 1141B); **4.** *organized body, society*, Clem.*str*.4.36(p.325.4; M.8.1381A); εἶδον μοναχῶν πολιτεύματα ‡Pall.*h.mon*.12.7(p.64.12); of Roman empire, Sophr.H.*ep.syn*.(M.87.3200A); πόλισμα πρὸς ταῖς ἐσχατιαῖς τοῦ π. κείμενον Evagr.*h.e*.5.9(p.204.14; M.86.2809A); *ib*.5.22(p.217. 15; 2837A); **5.** *membership of society, citizenship of a state*, of Christian's heavenly citizenship (Phil.3:20) οἱ ἐπὶ γῆς περιπατοῦντες, καὶ ἐν οὐρανοῖς τὸ π. ἔχοντες ‡Ath.*dial.Trin*.3.27(M.28.1245C); οὐράνιον π. as gift of H. Ghost, Bas.*Spir*.23(3.20C; M.32.109C); ἡ διάνοια, ὑψηλὰ...φρονοῦσα, οἷα δὴ τὸ π. ἔχουσα ἐν οὐρανοῖς †Bas.*parad*.7(1. 350A; M.30.68C); πᾶσι μία τοῖς ὑψηλοῖς πατρίς,...ἡ ἄνω Ἱερουσαλήμ, εἰς ἣν ἀποτιθέμεθα τὸ π. Gr.Naz.*or*.33.12(M.36.229A); ἡμεῖς γὰρ ἐπὶ γῆς ὄντες, ἐν οὐρανοῖς ἔχομεν τὸ π., εἰς ἐκεῖνον τὸν κόσμον ἔχοντες τὴν διαγωγὴν καὶ τὴν πολιτείαν Mac.Aeg.*hom*.17.4(M.34.625C); **6.** *mode of life, conduct* κόσμου...ἡ κατασκευὴ καλή, τὸ δὲ ἐν αὐτῷ π. φαῦλον Tat.*orat*.19(p.21.12; M.6.849A); τὸ ἀστικὸν π. ἐζηλωκότες Clem.*paed*. 2.10(p.220.10; M.8.521C); Meth.*res*.2.1(p.330.4; M.18.297A); τοῦ κατὰ θεὸν π. διηγηματικὸς ἡμῖν λόγος Eus.*h.e*.5 proem.4(M.20.408B); αἱ τῶν εὐαγγελικῶν π. ὑποτυπώσεις Bas.*Spir*.35(3.28D; M.32.128D); πονηροῖς...χαίροντες π. Procl.CP *annunt*.2(M.85.432B); Bas.Sel.*or*. 4.1(M.85.64B); ‡Proc.G.*Pr*.4:3(M.87.1253C).

πολιτευτής, ὁ, 1. *decurion*, Eus.*v.C*.3.1(p.77.23; M.20.1056A); Ath.*h.Ar*.31(p.200.18; M.25.729A); *ib*.54(p.214.3; 757D); Gr.Naz. *ep*.141(M.37.241B); **2.** *one who behaves, conducts himself* εὐχὰς ποιησόμενοι...ὅπως καταξιωθῶμεν τὰ ἀληθῆ μαθόντες καὶ δι' ἔργων ἀγαθοὶ πολιτευταὶ...εὑρεθῆναι Just.*1apol*.65.1(M.6.428A); abs., *follower of Christian life, devotee*, ‡Petr.I Al.*phys*.3(p.34) = *Phys*. A 36(p.117.5).

πολιτεύ-ω, med., **A.** *be a citizen* οὐδὲ γὰρ ⟨ἐπιθυμεῖ⟩ πολιτείας ὀρθῆς, ἀλλὰ τοῦ ~εσθαι Clem.*str*.7.7(p.29.24; M.9.453C); ref. Phil. 3:20 ἐπὶ γῆς διατρίβουσιν, ἀλλ' ἐν οὐρανῷ ~ονται *Diogn*.5.9; τὸν ἀέρα διαβαίνουσι, καὶ ἐν οὐρανῷ ~ονται ‡Ath.*pass*.29(M.28.233D); ἡ ἄνω Ἱερουσαλήμ, ἡ μὴ βλεπομένη, νοουμένη δὲ πόλις, ἐν ᾗ ~όμεθα Gr.Naz.*or*.8.6(M.35.796B); Cyr.*Is*.1.2(2.57C).

B. *govern* τοῦ θεοῦ ἁγίας ἐκκλησίας τῶν Ναυατῶν ἐν ᾗ κὲ ἐπολιθεύσατο *MAMA* 1.172 (Laodicea Combusta); ὁ σταυρὸς τοῦ Χριστοῦ... πανταχοῦ βασιλεύει, πανταχοῦ ~εται *Dial.Christ.et Jud*.10(p.62.19).

C. *conduct, carry on*, Gr.Nyss.*or.catech*.27(p.102.19; M.45.72A); ‡Chrys.*ascens*.2(3.779E); Basilisc.*antencycl*.(p.52; M.86.2609C); καινήν τινα θεανδρικὴν ἐνέργειαν ἡμῖν πεπολιτευμένος Dion.Ar.*ep*.4(M.3. 1072C).

D. *conduct oneself*; **1.** *live as member of community, share a particular mode of life*, Athenag.*res*.11(p.60.29; M.6.996A); of Jews τοὺς κατὰ τὸν νόμον τὸν Μωϋσέως ~σαμένους Just.*dial*.45.3(M.6.572C); Eus.*d.e*.1.6(p.34.30; M.22.68B); Thdr.Mops.*Gal*.3:21(p.50.23; M.66. 904D); **2.** *live, be active*, in gen. ὁ θεὸς ἐν οὐρανοῖς ~εται *Diogn*.10.7; Ath.*Ar*.2.65(M.26.285B); Chrys.*oppugn*.3.3(1.80D); Ἰσραὴλ...δυσσεβῶς ~όμενος Thdt.*qu.22 in 4Reg*.(1.527); **3.** esp. of Christian life and conduct ὁσίως ~σαμένοις *1Clem*.6.1; καλῶς ~όμενος *ib*.44.6; μετὰ φόβου καὶ ἀγάπης ~όμενοι *ib*.51.2; ἐὰν ~σώμεθα ἀξίως αὐτοῦ Polyc.*ep*.5.2; π. καλῶς καὶ ἁγνῶς Herm.*sim*.5.6.6; ἐν ἁγίῳ πνεύματι ~σαμένη Polycr.ap.Eus.*h.e*.3.31.3(M.20.280B); ἵνα...~σώμεθα καθ' ὑπακοὴν Clem.*str*.1.10(p.30.21; M.8.744A); κατὰ θεὸν ~εται *ib*.3.4 (p.210.8; M.8.1136B); *ib*.7.14(p.63.18; M.9.524A); ~ονται γὰρ παρρησιαζόμενοι ἐν τῷ σταυρῷ τοῦ Χριστοῦ Or.*Jo*.2.34(28; p.93.23; M.14. 177A); τοὺς ἰσάγγελον βίον ~ομένους Cyr.H.*catech*.4.1; δὸς τὸν λαὸν καθαρῶς ~εσθαι Serap.*euch*.5.3; τῶν λόγῳ ~ομένων καὶ συνέσει Pall. *h.Laus*.proem.(p.13.24; M.34.1003); ἵνα ~οιντο...εὐαγγελικῶς Cyr. *Is*.1.1(2.15A); ~εται γὰρ οὐδεὶς εὐαγγελικῶς μὴ οὐχὶ πρότερον τὴν διὰ τοῦ...βαπτίσματος καταπλουτήσας κάθαρσιν *ib*.3.3(475C); κατὰ τὸ εὐαγγέλιον ~σαμένη ψυχή Marc.Er.*opusc*.5.1(M.65.1029A); τὰ θεῖα θελήματα...καθ' ἃ χρὴ τοὺς πάντας...~εσθαι Max.*myst*.24(M.91.705D); specifically of monastic life, Dor.*doct*.1.14(M.88.1636A); hence *perform ascetic exercises* πλέον τι τῶν...ἀδελφῶν ~εσθαι Nil.*epp*. 3.46(M.79.413D); **4.** of Christ's earthly life ὁ ψυχικὸς Χριστός... ἀόρατος ἦν, ἔδει δὲ τὸν εἰς κόσμον ἀφικνούμενον, ἐφ' ᾧτε ὀφθῆναι,... ~σασθαι, καὶ αἰσθητοῦ σώματος ἀνέχεσθαι Clem.*exc.Thdot*.59(p.126. 23; M.9.688B); θεὸν...σὺν ἀνθρώποις ἐπὶ γῆς ~εσθαι Eus.*d.e*.7 proem. (p.297.1; M.22.485B); κατὰ τὸ ἀνθρώπινον ἐπὶ γῆς ~σάμενος ὁ τοῦ θεοῦ λόγος Apoll.*fid.sec.pt*.12(p.171.7; M.10.1109A); σαρκὶ ἐπὶ γῆς ~σασθαι ‡Ath.*Apoll*.1.7(M.26.1104C); *Const.App*.6.11.4; Sophr.H.*or*.2.40(M. 87.3269C).

E. *be concerned with, occupied in* ~εσθαι τῇ πρώτῃ κρίσει *Hom. Clem*.2.11; Bas.*ep*.41.1(3.124E; M.32.345C); ~σώμεθα ταῖς εὐχαῖς Gel.Cyz.*h.e*.2.31.1(M.85.1316A).

F. *occur*; **1.** lit., *be current*; of coins, ‡Nil.*narr*.3(M.79.617C); **2.** in gen., *be prevalent* μία τις ἐν ἡμῖν...γνώμη ~εται Eus.*v.C*.2.71(p.70. 26; M.20.1045B); τὴν...ἐν βαρβάροις ~σαμένην ἀλήθειαν *Hom.Clem*. 1.11; οὐ γὰρ ἂν τῶν...ἁμαρτημάτων οὐδὲν ἐπολιτεύετο Tit.Bost.*Man*. 1.24(M.18.1101B); εἴ τις ἐπίσκοπος ὀξύχολος εὑρίσκοιτο, ὅπερ οὐκ ὀφείλει ἐν τοιούτῳ ἀνδρὶ ~εσθαι CSard.*can*.14; ὅρα πόση τὸ παλαιὸν ἐπολιτεύετο παρ' αὐτοῖς ἡ φιλοσοφία Chrys.*hom.38.4 in Gen*.(4.388D); ἀρεταὶ ~ονται ‡Cyr.*Trin*.28(6³.34B; M.77.1173A); ἀπαθείας δὲ ~ομένης, χώραν οὐκ ἔσχεν ἡ ἁμαρτία Thdt.*Ps*.50:7(1.937); τὰ ~όμενα κακά id. *Rom*.1:31(3.28); οὐδὲ προσωποληψία τις παρ' αὐτῷ ~εται Sophr.H. *or*.4(M.87.3304B).

G. *be a decurion* (πολιτευτής), Soz.*h.e*.4.24.15(M.67.1193B); Thdt. *ep*.125 tit.(4.1208); Jo.Mal.*chron*.12 p.294(M.97.445A); *Chron.Pasch*. p.300(M.92.752B); *ib*.p.320(817A); Ἑλλαδίου πρε[σ]β(υτέρου) [κ]ὲ πολιτε[υομένου] *CIG* 4.8838 (Mysia, saec. vi).

πολίτης, ὁ, *citizen*; **1.** in gen., of Christians in civil society μετέχουσι πάντων ὡς π., καὶ πάνθ' ὑπομένουσιν ὡς ξένοι *Diogn*.5.5; Christians' duty to train earthly citizens for membership of heavenly commonwealth, Or.*Cels*.8.74(p.291.23; M.11.1629A); **2.** of Jo. Bapt. ὁ τῆς ἐρήμου π. ‡Thdt.*nativ.Jo.Bapt*.(5.101); **3.** of Christians as citizens of heavenly country or spiritual Jerusalem οὐρανοῦ π. εἶναι δυνάμενος Clem.*prot*.10(p.68.4; M.8.205A); πολίτας τῶν μακαρίων ἐκείνων αἰώνων Meth.*symp*.8.6(p.88.16; M.18.148B); ἡ ἄνω Ἱερουσαλὴμ...νοουμένη...πόλις ἐν ᾗ πολιτευόμεθα καὶ πρὸς ἣν ἐπειγόμεθα· ἧς π. Χριστός, καὶ συμπολῖται πανήγυρις καὶ ἐκκλησία πρωτοτόκων ἀπογεγραμμένων ἐν οὐρανοῖς Gr.Naz.*or*.8.6(M.35.796B); οὐδὲν κοινὸν τι πρὸς τὴν γῆν ἐστιν αὐτοῖς, ἀλλὰ τῶν οὐρανῶν γεγόνασι π. Chrys.*hom.82.1 in Jo*.(8.483D); Thdt.*h.rel*.15(3.1221); Cosm.Ind. *top*.2(M.88.72C).

πολιτικός, *of* or *pertaining to a citizen, civil*; hence **1.** *secular*, opp. ecclesiastical νόμοι...οἱ π. Clem.*str*.7.3(p.14.18; M.9.424C); π. ἐξουσιῶν *Ep.Lugd*.ap.Eus.*h.e*.5.1.30(M.20.420B); **2.** *worldly, secular*, opp. religious or sacred, Gr.Thaum.*pan.Or*.15(p.34.26; M.10. 1096A); Eus.*d.e*.1.8(p.39.31; M.22.77A); hence *pertaining to this world* τὰς π. λεγομένας ἀρετάς Const.*or.s.c*.11(p.169.6; M.20.1265B); opp. monastic or ascetic ἀσκητικὴν...καὶ π. ἐκέρασεν ἀρετήν Thdt. *h.rel*.2(3.1127); *ib*.(1132); διαπρέψας βίῳ, τῷ τε π. καὶ ἐρημικῷ *ib*.25 (3.1264); **3.** as epithet of Mac. Al. distinguishing him, as *belonging to the city*, from Mac. Aeg., *Apophth.Patr*.(M.65.269D); ‡Pall.*h.mon*. 30.2(p.92.10); Soz.*h.e*.3.14.1(M.67.1068D); **4.** ἄρτος π. *public dole of bread* κτήτωρ τις...Ἀντιοχείας...ὀνόματι Ἀρταβάνης...ῥίψας...τῷ δήμῳ καλαμίων συντόμια πολλὰ ἄρτων διαιωνιζόντων, καλέσας τοὺς αὐτοὺς ἄρτους π. διὰ τὸ τῇ ἰδίᾳ αὐτοῦ πόλει τούτους χαρίσασθαι Jo.Mal. *chron*.12(p.289; M.97.437A); *Chron.Pasch*.p.263(M.92.641B); ἀπητήθησαν οἱ κτήτορες τῶν π. ἄρτων διὰ διαγραφῶν καθ' ἕκαστον ἄρτον νομίσματα γʹ. καὶ μετὰ τὸ παρασχεῖν πάντας...ἀνηρτήθη τελείως ἡ χορηγία τῶν αὐτῶν π. ἄρτων *ib*.p.389(997A); of bequest to a monastery δωρησάμενος τῷ αὐτῷ μοναστηρίῳ...ἄρτους π. καὶ κειμήλια Sergia *Olymp*.3(p.45.24); **5.** *usual, common, prevalent*, Clem.*paed*.3. 3(p.249.7; M.8.584C); Jo.Clim.*past*.12(M.88.1196C).

πολιτικῶς, *in secular fashion*, Bas.Sel.*v.Thecl*.2.30(M.85.617A).

πολιτισμός, ὁ, 1. *urbanity, elegance*, Gr.Nyss.*ep*.19(M.46.1077C); **2.** *wit, facetiousness* γέλως γέγονε τὰ ἡμέτερα καὶ π. καὶ ἀστειότης Chrys.*hom.15.4 in Heb*.(12.155A).

***πολίτισσα, ἡ,** = πόλιτις, *female citizen*, Jo.Mal.*chron*.12 p.294 (M.97.445B).

πολιτογραφ-έω, *enrol as citizen, naturalize*, met.; **1.** of unredeemed men ὁ σωτὴρ...ἦλθεν τοὺς...~ηθέντας ἐν τοῖς κάτω μεταστῆσαι ἐπὶ τὰ ἄνω Or.*Jo*.19.20(5; p.322.8; M.14.565A); **2.** of Christians as citizens of kingdom of heaven; ref. baptism, Bas. *hom.in Ps*.45(1.173A; M.29.421B); ref. Jo. Bapt. ἐπολιτογράφησεν ὁ θεός, ὃν οὐκ ἐβλάστησε γαστήρ Antip.Bost.*Jo.Bapt*.6(M.85.1769A); ~ηθέντες εἰς τὴν βασιλείαν τῶν οὐρανῶν Leont.B.*parasc*.(M.86.1993C); **3.** pass., of baptized as enrolled members of Church, Ephr.2.378E.

***πολιχνιωτικός**, *of a town, municipal* (Lat. *municipalis*), *Cod. Afr.*69; *ib.*93.

***πολλακισμύριοι**, *myriads*, Synes.*provid.*10(M.66.1229A).

πολλαχόσε, *in many places*, Isid.Pel.*epp.*1.198(M.78.405B).

πολλοστός, **1.** *numerous, manifold* ὁ κόκκος τοῦ σίτου...π. ἐγέρθη διὰ τοῦ πνεύματος Iren.*haer.*5.2.3(M.7.1127A); ὁ...εἷς ὅτε ἁμαρτάνει, π. ἐστιν, ἀποσχιζόμενος ἀπὸ θεοῦ...καὶ τῆς ἑνότητος ἐκπίπτων Or. *comm.in Os.*ap.*philoc.*8(p.53.24; M.13.828C); ὁ δίκαιος π. λέγεται, ὡς ἐννενήκοντα ἐννέα ἐν παραβολῇ πρόβατα Nil.*epp.*1.201(M.79.157B); εἷς μὲν...Χριστός, πλὴν ὡς ἐν εἴδει δράγματος π. νοεῖται...διὰ τὸ πάντας ἔχειν ἐν ἑαυτῷ τοὺς πιστεύοντας Cyr.*glaph.Num.*(1.398C); **2.** *composed of several* ὑποστάσεις, Epiph.*haer.*77.23(p.436.26; M.42.673D).

πολυαγάπητος, *much-beloved*, Ign.*Eph.*1.1.

***πολυάγρυπνος**, *very wakeful, much inclined to sleeplessness*, Geo.Al.*v.Chrys.*28(p.192.11).

πολύαθλος, *much contending, sorely tried*; of Job, *T.Job* tit. (p.104n.); Eus.Al.*serm.*4(M.86.340B); Eustrat.*v.Eutych.*3(M.86. 2277A); of martyrs, *V.Olymp.*(p.410); Evagr.*h.e.*3.8(p.107.31; M.86. 2612B); ‡Jo.D.*Artem.*7(M.96.1257C).

πολυάκανθος, *with many thorns*; met., of sin, Ast.Am.*prod.* (p.109.33).

***πολυαμάρτητος**, *sinning often, guilty of much sin*, Bas.*renunt.*1 (2.202E; M.31.628B); Nil.*epp.*4.39(M.79.569A); ἐνδέχεται...τὸν ὀλιγαμάρτητον...μέγα λαβεῖν ἐπιτίμιον...τὸν δὲ π. ... μικρόν, ἵνα μὴ καταποθεὶς...ἀφήσῃ πάντα †Jo.Jej.*serm.*(M.88.1925D); †Jo.Jej.*poenit.* (1908B); *Mir.Geo.*4(p.28.18).

***πολυαμύθητος**, *incalculably vast*, Ephr.3.494E.

πολυανδρία, ἡ, *populousness, multitude*, Eust.*fr.in Pr.8*:22(M. 18.676C)ap.Thdt.*h.e.*1.8.1; Synes.*ep.*139(M.66.1529B).

πολύανθος, *with many flowers*, of BMV π. ἄνθος ‡Jo.D.*hom.*5(M. 96.649B).

***πολυανθρώπινος**, *populous*, Bas.Sel.*v.Thecl.*2.17(M.85.593C).

***πολυάντυξ**, *much-indented*, Paul.Sil.*ambo*.198(M.86.2259A).

***πολυάρετος**, *very virtuous*, Bas.*renunt.*3(2.205A; M.31.632D).

***πολυαρχέομαι**, *be ruled democratically*, Eus.*p.e.*1.4(10B; M.21. 37A).

πολυαρχία, ἡ, *government shared by many*; **1.** in gen.; of divided rule in period before advent of Christ and Augustus, Eus.*p.e.* 1.4(10A; M.21.37C); id.*d.e.*7.2(p.332.7; M.22.541B); *ib.*8.3(p.393.33; 636D); υἱὸν ἀνθρώπου...συντρίβοντα πολυαρχίαν τοπαρχιῶν καὶ πολυθεΐαν ἀθέων, κηρύσσοντα δὲ τὸν ἕνα θεὸν καὶ χειροτονοῦντα τὴν Ῥωμαίων μοναρχίαν *Const.App.*5.20.11; **2.** of polytheism ἡ μὲν μοναρχία ὁμονοίας ἐστὶ παρεκτική, ἡ δὲ π. πολέμων ἐξεργαστική *Hom.Clem.*9.2; cf.Dion.Al.*fr.*(p.185.9); Gr.Naz.*or.*29.2(p.74.13; M. 36.76A); **3.** not a consequence of relationship of Logos to Father, ‡Ath.*Ar.*4.1(p.44.8; M.26.468B) cit. s. δυαρχία; or of coexistence of three Persons, Gr.Naz.*or.*31.13(p.161.9; M.36.148B).

πολυάρχιος, *invented by Polyarchus* the physician, hence as name for a medical unguent ἀποστεῖλαι τὸ π. Chrys.*ep.*34(3.613B).

πολύαρχος, *ruling through many governors*; of pagan gods, Gr. Naz.*carm.*1.1.3.80(M.37.414A); neut. as subst., *rule of many*, ref. polytheism τό τε π. στασιῶδες id.*or.*29.2(p.74.15; M.36.76A).

πολυάσχολος, *burdensome, troublesome* π. ματαιότης Bas.*hex.*1.3 (1.4C; M.29.9C); στυγνοποιὸν πρᾶγμα ἡ ὀρφανία, καὶ π. id.*ep.*184(3. 266D; M.32.661A); Areth.*Apoc.*2:25(M.106.545A).

***πολυαυγής**, *glittering*, Eus.*l.C.*66(M.20.344B).

πολυαῦλαξ, *with many furrows, fertile*, *Orac.Sib.*4.72.

πολύβιβλος, **1.** *voluminous, in many books*, Or.*Jo.*10.16(13; p.186. 9; M.14.333A); *ib.*10.17(13; p.187.15; 336A); of heretical works προφάσει γνώσεως ἐπανισταμένων τῶν ἑτεροδόξων τῇ...ἐκκλησίᾳ καὶ π. συντάξεις φερόντων *ib.*5.8(p.105.5; 196A); Eus.*v.C.*1.10(p.12.6; M.20. 924A); **2.** *possessing many books*, Jo.Mosch.*prat.*172(M.87.3040C).

πολυβλέπων, *seeing much*, euphemistically applied to the blind; hence as example of perversity οἱ τυφλοὶ πολυβλέποντας κικλήσκουσιν ἑαυτούς Nil.*epp.*2.21(M.79.209A); cf.Gr.Nyss.*hom.8 in Cant.*(M. 44.949D).

***πολύβλυστος**, neut. as subst., *abundant*, Epiph.*haer.*59.1(p.364. 9(M.41.1017C).

***πολυβλύστως**, *abundantly*, Epiph.*haer.*69.27(p.177.14; M.42. 245C).

***πολυγαμέω**, **1.** *practise polygamy*, Bardesanes ap.Eus.*p.e.*6.10 (278B; M.21.473A); **2.** *marry many times*, Phot.*nomoc.*13.2(M.104. 1168B).

πολυγαμία, ἡ, *polygamy*; **1.** in gen., allowed in OT but contrary to Christ's teaching κύριος...οὐ π. ἔτι συγχωρεῖ...μονογαμίαν δὲ εἰσάγει Clem.*str.*3.12(p.233.22; M.8.1184A); necessary in patriarchal times, Isid.Pel.*epp.*2.274(M.78.704B); but Lamech's two marriages not permitted τὸ δὲ ἑαυτῷ λαβεῖν ἐστι τὸ μὴ κατὰ θέλημα θεοῦ. τὴν π. οὖν ἔλεγεν γάμου μὲν ἔχειν ὄνομα, εἶναι δὲ φιλευπρόσωπον πορνείαν ‡Pion.*v.Polyc.*14 = †Bas.*contub.*10(M.30.825A); **2.** of third and subsequent marriages περὶ τριγάμων καὶ πολυγάμων τὸν αὐτὸν ὥρισαν κανόνα, ὃν καὶ ἐπὶ τῶν διγάμων...ὀνομάζουσι δὲ τὸ τοιοῦτον οὐκ ἔτι γάμον, ἀλλὰ π. Bas.*ep.*188 *can.*4(3.271D; M.32.673A); cf.*Const. App.*3.2.2.

πολύγαμος, *polygamous*, i.e. marrying several times in succession, Or.*comm.in Mt.*17.30(p.670.29; M.13.1568B); equated with τρίγαμος, Bas.*ep.*188 *can.*4(3.271D; M.32.673A).

***πολύγελος**, *accompanied by much laughter*, Ephr.3.23B.

***πολυγλωσσία, ἡ**, *variety of tongues*; of gift of glossolalia, Cyr. *Joel.*35(3.227B); of confusion of tongues, id.*Juln.*4(6[2].139A).

πολυγνώμων, **1.** *of many opinions*; of pagan religion, Eus.*p.e.* 5.3 tit.(177; M.21.316C); of semi-pagan Christians, Cyr.*Ps.*67:7(M. 69.1145C); id.*hom.pasch.*15(5[2].202C); **2.** *rich in thought* π. ἐν ἡμῖν ἡ καρδία id.*Ps.*103:25(1264D).

πολυγον-έω, *be fertile*, Gr.Nyss.*hom.opif.*18.2(M.44.192C); id.*hom. 7 in Cant.*(M.44.925A); met. ~οῦσα...ἡ κακία id.*res.*1(M.46.608D); med. ~εῖται τὰ ποίμνια id.*Apoll.*1(M.45.1125A).

***πολυγύρευτος**, *travelling about frequently*; neut. as subst., Thdr. Stud.*epp.*1.10(M.99.941B).

πολυδάκρυτος, *much-lamented*, *Orac.Sib.*11.139.

***πολυδαπάνητος**, *very expensive*, Jo.Mal.*chron.*11 p.278(M.97. 420B).

***πολύδετος**, *firmly binding*, Eus.*h.e.*10.4.13(M.20.853A).

πολυδημώδης, *of many people, thronging*, ‡Pion.*v.Polyc.*7.

***πολυδίδακτος**, *learned*, ref. quality for episcopal office, *Const. App.*3.5.4.

***πολυδιεξόδευτος**, *much given to straying*, Thdr.Stud.*epp.*1.10(M. 99.941B).

***πολυδόνητος**, *readily disturbed* π. γνώμη Isid.Pel.*epp.*1.419(M. 78.416B).

πολυδοξία, ἡ, *high reputation*, Gr.Thaum.*Eccl.*6:2(M.10.1004A).

πολύδροσος, *much-bedewed*, *Orac.Sib.*3.322.

πολυδύναμος, *abundantly powerful*; in gen., Isid.Pel.*epp.*1.59(M. 78.220C); *ib.*1.133(272A); of operation of God, Cyr.H.*catech.*9.9; of Logos, Eus.*l.C.*12(p.233.12; M.20.1393A); of H. Ghost, Cyr.H.*catech.* 4.16; of grace of Christ, Gel.Cyz.*h.e.*1.5.7(M.85.1205A); of Cross ἔστι σταυρὸς π. δύναμις Jo.D.*hom.*3.1(M.96.589A).

πολυειδής, *of many varieties, diverse*, of primal man in theory of Monoïmus κεραία μία ἀσύνθετος, ἁπλῆ, μονὰς εἰλικρινὴς ἐξ οὐδενὸς ὅλως τὴν σύνθεσιν ἔχουσα, συνθετή, π., πολυσχιδής, πολυμερής Hipp. *haer.*8.12(p.232.23; M.16.3358C); of Arian Trinity τῆς π. καὶ πολυμεροῦς τῶν αἱρετικῶν θεότητος Ath.*Ar.*3.15(M.26.353B); οὐδὲ ὁ υἱὸς π. καὶ συγκείμενος, ἀλλ' ὅμως οὐ διὰ τοῦτο ἀγέννητος Gr.Nyss.*Eun.*12 (1 p.228.7; M.45.924B).

πολυέλαιος, *yielding much oil*, met. τῷ λιπαρῷ τοῦ γάλακτος, ὃ δὴ βούτυρον καλοῦσιν, καταχρῶνται εἰς λύχνον, τὸ π. τοῦ λόγου δι' αἰνίγματος ἀριδήλου σαφηνίσαντες Clem.*paed.*1.6(p.121.1; M.8.312A).

πολυέλεος, *rich in mercy*; of God, Just.*dial.*108.3(M.6.728A); Clem.*str.*2.13(p.143.27; M.8.996A); Cyr.*Jo.*6.1(4.593C); of Christ, *ib.*4.2(360B).

***πολυέπεια, ἡ**, *much speaking*, Olymp.*Eccl.*5:6(M.93.541C).

πολυεπής, *verbose, wordy*; of pseudo-Clementine literature, Eus. *h.e.*3.38.5(M.20.293D); of Marcellus' work, id.*e.th.*proem.(p.60.3; M. 24.824C); *containing many words*, Olymp.*Eccl.*12:12(M.93.625A).

πολυετέω, *pass many years*, ref. persecuted believers οὔπω ἐπολυετήσαμεν κατὰ τοὺς προλαβόντας ὁμολογητάς Thdr.Stud.*epp.* 2.37(M.99.1228B).

***πολυευζωΐα, ἡ**, *long and happy life*, ‡Jo.D.*ep.Thphl.*9(M.95. 356C).

***πολυευπρέπης**, *very handsome*, ‡Hesych.H.*m.Long.*15(M.93. 1557C).

***πολυευσπλαγχνία, ἡ**, *great compassion*, Herm.*sim.*8.6.1; ‡Ath. *doct.Ant.*9(M.28.568A).

***πολυεύσπλαγχνος**, *rich in mercy*, Herm.*sim.*5.4.4; Nil.*epp.*2.140 (M.79.264A); *Hymn.*(*AS* 1 p.569).

***πολυεύτακτος**, *very orderly*; neut. as subst., Ign.*Magn.*1.1.

***πολύζαλος**, *stormy*, ‡Caes.Naz.*dial.*1(M.38.853).

***πολυζητησία, ἡ**, *state of being much sought after*; of monastic *cellarius*, Thdr.Stud.*iamb.*12(M.99.1784D).

***πολυζήτητος**, *eagerly inquired after*, Anast.S.*qu.et resp.*95 tit. (M.89.733A).

***πολυζώητος**, *long-lived*, Melet.*nat.hom.*7(M.64.1184C).

*****πολύζωμος**, *much-fermented*, Anast.S.*qu.et resp.*94(M.89.732C).

*****πολυήλατος**, *much-hammered*, irreg. dat. πολυήλατι χαλκῷ *Orac. Sib.*5.218.

*****πολυημερία**, ἡ, *great number of days*, i.e. *long life*, Gr.Thaum. *Eccl.*6:3(M.10.1004A).

πολυήσυχος, *very peaceful*, *Orac.Sib.*14.332.

πολυθαμβής, *greatly frightened* or *astonished*, Nonn.*par.Jo.*12:30 (M.43.856A).

πολυθαύμαστος, *very wondrous, miraculous*; of Abgar's image of Christ, *A.Thadd.*5(p.276n.); of Christ's conception, Sophr.H.*or.*2. 24(M.87.3244D); of Ascension, id.*ep.syn.*(M.87.3176B).

πολυθεάμων, *of* or *for seeing much, contemplative* τῆς...πολυπόρου καὶ π. δυνάμεως [sc. of seraphim] Dion.Ar.*c.h.*13.4(M.3.305A); id. *e.h.*4.3.7(M.3.481A) cit. s. σεραφίμ.

*****πολυθεέω**, *be a polytheist*, Anast.Ap.*a.Max.*2.14(M.90.149D).

πολυθεΐα, ἡ, **1.** *multiplicity of gods* (pagan) ἡ...τοῦ σωτῆρος ἡμῶν δύναμις τὰς τῶν δαιμόνων πολυαρχίας καὶ π. καθεῖλε Eus.*l.C.*16(p.249. 31; M.20.1424B); Epiph.*haer.*62.7(p.396.15; M.41.1060C); διάβολος... τῇ π. βρομῶν Ast.Soph.*Ps.*7(M.40.472C); Cyr.*Juln.*3(6².91D); Nil. *epp.*1.248(M.79.173C); τὸν ἕνα θεὸν διεμέρισαν εἰς π. Philox.*ep.*32 (p.180); **2.** *belief in many gods, polytheism*, in rel. to Christian theology ἑκάστην τῶν ὑποστάσεων μοναχῶς ἐξαγγέλλομεν· ἐπειδὰν δὲ συναριθμῆσαι δέῃ, οὐχὶ ἀπαιδεύτῳ ἀριθμήσει πρὸς πολυθεΐας ἔννοιαν ἐκφερόμεθα Bas.*Spir.*44(3.38A; M.32.149A); ἐποίησεν ὁ θεὸς τὸν ἄνθρωπον. οὐχί, ἐποίησαν. ἔφυγεν ἐνταῦθα τὸν πληθυσμὸν τῶν προσώπων...ἵνα καὶ υἱὸν νοῇς μετὰ πατρός, καὶ τῆς π. ἐκφύγῃς τὸ ἐπικίνδυνον id.*hex.*9.6(1.88C; M.29.208A); ref. Arianism ὁ μονογενὴς βλασφημεῖται...τὸ πνεῦμα...ἀθετεῖται...π. κεκράτηκε id.*ep.*243(3. 375C; M.32.909A); Amph.*ep.syn.*(M.39.97A); Isid.Pel.*epp.*2.143(M. 78.588D); ref. Gnost. pluralism πῶς οὖν π. ἔσται καὶ πολλαὶ ἀρχαί, εἰ [1Cor.8:6b]; Epiph.*haer.*56.3(p.342.14; M.41.993B); ref. Noëtus' conception of Trin. orthodoxy μὴ πολυθεΐαν ἡγήσοιντο οἱ τὸ σέβας ἀληθινῶς τῇ τριάδι προσφέροντες *ib.*57.4(p.349.8; 1001A); fear of polytheism must not produce Sabellianism, Gr.Naz.*or.*20.6(M.35. 1072B); cf. a too strict orthodoxy called πολυθεΐα, *ib.*2.37(444C); pagans accuse Christians of polytheism, Chrys.*hom.17.4 in Jo.*(8. 102B); ref. 1Tim.2:5 εἷς καὶ εἷς. οὐ τίθησι δύο· ἐπειδὴ γὰρ περὶ πολυθεΐας διελέγετο, ἵνα μή τις ἁρπάσῃ τῶν δύο τὸν ἀριθμὸν εἰς π. id. *hom.7.2 in 1Tim.*(11.586C); τὸ γὰρ ἑνικὸν αὐτοῦ τῆς οὐσίας καὶ φύσεως ἀριθμεῖσθαι...οὐκ ἀνέχεται, ἵνα μὴ καὶ διαφορὰν εἰσοίσῃ θεότητος, καὶ...π. τὴν μοναρχίαν ἐργάσοιτο Sophr.H.*ep.syn.*(M.87.3156B); οὐ λέγουσιν, ἅγιοι, ἅγιοι, ἅγιοι...ἀλλὰ τρὶς μὲν διδόασι τὴν ἁγιαστίαν, μονοειδῶς δέ, ἑνικῶς ἀποφθέγγονται τὸν λόγον, ἵνα μὴ π. ὀνομάσωσιν Jo.D.*trisag.*25(M.95.56B); ref. monothelite doctrine ἐὰν εἴπῃς τὴν ὡς ἑνὸς μίαν θέλησιν...ἀναγκασθήσῃ τὴν ὡς ἑνὸς τοῦ πατρός, καὶ τὴν ὡς ἑνὸς τοῦ πνεύματος εἰπεῖν...θέλησιν...καὶ εὑρεθήσεται εἰς π. ἐκπίπτων ὁ λόγος Max.*opusc.*(M.91.269B).

*****πολυθεοαθεότης**, ἡ, v. ἀθεότης.

*****πολυθεομανία**, ἡ, *madness of polytheism*, *Hom.Clem.*3.3, written *divisim* πολυθεοῦ μανία *GCS* p.57.23.

πολύθεος, **1.** *of many gods* τῆς π. στρατιᾶς Eus.*l.C.*7(p.214.13; M. 20.1356A); **2.** *believing in many gods, polytheist*, of persons εἰδωλολάτραι, π. ὀνομαζόμενοι Or.*Ps.*15:4(p.469); π. ὄντες καὶ ἄθεοι *ib.*65:12 (p.77); προφάσει τοῦ εἶναι π. ὄντες ἄθεοι id.*mart.*5(p.6.30; M. om.); Max.*opusc.*(M.91.28C); **3.** *polytheistic*; of belief, opinion, etc., *A.Andr.*A 6(p.49.19); π. γνώσεως *Hom.Clem.*11.5; Gr.Nyss.*Eun.*5 (2 p.103.24; πολυθεΐαν M.45.681D); Epiph.*haer.*42.12(p.167.8; M.41. 789C); Cyr.*ador.*3(1.93E); ref. Const. πᾶσαν π. πλάνην καθελόντος Eus.*v.C.*4.75(p.148.15; M.20.1229B); Cyr.*Is.*2.3(2.272D); ποιηταὶ...π. πλάνης κήρυκες *ib.*4.1(549A); id.*Os.*5(3.23E); ref. Christian heresy εἰ οὖν εἰς πλῆθος ἐκτείνειν τὸν ἀριθμὸν τῶν θεοτήτων μόνον τῶν τὴν π. πλάνην νενοσηκότων ἐστί· τὸ δὲ καθόλου ἀρνεῖσθαι τὴν θεότητα, τῶν ἀθέων ἂν εἴη Gr.Nyss.*Trin.*4(p.74.15; M.32.688C); εἰ δὲ φύσει θεὸς ὁ Χριστός, καθὸ φύσει Χριστός, π. ὁ ταῦτα λέγων· ἄλλην πατρὸς ὡς θεοῦ φύσιν, οὐκ ὄντος φύσει Χριστοῦ Max.*opusc.*(M.91.28C).

*****πολυθεότης**, ἡ, *polytheism*, Or.*Cels.*1.1(p.56.15; M.11.653A) cit. s. ἄθεος; *ib.*3.73(p.265.10; 1016B); Ὀρφεύς γ' οὖν, ὁ τῆς π. ὑμῶν... πρῶτος διδάσκαλος ‡Just.*coh.Gr.*15(M.6.269A); in rel. to Arianism οἱ Ἀρειομανῖται δικαίως ἂν σχοῖεν τὸ ἔγκλημα τῆς π. ἢ καὶ ἀθεότητος, ὅτι ἔξωθεν τὸν υἱὸν κτίσμα καὶ πάλιν τὸ πνεῦμα ἐκ τοῦ μὴ ὄντος βαττολογοῦσιν Ath.*Ar.*3.15(M.26.353A); id.*ep.Serap.*1.28(M.26.596B); ἐκπεσόντες τῆς περὶ τοῦ ἑνὸς θεοῦ ἐννοίας, εἰς π. κατῆλθον id.*ep.Aeg. Lib.*14(M.26.569B); in Sabellian accusation against orthodox, ‡Ath. *Sabell.*1(M.28.97A).

πολύθεστος, *much-desired*, †Apoll.*met.Ps.*104:34(M.33.1472A).

*****πολυθεώρητος**, *much-considered*, Mac.Mgn.*apocr.*4.16(p.189.27).

*****πολύθλιπτος**, *full of tribulation*, Ephr.2.202C; Thdr.Stud.*epp.*1.6 (M.99.928B).

πολυθρέμμων, *feeding many*, Gr.Naz.*carm.*1.2.10.498(M.37.716A).

πολυθρήνητος, *much given to lamenting*; of Jeremiah, Thdr.Stud. *cant.*3.8(p.342).

πολυθρύλ(λ)ητος, **1.** *famous, well-known, much talked of*, in gen. τὰ Ἐφέσια καλούμενα γράμματα...π. ὄντα Clem.*str.*5.8(p.356.2; M.9. 72C); τῆς π. πεντηκοστῆς ‡Hipp.*fr.9 in Pss.*(p.138.10; M.10.713B); Meth.*symp.*4.5(p.51.16; M.18.96A); Isid.Pel.*epp.*1.13(M.78.188B); Ἀθανάσιος...ὁ π. Thdt.*eran.*1(4.43); τὸ π. ζῶον τὸν ἄνθρωπον Jo.D. *hom.*4.6(M.96.608C); **2.** *notorious* Ἐπιφάνης...ἐν...τῷ π. βιβλίῳ, τῷ περὶ δικαιοσύνης Clem.*str.*3.2(p.199.30; M.8.1109B); Bas.Sel.*v.Thecl.*1 (M.85.541B); **3.** *much-discussed* π. ... ζητήματος τοῦ πόθεν ἡ κακία Eus.*h.e.*5.27(M.20.509B); Bas.*hom.*24.4(2.193B; M.31.608C); τὴν π. κρᾶσιν καὶ σύγχυσιν Thdt.*eran.*2(4.113); **4.** *much-quoted, trite* τὸ π. ... ἐπίφθεγμα...τὸ γνῶθι σαυτόν Or.*Cant.*2(p.141.28; M.17.256D); τὸ π. ...εἰρημένον, κτίσμα ἐστὶν ὁ υἱός Ath.*Ar.*2.50(M.26.252B); Proc.G. *Dt.*12:5(M.87.908D); Dion.Ar.*d.n.*4.28(M.3.729A); Anast.S.*hod.*8(M. 89.132B); **5.** *much-vaunted, boasted* π. ταύτης ἀστρολογίας Clem.*prot.*6 (p.51.22; M.8.172C); π. κατὰ τὰς ἐκκλησίας αὐτῶν πρωτοκαθεδρίας id. *str.*7.16(p.69.20; M.9.536B); οἱ π. ὕπατοι Ast.Am.*hom.*4(M.40.221C); **6.** *much-valued* συλλέγων...καθάπερ καὶ τὰ λιθίδια ταῦτα τὰ π. οἱ τούτων ἔμποροι Bas.Sel.*v.Thecl.*2.30(M.85.616C).

πολυκαμπής, *frequently encircled* π. νύσσῃ Nonn.*par.Jo.*8:57(M. 43.821D).

*****πολυκάνδηλον**, τό, *candelabrum*, Thdr.Stud.*poen.*1.74(M.99. 1741D).

*****πολυκάρτερος**, *enduring much*, Thdr.Stud.*cant.*6.1(p.346).

πολυκέντητος, *much-patched*, Gr.Nyss.*Eun.*7(2 p.159.11; M.45. 748C).

πολύκεστος, *much-embroidered*, hence *much-adorned* ἕλιξ πολύκεστος ἀκάνθης Paul.Sil.*Soph.*659(M.86.2144B); *ib.*739(2147B).

*****πολυκευθής**, *concealing much*, Clem.*str.*6.15(p.498.21; M.9.356B).

*****πολυκεφάλαιος**, *many-headed*, Anast.S.*hex.*12(M.89.1073A).

πολυκίνδυνος, *much in peril*, Isid.Pel.*epp.*1.50(M.78.213A); ‡Caes.Naz.*dial.*20(M.38.876); *ib.*134(M.38.1040).

πολυκινησία, ἡ, *manifold motion*, Dion.Ar.*d.n.*4.4(M.3.697D).

πολυκλήϊστος, *celebrated*, Nonn.*par.Jo.*6:31(M.43.800A); *ib.*11:55 (849A).

*****πολυκλήματος**, *many-branched*, Meth.*res.*1.41(p.285.14; M.18. 269A).

*****πολυκλόνητος**, *in continual movement*; of heavenly bodies, Synes.*provid.*9(M.66.1228A).

*****πολύκλονος**, *much-agitated* δένδρον...ὑψηλὸν καὶ π. *A.Mt.*4(p.220. 9, v.l. πλατύν); *thronged and noisy*; of a theatre, †Cyr.*hom.div.*11 (5².379A).

*****πολυκόκκινος**, *with many grains*, Ph.Carp.*Cant.*188(M.40.120B).

*****πολύκοκκος**, = foreg., Ph.Carp.*Cant.*215(M.40.133D); ‡Chrys. *hom.*13(13.251B).

*****πολυκόλλητος**, *much-patched*, Gr.Nyss.*bapt.Chr.*(M.46.593B); id.*bapt.diff.*(M.46.420C).

πολύκομπος, *boastful*, Epiph.*haer.*35.3(p.43.4; M.41.632B).

*****πολύκοπρος**, *insanitary*, ‡Ath.*qu.Ant.*103(M.28.661A).

πολύκρανος, *many-headed*; met., of rule exercised by many governors, *Orac.Sib.*3.175; of philosophy; as disputed among many sects, Just.*dial.*2.2(M.6.476B).

[*]**πολύκρεος**, = sq., *abounding in meat*, Anast.S.*qu.et resp.*94 (M.89.732C).

πολύκρεως, *abounding in flesh*; of Leviticus, i.e. *containing much about animal sacrifices*, Anast.S.*hod.*22(M.89.285A).

*****πολυκτηδών**, *with many layers*; of cornea of eye, Hipp.*haer.*8.10 (p.230.5; M.16.3354D).

πολυκτησία, ἡ, *great wealth*, Bas.*renunt.*1(2.202B; M.31.625C).

*****πολυκυδήεις**, *very celebrated*, †Apoll.*met.Ps.*10:4(M.33.1325A).

*****πολυκυδής**, s.v.l., *most glorious*, †Apoll.*met.Ps.*76:4(M.33. 1421B; πολυγηθής *delightful, gladsome*, *Teub.*).

*****πολύκυδος**, *famous*, ‡Jo.D.*Const.*16(M.95.332C).

πολυλαλία, ἡ, *much talking*, *Hom.Clem.*18.11.

*****πολυλεξία**, ἡ, *chatter*, Socr.*h.e.*4.7.9(M.67.473A).

*****πολυλογητέον**, *one must speak at length*, Clem.*paed.*2.7(p.192. 20; M.8.461C).

πολυλογία, ἡ, *much speaking*, Or.*Jo.*5.5(p.102.29f.; M.14.192A); Ath.*syn.*32(p.260.17; M.26.749B); Jo.Clim.*scal.*18(M.88.932D).

πολύλογος, *of many words*; of prayer, Clem.*str.*7.7(p.37.10; M.9. 469B); of God π. ἐστιν ἡ ἀγαθὴ πάντων αἰτία, καὶ βραχύλεκτος ἅμα καὶ ἄλογος Dion.Ar.*myst.*1.3(M.3.1000C); cf. Pachymeres ad loc.: τὸ δὲ πολύλογος προπαροξυτόνως, πολυλόγος γὰρ ὁ πολλὰ λέγων, πολύλογος δὲ ὁ πολλῶν λόγων δεόμενος (M.3.1021A).

***πολυλοίδορος**, *very abusive*, Steph.Diac.*v.Steph.*(M.100.1148B).

***πολυλουσία**, ἡ, *much bathing*, Jo.D.*fr.*(M.95.236D).

***πολυμάγγανος**, *full of seduction*; of illicit unions, †Jo.Jej.*poenit.*(M.88.1893D).

***πολυμαθῶς**, *very learnedly*, Clem.*ecl.*29(p.146.6; M.9.713B); Or.*Cels.*1.16(p.68.16; M.11.688B).

πολυμάκαρ, *greatly blessed*, Jo.D.*trisag.*(M.95.32A).

πολυμανής, *exceedingly mad*; of Simon Magus, *Hom.Clem.*2.25.

***πολυμέθοδος**, *manifold*, Thdr.Stud.*epp.*1.14(M.99.956B).

πολυμεμφής, *much given to blaming*, Nonn.*par.Jo.*10:32(M.43.837A).

πολυμέρεια ([*]-μερία), ἡ, **1.** *multiplicity of parts*, Dion.Ar.*c.h.*15.3(M.3.332A); ‡Caes.Naz.*dial.*140(M.38.1088); **2.** ? error for πολυημέρεια *great number of days* διὰ τῆς ἐν τῇ πεντηκοστῇ π. Thdr.Stud.*epp.*1.13(M.99.953B).

πολυμερής, *of many parts, composite, manifold*; **1.** in gen. τὸ σῶμα τοῦ ἀνθρώπου π. ὄν Arist.*apol.*13.5; τῆς π. καὶ ποικίλης ὕλης Clem.*exc.Thdot.*50(p.123.9; M.9.681D); π. ... ἡ φρόνησις id.*str.*6.17 (p.511.25; M.9.388A); **2.** theol.; **a.** of name Christ (Marcosian) τὸ δὲ παρὰ τοῖς αἰῶσι τοῦ πληρώματος πολυμερὲς τυγχάνον Iren.*haer.*1.14.4 (M.7.604A); **b.** ref. primal man of Monoïmus, Hipp.*haer.*8.12(p.232.24; M.16.3358C) cit. s. πολυειδής; **c.** Arian τῆς πολυειδοῦς καὶ π. τῶν αἱρετικῶν θεότητος Ath.*Ar.*3.15(M.26.353B); Ἄρειον...π. καὶ πολυσύνθετον λέγοντα τὸν θεὸν τῶν ὅλων Philost.*h.e.*10.2(M.65.584C).

***πολυμεριμνία**, ἡ, *manifold anxiety*, Hipp.*haer.*4.45(p.68.1; M.16.3110A).

πολυμέριμνος, **1.** *laborious* τήν τε π. αὐτῶν...μαντικήν Hipp.*haer.*4.27(p.53.21; M.16.3090A); **2.** *busy, full of worldly cares* μὴ τοῖς π. καὶ φιληδόνοις ἀνθρώποις ἐμπιστεύσητε τὰ λόγια τοῦ κυρίου Nil.*epp.*2.5(M.79.204C); **3.** *burdened with care* ἀπολελυμένους...τῶν π. φροντίδων Eus.*d.e.*1.9(p.42.6; M.22.81A); Ephr.1.35F; τὴν π. ταύτην ζωήν ‡Gr.Nyss.*or.2 in Gen.*1:26(M.44.284D); φιλαργυρία...π. κακία †Nil.*vit.*3(M.79.1141D).

πολύμικτος, *much-mixed*, Gr.Naz.*carm.*1.2.5.7(M.37.642A).

***πολύμιξ**, *promiscuous*, Epiph.*anc.*103(p.123.26; M.43.201C).

πολυμιξία, ἡ, **1.** *polygamy*, ref. Lamech's marriages ἔκτοτε ἀρχὴ ἐγένετο τῆς π., ἀλλὰ καὶ τῆς μουσικῆς Thphl.Ant.*Autol.*2.30(M.6.1100A); **2.** *promiscuity*; ref. stories of pagan gods, *ib.*3.8(1133B); among Gnostics, Epiph.*haer.*24.3(p.261.6; M.41.313A); *ib.*26.3(p.279.3; 336B); fig., of Marcion's assault on scriptural truths καινὴ Σοδόμων π. *ib.*42.12(p.169.26; 793D); of Collyridian heresy, *ib.*79.4 (p.479.15; M.42.745C); **3.** met., *hotch-potch* π. κενοφωνίας *ib.*32.3 (p.442.3; M.41.548A); *ib.*39.3(p.74.13; 669A).

πολύμισθος, *rich in reward*; of alms-deeds, Chrys.*poenit.*7.6(2.336E).

πολύμορφος, *multiform, manifold*, of an evil spirit ὁρκίζω σε πνεῦμα π. *A.Mt.*15(p.235.10); of Hecate, *Hymn.*ap.Hipp.*haer.*4.35(p.62.7; M.16.3102A); of Attis, Hipp.*haer.*5.9(p.99.24; 3155A); Basilidean σπέρμα...ἐν ὃν ὅμως ἔχει ἐν ἑαυτῷ πολλὰς οὐσιῶν π. ... καὶ πολυσυστάτων ἰδέας...σπέρμα τοῦ κόσμου π. ὁμοῦ καὶ πολυούσιον *ib.*7.21(p.197.13; 3303C).

πολυμόρφως, *in many forms*, Cosm.Mel.*schol.*(M.38.488) in Gr.Naz.*carm.*2.2(poem.)7.103ff.

πολύμυθος, *famous, celebrated*, Or.*exp.in Pr.*3:19(M.17.169A).

***πολυνοήμων**, *rich in ideas*, Agath.*v.Gr.Ill.*169.

πολύνοια, ἡ, *thought about many things, mental distraction*, Marc.Er.*opusc.*4(M.65.1016C).

***πολυνοσέω**, *be ill with many diseases*, Or.*sel.in Ps.*50:3(M.12.1456A).

πολύνυμφος, *with many brides*; of Christ as spouse of virgins, Thdr.Stud.*epp.*2.150(M.99.1468C).

πολυοδία, ἡ, *multiplicity of paths, maze*; met., of earthly life ταῖς π. τοῦ βίου τούτου ἐναμηχανοῦντες Gr.Nyss.*hom.6 in Eccl.*(M.44.701C); ἐν ταῖς π. ... τοὺς ὁδοιπόρους ὁρῶμεν τῆς εὐθείας οὐχ ἁμαρτάνοντας id.*virg.*7(p.281.15; M.46.352C); of ways of wickedness, Olymp.*fr.Jer.*6:25(M.93.644A); of erroneous arguments, Gr.Nyss.*Eun.*10(2 p.236.22; M.45.837D); Const.Diac.*laud.*21(M.88.504B).

πολυόλβιος, *blissful*, Jo.D.*trisag.*(M.95.32A).

***πολυολκής**, *burdensome*, Pall.*v.Chrys.*11(p.65.15; M.47.37).

πολυομβρία, ἡ, *much rain*, Proc.G.*Gen.*2:5(M.87.149B); Anast.S.*qu.et resp.*20(M.89.521B).

πολυόμματος, *many-eyed*; **1.** in gen., ref. Cant.4:9 τυφλὸς μέν ἐστιν ὁ π., ὁ πρὸς τὰ μάταια πολλοῖς ὀφθαλμοῖς βλέπων Gr.Nyss.*hom.8 in Cant.*(M.44.952A); τὸ π. τῆς ψυχῆς id.*infant.*(M.46.164A); **2.** of cherubim and seraphim π. ἑξαπτέρυγα χερουβίμ τε καὶ σεραφίμ ‡Hipp.*consumm.*39(p.305.16; M.10.941B); in visions of Isaiah and Ezekiel, ‡Just.*qu.et resp.*44(M.6.1288C); Procl.CP *annunt.*2(M.85.429A); Dion.Ar.*c.h.*6.2(M.3.200D); compared with deacons as 'bishop's eyes', Isid.Pel.*epp.*1.29(M.78.200C); **3.** abs., as distinct order of angelic hierarchy ἡ δύναμις τῶν ἀγγέλων καὶ τῶν π. *1 Apoc.Jo.*17(p.84); ‡Rom.Mel.(*AS* 1 p.229); **4.** of BMV ἐπαινείσθω ἡ πολυώνυμος ὄντως καὶ π. ‡Jo.D.*hom.*5(M.96.648C).

πολυόμφαλος, *with many bosses*, in mysteries πόπανα π. Clem.*prot.*2(p.17.6; M.8.88B).

πολυορκία, ἡ, *much swearing of oaths*; forbidden to Christians, *Const.App.*2.36.5.

πολύορκος, *swearing many oaths*, Bas.*renunt.*6(2.208B; M.31.640C).

πολυούσιος, *manifold in substance*, Hipp.*haer.*7.21(p.197.16; M.16.3303C) cit. s. πολύμορφος.

πολυοχλία, ἡ, *thronging of people, crowdedness*, *Pet.Ar.*3(M.26.820D); Bas.*hom.*20.7(2.162B; M.31.537C); μοναστήρια...καθαρὰ...πολυοχλίας Chrys.*hom.14.3 in 1Tim.*(11.629A); Nil.*exerc.*62(M.79.793D).

πολύοχλος, *populous*, ‡Ath.*qu.Ant.*103(M.28.661A).

πολυπάθεια, ἡ, **1.** *subjection to many passions*, or *physical sensations*; of animal body opp. rational soul, Nemes.*nat.hom.*1(M.40.524B) = Melet.*nat.hom.*synops.(M.64.1101C); Nil.*epp.*3.33(M.79.388D); **2.** *variety of passions* τὰς τῶν ᾀσμάτων...ἑταιρικὰς π. Dion.Ar.*ep.*9.1(M.3.1105B).

πολυπαθής, **1.** *subject to many passions* χοιρώδη βίον καὶ π. τὴν ψυχὴν βιοτεύειν Meth.*creat.*1(p.494.14; M.18.333B); **2.** *subject to much suffering*; of Jeremiah, Isid.Pel.*epp.*2.298(M.78.356C); of Christ ὢν κατὰ φύσιν ἀπαθής, γέγονε δι' οἶκτον π. Procl.CP *or.laud.BMV* 4 (p.104.21; M.65.684C); of the body τὸ π. τῆς ὕλης ἱμάτιον id.*Arm.*3 (p.188.18; M.65.857B); of physical life, Jo.Mon.*hymn.Blas.*9(M.96.1405D); Melet.*nat.hom.*30(M.64.1277A); of an eye damaged by an evil spirit, *T.Sal.*18.39(M.122.1345D).

[*]**πολυπάμμων**, *exceedingly wealthy*, *Orac.Sib.*2.342.

***πολυπαμποίκιλος**, *very varied, manifold*, ‡Ath.*diab.*3(p.6.12).

***πολυπάνσοφος**, *exceedingly wise*, *Orac.Sib.*2.1.

***πολυπεριούσιος**, *of much substance, wealthy* πλούσιος λέγεται...οἷόν τις π. πολλὴν ἔχων περὶ αὐτὸν οὐσίαν Jo.D.*Man.*1.14(M.94.1517B).

πολυπερίσπαστος, *much-distracted*, Gr.Agr.*Eccl.*3.29(M.98.908A).

***πολυπευστέω**, *make many inquiries, investigate fully*, Eust.*engast.*12(p.36.8; M.18.640B); *Const.App.*3.14.2.

***πολυπήγητος**, *poured forth abundantly*, †Hipp.*theoph.*1(p.257.8; M.10.852A).

***πολυπλασία**, ἡ, *multiplicity, compound character, complexity*, ‡Caes.Naz.*dial.*138(M.38.1044); *ib.*155(1108).

πολυπλασιάζω, *multiply* a number *by itself, square*, Anat.Laod.*decad.*(p.40).

πολυπλασιασμός, ὁ, *multiplication* of a number *by itself, squaring*, Anat.Laod.*decad.*(p.30).

***πολυπλασίως**, *many times over*, *Hom.Clem.*3.70.

πολύπλεκτος, *much wound round*, Nonn.*par.Jo.*19:40(M.43.908A).

πολυπληθέω, *abound in*, ref. Lev.11:42 πολυπληθεῖ δὲ ποσὶν ὁ πέριξ τῶν σωματικῶν περιεχόμενος Nil.*exerc.*14(M.79.736C).

πολυπληθής, *very numerous*, *Orac.Sib.*12.62.

πολυπλοκία, ἡ, *cunning, craft*, ref. Devil, Herm.*mand.*4.3.4.

πολυπλόκως, *in a tangled* or *complex way*, Afric.*ep.Arist.*2(p.58.22; M.10.56B).

[*]**πολυπνία**, v. πολυυπνία.

***πολύπνοια**, ἡ, *much wind*, *Orac.Sib.*8.180.

πολυπόθητος, **1.** *much-loved*, in address to congregation ὦ π. τέκνα Chrys.*hom.7.1 in Jo.*(8.44C); of Jairus' daughter, Eus.Al.*serm.*15(M.86.388A); of Christ, Diad.*perf.*38(p.44.12); *ib.*59(p.66.17); of God τὸ π. κάλλος Jo.D.*Trin.*3(M.95.13B); ref. significance of τρίς in τρισάγιον: τριπόθητος ὁ π. id.*trisag.*4(M.95.29C); **2.** *much-valued, much sought after* π. ὑγιείας Isid.Pel.*epp.*3.192(M.78.880A).

πολυποίκιλος, *very varied, manifold, variegated* ὀργὴ π. *Orac.Sib.*8.120; γαίην π. *ib.*12.149; Hipp.*haer.*8.9(p.228.13; M.16.3351B); of a demon ἔχω δὲ π. τρόπον *T.Sal.*4.4(M.122.1321A); of wisdom τῷ π. νοητῷ κάλλει αὐτῆς Or.*Jo.*1.9(11; p.14.28; M.14.40D); ref. Eph.3:10, *ib.*19.22(5; p.324.6; 568C); ἡ ἁπλῆ καὶ π. σοφία καὶ τοὺς ἀσκεπεῖς ἀμφιέννυσι Dion.Ar.*c.h.*15.4(M.3.333A).

πολυποίκιλτος, *of varied hue*, ‡Jo.D.*hom.*5(M.96.656C).

***πολυποκέω**, *be rich in fleece*, Tim.Ant.*caec.*14(M.28.1021B).

***πολυπόλεμος**, *much warring, experienced in war*; of Goliath, ‡Ath.*sem*.11(M.28.157B).

πολύπορος, *with many ways, many-sided* τῆς ἀεικινήτου καὶ π. ... νοήσεως [sc. of seraphim] Dion.Ar.*e.h*.4.3.7(M.3.481A); id.*c.h*.13.4 (M.3.305A).

πολυπραγμον-έω, **A.** in good sense; **1.** *be busy about, concern oneself with, take trouble over* ὁ ἐκζητῶν τὸν θεὸν τὴν ἰδίαν ∼εῖ σωτηρίαν Clem.*prot*.10(p.76.19; M.8.224A); Cyr.H.*catech*.2.3; ἠμελημένοι, καὶ οὐδένα τὸν ∼οῦντα ἔχοντες...οὐδενὸς ὄντος τοῦ τὰς φιλίας αὐτῶν ∼οῦντος Chrys.*hom.4.3 in Tit*.(11.753B,C); Nil.*epp*.2.167(M.79.284A); Bas.Sel.*or*.14.1(M.85.181B); **2.** *study* διδασκαλίαν ἔτι,...πρὸς δὲ καὶ Ἰωνίαν ∼οῦντας Clem.*prot*.11(p.79.9; M.8.229A); τὰ τῶν θηρίων ∼οῦντες ἔθη Cyr.*Am*.27(3.277A); of believer's study of Christ, Clem.*prot*.1(p.10.12; M.8.68A); **3.** *investigate, inquire into*; **a.** in gen., *ib*.2(p.28.7; 116B); τὴν γένεσιν τοῦ κόσμου π. id.*str*.1.14(p.38.21; M.8.760B); ἥτις εἴη...ἐπολυπραγμόνει Eus.*m.P*.11(p.938.2; M.20.1504B); of those who might seek baptism in order to discover Christians' practices νομίζεις ὅτι σὺ μὲν ∼εῖς τὰ γιγνόμενα, θεὸς δέ σου οὐ ∼εῖ τὴν καρδίαν; Cyr.H.*procatech*.2; τὴν αἰτίαν...∼ῶν Bas.*jud*.2(2.214B; M.31.656A); τὴν τοῦ ὄντος ∼ῶν φύσιν Gr.Naz.*or*.28.9(p.36.5; M.36.37A); σφᾶς δὲ αὐτοὺς ∼εῖν...οὐκ ἠδύνατο Soz.*h.e*.2.32.3(M.67.1028A); **b.** of investigation and searching into scriptures βαθυτέρας...∼εῖν θεωρίας Eus.*h.e*.6.2.9(M.20.525A); ∼εῖν...τὴν ...γραφήν Cyr.*ador*.1(1.6B); id.*glaph.Gen*.2(1.52C); id.*Os*.32(3.57E); Ammon.*Ac*.16:7(M.85.1556B); **c.** of theological inquiry, ‡Ath.*dial. Trin*.1.20(M.28.1148B); Gr.Naz.*or*.20.10(M.35.1077A); τὸ τῆς...τριάδος ∼ῶμεν μυστήριον Cyr.*Is*.1.5(2.132A); ἐπὰν...τὸ τῆς ἐνανθρωπήσεως ∼ῆται μυστήριον id.*Jo*.4(4.376B); **d.** of inquiry into Church affairs, discipline, etc. διάκονοι...ἑκάστου τῆς ἐκκλησίας ∼οῦντες τὰς πράξεις *Clem.ep*.12(M.2.48A); Ath.*apol.sec*.5(p.91.23; M.25.257A); of examination of ordinands, Bas.*ep*.54(3.148B; M.31.400B).

B. in bad sense; **1.** *be unduly concerned about, seek too eagerly* τὰς διαποντίους ∼ούντων ἐδωδάς Clem.*paed*.2.1(p.155.5; M.8.380B); Hipp.*haer*.6.8(p.135.10; M.16.3207A); **2.** *take unnecessary trouble over, deal with unnecessarily*, Tat.*orat*.24(p.26.15; M.6.860A); οὐδὲ ἡ σύνοδος τοιοῦτο ἐπολυπραγμόνησε δόγμα †Leont.B.*sect*.10.3(M.86.1264A); **3.** *be inquisitive about, inquire too inquisitively into*, esp. of matters beyond human understanding τὴν συντέλειαν τοῦ παντὸς κόσμου ∼ήσῃς Hipp.*Dan*.4.22.1; μὴ ∼οῦσα τῆς προνοίας τὰ κρίματα Or.*fr.75 in Lam*.(p.265.6; M.13.645A); μηδὲν ∼εῖν, μηδὲ περιεργάζεσθαι τῶν γινομένων Chrys.*hom.10.7 in Mt*.(7.148B); ἐκεῖνα δὲ ∼ούντων...ἃ μηδ' εὑρεῖν οἷόν τε, καὶ τὸ θεῖον παροξύνει ζητούμενα Isid.Pel.*epp*.2.93 (M.78.537B); τῆς...κυρίου παρουσίας μὴ ∼εῖν τὸν καιρόν Thdt.*1 Thess*. proem.(3.503); ∼εῖν...τὰ ὑπὲρ νοῦν Gel.Cyz.*h.e*.2.21.22(M.85.1288B).

πολυπραγμονητέον, **1.** *one must concern oneself with, give one's mind to*, c. acc., Clem.*paed*.2.2(p.174.17; M.8.425A); id.*str*.6.17(p.509.24; M.9.381B); **2.** *one must inquire into*, Gennad.*fr.Gen*.1:1(M.85.1624C).

***πολυπραγμονία**, **ἡ**, *inquisitiveness*, Pall.*v.Chrys*.(133.21; M.47.74).

***πολυπραγμονικῶς**, *with over-eager curiosity*, ref. disciples touching risen Christ ἀκριβέστερόν τε καὶ πολυπραγμονικώτερον διὰ τῆς ἀφῆς...ψηλαφᾶσθαι Leo Mag.*ep*.28.5(p.17.4; M.*PL*.54.774A).

πολυπραγμοσύνη, **ἡ**, **A.** in good sense; **1.** *pursuit, study* ἔοικε γὰρ οὐδ' ἄλλο τι γεγονέναι προοίμιον φιλοσοφίας, ἢ π. γνώσεως Synes. *Dion* 4(p.245.14; M.66.1125A); **2.** *disposition to seek for knowledge, curiosity* τὴν ἄστατον τοῦ νοῦ π. Gr.Nyss.*hex*.1(M.44.64A); πολυπραγμοσύνῃ τῆς διανοίας πρὸς τὸ ἀθέατον id.*v.Mos*.(M.44.377A); περαιτέρω προελθεῖν διὰ τῆς π. οὐ δύναται id.*hom.11 in Cant*.(M.44.1009C); ref. Jo.14:10 σημαίνων ὅτι ὁ ὑπερβὰς τὸν υἱὸν τῇ π. καὶ τὴν περὶ τοῦ πατρὸς ἔννοιαν συμπαρέρχεται id.*Eun*.9(2 p.222.2; M.45.821A); *curiosity* τῇ π. τοῦ νοῦ πρὸς τὸ σαφέστερον ἐκκαλυπτόμενον Leont.B.*Nest.et Eut*.2(M.86.1324C); τὸ τῇ αἰσθήσει δόξαν εἶναι ἁπλοῦν, τῇ π. τοῦ νοῦ πολυμερές τε καὶ ποικίλον ἀναφαίνεσθαι id.*arg.Sev*.(M.86.1932A); **3.** *searching, inquiry*; of investigation of hidden sense of scripture, Or.*fr.in Mt*.7:7(p.70.17; M.17.292B).

B. in bad sense; **1.** *officiousness, fussiness*; of Jews, *Diogn*.4.6; **2.** *idle pursuit* of, *vain preoccupation* with ὦ τῆς κενῆς π. ὦ τῆς ματαίας δοξομανίας Clem.*paed*.2.12(p.232.10; M.8.549A); τῆς κατὰ τὸν βίον π. Gr.Thaum.*pan.Or*.11(p.26.20; M.10.1084A); φιλοπραγμοσύνας ...ἐξ ὧν τίκτονται π. ἢ κακοπραγμοσύναι ἀπελαύνουσαι καλοπραγμοσύνην, τὴν μητέρα τῆς ἰδιοπραγμοσύνης Pall.*h.Laus*.proem.(p.12.5; φιλοπραγμοσύναι M.34.1003); τὰς πέρα τοῦ μέτρου π. ἀστρονομικὴν... καὶ γεωμετρικήν Thdt.*provid*.5(4.545).

πολυπράγμων, **1.** *inquisitive, preoccupied with vain questions*, ref. human reasoning opp. Christian faith φροντίδι πολυπραγμόνων ἀνθρώπων μάθημα...εὑρημένον *Diogn*.5.3; τοὺς περὶ ὁτιοῦν π. σοφοὺς ἅμα καὶ σοφιστὰς...κεκλήκασι Clem.*str*.1.3(p.15.21; M.8.713B); of Greek philosophers, *ib*.5.14(p.417.9; M.9.197A); **2.** *meddlesome, who is a busybody*, Bas.*ep*.114(3.206E; M.32.528B).

***πολύπρατος**, *to be sold for much*, Ephr.3.445F.

πολύπρεμνος, *having many trees*; superl., ‡Jo.D.*Artem*.51(p.87.6; M.96.1297D).

***πολυπρόοδος**, *frequently going out*; neut. as subst., Thdr.Stud. *epp*.1.10(M.99.941B).

***πολυπροσκύνητος**, **1.** *greatly revered*; of Cross, ‡Jo.D.*hom*.5(M.96.656D); **2.** *worshipping many* divine beings, *worshipping polytheistically*, in iconoclastic argument τὸ σέβας ἡμῶν π. διὰ τῆς εἰκονικῆς ἀναστηλώσεως ἀποδέδεικται Thdr.Stud.*antirr*.1.2(M.99.329B).

πολυπρόσωπος, **1.** *with many faces* τὸ...π. τῶν ἀνθρώπων πληθύν Cyr.*Ps*.103:25(M.69.1264C); of angels, Dion.Ar.*c.h*.2.1(M.3.137A); of cherubim and seraphim τὰ π. καὶ πολυόμματα ‡Chrys.*hom*.9(13.233B) ∞ Gr.Ant.*bapt*.2.3(M.88.1873B); of Devil πολυκέφαλος καὶ π. θήρ Meth.*symp*.8.12(p.97.6; M.18.157D); **2.** *taking many forms, varied* in *appearance*, of Devil εἴωθε...ὁ θὴρ εἰς π. ἑαυτὸν ἐξαλλάττειν ἰδέας Eust.*engast*.4(p.21.25; M.18.621A); of Christ's preaching, ‡Chrys.*hom*.8(13.226D); of varied forms of Arian and Eunomian heresy π. ... πλανή Cyr.*thes*.proem.(5^1.2C); (Monoïmus) ἡ π. καὶ μυριόμματος...μία τοῦ ῑ κεραία, ἥτις ἐστὶν εἰκὼν τοῦ τελείου ἀνθρώπου ...τοῦ ἀοράτου Hipp.*haer*.8.12(p.232.24; M.16.3358D); of Christ's intercourse with disciples, *A.Jo*.91(p.196.8); of Godhead (Sabellian) ἓν πρᾶγμα π. ... πατέρα καὶ υἱὸν καὶ ἅγιον πνεῦμα Bas.*ep*.210.3 (3.115A; M.32.772B).

***πολύπτορθος**, *with many shoots*, Nonn.*par.Jo*.15:4(M.43.873A); Paul.Sil.*ambo*.125(M.86.2256B).

πολύρραφος, **1.** *well sewn*, Nonn.*par.Jo*.9:38(M.43.832A); **2.** *much-sewn, much-patched*, ‡Pall.*h.mon*.13.6(p.66.17; M.34.1161D); *Apophth. Patr*.(M.65.225B); †Jo.D.*B.J*.18(M.96.1020A); fig., Nil.*exerc*.65(M.79.797D).

***πολυρρεής**, *much flowing*, Chrysipp.*enc.in Jo.Bapt*.1(p.30.11).

πολύρρητος, *loquacious*, *Schol*.2 in Jo.Clim.*scal*.7(M.88.817B).

πολύς, *much, manifold*, of God αὐτὸς δὲ μόνος ὢν π. ἦν, οὔτε γὰρ ἄλογος οὔτε ἄσοφος οὔτε ἀδύνατος, οὔτε ἀβούλευτος ἦν· πάντα δὲ ἦν ἐν αὐτῷ, αὐτὸς δὲ ἦν τὸ πᾶν Hipp.*Noët*.10(p.251.17; M.10.817A); πρόσφατον γὰρ ἅπαν τὸ ἀρχὴν εἰληφός, ἐπειδὴ π. καὶ ἄμετρος ὁ πρὸ τῶν αἰώνων Apoll.*fid.sec.pt*.12(p.170.22; M.10.1108D).

***πολυσαλεύτως**, *being greatly shaken, with rapid beating* of the heart, *A.Xanthipp*.7(p.62.17).

***πολυσαρκέω**, *be gross*, Bas.*ascet*.3(3.321C; M.31.876D).

πολύσεμνος, *very august*, Max.*ambig*.(M.91.1388A).

πολύσεπτος, **1.** *much-revered* π. βίβλων Eudoc.*Cypr*.1.296(M.85.844B); **2.** *worshipped as plural* οὐ θεότητα τέμνει, ὄφρα κεν οἷον ἔχῃς κράτος, οὐ π. Gr.Naz.*carm*.1.1.3.59(M.37.412A).

πολυσήμαντος, *having many meanings* π. τὸ ὄνομα τῆς παραβολῆς ‡Hipp.*fr.32 in Pr*.(p.169.1); Chrys.*hom.3.2 in Phil*.(11.214B); *Disp. Phot*.(M.88.556A).

πολύσημος, = foreg., of words: ἀρχή, Or.*Jo*.1.16(p.20.6; M.14.49B); λόγος, Eus.*e.th*.2.13(p.114.11; M.24.925C); δόξα, †Bas.*Is*.237(1.560B; M.30.536B); ζωή, Gr.Nyss.*Eun*.8(2 p.201.29; M.45.797C); of oracles of OT prophets, *Clem.ep.Petr*.1(M.2.25B).

***πολυσήμως**, *so as to have many meanings*, Clem.*ecl*.32(p.147.1; M.9.716B).

πολυσιτία, **ἡ**, *abundance of corn* or *food*, Isid.Pel.*epp*.1.424(M.78.1417C).

***πολυσκέδαστος**, *much-scattered*, Isid.Pel.*epp*.1.451(M.78.1429D).

***πολυσκελής**, *many-legged*, Clem.*str*.5.8(p.362.4; M.9.84A).

***πολύσκοτος**, *very dark*; met., of incest, †Jo.Jej.*poenit*.(M.88.1893D).

πολυσμάραγος, *loud-roaring*; of rivers, †Apoll.*met.Ps*.17:17(M.33.1332D); of sea, *ib*.138:9(1521C).

πολυσπέρματος, *with many seeds, well planted*; of a garden, Hipp.*haer*.5.9(p.102.5; M.16.3158C).

***πολύσπιλος**, *deeply stained*, Nil.*epp*.2.167(M.79.280C).

***πολυσπλαγχνία**, **ἡ**, *great compassion*; of Christ, Herm.*vis*.1.3.2; of God, Just.*dial*.55.3(M.6.596C).

πολύσπλαγχνος, *very compassionate*; of God, Herm.*sim*.5.7.4; Clem.*q.d.s*.39(p.186.3; πολυεύσπλαγχνος M.9.645); of gifts of God's mercy ἡ π. αὐτοῦ ἀνάπαυσις *A.Thom*.A 119(p.229.11).

πολύστημος, *with many ribs* or *upright timbers*, hence *well* or *strongly built* πλοίοις Θάρσις, οἱονεὶ π. Or.*Ps*.47:8(p.46).

πολύστομος, *uttered by many mouths*, Nonn.*par.Jo*.7:40(M.43.812B).

***πολυσύνακτος**, *gathered in abundance*, Eus.Al.*serm*.21.12(M.86.437C).

πολυσύνθετος, *compounded of many elements*; of the universe, Eus.*l.C*.12(p.233.1; M.20.1392C); ref. false division of man into many elements, suggested by Apollinarius' trichotomy, Gr.Nyss.*Apoll*.8(M.45.1140B); of a picture, ‡Nil.*fr.pasch*.2(M.79.1496D); of Eunomian conception of Trin., Gr.Nyss.*Eun*.9(2 p.207.17; M.45.804D) cit. s. διφυής; πολυειδῆ τινά φησι τὴν θείαν φύσιν καὶ π. *ib*.12 (1 p.301.20; M.45.1013A); ref. Arian teaching πολυμερῆ καὶ π.... τὸν θεὸν τῶν ὅλων. οὐ γὰρ ὅσον ἐστὶν ὁ θεὸς καταλαμβάνεσθαι...ἀλλ' ὅσον ἡ ἑκάστου δύναμις πρὸς κατάληψιν ἔρρωται Philost.*h.e*.10.2(M.65.584C).

***πολυσύντακτος**, *compiled out of many materials*; of a book, Thdr.Lect.*fr*.(p.397).

***πολυσύστατος**, *compounded of many elements*, Hipp.*haer*.7.21 (p.197.14; M.16.3303C) cit. s. πολύμορφος.

πολυσφρήγιστος, *well secured*, Nonn.*par.Jo*.15:11(M.43.873C).

[*]πολυσχεδής, = πολυσχιδής, *much-divided*, Gr.Agr.*Eccl*.6.4(M.98.988B); π. ... ἡ τῆς ἐπιθυμίας ἡδονή Jo.D.*spir.neq*.(M.95.89C); of pentecostal tongues, id.*hom*.11.4(M.96.765C).

[*]πολυσχεδῶς, *in many different ways*, Nil.*epp*.3.261(M.79.513D); Jo.D.*f.o*.3.1(M.94.981B); v. πολυσχιδῶς.

πολύσχημος, *in many forms*, Melet.*nat.hom*.4(M.64.1180D); of God as depicted in scripture, Dion.Ar.*d.n*.9.1(M.3.909B).

πολυσχιδής, cf. πολυσχεδής, *split into many parts*; hence of a book, *having many pages*, Thdr.Stud.*epp*.2.162(M.99.1516A).

***πολύσχιδος**, *much divisible*; fig., ref. Arian heresy ὕδραν τὴν... π. Epiph.*haer*.69.81(p.229.27; M.42.333D).

πολυσχιδῶς, **1.** *with many branches*; ref. veins in plants, Ast.Am.*hom*.3(M.40.208C); ref. human veins, Melet.*nat.hom*.26(M.64.1249B); **2.** *in many ways*, Clem.*paed*.3.4(p.251.21, v.l. πολυσχεδῶς M.8.592B); Gr.Nyss.*Eun*.12(1 p.313.4; M.45.1025D).

***πολυτεκνογονία, ἡ**, *much bringing forth of children*, ‡Chrys.*hom*.10(13.239E).

πολυτέλεια, ἡ, **1.** *great richness, sumptuousness* π. ἐδεσμάτων Herm.*mand*.6.2.5; π. ἱματίων Or.*hom.11.4 in Jer*.(p.81.29; M.13.372C); plur., Bas.*reg.fus*.20.1(2.364C; M.31.972B); **2.** *cost, expense*, Pall.*v.Chrys*.5(p.32.12; M.47.20).

πολυτελεύομαι, *feast luxuriously*, Meth.*res*.1.60(p.325.2; M.41.1157B).

***πολύτιλτος**, *spotted, discoloured*, ‡Hesych.H.*m.Long*.(M.93.1545B).

πολυτίμιος, *very expensive*, *Hom.Clem*.8.12.

πολύτιμος, *highly prized* or *honoured* πολυτιμότεροι γεγόνασιν μάγειροι γεωργῶν Clem.*paed*.2.1(p.160.13; M.8.393A); Hipp.*haer*.5.9 (p.102.9; M.16.3158C).

πολυτοκία, ἡ, *high yield of interest*, *Mir.Artem*.38(p.62.8).

πολυτράχηλος, *with many necks*, of sect of Acephaloi τὴν π. ἐκτεμεῖν πλάνην, πολλοὶ γάρ εἰσι τῶν Ἀκεφάλων αὐχένες Geo.Pis.*Sev*.64(M.92.1625B).

πολύτρεπτος, *much turning, changeable* καιροῖο π. Gr.Naz.*carm*.2.1.13.82(M.37.1234A); π. ... ἀπιστίαν Isid.Pel.*epp*.1.31(M.78.201B).

πολύτροπος, *turning many ways*, hence *wily, crafty*; of Devil, Meth.*symp*.8.10(p.92.4; M.18.152C); *Const.App*.3.12.2; Nonn.*par.Jo*.16:11(M.43.880A).

πολυτροφία, ἡ, *plentiful nourishment* π. τοῦ πνεύματος τοῦ ἁγίου Chrysipp.*enc.in Jo.Bapt*.5(p.35.11).

πολυτρόφος, *supplying food* π. ἄστυ *Orac.Sib*.14.139.

πολύυδρος, *flowing abundantly* π. ... πηγῆς Just.*dial*.102.5(M.6.713C).

πολύυλος, **1.** *rich in resources*; lit., *wealthy* τίς γὰρ τοῖς π. κοινωνία πρὸς τοὺς ἀκτήμονας; Nil.*Magn*.31(M.79.1005D); Eulog.*palm*.13(M.86.2937A); met. μόνος τῶν λογισμῶν ὁ τῆς κενοδοξίας ἐστὶ π. †Nil.*mal.cog*.15(M.79.1216D); πολυπείρων τε καὶ π. λογισμῶν τῆς κακίας Jo.Carp.*cap*.37(M.85.1844); **2.** *lengthy*; of a discourse, ‡Bas.*struct.hom*.2.6(1.341A; M.30.48B).

πολυύμνητος, **1.** *often sung*; of *Gloria in excelsis*, Dion.Ar.*c.h*.4.4 (M.3.181C); of *Ter sanctus*, *ib*.7.4(212B); *Lit.Jac*.(p.164.16); **2.** *greatly praised*; of Trin., Bas.*Spir*.45(3.38C; M.32.152A); Jo.D.*hom*.4.21(M.96.620B); Thdr.Stud.*epp*.2.8(M.99.1132A); of Christ, ‡Chrys.*hom*.6 (13.214C) cit. s. προμαχεών; **3.** *celebrated, greatly honoured, famous*; of persons, Clem.*prot*.12(p.83.19; M.8.237C); Bas.Sel.*or*.11.1(M.85.148B); of Christ's miracles, Eus.*d.e*.3.4(p.115.14; M.22.197B); of miracles of James of Nisibis, Thdt.*h.e*.2.30.3(3.905); iron. πολυύμνητον...ταύτην σοφιστικήν Gr.Naz.*or*.22.3(M.35.1133C).

πολυ(υ)πνία, ἡ, *sleeping much*, Jo.Clim.*scal*.19(M.88.937A); Anast.S.*qu.et resp*.8(M.89.392A).

πολυφαγ-έω, *eat many kinds of food* νηστεία...ἐστιν...τὸ μὴ ~ῆσαι. ἄσκησις γάρ ἐστιν ἐν μονοειδεῖ τροφῇ συνεσταλμένη τράπεζα Ant.Mon.*hom*.7(M.89.1453A).

***πολυφάνταστος**, *with many hallucinations*, Bas.*ep*.210.6(3.317C; M.32.777A).

***πολυφθογγία, ἡ**, *diversity of speech*; ref. Babel, Just.*dial*.102.4 (M.6.713C).

πολύφθορος, *corrupt in many ways* τὴν π. τῶν ἀνθρώπων φύσιν Isid.Pel.*epp*.2.139(M.78.584A).

πολυφίλητος, *much-loved*, Chrys.*fr.in Jer*.7:7(M.64.836C).

***πολύφλεβος**, *abundant* πηγὴν π. *Mir.Artem*.34(p.54.8).

πολύφλογος, *consuming*, ‡Chrys.*hom*.6(13.215A).

πολύφλοισβος, **1.** *loud-roaring*; met., *tumultuous* π. ... μύθῳ Nonn.*par.Jo*.10:20(M.43.836A); π. ... κόσμῳ *ib*.16:33(884B); π. μελάθρου 18:28(893C); **2.** *overflowing*, hence, met., *abundant* π. τραπέζης *ib*.6:12(796A).

πολύφροντις, **1.** *full of thought, thinking much*, Thdt.*rect.conf*.8 (M.6.1221A); **2.** *full of care, anxious*; of earthly life, id.*h.rel*.15(3.1221); of worldly affairs, Nil.*exerc*.67(M.79.800D).

πολυφυής, *very productive*; of land, Gr.Thaum.*pan.Or*.7(p.19.1; M.10.1073B).

***πολύφυρτος**, *thoroughly mixed*, Sophr.H.*or*.2.6(M.87.3224C).

***πολυφώνημα, τό**, *gossip*, *Pet.Ar*.3(M.26.820D).

***πολύφωτος**, **1.** *brightly shining, glorious* π. ἀκτῖνα τῆς θεαρχικῆς ἡλιοβολίας Dion.Ar.*c.h*.15.8(M.3.337A); id.*d.n*.3.1(M.3.860C); id.*ep*.8.6(M.3.1100A); **2.** *glorious, splendid*; of priesthood, Isid.Pel.*epp*.1.151(M.78.284C); of Church, Anast.S.*hex*.12(M.89.1072D); of Christ's disciples, Sophr.H.*triod*.(M.87.3905A); of BMV οὐρανὲ π. Jo.Mon.*hymn.Chrys*.6(M.96.1381C); **3.** *well illuminated*, hence, of the eye, *giving good vision*, Melet.*nat.hom*.2(M.64.1169D).

πολυχαρής, *joyful*, Melet.*nat.hom*.30(M.64.1277A).

***πολυχείμαστος**, *stormy*, Meth.*res*.2.25(p.381.9; M.18.328C).

***πολυχρονέω**, **1.** *tarry long*, Leont.N.*v.Sym*.12(M.93.1685A); **2.** *live long*, ‡Ath.*qu.Ant*.79(M.28.648A); Anast.S.*qu.et resp*.96(M.89.745D).

πολυχρόνιος, **1.** *long-continued* π. λιμόν Clem.*str*.1.23(p.93.16; M.8.896A); Or.*comm.in Ex*.4(p.246.9; M.12.269C); αἰχμαλωσίαν π. id.*hom.11.1 in Jer*.(p.79.7; M.13.368C); **2.** *of long duration* π. ἦμαρ *Orac.Sib*.1.69; ‡Jo.D.*ep.Thphl*.9(M.95.356D); **3.** *long-lasting, long enduring* φιλοσοφία...π. ἐστι συμβουλή Clem.*prot*.11(p.79.26; M.8.229B); Ath.*decr*.19(p.16.1; M.25.'456'(448)D); Bas.*iud*.2(2.214B; M.31.653C); **4.** *long living*, Or.*hom.12.10 in Jer*.(p.97.1; M.13.392D); Meth.*symp*.8.15(p.103.17; M.18.168A); id.*res*.2.22(p.376.12; M.18.328B).

πολυχρονίως, *for a long time* π. βιοῦν Tat.*orat*.14(p.16.2; M.6.837A); Clem.*str*.6.3(p.444.14; M.9.244C); τὰ π. καὶ χιλιοστῶς ἐκτελούμενα Areth.*Apoc*.1:1(M.106.501B).

πολύχωρος, *containing much, spacious, capacious* τὰ κυκλικὰ σχήματα...πολυχωρότερα Melet.*nat.hom*.1(M.64.1160D); of the mind πολυχωροτάτη ψυχὴ ταῖς ἁπάντων ἀρκοῦσα φροντίσιν Synes.*ep*.57(M.66.1397C); of hand of God, Gr.Nyss.*Apoll*.16(M.45.1156B).

***πολύψοφος**, *rattling*, ‡Paul.Sil.*therm.Pyth*.(M.86.2264).

πολυώδυνος, **1.** *suffering much pain*, *Orac.Sib*.3.504; ‡Sophr.H.*triod*.(M.87.3865D); **2.** *painful*; of illness, Nil.*epp*.1.245(M.79.173A); of earthly life, Ephr.3.533B; Isid.Pel.*epp*.1.181(M.78.301A); Melet.*nat.hom*.30(M.64.1277A).

***πολυώνητος**, *dearly bought*, Petr.II Al.*encycl*.6 ap.Thdt.*h.e*.4.22.21(M.33.1285A).

πολυωνυμία, ἡ, *multitude of names*; of divine appellations, Dion.Ar.*d.n*.1.8(M.3.597C).

πολυώνυμος, *with many names*; **1.** in gen. ὕβρις...ἡ π. καὶ πολυειδής Clem.*paed*.2.10(p.213.14; M.8.508B); of opinions about Christ, Isid.Pel.*epp*.1.235(M.78.328C); **2.** of gods of polytheism, Arist.*apol*.2.1; **3.** of God ὁ ὑπὲρ πᾶν ὄνομα ὤν, ἡμῖν π. γίνεται Gr.Nyss.*Eun*.10(2 p.230.7; M.45.832A); τὸ ὑπὲρ πᾶν ὄνομα, τὸ ἀνώνυμον ...π. δέ,...ἡ ζωή, τὸ φῶς, ὁ θεός, ἡ ἀλήθεια Dion.Ar.*d.n*.1.6(M.3.596A); **4.** of BMV ἡ π. ὄντως ‡Jo.D.*hom*.5(M.96.648C); **5.** (Naassene) of Spirit or Word, Hipp.*haer*.5.9(p.98.15; M.16.3154B); cf. Philo ap.Eus.*p.e*.11.15(533C; M.21.885B).

***πολυωνύμως**, *under many names* τῶν πάντων αἴτιον οἱ θεόσοφοι π. ... ὑμνῶσιν Dion.Ar.*d.n*.1.6(M.3.596A); Andr.Caes.*Apoc*.57(M.106.397D).

πολυωρέω, *treat with much care*, c. acc., Didym.*Ps*.11:8(M.39.1216B).

πολυώψ, *with many faces* τὸν χερουβικὸν ἔχων π. θρόνον Didym.*Trin*.1.26(M.39.392C).

[*]πομάριον (πωμάριν), τό, (Lat. *pomarium*) *orchard*, Pach.*reg*.A (p.16.19); πωμάριν ῥωμαϊστί ἐστιν ἡ λέξις, 'πώμαρα' γὰρ λέγουσιν τὰ κηπία Anast.S.*hod*.2(M.89.85A).

πομπεύς, ὁ, *guide*, of Jo. Bapt. π. κελεύθου Nonn.*par.Jo*.3:28(M.43.772B).

πομπεύ-ω, 1. *take part in a religious procession* ~ειν τῷ Διονύσῳ Hipp.*antichr*.49(p.33.6; M.10.769A); **2.** *escort in triumph*; pass., *be accorded a triumph, be fêted*, of S. Paul εἶπε περὶ τῶν πειρασμῶν...καὶ ὅτι πανταχοῦ ~εται παρὰ τοῦ θεοῦ ἐν τῷ Χριστῷ Chrys.*hom.6.1 in 2Cor*.(10.473E); with play on sense 8 infra τῆς κεφαλῆς ἀπετμήθη...ἐπομπεύθη δὲ μετὰ θάνατον, μᾶλλον ἢ ὅτε φερόμενος ἐπὶ τοῦ δίφρου Ast.Am.*hom*.4(M.40.224C); **3.** *go in triumph* μάρτυρα ~οντα ἀπὸ Πόντου Chrys.*pan.Phoc*.1(2.704A); κύριος...ἐπὶ γῆς ~ει ‡Meth.*Sym. et Ann*.1(M.18.349A); met., of mortal life, ‡Nil.*perist*.12.13(M.79.965C); **4.** *make show of, flaunt* ἀκολασίᾳ ἐπομπεύετο ‡Chrys.*Petr.et El*.2(2.733B); ~ων ἅπερ αὐτὸς οὐκ ἐγέννησεν Max.*ambig*.(M.91.1405A); **5.** *boast, make a show*, Tat.*orat*.26(p.28.12; M.6.864A); ἠγοράσατε...καινὸν φρόνημα...καὶ ἐν αὐτῷ ~ετε Ath.*Ar*.2.47(M.26.248B); **6.** *lead in triumph, lead captive* ἐκείνην ὁ δαίμων ~ει Bas.Sel.*or*.20.2(M.85.249A); **7.** *show openly, make spectacle of*, *Chron.Pasch*.p.46(M.92.168A); **8.** *be taken in procession, be publicly exhibited* in disgrace, of martyrs ὑπὸ φρουρὰν ~οντες ἐν τῷ κόσμῳ Or.*mart*.42(p.39.21; M.11.617C); in gen., Epiph.*haer*.76.1(p.340.20; M.42.516C); Jo.Mal.*chron*.2 p.24(M.97.89B).

πομπή, ἡ, 1. *procession*, pagan, at Kalends of January μετὰ παμμεγέθους π. προέρχονται *M.Das*.3.2; cf.Gr.Nyss.*or.catech*.18(p.75.11; M.45.53D); **2.** *solemnity*, of eucharistic worship πομπὰς καὶ ὕμνους πέμπειν Just.*1apol*.13.2(M.6.345B); **3.** *display, show*, Clem.*paed*.3.5(p.254.23; M.8.600B); theatrical, etc., Cyr.H.*catech*.19.6; θέατρα καὶ Ἑλληνικὰς π. *Const.App*.2.62.2; Chrys.*hom.83.4 in Mt*.(7.796A); **4.** *pomp* of Devil ἀποτάσσομαί σοι, σατανᾶ...καὶ πάσῃ τῇ π. αὐτοῦ. π. δὲ διαβόλου ἐστὶ θεατρομανίαι καὶ ἱπποδρομίαι, κυνηγεσία καὶ πᾶσα τοιαύτη ματαιότης Cyr.H.*catech*.19.6; καταγελάσατε τῆς σατανικῆς π. καὶ τῆς διαβολικῆς τέχνης Chrys.*hom.30.6 in Mt*.(7.356C); †Gregent.*leg.Hom*.17(M.86.589B); ass. pagan ritual processions, dances, etc., *M.Das*.3.3; †Gregent.*leg.Hom*.34(600B); in baptismal renunciation, *M.Das*.3.3; Cyr.H.*catech*.19.6; *Const.App*.7.41.2; Cyr.*glaph.Gen*.5(1.177A); **5.** *disgrace* ζημία χρημάτων,...ἀτιμία, οὔτε ἡ τοσαύτη π. Chrys.*stat*.13.2(2.136B).

πομπικῶς, *for making an impression*, Max.*ep*.6(M.91.432B).

πομπός, ὁ, *guide*; of guardian angel, Gr.Thaum.*pan.Or*.5(p.14.16; M.10.1068C); met. μετὰ πάσης...σοφίας ὥσπερ τινὸς ἀγαθοῦ π. καὶ ἱερέως...προσίωμεν τῷ θεῷ *ib*.12(p.28.25; 1085C).

πομφολυγώδης, *frothy, like bubbles*; met., *unsubstantial*, Gr.Nyss.*or.dom*.1(p.14.18; M.44.1128C); id.*Eun*.7(2 p.159.27; M.45.748D).

***πονημάτιον, τό,** *short treatise*, Aët.*synt*.ap.Epiph.*haer*.76.11(p.352.1; M.42.545C); Didym.*Trin*.2.8(M.39.608C); Cosm.Ind.*top*.7(M.88.340D).

πονηρεύ-ω, *act wickedly* ~ειν τι ἐν τῇ ἐξηγήσει Just.*1apol*.61.1(v.l. ~εσθαι; M.6.420B); but usu. med. ἄνθρωπος ἀγαπῶν τὸν ~όμενον *T.Aser* 2.3; μὴ ~εσθε ὀπίσω τῶν ἐπιθυμιῶν ὑμῶν *T.Jud*.13.2; γλώσσης, ἐν ᾗ ~εται Herm.*vis*.2.2.3; ~εται ὅτι λυπεῖ τὸ πνεῦμα τὸ ἅγιον id.*mand*.10.3.2; ἀγγέλους...~σαμένους καὶ ἀποστάντας τοῦ θεοῦ Just.*dial*.79.1(M.6.661B); of Devil φρονίμως ~όμενος Clem.*str*.2.13(p.143.25; M.8.996A); οἱ...τοιαῦτα ~όμενοι Ath.*decr*.2(p.2.11; M.25.'425'(417)C); ἐπονηρεύσατο ποιῆσαι τῷ πλησίον Diod.*Ps*.53:6(M.33.1591C); Cyr.*Am*.73(3.333C).

πονηρία, ἡ, A. *wickedness, evil, malice*; **1.** def. and descriptions τυφλὸν γάρ τί ἐστιν ἡ π. καὶ βουλομένη ὡς ἰσχυροτέρα τοῦ χρεὼν νικᾶν αὐτὸ Or.*Cels*.1.61(p.112.1; M.11.772B); cf. *definiunt quidam* πονηρίαν *...spontaneam vel voluntariam esse malitiam*, id.*sel.in Ps*.36:4(M.12.1332C); not self-existent οὐ γάρ ἐστιν ὑφεστώς, ὥσπερ τι ζῷον, ἡ π. Bas.*hom*.9.5(2.78A; M.31.341B); *ib*.9.8(2.80C; 348A); οὐ γὰρ τῶν ἐκ φύσεως, ἀλλὰ τῶν ἐκ προαιρέσεως ἐπιγινομένων ἐστὶν ἡ π. Chrys.*hom. 19.6 in Mt*.(7.254A); τοιοῦτον γὰρ ἡ π. οὐδενὶ βούλεται εἴκειν, πρὸς ἓν βλέπει μόνον, ὥστε τὸν ἐπιβουλευόμενον ἀνελεῖν id.*hom.51.3 in Jo*.(8.302B); π. ἐστιν ἐπιστήμη, μᾶλλον δὲ ἀσχημοσύνη δαιμονιώδης, ἀληθείας ἀποστερηθεῖσα, καὶ τοὺς πολλοὺς λανθάνειν δοκοῦσα...π. ἐστιν εὐθύτητος ἐναλλαγή, πεπλανημένη ἔννοια...δαιμονιώδης βίος Jo.Clim.*scal*.24(M.88.981B,C); **2.** in gen., *2Clem*.13.1; *Barn*.4.12; Chrys.*hom. 83.3 in Jo*.(8.492E); esp. of heretics, Ath.*hom.in Mt.11*:27(M.25.213C); id.*ep.Jov*.1(M.26.816A)ap.Thdt.*h.e*.4.3.4; personified, Herm.*sim*.9.15.3; dist. from κακία: τὴν ἐφεξῆς γεγενημένην π. ἐν τῇ κακίᾳ Thdt.*Jer*.11:8(2.469); **3.** origin demonic, Mac.Aeg.*hom*.24.3(M.34.664D); assisted by passions, *ib*.25.4(669C); ἑρπετῶν πνευμάτων πονηρίας ἐν αὐτῇ [sc. ψυχῇ] καταλυόντων *ib*.28.1(712A); working from within, *ib*.42.3(772A); demons called ἄγγελοι πονηρίας, Herm.*mand*. 6.2.1; τῆς...π. ... ἀπαυγάσματα Tat.*orat*.15(p.17.2; M.6.840A); πνεύματα πονηρίας Mac.Aeg.*hom*.21.2(M.34.656D); *ib*.21.3(657A); Devil ἄρχων τῆς π. *ib*.5.1(496A); τῶν ὀκτὼ πνευμάτων τῆς π. Nil.*spir.mal*. tit.(M.79.1145); **4.** effects: destruction of life, Herm.*mand*.2.1; deprivation of knowledge of God, Or.*Jo*.19.3(1; p.301.9f.; M.14.529A); brutalizing soul, id.*princ*.1.8.4(p.104.10; M.11.180C); but also means of purification ὁ κύριος ἐν τῇ πιστῇ ψυχῇ γινόμενος, καὶ διαπερῶν αὐτὴν...τὰ ἄγρια τῆς π. κύματα Mac.Aeg.*hom*.44.7(M.34.784B); ἡ γὰρ π. οὐ συγχωρεῖ διὰ μετανοίας ἀναστῆσαι τοῦ πτώματος *Schol*.5 in Jo.Clim.*scal*.24(M.88.985B); **5.** remedies: faith, though not always efficacious ἐπίστευσαν δὲ ἐν ὑποκρίσει, καὶ πᾶσα π. οὐκ ἀπέστη ἀπ' αὐτῶν Herm.*vis*.3.6.1; spiritual regeneration, Clem.*paed*.1.6(p.109.19; M.8.289A); Christ's passion, Just.*dial*.41.1(M.6.564B); cf.*ib*.114.4(740C); punishment, Meth.*res*.1.31(p.265.8; M.41.1141B); though not to be totally uprooted in this life, *ib*.1.44(p.293.14; 1116A); spiritual heaven, Mac.Aeg.*hom*.24.4(M.34.665A); **6.** in rel. to God οὐδὲν φαῦλον ὑπὸ τοῦ θεοῦ πεποίηται, τὴν π. ἡμεῖς ἀνεδείξαμεν Tat.*orat*.11(p.12.16; M.6.829B); ὁ διάβολος δέδεικται ὅτι τοιοῦτος μὲν οὐκ ἐκτίσθη, ἐξ ἰδίας δὲ π. εἰς τοῦτο κατέπεσε Or.*princ*.1.8.3(p.100.5); λιθίνη γὰρ οὐδενὶ ἔκτισται ὑπὸ θεοῦ καρδία, ἀλλ' ἀπὸ τῆς π. τοιαύτη γίνεται *ib*.3.1.14(p.219.6; M.11.276A); τὸ θεῖον, ἀνεννόητον ἄρα πονηρίας Meth.*symp*.8.16(p.104.14; M.18.168B); **7.** in dualist heresies, Valent. ἐκ δὲ τῆς λύπης τὰ πνευματικὰ τῆς π. διδάσκουσι γεγονέναι· ὅθεν τὸν διάβολον τὴν γένεσιν ἐσχηκέναι...καὶ πᾶσαν τὴν πνευματικὴν τῆς π. ὑπόστασιν. ἀλλὰ τὸν μὲν δημιουργὸν υἱὸν τῆς μητρὸς αὐτῶν λέγουσι, τὸν δὲ κοσμοκράτορα κτίσμα τοῦ δημιουργοῦ· καὶ τὸν μὲν κοσμοκράτορα γινώσκειν τὰ ὑπὲρ αὐτόν, ὅτι πνεῦμά ἐστι τῆς π. Iren.*haer*.1.5.4(M.7.497A,B); Clem.*exc.Thdot*.81(p.132.1; M.9.696B).

B. *evil deed* or *thought* τῶν π. ὧν εἰργάσαντο Herm.*vis*.3.7.2; αἱ π. αὐτῶν ἐν ταῖς καρδίαις ἐμμένουσιν *ib*.3.6.2; incl. μοιχεία, ὑπερηφανία etc., id.*mand*.8.3; ἀποβάλλετε τὰς π. τοῦ αἰῶνος τούτου id.*sim*.6.1.4.

***πονηροποιός,** *causing, making evil*, Epiph.*haer*.26.11(p.290.12; M.41.349B); *ib*.66.53(p.90.4; M.42.109A).

πονηρός, 1. *imperfect, maimed* παραλυτικοὺς καὶ ἐκ γενετῆς πονηροὺς ὑγιεῖς πεποιηκέναι Just.*1apol*.22.6(M.6.364A) s.v.l., cf. τοὺς ἐκ γενετῆς καὶ κατὰ τὴν σάρκα πηρούς id.*dial*.69.6(M.6.640A); **2.** *wretched, dreadful, evil* ἀποθανεῖτε θανάτῳ π. *T.Reub*.6.6; π. τῶν Αἰγυπτίων δουλείας Cyr.H.*catech*.19.1; Chrys.*hom.32.4 in Mt*.(7.370C); of present dispensation or life, cf.*4Esdr*.7.12; διατηρήσειέ σε ἀπὸ τοῦ ἐνεστῶτος αἰῶνος π. Hegem.*Arch*.5(p.6.1; M.10.1433B); of Day of Judgement τὴν δὲ π. ἡμέραν κακώσεως ἡμέραν ὁ Σύμμαχος εἴρηκεν. αἰνίττεται δὲ...τὴν τῆς κρίσεως ἡμέραν Thdt.*Ps*.40:2(1.865); **3.** *wicked, morally evil*; **a.** of persons, Just.*1apol*.27.1(M.6.369B); Athenag.*leg*.29.2(M.6.957C); Or.*princ*.3.1.11(p.213.7; M.11.268B); **b.** of things, qualities, etc. δόλῳ π. Ign.*Eph*.7.1; Herm.*mand*.3.5; ἐπιθυμίαι π. *ib*.12.2.2; ἐν συνειδήσει π. *Barn*.19.12; Just.*dial*.93.1(M.6.697A); Athenag.*leg*.36.1(M.6.969B); τὰ π. τῆς τρυφῆς συμπόσια Chrys.*hom.39.9 in 1Cor*.(10.378A); of 'evil' eye (cf. Mt.6:23) πάντα ὁρᾷ ἐν εὐθύτητι καρδίας μὴ ἐπιδεχόμενος ὀφθαλμοὺς π. ἀπὸ τῆς πλάνης τοῦ κόσμου *T.Isach*.4.6; **c.** of evil demiurge Μαρκίων...καὶ Κέρδων...ὁρίζουσιν εἶναι τρεῖς τὰς τοῦ παντὸς ἀρχάς, ἀγαθόν, δίκαιον, ὕλην· τινὲς δὲ τούτων μαθηταὶ προστιθέασι τετάρτην λέγοντες ἀγαθόν, δίκαιον, π., ὕλην· οἱ δὲ πάντες τὸν μὲν ἀγαθὸν οὐδὲν ὅλως πεποιηκέναι, τὸν δὲ δίκαιον οἱ μὲν τὸν π., οἱ δὲ μόνον δίκαιον ὀνομάζουσι...Ἀπελλῆς...ἕτερον...τὸν δημιουργὸν τοῦ παντός,...ἕτερον δὲ πύρινον τὸν φανέντα, ἕτερον δὲ π. Hipp.*haer*.10.19,20(p.280.2,22; M.16.3435C; 3438B); εἰ μὲν γὰρ ἀπογραψάμενός τις...ἵστατο πρὸς τὸ π. εἶναι τὸν δημιουργόν, ἄλλων ἔδει λόγων πρὸς αὐτὸν Or.*princ*.3.1.9(p.209.11; M.11.264A); δύο σέβει [sc. Manes] θεούς...τὸν μὲν ἀγαθόν, τὸν δὲ π. εἰσηγεῖται Hegem.*Arch*.7(p.9.13; M.10.1437A); Jo.D.*Man*.1.2(M.94.1508B); v. δημιουργός; **d.** of evil spirits ἔστιν γὰρ ἐν αὐτῷ [sc. οἴνῳ] τέσσαρα πνεύματα π. *T.Jud*.16.1; ἄγγελος π. ἐσόφιζεν αὐτούς *Barn*.9.4; π. καὶ πλάνων πνευμάτων Just.*dial*.30.2(M.6.540A); π. δαιμόνων Tat.*orat*.22(p.24.19; M.6.856A); **e.** of Devil ψυχὴ...βασανίζεται ὑπὸ τοῦ π. πνεύματος *T.Aser* 6.5; Eus.*h.e*.3.27.1(M.20.273A); ἀποτάσσομαί σοι, σατανᾶ, σοὶ τῷ π. καὶ ὠμοτάτῳ τυράννῳ Cyr.H.*catech*.19.4; hence **4.** ὁ π. *the Devil*; **a.** as enemy of Christians, *Barn*.19.11; Clem.*paed*.1.7(p.123.29; M.8.317C); Or.*hom.1.15 in Jer*.(p.14.12; M.13.273C); conquered by Christ as second Adam, Meth.*symp*.3.6(p.33.9; M.18.69B); δι' ἕκαστον ὑμῶν ὁ π. αὐτῷ μόνῳ τὸ πλεῖον ἐχθραίνων προσπολεμεῖ *Clem.ep*.17(M.2.53A); τὰ μυστικὰ σύμβολα...ἀποτρόπαια...τῶν κατ' ἐπιβουλὴν τοῦ π. τοῖς πεπιστευκόσιν ἐπαγομένων Gr.Nyss.*Eun*.11(2 p.271.9; M.45.880D); πολλὰ γὰρ τὰ δίκτυα τοῦ π. *Const.App*.1.9.1; πονηρὸν...τὸν διάβολον καλεῖ, κελεύων ἡμᾶς ἄσπονδον πρὸς αὐτὸν ἔχειν πόλεμον Chrys.*hom.19.6 in Mt*.(7.253E); φθονήσας τῷ ἀνθρώπῳ ὁ π. ...ἠπάτησεν αὐτὸν Anast.S.*hod*.4(M.89.93C); as enemy of martyrs,

*M.Polyc.*17.1; **b.** as author of error, *Barn.*2.10; esp. of heresy, Eus. *h.e.*3.27.1(M.20.273A); Eulog.*fr.Trin.*1.3(p.363); **c.** ref. origin of Devil; not created evil, *Hom.Clem.*19.16,17; *ib.*20.8; uncreated (Manich.), Serap.*Man.*26(p.41; M.18.1120D); Jo.D.*Man.*1.46(M.94. 1548B); **d.** ref. his destiny; delay in his destruction serves to test the righteous, Mac.Aeg.*pat.*2(M.34.868A); **e.** ref. trinity of evil acc. Origen *ἐπὰν τὸ πνεῦμα τοῦ π. βλέπωμεν ἀντιπρᾶττον ἡμῶν τοῖς πράγμασιν...ταῦτα πάσχοντες τρεῖς φυλακὰς τῆς νυκτὸς τοῦ ἐν τοῖς πειρασμοῖς σκότους διανύσωμεν...ἀγωνιζόμενοι καλῶς...πρώτην φυλακὴν τὸν πατέρα τοῦ σκότους...καὶ δευτέραν τὸν υἱὸν αὐτοῦ τὸν ἀντικείμενον...καὶ τρίτην τὸ ἐναντίον τῷ ἁγίῳ πνεύματι πνεῦμα* Or.*comm.in Mt.*11.6(p.44.4; M.13.920C); *τῇ τρίτῃ δὲ ἡμέρᾳ...ἀνέστη, ἵνα ῥυσάμενος ἀπὸ τοῦ π. καὶ τοῦ υἱοῦ αὐτοῦ, ἐν ᾧ τὸ ψεῦδος ἦν καὶ...πάντα τὰ ἐναντία οἷς ἐστιν ὁ Χριστός,...περιποιήσῃ τοῖς ῥυσθεῖσι βαπτίσασθαι τὸ πνεῦμα καὶ τὴν ψυχὴν καὶ τὸ σῶμα* *ib.*12.20(p.115.22; 1029B); **5.** neut. as subst., *evil*; **a.** in gen., *Barn.*20.2; Meth.*res.*2.2(p.332. 18; M.18.300B); *Hom.Clem.*19.23; **b.** ref. 'knowledge of good and evil', Meth.*symp.*3.7(p.34.11; M.18.72A); Manich. *τὸ δὲ ἐν παραδείσῳ φυτὸν...αὐτός ἐστιν ὁ Ἰησοῦς, ἡ γνῶσις αὐτοῦ, ἡ ἐν τῷ κόσμῳ· ὁ δὲ λαμβάνων διακρίνει τὸ καλὸν καὶ τὸ π.* Hegem.*Arch.*11(p.18.5; M.10. 1445A); *τὸ δὲ καὶ τὸν θεὸν ἀπαγορεύειν τὴν διάγνωσιν καλοῦ τε καὶ φαύλου...ἆρ' οὐχ ὑπερβολὴν ἀτοπίας ἔχει; τί γὰρ ἂν ἠλιθιώτερον γένοιτο, τοῦ μὴ δυναμένου διαγινώσκειν καλὸν καὶ π.;* Juln.ap.Cyr. *Juln.*3(6².89A); **6.** ref. Lord's Prayer, interprns. of *τοῦ π.*; **a.** as *from the Evil One*, Or.*or.*30.1(p.393.10; M.11.545C); cf.id.*sel.in Ps.* 36:9(M.12.1332C); *Hom.Clem.*19.2; Cyr.H.*catech.*23.18; Gr.Nyss.*or. dom.*5(p.114.7; M.44.1192B); *Lit.*ap.*Const.App.*8.10.19; Petr.Laod. *or.dom.*(p.111.8; M.86.3329C); **b.** as *from evil*, Chrys.*hom.in Mt.*7:14 (3.31D); incl. evil caused both by Satan and by men, ‡Chrys.*or. dom.*(8.150A); **c.** both senses allowed, Max.*or.dom.*(M.90.904Cff.).

***πονηρόφρων**, *evil-minded*, *Did.*3.6; *Const.App.*7.7.2.

πονικός, *working, labouring*, *Apophth.Patr.*(M.65.120B); *ib.* (209D); Jo.Mosch.*prat.*178(M.87.3048B).

πονικῶς, *laboriously*, *A.Petr.et Andr.*1(p.117.14).

πόνος, ὁ, *toil, suffering*, of spiritual struggle *π. καρδίας ἐγὼ ἀλγῶ T.Jos.*7.2; *τοὺς δίχα πόνων εἰληφότας τῶν ἁμαρτημάτων τὴν ἄφεσιν* Thdt.*Ps.*50:1(1.932); of mental labour, *Hom.Clem.*17.6; of ascetic discipline *τῶν τῆς ἀσκήσεως π.* Pall.*v.Chrys.*5(p.29.6; M.47.18); id. *h.Laus.*(M.34.1043B); Mac.Aeg.*or.*5(M.34.856C); *κενοδοξία, τοὺς π. κατατοξεύουσα* Nil.*Eulog.*14(M.79.1112A); *εἰδέναι...τότε φαμὲν τούς τινων π., τοὺς διὰ...προσευχῆς καὶ ἀσκήσεως τὸν τῶν ὅλων θεόν, ὅτε κατανεύει τοῖς αἰτήμασιν αὐτῶν...ἐλεεῖ γὰρ ἑτοιμῶς τοὺς αὐτόκλητον ποιουμένους τὴν διὰ πόνου ταπείνωσιν* Cyr.*Is.*5.3(2.814C).

ποντίζω, reflex., *plunge, immerse* oneself, c. *εἰς*, Nil.*epp.*4.1(M. 79.544B).

ποντικός, ὁ, *weasel*, Gr.Mag.*dial.*(tr.Zach.)3.4(M.*PL.*77.226A).

***ποντισμός, ὁ**, *sinking, engulfing*, Jo.D.*Man.*1.41(M.94.1545A).

***ποντιστήριον, τό**, *depth of the sea*, fig. *κατεπόντισέν με εἰς τὰ π. τῶν αὐτοῦ διδαγμάτων* Ephr.2.293A.

***ποντογείτων**, *near the sea*; of Danube in lower reaches, Geo.Pis. *bell.Avar.*30(M.92.1266A, v.l. *παντο-*).

***ποντογέφυρα, ἡ**, *pontoon*, Thphn.*chron.*p.269(M.108.668A).

***ποντοπόρεια, ἡ**, *sea-journey*, Epiph.*haer.*37.9(p.62.5; M.41. 653B); Nil.*Eulog.*1(M.79.1096A).

***ποντοπορεύς**, *sea-going*, Gr.Naz.*carm.*2.1.17.5(M.37.1262A).

ποντόω, **1.** *journey by sea*, Jo.Mon.*hymn.Petr.*3(M.96.1392C); **2.** *drown*, Pall.*v.Chrys.*20(p.126.11; M.47.71); Nil.*Alb.*(M.79.705D).

πόππυσμα, τό, *clucking*; of barbarian speech, Jo.D.*carm.pent.*79 (p.216; M.96.836C).

ποππυσμός, ὁ, = foreg.; to coax a horse, Thdr.Stud.*epp.*1.49 (M.99.1088A); *kiss*, *ib.*2.144(1453A).

πορεία, ἡ, *journey*; **1.** of heavenly bodies, *course* *ὁ διατάξας ἐν π. φωστῆρας Pss.Sal.*19.2; Arist.*apol.*4.2; *Hom.Clem.*2.23; **2.** medic. *διάχυσις λέπρας ἐστὶν ὡσανεὶ βάδισις καὶ π. ῥευστική* Clem.*fr.*34(p.218. 9); **3.** of soul's journey, in death *τὴν κοινὴν στειλαμένου π.* Evagr. *h.e.*3.23(p.121.1; M.86.2645A); in heavenly ascent, Tat.*orat.*16(p.17. 22; M.6.840C); Or.*Cels.*7.3(p.155.11; M.11.1424C) cit. s. *ἄνοδος*; Eus. *v.C.*4.55(p.140.21; M.20.1208A); *τὴν πρὸς τὸν...θεὸν π.* *ib.*4.63(p.144.5; 1220A); *τὴν τὰ ἄνω π.* Bas.*hom.in Ps.*1(1.91D; M.29.213C); **4.** of Christ's Ascension, Eus.*v.C.*3.43(p.95.30; M.20.1104A); Cyr.*Jo.*11(4. 932D); of descent to Hades, Or.*Jo.*6.35(18; p.144.9; M.14.260B); **5.** *way, course*, of life and conduct *κατευθύνοντες τὴν π. ... ἐν ὁσιότητι 1Clem.*48.4; *ib.*62.1; Eus.*d.e.*9.13(p.432.19; M.22.697A); *μεταμάθωμεν τὴν θείαν π.* Thdt.*Ezech.*18:41(2.815); Proc.G.*Num.* 21:1(M.87.856C).

πορεύ-ω, med.; **1.** *go*; of departure from life, *1Clem.*5.4; **2.** met., *walk, behave, conduct one's life* *∼εσθαι ὑπηκόους ὄντας* *ib.*13.3; *∼ώμεθα ἐν ταῖς ἐντολαῖς* Polyc.*ep.*2.2; *∼όμενοι κατὰ τὴν ἀλήθειαν* *ib.*5.2; *∼ομένων ἐν ὁδῷ θανάτου Barn.*19.2; *κατ' ἀξίαν τῶν πράξεων ∼εσθαι* Just.*1apol.*12.1(M.6.341C); *Ep.Lugd.*ap.Eus.*h.e.*5.1.9(M.20. 412A); **3.** of time, *advance*, Philost.*h.e.*9.12(M.65.577A); **4.** as fut. auxiliary *ὅπερ εἰμί, καὶ διαμεῖναι ∼ομαι M.Scill.*9.

πορθμευτής, ὁ, *conveyer, conductor*; of Christ, Synes.*hymn.*5.8 (p.35; M.66.1608).

***πορνάς, ἡ**, *harlot*; of Helena, consort of Simon Magus *τὴν δὲ σύζυγον π. πνεῦμα ἅγιον εἶναι τετόλμηκεν λέγειν* Epiph.*haer.*21.2 (p.240.1; M.41.288B); Tim.CP *haer.*(M.86.25C); met. (in contrast to Church as bride) of Jewish and heret. bodies, Anast.S.*hex.*12(M.89. 1072C).

πορνεία, ἡ, *fornication, unchastity, sexual impurity*; **1.** fanciful etym. *π. ἢ διὰ τὸ πυροῦν τὴν νεότητα, ἢ διὰ τὸ πηροῦν, ἢ ὡς ἐκτυφλοῦν, τὸν νοῦν, ἢ διὰ τὸ πόρρωθεν νεύειν* ‡Ath.*def.*11(M.28.552A); **2.** *illicit intercourse* in gen. *μὴ ἀναβαινέτω σου ἐπὶ τὴν καρδίαν περὶ γυναικὸς ἀλλοτρίας ἢ περὶ π. τινός* Herm.*mand.*4.1.1; Or.*fr.*2 *in Jer.*(p.199.15; M.13.545A); ref. Jo.8:41 *σύ, ὁ φάσκων μὲν ἐκ παρθένου γεγεννῆσθαι, ἐκ π. δὲ γεγεννημένος...τάχα δὲ διὰ τὸ τῶν ἀνθρώπων τινὰς μὲν εἶναι ἐκ τοῦ διαβόλου, ἑτέρους δὲ γεγεννῆσθαι ἐκ τοῦ θεοῦ, πάντας ἂν ὑγιῶς λέγοιμεν τοὺς μὴ γεγεννημένους ἐκ θεοῦ, ἐκ π. γεγεννῆσθαι, οὐ γὰρ ἐκ νύμφης, ἀλλ' ἐκ πόρνης, τῆς ὕλης, οὓς γεννᾷ ὁ διάβολος* id.*Jo.*20.16(14; pp.347.16,348.3; M.14.608C,609A); *ἥ τε π. φθορὰ τῆς οἰκείας ἐστὶ σαρκός, οὐκ ἐπὶ παιδοποιΐᾳ γινομένη, ἀλλ' ἡδονῇ χαριζομένη τὸ πᾶν, ὅπερ ἐστὶν ἀκρασίας σύμβολον Const.App.*6.28.3; *καλεῖ π. μὲν τὴν οὐ κατὰ γάμον γινομένην συνουσίαν* Thdt.*Rom.*1:31(3.27); punished by deprivation in case of clergy, *Can.App.*25; disqualifies from ordination, *ib.*61; in rel. to marriage *ἡ π. γάμος οὐκ ἔστιν. ἀλλ' οὐδὲ γάμου ἀρχή· ὥστε, ἐὰν ᾖ δυνατὸν τοὺς κατὰ πορνείαν συναπτομένους χωρίζεσθαι, τοῦτο κράτιστον. ἐὰν δὲ στέργωσιν ἐκ παντὸς τρόπου τὸ συνοικέσιον, τὸ μὲν τῆς π. ἐπιτίμιον γνωριζέτωσαν· ἀφιέσθωσαν δέ, ἵνα μή χεῖρόν τι γένηται* Bas.*ep.*199 *can.*26(3.293E; M.32.724B); *γάμος δὲ πορνείας ἀναιρετικὸν φάρμακον* Chrys.*hom.in 1Cor.*7:2(3.195A); marriage regarded as *π.* by Tatian, Iren.*haer.*1.28.1(M.7.691A); view condemned as blasphemy, Clem.*str.*3.12(p.237.7; M.8.1189B); **3.** specifically, *prostitution*, ref. exposed children *τοὺς πάντας σχεδὸν ὁρῶμεν ἐπὶ πορνείᾳ προάγοντας* Just.*1apol.*27.1(M.6.369B); *ἀγορὰν στήσαντες πορνείας καὶ καταγωγὰς ἀθέσμους πεποιημένοι* Athenag.*leg.*34.1(M.6.968A); **4.** linked with adultery, but dist. therefrom *μοιχεία...καὶ π. καὶ ἀνδροφονία* Just.*dial.*93.1(M.6.697A); Or.*or.*28.10(p.381.14; M.11.529B); id.*hom.*5.5 *in Jer.*(p.36.4; M.13. 304B); as object of Devil's desire, id.*Jo.*20.22(20; p.354.16; M.14. 620B); *Can.App.*61; *Const.App.*6.27.8; linked with adultery as ground of divorce after which remarriage is allowable *τὸν δὲ μὴ δυνηθέντα τῇ μιᾷ ἀρκεσθῆναι τελευτησάσῃ ἢ ἕνεκέν τινος προφάσεως, ἢ π. ἢ μοιχείας ἢ ἄλλης αἰτίας, χωρισμοῦ γενομένου, συναφθέντα δευτέρᾳ γυναικὶ ἢ γυναῖκα δευτέρῳ ἀνδρί, οὐκ αἰτιᾶται ὁ θεῖος λόγος οὐδὲ ἀπὸ τῆς ἐκκλησίας καὶ τῆς ζωῆς ἀποκηρύττει, ἀλλὰ διαβαστάζει διὰ τὸ ἀσθενές* Epiph.*haer.*59.4(p.368.17; M.41.1024C); marital infidelity not *π.* but *μοιχεία*, Chrys.*hom.in 1Cor.*7:2(3.198C); distinction defined *π. μὲν εἶναι...τὴν χωρὶς ἀδικίας ἑτέρου γινομένην τισὶ τῆς ἐπιθυμίας ἐκπλήρωσιν· μοιχείαν δέ, τὴν ἐπιβουλήν τε καὶ τὴν ἀδικίαν τοῦ ἀλλοτρίου* Gr.Nyss.*ep.can.*4(M.45.228C); **5.** of illicit intercourse committed by married people, hence incl., or identified with, adultery; **a.** by either party, Bas.*moral.*73.1(2.308A; M.31.849D); **b.** by married man (who by custom is not divorced by his wife), id. *ep.*188 *can.*9(3.273E; M.32.677B); with unmarried woman, *ib.*199 *can.* 21(3.292E; M.721A); Chrys.*hom.*19.2 *in 1Cor.*(10.161E); *μετὰ τὴν π. ὁ ἀνὴρ οὐκ ἔστιν ἀνήρ* *ib.*19.3(162D); with married woman, cf.id. *hom.*17.4 *in Mt.*(7.228B); **c.** by married woman *ἐὰν...ἐπιμένῃ τῇ π. αὐτῆς καὶ συνζῇ ὁ ἀνὴρ μετ' αὐτῆς, ἔνοχος γίνεται τῆς ἁμαρτίας αὐτῆς καὶ κοινωνὸς τῆς μοιχείας αὐτῆς* Herm.*mand.*4.1.5; of offence of which Joseph suspected BMV, Just.*dial.*78.3(M.6.657C); **d.** in opinion of some rigorists all *π.* is really *μοιχεία* since only permissible union is in marriage, Gr.Nyss.*ep.can.*4(M.45.228B); **6.** of marriages contracted without permission by those who are not of free condition; **a.** by girls under parental authority, cf.Bas.*ep.*199 *can.*38(3.295D; M.32.728C); **b.** by slave women, *ib.can.*40(296A; M. 729A); cf. *οἱ ἄνευ τῶν κρατούντων γάμοι π. εἰσιν* *ib.can.*42(296B; M. 729A); **7.** of illicit union with heathens, cf.Just.*dial.*132.1(M.6.781C); v. *πορνεύω*; **8.** of polygamy, Clem.*str.*3.12(p.237.11; M.8.1189B); including many successive marriages *τὸ δὲ ὑπὲρ τὴν τριγαμίαν προφανὴς π. Const.App.*3.2.2; Bas.*ep.*188 *can.*4(3.271D; M.32.673A); **9.** ref. Mt.19:9 and Mt.5:32(cit.ap.Thphl.Ant.*Autol.*3.13(M.6.1140B), etc.); interpreted as *adultery*, Clem.*str.*2.23(p.193.6; M.8.1096B);

Bas.*ep*.199 *can*.48(3.297B; M.32.732B); Chrys.*hom*.*17.4 in Mt*.(7.228A) etc.; as *prostitution* by married woman, perh., Gr.Naz.*or*.37.8(M. 36.292B); Chrys.*Jud*.2.3(1.604D); discussed *ζητηθείη δ' ἄν, εἰ διὰ τοῦτο ⟨μόνον⟩ κελεύει τὴν γυναῖκα ἀπολῦσαι, ⟨τί ἔσται⟩ ἐὰν μὴ ἐπὶ πορνείᾳ μὲν ἁλῷ, φέρε δ' εἰπεῖν ἐπὶ φαρμακείᾳ ἢ ἀναιρέσει...παιδίου ...εἰ εὐλόγως τὴν τοιαύτην ἀποβαλεῖ, ὡς τοῦ σωτῆρος κωλύοντος 'παρεκτὸς λόγου πορνείας' ἀπολῦσαι...ἐφίστημι τοίνυν διὰ τί μὲν οὐκ εἶπε· 'μηδεὶς ἀπολυέτω τὴν γυναῖκα αὐτοῦ παρεκτὸς λόγου π.', φησὶ δὲ 'ὃς ἂν ἀπολύσῃ...ποιεῖ αὐτὴν μοιχευθῆναι'. ποιεῖ...γὰρ...μοιχευθῆναι τὴν γυναῖκα ὁ ἀπολύων αὐτὴν μὴ πορνεύσασαν. ... τὴν δ' ἁλοῦσαν φαρμακίδα...ἀπολογίαν ἔχειν ἢ μή, καὶ σὺ ζητήσαις ἄν. δύναται γὰρ καὶ παρ' ἄλλας αἰτίας παρὰ τὴν ἀπόλυσιν ποιεῖν ὁ ἀνὴρ μοιχευθῆναι τὴν ἑαυτοῦ γυναῖκα* Or.*comm.in Mt*.14.24(p.342.25; M.13.1248A); **10.** *unchastity, lewdness*; in gen., *Did*.3.3; *οἱ πάλαι μὲν πορνείαις χαίροντες, νῦν δὲ σωφροσύνην μόνην ἀσπαζόμενοι* Just.*1apol*.14.2(M.6.348B); id. *dial*.116.1(M.6.744B); Clem.*ecl*.39(p.148.24; M.9.717C); Or.*hom.1.14 in Jer*.(p.12.20; M.13.272B); *Const.App*.4.11.4; *πολλὰ τῆς ἀκολασίας εἴδη· οὐ δὴ χάριν οὐκ ἔφη πορνείας, ἀλλὰ ἀπὸ πάσης π.* Thdt.*1Thess*. 4:3(3.516); **11.** met., of sin and rebellion against God, esp. of idolatry, Or.*mart*.9(p.10.5; M.11.576B); *οὐ γὰρ ἡ περὶ σῶμα μόνον ἁμαρτία, π. καὶ μοιχεία λέγεται, ἀλλὰ καὶ ὁτιοῦν ἥμαρτες, καὶ μάλιστα ἡ περὶ τὸ θεῖον παρανομία* Gr.Naz.*or*.37.19(M.36.304C); Cyr.*Is*.1.1(2. 23D); *π. ... τὴν εἰδωλολατρείαν καλεῖ* Thdt.*Ps*.72:27(1.1121); *ἐπειδὴ γὰρ τῷ θεῷ συνημμένοι τὴν ἐκείνων θεραπείαν ἠγάπησαν, τὴν δεισιδαιμονίαν εἰκότως π. ἐκάλεσεν ib*.105:39(1363); *πορνεία γῆς, οἱ τοῖς γηΐνοις προστετηκότες* Areth.*Apoc*.17:4(M.106.717D); of false teaching, Or. *fr.in Ezech*.16:31(p.546).

πορνεύ-ω, 1. *fornicate*, Or.*hom.20.9 in Jer*.(p.191.20; M.13.521B); id.*Jo*.32.2(p.429.1; M.14.745B); Meth.*res*.1.61(p.326.19; M.41.1160B); ref. irregular union with heathens, Just.*dial*.132.1(M.6.781C); **2.** linked with, but dist. from, *μοιχεύω* in catechetical instruction, *Did*.2.2; *Barn*.19.4; Arist. *apol*.15.4; **3.** ref. illicit intercourse committed by married people, hence = *commit adultery*, ref. Mt.5:32, Or.*comm.in Mt*.14.24(p.343.27; M.13.1248B); *ὁ μέντοι ∼σας οὐκ ἀποκλεισθήσεται τῆς πρὸς γυναῖκα ἑαυτοῦ συνοικήσεως* Bas.*ep*.199 *can*.21 (3.293A; M.32.721A); Chrys.*hom.17.4 in Mt*.(7.228B); **4.** of a woman who presumes her husband's death and re-marries *ἐπόρνευσε μέν, ἐν ἀγνοίᾳ δέ· γάμου οὖν οὐκ εἰρχθήσεται* Bas.*ep*.199 *can*.46(3.296D; M. 32.729C); **5.** of those marrying irregularly *αἱ κόραι, αἱ παρὰ τὴν γνώμην πατρὸς ἀκολουθήσασαι, ∼ουσι· διαλλαγέντων δὲ τῶν γονέων, δοκεῖ θεραπείαν λαμβάνειν τὸ γεγονός ib.can*.38(3.295D; M.32.728C); *ἡ παρὰ γνώμην τοῦ δεσπότου ἀνδρὶ ἑαυτὴν ἐκδιδοῦσα, ἐπόρνευσεν· ἡ δὲ μετὰ ταῦτα πεπαρρησιασμένῳ γάμῳ χρησαμένη, ἐγήματο. ὥστε ἐκεῖνο μὲν πορνεία, τοῦτο δὲ γάμος. αἱ γὰρ συνθῆκαι τῶν ὑπεξουσίων οὐδὲν ἔχουσι βέβαιον ib.can*.40(3.295E; M.728C); **6.** dist. from polygamous marrying of patriarchs, Just.*dial*.141.4(M.6.800A); **7.** *behave unchastely*; of lewd behaviour in gen., Gr.Naz.*carm*.1.2.6. 35(M.37.646A); *ib*.1.2.30.10(909A); **8.** met., *be unfaithful* to God; *apostatize*, Or.*mart*.10(p.10.16; M.11.576C); of unfaithful conduct of synagogue (the 'former wife' of Christ), exeg. Mt.19:3 *οὐκ ἀπέλυσεν ὁ Χριστὸς τὴν προτέραν...γυναῖκα αὐτοῦ (τὴν προτέραν συναγωγήν) κατ' ἄλλην αἰτίαν...ἢ ὅτε ἐπόρνευσεν ἐκείνη ἡ γυνὴ μοιχευθεῖσα ὑπὸ τοῦ πονηροῦ...ἐκείνη οὖν ἑαυτὴν ἀπέστησε μᾶλλον ἢ ὁ ἀνὴρ αὐτὴν ἀπέστειλεν ἀπολύσας* id.*comm.in Mt*.14.17(p.325.14; M.13.1229C); *τὸν ἀπὸ τοῦ κυρίου πορνεύσαντα* Gr.Nyss.*Eun*.1(1 p.48.23; M.45.277A); exeg. Jo.14:17 *ἦν γὰρ αὐτῆς ὁ ἀνὴρ ἐν τῷ αἰῶνι...τὴν ὑλικὴν πᾶσαν κακίαν δηλοῦσθαι διὰ τῶν ἐξ ἀνδρῶν, ᾗ συνεπέπλεκτο καὶ ἐπλησίαζεν παρὰ λόγου ∼ουσα καὶ ἐνυβριζομένη...ὑπ' αὐτῶν* Heracleon ap.Or.*Jo*. 13.11(p.236.6; M.14.416C); *ib*.13.15(p.239.12; 421B).

πόρνη, ἡ, A. *harlot*; **1.** in gen. *τὰ τῆς παροιμίας ἡ π. τὴν σώφρονα* Athenag.*leg*.34.1(M.6.968A); harlots often portrayed in pagan art, Tat.*orat*.34(p.36.11; M.6.877A); *δρῦς ἐστιν ἡ π. ... βαλάνους ἐκφέρουσα, χοίρων ἀλόγων τροφήν* Chrys.*poenit*.8.1(2.342B); **2.** of siren as type of pleasure, Clem.*prot*.12(p.83.20; M.8.237C); **3.** of Rahab; as prophetess foretelling redemption by Christ's blood, *1Clem*.12. 1–8; esp. redemption of *πόρνοι καὶ ἄδικοι ἐκ πάντων τῶν ἐθνῶν* Just. *dial*.111.4(M.6.733A); Iren.*haer*.4.20.12(M.7.1043A); Proc.G.*Jos*.2:1 (M.87.1000B); as type of Church, cf. *videamus, quae sit ista meretrix. Raab dicitur, Raab vero interpretatur latitudo. quae ergo est latitudo, nisi ecclesia haec Christi, quae ex peccatoribus velut ex meretricatione collecta est?*, Or.*hom.3.4 in Jos*.(p.304.26; M.12.840A); cf.Chrys. *poenit*.7.5(2.334C); Thdt.*qu.2 in Jos*.(1.302); cf.Proc.G.*Jos*.2:1(M. 87.1000B); **4.** ref. Zach.3:4 *ῥυπαρὰ ἱμάτια ἐφάνη φορῶν διὰ τὸ γυναῖκα π.* [i.e. foreign wife?] *λελέχθαι εἰληφέναι αὐτόν* Just.*dial*.116.3(M.6. 744D); **5.** of woman of Lc.7:37 interpreted as representing gentile converts, Or.*hom.15.5 in Jer*.(p.129.23; M.13.436A); **6.** spiritual; **a.** of mind of woman who adorns herself elaborately *οὐ γὰρ τὴν εἰκόνα τοῦ θεοῦ κατοικοῦσαν ἔνδον εὑρήσει...π. δ' ἀντ' αὐτῆς καὶ μοιχαλὶς τῆς ψυχῆς κατείληφε τὸ ἄδυτον* Clem.*paed*.3.2(p.238.25; M.8. 561A); **b.** of soul unfaithful to God and united with demons, Or. *hom.8.5 in Ex*.(p.227.28; cf.M.12.357A); **7.** of matter opp. God *πάντας ἂν...λέγοιμεν τοὺς μὴ γεγεννημένους ἐκ τοῦ θεοῦ ἐκ πορνείας γεγεννῆσθαι· οὐ γὰρ ἐκ νύμφης, ἀλλ' ἐκ π., τῆς ὕλης, οὓς γεννᾷ ὁ διάβολος...οἵτινες καὶ...κολλῶνται τῇ π. ὕλῃ, γινόμενοι πρὸς αὐτὴν ἓν σῶμα, τῶν ἐκ τοῦ θεοῦ γεγεννημένων ἀφισταμένων τῆς π. ὕλης, καὶ κολλωμένων τῷ κυρίῳ* Or.*Jo*.20.16(14; p.348.4; M.14.609A).

B. *adulterous wife*, Clem.*str*.2.23(p.193.27; M.8.1097A); ref. Mt. 19:3 *συγχωρεῖ μὲν μόνον χωρίζεσθαι τῆς π., τὰ δὲ ἄλλα πάντα φιλοσοφεῖν κελεύει. καὶ τὴν π., ὅτι νοθεύει τὸ γένος* Gr.Naz.*or*.37.8(M.36. 292B); of Potiphar's wife, Chrys.*a.exil*.2.1(3.422B).

πορνίδιον, τό, *harlot* (dim. of *πόρνη*); of siren as type of pleasure, Clem.*prot*.12(p.83.16; M.8.237C).

πορνικός, 1. *of harlots, lewd, lascivious*, Tat.*orat*.33(p.34.20; M.6. 873C); Clem.*paed*.3.3(p.245.3; M.8.577A); Serap.*Man*.5(p.31; M.40. 904C); *φρόνημα*, Epiph.*haer*.80.1(p.485.1; M.42.756B); *π. ᾄσματα* Chrys.*hom.37.5 in Mt*.(7.421B); id.*hom.4.4 in 1Thess*.(11.463C); **2.** *covetous*, of Dathan and Abiram *π. ὀφθαλμῷ τοῦ ἀξιώματος ἐρασθέντες* Pall.*v.Chrys*.1(p.5.10; M.47.6).

πορνοβοσκ-έω, *prostitute φθείρων, ὑφέλκων, ∼ῶν τὴν φύσιν* Geo. Pis.*res*.49(M.92.1377B).

πορνογέννητος, *born of a harlot, Chron.Pasch*.p.113(M.92.297C).

πορνοκόπος, ὁ, *fornicator*, ‡Ign.*Ant*.11(v.l. *πορνοσκόπος*).

πορνομανής, *harlot-mad*, Isid.Pel.*epp*.1.464(M.78.437B).

***πορνομοιχής,** *adulterous*, †Cyr.*hom.div*.14(5².414E).

***πορνοποιός,** *causing fornication*, Thdr.Stud.*epp*.2.131(M.99. 1425A).

πόρνος, ὁ, 1. *fornicator*, ref. Mt.5:46 *καὶ γὰρ οἱ π. τοῦτο ποιοῦσιν* Just.*1apol*.15.9(M.6.352A); in gen., id.*2apol*.2.16(M.6.445B); *λέγοντες ...τὸν π. καὶ ἀσελγῆ ἀπολαυστικόν τινα καὶ ἀνειμένον* Bas.*hom.in Ps*.61 (1.195D; M.29.476B); of married man who consorts with unmarried woman, and may be received back by his wife, id.*ep*.199 *can*.21(3. 292E; M.32.721A); ref. Mohammedan teaching *ὁ θεὸς προσέταξεν, ὡς σὺ λέγεις, τὸν π. πορνεύειν* Jo.D.*disp*.(M.94.1592A); **2.** in gen., *unchaste, sensual person*, Jo.D.*anacr*.(M.96.855C).

πορνότριψ, ὁ, *fornicator*, Synes.*ep*.32(M.66.1360C).

πορνοτρόφος, ὁ, *brothel-keeper*, Pall.*v.Chrys*.5(p.31.20; M.47.20).

***πορνοφόνος,** *harlot-slaying*, Gr.Naz.*carm*.2.1.15.22(M.37.1252A).

***πόρτα, ἡ,** (Lat. *porta*) *gate, A.Petr.et Paul*.80(p.213.9); *V.Aberc*. 52(p.37.21); ‡Ath.*comm.essent*.6(M.28.33D); Jo.Mal.*chron*.5 p.99(M. 97.185C); Leont.N.*v.Sym*.5(M.93.1708C).

***πορτάριος, ὁ,** (Lat. *portarius*) *gate-keeper*, Jo.Mal.*chron*.7 p.184 (M.97.293B); Thdr.Stud.*epp*.2.34(M.99.1209A).

***πόρτικος, ὁ,** (Lat. *porticus*) *portico, Chron.Pasch*.p.337(M.92. 876C); Thphn.*chron*.p.157(M.108.424C).

***πορτίξ, ὁ,** *porch*, Jo.Mosch.*prat*.185(M.87.3060B).

***πόρτος, ὁ,** (Lat. *portus*) *harbour*, Ath.Scholast.*coll*.4.3(p.52).

πορφύρα, ἡ, 1. *purple*, proverb *πορφύραν ἐξ ἀντιπαραθέσεως ἄλλης πορφύρας ἐκλεγόμεθα* Clem.*str*.6.10(p.472.7; M.9.301B); **2.** *purple robe*; **a.** of emperor, Eus.*v.C*.4.66(p.145.9; M.20.1221B); *ἐγώ τε καὶ τὸ πορφύρας κράτος κιγκλίδος ἦμεν τῆς σεβασμίας ἔσω* Gr.Naz.*carm*.2. 1.11.1360(M.37.1122A); *Θεοδόσιος ἐν τῇ π. ἐτέχθη* Marc.Diac.*v.Porph*. 44; **b.** met.; **i.** of triumphal robe obtained through asceticism, Nil. *Eulog*.2(M.79.1096D); **ii.** of Christ's humanity *ἐνδυσάμενος...τὴν τῆς φύσεως ἡμῶν π.* Mod.*dorm*.13(M.86.3309B); *ὁ βασιλεὺς τῆς δόξης τὴν τῆς σαρκὸς π. περιβαλλόμενος* ‡Jo.D.*hom*.6.4(M.96.668A); **iii.** of BMV *ἡ βασιλικὴ π., τὸν οὐρανοῦ καὶ γῆς ἐνδύσασα βασιλέα τὸ...τοῦ σώματος πορφυροειδὲς ἔνδυμα* ‡Epiph.*hom*.5(M.43.496B); Thdr.Stud. *nativ.BMV* 7(M.96.693C).

***πορφυραυγής,** *bright purple*, Geo.Pis.*carm*.107.19 cit. s. *γράφω*.

πορφύρεος, 1. *of purple colour*; of wine in chalice made by Marcus to appear as blood when consecrated, Iren.*haer*.1.13.2(M.7. 580A); Hipp.*haer*.6.39(p.171.2; M.16.3258A); **2.** *of porphyry*, Philost. *h.e*.2.17(M.65.480A).

πορφυρευτής, ὁ, *fisher for purple fish*, Clem.*paed*.2.10(p.225.33; M.8.536A).

***Πορφυριανός, ὁ,** *disciple of Porphyry*; name given to Arians by Const., as being enemies of Christianity, Const.ap.Gel.Cyz.*h.e*.2.36. 1(M.85.1340C); *Ἀρειανούς, οὓς ἐκεῖνος Π. ὠνόμασε* Ath.*h.Ar*.51(p.212. 12; M.25.753D); *Cod.Thds*.16.5.66(p.68.15; H.1.1716D); Phot.*nomoc*. 12.3(p.604; M.104.872C).

***πορφυροβαφέω,** *dye purple*, Anast.S.*hod*.17(M.89.265A) cit. s. *συμπορφυροβαφέω*.

πορφυροειδής, *of purple hue*, ref. Christ's 'robe' of humanity, ‡Epiph.*hom*.5(M.43.496B).

***πορφυροποίκιλτος**, *purple-embroidered*, ‡Jo.D.*hom*.5(M.96.649B).

πορφυροπώλης, ὁ, *dealer in purple*, Chrys.*hom.1 in Rom.16:3*(3.177B).

***πορφυροφορέω**, *wear purple*, Thdr.Stud.*epp*.2.181(M.99.1560D).

***πορφυροφόρος**, *clothed in purple*, Cyr.H.*catech*.2.11; Jo.Mosch.*prat*.46(M.87.2900D); of BMV, †Anast.S.*relat*.42(*OC* 3 p.63).

***πορφυροχρυσόμικτος**, *entwined with purple and gold*, Thdr.Stud.*nativ.BMV* 7(M.96.693C).

ποσάκις, *how many times?* Clem.*str*.1.5(p.18.21; M.8.720B).

ποσαπλοῦς, *how manifold?* Ath.*apol.sec*.4(p.90.35; M.25.256A).

ποσαπλῶς, *how much?, how intensely?* τὸ π. ... τὴν ἐπίτασιν τοῦ πόθου σημαῖνον Thdt.*Ps*.62:2(1.1019).

ποσότης, ἡ, *size, quantity, amount*; **1.** in gen. ὁ...πατὴρ...γινώσκει τὴν π. ... αὐτῶν *1Clem*.35.3; τὴν π. τῆς δαπάνης Herm.*sim*.5.3.7; ἐν διπλῇ π. ἀπαιτείσθω τὸν μισθόν †Gregent.*leg.Hom*.52(M.86.608C); Leont.N.*v.Jo.Eleem*.27(p.57.17); **2.** of abstracts, *degree, quantity* πίστεως...π. *Hom.Clem*.9.11; τὴν ποιότητα καὶ π. καὶ πηλικότητα τῶν ἁμαρτημάτων Isid.Pel.*epp*.2.172(M.78.624B); πνευματικῆς π. τῆς ὡς ἔν γε ταῖς ἀρεταῖς νοουμένης Cyr.*Ps*.50:21(M.69.1104A); ἐν π. τῆς ἀρετῆς id.*Joel*.35(3.229C; ποιότητι Aubert); **3.** Christol. εἰ μὴ ψιλὴν ἐκήρυττε τὴν διαφοράν, οὐ παρῃτεῖτο λέγειν ἐν Χριστῷ μετὰ τὴν ἕνωσιν τὴν ἄτμητον καὶ ἀδιαίρετον τῶν διαφερόντων ποιότητα [l. ποσότητα], γινώσκων ὅτι πάσῃ διαφορᾷ πάντως συνεισάγεται π.· καὶ πάσῃ π., συνέζευκται ὁ δηλωτικὸς αὐτῆς ἀριθμός. ἀμήχανον γάρ, ἢ διαφορὰν ποσότητος εἶναι χωρίς, ἢ π. δίχα τοῦ δηλοῦντος αὐτὴν ἀριθμοῦ διαγνωσθῆναι Max.*opusc*.(M.91.41B); *ib*.(45C).

ποσόω, *determine quantitatively* ἡ θεία φύσις οὐ πεπόσωται Cyr.*Jo*.1.3(4.21E); οὐ γὰρ πεποσῶσθαι τὸ θεῖον *ib*.2.8(230E); id.*ador*.6(1.213B); id.*Nest*.1.2(p.21.3; 6[1].13E); πεπόσωται παρ' αὐτοῖς ἡ οὐσία τοῦ θεοῦ id.*resp*.(p.577.13; 6[2].385E).

ποστημόριον, τό, *fraction*, Or.*comm.in Gen*.ap.Eus.*p.e*.6.11(294C; M.12.80A); Epiph.*mens*.24(M.43.281A); Proc.G.*Gen*.1:15(M.87.89A); δύναται...κιβωτὸς π. τῶν ἐπὶ γῆς χωρῆσαι ζῴων *ib*.6:16(277A); Leont.B.*Nest.et Eut*.1(M.86.1277A).

[*]ποταμήρρυτος, *washed down by rivers*, Paul.Sil.*Soph*.1013(cj. ποταμό-; M.86.2158A).

***ποταμῖτις**, *plying on rivers* φορτίδα...π. Paul.Sil.*Soph*.626(cj. for ποταμήτιδα; ποταμῆϊδα M.86.2143A).

***ποταμόπνικτος**, *drowned in a river*, Thphn.*chron*.p.306(M.108.744C).

***ποταμοριφής**, *cast into a river*; of Moses, Ephr.3.302C.

ποταμός, ὁ, *river*;

A. lit.; **1.** origin and purpose of rivers ὄψει τοῦ θερμοῦ τὴν δύναμιν τοῖς ἐν γενέσει καὶ φθορᾷ πᾶσιν ἐνδυναστεύουσαν. διὰ τοῦτο πολὺ τὸ ὕδωρ ὑπὲρ γῆς κεχυμένον...ὅθεν...ποταμῶν ῥεύματα...ὑπὲρ τοῦ ἐν πολλοῖς... ταμείοις διατηρεῖσθαι τὴν ὑγρασίαν Bas.*hex*.3.6(1.27E; M.29.68B); τῷ π. μὲν οὐ λείπει ἡ χορηγία τοῦ ὕδατος, τῆς γῆς πρὸς τοῦτο μεθισταμένης Gr.Nyss.*hex*.62(M.44.112D); formed from tears of Sophia (Valent.), Iren.*haer*.1.4.3(M.7.484B); their movements as likely to influence human life as those of stars (in argument against astrology), Gr.Nyss.*fat*.(M.45.160D); **2.** rivers worshipped by pagans, Just.*1apol*.24.1(M.6.364B); Clem.*prot*.4(p.35.15; M.8.133B); esp. in Egypt, Ath.*gent*.24(M.25.48C); **3.** as abode of demons in pre-Christian times, Ath.*inc*.47.2(M.25.180C); **4.** rivers of Eden so designed as to prevent discovery of earthly paradise by one following their course, Thdt.*qu.29 in Gen*.(1.43); their geography discussed, Proc.G.*Gen*.2:8–9(M.87.157Dff.); **5.** rivers of paradise (i.e. abode of righteous souls); **a.** to be passed before entering abode of blessed, thirty miles wide and deep as the abyss, *V.Zos*.4(p.98.22); **b.** river of Ocean, encircling earth, by which souls of righteous dwell, *Apoc.Paul*.21(p.50); **c.** four rivers encircling city of God (of honey, milk, oil, and wine), *ib*.23(p.52); prophets dwell by the first, Holy Innocents by second, *ib*.25(p.53); *ib*.26(p.54); those devoted to God by third, *ib*.28(p.54); perh. the φιλόξενοι by fourth, *ib*.27(p.54); corresponding to four rivers of earthly paradise, *ib*.45(p.64); cf. τοὺς π. τοὺς ἐλαίου δίκην ἀψοφητὶ ῥέοντας Chrys.*hom.23.5 in 1Cor*.(10.208D); **6.** rivers of Hades; **a.** river of Ocean beyond which lies dark abode of souls of unrighteous, *Apoc.Paul*.31(p.57); **b.** ποταμὸς κοχλάζων in which wicked are tormented, *T.Abr*.A 19(p.101.13,32); *Apoc.Paul*.31(p.57); *Apoc.BMV* 23(p.122.25ff.); **c.** river of fire ἐπέρρεεν π. πύρινος καὶ ἦν ἐκεῖ πλῆθος πολλῶν ψυχῶν *Apoc.Paul*.32(p.57); esp. for punishment of clergy, *1Apoc.Jo*.24(p.90); τὰς καμίνους τὰς ἀφορήτους, τοὺς πυριφλεγέθοντας π. Chrys.*hom.23.6 in 1Cor*.(10.210A); **7.** river of fire connected with Judgement (cf. Dan.7:10), cf.*Orac.Sib*.2.252; *Apoc.En*.14.19; π. ἐκπορεύεται πυρὸς ὑποκάτω τοῦ θρόνου τοῦ Τόπου, καὶ ῥεῖ εἰς τὸ κενὸν τοῦ ἐκτισμένου, ὅ ἐστιν ἡ γέεννα...καὶ αὐτὸς ὁ Τόπος πύρινός ἐστι Clem.*exc.Thdot*.38(p.118.29; M.9.677A); cf. *stabit in igneo flumine dominus Jesus Christus...ut quicumque...ad paradisum transire desiderat et purgatione indiget, hoc eum omne baptizet...eum vero, qui non habet signum priorum baptismatum, lavacro igneo non baptizet. oportet enim prius aliquem baptizari aqua et spiritu, ut, cum ad igneum fluvium venerit, ostendat se et aquae et spiritus lavacra servasse*, Or.*hom.24 in Lc*.(p.158.20; M.13.1864C); Ephr.2.229F; regarded as place of punishment for wicked after Judgement πόρρω γενέσθαι τοῦ π. τοῦ πυρὸς τοῦ συρομένου...πρὸ τοῦ βήματος τοῦ φρικτοῦ. τὸν γὰρ ἅπαξ ἐμπεσόντα ἐκεῖ, χρὴ μένειν διὰ παντός Chrys.*hom.12.3 in Jo*.(8.71B); πόσοι π. πυρὸς ἀρκέσουσι τῇ τοιαύτῃ ψυχῇ; id.*hom.11.6 in Rom*.(9.539C); πυρὸς ἕλκεται π. πρὸ προσώπου αὐτοῦ, βίβλοι...ἀνοίγονται id.*hom.3.2 in 2Tim*.(11.675B); **8.** fiery river destroying all things at end of world καὶ τότε δὴ π. τε μέγας πυρὸς αἰθομένοιο ῥεύσει ἀπ' οὐρανόθεν καὶ πάντα τόπον δαπανήσει *Orac.Sib*.2.196; cf.*ib*.3.54,84; *ib*.7.243; ὁ δὲ πύρινος π. ἐξερχόμενος μετὰ θυμοῦ ὥσπερ ἀγρία θάλασσα, καὶ κατακαύσει ὄρη καὶ βουνούς ‡Hipp.*consumm*.37(p.304.15; M.10.940B); ὅταν ἴδωμεν τὸν πύρινον π. ἐξερχόμενον μετὰ θυμοῦ, ὥσπερ ἀγρίαν θάλασσαν, καὶ κατεσθίοντα ὄρη καὶ νάπας Ephr.2.192F; id.2.213D; id.3.145D; **9.** rivers as illustrations of heavenly entities ἐπισκεπτέον δὲ καὶ τὸ ποταμοὺς εἰρῆσθαι καὶ...ἅρματα συνημμένα ταῖς οὐρανίαις οὐσίαις. οἱ μὲν γὰρ ἐμπύριοι π. σημαίνουσι τοὺς θεαρχικοὺς ὀχετούς, ἄφθονον αὐταῖς καὶ ἀνέκλειπτον ἐπίρροιαν χορηγοῦντας, καὶ ζωοποιοῦ θρεπτικοὺς γονιμότητος Dion.Ar.*c.h*.15.9(M.3.337C); cf.*ib*.15.5(329A); **10.** exeg.; **a.** in gen., cf. *novi ego differentias fluminum, et scio flumina in quibus draco sedeat, super quae flumina hi qui de Israel capti fuerant, sedentes...flebant, et scio aliud flumen, cujus impetus laetificat civitatem dei...Jesus Christus...est fluvius...iste est qui ait per Isaiam: ecce ego declino in vos quasi fluvius pacis...habes igitur fluvios sanctos a quibus procul est draco. ... est autem quidam fluvius quem draco fecit: dicit quippe draco...mea sunt flumina, et ego feci illa. audi haereticum...praedicantem necdum venisse Jesum Christum. ... idcirco diligenter attende cum aquam biberis, ne forte de illo fluvio bibas in quo sedet draco; sed bibe ex aqua viva et de eo fluvio in quo est sermo dei*, Or.*hom.13.4 in Ezech*.(p.449.24; M.13.764C); Dion.Ar.*c.h*.2.5(M.3.144D); **b.** Ps.45:5; π. interpreted; **i.** of Christ, cf. Or.*hom.13.4 in Ezech*.(p.449.31; M.13.764D); id.*hom.17.4 in Num*.(p.161.8; M.12.707D); Eus.*e.th*.1.20(p.94.20; M.24.889B); πόλιν θεοῦ ἤτοι τὴν ἐκκλησίαν...εὐφραίνουσι τὰ ὁρμήματα τοῦ π.· π. δέ ἐστιν ὁ τοῦ θεοῦ λόγος, ὁ ἐξ Ἐδὲμ τῆς θείας τρυφῆς ἐκπορευόμενος Didym.*Ps*.45:5(M.39.1373B); Cyr.*Ps*.45:5(M.69.1048B); **ii.** of H. Ghost in Church, Eus.*Ps*.45:5(M.23.408D); τίς δ' ἂν εἴη ὁ π. τοῦ θεοῦ, ἢ τὸ πνεῦμα τὸ ἅγιον, ἐκ τῆς πίστεως τῶν εἰς Χριστὸν πεπιστευκότων ἐγγινόμενον τοῖς ἀξίοις; Bas.*hom.in Ps*.45(1.173A; M.29.421C); **iii.** of preaching of gospel π. τὸν εὐαγγελικὸν λόγον φησίν, ὃς καὶ εὐφραίνει τὴν ἐκκλησίαν Ath.*exp.Ps*.45:5(M.27.216A); π. δὲ ἐνταῦθα τὸ εὐαγγελικὸν προσηγόρευσε κήρυγμα Thdt.*Ps*.45:5(1.900); **iv.** of divine providence and gifts, Chrys.*exp.in Ps*.45:5–6(5.184C); **c.** Ps.92:3, interpreted; **i.** of words of scripture δυνατὸν δὲ καὶ τοὺς λόγους αὐτοὺς τῶν θεοπνεύστων γραφῶν...π. ⟨λέγειν⟩, διὰ τὸ τίμιον καὶ ζωτικὸν καὶ καρποφορίας αἴτιον Didym.*Ps*.92:3(M.39.1501B); **ii.** of preachers of gospel, esp. apostles, Eus.*Ps*.92:3(M.23.1888C); Ath.*exp.Ps*.92:3(M.27.408B); Cyr.*Ps*.92:3(M.69.1229D); id.*Jo*.5.1(4.469D); Proc.G.*Is*.32:1–8(M.87.2277A); **d.** Ps.136:1, cf. *si quis ergo inter ista flumina fuerit Babylonis, si quis rheumatibus libidinis inundatur, et luxuriae aestibus circumluitur, iste non dicitur stare, sed sedere*, Or.*hom.15.1 in Num*.(p.130.14; M.12.685A); *gravis autem est hujus saeculi fluvius...de anima significat, quae in vitae istius inciderit turbines...ita sunt flumina Babylonis, juxta quae sedentes et reminiscentes patriae coelestis lugent...ubi suspendunt organa sua, in salicibus legis et mysteriorum dei* id.*hom.1.5 in Ezech*.(p.330.1; M.13.674A); cf. ἐν ταῖς ἐπιθυμίαις τῆς συγχύσεως. τοῦτο γὰρ ἑρμηνεύεται Βαβυλῶνος Hesych.H.*Ps.tit*.136(M.27.1273C); **e.** Cant.4:16 τοιοῦτος π. ἀρωμάτων ἦν, ἐκ τοῦ κήπου τῆς ἐκκλησίας ῥέων διὰ τοῦ πνεύματος, ὁ μέγας Παῦλος Gr.Nyss.*hom.10 in Cant*.(M.44.985B); **f.** Is.18:1 ποταμοὺς λέγων τῶν εἰς θεὸν ἐπιστρεφόντων τὸ πλῆθος Proc.G.*Is*.18:1–7(M.87.2133A); **g.** Is.19:5, interpreted of ancient philosophy of Egypt, *ib*.19:1–15(2149D); **h.** Is.33:21, interpreted of angels, *ib*.33:21(2304B); of apostles and others, *ib*.(2304D); **i.** Is.42:15 τὰς παρ' αὐτοῖς δὲ νομικὰς διδασκαλίας ποταμοὺς εἰπών, ...καὶ τὰ παρ' αὐτοῖς δὲ λιμνάζοντα λογικῶν ὑδάτων χωρία... ξηρανῶ *ib*.42:10–25(2376D); **j.** Is.43:2, interpreted of temptations encountered by believers, Cyr.*Is*.4.1(2.559A); Proc.G.*Is*.43:1–13(M. 87.2385C); **k.** Is.50:2, interpreted of idolatrous nations, *ib*.50:1–11 (2438D); **l.** Is.66:12, interpreted of Christ, cf.Or.*hom.13.4 in Ezech.* (p.450.2; M.13.764D); **m.** Ezech.47:7; interpreted of baptism, *Barn.* 11.10,11; of preaching of gospel, proceeding by way of Galilee of gentiles (cf. Ezech.47:8) to barbarian lands, Thdt.*Ezech*.47:5–8 (2.1040,1041); **n.** ref. Joel 3:18, interpreted of Christ, Cyr.*Joel.* 44(3.244B); **o.** Jo.7:38, interpreted; **i.** of Christ's teaching, proceeding from his faithful followers (connected with wells filled by Philistines, Gen.26:15), cf.Or.*hom.13.3 in Gen.*(p.118.28ff.; M. 12.234B); cf.id.*hom.12.1 in Num.*(p.94.24; M.12.657A); id.*hom.13.4 in Ezech.*(p.450.2; M.13.764D); **ii.** of Christian preachers or of grace of H. Ghost, Cyr.*Jo*.5.1(4.469D–470B); **iii.** of H. Ghost, cf.Or.*hom.17.4 in Num.*(p.161.10; M.12.708A); Bas.*hom.in Ps*.45(1. 173A; M.29.421C); **p.** miscellaneous figures; **i.** Num.24:6, interpreted of scriptures or of angelic powers, cf.Or.*hom.17.4 in Num.* (p.161.4; M.12.707D); **ii.** of Israel's camp near Jordan (Num. 33:48), cf. *omnis namque hic cursus propterea agitur...ut perveniatur ad flumen dei, ut proximi efficiamur fluentis sapientiae et rigemur undis scientiae divinae*, Or.*hom.27.12 in Num.*(p.279.13; M.12.800A); **iii.** ref. Jos.3:16 τοῦτον τὸν π. τῆς ὕλης...διέκοψαν καὶ διέστησαν ...προφῆται...περατουμένης τῆς ὕλης καθ' ἑκάτερον διάστημα ὕδατος βουλήσει τοῦ θεοῦ Clem.*ecl*.6(p.138.20; M.9.701A); **iv.** ref. 4Reg. 6:6; casting of wood into river Jordan interpreted of baptism and redemption through Cross, Just.*dial*.86.6(M.6.681B); **v.** ref. Pr.9:18 ἡμῖν δὲ παριέναι π. ἀλλότριον ὁ θεῖος παραινεῖ παιδαγωγός, τὴν ἀλλοτρίαν γυναῖκα, τὴν μάχλον, π. ἀλλότριον ἀλληγορῶν...πᾶσι δι' ἀσέλγειαν πορνικὴν εἰς τρυφὴν ἐκχεομένην Clem.*paed*.3.2(p.241.21; M.8.569A); **vi.** ref. Apoc.12:15 π. τὸν πειρασμὸν ἡ θεία ἀλληγορεῖ γραφή...π. οὖν λέγει τὸν ἐπὶ τῷ πάθει τοῦ κυρίου πειρασμόν Oecum. *Apoc*.12:15(p.147); **vii.** ref. etym. of 'Jordan' ἑρμηνεύεται δὲ Ἰορδάνης 'καταβαίνων'. καταβαίνων γάρ ἐστιν ἀληθῶς ὁ π. τοῦ θεοῦ, τὸ ὕδωρ τὸ ἀληθινόν Or.*hom.21 in Lc.*(p.139.13; cf.M.13.1855B); **viii.** as fig. title of Christ, Eus.*e.th*.1.20(p.96.30; M.24.893B); **ix.** as Trin. illustration, cf. ὕδωρ ἐκ πηγῆς Hipp.*Noët*.11(p.253.10; M.10. 817C); μέμνημαι πλείονα προσθεὶς τῶν συγγενῶν ὁμοιώματα·...καὶ π. ἀπὸ πηγῆς ῥέοντα ἕτερον σχῆμα καὶ ὄνομα μετειληφέναι, μήτε γὰρ τὴν πηγὴν π. μήτε π. πηγὴν λέγεσθαι, καὶ ἀμφότερα ὑπάρχειν, καὶ τὴν μὲν πηγὴν οἱονεὶ πατέρα εἶναι, τὸν δὲ π. εἶναι ἐκ τῆς πηγῆς ὕδωρ Dion.Al. ap.Ath.*Dion*.18(p.60.2; M.25.505C); ὥσπερ π. ἀπὸ πηγῆς ἔρρευσε Dion.Al.*ib*.(p.60.9; 508A); πατὴρ...αἴτιος τοῦ υἱοῦ αὐτοῦ, ὡς πηγὴ ποταμοῦ ‡Caes.Naz.*dial*.2(M.38.857).

B. met.; **1.** of life π. ... ὁ βίος ἡμῶν, ῥέων ἐνδελεχῶς Bas.*hom*.21. 11(2.172E; M.31.561C); cf.Chrys.*hom.30.4 in 1Cor.*(10.275C); cf.id. *hom.9.5 in Heb.*(12.100D); **2.** of earthly body π. ὠνόμασται τὸ σῶμα, διότι ὡς πρὸς τὸ ἀκριβὲς τάχα οὐδὲ δύο ἡμερῶν τὸ πρῶτον ὑποκείμενον ταὐτόν ἐστιν ἐν τῷ σώματι ἡμῶν Meth.*res*.1.22(p.244.21; M.41.1089D); **3.** of a crowd π. ἔδειξε λογικὸν τὸν παραρρέοντα μιμούμενον π. Thdt. *h.e*.5.35.4(3.1077); **4.** of Christianity μία μὲν οὖν ἡ τῆς ἀληθείας ὁδός, ἀλλ' εἰς αὐτὴν καθάπερ εἰς ἀέναον π. ἐκρέουσι τὰ ῥεῖθρα ἄλλα ἄλλοθεν Clem.*str*.1.5(p.18.9; M.8.720A).

ποταμώδης, *by a river* ἐπὶ τόπου π. *V.Zos*.2(p.97.14).

ποταπός, *of what sort?*; μηδὲ ποταπόν *not at all* μηδὲ π. ἐκάθισα ἐν τῷ...θρόνῳ Thphn.*chron*.p.385(M.108.921C).

ποτήριον, τό, *cup*; **1.** in gen., ref. Mt.10:42 κἂν π. ψυχροῦ ὕδατος δῷς, ἔνθα οὐδέν ἐστι δαπανῆσαι, καὶ τούτου κείσεταί σοι μισθός Chrys. *hom.35.2 in Mt.*(7.401B); σὺ Θάσιον οἶνον, ἐκείνῳ δὲ οὐδὲ ψυχρὸν ἐπέδωκας π. διψῶντι *ib*.48.6(501B); π. χρυσοῦν ποιεῖς, καὶ π. ψυχροῦ οὐ δίδως; *ib*.50.4(518E); ref. Mt.23:25, cf. *omnes falsi dogmatis professores calices sunt a foris quasi mundati...ab intus autem pleni rapina*, Or.*comm.ser.21 in Mt.*(p.37.26; M.13.1627D); ἄλλως δὲ οὐδὲ περὶ π. καὶ παροψίδος λέγει, ἀλλὰ περὶ ψυχῆς καὶ σώματος Chrys.*hom. 73.2 in Mt.*(7.710A); ref. ceremonial cleansings of Hemerobaptists ποτήρια...ἐὰν μὴ καθάρωσιν ὕδατι, οὐδενὶ χρῶνται *Const.App*.6.6.5; **2.** of cup of suffering, ref. Mt.20:22 ζητήσει τις τί τὸ π. καὶ τί τὸ βάπτισμα...οἱ πολλοὶ μὲν οὖν τὰ ἀμφότερα ἄγουσιν εἰς τὴν κατὰ τὸ μαρτύριον οἰκονομίαν...ἡμεῖς δὲ οὐκ ἀποδοκιμάζομεν μὲν καὶ ταύτην τὴν ἐκδοχήν, ἐφίσταμεν δὲ εἰ δύναται καὶ ἄλλο τι δηλοῦν...τὰ δύο ὀνόματα. ...σαφῶς δὲ ἐδίδαξεν ἐν τούτοις ὅτι τὸ π. ⟨τὸ μαρτύριόν⟩ ἐστιν ὁ ἐπαγαγὼν τοῖς κατὰ τὸ π. τὸ 'τίμιος ἐναντίον κυρίου ὁ θάνατος τῶν ὁσίων αὐτοῦ'. τῇ δ' ἐπινοίᾳ τὸ μαρτύριον δύο ἐστίν, ὧν τὸ μὲν ἓν καλεῖται π. σωτηρίου, τὸ δὲ λοιπὸν βάπτισμα. καὶ καθὸ μὲν ὑπομένει τις τοὺς πόνους, π. ἐστιν ἐκπινόμενον ὑπὸ τοῦ φέροντος πάντα τὰ προσαγόμενα εἰς ἑαυτόν Or.*comm.in Mt*.16.6(p.481.26; M.13.1381A); ὥσπερ ἔστι τι βρῶμα τοῦ σωτῆρος...[Jo.4:34], οὕτως ἀνάλογόν ἐστι π. ἐκείνῳ τῷ βρώματι...λέγοι γὰρ ἂν τις ὅτι ἀληθῶς μὲν βρῶσις ἡ πρᾶξις, ἀληθῶς δὲ πόσις ἡ θεωρία, καὶ...διὰ τοῦτο πρῶτον δίδωσι τὸν ἄρτον...ἐπεὶ πρώτη ἐστὶν ἡ πρᾶξις, καὶ μετὰ τοῦτο λαβὼν π. ... ἔδωκεν αὐτοῖς *ib*. 16.7(p.487.5; 1385B); δύνασθε πιεῖν τὸ π. ... ἐδήλου δὲ τὸν θάνατον, ὃν κατεδέχετο ὑπὲρ τῆς τοῦ κόσμου σωτηρίας †Bas.*hom.in Ps*.115(1. 374B; M.30.109C); οὐδὲ γὰρ εἶπε...δύνασθε τὸ αἷμα ὑμῶν ἐκχεῖν; ἀλλὰ πῶς; δύνασθε πιεῖν τὸ π.; εἶτα ἐφελκόμενός φησιν· ὃ ἐγὼ μέλλω πίνειν, ἵνα τῇ πρὸς αὐτὸν κοινωνίᾳ προθυμότεροι γένωνται Chrys.*hom.65.2 in Mt.*(7.646B); connected with martyrdom in gen. λαβεῖν μέρος ἐν ἀριθμῷ τῶν μαρτύρων ἐν τῷ π. τοῦ Χριστοῦ *M.Polyc*.14.2; **3.** ref. Ps. 15:5 γίνεται δὲ καὶ ἄρτος ὁ κύριος, παρέχων διδασκαλίαν, καὶ στηρίζων τοῦ ἐσθίοντος τὴν καρδίαν· π. δὲ κατὰ θεωρίαν τῆς ἀληθείας, παρέχον εὐφροσύνην τῆς γνώσεως τῷ διὰ συγκαταθέσεως πίνοντι Or.*sel.in Ps.* 15:5(M.12.1213B); τῆς ἐμῆς ἐκκλησίας, ἥτις ἐστὶν ἡ κληρονομία μου, μερίς ἐστιν ὁ κύριος· ὁ αὐτὸς δὲ καὶ τοῦ π. μου, τουτέστι τοῦ θανάτου, μερὶς γεγενημένος ὁ αὐτός Eus.*Ps*.15:5(M.23.160A); τὸ γὰρ π. τὸν θάνατον σημαίνει Ath.*exp.Ps*.15:5(M.27.104B); ὡς εὐφραινούσης τοίνυν αὐτὸν τῆς ἐκκλησίας ποτήριον ὀνομάζει Cyr.*Ps*.15:5(M.69.809D); **4.** ref. Ps.115:4 interpreted of martyrdom, Or.*sel.in Ps*.115:8(M.12. 1577Bff.); linked with θυσία αἰνέσεως and interpreted of eucharist, Eus.*Ps*.115:17(M.23.1360Dff.); Cyr.H.*catech*.22.5; of martyrdom, †Bas.*hom.in Ps*.115(1.374B; M.30.109C); τὸ ἐν τοῖς ἀγῶσι τοῖς ὑπὲρ εὐσεβείας, τὸ μέχρι θανάτου πρὸς τὴν ἁμαρτίαν ἀντικαταστῆναι, τὸ π. λέγων Didym.*Ps*.115:4(M.39.1556A); π. σωτηρίου λήψομαι...οἱ μὲν οὖν κατὰ ἀναγωγὴν τὸ εἰρημένον ἐκλαμβάνοντες, τῶν μυστηρίων τὴν κοινωνίαν φασίν· ἡμεῖς δὲ τῆς ἱστορίας τέως ἐχόμενοι, σπονδὰς αὐτὸν λέγειν...καὶ θυσίας καὶ εὐχαριστηρίους ὕμνους λέγομεν. καὶ γὰρ διάφοροι τὸ παλαιὸν ἦσαν θυσίαι Chrys.*exp.in Ps*.115:4(5.314A); σωτηρίου γὰρ ὄντως ἐστὶ π. τὸ ὑμνολογεῖν τὸν τῶν ὅλων σωτῆρα θεόν Cyr.*Ps.* 115:4(M.69.1269B) = Hesych.H.*fr.Ps*.115:4(M.93.1333C); **5.** ref. Ps. 22:5 μὴ μόνον τράπεζαν ἡτοίμασεν ἡ σοφία, ἀλλὰ καὶ κράτος ἐκέρασε τὸν ἑαυτῆς οἶνον...καταμίξασα τὰ θεῖα νοήματα λέξεσιν ἀνθρωπίναις, ἐκ τοῦ τοιούτου κρατῆρος μερίζουσα ἑκάστῳ δίδωσι π. Or.*sel.in Ps.* 22:5(M.12.1264B) = Didym.*Ps*.22:5(M.39.1293A); τὸ π. ... πάλιν τὴν μυστικὴν εὐφροσύνην φησίν Ath.*exp.Ps*.22:5(M.27.140C); interpreted of eucharistic cup, Cyr.H.*catech*.22.7; **6.** of ritual cup; **a.** in pagan mysteries ἐν τοῖς τοῦ Μίθρα μυστηρίοις...π. τοῦ ὕδατος τίθεται Just. *1apol*.66.4(M.6.429A); **b.** in eucharist, Ign.*Philad*.4.1 cit. s. εὐχαριστία; οὕτως εὐχαριστήσατε· πρῶτον περὶ τοῦ π.· εὐχαριστοῦμέν σοι... ὑπὲρ τῆς ἁγίας ἀμπέλου Δαυεὶδ τοῦ παιδός σου...περὶ δὲ τοῦ κλάσματος· εὐχαριστοῦμέν σοι κτλ. *Did*.9.2,3; προσφέρεται τῷ προεστῶτι τῶν ἀδελφῶν ἄρτος καὶ π. ὕδατος καὶ κράματος Just.*1apol*.65.3(M.6.428A); τοῦ π. ... τῆς εὐχαριστίας id.*dial*.41.3(M.6.564C); cf. φαγεῖ ἄρτον ζωῆς εὐλογημένον, καὶ πιεῖ π. ἐμπεπλησμένον ἀθανασίας *Asen*.15(p.61.6); τὸ ἀπὸ τῆς κτίσεως π. αἷμα ἴδιον ὡμολόγησε, ἐξ οὗ τὸ ἡμέτερον δεύει αἷμα Iren.*haer*.5.2.2(M.7.1125A); as used by Marcus ποτήρια οἴνῳ κεκραμένα προσποιούμενος εὐχαριστεῖν, καὶ ἐπὶ πλέον ἐκτείνων τὸν λόγον τῆς ἐπικλήσεως, πορφύρεα καὶ ἐρυθρὰ ἀναφαίνεσθαι ποιεῖ· ὡς δοκεῖν τὴν ἀπὸ τῶν ὑπὲρ τὰ ὅλα χάριν τὸ αἷμα τὸ ἑαυτῆς στάζειν ἐν τῷ ἐκείνῳ π. διὰ τῆς ἐπικλήσεως αὐτοῦ *ib*.1.13.2(580A); Hipp.*haer*.6.39(p.170.14; M.16.3258A); τὸν σωτῆρα...ἑορτάζοντα μετὰ τῶν μαθητῶν καὶ διδόντα αὐτοῖς π., περὶ οὗ γέγραπται οὐχ ὅτι ἐκέρασεν· ὁ Ἰησοῦς γὰρ εὐφραίνων τοὺς μαθητὰς ἀκράτῳ εὐφραίνει Or.*hom.12.2 in Jer.*(p.87.28; M.13. 380C); εἴ τις ἑορτάζει μετὰ τοῦ Ἰησοῦ, ἄνω ἐστὶν ἐν ἀναγαίῳ κεκοσμημένῳ...ἐὰν δὲ ἀναβῇς μετ' αὐτοῦ...δίδωσί σοι τὸ π. τῆς διαθήκης τῆς καινῆς, δίδωσί σοι καὶ τὸν ἄρτον τῆς εὐλογίας, τὸ σῶμα ἑαυτοῦ καὶ τὸ αἷμα ἑαυτοῦ χαρίζεται *ib*.*19.13*(p.169.31; 489C); προσφέρομέν σοι... τὸν ἄρτον...καὶ τὸ π. κατὰ τοῦτο *Lit*.ap.*Const.App*.8.12.38; ὁ δὲ διάκονος κατεχέτω τὸ π. καὶ ἐπιδιδοὺς λεγέτω· αἷμα Χριστοῦ, π. ζωῆς *Lit.ib*.8. 13.15; οὐ γὰρ μέγα ἡγῇ τὸ π. κατασχεῖν, ἐξ οὗ πίνειν ὁ Χριστὸς μέλλει, καὶ προσάγειν τῷ στόματι; οὐχ ὁρᾷς ὅτι τῷ ἱερεῖ μόνῳ θέμις τὸ τοῦ αἵματος ἐπιδιδόναι π.; Chrys.*hom.45.3 in Mt.*(7.479B); id.*hom.15.3 in Jo.*(8.89B); ἡμᾶς παρισταμένους τῇ τραπέζῃ τῇ βασιλικῇ, καλοὺς τῷ εἴδει εἶναι δεῖ τῷ τῆς ψυχῆς...ὁ τοιοῦτος προσίτω, καὶ π. ἀπτέσθω βασιλικῶν id.*hom.17.5 in Heb.*(12.171C); Cyr.*Nest*.4(p.90.29; 6[1]. 118B); δίσκον ἕνα καὶ π. ἓν γενέσθαι εἰς λόγον τῶν θείων μυστηρίων Chosroes ap.Evagr.*h.e*.6.21(p.238.1; M.86.2876C); δισκάρια καὶ π. καὶ ἄλλα ἱερὰ σκεύη *Chron.Pasch*.p.390(M.92.1001C); ἐλθόντος τοῦ ἁγίου π., μετέλαβεν τοῦ ἁγίου σώματος καὶ αἵματος τοῦ μεγάλου θεοῦ καὶ σωτῆρος ἡμῶν Jo.Mosch.*prat*.48(M.87.2904B); τὸ π. ἐστιν ἀντὶ τοῦ σκεύους οὗ ἐδέξαντο τὸ ἐκβλυσθὲν τῆς αἱμαχθείσης ἀχράντου πλευρᾶς καὶ χειρῶν καὶ ποδῶν τοῦ Χριστοῦ ἀπομύρισμα. ἔστι δὲ πάλιν τὸ π. κατὰ τὸν κρατῆρα ὃν γράφει κύριος ἤτοι ἡ σοφία καὶ ὁ υἱὸς τοῦ θεοῦ ἐκέρασε τὸ ἑαυτοῦ αἷμα ἀντὶ τοῦ οἴνου ἐκείνου καὶ προέθηκε ἐν τῇ αὐτοῦ ἁγίᾳ τραπέζῃ ‡Bas.*h.myst*.53(p.391.20); τὸ δὲ ἐν τῷ π. ποιῆσαι τύπον σταυροῦ καὶ αὐτὸν τρίτον, ἁγιασθῆναι δηλοῖ τὸν τετραπέρατον ἅπαντα κόσμον παρὰ τῆς...ἐνσάρκου οἰκονομίας καὶ παρὰ τοῦ...πάθους Χριστοῦ

‡Germ.CP *contempl.*(M.98.448C); of chalice alleged to have been broken by Athanasius, Const.ap.Ath.*apol.sec.*68(p.146.18; M.25.369C); περὶ π. κυριακοῦ κεκλασμένου *Ep.Mareot.*2(p.156.4; M.25.385B); π. δὲ κατέαξε μυστικόν Socr.*h.e.*1.27.15(M.67.156B); for π. εὐλογίας v. εὐλογία; **7.** fig.; **a.** Peratic τὸ δὲ οὐδέν ἐστιν ὃ χωρὶς αὐτοῦ γέγονεν, ὁ κόσμος ὁ ἰδικός...τοῦτο...ἐστὶ τὸ π. τὸ κόνδυ ἐν ᾧ βασιλεὺς πίνων οἰωνίζεται. τοῦτο...κεκρυμμένον εὑρέθη ἐν τοῖς καλοῖς τοῦ Βενιαμὶν σπέρμασι...τοῦτο...τὸ τοῦ Ἀνακρέοντος π. ἀλάλως λαλοῦν μυστήριον ἄρρητον...καὶ τοῦτό ἐστι τὸ ὕδωρ...ὃ...ὁ Ἰησοῦς ἐποίησεν οἶνον Hipp.*haer.*5.8(p.90.3; M.16.3142A); **b.** of cup of reward or punishment ἐν τῇ δεξιᾷ χειρὶ τοῦ θεοῦ τὸ π. τῶν ἀγαθῶν σου τῶν ἔργων, εἶτα ἔστω τὸ π. σου τῶν ἁμαρτημάτων ἐν τῇ ἀριστερᾷ χειρὶ τοῦ θεοῦ. ὅταν οὖν μέλλῃς κολάζεσθαι διὰ τὰ ἁμαρτήματα, ἐπεὶ καὶ χρηστότερά σοι ἔργα γεγένηται...οὔτε γὰρ μόνον δύνασαι πιεῖν τὸ τῶν ἀγαθῶν π., ὡς οὐ μόνον ἀγαθὰ ἔργα πεποιηκώς, οὔτε δύνασαι πιεῖν μόνον τὸ τῶν ἁμαρτημάτων π., χρηστὰ γάρ σοι πέπρακταί τινα Or.*hom.12.2 in Jer.*(p.88.18; M.13.381A); π. ... τὴν τιμωρίαν ὀνομάζει... τοῦτο τὸ π. ... Ἱερεμίας τοῖς ἔθνεσι προσενεγκεῖν ἐκελεύθη Thdt.*Ps.*10:7(1.673); cf.id.*Jer.*25:15f.(2.523f.).

ποτηροπλύτης, ὁ, *bowl for washing cups*, Chrys.*fr.in Jer.*52:19(M.64.1073A).

ποτίζ-ω, 1. *give to drink*; fig., Jul.Papa *ep.Alex.*(p.134.14; M.25.345B); τὰ βδελύγματα...οἷς ἡ φιλαμαρτήμων πληθὺς ∼εται Areth.*Apoc.*17:4(M.106.717D); **2.** *water*; fig., of a teacher, Gr.Thaum.*pan.Or.*7(p.19.21; M.10.1073D); Isid.Pel.*epp.*1.173(M.78.296B).

πότιμος, *drinkable*; superl., met., of Christ's teaching, Or.*fr.in Ps.*105:32(p.92).

ποτισμός, ὁ, *water supply*, Ath.*v.Anton.*50(M.26.916C).

ποτιστήριον, τό, *drinking-trough*, ref. Gen.30:38, Gr.Nyss.*hom.15 in Cant.*(M.44.1108C); ἐπιβουλεύοι δὲ τῷ πνευματικῷ π. id.*Apoll.*1(M.45.1125A).

ποτιστής, ὁ, *one who gives to drink*, Nil.*epp.*2.49(M.79.220C).

ποτνιασμός, ὁ, *lamentation*, Ant.Mon.*hom.*18(M.89.1485A).

ποτνι-άω, 1. *cry out in horror* or *grief* ἔλαθέν με ∼ῶν ὁ πτωχός Ast.Am.*hom.*1(M.40.172C); Marc.Er.*opusc.*7.14(M.65.1092B); Thdr.Stud.*epp.*2.209(M.99.1632B), but usu. med.; ref. Christ's agony τί οὖν ∼ᾶται καὶ ὀδύρεται; Cels.ap.Or.*Cels.*2.24(p.153.7; M.11.841D); **2.** med., *implore, entreat* ἀνεκαλεῖτο...ἐν εὐχαῖς τοῦτον...∼ώμενος φῆναι αὐτῷ ἑαυτὸν ὅστις εἴη Eus.*v.C.*1.28(p.21.5; M.20.944A); πρὸς πατέρα...∼ώμενοι Gr.Naz.*or.*5.27(M.35.697B); Mac.Aeg.*carit.*6(M.34.912D); Thdt.*affect.*10(p.251.10; 4.959); τὸν θεὸν ∼ώμενος Euthal.Diac.*epp.cath.*(M.85.668A); πᾶσαν κτίσιν ∼ᾶσθαι αὐτῷ παιδεύων ‡Caes.Naz.*dial.*29(M.38.889); ∼ωμένῳ...τὸ ἀγαθὸν εὑρεῖν †Jo.D.*B.J.*5(M.96.896B).

ποῦ, 1. *whither?* ἐμάθετε ποῦ ὁ Παῦλος κατήχθη *A.Xanthipp.*12(p.65.21); **2.** *how?* εἰ καὶ σημεῖα ἐγένοντο, ποῦ οὐκ ἂν ἐγένετο ῥήγματα; Chrys.*hom.32.7 in Mt.*(7.375E); ποῦ...κεκένωκεν ἑαυτόν Cyr.*expl.xii cap.*4(p.19.26; 6¹.150D).

***πουβλικός** (*πουπλ-), (Lat. *publicus*) *public, notorious*, πουπλ-, Hipp.*haer.*9.12(p.246.18; M.16.3379C); *Cod.Afr.*43.

***πούλπιτον, τό,** (Lat. *pulpitum*) *stage, platform*, Jo.Mal.*chron.*15 p.387(M.97.576A).

πουλυέλικτος, metr. gr. for πολυέλικτος, *moving far on* π. ... ἴχνος Nonn.*par.Jo.*8:21(M.43.816B); αἰὼν π. *ib.*13:8(861A).

***πουλυέτηρος,** metr. gr. for ⟨πολυέτηρος⟩, *long-lived*, Nonn.*par.Jo.*8:57(M.43.824A).

πουλυμέλαθρος, metr. gr. for πολυμέλαθρος, *with many halls*, Nonn.*par.Jo.*14:2(M.43.868A).

πουλυπόδης, ὁ, metr. gr. for πολυ-, *polypus*, Gr.Naz.*carm.*1.2.9.44(M.37.670A).

[*]πουλύχοος, metr. gr. for πολύχοος, *pouring forth much, prolific, abundant*, Gr.Naz.*carm.*1.2.9.88(M.37.674A).

***πουπλικός,** v. *πουβλικός.

πούς, ὁ, *foot*; **1.** purpose of feet πόδες ἐδόθησαν, ἵνα τρέχῃς εἰς καλὰ ἔργα Chrys.*diab.*2.3(2.264A); id.*hom.10.5 in Phil.*(11.281C); objection discussed that resurrection body will not need feet, Gr.Nyss.*anim.et res.*(M.46.144C); **2.** of aspiration of worshipper to heavenly sphere τούς τε πόδας ἐπεγείρομεν κατὰ τὴν τελευταίαν τῆς εὐχῆς συνεκφώνησιν, ἐπακολουθοῦντες τῇ προθυμίᾳ τοῦ πνεύματος εἰς τὴν νοητὴν οὐσίαν Clem.*str.*7.7(p.30.20; M.9.456B); fig., in spiritual life ἀνατεινόμενοι δὲ ἄνω τῇ ἐννοίᾳ...ὀλίγῳ π. ἐφαπτόμενοι τῆς γῆς id.*paed.*1.5(p.99.32; M.8.269A); **3.** ref. washing of feet; **a.** as social custom ἰδὼν δὲ τὸν ξένον μάλα κεκμηκότα, ἄγε δή, πρὸς τὴν θυγατέρα ἔφη, ὅπως τοῦ ἀνδρὸς τοὺς π. νίψῃς Soz.*h.e.*1.11.10(M.67.889B); **b.** met. ἐπεμβαίνειν τολμήσαντες ἀνίπτοις τοῖς ποσὶ (τοῦτο δὴ τὸ τοῦ λόγου) ἀκοαῖς, αἷς...ὁ θεῖος λόγος οὐδὲν ἐσκεπασμένοις...τοῖς π. ὥσπερ ὑπὸ παχέων τινῶν δερμάτων τῶν...ἀσαφῶν λέξεων, ἀλλὰ γυμνοῖς...σαφὴς ...ἐμβατεύων ἐνεπιδημεῖ Gr.Thaum.*pan.Or.*2(p.5.17; M.10.1056C); **c.** ref. Jo.13:6ff., cf. *ipsum verbum per seipsum sordes abluit filiarum Sion, manibus suis lavans pedes discipulorum. hic est enim finis humani generis haeredificantis deum...uti...qui ab initio discipuli, emundati et abluti quae sunt mortis, in vitam veniant dei*, Iren.*haer.*4.22.1(M.7.1046B); ἀπονίπτων τοὺς π. τῶν μαθητῶν εἰς τὰς καλὰς πράξεις ἀποστέλλων αὐτούς, τὴν ὁδοιπορίαν αὐτῶν τὴν εἰς τὰς εὐεργεσίας τῶν ἐθνῶν ᾐνίξατο εὐπρεπῆ καὶ καθαρὰν προπαρασκευάσας τῇ ἰδίᾳ δυνάμει Clem.*paed.*2.8(p.195.12; M.8.468B); cf. *aqua quam mittebat Jesus in pelvim, ros erat gratiae coelestis, ex quo lavabat pedes discipulorum...et nos, modo si praebeamus pedes nostros, paratus et dominus lavare pedes animae...et purgare eos...gratia spiritus sancti, verbo doctrinae*, Or.*hom.8.5 in Jud.*(p.514.15; M.12.985B); τί δὲ ἦν ὃ ἐποίει νίπτων τοὺς π. τῶν μαθητῶν ὁ Ἰησοῦς; ἢ εἰργάζετο διὰ τοῦ νίπτειν αὐτῶν τοὺς π. ... ὡραίους αὐτούς, μελλόντων αὐτῶν εὐαγγελίσασθαι τὰ ἀγαθά; ὅτε γὰρ ἔνιψεν τοὺς π. ... τότε... πεπλήρωται τὸ περὶ τῶν ἀποστόλων αὐτοῦ προφητικῶς εἰρημένον, ὡς ὡραῖοι οἱ π. τῶν εὐαγγελιζομένων τὰ ἀγαθά id.*Jo.*32.7(6; p.436.30; M.14.760A); cf. *salvator...mittit spiritalem aquam in pelvim secundum scripturas et lavat pedes discipulorum...ut cum mundi fuerint, ascendant ad dicentem, ego sum via. ... qui vere...sunt episcopi... mittunt aquam de scripturis in pelvim animae...et tentant pedum discipulorum sordes lavare*, id.*hom.6.5 in Is.*(M.12.241B); πῶς ἀλαζὼν ὁ...νίπτων ἑκάστου τοὺς π.; id.*Cels.*2.7(p.133.4; M.11.804C); Ephr.3.423B; καὶ εἰ καθαροί εἰσι, τίνος ἕνεκεν νίπτεις τοὺς π.; ὥστε ἡμᾶς μετριάζειν μαθεῖν Chrys.*hom.70.2 in Jo.*(8.416A); τοσαύτην ὑπέστη τὴν ταπείνωσιν ὡς...τῶν...μαθητῶν ἀπονίζειν τοὺς π. Cyr.*Jo.*9(4.721D); καὶ αὐτοῦ [sc. Judas] π. ἔνιψεν, ἀπροφάσιστον αὐτοῦ τὴν δυσσέβειαν ἀποτελῶν, ἵνα καρπὸς τῆς ἐνούσης αὐτῷ πονηρίας ἡ ἀπόστασις φαίνηται *ib.*(726A); διὰ τῆς ἀφῆς ἐκαθάρισεν αὐτῶν τοὺς π. εἰς ἑτοιμασίαν τοῦ εὐαγγελίου· ἄγει δὲ καὶ εἰς ταπεινοφροσύνην Ammon.*Jo.*13:6(M.85.1481B); τούτων τοὺς π. ὡραίους ἀποκαλεῖ, ὡς τὸν καλὸν τρέχοντας δρόμον, ὡς ὑπὸ τῶν δεσποτικῶν ἀπονιφθέντας χειρῶν Thdt.*Rom.*10:15(3.114); related to baptism ἔνιψεν τοὺς π., ἐπεὶ ἦσαν ὡς ἐν ἀνθρώποις καθαροὶ ἀλλ' οὐχὶ καὶ παρὰ θεῷ· χωρὶς γὰρ Ἰησοῦ οὐδεὶς παρὰ θεῷ καθαρὸς γίνεται...τοῖς δ' ὡς ἐν ἀνθρώποις καθαροῖς ἤδη γεγενημένοις καὶ λουσαμένοις τὸ τοῦ Ἰησοῦ βάπτισμα, καὶ νιψαμένοις ὑπ' αὐτοῦ τοὺς π., ἐνοικεῖν καὶ τὸ ἅγιον δύναται πνεῦμα Or.*Jo.*32.7(6; p.436.17ff.; M.14.757C); καλὸν καὶ τὰς χεῖρας τελειοῦσθαι, καὶ τοὺς π. ... τοὺς δέ, μὴ ὀξεῖς εἶναι πρὸς τὸ ἐκχέειν αἷμα...ἀλλ' ἑτοίμους εἰς τὸ ...Χριστὸν ὑπονίπτοντα καὶ καθαίροντα δέχεσθαι Gr.Naz.*or.*40.39(M.36.416A); cf. ἐκδυσαμένη [sc. ἡ ψυχή] τὸν δερμάτινον χιτῶνα...καὶ ἀπονιψαμένη τῶν π. τὸ γεῶδες, ᾧ ἐνειλήθη ἀπὸ τῆς ἐν παραδείσῳ διαγωγῆς εἰς τὴν γῆν ἀναλύσασα...τὸν παλαιὸν λέγω ἄνθρωπον, ὃν ἐκδύσασθαι καὶ ἀποθέσθαι κελεύει ὁ...ἀπόστολος τοὺς μέλλοντας τῷ λουτρῷ τοῦ λόγου τὸν ῥύπον τῶν βασέων τῆς ψυχῆς ἀποκλύσασθαι Gr.Nyss.*hom.11 in Cant.*(M.44.1004D); Thdr.Mops.*Jo.*13:10(p.380.9; M.66.772D); Cyr.*Jo.*9(4.723B,C); Ammon.*Jo.*13:10(M.85.1481C); **4.** of removal of shoes from feet οὐδὲ γὰρ Μωυσῆς τῷ θείῳ προστάγματι τῆς νεκρᾶς τῶν δερμάτων περιβολῆς ἐλευθερώσας τοὺς π. ... πάλιν ἱστορεῖται διαλαβὼν τοὺς π. τοῖς ὑποδήμασιν...ἀλλ' ἦν καλλωπισμὸς τοῦ ἱερατικοῦ π. τὸ γυμνὸν εἶναι πάσης περιβολῆς Gr.Nyss.*hom.11 in Cant.*(M.44.1005C); related to putting off of shoes in baptism and to Jo.13:6ff., *ib.*(1008B), cf. *solve calceamentum e pedibus tuis; quidam opinantur his verbis juberi Mosen dimittere uxorem... quidam aiunt hanc praemonitionem fuisse monumentum legis dandae, secundum quam sacerdotes discalceati rem divinam facerent... quidam volunt deum istud imperasse...ut Judaei...discerent majore cautela versari et ambulare coram deo...quidam...deum...significare Mosi fore ut proterat et conculcet Aegyptios...infert alius...qui sub calceamento intelligit pedem, quasi deus diceret, Move pedem tuum contra hostes...verumtamen deus ipse subdit causam, inquiens, locus in quo stas, terra sancta est. at quid inquinabit sanctam terram?... omnis enim locus in quo fuerit Christus, locus sacer indicatur. ... ad hanc celsitudinem et lucem deitatis non licet scandere pedibus quos calceamenta onerant. solvendus...est amictus, qui constat ex terrenis et mortuis pellibus*, Proc.G.*Ex.*3:2(M.87.526–7); cf.Nil.ap.eund.*Cant.*5:3(M.87.1680C); **5.** of 'feet' of God πόδες, ἡ παρουσία, ἐπειδὴ ποσὶ παραγινόμεθα οὗ ἐὰν δοκῇ Diod.*Gen.*6:6(M.33.1571A); Gennad.*fr.Gen.*1:26(M.85.1633B); Jo.D.*f.o.*1.11(M.94.814A); of angels τοὺς π. δέ, τὸ κινητικόν, καὶ ὀξὺ καὶ ἐντρεχὲς τῆς ἐπὶ τὰ θεῖα πορευτικῆς ἀεικινησίας Dion.Ar.*c.h.*15.3(M.3.332C); **6.** of those who comprise the 'feet' of Church as body of Christ, ref. Ps.18:6 interpreted of Church triumphant οἱ μὲν ὡς κεφαλή...οἱ δὲ ὡς πόδες ἐν ἡλίῳ τεθήσονται φωτεινοί Clem.*ecl.*56(p.153.11; M.9.725A); **7.** of feet of paschal lamb, allegorically interpreted, Cyr.*glaph.Ex.*2(1.273A); id.*hom.pasch.*22(5².275Eff.); Ammon.*Jo.*19:36(M.85.1513B); cf. *qui adhibiti sunt epulo pedum Christi, non sunt amplius...cunctatores, immo festinanter currunt ad palmam supernae vocationis Christi,* Proc.G.*Ex.*12:9(M.87.571A); **8.** of 'foot' of the soul εἴπερ ἐσθίειν μέλλομεν τὸ πάσχα τὸ μυστικόν, τοὺς τῆς ψυχῆς κατασφαλισώμεθα π. τῇ ἐγκρατείᾳ Nil.*epp.*4.55(M.79.576A); **9.** phrase ἐκ ποδός *standing,* Agath.*v.Gr.Ill.*158(p.80); **10.** as an oath ναί, τῶν π. ἡμῶν CEph.(449) *act.*(*ACO* 2.1.1 p.188.42; H.2.237A); CChalc.*act.*4(*ACO* 2.1.2 p.110.22; H.2.413E).

πρᾶγμα, τό, [acc. πράγμαν *Mir.Geo.*6(p.72.8)]; **1.** *action, thing;* **2.** *creature,* Clem.*str.*1.28(p.109.7; M.8.924A); οὐδὲν γὰρ αὐτό τι καθ' ἑαυτὸ τῶν π. ἡγητέον εἶναι κακόν Meth.*symp.*2.5(p.21.16; M.18.56A); θεὸς...πάντων π. πατήρ Const.ap.Gel.Cyz.*h.e.*2.7.8(M.85.1233C); **3.** *object, reality,* opp. *name* τὰ ὀνόματα καθ' ὑποκειμένων κατηγορεῖσθαι πραγμάτων Athenag.*leg.*5.1(M.6.900B); ἐπεὶ...δύο εἰσὶν ἰδέαι τῆς ἀληθείας, τά τε ὀνόματα καὶ τὰ π., οἱ μὲν τὰ ὀνόματα λέγουσιν, οἱ περὶ τὰ κάλλη τῶν λόγων διατρίβοντες, οἱ παρ' Ἕλλησι φιλόσοφοι, τὰ π. δὲ παρ' ἡμῖν ἐστι τοῖς βαρβάροις Clem.*str.*6.17(p.509.31; M.9.381C); Πυθαγόρας ἠξίου...πρεσβύτατον ἡγεῖσθαι τῶν σοφῶν τὸν θέμενον τὰ ὀνόματα τοῖς π. id.*ecl.*32(p.146.25; M.9.716A); τρία ἐστὶ περὶ τὴν φωνήν· τά τε ὀνόματα σύμβολα ὄντα τῶν νοημάτων...καὶ...τῶν ὑποκειμένων, δεύτερον δὲ τὰ νοήματα ὁμοιώματα...τῶν ὑποκειμένων ὄντα...τρίτον δὲ τὰ ὑποκείμενα π., ἀφ' ὧν ἡμῖν τὰ νοήματα ἐντυποῦνται id.*str.*8.8(p.94.11; M.9.589A); τὰ γὰρ π. τῶν ὀνομάτων ἰσχυρότερα Didym.(‡Bas.)*Eun.*4(1.285A; M.29.685A); opp. falsehood and fiction ἀφαιρεῖται δὲ ἄλλος δεισιδαιμονίαν διὰ τῆς ἐπιγνώσεως τῶν π. Clem.*ecl.*28(p.145.22; M.9.713A); [Mt.12:36] ἀργὸν δέ, τὸ μὴ κατὰ πράγματος κείμενον, τὸ ψευδές, τὸ συκοφαντίαν ἔχον Chrys.*hom.42.2 in Mt.*(7.453D); φοβοῦμαι δὲ μὴ κατὰ πραγμάτων ᾖ τὰ λεγόμενα ῥήματα id.*hom.3.3 in 1Tim.*(11.565C); in gen. τρία...τῆς γνωστικῆς δυνάμεως ἀποτελέσματα, πρῶτον τὸ γινώσκειν τὰ π. Clem.*str.*7.1(p.5.7; 408A); φύσις ἐστὶν ἡ τῶν π. ἀλήθεια, ἡ τούτων τὸ ἐνούσιον id.*fr.*37 (p.219.19; M.9.752A); διδασκαλίαι...καινοτέρων οὖσαι πραγμάτων ἀπαγγελτικαί Cyr.H.*catech.*20.1; τίς τοῦτο εἴποι ἂν περὶ ἀνθρώπου; οὐ τῷ π., φησί, λέγω Chrys.*hom.12.1 in Heb.*(12.121D); θεὸς καὶ ἄνθρωπός ἐστιν...πράγματι καὶ ἀληθείᾳ Max.*ep.*17(M.91.581C); **4.** *object, entity,* Trin. and Christol. θρησκεύομεν οὖν τὸν πατέρα τῆς ἀληθείας καὶ τὸν υἱὸν τὴν ἀλήθειαν, ὄντα δύο τῇ ὑποστάσει π. ἓν δὲ τῇ ὁμονοίᾳ Or.*Cels.*8.12(p.230.1; M.11.1533C); τρία ὁμολογοῦντες π. καὶ τρία πρόσωπα τοῦ πατρὸς καὶ τοῦ υἱοῦ καὶ τοῦ ἁγίου πνεύματος *Symb.Ant.*(345)4(p.252.22; M.26.729B); ref. Sabellius ὁ...ἓν π. πολυπρόσωπον λέγων πατέρα καὶ υἱὸν καὶ ἅγιον πνεῦμα Bas.*ep.*210.3(3.315A; M.32.772B); ἓν π. πολυώνυμον...καὶ μίαν ὑπόστασιν ὑπὸ τριῶν προσηγοριῶν ἐκφωνουμένην *ib.*226.4(349A; M.849C); τοῖν δυοῖν π. τὴν εἰς ἓν ἀναπλοκήν, τοῦ τε ἀνθρωπίνου...καὶ τοῦ θεϊκοῦ Cyr.*Jo.*11.9(4.969D); ἐκ δυοῖν μὲν π. ... θεότητός τε καὶ ἀνθρωπότητος ὁ Ἐμμανουήλ id.*ep.*1(p.18.19; 5².13A); id.*Thds.*44(p.72.22; 5².41D); id.*apol.orient.*3(p.40.27; 6¹.167C); ἀσύγχυτοι γὰρ αἱ δύο φύσεις ἐν τῷ Χριστῷ, τὰ δύο αὐτοῦ γένη, τουτέστι τὰ δύο αὐτοῦ π., τὸ κτιστὸν καὶ τὸ ἄκτιστον Eulog.*fr.Trin.*4.8(p.371); **5.** *law-suit,* π. *Graecum est, quod Latine dicitur causa,* Isid.H.*etym.*5.21.22; ἐὰν ἐπισκόπων τις ἄντικρυς ἀδελφοῦ ἑαυτοῦ καὶ συνεπισκόπου π. σχοίη CSard.*can.*3; CChalc.*can.*9; πράγματα παρέχειν *bring an action,* Chrys.*hom.18.2 in Mt.*(7.236A); or, *hold responsible, lay charge against* ὁ δὲ τῷ θανάτῳ πράγματα παρέχων, πολλῷ μᾶλλον τοῖς σταυρώσασιν id.*hom.6.2 in Ac.*(9.50B); πρᾶγμα ἔχειν *be held responsible, be charged with a fault* οὐκ ἔχει π. ὁ ἀναχωρητής, ἀλλ' ἐψευσάμην κατ' αὐτοῦ *Apophth.Patr.*(M.65.260B); *ib.*(285C); Dor.*doct.*4.10(M.88.1672A); ἐγὼ π. οὐκ ἔχω *V.Dan.*(p.259.7).

πραγματευτής, ὁ, *trader, commercial traveller, agent, A.Thom.*B 7 (p.29.18); Jo.Disc.*v.Epiph.*2(M.41.25B); Pall.*h.Laus.*13(p.36.12; M.34.1035B); Jo.Mosch.*prat.*75(M.87.2928A); met. σὺ...τῆς ἀγγελικῆς διαγωγῆς π. Bas.*renunt.*2(2.204A; M.31.629D).

πραγματευτικός, 1. *trading* π. σκάφη *merchant ships,* Thphn.*chron.*p.323(M.108.781B); **2.** *concerned with trade,* of tax levied on traders π. χρυσίου Bas.*ep.*88(3.179E; M.32.469A).

***πραγματευτικῶς,** *in the manner of tradesmen,* Thdr.Stud.*epp.*1.11(M.99.949A).

***πραγματίδια, τά,** *small fortune, estate, Mir.Artem.*36(p.58.18).

πραγματικός, 1. *active, practical,* opp. *contemplative* πρακτικόν Or.*hom.1 in Lc.*(p.9.17, v.l. πραγματικόν); **2.** *real, effectual,* opp. *conceptual,* Christol. οὔτε θελήματος διαφορὰν ἢ γνώμης, ἢ ἐνεργείας, ἢ δυνάμεως, ἤ τινος ἑτέρου, ἅτινα τὴν π. ... ἐν ἡμῖν γεννῶσι διαίρεσιν ‡Cyr.*Trin.*10(6³.15E; M.77.1144B); τὴν ἐν ποιότητι φυσικῇ διαφορὰν τῇ π. καὶ κατὰ φύσιν Max.*opusc.*(M.91.40B); ἕνωσιν φυσικὴν ἤγουν...π. id.*ep.*15(M.91.556C); *ib.*(572C); Cyrus Al.*cap.*7(H.3.1341D); opp. *figurative* or *sacramental,* of martyrdom in rel. to baptism οὐκ ἠλλοτρίωται ὁ μυστικὸς ἡμῶν θάνατος τοῦ π., κἂν εἰ τελειοῦται ἐν τῷ π. Eutych.*pasch.*5(M.86.2397A); **3.** π. τύπος, or as subst. τὸ π., *imperial mandate,* sanctio pragmatica τοῦ θείου π. Thds.Imp.*cod.*9.45.4(p.67.2; H.1.1720D); θείου...καὶ προσκυνουμένου τύπου π. Phot.Tyr.*supplic.*(p.105.4; H.2.437C); CChalc.*can.*12.

πραγματικῶς, 1. *really, in actual fact;* **a.** opp. *conceptually, verbally,* Christol. τῇ μὲν οὖν ἐνεργείᾳ, καὶ ὡς ἄν τις εἴποι π., οὐδ' ἡμεῖς διαιροῦμεν τὰς φύσεις· τῇ δ' ἐπινοίᾳ διΐστανται Eust.Mon.*ep.*(M.86.921D); οὐ π. ... διΐστανται τὰ ἐξ ὧν...Χριστὸς συνετέθη Justn.*conf.*(p.82.25; M.86.1005C); Max.*ambig.*(M.91.1049D); **b.** opp. *symbolically, typically, sacramentally,* Clem.*str.*2.1(p.113.15; M.8.932A); Or.*Cels.*6.2(p.71.15; M.11.1289C); μυστικῶς...ἀποθνήσκομεν ἐν τῷ βαπτίσματι ...ἐν μαρτυρίῳ δὲ...π. Eutych.*pasch.*5(M.86.2397A); παραβολικῶς καὶ τυπικῶς, ἀλλ' οὐ π. Anast.S.*qu.et resp.*91(M.89.721C); **2.** *essentially, absolutely* τήν τε διαφορὰν καὶ τὴν ἕνωσιν...τὴν μὲν ἐν τῷ φυσικῷ λόγῳ π. καὶ τελείως συντηρουμένην, τὴν δὲ...ἐν τῷ οἰκονομικῷ τρόπῳ ...ὑποστατικῶς σωζομένην Max.*opusc.*(M.91.84A); *ib.*(152A); **3.** *in activity, in relation to action, in deed* τὸ 'ἐκεῖ' π. νοούμενον, καὶ οὐχὶ δὴ μᾶλλον τοπικῶς Cyr.*Os.*67(3.101C); ζητεῖται γὰρ παρ' ἡμῖν ὁ θεὸς οὐχὶ μᾶλλον τοπικῶς, ἀλλ' οἶμαι π. id.*Soph.*4(3.583A); id.*thes.*32(5¹.320D); *ib.*21(214E); ἐπεὶ...ἡ πρακτικὴ ἀρετὴ...δικαιοσύνη καλεῖται, ταύτην ἀναγγέλλειν π. μόνοι ἴσασιν οἱ οὐρανοί, ὄντες ἄνδρες δίκαιοι id.*Ps.*96:6(M.69.1249C); ὡς λογικῶς τε καὶ π. ἀρνουμένου Χριστοῦ Thdr.Stud.*epp.*2.49(M.99.1257A).

***πραγματιωδῶς (πραγματωδῶς),** *really, in fact,* opp. nominally or conceptually, Christol. τὸ τῆς ἑνώσεως ἄφραστον δώρημα πραγματωδῶς ἐστιν Leont.H.*Nest.*3.1(M.86.1604B); *ib.*3.5(1616A); φύσει καὶ π. *ib.*3.6(1620C); σώζεσθαι π. κατὰ φύσιν τὰ ἑνωθέντα μετὰ τὴν ἕνωσιν Max.*ep.*13(M.91.524D).

***πραγματογραφέω,** *describe in material terms* or *literally,* Sever.*sigill.*4(M.63.537).

***πραετεριτίων, ἡ,** (Lat. *praeteritio*) *passing over* in a will, Ath.Scholast.*coll.*9 paratit.10(p.110).

***πραῖδα (*πρέδα), ἡ,** (Lat. *praeda*) *booty, plunder* εἰς πρέδαν δέδωκε τὴν ἐκκλησίαν Ath.*ep.encycl.*4(p.173.2; M.25.229B); μερισάμενοι τὴν π. Jo.Mal.*chron.*5 p.108(M.97.200A); *Chron.Pasch.*p.247(M.92.593B); Thphn.*chron.*p.152(M.108.409C); *ib.*p.380(909C); as though acc. of ⟨πραῖς⟩, *plundering raid* ὅταν...ὁ τῶν Σαρακηνῶν φύλαρχος τὴν πραῖδα (s.v.l.) πεποίηκεν Jo.Mosch.*prat.*155(M.87.3024B).

πραιδεύ-ω, (cf. Lat. *praedor*) *plunder,* CSyr.*act.*(p.103.1; H.2.1381D); Cyr.S.*v.Sab.*(p.172.4); ~θέντων Χριστιανῶν *ib*(p.175.11); Jo.Mal.*chron.*2 p.30(M.97.100A).

***πραίκεπτον, τό,** (Lat. *praeceptum*) *precept, instruction,* Martin.*ep.*5(M.*PL.*87.156D); Max.*ep.Anast.*(M.90.132C).

πραίκων, ὁ, (Lat. *praeco*) *herald, A.Pil.*A 1.2(p.217).

πραιπόσιτος ([*]πρεπόσιτος), ὁ, (Lat. *praepositus*) *one set in authority, prefect;* **1.** as military title, praefectus castrorum, *PLond.*1914.17; Ath.*h.Ar.*72(p.222.21; M.25.780A); **2.** *civil magistrate* γράψαι ...πρὸς τοὺς λογιστὰς καὶ τοὺς στρατηγοὺς καὶ τοὺς π. τοῦ πάγου ἑκάστης πόλεως Sabinus ap.Eus.*h.e.*9.1.6(M.20.801A); of a city treasurer, Bas.*ep.*237.1(3.365A; M.32.885B); **3.** praepositus sacri cubiculi, *Lord Chamberlain* πρεπόσιτος Cyr.S.*v.Thds.*(p.240.19); dignity and office reserved to eunuchs, Pall.*h.Laus.*63(p.158.6; M.34.1235B); Cyr.*ep.*44(p.37.6; 5².134D); for long, head of all *cubicularii* τὸν δὲ π. τοῦ παλατίου αὐτοῦ ὀνόματι Ῥοδανόν, ἄνδρα δυνατώτατον καὶ εὔπορον καὶ διοικοῦντα τὸ παλάτιον. ὡς πρῶτον ὄντα ἀρχιευνοῦχον καὶ ἐν μεγάλῃ τιμῇ ὄντα Jo.Mal.*chron.*13 p.339(M.97.505C); position leading to great influence and highest honours, e.g. in case of Eutropius, cf.Chrys.*Eutrop.*1.2(3.382D); playing a leading part in court ceremonial, e.g. coronation, *Euchol.*(p.727).

***πραισεντεύω,** (from Lat. *praesens*) *be at hand,* Jo.Mal.*chron.*7, p.176(M.97.281B).

***πραίσεντον, τό,** a body of troops called *praesens militia, bodyguard* στρατηγοῖς τοῦ θείου π. CSyr.*act.*(*ACO* 3 p.101.30; H.2.1380D); Jo.Mal.*chron.*14 p.375(M.97.560A); *ib.*16 p.398(589B); Evagr.*h.e.*4.3 (p.154.14; M.86.2705B); κόμητα πραισέντου Thphn.*chron.*p.141(M.108.384A).

***πραισόριον (*πρησώριον), τό,** (Lat. *pressorium*) *press, M.Pers.*8.10(p.460.8); πρησώ-, Call.*v.Hyp.*(p.77).

***πραίτωρ, ὁ,** Lat. *praetor,* Thphn.*chron.*p.59(M.108.200C).

***πραιτωριοκτυπέω,** *knock at door of praetorium, canvass the palace,* Pall.*v.Chrys.*5(p.29.21, v.l. πραιτώρια κατατρίβοντες; M.47.19).

πραιτώριον ([*]πρετ-), τό, (Lat. *praetorium*); **1.** *governor's residence and seat of his jurisdiction;* of Pilate's praetorium (Jo.

18:28), Clem.*fr*.28(p.217.5; M.9.757B); Jo.D.*hom*.3.3(M.96.592D); in gen., *M.Thdot.1* 22(p.75.5); *Chron.Pasch*.p.308(M.92.785A); *ib*.p.337 (877A); **2.** *palace* ἡ φυλακὴ ἐμοὶ γέγονεν π. *M.Perp*.3(p.67.1); π. βασιλικά *A.Thom*.A 3(p.103.11); πρετ-, Cyr.S.*v.Abr*.(p.247.15); **3.** ἔπαρχος τοῦ π. *praetorian prefect*, *Ep.Mareot*.2 ap.Ath.*apol.sec*.76(p.155.36; M.25.385A); cf. ἔπαρχος τῶν πραιτωρίων *ib*.infra.

***πραιτώριος**, (Lat. *praetorius*) *of* or *belonging to the emperor's guard*, *praetorian*; **1.** of praetorian guard, Socr.*h.e*.1.2.1(M.67.36A); **2.** ἔπαρχος τῶν π. *praetorian prefect*, Pall.*v.Chrys*.3(p.19.18; M.47.14); *ib*.11(p.66.28; M.47.38); CChalc.*act*.1(*ACO* 2.1.1 p.55.9; H.2.53B); Philost.*h.e*.3.28(M.65.513D); Cyr.S.*v.Sab*.54(p.146.1).

***πραίφεκτος, ὁ,** (Lat. *praefectus*) *prefect*, Antoninus Imperator ap.Just.*1apol*.71(M.6.440B); *A.Paul*.3(p.112.4); πρέφ-, *Trad.Pil*.10 (p.455).

πρακτεῖον, τό, *revenue-office* ἐδωρήσατο χρημάτων δόσιν τὰ γενόμενα ἐκ τοῦ πρακτίου *CIG* 8619 (Chers. Taurica, 476).

πρακτέος, *to be done*; neut. as subst., *deed* τῇ ἐφεκτικῇ...τῶν ἡδέων καὶ τῇ κατορθωτικῇ τῶν π. Clem.*str*.7.7(p.33.27; M.9.464B); τῶν π. τὰς ἀμοιβάς ‡Just.*qu.et resp*.93(M.6.1336A); Thdr.Stud.*epp*.1.56(M.99.1112C); ὡς μακάριά σου τὰ π. *ib*.2.70(1300B).

***πρακτεύω,** *perform*, Thdr.Stud.*or*.11.5.27(M.99.829C) prob. for τρακτεύω.

πρακτήρ (πρηκτήρ), ὁ, *tax-collector*; in gen., πρηκτήρ Gr.Naz.*carm*.2.1.1.149(M.37.981A); Ast.Am.*hom*.4(M.40.220B); Nil.*epp*.3.43(M.79.413A); of collectors of temple-tax (Mt.17:24), Cyr.*Jo*.2.5 (4.189C); of collectors of revenue for Montanist sect, Apollon.ap. Eus.*h.e*.5.18.2(M.20.476B).

πρακτήριος, neut. as subst., *practice*, *activity*, Thdr.Stud.*epp*.2.187(M.99.1573C).

***πρακτίκευμα, τό,** ? *difficulty* ἐπὶ τῶν αὐτῶν...π. Thdr.Stud.*epp*.2.142(M.99.1448C).

πρακτικεύομαι, *operate*, Dion.Ar.*d.n*.4.10(M.3.708B).

πρακτικός, *practical*, *active*; **1.** of practical opp. theoretical knowledge θεωρητικὸν μὲν τὸ κατὰ νοῦν, ὡς ἔχει τὰ ὄντα, π. δὲ τὸ βουλευτικόν, τὸ ὁρίζον τοῖς π. τὸν ὀρθὸν λόγον. καὶ καλοῦσι τὸ μὲν θεωρητικὸν νοῦν, τὸ δὲ π. λόγον, καὶ τὸ μὲν σοφίαν, τὸ δὲ φρόνησιν Max.*ambig*.(M.91.1109B); **2.** of active opp. contemplative qualities and way of life; **a.** as mutually complementary ὁ λόγος...σὰρξ γενόμενος τὴν αὐτὴν ἀρετὴν π. ἅμα καὶ θεωρητικὴν ἐπιδεικνύς Clem.*paed*.1.3(p.95.21; M.8.260B); ἡ γὰρ ἀρετὴ ἡ γνωστική...θεωρητικὸν ὁμοῦ καὶ π. id.*ecl*.37(p.148.11; M.9.717A); διχῶς δὲ ἡ ὁδὸς κυρίου εὐθύνεται, κατά τε τὸ θεωρητικὸν...καὶ κατὰ τὸ π. μετὰ τὴν ὑγιῆ θεωρίαν Or.*Jo*.6.19(11; p.127.29; M.14.232D); τὴν...χήραν λεπτὰ βάλλουσαν δύο τάχα τῷ γνωστικῷ τόπῳ ἢ τῷ π. *ib*.19.8(2; p.307.32; 541A); ref. Cant.2:17 ὁ λόγος ὁμοιοῦται, ἐν μὲν τοῖς ἀνακειμένοις τῇ θεωρίᾳ, δόρκωνι· ἐν τοῖς πρακτικωτέροις δὲ καὶ καθαιρετικοῖς τῶν ἀντικειμένων δυναμέων, ἐλάφων νεβρῷ id.*schol.in Cant*.2:17(M.17.268C); Eus.*d.e*.9.13(p.432.18; M.22.697A); Didym.*Ps*.4:1(M.39.1165A); **b.** but practical qualities often contrasted with and sometimes subordinated to contemplative διὰ τοῦ 'αὐτόπται' δηλώσῃ τὸ θεωρητικόν, διὰ δὲ τοῦ 'ὑπηρέται' τὸ π. αὐτῶν παραστήσῃ...πρᾶξις γὰρ θεωρίας ἀνάβασις Or.*hom.1 in Lc*.(p.9.18); ref. Jo.1:38ff. διὰ τοῦ μὲν 'ἔρχεσθε' ἐπὶ τὸ π. αὐτοὺς παρακαλῶν, διὰ δὲ τοῦ 'ὄψεσθε' τὴν ἀκολουθοῦσαν τῇ κατορθώσει τῶν πράξεων θεωρίαν πάντως ἔσεσθαι τοῖς βουλομένοις id.*Jo*.2.36(29; p.95.9; M.14.180B); σύμβολόν ἐστι Μαρία μὲν τοῦ θεωρητικοῦ βίου, Μάρθα δὲ τοῦ π. id.*fr.80 in Jo*.(p.547.24); ἀντὶ δὲ τοῦ 'Ιακὼβ ὁ θεὸς αὐτῷ τὸ τοῦ 'Ισραὴλ ὄνομα δωρεῖται, τὸν...π. ἐπὶ τὸν θεωρητικὸν μεταστησάμενος Eus.*p.e*.11.6(519A; M.21.860D); ref. order of commandments (Mt.22:37–39) δείκνυσιν ἐν μὲν τῇ πρώτῃ τὴν θεωρητικὴν ἀρετὴν κατορθουμένην· ἐν δέ γε τῇ δευτέρᾳ τὴν π. Thdt.*Rom*.13:10(3.138); κατανύξεως μὲν πόμα πίνει ὁ π. ἐν εὐχῇ· ποτηρίῳ δὲ κρατίστῳ μεθύσκεται ὁ θεωρητικός ‡Max.*cap.al*.146(M.90.1433D); ἐν πύλαις μὲν εἰσέρχονται οἱ π. τῶν ἐντολῶν τοῦ θεοῦ ἐν τῷ εὔχεσθαι· ὡς ἐν αὐλαῖς δὲ ἀρετῶν ἐν ὕμνοις, οἱ θεωρητικοί *ib*.148(1436A); Ζοροβάβελ ἐστὶν ὁ π. νοῦς· καὶ 'Ιησοῦς ὁ θεωρητικός Max.*qu.Thal*.56(M.90.581B); **3.** in rel. to ἀγάπη, Thdt.*Rom*.13:10(3.138); ἀγάπη πάσης ἐντολῆς π. περιεκτική id.*Col*.1:4(3.474); δηλοῖ ἡ μὲν πίστις τῆς εὐσεβείας τὸ βέβαιον· ἡ δὲ ἀγάπη τὴν π. ἀρετήν id.*1Thess*.3:7(3.513); **4.** related to human and earthly, opp. heavenly, life μηδὲ π. καὶ ἀνθρωπίνης ἀρετῆς νόμους ἔστιν εὑρεῖν ἐν ἀφθάρτῳ σώματι Leont.B.*Nest.et Eut*.2(M.86.1349C); **5.** fem. as subst., *active life of good works*, almost = ἄσκησις: ἥ γε π. ἐστι διδασκαλία πνευματικὴ τὸ παθητικὸν μέρος τῆς ψυχῆς ἐκκαθαίρουσα Or.*Ps*.2:12(p.449); *ib*.39:11(p.37); Cyr.*Ps*.23:4(M.69.845A); Leont.B.*Nest.et Eut*.3(M.86.1361C); Max.*ambig*.(M.91.1068C); neut. as subst., Or.*comm.in Mt*.16.7(p.488.3; M.13.1388A); id.*Jo*.6.19 (11; p.127.31; M.14.232D); id.*dial*.9(p.140.21); Esaias *or*.16.8(p.97); **6.** of persons, *practising*, *active in*, *productive of* π. τῶν ἀρετῶν Or.*princ*.3.1.15(p.221.16; M.11.280A); ἡ ἐν σοφίᾳ πορεία καὶ π. τῶν σῳζομένων ἐν αὐτῷ γινομένη id.*Jo*.1.27(26; p.34.6; M.14.73A).

πρακτορεύομαι, *engage in business*, Thdr.Stud.*epp*.1.11(M.99.945B).

***πρακτοψηφιστής, ὁ,** *calculator of finances*, *tax-inspector*, in list of Devil's hierarchy οἱ κοσμοκράτορες τῆς πονηρίας, οἱ τελωνάρχαι, καὶ λογοθέται, καὶ π. τοῦ ἀέρος †Cyr.*hom.div*.14(5^2.405B).

πράκτωρ, ὁ, *tax-collector*, Gr.Naz.*carm*.2.1.11.444(M.37.1060A); Soz.*h.e*.5.5.4(M.67.1228A); Thphn.*chron*.p.280(M.108.693A); of exactors in gen., ref. Is.3:12 πράκτορας δὲ ἐνταῦθα δοκεῖ μὲν τοὺς ἀπαιτοῦντας λέγειν· ἐγὼ δὲ οἶμαι τοὺς ἅρπαγας...αὐτῶν αἰνίττεσθαι· εἰ δὲ μὴ τοῦτο, ἀλλὰ τοὺς φορολογοῦντας Chrys.*Is.interp*.3:12(6.40C); ref. Ps.108:11 Σύμμαχος οὕτως, συγκρούσαι πράκτωρ πάντα τὰ ὑπάρχοντα αὐτῷ· πράκτωρες δὲ καὶ οἱ 'Ρωμαίων βασιλεῖς, τὸν ἐπικείμενον εἰσπραττόμενοι φόρον Thdt.*Ps*.108:11(1.1384).

***πρανδιάρα, ἡ,** *dining-hall*, *Chron.Pasch*.p.308(M.92.781B).

***πράνδιος, ὁ,** *ribbon*, *fillet*, *headband*, Thphn.*chron*.p.196(M.108.508C).

πρᾶξις, ἡ, **1.** *conduct*; **a.** Christian ἡ μαρτυρία τῆς ἀγαθῆς π. ἡμῶν διδόσθω ὑπ' ἄλλων *1Clem*.30.7; οὐκ ἔσται ὁ λόγος σου ψευδής...ἀλλὰ μεμεστωμένος πράξει *Did*.2.5; ἐντολὴ καὶ π. Just.*dial*.44.2(M.6.569B); necessary to salvation, Iren.*haer*.1.6.2(M.7.505A); τὴν ἑπομένην ἀκολούθως τῷ θεῷ πρᾶξιν στελλόμεθα Clem.*str*.2.18(p.155.11; M.8.1020B); ὁ γνωστικὸς...κατορθοῖ...καὶ ἐν λόγῳ καὶ ἐν π. id.*str*.7.9(p.40.10; M.9.477B); Meth.*symp*.3.1(p.26.13; M.18.60D); esp. of active life opp. contemplation, ref. Jo.4:34 ἀληθῶς μὲν βρῶσις ἡ π., ἀληθῶς δὲ πόσις ἡ θεωρία...διὰ τοῦτο πρῶτον δίδωσι τὸν ἄρτον εὐλογήσας...ἐπεὶ πρώτη ἐστὶν ἡ π. ... ἐπεὶ δεῖ τὰ τῶν π. ῥυθμίσαντα καὶ τὸ πρακτικὸν κατορθώσαντα οὕτως ὁδεύειν διὰ τῶν πραγμάτων καὶ ἐπὶ τὴν θεωρίαν αὐτῶν Or.*comm.in Mt*.16.7(p.487.24; M.13.1388A); ὥσπερ τὸ πρόβατον τρέφεται χλόῃ καὶ ὕδατι, οὕτω ὁ ἄνθρωπος ζωοποιεῖται π. καὶ γνώσει id.*sel.in Ps*.22:1(M.12.1260C); π. γὰρ θεωρίας ἀνάβασις id.*hom.1 in Lc*.(p.9.26); **b.** of evil conduct τῶν τὰ φαῦλα πεποιηκότων διὰ τὸ ἐκτίσθαι αὐτοὺς σκεύη ἀτιμίας ἐπὶ τοῦτο πράξεως ἐληλυθότων id.*princ*.3.1.20(p.237.6; M.11.296B); **2.** *action*; **a.** in gen. τριῶν γέ τοι τούτων περὶ τὸν ἄνθρωπον ὄντων, ἠθῶν, πράξεων, παθῶν Clem.*paed*.1.1(p.90.3; M.8.249A); διάκονοι...ἑκάστου τῆς ἐκκλησίας πολυπραγμονοῦντες τὰς π. *Clem.ep*.12(M.2.48A); **b.** of good works π. ἀγαθὰς ἐπιδεικνύουσιν Athenag.*leg*.11.3(M.6.913A); τὰ δὲ μετέχοντα τῆς γνώσεως ἔργα αἱ ἀγαθαὶ καὶ καλαὶ π. εἰσίν Clem.*str*.6.12(p.481.31; M.9.320C); in rel. to justification οὐχ ἡ τῶν π. ἀποχὴ δικαιοῖ τὸν πιστόν, ἀλλ' ἡ τῶν ἐννοιῶν ἁγνεία καὶ εἰλικρίνεια id.*fr*.65(p.228.20); eternal punishment or salvation acc. merit of works, Just.*1apol*.12.1(M.6.341C); τὸ κατ' εἰκόνα αἱ π. χαρακτηρίζουσι Or.*sel.in Gen*.1:26(M.12.96A); προτρέπεται αὐτὴν ὁ νυμφίος πᾶν νόημα καὶ π. μορφῶσαι τῷ ἑαυτοῦ χαρακτῆρι· ποιεῖν δὲ ταῦτά φησιν...ἀγάπην id.*schol.in Cant*.8:6 (M.17.285B); τὴν ἀνάστασιν εἶναι τὴν σκηνοπηγίαν...καὶ τὰ εἰς τὴν σύνθεσιν παραλαμβανόμενα τῆς σκηνῆς τὰς π. εἶναι τῆς δικαιοσύνης Meth.*symp*.9.3(p.116.27; M.18.181C); **c.** of evil deeds, *T.Jos*.5.2; Herm.*vis*.5.3.1; Arist.*apol*.11.7; Just.*dial*.116.1(M.6.744B); νόημα... ἀναπαυόμενον ἀπὸ πάσης λαλιᾶς τε καὶ π. Clem.*fr*.44(p.222.17); Or. *sel.in Gen*.1:26(96B); Cyr.H.*catech*.19.8; **d.** of impulse to do a deed, personified ἡ κακή μου π. λέγει μοι· λάβε καὶ τὸ ὀθόνιον αὐτοῦ Jo. Mosch.*prat*.77(M.87.2932C); **3.** *official duty*, exercise of office οἱ δὲ δημοσιεύοντες ὑπὸ τῶν π. ἤγοντο Dion.Al.ap.Eus.*h.e*.6.41.11(M.20.608B); Eus.*ib*.8.11.2(769A); ἀπὸ τῆς π. τῆς ἐπισκοπῆς ἀποκινεῖ CChalc.*can*.29; **4.** *work* of literature, Eus.*h.e*.5.28.7(M.20.513B); **5.** *deposition*, Phot.*nomoc*.13.3(p.612; M.104.904C); **6.** *acts*, *transactions*, of historical record τὰς τῶν βασιλέων π. ἐκτιθέμενος Tat.*orat*.38(p.39.9; M.6.881A); as title of book; **a.** of *Acts of Apostles*, cf.Iren.*haer*.3.12.11(M.7.905A); Clem.*paed*.2.1(p.165.18; M.8.404A); id.*fr*.4(p.196.6) ap.Eus.*h.e*.1.12.1(M.20.117B); τὴν ἑρμηνείαν...τῶν Πράξεων Clem.*fr*.22(p.201.22)*ib*.6.14.2(549B); Or.*Cels*.3.46(p.243.2; M.11.980D); Ath. *ep.fest*.39(M.26.1437B); rejected by Severians, Eus.*h.e*.4.29.5(401A); Thdt.*haer*.1.21(4.313); **b.** of apocryphal acts τῶν Παύλου Πράξεων ἡ γραφή Eus.*h.e*.3.25.4(M.20.269A); τῶν ἄλλων ἀποστόλων πράξεις *ib*.3.25.6(269B); Epiph.*haer*.47.1(p.216.6; M.41.852B).

πρᾶος (πραΰς), *gentle*, *mild*; **1.** in gen. ἔσῃ π. *Barn*.19.4; Herm. *mand*.6.2.3; Arist.*apol*.15.5; Athenag.*leg*.12.1(M.6.913A); Clem. *paed*.3.11(p.280.18; M.8.657C); as quality of 'gnostic' virtue, id. *ecl*.37(p.148.9; M.9.717A); *Const.App*.2.1.5; *ib*.7.7.3; μήτηρ τις εἶναι τῆς κατὰ τὸ π. ἕξεως ἡ τῆς ταπεινοφροσύνης κατάστασις Gr.Nyss.*beat*.2(M.44.1217B); Chrys.*hom.61.1 in Jo*.(8.361B); ὁ π. ὀρφανῶν πατήρ, χηρῶν προστάτης, πενίας κηδεμών, ἀδικουμένων βοηθός, πανταχοῦ ποιῶν τοῦ δικαίου τὸ κράτος ‡Chrys.*mans*.(12.422D); **2.** of Christ, cf.

Zach.9:9 ὁ σωτὴρ τῶν ἐθνῶν· ἐστὶ γὰρ...π. καὶ ταπεινός *T.Dan* 6.9; of H. Ghost's appearance as dove, Clem.*fr.*57(p.226.25; M.9.765C); **3.** exeg. Mt.5:5 τί τὸ π.; καὶ περὶ τί τὸ π. μακαρίζει ὁ λόγος; οὐ γάρ μοι δοκεῖ πάντα ἐπίσης ἀρετὴν οἴεσθαι δεῖν, ὅσα ἂν ἐν πραότητι γίνεται, εἰ τὸ...βραδὺ μόνον διὰ τῆς λέξεως ταύτης σημαίνοιτο. οὔτε γὰρ ἐν δρομεῦσιν ὁ π. ἀμείνων τοῦ ἐπισπεύδοντος Gr.Nyss.*beat.*2(M.44.1212C); ref. righteous in future life αὕτη ἐστὶν ἡ γῆ τῶν π. ... γέγραπται [Mt.5:5] *Apoc.Paul.*21(p.50); Thdt.*Is.*33:17(2.313); ἐν γῇ τῶν π. πάντων αὐλίζεσθαι τὸν προκεκοιμημένον σωτὴρ εὐδόκησον *Euchol.* (p.428); **4.** ref. advantages of gentleness ἱκανὸν εἰς μακαρισμὸν τὸ π. εἶναι Gr.Nyss.*beat.*2(M.44.1216A); ὁ π. φίλος μὲν τοῖς ὁρῶσι, φίλος δὲ καὶ τοῖς ἀκοῇ γνωρίμοις ‡Chrys.*mans.*(12.423A); **5.** of gentleness opp. ὀργή, Ign.*Eph.*10.2; πονηρία, †Bas.*Is.*17(1.389B; M.30.144C); ref. ἀπαθής, Gr.Nyss.*beat.*2(M.44.1216A).

πραότης (πραΰτης), ἡ, *mildness, gentleness*; **1.** def. τοῦτο δέ ἐστι π., ἡ πρὸς τὰς τοιαύτας τῆς φύσεως ὁρμὰς βραδεῖά τε καὶ δυσκίνητος ἕξις Gr.Nyss.*beat.*2(M.44.1213C); **2.** divine ἐν ἐπιεικείᾳ καὶ π. ὡς βασιλεὺς πέμπων υἱὸν βασιλέα ἔπεμψεν *Diogn.*7.4; taught by Christ, cf.*T.Jud.*24.1; π. ... διδάσκει διὰ τῶν ἔργων Chrys.*hom.in Mt.*7:14 (3.23A); coupled with ἐπιείκεια, id.*hom.*83.5 *in Jo.*(8.496D); **3.** in gen., *1Clem.*21.7; μακροθυμήσατε οὖν μετ' ἀλλήλων ἐν π. Ign.*Polyc.* 6.2; *Did.*5.2; Herm.*mand.*5.2.6; Clem.*q.d.s.*3(p.162.4; M.9.608B); Meth.*symp.*proem.(p.5.10; M.18.32B); **4.** as virtue esp. pleasing to God, Chrys.*hom.*61.1 *in Jo.*(8.361B); *ib.*78.4(464B); διὰ πραότητος τῷ θεῷ λειτουργεῖν, ὡς ταύτην μᾶλλον ἀσμένως δεχομένῳ τὴν λειτουργίαν ἢ τὰς ἄλλας ἁπάσας ἀρετάς ‡Chrys.*mans.*(12.427B); greatest of virtues, *ib.*(425B); ἡ π. θεραπεύει τὸ θεῖον. καὶ γὰρ ὁ Μωϋσῆς διὰ τὸ εἶναι αὐτὸν πραότατον παρὰ πάντας, θεράπων θεοῦ ἐκλήθη, καὶ θεοπτίας ὑπὲρ πάντας προφήτας ἠξίωται...ἡ γὰρ κατὰ θεὸν π., ἔργον ἐστὶ θεάρεστον Ant.Mon.*hom.*115(M.89.1792A); **5.** esp. as virtue of clergy; of bishop ἡ δὲ π. αὐτοῦ δύναμις Ign.*Trall.*3.2; τοὺς λοιμοτέρους ἐν π. ὑπότασσε id.*Polyc.*2.1; Gr.Naz.*or.*9.5(M.35.825A); *Const.App.*2.1.3; and of ascetics πραότητος δεῖ ὅτι μάλιστα ἔμπλεον εἶναι τὸν ἀσκητήν· ἐπειδὴ τοῦ πνεύματος τῆς π. ἢ μετέσχηκεν, ἢ μετασχεῖν ἐφίεται ‡Bas. *const.*13(2.557E; M.31.1376B); πρεσβύτην πραότητι πάντας ἀνθρώπους ὑπερβάλλοντα, ὀνόματι ἀββᾶ Βῆν ‡Pall.*h.mon.*4.1(p.28.4; M.34.1132D); **6.** as quality of emperor, Constantius ap.Ath.*apol.sec.*54(p.135.7; M.25.348B); *ib.*55(p.135.36; 349A); τὴν ὑπατείαν τῆς αὐτοῦ θεοσόφου π. CCP(681)*act.*4(H.3.1072C); **7.** opp. vices: θυμός, Gr.Nyss.*beat.*2 (M.44.1216C); ὀργή, Chrys.*hom.*15.4 *in Ac.*(9.124D); indolence, ‡Bas. *const.*13(2.558C; M.31.1377A); Max.*ambig.*(M.91.1249B); **8.** effects: other virtues such as ἀνεξικακία, χρηστότης, ἀγάπη, ‡Bas.*const.* 13(2.558C; M.31.1377A); establishing of soul in peace, Chrys.*hom.* 34.1 *in Gen.*(4.340B); π. more effective in disputes than fierceness, id.*hom.*6.2 *in 2Tim.*(11.694A); τοῦ θεοῦ μιμητὰς ἡ π. ποιεῖ ‡Chrys. *mans.*(12.425B).

***πρασινοβένετοι, οἱ,** *the greens and the blues* (factions of the circus and of politics), Thphn.*chron.*p.194(M.108.504B).

πράσινος (πράσιος), 1. as subst., *green, emerald*, Epiph.*gemm.*3 (M.43.296B); in adornment of Temple, *T.Sal.*10.5(p.38.8; M.122. 1332B); τίς δὲ λίθος ὁ π.; οὐχὶ ἡ ἑκούσιος τῆς σωματικῆς αὐτοῦ νεκρώσεως ὠχρότης; Procl.CP *or.*6.1(M.65.721C); Areth.*Apoc.*4:3 (πρασίῳ M.106.569A); **2.** of green faction in circus and in Byzantine politics Χριστιανῶν βασιλέων καὶ πρασίνων πολλὰ τὰ ἔτη *IGC As. Min.*114[3](602 or 610); *ib.*114[1](613); *Chron.Pasch.*p.112(M.92.296A); *ib.* p.320(817A); *ib.*p.339(884B).

πράσσω, *do*, **1.** dist. from ποιέω by Aristotle, Clem.*str.*5.13(p.383. 3; M.9.128A); **2.** *study* ἀπήλθομεν...ἵνα πράξωμεν Jo.Mosch.*prat.*77 (M.87.2929D); *ib.*(2932C); ἔστι δὲ καὶ αὐτὸς [sc. Hesiod] τῶν πραττομένων ποιητῶν, οὗτινος τρία ποιήματα πράττονται Cosm.Mel.*schol.* (M.38.491) in *carm.*2.2(poem.)7.241.

πρασώδης, *leek-green*; of the sea, Tat.*orat.*20(p.22.28; M.6.852B).

πραΰθυμος, *of gentle mind* οἶνος...π. ... τοὺς ἀνθρώπους ἐργάζεται †Dion.Al.*fr.Eccl.*2:2(p.215.1; M.10.1580C); Chrys.*fr.in Pr.*14:24(M. 64.701C).

πραϋλόγος, *soothing*, Synes.*hymn.*6.33(p.42; M.66.1609).

πραϋπάθεια, ἡ, *gentleness*, Ign.*Trall.*8.1; Max.*qu.Theop.*(M.90. 1400A); π. καθ' ἣν καὶ πάσχοντες ἀναλλοίωτοι μένομεν πρὸς τοὺς δρῶντας κακῶς id.*ep.*2(M.91.396A).

***πραϋπαθῶς,** *gently*, Didym.*Trin.*2.17(M.39.724B).

πραΰς, πραΰτης, v. πρᾶος, πραότης.

***πραΰφρων,** *of gentle disposition*, Sophr.H.*carm.*19.65(M.87. 3816A).

***πρέδα, ἡ,** v. *πραῖδα.

***πρεμνογονέω,** *inseminate by male trees*; of fertilization of figs, Ephr.2.277B.

[*]**πρεπόσιτος, ὁ,** v. πραιπόσιτος.

***πρεπωδῶς,** *becomingly*, *Mir.Geo.*(p.151.4).

πρεσβεία, ἡ, A. *rank, dignity* ἄλλης ὑπὲρ ἐκεῖνα οὐσίας πρεσβείᾳ καὶ δυνάμει Or.*Jo.*13.21(p.244.22; M.14.432C).

B. *embassage, advocacy*; **1.** of work of Christians as God's or Christ's ambassadors; in gen. οἱ...τὴν...θειοτέραν π. ὑπὲρ Χριστοῦ πρεσβεύοντες Or.*Cels.*8.6(p.225.19; M.11.1528B); of special commissions performed in service of Church πρέπον ἐστὶν ὑμῖν...χειροτονῆσαι διάκονον εἰς τὸ πρεσβεῦσαι ἐκεῖ θεοῦ π. Ign.*Philad.*10.1; ἡμᾶς... ἐπιθυμίᾳ...τῆς πρὸς ἀλλήλους ἡμῶν συναφείας τῶν ὁμονοούντων εἰς τὰ πρὸς τὸν κύριον, ἐπὶ τὴν π. ταύτην καὶ μεσιτείαν ἀφικομένους Bas.*ep.*82 (3.176A; M.32.460D); hence **2.** *request, entreaty*; **a.** in gen. ταύτην ἐθαρρήσαμεν τὴν π. προσαγαγεῖν Gr.Naz.*ep.*21(M.37.56C); Evagr.*h.e.* 3.4(p.100.28; M.86.2597B); **b.** of prayer, ref. Jo.17:21–24 αὕτη ἡ μεγάλη τοῦ σωτῆρος ἡμῶν ὑπὲρ ἡμῶν π. Eus.*e.th.*3.18(p.179.23; M. 24.1041B); Didym.*Ps.*12:1(M.39.1216C); **c.** esp. of intercession and advocacy on man's behalf; **i.** of angels, id.*Trin.*2.8(M.39. 589C); Eus.Al.*serm.*21.23(M.86.452B) cit. infra; **ii.** of saints θέας... ἧς καὶ ἡμεῖς ἀξιωθείημεν εὐχαῖς καὶ π. πάντων τῶν ἁγίων Eus.*Is.*66:24 (M.24.525A); γίνεσθε οὖν πρεσβευταὶ...ὅπως εὑρεθῶ ἐκεῖ δι' ὑμετέρων π. σωζόμενος Ephr.3.254B; Gr.Naz.*or.*43.25(M.36.532A); τὴν τῶν ἁγίων π. ἐπεκαλέσατο Gr.Nyss.*mart.*3.8(M.46.784C); Chrys.*hom.*44.2 *in Gen.*(4.449C); ἀξιωθῶμεν ἰδεῖν τὸν διδάσκαλον [sc. S. Paul], καὶ διὰ τῆς ἐκείνου π. ... ἀπολαύσωμεν εὐμενείας Thdt.*Rom.*16:24(3.162); id. *h.rel.*2(3.1136); οὐ ταῖς π. καταξιῶσαι ἡμᾶς Χριστὸς...τῆς...αὐτοῦ βασιλείας *M.Tim.fr.*(p.144); δοθῆναι παῖδα ταῖς τοῦ Βαπτιστοῦ π. αὐτῇ Niceph.Ur.*v.Sym.*4(M.86.2992A); **iii.** of BMV ἀξιωθῆναι πρεσβείαις τῆς...δεσποίνης ἡμῶν...Μαρίας, τῶν φωτοειδῶν ἀγγέλων καὶ πάντων τῶν ἁγίων Eus.Al.*serm.*21.23(M.86.452B); πρεσβείαις τῆς δεσποίνης ἡμῶν τῆς θεοτόκου *Pap.Chr.*(p.419); *Euchol.*(p.446); cf. *Lit.Chrys.* (p.364.8); **3.** *favour, gift*, Ath.Scholast. *coll.*3.3(p.46).

πρεσβεῖον, τό, 1. *old age* τὸν ἐκ νεαρᾶς γὰρ ἡλικίας...παιδευόμενον... ἕως γήρους καὶ π. οὐ μὴ ἐγκαταλίπῃ ὁ θεός Ant.Mon.*hom.*82(M.89. 1681A); **2.** *privilege of age, seniority* τὸ π. τῆς ἡλικίας, τὸν πολιὲα Clem.*paed.*3.3(p.246.17; M.8.580A); Bas.*hom.*6.4(2.46E; M.31.268D); τῶν πρωτοτοκίων ἔχουσι τὰ π. Thdt.*qu.*37 *in 2Reg.*(1.441); τοῖς... τοῦ χρόνου π. id.*haer.*5.9(4.415); of Christians' baptismal privilege τὰ π. τῆς γενέσεως Bas.*ep.*199 *can.*20(3.292E; M.32.721A); hence **3.** *presbyterate*, as grade of ministry πρεσβείου χειροθεσίαν...ἀναλαμβάνει Eus.*h.e.*6.23.4(πρεσβυτερίου M.20.576C); Διονύσιον, τότε μὲν πρεσβείου ἠξιωμένον *ib.*7.7.6(652A); πρεσβείων τὸν Ὠριγένην...ἄξιον εἶναι δοκιμάσαντες *ib.*6.8.4(537A); id.*m.P.*11(p.934.2; M.20.1500A); τιμηθέντα...τῆς Ἀντιοχέων ἐκκλησίας πρεσβείῳ id.*Marcell.*1.4(p.18.3; M.24.752A); **4.** *privilege, superiority*; in gen., of a marvellous thing τὰ π. κατὰ πάντων ἔχον Evagr.*h.e.*1.21(p.31.2; M.86.2480B); of privileges of clergy οἱ δὲ λεγόμενοι κληρικοὶ τούτων καίτοι τὰ π. παρὰ τῶν λαῶν ἐκδικοῦντες Ath.*syn.*2(p.232.16; M.26.684C); of status of H. Ghost τιμῇ μὲν καὶ δόξῃ καὶ πρεσβείοις ὑπερέχον καί...ἀνώτερον πάσης τῆς νοερᾶς καὶ λογικῆς τυγχάνον οὐσίας Eus.*e.th.*3.5(p.162.29; M. 24.1012B); of Father οὐ γὰρ ἱκανὸν τὸ τοῦ πατρὸς ὄνομα δεῖξαι τὰ π. τοῦ πατρός; Chrys.*hom.*7.1 *in Phil.*(11.246A); **5.** esp. of eccl. privileges, *prerogatives* of churches τὰ π. σώζεσθαι ταῖς ἐκκλησίαις CNic.(325) *can.*6; CCP(381)*can.*2; τὸν μέντοι Κωνσταντινουπόλεως ἐπίσκοπον ἔχειν τὰ π. τῆς τιμῆς μετὰ τὸν τῆς Ῥώμης ἐπίσκοπον, διὰ τὸ εἶναι αὐτὴν νέαν Ῥώμην *ib.*3; τὴν βασιλείᾳ καὶ συγκλήτῳ τιμηθεῖσαν πόλιν καὶ τῶν ἴσων ἀπολαύουσαν π. τῇ πρεσβυτέρᾳ βασιλίδι Ῥώμῃ, καὶ ἐν τοῖς ἐκκλησιαστικοῖς...μεγαλύνεσθαι πράγμασι CChalc.*can.*28; ἐδόκει δὲ καὶ τὸν θρόνον τῆς νέας Ῥώμης ἐκ τῶν δευτερείων τῆς πρεσβυτέρας Ῥώμης τῶν ἄλλων τὰ π. φέρειν Evagr.*h.e.*2.4(p.50.28; M.86.2509B).

πρεσβευτής, ὁ, *ambassador*; **1.** from God to men; **a.** of Christ ὁ π. ὁ ἀπὸ τοῦ ὕψους ἀποσταλεὶς καὶ ἕως τοῦ ᾅδου καταντήσας *A.Thom.* A 10(p.115.4); **b.** of God in dealings with prophets, Thdt.*qu.*54 *in 3Reg.*(1.501); **c.** of an apostle ὁ τῆς ἀληθείας π. ὃ ἂν δήσῃ ἐπὶ γῆς, δέδεται καὶ ἐν οὐρανῷ *Clem.ep.*6(*GCS* p.10.9; πρεσβύτης M.2.41A); *Hom.Clem.*1.16; **2.** from men to God, hence *intercessor*; **a.** of Christ οὐκ αὐτοὶ τυχεῖν τῶν διαλλαγῶν ἱκετεύσαντες, ἀλλὰ τὸν μονογενῆ δεξάμενοι π. Thdt.*carit.*(3.1303); **b.** of angels π. ... τοῦ ἀνθρώπων γένους Didym.*Trin.*2.8(M.39.592A); **c.** of a prophet Ἡσαΐαν γενέσθαι π. ἠντιβόλησεν Thdt.*qu.*52 *in 4Reg.*(1.545); **d.** of saints, esp. martyrs π. δυνατώτατοι Bas.*hom.*19.8(2.156B; M.31.524C); ὁ...τοσούτους ἔχων π., οὔποτ' ἂν ἄπρακτος ἀπέλθοι προσευχῆς Gr.Nyss.*mart.*2.9(M.46.788A); Ast.Am.*hom.*10(M.40.317C); π. ὑπὲρ ὑμῶν πρὸς τὸν θεὸν ἀπέρχομαι *M.Thdot.*3(p.141.18); τοῖς ἐν ἀρετῇ τελείοις οἱ ἀτελεῖς χρώμεθα π. Thdt.*qu.*1 *in Lev.*(1.182); οὐχ ὡς θεοῖς αὐτοῖς προσιόντες, ἀλλ' ὡς θείους ἀνθρώπους...γενέσθαι π. ὑπὲρ σφῶν παρακαλοῦντες id.*affect.*8(p.217. 14; 3.921).

πρεσβευτικός, *interceding* χεῖρα π. Thdr.Stud.*epp*.2.9(M.99.1141A).

πρεσβεύ-ω, **A.** *be elder, have precedence in age.*

B. ? *assign precedence to* ἀρξώμεθα δὲ ἀπὸ τῆς Γενέσεως, ἵνα δὴ καὶ ~ωμεν μᾶλλον τὴν γραφήν Meth.*symp*.2.1(p.15.13; M.18.48C).

C. *act as ambassador*; **1.** of Christ τὸν ὑπὲρ τοῦ πατρὸς ~οντα μεσίτην Max.*qu.Thal*.61(M.90.637C); **2.** of envoy of a church, Polyc.*ep*.13.1.

D. *plead, intercede, pray*; **1.** in gen. ὑπὲρ τῆς τῶν ἐκκλησιῶν εἰρήνης ...ἐπρέσβευεν Eus.*h.e*.5.24.18(M.20.508A); Gr.Naz.*ep*.22(M.37.57A); Euthal.Diac.*epp.Paul*.(M.85.705C); π. καὶ δέομαι, ἵνα μὴ...ὑφέξω Sophr.H.*ep.syn*.(M.87.3197B); **2.** towards God; **a.** of intercessory prayer in gen. ~ων ὑπὲρ σοῦ πρὸς θεόν Clem.*q.d.s*.41(p.187.18; M.9.648A); τοὺς ἱεροὺς ἄνδρας, τοὺς περὶ τῆς εἰρήνης αὐτοῦ [sc. Gallus]... ~οντας πρὸς τὸν θεόν Dion.Al.ap.Eus.*h.e*.7.1(M.20.640A); **b.** of intercession for men; by Christ μόνος ἦν δυνατὸς...~σαι περὶ πάντων πρὸς τὸν πατέρα Ath.*inc*.7.5(M.25.109A); by BMV σώζει...τοὺς ὁμολογοῦντάς σε θεοτόκον, ὁ μυσταγωγήσας σε θεὸς γενέσθαι πρὸς αὐτόν, τοῦ ~ειν ὑπὲρ ἡμῶν Mod.*dorm*.10(M.86.3301C); ~ουσα τῷ σῷ υἱῷ καὶ θεῷ ἡμῶν Jo.Thess.*dorm.BMV* 2.14(p.435.29); θεοτόκε...~ε τὸν υἱόν σου ...ὅπως ἐλεήσῃ με Jo.V H.*icon*.14(M.96.1360C); ~ειν μητρικῶς τῷ αὐτῆς υἱῷ καὶ κυρίῳ ὑπὲρ παντὸς τοῦ κόσμου Thdr.Stud.*epp*.2.166 (M.99.1528C); by angels, Didym.*Trin*.2.8(M.39.589D); by saints, esp. martyrs ὦ...Βασίλειε...~ε ὑπὲρ ἐμοῦ τοῦ σφόδρα ἐλεεινοῦ, καὶ ἀνακάλεσαί με ταῖς πρεσβείαις σου, πατέρ Ephr.2.296E; ἀθλοφόροι μάρτυρες...πρεσβεύσατε ἅγιοι ὑπὲρ ἡμῶν τῶν χαύνων id.3.251E; *ib*.3.253E; παθὼν διὰ Χριστόν, ~σον ὑπὲρ πάθους καὶ νόσου Ast.Am.*hom*.10 (M.40.317D); κάθευδε...ἐν εἰρήνῃ...~ων ὑπὲρ ἐμοῦ πρὸς τὸν θεόν ‡Pall.*h.mon*.11.14(p.57.17; M.65.452C); ὁ δὲ ἐδέετο αὐτοῦ καὶ ἱκέτευε ~ειν ὑπὲρ αὐτοῦ πρὸς τὸν θεόν *ib*.11.15(p.58.2; 452D); διὰ τὰ σὰ παθήματα δεόμεθα, ὥστε ~σαί σε ὑπὲρ τῶν ἡμαρτημένων †Bas.Sel.*or*.41(M.85.473B); τὴν μὲν ἐκείνου μακαρίαν ψυχὴν θεραπεύσετε· ἥτις ἐγγύτερον θεοῦ γενομένη, ὅσῳ...καὶ παρρησίαν ἐκ τῶν οἰκείων ἀγαθῶν ἐκτήσατο ἔργων, ~ει ὑπὲρ τῆς εἰρήνης καὶ σωτηρίας τῆς ὑμετέρας εὐσεβείας *Ep.* ap.CCP(536)*act*.1(*ACO* 3 p.133.15; H.2.1197A); νῦν ἔστιν ἐν τῷ παραδείσῳ τῆς τρυφῆς, ~ων μετὰ πάντων τῶν ἁγίων ὑπὲρ ἡμῶν, ὧν ταῖς εὐχαῖς ἐλεήσῃ ἡμᾶς ὁ...θεός Marc.Diac.*v.Porph*.103.

E. *advocate, espouse the cause of*, hence *cultivate, honour, have regard to* περὶ δικαιοσύνης ~οντες Or.*Cels*.2.8(p.134.4; M.11.805B); εἴ τι τῆς...ἀληθείας ἐπρέσβευεν *ib*.3.22(p.218.21; 945A); π. τὸν Χριστιανισμόν *ib*.3.54(p.249.18; 992B); ἐπρέσβευε περὶ τῶν πενήτων id.*comm.in Mt*.11.9(p.49.22; M.13.932C); ἐπρέσβευον τὰ Χριστοῦ Ath.*syn*.45(p.269.23; M.26.772A); Gr.Nyss.*Apoll*.44(M.45.1229C); τοῦτο ~ει πανταχοῦ τῆς ἀκριβοῦς πίστεως ὁ λόγος Cyr.*ep*.4(p.28.17; 5².24E); τὸ ἑτεροούσιον ~ειν Philost.*h.e*.2.6(M.65.469B); καθὸ τριὰς ὁ εἷς θεός ἐστι...καὶ ὑποστάσεις τρεῖς καταγγέλλεται, καὶ εἰς τρία ~εται πρόσωπα Sophr.H.*ep.syn*(M.87.3153B).

πρέσβις, **ὁ**, *ambassador*; in gen., Thphyl.*exc.Rom*.5(p.224.18; M.113.932B); of Christ ἐξαπέστειλας τὸν...υἱὸν εἰς τὸν κόσμον πρέσβιν *Lit.Jac*.(*NBP* 10² p.109).

πρέσβις, **ἡ**, *ambassadress*, hence *intercessor* (fem.), of BMV π. καὶ μεσιτείαν Jo.Mon.*hymn.Bas*.10(M.96.1377B); ‡Gr.Naz.*Chr.pat*.2570(M.38.335A).

πρέσβυς, **1.** *senior, chief* τὸν π. τῶν ἱερέων *Pers*.(p.4.3); **2.** ? for πρεσβύτερος *presbyter* Ἵμηρος πρέσβυς ἀνέστησα τοῦ γλυκυτάτου υἱοῦ ...μνήμης χάριν *CIG* 3989 i (Laodicaea saec. iii–iv), so interpreted and catalogued as Christian by Cumont, *Mélanges d'archéologie et d'histoire*, 15, Rome 1895 p. 279 no. 220 cf. p.260; **3.** fem., of empress Helena ἧκεν δὴ σπεύδουσα νεανικῶς ἡ π. Eus.*v.C*.3.42(p.95.15; M.20.1101B); *ib*.3.43(p.96.10; 1104B); **4.** *ambassador*, Mont.*fr*.ap.Epiph.*haer*.48.11(p.235.2; M.41.872D) cit. s. πατήρ; of angels, *Pap.Chr*. (p.447); **5.** comp., v. πρεσβύτερος.

πρεσβυτέρα, **ἡ**, fem. of comp. of πρέσβυς, as subst.; **1.** *old woman*, for whom subsistence is provided by the church; analogous or equivalent to a widow, *Const.App*.2.28.1; **2.** female *presbyter* γυνὴ οὐ γίνεται π. Phot.*nomoc*.1.37(p.481; M.104.1025D); **3.** *head* or *senior member of women's community*, to be present at confessions made by its members εὐσχημονέστερον...μετὰ [v.l. διὰ] τῆς π. πρὸς τὸν πρεσβύτερον ἡ ἐξαγόρευσις γενήσεται Bas.*reg.br*.110(3.453C; M.31.1157A); **4.** ἡ π. [sc. διαθήκη] *the Old Testament*, Sophr.H.*or*.7.12(M.87.3340D).

***πρεσβυτερεία**, **ἡ**, *office of presbyter*, †Leont.B.*sect*.4.6(M.86.1225B).

***πρεσβυτερεύ-ω**, *be senior* τοῦ γὰρ οὐσιωδῶς ἐξεικονίζοντος τὸν θεόν...οὐδεὶς ὑπέρκειται, οὐδὲ ~ει Didym.*Trin*.1.15(M.39.328B); *ib*.3.34(961B).

***πρεσβυτερικός**, *of* or *belonging to presbyters, priestly* π. τάγματι v.l. for πρεσβυτερίῳ, Pall.*v.Chrys*.16(p.94.2; M.47.53).

πρεσβυτέριον (**πρεσβυτερεῖον**), **τό**, **I.** *body of elders*; **A.** Jewish (cf. Lc.22:26), *Const.App*.5.14.9.

B. Christian; **1.** exeg. 1Tim.4:14; of ruling body of presbyters in apostolic Church π. δὲ ἐνταῦθα, τοὺς τῆς ἀποστολικῆς χάριτος ἠξιωμένους [sc. ἐκάλεσε] Thdt.*1Tim*.4:14(3.662); cf.Chrys.*hom.13.1 in 1Tim*.(11.618B) cit. s. πρεσβύτερος; or of college of apostles conferring ordination, Thdr.Mops.*1Tim*.4:14(M.66.941D); **2.** of college of presbyters assisting bishop in worship and administration of church ὑποτασσόμενοι τῷ ἐπισκόπῳ...ὁμοίως καὶ τῷ π. Ign.*Trall*.13.2; id.*Smyrn*.12.2; κατέστησεν αὐτὸν εἰς τὸ π. ‡Pion.*v.Polyc*.17; ὁ...τῆς προεδρίας ἀξιωθείς, καὶ ἐγκαταλεγεὶς τῷ π. †Bas.*Is*.103(1.450D; M.30.285A); παρακαλοῦμεν...ὑπὲρ παντὸς τοῦ π. *Lit*.ap.*Const.App*.8.12.41; ἱερατεύσας ἐν τῷ π. Pall.*v.Chrys*.16(p.94.2, v.l. πρεσβυτερικῷ τάγματι; M.47.53); its agreement with bishop necessary for all activity in church, Ign.*Eph*.4.1; id.*Trall*.7.2; likened to apostles ὑποτάσσεσθε καὶ τῷ π. ὡς τοῖς ἀποστόλοις Ἰησοῦ Χριστοῦ *ib*.2.2; id.*Philad*.5.2; id.*Smyrn*.8.1; and, in their rel. to bishop, to Christ in rel. to Father ὑποτάσσεται τῷ ἐπισκόπῳ ὡς χάριτι θεοῦ καὶ τῷ π. ὡς νόμῳ Ἰησοῦ Χριστοῦ id.*Magn*.2; seated in church on either side of bishop, *Const.App*.2.57.4; associated with eucharistic offering, Ign.*Philad*.4; participating in appointment of bishops, *Const.App*.8.4.2; **3.** of body of elders (in which women were included) in Montanist sect, Epiph.*haer*.49.3(p.243.19; M.41.881B); **4.** of heavenly π. (of which earthly order of presbyters is a copy) in which 'gnostic' will be included, even though only a layman on earth, Clem.*str*.6.13(p.486.2; M.9.329A); cf.Proc.G.*Jos*.13:1(M.87.1024B).

II. *office of elder, priesthood*, Eus.*h.e*.5.15(M.20.464A); Socr.*h.e*.7.41.2(M.67.829C).

III. *place assigned to elders in church* οὐκ αὐτὸ τὸ καθέζεσθαι ἐν π. ἐστίν, ἀλλὰ τὸ βιοῦν ἀξίως τοῦ τόπου Or.*hom.11.3 in Jer*.(p.81.2; M.13.369D); id.*fr*.50 *in Jer*.36:21(p.223.22; M.13.580A).

***πρεσβυτερίς**, **ἡ**, *female presbyter*, Epiph.*haer*.79.4(p.478.29; M.42.745A) cit. s. πρεσβῦτις.

***πρεσβυτέρισσα**, **ἡ**, *wife of a presbyter* ἱερωμέναι, ἤγουν πρεσβυτέρισσαι ἢ ἐμβάθμων διακόνων γυναῖκες †Jo.Jej.*poenit*.(M.88.1912B).

πρεσβύτερος, **I.** as adj., comp. of πρέσβυς; **1.** *older* (in years), *Barn*.13.5; τὸ πνεῦμα ὑμῶν π. καὶ ἤδη μεμαρασμένον Herm.*vis*.3.11.2; Meth.*symp*.proem.(p.7.2; M.18.36A); Philost.*h.e*.3.1(M.65.480B); **2.** *suitable for an older person* τὸ δὲ [sc. βρέφος] ἔτι ἀδυνατεῖ τὴν αὐτοῦ π. δέξασθαι τροφήν Iren.*haer*.4.38.1(M.7.1105B); **3.** *more mature, advanced* in knowledge or piety, Gr.Nyss.*hom.1 in Eccl*.(M.44.629D); π. ... φαμεν οὐ τὸν κατὰ χρόνον...ἀλλὰ τὸν κατὰ σύνεσιν Cyr.*Is*.1.2 (2.55D); **4.** *antecedent in time*; **a.** of persons Μωϋσέως, τοῦ...πρώτου προφήτου καὶ π. τῶν ἐν Ἕλλησι συγγραφέων Just.*1apol*.59.1(M.6.416C); Athenag.*leg*.17.1(M.6.921C); π. ... τῷ χρόνῳ Ἡσαΐᾳ ὁ Δαυΐδ Or.*sel.in Ps*.3:1(M.12.1120A); Μωϋσέως, τοῦ...πολλῷ τῶν Ἰλιακῶν π. id.*Cels*.4.36(p.307.6; M.11.1084C); **b.** of things γράμματα π. τῶν Βίκτορος χρόνων †Hipp.*Artem*.ap.Eus.*h.e*.5.28.4(M.20.512C); Chrys.*hom.1.1 in Col*.(11.323A); Thdt.*Ps*.25:2(1.764); of the older Israel and covenant opp. Church and NT, Clem.*paed*.1.7(p.124.30; M.8.321A); τῆς μὲν πρεσβυτέρας [sc. διαθήκης] τέλος...τῆς δὲ νεωτέρας ἀρχὴ καὶ προοίμιον [i.e. Jo. Bapt.] Sophr.H.*or*.7.12(M.87.3340D); of Rome in rel. to CP, CChalc.*can*.28; Evagr.*h.e*.4.38(p.186.23; M.86.2772B); **5.** *prior, logically antecedent* ὄνομα τῷ...πατρὶ θετόν, ἀγεννήτῳ ὄντι, οὐκ ἔστιν. ᾧ γὰρ ἂν καὶ ὄνομά τι προσαγορεύηται, π. ἔχει τὸν θέμενον τὸ ὄνομα Just.*2apol*.6.1(M.6.453A); ὡς ἀγέννητον ἑαυτοῦ π. μηδὲν ἔχον *Hom.Clem*.14.4; τί ἄτοπον...νοεῖν π. αἴτια τοῦ τὸν Ἰακὼβ ἠγαπῆσθαι καὶ τὸν Ἠσαῦ μεμισῆσθαι γεγονέναι; Or.*princ*.3.1.22(p.238.11; M.11.297A); θεὸς...οὔτε γίνεται, οὔτε ἔχει τι π. Chrys.*hom.4.2 in Jo*.(8.29C); hence **6.** *more important* ὁπόσα λέγομεν μαθόντες παρὰ τοῦ Χριστοῦ καὶ τῶν...προφητῶν, μόνα ἀληθῆ ἐστι καὶ π. πάντων...συγγραφέων Just.*1apol*.23.1(M.6.364A); π. τὰ ἀσώματα τῶν σωμάτων Athenag.*leg*.36.2(M.6.972A); Meth.*symp*.8.14 (p.100.16; M.18.164A).

II. as subst.; **A.** *venerable person* (in years or rank); **1.** *old person, elder*, Herm.*vis*.3.12.2; *ib*.2.1.3; Thdt.*1Tim*.5:1(3.662); **2.** *veteran* soldier, Cyr.S.*v.Sab*.9(p.92.29); **3.** *teacher*, Clem.*paed*.3.8(p.262.3; M.8.616A); of ancient authors, id.*ecl*.50(p.150.21; M.9.720D); **4.** *elder* in village community, Pall.*h.Laus*.31(p.86.19; M.34.1098D); **5.** of members of Roman Senate, Soz.*h.e*.2.3.47(M.67.940A); **6.** of Jewish elders, Just.*dial*.40.4(M.6.564A); Clem.*paed*.1.9(p.139.15; M.8.349C); *Const.App*.2.24.6; **7.** of LXX interpreters, Just.*dial*.68.7(M.6.636A); *ib*.84.3(M.6.673C).

B. in Christian ministry (in early writers π. is most often used in vague sense of *venerable man, one respected* on account of age, or authority in Church, and may be applied to an apostle, a member of a college of ἐπίσκοποι, a 'monarchical bishop', a teacher, an early witness to eccl. tradition, or any respected member of Church; it is difficult to distinguish between this gen. use of π., and its technical use to denote a member of a particular ministerial order); **1.** *old man* (not ref. ministerial rank), Herm.*vis*.3.1.8; ref. 1Tim.5:1, cf. ἄρα τὸ ἀξίωμα νῦν φησιν; οὐκ ἔγωγε οἶμαι, ἀλλὰ περὶ παντὸς γεγηρακότος Chrys.*hom.13.2 in 1Tim*.(11.618F); cf. οὐ τὸν ἱερέα ἐνταῦθα λέγει, ἀλλὰ τὸν γεγηρακότα Thdt.*1Tim*.5:1(3.662); **2.** *elder, venerable man*, of early teachers and fathers εἰ δέ που καὶ παρηκολουθηκώς τις τοῖς π. ἔλθοι, τοὺς τῶν πρεσβυτέρων ἀνέκρινον λόγους, τί Ἀνδρέας ἢ τί Πέτρος εἶπεν Papias ap.Eus.*h.e*.3.39.4(M.20.297A); Iren.*haer*.4.26.5(M.7.1055C); Clem.*fr*.22(p.201.26)ap.Eus.*h.e*.6.14.4(M.20.552A); of S. John, cf.id.*fr*.24(p.210.1; M.9.733D); of early, prob. heterodox, writers cited by Cels.ap.Or.*Cels*.6.40(p.109.14; M.11.1357B); associated with παράδοσις of apostolic doctrine ἐκβιασθῆναι ὁμολογεῖ [sc. Clem.] πρὸς τῶν ἑταίρων ἃς ἔτυχεν παρὰ τῶν ἀρχαίων π. ἀκηκοὼς παραδόσεις γραφῇ τοῖς μετὰ ταῦτα παραδοῦναι, μέμνηται δ' ἐν αὐτῷ [sc. τῷ λόγῳ] Μελίτωνος καὶ Εἰρηναίου Eus.*h.e*.6.13.9(M.20.549A); ἐν τοῖς αὐτοῖς ὁ Κλήμης βιβλίοις περὶ τῆς τάξεως τῶν εὐαγγελίων παράδοσιν τῶν ἀνέκαθεν π. τέθειται *ib*.6.14.5(552A); and with παρακαταθήκη of scriptural teaching, Clem.*ecl*.27(p.145.3; M.9.712C); **3.** *elder* (i.e. one who holds position of authority in Church; but still including idea of *old man* opp. νεός) ὑποτασσόμενοι τοῖς ἡγουμένοις ὑμῶν καὶ τιμὴν τὴν καθήκουσαν ἀπονέμοντες τοῖς παρ' ὑμῖν π.· νέοις τὰ μέτρια καὶ σεμνὰ νοεῖν ἐπετρέπετε *1Clem*.1.3; τοὺς π. [sc. ἡμῶν] τιμήσωμεν, τοὺς νέους παιδεύσωμεν *ib*.21.6; hence Is.3:5 ἐπηγέρθησαν...οἱ νέοι ἐπὶ τοὺς π. cited to describe unlawful deposition of Corinthian elders, *ib*.3.3; association of age with office persists even when π. has acquired definite meaning of *priest* in threefold ministry τὰ δὲ κατὰ τοὺς π. ἔστω τάδε. πρὸ πάντων τοὺς νέους...ζευγνύτωσαν *Clem. ep*.7(M.2.41A); bishop may well be younger than his presbyters, Ign. *Magn*.3.1; advanced age specified as qualification for priesthood, *Ordo Eccl.App*.18; †Bas.*Is*.104(1.451B; M.30.285C); **4.** equivalent to ἐπίσκοπος; as member of higher order of twofold ministry of πρεσβύτεροι (or ἐπίσκοποι) and διάκονοι (cf. Ac.20:28; Phil.1:1); at Corinth, *1Clem*.21.6 cit. supra; οἱ ἀπόστολοι...ἔγνωσαν...ὅτι ἔρις ἔσται περὶ τοῦ ὀνόματος τῆς ἐπισκοπῆς...ἁμαρτία γὰρ...ἔσται, ἐὰν τοὺς ...ὁσίως προσενεγκόντας τὰ δῶρα τῆς ἐπισκοπῆς ἀποβάλωμεν. μακάριοι οἱ προοδοιπορήσαντες π. ... οὐ γὰρ εὐλαβοῦνται, μή τις αὐτοὺς μεταστήσῃ ἀπὸ τοῦ...τόπου *ib*.44.1,4,5; τὸ ποίμνιον...εἰρηνευέτω μετὰ τῶν καθεσταμένων π. *ib*.54.2; *ib*.57.1; at Philippi, Polyc.*ep*.5.3 cit. infra; at Rome, Herm.*vis*.2.4.2; τῶν π. τῶν προϊσταμένων τῆς ἐκκλησίας *ib*.2.4.3; cf. τοῖς προηγουμένοις *ib*.2.2.6; *ib*.3.9.7, prob. of a collegiate episcopate or presbytery; presbyter-bishops and deacons typify, or represent, God and Christ ὑποτασσομένους τοῖς π. καὶ διακόνοις ὡς θεῷ καὶ Χριστῷ Polyc.*ep*.5.3; in twofold ministry, cf.*Did*.15.1 cit. s. ἐπίσκοπος; **5.** accurate distinction between above sense and that of *priest* in threefold ministry is rendered difficult by long survival of inexact or untechnical terminology, by which πρεσβύτερος = *ruler in a church* and often denotes a 'monarchical' bishop, being used interchangeably with ἐπίσκοπος; cf. *per successiones presbyterorum*, Iren.*haer*.3.2.2(M.7.847A); *per successiones episcoporum*, *ib*.3.3.2(848B); of early bishops of Rome οἱ πρὸ Σωτῆρος π. id.*ep.Vict*.ap.Eus.*h.e*.5.24.14(M.20.505A); of a bishop in Asia, Clem.*q.d.s*.42(p.188.14; M.9.648C); of bishops exercising *ordinandi potestatem*, cf.Firmilian *ep*.int.opp.Cypr.*ep*.75.7(M.*PL*.3.1209A) where πρεσβύτεροι is translated *majores natu* instead of *presbyteri*, so as not to suggest ascription of power of ordination to *presbyters* in restricted sense; hence Is.60:17 [δώσω τοὺς ἄρχοντάς σου ἐν εἰρήνῃ, καὶ τοὺς ἐπισκόπους ἐν δικαιοσύνῃ] applied to πρεσβύτεροι of Church, Iren.*haer*.4.26.5(M.7.1055C); **6.** actual identity of πρεσβύτεροι and ἐπίσκοποι in certain NT passages, and subsequent verbal interchangeability of these terms, cause variety of interpretation in comment on NT; **a.** interchangeability recognized οἱ π. παλαιὸν ἐκαλοῦντο ἐπίσκοποι καὶ διάκονοι Χριστοῦ, καὶ οἱ ἐπίσκοποι π. Chrys.*hom.1.1 in Phil*.(11.195B); ἐπισκόπους δὲ τοὺς π. καλεῖ· ἀμφότερα γὰρ εἶχον κατ' ἐκεῖνον τὸν καιρὸν τὰ ὀνόματα Thdt.*Phil*.1:1(3.445); cf.id.*1Tim*.3:1(3.652) cit. s. ἐπίσκοπος; λανθάνει τοὺς πολλοὺς ἡ συνήθεια, μάλιστα τῆς καινῆς διαθήκης, τοὺς ἐπισκόπους π. ὀνομάζουσα, καὶ τοὺς π. ἐπισκόπους Oecum.*Ac*.20:17(M.118.256D); τὸ τοῦ π. ὄνομα καὶ τὸν ἐπίσκοπον δηλοῖ· ἐπίσκοπον δὲ καὶ ὁ π.· καὶ τοῦτο δηλοῦται ἐν ταῖς Πράξεσιν Max.schol.*d.n*.1.1(M.3.185A); **b.** threefold ministry inferred from all NT passages, and apparent identity of ἐπίσκοποι and π. explained by close relationship existing between the two orders διαλεγόμενος περὶ ἐπισκόπων...τὸ τῶν π. τάγμα ἀφείς, εἰς τοὺς διακόνους μετεπήδησε. ... ὅτι οὐ πολὺ τὸ μέσον. ... καὶ ἃ περὶ ἐπισκόπων εἶπε, ταῦτα καὶ περὶ πρεσβυτέρων ἁρμόττει. τῇ γὰρ χειροτονίᾳ μόνον αὐτῶν ἀναβεβήκασι, καὶ...δοκοῦσι πλεονεκτεῖν τοὺς π. Chrys.*hom.11.1 in 1Tim*.(11.604C); **c.** identity in NT of the two orders explicitly or implicitly denied, cf. *in Mileto...convocatis episcopis et presbyteris qui erant ab Epheso et a reliquis proximis civitatibus*, Iren.*haer*.3.14.2(M.7.914B); τοῖς Παύλου κανόσι...οὓς περὶ ἐπισκόπων καὶ π. ἔταξε Gr. Naz.*or*.2.69(M.35.477C); οὐ περὶ πρεσβυτέρων φησὶν ἐνταῦθα [sc. 1Tim.4:14], ἀλλὰ περὶ ἐπισκόπων· οὐ γὰρ δὴ πρεσβύτεροι τὸν ἐπίσκοπον ἐχειροτόνουν Chrys.*hom.13.1 in 1Tim*.(11.618B); cf.Thdr.Mops. *1Tim*.4:14; **d.** identity in NT of the two orders affirmed by Aërius ὁ ἀπόστολος γράφει πρεσβυτέροις καὶ διακόνοις καὶ οὐ γράφει ἐπισκόποις...πάλιν δὲ ἐν ἄλλῳ τόπῳ, ἐπισκόποις καὶ διακόνοις, ὡς εἶναι ...τὸν αὐτὸν ἐπίσκοπον, τὸν αὐτὸν π. Epiph.*haer*.75.4(p.336.11; M.42.509A); denied by Epiph. ὅπου μὲν ἦσαν ἐπίσκοποι ἤδη κατασταθέντες, ἔγραφεν ἐπισκόποις καὶ διακόνοις. οὐ γὰρ πάντα εὐθὺς ἠδυνήθησαν οἱ ἀπόστολοι καταστῆσαι...πλήθους δὲ μὴ ὄντος οὐχ εὑρέθησαν ἐν αὐτοῖς πρεσβύτεροι κατασταθῆναι, καὶ ἠρκέσθησαν ἐπὶ τῷ...μόνῳ ἐπισκόπῳ *haer*.75.4(p.336.24; M.42.509A); **7.** *priest*, in regular threefold ministry ἄνευ τοῦ ἐπισκόπου καὶ τῶν π. μηδὲν πράσσετε Ign.*Magn*.7.1; σὺν τῷ ἐπισκόπῳ καὶ τοῖς σὺν αὐτῷ π. καὶ διακόνοις id.*Philad*. proem.; *ib*.10.2; Polyc.*ep*.proem.; *Clem.ep*.proem.(M.2.33A); in comparison of Church with a ship παρεικάσθω...ὁ πρωρεὺς ἐπισκόπῳ, οἱ ναῦται πρεσβυτέροις, οἱ τοίχαρχοι διακόνοις *ib*.14(49A); **8.** ref. functions; **a.** πρεσβύτεροι represent or typify: **i.** the Twelve προκαθημένου τοῦ ἐπισκόπου εἰς τόπον θεοῦ καὶ τῶν π. εἰς τόπον συνεδρίου τῶν ἀποστόλων καὶ τῶν διακόνων...πεπιστευμένων διακονίαν Ἰησοῦ Χριστοῦ Ign.*Magn*.6.1; id.*Trall*.3.1 cit. s. διάκονος; *Const.App*.2.26.7; hence apostles represented as installing twelve presbyters in each church, *Hom.Clem*.11.36; **ii.** the seventy elders (Num.11:16–25), Serap.*euch*.27(p.190.4); *Const.App*.8.16.4; **iii.** OT priests ἐν τούτοις τοῖς ἱερεῦσι (δείκνυμι δὲ τοὺς π. ἡμᾶς) Or.*hom.12.3 in Jer*.(p.89.22; M.13.381D); *Const.App*.2.26.3; (in gen. comparison of OT hierarchy with ordering of Church, *1Clem*.40.5, ἱερεῖς do not specifically correspond with πρεσβύτεροι); hence in later writers ἱερεύς denotes presbyter as well as bishop, Chrys.*sac*.4.8(p.124.13; 1.414A); ‡Cyr.*fr.Jac*.5:7(M.74.1012C); Thdt.*1Tim*.5:1(3.662); and sts. distinguishes presbyter from bishop, v. ἱερεύς; **iv.** cherubim, ‡Sophr.H.*liturg*.6(M.87.3988A); **v.** the twenty-four elders (Apoc. 4:4), *Ordo Eccl.App*.18; **b.** office includes; **i.** ruling, *1Clem*.57.1; Polyc.*ep*.5.3; Herm.*vis*.2.4.3; **ii.** exercise of discipline, *Clem.ep*.7(M.2.41B); and of arbitral jurisdiction under episcopal supervision, *ib*.10(45A); ἐπὶ τῶν π. συμβιβαζέσθωσαν· τὸν δὲ συμβιβασμὸν οἱ π. τῷ ἐπισκόπῳ προσαναφερέτωσαν *Hom.Clem*.3.67; **iii.** chiefly, assisting bishop; in gen., and as his council, Ign.*Trall*.12.2; *Hom.Clem*.3.67; σύμβουλοι τοῦ ἐπισκόπου *Const.App*.2.28.4; Socr.*h.e*.1.5.1(M.67.41A); hence presbyter occupies 'second throne', Const.ap.Eus.*h.e*.10.5.23(M.20.889C); Gr.Naz.*carm*.2.1.11.344(M.37.1053A); cf.*ib*.2.1.14.51(1249A); liturgically, ‡Hipp.*can*.20; *Ordo Eccl.App*.18; *Const.App*.2.57.7 cit. s. διάκονος; Dor.*doct*.9.2(M.88.1717D); in administration of church finance, CAnt.(341)*can*.24; *ib*.25; **iv.** baptizing, *Const.App*.3.20.2; τοῖς μὲν ἀφελεστέροις τῶν π. τοῦτο ἐγχειρίζομεν, τὸν δὲ διδασκαλικὸν λόγον τοῖς σοφωτέροις Chrys.*hom.3.3 in 1Cor*.(10.19A); **v.** celebrating eucharist independently of bishop, cf.Ign.*Smyrn*.8.1 (cf.*1Clem*.44.4); CAnc.(314)*can*.1; προστάσσομεν...τὸν π. ... ἀναφέρειν *Const.App*.3.20.2; **vi.** blessing τίνι γὰρ ὁ π. ἐπιθήσει χεῖρα; τίνα δὲ εὐλογήσει; Clem.*paed*.3.11(p.271.21; M.8.637B); *Const.App*.3.20.2; π. εὐλογεῖ, οὐκ εὐλογεῖται *ib*.8.28.3; **vii.** reconciling penitents, cf. *sacerdoti indicare peccatum...vocet presbyteros ecclesiae*, Or.*hom.2.4 in Lev*.(pp.296.20,297.1; M.12.418B,419A); Serap.*euch*.27.1; χειροθετεῖ, οὐ χειροτονεῖ (referring either to reconciliation or blessing) *Const. App*.8.28.3; penitentiary presbyter added to clergy-list at Constantinople after Decian persecution ὅπως ἂν οἱ μετὰ τὸ βάπτισμα πταίσαντες ἐπὶ τοῦ προβληθέντος τούτου π. ἐξομολογῶνται τὰ ἁμαρτήματα Socr.*h.e*.5.19.2(M.67.616A); ἐν δὲ τῇ Κωνσταντινουπόλει ἐκκλησίᾳ, ὁ ἐπὶ τῶν μετανοούντων τεταγμένος π. ἐπολιτεύετο Soz.*h.e*.7.16.8(M.67.1461A); but abolished by Nectarius, Socr.*h.e*.5.19.1(M.67.613A); Soz.*h.e*.7.16.1(1457D); **viii.** teaching and preaching ἐν τῷ νουθετεῖσθαι ἡμᾶς ὑπὸ τῶν π. *2Clem*.17.3; συγκαλέσας τοὺς π. καὶ διδασκάλους Dion.Al.ap.Eus.*h.e*.7.24.6(M.20.696A); cf. *presbyteri doctores*, *M.Perp*.(Lat.)13; Cypr.*ep*.24(M.*PL*.4.294C); CAnc.(314) *can*.1; προστάσσομεν...τὸν π. διδάσκειν *Const.App*.3.20.22; but preaching by presbyters forbidden at Alexandria after disturbance caused by Arius, Socr.*h.e*.5.22.58(M.67.640B); **ix.** joining with bishop in imposition of hands at ordination, cf.Hipp.*trad.ap.* 8.1; ‡Hipp.*can.*5; **x.** assisting in selection and approval of new clergy, Chrys.*sac.*3.15(p.76.23; 1.393A); cf.Thphl.Al.*common.*6(M. 65.40B); **c.** presbyters cannot ordain *ἐπίσκοπος…χειροθετεῖ, χειροτονεῖ…π. … χειροθετεῖ, οὐ χειροτονεῖ Const.App.*8.28.2f.; *τὸ λέγειν αὐτὸν* [sc. *Ἀέριον*] *ἐπίσκοπον καὶ π. ἴσον εἶναι. καὶ πῶς ἔσται δυνατόν; ἡ μὲν γάρ ἐστι πατέρων γεννητικὴ τάξις· πατέρας γὰρ γεννᾷ τῇ ἐκκλησίᾳ, ἡ δὲ…τέκνα γεννᾷ τῇ ἐκκλησίᾳ, οὐ μὴν πατέρας* Epiph.*haer.*75. 4(p.336.3; M.42.508D); Chrys.*hom.11.1 in 1Tim.*(11.604D); *ib.13.1* (11.618B); **d.** presbyters as parish priests, in Egypt *ὁ τῶν τόπων π.* Ath.*apol.sec.*63(p.143.1; M.25.364A); *ἕκαστος…τῶν π. ἔχει τὰς ἰδίας κώμας μεγίστας ib.*85(p.163.23; 400C); of Arius *π. γεγονότα, ὃς προΐστατο τῆς ἐκκλησίας τῆς Βαυκάλεως…ὅσαι γὰρ ἐκκλησίαι…ἐν Ἀλεξανδρείᾳ ὑπὸ ἕνα ἀρχιεπίσκοπον τυγχάνουσιν οὖσαι καὶ κατ' ἰδίαν ταύταις ἐπιτεταγμένοι εἰσὶ π.* Epiph.*haer.*69.1(p.152.20; M.42.201D); in Cappadocia, Bas.*ep.*36(3.114B; M.32.321D); in charge of martyr-chapels, *POxy.*1311; **e.** presbyters' functions summed up *οἰκονομῆσαι τὸν λαόν…καὶ πρεσβεύειν τὰ θεῖα…λόγια, καὶ καταλλάξαι τὸν λαόν* Serap.*euch.*27.1; *Const.App.*3.20.2; *ib.*8.28.3; their work superior to that of deacons *τῆς γὰρ περὶ τοὺς ἀνθρώπους θεραπείας ἡ μὲν βελτιωτική, ἡ δὲ ὑπηρετική…κατὰ τὴν ἐκκλησίαν τὴν μὲν βελτιωτικὴν οἱ π. σώζουσιν εἰκόνα, τὴν ὑπηρετικὴν δὲ οἱ διάκονοι* Clem.*str.*7.1 (p.4.19; M.9.405A); regarded as equal to that of bishop, save for 'throne' and power to ordain, ‡Hipp.*can.*4; **9.** qualifications for office; **a.** spiritual and moral, Polyc.*ep.*6.1; Or.*hom.11.3 in Jer.* (p.80.19; M.13.369C); *Ordo Eccl.App.*18; †Bas.*Is.*103(1.450E; M.30. 285A); Gr.Naz.*or.*2.69(M.35.477C); **b.** minimum age fixed at thirty, corresponding with Christ's age at baptism, CNeocaes.*can.*11; cf. Justn.*nov.*123.1.1(p.594.23); CTrull.*can.*14; cf.Eustrat.*v.Eutych.*15 (M.86.2292B); **c.** women excluded, Phot.*nomoc.*1.37(M.104.1025D); **10.** ordination and appointment; by one bishop only, *Can.App.*2; ordination without title forbidden, CChalc.*can.*6; ordination *per saltum* forbidden, CSard.*can.*10; cf.Eustrat.*v.Eutych.*15(M.86. 2292A); deposition (and therefore, probably, election) apparently effected by community in primitive times, *1Clem.*54.2; **11.** special uses; **a.** in conjunction with another title, of priests appointed to particular offices in churches and monasteries *τῷ π. ξενοδόχῳ* Pall. *h.Laus.*1(p.15.9; M.34.1009A); cf.Gr.Naz.*ep.*211(M.37.348C); *δὶς γενόμενος πρεσβ(ύτερος) καὶ παραμονάριος CIG* 9259 (Galatia); **b.** of Ebionite elders, in ministry closely related to that of the Jews *πρεσβυτέρους γὰρ οὗτοι ἔχουσι καὶ ἀρχισυναγώγους, συναγωγὴν δὲ καλοῦσι τὴν ἑαυτῶν ἐκκλησίαν* Epiph.*haer.*30.18(p.357.17; M.41. 436A); **c.** of head of monastery, Bas.*reg.br.*110(2.453C; M.31.1157A); *Apophth.Patr.*(M.65.144D); *ib.*(176A); **d.** office combined with secular employment *Διονυσίου ἰατροῦ πρεσβυτέρου Hesp.*16 p.32 n.167 (saec. iv–vi); *Παύλου πρεσβ(υτέρου) καὶ ζωγράφου ib.*; **e.** of 'gnostic' as being truly a *π. τῆς ἐκκλησίας* and, even if not assigned the *πρωτοκαθεδρία* on earth, to be numbered among the twenty-four elders in heaven, Clem.*str.*6.13(p.485.10; M.9.327B).

πρεσβύτης, ὁ, *aged man*; **1.** in gen.; as object of reverence, Herm.*mand.*8.10; as supervisors of young, Clem.*paed.*2.7(p.191.22; M.8.460C); as object of care by deacons, *Const.App.*2.58.6; ref. selection of clergy *οὐ χρὴ…τὸν π. ἀπὸ τῆς πολιᾶς δοκιμάζειν* Chrys. *sac.*2.8(p.46.20; 1.380B); **2.** of a Christian of very early times, cited by Iren. as source of orthodox teaching and apostolic tradition *ὁ θεῖος π. καὶ κῆρυξ τῆς ἀληθείας* Iren.*haer.*1.15.6(M.7.628A); cf.*ib.*4.27.1 (1056B); *ib.*4.31.1(1068A); **3.** in gen., of an ancient teacher, Clem. *ecl.*50(p.150.21; M.9.720D); or a senior man of authority *μεταπεῖσαι ἄνδρα σοφόν, καὶ ταῦτα π. Hom.Clem.*16.2; **4.** perh. in sense of *πρεσβεύτης*, of Manich. saviour *ὁ π. ὅταν προφάνῃ αὐτοῦ τὴν εἰκόνα… αἱ δὲ προβολαὶ πᾶσαι, ὁ Ἰησοῦς ἐν τῷ μικρῷ πλοίῳ, καὶ…ὁ π. ὁ τρίτος ὁ ἐν τῷ μεγάλῳ πλοίῳ…πρὸς τὸν μικρὸν φωστῆρα οἰκοῦσιν* Hegem. *Arch.*13(p.21.5; M.10.1448C).

πρεσβῦτις, ἡ, *aged woman*;

A. in gen., Tat.*orat.*32(p.33.9; M.6.872B); Dion.Al.ap.Eus.*h.e.*7. 11.20(M.20.669B); *A.Xanthipp.*35(p.82.11); of aged lady representing Church in Hermas' vision, Herm.*vis.*1.2.2; of a pagan goddess, Tat.*orat.*21(p.23.10; 853A); as used of Christians hard to distinguish from technical sense of a woman possessing eccl. status, e.g. *ἡ σεμνοτάτη π. Μερκουρία* Dion.Al.ap.Eus.*h.e.*6.41.18(609C).

B. eccl.; **1.** *senior widow*; recipient of relief, *Const.App.*2.28.3; occupying prominent position among congregation at worship, *ib.* 2.57.12; not to speak on doctrine to the unconverted, *ib.*3.5.6; status not involving priesthood or priestly functions *χήρας τε ὠνόμασε καὶ τούτων τὰς ἔτι γραοτέρας πρεσβύτιδας, οὐδαμοῦ δὲ πρεσβυτερίδας ἢ ἱερίσσας προσέταξε* Epiph.*haer.*79.4(p.478.29; M.42. 745A); cf. *πρεσβύτιδας…τὰς γεγηρακυίας οὕτως ὠνόμασεν, οὐ τὰς λειτουργίας τινὸς ἠξιωμένας* Thdt.*Tit.*2:3(3.703); **2.** *female presbyter* *κατέστησεν ὁ Ματθαῖος τὸν μὲν βασιλέα πρεσβύτερον…καὶ τὸν υἱὸν τοῦ βασιλέως κατέστησεν διάκονον…καὶ τὴν γυναῖκα…κατέστησεν π., καὶ τὴν γυναῖκα τοῦ υἱοῦ αὐτοῦ…διακόνισσαν A.Mt.*28(p.259.4); cf. *Ἄγγελος Ἐπικτοῦς πρεσβύτιδος IGC As.Min.*167 (saec. iii–iv); perh. of heads of religious communities *γυναικῶν πρεσβυτίδων* ‡Pall.*h. Laus.*proem.(p.3.5; M.34.995); appointment of female elders forbidden, CLaod.*can.*11.

[*]**πρετώριον, τό,** v. *πραιτώριον.*

***πρεφεκτορία, ἡ,** (Lat. *praefectura*) *office of prefect*, Ath.Scholast. *coll.*8.1(p.91).

***πρέφεκτος, ὁ,** v. **πραίφεκτος.*

πρηκτήρ, ὁ, v. *πρακτήρ.*

***πρηνηδόν,** *down to the ground* *ῥιπτούμενον οἶκον π. πυρὶ τεγγόμενον Orac.Sib.*5.399; Nonn.*par.Jo.*4:23(M.43.777C).

πρηνής, 1. *prone*; of falling on one's face in awe, Thdt.*Dan.* 10:9(2.1260); in prayer, Just.*dial.*90.5(M.6.692B); **2.** *headlong*, ref. Jo.18:6 *πρηνεῖς ἐποίησεν καταπεσεῖν* Mac.Mgn.*apocr.*3.8(p.64.19); ref. Judas (Ac.1:18) '*π. γενόμενος ἐλάκισε*'…*τοῦτο δὲ…ἱστορεῖ Παπίας…λέγων…πρησθεὶς γὰρ ἐπὶ τοσοῦτον τὴν σάρκα, ὥστε μὴ δύνασθαι διελθεῖν ἁμάξης…διερχομένης, ὑπὸ τῆς ἁμάξης πταισθέντα τὰ ἔγκατα ἐκκενωθῆναι* Apoll.ap.*cat.Mt.*27:3(p.231.13); applied to death of Arius, Ath.*ep.mort.Ar.*3(p.179.26; M.25.688C); met. *εἰς τὴν ὁδὸν τῆς ἀπωλείας π. ἀπέλθοι* Const.ap.Ath.*apol.sec.*68(p.146.27; M. 25.369D); *ἐν τούτοις κατεπεπτώκεισαν ὅλοι π.* Ath.*gent.*26(M.25.52C); *πέτρα…ἐπὶ τοῦ πρηνοῦς ἐνεχθεῖσα* ‡Jo.D.*Artem.*60(M.96.1308C).

πρηνίζω, *cast down to the ground, raze*, *Orac.Sib.*4.59; *ib.*4.108; Nonn.*par.Jo.*19:32(M.43.905A).

***πρηνισμός, ὁ,** *casting down to the ground, razing*, *Orac.Sib.*4.69; *ib.*12.241; *ib.*14.124.

***πρησμός, ὁ,** *burning*, *Vaticin.*2(p.51).

***πρηστήριος,** *effected by burning* *τῇ τῶν σεραφὶμ ὁμωνυμίᾳ κληθῆναι, διὰ τὴν π. τῶν…ἁμαρτιῶν ἀναίρεσιν* Dion.Ar.*c.h.*13.2(M.3. 300B).

***πρηστηρίως,** *by burning* *τὸ π. καὶ ὁλοκαύτως καθαρτικόν* Dion. Ar.*c.h.*7.1(M.3.205C).

***πρηστηροειδής,** *like lightning*, Nil.*epp.*3.33(M.79.388B).

***πρηστηροκράτωρ, ὁ,** *ruler of lightning*; of God, Synes.*hymn.*3. 161(p.11; M.66.1596).

***πρησώριον, τό,** v. **πραισόριον.*

πριβᾶτος** (πριουᾶτος**), (Lat. *privatus*); **1.** *private*; plur., *res privatae* of emperor, *privy purse*, in title *κόμης πριβάτων* Bas.*ep.*15 tit.(3.94D; M.32.277D); *κόμης ἦν τῶν λεγομένων πριουάτων* Philost. *h.e.*3.12(M.65.500C); *τῆς βασιλικῆς οἰκίας προεστὼς (κόμητας πριουάτων ἡ Ῥωμαίων γλῶττα καλεῖ) ib.*7.10(548B); *τῶν ἰδίων τοῦ βασιλέως χρημάτων τε καὶ κτημάτων τὴν ἡγεμονίαν πεπιστευμένος· κόμητα δὲ πριβάτων τὸν τοιοῦτον Ῥωμαῖοι προσαγορεύειν εἰώθασιν* Thdt.*h.e.*3.12. 2(3.925); Malchus *exc.gent.*5(p.573.20; M.113.788C); *τοὺς τῶν θείων π. καὶ τοὺς τοῦ θείου πατριμονίου* Ath.Scholast.*coll.*4.13(p.58); **2.** *πριβάτων* for *πριμάτων*, *Schol.* in CTrull.*can.*2(*Mon.*2 p.651); v. *πριμάς.*

πριβιλέγιον** (πριβιλήγ-**, ***πριβηληγ-**), **τό,** v. **πριμιλίγιον.*

πρίγκιψ ([*]**πρίγκιπος**, [*]**πριγκίπιος**), **ὁ,** (Lat. *princeps*) *imperial official, head of a group of bureaux*, Pall.*v.Chrys.*8(p.43.20; M.47. 26); cf. *ἀλλὰ πρίγκιψ ἐστὶν ἀξιόλογος· εἰ δὲ οὐ θέλεις, ἄρχων εἰμί M. Pion.*15.5; *πρίγκιπος*, Nil.*epp.*3.41 tit.(M.79.408A); Thdr.Stud.*epp.* 2.125 tit.(M.99.1405C); cf. *τὸν μακάριον πριγκίπιον* Thdt.*ep.*110(4. 1180) where prob. a proper name.

§**πριμάς, ὁ,** *primate*; of Numidian primate, Martin.ap.CLater.*act.* 2(H.3.736D); *τῶν ἐν Ἀφρικῇ πριβάτων, τουτέστι τῶν πρωτευόντων Schol.* in CTrull.*can.*2(*Mon.*2 p.651); Phot.*nomoc.*1.5(p.462; *πριβάτων* M.104.985D); cf. s. *πριβᾶτος.*

πριμιγίλιον** (πριμηγίλιον**), **τό,** v. **πριμιλίγιον.*

***πριμικηρᾶτος, ὁ,** *office of πριμικήριος*, Jo.Mal.*chron.*18 p.474(M. 97.689A).

***πριμικήριος, ὁ,** (Lat. *primicerius*) *head of a government department* *πρεσβύτερος Ἀλεξανδρείας καὶ π. νοταρίων* CEph.(431)*act.*1 (*ACO* 1.1.2 p.7.34, v.l. *πριμμι-* H.1.1356C); Nil.*epp.*2.238 tit.(M.79. 321B); *ἀρχιδιάκονος καὶ π. νοταρίων* Evagr.*h.e.*2.18(p.74.8; M.86. 2560A); Anast.Ap.*a.Max.*1.3(M.90.113D); Thphn.*chron.*p.384(M.108. 917C).

πριμιλίγιον** (πριμιλέγ-**, ***πριμιγίλιον, πριμηγίλ-**, ***πριβιλέγ-**, ***πριβιλήγ-**, ***πριβηλήγ-**), **τό,** (Lat. *privilegium*) *privilege*, eccl. *τὰ πριβιλέγια τῆς Ῥωμαϊκῆς ἐκκλησίας Cod.Afr.*138(H.1.948C); civil *προσδοκήσας τῶν πριμιγιλίων τῆς…σχολῆς* [sc. *τῶν μαγιστριανῶν*] ἀξιοῦσθαι Thdr.Al.*libell.*(p.15.43, v.l. πριμηγιλ-; πριβηλην- H.2.324A); τὰ π. τῆς πόλεως Valent.Imp.*ep.Nic.*2(p.61.24, v.l. πριμιλέγ-; πριβιλήγ- H.2.569B).

πριμισκρίνιος, ὁ, (Lat. *primiscrinius*) *chief clerk*, Nil.*epp.*1.239 tit.(M.79.169C); *ib.*2.153 tit.(272C); προμοσ-, Thphn.*chron.*p.411(M.108.976B).

***πρῖμος,** (Lat. *primus*) *first*; name of first month (March), Jo.Mal.*chron.*7 p.187(M.97.297B); *Chron.Pasch.*p.110(M.92.292A).

πρίν, *before*; *of old*, in phrase ἐκ πρὶν καὶ δεῦρο *Pers.*(p.10.4).

***πρινή,** = πρὶν ἤ, *before* πρινὴ γένηται Didym.*Trin.*3.3(M.39.820C); πρινὴ...ἀναγεννηθῆναι *ib.*3.39(980C); ‡Nil.*Epict.*64(M.79.1309A); †Jo.D.*B.J.*6(M.96.897B).

πριονοειδής, *like a saw, serrated*, Thdt.*Is.*41:15f.(p.162.33; 2.332); id.*Am.*1:3(2.1412).

***πριοποι-έω,** *fashion like a workman with a saw*; etym., of 'Priapus', acc. Naassenes διὰ τοῦτο καλεῖται Πρίαπος, ὅτι ἐπριοποίησε τὰ πάντα...~ήσας τὴν κτίσιν πρότερον οὐκ οὖσαν Hipp.*haer.*5.26(p.132.4; M.16.3202C).

***πρίορες, οἱ,** (Lat. *priores*) *officers* in army, Phot.*nomoc.*13.3 (p.612; M.104.904C).

***πριουᾶτος,** v. *πριβᾶτος.

πριστηροειδής, *saw-toothed*, Thdr.Heracl.*Is.*41:15(M.18.1333B); Nil.*epp.*2.137(M.79.257B).

πρίων, ὁ, *saw*; hence *saw-fish*, ‡Bas.*struct.hom.*1.11(1.329D; M.30.21D); ‡Petr.I Al.*phys.*5 tit.(p.35); ‡Caes.Naz.*dial.*102(M.38.968).

πρό, *before*; **1.** adv. of time ἀεὶ...ἔρως εἰσέρχεται πρὸ ταῖς ὑπαρξάσαις θεωρίαις Didym.*Ps.*5:4(M.39.1169B); Jo.Mosch.*prat.*124(M.87.2985C); **2.** prep. of place, *above* ἐπάνω τῆς κεφαλῆς...ἡ...γραφὴ ἣν Πιλᾶτος πρὸ τῆς κυριακῆς ἔπηξε κεφαλῆς Jo.D.*fr.Mt.*27:37(M.96.1412B); **3.** conjunction πρὸ τοῦ c. subj., Jo.Mosch.*prat.*127(M.87.2989D); Sophr.H.*mir.Cyr.et Jo.*44(M.87.3589A); πρὸ τοῦ ἑνωθῶσιν αὐτοῖς οἱ τρισχίλιοι Thphn.*chron.*p.265(M.108.660A).

***προαγαπ-άω,** *love beforehand* (i.e. love before one is loved) πῶς ἀγαπήσεις τὸν οὕτως ~ήσαντά σε; *Diogn.*10.3; ὑπὸ τούτου...~ηθέντας ...οὐχ ὅσιον ἄλλο τι πρεσβύτερον ἄγειν Clem.*q.d.s.*27(p.178.11; M.9.633A); of Church as bride κατηξιώθη ~ηθεῖσα ὑπὸ τοῦ κυρίου ἀγαπῆσαι τὸν κύριον Ph.Carp.*Cant.*15(M.40.49A).

προαγγελία, ἡ, *announcement in advance*, Just.*dial.*53.4(M.6.593A); *ib.*104.1(720B); *ib.*105.1(720C).

προάγγελμα, τό, *previous announcement*, Cyr.*ador.*2(1.72E).

προάγγελος, 1. adj., *announcing beforehand, foretelling*, Nonn.*par.Jo.*14:29(M.43.872C); *ib.*19:31(904C); of prophecy μολπὴ χρωτὸς ἀμωμήτοιο προάγγελος *ib.*19:36(905B); **2.** subst., *harbinger*; of Jo. Bapt., Gr.Naz.*carm.*1.2.1.420(M.37.554A).

***προαγγελτικός,** *foretelling, prophetic*, of OT prophecies τὸ γὰρ 'πλύνων τὴν στολὴν...' π. ἦν τοῦ πάθους Just.*1apol.*32.7(M.6.380B); τὸ οὖν εἰρημένον ῥάβδον δυνάμεως...π. τοῦ λόγου...ὃν...οἱ ἀπόστολοι... ἐκήρυξαν *ib.*45.5(397A); *ib.*36.2(προαγγελτικῶς M.6.385A); Cyr.*Jo.*8 (4.709B); of NT prophecies ἥντινα τῶν εὐαγγελίων θείαν βίβλον συνήθως εἰς χεῖρας ἀναλαβών, τὰς τούτου [sc. vision of Cross in Jerusalem] κειμένας π. μαρτυρίας ἐγγράφους εὑρήσεις Cyr.H.*ep.Const.*6(M.33.1172B).

***προαγιάζω,** *consecrate beforehand, presanctify*, in Mass of Presanctified ἐν πάσαις τῆς ἁγίας τεσσαρακοστῆς τῶν νηστειῶν ἡμέραις, παρεκτὸς σαββάτου καὶ κυριακῆς καὶ τῆς ἁγίας τοῦ εὐαγγελισμοῦ ἡμέρας, γινέσθω ἡ τῶν προηγιασμένων ἱερὰ λειτουργία CTrull.*can.*52; regulations of Sergius (645) ἀπὸ τῆς α' ἑβδομάδος τῶν νηστειῶν ἰνδικτιῶνος δ' ἤρξατο ψάλλεσθαι μετὰ τὸ 'κατευθυνθήτω', ἐν τῷ καιρῷ τοῦ εἰσάγεσθαι τὰ προηγιασμένα δῶρα εἰς τὸ θυσιαστήριον ἀπὸ τοῦ σκευοφυλακίου μετὰ τὸ εἰπεῖν τὸν ἱερέα, 'κατὰ τὴν δωρεὰν τοῦ Χριστοῦ σου', εὐθέως ἄρχεται ὁ λαός· 'νῦν αἱ δυνάμεις τῶν οὐρανῶν...ἀλληλούϊα'. τοῦτο δὲ οὐ μόνον ἐν ταῖς νηστείας προηγιασμένων εἰσαγομένων ψάλλεται, ἀλλὰ καὶ ἐν ἄλλαις ἡμέραις, ὁσάκις ἂν προηγιασμένα γίνηται *Chron.Pasch.*p.385(M.92.989A,B); νῦν πρὸ τῶν ἄλλων ἡ ἱερουργία τοῦ ...Βασιλείου καὶ...Χρυσοστόμου κρατεῖ μετὰ τῶν προηγιασμένων, ἥν τινες 'Ιακώβου μὲν εἶναί φασιν τοῦ...ἀδελφοῦ τοῦ κυρίου, ἕτεροι δὲ Πέτρου ‡Sophr.H.*liturg.*1(M.87.3981D); μίαν προνήστιμον ἑβδομάδα, ἐν ᾗ...ἡ μέχρις ἑσπέρας νηστεία ἐπετελεῖτο, μηδαμῶς τρίτης ἢ ἕκτης, ἢ ἐννάτης, ἢ τῆς τῶν ἁγίων προηγιασμένων τελετῆς γενομένης Jo.D.*jej.*5(M.95.69D); *Lit.Praesanct.*(pp.345.20; 346.21; 351.11; 352.11); *Euchol.*(pp.161–8); interprn. of rite, Thdr.Stud.*praesanct.*(M.99.1688–9).

***προαγνίζω,** *purify, hallow beforehand* ἕτοιμος ὁ τόπος προαγνισθεὶς ταῖς προγενομέναις εὐχαῖς, ζητῶν παρουσίαν τῆς σῆς εὐσεβείας Ath.*apol.Const.*18(M.25.620A); Cyr.*ador.*11(1.406D); *ib.*(410A).

προαγνοέω, *be ignorant of previously*; perf. ptcpl. pass., of errors committed in ignorance before conversion, Eus.*d.e.*4.12(p.170.25; M.22,284D).

***προαγόντως,** *previously*, Epiph.*haer.*42.16(p.185.13; M.41.816C).

προαγοράζ-ω, *purchase in advance, forestall*, ‡Ath.*syntag.*3.5 (p.124; cj. for προσαγόραζε M.28.840C); κληρικοὺς...~οντας τῶν χειροτονουμένων ἀρχόντων τὰς προαγωγὰς ἐν τῇ Αἰγυπτιακῇ διοικήσει Pall.*v.Chrys.*7(p.41.11; M.47.25).

προαγοραστής, ὁ, *buyer of stores for the king, officer responsible for public purchases*; of Tobit, ‡Ath.*synops.*44(M.28.372B), cf. Tob.1:13 ἀγοραστής.

προαγόρευσις, ἡ, *prediction, prophecy*, of OT prophecy and predictions by Christ πνεῦμα...παρὰ δέ τισι τοῖς δικαίως πολιτευομένοις καταγινόμενον καὶ συμπεριπλεκόμενον τῇ ψυχῇ διὰ προαγορεύσεων ταῖς λοιπαῖς ψυχαῖς τὸ κεκρυμμένον ἀνήγγειλε Tat.*orat.*13(p.15.3; M.6.836A); Clem.*str.*4.11(p.283.7; M.8.1288B); Cyr.*Joel.*15(3.214B); of prophecies concerning Christ from pagan sources, ‡Jo.D.*Artem.*46 (p.163.23; M.96.1293C).

προαγορευτής, ὁ, *foreteller, prophet* Δανιὴλ...ἐνανθρωπήσεως θεοῦ προαγορευτής Bas.*renunt.*7(2.208D; M.31.641A); Cyr.*Is.*4.3(2.648C); id.*Abac.*1(3.518B); of Zacharias, ‡Thdt.*nativ.Jo.Bapt.*(5.94).

προαγορεύω, *predict, prophesy*; **1.** pagan ὄρνιθες π. Tat.*orat.*19 (p.21.23; M.6.849B); Clem.*str.*1.21(p.82.9; M.8.868A); of pagan foreshadowings of Christian truths Δίφιλος...τὴν ἐσομένην προηγόρευσε κρίσιν Thdt.*affect.*6(p.156.23; 4.855); of Druidical predictions, Hipp.*haer.*1.25(p.29.22; M.16.3053A); **2.** of OT prophecy 'Ησαίας... προηγόρευε τὸ βάπτισμα Just.*dial.*14.1(M.6.504C); Eus.*d.e.*4.16(p.185.8; M.22.309A); προηγόρευσε γὰρ ὁ νόμος τὰ ἐσόμενα Cyr.*ador.*10(1.329C); of Is.17:7–8 as prophecy of Const.'s reign, Thdt.*affect.*10 (p.258.27; 4.968); **3.** of predictions by Christ, Cels.ap.Or.*Cels.*6.42 (p.111.1; M.11.1360B); **4.** of prophesying through H. Ghost in rel. to activity of other Persons μόνον ὑποληψόμεθα τὸ πνεῦμα...προσαγορεύειν [l. προαγορεύειν] τὰ μέλλοντα, καὶ μὴ ἐκ πατρὸς δι' υἱοῦ... προφητείαν κατάρχεσθαι Didym.(‡Bas.)*Eun.*5(1.311B; M.29.745C).

προάγ-ω, 1. *lead forward*, exeg. Mt.26:32 προάξω ὑμᾶς, λέγει,... εἰς τὴν Γαλιλαίαν· αὐτὸς γὰρ ~ει πάντα, καὶ τὴν ἀφανῶς σῳζομένην ψυχὴν ἀναστήσειν ᾐνίσσετο καὶ ἀποκαταστήσειν οὗ νῦν ~ει Clem.*exc.Thdot.*61(p.127.12; M.9.688C); cf. *praecedente eos in Galilaeam, qui se sequi voluerint in Galilaeam gentium, ut 'populus qui sedebat in tenebris videat lumen magnum'*, Or.*comm.ser.*87 *in Mt.*(p.201.9; M.13.1738A); προάξω ὑμᾶς...οὐδὲ γὰρ ἀπὸ οὐρανοῦ φαίνεται εὐθέως, οὐδὲ εἰς μακράν τινα χώραν ἄπεισιν, ἀλλ' ἐν αὐτῷ τῷ ἔθνει ἐν ᾧ καὶ ἐσταυρώθη...ὥστε καὶ ἐντεῦθεν αὐτοὺς πιστώσασθαι Chrys.*hom.82.2 in Mt.*(7.785A) = Cyr.*fr.Mt.*26:32(M.72.453C); **2.** *bring forward*; **a.** *present*, eucharistic offerings μετὰ τὰ ἀναγνώσματα...παρακαλέσας Πανοσόφιον...~αγεῖν τὰ δῶρα Pall.*v.Chrys.*14(p.85.9; M.47.48); **b.** *bring forward* as a witness ὀμνύντα τινὰ ~ετε ἑωρακέναι...ἀνερχόμενον εἰς τὸν οὐρανὸν...καίσαρα Just.*1apol.*21.3(M.6.360B); **3.** *produce*, of God in Creation τὸ μηδαμῶς ὑπάρχον ἐκ τοῦ μὴ ὄντος εἰς τὸ εἶναι ~αγεῖν Eus.*e.th.*1.12(p.71.5; παράγειν M.24.845D); *ib.*3.3(p.156.7; 1000C); ἐργάζεται δὲ οὐκ ἐξ αὐτοῦ ~ων τὰ δημιουργήματα, ἀλλ' ἐνεργητικῶς . ὑφιστάς Didym.(‡Bas.)*Eun.*5(1.307A; M.29.736B); (Gnost.) of emanation of aeons ἡ μήτηρ αὖθις τὸν τῆς οἰκονομίας προηγάγετο ἄρχοντα Clem.*exc.Thdot.*33(p.117.27; M.9.676B); αὐτὸς ἑαυτὸν ἀπὸ ἑαυτοῦ ~αγὼν ἐφανέρωσεν ἑαυτῷ τὴν ἰδίαν ἐπίνοιαν Hipp.*haer.*6.18(p.144.26; M.16.3222B); ἐπεὶ δὲ ἦν γόνιμος, ἔδοξεν αὐτῷ...ὃ εἶχεν ἐν ἑαυτῷ, γεννῆσαι καὶ ~αγεῖν *ib.*6.29(p.156.14; 3238A); cf. τοῦ δὲ πατρὸς...ἡ οὐσία ἐστὶν ἀφθαρσία...ἡ δὲ τούτου οὐσία διττὴν μέν τινα δύναμιν προήγαγεν Ptol.*ep.*ap.Epiph.*haer.*33.7(p.457.7; M.41.568B); pass., denied of Son ὁ...γενητὸν ἐξ οὐκ ὄντων καὶ κτίσμα προηγμένον ἐκ τοῦ μὴ ὄντος τὸν υἱὸν ὁριζόμενος λέληθεν...τὸ...ἀληθῶς υἱὸν εἶναι ἀρνούμενος Eus.*e.th.*1.9(p.68.9; M.24.841A); but asserted in sense of *be begotten* εἰς τὸ εἶναι, εἰ καὶ ἀχρόνως καὶ ἀεί, ~ει ὁ πατὴρ τὸν υἱόν Leont.H.*Nest.*4.37(M.86.1709B); **4.** *bring forth, produce* in order to communicate to others τὰς οἰκείας προνοητικὰς ἐνεργείας ἐκ τοῦ κρυφίου καὶ εἰς ἡμᾶς προήγαγεν ἡ πάσης αἰτία καὶ δημιουργὸς καθάρσεως Dion.Ar.*c.h.*13.4(M.3.308A); οἱ πρῶτοι τῆς καθ' ἡμᾶς ἱεραρχίας καθηγεμόνες, ἐκ τῆς ὑπερουσίου θεαρχίας, αὐτοί τε ἀναπλησθέντες τοῦ ἱεροῦ δώρου, καὶ εἰς τὸ ἑξῆς αὐτὸ ~αγεῖν ὑπὸ τῆς θεαρχικῆς ἀγαθότητος ἀπεσταλμένοι id.*e.h.*1.5(M.3.376D); τήν...κρυφιότητα θεόν, ἢ ζωὴν... οὐδὲν ἕτερον νοοῦμεν, ἢ τὰς εἰς ἡμᾶς ἐξ αὐτῆς ~ομένας δυνάμεις id.*d.n.*2.7(M.3.645A); τοῖς...ἀσεβοῦσιν...ἄφεσιν ~ει παρὰ τοῦ πατρός id.*ep.*8.4(M.3.1096B); ἀγγέλους δι' αἰνιγμάτων τὰ θεῖα μυστικῶς ~οντας ὁρῶμεν *ib.*9.1(1108A); τῆς μὲν ἀγάπης...θεὸν προβολέα φησί...αὐτὸς γὰρ ταῦτα ἐν ἑαυτῷ ὄντα προήγαγεν εἰς τὰ ἐκτός, τουτέστι τὰ περὶ τὰ κτίσματα Max.*schol.d.n.*4.14(M.4.265C); **5.** *prostitute*, Just.*1apol.*27.1(M.6.369B); **6.** *promote, prefer*, esp. of ordination to priesthood;

a. of OT priests τὸν...προηγμένον ἱερέα χρίων Eus.*d.e.*4.15(p.180.10; M.22.300C); **b.** of Christian clergy, CAnc.(314)*can.*12; CNeocaes. *can.*9; CNic.(325)*can.*1; ὁ διὰ τῆς ἐκείνου χειρὸς προαχθεὶς Bas.*ep.*251. 3(3.387B; M.32.936B); of a reader, ‡Pall.*h.mon.*86.2(p.106.9; M.34. 1188C); **7.** pass., *be advanced* or *promoted* beyond zero point of indifference (Stoic), of things εἰσὶ γὰρ οὖν καὶ μεσότητές τινες καὶ προηγμένα καὶ ἀποπροηγμένα ἐν τοῖς μέσοις Clem.*str.*4.26(p.321.19; M. 8.1373C); **8.** *precede*; **a.** in time πίστιν...ἐπακολουθούσης τῆς ἐλπίδος, ~ούσης τῆς ἀγάπης Polyc.*ep.*3.3; *M.Polyc.*1.1; ἔτεσι...χιλίοις ~ει Μωϋσῆς τῆς τοῦ Ἰλιακοῦ ἁλώσεως Thphl.Ant.*Autol.*3.29(M.6.1164D); ἐὰν...αἱ ~ουσαι ἡμέραι βελτίους ὦσι τῶν μετὰ ταῦτα †Bas.*Is.*17(1.389C; M.30.145A); Marc.Diac.*v.Porph.*21; cf. exeg. Mt.21:9 οὐκ ἀπίθανόν ἐστιν ἐφαρμόσαι τοὺς μὲν ~οντας...τοῖς προφήταις, τοὺς δ' ἀπακολουθοῦντας τοῖς...ἀποστόλοις Or.*Jo.*10.29(18; p.202.27; M.14.360B); **b.** logically, *be prior to* τὰ νοητὰ ~ει τῶν αἰσθητῶν Athenag.*leg.* 36.2(M.6.972A); **9.** impers., *be preferable* ~ει οὖν...ἵνα μία πόλις ἀπόληται καὶ μὴ τὸ βασίλειόν σου *A.Petr.et Paul.*15(p.185.14).

προαγωγεύς, ὁ, 1. *one who leads forth, one who sends out* in order to impart to others; of God in his self-communication to the soul κίνησιν θείαν, ἐν ᾗ κινεῖται καὶ αὐτοῦ ἐστι π. καὶ κινητικὸς ὁ θεός Max.*schol.d.n.*4.14(M.4.268A); **2.** *one who produces*, of God π. εἰς τὸ ὂν τῶν μὴ ὄντων *cat.Apoc.*19:3(p.450.5); **3.** *prostitutor*, Thphn. *chron.*p.43(M.108.164A); **4.** *collector* of revenue, Malchus *exc.gent.*6 (p.573.27; M.113.788D).

προαγωγία, ἡ, *attraction, allurement*, of God in rel. to soul which he attracts into union with himself προαγωκικὸν...πρὸς ἐρωτικὴν συνάφειαν τὴν ἐν πνεύματι τὸν θεὸν εἶναί μοι νόει...τὸ δὲ τῆς π. ὄνομα, εἰ καὶ παρὰ τοῖς τῶν ἔξωθεν πρᾶγμα σημαίνει οὐκ εὐαγές, ἀλλ' ἐνταῦθα τὴν πρόξενον τῆς ἐν θεῷ ἑνώσεως μεσιτείαν φησί Max.*schol.d.n.*4.14 (M.4.268A).

προαγωγικός, *leading forth, sending out*, in order to impart to others, of God in his self-communication to soul ποτὲ μὲν ἔρωτα καὶ ἀγάπην αὐτόν φασι, ποτὲ δὲ ἐραστὸν...καὶ τῷ μὲν κινεῖται, τῷ δὲ κινεῖ· ἢ ὅτι αὐτὸς ἑαυτοῦ καὶ ἑαυτῷ ἐστι π. καὶ κινητικός Dion.Ar.*d.n.*4.14 (M.3.712C); ref. illustrations of Son's generation ἀπαυγασμάτων προαγωγικὰς φωτογονίας id.*ep.*9.1(M.3.1105A).

***προαγωκικῶς,** *alluringly*, Sophr.H.*v.Anast.*(M.92.1717C).

προαγών, ὁ, *preliminary contest*; met., of propaedeutic instruction to 'gnostics', Clem.*str.*1.1(p.11.21; M.8.704D).

***προαδολεσχέω,** *commune with*, Dan.Raith.*v.Jo.Clim.*(M.88. 601C).

προᾴδ-ω, 1. *sing of beforehand*; of OT prophets foretelling Inc., Meth.*arbitr.*1(p.146.19; M.18.241A); **2.** *sing forth*, of Devil in Temptations δευτέραν...καὶ τρίτην...πεῖραν ~ει Thdt.*pental.*(5.126).

προαθλέω, *contend beforehand* τὴν τῶν προηθληκότων μνήμην *M.Polyc.*18.2; Ast.Am.*hom.*12(M.40.341C).

***πρόαθλος, ὁ,** *former fighter*; of departed saints, *Hymn.*(*AS* 1 p.632).

προαικίζομαι, *maltreat beforehand*, Eus.*d.e.*10.1(p.448.12; M.22. 721A).

προαινίσσομαι, *foretell in a figure*, Bas.Sel.*or.*19.2(M.85.244A).

προαίρεσις, ἡ, I. *faculty of free choice*; *deliberate choice*;

A. def. and explanations τὸ κατὰ π. dist. from τὸ ἑκούσιον: π. dist. from ὄρεξις, βούλησις, δόξα, βούλευσις, and explained as μικτόν τι ἐκ βουλῆς καὶ κρίσεως καὶ ὀρέξεως, or as ὄρεξις βουλευτικὴ τῶν ἐφ' ἡμῖν Nemes.*nat.hom.*33(M.40.732A–736A); dist. from θέλησις, Max.*opusc.*(M.91.13A) cit. s. θέλησις; dist. from βούλησις *ib.*(13C) cit. s. βούλησις; defined as ὄρεξις βουλευτικὴ τῶν ἐφ' ἡμῖν πρακτῶν *ib.*(13B); dist. from βούλευσις: ἡ μὲν βούλευσις ἐπὶ τοῖς ἔτι ζητουμένοις ἐστίν· ἡ δὲ π., ἐπὶ τοῖς ἤδη προκεκριμένοις *ib.*(16B); cf.*ib.*(20C); π. γάρ ἐστι, δύο προκειμένων, τὸ μὲν αἱρεῖσθαι, καὶ ἐκλέγεσθαι τοῦτο πρὸ τοῦ ἑτέρου Jo.D.*f.o.*2.24(M.94.945B); cf. τοῦτο δέ ἐστιν ἡ π., ἀδούλωτόν τι χρῆμα καὶ αὐτεξούσιον, ἐν τῇ ἐλευθερίᾳ τῆς διανοίας κείμενον Gr.Nyss. *or.catech.*30(p.112.12; M.45.77A).

B. as human endowment; **1.** in gen. βουλόμενος γὰρ τούτους ἐν ἐλευθέρᾳ π. ... γενομένους, τούς τε ἀγγέλους καὶ τοὺς ἀνθρώπους, ὁ θεὸς πράττειν ὅσα ἕκαστον ἐνεδυνάμωσε δύνασθαι ποιεῖν, ἐποίησεν Just. *dial.*88.5(M.6.685C); αὐτεξούσιοι ὄντες οἱ ἄνθρωποι, τῷ π. ἐλευθέραν ἔχειν Or.*fr.43 in Jo.*(p.518.13); opp. nature of animals, Ath.*Ar.*3.18 (M.26.361A); Gr.Nyss.*hom.2 in Cant.*(M.44.796D); τοῦτο μάλιστα δείκνυσιν ἡμῖν τὴν π. ... ἡ ἀθρόα μεταβολή Chrys.*hom.41.3 in Ac.*(9. 312B); τῆς οἰκείας π. ἕκαστος ἔχει τὴν ἐξουσίαν Cyr.*Jo.*1.7(4.63A); gen. in respect of moral choice π. ἐλευθέρᾳ πρὸς τὸ φεύγειν τὰ αἰσχρὰ καὶ αἱρεῖσθαι τὰ καλὰ δύναμιν ἔχει τὸ ἀνθρώπινον γένος Just.*1apol.*43. 3(M.6.393A); rendering reward or punishment just and fitting, Tat. *orat.*7(p.7.14; M.6.820B); τὴν ἡμετέραν π., κλίνουσαν ἐπὶ τὰ κρείττονα ἢ ἐπὶ τὰ χείρονα Or.*princ.*3.1.24(p.244.2; cf.M.11.303A); ἀνθρώπων εἰς ἀμφότερα νεύειν δυναμένην π. Ath.*inc.*3.4(M.25.101C); Cyr.H. *catech.*19.8; **2.** opp. determined character of inanimate nature τὸ μὲν γὰρ δένδρον φύσει κινεῖται, σὺ δὲ προαιρέσει πολιτεύῃ Tit. Bost.*fr.Lc.*6:43(p.163); opp. ἀνάγκη from which Christians are delivered μὴ ἀνάγκης τέκνα...μένωμεν, ἀλλὰ προαιρέσεως Just.*1apol.*61. 10(M.6.421A); opp. astrological determinism, Eus.*p.e.*6.1(238A; M. 21.408A); cf. discussion of subject, *ib.*6.6(243D; M.416A).

C. in rel. to sin and responsibility for sin; **1.** ref. Devil ἐκ π. ἔχων τὴν πονηρίαν, οὐ φύσις ἀντικειμένη τῷ ἀγαθῷ Bas.*hom.*9.8(2.80C; M. 31.348A); Cyr.H.*catech.*2.4; Bas.Sel.*or.*23.1(M.85.269C); ‡Caes.Naz. *dial.*123(M.38.1016); Petr.Laod.*or.dom.*(p.111.9; M.86.3333C); **2.** of demons; as angels, Cyr.H.*catech.*2.4 cit. s. ἁμαρτητικός; †Jo.D.*B.J.* 7(M.96.908A,B) cit. s. δαίμων; as sinful only by deliberate choice, Serap.*Man.*29(p.44; M.18.1116A); cf.Bas.*Eun.*2.27(1.264B; M.29. 636B); **3.** of men οὔτε δὲ οἱ ἔπαινοι οὔτε...αἱ κολάσεις δίκαιαι, μὴ τῆς ψυχῆς ἐχούσης τὴν ἐξουσίαν τῆς ὁρμῆς...τῶν ἁμαρτημάτων π. καὶ ὁρμὴ κατάρχει Clem.*str.*1.17(p.54.17; M.8.800A); καθάπερ ἐν ἐρημίᾳ τῇ πόλει βιοῖ, ἵνα μὴ ὁ τόπος αὐτὸν ἀναγκάζῃ, ἀλλ' ἡ π. δεικνύῃ δίκαιον *ib.*7.12(p.55.7; M.9.505B); οὐ γὰρ φύσις ἐν ἡμῖν αἰτία τῆς πονηρίας, ἀλλὰ π. ἑκούσιος οὖσα κακοποιητική Or.*comm.in Mt.*10.11(p.12.24; M.13.860C); Mac.Mgn.*apocr.*4.18(p.197.26); [that 'a corrupt tree cannot bring forth good fruit' is no excuse for yielding to sin] εἰ γὰρ φύσει κακὸς τυγχάνεις, τί μανθάνεις; εἰς τί διδάσκῃ; τὸ γὰρ φύσει ὂν ἀμετάβλητόν ἐστιν. εἰ δὲ ἡ διδασκαλία μεταβάλλει τὴν διάνοιαν...ἡ μὲν ὑποψία τῆς ἀνάγκης ἐκβάλλεται, τὸ δὲ δόγμα τῆς π. ὁμολογεῖται Tit. Bost.*fr.Lc.*6:43(p.163); δεινὸν ἡ ἁμαρτία...κακὸν αὐτεξούσιον, βλάστημα προαιρέσεως Cyr.H.*catech.*2.1; ref. Mt.18:7 οὐ τὴν ἐλευθερίαν τῆς π. λυμαινόμενος, οὐδὲ ἀνάγκην τινὰ καὶ βίαν ἐφιστὰς τῷ βίῳ, ἀλλὰ τὸ πάντως ἐσόμενον ἐκ τῆς πονηρᾶς τῶν ἀνθρώπων γνώμης προλέγων Chrys.*hom.27.2 in 1Cor.*(10.242B); οὐκ ἔστι φύσεως τὰ τῆς πονηρίας· προαιρέσει τετιμήμεθα καὶ ἐλευθερίᾳ id.*dimiss.Chan.*2(3.434D); αἱ δὲ φαντασίαι ἐκ π. ἔρχονται καὶ τῆς κακῆς γνώμης ἐστὶ τεκμήριον ‡Pall.*h. mon.*22(p.82.12; M.34.1172B); οὐκ ἄρα ὁ θεός ἐστιν αἴτιος τοῦ εἶναι ἡμᾶς ἀγαθοὺς ἢ κακούς, ἀλλ' ἡ π. ‡Just.*qu.et resp.*8(M.6.1257C); πέφυκε δὲ ἁμαρτάνειν ὁ κατὰ τὴν αὐθαίρετον π. ἄγων ἑαυτὸν εἰς τὸ πράττειν ἃ βούλεται, εἴτε ἀγαθά, εἴτε φαῦλα *ib.*88(1329C); καλὰ τὰ τῇδε πάντα...καὶ...κακὸν κατ' οὐσίαν οὐδέν ἐστιν ἐν αὐτοῖς...ἀλλὰ κατὰ τὴν ἑκούσιον π. τῶν ἀνθρώπων...συγχωρεῖ δὲ [sc. ὁ θεός] ἡμᾶς πράττειν ἃ ἑκουσίως αἱρούμεθα κακά, οὐ διὰ τὴν ἀσθένειαν τῆς αὐτοῦ δυνάμεως, ἀλλ' ἵνα τὸ ἡμῶν αὐθαίρετον...δειχθῇ ‡Just.*qu.Chr.*1.5(M.6.1412D); asserted agst. pagan view that τὰ πολλὰ οὐ κατὰ π. ἁμαρτάνει ὁ ἄνθρωπος, ἀλλὰ κατὰ φύσιν *V.Aberc.*38(p.70.16); Petr.Laod.*or.dom.* (p.111.10; M.86.3333C).

D. in rel. to virtuous living; **1.** necessary for moral action, Clem.*str.*4.6(p.264.11; M.8.1248B); *ib.*7.12(p.53.1; M.9.501B); Chrys. *sac.*2.3(p.33.4; 1.374C); Gennad.*fr.Rom.*5:12ff.(p.362.27; M.85. 1672C); **2.** in gen., Clem.*str.*6.11(p.478.21; M.9.313B); τῆς...π. ... τῆς ἐγγιζούσης τῷ θελήματι αὐτοῦ Or.*comm.in Eph.*2:13(p.406); θεοῦ κατόρθωμα γέγονε μέγιστον, ὥστε τὸ συνειδὸς ἡμῶν καὶ τὴν π. τέως καὶ πρὸ τῆς πράξεως οἰκειῶσαι μὲν τῇ ἀρετῇ, ἐκπολεμῶσαι δὲ τῇ πονηρίᾳ... πάλιν τὴν π. ὁλόκληρον ἀναδέξασθαι τὸ φορτίον οὐκ εἴασε...ἀλλ' ὑπαγορεύει μὲν αὐτῇ τὸ συνειδὸς τὰ πρακτέα Chrys.*stat.*13.3(2.137D,E); ref. counsels of perfection 'εἰ θέλεις τέλειος εἶναι...πώλησόν σου τὰ ὑπάρχοντα.' ἐπὶ τῇ σῇ τίθημι γνώμῃ, σὲ κύριον ποιῶ τῆς π., οὐκ εἰς ἀνάγκην ἄγω *ib.*2.5(2.27B); ref. 2Tim.2:21 διὰ τὰς π. τινὰς μὲν ἐκ χειρόνων εἰς κρείττονα προκόπτειν, ἑτέρους δὲ ἀπὸ κρειττόνων εἰς χείρονα καταπίπτειν Or.*princ.*3.1.23(p.241.11; M.11.300B); *ib.*3.1.24 (p.244.2; 303A); cf. *quod illic materia naturalis, facit hic arbitrium—qui enim se a deterioribus segregaverit est vas utile; hoc autem in nostro est positum arbitrio et potestate*, Thdr.Mops.*2Tim.*2:21(p.210. 18); ref. love for enemies εἰρηνεύειν δὲ οὐ πρὸς ἅπαντας ἔνεστι· τῆς γὰρ κοινῆς τοῦτο π. δεῖται Thdt.*2Tim.*2:22(3.686); οὐ γὰρ θεός σε σωφρονεῖν ἀναγκάσει· ἐν τῇ π. δὲ καὶ γνώμῃ βροτῶν τὸ σωφρονεῖν ἔνεστιν εἰς τὰ πάντ' ἀεί ‡Gr.Naz.*Chr.pat.*263(M.38.157A); **3.** in rel. to faith εἰ μὲν οὖν π. ἐστιν...ἡ ὄρεξις νῦν διανοητική, ἐπεὶ δὲ πράξεως ἀρχὴ ἡ π., πίστις εὑρίσκεται ἀρχὴ πράξεως, θεμέλιος ἔμφρονος προαιρέσεως Clem.*str.*2.2(p.117.15; M.8.940B); faith not bestowed without man's π., Chrys.*hom.1 in 2Cor.*4:13(3.264D); **4.** in rel. to communion with God ἔστι γὰρ [sc. ὁ θεός] αὐτοσοφία καὶ δικαιοσύνη· ἡμεῖς δὲ κατὰ μέθεξιν σοφοί τε καὶ δίκαιοι, κατὰ π. τε καὶ δύναμιν Or.*schol.in Cant.* 1:1(M.17.253B); ‡Ath.*Ar.*4.5(p.49.13; M.26.473D); ἐπειδὴ γὰρ παντὸς ἀγαθοῦ πηγὴ καὶ ἀρχὴ...ἐν τῇ ἀκτίστῳ θεωρεῖται φύσει, πᾶσα δὲ πρὸς ἐκεῖνο νένευκεν ἡ κτίσις, διὰ τῆς κοινωνίας τοῦ πρώτου ἀγαθοῦ τῆς ὑψηλῆς φύσεως...μετέχουσα...τῶν μὲν πλειόνως τῶν δὲ ἐλαττόνως κατὰ τὸ αὐτεξούσιον τῆς π. μεταλαμβανόντων Gr.Nyss.*Eun.*1(1 p.101.

3; M.45.333D); ἕκαστος τῶν ἐπιεικῶς ζῆν βουλομένων π. οἰκείᾳ μένει ἐν τῇ ἀμπέλῳ ἑνούμενός τε αὐτῇ διὰ τῆς ἀγάπης Thdr.Heracl.ap.*cat.* *Jo.*15:4(p.354.34); **5.** in rel. to grace εἰλήφαμεν χάριν τὴν θειοτέραν καὶ...προφητικὴν ἀντὶ χάριτος τῆς κατὰ τὴν π. ἡμῶν ἀποδεχθείσης παρ' αὐτοῦ Or.*Jo.*6.6(3; p.114.8; M.14.209C); οὔτε γὰρ...ἡ τοῦ πνεύματος χάρις τὴν ἡμετέραν προφθάνει π. Chrys.*hom.1 in 2Cor.4:13*(3.264D); τὸ κατορθῶσαι οὐκ ἐν ἡμῖν, ἀλλ' ἐν τῇ τοῦ θεοῦ βοηθείᾳ· τὸ δὲ ἑλέσθαι ἐν ἡμῖν καὶ ἐν τῇ ἡμετέρᾳ π. id.*hom.in Jer.10:23*(6.166A); hence Rom.9:21 not to be understood as abolishing freedom of choice φαίνεται δὲ καὶ ὁ Παῦλος οὕτως αὐτὸς ἑαυτῷ μαχόμενος ὁ πανταχοῦ τὴν π. στεφανῶν id.*hom.16.8 in Rom.*(9.615D); ref. baptismal grace διττὸς ἐν ἡμῖν τῆς ἐκ θεοῦ γεννήσεως ὁ τρόπος· ὁ μὲν πάσῃ δυνάμει παροῦσαν τοῖς γεννωμένοις διδοὺς τὴν χάριν τῆς υἱοθεσίας· ὁ δὲ κατ' ἐνέργειαν ὅλην παροῦσαν καὶ τοῦ θεοῦ γεννωμένου πᾶσαν πρὸς τὸν γεννῶντα θεὸν π. γνωμικῶς μεταπλάττουσαν εἰς αὐτόν Max.*qu.Thal.* 6(M.90.280C); **6.** in rel. to 'counsels' opp. 'precepts' τὰ μὲν ἐκ προστάγματος, τὰ δὲ κατὰ ἀποδοχὴν προαιρέσεως Epiph.*exp.fid.*21(p.521.31; M.42.824A).

E. in rel. to salvation ἐπιδέχεται ἡ φύσις τὴν σωτηρίαν, ζητεῖ δὲ τὴν π. Cyr.H.*catech.*2.5; τὰ δὲ ἔργα τὰ τὴν ψυχὴν σώζειν δυνάμενα π. μόνης δεῖται. εἴτε γὰρ νέος τίς ἐστιν εἴτε πρεσβύτης...δυνατός ἐστι μὴ μοιχεύειν...καὶ ἁπλῶς πάντα πράττειν ἃ ὁ κύριος...παρήγγειλεν *V.Aberc.*36(p.69.29).

F. π. corrupted through sin, Gr.Nyss.*ep.*3(M.46.1021A); but will be made incorruptible in resurrection, ‡Proc.G.*Pr.*16:11(M.87.1384C).

G. of God; **1.** in dealings with men οὔκουν ὁ θεὸς ἀνάγκῃ ἀγαθοποιεῖ, κατὰ προαίρεσιν δὲ εὖ ποιεῖ τοὺς ἐξ αὑτῶν ἐπιστρέφοντας Clem.*str.*7.7(p.32.7; M.9.460A); denial that οὐκ ἐκ τοῦ ἐφ' ἡμῖν τὸ σώζεσθαι, ἀλλ'...ἐκ π. τοῦ ὅτε βούλεται ἐλεοῦντος Or.*princ.*3.1.18(p.229.12; M.11.288A); μείζονα λέξεις τοῦ θεοῦ τὰ κακά, νικῶντα τῆς π. αὐτοῦ τὴν ὁρμήν· ὅπερ ἄτοπον εἶναί μοι λέγειν περὶ θεοῦ δοκεῖ Meth.*arbitr.*11(p.175.7); τοῦτο...μόνον ἐστὶ τὸ κακόν, ὃ παρὰ τὴν τοῦ θεοῦ π. γίνεται *ib.*17(p.190.7); **2.** not properly predicated of God ἐπὶ θεοῦ βούλησιν μὲν λέγομεν, π. δὲ κυρίως οὐ λέγομεν. οὐ γὰρ βουλεύεται θεός· ἀγνοίας γάρ ἐστι τὸ βουλεύεσθαι Jo.D.*f.o.*2.22(M.94.945C); **3.** ref. Son's generation ἡ μὲν αὐγὴ οὐ κατὰ προαίρεσιν τοῦ φωτὸς ἐκλάμπει ...ὁ δὲ υἱὸς κατὰ γνώμην καὶ π. εἰκὼν ὑπέστη τοῦ πατρός Eus.*d.e.* 4.3(p.153.12; M.22.256B); view refuted by orthodox εἰ δι' ἡμᾶς ἔκτισε τὸν υἱὸν ὁ πατήρ, οὐ πάντως ἐκ π. τοῦτο ποιεῖ, ἀλλ' ὡς ἐξ ἀνάγκης δι' ἡμᾶς Cyr.*thes.*12(5^{1}.153E).

H. of Christ, ref. 1Cor.15:28 τὴν ἐξ αὐθεκουσίου π. ὑπακοὴν καὶ τὴν δόξαν...ἣν ἀποδώσει αὐτῷ τὰ πάντα οἷα σωτῆρι Eus.*e.th.*3.15(p.172.18; M.24.1029A); ref. problem of divine nature as ἄτρεπτος: (Arian) αὐτεξούσιός ἐστι καὶ ἰδίᾳ π. οὐ τρέπεται, τρεπτῆς οὖν φύσεως Ath.*Ar.*1.22(M.26.57C); προαιρέσει...καλός ἐστι...τρεπτῆς ὢν φύσεως· ἢ ὡς λίθος καὶ ξύλον οὐκ ἔχει τὴν προαίρεσιν ἐλευθέραν *ib.*1.35(84B); προαιρέσει δὲ πράξας, τρεπτῆς ἐστι...φύσεως *ib.*1.37(88C); problem discussed and distn. drawn τὸ μὲν οὖν προαιρέσεως ἁπτόμενον, καὶ πρὸς κακίαν ἀπὸ τῆς ἀρετῆς μεταστρέφον, ἀληθῶς πάθος ἐστί· τὸ δ' ὅσον ἐν τῇ φύσει κατὰ τὸν ἴδιον εἱρμὸν πορευομένη διεξοδικῶς θεωρεῖται, τοῦτο κυριώτερον ἔργον ἂν μᾶλλον ἢ πάθος προσαγορεύοιτο Gr.Nyss.*or.catech.*16(p.67.6; M.45.49B); hence π. denied in respect of Christ's earthly conduct εἰ μὲν ὡς προαιρέσει καλλίων, τοῦτο δεδύνηται πῶς; π. γὰρ ἀνθρώπου δικαιοσύνην ἀληθινὴν οὐ κατορθοῖ. εἰ δὲ ὡς φύσει δίκαιος, θεός ἐστιν Apoll.*anac.*25(p.245.6; M.28.1277B); ‡Cyr.*Trin.*15(6^{3}.21C; M.77.1152D) cit. s. προαιρετικός; τὸ γὰρ ἀνθρώπινον τοῦ θεοῦ κατὰ προαίρεσιν ὡς ἡμεῖς οὐ κεκίνηται, διὰ βουλῆς πεποιημένον καὶ κρίσεως τὴν τῶν ἀντικειμένων διάγνωσιν· ἵνα μὴ φύσει κατὰ π. νομισθείη τρεπτόν Max.*opusc.*(M.91.32A); οὔτε δὲ ἐπὶ τῆς τοῦ κυρίου ψυχῆς φαμεν βουλὴν ἢ π. οὐ γὰρ εἶχεν ἄγνοιαν Jo.D.*f.o.*2.22(M.94.948A); in rel. to Nativity, Leont.H.*Nest.*4.25f.(M.86.1689Dff.).

II. *motive, intention, disposition*;

A. of God ἑτεροδόξους, λεξιθηροῦντας μὲν τὰ ἀπὸ τῆς παλαιᾶς διαθήκης τοιαῦτα, ἔνθα ἐμφαίνεται, ὡς...λέγουσιν, ὠμότης τοῦ δημιουργοῦ ἢ ἀμυντικὴ καὶ ἀνταποδοτικὴ τῶν χειρόνων π. Or.*princ.*3.1.16(p.224.13; M.11.281B).

B. of men; **1.** of motive or intention in moral action οὐδὲ...τῷ τέλει παραμετρεῖται μόνῳ τὰ πράγματα, ἀλλὰ καὶ τῇ ἑκάστου κρίνεται π. Clem.*str.*2.6(p.127.12; M.8.961B); *ib.*4.6(p.265.16; 1249B); κρίνωμεν τὰ πράγματα προαιρέσει καὶ μὴ τῷ βλέπειν πολλοὺς συναγομένους Or.*hom.4.3 in Jer.*(p.25.17; M.13.288D); Gr.Nyss.*infant.*(M.46.165A); ἀρκεῖ γὰρ πολλαχοῦ καὶ π. μέγα ποιῆσαι ἀγαθόν Chrys.*hom.55.3 in Jo.*(8.325C); *ib.34.2*(8.196E); Dor.*doct.*8.5(M.88.1713D); Max.*ambig.*(M.91.1389B); ref. disposition of candidates for baptism τὴν ἀπὸ τοῦ βαπτίσματος ὠφέλειαν ἔχεσθαι τῆς π. τοῦ βαπτιζομένου Or.*Jo.*6.33(17; p.142.21; M.14.256D); εἰ δὲ ἐπιμένῃς κακῇ π. ... μὴ προσδόκα λήψεσθαι τὴν χάριν Cyr.H.*procatech.*4; of reader of scripture, Cyr.*Jo.*1 proem.(1.7B); in prayer, Or.*or.*11(p.323.29; M.11.452A); **2.** *intention, policy, principle*, cf.Cyr.H.*procatech.*10; συμφώνως τῇ π. τὴν ζωὴν διεξάγειν Bas.*ep.*293(3.431E; M.32.1036A); *ib.*305(3.440E; M.1053C); **3.** *way, mode*; of life, *occupation, pursuit* λογισμὸν τῆς π. ἡμῶν παρέχω Athenag.*leg.*18.1(M.6.925B); τρόπον καὶ...π. τοῦ βίου Eus.*p.e.*1.2(4D; M.21.28C); Juln.Imp.ap.Cyr.*Juln.*7(6^{2}.238C); Gr.Naz.*ep.*14(M.37.48B); εἴτε εὔχονται εἴτε ἀναγινώσκουσι...οὕτως δύναται εὐδοκία κυρίου γενέσθαι εἰς ἐκείνας τὰς π. Ephr.3.314D = Mac.Aeg.*hom.*3.1(M.34.468C); **4.** *character, temperament* λεοντώδη τὴν π. ἔχων Cyr.H.*catech.*2.17; *ib.*2.18; **5.** *opinion, doctrine*, *Hom.Clem.*1.17; δῆλος ἂν εἴη ὁποίας αὐτὸς ὑπῆρχε π. Eus.*Marcell.*1.4(p.30.27; M.24.773C); Didym.*Trin.*2.19(M.39.548B); Synes.*Dion* 2(p.238.14; M.66.1117D); **6.** *sense, purport* of a book, Didym.*Trin.*2.4(M.39.481A).

προαιρετικός, **A.** *able to choose freely*, ref. power of free choice; **1.** a human faculty τὴν π. δὲ τὸ ἡγεμονικὸν ἔχει δύναμιν Clem.*str.*6.16(p.500.21; M.9.360B); τὸ ζῷον γένος ἐστὶν κατ' εἶδος κατηγορούμενον, τουτέστιν κατά γε ἀνθρώπου καὶ τῶν ὁμοίων, ὅσα τε ἔμψυχα ὄντα τὴν π. κίνησιν ἔχει Meth.*arbitr.*13(p.179.5); Bas.*hom.*9.7(2.79E; M.31.345B) cit. s. ἀνόρμητος; Max.*ambig.*(M.91.1237A); neut. as subst., *ib.*(1109A) etc.; **2.** question discussed whether fate is endowed with this faculty (in pagan thought), Gr.Nyss.*fat.*(M.45.149B); *ib.*(153C); **3.** in Logos, accompanied by omnipotence εἰ οὖν ζῇ ὁ λόγος, ὁ ζωὴ ὤν, καὶ π. δύναμιν ἔχει πάντως. οὐδὲν γὰρ ἀπροαίρετον τῶν ζώντων ἐστί. τὴν δὲ προαίρεσιν ταύτην καὶ δυνατὴν εἶναι...εὐσεβές ἐστι λογίζεσθαι Gr.Nyss.*or.catech.*1(p.9.16; M.45.13D); λόγον...π. ... καὶ παντοδύναμον Jo.D.*f.o.*1.7(M.94.805A); **4.** in rel. to incarnate Christ οὐδὲ προαίρεσις ἡ ἀμφιρρεπὴς ἦν ἐν Χριστῷ· π. μὲν γὰρ ἦν ὡς αὐτεξούσιος καὶ κατὰ τὸ ἀνθρώπινον ὁ Χριστός, ὅτι καὶ λογικός (πᾶν γὰρ λογικόν, αὐτεξούσιον· πᾶν δ' αὐτεξούσιον, π.). βουλῆς δὲ καὶ...γνώμης καὶ προαιρέσεως ὥσπερ ἡμεῖς ἔχρῃζεν οὐδαμοῦ ‡Cyr.*Trin.*15(6^{3}.21C; M.77.1152D); agst. monothelite view εἰ δὲ π. [sc. ἓν θέλημα] ὅπερ καλοῦσι γνωμικόν, ἢ κατὰ φύσιν ἔσται πάντως...ἐγκρατὴς...παθῶν κατ' αὐτοὺς ὁ Χριστὸς ὑπάρχων δειχθήσεται· καὶ κατὰ προκοπὴν ἀγαθός Max.*opusc.*(M.91.28D); ἓν γὰρ θέλημα Χριστοῦ φυσικόν, ἢ π., οὐ μόνον διὰ τὴν δειχθεῖσαν ἀτοπίαν δέος εἰπεῖν τοὺς εὐσεβεῖν ἐσπουδακότας, ἀλλ' ὅτι καὶ μηδεὶς τῶν ἁγίων διδασκάλων πώποτε τοῦτο φήσας πέφανται *ib.*(32C); id.*Pyrr.*(M.91.329D) cit. s. θέλημα; **5.** of H. Ghost καθ' ὑπόστασιν οὖσαν, ζῶσαν, π. Jo.D.*f.o.*1.7(M.94.805B).

B. *freely choosing*; of those who voluntarily live as Christians, Clem.*paed.*1.10(p.145.31; M.8.361B); in rel. to problem of evil διὰ τί μὴ ἀγαθῶν π. ἐποίει τὴν ἑκάστου κρᾶσιν; *Hom.Clem.*19.12; in rel. to acceptance of divine revelation ὡς ἕκαστον δηλονότι ἢ κατὰ τὸ θέλημα...ἢ παρὰ τὸ θέλημα...π. κίνησις τῆς θείας ἀκοῦσαι φωνῆς παρεσκεύασε Max.*ambig.*(M.91.1085C); *ib.*(1136A); neut. as subst., *free choice, deliberate purpose*, in rel. to suffering μόνον τὸ π. καὶ τὴν ἀγάπην σώζωμεν, ἐν παντὶ θλιβόμενοι ἀλλ' οὐ στενοχωρούμενοι Clem.*str.*4.21(p.306.7; M.8.1341B); τοῦ μὲν θλίβεσθαι...ἐπὶ τοῦ ἀπροαιρέτως συμβαίνοντος περιστατικοῦ, τοῦ δὲ στενοχωρεῖσθαι ἐπὶ τοῦ π. Or.*or.*30(p.393.20; M.11.545D).

C. of object of free choice, *freely chosen, within scope of free choice*; in gen., of moral action, Clem.*str.*2.14(p.146.8; M.8.1000B); Or.*sel.in Ps.*4:6(M.12.1149D); τῶν γὰρ ἀρετῶν αἱ μέν εἰσι π., αἱ δὲ περιστατικαί Pall.*h.Laus.*15(p.40.10; M.34.1041B); of religious life as ὁ καθ' ἡμέραν π. θάνατος Thdr.Stud.*epp.*2.98(M.99.1352A); in rel. to sin οὐ τοίνυν φυσικὸν...ἀνθρώποις τὸ ἁμαρτεῖν, ἀλλὰ π. τὸ κακοπραγεῖν Tit.Bost.*Man.*2.5(M.18.1141C); φυσικὸς καὶ κοινὸς θάνατος, πρὸς ἀντιδιαστολὴν τοῦ π. θανάτου, τοῦ τῆς ψυχῆς Cyr.*Ps.*22:4(M.69.841B); τὸν Ἰούδαν τῇ π. κακίᾳ ἐάσας ἀπολέσθαι Ammon.*Jo.*18:9(M.85.1505B); in rel. to problem of evil, exeg. Jo.1:9 εἴπερ οὖν ἡ κτίσις κατὰ φύσιν τὸ φῶς...πῶς οὐκ ἔρχεται πρὸς τὸ φῶς; ἢ πῶς ἀγαπᾷ τὸ σκότος, ὡς οὐκ ἔχουσα...κατὰ φύσιν τὸ εἶναι φῶς ἀληθινόν, π. δὲ μᾶλλον ποιουμένη τὴν ἐπὶ τὸ ἄμεινον ἢ τὰ χείρω ῥοπήν; Cyr.*Jo.*1.8(4.68E); ref. union of believer with God, contrasted with natural unity of Son and Father, id.*thes.*12(5^{1}.122B); of Christian faith π. ἅπασι τὸ πιστεύειν ἐστί id.*Lc.*14:23(M.72.792C); in rel. to grace, of BMV ὁ καρπὸς οὐ τῆς ἐμῆς προαιρέσεως κατόρθωμα, ἀλλὰ θεοῦ τοῦ θαυματουργοῦντος ἐν ἐμοὶ τὰ ὑπὲρ φύσιν...χρὴ δέ με καὶ προαιρέσεως καρπὸν προσενεγκεῖν, ἵνα...ἡ ψυχή μου τὸν π. καρπὸν τῷ...θεῷ προσαγάγῃ Antip.Bost.*hom.*2.18(M.85.1788B); in rel. to evil as experienced by incarnate Christ σῶμα ἀνείληφεν...πόνων δεκτικὸν... καὶ τῶν...ἀνιαρῶν, εἰ τοῦ ἀνιαροῦ μὴ ὡς π. ἀκούοιμεν Or.*Cels.*2.23(p.152.22; M.11.841C).

προαιρετικῶς, *deliberately, voluntarily, of deliberate choice*; **1.** in gen., of God παντὸς...π. σπεύσει πρὸς σωτηρίαν Clem.*str.*7.7(p.32.4;

M.9.460A); of men τοῖς μὲν τῷ τοῦ εἶναι λόγῳ κατὰ φύσιν π. χρησαμένοις Max.*ambig.*(M.91.1392D); Jo.D.*hom.*2.1(M.96.577B); **2.** in rel. to origin of evil σκότος ἦν...ἐπάνω τῆς ἀβύσσου. σκότος τοῦτο, οὐ κτισθὲν σκότος, ἀλλὰ π. ἀρξάμενον εἶναι σκότος τῇ τοῦ φωτὸς στερήσει Meth.*fr.Job* 17(p.516.12); **3.** in rel. to grace τῶν ἀρετῶν τὸ μὲν... ἔχομεν...παρ' ἑαυτῶν, ὃ π. κτώμεθα, τὸ δὲ ἐκ θεοῦ. ... ἡ γὰρ λέξις ἡ 'πρόσθες' σημαίνει ἀπαιτεῖν αὐτοὺς θεοδώρητον πίστιν πρὸς ᾗ εἶχον π. ... ἐπεὶ οὖν ἡ ἀρετὴ χάρις ἐστὶ κεχαριτωμένον ποιοῦσα τὸν ἔχοντα, ὅταν ἡμῖν π. κατορθωθῇ αὐτή, τηνικαῦτα τὸ ἐκ θεοῦ παραγίνεται Or.*fr.11 in Jo.*(p.493.19); διοικεῖται μὲν γὰρ ὁ ἄνθρωπος π. καὶ τὰς ἡνίας πεπίστευται τῆς αὐτοῦ διανοίας, ὥστε ἐφ' ὅπερ ἂν βούλοιτο τρέχειν, εἴτε πρὸς τὸ ἀγαθόν, εἴτ' οὖν πρὸς τὸ ἐναντίον Cyr.*dogm.*2(6^2.368B).

προαίρω, *remove in advance*, ‡Just.*qu.et resp.*107(M.6.1353C).

***προαιχμαλωτίζω**, *make captive beforehand*, Or.*sel.in Ezech.*14:22 (M.13.809B).

***προαιών, ὁ**, *age before the ages* υἱὸς...πρὸ τῶν π. ὑπάρχων ‡Ath. *dial.Trin.*2.26(M.28.1197A).

προαιώνιος, *from before the ages, eternal*;

A. of God, Gr.Nyss.*Eun.*1(1 p.74.16; M.45.304D); Eulog.*fr.Trin.* (M.86.2941A); μία θεότης, οὐσία...π. ‡Cyr.*Trin.*1(6^2.1A; M.77.1120A); ‡Caes.Naz.*dial.*3(M.38.860); Jo.D.*fid.Nest.*18(p.566); of God's counsel τῇ π. προγνωστικῇ βουλῇ τοῦ θεοῦ προορισθεῖσα [sc. *Μαρία*] Jo.D.*f.o.*4.14(M.94.1156A).

B. of Son; **1.** of his status ἀναθεματίζοντες...τοὺς τὸν θεὸν λόγον τὸν υἱὸν τοῦ θεοῦ, π. καὶ συναΐδιον τῷ πατρὶ καὶ ἐνυπόστατον...υἱὸν καὶ θεὸν μὴ ὁμολογοῦντας Photinus et al.*ep.*ap.Epiph.*haer.*72.11(p.266. 7; M.42.397C); οἱ ἀπὸ Μαρκέλλου καὶ Σκοτεινοῦ...οἳ τὴν π. ὕπαρξιν τοῦ Χριστοῦ...ἀθετοῦσιν *Symb.Ant.*(345)6(p.253.2; M.26.732A); ref. Jo. 1:1 τὸ δέ, ἦν τὴν...π. ὕπαρξιν [sc. σημαίνει] Bas.*Eun.*2.17(1.252D; M. 29.608A); οἱ μὲν [sc. διοριζόμενοι] π. τὴν ὕπαρξιν, οἱ δὲ ἀπὸ Μαρίας τὴν ἀρχὴν ἐσχηκέναι id.*ep.*260.8(3.400D; M.32.965B); ὁ τοῦ θεοῦ λόγος ὁ π. Gr.Naz.*or.*38.13(M.36.325B); ref. Jo.1:1 περὶ τῆς...π. ἡμῖν ὑπάρξεως διαλέγεται νῦν. διὰ τοῦτο τὸ 'ἐποίησεν' ἀφείς, τὸ 'ἦν' ἔθηκεν Chrys. *hom.3.4 in Jo.*(8.21E); *ib.8.1*(48E); id.*hom.6.2 in Phil.*(11.235A); ref. Mich.5:2 αἱ ἔξοδοι αὐτοῦ ἀπ' ἀρχῆς...τὴν π. ἐδήλωσεν ὕπαρξιν id.*Jud.et gent.*3(1.561C); π. γὰρ ὁ υἱός, καὶ αὐτός ἐστι τῶν αἰώνων ὁ ποιητής Cyr.*Jo.*1.3(4.25D); id.*Mich.*46(3.436C); θεὸς π. ὁ...Χριστός Thdt.*eran.*1(3.39); Leont.H.*Nest.*2.16(M.86.1573C); π. τοίνυν τὸν θεὸν λόγον δοξάζοντες καὶ τῷ πατρὶ συναΐδιον Sophr.H.*ep.syn.*(M.87. 3177C); Jo.D.*hom.*1.18(M.96.572C); **2.** of his generation, ref. Jo.1:1 τὸ 'ἦν' ἀναγκαίως ἐπιφέρων διὰ τὴν π. γέννησιν αὐτοῦ Cyr.*Jo.*1.2(4.15C); τὴν ἄρρητον αὐτοῦ καὶ π. γέννησιν *ib.*11.7(965A); id.*Pulch.*38(p.47.35; 5^2.160B); id.*Ps.*2:7(M.69.721A); τὰς δύο γεννήσεις, τήν τε π. ἀσωμάτως ἐκ τοῦ πατρός, καὶ τὴν χρονικὴν ἐκ μητρὸς...σωματικῶς...γεγενημένην Max.*ep.*13(M.91.525A); τῆς ἄνω ἐκ τοῦ πατρὸς π. γεννήσεως id.*ambig.*(M.91.1141D); ref. Ps.2:7 τὸ δὲ 'σήμερον' ἐπὶ τῆς π. γεννήσεως χώραν οὐκ ἔχει· ἐκείνη γὰρ ἄχρονος ‡Jo.D.*hom.*6.3(M.96.665C); ‡Jo.D.*Jacob.*79(M.94.1476C); **3.** in rel. to Inc. ἀπέκρυβε τὰ σημεῖα τῆς αὐτοῦ θεότητος, καίπερ θεὸς ἀληθὴς π. ὑπάρχων Mel.*fr.*6(p.310; M. 5.1221A); ref. Jo.6:58 τὸ ῥητὸν οὐ τὴν π. ... ζωὴν ὀνομάζει...ἀλλὰ ζωὴν ταύτην τὴν ἐν σαρκί Evagr.Pont.*ep.*4(M.32.253A); ref. Ac.2:36 οὐ τὴν π. ὕπαρξιν τοῦ κυρίου διὰ τοῦ 'ἐποίησε' ῥήματος παρίστησιν...ἀλλὰ τὴν τοῦ ταπεινοῦ πρὸς τὸ ὑψηλὸν μεταποίησιν Gr.Nyss.*Eun.*5(2 p.116.24; M.45.697B); τὸν ἐκ γυναικὸς γεννηθέντα, καὶ θεὸν π., καὶ ἐπ' ἐσχάτων ἡμερῶν ἄνθρωπον *ib.*6(2 p.132.27; 716D); τὸν ἐκ πατρὸς π. υἱὸν ἐν ἐσχάτοις τοῦ αἰῶνος καιροῖς...ἑνωθῆναι σαρκί Cyr.*apol.Thdt.*1(p.113. 10; 6^1.207A); ἄνθρωπος δι' οἰκονομίαν γεγονώς, αὐτὸ δὴ τοῦτο νομίζομαι μόνον ὅπερ ὁρῶμαι, καὶ οὐ πολλοῖς π. ὢν υἱὸς γινώσκομαι id.*thes.*30 (5^1.259B); id.*Ps.*2:7(M.69.721A); π. μένων εἶναι ἤρξατο ἀπὸ χρόνου Leo Mag.*ep.*28.4(p.14.16; M.*PL.*54.768A); παιδίον θεόν, τεσσαρακονθήμερον καὶ π. ‡Cyr.H.*occurs.*4(M.33.1192A); Bas.Sel.*or.*10.2(M.85. 141B); Oecum.*Apoc.*1:14(p.41); ἡ οὖν ἀρχὴ τοῦ εἶναι ταύτης τῆς συνθέτου φύσεως, πότε τε καὶ ὅπως;...εἰ δὲ ἀπὸ τῆς προσφάτου ἑνώσεως ἡ ταύτης ἀρχή, πῶς...π. ... ὁμολογήσοιμεν τὴν ἐπὶ τῶν Αὐγούστου χρόνων προελθοῦσαν εἰς τὸ εἶναι φύσιν; Leont.H.*monoph.*5 (M.86.1772C); Max.*ep.*13(M.91.525A); ὁ Ἰουδαῖος εἶπεν...εἰ γὰρ ἐγεννήθη οὐκ ἔτι π. ὑπῆρχεν *Dial.Tim.et Aquil.*80 r°(p.68); Jo.D.*disp.*(M. 96.1345A); δέσποινα, γεννήσασα βρέφος π. Jo.Mon.*hymn.Chrys.*5(M. 96.1381A); τὸν ἐν νηπιότητι π. ‡Meth.*Sym.et Ann.*6(M.18.360C); **4.** of his kingdom ὁ αὐτὸς καὶ ὢν Χριστὸς καὶ γενόμενος· ὢν μὲν κατὰ τὴν π. βασιλείαν, γενόμενος δὲ ὅτε εὐηγγελίζοντο τοῖς ποιμέσιν οἱ ἄγγελοι τὴν ...χαράν Gr.Nyss.*Apoll.*55(M.45.1257B); π. ἔχοντα τὸν τῆς θεότητος θρόνον...καὶ βασιλείαν δεχόμενον ἀνθρωπίνως ἐν χρόνῳ Cyr.*Ps.*2:7(M. 69.721A); π. τὴν βασιλείαν ἔχων, ὡς ὁ γεννήσας αὐτόν ‡Meth.*palm.*5 (M.18.393A); ‡Chrys.*hom.in Ps.96:1*(5.611E); **5.** of his heavenly flesh, acc. doctrine ascribed to Apollinarius σάρκα ἐκείνην, ἣν ἐν τοῖς οὐρανοῖς ἔχων ἐτύγχανε, π. τινα καὶ συνουσιωμένην Gr.Naz.*ep.* 203(M.37.332C); Gr.Nyss.*Apoll.*3(M.45.1128D); *ib.*(1129A); εἰ π. ἡ σάρξ,...ἄρα καὶ πρὸ τοῦ Ἀδὰμ ἡ Μαρία *ib.*13(1148C); ref. Heb.1:1 ἀπόδειξίς ἐστι, φησί [sc. Ἀπολινάριος], τὸ ἀνθρώπινον τοῦ φανέντος ἡμῖν θεοῦ προαιώνιον εἶναι *ib.*18(1157B); *ib.*19(1161D); *ib.*24(1173B).

C. of H. Ghost ἡ...π. ὕπαρξις Bas.*Spir.*63(3.53A; M.32.184B); Gel.Cyz.*h.e.*1 proem.(p.3.4; M.85.1193C); of procession of H. Ghost ‡Ath.*Lat.*1(M.28.825A).

***προαιωνίως**, *eternally, before the ages*; ref. God's being, Dion.Ar. *d.n.*5.4(M.3.817D); and counsel π. οὖν ἐν αὐτῷ προεγνωσμένα [sc. creatures] προϋφέστηκε Max.*schol.d.n.*1.4(M.4.200B); ref. eternal existence of Son's divine nature, Jo.D.*nat.*6(M.95.120D).

προακροβολίζ-ομαι, *skirmish with missiles before battle*; met., Chrys.*hom.20.4 in 1Cor.*(10.175A); ~όμεθα πρὸς τοὺς λέγοντας...τὴν δημιουργίαν πονηρὰν εἶναι id.*comm.in Gal.*5:12(10.717E).

προακτέον, *one must raise* or *promote* οὐ μὴν π. εἰς τὸν ἀφ' οὗ εἴρχθη διὰ τὴν παράβασιν βαθμόν, ἕως τοῦ δέοντος καιροῦ Thdr.Stud. *epp.*2.211(M.99.1637B).

προακτικός, *bringing out*; **1.** of creative Logos, Leont.H.*Nest.*1. 13(M.86.1452B) cit. s. διατηρητικός; **2.** *educative* κεκλήσθω...οὗτος... παιδαγωγός, π., οὐ μεθοδικὸς ὤν, ᾗ καὶ τὸ τέλος αὐτοῦ βελτιῶσαι τὴν ψυχήν ἐστιν, οὐ διδάξαι Clem.*paed.*1.1(p.90.19; M.8.249B).

προαλής, **1.** lit., *prominent*, Hipp.*haer.*4.20(p.51.24; M.16.3086C); of hair, *standing up*, *ib.*4.21(p.52.4; 3086C); *ib.*4.23(p.52.21; 3087B); **2.** met.; **a.** *rash, hasty* μὴ εἶναι...π., πρὸ καιροῦ καιρὸν ἐπιζητοῦντα id. *Dan.*4.15.1; Cyr.*ador.*3(1.115A); **b.** *prone* to π. γὰρ ἀεὶ τὸ βάρβαρον εἰς ὀργάς id.*Jon.*3(3.370E); id.*Is.*2.1(2.198D); **c.** neut. as subst., *rapid growth, hasty springing up*, Eus.*d.e.*3.4(p.117.18; M.22.201A).

προάλλ-ομαι, *rush forward, spring forth, be impetuous*; **1.** Valent., ref. fall of Sophia προήλατο δὲ πολὺ ὁ τελευταῖος...τῆς δωδεκάδος... αἰὼν...καὶ ἔπαθε πάθος Iren.*haer.*1.2.2(M.7.453A); **2.** of S. Peter θερμότερον ὄντα, καὶ ~όμενον ἐν τοῖς κινδύνοις Chrys.*comm.in Gal.*2:11 (10.687A); **3.** of Paraclete προαλεῖται γὰρ ὥσπερ, φησί, καὶ φθάσει μὲν τάχα τὴν τοῦ μεσιτεύοντος αἴτησιν Cyr.*Jo.*11.2(4.939D).

***προαλῶς**, *rashly, hastily*, ref. attitude of Basilides to martyrdom δεῖ τοίνυν ἀρνεῖσθαι καὶ μὴ π. ἀποθνήσκειν Epiph.*haer.*24.4 (p.262.2; M.41.313B); π. καὶ προπετῶς ἀνέκυψαν *ib.*69.25(p.174.30; M. 42.241B); Synes.*ep.*143(M.66.1536C); τὸ π. τι καὶ προχείρως εἰπεῖν Cyr.*Jo.*9(4.724A); προαλέστερον εἰρηκότος id.*Os.*3(3.13A).

προαμαρτάνω, *commit sin in the past*; perf. ptcpl. pass. neut., *past sin*; **1.** in gen. θάνατον, ὃν ὤφειλες ἐπὶ τοῖς προημαρτημένοις Clem.*q.d.s.*23(p.175.15; M.9.628D); *ib.*40(p.186.11; 645A) cit. s. ἀπαλείφω; id.*ecl.*9(p.139.13; M.9.701C); ὁ...προαμαρτήσας, ἀκριβῶς δὲ μετανοήσας Or.*hom.5.10 in Jer.*(p.39.16; M.13.308C); μισθὸν παρὰ τοῦ πατρὸς τοῦτ' εἰληφώς, λέγω δὴ τὸ ἀφιέναι ἁμαρτίας τοῖς προημαρτηκόσι Eus.*Is.*53:12(M.24.461B); **2.** of sins remitted in baptism, Just.*1apol.*61.2,10(M.6.420C,421A); and expiated by faith of martyr, Clem.*str.*4.12(p.285.33; M.8.1293C); **3.** of sin committed in previous state of existence τῷ Βασιλείδῃ ἡ ὑπόθεσις προαμαρτήσασάν φησι τὴν ψυχὴν ἐν ἑτέρῳ βίῳ τὴν κόλασιν ὑπομένειν ἐνταῦθα *ib.*(p.285.4; M.8.1292C); τὴν ψυχὴν ἐνδεθῆναι τῷ σώματι, ὑπὲρ τῶν αὐτῇ προημαρτημένων τιμωρουμένην Bars.*resp.*(M.86.897D); Max.*ambig.*(M.91.1069A).

***προαναβιβάζω**, *exalt, promote*, Thphn.*chron.*p.271(M.108.672A).

προαναβλέπω, *foresee*, Cyr.*Is.*3.2(2.418A).

***προανάβλεψις, ἡ**, *prevision, foresight*; of God's providence, Cyr. *Is.*1.2(2.46C).

***προαναβράσσω**, *throw off*, Cyr.*hom.pasch.*13(5^2.179A).

προαναγγέλλω, *announce beforehand*, Meth.*symp.*proem.(p.3.11, v.l. προαγγείλαντος; M.18.29A); Thphn.*chron.*p.238(M.108.600A).

***προανάγγελμα, τό**, *announcement*, Leont.N.*serm.*2(M.93.1588C).

προαναγιγνώσκω, **1.** *read beforehand*, Cyr.*Os.*27(3.50C); id.*Soph.* 38(3.615C); of liturgical Gospel φώτισον τὰς ψυχὰς ἡμῶν...εἰς τὴν τῶν προαναγνωσθέντων κατάληψιν *Lit.Jac.*(p.174.27); **2.** *read what has gone before, read previous passage*, Cyr.H.*catech.*6.28; *Dial.Tim.et Aquil.*122 v°(p.94).

***προαναγόρευσις, ἡ**, *prediction*, Cyr.*ador.*11(1.404C).

***προαναγορεύ-ω**, **1.** *announce beforehand, prophesy* τὸν ἀντίχριστον...λέοντα προανηγόρευσαν αἱ γραφαί Hipp.*antichr.*6(p.8.1; M. 10.733B); λίθος...τῇ Σιὼν ~θείς ‡Meth.*Sym.et Ann.*6(M.18.361B); **2.** *proclaim previously* ~σας...τὸν ἀδελφὸν βασιλέα Thphn.*chron.*p.46 (M.108.172A).

προαναγράφω, **1.** *write beforehand*; of synoptic gospels in relation to fourth, Eus.*h.e.*3.24.7(M.20.265B); **2.** *record before the event, prefigure* ὅταν εἰσπορεύωνται εἰς τὴν σκηνὴν...νίψονται ὕδατι. ... ἡ διὰ τοῦ ἁγίου βαπτίσματος ὡς ἔν γε δὴ τούτῳ προανεγράφετο χάρις Cyr. *ador.*9(1.312A).

*__προαναδείκνυμι__, *show forth beforehand* in type, Cyr.*glaph.Gen.* 2(1.36B); id.*Lc.*9:30f.(p.80.5; M.72.653B).

*__προανάδειξις__, ἡ, *foreshowing, foreshadowing* ὁ Ἀαρὼν τύπος ἂν εἴη Χριστοῦ, καὶ τῆς...νοουμένης ἱερωσύνης οἱονεὶ π. Cyr.*ador.*11(1. 376E); id.*glaph.Gen.*2(1.60D); *ib.*7(211E).

*__προαναδέομαι__, *win* good opinions, praise, Thdr.Stud.*epp.*2.157 (M.99.1493A).

__προαναδίδωμι__, *vouchsafe beforehand*, Cyr.*Ps.*17:9(M.69.821C).

*__προαναζητέω__, *seek out before*, Cyr.*ador.*5(1.157A).

__προαναζωγραφ-έω__, *portray in advance, foreshadow*, Bas.*Spir.*5(3. 5B; M.32.76B); of use of theological imagery τούτῳ τῷ λόγῳ...~ῶν τὴν οἰκονομίαν τοῦ θεοῦ λόγου Sever.*sigill.*6(M.63.542); of typology, Cyr.*Jo.*2.5(4.212A); Tim.Ant.*descr.BMV* 8(M.28.956B); id.*cruc.*(M. 86.257A).

*__προαναζώννυμι__, *gird up beforehand*, Cyr.*Ps.*26:1(M.69.853A).

*__προαναθεματίζω__, *anathematize in advance*, Anast.S.*hod.*1(M.89. 41A); *ib.*5(100A).

*__προαναθεωρέω__, *perceive beforehand*, Cyr.*ador.*12(1.446C); id. *Mich.*66(3.460D).

__προαναθρέω__, *perceive, contemplate beforehand*, Cyr.*ador.*7(1.241D); id.*glaph.Gen.*1(1.8D); *ib.*7(220E); αὐτοὺς διὰ πίστεως...δεδικαιωμένους προαναθρήσας id.*Is.*3.5(2.524D).

__προαναθρῴσκ-ω__, *rush forward eagerly* ~ων...πρὸς τὸ συνιέναι θερμῶς τοῦ λόγου τὸ πέρας Cyr.*ador.*1(1.22A); *spring up* ~ουσιν ἐν ἡμῖν...αἱ ἡδοναί *ib.*15(539A).

*__προανακηρυκτός__, *announced beforehand*, ‡Sophr.H.*liturg.*11(M. 87.3992C).

__προανακήρυξις__, ἡ, *proclamation in advance, prophecy* ἡ ἀπαλλαγὴ τοῦ κήτους τῆς ἀναστάσεως...π. ἦν Chrys.*hom.div.*3.3(12.338B).

__προανακηρύσσ-ω__, *proclaim beforehand, prophesy*, Chrys.*hom. 8.2 in Mt.*(7.122B); *ib.10.3*(142C); id.*hom.20.1 in Jo.*(8.116C); ~ει γὰρ ὁ νόμος, τῆς διὰ Χριστοῦ καθάρσεως τὸν καιρόν Cyr.*ador.*4(1. 123E); τῷ τὰ πάντα προανακηρύξαντι νόμῳ id.*Jo.*10.2(4.908B).

__προανακοιν-όομαι__, *join oneself to beforehand, participate with beforehand* Μωσῆς οὐκ εὐθυδρομεῖ πρὸς τοῦτο τὰ ἐν κόσμῳ μεθείς, μερίζεται δὲ εἰς φροντίδα σαρκικήν, καὶ τοῖς κατὰ γένος ~οῦται τὴν ἀποδημίαν Cyr.*ador.*2(1.75D).

__προανακόπτω__, *cut off in advance, preclude*, Clem.*str.*3.12(p.233.13; M.8.1181D); of S. Stephen's vision of Son as precluding Sabellian heresy, Ast.Am.*hom.*12(M.40.349D); Cyr.*ador.*2(1.54D); Cosm.Ind. *top.*10(M.88.440A).

*__προανακράζω__, (perf. only), *cry out beforehand, proclaim in advance* Ἡσαΐας προανακεκράγει λέγων ὡς ἐκ προσώπου τῆς ἐκκλησίας Cyr.*ador.*11(1.378D); ὁ λόγος τοιοῦτος τὴν τοῦ πνεύματος ἐνέργειαν εἰς ἡμᾶς ἐσομένην προανακεκράγει *ib.*16(557B); Χριστὸς...διὰ φωνῆς τοῦ Δαβὶδ...προανακεκράγει id.*Is.*3.3(2.443A); Thdt.*Is.*6:3(2.208); Sophr.H.*or.*2.41(M.87.3272B).

__προανακρού-ομαι__, **1.** *forestall, prevent* ὅπως...~ωνται νουθετούμενοι Clem.*str.*4.24(p.316.24; M.8.1364A); **2.** *introduce, play prelude to* ~όμεθά τινας ἀγῶνας Chrys.*comm.in Gal.*5:12(10.717E); ~εται τὸν περὶ ἀγάπης λόγον id.*hom.20.2 in 1Cor.*(10.170B); id.*hom.1.3 in 2Cor.*(10.421E).

*__προαναλάμπω__, *shine out before*, Cyr.*ador.*6(1.173D); id.*Mal.*45 (3.868E); id.*dogm.*(Aubert; v.l. for ἀναλάμψαντος 6^2.376D).

__προαναλέγω__, [aor. προανεῖπον], *prophesy*, Philost.*h.e.*7.14(M.65. 552D).

*__προαναμανθάνω__, *learn beforehand*, Cyr.*Am.*43(3.297A); id. *Abac.*8(3.524A); id.*Nah.*28(3.506B).

__προαναμέλπω__, *foretell in song*; of David prophesying, Leont.N. *serm.*1(M.93.1581A).

*__προαναμορφόω__, *prefigure*, Cyr.*Is.*1.4(2.107C); *ib.*3.5(517D).

__προαναπαύομαι__, *die before*, Dion.Al.ap.Eus.*h.e.*7.24.4(M.20. 693B); *IGC As.Min.*108 (c. 535); *Lit.Bas.*(M.31.1641C).

*__προαναπείθω__, *assure in advance*, Cyr.*ador.*2(1.68A); *ib.*(73A); id. *Abac.*2(3.519A).

*__προαναπέτομαι__, *fly away first*, Gr.Naz.*or.*21.25(M.35.1112A).

__προαναπηδάω__, *precede*, Cyr.*hom.pasch.*8(5^2.92E); id.*Jo.*1.1(4.11B).

*__προαναπίμπλημι__, *fill beforehand*, Valent.Imp.*ep.Nic.*1(p.61.6; H.2.568E); Cyr.*Ps.*60:5(M.69.1113C).

__προαναπλάσσ-ω__, **1.** *imagine as previously existing* ἑτέρας τινὸς ὑποστάσεως πρεσβυτέρας τοῦ μονογενοῦς προαναπλασθείσης Gr.Nyss. *Eun.*1(1 p.94.16; M.45.328A); ἐνέργειάν τινα ~οντες τῆς τοῦ Χριστοῦ ὑποστάσεως ἐκείνης ἔργον αὐτὸν καὶ ἀποτέλεσμα λέγουσιν *ib.*(p.99.1; 332C); τῆς ἀνθρωπείας [sc. φύσεως] κατ' ἐπίνοιαν ~ομένης αὐτοῖς πρὸ τῆς ἑνώσεως Leont.H.*monoph.*24(M.86.1785A); **2.** *prefigure*; of horns of altar prefiguring Cross, Cyr.*ador.*9(1.305E).

__προαναπληρόω__, *fill up beforehand* τὸ...ἐκείνῳ παραλελειμμένον, ὁ Μάρκος προανεπλήρωσεν Vict.*Mc.*16:1(p.445.23), prob. for προσ-.

*__προαναποφωνέω__, *proclaim beforehand*, Cyr.*Jo.*10.2(4.908C).

*__προαναπτύσσω__, *unfold before*, Cyr.*Is.*4.2(2.607A).

__προαναρπάζω__, *snatch away before* ἀπεκρίθη ὁ ᾅδης...σημεῖον οὐκ ἀγαθόν μοι δοκεῖ ὁ προαναρπασθεὶς Λάζαρος ἀπ' ἐμοῦ *A.Pil.*B 20 (p.327); of removal by untimely death ἐὰν προαναρπασθῇς τοῦ βαπτίσματος Bas.*hom.*13.8(2.122B; M.31.444B); προαναρπαγεὶς τοῦ προσήκοντος καιροῦ Chrys.*hom.24.7 in 1Cor.*(10.320C); id.*hom.7.3 in 2Tim.*(11.704B); ‡Proc.G.*Pr.*28:10(M.87.1505C); abs. εἰ δὲ τὸν παρόντα καιρὸν προϊέμενοι ἀθρόον προαναρπασθείημεν Chrys.*hom.43.1 in Gen.*(4.436C); id.*hom.9.2 in Mt.*(7.132E); Philost.*h.e.*11.7(M.65. 601C); Areth.*Apoc.*3:10(M.106.557C).

*__προανάρρησις__, ἡ, *prediction*, Cyr.*glaph.Gen.*3(1.66B); id.*Is.*1.2 (2.39D); Dion.Ar.*e.h.*3.3.4(M.3.429C).

*__προαναρχικός__, *before the beginning*, Anast.S.*hod.*4(M.89.93B).

*__προάναρχος__, *before all eternity*; **1.** of God, ‡Ath.*templ.*(p.111.12; M.28.1429D) cit. s. προκηρύσσω; ἡ πατρική τε καὶ ἀρχική, μᾶλλον δὲ π. μονάς Proc.G.*ep.*104(M.87.2792^{n}A); ὁ π. καὶ προαιώνιος ὁ ἄκτιστος θεός Eulog.*fr.Trin.*(M.86.2941A); π. οὐσίαν Const.Diac.*laud.*16(M. 88.497B); **2.** of Son's generation, Hier.H.*Trin.*(M.40.853C); Domit. *Jo.Bapt.*14(p.324).

*__προανάρχως__, *before all eternity* π. ὁ θεὸς ἐγέννησε τὸν υἱόν Hier.H.*Trin.*(M.40.852C).

*__προανασειράζ-ω__, *check in advance* ~ων ἀσυνέτους ὑπονοίας Cyr. *Jo.*11.11(4.995A); Gr.Agr.*Eccl.*2.6(M.98.824B).

__προανασκευάζω__, *forestall, refute in advance*, Gr.Agr.*Eccl.*2.6(M. 98.824A).

*__προαναστέφω__, *crown beforehand*, Eus.*p.e.*7.8(311B; M.21.525C).

__προαναστομόω__, *silence in advance*, Ephr.Ant.*fr.*(M.86.2109C).

__προανατάσσω__, **1.** *prefer in advance*, Meth.*symp.*4.5(p.51.4; M.18. 93B); ψυχῶν, ἃς προανατάξασθαι πρώτας...θεὸς ἐπαγγέλλεται *ib.*(p.51. 19; 96A); **2.** *set before* γένεσιν προανέταξεν τῆς ἐνανθρωπήσεως ὁ εὐαγγελιστής Didym.*Trin.*2.7(M.39.572A).

__προανατείν-ω__, *hold* or *lift up before* ὥσπερ ἔρυμα ~οντες ἀκρασίας τό τε εἶπεν ὁ θεός· αὐξάνεσθε Meth.*symp.*3.10(p.38.14; M.18.76D); ὥσπερ εἰ πυρσοὺς τὰς ἑαυτῶν ~οντες φωνάς Eus.*h.e.*1.1.3(M.20.52A); id.*d.e.*2.3(p.80.34; M.22.144D); ἱκετηρίαν ~ωμεν Cyr.*ador.*1(1.8E).

*__προανατείχισμα__, τό, *bulwark* καθάπερ π. τὴν ἐπὶ θεῷ πίστιν ἑλόντες εἰς νοῦν Cyr.*ador.*6(1.173D).

__προανατέλλ-ω__, **1.** *rise previously*; **a.** lit. πάλιν ἐπανατείλας ὁ προανατείλας ἥλιος Dion.Al.ap.Eus.*h.e.*7.23.2(M.20.692B); **b.** met., *arise before* ~ουσα γὰρ ἡδονὴ καταγοητεύει τὸν νοῦν Cyr.*ador.*1(1. 10D); id.*Jon.*13(3.378B); id.*Jo.*1.1(4.10E); **2.** *precede*, Bas.Sel.*or.*33.2 (M.85.364B).

__προανατρέχω__, *run away before, escape from before*, Cyr.*Jo.*1.1(4. 11B).

__προανατυπ-όω__, *prefigure* ~οῖ [sc. ὁ νόμος] τῆς ἐν Χριστῷ λατρείας τὸ ἀληθὲς μυστήριον Thdr.Heracl.ap.*cat.Mt.*23:5(p.189.25); id.*Is.* 30:19(M.18.1324A); Cyr.*ador.*1(1.41D); τὸ Χριστοῦ μυστήριον καταθρῆσαι τις ἂν ~ούμενον ἐν ἀρχαῖς ὡς ἐν σκιᾷ τῷ συμβεβηκότι id.*glaph. Gen.*1(1.17D); ἱλαστήριον ὡς ἐν αἰνίγμασι νομικοῖς ~ούμενον τουτέστι Χριστόν id.*Abac.*36(3.552C); id.*Jo.*1.9(4.92E); τὸ μυστήριον ~οῦσθαι προστέταχεν ὁ θεὸς id.*hom.pasch.*18(5^2.244C); id.*Juln.*8(6^2.281A).

*__προανατύπωσις__, ἡ, *prefiguration* τῆς ἐκκλησίας τὴν τάξιν...τὴν ἐν νόμῳ π. Cyr.*ador.*13(1.454A); id.*1Cor.*10:1(p.278.21; cf.M.74.880A); κἂν εἰ γέγονεν ἐκεῖνος [sc. Ἀδάμ] π. ὥσπερ τι καὶ μέρος τῆς ἐπ' αὐτῷ θεωρίας id.*Heb.*2:9(p.391.7n.).

__προαναφαίν-ω__, *show forth in advance* ~ων τῆς Ἰουδαϊκῆς πολιτείας τὴν ἀναίρεσιν Isid.Pel.*epp.*3.249(M.78.929B); τύποις ~οντες Cyr. *ador.*1(1.5E); μυστήριον ὡς ἐν σκιαῖς ἔτι ~ουσα *ib.*10(329E); id.*Am.*27 (3.277C); id.*Abac.*2(3.518E).

__προαναφέρω__, *mention before*, Hier.*vir.ill.*(tr.Sophr.Pal.)18(p.20. 29; M.*PL*.23.638A).

__προαναφων-έω__, **1.** *proclaim in advance*, Cyr.H.*ep.Const.*6(M.33. 1172B); Cyr.*Jo.*4.1(4.345E); Proc.G.*Gen.*2:2(M.87.140D); **2.** *proclaim before* ὁ νόμος...τῆς τοῦ κυρίου...φωνῆς προαναπεφώνηκεν Clem.*str.*3. 11(p.228.14; προσανα- M.8.1172C); **3.** *utter a prediction* Δαβὶδ προαναπεφωνήκει περὶ αὐτοῦ Iren.*haer.*3.22.2(M.7.957A); Eus.*qu.Steph.*10 (M.22.969A); διὰ τῶν μετὰ ταῦτα...προανεφωνεῖτο δι' ἡμᾶς Chrys.*hom. 23.3 in 1Cor.*(10.204C); Cyr.*Nah.*3(3.477A); **4.** *prophesy, predict*, of OT prophecy ἀπόδειξιν οὖν λαβὼν τῶν...προαναπεφωνημένων Thphl. Ant.*Autol.*2.14(M.6.1045A); Or.*hom.10 in Lc.*(p.72.8; M.17.324B); Ἰουδαῖοι...τὰ ἡμέτερα προανεφώνησαν Meth.*symp.*5.8(p.62.15; M. 18.112A); Eus.*d.e.*1.10(p.47.32; M.22.89D); id.*h.e.*1.3.6(M.20.69C); προανεφώνει τὸ πνεῦμα ἐν...ψαλμῷ Ath.*Ar.*1.41(M.26.97C); †Bas.*Is.*

65(2.426C; M.30.232A); νόμον...πνευματικόν, ὃς...ἀνακαλύπτει τῶν ~ηθέντων τὴν ἔκβασιν Melit.Ant.hom.ap.Epiph.haer.73.29(p.304.2; M.42.457D); Chrys.hom.1.2 in Rom.(9.431D); Cyr.ador.8(1.278D); of predictions of Christian truth by pagan writers, Clem.str.6.10(p.473.18; M.9.304B); ‡Just.coh.Gr.26(M.6.289A).

προαναφώνημα, τό, prophecy, Jo.D.hom.11.2(M.96.764C).

προαναφώνησις, ἡ, prediction; of OT prophecy in gen., Thphl.Ant.Autol.3.10(M.6.1136C); Clem.str.1.19(p.60.19; M.8.809B); Chrys.hom.51.1 in Gen.(4.500D); of Creation as foreshadowing end of world, Bas.hex.1.3(1.4B; M.29.9B); of Babel as prefiguring Pentecost, Cyr.glaph.Gen.2(1.45B); of altar as type of spiritual sacrifices, id.ador.9(1.304E); of details of parable of Lazarus as prophecy of general resurrection of body, Gr.Nyss.res.3(M.46.677C); of prophecies in Apocalypse, cat.Apoc.13:15(p.382.15).

*προανδρίζω, strengthen in preparation, Cyr.glaph.Ex.2(1.279A).

*προανεννόητος, surpassing all thought; Gnost., of προαρχή, source of deity, Iren.haer.1.11.3(M.7.565A); ib.1.11.4(565B); τινὲς ἐξ αὐτῶν...τὸν Προπάτορα καὶ...π., Ἄνθρωπον λέγουσι καλεῖσθαι ib.1.12.4(577A).

*προανευφημέω, extol in advance, ‡Meth.Sym.et Ann.6(M.18.361D).

προανέχ-ω (προανίσχω), 1. excel μηδεὶς...καυχάσθω ἐν ἀνθρωπίνῃ ~ων διανοίᾳ Clem.str.1.11(p.32.24; M.8.748B); 2. precede, Synes.regn.16(p.37.2; M.66.1084A); ψυχὴ μὲν καὶ σῶμα πρὸς ἀνθρώπου γένεσιν καὶ οὐκ ἂν προανίσχει θατέρου θάτερον Cyr.Diod.(p.497.19; M.76.1452C); id.Jo.1.1(4.10E); προανίσχουσι τῶν ἀποτελεσμάτων αἱ ἡδοναί id.ador.15(1.539A); id.Ps.7:15(M.69.756A).

*προανίπταμαι, leap up in front of, Cyr.Nah.4(3.480A).

*προανιστορέω, quote before, Just.dial.32.2(M.6.544A); ib.39.7(561B); ib.63.2(620B).

προανίσχω, v. προανέχω.

*προανούσιος, before all being, Synes.hymn.2.72(p.46; M.66.1593); ib.3.152(p.11; M.1596).

*προάξιμος, ὁ, a public servant, officer, V.Dan.(p.388.29).

*προαξιόω, make request for beforehand, ‡Dion.Al.fr.in Lc.22:42(p.239.7; M.10.1592A).

προαπαλείφω, wipe away previously τοὺς τῆς ἀγνοίας χαρακτῆρας προαπαλείψαντες, τόν...τῆς γνώσεως νόμον ἐν πτυκτίῳ τῆς καρδίας... μετεγγράψομεν Const.Diac.laud.33(M.88.517A).

*προαπαριθμέω, enumerate previously, Gennad.fr.Rom.8:38f.(p.386.8; M.85.1705C).

*προαπαρνέομαι, deny previously, Anast.S.hod.13(M.89.232A).

*προαπατάω, deceive first, Gr.Nyss.or.catech.26(p.98.12; M.45.68D).

προαπειλέω, threaten beforehand; 1. of prophetic forewarnings, Proc.G.Is.27:1–11(M.87.2237A); 2. of threatening by God of penalty consequent on Adam's disobedience, Ath.inc.4.4(M.25.104B); and threat of hell for wicked, Chrys.stat.20(2.202E).

προαπελαύνω, drive away before, Proc.G.Is.52:1ff.(M.87.2501A).

*προαπελέγχω, refute in advance, Eus.Hierocl.1(511B; M.22.797A).

*προαποβύ-ω, stop up in advance τῇ φιλαργυρίᾳ τὰ ὦτα ~σας Bas.hom.6.6(2.49C, v.l. προαποκλείσας; M.31.276A).

*προαπογυμνόω, lay bare beforehand, Cyr.Is.5.3(2.812B).

προαποδείκνυμι, demonstrate beforehand; 1. in gen., Just.dial.88.2(M.6.685B); Clem.str.2.2(p.117.17; M.8.940B); Or.Jo.1.1(p.4.30; M.14.24B); Ath.decr.18(p.15.31; M.25.'456'(448)C); Cyr.ador.13(1.457D); 2. of scriptural prophecy, Hipp.Dan.2.33.5(M.10.680B).

*προαπόδειξις, ἡ, previous demonstration, Clem.str.2.6(M.8.964A; πρὸ ἀποδείξεως p.127.29).

*προαποδημέω, depart this life earlier, Gr.Naz.or.8.21(M.35.813B); Max.ep.13(M.91.532C).

προαποδίδωμι, 1. set out before, explain previously, Or.Jo.1.3(5; p.6.18; M.14.28A); Eus.d.e.7.1(p.327.6; M.22.533C); †Bas.Is.135(2.473B; M.30.337A); Gr.Nyss.Apoll.44(M.45.1228C); Cyr.ador.11(1.399C); Dion.Ar.c.h.13.2(M.3.300B); 2. admit as premiss, allow before εἰ δὲ προαποδεδώκαμεν ἐν τῷ παντὶ...εἶναι τοῦτον, τί ἄπιστον εἰ...καὶ ἐπιφαίνει; Ath.inc.42.5(M.25.169C).

*προαποδύομαι, put off before, Clem.str.4.4(p.254.7; M.8.1225B); Cyr.Jo.10.2(4.868A).

*προαποκαθαίρ-ω, purify previously, Eus.h.e.10.4.36(M.20.864B); Cyr.ador.4(1.122E); ~εσθαι δεῖν ταῖς εἰς πᾶν ἔργον ἀγαθὸν ἐπιθυμίαις, τοὺς ἐγγίζειν ἐθέλοντας τῷ Χριστῷ διὰ τῆς πίστεως id.Jo.4.3(4.379B).

*προαποκαλύπτω, reveal beforehand, Chrys.hom.29.3 in Mt.(7.345A); Proc.G.Is.37:1–7(M.87.2316B); Chrysipp.enc.in Thdr.(p.63.16).

προαπόκειμαι, 1. be laid down in advance μὴ προαποκειμένων γὰρ ἐντολῶν, οἰκοδομηθῆναι τὴν...γνῶσιν ἀδύνατον Or.schol.in Cant.4:4(M.17.272B); 2. be laid or stored up beforehand δεῖ γὰρ προαποκεῖσθαι τὸ ἀγαθὸν ἐν τῷ θησαυρῷ, εἶτα προφέρεσθαι διὰ στόματος id.Ps.48:4(AS 3 p.48); ταῦτα [sc. OT prophecies]...προαπέκειτο τῷ Χριστῷ Eus.d.e.8.1(p.364.31; M.22.592D); Leont.H.Nest.4.17(M.86.1684B); of food already eaten, Synes.ep.120(M.66.1500A); 3. exist beforehand νουθετεῖν ἀνθρώπους...εἰς ὃ χρήσασθαι προαποκειμένῃ τῇ παρασκευῇ τῆς γλώττης Synes.Dion 2(p.238.1; M.66.1117C).

*προαποκείρ-ω, cut off, Cyr.Nah.35(3.511E); τοῦ πάθους τὴν ῥίζαν, τουτέστι τὴν ἁμαρτίαν, ~ειν id.Lc.5:18(M.72.565D).

*προαποκερδαίνω, gain in advance, Cyr.glaph.Gen.3(1.102C).

*προαποκλίν-ω, 1. turn aside beforehand πολυμόρφους λογισμούς... ~ειν δι' εὐσεβοῦς ἀντιλογίας Ant.Mon.hom.81(M.89.1677C); 2. pass., be previously favourably inclined Μακεδόνιον,...τοῖς περὶ Εὐνόμιον προαποκεκλιμένον Philost.h.e.4.9(M.65.524A).

*προαποκρούομαι, repel beforehand, Synes.insomn.13(p.171.4; M.66.1305A).

*προαποκτάομαι, surrender beforehand, Jo.D.hom.11.7(M.96.768D).

*προαπολογέομαι, make one's defence beforehand, Or.Cels.2.8(p.133.28; M.11.805B); Isid.Pel.epp.5.87(M.78.1376D); Thdr.Stud.epp.2.39(M.99.1233C).

*προαπολυθέω, be set free, Ephr.3.xxviiF.

προαπολύομαι, solve beforehand, Clem.str.1.1(p.11.18; M.8.704C).

*προαπομνημονεύω, record beforehand, v. προσαπομνημονεύω.

*προαπονέμ-ω, apportion before, Serap.Man.46(p.64, v.l. προσαπο- M.18.1233B); τῆς στερεωτέρας τροφῆς ~ειν τὸ γάλα Cyr.hom.pasch.16(5^2.215A).

*προαπονευρόω, weaken, enervate beforehand, Cyr.Ps.9:30(M.69.784C); id.Nah.28(3.506B); id.Jo.10.2(4.915C).

*προαπονεύρωσις, ἡ, unnerving, weakening, Cyr.Ps.118:67(M.69.1272B).

*προαπονεύω, turn aside, Cyr.ador.1(1.17A).

[*]προαπονίζ-ω (-νίπτω), cleanse beforehand ~ων ὕδατι τοὺς εἰς τὰ ἅγια...εἰστρέχοντας Cyr.ador.10(1.337D); προαπενίζοντο γοῦν καίτοι κατὰ νόμον ἡγιασμένοι ib.9(1.312C); ref. moral purification of Christian before admission into Church, id.glaph.Ex.1(1.263E); id.hom.pasch.26(5^2.305A); met., in gen. τῷ βίῳ προαπονίψαι...τὴν ψυχὴν ὀφείλει Ath.inc.57.2(M.25.196D); Cyr.Am.45(3.298E).

*προαποπειράομαι, try before, Clem.ecl.36(p.148.7; M.9.717A).

*προαποπεραίνω, complete before, Cyr.glaph.Ex.2(1.265D).

*προαπορρίζω, uproot first, Cyr.Jo.3.2(4.261D).

*προαποσαρκ-όω, make fleshly beforehand, ref. theory of Christ's 'heavenly flesh', ascribed to Apollinarius μᾶλλον δὲ αὐτὸν ~οῖ τὸν λόγον οὐκ οἰκονομικῶς ἐπ' ἐσχάτων ἡμερῶν τὴν ἡμετέραν ὑπελθόντα μορφήν, ἀλλ' ἀεὶ τοῦτο ὄντα Gr.Nyss.Apoll.40(M.45.1216A).

προαποσημαίνω, signify beforehand; of OT types, Bas.Spir.31(3.26A; M.32.121C).

*προαποσκευάζομαι, rid oneself of beforehand, Gr.Nyss.mort.(M.46.520A); Philost.h.e.12.3(M.65.609A).

προαποστερέω, take away in advance, Ptol.ep.ap.Epiph.haer.33.3(p.451.16; M.41.557C).

προαποτέμνω, cut away in advance, Cyr.Ag.2(3.628C); id.Jo.3.4(4.291C).

προαποτίθημι, 1. put away beforehand Ἰὼβ...προαπέθετο πάντα διὰ τῆς πρὸς τὸν κύριον ἀγάπης Clem.str.7.12(p.57.21; M.9.512B); τὴν ἀνελεημοσύνην προαπόθου Chrys.hom.11.7 in Mt.(7.158A); Cyr.ador.6(1.173D); an argument, reject previously, Gr.Nyss.tres dii(M.45.124D); 2. provide beforehand, provide for the future, Bas.hex.3.5(1.27B; M.29.65A); ἐν τῷ παρόντι αἰῶνι προαποθήσεις τὰς τοῦ μέλλοντος ἀναπαύσεις ib.9.3(83A; M.193C); Chrys.pan.Bern.6(2.643B); ἑαυτοῖς ὑπόθεσιν προαποθέσθαι εὐνοίας id.hom.6.1 in Mt.(7.85B); †Jo.D.B.J.14(M.96.984A).

*προαποτινάσσω, shake off in advance προαποτινάξασθαι τὸ χοϊκὸν καὶ γεῶδες φρόνημα Cyr.Is.5.1(2.726D).

*προαποτρίβ-ομαι, rub off beforehand τὸν ἐκ τῆς ἁμαρτίας ~εσθαι ῥύπον Cyr.glaph.Ex.1(1.263E); id.Jo.4.7(4.437C); id.hom.pasch.17(5^2.225D).

*προαποτυπόω, prefigure, Bas.Spir.33(3.27B; M.32.125B).

προαποφέρω, carry off beforehand, Chrys.hom.12.3 in 1Tim.(11.614C).

*προαποφιμόω, put to silence in advance, ‡Ath.qu.Ant.53(M.28.632A).

προαποφοιτάω, depart from beforehand, Cyr.Is.5.3(2.815C).

*προαποψύχω, make cool in advance, Cyr.Jo.10.2(4.914A).

***προαρδεύ-ω**, *water beforehand* καθάπερ δ' οἱ γεωργοὶ ~σαντες τὴν γῆν, οὕτω δὴ καὶ ἡμεῖς τῷ ποτίμῳ τῶν παρ' Ἕλλησι λόγων ~ομεν τὸ γεῶδες αὐτῶν Clem.*str*.1.1(p.12.26; M.8.708A); ἡ δὲ τοῦ πνεύματος... δύναμις...ἐκάθηρέ τε καὶ ἡγίασε, καὶ οἱονεὶ προήρδευσε Jo.D.*hom*.8.3 (M.96.704A).

***προαρέσκω**, *please beforehand*, Didym.*Trin*.3.29(M.39.948B).

***πρόαρθρον, τό**, *prefixed particle*; of Hebr. אֵת rendered σύν by Aquila, Hier.*ep*.57.11(M.*PL*.22.578).

προαριθμέω, *enumerate first*, Gr.Naz.*or*.31.20(p.69.17; M.36.156B).

***προαρκτικός**, *antecedent*, Leont.H.*Nest*.1.1(M.86.1408A).

***προαρραβωνίζ-ομαι**, *guarantee by first instalment* τὰ πρωτόλεια τῶν ἐπάθλων ἐνθένδε ~εται Eus.*v.C*.1.3(p.8.30; M.20.916A); id.*d.e*.5. 13(p.237.17; M.22.392B).

***προαρρωστέω**, *be previously infected*, Cyr.*ep*.50(p.96.25, v.l. προσα- 5².166B).

προαρτάω, *attach* to, *make to depend* upon τὴν προηρτημένην τῷ σταυρῷ ἀΐδιον...ζωήν †Ath.*fr.Mt*.(M.27.1372B).

***προαρχή, ἡ**, name of primal monad (Valent.), the cosmic first principle, Iren.*haer*.1.5.3(M.7.565A); *ib*.1.5.4(565B); Hipp.*haer*.6.38 (p.169.4; M.16.3255A).

***προάρχιος**, *existing from before the beginning* τῆς υἱοθεσίας τὸ π. πέρας Geo.Pis.*hex*.1770(M.92.1571A).

προάρχ-ω, **1.** *begin first, originate* γένους ~ειν κρεῖσσον, ἢ λύειν γένος Gr.Naz.*carm*.1.2.33.143(M.37.938A); med. ἑκάστῳ δὲ τῶν προαρξαμένων τὰ ἴδια ἀποδιδόντες Hipp.*haer*.proem.(p.4.9; M.16. 3021B); τὸν τῆς τιμῆς προαρξάμενον νικῶν ταῖς ἀντιδόσεσι Eus.*v.C*.4.8 (p.120.30; M.20.1157A); **2.** *preside* over τοῖς...προάρξασι τῆς μοιχοκυρώτου συνόδου Thdr.Stud.*epp*.1.37(M.99.1040D).

***προασμενίζω**, *accept in preference*, Eus.*p.e*.11 proem.(508A; M. 21.844D).

***προασπάζ-ομαι**, **1.** *be the first to embrace*, Or.ap.Proc.G.*Cant*.6:7 (M.87.1721D); Marc.Diac.*v.Porph*.39; **2.** met., *embrace by preference* ἰδιωτικὸν ~ομένους βίον Eus.*h.e*.8.4.2(M.20.749B).

προασπίζ-ω, *hold a shield before*; hence *act as champion, be a defender*; **1.** in gen. ταύτης...τῆς γνώμης οὗτος ἐδόκει ~ειν Eus. *h.e*.5.20.1(M.20.484A); Sophr.H.*ep.syn*.(M.87.3193B); **2.** of God, as champion of Israel, Cyr.*glaph.Num*.(1.388E); id.*Os*.120(3.151B); id. *Nah*.28(3.497D); ~ούσης χειρός ‡Nil.*perist*.12.7(M.79.953A); as protector of a martyr, Bas.Sel.*v.Thecl*.1(M.85.544D); and of Christians in gen., Thdt.*2Cor*.4:9(3.310); **3.** of Christ as champion of faithful against evil, Cyr.*Os*.27(3.51C); ~ει...τῆς τῶν ἀποστόλων σωτηρίας ὁ κύριος id.*Jo*.11.12(4.1014E).

προασπιστήρ, ὁ, *defender*, Nonn.*par.Jo*.17:11(M.43.885A).

προασπιστής, ὁ, *champion* τοὺς αὐτῶν θεοὺς...προασπιστὰς ἀντιπαρατάττοντες τῷ ἡμετέρῳ Eus.*l.C*.17(p.254.23; M.20.1432A); of God as Constantine's champion, *ib*.18(p.259.11; 1440A); as Israel's champion, Cyr.*ador*.5(1.157D); of a martyr, Bas.Sel.*v.Thecl*.1(M.85. 541C); of a leader of heresy, Jo.D.*haer*.83(M.94.744B); of a pagan priest as champion of idolatry, †Jo.D.*B.J*.29(M.96.1132C).

προάστειον, τό, **1.** *suburb* (including area as far from city as Canopus from Alexandria, Ath.Presb.*libell*.(p.21.21; H.2.333A); and Daphne from Antioch, Soz.*h.e*.5.19.7(M.67.1273A)); *Hom.Clem*. 8.1; Eus.*h.e*.2.12.3(M.20.165B); Chrys.*hom.1.5 in Ac.princ*.(3.59C); where separate congregations exist under jurisdiction of city bishop, Dion.Al.ap.Eus.*h.e*.7.11.17(M.20.668B); **2.** *suburban house*, †Polyb.*v.Epiph*.61(M.41.101B); Chrys.*hom.65.3 in Jo*.(8.393D); π. αὐτῆς...πρὸ πέντε μιλίων τῆς πόλεως ὄν id.*ep*.14.2(3.597C); of residences of Christians used as martyrs' burial places, *M.Ner.et Ach*.18(p.17.27); *ib*.24(p.23.4); **3.** *temple outside city walls* τῷ π. τοῦ Διός *M.Con*.1.1.

προάστειος, *suburban*; as subst., name given to subordinate, or remoter, aeons in Peratic system τοπάρχας καὶ π. καὶ ἄλλα πλεῖστα ὀνόματα Hipp.*haer*.4.2(p.33.7; M.16.3059B); οὗτοί εἰσιν οἱ π. ἕως αἰθέρος *ib*.5.14(p.110.12; 3170B); *ib*.5.15(p.110.22; 3170C); *ib*.5.16 (p.111.14; 3171A).

προασφαλίζ-ομαι, **1.** *take precautions, be on one's guard beforehand* εἰς τὸ γινώσκειν τὰ δεινὰ καὶ...~εσθαι Epiph.*haer*.proem.2.3(p.171. 17; M.41.177B); προησφαλισάμην τῇ διανοίᾳ μου ἑαυτῷ Hesych.H. *Ps.tit*.76(M.27.964C); **2.** *be on one's guard against beforehand* δεῖ ἡμᾶς ~εσθαι τὸν μονοφυσίτην Anast.S.*hod*.1(M.89.41B); †Jo.D.*creat*. 5(p.127); **3.** *make secure, fortify in advance* προησφαλίζετο τὸν Ἰουδαίων λαὸν ὁ...λόγος Ath.*gent*.45(M.25.89B); ~εταί σε ἡ πίστις Cyr.H.*catech*.10.4; Epiph.*haer*.38.6(p.69.21; M.41.664A); Mac.Aeg. *hom*.7.8(M.34.528B); Ast.Am.*hom*.12(M.40.349D); **4.** *safeguard, secure, ensure in advance* βουλόμενος ὁ κύριος προασφαλίσασθαι τὴν σωτηρίαν τῶν ποτὲ αὐτὸν βλασφημησάντων Epiph.*haer*.54.2(p.319.11, v.l. ἀσφαλίσασθαι M.41.964C); θεῷ τῷ προασφαλισαμένῳ...ἐν τῇ... γραφῇ παριστᾶν πάσης γραφῆς τὴν ἀλήθειαν Epiph.*ep.Arab*.ap.*haer*. 78.9(p.459.24; M.42.712C); Rom.Mel.(*AS* 1 p.112).

***προασχολ-έομαι**, *devote time to, engage in*, Isid.Pel.*epp*.1.220 (M.78.321A); θελημάτων τῆς σαρκὸς...καὶ τῶν ~ουμένων τούτοις... ἀκαθάρτων πνευμάτων Jo.Carp.*cap*.5(M.85.1839).

προαύλιος, *before a court* or *house*, of outer room of baptistery where candidates were prepared for baptism τὸν π. τοῦ βαπτιστηρίου (v.l. βαπτίσματος) οἶκον Cyr.H.*catech*.19.2; neut. as subst., *place before a court* or *house*; **1.** *out-building* τοὺς...κριοὺς...ἐλθὼν εἰς μικρὸν π. ἀπέδειρε Pall.*h.Laus*.19(p.59.12; ἐναύλιον M.34.1066A); **2.** *fore-court, antechamber* τὰ τοῦ οἴκου π. [i.e. of a church] Sophr.H. *v.Mar.Aeg*.22(M.87.3713A); ἐν τῷ π. τῆς μεγάλης ἐκκλησίας ‡Jo.D. *ep.Thphl*.6(M.95.353A); fig., ref. status of catechumens περὶ τὸ π. τῶν βασιλείων γεγόνατε Cyr.H.*procatech*.1(τὴν πρόαυλιν M.33.332A); **3.** met. π. ... τῆς εὐαγγελικῆς παιδεύσεώς τε καὶ πολιτείας ἡ νομική Cyr.*Jo*.12(4.1070D).

***προαφαγνίζω**, *purify beforehand*, Cyr.*ador*.11(1.391B); id.*Jo*.4.6 (4.422D).

***προαφήγησις, ἡ**, *prophetic description*, Cyr.*Am*.3(3.252A); id. *Nah*.31(3.508C).

προβαδίζ-ω, *go before* τὸ ~ειν ἢ συμβαδίζειν πολλὰ πεποίηκε τὰ συντρίμματα ἡμῶν διακενῆς Gr.Naz.*or*.26.15(M.35.1248C); ~ει... ἡμῶν ὁ Χριστός Cyr.*ador*.5(1.158C); ἡ κιβωτὸς εἰς τύπον θεοῦ ~ουσα id.*Am*.55(3.308E); of prophets as forerunners of Christ, id.*Nah*.4(3. 480A); of Jo. Bapt., id.*Jo*.3.1(4.251C); id.*thes*.11(5¹.96A).

[*]**προβαθής**, *very deep*, Didym.*Trin*.1.18(M.39.348B).

προβάλλ-ω, *put forward, bring forward, send forth*;

A. in gen.; **1.** *move up, send to front*, in war οἱ...μεγιστᾶνες... ἀπομένουσι· λοιπὸν ~ονται οἱ τίρωνες Mac.Aeg.*hom*.43.8(M.34.777A); **2.** *exhibit ostentatiously, make a show of* ~εσθε ῥημάτων εὐπρέπειαν Tat.*orat*.1(p.1.17; M.6.805A); [sc. Βραχμᾶναι] βίον μὲν αὐτάρκη ~ονται Hipp.*haer*.1.24(p.28.1; M.16.3052A); of Messalian monks κόμαις γυναικικαῖς ⟨χρῆσθαι⟩ ~όμενοι Epiph.*haer*.80.6(p.491.21; M. 42.765C); of false ascetics κατὰ ἀνθρωπαρέσκειαν ταῦτα ποιοῦσι, καὶ ~ουσι σακκοφορίαν Eus.Al.*serm*.22.6(M.86.460A); **3.** *reject, drive away* εἰ μισητέον τοὺς πρὸς αἵματος, πολὺ μᾶλλον τοὺς ἐχθροὺς ~εσθαι κατιὼν ὁ λόγος διδάσκει Clem.*q.d.s*.22(p.174.20; ἀποβάλλεσθαι M.9. 628B).

B. *put forth*; **1.** ref. Creation, *produce, bring into being* ὁ θεός,... μέλλων τὴν λογικὴν πᾶσαν ~εσθαι κτίσιν Eus.*d.e*.4.1(p.150.21; M.22. 252A); *Hom.Clem*.19.12; ἡ ἐν τοῖς κτίσμασι καὶ τοῖς ὑπ' αὐτοῦ προβεβλημένοις...μεγαλειότης Gr.Naz.*or*.28.3(p.25.7; M.36.29A); προεβάλετο τὰ ὄντα εἰς τὸ εἶναι Leont.H.*Nest*.2.30(M.86.1589A); οὔτε γὰρ ἄναρχος ἡ ὕλη...γενητὴ δὲ καὶ...ὑπὸ τοῦ πάντων δημιουργοῦ προβεβλημένη Tat.*orat*.5(p.6.15; M.6.817B); τί δέ, εἰ ἡ ὕλη αὐτῷ σύγχρονος οὖσα...ὡς ἐχθρὰ ~ει αὐτῷ ἡγεμόνας, ἐμποδίζοντας αὐτοῦ τοῖς βουλήμασιν; *Hom.Clem*.19.14; χάος...ὅπερ Ὀρφεὺς ᾠὸν λέγει γενητόν, ἐξ ἀπείρου τῆς ὕλης προβεβλημένον *ib*.6.3; ref. Valent. theory of Creation προβαλεῖν τὰ παρὰ τοῦ σωτῆρος μαθήματα Iren.*haer*.1.5.1 (M.7.492A); *ib*.1.8.5(532B); **2.** of divine grace ὁ ~ων ἐφ' ἑαυτοῦ τοὺς οἰκτιρμοὺς τοὺς ἀναριθμήτους *A.Phil*.132(p.63.18); **3.** of emanation of aeons (Gnost.) ἐννοηθῆναί ποτε ἀφ' ἑαυτοῦ προβαλέσθαι τὸν Βυθὸν τοῦτον ἀρχὴν τῶν πάντων, καὶ καθάπερ σπέρμα τὴν προβολὴν ταύτην (ἣν προβαλέσθαι ἐνενοήθη), καὶ καθέσθαι, ὡς ἐν μήτρᾳ, τῇ συνυπαρχούσῃ ἑαυτῷ Σιγῇ Iren.*haer*.1.1.1(M.7.445A); αἰῶνας εἰς δόξαν τοῦ Πατρὸς προβεβλημένους,...προβαλεῖν προβολὰς ἐν συζυγίᾳ *ib*.1.1.2 (449A); *ib*.1.2.4(457A); of emanation of 'psychic' Christ, *ib*.1.7.2 (513A); Clem.*exc.Thdot*.47(p.121.23; M.9.681A); Μονογενῆ...ἐν ᾧ τὰ πάντα ὁ Πατὴρ προέβαλε σπερματικῶς. ὑπὸ δὲ τούτου...τὸν Λόγον προβεβλῆσθαι Iren.*haer*.1.8.5(532B); *ib*.1.11.1(561A); προέβαλεν...ὁ Πατήρ, ὥσπερ ἦν μόνος, Νοῦν καὶ Ἀλήθειαν Hipp.*haer*.6.29(p.156.15; M.16.3238A); ὑπὸ νοῦ καὶ ἀληθείας προβεβλῆσθαι λόγον καὶ ζωήν Or.*Jo*.2.24(19; p.81.2; M.14.156C); Epiph.*haer*.24.1(p.257.9; M.41. 309A); φάσκουσι [sc. Ophites] γὰρ ἀπὸ τοῦ ἄνω Αἰῶνος προβεβλῆσθαι αἰῶνας καὶ κατώτερον γεγενῆσθαι τὸν Ἰαλδαβαώθ· τοῦτον δὲ προβεβλῆσθαι κατὰ ἀδράνειαν καὶ ἄγνοιαν τῆς...μητρὸς τουτέστι τῆς ἄνω Προυνίκου *ib*.37.3(p.54.1; 645B); Σηθιανοὶ...τὸν Σὴθ δοξάζουσι φάσκοντες αὐτὸν εἶναι ἐκ τῆς ἄνω μητρός, μεταμεληθείσης ἐφ' οἷς τοὺς περὶ Κάϊν προεβάλετο Jo.D.*haer*.39(M.94.701A); Manich. γνόντα δὲ τὸν ἀγαθὸν πατέρα τὸ σκότος ἐν τῇ γῇ αὐτοῦ ἐπιδεδημηκός, ~ειν ἐξ αὐτοῦ δύναμιν, λεγομένην μητέρα τῆς ζωῆς, καὶ αὐτὴν προβεβληκέναι τὸν πρῶτον ἄνθρωπον τὰ πέντε στοιχεῖα Hegem.*Arch*.7(p.10.5; M.10. 1437B); ὁ ἄρχων ὁ μέγας ~ει τὰς νεφέλας ἐξ αὐτοῦ, ὅπως σκοτίσῃ τῇ ὀργῇ αὐτοῦ τὸν κόσμον *ib*.9(p.14.8; 1441A); Epiph.*haer*.66.45(p.82. 14; M.42.97A); *Disp.Phot*.40(M.88.565D); **4.** Valent., of production by Sophia of *πνευματικὸν σπέρμα* with which Saviour descended to earth, Clem.*exc.Thdot.*1(p.105.6; M.9.653A); **5.** Valent., of production of angels *ἐν ἑνότητι μέντοι γε προεβλήθησαν οἱ ἄγγελοι ἡμῶν...εἷς ὄντες, ὡς ἀπὸ ἑνὸς προελθόντες* ib.36(p.118.20; 677A); of production of souls by demiurge, Hipp.*haer.*6.34(p.163.5; M.16.3246C); **6.** of generation of Logos, in comparison with utterance of human speech *λόγον γάρ τινα ~οντες, λόγον γεννῶμεν, οὐ κατὰ ἀποτομήν, ὡς ἐλαττωθῆναι τὸν ἐν ἡμῖν λόγον, ~όμενοι* Just.*dial.*61.2(M.6.616A); *τὸ τῷ ὄντι ἀπὸ τοῦ πατρὸς προβληθὲν γέννημα πρὸ πάντων τῶν ποιημάτων συνῆν τῷ πατρί* ib.62.4(617C); *οὐκ ἔστιν ἀνθρώπινον ἔργον, ἀλλὰ τῆς βουλῆς τοῦ ~οντος αὐτὸν πατρός* ib.76.1(653A); Gnost., Iren.*haer.*1.7.2(M.7.513A); ib.1.8.5(532B); *ὁ μὲν μείνας μονογενὴς υἱὸς εἰς τὸν κόλπον τοῦ πατρός, τὴν ἐνθύμησιν διὰ τῆς γνώσεως ἐξηγεῖται τοῖς αἰῶσιν, ὡς ἂν καὶ ὑπὸ τοῦ κόλπου αὐτοῦ προβληθείς* Clem.*exc.Thdot.*7(p.108.10; M.9.657B); *ἔπρεπεν γὰρ τῷ ἐπὶ πάντων θεῷ πρὸ παντὸς γενητοῦ καὶ πρὸ πάντων αἰώνων τὸ μονογενὲς τοῦτο προβαλέσθαι γέννημα* Eus.*e.th.*1.8(p.66.27; M.24.837C); Sabellian, ‡Ath.*Ar.*4.11(p.54.16; M.26.481A); such language rejected, cf.Or.*princ.*1.2.6(p.35.10; M.11.134D); ib.4.4.1(28; p.348.8; M.11.401B); idea of division in Godhead excluded from its meaning *οὐ κατὰ διάστασιν ἢ τομὴν ἢ διαίρεσιν ἐκ τῆς τοῦ πατρὸς οὐσίας προβεβλημένον* Eus.*d.e.*4.3(p.154.18; M.22.257B); ib.5.1(p.212.15; 352D); Leont.H.*Nest.*4.9(M.86.1668C).

C. *send out*; of sending of Son into world, Or.*Jo.*2.11(6; p.66.32; M.14.132B); of demons sending evil into world, Eus.*d.e.*4.10(p.165.8; M.22.276B).

D. *put forward* for office, *appoint*; in gen., Thdt.*Ezech.*33:5(2.954); *Chron.Pasch.*p.285(M.92.712B); bishops *τινὰ δόκιμον...προβαλέσθαι τῆς πόλεως προστάτην* Bas.*ep.*190.1(3.282C; M.32.697B); ib.217 *can.*1(3.325B; M.796A); Gr.Naz.*or.*18.34(M.35.1029B); id.*ep.*182(M.37.297A); Thdt.*h.e.*4.7.1(3.954); id.*h.rel.*15(3.1220); Eustrat.*v.Eutych.*23(M.86.2301A); an archimandrite, Cyr.S.*v.Sab.*30(p.115.16); ib.36(p.125.16); an apostle, Thdt.*Tit.*1:1(3.699); high priest, in comparison with Christ *ἄνθρωπος ὑπὲρ ἀνθρώπων ἀρχιερεὺς ~εται* id.*Heb.*5:6(3.573).

***προβαπτίζω**, *baptize beforehand*, Gnost. *ἐν τῇ χειροθεσίᾳ λέγουσιν ἐπὶ τέλους, εἰς λύτρωσιν ἀγγελικήν, τουτέστιν ἣν καὶ ἄγγελοι ἔχουσιν, ἵν' ᾖ ὁ βεβαπτισμένος ὁ τὴν λύτρωσιν κομισάμενος τῷ αὐτῷ ὀνόματι, ᾧ καὶ ὁ ἄγγελος αὐτοῦ προβεβάπτισται* Clem.*exc.Thdot.*22(p.114.11; M.9.669A); ref. question of sense in which patriarchs were baptized *ὁ Ἀβραὰμ καὶ Ἰσαὰκ καὶ Ἰακὼβ καὶ οἱ λοιποὶ πρὸ Χριστοῦ ἅγιοι εἰσερχόμενοι εἰς τὴν βασιλείαν τῶν οὐρανῶν, εἰ μὴ προεβαπτίσθησαν, οὐκ ἂν ἐσῴζοντο* Jo.D.*disp.*(M.96.1340C).

προβασιλεύω, *reign before*, Justn.*typ.Thdr.Mops.*(M.86.1035B).

πρόβασις, ἡ, 1. *progression* *κατὰ πρόβασιν χρόνων* Meth.*symp.*7.4(p.75.7; M.18.129B); of emanations of aeons (Valent.) *οὐκέτι μὲν κατὰ χρόνους τάττων διαδοχῆς τὴν σύνταξιν, ἀλλὰ κατὰ πρόβασιν ἀφ' ἑτέρας εἰς ἑτέραν διερχόμενος* Epiph.*haer.*31.1(p.383.3; M.41.473B); **2.** *progress* (moral) *εἰς παρθενίαν ἐκ π. προκόψαι τὸν ἄνθρωπον* Meth.*symp.*2.1(p.15.6; M.18.48B).

***προβατέμπορος, ὁ,** *trader in sheep*, Thdr.Stud.*epp.*1.7(M.99.932D).

προβατεύς, ὁ, *shepherd*, Thdt.*Ps.*77:70(1.1165); id.*h.rel.*15(3.1219).

προβατεών, ὁ, *sheepfold* *ἄλλα, φησὶν ὁ κύριος, ἔχω ἅπερ οὐκ ἔστιν ἀπὸ τούτου τοῦ π.* Cael.*ep.Nest.*5(p.80.25; M.*PL.*50.478B).

προβατικός, *of sheep*; **1.** epithet of pool in Jerusalem, exeg. Jo.5:2 *π. δὲ κολυμβήθρα ἐλέγετο ἀπὸ τοῦ τὰ...πρόβατα...ἐκεῖ συναθροίζεσθαι, καὶ ἀπὸ τῶν θυομένων τῶν προβάτων ἐν ἐκείνῳ πλύνεσθαι τῷ ὕδατι τὰ ἔγκατα* Or.*fr.61 in Jo.*(p.533.3); Ammon.*Jo.*5:2(M.85.1428D); *ἐν εὐύδρῳ προβατικῇ* Nonn.*par.Jo.*5:2(M.43.784C); as type of baptism, Chrys.*hom.36.1 in Jo.*(8.207B); **2.** fem. as subst., *sheepfold* as birth-place of BMV *τίκτεται δὲ ἐν τῷ τῆς π. τοῦ Ἰωακεὶμ οἴκῳ* Jo.D.*f.o.*4.14(M.94.1157B); *χαίροις, π., τῆς τοῦ θεοῦ μητρὸς τὸ... τέμενος· χαίροις, π. τῆς βασιλίδος τὸ προγονικὸν καταγώγιον· χαίροις, π. τῶν τοῦ Ἰωακεὶμ προβάτων τὸ πάλαι σηκός, νῦν δὲ τῆς λογικῆς τοῦ Χριστοῦ ποίμνης οὐρανομίμητος ἐκκλησία* ‡Jo.D.*hom.*6.11(M.96.677C).

***προβατικῶς**, *in the manner of sheep*, ref. Jo.10:16 *ἀνθρωπικῶς, ὡς δ' ἄν τις εἴποι π., ἡμῖν διαλέγεται* Gr.Nyss.*Apoll.*16(M.45.1153C).

πρόβατον, τό, *sheep*; **1.** of Christ; passover sheep as type of Christ, Just.*dial.*40.1(M.6.561B) cit. s. *αἷμα*; *ὁ ἀκούων τῶν περὶ τοῦ πάσχα νενομοθετημένων κεκρυμμένως, ἐσθίει ἀπὸ τοῦ π. Χριστοῦ...καὶ εἰδὼς τὴν σάρκα τοῦ λόγου ὁποία ἐστί, καὶ εἰδὼς ὅτι ἀληθής ἐστι βρῶσις, μεταλαμβάνει ταύτης* Or.*hom.12.12 in Jer.*(p.99.28; M.13.396C); *θυομένου πρὸς ἑσπέραν, τουτέστιν, ἐπὶ συντελείᾳ τοῦ αἰῶνος, τοῦ ἀληθινοῦ π. Χριστοῦ οὗ ἡ σὰρξ ἀληθῶς ἐστι βρῶσις* †Bas.*Is.*27(1.401B; M.30.172C); *π. δέ, ὡς σφάγιον· ἀμνὸς δέ, ὡς τέλειον* Gr.Naz.*or.*30.21(p.143.6; M.36.132C); *λαμβάνεται π. μέν, διὰ τὴν ἀκακίαν, καὶ τὸ ἔνδυμα τῆς ἀρχαίας γυμνώσεως. τοιοῦτον γὰρ τὸ ὑπὲρ ἡμῶν σφάγιον, ἔνδυμα ἀφθαρσίας* ib.45.13(M.36.640C); *αὐτὸς ἀρχιερεύς, αὐτὸς π., αὐτὸς ἀρνίον* Epiph.*haer.*55.4(p.330.4; M.41.980C); **2.** of Christians; **a.** in gen. as Christ's sheep, Herm.*sim.*6.1.6; *μαθητὴς ποιμένος ἁγνοῦ, ὃς βόσκει προβάτων ἀγέλας ὄρεσι πεδίοις τε* Aberc.*epitaph.*4; ref. unity of Church **π.** *φησιν ὡς ἑνὸς πεπλανημένου. ... οἱ γὰρ πάντες ἓν σῶμά ἐσμεν καὶ ἓν π.·...ὁ δὲ ποιμὴν ἐλθὼν συνήγαγεν...καὶ... ἀνέλαβεν ἐπὶ τὴν χώραν αὐτοῦ. ... πλανώμενον δὲ π. ὁ μὴ τυγχάνων τῆς τοῦ καθήκοντος θήρας ἔν τε λόγῳ καὶ πράξει ἢ τῷ μὴ ζητεῖν ἢ τῷ μὴ εὑρεῖν* Or.*fr.28 in Jer.*27:17(p.212.20); *τοὺς μὲν γὰρ προσπεφευγότας τῇ ἐπιστασίᾳ αὐτοῦ, καὶ τὸ εὐμετάδοτον δι' ἀνεξικακίας κατωρθωκότας, πρόβατα λέγει, καὶ ποιμὴν εἶναι τῶν τοιούτων ὁμολογεῖ...βασιλεὺς δὲ τῶν ὑπεραναβεβηκότων ἤδη* Bas.*Spir.*17(3.14E; M.32.97A); *κἂν μυρία ...πάθῃς, μένε π. ὄν, καὶ οὕτω περιέσῃ τῶν λύκων. ... τί προβάτου ἡμερώτερον; τί δὲ λύκου ἀγριώτερον; ἀλλ' ὅμως τοῦτο ἐκείνου περιέσται* Chrys.*exp.in Ps.*119:7(5.333D); *ὑπείκειν ὀρθῶς τῇ τοῦ ποιμαίνοντος φωνῇ τὴν τῶν π. ἀγέλην εὖ μάλα διϊσχυρίζεται* Cyr.*Jo.*6.1(4.638B); *ἔμπροσθεν τῶν π. οὗτος* [sc. *Χριστὸς*] *περιπατεῖ, δεικνύς, ὅτι αὐτὸς ὁδηγεῖ πάντας πρὸς τὴν ἀλήθειαν* Ammon.*Jo.*10:4(M.85.1460C); **b.** ref. humanity as 'lost sheep', Gr.Nyss.*Eun.*4(2 p.64.1; M.45.636B); *ὁ πᾶσαν τὴν λογικὴν κτίσιν ποιμαίνων...τὸ πεπλανημένον π., τὴν ἡμετέραν λέγω φύσιν, ὑπὸ φιλανθρωπίας μετέρχεται* ib.12(2 p.278.15; 889A); **c.** ref. Jo.10:8 *πάντα ψεκτὰ τὰ ἐν ἀνθρώποις, ἅτε ἐνδεῆ καὶ ἐλλιπῆ, οἷς τελείως οὐχ ὑπακούει τὰ ἐν ἡμῖν ἄλογα π., τροπικώτερον εἰρημένα* Or.*Jo.*1.37(42; p.48.28; M.14.97D); **d.** ref. Jo.10:16 '*ἄλλα π. ἔχω, ἃ οὐκ ἔστιν ἐκ τῆς αὐλῆς ταύτης*', *τουτέστιν τοὺς ἀνθρώπους τοὺς ὁμοιουμένους τῶν ἀγγέλων διὰ τῆς ἐναρέτου αὐτῶν πολιτείας* *Apoc.Jo.*27(p.92); interpreted as gentiles, Bas.*hom.in Ps.*28(1.116E; M.29.288B); Ammon.*Jo.*10:16(M.85.1461C); **e.** ref. 'unbranded sheep', i.e. person unsealed (by baptism) *π. ἀσημείωτον ἀκινδύνως ἐπιβουλεύεται* Bas.*hom.*13.4(2.117C; M.31.432C); *ἀσφράγιστον γὰρ π. εὐάλωτον τοῖς λύκοις* Didym.*Trin.*2.15(M.39.717B); **f.** of righteous at Judgement, Chrys.*hom.79.1 in Mt.*(7.758C); **g.** of sheep representing allegorically various types of Christian, Herm.*sim.*6.1.6ff.; **3.** partic., of laity as bishop's flock *ὅπου δὲ ὁ ποιμήν ἐστιν, ἐκεῖ ὡς πρόβατα ἀκολουθεῖτε* Ign.*Philad.*2.1; *ποιμένες...οἱ τῶν ἐκκλησιῶν προηγούμενοι κατ' εἰκόνα τοῦ ἀγαθοῦ ποιμένος, τὰ δὲ π. ἡμεῖς* Clem.*paed.*1.6(p.112.18; M.8.293D); *Const.App.*2.19.1; divided into two *τάγματα*, baptized and catechumens, Eus.*d.e.*2.3(p.77.25; M.22.140B); **4.** first-fruits of flocks to be offered to priests, *Const.App.*7.29.1; **5.** as object of pagan worship, Arist.*apol.*12(*TS* p.108.5); **6.** in eschatological prophecy *ἐν γὰρ ταῖς ἐσχάταις ἡμέραις...στραφήσονται τὰ π. εἰς λύκους* *Did.*16.3.

***προβατόσχημος**, *in sheep's clothing*, Chrys.*ep.*125(3.670D).

[*]**προβατουρία, ἡ,** (Lat. *probatoria* sc. *epistola*) *imperial letter of commendation*, Ath.Scholast.*coll.*4.4(p.54).

***προβατώδης**, *sheep-like*, Eus.*d.e.*7.1(p.314.5; M.22.513B).

προβιάζομαι, *extort by force*, of earnest prayer *ἀληθινὴν ἀγάπην... ἣν προεβιάσατο καὶ ἐζήτησε* Mac.Aeg.*cust.cor.*14(M.34.840D).

***προβιοτεύω**, *live in previous existence*; of pre-existence of souls, Gr.Nyss.*hom.opif.*28.2(M.44.229D).

προβιοτή, ἡ, *previous existence*; of soul, in Greek thought, Cosm.Ind.*top.*5(M.88.280D); Olymp.*Eccl.*4:2–3(M.93.525B); in Origenist theology, Sophr.H.*or.*2.20(M.87.3240C).

***προβιότης, ἡ,** *previous existence*; of life before conversion, Clem.*str.*2.13(p.144.12; M.8.996C).

προβιόω, A. *live previously*; **1.** of life before conversion *μετανοήσαντες ἐφ' οἷς κακῶς προβεβιώκασιν* Clem.*str.*4.6(p.265.6; M.8.1249A); **2.** of past life and moral achievement in rel. to further progress *μὴ ἐπαμεριμνεῖν τοῖς προβεβιωμένοις ἀγαθοῖς, ἀλλ'...εἰς τὸ πρόσω προκόπτειν* †Bas.*ep.*42.1(3.125D; M.32.348C); **3.** of pre-existence of soul, Aen.*dial.*(M.85.877C).

B. *live before* *τὰς...ψυχὰς οὐ νῦν δημιουργεῖσθαί φατε...προβιῶναί τε αὐτὰς τῶν σωμάτων* Zach.Mit.*opif.*(M.85.1072C).

***προβλέπτης, ὁ,** *seer*, Jo.Clim.*scal.*24(M.88.984B).

προβλεπτικός, *able to foresee* *ὁ π. νοῦς προβλέπει...τῆς ἀντικειμένης δυνάμεως τὰς τέχνας* Mac.Aeg.*cust.cor.*6(M.34.825A); Geo.Pis.*hex.*95(M.92.1439A); of David's prophetic vision *προβλεπτικοῖς...προορώμενος ὄμμασι* Jo.D.*hom.*1.3(M.96.549B).

***προβλεπτικῶς**, *with foresight*, Jo.D.*hom.*8.9(M.96.713B).

προβλέπ-ω, 1. *foresee*; of God's purpose and election, *Barn.*3.6; ib.6.14; Cyr.*Ps.*36:12(M.69.932C); of prophetic foresight, *Barn.*9.7; *A.Barth.*2(p.132.19); Cyr.H.*procatech.*6; **2.** *see before one* *ἐν τῷ ἁμαρτάνειν οὐ πάρεστι ~ειν τὸν τοῦ θεοῦ φόβον* Or.*exp.in Pr.*7:20(M.17.181D); Jo.D.*fr.Mt.*17:2(M.96.1409A).

πρόβλημα, τό, 1. *defence, protection,* ref. Adam and Eve δίχα παντὸς ἐπικαλύμματος καὶ π. Gr.Naz.*or*.45.8(M.36.632C); ἀρωγὲ Χριστέ, τὸν βροτοῖς ἐναντίον π., τὴν σάρκωσιν ἀρρήτως ἔχων Jo.D. *carm.theog*.92(p.207; M.96.824A); **2.** *excuse, screen* κακία, π. ἑαυτῆς τῶν πράξεων τὰ προσόντα τῇ ἀρετῇ...περιβαλλομένη Just.*2apol*.11.7 (M.6.461C); **3.** *obstacle* put forward ἐπιπροσθεῖ νέφος σαρκὸς παχείας, δυσμενοῦς π. Gr.Naz.*carm*.1.2.10.94(M.37.687A); **4.** *anything proffered,* ref. deception of Devil in Atonement ἀπατᾶται γὰρ καὶ αὐτὸς τῷ τοῦ ἀνθρώπου π. Gr.Nyss.*or.catech*.26(p.98.12; M.45.68D); **5.** *point advanced* in argument and discussion; **a.** *accusation,* Or.*Ps*.37:15 (p.25); **b.** *argument, dialectical point,* id.*Cels*.5.18(p.19.7; M.11. 1205D); Gr.Naz.*or*.21.23(M.35.1108B); αἱρετικῶν δὲ πρῶτόν ἐστιν ἀσεβέστατον καὶ ἀποτομώτατον π., τὸ...γεγραμμένον 'κύριος ἔκτισέν με' κτλ. Didym.*Trin*.3.3(M.39.805C); *ib*.(828A); *ib*.3.4(828C); Νεστορίῳ προσποιούμενοι πολεμεῖν, τοῖς αὐτοῦ π. κέχρηνται Eulog.*fr.dogm*. (M.86.2949A); οἷς γὰρ π. διαιρουμένην ὑπὸ τῶν προτέρων ἔστιν ἰδεῖν τὴν τριάδα, τούτοις συγχεομένην ὑπὸ τῶν ὑστέρων εὑρίσκομεν τὴν οἰκονομίαν Leont.B.*Nest.et Eut*.1(M.86.1276C); **c.** *question* put forward, *subject-matter* for discussion, *problem,* Just.*dial*.65.3(M.6. 625C); Clem.*str*.6.4(p.450.7; M.9.256B); Or.*princ*.3.1.1(p.195.9; M.11. 249A); Eus.*d.e*.4.16(p.190.22; M.22.317B); Chrys.*hom.62.1 in Mt*.(7. 619E); as title of work by Tatian Προβλημάτων βιβλίον Rhod.ap. Eus.*h.e*.5.13.8(M.20.461B); **d.** *riddle* τὰ μὲν ἐν αἰνίγμασι τὰ δ' ἐν τοῖς... σκοτεινοῖς λόγοις...τὰ δὲ διὰ παραβολῶν καὶ ἄλλα διὰ π. Or.*Cels*.3.45 (p.242.4; M.11.980A); σκοτεινοῖς ἐχρῆτο π. Eus.*Marcell*.1.3(p.16.32; M.24.749A); id.*p.e*.11.5(513B; M.21.852B); Thdt.*affect*.3(p.86.10; 4. 777); **e.** any *statement,* Ephr.3.405F; **6.** *product* προσευχή ἐστι χαρᾶς καὶ εὐχαριστίας π. Evagr.Pont.*or*.15(M.79.1169D); cf.Jo.D.*Man*.1.55 (M.94.1552A) cit. infra; hence, **a.** Gnost., *emanation* ἕνα ἕκαστον τῶν αἰώνων...προβαλέσθαι προβλήματα εἰς τιμὴν καὶ δόξαν τοῦ Βυθοῦ Iren.*haer*.1.2.6(M.7.465A); **b.** of Son, denied by Origen against Valentinians εἰ γὰρ π. ἐστιν ὁ υἱὸς τοῦ πατρὸς καὶ γέννημα γεγεννημένον ἐξ αὐτοῦ, ὁποῖα τὰ τῶν ζῴων γεννήματα, ἀνάγκη σῶμα εἶναι τὸν προβαλόντα καὶ τὸν προβεβλημένον Or.*princ*.4.4.1(28; p.348.8; προβολή M.11.401B); **c.** of H. Ghost ὁ μὲν γεννήτωρ καὶ προβολεύς,...τῶν δέ, τὸ μὲν γέννημα, τὸ δὲ π., ἢ οὐκ οἶδ' ὅπως ἄν τις ταῦτα καλέσειεν Gr. Naz.*or*.29.2(p.75.11; M.36.76B); τὸ πνεῦμα, ἐνυπόστατον ἐκπόρευμα καὶ π. Jo.D.*trisag*.28(M.95.60D); πάντων λεγόντων τὸ πνεῦμα π. πατρός, συνεπινοεῖται καὶ τὸ ἐκ μόνου τοῦ πατρὸς τὸ πνεῦμα, κατὰ τὴν προαιώνιον πρόβλησιν ‡Ath.*Lat*.1(M.28.825A); **d.** of creatures ἵνα γὰρ ἐγκολπώσηται τὰ ἴδια π. ἡ θεότης, ἥτις λόγῳ ἀληθείας ἀπεκύησεν ἡμᾶς...μακρὰν αὐτῆς ἀπεσχοινισμένα, διὰ τῆς αὐτῆς τῶν τριῶν μιᾶς ὑποστάσεως ἑαυτῆς, δι' ἧς καὶ προεβάλετο τὰ ὄντα εἰς τὸ εἶναι, ἀνελάβετο πάλιν αὐτὰ εἰς ἑαυτήν Leont.H.*Nest*.2.30(M.86.1589A); πῶς οὖν προεβάλλετο τὰ ἑαυτῆς π. ἡ κακία, ἄζωος καὶ ἀναίσθητος; πῶς οὖν αἰσθάνεται τοῦ ἀγαθοῦ, καὶ τῶν τοῦ ἀγαθοῦ π.; Jo.D.*Man*.1.55(M.94. 1552A); **7.** *advancement, promotion to office* εἰ δὲ διὰ τὸ π. καὶ ὅπερ ἐκ τούτου κέρδος τῆς φιλοχρηματίας ἐσχήκασι...οὐ τολμῶσιν ἀρνεῖσθαι τὸ 'ὁ λόγος σὰρξ ἐγένετο' Ath.*Ar*.1.53(M.26.124A).

***πρόβλησις, ἡ, 1.** *emission,* of procession of H. Ghost ἀπὸ τοῦ ἑνὸς...πατρὸς γέννησις τοῦ υἱοῦ, καὶ ἀπὸ τοῦ αὐτοῦ π. τοῦ...πνεύματος †Proc.G.*Procl*.(M.87.2792[h]A); τὸ ἐκ μόνου πατρὸς τὸ πνεῦμα κατὰ τὴν προαιώνιον π. ‡Ath.*Lat*.1(M.28.825A); **2.** *impulse* προβλήσεις δέχονται τὰς ἐπ' ἀγαθοῖς Cyr.*Ps*.33:3(M.69.885B); **3.** *exhibition* καὶ π. ἐκ τῶν ἀργυροπρατῶν καὶ φῶτα πάμπολλα ἐγένετο Jo.Mal.*chron*.18 p.492(M. 97.712A).

προβοάω, *proclaim in advance*; pass., of Christ ὁ διὰ νόμου προβοώμενος Cyr.*Jo*.6.1(4.625B).

προβόλαιος, neut. as subst., *defence, shield,* Gr.Nyss.*or.2 in Gen.1*:*26*(M.44.296D).

προβολεύς, *producer, originator*; **1.** in gen., Ephr.3.406C; Dion. Ar.*d.n*.4.14(M.3.712C); **2.** *creator* αὐτὸν π. γενέσθαι τῶν τεσσάρων οὐσιῶν *Hom.Clem*.19.12; **3.** *parent,* Sophr.H.*or*.7.12(M.87.3340D); **4.** *originator*; Gnost., of the primal monad in rel. to aeons οἱ... αἰῶνες...ἐπεπόθουν τὸν π. τοῦ σπέρματος αὐτῶν ἰδεῖν Iren.*haer*.1.2.1 (M.7.453A); Epiph.*haer*.31.2(p.384.20; M.41.476B); (Valent.) of sources of ὕλη and σάρξ, *ib*.31.7(p.397.7; 488B); **5.** of God in rel. to procession of H. Ghost, opp. his fatherhood in rel. to Son, Gr.Naz. *or*.23.7(M.35.1160A); ὁ μὲν γεννήτωρ καὶ π....τὸ μὲν γέννημα, τὸ δὲ πρόβλημα *ib*.29.2(p.75.10; M.36.76B); *Const.App*.8.37.2(some MSS only); ‡Ath.*Trin*.(M.28.1605A); ‡Cyr.*Trin*.7(6³.9A; M.77.1132C); Thal.*cent*.4.92(M.91.1468D); ‡Caes.Naz.*dial*.3(M.38.861); Jo.D.*f.o*.1. 8(M.94.809B); ‡Ath.*Lat*.1(M.28.824B).

προβολή, ἡ, 1. *putting forward* of a weapon, hence met. π. ἔχειν *hold in readiness* (like a lance in rest), Didym.*Trin*.3.23(M.39. 924A); **2.** *protection* ὧν δὲ οἱ καρποὶ στεγανώτεροι, ἐλαφρὰ τῶν φύλλων ἡ π. Bas.*hex*.5.8(1.47D; M.29.112D); met., *screen, excuse,* Meth.*res*.1. 28(p.256.17; cj. for προσβ- M.41.1133D); **3.** *projection, jutting forward,* ‡Bas.*struct.hom*.2.16(1.347A; M.30.61A); **4.** *onrush* of wind, Or.*Ps*.67:3(p.79); of an attack ταῖς τῶν πειρασμῶν π.,...τῇ π. τῶν λυπούντων Gr.Nyss.*v.Mos*.(M.44.341C); **5.** *exercise, putting forth* of power of sight μεγάλη γάρ, ἵν' οὕτως εἴπω, π. βλέψεως τοῦ πάντων κρυπτοῦ γνῶσιν ἔχειν Diod.*Ps*.52:3(M.33.1590D); **6.** *advancement* or *appointment* to office ἐστασίαζεν ἡ Καισαρέων πόλις περὶ προβολὴν ἀρχιερέως Gr.Naz.*or*.18.33(M.35.1028B); ἔθος ἐν ταῖς τῶν ἐπισκόπων...π., τὸ μὴ ὑφ' ἑνός, ἀλλ' ὑπὸ πλειόνων τὰς τοιαύτας ἐν τῇ ἐκκλησίᾳ χειροτονίας πληροῦσθαι Thdr.Mops.*1Tim*.4:14(p.150.19; M.66.944A); Cyr.*Jo*.3.1(4.251C); μηδὲν...ὠφελείσθω χειροτονίας ἢ π. CChalc.*can.2*; τοὺς ἡγουμένους...τῆς ἐκκλησίας πρὸ τῶν...χειροτονιῶν διανυκτερεύειν ἐν προσευχῇ, ὅπως μὴ ματαία γένηται αὐτοῖς ἡ π. Vict. *Mc*.3:13(p.296.28); Eustrat.*v.Eutych*.9(M.86.2284C); Sophr.H.*mir. Cyr.et Jo*.9(M.87.3444D); **7.** *presentation of case* in court, Max.*qu. Thal*.54(M.90.509C); **8.** *discharge, shedding* ὁ κύριος τῇ μὲν π. τοῦ αἵματος τὴν βεβαιότητα τῆς σαρκὸς ἐπεδείκνυτο ‡Ath.*Apoll*.1.18(M. 26.1125B); **9.** *issue, product* σάρκα...φησιν ἐκείνην τὴν ἀσθένειαν, τὴν ἀπὸ τῆς ἄνω γυναικὸς π. Clem.*exc.Thdot*.67(p.129.3; M.9.689C); **10.** *emanation*; **a.** Gnost. ἐννοηθῆναί ποτε ἀφ' ἑαυτοῦ προβαλέσθαι τὸν Βυθὸν...καὶ καθάπερ σπέρμα τὴν π. ταύτην...καθέσθαι...τῇ συνυπαρχούσῃ ἑαυτῷ Σιγῇ Iren.*haer*.1.1.1(M.7.445B); Val.Gn.*ib*.1.8.5 (533A) cit. s. ἕνωσις; οἱ μὲν οὖν ἀμφὶ τὸν Οὐαλεντῖνον ἄνωθεν ἐκ τῶν θείων π. τὰς συζυγίας καταγαγόντες Clem.*str*.3.1(p.195.4; M.8. 1097B); διὰ μὲν τοῦ 'μητροπάτωρ'...δέδωκεν...ἀφορμὰς τοῖς τὰς π. εἰσάγουσι...καὶ σύζυγον νοῆσαι τοῦ θεοῦ *ib*.5.14(p.411.17; M.9.185C); τῷ 'κατ' εἰκόνα θεοῦ ἐποίησεν αὐτούς, ἄρσεν καὶ θῆλυ...' τὴν π. τὴν ἀρίστην φασὶν οἱ Οὐαλεντινιανοὶ τῆς Σοφίας λέγεσθαι id.*exc.Thdot*. 21(p.113.19; M.9.668B); cf. προβολήν...*id est prolationem rei alterius ex altera, quod facit Valentinus, alium atque alium Aeonem de Aeone producens,* Tert.*adversus Praxeam* 8(M.*PL*.2.186A); παυσάσθων τοίνυν οἱ τῶν αἱρεσιαρχῶν δογματισταί, οἳ δυνάμεις καὶ αἰῶνας καὶ π. ὀνομάζοντες κενὰ τεραταλογήματα ἐφευρίσκουσιν Hipp.*Dan*.2.30.5; σχεδὸν πᾶσα αἵρεσις...ἐφεῦρεν...αἰώνων τινὰς π. id.*haer*.4.51(p.74.17; M.16.3118D); ἡ ἐκ τοῦ πατρὸς πᾶσα π. τῶν αἰώνων *ib*.6.37(p.168.4; 3254A); *ib*.6.38(p.169.2; 3254B); ἐπεὶ δὲ ἦν ἄπορον εἰπεῖν π. τινα τοῦ μὴ ὄντος θεοῦ γεγονέναι τὸ οὐκ ὄν—φεύγει γὰρ καὶ πάνυ καὶ δέδοικε τὰς κατὰ προβολὴν τῶν γεγονότων οὐσίας ὁ Βασιλείδης—ποίας γὰρ π. χρεία...ἵνα κόσμον θεὸς ἐργάσηται; *ib*.7.22(p.198.2; 3306A); κατὰ τοὺς μύθους Οὐαλεντίνου...προβολὰς καὶ αὐτὸς [sc. Τατιανός] εἰσηγήσατο Epiph.*haer*.46.1(p.204.10; M.41.840B); Jo.D.*haer*.35(M.94.700B); Manich. αἱ δὲ π. πᾶσαι, ὁ Ἰησοῦς ἐν τῷ μικρῷ πλοίῳ, καὶ ἡ μήτηρ τῆς ζωῆς, καὶ οἱ δώδεκα κυβερνῆται κτλ. Hegem.*Arch*.13(p.21.9; M. 10.1448C); πῶς δὲ καὶ αὔξησις τῆς κακίας γένοιτ' ἂν ἢ προσθήκη τῶν π.; Tit.Bost.*Man*.1.15(M.18.1089A); Jo.D.*Man*.2(M.96.1321D); **b.** of Logos; **i.** orthodox use defended, cf. *hoc si qui putaverit me* προβολήν *aliquam introducere...non ideo non utitur et veritas vocabulo isto...quia et haeresis potius ex veritate accepit. ... prolatus est sermo dei, annon?...si prolatus est, cognosce probolam veritatis,* Tert. *adversus Praxeam* 8(M.*PL*.2.186A); **ii.** rejected, cf.Or.*princ*.4.4.1 (28; p.348.8; M.11.401B); by Arians Φιλογονίου καὶ Ἑλλανικοῦ καὶ Μακαρίου...λεγόντων οἱ μὲν ἐρυγήν, οἱ δὲ π. Ar.*ep.Eus*.(p.2.7; M. 42.212A); γέννημα, ἀλλ' οὐχ ὡς ἕν τῶν γεγεννημένων, οὐδ' ὡς Οὐαλεντῖνος π. τὸ γέννημα τοῦ πατρὸς ἐδογμάτισεν id.*ep.Alex*.(p.12.11; M.26. 709A); τῶν αἱρετικῶν τὴν ἀσέβειαν, οἳ σωματικήν τινα καὶ παθητικὴν κατεψεύσαντο τοῦ θεοῦ τὴν τεκνογονίαν, τὰς π. δογματίζοντες Ast.Soph. *fr*.18 ap.Eus.*Marcell*.1.4(p.19.20; M.24.756A); ἔφασαν [sc. Arians at Nicaea] ὁμοούσιον εἶναι, ὃ ἔκ τινός ἐστιν, ἢ κατὰ μερισμόν, ἢ κατὰ ῥεῦσιν, ἢ κατὰ π.· κατὰ π. μέν, ὡς ἐκ ῥιζῶν βλάστημα Socr.*h.e*.1.8.32 (M.67.68C); by others οὐ κατὰ π., ἢ κατὰ διαίρεσιν, ἢ τομήν, ἢ μείωσιν, ἢ κατά τι τῶν ἐν σώμασιν ὑπονοουμένων Eus.*d.e*.4.15(p.181.21; M.22. 301C); γέννημα θεοῦ αὐτὸ εἶναι φαμέν,...ἐπεὶ μήτε κατὰ π. μήτε κατὰ διάστασιν...τὴν γενεσιουργίαν ἐπινοοῦμεν *ib*.5.1(p.211.25); οὐ τμῆσιν τῆς ἀπαθοῦς φύσεως, οὔτε π., ἀλλ' υἱὸν αὐτοτελῆ †Ath.*exp.fid*.1(M.25.201A).

πρόβολος, ὁ, 1. *promoter* πρόβολοι...γίνονται γάμου Chrys.*fem. reg*.8(1.265C); **2.** *offspring* ὁ τοῦ Δαυὶδ π. Jo.Eub.*concept.BMV* 8(M. 96.1473A).

προβούλευσις, ἡ, *previous deliberation,* Gr.Nyss.*Eun*.10(2 p.237. 9; M.45.840A).

προβούλια, τά, *deliberation, forethought* ληπτοὺς τοῖς προβουλίοις τοὺς ἀνθρώπους εὕρατο Eus.*d.e*.4.9(p.163.8; M.22.272C); of Adam προβουλίοις ἐτίμα καὶ αὐτουργίᾳ τὸ τέχνημα Cyr.*glaph.Gen*.1(1.5C); τετίμηται...προβουλίοις ἡ ἀνθρώπου φύσις id.*Juln*.1(6².22E).

πρόβουλος, *taking counsel beforehand,* Serap.*Man*.18(p.36; M.40. 913C); ‡Gr.Naz.*Chr.pat*.2367(M.38.322A).

***προβραχέων**, *a little before*, Bas.Sel.*or*.29.2(M.85.332B).

***προβραχέως**, *just now, a little while ago*, Cyr.*hom.div*.12(5^2.385E).

προγαμιαῖος, *ante-nuptial*, *Pers*.(p.17.9).

***προγενεαλογέω**, *include in preceding genealogy*, Gr.Nyss.*Eun*.12 (1 p.390.21; M.45.1120D).

***προγένεθλος**, *born earlier*, Nonn.*par.Jo*.1:14(M.43.752B).

προγενής, *born before, older in years*; hence *prior to*; **a.** in gen. *τῆς τῶν...προφητῶν ἡλικίας...προγενεστέρα ἂν εἴη ἡ ὀλυμπιὰς ἡ πρώτη* Clem.*str*.1.21(p.80.18; M.8.861B); *τὴν παρὰ βαρβάροις προγενεστάτην ἀλήθειαν ib*.1.29(p.110.26; 928A); *προγενεστέρων οὐσῶν τῶν παρ' ἡμῖν γραφῶν ib*.2.1(p.113.8; 932A); Meth.*symp*.8.14(p.100.7; M.18.164A); Proc.G.*Ex*.17:5(M.87.593A); **b.** of Catholic Church as antecedent to heretical bodies, Clem.*str*.7.17(p.76.2; M.9.552A); **c.** of first Adam in relation to second, ‡Ath.*Apoll*.1.8(M.26.1105B); **d.** of Son *υἱὸς...πάσης τῆς κτίσεως αὐτοῦ προγενέστερός ἐστιν* Herm. *sim*.9.12.2; ref. Marcellus' exegesis of Pr.8:22 *Χριστὸς...τῶν προφητῶν καὶ τῶν ἔτι ἀνωτέρω...ὧν πρεσβύτερος, ἀλλ' οὐχὶ ἡ σὰρξ ἣν ἀνείληφεν ἐκείνων ἁπάντων ὑπῆρχεν προγενεστέρα* Eus.*e.th*.3.3(p.146.12; M.24.984B); against Arians *πῶς ἂν ποίημα, ἢ...προγενέστερον ἔχοντα...προσομολογήσει* Didym.*Trin*.1.15(M.39.328C); *ἵστωρ οὖν γενόμενος τῆς παρόδου τῶν φύσεων ὑπαριθμεῖ τὴν τάξιν αὐτῶν ὁ προγενέστερος αὐτῶν* Gel.Cyz.*h.e*.2.17.33(M.85.1272D).

προγενν-άομαι, **1.** in gen., *be born before*, Sophr.H.*or*.7(M.87.3332D); **2.** *be begotten before*, of Son's generation before Creation *ἐν μὲν τὸ ἀγέννητον...ἓν δὲ καὶ ~θέν, δι' οὗ τὰ πάντα ἐγένετο* Clem.*str*.6.7 (p.461.7; M.9.280B); *~θέντα καὶ ἔσεσθαι καὶ εἶναι τὸν αὐτόν* Meth. *symp*.8.9(p.91.11; M.18.152B); ref. Marcellus' exegesis of Pr.8:22 *διὰ τὸ προγεγεννημένην εἶναι αὐτὴν τῆς τῶν ἀποστόλων ἐκλογῆς* Eus. *e.th*.3.3(p.154.14; M.24.997A); '*σήμερον γεγέννηκά σε*', *καίτοι προγεγεννημένον καὶ ἀεὶ συνόντα* ‡Gr.Nyss.*Ar.et Sab*.4(M.45.1285C); *οὐδὲ συγγεγεννημένος ἢ προγεγεννημένος ἢ μεταγεγεννημένος υἱὸς ἕτερος τοῦ θεοῦ τῷ...υἱῷ αὐτοῦ θεῷ λόγῳ* Gel.Cyz.*h.e*.2.19.8(M.85.1277B); Leont.H.*Nest*.4.6(M.86.1664A); of Christ as first-born of baptized believers *ὁ τοῦ καινοῦ τῆς παλιγγενεσίας τόκου ~θεὶς ἐν τῷ ὕδατι* Gr. Nyss.*Eun*.4(2 p.64.16; M.45.636C); **3.** *precede, be antecedent to εἰ καὶ προγεγέννηται ταῦτα cat.Apoc*.6:2(p.263.6).

***προγέννητος**, *antecedent*, *cat.Apoc*.6:2(p.263.5).

***προγευστικῶς**, *by way of foretaste*, Eus.*Ps*.144:9(M.24.60B).

προγι(γ)νώσκ-ω, **1.** *make known beforehand*, ref. prophets *γνῶσις τῶν ἐκείνοις προεγνωσμένων ὑπὸ τοῦ προφαίνοντος τὰ πάντα κυρίου* Clem.*str*.2.12(p.142.14; M.8.992B); **2.** *know in advance, have foreknowledge of*; **a.** in gen. *προδηλῶσαί σοι τὴν θλῖψιν, ἵνα προγνοὺς αὐτὴν ὑπενέγκῃς ἰσχυρῶς* Herm.*sim*.7.5; *ἐν πᾶσιν οὖν τοῖς ζητουμένοις ἔστι τι ~όμενον* Clem.*str*.8.3(p.84.30; M.9.569A); Or.*Jo*.6.14(7; p.123.16; M.14.225A); of Moses, *Hom.Clem*.3.44; **b.** of divine foreknowledge; **i.** in gen. *ὁ κύριος, πάντα ~ων* Herm.*mand*.4.3.4; Just.*dial*.77.3(M.6.656B); Clem.*str*.6.7(p.461.13; M.9.280C); *φῶς ἀπρόσιτον...πάντα εἰδός, ~ον πάντα* id.*ecl*.21(p.142.24; M.9.708B); in rel. to evil, Or.*princ*.3.1.13(p.218.3; M.11.273A); ref. reason for Inc. *εἰ δὲ ἐκ μεταμέλου φαίη τοῦτο πεποιηκέναι τὸν θεόν...ἀσθενὴς αὐτῷ ὁ λόγος, μεταγινώσκοντα τὸν θεὸν εἰσάγων. ἀλλ' οὔτε ἀσύνετος τοῦ μέλλοντος ὁ θεὸς οὔτε κακοποιός, ἀλλὰ καὶ ἄκρως ἀγαθὸς καὶ ~ων τὰ μέλλοντα* Meth.*res*.1.39 (p.284.4; M.41.1108B); *τοῖς δὲ ὑπολαμβάνουσιν, ὅτι ὁ θεὸς οὐ ~ει, ἔφη· οἶδε γὰρ ὁ πατὴρ...ὅτι χρῄζετε...πρὶν αὐτὸν ἀξιώσετε Hom.Clem*.3.55; Didym.(‡Bas.)*Eun*.4(1.282D; M.29.680B); **ii.** in rel. to predestination *μή τινες...δοξάσωσι καθ' εἱμαρμένης ἀνάγκην φάσκειν ἡμᾶς τὰ γινόμενα γίνεσθαι, ἐκ τοῦ προειπεῖν προεγνωσμένα...ἐπεὶ εἰ...καθ' εἱμαρμένην πάντα γίνεται, οὔτε τὸ ἐφ' ἡμῖν ἐστιν ὅλως* Just.*1apol*.43.1 (M.6.392C); ref. Judas *εἰ μὲν ὡς θεὸς προέγνω καὶ οὐχ οἷόν τε ἦν αὐτοῦ τὴν πρόγνωσιν ψεύσασθαι, οὐχ οἷόν τε ἦν οὔτε τὸν ἐγνωσμένον ὡς προδώσοντα μὴ προδοῦναι οὔτε τὸν ἐλεγχθέντα ἀρνησόμενον μὴ ἀρνήσασθαι* Or.*Cels*.2.18(p.147.11; M.11.833B); *οὔ φαμεν ὅτι ὁ ~ων, ὑφελὼν τὸ δυνατὸν εἶναι γενέσθαι καὶ μὴ γενέσθαι, οἱονεὶ τοιοῦτόν τι λέγει· τόδε πάντως ἔσται, καὶ ἀδύνατον ἑτέρως γενέσθαι ib*.2.20(p.148.28; 836B); *ἄξιος οὖν τοῦ πιστευθῆναι ὤν, εἰ καὶ προεγνώσθη μεταπεσούμενος, ἐπιστεύθη* id.*Jo*.32.14(8; p.448.18; M.14.777B); *εἰκὸς δὲ τῷ θεῷ οὐ μόνον προεγνῶσθαι τὰ ἐσόμενα ἀλλὰ καὶ προδιατετάχθαι, καὶ μηδὲν αὐτῷ παρὰ τὰ προδιατεταγμένα γίνεσθαι* id.*or*.5(p.309.12; M.11.432A); *πολλοὶ τῶν Ἑλλήνων, οἰόμενοι κατηναγκάσθαι τὰ πράγματα, καὶ τὸ ἐφ' ἡμῖν μηδαμῶς σώζεσθαι, εἰ ὁ θεὸς ~ει τὰ μέλλοντα, ἀσεβὲς δόγμα ἐτόλμησαν...προσέσθαι τό, ὥς φασιν...ἔνδοξον μὲν περὶ θεοῦ, ἀναιροῦν δὲ τὸ ἐφ' ἡμῖν, καὶ διὰ τοῦτο ἔπαινον καὶ ψόγον* id.*comm.in Gen*.ap. Eus.*p.e*.6.11(286D; M.12.61C); *οὐχ ἡ πρόγνωσις τοῦ θεοῦ γέγονεν αἰτία αὐτῷ τῷ διαβόλῳ τοῦ κακὸν ἔσεσθαι, δῆλον· οὐδὲ γὰρ ὁ ~ων ἰατρὸς τὴν ἐσομένην νόσον αἴτιός ἐστι τῆς νόσου* Jo.D.*Man*.1.37(M.94.1544B); **iii.** in rel. to election *~ει γάρ τινας ἐκ μετανοίας σωθήσεσθαι μέλλοντας, καί τινας μηδέπω ἴσως γεννηθέντας* Just.*1apol*.28.2(M.6.372B); *ἀληθέστεροι οἱ ἀπὸ τῶν ἐθνῶν καὶ πιστότεροι προεγινώσκοντο ib*.53.10 (408B); *τῶν εἰς αὐτὸν πιστεύειν προεγνωσμένων* id.*dial*.42.4(M.6.565C); Or.*princ*.3.1.17(p.227.6; M.11.285A); *οὐ γὰρ διστάζει ὁ θεός, ἵνα λέγῃ τὸ ἴσως ἀκούσονται...ἀλλ' ἵνα...μὴ εἴπῃς· εἰ προέγνω με ἀπολλύμενον ἀπολέσθαι με δεῖ, εἰ προέγνω με σωθησόμενον σωθήσεσθαι πάντως με χρή...ἵνα τηρήσῃ σου τὸ αὐτεξούσιον τῷ μὴ προειληφέναι μηδὲ προεγνωκέναι, πότερον μετανοήσεις ἢ μή* id.*hom.18.6 in Jer*.(p.160.5; M.13.477B); *τὸ τοῦ σωτῆρος...πάθος ἐπὶ καθαρισμῷ τῶν προεγνωσμένων ἐγίνετο ἐν οἷς ὁ κόσμος κρίνεσθαι ἔμελλε* id.*fr.90 in Jo*.(p.553.9); Chrys.*hom.60.1 in Jo*.(8.352D); **iv.** Trin. *οἱ μὲν γὰρ* [sc. Arians] *κατὰ τὸ ~ειν ἑκάτερον ἔφασαν, οἱ δὲ κατὰ τὴν φύσιν, θεόν* Philost. *h.e*.10.3(M.65.585A).

προγνωσία, ἡ, *foreknowledge*; of God, Epiph.*haer*.74.13(p.331.27; M.42.500D); ref. predestination *ὧν προέγνω τὴν πρόθεσιν, τούτους προώρισεν ἄνωθεν...ἀλλὰ μηδεὶς τὴν π. αἰτίαν εἶναι τούτων λεγέτω* Thdt.*Rom*.8:30(3.93).

πρόγνωσις, ἡ, I. *foreknowledge*;

A. descriptions and def. *ἡ γνῶσις καὶ ἡ π. διττὴ λέγεται, ἡ μὲν ἀπηκριβωμένην ἔχουσα τὴν ἑαυτῆς φύσιν, ἡ δὲ ἐλλιπὴ* Clem.*str*.2.11 (p.138.22; M.8.984C); *ἡ προφητεία π. ἐστιν, ἡ δὲ γνῶσις προφητείας νόησις ib*.2.12(p.142.13; 992B); *π. λέγεται διχῶς, ἡ μὲν ἐπιστημονική τε καὶ βεβαία, ἄλλη δὲ μόνον ἐλπιστική ib*.8.3(p.82.15; M.9.564B); *ὥσπερ γὰρ ἡ γνῶσις τῶν ὄντων ἐστίν, οὕτω καὶ π. τῶν πάντων ἐσομένων ἐστί* Jo.D.*Man*.1.73(M.94.1572D).

B. in paganism; **1.** through astrology *ἐξεῦρον...Κᾶρες τὴν διὰ τῶν ἄστρων π.* Tat.*orat*.1(p.1.5; M.6.804A); Clem.*str*.1.16(p.48.5; M.8.784B); *δεῖ καθόλου πάσης ἀσεβοῦς π. μὴ ἀνέχεσθαι· εἰ γὰρ ἀστέρες τυχὸν ἐνεργοῦσι, μάτην εὐχόμεθα* Or.*fr.49 in Jer*.36:8(p.223.12); *τῶν ὑπόγυιον καταστερισθέντων, Λέοντος...καὶ τῶν ἄλλων, ἐξ ὧν εἰσηγεῖσθε κατακοσμηθέντων τοὺς πολλοὺς κατειληφέναι τὴν μαθηματικὴν ταύτην, μᾶλλον δὲ καταθεματικήν, π.* Meth.*symp*.8.15(p.103.7; M.18.165C); **2.** through magic of various kinds, Hipp.*haer*.4.36(p.62.18; M.16.3102B); and hepatoscopy *Μάγων θυτική, καὶ π. ἔντομος* Gr.Naz.*or*. 39.5(M.36.340A); **3.** by philosophers, esp. Pythagoras, Clem.*str*.1.21 (p.82.23; M.8.868B).

C. Christian; as divine gift, Or.*fr.49 in Jer*.36:8(p.223.16); *Const. App*.8.1.12; bestowed by H. Ghost *ὁ μὲν γὰρ λαμβάνει συνέσεως πνεῦμα,...ὁ δὲ προγνώσεως* Just.*dial*.39.2(M.6.560C); *τὸ τῆς π. ἅγιον οὐκ εἶχεν πνεῦμα Hom.Clem*.3.14; given to prophets, Iren.*haer*.2. 32.4(M.7.829B); *Hom.Clem*.12.28; Cyr.*Abac*.2(3.518E); absent from false prophets, Eust.*engast*.8(p.26.14; M.18.628A); in true prophet must co-exist with right judgement, *Hom.Clem*.12.27; given to apostles for determining church order, *1Clem*.44.2; not to replace exercise of pastoral judgement, Chrys.*hom.32.5 in Mt*.(7.372C); in gen., *A.Xanthipp*.9(p.64.2); apparent in scriptural types, Just. *dial*.134.4(M.6.788A); and prophecies, Epiph.*mens*.1(M.43.237B); bestowed on Constantine through theophanies, Eus.*v.C*.1.47(p.30.2; M.30.961B).

D. of angels, ref. Gnost. doctrines of Creation, Clem.*str*.2.8(p.133.18; M.8.973B).

E. of God; **1.** in gen. *συκοφαντηθήσεται ὁ θεός, ὡς μήτε π. ἔχων* Just.*dial*.92.5(M.6.696C); *τί...μεταμέλεται, ἅπαντα πρὸς τὴν π. τὴν οἰκείαν οἰκονομῶν* Or.*adnot.in Gen*.7:4(M.17.12B); id.*fr.105 in Jo*. (p.560.21); *εἰ δὲ...αἱ ψυχαί...ἄνωθεν ἐλθοῦσαι φαίνονται...εἰ δὲ ἀπεστάλησαν...ἵνα δίκαιόν τι πράξωσι, πονηρὸν δὲ εἰργάσαντο, ὀφθήσεται ὁ ἀποστείλας αὐτὰς π. ἂν μὴ ἔχων* Epiph.*haer*.44.5(p.197.1; M.41.829A); Thdt.*qu.65 in Gen*.(1.78); *ib.24*(1.39); **2.** in rel. to predestination and election *ποιεῖ...ὁ δημιουργὸς σκεύη τιμῆς καὶ σκεύη ἀτιμίας οὐκ ἀρχῆθεν κατὰ τὴν π., ἐπεὶ μὴ κατ' αὐτὴν προκατακρίνει... ἀλλὰ σκεύη τιμῆς τοὺς ἐκκαθάραντας ἑαυτοὺς καὶ σκεύη ἀτιμίας τοὺς ἀπερικαθάρτους ἑαυτοὺς περιϊδόντας* Or.*princ*.3.1.21(20; p.238.4; M.11.297A); *ὁ μὲν Κέλσος οἴεται διὰ τοῦτο γίνεσθαι τὸ ὑπό τινος π. θεσπισθέν, ἐπεὶ ἐθεσπίσθη· ἡμεῖς δὲ...φαμὲν οὐχὶ τὸν θεσπίσαντα αἴτιον εἶναι τοῦ ἐσομένου* id.*Cels*.2.20(p.148.21; M.11.836B); *ταύτης δὲ... εἰκόνος...συμμόρφους προώρισεν γενέσθαι ὁ θεός, οὓς διὰ τὴν περὶ αὐτῶν π. προώρισεν. οὐ νομιστέον...εἶναι τῶν ἐσομένων αἰτίαν τὴν π. τοῦ θεοῦ* id.*comm.in Rom*.1:1(*JTS* 13 p.211); *ἕως μὲν γὰρ ἦσαν ἐν τῇ π.* [sc. elect] *οὐδενὶ ἦσαν δῆλοι· ἐπειδὴ δὲ ἐσφραγίσθησαν, δῆλοι γεγόνασιν* Chrys.*hom.2.2 in Eph*.(11.10F); *ἀλλ' οὐχ ἡ π. τοῦ θεοῦ, ἢ τὸν Φαραὼ πονηρόν, ἢ τὸν Ἱερεμίαν πεποίηκεν ἅγιον· ἀλλὰ τὸ μέλλον ἔσεσθαι προέγνω ὡς θεός* Thdt.*Ps*.57:4(1.984); Euthal.Diac.*Ac*.(M.85.657D); *κατὰ μὲν πρόγνωσιν οἱ τεταγμένοι εἰς ζωήν, οὗτοι ἐπίστευσαν, πλὴν οἰκείᾳ γνώμῃ καὶ προαιρέσει· ἡ γὰρ τοῦ θεοῦ π. οὐκ ἀναιρεῖ τῆς ἡμετέρας βουλήσεως τὸ αὐτεξούσιον* Ammon.*Ac*.13:48(M.85.1544A);

ἡ τοῦ θεοῦ π. οὐ βλάπτει τὴν μετάνοιαν Hesych.H.*fr.Ps.*80:9–10(M.93.1257A); **3.** ref. generation of Son εἴ τις κατὰ πρόγνωσιν πρὸ Μαρίας λέγει τὸν υἱὸν εἶναι καὶ μὴ πρὸ αἰώνων ἐκ τοῦ πατρὸς γεγεννημένον... ἀ. ἔ. *Symb.Sirm.*1 *anath.*5; προεθεμελίωσε τὸν ἑαυτοῦ υἱὸν ὅσον εἰς τὴν οἰκείαν π. Cyr.*thes.*15(5¹.172E); **4.** ref. Inc. ὁ πρὸ τοῦ αἰῶνος θεμελιωθεὶς εἰς τὰ ἀπόκρυφα τῆς πατρῴας διανοίας ἐν π. ἣν ὃν ἔμελλεν ἐκ Μαρίας κυριακὸν ἄνθρωπον κτίζειν ‡Ath.*serm.fid.*31(p.28; M.26.1285C); εἶχέν τε καὶ ῥοπὴν οὐ τὴν τυχοῦσαν πρὸς τὰ κρείττω τῇ πρὸς τὸν...λόγον ἑνώσει, ἧς ἠξίωτο κατὰ πρόγνωσιν τοῦ θεοῦ λόγου, ἄνωθεν αὐτὸν ἑνώσαντος ἑαυτῷ Thdr.Mops.*fr.inc.*7(p.296.33; M.66.977B); κατὰ πρόγνωσιν τοῦ ὁποῖός τις ἔσται, ἑνώσας αὐτῷ ὁ θεὸς λόγος ἑαυτῷ ἐν αὐτῇ διαπλάσεως ἀρχῇ *ib.*(p.298.3; 980B); Nestorian κοινὸν ἄνθρωπον...ὡς ἐξ ἰδίας τε καὶ ἀνθρωπίνης ἀρετῆς ἄξιον ἑαυτὸν παραστήσαντα τοῦ χρῆναι τιμᾶσθαι καὶ συναφείᾳ προσώπου τῇ πρὸς τὸν...λόγον, καὶ ἀπόλεκτον γενέσθαι κατὰ πρόγνωσιν Cyr.*Arcad.*(p.69.31; 5².54A).

F. of Christ οἱ ἐχθροὶ τοῦ Ἰησοῦ μέρος τι τῶν πάντων ἦσαν οὓς ᾔδει, ὅσον ἐπὶ τῇ π., δεδόσθαι...αὐτῷ Or.*Jo.*32.3(p.429.18; M.14.745D); ref. treachery of Judas, id.*Cels.*2.20(p.148.21ff.; M.11.836Bff.); Chrys. *hom.*47.2 *in Jo.*(8.278E); ref. Mt.12:32 οὐκ ἐπαινῶν τοὺς βλασφημοῦντας αὐτόν, ἀλλὰ τὴν αὐτοῦ π. ... δεικνύς, προασφαλιζομένην τὴν σωτηρίαν τῶν ἀπὸ βλασφημίας αὐτοῦ μετανοούντων Epiph.*haer.*54.2 (p.319.19; M.41.964D); ἡ σοφία τοῦ θεοῦ π. ἔχει ἢ οὔ;...ἔχει. ... ἡ σοφία...ὁ υἱὸς τοῦ θεοῦ ἐστιν Gel.Cyz.*h.e.*2.18.2(M.85.1273B).

II. *knowledge in preparation, preliminary knowledge,* Thdt.*Is.* 37:19(2.322 but cf. p.147.16).

III. *prognostication, prophecy* (pagan) μαντείας μὲν καὶ χρησμοὺς καὶ μελλόντων προγνώσεις...ἐπηγγέλλοντο Eus.*l.C.*9(p.218.11; M.20.1364A); Synes.*insomn.*12(M.66.1301C; p.167.16n.).

προγνώστης, ὁ, *one who foreknows;* **1.** in paganism π. ὁ Ἀπόλλων Tat.*orat.*19(p.21.21; M.6.849B); μάντεις καὶ π. γεγενῆσθαι κατὰ τοὺς συγγραφεῖς Thphl.Ant.*Autol.*3.17(M.6.1144C); of oracles μᾶλλον στοιχασταί εἰσιν ἢ π. Ath.*v.Anton.*33(M.26.892B); of false prophets, Cyr.*Is.*4.3(2.648C); **2.** of God, in gen. π. γάρ ἐστιν τῶν πάντων καὶ εἰδὼς ἡμῶν τὰ ἐν καρδίᾳ *2Clem.*9.9; οὐδεὶς...τολμήσει εἰπεῖν ὅτι μὴ καὶ π. τῶν γίνεσθαι μελλόντων ἦν καὶ ἔστιν ὁ θεός Just.*dial.*16.3(M.6.509B); φιλάνθρωπον καὶ π. καὶ ἀνενδεῆ *ib.*23.2(525C); π. ἐστὶ τῶν μελλόντων Cyr.H.*catech.*4.5; Gnost. τρεῖς...ἀρχὰς...ἀγεννήτους, ἀρρενικὰς δύο, θηλυκὴν μίαν. τῶν δὲ ἀρρενικῶν ἡ μέν τις ἀρχὴ καλεῖται ἀγαθός...π. τῶν ὅλων Hipp.*haer.*10.15(p.276.13; M.16.3431A); ref. Creation and providence εἰ τῆς ἑκάστου βιώσεως π. ὁ δεσπότης...διὰ τί μὴ τῶν εὐσεβῶν τὰς ψυχὰς ἐν σώμασιν εὐσθενέσιν εἰσῴκισεν; ‡Just. *qu.et resp.*124(M.6.1373A); ref. conversion ᾔδει ὁ θεός, ἅτε π. ὤν, μὴ πιστεύσοντα τοῦτον Clem.*str.*6.14(p.487.9; M.9.333A); ref. problem of divine 'repentance' θεὸς...π. ὢν τῶν μελλόντων, οὐ δύναται μὴ καλῶς βεβουλεῦσθαι, καὶ παρὰ τοῦτο μετανοεῖν Or.*hom.18.6 in Jer.* (p.157.32; M.13.473C); ref. prayer εἰ π. ἐστιν ὁ θεὸς τῶν μελλόντων, καὶ δεῖ αὐτὰ γίνεσθαι, ματαία ἡ προσευχή Or.*or.*5(p.311.9; M.11.433C); **3.** of Christ Ἰησοῦν καὶ τῶν μετ' αὐτὸν γενησομένων π. ἐπιστάμεθα Just.*dial.*35.7(M.6.552B); εἰδὼς ὁ δεσπότης...ὡς π. τὸ τί ἔμελλον ποιεῖν οἱ μαθηταί †Or.*fr.247 in Mt.*12:1ff.(p.115); π. ὢν ὡς θεός Epiph.*haer.*71.4(p.253.30; M.42.380D); ἐγίνωσκε γὰρ ὡς π. θεὸς τὸ ἐσόμενον Cyr.ap.*cat.Lc.*19:2ff.(p.137.15) cf.id.*Lc.*19:5(M.72.868A); τὸν ἀληθῆ π. καὶ βασιλέα προσκυνείτω Isid.Pel.*epp.*3.94(M.78.800B); of Son as Wisdom, Gel.Cyz.*h.e.*2.18.9(M.85.1276A); **4.** of H. Ghost εἰ τοὺς προφήτας καὶ ἀποστόλους...ἀπεσταλκέναι καθ' ὁμοιότητα τοῦ πατρὸς καὶ τοῦ υἱοῦ μεμαρτύρηται, ὡς θεός...καὶ ὡς π. καὶ τῆς κτίσεως δεσπότης ταῦτα πεποίηκεν Didym.*Trin.*3.2(M.39.804A).

προγνωστικός, *having foreknowledge, prescient;* **1.** in gen., of Anaxagoras τοῦτον λέγουσι καὶ π. γεγονέναι Hipp.*haer.*1.8(p.15.2; M.16.3033D); of Druids τούτους Κελτοὶ ὡς προφήτας καὶ π. δοξάζουσι *ib.*1.25(p.29.21; 3053A); of Peratic Gnostics π. ἑαυτοὺς φάσκοντες ἔσθ' ὅτε διὰ τοῦ πολλὰ μαντεύεσθαι ἐν ἐπιτυγχάνοντες *ib.*4.13(p.45.15; 3075D); and Elchezaites π. ἑαυτοὺς λέγειν...μέτροις καὶ ἀριθμοῖς τῆς ...Πυθαγορείου τέχνης ἀφορμαῖς χρωμένους *ib.*9.14(p.252.25; 3390B); Thdt.*haer.*2.7(4.333); of prophets ποίῳ νῷ ὁ προφήτης...λέγει ὁπόσα ἀναγέγραπται ἐν ταῖς προφητείαις· ἆρα γὰρ προγνωστικῷ μελλόντων ἢ οὔ; εἰ μὲν γὰρ π. μελλόντων, θεῖον εἶχον πνεῦμα οἱ προφῆται Or.*Cels.*1.35(p.87.9; M.11.728C); Φαιδίμου...τῆς Ἀμασαίων ἐκκλησίας καθηγουμένου· ᾧ θεόθεν ἐξ ἁγίου πνεύματος π. τις δύναμις ἦν Gr.Nyss. *v.Gr.Thaum.*(M.46.909A); of false prophets ἄγε πρὸς ἐμὲ τὸν ἄνδρα τὸν μάγον, εἴ τινα ἔχει δύναμιν π., εἰπάτω τί μοι συμβήσεται Chrys. *hom.*8.5 *in 2Tim.*(11.712F); of an apostle, Isid.Pel.*epp.*1.181(M.78.300C); of scripture, Tat.*orat.*29(p.30.10; M.6.868A); of Christ's prophecies of Jerusalem's destruction, Eus.*h.e.*3.7.3(M.20.233B); **2.** of God π., τέλειος, ἀνενδεὴς *Hom.Clem.*3.38; τῇ προαιρέσει τῇ διὰ τῆς π. δυνάμεως γνωρισθείσῃ Gr.Nyss.*infant.*(M.46.185C); Ἰουδαίους... οἱ τῇ π. τοῦ θεοῦ προνοίᾳ ἐν πεπλανημένοις ἐλογίσθησαν Cyr.*Ps.*57:4 (M.69.1109C); τῇ προαιωνίῳ π. βουλῇ τοῦ θεοῦ προορισθεῖσα [sc. Μαρία] Jo.D.*f.o.*4.14(M.94.1156A); of good principle in Peratic system, Hipp.*haer.*5.26(p.126.31; M.16.3194C); **3.** of Logos, Tat.*orat.*7(p.7.20; M.6.820C) cit. s. αἱρέω; of Christ εἰπὼν δὲ 'ἀνάγκη', οὐκ ἀναιρεῖ τὸ αὐτεξούσιον, ἀλλὰ τὸ π. τοῦ πάντως ἐσομένου δηλοῖ Or.*fr.375 in Mt.*18:5ff.(p.161.2; M.17.297C); **4.** of phantoms and demonic apparitions, Or.*Cels.*7.5(p.157.4; M.11.1428A); *V.Pach.A* 25(p.152.23).

προγνωστικῶς, *with foreknowledge,* ref. prophets π. ἀπαγγέλλουσι περὶ τῆς κηρύξεως τοῦ εὐαγγελίου Or.*Cels.*1.62(p.114.22; M.11.776C); of God's providence πάντα τῇ βουλήσει τοῦ θεοῦ π. κατὰ τὴν ἄπειρον αὐτοῦ δύναμιν...περιέχεσθαι Max.*ambig.*(M.91.1328C); against Marcellus, of Son οὐ π. συνόντα καὶ συνδιατρίβοντα πρὸ αἰώνων τῷ ἑαυτοῦ πατρί Symb.Ant.(345)6(p.253.5; M.26.732B).

προγονικός, 1. *derived from ancestors;* **a.** in gen. τὴν συγγενικὴν καὶ π. ζηλώσας παιδείαν Clem.*str.*1.23(p.96.4; M.8.900B); *ib.*2.21 (1076B; τριγενικήν p.184.3); ἔχει ἐν ἑαυτῷ π. τε καὶ συγγενικοὺς λόγους ὁ σπείρων, ὁτὲ μὲν κρατεῖ ὁ αὐτοῦ λόγος...ὁτὲ δὲ ὁ λόγος τοῦ ἀδελφοῦ τοῦ σπείραντος Or.*Jo.*20.5(p.332.34; M.14.584B); ἀποστάτην π. παραγγελίας Mac.Mgn.*apocr.*3.29(p.123.20); μὴ ἀπολαύσητε...τοῦ πλούτου καὶ τῶν π. πραγμάτων Pall.*h.Laus.*54(p.147.14; M.34.1227B); met., of apostolic teaching τὰ π. ἐκεῖνα καὶ ἀποστολικὰ...σπέρματα Clem.*str.*1.1(p.9.7; M.8.700A); of teaching of fathers, Paul.Em. *hom.*2(*ACO* 1.1.4 p.14.14; M.77.1444B); **b.** of original sin μηδὲν ἐκ τοῦ Ἀδὰμ ἕλκειν π. ἁμαρτίας *Cod.Afr.*110 (Lat. *originalis*); μνήμην ...τῆς π. παρακοῆς Jo.VI H.*v.Jo.D.*29(M.94.469A); **c.** ref. Valent. saviour οἱ δὲ ἐκ...τῶν δέκα αἰώνων...προβεβλῆσθαι αὐτὸν λέγουσιν, τὰ π. ὀνόματα διασῴζοντα Iren.*haer.*1.12.4(M.7.576B); **2.** *belonging to ancestors* π. εὐσέβειαν...νικῶντος Cyr.H.*ep.Const.*3(M.33.1168B); of Adam's sovereignty over creation recovered by man through Christ ἀνενεώσαντο τὴν π. ἀρχήν Isid.Pel.*epp.*3.95(M.78.804C); Cyr. *Os.*138(3.171E); id.*Am.*4(3.254C); of a family friend εἶναι αὐτὸν π. ἡμῶν Anast.Ap.*a.Max.*2.24(M.90.161A); **3.** *given to ancestors* τῆς π. ἀπήλαυσαν ὑποσχέσεως Thdt.*qu.*40 *in Ex.*(1.152); ἐπέθηκε...τῇ π. προρρήσει τὸ τέλος id.*qu.23 in 2Reg.*(1.421).

πρόγραμμα, τό, 1. *public announcement, official notice,* in gen. προγράμματι κηρύξαι τὴν ὑποχώρησιν Gr.Naz.*ep.*203(M.37.336A); of credal statement μέγα...π. ... καὶ κήρυγμα τῆς ὀρθοδοξίας *ib.*102 (200B); of imperial edict ἀνίησί τε αὐτίκα διὰ προγραμμάτων τὸν... διωγμόν Eus.*h.e.*7.13(M.20.673C); *ib.*8.16.1(789A); Philost.*h.e.*7.1(M.65.537A); Const.Diac.*laud.*5(M.88.485A); **2.** *official letter, manifesto,* Dion.Al.ap.Eus.*h.e.*7.6.1(M.20.648A); **3.** *example* τύπον καὶ π. τοῖς πιστεύουσιν εἰς αὐτόν Max.*ambig.*(M.91.1333C).

προγραμμός, ὁ, *example,* †Bas.Sel.*or.*41(M.85.465B); *ib.*(472C); ‡Meth.*Sym.et Ann.*10(M.18.372B).

προγραφή, ἡ, *title,* of a Psalm 'ὑπὲρ τῶν ληνῶν' τὴν π. περιέχει Eus.*Ps.*8:1(following Or., cf.*AS* 2 p.459); id.*d.e.*4.15(p.180.28; M.22.301A); id.*e.th.*1.20(p.95.25; M.24.892B); Cyr.*Ps.*33:1(M.69.884D); Thdt.*Ps.*44:2(1.887); of a scriptural book, Thdr.Mops.*Abd.*1:1(M.66.309A); including salutation introducing an epistle, id.*Eph.*1:1 (p.118.23); Thdt.*Cant.*1 proem.(2.21); of a section of a prophetical book ἔστι π. 'ἃ προεφήτευσεν Ἱερεμίας ἐπὶ πάντα τὰ ἔθνη' τῇ 'Αἰλάμ', τῇ 'Δαμασκῷ' Or.*hom.1.12 in Jer.*(p.10.10); *opening words* of any letter, Thdr.Stud.*epp.*2.79(M.99.1317C).

προγράφω, *set forth, show manifestly, Orac.Sib.*8.249; ref. Gal.3:1 οὐκ εἶπεν 'ἐσταυρώθη' ἀλλὰ 'προεγράφη ἐσταυρωμένος', δηλῶν ὅτι τοῖς τῆς πίστεως ὀφθαλμοῖς ἀκριβέστερον ἐθεώρησαν τῶν παρόντων Chrys. *comm.in Gal.*3:1(10.696A); Thdt.*Gal.*3:1(3.373); τὸ δέ, π. ... εἴρηκε, δεικνὺς τὸν ἄπληστον αὐτῶν πρότερον περὶ τὸν Χριστὸν πόθον, ὡς διὰ παντὸς ἐν ὀφθαλμοῖς ὁρᾶν τὸ μυστήριον Jo.D.*Gal.*3:1(M.95.792C).

προγυμνασία, ἡ, *preparatory training,* Clem.*str.*1.6(p.21.24; M.8.728B); π. γὰρ βασιλείας...ἡ ποιμενική *ib.*1.23(p.98.17; 904B); Anast. S.*hod.*1 tit.(M.89.40A).

προγύμνασμα, τό, *preparatory exercise* or *training* ταῦτα γνωστικῆς ἀσκήσεως προγυμνάσματα Clem.*str.*4.21(p.306.33; M.8.1344A); *ib.*6.10 (p.473.6; M.9.304A); ref. Sibylline oracles ἔσται γὰρ ὑμῖν ἀναγκαῖον π. ἡ τούτων γνῶσις τῆς τῶν ἱερῶν ἀνδρῶν προφητείας ‡Just.*coh.Gr.* 38(M.6.312A); of Passover as a type π. πίστεως τὸ δρώμενον Cyr. *glaph.Ex.*2(1.282E); π. ... τῆς ἐν πνεύματι λατρείας τὸ γράμμα ἐστὶ τὸ Μωσαϊκόν id.*Jo.*2.1(4.157A); *ib.*4.6(423E).

***προγυμναστέον,** *one must exercise beforehand,* Clem.*str.*7.12(p.51.15; M.9.500A).

προγυμνόω, *expose in advance,* Gr.Nyss.*bapt.diff.*(M.46.425B).

***προδαμάζω,** *subdue beforehand,* Gr.Nyss.*v.Ephr.*(M.46.836D).

προδαπαν-άω, *spend, use up in advance,* in argument on division of substance of Godhead ~ᾶται τῆς τοῦ Ἀβραὰμ ὑποστάσεως ἡ τοῦ

Ἀδὰμ οὐσία Gr.Nyss.*Eun*.2(2 p.321.21; M.45.496A); Synes.*provid*.2.6 (p.126.14; M.66.1276B); Cyr.*Jo*.9(4.748E).

***προδειλιάω**, *be the first to show fear*, Jo.Clim.*scal*.21(M.88.945D).

***προδέομαι**, **1.** *stand in need of*, Gr.Nyss.*v.Mos*.(M.44.321); **2.** *be required* προεδεήθησαν ἄκοντα αὐτὸν ἀπαντῆσαι εἰς τὴν δίκην Pall.*v.Chrys*.8(p.50.1, v.l. προσεδεήθησαν; M.47.29).

***προδερέλικτος**, (Lat. *pro derelictus* [sc. *habeor*]) *regarded as lost* ἐπὶ τῶν π. οἰκετῶν Ath.Scholast.*coll*.10.2(p.114).

προδεσμ-έω, *bind beforehand* λογισμὸς ἐμπαθὴς αἰσθητοῖς πράγμασι τὸν νοῦν ~ῶν Or.*sel.in Ps*.1:1(M.12.1085A).

***προδεσπόζω**, *be in charge previously*; of one who was former occupant of a see, *Schol.* in CChalc.*can*.17(*Mon*.2 p.645).

***προδηλοποιέω**, *show forth before*, †Gregent.*disp*.1(M.86.636C).

προδηλ-όω, **1.** *reveal in advance*, Herm.*sim*.7.5; ὁ θεὸς ~οῖ καὶ προκαταγγέλλει Cels.ap.Or.*Cels*.4.23(p.292.22; M.11.1060B); Or.*Cels*.4.93(p.366.21; 1172C); **2.** *show beforehand* or *above* (i.e. in a treatise), Just.*dial*.105.1(M.6.721A); hence προδεδηλωμένος, *aforesaid*, *1Clem*.62.2; Just.*1apol*.33.6(M.6.381B); Clem.*prot*.4(p.37.16; M.8.140A); Hipp.*haer*.7.27(p.207.10; M.16.3319B).

***προδήλωμα, τό**, **1.** *public announcement*, Anast.S.*hod*.10(M.89.161B); **2.** *proof in advance*, Thdr.Stud.*epp*.2.107(M.99.1368B).

προδημιουργέω, *create before*, *1Clem*.33.3; εἰσί τινες, οἳ προδεδημιουργῆσθαι οὐρανοῦ καὶ γῆς ἔφασαν τοὺς ἀγγέλους, Πλάτωνος...τοῖς μύθοις...ἐξακολουθήσαντες Gennad.*fr.Gen*.1:1(M.85.1624C).

προδιαβαίνω, *pass by before*, Didym.*Ex*.33:19(M.39.1113D).

προδιαγράφ-ω, **1.** *delineate in advance*, ref. OT prophecies and types τοῦ...γεννητοῦ υἱοῦ [sc. of Adam] εἰκόνα ~οντος τοῦ γεννητοῦ υἱοῦ καὶ λόγου τοῦ θεοῦ Meth.*fr.Job*(p.521.7; M.18.408B); τὸν γὰρ τοῦ σώματος Ἰησοῦ ναὸν π. ὁ ἄψυχος καὶ ἄνους καὶ ἀθελὴς τοῦ Σολομῶντος ναός Apoll.*fr*.2(p.204.16)ap.Anast.S.*monoph*.(M.89.1184A); τὰς...μελλούσας ἐπιτελεῖσθαι...οἰκονομίας...π. οἱ τύποι ὡς τύποι Chrys.*hom.14.3 in Jo*.(8.82C); id.*hom.23.3 in 1Cor*.(10.204C); προφητῶν ~όντων ...καὶ ἀνακηρυττόντων *ib.38.3*(354D); Cyr.*Zach*.17(3.672D); Thdt.*qu.2 in Jos*.(1.304); Anast.S.*hex*.7(M.89.937A); καθὼς π. ἐν τῇ προσφορᾷ τοῦ δράγματος τῆς ἀπαρχῆς, οὕτως ἀνέστη *Chron.Pasch*.p.223 (M.92.541C); πέμπτος τρόπος εἰκόνος λέγεται, ὁ...~ων τὰ μέλλοντα, ὡς ἡ βάτος...τὴν παρθένον Jo.D.*imag*.3.22(M.94.1341C); ‡Meth.*Sym.et Ann*.9(M.18.369B); **2.** *picture, portray* ~ει τὴν σοφίαν ὁ λόγος ῥήσεις τινὰς ἐξ οἰκείου διεξιοῦσαν προσώπου Gr.Nyss.*Eun*.3(2 p.11.8; M.45.576A); ~ει ἐν τῷ νῷ οἰνεῶνας Mac.Aeg.*hom*.26.11(M.34.681B); ἐν... ταύτῃ ζωῇ τὴν ἀθάνατον ~ω ζωήν Thdt.*Gal*.2:20(3.372).

***προδιάγραψις, ἡ**, *prophetic delineation*, Anast.S.*serm.imag*.3(M.89.1160D).

προδιαζεύγνυμι, *separate previously* ἡ τοῦ πρὸς ἐπισκοπῆς προεδρίαν ἀναγομένου γυνή, κατὰ κοινὴν συμφωνίαν τοῦ οἰκείου ἀνδρὸς προδιαζευχθεῖσα, μετὰ τὴν ἐπ' αὐτῷ τῆς ἐπισκοπῆς χειροτονίαν ἐν μοναστηρίῳ εἰσίτω CTrull.*can*.48.

***προδιαζωγραφέω**, *depict previously*, †Gr.Nyss.*nativ*.(M.46.1128A); Gr.Agr.*Eccl*.1.21(M.98.801D).

προδιαιρέω, *divide beforehand*, Cyr.*apol.orient*.8(p.50.9; 6¹.180A).

***προδιαιτέομαι**, = προδιαιτάομαι, pass., *be weighed*, or *considered, beforehand*, Thdr.Stud.*epp*.2.106(M.99.1365A).

προδιακαθαίρ-ω, *clear out of the way beforehand* ~ων τὴν ἐνοχλοῦσάν τισιν ἀπιστίαν Athenag.*res*.11(p.60.14; v.l. for προκαθαίρων M.6.993C); Chrys.*hom.19.3 in Mt*.(7.248E).

προδιακρίνω, *analyse, explain in advance*, ‡Sophr.H.*liturg*.8(M.87.3988D).

προδιαμαρτάνω, *sin before* (i.e. in previous existence), Aen.*dial*.(M.85.926A).

προδιαμαρτύρ-ομαι, **1.** *give warning in advance*, Or.*hom.1.1 in Jer*.(p.1.3; M.13.256A); Thdr.Heracl.ap.*cat.Jo*.8:24(p.276.24); **2.** *proclaim beforehand, testify to beforehand* ἐσθῆτος...~ομένης τὸ ἐπάγγελμα τῆς κατὰ θεὸν ζωῆς Bas.*reg.fus*.22.3(2.367E; M.31.980B); Cyr.*Soph*.37(3.614A).

***προδιαμορφόω**, *prefigure*, Bas.*Spir*.31(3.25E; M.32.121B).

***προδιαναθλέω**, *be foremost athlete*; of a martyr, Thdr.Stud.*cant*.16.9(p.373).

προδιαναπαύω, *order previous cessation of work*, Proc.G.*Gen*.1:5 (M.87.57C).

***προδιανοίγω**, *open in advance* προδιανοιχθείσης τῆς ἀκοῆς τῆς παρθένου διὰ τῆς ἀρχαγγελικῆς φωνῆς ‡Ath.*annunt*.8(M.28.928A); ‡Meth.*Sym.et Ann*.4(M.18.356C).

***προδιανυκτερεύ-ω**, *pass previous night*, of spending a vigil before a feast οἱ δὲ ἀπὸ Βασιλείδου καὶ τοῦ βαπτίσματος αὐτοῦ τὴν ἡμέραν ἑορτάζουσι ~οντες ἐν ἀναγνώσεσι Clem.*str*.1.21(p.90.22; M.8.888A).

προδιανύω, **1.** *accomplish previously* λήθην τῶν προδιηνυσμένων ποιούμενος Gr.Nyss.*hom.12 in Cant*.(M.44.1036C); **2.** *treat of previously*, Clem.*prot*.8(p.59.7; M.8.185C); id.*str*.5.1(p.328.21; M.9.13B); Meth.*symp*.2.5(p.21.1; M.18.53B); Gr.Nyss.*hom.5 in Cant*.(M.44.857D).

***προδιάπλασις, ἡ**, *previous formation*, of human nature of Christ before union of natures οὐ...διὰ τὸ ἀδύνατον, ἀλλὰ διὰ τὸ πρέπειν ψιλήν ποτε καὶ ἄνευ θεότητος εἶναι...τὴν ἀνθρωπότητα, τὴν π. ἐκβάλλομεν· τοῖς δὲ λέγουσιν, ἐξ ὑποστάσεων ἕπεται ἡ π., καὶ...ἄλλον καὶ ἄλλον τὸν Χριστὸν καὶ τὸν λόγον ἐπίστασθαι...τοῦ δὲ ταῦτα ἐννοεῖν ...οὐδὲν ἂν διαιρετικώτερον Leont.B.*arg.Sev*.(M.86.1944D); εἰ καὶ... Χριστὸν ἐκ δύο φύσεων λέγουσιν οἱ πατέρες, οὐκ ἀνάγκη π. ἐπὶ τοῦ ἀνθρώπου αὐτοῦ δοξάζειν, ἵνα μὴ εἰς τὸ Παύλου καὶ Νεστορίου ἐμπέσωσιν ἀσέβημα Pamph.H.*panopl*.5.2(p.613).

προδιαπλάσσω, *form in advance*, of human nature of Christ πότε γὰρ διῃρημένας τὰς φύσεις, καὶ καθ' ἑαυτὰς ὑποστάσας ἔγνως, ἵνα ταύτας συνάψας ἐξ ὑποστάσεων αὐτὸν εἶναι δογματίσῃς; οὔτε γὰρ πρὸ τῆς ἑνώσεως τοῦτο λέγειν θεμιτόν· εἴπερ μὴ προδιαπεπλάσθαι τὸν ἄνθρωπον, εἶθ' ὑποδεδυκέναι θεὸν λέγειν τολμᾷς Leont.B.*arg.Sev*.(M.86.1933A); *ib*.(1944C,D); οὐ προδιαπλασθέντι ἀνθρώπῳ ἡνώθη, καθάπερ ἡ Νεστορίου καὶ Θεοδώρου παραδέδωκεν ἀσέβεια Justn.*ep.Thdr.Mops*.(p.56.36; M.86.1065A); τὴν δὲ ἀνθρωπίνην...οὐσίαν οὐχ ὑποτίθεται ὁ τῆς εὐσεβείας λόγος προδιαπεπλάσθαι τῆς...ἑνώσεως Pamph.H.*panopl*.5.1(p.612); οὐχί τινος ἀνθρώπου ψιλοῦ...δίχα τῆς πρὸς τὸν λόγον ἑνώσεως προδιαπλασθέντος Max.*ep*.12(M.91.504A); ἡνίκα λέγετε, ἐκ...δύο προσώπων συνετέθη, δῆλον, ὅτι προδιεπλάσθη ἡ σὰρξ καὶ τότε ἐνῴκησεν εἰς αὐτὴν ὁ...λόγος Anast.S.*hod*.10(M.89.189B); γεννηθεὶς δὲ σωματικῶς...οὐ προδιαπλασθέντι ἀνθρώπῳ ἐνοικήσας, ὡς ἐν προφήτῃ Jo.D.*f.o*.3.12(M.94.1029B).

***προδιαστρέφω**, *pervert previously*, Bas.*hom.in Ps*.44(1.164C; M.29.401A).

***προδιαστροφή, ἡ**, *previous distortion*, Clem.*str*.2.20(p.173.5; M.8.1053C).

προδιατάσσομαι, *arrange in advance*, of divine ordering of universe in rel. to problem of prayer, Or.*or*.5(p.309.13; M.11.432A) cit. s. προγιγνώσκω; *ib*.(p.311.3; 433B); ἐν τῷ προδιατεταγμένῳ χρόνῳ ἔσται ἡ ῥίζα τοῦ Ἰεσσαί †Bas.*Is*.247(1.567D; M.30.553A).

προδιατίθημι, **1.** *take steps to compose* ἀμφιβόλα π. Soz.*h.e*.4.17.1 (M.67.1161A); **2.** *dispose of affairs beforehand, make testamentary dispositions in advance*, Ath.Scholast.*coll*.1.13(p.21).

***προδιατρανόω**, *make clear beforehand*, Cyr.*Zach*.4(3.745C).

προδιατυπ-όω, *prefigure* προδιατετυπωμένων τῶν προϊστορηθῆναι δεόντων Clem.*str*.4.1(p.249.9; M.8.1216C); ἡ κατὰ τὸν ὕπνον ἔκστασις ...~ουμένη τὴν ἐπὶ τῆς φιλοτησίας θέλξιν τοῦ ἀνδρός Meth.*symp*.2.2 (p.16.13; M.18.49A); Gr.Nyss.*hom.7 in Cant*.(M.44.929D); διὰ τοῦ τυμπάνου τὴν παρθενίαν ἔοικεν ὁ λόγος αἰνίττεσθαι ὑπὸ τῆς Μαρίας πρώτης κατορθωθεῖσαν δι' ἧς οἶμαι καὶ τὴν θεοτόκον ~οῦσθαι Μαρίαν id.*virg*.19(p.323.2; M.46.396B); εἰ δὲ βάθος προδιατυποῖ τὸ θεοτόκον σῶμα τῆς παρθένου id.*nativ*.(M.46.1136C); Epiph.*haer*.48.9(p.231.15; προετύπου M.41.868D); Chrys.*hom.66.2 in Mt*.(7.655B); id.*hom.53.1 in Jo*.(8.310D); τὴν οὖν ἕνωσιν τοῦ ἱερείου τὴν ἀδιαίρετον ἀναγκαίως ὁ νόμος εἰς Χριστὸν προετύπου ἐν ταύτῃ καὶ τὴν ἐκκλησίας ἕνωσιν ~ῶν ‡Chrys.*pasch*.1(8.252D); διὰ τῆς...τῶν κτηνογενῶν δερμάτων ἐνδύσεως καὶ ἡ ἔνσαρκος οἰκονομία τοῦ Χριστοῦ προδιετυποῦτο Anast.S.*hex*.12(M.89.1053A); Ἐλισσαῖος...ὡς παροῦσαν τὴν μήπω οὖσαν ~ῶν ‡Meth.*Sym.et Ann*.9(M.18.372A).

***προδιατύπωσις, ἡ**, **1.** *preliminary outline* ἀσκητικὴ π. Bas.*inst.ascet*.tit.(2.199A; M.31.620A); **2.** *prefiguration* μή τι οὖν ὁμολογήσουσιν ἄκοντες τὸν λόγον...κατὰ τὴν οἰκονομικὴν π. ἀναγεννηθῆναι τελείως; Clem.*paed*.1.6(p.105.12; M.8.280C); τὸ εὐαγγέλιον εἶναι τοῦ ἐξ ἀναστάσεως βίου π. Bas.*Spir*.35(3.29E; M.32.132A); Gr.Nyss.*res*.1 (M.46.600C); περὶ τὸν ἄνθρωπον προνοίας εἴδη τε καὶ μυστήρια... προοδοποίησίν τινα καὶ π. τῶν μελλόντων Max.*ambig*.(M.91.1256B); τῶν δύο τοῦ Χριστοῦ οὐσιῶν τὴν π. Anast.S.*serm.imag*.3(M.89.1160D).

προδίδ-ωμι, **1.** *give beforehand, pay in advance* ~οὺς ταῖς γαμουμέναις ὅσα ἐχρῆν τοῖς λαμβάνουσι πρὸς γάμου κοινωνίαν εἰσφέρειν Eus.*v.C*.1.43(p.28.7; M.20.957B); Chrys.*dimiss.Chan*.8(3.439D); Thdt.*h.rel*.17(3.1224); **2.** *abandon, forsake* προδεδομένοι [sc. Ἰουδαῖοι] κατὰ τὸν τῆς σωτηρίας λόγον Chrys.*hom.7.1 in Rom*.(9.483D); *ib.17.5* (629D); προδεδομένους ἀπὸ τῶν ἔργων χάριτι ἔσωσεν id.*hom.4.2 in Eph*.(11.28C); **3.** *betray* οἱ ~όντες αὐτὸν οἰκεῖοι ὑπῆρχον *M.Polyc*.6.2; of heretics compared with apostates οὐχ οἱ κλίναντες εἰς εἴδωλα μόνον κατεκρίθησαν...ἀλλὰ καὶ οἱ προδεδωκότες τὴν ἀλήθειαν Ath.*ep.Aeg.Lib*.21(M.25.588A); ref. unchastity λέχη προδοῦσαν Meth.*symp*.11.2(p.135.12; M.18.212B); of Judas, *Const.App*.5.14.3.

***προδιελέγχω,** *refute in advance,* Gr.Nyss.*Eun.*11(2 p.269.11; M. 45.877C).

προδιεξοδεύω, *treat of beforehand,* Eus.*h.e.*5.7.1(M.20.445C); *ib.* 10.1.2(841B); id.*d.e.*8 proem.(p.349.7; M.22.568B).

***προδιετία, ἡ,** *space of the preceding two years,* Gr.Mag.*dial.*(tr. Zach.)4.55(M.*PL.*77.418A, MS πρὸ τῆς διετίας).

***προδικαιόω,** *prejudge,* Or.*princ.*3.1.21(p.238.4; M.11.297A).

πρόδικος, *judged first,* hence *easily reversed, changeable* τοιοῦτος ἡμῶν ὁ βίος...καὶ εἴ τι τῶν λεχθέντων προδικώτερον Ast.Am.*hom.*2(M. 40.184B).

***προδιορατικός,** *endowed with prophetic insight,* Gr.Mag.*dial.* (tr.Zach.)2.20(M.*PL.*66.171B).

προδιορθ-όω, 1. *correct in advance* ἵνα μηδεὶς εἴπῃ, ἀκούων ὅτι ἐκδημοῦμεν ἀπὸ τοῦ κυρίου, τί ταῦτα λέγεις;...προδιώρθωσε τοῦτο εἰπών, διὰ πίστεως γὰρ περιπατοῦμεν Chrys.*hom.10.2 in 2Cor.*(10. 508C); med. ~οῦται πρότερον τὴν ἐπιχείρησιν Meth.*symp.*3.2(p.28.17; M.18.61C); Chrys.*bapt.*3(2.371E); id.*hom.12.1 in Mt.*(7.161A); **2.** *inform in advance,* Ammon.*Ac.*23:16(M.85.1592A).

προδιορισμός, ὁ, *previous limitation,* Chrys.*stat.*1.4(2.6E).

***προδιορύσσω,** *undermine before,* Chrys.*hom.5.3 in Rom.*(9. 465A).

***προδισχ-έω,** *assure beforehand* οὐδὲ ἀνέμενεν αὐτὸς [sc. risen Christ] φανῆναι αὐτοῖς, ἀλλὰ τοῖς εὐαγγελίοις ~εῖ Chrys.*fr.in Jer.* 25:11(M.64.953D).

προδοσία, ἡ, 1. *treachery,* ref. Judas τοῦτο ἄρα ἦν ὃ προεφήτευον οἱ μυριζόμενοι πόδες, τὴν Ἰούδα π. εἰς πάθος ὁδεύοντος κυρίου Clem.*paed.* 2.8(p.195.11; M.8.468B); Or.*Jo.*1.11(12; p.17.2; M.14.44D); Chrys. *hom.80.3 in Mt.*(7.769D); Isid.Pel.*epp.*1.56(M.78.220A); of treachery of Judas in Cainite speculation, Iren.*haer.*1.31.1(M.7.704B) = Thdt. *haer.*1.15(4.309); ref. Wednesday fast as commemoration of betrayal of Christ by counsel of Judas and chief priests, Petr.I Al. *ep.can.*15(M.18.508B); *Const.App.*5.13.20; **2.** *previous bestowal,* Thdr. Stud.*epp.*2.106(M.99.1365A).

προδότης, ὁ, *one who betrays, traitor*; **1.** in gen. π. γονέων Herm. *vis.*2.2.2; *Const.App.*2.43.4; **2.** of one who betrays Christianity; **a.** by sinful conduct πᾶς ὁ τῶν μαθητῶν Ἰησοῦ π., Ἰησοῦ π. εἶναι λελόγισται Or.*Jo.*1.11(12; p.17.6; M.14.44D); esp. actual apostasy ἀποστάται καὶ π. τῆς ἐκκλησίας Herm.*sim.*8.6.4; ἀποστάται καὶ βλάσφημοι εἰς τὸν κύριον καὶ π. τῶν δούλων τοῦ θεοῦ *ib.*9.19.1; κεῖται δὲ αὐτοῖς μετάνοια διὰ τὸ μὴ γενέσθαι αὐτοὺς βλασφήμους μηδὲ π. *ib.* 9.19.3; π. Χριστιανοῦ...καὶ ἐπίβουλος τῆς...θεοσεβείας Or.*Jo.*28.23 (18; p.418.11; 729A); **b.** by violating *disciplina arcani* χρὴ γὰρ ἐν τοῖς μυστικοῖς μὴ π. εἶναι, ἀλλ' ἀσφαλῆ *Const.App.*3.5.5; **3.** of Judas, Or.*Jo.*32.23(15; p.466.8; M.14.805C); *ib.*32.24(16; p.467.7; 808B); compared with *sacrificati* οὐχ οἱ κλίναντες εἰς εἴδωλα μόνον κατεκρίθησαν...ἀλλὰ καὶ οἱ προδεδωκότες τὴν ἀλήθειαν. Ἰούδας γοῦν οὐ θύσας ἀπεβλήθη τῆς ἀποστολικῆς τιμῆς, ἀλλὰ π. γενόμενος Ath.*ep. Aeg.Lib.*21(M.25.588A); *Const.App.*5.14.3; *ib.*6.12.1; Chrys.*hom. 71.2 in Jo.*(8.418D); *ib.*(419C).

προδότις, ἡ, *traitress*; of Eve, *Orac.Sib.*1.42.

***προδουλεύω,** *be formerly a servant,* Ant.Mon.*ep.Eust.*(M.89. 1425C).

***προδοχεύς, ὁ,** *one who receives on another's behalf,* ‡Meth.*Sym. et Ann.*14(M.18.381C).

***προδρομία, ἡ, 1.** *precursor, preliminary,* of Second Advent ἀντιχριστικὴ π. Thdr.Stud.*epp.*1.34(M.99.1025C); *ib.*1.36(1032C); **2.** *emulation,* Nil.*epp.*3.189(M.79.472D).

πρόδρομος, ὁ, A. *courier,* esp. of light troops used as scouts or escorts ἀπέστειλεν ἄνδρας δυνατοὺς εἰς πόλεμον...ἑξακοσίους καὶ π. ν' *Asen.*24(p.77.23); *ib.*26(p.80.11); τῶν τοῦ βασιλέως π., οὓς κούρσωρας εἰώθασιν οἱ Ῥωμαῖοι καλεῖν *V.Const.*36(p.566.7).

B. *precursor,* also as adj., *going before, preceding*; **1.** in gen. γέλωτα...πορνείας π. Clem.*paed.*3.4(p.253.17; παράδρομον M.8.597A); ἀνάγνωσιν νόμου τε καὶ προφητῶν π. τῆς χάριτος ‡Pion.*v.Polyc.*18; π. ... τῆς ἀφίξεως τὴν ἐπιστολήν Firm.*ep.*19(M.77.1496A); **2.** of precursors of Christ; **a.** OT prophets, etc. κυρίου ἥκοντος...μυρίοι σημάντορες,...ἑτοιμασταί, π. ἄνωθεν ἐκ καταβολῆς κόσμου Clem.*str.*6. 18(p.517.31; M.9.400A); of Three Holy Children χάριτος πρόδρομοι Thdt.*provid.*8(4.627); of prophets as Christ's precursors in Hades, Or.*engast.*8(p.291.29; M.12.1025A); **b.** of Jo. Bapt. π. Ἰωάννης καὶ ἡ φωνὴ π. τοῦ λόγου Clem.*prot.*1(p.9.19; M.8.65A); id.*str.*6.18(p.517.34; M.9.400B); ἡ Ἰωάννου μαρτυρία π. ἑκάστη τῶν τοῦ Χριστοῦ ἐπινοιῶν Or.*Jo.*2.37(30; p.97.12; M.14.184A); Meth.*symp.*11.2(p.135.18; M.18. 212B); λόγου καὶ φωτὸς π. Gr.Naz.*or.*6.7(M.35.729B); Ζαχαρίας, ὁ πατὴρ τοῦ π. id.*carm.*1.2.3.24(M.37.634A); Chrys.*hom.14.1 in Mt.*(7. 178B); as Christ's precursor in Hades, Cyr.*Lc.*7:17(M.72.612D); Ἠσαΐας, τὸν π. ἡμῖν καὶ προάγγελον εἰσφέρων id.*Jo.*1.10(4.108D); Cosm.Ind.*top.*5(M.88.212B); Sophr.H.*mir.Cyr.et Jo.*8(M.87.3437A); Ἰουνίου κδ' ἡ γέννησις τοῦ π. Jo.Nic.*nativ.*(M.96.1445B); Ἰωάννου τοῦ ἐνδόξου προφήτου, π. καὶ βαπτιστοῦ *Lit.Jac.*(p.188.20); **c.** of Cross σὺ εἶ ἐκεῖνος οὗ π. ἔτυχεν ὁ σταυρός, ὁ ἄνω μόνος ἐκ μόνου πατρός *A.Xanthipp.*15(p.69.5); **d.** of S. John Evangelist as pioneer of doctrine of Logos ὁ τοῦ λόγου π. Gr.Naz.*or.*28.20(p.52.9; M.36.53A); Max.*ambig.*(M.91.1252C); **e.** of precursors of Second Advent π. τινες ἀναφαίνονται ψευδόχριστοι καὶ ψευδοπροφῆται Cyr.ap.*cat.Lc.*21:5 (p.150.20) for προδραμοῦνται, id.*Lc.*21:5(M.72.896C); of Enoch and Elijah, Oecum.*Apoc.*11:3(p.128); **3.** of heresies and heretics as precursors of antichrist or of the 'man of lawlessness', Alex.Al.*ep. encycl.*1(p.7.1; M.18.572B); Ἀρειανὴν αἵρεσιν...τοῦ ἀντιχρίστου π. Ath.*apol.sec.*90(p.168.9; M.25.409D); id.*Ar.*1.1(M.26.13A); Cyr.*hom. pasch.*20(5^2.259B); **4.** of Christ as man's precursor into heaven, Cyr. *hom.pasch.*16(5^2.222A); π. ὑπὲρ ἡμῶν εἰς οὐρανοὺς ἀναβάς id.*Ps.*24:1 (M.69.845D); ἐν ᾧ μέλλοντι κόσμῳ εἰσῆλθεν πρῶτος π. ὑπὲρ ἡμῶν Χριστός Cosm.Ind.*top.*2(M.88.92A); †Anast.S.*relat.*47(*OC* 3 p.68).

C. *forecourt* of house, *Asen.*19(p.69.2,4).

***προδροσίζω,** *dampen in advance* ἐὰν μὴ προδροσίσωμεν ἐν δάκρυσιν τὴν φλόγα [i.e. of Gehenna] Ephr.3.85D.

***προδύναμαι,** *be able to perform beforehand* or *from of old,* of Logos in Creation πάντα μὲν προειδὼς καὶ προδυνάμενος Didym.*Trin.* 3.3(M.39.809C).

***προεγγυμνάζω,** *practise beforehand,* Or.*comm.in Mt.*10.9(p.11.6; M.13.857A).

προεγείρω, med., *rise* from table *before* end of meal, Thdr.Stud. *poen.*2.36(M.99.1753B).

προέγκειμαι, *be paramount,* Cyr.*ador.*7(1.244A); Marc.Er.*opusc.*1. 182(M.65.928B).

***προεγκρατεύομαι,** *practise self-restraint early,* Bas.*hom.*1.10 (2.9D; M.31.181C).

προεδρεύ-ω, *preside* [f.l. for προσε-, Cyr.*hom.pasch.*19(5^2.249B)]; **1.** of church officials in gen., ref. Mt.18:17 εἰπὲ τῇ ἐκκλησίᾳ, τουτέστι τοῖς ~ουσιν Chrys.*hom.60.2 in Mt.*(7.607D); **2.** *be a bishop,* Gr. Naz.*or.*43.26(M.36.532B); *ib.*43.37(545C); Bas.Sel.*v.Thecl.*2.15(M.85. 592B); Evagr.*h.e.*3.30(p.126.23; M.86.2657B); Jo.Mosch.*prat.*197(M. 87.3084B); **3.** *take the lead, be pre-eminent* πόλις...~ουσα δὲ καὶ προκαθεζομένη πάσης Ἰσαυρίδος πόλεως Bas.Sel.*v.Thecl.*1(M.85. 556C).

προεδρία, ἡ, A. *precedence, privileged position, high rank*; **1.** of privilege of birth τὴν ἀπὸ τῆς φύσεως...π. χαρισθεῖσαν, τὴν τῶν πρωτοτόκων Chrys.*hom.20.4 in Gen.*(4.178A); **2.** of high rank; in gen., Isid.Pel.*epp.*5.131(M.78.1401C); †Nil.*vit.*4(M.79.1144C); in Jewish hierarchy ἱερωσύνη τε καὶ διδασκάλων π. Eus.*d.e.*6.13(p.263.7; M.22. 432D); in Church, Gr.Naz.*or.*26.15(M.35.1248B); ὡς ὄφελόν γε μηδὲ ἦν π., μηδέ τις τόπου προτίμησις *ib.*(1248C); Thdt.*1Tim.*3:6(3.655); ref. righteous in heaven τὴν π. ἕξεις τὴν μετὰ τῶν ἀρνῶν Chrys.*hom. 18.7 in Rom.*(9.641B); ref. Christ's high priesthood πᾶσαν ὑπερβαλλούσῃ...τὴν ἐν ἀνθρώποις π. Eus.*h.e.*1.3.2(M.20.69A); ref. preeminence in Godhead οὐ σωματικῶς τοῦ δεξιοῦ λαμβανομένου...ἀλλ' ἐκ τῶν τιμίων τῆς π. ὀνομάτων τὸ μεγαλοπρεπὲς τῆς περὶ τὸν υἱὸν τιμῆς παριστῶντος τοῦ λόγου...ὁ γὰρ τῷ πατρὶ τὴν ἄνω χώραν εἰς π. ἀποδιδούς, τὸν δὲ μονογενῆ υἱὸν ὑποκαθῆσθαι λέγων, πάντα ἀκολουθοῦντα ἕξει τὰ σωματικὰ συμπτώματα τῷ ἑαυτοῦ ἀναπλασμῷ Bas. *Spir.*15(3.11D,12B; M.32.89C,92C).

B. *presidency,* in Church; **1.** of presbyter's office τῆς π. ἀξιωθείς, καὶ ἐγκαταλεγεὶς τῷ πρεσβυτερίῳ †Bas.*Is.*103(1.450D; M.30.285A); **2.** of bishop's office π. καὶ ἐπισκοπή *V.Aberc.*1(p.3.1); Bas.*ep.*92.2(3. 184D; M.32.480B); *ib.*188 *can.*1(269A; M.665A); Gr.Naz.*or.*43.26(M. 36.532C); οὐκ ἀπείληφε τὴν π. καὶ τὴν εἴσοδυσιν τῆς ἐκκλησίας Epiph. *haer.*42.1(p.95.4; M.41.696D); ἀρχιερατικῆς π. ἀξιωθῆναι Thdt.*h.rel.*3 (3.1139); Gel.Cyz.*h.e.*2.34.1(M.85.1340A); Jo.Mosch.*prat.*197(M.87. 3084B); hence **3.** synon. with καθέδρα, *see* τῆς ἐκκλησίας τῆς Ἀλεξανδρείας τὴν π. Pall.*v.Chrys.*2(p.8.23; M.47.8); τὴν π. ἔλαβεν Ἡρακλείας *ib.*8(p.50.5; M.47.29); Thdt.*h.e.*1.7.10(3.756); *ib.*3.19.1(3.935); **4.** of apostleship, Chrys.*hom.3.4 in Col.*(11.349D).

C. *front seat, place of honour*; in church, *Const.App.*2.58.4.

πρόεδρος, ὁ, *president, leading official, leader*; **1.** of leading officials in Church; **a.** of clergy in gen. τὸ 'πώλησόν σου τὰ ὑπάρχοντα, καὶ δὸς πτωχοῖς'...πρὸς τοὺς τῆς ἐκκλησίας π. ... καιρὸν ἂν ἔχοι λέγεσθαι Chrys.*hom.85.4 in Mt.*(7.810A); *ib.*60.2(608A); id.*hom.4.5 in Heb.*(12.47D); **b.** of bishops (from 5th cent. chiefly of patriarchs) ἀποστόλων...ἐκ δὲ τῆς ἐκείνων διαδοχῆς...πρόεδροι τῆς...ἐκκλησίας Eus.*Is.*2:27(M.24.100C); τὸ πρῶτον τῶν π. τάγμα, καὶ τὸ δεύτερον τῶν πρεσβυτέρων *ib.*19:18(232C); id.*d.e.*2.3(p.77.28; M.22.140B); θρόνοις

...τοῖς ἀνωτάτω εἰς τὴν τῶν π. τιμήν id.*h.e.*10.4.44(M.20.865C); id. *v.C.*2.2(p.41.1; M.20.980C); Gr.Naz.*carm.*2.1.11.1586(M.37.1139A); Gr.Nyss.*paup.*(M.46.453A); Ast.Am.*hom.*8(M.40.264A); π. δήμου [Alexandria] Synes.*ep.*12(M.66.1349A); τῆς πόλεως π. [Jerusalem] Thdt.*h.e.*1.18.4(3.794); id.*ep.*11(4.1189) [Alexandria]; Eulog.*fr.Trin.*(M.86.2944A) [CP]; Ἀντιοχείας π. Evagr.*h.e.*1.10(p.17.25; M.86.2445B); τῆς Ἀντιοχέων π. Tim.CP *haer.*(M.86.48A); τῶν ἀνατολικῶν π. Sophr.H.*ep.syn.*(M.87.3188C); *ib.*(3188D) [CP]; Niceph.Ur.*v.Sym.* 190(M.86.3160C) [CP]; τῷ Ῥωμαίων προέδρῳ Thdr.Stud.*epp.*1.53(M.99.1105C); **2.** *leading person, chief*; **a.** of leading bishops at CNic. (325) παρεδίδου [sc. Const.] τὸν λόγον τοῖς τῆς συνόδου π. Eus.*v.C.*3.13(p.83.14; M.20.1069B); **b.** of Arius as leader of heresy, Const.ap. Gel.Cyz.*h.e.*3.19.5(M.85.1345B); **c.** of S. Peter τῆς ἐκκλησίας ἐπάξιον π. Jo.D.*hom.*1.6(M.96.553D); **d.** of Rome τὴν ἑσπέραν πᾶσαν δέουσα τῷ σωτηρίῳ λόγῳ, καθὼς δίκαιον τὴν π. τῶν ὅλων Gr.Naz.*carm.*2.1.11.571(M.37.1068A).

***προεικονίζ-ω**, *represent in advance, foreshadow* Μωϋσῆς σαφῶς ταύτην ∼ει διὰ τῆς...πέτρας ‡Anast.S.*Jud.disp.*3(M.89.1244C); ἡ τράπεζα [sc. of Melchizedek] ταύτην τὴν μυστικὴν ∼ε τράπεζαν Jo.D.*f.o.*4.13(M.94.1149C); πέμπτος τρόπος εἰκόνος λέγεται, ὁ ∼ων καὶ προδιαγράφων τὰ μέλλοντα, ὡς ἡ βάτος...τὴν παρθένον id.*imag.*3.22(M.94.1341C).

***προεικόνισμα, τό**, *foreshadowing*; of prayer as a foretaste of blessedness of kingdom of heaven, †Jo.D.*B.J.*20(M.96.1041A).

πρόειμι, (εἶμι *ibo*), *go forward, advance, proceed*; theol.; **1.** of Logos or Son πατέρα θεόν, ἐξ οὗ προϊών, εἰκότως τοῦ...πατρὸς ἑρμηνεὺς καὶ ἄγγελος λέγεται Ath.*gent.*45(M.25.89A); acc. Marcellus λόγον...ποτὲ μὲν ἡσυχάζοντα, ποτὲ δὲ σημαντικῶς ἐνεργοῦντα, μόνῃ τε ἐνεργείᾳ προϊόντα τοῦ πατρός Eus.*Marcell.*2.1(p.32.1; M.24.777A); ποτὲ μὲν ἔνδον εἶναι ἐν τῷ θεῷ...ποτὲ δὲ προϊέναι τοῦ θεοῦ id.*e.th.*2.8(p.107.9; M.24.913C); οὐ κατὰ τὸν προφορικὸν ἀνθρώπων λόγον...οἷα δὲ μονογενὴς...υἱὸς ζῶν καὶ ὑφεστὼς πρόεισιν μὲν τῆς πατρικῆς θεότητος *ib.*2.17(p.121.12; 940A); οὐκ ἐν χρόνῳ πρόεισι τὸ προϊὸν ἐκ θεοῦ Didym.(‡Bas.)*Eun.*5(1.307B; M.29.737A); **2.** of H. Ghost τὸ πνεῦμα προϊὸν ἐκ τοῦ πατρός Gr.Naz.*or.*20.11(M.35.1077C); τοῦ...ἀγεννήτως προελθόντος ἢ προιόντος [sc. ὄνομα], τὸ πνεῦμα τὸ ἅγιον *ib.*30.19(p.138.11; M.36.128C); *ib.*39.12(348B) cit. s. ἐκπορευτῶς; εἰ γὰρ καὶ πρόεισιν ἐκ πατρὸς τὸ πνεῦμα, ἀλλ' ἔρχεται δι' υἱοῦ, καὶ ἴδιόν ἐστιν αὐτοῦ Cyr.*Jo.*9.1(4.824B).

πρόειμι, (εἰμί *sum*), *be before, pre-exist*; **1.** of Father, Geo.Pis.*carm.*107.33(14 p.68); **2.** ref. work of Logos in Creation δυνατὸν γὰρ καὶ τὸν ὄντα ποιεῖν καὶ τὰ μὴ ὄντα καὶ τὰ ὄντα καὶ τὰ προόντα Ath.*Ar.*1.24(M.26.61A); **3.** of Son τοῦ ἐν ἀρχῇ ὄντος καὶ π. λόγου· ἐπεφάνη δὲ ἔναρχος ὁ προὼν σωτήρ Clem.*prot.*1(p.7.28; M.8.61C); τὸ δὲ 'ἐγὼ σήμερον γεγέννηκά σε' ὅτι προόντα ἤδη πρὸ τῶν αἰώνων Meth.*symp.*8.9(p.91.12; M.18.152B); Eus.*d.e.*7.3(p.344.13; M.22.561A); id.*h.e.*1.2.8(M.20.57B); id.*l.C.*1(p.198.23; M.20.1324A); οὐδὲ γὰρ ζητεῖν οὐδ' ἀμφιβάλλειν...αὐτοῖς [sc. Sabellians] εἰ ἦν καὶ προῆν ὁ...υἱὸς...ὁ τῆς ἐκκλησίας ἐπιτρέποι ἂν θεσμός id.*Marcell.*1.1(p.4.29; M.24.720A); in Marcellus' teaching τοῦ προόντος ἐν θεῷ λόγου ἀφοριζομένου μὲν τοῦ σώματος *ib.*(p.6.16; προσόντος 724A); but πρὶν ἢ γενέσθαι ἐκ γυναικός, υἱὸν ὄντα καὶ προόντα ἀπέστειλεν ὁ πατήρ *ib.*(p.7.9; 724C); Σαβέλλιος ...μὴ καὶ υἱὸν...ζῶντα καὶ ὑφεστῶτα ὄντα τε καὶ προόντα τῆς σαρκὸς ὡμολόγει id.*e.th.*1.16(p.77.2; M.24.857C); *ib.*1.20(p.90.17; cod. περιόντος M.24.881C); ἐτόλμησαν [sc. heretics]...εἰπεῖν, ὅτι οὐχ ὁ προὼν λόγος, οὗτος ἐνηνθρώπησεν· ἀλλὰ ἄνθρωπός τις προκόψας, οὗτος ἐστεφανώθη Cyr.H.*catech.*12.3; τὸν αὐτὸν ἀεὶ μένοντα ἄνθρωπον, καὶ προόντα θεόν ‡Chrys.*hom.*9(13.235B); ref. Inc. in terms of πνεῦμα: τὸ πνεῦμα τὸ ἅγιον τὸ προόν, τὸ κτίσαν πᾶσαν τὴν κτίσιν, κατῴκισεν ὁ θεὸς εἰς σάρκα ἣν ἐβούλετο Herm.*sim.*5.6.5; **4.** denied of matter, Meth.*arbitr.*10(p.170.13; M.18.257B); and men, Clem.*ecl.*17(p.141.19; M.9.705C); but ἕκαστον...τῶν νοερῶν τε καὶ λογικῶν ἀγγέλων τε καὶ ἀνθρώπων...μοῖρα...ἐστι θεοῦ, διὰ τὸν αὐτοῦ προόντα ἐν τῷ θεῷ... λόγον Max.*ambig.*(M.91.1080B); **5.** Gnost., of primal aeon, Iren. *haer.*1.1.1(M.7.445A); Ἄνθρωπον...ὅτι ἦν ἀντίτυπος τοῦ προόντος Ἀγεννήτου Val.Gn.ap.Epiph.*haer.*31.5(p.391.7; M.41.481C); of Father ἐγὼ υἱὸς ἀπὸ πατρός, πατρὸς προόντος, υἱὸς δὲ ἐν τῷ παρόντι Heracleon ap.Epiph.*haer.*36.3(p.46.16; M.41.636B); of soul (Naassene) ἀποροῦσιν...πότερόν ποτε ἐκ τοῦ προόντος ἐστὶν ἢ ἐκ τοῦ αὐτογενοῦς ἢ ἐκ τοῦ ἐκκεχυμένου χάους Hipp.*haer.*5.7(p.81.3; M.16.3130B); in orthodox complaint against Ptolemaeans ὡς γὰρ παρόντες καὶ τῶν ἐπουρανίων τὰς φύσεις θεασάμενοι καὶ ὡς αὐτοῦ προόντες τοῦ...Βυθοῦ...ἐπαγγέλλεσθε τὴν εἴδησιν ἡμῖν ὑποδεικνύναι Epiph.*haer.*33.8(p.458.23; M.41.569B).

***προεισαγωγή, ἡ**, *introduction* π. τις ἐστὶ τῆς εἰς ἀρετὴν τελειότητος ἡ περιτομή [sc. of Abraham] Cyr.*Jo.*4.7(4.433A); of Solomon's writings as introduction to prophetic books, Dion.Ar.*d.n.*4.12(M.3.709B); π. καλεῖ τῆς θείας γραφῆς τὰ Σολομῶντος Max.*schol.d.n.*4.12(M.4.265A).

***προεισβαίνω**, *enter before*, Cyr.*Nest.*2.2(p.37.9; 6^{1}.37C); id.*Juln.*3(6^{2}.108E,109C).

***προεισβολή, ἡ**, **1.** *entrance, approach*; of outer part of tabernacle as approach to Holy of Holies, Cyr.*ador.*10(1.333E); id.*hom. pasch.*16(5^{2}.216D); **2.** met.; of chastity in rel. to spiritual glory, id.*ador.*7(1.240B); of envy in rel. to murder, id.*glaph.Gen.*1(1.17A); of types in rel. to realities, *ib.*5(140C); purgation in rel. to faith, id. *Is.*1.2(2.37A); faith in rel. to life in Christ, id.*Os.*55(3.85B); law in rel. to gospel, id.*Jo.*12(4.1070D); John's baptism in rel. to Christian faith, id.*hom.pasch.*30(5^{2}.344D); of Nativity as beginning of Christ's assimilation to man in Inc., id.*Chr.un.*(5^{1}.721B).

***προεισδέχομαι**, *receive beforehand*, Cyr.*Ps.*7:15(M.69.756A); id. *apol.Thdt.*1(6^{1}.206E).

προεισελαύνω, *enter in before, be introduced first* τὸ μὴ ἐν ἀρχαῖς... δεδόσθαι τὴν χάριν, τὸ δὲ προεισελάσαι...τὴν διὰ Μώσεως ἐντολήν Cyr. *hom.pasch.*29(5^{2}.339C).

***προεισθέω**, *precede*, Cyr.*hom.pasch.*16(5^{2}.216B).

***προεισκαλέω**, *call in first*, Cyr.*Am.*4(3.349A); id.*Juln.*3(6^{2}.105C, 109B).

***προεισκρίν-ω**, *introduce before* ὁπηνίκα ἂν εὐαγγελίζωνται οἱ ἄγγελοι τὰς στείρας, οἷον ∼ουσι τῆς συλλήψεως τὰς ψυχάς Clem.*ecl.*50(p.151.6; M.9.721A); Cyr.*hom.pasch.*16(5^{2}.214C,215A).

***προεισοδικόν, τό**, *vestibule*, Pall.*h.Laus.*35(p.102.1; M.34.1113C).

προεισόδιος, **1.** *preparatory, introductory*, ref. feast of Nativity of Jo. Bapt. π. τὰ γενέσια τῶν Χριστοῦ γενεθλίων Thdr.Stud.*or.*8.10(M.99.757B); π. τῆς τοῦ ἀντιχριστοῦ παρουσίας id.*epp.*2.12(M.99.1153A); **2.** as subst., *vestibule*, Gr.Nyss.*hom.3 in Eccl.*(M.44.656B).

***προεισοικίζομαι**, *introduce into one's house before, establish beforehand*; **1.** lit. Ἰακὼβ...τὴν Λείαν προεισοικισάμενος Cyr.*glaph. Gen.*6(1.180A); **2.** met. μαθημάτων εἰς νοῦν...προεισοικίσασθαι τὰ στοιχεῖα id.*hom.pasch.*16(5^{2}.215A); id.*Juln.*1(6^{2}.19B); *ib.*5(172C).

***προεισπνέω**, *inhale first*, Geo.Pis.*hex.*900(M.92.1503A).

***προειστρέχ-ω**, *enter into before, precede*, Cyr.*ador.*1(1.29C); *ib.*13(457C); οὐκ ἂν ἑτέρως νοοῖτο θεοτόκος, εἰ μὴ κατὰ τοῦτον αὐτὸν τὸν τρόπον, ὥστε ∼ει πάντως ἡ τῆς ἐνανθρωπήσεως ὁμολογία id.*hom.div.*15.3(p.14.27; M.77.1095B).

προεισφέρω, **1.** *offer in advance* μηδὲν γὰρ προεισενεγκοῦσι παρέχω ὑμῖν εὐεργεσίαν σωτήριον ‡Proc.G.*Pr.*4:2(M.87.1253B); Chrysipp. *enc.in Thdr.*(p.51.5); **2.** *introduce first* εὐαγγελιστὴς σάρκα γεγονότα προεισενεγκὼν τὸν λόγον Cyr.*Chr.un.*(5^{1}.760A).

***προεισφρέω**, *make one's way into*, Cyr.*glaph.Gen.*7(1.223E).

***προεκδειματόω**, *terrify first*, Cyr.*Mich.*2(3.444D).

***προεκδημέω**, *predecease*, Gr.Naz.*or.*18.3(M.35.988C); Niceph.Ur. *v.Sym.*111(M.86.3089C); †Jo.D.*B.J.*22(M.96.1061C).

προεκδρομή, ἡ, v. προσεκδρομή.

***προεκδύω**, *strip off in advance*, Jo.D.*hom.*12(M.96.801D).

***προεκθερίζω**, *cut off in advance*, Gr.Nyss.*v.Ephr.*(M.46.828A); Philost.*h.e.*12.2(M.65.608A).

***προεκθλίβω**, *crush out of existence beforehand*, Cyr.*hom.pasch.*17(5^{2}.225A).

***προεκθνήσκω**, *be dead to in advance* προεκτεθνεῶτας τῷ κόσμῳ Cyr.*ador.*16(1.561C).

προεκθρώσκω, **1.** *be born first*, Cyr.*glaph.Gen.*6(1.201A); **2.** *come to pass*, Synes.*insomn.*17(p.182.14; M.66.1313D).

***προεκκαλύπτω**, *reveal beforehand*, Cyr.*Is.*4.1(2.568B); Chrysipp. *enc.in Thdr.*(p.65.3); id.*enc.in BMV* 2(p.339.9).

***προεκκύπτ-ω**, *issue forth from*, in similes of Son's generation τῷ ἐκ φωτὸς ἀπαυγάσματι, τὸ ἐξ οὗπερ ἐξηστράφθη φῶς· ἐν γὰρ τοῖς τοιούτοις χωρίζεσθαι μέν πως ἐπινοίᾳ δοκεῖ τὸ γεννῶν τοῦ γεννωμένου καὶ ∼οντος ἀμερίστως Cyr.*Jo.*1.5(4.48C); ὥσπερ ἡ ἐξ ἀνθέων εὐωδία... οὐσιωδῶς ∼ουσα...οὕτω καὶ ὁ υἱὸς ὀσμή τις ὑπάρχων τῆς πατρῴας οὐσίας id.*thes.*32(5^{1}.274D).

***προεκπηδητέον**, *one must rush forward*, Clem.*paed.*2.7(p.191.1; M.8.460A).

προεκτείνω, *draw out, expand previously*, Gr.Nyss.*Eun.*5(2 p.105.9; M.45.684D); *ib.*(p.105.27; 685A); *ib.*8(2 p.188.24; 784A); *ib.*11(2 p.265.19; 873C).

***προεκτικός**, *holding out, offering* ἀγαθοῦ δὲ ὄντος τοῦ κόσμου τὴν τῶν ἀγαθῶν π. τε καὶ ποιητικὴν δύναμιν αἰτίαν εἶναι Gr.Nyss.*or.catech.*5(p.21.12, v.l. ὀρεκτήν M.45.21A).

***προεκτρίβω**, *rub off early*, Cyr.*ador.*14(1.480C).

προεκτυπόω, *prefigure*, Meth.*symp.*11.2(p.134.5; M.18.209C).

***προεκτύπωμα, τό**, *prefiguration*, Germ.CP *or.*8(M.98.364C).

***προεκφαίνομαι,** *appear before,* Gr.Nyss.*hex*.9(M.44.72C).
***προέκφημι,** *mention before,* Mod.*dorm*.9(M.86.3300A).
***προεκφύω,** *be produced, be born, Hom.Clem*.5.24.
προεκφωνέω, *prophesy,* Gr.Nyss.*anim.et res*.(M.46.132A).
προελέγχω, *refute beforehand,* Epiph.*haer*.24.1(p.257.6; M.41. 309A).
προέλευσις, ἡ, *coming forth*; **1.** in gen.; of setting out on a journey, Const.ap.Gel.Cyz.*h.e*.3.18.4; of a monk going out in public πᾶσαν π. παραιτοῦ Bas.*renunt*.5(2.206C; M.31.636C); **2.** *way* or *manner of coming out* ὁρᾶτε τὴν π. μου τί ἐνδύομαι *T.Job* 39(p.128.12); **3.** *procession* τῆς π. καὶ τῆς ἐν τῷ θείῳ θυσιαστηρίῳ θείας εἰσόδου †Gregent.*leg.Hom*.proem.(M.86.569B); *Lit.Jac*.(p.160.27); *ib*.(p.164. 21); **4.** *appearance in order, sequence* δύο...γενικαὶ ἔστωσαν προφητεῖαι, ἡ μὲν ἀρσενική...ἡ δὲ δευτέρα θῆλυς οὖσα πρώτη ὡρίσθη ἔρχεσθαι ἐν τῇ τῶν συζυγιῶν π. *Hom.Clem*.3.22; **5.** *coming forth,* of Son's generation ἐγεννήθη τοίνυν ἀμερίστῳ π. Const.ap.Gel.Cyz.*h.e*.suppl.1 (p.193.10); of his coming forth in the two 'generations', eternal and human, Leont.H.*Nest*.4.3(M.86.1657D); of Inc. π. σαρκικῇ ἐκ τῆς... παρθένου τεχθῆναι *ib*.4.9(1669B); τὴν θεανδρικὴν...ἐκ τῆς...Μαρίας π. ‡Caes.Naz.*dial*.20(M.38.876); **6.** *promotion* ἡ εἰς τὴν προεδρίαν π. Jo. Mosch.*prat*.197(M.87.3084B); **7.** *coming in advance* π. ἣν προελήλυθεν ...Χριστοῦ...᾿Ιωάννης ὁ βαπτιστής Just.*dial*.50.2(M.6.585C); v. προσέλευσις.
προελεχθῇ, f.l. for προλεχθῇ, Didym.*Ps*.4:1(M.39.1165B) v. προλέγω.
προεμβάλλ-ω, 1. *project, hurl into* σφᾶς αὐτοὺς...παρεμβεβληκότες ἀφύκτῳ δίκῃ Cyr.*hom.pasch*.24(5^2.289E); **2.** *interpose,* ref. mediation between divine and human εἰκότως ὁ...θεὸς...μέσην τινὰ ~ει τὴν τοῦ μονογενοῦς αὐτοῦ λόγου θείαν καὶ παναλκῆ δύναμιν Eus.*l.C*.11(p.227. 16; παρεμ- M.20.1381B), but cf.id.*d.e*.4.6(p.159.1; M.22.265A).
προεμμελετάω, *occupy oneself with in advance,* c. dat., Eus.*l.C*. 6(p.209.15; M.20.1345C); id.*d.e*.4.15(p.176.14; M.22.293B).
***προεμπορεύομαι,** *acquire in advance,* Gr.Nyss.*hom.opif*.22.8(M. 44.209A).
προεμφαίνω, *show forth in advance*; of prophets, Chrys.*hom.85.3 in Mt*.(7.808A).
***προεμφράσσω,** *stop up beforehand,* Clem.*paed*.2.6(p.188.1; M.8. 453A).
***προεναλείφω,** *anoint beforehand, Hom.Clem*.20.16.
***προεναπόκειμαι,** *be previously stored up,* Bas.*hom*.12.9(2.105E; M. 31.405B).
προενάρχομαι, *begin before,* Chrys.*hom.16.3 in 2Cor*.(10.556B); *cat.2Cor*.8:6(p.401.17).
***προενατενίζ-ω,** *gaze upon, fix attention on beforehand,* Or. *comm.in Rom*.1:1(*JTS* 13 p.211); †Bas.*Is*.208(2.534E; M.30.477A); τῇ ὀξυωπίᾳ τῆς διανοίας ~ειν τῷ μέλλοντι *ib*.254(573E; M.568A).
***προεναυλίζομαι,** *inhabit previously,* Cyr.*ador*.10(1.360B).
προένειμι, *exist in beforehand* προένεστι τὰ τῶν αἰτιατῶν τοῖς αἰτίοις Dion.Ar.*d.n*.2.8(M.3.645D); θεῷ...ἐν ᾧ ὁ τοῦ εἶναι αὐτοῦ λόγος προένεστι, ὡς ἀρχὴ καὶ αἰτία Max.*ambig*.(M.91.1080C); οὐδὲν...ἔστι τῶν ὄντων οὗ μὴ παρὰ τῷ θεῷ πάντως ὁ λόγος προένεστιν *ib*.(1329B).
***προένεξις, ἡ,** *previous implication,* Germ.CP *vit.term*.17(M.98. 121A).
***προενηχ-έω,** *instruct in advance* ~οῦντος αὐτοῖς [sc. prophets] τοῦ...πνεύματος...γνῶσιν Cyr.*Abac*.59(3.574A).
προενθύμησις, ἡ, *previous thought,* Isid.Pel.*epp*.3.66(M.78.773C).
***προενθυμητέον,** *one must consider beforehand, Symb.Ant*.(345)3 ap.Ath.*syn*.26(p.252.14; M.26.729A).
***προενόω,** *unite with in advance,* Bas.*reg.fus*.7.1(2.346A; M.31. 929A); τῷ σώματι π. ὁ λόγος Leont.H.*Nest*.2.20(M.86.1580D).
***προενριζόω,** *root in first* εἴδησιν π. αὐτοῖς Cyr.*ador*.7(1.235C).
***προεντέλλομαι,** *enjoin before,* Cyr.*ador*.7(1.234E).
προεντίθημι, *set within beforehand* τῇ φύσει προενθεὶς...τὴν γνῶσιν Tit.Bost.*Man*.2.2(M.18.1133C); *ib*.2.3(1140A); τὴν προεντεθεῖσαν τῷ σώματι...βλάβην Gr.Nyss.*or.catech*.37(p.142.12; M.45.93B); Epiph. *haer*.66.10(M.42.44C; corr. προεκέκτητο p. 31.2).
***προεντρυφάω,** *revel in before,* Cyr.*Jo*.6.1(4.625C).
***προεντύνω,** *raise forth,* Paul.Sil.*ambo*.112(M.86.2256A).
προεντυπόω, *impress on beforehand,* Gr.Nyss.*Eun*.8(2 p.185.6; M.45.777D).
***προεξαπατάω,** *deceive thoroughly beforehand,* Or.*Cels*.1.30(p.82. 5; M.11.717B).
***προεξαρπάζ-ω,** *snatch away* from *beforehand* ὕβρεως ἑαυτὴν ~ει Chrys.*pan.Pelag.Ant*.1.1(2.585C); id.*hom.9.3 in 2Cor*.(10.503A); ‡Chrys.*hom*.8.6(12.379D).
***προεξεικονίζω, 1.** *depict previously,* Thdr.Stud.*epp*.2.199(M.99. 1609B); **2.** *prefigure* ὁμοίωμα...τοῦ υἱοῦ τοῦ θεοῦ ἐν τῷ καμίνῳ τῶν παίδων προεξεικονίσθη Ephr.Ant.*fr*.(M.86.2108B); of rock of Ex.17:6 prefiguring BMV, ‡Meth.*Sym.et Ann*.8(M.18.369B).
***προεξευμαρίζω, 1.** *make easy beforehand* πορείαν...προεξευμαρίσαντος τοῦ θεοῦ Eus.*d.e*.3.7(p.146.8; M.22.245B); of Christ's teaching facilitating Roman pacification of world, id.*l.C*.16(p.250.6; M.20. 1424C); Cyr.*Jo*.2.5(4.194E); id.*Is*.5.4(2.818E); **2.** *smooth away* π. φόβον id.*Jo*.10.2(4.914A).
***προεξευμενίζομαι,** *propitiate beforehand,* Isid.Pel.*epp*.4.184(M. 78.1276B).
προεξευρίσκω, *find out, devise beforehand* Ἄρειος...πάθος καὶ τομὴν καὶ ῥεῦσιν προεξεῦρεν ‡Ath.*Apoll*.1.21(M.26.1129B); Aen.*dial*.(M.85. 972A); Cyr.*Juln*.2(6^2.54B).
***προεξήγημα, τό,** *preliminary observation,* Meth.*symp*.10.1(p.121. 16; M.18.192C).
***προεξήγησις, ἡ,** *preliminary observation,* Anast.S.*hod*.21(M.89. 281D).
***προεξομολογ-έομαι,** *confess beforehand* κατὰ κυριακὴν...συναχθέντες...εὐχαριστήσατε ~ησάμενοι τὰ παραπτώματα ὑμῶν *Did*.14.1; †Jo. Jej.*poenit*.(M.88.1929B).
***προεξοπλίζομαι,** *arm oneself thoroughly,* Cyr.*Jo*.6.7(4.436A).
***προεξυπνίζομαι,** *awake first,* Thphn.*chron*.p.89(M.108.268C).
προεορτάζω, *keep festival beforehand,* Gr.Naz.*or*.39.14(M.36. 349B); id.*ep*.115(M.37.212C).
προεόρτιος, *for a festival,* ref. pre-paschal fast τὴν συννέκρωσιν Χριστοῦ τοῦτο δύναται, καὶ κάθαρσίς ἐστι π. Gr.Naz.*or*.40.30(M.36. 401B); of Easter Eve ceremonies οἷον εὐφροσύνη τις π. *ib*.45.2(625A); of first evening of sabbath π. ἑορτή Proc.G.*Gen*.1:5(M.87.57C); of Palm Sunday as festival preparatory for festival of Easter, Sophr. H.*v.Mar.Aeg*.8(M.87.3704B); of mid-Pentecost in rel. to Ascension Day, Leont.N.*serm*.2(M.93.1584B); of feast of Nativity of Jo. Bapt. as preparation for feast of Christ's Nativity, Thdr.Stud.*or*.8.10 (M.99.757B).
προέορτος, = foreg.; of Lent, Eus.*pasch*.4(M.24.697C); Ath. *apol.Const*.15(M.25.613A).
***προεπᾴδω,** *utter preliminary warning,* ref. those desiring to become catechumens προβασανίσαντες τῶν ἀκούειν σφῶν βουλομένων τὰς ψυχὰς καὶ κατ' ἰδίαν αὐτοῖς προεπᾴσαντες Or.*Cels*.3.51(p.247. 6; M.11.988A).
***προεπεύχομαι,** *petition beforehand,* ‡Caes.Naz.*dial*.140(M.38. 1068).
***προεπιδίδωμι,** *make good progress,* Clem.*str*.6.17(p.514.24; M.9. 393A).
***προεπίδοσις, ἡ,** a *being foremost in giving* φιλιάζειν...πρὸς ἅπαντας διὰ τῆς εὐμεταδότου καὶ φιλοφρόνου δεξιώσεως καὶ π. Thdr. Stud.*epp*.1.11(M.99.948B).
***προεπικαλέω,** *invite,* Polyc.*ep*.3.1.
προεπινο-έω, 1. *conceive as preceding* ἐπεὶ οὖν προκεῖται τὸ 'ἐν ἀρχῇ ἦν ὁ λόγος', σαφῶς ἰδεῖν, ἀρχὴ δὲ...ἀποδέδοται εἰρῆσθαι ἡ σοφία, καὶ ἔστι ~ουμένη ἡ σοφία τοῦ αὐτὴν ἀπαγγέλλοντος λόγου, νοητέον τὸν λόγον ἐν τῇ ἀρχῇ, τουτ' ἔστι τῇ σοφίᾳ, ἀεὶ εἶναι Or.*Jo*.1.39(42; p.51.7; M.14.101C); *ib*.2.12(6; p.68.5; 133B); Ath.*decr*.8(p.7.27; M.25.'457' (429)B); τοῦ αἰτιατοῦ π. τὸ αἴτιον Bas.*Eun*.1.20(1.232B; M.29.557B); *ib*.2.12(247C; M.593C); †Bas.*ep*.362(3.464D; M.32.1104B); τίς οὕτως ἄθεος ὥστε π. τοῦ θεοῦ τὸ μὴ εἶναι; Gr.Nyss.*Eun*.8(2 p.190.10; M.45. 785A); id.*hex*.proem.5(M.44.65D); of the divine activity, not to be predicated of separate Persons of Trin. in isolation οὐκ ἄναρχος δὲ ἡ τοῦ ἀγαθοῦ κίνησις ἐκ τοῦ πνεύματος· ἀλλ' εὑρίσκομεν ὅτι ἡ ~ουμένη ταύτης δύναμις ἥτις ἐστὶν ὁ μονογενὴς θεός, πάντα ποιεῖ...καὶ αὐτὴ πάλιν τῶν ἀγαθῶν ἡ πηγή, ἐκ τοῦ πατρικοῦ βουλήματος ἀφορμᾶται id.*tres dii*(M.45.129A); τῆς ἀρχῆς οὐδέν τι ἐστὶ πρεσβύτερον...ἢ πάντως ἐκβήσεται τοῦ εἶναι κατὰ ἀλήθειαν ἀρχή, ~ουμένου τινὸς ἑτέρου καὶ προανίσχοντος αὐτῆς Cyr.*Jo*.1.1(4.10E); of Christ's natures λαβόντες ἐκ τῆς μετὰ τὴν ἕνωσιν θεωρίας...τὴν διάγνωσιν, ὡς δύο φύσεων...ταύτας καὶ ~οῦσιν αὐτοῦ Leont.H.*monoph*.24(M.86.1785A); Max.*ambig*.(M.91.1036C); τῶν ἐκ θεοῦ γενομένων...ἡ γένεσις τῆς κινήσεως ~εῖται *ib*.(1072A); *ib*.(1180B); **2.** *devise, think out,* Thdt. *Rom*.1:31(3.28).
προεπισημαίνω, *point out in advance,* Eus.*ecl*.3 proem.(M.22. 1120D); id.*Ps*.37:5–12(M.23.344B) = †Bas.*hom.in Ps*.37(1.368A; M. 30.96B).
προεπιστέλλω, *send letter in advance,* Gr.Naz.*ep*.19(M.37.53A).
***προεπιστορέννυμι,** *spread out before,* Rom.Mel.3.58(*SBBAW* 1898^2,p.137).
***προεπιστρεπτικός,** *leading to conversion,* Or.*sel.in Ps*.2:5(M.12. 1108A).

***προεπιτάσσω**, *enjoin before*, Cyr.*ador*.7(1.219C).

***προεπιτείνω**, *extend*, Didym.*Pr*.30:15(M.39.1641B).

***προέργω**, *exclude previously*; from sacred functions, Thdr.Stud. *epp*.2.211(M.99.1637A).

προερμηνεύω, *explain previously*, ‡Chrys.*pasch*.6.1(p.119.9; 8.264E); Thdt.*Is*.40:7(2.327; προμηνεύει p.156.4); Anast.S.*hod*.14(M.89.253A).

προέρχ-ομαι, **A**. in gen., **1**. *go forth, walk abroad*, Epiph.*haer*.16.1(p.211.5; M.41.249A); ref. sabbath law οὐδὲ γὰρ ἐξῆν προελθεῖν Chrys.*hom.89.1 in Mt*.(7.832B); **2**. *go out*, of monks and nuns from monasteries οὐ χρείαν ἔχω, ἵνα μὴ ἀναγκασθῶ καὶ προελθεῖν. αἱ μὲν γὰρ ἄλλαι πᾶσαι κατὰ κυριακὴν ~ονται ἐν τῇ ἐκκλησίᾳ χάριν τῆς κοινωνίας Pall.*h.Laus*.59(p.153.20; M.34.1236B); οὐ...φέρει σοι τὸ ~εσθαι τοιαύτην ὠφέλειαν, ὅσον τὸ καθέζεσθαι *Apophth.Patr*.(M.65.417A); of catechumens, etc., leaving church before Mass of Faithful προέλθετε, οἱ κατηχούμενοι, ἐν εἰρήνῃ *Lit*.ap.*Const.App*.8.6.14; π., οἱ ἐνεργούμενοι *ib*.8.7.9; of king leaving palace, compared with Christ leaving invisible state at Second Advent, ‡Jo.D.*Const*.13(M.95.329C); **3**. *make official progress, appear publicly*; of high officials, *Chron.Pasch*.p.293(M.92.736A); *ib*.p.383(984A); **4**. *come into being, appear, happen* αἰώνιός ἐστι μετὰ τὸν Μωϋσέως θάνατον προελθοῦσα ἡ προφητεία Just.*dial*.30.1(M.6.540A); τὰ σύμπαντα...εἰς τὸ εἶναι προελθόντα Eus.*e.th*.3.2(p.142.12; M.24.977A); ἡ μὲν κατάρα προῆλθεν Apoll.*fr*.125(p.238.6)ap.Thdt.*eran*.2(4.170); μὴ φυσικῇ τινι ταῦτα προελθεῖν ἀκολουθίᾳ Philost.*h.e*.12.9(M.65.617C); **5**. *precede* τῶν προελθόντων με Ign.*Rom*.10.2; τῶν προελθόντων αὐτοῦ προφητῶν Just. *1apol*.23.1(M.6.364A); Ἰωάννης...προελήλυθε βοῶν...μετανοεῖν id. *dial*.51.2(M.6.588C).

B. theol., *come forth, proceed*; **1**. of Son's generation Χριστὸν τὸν ἀφ' ἑνὸς πατρὸς προελθόντα Ign.*Magn*.7.2; λόγος, προελθὼν ἐκ τῆς τοῦ πατρὸς δυνάμεως Tat.*orat*.5(p.6.2; M.6.817A); ref. pagan adumbrations of Christian Logos doctrine προελθὼν ὁ λόγος δημιουργίας αἴτιος, ἔπειτα καὶ ἑαυτὸν γεννᾷ, ὅταν ὁ λόγος σὰρξ γένηται, ἵνα καὶ θεαθῇ Clem.*str*.5.3(p.336.12; M.9.33A); προελθὼν γνῶσις, τουτέστιν ὁ υἱός id.*exc.Thdot*.7(p.108.4; M.9.657B); οὐ βούλεται [sc. Marcellus]...τὸν υἱὸν ἐκ τοῦ πατρὸς γεγεννῆσθαι...οἷα δὲ λόγον αὐτὸν σημαντικόν τινος...προελθεῖν τοῦ θεοῦ φάσκει Eus.*Marcell*.2.8(p.106.28; M.24.913B); γέννημα γὰρ τὸ προελθὸν τοῦ προεμένου γίγνεται πατρός Marcell.*fr*.31 *ib*.(p.106.31; 913B); ὁ λόγος προελθὼν ἐγίνετο τοῦ κόσμου ποιητής, ὁ καὶ πρότερον ἔνδον νοητῶς ἑτοιμάζων αὐτόν Marcell.*fr*.54 *ib*.(p.107.28; 916A); ὁ...λόγος προῆλθεν μὲν τοῦ πατρός, ἵνα πάντα δι' αὐτοῦ γένηται Marcell.*fr*.108 *ib*.2.2(p.42.16; 796A); προῆλθεν ὁ λόγος δραστικῇ ἐνεργείᾳ Marcell.*ib*.(p.42.23; 796A); τίς οὕτω κτηνώδης, ὥστε ἀκούων θεὸν λόγον ἐκ θεοῦ προελθόντα...πρὸς τὰ σώματος πάθη τοῖς λογισμοῖς καταπίπτειν; Bas.*Eun*.2.5(1.241E; M.29.581B); υἱὸν...αὐτοάγαθον ἐκ τῆς...πηγῆς τῆς πατρικῆς ἀγαθότητος προελθόντα *ib*.2.25(261E; M.629B); in Sabellian view διὰ τὴν λειποταξίαν ἀνθρωπίνην προεληλυθέναι τὸν υἱὸν ἐκ τοῦ πατρὸς προσκαίρως ‡Gr.Nyss.*Ar.et Sab*.6(M.45.1289B); γέννημα...οὐκ ἀπορρεῦσαν ἐκ πατρός, οὐδὲ ἀποτμηθέν τε καὶ διαιρεθέν, ἀλλ' ἀπαθῶς καὶ ὁλοκλήρως προελθὸν ἐκ τοῦ μηδὲν ἀποβεβληκότος ὧν εἶχε Melit.Ant.*hom*.ap. Epiph.*haer*.73.30(p.305.18; M.42.461A); ὁ υἱὸς προελθών, ἀεὶ ὢν παρὰ τῷ πατρί Epiph.*haer*.69.54(p.201.10; M.42.285D); οὐκ ἀλλαχόθεν οὐδὲ ἐξ οὐκ ὄντων, ἀλλὰ ἐκ πατρὸς προελθόντα *ib*.73.36(p.310.25; 469A); οὐσία...ἐνυπόστατος, ἐξ αὐτοῦ προελθοῦσα ἀπαθῶς τοῦ πατρὸς Chrys. *hom.4.1 in Jo*.(8.27D); ἐκ τῆς τοῦ πατρὸς οὐσίας προῆλθεν ὁ υἱός Cyr. *thes*.12(5^1.109A); Thdt.*affect*.2(p.63.22; 4.755); Jo.D.*f.o*.1.6(M.94.804A); **2**. of Inc. παρθένον τινά,...καὶ ἐξ αὐτῆς προῆλθεν ἀμνός *T.Jos*.19.8; Just.*dial*.43.1(M.6.568A); θεὸν ἄνωθεν προελθόντα καὶ ἄνθρωπον ...γενόμενον *ib*.64.7(625A); οὗτος ὁ προελθὼν εἰς τὸν κόσμον, θεὸς καὶ ἄνθρωπος ἐφανερώθη Hipp.*fr.18 in Pss*.(p.146.2; M.10.608C); ἐγὼ καὶ ὁ πατὴρ ἕν ἐσμεν...οὐκ εἰς τὸν ἄνθρωπον ὃν ἀνείληφεν ἀποβλέπων ...φησιν, ἀλλ' εἰς τὸν ἐκ τοῦ πατρὸς προελθόντα λόγον Marcell.*fr*.65 ap.Eus.*Marcell*.2.2(p.39.16; M.24.789C); τοῦ...τεχθησομένου καὶ ἐκ σπέρματος Δαυὶδ...προελευσομένου Eus.*ib*.2.1(p.32.18; 777C); προῆλθεν ἄνθρωπος, μένων ὡς ἦν θεός Ath.*exp.Ps*.88:20(M.27.388C); Leont.H. *Nest*.4.14(M.86.1677D); τὴν ἐπὶ τῶν Αὐγούστου χρόνων προελθοῦσαν ...φύσιν id.*monoph*.5(M.86.1772C); **3**. of H. Ghost; **a**. in gen. Χριστός, οὗ...κῆρυξ προῆλθε τὸ ἐν Ἠλίᾳ γενόμενον πνεῦμα τοῦ θεοῦ, ἐν Ἰωάννῃ Just.*dial*.49.3(M.6.584B); Gnost. τὸ...τῆς ἀγάπης πνεῦμα κέκραται τῷ τῆς γνώσεως, ὡς πατὴρ υἱῷ καὶ ἐνθύμησις ἀληθείᾳ, ἀπ' ἀληθείας προελθὸν ὡς ἀπὸ ἐνθυμήσεως ἡ γνῶσις Clem.*exc.Thdot*.7(p.108.7; M.9.657B); **b**. of procession of H. Ghost, ref. Jo.20:22 δῆλον ὅτι ἐκ τοῦ λόγου τὸ πνεῦμα ἐξῆλθεν. πῶς οὖν, εἰ ἐκ τοῦ λόγου τὸ πνεῦμα προῆλθεν, πάλιν τὸ αὐτὸ ἐκ τοῦ πατρὸς ἐκπορεύεται; Marcell.*fr*.60 ap.Eus.*e.th*.3.4(p.158.30; M.24.1004D); τὸ πνεῦμα...ἐκ στόματος θεοῦ προεληλυθέναι Didym.(‡Bas.)*Eun*.5(1.307D; M.29.737B); μόνον τὸ ἅγιον πνεῦμα ἐκ πατρὸς προῆλθε καὶ τοῦ υἱοῦ ἔλαβε. τὰ δὲ ἄλλα πάντα κτιστὰ καὶ οὔτε προελθόντα ἐκ πατρός Epiph.*haer*.69.34(p.182.32; M.42.256B); υἱός...γεννητὸς ἐκ πατρὸς καὶ πνεῦμα προελθὸν ἐκ πατρός *ib*.74.12(p.330.14; 497C); δύναμιν οὐσιώδη...τοῦ πατρὸς ~ομένην Jo.D.*f.o*.1.7(M.94.805B); **4**. of second and third Persons προῆλθεν ὁ θεὸς λόγος καὶ τὸ ἅγιον...πνεῦμα Epiph.*haer*.76.47(p.401.3; M.42.616B); **5**. of aeons, ref. production of Valent. Jesus ἀπὸ...τῆς πρώτης τετράδος, ἐν θυγατρὸς τρόπῳ προῆλθεν ἡ δευτέρα τετράς Iren.*haer*.1.15.2(M.7.616A); ὅσα ἐκ συζυγίας ~εται, πληρώματά ἐστιν Clem.*str*.4.13(p.287.30; M.8.1297B); **6**. ref. pagan theogonies προῆλθε δὲ καὶ θεός τις δισώματος Athenag.*leg*.18.3(M.6.928B).

προερωτάω, *ask previously*, Max.*schol.c.h*.2.5(M.4.48C).

προεστία-ω, *make festive beforehand*; pass., of prophets declaring future blessings, Thdr.Heracl.*Is*.61:10(M.18.1365C); ~θεὶς...προφήτης τῇ μελλούσῃ...σωτηρίᾳ Proc.G.*Is*.49:1–13(M.87.2476A); *ib*.65:13–25(2708C).

προετοιμάζ-ω, *prepare in advance*; **1**. of God's purposes and providence προετοιμάσας τὰς εὐεργεσίας αὐτοῦ πρὶν ἡμᾶς γεννηθῆναι *1Clem*.38.3; ὄντες λίθοι ναοῦ προητοιμασμένοι εἰς οἰκοδομὴν θεοῦ πατρός Ign.*Eph*.9.1; *M.Polyc*.14.2; θεὸς...τὰ ἄξια ἑκάστῳ ~ων Just. *dial*.16.3(M.6.509B); *ib*.131.2(780C); *A.(Pass.)Andr*.10(p.24.24; M.2.1236B); ref. Creation, Meth.*res*.1.34(p.271.7; M.41.1097B); Eus.*e.th*.3.3(p.155.31; M.24.1000B); ref. Christian's reward βασιλεῖ δ' ἀγαθῷ ...μείζονα προετοιμάσθαι κηρύττει τῶν ἐπάθλων τὰ γέρα id.*l.C*.6(p.209.24; M.20.1345D); Chrys.*hom.3.2 in Philm*.(11.790C); **2**. of Christian's self-preparation ἐὰν οὖν προετοιμάσησθε καὶ μετανοήσητε...πρὸς τὸν κύριον Herm.*vis*.4.2.5; Clem.*fr*.28(p.216.32; M.9.757A); *A.(Pass.) Andr*.7(p.17.19; M.2.1229B); **3**. of Jo. Bapt. φωνὴ...~ουσα εἰς σωτηρίαν Clem.*prot*.1(p.9.20; M.8.65A); προοδοποιῶν παρεγένετο καὶ ~ων Chrys.*hom.10.3 in Mt*.(7.142E).

προετοιμασία, ἡ, *previous preparation*; of preparation of Passover, Clem.*fr*.28(p.216.30; M.9.757A); *Chron.Pasch*.p.218(M.92.532C); of Jo. Bapt.'s mission of repentance symbolizing believer's preparation to receive πνευματικὸν λόγον, Or.*Jo*.6.43(26; p.152.30; M.14.276B); of preparation of sabbath, Jo.D.*hom*.4.29(M.96.629D).

***προετοιμαστής**, ὁ, *one who prepares before*, Epiph.*haer*.42.11 (p.136.13; M.41.744C); *ib*.66.75(p.116.16; M.42.148B).

προευλογέω, *bless beforehand*; of human nature as blessed before its creation by divine purpose of redemption, Cyr.*thes*.15(5^1.174D).

***προευπάσχω**, *be well treated previously* τοῦ θεοῦ χάρις ἦν, οὐ γὰρ προευπαθὼν εὐηργέτησεν...προευπαθόντες ἡμεῖς παρὰ τοῦ θεοῦ Chrys. *hom.4.2 in 2Tim*.(Gaume; πρὸ εὖ π. 11.681E) but cf. κακοπαθοῦντα *ib*.(681A).

προευτρεπίζ-ω, *make ready beforehand*; **1**. in gen.; of baptismal water preparing way for reception of H. Ghost by faithful, Or.*Jo*.6.33(17; p.143.4; M.14.257A); of a doctrine preparing way for heresy, Bas.*Eun*.1.5(1.216A; M.29.520A); of baptismal formula in rel. to grace, Gr.Nyss.*bapt.diff*.(M.46.425A); of gratitude to God in rel. to παρρησία, Chrys.*hom.26.5 in Gen*.(4.253B); ἁγνὰ σκεύη ~ομαι Synes.*ep*.126(M.66.1508A); αὐτὸς ἑαυτῷ ~ει τὴν φλόγα Aen.*dial*.(M.85.921C); **2**. of divine providence and purposes ἡ τοῦ Χριστοῦ παρουσία οὐ μόνοις Ἰουδαίοις ἀλλὰ καὶ τοῖς...ἔθνεσιν σωτήριος ἔσεσθαι προηυτρεπίζετο Eus.*d.e*.2.2(p.60.16; M.22.112A); ὁ προνοητικὸς γεωργὸς πάντα προευτρεπίσας †Bas.*Is*.142(1.478E; M.30.349A); Cyr. *glaph.Ex*.3(1.312D); νομὴν ὥσπερ τινὰ καὶ τόπον προευτρεπίσων ὑμῖν id.*Jo*.9(4.763E); ref. Creation, Thdt.*qu.13 in Gen*.(1.16); ref. salvation ~ων τῷ γένει τῆς σωτηρίας τὸ φάρμακον *ib.37*(51); ταῦτα τῆς προνοίας προευτρεπισάσης Socr.*h.e*.1.29.5(M.67.160C); ὁ ἀγαθὸς νομοθέτης...ἰάσεις πρὸ τῶν νοσημάτων τῇ γῇ ~ειν κελεύει Aen.*dial*.(M.85.945B); ref. heavenly reward τῷ τῆς...δόξης...προηυτρεπισμένῳ αὐτῷ στεφάνῳ †Jo.D.*B.J*.40(M.96.1237A); of Christ τοῖς...οὐδέπω τεχθησομένοις ~ειν τὴν χάριν Cyr.*Jo*.2.1(4.135A); **3**. of preparation of men for spiritual gifts and perfection, Or.*Jo*.6.38(22; p.147.5; M.14.265B); οὐδὲ αὐτὸς μὴ προευτρεπισθεῖσιν πρὸς τὸ λαβεῖν αὐτὸν οὕτως ἂν σπουδαίως ἐπεδήμησεν *ib*.13.56(55; p.287.12; 505C); χρὴ ~ειν ἑαυτόν, ὅσον δυνατὸν εἰς τὸ ἀγαθόν· ἐνίοτε γὰρ γίνεται πρὸς αὐτὸν ἡ θεία χάρις αἰτοῦντα Mac.Aeg.*hom*.19.6(M.34.648A); τὴν ψυχὴν τῶν πολλῶν ~ων τῷ φόβῳ Chrys.*hom.23.2 in Rom*.(9.688C); Cyr.*Jo*.9(4.748D); ἡ φύσις τῆς κτίσεως...~ομένη πρὸς τὴν κοινὴν ἀναγέννησιν Gennad.*fr.Rom*. 8:22(p.381.14; M.85.1697B).

προευτρεπισμός, ὁ, *preparation*, Cyr.*ador*.7(1.234C).

***προευτρεπιστής**, ὁ, *one who prepares*, Cyr.*glaph.Ex*.3(1.320B).

***προευχαριστέω**, *give thanks in advance*, Cyr.*Jo*.12(4.1065A).

***προεύχομαι**, *pray for beforehand*, Max.*qu.Thal*.50(M.90.469A).

προεφοδεύω, *previously conduct on the way*, *cat.Apoc.*19:17(p.464.13).

προεφοδιάζομαι, *be set on the way, be instructed*, *Hom.Clem.*2.40.

***προεχθές**, *the day before yesterday*, *A.Pil.*B 15.5(p.321); Geo.Pis. *carm.*1.18(13 p.1).

***προεωσφόρος, ὁ**, *he who is before the day-star*; of Christ, ‡Chrys. *pasch.*6.5(8.272E; πρὸ ἑωσφόρου p.183.7); *Didasc.Jac.*1.14(p.752.4); *ib.*1.16(p.753.6).

***προζύμη, ἡ**, *leaven*, ‡Jo.D.*azym.*1(M.95.389C).

προζύμιον, τό, *leaven* τοῦ π. τοῦ ἐπουρανίου, ὅπερ ἐστὶν ἡ τοῦ θεοῦ πνεύματος δύναμις Mac.Aeg.*hom.*24.3(M.34.664C); of Israel as leaven of world κεκώλυτο γὰρ Ἕλλησιν ἐπιμίγνυσθαι Ἰουδαίους...ἔδει γὰρ τὸ π. ἰσχυρὸν γενέσθαι, ἵν' οὕτως τὸ ὅλον τοῦ κόσμου ζυμωθῇ Sever.*Eph.*2:14f.(p.309.5).

***προζωγραφ-έω**, **1.** *prefigure, depict beforehand*, Chrys.*comm.in Gal.*4:22(10.709D); ἀεὶ...θεός, ὅταν μέλλῃ πρᾶγμα μέγα διοικεῖν παρὰ τοῖς ἀνθρώποις...τὴν σκιὰν αὐτοῦ ~εῖ ‡Chrys.*Abr.*3(2.745E); of pool of Bethesda as type of baptism, Chrys.ap.*cat.Jo.*5:2(p.228.6) for προγρ-, id.*hom.36.1 in Jo.*(8.207B); Bas.Sel.*or.*13.1(M.85.173A); of double paternity of Joseph foreshadowing divine and human origins of Christ, ‡Just.*qu.et resp.*66(M.6.1308C); προζωγράφησεν ἐν τῇ κιβωτῷ τὴν ἄχραντον...αὐτοῦ σάρκα *Chron.Pasch.*p.199(M.92.489B); of crossing of Red Sea prefiguring Virgin birth, Jo.Mon. *hymn.Blas.*1(M.96.1372B); **2.** *imagine in advance* τῶν νεκρῶν...ἐν τοῖς τάφοις ἔτι κειμένων, ἡ πίστις ἡμῖν ~εῖ τὴν ἀνάστασιν Thdt.*Heb.*11:1(3.613).

προηγ-έομαι, **1.** *lead, go before* ἐὰν ᾖ ἀγαθός, ἡ δικαιοσύνη αὐτοῦ ~ήσεται αὐτοῦ *Barn.*4.12; αὐτὸς [sc. Origen as teacher] δὲ συνεισῄει ~ούμενος καὶ χειραγωγῶν Gr.Thaum.*pan.Or.*14(p.33.5; M.10.1093A); ref. Const.'s divine guide at founding of CP δύναμις αὐτοῦ τις οὐρανία ~οῖτο Philost.*h.e.*2.9(M.65.472B); *lead a procession*, Marc. Diac.*v.Porph.*47; ‡Sophr.H.*liturg.*21(M.87.4001A); **2.** ptcpl., *previous* or *preliminary* ὑπερβὰς τὸ ~ούμενον τῆς φιλοσοφίας τῆς Ἑλληνικῆς...ὥρμησεν ἐπὶ τὴν ἀληθῆ διδασκαλίαν Clem.*str.*7.2(p.9.18; M.9.416A); ~ουμένης πολυβίβλου συγγραφῆς Or.*Jo.*10.17(13; p.187.15; M.14.336A); hence *previously mentioned*, Clem.*str.*1.21(p.85.24; M.8.873A); Eus.*d.e.*4.10(p.165.5; M.22.276A); **3.** *precede, come before* ~εῖται...πάντων τὸ βούλεσθαι Clem.*str.*2.17(p.153.21; M.8.1016A); Or. *Jo.*13.62(60; p.295.8; M.14.520A); ref. Creation οὐκ αὐτομάτως αὐτὰ γεγενῆσθαι...ἀλλ' αἰτίαν τούτων ~εῖσθαι Ath.*inc.*2.2(M.25.100A); τὸ δὲ ~εῖσθαι τὴν διὰ τῆς εὐχῆς κλῆσιν τῆς θείας οἰκονομίας Gr. Nyss.*or.catech.*34(p.127.13; M.45.85B); **4.** *take the initiative, be the first* to ἐπὶ τῷ τοὺς σφᾶς ἀποστερεῖν ~ουμένους ἀμνησικάκως φέρειν Eus.*d.e.*3.4(p.116.25; M.22.200B); **5.** *be superior* or *pre-eminent, rule*; **a.** *be a leader* or *ruler*, in Church; **i.** of descendants of Jude at Jerusalem ~οῦνται πάσης ἐκκλησίας ὡς μάρτυρες καὶ ἀπὸ γένους τοῦ κυρίου Heges.ap.Eus.*h.e.*3.32.6(M.20.284A); **ii.** of clergy in gen., prob. with special reference to presbyter-bishops τοὺς ~ουμένους ἡμῶν αἰδεσθῶμεν *1Clem.*21.6; ἐρεῖς...τοῖς ~ουμένοις τῆς ἐκκλησίας ἵνα κατορθώσωνται τὰς ὁδοὺς αὐτῶν ἐν δικαιοσύνῃ Herm.*vis.*2.2.6; ~ουμένοις τῆς ἐκκλησίας καὶ τοῖς πρωτοκαθεδρίταις *ib.*3.9.7; **iii.** of senior clergy, esp. teachers ποιμένες ἐσμὲν οἱ τῶν ἐκκλησιῶν ~ούμενοι Clem. *paed.*1.6(p.112.17; M.8.293C); id.*str.*6.17(p.510.29; M.9.385A); **iv.** of bishops τῷ ταύτης [sc. ἐκκλησίας] ~ουμένῳ Πολυκάρπῳ Eus.*h.e.*3.36.10(M.20.289B); *Const.App.*2.46.3; Chrys.*hom.10.2 in 1Tim.*(11.601C); **v.** of a prior of a monastery, Thdr.Stud.*epp.*1.22(M.99.977B); **b.** of advanced Christians, ref. Canaanite woman ἀπὸ τούτου οὖν τοῦ μέτρου τῆς δυνάμεως ἐταμιεύετο, τοῖς μὲν ~ουμένοις πλείονα ἐπιδιδοὺς καὶ καλουμένοις υἱοῖς, τοῖς δὲ μὴ τοιούτοις ἐλάττονα Or.*comm.in Mt.*11.17(p.66.7; M.13.964A); **c.** of heavenly life, id.*Jo.*1.26(24; p.33.12; M.14.72B); *ib.*2.18(12; p.75.10; 145C); **d.** of Christ μαρτυρία τοῦ...βαπτιστοῦ περὶ Χριστοῦ...τὴν ~ουμένην αὐτοῦ ὑπόστασιν ἔτι διδάσκουσα διήκουσαν ἐπὶ πάντα τὸν κόσμον *ib.*2.35(29; p.94.13; M.14.177C); τῆς ~ουμένης οὐσίας Χριστοῦ *ib.*6.30(15; p.140.10; 252D); **6.** ptcpl., *of chief importance*, of things μηδὲ ταῦτα ὡς ~ούμενα, ἐκ δὲ τῆς κατὰ τὸν βίον κοινωνίας ὡς ἀναγκαῖα...προσιέμενος Clem.*str.*6.9(p.471.15; M.9.300B); ~ουμένη...ἡ γνῶσις *ib.*(p.471.17; 300C); ταῦτα γὰρ μάλιστα ~ούμενα ἐν τῇ...ψυχῇ κατέχω Const.ap.Ath.*apol.sec.*68(p.146.7; M.25.369B); ~ούμενον γὰρ πρόσταγμα τοῦ κυρίου ἐστὶ τὸ 'πώλησόν σου τὰ ὑπάρχοντα' Bas.*reg.br.*101(2.451B; M.31.1153A); Chrys.*hom.22.3 in Mt.*(7.278B); **7.** ptcpl., *primary* πάντων...αἴτιος τῶν καλῶν ὁ θεός, ἀλλὰ τῶν μὲν κατὰ ~ούμενον ὡς τῆς τε διαθήκης...τῶν δὲ κατ' ἐπακολούθημα ὡς τῆς φιλοσοφίας Clem.*str.*1.5(p.17.36; M.8.717D); οὐ περὶ αἰσθητῶν ποταμῶν ὁ ~ούμενος λόγος ἐστὶν τῷ ἐν...γραφαῖς λαλοῦντι πνεύματι Or.*Jo.*6.48(29; p.157.1; M.14.284A); τῷ ~ούμενον μὲν σημείων εἶναι τοῦ υἱοῦ τοῦ θεοῦ τὴν εὐφροσύνην *ib.*10.12(10; p.183.2; 328A); ὁ ~ούμενος τῆς διανοίας σκοπὸς Eus.*d.e.*9.1(p.406.1; M.22.653D); ref. Mosaic divorce law οὐ ~ούμενος οὗτος ὁ νόμος ἦν Chrys.*hom.17.4 in Mt.*(7.227B); τὰ χρηστὰ...τῆς ~ουμένης τοῦ θεοῦ γνώμης ἐστί id.*hom.3.1 in Rom.*(9.448A); αὐτοῦ βούλημα ἦν, οὐχὶ ~ούμενον μέν, βούλημα δ' οὖν ὅμως id.*hom.28.1 in 2Cor.*(10.634E); **8.** ptcpl., *essential, true* πρὸ τοῦ κενῶσαι ἑαυτὸν ἐν τῇ ~ουμένῃ ὑπάρχοντα θεοῦ μορφῇ Or.*Jo.*20.18(16; p.350.27; M.14.613B); ἡμῶν δὲ ἡ π. ὑπόστασίς ἐστιν ἐν τῷ κατ' εἰκόνα τοῦ κτίσαντος *ib.*20.22(20; p.355.9; 621B); id.*princ.*4.3.5(21; p.331.9; M.11.385A); **9.** ptcpl., *universal, general* ἕκαστον ἐν μέρει μιᾷ προσβολῇ προσβλέπει, οὐ πάντα μέντοι κατὰ τὴν ~ουμένην ἐπέρεισιν Clem.*str.*6.17(p.512.26; M.9.388C).

***προηγητικῶς**, *initially, of one's initial purpose*, Iren.*haer.*5.27.2(M.7.1196C).

προηγουμένως, **1.** *primarily, principally* ἔστι δὲ αὐτοῖς π. βιβλίον ἐπιγραφόμενον Βαρούχ Hipp.*haer.*5.27(p.133.18; M.16.3203C); ἄνθρωπος π. γέγονεν εἰς ἐπίγνωσιν θεοῦ Clem.*str.*6.8(p.464.28; M.9.288B); ἔστω δὲ π. κοινὴ πᾶσιν αὕτη σπουδὴ Ath.*v.Anton.*16(M.26.868A); ψυχῇ π. μὲν καρπὸς ἡ ἀλήθεια Bas.*leg.lib.gent.*2(p.44; M.31.568B); π. γὰρ τὸ εἰδοποιοῦν τὴν ψυχὴν οὐδὲν ἄλλο ἐστίν, ἀλλ' ἢ ἡ ζωή Nemes.*nat.hom.*2(M.40.564B); νοσήματα πολλὰ ἔχομεν ψυχῶν, καὶ ταῦτα π. βούλεται θεραπεύειν Chrys.*hom.14.3 in Mt.*(7.181D); τὰ σημεῖα π. τῆς ψυχῆς ἕνεκεν ἐγένετο id.*hom.35.2 in Jo.*(8.205A); δεῖ π. βίον σεμνὸν καὶ τὸ πνεῦμα...ἔνοικον ἔχειν Anast.S.*hod.*1(M.89.40A); **2.** *excellently* τοὺς...ἐν δικαιοσύνῃ καὶ π. βεβιωκότας Clem.*str.*6.6(p.454.24; M.9.268B); **3.** *originally, in the first place* οὐ π. ὄντες ἄνθρωποι, ὡς ἄνθρωποι ἀποθνήσκουσιν Or.*Jo.*32.18(11; p.457.11; M.14.792C); οὐ π. τὴν...εἰσῆγε νομοθεσίαν, ἀλλὰ πρότερον συντίθησιν ἀπολογίας Chrys.*hom.16.2 in Mt.*(7.205B); ἡδονὴ καὶ λύπη...τῇ φύσει τῶν ἀνθρώπων π. οὐ συνεκτίσθη Max.*cap.*1.65(M.90.1204C); **4.** *of one's primary purpose, of one's original choice* οὐκ εὐθὺς δ' εἴ τις μὴ π. ἐπιτελεῖ, κατὰ περίστασιν αὐτὸ ποιεῖ Clem.*str.*1.1(p.12.22; M.8.708A); Chrys.*hom.39.1 in Mt.*(7.431E); οὐδὲ...π. ... ἔρχεται, ἀλλὰ παριὼν id.*hom.31.2 in Jo.*(8.177B); **5.** *emphatically, definitely* δύναται γὰρ πτωχὸς μὲν...εἶναι...ἐπιθυμεῖν δὲ...ὃ π. οὐ χρὴ *Hom.Clem.*15.10; **6.** *essentially, in respect of one's essential nature* οὐδὲ γὰρ ὁ λόγος...π. σὰρξ γέγονε Iren.*haer.*1.9.3(M.7.541B); ἐσθίει καὶ πίνει καὶ γαμεῖ οὐ π., ἀλλὰ ἀναγκαίως Clem.*str.*7.12(p.51.3; M.9.497C); πάντα φασκόντων σώματα τὰ π. ὑφεστηκότα Or.*Cels.*3.47(p.243.20; M.11.981B); π. μὲν οὖν ἕστηκεν ὁ πατὴρ ἄτρεπτος...ὢν id.*Jo.*6.38(22; p.147.7; M.14.265B); μονογενὴς π. τὸ καθ' ἑαυτὸν υἱὸς τοῦ θεοῦ ἐστί Cyr.*inc.unigen.*(5[1].680B); **7.** *as a leader* τὸν π. εἰς ἐπισκοπὴν κατασταθησόμενον Or.*Cels.*3.48(p.244.25; M.11.984A).

***προηλόω**, *crucify*, Leont.H.*monoph.*46(M.86.1797A).

***προημερόω**, *soothe first*, Bas.*Eun.*2.11(1.246B; M.29.592B).

***προθαυμάζω**, *admire beforehand*, Hipp.*haer.*9.9(p.242.12; M.16.3374A).

***προθαυματουργέω**, *effect miraculously before*, Sev.Ant.*res.*(p.800.9; M.46.629C).

***προθέλω**, *will beforehand* πάντα...αὐτῷ τὰ...ὄντα ἢ γενησόμενα κατὰ τὴν οὐσίαν προτεθέληται Max.*ambig.*(M.91.1328B).

πρόθεμα, τό, *edict* ἐκ τοῦ προθέμματος γνώμη *CG–CI* I 5 (Corinth, saec. iv–v); †Gregent.*leg.Hom.*61(M.86.613C); Jo.Mal.*chron.*13 p.338(M.97.504B); Evagr.*h.e.*2.18(p.79.23; M.86.2568A).

***προθεματίζω**, *lay down as a proposition, presuppose*, Leont.H. *monoph.*testimonia(M.86.1892B).

προθεμελιόω, *lay as foundation beforehand*, Cyr.*thes.*15(5[1].172E); *ib.*(174B); met. τὸν περὶ μοναρχίας τοῦ θεοῦ λόγον π. τῇ καρδίᾳ Cyr.H. *catech.*4.6.

***προθεολογέω**, *speak of previously as God*, Diod.*Ps.*88:11(M.33.1620D).

***προθεσία, ἡ**, v. προθεσμία.

πρόθεσις, ἡ, **I.** *purpose, intention, inclination*;

A. of men; **1.** *free choice, inclination*; **a.** in gen., Clem.*str.*3.12(p.231.23; M.8.1177C); Galerius ap.Eus.*h.e.*8.17.7(M.20.793A); οἰκεία π. τῷ...Χριστῷ θυσία γενέσθαι *M.Das.*5.2; **b.** of human free will κατὰ π. αὐτεξουσίου ψυχῆς Meth.*symp.*3.13(p.42.15; M.18.81C); οὐσίᾳ μὲν καὶ φύσει ἄνθρωπος καλός..., ἀγαθὸς δὲ ἢ...κακὸς προθέσει Tit. Bost.*Man.*2.4(M.18.1140A); οὕτω τὸν ἄνθρωπον τετίμηκεν ὁ θεὸς...ἵν' ...ὁ ἄνθρωπος ἐλευθεριότητι προθέσεως ζηλωτὴς ὑπάρχῃ θεοῦ. ... ὅσα μὲν γὰρ φύσεως ἀνάγκῃ δρῶμεν, τούτων μεταβολὴν οὐκ ἐπιδεχόμεθα· ὅσα δὲ λόγῳ προθέσεως ποιοῦμεν, ταῦτα ἄλλοτε ἄλλως ἐν ἡμῖν ἔχει πρὸς τὰς ἐγγινομένας τῇ π. ῥοπάς *ib.*2.5(1141C); ἡ δὲ π. ἐφ' ὃ βούλεται ῥέπει ...οὕτως ἡ μὲν πρᾶξις ἀφώρισται τῇ αἱρέσει τῆς π. *ib.*2.6(1144B,C); **2.** *disposition* ἐν ὁσίᾳ καὶ ἀμώμῳ π. δουλεύοντας τῷ θεῷ *1Clem.*45.7; ὅταν ὁλοψύχῳ π. ποιῶμεν τὰς αὐτοῦ ἐντολάς Clem.*fr.*44(p.223.7);

δυνατόν τινα κατὰ π. βελτίστην λέγειν...τὰ μηδαμῶς...συμφέροντα Or.*Jo*.32.5(p.433.14; M.14.753A); ἀσεβῆ π. δείκνυσιν Ath.*apol.sec*.85 (p.163.20; M.25.400B); in catechumens π. ἀγαθή, καὶ ἐλπὶς ἐπακολουθοῦσα Cyr.H.*procatech*.1; ἡ π. γνησία οὖσα, κλητόν σε ποιεῖ *ib*.; Tit. Bost.*Man*.2.13(M.18.1160B); ref. Judas διάβολος ἤδη γενόμενος τῇ προαιρέσει Chrys.*hom.81.3 in Mt*.(7.776D; cj. προθέσει Gaume); Didym.*Ps*.3:8(M.39.1164C); plur. π., δόγματα, κρίσεις as elements constituting spiritual life of 'gnostic', Clem.*str*.2.17(p.153.24; M.8. 1016B); ref. motives of converts, Or.*Jo*.19.12(3; p.311.30; M.14. 548B); ἄπειροι γὰρ ἡμῖν...αἱ ψυχαί,...καὶ πλεῖστα ὅσα τὰ κινήματα καὶ αἱ π. καὶ αἱ ἐπιβολαὶ καὶ αἱ ὁρμαί id.*princ*.3.1.14(p.220.9; M.11.276C); **3.** *persuasion* εἰ ἐπιμένοιεν τῇ τοῦ Χριστιανισμοῦ π. Eus.*h.e*.8.2.4(M. 20.748A); οἵτινες τῶν γονέων τῶν ἑαυτῶν καταλελοίπασι τὴν αἵρεσιν, εἰς ἀγαθὴν π. ἐπανέλθοιεν Galerius *ib*.8.17.7(M.20.793A); τεθάρρηκα τῇ περὶ πάντων ὑμῶν ὀρθῇ π. Alex.Al.*ep.Alex*.12(p.27.23; M.18.565D); **4.** *tenor* ὅταν...κατὰ τὴν π. τῆς ὑγιοῦς διδασκαλίας κοινωνικὸς ᾖς Or.*hom.5.14 in Jer*.(p.44.1; M.13.317A); **5.** *purpose, intention, plan*, Clem.*str*.4.1(p.249.4; M.8.1216B); ἀλλὰ μὲν π. τὴν ἀρχὴν...ὑπηγορεύσαμεν ἄλλη δὲ τὰ μετὰ τὴν ἀρχήν Or.*Cels*.proem.6(p.54.36; M.11.649B); ἔστι γὰρ ὁ θυμὸς τῆς π. τῆς τοῦ θυμῷ ἐλέγχοντος, βουλομένης τὸν ἐλεγχόμενον...ἐπιστρέφειν id.*hom.20.1 in Jer*.(p.177.5; M.13.500D); Meth.*symp*.3.14(p.44.14; M.18.85A); of partic. intention κατὰ πρόθεσιν εὐνουχίας ὁμολογήσας μὴ γῆμαι Clem.*str*.3.15(p.241.4; M.8.1197A); τῆς περὶ τὰ κρείττω π. Eus.*d.e*.1.9(p.40.29; M.22.77D); ὅσοι...προθέσει εὐλογιῶν πολιτεύονται Nil.*epp*.1.68(M.79.112B); phrases ποιῆσαί τι παρὰ πρόθεσιν Or.*princ*.3.1.4(p.199.3; M.11.253A); Max.*carit*.3.85(M. 90.1044B); ἐν π. Jo.Mal.*chron*.11 p.277(M.97.420A); **6.** *policy* μὴ καὶ τὴν π. τῆς δωροφορίας [i.e. people's offerings for charity] ὑβρίσῃς, τὸν τρόπον τῆς δαπάνης αὐτῆς ἐρευνῶν Isid.Pel.*epp*.1.187(M.78.304A).

B. of God, *purpose, counsel*; **1.** ref. Creation οὐδὲ...ποιῆσας τὸ φῶς, ἔπειτα ἰδών, καλὸν εἶπεν· ὃ δέ, καὶ πρὶν ἢ ποιῆσαι, οἷον ἔσται, εἰδώς, τοῦτο ἐπῄνεσεν· τὸ δ' ἐγένετο δυνάμει ποιοῦντος καλὸν ἄνωθεν διὰ τῆς ἀνάρχου π. τὸ ἐσόμενον ἐνεργείᾳ καλόν Clem.*str*.6.12(p.483.3; M.9.324A); πάντων...ὄντων...ἐν τῷ θεῷ προϋπάρχουσι...οἱ λόγοι, καθ' οὓς καὶ εἰσὶ τὰ πάντα...καὶ διαμένουσιν ἀεὶ τοῖς ἑαυτῶν κατὰ πρόθεσιν λόγοις Max.*ambig*.(M.91.1329A); **2.** ref. predestination ἐπίστησον εἰ προορισμὸς καὶ π. διαφέρει, ὡς μετὰ τοῦ προορισμοῦ τὴν π. γενέσθαι· ὥστε κατὰ τὰ ἐννοήματα τοῦ θεοῦ γίνεσθαι τὸν προορισμόν, κατὰ δὲ ταὐτὰ τὴν περὶ ὧν προώρισε π. οὐσιωμένων πως ἐπακολουθεῖν καὶ εἰς ἔργον ἐχομένων τοῦ προορισμοῦ Or.*comm.in Eph*.1:9(p.240); **3.** ref. election ὁ κατὰ πρόθεσιν τὸν ἐκλεκτὸν καὶ πρὸ τῆς γενέσεως τό τε ἐσόμενον ὡς ἤδη ὑπάρχον ἐγνωκώς Clem.*str*.7.7(p.29.11; M.9.453B); οὐ κατὰ τὰ ἔργα ἡμῶν...ἀλλὰ κατ' ἰδίαν π. Chrys.*hom.2.1 in 2Tim*. (11.666E); **4.** ref. prayer αὐτόθεν δὲ ἀπεμφαίνει, ἀτρέπτου ὄντος τοῦ θεοῦ καὶ τὰ ὅλα προκατειληφότος μένοντός τε ἐν τοῖς προδιατεταγμένοις, εὔχεσθαι, οἰόμενον μετατρέψειν διὰ τῆς εὐχῆς αὐτοῦ τὴν π. Or.*or*.5(p.311. 4; M.11.433B).

C. of Logos τοσαύτην εἶναι...τὴν δύναμιν, ὅση ἐστὶ καὶ ἡ π. Gr.Nyss. *or.catech*.1(p.10.8; M.45.16A); of purpose of Son in Inc., *ib*.32(p.115. 12; 80A).

D. of H. Ghost δύναμιν...πρὸς πᾶσαν π. σύνδρομον ἔχουσαν τῇ βουλήσει τὴν δύναμιν Jo.D.*f.o*.1.7(M.94.805B).

E. of disposition of Christ's human nature ἀσχέτῳ δὲ στοργῇ πρὸς τὸ καλὸν ἑαυτὸν συνάψας, ἀνάλογόν τε τῇ οἰκείᾳ π. καὶ τὴν τοῦ θεοῦ λόγου συνέργειαν δεχόμενος Thdr.Mops.*fr.inc*.7(p.296.36; M.66. 977B); ὅθεν καὶ τὴν περὶ τὰ καλὰ π. ἀκέραιον αὐτῷ διεφύλαττεν. οὐ γὰρ δὴ τοῦτο φήσομεν ὅτι περ ὁ ἄνθρωπος π. εἶχεν οὐδεμίαν, ἀλλ' ὅτι προὐτεθεῖτο μὲν αὐτῷ τὸ καλόν· μᾶλλον δὲ πλείστη αὐτῷ τῆς κατὰ πρόθεσιν προσῆν ἥ τε τοῦ καλοῦ στοργὴ καὶ τὸ τοῦ ἐναντίου μῖσος· διεφυλάττετο δὲ αὐτῷ τὰ τῆς π. ἀκέραια ὑπὸ τῆς θείας χάριτος *ib*.14 (p.308.21; 989D).

F. of Devil's purpose in accomplishing Christ's death, Oecum. *Apoc*.12:15(p.147).

II. ἄρτοι τῆς προθέσεως *shewbread*;

A. in OT, Bas.*hom.in Ps*.33(1.142D; M.29.349B), etc.; interpreted as signifying tribes of Israel, cf.Or.*hom.13.3 in Lev*.(p.471.13; M.12. 547A); Christ as sacrificed, *ib*.(p.471.23; 547B); commemoration in eucharist of Christ's sacrifice, *ib.13.5*(p.476.10ff.; 550C,D); twelve orders of creation, *ib.13.4*(p.474.22; 549C); twelve apostles, Cyr.*ador*. 10(1.346A); fruits of the earth, Thdt.*qu.60 in Ex*.(1.164); twelve months of year, Cosm.Ind.*top*.2(M.88.92B); their method of composition signifying unity of substance and diversity of Person of Father and Son, cf.Or.*hom.13.4 in Lev*.(p.473.14ff.; 548C); table of shewbread denoting τὴν ἀναίμακτον θυσίαν, δι' ἧς εὐλογούμεθα τὸν ἄρτον ἐσθίοντες τὸν ἐξ οὐρανοῦ, τουτέστι Χριστόν Cyr.*ador*.13(1.457E); shewbread itself as type of eucharist, Jo.D.*f.o*.4.13(M.94.1149C).

B. designating eucharistic bread ἡμεῖς ἐπὶ σινδόνος τὸν ἄρτον τῆς π. ἁγιάζοντες, σῶμα Χριστοῦ ἀδιστάκτως εὑρίσκομεν Isid.Pel.*epp*. 1.123(M.78.265A); ματαιάζουσιν οἱ τὸν τῆς π. ἄρτον καὶ τὸ κερασθὲν ἀρτίως ποτήριον, τῷ ἁγίῳ θυσιαστηρίῳ προσάγειν μελλούσης τῆς λειτουργικῆς τάξεως, ὕμνον...λέγειν παραδεδωκότες τῷ λαῷ, τῷ γινομένῳ πράγματι πρόσφορον...βασιλέα δόξης προσφέρειν ἢ καὶ προσαγορεύειν τὰ εἰσφερόμενα καὶ μηδέπω τελειωθέντα, διὰ τῆς ἀρχιερατικῆς ἐπικλήσεως Eutych.*pasch*.8(M.86.2400C); ὁ ἄρτος τῆς π. λέγεται ἤγουν ἀποκαθαιρόμενος καὶ ἐμφαίνει τὸν ὑπερβάλλοντα πλοῦτον τῆς χρηστότητος τοῦ θεοῦ, ὅτι ὁ υἱός...ἄνθρωπος γέγονε ‡Bas.*h.myst*.28 (p.263.21); Jo.D.*f.o*.4.13(M.94.1145A).

III. eucharistic; **A.** *setting forth* of eucharistic offering θεὸς ὁ εὐλογῶν καὶ ἁγιάζων πάντας ἡμᾶς ἐπὶ τῇ π. τῶν θείων καὶ ἀχράντων μυστηρίων *Lit.Jac*.(p.182.2).

B. *offertory* τὴν εὐχὴν τῆς π. *Lit.Jac*.(p.180.14); *Lit.Marc*. (Brightman p.124.21); *Lit.Chrys*.(p.360.28).

C. part of church where πρόθεσις takes place, i.e. sacristy or north side of *bema* ἀνηγέρθη ἐκ θεμελίων ἡ ἁγία τοῦ θεοῦ ἡμῶν π. *IGC As.Min*.118 (saec. v–vi); typifying Golgotha, Jo.Jej.*liturg*.(p.441); ‡Sophr.H.*liturg*.2(M.87.3984B); *ib*.8(3988D); of greater sanctity than Holy of Holies, as representing Bethlehem and Upper Room, *ib*.9 (3989B); *ib*.21(4001B); ἡ ἀποκαθίστασις τῶν δώρων ἐν τῇ π. Thdr.Stud. *praesanct*.(M.99.1689C); *Lit.Chrys*.(p.356.15).

D. *credence-table* on which πρόθεσις was performed προσκυνήματα τρία ἔμπροσθεν τῆς π. ποιήσαντες *Lit.Chrys*.(p.356.16).

E. eucharistic elements as set forth (= ἄρτοι τῆς π.) εὐλόγησον τὴν π. ταύτην *Lit.Jac*.(p.180.17); *Lit.Chrys*.(p.360.23,34).

IV. *preposition* in theol. controversy, ref. Marcellus' citation of Rom.1:4 as τοῦ προορισθέντος υἱοῦ θεοῦ: οὐ τὴν λέξιν μόνην τὴν ἀποστολικὴν παρέφθειρεν, ἀλλὰ καὶ τὴν διάνοιαν αὐτὴν διὰ τῆς προσθήκης τῆς τοῦ πρὸ προθέσεως Eus.*Marcell*.1.2(p.12.7; M.24.737C); οὐ γὰρ ὑπ' αὐτοῦ φησιν, οὐδ' ἐξ αὐτοῦ τὰ πάντα γεγενῆσθαι, ἀλλὰ δι' αὐτοῦ. ἡ δὲ διὰ πρόθεσις τὸ ὑπηρετικὸν σημαίνει id.*e.th*.2.14(p.116.2; M.24.929B); ref. Pr.8:27a ἡ γὰρ 'σύν' π. ... τὴν κατὰ τὸ αὐτὸ σὺν ἑτέρῳ παρουσίαν δηλοῖ *ib*.3.3(p.156.30; 1001A); ref. 2Cor.13:13, Rom.15:30 εἰ τοίνυν ἀντὶ τῆς 'καί' τῇ 'σύν' ἐθελήσαιμεν χρήσασθαι, τί διάφορον πεποιηκότες ἐσόμεθα; Bas.*Spir*.59(3.50A; M.32.176C); ref. Rom.11:36 ἔδειξε...ὁ ἀπόστολος ὡς οὐκ οἶδε τῆς 'ἐξ οὗ' καὶ τῆς 'δι' οὗ' π. διαφοράν, καὶ τὴν μὲν ὡς μεῖζόν τι σημαίνουσαν, προσήκουσαν τῷ πατρί, τὴν δέ, ὡς ἔλαττόν τι διδάσκουσαν, ἁρμόττουσαν τῷ υἱῷ Thdt.*Rom*. 11:36(3.127); πάλιν μέντοι τὴν 'διά' π. ἐπὶ τοῦ πατρὸς τέθεικεν id.*Col*. 1:1(3.473).

προθεσμία, ἡ, 1. *appointed time*, of eschatological expectation of prophet οἶδεν εἰς ποίαν π. προσεδόκα Epiph.*anc*.99(p.120.6; M.42. 196C); **2.** *time limit* ὁρισθεῖσαν ἐπ' αὐτῷ [sc. τῷ κόσμῳ] π. †Dion.Al. *fr.Eccl*.3:11(p.226.16; M.10.1588C); Χριστὸς π. τῷ παροργισμῷ ἔδωκεν Adam.*dial*.1.13(p.30.11; M.11.1740B); ref. Marcellus' doctrine of temporary kingdom of Christ ὅρον...καὶ π. τῆς βασιλείας αὐτοῦ δηλοῦσθαι Eus.*e.th*.3.13(p.169.29; M.24.1024D); στενὴν τὴν π. τῆς συνόδου ὡρίσαμεν Jul.Papa *ep.Dian*.ap.Ath.*apol.sec*.25(p.106.9; M. 25.289C); Jo.D.*fr.Mt*.28:20(M.96.1413A); **3.** *allotted span* of life ἵνα ἐν τῇ π. τὸν ἀγῶνα τελέσωμεν Mac.Mgn.*apocr*.2.7(p.5.2); π. βίου Bas. *hom*.23.1(2.185D; M.31.589C); Chrys.*oppugn*.3.17(1.106E); **4.** *interval, delay, respite*; of time accorded for repentance, Bas.*jud*.7(2. 221B; M.31.669D); τὰ ζιζάνια ἀφεθῆναι ἐκέλευσε, διδοὺς π. μετανοίας Chrys.*hom.29.3 in Mt*.(7.346B); id.*hom.12.4 in Ac*.(9.102A); Nil. *epp*.3.177(M.79.468A); Thdt.*Ezech*.22:4(2.851); in gen., Gr.Naz.*ep*. 155(M.37.261C); Bas.Sel.*or*.2.4(M.85.48A); ref. man born blind ἐν σκότῳ τεχθεὶς νυκτός, π. οὐκ ἔχων ἐν ὄμμασιν *ib*.25.1(288C); of lifespan as respite allotted for performance of good works before judgement, Chrys.*hom.24.3 in Ac*.(9.196A); προθεσία, Ath.Scholast. *coll*.4 paratit.9(p.68); **5.** *fore-ordaining, previous appointment*, Eus. *h.e*.1.4.2(M.20.77A); ἡ ἄρρητος τοῦ κυρίου βουλή, καὶ ἡ π. αὐτοῦ Euthal.Diac.*epp.Paul*.1(M.85.700A).

προθεσπίζ-ω, 1. *foretell*, of inspired prophecy: S. Peter's utterance at Transfiguration οὐ λογισμῷ ταῦτα...ἐφθέγγετο, ἐπιπνοίᾳ δὲ τοῦ τὰ μέλλοντα ~οντος πνεύματος Jo.D.*hom*.1.16(M.96.572A); angel's utterance at Annunciation, Clem.*prot*.1(p.9.22; M.8.65A); utterance of prophets Μωσῆς...τὸ ὄνομα καὶ τὴν παιδαγωγίαν ~ει [i.e. of Joshua] id.*paed*.1.7(p.125.27; M.8.324A); διὰ τοῦ ψαλμῳδοῦ ~ει τὸ πνεῦμα *ib*.2.8(p.194.17; 465C); Or.*fr.61 in Jer*.39:10(p.228.18; M.13. 584D); id.*Jo*.32.16(9; p.453.1; M.14.785A); Ἄγαβος...περὶ τοῦ μέλλειν ἔσεσθαι λιμὸν ~ει Eus.*h.e*.2.3.4(M.20.144B); Epiph.*haer*.30.20(p.360. 1; M.41.437B); Ἡσαΐαν...προθεσπίσαι αὐτοῦ τὰ σωτήρια πάθη Thdt. ap.Cyr.*apol.Thdt*.4(p.122.18; 6[1].216B); in text of scripture τὰ ἐν Ψαλμοῖς προθεσπισθέντα Eus.*h.e*.8.1.9(741C); ἐν ἄλλῳ τόπῳ λέγει

~ον τὸ ἅγιον πνεῦμα Epiph.*haer*.26.15(p.295.21; 356D); Philost.*h.e.* 7.14(M.65.552D); utterance made as result of prophetic dream, Eus.*h.e.*4.15.10(345C); **2.** *utter beforehand* βουλόμενος ὁ κύριος προασφαλίσασθαι τὴν σωτηρίαν...τὸν λόγον ~ει Epiph.*haer*.54.2(p.319. 13; M.41.964C); **3.** *proclaim previously* ἐν τῷ ἐκφωνηθέντι...ὅρῳ προεθέσπισεν ἡ...συναχθεῖσα σύνοδος Jo.VI CP.*ep*.(M.96.1425B).

***προθέσπισμα, τό,** *prediction*, Epiph.*inc*.4(p.232.4; M.41.280B).

προθεωρ-έω, 1. *observe previously*, Or.*Jo*.13.28(p.252.8; M.14. 448A); **2.** *consider, examine previously*, Gr.Nyss.*v.Mos*.(M.44.405B); Epiph.*haer*.42.13(p.182.26; M.41.812C); Jo.D.*f.o*.3.15(M.94.1049A); **3.** *foresee*; of prophets, Eus.*d.e*.7.1(p.298.2; M.22.488C); Cyr.*Ps*. 58:6(M.69.1112C); of God, ‡Nil.*tract*.4(M.79.1285A); προεθεώρει καὶ προώριζε τὸν δι' ἡμᾶς...ἐσόμενον ἄνθρωπον Cyr.*thes*.15(5¹.173A); οὐ γὰρ ἡ πρόγνωσις αὐτοὺς τοιούτους εἰργάσατο· ἀλλὰ πόρρωθεν ὁ θεὸς τὰ ἐσόμενα προεθεώρησεν ὡς θεός Thdt.*Rom*.8:30(3.93); id.*qu.19 in Gen*.(1.23); **4.** *regard as prior* ὡς γὰρ συνάπτεται τῷ πατρὶ ὁ υἱὸς καὶ τὸ ἐξ αὐτοῦ εἶναι ἔχων οὐχ ὑστερίζει κατὰ τὴν ὕπαρξιν, οὕτω πάλιν καὶ τοῦ μονογενοῦς ἔχεται τὸ πνεῦμα..., ἐπινοίᾳ μόνῃ κατὰ τὸν τῆς αἰτίας λόγον ~ουμένου τῆς τοῦ πνεύματος ὑποστάσεως Gr.Nyss.*Eun*.1(1 p.215.15; M.45.464C).

***προθεωρητικός,** *foreseeing* ἡ γὰρ πρόγνωσις, οὐκ ἔστιν ἀναγκαστική· ἀλλὰ π. τῆς τῶν πολιτευομένων ὁρμῆς Thdr.Mops.ap.*cat.Rom*.8:29f. (p.265.15) = Diod.*Rom*.8:29f.(p.95.11–19n.); ‡Meth.*palm*.3(M.18. 388C).

προθεωρία, ἡ, 1. *prevision, previous consideration*, Bas.*reg.fus*.24 (2.369C; M.31.984A); of God in Creation, Thdt.*qu.19 in Gen*.(1.24); **2.** *preface, introduction*, Or.*enarr.in Job* 3(M.17.65D); Thdt.*Pss*. proem.(1.608); Max.*schol.d.n*.1.1(M.4.185A).

***προθεωρός,** *foreseeing*, ‡Meth.*Sym.et Ann*.9(M.18.372A).

***προθήβη, ἡ,** *youthful vigour*, Cyr.*hom.pasch*.9(5².112C).

προθήκη, ἡ, 1. *show-case, stall* for displaying goods χρήματα... εἴρηται, οὐχ ἵνα οὕτω χρώμεθα αὐτοῖς, καθάπερ αἱ π. τῶν χρυσοχόων, ἀλλ' ἵνα ἐργαζώμεθά τι καλὸν ἐν αὐτοῖς Chrys.*hom.10.3 in Phil*.(11. 279C); τὰ χρυσία ταῖς πομπαῖς ἀφῶμεν, ταῖς σκηναῖς, ταῖς π. ταῖς ἐπὶ τῶν ἐργαστηρίων id.*hom.12.6 in Heb*.(12.266C); **2.** = διαθήκη, Nil. *Magn*.21(M.79.996C).

[*]προθρυλλέω, *noise abroad*, Apoll.*fr*.14(p.208.30)ap.Gr.Nyss. *Apoll*.4(M.45.1129C).

προθυμ-έομαι, 1. *be willing, eager*; in polite request ~ήθητι, πάτερ,...εἰπεῖν ἡμῖν Pall.*v.Chrys*.4(p.25.18; M.47.16); **2.** trans., *encourage*, Thdr.Stud.*epp*.2.118(M.99.1392B).

***προθυμοεργέω,** *be industrious*, Thdr.Stud.*epp*.2.132(M.99.1425B).

προθυμοποιέω, *encourage, stimulate*, Leont.N.*v.Sym*.7(M.93. 1677A); *cat.Apoc*.8:9(p.305.1); med., Gr.Nyss.*hom.2 in Cant*.(M.44. 792C); Chrys.ap.*cat.Mt*.19:12(p.152.30) for διορθούμενος, Chrys.*hom. 62.3 in Mt*.(7.623B); Thphn.*chron*.p.375(M.108.900A).

***προθυμοποιΐα, ἡ,** *encouragement*, *cat.Apoc*.8:9(p.305.3).

***προθυμοποιός,** *encouraging*, *cat.Apoc*.8:6(p.303.8).

***προθυμοτέρως,** *more zealously*, Call.*v.Hyp*.(p.47).

προθύραιος, *before the door*, of a servant employed as doorkeeper τῆς π. παιδός Cyr.*Jo*.11.12(4.1022D).

πρόθυρον, τό, (usu. plur.) *door, gate, forecourt*; **1.** lit. τὰ π. τῆς ἐκκλησίας Pall.*v.Chrys*.2(p.9.5; M.47.8); τὰ π. τῆς πόλεως *A.Xanthipp*. 7(p.62.13); CLater.*act*.1(H.3.697D); **2.** met. ἐπὶ προθύροις ὡς εἰπεῖν τοῦ πατρὸς προσεχεῖς τῷ μεγάλῳ ἀρχιερεῖ γενόμεναι Clem.*str*.7.7(p.34. 11; M.9.465A); ἐπὶ τὰ π. τοῦ ἀγαθοῦ δυναμένου τινὸς οὕτως ἐλθεῖν Or. *Cels*.7.44(p.194.28; M.11.1484C); π. καὶ προσχήματα καὶ πᾶσαν ὑποδυσάμενον τῆς ὑποκρίσεως τὴν σκευήν Meth.*res*.1.27(p.256.15; M.41. 1133C); πρῶτον...βαθμὸν εὐσεβείας ὡς ἐν εἰσαγωγαῖς καὶ προθύροις τῶν τελεωτέρων Eus.*d.e*.1.6(p.27.35; M.22.56C); π. ὥσπερ...ἐστὶ τῆς εἰς ἀρετὴν τελειότητος ἡ περιτομή Cyr.*Jo*.4.7(4.433A); ἐν π. ... ἡ προρρηθεῖσα τιμωρία φανήσεται Thdt.*Ezech*.12:23(2.756); πανάγιαι...δυναμεῖς...οἷον ἐν π. τῆς ὑπερουσίου τριάδος ἱδρυμέναι Dion.Ar.*d.n*.5.8(M. 3.821C).

***πρόθυρος, ὁ,** *porter*, *T.Job* 6(p.107.7).

***προικισμός, ὁ,** *giving of a dowry*, Epiph.*exp.fid*.6(p.502.5; M.42. 784B).

προικῷος, *belonging to a dowry* ἐν τοῖς γραμματείοις καὶ τοῖς π. ... ἄνω μὲν γράφεται πᾶσα ἡ διήγησις, εἰς τὸ τέλος δὲ τοῦ συγγράμματος, αὐτὸς ὑπογράφει ὁ κύριος τοῦ πράγματος Ast.Am.*hom*.15(M.40.389B); ἀνὴρ...ἐπειδὰν γυναῖκα θέλῃ λαβεῖν, ὑπαγορεύει τῷ νομογράφῳ τὰ π. ‡Chrys.*fid*.2(1.829D); γαμετὴν γυναῖκα, ὡς οἱ συμβολαιογράφοι ἐν τοῖς π. γράφουσι Isid.Pel.*epp*.3.176(M.78.868B); of tables of Law π. γραμματέων τύπον εἶχον αἱ πλάκες Thdt.*qu.68 in Ex*.(1.172); of God's covenant as π. γράμματα, id.*Cant*.proem.(2.13); id.*ep*.8(4.1066).

προίξ, ἡ, *gift, dowry*; **1.** *gift* κορβᾶν...ὅπερ οὐκ ἔστι δωρεὰ καὶ π., ἀλλὰ προσφορά Chrys.*hom.51.2 in Mt*.(7.522C); **2.** *dowry*; given by woman to man; **a.** among Peratic Gnostics in imitation of Edem's self-offering to Elohim in primal marriage, Hipp.*haer*.5.26 (p.128.13; M.16.3195C); **b.** in normal practice πενιχρά ἐστι...οὐκ ἔχει π. ἐπιδοῦναι; Chrys.*hom.12.4 in Col*.(11.418C); **3.** met. νυμφεύομαι τῷ λόγῳ καὶ τὸν ἀΐδιον τῆς ἀφθαρσίας π. λαμβάνω στέφανον Meth. *symp*.6.5(p.69.18; M.18.120C); δύο...ἡμῖν γενικαὶ...προφητεῖαι...ἡ μὲν οὖν...θήλεια...ὡς ὅλα ἴδια συνεκφέρει τὰ γεννήματα, καὶ τὸν παρόντα ἐπίγειον πλοῦτον ὡς π. δώσειν ἐπαγγέλλεται *Hom.Clem*.3.23; of gifts to Church ὡσανεὶ γυναῖκα ἀγαγὼν...οὕτω τῇ ἐκκλησίᾳ διάκεισο· π. ἐπίδος αὐτῇ Chrys.*hom.18.4 in Ac*.(9.150A); of creation as Eve's dowry, Bas.Sel.*or*.3.3(M.85.53C); **4.** προῖκα as adv., *freely*, ‡Nil.*narr*. 3(M.79.617C cj. for f.l. προίκοι); ‡Nil.*Epict*.17(M.79.1292B); **5.** προικός = προῖκα: προικὸς ἐμὲ στυγέεσκον Nonn.*par.Jo*.15:25(M.43.877A).

***προϊππικός,** *before a horse race*, ‡Chrys.*circ*.(8.88D).

προΐστημι (προϊστάω), A. trans.; **1.** med., *set before one as one's aim* προὐστησάμην τοῦ βίου τέχνας δύο, φυτηκομεῖν τε καὶ κυνοκομεῖν Synes.*calv*.4(p.197.3; M.66.1173C); **2.** med., *appoint, put forward for office* Γάλλον...Καίσαρα προστησάμενος ‡Jo.D.*Artem*.12(p.51.27; M. 96.1261C); **3.** med., *put first, give prominence to* οἶμαι αὐτοὺς οὐ πάνυ πρὸς τὸν Τιμόθεον ἔχειν ἀπεχθῶς, ὅθεν καὶ αὐτὸν προεστήσατο. 'γινώσκετε' γάρ, φησί, '...Τιμόθεον ἀπολελυμένον, μεθ' οὗ...ὄψομαι ὑμᾶς' Chrys.*hom.34.2 in Heb*.(12.315A).

B. intrans.; **1.** *be exhibited publicly*; as prostitute, Clem.*str*. 3.4(p.208.27; M.8.1133A); Or.*Cels*.4.63(p.334.25; M.11.1132A); Θεσσαλίδα, δραπέτριαν, προεστῶσαν καλοῦσα Chrys.*hom.15.3 in Eph*.(11. 113B); **2.** *be champion, protector, patron*; **a.** in gen. εἰ δὲ Χριστὸς οὐδὲν ὠφελεῖ τοὺς μὴ βουλομένους ἑαυτοῖς προσέχειν, πῶς ἄνθρωπος προστήσεται; Chrys.*hom.9.5 in Mt*.(7.137A); *ib*.66.3(658A); ἐκεῖ κόλασίς ἐστιν ἀθάνατος...ὁ προστησόμενος οὐδεὶς id.*hom.9.5 in 1Thess*. (11.494A); **b.** of God ἐν πᾶσι δὲ τούτοις προΐσταται καὶ ἐν διαφόροις τρόποις παρακαλεῖ *T.Jos*.2.6; cf. ἄν τε προΐστᾶται, ἄν τε μή, πιστεύειν αὐτῷ Chrys.*hom.6.3 in Heb*.(12.67D); **c.** of BMV cf. θεοτόκε, προΐστα καὶ κυβέρνησον τὴν πόλιν ταύτην *IGC As.Min*.151 (Mitylene); δέσποινα ...πρόστηθι, καὶ ῥῦσαι δὲ πυρὸς καὶ σκότους ‡Gr.Naz.*Chr.pat*.2593 (M.38.337A); **d.** of angels οἱ ἄγγελοι τῶν ἐν τῇ ἐκκλησίᾳ μικρῶν καὶ τεταγμένοι εἰς τὸ προΐστασθαι αὐτῶν Or.*Cels*.6.41(p.110.16; M.11. 1360A); hence **3.** *be advocate, intercessor* for, of SS. Peter and Paul ὁ τὴν ἁλουργίδα περικείμενος...ἕστηκε δεόμενος τῶν ἁγίων, ὥστε αὐτοῦ προστῆναι παρὰ τῷ θεῷ Chrys.*hom.26.5 in 2Cor*.(10.625B); met., *excuse, plead in favour* of οὐδὲν τούτων αὐτοῦ προστήσεται id. *hom.48.4 in Mt*.(7.499A); **4.** *support cause* of, *advocate* δόγματος ἀνθρωπίνου προεστᾶσιν *Diogn*.5.3; Clem.*str*.2.20(p.176.22; M.8.1061A); Or.*or*.5(p.308.19; M.11.429B); ἰατρικῆς...προστήσεται Eus.*d.e*.4.5 (p.156.23; M.22.261B); of Christian teacher τὸν προϊστάμενον τοῦ λόγου Or.*Cels*.6.7(p.77.15; M.11.1300B); **5.** *offend, be obstacle to* μὴ προστῆναι...τοῖς ἀκούουσιν...τὸ λεχθὲν Chrys.*hom.26.4 in Mt*.(Gaume; cj. προσίστατο 7.319B); μὴ...προστῇ τὸ λεγόμενον id.*hom.44.1 in Jo*. (8.260C); ἐὰν περὶ τῆς δίκης τῶν διαγνωστῶν προΐσταται αὐτῷ πρὸς τὰς συνόδους τῆς ἰδίας ἐπαρχίας...ἐκκαλέσασθαι *Cod.Afr*.138(H.1.949B); Thdr.Stud.*epp*.2.218(M.99.1660B); hence *be raised as an objection* εἰ δέ τινι προΐσταται μὴ εἶναι θυγατριδοῦν τοῦ Ναβουχοδονόσορ τὸν Δαρεῖον, ἀλλ' υἱδοῦν Thdt.*Dan*.5:31(2.1175); **6.** *be leader, be superior, be in command*, esp. in ptcpl.; **a.** of Jewish authorities, Cyr.*Lc*. 7:32(M.72.620C); of local head of Essenes, Hipp.*haer*.9.20(p.257.2; M.16.3398A); **b.** in Church; **i.** of celebrant of eucharist προσφέρεται τῷ προεστῶτι τῶν ἀδελφῶν ἄρτος καὶ ποτήριον ὕδατος καὶ κράματος, καὶ οὗτος λαβὼν αἶνον καὶ δόξαν τῷ πατρὶ...διὰ τοῦ ὀνόματος τοῦ υἱοῦ καὶ τοῦ πνεύματος τοῦ ἁγίου ἀναπέμπει καὶ εὐχαριστίαν Just.*1apol*. 65.3(M.6.428A,B); ὁ προεστὼς διὰ λόγου τὴν νουθεσίαν καὶ πρόκλησιν ...ποιεῖται...καὶ ὁ π. εὐχὰς ὁμοίως καὶ εὐχαριστίας...ἀναπέμπει *ib*.67. 4,5(429B,C); ἐν τῇ ἐκκλησίᾳ ὁ προεστὼς δίδωσιν εἰρήνην Chrys.*hom. 32.6 in Mt*.(7.373A); ὁ τῆς ἐκκλησίας προεστὼς εὐθέως λέγει· εἰρήνη πᾶσιν id.*hom.3.3 in Col*.(11.348C); **ii.** of presbyters τῶν πρεσβυτέρων τῶν προϊσταμένων τῆς ἐκκλησίας Herm.*vis*.2.4.3; **iii.** of church leader, perh. bishop, but official status not clearly indicated π. ... τῆς ἐκεῖ [sc. ἐν τῇ Συρίᾳ] ἐκκλησίας Hipp.*Dan*.4.18.2; **iv.** of bishops with other clergy, cf. αὐχοῦσι [sc. heretics] προΐστασθαι διατριβῆς μᾶλλον ἢ ἐκκλησίας Clem.*str*.7.15(p.65.35; M.9.528C); ‡Ath.*sem*.4(M. 28.149A); as τοῖς προεστηκόσι τοῦ βίου τῆς εὐσεβείας Gr.Nyss.*or. catech*.proem.(p.1.2; M.45.9A); μὴ δῷς τοῖς προεστῶσι τῆς ἐκκλησίας διανεῖμαι Chrys.*hom.14.3 in 1Tim*.(11.628B); *ib*.15.2(636C); *Chron. Pasch*.p.292(M.92.729B); **v.** of bishops, Iren.*haer*.1.10.2(M.7.553A); οἱ πρὸ Σωτῆρος πρεσβύτεροι, οἱ προστάντες τῆς ἐκκλησίας...Ἀνίκητον λέγομεν καὶ Πίον id.*ep.Vict*.ap.Eus.*h.e*.5.24.14(M.20.505A); εἰσὶν ὁμόφρονες οἱ πανταχοῦ προεστῶτες Dion.Al.ap.Eus.*h.e*.7.5.1(M.20.

644A); τῆς ἐπισκοπῆς...Πίου μεταλλάξαντος, Ἀνίκητος τῶν ἐκεῖσε προΐσταται Eus.*h.e.*4.11.7(M.20.329C); *ib.*5.24.9(497A); of bishop as π. τῆς λειτουργίας *ib.*5.28.7(513A); *Clem.ep.*6(M.2.41A); *ib.*11(48A); Marcell.*ep.*ap.Epiph.*haer.*72.2(p.257.1; M.42.384C); ἐπίσκοποι καὶ π. τοῦ σωτηρίου λόγου Valent.Imp.*ep.episc.*ap.Thdt.*h.e.*4.8.3(3.957); *Const.App.*2.28.9; Chrys.*hom.2.1 in Tit.*(11.737E); Eustrat.*v.Eutych.* 83(M.86.2368D); **vi.** of προστάτης τοῦ ἱεροῦ cleric in charge of local church (i.e. the building) μετασχηματισάμενος ὁ...ἐπίσκοπος τὸ ἱερὸν τοῦτο εἰς τόπον τοῦ ἁγίου Στεφάνου...ἐπὶ τοῦ εὐλαβεστάτου Ποσίου διακόνου καὶ προεστῶτος *CIG* 8647 (Egypt, saec. vi); **vii.** of superiors in monasteries, *PLond.*1913.2; Ephr.1.323E; id.1.333E; Bas.*reg.fus.* 35.3(2.380B; M.31.1005C); **c.** of head of philosophical school Μαλχίων ...τῶν ἐπ' Ἀντιοχείας Ἑλληνικῶν παιδευτηρίων διατριβῆς π. Eus.*h.e.* 7.29.2(M.20.708C).

προκαθαιρέω, **1.** *abolish first,* Eus.*l.C.*16(p.250.1; M.20.1424B); Chrys.*hom.5.3 in Rom.*(9.464E); **2.** *depose before* from bishopric, Thphn.*chron.*p.107(M.108.312A).

προκαθαίρ-ω, **A.** *cleanse in advance*; **1.** *clear beforehand,* Clem. *str.*1.1(p.11.19; M.8.704C); **2.** *purify in advance* φιλοσοφία δὲ ἡ Ἑλληνικὴ οἷον ~ει...τὴν ψυχὴν εἰς παραδοχὴν πίστεως *ib.*7.3(p.14.21; M. 9.424C); ψυχὰς ~ειν...ἀπὸ τῶν φαύλων...δογμάτων *ib.*7.4(p.20.12; 436B); μετὰ τὰς Ἰωάννου διδασκαλίας...τοῖς...ἐπιδημεῖν προκεκαθαρμένοις διὰ τῶν ἡττόνων καὶ τὸν τέλειον λόγον Or.*Jo.*6.38(22; p.147.6; M.14.265B); τούτοις τοῖς νόμοις οἱονεὶ προκαθαρθεὶς τὴν διάνοιαν, ἐπὶ τὴν τελεωτέραν μυσταγωγίαν παράγεται Gr.Nyss.*v.Mos.*49(M.44. 317C); πάσης αἰσθητικῆς τε καὶ ἀλόγου κινήσεως προκαθᾶραι τὸν τρόπον *ib.*(373D); πάντων τῶν παθῶν τὴν ψυχὴν π. †Jo.D.*B.J.*20(M.96.1041B); ref. BMV κυηθεὶς...ἐκ τῆς παρθένου, καὶ ψυχὴν καὶ σῶμα προκαθαρθείσης τῷ πνεύματι Gr.Naz.*or.*38.13(M.36.325B); οὐδεὶς κατὰ σὲ προκεκάθαρται Sophr.H.*or.*2.25(M.87.3248A); τὴν ψυχὴν ἁγιασθεῖσα, καὶ τὸ σῶμα προκαθαρθεῖσα Jo.Mon.*hymn.Bas.*5(M.96.1373C); **3.** *purge in advance,* Synes.*ep.*44(M.66.1368B).

B. *clear away beforehand,* Athenag.*res.*1(p.49.10; M.6.976C); Clem.*str.*4.1(p.249.9; M.8.1216C).

***προκαθεδράω,** pass., *be placed as bishop,* CCarth.*act.*(H.1.165D).

προκαθέζ-ομαι, *sit before others*; **1.** *sit out in public,* as a prostitute νόμος...τῶν Ἀμορραίων τὴν χηρεύουσαν ~εσθαι ἐν πορνείᾳ *T.Jud.* 12.2; of Phoenician temple-prostitutes, Ath.*gent.*26(M.25.52A); **2.** *preside over*; **a.** in gen. οἱ τοῖς ματαίοις...τοῦ αἰῶνος τούτου ~όμενοι πράγμασιν Or.*Ps.*61:10(p.70; ? l. προσκ-); **b.** as judge in court, met. ὑψηλὸς ~εταί σου ὁ νοῦς πεπιστευμένος τὸ δικαστήριον Bas.*hom.*12.9(2.106B; M.31.405C); Σεβῆρος...π. δικαστὴς καὶ κριτὴς τῶν ἁγίων πατέρων Anast.S.*hod.*6(M.89.104B); **c.** of governor, Synes. *ep.*57(M.66.1393B); **d.** as president of council Γεώργιον τὸν Ἀλεξανδρείας συνεδρίου...~όμενον Philost.*h.e.*7.2(M.65.537B); †Jo.D.*B.J.* 32(M.96.1169D); **e.** of presidents of Church; **i.** clergy in gen. ἡμᾶς... οἱ δοκοῦμεν εἶναι ἀπὸ κλήρου τινὲς ~όμενοι ὑμῶν Or.*hom.11.3 in Jer.* (p.80.17; M.13.369C); **ii.** bishops, Clem.*q.d.s.*42(p.189.11; M.9.649A); Eus.*v.C.*3.58(p.105.16; M.20.1125A); *Hom.Clem.*3.64; bishop as τὸν ἀληθείας ~όμενον *Clem.ep.*2(M.2.36B); μεγάλου ποιμένος, τοῦ τῆς λαμπρᾶς ~ομένου πόλεως Gr.Naz.*or.*13.2(M.35.853C); ref. Cyprian οὐ γὰρ τῆς Καρχηδονίων π. μόνον ἐκκλησίας, οὐδὲ...Ἀφρικῆς, ἀλλὰ καὶ πάσης τῆς ἑσπερίου, σχεδὸν δὲ καὶ τῆς ἑῴας αὐτῆς *ib.*24.12(M.35. 1184B); ἐπίσκοπος ~έσθω ὑμῶν ὡς θεοῦ ἀξίᾳ τετιμημένος *Const.App.* 2.26.4; **f.** of God ὃς καὶ τῆς ζωῆς ~εται Const.ap.Ath.*apol.sec.*61 (p.141.8; M.25.360B); *Hom.Clem.*2.46; **g.** of primal substance of universe (Orphic) ὥσπερ ἐπ' ἀκρωρείας οὐρανοῦ ~εται *ib.*6.6; **3.** *be superior, have pre-eminence*; **a.** of capital city πόλις...~ομένη πάσης Ἰσαυρίδος πόλεως Bas.Sel.*v.Thecl.*1(M.85.556C); **b.** of metropolitan church, Oecum.*Apoc.*2:1(p.46); **c.** met. ἡ γὰρ ἰατρικὴ τῶν ἰαμάτων ~εται Eus.*v.C.*2.59(p.65.10; M.20.1033B); τούτων δὲ δύο ὁδῶν ~εται ἀπιστία καὶ πίστις *Hom.Clem.*7.7; **d.** hence *dominate* τοὺς πολεμίους τοὺς τῆς χώρας ~ομένους Clem.*str.*1.24(p.101.21; M.8.909A).

προκαθηγ-έομαι, **1.** *lead the way, be a guide*; **a.** lit., Bas.*hex.*8.5(1. 75A; M.29.176B); **b.** met. ὁρμή τε ἡ ~ουμένη τούτων Clem.*str.*2.3 (p.118.28; M.8.941C); ἡ διὰ τοῦ λουτροῦ π. κάθαρσις Gr.Nyss.*or. catech.*35(p.138.9; M.45.92B); τὸ μόνην τῆς αὐτοῦ κατὰ σάρκα γεννήσεως τὴν θείαν ~ήσασθαι θέλησιν δηλοῦν αὐτὸν οἶμαι Max.*opusc.*(M. 91.244A); **2.** *be in command* ἡ ἀλήθεια...καθάπερ τις στρατηγὸς ~ουμένη τῶν ἡμετέρων λόγων Gr.Nyss.*Eun.*12(1 p.216.13; M.45. 909A); hence προκαθηγούμενος, ὁ, *superior* of monastery, Bas.*ascet.* 1.5(2.323C; M.31.881A); fem. ἡ ἀδελφότης τὰ παραγγέλματα τῆς ~ουμένης ἀδιακρίτως δεχέσθω *ib.*2.2(326D; M.888C).

***προκαθήγησις, ἡ,** *leading,* Max.*ambig.*(M.91.1240A).

***προκαθηγουμένως,** *primarily,* Meth.*res.*1.38(p.280.6; M.41. 1104C).

προκάθη-μαι, *preside*; **1.** of bishop ~μένου τοῦ ἐπισκόπου εἰς τύπον θεοῦ Ign.*Magn.*6.1; and senior clergy ἑνώθητε τῷ ἐπισκόπῳ καὶ τοῖς ~μένοις *ib.*6.2; ἡμῶν τῶν τοῦ λαοῦ ~μένων Chrys.*hom.30.4 in 1Cor.*(10.275B); περὶ τοῦ μὴ δεῖν τὰς λεγομένας πρεσβύτιδας ἤτοι ~μένας ἐν ἐκκλησίᾳ καθίστασθαι CLaod.*can.*11; of Constantius at Church council μεταξὺ ~μένου τοῦ βασιλέως...τῶν ἐπισκόπων καὶ ἄρχειν καὶ τῶν ἐκκλησιῶν ἐθέλοντος Philost.*h.e.*7.6(M.65.636A); **2.** of a city, *be pre-eminent, be capital* Καρχηδόνα, τὴν τῆς Λιβύης ~μένην Thdt.*Ps.*71:10(1.1106); id.*Jon.*1:1(2.1463); of Rome ἡ γὰρ αὐτὴ πασῶν μεγίστη...καὶ τῆς οἰκουμένης ~μένη id.*ep.*113(4.1187); **3.** of a church ~ται ἐν τόπῳ χωρίου Ῥωμαίων...καὶ ~μένη τῆς ἀγάπης Ign.*Rom.*proem.

προκαθιδρύω, *establish beforehand,* Meth.*symp.*4.5(p.51.4; καθιδρύων M.18.93B); Nil.ap.Proc.G.*Cant.*2:4(M.87.1584A).

προκαθιερ-όω, *consecrate in advance* οἱ καλλίνικοι μάρτυρες οἱ τὰς ψυχὰς θεῷ ~ώσαντες, εἶτα καὶ τὰ σώματα θύσαντες Const.Diac.*laud.*8 (M.88.487B); Thdr.Stud.*epp.*2.192(M.99.1584B).

προκαθίζω, **1.** *put forward, appoint*; of congregation appointing Levites, Cyr.*ador.*11(1.409E); Call.*v.Hyp.*(p.67); **2.** *preside* over οἰκουμενικῇ προκαθίσας συνόδῳ Thdt.*ep.*112(4.1184); Call.*v.Hyp.* (p.70).

προκακόομαι, *be afflicted before,* Clem.*str.*2.20(p.173.5; M.8.1053B).

προκάλυμμα, τό, *veil, cloak,* of Christ's humanity τῷ π. τῆς φύσεως ἡμῶν ἐνεκρύφθη τὸ θεῖον Gr.Nyss.*or.catech.*24(p.93.1; M.45. 65A); χρησάμενος οἷόν τινι παραπετάσματι, τῷ τῆς σαρκὸς π. Thdt. *eran.*1(4.23); οὐ γὰρ π. τῆς θεότητος χρώμενος ἀνέλαβε τὴν τοῦ σώματος φύσιν, κατὰ τὴν Ἀρείου...φρενοβλάβειαν...ἀλλ' ἠβουλήθη αὐτὴν τὴν ἡττηθεῖσαν φύσιν καταγωνίσασθαι τὸν ἀντίπαλον id.*haer.*5.11(4. 422); ῥᾷστον μὲν γὰρ ἦν αὐτῷ καὶ δίχα τοῦ τῆς σαρκὸς π. πραγματεύσασθαι τῶν ἀνθρώπων τὴν σωτηρίαν id.*affect.*6(p.175.21; 4.877); ὅπως ἂν μὴ λάθῃ ὅτιπερ τῷ π. τῆς σαρκὸς ἡ θεότης ἐκρύπτετο, ἡ τοῦ πατρὸς φωνὴ ἐξ οὐρανῶν ἐπιβοῶσα Leo Mag.*ep.*28.4(p.15.15; M.*PL.*54.770A).

***προκαρποφορέω,** *bear fruit before,* Cyr.*glaph.Gen.*3(1.103B).

προκαταβάλλ-ω, **1.** *lay foundation beforehand*; **a.** lit., in simile of growth of Church τοὺς...ἐκκλησιῶν προκαταβληθέντας...θεμελίους Eus.*h.e.*3.37.1(M.20.292D); **b.** met. ἀγαθὴν προκατεβάλοντο τῶν πραγμάτων κρηπῖδα id.*v.C.*2.25(p.51.23; M.20.1004A); τὸ ἄθεον τοῦτο παρὰ τοῦ διαβόλου προκαταβέβληται κήρυγμα Gr.Nyss.*Eun.*11(2 p.273.11; M.45.884A); id.*Apoll.*54(M.45.1256A); Chrys.*hom.5.3 in Jo.*(8.39A); ‡Proc.G.*Pr.*1:20(M.87.1229C); **2.** *put down, sow in advance*; of seeds, Gr.Nyss.*or.catech.*26(p.97.20; M.45.68C); met., Chrys.*hom. 15.7 in Mt.*(7.197A); τοὺς ὡρισμένους ἐπὶ τοῖς στεφάνοις οὐ ~όμενος ἀγῶνας καὶ πόνους ‡Bas.*const.*24.1(2.575A; M.31.1413A); πόνος διὰ τὴν τῶν καρπῶν ἐλπίδα ~εται Mac.Aeg.*or.*5(M.34.857A); **3.** *lay down* τὸ θέλειν τὸ καλόν,...ἄνωθεν ἦν προκαταβεβλημένον Chrys.*hom.13.2 in Rom.*(9.560C); **4.** *pay down in advance,* met. προκαταβαλέσθαι τοῖς ἠδικημένοις τὸν τῆς συμπαθείας ἔρανον Bas.*ep.*65(3.158D; M.32.424A); **5.** *introduce* a subject *in advance,* Chrys.*hom.11.6 in Mt.*(7.157A); τὸν περὶ τοῦ πάθους ~εται λόγον *ib.*30.4(352D); *ib.*57.4(581A); id. *hom.8.5 in Rom.*(9.503E); Socr.*h.e.*3.10.1(M.67.405B); **6.** *state beforehand,* Thdt.*h.rel.*2(3.1120); **7.** *institute in advance* ~εται προοίμια τῶν ἐθνῶν Chrys.*hom.80.1 in Jo.*(8.473C); **8.** *abase beforehand* τοὺς ὀκνοῦντας πρὸς ἀρετὴν ὁ τῶν κακῶν φόβος ~ει Or.*exp.in Pr.*18:8(M.17. 204B); προκαταβαλὼν γὰρ ἑαυτὸν διὰ ταπεινοφροσύνης...εὐπαράδεκτος ἔσῃ Bas.*ep.*2.5(3.74A; M.32.232A); Chrys.*hom.6.2 in Rom.*(9. 474E); **9.** *cast down, dismay in advance* πάντες δὲ τῷ φόβῳ τῶν προσδοκωμένων προκατεβέβληντο Gr.Nyss.*Eun.*1(1 p.65.10; M.45.293C); Chrys.*hom.72.3 in Jo.*(8.426B).

***προκατάβασις, ἡ,** *previous descent,* Chrysipp.*enc.in Jo.Bapt.* (p.30.14).

προκαταγγέλλ-ω, *announce in advance* τὴν προκατηγγελμένην... γῆν Clem.*str.*3.11(p.228.30; M.8.1173B); φάσκουσιν ὅτι πάντα ἡμῖν ὁ θεὸς...~ει Cels.ap.Or.*Cels.*4.23(p.292.23; M.11.1060B); ἔχοιεν διὰ τῶν αἰσθητῶν τὴν εἰκόνα τῶν θείων ~ειν πραγμάτων Meth.*symp.*5.7(p.62. 2; M.18.109B); of OT prophecies, Ath.*inc.*33.5(M.25.153B); ὁ παρὼν καιρὸς οὗτός ἐστιν ἐκεῖνος ὁ πάλαι ~όμενος Ath.*Ar.*2.16(M.26.180B); ἡ δὲ τοῦ νομοθέτου μάθησις ἐπίγνωσις τοῦ ~ομένου Serap.*Man.*36(p.53; M.18.1213D); τοῖς προκατηγγελμένοις παρὰ τῶν ἁγίων [i.e. orthodox doctrine] Bas.*Eun.*2.8(1.243E; M.29.585B); προφῆται καὶ πάντες οἱ τὰ θαύματα περὶ τοῦ κυρίου ~οντες Gr.Nyss.*Apoll.*45(M.45.1232C); παρέσται κατὰ καιροὺς ὁ προκατηγγελμένος Cyr.*Abac.*20(3.534C); Jo. Eub.*concept.BMV* 11(M.96.1476C).

***προκαταγγελτικός,** *prophetic*; of OT types, Meth.*symp.*9.2 (p.115.25; M.18.180C).

***προκαταγγελτικῶς,** *prophetically,* Epiph.*haer.*71.2(p.251.11; M. 42.377A); Jo.D.*haer.*65(M.94.717A).

***προκατάγγελτος**, *announced beforehand*, ‡Jo.D.*hom*.5(M.96.649B).

***προκαταγγέλτωρ, ὁ**, *one who announces in advance*, Epiph.*haer*.66.75(p.116.17; M.42.148B).

***προκαταγνωστέον**, *one must condemn beforehand*, Clem.*str*.6.8 (p.465.15; M.9.288C).

***προκαταγοητεύω**, *bewitch beforehand*, Nil.*epp*.3.82(M.79.425B).

προκαταγράφ-ω, *depict beforehand*, Cyr.*glaph.Gen*.3(1.66B); ἐλυτρώσατό ποτε τοὺς ἐξ Ἰσραήλ, ὡς ἐν σκιαῖς καὶ τύποις ~ων ἡμῖν τοῦ Χριστοῦ τὸ μυστήριον id.*Ps*.68:19(M.69.1169B); id.*hom.pasch*.20 (5[2].257D).

***προκαταδείκνυμι**, *point out before*, Cyr.*ador*.9(1.313B); id.*Is*.4.1 (2.568B).

***προκαταδηόω**, *ravage beforehand*, Cyr.*Nah*.13(3.490E).

προκαταθήγω, *make keen, stimulate in advance*, Cyr.*ador*.6(1.173A).

***προκαταικίζω**, *torture previously*, *Ep.Lugd*.ap.Eus.*h.e*.5.1.28(M.20.420A).

προκατακλ-άω, *shatter before* ~ῶντες εἰς φόβον τοὺς ἐν αὐταῖς Cyr.*Soph*.7(3.587A; προκαλοῦντες Aubert); ~ῶντος τῷ φόβῳ τοὺς μαθητάς id.*Jo*.9(4.748D; προσκ- Aubert).

***προκατακοιμίζω**, *lull to sleep before*, Clem.*paed*.2.2(p.171.14; M.8.420A).

προκατακρίν-ω, **1.** *condemn in advance*, ref. predestination ποιεῖ ...σκεύη τιμῆς καὶ σκεύη ἀτιμίας οὐκ ἀρχῆθεν κατὰ τὴν πρόγνωσιν, ἐπεὶ μὴ κατ' αὐτὴν ~ει Or.*princ*.3.1.21(p.238.4; M.11.297A); ref. Pilate ἐξουσίαν ἔχων σταυρῶσαί σε. ὁρᾷς πῶς ἑαυτὸν ~ει; Chrys. *hom.84.2 in Jo*.(8.500C); ῥᾳστώνης πῶς ἄν τις ἴδοι τὴν ἄφεσιν, οὐ ~αντος ἡμᾶς τοῦ νόμου Cyr.*ador*.2(1.54C); **2.** *condemn formerly* τὸ αὐτὸ τῷ...προκατακριθέντι [i.e. in OT times] τολμήσας Bas.*reg.br*.47 (2.431C; M.31.1116A).

προκαταλαμβάνω, **1.** *attain before* πρὸ γὰρ τῆς ἐμῆς ἀφίξεως τοῦ βίου προκατειλήφει τὸ τέρμα Thdt.*h.rel*.24(3.1259); **2.** *anticipate*, ref. prophets, etc., who did not pray to God as Father ἵνα μὴ προκαταλάβωσιν τὴν διὰ τοῦ Ἰησοῦ ἐκκενουμένην παντὶ τῷ κόσμῳ χάριν Or.*Jo*. 19.5(p.304.3; M.14.533B); **3.** *seize upon in advance* so as to condemn τὰ πράγματα προκατείληπται Chrys.*hom.3.4 in Ac*.(9.29D); **4.** *determine beforehand* φθάνειν τὴν τοῦ θεοῦ γνῶσιν ἐπὶ τοὺς προγνώσει τοῦ θεοῦ προκαταληφθέντας ὅτι ἀξίως βιώσουσι τοῦ ἐγνωσμένου Or.*Cels*. 7.44(p.195.7; M.11.1484C); ref. prayer εἰ...τὸ ἑκάστου ἐφ' ἡμῖν αὐτῷ ἔγνωσται, καὶ διὰ τοῦτο προεωραμένον αὐτῷ διατάττεσθαι ἀπὸ τῆς προνοίας τὸ κατ' ἀξίαν παντὶ τῷ εὔλογον καὶ τὸ τί εὔξηται...καὶ τί βουλόμενος αὐτῷ γενέσθαι προκατειλῆφθαι· οὗ προκαταληφθέντος, καὶ τοιοῦτόν τι ἀκολούθως ἐν τῇ διατάξει τετάξεται id.*or*.6(p.313.19; M.11.437A).

***προκαταλεαίνω**, *smooth down before*, Bas.*ep*.2.2(3.72A; M.32.225B); Chrys.*hom.10.1 in 1Cor*.(10.80D).

προκατάληψις, ἡ, *anticipation*; hence *prevention* ἀντίδοτον ἰατρικὴν...εἰς παθῶν π. Epiph.*haer*.47.3(p.219.3; M.41.856A).

προκαταμανθάνω, *learn beforehand*, Gr.Nyss.*Apoll*.25(M.45.1177D).

***προκαταμηνύω**, **1.** *indicate previously*, Cyr.*ador*.14(1.510C); **2.** *prophesy*, id.*glaph.Gen*.2(1.53C); id.*Ps*.41:4(M.69.1001D); id.*Os*.4 (3.22B); id.*Nest*.5.5(p.101.40; 6[1].136B).

προκατανο-έω, *observe beforehand* τὰ πάντα ~ῆσθαι τῇ τοῦ θεοῦ σοφίᾳ Gr.Nyss.*hex*.13(M.44.76B); id.*fat*.(M.45.164A).

προκαταπίνω, *swallow beforehand*, in comparison of Jonah with Christ οὐδὲ καταποθεὶς ὁ Ἰωνᾶς ἀνήγαγε τοὺς προκαταποθέντας ὑπὸ τοῦ κήτους Ath.*Ar*.3.23(M.26.369C); ὁ θάνατος κατέπιεν τὴν ζωήν, καὶ ναυτιάσας ἔμεσεν καὶ τοὺς προκαταποθέντας Ast.Soph.*hom.5 in Ps.5* (M.40.436A).

***προκαταπλουτ-έω**, *be previously enriched*, of apostles and evangelists τὸν θεῖον...ἀναβρύουσι λόγον ~οῦντες ἄνωθεν αὐτοὶ τὴν χάριν Cyr.*Is*.3.2(2.431B).

***προκαταπτοέω**, *terrify beforehand*, Cyr.*Is*.3.2(2.399D); *ib*.(425A); *ib*.2.3(250D); id.*Jo*.4.3(4.372D).

***προκαταραφή, ἡ**, *first row* in plaiting a basket, *Apophth.Patr*. (M.65.192C).

προκαταρκτικός, **1.** *initial* τοῦ ὀνόματος τὸ π. στοιχεῖον τὸ α Cyr. *syn.def*.(M.76.1421A); **2.** *primary, immediate*, of causes τῶν αἰτίων τὰ μὲν π., τὰ δὲ συνεκτικά Clem.*str*.8.9(p.95.27; M.9.592C); τὰ μὲν π. λέγουσι τῶν αἰτίων εἶναι, τὰ δὲ συνεργὰ ἢ συναίτια Bas.*Spir*.5(3.5A; M.32.76A); **3.** *belonging to initial stages* διττὸς ὁ φόβος, ὁ μὲν π., ὁ δὲ τελειωτικός, καὶ τοῦ μὲν π. τοῖς οὔπω τὴν ἀθῴωσιν εἰληφόσι συνόντος, τοῦ τελειωτικοῦ δὲ τοῖς ἤδη ὑπὸ θεοῦ ἀνειλημμένοις Areth.*Apoc*.11:16 (M.106.657A); **4.** *originating, causative* τὰ αἴτια καὶ π. τῆς ἁμαρτίας Meth.*lepr*.7(p.460.1); νοῦς...τῶν ἐν αὐτῷ κινήσεων καὶ ἐννοιῶν π. Melet.*nat.hom*.31(M.64.1308C); **5.** theol.; **a.** ref. creation γενηθήτω στερέωμα. αὕτη ἡ φωνὴ τῆς π. αἰτίας Bas.*hex*.3.4(1.26C; M.29.64A) = Proc.G.*Gen*.1:6(M.87.72A); ἀρχὴ γὰρ τῆς κτίσεως ἡ π. αἰτία καὶ ἄκτιστος Andr.Caes.*Apoc*.9(M.106.249A); **b.** ref. Trin. μήτε ἀπηλλοτριῶσθαι πατὴρ υἱοῦ ᾗ πατήρ, π. γάρ ἐστι τῆς συναφείας τὸ ὄνομα Dion.Al.ap.Ath.*Dion*.17(p.58.19; M.25.504D); ref. work of Persons in Creation τὴν π. αἰτίαν τῶν γινομένων, τὸν πατέρα, τὴν δημιουργικήν, τὸν υἱόν, τὴν τελειωτικήν, τὸ πνεῦμα Bas.*Spir*.38(3.31D; M.32.136B); 'διὰ τοῦ υἱοῦ' δημιουργεῖν τὸν πατέρα...ὥστε ἡ 'δι' οὗ' φωνὴ ὁμολογίαν τῆς π. αἰτίας ἔχει *ib*.21(18D; M.105C).

***προκαταρκτικῶς**, *in respect of origin*, Cyr.*Jo*.2.6(4.219C).

προκάταρξις, ἡ, **1.** *first beginning*, ‡Bas.*struct.hom*.2.10(1.343D; M.30.53B); CLater.*act*.1(H.3.692E); **2.** *formal entering of a suit in law*, litis contestatio ὅπου γὰρ γέγονε π., ἐκεῖ καὶ τὸ πέρας [τῆς δίκης] γυμνάζεται Ath.Scholast.*coll*.1.2(p.11).

***προκαταρρωστέω**, *to be ailing before*, Cyr.*ador*.15(1.553A).

***προκαταρτισμός, ὁ**, *preliminary performance*, Max.*qu.Thal*.47 (M.90.429B).

προκατάρχ-ω, **1.** *exist before*, of causes τὸ γὰρ ποιητικὸν αἴτιον ~ειν τῶν γιγνομένων ἀνάγκη Athenag.*leg*.19.3(M.6.929B); of Marcion's good deity opp. creator ἡ τοῦ σῴζοντος βούλησις οὐκ ἀπολείπεται τοῦ ἀγαθοῦ ἥ γε προκατάρξασα Clem.*str*.5.1(p.328.19; M.9.13B); **2.** *originate, be first cause* of τὸ σκώπτειν ὕβρεως ~ον Clem. *paed*.2.7(p.189.18; M.8.456B); ἄγνοια προκατῆρξε τῆς ἐκπλήξεως id. *str*.2.8(p.133.3; M.8.973A); οἱ χρόνοι δὲ τῶν προκαταρξάντων τῆς φιλοσοφίας αὐτῶν...λεκτέοι *ib*.1.14(p.41.6; 765A); of Eve ἡ προκατάρξασα τῆς παραβάσεως 'ζωὴ' προσηγορεύθη *ib*.3.9(p.225.29; 1168A); ὁ μὲν γὰρ εὐεργέτης ~ει τῆς εὐποιΐας *ib*.7.3(p.15.15; M.9.425B); ὁ ἅγιος ζῇ πνεύματι, ~οντι τῶν ἐν τῷ ζῆν καὶ πάσης πράξεως καὶ εὐχῆς Or.*Jo*. 32.18(11; p.456.5; M.14.789C); Ἀσκλήπιον τὸν προκατάρξαντα καθ' ὑμᾶς τῆς ἰατρικῆς ἐπιστήμης ‡Jo.D.*Artem*.28(p.160.15; M.96.1277A); of Father προκατήρξατο γὰρ εὐδοκήσας ὁ πατήρ· ἐδημιούργησεν δὲ ὁ μονογενής Didym.*Trin*.2.1(M.39.449B); πῶς γὰρ ἂν αὐτὸς ἰδίᾳ καὶ μόνος προκατάρξαιτό ποτε, δύναμιν ἔχων τὴν ἐφ' ἅπασιν ἐνεργετικὴν τὸν υἱόν, συνυπάρχοντα μὲν ἀϊδίως αὐτῷ; Cyr.*Jo*.2.6(4.221D); of grace preceding human intention, Didym.*Trin*.2.14(M.39.712B); **3.** *be origin* of τὴν παρ' αὐτοῖς [sc. Ἰουδαίοις] φιλοσοφίαν...γενομένην προκατάρξαι τῆς παρ' Ἕλλησι φιλοσοφίας Clem.*str*.1.15(p.46.16; M.8.781A); **4.** *begin, initiate*, Athenag.*leg*.11.2(M.6.912B); προκατήρχετο τοῦ ὕμνου Clem.*str*.5.8(p.359.3; M.9.77A); ~ομένου τοῦ ἔργου Or.*Jo*. 13.50(49; p.278.9; M.14.489C); παραχωρεῖν τοῦ προκατάρξασθαι τῷ νεωτέρῳ θεῷ Synes.*ep*.116(M.66.1497A); Proc.G.*Jos*.1:2(M.87.993A); c. infin., Philost.*h.e*.7.5(M.65.544A); **5.** *take lead in* οἱ τῆς ἐναντίας ~οντες λήξεως Eus.*v.C*.2.10(p.45.7; M.20.989A); **6.** *predispose* ἀσυμπαθὴς τρόπος προκαταρξάμενος εἰς μισανθρωπίας ἔγκλημά με ῥίπτει Bas.*ep*.45.1(3.133A; M.32.365A); **7.** *be pre-eminent over* πάντων μὲν ~ειν τάξας τῶν κτισμάτων †Jo.D.*B.J*.17(M.96.1009C).

προκατασεί-ω, *shake, overthrow in advance*, Chrys.*hom.11.3 in 1Cor*.(10.90C); Cyr.*ador*.5(1.142B); φρίττω καὶ ~ομαι Anast.S.*Ps.6* (M.89.1089B).

προκατασκευάζω, **1.** *prepare in advance*; of Greek philosophy preparing way for Christian doctrine, Clem.*str*.1.16(p.52.21; M.8.796A); of God preparing remedy for future sins, Ast.Am.*hom*.12(M.40.349C); of construction of arguments or theories in advance of discussion, Gr.Nyss.*anim.et res*.(M.46.36B); Epiph.*haer*.69.19(p.169.5; M.42.232B); hence **2.** pass., *be accepted as proved* (i.e. before or without discussion) τὸ μηδενὶ λόγῳ μήτε δειχθὲν μήτε δειχθῆναι δυνάμενον ὡς προκατεσκευασμένον θαρσῶν ἀποφαίνεται Gr.Nyss.*Eun*. 1(1 p.88.25; M.45.320D).

προκατασκευαστικός, *preliminary* προοιμιώδη ταῦτα καὶ π. τῶν λόγων Meth.*symp*.9.1(p.113.4; M.18.176C); Chrys.*hom.7.2 in Col*. (11.373D).

***προκατασκευαστικῶς**, *as a preliminary*, Epiph.*haer*.69.60(p.208.28; M.42.300A).

προκατασκευή, ἡ, **1.** *preface, introduction*, Eus.*h.e*.1.5.1(M.20.80D); id.*p.e*.1.1(4A; M.21.25D); Isid.Pel.*epp*.4.12(M.78.1060C); **2.** *preparation* π. ἐστι τοῦ...χειροτονηθῆναι Chrys.*hom.8.1 in Heb*.(12.82D).

***προκατασκοπέω**, *watch beforehand*, *Hom.Clem*.14.2.

***προκατασπάω**, *pull down, demolish beforehand*; a theory, Chrys. *hom.12.1 in 1Tim*.(11.611A).

***προκαταστίζομαι**, *suffer compunction beforehand*, Cyr.*hom. pasch*.13(5[1].183C).

***προκατασωρεύω**, *heap up beforehand*, Cyr.*Is*.5.2(2.782E).

προκατα-τίθημι, *lay down beforehand* as foundation, met. ~θέντες τῇ πίστει τὴν ἕνωσιν οἷά τινα κρηπῖδα καὶ θεμέλιον Cyr.*schol.inc.*35 (p.225.32; cf.5[1].799c).

***προκαταυγάζω**, *be first illuminated*, Gr.Nyss.*diff.ess.*4(M.32.329c); προκαταυγασθέντα τῷ πνεύματι id.*Steph.*1(M.46.717a).

προκατηχ-έω, *give preliminary instruction* (*to*) of God 'tempting' Israel 'ἐπείραζεν' ἀντὶ τοῦ 'προκατήχει' Proc.G.*Ex.*15:23(M.87.589a); pass., *receive preliminary instruction*, esp. in Christian faith τὰ πάτρια ὑμᾶς...ἔθη ~ημένους Clem.*prot.*10(p.70.17; προκατεσχημένους M.8.209b); of preliminary teaching received by Christ's disciples concerning the Passion, Or.*comm.in Mt.*12.17(p.107.30; M.13.1021a); of catechizing received by heretics on admission to Church, Dion. Al.ap.Eus.*h.e.*7.5.5(M.20.645a); Gr.Nyss.*v.Gr.Thaum.*(M.46.921d); Cyr.*ador.*3(1.87e); ref. Cornelius οὐκ ἂν ἄλλως ἐπέπεσε τὸ πνεῦμα...εἰ μὴ ~ηθέντας τὸν τῆς πίστεως λόγον Ammon.*Ac.*10:44(M.85.1537d); κεκράτηκεν ἐν πολλαῖς ἐκκλησίαις τῇ τετράδι τῆς ἁγίας ἑβδομάδος ~εῖσθαι τὰ νῦν, ὡς εἰπεῖν ἀκούοντας 'ἑτοιμάζεσθε ἑαυτοῖς ἐπισιτισμόν. ἔτι γὰρ γ' ἡμέρας ὑμεῖς διαβήσεσθε τὸν 'Ιορδάνην' Proc.G.*Jos.*1:11(M.87.996c); of instruction to be given to Meletian schismatics in order that they may recognize antichrist in Arius, Ath.*h.Ar.*78 (p.227.14; M.25.789a).

προκατήχησις, ἡ, *preliminary instruction*, Cyr.H.*procatech.*tit.; of God's revelation in OT types ὡς ἐν αἰνίγμασι καὶ μονονουχὶ π. καὶ προεισβολὴν εἰς σύνεσιν Cyr.*glaph.Gen.*5(1.140c); of Law προγύμνασμα γάρ τι καὶ π. τῆς ἐν πνεύματι λατρείας τὸ γράμμα id.*Jo.*2.1 (4.157a); τὸ ἐν...μ' ἔτεσι μὴ ἐκτριβῆναι τὰ ἱμάτια τοῦ λαοῦ...π. ἦν τῆς μελλούσης ἀσφαλείας Proc.G.*Gen.*9:4(M.87.289a).

προκατονομάζω, *set forth the name* or *definition of* Παῦλος... ἔγραψεν...ἡ κοινωνία τοῦ ἁγίου πνεύματος...ἥντινα...κοινωνίαν καὶ τὰ καθολικὰ προκατωνόμασεν χαράγματα οὕτως. ἵνα γένησθε θείας κοινωνοὶ φύσεως Didym.*Trin.*2.12(M.39.688a).

***προκατοπτρίζομαι**, *see beforehand as in a mirror*; of prophetic vision προορῶν Pall.*v.Chrys.*5(p.28.12; M.47.18; v.l. προκατοπτριζόμενος).

προκατορθόω, **1.** *correct in advance*, *Hom.Clem.*1.6; **2.** *accomplish successfully beforehand*, Bas.*reg.br.*237(2.495b; M.31.1241b); Cyr.*Is.*5.3(2.815d); id.*ador.*2(1.72b); †Jo.D.*B.J.*33(M.96.1181a); **3.** *live rightly beforehand*, Gr.Nyss.*v.Mos.*13(M.44.304a).

πρόκει-μαι, **1.** *be set forth*, of eucharistic elements on altar πάντα πνευματικὰ γίνεται τὰ ~μενα...οὐκ εἰς κνῖσαν διαχεῖται ἡ θυσία, ἀλλὰ λαμπρὰ καὶ φαιδρὰ ἐργάζεται τὰ ~μενα Chrys.*hom.14.2 in Heb.* (12.141c); οὐ γὰρ ἄνθρωπός ἐστιν ὁ ποιῶν τὰ ~μενα γενέσθαι σῶμα καὶ αἷμα τοῦ Χριστοῦ. ... 'τοῦτό μού ἐστι τὸ σῶμα'...τοῦτο τὸ ῥῆμα τὰ ~μενα μεταρρυθμίζει id.*prod.Jud.*2.6(2.394a); ref. Nest.'s Christology in its eucharistic consequences φησιν ὅτι...ἐν τοῖς μυστηρίοις σῶμά ἐστιν ἀνθρώπου τὸ ~μενον Cyr.*ep.*11a(p.171.29; M.77.88b); ἐξαπόστειλον ἐφ' ἡμᾶς καὶ ἐπὶ τὰ ~μενα ἅγια δῶρα ταῦτα τὸ πνεῦμά σου τὸ πανάγιον *Lit.Jac.*(p.204.23); *Lit.Chrys.*(p.329.18); **2.** προκείμενον, τό, *proper antiphon* or *gradual* preceding reading of Epistle, ‡Sophr.H. *liturg.*17(M.87.3997b); τὸ π. μηνύει τῶν προφητῶν τὴν ἐκφαντορίαν ‡Bas.*h.myst.*39(p.387.2); τὸ π. τοῦ ἀποστόλου *Lit.Chrys.*(p.371.4).

***προκείρω**, *cut off before*, Geo.Pis.*carm.vit.*77.

***προκελαδέω**, *announce beforehand*, †Gregent.*disp.*(M.86.760d).

προκέλευθος, *heralding*, *introducing*, Nonn.*par.Jo.*1:8(M.43.752a); *ib.*1:31(756a); Paul.Sil.*Soph.*959(M.86.2155b).

***πρόκενσος, ὁ**, (Lat. *processus*); **1.** *imperial progress*, Const. ap.Gel.Cyz.*h.e.*3.18.4; †Polyb.*v.Epiph.*61(M.41.101b); *M.Pers.*3.6 (p.444.11); **2.** *temporary residence* of emperor outside capital (sometimes indistinguishable from former sense) ἐποίησεν ἐκεῖ π. μῆνας ἐξ *Chron.Pasch.*p.324(M.92.829a); **3.** *place of temporary residence*, *ib.*p.376(964a).

προκέντημα, τό, **1.** *pattern*, *example* ἔχων π. τὸ ἐπὶ τῶν τριῶν παίδων γεγενημένον Hipp.*Dan.*3.21.1; **2.** *type*, of Passover as type of Redemption ἵνα τὸ μέλλον ἐγείρεσθαι...διὰ μικροῦ καὶ φθαρτοῦ π. ὁραθῇ Mel.*pass.*36 p.6.11; of Israel as type of Church, *ib.*40 p.6.31.

προκήρυγμα, τό, *proclamation beforehand*, *prophecy*; of OT types foreshadowing Christ, Just.*dial.*131.5(M.6.781b); of Jo. Bapt. ᾧ ἐδόθη τὸ μήνυμα τοῦ π. Epiph.*haer.*62.5(p.394.2; M.41.1056d); τοῦ προφήτου διὰ τοῦ πνεύματος τὰ π. ‡Meth.*Sym.et Ann.*2(M.18.352a).

***προκῆρυξ, ὁ**, *fore-announcer*, Cyr.*Jo.*2.1(4.159a).

προκήρυξις, ἡ, *proclamation in advance*, *prophecy*, Just.*dial.*125.5 (M.6.768b); *ib.*134.2(785c).

προκηρύσσω, *proclaim in advance* οἱ προφῆται οἱ προκηρύξαντες τὴν ἔλευσιν τοῦ κυρίου Polyc.*ep.*6.3; προφῆται, δι' ὧν τὸ προφητικὸν πνεῦμα π. τὰ γενήσεσθαι μέλλοντα Just.*1apol.*31.1(M.6.376a); διὰ τῶν προφητῶν προεκεκήρυκτο [sc. Χριστός] *ib.*56.1(413a); id.*dial.*106.1(M.6.724a); Clem.*prot.*10(p.78.15; M.8.228a); προκεκηρύχει δὲ καὶ Κῦρος τὴν 'Εβραίων ἀποκατάστασιν id.*str.*1.21(p.77.26; M.8.853a); id.*exc. Thdot.*59(p.126.20; M.9.688a); ref. descent into Hades κατελήλυθεν ἐκεῖ προκηρυχθεὶς ὑπὸ τῶν προφητῶν ἢ οὔ; ἀλλ' ἐνθάδε μὲν προεκηρύχθη ὑπὸ τῶν προφητῶν, ἀλλαχοῦ δὲ κατέρχεται οὐ διὰ προφητῶν; Or.*engast.*6(p.289.10; M.12.1021a); οἱ τῶν 'Ελλήνων παῖδες προεφήτευσαν, καὶ τὸν προάναρχον θεόν, καὶ τὸν συνάναρχον αὐτοῦ υἱόν...καὶ τὸ σύνθρονον αὐτοῦ...πνεῦμα προεκήρυξαν ‡Ath.*templ.*(p.111.13; M. 28.1432a); Chrys.*hom.1.2 in Rom.*(9.431c); *Chron.Pasch.*p.238(M. 92.576a); abs. ὁ νόμος καὶ οἱ προφῆται ἕως 'Ιωάννου προεκήρυξαν [cf.Mt.11:12], *ib.*p.237(573c).

***προκισσάω**, *engender*, Epiph.*haer.*37.1(p.51.15; M.41.641d).

προκιχρ-άω, *lend in advance*, of God's action in Inc. ~ᾷ τῇ φύσει τῶν ἀνθρώπων τὸν υἱόν, καὶ τόκον εἰσπράττεται δι' αὐτοῦ, πάσης ψυχῆς τὴν ἐξουσίαν Ephr.2.271e; monastic system ἔχει τὴν ζωὴν τὴν ἐπὶ τοῦ παρόντος θεῷ διακονοῦσαν, καὶ ~ᾷ ταύτην, ἵνα τὸν τόκον ζωὴν αἰώνιον ἀπολάβῃ *ib.*412d; μηδ' ὅτι νεκρὸν ἐγκλίνιον βλέπομεν, σχετλιάζωμεν· ἀλλ' ἐννοῶμεν ὅτι τὸ δάνειον ὁ ~ῶν ἑκάστῳ τὴν πνοήν, ὁπότε βεβούλητο εἰσεπράξατο Andr.Cr.*or.*21(M.97.1284b).

προκοιμ-άομαι, *fall asleep before*, *predecease*, perf. and aor. ptcpl. οἱ ἀπόστολοι καὶ οἱ διδάσκαλοι οἱ κηρύξαντες τὸ ὄνομα τοῦ υἱοῦ τοῦ θεοῦ, κοιμηθέντες...ἐκήρυξαν καὶ τοῖς προκεκοιμημένοις Herm.*sim.*9. 16.5; ἡ πρὸς τὸν πλησίον ἀγάπη· ἣν πολλῷ μᾶλλον προσεῖναι τοῖς προκεκοιμημένοις ἁγίοις πρὸς τοὺς ἐν βίῳ ἀγωνιζομένους ἀναγκαῖον νοεῖν Or.*or.*11.2(p.322.15; M.11.449a); οἱ προκεκοιμημένοι ἅγιοι προσδοκῶντες καὶ τὴν ἐν σώματι τοῦ Χριστοῦ ἐπιδημίαν id.*Jo.*13.59(58; p.290. 4; M.14.509c); προκεκοιμημένους πατριάρχας *ib.*28.21(16; p.415.32; 725a); commemoration of departed at eucharist μνημονεύομεν καὶ τῶν προκεκοιμημένων...ὅπως ὁ θεὸς ταῖς εὐχαῖς αὐτῶν...προσδέξηται ἡμῶν τὴν δέησιν. εἶτα καὶ ὑπὲρ τῶν προκεκοιμημένων ἁγίων πατέρων καὶ ἐπισκόπων, καὶ πάντων ἁπλῶς τῶν ἐν ἡμῖν προκεκοιμημένων Cyr.H.*catech.*23.9; *Lit.Jac.*(p.194.16); τῶν ἐν πίστει καὶ σφραγῖδι Χριστοῦ ~ηθέντων *ib.*(p.218.22).

***προκοιτάω**, for προκοιτέω, *sleep in front of*, *guard*, Bas.Sel.*v. Thecl.*1(M.85.505c, v.l. προκοιτοῦσαι).

προκολάζω, *punish in advance*, Thphn.*chron.*p.243(M.108.612c).

προκομιδή, ἡ, **1.** *carrying forth* for burial, *funeral procession*, Eus. *v.C.*1.22(p.18.25; M.20.937b); *V.Pach.A* 5(p.128.6); **2.** *production* of documents ἅπαξ τοῦ ὁσιωτάτου ἀρχιεπισκόπου ἡμῶν κελεύσαντος προκομισθῆναι τὴν πρᾶξιν τῶν ὑπομνημάτων, οὐδεμίαν δεῖ ἀναβολὴν περὶ τὴν π. γενέσθαι CCP(448)*act.*(p.155.13; H.2.180e).

προκομίζ-ω, **1.** *carry out* for burial, *A.Thom.*56(p.173.9); *Chron. Pasch.*p.287(M.92.716c); Ath.Scholast.*coll.*15 paratit.7(p.157); **2.** *adduce* in evidence, of writing by Nepos adduced in support of chiliasm, Dion.Al.ap.Eus.*h.e.*7.24.4(M.20.693a); τὴν μὲν ἐπιστολήν...οὐκ ἔχω προκομίσαι id.ap.Ath.*decr.*25(p.21.23; M.25.461b); Ath.*apol.sec.* 28(p.107.32; M.25.293d); οὐ φεύγομεν τὴν...αὐθεντικὴν πίστιν...~οντες αὐτήν Acac.Caes.ap.eund.*syn.*29(p.257.34; M.26.744b); **3.** *bring forward* as matter of accusation, Philost.*h.e.*2.11(M.65.476b); **4.** pass., of a law, *be brought in*, *promulgated*, (tr. Lat. *lata*) *Cod.Afr.*99.

προκοπή, ἡ, **A.** *advance*, *progress*; **1.** in gen. τὰ μὲν τῆς τοῦ σωτῆρος ἡμῶν διδασκαλίας τε καὶ ἐκκλησίας...ἐπὶ μεῖζον ἐχώρει προκοπῆς Eus.*h.e.*4.2.1(M.20.303c); of advance of time, Ammon.*Ac.* 13:48(M.85.1544a); **2.** of spiritual and moral progress ἕκαστος γὰρ κατὰ τὴν ἰδίαν π. οἰκείαν ἔχει τὴν περὶ θεοῦ γνῶσιν Clem.*ecl.*57(p.153. 28; M.9.725c); ref. angelic beings οὐδ' ὑπολείπεταί τις αὐτοῖς π., ἐξ ἀρχῆς ἀπειληφότων τὸ τέλειον ἅμα τῇ πρώτῃ γενέσει παρὰ τοῦ θεοῦ διὰ τοῦ υἱοῦ id.*exc.Thdot.*10(p.109.30; M.9.660c); of Jo. Bapt. ref. Jo. 1:29 'Ιησοῦς ἤδη βλέπεται ὑπὸ τοῦ μαρτυρήσαντος, ἐρχόμενος πρὸς αὐτὸν ἔτι προκόπτοντα...ἧς π. ... σύμβολον ἡ ὠνομασμένη αὔριον Or. *Jo.*6.49(30; p.159.4; M.14.288a); ἐπιγινομένης τῆς π. καὶ ὁδευούσης ἐπὶ τὴν τελειότητα *ib.*32.15(9; p.449.34; 780b); ἐκκλησία...δυναμένη τῇ πλείονι π. κατανοεῖν αὐτοῦ τὴν θεότητα id.*schol.in Cant.*6:4(M.17. 276d); π. ... ἡ παρὰ τῆς σοφίας μεταδιδομένη τοῖς ἀνθρώποις θεοποίησις καὶ χάρις Ath.*Ar.*3.53(M.26.433b); δὸς ἔλεος καὶ οἰκτιρμὸν καὶ π. Serap.*euch.*11.4; ἐκ π. λαμβάνεις τὴν χάριν Cyr.H.*catech.*3.14; of manna as ἄρτος προκοπῆς opp. bread of Joshua's passover typifying bread of perfection, Or.*Jo.*6.45(26; p.154.31; M.14.280a); **3.** denied of God οὔτε π. οὔτε μείωσιν ἐπιδεχόμενον Alex.Al.*ep.Alex.* 12(p.27.2; M.18.565a); τριάδα ἄκτιστον...μηδὲν ἐπείσακτον ἔχουσαν... ἢ ἐκ π. εἰς τὸ εἶναι ἐπανελθόν ‡Chrys.*Trin.*1(1.832b); **4.** of Son (ref. Sonship as attained κατὰ προκοπήν or ἐκ π.); **a.** asserted by Ebionites λιτὸν μὲν γὰρ αὐτὸν καὶ κοινὸν ἡγοῦντο, κατὰ π. ἤθους αὐτὸ μόνον ἄνθρωπον δεδικαιωμένον Eus.*h.e.*3.27.2(M.20.273a); υἱὸν δὲ θεοῦ κατὰ π. Epiph.*haer.*30.18(p.358.4; M.41.436b); by Cerinthians 'Ιησοῦν δὲ κατὰ π. Χριστὸν καλεῖσθαι λέγοντες id.*anac.*28(p.236.8; M. 41.284b); by Alogi εἶναι μὲν πρότερον ψιλὸν ἄνθρωπον, κατὰ π. δὲ εἰληφέναι τὴν τοῦ υἱοῦ τοῦ θεοῦ προσηγορίαν id.*haer*.51.18(p.275.19; M.41.924A); in opinion ascribed to Paul. Sam. ἅγιος...γέγονεν ἡμῶν ὁ σωτὴρ ἀγῶνι καὶ πόνῳ τῆς τοῦ προπάτορος ἡμῶν κρατήσας ἁμαρτίας, οἷς κατορθώσας τὴν ἀρετὴν συνήφθη τῷ θεῷ, μίαν καὶ τὴν αὐτὴν πρὸς αὐτὸν βούλησιν καὶ ἐνέργειαν ταῖς τῶν ἀγαθῶν π. ἐσχηκώς ‡Paul.Sam. *fr*.3(p.339.15); οἱ ἀπὸ Παύλου...ὕστερον αὐτὸν μετὰ τὴν ἐνανθρώπησιν ἐκ π. τεθεοποιῆσθαι λέγοντες *Symb.Ant*.(345)4(p.252.29; M.26.729C); by Thdr. Mops. προέκοπτεν παρά τε θεῷ καὶ ἀνθρώποις, τῶν μὲν ὁρώντων τὴν π., τοῦ δὲ οὐχ ὁρῶντος μόνον, ἀλλὰ καὶ ἐπιμαρτυροῦντος καὶ συνεργοῦντος τοῖς γινομένοις Thdr.Mops.*fr.inc*.7(p.297.36; M.66.980A); CCP(553)*anath*.12 = Justn.*conf.anath*.11(p.92.27; M.86.1017A); by Nestorius ἕτερόν τινα παρ' αὐτὸν ἄνθρωπον...χρηματίσαι καὶ ἀπόστολον καὶ ἀρχιερέα καὶ κατὰ π. εἰς τοῦτο ἐλθεῖν, καὶ οὐχ ὑπέρ γε μόνων ἡμῶν, ἀλλὰ καὶ ὑπὲρ ἑαυτοῦ προσενεγκεῖν ἑαυτόν Cyr.*expl. xii cap*.10(p.24.18; 6[1].156A); τὸν κατὰ π. παρ' αὐτοῦ θεοποιούμενον ἄνθρωπον Max.*opusc*.(M.91.45D); **b.** denied by orthodox υἱότητα, οὐ τρόπων ἐπιμελείᾳ καὶ προκοπῆς ἀσκήσει, ἀλλὰ φύσεως ἰδιώματι ταύτην λαχόντος Alex.Al.*ep.Alex*.8(p.25.2; M.18.560B); Ath.*decr*.16 (p.13.24; M.25.'449'(441)D); id.*Ar*.1.38(M.26.89B); ref. Phil.2:5–11 ποία π. καὶ βελτίωσις ἐν ταπεινώσει; *ib*.1.40(93D); Χριστὸς ἀληθής, οὐκ ἐξ ἀνθρώπων ἐκ π. εἰς ἱερωσύνην ἀνελθών Cyr.H.*catech*.11.1; οὐκ ἐκ δουλείας εἰς π. υἱοθεσίας ἐλθόντα *ib*.11.4; οὐκ ἐκ π. αὐξηθείς, ἀλλὰ τοῦτο γεννηθεὶς ὅπερ ἐστὶ νῦν *ib*.11.13; μὴ...νομισθῇ...εἰς π. ἐλθεῖν θεότητος *ib*.11.15; οὐδὲ ἐκ π. ἡ θέωσις Gr.Naz.*or*.25.16(M.35.1221B); ἀεὶ βασιλεύς, ἀεὶ κύριος...οὐδὲν τούτων ἐκ π. γενόμενος Gr.Nyss.*Eun*.6(2 p.150.12; M.45.736D); denied by Eunomius οὐ κατὰ π. γενόμενος κύριος [but cf. τοῦτον...κύριον...ἐποίησεν ὁ θεός] Eun. *ib*.5(2 p.109.29; 689A); κατὰ τὴν ὁμολογίαν τοῦ Εὐνομίου, οὐχὶ τῆς θεότητος κατὰ π. τι προσλαμβανούσης Gr.Nyss.*ib*.(p.135.4; 720A); Amph.*fr*.12(M.39.109A) cit. s. ἔκπτωσις; ref. Col.1:13 οἱ ληροῦντες ἐνταῦθα, μὴ νοοῦντες τὴν λέξιν, κατὰ π. ἀγάπης θεοῦ εἶναι τὸν υἱόν φασι Epiph.*anc*.50(p.59.15; M.43.104C); οὐκ ἄνθρωπος ἐλθὼν ἐν π. θεότητος *ib*.93(p.114.6; 185C); οὐδὲ...κατὰ π. ἐξ ἀνθρώπου γέγονε θεός †Chrys.*nativ*.(6.392B); οὐκ ἐκ π. θεὸς...ἀλλὰ δι' εὐσπλαγχνίαν ἄνθρωπος Procl.CP *ep*.2.14(M.65.872B); **5.** asserted of Christ as man, cf.Or.*hom.20 in Lc*.(p.135.9; M.13.1855B); ἐν αὐτῷ γὰρ ἦν ἡ σὰρξ ἡ προκόπτουσα καὶ αὐτοῦ λέγεται· καὶ τοῦτο ἵνα πάλιν ἡ τῶν ἀνθρώπων π. ἄπτωτος διὰ τὸν συνόντα λόγον διαμείνῃ...ὡς εἶναι τῆς ἀνθρωπίνης φύσεως τὴν π. Ath.*Ar*.3.53(M.26.436A); τῆς φύσεως ἡμῶν ἴδια...τὴν βρῶσιν, τὴν πόσιν...τὴν π. τῆς σωματικῆς ἡλικίας Gr.Nyss.*ep*.3(M.46.1020D); cf.Or.*hom.14.10 in Jer*.(p.114.29; M.13.416B); cit. s. προκόπτω; Cyr.*Lc*.2:40(M.72.508B,C).

B. *stage of development* or *progress* εἰς τὸ συγγενὲς τῆς ψυχῆς θεῖόν τι καὶ ἅγιον μετοικίζει καὶ διά τινος οἰκείου φωτὸς διαβιβάζει τὰς π. τὰς μυστικὰς τὸν ἄνθρωπον Clem.*str*.7.10(p.41.28; M.9.480C); Or.*Cels*.3.71 (p.263.18; M.11.1013B); τῶν ἐν ἑκάστῃ ἀρετῇ π. ὁμωνύμως τῇ τελείᾳ ὀνομαζομένων id.*Jo*.32.15(9; p.450.22; M.14.781A); Cyr.H.*catech*.11.4; Mac.Aeg.*ep*.(M.34.417B).

C. *preferment, position of dignity*; **1.** in gen. εἰλήφασι τὴν παρ' αὐτοῖς καλουμένην π. τοιαύτην ὥστε ἀποτεμεῖν ἀνθρώπων κεφαλάς Or. *hom.12.8 in Jer*.(p.94.22; M.13.389B); τῶν ἐν Ῥωμαϊκαῖς προκοπαῖς οὐ μικρᾶς ἐπειλήπτο ἀξίας Eus.*m.P*.14(p.942.25; M.20.1453C); id.*h.e*. 7.15.2(M.20.676C); **2.** of eccl. ranks αἱ...κατὰ τὴν ἐκκλησίαν π. ἐπισκόπων, πρεσβυτέρων, διακόνων Clem.*str*.6.13(p.485.28; M.9.328C); cf.Chrys.*hom.11.1 in 1Tim*.(11.605C).

***προκοπτικῶς**, *progressively*, or perh. *advantageously*, Didym.*Ps*. 2:10(M.39.1161B).

προκόπτ-ω, A. *advance, make progress*; **1.** trans., *advance*, i.e. help forward the process of making ~εις τὴν ὕλην τῷ τύπῳ Mel.*pass*. 38 p.6.21; **2.** of moral and spiritual progress ~ειν ἐν ταῖς ἐντολαῖς τοῦ κυρίου *2Clem*.17.3; Just.*dial*.2.6(M.6.477C); ὁ γὰρ σωτὴρ...ἐστι τῷ μὲν μηδέπω φθάσαντι ἐπὶ τὸ τέλος ἀλλ' ἔτι ~οντι ὁδός Or.*Jo*.6.19(11; p.128.26; M.14.233C); οὔτε ἡ ἐπιστήμη τοῦ θεοῦ ~ειν ἡμᾶς ἀναγκάζει, ἐὰν μὴ καὶ ἡμεῖς ἐπὶ τὸ ἀγαθόν τι συνεισαγάγωμεν id.*princ*.3.1.23 (p.243.11; M.11.301B); id.*Cant*.2:13(p.240.29; M.17.265B); δεύτερον τὸ κῆπος κεκλεισμένος ἐρρέθη, τὸ μὲν ἐπὶ ~οντος, τὸ δὲ ἐπὶ τελείου id. *schol.in Cant*.4:12(M.17.272D); Meth.*symp*.1.2(p.10.17; M.18.41A); of progress of gospel, Eus.*d.e*.3.7(p.146.16; M.22.245C); **3.** ref. Sonship of Christ, heret. view that it was consequence of human progress denied, ref. doctrines of Paul of Samosata and others in rel. to Arianism τί γὰρ ἂν προκόψαι ἔχοι ἡ τοῦ θεοῦ σοφία; Alex.Al.*ep. Alex*.7(p.24.13; M.18.557D); ἐτόλμησαν γὰρ εἰπεῖν, ὅτι οὐχ ὁ προὼν λόγος, οὗτος ἐνηνθρώπησεν· ἀλλὰ ἄνθρωπός τις προκόψας, οὗτος ἐστεφανώθη Cyr.H.*catech*.12.3; asserted ref. high priesthood ἐγένετο γὰρ οὗτος, οὐκ ἀϊδίως προῆν—οὗτος ὁ κατὰ μικρὸν εἰς ἀρχιερέως προκόψας ἀξίωμα Nest.*hom.in Heb.3:1*(p.235.9; M.64.484B); **4.** of Christ as man, ref. Lc.2:52 εἰ γὰρ ἐκένωσεν ἑαυτὸν καταβαίνων ἐνταῦθα καὶ κενώσας ἑαυτὸν ἐλάμβανε πάλιν ταῦτα ἀφ' ὧν ἐκένωσεν ἑαυτόν, ἑκὼν κενώσας ἑαυτόν, τί ἄτοπον αὐτὸν καὶ προκεκοφέναι; Or. *hom.1.7 in Jer*.(p.6.28; M.13.264B); οὐ γὰρ καθ' αὐτὸν μόνον ὁ Ἰησοῦς προέκοπτεν..., ἀλλὰ καὶ ἐν ἑκάστῳ τῶν τὴν προκοπὴν ἐν σοφίᾳ καὶ ἡλικίᾳ καὶ χάριτι παραδεχομένων ~ει Ἰησοῦς ἐν σοφίᾳ κτλ. *ib.14.10*(p.114.28; 416B); τὸ ἐν σοφίᾳ ~ειν, οὐκ ἔστι τὴν σοφίαν αὐτὴν ~ειν, ἀλλὰ τὸ ἀνθρώπινον μᾶλλον ἐν αὐτῇ ~ειν. [Lc.2:52] αὐτὸς ἐν ἑαυτῷ προέκοπτε. 'ἡ σοφία γὰρ ᾠκοδόμησεν ἑαυτῇ οἶκον', καὶ ἐν ἑαυτῇ τὸν οἶκον ~ειν ἐποίει Ath.*Ar*.3.52(M.26.433B); ὥσπερ...σαρκὶ πέπονθεν,...οὕτω καὶ ...σαρκὶ προέκοπτεν...ἐν αὐτῷ γὰρ ἦν ἡ σὰρξ ἡ ~ουσα καὶ αὐτοῦ λέγεται ...διὸ οὐδὲ εἶπεν, ὁ λόγος προέκοπτεν, ἀλλ' ὁ Ἰησοῦς...ὡς εἶναι τῆς ἀνθρωπίνης φύσεως τὴν προκοπὴν *ib*.3.53(433Cff.); τὸ γὰρ γεννηθὲν ἡμῖν παιδίον Ἰησοῦς, ὁ ἐν τοῖς δεξαμένοις αὐτὸν διαφόρως ~ων...καθὼς ἂν ὁ χωρῶν αὐτὸν ἱκανῶς ἔχῃ, τοιοῦτος φαίνεται, ἢ νηπιάζων, ἢ ~ων, ἢ τελειούμενος Gr.Nyss.*hom.3 in Cant*.(M.44.828D); discussion, Thdr. Mops.*fr.inc*.7(p.297.30ff.; M.66.980A,B); ἐν σοφίᾳ ~ειν ἂν λέγοιτο, οὐ προσθήκην σοφίας δεχόμενος, καθ' ὃ νοεῖται θεὸς ὁ ἐν πᾶσι παντέλειος ...ἀλλὰ τοῦ...λόγου τῇ τοῦ σώματος ἡλικίᾳ συνεκτείνοντος κατὰ βραχὺ τῆς σοφίας τὴν ἔκφανσιν. ~ει δὲ ἡλικίᾳ μὲν σῶμα, σοφίᾳ δὲ ψυχή· θεότης γὰρ οὐδετέραν ἐπίδοσιν ἐπιδέχεται Cyr.*Lc*.2:40(M.72.508B); οὐ καθὸ λόγος ἐστὶ ~ειν λέγεται, ἀλλὰ καθὸ γέγονεν ἄνθρωπος· καὶ φύσιν πεφόρηκε τὴν τούτου δεκτικήν id.*thes*.28(5[1].249B); ὥσπερ δι' ἡμᾶς ἐταπείνωσεν ἑαυτόν, οὕτω δι' ἡμᾶς ἐπιδέχεται τὸ ~ειν, ἵνα πάλιν ἡμεῖς ἐν αὐτῷ προκόπτωμεν ἐν σοφίᾳ *ib*.(251A); ἡ τὴν ἀνθρώπου φύσιν ἐνδυσαμένη σοφία...τὸν ἀναληφθέντα ναὸν ~ειν......ἐποίει...οὕτως ἐν σοφίᾳ προέκοπτεν ἡ ἀνθρωπότης...προέκοπτεν οὖν ἡ φύσις ἡμῶν ἐν τῇ σοφίᾳ ...ἐπειδὴ γὰρ τῇ σαρκὶ τὸ ~ειν ὀφείλεται, λεγέσθω ~ειν ὡς ἐν αὐτῇ γενόμενος...οὕτω κἂν ~ειν λέγηται, προκοπὴν οὐδεμίαν ἐπιδεχόμενος ὡς θεός, διὰ τὸ ~ειν ἐν αὐτῷ τὴν ἰδίαν ἑαυτοῦ σάρκα τοῦτο λέγεται *ib*. (251Eff.); μηδ' αὖ ἐκεῖνο...τολμήσῃς εἰπεῖν, ὅτι τὸ ~ειν...τῷ ἀνθρώπῳ προσάψομεν. τοῦτο γάρ...ἐστὶν ἕτερον οὐδὲν ἢ διελεῖν εἰς δύο τὸν ἕνα Χριστόν. ... ~ειν...λέγεται...τὰ τῆς ἀνθρωπότητος ἴδια διὰ τὴν εἰς ἄκρον ἕνωσιν εἰς ἑαυτὸν εἰκότως ἀναλαβών id.*hom.pasch*.17(5[2] 230Aff.).

B. *be promoted*, of angels προκόψουσιν εἰς ἣν ἐκεῖνοι ἀπολελοίπασι τάξιν Clem.*ecl*.56(p.153.23; M.9.725B); of S. Peter σκηνοποιὸς ἐξ ἁλιέων προέκοπτε Procl.CP *or*.8.2(M.65.765B); of eccl. rank οὐκ ἔτι τὸν ἀναγνώστην περαιτέρω ~ειν, ἀλλὰ μένειν ἀπρόκοπον †Jo.Jej.*poenit*. (M.88.1909B).

***προκορυφαῖος, ὁ,** *first leader*; of S. Andrew, *Hymn*.(*AS* 1 p.556).

***προκοσμέω**, *adorn beforehand* θυγατέρα δὲ καλοῦσιν τὴν ἐκκλησίαν, ἅτε δὴ αὐτὴν προκοσμιθεῖσαν τῷ οὐρανίῳ νυμφίῳ Or.*Ps*.44:11–14 (p.43; perh. for προκοσμισθεῖσαν).

προκόσμιον, τό, *ornament*, Gr.Nyss.*or.dom*.1(p.24.10; M.44.1133C).

προκόσμιος, *before the worlds*, of Logos φῶς τὸ π. καὶ τὴν πρὸ αἰώνων...σοφίαν Eus.*h.e*.1.2.3(M.20.53B); οὐσία τις π. ζῶσα καὶ ὑφεστῶσα *ib*.1.2.14(60B); μόνος...λόγος ὢν θεοῦ π. id.*d.e*.1.10(p.47.3; M.22.89A); λόγος ὢν π. καὶ σωτὴρ id.*l.C*.2(p.199.19; M.20.1325B); of glory of Logos τὴν δοθεῖσαν αὐτῷ ἐξουσίαν Ἀστέριος δόξαν ὀνομάζει, καὶ οὐ δόξαν μόνον ἀλλὰ καὶ π. δόξαν, οὐκ ἐννοῶν ὅτι μήπω τοῦ κόσμου γεγονότος οὐδὲν ἕτερον ἦν πλὴν θεοῦ μόνου Marcell.*fr*.93 ap.Eus. *Marcell*.2.2(p.40.6; M.24.792A); ἡ δὲ π. ... δόξα, ᾗ ὁ μονογενὴς θεὸς ἐνδοξάζεται, οὐκ ἂν ἄλλη τις εἴη...παρὰ τὴν δόξαν τοῦ πατρός Gr.Nyss. *Apoll*.53(M.45.1252D); Christol. οὐ γάρ τοι φαῖεν ἄν οἶμαί που π. δόξαν ὡς ἰδίαν αἰτεῖν τὸν ἐκ σπέρματος τοῦ Δαβίδ...τεχθέντα Cyr.*Chr. un*.(5[1].742C); πῶς ὡς δόξης ἐπιδεὴς τὴν π. αὐτοῦ δόξαν αἰτεῖ; ἐπειδὴ γὰρ γέγονεν ἄνθρωπος id.*apol.Thdt*.55(p.131.13; 6[1].225C); Leont.H. *Nest*.5.1(M.86.1724D); of Christ's divine nature, Thdt.*eran*.3(4.213); ref. Nestorius' teaching πῶς οὖν...π. ὁ ἐκ τῆς...παρθένου κατὰ σὲ νοούμενος ἄνθρωπος ἰδικῶς; Cyr.*Nest*.5.1(p.94.21; 6[1].124C); in *reductio ad absurdum* of Eunomian exegesis of Ac.2:36 ἡ π. ὁ σταυρός; Gr.Nyss.*Eun*.6(2 p.144.28; M.45.129D); of H. Ghost τὸ προαιώνιον καὶ π. πνεῦμα τοῦ θεοῦ Didym.*Trin*.2.7(M.39.576A).

***προκουράτωρ, ὁ,** (Lat. *procurator*) **1.** *procurator*, *financial agent* ἐπίσκοποι καὶ πρεσβύτεροι καὶ διάκονοι...μὴ γένωνται...π., μηδὲ ἐκ τινος αἰσχροῦ ἢ ἀτίμου πράγματος τροφὴν πορίζωνται *Cod.Afr*.16; **2.** *church official*, ? in charge of church funds προνοοῦντος κυριακοῦ τοῦ...πατριάρχου καὶ Ῥομάνου τοῦ...πρεσβυτέρου, π. καὶ ἐκκλησιεκδίκου τῆς μεγάλης ἐκκλησίας Κουνσταντινουπόλεως *IGC As.Min*.225 (Didyma 602).

***πρόκουρσον, τό,** (cf. Lat. *procursus*) *vanguard*, *Chron.Pasch*. p.392(M.92.1005B).

προκρατ-έω, 1. *be prevalent beforehand* ἡ κιβωτὸς...ἤρκεῖτο...ἀντὶ πάσης παρατάξεως εἰς βοήθειαν, εἰ μή τις ἦν...~ήσασα ἁμαρτία Ath.

*ep.Marcell.*32(M.27.44D); **2.** *prevail formerly* τὴν ∼ήσασαν εὐαγῆ διαγωγὴν τῆς ζωῆς Thdr.Stud.*epp.*2.146(M.99.1457D).

πρόκριμα, τό, *prejudgement* τί ἂν γένοιτο π. χεῖρον οὕτω φανερῶς ...ἐπιφερόμενον τῇ ἐκείνων δίκῃ, ἢ τὸ τούτους, οὓς ἀνῃρῆσθαι ἔλεγον, ζῆν τε καὶ τοῦ βίου ἀπολαύειν Const.ap.Ath.*apol.sec.*68(p.146.14; M. 25.369B); ἡμεῖς ὑπὲρ ἀκριβείας οὔτε ὑμῖν οὔτε τοῖς ὑπὲρ αὐτῶν γράψασι π. ποιοῦντες προετρεψάμεθα τοὺς γράψαντας ἐλθεῖν Jul.Papa *ep.Dian. ib.*23(p.104.38; 288A); κἂν ὀλίγοι τινὲς ἀντιλέγωσι ταύτῃ τῇ πίστει, οὐ δύνανται π. ποιεῖν πάσῃ τῇ οἰκουμένῃ Ath.*ep.Jov.*2(M.26.817A)ap. Thdt.*h.e.*4.3.9; οὐδὲ γὰρ π. τι ἠδυνήθη γενέσθαι ὑπὸ τοῦ ἀριθμοῦ τῶν ἐν Ἀριμηνῷ συναχθέντων Dam.Papa *ep.Illyr.*ap.Thdt.*h.e.*2.22. 9(3.883); αὐτῷ τῷ συμβόλῳ τῷ παρὰ τῶν ἀποστόλων εἰσηγηθέντι π. φέρειν Leo Mag.*ep.*45.2(p.47.32; M.*PL.*54.836B); τὰ ἐξ ἀνάγκης λεγόμενα, οὐδὲ εἰς νόμον γίνονται, οὔτε εἰς π. τῆς ἐκκλησίας Anast.S.*hod.* 11(M.89.193D).

προκριματίζ-ω, *prejudice,* (tr. Lat. *praejudico*) *Cod.Afr.*119; οὐδαμῶς...τοῦ ἐκκλησιαστικοῦ ∼ομένου κανόνος Martin.*ep.*9(M.*PL.* 87.171D).

πρόκρισις, ἡ, *preliminary judgement*; of God's frequent judgements opp. final judgement, Clem.*str.*7.2(p.10.4; M.9.416B); καλὴ ἡ κρίσις τοῦ θεοῦ, ἥ τε διάκρισις ἡ τῶν πιστῶν ἀπὸ τῶν ἀπίστων ἥ τε π. ὑπὲρ τοῦ μὴ μείζονι περιπεσεῖν κρίσει ἥ τε κρίσις παίδευσις οὖσα id.*ecl.* 40(p.148.28; M.9.717C).

***προκριταία, ἡ,** *previous choice,* Ephr.3.195F.

πρόκριτος, *chosen before* others; **1.** masc. as subst., *chief, leader*; of S. Peter ὁ π. τῶν ἀποστόλων Petr.Al.*ep.can.*9(M.18.484D); Didym. *Ps.*9 proem.(M.39.1188C); Nil.*Magn.*8(M.79.980C); νομικός...καὶ προκριτότερος Dam.*troph.*4.1(p.216.6); **2.** neut. as subst., *preeminence* τὸ π. τῆς παρθενίας Epiph.*anc.*98(p.119.16; M.43.196A); Cyr.*Am.*60 (3.317B; πολλοί Aubert).

προκρούω, *offend,* Isid.Pel.ap.*cat.Lc.*18:10(p.133.14,18); conj. for προσκεκρουκότας, Anast.S.*hex.*12(M.89.1052B).

***προκτεατίζομαι,** *possess formerly,* †Apoll.*met.Ps.*73:2(M.33. 1417A).

***προκτίζω,** *create before* ἐγὼ Ἰακὼβ...ἄγγελος θεοῦ εἰμι ἐγώ, καὶ... Ἀβραὰμ καὶ Ἰσαὰκ προεκτίσθησαν πρὸ παντὸς ἔργου Jewish apocryphon ap.Or.*Jo.*2.31(25; p.88.25; M.14.168D); ref. Son πρωτότοκος δὲ πάσης κτίσεως, οὐ διὰ τὸ προεκτίσθαι αὐτῆς (ἐπεὶ ἂν πρωτόκτιστος ἐκλήθη) ἀλλ' ὡς τῇ προγνώσει...πρὸ παντὸς δημιουργήματος ἀπὸ τῆς ἁγίας παρθένου τεχθείς Didym.*Trin.*3.4(M.39.832A); φατε [sc. Arians] ἀσεβῶς βλασφημοῦντες εἰς ποίησιν τῶν κτιστῶν φυσέων προκεκτίσθαι αὐτόν Gel.Cyz.*h.e.*2.15.2(M.85.1257C).

***προκυλίνδημα, τό,** *unrolling, unfolding,* Synes.*insomn.*15(p.178. 3; M.66.1309D).

***προκυοφορέω,** *engender,* Cyr.*glaph.Gen.*3(1.79C); id.*Jo.*4.7(4. 431E).

προκύπτ-ω, *emerge*; of begetting of Son, Cyr.*Jo.*1.3(4.29A); σοφίας τοῦ θεοῦ...ἰδίως μὲν καὶ καθ' ἑαυτὴν ὑφεστώσης, ∼ούσης δ' οὖν ὅμως κατὰ τὸν ἄρρητον τῆς γεννήσεως τρόπον ἐκ πατρὸς *ib.*1.5(45B); τὸ θεῖον ἐκ πατρὸς προέκυψε γέννημα *ib.*1.10(105E); λόγος ἐκ τοῦ γεννήσαντος νοῦ ∼ων *ib.*2.5(197C).

προκυρόω, *sanction beforehand,* Eus.*p.e.*10.4(468D; M.21.780C); Ephr.2.271E.

πρόκωπος, *drawn* (of a sword), Gr.Nyss.*Eun.*12(1 p.217.8; M.45. 909B).

***πρόλαβα, τά,** *anticipations* τοῦ ἀντιχρίστου τὰ π. φέρουσι Thdr. Stud.*epp.*1.50(M.99.1093D).

προλαμβάν-ω, 1. *prefer, take by preference,* of S. John in rel. to Synoptists Ἰωάννης...∼ει τῶν ῥηθέντων τὰ μὴ ῥηθέντα Epiph.*haer.* 51.19(p.276.8; M.41.924B); of gentiles in rel. to Jews παιδευθέντες γὰρ οἱ ἐξ Ἰουδαίων τὸ μυστήριον...ἐξέπεσον· οἱ δὲ οὐδέποτε ἀκηκοότες οἱ ἐξ ἐθνῶν, προελήφθησαν Cyr.*Ps.*35:7(M.69.920A); **2.** *anticipate* προλαβοῦσα ἡ κακία...προαπέστειλε Σίμωνα *Hom.Clem.*3.59; προλαβὼν γὰρ αὐτὸς ἑαυτοῦ ταύτην ἀφείλετο τὴν ἀπολογίαν Chrys.*sac.*4.1 (p.97.3; 1.402A); ‡Nil.*perist.*11.3(M.79.908C); of God anticipating human prayer ἑκούσιος δὲ ἡ τῶν ἀγαθῶν μετάδοσις αὐτῷ, κἂν ∼ῃ τὴν αἴτησιν Clem.*str.*7.7(p.32.2; M.9.457C); ∼εις ἀεὶ τὰς αἰτήσεις Thdt. *Ps.*58:11(1.995); of God in Creation τὰ μὴ ὄντα προλαβὼν...ὡς ἤδη ὄντα...θεωρεῖ Eus.*e.th.*2.6(p.103.29; M.24.908A); of prophetic anticipation ἃ γὰρ προλαβὼν μέλλειν γίνεσθαι...ἔφη Just.*dial.*35. 2(M.6.549C); Eus.*d.e.*6.15(p.269.31; M.22.444B); of anticipating a formal judgement, Jul.Papa *ep.Dian.*ap.Ath.*apol.sec.*30(p.109.7; M.25.297B); *ib.*34(p.112.17; 305A); Chrys.*hom.84.3 in Mt.*(7.801B); **3.** *take initiative in* προέλαβον παρακαλεῖν ὑμᾶς Ign.*Eph.*3.2; τοῖς ψευδῶς προειληφόσιν εἰδέναι τὸ τοῦ ἀντιχρίστου ὄνομα Iren.*haer.*5.30.1 (M.7.1204C); Ἐβίων καὶ οἱ ἀμφ' αὐτὸν προὔλαβον ἑαυτοὺς κατατέμνοντες Epiph.*haer.*30.26(p.369.18; M.41.452A); of God in typological revelations ∼οντος πρὸ τῶν ἰδίων καιρῶν τὰ μυστήρια χαρίζεσθαι ὑμῖν τοῦ θεοῦ Just.*dial.*131.4(M.6.781A); **4.** *prevent, forestall,* Chrys.*pan. Macc.*1.1(2.629E); προσκυνεῖται...πολλὰ τῶν ἀλόγων· οὐκοῦν πάντα ἂν προσεκυνήθη, μὴ προλαβούσης τῆς κρεωφαγίας Diod.*Gen.*9:3(M.33. 1572D); **5.** *arrive before time* τῶν ∼όντων εἰς τὰ δεῖπνα Chrys.*hom.7.2 in Col.*(11.373D); **6.** pass., *be preoccupied* οὐδ' οἰκίας οὐδὲ πόλεις... εὐχερῶς βούλονται καταλιπεῖν οἱ προληφθέντες αὐτοῖς Or.*Cels.*1.52 (p.103.12; M.11.757A); Chrys.*hom.6.4 in 2Tim.*(11.697E); esp. with evil things τί οὖν ἐὰν προληφθῶ; φησί. κάθαρον σαυτόν id.*hom.51.5 in Mt.*(7.526D); id.*hom.24.1 in Heb.*(12.220C); Philox.*ep.*24(p.175); hence *be prejudiced* προείληπτο τῇ κατὰ τοῦ δόγματος ἡμῶν διαβολῇ Gr.Nyss.*Eun.*1(1 p.60.2; M.45.288D); **7.** *take for granted, assume* χρὴ δὲ προειληφέναι τοὺς ἐπὶ σωτηρίᾳ σπεύδοντας ὡς ἄρα χρήσεως... ἕνεκεν ἡ πᾶσα ἡμῖν κτίσις Clem.*paed.*2.3(p.180.21; M.8.437B); Meth. *arbitr.*5.1(p.157.7; M.18.249B); *Hom.Clem.*2.36; **8.** *precede,* Clem.*str.* 4.21(p.306.2; M.8.1341A); ἐν τῷ προλαβόντι ψαλμῷ Or.*Ps.*18:12(p.474); αἰτοῦμαι...μὴ...τῇ τάξει τῶν προλαβόντων τὸ πλέον νέμοντας, ἀποφράττειν τὰς ἀκοὰς τοῖς ὑστέροις Eun.ap.Bas.*Eun.*1.3(1.210C; M.29.508A); κατὰ τὴν προλαβοῦσαν ἀκολουθίαν Gr.Nyss.*hex.*(M.44.85B); id.*infant.* (M.46.164C); δοκεῖ μὴ ἀκολουθεῖν τοῖς προλαβοῦσιν ὁ...λόγος Cyr.*Ps.* 18:8(M.69.832A); προλαβόντων ἐξηγητῶν id.*Is.*4.4(2.668A); ἵνα τοῖς προλαβοῦσι τὰ ἐσόμενα βεβαιώσῃ Thdt.*Jon.*proem.(2.1461); of the departed ποῦ...εἰσὶν αἱ προλαβοῦσαι τῶν ἀνθρώπων ψυχαί; ‡Ath. *qu.Ant.*19(M.28.609A); οἱ ἐκεῖ προλαβόντες Anast.S.*defunct.*(M.89. 1196B); **9.** ptcpl., of time, *past* ἐν τῷ προλαβόντι χρόνῳ Thdt.*Jer.* 49:8(2.603); Jo.Mal.*chron.*18 p.429(M.97.633B).

προλάμπω, 1. *shine forth,* met. ∼ειν τῆς προρρήσεως τὴν ἰσχύν Chrys.ap.*cat.Mt.*24:22(p.199.32) for διαλ- id.*hom.76.2 in Mt.*(7. 634B); Ζεβεδαίου...παῖς καὶ Σαλώμης προέλαμψεν Sophr.H.*or.*9(M.87. 3364B); Thphyl.*exc.gent.*3(p.480.17; M.113.940B); **2.** *shine out from amongst* οὐκ ἀρχιερέων ∼ουσι μόνον, ἀλλὰ καὶ τῶν μαρτύρων διακοσμοῦσι χορόν Thdt.*ep.*145(4.1252); **3.** *shine in front of* ∼ειν τῶν πραττομένων ὑπομνημάτων τυπώσαντες τὸ θεοφιλὲς γράμμα τῆς ὑμετέρας εὐσεβείας [i.e. emperor] CEph.(431)*act.*1(*ACO* 1.1.3 p.4.17; H.1. 1441D); **4.** *be clear in advance* καὶ τὰ λοιπά, ὥσπερ ∼ει *ib.*(H.1.1396C; *ACO* 1.1.2 p.36.15 om.); **5.** *outshine* ∼ει τῶν ἀστέρων *Ev.Barth.*4.5 (*RB* p.327); *Hymn.*(*AS* 1 p.545); Thdr.Stud.*epp.*1.16(M.99.960C); **6.** *be distinguished before* ἐνίας τῶν προλαμψάντων φωνὰς παραιτεῖσθαι Leont.B.*arg.Sev.*(M.86.1929C); Jo.Thess.*dorm.BMV* 1.3(p.379.17).

***προλανθάνω,** *go unobserved,* †Apoll.*met.Ps.*138:3(M.33.1521B).

προλεαίν-ω, 1. *make smooth in advance* ∼ούσης τὴν...ὁδὸν τοῦ βίου †Chrys.*hom.prec.*1(2.779E); **2.** *conciliate beforehand* π. ... τοῦ ἀκροατοῦ τὴν ψυχήν Chrys.*hom.16.10 in Mt.*(7.219C); id.*hom.11.5 in 1Cor.*(10.94B); Thdt.*Col.*1:4(3.474).

προλέγ-ω, 1. *speak of as prior, assign priority to* Πλωτῖνος...τὴν ὕλην σαφῶς πάνυ ∼ει, καὶ τὸν Ἀναξαγόραν κωμῳδεῖ ὅτι μὴ ∼ει Aen. *dial.*(M.85.964A); **2.** *prophesy*; of OT prophets, *1Clem.*34.3; προλέλεκται ἐν ταῖς...προφητείαις Just.*1apol.*54.9(M.6.409C); Tat.*orat.* 20(p.23.3; M.6.852B); of David, Didym.*Ps.*4:1(M.39.1165B).

προλείπω, *forsake,* of dying κόσμου πλάνην προλιπών *IG* 14.463 (Rome); Philost.*h.e.*11.2(M.65.596B).

***προλειτουργέω,** *exercise sacred ministry previously,* Pulch.*ep. Leon.*(p.9.38; M.*PL.*54.908B).

***προλεκτικός,** *prophetical,* ‡Paul.Sil.*therm.Pyth.*(M.86.2264).

πρόλεξις, ἡ, *prophecy, M.Perp.*21(p.93.7).

προλευκαίνω, *whiten beforehand*; of artists who whiten walls in preparation for frescoes, Bas.Sel.*or.*1.2(M.85.29C).

πρόλημμα, τό, 1. *anticipation of gain* or *reward,* Tat.*orat.*3(p.4. 17; M.6.812B); ‡Just.*ep.Zen.et Ser.*4(M.6.1188A); **2.** *advantage* τὸ τῶν Ῥωμαίων βασίλειον πολλὰ π. ἔχει ἐν τούτῳ, ὡς καὶ πρῶτον ὄν, καὶ πρῶτον πιστεῦσαν εἰς Χριστόν Cosm.Ind.*top.*2(M.88.113D); **3.** *preconception, prejudice,* Tat.*orat.*27(p.28.24; M.6.864B); μηδὲ τοῖς π. πιστεύσητε Jul.Papa ap.Ath.*apol.sec.*34(p.112.25; M.25.305B); ‡Just. *ep.Zen.et Ser.*1(M.6.1184A, v.l. πρόβλημα); **4.** *predisposition* ἔνδυμα οὖν εἰ βούλεσθε γενέσθαι θείου πνεύματος, σπουδάσατε πρῶτον ἐκδύσασθαι τὸ ῥυπαρὸν ὑμῶν π. *Hom.Clem.*8.23.

προληπτικός, 1. *anticipatory* τὰ προληπτικῷ παρατεθειμένα *cat. Apoc.*2:23(p.214.21 conj. προληπτικῶς); **2.** *inclined to be prejudiced* τὸν φιλέριστον καὶ π. τρόπον Adam.*dial.*4.13(p.170.2; M.11.1828D).

προληπτικῶς, *by anticipation,* Or.*comm.in Mt.*14.7(p.290.35; M. 13.1200A); Philox.*ep.*24(p.175).

πρόληψις, ἡ, 1. *preconception* τῶν κατὰ κοινὴν π. ... ὀνομαζομένων θεῶν Athenag.*leg.*5.1(M.6.900A); πᾶν μὲν ἔθνος...μίαν ἔχει καὶ τὴν αὐτὴν π. περὶ τοῦ καταστησαμένου τὴν ἡγεμονίαν Clem.*str.*5.14(p.417.6; M.9.197A); εἰ δὲ ἀλλοῖα φαίνεται, οὐκ ἔτι ἔμεινεν ἐπὶ τῆς π., ἐλέγξαντος αὐτὰ τοῦ λόγου Dion.Al.ap.Eus.*p.e.*6.9(272A; M.21.461B); τὰ δὲ τοῦ νόμου ἰδίᾳ π. ἀλληγορεῖ *Hom.Clem.*2.22; πρὸς τὰς π. ἡ ἑκάστου ψυχὴ ἰδέας δαιμόνων ἀπεικονίζει *ib.*9.16; κοινὴ ἡ π. πᾶσιν ὁμοίως Χριστιανοῖς ἐνυπάρχει...περὶ τοῦ φῶς εἶναι τὸν υἱόν Bas.*Eun.*2.25(1.261E; M.29.629A); τὰς κοινὰς περὶ θεοῦ π. Proc.G.*Is.*2:1–4(M.87.1873C); Dion.Ar.*d.n.*4.12(M.3.709B); in Epicurus' definition of πίστις: π. διανοίας αὐτὴν εἶπε. τὴν δὲ π., προσλαβοῦσαν τὴν γνῶσιν, κατάληψιν γίνεσθαι Thdt.*affect.*1(p.26.11; 4.717); **2.** *preoccupation* μηδεμίαν π. ἔχωμεν κατὰ διάνοιαν· τότε γὰρ ἡ χάρις τοῦ...πνεύματος ἀνάπαυσιν εὑροῦσα ἐν ἡμῖν...φωτιεῖ τὰς καρδίας Ephr.1.226F; ἡνίκα ψυχὴ πάθη πρόληψιν ὑπὸ τῶν αἰσθητῶν id.1.263F; Max.*ep.*22(M.91.605C); **3.** *predisposition* τὴν προαίρεσιν ἀπαγγέλλεις τὴν σήν, ὡς οὐ προλήψει κρατούμενος Meth.*arbitr.*4(p.156.3; M.18.248D); συνηθείᾳ καὶ π. πολλῇ Mac.Aeg.*hom.*4.8(M.34.477D); Chrys.*hom.20.2 in Heb.*(12.189B); πολεμήσωμεν πάθεσι τοῖς κατὰ πρόληψιν Marc.Er.*opusc.*1.139(M.65.921D); ἔστι κακία καρδιακῶς κατέχουσα διὰ τὴν χρονίαν π. *ib.*1.184(928B); Jo.Clim.*scal.*18(M.88.932B); Thal.*cent.*3.6(M.91.1448C); **4.** *prejudice* μὴ προλήψει μηδ' ἀνθρωπαρεσκείᾳ...κατεχομένους Just.*1apol.*2.3(M.6.329B); κακῆς π. αἴτιοι id.*dial.*17.1(M.6.512B); χαλεπὸν γὰρ φιλονεικία καὶ π. πρὸς τὸ ποιῆσαι καὶ τοῖς ἐναργέσιν ἀντιβλέψαι Or.*Cels.*1.52(p.103.5; M.11.757A); τὴν π. ἀποθέμενος, εὐγνωμόνως πρὸς ἕκαστον...ἀποκρίνου Adam.*dial.*4.3(p.142.11; M.11.1809B); πᾶσαν ἀπεδυσάμην π. Ἰουδαϊκήν Chrys.*comm.in Gal.*1:14(10.673B); Thdt.*eran.* proem.(4.4); Jo.D.*Gal.*1:1(M.95.776D); **5.** *anticipation*, Clem.*paed.*1.6(p.107.5; M.8.284B); πίστις δὲ...π. ἑκούσιός ἐστι id.*str.*2.2(p.117.9; M.8.940A); προλήψει φιλεῖν [i.e. in hope of reward] Chrys.*hom.1.2 in 1Thess.*(11.427C); of Inc. οὐκέτι κατὰ ἀνάγκην ἐφαίνετο...ἀλλὰ κατὰ χάριν, οὐ φόβῳ καὶ π. παρὰ προσδοκίαν...εἰς τὸ δῆλον καθιστῶν τὴν ἑαυτοῦ ὀπτασίαν Epiph.*haer.*26.12(p.291.23; M.41.352B); **6.** a rhetorical figure, cf. *prolempsis est praesumptio, ubi ea quae sequi debent, anteponuntur*, Isid.H.*etym.*1.36.2; **7.** *taking in addition, assumption* of humanity by Son τὸν αὐτὸν ἐν π. ψυχῆς καὶ σώματος Flav.CP ap.Leont.H.*monoph.*(M.86.1888A) for προσλήψει id.*ep.Thds.*(p.35.17; M.65.892B); ἐπίβλεψον τῷ μαργαρίτῃ, καὶ βλέπεις τὰς δύο φύσεις συνέχοντα· φαιδρότατός ἐστι διὰ τὴν θεότητα, λευκὸς διὰ τὴν π. Ephr.Ant.*fr.*(M.86.2109B); ἵνα μὴ ταῖς...φρενοβλαβείαις περιπέσωμεν, ὁρῶντες...εἰς τὸν κυριακὸν ἔνθεον ἄνθρωπον τὰς...τοσαύτας...ἐναλλαγάς τε καὶ π. Anast.S.*hod.*13(M.89.228A); εἷς γὰρ ὁ...λόγος...καὶ μετὰ τὴν π. τῆς σαρκὸς ὑποστατικῶς Jo.D.*disp.*(M.96.1345B).

προλογισμός, ὁ, *forethought*, Hipp.*haer.*10.14(p.275.29; M.16.3430C).

πρόλογος, ὁ, 1. *preface*, ‡Ath.*dial.Trin.*2.29(M.28.1201B); **2.** *proper antiphon* or *gradual*, sung before Gospel ὁ π. τοῦ ἀλληλούια *Lit.Marc.*(Brightman, p.118.19).

προλυπέω, *grieve* or *injure previously*, Gr.Nyss.*or.dom.*5(p.110.20; M.44.1189B); id.*Trin.*2(p.72.9; M.32.685B).

***προλύπη, ἡ,** *distress*, Ath.Scholast.*coll.*10.2(p.114).

προλυσσάω, *suffer from mad craving*, Gr.Nyss.*hom.4 in Eccl.*(M.44.672B).

***προμάζιον, τό,** *apron*, Ephr.2.298C.

***προμακαρίζομαι,** *be called blessed beforehand*, Eus.*fr.Lc.*1:55(M.24.536C).

***προμακροημερεύω,** *live a long life*, Thdr.Stud.*epp.*1.29(M.99.1005C).

***προμαλακτήρ, ὁ,** *one who softens* or *weakens in advance*, met. πορνεία...π. καρδίας ‡Nil.*vit.*2(M.79.1141B).

προμαλάσσω, *soften beforehand, make supple beforehand*, ref. conversion of S. Paul οὐκ εὐθέως πάντα αὐτῷ ἀποκαλύπτει, ἀλλὰ μόνον π. αὐτοῦ τὴν διάνοιαν Chrys.*hom.19.3 in Ac.*(9.156D); προμαλάσσων, ὁ, *massage-room* where bathers were rubbed before bathing, Thdr.Lect.*fr.*(M.86.221B).

προμάντιον, τό, *prediction*, *Orac.Sib.*3.227.

***προμάξιον, τό,** *towel*, Ephr.3.289A.

***προμάρτυρ, ὁ,** *previous witness*, Jo.D.*haer.*101(M.94.768B; ? for προμάρτυς).

***προμαρτυρ-έω, 1.** *testify to in advance*, Tit.Bost.*Man.*1.17(M.18.1089D); **2.** med., *make representations beforehand* ~ούμενοι τῷ βασιλεῖ τὰ...συμφωνηθέντα μὴ διαστραφῆναι Thphn.*chron.*p.305(M.108.744A, v.l. προμαρτυρόμενοι); **3.** *warn previously*, Jo.Scholast.*coll.cap.*71(p.389).

***προμαρτυρία, ἡ,** *protestation* (tr. Lat. *protestatio*), *Cod.Afr.*97.

προμαρτύρομαι, 1. *testify to beforehand*, Eus.*l.C.*17(p.256.33; M.20.1436A); Bas.Sel.*or.*1.2(M.85.32A); †Gr.II Papa *ep.Leon.*2(H.4.13A); **2.** med., *make representations beforehand* (tr. Lat. *protestatos*), *Cod.Afr.*97.

***προμάρτυς, ὁ,** *first martyr*, Or.*mart.*14(p.14.3).

***προμαστίζω,** *punish beforehand*, Thphn.*chron.*p.354(προσμ- M.108.852B); Thdr.Stud.*epp.*2.59(M.99.1273B).

προμαχεών, ὁ, *champion*, of Christ τὸν πολυύμνητον π. ‡Chrys.*hom.*6(13.214C).

προμάχομαι, *fight previously*, Proc.G.*2Reg.*21:15(M.87.1141B).

***προμεθίστημι,** intrans., *die previously* προμεταστάντι...σοι *Hymn.*(*AS* 1 p.623).

προμελετ-άω, 1. *practise beforehand*, Clem.*ecl.*29(p.146.9; M.9.713C); Ath.*gent.*10(M.25.21B); Ἱερουσαλὴμ ἐπὶ τοσοῦτον συνειστήκει, ἵν' ἐκεῖ ~ῶσι τῆς ἀληθείας τοὺς τύπους id.*inc.*40(M.25.165A); ref. baptism τὸ ἐν τῷ ὕδατι ~ῆσαι τὴν τῆς ἀναστάσεως χάριν Gr.Nyss.*or.catech.*35(p.136.7; M.45.89D); ~ᾶν τὸν ἐλπιζόμενον βίον διὰ τῆς ἐν τῷ κόσμῳ ζωῆς id.*hom.4 in Cant.*(M.44.856D); **2.** *dwell upon, meditate on beforehand*, Clem.*str.*6.18(p.517.34; M.9.400B); Cyr.*Jo.*9(4.748E).

***προμελέτησις, ἡ,** *preliminary training* ἡ προπαρασκευὴ ἡ διὰ τοῦ νόμου, καὶ π. εἰς εὐσέβειαν †Bas.*Is.*142(1.479A; M.30.349C); of Law, Cyr.*ador.*8(1.272B); of OT types, id.*Jo.*2.1(4.157A); of shepherd's life as training for human sovereignty, id.*glaph.Gen.*1(1.15B).

***προμελῳδέω,** *sing of in expectation*, ‡Caes.Naz.*dial.*128(M.38.1025).

προμεριμνάω, *think out beforehand*, Hipp.*haer.*6.52(p.184.14; M.16.3282B); *ib.*8.15(p.235.23; 3363A).

***προμεσονύκτιον, τό,** *time before midnight*, Thdr.Stud.*poen.*1.99(M.99.1745C).

***προμεταγινώσκω,** *change one's mind beforehand*, Proc.G.*Gen.*1:26(M.87.112A).

προμήθεια, ἡ, *forethought, consideration*; **1.** in gen.; exercised by Christian teacher in respect of pupils, Gr.Thaum.*pan.Or.*4(p.10.19; M.10.1064A); by bishops as pastors, Jo.Ant.*ep.pop.CP*(p.128.28; M.83.1448D); **2.** of God ἐγὼ γὰρ ὁ σὸς ἄνθρωπος ἵλεων ἔχων τὴν παρὰ σοῦ π. Const.ap.Gel.Cyz.*h.e.*3.19.18(M.85.1349A); ἀλληγορίαν ἔχει... Προμηθεὺς ἡ π. ὑφ' ἧς τὰ πάντα ἐγένετο *Hom.Clem.*6.14; ‡Nil.*perist.*4.11(M.79.837A); Thdt.*qu.65 in Gen.*(1.78); ὑπὲρ μὲν τῶν ὑπαρξάντων χάριν ὁμολογοῦντας, αἰτοῦντας δὲ τὴν ἔπειτα π. id.*Rom.*11:36(3.127).

***προμήνυμα, τό,** *previous indication*; of OT types, Gr.Nyss.*bapt.diff.*(M.46.421A); *Didasc.Jac.*2.3(p.46.17).

προμήνυσις, ἡ, 1. *previous indication*, ‡Just.*qu.et resp.*2(M.6.1252C); ἡ διὰ παλμοῦ π. τοῦ πλούτου *ib.*19(1265B); ‡Sophr.H.*liturg.*17(M.87.3997B); **2.** *declaration, showing forth* ποίησον...χερουβὶμ...εἰς π. τῆς ἐμῆς εἰκόνος ‡Ath.*proph.*8(M.28.1072B, v.l. προσκύνησιν).

***προμηνυτικός,** *previously indicating*, ‡Just.*qu.et resp.*83(M.6.1324D).

***προμηνυτικῶς,** *so as to predict*, ‡Chrys.*pasch.*5(8.262E).

προμηνύ-ω, 1. *mention previously* τὸν Χριστὸν...προεμηνύσαμεν λόγον ὄντα Just.*1apol.*46.2(M.6.397B); *ib.*63.1(424A); Clem.*str.*1.17(p.56.8; M.8.801B); ἐν τῇ προτέρᾳ ἣν ἐπιστολῇ ~σας Chrys.*hom.2.2 in 2Cor.*(10.430A); **2.** *foretell, prophesy*, of pagan prophecies of Christ οἱ μάγοι οἱ μαγείᾳ καὶ τοῦ σωτῆρος προεμήνυσαν τὴν γένεσιν Clem.*str.*1.15(p.45.24; M.8.777B); in gen. Σεμνοὶ τῶν Ἰνδῶν γυμνοὶ ...περὶ τῶν μελλόντων ~ουσι *ib.*3.7(p.224.4; 1164B); of comet presaging Constantine's death, ‡Jo.D.*Artem.*7(p.26.10; M.96.1257B); of Sibylline Oracles, Clem.*prot.*4(p.38.28; M.8.141B); of divine foretelling through prophets and apostles, *ib.*1(p.8.13; M.8.64A); ‡Just.*qu.et resp.*2(M.6.1252C); in revelation to Abraham, Thdt.*qu.3 in Jos.*(1.306); to prophet, id.*Jon.*1:1(2.1463); of OT prophecy, Just.*dial.*17.1(M.6.512B); Hipp.*Dan.*4.3.8(M.10.681C); Eus.*d.e.*1 proem.(p.2.17; M.22.16A); Ath.*inc.*33.3(M.25.153A); of OT types, Just.*dial.*54.2(596A); Ἐνὼχ...μετετέθη, τὴν μετάθεσιν τῶν δικαίων ~ων Iren.*haer.*5.5.1(M.7.1134B); of BMV as prototype revealing redemption of mankind, ‡Meth.*Sym.et Ann.*7(M.18.365A); of apostle prophesying future heresies, ref. 1Tim.4:1, Ath.*ep.Aeg.Lib.*20(M.25.585A); of Christ, Just.*1apol.*28.1(M.6.372B); id.*dial.*141.2(797C); Clem.*paed.*1.5(p.97.20; M.8.264B); **3.** *forewarn* Παῦλος ~θεὶς ὑπὸ τοῦ θεοῦ *A.Xanthipp.*13(p.66.28); **4.** *show forth* ἀγαθὰς καὶ κακὰς πράξεις...~ω ὑμῖν ὡς ὁδοὺς δύο *Hom.Clem.*7.7.

προμήτωρ, ἡ, 1. *first mother*; of Eve, Jo.D.*f.o.*4.14(M.94.1160C); ‡Jo.D.*hom.*6.1(M.96.661C); **2.** *grandmother*, Thdr.Stud.*epp.*1.18(M.99.964D); of Anna as π. τοῦ κυρίου ‡Hipp.Th.*fr.*16(p.48.8).

προμνημονεύω, *mention previously*, Eus.*h.e.*4.17.13(M.20.373A); Jo.Eub.*concept.BMV* 22(M.96.1497C).

προμνηστεύ-ομαι, 1. *betroth to oneself before*, Thphn.*chron.*p.391(M.108.932C); **2.** *solicit, endeavour to obtain*, of a bishop ἀλλοτρίαν καθέδραν ἑαυτῷ ~σθαι CSard.*can.*11.

***προμνηστεύτρια, ἡ,** *match-maker, woman who arranges a marriage*, Chrys.*vid.*2.1(1.349D).

προμνήστρια, ἡ, *woman who arranges a marriage, match-maker*, hence *one who obtains* or *brings something about*, of BMV *αὕτη πάντων τῶν ἀγαθῶν ἡμῖν π. γέγονεν* Jo.D.*hom*.9.16(M.96.744C); met. *π. ... χειρόνων ἡ πλάνησις* Cyr.*glaph.Ex*.3(1.336D); id.*Os*.54(3.84D); *ἡ εἰς θεὸν ἐλπίς, σωτηρίας...π.* id.*Ps*.30:20(M.69.864D); *πλείστων... ἀγαθῶν π. γέγονεν ἡ πίστις ib*.46:1(1052A); Christol. *τιμῆς ἄρα καὶ δόξης αὐτῷ π. γενέσθαι φαίη τις ἂν τὴν κένωσιν; εἶτα πῶς ἔτι κένωσις τὸ χρῆμά ἐστιν;* id.*apol.orient*.10(p.56.1; 6[1].188B).

***προμνήστωρ, ὁ,** *arranger of a marriage*, Gr.Nyss.*bapt.Chr*.(M.46.588D); ref. union of Christ and Church *οἱ...τῆς παρθένου π., πατριάρχαι τε καὶ προφῆται* id.*hom.1 in Cant*.(M.44.772B).

***προμονάζω,** *be a monk previously*, Phot.*nomoc*.1.11(p.469; M.104.500C) v. *προσμονάζω*.

***προμορφ-όω, 1.** *form in advance*, of Christ's body *σαρκοῦται...ὁ λόγος...οὐ...~ωθέντι καὶ κατ' αὐτὸ προϋποστάντι ποτὲ προσπλεκόμενος σώματι* Sophr.H.*ep.syn*.(M.87.3161B); *προϋποστὰν καὶ ~ωθὲν ἐν τῇ μήτρᾳ τῆς παρθένου λέγεις τὸ σῶμα Χριστοῦ* Anast.S.*hod*.22(M.89.293A); **2.** *prefigure ἐν διαφόροις σκεύεσιν ἐν τῇ ἁγίᾳ σκηνῇ προεμορφοῦτο Χριστός* Cyr.*ador*.10(1.330E).

***προμοσέλλα, ἡ,** *carriage τοὺς ἵππους καὶ τὴν βασιλικὴν π. λαβών* Thphn.*chron*.p.400(M.108.953A).

[*]προμοσκρίνιος, ὁ, v. *πριμισκρίνιος*.

προμυ-έω, *initiate beforehand ἐπιστολὴ...γεγραμμένη πρὸς τοὺς ἤδη τὰ θεῖα ~ηθέντας* †Oecum.*Rom*.proem.(M.118.317A)ap.*cat.Rom*.(p.1.7).

***προμυθολογέω,** *tell myths beforehand*, Cyr.H.*catech*.15.11.

***προμυκτήρ, ὁ,** *beak*, *Phys*.B 8(p.192.1); cf.‡Epiph.*phys*.6(M.43.524A).

***προμυσταγωγέω,** *instruct beforehand*, Cyr.*glaph.Ex*.3(1.318A); id.*Jo*.4.6(4.423A).

***προναρκάω,** *grow numb beforehand*, Eus.*h.e*.8.3.1(M.20.748B); id.*m.P*.1.3(p.908.7; M.20.1464A).

***προνεδετίων, ἡ,** *action as heir* (Lat. *pro haerede gestio*), Ath.Scholast.*coll*.9.1(p.97).

προνηστεύ-ω, *fast before πρὸ δὲ τοῦ βαπτίσματος ~σάτω ὁ βαπτίζων καὶ ὁ βαπτιζόμενος καὶ εἴ τινες ἄλλοι δύνανται Did*.7.4; *οὐχ ὡς ἔτυχεν ἐχειροτόνουν τοὺς διακόνους, ἀλλὰ ~οντες* Ammon.*Ac*.13:2(M.85.1541A).

***προνήστιμος,** *of preliminary fasting*, Jo.D.*jej*.5(M.95.69D).

προνο-έω, 1. *foresee*, hence *preconceive ἐν αὐτῷ ζῇ τὰ πάντα, καὶ ἐν αὐτῷ ~εῖται cat.Jo*.1:4(p.181.4); **2.** *conceive as being before τίς οὗτος ὁ ~ούμενος τοῦ Ἀδὰμ ἄνθρωπος;* Gr.Nyss.*Apoll*.3(M.45.1128D); **3.** *provide Ἰησοῦς...αἰώνιον βασιλείαν ~ῆσαι ἐπήγγελται* Just.*dial*.116.2(M.6.744C); **4.** *provide for, care for*; **a.** in gen. *χήρας ~ουμένης ὑπὸ τῆς ἐκκλησίας* Or.*or*.28(p.377.17; M.11.524C) etc.; **b.** of divine providence; **i.** pagan *οἱ πλεῖστοι οὐδὲ τούτου πεφροντίκασιν, εἴτε εἷς εἴτε καὶ πλείους εἰσὶ θεοί, καὶ εἴτε ~οῦσιν ἡμῶν ἑκάστου εἴτε καὶ οὔ* Just.*dial*.1.4(M.6.473C); ref. possibility of another deity besides true God *ἀλλὰ ~εῖ; καὶ μὴν οὐδὲ ~εῖ, εἰ μὴ πεποίηκεν, εἰ δὲ μὴ ποιεῖ μήτε ~εῖ... εἷς...ὁ ποιητὴς τοῦ κόσμου θεός* Athenag.*leg*.8.4(M.6.905C); in Plato's doctrine *θεὸν...τὸν ποιητὴν καὶ διακοσμήσαντα τόδε τὸ πᾶν καὶ ~ούμενον αὐτοῦ* Hipp.*haer*.1.19(p.19.6; M.16.3041A); Stoic, Athenag.*leg*.19.2(M.6.929A); **ii.** Christian *πάντ' ἐρῶ γὰρ μᾶλλον ἢ κακὸν τὸ ~οῦν ἐρῶ* Basilides ap.Clem.*str*.4.12(p.284.27; M.8.1292B); cf.*ib*.2.20(p.175.15; 1060A); *τὸ ~οῦν τῆς αὐτῆς οὐσίας λέγοντες εἶναι τοῖς ~ουμένοις γενικῷ λόγῳ, τέλειον ἀλλ' οἷον τὸ ~ούμενον. παρεδέξαντο δὲ τὰ ἀπαντῶντα τῷ λόγῳ αὐτῶν ἄτοπα οἱ θέλοντες εἶναι σῶμα τὸν θεόν* Or.*Jo*.13.21(p.244.33f.; M.14.433A); *οἰκονομεῖ ὁ θεὸς μὴ εἶναι μετ' ἀλλήλων τοὺς φαύλους, τάχα καὶ αὐτῶν ~ῶν, ἵνα μὴ συναυξήσῃ αὐτῶν ἡ κακία* id.*hom.12.4 in Jer*.(p.91.15; M.13.384D); *δικαστὴς... ~ούμενος καὶ τοῦ ἑνός, πλεῖον δὲ ~ούμενος τῶν πολλῶν ib.12.5*(p.92.14; 385C); of divine wisdom in Creation and sustaining of universe, Meth.*res*.2.9(p.349.2); *τῇ τοῦ ~οῦντος κελεύσει* Const.*or.s.c*.15(p.176.6; M.20.1280A); *Χριστὸν δι' οὗ τὰ πάντα ὁ πατὴρ...συνέχει, καὶ ~εῖται τῶν ὅλων* Ath.*gent*.47(M.25.96B); *σοφίας...καθ' ἣν ἀγγέλων καὶ ἀρχαγγέλων καὶ τῶν ἄνω ~εῖ δυνάμεων* Chrys.*incomprehens*.1.5(1.449B); *ἡ τῶν ~ουμένων φύσις ἐπιδέχεται τὰς τῆς ὅλης...προνοίας ἐκδιδομένας... προνοητικὰς ἀγαθότητας* Dion.Ar.*d.n*.4.33(M.3.733C); *~εῖ καὶ...καλῶς ~εῖ...ὡς οὖν ἀγαθός, ~εῖ, ὁ γὰρ μὴ ~ῶν οὐκ ἀγαθός* Jo.D.*f.o*.2.29(M.94.964B); **iii.** of Son *ὁ μονογενὴς τοῦ θεοῦ λόγος...πάντων ἐξ ἴσης τῆς σωτηρίας ~εῖ* Eus.*d.e*.4.6(p.159.29; M.22.265C); *εἰ δὲ ~εῖ μὲν ὁ πατὴρ τῶν ἁπάντων, ~εῖ δὲ ὡσαύτως καὶ ὁ υἱός..., ἡ τῶν προαιρέσεων ταὐτότης τὸ κοινὸν τῆς φύσεως...ἐνδείκνυται* Gr.Nyss.*Eun*.1(1 p.147.12; M.45.388A); **c.** ref. liturgical duties *οἱ ἐκ δεξιῶν πρεσβύτεροι ~ήσονται τῶν ἐπισκόπων πρὸς τὸ θυσιαστήριον, ὅπως τιμήσωσι καὶ ἐντιμηθῶσιν εἰς ὃ ἂν δέῃ· οἱ ἐξ ἀριστερῶν πρεσβύτεροι ~ήσονται τοῦ πλήθους, ὅπως εὐσταθήσῃ καὶ ἀθόρυβον ᾖ Ordo Eccl.App*.18.

προνοησία, ἡ, *providence*, Epiph.*haer*.76.52(p.407.6; M.42.625C).

προνοητεύω, *govern*, *Apoc.Dan*.C(p.117).

προνοητής, ὁ, *one who foresees and provides, controller*; **1.** of men *κρατήσουσιν ἐπὶ τὴν ἀνατολὴν π. τρεῖς Apoc.Dan*.C(p.117); **2.** of God *μεμάθηκεν...ἐκ...τῆς δημιουργίας καὶ προνοίας τὸν δημιουργὸν καὶ π.* Or.*exc.in Ps*.17:12(M.17.112C); *μεμαθήκαμεν...ἐξ ἀρχῆς εἰς ἕνα θεὸν ...πιστεύειν, τὸν πάντων νοητῶν τε καὶ αἰσθητῶν δημιουργόν τε καὶ π.* *Symb.Ant*.(341)1(p.249.1; M.26.721A); *ὁ π., ὁ κηδεμὼν Lit*.ap.*Const.App*.8.5.2; *π. τῶν ὅλων ὑπάρχων* Didym.*Ac*.9:6(M.39.1672A); *κύριος π. τῶν εἰς αὐτὸν καταφευγόντων κατὰ πάντα γίνεται* Mac.Aeg.*hom*.48.1(M.34.808D); *ἐπὶ παντὶ θλιβερῷ ἐπερχομένῳ ἡμῖν, λίαν ἐπωφελές, καὶ πάνυ ἀναγκαῖον τὸ εὐχαριστεῖν τῷ θεῷ τῷ π. καὶ κριτῇ τῆς τῶν ἀνθρώπων ζωῆς* Nil.*epp*.3.118(M.79.437B); *ἔφορον καὶ π.* Isid.Pel.*epp*.2.299(M.78.725D); *εἷς θεὸς πάντων ποιητὴς ὁρατῶν τε καὶ ἀοράτων, πάντων π.* Taras.*ep*.5(M.98.1461D); **3.** of Christ *ὁ...π. τοῦ κόσμου Χριστός A.Xanthipp*.9(p.63.24); *τὸν μεσίτην, τὸν π., τὸν νομοθέτην Const.App*.7.36.6; ref. eternity of Son *εἰ μὴ προῆν ἀδημιουργήτως ὁ...π., οὐκ ἂν ὑπῆν δημιουργικῶς τὰ...προνοούμενα* Didym.*Trin*.3.5(M.39.841B); **4.** of Satan as worshipped by pagans, *A.Xanthipp*.8(p.63.7); of pagan gods *τοῦ ἀνθρωπείου γένους π. τε καὶ κηδεμόνας τυγχάνοντας* ‡Jo.D.*Artem*.32(M.96.1281A).

προνοητικός, 1. *provident, far-seeing, careful*; of those born under Aries, Hipp.*haer*.4.15(p.49.18; M.16.3083B); *ὁ π. γεωργός* †Bas.*Is*.142(1.478E; M.30.349A); of Christ performing miracle and previously remitting sins, Chrys.*paralyt*.4(3.39B); **2.** *providing for, taking care for π., ὥσπερ ὁ ἀγαθὸς ποιμήν* Clem.*exc.Thdot*.73(p.130.10; M.9.692D); *τῷ ἀνδρὶ καὶ τῇ γυναικὶ...τὴν προσήκουσαν ἀπονέμων χώραν, τούτῳ μὲν τὴν ἀρχικὴν καὶ π., ἐκείνῃ δὲ τὴν ὑποτακτικήν* Chrys.*hom.20.1 in Eph*.(11.144A); **3.** *providential*; **a.** of God and his attributes, Iren.*fr*.5(M.7.1232B) cit. s. *ἐνέργεια*; Clem.*str*.2.2(p.115.2; M.8.933C) cit. s. *διοίκησις*; *τῇ...π. αὐτοῦ δυνάμει* id.*fr*.42(p.220.32; M.9.768B); *ἡ σοφία...ἀρχὴ τῶν ὁδῶν τοῦ θεοῦ γέγονε τῶν ποιητικῶν καὶ π.* Or.*exp.in Pr*.8:22(M.17.185A); *θείαν...φύσιν...π. τῶν ὄντων* Eus.*Hierocl*.6(516A; M.22.805C); *ὁδοὺς...π. τῶν ὅλων* id.*e.th*.3.3(p.146.18; M.24.984B); *διὰ προνοητικῆς ἀνθρώπων ἐκ τῆς αὐτοῦ φιλανθρωπίας ἐπιμελείας* Epiph.*haer*.70.12(p.246.9; M.42.368A); *ἡ τῶν προνοουμένων φύσις ἐπιδέχεται τὰς τῆς ὅλης...προνοίας ἐκδιδομένας ἀναλόγως ἑκάστῳ π. ἀγαθότητας* Dion.Ar.*d.n*.4.33(M.3.733C); *θεὸν...ἀρχὴν...πάντων προνοητικήν* ‡Cyr.*Trin*.7(6[3].8B; M.77.1132A) = Jo.D.*f.o*.1.8(M.94.808C); *οὐ γὰρ οἷόν τέ ἐστιν ἀγαθὸν ὄντα τὸν θεὸν μὴ...εὐεργετικὸν ὄντα μὴ καὶ π. ὄντα πάντως εἶναι* Max.*ambig*.(M.91.1189A); *ἡ ποιητικὴ δὲ αὐτοῦ δύναμις, καὶ ἡ συνεκτική, καὶ ἡ π., ἡ ἀγαθὴ αὐτοῦ θέλησίς ἐστιν* Jo.D.*f.o*.2.29(M.94.964B); **b.** of Christ *τὴν...π. αὐτοῦ χεῖρα* Or.*fr.50 in Jo*.(p.525.17); ref. titles *οὐ γὰρ ὥσπερ υἱὸν τοῦ πατρός, οὕτως ἢ λίθον ἢ ἀνάστασιν...λέγομεν, ἀλλ' ἔστιν οἷον τέχνῃ τινὶ...διελέσθαι τῶν θείων ὀνομάτων τὴν σημασίαν· τὰ μὲν γὰρ τῆς...δόξης τὴν ἔνδειξιν ἔχει, τὰ δὲ τὸ ποικίλον τῆς π. οἰκονομίας ἐνδείκνυται* Gr.Nyss.*Eun*.3(2 p.44.1; M.45.612C); ref. Nestorian division of Christ *πῶς οὐ δύο υἱοὺς... δοξάζετε; πῶς δὲ οὐ θάτερον μὲν θεὸν οὐδὲν εἰς ἀνθρώπους κατ' οὐσίαν κενωθέντα, ἀλλὰ μόνον κατὰ τὴν...π. αὐτοῦ ἐνέργειαν;* Leont.H.*Nest*.3.6(M.86.1621A); **4.** neut. as subst., *providence πῶς οὐ καταγέλαστον, τὸ δημιουργικὸν οὐσίαν εἶναι λέγειν; ἢ τὸ π. πάλιν οὐσίαν;* Bas.*Eun*.1.8(1.219E; M.29.528B); *ὁ θεὸς ἦν ἐν τῷ κόσμῳ, κατ' οὐσίαν, ἀλλ' οὐ κατὰ τὸ π.* Ammon.*Jo*.1:10(M.85.1396D).

προνοητικῶς, *providentially, with care τὸ 'αὐξάνεσθε' ἐν ῥῆμα σοφῶς λεχθέν, π. οἰκονομεῖται* ‡Bas.*struct.hom*.1.18(1.331B; M.30.25C); *τὰ ἥττω τῶν κρειττόνων ἐπιστρεπτικῶς ἐρῶσι...καὶ τὰ κρείττω τῶν ἡττόνων π.* Dion.Ar.*d.n*.4.10(M.3.708A); id.*ep*.8.1(M.3.1088B); *πάντα σοφῶς τε καὶ π. ... δεδημιουργημένα* Max.*ambig*.(M.91.1176B); *δραστήριος γὰρ δύναμις...ἕλκει τὰ κινούμενα π. ὡς τέλος ib*.(1260A).

***προνοήτρια, ἡ,** *provider, guardian τὴν θεοτόκον κουράτορα καὶ π.* Leont.N.*v.Jo.Eleem*.34(p.67.1).

πρόνοια, ἡ, *forethought, care*;

A. of men; **1.** *forethought τῶν ὑπὸ λόγου καὶ π. κατακοσμουμένων* Or.*Jo*.13.21(p.244.32; M.14.432D); **2.** *care*, in gen. *χρὴ...τὸν ἀποδεικτικὸν ἄνδρα τῆς μὲν ἀληθείας [ὡς] τῶν λημμάτων πολλὴν ποιήσασθαι π.* Clem.*str*.8.3(p.84.16; M.9.568C); *τῆς...ἀθανασίας τῶν δημιουργημάτων π. ποιοῦνται* Meth.*res*.1.35(p.274.12; M.41.1100C); *προσφέρειν δεῖ...νοσοῦντι π. Hom.Clem*.11.4; *εἰ παρὰ ἀνθρώποις τοσαύτη π. καὶ τάξις...πολλῷ μᾶλλον παρὰ θεῷ* Chrys.*hom.60.4 in Jo*.(8.357D); *τί μὴ τοσαύτην ἀπονέμεις τῇ ψυχῇ π. ὅσην τῷ σώματι; ib.69.3*(411D); of Christ looking on S. Peter *καὶ δεδεμένος πολλὴν ἐποιεῖτο τοῦ μαθητοῦ π. ib.83.3*(494A); ref. Jo.19:27 *εἰ γὰρ μὴ ἐγεννήθη κατὰ σάρκα, μηδὲ μητέρα ἔσχε, τίνος ἕνεκεν τοσαύτην περὶ αὐτὴν...ποιεῖται π.; ib.85.2*(506D); ref. 1Tim.5:8 *π. πᾶσαν λέγει, τὴν κατὰ ψυχήν, τὴν κατὰ σῶμα, ἐπεὶ καὶ αὕτη π. ἐστιν* id.*hom.14.1 in 1Tim*.(11.625A);

Παῦλος ὑπὲρ δραπέτου...τοσαύτην ποιεῖται π. id.*hom.in Philm.* proem.(11.773C); αἱ π. τῶν ὑπερτέρων Dion.Ar.*d.n.*4.7(M.3.704B); displayed by S. Mark in composing gospel ἑνὸς γὰρ ἐποιήσατο π., τοῦ μηδὲν ὧν ἤκουσεν παραλιπεῖν ἢ ψεύσασθαί τι ἐν αὐτοῖς Papias *fr.*2. 15; of church builder συναγωγὴ Μαρκιανιστῶν κώμης Λεβάβων...π. Παύλου πρεσβυτέρου *CG–CI* I p.18 (Lebaba 318); **3.** *pastoral care* τῆς τοῦ ἐπισκοποῦντος π. ἐστέρησθε Const.ap.Ath.*apol.sec.*55(p.135.22; M.25.348C); **4.** *act of foresight* παραδόξῳ π. τινὶ ὁ Χαγάνος πρὸς τοὺς Ῥωμαίους πρεσβεύεται Thphyl.*exc.gent.*15(p.488.11; M.113.952A)

B. divine, *providential care, providence*; **1.** in paganism; **a.** denied of pagan gods ὅτε γὰρ περὶ τῆς ἰδίας σωτηρίας οὐδὲν ἰσχύουσι, πῶς τῶν ἀνθρώπων π. ποιήσονται; Arist.*apol.*13.2; **b.** in Stoicism δισσοῦ αἰτίου κατ' αὐτοὺς ὄντος, τοῦ μὲν δραστηρίου καὶ καταρχομένου, καθὸ ἡ π., τοῦ δὲ πάσχοντος...καθὸ ἡ ὕλη Athenag.*leg.* 19.2(M.6.929A); **c.** various pagan views discussed ἕτεροι δ' αὖ εἶπον π. εἶναι...Ἄρατος μὲν οὖν φησιν ἐκ Διὸς ἀρχώμεσθα, κτλ. ... τίνι οὖν πιστεύσωμεν, πότερον Ἀράτῳ...ἢ Σοφοκλεῖ λέγοντι· π. δ' ἐστὶν οὐδενὸς σαφής. ... ἀσύμφωνα ἑαυτοῖς ἐξεῖπον...καὶ π. εἶναι τοῖς λέγουσιν, ἀπρονοησίαν τἀναντία εἰρήκασιν Thphl.Ant.*Autol.*2.8(M.6.1060B); Xenocrates μέχρι τῆς σελήνης αὐτῆς διορίζων τὴν π. Clem.*prot.*5 (p.51.3; M.8.172A); ἀμαθῶς ὅρον τῇ π. θείς [sc. Aristotle] Tat.*orat.* 2(p.2.24; M.6.808A); **d.** denied by Epicureans, Thphl.Ant.*Autol.* l.c.(1061B); Clem.*str.*1.11(p.33.10; M.8.748C); ὁμολογῶν Ἐπικούρειος εἶναι οὐκ ἂν ἔχοι τὸ ἀξιόπιστον ἐν τῷ κατηγορεῖν τῶν ὅπως ποτὲ πρόνοιαν εἰσαγόντων καὶ θεὸν ἐφιστάντων τοῖς οὖσι Or.*Cels.*1.8(p.61. 5; M.11.669C); *ib.*1.10(p.63.12; 676A); Ἐπικουρείους, τοὺς πάντῃ π. ἀναιροῦντας *ib.*2.13(p.142.8; 820B); Gr.Nyss.*anim.et res.*(M.46.21B); **e.** and astrologers ἐκβάλλουσι π. τὴν οἰκονομοῦσαν τὰ τῶν ἀνθρώπων †Bas.*Is.*275(1.589A; M.30.604A); **2.** belief in it established by Christianity as against Epicureanism φιλοσοφίας...τῆς ἀναιρούσης τὴν π., κατὰ τὴν παράδοσιν τῶν ἀνθρώπων· ἡ γὰρ κατὰ τὴν θείαν παράδοσιν φιλοσοφία ἵστησι τὴν π. καὶ βεβαιοῖ Clem.*str.*1.11(p.34. 5; M.8.749B); **3.** of God's providence in Christian thought; **a.** in gen.; **i.** its nature ἡ τοῦ θεοῦ π. ἐμποιοῦσα τοῖς γινομένοις τὸ εἶναι καὶ τὸ πῶς εἶναι Clem.*fr.*37(p.219.21; M.9.752A); π. ... ἐστὶν ἐκ θεοῦ εἰς τὰ ὄντα γινομένη ἐπιμέλεια. ὁρίζονται δὲ αὐτὴν καὶ οὕτω· π. ἐστι βούλησις θεοῦ, δι' ἣν πάντα...τὴν πρόσφορον διεξαγωγὴν λαμβάνει Nemes.*nat.hom.*43(M.40.792B) = Max.*ambig.*(M.91.1189B); Max.*ambig.*(M.91.1133D); **ii.** its operation in gen., ref. Mt.13:3 ἐκ τῆς διαλύσεως ἡ μεγαλειότης τῆς π. τοῦ δεσπότου ἀνίστησιν αὐτά, καὶ ἐκ τοῦ ἑνὸς πλείονα αὔξει *1Clem.*24.5; τῇ ἰδίᾳ σοφίᾳ καὶ π. κτίσας τὴν ἁγίαν ἐκκλησίαν αὐτοῦ Herm.*vis.*1.3.4; ἐγὼ...π. θεοῦ ἦλθον εἰς τόνδε τὸν κόσμον Arist.*apol.*1.1; τῇ καθολικῇ τοῦ θεοῦ π. διὰ τῶν προσεχέστερον κινουμένων...εἰς τὰ ἐπὶ μέρους διαδίδοται ἡ δραστικὴ ἐνέργεια Clem.*str.*6.16(p.508.18; M.9.380B); ἡ θεία π. οὐ καταστρέφει ἐπὶ μόνους τοὺς ἐν σαρκί id.*ecl.*48(p.150.7; M.9.720B); ποικίλης π. τοῦ θεοῦ Or.*princ.*3.1.17(p.228.2; M.11.285B); πάντα ἡ θεία περιείληφε π. id.*Cels.*8.70(p.287.20; M.11.1624A); τῆς ἐνθέου π. καὶ δυνάμεως ἐναργῶς ἀποφαινούσης ἑαυτὴν ἔκ τε τῶν καθόλου πανσόφων καὶ τεχνικῶν ἀποτελεσμάτων, ἔκ τε τῶν καθ' ἡμᾶς...τὴν ἐλευθέραν...τῆς λογικῆς ψυχῆς δύναμιν παραδεικνυμένων Eus.*p.e.*6.6(252D; M.21.429B); ref. Logos ὃν...ὁ πατὴρ προνοίᾳ τῶν ὅλων πρὸ τῶν ἄλλων ἁπάντων συνεστήσατο id.*d.e.*4.6(p.159.23; M.22.265C); π. ... οἰακισμός, ᾧ φέρει τὸ πᾶν θεός Gr.Naz.*carm.*1.2.34.265(M.37.964A); ἡ πόλις [sc. Νινευί]...λιμήν τις...τοῖς ἁμαρτάνουσιν...γέγονεν...καλοῦσα ἅπαντας εἰς μετάνοιαν...δι' ὧν ἀπήλαυσε τῆς τοῦ θεοῦ π. Chrys.*stat.*5.5(2.67A); ὄψονται δὲ οὐ τὴν π. μου δίκην φωτὸς ἐπιφαινομένην ἀλλὰ τὴν τιμωρητικὴν δύναμιν Thdt.*Is.*5:30(p.29.28; 2.206); ref. Creation τὸ δὲ προνοίας ἐστὶν ἔργον, τῆς τόδε τὸ πᾶν ἐκ διαφόρων...μερῶν ποιησάσης ‡Just.*confut.*53(M.6.1549C); οὐ γὰρ τῇ δυνάμει ὁ κόσμος γεγένηται, τούτου καὶ τῇ π. διοικεῖται ‡Just.*qu.et resp.*126(M.6.1376C); δημιουργίᾳ καὶ π. τῶν ὄντων *Disp.Phot.*(M.88.568A); ἡ δὲ τοῦ θείου συμβόλου τῆς πίστεως γινομένη...ὁμολογία τὴν...τῆς...περὶ ἡμᾶς τοῦ θεοῦ π. γενησομένην μυστικὴν εὐχαριστίαν...προσημαίνει Max.*myst.*18(M.91. 696B); **iii.** π. equated with divine character εἰς τὸ ἐξομοιοῦσθαι...τῇ ἀγαθότητι τῆς τοῦ θεοῦ π. διά τε τῆς ἀνεξικακίας διά τε τῆς ἀμνησικακίας Clem.*str.*7.14(p.62.1; M.9.520C); **iv.** π. κατὰ τὴν διαμονήν contrasted with δημιουργία, Chrys.*hom.*5.3 *in Jo.*(8.39A); **v.** π. as virtually synonymous with θεός, Clem.*str.*4.12(p.286.36; M.8. 1296B); ἐπὶ τῶν τῆς ἁπτομένης τοῦ παντὸς κόσμου π. ἔργων, τινὰ μὲν ἐναργέστατα φαίνεται, ᾗ προνοίας ἐστὶν ἔργα, ἕτερα δὲ οὕτως ἀποκέκρυπται ὡς ἀπιστίας χώραν παρέχειν δοκεῖν Or.*princ.*4.1.7(p.303.4; M.11.353B); τῆς ἐπιδιδούσης τὴν ὑπὲρ ἄνθρωπον σοφίαν ἱερᾶς π. διὰ τῶν γραμμάτων τῷ γένει τῶν ἀνθρώπων id.*sel.in Ps.*1(M.12.1081B); ἐπὰν... τὰ ἀπὸ τῆς π. γίνηται πάντα εἰς ἡμᾶς, ἵνα συντελεσθῶμεν...ἡμεῖς δὲ μὴ παραδεχώμεθα τὰ τῆς π. τῆς ἐπὶ τελειότητα ἡμᾶς ἑλκούσης id.*hom.*6.2 *in Jer.*(p.50.7; M.13.328A); ἡ π., ἐν ἁγίαις γραφαῖς δεδωκυῖα πάσαις ταῖς...ἐκκλησίαις οἰκοδομήν id.*ep.*1.4(M.11.60A); ἡ πανάγαθος καὶ φιλανθρωποτάτη τῶν ὅλων π. Eus.*h.e.*2.14.6(M.20.172A); οἱ δέ, ὥσπερ ἐξ ἐπιτάγματος τῆς π. προθύμως αὐτὸν ἐδέξαντο Ath.*v.Anton.*49(M.26. 916A); βασιλεύειν οὖν τεταγμένοι παρὰ θεοῦ...τῇ τε π. καὶ ἀνθρώποις μεσιτεύοντες Thds.Imp.*ep.Cyr.*2(p.115.5; H.1.1344C); πλουτείτω... τέως ὁ πονηρός, φησὶν ἡ τῆς π. φιλανθρωπία Aen.*dial.*(M.85.921C); ἀπὸ δὲ τῆς τὸ πᾶν σοφῶς διοικούσης π. τὰς ἀρετὰς κατορθοῦν διδασκόμενος Max.*ambig.*(M.91.1149D); **vi.** in rel. to human virtue συμπλακεῖσα τῇ μακαρίᾳ π. ἡ τοῦ γνωστικοῦ ὁσιότης κατὰ τὴν ἑκούσιον ὁμολογίαν τελείαν τὴν εὐεργεσίαν ἐπιδείκνυσι τοῦ θεοῦ Clem.*str.*7.7 (p.31.28; M.9.457C); τὸ πλέον νέμων τῇ τοῦ θεοῦ π., τὸ δὲ αὐτοῦ συστέλλων, πλὴν ὅσον μὴ λυμήνασθαι...τὴν αὐτεξουσίαν Chrys.*hom.* 3.1 *in 1Tim.*(11.562C); τὸ γὰρ φθεῖραι φύσιν οὐκ ἔστι προνοίας Dion. Ar.*d.n.*4.33(M.3.733B); **vii.** ref. evil αἱ τῶν ἀποστατησάντων βουλαί τε καὶ ἐνέργειαι...κυβερνῶνται...ὑπὸ τῆς καθόλου π. ἐπὶ τέλος ὑγιεινόν, κἂν νοσοποιὸς ᾖ ἡ αἰτία Clem.*str.*1.17(p.55.22; M.8.801A); εἰ δὲ ταῦτα κακὰ κυρίως ὑπάρχει, καὶ οὐ μᾶλλον παιδευτικὰ ἐκ θεοῦ προνοίας πρὸς σωφρονισμὸν ἀνθρώπων ἐξευρημένα *Disp.Phot.*(M.88.576C); πῶς ὅλως τὰ κακὰ προνοίας οὔσης;...οὐδὲν...τῶν ὄντων ἐστέρηται καθόλου τοῦ ἀγαθοῦ, ἐν πᾶσι τοῖς οὖσιν ἡ θεία π. ... ἀλλὰ καὶ τοῖς γινομένοις κακοῖς ἀγαθοπρεπῶς ἡ π. κέχρηται, πρὸς τὴν αὐτῶν, ἢ ἄλλων...ὠφέλειαν Dion.Ar.*d.n.*4.33(M.3.733B); **viii.** ref. inequality of opportunity for good living τὰς δὲ περὶ τούτων αἰτίας πάντως μὲν εἰκὸς εἶναι ἐν τοῖς τῆς π. λόγοις, πίπτειν δὲ αὐτὰς εἰς ἀνθρώπους οὐκ εὐχερές Or.*Cels.*3.38 (p.235.4; M.11.969B); for hearing gospel, id.*princ.*3.1.17(p.228.9; M. 11.285B); of reward and punishment; Basilides' view discussed, Clem.*str.*4.12(p.285.8ff.; M.8.1293Aff.); **ix.** contrasted with pagan conception of fate, Clem.*exc.Thdot.*74(p.130.22; M.9.693A) cit. s. εἱμαρμένη; ὁ δὴ τὴν εἱμαρμένην εἰσάγων ἄντικρυς θεὸν καὶ θεοῦ π. ἐξωθεῖ Eus.*p.e.*6.6(252A; M.21.428C); *Hom.Clem.*11.34 cit. s. διοικέω; **x.** belief in π. asserted against Epicureans, Clem.*str.*1.11(p.34.10; M.8.749C); Or.*Cels.*1.8(p.61.5; M.11.669C); *ib.*4.3(p.276.20; 1033A); id.*Jo.*2.3(p.57.7; M.14.113B); εἰς ἀθεότητα ἐκπίπτουσι, μήτε ἐκ προνοίᾳ θεοῦ διοικεῖσθαι τὸ πᾶν, μήτε εἰ αὐτομάτως φέρεται συντιθέμενοι †Bas.*Is.*172(1.503E; M.30.405C); ἐκείνων ἔστι καὶ τῆς π. κατηγορεῖν καὶ τῆς τῶν πραγμάτων καταστάσεως, οὐκ ἐθελόντων ἐμμένειν τοῖς νόμοις Chrys.*fr.in Pr.*22:12(M.64.728B); **xi.** ass. emperor's τύχη: τῇ τοῦ δεσπότου θ[εο]ῦ π. καὶ τύχῃ τῶν εὐσεβεστάτων ἡμῶν δεσποτῶν *CG–CI* p.23 (Phylae 577); **b.** special providence, ref. prophecies of Christ θαυμαστὴ π. θεοῦ τοῦτο γέγονεν, ἵνα ἡμεῖς ὑμῶν...συνετώτεροι...εὑρεθῶμεν Just.*dial.*118.3(M.6.749C); τὴν π. μεχρὶ τῶν κατὰ μέρος ἄγει Clem.*str.*1.11(p.34.10; M.8.749C); ἡ θεία π. σε διαφυλάττοι Ursac.*ep.Ath.*ap.Ath.*apol.sec.*58(p.138.28; M.25.356A); ἦν...τοῦτο τῆς π. ἔργον, ἵνα...τὸ...καθαρὸν τῆς πίστεως δειχθῇ φρόνημα Ath.*syn.* 2(p.232.7; M.26.684B); σοφίας...τῆς ἐν π. φαινομένης, τῆς καθόλου λέγω, καθ' ἣν ἀγγέλων καὶ ἀρχαγγέλων καὶ τῶν ἄνω προνοεῖ δυνάμεων· ἀλλ' ἐκεῖνο τῆς π. τὸ μέρος ἐξετάζων, καθ' ὃ προνοεῖ τῶν ἐν τῇ γῇ ἀνθρώπων, καὶ ταύτης πάλιν αὐτῆς μέρος Chrys.*incomprehens.*1. 5(1.449B); θεία π. παραδόξως τοῦτον [sc. Tiberius] διέσωσε Evagr. *h.e.*5.11(p.207.29; M.86.2813C); ὑπὸ πρόνοιαν θεοῦ ἐστι καὶ μεχρὶ τῶν εὐτελεστάτων τὰ καθ' ἡμᾶς Dor.*doct.*17.3(M.88.1804B); **c.** Son as source of divine π., Clem.*str.*7.2(p.6.10; M.9.409A); ὁ πατὴρ...ἀνακεφαλαιούμενος ἐν αὐτῷ...τὴν διάταξιν τοῦ παντός...ὡς μὴ μόνον τὰ σύμπαντα δι' αὐτοῦ συστῆναι ἐκ τοῦ μὴ ὄντος εἰς τὸ εἶναι προελθόντα, ἀλλὰ καὶ τῆς τῶν ὅλων διοικήσεως τὴν π. ἀναδέχεσθαι αὐτὸν ἅτε λόγον ὄντα Eus.*e.th.*3.2(p.142.13; M.24.977A); θεοῦ λόγος...οὗτος ἡ καθόλου π. id.*l.C.*12(p.231.18; M.20.1389B); ὁ υἱὸς εὐδοκίᾳ τοῦ πατρὸς καὶ συνεργείᾳ τοῦ...πνεύματος πᾶσαν τὴν τῶν ὄντων π. ἀναδεδεγμένος ‡Ath.*annunt.*5(M.28.924B); as fulfiller of Father's π., Ath.*decr.*16 (p.13.34; M.25.'452'(444)A); exercising π. during earthly life, Chrys. *hom.*60.4 *in Jo.*(8.356A); **d.** divine π. exercised by angels, Just. *2apol.*5.2(M.6.452B); Nil.*epp.*1.59(M.79.109A); general providence exercised by God, special providence committed to angels, Athenag. *leg.*24.3(M.6.948A) cit. Meth.*res.*1.37(p.278.6; M.41.1104A); **e.** heret. teaching; ref. docetic view of Inc. τὸν σωτῆρα ἐνδύσασθαι σῶμα ψυχικόν, ἐκ τῆς οἰκονομίας κατεσκευασμένον ἀρρήτῳ π. Iren.*haer.*1.9. 3(M.7.544A); Basilidean ἡ π. δὲ εἰ καὶ ἀπὸ τοῦ Ἄρχοντος, ὥς φασιν, κινεῖσθαι ἄρχεται Clem.*str.*4.12(p.287.1; M.8.1296C); Ophite τῷ δὲ δευτέρῳ κύκλῳ ἐνεγέγραπτο, περιπεπλεγμένῳ καὶ ἐμπεριειληφότι ἄλλους δύο κύκλους καὶ ἄλλο σχῆμα ῥομβοειδές, σοφίας π. Or.*Cels.*6.38 (p.107.16; M.11.1353D); ref. Arian doctrine ψευδὴς κατ' αὐτοὺς καὶ τῆς π. ὁ λόγος καὶ τῆς κρίσεως καὶ...πάντων τῶν παρὰ τοῦ μονογενοῦς γεγενῆσθαι...πεπιστευμένων Gr.Nyss.*Eun.*1(1 p.105.18; M.45.340A).

***προνόμευσις**, ἡ, *plundering*, Cyr.*Is.*2.5(2.336E).

προνομία, ἡ, **1.** *privilege, special honour*, Eus.*h.e.*7.32.7(M.20.

724B); τυχεῖν προνομίας τῆς παρ' αὐτῷ τῷ βασιλεῖ id.*Marcell.*2.4(p.58. 22; M.24.824B); Ῥωμαῖος γὰρ ἦν...μεγάλην εἶχον ταύτην τότε π. οἱ ἀξιούμενοι οὕτω καλεῖσθαι Chrys.*hom.48.1 in Ac.*(9.359A); ref. eccl. dignities, Gr.Naz.*or.*26.15(M.35.1248C); Gr.Nyss.*ep.*1(M.46.1008D); of divine privileges, Ephr.3.406B; **2.** *honour, dignity*; in gen., Clem.*paed.*1.5(p.98.8; M.8.265A); οἱ παρ' Ἕλλησιν...ἐκ τῆς...φιλοσοφίας τῷ...τῶν καλλίστων αἰτιωτάτῳ τὴν π. ἔδοσαν id.*str.*5.14(p.417. 12; πρόνοιαν M.9.197B); πολλαχοῦ...τῆς γραφῆς διαφερούσης προνομίας τετευχότα τὸν δέκα ἀριθμόν Or.*Jo.*10.1(p.171.7; M.14.308A); Ἰούδα... προνομίας ἠξιωμένην Eus.*d.e.*8.1(p.359.11; M.22.584C); τὴν τοῦ Ἰησοῦ προσηγορίαν...ἐξαιρέτου π. ... ἀξιοῖ id.*h.e.*1.3.3(M.20.69A).

προνόμιον, τό, 1. *privilege*, of city τά τε τῆς πόλεως [sc. Antioch] ἀφείλετο [sc. Theodosius] π. καὶ τῇ γειτονευούσῃ πόλει τὴν ἡγεμονίαν δέδωκε Thdt.*h.e.*5.20.2(3.1053); προτιμήσει τὴν Ἱερουσαλήμ, καὶ τὰ παλαιὰ παρέξει π. id.*Zach.*1:16(2.1601); eccl., ref. privileges of Roman church exercised by Julius in dealing with case of Athanasius etc., Socr.*h.e.*2.15.3(M.67.212B); ref. privileges secured by Theodosius to Novatianist churches, *ib.*5.10.28(593A); ref. consecration of bishop of CP Δημόφιλος...ἐγκαθίσταται τῇ Κωνσταντινουπόλει ὑπὸ...τοῦ Ἡρακλείας ἐπισκόπου. ἐδόκει γὰρ τὸ π. οὗτος ἔχειν τῆς τοιαύτης ἱερουργικῆς ἐνεργείας Philost.*h.e.*9.10(M.65.576C); ref. consecration of bishop of Ephesus οἱ κληρικοὶ Κωνσταντινουπόλεως ἐβόησαν, τὰ τῶν ἁγίων πατέρων τῶν ρ̅ν̅ κρατείτω. τὰ π. Κωνσταντινουπόλεως μὴ ἀπόληται. ἡ χειροτονία κατὰ τὸ ἔθος ὑπὸ τοῦ ὧδε ἀρχιεπισκόπου γένηται CChalc.*act.*12(*ACO* 2.1.3 p.53.6; H.2. 557E); ref. grant of privileges to church at Gaza by bishop of Caesarea, Marc.Diac.*v.Porph.*53; ref. right of sanctuary, Jo.Mal.*chron.*10 p.234(M.97.359C); in gen. τοῖς τῆς φύσεως π. τετίμηνται Thdt.*Eph.*6:9(3.438); ἐπειδὴ γὰρ ἀθάνατον ἐποίησε τὴν ψυχήν, τὸ δὲ σῶμα θνητόν, ἀπένειμε τῷ σώματι τὰ τοῦ χρόνου π. id.*haer.*5.9(4.415); Ath.Scholast.*coll.*1.4(p.16); **2.** *prelude*, Synes.*calv.*4(p.197.10; M.66. 1173C).

***προνυμφεύ-ω,** *betroth* to oneself *beforehand* πνεύματος ἁγίου ~σαντος καὶ ἁγιάσαντος [sc. BMV] ‡Meth.*Sym.et Ann.*3(M.18.353C).

προξεν-έω, 1. *procure, effect, secure for* ζωὴν αὐτοῖς ἀλλ' οὐ θάνατον π. Eus.*theoph.*6(p.19*.26; M.24.628A); διάβολος...γέενναν ~ῶν Chrys.*hom.66.3 in Mt.*(7.657C); id.*hom.10.1 in 1Cor.*(10.80E); ὁ υἱὸς...τῇ τοῦ ἀνθρώπου φύσει ~ῶν τὸ...πνεῦμα Cyr.*Ps.*44:8(M.69.1040A); εἴ τι λέγοιτο λαβεῖν ἀνθρωπίνως παρὰ τοῦ πατρός, τοῦτο τῇ ἡμετέρᾳ προὐξένησε φύσει id.*Pulch.*18(p.35.7; 5².141B); ὁ κατὰ θεοῦ στρατευόμενος καὶ τὴν αὐτοῦ ῥοπὴν ~ῶν τοῖς βαρβάροις Thphn.*chron.*p.53(M. 108.188B); esp. of Christian gospel, conduct, and institutions procuring spiritual benefit, Eus.*p.e.*1.1(2A; M.21.24B); Gr.Naz.*or.*22.15 (M.35.1149A); ἐλεημοσύνη...ζωὴν αἰώνιον ~εῖ Chrys.*hom.52.3 in Mt.* (7.534A); τὸ μὴ ταῦτα [sc. silver and gold] ἔχειν, τοῦτο αὐτῷ τὸν οὐρανὸν προὐξένησε *ib.*90.4(844D); βάπτισμα...τὴν ἐν πνεύματι πρὸς θεὸν οἰκείωσιν ~οῦν Cyr.*Os.*55(3.85C); Ἰωάννης...τὸ ἐν ὀρθῇ τῇ πίστει φυλάττεσθαι ~ῶν id.*Jo.*1.2(4.15A); ἡ ἀγάπη...~εῖ τὸ φῶς *ib.*1.8(72D); Thdt.*Ag.*2:10(2.1587); νοητὴν τροφὴν...ἣν ἡ εἰς Χριστὸν πίστις ~εῖ Ammon.*Jo.*6:27(M.85.1433B); λύπην κατὰ θεὸν...~οῦσαν ζωὴν αἰώνιον Jo.Eub.*concept.BMV* 6(M.96.1468B); **2.** *recommend* ἡμετέρας εὐχὰς ...τῇ σῇ π. φιλανθρωπίᾳ Gr.Naz.*ep.*105(M.37.205B); πενία...οἵαν προεξένει τότε τῷ πλουσίῳ ἐκείνῳ [Mt.19:21] Chrys.*hom.34.6 in 1Cor.* (10.319C).

προξενητής, ὁ, *agent, one who effects*, Cyr.*hom.div.*19(M.77.1108C).

προξενίζω, *secure for another*, Soz.*h.e.*8.25.3(M.67.1581A); Cyr.ap. *cat.Jo.*10:33(p.305.21) for προξενήσας id.*Jo.*7(4.669D).

πρόξενος, subst. and adj., *one who effects* or *secures for another, agent*; *effecting, productive* of; **1.** in gen. ὅσῳ γὰρ ἂν φθονῇς, τοσούτῳ γίνῃ μειζόνων πρόξενος ἀγαθῶν τῷ φθονουμένῳ Chrys.*hom.40.4 in Mt.* (7.442A); τύραννοι...ἄκοντες...ἡμῖν...γίνονται...ἀγαθῶν π. id.*hom.15.2 in Rom.*(9.596A); ἐμαυτῷ...π. ἐγενόμην κακῶν Thdt.*Ps.*50:6(1.935); εἰ...χαρὰ γίνεται ἐν οὐρανῷ δι' ἐπιστροφὴν ἁμαρτωλοῦ, τῷ π. τῆς ἐπιστροφῆς οὐ μέγας ἐποφείλεται μισθός; †Jo.D.*B.J.*30(M.96.1148B); **2.** of Christ ἐκπέμπει...τοὺς μαθητὰς...ἵνα...ὠφελείας γένηται π. *cat. Lc.*9:51(p.80.26); Χριστὸς τοῖς ἐξ αὐτοῦ...γέγονε π. δικαιοσύνης Chrys. *hom.10.1 in Rom.*(9.520D); π. αἰωνίου ζωῆς Cyr.*Jo.*2 proem.(4. 114B); σωτηρίας ἀκαταλύτου π. *ib.*2.1(152A); π. παντὸς ἀγαθοῦ τῇ τοῦ ἀνθρώπου φύσει id.*dogm.*10(6².378A); πάσῃ τῇ ἀνθρωπείᾳ φύσει π. τῆς νίκης Cosm.Ind.*top.*2(M.88.124B); **3.** of Cross ὁ...σταυρὸς γέγονε π. τοῦ συνενεχθῆναι πρὸς ὁμοπιστίαν τοὺς ἀνὰ πᾶσαν τὴν γῆν Cyr.*Is.*2.1 (2.205E); ξύλον...π. ζωῆς αἰωνίου γενήσεται Jo.Eub.*concept.BMV* 21 (M.96.1496B); **4.** of Christian ministers, doctrine, and institutions; apostles as π. πάσης θεοσεβείας Proc.G.*Is.*1:7–9(M.87.1840B); μέγα τὸ τῆς διακονίας ἔργον, καὶ βασιλείας οὐρανῶν π. Bas.*renunt.*9(2.210D; M.31.645B); αἰωνίου ζωῆς οὐρανίου τε βασιλείας μαθήματα π. Eus.*l.C.* 17(p.258.1; M.20.1436D); βάπτισμα...βασιλείας π. Cyr.H.*procatech.* 16; cf. ζωοποιὸν γὰρ τὸ ὕδωρ καὶ ἁπάσης π. εὐκαρπίας Cyr.*Is.*3.3(2. 451B); of Christ's commandments as ζωῆς π. Chrys.*hom.63.1 in Mt.*(7.629B); **5.** ref. function of Law δεικτικὸς οὖν ἄρα τῆς ἁμαρτίας ὁ νόμος, οὐκ αὐχήματος τοῦ εἰς ἀρετὴν π. Cyr.*ador.*2(1.52C); **6.** of Christian virtues and spiritual conditions; of image of God implanted in man τῶν ἄνω πρόξενον Gr.Naz.*or.*14.2(M.35.860C); of martyrdom as productive of heavenly rewards, *M.Thdot.*1 21(p.74. 21); of ascetic life π. αἰωνίου τρυφῆς Bas.*hom.in Ps.*61(1.197B; M. 29.480A); πρᾶξις γὰρ θεωρίας πρόξενος Gr.Naz.*or.*40.37(M.36.412C); of poverty as βασιλείας π. Chrys.*hom.10.5 in Phil.*(11.280F); τῶν μελλόντων αἰώνων ἀπολαύσεως π. ἡμῖν ἡ υἱοθεσία γίνεται id.*hom.9.3 in Heb.*(12.98A); of knowledge of Christ as productive of eternal life, Cyr.*ador.*2(1.58E); of love of God as π. τρυφῆς καὶ εὐημερίας id. *Os.*134(3.167A); obedience as τῆς ἀνωτάτω τιμῆς π. id.*Ps.*98:7(M.69. 1257D); στέρξομεν τὴν ἀδικίαν, ὡς τῆς τῶν οὐρανῶν πρόξενον βασιλείας Thdt.*ep.*91(4.1162); τὴν σωτήριον ὁμολογίαν δικαιοσύνης π. Proc.G.*Is.* 59:19–21(M.87.2616C); ἡ βασιλεία τῶν οὐρανῶν, ἧς π. γίνονται ἀπάθεια καὶ γνῶσις Thal.*cent.*2.34(M.91.1441A); **7.** of heathen institutions, vices, etc., as effecting spiritual penalties; of wealth as χορηγὸς καὶ π. θανάτου Clem.*q.d.s.*26(p.177.18; M.9.632B); ill-treatment of poor as γεέννης π. Chrys.*hom.48.6 in Mt.*(7.502B); riches etc., as π. ἀσεβείας Cyr.*hom.pasch.*8(5².98B); ἡλίκων π. ἡ ἁμαρτία κακῶν Thdt. *qu.34 in Gen.*(1.46); οἱ δὲ ἀπιστήσαντες π. ἑαυτοῖς τῆς γεέννης γεγένηνται id.*qu.12 in Ex.*(1.129); ἐφοὺδ...τῷ...λαῷ π. παρανομίας ἐγένετο id. *qu.17 in Jud.*(1.335); βωμοὶ τῶν εἰδώλων...π. δυσσεβείας id.*Os.*10:7 (2.1358); θερμότης ἀχαλίνωτος μεγίστων κακῶν π. Nil.*epp.*1.11(M.79. 85D); **8.** of Satan as agent of death, Cyr.*Ps.*15:4(M.69.809B).

***πρόξιμος, ὁ,** (Lat. *proximus*) *first secretary* τοῦ περιβλέπτου κόμητος καὶ π. τοῦ θείου σκρινίου τῶν λιβέλλων καὶ τῶν θείων κογνιτιόνων CCP(449)*act.*3(*ACO* 2.1.1 p.177.4; H.2.210D); ἕνα ξιφήρη ἄνδρα, τῇ τοῦ π. ἀξίᾳ καταλεγόμενον Steph.Diac.*v.Steph.*(M.100.1169C).

προοδεύ-ω, *precede*; **1.** lit., *go before*, *Hom.Clem.*8.3; Ath.*h.Ar.*48 (p.211.12; M.25.753A); **2.** in gen. πατέρας γὰρ ἴσμεν τοὺς μακαρίους ἐκείνους τοὺς ~σαντας...Πάνταινον...καὶ...Κλήμεντα Alex.H.ap.Eus. *h.e.*6.14.9(M.20.552C); Eus.*h.e.*1.1.3(M.20.49B); *Hom.Clem.*2.18; Ἰωάννης...προχειρισθεὶς εἰς τὸ ~σαι τοῦ κυρίου Ath.*Ar.*2.54(M.26. 261B); Gr.Nyss.*hom.2 in Cant.*(M.44.805A); ἀναγκαῖον καὶ τὰς ὁδοὺς τῶν ~σάντων μοναχῶν ὀρθῶς διερωτᾶν Evagr.Pont.*cap.pract.*B 91 (M.40.1249A); **3.** *predecease*; ptcpl., *departed* τῶν προοδευκουσῶν (sic) μητέρων Gr.Mag.*dial.*(tr.Zach.)4.13(M.*PL.*77.342B) cf. προοδοιπορέω.

προοδηγός, *going before to show the way*, *Orac.Sib.*8.24.

προοδικῶς, *by way of procession*, ref. H. Ghost π. ὂν ἐκ θεοῦ δι' υἱοῦ ‡Ath.*ref.*(M.28.88C); τοῦ μὲν γεννητικῶς, τοῦ δὲ π., εἴτουν ἐκπορευτικῶς Zach.Mit.*opif.*(M.85.1116D).

προοδοιπορ-έω, 1. *go before*, of the departed μακάριοι οἱ ~ήσαντες πρεσβύτεροι *1Clem.*44.5; **2.** *precede*, Afr.*ep.Or.*2(p.80.7; M.11.48A).

προοδοιπόρος, ὁ, *one who travels before*, *2Clem.*10.1.

προοδοποι-έω, 1. *precede* προπαρασκευάζει...ἡ φιλοσοφία ~οῦσα τὸν ὑπὸ Χριστοῦ τελειούμενον Clem.*str.*1.5(p.18.4; M.8.720A); ταῦτα πάντα ἀνῄρει ~οῦσα ἡ χάρις Chrys.*hom.28.5 in Gen.*(4.276D); **2.** *prepare the way for* ἐντολὴ δευτέρα...ἐκείνην ~εῖ Chrys.*hom.71.1 in Mt.* (7.694D); ἵνα τῇ γνώσει ἡ ἀνάγνωσις ~οῦσα ᾖ *ib.*1.6(13B); of John's baptism as preparation for Christ's, *ib.10.2*(141D); ἡ τοῦ πνεύματος χάρις...αὐτοῖς πανταχοῦ ~εῖ id.*hom.3.5 in Ac.princ.*(3.80A); οὐδὲ ἄλλην τινὰ αἰτίαν εἶχεν ἐκεῖνο τὸ λουτρὸν [sc. of John] ἢ ~ῆσαι τὴν τοῦ Χριστοῦ πίστιν τοῖς ἄλλοις ἅπασιν Ammon.*Jo.*1:30(M.85.1401D); ~οῦντός μοι καὶ ποδηγοῦντος...θεοῦ λόγου Gel.Cyz.*h.e.*1 proem.25(M. 85.1197B); καὶ Ἕλλησιν ὁ θεὸς συνεχώρει χρηματίζεσθαι...πᾶσι ~ῶν κατὰ πρόνοιαν Max.*ep.*26(M.91.616A); εὐαγγελιστὴν Ἰωάννην πρόδρομον, ἐν ᾧ συνέταξεν εὐαγγελίῳ ~οῦντι τὴν διάνοιαν πρὸς παραδοχὴν τοῦ τελεωτέρου λόγου id.*ambig.*(M.91.1252C); ref. Law ὁ δὲ παιδαγωγὸς οὐκ ἐναντίος τῷ διδασκάλῳ ἀλλὰ ~ῶν αὐτῷ Jo.D.*Gal.*3:24(M.95. 800B); **3.** *prepare in advance* αὐλακηδὸν τὰ τῆς ψυχῆς βάθη ~ῶν [sc. νόμος] ‡Chrys.*pasch.*6(p.137.16; 8.267B).

***προοδοποίησις, ἡ,** *preparation of way*, of John's baptism παρασκευὴ τοῦτό ἐστιν ἐκείνου καὶ π. Chrys.*hom.16.3 in Jo.*(8.94B); of deacons' action in liturgy ὁ χερουβικὸς ὕμνος ἐμφαίνει διὰ τῆς τῶν διακόνων π. καὶ τῆς τῶν ῥιπιδίων σεραφικῶν ἀπεικονισμάτων ἱστορίας τὴν εἴσοδον τῶν ἁγίων ‡Bas.*h.myst.*49(p.390.18).

προοδοποιός, *preparing the way*; of false prophet preparing way for antichrist as Jo. Bapt. for Christ, *cat.Apoc.*19:21(p.467.23).

πρόοδος, ὁ, 1. *courier*, *Hom.Clem.*3.58; *ib.*8.2; **2.** *precursor, preparer of the way* π. γενήσεσθαι τὸν Ἠλίαν Just.*dial.*49.2(M.6.584A); Ἰωάννης...ἐγένετο π. *Hom.Clem.*2.23; τὸ λεγόμενον ὄνομα [sc. of

God] τοῦ μὴ λεγομένου π. ἐστιν *ib*.16.18; of H. Ghost παντὸς ἀγαθοῦ νοῦ π. Didym.*Trin*.2.1(M.39.452C).

πρόοδος, ἡ, I. *going forth, advance*;

A. in gen.; **1.** of going out from one's house βρῶσιν, πόσιν, π. ποιεῖν εἰς δόξαν Χριστοῦ Mac.Mgn.*apocr*.1.43(p.149.15); of 'going out and coming in' (i.e. daily conduct) τὰς π. αὐτοῦ καὶ τὰς εἰσόδους καὶ τὸν χαρακτῆρα τοῦ βίου Iren.*ep.Flor*.ap.Eus.*h.e*.5.20.6(M.20.485A); of monks leaving monasteries κωλυέσθω καὶ τῆς συγκεχωρημένης π. Bas.*reg.br*.141(2.463D; M.31.1177A); μὴ ταῖς πυκνοτέραις π. τὰ διὰ τῶν αἰσθήσεων τῇ διανοίᾳ ἐγγινόμενα τραύματα ἀναξαίνειν Nil.*epp*.3.223(M.79.485C); Jo.Mosch.*prat*.171(M.87.3040B); **2.** *coming forth in public, public appearance* τὴν π....τῶν ἀποστόλων Eus.*d.e*.2.3(p.76.27; M.22.137C); ὁ...υἱὸς Δαβὶδ τὴν π. ἐξ αὐτῆς [sc. Bethlehem] ἐποιήσατο *ib*.7.2(p.336.8; 548C); esp. of official progresses τὸ ὑπήκοον ἐνδεικνύμενοι κατὰ τὴν π. Gr.Nyss.*Maced*.9(M.45.1312C); ἅμιλλα μὴ ἧττονα τῶν λοιπῶν ἐν ταῖς π. ἐπισύρεσθαι ἀνδράποδα Nil.*exerc*.24(M.79.752C); ἐν...δόξῃ βασιλικῆς π. *Chron.Pasch*.p.287(M.92.717A); **3.** *emergence* from grave; of Resurrection, Gr.Ant.*mul.ung*.10(M.88.1860C); **4.** *departure* from π. τῆς ζωῆς Mac.Mgn.*apocr*.4.14(p.181.22); **5.** ref. 2Cor.12:2, Gr.Naz.*or*.28.20(p.51.12; M.36.52C) cit. s. ἀνάβασις.

B. *emergence into existence*, Diod.*fat*.ap.Phot.*cod*.223(M.103.861B); τὴν ὕπαρξιν καὶ τὴν π. διὰ τοῦ θείου ἐμφυσήματος ἡ...ψυχὴ ἔσχεν Anast.S.*serm.imag*.3(M.89.1164C); *process of becoming* ὁ ἀΐδιος ...ἔν τε ταῖς π. καὶ ταῖς ἐπιτροφαῖς κύκλος σώζεται...καὶ ἄλλη τηνικαῦτα π. ἔσται, καθ' ἣν ἔσται ὁ θεὸς τὰ πάντα ἐν πᾶσι †Proc.G.*Procl*.(M.87.2792ʰC,D).

C. *coming forth* in birth, Bas.*Eun*.2.5(1.241E; M.29.581B); ‡Nil.*fr.pasch*.1(M.79.1493A); of Inc. ‡Ath.*Ar*.4.28(p.76.14; M.26.512B); Cyr.*Is*.5.1(2.748B); Max.*opusc*.(M.91.240B).

D. *progress* προτροπὴ τῆς ἐν πίστει π. Euthal.Diac.*epp.Paul*.(M.85.780A); ἡ διὰ μετανοίας π. Areth.*Apoc*.3:18(M.106.565A); δραστικωτέρᾳ π. πραγμάτων χρώμενος *ib*.19:17(745B); hence *benefit, profit*, Chrys.*terr.mot*.(2.718A).

E. *procession, issuing forth, emanation*; **1.** in gen. πᾶσα γὰρ π. διὰ τῶν ἴσων καὶ ὁμοίων ἐπιτελεῖται Didym.*Trin*.3.38(M.39.976A); υἱὸς μὲν κυρίως ἐστὶ δευτερότης ὑποστάσεως ἐν ταυτότητι φύσεως, ἡ...π. φύσεως εἰς συγγένειαν γνωριζομένη Anast.S.*hod*.2(M.89.56A); **2.** of sending forth of divine grace and revelation φάσκειν τὴν δύναμιν τὴν παρὰ τοῦ πατρὸς...φανεῖσαν τῷ Μωϋσεῖ...ἄγγελον καλεῖσθαι ἐν τῇ πρὸς ἀνθρώπους π., ἐπειδὴ δι' αὐτῆς τὰ παρὰ τοῦ πατρὸς τοῖς ἀνθρώποις ἀγγέλλεται Just.*dial*.128.2(M.6.776A); πᾶσα πατροκινήτου φωτοφανείας π. εἰς ἡμᾶς ἀγαθοδότως φοιτῶσα Dion.Ar.*c.h*.1.1(M.3.120B); ἀγαθουργοὺς τῆς θεαρχίας π. id.*d.n*.1.4(M.3.589D); τὴν οὐσιοποιὸν εἰς τὰ ὄντα πάντα τῆς θεαρχικῆς οὐσιαρχίας π. *ib*.5.1(816B); **3.** of Son's generation, Or.*Jo*.1.38(42; p.50.5; M.14.100D); εἰ γὰρ ἡ π. αὐτοῦ γέννησίς ἐστιν, ἡ ἀναδρομὴ πάλιν παῦλα τῆς γεννήσεως ‡Ath.*Ar*.4.12(p.56.14; M.26.484B); ἓν καὶ μόνον ἀπογέννημα, ἀδιαιρέτῳ καὶ ἀσωμάτῳ π. †Apoll.*ep.Bas*.1(M.32.1104D); ἐκ τῆς οὐσίας τοῦ θεοῦ καὶ πατρὸς θεοῦ λόγου π. Cyr.*Ps*.44:2(M.69.1028A); ἐν ἐξ ἑνός, ἀμερίστῳ τινὶ καὶ ἀδιαστάτῳ π. προκύπτον id.*Jo*.1.3(4.29A); ἀναχωρήσει μὲν γὰρ οὐκ εἰς ἰδιότητα παντελῶς...κεχωρισμένην,...ἀλλ' ὢν ἐν πατρὶ κατὰ λόγον, ἤτοι σχέσιν ἀδιάστατον τὴν ὡς ἐν ὁμοουσιότητι, καὶ ἐξ αὐτοῦ νοηθήσεται κατὰ πρόοδον ἀπορρήτως τὴν ἐκφαντικήν, ἤτοι τὴν ὡς ἐν ἀπαυγάσματι *ib*.3.5(306E); γεγέννημαι...τῆς οὐσίας αὐτοῦ, κατὰ πρόοδον μὲν τὴν πρὸς τὸ εἶναί τε καὶ νοεῖσθαι τυχὸν ἰδιοσυστάτως, οὐ μὴν εἰς ἅπαν διῃρημένως *ib*.11.2(939D); plur., Max.*ambig*.(M.91.1400C) cit. s. ἀνεκφοιτήτως; of Son and H. Ghost θεία π. ἄναρχος καὶ ἀτελεύτητος μόνη ἂν λέγοιτο ἡ ἀπὸ τοῦ...πατρὸς γέννησις τοῦ...υἱοῦ, καὶ ἀπὸ τοῦ αὐτοῦ πρόβλησις τοῦ...πνεύματος †Proc.G.*Procl*.(M.87.2792ᵉC); τὴν πατρικὴν...π. εἰς ἔκφανσιν τοῦ υἱοῦ καὶ τοῦ ἁγίου πνεύματος Max.*schol.d.n*.1.4(M.4.196B); **4.** of procession of H. Ghost μηδὲ τοῦ πνεύματος περιεργάζου τὴν π. Gr.Naz.*or*.20.10(M.35.1077A); τὸ καλὸν γέννημα, καὶ τὴν θαυμασίαν π. *ib*.23.7(1160A); μίαν...φύσιν θεότητος, ἀνάρχῳ, καὶ γεννήσει, καὶ π. γνωριζομένην *ib*.23.11(1161C); ἵνα καὶ τοῦτο θεϊκὸν ἔχωσι τὸ μοναδικόν, ὁ μὲν τῆς υἱότητος, τὸ δὲ τῆς π. καὶ οὐχ υἱότητος *ib*.25.16(1221A); Apoll.*quod.un.Chr*.2(p.295.20; M.28.124B); Didym.*Trin*.2.2(M.39.460B); μὴ γέννησις ἡ τοῦ πνεύματος π. κέκληται id.(‡Bas.)*Eun*.5(1.306D; M.29.736A); εἰ γὰρ μὴ τὴν φυσικὴν ἐκεῖθεν π. ἔλεγεν διὰ τοῦ 'ἐκπορεύεται' ἀλλά τινα ἀποστολὴν ἔξωθεν γινομένην, ἄπορον περὶ τίνος λέγει, πολλῶν ὄντων...ἀποστελλομένων πνευμάτων Thdr.Mops.*Jo*.15:26(p.398.16; M.66.780B); Cyr.*Is*.5.3(2.809E); †Proc.G.*Procl*.(M.87.2792ᵉC).

F. *process* of law ἣν ἂν ὥραν ἔλθῃ ὁ ἡγεμών, καὶ ἔλθω εἰς π., ἀποθανεῖν ἔχω Jo.Mosch.*prat*.189(M.87.3068D); Πηγάσιος...σὺν τοῖς τέκνοις αὐτοῦ ἐν π. ἐξητάσθησαν Thphn.*chron*.p.153(M.108.416A); †Anast.S.*relat*.49(*OC* 3 p.69.14).

II. *shoot, branch*, Manich. δύο γὰρ ἦσαν ῥίζαι, καὶ δύο προῆλθον π., αἱ π. κατάλληλοι ταῖς ῥίζαις Serap.*Man*.26(p.41; M.18.1121A).

III. *entrance* ἐκέλευσεν ἐν π. στῆναι *Trad.Pil*.2(p.450).

προοικει-όομαι, 1. *make one's own previously* οὐδ' ἂν εἴρητο πεινῆσαι...μὴ οὐχὶ ~ωσάμενος σῶμα, τὸ πεινᾶν τε καὶ κοπιᾶν πεφυκός Cyr.*Chr.un*.(5¹.719E); **2.** pass.; *be made familiar with, accustomed to*, Chrys.*hom.11.1 in Jo*.(8.62C); *ib.23.1*(132D).

προοικονομ-έω, *provide, arrange in advance*; **1.** in gen. ἀντερεῖ πάνθ' ὅσα ~ηθῆναι καθήκει τῆς κατὰ τὴν ἐποπτικὴν θεωρίαν γνώσεως Clem.*str*.1.1(p.11.13; M.8.704C); *A.Jo*.113(p.212.9); Chrys.*hom.72.1 in Mt*.(7.701D); id.*hom.2.2 in 1Cor*.(10.11C); med. Ἰησοῦς...~ησάτω εἰς πίστιν τὰς καρδίας Serap.*euch*.2.2; **2.** of God's counsels, *ordain previously*, *Hom.Clem*.13.11; Proc.G.*Gen*.11:31(M.87.317C).

πρόοικος, ὁ, *major-domo, mayor of the palace* (of Frankish king), Thphn.*chron*.p.337(M.108.813A).

προοιμιάζ-ω, usu. med.; **1.** *make a preface, say by way of preface* ὁ ἀγαπητὸς τοῦ θεοῦ, ὑπὲρ οὗ ἐπὶ τῆς προφητείας συνέσεως δεῖν ὁ ψαλμὸς ἡμῖν ~εται Eus.*d.e*.4.15(p.181.12; M.22.301C); †Bas.*Is*.8(1.384B; M.30.132C); ~ων...ἔλεγεν ὁ Σαλομών ‡Meth.*Sym.et Ann*.5(M.18.360B); **2.** *introduce beforehand, foreshadow* οὐχ ὁρᾷς τὴν ἀνάστασιν τῶν νεκρῶν ἤδη ~ομένην Or.*hom.1.16 in Jer*.(p.15.5; M.13.276A); Eus.*d.e*.5.19(p.242.14; M.22.400B); of those translated to paradise as being 'first instalment' or anticipation of general resurrection, Iren.*haer*.5.5.1(M.7.1135B); **3.** *make preliminary* to, *treat as prelude* to τῶν θησαυρῶν ἔχειν τὴν ἐπιμέλειαν· ἐντεῦθεν γὰρ αὐτῷ τὰς μείζους ἀρχὰς βασιλεὺς ~εται Gr.Naz.*or*.7.15(M.35.773A); **4.** *be prelude* to ἡ ποιμαντικὴ ~εται τὴν ἑαυτοῦ τε καὶ ἄλλων ἀρχὴν Proc.G.*Gen*.4:2(M.87.236A).

προοιμιακός, 1. *introductory*; of hymns used in preparation for liturgy, Jo.Clim.*scal*.19(M.88.937B); **2.** *of* or *belonging to Proverbs*, Gr.Nyss.*Apoll*.41(M.45.1217B).

προοιμιαστικός, *introducing* ἡ ἄνωθεν ἡμέρα, τουτέστιν ἡ π. καὶ αἰτία τῆς παραβάσεως Olymp.*Job* 3:1–3(M.93.53C).

προοίμιον, τό, 1. *prelude, preface*; of a preamble to a will, ‡Nil.*perist*.9.1(M.79.864A); of John's baptism as prelude to gospel, ‡Just.*qu.et resp*.37(M.6.1284B); of Christ's birth οὐ γὰρ...ὁ τόκος ἀρχὴ θεότητος γέγονεν, ἀλλὰ π. ἦν τοῦ σάρκα γενέσθαι τὸν λόγον Thdot.Anc.*exp.fid*.22(M.77.1345B); of miracle of Cana θαυμάτων ἁπάντων π. Thdt.*Is*.9:1(p.47.19; 2.231); of heathen rulers as prelude to coming of antichrist, Areth.*Apoc*.13:2(M.106.672C); of prayer as π. τῆς ἀΰλου...γνώσεως Evagr.Pont.*or*.85(M.79.1185B); **2.** *preliminary stage* π. ἄττα καὶ στοιχεῖα θεοσεβείας εἰς ἀνθρώπους καταβαλλόμενος Eus.*l.C*.13(p.240.33; M.20.1408A); ref. Christian life τὰ π. μόνον εἶδες τῆς ὁδοῦ Chrys.*Laz*.7.5(1.798B); ἐπέθετο ἐν προοιμίοις ὁ τῆς πορνείας πόλεμος Pall.*h.Laus*.45(p.133.2; M.34.1217C); **3.** *foretaste* π. ἐπιδείκνυνται ὧν ὑπισχνεῖται τὸ πῦρ Clem.*prot*.4(p.41.15; M.8.148A); Meth.*res*.2.23(p.378.10; M.18.316B); **4.** *preparatory psalm* in preparation for liturgy, *Lit.Praesanct*.(p.345.10); Thdr.Stud.*praesanct*.(M.99.1688C); at Vespers, *Const.Stud*.9(M.99.1708B); of liturgy up to Gospel, *Schol*. in CCarth.*can*.103(*Mon*.2 p.650); of ceremonies of Easter leading up to liturgy, Anast.*temp*.(p.280); **5.** *outskirts, borders* τῆς Πισιδῶν καὶ Φρυγῶν χώρας ἐν π. κειμένη Bas.Sel.*v.Thecl*.1(M.85.481D); *ib*.(556C); **6.** ἐκ προοιμίων *to begin with, from the first*, Proc.G.*Gen*.3:24(M.87.229D); Evagr.*h.e*.4.18(p.168.30; M.86.2736C); Thphn.*chron*.p.84(M.108.257A).

***προοιμιώδης,** *introductory*, Meth.*symp*.9.1(p.113.3; M.18.176C).

***προόλλυμι,** *destroy previously*, Gr.Nyss.*v.Mos*.(M.44.325A).

***προομαλίζ-ω,** *level* the ground *in advance*, hence *prepare beforehand*, Gr.Nyss.*v.Ephr*.(M.46.820A); ἔδει προομαλισθῆναι διὰ τῆς ἐν τύποις ἐντολῆς τὴν τῶν παιδαγωγουμένων καρδίαν Cyr.*Is*.3.2(2.404C); ref. miracles of Moses δεικνύειν...ὅτι πιστὸς ἦν τῷ θεῷ...~ων αὐτοὺς καὶ προπαρασκευάζων εἰς τὸ εὐπαράδεκτος αὐτοῖς εἶναι Cosm.Ind.*top*.3(M.88.140C); of week added to seven weeks of Lenten fast διὰ τὸ...~εσθαι τοὺς μέλλοντας εἰσελθεῖν εἰς τὸν κόπον τῶν νηστειῶν Dor.*doct*.15.1(M.88.1788C).

***προομαλισμός, ὁ,** *levelling* of ground *in advance*, hence *preparation* τὰ γραφέντα πρὸς αὐτοῦ [sc. S. John] π. τίς ἐστι τοῦ τελεωτέρου καὶ τέως ἀχωρήτου λόγου Max.*ambig*.(M.91.1252C).

***προομαλιστής, ὁ,** *one who levels* the ground *beforehand*; of the Law, Cyr.*Is*.3.2(2.404D).

προομολογ-έω, 1. *acknowledge, confess beforehand* Ἀβραὰμ...ἤδη προωμολόγει...τὸ μέλλον μυστήριον Nil.*epp*.2.243(M.79.325C); **2.** *acknowledge in first instance*, ref. 2Thess.3:5 ὁ δὲ κύριος κατευθύναι ὑμῶν τὰς καρδίας εἰς τὴν ἀγάπην τοῦ θεοῦ καὶ εἰς τὴν ὑπομονὴν τοῦ Χριστοῦ...εἰ μὲν γὰρ τὸν πατέρα προτάξειας, θεός ἐστι τὸ πνεῦμα· εἰ δὲ τὸ πνεῦμα ~ήσειας, κύριος τυγχάνει ‡Ath.*disp*.43(M.28.497B); **3.** *utter previously*, Dion.Ar.*e.h*.3.2(M.3.425C).

***προονομάζω**, 1. *name beforehand* Μωυσῆς ἄγγελον προονομάσας αὐτὸν εἶναι τὸν ὄντα τοῖς ἐφεξῆς ἐκδιδάσκει λόγοις Gr.Nyss.*Eun.*11(2 p.263.29; M.45.872C); ref. Marcion's interpretation of Lc.22:8 μὴ λέγε ὅτι ὁ ἔμελλε μυστήριον ἐπιτελεῖν, τοῦτο προωνόμαζε λέγων, θέλω...φαγεῖν τὸ πάσχα Epiph.*haer.*42.11(p.149.9; M.41.764B); Max. *schol.c.h.*4.4(M.4.57B); 2. *name before* others ὁ πατὴρ...ἐπειδὴ... πηγή τις ἐστίν,...οἰκονομικῶς προωνόμασται Cyr.*Abac.*35(3.549E); 3. *mention previously*, Just.*dial.*19.5(M.6.517A); Eus.*d.e.*1.6(p.23. 34; M.22.49C); ὁ...προονομασθεὶς ἄρχων *Mir.Geo.*8(p.93.6).

***προοπλίζω**, *arm in advance*, *Hom.Clem.*2.3.

***προοπτεύ-ω**, *keep a look-out forward for*, of S. Phocas πολλάκις μὲν γὰρ ὤφθη...ἀπὸ τῆς πρώρας ~ων τὰ βράχη Ast.Am.*hom.*9(M.40. 312A).

προόπτης, ὁ, *one who sees beforehand*; of a prophet, ‡Rom.Mel. (*AS* 1 p.296).

***προόπτως**, *eagerly looking ahead*, †Jo.Jej.*paraen.*(p.236).

προορίζ-ω, 1. *predetermine*; of counsel of God; a. dist. from προγινώσκω: πάντα μὲν προγινώσκει ὁ θεός, οὐ πάντα δὲ ~ει. προγινώσκει γὰρ τὰ ἐφ' ἡμῖν, οὐ ~ει δὲ αὐτά. ... ~ει δὲ τὰ οὐκ ἐφ' ἡμῖν κατὰ τὴν πρόγνωσιν αὐτοῦ Jo.D.*f.o.*2.30(M.94.972A); id.*Man.*1.79(M.94. 1577B); b. ref. Inc., acc. Paul of Samosata θεὸν ὁμολογεῖν τὸν ἐκ τῆς παρθένου, πρὸ αἰώνων μὲν προορισθέντα, ἐκ δὲ Μαρίας τὴν ἀρχὴν τῆς ὑπάρξεως ἐσχηκότα Paul.Sam.*fr.*D 2(p.338.2)ap.‡Ath.*Apoll.*1.20(M. 26.1128B); ref. Pr.8:23 τὴν κατὰ σάρκα αὐτοῦ προορισθεῖσαν οἰκονομίαν Marcell.*fr.*14 ap.Eus.*e.th.*3.3(p.147.14; M.24.985A); προώρισεν ἑαυτῷ τὴν ἐνανθρώπησιν ὁ θεός ‡Caes.Naz.*dial.*170(M.38.1133); ‡Jo.D. *hom.*6.10(M.96.677A); c. ref. election; i. in gen. πληρωθέντος τοῦ ἀριθμοῦ, οὗ αὐτὸς παρ' αὐτῷ προώρισε, πάντες...ἀναστήσονται Iren. *haer.*2.33.5(M.7.834A); of 'gnostic' τὸν φίλον τοῦ θεοῦ, ὃν προώρισεν ὁ θεὸς πρὸ καταβολῆς κόσμου Clem.*str.*6.9(p.469.25; M.9.296C); τὴν ἑαυτοῦ διένειμεν εὐεργεσίαν, Ἕλλησί τε καὶ βαρβάροις καὶ τοῖς ἐκ τούτων προωρισμένοις μέν, κατὰ δὲ τὸν οἰκεῖον καιρὸν κεκλημένοις *ib.*7.2 (p.6.27; 409C); Marcell.*fr.*16 ap.Eus.*Marcell.*1.2(p.11.32; M.24.737C); ref. Mt.25:34 αἱ ἀθλήσεις προωρίσθησαν, καὶ ἀρεταὶ τῶν διὰ τῶν ἄθλων προερχομένων προεθεωρήθησαν ‡Nil.*tract.*4(M.79.1285A); εἰς υἱοθεσίαν ἡμᾶς ~ει δι' αὐτοῦ Cyr.*thes.*15(5¹.174C); ii. of BMV τῇ προαιωνίῳ προγνωστικῇ βουλῇ τοῦ θεοῦ προορισθεῖσα Jo.D.*f.o.*4.14(M.94.1156A); ‡Jo.D.*hom.*5(M.96.649A); iii. of Church, Ign.*Eph.*proem.; τὴν ἐκκλησίαν πάλαι προωρίσατο ὁ παντοκράτωρ θεός Marcell.*fr.*16 ap.Eus. *Marcell.*1.2(p.11.30; M.24.737C); d. ref. scope permitted to Devil τοὺς προωρισμένους τοῦ θεοῦ πρὸ καταβολῆς κόσμου ὁρισμούς, λέγω δὲ ἐπὶ ποίαις κακαῖς πράξεσι τοὺς ἀνθρώπους ἔταξεν ὑπὸ τοῦ τῆς κακίας ἡγεμόνος κακοῦσθαι *Hom.Clem.*7.6; e. ref. predetermined number of human race, Meth.*symp.*2.1(p.15.22; M.18.48C); τὸν σύμμετρον τῶν ἀνθρώπων χρόνον κατενόησεν τῇ κατασκευῇ ὥστε τῇ παρόδῳ τῶν προορισθεισῶν ψυχῶν συναπαρτηθῆναι αὐτόν ‡Caes.Naz.*dial.*156(M.38. 1116); f. ref. question whether length of individual lives is fixed, Anast.S.*qu.et resp.*88(M.89.713B); 2. *arrange in advance*, *Hom.Clem.* 6.1; 3. *limit, define in advance* τίς ἐστι πλησίον; οὐ τὸν αὐτὸν τρόπον Ἰουδαίοις προωρίσατο τὸν πρὸς αἵματος, οὐδὲ τὸν πολίτην οὐδὲ τὸν προσήλυτον Clem.*q.d.s.*28(p.178.21; M.9.633B); 4. *define previously*, Or.*sel.in Ps.*4:5(M.12.1141C).

***προόρισις, ἡ**, *predetermining*; of God's predetermination of total number of mankind, Iren.*haer.*2.33.5(M.7.834B); ref. birth of saint εἰ καὶ μὴ ἐξ ἐπαγγελίας, ἀλλὰ θείας προγνώσεως καὶ π. Jo.VI H. *v.Jo.D.*7(M.94.440A); in rel. to prayer, Gr.Mag.*dial.*(tr.Zach.)1.8 (M.*PL.*77.187B).

***προωρισμένως**, *in accordance with God's predetermination*, Clem.*str.*6.9(p.469.29; M.9.297A).

προορισμός, ὁ, *predetermination*; 1. def. πρόγνωσις...τὸ εἰδέναι τὰ ἐσόμενα, πρὶν γενέσεως αὐτῶν· ἐπίγνωσις δέ ἐστιν, ἡ μετὰ ψευδῆ ἐπιγινομένη ἀληθὴς γνῶσις· καὶ ὁρισμὸς μέν ἐστι κρίσις καὶ ἀπόφασις ἐπὶ τοῖς γεγενημένοις· π. δέ, κρίσις καὶ ἀπόφασις ἐπὶ τοῖς ἐσομένοις Jo.D. *Man.*1.78(M.94.1577A); 2. ref. God's counsel; a. in gen. παραδείγματα δέ φαμεν εἶναι τοὺς ἐν θεῷ τῶν ὄντων οὐσιοποιοὺς καὶ ἑνιαίως προϋφεστῶτας λόγους, οὓς ἡ θεολογία π. καλεῖ Dion.Ar.*d.n.*5.8(M.3. 824C) cit. ap. Max.*ambig.*(M.91.1085A); τῆς θείας κελεύσεως ἔργον ἐστὶν ὁ π. Jo.D.*f.o.*2.30(M.94.972A); b. as shared by Son, †Diad.*Ar.*6 (M.65.1160C); c. ref. election ἔστιν αὐτῷ ἀρχὴ τῆς κλήσεως καὶ τῆς δικαιώσεως οὐχ ὁ π.· οὗτος γὰρ εἰ ἦν ἀρχὴ τῶν ἑξῆς, κἂν πιθανώτατα ἐκράτουν οἱ παρεισάγοντες τὸν περὶ φύσεως ἄτοπον λόγον· ἀνωτέρω δέ ἐστι τοῦ π. ἡ πρόγνωσις Or.*comm.in Rom.*1:3(*JTS* 13 p.211); contrasted with πρόθεσις: ἐπίστησον εἰ π. καὶ πρόθεσις διαφέρει, ὡς μετὰ τὸν π. τὴν πρόθεσιν γενέσθαι· ὥστε κατὰ τὰ ἐννοήματα τοῦ θεοῦ γίνεσθαι τὸν π., κατὰ δὲ ταῦτα τὴν περὶ ὧν πρόθεσιν οὐσιωμένων πως ἐπακολουθεῖν καὶ εἰ ῤγον ἐρχομένων τοῦ π. id.*comm.in Eph.*1:9 (p.240f.); d. ref. predetermination of length of man's life πρὸς δὲ τοὺς φιλονεικοῦντας...προορισμὸν παρὰ τῷ θεῷ δεῖξαι ἐτῶν παντὸς ἀνθρώπου,...ἐροῦμεν ὅτι εὑρεθήσεται ὁ θεὸς...ποιῶν ὅπερ ἄτοπόν ἐστι ...καὶ πάλιν εἰ προπεπηγμένος...ἐστι π. τῶν ἑκάστου χρόνων, μηδεὶς ἀσθενῶν εἰς ἀντίληψιν ἁγίους ἐπικαλέσεται Anast.S.*qu.et resp.*88(M. 89.713B); e. ref. what is purposed by God but not yet realized; i. man's resurrection τό, συνήγειρε,...κατὰ πρόγνωσιν καὶ π. θεοῦ Or.*comm.in Eph.*2:6(p.405); ii. existence of Son acc. Paul. Sam. θεὸν ἐκ τῆς παρθένου ὁμολογεῖ...ἐντεῦθεν τῆς ὑπάρξεως τὴν ἀρχὴν ἐσχηκότα...τῷ μὲν π. πρὸ αἰώνων ὄντα, τῇ δὲ ὑπάρξει ἐκ Ναζαρὲτ ἀναδειχθέντα ‡Ath.*Apoll.*2.3(M.26.1136B); cf. Paul.Sam.*fr.*D 2 (p.338.2).

***προοριστικῶς**, *in* God's *predetermined counsel*, of Son in teaching of Photinus πίστιν τὴν λέγουσαν ἀπὸ Μαρίας καὶ ὧδε εἶναι τὸν υἱόν, μὴ εἶναι δὲ αὐτὸν πρὸ τούτου, ἀλλὰ π. λέγεσθαι ἐν ταῖς γραφαῖς, ἀπὸ δὲ Μαρίας εἶναι αὐτὸν μόνον κατὰ τὴν θεότητα ‡Bas.*exp. fid.Nic.*(p.309; προωρικῶς M.28.1638A); ref. Arian proof-texts εἰ δέ που π. αἱ θεῖαι γραφαὶ λέγουσιν αὐτὸν ὥσπερ κτίσμα, τὸ κατὰ σάρκα πληροῦσθαι καταλαμβάνομεν *ib.*(p.310; 1639A); of Photinus' doctrine that Christ became Son of God at Inc. and before then is described in scripture as Son only π., *Didasc.Patr.*proem.(p.8.11).

προούσιος, *before all being* τὸ...πνεῦμα...ἀπὸ τῆς...ὑπερουσίου καὶ π. ... προῆλθεν...πατρικῆς ὑποστάσεως Didym.*Trin.*2.4(M.39.484A).

***προοχυρόω**, *make secure, fortify beforehand*, Jo.D.*Man.*1.29(M. 94.1533A).

προπάθεια, ἡ, *first stage of emotion* ἀπροαίρετον, ὃ καλοῦσί τινες π. γενομένην, ἐπί τισι δὲ ἐρεθισμοῖς ἕλκουσαν ἐφ' ἣν προωρισάμεθα ὀργήν Or.*sel.in Ps.*4:5(M.12.1141C); τὸ ἀπροαίρετον τὸ κατὰ τὴν π. γινόμενον *ib.*(1144A); κἂν κατ' ἀρετήν τις προκόπτῃ, οὐκ ἀφανιζομένου τοῦ παθητικοῦ, συμβαίνει ἐν τῇ λεγομένῃ π. γενέσθαι Diod.*Ps.* 54:6(M.33.1592B); ἐν...ταῖς τοῦ νοῦ π., καὶ...προαπονευρώσεσιν ταῖς διὰ νοημάτων φυσικῶν Cyr.*Ps.*118:67(M.69.1272B).

***προπαιδαγωγ-έω**, *give preliminary instruction* ~ῶν...διὰ τῶν ἐντολῶν Mac.Mgn.*apocr.*3.12(p.80.7); Cyr.*Jo.*4.2(4.363A); pass., *be given preliminary instruction* τοῖς ἐν τούτῳ [sc. τῷ νόμῳ] ~ηθεῖσι Eus.*d.e.*1.6(p.33.27; M.22.65A).

προπαιδεία, ἡ, *preliminary training*, of basic moral instruction αἱ δὲ ὁδοὶ τῶν δικαίων...εἶεν δ' ἂν καὶ αἱ ἐντολαὶ καὶ αἱ π. ὁδοὶ καὶ ἀφορμαὶ τοῦ βίου Clem.*str.*1.5(p.18.16; M.8.720B); of pagan philosophy as introduction to Christianity φιλοσοφίας καὶ τῆς ἄλλης π. *ib.* 1.1(p.11.22; 705A); ἦν...εἰς δικαιοσύνην Ἕλλησιν ἀναγκαία φιλοσοφία, νυνὶ δὲ χρησίμη πρὸς θεοσέβειαν γίνεται, π. τις οὖσα τοῖς τὴν πίστιν δι' ἀποδείξεως καρπουμένοις *ib.*1.5(p.17.33; 717C); π. ἡ Ἑλληνική *ib.*1.7 (p.24.8; 732B); φιλοσοφίαν...π. ... ὁμολογοῦμεν τοῦ γνωστικοῦ *ib.*1.20 (p.63.9; 816C); τὴν π. Ἑλλήνων τε καὶ Ἰουδαίων [signified by loaves and fishes of Jo.6:9–11] *ib.*6.11(p.479.4; M.9.316A); ἦν δ' οὗτος [sc. Dorotheus] τῶν μάλιστα ἐλευθερίων προπαιδείας τε τῆς καθ' Ἕλληνας οὐκ ἄμοιρος Eus.*h.e.*7.32.3(M.20.721B).

προπαίδευμα, τό, *preparatory instruction*, ref. Gen.16:4 πέφυκεν ἀτιμάζεσθαι ἀρετή, ἡνίκα τὰ π. γεννήσῃ Or.*sel.in Gen.*16:4(M.12.116A); γεωμετρίαν καὶ ἀριθμητικὴν καὶ τἄλλα π. Eus.*h.e.*6.18.3(M.20.561A); ἵνα μοι μετὰ τοὺς τῆς γενναίας φιλοσοφίας προστάτας ἀπάρχοιτό ποτε καὶ τοῖς πολιτικοῖς τοῦ Δίωνος γράμμασι, μεθόριον αὐτὰ ἡγούμενος τῶν π. τε καὶ τῆς ἀληθινωτάτης παιδείας Synes.*Dion* 4(p.244.17; M. 66.1124C).

προπαίδευσις, ἡ, *preliminary instruction* σοφὸν ἐκ π. γενέσθαι Gr. Nyss.*Eun.*3(2 p.9.25; M.45.573A); ref. pentecostal gift οὐκ ἐκ π. ... ἀλλ' ἐξ ἐπιπνοίας τοῦ πνεύματος...ἡ τοῦ φθέγγεσθαι δύναμις προσεγένετο id.*Steph.*1(M.46.704D); παιδείᾳ γὰρ οὐ τῇ τυχούσῃ ὁ ἀνὴρ [sc. Apollinarius] ἐξήσκηται, ἀπὸ τῆς τῶν λόγων π. τε καὶ Ἑλληνικῆς διδασκαλίας ὁρμώμενος Epiph.*haer.*77.24(p.437.27; M.42.676D).

προπαιδεύ-ω, 1. *give preliminary instruction* ὁ θεῖος νόμος...~ει ἡμᾶς εἰς τὴν περιποίησιν τῆς ἐγκρατείας Clem.*str.*2.20(p.170.19; M.8. 1049A); ἐκ νόμου καὶ προφητῶν ~εσθαι διὰ κυρίου τῷ θεῷ συμφέρειν ἔδοξεν *ib.*2.8(p.132.19; 972C); διδασκάλους πρὸς φιλοσοφίαν ~οντας Or.*Cels.*3.58(p.253.14; M.11.997B); παῖδας πρὸ τῆς ἐπιθυμίας διὰ τῶν σωφρονιζόντων βιβλίων ~ειν *Hom.Clem.*5.25; 2. *teach as preliminary* ~ει γὰρ τῷ κυριακῷ λόγῳ τὰ κατὰ τοὺς προσήκοντας καιροὺς ἑκάστῃ γενεᾷ συμφερόντως δεδομένα Clem.*str.*1.5(p.19.7; M.8.721A); 3. *prepare the mind of* τοσούτοις αὐτὸν προεπαίδευσε φαρμάκοις Chrys.*hom. 61.3 in Mt.*(7.615B).

***προπαίω**, *smite previously*, Alex.Sal.*Barn.*proem.5(437C).

***προπάνδημος**, *made public*, Bars.*resp.*(M.88.1821B).

***προπανυπέρτατος**, *most sublime*, Iren.*haer.*1.15.5(M.7.625B).

***προπαραινετικός**, *warning beforehand*, *cat.Rom.*7:18(p.108.33).

προπαρατίθημι, *set out previously, state beforehand*, Clem.*str.*1.1

(p.11.17; M.8.704C); Or.Jo.2.30(24; p.87.29; M.14.168A); Eus.d.e.7.3 (p.340.19; M.22.556A); Max.schol.d.n.1.4(M.4.200C).

***προπαραφυλάσσομαι**, *guard against in advance*, tr. Lat. *praecaveo*, Cod.Afr.134(H.1.941A).

προπαρεγγυάω, *guarantee beforehand*, Cyr.glaph.Ex.3(1.330A).

προπαρέρχομαι, *pass over previously* οὐ γὰρ ἔστιν ἑτέρως δύνασθαι ...τὴν ἄζυμον...τῶν εὐαγγελικῶν κηρυγμάτων εὑρέσθαι τροφήν, μὴ προπαρελθόντας μὲν τὸν μυστικὸν Ἰορδάνην Cyr.Jo.4.7(4.437C).

***προπαρηγορέω**, *quieten first*, ‡Ath.sem.16(M.28.165A).

***προπαρίστημι**, *establish beforehand*, Or.fr.27 in Lam.(p.247.26; M.13.621D); Eus.d.e.4.16(p.193.7; M.22.321B); ib.9.3(p.411.7; 661D).

προπατέω, *advance*, ‡Ath.qu.script.125(M.28.769C).

προπατήρ, ὁ, *forefather*, hence *predecessor* τοὺς τοῦ...ἀποστολικοῦ καὶ σεβασμίου θρόνου π. Jo.VI CP ep.(M.96.1420C).

***προπατορικός**, *ancestral*; **1.** of original sin ἐπὶ δὲ τῶν πιστῶν τὸ ἅγιον βάπτισμα καθαρίζει ἡμᾶς ἀπὸ πάσης π. ἁμαρτίας ‡Ath.qu.Ant.67 (M.28.636A); Χριστοῦ οὖν συγχωρήσαντος ταύτην διὰ τοῦ λουτροῦ τῆς ἀφέσεως, ἐκαθαρίσθη μὲν ἡ π. ἁμαρτία Olymp.fr.Jer.31:30(M.93.689D); δίχα τὸν κύριον εἶναι τῆς π. ἁμαρτίας ὡς ἄνθρωπον Max.opusc.(M.91.136A); ἐκ τῆς π. καταδίκης θλίψιν id.myst.(M.91.709D); **2.** of original virtue restored to man by Inc. π. παρθενίαν Jo.Mon.hymn.Blas.8(M.96.1405C).

***προπάτορος, ὁ**, *ancestor* πνεῦμα ἅγιον...οὐ γεννητόν, οὐ κτιστόν, οὐ συνάδελφον, οὐ π., οὐκ ἔκγονον Epiph.haer.74.12(p.330.20; M.42.497D); ib.76.39(p.394.5; 604A); ib.73.36(p.310.27; προπάτορα M.42.469B); id.anc.7(p.14.19; M.43.29A).

προπάτωρ, ὁ, *ancestor, forefather*; **1.** of Osiris as ancestor of Egyptian kings, Clem.prot.4(p.37.24; M.8.140A); **2.** of Adam and Eve οἱ πρῶτοι τοῦ γένους π. ξύλου γεύσει τὸν πολυώδυνον κατεδικάσθησαν καὶ βίον καὶ θάνατον Isid.Pel.epp.1.181(M.78.301A); ref. Euchite doctrine ἕλκειν γὰρ ἕκαστον τῶν τικτομένων...ἐκ τοῦ π. [sc. Adam], ὥσπερ τὴν φύσιν, οὕτω δὴ καὶ τὴν τῶν δαιμόνων δουλείαν Thdt.h.e.4.11.7(3.966); ref. temptation of Christ ὁ διάβολος...ὡς τοῦ π. τὸ πάθος ἐν αὐτῷ θεωρήσας Thdt.pental.(5.124); Thdr.Stud. epp.1.18(M.99.964D); **3.** of patriarchs, T.Lev.9.1; Just.1apol.32.3(M.6.377C); Or.Cels.5.48(p.52.13; M.11.1256B); Eus.d.e.5.15(p.238.27; M.22.393C); Abraham as π. of Christians, Const.App.7.33.4; ὁ π. ...ἐν τῇ δρυῒ τῇ Μαμβρῇ τὴν ἁγίαν...προσκυνήσας τριάδα Didym.Trin. 2.23(M.39.744C); τὰς ιβʹ φυλὰς ἐξ ἑνὸς π. ... καταγομένας Cosm.Ind. top.5(M.88.213C); **4.** met., of clay from which man is formed τὸν χοῦν τὸν π. Thdt.Soph.2:3(2.1568); id.provid.6(4.576); **5.** *originator*, of founders of heresies οἱ π. τῶν δογμάτων Clem.str.3.1(p.196.21; M.8.1104A); Eus.h.e.2.1.12(M.20.137C); **6.** Trin. τὸν υἱὸν...γεγεννημένον, οὐ συνάδελφον, οὐ π. Epiph.haer.73.36(M.42.469B; cj. προπάτορον p.310.27); **7.** of source of pleroma, Bythus; Valent., Iren. haer.1.1.1(M.7.445A); ib.1.2.1(452B); Ptolemaean τινὲς ἐξ αὐτῶν ῥαψῳδοὶ τὸν π. τῶν ὅλων καὶ προαρχὴν...ἄνθρωπον λέγουσι καλεῖσθαι ib.1.12.4(577A); Marcosian ὅλου τοῦ ὀνόματος τὸν βύθον τῶν γραμμάτων, ἐξ ὧν τὸν π. ἡ Μάρκου Σιγὴ συνεστάναι ἐδογμάτισε ib.1.14.2 (600B); Hipp.haer.6.43(p.176.11; M.16.3266B); ib.6.48(p.180.13; 3275A); cf. *appellant, personaliter vero* π. *et* προαρχήν Tert.adversus Valentinianos 7(M.PL.2.586A); **8.** met., of Stephen as 'ancestor' of martyrs, Chrysipp.enc.in Thdr.(p.55.16); **9.** as mode of address, to bishop μακαριώτατε π. Thdr.Stud.epp.2.41(M.99.1240D).

προπεμπτήριος, *escorting*; hence *of or belonging to a funeral* οἱ δὲ ἐξιτήριοι λόγοι καὶ π. Thdr.Stud.or.13.7(M.99.892C); neut. plur. as subst., *obsequies*, Gr.Naz.or.8.22(M.35.813C); id.ep.155(M.37.261B).

προπέμπ-ω, **1.** *send forward, send forth* δυνάμεις...οὐκ ἀπεσταλμέναι οὐδὲ ὑπὸ τοῦ θείου βουλήματος προπεμφθεῖσαι Or.Jo.20.19(17; p.351.30; M.14.616B); **2.** *escort* ἀπὸ τῶν κοιμητηρίων προπέμψαντες τοὺς μάρτυρας ἠρχόμεθα ἐπὶ τὰς συναγωγάς Or.hom.4.3 in Jer.(p.25.20; M.13.288D); ἐν ταῖς ἐξόδοις τῶν κεκοιμημένων ψάλλοντες ~ετε αὐτούς Const.App.6.30.2; Bas.Sel.or.10.2(M.85.144C); of angels escorting ascending Christ οἱ δὲ ~οντες αὐτὸν τοῖς ἐπὶ τῶν οὐρανίων πυλῶν τεταγμένοις φασὶν τό, ἄρατε πύλας Or.Jo.6.56(37; p.165.3; M.14.297B); **3.** *conduct* οὐ...μόνον τὸν κόσμον, ἀλλὰ καὶ τὴν ἐκλογὴν διακρίνας ὁ ἐπὶ πᾶσι ~ει Clem.str.2.8(p.132.6; M.8.972B); id.q.d.s.25(p.176.8; M.9.629B).

***προπεριέχ-ω**, pass., *be previously contained in* μηδὲ γὰρ οἴεσθαι δεῖν...τὸν θεὸν τὰ κατὰ πρόγνωσιν ἀπειροδυνάμως ἐν ἑαυτῷ...~όμενα ἕκαστα μανθάνειν διὰ τῆς εἰς τὸ εἶναι παραγωγῆς Max.ambig.(M.91.1328C).

***προπεριτέμνω**, *circumcise before*, Cyr.hom.pasch.9.6(5[2].124B).

***προπετάζω**, *spread in front*, Sophr.H.v.Anast.(M.92.1709D).

προπετεύ-ομαι, **1.** *act rashly, presumptuously* τῶν ἰδιωτῶν ~σαμένων περὶ τῆς τοιούτων διηγήσεως Or.Cels.6.62(p.132.12; M.11.1392C); εἰ ~σαιντο πρὸς ὑμᾶς ἐλθεῖν Alex.Al.ep.encycl.(p.10.12; M.18.577B); Ath.apol.Const.2(p.280.12; M.25.597B); μὴ ~εσθαι μὲν ἐν τῷ πειράζειν τὸν κύριον id.fug.22(p.83.15; M.25.672D); ἐπὶ μείζονί σου μὴ ~σῃ καθίσαι Bas.renunt.8(2.209B; M.31.644A); οὐ περπερεύεται· τουτέστιν, οὐ ~εται Chrys.hom.33.1 in 1Cor.(10.300B); τί ταπειναῖς ἐννοίαις ~εσθαι θέλεις; Procl.CP or.8.2(M.65.765B); **2.** *use rashly* τὴν τοιάνδε φωνὴν μὴ ~έσθωσαν Leont.H.monoph.62(M.86.1804B).

προπηδ-άω, *leap forward*; **1.** in gen. ~ῶσιν μὲν αὐτῷ [sc. Galerius] τὰ ὄμματα Eus.h.e.9.10.15(M.20.836D); id.v.C.1.59(p.35.20; M.20.973B); **2.** *rush forward eagerly*, of Jo. Bapt. πανταχοῦ ~ᾷ Chrys. hom.10.4 in Mt.(7.144D); of S. Peter at tomb οὐκ ἠνέσχετο μετὰ τῶν ἄλλων ἐλθεῖν, ἀλλὰ προεπήδησεν ib.50.1(515A); in argument ἀπὸ τούτου ~ήσαντες καὶ ἄλλα τινὰ ἐφηύραντο Epiph.haer.59.3(p.366.7; M.41.1021A); **3.** *rush forward before* Πέτρος, ὁ...θερμὸς καὶ ἀεὶ τῶν ἄλλων ~ῶν Chrys.hom.50.1 in Mt.(7.515A); Πέτρος...~ῶν ἀεὶ τοῦ χοροῦ τῶν ἀποστόλων id.paralyt.2(3.35E); τῶν ἄλλων προεπήδησε [sc. Epaenetus] καὶ ἐπίστευσε id.hom.31.1 in Rom.(9.746A); ref. S. Peter's confession ~ᾷ...τῶν ἄλλων...καὶ παντὸς τοῦ χοροῦ γίνεται στόμα Cyr.Lc.9:18(M.72.648B); hence **4.** in gen., *precede* ~ησάτω ὁ τῆς παρακλήσεως λόγος τῶν λοιπῶν σου ῥημάτων Bas.renunt.8(2.209D; M.31.644B); Cyr.glaph.Gen.1(1.14D); **5.** *press forward, be eager*, Meth.symp.6.1(p.64.5; M.18.113A); Dion.Al.fr.(p.91.1); CCP(360)ep. ap.Thdt.h.e.2.28.4(3.900); **6.** *seek to surpass* φιλονεικεῖν...καὶ ~ᾶν ὡς οἱ διδάσκαλοι Meth.res.1.27(p.256.4; M.41.1133C); εἰς κατὰ τοῦ ἑτέρου ἐπαιρόμεθα, ἢ ἀλλήλους ~ῶμεν Ephr.1.114B; ~ᾶν ἀλλήλους καὶ ἐξουθενεῖν...ἐπειγόμεθα id.1.114E; **7.** *proceed forth*, of generation of Logos ὁ πατήρ, ὅταν βούληται, λέγουσι, δύναμιν αὐτοῦ ~ᾶν ποιεῖ, καὶ ὅταν βούληται πάλιν ἀναστέλλει εἰς ἑαυτόν Just.dial.128.3(M.6.776A); θελήματι δὲ τῆς ἁπλότητος αὐτοῦ ~ᾷ λόγος Tat.orat.5(p.5.22; M.6.813C); ἕτερος γενόμενος τοῦ ἐν καρδίᾳ λόγου ὁ διὰ γλώσσης νοῦς ~ῶν Dion.Al.ap.Ath.Dion.23(p.63.9; M.25.513B); ὁ δὲ λόγος νοῦς ~ῶν id.ib.(p.63.19; 513C).

***προπιαίν-ω**, ? *emphasize, enhance effect of* ὁ τῶν πρέσβεων ἐπιφανέστερος ~ων τῷ δακρύῳ τὸν λόγον...τῶνδε τῶν λόγων ἀπήρξατο Thphyl.exc.gent.6(p.484.16; M.113.945B).

προπινάριος, ὁ, (Lat. *popinarius*) *victualler*, Cyr.S.v.Sab.58 (p.160.3).

προπίν-ω, **1.** *drink in compliment to*; hence *offer as gift* οὐδὲ... ἡδονῆς φάρμακα τοῖς τῶνδε ~οῦμαι φίλοις Eus.l.C.proem.(p.195.4; M.20.1317A); **2.** *offer chalice to, communicate* τοῦτο [sc. τὸ μυστικὸν ποτήριον] ὑμεῖς νομίμως ~ετε τοῖς λαοῖς CAlex.ep.ap.Ath.apol.sec.11 (p.96.30; M.25.268C); met., ref. Ps.74:9 περὶ ποίου ποτηρίου φησίν; ὃν τοῖς ἀνθρώποις θεόθεν προποθέντα λόγον...ἐν παλαιᾷ διαθήκῃ καὶ νέᾳ Synes.hom.1(p.280.11; M.66.1561C); **3.** *give away, sacrifice heedlessly* τὴν ἐλευθερίαν τῆς ἑαυτῶν ψυχῆς ἄλλοις ~οντες Ath.decr.4(p.3.30; M.25.'429'(421)B); id.syn.13(p.240.23; M.26.704B); Bas.Eun.1.2 (1.210B; M.29.505B); Chrys.hom.12.6 in 1Cor.(10.106C); ‡Nil.perist. 9.8(M.79.881A).

προπλάσσω, *form previously*, ref. union of soul and body ἡ τῶν ἀγγέλων πρὸς τὸ ἐνσπείρεσθαι ψυχὰς σώμασιν λειτουργία, δύο τινὰ συναγόντων...καὶ ἐν καιρῷ τῷ τεταγμένῳ ἀρχομένων τε τὴν περὶ ἑκάστου ποιεῖν οἰκονομίαν καὶ εἰς τελεσφόρησιν προαγόντων τὸν προπεπλασμένον Or.Jo.13.50(49; p.277.26; M.14.489A); ref. flesh of Christ σαρκοῦται γοῦν ὁ λόγος...οὐ προπλασθείσῃ σαρκὶ συναπτόμενος Sophr.H.ep.syn.(M.87.3161B); ref. union of natures συνεπλάσθη καθ' ὑπόστασιν, ἀλλ' οὐ προεπλάσθη ὁ τοῦ θεοῦ λόγος, τὴν σκηνώδημον φύσιν Anast.S.hex.12(M.89.1053B; perh. for προσ-).

προπλέκω, med., *enfold*, Bas.Sel.or.1.2(M.85.32C).

***προπλουτέω**, *be rich previously*, Cyr.glaph.Gen.3(1.101A).

***προπόδιος**, *right at the foot*; as subst., *foot* of a hill, Hesych.H. qu.ev.36(M.93.1424D).

***προποδών**, *lying before*, V.Const.27(p.559.2).

προποιέω, *do before*; hence *precede*, Thphn.chron.p.267(M.108.661C).

***προποιόω**, pass., *be affected beforehand* νοῦς...προπεποίωται... τοῖς...πάθεσιν Evagr.Pont.or.30(M.79.1173B).

προπολεμέω, *fight against* ἄνδρα...προπολεμήσαντα τοὺς...Ἄραβας Thphn.chron.p.337(M.108.813B).

προπόλεος, *suburban*, of martyr's shrine τὸν π. κόσμον Bas.hom. 18.1(2.141D; M.31.489C).

πρόπομα, τό, *drink taken before meals* σίκερα ὁ Σύμμαχος καὶ ὁ Ἀκύλας 'μέθυσμα' ἡρμήνευσεν. ἐγὼ δὲ οἶμαι...σημαίνεσθαι τὰς τῶν π. ⟨κατα⟩σκευάς Thdt.Is.5:11(p.26.9; 2.201); as preventative against poison, Isid.Pel.epp.5.454(M.78.1589C).

προπομπεύ-ω, **1.** *lead in procession*, of cross as standard in

Const.'s army τοῦ σωτηρίου τροπαίου ~οντος τῆς ἀμφ' αὐτὸν φάλαγγος Eus.*v.C.*2.6(p.44.4; M.20.988A); ἐποίει...τοῦ...στρατοῦ ~ειν χρυσῶν μὲν ἀγαλμάτων, ὁποῖα πρότερον...ἔθος ἦν, τὸ μηθὲν μόνον δὲ τὸ σωτήριον τρόπαιον *ib.*4.21(p.125.18; 1168C); τοῦ χοροῦ...~ουσα [sc. Miriam] Gr.Nyss.*virg.*19(p.322.27; M.46.396A); in funeral procession, Philost.*h.e.*6.6(M.65.537A); **2.** *escort* δίφρων ὑπεραίρεσθαι... ~εσθαί τε Gr.Naz.*or.*42.24(M.36.488A); **3.** *go in triumph*, hence *triumph* over, of Christ κατὰ τοῦ ἐχθροῦ ~ων ‡Chrys.*pasch.*6(p.183.2; 8.272E).

προπομπή, ἡ, *procession*; **1.** of column of troops, Bas.*hex.*8.5(1.75B; M.29.176C); **2.** of funeral procession, ‡Chrys.*hom.*1(13.202E); ‡Nil.*narr.*1(M.79.596C); **3.** of festival procession, Jo.Mon.*hymn. Chrys.*5(M.96.1381A).

***προπόμπιος,** *of a funeral procession* τῆς π. τιμῆς Gr.Naz.*or.*5.17 (M.35.685B); Thdt.*h.e.*1.21.5(3.802) = Gel.Cyz.*h.e.*3.16.16.

***προπόρευσις, ἡ,** *coming before*, of Exaltation of Cross preceded by dedication of Church of Resurrection at Jerusalem τοὺς ἐκ τῶν περάτων ἀφικνουμένους πρὸς τὴν...προσκύνησιν τῆς...π. εἶναι τὸ αἴτιον Sophr.H.*or.*4(M.87.3205B).

***προποσία, ἡ,** *first draught*, Meth.*symp.*5.6(p.60.10; M.18.108B); id.*Porph.*1(p.503.5; M.18.397C).

***προπότιον, τό,** = πρόπομα q.v.; met., of Christ's Resurrection as preventative against poison of Origenist teaching on future life, Epiph.*haer.*64.72(p.522.21; M.41.1197D).

πρόπους, ὁ, 1. *foot*, Gr.Naz.*carm.*1.2.9.58(M.37.672A); **2.** *approach* ὑπὸ προπόδεσσι γάμοιο ἐσθλοὺς ἄνδρας ὄπασσας *ib.*2.2(poem.)3.168 (M.37.1492A); *ib.*2.2(poem.)6.99(1549A).

προπταίω, *sin previously*; perf. ptcpl. pass., *past sin* τὰς τῶν ἤδη π. ἀπολύειν αἰτίας Cyr.*Os.*159(3.192C); τὴν ἐν πίστει δικαίωσιν... ἀφανίζουσαν...τῶν ἤδη π. τὴν κατάκρισιν id.*hom.pasch.*24(5^2.290D); of pre-baptismal sins, id.*Is.*1.1(2.18C).

πρόπυλον, τό, *porch*; of church, *MAMA* 1.170 (c. 340).

προπύργιον, τό, *bulwark* τὴν γέφυραν καὶ τὰ ἐν αὐτῇ π. Thphn. *chron.*p.262(M.108.652B); met., of baptism τεῖχος ἡμῖν ἐστιν ἀσφαλὲς καὶ π. †Jo.D.*B.J.*11(M.96.952A); of BMV τῶν πιστῶν ἀνακτόρων π. *Hymn.*(Maas, *KlT* p.9.30); ὦ τῆς Χριστιανῶν π. πίστεως Andr.Cr.*or.* 14(M.97.1108B).

***προπύργιος,** *like a bulwark, defensive* ἡ τοῦ ὑψίστου δεξιά, ἡ προπύργιος ἀσφάλεια τῶν ἀγαπώντων αὐτόν †Gregent.*disp.*(M.86.689B).

προπυρόω, *heat*, hence *temper, in advance*, Jo.Clim.*scal.*19(M.88.937C).

***προπυρσεύω,** *kindle beforehand*, ‡Nil.*perist.*3.1(M.79.824B).

πρόρρησις, ἡ, 1. *prediction*; **a.** in gen., Eus.*h.e.*4.16.7(M.20.368A); Thdt.*eran.*3(3.193); Jo.Mosch.*prat.*127(M.87.2989C); dist. from true prophecy ἃ γὰρ οἱ ἰατροὶ προλέγουσιν...καὶ οἱ μὲν πτηνά, οἱ δὲ θύματα, καὶ ἄλλοι ἄλλας ὕλας...ὑποβεβλημένας ἔχοντες προλέγουσιν... εἰ δὲ βουληθείη τις λέγειν, τὴν διὰ τῶν τοιούτων π. τῇ ὄντως ἐμφύτῳ προγνώσει ὁμοίαν εἶναι, πολὺ ἠπάτηται *Hom.Clem.*3.12; **b.** of oracles and divination τὰ πάντα...ἤλω...τῆς π. ἀποπεπτωκότα Eus.*p.e.*4.2 (133B; M.21.233C); ἡ φθοροποιὸς...φύσις...π. τισὶ καὶ ἰατρείαις τὸν... τῆς ἀπάτης λόγον ἐπικαλύπτουσα Gr.Nyss.*fat.*(M.45.172B); τὸ δέ γε πλάνον ἐν ταῖς π. ἀληκτόν ἐστι τῶν ἀλινδουμένων εἰς ὕλην, ἐμπαθὲς καὶ φιλότιμον Synes.*insomn.*10(p.164.2; M.66.1300A); practised by Peratic Gnostics, Hipp.*haer.*4.28(p.56.20; M.16.3091D); **c.** of OT prophecy; ref. Ps.28:3 applied to Christ's baptism, †Hipp.*theoph.* 7(p.261.16; M.10.857C); αἱ περὶ τῆς εἰς ἀνθρώπους ἐπιφανείας αὐτοῦ π. Eus.*d.e.*3 proem.(p.94.12; M.22.164A); Bas.*hom.in Ps.*1(1.91C; M. 29.213B); εἰς δέκα γὰρ διῄρηνται θεωρίας αἱ προφητεῖαι...διδασκαλίας, θεωρίας, προτροπάς, ἀπειλάς, ὀλοφυρμούς, θρήνους, εὐχάς, ἱστορίας, π. Epiph.*mens.*1(M.43.237A); τὰς τῶν μελλόντων π. ταῖς ἀρχαιοτέραις ἐνυφῆναι γραφαῖς Isid.Pel.*epp.*2.63(M.78.505D); αὕτη μὲν γὰρ [sc. ἡ πίστις] προφητῶν ἐστι π., ἀποστόλων δὲ κήρυγμα Cyr.*deip.BMV* 30 (p.32.19; M.76.289D); τῶν δώδεκα προφητῶν τὰς τῇ ἀσαφείᾳ κεκρυμμένας π. Thdt.*Pss.*proem.(1.602); ἐκ τῆς π. τοῦ πατρὸς Νῶε Λαμὲχ ...[Gen.5:29] Cosm.Ind.*top.*2(M.88.92C); ‡Meth.*Sym.et Ann.*2(M.18. 349C); **d.** of prophetic sayings of Christ, Dion.Al.ap.Eus.*h.e.*6.41. 10(M.20.609A); Eus.*d.e.*3.5(p.125.14; M.22.213B); Ath.*ep.Aeg.Lib.*1 (M.25.540B); Chrys.*hom.26.4 in Mt.*(7.319D); id.*hom.33.2 in Jo.*(8. 192D); προστάξας...'Ιουλιανὸς τὰ 'Ιεροσόλυμα ἀνοικοδομεῖσθαι, ὡς ἂν τὰς περὶ αὐτῶν δεσποτικὰς π. ἀκύρους ἐλέγξῃ Philost.*h.e.*7.14(M.65. 552B); **e.** of Agabus' prophecy, Eus.*h.e.*2.8.1(M.20.156C); and predictions by apostles, Ath.*ep.Aeg.Lib.*20(M.25.585A); Euthal.Diac. *epp.cath.*(M.85.684A); **2.** *previous instruction* αἱ τελεταὶ τοῖς ἐντυγχάνουσιν ἀνέδην οὐ δείκνυνται, ἀλλὰ μετά τινων καθαρμῶν καὶ π. Clem. *str.*5.4(p.339.7; M.9.40A); **3.** *lection* πανταχοῦ εἰρήνην αἰτοῦμεν...ἐν ταῖς ἐκκλησίαις εἰρήνην, ἐν ταῖς εὐχαῖς, ἐν ταῖς λιταῖς, ἐν ταῖς π.· καὶ ἅπαξ καὶ δὶς καὶ...πολλάκις αὐτὴν δίδωσιν ὁ τῆς ἐκκλησίας προεστὼς Chrys.*hom.3.3 in Col.*(11.347D).

§**προρρίπτω,** *reject*, Ath.*v.Anton.*81(M.26.956B, v.l. ἀπορριφθέντες).

***προρρυπόω,** pass., *be previously defiled*, Bas.*hom.in Ps.*28(1.123C; M.29.304B).

πρός, A. c. acc.; **1.** *with* ἀμιγοῦς πρός τι ἕτερον ζωῆς Or.*Jo.*1.27 (25; p.34.32; M.14.73D); ref. Jo.1:1 (distinction between 'coming' of Logos 'to' a prophet and 'being' of Logos πρὸς τὸν θεόν) πρὸς μὲν τοὺς ἀνθρώπους πρότερον οὐ χωροῦντας τὴν τοῦ υἱοῦ τοῦ θεοῦ... ἐπιδημίαν ὁ λόγος γίνεται· πρὸς δὲ τὸν θεὸν οὐ γίνεται, ὡς πρότερον οὐκ ὢν πρὸς αὐτόν, παρὰ δὲ τὸ ἀεὶ συνεῖναι τῷ πατρὶ λέγεται· καὶ ὁ λόγος ἦν πρὸς τὸν θεόν *ib.*2.1(p.53.14; 105C); τὸν ὄντα ἐν ἀρχῇ πρὸς τὸν θεόν *Symb.Ant.*(341)2(p.249.18; M.26.721C); ὄντα πρὸς τὸν θεὸν ἐν ὑποστάσει *Symb.Ant.*(341)3(p.250.12; 724C); explained as though meaning *in relation to* (v. 3 infra) τὸ ἦν πρὸς τὸν θεὸν παριστᾷ ἣν υἱὸς ἔχει πρὸς θεὸν πατέρα φύσεως οἰκειότητα Didym.*Trin.*1.15(M.39. 300A); ἕν ἐστιν πρὸς τὸν...πατέρα διὰ τὴν ταυτότητα τῆς οὐσίας Cyr. *ep.*17(p.38.11; 5^2.73B); Christol. ἐν γὰρ μάλιστα μετὰ τὴν οἰκονομίαν γεγένηται πρὸς τὸν λόγον τοῦ θεοῦ ἡ ψυχὴ καὶ τὸ σῶμα 'Ιησοῦ Or.*Cels.* 2.9(p.136.31; M.11.809D); **2.** intent *upon* ὁ ζητῶν...πρὸς ἐκεῖνο γίνεται μόνον τὸ ζητούμενον Chrys.*hom.23.4 in Mt.*(7.289B); ὁ ἀπόστολος πρὸς τοῦτο ἦν id.*hom.11.3 in Eph.*(11.83F; Gaume cj. τούτῳ); **3.** *in relation to*; hence πρός τι *relatively*, Chrys.*hom.3.2 in Tit.*(11.746E); *ib.*5.2(759D); **4.** *to the extent of* πρὸς τὸ πολλοστὸν μέρος τὴν δουλείαν... ἐπιδεικνύμεθα id.*hom.16.2 in 1Tim.*(11.645C); id.*hom.14.2 in Heb.* (12.184B); hence, *as much as, equivalently to* ὡς κάμνειν αὐτὸν πρὸς τρία ὀνόματα (*toil as hard as three people*) Call.*v.Hyp.*(p.85); **5.** *at the rate of*, *Apophth.Patr.*(M.65.92B); **6.** *in addition to* πρὸς τὸ ταῦτα μὴ ποιεῖν Diod.*Ps.*67:20(M.33.1605A).

B. adverbially; *moreover, besides* πρὸς ἐπὶ τούτοις Eus.*h.e.*1.1.2 (προσέτι M.20.49A); Epiph.*haer.*26.4(p.281.3; M.41.337C); *ib.*66.40 (p.77.28; M.42.89B).

προσάββατον, τό, *eve of Sabbath, Friday*, Eus.*m.P.*6(p.920.6; M. 20.1480B); ref. Friday fast ἐν παντὶ μὲν π. τοῦ σωτηρίου πάθους τὴν ἀνάμνησιν ποιούμενοι διὰ νηστείας id.*pasch.*12(M.24.705C); πεφιλοτίμηται μᾶλλον ἐν κυριακῇ νηστεύειν [sc. Aërians], τετράδα δὲ καὶ π. ἐσθίειν Epiph.*haer.*75.3(p.335.16; M.42.508B); ἐν πᾶσι κλίμασι τῆς οἰκουμένης...τετρὰς καὶ π. νηστεία ἐστὶν ἐν τῇ ἐκκλησίᾳ ὡρισμένη *ib.* 75.6(p.338.8; 512C); συνάξεις...ταχθεῖσαί εἰσιν...τετράδι καὶ π. καὶ κυριακῇ· τετράδι δὲ καὶ π. ἐν νηστείᾳ ἕως ὥρας ἐνάτης...δίχα μόνης τῆς πεντηκοστῆς ὅλης τῶν πεντήκοντα ἡμερῶν, ἐν αἷς...οὔτε νηστεία προστέτακται, ἀντὶ δὲ τῶν πρὸς τὴν ἐνάτην συνάξεων τετράδι καὶ π., ὡς ἐν ἡμέρᾳ κυριακῇ, κατὰ τὰς πρωϊνὰς αἱ συνάξεις ἐπιτελοῦνται id.*exp. fid.*22(p.522.27; M.42.825B).

***προσάββατος,** *pre-Sabbath, of the eve of the Sabbath*, Nonn. *par.Jo.*19:14(M.43.900C); *ib.*19:42(908B).

προσαγοράζω, *buy besides*, ‡Ath.*syntag.*3.5(p.124; M.28.840C; cj. προαγ-).

***προσάγχω,** *be exhausted*, Sophr.H.*v.Anast.*(M.92.1721B).

προσάγ-ω, 1. *lead on to, introduce to*, esp. of leading to knowledge and spiritual improvement and of man being led to God ἔστι γάρ... φιλοσοφία...κτῆμα...τιμιώτατον τῷ θεῷ, ᾧ τε ~ει καὶ συνίστησιν ἡμᾶς μόνη Just.*dial.*2.1(M.6.476B); ὁ γνωστικὸς Μωϋσῆς...~ων εἰς ἔννοιαν τοῦ θεοῦ τοὺς 'Εβραίους Clem.*str.*5.11(p.376.8; M.9.112C); πλησιαίτερον τῇ κτιζούσῃ δυνάμει ~ουσα [sc. astronomy] τὴν ψυχήν *ib.*6.11(p.477.10; 312B); ὁ δημιουργὸς...φῶς ἐποίησεν, τουτέστιν ἐφανέρωσεν καὶ εἰς φῶς καὶ ἰδέαν προσήγαγεν id.*exc.Thdot.*48(p.122. 11; M.9.681B); ἵνα...ἐλευθερώσας τῶν τύπων ~άγῃ τῇ ἀληθείᾳ Or.*Jo.* 13.18(p.242.27; M.14.429A); ἡ ἀρχέτυπος εὐσέβεια...ἀπὸ τῆς πρώτης στοιχειώσεως τῆς κατὰ Μωσέα λατρείας ἐπὶ τὸν κρείττονα καὶ τελειότερον ~ουσα τοὺς προσιόντας αὐτῇ βίον Eus.*d.e.*1.6(p.29.16; M.22. 60A); ὁ ἀχώριστος τοῦ πατρὸς υἱὸς ~αγόμενος ἡμᾶς πρὸς ἑαυτόν... αἴτιος γέγονε τοῦ προσαχθῆναι θεῷ Apoll.*Rom.*5:1–6(p.62.9); διὰ τῶν ἀποστόλων προσήχθημεν Chrys.*hom.66.2 in Mt.*(7.656B, v.l. τὴν δι' αὐτῶν προσένεξιν τῶν ἐθνῶν); αὐτὸς [sc. Christ] γάρ ἐστιν ἡ ὁδὸς ἡ ~ουσα εἰς τὸν πατέρα id.*hom.6.1 in Col.*(11.365B); ἦσάν τινες οἱ λέγοντες, οὐ δεῖ ἡμᾶς διὰ τοῦ Χριστοῦ ~εσθαι *ib.*7.1(372A); **2.** *bring forward* in argument, Or.*or.*15(p.335.4; M.11.465C); ἐνίοτε λόγους ⟨τοῖς⟩ ἀπὸ τῶν ἐθνῶν ~ομεν βουλόμενοι αὐτοὺς ~αγεῖν τῇ πίστει id.*hom.20.5 in Jer.*(p.184.32; M.13.512B); Chrys.*hom.81.2 in Mt.*(7. 775B); **3.** *apply* ἐπὶ τοῦ οἰκείου προσώπου ~ειν τὴν ἐξουδένωσιν Chrys. *hom.8.3 in 1Cor.*(10.69A); λόγους π. *negotiate*, Men.*exc.Rom.*9(p.195. 27; M.113.889A); **4.** med., *admit*, penitents διὰ τοὺς οἰκτιρμοὺς καὶ τὴν ἀγαθότητα τοῦ θεοῦ ~εσθαι τῇ κοινωνίᾳ CLaod.*can.*2; of admission to clerical orders μὴ δεῖν πρόσφατον φωτισθέντας ~εσθαι ἐν τάγματι ἱερατικῷ *ib.*3(? for προαγ-); **5.** med., *attract, draw to oneself* οὐ βίᾳ ...ἀλλὰ πειθοῖ ~εται Chrys.*hom.4.1 in Eph.*(11.26C); τοῦτο τῆς τοῦ θεοῦ φιλανθρωπίας, τὸ μὴ τυραννικῶς ~εσθαι id.*hom.5.2 in Col.*(11. 359D); *ib.10.4*(401B); **6.** *offer, present*; **a.** in gen., *T.Isach.*2.5; τοῦ ἀποκτεινννόντος...ἔνοχος καθίσταται ὁ ἑαυτὸν ~ων τῷ δικαστηρίῳ Clem.*str.*4.10(p.282.23; M.8.1285B); ἑαυτοὺς ἔλαθον ~όμενοι τῷ θεῷ *ib.*4.23(p.315.30; 1361A); οἷον εἰρήνης πρύτανιν ἐμαυτὸν...~ω Const. ap.Eus.*v.C.*2.68(p.68.11; M.20.1041A); ~ει τῷ θεῷ διὰ τῆς ἱερωσύνης τὸν ἄνδρα Gr.Nyss.*v.Gr.Thaum.*(M.46.937C); ἐμαυτὸν ἐγὼ τῇ σῇ προνοίᾳ ~ω Thdt.*Jer.*17:14(2.497); **b.** *pay* respect, etc. εὐλάβειαν ~ει τῷ θείῳ νόμῳ Clem.*str.*2.22(p.186.4; M.8.1081A); **c.** *put* question ἐρωτήσεις τινὰς ~αγών Thdt.*Dan.*1:20(2.1075); **d.** of Christ's offering of his body in Atonement, Ath.*inc.*8.4(M.25.109C); **e.** *offer* worship, esp. in sacrifice, *1Clem.*31.3; εἰ δὲ...τὴν θρησκείαν ~ουσιν αὐτῷ ταύτην, διαμαρτάνουσιν *Diogn.*3.2; δέον ἀναίμακτον θυσίαν τὴν λογικὴν ~ειν λατρείαν Athenag.*leg.*13.2(M.6.916C); λέγονται...τινὲς βουθυσίας ...τοῖς τοῦ Ἰησοῦ προσαγηοχέναι Eus.*d.e.*3.7(p.145.3; M.22.244C); τὰ ὅμοια θύοντες, τὰ αὐτὰ ~ειν δοκοῦσι Ath.*gent.*24(M.25.48C); οὐ ~εται τῷ δεσπότῃ τῷ σῷ. ὃ γὰρ θύει...τὰ ἔθνη, δαιμονίοις θύει Chrys.*hom. 24.3 in 1Cor.*(10.214E); τὴν Κωνσταντίνου εἰκόνα...θυσίαις τε ἱλάσκεσθαι...καὶ εὐχὰς ~ειν ὡς θεῷ...τοὺς Χριστιανοὺς κατηγορεῖ Philost. *h.e.*2.17(M.65.480A); ref. Sym. Styl. τὰς ὑπὲρ τῶν ἀνθρώπων πρεσβείας τῷ θεῷ ~ων Evagr.*h.e.*1.13(p.21.14; M.86.2453C); of eucharistic offering διὰ τοῦ κράματος τοῦ ποτηρίου, οὗ προσφέρουσιν οἱ μονοφυσῖται, οἶνον ἄκρατον...~οντες, ἐλέγχονται Anast.S.*hod.*1(M.89. 41B); τὸ γοῦν ~όμενον πολλοῖς ὀνόμασιν ὀνομάζεται· καλεῖται γὰρ εὐλογία, προσφορά, ἀπαρχή, ἄρτος ‡Sophr.H.*liturg.*9(M.87.3989A); **7.** intrans.; **a.** *approach, draw near* τῇ νοήσει τοῦ παντοκράτορος ἀμῇ γέ πῃ ~οιμεν Clem.*str.*5.11(p.374.14; M.9.109A); **b.** *move against, attack* προσάξαντες πρὸς αὐτοὺς ἐν κραταιᾷ μαχαίρᾳ περιεγενόμεθα αὐτῶν *T.Jud.*6.3; **c.** *continue* μᾶλλον προσῆγε λέγων *A.(Pass.)Andr.* 12(p.28.10; μᾶλλον προσετίθει τοῦ λέγειν M.2.1240B).

προσαγωγεύς, ὁ, 1. *one who brings into being*, of God as creator, Areth.*Apoc.*4:10(M.106.576B); **2.** *one who secures access*, of Sophia in prayer of Marcosians ὦ πάρεδρε θεοῦ καὶ...σιγῆς,...ἣν τὰ μεγέθη διαπαντὸς βλέποντα τὸ πρόσωπον τοῦ Πατρός, ὁδηγῷ σοι καὶ π. χρώμενα, ἀνασπῶσιν ἄνω τὰς αὐτῶν μορφὰς Iren.*haer.*1.13.6 (M.7.589A); of Christ προσαγωγέα καὶ ἀρχιερέα Gr.Naz.*or.*4.78(M. 35.604B).

προσαγωγή, ἡ, 1. *production*, in gen. τὸν καιρὸν ζητεῖν τῆς π. τῶν τοιούτων δογμάτων Or.*Jo.*20.2(p.328.27; M.14.576A); of Creation τῇ ἐνιαίᾳ τῶν ὅλων π. Dion.Ar.*d.n.*2.11(M.3.649B, v.l. παραγ-); **2.** *leading on, advancement, progression*, Clem.*paed.*2.9(p.207.14; M.8.496B); ὄντως γὰρ ἀτρέπτῳ πρὸς τὸ ἄτρεπτον ἡ π. id.*str.*2.11(p.141.7; M.8. 988B); θεμέλιος γνώσεως ἡ...ἐγκράτεια καὶ π. τις ἐπὶ τὸ βέλτιον *ib.*7.12 (p.50.19; M.9.497A); id.*q.d.s.*4(p.162.13; M.9.608C); τῶν ἀγνοουμένων καὶ προσαγωγῆς εἰς ἐπίγνωσιν δεομένων Dion.Al.ap.Ath.*Dion.*18 (p.60.7; M.25.508A); ref. Cant.5:8 εἶδες τοῦ πολέμου τὸ κατόρθωμα, τὴν π. τῶν πρὸ τούτου στασιαζόντων Cyr.*Ps.*44:6(M.69.1037A); **3.** *access* διὰ τοῦ συνθρόνου...τῆς θείας σοῦ φύσεως τὴν πρὸς σὲ καταλλαγὴν καὶ π. ἐν πεποιθήσει ἐφιλοτιμήσω ‡Meth.*Sym.et Ann.*8(M.18. 368A); **4.** *approach, manner of approaching* χρὴ...τὰς προσελεύσεις [sc. of children to Christ and children to Elisha] ἱστορῆσαι, καὶ εἰ μὲν ἴσαι εἰσὶν αἱ π., εὖ ἂν ἔχοι Adam.*dial.*1.16(p.32.29; M.11.1741C); **5.** *introduction* ἡ γραφὴ...τῶν ὀνομάτων ποιεῖται τὴν π. ‡Ath.*Apoll.* 2.2(M.26.1133C); **6.** *offering* ἐν ταῖς τῶν θυσιῶν π. παρὰ τῷ νόμῳ οἱ τῶν ἱερείων μωμοσκόποι Clem.*str.*4.18(p.299.32; M.8.1325B); ἡ δι' αἵματος λατρεία καὶ π. Cyr.*Is.*5.1(2.732C); ὁ...νόμος πλείστην ἔχει τὴν ἐπιτήρησιν περὶ θυσιῶν καὶ προσαγωγῆς id.*Soph.*32(3.609C); ἐπειδὴ ζωὴ...ὁ θεός, ταῖς τῶν ἐμψύχων π. ἐπιγάννυται Juln.Imp.ap.Cyr.*Juln.* 10(6^2.348B) = Proc.G.*Gen.*4:2(M.87.236C); **7.** *addition, accession*, of conversions to Christianity προσαγωγὰς...προσέφερε τῷ τοῦ θεοῦ νόμῳ *Hom.Clem.*11.34; of Christ's acquisition of human name, ‡Ath.*Apoll.*2.12(M.26.1152C).

*προσαγωγικός, *leading forward* (to), *introducing* (to) τὸ πρὸς τὰ θεῖα καὶ τὰ μυστικὰ θεάματα π. Dion.Ar.*c.h.*15.4(M.3.333A); id.*e.h.* 6.3.1(M.3.533C); ἀγάπην...ἐκστατικὴν οὖσαν τῶν ἐξ αὐτῆς καὶ προσαγωγικὴν τῶν δι' αὐτῆς Max.*ambig.*(M.91.1249B).

*προσαδολεσχέω, *be conversant with*, c. dat., Chrys.*hom.2.6 in 2Cor.*(10.437E); Dan.Raith.*v.Jo.Clim.*(M.88.601C).

προσαθύρ-ω, *play with*, Synes.*astrolab.*3(p.136.5; M.66.1581B); θεὸν...ταῖς ἀκακίαις μάλιστα τῶν ἁγίων ψυχῶν μονονουχὶ ~οντα Cyr. *Jon.*27(3.388B).

*προσαιτήτρια, ἡ, *beggar-woman*, *Hom.Clem.*12.23.

προσαῖτις, ἡ, = foreg., Mac.Aeg.*hom.*42.2(M.34.769D).

*προσακοντ-έω, *hurl lance against*, met. τὸ δὲ κακὸν ~οῦσιν Or. *exp.in Pr.*24:7(M.17.225C).

προσακοντίζω, *toss to*; of tossing a bone to a dog, Nil.*exerc.*19(M. 79.744C).

*προσακροάομαι, *be a hearer* (i.e. in a class of penitents), Jo. Clim.*scal.*12(M.88.856A).

*προσακτικός, *productive* of, Gr.Nyss.*hex.*9(M.44.72C).

*προσαλγέω, *feel pain*, Geo.Pis.*Pers.*1.31(M.92.1200A).

προσαλεύω, 1. *shake in advance* τοὺς νεκροὺς προεσάλευσαν of angels at Christ's entry into Jerusalem, Procl.CP *or.*9.3(M.65. 776A); **2.** *brandish before* προεσάλευε τῶν ὅπλων τὴν...κατὰ τοῦ θεοῦ γλωσσαλγίαν Cyr.*ador.*1(1.18E).

*προσαλλοίωσις, ἡ, *alteration* of countenance in feigning madness, Or.*sel.in Pss.*proem.(M.12.1069A).

*προσαμ-άομαι, *gather together* in harvest πολύχουν τῷ δεσπότῃ τὸν στάχυν ~ώμενοι Jo.D.*hom.*1.14(M.96.568C, edd. προσανιμώμενοι).

προσαμιλλάομαι, *contend against*, *Clem.ep.*18(M.2.53B).

*προσαναβλέπω, *look up to*, c. dat. Sophr.H.*v.Anast.*(M.92. 1724B).

προσανάγω, *carry up to*; of angels carrying martyr up to Christ, *M.Thdot.*3(p.139.8).

*προσαναδείκνυμι, *proceed to show*, Tit.Bost.*Man.*2.3(M.18. 1140A; perh. for προαν-).

*προσαναδενδρόομαι, *spring up besides*, Nil.*exerc.*55(M.79.788C).

*προσαναθλίβω, *compress*, Clem.*paed.*2.10(p.209.15; M.8.500B).

*προσαναισχυντέω, *behave with fresh impudence*, Philost.*h.e.*2.11 (M.65.476A).

*προσανακαινόομαι, *begin afresh*, Cyr.ap.*cat.Lc.*9:51(p.81.17) for προσανακοιν-, Cyr.*Lc.*9:61f.(*TU* p.98.10).

προσανάκειμαι, *be devoted to*, Clem.*str.*6.10(p.471.20; M.9.300C); ἡ πᾶσα τῶν Ἐδεσσηνῶν πόλις τῇ Χριστοῦ προσανάκειται προσηγορίᾳ Eus.*h.e.*2.1.7(M.20.137A); Μαγνέντιον...καὶ τοὺς σὺν αὐτῷ...τῇ τῶν δαιμόνων θεραπείᾳ προσανακειμένους Philost.*h.e.*3.26(M.65.513A).

*προσανακλαίω, **1.** *mourn in company* with, Synes.*ep.*29(M.66. 1357C); *ib.*57(1392C); *ib.*73(1437A); **2.** *utter lamentations*, Niceph. Ur.*v.Sym.*39(M.86.3021C).

προσανακλίν-ω, pass., **1.** *lie down on* τῇ κλίνῃ προσανακλιθεὶς Niceph.Ur.*v.Sym.*196(M.86.3165B); **2.** *keep one's bed* τρίτον...ἔτος ἱεροῖς ~όμενος οἴκοις *ib.*100(3080B); **3.** met., *rest upon, rely upon* ἀνθρωπίνοις ἐντάλμασι π. Cyr.*ador.*5(1.166C).

προσανακοιν-όομαι, *consult, take counsel* with ~οῦσθαι...τοῖς κατὰ γένος οἰκείοις Cyr.*Lc.*9:61f.(*TU* p.98.10).

προσαναλύω, *dissolve into*, c. dat., ‡Caes.Naz.*dial.*109(M.38.984).

*προσανάλωμα, τό, *wasteful expenditure*, †Dion.Al.*fr.Eccl.*2:1 (p.221.13; M.10.1585A).

*προσαναμάσσομαι, *be besmirched*, Bas.*hom.in Ps.*1(1.96B; M.29. 225A).

προσαναμένω, *continue with, dwell on*, c. dat., Cyr.*Ps.*76:19(M.69. 1193C).

*προσαναπαράγω, v. *προσαντιπαράγω.

προσαναπείθω, *persuade besides*, Cyr.*ador.*6(1.199C).

προσαναπλάσσ-ω, 1. *form in addition* τοὺς μηχανικοὺς...τῶν μεγάλων...οἰκοδομημάτων ἐν ὀλίγῳ κηρῷ...τοὺς τύπους ~ουσιν Gr. Nyss.*res.*3(M.46.665D ? for προαν-); **2.** *invent in addition* μοῖραν μοίρας, καὶ ἀνάγκης ἀνάγκην ~ων id.*fat.*(M.45.161C); **3.** s.v.l., *dash against* τοῦτον δὲ εἶναι τὸν πλοῦν...οὐκ ἄν, εἴ γε παρὰ τὰς ἀκτὰς ἐπλέομεν· προσαναπεπλάσθαι γὰρ ἂν τῇ γῇ Synes.*ep.*4(M.66.1332B; perh. for ⟨προσαναπεπλῆσθαι⟩).

προσαναπληρόω, 1. *fill up*, Athenag.*leg.*17.2(M.6.924A); **2.** *complete*, Clem.*paed.*1.3(p.94.22; M.8.257B); Pall.*v.Chrys.*1(p.3.30; M. 47.5); Jo.D.*f.o.*4.14(M.94.1156A).

*προσαναπνέω, *breathe freely again*, Dion.Al.ap.Eus.*h.e.*6.41.9 (M.20.608B).

*προσανάρρησις, ἡ, *utterance* προφητῶν π. Cyr.*Juln.*7(6^2.239C; prob. for προαν-).

*προσανασύρω, *hold up*, Philost.*h.e.*7.10(M.65.549A).

προσανατείν-ω, 1. *lift up*; pass., of ear of corn springing from stalk, †Ath.*fr.Mt.*(M.27.1372B); of spiritual aspiration ~ομεν τὴν κεφαλὴν καὶ τὰς χεῖρας εἰς οὐρανὸν αἴρομεν Clem.*str.*7.7(p.30.19; M.9. 456B); **2.** *present* appeal to emperor, CCP(449)*act.*(*ACO* 2.1.1 p.157. 5; H.2.181E).

προσανατρέπω, *overthrow*, Epiph.*haer.*56.3(p.342.24; M.41.993C).

*προσαναφαίνω, for προαν-, Cyr.*ador.*10(1.328C); id.*hom.pasch.* 14(5^2.187D).

προσαναφέρ-ω, 1. *offer* worship to God ἑνὶ θεῷ...ποιῶ τὴν πᾶσαν ~ων τιμὴν *Hom.Clem.*16.12; εὐχὰς τῷ θεῷ ~οντες Eus.*v.C.*4.45(p.136.

21; M.20.1196B); 2. *report* προσανήνεγκεν δὲ αὐτῷ περὶ τοῦ τέκτονος ὃν μετ' αὐτοῦ ἤγαγεν *A.Thom.*17(p.124.7); in lawsuits between Christians ἐπὶ τῶν πρεσβυτέρων συμβιβαζέσθωσαν. τὸν δὲ συμβιβασμὸν οἱ πρεσβύτεροι τῷ ἐπισκόπῳ ~έτωσαν *Hom.Clem.*3.67; *ib.* 20.13; Const.ap.Eus.*h.e.*10.6.5(M.20.893A); τὴν ἡμετέραν πίστιν ὑμῖν ~ομεν Eus.*ep.Caes.*(p.43.8; M.20.1537B).

***προσαναφωνέω**, prob. for προανα- q.v., Clem.*str.*3.11(M.8.1172C; προ- p.228.14); Didym.*Trin.*2.21(M.39.553B); Gel.Cyz.*h.e.*2.16.19 (M.85.1264D προ-).

***προσαναχαιτίζω**, ?*flow up to*, of healing of blind person τὴν κεφαλὴν τοῦ πηροῦ ἐξύρησεν, ἵνα τὸ ῥεῦμα προσαναχαιτίσῃ Leont.B. *mesopent.*(M.86.1984B).

προσανέχ-ω, 1. *attach, fix upon* τὴν ἐλπίδα...ταῖς τῶν μορίων ἀναισχυντίαις ~οντες Clem.*str.*3.18(p.246.30; M.8.1212C); 2. *attend to, devote oneself to*, *ib.*1.21(p.82.23; M.8.868B); ἀπόστολοι...τῷ κηρύγματι ~οντες *ib.*3.6(p.220.20; 1157A); μὴ τοῖς αἰσθητοῖς ~ωμεν *ib.*5.5(p.344. 11; M.9.49B); Μαρίαν δὲ τῇ θεωρίᾳ μόνῃ...~ουσαν Or.*fr.39 in Lc.* 10:38(p.252; M.17.353A); Gr.Thaum.*pan.Or.*14(p.31.6; M.10.1089B); Mac.Aeg.*perf.*13(M.34.849C); Chrys.*hom.13.2 in 1Tim.*(11.620A); Synes.*Dion* 1(p.237.17; M.66.1117B); 3. *trust in, put one's confidence in*; idols etc., Clem.*prot.*4(p.45.25; M.8.157A); εἰ γάρ τις ὑπὸ τῆς ὕλης θεραπεύεται πιστεύων αὐτῇ, θεραπευθήσεται μᾶλλον αὐτὸς δυνάμει θεοῦ ~ων Tat.*orat.*18(p.19.28; M.6.845A); Eus.*d.e.*4.10(p.167.13; M. 22.277D).

[*]**προσανιάω**, *cause distress*, Synes.*ep.*46(M.66.1376A).

[*]**προσαντιβάλλ-ω**, 1. *bring to notice of* τοὺς δὲ...νοσοῦντας μανθανέτωσαν [sc. οἱ διάκονοι], καὶ τῷ ἀγνοοῦντι πλήθει ~έτωσαν *Clem.ep.*12(M.2.48B); 2. *put up in defence* πάλους ~ειν Geo.Pis.*bell. Avar.*273(M.92.1280A).

***προσαντικρούω**, *dash against*, Geo.Pis.*Pers.*2.115(M.92.1219B).

***προσαντιλέγω**, *speak in opposition*, Pall.*h.Laus.*32(p.92.8; M.34. 1100C); id.*v.Chrys.*15(p.89.20; M.47.51).

***προσαντιπαράγω**, *introduce by way of a digression*, Hipp.*haer.*9. 8(p.241.12; προσαναπαραχθῆναι M.16.3371B).

***προσαντιτείνω**, *resist*, c. dat., Geo.Pis.*bell.Avar.*391(M.92.1286A).

***προσαξία**, ἡ, *offering*, Thdot.Anc.*hom.BMV et Sym.*3(M.77. 1393A).

προσαπαντάω, *go to meet*; c.acc., *T.Isach.*1.3(v.l. προαπ-); c. dat., *A.Phil.*124(p.53.8); *cat.Lc.*15:20(p.119.14); cf.Clem.*str.*6.9(M.9.297B; ed. προαπ- p.470.5).

προσαπαρτίζω, *complete by the addition* of, Gr.Nyss.*Eun.*7(2 p.171.6; M.45.761C).

προσαπειλέω, *threaten further*, Clem.*paed.*3.12(p.286.21; M.8. 672A).

***προσαπεκδύομαι**, *strip further*, Gr.Naz.*or.*4.124(M.35.664B).

προσαπερείδω, 1. act., *make to rest upon*, hence *apply to* τῷ δὲ σώματι μόνῳ τὸν λογισμὸν προσαπήρεισε [sc. Audaeus] Thdt.*haer.* 4.10(4.364); 2. med., *rest upon*, Synes.*insomn.*15(p.177.20; M.66. 1309C).

***προσαπλόω**, *make level with*, Sophr.H.*v.Anast.*(M.92.1720A).

***προσαποκαλύπτω**, *reveal*, Nil.*epp.*2.230(M.79.320A).

***προσαπολιμπάνω**, *leave to, leave in* someone's *hands*, Philost. *h.e.*6.3(M.65.536A).

***προσαπολογέομαι**, *apologize*; of judge apologizing for a person's wrongful arrest, Pall.*h.Laus.*46(p.135.16; ἀπελογήσατο M.34. 1225D); Thphn.*chron.*p.387(M.108.924D).

***προσαπομένω**, *remain fixed*, Bas.*hex.*3.9(1.31B; M.29.73D).

***προσαπομνημονεύω**, *mention besides*, Vict.*Mc.*10:32(p.383.25, v.l. προαπ-).

προσαπονέμω, *attribute*, Eustrat.*stat.anim.*5(p.350); v. προαπονέμω.

***προσαπονίζω**, *proceed to cleanse*, Cyr.*ador.*9(1.312B).

***προσαποπληρόω**, *complete besides*, Clem.*str.*4.1(p.248.5; M.8. 1216A).

προσαποσείω, med., *shake off besides*, Cyr.*ador.*4(1.119A).

***προσαποτείνω**, med., *inveigh against*, c. dat., Clem.*str.*3.11 (p.230.8; M.8.1176B).

***προσαποτινάσσω**, *shake off*, Bas.Sel.*or.*37.4(M.85.397A).

προσαπόφημι, *declare in addition*, Sev.Ant.ap.Leont.H.*monoph.* (M.86.1848B; perh. for προαπ-).

προσαποφωνέω, *declare besides*, Cyr.*hom.pasch.*26.2(5[2].307E).

***προσαποχράομαι**, *abuse*, c. dat., Bas.Sel.*or.*35.1(M.85.376A) cit. s. αὐτεξούσιος.

προσάπτ-ω, 1. *attribute* τούτῳ καὶ ἡ αἰτία...~εται Clem.*str.*1.17 (p.53.20; M.8.797A); ὕλην αὐτῷ [sc. θεῷ] ~ειν Meth.*arbitr.*8(p.165.7); *Hom.Clem.*10.9; τὰς ἀνθρώπων θεοῖς π. ἐννοίας Ath.*gent.*16(M.25. 33B); τὰ ἀνθρωπολογούμενα οἱ ἀμαθέστατοι τῇ θεότητι ἀσεβῶς ~ουσι Didym.(‡Bas.)*Eun.*5(1.313B; M.29.752A); Cyr.*expl.xii cap.*4(p.20.2; 6[1].150D) cit. s. ἀνθρώπινος; 2. med., *have to do with, participate in*, ref. necessity for Christ's death εἰ...δύο πέρασι τῆς...ζωῆς διειλημμένης, ἐν τῷ ἑνὶ γενόμενος τοῦ ἐφεξῆς μὴ προσήψατο, ἡμιτελὴς ἂν ἡ πρόθεσις ἔμεινε Gr.Nyss.*or.catech.*32(p.115.12; M.45.80A).

προσαπωθέω, *reject, push away besides*, Pall.*v.Chrys.*20(p.141.25; M.47.79).

***προσαρμοστέον**, *one must accommodate*, Didym.(‡Bas.)*Eun.*5 (1.306B; M.29.734C).

***προσαρόω**, *cultivate with a view to* προσαρώσαντες ἑαυτοὺς τοῦ βαπτίσματος Gr.Naz.*or.*40.22(M.36.388C).

***προσάρραξις**, ἡ, *assault*, CCP(681)*or.imp.*(H.3.1420A).

***προσαρρωστέω**, *be infected further*, Cyr.*Ag.*16(3.646D); v. *προαρρωστέω.

προσάρτημα, τό, *appendage*, Clem.*str.*2.20(p.174.6; M.8.1056B); *ib.*(p.175.1; 1057B).

***προσαρτίζω**, *make fast to*, Thphn.*chron.*p.372(M.108.892C).

***προσάρτυσις**, ἡ, *seasoning*, Nil.*epp.*3.106(M.79.433C).

προσασκέω, *exercise towards, direct* the eye *towards*, †Jo.Jej. *paraen.*(p.236).

προσαστράπτ-ω, *shine upon* δόξης...~ούσης ταῖς ἡμετέραις ψυχαῖς Gr.Naz.*or.*8.23(M.35.816C); *ib.*31.32(p.188.8; M.36.169C); id.*carm.*1. 2.8.139(M.37.659A).

***προσασφαλίζομαι**, *make secure*, Max.*schol.myst.*4(M.4.428D).

προσασχολ-έω, 1. intrans., *be occupied with, be engaged in* τῇ πρὸς τὸ παρὸν ἀεὶ περὶ τὰ καλὰ διασκέψει ~εῖν ‡Bas.*const.*17.1(2. 559E; M.31.1380B); med. ~εῖσθαι τῇ θεωρίᾳ Ephr.1.273A; id.3.116D; Gr.Nyss.*hex.*4(M.44.65A); 2. trans.; a. *compel attention to, engage* a person *upon* ἡ ἀρετὴ τῆς γυναικὸς...ἰδίοις ἀλγήμασι ~ήσασα τὸν ἀλάστορα [i.e. of Sarah and Pharoah] ‡Nil.*perist.*11.6(M.79.912D); b. *turn* the mind *towards* μηδενὶ τῶν βιωτικῶν πραγμάτων ~εῖν τὴν διάνοιαν Gr.Nyss.*virg.*6(p.280.5; M.46.349D); Nil.*epp.*2.257(M.79. 332C); id.*Magn.*55(M.79.1041A).

***προσατενίζω**, *gaze steadfastly at*, c. dat., *Asen.*8(p.49.15).

***προσατιμάζω**, *disgrace in addition*, Thphn.*chron.*p.389(M.108. 929A).

προσαύξησις, ἡ, *increase* in amount, Ath.Scholast.*coll.*10.6 (p.123).

***προσαυτομολέω**, *desert to* the enemy, c. dat., Geo.Pis.*Pers.*3. 145(M.92.1243B).

***προσαφαρπάζω**, *seize besides*, †Jo.D.*B.J.*23(M.96.1068A).

[*]**προσαφίημι**, 1. *leave to*, Bas.*reg.fus.*9.1(2.351C; M.31.941B); 2. *give up in addition*, †Bas.*bapt.*1.2.12(2.637E; M.31.1545B); 3. *forgive*, Max.*ep.*9(M.91.448B).

προσβάλλ-ω, 1. *encounter, come into contact with* τότε...ὁ νοῦς ~ει χωρὶς αἰσθήσεως τοῖς νοητοῖς Or.*or.*25(p.358.11; M.11.497B); id. *fr.45 in Jo.*(p.521.4); οὐδενὸς τῶν γενητῶν προσβαλεῖν αὐτῷ χωρὶς ὁδηγοῦ δυναμένου id.*Jo.*1.38(42; p.49.7; M.14.100A); τὸ φῶς τὸ θεῖον ...ᾧ μὴ δύναται προσβαλεῖν μηδέν Max.*schol.d.n.*7.1(M.4.341A); 2. *attend to* ταῖς τοιαύταις ζητήσεσιν οὐ ~ω Just.*dial.*71.2(M.6.644A); Eus.*v.C.*2.23(p.50.22; M.20.1001A); *Pers.*(p.6.5); 3. *attain to understanding* of δυσέφικτον...τὸ προσβαλεῖν...τοῖς ὧδε διεσταλμένοις Cyr. *ador.*4(1.115E); id.*Is.*1.4(2.104B); 4. *arrive at* ~ει τῇ πόλει Chrys. *hom.65.1 in Mt.*(7.643D); 5. *bring into contact with* σάρκα περιεβάλετο, ἵνα μὴ γυμνῇ τῇ θεότητι προσβαλὼν ἅπαντας ἀπολέσῃ id.*hom. 6.1 in Jo.*(8.43A); 6. *come near to, resemble* ἥλιος δικαιοσύνης ὁ σωτὴρ λέγεται...ὁ ~ων τῷ ὑπερέχοντι τῶν αἰσθητῶν Didym.*Ps.*18:6 (M.39.1269A).

***προσβαρέομαι**, *be weighed down, encumbered*, Thdr.Stud.*epp.*2. 134(M.99.1429D).

***προσβάσιμος**, *facing towards*, Cyr.*Jo.*4.5(4.397A).

πρόσβασις, ἡ, 1. *progression* τὸν γηγενῆ εἰς ἅγιον καὶ ἐπουράνιον μεταπλάσας ἐκ π. ἄνθρωπον Clem.*paed.*1.12(p.148.22; M.8.368A); 2. *succession* κατὰ πρόσβασιν ἀριθμοῦ Iren.*haer.*1.15.2(M.7.617A); Cosm.Ind.*top.*2(M.88.100C); Anast.S.*qu.et resp.*96(M.89.748A).

***προσβασκανία**, ἡ, *witchery*, *Pap.Chr.*(p.420).

προσβολή, ἡ, 1. *ray* of light φωτὸς ἡλίου...π. Eus.*d.e.*4.5(p.157.11; M.22.261C); *ib.*4.6(p.159.13; 265B); ‡Eust.*hex.*(M.18.721D); of divine illumination, Cyr.*ador.*10(1.353D); 2. *glance* πάντα...μιᾷ π. προσβλέπει Clem.*str.*6.17(p.512.25; M.9.388C); τὴν π. τῆς θεωρίας *ib.*7.7 (p.33.22; 464B); ὁ νοῦς...ἰδεῖν τὸν θεὸν οὐ δύναται κατὰ προσβολὴν νοήσεως Or.*fr.13 in Jo.*(p.495.20); πρώτῃ ὄψεως π. *ib.45*(p.521.6); Didym.*Trin.*3.16(M.39.873B); 3. *outburst* of tears, Thdr.Stud.*epp.* 1.42(M.99.1061D); 4. *encounter*, hence *acquaintance, understanding* ταῖς πρώταις τῶν τεττάρων εὐαγγελίων τοῦ γράμματος προσβολαῖς ἐμβιβάζων Eus.*h.e.*10.4.63(M.20.876A); **5.** *approach*, Cyr.*ador.*13(1.467D); **6.** *attack, assault*, esp. of sin and evil and as synon. for *temptation*, Clem.*ecl.*9(p.139.14; M.9.701C); Meth.*res.*2.1(p.330.1; M.18.297A); τὴν τῆς ἁμαρτίας...π. Ath.*exp.Ps.*44:5(M.27.209B); Χριστὸς τὴν π. τῶν λογισμῶν ἀπεκώλυσε τῆς καρδίας Marc.Er.*opusc.*4(M.65.1000A); δεδόσθω ὅτι τὴν παράβασιν θελήματι ἔσχεν ὁ Ἀδάμ...μὴ καὶ τὴν π. θελήματι ἔσχεν; ναί. τὴν π. κατὰ ἀνάγκην ἔσχεν. ἀλλ' ἡ π. οὔτε ἁμαρτία ἐστίν, οὔτε δικαιοσύνη, ἀλλ' ἔλεγχος τοῦ αὐτεξουσίου ἡμῶν θελήματος. διὸ καὶ προσβάλλειν ἡμῖν παρεχωρήθη, ἵνα τοὺς μὲν...ἀποδείξῃ ὡς πιστούς, τοὺς δὲ...ὡς ἀπίστους *ib.*(1020A); ἐκ π. πολλοὶ λογισμοί, ἐκ δὲ τούτων ἡ πονηρὰ αἰσθητὴ πρᾶξις Hesych.S.*temp.*1.86 (M.93.1508A).

***προσβόλιον, τό,** *point of contact* ἡ ἀνάλυσις [sc. of snake's head] τοῖς τῶν λεπίδων π. ἀντισπωμένη Nil.*epp.*3.130(M.79.444C).

***προσβρέχω,** *rain* tears, *A.Jo.*24(p.164.11).

***προσγεγονότως,** *by way of addition*, Cyr.*Jo.*2.2(4.163E).

προσγενής, ὁ, *kinsman*, Cyr.*ador.*4(1.138E); Philost.*h.e.*8.6(M.65.561A); Evagr.*h.e.*5.1(p.196.2; M.86.2789B).

***προσγεννάω,** *beget in addition*, of Son acc. Eunomians οὐδὲ ἀκούειν δοκῶν οὕτως ἡμῖν...ἐμβοῶντος τό, ἦν, οὐκ ὤν, φησίν, ἐγεννήθη· οὐκοῦν ὕστερον προσγεγέννηται Bas.*Eun.*2.15(1.250E; M.29.604A); *cat. Apoc.*16:2(p.410.22; for προσγενήσεται); v. προσγίγνομαι.

προσγί(γ)ν-ομαι, *come into existence in addition, accrue*; theol., of Son's generation ἕως ἂν...μηδεμίαν ἔχῃς αἰτίαν εἰπεῖν, καθ' ἣν εὐσεβές ἐστιν ὕστερον τῷ πατρὶ τὸν υἱὸν προσγεγενῆσθαι λέγειν Gr. Nyss.*Eun.*9(2 p.211.8, v.l. προσγεγεννῆσθαι; M.45.809A); τῶν ὕστερον τῷ θεῷ διὰ κτίσεως τὸν υἱὸν προσγεγενῆσθαι λεγόντων τὴν βλασφημίαν ἐλέγχεσθαι *ib.*(p.225.14; 825A); εἰ ἡ μὲν ὑποστᾶσα φύσις ἔξωθεν προσεγένετο ἀπαράλλακτος εἶναι οὐ δύναται ‡Ath.*dial.Trin.*2.12(M.28.1177A); Jo.D.*f.o.*1.7(M.94.805A); of Inc. οὐ γὰρ ἀσώματον εἶδος αὐτῷ ἀσωμάτου οὐσίας προσεγένετο ὅπερ ἦν αὐτός, ἀλλὰ τὸ σωματικόν Gel.Cyz.*h.e.*2.24.11(M.85.1300D); οὐ διὰ μέσης σαρκὸς ἀψύχου λογικὴν ψυχὴν προσδέξασθαι ~ομένην Max.*ambig.*(M.91.1341B).

***προσγόνιμος,** *procreative*, Or.*fr.in Ps.*1(p.71).

***προσδεκτικός,** *willing to receive, receptive*, Clem.*paed.*3.11(p.268.15; M.8.629A).

προσδεκτός, *acceptable* to God ἴδωμεν τί καλὸν καὶ...τί π. ἐνώπιον τοῦ ποιήσαντος ἡμᾶς *1Clem.*7.3; ἡ ἔντευξις τοῦ πένητος π. ἐστι...πρὸς τὸν θεόν Herm.*sim.*2.6; of martyr's death as acceptable sacrifice, *M.Polyc.*14.2; of purification of soul as acceptable sacrifice typified by levitical offerings of dove or pigeon, Clem.*str.*7.6(p.24.24; M.9.445A).

προσδέχ-ομαι, A. *receive*; **1.** into communion, ref. lapsed in persecution εἰ δὲ καὶ ἐκωλύθησαν ὑπό τινος, περισσοτέρας ἀκριβείας ἕνεκεν ἢ καί τινων ἀγνοίᾳ, εὐθὺς προσδεχθῆναι CAnc.(314)*can.*3; ref. admission of heretics περὶ τοὺς ἐκ τῶν...Ναυατιανῶν ἤτοι Φωτεινιανῶν ἢ Τεσσαρεσκαιδεκατιτῶν ἐπιστρεφομένους...τοὺς παρ' ἐκείνοις μὴ ~εσθαι, πρὶν ἀναθεματίσωσι πᾶσαν αἵρεσιν CLaod.*can.*7; ref. penitents, *Const.App.*2.12.4; *ib.*2.21.7; ref. energumens ἐὰν δέ τις δαίμονα ἔχῃ, διδασκέσθω μὲν τὴν εὐσέβειαν, μὴ ~έσθω δὲ εἰς κοινωνίαν, πρὶν ἂν καθαρισθῇ· εἰ δὲ θάνατος κατεπείγοι, ~έσθω *ib.*8.32.6; ἐάν τις δαίμονα ἔχῃ, κληρικὸς μὴ γινέσθω, ἀλλὰ μηδὲ τοῖς πιστοῖς συνευχέσθω· καθαρισθεὶς δὲ ~έσθω, καὶ ἐὰν ᾖ ἄξιος, γινέσθω *Can.App.*79; **2.** *receive as, interpret as* δόγματα...κατ' ἐπιθυμίαν τῆς σαρκὸς ὡς περὶ βρώσεως προσεδέξαντο *Barn.*10.9; **3.** *admit*, ref. Christ's natures μὴ ἀφορᾶν εἰς ἕνα μὲν οὐ προσκυνητόν· μηδὲ ἐν αὐτῷ εἶναι τὸν μὲν οὐκ ἀνεχόμενον προσκυνεῖσθαι, τὸν δὲ ~όμενον τὴν...προσκύνησιν Apoll.*fr.*9(p.207.1)ap.Leont.B.*Apoll.*(M.86.1973B); theol. χωρισμὸν ἡ τριὰς οὐ ~εται Didym.(‡Bas.)*Eun.*5(1.304A; M.29.729A); in gen. δέδοικα τὸν τοιοῦτον προσδέξασθαι λόγον Max.*ambig.*(M.91.1341A); **4.** *receive, be subjected to* π. τὰς ἐπιφορὰς τοῦ τῆς ἀνοίας...κύματος Meth.*symp.*4.2(p.47.7; M.18.88D); **5.** *accept*; **a.** as valid; of Donatist acceptance of Maximianists' baptisms, tr. Lat. *acceptaverunt*, *Cod. Afr.*69; **b.** of God ἕως πάλιν...οἰκτειρήσῃ καὶ προσδέξηται ὑμᾶς *T.Lev.*16.5; δῶμεν...αὐτῷ αἶνον αἰώνιον...ἵνα ἡμᾶς προσδέξηται ὡς υἱούς *2Clem.*9.10; οὐ δέεσθαι τῆς...ὑλικῆς προσφορᾶς προσειλήφαμεν τὸν θεόν,...ἐκείνους δὲ ~εσθαι...τοὺς τὰ...ἀγαθὰ μιμουμένους Just.*1apol.*10.1(M.6.340C); ref. acceptance of sacrifices, id.*dial.*117.2(M.6.745B); *Const.App.*7.5.5; of prayer, *Lit.*ap.*Const.App.*8.6.5; of incense in liturgy, *Lit.Jac.*(p.170.6); of eucharistic oblation, *ib.*(p.224.4); ref. martyr's death as a sacrifice, *M.Polyc.*14.2.

B. *await, expect* Χριστιανοὶ...τὴν...ἀφθαρσίαν ~όμενοι *Diogn.*6.8; αἱ γνωστικαὶ ψυχαί, ἃς ἀπείκασεν τὸ εὐαγγέλιον ταῖς...παρθένοις ταῖς ~ομέναις τὸν κύριον Clem.*str.*7.12(p.52.11; M.9.500C).

προσδιαιρέω, *distribute, apportion* among, Bas.*renunt.*6(2.208A; M.31.640B).

***προσδιαμαρτύρομαι,** *raise objection*, Cyr.*ador.*2(1.53E).

***προσδιασαφηνίζω,** *make more abundantly clear*, ‡Chrys.*Spir.*2(3.799C).

προσδιαστέλλω, *add*; of heret. doctrine added to Christian gospel, Serap.Ant.ap.Eus.*h.e.*6.12.6(M.20.545C); in gen., Bas.*ep.*125.3(3.217A; M.32.549D).

***προσδιαστολή, ἡ,** *separation*, Cyr.*glaph.Lev.*(1.362E).

***προσδιωρισμένως, 1.** *making a distinction*, Max.*qu.Thal.*51(M.90.477B); **2.** *with qualification* οὐσία...πάντων τῶν ἀρετῶν αὐτός ἐστιν ὁ κύριος...ὡς γέγραπται· ὃς ἐγενήθη...σοφία, δικαιοσύνη...ἀπολύτως ταῦτα...ἐπ' αὐτοῦ λεγόμενα ἔχων, ὡς αὐτοσοφία καὶ δικαιοσύνη...ὤν, καὶ οὐχ ὡς ἐφ' ἡμῶν π., οἷον ὡς...δίκαιος ἄνθρωπος id.*ambig.*(M.91.1081D).

προσδοκ-άω, *expect*; **1.** of expectation of Christ, in OT οἱ προφῆται...ὡς διδάσκαλον αὐτὸν προσεδόκων Ign.*Magn.*9.2; eschatol., id.*Polyc.*3.2; ref. Gen.49:10–11 ἐκ πάντων τῶν ἐθνῶν ~ήσουσιν αὐτὸν...ἐκ πάντων γὰρ γενῶν ἀνθρώπων ~ῶσι τὸν ἐν Ἰουδαίᾳ σταυρωθέντα Just.*1apol.*32.4(M.6.377C); τὰ ἔθνη, πιστεύοντα ἐπὶ τὸν παθητὸν Χριστόν, πάλιν παραγενησόμενον προσδοκήσει id.*dial.*52.1(M.6.589B); of Christ's promises, *ib.*53.1(592C); **2.** of future life ~ῶντες ἀνάστασιν νεκρῶν καὶ ζωὴν τοῦ μέλλοντος αἰῶνος Arist.*apol.*15.3; Clem.*str.*2.20 (p.172.19; M.8.1053A); Meth.*res.*3.5(p.394.5; M.18.317C); τῆς μελλούσης εὐδαιμονίας τὴν ἐλπίδα οὐ μόνον ~ῶμεν ἀλλ' ὥσπερ τινὶ τρόπῳ ἤδη κατέχομεν Const.ap.Gel.Cyz.*h.e.*2.7.20(M.85.1236D); ὁ δὲ...ἀκόλαστος βίος οὐχὶ ~ωμένην εἰς ὕστερον, ἀλλ' ἤδη παροῦσαν προτείνεται τὴν ἀπόλαυσιν Bas.*hom.in Ps.*1(1.95D; M.29.224A); Gr.Nyss. *v.Mos.*(M.44.369B); **3.** of judgement, *Hom.Clem.*3.61; *ib.*19.19; **4.** of Jewish nationalist expectation, Meth.*symp.*4.4(p.50.14; M.18.93A).

προσδοκία, ἡ, A. *expectation*; **1.** in rel. to faith ἡ μὲν πίστις ὑπόληψις ἑκούσιος καὶ πρόληψις εὐγνώμων πρὸ καταλήψεως, π. δὲ [δόξα] μέλλοντος· ἡ δὲ τῶν ἄλλων π. δόξα ἀδήλου Clem.*str.*2.6(p.128.2; M.8.964A); and hope, *ib.*2.9(p.134.17; 976B) cit. s. ἐλπίς; **2.** of expectation of Christ among Jews and Greeks, Eus.*d.e.*2.1(p.53.3; M.22.97C); **3.** ref. future life, Clem.*str.*3.12(p.236.15; M.8.1188C); and judgement, *Hom.Clem.*4.14.

B. *object of expectation*; of Christ [Χριστὸς] ἡ π. τῶν ἀπὸ πάντων τῶν ἐθνῶν ἀναμενόντων τὰ παρὰ τοῦ θεοῦ ἀγαθά Just.*dial.*11.4(M.6.500A); *Didasc.Jac.*(p.760.12); of BMV, Jo.Thess.*dorm.BMV* 2.4 (p.411.30).

***προσδροσίζω,** *damp down*, Ephr.3.85D.

***προσδυσωπέω,** *beseech earnestly*, Jo.VI H.*v.Jo.D.*30(M.94.469C).

προσδωρέομαι, *give in addition*, Marc.Er.*opusc.*4(M.65.1008B); Thdot.Anc.*hom.BMV et Sym.*4(M.77.1396A).

***προσεγγιάζω,** *secure access to*, Diod.*Ps.*54:2(M.33.1591D).

προσεγγίζ-ω, 1. *approach*; ref. contact of Devil with Christ resulting in defeat of evil through Atonement, Gr.Nyss.*or.catech.*26 (p.99.1; M.45.68D); of approach of soul to God, Or.*Cant.*1:8(p.143.30; M.17.257A); πλησίον γίνεται τῆς δεσποτικῆς ἀγαθότητος, διὰ τῆς πρὸς τὸν πλησίον ἀγάπης τῷ θεῷ προσεγγίσασα Gr.Nyss.*hom.7 in Cant.*(M.44.917B); φόβῳ δουλικῷ, καὶ οὐχὶ ἔρωτι νυμφικῷ τῷ ἀγαθῷ ~ουσαν, παλλακὴν ἀντὶ τῆς βασιλίδος *ib.15*(1115B); through good works, Bas.*reg.fus.*proem.1(2.328A; M.31.892B); ref. divine grace casting into greater sin those who approach God wrongly, Gr.Naz.*or.*9.2(M.35.821B); ref. divine approach to man ἐξελέξατο κύριος ~ειν αὐτῷ *T.Jud.*21.5; **2.** *have sexual intercourse* with, *V.Dan.*(p.375.1).

***προσεγγισμός, ὁ, 1.** *drawing near, approach*; **a.** in gen. †Bas.*Is.*27(1.400D; M.30.172A); πῦρ διὰ τοῦ π. τὴν πονηρὰν φλόγα κατεργαζόμενον Gr.Nyss.*v.Mos.*(M.44.424C); τὸ ἀπρόσιτον τὸν τοῦ ἐναντίου π. οὐ προσίεται id.*Eun.*12(2 p.282.32; M.45.893D); Max.*ambig.*(M.91.1201C); **b.** astrol. ὁ...ἐπεσκεμμένος...τί δὲ ἡ σύνοδος αὐτῶν [sc. ἄστρων] ἐκ τῆς ποιᾶς πρὸς ἄλληλα κράσεως ἀπεργάζεται, τῆς κατὰ δύναμιν ἑκάστου αὐτῶν ἰδιότητος μιχθείσης τε τῷ π. πρὸς τὴν ἑτέραν, καὶ ἀποκριθείσης διὰ τῆς ἀποστάσεως Gr.Nyss.*fat.*(M.45.149C); ἡ ποικίλη κατὰ τοὺς π. αὐτῶν καὶ τὰς ἀποστάσεις γινομένη τῶν διαφόρων ἰδιωμάτων συμπλοκή *ib.*(152D); **c.** mental and spiritual προφῆτις ἡ Μαρία, ᾗ προσῆλθε κατὰ τὸν π. τὸν διὰ τῆς γνώσεως ὁ Ἡσαΐας †Bas.*Is.*208(1.535A; M.30.477B); ref. object of soul's quest πάντως ἐξώτερος ἦν, τὸν π. τῆς διανοίας διαδιδράσκων Gr.Nyss.*hom.12 in Cant.*(M.44.1028B); φησὶ πρὸς αὐτὴν ὁ λόγος, ὅτι γέγονας ἤδη καλὴ πλησιάσασα τῷ ἐμῷ φωτί, διὰ τοῦ π. τὴν κοινωνίαν ἐφελκομένη τοῦ κάλλους *ib.4* (833C); of approach of evil to soul, id.*virg.*21(p.328.20; M.46.401A); **d.** ref. approach of God to man, in Inc. τί κωλύει θείας φύσεως ἕνωσίν τινα καὶ π. κατανοήσαντας, πρὸς τὸ ἀνθρώπινον τὴν θεοπρεπῆ διάνοιαν καὶ ἐν τῷ π. διασῴζεσθαι, πάσης περιγραφῆς ἐκτὸς εἶναι τὸ θεῖον πιστεύοντας, κἂν ἐν ἀνθρώπῳ ᾖν; id.*or.catech.*10(p.57.2; M.45.

41D); περικεκάλυπται τῇ σαρκὶ ἡ θεότης, ὡς...μὴ πτοηθείη τὸν π. τῆς ...δυνάμεως *ib.*23(p.90.1; 64A); *ib.*26(p.99.15; 69A); in gen. ἐν οἷς ἐστε τόποις, αἰνέσατε αὐτόν· θεοῦ γὰρ προσεγγισμὸν τοπικὴ μετάστασις οὐ κατεργάζεται id.*ep.*2(M.45.1013C); ὁ π. τῆς ὀσμῆς τοῦ ἁγίου πνεύματος ἐξελάσει...τὸ φιλήδονον πνεῦμα Nil.*epp.*4.2(M.79.552B); **2.** *putting together*, ref. Is.5:8 ὁ...καταφυτεύσας τὸ ἑαυτοῦ ἡγεμονικὸν πάσῃ καρποφορίᾳ πνευματικῇ καὶ...ἐπιβαλὼν τὰ ἐκ τοῦ πονηροῦ γεωργοῦ, οὗτός ἐστιν ὁ διὰ τὸν...π. ἀγροῦ πρὸς ἀγρὸν ὑπὸ τοῦ λόγου ταλανιζόμενος †Bas.*Is.*153(1.488A; M.30.369C).

προσεγγράφ-ω, *enter, insert* on roll, Dion.Al.ap.Eus.*h.e.*7.21.9(M.20.685C); ref. insertion of ὁμοούσιον into creed ταύτης ὑφ᾽ ἡμῶν ἐκτεθείσης τῆς πίστεως...ὁ...βασιλεὺς...οὕτω τε καὶ ἑαυτὸν φρονεῖν συνωμολόγησε καὶ ταύτῃ τοὺς πάντας συγκαταθέσθαι...παρεκελεύετο, ἑνὸς μόνου ~έντος ῥήματος τοῦ ὁμοουσίου Eus.*ep.Caes.*4(p.44.3; M.20.1540A).

προσεγγυάω, *give a pledge*, Cyr.*Ps.*49:7(M.69.1081D); Jo.Jej.*doct.*1(p.228).

***πρόσεγγυς,** *near*, superl. adv. ἦσαν...τῇ κλίνῃ προσέγγιστα δοῦλοι δέκα *A.Phil.*80(p.32.8).

***προσεγκρίνω,** *include in addition*; of Esther in canon, Amph.*Seleuc.*288(M.37.1596A).

[*]**προσεδαφίζ-ω, 1.** *dash to ground* οὗτός [sc. refuter of heresies] ἐστιν ὁ τὰ Βαβυλώνια νήπια [sc. heresies] τῇ πέτρᾳ ~ων †Bas.*Is.*272(1.587A; M.30.597C; v.l. ἐδαφίζεται); **2.** *found upon* πάντα λογισμὸν αὐτῷ ~οντες Marc.Er.*opusc.*4(M.65.1001A).

***προσέδρα, ἡ,** *watchfulness*, Gr.Nyss.*hom.in 1Cor.6:18*(M.46.492B; for προσεδρεία).

προσεδρεία (-ία), ἡ, 1. *besieging, assault* ὅτε πειρασμὸς...ἐπιγίνηται, οἷά τις λύπη...καὶ πολεμίων τινῶν π. ‡Proc.G.*Pr.*1:27(M.87.1232D); **2.** *watchfulness*, ref. bishop's care of churches φεύγει...τὴν ἐκκλησιαστικὴν π. Nil.*Alb.*(M.79.701B; prob. for προε-); **3.** *attention* διὰ τῆς φιλοπονωτέρας π. μὴ διαμαρτεῖν Gr.Nyss.*hex.*45(M.44.104A); **4.** *waiting* τῆς ἐν Ἀριμίνῳ συνόδου τῇ π. ταλαιπωρουμένης Soz.*h.e.*4.19.9(M.67.1172A); upon God ἐν τεσσαράκοντα ἡμερῶν προσεδρείᾳ τὰς πλάκας κομίζεται πάλιν Gr.Nyss.*v.Mos.*(M.44.322B); **5.** *assiduity, perseverance, diligence*; **a.** in gen. of Moses μετὰ τοὺς μυρίους πόνους καὶ...τὴν ἐν τεσσαράκοντα ἔτεσι π. Chrys.*hom.5.4 in Mt.*(7.80A); ἕνεκα...τῆς ἐν στρατείᾳ π. κἂν ἐπροστάτησε Synes.*ep.*75(M.66.1441B); **b.** in prayer and devotion, Or.*fr.500 in Mt.*(p.205; M.17.305B); Ath.*exp.Ps.*62:2(M.27.277C); τεσσαράκοντα ἡμερῶν π. νηστεύοντος...τοῦ θεράποντος ἄχρηστον ἀπέδειξεν οἰνοφλυγία μία Bas.*hom.*1.5(2.4D; M.31.169C); τῆς εἰς τὰ ἅγια π. †Bas.*Is.*26(1.399D; M.30.169A); ref. delayed answer to prayer ἴσως διὰ τοῦτο ἀναβάλλεται διδόναι, τὴν πρὸς αὐτὸν π. σου σοφιζόμενος ‡Bas.*const.*1.6(2.540B; M.31.1337A); cf.Chrys.*hom.10.7 in Mt.*(7.147D); τὴν...π. τῆς περὶ τὰ θεῖα μαθήματα προσοχῆς Gr.Nyss.*hom.13 in Cant.*(M.44.1060C); ref. Mary of Bethany (Lc.10:42) ὁρᾷς π. ὑπὲρ ἀγάπης Mac.Aeg.*hom.*12.16(M.34.568A); κεφάλαιον πάσης ἀγαθῆς σπουδῆς...ἡ προσευχῆς ἐστι π. id.*or.*1(M.34.853A); πολλὰ τῇ π. τῆς εὐχῆς ὑπεῖναι τὰ τῆς κακίας ἐμπόδια *ib.*3(856A); ἀνάξιος εἶ; γενοῦ τῇ π. ἄξιος. ὅτι γὰρ καὶ τὸν ἀνάξιον δυνατὸν ἄξιον ἐκ τῆς π. γενέσθαι, καὶ δι᾽ ἡμῶν αὐτῶν μᾶλλον ἢ δι᾽ ἑτέρων παρακαλούμενος ὁ θεὸς ἐπινεύει...πειράσομαι ποιῆσαι φανερά Chrys.*hom.in Phil.1:18*(3.309B); ἵνα τῇ π. δυνηθῶμεν τὴν...κόλασιν διαφυγεῖν id.*hom.20.4 in Gen.*(4.176D); οὐχ ἁπλῶς αἰτεῖν ἐκέλευσεν, ἀλλὰ μετὰ π. πολλῆς καὶ εὐτονίας id.*hom.23.4 in Mt.*(7.289A); ἐθρήσκευον ἀπερισπάστῳ π. τὸ θεῖον Nil.*Magn.*20(M.79.996B); τῇ τοῦ θεοῦ π. ... τὸ κέρδος ἐλάμβανον...οὐ τοίνυν ἁπλῶς ἡ ἀργία ζωοποιός· ἀλλ᾽ ἡ τοῦ θεοῦ π. Thdt.*Ezech.*20:12(2.825); ἐκτὸς μὲν γὰρ σχολῆς καὶ πολλῆς π. ἐν ταῖς προσευχαῖς, καὶ ἐν ταῖς θείαις τῶν γραφῶν ἀναγνώσεσιν, οὐκ ἔστιν...τὸν θεὸν ἀληθῶς ἐπιγνῶναι Anast.S.*synax.*(M.89.828A); πάσῃ δυνάμει ὄκνον ἡμῖν ἐμποιεῖν σπουδάζουσιν εἰς τὴν τῆς προσευχῆς π. Jo.Carp.*cap.*76(M.85.1852); **6.** *importunity, pertinacity* τὸν καθεύδοντα...ἀναστήσαντα, οὐ διὰ τὴν φιλίαν ἀλλὰ διὰ τὴν π. Chrys.*hom.19.4 Mt.*(7.249B); τοὺς κύνας οὐ...φεύγομεν...ὅτι τῇ πολλῇ π. ἡμᾶς ἐκβιάζονται id.*hom.13.5 in 1Cor.*(10.116A); **7.** *attendance* in court εἰ ὀμόσῃ μὴ εὐπορεῖν ἐγγυῶν, ἐξομνυέσθω περὶ τῆς π. Ath.Scholast.*coll.*4.22(p.63); *ib.*5.2(p.72).

***προσεδρευτέον,** *one must wait upon*, Cyr.*ador.*11(1.400B).

προσεδρεύ-ω, 1. *sit*; of antichrist in Temple, Thdt.*haer.*5.23(4.458); **2.** *lie in wait for, ambush*, Chrys.*sac.*2.2(p.30.13; 1.373C); ὁ...τῆς ἁγιωσύνης ἐχθρὸς ἀεὶ καὶ μᾶλλον αὐταῖς ἐφέστηκε καὶ ~ει *ib.*3.17(p.89.9; 398C); **3.** *be devoted to, give attention to*; of wife caring for husband in sickness, Clem.*str.*2.23(p.190.21; M.8.1089B); in gen. χρὴ τὸν ὀφθαλμὸν τῷ πληρώματι τῶν πνευματικῶν ὑδάτων ~οντα τῷ ἀπλανεῖ...λούεσθαι γάλακτι Gr.Nyss.*hom.14 in Cant.*(M.44.1064A); of clergy τοὺς τῇ ἐκκλησίᾳ ~οντας *Const.App.*2.25.14; μάθοιτε δέ, εἰ τοῖς κατὰ θεὸν σοφοῖς προσεδρεύσοιτε· προσεδρεύσοιτε δέ, εἰ κακίαν φύγοιτε Isid.Pel.*epp.*2.153(M.78.608C); ἐλευθέρῳ τῷ λογισμῷ τῇ τῶν πάντων κρειττόνων ~ουσιν ἐργασίᾳ Nil.*Magn.*1(M.79.969C); ~ων ἀεὶ τοῖς τύποις Cyr.*glaph.Gen.*1(1.20A); διδασκάλῳ δεῖ προσκαθέζεσθαι τῷ Χριστῷ, καὶ ~ειν ἀδιαλείπτως...αὐτῷ id.*Jo.*4.4(4.384A); τὰ τῆς τῶν Ἑβραίων πολιτείας ἐξαίρετα...τὸν νομοθέτην ~ειν ἐδίδασκεν Thdt.*qu.65 in Ex.*(1.170); τῇ πνευματικῇ ~ειν διδασκαλίᾳ id.*1Tim.*4:6(3.660); οἱ ἁμαρτωλοὶ γήινοι ὄντες ~ουσι τῇ γῇ Proc.G.*Gen.*4:17(M.87.253D); **4.** *serve, wait upon* τῷ κυρίῳ τε ~ειν ἀρξάμενος...ὅλος ἐξ ὅλου τις ~ειν τῷ θεῷ Mac.Aeg.*libert.ment.*30(M.34.964A,B); ἐν παντὶ...καιρῷ θεῷ ~ειν Cyr.*ador.*11(1.400B); **5.** *attend upon, be assiduous at, frequent* ~ω τῷ ναῷ κυρίου *Protev.*23.1(p.45); τοῖς τῷ θυσιαστηρίῳ ~ουσι Chrys.*hom.66.3 in Mt.*(7.658B); τὸν δικαστηρίῳ ~οντα id.*sac.*1.3(p.4.14; 1.363B); **6.** *be in attendance*, CCP(449)*act.*(*ACO* 2.1.1 p.151.8,11; H.2.176C); **7.** *be importunate*, ref. Mt.15:26 κἂν γὰρ κύων ᾖς, ~ων προτιμηθήσῃ τοῦ τέκνου ῥᾳθυμοῦντος Chrys.*hom.22.5 in Mt.*(7.282A).

προσεθισμός, ὁ, *habituation*, Gr.Nyss.*virg.*5(p.278.7; M.46.349A); *ib.*9(p.286.14; 357B); id.*ep.*19(M.46.1077A).

πρόσειμι, (*sum*); **1.** *belong to, be a characteristic* or *an attribute of*; **a.** in gen., Just.*1apol.*7.5(M.6.337B); Clem.*paed.*1.9(p.141.23; M.8.356A); οὐ γὰρ προσεῖναι τοῖς οὐρανίοις...ὀρέξεις βδελυκτάς Meth.*symp.*8.16(p.105.3; M.18.168C); **b.** of God βία γὰρ οὐ πρόσεστι τῷ θεῷ *Diogn.*7.4; τοὺς τὰ προσόντα αὐτῷ μιμουμένους, σωφροσύνην καὶ δικαιοσύνην καὶ φιλανθρωπίαν Just.*1apol.*10.1(M.6.340C); ἐσφάλη Παῦλος...τὸ ἄφθαρτον καὶ ἀόρατον αὐτῷ μόνῳ προσεῖναι διδάξας, καὶ μὴ τὸ ἀγέννητον ‡Ath.*dial.Trin.*2.17(M.28.1184D); εἰ στέρησίς ἐστιν ἕξεως [sc. τὸ ἀγέννητον], πῶς ἂν τὸ μὴ προσὸν τῷ θεῷ συναριθμηθήσεται; *ib.*2.21(1189C); τὰ μόνῳ προσόντα τῷ πατρὶ ὡς θεῷ, καὶ οὐχ ὡς πατρί, καὶ τῷ υἱῷ ὡς θεῷ, καὶ οὐχ ὡς υἱῷ, ταῦτα μόνῳ πρόσεστι τῷ πνεύματι, οὐκέτι δὲ καὶ τῇ κτίσει Didym.(‡Bas.)*Eun*:5(1.296B; M.29.712A); of divine attributes in connexion with theologies of affirmation and negation, Gr.Nyss.*Eun.*12(2 p.252.19; M.45.953B); Cyr.*dial.Trin.*1(5^1.415B); Thdt.*affect.*2(p.63.5f.; 4.755); **2.** *be near to* πῶς γὰρ ἐν γῇ ἀλλοτρίᾳ τῆς ψυχῆς μου, ἔνθα μένοντας οὐκ ἔστι προσεῖναι θεῷ; Gr.Thaum.*pan.Or.*16(p.37.11; M.10.1100A).

πρόσειμι, (*ibo*) *approach*;

A. of persons; **1.** as converts τοιαῦτα ὑπ᾽ αὐτῶν [sc. Χριστιανῶν] προστάσσεσθαι· μηδεὶς προσίτω πεπαιδευμένος...ἀλλ᾽ εἴ τις ἀμαθὴς...θαρρῶν ἡκέτω Cels.ap.Or.*Cels.*3.44(p.239.27; M.11.976D); τινὲς δὲ προσηλύτους εἰρήκασι τοὺς οὐ γνησίως οὐδὲ καθαρῶς προσιόντας Proc.G.*Is.*54:1–17(M.87.2545A); **2.** *resort to* as member of audience ἐπὶ τοῦ ὀρεγομένου ἐπισκοπῆς διὰ τὴν παρὰ ἀνθρώποις δόξαν ἢ...τὸν ἀπὸ τῶν προσιόντων τῷ λόγῳ πορισμόν Or.*comm.in Mt.*11.15(p.59.13; M.13.953B); **3.** *draw near* to, *approach* God τοὺς ἐν περιτομῇ προσιόντας αὐτῷ τοῦτ᾽ ἔστι πιστεύοντας αὐτῷ καὶ τὰς εὐλογίας παρ᾽ αὐτοῦ ζητοῦντας Just.*dial.*33.2(M.6.545C); εἴτε, ὡς ὁ Πλάτων φησί, τέχνη τοῦ θεοῦ [sc. ὁ κόσμος], θαυμάζων αὐτοῦ τὸ κάλλος τῷ τεχνίτῃ πρόσειμι Athenag.*leg.*16.2(M.6.921A); ὁ θεῖος λόγος ἐπαγγέλλεται τῶν προσιόντων τὴν κακίαν ἐξαιρεῖν Or.*princ.*3.1.15(p.222.16; M.11.280B); χρὴ τοὺς εἰς τὸ πλήρωμα τῆς οὐρανοπόλεως ἀναληφθησομένους τῷ ἁρμοσαμένῳ Χριστῷ...καθαροὺς προσιέναι Meth.*lepr.*10(p.464.17); in prayer ἕκαστος οὖν τῶν ἐχόντων...σπίλον...εὐθέως προσίτω τῷ ἀρχιερεῖ, λέγω διὰ προσευχῆς *ib.*6(p.458.23); ἐν παντὶ καιρῷ πρόσιθι Chrys.*hom.24.3 in Eph.*(11.183C); in eucharistic prayer οὐδὲ εἰκῇ μνήμην ποιούμεθα τῶν ἀπελθόντων ἐπὶ τῶν...μυστηρίων, καὶ ὑπὲρ αὐτῶν πρόσιμεν id.*hom.41.4 in 1Cor.*(10.392E); προσιόντες γάρ, πρότερον ὑπὲρ τῆς οἰκουμένης καὶ τῶν κοινῶν εὐχαριστοῦμεν ἀγαθῶν id.*hom.2.5 in 2Cor.*(10.434D); to Christ, id.*hom.24.5 in 1Cor.*(10.218C); in paganism οἱ δαίμονες...ἐνήργησαν καὶ ῥαντίζειν ἑαυτοὺς τοὺς...προσιέναι αὐτοῖς μέλλοντας Just.*1apol.*62.1(M.6.421B); Athenag.*leg.*15.1(M.6.920A); **4.** *approach* a sacrament; **a.** baptism ἀλείφομεν...τοὺς προσιόντας...τῇ θείᾳ...ἀναγεννήσει Serap.*euch.*22.1; Thdt.*Is.*54:15(p.217.4; 2.362); **b.** eucharist; freq. abs., *come to communion* ἡ θυσία...κελεύουσα ἡμῖν μεθ᾽ ὁμονοίας αὐτῇ μάλιστα προσιέναι...καὶ ὑψηλὸν εἶναι δεῖ τὸν προσιόντα τῷ σώματι τούτῳ Chrys.*hom.24.3 in 1Cor.*(10.216C); *ib.24.5*(218B); μηδεὶς τοίνυν Ἰούδας ταύτῃ προσίτω τῇ τραπέζῃ, μηδεὶς Σίμων id.*hom.50.3 in Mt.*(7.517E); id.*hom.6.4 in Eph.*(11.44C); id.*hom.5.3 in 1Tim.*(11.577E).

B. of things; **1.** of divine providence in dealing with soul, Clem.*str.*2.20(p.175.17; M.8.1060A); **2.** *come to, fall to one's lot* πονηρὰ...τὰ προσιόντα γυμνάσια *ib.*7.12(p.52.19; M.9.501A); **3.** *come in besides, be added* αὐτοτελὴς...ἡ κατὰ τὸν σωτῆρα διδασκαλία...προσιοῦσα δὲ φιλοσοφία ἡ Ἑλληνικὴ οὐ δυνατωτέραν ποιεῖ τὴν ἀλήθειαν *ib.*1.20(p.63.

31; M.8.817A); **4.** *accede to, assent to,* Athenag.*leg.*14.1(M.6.916C); Chrys.*hom.7.8 in 1Cor.*(10.62B).

***προσειρηνεύ-ω,** *be at peace in regard to* τῇ κακίᾳ ~σει Or.*exp.in Pr.*26:20(M.17.240C).

προσεισκρίν-ω, *introduce besides,* ref. man's creation ἐπεισκρίνεται δὲ ἡ ψυχή, καὶ ~εται τὸ ἡγεμονικόν Clem.*str.*6.16(p.500.9, v.l. προεισ- M.9.360B).

***προσεισπέμπω,** *bring in besides,* ‡Chrys.*pasch.*5(8.262C).

***προσεκδρομή, ἡ,** *shooting forth* of vine tendrils, Cyr.*hom.pasch.* 9.2(5².109B, v.l. προεκ-).

προσέκκειμαι, *be outstanding, be a leader* ἀνεκομίσθησαν...ἐκ τῆς Βαβυλωνίων οἱ ἐξ Ἰσραὴλ...ἐν κόσμῳ τε καὶ τάξει...προσεκκειμένους ἔχοντες Cyr.*Zach.*33(3.704D; conj. Aubert προεκ-).

προσεκπέμπω, *expel,* Cyr.*hom.pasch.*14(5².187C).

***προσεκπετάννυμι,** *stretch out to,* Eust.*fr.in Pr.8*:22(M.18.681A).

***προσεκπλήσσω,** *shock yet further,* Clem.*q.d.s.*1.3(p.159.14; προσεμπλήσσουσιν M.9.605A).

προσεκπνέω, *expire,* Pall.*v.Chrys.*20(p.129.12; M.47.72).

προσεκπονέω, 1. *toil further,* Clem.*str.*1.18(p.58.8; M.8.805B); **2.** *work out in addition, ib.*4.2(p.249.29; 1217A); *ib.*7.14(p.60.10; M. 9.517A).

***προσεκτραγῳδέω,** *exaggerate like a tragic actor,* Or.*Cels.*2.24 (p.153.15; M.11.844A).

προσέλευσις, ἡ, 1. *approach*; of convert to God, Dion.Ar.*e.h.* 2.2.5(M.3.396A); through life of prayer, Thdr.Stud.*epp.*2.116(M.99. 1385A) cit. s. προσευκτικός; Adam.*dial.*1.16(p.32.28; M.11.1741B) cit. s. προσαγωγή; of communicant to altar, Chrys.*nativ.*7(2. 365B); **2.** *access* to emperor as suppliant, hence *petition,* †Bas.*ep.* 41.2(p.285.18; M.32.345C); Socr.*h.e.*3.25.1(M.67.452A, codd. προε-); **3.** *advent,* tr. Lat. *accessus, Cod.Afr.*85; of entry into congregation of the *lapsi* after persecution, Petr.I Al.*ep.can.*1(M.18.468B); **4.** *onset,* Epiph.*haer.*80.7(p.492.13; M.42.768A).

***προσελθετέον,** *one must approach,* Or.*Jo.*10.18(13; p.189.10; M. 14.357B).

***προσεμέω,** *spit upon,* Const.Diac.*laud.*2(M.88.480B).

***προσεμπαλόω,** (for προσεμβάλλω) *patch* a garment, Thdr.Stud. *poen.*1.62(M.99.1741A).

προσεμπεδόω, *confirm further,* Cyr.*Juln.*3(6².93B); id.*hom.pasch.* 19(5².256A); id.*Is.*1.3(2.79A).

***προσεμπείρομαι,** *be involved* in, *forced* into προσεμπαρῆναι εἰς πάθος αὐτὸ τὸ...ἀπαθές Thdr.Stud.*epp.*1.52(M.99.1100D).

προσεμπίμπρημι, *set on fire besides,* Or.*Jo.*6.58(37; p.167.1; M.14. 301A); †Bas.*Is.*121(1.463B; M.30.313B); Cyr.*Nah.*13(3.490D).

***προσεμπλέκω,** *grapple with,* c. dat., Gr.Nyss.*Apoll.*6(M.45. 1133C).

***προσεμποδίζω,** *put an obstacle in the way of,* †Ath.*fr.Mt.*(M. 27.1372B); Pall.*h.Laus.*41(p.128.9; M.34.1233C).

προσεμφορέω, *fill in addition* προσεμφορηθῆναι τῆς ἀταξίας τοῦ βίου Mac.Mgn.*apocr.*4.25(p.210.14) ? for προεμ-.

***προσεναντίωμα, τό,** *opposition,* †Ath. *fr.*(M.26.1241C).

***προσένδον,** *nearly, approximately,* Gr.Mag.*dial.*(tr.Zach.)4.10 (M.*PL.*77.334B).

***προσενδύ-ομαι,** *be clothed with in addition,* of one entering monastery φωτὶ φῶς ~όμενος Steph.Diac.*v.Steph.*(M.100.1089B).

***προσένεξις, ἡ,** *offering*; **1.** in gen., Chrys.*hom.66.2 in Mt.*(7.656B) v. προσάγω; τὴν Ἄννα ἐπὶ τῇ π. Σαμουὴλ...μιμούμενοι Sophr.H.*v.Cyr. et Jo.*1(M.87.3381A); of service to God, CCP(681)*or.imp.*(H.3.1417A); **2.** of Christ's sacrifice, Sophr.H.*or.*7.5(M.87.3329C); **3.** eucharistic ἐν τῇ ὥρᾳ τῆς π. Jo.Disc.*v.Epiph.*38(M.41.72D); Call.*v.Hyp.*(p.27); ἐπὶ προσενέξει τῆς ἁγίας καὶ ἀναιμάκτου θυσίας *Lit.Jac.*(p.208.12).

***προσενοίκησις, ἡ,** *dwelling among,* Thdt.*Jer.*9:26(2.462).

προσεν-όω, 1. *unite, join,* Sophr.H.*mir.Cyr.et Jo.*53(M.87.3621B); Christol., Leont.H.*Nest.*3.5(M.86.1616A); pass., of Christians in Christ, Cyr.*Jo.*11.12(4.1001D); abs. τῆς Αἰγυπτιακῆς διοικήσεως καὶ τῆς προσηνομένης (sic) ἑκατέρας Λιβύης Ath.Scholast.*coll.*7.2(p.83); **2.** perf. pass., *be devoted* to πρὸς...διακονίαν...π. Eus.*p.e.*7.18(332B; M.21.561A); τὸν νοῦν...προσηνῶσθαι τῷ σκοπῷ †Bas.*bapt.*1.2.25(2. 647D; M.31.1568D).

***προσεντρίβομαι,** *be rubbed in*; met., of heretical doctrine sinking into the mind, Epiph.*haer.*55.9(p.337.17; M.41.989A, v.l. προστριβομένη).

***προσεντυπόω,** *impress upon, Hom.Clem.*5.26.

***προσένωσις, ἡ,** *union with,* Leont.H.*Nest.*1.18(M.86.1472A).

***προσεξαιτέομαι,** pass., *have required of one in addition,* Cyr.*ador.* 8(1.255A).

***προσεξαποστέλλω,** *send out against,* Socr.*h.e.*7.18.15(M.67.776B).

***προσεξεργαστέον,** *one must accomplish besides,* Cyr.*Ps.*7:15(M. 69.753D).

***προσεξευμαρίζω,** *make easy besides,* Eus.*l.C.*16(p.250.6; M.20. 1424C).

***προσεξογκόω,** *puff up,* Gr.Agr.*Eccl.*6.15(M.98.1012A).

προσεξυφαίν-ω, *weave in addition*; met., of exegetes ~ουσι δὲ καὶ τοιόνδε τινα νοῦν Cyr.*Is.*4.4(2.668B).

***προσεξωθέω,** *expel besides,* Chrys.*hom.15.3 in 1Cor.*(10.129C).

προσεπάγ-ω, 1. *add,* Clem.*paed.*3.10(p.265.10; M.8.621B); Chrys. ap.*cat.Col.*1:21(p.311.10) for ἐπάγει, id.*hom.4.1 in Col.*(11.350D); προσεπάγει πολλάκις ταῖς μυσταγωγίαις τὰς μεγαλουργίας Cyr.*Lc.* 4:31(M.72.545B); ~ει καί φησιν id.*apol.Thdt.*4(p.124.10; 6¹.217E); *Dial.Tim.et Aquil.*126 r°(p.96); **2.** pass., *be brought forward in addition* οἴει...~εσθαι δεῖν τὸν...λόγον Cyr.*ador.*10(1.327B).

***προσεπαγωνίζομαι,** *bring forward to support a contention,* Cyr. *Jo.*10.2(4.900B).

προσεπᾴδω, *chant,* Andr.Cr.*or.*14(M.97.1092A).

***προσεπαθρητέον,** *one must further observe,* Cyr.*glaph.Gen.*2(1. 50B).

***προσεπανάπτομαι,** *rekindle* ἡ τοῦ θείου πυρὸς ἐνέργεια...τὸ τοῦ θερμοῦ ἀγγεῖον προσεπανήπτετο καὶ διεπυροῦτο *Mir.Geo.*4(p.37.19, v.l. προσεπανῆπτεν καὶ διεπύρωσεν).

***προσεπανίσταμαι,** *come upon* someone *in addition,* c. dat., Eus. *h.e.*9.8.2(M.20.816B).

***προσεπανορθόω,** *set in a straight path for,* Cyr.*ador.*12(1.420D).

***προσεπαντλέω,** *pour upon,* Cyr.*ador.*11(1.399C).

***προσεπείγομαι,** *make haste, Mir.Geo.*11(p.108.1).

***προσεπεισφρ-έω,** *rush in upon* or *to* τῶν παρά τινων...~ησάντων σοι...λογυδρίων Thdr.Stud.*epp.*1.8(M.99.937B).

προσεπεκτείνομαι, *press on towards,* c. dat., ‡Sophr.H.*triod.*(M. 87.3864D).

***προσεπεμβαίν-ω,** *trample on besides,* Gr.Naz.*or.*14.29(M.35. 897A); μὴ ~ωμεν αὐτοῦ ταῖς συμφοραῖς Chrys.*Laz.*2.6(1.735E); εὐπορία ~όντων, προσπλησσόντων Thdr.Stud.*epp.*1.12(M.99.949C).

***προσεπενδύω,** *clothe with in addition,* ‡Sophr.H.*triod.*(M.87. 3917D).

προσεπεξεργάζομαι, *bring out meaning of more fully,* Dion.Al.ap. Eus.*p.e.*14.26(778D; M.21.1281A); Eus.*e.th.*2.16(p.119.30; M.24.936C).

***προσεπεξηγέομαι,** *explain further,* Clem.*paed.*3.11(p.282.12; M. 8.661C).

***προσεπεργάζομαι,** = προσεπεξεργάζομαι, Iren.*haer.*1.10.3(M.7. 556A).

***προσεπερείδω,** *make to rest upon,* ‡Ath.*occurs.*(M.28.988A).

προσεπεύχομαι, *pray besides,* Just.*2apol.*15.4(M.6.469A).

***προσεπιβαίνω,** *trample upon besides,* c. dat., Or.*enarr.in Job* 19:4(M.17.72A).

προσεπιβάλλω, *cast up to,* Sophr.H.*v.Anast.*(M.92.1728B).

***προσεπιδιατάσσω,** *make further dispositions*; of making codicil to a will, ‡Nil.*perist.*9.2(M.79.865A).

***προσεπιδιδάσκω,** pass., *learn besides,* Clem.*str.*6.18(p.516.8; M.9. 396B).

***προσεπιθρύπτομαι,** *be enervated besides,* Clem.*paed.*2.2(p.176. 21; M.8.420B).

***προσεπικαλλωπίζω,** *adorn further, Const.App.*1.3.8.

***προσεπικλίνω,** *bend towards,* ‡Ath.*occurs.*11(M.28.988A).

***προσεπικύπτω,** *bend down over,* c. dat., ‡Jo.D.*fid.dorm.*26(M.95. 273A).

***προσεπιλύομαι,** *express freely,* ‡Pall.*h.mon.*1.9(M.34.1108D; προσεπέμπετο p.6.21).

***προσεπινομοθετέω,** *legislate further,* Cyr.*ador.*10(1.338E).

***προσεπιπνέω,** *breathe upon besides,* c. dat., Clem.*str.*5.13(p.384. 5; M.9.129A).

προσεπισύρ-ω, med., *sweep along besides,* of heretics who fast forty days at Christmas ('fast of S. Philip') οὐ μόνον ἑαυτοὺς θέλουσιν εἶναι μόνους πεπλανημένους, ἀλλὰ ~ονται καὶ πλήθη ἰδιωτικά ‡Anast. Ant.*serm.*4(M.89.1392B).

προσεπισφίγγω, *bind still more tightly,* Gr.Naz.*carm.*2.2(epigr.)24. 6(M.38.96A).

προσεπιτείν-ω, 1. *intensify* Clem.*q.d.s.*12(p.167.19; M.9.616C); ~ει δὲ τὴν εἰς τὸν τόπον ἀπορίαν καὶ ὁ Ἰωάννης Or.*Jo.*19.1(p.299.2; M. 14.525B); **2.** *press home* a point, *urge* ὁ προφήτης ~ει λέγων ὅτι... πικρίας ἐνεπλήσθην id.*hom.14.16 in Jer.*(p.123.16; M.13.425C); *ib. 13.1*(p.102.7; 400A); id.*enarr.in Job* 22:6(M.17.81B).

***προσεπιτερατεύομαι,** *attach miraculous quality* to, Clem.*prot.*2 (p.15.6; M.8.81A).

***προσεπιτήδειος,** *specially suitable,* Socr.*h.e.*7.29.2(M.67.804A).

***προσεπιτίκτω**, *produce besides*, Didym.*Trin*.1.27(M.39.401A).

προσεπιτιμάω, *add as penalty*, Petr.I Al.*ep.can*.1(M.18.168B).

***προσεπιτούτοις**, *in addition*, Nect.*Thdr*.1(M.39.1821B); Eustrat.*v.Eutych*.18(M.86.2296A); Max.*ambig*.(M.91.1341A).

***προσεπιφύομαι**, *grow as an accretion upon*, c. dat., Clem.*str*.2.20(p.174.9; M.8.1056B).

προσερανίζω, med., *collect more*, Synes.*ep*.44(M.66.1373C).

***προσερπύζω**, *creep up to*, Gr.Naz.*or*.15.8(M.35.925A).

***προσερριμμένως**, *in the manner of something thrown in, as a casual expression* or *utterance* τό, πλήν,...ἐν τοῖς ψαλμοῖς οὐ κατά τινα κεῖται διάνοιαν, ἀλλὰ π. ἀπὸ Ἑβραϊκοῦ ἰδιώματος Thdr.Mops.*Ps*.48:16(p.322.8).

προσέρχ-ομαι **1.** *draw near, approach*; **a.** a person for instruction ἄλλοις δὲ ὅσῃ δύναμις ἀποδεικτικῶς δι' ἐρωτήσεων καὶ ἀποκρίσεων ~όμεθα Or.*Cels*.6.10(p.80.26; M.11.1305B); **b.** the faith as a convert πολλοὶ ὡσπερεὶ ἄκοντες προσεληλύθασι Χριστιανισμῷ *ib*.1.46(p.96.9; 745A); τὸ πλῆθος τῶν ~ομένων τῷ λόγῳ *ib*.3.9(p.210.5; 932A); αἱ ἐκκλησίαι ἔχουσι μὲν ἀνάλογον τοῖς πλήθεσιν ὀλίγους σοφοὺς προσελθόντας *ib*.6.14(p.85.3; 1312B); ἀνθρώπους ἀπὸ ἐθνικοῦ βίου ἄρτι προσελθόντας τῇ πίστει CNic.(325)*can*.2; βιβλία...τετυπωμένα...ἀναγινώσκεσθαι τοῖς ἄρτι ~ομένοις ⟨καὶ βουλομένοις⟩ κατηχεῖσθαι Ath.*ep.fest*.39.11(p.88; M.26.1437C); Thdt.*Ezech*.36:27(2.990); **c.** of schismatics entering Church περὶ τῶν ὀνομαζόντων μὲν ἑαυτοὺς Καθαρούς ποτε, ~ομένων δὲ τῇ καθολικῇ...ἐκκλησίᾳ CNic.(325)*can*.8; **d.** of those coming to baptism προσῆλθέ ποτε καὶ Σίμων τῷ λουτρῷ...γέγραπται δὲ πρὸς νουθεσίαν τῶν μέχρις σήμερον ~ομένων Cyr.H.*procatech*.2; Chrys.*hom.6.4 in Eph*.(11.44C); **e.** to Communion, Cyr.H.*catech*.23.22; μήτις τῶν μὴ δυναμένων προσελθέτω *Lit*.ap.*Const.App*.8.10.1; Chrys.*hom.24.5 in 1Cor*.(10.218D); *ib.28.1*(250C); τοῦτο γὰρ τὸ δεινόν, ὅτι...τοῦτο εὐλάβειαν εἶναι νομίζεις τὸ μὴ πολλάκις προσελθεῖν, οὐκ εἰδὼς ὅτι τὸ ἀναξίως προσελθεῖν, κἂν ἅπαξ γένηται ἐκηλίδωσε, τὸ δὲ ἀξίως, κἂν πολλάκις, ἔσωσεν id.*hom.5.3 in 1Tim*.(11.577C); ἐννόησον...ποίᾳ ⟨μέλλεις⟩ ~εσθαι τραπέζῃ id.*nativ*.7(2.365A); μετὰ φόβου θεοῦ πίστεως καὶ ἀγάπης προσέλθετε *Lit.Chrys*.(p.395.40); **f.** of man's approach to God τὰς χάριτας αὐτοῦ ἀποδιδοῖ τοῖς ~ομένοις αὐτῷ ἁπλῇ διανοίᾳ *1Clem*.23.1; προσέλθωμεν οὖν αὐτῷ ἐν ὁσιότητι ψυχῆς *ib*.29.1; Or.*hom.4.5 in Jer*.(p.28.18; M.13.292D); Meth.*symp*.10.4(p.126.15; M.18.200A); ἐάν...μὴ...ἀμβλύνηται τὸ ἁμάρτημα μετὰ τὸ προσελθεῖν καὶ συγγνώμην αἰτήσασθαι παρὰ τοῦ θεοῦ id.*lepr*.10(p.464.8); to Christ, Or.*princ*.3.1.15(p.223.2; M.11.280B); id.*hom.12.12 in Jer*.(p.100.24; M.13.397B); id.*Cels*.7.51(p.202.17; M.11.1496B); of approach of worshipper to pagan images, Athenag.*leg*.15.1(M.6.920A); **g.** of divine approach to man εὐκατάληπτον ἔσται τὸ θεῖον τῆς ἀθανατιζούσης τὰς ψυχὰς ⟨δυνάμεως⟩ ὑμῖν προσελθούσης Tat.*orat*.16(p.17.24; M.6.841A); **2.** *come forward* to speak, of false prophets ἐν ὀνόματι τοῦ Ἰησοῦ προσελθόντες (cf. Mt.24:5), Just.*dial*.35.4(M.6.552A); **3.** *apply oneself to*; in gen., Clem.*paed*.3.10(p.264.28; M.8.621A); φιλοσοφήσει προσελθεῖν Gr.Thaum.*pan.Or*.14(p.31.4; M.10.1089B); to religion οὐ προσελεύσῃ ἐπὶ προσευχήν σου ἐν συνειδήσει πονηρᾷ *Did*.4.14; πυκνότερον ~όμενοι πειρώμεθα προκόπτειν ἐν ταῖς ἐντολαῖς τοῦ κυρίου *2Clem*.17.3; to ascetic life, *V.Alex.Acoem*.20(p.673.7); **4.** *strive towards* ᾧ δὲ οὐδὲ τὸ τυχὸν προσελθεῖν ἔστιν εἰς ὕψος ἄνευ τοῦ ἐν τοῖς ἀναγκαίοις εἶναι Clem.*str*.4.4(p.256.25; M.8.1232A); **5.** *go forward, take place* εἴτις τῶν...ἀρχόντων...κωλύσῃ διαθήκην γενέσθαι...ἢ γάμον προσελθεῖν Ath.Scholast.*coll*.4.22(p.62).

***προσευαγγελίζομαι**, *declare good tidings to*, Thdr.Mops.*Ps*.32:1(p.142.20; M.66.669A).

***προσευκτέον**, *one must pray*, Cels.ap.Or.*Cels*.8.25(p.241.23; M.11.1553C); Or.*or*.15.1(p.334.5; M.11.465A).

προσευκτήριος, *for prayer*, ‡Nil.*perist*.4.5(M.79.829B); neut. as subst., *oratory, church*, Eus.*h.e*.7.32.32(M.20.736B); *ib*.10.4.14(853B); id.*l.C*.11(p.224.8; M.20.1376B).

προσευκτικός, *of* or *pertaining to prayer* τῇ ἐρημικῇ μονώσει καὶ τῇ π. προσελεύσει Thdr.Stud.*epp*.2.116(M.99.1385A).

***προσευχαριστ-έω**, *add thanksgivings*, Dion.Al.ap.Bas.*Spir*.72(3.60E; M.32.201B); τοσοῦτον...ἀπέχειν λύπης ὡς καὶ ~εῖν ἐπὶ τῷ φόνῳ Pall.*h.Laus*.15(p.40.2; M.34.1041B).

προσευχή, ἡ, **1.** *prayer*, v. εὐχή; **2.** *place of prayer* (Jewish) ὅρα πάλιν Ἰουδαΐζοντα τὸν Παῦλον...οὐ ἐνομίζετο φησί, π. εἶναι. οὐ γὰρ δὴ ἔνθα συναγωγὴ ἦν μόνον, ἀλλὰ καὶ ἔξω ηὔχοντο, ὥσπερ τόπον τινὰ ἀφορίζοντες Chrys.*hom.35.1 in Ac*.(9.268E); μᾶλλον μὴ οὔσης ἐκεῖ συναγωγῆς διὰ τὸ σπάνιον, παρὰ τὸν ποταμὸν ἔξω τῆς πόλεως λάθρα συνήγοντο οἱ δῆθεν θεοσεβεῖς Ammon.*Ac*.16:13(M.85.1556D).

***προσεφαρμόζ-ω**, *adapt to, suit*, Or.*sel.in Ezech*.6:9(M.13.785D); εἰ δὲ ἐν ἑκάτερόν ἐστι κατὰ τὴν ἕνωσιν καὶ τὴν σύνοδον καὶ τὴν σύνθεσιν τὴν ἀνθρωποειδῆ, ἓν καὶ τὸ ὄνομα τῷ συνθέτῳ ~εται, ἀπὸ μὲν τῆς θεότητος τὸ ἄκτιστον, ἀπὸ δὲ τοῦ σώματος τὸ κτιστόν Apoll.*ep.Dion*.9(p.260.2; M.*PL*.8.934B).

***προσεφευρίσκω**, *find in addition*, Clem.*str*.4.2(p.249.28; M.8.1217A).

προσέχεια, ἡ, *attention*, Tit.Bost.*Man*.2.7(M.18.1145D); ‡Pall.*proem*.(p.4.14; M.34.996); διὰ πολλῆς π. καὶ νοῦ ἐπιστασίας...εὑρὼν τὰ τοῖς πολλοῖς ἀγνοούμενα...κακά Marc.Er.*opusc*.5.13(M.65.1049B); Max.*ep*.12(M.91.465C).

***προσεχεστέρως**, adv., formed from comp. of προσεχής, *more directly* ἡ δύναμις τοῦ κυρίου...π. ... ἐνεργοῦσα [sc. τὸν ἴδιον σῶμα] Leont.H.*Nest*.5.2(M.86.1725B).

προσεχής, **1.** *close at hand, near*; of believer's relationship to God ἕως τῆς ἐπαναβεβηκυίας καὶ π. τοῦ κυρίου ἐν ἀϊδιότητι θεωρίας Clem.*str*.7.2(p.9.8; M.9.413C); ὁ γνωστικὸς...π. τῇ πανσθενεῖ δυνάμει γενόμενος, πνευματικὸς εἶναι σπουδάσας διὰ τῆς ἀορίστου ἀγάπης ἥνωται τῷ πνεύματι *ib*.7.7(p.33.18; 464B); ἐπὶ προθύροις...τοῦ πατρὸς π. τῷ μεγάλῳ ἀρχιερεῖ γενόμεναι [sc. ψυχαί] *ib*.(p.34.16; 465A); γνωστικὸς...ἔργῳ καὶ λόγῳ καὶ αὐτῷ τῷ πνεύματι π. γενόμενος τῷ κυρίῳ *ib*.7.14(p.63.1; 521C); of God in rel. to believer ὅσῳ τις...γνωστικώτερος γίνεται, προσεχέστερον τούτῳ τὸ πνεῦμα τὸ φωτεινόν *ib*.4.17(p.295.22; M.8.1316A); **2.** *appropriate*, *ib*.8.6(p.93.9; M.9.585D); ‡Proc.G.*Pr*.1:7(M.87.1225A); **3.** *closely related, akin* ἡ υἱοῦ φύσις ἡ τῷ μόνῳ παντοκράτορι προσεχεστάτη Clem.*str*.7.2(p.5.22; M.9.408B); **4.** *direct, immediate*, *ib*.3.2(p.199.28; M.8.1109B); τῆς τοῦ κυρίου π. κατὰ τὴν νέαν διαθήκην φωνῆς *ib*.3.11(p.228.13; 1172C); ἡ τοῦ λόγου δύναμις...διὰ φωτεινῆς καὶ π. διακονίας ἐνήργει *ib*.6.3(p.448.17; M.9.252C); ἡ δὲ διαφωνία προσεχὲς αἴτιον τῆς ἐποχῆς *ib*.8.7(p.93.29; 588B); πάντα δι' αὐτοῦ ἐγένετο, κατὰ τὴν π. ἐνέργειαν τοῦ ἐν ταὐτότητι λόγου id.*exc.Thdot*.8(p.108.22; M.9.657C); ἀστρονομία...π. πορθμεῖον τῆς ἀπορρήτου θεολογίας Synes.*astrolab*.4(p.138.1; M.66.1581D); **5.** *attentive* ἵνα ἡ τοῦ λέγοντος ἀξιοπιστία...καταστήσῃ...π. τοὺς ἀκούοντας ‡Hipp.*fr.33 in Pr*.(p.170.11; M.10.616B); π. πρὸς ἀκρόασιν ἐποίει τὸν βάρβαρον Thphyl.*exc.Rom*.5(p.224.22; M.113.932C); **6.** *attendant upon, concerned with* αἱ π. τῆς προνοίας ἐνεργοῦνται οἰκονομίαι Clem.*str*.7.7(p.32.10; M.9.460A); Πλάτων θεὸν...φησὶ τἀγαθόν· ἐξ αὐτοῦ τε...ἀναλάμψαι νοῦν, καὶ τοῦτον εἶναι τὸν π. τῷ κόσμῳ δημιουργόν Cyr.*Juln*.4(6^2.147A); abs., of angels, Clem.*str*.7.2(p.10.3; 416B); ἡ κατὰ διαθήκην τῶν πρωτοκτίστων ἀγγέλων ἐνέργεια π. id.*ecl*.51(p.151.13; M.9.721B); **7.** *prone to* φιλαργυρίᾳ δὲ πάνυ π. ἦν Tat.*orat*.19(p.21.2; M.6.848B).

προσέχ-ω, **1.** *apply to* αἱ θεαὶ γυμναὶ προσεῖχον τῷ ποιμένι, εἴ τις αὐτῷ δόξει καλή Clem.*prot*.2(p.25.9; M.8.109B); **2.** *take notice* φεύγειν προφάσει τοῦ τετάσθαι ἐπί τι σπουδαῖον καὶ μὴ προσεσχηκέναι ‡Pion.*v.Polyc*.7; προσσχὼν εὐφυῆ τὸν νεανίσκον Pall.*v.Chrys*.5(p.28.10; M.47.18); **3.** *pay heed to, attend to* ~οντες τοὺς λόγους αὐτοῦ ἐπιμελῶς *1Clem*.2.1; τῷ ἐπισκόπῳ ~ετε, ἵνα καὶ ὁ θεὸς ὑμῖν Ign.*Polyc*.6.1; μόνῳ δὲ ~ειν θεῷ καὶ τοῖς τούτου προφήταις Gr.Thaum.*pan.Or*.15(p.33.16; M.10.1093B); ref. interpretation of scripture ὁ γὰρ κατά τι μόριον φυλασσόμενος καὶ ~ων, κατά τι περισπώμενος...ὅλος οὐκ ἀνάκειται θεῷ Meth.*symp*.5.2(p.54.1; M.18.97C); ref. reading of gospels οὐδὲν ἧττον αὐτῷ [sc. Luke] καὶ Μάρκῳ ~ομεν ἢ Ματθαίῳ καὶ Ἰωάννῃ Thdt.*h.rel*.proem.(3.1107); in liturgy, *pay attention* ἕστηκεν ὁ διάκονος [i.e. before reading of lessons] μέγα βοῶν καὶ λέγων πρόσχωμεν...μετ' ἐκεῖνον ἄρχεται ὁ ἀναγνώστης τῆς προφητείας Ἡσαΐου· καὶ οὐδὲ οὕτω ~ει τις Chrys.*hom.19.5 in Ac*.(9.159E); *Lit.Jac*.(p.172.22); *Lit.Marc*.(Brightman p.118.17); **4.** *observe* ἃ ἐνετείλατο ~ετε *Barn*.7.6; Meth.*symp*.8.17(p.112.2; M.18.173C); id.*res*.1.43(p.289.17; M.18.272A); Jo.Mal.*chron*.5 p.136(M.97.233A); **5.** *regard as* ὡς στασιασταῖς προσεῖχον αὐτοῖς Chrys.*hom.75.3 in Mt*.(7.726B); ἵνα μὴ ὡς ἐχθροῖς αὐτοῖς ~ῃ id.*hom.7.2 in 1Tim*.(11.585E); ref. eucharistic elements μὴ ~ε οὖν ὡς ψιλοῖς τῷ ἄρτῳ καὶ τῷ οἴνῳ Cyr.H.*catech*.22.6; **6.** *look, face towards* ἐν φωλεῷ...πρὸς ἀνατολὴν ~οντι Epiph.*haer*.53.2(p.316.22; M.41.961A).

προσεχῶς, **A.** *nearly, closely*; **1.** of time, *recently* διὰ τῆς ἐν ταύτῃ τῇ πόλει γενομένης παρὰ Σεργίου ἐκθέσεως καὶ διὰ τοῦτο π. ἐπὶ τῆς ἕκτης ἰνδικτιῶνος ἐκτεθέντος τύπου Anast.Ap.*a.Max*.1(M.90.120D); **2.** *closely, near at hand* φιλοσοφία...διατείνουσα ἐπὶ τὴν π. ἁπτομένην τῆς ἀληθείας τὴν καθ' ἡμᾶς εἴδησιν Clem.*str*.1.20(p.62.34; M.8.816B); τῇ ἐξ ἀσκήσεως ἕξει τούτῳ προσεχέστερον συνεγγίζων *ib*.6.9(p.468.2; M.9.293B); προσεχέστερον δὲ ὁ γνωστικὸς οἰκειοῦται θεῷ *ib*.7.7(p.28.1; 452A); fig. ἀπὸ τοῦ παραδείγματος τῆς εἰκόνος τοῦ βασιλέως προσεχέστερόν τις κατανοεῖν δυνήσεται Ath.*Ar*.3.5(M.26.332A).

B. *immediately, directly* πάντων δὲ ἀνθρώπων ὁ θεὸς κύριος, προσεχέστερον δὲ τῶν ἐγνωκότων πατήρ Clem.*str*.6.6(p.455.21; M.9.269B); δι' ἀγγέλου π. μυσταγωγεῖται *ib*.5.11(p.375.22; 112A); π. τῆς τοῦ πατρὸς ἀπολαύων δυνάμεως id.*exc.Thdot*.10(p.109.25; M.9.660C);

ψυχὴ...ἐμψυχουμένη ὡς εἰπεῖν ὑπὸ τοῦ λόγου π. ἤδη *ib.*27(p.116.5; 673A); ὁ παράκλητος ὁ π. ἐνεργῶν νῦν ἐν τῇ ἐκκλησίᾳ τῆς αὐτῆς οὐσίας ἐστὶ καὶ δυνάμεως τῷ π. ἐνεργήσαντι κατὰ τὴν παλαιὰν διαθήκην *ib.*24 (p.115.7; 672A); τὸν μὲν π. δημιουργὸν εἶναι τὸν υἱόν Or.*Cels.*6.60 (p.130.21; M.11.1389C); εἰ δὲ ἀνυπόστατον ἐροῦσιν αὐτόν, οὐδενὸς μεσολαβοῦντος ἔτι καὶ διατειχίζοντος τὸν υἱόν, πῶς ἔσται τρίτος ἐκ πατρός, καὶ οὐχὶ μᾶλλον π., ὡς υἱὸς πρὸς πατέρα; Cyr.*Jo.*1.4(4.38D); ἐν αὐτῷ μένοντός τε καὶ ὄντος ἀεί, π. τε ἅμα καὶ οἷον μεμερισμένως *ib.*11. 10(987B); μόνος...ὁ υἱὸς ἐκ τοῦ πατρὸς π. ἐστιν. οὐκοῦν τὸ πνεῦμα...ἐκ τοῦ πατρὸς οὐκ ἔστι π. ἔστι δὲ καὶ κοινὴ ἔννοια, ὅτι ὅπερ οὖν ἐστιν ἀπό τινος, ἀπό τινός ἐστι π. ἐπειδὴ οὖν τὸ πνεῦμα...ἀπό τινός ἐστι π.· ἀλλ' οὐκ ἔστιν ἀπὸ τοῦ πατρὸς π. ... οὐκοῦν ἀπὸ τοῦ υἱοῦ π. Gr.II Papa *conf.*(M.91.1020D).

C. *carefully, attentively*, Clem.*str.*6.11(p.476.6; M.9.309B).

***προσεψέω**, *boil together*, Thdr.Stud.*iamb.*14(M.99.1785B).

προσηγορία, ἡ, A. *salutation, greeting* ἠπιά σοι πρὸς τοὺς ἀπαντῶντας ἔστω τὰ ῥήματα καὶ π. γλυκεῖαι Clem.*fr.*44(p.221.29); οὐ γὰρ κατ' ἀποκλήρωσιν δώσετε τὴν π., ἀλλ' ὑμεῖς μὲν τὸν λόγον δώσετε Tit.Bost. *fr.Lc.*10:6(p.189); ref. Rom.1:7 ὦ προσηγορίας μυρία φερούσης ἀγαθά Chrys.*hom.1.4 in Rom.*(9.434E); of liturg. greeting Ἰωάννης... εἰσῆλθεν εἰς τὴν ἐκκλησίαν σὺν τοῖς ἐπισκόποις...δοὺς δὲ τῷ λαῷ τὴν συνήθη τῆς εἰρήνης π. Pall.*v.Chrys.*14(p.84.26; M.47.48); of personal greetings at close of Pauline epistle, Thdt.*Rom.*16:14(3.159).

B. *allocution*, CSyr.*act.*(*ACO* 3 p.98.34; H.2.1376B).

C. *mode of speech* τίς γάρ ποτε Ἑλλήνων ἐχρήσατο τῇ 'ἐνωτίζου' π. ... ἀντὶ τοῦ 'εἰς τὰ ὦτα δέξαι';...ἰσομοία τῇ 'ἐπιούσιον' π. ἐστὶ... γεγραμμένη...'λαὸς περιούσιος' Or.*or.*27(p.367.6; M.11.509C).

D. *appellation, designation, title*; **1.** in gen., of designations of letters of alphabet, *Ev.Thom.*B 7(p.161); μολύνει τὴν ἀνθρώπου π. Clem.*str.*4.13(p.289.19; M.8.1300D); ἡ 'εὐαγγέλιον' π. Or.*Jo.*1.5(7; p.9.23; M.14.32C); τοῦ κακῶς λέγεσθαι τὴν π. λαμβάνει Meth. *arbitr.*13(p.180.9); οὔτε ὁ υἱὸς ἀπῴκισται τοῦ πατρός. ἡ γὰρ πατὴρ π. δηλοῖ τὴν κοινωνίαν Dion.Al.ap.Ath.*Dion.*17(p.58.20; M.25.505A); of designation 'God' implicitly assigned to Christ by S. Paul, Chrys. *paralyt.*6(3.44C); μηδενὶ...τῶν φωστήρων νέμειν τὴν θεοῦ π. Thdr. Mops.*Os.*13:4–6(M.66.201B); **2.** of title 'Christian' εἰ μηδὲν διά τε τὴν π. τοῦ ὀνόματος εὑρισκόμεθα ἀδικοῦντες Just.*1apol.*4.2(M.6.332B); ἀπολωλεκότες δὲ τὴν πάντιμον καὶ ἔνδοξον καὶ ζωοποιὸν π. *Ep.Lugd.*ap. Eus.*h.e.*5.1.35(M.20.421B); οἱ πιστοὶ...τῆς π. ἄξιοι, ἣν ὥσπερ διάδημα περίκεινται Clem.*q.d.s.*36(p.183.16; M.9.641A); Χριστοῦ προσηγορίαν λάβητε Cyr.H.*procatech.*15; **3.** of designation θεός as incommunicable to any other, Ath.*gent.*17(M.25.36C); **4.** of term θεός applied to men, ref. Ps.81:6 μέλλουσιν ἄνθρωποι θεοῦ π. λαμβάνειν Cyr.H.*procatech.* 6; applied to baptized in sense that they are πιστοί and πιστὸς ὁ θεός *ib.*; ὥσπερ γὰρ καλεῖται θεὸς ἀγαθός...οὕτω καὶ πιστός. λογίσαι τοίνυν εἰς ὁποῖον ἀξίωμα ἀναβαίνεις, θεοῦ μέλλων προσηγορίας γίνεσθαι κοινωνός id.*catech.*5.1; of man's designation as εἰκὼν θεοῦ, Chrys. *stat.*3.6(2.46B); **5.** of titles (expressive of divine nature and attributes) of Son ὡς...αἰδοῦμαι μὲν τὰς τοῦ λόγου π., τοσαύτας τε οὔσας, καὶ οὕτως ὑψηλὰς καὶ μεγάλας...αἰδοῦμαι...τὴν ὁμοτιμίαν τοῦ πνεύματος Gr.Naz.*or.*34.11(M.36.252A); (expressive of inferiority), *ib.*23.10(M.35.1161B); εἰκότως φαίη τις ἂν τὴν κυριωτάτην...καὶ μόνην ἐνεργείᾳ τοῦ πατρὸς ὑποστᾶσαν οὐσίαν εἰς ἑαυτὴν δέχεσθαι τὰς τοῦ γεννήματος καὶ ποιήματος καὶ κτίσματος π. Eun.ap.Gr.Nyss.*Eun.*4 (2 p.71.15; M.45.644D); πάντα τὰ τῆς θεολογίας ὀνόματα κατὰ τὸ ἴσον ἐπί τε τοῦ πατρὸς καὶ τοῦ υἱοῦ λέγεται, ὥστε εἰ τὸ παρηλλαγμένον τῶν π. τὴν διαφορὰν σημαίνει τῶν φύσεων, ἡ κοινότης τῶν ὀνομάτων τὸ κοινὸν τῆς οὐσίας πάντως ἐνδείξεται Gr.Nyss.*Eun.*7(2 p.166.1; 756C); τί...θεὸν αὐτὸν ἀλλὰ μὴ σάρκα προσαγορεύετε [sc. monophysites]; ἁρμόττει γὰρ τῇ ἀλλοιώσει τῆς φύσεως ἡ τῆς π. Thdt.*eran.*1(4.12); Gennad.*fr.in Ps.1*(M.85.1668D); **6.** of an eccl. title τῆς τοῦ καθολικοῦ ...π. CHier.(536)*act.*(*ACO* 3 p.187.24; H.2.1416E).

E. *personal name*, Or.*hom.9 in Lc.*(p.65.4; M.17.321D); *Hom. Clem.*4.7; τὴν π. ... τοῦ μακαρίου Ἰωάννου ταῖς μυστικαῖς δέλτοις ἐγγραφῆναι Attic.*ep.Cyr.*(p.23.27; M.77.349C); θεός, ὁ εἰδὼς ἑκάστου τὴν ἡλικίαν καὶ τὴν π. *Lit.Bas.*(p.408.24); of name of Christ in exorcism, Eus.*Hierocl.*4(514A; M.22.801C); of names of three Persons ἤρετο εἰ πιστεύει τῷ πατρὶ καὶ τῷ...υἱῷ καὶ τῷ...πνεύματι. τοῦ δὲ πιστεύειν ὁμολογήσαντος, ταύταις, ἔφη, ταῖς π. πιστεύων ἀνάστηθι Thdt.*h.rel.*26(3.1276).

F. *term* οἱ μὲν ἅγιοι τῆς μοναχικῆς φιλοσοφίας...τὰς π. ἁρμοδίας τοῖς πράγμασι...ἔθεντο, 'ἀποταγὴν'...καὶ 'ὑποταγήν' Isid.Pel.*epp.*1.1(M. 78.177A).

G. *naming, mention* ἐπὶ τῶν λοιπῶν συζυγιῶν ἠρκέσθη τῇ τῶν ἀρρένων π. Iren.*haer.*1.9.1(M.7.540A); ἡ δεκάλογος...π. σωτήριον ἁμαρτιῶν περιγράφουσα Clem.*paed.*3.12(p.285.2; M.8.668A).

προσηγορικῶς, *by way of a mere appellation*, opp. κυρίως or ἀληθῶς; in arguments of Pneumatomachoi τὰ ἀλληγορικῶς ἢ π., ἢ μεταφορικῶς, ἢ ὁμωνύμως λεγόμενα, οὐ χρὴ εἰς δόγματος ἀκρίβειαν παραλαμβάνειν...εἰ φύσει ἄνθρωποι, π. ναός εἰσιν, καὶ οὐχὶ δῆθεν ἀληθῶς Didym.*Trin.*2.10(M.39.645A).

προσήγορος, *familiar* φωνὴν...προσήγορον τοῖς ἁγίοις Bas.*Spir.* 75(3.64A; M.32.209A).

***προσηκόντως**, *fittingly*, Clem.*str.*2.19(p.169.19; M.8.1048B); ref. Gen.1:28 πληροῦται π. εἰς μέγεθος...αὐξανομένης [sc. τῆς ἐκκλησίας] Meth.*symp.*3.8(p.35.19; M.18.73A); Eus.*d.e.*1.10(p.45.16; M.22.85D).

προσήκ-ω, 1. *belong to, befit*, as Stoic term τὸ δὲ κατορθούμενον κατὰ τὴν τοῦ λόγου ὑπακοὴν ~ον καὶ καθῆκον Στωϊκῶν ὀνομάζουσι παῖδες Clem.*paed.*1.13(p.151.13; M.8.373A); **2.** med. or pass. ? *approve* ἡ δὲ Ῥώμη ταῦτα οὐ ~ατο Thdr.Stud.*epp.*1.38(M.99.1044C).

προσηλ-όω, A. *nail to, rivet to*; **1.** in gen. ref. martyr nailed to stake for burning, *M.Polyc.*13.3; ref. Symeon Stylites ἅλυσιν... κατασκευάσας, καὶ ταύτης θατέραν μὲν ἀρχὴν πέτρᾳ...~ώσας, θατέραν δὲ τῷ δεξιῷ ποδὶ προσαρμόσας Thdt.*h.rel.*26(3.1271); **2.** to cross (often abs., *crucify*); **a.** ref. Crucifixion of Christ ὁ διδάσκαλος ~ωθεὶς ηὔχετο τῷ πατρί *Hom.Clem.*11.20; Ath.*exp.Ps.*2:4(M.27. 65A); Chrys.*hom.85.2 in Mt.*(7.806C); id.*hom.24.4 in 1Cor.*(10.217A); ἐπειδὴ δὲ ~ώθη...ἀπεξεδύσατο μὲν τὸ λανθάνειν, γυμνῇ δὲ τῇ κεφαλῇ ὁρᾶν τὴν θεότητα...ἐδείκνυεν Sever.*Col.*2:14–15(p.324.17); πῶς οὐκ ἔφριξαν σταυρῷ ~ῶσαι, ὃν σταυρούμενον ἰδὼν ὁ ἥλιος ἔφυγε; Gr. Ant.*mul.ung.*6(M.88.1856B); ref. questions of suffering of Logos and purpose of Inc. ἄνθρωπος ἐγένετο καὶ ~ώθη τῷ σταυρῷ οἰκονομούμενος Meth.*Porph.*1(p.503.14; M.18.397D); ἄτρωτός γε ἔμεινεν ἡ σοφία καὶ ἀπαθής...κἂν τεμνομένῳ συνῆν καὶ ~ωμένῳ τῷ σώματι *ib.* 2(p.506.4; 404B); σταυρῷ ~ώθη ὁ ἀπαθὴς *Lit.*ap.*Const.App.*8.12.33; **b.** of Christ crucifying hostile demons τίς γὰρ οὕτως εἰρηνικὸς ὡς ὁ ἀποκτείνας τὴν ἔχθραν καὶ τῷ σταυρῷ ~ώσας τοὺς ἐχθροὺς ἑαυτοῦ Gr.Nyss.*hom.7 in Cant.*(M.44.908A); **c.** ref. Col.2:14, of nailing to cross of χειρόγραφον τοῖς δόγμασιν· οὐδὲ οὕτως ἐφύλαξεν, ἀλλὰ καὶ διέρρηξεν αὐτὸ ~ώσας τῷ σταυρῷ Chrys.*hom.2.2 in Col.*(11.368A); cf. *bene autem dixit, configens illam cruci, eo quod secundum praesentem vitam lex utilis est nobis, quando et peccare possumus; finis vero hujus vitae mors est. confixit illam cruci, mortuus enim finem legi dedit*, Thdr.Mops.*Col.*2:14(p.290.18); ἡγοῦμαι τοίνυν καὶ τὸ σῶμα ἡμῶν καλεῖσθαι χειρόγραφον...ὁ τοίνυν θεὸς λόγος, τὴν ἡμετέραν φύσιν ἀναλαβών...ταύτην δὲ συγχωρήσας τῷ σταυρῷ ~ωθῆναι, τὸ πάντων ἡμῶν ἐξέτισε χρέος Thdt.*Col.*2:14(3.488); ἔγραψε δὲ καὶ τίτλον ὁ Πιλάτος. ... τοῦτό ἐστι τὸ χειρόγραφον ὃ ~ωσε τῷ σταυρῷ ἡ κατὰ τοῦ Ἀδὰμ ἀπόφασις, ὅπερ ὁ διάβολος κατέχων, πάντας ἀνθρώπους ἀπέφερεν εἰς θάνατον Ammon.*Jo.*19:19(M.85.1512C); Cosm.Ind.*top.*2(M.88. 124B); **d.** of crucifixion of martyrs, Eus.*h.e.*8.8(M.20.760A).

B. *fasten, bind*; met.; of Israelites bound as serfs to labour in Egypt τῇ πλίνθῳ ~ωμένοι ‡Chrys.*Abr.*3(2.746E); of works of creator τὰ μὲν σκιρτῶντα ταῖς μεταβάσεσι, τὰ δὲ δεσμῷ φύσεως ~ωμένα τῇ γῇ Bas.Sel.*or.*1.3(M.85.33B); τῇ φύσει δεθείς, καὶ τῷ πόθῳ ~ωθεὶς *ib.*7.2(105C); ~οῦσθαι τῇ κλίνῃ *be confined to bed*, Chrys. *ep.*120(3.661A); id.*terr.mot.*(2.717B); βέλτιον νοσεῖν, εἴ γε μέλλοι τις διὰ τοῦτο ὑγιαίνειν, ἵνα πάλιν τῇ κλίνῃ ~ώσῃ ἑαυτόν id.*hom.3.2 in Philm.* (11.788E).

C. met., *attach to, fix one's mind* or *attention upon* δαίμονες... τοὺς μὲν τῆς γῆς μὴ ἐπαίρεσθαι δυναμένους τοῖς γηΐνοις καὶ χειροποιήτοις ~ωσαν Just.*1apol.*58.3(M.6.416B); τὸν εὐχόμενον...τοῖς ὑψηλοῖς ~ῶν χωρίοις Chrys.*hom.19.4 in Mt.*(7.249E); τῶν ἐπὶ τῆς γῆς ἀπάγων, καὶ τῷ θεῷ ~ῶν *ib.63.1*(628D); οὐ τοίνυν εἰς ἀργίαν αὐτὴν [sc. Μάρθαν] ἐμβάλλων, ταῦτα ἔλεγεν, ἀλλὰ ~ῶν τῇ ἀκροάσει id.*hom.44.1 in Jo.*(8. 259D); μέγα δὲ οὐδὲν...ἐνδείκνυνται, τῷ...τῷ πηλῷ ~οῦν ἑαυτοὺς *ib.* *1.1*(3B); Thdt.*Ezech.*20:25(2.829); τῇ τοῦ θεοῦ μνήμῃ ~ώσας τὸν νοῦν id.*h.rel.*21(3.1236); pass., *be devoted* to, *engrossed* in, Clem.*paed.*3.12 (p.283.9; M.8.664C); Or.*Cels.*8.60(p.276.16; M.11.1608A); τοῖς θείοις λογίοις ~ῶσθαι Ath.*exp.Ps.*1:2(M.27.61A); τοὺς τῷ πηλῷ...~ωμένους Chrys.*hom.68.4 in Mt.*(7.675C); with explicit metaphor of fixing ψυχὴ ἐὰν μὴ ἔχῃ τὴν πλάστιγγα τῶν...λογισμῶν πεπηγυῖαν καὶ ~ωμένην ἀσφαλῶς τῷ νόμῳ τοῦ θεοῦ id.*hom.5.3 in 2Tim.*(11.689B); ψυχαί...τῷ σταυρῷ τούτου ~ωμέναι Mac.Aeg.*carit.*25(M.34.928C); πλῆθος τὸ...ἀνοίᾳ ~ωμένον Cyr.*Ps.*4:7(M.69.740A); of personal devotion, ref. multitude's adherence to Christ in gospels, Chrys.*hom. 25.1 in Mt.*(7.307B); ἰδὼν...Ἀφραάτην ~ωμένον ἡμῖν id.*ep.*51(3. 620E); Thdt.*h.e.*2.27.9(3.896); μὴ δύνασθαι καρποφορεῖν, εἰ μὴ μόνους τοὺς ~ωμένους αὐτῷ Ammon.*Jo.*15:5(M.85.1493D); ‡Proc.G.*Pr.*3:24 (M.87.1249B).

***προσήλυσις, ἡ,** *coming over to* the Christian faith, *conversion*, Just.*dial.*28.2(M.6.536A).

προσηλυτεύ-ω, *become a convert to Judaism*, Eus.*d.e.*6.20(p.286.33; M.22.472B); Ἀντίπατρος...ἀπὸ τοῦ ἐπιτροπεύειν ~ει Epiph.*haer.* 20.1(p.225.10; M.41.272A); Ἀκύλας...τὸν Χριστιανισμὸν ἀρνησάμενος ...~ει id.*mens.*15(M.43.261D); Diod.*Ps.*51:7(M.33.1589B); Proc.G. *Is.*56:1–11(M.87.2569B).

προσήλυτος, ὁ, 1. *stranger, sojourner* in Israel; of Solomon's workmen, ‡Ath.*synops.*15(M.28.317C); with play on ἐπήλυτος: ὁ πολεμήσας τὸν λαὸν ἐκεῖνον ἐπήλυτος ἦν, καὶ οὐ π. Or.*enarr.in Job* 20:25(M.17.76B); **2.** *proselyte, convert to Judaism*, cf. *proselytus, id est advena et circumcisus qui miscebatur populo dei, Graecum est*, Isid.H.*etym.*7.14.10; in gen., Just.*dial.*23.3(M.6.525C); ἀπὸ τοῦ ἡμετέρου γένους ἢ καὶ τῶν π. *ib.*80.1(664B); *ib.*122.1(760A); Θεοδοτίων ...καὶ Ἀκύλας...'Ιουδαῖοι π. Iren.*haer.*3.21.1(M.7.946B); ὁ ἐξ ἐθνῶν ἐπιστρέφων...ὅς ὁ π. προεφητεύετο Clem.*str.*6.6(p.457.7; M.9.272C); πυνθανομένου δὲ τοῦ προσδιαλεγομένου τίς ἐστιν πλησίον; οὐ τὸν αὐτὸν τρόπον 'Ιουδαίοις προωρίσατο τὸν πρὸς αἵματος οὐδὲ τὸν πολίτην οὐδὲ τὸν π. οὐδὲ τὸν ὁμοίως περιτετμημένον οὐδὲ τὸν ἑνὶ καὶ ταὐτῷ νόμῳ χρώμενον id.*q.d.s.*28(p.178.22; M.9.633B); μέμνημαι...ἔν τινι πρὸς τοὺς λεγομένους παρὰ 'Ιουδαίοις σοφοὺς [ἐν] ζητήσει ταῖς προφητείαις χρησάμενος, ἐφ' οἷς ἔλεγεν ὁ 'Ιουδαῖος ταῦτα πεπροφητεῦσθαι ὡς περὶ ἑνὸς τοῦ ὅλου λαοῦ...ἵνα πολλοὶ π. γένωνται τῇ προφάσει τοῦ ἐπεσπάρθαι 'Ιουδαίους τοῖς λοιποῖς ἔθνεσιν Or.*Cels.*1.55(p.106.6; M.11.761B); γυνὴ ...'Ιουδαίας π. *Hom.Clem.*13.7; **3.** of converts to Christianity; **a.** Jewish term applied to Christian converts exeg. OT prophecy π. καλεῖ τοὺς καθ' ἑκάστην...ἡμέραν ἐκ τῶν ἐθνῶν ἀγρευο⟨μέ⟩νους, καὶ τῷ θείῳ προσιόντας βαπτίσματι Thdt.*Is.*54:15(p.217.2; 2.362); π. προσελεύσονται, φησί,...τοὺς...προσιόντας τῇ πίστει δηλῶν ἐξ ἐθνῶν, ἢ καὶ ἐξ αὐτῶν 'Ιουδαίων...καὶ γεγόνασι π. τοῖς ἐξ ἐθνῶν, οἱ πάλαι τούτους π. δεχόμενοι...τινὲς δὲ π. εἰρήκασι τοὺς οὐ γνησίως...προσιόντας, ἀλλὰ...τινος χάριν ὠφελείας· οὓς καὶ παροικήσειν, ἀλλ' οὐ κατοικήσειν φησίν Proc.G.*Is.*54:1–17(M.87.2544D); **b.** Jewish term used contemptuously of Christian neophyte οἱ δὲ τὸν ἀλλογενῆ καὶ οὔτω π. ἁρπάζοντες, καὶ...τῷ τῆς ἱερωσύνης καταστέφοντες ἀξιώματι τὸν οὔπω κατηχούμενον, πρὸς μεγάλους ἐν ἡμέρᾳ κρίσεως εὐτρεπιζέσθωσαν λόγους Cyr.*Jo.*2.5(4.192E); **c.** as Christian term, ref. 1Cor. 6:9 οὐ τοὺς κατὰ πίστιν μόνον, ἀλλὰ καὶ τοὺς π. λέγων Clem.*str.*7.14 (p.61.20; M.9.520B).

προσήλωσις, ἡ, 1. *nailing*, hence, abs., *crucifixion*; of martyrs, Eus.*h.e.*8.14.13(M.20.785A); id.*v.C.*1.58(p.35.2; M.20.972C); of Christ, ref. impassibility of Logos θεὸς μὲν λόγος ἐν ἐπιδείξει τῆς ἀθανασίας ...ἄνθρωπος δὲ τῇ π. τοῦ σταυροῦ ‡Ath.*Apoll.*2.18(M.26.1164C); ἡ γὰρ ιδ' εὑρίσκεται οὐχ ἡ ἀνάστασις, ἀλλ' ὁ καιρὸς τῆς...π. τῆς ἐν τῷ σταυρῷ *Chron.Pasch.*p.220(M.92.537A); **2.** *attachment*, met. ἐπὶ τὰ φαυλότερα π. Leont.H.*Nest.*4.32(M.86.1697C).

***προσημάντωρ, ὁ,** *one who indicates in advance, seer*, ‡Ath.*pass.*9 (M.28.201A).

***προσημείωσις, ἡ,** *prognostication*, Eus.*h.e.*8 suppl.3(M.20.796A).

***προσημερόω,** *make gentle*, Gr.Naz.*or.*11.3(M.35.833C); Gr.Nyss. *hom.opif.*1(M.44.132B).

προσήνεια, ἡ, *gentleness* μετὰ κολακείας καὶ π. ... πρὸς τὰ παιδία ταῦτα διαλεξόμεθα Chrys.*oppugn.*1.3(1.48C); id.*hom.34.3 in Gen.*(4.343B); οὐ γὰρ πανταχοῦ ἡ π. καλόν id.*hom.53.3 in Mt.*(7.542B); ἡ θεῷ διακονοῦσα π. Isid.Pel.*epp.*1.47(M.78.212B); οὐ γὰρ βίᾳ...ἀλλὰ πειθοῖ καὶ π. ἡ τῶν ἀνθρώπων σωτηρία κατασκευάζεται *ib.*2.129(573B).

προσηνής, 1. *gentle, kind* τὸ θεῖον ἀγαπᾶν μὲν ὡς π. καὶ εὐμενὲς τοῖς ὁσίοις Clem.*str.*5.5(p.346.24; M.9.56B); **2.** *pleasant* (i.e. acceptable) of spiritual sacrifices offered through eucharist, Eus.*d.e.* 1.10(p.48.4; M.22.92A); through observance of commandments, *ib.* 3.3(p.110.26; 189D).

πρόσθετος, *assigned*, hence *sacrosanct*, Gr.Naz.*carm.*2.2(epigr.) 70.3(M.38.118A).

***πρόσθεττε,** for πρόσθες τε, †Andr.Cr.*cycl.*(M.19.1329B).

προσθήκη, ἡ, 1. *addition, increase*; **a.** in gen. διὰ τὴν π. τῶν ἁμαρτημάτων συγκρινομένων τοῖς ἁμαρτήμασι τοῦ 'Ισραὴλ δικαιοσύνην εὑρῆσθαι ἐν τῷ 'Ισραὴλ παρὰ τὸν 'Ιούδαν Or.*hom.4.1 in Jer.*(p.22.26; M.13.285A); εἰς βεβαίωσιν καὶ π. πίστεως *Lit.Marc.*(*PDêr-Baliz.*3 r° 3, p.30); μείζων ἑαυτοῦ καταστὰς τῇ π. τῶν μυστικῶν μαθημάτων Gr. Nyss.*v.Mos.*(M.44.320D); πάσης...διδασκαλίας ὁ μὲν ἀγαθὸς καρπὸς... ἡ π. τῶν κατὰ τὴν ἐκκλησίαν σωζομένων ἐστίν id.*Apoll.*1(M.45.1124A); π. ... τοῖς ἀποστολικοῖς...κηρύγμασιν Gel.Cyz.*h.e.*3.9.2; **b.** of *accompaniments* of worship ναοὺς...οἰκοδομοῦντες καὶ...αὔξοντες...τῆς προσκυνήσεως τὰς π. Const.ap.Gel.Cyz.*h.e.*2.7.31(M.85.1240A); **c.** of addition of article to noun, ref. Jo.1:1 ὁ αὐτὸς δὲ 'Ιωάννης ἐν τῇ Ἀποκαλύψει καὶ μετὰ τῆς π. αὐτὸν ὀνομάζει τῆς θεοῦ λέγων...τὸ ὄνομα αὐτοῦ λόγος τοῦ θεοῦ Or.*Jo.*2.5(4; p.58.33; M.14.116D); οὐχ ἁπλῶς δὲ αὐτὸν λόγον εἴρηκεν, ἀλλὰ μετὰ τῆς τοῦ ἄρθρου π., τῶν λοιπῶν αὐτὸν καὶ ταύτῃ χωρίζων Chrys.*hom.2.4 in Jo.*(8.12E); ref. 1Cor.1:24 οὐ γὰρ εἶπεν ὁ...Παῦλος Χριστὸν κηρύσσειν τὴν ἰδίαν αὐτοῦ δύναμιν ἢ τὴν σοφίαν αὐτοῦ,...ἀλλὰ δίχα τῆς π. δύναμιν θεοῦ καὶ θεοῦ σοφίαν· ἄλλην μὲν εἶναι τὴν ἰδίαν αὐτοῦ τοῦ θεοῦ δύναμιν, τὴν ἔμφυτον αὐτῷ...κηρύσσων Ast.Soph.*fr.*1 ap.Ath.*syn.*18(p.246.2; M.26.77A); **d.** of additions to *Symb. Nic.*(325), Maced. ὑπογράφεις οὖν τῇ ἐκθέσει Λουκιανοῦ; orth. τί γὰρ κατέγνως τῆς...ἐν Νικαίᾳ...ἐκτεθείσης...; Maced. σὺ γὰρ τί κατέγνως τῆς τοῦ Λουκιανοῦ; orth. κατέγνων τῆς π. ἧς προσεθήκατε... Maced. ὑμεῖς γὰρ οὐ προσεθήκατε τῇ ἐν Νικαίᾳ; orth. ἀλλ' οὐκ ἐναντία αὐτῇ ‡Ath.*dial.Trin.*3.1(M.28.1204A); **e.** of dogmatic additions to teaching of scripture and fathers, Jo.Ant. *ep.Cyr.*2(p.8.20; M.77.172C); **f.** Trin. εἰ γὰρ οὐκ ἀϊδίως σύνεστιν ὁ λόγος τῷ πατρί, οὐκ ἔστιν ἡ τριὰς ἀΐδιος· ἀλλὰ μονὰς μὲν ἦν πρότερον, ἐκ π. δὲ γέγονεν ὕστερον τριάς Ath.*Ar.*1.17(M.26.48A); ποῦ οὖν πλεῖον εἶχεν ὑψωθῆναι ὁ ἐν τῷ πατρὶ ὤν...; οὐκοῦν πάσης π. ἀπροσδεής ἐστι, καὶ οὐκ ἔστιν ὡς ὑπονοοῦσιν οἱ Ἀρειανοί *ib.*1.40(96A); in rel. to Inc., ref. heret. view that recognition of humanity of Christ's body implies quaternity of Godhead ἐὰν δὲ ἀνθρώπινον εἴπωμεν τὸ ἐκ Μαρίας σῶμα, ἀνάγκη ξένου ὄντος κατ' οὐσίαν τοῦ σώματος καὶ ὄντος ἐν αὐτῷ τοῦ λόγου, τετρὰς ἀντὶ τριάδος γίνεται διὰ τὴν τοῦ σώματος π. Ath.*ep.Epict.*8(p.14.3; M.26.1064C); πολὺ πλανῶνται... ὑπονοοῦντες δύνασθαι τὴν θεότητα προσθήκην λαμβάνειν...πῶς οὖν οἴονται τὸ διὰ τοῦ λόγου λυτρωθὲν σῶμα...προσθήκην εἰς θεότητα τῷ ...λόγῳ ποιεῖν; μᾶλλον γὰρ αὐτῷ τῷ ἀνθρωπίνῳ σώματι π. μεγάλη γέγονεν ἐκ τῆς τοῦ λόγου...ἑνώσεως. ... ἡ...τριὰς καὶ λαβόντος ἐκ Μαρίας σῶμα τοῦ λόγου τριάς ἐστιν οὐ δεχομένη π. οὐδὲ ἀφαίρεσιν *ib.* 9(p.15.2ff.; 1065Af.); μὴ...λέγε προσθήκην σεβάσματος Didym.(‡Bas.) *Eun.*5(1.317B; M.29.760C); μηδὲ μιᾶς γενομένης π. τῇ ἁγίᾳ τριάδι... ἐκ τῆς τοῦ λόγου σαρκώσεως Max.*ep.*12(M.91.468D); ἡ...γέννησις ἄναρχος καὶ ἀΐδιος...ἵνα μὴ θεὸς πρῶτος, καὶ θεὸς ὕστερος εἴη, καὶ π. δέξηται Jo.D.*f.o.*1.8(M.94.813A); **g.** Christol. εἰ δοξασθῆναι...αἰτῶν ὁ υἱός, θεϊκῶς καὶ οὐκ ἀνθρωπίνως ᾔτει· ὃ οὐκ εἶχεν ᾔτει. καὶ ψεύδεται... ὁ Δαβίδ· καὶ εἰσελεύσεται ὁ βασιλεὺς τῆς δόξης· οὐ π. οὖν δόξης αἰτεῖ, ἀλλὰ τῆς οἰκονομίας τὴν φανέρωσιν γενέσθαι Didym.(‡Bas.)*Eun.*4(1.292B; M.29.701A); **2.** *interest* on money, Bas.*hom.*6.3(2.45D; M.31.265C); met. ἀνάγκη, τὸν κατάρξαντα κακοῦ μετὰ προσθήκης ἀποτῖσαι τὰ ὀφειλόμενα id.*ep.*260.2(3.396B; M.32.956C); **3.** *aid, assistance* of grace π. τῆς παρὰ θεοῦ δυνάμεως Clem.*q.d.s.*21(p.173.18; M.9.625B); **4.** *advance* ἡ διὰ τῶν μαθημάτων εἰς τελείωσιν π. ‡Bas.*struct.hom.* 2.2(1.338E; M.30.41D); **5.** that part of a church which is additional to the sanctuary οἶκος ἁγίων...μαρτύρων...ἐκτίσθη ἐκ θεμελίων, τὸ ἱερατεῖον καὶ τὴν π. τοῦ ναοῦ *CIG* 8609.

προσθλίβω, *press against*, Epiph.*haer.*53.2(p.316.22; M.41.961A).

***προσθυμία, ἡ,** *eagerness*, Gr.Naz.*carm.*1.2.34.38(M.37.948A).

***προσθύω,** *offer in sacrifice* to, Eus.*p.e.*4.15(154D; M.21.269A); of oblation of eucharist to God, Gr.Mag.*dial.*(tr.Zach.)4.55(M.*PL.*77. 418C).

***προσθωρακίζω,** pass., *wear a breastplate*, ‡Caes.Naz.*dial.*191(M. 38.1169).

***προσιαλισμός, ὁ,** *slobbering, spitting upon*, Ephr.1.223C.

***προσιδιοποιέω,** *attribute as a property*, Apoll.*fid.sec.pt.*3(p.168. 18; M.10.1105C).

προσίημι, *accept*; **1.** in gen., *accept so as to comply with, accept as reasonable* or *true*, hence dist. from δέχομαι: τὸ θεῖον γράμμα δεξάμενος οὐ προσήκατο Gel.Cyz.*h.e.*3.15.20; ὅστις...εὐχὴν μὴ προσίεται Or.*or.*5(p.308.13; M.11.429A); ἐκήρυσσε τοίνυν τὸν λόγον, οὐδεὶς προσίετο τὰ λεγόμενα id.*hom.14.3 in Jer.*(p.108.1; M.13.405D); τὸ γὰρ θεοπρεπὲς τῆς...ἀναστάσεως διὰ τὸ περὶ τὸν θάνατον ἀπρεπὲς οὐ προσίενται Gr.Nyss.*or.catech.*9(p.53.6; M.45.40D); τὰς εὐφημίας οὐ δεῖ προσίεσθαι Chrys.*hom.14.4 in Ac.*(9.118B); ὁ κόσμος...τὴν ἐκ πίστεως δικαιοσύνην οὐ προσηκάμενος Cyr.*Jo.*10.2(4.921D); μηδὲν προσηκάμενος τῆς πρεσβείας Thphyl.*exc.gent.*12(p.487.6; M.113. 949B); **2.** *accept as canonical*, Or.*ep.*1.9(M.11.72A); **3.** *accept* persons with favour; of men accepting Christ οὐκ ἐπὶ τούτῳ μᾶλλον αὐτὸν θαυμάζομεν; οὐκ ἐπὶ τούτῳ μᾶλλον προσιέμεθα; Chrys.*hom.6.3 in 2Tim.*(11.696C, v.l. ἐκπληττόμεθα Gaume); τὸ μὴ προσίεσθαι τὸν υἱόν Cyr.*ador.*7(1.235B); of God accepting men τοὺς ἑαυτῶν ἐπὶ τοῖς ἡμαρτημένοις κατεγνωκότας...προσίεται τῆς μετανοίας χάριν ὁ θεός Or.*Cels.*3.71(p.263.14; M.11.1013B); *Hom.Clem.*2.44; of God's acceptance of praise from creation, Didym.(‡Bas.)*Eun.*4(1.286E; M.29. 689A); of Christ τοὺς εἰς αὐτὸν καὶ δι' αὐτοῦ πιστεύοντας προσιέμενος Clem.*str.*1.24(p.100.24; M.8.908B); of admittance to Church τοὺς δὲ ἀκροᾶσθαι βουλομένους πάντας...προσιέμεθα Tat.*orat.*32(p.33.9; M.6.872B); Or.*Cels.*3.51(p.248.3; M.11.988C); of admission of penitents, *Hom.Clem.*18.23; persons excommunicated by one bishop not to be admitted by another, CNic.(325)*can.*5; of admission of former heretics, Dion.Al.ap.Eus.*h.e.*7.7.4(M.20.649A); Liber.*ep. Maced.*ap.Socr.*h.e.*4.12.37(M.67.493C); of admission to clerical office, CNic.(325)*can.*1; *ib.*9; **4.** f.l. for πρόσειμι, Chrys.*hom.54.1 in Mt.* (Gaume; προσῄεσαν 7.546C); *ib.82.4*(7.788A); id.*hom.27.5 in 1Cor.* (10.248E; Gaume om.).

προσικετεύω, v. προσπίπτω.

***προσιλαρεύομαι,** *welcome gladly,* ‡Pall.*h.mon.*1.13(p.8.5; M.34.1115B).

***προσιλιγγι-άω,** *be greatly agitated about* εἰ δέ τις Χριστιανὸς χρηματίζειν δοκεῖ, καὶ πρὸς τὴν θεοτόκον...ἀσχάλλει καὶ ~ᾷ Thdot. Anc.*hom.BMV et Sym.*5(M.77.1396B).

προσινής, *hostile, evil,* Jo.Jej.*canonar.*1(*SS* 4 p.438; προσηνεῖ p.115B).

προσιστορέω, *give further instructions, Can.App.*85.

***προσιτίζω,** *feed up in advance*; of Donatists' behaviour towards intending 'martyrs' (by suicide, etc.) compared with feeding and fattening of sacrificial victims, Thdt.*haer.*4.6(4.360).

προσιτός, *approachable*; of God, ref. ascent to Sinai of Moses and Joshua αὐτοῖς τοῖς ἁγίοις προφήταις δι' υἱοῦ π. ὁ πατήρ Cyr.*ador.*9(1.290E); οὐ γὰρ π. ἑτέρως ὁ πατὴρ εἰ μὴ δι' υἱοῦ *ib.*10(328E); ἀπρόσιτος οὖν διὰ νομικῆς λατρείας ὁ θεός, π. δ' ἂν γένοιτο διὰ μόνου Χριστοῦ id. *glaph.Ex.*2(1.280D); π. οὐχ ἑτέρως...εἰ μὴ διὰ μόνου τοῦ κατὰ φύσιν υἱοῦ *ib.*3(316A); οὐδὲ...Μωσῇ π. γέγονεν ὁ πατήρ, δίχα τῆς αὐτοῦ μεσιτείας *ib.*(333A); Χριστόν, δι' οὗ καὶ ἐν ᾧ π. τε ἅμα καὶ γνωστὸς ὁ πατήρ id.*Os.*38(3.69E).

προσκαθέζ-ομαι, *sit down before*; hence **1.** *sit at feet of* a teacher ἑνὶ καὶ μόνῳ διδασκάλῳ δεῖ ~εσθαι τῷ Χριστῷ Cyr.*Jo.*4.4(4.384A); **2.** *attend carefully* to, Clem.*paed.*3.2(p.239.4; M.8.561A); id.*q.d.s.*10 (p.166.20; M.9.613D); Or.*hom.10.6 in Jer.*(p.77.2; M.13.365B).

προσκαθεύδ-ω, *rest idly upon* μὴ τῷ γράμματι ~οντας σφᾶς τῶν θειοτέρων ἀποκλείσωμεν ‡Caes.Naz.*dial.*36(M.38.900).

***προσκαθηλόω,** *nail fast in place*; *fasten* to; pass., Clem.*prot.*4 (p.40.4; M.8.144B); met. ὅλον σεαυτὸν π. πόνοις Geo.Pis.*carm.*4.100 (p.14).

πρόσκαιρος, **1.** *timely, opportune,* exeg. πρὸς καιρόν 1Cor.7:5 ἡ δὲ ἐπιφορὰ τοῦ ἀποστόλου, καὶ πάλιν ἐπὶ τὸ αὐτὸ γίνεσθαι διὰ τὸν σατανᾶν,...οὐ...ἀποκρούεται τέλεον τὰς τῆς φύσεως ὀρέξεις δυσωποῦσα ἡ π. συμφωνία, δι' ἃς εἰσάγει πάλιν τὴν συζυγίαν τοῦ γάμου Clem.*str.*3.12(p.233.15; M.8.1121C); τὸ ἀγαθὸν...ὃ διαρκές ἐστι καὶ π. †Dion.Al.*fr.Eccl.*2:3(p.215.11; M.10.1580C); **2.** = καίριος *mortal,* of a blow or wound ὁ θεὸς...τὸν ἑαυτοῦ νεὼν τὸν ἄνθρωπον...διέλυσε θανάτου π. προσβολαῖς ἀποκτέννων Meth.*res.*1.41(p.286.7; M.41.1109B); **3.** *temporary, transient*; **a.** in gen. τὰ π. καὶ ἐπίγεια καὶ εὔφθαρτα Hipp.*Dan.*4.60.2; τὴν τῶν πονηρευομένων π. εὐημερίαν Or.*exc.in Ps.*36:1(M.17.120A); μὴ π. ἔχειν ζωήν, ἀλλὰ μετὰ ταῦτα διαμεῖναι ζῶντες ἐν Χριστῷ Ath.*Ar.*2.76(M.26.309A); τρυφῆς ἀπόλαυσις πρόσκαιρος Bas.*ep.*45.1(3.133C; M.32.365A); τὴν π. αὐτῶν θερμότητα εἰδὼς...οὐκ ἐνεχείριζε πάντα τὰ δόγματα αὐτοῖς [sc. apostles] ὡς ἤδη βεβαίως πιστοῖς γενομένοις Chrys.*hom.24.1 in Jo.*(8.137D); π. μὲν τὴν λύπην, διηνεκῆ δὲ τὴν χαράν *ib.79.1*(466C); ἄνθους π. ὀλιγοχρονιωτέρα ἡ δόξα ἡμῶν *M.Thdot.*3(p.135.13); ὑπὲρ ὀδύνης π. ἀτελεύτητον δωρεῖται ἄνεσιν *ib.*(p.141.10); of sleep as π. θάνατος, Cyr.*Jo.*7(4.679C); **b.** of Law and OT institutions π. ἦν καὶ αὐτὴ ἡ ἐντολή [sc. Passover as typical of Christ] Just.*dial.*40.1(M.6.561C); of Joshua's division of Canaan among tribes, superseded by eternal inheritance bestowed by Christ on faithful, *ib.*113.4(736C); ὁ νόμος διὰ Μωσέως ἐδόθη...διὸ καὶ π. ἐγένετο, ἡ δὲ ἀΐδιος χάρις...διὰ...Χριστοῦ ἐγένετο Clem.*paed.*1.7(p.125.20; M.8.321C); of Levitical washings contrasted with baptism, Cyr.*Ps.*18:14(M.69.833B); of life on sensible opp. intellectual plane, symbolized by Samaritan woman (Jo.4:17), Heracleon ap.Or.*Jo.*13.10(p.234.8; M.14.413A); **c.** ref. Arian doctrine οὐ...κατὰ τὸν δυσσεβῆ τοῦτον Ἀρειανόν, χρονικὸν ἢ π. δοξάζοντες τὸν υἱόν Petr.II Al.*encycl.*5(M.33.1284A)ap.Thdt.*h.e.*4.22.17; **d.** ref. Sabellian doctrine οὐδ' ἡ εὐαγγελικὴ φωνή σε πείθει οὐ π. εἶναι τὸν υἱόν, ἀλλ' ὅτι καὶ ἡ ἐν τῷ μέλλοντι αἰῶνι κατὰ πάντων δίκη ἐγκεχείρισται τῷ υἱῷ; ‡Gr.Nyss.*Ar.et Sab.*6(M.45.1289C); ref. doctrine of Marcellus νεωτερίζεις...ἀρχὴν τε π. ... τῇ βασιλείᾳ τοῦ Χριστοῦ διδούς Eus.*Marcell.*2.4(p.56.19; M.24.820A); **4.** *temporal, belonging to present world* (often combined with, or indistinguishable from, sense 3); **a.** explicitly opp. αἰώνιος; of τὸ πῦρ τὸ π. opp. τὸ πῦρ τὸ αἰώνιον, *Diogn.*10.8; of God as creator of τὰ μὲν π., τὰ δὲ αἰώνια Iren.*haer.*1.10.3(M.7.556A); of present life opp. ζωὴ αἰώνιος, *ib.*5.3.3(1132A); Eus.*Lc.*17:31(M.24.585B); Chrys.*hom.44.1 in Jo.* (8.260B); of this world's affairs, Clem.*str.*3.6(p.222.4; M.8.1160B); μεταβάλλεσθε τὸν τρόπον...ἀπὸ τῶν π. ἐπὶ τὰ αἰώνια *Hom.Clem.*1.7; ‡Proc.G.*Pr.*11:23(M.87.1332A); Heracleon ap.Or.*Jo.*13.60(59; p.291.21; M.14.513A) cit. s. βασιλικός; of martyr's sufferings contrasted with eternal torment, *Ep.Lugd.*ap.Eus.*h.e.*5.1.26(M.20.417B); *M.Thdot.3*(p.139.25); of earthly pleasure leading to death hereafter, Bas.*hom.in Ps.*61(1.197B; M.29.480A); of physical opp. spiritual death, Chrys.*hom.27.2 in Jo.*(8.155C); **b.** in gen. ὅτε χοϊκοὶ ἦμεν, Καίσαρος ἦμεν. Καῖσαρ δέ ἐστιν ὁ π. ἄρχων, οὗ καὶ εἰκὼν ἡ χοϊκὴ ὁ παλαιὸς ἄνθρωπος Clem.*ecl.*24(p.143.12; M.9.709A); ὁ τῶν βλεπομένων πολίτης καὶ παρερχομένων καὶ π. ἐκ τῶν κάτω ἐστίν Or.*Jo.*19.20(5; p.322.1; M.14.564D); δύο οὖν ἡμῖν γενικαὶ ἔστωσαν προφητεῖαι...ἡ...δευτέρα θῆλυς οὖσα...ἐπὰν δὲ συλλαβοῦσα τοὺς π. τίκτῃ βασιλεῖς...ἐγείρει πολέμους *Hom.Clem.*3.24; καλὴ ἡ γυνὴ...ἡ τῶν π. ἐπιθυμιῶν λελυμένη *ib.*13.16; δύο βασιλεῖς ἐτάχθησαν, ὧν ὁ μὲν τοῦ...π. κόσμου νόμῳ βασιλεύειν χειροτονεῖται,...ὁ δὲ ἕτερος...βασιλεὺς ὑπάρχων τοῦ ἐσομένου αἰῶνος *ib.*20.2; τοῦ π. ζῆν καταφρονήσαντες [sc. martyrs] Eus.*h.e.*8.8(M.20.757C); θνητῆς καὶ π. ζωῆς id.*l.C.*12(p.231.9; M.20.1389A); ἡ ψυχὴ...ἐνόμισε...μόνα τὰ π. καὶ τὰ σωματικὰ εἶναι τὰ καλά Ath.*gent.*8(M.25.16D); τῶν ἐπιγείων πραγμάτων καὶ π. ἐπιθυμιῶν Cyr.*Abac.*17(3.532C); of Christ ἐπίγειον καὶ οὐράνιον, π. καὶ ἀθάνατον Gr.Naz.*or.*38.11(M.36.324A).

προσκαίρως, *for a particular occasion*; theol., ref. 'Sabellian' (Marcellan) doctrine οἰόμενοι διὰ μὲν λειτοταξίαν ἀνθρωπίνην προεληλυθέναι τὸν υἱὸν ἐκ τοῦ πατρὸς π. ‡Gr.Nyss.*Ar.et Sab.*6(M.45.1289B); ref. Son's assumption of humanity εἴ τι τοίνυν π. δέχεται ὁ Χριστός, κατὰ τὴν ἀνθρωπότητα δέχεται, ᾗ τινι, ταῦθ' ἅπερ οὐκ εἶχεν προσφέρεται· κατὰ γὰρ τὴν δύναμιν τῆς θεότητος...πάντα ὅσα ἔχει ὁ πατήρ, ἔχει καὶ ὁ υἱός Leo Mag.*ep.*165.8(p.60.38; M.*PL.*54.1168C).

***προσκακοπαθέω,** *be distressed at,* Gr.Naz.*or.*39.17(M.36.353C).

προσκακουργέω, *do* one *an ill turn besides,* Synes.*provid.*18(p.107.10; M.66.1256B).

προσκαλ-έω, **1.** *call on, summon* προσεκάλουν αὐτοὺς μὴ ποιῆσαι τὴν ἁμαρτίαν *T.Zab.*1.7; **2.** *call, invite*; **a.** of divine vocation διὰ τοῦ πνεύματος τοῦ ἁγίου οὕτως ~εῖται ἡμᾶς *1Clem.*22.1; ἐν τῷ πάθει αὐτοῦ ~εῖται ὑμᾶς Ign.*Trall.*11.2; τοῖς ἔξω ἀναγινώσκομεν τοὺς λόγους τοῦ θεοῦ ~ούμενοι αὐτοὺς ἐπὶ σωτηρίαν Or.*hom.9.4 in Jer.*(p.68.22; M.13.353C); οἱ...προσκληθέντες μὲν ὑπὸ τῆς χάριτος CNic.(325)*can.*12; ref. Rom.1:1, Ac.22:13, and Ac.13:2 εἰ δὲ ἐκλέγεται μὲν αὐτὸν κύριος ὁ θεὸς...ὁ δὲ υἱὸς προσεκαλέσατο τὸν αὐτὸν δὲ ἀφορίζει τὸ πνεῦμα...πῶς ἑτερότης οὐσίας ἐν τῇ τριάδι...εὑρίσκεται; Didym.(‡Bas.)*Eun.* 5(1.300C; M.29.720D); ὑπὸ τῆς θείας χάριτος προσκληθεὶς ὡς ἂν καὶ ἑτέρους...εἰς τὴν αὐτὴν παιδοτριβήσειεν ἀρετήν Thdt.*h.rel.*2(3.1126); **b.** of enticement of sin, Meth.*res.*2.2(p.331.4; M.41.1164B); **3.** *summon* to contest, *challenge,* of Christ ἐπ' ὄψει πάντων ~εσάμενος αὐτόν [sc. θάνατον] Ath.*inc.*23.4(M.25.137A); **4.** pass., *be called away, die,* Gr.Naz.*or.*8.8(M.35.797C).

***προσκαρτερητέον,** *one must cleave to,* Nil.*epp.*3.274(M.79.520C).

***προσκατάγνυμι,** *break against,* c. dat., Synes.*calv.*13(p.215.8; M.66.1192A).

***προσκατακλίνω,** *bow down towards* κεφαλὴν τῇ γῇ προσκατέκλινεν Sophr.H.*v.Anast.*(M.92.1700C).

προσκατασκευάζω, *prove besides,* Cyr.*Jo.*12(4.1076E).

προσκατασύρω, *draw down besides,* †Bas.*Is.*156(1.489E; M.30.373C).

***προσκατεμπίμπρημι,** *set on fire in addition,* Cyr.*Nah.*3(3.478A).

προσκατέχ-ω, *hold firmly to* ψυχαὶ...~ονται τῇ ζωῇ ταύτῃ Bas.*hom.* 5.5(2.38B; M.31.249A).

***προσκαύησις, ἡ,** *worship by offering of incense, A.Andr.*A 11 (p.53.3, conj. προσκύνησιν).

πρόσκαυμα, τό, *soot,* ref. Nah.2:10, Joel 2:6 μηκέτι διὰ τὰς ἁμαρτίας τὸ πρόσωπον τοῦ ἔσω ἀνθρώπου ὡς π. χύτρας ἔχειν †Bas.*bapt.*1.2.10(2.636E; M.31.1544A).

πρόσκει-μαι, *be added to* canon of scripture ἐπειδή τινές φασι, περιττὸν εἶναι τὸ καὶ ταύτην ~σθαι τὴν ἐπιστολήν Chrys.*hom.in Philm.*proem.(11.772C); id.*hom.31.1 in Rom.*(9.745C; conj. προφερόμενον).

προσκενόω, **1.** *discharge upon, empty out on,* c. dat., Epiph.*haer.* 30.8(p.343.27; M.41.420B); **2.** *discharge completely,* medic., Sophr.H.*mir.Cyr.et Jo.*42(M.87.3585D).

***προσκέπασμα, τό,** *cave in front* of Holy Sepulchre, existing before Constantine's adornment of the tomb and pointed to as fulfilment of Cant.2:14, Cyr.H.*catech.*14.9.

προσκεπαστής, ὁ, *protector,* one of imperial bodyguard, Men. *exc.Rom.*19(p.216.27; M.113.920C).

προσκέπτομαι, *consider beforehand,* Clem.*ecl.*27(p.144.28; M.9.712B).

***προσκευάζομαι,** *prepare beforehand,* Cyr.*Jo.*10.2(4.912C).

***προσκέφαλα**, *at* or *near the head* of ἔκειτο δὲ π. τοῦ λειψάνου Jo. Mal.*chron*.10 p.250(M.97.381A); cf., s.v.l., *Apophth.Patr*.(M.65.220A).

***προσκιαγραφέω**, *sketch beforehand*, Chrys.*hom.82.1 in Mt*.(7.782B).

***προσκίασμα, τό**, *foreshadowing* ἀλλ' οὐδὲ εἰκὼν ἦν ὁ νόμος, ἀλλ' εἰκόνος προσκίασμα Jo.D.*imag*.1.15(M.94.1244D).

***προσκιόνιον, τό**, *portico*, Thphn.*chron*.p.154(M.108.417B).

***προσκιρτ-άω**, **1.** *leap before*, of Jo. Bapt. ∼ῶντι τοῦ λόγου, δι' ὃν ἐγένετο Gr.Naz.*or*.29.19(p.103.8; M.36.100B); *ib*.39.15(352C); Max. *ambig*.(M.91.1068A); **2.** *leap upon, be dashed upon*, of a ship προεσκίρτησε πετραίῳ πάγῳ Geo.Pis.*Pers*.1.180(M.92.1210A).

***προσκισσάω**, *long for*, Tit.Bost.*Man*.1.12(M.18.1085A).

[*]**προσκιχράω**, *put at one's disposal*, Ath.*ep.Aeg.Lib*.22(M.25.589A).

προσκλαί-ω, **1.** *mourn before* God ὁμοίως Νινευίταις προσκλαύσητε τῷ θεῷ Just.*dial*.108.1(M.6.725C); Thphn.*chron*.p.26(M.108.124B); **2.** *be a mourner* before church door, one of the first grade of penitents χρὴ τῷ πρώτῳ ἐκβάλλεσθαι τῶν προσευχῶν, καὶ ∼ειν αὐτοὺς τῇ θύρᾳ τῆς ἐκκλησίας· τῷ δευτέρῳ δεχθῆναι εἰς ἀκρόασιν Bas. *ep*.199 *can*.22(3.293C; M.32.724A); ἐν τέσσαρσιν ἔτεσι ∼ειν ὀφείλει, ἔξω τῆς θύρας ἑστὼς τοῦ εὐκτηρίου οἴκου, καὶ τῶν εἰσιόντων πιστῶν δεόμενος εὐχὴν ὑπὲρ αὐτοῦ ποιεῖσθαι, ἐξαγορεύων τὴν ἰδίαν παρανομίαν id.*ep*.217 *can*.56(3.326B; M.797A) = CCP(381)†*can*.1; *ib.can*.57(326C; M.797B); *Const.App*.2.10.4; *ib*.2.18.7; *ib*.3.8.3; CTrull.*can*.87.

***πρόσκλαυσις, ἡ**, *mourning* before church door (first degree of penitence) ἡ π. ἔξω τῆς πύλης τοῦ εὐκτηρίου ἐστίν· ἔνθα ἑστῶτα τὸν ἁμαρτάνοντα χρὴ τῶν εἰσιόντων δεῖσθαι πιστῶν, ὑπὲρ αὐτοῦ εὔχεσθαι Gr.Thaum.*ep.can*.11(M.10.1048A); ἀποχὴ τῶν ἁγιασμάτων, μετὰ προσκλαύσεως, καὶ ἐπιπόνου δεήσεως· ἐπὶ μὲν τῶν πρώτων, τριετίζουσα Thdr.Stud.*epp*.2.49(M.99.1257C).

προσκλείω, *shut to*; Gen.19:10 (LXX ἀπέκλεισαν) cited as τὴν θύραν...προσέκλεισαν Just.*dial*.56.19(M.6.604C); Chrys.*hom.11.1 in 1Thess*.(11.502E).

***προσκλήρωσις, ἡ**, *attachment, adherence* διὰ τῆς τῶν...εἰδώλων ἀποχῆς καὶ τῆς πρὸς τὸν...πατέρα τῶν ὅλων π. [v.l. προσκλήσεως; cj. προσκλίσεως; but cf. Philo *De Fortitudine* 7] Clem.*str*.2.18(p.154.4; M.8.1016C).

πρόσκλησις, ἡ, *invitation*, Cyr.*Zach*.16(3.671D); to combat, *challenge* τὴν τοῦ Ἕκτορος περὶ τῆς μονομαχίας π. ‡Just.*coh.Gr*.30(M.6.297C); to evil, *temptation*, †Bas.*bapt*.2.10.1(2.669B; M.31.1617C).

***προσκλητέος**, *to be called* or *summoned*, Gr.Mag.*dial*.(tr.Zach.) 4.2(M.*PL*.77.322A).

προσκλινής, **1.** *prejudiced, biased*, Cyr.ap.*cat.Lc*.11:42(p.97.1) for ἀπροσκλινής Cyr.*Lc*.11:42(M.72.716A); **2.** ? *resting*, hence *inactive* ἔλαβεν ἀρραβῶνα τὴν πίστιν τῆς νεανίδος, καὶ οὐκέτι π. ἦν ἡ χάρις· ἀλλὰ περιεῖχεν αὐτῇ τῆς ἀφθαρσίας τὴν δύναμιν Ephr.2.270E.

πρόσκλισις, ἡ, **1.** *inclination, proclivity*, Clem.*str*.1.18(p.57.11; M.8.804B); αἵρεσίς ἐστι π. δογμάτων ἤ...π. δόγμασι πολλοῖς *ib*.8.5(p.89.24; M.9.581A); τῆς προαιρέσεως διὰ τῆς πρὸς τὴν κακίαν π. τὸν ἐκμαλάσσοντα τὴν ἀντιτυπίαν λόγον οὐ δεχομένης Gr.Nyss.*v.Mos*.(M.44.348C); ref. Valent. tripartite division of man τὸ δὲ ψυχικόν...ἅτε μέσον ὂν τοῦ τε πνευματικοῦ καὶ ὑλικοῦ, ἐκεῖσε χωρεῖν, ὅπου ἂν καὶ τὴν π. ποιήσηται Iren.*haer*.1.6.1(M.7.504A); **2.** *personal attachment, partiality, favour*, *1Clem*.21.7; πνευματικῶς ἐπέστειλεν ὑμῖν περὶ αὐτοῦ τε καὶ Κηφᾶ τε καὶ Ἀπολλώ, διὰ τὸ καὶ τότε π. ὑμᾶς πεποιῆσθαι. ἀλλ' ἡ π. ἐκείνη ἥττονα ἁμαρτίαν...προσήνεγκεν· προσεκλίθητε γὰρ ἀποστόλοις *ib*.47.3,4; ἐν ἀγάπῃ...δίχα π. ἀνθρωπίνης *ib*.50.2; οὔτε πρόσωπα λαμβάνων...οὔτε ποιῶν κατὰ πρόσκλισιν Bas.*hom*.12.9(2.105D; M.31.405A); id.*ep*.156.2(3.246C; M.32.616C); Cyr.*Mal*.4(3.820B).

προσκνάομαι, *itch*; met. (cf. 2Tim.4:3), Gr.Naz.*or*.27.1(p.1.3; M.36.12A).

προσκνήθομαι, *scratch*; of horses pawing the ground, Max. *ambig*.(M.91.1212A).

προσκολλ-άω, **1.** *join to* προσεκόλλησε τῷ πρασίνῳ μέρει...τὸ λευκὸν...καὶ τῷ βενέτῳ μέρει...προσεκόλλησε...τὸ Ῥούσιον μέρος Jo. Mal.*chron*.7 p.176(M.97.281B); **2.** med. and pass., *cleave to, adhere to, be joined to* πῶς γάρ τις ∼ηθήσεται τῷ κυρίῳ, μὴ τοῦ πνεύματος τὴν συνάφειαν...ἐνεργοῦντος; Gr.Nyss.*Maced*.23(M.45.1329B); Λευί, κολλητός, τουτέστι θεῷ ∼ώμενος Nil.*epp*.1.90(M.79.121C); to BMV, Sergia *Olymp*.2(p.50.13); theol. πότερον οὖν [sc. ὁ Χριστὸς] ἀφ' ἑαυτοῦ ὑπέστη, καὶ ὑποστὰς προσκεκόλληται τῷ πατρί; ‡Ath.*Ar*.4.3(p.46.13; M.26.472A); of Inc. κατῆλθεν ὁ λόγος ∼ηθησόμενος τῇ γυναικί Meth.*symp*.3.8(p.35.12; M.18.73A); καταβὰς ἐξ οὐρανῶν καὶ ∼ηθεὶς τῇ ἑαυτοῦ γυναικί, τῇ ἐκκλησίᾳ *ib*.(p.36.3; 73B).

προσκόλλησις, ἡ, *joining, uniting*, of Church's union with Christ τὴν π. τῶν δύο εἰς ἑνὸς σώματος κοινωνίαν τὸ μέγα μυστήριον εἶναι λέγει Gr.Nyss.*hom.4 in Cant*.(M.44.836D); of soul's adherence to God, id.*Maced*.23(M.45.1329B); in gen. ἡ τῶν κακοτρόπων ἀνδρῶν ...συντυχία καὶ π. βλάψαι καὶ αὐτοὺς τοὺς προσέχοντας ἑαυτοῖς Leont.N.*v.Jo.Eleem*.1(p.4.5).

προσκομιδή, ἡ, **1.** *supply, provision* Κωνσταντινούπολις...τὰ πολλὰ εὐθηνεῖται τῷ...διὰ θαλάσσης ἔχειν τῶν πανταχόθεν ἐπιτηδείων τὴν π. Socr.*h.e*.4.16.8(M.67.501B); of provisions given to poor as being form of divine service, Nil.*epp*.3.7(M.79.369A); **2.** *offering*; **a.** in gen., of offering of vinegar to Christ as an insult, Chrys.*hom. 87.1 in Mt*.(7.818A); **b.** *sacrificial offering*; **i.** ref. sacrifice of Isaac ἀπέδειξε γάρ, ὅτι παρὲκ θεοῦ ἄλλο τι οὐκ ἠγάπησε διὰ τῆς τοῦ μονογενοῦς π. Mac.Aeg.*hom*.5.6(M.34.509A); Thdt.*Cant*.8:7(2.157); **ii.** of alms πολλοὶ δὲ ἡμῖν καὶ περὶ ὀβολῶν ἐν καιρῷ μικρολογοῦνται προσκομιδὴν ‡Chrys.*pan.Macc*.3(2.633A); Nil.*epp*.3.243(M.79.500B); **iii.** of OT sacrifices contrasted with self-offering of Christians as λογικὴ λατρεία, Thdr.Mops.*Rom*.12:1(p.160.28; M.66.861A); **iv.** of Hebrew free-will offering, Cyr.*ador*.4(1.130A); **v.** of Abel's sacrifice, Gennad.*fr.Gen*.4:4(M.85.1640C); **vi.** eucharistic, of service as a whole, *A.Mt*.B 25(p.254.14); εἰ χρὴ εἰς κοινὸν οἶκον π. γίνεσθαι Bas. *reg.br*.310 tit.(2.525D; M.31.1304B); Pall.*h.Laus*.57(M.34.1250C; p.150.21 om.); ἤτησεν ἐκεῖ γενέσθαι τὴν τοῦ θείου δώρου π. Thdt.*h.rel*.20(3.1234); ἐν τῷ καιρῷ τῆς θείας π. Cyr.S.*v.Sab*.32(p.117.24); of preparation of elements ἡ π. ἡ γενομένη ἐν τῷ σκευοφυλακίῳ ἐμφαίνει τὸν κρανίου τόπον ‡Bas.*h.myst*.48(p.389.26); ‡Sophr.H.*liturg*.21(M.87.4001A); of anaphora, †Gregent.*leg.hom*.(M.86.617A); ἀδελφὸς...ὃς ἦν μαθὼν τὴν π. τῆς ἁγίας ἀναφορᾶς...καὶ...εἶπεν τὴν π. ὡς ἐν τάξει τῆς στιχολογίας Jo.Mosch.*prat*.25(M.87.2869D); ἀπαγγέλλειν δὲ καὶ τὴν ἁγίαν π. τὴν ἐπὶ τῇ ἁγίᾳ κοινωνίᾳ γενομένην Ath.Scholast.*coll*.1.17 tit.(p.23); ἐν τῇ ἁγίᾳ π. ὁ ἱερεὺς...δυσωπεῖ τὸν θεὸν λέγων· μνήσθητι, κύριε, πάσης ψυχῆς Anast.S.*qu.et resp*.110(M.89.764B); Niceph.Ur. *v.Sym*.156(M.86.3132B); εἰ μή τινες εὐεργεσίας μετεῖχον...οὐκ ἂν ἐν τῇ π. ἐμνημονεύοντο ‡Ath.*qu.Ant*.34(M.28.617B); Jo.D.*haer*.86(M.94.756B); id.*trisag*.27(M.95.57C).

προσκομίζ-ω, **1.** *carry* or *convey to* τὸ τοῦ πατρὸς σκῆνος...τῇ πόλει προσεκόμιζεν Eus.*v.C*.4.70(p.146.29; M.20.1225A); **2.** *address* speech, Cyr.*Ps*.34:19(M.69.908D); **3.** *offer*; **a.** in gen. χρυσὸν αὐτῷ γεννηθέντι ...προσεκόμισαν οἱ μάγοι Clem.*paed*.2.8(p.196.1; M.8.469A); Ephr. 1.221A; παράδοξα ἀεὶ ἡμῖν ἡ θεία μητροπαρθένος ἐν ἁγίαις αὐτῆς ἐπιλάμψεσι ∼εται Thdot.Anc.*hom.BMV et Sym*.4(M.77.1396A); **b.** of sacrifice to God; **i.** of OT sacrifices, Clem.*str*.2.11(p.140.9; M.8.988A); Cyr.*ador*.4(1.129E); id.*Mal*.9(3.826D); **ii.** of sacrifice of Isaac likened to self-sacrifice of martyrs, *M.Glyc*.7(p.13*F); **iii.** of Christ's self-offering ἴδιον αὐτοῦ σῶμα τὸ ὑπὲρ ἡμῶν εἰς ὀσμὴν εὐωδίας τῷ θεῷ καὶ πατρὶ προσκεκομισμένον Cyr.*Arcad*.7(p.64.17; 5².46A); οὐκ ἐπίγειον τινὰ θυσίαν ∼οντα τῷ πατρί, θείαν δὲ μᾶλλον id. *Nest*.3.2(p.62.9; 6¹.74E); προσκεκόμικε μὲν ὁ Χριστὸς ἑαυτὸν ὑπὲρ τοῦ κατὰ σάρκα γένους *ib*.3.6(p.74.20; 93B); **iv.** of Christ's intercessory presentation of prayers to Father ∼ει τῷ πατρὶ τὰς ὑπὲρ ἡμῶν ἱκετηρίας id.*Jo*.11.2(4.937A); **v.** of Christians' offering of worship ἐν παντὶ τόπῳ ∼οντες αὐτῷ τὸν εὐώδη καρπὸν τῆς παναρέτου θεολογίας Eus.*d.e*.1.10(p.49.3; M.22.92D); τὴν ὑπὲρ σωτηρίας ἡμῶν εὐχαριστίαν δι' εὐσεβῶν ὕμνων τε καὶ εὐχῶν τῷ θεῷ ∼οντες *ib*.(p.49.10; 92D); ἥξουσι...εἰς τὴν...ἐπουράνιον Ἱερουσαλήμ, ἐκεῖ προσκομιοῦσι θεῷ πνευματικὰς θυσίας Cyr.*Nah*.18(3.498A); ∼όντων αὐτῷ τὰς πνευματικὰς λατρείας...πίστιν, ἐλπίδα, ἀγάπην id.*Mal*.12(3.830B); **vi.** and self-offering through Christ, id.*Juln*.8(6².258B); **vii.** of eucharistic offering ὑπὲρ τοῦ δώρου τοῦ προσκομισθέντος...τῷ θεῷ...δεηθῶμεν, ὅπως ὁ...θεὸς προσδέξηται αὐτὸ...εἰς τὸ ἐπουράνιον αὐτοῦ θυσιαστήριον εἰς ὀσμὴν εὐωδίας *Lit*.ap.*Const.App*.8.13.3; κἂν γὰρ πιστεύσῃς ὡς ἀληθὲς εἴη τὸ σῶμα τοῦ Χριστοῦ καὶ προσκομίσῃς τῷ θυσιαστηρίῳ πρὸς μεταποίησιν Thdt.*eran*.2(4.145); ἐπιφανεὶς ὁ Χριστός...ἔν ἄρτῳ τε καὶ οἴνῳ πνευματικῶς προσκομίσας Niceph.Ur.*v.Sym*.115(M.86.3093B); μνήσθητι κύριε τῶν τὰ δῶρα ταῦτα προσκομισάντων *Lit.Bas*.(p.332.16); οἱ τὰ ἄζυμα ∼οντες, νεκρὰν σάρκα, καὶ οὐχὶ ζῶσαν προσφέρουσιν ‡Jo.D.*azym*.proem.(M.95.388A); hence = *celebrate* χρὴ τοὺς ∼οντας ...ἐκφωνεῖν τὰς εὐχὰς καὶ τὴν προσκομιδὴν Ath.Scholast.*coll*.1.17 (p.24); ἐν τῷ ∼ειν τὸν ἀββᾶν Jo.Mosch.*prat*.25(M.87.2872A); ∼οντα αὐτὸν ἔφθασα *ib*.108(2972A); ταύτῃ τῇ κυριακῇ μὴ προσκομίσῃς *ib*.150 (3013D).

προσκομιστέον, *one must supply*, Clem.*str*.1.6(p.22.19; M.8.729A).

πρόσκομμα, τό, **1.** *occasion of stumbling*, met. ὀνειδισμὸν ἑαυτῷ φέρει παρὰ τοὺς υἱοὺς τῶν ἀνθρώπων καὶ π. τῷ Βελίαρ *T.Reub*.4.7; π. λογικῆς φύσεώς ἐστι λογισμὸς ἀκάθαρτος, ἢ γνῶσις ψευδὴς Or.*exp.in Pr*.3:23(M.17.169A); **2.** *obstacle, stumbling-block* ἡ γὰρ στρεβλὴ ὁδὸς ...ἔχει...π. πολλά Herm.*mand*.6.1.3; met., *hindrance, obstacle* ἔθηκα π. τῇ εὐθύτητί μου *A.Phil.*140(p.75.8); of scriptural difficulties οὐδὲν οὖν π. κατὰ τὸν τόπον ἐστίν Or.*engast.*10(p.294.10; M.12.1028C); ἐὰν δέ ποτε ἀναγινώσκων τὴν γραφὴν προσκόψῃς νοήματι ὄντι καλῷ λίθῳ προσκόμματος...αἰτιῶ σαυτόν. μὴ ἀπελπίσῃς γὰρ τὸν λίθον τοῦτον τοῦ π. ... ἔχειν νοήματα ὥστ' ἂν γενέσθαι κατὰ τὸ εἰρημένον· καὶ ὁ πιστεύων οὐ καταισχυνθήσεται id.*fr.hom.21 in Jer.*(p.196.10; M.14.1310C); τὰ ἐκ τῆς γραφῆς π. λύειν καὶ διαρθροῦν Gr.Naz.*or.*42.18(M.36.480B); **3.** *offence, scandal*; **a.** in gen., Herm.*mand.*2.4; εἰσιν οἱ γεννήσαντες τὴν ἀδοξίαν τῇ προνοίᾳ, τὰ π. τῷ θεῷ Or.*hom.12.11 in Jer.*(p.98.3; M.13.393B); *Const.App.*2.17.1; μὴ γενόμενος π. τοῖς ἀσθενέσι Pall.*v.Chrys.*18(p.112.2; M.47.62); Nil.*Magn.*37(M.79.1013D); of scandal of Christ, *Orac.Sib.*8.246; ref. Pauline teaching on sacrificial food ἐὰν διὰ προσκόμματος ἐσθίῃ Clem.*str.*3.12(p.235.17; M.8.1185C); **b.** ref. λίθος προσκόμματος (Is.8:14; Rom.9:33); **i.** interpreted of Christ, cf. *Jesus, quem plurimis, sed bonis... nominibus compellari invenimus, mirum fortasse videatur cur in hoc loco...lapis offensionis...nominetur...offensio et scandalum unum prope atque idem significat...quia igitur hi qui erant in Sion, vias non bonas incedentes iter perditionis...currebant, malis suis faventes invicem...veniens dominus...impedire coepit vias perditionis eorum, et effectus est lapis offensionis,* Or.*Rom.*7.19(M.14.1156A–C); †Bas.*Is.*214(2.540B; M.30.489B); εἰς Χριστός· ἀλλ' εἰς πτῶσιν κεῖται καὶ ἀνάστασιν· πτῶσιν μὲν τοῖς ἀπίστοις, ἀνάστασιν δὲ τοῖς πιστεύουσι· καὶ τοῖς μὲν ἔστι πέτρα προσκόμματος...τοῖς δὲ λίθος ἀκρογωνιαῖος Gr.Naz.*or.*17.7(M.35.973B); προσκόμματος δὲ λίθον...φησὶν ἀπὸ τῆς γνώμης καὶ τοῦ τέλους τῶν μὴ πιστευσάντων Chrys.*hom.16.10 in Rom.*(9.620D) = Jo.D.*Rom.*9:33(M.95.521A); Thdr.Mops.*Rom.*9:33(p.150.8ff.; M.66.845A); ἁγιαζέσθω...ὁ Χριστὸς...καὶ φοβερὸς ἔστω παρ' ὑμῖν. ἔσται γὰρ οὕτως ὑμῖν ἁγίασμα, καὶ οὐχ ὡς λίθου προσκόμματι συναντήσετε αὐτῷ Cyr.*Is.*1.5(2.141B); cf. Ἰουδαῖοι περὶ...τὰ περιττὰ τοῦ νόμου κεχηνότες, τὸν ὑπὸ τῶν προφητῶν προαγορευθέντα λίθον ἰδεῖν οὐκ ἠθέλησαν Thdt.*Rom.*9:33(3.110); ὁ αὐτὸς δὲ κύριος, τοῖς μὲν ἁγίασμα, τοῖς δὲ π. γίνεται. καὶ π. μὲν ἴσως Ἕλλησιν τοῖς σοφίαν ζητοῦσιν, ἡ μωρία τοῦ κηρύγματος...διὰ τοῦτο δέ, φησίν, ἀδυνατήσουσιν ἐν αὐτοῖς πολλοί, δῆλον δι' ὅτι γέγονεν αὐτοῖς εἰς λίθον προσκόμματος Proc.G.*Is.*8:11–15(M.87.1988B–D), based on †Bas. ad loc.; **ii.** esp. ref. Christ's birth πῶς οὖν ἐγένετο λίθος π. ... Ἐμμανουήλ; διὰ τῆς ἐκ παρθένου κυήσεως. ὅθεν καὶ ὁ θεῖος ἀπόστολος ταῦτα διδάσκων ἔλεγεν, Ἰουδαίοις μὲν σκάνδαλον, Ἕλλησι δὲ μωρία. οἱ τοίνυν ἀπειθοῦντες τῇ ἰσχυρᾷ χειρὶ κυρίου ἔσχον αὐτὸν λίθον π. Eus.*Is.*8:12(M.24.145A); **iii.** esp. ref. Cross, Thdt.*Is.*8:13–15(p.44.22; 3.227–8); **iv.** with distn. bet. two passages of Is. combined by S. Paul κεῖται ἡ...λέξις ἐν ταῖς Ἡσαΐου προφητείαις διεσπαρμένως, οὐχ ὡς εἴρηται νῦν ὑπὸ τοῦ ἀποστόλου, συνηθροισμένως. · περὶ μὲν ἀρχὴν τῆς βίβλου γέγραπται περὶ τοῦ κυρίου κατὰ τὴν ἔκδοσιν τὴν Ἀκύλα ᾗ συμπεφώνηκε καὶ ἡ ἀποστολική·...ἔσται εἰς ἁγίασμα καὶ εἰς λίθον π. ... μετὰ πολλὰ δὲ ἔστιν ὅτι ἰδοὺ ἐμβάλλω...λίθον πολυτελῆ. ... καὶ ἔστι... κατανοῆσαι σαφῶς τὸν ἐν τῷ ἑτέρῳ λίθον ἁπλῶς εἰρημένον, ἐν τῷ ἑτέρῳ τὸν κύριον ἡρμηνευομένον ἐπὶ τοῦ θεϊκοῦ ἀξιώματος Apoll.*Rom.*9:33(p.69.6) = Gennad.*fr.Rom.*9:33(M.85.1712B–C).

προσκόπτ-ω, **1.** *stumble against*; abs., *stumble*, Jo.Mal.*chron.*4 p.89(M.97.173A); **2.** *offend* μᾶλλον ἀνθρώποις ἄφροσι...προσκόψωμεν ἢ τῷ θεῷ *1Clem.*21.5; Clem.*str.*2.12(p.142.11; M.8.992A); σοὶ τῷ θεῷ ~ειν Or.*hom.14.15 in Jer.*(p.121.20; M.13.424C); *Didasc.Jac.*2.6(p.48.28); abs., ref. original sin ἐν μὲν γὰρ τῷ πρώτῳ Ἀδὰμ προσεκόψαμεν Iren.*haer.*5.16.3(M.7.1168B); ~ειν ποιεῖ διαλογισμοῖς ματαίοις Mac.Aeg.*hom.*5.2(M.34.496B); **3.** *take offence, find difficulty* or *perplexity* ἐπεὶ ~ουσιν οἱ ἀδελφοὶ ἡμῶν δύο εἶναι θεούς Or.*dial.*2(p.124.7); ἄνελε τὴν κακίαν, καὶ οὐ ~εις τῇ προνοίᾳ id.*hom.12.11 in Jer.*(p.97.28; M.13.393B); ἐάν ποτε ἀναγινώσκων τὴν γραφὴν προσκόψῃς νοήματι ὄντι καλῷ λίθῳ προσκόμματος...αἰτιῶ σαυτόν· μὴ ἀπελπίσῃς γὰρ τὸν λίθον τοῦτον τοῦ προσκόμματος...ἔχειν νοήματα ὥστ' ἂν γενέσθαι τὸ εἰρημένον· καὶ ὁ πιστεύων οὐ καταισχυνθήσεται id.*fr.hom.39 in Jer.*(p.196.19; M.13.541D); κατὰ μὲν τὴν καινὴν [sc. διαθήκην] οὐ ~οντες ἀλλ' ἀπολογίαν ζητοῦντες, κατὰ δὲ τὴν παλαιὰν περὶ τῶν παραπλησίων, δέον ἀπολογεῖσθαι ὁμοίως τοῖς ἀπὸ τῆς καινῆς, κατηγοροῦντες id.*princ.*3.1.16(p.225.8; M.11.281C); μὴ ~ε τοίνυν, εἰ...τις λέγοι Meth.*res.*1.23(p.246.12; M.41.1092C); **4.** impers., *be an obstacle* or *difficulty*, ref. Is.7:16 οὐ ~ει σοι ταῦτα λέγειν περὶ τοῦ μονογενοῦς Or.*hom.1.8 in Jer.*(p.7.2; M.13.264B); εἰ δέ τινι ~ει τοὺς ἀνθρωπίνους τεχνίτας μὴ δύνασθαι παραδέξασθαι τὸν θεὸν χωρὶς ὕλης...ὑποκειμένης κατασκευάζειν τὰ ὄντα id.*comm.in Gen.*ap.Eus.*p.e.*7.20(334D; M.12.48A); **5.** ? *be struck, knocked about* ὥσπερ γὰρ ἐν τῷ σινίῳ ὁ σῖτος ὑπὸ τοῦ σινιάζοντος ~ει Mac.Aeg.*hom.*5.2(M.34.496B) perh. for ~εται; **6.** f.l. for προκόπτειν, Nil.*exerc.*32(M.79.761A); ‡Nil.*perist.*9.8(M.79.880C).

***προσκορέω**, *be satiated*, Or.*exc.in Ps.*77:31(M.17.140C).

***προσκοσμέω**, reflex., *adorn oneself* for ἀρετὴν γὰρ τῇ σοφίᾳ συνήρμοσεν καὶ οὕτως ἐν τούτοις ἑαυτὴν...τῷ σωτῆρι Σωτερὶς προσεκόσμησεν Pamph.Mon.*Soter.*3(p.119.28).

***προσκουλκάτωρ**, ὁ, *advanced scout* (? for προσπεκουλάτωρ), Jo.Mal.*chron.*13 p.330(M.97.492C).

πρόσκρουσις, ἡ, **1.** *offence* προσέκρουσας τῷ θεῷ, καὶ ἐπιλανθάνῃ; δευτέρα αὕτη π. Chrys.*hom.22.3 in 2Cor.*(10.592D); **2.** *opposition* εἰ μὴ ἐν π. ὁ τοῦ Χριστοῦ πατήρ, ὡς ὁ Μαρκίων λέγει, πρὸς τὸν ἴδιον αὐτοῦ υἱὸν γεγένηται Epiph.*haer.*42.16(p.185.19; M.41.816C).

προσκρουσμός, ὁ, *offence*, Ast.Am.*hom.*5(M.40.228B); Chrys.*hom.17.3 in 1Tim.*(11.651A).

***προσκρουστικῶς**, *offensively*, Or.*Jo.*20.16(14; p.347.26; M.14.608D).

προσκρού-ω, **1.** *collide*, ref. theory of Leucippus ὅταν εἰς μέγα κενὸν...ἀθροισθῇ πολλὰ σώματα...~οντα ἀλλήλοις συμπλέκεσθαι τὰ ὁμοιοσχήμονα καὶ παραπλήσια τὰς μορφὰς Hipp.*haer.*1.12(p.16.20; M.16.3037A); ~ομένων τῶν νεφελῶν...γίνεται ἡ ἀστραπή Or.*hom.8.4 in Jer.*(p.60.5; M.13.341C); **2.** *offend*, c. dat., *T.Gad* 5.5; Or.*hom.13.1 in Jer.*(p.102.6; M.13.400A); Chrys.*hom.62.5 in Jo.*(8.374C); τὰ... προσκρούσματα, ἃ καθ' ἑκάστην ~ομεν τὴν ἡμέραν id.*hom.19.7 in Mt.*(7.255C); id.*hom.86.4 in Jo.*(8.518D); ἁγίῳ ἀνδρὶ προσκεκρουκὼς Isid.Pel.*epp.*5.22(M.78.1340A); Thdt.*Rom.*8:34(3.95); **3.** *be offensive* ἐπεὶ πατέρα ἴδιον ἔλεγεν τὸν θεὸν...εἰκὸς αὐτοὺς ἐπιφέρειν πάλιν ~οντας τὸ ἕνα πατέρα ἔχομεν, τὸν θεόν Or.*Jo.*20.16(14; p.347.14; M.14.608C).

προσκτίζω, *create in addition* ἐγεννήθη ὁ υἱός...οὐχὶ προγενόμενος ὑπάρχων πρὸ τῶν αἰώνων, οὐχὶ προσκτισθεὶς ὕστερον Nil.*epp.*2.323(M.79.357C).

προσκυλινδ-έομαι, *roll before*; hence **1.** *fall prostrate before* ἐδεξιοῦντο αὐτὸν ~ούμενοι τοῖς τούτου ποσὶ βρώσεως μεταλαβεῖν *A.Jo.*6(p.154.30); *M.Ner.et Ach.*13(p.13.5); Nil.*epp.*2.140(M.79.260D); **2.** *wallow*, of a lunatic προσεκυλινδεῖτο τῇ γῇ Sophr.H.*v.Anast.*(M.92.1729A); **3.** *grovel before*, in contemptuous ref. to martyr-cults καίτοι οὐκ εἴρηται παρ' ὑμῖν οὐδαμοῦ τοῖς τάφοις ~εῖσθαι Juln.Imp.ap.Cyr.*Juln.*10(6^{2}.335C); ὑπὲρ τίνος ~εῖσθε τοῖς μνήμασι; id.*ib.*(339E).

προσκυν-έω, **1.** *make obeisance* πεσόντες πάντες ἐπὶ πρόσωπον προσεκύνησαν τρίτον τῷ ἀποστόλῳ *A.Phil.*93(p.36.11); ὁ παῖς προσεκύνησεν τῷ Πέτρῳ *M.Ner.et Ach.*12(p.12.16); ‡Ath.*dial.Trin.*3.12(M.28.1220C); to emperor, *Chron.Pasch.*p.324(M.92.829B); in gen. ἰδὼν ἡμᾶς προσεκύνησε...ἐπὶ τὴν γῆν ἑαυτὸν ἐξαπλώσας ‡Pall.*h.mon.*8.48(p.46.19; M.34.1147A); Cyr.S.*v.Sab.*24(p.108.23); **2.** *make act of reverence, bow*, in liturgy ὁ διάκονος ~ήσας ἅπαξ λαμβάνει παρὰ τοῦ ἱερέως τὸ ἅγιον ποτήριον *Lit.Chrys.*(p.395.38; M.63.921); *ib.*(p.396.33; 921); **3.** *greet, salute* ~ηθῆναι αὐτὴν παρά τινος οὐ συγχωρεῖ *M.Ner.et Ach.*7(p.5.27); δυνησόμεθα εἰρηνικοῖς γράμμασιν ἑαυτοὺς ~εῖν CIllyr.*ep.*ap.Thdt.*h.e.*4.9.8(3.962); **4.** *entreat, beg*, Isid.Pel.*epp.*1.490(M.78.449A); **5.** *hold in honour, respect* μεταλαβὼν δὲ ὁ βασιλεὺς ...τὰ περὶ τοῦ Δημητρίου, ~ήσας ἐκέλευσε μεγάλην ποιεῖσθαι τῶν βιβλίων ἐπιμέλειαν Aristeas ap.Eus.*p.e.*8.5(355A; M.21.597A); ἐάν σοι εἴπω, θέλων ἔπαθεν [sc. Χριστός], ἵνα μοι εἴπῃς, ἄπελθε, ~ησον τοὺς Ἰουδαίους, ἐπειδὴ τὸ θέλημα τοῦ θεοῦ ἐποίησαν Jo.D.*disp.*2(M.96.1340D); **6.** *venerate, revere, adore, worship*; **a.** ref. pagan and idolatrous worshippers, Just.*dial.*20.4(M.6.520B); ἥλιον καὶ τὴν σελήνην, ἃ γέγραπται τοῖς ἔθνεσι συγκεχωρηκέναι τὸν θεὸν ὡς θεοὺς ~εῖν *ib.*55.1(596A); θύεις πρόβατον, τὸ δ' αὐτὸ καὶ ~εῖς Tat.*orat.*10(p.11.14; M.6.828B); τὰς ἀντιδόσεις ~οῦντες καὶ τὰς συμφοράς. ἐντεῦθεν τὰς Ἐρινύας καὶ τὰς Εὐμενίδας...ἀναπεπλάκασιν Clem.*prot.*2(p.19.20; M.8.96A); κατὰ χρόνους ὕστερον ἀνέπλαττον θεούς, οἷς ~οῖεν *ib.*3(p.33.26; 129B); θεοὺς δὲ δὴ τοὺς ὁρατοὺς καὶ τὸν σύγκλυδα τῶν γενητῶν τούτων ὄχλον ὁ ~ῶν...αὐτῶν ἐκείνων τῶν δαιμόνων ἀθλιώτερος μακρῷ *ib.*10(p.71.3; 212A); ref. cults of hero-tombs ἐπιόντι μοι τοὺς ~ουμένους ὑμῖν τάφους, ἐμοὶ μὲν οὐδ' ὁ πᾶς ἂν ἀρκέσαι χρόνος *ib.*3(p.35.4; 133A); of image-cults ἡ τέχνη...προσάγουσα...ἐπὶ τὸ...~εῖν τά τε ἀγάλματα καὶ τὰς γραφὰς *ib.*4(p.45.14; 156C); ref. cults of divine rulers νῦν μὲν τὸν Μακεδόνα τὸν...Ἀμύντου Φίλιππον ἐν Κυνοσάργει νομοθετοῦντες ~εῖν *ib.*(p.42.22; 149B); ref. worship of deified men τὰ ~ούμενα παρὰ τοῖς ἔθνεσι τὰ μὲν ~εῖται ὡς θεοί, τὰ δὲ ὡς ἥρωες...Ἡρακλέα ~οῦσιν οὐχ ὡς γεγεννημένον θεόν, ἀλλ' ὡς ἐξ ἀνθρώπου εἰς θεὸν μεταβληθέντα... ὅταν δὲ ~ῶσι τοὺς πατέρας τούτων ὀνομαζομένους παρ' αὐτοῖς θεούς, ~οῦσιν οὐχ ὡς μεταβαλόντας ἐξ ἀνθρώπων εἰς θεούς, ἀλλ' ὡς...θεοὺς ἀρχῆθεν ὄντας Or.*hom.5.3 in Jer.*(p.33.19ff.; M.13.300C); ἐάν τις ἐν τῇ γῇ τοῦ θεοῦ, τῇ ἐκκλησίᾳ, τυγχάνων ~ήσῃ θεοῖς ἀλλοτρίοις θεοποιῶν τὰ μὴ θεοποιεῖσθαι ἄξια, ἐκβληθήσεται εἰς γῆν ἀλλοτρίαν καὶ ~είτω τοὺς θεούς, οὓς ἔνδον προσεκύνησεν γενόμενος *ib.*7.3(p.53.34; 333A); οὔτε ὡς Αἰθίοπες...Δία καὶ Διόνυσον...μόνους ~ήσομεν...οὔθ' ὡς οἱ Ἀράβιοι τὴν Οὐρανίαν καὶ τὸν Διόνυσον...ὡς θήλειαν γὰρ Ἀράβιοι τὴν Οὐρανίαν ~οῦσι, καὶ ὡς ἄρρενα τὸν Διόνυσον...εἰ δὲ καὶ Ναυκρατίταις ἄλλα μὲν ἔδοξε σέβειν τοῖς πρεσβυτέροις, τὸν Σάραπιν δὲ τοῖς χθὲς καὶ πρώην ἀρξαμένοις, τὸν οὐ πώποτε γενόμενον θεόν, ~εῖν· οὐ παρὰ τοῦτο καὶ ἡμεῖς νέον τὸν οὐ πρότερον ὄντα θεὸν...φήσομεν εἶναι id.*Cels.* 5.37(p.41.9; M.11.1237C); ref. Dt.4:19, cf.Just.*dial.*55.1 cit. supra ἀλλ' εἰκὸς ὅτι θελήσει ἡμᾶς κατασοφίσασθαι δι' ὧν ἂν δύνηται ὁ ἐχθρὸς πρὸς τὸ ~ῆσαι τῷ ἡλίῳ...κτλ. ἀλλ' ἡμεῖς ἐροῦμεν ὅτι ὁ τοῦ θεοῦ λόγος ταῦτα οὐ προσέταξεν. ... καὶ οὐδ' αὐτός γ' ἂν θέλοι ὁ ἥλιος ~εῖσθαι ὑπὸ τῶν ἀπὸ τῆς τοῦ θεοῦ μερίδος, εἰκὸς δὲ ὅτι οὐδὲ ὑπὸ ἄλλου τινός· ἀλλὰ...ὡσπερεὶ φήσει τῷ ~εῖν αὐτὸν ἐθέλοντι· τί...με ~εῖς; κύριον γὰρ τὸν θεόν σου ~ήσεις. ... τί βούλει ~εῖν τὸν ~οῦντα; κἀγὼ γὰρ τῷ θεῷ καὶ πατρὶ ~ῶ καὶ λατρεύω id.*mart.*7(p.8.25; M.11.573A); παραβάτης ἐκ Χριστιανῶν καὶ εἴδωλα ἀναισχύντως ~ῶν Ath.*ep.encycl.*5 (p.174.23; M.25.233B); Bas.*ep.*243.2(3.373D; M.32.905A); ref. pagan image-worship compared with avarice ὥσπερ τὸ ξόανον περιέπει ὁ Ἕλλην· οὕτω σὺ τὸ χρυσίον θύραις πιστεύεις καὶ μοχλοῖς, ἀντὶ ναοῦ τὸ κιβώτιον κατασκευάζων...ἀλλ' οὐ ~ῶ τὸ χρυσίον, φησίν· οὐδὲ ἐκεῖνος τὸ εἴδωλον, φησί, ~εῖ ἀλλὰ τὸν ἐνοικοῦντα δαίμονα. οὕτω καὶ σύ, κἂν μὴ τὸ χρυσίον ~ῇς, ἀλλὰ τὸν ἀπὸ τῆς ὄψεως τοῦ χρυσίου καὶ τῆς ἐπιθυμίας ἐπιπηδῶντά σου τῇ ψυχῇ δαίμονα Chrys.*hom.65.3 in Jo.*(8.392E); **b.** ref. veneration of idols and all created things, forbidden to Christians τῷ δὲ καὶ μὴ δεῖν χειρῶν ἀνθρωπίνων ἔργοις ~εῖν Μενάνδρῳ τῷ κωμικῷ καὶ τοῖς ταῦτα φήσασι ταὐτὰ φράζομεν Just.*1apol.*20.5(M.6.357D); οὐ διακρίνοντες...τὸ ἀγένητον καὶ τὸ γενητόν, τὸ ὂν καὶ τὸ οὐκ ὄν, τὸ νοητὸν καὶ τὸ αἰσθητόν...~ήσομεν τὰ ἀγάλματα; Athenag.*leg.* 15.1(M.6.920A); Or.*mart.*7(p.9.1; M.11.573A); hence Arian doctrine of Son condemned κτίσμα γὰρ κτίσματι οὐ ~εῖ. ... οὐκ ἂν δὲ οὐδὲ αὐτὸς προσεκυνήθη...εἰ ὅλως τῶν κτισμάτων ἦν Ath.*Ar.*2.23,24(M.26.196A,197A); ref. attempted distinction between π. and λατρεύω based on Ex.20:4 εἴπερ δὲ ὁ φάσκων· οὐ ποιήσεις σεαυτῷ...καὶ τὰ ἑξῆς, ὡς διαφερόντων πρὸς ἄλληλα τοῦ 'οὐ ~ήσεις αὐτοῖς' καὶ τοῦ 'οὐδὲ μὴ λατρεύσῃς αὐτοῖς', ταῦτα λέγει, μή ποτε ὁ μὲν διακείμενος πρὸς τὰ εἴδωλα λατρεύῃ αὐτοῖς· ὁ δὲ μὴ διακείμενος ἀλλὰ διὰ δειλίαν...καθυποκρινόμενος αὐτὰ ὑπὲρ τοῦ δοκεῖν ὁμοίως τοῖς πολλοῖς εὐσεβεῖν οὐ λατρεύει μὲν ~εῖ δὲ τοῖς εἰδώλοις. καὶ εἴποιμ' ἂν ὅτι οἱ...ἐξομνύμενοι τὸν Χριστιανισμὸν...οὐ λατρεύουσι μὲν ~οῦσι δὲ τοῖς εἰδώλοις, λαμβάνοντες τὸ ὄνομα κυρίου...τό, θεός, ἐπὶ ματαίῳ...ὕλῃ· προσεκύνουν δὲ οὕτως καὶ οὐκ ἐλάτρευον εἰδώλοις ὁ βεβηλωθεὶς λαὸς εἰς τὰς θυγατέρας Μωάβ. ... τάχα δὲ οὕτως...προσεκύνησαν οὐ λατρεύσαντες τῷ μόσχῳ, ὃν γινόμενον ἐθεάσαντο Or.*mart.*6(p.7.15; M.11.569B); distinction recognized and equated with that between outward and inward reverence ἐπειδὴ συμβαίνει τινὰς ~ῆσαι μὲν διὰ φόβον ἀνθρώπινον, οὐ μὴν καὶ λατρεῦσαι κατὰ ψυχήν, ἐδίδαξεν ὡς ἑκάτερον ἀσεβές Thdt.*qu.38 in Ex.*20:3(1.149); for this distinction in Christian controversy v. infra and s. εἰκών; **c.** of emperor, refused by Christians μᾶλλον τιμήσω τὸν βασιλέα, οὐ ~ῶν αὐτῷ, ἀλλ' εὐχόμενος ὑπὲρ αὐτοῦ. θεῷ...~ῶ, εἰδὼς ὅτι ὁ βασιλεὺς ὑπ' αὐτοῦ γέγονεν. ἐρεῖς οὖν μοι· διὰ τί οὐ ~εῖς τὸν βασιλέα; ὅτι οὐκ εἰς τὸ ~εῖσθαι γέγονεν, ἀλλὰ εἰς τὸ τιμᾶσθαι τῇ νομίμῳ τιμῇ· θεὸς γὰρ οὐκ ἔστιν, ἀλλ' ἄνθρωπος, ὑπὸ θεοῦ τεταγμένος, οὐκ εἰς τὸ ~εῖσθαι, ἀλλὰ εἰς τὸ δικαίως κρίνειν Thphl.Ant.*Autol.*1.11(M.6.1041A); ref. God's dealings with Nebuchadnezzar τοὺς τὴν παρὰ πάντων ἀπαιτοῦντας προσκύνησιν τοὺς ἁγίους αὐτοῦ θεράποντας ~εῖν ἀναγκάζει Thdt.*Dan.*2:45(2.1100); of emperor's image under Christian empire εἰκὼν βασιλέως πληροῖ χώραν βασιλέως· καὶ ~οῦσιν ἄρχοντες...καὶ δῆμοι ~οῦσιν, οὐ πρὸς τὴν σανίδα βλέποντες, ἀλλὰ πρὸς τὸν χαρακτῆρα τοῦ βασιλέως †Sever.*cruc.*(p.898.43); Constantine's statue ἐπεγείρεσθαι [sc. subsequent emperors] τὸν κατὰ καιρὸν βασιλέα καὶ ~εῖν τὴν στήλην τοῦ αὐτοῦ βασιλέως...καὶ αὐτῆς τῆς τύχης τῆς πόλεως *Chron.Pasch.*p.285(M.92.712B); in comparison of emperor's robe with Christ's flesh ὁ βασιλεὺς καὶ γυμνὸς ~εῖται καὶ ἐνδεδυμένος, καὶ ἡ ἁλουργίς, ὡς μὲν ψιλὴ ἁλουργίς, πατεῖται ...βασιλικὸν δὲ γενομένη ἔνδυμα, τιμᾶται Jo.D.*f.o.*4.3(M.94.1105A); id.*imag.*3.38(M.94.1356B); Taras.*ep.*1(M.98.1433D); **d.** of God; alone worshipped by Christians, Athenag.*leg.*16.2(M.6.921A); Thphl.Ant. *Autol.*1.11(M.6.1041A); Or.*Cels.*3.77(p.268.27; M.11.1021A); τὸ ἐναντίον ποιῆσαι, ὡς ἐποίησαν οἱ υἱοὶ Ἰσραὴλ...ἐκεῖνοι μὲν γὰρ [τὰ ἀλλότρια] ἐν τῇ γῇ τῇ ἁγίᾳ ἀλλοτρίοις προσεκύνησαν· ἡμεῖς δὲ ἐν ἀλλοτρίᾳ γῇ τὸν ἀλλότριον τῆς γῆς ~οῦμεν θεόν, ἀλλότριον τῶν ἐπὶ γῆς πραγμάτων...ἦλθεν ἐπὶ ταύτην φορέσας σῶμα...ἵνα...δυνηθῶ ~ῆσαι τὸν θεὸν ἐνθάδε καὶ μετὰ τοῦτο ~ήσω ἐν τῇ γῇ τῇ ἁγίᾳ id.*hom.7.3 in Jer.* (p.54.14; M.13.333C); ref. Arian doctrine of Son οὐκοῦν θεοῦ ἐστι μόνου τὸ ~εῖσθαι Ath.*Ar.*2.23(M.26.196B); ref. Gen.18:1–2 τίνι προσεκύνησεν ἐπὶ τὴν γῆν, ἢ τοῖς ἀνδράσιν; εἶπον ὅτι δύο ἄγγελοι ἦσαν μετὰ τοῦ θεοῦ, καὶ προσεκύνει δηλονότι τῷ θεῷ ‡Ath.*dial.Trin.*3.9(M.28.1216C); of Trin., Gr.Naz.*or.*37.24(M.36.308C); Gr.Nyss.*Apoll.*44 (M.45.1228C); by angels ἤγγισεν δὲ ἡ ὥρα τῶν ἀγγέλων τῶν φυλασσόντων τὴν μητέρα ὑμῶν τοῦ ἀναβῆναι καὶ ~ῆσαι τὸν κύριον *Apoc. Mos.*7(p.4); **e.** of divine attributes, etc. τὴν χεῖρα τοῦ θεοῦ...~εῖν *A.Jo.*7(p.155.13); ~εῖν αὐτοῦ τὴν φιλανθρωπίαν Bas.*ep.*5.2(3.78B; M.32.240C); **f.** of Christ, contrasted with martyrs τοῦτον μὲν γὰρ υἱὸν ὄντα τοῦ θεοῦ ~οῦμεν, τοὺς δὲ μάρτυρας ὡς...μιμητὰς τοῦ κυρίου ἀγαπῶμεν *M.Polyc.*17.3; in gen. ὁδός ἐστιν ὁ κύριος...στενὴ ἐπὶ γῆς ὑπερορωμένη, πλατεῖα ἐν οὐρανοῖς ~ουμένη Clem.*prot.*10(p.72.20; M.8.213C); ὁ κύριος, ὄψει καταφρονούμενος, ἔργῳ ~ούμενος *ib.*(p.78.12; 228A); of Sophia acc. Valentinians ἰδοῦσα δὲ αὐτὸν ἡ Σοφία ὅμοιον τῷ καταλιπόντι αὐτὴν φωτὶ ἐγνώρισεν καὶ προσέδραμεν καὶ...προσεκύνησεν id.*exc.Thdot.*44(p.120.21; M.9.680C); οὐ...~ήσομεν τοὺς ~οῦντας ὡς οὐδὲ Μωϋσέα καὶ τοὺς μετ' αὐτὸν ἐκ θεοῦ προφητεύσαντας...ἀλλὰ...τὸν διάκονον αὐτῶν λόγον τοῦ θεοῦ ~ήσομεν Or.*Cels.*5.12(p.13.27; M.11.1200B); hence, as ambassadors of Sparta refused to prostrate themselves before Persian king (Herodotus 7.136), Christ's ambassadors will worship no other power, *ib.*8.6(p.225.17; 1528B); ref. Magi οἷα θεῷ προσκυνῆσαι τῷ τεχθέντι Eus.*h.e.*1.8.1(M.20.100B); τοῦ σταυροῦ γενομένου, πᾶσα μὲν εἰδωλολατρεία καθῃρέθη...καὶ μόνος ὁ Χριστὸς ~εῖται Ath.*gent.*1(M.25.5A); Trin. ~εῖται παρ' αὐτῶν [sc. ἀγγέλων], οὐχ ὡς τῇ δόξῃ μείζων, ἀλλ' ὡς ἄλλος παρὰ πάντα τὰ κτίσματα καὶ παρ' ἐκείνους ὤν...οὐκ ἂν δὲ οὐδὲ αὐτὸς προσεκυνήθη, οὐδὲ ταῦτ' ἐλέγετο περὶ αὐτοῦ, εἰ ὅλως τῶν κτισμάτων ἦν. νῦν δέ, ἐπειδὴ οὐκ ἔστι κτίσμα, ἀλλ' ἴδιον τῆς οὐσίας τοῦ ~ουμένου θεοῦ γέννημα...διὰ τοῦτο ~εῖται id.*Ar.*2.23,24(M.26.196A,197A); ref. Jo.11:47 ἄνθρωπον αὐτὸν ἔτι καλοῦσιν, οἱ τοσαύτην λαβόντες ἀπόδειξιν τῆς αὐτοῦ θεότητος. τί ποιοῦμεν; πιστεῦσαι ἔδει καὶ...~ῆσαι, καὶ μηκέτι νομίζειν ἄνθρωπον Chrys.*hom.64.3 in Jo.*(8.386D); ἐγώ σε ἐδόξασα ἐπὶ τῆς γῆς...ἐν γὰρ τῷ οὐρανῷ δεδόξαστο, ἔν τε τῇ φύσει τὴν δόξαν ἔχων, καὶ παρὰ τῶν ἀγγέλων ~ούμενος *ib.80.2*(475A); ref. mocking of Christ μετὰ χλεύης αὐτῷ προσεκύνουν *ib.83.5*(496D); Christol. οὐ ~οῦμεν ἡμεῖς τὸν κύριον μετὰ τῆς σαρκός· ἀλλὰ διαιροῦμεν τὸ σῶμα, καὶ μόνῳ τούτῳ λατρεύομεν; Ath.*ep.Adelph.*5(M.26.1077D); Apoll.*ep.Jov.*(p.251.2; M.28.28A) cit. s. προσκύνησις; ~εῖν ὁμολογεῖ Χριστὸς κατὰ τὴν σάρκα τὸν πατέρα...καὶ οὐ χωρίζεται ἡ θεότης. ~εῖται κατὰ τὴν θεότητα καὶ οὐ μερίζεται τὸ σῶμα τῇ τῆς θεότητος προσκυνήσει. οὔτε ἀφιστῶμεν τὸ σῶμα, ὅτε ~οῦμεν Apoll.*ep.Dion.*12(p.261.10; M.*PL.*8.935Af.); ἡ σὰρξ τοῦ κυρίου ~εῖται, καθὸ ἕν ἐστι πρόσωπον καὶ ἓν ζῶον μετ' αὐτοῦ id.*fr.*85(p.225.19)ap.Gr.Nyss.*Apoll.* 44(M.45.1228C); Nest.*fr.*C9(p.262.4)ap.Cyr.*apol.orient.*3(p.39.10; 6[1].165C) cit. s. προσκύνησις; ἕνα ~οῦμεν υἱὸν καὶ κύριον...Χριστόν Cyr.*ep.*17(p.35.27; 5[2].70C); id.*Arcad.*6(p.64.1; 5[2].45C); id.*Nest.*2.13 (p.52.12; 6[1].59E); τὴν ζύμην τοῦ ἀνθρωπίνου φυράματος καθαρίσας, καὶ ὥσπερ ἐξοπτήσας τῷ οἰκείῳ πυρὶ τῆς θεότητος, καὶ εἰς ἓν σὺν αὐτῇ γεγονὼς πρόσωπον καὶ μίαν ~ουμένην ὑπόστασιν Isid.Pel.ap.*cat.Jo.* 6:35(p.250.11); τὴν μὲν διαφορὰν τῶν φύσεων γνωρίζομεν, φύσεις δὲ οὐ ~οῦμεν, ἀλλὰ τὸ ἓν αὐτοῦ πρόσωπον ἤτοι τὴν μίαν ὑπόστασιν, μιᾷ προσκυνήσει ~οῦμεν Pamph.H.*panopl.*10.1(p.636); ἡ σάρξ, κατὰ μὲν τὴν ἑαυτῆς φύσιν, οὐκ ἔστι προσκυνητή, ~εῖται δὲ ἐν τῷ σεσαρκωμένῳ θεῷ λόγῳ...καὶ οὔ φαμεν, ὅτι σάρκα ~οῦμεν ψιλήν, ἀλλὰ σάρκα θεοῦ, ἤτοι σεσαρκωμένον θεόν Jo.D.*f.o.*4.3(M.94.1105B); in doxology, ‡Ath. *imag.Beryt.*7(M.28.805B); **g.** of H. Ghost πνεῦμα δὲ τὸ προφητικὸν σεβόμεθα καὶ ~οῦμεν Just.*1apol.*6.2(M.6.337A); Trin. τίς προσεκύνησε τῷ πνεύματι, φησίν;...ποῦ τὸ χρῆναι ~εῖν...γέγραπται;...τὸ πνεῦμά ἐστιν, ἐν ᾧ ~οῦμεν καὶ δι' οὗ προσευχόμεθα...τὸ οὖν ~εῖν τῷ πνεύματι ...οὐδὲν ἄλλο εἶναί μοι φαίνεται, ἢ αὐτὸ ἑαυτῷ...προσάγειν καὶ τὴν προσκύνησιν Gr.Naz.*or.*31.12(p.159.8ff.; M.36.145B); ~ῶ πατέρα, ~ῶ τὸν υἱόν, ~ῶ τὸ πνεῦμα τὸ ἅγιον *ib.*37.24(308C); Gr.Nyss.*Maced.*24 (M.45.1332B); **h.** of angels; not to be worshipped, Ath.*Ar.*2.23(M.26.196B); ‡Ath.*dial.Trin.*3.9(M.28.1216C); Oecum.*Apoc.*19:10(p.205); **i.** of BMV, Leont.H.*Nest.*4.37(M.86.1712B); Leont.N.*serm.*3(M.93.1608C); Jo.D.*imag.*3.33(M.94.1352A); *ib.*3.34(1353C); *ib.*3.41(1357A); **j.** of martyrs and saints; **i.** ἀγάπη for martyrs contrasted with προσκύνησις of Christ, *M.Polyc.*17.3; reverence for martyrs contrasted with pagan cults οὐ γὰρ ~ῶ μάρτυρας, οὐδὲ νομίζω θεούς· σὺ δὲ...ἀνθρώπους...οὐ θεοὺς ~ῶν ἀποδέδειξαι Ast.Am.*hom.*10(M.40.324C); ἡμεῖς μάρτυρας οὐ ~οῦμεν, ἀλλὰ τιμῶμεν ὡς γνησίους προσκυνητὰς θεοῦ *ib.*(321D); **ii.** veneration of martyrs, by Montanists Ἀλέξανδρον, τὸν λέγοντα ἑαυτὸν μάρτυρα,...ᾧ ~οῦσιν καὶ αὐτῷ πολλοί Apollon.ap.Eus.*h.e.*5.18.6(M.20.477B); of saints by orthodox, Jo.D. *imag.*3.33(M.94.1352A); Thdr.Stud.*ep.imag.*(M.99.504B); **iii.** saints' relics ὅσιε Ἐπιφάνιε, ποίησον ἀναβλέψαι, ὅπως καὶ ἡμεῖς ~ήσωμεν τὸ τίμιόν σου λείψανον. καὶ εὐθέως ἀνέβλεψαν, καὶ εἰσελθόντες ἐν τῇ πόλει προσεκύνησαν τὸ τίμιον λείψανον τοῦ ὁσίου πατρός †Polyb.*v. Epiph.*66(M.41.112B); **k.** other relics, autograph of Fourth Gospel ὅπερ μέχρι νῦν πεφύλακται...ἐν τῇ Ἐφεσίων...ἐκκλησίᾳ καὶ ὑπὸ τῶν πιστῶν ἐκεῖσε ∼εῖται *Chron.Pasch.*p.219(M.92.533B); various, cf. Jo.D.*imag*.1.16(M.94.1245B); holy places ἔνθα ἐπέβη, ἢ κεκάθικεν ἢ ἐπέφανεν...∼οῦμεν ὡς τόπον θεοῦ Leont.N.*serm*.3(M.93.1600B); Jo.D. *imag*.3.34(M.94.1353A); holy sepulchre, Ath.*exp.Ps*.108:29(M.27. 461A); Cross, Juln.Imp.ap.Cyr.*Juln*.6(6².194C) cit. s. σταυρός; Ast. Am.*hom*.11(M.40.537B); Dor.*doct*.4.9(M.88.1669A); Taras.*ep*.1(M.98. 1433C); τὸν δὲ σταυρὸν...ὅτι διὰ τὸν σταυρωθέντα ἐν αὐτῷ Χριστὸν ∼οῦμεν οἱ πιστοὶ...τὸν...σταυροῦ τύπον ἐκ δύο ξύλων συνάπτοντες ∼οῦμεν. ἡνίκα δέ τις ἡμῖν τῶν ἀπίστων ἐγκαλέσειεν, ὡς ξύλον ∼οῦντας δυνάμεθα τὰ δύο ξύλα χωρίσαντες, καὶ τὸν τύπον...διαλύσαντες, ὡς ἀργὰ ταῦτα ἡγεῖσθαι ξύλα...καὶ τὸν ἄπιστον πεῖσαι, ὅτι οὐ τὸ ξύλον σεβόμεθα, ἀλλὰ τὸν τοῦ σταυροῦ τύπον ‡Ath.*qu.Ant*.39,41(M.28.621D, 624B); ∼οῦμεν...καὶ τὸν τύπον τοῦ τιμίου σταυροῦ...ὡς Χριστοῦ σύμβολον Jo.D.*f.o*.4.11(M.94.1132B); sacred books, id.*imag*.3.35(M.94. 1353C); **l.** of images (v. προσκύνησις); **i.** by Carpocratians, Epiph. *haer*.27.6(p.311.6; M.41.376A); **ii.** by orthodox, †Bas.*ep*.360(3.463A; M.32.1100C); *A.Thadd*.4(p.275.1); Jo.Mosch.*prat*.45(M.87.2900B); **iii.** forbidden by inconoclasts, CCP(754)*decr*.ap.CNic.(787)*act*.6 (H.4.417B); Steph.Diac.*v.Steph*.(M.100.1084C); **iv.** defended, *Dial. Christ.et Jud*.(p.74.16); Sym.Styl.J.*imag*.(M.86.3220A); Leont.N. *serm*.3(M.93.1597C,1600A); ‡Ath.*qu.Ant*.39(M.28.621B); Jo.D.*imag*. 1.21(M.94.1252C,D); ‡Jo.D.*Const*.9(M.95.325A); εἴ τις ∼ῶν τὴν εἰκόνα Χριστοῦ, ἐν αὐτῇ φυσικῶς τὴν θεότητα ∼εῖσθαι λέγοι, ἀλλὰ μὴ καθ' ὅσον ἐστὶ σκιὰ τῆς ἑνωθείσης αὐτῇ σαρκός...αἱρετικός ἐστιν Thdr. Stud.*antirr*.1.20(M.99.349D); id.*ep.imag*.(M.99.504C); **v.** with distinction of π. and λατρεύω (q.v.): πόσα τὰ ∼ούμενα εὑρίσκομεν ἐν τῇ γραφῇ. ... πρῶτον μέν, ἐφ' οἷς ἀναπέπαυται ὁ θεός...ὡς τῇ ἁγίᾳ θεοτόκῳ καὶ πᾶσι τοῖς ἁγίοις...δεύτερος τρόπος, καθ' ὃν ∼οῦμεν κτίσματα, δι' ὧν καὶ ἐν οἷς ἐνήργησεν ὁ θεὸς τὴν σωτηρίαν ἡμῶν...τρίτος τρόπος, καθ' ὃν ∼οῦμεν τὰ τῷ θεῷ ἀνακείμενα, τὰ ἱερὰ...εὐαγγέλια καὶ τὰς λοιπὰς βίβλους...τέταρτος τρόπος, καθ' ὃν ∼οῦνται αἱ εἰκόνες αἱ ὀφθεῖσαι τοῖς προφήταις...καὶ αἱ τῶν ἐσομένων εἰκόνες, ὡς ἡ ῥάβδος Ἀαρών...πέμπτος τρόπος, καθ' ὃν ∼οῦμεν ἀλλήλοις, ὡς μοῖραν θεοῦ ἔχουσι...ἕκτος τρόπος, τῶν ἐν ἀρχαῖς καὶ ἐξουσίαις ὄντων...ἕβδομος τρόπος, καθ' ὃν τοῖς δεσπόταις οἱ δοῦλοι, καὶ τοῖς εὐεργέταις...ἀλλ' οὐδενὶ δεῖ ∼εῖν ὡς θεῷ, εἰ μὴ μόνῳ τῷ φύσει θεῷ Jo.D.*imag*.3.33–40 (M.94.1352A–1356C); ∼ήσωμεν καὶ λατρεύσωμεν μόνῳ τῷ κτίστῃ...ὡς φύσει προσκυνητῷ θεῷ. ∼ήσωμεν καὶ τῇ ἁγίᾳ θεοτόκῳ, οὐχ ὡς θεῷ, ἀλλ' ὡς μητρὶ θεοῦ κατὰ σάρκα· ἔτι ∼ήσωμεν καὶ τοὺς ἁγίους ὡς ἐκλεκτοῖς φίλοις θεοῦ...εἰ γὰρ βασιλεῦσι...καὶ τοῖς ὑπ' αὐτοῦ χειροτονουμένοις ἄρχουσι...∼οῦσιν οἱ ἄνθρωποι...πόσῳ μᾶλλον ἐχρῆν ∼εῖν τῷ βασιλεῖ τῶν βασιλευόντων...καὶ τοῖς αὐτοῦ δούλοις καὶ φίλοις; *ib*.3.41 (1357A); εἰκόνας τοῦ...Χριστοῦ...τῆς τε...θεοτόκου, ἁγίων τε ἀγγέλων ...καὶ πάντων τῶν ἁγίων...ἡ...ἐκκλησία παρέλαβε...∼εῖν, ἤτοι ἀσπάζεσθαι· ταυτὸν γὰρ ἀμφότερα· κυνεῖν γὰρ τῇ Ἑλλαδικῇ ἀρχαίᾳ διαλέκτῳ τὸ ἀσπάζεσθαι καὶ τὸ φιλεῖν σημαίνει· καὶ τὸ τῆς πρὸς προθέσεως ἐπίτασίν τινα δηλοῖ τοῦ πόθου, ὥσπερ φέρω καὶ προσφέρω ...κυνῶ καὶ ∼ῶ...ὁ γάρ τις φιλεῖ, καὶ ∼εῖ· καὶ ὃ ∼εῖ, πάντως καὶ φιλεῖ Taras.*ep*.1(M.98.1432D); Thdr.Stud.*epp*.2.85(M.99.1329A); **m.** of eucharistic elements μένει γὰρ ἐπὶ τῆς προτέρας οὐσίας... νοεῖται δ' ἅπερ ἐγένετο, καὶ πιστεύεται, καὶ ∼εῖται, ὡς ἐκεῖνα ὄντα ἅπερ πιστεύεται Thdt.*eran*.2(4.126); **n.** of Inc. ἐπιφανείας...ἦν...ἡμεῖς ...∼οῦμεν Ath.*inc*.1.1(M.25.97A).

προσκύνημα, τό, 1. *salutation* ἡμῖν λέγοντος τοῦ λόγου· ἐάν τις διὰ τοῦτο ἐκ δευτέρου καταφιλήσῃ, ὅτι ἤρεσεν αὐτῷ...οὕτως οὖν ἀκριβώσασθαι τὸ φίλημα μᾶλλον δὲ τὸ π. δεῖ Athenag.*leg*.32.3(M.6.964C); **2.** *reverence, act of adoration*, liturg. π. τρία ἔμπροσθεν τῆς προθέσεως ποιήσαντες *Lit.Chrys*.(p.356.15; M.63.904); Trin. οὐ χρεία τρισὶ π. τὰς τρεῖς θείας ὑποστάσεις προσκυνεῖν, ἀλλὰ μιᾷ προσκυνήσει ἡ ὁλότης τοῦ προσκυνητοῦ θεοῦ φύσει προσκεκύνηται Leont.H.*Nest*.1.44(M.86. 1504B); before images ποιοῦσιν...π. τρία ἔμπροσθεν τοῦ εἰκόνος τοῦ σωτῆρος καὶ τῆς...θεοτόκου *Lit.Chrys*.(p.353.7; M.901); **3.** *object of adoration* γέγονεν ἡμῖν...τὰ ποιήματα εἰς π. ‡Ath.*diab*.1(p.5.9).

***προσκυνήσιμος**, *involving adoration* σήμερον...π. ἡμέρα τοῦ τιμίου σταυροῦ καθέστηκε ‡Chrys.*ador*.1.1(3.819B).

προσκύνησις, ἡ, 1. *obeisance, act of reverence*, in prayers τὰς ἀπὸ τοῦ πάσχα ἡμέρας ἕως τῶν Ἁγίων Πάντων μὴ γονυκλιτεῖν ἐν ταῖς εὐχαῖς, ἀλλὰ μόνον προσκυνήσεις ποιεῖν κατὰ πάντα (ref. penitents) †Jo.Jej.*poenit*.(M.88.1916D); as act of penitence προσκυνήσεις ποιείτωσαν χωρὶς μετανοιῶν *ib*.(1904C); **2.** *salutation, greeting*, (tr. Lat. *salutatio*) *Cod.Afr*.138; **3.** *adoration, veneration, worship*; **a.** pagan τῆς τῶν πολυωνύμων θεῶν λατρείας καὶ π. Arist.*apol*.2.1; εἰ δύνανται... ἄξιοι εἶναι σεβασμῶν καὶ π. σπαραττόμενοι ὑπὸ Τιτάνων Or.*Cels*.3.23 (p.219.25; M.11.945D); τά...ἤτοι ὡς μὴ ὄντα ἢ ὡς ὄντα μὲν καὶ τιμῆς ἄξια οὐ μὴν καὶ π. καὶ σεβασμοῦ *ib*.1.11(p.63.18; 676B); **b.** Christian, defined τοῦτό ἐστιν ἡ π., ἡ μετὰ ἱκεσίας καὶ ταπεινότητος τῶν καταθυμίων τινὸς αἴτησις γινομένη Gr.Nyss.*Maced*.25(M.45.1333B); **c.** of God, Just.*dial*.86.6(M.6.681C); τῷ θεῷ πατρὶ πρέπει δόξα, τιμὴ καὶ π. σὺν τῷ συνανάρχῳ αὐτοῦ υἱῷ καὶ λόγῳ ἅμα τῷ παναγίῳ...πνεύματι Ath.*decr*.32(p.28.25; M.25.476C); θεόν, ᾧ πᾶσα δόξα καὶ π., νῦν καὶ ἀεί Bas.*hex*.3.10(1.32E; M.29.77C); τὴν τῷ θεῷ χρεωστουμένην λατρείαν καὶ π. τῷ ἀντικειμένῳ προσῆγον...οἱ ἄνθρωποι Gr.Nyss.*Eun*.2(2 p.343.18; M.45.520B); ref. Jo.4:24 λέγει δὲ περὶ τῆς ἐκκλησίας, ὅτι ἡ ἀληθὴς π. καὶ θεῷ πρέπουσα αὕτη ἐστὶν...καθὼς καὶ ὁ Παῦλός φησιν,...τὴν λογικὴν λατρείαν ὑμῶν Chrys.*hom.33.2 in Jo*.(8.191C); Χριστοῦ, μεθ' οὗ τῷ πατρὶ ἅμα τῷ ἁγίῳ πνεύματι δόξα, κράτος, τιμή, καὶ π. νῦν καὶ ἀεί Eus.Al.*serm*.3(M.86.332C); τὴν ὀφειλομένην π. τῷ θεῷ Cosm.Ind. *top*.3(M.88.148D); by soul of departed ψυχὴν...οἱ ἄγγελοι...ἔστησαν ...εἰς π. τοῦ θεοῦ καὶ πατρός *T.Abr*.A 20(p.103.28); ref. Jo.4:24 ἐπὰν δὲ ἐνστῇ τὸ πλήρωμα τοῦ χρόνου, τότε οὐχ ἡγητέον τὴν ἀληθινὴν π. καὶ τελείαν θεοσέβειαν τελεῖσθαι ἐν Ἱεροσολύμοις ἔτι, ὅταν τις γένηται μηδαμῶς ἐν σαρκὶ ἀλλ' ἐν πνεύματι, καὶ μηδαμῶς ἐν τύπῳ, ἀλλὰ πᾶς ἐν ἀληθείᾳ...δὶς δὲ τό, ἔρχεται ὥρα, γέγραπται...καὶ οἶμαί γε τὸ μὲν πρότερον δηλοῦν τὴν ἔξω σωμάτων π. ἐνστησομένην κατὰ τὴν τελειότητα· τὸ δὲ δεύτερον τὴν τῶν ἐν βίῳ τούτῳ...τελειουμένων Or.*Jo*.13.13–14(p.238.12; M.14.420B); τοῖς μὲν ἐξ ἀρετῆς κατορθώμασιν εὐαγγελικῶς διαλάμποντα, τῇ δὲ τῶν θείων δογμάτων ὀρθότητι τὴν ὄντως ἀληθῆ πληροῦντα π. Cyr.*Jo*.2.5(4.191C); οἱ γὰρ Ἰουδαῖοι, σωματικώτερον περὶ θεοῦ φρονοῦντες, τὴν π. ἐπὶ τὰ Ἱεροσόλυμα...ἐποιοῦντο...οἱ δὲ Χριστιανοὶ οὐχ οὕτως, ἀλλὰ μονότροπον μίαν π. πνευματικήν, ὡς ἀπεριγράφου ὄντος τοῦ θεοῦ, ἐπὶ ἀνατολὰς ποιοῦνται Cosm.Ind.*top*.5 (209A); **d.** of Christ: by Magi, Chrys.*hom.8.3 in Mt*.(7.123C); refused by Jews τὸν θεοῦ τοῦ καὶ αὐτὸν τοῦτον ποιήσαντος λατρευταὶ ὄντες, οὐ δεόμεθα τῆς ὁμολογίας αὐτοῦ, οὐδὲ τῆς π. Just.*dial*.64.1(M.6. 621C); Trin. δοξάσῃς πατέρα ἐν υἱῷ, καὶ υἱὸν ἐν πνεύματι ἁγίῳ...μὴ σχίζων τὴν π., ἀλλ' ἑνῶν τὴν θεότητα ‡Bas.*struct.hom*.1.2(1.325C; M. 30.13B); τὸ μὲν ἕν, τῇ οὐσίᾳ γινώσκοντες, καὶ τῷ ἀμερίστῳ τῆς π. Gr. Naz.*or*.42.16(M.36.477A); μία τριὰς καὶ μία θεότης καὶ μία π. Epiph. *haer*.76.27(p.376.12; M.42.572C); δέον οὖν τρισὶ μὲν ὁμοτίμοις π. τὰς τρεῖς ὑποστάσεις τὰς θείας προσκυνεῖν Leont.H.*Nest*.1.44(M.86. 1504C); μιᾷ π. λατρεύομεν μίαν τρισυπόστατον θεότητα ‡Meth.*palm*.5 (M.18.393A); Christol. εἶναι τέλειον αὐτὸν υἱὸν θεοῦ καὶ αὐτὸν υἱὸν ἀνθρώπου, ἓν πρόσωπον καὶ μίαν τὴν π. τοῦ λόγου καὶ τῆς σαρκὸς ἣν ἀνέλαβεν. καὶ ἀναθεματίζομεν τοὺς διαφόρους π. ποιοῦντας, μίαν θεϊκὴν καὶ μίαν ἀνθρωπίνην Apoll.*fid.sec.pt*.27(p.177.8; M.10.1116C); οὐ δύο φύσεις τὸν ἕνα υἱόν, μίαν προσκυνητὴν καὶ μίαν ἀπροσκύνητον, ἀλλὰ μίαν φύσιν τοῦ θεοῦ λόγου σεσαρκωμένην καὶ προσκυνουμένην μετὰ τῆς σαρκὸς αὐτοῦ μιᾷ π.· οὐδὲ δύο υἱούς...προσκυνούμενον...μὴ προσκυνούμενον id.*ep.Jov*.(p.251.3; M.28.28A); διὰ τί οὐ λογίζεσθε, ὅτι καὶ ποιηθὲν τὸ σῶμα τοῦ κυρίου οὐ κτιστὴν ἀποφέρεται τὴν π.; τοῦ γὰρ ἀκτίστου λόγου γέγονε σῶμα· οὐ γὰρ σῶμα γέγονε, τούτῳ προσάγετε καὶ τὴν π. ‡Ath.*Apoll*.1.6(M.26.1101C); διὰ τὸν κεκρυμμένον προσκυνῶ τὸν φαινόμενον...χωρίζω τὰς φύσεις, ἀλλ' ἑνῶ τὴν π. Nest.*fr*.C 9(p.262. 6)ap.Cyr.*apol.orient*.3(p.39.12; 6¹.165C); ἀρνεῖται γὰρ [sc. Nest.]...τὴν ἕνωσιν, καθ' ἣν οὐχ ὡς ἕτερος ἑτέρῳ συμπροσκυνεῖταί τις...ἀλλ' εἷς νοεῖται Χριστὸς Ἰησοῦς υἱὸς μονογενής, μιᾷ π. τιμώμενος μετὰ τῆς ἰδίας σαρκός Cyr.*ep*.17(p.37.8; 5².72A); εἴ τις τολμᾷ λέγειν τὸν ἀναληφθέντα ἄνθρωπον συμπροσκυνεῖσθαι δεῖν τῷ θεῷ λόγῳ...ὡς ἕτερον ἑτέρῳ...καὶ οὐχὶ δὴ μᾶλλον μιᾷ π. τιμᾷ τὸν Ἐμμανουὴλ...ἀνάθεμα ἔστω *ib.anath*.8 (p.41.15; 5².76E); id.*expl.xii cap*.8(p.23.12; 6¹.154D); ἡμεῖς δὲ μιᾷ π. τιμᾶν εἰθίσμεθα τὸν Ἐμμανουήλ, οὐ διϊστάντες τοῦ λόγου τὸ ἑνωθὲν αὐτῷ καθ' ὑπόστασιν σῶμα id.*Nest*.2.10(p.47.29; 6¹.53A); *ib*.2.14(p.52.37; 60E); τὴν παρὰ πάσης τῆς κτίσεως δέχεται π. ὡς ἀχώριστον πρὸς τὴν θείαν φύσιν ἔχων τὴν συνάφειαν, ἀναφορᾷ θεοῦ καὶ ἐννοίᾳ πάσης αὐτῷ τῆς κτίσεως τὴν π. ἀπονεμούσης Thdr.Mops.*symb*.(p.98.27; M.66. 1017C); ὥσπερ...οὐ χρεία τρισὶ προσκυνήμασι τὰς τρεῖς θείας ὑποστάσεις προσκυνεῖν, ἀλλὰ μιᾷ π. ἡ ὁλότης τοῦ προσκυνητοῦ θεοῦ φύσει προσκεκύνηται, οὕτως ἐπὶ τῆς οἰκονομίας· εἰ ὡς ὑποστάσει τῇ τοῦ λόγου τοῦ σεσαρκωμένου προσάγοιμεν τὴν π., οὐ δέον τι λέγειν ἕτερον ἑτέρῳ συμπροσκυνεῖσθαι ἐν Χριστῷ, ἀλλὰ μιᾶς ὑποστάσεως προσκυνήσει τιμᾶσθαι τὸ τοῦ λόγου πρόσωπον ἓν Leont.H.*Nest*.1.44(M.86. 1504B); εἴ τις...τῶν παρ' αὐτοῦ εἰσαγομένων δύο προσώπων ἐν πρόσωπον λέγει κατ' ἀξίαν καὶ τιμὴν καὶ π. CCP(553)*anath*.5; exeg. Phil.2:10 ὅταν λέγῃ ὅτι 'αὐτῷ κάμψει πᾶν γόνυ ἐπουρανίων...' οὐ γόνατα καὶ ὀστᾶ περιτιθεὶς τοῖς ἀγγέλοις ταῦτα λέγει...ἀλλὰ τὴν ἐπιτεταμένην π. διὰ τοῦ παρ' ἡμῖν σχήματος αἰνίξασθαι βούλεται Chrys.*hom.32.3 in 1Cor*.(10.290B); Christ not to be venerated by means of images (ref. prohibition of images by Philoxenus) εἶναι δὲ μόνην αὐτῷ προσδεκτὴν...τὴν ἐν πνεύματι καὶ ἀληθείᾳ π. Jo.Diacr. *fr.h.e*.ap.CNic.(787)*act*.5(H.4.305D); **e.** of H. Ghost, Ath.*decr*.32 (p.28.25; M.25.476C) cit. 3.c supra; ‡Bas.*struct.hom*.1.2(1.325C; M. 30.13B) cit. 3.d supra; τί ζυγομαχοῦσι πρὸς ἡμᾶς [sc. Macedonians] περὶ λατρείας καὶ π.; τί κατειρωνεύονται διὰ τοῦ τῆς λατρείας ὀνόματος κατὰ τῆς θείας...φύσεως; Gr.Nyss.*Maced.*23(M.45.1329C); Eus.Al. *serm.*3(M.86.332C) cit. 3.c supra; **f.** of BMV, disallowed *παρθένος καὶ τετιμημένη, ἀλλ' οὐκ εἰς π. ἡμῖν δοθεῖσα, ἀλλὰ προσκυνοῦσα τὸν ἐξ αὐτῆς γεγεννημένον* Epiph.*haer.*79.4(p.479.18; M.42.745C); but v. *προσκυνητός*; **g.** of angels, contrasted with worship of God *βουλομένου γὰρ τὸν θεῖον ἄγγελον προσκυνῆσαι τοῦ εὐαγγελιστοῦ, καὶ οὐχ ὡς θεὸν προσκυνῆσαι...ὅμως καὶ αὐτὴν τὴν ὡς ἀγγέλου π. φαίνεται παραιτούμενος, ἐπειδὴ ὅλως ἐστὶ π.* Oecum.*Apoc.*19:10(p.205); **h.** of an inspired prophet, Thdt.*Dan.*2:45(2.1100); **i.** of Cross *ἡμέρα...τὸν ...σταυρὸν προσκομίζουσα, καὶ τοῦτον προτιθεμένη εἰς π.* ‡Chrys.*ador.* 1.1(3.819B); *ἡ δὲ τοῦ θείου σταυροῦ καθαρωτάτη π. τὸν νοῦν ἡμῶν ἀπάγουσα τῆς τῶν αἰσχίστων ἔργων συγχύσεως* Sophr.H.*or.*5(M.87.3312D); *καὶ νῷ καὶ λόγῳ καὶ αἰσθήσει τὴν π. αὐτῷ ἀπονέμοντες τοὺς ἐν τῷ ἐδάφει τοῦ σταυροῦ τύπους...κατασκευαζομένους ἐξαφανίζεσθαι... προστάττομεν* CTrull.*can.*73; *Symb.Nic.*(787)(H.4.456B); *προσάγειν τῷ θεῷ τὸ σέβας διὰ τῆς τοῦ σταυροῦ π.* †Jo.D.*B.J.*33(M.96.1176D); **j.** of shrines, relics, holy places *τοῖς βήμασι τοῖς σωτηρίοις τὴν πρέπουσαν ἀπεδίδου π.* Eus.*v.C.*3.42(p.95.18; M.20.1101B); *τῆς ἐκδημίας δὲ σκοπὸς ὑπῆρχε καὶ πρόφασις ἡ εἰς Μηνᾶν τὸν ἅγιον τὸν ἐν τῇ Μαρεώτῃ π.* Sophr.H.*mir.Cyr.et Jo.*51(M.87.3613C); Jo.D.*imag.*1.16 (M.94.1245C); *πλῆθος...εἰς π. ... συνέρρεον τῶν μακαρίων σωμάτων* †Jo.D.*B.J.*40(M.96.1240A); **k.** of images (v. *προσκυνέω*); veneration defended *τὴν νοερὰν π. τῶν ἁγίων καὶ σεπτῶν εἰκόνων ἀποκαταστῆσαι* Steph.Diac.*v.Steph.*(M.100.1117B); with distinction between *π.* and *λατρεία* (q.v.): *ἀφέντες τὰς π. τοῦ διαβόλου, ταύτας* [sc. icons] *προσεκύνησαν οὐ λατρευτικῶς, ἀλλὰ σχετικῶς* †Gr.II Papa *ep.Leon.*1(H.4.5C); *οἶδα διαφορὰν προσκυνήσεως. προσεκύνησε ποτὲ Ἀβραὰμ τοῖς υἱοῖς Ἐμμώρ...προσεκύνησε μέν, ἀλλ' οὐκ ἐλάτρευσε* Jo.D.*imag.*1.8 (M.94.1240B); *ἡ π. ... τιμῆς ἐστι σύμβολον· καὶ ταύτης διαφόρους ἔγνωμεν τρόπους· πρώτην, τὴν κατὰ λατρείαν ἣν προσάγομεν μόνῳ... θεῷ. ἔπειτα, τὴν διὰ...θεὸν προσαγομένην τοῖς αὐτοῦ φίλοις...ἢ τοῖς θεοῦ τόποις...καὶ τοῖς αὐτοῦ ἀναθήμασιν...καὶ...τοῖς ὑπ' αὐτοῦ χειροτονηθεῖσιν ἄρχουσιν. ... οἶδα καὶ κατὰ τιμὴν τὴν πρὸς ἀλλήλους π. ὡς Ἀβραὰμ τοῖς υἱοῖς Ἐμμώρ· ἢ τοίνυν πᾶσαν π. ἄνελε, ἢ πάσας δέχου, μετὰ τοῦ ὀφείλοντος λόγου καὶ τρόπου* *ib.*1.14(1244A,B); *φόβου καὶ πόθου καὶ τιμῆς ἐστιν ἡ π. σύμβολον, ὑποπτώσεώς τε καὶ ταπεινώσεως. ἀλλ' οὐδενὶ δεῖ προσκυνεῖν ὡς θεῷ, εἰ μὴ μόνῳ τῷ φύσει θεῷ* *ib.*3.40 (1356C); *προσκυνοῦμεν οὖν ταῖς εἰκόσιν, οὐ τῇ ὕλῃ προσφέροντες τὴν π., ἀλλὰ δι' αὐτῶν τοῖς ἐν αὐταῖς εἰκονιζομένοις* *ib.*3.41(1357C); *εἰ δὲ καὶ πολλάκις εὕρηται ἡ π. ἐν τῇ θείᾳ γραφῇ, καὶ τοῖς ἀστειολόγοις ἁγίοις πατράσιν ἡμῶν ἐπὶ τῆς ἐν πνεύματι λατρείας, ὡς πολύσημος οὖσα ἡ φωνὴ μίαν τῶν αὐτῆς σημαινομένων ἐμφαίνει τὴν κατὰ λατρείαν π. ἔστι γὰρ π. καὶ ἡ κατὰ τιμὴν καὶ πόθον καὶ φόβον...ἔστιν ἑτέρα κατὰ φόβον μόνον...ἔστι καὶ κατὰ χάριν...ἔνθεν καὶ ἡ...γραφὴ...'κύριον... προσκυνήσεις, καὶ αὐτῷ μόνῳ λατρεύσεις'· τὴν μὲν π. ἀπολύτως καὶ οὐ μόνῳ εἴρηκεν, ὡς διάφορα σημαινόμενα ἔχουσαν καὶ ὁμώνυμον οὖσαν τὴν φωνήν· τὸ δὲ λατρεύσεις αὐτῷ μόνῳ εἴρηκε· καὶ γὰρ μόνῳ θεῷ τὴν λατρείαν ἡμεῖς ἀναφερόμεν* Taras.*ep.*1(M.98.1433cff.); Thdr.Stud. *antirr.*1.20(M.99.349C) cit. s. *σχετικός*; id.*ep.imag.*(M.99.504B); *ἐπ' αὐτοῦ δὴ Χριστοῦ λατρευτικὴ ἡ π. προσκυνῶν γὰρ αὐτὸν συμπροσκυνῶ τὸν πατέρα καὶ τὸ ἅγιον πνεῦμα...ὅπερ ἐστὶν ἡ τριαδικὴ ἡμῶν π. καὶ λατρεία· ἐπὶ δὲ τῆς εἰκόνος, ἡ αὐτὴ μὲν...σχετικὴ δὲ ὅμως, ἤγουν ὁμωνυμική* id.*epp.*2.85(M.99.1328D); veneration approved *καλῶς εἶναι...τὴν ὀφειλομένην π. ἀπονέμειν· εἴτε οὖν ἀσπασμόν τινι τοῦτο φίλον καλεῖν ἢ π. ... εἰ μή πού τὴν κατὰ λατρείαν π. τις ἐννοήσειεν· ἄλλη γὰρ αὕτη* CNic.(787)*act.*6(H.4.441C); *ἀσπασμὸν καὶ τιμητικὴν π. ἀπονέμειν, οὐ μὴν τὴν κατὰ πίστιν ἡμῶν ἀληθινὴν λατρείαν, ἣ πρέπει μόνῃ τῇ θείᾳ φύσει* *Symb.Nic.*(787)(H.4.456B).

προσκυνητέον, *one must venerate* *οὐδαμῶς γὰρ π. τὰ κτίσματα* Or. *mart.*7(p.9.1; M.11.573A).

[*]**προσκυνητήριον, τό**, *place of worship*, Thphn.*chron.*p.281(M. 108.693C).

προσκυνητής, ὁ, 1. *one who holds in reverence* *οἱ τἀγαθοῦ π.* Clem. *prot.*9(p.65.24; M.8.200B); *οἱ τῆς ἀληθείας π.* Cyr.*Jo.*1.2(4.19A); *ὁ τῆς Χριστοῦ θυσίας π.* Bas.Sel.*or.*27.2(M.85.313B); **2.** *one who makes obeisance, suppliant* *πολεμίους π. ἀποφήναντι* Thdt.*Ps.*128:2(1.1500); **3.** *worshipper* *οἱ τῶν παρ' ὑμῖν λεγομένων θεῶν π.* Arist.*apol.*2.1; *οἱ τῶν λίθων π.* Clem.*prot.*4(p.40.14; M.8.145A); *ib.*10(p.71.11; 212B); *π.* [sc. man] *μικτόν, ἐπόπτην τῆς ὁρατῆς κτίσεως,...βασιλέα τῶν ἐπὶ γῆς* Gr.Naz.*or.*38.11(M.36.324A) = *ib.*45.7(632A); *πατὴρ ἐποίησε διὰ υἱοῦ, καὶ υἱὸς ἐκτίσατο πατρῴῳ θελήματι...οὕτω κοινὸν γέγονας ἔργον, ἵνα καὶ κοινὸς π. ἀμφοτέρων ᾖς* ‡Bas.*struct.hom.*1.2(1.325C; M.30.13B); *τὸν λαὸν...τέλειον τελείας τῆς τριάδος π.* Gr.Naz.*or.*21.37(M.35.1128B); of martyr as *π. θεοῦ* who must not receive worship due to God, Ast.Am.*hom.*10(M.40.321D); *π. τῆς ἁγίας τριάδος, καὶ τῆς Χριστοῦ εἰκόνος* ‡Jo.D.*ep.Thphl.*28(M.95.381A); *π. εἰμι σχετικῶς ἀλλ' οὐ λατρευτικῶς* *Euchol.*(p.255); ref. Jo.4:23 *ὅταν τις γένηται μηδαμῶς ἐν σαρκὶ ἀλλ' ἐν πνεύματι...ὥστε ἐξομοιοῦσθαι αὐτὸν οἷς ζητεῖ προσκυνηταῖς ὁ θεός* Or.*Jo.*13.13(p.238.15; M.14.420B); *οἱ ἀληθινοὶ π. ἀφομοιοῦνται τῇ δόξῃ τοῦ θεοῦ* *M.Carp.*7(p.11.15); *τίνες οὖν εἰσιν οἱ ἀληθινοὶ π.; οἱ μήτε τόπῳ περικλείοντες τὴν λατρείαν, καὶ θεὸν ἐν πνεύματι θεραπεύοντες* Chrys.*hom.33.2 in Jo.*(8.191D); *τὸν ἀληθινὸν π., τὸν ἄνθρωπον δηλονότι τὸν πνευματικόν...διά τοι τοῦτο δικαίως τὸν πνευματικὸν ἀποδέχεται π., οὐκ ἐν μορφώσει καὶ τύποις φοροῦντα τῆς εὐσεβείας τὴν μόρφωσιν Ἰουδαϊκῶς, ἀλλὰ...τῇ τῶν θείων δογμάτων ὀρθότητι τὴν...ἀληθῆ πληροῦντα προσκύνησιν...οἱ ἀληθινοὶ π. τὴν ἐν πνεύματι λατρείαν προσοίσουσι τῷ θεῷ* Cyr.*Jo.*2.5(4.191B); id.*Lc.*6:12 (M.72.580B); of worshippers of Christ, Chrys.*hom.7.5 in Mt.*(7. 112B).

***προσκυνητικός**, *offering worship*, Cyr.ap.*cat.Lc.*6:12(p.49.11) for *προσκυνητάς* Cyr.*Lc.*6:12(M.72.580B).

προσκυνητός, 1. *to be worshipped*; **a.** of God *τὸ...λουτρὸν...τῷ ἐμπαρέχοντι ἑαυτὸν τῇ θειότητι τῆς δυνάμεως τῶν τῆς π. τριάδος ἐπικλήσεών ἐστιν ἡ χαρισμάτων...πηγή* Or.*Jo.*6.33(17; p.142.30; M. 14.257A); *ἑνωθῆναι καὶ εὐαρεστῆσαι τῇ θείᾳ καὶ π. οὐσίᾳ τῆς θεότητος* ‡Tit.Bost.*palm.*4(M.18.1269C); *πρὸ τῆς ἁγίας ἐπικλήσεως τῆς π. τριάδος* Cyr.H.*catech.*19.6; *ἡ τριὰς ἡ π.* Apoll.*fid.sec.pt.*37(p.181.22; M. 10.1120B); *θεὸν καὶ λόγον καὶ πνεῦμα, μίαν οὖσαν θεότητα, τὴν καὶ μόνην π.* Didym.(‡Bas.)*Eun.*5(1.306B; M.29.733C); *μιᾶς τρισυποστάτου καὶ π. θεότητος* Cosm.Ind.*top.*proem.(M.88.52A); *καθ' ἕκαστον ὄνομα τῆς ἁγίας καὶ ὁμοουσίου καὶ π. τριάδος* Jo.Mosch.*prat.*176(M.87. 3045A); *πᾶσα προσκύνησις διὰ τὸν φύσει π. θεόν ἐστι* Jo.D.*imag.*1.14 (M.94.1244A); *ib.*3.15(1337A); *σὺ γὰρ π. καὶ δεδοξασμένος ὑπάρχεις ὁ θεὸς ἡμῶν, καὶ ὁ...υἱὸς καὶ πνεῦμά σου τὸ πανάγιον* *Lit.Jac.*(p.226. 12); **b.** of Christ, ref. Ps.44:7–13 *ὅτι γοῦν καὶ π. ἐστι καὶ θεὸς καὶ Χριστὸς ὑπὸ τοῦ ταῦτα ποιήσαντος μαρτυρούμενος, καὶ οἱ λόγοι οὗτοι... σημαίνουσι* Just.*dial.*63.5(M.6.621B); *Χριστὸς καὶ θεὸς π. διὰ Δαυείδ* *ib.*126.1(768C); Trin. *προσκυνεῖται...διὰ τοῦ εἶναι αὐτὸν υἱὸν τοῦ π. πατρός, ἡμεῖς δὲ προσκυνοῦμεν...διὰ τὸ εἶναι ἡμᾶς κτίσματα* Ath.*decr.* 11(p.10.20; M.25.'444'(436)B); *εἰ δὲ μήγε* [sc. *ὁμοούσιος*], *οὐδὲ π. οὐδὲ γὰρ προσκυνήσεις θεῷ ἀλλοτρίῳ* Didym.(‡Bas.)*Eun.*5(1.317A; M.29. 760C); *ἀντιμάχεται γάρ σοι* [sc. Origen] *καὶ τὸ φρόνημα καὶ ὁ λόγος. πᾶν γὰρ τὸ κτιστὸν οὐ π. ... εἰ δὲ ὅλως π., πολλῶν ἄλλων ὑπαρχόντων κτιστῶν οὐδὲν ἂν διοίσει τὸ καὶ ἡμᾶς μετὰ τοῦ ἑνὸς κτιστοῦ τὰ ὅλα προσκυνεῖν, σύνδουλα ὄντα καὶ τῇ αὐτῇ ἀγωγῇ τῆς ὀνομασίας ὑποπεπτωκότα* Epiph.*haer.*64.8(p.418.7; M.41.1084B); *εἰ γὰρ οὐκ ἔστιν ἀληθινὸς θεός, οὔτε π. ἐστι...καὶ εἰ οὐκ ἔστι π., πῶς ἄρα θεολογεῖται;* *ib.*69.31(p.180.15; M.42.252B); *ἄλλην τὴν προσκυνουμένην κτίσιν παρὰ τὸν π. κύριον, υἱὸν τοῦ θεοῦ...διὰ γὰρ τὸ ἐξ αὐτοῦ γεγεννῆσθαι ὅμοιον αὐτῷ καὶ ὄντα υἱόν· διὰ τοῦτο γὰρ καὶ π. παρὰ πᾶσι* *ib.*76.8(p.349.13; M.42.529C); *ib.*76.27(p.376.5; 572B); Christol. *σῶμα οὐκ ἀλλότριον τοῦ ἡμετέρου...τοῦ λόγου γεγονὸς ἔνδυμα π.* †Ath.*fr.*(M.26.1245B); *οὐδὲν οὕτως ἥνωται πρὸς θεὸν ὡς ἡ σὰρξ ἡ προσληφθεῖσα· τὰ μὴ οὕτως ἡνωμένα οὐδ' οὕτως π. οὐδὲν δὲ οὕτως π. ὡς ἡ σὰρξ τοῦ Χριστοῦ* Apoll.*fr.*84(p.225.2)ap.Gr.Nyss.*Apoll.*44(M.45.1228B); *εἰ μηδὲν ποίημα π. μετὰ τοῦ κυρίου ὡς ἡ σὰρξ αὐτοῦ* *ib.*86(p.225.24; M.45. 1229A); id.*ep.Jov.*(p.251.1; M.28.28A) cit. s. *ἀπροσκύνητος*; *ἔσται δὲ οὐχ ἑτέρως π., ἐὰν μὴ πιστεύσωμεν ὅτι αὐτὸς ὁ ἐκ θεοῦ λόγος ὁ παρὰ πάσης κτίσεως προσκυνούμενος σὰρξ ἐγένετο* Cyr.*Arcad.*6(p.64.1; 5².45C); *πῶς ἔσται π., ὁ τοῖς προσκυνοῦσι συντεταγμένος;* id.*inc.unigen.*(5¹.701E); *ὅσον μὲν ἦν δεκτικὸν θείων αὐχημάτων τὸ ἀνθρώπινον τοῦ Χριστοῦ, μετέσχεν ὑπ' αὐτοῦ τοῦ λόγου διὰ τὴν ἕνωσιν, δι' ἣν καὶ σεπτόν ἐστι καὶ π.* ‡Cyr.*Trin.*17(6³.24B; M.77.1156D); *ἡ σάρξ, κατὰ μὲν τὴν ἑαυτῆς φύσιν, οὐκ ἔστι π., προσκυνεῖται δὲ ἐν τῷ σεσαρκωμένῳ θεῷ λόγῳ* Jo.D.*f.o.*4.3(M.94.1105B); **c.** of H. Ghost *κατὰ τὸ ἕκτον... τῶν εἰς τὸ κατὰ Ἰωάννην εὐαγγέλιον ἐξηγητικῶν* [sc. *Ὠριγένης*], *καὶ π. αὐτὸ φανερῶς ἀπεφήνατο* (cf. 1.a supra) Bas.*Spir.*73(3.61D; M.32. 204B); *σὺν τῷ π. καὶ παναγίῳ καὶ ζωοποιῷ...πνεύματι* Chrys.*hom.45.4 in Jo.*(8.268D); *Ἀμφιλόχιος...ὑπόγυόν μοι λόγον ἀνέγνω περὶ τοῦ ἁγίου πνεύματος, ὅτι θεὸς καὶ π. ἐστιν, ἅτε δὴ παντοκράτωρ* Hier. *vir.ill.*(tr.Sophr.Pal.)133(p.61.20; M.*PL*.23.716B); †Diad.*Ar.*9(M.65. 1165C); **d.** of divine glory, ‡Meth.*Sym.et Ann.*2(M.18.352C); **e.** of BMV *μήτηρ θεοῦ, ἡ π. εἰς τοὺς αἰῶνας* ‡Jo.D.*hom.*5(M.96.653C); *σὺ π. καὶ πάσαις οὐρανίαις δυνάμεσιν* Thdr.Stud.*nativ.BMV* 7(M.96. 696A); **2.** *to be venerated, venerable*; **a.** of saints *ὡς τοῦ φύσει θεοῦ μέτοχοι, οὕτως εἰσὶ π., οὐχὶ φύσει, ἀλλ' ὡς τὸν φύσει π. ἐν ἑαυτοῖς ἔχοντες* Jo.D.*imag.*3.33(M.94.1352C); **b.** of images; **i.** pagan *ἀγάλματα...π. παρεισάγουσι* Epiph.*haer.*79.4(p.479.13; M.42.745C); **ii.** Christian *σεβασμίων καὶ π. εἰκόνων* Jo.V H.*icon.*2(M.96.1349D); *ib.*3(1352B); v. *προσκυνέω, προσκύνησις*; **c.** of Cross, Cyr.*Is.*2.4(2. 294E); Jo.V H.*icon.*3(M.96.1352B); **d.** of events in gospel history,

Nest.*ep*.5(p.32.2, v.l. προσκυνητῶς M.77.56B); π. αὐτοῦ ἀναστάσεως Procl.CP *or*.12.2(M.65.789B); **e.** of festival (Annunciation) πανσεβάσμιος καὶ π. Jo.Eub.*concept.BMV* 10(M.96.1476A); **f.** of Christian faith as π. νόμος, Const.ap.Ath.*apol.sec*.87(p.106.14; M.25.405B); **g.** of synodal definitions of faith σωτηριώδη ὅρον καὶ τὴν π. σκέψιν διαφθεῖραι Dam.Papa *ep.Illyr*.ap.Thdt.*h.e*.2.22.7(3.883); Gel.Cyz. *h.e*.1 proem.18,19(M.85.1196D,1197A); *ib*.2.25.3(1305B); **3.** *reverend* Ἀναστασίῳ, τῷ π. ἁγίῳ τῆς ἀποστολικῆς καθέδρας ἐπισκόπῳ (tr. Lat. *venerabili*) *Cod.Afr*.56.

προσκυνητῶς, **1.** *in worship* τῇ μιᾷ τριάδι π. τὸ σέβας νέμειν Epiph.*haer*.76.38(p.391.5; M.42.597B); **2.** *adorably*, Nest.*ep.Cyr*.2(M.77.56B; προσκυνητά p.32.2); π. κατασπαζόμενος Thdr.Stud.*epp*.1.34 (M.99.1028C).

προσκύπτ-ω, **1.** *lean towards* to whisper, Clem.*str*.1.23(p.96.16; M.8.901A); **2.** *decline upon*, c. genit. εἶδον ἄρτι τοῦ ὁρίζοντος τὸν ἑωσφόρον ~οντα ‡Nil.*narr*.7(M.79.684C); abs., Vict.*Mc*.16:1(p.444.12; f.l. for προκεκοφυῖαν); **3.** *be devoted to, preoccupied with* πολλὰ τῇ ψυχῇ προσκεκυφὼς Synes.*ep*.126(M.66.1505C); **4.** *be placed under, be subject to* ban of excommunication ὅν γε εἰκὸς ἀτολμότερον ἔσεσθαι προσκεκυφότα ταῖς ἐκκλησίαις *ib*.72(1436A).

προσκυρ-όω, *assign to, make over to*; π. ἑαυτῷ *claim* for oneself τὰ χρήματά σου τῷ ταμιείῳ ~ωθήσεται *M.Thdot*.1 8(p.66.13); (tr. Lat. *pertineo*) *Cod.Afr*.121; ὁ γὰρ ἀρνούμενος τὸν ἀληθινὸν ἄνθρωπον τοῦ κυρίου...πλείστων ὅσων ἐμπαιγμάτων πληροῦται τοῦ διαβόλου καὶ τοῦτον ὡς οἰκεῖον Ἀπολινάριος ἔχει ἢ Βαλεντῖνος ἑαυτῷ ~οῖ Leo Mag. *ep*.35(p.41.4; M.*PL*.54.806B); ref. objections to *Theotokos* δέον ἢ ἐν ἀμφοῖν [sc. Father and BMV] ὁμοίαν θεωρεῖσθαι γέννησιν αὐτοῦ, ἢ τῇ κυριωτέρᾳ ~ωθῆναι τὸ ὄνομα [i.e. for the divine generation] Leont.H.*Nest*.4.37(M.86.1709B); τὴν δὲ αὐτῆς περιουσίαν τῇ ἑαυτοῦ προσεκύρωσεν λαύρᾳ Cyr.S.*v.Sab*.25(p.109.13).

***προσκωμῳδέω**, pass., *be ridiculed*, ‡Nil.*perist*.9.9(M.79.881C).

προσλαλ-έω, **1.** *speak to, address* ὁμιλία πρὸς τὸν θεὸν ἡ εὐχή· κἂν...μετὰ σιγῆς ~ῶμεν Clem.*str*.7.7(p.30.17; M.9.456B); Cyr.*inc. unigen*.(5[1].696D); *ib*.(706C); **2.** *address* by letter, Ign.*Eph*.3.1; id. *Magn*.1.1; **3.** *tell, instruct* ταῖς ἀδελφαῖς μου ~ει ἀγαπᾶν τὸν κύριον id. *Polyc*.5.1; **4.** *address oneself to* ~ήσαντας σοφῶν βίβλοις Gr.Naz. *carm*.1.2.10.163(M.37.692A).

προσλαλία, ἡ, *talk*, *Orac.Sib*.1.27.

προσλαμβάν-ω, **1.** *receive in addition, take besides* ὕδωρ, καὶ τὸ ἐξορκιζόμενον καὶ τὸ βάπτισμα γινόμενον, οὐ μόνον χωρίζει τὸ χεῖρον, ἀλλὰ καὶ ἁγιασμὸν ~ει Clem.*exc.Thdot*.82(p.132.14; M.9.696C); προσλαβεῖν κοινωνὸν Philost.*h.e*.8.8(M.65.561C); Trin. τί γὰρ ἂν προκόψαι ἔχοι ἡ τοῦ θεοῦ σοφία, ἢ τί προσλαβεῖν ἡ αὐτοαλήθεια; Alex. Al.*ep.Alex*.7(p.24.13; M.18.557D); εἰ σπερματικῶς ἦν ἐν τῷ ἀγεννήτῳ θεῷ τὸ γέννημα, μετὰ τὴν γέννησιν ἔξωθεν προσλαβὸν ὡς ἂν εἴποι τις ἠνδρώθη· τέλειος οὖν ἐστιν ὁ υἱὸς οὐκ ἐξ ὧν ἐγεννήθη, ἀλλ' ἐξ ὧν προσέλαβε. τὰ γὰρ συγγενικῶς ~οντα ὡς ἐξ ἐκείνων συνεστῶτα, τὸ τοῦ τελείου ὄνομα διαφόρως προσίεσθαι πέφυκεν Aët.*synt*.9 ap.Epiph. *haer*.76.26(p.373.8; M.42.565D); Christol. τὸ δὲ θνητὸν αὐτοῦ σῶμα καὶ τὴν ἀνθρωπίνην ἐν αὐτῷ ψυχὴν τῇ πρὸς ἐκεῖνον...ἀνακράσει τὰ μέγιστά φαμεν προσειληφέναι καὶ...εἰς θεὸν μεταβεβληκέναι Or.*Cels*.3.41(p.237.9; M.11.975A); οὐχὶ τῆς θεότητος κατὰ προκοπήν τι ~ούσης Gr.Nyss.*Eun*.6(2 p.135.5; M.45.720B); **2.** *acquire, obtain*, Tat.*orat*.5 (p.5.25; M.6.816A); τὰ τῆς γνώσεως τὰ μὲν ἤδη μετέχομεν...οὔτε γὰρ πᾶν κεκομίσμεθα...ἀλλ' οἷον ἀρραβῶνα τῶν αἰωνίων ἀγαθῶν... προσειλήφαμεν Clem.*ecl*.12(p.140.1; M.9.704B); ἄρχεται...βεβαιότητα τῶν θορύβων ὁ νοῦς ~ειν Meth.*symp*.5.2(p.55.14; M.18.100C); τὴν ἐκτύπωσιν...τοῦ Χριστοῦ ~ουσιν οἱ φωτιζόμενοι *ib*.8.8(p.90.9; 149B); οὐδεμίαν ὄνησιν...προσλήψεται Thdt.*Os*.5:13(2.1336); **3.** *assume*, Christol. κενωθεὶς γὰρ καὶ τὴν μορφὴν τοῦ δούλου προσλαβὼν εἰς τὴν ἑαυτοῦ τελειότητα πάλιν ἀνεπληρώθη Meth.*symp*.8.11(p.95.18; M.18.157A); οὐκ ἄρα ὁ λόγος ἐστίν, ᾗ λόγος ἐστὶ καὶ σοφία, ὁ τῷ παρ' αὐτοῦ διδομένῳ πνεύματι χριόμενος, ἀλλ' ἡ προσληφθεῖσα παρ' αὐτοῦ σάρξ ἐστιν, ἡ ἐν αὐτῷ καὶ παρ' αὐτοῦ χριομένη Ath.*Ar*.1.47(M.26.109C); τὴν τοίνυν προσληφθεῖσαν ὑπὸ τοῦ λόγου σάρκα...πῶς οἱ ταύτην ἐξουδενοῦντες, ἢ οἱ διὰ ταύτην κατηγοροῦντες τοῦ υἱοῦ...ὡς ποιήματος, οὐκ ἀχάριστοι φαίνονται; id.*ep.Adelph*.5(M.26.1079B); εἰ γὰρ ἄλλο μὲν ἦν τὸ βασιλευόμενον ὑπὸ τοῦ θανάτου, ἄλλο δὲ τὸ παρὰ τοῦ κυρίου προσληφθέν, οὐκ ἂν μὲν ἐπαύσατο τὰ ἑαυτοῦ ἐνεργῶν ὁ θάνατος Bas.*ep*.261.2 (3.402A; M.32.969B); θεὸς μὲν...τῷ πνεύματι τῷ σαρκωθέντι, ἄνθρωπος δὲ τῇ ὑπὸ τοῦ θεοῦ προσληφθείσῃ σαρκί Apoll.*fr*.19(p.209.26) ap.Gr.Nyss.*Apoll*.7(M.45.1136D); *ib*.67(p.220.13; M.45.1200B) cit. s. ἄνθρωπος; ἓν ἐκ τῶν δύο γενέσθαι ἀνασχόμενος, θεὸς γὰρ ἀμφότερα, τό τε προσλαβὸν καὶ τὸ προσληφθέν· δύο φύσεις εἰς ἓν συνδραμοῦσαι, οὐχ υἱοὶ δύο Gr.Naz.*or*.37.2(M.36.285A); οὐχ ὃ ἦν μεταβαλών (ἄτρεπτον γάρ) ἀλλ' ὃ οὐκ ἦν προσλαβών (φιλάνθρωπος γάρ) *ib*.39.13(349A); *ib*.2.23(M.35.432B); ὧν γὰρ ὅπερ ἦν, καὶ θεὸς καὶ λόγος...ἐν τῷ προσληφθέντι ἀνθρώπῳ, ὃς οὐδὲν τούτων ἦν, τά τε ἄλλα ἐγένετο, ὅσα ὁ λόγος ἦν, καὶ μετὰ τῶν ἄλλων καὶ Χριστὸς καὶ κύριος Gr.Nyss.*Eun*.6 (2 p.134.30; M.45.720A); ὁ...θεὸς...οὔτε ὃ ἦν τραπείς, καὶ ὃ οὐκ ἦν προσλαβὼν Isid.Pel.*epp*.1.323(M.78.369B); ὃ γὰρ μὴ προσείληπται, οὐδὲ σέσωσται Cyr.*Jo*.8(4.705A); ἡμεῖς δὲ οὐκ ἄνθρωπον θεῷ ἑνωθέντα, ἀλλὰ θεὸν τὰ ἀνθρώπινα προσλαβόμενον οἴδαμεν τὸν Χριστόν id.*deip. BMV* 9(p.23.6; M.76.265C); τὴν ἡμετέραν ὁμοίωσιν ἀναλαβών, καὶ γενόμενος ἄνθρωπος...οὐχ ὅπερ ἦν ἀναλαβών, ἀλλ' ὅπερ οὐκ ἦν προσλαβών id.*hom.pasch*.1.6(5[2].15B); τὸν θεὸν λόγον...γεννηθῆναι θεὸν μετὰ τοῦ προσλήμματος, οὐχ ὅπερ ἦν ἀποβαλόντα, τροπῆς γὰρ πάσης τὸ θεῖον ἐλεύθερον· ἀλλὰ προσειληφότα τὸ γενέσθαι καὶ ἄνθρωπον †Thdt.*Nest*.(4.1046); Νεστόριος...τὴν θεότητα τοῦ λόγου χωρίζων ἀπὸ τῆς οὐσίας τοῦ προσληφθέντος ἀνθρώπου Leo Mag.*ep*.35(p.40.29; M.*PL*.54.806A); ἡ θεότης τοῦ γεννηθησομένου παιδίου...ἀδιαίρετος μείνασα προσληφθείσης σαρκὸς σὺν αὐτῇ γεννηθήσεται ‡Gr.Nyss.*hom. 1.4 in Jo*.(p.94.21); τῆς ἐξ ἡμῶν νοερῶς τε καὶ λογικῶς ἐψυχωμένης, ὑπ' αὐτοῦ...προσληφθείσης, καὶ αὐτῷ κατὰ μίαν καὶ τὴν αὐτὴν ὑπόστασιν ἑνωθείσης ἁγίας σαρκός Max.*opusc*.(M.91.93A); **4.** *assume* in argument ~ει γὰρ τὸ ζητούμενον τῇ ἀποφάσει Nemes.*nat.hom*.2(M.40.548B); **5.** *accept, admit* οὐ δέεσθαι τῆς παρὰ ἀνθρώπων ὑλικῆς προσφορᾶς προσειλήφαμεν τὸν θεόν Just.*1apol*.10.1(M.6.340C); οὐδὲ γὰρ τὸ βάπτισμα ἐκεῖνο τὸ ἀνωφελὲς τὸ τῶν λάκκων ~ομεν id.*dial*. 19.2(M.6.516C); **6.** *take as helper, obtain assistance of* δαίμονες... ~όντες τὰς ψευδοδόξους...τῆς ψυχῆς κινήσεις Athenag.*leg*.27.2(M.6.953A); hence *take advantage of, use to one's advantage* ἔγνων καὶ τοὺς ἁγίους πρεσβυτέρους οὐ προσειληφότας τὴν φαινομένην νεωτερικὴν τάξιν [sc. of the bishop] Ign.*Magn*.3.1; **7.** *take up* an objector τὴν ἀντίθεσιν προσλαβὼν ἐκεῖνον τέθεικεν Chrys.*hom.13.4 in Rom*.(9.548A); or his argument, *ib.9.2*(500B); id.*hom.10.1 in 2Cor*.(10.505E); **8.** *fasten, bind*, met. ὅρκῳ τινὶ προσληφθεὶς...ἀπαίρειν τῆς πόλεως Thdt.*h.rel*.21(3.1241); hence *fix attention on, study* πρὸς βασιλέα ἀνῆλθε προσλαβεῖν τοὺς νόμους βουλόμενος, ὅπως προέλθῃ ῥήτωρ Proc.G.*ep*.148(89; M.87.2788B); **9.** *receive, accept* someone; **a.** of God accepting men ἐν ἀγάπῃ προσελάβετο ἡμᾶς ὁ δεσπότης *1Clem*. 49.6; *Lit*.ap.*Const.App*.8.12.21; of Christ's acceptance of Judas, Chrys.ap.*cat.Jo*.13:18(p.339.14) for συλλαμβάνεται id.*hom.71.2 in Jo*.(8.419E); in baptism ὑπ' αὐτοῦ τοῦ κυρίου ~όμενος Bas.*hom*.13. 2(2.114C; M.31.425B); **b.** of hospitality among men, Just.*dial*.47.2 (M.6.577A); τοὺς διωκομένους δὲ διὰ τὴν πίστιν...~εσθε *Const.App*. 5.3.1; **c.** of reception of penitents into Church, *ib*.2.12.1; τοὺς ἐφ' ἁμαρτίας λέγοντας μετανοεῖν ἀφορίζειν χρόνον ὡρισμένον...ἔπειτα μετανοοῦντας ~εσθαι *ib*.2.16.4; **10.** *adopt* a child, *ib*.4.1.1; **11.** *pick up* a child, liturg., in deacon's warning before Mass of Faithful τὰ παιδία ~εσθε, αἱ μητέρες *Lit*.ap.*Const.App*.8.12.2.

πρόσλημμα, τό, **1.** *addition*, of addition of self-will to soul ἄζυμον δέ ἐστι ψυχὴ μὴ ἔχουσα π. τοῦ ἑαυτῆς θελήματος Jo.Clim.*past*. 14(M.88.1201B); **2.** *acquisition*, of human nature assumed by Christ in Inc., ref. Ps.77:6 κοινοποιεῖ τὸν λόγον, καί, ἠκούσαμεν, εἶπε, διὰ τὸ π. ... τῶν πατέρων ἡμῖν διηγησαμένων, Μωσέως, φημί, καὶ τῶν προφητῶν. τούτων γὰρ υἱὸς ὁ Χριστὸς διὰ τῆς μητρὸς Or.*Ps*. 77:3–6(p.112); υἱὸν...ἀπαθῆ θεότητι, παθητὸν τῷ π. Gr.Naz.*or*.40.45 (M.36.424B); εἴ τις ἀποτεθεῖσθαι νῦν τὴν ἁγίαν σάρκα λέγοι, καὶ γυμνὴν εἶναι τὴν θεότητα τοῦ σώματος, ἀλλὰ μὴ μετὰ τοῦ π. καὶ εἶναι καὶ ἥξειν μὴ ἴδοι τὴν δόξαν τῆς παρουσίας αὐτοῦ id.*ep*.101(M.37.181A); εἰ μὴ σέβοιεν, ὡς ἕν, ἄνθρωπον θεόν, τὸν προσλαβόντα σύν γε τῷ π. id.*carm*.2.1.11.648(M.37.1074A); οὐ τὴν θεότητα πεπονθέναι...ἥτις ἐστὶ κύριος τῆς δόξης ἀλλὰ τὸ π. †Ath.*fr*.(M.26.1224C); γενόμενον ἄνθρωπον, γεννηθῆναι θεὸν μετὰ τοῦ π. †Thdt.*Nest*.(4.1046); (ref. Gr. Naz.*or*.30.8) ὁ...Γρηγόριος...τὰ δύο εἰς τὸν Χριστὸν ἐδέξατο· πατέρα μὲν τοῦ λόγου, θεὸν δὲ τοῦ π. Oecum.*Eph*.1:17(p.448.7); εἰς δήλωσιν τοῦ θησαυρίσματος τῆς θεότητος, ἀλλ' οὐκ ἀναίρεσιν καὶ μεταστοιχείωσιν τοῦ π. τεθαυματούργηκεν Leont.B.*Nest.et Eut*.2(M.86.1336C); θεὸς ἀνθρώποις ἐκ παρθένου πεφανέρωται μορφωθεὶς τὸ καθ' ἡμᾶς· καὶ θεώσας τὸ π. Sophr.H.*trop*.(M.87.4005A); μηδὲν τοῦ π. φυσικὸν παντελῶς ἀπομειώσας, πλὴν τῆς ἁμαρτίας Max.*opusc*.(M.91.32B); γεγονότος [sc. Adam]...συνέδρου τῷ...πατρί, διὰ τῆς ἀπαρχῆς ταύτης καὶ τοῦ π. Germ.CP *or*.2(M.98.260B); ἐξ ἡμῶν προσλήμματι τὴν ἡμετέραν παρακοὴν ἰώμενος Jo.D.*f.o*.3.1(M.94.984C); θεοῦντι τὸ π. *ib*.3.12(1032C); ἡ μὲν φύσις τῆς σαρκὸς θεοῦται, οὐ σαρκοῖ δὲ τὴν φύσιν τοῦ λόγου· θεοῖ μὲν τὸ π., οὐ σαρκοῦται δέ id.*Jacob*.52(M.94.1461C); ὁ θεότητος ἐλπίδι δελεάσας τὸν ἄνθρωπον, σαρκὸς προσλήμματι εἰκότως δελεασθήσεται id.*hom*.1.10(M.96.561C); ὃ μὲν ἐθέωσεν, ὃ δὲ ἐθεώθη, τουτέστι τὸ π. ὃ διὰ τὴν ἀξίαν τοῦ προσενέγκαντος... ἐδέξατο...ὁ θεός ‡Bas.*h.myst*.38(p.267.2).

προσληπτικός, *additional*, of incarnate Christ τὰ ἀνθρωποπαθῆ περὶ αὐτοῦ καὶ τῆς ἐνσάρκου αὐτοῦ παρουσίας προσληπτικὰ τῆς δόξης...λέγεται Epiph.*haer*.69.73(p.222.12; M.42.321C); ref. Son's divinity μηδὲν χρείαν ἔχοντι π. ἐπιδόσεως *ib*.76.26(p.373.25; 568B); οὔτε γὰρ...ἀποκληρώσεως ἕνεκεν ἢ π. τινος ὀνομασίας ἢ προσθήκης τῷ ἀξιώματι ἑαυτῷ ἐπενόησεν ὁ πατὴρ δι' υἱοῦ μὲν κτίσαι οὐρανὸν καὶ γῆν *ib*.76.38(p.391.12; 597C).

*__προσληπτός__, *assumed* περὶ δὲ τῆς τοῦ δούλου μορφῆς π. ἀπέφηνε καὶ οὐκ εἶπεν αὐτοῦ ἰδίαν οὖσάν ποτε Epiph.*haer*.65.7(p.10.25; M.42.24D).

*__προσλήψιμος__, *needing to be assumed*; of human νοῦς as focus of man's Fall, requiring to be assumed by Christ, Gr.Naz.*carm*.2.1.11.625(M.37.1072A).

πρόσληψις, ἡ, **1.** *addition* τροφὴν...γενέσθαι π. εἰς οὐσίαν Athenag.*res*.6(p.54.5; M.6.984C); ref. human, opp. divine, generation ὁ υἱὸς ...τέλειος ἐγεννήθη. ... ἀτελής, ἄνθρωπε, ἡ σὴ γέννησις· ἐκ προκοπῆς γὰρ ἡ π. Cyr.H.*catech*.11.7; οὔτε δὲ κατὰ προκοπὴν ἀρετῆς, καὶ π. δικαιοσύνης ‡Ath.*Apoll*.1.16(M.26.1124A); εἶχε γὰρ ἐν ἑαυτῷ τὸ ἀεὶ δημιουργικὸν καὶ τέλειον καὶ μηδεμιᾶς ἐπιδεόμενον προσλήψεως δόξης Epiph.*haer*.76.38(p.391.22; M.42.600A); **2.** *acquisition* νομικοῦ μὲν τελείωσις γνωστικὴ εὐαγγελίου πρόσληψις Clem.*str*.4.21(p.305.26; M.8.1340C); **3.** *introduction, bringing in to use* εἰ δὲ πάθος ἐν θεῷ γεννῶντι φοβεῖταί τις, ἔστι καὶ κτίζοντος φοβηθῆναι κίνησιν...καὶ π. ὕλης, καὶ χρείαν ὀργάνων Didym.(‡Bas.)*Eun*.5(1.316D; M.29.760A); **4.** *assumption* of humanity by Logos ἐπεδήμησε γὰρ ὁ θεὸς λόγος σὰρξ γεγονώς, προσλήψει σαρκός Eus.*Ps*.5:12(M.23.117C); εἰ διὰ τὴν π. τῆς σαρκὸς τὸ 'ἐταπείνωσε' γέγραπται, δῆλόν ἐστιν ὅτι καὶ τὸ 'ὑπερύψωσε' δι' αὐτήν ἐστι Ath.*Ar*.1.41(M.26.96C); ἡ π. τῆς σαρκὸς οὐκ ἐδούλου τὸν λόγον φύσει κύριον ὄντα· ἀλλὰ...ἐλευθέρωσις μὲν ἦν ἡ γινομένη... πάσης τῆς ἀνθρωπότητος *ib*.2.14(176C); ὁμολογοῦμεν ὅτι ὁ υἱὸς τοῦ θεοῦ καὶ ἄνθρωπος γέγονε χωρὶς ἁμαρτίας, κατὰ πρόσληψιν πάσης τῆς ἀνθρωπείας φύσεως, τουτέστι ψυχῆς λογικῆς καὶ νοερᾶς καὶ σαρκὸς ἀνθρωπίνης Photinus et al.*ep*.ap.Epiph.*haer*.72.12(p.266.18; M.42.397D); Apoll.*fr*.76(p.222.21)ap.Gr.Nyss.*Apoll*.40(M.45.1213C) cit. s. ἐπιστημοσύνη; περὶ τὴν Χριστοῦ σάρκωσιν, ἤτοι π. Gr.Naz.*or*.21.3(M.35.1085A); Gr.Nyss.*Apoll*.34(M.45.1200A); οὐκέτι γὰρ ἴδιον υἱὸν εὑρίσκεται δοὺς ὑπὲρ ἡμῶν ὁ πατήρ, εἴπερ ἐστὶν ἄνθρωπος διῃρημένως, καὶ οὐχὶ δὴ μᾶλλον ὡς ἐν π. σαρκὸς ὁ ἐκ θεοῦ λόγος Cyr.*Arcad*.(p.103.17; 5^2.104A); διαβεβαιούμεθα τοίνυν τὸν ἐκ...πατρὸς λόγον ἐν π. γεγονότα τῆς ἁγίας τε καὶ ἐμψύχου σαρκός id.*apol.Thdt*.1(p.112.21; 6^1.206D); τῆς θείας φύσεως συγκαταβάσεσι πρὸς τὸ ἡμέτερον σχῆμά τε καὶ εἶδος ἀλλοιωθείσης, οὐ κατὰ βολήν, ἀλλὰ κατὰ π. id.*Ps*.76:11(M.69.1192C); θεὸν τέλειον καὶ ἄνθρωπον τέλειον τὸν αὐτὸν ἐν π. ψυχῆς λογικῆς καὶ σώματος Flav.CP *ep.Thds*.(p.36.16; M.65.892B); οὐ γὰρ δοῦλος ὁ μονογενής,...κατὰ τὴν π. δὲ δοῦλος Thdt.*Ezech*.37:24(2.1000); Βήρων γάρ τις...μεθ' ἑτέρων τινῶν...λέγοντες τὴν μὲν προσληφθεῖσαν τῷ λόγῳ σάρκα γενέσθαι ταυτουργὸν τῇ θεότητι διὰ τὴν π. ‡Hipp.*Ber.Hel*.5(p.324.13; M.10.836D); βασιλεὺς...νυνὶ δέ, καὶ μετὰ τῆς π., καὶ εἰς τὸ διηνεκές ‡Meth.*palm*.5(M.18.393B); υἱὸς θεοῦ κατὰ τὴν προαιώνιον...γέννησιν, υἱὸς ἀνθρώπου ὁ αὐτὸς κατὰ τὴν...σάρκωσίν τε καὶ π. Jo.D.*rect.sent*.2(M.94.1425A); **5.** = πρόσλημμα *that which is assumed* προελθὼν δὲ θεὸς μετὰ τῆς π. Gr.Naz.*or*.38.13(M.36.325B) = *ib*.45.9(633D) = Jo.D.*Jacob*.83(M.94.1481C); ὁ λόγος ἐστίν, εἰ καὶ ἀνέλαβε τὴν ἡμῶν π. ‡Quint.*ep*.(p.16.8; M.85.1737A); **6.** *assumption* in argument, Nemes.*nat.hom*.2(M.40.548A); **7.** *acceptance, reception* of converts into Church, Meth.*symp*.8.6(p.88.9; M.18.148B); of faithful by God, Marc.Er.*opusc*.7.3(M.65.1076A); of penitents by bishop, *Const.App*.2.13.5.

προσλιπαίνω, *amplify*, Chrys.*hom*.4.3 *in 1Thess*.(11.454D).

*__προσμαρτυρία__, ἡ, *additional witness*, Sophr.H.*v.Anast*.(M.92.1709A).

*__προσμάσθιος__, *at the breast* βρέφος π. *Mir.Artem*.11(p.11.14).

*__προσμαστίζω__, v. *προμαστίζω.

*__προσμεταβάλλομαι__, *exchange qualities mutually*, Leont.H.*Nest*.1.51(M.86.1516D).

*__προσμίμημα__, τό, *imitation*, Hipp.*haer*.4.37(p.63.4; M.16.3102C).

*__προσμονάζω__, *dwell as a monk*, Thphn.*chron*.p.134(v.l. προμ- M.108.368B).

*__προσμονάριος__, ὁ, *one who stays in church building, person devoted to guardianship of a church*, CChalc.*can*.2 (v.l. for παραμονάριον *ACO* 2.1.2(p.158.14)); Anton.Hag.*v.Sym.Styl*.14(p.38.16); τῷ π. αὐτοῦ τοῦ σεπτοῦ οἴκου Sergia *Olymp*.1.11(p.417); *Mir.Artem*.15(p.15.19); *Mir.Geo*.4(p.20.5); *Mir.Mich*.4(p.550.11).

*__προσμονέω__, *dwell in*, *Hymn*.ap.*Mir.Geo*.(p.152.25).

*__προσναυτιάω__, *be nauseated* by, *feel disgust* at, Gr.Nyss.*Eun*.1(1 p.28.7; M.45.256C).

*__προσοβέω__, *scare*, Synes.*regn*.3(p.8.13; M.66.1057A).

προσογκ-έω, *increase* ὤφθη...~ουμένου χειμῶνος διεγείρων τὸν κυβερνήτην Ast.Am.*hom*.9(M.40.309B, v.l. προσδοκωμένου).

προσοδεύ-ω, **1.** *bring in as profit* οἱ Στρωματεῖς ἡμῶν, κατὰ τὸν γεωργὸν Τιμοκλέους σῦκα, ἔλαιον...~ουσι Clem.*str*.4.2(p.251.1; M.8.1220A); Or.*exp.in Pr*.28:16(M.17.244C); Mac.Aeg.*hom*.27.6(M.34.697B); **2.** med., *receive income*, *ib*.(697A).

πρόσοδος, ἡ, **1.** *approach*; **a.** to God in prayer (pagan) τὰς π. ἃς...προσίασιν καὶ τὰς θυσίας ἐπ' ἐκείνους ἀναφέρεσθαι Athenag.*leg*.18.1(M.6.925A); Christian οὐδεμίαν ἀφορμὴν παραλειπτέον τῆς π. τῆς πρὸς τὸν θεόν Clem.*str*.7.7(p.31.27; M.9.457C); **b.** to Communion καιρὸν...προσόδου καὶ κοινωνίας Chrys.*hom*.28.1 *in 1Cor*.(10.250D); id.*hom*.3.4 *in Eph*.(11.22B); δεινόν, ὅτι οὐ καθαρότητι διανοίας, ἀλλὰ διαστήματι χρόνου τὴν ἀξίαν διορίζεις τῆς π. id.*hom*.5.3 *in 1Tim*.(11.577C); **2.** *advent*, Eus.*d.e*.2.3(M.22.113B; πρόοδος p.61.26n.); of birth of Jo. Bapt. αὐτοῦ τῇ π. πᾶν εἴ τι κάλλιστον...συμπρόεισιν ‡Thdt. *nativ.Jo.Bapt*.(5.96); **3.** *revenue, income, profit* αἱ π. τοῦ πονηροῦ βασιλέως εἰσὶν αἱ κακίαι καὶ τὰ ψευδῆ δόγματα Or.*exp.in Pr*.28:16(M.17.244C); Chrys.*laud.Paul*.1(2.480C); of reward for alms-deeds ἡ μὲν γὰρ δαπάνη ἐν χρήμασι γίνεται· ἡ π. δὲ οὐκ ἔτι ἐν χρήμασι μόνον, ἀλλὰ καὶ ἐν ἁμαρτημάτων ἀφέσει id.*hom*.1.10 *in 2Cor*.4:13(3.268A); id.*hom*.21.1 *in Heb*.(12.195C); ὡς π. ἔχον τὴν βασιλείαν τῶν οὐρανῶν Thdt.*Dan*.4:34(2.1156); id.*h.rel*.4(3.1150).

προσοικει-όω, **1.** *adapt, make appropriate to* ὅσα τοῖς ἐκτὸς τοῦ πληρώματος αὐτῶν ~οῦν πειρῶνται ἐκ τῶν γραφῶν Iren.*haer*.1.8.2(M.7.524A); †Bas.*Is*.147(1.483A; M.30.360A); pass., *be appropriate* ἴσασιν οἱ δαίμονες τὰ ὄντως πρὸς ἕκαστον πάθος προσῳκειωμένα βοηθήματα *Hom.Clem*.9.16; τοῦ κοινωνῆσαι ἐπιτηρήσιμοι ἡμέραι προσῳκείωνται *ib*.19.22; **2.** *make one's own, appropriate, associate with oneself*, Thdt.*Dan*.9:18(2.1235); προσῳκειώσαμεν...τὸν ἄνθρωπον, οἷον εἰπεῖν, ἰδιοποιήσαμεν Dor.*doct*.22.4(M.88.1825C); of God ἐκκλησίαν...~οῦται Bas.*hom.in Ps*.44(1.167C; M.29.409A); id.*Eun*.2.23(1.259C; M.29.624B); **3.** *unite, associate*; **a.** in gen. αὐτὰ ἡ φιλία...~οῖ τῷ παντί, ἵνα μένῃ τὸ πᾶν ἕν Hipp.*haer*.7.29(p.212.4; M.16.3326C); **b.** of union of believer with God ὡς οἱ ~ωθέντες τῷ θεῷ σεμνυνόμεθα Or.*comm.in Rom*.5:5ff.(*JTS* 13 p.363); ἄνδρας εὐτελεῖς ἐξ ἁλιείας καὶ ταπεινοῦ βίου ~ωσάμενος Eus.*d.e*.3.7(p.141.5; M.22.237B); μελλόντων τῷ θεῷ...ἁπάντων ἀνθρώπων...~οῦσθαι id.*v.C*.2.45(p.60.13; M.20.1021C); ‡Eust.*Laz*.6(p.31.14); ἡ μορφὴ τοῦ δούλου, ἣν αὐτὸς ὁ λόγος ἰδιοποιήσατο φυσικῇ γεννήσει,...καὶ ἡμᾶς ~οῦται...συμπολίτας τῶν ἁγίων καὶ οἰκείους θεοῦ γενομένους ‡Ath.*Apoll*.1.12(M.26.1113A); πάντα χρὴ τάξει τινὶ...τῇ θείᾳ ~ωθῆναι φύσει Gr.Nyss.*anim.et res*.(M.46.105A); Bas.*hom*.13.5(2.118B; M.31.433C); χάρις ~οῦσα δι' ἁγιασμοῦ τῷ θεῷ Cyr.*Ps*.35:8(M.69.920C); id.*Is*.1.3(2.70C); τὸν διὰ πίστεως ~ωθέντα Χριστῷ id.*Jo*.4.6(4.437E); τὸ εὐαγγελικὸν... κήρυγμα...τὸ δυνάμενόν σε...~ῶσαι τῷ θεῷ Oecum.*Apoc*.3:18(p.66); Max.*ambig*.(M.91.1196A); ἅγιοι...ὅσον κτῶνται διὰ τῶν ἐντολῶν τὰς ἀρετάς, τοσοῦτον ~οῦνται τῷ θεῷ Dor.*doct*.23.3(M.88.1833D); in eucharist, *Lit*.ap.*Const.App*.8.15.2; τῆς μυστικῆς εὐλογίας τὴν μέθεξιν, δι' ἧς τῷ ζῶντι καὶ ζωοποιῷ ~ούμεθα λόγῳ Cyr.*Jo*.11.5(4.953D); **c.** of Christ in Inc. τὸν γὰρ καινὸν ἐκεῖνον ἄνθρωπον...διὰ καθαρότητος τῇ συγγενείᾳ τοῦ πατρὸς τῆς φύσεως ἡμῶν ~ώσας πᾶσαν τὴν κοινωνὸν τοῦ σώματος αὐτοῦ καὶ συγγενῆ φύσιν πρὸς τὴν αὐτὴν χάριν συνεφειλκύσατο Gr.Nyss.*Eun*.12(2 p.279.2; M.45.889C); **d.** of man with Christ, Clem.*paed*.1.6(p.119.22; M.8.308C); **e.** with Devil ἡ ἐργασία τῆς ἁμαρτίας ἀπαλλοτριοῖ τοῦ κυρίου, καὶ ~οῖ τῷ διαβόλῳ Bas.*moral*.22(2.254E; M.31.741B); cf.Gr.Nyss.*hom*.2 *in Cant*.(M.44.789C); **4.** *unite, bring into association*, Sophr.H.*v.Anast*.(M.92.1685D); **5.** pass., *be closely related to, have affinity with*, Clem.*str*.2.20(p.174.14; M.8.1056C); προσῳκείωται δὲ τῇ μονάδι τὸ φῶς, τῇ δὲ δυάδι τὸ σκότος Hipp.*haer*.4.43(p.66.26; M.16.3107B); Or.*Jo*.10.39(23; p.216.27; M.14.384A); τῷ φωτὶ φῶς ~οῦται Gr.Nyss.*or.dom*.2(p.34.22; M.44.1141B); οὐκ ἔστιν...πονηρὸν ἀγαθῷ ~ωθῆναι *ib*.5(p.92.34; 1177C); Trin. ὁ μὲν υἱὸς τῷ πατρὶ προσῳκείωται, καὶ τὸ γεννηθὲν τῷ γεννήσαντι id.*Eun*.4(2 p.83.14; M.45.657D); **6.** pass., *be devoted* to, *given up* to, Eus.*d.e*.1.8(p.39.16; M.22.76C); *Lit*.ap.*Const.App*.8.9.5; Justn.*Or*.(p.200.12; M.86.965D).

προσοικείωσις, ἡ, *association*, Meth.*symp*.3.7(p.34.13; M.18.72B).

*__προσοικειωτέον__, *one must attach* to, Clem.*str*.7.16(p.71.12; M.9.540B).

προσοικίζ-ω, *attach* to, *make the property* of ὁ ἀνθρωπίνην σάρκα, καὶ ταύτην ἔμψυχον, ~ων τῷ λόγῳ, οὐδὲν ἕτερον, ἢ ὅλον συνάπτει τὸν ἄνθρωπον Gr.Nyss.*Apoll*.7(M.45.1137B).

προσοικοδομ-έω, *build up into* προσοικοδομηθήσῃ Χριστῷ *Const.App*.1.6.12; ψυχὴ...~εῖται τῇ ἐκκλησίᾳ Mac.Aeg.*hom*.38.9(M.34.756C).

[*]**προσοικονομ-έομαι**, *manage to secure for oneself* ~οῦνται σφίσιν

οἱ κακοὶ τὸ πάντῃ τε καὶ πάντως τὰς τιμωρίας διαφεύγειν Clem.*str*.6.17 (p.511.24; M.9.385C).

***προσοί-ομαι**, *intend, plan* ὁ γὰρ καταλήμψεσθαι τὴν οἰκουμένην... ~όμενος [sc. ὁ Βελίαρ] ὑπὸ γυναίου ἐμπαίζεται Pamph.Mon.*Soter*.1 (p.115.6).

προσομιλ-έω, **1.** *come into contact with* πεπηγόσιν ὕδασιν ὑπὸ τοῦ κρυμοῦ γυμνῇ τῇ γαστρὶ ~οῦντες Chrys.*hom.21.5 in 1Cor*.(10.187E); ~ῶν τῷ πυρί Thdt.*Os*.7:8(2.1343); ἄμμος ~οῦσα πυρί id.*eran*.1(4.11); ref. S. James the Just οὐδὲ...λουτροῖς προσωμίλησεν Hier.*vir. ill*.(tr.Sophr.Pal.)2(p.4.2; M.*PL*.23.610B); eucharistic μηδὲν...ἐκβαλλέτω ἀηδὲς ἢ τῷ θείῳ σώματι ~οῦσα γλῶσσα Chrys.*hom.6.2 in 1Tim*.(11.580B); ref. monophysite Christology ἀνθρωπίνῳ σχήματι προσπελάσας ἡμῖν, ἀλλ' οὐκ ἀνθρωπίνῃ φύσει προσομιλήσας Max. *ambig*.(M.91.93C); **2.** *enter upon*; baptism, Didym.*Trin*.2.14(M.39.700B); marriage, ‡Epiph.*epit.haer*.1.30(p.360.6); **3.** *meet with, experience*, Nil.*epp*.2.319(M.79.356C); of Christ σαρκὶ δὲ θανάτῳ προσομιλήσαντα Attic.*ep.Eups.fr*.(p.115.20)ap.Thdt.*eran*.2(4.167); **4.** *associate oneself with* οἱ δὲ τὸν υἱόν...ἀρνούμενοι...τί καὶ παρενοχλοῦσιν μάτην τῇ ἐκκλησίᾳ, ταῖς Ἰουδαίων ~εῖν συναγωγαῖς δέον; Eus.*e.th*.1.4(p.64.11; M.24.833A); **5.** *keep company with* προσομιληθεῖσα...ἀνδρὶ...εὐδαιμονεστέρῳ Bas.Sel.*v.Thecl*.1(M.85.484A); **6.** *converse with*; **a.** in gen., Just.*dial*.1.2(M.6.473A); Gr.Thaum.*pan.Or*.13 (p.29.17; M.10.1088B); *Hom.Clem*.14.3; **b.** by letter, Ign.*Eph*.9.2; ἐγγράφως Καίσαρι ~ῶν Just.*dial*.120.6(M.6.756B); Tat.*orat*.5(p.6.5; M.6.817A); **c.** of Father's converse with pre-existent Son πρὸ πάντων τῶν ποιημάτων συνῆν τῷ πατρί, καὶ τούτῳ ὁ πατὴρ ~εῖ Just. *dial*.62.4(M.6.617C); asserted against teaching of Marcellus τίνι δ' ἂν καὶ ὡμίλησεν μὴ παρόντος τινός; ἀλλ' αὐτὸς ἑαυτῷ προσωμίλει φωνῇ καὶ διαλέκτῳ χρώμενος, ὡς καὶ τὸν λόγον ἐξ αὐτοῦ προελθεῖν; Eus.*e.th*.3.3(p.157.12; M.24.1001C); **d.** of incarnate Christ addressing Father, Ath.*Ar*.3.19(M.26.364B); **e.** cf converse of Father and Son with men, Just.*dial*.60.4(M.6.613A); ref. scriptural difficulties οὕτω φίλον ὂν τῷ θεῷ ~εῖν ἀνθρώποις, ὡς μὴ καὶ ἀναξίαν ψυχὴν... γυμνὸς καὶ ἀσκεπὴς ὁ θεῖος εἰσίῃ λόγος Gr.Thaum.*pan.Or*.15(p.33.19; M.10.1093B); **f.** of man's converse with God αὕτη...ἡ ἐνέργεια τοῦ τελειωθέντος γνωστικοῦ, ~εῖν τῷ θεῷ διὰ τοῦ μεγάλου ἀρχιερέως Clem.*str*.7.3(p.10.17; M.9.417A); ἄχραντον τὴν ψυχὴν ἔχειν χρή...τὸν ~οῦντα τῷ θεῷ *ib*.7.7(p.36.28; 469A); of Const. μόνος μόνῳ τῷ αὐτοῦ προσωμίλει θεῷ Eus.*v.C*.4.22(p.125.22; M.20.1169A); εἰ καλὴ γὰρ συντυχία ἀνδρὸς ἀγαθοῦ βελτιοῖ τὸν συντυγχάνοντα· πόσῳ μᾶλλον καὶ ἐν νυκτὶ καὶ ἐν ἡμέρᾳ ~εῖν τῷ θεῷ; †Jo.Jej.*poenit*.(M.88.1973A); **g.** of men with H. Ghost, ref. scriptural writers σφόδρα προσομιλήσαντες τῷ θεϊκῷ πνεύματι Didym.*Trin*.1.18(M.39.353A); **7.** *preach*, *Hom.Clem*.11.26; ref. lay preachers οἱ ἐπιτήδειοι πρὸς τὸ ὠφελεῖν τοὺς ἀδελφοὺς...παρακαλοῦνται τῷ λαῷ ~εῖν ὑπὸ τῶν...ἐπισκόπων Alex.H.ap.Eus.*h.e*.6.19.18(M.20.569C); πρεσβύτερος ἐν Ἀλεξανδρείᾳ οὐ ~εῖ [but only bishop] Socr.*h.e*.5.22.58(M.67.640B); ἔθος τοῖς Ἰουδαίοις...μετὰ τὴν...ἀνάγνωσιν ~εῖν καὶ ἐξηγεῖσθαι Ammon.*Ac*. 13:15(M.85.1541B); Jo.Mal.*chron*.10 p.247(M.97.377A); ἀνέβη προσομιλῆσαι *Chron.Pasch*.p.318(M.92.809B).

***προσομίλησις, ἡ,** *contact, communion*; of soul with God, Clem. *paed*.2.9(p.207.27; M.8.496C).

προσομιλία, ἡ, *address, sermon* μετὰ τὴν π. εὔξασθαι ὑπὲρ τῶν πασχόντων *Hom.Clem*.9.19; *ib*.12.24; Eus.*v.C*.4.45 tit.(p.116.16; M.20.1196B); Cyr.H.*procatech*.11; ἐν ἐκκλησίᾳ π. λεγομένων, οὐκ οἴδασι τί ἀκούουσι †Bas.*contub*.11(M.30.825D); ref. Nestorius ὁ τὴν...ἐκκλησίαν διεστραμμέναις π. ταράττειν ἐπιχείρων Cael.*ep.Cyr*.1(p.75.6; 5[2].40B); *ib*.(p.76.1; 41A).

***προσοπλίζω**, pass., *be thoroughly armed*, Isid.Pel.*epp*.1.218(M.78.320C).

***προσοφίζομαι**, *devise craftily beforehand*, Hipp.*haer*.8.11(p.231.24; M.16.3358A); Bas.Sel.*or*.16.2(M.85.209B).

προσοχή, ἡ, 1. *attention, application, diligence*, esp. in study and in pursuit of virtue ἵν' εὐλαβείᾳ καὶ π. τὴν ἀμεριμνίαν ὁ φιλόσοφος κτήσηται Clem.*str*.2.20(p.178.12; M.8.1065A); μετ' ἐπιμελείας καὶ π. ἐντυγχάνων τοῖς προφητικοῖς λόγοις Or.*princ*.4.1.6(p.302.3; M.11.353A); πωλοῦσι δὲ τὸ ἔλαιον οἱ διδάσκοντες μισθοῦ προσεδρίας, π., φιλομαθίας id.*fr. in Mt*.25:1–9(p.205.19; M.17.305B); ἐν τῇ π. καὶ τηρήσει τοῦ λόγου id.*Jo*.20.39(31; p.382.21; M.14.668C); Bas.*reg.br*. 180 tit.(2.476B; M.31.1204A); ἀρχαὶ...καὶ ἐξουσίαι, καὶ πᾶσα ἡ τοιαύτη κτίσις, ἐκ π. καὶ ἐπιμελείας τὸν ἁγιασμὸν ἔχουσαι id.*Eun*.3.2 (1.274A; M.29.660B); τῷ ὑψηλοτέρῳ βίῳ διὰ π. καὶ ἐπιμελείας αὐτοὺς οἰκειώσαντες Gr.Nyss.*v.Mos*.(M.44.337D); ζητεῖν κατὰ πᾶσαν π. ... τὸ εὐσεβῶς διὰ τοῦ λεγομένου νοούμενον id.*Eun*.3(2 p.15.20; M.45.580B); δεήσει...τῆς πρὸς τὸ ἀγαθὸν π. Arsen.*doct*.2(M.66.1620D); ἐκ μιᾶς οὖν π. ὑπάρξει σοι, κἀμοὶ καὶ τοῖς νόμοις χαρίσασθαι Synes.*ep*. 42(M.66.1365B); π. ἐστι, καρδιακὴ ἀδιάλειπτος ἡσυχία ἀπὸ παντὸς λογισμοῦ, Χριστὸν...ἀναπνέουσα Hesych.S.*temp*.1.5(M.93.1481C); **2.** *care* τοῖς μακρᾷ νόσῳ πεπονηκόσι σώμασι διαίτης χρεία καὶ προσοχῆς πλείονος Clem.*q.d.s*.40(p.186.20; M.9.645B); περὶ π. τῆς εἰς Χριστὸν πίστεως Euthal.Diac.*epp.cath*.(M.85.689C); of God's care for man, Meth.*symp*.5.3(p.56.4; M.18.101A); Chrys.*hom.25.2 in Rom*. (9.702E); **3.** *reverent care* οὐχ ἁπλῶς εὔχεται...ἀλλὰ μετὰ π. θεὶς τὰ γόνατα id.*hom.18.2 in Ac*.(9.145B); *Lit.Chrys*.(p.378.35); **4.** *application* μετὰ προσθήκης τῆς πρὸς τὸ ἐνέργημα π. *cat.Apoc*.10:9(p.333.21).

***προσοχθέω**, *be vexed with, detest*, *Asen*.9(p.50.10); Cyr.*Ps*.35:5 (M.69.917A); *Dial.Tim.et Aquil*.108 r°(p.85).

προσοχθίζω, *be angry at*, *T.Jud*.18.5; Herm.*sim*.9.7.6; κακίᾳ δὲ οὐ προσώχθισε τουτέστιν, οὐκ ἐμίσησε τὴν κακίαν Thdt.*qu.3 in 4 Reg*.(1.513); προσοχθίσας τοῖς ἑαυτοῦ ὁμοθρήσκοις Socr.*h.e*.5.24.3(M.67.648C); τῆς φαύλης προσοχθίσας κακοδοξίας *V.Max*.9(M.90.77B).

προσόχθισμα, τό, *detestable thing, abomination* οἱ τῶν δαιμόνων θεραπευταὶ ἐν τοῖς μυσαροῖς καὶ βδελυκτοῖς καὶ ἀκαθάρτοις π. αὐτῶν *Const.App*.2.28.8; π. ... τὰ εἴδωλα προσαγορεύειν εἴωθεν ἡ...γραφή· ...τὸ γὰρ π. τὸ μῖσος δηλοῖ Thdt.*qu.3 in 4Reg*.(1.513); Const.Diac. *laud*.7(M.88.487A).

***προσοχικός**, *diligent*, Hesych.S.*temp*.2.13(M.93.1516B).

πρόσοχος, *attentive*, Isid.Pel.*epp*.1.84(M.78.241A).

***προσοψίζομαι**, *be face to face* with, *confront*, c. dat., Max.*Pyrr*. tit.(M.91.288A).

πρόσοψις, ἡ, *vision*, Clem.*exc.Thdot*.38(p.118.32; M.9.677B).

προσπάθεια, ἡ, 1. *inclination, propensity, attraction*, opp. ἀντιπάθεια: οὐ γὰρ ἀποξύνεσθαι τὸ γάλα ἐᾷ ἡ πρὸς τὸ ὕδωρ κοινωνία, οὐκ ἀντιπαθείᾳ τινί, προσπεπαινομένου δὲ προσπαθείᾳ Clem.*paed*.1.6 (p.120.16; M.8.309B); π. μὲν οὐκ ὀξυδορκεῖ, ἀντιπάθεια δὲ ὅλως οὐχ ὁρᾷ Isid.Pel.*epp*.1.310(M.78.361B); τὰ τῆς ἀπιστίας σημεῖα...προσπάθειαι, ἀντιπάθειαι Jo.D.*hom*.2.6(M.96.585A); π. here meaning *undue favour, partiality*, v. infra; **2.** *natural attachment*, Bas.*renunt*.2(2.204B; M.31.632A); π. φυσικὴν ἡ αἴσθησις ἔχει πρὸς τὰ αἰσθητά Thal. *cent*.2.42(M.91.1441B); γυνή τε καὶ τέκνα...ὧν τῇ π. κεκολλημένοι δυσαποσπάστως ἔχομεν †Jo.D.*B.J*.13(M.96.980C); **3.** *passionate inclination, craving*; **a.** in good sense τί δ' ἂν εἴη πρὸ τῆς ἐν λόγοις τε καὶ περὶ λόγους διατριβῆς; τίς ἡδονὴ καθαρωτέρα; τίς ἀπαθεστέρα π.; Synes.*Dion* 8(p.253.2; M.66.1133A); **b.** usu. in bad sense τὰς...π. τὰς σαρκικὰς πολὺ τῆς ἡδονῆς τὸ φίλτρον ἐχούσας Clem.*str*.7.12(p.56.32; M.9.509B); πᾶσαν τὴν πρὸς ὕλην καὶ σώματα π. ... ἀπολείψαντες Or. *Jo*.20.22(20; p.355.16; M.14.621B); ἐξορίσωμεν ἀφ' ἑαυτῶν πᾶσαν π. βιωτικήν Ephr.1.226F; πλεονεξία, φιλοϋλία, π. id.3.426C; λυθῆναι οὖν δεῖ τῶν δεσμῶν τῆς π. τοῦ βίου Bas.*reg.fus*.5.2(2.342B; M.31.921A); περὶ τὰ ὑλικὰ π. †Bas.*Is*.167(1.499B; M.30.396B); τὸ ἐπιθυμητικόν... μετατεθὲν ἀπὸ τῆς ὑλικῆς π. πρὸς τὴν ἄϋλον σχέσιν Gr.Nyss.*hom.1 in Cant*.(M.44.768C); ματαίαν πρὸς τὰ χρήματα τῶν ἀνθρώπων π. id. *mort*.(M.46.500D); τὸ προσπαθείᾳ τῶν γηίνων ἁλῶναι Mac.Aeg.*pat*.21 (M.34.881D); μέγα τοῖς πρὸς ἀρετὴν ἐπειγομένοις ἐμπόδιον ἡ τῶν κοσμικῶν πραγμάτων π. Nil.*exerc*.13(M.79.733B); τὴν ἐν τῷ λογισμῷ π. τῶν φαύλων ἐννοιῶν id.*Magn*.7(M.79.977C); ἑαυτὸν τῆς τῶν ὁρωμένων ἐξέδυσε π. *Ep.Dor*.1(M.88.1613C); of undue attachment to persons ἔχων π. πρός τινα Dor.*doct*.7.1(M.88.1697A); Jo.D.*haer*.83(M.94.741A); †Jo.D.*B.J*.13(M.96.980B); **4.** abs., *evil desire*, Clem.*str*.1.1 (p.7.23; M.8.696B); ἀφίστασθαι κελεύει...πάσης π. id.*ecl*.47(p.150.6; M.9.720B); Or.*adnot.in Dt*.16:19(M.17.28B); Bas.*moral*.70.29(2.303A; M.31.840C); Isid.Pel.*epp*.1.379(M.78.396D); **5.** *partiality, favour, prejudice in favour* of someone or something χωρὶς π. καὶ διαφορᾶς χρώμεθα Clem.*paed*.2.12(p.229.28; M.8.544B); Gr.Nyss.*hom.7 in Cant*.(M.44.909A); Justn.*conf*.(p.100.7; M.86.1023C).

προσπαθής, 1. *passionately desirous* of evil things προσπαθεῖς τοῖς ὑλικοῖς πράγμασιν Or.*Jo*.20.22(20; p.354.31; M.14.620D); ἁμαρτίας τῆς οὐκ ἐν...λόγοις μόνον, ἀλλὰ καὶ προσπαθοῦς ἐνθυμήσεως †Bas. *bapt*.1.2.15(2.640B; M.31.1552A); **2.** neut. as subst., *prejudice in favour*, Thdr.Stud.*epp*.1.49(M.99.1088B).

***προσπαθητικός**, *vicious* τῇ π. σχέσει τοῦ διγαμοῦντος Thdr.Stud. *epp*.1.50(M.99.1096C).

προσπαθῶς, *with strong affection* or *attachment* οὐ π. τῇ κτίσει χρώμενοι Clem.*str*.3.14(p.240.10; M.8.1196B); *ib*.4.16(p.261.28; 1241C); ἀδύνατον μαθητὴν τοῦ κυρίου γενέσθαι τὸν π. ἔχοντα πρός τι τῶν παρόντων Bas.*moral*.2.2(2.237A; M.31.705A); οὐ τὸ ἔχειν βλάπτει, ἀλλὰ τὸ π. ἔχειν Zos.*alloquia* 14(M.78.1700C).

***προσπαιδαγωγ-έω**, *lead on by instruction* ὁ νόμος ~ῶν εἰς τὸ τέλειον Cyr.*ador*.8(1.264A).

***προσπαραβαίνω**, *pass on to attack*, Nil.*epp*.1.25(M.79.92B).

προσπαράκειμαι, 1. *be adjacent*, Eus.*d.e*.1.4(p.20.6; M.22.44B);

*Chron.Pasch.*p.308(M.92.781B); **2.** *be appended* or *attached*, Juln. Imp.ap.Cyr.*Juln.*9(6^2.290C).

προσπαράληψις, ἡ, *taking as additional aid*, Clem.*str.*7.8(p.37. 21; M.9.472A).

***προσπαρεγγυάω,** *exhort*, Cyr.*Am.*73(3.333B; *παρεγγυᾷ* Aubert).

***προσπαρεισκρίνω,** *introduce in addition*, Gr.Agr.*Eccl.*1.5(M.98. 769C).

προσπαροινέω, *add further insults*, Thdt.*qu.58 in 1Reg.*(1.394).

προσπάσχ-ω, 1. *be fond of ἀστράγαλοι καὶ σφαῖραι τῆς παιδιᾶς ἐστιν ὕλη, καὶ τούτοις προσπεπόνθασι* Nil.*exerc.*63(M.79.796C); **2.** *sympathize with τὸ πᾶσι κατὰ τὴν ἑαυτῶν ἀξίαν* ~ειν Jo.Clim.*past.* 2(M.88.1169C); **3.** *be addicted to, have a craving for*, Athenag.*res.*25 (p.79.1; M.6.1021D); *τοῖς σωματικοῖς προσπεπονθότες* Or.*Jo.*20.16 (14; p.348.5; M.14.609A); Nil.*serm.*1(M.79.1265A); Dion.Ar.*d.n.*4.11 (M.3.708C); **4.** *be partial to, show favour to*, Nil.*paraen.*100(M.79. 1257C); Socr.*h.e.*1.10.5(M.67.101B).

προσπάω, *draw towards one*, Gr.Naz.*carm.*1.1.8.29(M.37.449A).

πρόσπεινος, *hungry*, *A.Andr.et Mt.*22(p.97.9); Gr.Nyss.*hom.11 in Cant.*(M.44.992A).

***προσπειράομαι,** *endeavour besides*, Cyr.*ador.*4(1.119A).

***προσπείρω,** *nail to*; of the *χειρόγραφον* nailed to Cross (Col. 2:14), Chrys.*hom.6.3 in Col.*(11.368B); pass., *be crucified*; of Christ, Leo Mag.*ep.*165.7(p.60.1; M.*PL.*54.1166B).

προσπελάζ-ω, 1. *approach τὴν αἴσθησιν τοῦ* ~οντος *κακοῦ προσλαμβάνει* Meth.*arbitr.*11(p.174.13; M.18.260B); Petr.II Al.*encycl.*7(M. 33.1288A)ap.Thdt.*h.e.*4.22.26; ‡Jo.D.*Artem.*24(p.83.19; M.96.1273A); of time *ἤδη γὰρ προσεπέλαζε τῆς ἡμέρας τὸ σέβας* Men.*exc.Rom.*3 (p.183.12; M.113.869C); **2.** *come over to ἔθνος...ἑκουσίως προσεπέλασεν ἡμῖν ib.*(p.179.1; 864B); **3.** *have recourse to προσπελάσουσι τῇ πανουργίᾳ T.Isach.*6.1; Adam.*dial.*5.16(p.206.4; M.11.1853D); Bas. *hom.*21.3(2.165E; M.31.545C); **4.** *come in contact with, experience πείνῃ* ~ειν Epiph.*exp.fid.*17(p.518.11; M.42.816A); **5.** *be attached to δεῖ γὰρ μᾶλλον τῷ διαφέροντι ὀνόματι προσπελάσαι ἢ τῷ ἥττονι* Adam.*dial.*1.8 (p.18.5; M.11.1729B); **6.** reflex., *gain access to προσπελάσας ἑαυτὸν ὁ Μακριανὸς τῆς ἐφεστώσης Γαλλιήνου βασιλείας* Dion.Al.ap.Eus.*h.e.* 7.23.2(M.20.692B).

***προσπεπαίνομαι,** *be mellowed*, Clem.*paed.*1.6(p.120.15; M.8. 309B).

προσπεφυκότως, *being naturally attached to* something, Cyr.*dial. Trin.*5(5^1.558D).

προσπήγνυμι, 1. *fix to*, hence *crucify*; Father in Patripassian theology, Hipp.*haer.*9.10(p.245.6; M.16.3378B); S. Andrew, *A.(Pass.) Andr.*4(p.8.26; M.2.1224A); Christ *ἔπαθε γὰρ σαρκὶ τῷ σταυρῷ προσπαγεὶς ὁ λόγος* Meth.*Porph.*3(p.506.23; M.18.401B); **2.** intrans., *stick fast to, adhere to*, Chrys.*hom.90.2 in Mt.*(7.840B); met. *ὁ ἀνθρώπινος νοῦς...προσπέπηγε τοῖς γεωδεστέροις* Cyr.*Lc.*16:1(M.72.812B); **3.** pass., *be congealed*, *A.Petr.et Paul.*53(p.202.6).

***πρόσπηξις, ἡ,** *fixing* hence *crucifixion*, *Const.App.*5.5.3.

***προσπιλέω,** *press close to λαμπάδων...ταῖς πλευραῖς...προσπιληθεισῶν* Pall.*v.Chrys.*20(p.129.11, v.l. *προσπιλωθεισῶν* M.47.72) perh. for *προσπελασθεισῶν*.

προσπίπτω, *fall before* in supplication, *1Clem.*9.1; *προσπέσωμεν τῷ δεσπότῃ ib.*48.1; Chrys.*hom.14.7 in Rom.*(9.586B); ‡Pall.*h.mon.* 8.31(p.42.3; *προσικέτευσεν* M.34.1145A); Jo.Mal.*chron.*18 p.476(M. 97.692B); *προσπίπτομεν τῇ ἀγαθότητί σου, δέσποτα Lit.Jac.*(p.194. 27).

προσπλέκ-ω, 1. *mingle, combine* with *τὴν τοῦ θεοῦ δύναμιν ἀσθενείᾳ προσπλακῆναι* [i.e. in Arian theology] Alex.Al.*ep.Alex.*7 (p.24.16; M.18.557D); Petr.II Al.*encycl.*7(M.33.1285C)ap.Thdt.*h.e.*4. 22.25; Epiph.*haer.*66.5(p.24.14; M.42.37B); **2.** *introduce* an argument, Const.ap.Gel.Cyz.*h.e.*3.19.14(M.85.1348C); **3.** *associate oneself with διανοεῖται προσπλέξαι πρὸς τὸν ἄνδρα* Epiph.*haer.*66.5(p.25.7; M. 42.37C); **4.** pass., *be involved in*, Just.*dial.*80.1(M.6.664A); Bas.*Eun.* 1.5(1.216D; M.29.521A); **5.** pass., *be united with*; ref. sexual relations, Hipp.*haer.*5.26(p.131.12; M.16.3202A); Epiph.*haer.*38.2(p.65.4; M.41. 657A); Chrys.*hom.20.8 in Eph.*(11.156B); Thdt.*affect.*12(p.315.10; 4.1030); ref. Inc. *ὁ λόγος...οὐ...προμορφωθέντι...*~ώμενος *σώματι* Sophr.H.*ep.syn.*(M.87.3161B); **6.** *attach ταῦτα...οἷς οὔτε ψόγος οὔτε κακοδοξία τις δυνήσεται προσπλακῆναι* Const.ap.Ath.*apol.sec.*86(p.165. 33; M.25.405A); Ath.*inc.*44.4(M.25.176A); id.*Ar.*2.17(M.26.184A).

προσπλήσσω, *strike*, Gr.Naz.*or.*45.12(M.36.640A).

προσπλοκή, ἡ, *admixture*, Iren.*haer.*1.7.4(M.7.517A).

πρόσπνευσις, ἡ, *rough breathing, aspiration*, Or.*mart.*46(p.42.15; M.11.628A).

προσποθέω, *desire earnestly*, Sophr.H.*mir.Cyr.et Jo.*38(M.87. 3568A).

προσποίησις, ἡ, *pretence*, of certain aspects of Christ's conduct as man *τὰ μὲν γὰρ αὐτῶν κατὰ φύσιν οἰκονομικῶς πέπρακται...οἷον ὁ ἐκ παρθένου τόκος...τὰ δὲ κατὰ π.· οἷον τὸ ἐρωτᾶν· ποῦ τεθείκατε Λάζαρον; ὁ ὑπὸ τὴν συκῆν δρόμος· τὸ ὑποδύεσθαι ἤγουν ὑπαναχωρεῖν· ἡ προσευχή* ‡Cyr.*Trin.*25(6^3.31A; M.77.1168C).

προσποιητός, *simulating*; masc. as subst., *pretender*, Gr.Mag. *dial.*(tr.Zach.)3.14(M.*PL.*77.243D).

***προσπορέω,** *provide*, ‡Ath.*syntag.*6.9(p.126; M.28.844A).

***πρόσπτυξις, ἡ,** *embrace π. τε τιμίου λειψάνου* Thdr.Stud.*epp.*2. 176(M.99.1545D).

πρόσπτωσις, ἡ, 1. *falling before* someone *as a suppliant*, hence *supplication*, Gr.Nyss.*ep.*19(M.46.1076C); Chrys.*hom.23.5 in 1Cor.* (10.207D); **2.** *fall*, Cyr.*Ps.*44:6(M.69.1037A); **3.** *attack*, *Const.App.*4. 3.3; *χαλεπῶν δαιμόνων τὰς μυρίας π.* Nil.*epp.*2.137(M.79.257A).

***προσπωρόω,** pass., *be hardened upon, become habitual to οἷς δὲ προσεπωρώθη τὰ πάθη* Gr.Nyss.*or.catech.*35(p.138.12; M.45.92B).

προσρέω, 1. *flow onwards*, *Hom.Clem.*8.8; **2.** aor., *betake oneself, accede, attach oneself* to *τοὺς σοὺς πόνους τίμησον, οἷς προσερρύης* Gr.Naz.*carm.*2.1.11.1793(M.37.1155A); *προσρυέντι Ῥωμαίοις* Jo.Mal. *chron.*18 p.427(M.97.629A); **3.** ? *turn towards πάντων τὰ πρόσωπα ἐπὶ γῆς δοθέντα, ἔγνω αὐτοὺς μηδαμῶς δύνασθαι προσρυέσθαι αὐτῷ Pers.* (p.4.11); *be assimilated* to, †Anth.*eccl.fr.*(p.97.10); *go over to* enemy, †Anast.S.*relat.*40 suppl.(*OC* 2 p.87.24).

***πρόσρηγμα, τό,** *dashing against*; of shipwreck, *Clem.ep.*14(M.2. 49B); Cyr.*Abac.*6(3.522C).

προσρήγνυμι, A. trans., *dash against*, exeg. Ps.136:8–9 *νήπια... Βαβυλῶνος...εἰσὶν συγχυτικοὶ λογισμοὶ οἱ ἀπὸ κακίας· ὧν ὁ κρατῶν, ὡς καὶ τῷ στερεῷ...τοῦ λόγου προσρῆξαι αὐτῶν τὰς κεφαλάς, ἐδαφίζει τὰ νήπια...πρὸς τὴν πέτραν* Or.*Cels.*7.22(p.174.14; M.11.1453A).

B. intrans.; **1.** *be dashed against*, of ships *πολλάκις προσέρραξε τὸ σκάφος* Chrys.*hom.14.4 in Heb.*(12.147B); fig. *παιδίον, ὥσπερ σκάφος, εἰς θηριώδη...προσρῆξαι δίαιταν* Clem.*paed.*1.7(p.122.20; M.8.313C); *ὁ φαρισαῖος...τούτῳ προσέρρηξε τῷ σκοπέλῳ* [i.e. of boasting], Chrys. *hom.25.1 in 2Cor.*(10.612C); **2.** *burst forth, launch an attack*, Eus.*h.e.* 8.1.7(M.20.741B); Jo.Mon.*hymn.Geo.*4(M.96.1396C).

C. med.; **1.** *rush against* or *into*, of wind into a hollow, Clem.*str.* 6.3(p.447.21; M.9.252A); **2.** *dash against*; of waves, Chrys.*hom.24.3 in Mt.*(7.302D); met. *ἡ...τῶν δήμων προπέτεια, τῷ μὲν ἄρχοντι προσρηγνυμένη* Isid.Pel.*epp.*1.148(M.78.281C).

πρόσρησις, ἡ, 1. *designation, naming τῶν...ἀποστόλων...σαφὴς ἐκ τῶν εὐαγγελίων ἡ π.* Eus.*h.e.*1.12.1(M.20.117B); *ἐκ τῆς περὶ αὐτοὺς εἰκονικῆς τοῦ Χριστοῦ π. Χριστιανοὺς ἐπεφήμισεν ib.*1.3.10(72C); theol. *τὸ δὲ πατὴρ καὶ θεὸς καὶ κτίστης καὶ κύριος καὶ δεσπότης οὐκ ὀνόματά ἐστιν, ἀλλ' ἐκ τῶν εὐποιϊῶν καὶ τῶν ἔργων π.* Just.*2apol.*6.2 (M.6.453A); *μέχρι λόγου τὴν τοῦ υἱοῦ π. ἀποδεχόμενος* Eus.*e.th.*2.2 (p.101.19; M.24.904A); ref. pagan myths *καταβάλλειν εἰς αἰσχρὰς... ἀρρητολογίας τὴν σεβάσμιον τοῦ θεοῦ π.* id.*p.e.*3.13(122A; M.21.217C); **2.** *salutation, greeting*, Chrys.*hom.18.6 in Mt.*(7.243C); liturg., of greeting exchanged by newly consecrated bishop and congregation, *Lit.*ap.*Const.App.*8.5.12; in gen.; of liturg. greetings, Chrys. *hom.3.3 in Col.*(11.347D); in epistle, id.*hom.31.1 in Rom.*(9.745A); *ib.31.3*(748D); Thdt.*Rom.*16:15(3.159); of episcopal letters of communion, Thdt.*h.e.*5.34.12(3.1076); **3.** *address*, CHier.(350)*ep.*ap. Ath.*apol.sec.*57(p.137.9; M.25.352C); of imperial letter, Const.*ib.*62 (p.142.19; M.25.361C).

προσρήσσ-ω, 1. *drive on*, Ath.*gent.*27(M.25.56A); Petr.II Al. *encycl.*7(M.33.1285D)ap.Thdt.*h.e.*4.22.25; **2.** med., *come into collision* with ~ονται *ἑαυτοῖς ὡς μεθύοντες* Arist.*apol.*16.6; hence, *be shipwrecked* upon, met. *μὴ* ~ώμεθα *ὡς ἐπήλυτοι τῷ ἐκείνων νόμῳ Barn.*3.6.

***προσρητικός,** *of salutation, of personal greeting διὰ π. γραμμάτων* Epiph.*haer.*proem.2.2(p.170.26, v.l. *προφη-* M.41.176C); *ἐν μακροθυμίᾳ τε καὶ γραμμάτων ἀγάπῃ π.* Nest.*ep.Cyr.*1(p.25.14; M.77.44A).

προσρίπτ-ω, 1. *throw to*, *A.Jo.*53(p.177.22); *Ἰωνᾶν προσρίψαι τοῖς κύμασιν* Thdt.*serm.Chrys.*(5.102); met., of hurling insults at someone, Chrys.*hom.12.6 in 1Cor.*(10.105D); of casting afflictions before God in prayer, Serap.*euch.*5.1; **2.** *assign to, attribute to*, Chrys.*hom. 12.3 in 1Cor.*(10.100B); *ib.26.6*(237A); id.*scand.*4(3.472E); **3.** *apply to τὸ κύριος ὄνομα τῷ υἱῷ* ~ουσι id.*pan.Phoc.*4(2.709E); id.*comm. in Gal.*1:1(10.660B); Cyr.*Mal.*28(3.846C); **4.** *add*, Bas.*Eun.*1.5(1. 216B; M.29.520B); Gr.Nyss.*Eun.*9(2 p.207.2; M.45.804C); Cyr.*Juln.*4 (6^2.137C).

***προσστοιβάζω,** *build up in addition*, ‡Ath.*disp.*25(M.28.469B).

***προσσυμπάθεια, ἡ,** s.v.l., *craving, evil desire for*, Or.*fr.43 in Jer.*28:29(M.13.695A, v.l. for *προσπαθείας* p. 220.13).

προσσυνάπτω, *join on* to, Socr.*h.e.*5.7.1(M.67.573B).

προσσύρω, *drag along*; med., *crawl*, Bas.*hom*.8.3(2.65D; M.31.313A); Ast.Am.*hom*.6(M.40.244B).

προσσφίγγω, (also προσφ-) *bind to*, c. dat., Clem.*prot*.1(p.8.8; M.8.64A); Hipp.*haer*.7.13(p.191.10; M.16.3295B); †Bas.*Is*.proem.1(1.378B; M.30.120A).

***προσσώζω**, *reserve for*, c. dat., Thdt.*2Cor*.3:10(3.304).

προσσωρεύω, *heap up in addition*, hence *add*, CChalc.(451)*act*.16 (*ACO* 2.1.3 p.95.1; f.l. προ- H.2.636E).

πρόσταγμα, τό, *ordinance*; **1.** of men in gen., ref. Daniel οὐ... μόνον τὰς τοῦ θεοῦ ἐντολὰς...ἐφύλαττεν, ἀλλὰ καὶ τὰ τοῦ βασιλέως π. Hipp.*Dan*.3.19.7; ref. Herod's order for massacre of children, Eus. *h.e*.1.8.1(M.20.101A); of master's order to servants, Gr.Nyss.*Eun*.10 (2 p.243.26; M.45.845D); **2.** *edict* of emperor τὰ π. τῶν Αὐγούστων περὶ τοῦ δεῖν...σέβειν τοὺς θεοὺς τοὺς τὰ πάντα διοικοῦντας *M.Carp*.4; *ib*.45; Dion.Al.ap.Eus.*h.e*.6.41.1(M.20.605A); Const.ap.Gel.Cyz.*h.e*. 3.15.3; Socr.*h.e*.3.13.13(M.67.416A); summoning a council, Ath.*syn*. 1(p.231.9; M.26.681A); *ib*.10(p.237.3; 696B); **3.** *decree* of fate, Meth. *symp*.8.16(p.105.8; M.18.168D); **4.** *precept* of philosophy, Gr. Thaum.*pan.Or*.11(p.27.9; M.10.1084C); **5.** *commandment* of God, *T.Lev*.3.2; πορεύεσθε ἐν τοῖς π. αὐτοῦ πρώτοις καὶ ἐσχάτοις *T.Jud*. 24.3; *1Clem*.2.8; ἐν τοῖς νομίμοις τῶν π. αὐτοῦ πορεύεσθαι *ib*.3.4; ἀβύσσων τε ἀνεξιχνίαστα...τοῖς αὐτοῖς συνέχεται π. *ib*.20.5; μακάριοι οἱ τούτοις ὑπακούοντες τοῖς π. *2Clem*.19.3; τὰ στοιχεῖα...ἐκ τοῦ μὴ ὄντος παραχθέντα προστάγματι τοῦ ὄντως θεοῦ Arist.*apol*.4.1; θάλασσα...οὐχ ὑπερβαίνουσα τὸν οἰκεῖον τόπον...θεῖόν τι π. πεφοβημένη Meth.*arbitr*.2(p.148.13; M.18.244A); τὸν θεὸν οὐ δοκεῖ προτρέποντα τὸν ἄνθρωπον πείθεσθαι τοῖς π. ἀφαιρεῖν αὐτοῦ τὴν ἐξουσίαν τῆς προαιρέσεως *ib*.16(p.188.15; 264D); πῶς γὰρ ἂν ἡ φύσις τῷ π. μάχοιτο τοῦ θεοῦ; Juln.Imp.ap.Cyr.*Juln*.4(6².143C); ἐπὶ τῆς κτίσεως συνεξέλαμψε τὸ φῶς τῷ π. Gr.Nyss.*hom.8 in Cant*.(M.44.945D); ref. Creation οὔτε δὲ ἐν ἐκείνοις ῥῆμα νοοῦμεν τὸ π., ἀλλὰ βούλημά τε καὶ θέλημα Thdt.*haer*.5.9(4.410); Jo.D.*hom*.1.20(M.96.576A); of Mosaic Law αἰώνιος...νόμος ὁ Χριστὸς ἐδόθη καὶ ἡ διαθήκη πιστή, μεθ' ἣν οὐ νόμος, οὐ π., οὐκ ἐντολή Just.*dial*.11.2(M.6.497B); τὸ σάββατον ἐντέταλται ὁ θεὸς φυλάσσειν ἡμᾶς, καὶ τὰ ἄλλα π. προσετετάχει *ib*.21.1 (520B); Meth.*symp*.4.4(p.50.11; M.18.92C); Cosm.Ind.*top*.2(M.88. 96B); of Mosaic ordinances applied to Christian life ὁ λαϊκὸς ἄνθρωπος λαϊκοῖς π. δέδεται *1Clem*.40.4; in transferred sense, *thing commanded* by God ἐπεὶ οὖν...παρῆλθον θυσίαι, βασιλεῖαι, αἱ ἐν γεννητοῖς γυναικῶν προφητεῖαι...ὡς οὐκ ὄντα θεοῦ π. *Hom.Clem*.3.52; **6.** divine *precept* opp. counsel, Chrys.*hom.2 in Rom.16:3*(3.183A).

προστακτικῶς, *imperatively*, Hadr.*introd*.98(p.114; M.98.1300A).

***προστάλας**, *exceedingly wretched*, *Apoc.Dan*.C(p.122).

πρόσταξις, ἡ, **A.** *command, ordinance*; **1.** of emperor τοῦτο γὰρ ἀθέμιτον ἦν...πρὸ τῆς σῆς π. ποιῆσαι Ath.*apol.Const*.14(M.25.612B); τὴν ἡμετέραν π. φυλαχθῆναι βουλόμεθα Constantius ap.eund.*apol.sec*. 56(p.136.17; M.25.349C); **2.** of God σώματα κατὰ καιρὸν προστάξει θεοῦ ἀναστῆναι Just.*dial*.19.4(M.6.357A); Clem.*str*.7.2(p.6.18; M.9.409B); Ath.*gent*.27(M.25.53B).

B. *precept* of scripture πιστεύειν γὰρ ἡμᾶς οὐκ εἰς τὸν λόγον, ἀλλ' εἰς τὸν υἱὸν π. ἐστι...[Jo.3:36] ‡Ath.*Ar*.4.21(p.67.15; M.26.497D).

C. *authority* μὴ ἐξεῖναι γυναικὶ ἀναίδην ἐξ οἰκείας π. βίβλους συγγράφειν Didym.*Trin*.3.41(M.39.989A); οὐχ ὡς κατὰ πρόσταξιν λεγόμενοι, ἀλλ' ὡς παρ' αὐτῶν γνωσθέντες ‡Ath.*synops*.22(M.28. 345A).

***προσταπεινόομαι**, *be brought low*, Nil.*epp*.2.59(M.79.225C).

προσταράσσω, *vex further*, Chrys.*Laz*.2.6(1.735E).

προστασία, ἡ, **1.** *support, protection, patronage*; **a.** in gen. χρήσιμον δὲ πολλάκις καὶ ἡ παρὰ τοῖς κρατοῦσι π. Or.*fr.63 in Jer*. 45:4(p.229.19); Ath.*Ar*.1.10(M.26.32C); *ib*.2.43(240A); Gr.Naz.*or*.7. 11(M.35.768C); τέχνης κοινωνοὶ τοσαύτην ἐπιδείκνυνται π. Chrys. *hom.15.9 in Mt*.(7.200C); **b.** of patronage of angels κατά τε γὰρ τὰ ἔθνη καὶ πόλεις νενέμηνται τῶν ἀγγέλων αἱ π. Clem.*str*.6.17(p.513.6; M.9.389B); of martyrs τῆς π. αὐτῶν τῆς πρὸς τὸν θεὸν ἀπολαύομεν Ast.Am.*hom*.10(M.40.321D); ref. Lc.22:32 of S. Peter in rel. to disciples τὴν π. ἐνεπιστεύθη τῶν ἀδελφῶν Chrys.*hom.88.2 in Jo*.(8. 527C); of BMV, *Euchol*.(p.403); of Christ τούτων ἁπάντων [sc. saints] Χριστὲ Ἰησοῦ ἐφάνης βοήθεια καὶ π. *IGC As.Min*.282.3 [Cnossus, Lycia, saec. vi]; **2.** *charge, government, leadership*, Clem.*str*.7.9(p.38. 29; M.9.473B); of angels exercising charge over world of nature ascribed by pagans to demons, Or.*Cels*.8.31(p.246.26; M.11.1561D); of providential ordering of world, Meth.*res*.2.10(p.350.6); of eccl. office εἰς οὐδεμίαν ἀρχὴν καὶ π. τῆς...ἐκκλησίας τοῦ θεοῦ καταλέγοντες τοὺς φθάσαντας μετὰ τὸ προσεληλυθέναι τῷ λόγῳ ἐπταικέναι Or.*Cels*.3. 51(p.248.3; 988C); esp. episcopal office Πρῖμον μεταλλάξαντα δωδεκάτῳ τῇ: π. ἔτει διαδέχεται Ἰοῦστος Eus.*h.e*.4.4(M.20.308C); Bas.*ep*. 92.2(3.184D; M.32.480B); *ib*.102(197E; M.508C); of party-episcopates at Antioch in Meletian schism παῦσαι δὲ τὰς μερικὰς π. *ib*.66.2 (160B; M.425C); Chrys.*stat*.3.1(2.35C); Pall.*v.Chrys*.8(p.46.28; M.47. 28).

προστάσσ-ω, **1.** *appoint, assign* προσέταξε δύο μὲν στοιχεῖα εἰς τὸ ἄνω ἡμισφαίριον Hipp.*haer*.4.43(p.66.8; M.16.3106D); Or.*Cels*.8. 31(p.246.25; M.11.1561D); οἱ δὲ τὰ Ῥωμαίων σκῆπτρα κατέχοντες ~ουσι πανταχοῦ τοὺς ὑπ' αὐτῶν γενομένους καὶ στρατοπεδαρχοῦντας τοῖς Ῥωμαϊκοῖς στρατεύμασι *Mir.Geo*.4(p.21.4); **2.** *command, enjoin* ταῦτα...προσέταξεν εἶναι *1Clem*.20.11; τοῖς προστεταγμένοις καιροῖς ποιοῦντες τὰς προσφορὰς *ib*.40.4; περιτομὴν...ἂν...ἐφυλάσσομεν, εἰ μὴ ἔγνωμεν δι' ἣν αἰτίαν καὶ ὑμῖν προσετάγη Just.*dial*.18.2(M.6.516A); ὅπερ δὴ τοῖς ὑπηκόοις καὶ ~ομένοις ἁρμόττει Thdt.*affect*.2(p.54.20; 4.746); c. ἵνα, *A.Petr.et Paul*.51(p.200.16); ref. edicts κατὰ τὰ προσταχθέντα ἔθυσα *Pap.Chr*.(p.361).

προστάτης, ὁ, **1.** *champion, patron, supporter*; **a.** in gen., Bas.*ep*. 316(3.445C; M.32.1064C); of deacons as εὐσεβείας π., *Const.App*.3.19. 5; **b.** of God π., ἐπίκουρος *Lit*.ap.*Const.App*.8.11.5; ref. one taking sanctuary τῇ ἱερᾷ τραπέζῃ προσφεύγει, καὶ θεὸν ποιεῖται π. τῆς ἐπηρείας Gr.Naz.*or*.43.56(M.36.568A); **c.** of Christ τὸν π. καὶ βοηθὸν τῆς ἀσθενείας ἡμῶν *1Clem*.36.1; τῷ π. τῶν ἡμετέρων ψυχῶν Gr. Thaum.*pan.Or*.4(p.8.13; M.10.1060C); ὁ τῶν χήρων π. Bas.Sel.*or*.10.2 (M.85.145B); **d.** of angels τοῖς μὲν τῶν ἐθνῶν ἀοράτοις π., αὐτοῖς δὴ τοῖς ἀγγέλοις, τὰ ἔθνη πάντα...φησιν διανεμηθῆναι Eus.*d.e*.4.7(p.160. 33; M.22.268C); **e.** of saints τοῦ σκηνοποιοῦ καὶ τοῦ ἁλιέως προστατῶν καὶ τετελευτηκότων δεῖται ὁ τὸ διάδημα ἔχων Chrys.*hom.26.5 in 1Cor*. (10.625B); τίς κατηγορία προστάταις [i.e. martyrs] προσφεύγειν; Ast. Am.*hom*.10(M.40.324A); ὁ τῶν ἐκκλησιῶν π. Alex.Sal.*Barn*.proem. 6(p.438D); **f.** of pagan gods θεούς τε καὶ π. ἀγαθούς Juln.Imp.ap. Cyr.*Juln*.4(6².141C); **g.** of Satan as ὁ τοῦ ψεύδους π., *Const.App*. 7.32.2; **2.** *protector* of a virgin (i.e. perh. 'spouse' of a συνεισακτός) παρθένε, μὴ συνοίκει προστάτῃ, Χριστὸν ἔχουσα νυμφίον Gr.Naz. *carm*.1.2.3.67(M.37.638A); **3.** *leader, chief* οἱ νῦν π. τῆς αἱρέσεως Hipp. *haer*.9.8(p.241.8; M.16.3371B); Pall.*v.Chrys*.9(p.56.25; M.47.33); of S. Peter as μαθητῶν π., Bas.Sel.*or*.17.1(M.85.217A); **4.** *ruler*, of God τὸν μέγαν π. καὶ παμβασιλέα τῶν ὅλων Eus.*p.e*.1.1(2D; M.21.24C); of civil ruler, Thdt.*h.rel*.17(3.1225); of eccl. rulers, Just.*dial*.92.2(M.6. 696A); οἱ ἀπόστολοι, καὶ οἱ ἀρχαῖοι ἐπίσκοποι, οἱ τῆς ἐκκλησίας π. Cyr. H.*catech*.4.35; bishops, Bas.*ep*.214.4(3.323A; M.32.789C); Gr.Nyss. *v.Macr*.(p.385.17; M.46.973B); of a minor official, Photinus et al.*ep*. ap.Epiph.*haer*.72.11(p.265.13; M.42.397A); **5.** as adj. π. τὴν ὑπὲρ λίαν ὑπόθεσιν Alex.Sal.*Barn*.proem.1(p.436F).

προσταυρ-όω, *crucify beforehand* ~οῦντα ἢ ἀνασταυροῦντα τὸν υἱὸν τοῦ θεοῦ...εἴτε πρὸ τῆς...σωματικῆς τοῦ σωτῆρος ἡμῶν ἐπιδημίας εἴτε καὶ ὕστερον Or.*Jo*.20.12(p.341.29; M.14.600A); *ib*.(p.342.4; 600A); cf. *ib*.(p.342.11; 600B).

προστείχω, *go before, anticipate*, Eudoc.*Cypr*.1.264(M.85.841C).

***προστελείωσις, ἡ**, Gr.Nyss.*Eun*.4(M.45.640B; l. πρὸς τελείωσιν 2 p.67.10).

***προστήθιον, τό**, *breastplate* of high-priest, Gr.Nyss.*v.Mos*.(M.44. 388B).

***προστήρησις, ἡ**, *observation, watchful care*, exercised by bishop in determining duration of penitential discipline, Gr.Nyss.*ep.can*. 5(M.45.232B).

προστίθ-ημι, **1.** *add*, to doctrinal tradition φυλάξεις ἃ παρέλαβες, μήτε ~εὶς μήτε ἀφαιρῶν *Barn*.19.11; **2.** *attribute* τοῦτο...~ησι τῷ υἱῷ, τὸ πρεσβύτερον εἶναι τῆς κτίσεως Bas.*Eun*.2.14(1.248C; M.29. 597A); **3.** *go on, proceed* to do προσέθεντο αὐτῇ δοῦναι σημεῖον *1Clem*.12.7.

***πρόστιμον, τό**, *penalty*, Ath.Scholast.*coll*.20.1(p.171).

***προστοιβάζομαι**, *be piled up before* or *already*, Thdr.Stud.*epp*.2. 180(M.99.1557A).

προστοιχειόω, pass., *be given elementary instruction in advance* οἱ μὴ προστοιχειωθέντες ἀσφαλῶς ταῖς τοῦ Χριστοῦ περὶ αὐτοῦ [sc. antichrist] προρρήσεσι Andr.Caes.*Apoc*.54(M.106.380C).

προστραγωδέω, *add a further fable*, Bas.*ep*.51.1(3.143D; M.32. 389A).

προστρέφω, *feed up, nourish up*, †Dion.Al.*fr.Eccl*.2:25(p.224.4; M.10.1585D).

προστρέχ-ω, *have recourse to* θλιβόμενοι εἰς τὸ τὸν θεὸν ποιεῖν ἃ βούλεται ~ουσιν Meth.*res*.1.20(p.242.13; M.41.1088C); τῇ δὲ αὐτοῦ φιλανθρωπίᾳ προσδραμεῖν Thdr.Heracl.*Is*.28:16(M.18.1317C); π. εἰς τὴν θεογνωσίαν *ib*.52:15(1356B); Chrys.*hom.3.3 in Col*.(11.347A).

προστρίβ-ομαι, *inflict*, pass. σπῖλον ἢ ῥυτίδα, ἤ τι τῶν τοιούτων ~ομένων τῇ τοῦ Χριστοῦ ἐκκλησίᾳ Or.*sel.in Jer*.17:21ff.(*AS* 3 p.541).

πρόστριψις, ἡ, *conflict*, Just.*dial*.50.1(M.6.585B).

[*]**προστροπή, ἡ,** *pollution*, Synes.*ep*.44(M.66.1373C).

προστύφ-ω, *prepare wool for dyeing by application of mordants* τὰ βαπτόμενα τῶν ἐρίων ~εσθαι φιλεῖ εἰς βεβαίαν εὐτρεπιζόμενα τῆς βαφῆς παραδοχήν Clem.*paed*.1.9(p.135.27; M.8.344A); met. ἡ Ἑλληνικὴ φιλοσοφία...τὸ ἦθος...~ουσα εἰς παραδοχὴν τῆς ἀληθείας id. *str*.1.16(p.52.22; M.8.796A); ὥσπερ τὰ ἔρια πρὸς παραδοχὴν βαφῆς... ~εται...οὕτως ὁ...Παῦλος τῆς Ἰουδαϊκῆς ἀποτμηθεὶς ἀλογίας, τριημέρῳ προεστύφθη πηρώσει Isid.Pel.*epp*.1.346(M.78.380D).

***προσυγχωρέομαι,** *be agreed on before*, Or.*or*.28(p.379.8; M.11. 528A).

***προσυλλαμβάνω,** *grasp beforehand* οὐ γὰρ ἐκ τῶν ὄντων τὰ ὄντα μανθάνων, οἶδεν ὁ θεῖος νοῦς, ἀλλ' ἐξ αὐτοῦ...κατ' αἰτίαν τὴν πάντων εἴδησιν...καὶ οὐσίαν προέχει καὶ προσυνείληφεν Dion.Ar.*d.n*.7.2(M.3. 869B); Max.*schol.d.n*.7.2(M.4.348D).

προσυλλέγω, *collect beforehand*, Anast.S.*hod*.10(M.89.149D).

πρόσυλος, *belonging to matter, gross*, Dion.Ar.*c.h*.2.4(M.3.141D); Max.*qu.Thal*.31(M.90.372A); id.*opusc*.(M.91.69B); ἐμπαθὲς καὶ π. νόημα Jo.Mon.*hymn.Chrys*.4(M.96.1380B).

***προσύλως,** *in a material* or *gross fashion* τῶν ποιητῶν π. καὶ ἐμπαθῶς ἐναπομενόντων Dion.Ar.*ep*.7.2(M.3.1080B); Const.Diac.*laud*. 19(M.88.501C).

***προσυναγείρω,** *collect beforehand*, Cyr.*Ag*.5(3.630D).

***προσυνδιατρίβω,** *associate with before*, Thphn.*chron*.p.55(M.108. 192C; v.l. προσσ-).

***προσυντείνομαι,** *strain towards*, Cyr.*Jo*.3.6(3.315B).

προσυπακού-ω, 1. *understand* (gram.), *supply in thought*, Clem. *str*.7.14(p.63.15; M.9.524A); Or.*Cels*.6.62(p.132.23; M.11.1393A); Eus. *Ps*.13:4(M.23.145C); παντὸς ἀνδρὸς ἡ κεφαλὴ ὁ Χριστός ἐστιν...τοῦ πιστοῦ δεῖ ~ειν Chrys.*hom.26.2 in 1Cor*.(10.229A); ὁ νόμος ὀργὴν κατεργάζεται...ἐπειδὴ παρέβημεν, ~εται id.*hom.5.2 in Eph*.(11.34D); εἶπεν ὁ θεὸς τῷ Ἀδάμ·...εἰς γῆν ἀπελεύσῃ· οὐ προσέθηκε δέ· ἀφανισθήσῃ ...διὰ τοῦ ταῦτα παρασεσιωπῆσθαι, τὴν ἀνάστασιν προσυπήκουσα Isid. Pel.*epp*.4.149(M.78.1233D); πολλὰ γὰρ ἐν τῇ...γραφῇ τῷ λόγῳ τῆς ἐλλείψεως εὕρηνται κατὰ τὸν ποιητικὸν τρόπον, ἃ ~όμενα δέχονται τὴν ἀναπλήρωσιν παρὰ τῶν εὐγνωμόνων ἐξηγητῶν Gr.Agr.*Eccl*.1.16(M.98. 793B); κἂν γὰρ οὐκ ἔχῃ τὸ ῥητὸν σαφεστέραν τὴν ἔννοιαν, ἀλλὰ ~ομένην κατὰ τὸ ἰδίωμα τῆς γραφῆς *ib*.4.3(929A); **2.** *make response to* θεός, ᾧ τὸ καινὸν ᾆσμα μέλπωμεν ~οντες τῷ ποιοῦντι θαυμάσια Eus.*h.e*.10.4.9 (M.20.852B); id.*d.e*.10.8(p.490.12; M.22.788A).

***προσυπαναλίσκω,** *spend fully on*, c. dat., Ephr.2.312F.

προσυπαντάω, *go to meet*, Ast.Am.*prod*.(p.113.9).

***προσυπέρχομαι,** *approach*, Meth.*symp*.1.1(p.8.7; M.18.37B).

προσυπογράφω, *sign in addition*, Socr.*h.e*.1.6.32(M.67.52B).

προσφάγιον, τό, *relish* προσφέρονται [sc. Essenes] ἄρτον, ἔπειτα ἕν τι π., ἐξ οὗ ἑκάστῳ τὸ αὔταρκες μέρος Hipp.*haer*.9.21(p.257.16; M.16. 3398B); ‡Pall.*h.mon*.3.1(p.27.16; M.34.1131C).

πρόσφατος, *recent*, ref. Creation in rel. to Logos τὸ δὲ ἐξ οὐκ ὄντων δημιουργεῖσθαι τὸν κόσμον νεωτέραν ἔχει τὴν ὑπόστασιν καὶ π. τὴν γένεσιν Alex.Al.*ep.Alex*.4(p.22.18; M.18.553B); εἰ μὴ ἀΐδιος θεὸς ὁ υἱός, ἐξ ἀνάγκης π. ... ἀσεβῶν δὲ π. ... λατρεύειν. οὐκ ἔσται γάρ σοι, φησίν, θεὸς π. Didym.(‡Bas.)*Eun*.4(1.287A; M.29.689B); οὐδὲ π. τινα παραδέξασθαι θεὸν παρακελευόμεθα *ib*.5(317A; M.760C); οὐ π. ὑπάρχων θεός, ἀλλ' ἐκεῖνος αὐτὸς ὁ καὶ τοῦ...Ἀβραάμ Cyr.*Ps*.46:10(M.69. 1057B); οἱ νέον ἡμῖν καὶ π. εἰσφέροντες τὸν υἱόν id.*Jo*.1.1(4.10C); *ib*.2.1 (128B); θεὸς ἦν ὁ λόγος. ἐνταῦθα...ἀναιρεῖται τὸ π. εἶναι θεὸν τὸν υἱόν id.*thes*.32(5^1.313B); Ἄρειος...π. θεὸν τὸν υἱὸν...δογματίσας Socr.*h.e*. 4.33.8(M.67.553A); εἰ δὲ ἑτεροούσιός ἐστιν ἡ σὰρξ τῷ πατρί, καθότι αὕτη μὲν π., ὁ δὲ πατὴρ ἄχρονος, πῶς οὐχὶ π. καὶ ὁ λόγος; ‡Quint.*ep*. (p.16.10,11; M.85.1737A).

προσφέρ-ω, A. *bring to, present* bride to husband, met. τὸ ἀγαπᾶν ὡς νύμφη οὖσα ~εται ὡς νυμφίῳ τῷ φόβῳ *Hom.Clem*.12.33; converts to Christ, Chrys.*hom.66.2 in Mt*.(7.656B).

B. *bring forward, bring to one's notice*, Thdt.*1Thess*.5:27(3.526); id.*qu.3 in Jos*.(1.305); id.*affect*.2(p.55.22; 4.747).

C. *contribute* ἡ παρθένος οὐδὲν τῆς ἡμετέρας φύσεως τῷ σαρκωθέντι προσενεγκοῦσα θεῷ Thdt.*eran*.1(4.40).

D. *attribute*, Bas.Sel.*or*.4.2(M.85.68B).

E. *bring up against, urge against*, Chrys.*hom.29.4 in 1Cor*.(10. 265B); Marc.Er.*opusc*.2.166(M.65.956D).

F. *administer* oath, Thdt.*h.rel*.3(3.1147); baptism, Proc.G.*2Par*. 29:34(M.87.1217A).

G. *win over* οὐ σπονδῇ...κακούργων ~εται ὁ θεός ‡Just.*monarch*.4 (M.6.320A).

H. *produce*, of procession of H. Ghost ἅμα τῷ τόκῳ τῆς αὐτῆς οὐσίας, ἅγιον πνεῦμα προσήνεγκε...διὸ δὴ καὶ τέτοκε βουλόμενος καὶ προήγαγε δυνάμενος Aen.*dial*.(M.85.960B).

I. pass., *approach, enter upon* Εἰρηναῖος...τῷ ἐλέγχῳ προσενεχθεὶς Hipp.*haer*.6.42(p.173.13; M.16.3259D).

J. med., *set forth* food λόγῳ εὐχῆς καὶ εὐχαριστίας ἐφ' οἷς ~όμεθα πᾶσιν...αἰνοῦντες Just.*1apol*.13.1(M.6.345B); *ib*.67.2(429B); ref. Essene rites ~ονται ἄρτον, ἔπειτα ἕν τι προσφάγιον Hipp.*haer*.9.21 (p.257.16; M.16.3398B).

K. med., *address* ἤρξατο τούτους...~εσθαι Gr.Mag.*dial*.(tr.Zach.) 1.10(M.*PL*.77.206C).

L. *offer*; **1.** in gen.; of offering of gratitude to benefactors, Gr. Thaum.*pan.Or*.3(p.6.26,28; M.10.1057C); **2.** of sacrificial offering to God; **a.** OT sacrifices οὐ πανταχοῦ...~ονται θυσίαι ἐνδελεχισμοῦ ἢ εὐχῶν ἢ περὶ ἁμαρτίας καὶ πλημμελείας, ἀλλ' ἢ ἐν Ἱερουσαλὴμ μόνῃ *1Clem*.41.2; ἐντέταλται τῷ Ἰσραὴλ ~ειν δάμαλιν τοὺς ἄνδρας, ἐν οἷς εἰσιν ἁμαρτίαι τέλειαι *Barn*.8.1; Just.*dial*.41.1(M.6.564B); τραγέλαφος ...ὄν...κελεύει Μωσῆς ἡμᾶς ~εσθαι Or.*princ*.4.3.2(p.326.1; M.11. 380A); Κάϊν...οὐ προσεδέχθη...ἐν τῷ μὴ προσενέγκαι ὀρθῶς ‡Ath.*pat*.3 (M.26.1300D); οὐκ ἦν ἐξὸν ἀλλογενῆ, μὴ ὄντα λευΐτην, προσενέγκαι τι *Const.App*.2.27.1; τῷ Κάϊν βέλτιον ἦν μηδὲ ὅλως προσενεγκεῖν Chrys. *hom.73.3 in Jo*.(8.434A); id.*hom.18.1 in Heb*.(12.174A); of sacrifice of Isaac, *1Clem*.10.7; *Barn*.7.3; of Jephthah's daughter, Epiph.*ep. Arab*.ap.*haer*.78.23(p.473.24; M.42.736D); ref. Melchizedek, Thdt. *Ps*.109:4(3.1396); **b.** of pagan sacrifices, *Diogn*.2.8; contrasted with Christian offering of λογικὴ λατρεία, Athenag.*leg*.13.2(M.6.916C); **c.** of Christ's self-offering ὑπὲρ τῶν ἡμετέρων ἁμαρτιῶν ἔμελλεν τὸ σκεῦος τοῦ πνεύματος ~ειν θυσίαν *Barn*.7.3; ~ειν τὴν σάρκα *ib*.7.5; ὁ μόσχος Ἰησοῦς ἐστιν, οἱ ~οντες ἄνδρες ἁμαρτωλοὶ οἱ προσενέγκαντες αὐτὸν ἐπὶ τὴν σφαγήν *ib*.8.2; τί ἐστιν, ἁγιάζω ἐμαυτόν; ~ω σοι θυσίαν Chrys.*hom.82.1 in Jo*.(8.484B); ἀντὶ τῆς τῶν ἀλόγων σφαγῆς ἑαυτὸν ~ειν id.*hom.24.2 in 1Cor*.(10.213C); in context of eucharist αὐτὸς δὲ ἦν ὁ καὶ ~ων ἄρα καὶ ~όμενος Niceph.Ur.*v.Sym*.115(M.86.3093B); ‡Bas.*h.myst*.38(p.267.3); ἀρχιερεὺς γενόμενος ὡς υἱὸς ἀνθρώπου καὶ ~ων ἑαυτὸν καὶ ~όμενος εἰς τὸ ἀνενέγκαι ἁμαρτίας πολλῶν *ib* 48(p.390.14); **d.** of offering of worship and prayer to God, ref. Jews δοκοῦντες ἑαυτῶν πάσχα λατρείαν ~ειν τῷ θεῷ Or.*Jo*.28.25(20; p.422.20; M.14.736C); προσάγοντες τῷ θεῷ...τὰς εὐχὰς διὰ τοῦ μονογενοῦς αὐτοῦ· ᾧ πρῶτον ~ομεν αὐτάς id.*Cels*.8.13(p.230.24; M.11. 1536B); in eucharist ἕστηκεν ὁ ἱερεύς, καὶ δέησιν ~ει Chrys.*prod.Jud*. 2.6(2.394A); Bas.Sel.*or*.4.2(M.85.68B); ~ειν τῇ θεοτόκῳ τὸν ἔπαινον Procl.CP *annunt*.2(M.85.428C); by angels ~ουσι δὲ κυρίῳ...λογικὴν καὶ ἀναίμακτον προσφοράν *T.Lev*.3.6; **e.** of offering of virtues and good living, Const.ap.Gel.Cyz.*h.e*.2.7.41(M.85.1241B); Thdt.*Ps*.84:11 (1.1206); προσήνεγκαν οἱ πατέρες τῷ θεῷ...δῶρα τὴν παρθενίαν καὶ τὴν ἀκτημοσύνην Dor.*doct*.1.11(M.88.1629C); θεῷ τὰ τῆς φιλαδελφίας προσοίσομεν Jo.D.*fid.dorm*.8(M.95.253B); **f.** of self-offering in devotion, Eus.*d.e*.3.4(p.116.4; M.22.197D); **g.** of offering of candidate to God in baptism, Serap.*euch*.20.1; **h.** of offering of eucharistic gifts; **i.** by people in offertory, Just.*1apol*.65.3(M.6.428A) cit. s. εὐχαριστία; παυσαμένων ἡμῶν τῆς εὐχῆς ἄρτος ~εται καὶ οἶνος καὶ ὕδωρ, καὶ ὁ προεστὼς εὐχὰς ὁμοίως καὶ εὐχαριστίας...ἀναπέμπει *ib*.67.5(429B); cf. Hipp.*trad.ap*.23.1; connected with first-fruits and tithes paid to bishop τὰς θυσίας ὑμῶν ἤτοι προσφορὰς τῷ ἐπισκόπῳ ~ειν ὡς ἀρχιερεῖ, ἢ δι' ἑαυτῶν ἢ διὰ τῶν διακόνων. οὐ μὴν δὲ ἀλλὰ καὶ τὰς ἀπαρχὰς καὶ τὰς δεκάτας καὶ τὰ ἑκούσια αὐτῷ προσάγετε *Const.App*.2.27.6; Gr.Naz.*or*. 43.52(M.36.564A); Βάλης...τῷ θυσιαστηρίῳ τὰ εἰωθότα προσενήνοχε δῶρα Thdt.*h.e*.4.19.11(3.982); Cosm.Ind.*top*.7(M.88.385C) cit. s. εὐχαριστήριος; **ii.** of consecrated elements by celebrant ἁμαρτία... ἔσται, ἐὰν τοὺς ἀμέμπτως...προσενεγκόντας τὰ δῶρα τῆς ἐπισκοπῆς ἀποβάλωμεν *1Clem*.44.4; Iren.*haer*.1.13.2(M.7.581A); cf. *suis discipulis dans consilium, primitias deo offerre ex suis creaturis...ut ipsi ...nec ingrati sint, eum qui ex creatura panis est accepit...et calicem similiter, qui est ex ea creatura...suum sanguinem confessus est, et novi testamenti novam docuit oblationem; quam ecclesia...in universo mundo offert deo, ei qui alimenta nobis praestat, primitias suorum munerum in novo testamento...igitur ecclesiae oblatio, quam dominus docuit offerri in universo mundo, purum sacrificium reputatum est apud deum...offerre igitur oportet deo primitias ejus creaturae... oportet enim nos oblationem deo facere et in omnibus gratos inveniri fabricatori deo*, *ib*.4.17.5–18.4(1023B–1026C); ~ομεν δὲ αὐτῷ τὰ ἴδια *ib*.4.18.5(1028A); ~ειν σοι τὰ δῶρα τῆς ἁγίας σου ἐκκλησίας *Lit*.ap. *Const.App*.8.5.6; offering of gift as synonym for εὐχαριστία: μὴ πρότερον τὰ δῶρα ~ειν τοὺς ἐν διαφορᾷ τυγχάνοντας ἢ...τὰ πρὸς ἀλλήλους εἰρηνικῶς διαθέντας Eus.*v.C*.4.41(p.133.2; M.20.1189B); ἵνα ...μικροψυχίας ἀναιρουμένης τὸ δῶρον καθαρὸν ~ηται τῷ θεῷ CNic. (325)*can*.5; οὐ δεῖ τῇ τεσσαρακοστῇ ἄρτον ~ειν CLaod.*can*.49; *Lit*.ap. *Const.App*.8.12.38; ~ομέν σοι δῶρα...εἰς ἀθέτησιν τῶν...πλημμελημάτων *Lit.Jac*.(p.166.2); *ib*.(p.180.9); **iii.** of eucharist as sacrifice

(v. θυσία), cf. Just.*dial.*117.1(M.6.745A,B); παρακαλοῦμεν...ὑπὲρ πάντων βοηθείας δεομένων δεόμεθα πάντες...καὶ ταύτην ~ομεν τὴν θυσίαν Cyr.H.*catech.*23.8; *Lit.*ap.*Const.App.*8.12.38,39; προσενέγκας τὴν λογικὴν καὶ ἀναίμακτον θυσίαν τῷ θεῷ Eustrat.*v.Eutych.*84(M.86.2372A); ἱερέων τὴν θυσίαν ~όντων Anast.S.*synax.*(M.89.832A); **iv.** of elements as body and blood of Christ, dist. from other liturgical offerings ἵνα ἐν τοῖς ἁγίοις μηδὲν πλέον τοῦ σώματος καὶ τοῦ αἵματος τοῦ κυρίου προσενεχθείη...τουτέστιν ἄρτου καὶ οἴνου ὕδατι μεμιγμένου ...μηδὲν δὲ πλέον ἐν ταῖς ἀπαρχαῖς ~έσθω, ἢ ἀπὸ σταφυλῶν καὶ σίτου *Cod.Afr.*37; cf. *ut in sacramentis* [l. *sacramento*] *corporis et sanguinis domini, nihil amplius offeratur, quam ipse dominus tradidit, hoc est, panis et vinum aqua mixtum,* CCarth.(397)*can.*24; ~ομεν μέν, ἀλλ' ἀνάμνησιν ποιούμενοι τοῦ θανάτου αὐτοῦ· καὶ μία ἐστὶν αὕτη, οὐ πολλαί. ... ἐπειδὴ ἅπαξ προσηνέχθη ἐκείνη, εἰσηνέχθη εἰς τὰ ἅγια τῶν ἁγίων. τοῦτο ἐκείνης τύπος...τὸν γὰρ αὐτὸν ἀεὶ ~ομεν, οὐ νῦν μὲν ἕτερον πρόβατον, αὔριον δὲ ἕτερον, ἀλλ' ἀεὶ τὸ αὐτό...ἀλλ' εἷς πανταχοῦ ὁ Χριστός...ὥσπερ οὖν πολλαχοῦ ~όμενος ἓν σῶμά ἐστι, καὶ οὐ πολλὰ...οὕτω καὶ μία θυσία. ὁ ἀρχιερεὺς ἡμῶν ἐκεῖνός ἐστιν ὁ τὴν θυσίαν...προσενεγκών. ἐκείνην ~ομεν καὶ νῦν, τὴν τότε προσενεχθεῖσαν...τοῦτο εἰς ἀνάμνησιν γίνεται τοῦ τότε γενομένου...οὐκ ἄλλην θυσίαν...ἀλλὰ τὴν αὐτὴν ἀεὶ ποιοῦμεν· μᾶλλον δὲ ἀνάμνησιν ἐργαζόμεθα θυσίας Chrys.*hom.17.3 in Heb.*(12.168D); ~ει δὲ ἡ ἐκκλησία τὰ τοῦ σώματος αὐτοῦ καὶ τοῦ αἵματος σύμβολα, πᾶν τὸ φύραμα διὰ τῆς ἀπαρχῆς ἁγιάζουσα Thdt.*Ps.*109:4(3.1397); ἐκκλησίαν ἔνθα τὸ τίμιον σῶμα καὶ αἷμα Χριστοῦ ~εται Olymp.*fr.Jer.*31:12(M.93.688A); **v.** of eucharistic offerings as media of offering of ethical service in whole of life, Eus.*d.e.*1.10(p.48.5; M.22.92A); **vi.** π. = *celebrate* eucharist, CNeocaes.(c.320)*can.*9; ἐξουσίαν μὴ ἔχοντας ~ειν τοῖς ~ουσι διδόναι τὸ σῶμα τοῦ Χριστοῦ CNic.(325)*can.*18; ἑστηκέναι καὶ λειτουργεῖν καὶ π. Jul.Papa *ep.Dian.*ap.Ath.*apol.sec.*28(p.108.15; M.25.296C); CSard.*ep.Alex.*ap.Ath.*apol.sec.*37(p.116.27; 313B); ~ομέν σοι καὶ ὑπὲρ πάντων τῶν...ἁγίων...ἔτι ~ομέν σοι ὑπὲρ τοῦ λαοῦ τούτου *Lit.*ap.*Const.App.*8.12.43–44; διάκονος οὐ...~ει *Const.App.*8.28.4; ἡμῶν ὑπὲρ τῶν ἀπελθόντων ~όντων Chrys.*hom.41.5 in 1Cor.*(10.393A); Cyr.*ep.*79(5².211E); Thdr.Stud.*praesanct.*(M.99.1689B); **i.** heret. κολλυριδιανῶν τῶν τῇ Μαρίᾳ ~όντων Epiph.*haer.*79 tit.(p.475.26; M.42.740C); αὐτῇ ~ουσι τὴν κολλυρίδα αἱ ἀργαὶ αὗται γυναῖκες *ib.*79.9 (p.484.5; 753C); Aërian doctrine μὴ δεῖν ~ειν ὑπὲρ τῶν προκεκοιμημένων id.*anac.*75(p.231.14; M.42.337A); **j.** of other liturgical offerings; oil and water, Serap.*euch.*17.1; milk and honey, *Cod.Afr.*37; incense, *Lit.Jac.*(p.234.22).

προσφεύγ-ω, 1. *flee for refuge to* τῆς Ῥωμαϊκῆς οἰκουμένης ἐλαυνόμενοι Χριστιανοὶ καὶ βαρβάροις ~οντες προσετρίψαντο Eus.*v.C.*2.53(p.63.16; M.20.1029B); in taking sanctuary τῇ ἱερᾷ τραπέζῃ π. Gr.Naz.*or.*43.56(M.36.568A); of finding refuge in God, Just.*dial.*91.4(M.6.693B); *ib.*125.5(768B); in God's mercies, *1Clem.*20.11; in the gospel, Ign.*Philad.*5.1; in H. Ghost and Logos, Meth.*symp.*10.5 (p.128.10; M.18.201C); **2.** *have recourse to,* Clem.*prot.*10(p.67.5; M.8.204A); id.*str.*6.11(p.473.27; M.9.305A).

***προσφθάνω,** *come immediately,* ‡Jo.D.*ep.Thphl.*20(M.95.372C).

προσφθεγκτήριος, neut. plur. as subst., *salutations,* Thdot.Anc. *hom.BMV et Sym.*3(M.77.1393B).

προσφθείρ-ω, 1. *defile* κἂν δούλην προσφθείρῃ τις γυναῖκα ἔχων, οὐδὲν εἶναι δοκεῖ τοῖς νόμοις Chrys.*hom.12.5 in 1Cor.*(10.103C); pass., *be defiled with* παιδίσκας ἀγαπῶσιν καὶ ταύταις ~ονται *M.Ner.et Ach.* 3(p.3.2); Chrys.*hom.1.6 in Mt.*(7.14A); id.*hom.5.2 in 1Thess.*(11.462A); **2.** *meet with to one's hurt,* Clem.*q.d.s.*42(p.188.19; M.9.648C).

***προσφιλιόομαι,** *be made a friend,* Ast.Am.*hom.*5(M.40.236A); Thphn.*chron.*p.211(M.108.540C; προσεφιλώθη de Boor).

***προσφίλιος,** *dear, beloved,* Thdr.Stud.*epp.*1.2(M.99.912D).

προσφιλοπονέω, *give careful study to,* c. dat., Gr.Naz.*or.*37.7(M.36.292A).

προσφιλοσοφ-έω, 1. *speculate further upon,* Gr.Naz.*or.*28.9(p.35.11; M.36.37A); **2.** *meditate upon,* Bas.*ep.*45.1(3.133D; M.32.365B); Gr.Nyss.*Melet.*(M.46.861C); καθ' ἡσυχίαν ~εῖν τῇ θειοτέρᾳ ζωῇ id.*virg.* proem.(p.247.7; M.46.317A).

προσφιλοτιμέομαι, *be zealous about, be at great pains about, in addition,* c. dat., Or.*Cels.*6.22(p.92.22; M.11.1325A); *cat.Jac.*4:3(p.25.16); Nil.*Magn.*42(M.79.1020C).

[*]**προσφογγίζω,** = προσπογγίζω, *sponge beforehand, Exorc.*29 (p.341).

προσφορά, ἡ, 1. *bringing forward, producing,* Bas.Sel.*or.*2.1(M.85.37C); **2.** *setting forth;* of food, hence *meal* μίαν π. ἤσθιεν λεπτῶν εἴκοσι Jo.Mosch.*prat.*42(M.87.2896B); **3.** *offering, sacrifice;* **a.** OT τάς τε π. καὶ λειτουργίας...ἐπιτελεῖσθαι, καὶ οὐκ εἰκῇ...ἀλλ' ὡρισμένοις καιροῖς καὶ ὥραις *1Clem.*40.2; πεφανέρωκεν γὰρ ἡμῖν διὰ πάντων τῶν προφητῶν ὅτι οὔτε θυσιῶν οὔτε...π. χρῄζει...[Is.1:11–13] *Barn.*2.4; ἀρχιερεῖς...προσφέροντας τὰς π. Just.*dial.*27.5(M.6.533C); *ib.*40.1(561C); ἡ τῆς σεμιδάλεως δὲ π. *ib.*41.1(564B); θυσίαι καὶ π. καὶ ἑορταί *ib.*43.1(565C); Παῦλον...ξυράμενον καὶ π. ποιήσαντα Or.*Jo.*1.7(9; p.12.27; M.14.37A); θυσιαστήριον τὸ περικεκαλχωμένον εἰς ὃ τὰ ὁλοκαυτώματα ἀνεκομίζοντο καὶ αἱ π. Meth.*symp.*5.6(p.61.12; M.18.109A); Juln.Imp.ap.Cyr.*Juln.*10(6².347A); ὡς προσεδέξω τὴν π. Ἄβελ καὶ Νῶε...καὶ πάντων τῶν ἁγίων σου *Lit.Jac.*(p.182.12); as fruit of virtue of worshippers, Ath.*exp.Ps.*49 proem.(M.27.229B); **b.** Christ's sacrifice σῶμα προσάγων εἰς θάνατον...ἠφάνιζε τὸν θάνατον τῇ π. τοῦ καταλλήλου Ath.*inc.*9.1(M.25.112A); typified by that of Abraham's ram, Chrys.*hom.55.2 in Jo.*(8.323E); id.*cruc.*1.1(2.404B); **c.** martyr's sacrifice compared with OT animal sacrifice, *M.Polyc.*14.1; **d.** material sacrifices not offered by Christians ὁ καινὸς νόμος...μὴ ἀνθρωποποίητον ἔχῃ τὴν π. *Barn.*2.6; οὐ δέεσθαι τῆς...ὑλικῆς π. ... τὸν θεόν Just.*1apol.*10.1(M.6.340C); **e.** Christian sacrifice of worship and prayer Χριστὸν τὸν ἀρχιερέα τῶν π. ἡμῶν *1Clem.*36.1; εὐχαριστοῦσα...τῷ θεῷ ...διὰ ζητήσεως ἀληθοῦς, διὰ π. ἁγίας, δι' εὐχῆς μακαρίας Clem.*str.*6.14 (p.489.2; M.9.337A); ἀρχιερεὺς γὰρ τῶν π. ἡμῶν, καὶ πρὸς τὸν πατέρα παράκλητός ἐστιν ὁ υἱός Or.*or.*10(p.320.20; M.11.445D); ἀεὶ π. γίνεται θεῷ παντοκράτορι διὰ...Χριστοῦ, ὡς προσφόρου τῷ πατρί id.*dial.*4 (p.128.13); θεῷ διὰ θεοῦ π. γινέσθω *ib.*(p.130.2); ‡Pion.*v.Polyc.*23; **f.** of eucharist; **i.** of action as a whole; ref. Mal.1:11, Iren.*haer.*4.18.1(M.7.1024B); ἄρτῳ καὶ ὕδατι κατὰ τὴν π. χρωμένων Clem.*str.*1.19 (p.61.30; M.8.813A); cf.Hipp.*trad.ap.*23.13; τίνα αἶνον ἢ ποίαν π. ἢ τίνα εὐχαριστίαν κλῶντες τὸν ἄρτον τοῦτον ἐπονομάσωμεν ἀλλ' ἢ σὲ μόνον, κύριε Ἰησοῦ *A.Jo.*109(p.207.8); Meth.*lepr.*6(p.458.25); *Can.App.*8; CAnc.(314)*can.*5; CNic.(325)*can.*11; π. ἐποίησεν εἰς πλῆθος ἀδελφῶν ‡Pion.*v.Polyc.*26; τὴν ἁγίαν π. ἐπιτελεῖσθαι CLaod.*can.*19; *ib.*58; Jul.Papa *ep.Dian.*ap.Ath.*apol.sec.*28(p.108.17; M.25.296C); ἱερεῖς διαθήκης νέας...περιελεῖν δυνήσονται...ὀφειλήματα τῶν προοδευόντων ἐν ἁγίαις π. καὶ εὐχαῖς γλωσσῶν αὐτῶν Ephr.2.239E; Bas.*ep.*199 *can.*22(3.293C; M.32.724A); *ib.*217 *can.*75(328E; M.804C); Gr.Naz.*carm.*1.2.34.238(M.37.962A); π. καθ' ἑκάστην κυριακήν Chrys.*hom.18.4 in Ac.*(9.150B); ὅπερ οὐκ ἔπαθεν ἐπὶ τοῦ σταυροῦ, τοῦτο πάσχει ἐπὶ τῆς π. διὰ σέ, καὶ ἀνέχεται διακλώμενος ἵνα πάντας ἐμπλήσῃ id.*hom.24.2 in 1Cor.*(10.213D); ἐπὶ τῆς π. ἀναφέρομεν τὰ ἁμαρτήματα, καὶ λέγομεν...συγχώρησον id.*hom.17.2 in Heb.*(12.166C); ἡ μυστικὴ... τῆς π. ὑπὸ τοῦ ἱερέως εὐχαριστία Mac.Aeg.*carit.*29(M.34.932C); εἶχε δὲ ἔθος ὁ πρεσβύτερος ἔρχεσθαι καὶ ποιεῖν αὐτῷ τὴν ἁγίαν π. *Apophth.Patr.*(M.65.304A) contrast CLaod.*can.*58 and τὸ δέ γε δῶρον, ἤτοι τὴν π. ἣν τελοῦμεν μυστικῶς, ἐν ἁγίαις ἐκκλησίαις...χρὴ προσφέρεσθαι μόναις Cyr.*resp.*11(p.595.4; 6².380B); τίνος ἕνεκεν...ἐν τῇ οἰκίᾳ π. ἐτέλεσας; id.*ep.*11a(p.172.5; M.77.89A); Esaias *or.*3.4(p.13; cf.M.40.1111C); οὐκ αἰσθάνονταί τινος εὐεργεσίας καὶ αἱ τῶν ἁμαρτωλῶν ψυχαί, γινομένων ὑπὲρ αὐτῶν συναξέων καὶ εὐποιιῶν καὶ π.; ‡Ath.*qu.Ant.*34(M.28.617A); Jo.Mosch.*prat.*196(M.87.3081A); Dor.*doct.*9.2(M.88.1717D); **ii.** of eucharistic bread before consecration, cf.Hipp.*trad. ap.*23.1; *ib.*26.1; τοὺς ἐν ἀρτοποιείῳ ἐργαζομένους τὴν π. *V.Pach.Σ* 79 (p.256.4); τὴν...π. ἤτοι τὸν οὔπω ἁγιαζόμενον ἄρτον κωλῶθιν εἰώθασιν καλεῖν τὰ τῆς χώρας [sc. Amasea] παιδία Eustrat.*v.Eutych.*52(M.86.2333C); ἀντίτυπα...οὐ μετὰ τὸ ἁγιασθῆναι εἶπον, ἀλλὰ πρὶν ἁγιασθῆναι, τὴν π. οὕτω καλέσαντες Jo.D.*fr.Mt.*26:27(M.96.1409C); **iii.** of consecrated bread or of elements at consecration, representing first-fruits of God's creation, Iren.*haer.*4.18.2(M.7.1025A); ποιήσας γὰρ τὰς π., καὶ διανέμων ἑκάστῳ τὸ μέρος Corn.ap.Eus.*h.e.*6.43.18(M.20.625A); προσενέγκατε π. ἄρτον ἅγιον καὶ ἀπὸ τῆς ἀμπέλου τρεῖς βότρυας ἀποθλίψαντες ἐν ποτηρίῳ συγκοινωνήσατέ μοι ὡς ὁ κύριος...ὑπέδειξεν τὴν ἄνω π. τῇ τρίτῃ ἡμέρᾳ ἐγερθεὶς ἐκ νεκρῶν *A.Mt.*25(p.253.1); τὸν βότρυν ἀποθλίψατε...εἰς τὸ ποτήριον· καὶ μεταλαβόντες εἰς τὴν τρίτην ἡμέραν ἀναπέμψατε εἰς ὕψος τὸ ἀμήν, ἵνα γένηται τελεία π. *A.Phil.*143 (p.84.7); πῶς οἷόν τε ἦν π. προκεῖσθαι ἔνδον ὄντων τῶν κατηχουμένων; Jul.Papa *ep.Dian.*ap.Ath.*apol.sec.*28(p.108.16; M.25.296C); προσφορᾶς μεταλαμβάνειν CGangr.*can.*4; διδότω τὴν π. λέγων· σῶμα Χριστοῦ *Lit.*ap.*Const.App.*8.13.15; λαβεῖν τὴν π. *Apophth.Patr.*(M.65.276C); †CCP(381)*can.*1; τὸ...προσαγόμενον...καλεῖται...εὐλογία, π., ἀπαρχή, ἄρτος...π. δέ, ὡς ἐξ ὅλου τοῦ ἀνθρωπείου φυράματος, οἷα τῆς φιλοτιμίας τῷ θεῷ...εἰς τὰ τῶν ἁγίων ἅγια προσηνέχθημεν ‡Sophr.H.*liturg.*9(M.87.3989A); τὸ δὲ σφραγίζεσθαι τὴν π. ὁ...Βασίλειος παρέδωκεν· προσκομίζεται ἡ π. διὰ τὸ κοινωνεῖν τὸν λαὸν ἕκαστον μερίδα *ib.*(3989B); θεὶς τὴν...π. ἐν τῷ ἁγίῳ δίσκῳ ‡Bas.*h.myst.*31b (p.264.22); ὁ λόγος...ποιεῖ...τὸν ἄρτον καὶ τὸν οἶνον τῆς π. σῶμα αὐτοῦ καὶ αἷμα †Jo.D.*B.J.*19(M.96.1032A); **g.** of alms, etc. ἐπ' ὀνόματι προσφορῶν [sc. Montanus] τὴν δωροληψίαν ἐπιτεχνώμενος Apollon. ap.Eus.*h.e.*5.18.2(M.20.476B); αἱ τότε ἀπαρχαὶ καὶ δεκάται...νῦν π. αἱ διὰ τῶν...ἐπισκόπων προσφερόμεναι κυρίᾳ...οὗτοι γὰρ εἰσιν ὑμῶν οἱ ἀρχιερεῖς *Const.App.*2.26.2; Chrys.*hom.62.5 in Jo.*(8.374D); **4.** *propriety, suitability,* of the Word incarnate to human senses ἐκ τοῦ κατὰ τὴν π. αἰσθήτου λόγου ἐνηχούμενοι Leont.H.*Nest.*1.19(M.86.1476B).

***προσφοράριος, ὁ,** *messenger, errand-man*; in monastery, Cyr.S. *v.Sab.*58(p.159.30).

πρόσφορος, 1. *agreeable* τὴν π. ἀρετὴν ἔχουσιν αὐτῷ Clem.*str.*7.7 (p.30.4; M.9.453D); Meth.*symp.*3.13(p.42.15; M.18.81C); *ib.*9.1(p.113.11; 176C); **2.** *related to, resembling* προσφορὰ γίνεται θεῷ...διὰ... Χριστοῦ, ὡς π. τῷ πατρὶ τὴν θεότητα αὐτοῦ Or.*dial.*4(p.130.1); **3.** neut. as subst., eucharistic *oblation*, Serap.*euch.*13 tit.; εὐλόγησον τοὺς προσενεγκόντας τὰ π. *ib.*13.19.

***προσφράζω,** *declare in addition*, Leont.H.*monoph.*testimonia (M.86.1808C).

***προσφρέω,** *travel, proceed* οἱά τις ἀπαρχὴ τῆς ἀνθρωπότητος προσέφρησεν [sc. ὁ Χριστός] εἰς τὸν οὐρανόν Cyr.*glaph.Ex.*3(1.325D).

προσφύγιον, τό, *refuge, place of refuge*, Jo.Mal.*chron.*18 p.485(M.97.701C); *ib.*p.494(713C); †Jo.D.*B.J.*13(M.96.985B); met., Melet. *nat.hom.*proem.(M.64.1076C).

***προσφύλαξ, ὁ,** *guardian*, Const.ap.Gel.Cyz.*h.e.*1.11.22(M.85.1220B); Gel.Cyz.*h.e.*1.11.32(1221D); prob. for προφ-).

πρόσφυξ, ὁ, 1. *fugitive, refugee*, Eus.*Is.*30: 1–5(M.24.305A); of one taking sanctuary, Socr.*h.e.*6.5.5(M.67.673A); Gel.Cyz.*h.e.*1.11.20(M.85.1220B); **2.** *deserter*, Thphn.*chron.*p.306(M.108.745A); **3.** *client, suppliant*, Const.ap.Thdt.*h.e.*1.20.1(3.797); Isid.Pel.*epp.*2.269(M.78.697C); ‡Pall.*h.mon.*8.33(p.42.16; M.34.1145B); ὁ ὄφις...π. τῷ Νῶε προσέρχεται Bas.Sel.*or.*5.2(M.85.84B); of one consulting an oracle, Eus.*p.e.*4.2(134A; M.21.236B); id.*d.e.*proem.(p.203.24; M.22.337B); of one who has recourse to God or Christ, *A.Thom.*A 29(p.146.9); Eus.*l.C.*15(p.245.22; M.20.1416B); Mac.Mgn.*apocr.*3.12(p.81.24).

***προσφύσημα, τό,** *breathing upon*; of inbreathing of H. Ghost, Gr.Nyss.*Apoll.*28(M.45.1185B); id.*Eun.*2(2 p.273.12; M.45.553C).

***προσφύσησις, ἡ,** *breathing upon* π. τοῦ πνεύματος Gr.Nyss.*or. catech.*32(p.122.2; M.45.81D).

***προσφωνάριον, τό,** a kind of bag, Barth.Edess.*Agar.*(M.104.1425B).

προσφων-έω, 1. *address*; **a.** of a letter, Eus.*h.e.*4.23.9(M.20.388A); **b.** liturg. ὁ ἐπίσκοπος ∼ησάτω τῷ λαῷ οὕτω· τὰ ἅγια τοῖς ἁγίοις *Lit.*ap.*Const.App.*8.13.12; Cyr.*Jo.*12(4.1086C); ref. deacon's cries, *Const.App.*8.35.2; ὁ πᾶσι ∼ούμενος πνευματικὸς ἀσπασμός Max. *myst.*17(M.91.693D) = ‡Bas.*h.myst.*55(p.392.4); ∼εῖ λέγων· στῶμεν καλῶς Anast.S.*synax.*(M.89.836D); **c.** ref. OT prophecies addressing Christ ψαλμὸς...Χριστῷ...∼ῶν...ὁ θρόνος σου ὁ θεός Eus.*d.e.*4.15 (p.182.21; M.22.304C); id.*e.th.*1.11(p.70.9; M.24.845A); **2.** *tell, inform*, Eus.*v.C.*4.46(p.136.31; M.20.1197A).

***προσφωνή, ἡ,** *proclamation*, name given to Septuagesima when warning was given of Lenten fast τὴν τῆς π. ἑβδομάδα, ἐν ᾗ ἀναγινώσκεται τὸ...εὐαγγέλιον τοῦ τελώνου καὶ τοῦ Φαρισαίου *Catech.Stud.*8 (M.99.1697D).

προσφώνησις, ἡ, 1. *address* αὐτοκράτορι...τὴν π. καὶ ἔντευξιν πεποίημαι Just.*1apol.*1.1(M.6.329A); *ib.*68.3(432B); of imperial letter, Const.ap.Eus.*v.C.*2.71(p.70.13; M.20.1045A); of synodical letter, Jo. VI CP *ep.*(M.96.1417B); **2.** *invitation, summons* to prayer, uttered by deacon in liturgy, *Const.App.*8.38.1; **3.** *invocation, address to God*, Cyr.*Ps.*42:4(M.69.1017A); **4.** διὰ προσφωνήσεως *aloud, by word of mouth*, CLaod.*can.*19; *Chron.Pasch.*p.330(M.92.856A).

προσφωνητικός, *presenting an address*, speech *of address* to someone, ref. Just.*2apol.* λόγος...πρὸς Ἀντωνῖνον...π. Eus.*h.e.*4.18.2(M.20.373B); with λόγος understood π. παρὰ τῆς ἁγίας συνόδου πρὸς ...Μαρκιανόν CChalc.*ep.*(*ACO* 2.1.3 p.110.10; H.2.644D); ὁ παρὰ τῆς ...συνόδου...π. λόγος CCP(681)*act.*18(H.3.1416E); τοῖς μοναχοῖς... ἀπελογήσατο διὰ προσφωνητικοῦ Thphn.*chron.*p.133(v.l. π. λόγου M.108.364B); of bishop's address to diocese, Jo.D.*Jacob.*(M.94.1496C).

προσχαίρω, *rejoice at*, Gr.Nyss.*Eun.*3(2 p.22.21; M.45.588A); Sophr.H.*v.Anast.*(M.92.1720B).

***προσχαρής,** *pleasant, affable*, Hipp.*haer.*4.16(p.50.13; M.16.3083C); *ib.*4.23(p.52.22; 3087B); †Bas.*ep.*42.3(3.128A; M.32.353B).

***προσχαριώδης,** *cheerful*; of those born under Aries, Hipp.*haer.*4.15(p.49.19; M.16.3083B).

***προσχειρίζομαι,** *be ordained* προσεχειρίζετο Μωσῆς εἰς ἀποστολήν Cyr.*ador.*14(1.511D).

πρόσχεσις, ἡ, *promise*, Anast.S.*qu.et resp.*27(M.89.553D).

***προσχετλιάζω,** *complain about beforehand*, Gr.Nyss.*Eun.*2(1 p.316.29; M.45.1032A).

πρόσχημα, τό, 1. *outward appearance* or *character*, Eus.*Marcell.*2.1(p.31.26; M.24.776B); Ἰουδαϊκῷ π. Χριστομάχον συνεκρότησαν [sc. Arians] ἐργαστήριον Alex.Al.*ep.Alex.*4(p.20.6; M.18.549A); τὸ τῆς δουλείας π. σημαίνοντες *Lit.Marc.*(Brightman p.137.7); **2.** *semblance*, ref. 1Cor.9:9 τὰ δι' ἀνθρώπους γραφέντα ἐν π. τῷ περὶ ἀλόγων ζῴων φυσιολογίαν τινὰ παρέχει Or.*Cels.*5.36(p.40.4; M.11.1237A); ἐπὶ προσχήματι θεοῦ...τὸν υἱὸν τοῦ ἀνθρώπου...θρησκεύωσι Cels.*ib.*8.15 (p.232.19; 1537C); **3.** *likeness* Παῦλε...ἐκκλησιῶν τὸ καύχημα καὶ ἀγγέλων π. *Apoc.Paul.*49(p.67); **4.** *false appearance, pretence*, Meth.*symp.*10.5(p.127.6; M.18.200C); Eus.*h.e.*4.7.4(M.20.316C); Const.ap.Ath.*apol.sec.*86(p.165.34; M.25.405A); Thdt.*h.e.*3.28.2(3.944); **5.** monastic *habit*, id.*ep.*81(4.1140); CChalc.*can.*4; ἀξιοῦται... τοῦ τιμίου π. Marc.Diac.*v.Porph.*4; *ib.*36.

***προσχιδεύομαι,** *sketch out*, Anast.S.*hod.*proem.(M.89.36A).

***προσχλοάζω,** *be the first-fruits of*, ref. Innocents βρέφη τὸν τῶν μαρτύρων ἡμῖν προσεχλόαζε σῖτον Nest.*hom.tent.*3(p.354).

***προσχρεμετίζω,** *neigh to*, c. dat., Clem.*prot.*4(p.45.9; M.8.156B).

***προσχρεωστέομαι,** *be owed to in addition*, c. dat., Gr.Naz.*ep.*143 (M.37.245A).

***προσχρωτίζω,** *cleave closely, adhere*, Nil.*epp.*1.90(M.79.121C); *ib.*1.94(124B).

πρόσχυσις, ἡ, 1. *pouring upon* altar, *libation*; of blood of pagan sacrifices, Just.*2apol.*12.5(M.6.465A); *Hom.Clem.*2.44; **2.** *pouring forth* φλογὸς τῇ προσχύσει Geo.Pis.*hex.*251(διεκχύσει M.92.1453A).

προσχωρ-έω, pass., *pass to, be annexed to* τὰ πράγματα αὐτῶν...τῷ δημοσίῳ ∼ηθῆναι ταμείῳ Max.*ep.*12(M.91.465A).

προσχώρησις, ἡ, *advance, increase*, ‡Ath.*Apoll.*1.17(M.26.1124B, perh. for προ-).

***προσψάλλω,** *sing to*, c. dat., Diad.*perf.*37(p.42.22).

πρόσψαυσις, ἡ, *contact, touching*, Melet.*nat.hom.*15(M.64.1209B); of contact with relics and sacred objects, Sophr.H.*or.*5(M.87.3312C); Jo.Mon.*hymn.Blas.*9(M.96.1405D); †Jo.D.*B.J.*23(M.96.1065B).

***πρόσψημα, τό,** *extra dish, special addition to a meal*, ref. two kids served to Isaac, as proof of patriarch's vigorous appetite, Proc.G.*Gen.*27:9(M.87.417B).

προσῳδία, ἡ, *accent* which indicates modulation of the voice, ref. Antitactae κατὰ τὴν ἀνάγνωσιν φωνῆς τόνῳ διαστρέφοντες τὰς γραφὰς πρὸς τὰς ἰδίας ἡδονάς, καί τινων προσῳδιῶν καὶ στιγμῶν μεταθέσει τὰ παραγγελθέντα...βιαζόμενοι πρὸς ἡδυπαθείας τὰς ἑαυτῶν Clem.*str.*3.4(p.213.35; M.8.1144A); κατὰ προσῳδίαν *with accentuation* κατὰ π. ἔστιξαν τὰς γραφάς Epiph.*mens.*2(M.43.237B); τήν τε τῶν Πράξεων βίβλον...ἀναγνῶναί τε κατὰ π. Euthal.Diac.*Ac.*(M.85.633C).

προσωνυμία, ἡ, *appellation, name* ὀνόματος προσωνυμίᾳ οὔτε ἀγαθὸν οὔτε κακὸν κρίνεται ἄνευ...πράξεων Just.*1apol.*4.1(M.6.332B); ὀνόματος...Χριστιανοῦ π. ὁμολογοῦντα...ἐκόλασω id.*2apol.*2.16(M.6.445C); καλούμενοί εἰσιν ὑφ' ἡμῶν ἀπὸ τῆς π. τῶν ἀνδρῶν ἐξ οὗπερ ἑκάστη διδαχὴ...ἤρξατο id.*dial.*35.4(M.6.552A); τῆς τοῦ Διὸς π. πρωτότυπον στοιχεῖον Tat.*orat.*9(p.10.19; M.6.828A); Χριστὸν...ἐξ αὐτοῦ καὶ τῆς π. ἠξιώθημεν Eus.*h.e.*1.1.8(M.20.52C); πόλιν...ᾗ π. Νακώλεια Socr.*h.e.*4.5.2(M.67.469B).

προσωπεῖον, τό, 1. *mask* προσωπεῖα περικείμεναι αἱ ἑταῖραι ἐξεμίσθουν ἑαυτάς Or.*Cels.*4.63(p.334.18; M.11.1132A); fig. προσωπείου δίκην τὴν Πυθαγόρειον ἐπιμορφαζόμενος ἀγωγήν Eus.*Hierocl.*5(514D; M.22.804B); οἷον προσωπεῖον...γυμνωθεῖσαν ἀνακαλύπτεσθαι τὴν ἐγκειμένην δόξαν Gr.Nyss.*Eun.*7(2 p.155.1; M.45.744A); Ματθαῖος... ὥσπερ τι π. ἤμειψε τὸν βίον id.*bapt.Chr.*(M.46.596D); ref. Adam τὴν διὰ πνεύματος μόρφωσιν, π. ὥσπερ τι περικαλλὲς ἔλαχε Cyr.*Jo.*11.10 (4.988A); **2.** *disguise*, Clem.*prot.*2(p.20.28; M.8.100A); τῆς ἐνθάδε σκηνῆς ἀπέθεντο τὰ π. ‡Nil.*perist.*14(M.79.841C); ῥίψας τὸ π. τὸ ἀρχικόν, τὸ ἀδελφικὸν ἐπέδειξε πρόσωπον Thdt.*qu.106 in Gen.*(1.108); id.*qu.24 in 2Reg.*(1.425); hence *pretence* π. τῆς ἀληθείας Nil. *epp.*2.85(M.79.240D); Cyr.*apol.Thdt.*9(p.135.18; 6[1].229E); Ἑλληνισμὸν Χριστιανισμοῦ προσωπείῳ κρυπτόμενον Bas.Sel.*or.*27.1(M.85.309B); **3.** *part, character* διὰ...τὴν τῶν πολλῶν ὠφέλειαν τοῖς τῆς ὑποκρίσεως π. ἐχρήσατο Thdt.*ep.*3(4.1062); id.*Rom.*7:23(3.79); ref. God acc. Sabellians νῦν δὲ τὸ τοῦ πνεύματος ὑποδύεσθαι π. Bas.*ep.*214.3(3.322C; M.32.788D; v.l. πρόσωπον); **4.** *aspect*, ref. Inc. τὸ τοῦ ἀνθρώπου π. ἀναλαβὼν καὶ σαρκὶ ἀναπλασάμενος Clem.*prot.*10(p.78.15; M.8.228A); τῷ δουλικῷ π. διὰ σαρκὸς συναναστραφεὶς τοῖς ἀνθρώποις Gr.Nyss.*hom.13 in Cant.*(M.44.1048A); id.*Eun.*6(2 p.141.1; M.45.725D); **5.** *face* τοῦ ἐπιβεβλημένου τῷ π. τοῦ νομοθέτου καλύμματος *ib.*7(2 p.154.17; M.45.741D); Evagr.*h.e.*1.14(p.24.25; M.86.2461B).

***προσωπεύομαι,** *pretend*, ‡Caes.Naz.*dial.*131(M.38.1033).

***προσωπικός,** *of persons, in respect of persons, personal*; **1.** in gen. π. ... ἐγγύην Ath.Scholast.*coll.*5.4(p.74); *ib.*paratit.2(p.156); **2.** Trin. τὸν τῆς π. τριάδος ἀριθμόν, ἢ τῆς φυσικῆς μονάδος Leont.H. *Nest.*7.6(M.86.1768[d]C); μίαν...κυριότητα, ἄνευ π. ἀναχύσεως Sophr.H. *ep.syn.*(M.87.3152D); **3.** Christol. τό, θεός, καὶ φυσικὸν καὶ π. ὄνομα τῷ Χριστῷ Leont.H.*Nest*.2.18(M.86.1577B); ἑτέρα γὰρ ἕνωσις τοῦτο οὐ ποιεῖ· οὐδὲ ἡ δυὰς πάντως κατηγορηθεῖσά τινος, καὶ εἰς πρόσωπα διαιρεῖ τοῦτο, εἰ μὴ εἰς π. δίπλασιν εἴη ληφθεῖσα id.*monoph*.testimonia (M.86.1813D); φεύγων [sc. Nestorius] τὴν καθ' ὑπόστασιν ἕνωσιν, τὴν οὐσιώδη διαφορὰν π. ποιεῖται διαίρεσιν Max.*opusc*.(M.91.56C); ἐκ δύο φύσεων π. ὁ Χριστός Anast.S.*hod*.9(M.89.144B); καλοῦσι γὰρ τινες πρόσωπον τήν τινων σχέσιν πρὸς ἀλλήλους...λέγομεν γὰρ τὸ τοῦδε πρόσωπον ἀνειληφέναι τόνδε...κατὰ τοῦτο τὸ σημαινόμενον ὁ Νεστόριος τὴν π. ἐπρέσβευσεν ἕνωσιν Anast.Ap.*fr*.ap.*Doct.Patr*.6(p.38. 18); ἕνωσις λέγεται π., ὅταν τις τὸ ἑτέρου ὑποδυόμενος πρόσωπον, ἀντ' αὐτοῦ τοὺς ὑπὲρ αὐτοῦ ποιεῖται λόγους Jo.D.*dial*.65(M.94.664B); ἕνωσιν...οὐδ' αὖ πάλιν π. ... ὡς...ἔφη Νεστόριος id.*Jacob*.81(M.94. 1480A); Taras.*ep*.5(M.98.1464C); ref. Christ's wills πῶς δὲ τὴν φυσικὴν τῶν τοῦ...Χριστοῦ θελημάτων διαφορὰν εἰς π. μεταστρέφουσι τῶν τἀναντία θελόντων ἀλλήλοις προσώπων ἀντεισφοράν CLater.*act*.5(H.3. 905A); **4.** *individual* φύσεως...πολλάκις ἀντὶ οὐσίας καὶ ἀντὶ π. δὲ ὑποστάσεως λεγομένης Leont.H.*monoph*.testimonia(M.86.1808D); **5.** *outwardly manifest*, Anast.S.*hex*.12(M.89.1061C); π. θέαν, ἀλλ' οὐ φυσικὴν οὐσίαν θεοῦ ἑωράκασιν id.*hod*.8(M.89.132C).

***προσωπολεξία**, ἡ, *use of word* πρόσωπον: ἐπ' αὐτὴν τὴν κυρίως π. τὴν ἐν τῇ...γραφῇ τυγχάνουσαν, περὶ θεοῦ, χωρήσωμεν Anast.S.*hod*.8 (M.89.128D).

προσωποληπτέω, *have respect of persons, show partiality*, Or. *exp.in Pr*.19:6(M.17.208A); *Const.App*.2.58.4; Geo.Pis.*hex*.417(M. 92.1466A).

προσωπολήπτης, ὁ, *respecter of persons, partisan*; bishop warned against becoming such, *Const.App*.2.9.2; ref. God οὐ γάρ ἐστι π. Chrys.*compunct*.1.9(1.137E); Proc.G.*Is*.22:1–14(M.87.2173C); Leont.N.*v.Jo.Eleem*.4(p.10.14).

προσωποληψία, ἡ, *partiality* of any kind, whether *favouritism, prejudice*, or *snobbery*; to be avoided by presbyters, Polyc.*ep*.6.1; Clem.*paed*.1.6(p.108.19; M.8.288A); διὰ τὴν πρὸς τὸν βασιλέα...π. καταλελοίπατε τὴν...περὶ τῆς τοῦ πάσχα ἑορτῆς ἀκολουθίαν Epiph. *haer*.70.9(p.241.22; M.42.353B).

***προσωπόληψις**, ἡ, *respect of persons, partiality*, *Const.App*. 2.58.6.

***προσωπολογέω**, *speak of the external appearance of*, Anast.S. *hod*.8(M.91.132C).

πρόσωπον, τό, **I.** *face, countenance*;

A. in gen., in address to BMV χαῖρε, τὸ θεολαμπὲς...π. Thdot. Anc.*hom.BMV et Sym*.3(M.77.1393B); opp. προσωπεῖον: ἑταίρας... προσωπεῖα ποιούσας τὰ π. Clem.*paed*.3.2(p.242.27; M.8.572B).

B. of 'face of God'; **1.** in gen. οὐ γὰρ τὸ π. κυρίου ἐπιβλέπει, εἰρήνη καὶ ἀγαλλίασις Clem.*paed*.1.8(p.130.32; M.8.333B); ref. Ps.21:2 αἰτεῖ τὴν ἐποπτείαν τὴν παρὰ τοῦ πατρὸς...ἵνα...ἐφ' ἡμᾶς μεταγάγῃ τὸ π. τοῦ πατρός Ath.*exp.Ps*.21:2(M.27.132B); ἐπειδὴ τὸ τῆς θεότητος π. οὐδεὶς ἠδύνατο ἰδεῖν ζῶν, ἀνέλαβε τὸ τῆς ἀνθρωπότητος π. Cyr.H. *catech*.10.7; ἀποστρέφειν δὲ λέγεται τὸ...π. ὁ θεός, ὅταν...ἐκδότους ἀφίῃ τοῖς πειρασμοῖς Bas.*hom.in Ps*.29(1.129D; M.29.320A); τὴν δὲ ἐπισκοπήν, π. Gr.Naz.*or*.31.22(p.173.1; M.36.157C); κοινὸν π. δεικνῦσιν ἡ γραφὴ τοῦ πατρὸς καὶ τοῦ υἱοῦ καὶ τοῦ ἁγίου πνεύματος, καὶ εἰκόνα μίαν, καὶ ὁμοίωσιν τὴν αὐτήν [ref. Gen.1:26] Nil.*epp*.1.174(M. 79.152A); π. δὲ θεοῦ...τὴν εὐμένειαν ἐκάλεσε Thdt.*Dan*.3:41(2.1119); π. δέ, τὴν δι' ἔργων αὐτοῦ ἔνδειξίν τε καὶ ἐμφάνειαν, ἐκ τοῦ τὴν ἡμετέραν ἐμφάνειαν διὰ προσώπου γίνεσθαι Jo.D.*f.o*.1.11(M.94.841C); **2.** interpreted of Son π. δὲ τοῦ θεοῦ ὁ λόγος, ᾧ φωτίζεται ὁ θεὸς καὶ γνωρίζεται Clem.*paed*.1.7(p.124.3; M.8.320A); π. εἴρηται τοῦ πατρὸς ὁ υἱός, αἰσθήσεων πεντάδι σαρκοφόρος γενόμενος, ὁ λόγος ὁ τοῦ πατρῴου μηνυτὴς ἰδιώματος id.*str*.5.6(p.348.9; M.9.57B); id.*exc.Thdot*.10(p.110. 4; M.9.661A); π. δὲ θεοῦ, ὁ χαρακτὴρ τῆς ὑποστάσεως αὐτοῦ Or. *Ps*.20:7(p.476); Ath.*exp.Ps*.20:7(M.27.129A); ἡ τοῦ υἱοῦ ὑπόστασις οἱονεὶ μορφὴ καὶ π. γίνεται τῆς τοῦ πατρὸς ἐπιγνώσεως Gr.Nyss.*diff. ess*.8(M.32.340C); ὁ σωτήρ, π. ὢν θεοῦ, ἀπόκρυφον ἔχει πᾶν τὸ κατὰ τὴν θεότητα, ἐμφανὲς δὲ τὸ κατὰ τὴν οἰκονομίαν. ὅτ' ἂν οὖν ὁ λόγος... σκηνώσῃ ἐν ἡμῖν, κατακρυπτόμεθα ἐν τῷ ἀποκρύφῳ τοῦ π. αὐτοῦ Didym.*Ps*.30:20(M.39.1317A); π. ... τοῦ...πατρὸς τὸν υἱὸν εἶναί φησιν, ὅπερ ἐστὶ...ὁ χαρακτήρ Cyr.*Jo*.3.5(4.302C); καιρὸς δὲ προσώπου τοῦ πατρός, ὁ τῆς ἐνανθρωπήσεως νοοῖτο ἂν εἰκότως· π. γάρ ἐστι καὶ εἰκὼν ὁ υἱὸς τοῦ πατρός Proc.G.*Gen*.17:23(M.87.361A); **3.** of H. Ghost [Ps. 138:7–10] ὁ ὑμνῳδὸς...π. αὐτὸ καὶ χεῖρα θεοῦ προσαγορεύων Didym. (‡Bas.)*Eun*.5(1.309C; M.29.741B); τὸ πνεῦμα καὶ π. ἀποκαλεῖ τοῦ πατρὸς ὡς ἐξεικονίζον...τὴν...οὐσίαν Cyr.*thes*.34(5^1.340C).

C. of face of Christ, conjoined with sense of *person* εἰ οὐ τὸ π. τοῦ ...μονογενοῦς ἐνεπτύσθη, οὐκοῦν ἄλλο π. εἰ δὲ ἄλλο καὶ ἄλλο π., οὐδὲ κατὰ π. ἥνωνται Jo.D.*fid.Nest*.40(p.577).

II. *expression* (= *vultus*), *M.Polyc*.12.1; τοῖς παιδίοις π. ποιοῦμεν ...κατ' οἰκονομίαν φοβερόν Or.*hom.18.6 in Jer*.(p.160.15; M.13.477C); hence 'face', boldness ποίῳ π. τῷ κυρίῳ λέξεις, ἄφες μοι τὰς... ἁμαρτίας, αὐτὸς...μηδὲ τὰς ὀλίγας τῷ συνδούλῳ συγχωρήσας; Cyr.H. *catech*.1.6; *good countenance, assurance* π. τὰ ἀπρόσωπα ποιησάντων Nil.*epp*.3.284(M.79.524D).

III. *sight, presence* καταξιωθεὶς τοῦ π. σου Ign.*Polyc*.1.1; τῷ τοῦ Χριστοῦ π. τὰ τοῦ νόμου κεκινημένα Nest.*hom.in Heb*.3:1(p.237.19; M.64.485B); usu. with prep. ἀπέδρα ἀπὸ π. Ἡσαῦ *1Clem*.4.8; φανήσεται πρὸ προσώπου ἡμῶν Ign.*Eph*.15.3; γενόμενος ἐν ὑμῖν κατὰ πρόσωπον Polyc.*ep*.3.2; τὰ φαινόμενά σου εἰς π. κολακεύῃς Ign.*Polyc*. 2.2; προσηνέχθημεν εἰς π. τοῦ πατρὸς οἱ ἐκβεβλημένοι διὰ τὴν ἐν Ἀδὰμ παράβασιν Ath.*exp.Ps*.15:8(M.27.105A); so εἰς π. *face to face, personally* ἀγράφοις τε εἰς π. ζητήσεσι Eus.*h.e*.4.24(M.20.389B); *openly, publicly* ἐφοίτα δὲ καὶ εἰς π. ἐπισκόποις βασιλέως γράμματα *ib*.10.2. 2(845C); Ath.*apol.sec*.36(p.115.3; M.25.309C).

IV. *the part that shows*, e.g. *surface* of the ground, *Barn*.6.9; ref. Ac.17:26 interpreted as evidence against sphericity of the earth οὐκ ἐπὶ ἀντιπροσώπου τῆς γῆς εἶπεν, ἀλλ' ἐπὶ π. Cosm.Ind.*top*.2(M.88. 132A); *front* of a building, Eus.*v.C*.3.37(p.94.14; M.20.1097A); plur., *front* of battle-line, Thdt.*Zach*.10:3(2.1639); *top* of a cake, *Exorc*.19 (p.339).

V. *representation*;

A. *character* in drama or literature ἕνα μὲν τὸν...συγγράφοντα...π. δὲ τὰ διαλεγόμενα παραφέροντα Just.*1apol*.36.2(M.6.385A); ὑποκριταὶ οὐχ ὅπερ λέγουσίν ἐστιν, οὐδ' ὅπερ βλέπονται καθ' ὃ περίκεινται π. τοῦτο τυγχάνουσιν Or.*or*.20(p.344.13; M.11.480B); ἐγκαλεῖ τῷ Ἰησοῦ ὁ Κέλσος διὰ τοῦ Ἰουδαϊκοῦ π. id.*Cels*.2.41(p.164.23; M.11.861B); τὸ ἰδίωμα τῶν π. τῆς...γραφῆς id.*comm.min.in Cant*.ap.*philoc*.7.1(p.50. 22; M.13.36A); ref. Ac.8:34 ἐφοβεῖτο γὰρ μή, παρὰ πρόσωπον ἐκλαβὼν τὴν ἀνάγνωσιν, πλανηθῇ Ath.*Ar*.1.54(M.26.124C); ὑποκριτής ἐστιν ὁ ἐν τῷ θεάτρῳ ἀλλότριον π. ὑπελθών Bas.*hom*.1.2(2.2D; M.31.165B).

B. met., of fictitious characters in gen., Ath.*exp.Ps*.15:1(M.27. 100D); Bas.*ep*.2.5(3.74C; M.32.232A); Chrys.*hom.3.1 in 1Cor*.(10. 16C); τὸ π. τῆς πόλεως περιθέμενος ταῦτα ἔπασχεν id.*hom.9.3 in Phil*. (11.267F); ἀπὸ π., ἐκ π. τινός, *in character* of εἰπεῖν τὸν λόγον ὡς ἀπὸ π. πολλῶν Just.*dial*.42.2(M.6.565B); Or.*fr.in Ac*.ap.*philoc*.7.2(p.51. 25; M.14.832A) cit. s. προσωποποιέω; †Ath.*exp.fid*.3(M.25.205B); ᾄδει...ὁ Χριστὸς ἐκ π. τῆς ἀνθρωπότητος id.*exp.Ps*.21 proem.(M.27. 132B); Cyr.H.*procatech*.6; ref. Mt.27:46 ἀπὸ π. τῆς αὐτοῦ ἐνανθρωπήσεως ἀνθρωποπαθῶς προβάλλεται τὸ ῥῆμα Epiph.*haer*.69.64(p.213. 7; M.42.305A).

C. *guise, role* ὁ δὲ λόγος αὐτοῦ...ἀναλαμβάνων τὸ π. τοῦ πατρὸς... παρεγίνετο εἰς τὸν παράδεισον ἐν π. τοῦ θεοῦ Thphl.Ant.*Autol*.2.22(M. 6.1088A); ref. Pr.8:22 τῷ τοῦ σωτῆρος ἀναφέρει π. Eus.*e.th*.3.2(p.144. 34; M.24.981A); Ath.*apol.sec*.17(p.99.35; M.25.276B).

D. *pretence, false assumption* π. εἰρήνης ἔχοντες Herm.*vis*.3.6.3; Χριστιανοῦ μὲν π. περιτιθέντες ἑαυτοῖς, Ἰουδαΐζουσαν δὲ τὴν διάνοιαν ἔχοντες Cyr.*hom.div*.5(5^2.359E); μοναχοὺς...ἐν π. διάγοντας Philox.*ep*. 36(p.184).

E. with implication of certain mental or moral associations as pertaining to the *character* portrayed, *characteristics* οὐχ ἁρμοζόντως τῷ Ἰουδαϊκῷ π. Or.*Cels*.1.49(p.101.10; M.11.753B); οὐδὲ τὸ ἁρμόζον πάντῃ τῷ Ἰουδαίῳ π. ... τετήρηκε *ib*.1.28(p.79.19; 713A); παρατήρει...κατὰ τὸ 'ἱερατικὸν...π. ... τό, σὺ τίς εἶ;' id.*Jo*.6.8(5; p.117. 4; M.14.216A); πρὸς ὁμιλίαν ἐκκαλεῖται τῇ εὐτελείᾳ τοῦ π. Thdot.Anc. *hom*.3.3(M.77.1388C).

F. *illustration, figure, type* π. δὲ ἐκ τῶν φαινομένων ἐν κόσμῳ ἀπολαύσεων ἐνέγκωμεν...ἐκ παραδειγμάτων μερικῶς ὑποδεικνύντες Mac.Aeg.*hom*.19.7(M.34.640A); νόμου γὰρ π. ὁ Μωσῆς Cyr.*ador*.2(1. 63C); π. μὲν τῶν ἐξ ἐθνῶν Ἰοθόρ *ib*.3(95A); ἡ γυνὴ...εἰς π. πάσης ψυχῆς...λαμβάνεται Nil.*epp*.3.275(M.79.520D); Νῶε π. ἐστι τῆς ἀκτημοσύνης *Apophth.Patr*.(M.65.336C).

VI. *visible presentation, outward being*;

A. *individual self, person* ἐκζητήσεις...τὰ π. τῶν ἁγίων *Did*.4.2 = *Barn*.19.10; βασιλίσσης π. ... προτιμᾶται *M.Ner.et Ach*.6(p.4.28); τὰ γὰρ τοῦ σώματος αὐτοῦ εἰς τὸ αὐτοῦ π. λέγεται Ath.*inc.et c.Ar*.2(M. 26.988A); εἰς θεὸν...τὸν φύσει καὶ ἀληθῶς ἐν π. Χριστοῦ Cyr.*Thds*.32 (p.63.31; 5^2.29E); hence ἐκ π. *on behalf of*, Eus.*h.e*.3.38.1(M.20.293C); Ἀθανάσιος...ἐκ π. πάντων...ἐπισκόπων Ath.*ep.Jov*.tit.ap.Thdt.*h.e*. 4.3.1(3.948); Thphn.*chron*.p.312(M.108.757A); εἰς π. *to the account of* and of letters *to* such and such an *address* ὁ τὴν...σοφίαν εἰς αὐτοῦ π. ἀναθεὶς Eus.*p.e*.11.7(521D; M.21.865A); πλεῖστα...εἰς Ἀσσυρίων π. ... εἰρημένα id.*d.e*.7.1(p.310.13; M.22.508B); ταύτην εἰς ἡμέτερον π. γραφῶν διαπεμψάμενος id.*v.C*.2.45(p.60.19; M.20.1021C); διδασκαλίαν εἰς αὐτῶν π. διετίθετο *ib*.3.63(p.111.11; 1140B); μὴ εἰς π. τῶν νῦν καταλαμβανομένων γενέσθαι τὴν ἄφεσιν Bas.*ep*.104(3.199A; M.32.512A);

πάντα...εἰς π. τῆς ἑαυτοῦ σαρκὸς γινόμενα Leont.H.*Nest*.5.25(M.86.1748A); εἶχε...ἐξουσίαν εἰς π. τοῦ...ἀδελφοῦ Jo.Mal.*chron*.13 p.338 (M.97.504C); ἐπὶ προσώπου, *in the case* of ἐπὶ δὲ τοῦ Μελιτίου π. οὐκέτι τὰ αὐτὰ ἔδοξε CNic.(325)*ep*.(p.50.6; M.67.81B); Eust.*engast*.23 (p.52.11; M.18.660D); hence καταφεύγει...ἐπὶ τὸ τοῦ Χριστοῦ πρόσωπον (*to the case of Christ*) *ib*.17(p.44.8; 649B); τὸ τῆς κατηγορίας ἐγύμνωσε π. (*personal reference*) Thdt.*qu.64 in 3Reg*.(1.508); ‡Gr. Naz.*Chr.pat*.1420(M.38.249A).

B. of things, *outward form, appearance, expression* ἀγαθοῦ ζυγοῦ π. ἡμῖν...γνωρίσαντος τοῦ θεοῦ Clem.*paed*.1.8(p.132.2; M.8.336B); ἐκκλησία ἐν δυσὶ π. νοεῖται, τῷ συστήματι τῶν πιστῶν καὶ τῷ συγκρίματι τῆς ψυχῆς Mac.Aeg.*hom*.38.7(M.34.756A); πᾶν γὰρ τὸ ὑφεστὸς ἐφ' ὅσον ὑφίσταται, π. ἔχειν λέγεται τῆς οἰκείας φύσεως ἤτοι σχῆμα Gel.Cyz.*h.e*.2.21.29(M.85.1289A); τοῦ μὲν λόγου σοι γέγονε π. ὁ βίος, τοῦ δὲ βίου φύσις ὁ λόγος Max.*opusc*.(M.91.9A); ὑπόστασίς ἐστι πρᾶγμα ὑφεστός τε καὶ οὐσιῶδες, ἐν ᾧ τὸ τῶν συμβεβηκότων ἄθροισμα ὡς ἐν ἑνὶ ὑποκειμένῳ πράγματι καὶ ἐνεργείᾳ ὑφέστηκε...π. δέ ἐστιν, ὃ διὰ τῶν οἰκείων ἐνεργημάτων τε καὶ ἰδιωμάτων...περιωρισμένην τῶν ὁμοφυῶν αὐτοῦ παρέχεται τὴν ἐμφάνειαν Thdr.Raith.*praep*.(p.206.5); Jo.D.*dialect*.43(M.94.613A).

C. *real* opp. false *appearance* τὸ μὲν τῆς ἐπιεικείας ἀπεδύσατο προσωπεῖον, τὸ δὲ τῆς δυσσεβείας ἐγύμνωσε π. Thdt.*h.e*.3.15.6(3.931); εἰς π. τὸ προσωπεῖον μεταβληθέν id.*h.rel*.1(3.1113A).

VII. *particular individual*;

A. numerically, *person, party* στάσεως, ἣν ὀλίγα π. ... ἐξέκαυσαν *1Clem*.1.1; ἐν τοῖς προγεγραμμένοις π. τὸ πᾶν πλῆθος ἐθεώρησα Ign. *Magn*.6.1; ἔδει...Χριστὸν θεοῦ καὶ ἀνθρώπων μεσίτην γενόμενον παρ' ἀμφοτέρων ἀρραβῶνά τινα εἰληφέναι, ἵνα φανῇ δύο π. μεσίτης Hipp. *Bal*.(p.82.8; M.10.605B); Or.*Jo*.6.39(23; p.148.15; M.14.268B); π. δαιμονιζόμενα Eust.*engast*.8(p.26.22; M.18.628B); *Const.App*.2.47.3; τὰ φιλούμενα π. Chrys.*hom.10.1 in Col*.(11.396B); τὰ τῶν π. ὀνόματα Thdt.*Dan*.1:6(2.1070B); οὐ πᾶσαν τὴν φύσιν τῶν ἀποστόλων κατηράσατο, ἀλλ' ἐν π. Anast.S.*hod*.8(M.89.128C); οἱ...πατέρες ὑπόστασιν, καὶ π., καὶ ἄτομον τὸ αὐτὸ ἐκάλεσαν Jo.D.*dialect*.43(M.94.613B); of slaves τὰ...οἰκετικὰ π. προσαγαγέτωσαν †Gregent.*leg.Hom*.59(M.86.613B); Sophr.H.*v.Anast*.(M.92.1709B).

B. of things, *distinct item, object* πλειόνα...τῶν εἰρημένων παρεισφέροντες εὐαγγελίων π. Iren.*haer*.3.11.9(M.7.890B); Eus.*Marcell*.2.3 (p.49.8; M.24.805C); δύο...π. ἡμῖν εἰς διδασκαλίαν παρεισήγαγεν Epiph.*haer*.37.8(p.60.12; M.41.652B); δύο γὰρ π. συναπτόμενα, τέλειόν τι πρᾶγμα ἀπεργάζεται Mac.Aeg.*hom*.32.6(M.34.737A); πῶς δύναται τὰ δύο π. εἶναι ἐν τῇ καρδίᾳ, καὶ ἡ χάρις καὶ ἡ ἁμαρτία; *ib*.40.7(765D); and of persons classified as objects, ref. degrees of affinity ἐρωτᾶν ...εἰ ἐπεστράφησαν ἀπὸ τοῦ δευτέρου π. τῆς συγγενείας ἐπὶ τὸ πρῶτον πάλιν †Jo.Jej.*poenit*.(M.88.1912C); τοῦτο τὸ π. [sc. χήρα] ἐν πολλοῖς ...ἐλαττοῦται Olymp.*Job* 22:7(M.93.244C); in imaginary classifications ἀγάπη τὸν ἄνθρωπον εἰς τρία μερίζεται π.· ὁ μὲν διὰ θεὸν ἀγαπᾷ ὃν ἀγαπᾷ· ὁ δὲ ἐπεὶ πλούσιός ἐστι...ὁ δὲ ἐμπαθῶς Evagr.Pont.ap. Jo.D.*parall*.(M.95.1204A).

C. with more emphasis on qualitative aspect of individual than on purely numerical καιροῦ καὶ π. πρόφασις εἵλκυσεν αὐτὸν τοιαῦτα γράψαι Ath.*Dion*.4(p.49.3; M.25.485B); id.*Ar*.2.8(M.26.164B); τὸ τῶν π. ἀξιόπιστον Gr.Naz.*ep*.101(M.37.177A); ἀπὸ τῆς ποιότητος τοῦ π. Chrys.*hom.2.2 in Philm*.(11.780E); εἰσῆλθε μέγα π. δοῦναι εὐποιΐαν τοῖς ἐμβεβλημένοις Jo.Mosch.*prat*.189(M.87.3068B); and in phrases ass. προσωποληψία (*partiality to an individual*): οὐ λήμψῃ π. ἐλέγξαι τινά, *Did*.4.3 = *Barn*.19.4; οὐ...κατὰ πρόσωπον καλέσαι *ib*.4.10 = 19.7; μὴ π. θαυμάζειν Ath.*exp.Ps*.14:2(M.27.100C); Gr.Naz.*or*.9.5(M.35.824C); προσώποις χαριζόμενοι Socr.*h.e*.1.10.5(M.67.101B).

VIII. in quasi-legal usage; **A.** *standing, claim* ὁ μὴ ἔχων π. εἰς οἶκον θεοῦ εἰσιέναι Μωαβίτης Olymp.*fr.Jer*.48:11(M.93.705D).

B. *presentation of a case, plea* ἐκβάλλει αὐτῶν τὸ π. Chrys.*hom.50.2 in Ac*.(9.373B); π. ὑποδεικνύει τὸ τῆς κλοπῆς δρᾶμα Thdt.*provid*.8(4.620).

C. *account* ποίησον γραμμάτιον χρεωστικὸν...καὶ αἶρέ μοι αὐτὸ τὸ π. Jo.Mosch.*prat*.193(M.87.3073B); dat., *on account* of, *by virtue* of σώζεται τῷ π. τῆς μετανοίας Nil.*epp*.3.33(M.79.393C).

IX. Trin., *person* (not transitory or superficial presentation); ref. Jo.10:30 τὸ γὰρ 'ἐσμέν', οὐκ ἐφ' ἑνὸς λέγεται, ἀλλ' ἐπὶ δύο· ⟨δύο⟩ π. ἔδειξεν, δύναμιν δὲ μίαν Hipp.*Noët*.7(p.247.13; M.10.813A); δύο μὲν οὐκ ἐρῶ θεούς, ἀλλ' ἢ ἕνα, π. δὲ δύο, οἰκονομίᾳ, ⟨τὴν⟩ τε τρίτην τὴν χάριν τοῦ ἁγίου πνεύματος· πατὴρ μὲν γὰρ εἷς, π. δὲ δύο ὅτι καὶ ὁ υἱός, τὸ δὲ τρίτον τὸ ἅγιον πνεῦμα *ib*.14(p.257.1; 821A); τότε μὲν Χριστοῦ π., τότε δὲ πνεύματος ἁγίου, τότε δὲ τοῦ...θεοῦ ἦν...χρηματίζον Eus. *d.e*.5.13(p.236.21; M.22.389D); cf.Epiph.*anc*.39(p.49.8; M.43.88A); ref. monarchian doctrine of Callistus καλεῖσθαι πατέρα καὶ υἱὸν ἕνα θεόν, καὶ τοῦτο ἓν ὂν π. μὴ δύνασθαι εἶναι δύο Hipp.*haer*.9.12(p.249.7; M.16.3386A); πνεῦμα γάρ, φησίν, ὁ θεὸς οὐχ ἕτερόν ἐστι παρὰ τὸν λόγον ἢ ὁ λόγος παρὰ τὸν θεόν. ἓν οὖν τοῦτο π., ὀνόματι μὲν μεριζόμενον, οὐσίᾳ δὲ οὔ *ib*.10.27(p.283.18; 3442B); ref. Sabellian doctrine: **a.** not employed by Sabellians in sense of *mask* or *character*, nor are Sabellians usually said to speak of τρία πρόσωπα, cf. *unam eandemque subsistentiam patris ac filii asseverant,...unam tamen* ὑπόστασιν *subsistere, id est, unam personam duobus nominibus subjacentem*, Or.*fr.Tit*.(M.14.1304D); Ast.Soph.*fr*.28 ap.Eus.*e.th*.3.4 (p.158.21; M.24.1004C); Marcell.*fr*.68 ap.Eus.*e.th*.2.1(p.124.30; M.24.945B); τοὺς λέγοντας δὲ τὸν αὐτὸν εἶναι πατέρα καὶ υἱὸν καὶ ἅγιον πνεῦμα, καθ' ἑνὸς καὶ τοῦ αὐτοῦ πράγματός τε καὶ π. τὰ τρία ὀνόματα ἀσεβῶς ἐκλαμβάνοντας *Symb.Ant*.(345)7(p.253.15; M.26.732C); εἴ τις τὸν πατέρα καὶ τὸν υἱὸν καὶ τὸ ἅγιον πνεῦμα ἓν π. λέγει, ἀ. ἔ. *Symb. Sirm*.1 *anath*.19; π. ἓν πατρὸς καὶ υἱοῦ Bas.*hom*.24.1(2.190A; M.31.601A); cf.*ib*.24.2(190E; M.604A); μήτε...φύσει τέμνεσθαι· μήτε...εἰς ἓν π. περιγράφεσθαι Gr.Naz.*or*.34.8(M.36.249A); ὀνόματα...ψιλὰ καθ' ἑνὸς π. κείμενα Chrys.*hom.6.1 in Phil*.(11.234C); cf. τρεῖς ὀνομασίας,... τρεῖς...ἐνεργείας without ref. to πρόσωπα, Epiph.*haer*.62.1(p.389.13; M.41.1052B); τοὺς μὴ λέγοντας τὴν...τριάδα τρία π. ... αὐτοτελῆ Photinus et al.ap.Epiph.*haer*.72.11(p.266.4; M.42.397B); **b.** later allegations that Sabellians spoke of τρία π. in transitory sense, cf. μίαν...ὑπόστασιν τριπρόσωπον Eus.*e.th*.3.6(p.164.26; M.24.1016A); ἐπεὶ τόν γε ἀνυπόστατον τῶν π. ἀναπλασμὸν οὐδὲ ὁ Σαβέλλιος παρῃτήσατο, εἰπὼν τὸν αὐτὸν θεόν, ἕνα τῷ ὑποκειμένῳ ὄντα, πρὸς τὰς ἑκάστοτε παραπιπτούσας χρείας μεταμορφούμενον, νῦν μὲν ὡς πατέρα, νῦν δὲ ὡς υἱὸν...διαλέγεσθαι Bas.*ep*.210.5(3.317A; M.32.776C); Σαβελλίου... λέγοντος· ἕνα μὲν εἶναι τῇ ὑποστάσει τὸν θεόν, προσωποποιεῖσθαι δὲ ὑπὸ τῆς γραφῆς διαφόρως...καὶ νῦν μὲν τὰς πατρικὰς ἑαυτῷ περιτιθέναι φωνάς, ὅταν τούτου καιρὸς ᾖ τοῦ π.· νῦν δέ, τὰς υἱῷ πρεπούσας...νῦν δὲ τὸ τοῦ πνεύματος ὑποδύεσθαι προσωπεῖον, ὅταν ὁ καιρὸς τὰς ἀπὸ τοῦ τοιούτου π. φωνὰς ἀπαιτῇ· ἐὰν οὖν καὶ παρ' ἡμῖν φανῶσί τινες ἓν τῷ ὑποκειμένῳ πατέρα καὶ υἱὸν καὶ...πνεῦμα λέγοντες, τρία δὲ π. τέλεια ὁμολογοῦντες κτλ. *ib*.214.3(322C; M.788C); ἀναγκάζονται πρόσωπα μόνον ὁμολογεῖν διάφορα...μὴ φεύγοντες τὸ τοῦ Σαβελλίου κακόν...τὴν αὐτὴν ὑπόστασιν λέγων πρὸς τὴν ἑκάστοτε παρεμπίπτουσαν χρείαν μετασχηματίζεσθαι *ib*.236.6(364B; M.884C); cf. τρία π. οὐκ εἶναι διϊσχυριζόμενοι, ὥσπερ ἀνυπόστατον εἰσάγοντες π. Apoll.*fid.sec.pt*.13(p.171.21; M.10.1109C); ref. Paul. Sam. π. ἓν τὸν θεὸν ἅμα τῷ λόγῳ φασίν, ὡς ἄνθρωπον ἕνα καὶ τὸν αὐτοῦ λόγον Epiph.*haer*.65.3(p.5.17; M.42.16B); ref. Arianism οὔτε μὴν τρία ὁμολογοῦντες πράγματα καὶ τρία π. τοῦ πατρὸς καὶ τοῦ υἱοῦ καὶ τοῦ ἁγίου πνεύματος...τρεῖς διὰ τοῦτο θεοὺς ποιοῦμεν *Symb.Ant*.(345)4(p.252.22; M.26.729B); ref. 1Cor. 15:27, Gr.Nyss.*Eun*.1(1 p.78.25; M.45.309B); εἰς π. ἕτερον πάλιν τοῦ πατρός, ὑποτάσσοντος πάντα τῷ υἱῷ...οὐκέτι δὲ ἀπὸ π. πατρὸς μόνον, οὐδὲ ἀπὸ π. υἱοῦ μόνον, ἀλλὰ μεσαίτατα τῶν π. πατρὸς καὶ υἱοῦ φησιν, ἔσχατος ἐχθρὸς καταργεῖται...ἀπαρεμφάτως μετὰ τὸ π. τοῦ υἱοῦ καὶ τὸ π. τοῦ πατρὸς τὸ π. ὑπέφαινε τοῦ ἁγίου πνεύματος Epiph.*haer*.69.76(p.224.8; M.42.325A); in orthodox use: used by most anti-Sabellian writers as less metaphysical equivalent of ὑπόστασις; earlier writers prefer τρεῖς and ἕν, avoiding both use of π. and ὑπόστασις; later writers employ both, e.g. 'ποιήσωμεν ἄνθρωπον'... δευτέρου π. τοῦ ὑποδεικνυμένου μὲν μυστικῶς Bas.*hex*.9.6(1.87B; M.29.204C); διαιρεῖ τὰ π. φανερῶς ἐν τῷ λέγειν 'ὁ ἑωρακὼς ἐμέ'· δείκνυσι γὰρ ...τὸ ἴδιον αὐτοῦ π.· 'ἑώρακε τὸν πατέρα' ἀναφέρων ἐπὶ τὸ πατρικὸν π. id.*hom*.24.2(2.190C; M.31.601C); ἡ φωνὴ [i.e. ὁμοούσιος] καὶ τὸ τοῦ Σαβελλίου κακὸν ἐπανορθοῦται· ἀναιρεῖ γὰρ τὴν ταυτότητα τῆς ὑποστάσεως, καὶ εἰσάγει τελείαν τῶν π. τὴν ἔννοιαν id.*ep*.52.3(3.146A; M.32.393C); τρισὶ μέν, κατὰ τὰς ἰδιότητας, εἴτουν ὑποστάσεις...εἴτε π. (οὐδὲν γὰρ περὶ τῶν ὀνομάτων ζυγομαχήσομεν) Gr.Naz.*or*.39.11(M.36.345C); ἐν τῷ εὐαγγελίῳ τὰ τρία παραδέδοται π. τε καὶ ὀνόματα Gr. Nyss.*or.catech*.39(p.155.8; M.45.100A); τῶν ἐν τῇ ἁγίᾳ τριάδι πεπιστευμένων π. id.*tres dii*(M.45.124A); οὐ συνδιαιροῦντες δὲ τοῖς π. τὴν τῆς οὐσίας ἑνότητα id.*Eun*.1(1 p.164.5; M.45.405B); ἐν τρισὶ π. καὶ ὑποστάσεσι μηδεμίαν τὴν κατὰ τὸ εἶναι διαφορὰν πιστεύειν *ib*.(1 p.88.21; 320D); ἡ μὲν γὰρ τῶν ὑποστάσεων ἰδιότης τρανὴν τε καὶ ἀσύγχυτον ποιεῖται τὴν τῶν π. διαστολὴν *ib*.2(2 p.301.17; 472C); θεὸς εἷς ἐστιν, οὐδ' ἐν τοῖς π. τοῖς ἐν τῇ πίστει παραδεδομένοις ἐμμεριζόμενος *ib*.(p.355.11; 533A); π. μὲν γὰρ ἑκάστου τὸ εἶναι αὐτὸ καὶ ὑφεστάναι δηλοῖ, θεότης δὲ πατρὸς ἴδιον, καὶ ὁπότε μία τῶν τριῶν ἡ θεότης λέγοιτο, τὴν πατρὸς ἰδιότητα παροῦσαν υἱῷ τε καὶ πνεύματι μαρτυρεῖ· ὥστε εἰ μὲν ἐν τρισὶ π. μία ῥηθήσεται ἡ θεότης, καὶ ἡ τριὰς διαβεβαιοῦται καὶ τὸ ἓν οὐ διακόπτεται Apoll.*fid.sec.pt*.15(p.172.10; M.10.1109D); *ib*.24(p.175.25; 1113D); *ib*.25(p.176.3; 1116A); ἐν τρισὶ τελειοτάταις ὑποστάσεσιν, ἤγουν τρισὶ τελείοις π. CCP(381)*ep*.ap.Thdt.*h.e*.5.9.11(3.1031); ἐν ἑνὶ π. τὰ τρία κηρύσσουσι Didym.(‡Bas.)*Eun*.5(1.315B; M.29.756B);

ὁμολογοῦμεν δὲ πατέρα τέλειον προσώπῳ καὶ υἱὸν ὁμοίως, καὶ πνεῦμα δὲ ἅγιον ὡσαύτως Thdr.Mops.*symb.*(p.98.9; M.66.1017A); διαφορά, οὐ κατὰ τὴν οὐσίαν...ἀλλ' ἔξωθεν ἐπινοουμένη, δι' ἧς τὸ ἑκατέρου π. εἰσφέρεται ἐν ἰδιαζούσῃ μὲν ὑποστάσει κείμενον, εἰς ἑνότητα δὲ θεότητος διὰ ταυτότητος φυσικῆς σφιγγόμενον Cyr.*thes.*11(5[1].85C); μία γὰρ ἡ τῆς θεότητος φύσις, ἐν π. τε καὶ ὑποστάσει πατρός τε καὶ υἱοῦ καὶ ἁγίου πνεύματος id.*Jo.*9.1(4.806A); τὴν δέ γε ὑπόστασιν, π. τινὸς εἶναι δηλωτικὴν...τὴν γὰρ ὑπόστασιν, καὶ τὸ π., καὶ τὴν ἰδιότητα, ταὐτὸν σημαίνειν φαμέν Thdt.*eran.*1(4.8); τὸ ἀγέννητον καὶ γεννητὸν καὶ ἐκπορευτόν,...ἱκανὰ γὰρ ἡμῖν διακρίνειν τὰ π. id.*rect.conf.*3(M.6.1212A); τῶν ἰδικῶς ὑφισταμένων τριῶν θεαρχικῶν π. τὴν ὕπαρξιν ‡Gr. Nyss.*hom.6.79 in Jo.*(p.226.4); τῶν τριῶν ἁγίων π. Leont.H.*Nest.*1.6 (M.86.1421C); τριῶν ὄντων τῶν τῆς...τριάδος ὁμοουσίων π. *ib.*2.16 (1573C); ταῦτα μετάγειν ἐκ τοῦ ἑνὸς π. καὶ ἐπὶ τὰς ἑτέρας ὁμοουσίους ὑποστάσεις *ib.*4.23(1688C); μίαν θεότητα ἤτοι φύσιν καὶ οὐσίαν...ἐν τρισὶν ὑποστάσεσιν ἤτοι π. δοξάζοντες Justn.*conf.*(p.72.15; M.86.995A); ταὐτὸν δὲ τὸ λέγειν υἱὸν τοῦ πατρός, τῷ λέγειν υἱὸν τοῦ θεοῦ· ἐπειδὴ εἴ τί ἐστι τοῦ π., τοῦτό ἐστι καὶ τῆς τοῦ π. οὐσίας ‡Just.*qu.et resp.*18(M.6.1264D); π. δέ ἐστιν, ὃ διὰ τῶν οἰκείων ἐνεργημάτων τε καὶ ἰδιωμάτων ἀρίδηλον καὶ περιωρισμένην τῶν ὁμοφυῶν αὐτοῦ παρέχεται τὴν ἐμφάνειαν...καὶ αὕτη μὲν ἡ τοῦ π. ὑπογραφή· δοκεῖ δέ πως ταὐτὸν σημαίνειν τῇ ὑποστάσει, καὶ ἢ μικρὸν ἢ οὐδὲν διαλλάττειν Thdr.Raith. *praep.*(p.206.5); ὑπόστασις καὶ π. ταὐτόν ἐστιν Jo.D.*fid.Nest.*52 (p.582); μίαν θεότητα ἐν τρισὶν ὑποστάσεσιν ἤγουν π. προσκυνουμένην *ib.*2(p.561).

X. Christol.; **A.** = ὑπόστασις = φύσις: οἱ πατέρες...τὰς ὑποστάσεις πολλάκις ἀντὶ τῶν φύσεων...παραλαμβάνουσιν...ὅ τε...τῆς ἀθανασίας ἐπώνυμος καὶ π. ἐπὶ Χριστοῦ δύο εἶναι διϊσχυρίζεται Leont.B.*arg.Sev.* (M.86.1924C).

B. *person* φάσκουσι [sc. followers of Paul. Sam.]...ταῦτα [sc. Mt. 11:25ff.] περὶ ἑαυτοῦ ὁ ἄνθρωπος λέγει. ὁ πατὴρ γὰρ ἅμα τῷ υἱῷ εἷς θεός, ὁ δὲ ἄνθρωπος κάτωθεν τὸ ἴδιον π. ὑποφαίνει· καὶ οὕτως τὰ δύο π. πληροῦνται Epiph.*haer.*65.7(p.10.10; M.42.24B); ἐν π. σύνθετον ἐκ θεότητος...καὶ ἀνθρωπείας σαρκός ‡*Symb.Ant.*(269)(p.6.11; Hahn p.182); οὐκ ἐν διαιρέσει π. ἢ ὀνομάτων, ἀλλὰ φυσικῇ γεννήσει καὶ ἀλύτῳ ἑνώσει ‡Ath.*Apoll.*2.2(M.26.1133C); *ib.*2.10(1148C); μία φύσις ἐστίν, ἐπειδὴ π. ἓν οὐκ ἔχον εἰς δύο διαίρεσιν Apoll.*ep.Dion.*1.2(p.257.15; M.*PL.*8.929B); οὐκ εἰδότες διαίρεσιν τοῦ ἑνὸς π. *ib.*1.7(p.259.12; 934A); φυλάττων τὸ ἓν π. καὶ τὴν ἀμέριστον ἑνὸς ζῴου δήλωσιν id.*corp. et div.*10(p.189.15; M.*PL.*8.874C); ἡ σὰρξ τοῦ κυρίου...προσκυνεῖται, καθὸ ἕν ἐστι π. καὶ ἓν ζῷον μετ' αὐτοῦ id.*fr.*85(p.225.20)ap.Gr.Nyss. *Apoll.*44(M.45.1228C); οὐ μὴν ὅτι τὸ συναμφότερον ἐξ οὐρανοῦ, ἀλλ' ἡνωμένον τῷ οὐρανίῳ καὶ π. ἓν μετ' αὐτοῦ γεγονὸς οὐράνιον κατὰ τὴν ἕνωσίν ἐστιν id.*fr.*154(p.248.31)ap.Leont.B.*Apoll.*(M.86.1964A); εἰ δέ τις ἢ δύο π. λέγει τὸν υἱὸν ἢ τὴν σάρκα ὁμοούσιον τῷ θεῷ...ἀναθεματιζέσθω id.*fr.*163(p.255.11)*ib.*(1949C); οὔτε ὁμοούσιον τῷ θεῷ τὴν σάρκα καθό ἐστι σὰρξ καὶ οὐ θεός, θεὸς δὲ καθ' ὅσον εἰς ἓν π. ἥνωται τῇ θεότητι id.*fr.*164 *ib.*(1949A); Thdr.Mops.*ep.Domn.*(p.338.26; M.66.1012C) cit. s. ἕνωσις; τὸν υἱὸν τοῦ ἀνθρώπου καταβῆναί φησι, διχάζεσθαι μετὰ τὴν ἐνανθρώπησιν εἰς δύο π. παραιτούμενος Cyr.*Jo.*2.1(4.150E); τέλειος ὢν ἐν θεότητι, καὶ τέλειος ἐν ἀνθρωπότητι ὁ αὐτός, καὶ ὡς ἐν ἑνὶ π. νοούμενος id.*ep.*39(p.18.26; 5[2].107D); σωζομένης...τῆς ἰδιότητος ἑκατέρας φύσεως καὶ εἰς ἓν π. συνιούσης Leo Mag.*ep.* 28.3(p.13.11; M.*PL.*54.764A); τοῦ θεοῦ καὶ τοῦ ἀνθρώπου ἕν ἐστι π. *ib.*28.4(p.16.5; 772A); ref. Jo.1:14, Phil.2:7 ἐγένετο, εἶπε, καὶ... ἔλαβεν...ἵνα διὰ μὲν τοῦ προτέρου τὸ ἑνικὸν τοῦ π. παραστήσῃ, διὰ δὲ τοῦ ἑτέρου τὸ ἀναλλοίωτον τῆς φύσεως ἐκβοήσῃ Procl.CP *Arm.*6 (p.190.15; M.65.861C); ταύτην τὴν φύσιν...οὕτως ἑαυτῷ συνάψει τε καὶ ἑνώσει ὡς ἓν π. θεοῦ τε καὶ ἀνθρώπου νοεῖσθαι Thdt.*qu.19 in Gen.*(1.23); κοινὰ τοῦ π. γέγονε τὰ τῶν φύσεων ἴδια id.*eran.*3(4.226); τὰ θεῖα καὶ τὰ ἀνθρώπεια τὸ ἓν δέχεται π. ... ἵνα μὴ ἄλλο μὲν τὸ τῆς θεότητος, ἄλλο δὲ τὸ τῆς ἀνθρωπότητος π. νομισθῇ *ib.*(228); σωζομένης...τῆς ἰδιότητος ἑκατέρας φύσεως καὶ εἰς ἓν π. καὶ μίαν ὑπόστασιν συντρεχούσης, οὐκ εἰς δύο π. μεριζόμενον...ἀλλ' ἕνα καὶ τὸν αὐτὸν υἱόν *Symb.Chalc.*(451)(p.129.33; H.2.456C); τὸ ὑποστατικὸν π. Leont.H. *Nest.*2.16(M.86.1572C); ὑπόστασις...τόδε τι καθ' ἑαυτὴν ἀπόστασίς τις οὖσα καὶ διορισμὸς τῶν ἀδιορίστων οὐσιῶν εἰς τὸν κατὰ π. ἀριθμὸν ἑκάστου· διὸ δὴ καὶ π. ταύτην οἱ πατέρες νοοῦσι *ib.*2.1(1529D); ἐν Χριστῷ...τῷ ἑνὶ συντετελεσμένῳ π. *ib.*2.49(1601B); ἐν τῷ φυσικῷ π. τοῦ λόγου, φύσεώς ἐστιν ἡ ἕνωσις *ib.*2.34(1592C); *ib.*3.8(1636A); ref. Nestorian acceptance of Χριστοτόκος: ἀλλά...τὸ μὲν ἄνθρωπος φύσεως ὄνομα· τὸ δὲ Χριστὸς οὐ φύσεως, ἀλλὰ προσώπου· πῶς οὖν τὸ τῆς φύσεως ὄνομα...ἐκ τοῦ προσωπικοῦ σημάνωμεν; *ib.*4.20(1685C); εἰ μὲν τὴν μονάδα διὰ τὴν τοῦ π. ἑνότητα...καλῶς λέγετε,...ὡμολογημένου τοῦ κατ' αὐτὸ τὸ ἓν π. φυσικοῦ διαφόρου id.*monoph.*22(M.86.1784C); οὐ γὰρ ὡς τῇ φύσει ἀτελῆ ὄντα, μέρη ταῦτά φημι, ἀλλ' ὡς συμπληρωτικὰ τοῦ π. τῆς κατὰ Χριστὸν ὑποστάσεως Leont.B.*Nest.et Eut.*1(M.86.1289A); καὶ τὸ διάφορον τῶν ἡνωμένων, καὶ τὸ ταυτὸν τοῦ π., διὰ τῆς τῶν ἡνωμένων φύσεων εἰς μίαν ὑπόστασιν συνδρομῆς ἀνακεφαλαιούμενον *ib.*(1293B); ἔν μέν τι τούτων εἶναι τὸ ἀποτέλεσμα, ὃ εἴτε π., εἴτε ὑπόστασιν, εἴτε ἄτομον, εἴτε ὑποκείμενον...φίλον καλεῖν αὐτό, οὐ διαφέρομαι *ib.*(1305C); π. τὴν ἰδιοσύστατον τῆς ἑκάστου φύσεως ὕπαρξιν, καὶ...περιγραφήν, ἐξ ἰδιοτήτων τινῶν συγκειμένην Jo. Philop.*arb.*ap.*Doct.Patr.*36(p.274.10); τὴν...σάρκα τοῦ Χριστοῦ οὐ λέγομεν π., ἀλλ' οὐσίαν...ὑπόστασις γὰρ τὸ κεχωρισμένον π. λέγεται Anast.S.*hod.*2(M.89.61A); ταὐτὸν μὲν οὐσία καὶ φύσις· ταὐτὸν δὲ π. καὶ ὑπόστασις Max.*ep.*15(M.91.549B).

C. *character, representation,* cf. *utriusque naturae personam tractari in...Christo,* Hil.Pict.*De Trinitate* 9.14(M.*PL.*10.292B); ref. Phil.2:7 τὰ δουλοπρεπῆ ῥήματα, οὐκ ἀναβαίνοντα μὲν πρὸς τὴν οὐσίαν αὐτοῦ, ἀλλὰ τῷ τῆς ἐνανθρωπήσεως π. περικείμενα Cyr.*thes.*9(5[1].72A); ἐὰν μὴ τὸ...τοῦ δούλου ὑπέλθω π., ἀμήχανόν ἐστιν ὑμᾶς εἰς τὸν...τοῦ δεσπότου φθάσαι χαρακτῆρα Procl.CP *or.*6.14(M.65.748A); τὸ ἡμέτερον ...οἰκειούμενος π. Jo.D.*f.o.*4.18(M.94.1188A).

D. *concrete presentation* of an abstract οὐσία, *individual external appearance,* hence *individuality* Χριστὸς δύο ὑπάρχων φύσεις, ἀλλ' ἐν αὐταῖς ἀληθῶς γνωριζόμενος, μοναδικὸν ἔχει τῆς υἱότητος τὸ π. Gr. Nyss.*fr.*(M.46.1112C); controv. Apollinarius τίς ὢν ὁ σωτήρ; ὁ θεός, φησίν..., οὐ δύο π., ὡς ἑτέρου μὲν ὄντος θεοῦ, ἑτέρου δὲ τοῦ ἀνθρώπου id.*Apoll.*58(M.45.1265D); τὸν λόγον...τῇ ζωῇ τῶν ἀνθρώπων διὰ τοῦ δουλικοῦ π. καθομιλήσαντα *ib.*2(1128A); *ib.*14(1149A); εἰ...προτιμοτέρα ἡ θεία μορφὴ τοῦ δουλικοῦ π. *ib.*27(1181C); this terminology called forth accusation of teaching two π.: ἡμᾶς φησι δύο π. λέγειν, τὸν θεὸν καὶ τὸν...προσληφθέντα ἄνθρωπον *ib.*35(1200B); cf. Apollinarius' insistence on one π. in references sub B; abs., of humanity δύο...πράγματα περὶ ἓν π. ... παρὰ μὲν τῶν Ἰουδαίων τὸ πάθος, παρὰ δὲ τοῦ θεοῦ τὴν τιμήν, οὐχ ὡς ἄλλου μὲν πεπονθότος, ἑτέρου δὲ διὰ τῆς ἀνυψώσεως τετιμημένου id.*Eun.*5(2 p.116.14; M.45.697A); Thdr. Mops.*fr.inc.*8(p.299.21ff.; M.66.981B) cit. s. ἀπρόσωπος; in usage of Nestorius τὸ τῆς φύσεως κοινὸν...ἀναδέχεται ἵνα δείξας ἐν ἑαυτῷ τὸ τῆς φύσεως π. ἁμαρτίας ἐλεύθερον, γένηται...μεσίτης Nest.*hom. in Heb.3:1*(p.239.19; M.64.488C); θεὸς λόγος ὤν,...πτωχεύοντος δι' ὑμᾶς περιβέβλημαι π. id.*fr.*D 9(p.358.4)ap.Cyr.*Nest.*5.2(p.97.43; M.76.225B); τίθησι τὸ Χριστὸς ὡς τῆς ἀπαθοῦς καὶ παθητῆς οὐσίας ἐν μοναδικῷ π. προσηγορίαν σημαντικήν id.*ep.Cyr.*2(p.176.7; M.77.52C); τὴν μὲν τῶν φύσεων ἐπήνουν διαίρεσιν κατὰ τὸν τῆς ἀνθρωπότητος καὶ θεότητος λόγον καὶ τὴν τούτων εἰς ἑνὸς π. συνάφειαν *ib.*(p.176.17; 52C); cf. *dans les choses qui sont dites du prosôpon et de la forme de la nature, il est dit (être) ce qui le fait connaître, comme le prosôpon (fait connaître) l'essence. ce qui est naturellement n'est pas dit (du Verbe), parce que l'union n'a pas lieu selon l'essence et selon la nature, mais selon le prosôpon,* id.*Heracl.*1.3.231(p.139); *le fils unique de dieu et le fils de l'homme, le même (forme) de deux, est dit les deux, parce qu'il a attribué (les propriétés) de leurs prosôpons à son prosôpon et dorénavant il est désigné par celui-ci et par celui-là comme par son propre prosôpon, ib.*1.1.78(p.50); *on ne conçoit pas deux prosôpons des fils, ni encore deux prosôpons des hommes, mais d'un seul homme, qui est mû de la même manière même par l'autre. l'union des prosôpons a eu lieu en prosôpon, et non en essence ni en nature. on ne doit pas concevoir une essence sans hypostase, comme si l'union (des essences) avait eu lieu en une essence et qu'il y eût un prosôpon d'une seule essence. mais les natures subsistent, dans leurs prosôpons et dans leurs natures et dans le prosôpon d'union. quant au prosôpon naturel de l'une, l'autre se sert du même en vertu de l'union; ainsi il n'y a qu'un prosôpon pour les deux natures. le prosôpon d'une essence se sert du prosôpon même de l'autre. mais quelle essence vas-tu faire sans prosôpon?, ib.*2.1.304–5(p.193); *où donc ai-je dit du Christ qu'il était un simple homme, ou deux Christs, et qu'il n'y avait pas un seigneur Jésus-Christ, fils unique de dieu: de l'union des deux natures résulte un prosôpon?, ib.*1.3.214(p.129); *celui qui attribue ainsi à dieu le Verbe un prosôpon de deux natures n'attribue pas encore au prosôpon de l'humanité les propriétés de la divinité, de manière qu'il y ait un prosôpon de la divinité et de l'humanité: le prosôpon de la divinité et celui de l'humanité formant un prosôpon; l'un par diminution, l'autre par élévation, ib.*2.1.341 (p.218); *il y a un prosôpon de deux essences et deux essences d'un prosôpon. . . . l'essence n'est pas sans prosôpon; la nature n'est pas non plus sans prosôpon ni le prosôpon sans nature. car l'autre essence se sert de la même manière du prosôpon d'une essence et non d'un autre, à cause de l'union. il a fait siennes toutes nos propriétés, en donnant le sien à celui qui possède tout cela entièrement à l'exception du péché, ib.*2.1.342(p.219); *l'essence même de l'humanité se* *sert du prosôpon de l'essence de la divinité, mais non de l'essence, et l'essence de la divinité se sert du prosôpon même de l'humanité, et non de l'essence*, ib.2.1.439(p.282); *la divinité se sert du prosôpon de l'humanité et l'humanité, de celui de la divinité; de cette manière nous disons un seul prosôpon pour les deux*, ib.2.1.333(p.213); *par les prosôpons de l'union, l'un est dans l'autre, et cet 'un' n'est pas conçu par diminution, ni par suppression, ni par confusion, mais par l'action de recevoir et de donner, et par l'usage de l'union de l'un avec l'autre, les prosôpons recevant et donnant l'une et l'autre, mais non les essences*, ib.2.1.348(p.223); *pour l'union de la divinité et de la chair, dans le prosôpon de la divinité de dieu le Verbe, il n'est pas un autre et un autre, mais c'est le même; mais, dans les natures de la divinité et de l'humanité, il est autre et autre. c'est pourquoi le livre divin parle avec précaution du prosôpon de la divinité et désigne les deux (natures) par le prosôpon de l'union*, ib.2.1.361(p.232); *il n'est pas adoré dans son prosôpon, mais dans le prosôpon qui lui est uni et qui est commun à cause de l'union. c'est dans le prosôpon qu'a eu lieu l'union, de sorte que celui-ci soit celui-là, et celui-là celui-ci. à cause donc de celui qui l'a pris pour son prosôpon, celui qui a été pris obtient d'être le prosôpon de celui qui l'a pris*, ib.2.1.331 (p.211); *parce qu'il reste dans la nature humaine, il reçoit un nom qui l'emporte sur tous les noms; ce n'est ni par suite de la science et le la foi, mais c'est par une disposition bienveillante qu'il en a été ainsi, afin qu'il fût son image et son prosôpon, en sorte que son prosôpon est aussi le prosôpon de celui-ci. il est également dieu et également homme: forme de dieu dans la condescendance ... et forme de la chair comme homme*, ib.1.1.84(p.54); *il s'est humilié ... en se servant du prosôpon de celui qui est mort et a été crucifié comme de son propre prosôpon; et il s'est servi en son propre prosôpon de ce qui appartenait à celui qui est mort*, ib.1.1.85(p.55); *il est dans les deux, dans la forme du serviteur et dans la forme de dieu, et ... possède le même prosôpon de l'humanité et de l'exaltation*, ib.1.1.103(p.67); *l'union a lieu pour le prosôpon et non pour la nature. nous ne disons pas union des prosôpons, mais des natures, car, dans l'union, il n'y a qu'un seul prosôpon; mais dans les natures, un autre et un autre; de sorte que le prosôpon soit reconnu sur l'ensemble; c'est pour son prosôpon qu'il a pris la chair ... il donna sa propre forme à la forme du serviteur, et c'est de cette forme qu'il parlait comme de son prosôpon et de la divinité. le prosôpon (en effet) est commun, unique et le même. la forme du serviteur appartient à la divinité et celle de la divinité à l'humanité. un et le même (est le) prosôpon, mais (il n'en est pas de même pour) l'essence. car l'essence de la forme de dieu et l'essence de la forme du serviteur demeurent dans leurs hypostases*, ib.1.3.252(p.152); by π. Nest. means approximately what Cyr. means by an individual and particular *φύσις* or *οὐσία*; to Cyr. and others the *ὑπόστασις* is the external representation of the *οὐσία*; hence Nest.'s use of π. appears to Cyr. to signify *assumed character* or *dramatic part*, thus: *γέγονεν ἄνθρωπος...οὐδὲ ὡς ἐν προσλήψει προσώπου μόνου* Cyr.*ep*.4(p.27.1; 5².23B); *ὀνήσει δὲ κατ' οὐδένα τρόπον τὸν ὀρθὸν τῆς πίστεως λόγον εἰς τὸ οὕτως ἔχειν, κἂν εἰ προσώπων ἕνωσιν ἐπιφημίζωσί τινες· οὐ γὰρ εἴρηκεν ἡ γραφὴ ὅτι ὁ λόγος ἀνθρώπου π. ἥνωσεν ἑαυτῷ, ἀλλ' ὅτι γέγονε σάρξ* ib.(p.28.12; 24D); *ἐπειδὴ σκοπὸς ἐκείνοις δύο λέγειν Χριστοὺς...τὸν μέν, ἄνθρωπον ἰδικῶς, τὸν δέ, θεὸν ἰδικῶς, εἶτα μόνων τῶν π. ποιοῦσιν τὴν ἕνωσιν* ib.10 (p.110.31; 33D); acc. Nest. *πάντα...ὑπέταξεν ὑπὸ τοὺς πόδας αὐτοῦ· καὶ ἀπ' αὐτοῦ τῷ θείῳ λόγῳ, οὗ τὸ π. ἐπέχει* Leont.H.*Nest*.3.8(M.86. 1629B); *εἰς φανέρωσιν τοῦ λόγου ταύτην λέγοντες εἶναι τὴν ἕνωσιν, καὶ εἰς π. οὐκ οἶδα πῶς ἀποκαλοῦντες αὐτήν. τῷ γάρ, φησί, τὸ π. ἐπέχειν τοῦ λόγου τὸν Χριστόν, ταύτην ἴσμεν* ib.(1633D); cf. later Nestorian teaching *πολλάκις δὲ τὸ π. τῆς ὑποστάσεως διακρίνουσι, π. καλοῦντες τήν τινων σχέσιν πρὸς ἄλληλα...ἔνθεν καὶ οἱ τῶν Νεστορίου δογμάτων κατήκοοι οὔτε φύσιν μίαν ἐπὶ Χριστοῦ οὔτε ὑπόστασιν λέγειν ἀνεχόμενοι...ὅμως θαρροῦντως ἓν εἶναι τοῦ Χριστοῦ π. διϊσχυρίζονται, τὴν σχέσιν τοῦ θεοῦ λόγου πρὸς τὸν ἐκ Μαρίας ἄνθρωπον μίαν οὖσαν π. ἐν λέγοντες, ἐπεὶ πᾶσαν ἐκεῖνος τὴν...οἰκονομίαν εἰς π. ἐποιεῖτο τῆς τοῦ ...λόγου θεότητος* Jo.Philop.*arb*.ap.*Doct.Patr*.36(p.279); Anast.Ap. *fr*.ap.*Doct.Patr*.(p.38.18; M.74.749C); Jo.D.*dial*.65(M.94.664B); and use of *ὁ λαβών* and *ὁ ληφθείς* derived from Thdr. Mops. (cf.Thdr. Mops.*symb*.(p.99.3; M.66.1017D) cit. s. *συναναφέρω*) which suggested a doctrine of two distinct *ὑποστάσεις* or *πρόσωπα* incapable of true union; this rejected by Cyr. *ἑνὶ...π. τὰς ἐν τοῖς εὐαγγελίοις πάσας ἀναθετέον φωνάς, ὑποστάσει μιᾷ τῇ τοῦ λόγου σεσαρκωμένῃ* Cyr.*ep*.17 (p.38.21; 5².73D); usage of Thdt. (cf. B supra) *ὑπόστασιν καὶ τὸ π. καὶ τὴν ἰδιότητα ταὐτὸν σημαίνειν φαμέν* Thdt.*eran*.1(4.8); *εἰ τοίνυν ἑκατέρα φύσις τὸ τέλειον ἔχει, εἰς ταὐτὸν δὲ συνῆλθον ἀμφότεραι, τῆς τοῦ θεοῦ μορφῆς δηλονότι λαβούσης τὴν τοῦ δούλου μορφήν, ἓν μὲν π. καὶ ἕνα υἱὸν...ὁμολογεῖν εὐσεβές, δύο δὲ τὰς ἑνωθείσας ὑποστάσεις εἴτουν φύσεις λέγειν οὐκ ἄτοπον* id.ap.Cyr.*apol.Thdt*.3(p.117.16; 6¹. 211A); *θεότητος γὰρ ἡμεῖς καὶ ἀνθρωπότητος τοιαύτην κηρύττομεν ἕνωσιν, ὡς ἐννοεῖν ἐν π. ἀδιαίρετον, καὶ τὸν αὐτὸν θεόν τε εἰδέναι καὶ ἄνθρωπον...καὶ...πάντα ὅσα τῆς θεότητος καὶ τῆς ἀνθρωπότητος ὑπάρχει δηλωτικά, τῶν π. τῷ ἑνὶ προσαρμόττομεν* Thdt.*eran*.3(4. 203).

προσωποποι-έω, **1.** *introduce as a character* into drama or narrative *ὁ Κελσὸς οὐ ~εῖ Ἰουδαῖον πρὸς τοὺς ἀπὸ τῶν ἐθνῶν πιστεύοντας λέγοντα* Or.*Cels*.2.1(p.126.7; M.11.792C); *οὐκ ἂν ἐπροσωποποιήσατο τὸν Ἰουδαῖον* ib.(p.128.2; 796C); *ἀρετὴ μὲν ~οῦντός ἐστι τηρῆσαι τὸ βούλημα καὶ τὸ ἦθος τοῦ ~ουμένου* ib.7.36(p.187.1; 1472B); *~εῖ τὸ πνεῦμα...ἐν τοῖς προφήταις, καὶ ἐὰν ~ήσῃ τὸν θεόν, οὐκ ἔστιν ὁ θεὸς ὁ λαλῶν, ἀλλὰ τὸ...πνεῦμα ἐκ προσώπου τοῦ θεοῦ λαλεῖ* id.*fr.in Ac*.ap. *philoc*.7.2(p.51.23ff.; M.14.832A); Cyr.*Juln*.2(6².59C); ref. Sabellian doctrine *ἕνα μὲν εἶναι τῇ ὑποστάσει τὸν θεόν, ~εῖσθαι δὲ ὑπὸ τῆς γραφῆς διαφόρως, κατὰ τὸ ἰδίωμα τῆς ὑποκειμένης ἑκάστοτε χρείας* Bas.*ep*.214. 3(3.322C; M.32.788C); **2.** *speak in character, deliver a part* *τῷ μώλωπι αὐτοῦ ἡμεῖς ἰάθημεν...οἱ...ἰαθέντες...ταῦτα λέγουσι παρὰ τῷ προφήτῃ ...ἀπὸ ἁγίου πνεύματος ταῦτα ~ήσαντι* Or.*Cels*.1.55(p.106.20; M.11. 761C); Eus.*p.e*.7.12(321A; M.21.541C); **3.** med., *assume character of*, of Christ *τὸ τῶν ἀνθρώπων ~εῖται ταπεινόν* Mac.Mgn.*apocr*.3.9(p.71. 8); **4.** *represent the part of* *~ούμενος* [sc. *Συμεών*] *τὸν νόμον* ‡Meth. *Sym.et Ann*.11(M.18.376A); **5.** *represent as personal, personify*, Eus. *p.e*.3.10(104D; M.21.189B); Ast.Am.*hom*.4(M.40.216C); Chrys.*hom. 22.4 in Mt*.(7.279D); *Σιρὰχ...~ήσας τὴν σοφίαν* Isid.Pel.*epp*.4.228(M. 78.1324A); **6.** *make personal, endow with a personal subject*, Christol. *τῇ γὰρ ἰδίᾳ ὑποστάσει αὐτὴν* [sc. *σάρκα*] *ἀνειληφὼς ἐπροσωποποίησεν* Leont.H.*Nest*.5.25(M.86.1748A); *ἐξ ἀρχῆς ὑπάρξεως αὐτῆς ἐπὶ τῆς τοῦ λόγου ~ηθῆναι ὑποστάσεως εἰς Χριστόν* ib.1.29(1496A).

***προσωποποίησις**, **ἡ**, *speaking in person, making personal observations, Schol.* in Jo.Clim.*scal*.27(M.88.1101C).

προσωποποιΐα, **ἡ**, **1.** *dramatization*, Clem.*str*.3.6(p.222.10; M.8. 1160C); Or.*Cels*.1.34(p.85.16; M.11.725A); Thdt.*qu.68 in 3Reg*.(1. 511); **2.** *personification*; of inanimate objects, Chrys.*Is.interp*.3:26 (6.48C); Thdt.*Is*.5:14(p.26.17; 2.201); ref. scriptural anthropomorphisms *μολύνει δὲ τὰ ἐνδύματα αὐτοῦ, ὥσπερ ἐρυθρὰ γενέσθαι αὐτὰ λέγεται π. ἐμφατικῇ* Eus.*Is*.63:2(M.24.501D); Didym.*Rom*.7(p.1. 24); ib.(p.2.20); Proc.G.*Is*.1:20(M.87.1853A).

προσωποποιός, *representative*; of Anna (Lc.2:38) as representative of Church, ‡Meth.*Sym.et Ann*.11(M.18.376A).

προσωρεύω, *store up in advance*, Cyr.*glaph.Ex*.2(1.292A); id. *Juln*.2(6².38B).

προταλαιπωρέω, **1.** *suffer for* *τοῦ καλοῦ προταλαιπωρήσαντες* Gr. Naz.*or*.21.9(M.35.1089C); **2.** *suffer previously*, Malchus *exc.Rom*.1 (p.161.29; M.113.765D).

***προταπεινόομαι**, *be humbled first*, Nil.*exerc*.15(M.79.737B).

***προτέκτωρ**, **ὁ**, (Lat. *protector*) **1.** *member of magistrate's body of guards, serjeant* *ἀναγγέλλει...τῷ...ἐπάρχῳ, ὃς ὠμούς τινας...π. καὶ ταξεώτας...ἐξαπέστειλε* ‡Pall.*h.mon*.21.9(p.81.11; M.34.1171D); *π. ἀπὸ ἐπάρχων τυγχάνων* *A.Pil*.A proem.(p.210); *π. τῶν γενναιοτάτων ἀριθμοῦ Μαρτησίων* *CIG* 9449 (c. 518); **2.** *member of imperial bodyguard* *ὁ δέ γε τῶν μεθορίων λεγόμενος π.* (*δηλοῖ δὲ παρὰ Ῥωμαίοις τὸν ἐς τοῦτο καταλεγόμενον ἀξίας, τὸν βασίλειον προσκεπαστήν*) Men.*exc. Rom*.19(p.216.26; M.113.920C); *αἱ σχολαὶ καὶ οἱ π. καὶ οἱ ἀριθμοὶ καὶ πᾶσα ἡ σύγκλητος* Thphn.*chron*.p.197(M.108.512A).

προτελειόομαι, *be initiated previously*, Gr.Nyss.*Spir*.(M.46.697B).

προτέλειος, **1.** *beyond perfection*; of God and divine attributes, Dion.Ar.*c.h*.3.2(M.3.165C); ib.4.1(177D); *ὑπερτελὴς καὶ π.* id.*d.n*.2. 10(M.3.648C); ib.7.2(869A); ‡Cyr.*Trin*.4(6³.5E; M.77.1128B); Jo.D. *Jacob*.78(M.94.1476B); id.*hom*.1.8(M.96.560B); of incarnate Christ *ἐν πᾶσιν αὐτὸς τέλειος καὶ π.* Anast.S.*serm.imag*.3(M.89.1161A); **2.** neut. plur. as subst., *preliminary ceremonies*; of raising of Lazarus, in rel. to gen. resurrection *τὰ π. τῆς...ἀναστάσεως* Gr.Nyss.*hom.opif*.25 (M.44.220D).

προτέλεσμα, **τό**, plur., *preliminary ceremonies*, Gr.Naz.*or*.25.11 (M.35.1213B).

προτελ-έω, **1.** *celebrate* eucharist *before* *~εῖ τοῦ λαοῦ τὰ μυστήρια* Gr.Naz.*or*.18.29(M.35.1021A); **2.** *initiate before* *~ώμεθα τῷ λόγῳ* ib.39.10(M.36.345B); id.*ep*.173(M.37.284A); Proc.G.*Jos*.3:4(M.87. 1004D).

***προτένισμα**, **τό**, *that which is spread forth*, hence *canopy* of heaven, ‡Caes.Naz.*dial*.92(M.38.956).

προτερεύ-ω (**πρωτ-**), *be before* in time, *precede* *μόσχου* [i.e. Church] *πρωτερεύει ταῦρος* [i.e. Israel] *κατὰ τὸν χρόνον* Cyr.*Is*.2.1(2.199E); ref. Manich. principles of good and evil *σύγχρονα γὰρ ἄμφω καὶ* συναγέννητα ὄντα τὸν τοῦ ~ειν ἀλλήλοις διαφθείρει λόγον Tit.Bost. *Man.*1.7(M.18.1077D); ἐπεὶ...συμβεβηκός ἐστιν τὸ ἀγαθὸν ἐπὶ τῶν γενητῶν, πάντως ἐπὶ τούτων ~ει τὸ εἶναι τὸ ἀγαθόν *Disp.Phot.*(M.88. 573D); ref. Logos τῶν ὁμογενῶν ἐστι πρωτότοκος, ὡς ὁ Ῥουβὶμ τῶν μετ' ἐκεῖνον ἀριθμουμένων ~ων Gr.Nyss.*Eun.*4(2; p.62.3; M.45. 633A); id.*Apoll.*44(M.45.1229D); theol., ref. Son οὐ γὰρ ὥσπερ ~ω ἐγὼ...τοῦ ἐμοῦ υἱοῦ, οὕτω καὶ ὁ πατὴρ...προϋπάρχει τοῦ υἱοῦ Hier.H. *Trin.*(M.40.853B); εἰ δὲ λέγομεν τὸν πατέρα ἀρχὴν εἶναι τοῦ υἱοῦ... οὐ ~ειν αὐτὸν τοῦ υἱοῦ χρόνῳ...ὑποφαίνομεν Jo.D.*f.o.*1.8(M.94.820A); of flesh of Christ οὐδὲ ὡς ἐν ὀφθαλμοῦ ῥιπῇ ταύτην [sc. the union] ~ουσαν Sophr.H.*ep.syn.*(M.87.3161B).

προτέρημα, τό, 1. *superiority, advantage,* natural, social, or moral; of Jews under Law, Bas.*reg.fus.*8.2(2.349D; M.31.937B); Chrys.*hom.5.1 in Eph.*(11.32E); of Church opp. Israel, Or.*comm.in 1Cor.*5:5(*JTS* 9 p.364); Chrys.*hom.3.2 in Mt.*(7.36B); Christol., ref. adoptionist doctrine ψιλὸν ἄνθρωπον τῆς κοινῆς ἁπάντων φύσεως κατ' οὐδὲν κρείττονα ἢ ὅσον ἀρετῆς προτερήμασιν γεγονέναι αὐτόν Eus.*e.th.* 1.7(p.65.17; M.24.836B); **2.** *privilege,* of eating of shewbread τῶν ἱερέων ἦν τὸ π. Chrys.*hom.39.1 in Mt.*(7.432E).

***προτερίζω,** *lead forward* in the spiritual life ὁδὸν...τὴν ἐν τῷ ἁγίῳ αὐτοῦ κυρίῳ...ἐνεργοῦσαν καὶ προτερίζουσαν †Gregent.*disp.*(M.86. 752C).

***προτέρως,** *before, formerly, cat.Lc.*8:1(p.64.1).

προτεχνολογέω, *contrive* or *prepare beforehand,* Gr.Nyss.*fat.*(M. 45.173A).

προτηρέω, *observe, note in advance,* Eus.*h.e.*1.6.11(M.20.89B); id. *d.e.*8.1(p.355.19; M.22.577C); *ib.*10 proem.(p.446.17; 717C).

προτίθ-ημι, 1. med., *determine, purpose,* of God ἦλθε δὲ ὁ καιρὸς ὃν...προέθετο *Diogn.*9.2; Or.*princ.*3.1.9(p.208.11; M.11.264A); **2.** liturg., *set forth* in offertory ἄρτον ~έασι [sc. Collyridians] καὶ ἀναφέρουσιν εἰς ὄνομα τῆς Μαρίας Epiph.*haer.*79.1(p.476.18; M.42. 741A); Leont.H.*monoph.*testimonia(M.86.1900B); οἱ δὲ τῆς λειτουργικῆς διακοσμήσεως ἔκκριτοι σὺν τοῖς ἱερεῦσιν ἐπὶ τοῦ...θυσιαστηρίου ~έασι τὸν ἱερὸν ἄρτον καὶ τὸ...ποτήριον Dion.Ar.*e.h.*3.2(M.3.425C); *Lit.Marc.*(Brightman p.133.31); ‡Caes.Naz.*dial.*169(M.38.1132); *Lit. Bas.*(p.327.21).

προτίμησις, ἡ, *penalty,* CCP(381)*ep.*ap.Thdt.*h.e.*5.9.5(3.1028); Gel.Cyz.*h.e.*1.3.2(M.85.1201A).

***προτιμητέος,** *to be preferred, Hom.Clem.*4.1; Bas.*ep.*2.5(3.74A; M.32.229C).

προτιτρώσκω, *wound beforehand*; ref. 'wound of love', Or.*schol. in Cant.*3:1–4(M.17.268D).

προτολμάω, *venture upon* or *risk first,* Geo.Pis.*Pers.*3.66(M.92. 1239B).

προτονίζ-ω, *secure* or *brace* with halyards τὸ κέρας ἐτετρίγει, καὶ ἡμεῖς ᾠόμεθα ~ειν τὴν ναῦν Synes.*ep.*4(M.66.1337A).

***προτρανόομαι,** *be prefigured,* Or.*Jo.*1.19(22; p.24.6; M.14.56D).

προτρεπτικός, *hortatory, instructive* π. γὰρ ἡ πᾶσα θεοσέβεια Clem.*paed.*1.1(p.90.14; M.8.249B); τῷ συμβουλευτικῷ λόγῳ παράκειται τὸ π. καὶ παρακλητικὸν εἶδος *ib.*1.8(p.128.24; 329A); παροιμίαι ...εἰσὶ λόγοι π. ‡Hipp.*fr.33 in Pr.*(p.169.7; M.10.616B); Or.*Cels.*3.45 (p.240.28; M.11.977C); *ib.*8.47(p.262.13; 1588A); Ὠριγένης...διαπέμπεται τῷ πατρὶ προτρεπτικωτάτην περὶ μαρτυρίου ἐπιστολήν Eus.*h.e.* 6.2.6(M.20.524B); χαρίσματα π. εἰσι Mac.Aeg.*hom.*26.16(M.34.685A); opp. βιαστικός, Chrys.*hom.47.4 in Jo.*(8.281C) cit. s. ἐκλογή; Dor. *doct.*17.1(M.88.1800D).

προτρεπτικῶς, *in a hortatory manner,* Clem.*str.*7.11(p.46.3; M.9. 488C); ref. origin of Mc. ἐπιγνόντα τὸν Πέτρον π. μήτε κωλῦσαι μήτε προτρέψασθαι id.*fr.*8(p.196.26; M.9.749C); perh. l. πνευματικῶς, προφανῶς); Nil.*exerc.*31(M.79.760C); superl., Or.*Jo.*32.10(7; p.442.8; M. 14.768A).

προτρέπ-ω, 1. *urge, persuade,* c. dat., Clem.*str.*7.7(p.36.7; M.9. 468C); abs. λόγῳ τῷ ~οντι...χρῆται *ib.*(p.34.4; 464C); *Hom.Clem.*8. 21; Chrys.*hom.20.5 in Eph.*(11.149E); **2.** *invite, summon,* CSard.*ep. Alex.*ap.Ath.*apol.sec.*38(p.117.9; M.25.313D); Constantius Imp.*ib.*51 (p.133.1; 341C); Socr.*h.e.*1.27.8(M.67.153B); Nil.*epp.*2.46(M.79.217C); **3.** *warn, admonish,* CSard.*ep.Alex.*ap.Ath.*apol.sec.*39(p.118.5; M.25. 316C).

προτρίβω, pass., *be rubbed into previously*; fig., Cyr.*hom.pasch.*21 (5^2.265E).

***προτρομέω,** *tremble before,* Gr.Naz.*carm.*1.2.2.365(M.37.607A).

προτροπάδην, 1. *speedily, hastily,* Gr.Naz.*ep.*10(M.37.40A); Isid.Pel.*epp.*1.242(M.78.329D); Thdt.*haer.*5.27(4.471); **2.** *eagerly, zealously,* Meth.*res.*2.4(p.336.5; M.41.1168D); Cyr.*Is.*4.4(2.680C); τοῖς ἐπὶ θεὸν π. ἐπειγομένοις Max.*ambig.*(M.91.1117B).

***πρότυπος,** *prefigurative,* Adam.*dial.*4.5(p.182.23; M.11.1837C).

προτυπ-όω, 1. *impress,* hence fig.; **a.** *sign,* of making the sign of the cross τὸ μὲν σημεῖον δακτύλῳ τοῦ σταυροῦ προετύπωσε Thdt.*h.rel.* 3(3.1140); **b.** *form, mould previously* ἡ Ἑλληνικὴ φιλοσοφία...τὸ ἦθος ~οῦσα Clem.*str.*1.16(p.52.22; M.8.796A); **c.** *plan, devise beforehand* ὁ μὲν ἐκ μακροῦ καὶ προπάλαι τῷ λογισμῷ ταῦτα ~ούμενος Eus.*v.C.*4.60 (p.142.12, v.l. πρυτανευόμενος M.20.1212A); τὸν ἐσόμενον ἀνδριάντα τῇ ἑαυτοῦ προτυπώσας διανοίᾳ Marcell.*fr.*52 ap.Eus.*e.th.*2.15(p.119. 18; M.24.936B); οἱ αὐτοὶ [sc. συγγραφεῖς] ἀλεξητήρια...προετύπωσαν πρὸς ἀθέτησιν τῆς τῶν...ἑρπετῶν μοχθηρίας Epiph.*haer.*proem.3 (p.171.22; M.41.177C); **2.** *set forth as a type* ἡ τοῦ κυρίου σωτηρία καὶ ἀλήθεια ἐν τῷ λαῷ προετυπώθη Mel.*pass.*39 p.6.29; τὴν οὖν ἕνωσιν τοῦ ἱερείου τὴν ἀδιαίρετον ἀναγκαίως ὁ νόμος εἰς Χριστὸν προετύπου ‡Chrys.*pasch.*1(8.252D); *ib.*(253A); ὅνπερ καὶ ἀμνὸν προετύπωσεν ἐν Αἰγύπτῳ Μωϋσῆς ‡Bas.*h.myst.*5(p.259.1); pass., *be set forth as a type,* hence *serve as a type* ἡ Σωσάννα προετυποῦτο εἰς τὴν ἐκκλησίαν, Ἰωακεὶμ δὲ ὁ ἀνὴρ αὐτῆς εἰς τὸν Χριστόν Hipp.*Dan.*1.13.5(M.10. 689C); τρεῖς καιροὶ τοῦ ἐνιαυτοῦ προετυποῦντο εἰς αὐτὸν τὸν σωτῆρα id.*fr.3 in 1Reg.*(p.122.5; M.10.864C); πάντα κατά τινα λόγον εἰς νουθεσίαν τῷ μετὰ ταῦτα προετυποῦτο βίῳ Gr.Nyss.*hom.7 in Cant.*(M.44. 929C); **3.** *foreshow, foreshadow* προφήτας...τὸ μέλλον ἔσεσθαι ~ουμένους Eus.*d.e.*1.10(p.45.21; M.22.85D); περὶ οὗ Ἠλίας τυπικῶς προετύπωσεν Vict.*Mc.*9:3(p.356.25); ἐπὶ τοῦ ἁγίου πνεύματος καὶ τῆς ἐκκλησίας ~ούμενος [sc. ὁ Μωϋσῆς] Cosm.Ind.*top.*5(M.88.245B); **4.** *prefigure* ταῦτα πάλαι προετυποῦτο διὰ τῆς μακαρίας Σωσάννης δι' ἡμᾶς Hipp. *Dan.*1.16.4(διετυποῦτο M.10.693A); πῶς οὖν ἐξελέξατο, πρὶν γενέσθαι ἡμᾶς, εἰ μή, ὡς αὐτὸς εἴρηκεν, ἐν αὐτῷ ἦμεν προτετυπωμένοι; Ath.*Ar.* 2.76(M.26.308B); ὁ Μελχισεδὲκ...ἐξέβαλεν αὐτῷ ἄρτους καὶ οἶνον, ~ῶν τῶν μυστηρίων τὰ αἰνίγματα Epiph.*haer.*55.6(p.331.13; M.41.981A); ἄνωθεν αὐτὰ προτετυπῶσθαι Chrys.*hom.15.2 in Rom.*(9.595D); ~οῦσι δὲ καὶ οἱ ἱερεῖς οἱ αἴροντες τὴν κιβωτὸν τῆς διαθήκης κυρίου τὸν βαπτιστὴν Ἰωάννην Thdt.*qu.2 in Jos.*(1.304); πυρρὰν δὲ προσκομισθῆναι κελεύει δάμαλιν ἵνα ~ώσῃ τὸ γήινον σῶμα id.*qu.35 in Num.*(1.243); προετύπου διὰ τῆς ἐσωτέρας σκηνῆς τὴν ἄνοδον τοῦ δεσπότου Χριστοῦ κατὰ σάρκα Cosm.Ind.*top.*5(M.88.208B); ref. Ex.16:24 ὁ καιρὸς οὗτος τὸ τῆς ταφῆς τοῦ οὐρανίου ἄρτου προετύπου μυστήριον Germ.CP *or.*2 (M.98.264C); τὸν τίμιον σταυρὸν προετύπωσε τὸ ξύλον τῆς ζωῆς Jo.D. *f.o.*4.11(M.94.1132C); σὲ [sc. BMV] προετύπου στάμνος ἡ μαννοδόχος, ὑπέραγνε, τὴν θεοδόχον τράπεζαν Jo.Mon.*hymn.Nic.Myr.*3(M.96. 1384D); τὸ καταπέτασμα τὸ συσκιάζον κατὰ πρόσωπον τῆς προτυπωσάσης σε [sc. BMV] κιβωτοῦ διαθήκης ‡Meth.*Sym.et Ann.*5(M.18. 357D); **5.** *symbolize* τριμερὴς δὲ ἡ ψυχὴ ἡ ἐν αὐτῷ ~οῦσα τὴν ἁγίαν τριάδα Anast.S.*hod.*2(M.89.80B); **6.** *ordain, prescribe previously* εἴκειν πᾶσι τοῖς προτετυπωμένοις κανόσι καθ' ὁμοιότητα τῶν ἐπισκόπων Ἀμμωνιανοῦ Arsen.Hyps.*ep.*(p.147.20; M.25.372C); διὰ τῆς κβ' γραμμάτων ὑποθέσεως ἐξ ὧν ὁ νόμος τοῦ θεοῦ ἡμῶν παρέστη καὶ θεοῦ διδασκαλία ἡμῖν προτετύπωται Epiph.*mens.*24(M.43.280C); Socr.*h.e.* 2.37.17(M.67.304C); **7.** *conform* φύσει πᾶν ἐστι πλῆθος ἀνθρώπων δύσαρχόν τε καὶ δυσήνιον· καὶ μάλιστα τὸ μηδέπω τοῖς ἤθεσι τοῖς κάλοῖς ~ωθέν, ἢ νόμοις ὀρθοῖς εἰς ἀρίστην πολιτείαν ἐμβιβασθέν Athenod.*fr.* ap.Leont.et Jo.*sacr.*2(M.86.2089A).

προτύπωμα, τό, *prefiguration* νόμος ὁ διὰ Μωϋσέως, θεοσεβείας τὸ π. ‡Chrys.*pasch.*6(p.135.10; 8.267A); ὁμοίωμα καὶ π. τοῦ υἱοῦ τοῦ θεοῦ ἐν τῇ καμίνῳ τῶν παίδων προεξεικονίσθη Ephr.Ant.*fr.*(M.86.2108B); Anast.S.*qu.et resp.*78(M.89.708B); Germ.CP *or.*1(M.98.236A).

προτύπωσις, ἡ, *prefiguration* ὅλη γὰρ ἡ εἰκὼν ἐκείνη π. ἦν τῆς τοῦ ἀντιχρίστου παρουσίας Iren.*haer.*5.29.2(M.7.1202C); Adam.*dial.*1.11 (p.26.11; M.11.1736D); οὔτε ἡ ψυχὴ προϋπάρχει τοῦ σώματος π. οὖσα τῆς ἑνώσεως τοῦ κυρίου ‡Ath.*def.*5(M.28.545A) = Anast.S.*hod.*2(M.89. 69D); Bas.*Spir.*33(3.28A; M.32.128A); ἦν [sc. manna]...τοῦ παρόντος μυστηρίου π. Germ.CP *or.*2(M.98.264A); ἧς ἦν τῷ Μωσῇ παραδειχθεῖσα [sc. σκηνή] τύπος, μᾶλλον δὲ π. τύπου τῆς σήμερον ἐκκλησίας τύπος τυγχάνουσα Andr.Caes.*Apoc.*65(M.106.425B).

***προυνικεύ-ω,** *debauch,* ref. Gnost. teaching on Prunicus πᾶν γὰρ τὸ ~όμενον λαγνείας ὑποφαίνει τὸ ἐπώνυμον...ἐπὶ τοῖς γὰρ τὰ σώματα διακορεύουσιν Ἑλληνική τίς ἐστι λέξις τό, ἐπρουνίκευσε τήνδε Epiph.*haer.*25.4(p.271.7; M.41.325A); *ib.*37.6(p.58.12; 649A).

προυνικία, ἡ, *sexual desire* ἡ Ἀλήθεια μητρικὴν προενεγκαμένη π. ἐθήλυνε τὸν πατέρα ἑαυτῆς εἰς ἑαυτὴν καὶ συνήεσαν ἑαυτοῖς Val.Gn. ap.Epiph.*haer.*31.5(p.392.2; M.41.481C).

***Προύνικος, ἡ, 1.** name of aeon representing sexual knowledge, cf. *ex primo angelo, qui adstat Monogeni, emissum dicunt* [sc. Barbeliote Gnostics] *spiritum sanctum, quem et Sophiam et Prunicum vocant,* Iren.*haer.*1.29.4(M.7.693B); *virtutem...quam et sinistram, et Prunicon, et Sophiam, et masculo-feminam vocant* [sc. Ophites], *ib.*1.30.3(695C); *Adam...et Evam...corpora...demutasse in obscurius...quoadusque Prunicos miserata eorum, reddidit eis* *odorem suavitatis...post quos secundum providentiam Prunici dicunt generatum Seth*, *ib.*1.30.9(700A); Ἔννοιαν, ἥτις ἐστὶν αὐτὴ ἡ καὶ π. καὶ πνεῦμα ἅγιον καλουμένη Simon ap.Epiph.*haer.*21.2(p.240.5; M.41.288B); identified by Simonians with Helena, *ib.*(p.240.7; 288B); acc. Nicolaitans Π. δὲ ἄλλοι τιμῶντές τινα...τῆς Π. τὴν δύναμιν συλλέγομεν ἀπὸ τῶν σωμάτων, διά τε τῶν ῥευστῶν...γονῆς καὶ καταμηνίων *ib.*25.2(p.269.24; 324B); acc. Ophites Ἰαλδαβαὼθ... προβεβλῆσθαι κατὰ...ἄγνοιαν τῆς ἰδίας μητρὸς...τῆς ἄνω Π. *ib.*37.3 (p.54.3; 645B); ἀναδεικνύουσι [sc. Valentinians] δωδεκάδα Π. ἀρρενοθηλύντων *ib.*31.5(p.392.8; 484A); acc. Barbeliote Gnostics, Thdt. *haer.*1.13(4.305); **2.** π., ὁ, in phrase ἡ προυνίκου σοφία, *art of the stenographer*, Gr.Nyss.*Eun.*1(1 p.37.1; M.45.264C); *ib.*12(1 p.366.10; 1089C); κατὰ τὸν παιδευτὴν αὐτοῦ [sc. Eunomius] προύνικον *ib.*9 (2 p.212.16; 809D) perh. in allusion to speed of a hired porter (= π., *LS*).

***προϋπαγορεύομαι**, *be dictated, composed previously*, Or.*Jo.*6.2 (p.108.17,21; M.14.201B).

***προϋπαινίσσομαι**, *bear a hidden significance for the future* τοῦτο γὰρ [sc. Inc.] ἡ Μωϋσέως προϋπῃνίσσετο βάτος ‡Jo.D.*hom.*6. 10(M.96.677B).

***προϋπαρκτῖται, οἱ**, Origenist *believers in pre-existence* of soul, Thdr.Stud.*epp.*2.199(M.99.1601B).

***προϋπαρξις, ἡ, A.** *pre-existence*; **1.** of creator opp. creation, ‡Just.*qu.Chr.*7(M.6.1424D); **2.** of universe; denied in apostolic teaching, Cosm.Ind.*top.*5(M.88.284A); **3.** of souls in Origen's doctrine πατράσι...τὴν τῶν ψυχῶν π. ἀναιροῦσι Justn.*Or.*(p.194.19; M. 86.955C); *ib.*(p.196.11; 959B); εἴ τις τὴν μυθώδη π. τῶν ψυχῶν... πρεσβεύει· ἀ. ἔ. CCP(543)*anath.*1; †Leont.B.*sect.*10.5(M.86.1264D); *ib.*10.6(1265C); Cyr.S.*v.Sab.*30(p.124.28); Max.*ambig.*(M.91.1220C); ἡ...πέμπτη σύνοδος κατὰ...Ὠριγένους τοῦ φήσαντος π. ... ψυχῶν *CIG* 8963 (Bethlehem); **4.** of Christ, Eus.*d.e.*6.13(p.266.17; M.22.437B); *ib.*7.1(p.305.16; 500B); ref. Dan.2:35 τοῦ...ὄρους τὴν π. τῆς θεότητος αὐτοῦ σημαίνοντος id.*e.th.*1.20(p.94.25; M.24.889B); Thdr.Mops.*Ps.* 71:17(p.476.8; M.66.692B); Trin. Πλάτων φησὶν ὅτι πατρότης ἐστὶ π. υἱότητος Anast.S.*hod.*1(M.89.49D).

B. *state which is prior to all existence* ὕπαρξις μὲν κυρίως ἐπὶ θεοῦ οὐ λέγεται· καὶ γάρ ἐστι π., τουτέστι καὶ πρὸ αὐτῆς τῆς ὑπάρξεως Max. *schol.d.n.*2.1(M.4.212A).

***προϋπαρχόντως**, *in pre-existent state*, ‡Chrys.*pasch.*6(p.171.4; 8.271A).

προϋπάρχ-ω, A. *be present before*, Eus.*d.e.*2.1(p.53.19; M.22. 97D); Bas.*hom.in Ps.*61(1.196E; M.29.477C); Thdt.*1Tim.*2:1(3.646).

B. *exist before, pre-exist*; **1.** in gen. δεῖ...τὸ...ποιοῦν τοῦ γινομένου ∼ειν Eun.*apol.*7(M.30.841C); ref. S. Paul's spiritual children ὁ αὐτὸς...λέγοιτό τις τῶν...μαθητῶν προεῖναί τε τοῦ...πατρὸς...καὶ μετεῖναι...ἀλλὰ κατ' ἄλλο καὶ ἄλλο τὸν αὐτὸν τοῦ αὐτοῦ ∼ειν τε καὶ μεθυπάρχειν Leont.H.*Nest.*4.3(M.86.1657A); Max.*ambig.*(M.91. 1100C); **2.** of wisdom in rel. to Creation, Gel.Cyz.*h.e.*2.17.21(M.85. 1269B); of λόγοι of all things as pre-existent in God, Max.*ambig.*(M. 91.1329A); **3.** denied of created universe οὔτε προϋπάρξαντα, γενόμενα δὲ ἐξ οὐκ ὄντων Epiph.*exp.fid.*14(p.514.23; M.42.809A); **4.** of Father in rel. to Son, Eus.*d.e.*5.1(p.213.29; M.22.353D) cit. s. ἀνάρχως; acc. Arians ∼ειν τοῦ υἱοῦ τὸν πατέρα Marcell.*ep.*ap.Epiph.*haer.*72.2 (p.257.15; M.42.385B); οὐ γὰρ ἔκ τινος ἀρχῆς ∼ούσης ὁ πατὴρ καὶ ὁ υἱὸς ἐγεννήθησαν, ἵνα καὶ ἀδελφοὶ νομισθῶσιν Ath.*Ar.*1.14(M.26.41A); cf.id.*decr.*18(p.15.15; M.25.'456'(448)A); οὐ γὰρ ὥσπερ προτερεύω...τοῦ ἐμοῦ υἱοῦ, οὕτω καὶ ὁ πατὴρ...∼ει τοῦ υἱοῦ Hier.H.*Trin.*(M.40.853B); Cyr.*thes.*5 tit.(5^1.33B); Gel.Cyz.*h.e.*2.15.1(M.85.1257B); τριάδα ἀληθῶς τριάδα, καὶ μηδὲν ἐν αὐτῇ ∼ον *ib.*2.22.6(1292B); of Son's existence before Creation, Eus.*e.th.*3.3(p.151.22; M.24.992C); **5.** of Son in rel. to Inc. προϋπῆρχεν υἱὸς τοῦ ποιητοῦ...θεὸς ὤν, καὶ γεγένηται ἄνθρωπος διὰ τῆς παρθένου Just.*dial.*48.2(M.6.580B); θεὸν αὐτὸν ∼οντα *ib.* 87.2(684A); μήτε προϋπάρξαντα μετὰ ταῦτα τέλος ἐσχηκέναι Meth. *symp.*8.9(p.91.10; M.18.152B); denied by Ebionites, Eus.*h.e.*3.27.3 (M.20.273B); τὴν ἔνσαρκον ὑπέμεινεν οἰκονομίαν, προὼν μὲν αὐτῆς καὶ ∼ων id.*e.th.*1.13(p.74.2; M.24.852C); ref. Jo.1:15 δέδεικται...∼ων τῆς Ἰωάννου γενέσεως ὁ...ἔμπροσθεν αὐτοῦ γεγονώς *ib.*1.20(p.83.15; 869B); Ath.*Ar.*2.53(M.26.260A); Thdt.*eran.*2(3.99); **6.** of Christ's humanity, ref. Apollinarian doctrine καὶ ∼ει ὁ ἄνθρωπος Χριστὸς... ὡς τοῦ κυρίου ἐν τῇ τοῦ θεοῦ ἀνθρώπου φύσει θείου πνεύματος ὄντος Apoll.*fr.*32(p.211.25)ap.Gr.Nyss.*Apoll.*12(M.45.1145D); συνεπινοεῖ τῷ ἐν ἀρχῇ ὄντι λόγῳ τὸν φανέντα ἄνθρωπον, ὡς ∼οντα πρὸ τῆς φανερώσεως Gr.Nyss.*ib.*13(1148A); ἰδοὺ τοῦ αὐτοῦ...Χριστοῦ ἡ πρὸς πατέρα ἰσότης ∼ουσα, ἡ πρὸς ἀνθρώπους ὁμοιότης ἐπιγινομένη Apoll. *fr.*42(p.214.2, v.l. ὑπάρχουσα)*ib.*22(1168B); θεὸς προσέλαβε τὸ...νοερὸν αὐτοῦ σῶμα, οὐ προϋπάρξαν, ἀλλ' ἐν αὐτῷ ἐσχηκὸς τὴν ὕπαρξιν Mod. *dorm.*13(M.86.3309B); ref. Nestorianism οὐ γὰρ δή, ὡς Νεστόριος βούλεται, καὶ προϋπῆρξε τὸ ἀνθρώπινον τοῦ κυρίου, εἶτα ἑνοῦται Leont.H.*monoph.*52(M.86.1797C); ref. monophysitism ἡ σὰρξ ∼ει τῆς παρθένου, ἢ ὁ...λόγος μεθυπάρχει τῆς παρθένου id.*Nest.*4.10(M.86. 1672A); ἐροῦμεν ὡς ἐκ δύο μὲν τῆς τε θείας καὶ τῆς...ἀνθρωπείας ἄμφω ∼ουσῶν τῆς ἑνώσεως Χριστοῦ φαμεν id.*monoph.*58(1801B); **7.** acc. Simonians, of ∼ουσα δύναμις as first principle, Simon ap.Hipp. *haer.*6.18(p.144.20; M.16.3222A); **8.** of angels in rel. to Creation; denied, Thdt.*qu.3–4 in Gen.*(1.4ff.); **9.** of νοῦς δημιουργικός as pre-existent and bringing universe into being; doctrine anathematized, CCP(543)*anath.*6; **10.** of souls (Origenist), Justn.*Or.*(p.192.31; M.86. 953A); *ib.*(p.196.5; 959A); †Leont.B.*sect.*10.6(M.86.1265D); (Platonist) of souls of animals, *ib.*; τῶν ματαιοφρόνων ληρωδούντων ∼ειν τῶν σωμάτων ἡμῶν τὰς ψυχὰς ἐν οὐρανοῖς Eulog.*fr.Trin.*(M.86.2944B); **11.** of divine love ὁ ἀγαθοεργὸς τῶν ὄντων ἔρως, ἐν τἀγαθῷ καθ' ὑπερβολὴν ∼ων Dion.Ar.*d.n.*4.10(M.3.708B).

***προϋπαυγάζω**, *begin to shine*; ref. Cross as glory of the Lord, Germ.CP *or.*1(M.98.221D).

προϋπειμι, *exist previously*, Ammon.*Ac.*19:5(M.85.1573B); of divine unity αἱ διακρίσεις τῶν στοιχείων, προϋποῦσαι, σύνδρομοι γινόμεναι..., δευτέρας τὰς...ἑνώσεις ἐργάζονται· ἐπὶ δὲ τῶν θείων οὐχ οὕτως· ἐπὶ αὐτῶν γὰρ προϋποῦσα ἡ ἕνωσις τὰς διακρίσεις βουλήματι δευτέρας ποιεῖ Max.*schol.d.n.*2.11(M.4.233A); Trin. μηδὲ προϋπῆν ὁ πατὴρ τοῦ υἱοῦ id.*ambig.*(M.91.1264B); of soul τινες προϋπεῖναι τὴν ψυχὴν λέγουσι τοῦ σώματος. πῶς γὰρ...ἐνδέχεται λέγεσθαι ἀγαθὸν τὸν μηδὲ ὄντα;...ἐροῦμεν· εἰ προϋποῦσα ἡ ψυχή, διὰ τὴν ἐν ἀσωμάτῳ διαγωγῇ ἁμαρτίαν...ἐνεβλήθη εἰς τὸ σῶμα, ἵνα παιδευθῇ...πῶς μακαρία ἦν ἡ ἁμαρτοῦσα; Olymp.*Eccl.*4:2–3(M.93.525A).

***προϋπεξάγω**, *lead away secretly beforehand*, Gr.Naz.*or.*4.64(M. 35.585B).

***προϋπερβατικός**, *transcending*, ‡Gr.Nyss.*Ar.et Sab.*4(M.45. 1285B).

***προϋπέχω**, *interpose as defence*, ‡Caes.Naz.*dial.*109(M.38.984).

προϋποβάλλω, med., *lay as a foundation*; met., Gr.Nyss.*Eun.*1 (1 p.77.1; M.45.308B); pass., Or.*Cels.*4.13(p.283.8; M.11.1044A).

προϋποδείκνυμι, **1.** *show* or *point out beforehand*, Cyr.*Joel.*5(3. 202B); **2.** *announce beforehand*, Aen.*dial.*(M.85.916B).

προϋπόκειμαι, *be pre-existent, be in existence already*; **1.** of matter, acc. Greek thought εἰ...ὕλη τις προϋπέκειτο ἀγένητος οὖσα, τίς ἄρα ἦν ὁ ταύτην μετασκευάζων; Thphl.Ant.*Autol.*2.6(M.6.1056B); ἄλλοι δέ, ἐν οἷς...Πλάτων, ἐκ προϋποκειμένης καὶ ἀγενήτου ὕλης πεποιηκέναι τὸν θεὸν τὰ ὅλα διηγοῦνται· μὴ ἂν γὰρ δύνασθαί τι ποιῆσαι ...εἰ μὴ προϋπέκειτο ἡ ὕλη· ὥσπερ καὶ τῷ τέκτονι προϋποκεῖσθαι δεῖ τὸ ξύλον...τοῦτο λέγοντες...ἀσθένειαν περιτιθέασι τῷ θεῷ Ath.*inc.*2.3(M. 25.100A); Thdt.*Trin.*9(M.75.1157C); **2.** Trin., in comparison of generation of Logos with emission of scent by flowers οὔτι πω κατὰ ...διαίρεσιν τοῦ προϋποκειμένου Eus.*d.e.*4.3(p.154.5; M.22.257A); ref. objections to *homoousion*: ἐπιλέγουσιν· ἐὰν οὖν ὁ υἱὸς ὁμοούσιος... τῷ πατρί, ἀνάγκη προϋποκεῖσθαι αὐτῶν οὐσίαν, ἐξ ἧς καὶ ἐγεννήθησαν Ath.*syn.*51(p.275.3; M.26.784C); οὔτε γὰρ ἐξ οὐκ ὄντων τὸν υἱὸν λέγειν ...οὔτε μὴν ἐξ ἑτέρας τινὸς ὑποστάσεως παρὰ τὸν πατέρα προϋποκειμένης Symb.Ant.(345)3(p.252.12; M.26.729A); acc. Eunomians εἰ... τὸν υἱὸν ἐκ τῆς τοῦ πατρὸς οὐσίας προεληλυθότ αλέγειν, ἀνάγκη...προϋποκεῖσθαι τοῦτον ἐν αὐτῷ Cyr.*thes.*6(5^1.44C); **3.** of man's original goodness preceding Fall, id.*dogm.*5(p.555.13; 6^2.372B); **4.** ref. free will αὐτεξούσιον...γεγονέναι τὸν ἄνθρωπον· οὐχ ὡς προϋποκειμένου τινὸς ἤδη κακοῦ Meth.*arbitr.*17(p.189.10; M.18.265A); **5.** of faith which must precede baptismal grace, Gr.Nyss.*Maced.*19(M.45.1325A); **6.** of spiritual capacity necessary for reception of prophetic inspiration, †Bas.*Is.*proem.2(2.379B; M.30.121A).

***προϋπομιμνήσκω**, *give timely reminder*, Ath.*ep.encycl.*7(p.176. 30; M.25.237B); Cyr.*Am.*73(3.333C).

***προϋπονοέομαι**, *be conceived of previously*, Gr.Nyss.*Eun.*1(1 p.123.24; M.45.360B).

***προϋπόστατος**, *endued with previous personal existence* οὐ γὰρ π. καθ' ἑαυτὴν σαρκὶ ἡνώθη ὁ θεῖος λόγος Jo.D.*f.o.*3.2(M.94.985B).

***προϋποστολή, ἡ**, ? *supporting wall* of vault ἔπεσε τὸ ἀνατολικὸν μέρος τῆς π., καὶ συνέτριψε τὸ κιβούριον σὺν τῇ ἁγίᾳ τραπέζῃ Jo.Mal. *chron.*18 p.489(M.97.708C); Thphn.*chron.*p.197(M.108.509A).

προϋποτάσσω, *set out previously*, Epiph.*haer.*42.12(p.165.2; M.41. 788A).

προϋποτέμνω, *cut off, remove in advance*, Gr.Naz.*or.*4.48(M.35. 573A); Chrys.*pan.Laz.*(2.646B).

***προϋποτύπωσις, ἡ**, *preliminary account*, Or.*comm.in Mt.*12.16 (p.106.33; M.13.1020B).

προϋποφαίν-ω, **1.** *indicate beforehand*; of OT types ,Bas.*Spir.*31

(3.26A; M.32.121C); CTrull.*can.*82; **2.** med., *be just appearing* ὁ βαθὺς ὄρθρος ἴσως ~ομένην αὐγὴν ἑωθινὴν ἐμφανίζει Dion.Al.*ep.can.* (p.99.5; M.10.1276C).

***προϋποχαράττω**, *prefigure*; of manna remaining intact during sabbath as type of incorruptibility of Christ's body, Germ.CP *or.2* (M.98.264C).

***προϋποχρησμῳδέω**, *declare beforehand in an oracle*, Cyr.*Abac.* 19(3.534A).

προῦπτος, *manifest*, neut. as adv., Ammon.*Ac.*27:11(M.85.1600B).

προὔργου, *useful, worth while*, superl. προὐργιαίτατος Cyr.*1Cor.* 12:9(p.290.19).

***προϋφαίνω**, *compose in advance*, Thdt.*ep.*50(4.1108).

***προϋφηγέομαι**, *lead the way*, Meth.*symp.*11(p.131.12; v.l. προαφηγεῖσθαι M.18.208B).

προϋφίστημι, **A.** *establish, bring into existence previously* τί... τὰς ἄλλας λογικὰς δυνάμεις καὶ προϋπέστησεν ὁ θεὸς...τὰς δὲ τῶν ἀνθρώπων ψυχὰς...ἔτι καὶ νῦν προβάλλεται; Aen.*dial.*(M.85.945B); αὐτὸ...καθ' αὑτὸ τὸ εἶναι προϋπεστήσατο, καὶ τῷ εἶναι αὐτῷ πᾶν τὸ ὁπωσοῦν ὂν ὑπεστήσατο Dion.Ar.*d.n.*5.5(M.3.820B); Trin. ἔστι καὶ ἐν τοῖς Θεογνώστῳ πεπονημένοις...εὑρεῖν, ὅς φησι τὸν θεὸν βουλόμενον τόδε τὸ πᾶν κατασκευάσαι πρῶτον τὸν υἱὸν οἷόν τινα κανόνα τῆς δημιουργίας προϋποστήσασθαι Gr.Nyss.*Eun.*4(2 p.86.26; M.45.661D); Gel.Cyz.*h.e.*2.16.3(M.85.1260D).

B. intrans., *exist before, be pre-existent*; **1.** in gen. οὐσία ἐστὶν...τὸ προϋφιστάμενον τοῖς οὖσιν Or.*or.*27(p.368.5; M.11.512B); **2.** of matter, ref. Creation στοιχείων ἢ ὕλης...ἀγενήτως προϋφεστηκότων...ὁ θεὸς διακρίνας ἐτεχνάσατο τὰ πάντα Meth.*creat.*6(p.497.13; M.18.337B); **3.** of archetypes or principles in rel. to Creation ὁμοιώματα τυγχάνει τὰ πρὸς τοῦ υἱοῦ γιγνόμενα ἔργων ἀρχετύπων ἐν ἀπορρήτοις τοῦ πατρὸς λογισμοῖς προϋφισταμένων Eus.*e.th.*3.3(p.155.25; M.24.1000A); ἐν μονάδι πᾶς ἀριθμὸς ἑνοειδῶς προϋφέστηκε Dion.Ar.*d.n.*5.6(M.3.820D); Max.*ambig.*(M.91.1081C); *ib.*(1205C); **4.** of creation of intelligible world in rel. to man's creation τῆς νοητῆς κτίσεως προϋποστάσης... εἶτα κατεσκευάσθη τὸ γήϊνον πλάσμα τῆς ἄνω δυνάμεως ἀπεικόνισμα Gr.Nyss.*or.catech.*6(p.31.12; M.45.28A); of physical universe in rel. to man, Justn.*Or.*(p.193.33; M.86.955A); **5.** Trin.; of Father as antecedent to Son, Eus.*d.e.*5.1(p.213.29; M.22.353D) cit. s. ἀνάρχως; denied, Cyr.*dial.Trin.*2(5^1.446D); *ib.*(449B); ref. generation by Father's will ἐπειδὴ τὸ θέλειν ἐπράττετο σοφῶς δηλονότι...σοφία δέ ἐστι...ὁ υἱός, προϋφεστήξει τοῦ πατρός *ib.*(455A); of Son in rel. to Creation, Eus.*d.e.*4.4(p.154.26; M.22.257D); Cyr.*inc.unigen.*(5^1.685B); **6.** Christol.; **a.** ref. Christ's pre-existence in respect of Inc., denied by Beryllus of Bostra, Eus.*h.e.*6.33.1(M.20.593A); as Son; denied by Marcellus, id.*Marcell.*2.1(p.31.28; M.24.777A); πεφηνότι μὲν ἐν ἐσχάτοις τοῦ αἰῶνος καιροῖς...προϋφεστηκότι δὲ ὡς θεῷ Cyr.*glaph.Gen.*6(1.189B); **b.** ref. Christ's humanity παρὰ μὲν τῆς ὕλης λαβὼν τὸ σῶμα ἤδη προϋποστάσης Gr.Naz.*or.*38.11(M.36.321C); οὐ γὰρ προϋπέστησεν αὐτὸ [i.e. τὸ ἡμέτερον] καὶ τότε ἡνώθη, ἀλλὰ ἀδιαίρετον ἐκ μήτρας ἐποιήσατο τὴν ἕνωσιν *cat.Heb.*7:1(p.538.31); ὁ θεὸς λόγος...οὐ προϋποστάντι ἀνθρώπῳ ἡνώθη Justn.*conf.*(p.74.25; M.86.997B); εἰ δέ τις...ἐπιχειρήσει λέγων...τὴν ἀνθρωπίνην φύσιν...ἰδίαν ὑπόστασιν ἤτοι πρόσωπον ἴδιον ἔχειν, πρόδηλός ἐστιν...ὅτι προϋποστάντι ἀνθρώπῳ ἑνωθῆναι λέγει τὸν λόγον *ib.*(p.88.6; 1011B); σάρκα προσλαβὼν...οὐ προϋποστᾶσαν δὲ τῆς πρὸς αὐτὸν...συνθέσεως Sophr.H.*or.*2.46(M.87.3277C); Max.*ep.*13(M.91.525C); in simile of wood and fire, latter having no hypostatic existence independently of former, and former existing prior to its 'assumption' of latter, †Jo.D.*fr.*(M.95.412C).

***προῦχος**, **ὁ**, *leader, captain*, *M.Areth.*(p.30).

***προφανερόω**, *reveal beforehand*, *Barn.*3.6; *ib.*6.7; *M.Polyc.*14.2.

***προφασιλογία**, **ἡ**, *excuse*, Amph.*hom.*3.1(M.39.60D).

πρόφασις, **ἡ**, **1.** *open utterance, speaking out*, *A.Jo.*68(p.184.2); *ib.*85(p.193.11); **2.** *manner* εἰς τὸ δυνηθῆναι, οἵᾳ δήποτε π., τὴν ἀρετὴν τοῦ ἁγίου ἀνδρὸς διηγήσασθαι Marc.Diac.*v.Porph.*3.

προφασιστικός, *serving as an excuse* or *pretext*, Epiph.*haer.*69.39 (p.187.15; M.42.261D); *ib.*76.31(p.380.27; 580C).

***προφασίστρια**, **ἡ**, *occasioner* φιλαργυρία ἐστὶν...ἀσθενειῶν π. Jo.Clim.*scal.*16(M.88.924D).

***πρόφατον**, **τό**, *exordium, beginning*, tr. Lat. *praefatus*, *Cod.Afr.* 138.

προφέρ-ω, **A.** *bring forth, produce*; **1.** of God's activity in Creation σοφίαν τοῦ θεοῦ...πάντα εἰς τὸν κόσμον ~ειν Meth.*res.*2.9 (p.348.21; M.18.288C); Didym.*Trin.*1.15(M.39.301A); *ib.*2.7(572C); **2.** Valent.; of emission of aeons, Iren.*haer.*1.11.1(M.7.561B); Clem.*exc.Thdot.*2(p.106.4; M.9.653B); *ib.*40(p.119.13; 677C); Val.Gn.ap. Epiph.*haer.*31.5(p.391.8; M.41.481C); **3.** of generation of Logos acc. Marcellus, Bas.*ep.*263.5(3.407B; M.32.981A).

B. *utter*, in Trin. analogies τὴν μονάδα...φύσιν...ῥήμασιν οὔτε προοισθῆναι ἀνεχομένην Didym.*Trin.*2.5(M.39.505A); θεοῦ λόγον... οὐδὲ διὰ φωνῆς ~όμενον Jo.D.*f.o.*1.7(M.94.805A).

πρόφημι, **1.** *say previously*, Eus.*e.th.*1.20(p.85.32; M.24.875B); Max.*prol.Dion.*(M.4.16B); ‡Jo.D.*Artem.*51(p.86.29; M.96.1297C); **2.** *predict*, Eus.*p.e.*1.3(8A; M.21.33A).

προφητεία, **ἡ**, *prophecy*;

I. in gen. (non-religious), Gr.Naz.*ep.*146(M.37.249A); †Nil.*vit.* 3(M.79.1141D).

II. of religious prophesying; **A.** def. and descriptions π. ἐστὶν ἡ διὰ λόγου τῶν ἀφανῶν σημαντικὴ γνῶσις Or.*comm.in 1Cor.*14:6(*JTS* 10 p.36); distn. bet. two kinds of prophecy, the one represented by canonical prophecies of OT, ranking next after apostolic teaching, the other being exercised in primitive Church and resembling other spiritual *charismata*; hence difference in order in which prophecy is named in relation to other gifts in 1Cor.12:8–10, 27–28, id.ad loc.(p.31); various kinds of enthusiastic prophecies indicated by Celsus, in which prophet speaks in character of θεός or θεοῦ παῖς, or πνεῦμα θεῖον; dist. from genuine prophecy, Or.*Cels.*7.9 (p.160.33ff.; M.11.1433B); 'male' and 'female' prophesyings derived from Adam and Eve, *Hom.Clem.*3.23; dist. from dreams, Bas.*ep.* 210.6(3.317D; M.32.777B); χάρισμα δ' οἶδα πνεύματος θείαν δόσιν. κήρυγμ' ἀδήλων, τὴν π. λέγω Gr.Naz.*carm.*1.2.34.231(M.37.962A); εἰ γὰρ ἴδιον σοφίας ἐστὶν ἡ τῆς τῶν ὄντων ἀληθείας κατάληψις, π. δὲ τὴν τῶν μελλόντων περιέχει σαφήνειαν, οὐκ ἂν ἐν τῷ τελείῳ τις τῆς σοφίας εἴη χαρίσματι μὴ διὰ τῆς προφητικῆς συνεργείας συμπεριλαβὼν τῇ γνώσει καὶ τὸ ἐσόμενον Gr.Nyss.*Eun.*3(2 p.16.1; M.45.580C); ἡ π. ἡ διὰ τοῦ τύπου ἢ διὰ πραγμάτων ἐστὶ π., ἡ δὲ ἄλλη π. ἡ διὰ τῶν ῥημάτων ἐστὶ π. Chrys.*poenit.*6.4(2.323D); π. ... τὸ λέγειν, ἢ καὶ τυπικῶς δεικνύναι τὰ προλαβόντα, καὶ ὄντα καὶ ἐσόμενα id.*fr.in Jer.*proem.(M.64.740B); δύο π. εἴδη, καὶ διὰ ἔργων καὶ διὰ λόγων προαναφωνεῖν τὰ μέλλοντα †Chrys.*synops.*(6.317B); τὸ προφητικὸν ἅπαν εἶδος τριχῇ τέμνεται· εἴς τε τὸ μέλλον, τὸ ἐνεστὸς καὶ τὸ παρεληλυθός. π. μὲν γάρ ἐστι καὶ ἡ τοῦ Μωσέως διηγουμένου τὸ κατὰ τὸν Ἀδάμ, καὶ τοὺς ἀνέκαθεν χρόνους· π. δὲ καὶ ἡ τοῦ κεκρυμμένου εὕρεσις...· κυριωτέρα δέ ἐστι π. ἡ τὸ μέλλον προαγορεύουσα Diod.*proem.Pss.*(p.86.11ff.).

B. dist. from Wisdom; Marcellus often called Proverbs προφητεῖαι; Eus. replies: ὁ Σολομὼν σοφίας μὲν εἰληφὼς χάρισμα μεμαρτύρηται... οὔτε...ἐσχηκὼς...τὸν τῆς π. χαρακτῆρα, τὸν ἀπὸ τοῦ τάδε λέγει ὁ κύριος ...γνωριζόμενον Eus.*Marcell.*1.2(p.13.16; M.24.741B).

C. consisting esp. of prediction, cf. *prophetia est praedicatio futurorum, id est eorum quae post erunt praesignificatio*, Iren.*haer.* 4.20.5(M.7.1034C); *ib.*4.26.1(1052C); οὐδὲ γὰρ ἄλλο τί ποτέ ἐστι π., ἀλλ' ἢ τῶν μελλόντων πραγμάτων προαναφώνησις Chrys.*hom.2.3 in Is.*6:1(6.110C); but including also narration and explanation of past and present π. γάρ ἐστιν, οὐ τὰ μέλλοντα λέγειν, ἀλλὰ καὶ τὸ τὰ παρόντα id.*hom.5.1 in 1Tim.*(11.574D); οὐ μόνον δὲ τὰ μέλλοντα προφητείας ἐστὶν εἰπεῖν, ἀλλὰ καὶ τὰ παρελθόντα, ὅπερ μᾶλλόν ἐστι παρὰ Μωϋσῇ...ἔστι δὲ καὶ τὰ παρόντα προφητείας εἰπεῖν, ὅταν τι γίνηται μέν, κρύπτηται δέ †Chrys.*synops.*(6.317C); Diod.*proem.Pss.* (p.86.11ff.) cit. s. A supra; Thdt.*Pss.*proem.(1.604).

D. of OT prophesying; **1.** in gen., of Rahab οὐ μόνον πίστις, ἀλλὰ καὶ π. ἐν τῇ γυναικὶ γέγονεν *1Clem.*12.8; of continuity of prophecy in Israel αἰώνιός ἐστι μετὰ τὸν Μωϋσέως θάνατον προελθοῦσα ἡ π. Just.*dial.*30.1(M.6.540A); of prophecy of NT events contained in a psalm, Or.*Cels.*2.11(p.140.3; M.11.816B); †Bas.*bapt.*2.12.1(2.671E; M.31.1624B); Cyr.*hom.pasch.*14(5^2.193C); ref. prophesying of Deborah εἰς ἔλεγχον τῶν τότε ἀνδρῶν τῆς π. ἀξιωθῆναι Thdt.*qu.12 in Jud.*(1.330); id.*Pss.*proem.(1.603); id.*Jer.*20:7(2.504); **2.** including prophetic symbolism ἡ γὰρ δι' ἔργων π. τὸ ἀκουστὸν καθίστησιν ὁρατὸν καὶ τὸ μέλλον οἱονεὶ παρόν, ἐν τῷ μέρει δηλοῦσα τὸ ὅλον Or.*fr.61 in Jer.*(p.228.19); id.*fr.10 in Reg.*(p.298.24); **3.** inspired οἷς ἂν ὁ θεὸς ἄνωθεν ἐπιπέμψῃ τὴν χάριν αὐτοῦ, οὗτοι θεόσδοτον ἔχουσι τὴν π. Iren.*haer.*1.13.4(M.7.585A); Clem.*ecl.*16(p.141.9; M.9.705B); προφητείας, ἵνα δι' αὐτῶν ὁ ἀμφιβάλλων πληχθεὶς ὡς ἐνθέων...ἑαυτὸν ἐπιδῷ ...τοῖς λόγοις τοῦ θεοῦ Or.*princ.*4.1.7(p.302.12; M.11.353B); προφητείας...διὰ τοῦ πνεύματος Bas.*Spir.*39(3.33D; M.32.140B); τοῦ οἰκονομήσαντος πνεύματος γραφῆναι τὴν π. †Bas.*Is.*proem.1(1.378C; M.30.120B); **4.** purity of heart an essential condition for inspiration, *ib.*3(379E; M.124A); **5.** criteria for distinguishing true inspiration, Epiph.*haer.*48.3(p.223.15; M.41.860A); **6.** purpose; **a.** prediction of Christ, †Bas.*Is.*proem.7(1.383C; M.30.129D); Cyr.*Is.*5.6(2.917A); **b.** confirmation of faith, Andr.Caes.*Apoc.*57(M.106.400A); argument from prophecy contrasted with philosophical demonstration,

*Hom.Clem.*15.5; former being unassailable by sophistry, *ib.*1.21; and, unlike miracles, incapable of being ascribed to Devil, Chrys.*hom.19.2 in Jo.*(8.112B); **7.** obscurity of prophecy before its fulfilment *πᾶσα γὰρ π., πρὸ τῆς ἐκβάσεως, αἰνιγμά ἐστι καὶ ἀντιλογία τοῖς ἀνθρώποις* Iren.*haer.*4.26.1(M.7.1052C); *προφητειῶν, ἃς...ἴσμεν αἰνιγμάτων...πεπληρῶσθαι λόγων* Or.*princ.*4.2.3(p.310.7; M.11.361B); Chrys.*exp.in Ps.*117:22(5.325A); id.*proph.obscurit.*1.6(6.178A); **8.** cessation of prophecy from Israel, cf. *signata...prophetia, unctus est ...Christus,* Or.*comm.ser.40 in Mt.*(p.80.25; M.13.1658B); *ἐπεφάνη γὰρ ...ὁ...κύριος...πέπαυται παρ' αὐτοῖς τῆς π. ἡ χάρις* Cyr.*Is.*1.2(2.55A); *ἐσφράγισται ὅρασις καὶ π. κατὰ τὸν Δανιήλ. μέχρι γὰρ Ἰωάννου παρ' αὐτοῖς ὑπῆρχεν ἡ π.* Proc.G.*Is.*3:1–11(M.87.1897A); **9.** prophecies of OT indicated call of gentiles, Eus.*d.e.*6 proem.(p.251.24; M.22.413B); **10.** heret. attitude; some regarded as inspired by Achamoth, some by the 'seed', some by the demiurge (Valent.), Iren.*haer.*1.7.3(M.7.516B); inspired by evil powers responsible for Creation (Basilides), cf.*ib.*1.24.5(M.7.678A); *τὰς δὲ π., ἃς μὲν ἀπὸ τῶν κοσμοποιῶν ἀγγέλων λελαλῆσθαι, ἃς δὲ ἀπὸ τοῦ σατανᾶ* [i.e. acc. Saturninus] *ib.*1.24.2 ap.Hipp.*haer.*7.28(M.16.3323A); *προφήτας ἀπὸ τῶν κοσμοποιῶν ἀγγέλων ἐμπνευσθέντας εἰρηκέναι τὰς π.* [i.e. acc. Simonians] Hipp.*haer.*6.19(p.147.10; 3223C); ascribed by Apelles to evil spirit, Rhod.ap.Eus.5.13.2(M.20.460B).

E. of Christ's prophecies; **1.** his teaching in gen. *ὁ τῷ κυρίῳ πειθόμενος καὶ τῇ δοθείσῃ δι' αὐτοῦ κατακολουθήσας π. τελέως ἐκτελεῖται* Clem.*str.*7.16(p.71.20; M.9.540B); **2.** specific utterances; e.g. Mt.26:31, Or.*Jo.*32.5(p.434.6; M.14.753C); Jo.4:23, Chrys.*hom. 33.2 in Jo.*(8.191C); and actions, e.g. Christ's triumphal entry *ἐποίει δὲ τοῦτο, π. τὴν μὲν τυπῶν, τὴν δὲ πληρῶν...τὸ μὲν γάρ, χαῖρε ὅτι ὁ βασιλεύς σου ἔρχεται...π. πληροῦντος ἦν· τὸ δὲ ὄνον καθίσαι, μέλλον πρᾶγμα προδιατυποῦντος, ὅτι τὸ...τῶν ἐθνῶν γένος ἔμελλεν ὑποχείριον ἔχειν* *ib.66.1*(395C).

F. ref. Christ as exegete of uncomprehended prophecy, Just.*1apol.*32.2(M.6.377B).

G. of Christian prophesying *τὰ σημεῖα τοῦ πνεύματος, ἰάσεις καὶ π. διὰ τῆς ἐκκλησίας ἐπιτελοῦνται* Clem.*exc.Thdot.*24(p.115.5; M.9.672A); ref. ecstatic utterances of those claiming to be identified with Persons of Trin., Cels.ap.Or.*Cels.*7.9(p.160.33; M.11.1433A); Epiph.*haer.*48.2(p.221.17; M.41.857A); Thdt.*Trin.*26(M.75.1185C); *Νικῶν...προφητείας ἀξιώματι ὑπὸ θεοῦ τετιμημένος* Leont.N.*v.Sym.* 7(M.93.1677D); not a new *charisma* in apostolic Church, but continuous with OT prophecy, Chrys.*hom.35.7 in 1Cor.*(10.326C); superior to gift of tongues, as being conducive to edification, cf. *ib.35.1*(322A).

H. among Montanists *τῆς ψευδοῦς ταύτης τάξεως τῆς ἐπικαλουμένης νέας π. ἐβδέλυκται ἡ ἐνέργεια παρὰ πάσῃ τῇ ἐν κόσμῳ ἀδελφότητι* Serap.Ant.ap.Eus.*h.e.*5.19.2(M.20.481A); *ὑπὸ τῆς νέας ταύτης, οὐχ, ὡς αὐτοί φασιν, π., πολὺ δὲ μᾶλλον...ψευδοπροφητείας* Anon.*ib.*5.16.4 (465A); *τὰς μὲν φερομένας αὐτῶν π. ψευδεῖς οὔσας* Eus.*h.e.*5.18.1 (476B); *τῇ προσποιήτῳ αὐτοῦ π. ὁ Μοντανὸς ἐπικεχείρηκεν* *ib.*5.18.12 (480B).

I. Naassene, of Heracles as prophet, Hipp.*haer.*5.26(p.131.17; M.16.3202B).

J. of Cumaean Sibyl, ‡Just.*coh.Gr.*37(M.6.308C).

K. of prophecy uttered by unbelievers, Anast.S.*qu.et resp.*20(M.89.520A).

III. *prophecy,* written passage or book of prophetic character;

A. of passages of OT *ἐν ἄλλῃ π. λέγει...ὁ Ἰακὼβ* *Barn.*13.4; *μὴ νοήσαντες τὴν δεδηλωμένην π.* Just.*1apol.*33.3(M.6.381A); *ἑτέρας π. ἔχοντες εἰπεῖν* *ib.*53.1(405C); Or.*princ.*4.1.3(p.297.1; M.11.348A); id.*Cels.*8.72(p.289.11; M.11.1625A); Gr.Nyss.*Eun.*3(2 p.35.4; M.45.601B); Chrys.*hom.85.1 in Jo.*(8.505B).

B. of utterances of prophets as collected and arranged in books, Just.*1apol.*31.1(M.6.376A).

C. plur., of prophetic books of OT collectively *αἱ π. οὐδὲ ὁ νόμος* Ign.*Smyrn.*5.1; *ἡ π. the prophetic books,* Meth.*symp.*10.6(p.128.31; M.18.204A); Eus.*p.e.*11.13(531B; M.21.881C).

D. of books and passages not included in Hebr. prophetic canon *ἐκ τῆς π. τοῦ Λάμεχ* Cosm.Ind.*top.*2(M.88.96A); of Balaam's prophecies, said to have been written down by his disciples, Or.*adnot.in Num.*24:17(M.17.24A); of Jotham's parable, Meth.*symp.* 10.2(p.122.18; M.18.193B); of 1Reg. *παρὰ Ἑβραίοις καὶ παρὰ Σύροις π. Σαμουὴλ ὀνομάζεται* Proc.G.*1Reg.*proem.(M.87.1080C); of passages in Psalms, Or.*Cels.*2.11(p.140.3; M.11.816B); Meth.*res.*1.54(p.310.14; M.41.1129A); †Bas.*bapt.*2.12.1(2.671E; M.31.1624B); Gr.Nyss.*Eun.* 4(2 p.61.8; M.45.632C); of Proverbs, acc. Marcellus, but Eus. denies this and distinguishes prophecies from Wisdom literature, Eus.*Marcell.*1.2(p.13.2; M.24.741A) v. II.B supra; of Solomon's 'parables' (cf. 3Reg.4:28), id.*p.e.*11.7(521B; M.21.864D).

E. ref. interprn. of OT prophecies acc. historical and spiritual senses, Isid.Pel.*epp.*4.203(M.78.1289Dff.).

F. of prophetic utterance of Caiaphas, Chrys.*hom.83.2 in Jo.*(8.491D).

G. of recorded prophecy of Montanus, Epiph.*haer.*48.10(p.232.20; M.41.869C).

H. Church adds to canonical scriptures nothing *quasi prophetiam,* Or.*comm.ser.47 in Mt.*(p.96.9; M.13.1668C).

***προφητεῖον, τό,** *church dedicated in honour of a prophet,* Thdr.Lect.*h.e.*2.63(M.86.213B); CCP(536)*act.*3(*ACO* 3 p.166.30; H.2.1241B); *ib.*(p.167.25; 1244A).

προφητεύ-ω, *prophesy;*

A. of OT prophets; **1.** in gen. *οἱ προφῆται...εἰς αὐτὸν ἐπροφήτευσαν* *Barn.*5.6; *∼ων ἐπ' αὐτῷ* *ib.*5.13; *προεφητεύθη δὲ ὑπὸ Ζαχαρίου* Just.*dial.*53.3(M.6.593A); *∼ων περὶ τῆς τοῦ Ἰησοῦ ἐπιδημίας* Or.*Cels.*6.5(p.75.11; M.11.1296C); *ἀμφὶ Κῦρον δὲ...βασιλέα. οὗτος δ' ἦν ὁ χρόνος, ἐν ᾧ τῶν παρ' Ἑβραίοις προφητῶν οἱ πάντων ὕστατοι προεφήτευον* Eus.*p.e.*10.4(470C; M.21.781D); *προεφήτευον αἱ καθαραὶ καὶ διαυγεῖς ψυχαί* †Bas.*Is.*proem.3(1.379D; M.30.121C); ref. question how prophets could prophesy when H. Ghost had not been given (Jo.7:39), Chrys.*hom.51.1 in Jo.*(8.300C); **2.** incl. Moses and Law *νόμος τὴν ἀναγέννησιν ἡμῶν ∼ων* Clem.*str.*3.12(p.234.9; M.8.1184B); cf.*ib.*4.13(p.288.7; 1297C); *διὰ γραπτῆς νομοθεσίας οἱ τῆς ἀληθείας νόμοι ∼ονται* Or.*princ.*4.2.8(p.320.13; M.11.373A); Meth.*symp.*9.2(p.115.29; M.18.180C); Noah, Or.*Cels.*7.7(p.159.25; M.11.1432B); Jacob, Just.*dial.*54.1(M.6.593C); Chrys.*hom.33.2 in Jo.*(8.192B); Eldad and Medad *ἐγγὺς κύριος τοῖς ἐπιστρεφομένοις, ὡς γέγραπται ἐν τῷ Ἐλδὰδ καὶ Μωδάτ, τοῖς προφητεύσασιν ἐν τῇ ἐρήμῳ τῷ λαῷ* Herm.*vis.*2.3.4; Cyr.H.*catech.*16.26; the seventy elders, prophesying as result of temporary and special gift of prophetic *ἐνέργεια,* Thdt.*qu. 21 in 1Reg.*(1.371); Samuel and David, Cyr.H.*catech.*16.28; David, esp. as Psalmist, *Barn.*12.10; Procl.CP *or.*2.1(M.65.692C); Daniel, Cosm.Ind.*top.*2(M.88.109A); **3.** their inspiration *ἄξιος ἦν αὐτῶν ὁ...σεμνὸς βίος πνεύματος θεοῦ, τρόπῳ ∼οντος καινῷ* Or.*Cels.*7.7(p.160.6; M.11.1432B); *λέγει* [sc. Origen]*...οὐκ ἄλλως...ἢ κοινωνίᾳ τοῦ θείου πνεύματος· τῆς γὰρ αὐτῆς δυνάμεως δεῖ ∼ουσί τε καὶ ἀκροωμένοις προφητῶν· καὶ οὐκ ἂν ἀκούσαι προφήτου, ᾧ μὴ αὐτὸ τὸ πνεῦμα τὸ ∼σαν τὴν σύνεσιν τῶν αὐτοῦ λόγων ἐδωρήσατο* Gr.Thaum.*pan.Or.*15 (p.34.14,16; M.10.1093D); *τὸ πνεῦμα πεπροφητευκέναι* Meth.*symp.*2.3(p.18.16; M.18.52B); *ἐν ἁγίῳ πνεύματι ἐπροφήτευον* Cyr.H.*catech.*16.28; *φασὶ δέ τινες ἐξεστηκότας αὐτοὺς ∼ειν, ἐπικαλυπτομένου τοῦ...νοῦ παρὰ τοῦ πνεύματος. τοῦτο δὲ παρὰ τὴν ἐπαγγελίαν ἐστὶ τῆς θείας ἐπιδημίας, ἔκφρονα ποιεῖν τὸν θεόληπτον* †Bas.*Is.*proem.5(1.381A; M.30.125B); **4.** prophesying by symbols and allegories, as in law of unclean foods, Clem.*str.*5.8(p.361.4; M.9.81A); **5.** foretelling Christ, *Barn.*5.6, *ib.*5.13, Just.*dial.*53.3(M.6.593A) citt. s. 1 supra; *μείζων...τῶν προφητῶν πάντων ὁ ∼όμενος ὑπ' αὐτῶν* Or.*Jo.*20.44(33; p.388.20; M.14.677C); id.*Cels.*6.5(p.75.11; M.11.1296C); *Ἰησοῦν...ὑπὸ τῆς γραφῆς ∼θέντα* *Hom.Clem.*3.49; ref. Dt.18:18, *ib.*3.53; hence more impressive in their testimony than a contemporary teacher, Cyr.H.*catech.*12.5; Chrys.*hom.11.1 in Mt.*(7.149B); ‡Bas.Sel.*or.*38.1(M.85.400B); **6.** ref. rel. of OT to NT *θείων λογίων...∼θέντων μὲν τὸ πρῶτον, ἔπειτα δὲ καὶ σαφηνισθέντων* Clem.*str.*6.15(p.493.31; M.9.345C).

B. of Jo. Bapt., Chrys.*hom.11.1 in Mt.*(7.151B).

C. ref. cessation of prophecy among Jews *οὔτε νεώτεροι καὶ μετὰ τὴν Ἰησοῦ ἐπιδημίαν ἱστόρηνται ἐν Ἰουδαίοις τινὲς ∼σαντες* Or.*Cels.*7.8 (p.160.22; M.11.1432D).

D. of Christian prophets; **1.** of God inspiring Christians *αὐτὸς ἐν ἡμῖν ∼ων* *Barn.*16.9; **2.** ref. succession of prophets in Church, Eus.*h.e.*5.17.2(M.20.473A); **3.** of general endowment of prophecy in early Church, which was (as agst. Montanist view) temporary *ὅτε γὰρ ἦν χρεία προφητῶν...οἱ αὐτοὶ ἅγιοι τὰ πάντα ἐπροφήτευον* Epiph.*haer.*48.3(p.223.6; M.41.857D); *οἱ ἅγιοι προφῆται καὶ οἱ ἅγιοι ἀπόστολοι προεφήτευσαν* *ib.*48.8(p.229.19; 865C); **4.** of S. Paul, *ib.*(p.230.14; 868A); **5.** of Montanists *Μοντανὸν...παρὰ τὸ κατὰ παράδοσιν καὶ κατὰ διαδοχὴν ἄνωθεν τῆς ἐκκλησίας ἔθος...∼οντα* Anon.ap.Eus.*h.e.*5.16.8(M.20.468A); *∼ειν...προσποιουμένης τῆς Μαξιμίλλης* Eus.*ib.*5.18.13(480B); **6.** of Marcosians *φησὶν αὐταῖς* [sc. *ὁ Μάρκος*],...*ἡ χάρις κατῆλθεν ἐπὶ σέ...∼σον. τῆς δὲ γυναικὸς ἀποκρινομένης, οὐ προεφήτευσα πώποτε, καὶ οὐκ οἶδα ∼ειν· ἐπικλήσεις τινὰς ποιούμενος... φησὶν αὐτῇ, ἄνοιξον τὸ στόμα σου, λάλησον ὅ τι δήποτε, καὶ ∼σεις. ἡ δὲ...διαθερμανθεῖσα τὴν ψυχὴν ὑπὸ τῆς προσδοκίας τοῦ μέλλειν αὐτὴν ∼ειν...ἀποτολμᾷ λαλεῖν ληρώδη* Iren.*haer.*1.13.3(M.7.584A); *αὐτὸς ἐνομίζετο ∼ειν* Hipp.*haer.*6.41(p.172.15; M.16.3259A); **7.** of heret.

prophesying, as inspired by demons, Anast.S.*qu.et resp.*20(M.89.520C).

E. of Essene prophesying ἀσκεῖται δὲ ἐν αὐτοῖς τὸ ~ειν καὶ προλέγειν τὰ ἐσόμενα Hipp.*haer*.9.27(p.261.13; M.16.3406B).

F. of Sibylline oracle, *Orac.Sib*.1.2.

G. of pagan prophecy Πλάτων μονονουχὶ ~ων τὴν σωτήριον οἰκονομίαν ἐν τῷ δευτέρῳ τῆς Πολιτείας Clem.*str*.5.14(p.398.19; M.9.164B); of Pythia ~ειν...ἀπὸ τοῦ Ἀπόλλωνος πεπίστευται Or.*Cels*.7.3 (p.155.23; M.11.1425A); ‡Ath.*templ*.(p.111.12; M.28.1429D) cit. s. προκηρύσσω.

H. of false prophets οὗτοι ἐν ἐκστάσει προεφήτευον ὡς ἂν ἀποστάτου διάκονοι Clem.*str*.1.17(p.55.11; M.8.800C); *Hom.Clem*.3.24.

I. of prophesying by a demon, *T.Sal*.15.8(p.47.6; M.122.1337C).

προφήτης, ὁ, *prophet*;

I. of OT prophets; **A.** in gen. ἐγένοντό τινες...πάντων...τῶν... φιλοσόφων παλαιότεροι, μακάριοι καὶ δίκαιοι καὶ θεοφιλεῖς, θείῳ πνεύματι λαλήσαντες καὶ τὰ μέλλοντα θεσπίσαντες...π. δὲ αὐτοὺς καλοῦσιν Just.*dial*.7.1(M.6.492A); cf. *prophetia est praedicatio futurorum, id est eorum quae post erunt, praesignificatio. praesignificabant igitur prophetae quoniam videbitur deus ab hominibus*, Iren. *haer*.4.20.5(M.7.1034C); δίκαιοι ἄνδρες γεγένηνται φίλοι θεοῦ. οὗτοι π. κέκληνται διὰ τὸ προφαίνειν τὰ μέλλοντα Hipp.*haer*.10.33(p.290.26; M.16.3451A); π. δὲ ἀληθείας ἐστὶν ὁ πάντοτε πάντα εἰδώς, τὰ μὲν γεγονότα ὡς ἐγένετο, τὰ δὲ γινόμενα ὡς γίνεται, τὰ δὲ ἐσόμενα ὡς ἔσται, ἀναμάρτητος, ἐλεήμων, μόνος τὴν ἀλήθειαν ὑφηγεῖσθαι πεπιστευμένος...τοῦτο γὰρ προφήτου ἴδιον, τὸ τὴν ἀλήθειαν μηνύειν *Hom.Clem*.2.6; ὁ μὲν γὰρ παρέχων ἑαυτὸν ἄξιον ὄργανον τῇ ἐνεργείᾳ τοῦ πνεύματος π. ἐστίν †Bas.*Is*.proem.1(1.378D; M.30.120C); cf.*ib*.3(379D; M.121C); Thdt.*Dan*.proem.(2.1056); π. ὁ προφάσκων ἢ τὸ μέλλον, ἢ τὰ παρόντα λανθάνοντα Proc.G.*Is*.proem.(M.87.1817A); as seers, Or. *hom.4.3 in Gen*.(p.53.27; M.12.185D); τῶν ἀληθῶν ἡ θεωρία, διὰ τὸ ἐναργὲς καὶ ἀναμφίβολον ὅρασις προσηγορεύεται. δι' ὃ καὶ ὁρῶν ὁ π. ἐλέγετο, καὶ ἔμπροσθεν βλέπων, ὡς Ἀμώς τε καὶ Σαμουήλ· τὸ μέν, ὡς τὸ μέλλον ὁρῶν· τὸ δέ, ὡς θεωρητικὸς τοῦ θείου βουλήματος Proc.G. *Is*.1:1(1824B); ὁρῶντας τοὺς π. ὠνόμαζον, ὡς ἂν ἐπιταθείσης αὐτοῖς κατὰ νοῦν τῆς ὁράσεως *ib*.13:1–11(2068C); dist. from μάντεις by ethical content of prophecies and their rationality and intelligibility to prophet himself, Iren.*fr*.23(M.7.1244A); cf.Eus.*d.e*.5 proem.(p.207.36ff.; M.22.345A); Chrys.*exp.in Ps*.44:2(5.161B).

B. esp. as predictors ἐγνώρισεν γὰρ ἡμῖν ὁ δεσπότης διὰ τῶν π. τὰ παρεληλυθότα καὶ τὰ ἐνεστῶτα, καὶ τῶν μελλόντων δοὺς ἀπαρχὰς ...γεύσεως *Barn*.1.7; Thphl.Ant.*Autol*.2.9(M.6.1064B); οἱ...π. ὀφθαλμοὶ ἡμῶν ἐγένοντο, προορῶντες διὰ πίστεως τὰ τοῦ λόγου μυστήρια. ... οὐ μόνον τὰ παρῳχηκότα εἰπόντες, ἀλλὰ καὶ τὰ ἐνεστῶτα καὶ τὰ μέλλοντα ἀπαγγείλαντες· ἵνα μὴ μόνον πρὸς καιρὸν ὁ π. ὡς π. δειχθῇ, ἀλλὰ καὶ πάσαις γενεαῖς προλέγων τὰ μέλλοντα ὁ π. ὡς π. σημανθῇ Hipp.*antichr*.2(p.4.16; M.10.728C); id.*haer*.10.33(p.290.26; M.16.3451A) cit. supra; Or.*Cels*.1.36(p.87.18ff.; M.11.728Dff.); εἰ π. ἐστίν, καὶ δύναται εἰδέναι ὡς ἐγένετο ὁ κόσμος, καὶ τὰ ἐν αὐτῷ γινόμενα, καὶ τὰ εἰς τέλος ἐσόμενα· ἐὰν ἡμῖν ᾖ τι προειρηκώς, ὃ εἰς τέλος ἐγνώκαμεν γεγενημένον, καλῶς αὐτῷ ἐκ τῶν ἤδη γεγενημένων καὶ τὰ ἐσόμενα ἔσεσθαι πιστεύομεν, οὐ μόνον ὡς γινώσκοντι, ἀλλὰ καὶ προγινώσκοντι *Hom.Clem*.2.10; ἀληθῶς π. ἀποκαλεῖν τοὺς τοιούσδε παρὰ τὸ... προφωτίζειν ἐν αὐτοῖς τὸ θεῖον πνεῦμα μὴ μόνον τὰ παρόντα ἀλλὰ καὶ τῶν μελλόντων ἀληθῆ...γνῶσιν Eus.*d.e*.5 proem.(p.208.11; M.22.345B); τὰ μετὰ τοσαύτας γενεὰς μέλλοντα γίνεσθαι ὡς ἤδη γενόμενα ἑώρα ὁ π. Epiph.*haer*.79.6(p.481.3; M.42.749A); ἔθος ἅπασι τοῖς π., περὶ τῶν μηδέπω γεγενημένων ὡς γεγενημένων διαλέγεσθαι. ἐπειδὴ γὰρ τοῖς πνευματικοῖς ἑώρων ὀφθαλμοῖς τὰ μετὰ πολὺν ἐτῶν ἀριθμὸν μέλλοντα γίνεσθαι, διὰ τοῦτο ὡς ἤδη πρὸ τῶν ὀφθαλμῶν κείμενα κατοπτεύοντες τὰ πράγματα, οὕτως...διελέγοντο Chrys.*hom.10.3 in Gen*.(4.75D); ἔθος...προφήταις τὰ ἐσόμενα προαπαγγέλλειν, καὶ ἐν αὐταῖς ἔσθ' ὅτε γίνεσθαι ταῖς τῶν πράξεων φαντασίαις, ὥστε καὶ ὁρᾶν ἤδη δοκεῖν τὰ δρώμενα καὶ ἀκροᾶσθαι φωνῶν Cyr.*Joel*.42(3.240C); προφητῶν γὰρ ἴδιον τὸ προλέγειν τὰ μέλλοντα Thdt.*qu.in 1Par*. proem.(1.557); τί προφήτου ἴδιον εἶναι φατέ;...τὸ τὰ μέλλοντα προειδέναι τε καὶ προλέγειν id.*Dan*.proem.(2.1056); ὁ μὲν π., ἀποκαλύψει τοῦ πνεύματος προαγορεύει τὰ μέλλοντα· ὁ δὲ στοχαστὴς...ἐξ ὁμοίου παραθέσεως τὸ μέλλον τεκμαίρεται Proc.G.*Is*.3:1–11(M.87.1897B); Andr.Caes.*Apoc*.28(M.106.308C).

C. as revealers of hidden significance of present affairs ὁρῶσι δὲ οἱ π. οὐ τὰ μέλλοντα μόνον, ἀλλὰ καὶ τῶν παρόντων τὰ λανθάνοντα †Bas.*Is*.proem.4(1.380D; M.30.124C); Proc.G.*Is*.proem.(M.87.1817A) cit. s. A supra.

D. as revealers of God through prophetic symbolism, cf. *non solum autem per visiones...sed in operationibus visus est prophetis ut per eos...praemonstraret futura. propter quod et Osee propheta accepit uxorem fornicationis...id quod a propheta typice per operationem factum est, ostendit apostolus vere factum in ecclesia a Christo*, Iren. *haer*.4.20.12(M.7.1042A); Or.*hom.11.5 in Jer*.(p.83.5; M.13.373C).

E. prophets' inspiration; **1.** by Logos, Just.*1apol*.33.9(M.6.381C); λόγος γάρ...ἐστιν ὁ ἐν παντὶ ὤν, καὶ διὰ τῶν π. προειπὼν τὰ μέλλοντα γίνεσθαι id.*2apol*.10.8(M.6.461A); cf.Iren.*haer*.4.20.4(M.7.1034B); οἱ μακάριοι π. ... ὑπ' αὐτοῦ τοῦ λόγου...τετιμημένοι, ὀργάνων δίκην ἑαυτοῖς ἡνωμένοι ἔχοντες ἐν ἑαυτοῖς ἀεὶ τὸν λόγον ὡς πλῆκτρον, δι' οὗ κινούμενοι ἀπήγγελλον ταῦτα ἅπερ ἤθελεν ὁ θεός Hipp.*antichr*.2 (p.4.23; M.10.728C); by Christ, Ign.*Magn*.8.2; οἱ π., ἀπ' αὐτοῦ ἔχοντες τὴν χάριν, εἰς αὐτὸν ἐπροφήτευσαν *Barn*.5.6; Clem.*prot*.1(p.9.3; M.8.64C); id.*str*.1.17(p.53.2; M.8.796B); *ib*.(p.56.12; 801C); ref. Jer.11:19 ὁ σωτὴρ ἐν τῷ π. ... λέγει Or.*hom.10.1 in Jer*.(p.71.19; M.13.357C); τὸ ἐνεργῆσαν ἐν τοῖς π. πνεῦμα ἦν ὁ Χριστός id.*fr.116 in Lam*.(p.276.18; M.13.657D); hence καὶ πάλιν σὰρξ ἐγένετο διὰ προφητῶν ἐνεργήσας Clem.*exc.Thdot*.19(p.112.30; M.9.665D); **2.** by H. Ghost, as Spirit of Christ, Ign.*Magn*.9.2; as prophetic Spirit, Just.*1apol*.31.1(M.6.376A); *ib*.32.8(380B); π. ... θεοφορούμενος τῷ πνεύματι τῷ προφητικῷ *ib*.35.3(384B); *ib*.40.1(388D); id.*dial*.7.1(M.6.492A); ἔχομεν π. μάρτυρας, οἳ πνεύματι ἐνθέῳ ἐκπεφωνήκασι... πιστεύειν τῷ παρὰ τοῦ θεοῦ πνεύματι ὡς ὄργανα κεκινηκότι τὰ τῶν π. στόματα Athenag.*leg*.7.2f.(M.6.904C); π., οἱ κατ' ἔκστασιν τῶν ἐν αὐτοῖς λογισμῶν, κινήσαντος αὐτοὺς τοῦ θείου πνεύματος, ἃ ἐνηργοῦντο ἐξεφώνησαν, συγχρησαμένου τοῦ πνεύματος ὡς εἰ καὶ αὐλητὴς αὐλὸν ἐμπνεῦσαι *ib*.9.1(908A); οἱ δὲ τοῦ θεοῦ ἄνθρωποι, πνευματοφόροι πνεύματος ἁγίου καὶ π. γενόμενοι, ὑπ' αὐτοῦ τοῦ θεοῦ ἐμπνευσθέντες καὶ σοφισθέντες, ἐγένοντο θεοδίδακτοι...ὄργανα θεοῦ γενόμενοι Thphl.Ant. *Autol*.2.9(M.6.1064A); οἱ π. καὶ οἱ τοῦ πνεύματος μαθηταί Clem.*str*.1.9(p.30.6; M.8.741B); cf. π. ... ὄργανα θείας γενομένους φωνῆς *ib*.6.18(p.518.23; M.9.401A); Or.*Cels*.4.45(p.368.3; M.11.1173B); cf. *propheta deo plenus*, id.*hom.3.3 in Gen*.(p.42.19; M.12.177C); inspiration dist. from 'abiding' of H. Ghost in Christ, id.*hom.6.3 in Num*.(p.34.3; M.12.609B); οὐ γὰρ ἐν ψυχῇ 'Ηλίου φησίν...ἀλλ' ἐν πνεύματι καὶ δυνάμει 'Ηλίου. ἦν γὰρ ἐπὶ τὸν 'Ηλίαν πνεῦμα...εἴτ' οὖν πνευματικὸν χάρισμα, ὥσπερ καὶ ἐπὶ ἕκαστον τῶν π. id.*hom.4 in Lc*. (p.29.14; M.13.1811B); ὅσα γὰρ λαλεῖ π. πνεύματι ἁγίῳ, οὐκ αὐτὸς λαλεῖ, ἀλλ' ὁ κύριος ὑποβάλλει *ib.14*(p.101.7); Eus.*d.e*.5 proem.(p.208.29; M.22.345D); id.*e.th*.2.18(p.122.3; M.24.941A); id.*fr.Lc*.21:28(M.24.600A); πνεῦμα...ἦλθεν ἐπὶ πάντας δικαίους καὶ π. Cyr.H.*catech*.16.27; θεός, ὁ λαλήσας ἐν πνεύματι ἁγίῳ διὰ τῶν π. *ib*.17.38; *Symb.Hier*. (M.33.533B); H. Ghost's inspiration of prophets and apostles renders all scripture inspired, Didym.(‡Bas.)*Eun*.5(1.300D; M.29.721A,B); *Symb*.ap.Epiph.*anc*.118(p.147.14; M.43.232D); *Symb.Nic.–CP* (p.80.14; H.2.288B); π. γὰρ τὰ τῆς τοῦ πνεύματος ἐνεργείας φθέγγεται Chrys.*incomprehens*.3.3(1.465B); λαμβανόμενοι ὑπὸ τοῦ πνεύματος οὕτως ἔλεγον id.*Is.interp*.1:1(6.4B); ἐν γὰρ ταῖς ἐκκλησίαις...τὰς τῆς σωτηρίας συλλέγουσιν ἀφορμὰς οἱ τῶν ἁγιοπρεπῶν σπουδασμάτων ἐπιστήμονες· λαλεῖ γὰρ ἐν αὐτοῖς τὸ πνεῦμα...διὰ π. ἁγίων, διὰ φωνῆς ἀποστόλων καὶ εὐαγγελιστῶν Cyr.*Ps*.83:5(M.69.1208D); Proc.G.*Is*.3:1–11(M.87.1897B); **3.** its nature; **a.** in gen., illustrated by character of dreams, †Bas.*Is*.proem.3(1.380Bff.; M.30.124B,C); **b.** does not confer total sinlessness, cf.Or.*hom.6.3 in Num*.(p.34.10ff.; M.12.609Cff.); cf.id.*hom.20.8 in Jer*.(p.189.19; M.13.517C); **c.** continuous, and dist. from temporary possession manifested by pagan seers in frenzied and irrational utterances, *Hom.Clem*.3.13–14; dist. from irrational possession, Cyr.H.*catech*.16.15; cf.Chrys.*exp.in Ps*.44:2 (5.161C); **d.** confers knowledge of divine intentions, Gr.Naz.*or*.2.107(M.35.505B); not omniscience, but only knowledge of what divine grace reveals, Thdt.*qu.21 in 2Reg*.(1.416); id.*qu.16 in 4Reg*.(1.520); prophets being ἀγράμματοι καὶ ποιμένες καὶ ἰδιῶται Thphl. Ant.*Autol*.2.35(M.6.1109B); **e.** prophet's infallibility does not preclude human free will, Chrys.*hom.68.2 in Jo*.(8.406Dff.); **f.** accompanied by 'ecstasy', v. s. ἔκστασις; but contrasted with irrational ecstasy of false prophets, esp. Montanists, Anon.ap.Eus.*h.e*.5.17.3(M.20.473B) cit. s. παρέκστασις; cf.Clem.*str*.1.17(p.55.11; M.8.800C) cit. s. ἔκστασις; οὐκ ἐξιστάμενοι οἱ π. προεφήτευον...ἀλλ' ἐν τῷ κατὰ φύσιν ἱστάμενοι καὶ ἑκόντες καὶ εἰδότες ὑπούργουν τῷ πρὸς αὐτοὺς γιγνομένῳ λόγῳ Or.*hom.6.1 in Ezech*.(p.378.27; cf.M.13.709C); cf. φασὶ δέ τινες ἐξεστηκότας αὐτοὺς προφητεύειν, ἐπικαλυπτομένου τοῦ ἀνθρωπείου νοῦ παρὰ τοῦ πνεύματος. τοῦτο δὲ παρὰ τὴν ἐπαγγελίαν ἐστὶ τῆς θείας ἐπιδημίας, ἔκφρονα ποιεῖν τὸν θεόληπτον †Bas.*Is*. proem.5(1.381A; M.30.125B); ὁ π. πάντα μετὰ καταστάσεως λογισμῶν καὶ παρακολουθήσεως ἐλάλει...οὐχ ὡς ἐν ἐκστάσει διανοίας φερόμενος... ἀλλά...ἐρρωμένην ἔχων τὴν διάνοιαν...ταῦτα γὰρ τῶν ἀληθῶς π., ἐν ἁγίῳ πνεύματι ἐρρωμένην ἐχόντων τὴν διάνοιαν Epiph.*haer*.48.3(p.223.

16; M.41.860A); *ib.*48.7(p.228.14; 865A) cit. s. ἔκστασις; πάντα ἐν ἀληθείᾳ παρὰ τοῖς π. εἰρημένα καὶ ἐν...σώφρονι λογισμῷ, καὶ οὐκ ἐν παραπληξίᾳ *ib.*(p.229.15; 865C); οὐ κατὰ ἔκστασιν διανοίας...ὃ δὴ θείας ἐπιδημίας ἀνάξιον Proc.G.*Is.*proem.(M.87.1817A); **g.** prophetic *charisma* enabled prophets to predict Christ's advent when God was to be seen by men immediately in the flesh, Iren.*haer.*4.20.4(M.7.1034B); apprehension of Christ through prophets' inspiration contrasted with converse with him κατ' αἴσθησιν πνευματικήν, Or.*Cant.*1(p.91.30; M.13.85D); **4.** conditions required for inspiration; purity of heart, freedom from passions and τὸ ὁμαλὸν τῆς εὐσταθοῦς καταστάσεως, †Bas.*Is.*proem.3(1.379D,E; M.30.124A); purity and absence of sin and passion, Bas.*ep.*210.6(3.317C; M.32.777B); **5.** criteria of inspiration; Israelite people possessed *charisma* of διάκρισις πνευμάτων to dist. true from false prophets, Or.*hom.1 in Lc.*(p.3.12; M.13.1801A); true prophets' predictions are fulfilled, Epiph.*haer.*48.2(p.222.3; M.41.857B); Cyr.*ador.*6(1.186E); but H. Ghost can speak through false prophets in furtherance of God's counsels, Thdt.*qu.63 in 1Reg.*(1.399).

F. prophets and angels οἱ πρωτόκτιστοι ἄγγελοι ἐνήργουν εἰς τοὺς προσεχεῖς τοῖς π. ἀγγέλους διηγούμενοι δόξαν θεοῦ Clem.*ecl.*51(p.151.17; M.9.721B); ὥσπερ δὲ ἔρχεται ὁ υἱὸς τοῦ ἀνθρώπου...οὕτως ἄγγελοι γινόμενοι οἱ ἐν τοῖς π. λόγοι μετ' αὐτοῦ παραγίνονται Or.*comm.in Mt.*12.30(p.134.21; M.13.1049C); φίλους τοῦ νυμφίου...τοὺς ἁγίους ἀγγέλους ἢ ἀποστόλους τε καὶ π. id.*Cant.*3(p.184.28; M.13.153D).

G. methods used by prophets ποτὲ...οἱ π. σαφῶς λέγουσι τὰ δηλούμενα...ποτὲ δὲ διὰ συμβόλων...τινὰ δὲ καὶ συμπεπλεγμένως λέγεται· τῶν μὲν πρὸς λέξιν, τῶν δὲ πρὸς διάνοιαν εἰρημένων Proc.G.*Is.*proem.(M.87.1820A,B); use of types and parables, Just.*dial.*90.2(M.6.689B); cf.*ib.*68.6(636A); obscurity of sayings; significance of some prophecies not to be revealed until Last Day, Andr.Caes.*Apoc.*proem.(M.106.217A).

H. prophets foretold Christ, *Barn.*5.6; Just.*1apol.*52.1(M.6.404D); *ib.*61.13(421B); both his first and second Advent, id.*dial.*14.8(M.6.505C); esp. death and Resurrection, *ib.*106.1(724A); cf.Iren.*haer.*4.11.1(M.7.1001B); cf.*ib.*4.20.4(1034B); cf. *cum enim et ipsi membra essent Christi, unusquisque eorum secundum quod erat membrum, secundum hoc et prophetationem manifestabat; omnes et multi unum praeformantes...prophetae omnes quidem unum praefigurabant; unusquisque autem eorum secundum quod erat membrum, secundum hoc et dispositionem adimplebat, et eam quae secundum illud membrum erat, operationem Christi praeformabat, ib.*4.33.10(1079A); ζῶσιν ἐν ἡμῖν οἱ π., λαλοῦντες περὶ αὐτοῦ Or.*fr.116 in Lam.*(p.276.27; M.13.660A); πᾶσι...τοῖς π. τὸ περὶ τοῦ Χριστοῦ κατήγγελται μυστήριον id.*hom.10 in Lc.*(p.70.9); προφήτας ἀπὸ τοῦ πληρώματος Χριστοῦ τὴν δωρεὰν κεχωρηκέναι...ἐφθάκεισαν γὰρ κἀκεῖνοι ὑπὸ τοῦ πνεύματος χειραγωγούμενοι μετὰ τὴν ἐν τοῖς τύποις εἰσαγωγὴν ἐπὶ τὴν τῆς ἀληθείας θέαν. διόπερ οὐ πάντες οἱ π. ἀλλὰ πολλοὶ ἐπεθύμησαν ἰδεῖν, ἃ οἱ ἀπόστολοι ἔβλεπον. εἰ γὰρ ἦν προφητῶν διαφορά, οἱ τετελειωμένοι...οὐκ ἐπεθύμησαν ἰδεῖν...τεθεωρήκασι γὰρ αὐτά· οἱ δὲ μὴ φθάσαντες ὁμοίως τούτοις εἰς τὸ ὕψος ἀναβῆναι τοῦ λόγου ἐν ὀρέξει γεγόνασι τῶν τοῖς ἀποστόλοις διὰ Χριστοῦ ἐγνωσμένων id.*Jo.*6.3(2; p.109.21; M.14.204A); Meth.*symp.*7.1(p.71.12; M.18.124A); speaking of events of Christ's life and death as though already past, Chrys.*hom.in Mt.26:39*(3.17B); in order to accommodate teaching to hearers, id.*exp.in Ps.*44:6(5.173C,174A); Lc.10:34 does not imply that prophets failed to see Christ, id.*hom.7.1 in Jo.*(8.49Cff.); ἀναλάβετε τὴν διὰ Χριστοῦ [sc. ὁδόν]· ταύτην ὑμῖν ὁ τῶν ἁγίων π. προεκήρυττε χορός Cyr.*Jo.*1.10(4.109B); beheld Christ's glory, Or.*Jo.*1.7(9; p.11.30,12.1; 36C); were παιδαγωγοί to Christ, *ib.*(p.12.6; 36C); their task to send the spiritually sick to the true Jordan (Christ), illustrated by Elisha's treatment of Naaman, *ib.*6.47(28; p.156.7; 281B); their sufferings related to sufferings of Christ, id. *comm.in Mt.*12.30(p.134.21; M.13.1049B); were lights, contrasted with Christ as sun of righteousness, *ib.*16.3(p.470.22; 1372A); were represented by Elijah at Transfiguration, id.*fr.22 in Lc.*9:28(p.243.21).

I. prophets in relation to NT; opp. Marcion's teaching, their God is same God as revealed in Christ, cf.Iren.*haer.*4.20.5(M.7.1034C); cf. *neque patrem suum blasphemans...neque prophetas exhonorans, aut ab alio deo dicens esse eos, aut...ex alia et alia substantia fuisse prophetas, ib.*4.33.15(1083B); Christ appealed to Jerusalem (Mt.23:37) through prophets and through his personal presence, Clem.*str.*1.5(p.18.22; M.8.720B); τὸν ἕνα δείκνυσι θεὸν διὰ νόμου καὶ προφητῶν καὶ εὐαγγελίου κηρυσσόμενον *ib.*3.2(p.199.18; 1109A); τέλειος...καθαρισμὸς ἡ διὰ νόμου καὶ προφητῶν εἰς τὸ εὐαγγέλιον πίστις *ib.*4.25(p.318.26; 1368B); τὸν κύριον διά τε τῶν π. διά τε τοῦ εὐαγγελίου καὶ διὰ τῶν...ἀποστόλων...εἰς τέλος ἡγούμενον τῆς γνώσεως *ib.*7.16(p.67.17; M.9.532B); cf. *prophetae illius sunt dei, qui mundum fecit. ex ipsa ergo consequentia concluditur quoniam qui prophetas misit, de Christo quae praedicanda erant ipse praedixit,* Or.*princ.*2.4.1(p.127.7; M.11.198C); εἰς τὰς αὐτὰς σκηνὰς ἀνάγουσι νόμος καὶ προφῆται καὶ εὐαγγέλιον, τρεῖς μὲν ἀριθμούμεναι, πρὸς ἓν δὲ τέλος ὁρῶσαι id.*fr.24 in Lc.*9:33(p.244.11); κἄν ποτε τῶν αἱρετικῶν ἀκούσῃς τινὸς βλασφημοῦντος νόμον ἢ προφήτας, ἀντίφθεγξαι...οὐκ ἦλθεν Ἰησοῦς καταλῦσαι τὸν νόμον Cyr.H.*catech.*4.33; οἱ μέσοι Χριστοῦ καὶ νόμου π. Gr.Naz.*or.*2.23(M.35.432B); καθωδηγήθημεν ἐν νόμῳ καὶ ἐν προφήταις ἕως τῆς παρουσίας τοῦ διδασκάλου Epiph.*haer.*66.75(p.117.5; M.42.148D); οἱ λόγοι Μωσέως καὶ προφητῶν συντρέχουσι τῷ...εὐαγγελικῷ κηρύγματι Nil.*epp.*1.52(M.79.105C); hence closely ass. apostles, Polyc.*ep.*6.3; Clem.*str.*1.9(p.30.1; M.8.741B); *ib.*5.5(p.346.5; M.9.53B); *ib.*7.16(p.67.17; 532B); Or.*princ.*4.2.7(14; p.318.10; M.11.372A); id.*Cant.*3(p.184.28; M.13.153D); id.*Jo.*1.16(p.20.22; M.14.49D); Meth.*symp.*7.1(p.71.13; M.18.124A); id.*res.*3.5(p.394.13; M.18.317D); Eus.*e.th.*2.9(p.109.34; M.24.917D); Ath.*Ar.*3.10(M.26.341C); Cyr.H. *catech.*17.38; †Bas.*Is.*66(1.427D; M.30.233B); οἱ π. εἰσιν οἱ σπείραντες· ἀλλ' οὐκ αὐτοὶ ἐθέρισαν, ἀλλ' οἱ ἀπόστολοι Chrys.*hom.34.2 in Jo.*(8.197D); both possessed gift of H. Ghost, *ib.51.2*(300D–301A); ἔδει γὰρ δύο σκάφη συνδραμεῖν εἰς τὴν ἄγραν. ἐὰν γὰρ μὴ παρῇ χορὸς προφητῶν βοηθῶν τῇ ἀποστολικῇ χειρί, καὶ τῇ προφητικῇ προρρήσει μὴ ἀκολουθήσῃ τῶν ἀποστόλων ἡ ἔκβασις, οὐ θηρᾶται τὰ θηρώμενα ‡Chrys.*leg.*2(6.405C); Isaiah as both prophet and apostle, Cyr.*Is.*proem.(2.****B); and ass. gospel τοὺς π. δὲ ἀγαπῶμεν, διὰ τὸ καὶ αὐτοὺς εἰς τὸ εὐαγγέλιον κατηγγελκέναι Ign.*Philad.*5.2; cf.*ib.*9.2; Clem.*str.*3.2(p.199.18; M.8.1109A); *ib.*7.16(p.67.17; M.9.532B); Or.*comm.in Mt.*10.10(p.11.26; M.13.857C); Gr.Nyss.*Eun.*3(2 p.5.11); *ib.*5(2 p.101.15; 680A); cf. Chrys.*exp.in Ps.*44:3(5.165A).

J. ass. patriarchs, v. πατριάρχης.

K. Jews' failure to understand, and rejection of, prophets πατρὶς μὲν γὰρ τῶν π. ὁ ἐκ περιτομῆς λαός, παρ' οἷς οὔκ εἰσι δεκτοί· ἡμεῖς δὲ οἱ ἀλλότριοι...ἐδεξάμεθα τοὺς π. Or.*hom.33 in Lc.*(p.197.5; M.13.1884D); χρὴ γὰρ πατρίδα νομίζειν αὐτῶν τὴν Ἰουδαίαν...οὐκ ἔστιν οὖν π. ἄτιμος ἐν τοῖς ἔθνεσιν· ἢ γὰρ οὐδ' ὅλως οἴδασιν αὐτόν, ἢ... παραδεξάμενοι αὐτὸν π. τιμῶσιν...ἀτιμάζονται δὲ οἱ π. ... διωχθέντες... ὑπὸ τοῦ λαοῦ...μὴ πιστευομένης αὐτῶν τῆς προφητείας ὑπὸ τοῦ λαοῦ id. *comm.in Mt.*10.18(p.23.22; M.13.880C); Ἰουδαῖοι...πάντα σωματικὰ ...ἡγούμενοι τοὺς π. εἰρηκέναι Meth.*symp.*9.1(p.115.7; M.18.180A); hence prophecies relating to Christ often deliberately obscure, to prevent their destruction by Jews, Chrys.*Is.interp.*2:1f.(6.20A,B); id.*proph.obscurit.*1.5(6.177B); cf.Cyr.*Is.*3.1(2.383C); Thdt.*Ezech.*proem.(2.671); hence Jewish prophets silent after Inc. or appearance of John, Just.*dial.*87.3(M.6.684B); their silence typified by Zacharias' dumbness, Or.*hom.5 in Lc.*(p.30.24; M.13.1812B); id. *fr.50 in Lc.*11:11(p.257.23); cf.id.*comm.ser.40 in Mt.*(p.80.23; M.13.1658A); ἤρθησαν γὰρ ἐξ αὐτῶν...οἱ π.· οἱ π. δὲ λοιπὸν ἐν ἐκκλησίᾳ Cyr.H.*catech.*13.29; Chrys.*exp.in Ps.*8:3(5.82B,C); id.*Is.interp.*5:6(6.54B); id.*hom.51.2 in Jo.*(8.300E); ἐπειδὴ δὲ τετέλεσται τὸ προηγγελμένον, καὶ τὸ τοῦ νόμου καὶ τῶν π. ἀφῖκται τέλος Cyr.*Is.*1.2(2.55A); Israel never without prophets until rejection of Christ, after which they ceased, *ib.*1.3(82A,B); prophets' possession of Spirit transferred in fuller measure to apostles, Chrys.*hom.51.2 in Jo.*(8.301A); cf.Proc.G.*Is.*3:1–11(M.87.1897B).

L. their mission universal; not confined to Jews, Ath.*inc.*12.5(M.25.117B); though, unlike apostles, they were sent to men of one nation and language, Thdt.*Ezech.*3:6(2.700); were teachers of Greek philosophers, Just.*1apol.*44.8(M.6.396A).

M. were physicians of souls, Or.*hom.14.1 in Jer.*(p.106.13; M.13.404D); princes (ref. Num.21:17–18), id.*hom.12.2 in Num.*(p.99.4; M.12.660B); bestowed grace by personal contact, Thdt.*qu.18 in 1Reg.*(1.369); did not preach virginity, this being reserved for Christ, Meth.*symp.*1.4(p.12.15; M.18.44C).

N. 'sons of the prophets' interpreted as χοροὺς...μικρῶν προφητῶν assisting David in psalmody, Cosm.Ind.*top.*5(M.88.248C).

O. anointing of OT prophets, Clem.*str.*4.25(p.318.15; M.8.1368A); *ib.*5.13(p.382.8; M.9.125B); Chrys.*hom.3.5 in 2Cor.*(10.448B); Cyr. *Lc.*9:18(M.72.648C); Jo.D.*f.o.*4.14(M.94.1161A).

P. liberated from Hades by Christ, Cyr.H.*catech.*4.11.

Q. OT prophets include: Adam, Or.*princ.*1.3.6(p.58.5; M.11.152B); οὗτος...μόνος ἀληθὴς ὑπάρξας π., ἑκάστῳ ζῴῳ...τέθεικε τὰ ὀνόματα *Hom.Clem.*3.21; Chrys.*hom.15.3 in Gen.*(4.119C,D); cf.Cyr. *Joel.*35(3.227E); Abraham, Or.*hom.1.5 in Jer.*(p.3.29; M.13.260A); Meth.*symp.*7.6(p.77.15; M.18.133A); pre-Mosaic prophets in gen., Or.*Cels.*1.49(p.100.14; M.11.752C); Eus.*e.th.*3.3(p.148.10; M.24.985D);

Moses, Clem.*prot.*4(p.47.29; M.8.161B); ὁ ἀρχαιότατος ἡμῶν π. Or. *Cels.*6.21(p.91.21; M.11.1321C); cf.id.*hom.2.5 in Gen.*(p.35.24; M.12.172B); *ib.3.3*(p.42.17; 177C); *maximus...et eximius prophetarum*, id.*hom.6.3 in Num.*(p.34.15; M.12.609C); ὁ μέγας π. Meth.*res.*2.10 (p.349.14); Eus.*d.e.*5 proem.(p.206.6; M.22.341B); ‡Just.*coh.Gr.*9(M.6.257A); prophets in rel. to Law; coupled together in allegorical illustrations, cf.Or.*hom.7.6 inGen.*(p.76.24; M.12.203A); Meth.*symp.*10.6(p.128.27; M.18.204A); prophets' words are 'law', Or.*Jo.*19.3 (p.301.18; M.14.529B); scripture includes prophets under heading of 'law', Jo.D.*Rom.*3:19(M.95.464A); succeed Law and precede gospels, Gr.Nyss.*Eun.*5(2 p.101.15; M.45.680A); Aaron, *Const.App.* 8.1.13; cf. equation of Christian prophets with high priests, *Did.* 13.3; Joshua, Thdt.*qu.14 in Jos.*(1.312); David; esp. as Psalmist, Just.*1apol.*40.1(M.6.388C); Clem.*str.*7.10(p.42.18; M.9.481B); cf.Or. *hom.7.6 in Gen.*(p.77.5; M.12.203B); id.*Jo.*6.6(3; p.114.31; M.14.212A); Meth.*symp.*7.4(p.75.19; M.18.129D); Cyr.H.*catech.*16.28; Gr. Nyss.*Eun.*3(2 p.7.2); Cosm.Ind.*top.*5(M.88.248B); Asaphites, Thdt. *qu.1 in 1Par.*(1.565); cf.Cosm.Ind.*top.*5(M.88.248C); Solomon, Clem. *str.*1.21(p.72.3; M.8.837C); as author of Proverbs, *ib.*1.4(p.17.24; 717B); *ib.*3.17(p.244.4; 1208A); Meth.*symp.*7.4(p.75.19; M.18.129D); Marcell.*fr.*110,111 ap.Eus.*Marcell.*1.2(p.13.4,7; M.24.741A); title denied, Solomon exhibiting no marks of prophetic life and his gift being properly 'wisdom', Eus.*Marcell.*1.2(p.13.2ff.; 741Aff.); παροιμιαστής, ἀλλ' οὐ π. ἐστίν Didym.*Trin.*3.3(M.39.813C); Daniel vindicated as prophet against anti-Christian attacks, Thdt.*Dan.* proem.(2.1056); the twelve prophets collectively, Clem.*str.*3.16 (p.242.22; M.8.1201A); Cyr.H.*catech.*16.29; as one book, cf.Or.*Cant.* 2(p.169.21; M.13.143B); id.*comm.in Mt.*12.13(p.95.17; M.13.1009C); *A.Phil.*78(p.31.13); Eus.*e.th.*3.3(p.149.17; M.24.988D); Cyr.H.*catech.* 4.35; Ath.*ep.fest.*39.6(M.26.1177A).

R. rejection or false interprn. of OT prophets; **1.** by Samaritans νόμον δεχόμενοι μόνον, προφήτας οὐκέτι καταδέχονται Cyr.H.*catech.*18.11; Epiph.*haer.*9.2(p.198.10; M.41.225A); **2.** inspiration of H. Ghost denied by Ebionites, Meth.*symp.*8.10(p.93.6; M.18.153C); **3.** rejected, with apostles, by Elchezaites, Epiph.*haer.*53.1(p.315.22; M.41.960C); **4.** rejected, with Law, by Cerdon and Marcion, Thdt. *haer.*1.24(4.316); cf.Or.*Jo.*2.34(28; p.91.12ff.; M.14.173A) citing anonymous Gnost. fr.; **5.** Simonians ascribe their inspiration to κοσμοποιοὶ ἄγγελοι, Iren.*haer.*1.23.3 ap.Hipp.*haer.*6.19(M.16.3223C); similar doctrine of Basilides, cf.*ib.*1.24.5(M.7.678A); **6.** prophets assigned as ministers to seven aeons acc. Ophites, cf.*ib.*1.30.10–11(701A,B); **7.** inspiration ascribed by Manicheans to πνεῦμα ἀσεβείας, Hegem.*Arch.*11(p.18.14; M.10.1445B); said to be followers of god of darkness, *ib.*12(p.21.1; 1448B).

II. of Jo. Bapt. ἐν Ἰωάννῃ, τῷ γενομένῳ ἐν τῷ γένει ὑμῶν π., μεθ' ὃν οὐδεὶς ἕτερος λοιπὸς παρ' ὑμῖν ἐφάνη π. Just.*dial.*49.3(M.6.584B); *ib.*87.3(684B); ἐσκίρτησεν ἐν ἀγαλλιάσει τὸ βρέφος...καὶ οἱονεὶ ἤρξατο ἔκτοτε π. αὐτὸν ποιεῖν ὁ Ἰησοῦς Or.*hom.7 in Lc.*(p.46.3; M.13.1817B); as forerunner was filled with H. Ghost in manner unknown to earlier prophets, *ib.*(p.47.17); was π. but not ὁ π. (v. III.B infra), id.*Jo.*6.7(4; p.116.8; M.14.213B); Heracleon misunderstood this and denied he was π., *ib.*6.15(8; p.125.16; 229A); π. μὲν γὰρ ἦν· ὁ π. δὲ οὐκ ἦν Isid.Pel.*epp.*3.94(M.78.800A).

III. of Christ as prophet; **A.** in gen. ὡς ἐστιν ἀρχιερεύς, ὡς ἐστι σωτήρ, ὡς ἐστιν ἰατρός, οὕτως καὶ π. Or.*hom.1.12 in Jer.*(p.10.18; M.13.268D); τὸν ἐπὶ πᾶσι π. id.*Jo.*13.55(54; p.285.4; M.14.501C); π. ὢν ἐμφύτῳ καὶ ἀενάῳ πνεύματι πάντοτε ἐπιστάμενα τεθαρρηκῶς ἐξετίθετο *Hom.Clem.*3.15; ὤμοσεν ὁ π. εἰπών· ἀμὴν ὑμῖν λέγω, ἐὰν μὴ ἀναγεννηθῆτε *ib.*11.26; κύριος ἡμῶν καὶ π. *ib.*11.35; ὁ τῆς ἀληθείας π. *ib.*12.29; προφήτου ἀληθοῦς μαθητὴς ὢν [sc. Πέτρος], οὐ π. *ib.*18.7; ἑαυτὸν...ἀποδιορίζει σαφῶς τῆς τῶν π. ἀγέλης...τοῖς μὲν γὰρ...π. μερικὴ...διενεμήθη χάρις· ἐν δὲ τῷ...Χριστῷ πᾶν τὸ πλήρωμα...εὐδόκησε κατοικῆσαι Cyr.*Jo.*2.3(4.167C); εἰ δὲ π. ὠνόμασε τὸν...υἱὸν ὁ πατὴρ...μὴ θορυβηθῇς· ὅτε γὰρ γέγονεν ἄνθρωπος, τότε ἡρμόσθη αὐτῷ καὶ τὸ τοῦ π. ὄνομα *ib.*7(661C); id.*Chr.un.*(5[1].751A).

B. esp. ref. Dt.18:19 Μωσῆς γοῦν προφητεύων περὶ αὐτοῦ οὐχὶ π. μόνον, ἀλλὰ καὶ ἐξαιρέτως εἶπεν...π. ἐκ τῶν ἀδελφῶν...ἀναστήσει ὑμῖν κύριος...οὗτος οὖν ἐστιν ὁ καὶ π. εἰς ἔθνη τεθειμένος Or.*hom.1.12 in Jer.*(p.10.18; M.13.268D); ἦν μὲν γὰρ Ἰησοῦς καὶ π., ὡς δῆλον τῷ νοήσαντι τὸ 'π. ἐκ τῶν ἀδελφῶν...' πλὴν οὐχ ἡ ὑπεροχὴ αὐτοῦ ἐν τῷ π. αὐτὸν εἶναι ἦν, ἀλλ' ἐν τῷ υἱὸν θεοῦ id.*comm.in Mt.*17.14(p.622.25; M.13.1517B); ἐπεὶ δὲ πολλῶν π. γινομένων ἐν Ἰσραὴλ εἷς τις ὁ ὑπὸ Μωσέως προφητευθεὶς ἐξαιρέτως προσεδοκᾶτο...ἐρωτῶσιν οὐχὶ εἰ π. εἴη, ἀλλ' εἰ ὁ π. id.*Jo.*6.7(4; p.116.2; M.14.213A); *Hom.Clem.*3.53; Eus.*d.e.*9.11(p.428.3; M.22.689C); Epiph.*haer.*66.72(p.113.16; M.42.144B); argument against Jewish application of text to Joshua, Isid.Pel.*epp.*3.94(M.78.797C); Cyr.*Jo.*1.10(4.109A); text applied to prophets succeeding Moses, contrasted with pagan diviners, Or. *Cels.*1.36(p.87.33; M.11.729B).

IV. of Christian prophets; **A.** replaced Jewish prophets, Cyr.H. *catech.*13.29; more numerous in NT Church than in OT times, prophetic gift being widely distributed in every church, Chrys. *hom.31.1 in 1Cor.*(10.286B).

B. inspired by H. Ghost; **1.** in gen., *Did.*11.7; cf. Herm.*mand.* 11.9; Chrys.*hom.31.1 in 1Cor.*(10.286C); hence **2.** genuinely inspired prophet is not subject to trial or criticism, *Did.*11.7,11; being infallible, *Hom.Clem.*2.11; **3.** tests of genuine inspiration: **a.** moral character distinguishes true prophet, *Did.*11.8; Apollon.ap.Eus. *h.e.*5.18.8(M.20.477C); **b.** self-seeking convicts prophet of falsity πᾶς π. ὁρίζων τράπεζαν ἐν πνεύματι, οὐ φάγεται ἀπ' αὐτῆς, εἰ δὲ μήγε ψευδοπροφήτης ἐστί...ὃς δ' ἂν εἴπῃ ἐν πνεύματι· δός μοι ἀργύρια...οὐκ ἀκούσεσθε αὐτοῦ *Did.*11.9,12; prophet who exalts himself and desires πρωτοκεθεδρία, prophesying for profit, is false, Herm.*mand.* 11.12; **c.** luxurious and worldly living indicates false prophet, *ib.*; Apollon.ap.Eus.*h.e.*5.18.11(M.20.480B); **d.** prophet's inspiration produces rational teaching; cf. ἀγόμενον [sc. false prophet] καὶ μαινόμενον καὶ σκοτούμενον ὑπὸ τοῦ ἐν αὐτῷ πνεύματος λαλεῖν Jo.D. *1Cor.*12:2–3(M.95.664C); **e.** prophet to be suspected whose teaching has not been approved by S. James of Jerusalem, *Hom.Clem.*11.35; **4.** prophet's inspiration may be demonstrated in symbolic actions, *Did.*11.11.

C. office and functions; **1.** preaching under immediate inspiration, *Did.*11.7; Herm.*mand.*11.9; **2.** ass. apostles, *Did.*11.3; *Hom. Clem.*11.35; and teachers, *ib.*; **3.** dist. from teachers as being wholly inspired, Chrys.*hom.32.1 in 1Cor.*(10.286C); but equated with teachers of orthodoxy, cf. *qui ecclesiastice docent verbum, prophetae sunt Christi*, Or.*comm.ser.47 in Mt.*(p.97.14; M.13.1669A); cf. προφήτην ἀπίστους ἐλέγχοντα καὶ ἀνακρίνοντα (τοιοῦτος γάρ ἐστιν ὁ τῆς καινῆς διαθήκης π.) id.*comm.in Eph.*4:11–12(p.414); **4.** predictors, *Clem.ep.Petr.*2(M.2.28A); **5.** exercising liturg. functions τοῖς δὲ π. ἐπιτρέπετε εὐχαριστεῖν, ὅσα θέλουσιν *Did.*10.7; similar to those of bishops, *ib.*15.1; cf.Herm.*mand.*11.12; **6.** ass. martyrs in conferring absolution, Apollon.ap.Eus.*h.e.*5.18.7(M.20.477B); **7.** receiving maintenance, *Did.*13.1; and first-fruits as being high priests, *ib.*13.3.

D. NT prophets include: Elisabeth, cf.Or.*hom.6 in Lc.*(p.35.16; M.13.1814B); BMV, v. προφῆτις; Symeon and Anna, Or.*hom.17 in Lc.*(p.119.11); John the Evangelist as author of Apoc., Hipp. *antichr.*50(p.33.14; M.10.769B); Or.*Jo.*2.5(4; p.59.23; M.14.117B); id.*Apoc.*3(p.22.6); Andrew, *A.Xanthipp.*29(p.79.7); Paul τεθαρρηκότως λέγω ὅτι ἦν Παῦλος οὐ μόνον ἀπόστολος, ἀλλὰ καὶ π. (ref. 2Tim.3:2, 1Tim.4:1) Or.*comm.in 1Cor.*5:3–5(*JTS* 10 p.364).

E. Montanist prophets; **1.** Montanus, Hipp.*haer.*10.25(p.282.17; M.16.3439B); Epiph.*haer.*48.1(p.220.1; M.41.856B); **2.** as false prophets; not fulfilling Christ's sayings about prophets sent by him, Anon.ap.Eus.*h.e.*5.16.12(M.20.469A); Or.*comm.ser.28 in Mt.* (p.52.13; M.13.1637D); **3.** inspiration; prophesying ἐν παρεκστάσει, Anon.ap.Eus.*h.e.*5.17.3(M.20.473A) cit. s. παρέκστασις; μὴ δυναμένου [sc. Montanus] τὰ ὅμοια λέγειν προφήταις. οὔτε γὰρ πνεῦμα ἅγιον ἐλάλησεν ἐν αὐτῷ. τὸ γὰρ εἰπεῖν, ἐφίπταμαι καὶ πλήσσω καὶ...ἐξιστᾷ κύριος καρδίας, ἐκστατικοῦ ῥήματα ὑπάρχει...ἄλλον χαρακτῆρα ὑποδεικνύντος παρὰ τὸν χαρακτῆρα τοῦ...πνεύματος τοῦ ἐν προφήταις λελαληκότος Epiph.*haer.*48.4(p.225.6; M.41.861A); Didym.*Ac.*10:10 (M.39.1677A); **4.** ass. martyrs, Apollon.ap.Eus.*h.e.*5.18.7(M.20.477B); **5.** no succession of Montanist prophets, none having appeared after Maximilla, Anon.ap.Eus.*h.e.*5.17.4(M.20.473B); Epiph.*haer.*48.2(p.221.13; M.41.857A); **6.** Maximilla's prophecy μετ' ἐμὲ π. οὐκέτι ἔσται, ἀλλὰ συντέλεια Mont.*fr.*ap.Epiph.*haer.*48.2(p.222.1; v.l. προφῆτις M.41.857B), falsified by history acc. Epiph.; **7.** prophets accept rewards, contrary to scriptural teaching, Apollon.ap.Eus. *h.e.*5.18.4(M.20.477A); *ib.*5.18.11(480A).

F. prophets Barcabbas and Barcoph ass. Basilides, Eus.*h.e.*4.7.7(M.20.317A).

V. of false prophets; as prophets of Devil, Clem.*str.*1.17(p.55.5; M.8.800B); of impiety, Or.*mart.*8(p.9.15; M.11.573B); of antichrist; hence include Marcionite teachers, Or.*comm.ser.47 in Mt.*(p.97.15; M.13.1669A).

VI. of heathen prophets; **A.** oracle-priests, Eus.*p.e.*4.2(135C; M.21.237B); at Antioch under Maximinus Daia, id.*h.e.*9.11.6(M.20.840A).

B. Homer a prophet acc. Peratae, Hipp.*haer.*5.8(p.89.6; M.16.3139B).

C. Epimenides (ref. Tit.1:12), Clem.*str*.1.14(p.37.23; M.8.757B).

D. Egyptian prophets; as philosophers, Clem.*str*.1.14(p.39.23; M.8.761B); *ib*.1.15(p.45.21; 777A); in Egyptian liturg. rites, *ib*.6.4 (p.449.21; M.9.253C).

προφητικός, *prophetic*;

A. *like a prophet, prophetic in character*; of Moses, Clem.*str*.1.24 (p.99.16; M.8.905B); of Sibyl π. ... καὶ ποιητική id.*prot*.2(p.20.26; M. 8.100A); of Polycarp διδάσκαλος ἀποστολικὸς καὶ π. *M.Polyc*.16.2; of souls of prophets as represented by παλλακαί of Solomon, Meth. *symp*.7.4(p.75.22; M.18.129D).

B. *belonging to prophets* αἱμάτων...διψῶντας π. Chrys.*hom.11.1 in Mt*.(7.149E); *ib.36.1*(407D); π. ... σηκόν Thdt.*h.rel.21*(3.1239).

C. *consisting of prophets* χορὸς π. Clem.*prot*.1(p.8.22; M.8.64B); Eus.*Ps*.146:7(M.24.68A).

D. *characteristic of prophets* τὸν βίον τὸν π. Or.*hom.15.1 in Jer*. (p.125.15; M.13.428D); ref. Solomon οὔτε δὲ τὸν βίον π. ἐσχηκὼς οὔτε τὸν τῆς προφητείας χαρακτῆρα Eus.*Marcell*.1.2(p.13.15; M.24. 741B); ἀκρίβειαν π. Chrys.*hom.16.9 in Rom*.(9.618D).

E. *of* or *belonging to prophecy*; **1.** in gen. ἀνεβόα προφητικὰ ἡ Ἐλισάβετ Or.*hom.7 in Lc*.(p.48.4; M.17.320C); *ib*.(p.52.5; 321A); **2.** of writings or utterances λέγει...ὁ λόγος π. *2Clem*.11.2; λόγια πρὸς τοῖς π. ἐπιμνησθεὶς Just.*dial*.18.1(M.6.516A); οὐδὲν ἀπὸ τῶν π. ...λαβεῖν *ib*.112.4(736A); ῥήσεις π. ἢ λόγους ἀποστολικοὺς Iren.*haer*. 1.8.1(M.7.521A); μαρτυρίας π. Clem.*paed*.1.9(p.134.12; M.8.340C); θρῆνοι οἱ π. *ib*.2.8(p.195.1; 468A); id.*exc.Thdot*.47(p.122.1; M.9. 681A); Or.*princ*.3.1.12(p.214.8; M.11.269B); Eus.*d.e*.5 proem.(p.202. 14; M.22.336B); of a text from Pss., id.*v.C*.3.42(p.95.18; M.20. 1101B); Bas.*hom*.1.1(2.1A; M.31.164A); ὅπως συνᾴδοι τὰ π. τοῖς ἀποστολικοῖς καὶ τὰ ἀποστολικὰ τοῖς εὐαγγελικοῖς καὶ τὰ εὐαγγελικὰ τοῖς ἀποστολικοῖς καὶ τὰ ἀποστολικὰ τοῖς π. Epiph.*haer*.57.7(p.353. 6; M.41.1005C); πολλὰ...τῶν π. ἠφάνισται βιβλίων· καὶ ταῦτα ἐκ τῆς ἱστορίας τῶν Παραλειπομένων ἴδοι τις ἂν Chrys.*hom.9.4 in Mt*.(7. 135B); πληρῶν τὸ π. ἐκεῖνο id.*hom.84.2 in Jo*.(8.500A); μηδὲ τοῦ ὁμαλισμοῦ χάριν τῶν π. χωρίων εἰς ἀγυρτικὰς ἐμπίπτωμεν λογοποιΐας Isid.Pel.*epp*.4.203(M.78.1289D); ὁ πατὴρ...οὔτε λόγων χρῄζει π. Cyr. *Ps*.15:2(M.69.808C); τοῦτο π. Μαλαχίου ἐστίν...ἐπιτεμόμενος οὖν ὁ εὐαγγελιστής, ὡς ὑπὸ Ἡσαΐου εἰρημένας τὰς δύο χρήσεις παρέθηκεν... καὶ...οἱ λοιποὶ εὐαγγελισταὶ τοῦτο ποιοῦσιν, ἐπιτεμόμενοι τὰς π. ῥήσεις Vict.*Mc*.1:2(p.266.9); of prophetic teaching as symbolized by Levite in parable of Good Samaritan, Or.*hom.34 in Lc*.(p.202. 10); of apocryphal prophetic books used by Naassenes, Hipp. *haer*.5.27(p.133.17; M.16.3023B); π. κανόνος *Hom.Clem*.2.15; **3.** of prophetic vision, ref. docet. teaching εἰ οὖν καὶ νῦν τοιοῦτος ἐφάνη, μὴ ὢν ὅπερ ἐφαίνετο, π. τις ὀπτασία γέγονε τοῖς ἀνθρώποις, καὶ δεῖ καὶ ἄλλην ἐκδέχεσθαι παρουσίαν αὐτοῦ Iren.*haer*.5.1.2(M.7.1122B); ὅρασις δὲ π., καὶ διὰ νοῦ, καὶ τῶν ἔνδον ὀφθαλμῶν παραγίνεται, ὡς παρόντα βλεπόντων τὰ μέλλοντα θεοῦ τὸν νοῦν καταλάμποντος, οὐκ ἔκστασιν ὑπομενόντων, ὡς ἐπὶ τῆς δαιμονικῆς ἐνεργείας Proc.G.*Is*.13:1–11(M. 87.2068B); **4.** ref. prophetic inspiration; **a.** πνεῦμα π.: ὁ ἄγγελος τοῦ π. πνεύματος ὁ κείμενος πρὸς αὐτὸν πληροῖ τὸν ἄνθρωπον Herm.*mand*. 11.9; πνεῦμά τε τὸ π. σεβόμεθα καὶ προσκυνοῦμεν Just.*1apol*.6.2(M.6. 336C); πνεῦμά τε π. ἐν τρίτῃ τάξει ὅτι μετὰ λόγου τιμῶμεν ἀποδείξομεν *ib*.13.3(348A); προφῆται, δι' ὧν τὸ π. πνεῦμα προεκήρυξε τὰ...μέλλοντα *ib*.31.1(376A); id.*dial*.55.1(M.6.596A); συνᾴδει δὲ τῷ λόγῳ καὶ τὸ π. πνεῦμα Athenag.*leg*.10.3(M.6.909A); ref. Marcosian prophesying εἰ οὖν Μάρκος μὲν κελεύει...πρὸς τὰς ἰδίας ἐπιθυμίας ἑαυτοῖς μαντεύεσθαι, ἔσται ὁ κελεύων μείζων τε καὶ κυριώτερος τοῦ π. πνεύματος Iren.*haer*. 1.13.4(M.7.585B); cf. *torcular* [sc. Israel]...*receptaculum prophetici spiritus*, *ib*.4.36.2(1091A); Clem.*paed*.1.5(p.97.9; M.8.264A); κύριος [i.e. Christ] παντὸς π. πνεύματος id.*q.d.s*.6(p.164.8; M.9.612A); Hipp. *antichr*.2(p.4.22; M.10.728C); Or.*Cels*.2.9(p.136.12; M.11.809B); οἱ τοῦ π. πνεύματος ὑπηρέται καὶ οἱ τοῦ εὐαγγελικοῦ κηρύγματος διάκονοι id.*Jo*.6.1(p.106.14; M.14.197B); τῷ π. πνεύματι γνοὺς τὰ ἐσόμενα Ath. *exp.Ps*.72:18(M.27.332A); οὐ γὰρ ἔρημον π. πνεύματος εὑρήσομεν τὸν Ἀδάμ Cyr.*Joel*.35(3.227E); ref. Montanists πολλοὺς ἔχειν μάρτυρας... εἶναι τεκμήριον τοῦ παρ' αὐτοῖς λεγομένου π. πνεύματος Anon.ap. Eus.*h.e*.5.16.20(M.20.472B); needed for interpn. of OT prophets, Andr.Caes.*Apoc*.proem.(M.106.217B); ἡ γὰρ εἰς Χριστὸν...μαρτυρία, αὐτὴ χορηγός ἐστι π. πνεύματος *ib*.57(400B); **b.** π. συνεργία Gr.Nyss. *Eun*.3(2 p.16.3; M.45.580C); **c.** prophetic inspiration derived (contrary to Marcion's view) from Father-creator, Iren.*haer*.4.34.3 (M.7.1084C); **d.** π. χάρισμα: equated with πνεῦμα, Or.*hom.4 in Lc*. (p.30.10); symbolized by oil, Meth.*symp*.10.2(p.123.23; M.18.196A); in Church παρὰ γὰρ ἡμῖν καὶ μέχρι νῦν π. χαρίσματά ἐστιν Just.*dial*. 82.1(M.6.669B); cf.Iren.*haer*.2.32.4(M.7.829B); will remain in Church until parousia, Anon.ap.Eus.*h.e*.5.17.4(M.20.473B); γένοιτο δέ σε ἄξιον εἶναι καὶ π. χαρίσματος Cyr.H.*catech*.17.37; ἐν τῇ ἐκκλησίᾳ χάρισμά ἐστι π., διὰ τὸν θέμενον...πρῶτον ἀποστόλους, δεύτερον προφήτας †Bas.*Is*.102(1.450B; M.30.284C); many to possess it in times of antichrist, Andr.Caes.*Apoc*.48(M.106.360D); among Montanists εἰ γὰρ μετὰ Κοδρᾶτον καὶ...Ἀμμίαν...αἱ περὶ Μοντανὸν διεδέξαντο γυναῖκες τὸ π. χάρισμα, τοὺς ἀπὸ...τῶν γυναικῶν τίνες παρ' αὐτοῖς διεδέξαντο, δειξάτωσαν Anon.ap.Eus.*h.e*.5.17.4(M.20.473B); limit of time fixed for its exercise οἱ περὶ Μαξίμιλλαν ψευδοπροφῆται εὑρεθήσονται, μετὰ τὸν ὅρον τῶν π. χαρισμάτων τολμήσαντες οὐκ ἀπὸ ἁγίου πνεύματος, ἀλλ' ἀπὸ πλάνης δαιμονίων ἐνθουσιασθῆναι Epiph. *haer*.48.2(p.221.21; M.41.857A); **e.** π. χάρις Or.*Jo*.6.49(30; p.158.30; M.14.288A); Ath.*exp.Ps*.73:7(M.27.333D); ref. Adam, Chrys.*hom. 15.3 in Gen*.(4.119C,D); Thdt.*Jer*.20:9(1.505); departed from Jews after Jo. Bapt., Or.*comm.in Mt*.10.21(p.28.29; M 13.889B).

F. ἡ π. [sc. τέχνη] *prophecy*, Thdt.*Ps*.54:15(1.965).

***προφητικῶς**, **1.** *as a prophet* or *prophets* τὸ ἐνεργοῦν τοῖς ἐκφωνοῦσι π. ἅγιον πνεῦμα Athenag.*leg*.10.3(M.6.909A); Thdt.*eran*. 3(4.191); **2.** *in the style of a prophet, quoting a prophet's words* ἐγένοντο, π. εἰπεῖν, ὡσεὶ χόρτος δωμάτων Thdt.*haer*.proem.(4.281); **3.** *by means of prophecy* προμηνύων ἀρχῆθεν π., νῦν δὲ...ἐναργῶς Clem.*prot*.1(p.8.13; M.8.64A); Eus.*e.th*.1.19(p.80.24; M.24.864D); Thdt.*Ps*.49:15(1.928); **4.** *so as to foretell, prophetically* Ἀβραὰμ καὶ...προφῆται π. αὐτὸν ἔβλεπον Iren.*haer*.5.1.2(M.7.1122A); Clem. *paed*.1.7(p.125.25; M.8.321C); †Bas.*bapt*.1.2.13(2.638C; M.31.1548A); Chrys.*hom.41.2 in Jo*.(8.244D); Thdt.*Rom*.3:27(3.45).

προφῆτις, ἡ, *prophetess*; **1.** pagan τῆς ἐν Μιλήτῳ γενομένης π. Or. *Cels*.1.70(p.124.18; M.11.789C); at Delphi, *ib*.3.25(p.221.28; 949B); ἡ τοῦ Ἀπόλλωνος π. *ib*.7.3(p.155.14; 1424D); of Sibyl, *ib*.5.61(p.65.12; 1277C); **2.** of Elisabeth, Or.*schol.in Lc*.2:46(M.17.321D); **3.** of BMV, exeg. Is.8:3 π. ἡ Μαρία, ᾗ προσῆλθε κατὰ τὸν προσεγγισμὸν τὸν διὰ τῆς γνώσεως ὁ Ἡσαΐας...οὐ διστάσεις αὐτὴν εἰπεῖν καὶ π. διότι πνεῦμα κυρίου ἐπῆλθεν ἐπ' αὐτήν †Bas.*Is*.208(1.535A; M.30.477B); ref. views of Antidicomarianites, Epiph.*ep.Arab*.ap.*haer*.78.16 (p.466.29; M.42.725A); Nil.*epp*.2.180(M.79.293A); τέτοκεν ἡ παρθένος ἡ κατὰ τὸν Ἡσαΐαν π. τὸν Ἐμμανουὴλ...δι' ἀκοῆς συνέλαβεν ἡ Μαρία ἡ π. θεὸν ζῶντα Thdot.Anc.*hom.BMV et Sym*.2(M.77.1392D); **4.** of Anna, Or.*hom.17 in Lc*.(p.119.13); **5.** of Marcosian prophetesses, Iren.*haer*.1.13.3(M.7.584B); **6.** of Montanist prophetesses δείκνυμεν ...τὰς π. ταύτας, ἀφ' οὗ τοῦ πνεύματος ἐπληρώθησαν, τοὺς ἄνδρας καταλιπούσας Apollon.ap.Eus.*h.e*.5.18.3(M.20.476C); Priscilla and Maximilla, Hipp.*haer*.8.19(p.238.6; M.16.3366C); τοῦ Μοντάνου π. Eus.*h.e*.5.14(M.20.464A); Epiph.*haer*.48.1(p.220.2; M.41.856B); **7.** of Philumena, regarded as prophetess by Apelles, Hipp.*haer*.7.38 (p.224.8; M.16.3346A); **8.** of Eve as prototype of 'female prophecy' dealing with the things of this world, *Hom.Clem*.3.22.

***προφητοκράτωρ, ὁ**, *chief of the prophets*, Thdr.Stud.*nativ.BMV* 2(M.96.681B).

***προφητοκτονία, ἡ**, *slaughter of prophets*, Eus.*Is*.1:13ff.(M.24.96B).

***προφητοκτόνος**, *slaying prophets*; of Ahab, Cyr.H.*catech*.2.13; of Jews, Gr.Nyss.*res*.5(M.46.685C); Leont.N.*serm*.2(M.93.1588B); of Jerusalem προφητοκτόνῳ πόλει Sophr.H.*triod*.(M.87.3900B).

***προφητόφθεγκτος**, *uttered in prophecy*, Jo.D.*carm.pent*.86(p.216; M.96.837A).

***προφητοφόντης**, *murdering prophets*; of orthodox acc. Montanists, Anon.ap.Eus.*h.e*.5.16.12(M.20.469A); of Jews, Eus.*v.C*.4.27 (p.127.28; M.20.1176B); *Const.App*.6.25.1.

***προφθαδίην**, *in anticipation*, Nonn.*par.Jo*.16:19(M.43.880C).

προφθάνω, *have done* something *already*, c. infin. ἐὰν...προφθάσῃ ...αὐτὸ βαλεῖν *once he has cast it*, *2Clem*.8.2.

***προφιλοσοφέομαι**, *be studied before*, Or.*Cels*.7.39(p.189.23; M.11. 1476B).

προφοιβάω, *purify beforehand*, Nonn.*par.Jo*.11:55(M.43.849A).

***προφονεύω**, *kill previously*, Cyr.*glaph.Gen*.2(1.32C).

προφορά, ἡ, **1.** *utterance, expression*, Clem.*paed*.2.1(p.163.11; M. 8.400A); οὐ κατὰ τὴν π. ἀλλὰ κατὰ τὸ τῆς νοήσεως ἐπιτεταμένον Or. *fr.10 in Jo*.(p.491.27); λόγῳ, τῷ τε κατὰ διάνοιαν καὶ τῷ κατὰ π. Eus.*e.th*.2.15(p.118.23; M.24.933C); Cyr.*Ps*.37:19(M.69.968B); of expression of hands in gesture, Clem.*paed*.2.7(p.193.29; M.8.465A); **2.** *manner* or *form of expression*, Tat.*orat*.1(p.2.2; M.6.805A); of verbal form φωτὶ γὰρ πρὸς φῶς...οὐδεμία, οὔτε κατὰ τὴν π., οὔτε κατ' αὐτὴν τὴν ἔννοιαν, ἐστὶ παραλλαγή Bas.*Eun*.2.25(1.262A; M.29.629B); Gr.Nyss.*Eun*.1(1 p.203.7; M.45.449D); τῶν ὀνομάτων...τὰ μὲν ἔχει τὴν π. πληθυντικήν, ἑνικὴν δὲ τὴν σημασίαν, ὡς Θῆβαι Leont.B.*cap. Sev*.15(M.86.1905A); of *appellation* opp. reality, Aët.*synt*.16 ap. Epiph.*haer*.76.12(p.355.10; M.42.540A); **3.** *utterance, word*, ref. false theories of generation of Logos based on Ps.44:2 π. πατρικὴν οἱονεὶ ἐν συλλαβαῖς κειμένην εἶναι τὸν υἱόν Or.*Jo.*1.24(23; p.29.23; M.14.65B); **4.** *definition, formula*, Max.*ep.*12(M.91.473B); **5.** *fluency of speech, eloquence*, Or.*Jo.*1.8(10; p.13.28; M.14.40A); ἀπατᾶν τῇ τοῦ λόγου π. καὶ ἑτοιμολογίᾳ Epiph.*haer.*71.1(p.250.5; M.42.376A); Max.*ep.*20(M.91.601A).

προφορικός, *expressed, uttered*, opp. ἐνδιάθετος q.v.; cf. *sensatio... quae etiam in mente perseverans, verbum...appellabitur; ex quo emissibilis emittitur verbum* [i.e. λόγος] Iren.*haer.*2.13.2(M.7.742C); Clem.*str.*7.10(p.40.32; M.9.477D); Eus.*d.e.*5.5(p.228.17; M.22.377A); ἀνθρωπινωτέρως ὀνομάζεται λόγια θεοῦ π. ῥήματα Didym.(‡Bas.) *Eun.*5(1.303E; M.29.728C); ὁ λόγος...παντὸς ἀνθρώπου π. μέν ἐστι, γεννᾶται δὲ ἀτμήτως ἐκ τοῦ...νοῦ Gel.Cyz.*h.e.*2.21.31(M.85.1289B); τῷ ἐνδιαθέτῳ λόγῳ ποιήσασθαι τὴν διάλεξιν αἰνίττεται καθ' ἑαυτόν, ἥκιστα π. λόγῳ χρησάμενος Gr.Agr.*Eccl.*1.17(M.98.793C); Jo.D.*dial.*30(M.94.592A); of eloquent speech πλουτεῖν τῷ λόγῳ π. Or.*exc.in Ps.*36:16 (M.17.132A); theol., v. λόγος.

***προφράσσω**, *fortify in advance*, Eus.*fr.Lc.*6:20(M.24.537A); Marc. Diac.*v.Porph.*65.

προφυλακτικός, *prophylactic*, met. τὴν π. ἐπιμέλειαν Or.*adnot.in Ex.*28:30(M.17.17A); τῶν π. ... λόγων Chrys.*hom.*2.5 *in Jo.*(8.16A); c. genit. προφυλακτικὰς...αἱρέσεων...ἐφόδους Eus.*h.e.*4.7.5(M.20.317A).

***προφυλακτικῶς**, *so as to take precautions*, Ast.Am.*hom.*12(M.40.349C); Max.*schol.d.n.*4.30(M.4.301C).

***προφωνήσιμος**, prob. error for ⟨προσφωνήσιμος⟩ (cf. προσφωνή) *of the proclamation*, epithet of Septuagesima εἶναι δὲ...τὰς δύο ἑβδομάδας, τῆς τε Ἀποκρέου καὶ τῆς π. ἀκωλύτους ἅπαντας εἰς πάντα †Jo.Jej.*poenit.*(M.88.1913C).

***προφωράω**, *detect beforehand*, Gr.Nyss.*Eun.*6(2 p.142.1; M.45.728B).

***προφωτίζ-ω**, *enlighten beforehand*, ref. prophetic foreknowledge τὸ...∼ειν ἐν αὐτοῖς τὸ θεῖον πνεῦμα μὴ μόνον τὰ παρόντα, ἀλλὰ καὶ τῶν μελλόντων...γνῶσιν Eus.*d.e.*5 *proem.*(p.208.12; M.22.345B); ref. catechetical instruction preceding admission into mysteries τῆς...ψυχῆς διὰ τοῦ τῆς διδασκαλίας λόγου ∼ομένης Cyr.H.*catech.*18.32; ref. conversion preceding bodily healing πίστει προφωτισθεὶς τὴν ψυχήν Sophr.H.*mir.Cyr.et Jo.*37(M.87.3565B).

***προφώτισμα, τό**, *illumination beforehand*, of baptism preceding Easter festival τρία...δεῖπνα κατὰ τὸν τοῦ πάσχα καιρὸν πεποιηκότα εὑρίσκομεν...ἓν μὲν ἐν Γεθσημανῇ, ὃ καὶ τὸν νιπτῆρα περιέχει κατὰ τὴν τοῦ σαββάτου ἡμέραν...διὸ καὶ ἡμεῖς τηνικαῦτα ποιοῦμεν τὰ π. Eutych. *pasch.*1(M.86.2392A).

***πρόφωτος**, *existing before there was light*, of Christ οὗτος ἡ ἀκτὶς ἡ ἄκτιστος, ἐκ προφώτου ἡλίου γεννώμενος, ἀλλ' οὐ τεμνόμενος ‡Cyr.H.*occurs.*9(M.33.1196C).

***προχαιρετίζω**, *greet first*, *T.Abr.*A 2(p.78.21).

προχάραγμα, τό, 1. *preliminary sketch for picture*; met., of present life opp. eternity, Gr.Naz.*or.*17.9(M.35.976C); of Law, ref. Heb.10:1 ὁ νόμος...εἰκόνος ἐστὶ π. Jo.D.*imag.*1.15(M.94.1245A); **2.** *foreshadowing* ἡ στάσις ἦν...στήσῃ μετὰ τὸ βάπτισμα...τῆς ἐκεῖθεν δόξης ἐστὶ π. Gr.Naz.*or.*40.46(M.36.425A); π. τῶν ἀοράτων...τὰ ὁρώμενα id.ap.*cat.Heb.*8:6(p.582.18); *V.Max.*2(M.90.69B); of OT types ἡ δὲ σκηνοπηγία π. ἦν τῆς...ἀναστάσεως †Cyr.*coll.VT*(6⁴.22D; M.77.1208D); Max.*ambig.*(M.91.1300B); CTrull.*can.*82; **3.** *first picture*; of Abgar's portrait of Christ, *A.Thadd.*5(p.276n.).

προχαράσσ-ω, *delineate in advance* οἱ ταῖς σκιαῖς τὰ σώματα ∼οντες, δευτέρᾳ καὶ τρίτῃ χειρὶ ταύτας ἀπακριβοῦσιν Gr.Naz.*ep.*230 (M.37.372D); Eustrat.*v.Eutych.*9(M.86.2284C); ref. patriarchs οἱ... φυσικῶς ἐν ἑαυτοῖς τὸν γραπτὸν ἐν πνεύματι προχαράξαντες νόμον Max.*ambig.*(M.91.1149D); Ἀβραὰμ ὁ ἀρχιζωγράφος τῆς Χριστοῦ ταφῆς καὶ τῆς ἀναστάσεως. ἀμφότερα γὰρ ἐπὶ τῷ...παιδὶ προεχάραξεν Germ.CP *or.*2(M.98.280A).

***προχαρίζομαι**, *bestow in advance*, Iren.*haer.*5.2.3(M.7.1127C; perh. for προῖκα χαρίζεται).

***προχάρισμα, τό**, *gracious gift*, *Orac.Sib.*5.331.

προχειρίζ-ομαι, 1. *put forward*, Meth.*symp.*2.3(p.18.5; M.18.52A); Gr.Thaum.*pan.Or.*(p.15.7; M.10.1069A); **2.** *put forward for office, appoint*; **a.** civil ∼εται εἰς βασιλέα Λέων τις Thdr.Lect.*h.e.*1.7(M.86.169A); ‡Jo.D.*Artem.*12(p.51.30; M.96.1261D); **b.** eccl., *appoint to ministerial office*, Eus.*h.e.*2.1.10(M.20.137B); CAnc.(314)*can.*3; CNic.(325)*can.*10; Pall.*h.Laus.*38(p.117.3; M.34.1188C); Philost.*h.e.*2.11 (M.65.476B); Socr.*h.e.*2.9.1(M.67.197B); Leont.N.*v.Jo.Eleem.*2(p.7.18); **c.** ref. divine appointment: of apostles διδάσκαλοι τῆς οἰκουμένης προεχειρίζοντο Tit.Bost.*fr.Lc.*20:46(p.235); of Jo. Bapt. προχειρισθεὶς εἰς τὸ προοδεῦσαι Ath.*Ar.*2.54(M.26.261B); Cyr.*Ps.*49:4 (M.69.1077D); id.*Jo.*5.5(4.533C); προκεχείριστο μὲν εἰς ἀποστολὴν ὁ Μωσῆς id.*Rom.*9:24(M.74.841A); ἀπόστολοι, καὶ οἱ μετὰ τούτων τοῦ θείου κηρύγματος προχειρισθέντες διάκονοι Thdt.*Mich.*5:6(2.1503); of civil rulers οἱ μὲν...ὡς ἄξιοι...ὑπὸ θεοῦ ∼ονται· οἱ δὲ...ἀνάξιοι...κατὰ θεοῦ συγχώρησιν...∼ονται Anast.S.*qu.et resp.*16(M.89.476C).

προχείρισις (προχείρησις), ἡ, 1. *execution* of intention, -ησις, Max.*Pyrr.*(M.91.313B); -ησις, *ib.*(325A); **2.** *choice, selection* παραλόγους π. καὶ προβολὰς τῶν κρατούντων Gr.Agr.*Eccl.*9.9(M.98.1096C); of men by God, -ησις, Didym.(‡Bas.)*Eun.*5(1.300B; M.29.720C); Leont.H.*Nest.*4.37(M.86.1709C).

πρόχειρος, *ready to hand, obvious*; of lit. opp. spiritual sense of scripture, Or.*princ.*4.2.4(p.312.9; M.11.364B); Meth.*res.*1.21(p.243.14; M.41.1089A); Eus.*h.e.*7.25.6(M.20.697C); id.*d.e.*6.18(p.278.23; M.22.457C); τῆς ⟨νοητῆς⟩ Αἰγύπτου...καὶ...τῆς π. *ib.*9.4(p.413.10; 665C); id.*Marcell.*1.1(p.8.32; M.24.729A); καρπὸς μὲν...ἡ μυστικὴ καὶ πνευματικὴ τῶν γραφῶν διάνοια· φύλλα δὲ σκέποντα τὸν...καρπόν, αἱ π. λέξεις Didym.*Ps.*1:3(M.39.1160A); Isid.Pel.*epp.*1.360(M.78.388A); Thdt.*qu.31 in Dt.*(1.280); of a symbolical action ὁ Πέτρος τῷ προχειροτέρῳ ἐνιδών Or.*Jo.*32.6(5; p.434.33; M.14.756B).

προχειροτονέω, *ordain previously*, Jo.Clim.*past.*13(M.88.1193A).

προχορηγέω, pass., *be supplied*, Epiph.*haer.*42.12(p.169.19; M.41.793C).

προχράω, *lend, advance*, *T.Job* 11(p.110.11).

προχρηματίζω, *forewarn*, Epiph.*mens.*15(M.43.261B); ‡Meth. *Sym.et Ann.*2(M.18.352A).

***προχρησμῳδέω**, *give an oracle beforehand*; of OT prophesyings, ‡Gr.Nyss.*occurs.*(M.46.1165C); Isid.Pel.*epp.*2.212(M.78.653B); Cyr. *ador.*15(1.530D).

***προχρηστικῶς**, *by anticipation*, Epiph.*haer.*71.2(p.251.14; M.42.377A).

***προχρίομαι**, *be anointed beforehand*; of Moses as prototype of prophets, Cyr.*hom.pasch.*17(5².232B).

προχρονέω, *precede in order of time*, Clem.*str.*8.9(p.99.7; M.9.597A); *ib.*(p.99.8; M. *ib.*).

***προχρόνιος, 1.** *antecedent*, Gel.Cyz.*h.e.*2.22.13(M.85.1293A); **2.** *before time* ὅνπερ ἄν τις π. χρόνον...ὑπολάβῃ Didym.*Trin.*1.15(M.39.301B).

πρόχρονος, *before time*, of Valent. aeons π. φύσεις Gr.Naz.*carm.* 2.1.11.1165(M.37.1109A); of divine οὐσία, Gr.Nyss.*Eun.*1(1 p.74.19; M.45.304D).

προχωνεύω, *mix beforehand*, Cyr.H.*catech.*13.11.

προχώρημα, τό, *excrement*, Or.*Cels.*4.50(p.323.16; M.11.1109B).

***προψάλλω**, *sing in anticipation*, Ast.Soph.*hom.3 in Ps.*5(M.40.424A).

προωδίνω, *be in travail with first*, Cyr.*ador.*15(1.539B); Proc.G. *Gen.*17:23(M.87.361B).

προώλης, *bent upon destruction*, Just.*dial.*103.1(M.6.716B).

προώνυμος, *called by a name previously*, Nonn.*par.Jo.*9:7(M.43.825A).

***προωρικῶς**, v. *προοριστικῶς.

προώριος, *before the time*, Gr.Naz.*carm.*1.1.8.114(M.37.455A); Nonn.*par.Jo.*16:14(M.43.880B).

***προωρισμένως**, *predeterminately*, Clem.*str.*6.9(p.469.29; M.9.297A).

προωφελέω, pass., *be benefited before*, Or.*or.*10(p.320.12; M.11.445C); Eus.*e.th.*3.2(p.142.26; M.24.977B).

πρυμνήσιος, *of a stern*; neut. as subst., *helm*; met., Nonn.*par.Jo.* 17:2(M.43.884B).

***πρυμνήτης, ὁ**, *steersman*, Thphl.Ant.*Autol.*2.7(cj. πρυμνήτου for πρύμνιδι codd., M.6.1060A).

***πρυμνική, ἡ**, [sc. τέχνη] *art of navigation as exercised on the poop, watch astern*, Epiph.*haer.*61.4(p.384.20, v.l. πρύμνῃ M.41.1044D).

***πρύμνις, ἡ**, v. *πρυμνήτης.

πρυτανεῖον (πρυτάνιον), τό, *town hall, public table in town hall*, in comparison of shrines at which answers to prayer are bestowed with πρυτάνια from which doles are given, Didym.*Trin.*2.7(M.39.589B); met. κοινὸν...π. εὐσεβείας *V.Const.*37(p.567.24).

πρυτανεύ-ω, 1. *be in control of, rule*, Thdt.*Dan.*proem.(2.1061); ref. divine government, Sophr.H.*mir.Cyr.et Jo.*8(M.87.3440D); of virtues controlling life, Bas.*hom.*2.5(2.14A; M.31.192C); Epiph. *anc.*1(p.6.6; M.43.17B); **2.** *bestow, grant*, Meth.*res.*1.51(p.305.12; M.18.281B); Eus.*h.e.*10.8.1(M.20.893C); ἡ πανταχοῦ γῆς διὰ τῆς αὐτοῦ [sc. Const.] δυνάμεως ∼θεῖσα εἰρήνη id.*l.C.*17(p.257.18; M.20.1436B); Ath.*inc.*52.1(M.25.188C); Gr.Naz.*or.*4.47(M.35.572B); ἱερωσύνην... ∼ουσαν πᾶσι τὰ πρέποντα Isid.Pel.*epp.*2.52(M.78.496A); τὰ παρὰ τῆς ἀρρήτου σοφίας ∼όμενα Thdt.*ep.*15(4.1076).

πρύτανις, ὁ, 1. *governor*; of prefect of city, Ath.*apol.Const.*24 (M.25.625A); of God τῶν ὅλων ὁ π. Thdt.*qu.62 in Gen.*(1.75); id.

*Ps.*30:16(1.796); of Christ ἁπάντων...π. ὡς θεόν id.*eran.*1(4.17); δημιουργὸν τῶν ὅλων...καὶ π. id.ap.Cyr.*apol.Thdt.*4(p.121.11; 6[1]. 214E); θεοτόκε, δι' ἧς γαλακτοτροφεῖται ὁ...π. θεός ‡Jo.D.*hom.*5(M.96. 653B); **2.** *one who brings* a thing *about, promoter*, Clem.*paed.hymn.* 14(p.291; M.8.681B); εἰρήνης π. ἐμαυτὸν...προσάγω Const.ap.Eus. *v.C.*2.68(p.68.11; M.20.1041A); θεός, ὁ τῆς ἀληθείας π. †Gr.Thaum. *ep.Philagr.*(M.46.1108A); Χριστὸς ὁ πάντων ἡμῖν τῶν ἀγαθῶν καὶ δοτὴρ καὶ π. Cyr.*Ps.*6:11(M.69.748C); id.*Os.*87(3.118B); θεὸς...τῆς εἰρήνης ὁ π. Thdt.*1Cor.*14:33(3.263); of Telemachus intervening in amphitheatre τῆς εἰρήνης τὸν π. id.*h.e.*5.26.3(3.1067).

πρώην, *lately, the day before yesterday*; hence *before, previously* πολὺ τοῦ π. αἰδεσιμώτερος Leont.N.*v.Jo.Eleem.*28(p.62.3); ἐκ π. *from of old*, Gr.Mag.*dial.*(tr.Zach.)3.7(M.*PL.*77.230B).

πρωθύπνιον, πρώθυπνον, τό, v. πρωτοΰπνιον.

πρωθύστερος, *in reverse order* τὸ π. δοκεῖ σε ξενίζειν [i.e. apparent difficulty of glorification of Church before loosing of dragon] Ephr. 3.191E; *ib.*192C; Didym.*Trin.*3.18(M.39.884A); neut. as adv. π. ἐστι τὰ ῥήματα Thdr.Mops.*Ps.*9:35(p.61.22; M.66.656A); Proc.G.*Dt.*21:23 (M.87.928A).

***πρώθω**, *push* πρὸς τὸ κάταντες τῆς φάραγγος τοῦτον ἔπρωθον Steph.Diac.*v.Steph.*(M.100.1140A).

πρωΐθεν, *from early morning* οὕτως διάγοντες ἀπὸ π. ἕως ἑσπέρας Epiph.*mens.*3(M.43.241D).

πρώϊος, *early in the day*; fem. as subst.; **1.** *early morning, dawn*, Diod.*Ps.*54:18(M.33.1593C); εἴη δ' ἂν π. καὶ ὁ τῆς τοῦ σωτῆρος ἐπιδημίας καιρός Cyr.*Ps.*5:4(M.69.741B); met. π. εἰρηνικῆς ὀρθοδοξίας Thdr.Stud.*epp.*1.4(M.99.1124B); genit. πρωΐας as adv., Clem.*str.*7. 12(p.57.15; M.9.512A); **2.** ? *morning prayers* εἰς τὰς π. παρεστάναι Hesych.S.*temp.*1.9(M.93.1484C).

***πρωρική, ἡ,** [sc. τέχνη] *art of navigation exercised in fore-part of ship, watch ahead* (cf. πρυμνική), Epiph.*haer.*61.4(p.384.19; M.41. 1044D).

πρῷρον, τό, plur., *bows* of a ship, = πρῷρα, ἡ, *A.Phil.*34(p.17.10).

πρωτάγγελος, ὁ, ἡ, *first messenger*; of Jo. Bapt., Nonn.*par.Jo.* 1:15(M.43.752B); of Mary Magdalene as announcer of Resurrection, Cyr.*Jo.*12.1(4.1087B).

***πρωταγωγός**, *first, introductory*, Geo.Pis.*Sev.*522(M.92.1660B).

πρωταγωνιστής, ὁ, *first-line soldier*, Socr.*h.e.*5.25.13(M.67.653A).

πρωταίτιος, *originating, being the first cause*, Jo.D.*virt.*(M.95. 89A) = Ephr.3.427A,B.

***πρωταρχία, ἡ,** *headship, primacy of government*, in complimentary address to pope ὑπὸ τῆς θείας π. σου Thdr.Stud.*epp.*1.33(M.99. 1020C).

πρώταρχος, ὁ, *chief*, *M.Areth.*(p.13); Thdr.Stud.*epp.*2.162(M.99. 1509B); Πέτρον...πρώταρχον τῶν λοιπῶν ἀποστόλων *ib.*2.139(1444C); ἐπισκόπους...πρωτάρχους τῆς αἱρέσεως *ib.*1.38(1044A).

πρωτάρχων, ὁ, *initiator*; name of Barbeliote demiurge, Iren. *haer.*1.29.4 ap.Thdt.*haer.*1.13(4.305).

***πρωτεία, ἡ,** *supremacy, position of first importance* [poss. represented by *principalitas*, Iren.*haer.*3.3.2(M.7.849A)]; ref. Devil τῆς π. δι'...ἀλαζονείαν...ἐρρίφη Didym.*Trin.*3.32(M.39.957C).

πρωτεῖον, τό, 1. *chief rank*; plur., ref. eccl. offices, Herm.*sim.*8.7. 4; **2.** plur., *chiefs, leaders* τὰ δὲ π. τοῦ δήμου οὐ κατεδέξαντο τοῦτο Thphn.*chron.*p.246(M.108.617C); *ib.*p.293(717B).

***πρωτέμφασις, ἡ,** *primary significance*; of literal meaning of scripture, opp. spiritual sense, Chrysipp.*enc.in Mich.*(p.92.17).

πρωτεργάτης, ὁ, *originator, chief promoter*, of Phocas ὁ...συμφορῶν π. Geo.Pis.*Heracl.*2.7(M.92.1317A); of Justin φιλοσοφίας...π. id.*Sev.*544(M.92.1661B).

[*]πρωτερεύω, v. προτερεύω.

πρωτεύ-ω, 1. *precede, take precedence over* τὴν...ἐκ τοῦ πατρὸς γεγεννημένην ἀρχὴν...τῶν μετὰ ταῦτα γενητῶν ἁπάντων ~ειν Eus.*p.e.* 7.15(324D; M.21.549A); Eus.Em.*fr.Gal.*3:23(p.49.16); πολλάκις ὁ πένης τὸν πλούσιον ~ει ἐν τῇ εὐσεβείᾳ Chrys.*res.Chr.*3(2.442A); **2.** *take the lead, be pre-eminent*, Meth.*symp.*1.1(p.9.7; M.18.40A); of popes ὑμῖν τὸ ~ειν ἁρμόττει Thdt.*ep.*113(4.1187); τοὺς ἐν ἀγγέλοις ~οντας Andr.Caes.*Apoc.*67(M.106.432A); of eccl. primates οἱ ~οντες τῆς ἐπαρχίας *Cod.Afr.*13; of chiefs of the civil or military services, Nil. *epp.*1.174 tit.(M.79.152A); *ib.*1.219 tit.(164A); Thdt.*ep.*15 tit.(4.1075); **3.** ptcpl. as subst., *chief magistrates* of city ὁ δημεκδικῶν μετὰ τῶν εἰρηναρχῶν καὶ τῶν δύο ~όντων Marc.Diac.*v.Porph.*25.

***πρωτοαθλήτης, ὁ,** *first champion*; of S. Stephen, ‡Chrys.*Steph.* 2(12.811C).

***πρωτοασηκρήτης (-τις), ὁ,** *chief secretary, chief of chancellery* τὸ τοῦ πρωτοασηκρήτις...ἀξίωμα *Max.offic.*1(M.90.209B); Thphn. *chron.*p.321(v.l. πρωτοασηκρῆτις M.108.777A).

***πρωτόβαθμος**, *of the first rank*, of SS. Peter and Paul π. ἀπόστολοι *Hymn.*(*AS* 1 p.554).

πρωτόβαθρος, *chief*, of S. Peter as π. τῶν ἀποστόλων *Proem.*in Gr.Mag.*dial.*(M.*PL.*77.147C).

***πρωτόβιος**, *senior*, ‡Ath.*ep.Cast.*1.11(M.28.861C).

πρωτοβόλος, *shedding first* (*milk*) *teeth*, Jo.Mal.*chron.*12 p.288(M. 97.436A).

***πρωτογένεθλος**, *first-born*, Gr.Naz.*carm.*1.1.9.89(M.37.463A).

***πρωτογενεσία, ἡ,** *precedence in creation* πρωτογενεσίᾳ προτερεύουσιν οἱ ἄγγελοι Eustrat.*stat.anim.*18(p.489).

***πρωτογενέτειρα, ἡ,** *first mother*; of Valent., of ogdoad opp. subsequent aeons, Hipp.*haer.*10.13(p.274.4; M.16.3427B).

πρωτογενής, *first-begotten*, dist. from πρωτότοκος, cf. τὸ μὲν πρωτότοκον πρὸς τὸ μητρῷον γένος...τὸ δὲ π. πρὸς τὸ πατρῷον, γεννᾷ γὰρ ἄρρεν Philo ap.Leont.et Jo.*sacr.*2(M.86.2089C); of Logos, Gr. Thaum.*pan.Or.*4(p.8.14; M.10.1060C); denied of Son in exposition of πρωτότοκος, Isid.Pel.*epp.*3.31(M.78.749D) cit. s. πρωτόγονος.

***πρωτογέννημα, τό,** *firstling* παντὸς π. σου...πρόσφερε ἀπαρχάς *T.Lev.*9.14(v.l. -γενήματος); *T.Isach.*5.4(v.l. -γενήμασιν); οὐ ταὐτὸν εἶναι ἀπαρχὴν καὶ π.· μετὰ γὰρ τοὺς πάντας καρποὺς ἀναφέρεται ἡ ἀπαρχή, πρὸ δὲ πάντων τὸ π. ... τῶν γραφῶν...π. μὲν τὸν...νόμον, ἀπαρχὴν δὲ τὸ εὐαγγέλιον Or.*Jo.*1.2(4; p.6.15; M.14.25C).

πρωτογέννητος, *first-begotten*, ref. Son τῷ π. μαθητευόμενοι φωτί Or.*Jo.*1.25(24; p.31.25; M.14.68D).

πρωτόγονος, A. *first-born, first-begotten*; **1.** pagan τὸν Φάνητα... θεὸν ὄντα π. Athenag.*leg.*20.4(M.6.932B); cf. *Orpheus...deum verum et magnum, π., id est primogenitum, appellat*, Lactantius *divinarum institutionum* 1.5(M.*PL.*6.130A); **2.** of Son τοῦ ποιήσαντος θεοῦ καὶ τοῦ π. αὐτοῦ Χριστοῦ Just.*1apol.*58.3(M.6.416B); εἷς γὰρ τῷ ὄντι ἐστὶν ὁ θεός, ὃς ἀρχὴν τῶν ἁπάντων ἐποίησεν, μηνύων τὸν π. υἱόν ὁ Πέτρος γράφει Clem.*str.*6.7(p.461.9; M.9.280B); ὁ λόγος...ὁ π. πατρὸς παῖς Hipp.*haer.*10.33(p.290.25; M.16.3450C); in rel. to Adam ἥρμοζε γὰρ τὸ π. τοῦ θεοῦ καὶ πρῶτον βλάστημα...τὴν σοφίαν τῷ πρωτοπλάστῳ καὶ...πρωτογόνῳ τῶν ἀνθρώπων ἀνθρώπῳ κερασθεῖσαν ἐνηνθρωπηκέναι Meth.*symp.*3.4(p.30.20; M.18.65B); ὁ π. λόγος id.*Porph.* 1(p.504.16; M.18.400B); ἡ π. καὶ πρωτόκτιστος τοῦ θεοῦ σοφία Eus. *h.e.*1.2.21(64B); πρωτότοκος σοφία καὶ μονογενὴς καὶ π. τοῦ θεοῦ προϋπέστη λόγος id.*d.e.*5.1(p.215.12; M.22.357A); interpreted in act. sense πρῶτον τετοκέναι, τουτέστι, πεποιηκέναι τὴν κτίσιν, ἵν' ᾖ, τῆς τρίτης συλλαβῆς ὀξυνομένης, πρωτογόνος, οὐ πρωτογενής Isid.Pel.*epp.* 3.31(M.78.749D); **3.** of primal ὄφις as π. τῶν ὑδάτων (acc. Naassenes), Hipp.*haer.*5.19(p.120.14; M.16.3183C); **4.** of human first-born, Thdt. *Mich.*7:1(2.1510).

B. *first-produced, first-created*; **1.** of archangels ἑπτὰ μέν εἰσιν οἱ... π. ἀγγέλων ἄρχοντες Clem.*str.*6.16(p.504.19; M.9.369C); **2.** of Devil, Tat.*orat.*7(p.7.25; M.6.820C); **3.** of chaos, Gr.Naz.*carm.*1.2.1.63(M. 37.527A); **4.** of commandment given to Adam φῶς μὲν ἦν καὶ ἡ τῷ π. δοθεῖσα π. ἐντολή Gr.Naz.*or.*40.6(M.36.364D); **5.** of Israel ἐγὼ π. παντὸς ζῴου ζωουμένου ὑπὸ θεοῦ *Prec.Josephi* ap.Or.*Jo.*2.31(25; p.88. 27; M.14.169A); **6.** of Adam, Meth.*symp.*3.4(p.30.21; M.18.68A); Gr. Naz.*carm.*1.1.8.128(M.37.456A); τοῦ γὰρ...θύματος...πάσχοντος, ὁ ἐκ τοῦ πρωτοπλάστου λύεται θάνατος, καὶ σώζεται ὁ π. ἄνθρωπος ἐν ἡμῖν πᾶσιν ὤν ‡Chrys.*pasch.*2(8.254B); Nonn.*par.Jo.*19:17(M.43.901B).

C. *high-born, aristocratic*, *Orac.Sib.*14.263.

πρωτοδεύτερος, *of first and second rank*, ref. Trin. οὐδὲν π., οὐδὲν κυριόδουλον Eulog.*fr.Trin.*2.2(p.364); Jo.D.*haer.*epilog.(M.94.780A).

πρωτοδιάκονος, ὁ, 1. *first deacon*; of S. Stephen, Cosm.Ind.*top.*5 (M.88.297A); *Lit.Jac.*(p.214.20); Jo.D.*f.o.*4.15(M.94.1168B); **2.** *chief deacon, archdeacon* CQuerc.(M.103.108D); Προκόπιος...μοναχὸς καὶ π. CCP(536)*act.*3(*ACO* 3 p.168.3; H.2.1244B); τοὺς κεκοιμημένους παραπέμψαι ἐγγράφεσθαι τῷ π. ἐν τοῖς διπτύχοις Thdr.Stud.*poen.* 1.106(M.99.1748B); in Montanist sect Μοντανοῦ π. *MAMA* 4.321 (Pepuza, saec. v).

***πρωτοδίκαιος**, *first righteous*, of Abel π. ποιμὴν Χριστοῦ ποιμένος τύπος ‡Epiph.*hom.*2(M.43.452D).

***πρωτόδοτος**, *given first*; of immediate knowledge of God, Dion. Ar.*c.h.*7.3(M.3.209C); *ib.*10.1(272D).

***πρωτοδότως**, *so as to be given first*, Dion.Ar.*c.h.*7.3(M.3.209B); ἡ δὲ [sc. παραγωγή] κατ' ἔλλαμψιν...προβαίνει..., τοῖς μὲν π., τοῖς δὲ δευτεροδότως †Proc.G.*Procl.*1(M.87.2792[h]B); ‡Sophr.H.*triod.*(M.87. 3905A).

***πρωτοδόχως**, *so as to be the first to receive*, Leont.H.*Nest.*1.18(M. 86.1468C).

***πρωτοευνοῦχος, ὁ,** *chief eunuch*, Thphn.*chron.*p.306(M.108.745A).

***πρωτόθνητος**, *first to die*; of Abel, ‡Epiph.*hom.*2(M.43.452D).

πρωτόθρονος, ὁ, *chief bishop*, ‡Chrys.*serm.pasch.*(p.110); of metropolitan of Tyre, Thphn.*chron*.p.110(M.108.316C); ἡ κορυφαιοτάτη [i.e. Rome] τῶν ἐκκλησιῶν...ἧς Πέτρος π. Thdr.Stud.*epp*.2.86 (M.99.1332B).

***πρωτόθροος**, *speaking first, prophetic*; of Moses, Nonn.*par.Jo*. 5:45(M.43.792C); of Isaiah, *ib*.12:38(857A); of Jo. Bapt., *ib*.3:26 (772A).

***πρωτοιερεύς, ὁ**, *senior presbyter*, *Euchol*.(p.238).

πρωτοκαθεδρία, ἡ, *chief seat, presidency, highest office*; **1.** in gen. τὰς π. ἐν ταῖς συνελεύσεσι παραιτοῦ Bas.*renunt*.8(2.209D; M.31.644B); Jo.D.*spir.neq*.9(M.95.81D); **2.** of presidency of congregation, claimed by false prophets, Herm.*mand*.11.12; **3.** of office of presbyter, ref. 'gnostic' κἂν ἐνταῦθα ἐπὶ γῆς πρωτοκαθεδρίᾳ μὴ τιμηθῇ, ἐν τοῖς εἴκοσι καὶ τέσσαρσι καθεδεῖται θρόνοις Clem.*str*.6.13 (p.485.15; M.9.328B); **4.** of presbyters and bishops τὰς π. πεπιστευμένοι τοῦ λαοῦ ἐπίσκοποι καὶ πρεσβύτεροι Or.*comm.in Mt*.16.22(p.552. 29; M.13.1452A); **5.** of bishops; sought after by evil characters, Pall.*v.Chrys*.20(p.145.11; M.47.81); Thdr.Lect.*h.e*.2.34(M.86.201C); in sect of Theodotus and Asclepiodotus, †Hipp.*Artem*.ap.Eus.*h.e*. 5.28.12(M.20.513C); among Gnost. heretics, Clem.*str*.7.16(p.69.21; M.9.536B).

***πρωτοκαθεδρίτης, ὁ**, *occupant of chief seat, president*; plur., of presbyters in church, Herm.*vis*.3.9.7.

***πρωτοκάθεδρος, ὁ**, *president* τοῦ ἀποστολικοῦ χοροῦ π. Πέτρον Const.Pogon.*sacr*.3(M.*PL*.96.391A).

***πρωτοκαλλιγράφος, ὁ**, *chief writer* in charge of copyists in monastery, Thdr.Stud.*poen*.1.60(M.99.1740D).

***πρωτοκάμαρος**, *of the first chamber* or *vault* of the sky Εὐνώ· οὗτος οἰκονόμος τῆς π. ἀνατολῆς καὶ αἰθερίου, ὃν ἐκάλεσεν ἡ ἀγνωσία Ἶσιν [sc. in Peratic cosmology] Gnost.ap.Hipp.*haer*.5.14(p.109.18; M.16.3167D).

***πρωτοκήρυξ, ὁ**, *first herald, first preacher*, Eus.*e.th*.1.14(p.74.14; M.24.853A).

***πρωτόκλητος**, *first called*; of S. Andrew, *A.Andr*.B tit.(p.58.1); *Hymn*.(*AS* 1 p.555); of angels, Clem.*exc.Thdot*.27(p.116.12; M.9. 673A).

πρωτοκλισία, ἡ, *first seat at table*, Clem.*str*.7.16(p.69.22; M.9. 536B); Bas.*renunt*.8(2.209D; M.31.644B).

***πρωτόκλιτος, ὁ**, *occupant of chief seat, principal guest*, Thdt.*qu. 45 in 2Reg*.(1.454).

***πρωτοκόμιον, τό**, *first lock of hair*; met., *first-fruits* τὸ ἐξ Ἀβραὰμ ...γένος...π. τῶν ἄλλων ἐθνῶν Cyr.*Juln*.3(6².104A); id.*Joel*.8(3.206B).

***πρωτοκορυφαῖος, ὁ**, *chief leader*; of SS. Peter and Paul, *A.Petr. et Paul*.tit.(p.178n.).

***πρωτοκοσμοκράτωρ, ὁ**, *chief cosmic ruler* ἐξουσίας π. τοῦ σκότους τοῦ αἰῶνος ‡Ath.*doct.mon*.(M.28.1424C).

***πρωτοκούρσωρ, ὁ**, (cf. Lat. *cursor*) *chief courier*, Jo.Mal.*chron*. 14 p.352(M.97.525A); Thphn.*chron*.p.247(M.108.620B).

πρωτοκτίστης, ὁ, *first creator*, in explanation of πρωτότοκος: πρῶτον τετοκέναι...ἵν' ᾖ, τῆς τρίτης συλλαβῆς ὀξυνομένης, πρωτογόνος, οὐ πρωτογενής· π., οὐ πρωτόκτιστος Isid.Pel.*epp*.3.31(M.78.749D).

πρωτόκτιστος, **1.** *first created*; of unformed matter, Gr.Naz. *carm*.2.1.13.182(M.37.1241A); of light, Epiph.*haer*.76.26(p.374.2; M. 42.568C); Jo.D.*f.o*.2.7(M.94.888C); of angelic powers, Clem.*str*.5.6 (p.349.12; M.9.61A); id.*exc.Thdot*.10(p.109.17; M.9.660B); id.*ecl*.5.1 (p.151.13; M.9.721B); Max.*schol.c.h*.7.2(M.4.69C); of Devil, Didym. *Trin*.3.32(M.39.957C); of Wisdom, Clem.*str*.5.14(p.385.4; M.9.132A); and Logos, Eus.*h.e*.1.2.21(M.20.64B); but denied by orthodox who assert πρωτότοκος and μονογενής of Son, Gr.Nyss.*Eun*.4(2 p.97.18; M.45.673D); εἰ πρὸ τῆς κτίσεως ὁ υἱὸς οὐ γέννημά ἐστιν, ἀλλὰ κτίσμα· π. ἂν ἐλέγετο, καὶ οὐ πρωτότοκος Didym.(‡Bas.)*Eun*.4(1.292C; M.29. 701B); Epiph.*haer*.78.17(p.468.6; M.42.728A); Chrys.*hom.3.2 in Col*. (11.343F); Isid.Pel.*epp*.3.31(M.78.749D) cit. s. foreg.; Thdt.*Trin*.(M. 75.1160D); id.*Col*.1:15(3.477); Oecum.*Apoc*.3:14(p.64); of primal man, Gel.Cyz.*h.e*.2.17.27(M.85.1272A); **2.** *believer in Christ as πρωτόκτιστος*; nickname of Origenist sect, Cyr.S.*v.Sab*.89(p.197.15).

πρωτοκωμήτης, ὁ, *head man of village*, ‡Pall.*h.mon*.16.10(p.73. 14; M.34.1169B); Leont.N.*v.Sym*.46(M.93.1725B); Cyr.S.*v.Euthym*.12 (p.22.13).

πρωτόλ(ε)ιον, τό, **A.** *first-fruit*; **1.** as sacrificial offering; of Christ, Cyr.*ador*.17(1.611A); of prayers of saints offered at heavenly altar, Oecum.*Apoc*.8:3(p.104); **2.** as first instalment, earnest; of Christ as first-fruit of humanity in Resurrection, Cyr.*Is*.1.5(2.132C); π. τῶν κεκοιμημένων id.*hom.pasch*.13(5².186A); *ib*.26(311B); π. ... ἀνθρώπων ἐγέρσεως Oecum.*Apoc*.1:5(p.35); of apostles as first of Christian believers, Cyr.*Is*.3.1(2.388A); *ib*.4.5(695D); of S. Stephen as first of martyrs, id.*Abac*.30(3.546A); of martyrs as first of the saved, Oecum.*Apoc*.14:3(p.161); of trans-Jordan tribes as first of Assyria's Palestinian conquests, Cyr.*Os*.142(3.176B); **3.** as first reward of success ἁγνείαν...π. ὥσπερ τι τῆς εὐαγοῦς πολιτείας Cyr. *ador*.7(1.240B); **4.** as first prey or spoil, id.*Os*.69(3.105A); id.*Am*.88 (3.342B).

B. plur., *spoils, rewards of victory*, Eus.*v.C*.1.3(p.8.30; M.20.916A).

πρωτολογία, ἡ, **1.** *prosecutor's part*, †Bas.*hom.in Ps*.37(1.366A; M.30.92A); ref. Pr.18:17, Chrys.*Thdr*.1.18(1.31E); **2.** *antiphon* of psalm, Jo.Clim.*scal*.4(M.88.701C).

***πρωτομαίστωρ, ὁ**, ? *master-workman*, *T.Sal*.1.2(p.7.1; M.122. 1316D).

***πρωτομαντία, ἡ**, *divination*; as work of Devil renounced at baptism, Ephr.2.217B.

***πρωτομάρτυς, ὁ**, *first martyr*; **1.** of Christ, Gel.Cyz.*h.e*.2.19.26 (M.85.1280D); **2.** of S. Stephen, Gr.Nyss.*Steph*.2(M.46.725B); *Const. App*.2.49.2; Epiph.*haer*.25.1(p.267.15; M.41.321A); *ib*.70.6(p.238.7; M. 42.348C); Cosm.Ind.*top*.5(M.88.297A); Sophr.H.*or*.8.6(M.87.3361A); Jo.D.*f.o*.4.15(M.94.1168B); **3.** of Thecla, *A.Paul.et Thecl*.1(p.235. 1n.); *ib*.43(p.269.6n.); Isid.Pel.*epp*.1.160(M.78.289C); Bas.Sel. *v.Thecl*.1 tit.(M.85.478); Evagr.*h.e*.3.8(p.107.31; M.86.2612B); ‡Jo.D. *fid.dorm*.9(M.95.253C); **4.** plur., of first martyrs in a persecution, *Ep.Lugd*.ap.Eus.*h.e*.5.1.11(M.20.413A).

***πρωτομοιχειανός, ὁ**, *chief favourer of adultery*, Thdt.Stud.*epp*.1. 49(M.99.1089D).

***πρωτόνοια, ἡ**, *first thought*, or *movement of the mind* οὗτος προσευχὴν ἐπιτελεῖ, ὁ ἀεὶ τὴν π. ἑαυτοῦ πᾶσαν καρποφορῶν τῷ θεῷ Evagr.Pont.*or*.126(M.79.1193C); ref. temptations, Marc.Er.*opusc*.4 (M.65.1016B); *ib*.(1024C); ref. free will τὴν...π. κατ' οἰκονομίαν ἔχομεν ὥσπερ κἀκεῖνος [sc. Adam]· καὶ τὸ παρακοῦσαι ἢ μὴ παρακοῦσαι κατὰ θέλημα ἔχομεν, ὥσπερ κἀκεῖνος *ib*.(1025D); Nil.*epp*.4.49(M.79.573B).

***πρωτονοτάριος, ὁ**, *chief notary*, Sophr.H.*ep.syn*.(M.87.3200A); Thdr.Stud.*epp*.2.172 tit.(M.99.1540A).

πρωτόνυμφος, *who is the chief bride*; fig., of superior of convent, Thdr.Stud.*epp*.2.150(M.99.1468B).

πρωτοπάθεια, ἡ, *first impulse*, Olymp.*Eccl*.10:4(M.93.596D).

πρωτοπαθ-έω, *suffer first* ποῦ δίκαιον, ἐν οἷς π. τὸ σῶμα καὶ τὴν ψυχὴν ἕλκει πρὸς συμπάθειαν...αὐτὴν κρίνεσθαι μόνην; Athenag.*res*.21 (p.74.16; M.6.1016B); Ἐπίκουρος πᾶσαν χαρὰν τῆς ψυχῆς οἴεται ἐπὶ ~ούσῃ τῇ σαρκὶ γενέσθαι Clem.*str*.2.21(p.185.4; M.8.1077B); *ib*.6.16 (p.500.20; M.9.360B); συμπάσχει [sc. ὁ γνωστικός] τῷ σώματι... παθητῷ ἐνδεδεμένος, ἀλλ' οὐ π. κατὰ τὸ πάθος *ib*.7.7(p.45.5; M.9. 488A); τὸν νοῦν, οὐ πταίσαντα μόνον ἐν τῷ Ἀδάμ, ἀλλὰ καὶ ~ήσαντα Gr.Naz.*ep*.101(M.37.188B); ψυχῆς...προσειλημμένης διότι ~ήσασα Leont.B.*Nest.et Eut*.2(M.86.1324D); Max.*opusc*.(M.91.136B); Germ. CP *or*.2(M.98.256B); ref. Apollinarianism τί δὲ καὶ τῆς ἐνανθρωπήσεως ἀπωνάμεθα, τοῦ ~ήσαντος μὴ σεσωσμένου; Jo.D.*f.o*.3.18(M.94. 1072C); ref. monothelitism εἰ ἀνθρώπινον οὐκ ἀνέλαβε θέλημα, τὸ ~ῆσαν ἐν ἡμῖν οὐκ ἰάσατο id.*volunt*.28(M.95.161C).

***πρωτοπαπᾶς, ὁ**, *senior presbyter*, *Euchol*.(p.242).

πρωτοπατρίκιος, ὁ, *first patrician*, Malchus *exc.gent*.1(p.569.24; M.113.781C); Thphn.*chron*.p.318(M.108.769C).

πρωτοπάτωρ, ὁ, *chief father*; of bishop of Ephesus, Thdr.Stud. *epp*.2.70(M.99.1300C).

***πρωτόπιστος**, *first to believe*; of Abraham, Agath.*v.Gr.Ill*.105 (p.53).

***πρωτοπλαστία, ἡ**, *first moulding*; of man's creation, Tit.Bost. *Man*.3 proem.(M.18.1209C).

πρωτόπλαστος, *first-formed*; **A.** of Adam, cf. *protoplastus ille Adam de rudi terra et de adhuc virgine...habuit substantiam*, Iren. *haer*.3.21.10(M.7.954C); πρωτότοκον ἐκ παρθένου, ἵνα τὸν π. Ἀδὰμ ἐν ἑαυτῷ ἀναπλάσσων δειχθῇ Hipp.*Dan*.4.11.5(M.10.684B); ὁ π. καὶ προπάτωρ Ἀδὰμ *A.Pil*.B 19(p.325); Eus.*e.th*.3.2(p.143.3; M.24.977C); ref. Christ's body ἐξ ἐκείνης τῆς ὑποστάσεως τῆς τοῦ π. Ἀδὰμ Adam. *dial*.4.13(p.170.7; M.11.1829A); τὸν...πρῶτον Ἀδὰμ τὸν π. τοῦ κόσμου δηλοῖ· τὸν δὲ δεύτερον Ἀδὰμ τὸν κατὰ τὸν σωτῆρα νοούμενον ἄνθρωπον ‡Ath.*serm.fid*.25(p.22; M.26.1280A); μίμημα [sc. in baptism] ἐφέρετε τοῦ π. Ἀδὰμ Cyr.H.*catech*.20.2; Epiph.*haer*.66.51(p.88.7; M.42.105B); in comparison of Adam's 'birth' with Christ's (cf. supra), Procl.CP *or*.2.3(M.65.696A); πρώτη Ἰουδαία ἄνθρωπον ἔσχεν οἰκήτορα, τὸν π. Ἀδὰμ μετὰ τὸ ἐκβληθῆναι τοῦ παραδείσου Isid.Pel.*epp*.1.2(M.78.84A).

B. as subst.; **1.** = Adam, Clem.*str*.3.14(p.239.17; M.8.1193C); *ib*. 5.14(p.388.13; M.9.140A); Ἀβραὰμ εἰκοστὸς γεγέννηται ἀπὸ τοῦ π. Or. *Jo*.20.3(p.329.20; M.14.576C); Meth.*symp*.3.8(p.35.4; M.18.72C); id. *res*.1.39(p.282.5; M.18.268A); ὁ π. ἀπὸ τῆς γῆς ἤνεγκεν οἰκουμενικὸν θάνατον Cyr.H.*catech*.13.2; τὰ...πρωτότοκα, τύπος τοῦ π., ὃς ἐπειδὴ... ἡμῖν ἐνυπάρχει τῇ ἀκολουθίᾳ τῆς διαδοχῆς...διὰ τοῦτο ἐν τῷ Ἀδὰμ πάντες ἀποθνήσκομεν Bas.*Spir.*31(3.26B; M.32.124A); ὅλον με... κατακριθέντα ἐκ τῆς τοῦ π. παρακοῆς Gr.Naz.*or.*22.13(M.35.1145B); id.*carm.*1.2.10.427(M.37.711A); Gr.Nyss.*Eun.*1(1 p.193.15; M.45.440A); ref. question of Adam's salvation, denied by Tat., Epiph. *haer.*46.2(p.206.13; M.41.841A); διὰ τῆς τοῦ π. παρακοῆς ἔνοχοι κατέστημεν πάντες Mac.Aeg.*libert.ment.*27(M.34.960B); ἀθάνατον γενόμενον τὸν π. Chrys.*hom.46.4 in Gen.*(4.472B); συγκληρονόμοι γεγόναμεν τῶν συμβεβηκότων τῷ π. κακῶν Cyr.*Is.*2.1(2.194B); ἐν τῷ π. κατεκλίθημεν εἰς θάνατον id.*Jo.*4.2(4.354E); πέπαυται γὰρ ἐν Χριστῷ τὰ ἐν τῷ π. τῇ ἀνθρώπου φύσει συμβεβηκότα σωματικά τε καὶ ψυχικὰ τῶν ἀρρωστημάτων id.*Pulch.*36(p.45.27; 5^2.157A); **2.** plur., = Adam and Eve μετῳκίσθησαν ⟨γὰρ⟩ οἱ δαίμονες, ἐξωρίσθησαν δὲ οἱ π. Tat.*orat.*20(p.22.16; M.6.852A); οἱ π. οὐκ ἐγεννήθησαν, ἀλλ' ἐγενήθησαν Meth.*res.*1.47(p.297.5; M.41.1117C); ἐκρατήθησαν δὲ οἱ π. ἀλόγῳ δελεασθέντες ἡδονῇ *ib.*1.54(p.311.18; M.41.1145C); τραῦμα τοῖς π. ἐδόκει ἡ διὰ τῆς ἐντολῆς γενομένη τοῦ κακοῦ ἀπαγόρευσις·...φίλημα δὲ ἡ πρὸς τὸ ἡδὺ...προτροπή· ἀλλ' ἔδειξεν ἡ πεῖρα, ὅτι τὰ νομιζόμενα τοῦ φίλου τραύματα τῶν φιλημάτων ἦν τοῦ ἐχθροῦ λυσιτελέστερα Gr.Nyss.*hom.13 in Cant.*(M.44.1044C); δερματίνους ἐπιβάλλει χιτῶνας τοῖς π. ὁ κύριος id.*or.catech.*8(p.43.5; M.45.33C); ‡Chrys.*pasch.*2(8.254B); in comparison of their creation with virgin birth, Isid.Pel.*epp.*1.141(M.78.277A); ζωὴ...κατὰ τὰς ἡμέρας τοῦ ξύλου τῆς ζωῆς... τοιαύτη γὰρ ἦν πρὸ τῆς παραβάσεως ἐν τοῖς π. Cyr.*Is.*5.6(2.904E); Gel.Cyz.*h.e.*2.24.20(M.85.1301D); at eucharist εὐλογία μὲν ὡς τῆς ἀρᾶς τῶν π. ἀναίρεσις ‡Sophr.H.*liturg.*9(M.87.3989A).

***πρωτόπραστος**, *first-sold*; of serpent as sold under sin in the beginning, Germ.CP *or.*2(M.98.253B).

πρωτοπρεσβύτερος, ὁ, *senior presbyter* (cf. ἀρχιπρεσβύτερος, which denotes essentially the same official) Πέτρος τις π. ἦν τῆς ἐν Ἀλεξανδρείᾳ ἐκκλησίας Socr.*h.e.*6.9.3(M.67.692B); CQuerc.(M.103.112C); CNic.(787)*act.*4(H.4.189D); *Euchol.*(p.238).

πρῶτος, (also in superl. form πρώτιστος), **A.** *first*, also c. genit. *prior to*; **1.** of God οὖσα [sc. σοφία]...παρὰ τῷ πρωτίστῳ θεῷ *Hom. Clem.*2.25; ἀνωτάτω τοῦ π. Eus.*d.e.*5.6(p.229.20; M.22.380A); τὸ π. αἴτιον Gr.Naz.*or.*28.31(p.70.16; M.36.72B); ἡ ἀπόρροια τοῦ π. καλοῦ *ib.*30.13(p.129.15; M.36.121A); **2.** ref. Son δυνάμεως θεοῦ...ἐπιρρεούσης ταῖς...ψυχαῖς, ὑπὸ Ἰησοῦ διακονουμένης, ἧς π. ἐστιν, αὐτοδύναμις θεοῦ Or.*Jo.*1.33(38; p.43.9; M.14.89A); διδάσκει δὲ ὁ βαπτιστὴς πῶς ἔμπροσθεν αὐτοῦ γέγονεν Ἰησοῦς τῷ πρῶτος αὐτοῦ (ἐπεὶ πρωτότοκος πάσης κτίσεως) εἶναι *ib.*6.6(3; p.114.2; 209B); εἰ καὶ φύσει μονογενὴς υἱὸς καὶ θεὸς ἡμῶν ἀνευφημεῖται, ἀλλ' οὐχ ὁ π. θεός, πρῶτος δὲ τοῦ θεοῦ μονογενὴς υἱὸς καὶ διὰ τοῦτο θεός Eus.*d.e.*5.4(p.225.30; M.22.372D); π. ... ὡς ἐν γενητοῖς εὐσεβῶς εἶναι λέγει, τὴν ἄναρχον...καὶ τὴν ὑπὲρ τὸ π. οὐσίαν ἀπονέμων τῷ πατρί...μόνου τοῦ θείου λόγου πάντων τῶν γενητῶν π. χρηματίζοντος *ib.*5.6(p.229.16; 377D); εἰ...ἐποίησεν τοὺς αἰῶνας...οὐδὲν δὲ πρὸ τῶν...αἰώνων νοεῖσθαι δύναται, εἰ μὴ ἡ... πρωτίστη...φύσις, πῶς οὐκ ἀνάρχως...γεννηθῆναι πιστεύεται; Didym. *Trin.*1.15(M.39.308C); εἰ γέγονεν ὁ υἱὸς δι' ἡμᾶς...οὐκ ἔστιν οὐδὲ π. ἡμῶν παρὰ θεῷ Cyr.*thes.*15(5^1.153D); in rel. to angels τὸν πρεσβύτατον τῶν αἰώνων καὶ π. τῶν ἀρχαγγέλων Meth.*symp.*3.4(p.31.3; M.18.68A) where π. may = *prior to* (cf. τὸν πρὸ αἰώνων *ib.*(p.30.19; 65A)); πρεσβυτάτους ἀγγέλους εἶναί τινας, καὶ πρῶτον αὐτῶν τινα εἶναι. ... μήτε τῷ πρωτίστῳ τῶν ἀγγέλων ἐφικτὸν εἶναι τὸν τρόπον τῆς ἐνανθρωπήσεως Max.*schol.d.n.*2.9(M.4.225D); **3.** of first-made heaven as dwelling of God, opp. second or visible heaven, Cosm.Ind.*top.*2(M.88.81B); **4.** of first man τὸν πρεσβύτατον καὶ π. τῆς ἀνθρωπότητος ἄνθρωπον...τὸν Ἀδάμ Meth.*symp.*3.4(p.31.4; M.18.68A); Ἀδὰμ ...π. ἡμαρτηκὼς...Χριστὸς π. ἐκ νεκρῶν ἀναστάς Thdt.*Rom.*5:14(3.57); **5.** of Church πάντων π. ἐκτίσθη Herm.*vis.*2.4.1; **6.** πρώτη τοῦ σαββάτου, ref. paschal chronology ὡς γὰρ μία τῶν σαββάτων ἡ μετὰ τὸ σάββατον π. καλεῖται, οὕτως εἴποις ἂν καὶ τὴν πλησιάζουσαν ὄπιθεν τῷ σαββάτῳ, τουτέστι τῆς ἑβδομάδος ἕκτην, πρώτην τοῦ σαββάτου, τουτέστι πρὸ τοῦ σαββάτου Jo.Philop.*pasch.*(p.220.9); **7.** masc. plur. as subst., *ancients*, Eus.*h.e.*3.27.1(M.20.273A); **8.** adverbially οὐκ ἀνέχεσθαι...τούτους νομίζειν θεούς, ὅτι ἄνθρωποι ἦσαν καὶ πρῶτοι Cels. ap.Or.*Cels.*3.22(p.218.14; M.11.944C, perh. for πρῶτον).
B. *chief, most important*; of archangels, Max.*schol.d.n.*2.9(M.4.225D); as military rank = πρωτεύων· κυμητήριον Ἀθηνέου π. *CG-CI* 46 (Corinth, saec. iv–vi).
C. *best* τὰ π. μύρα χριόμενοι Gr.Nyss.*v.Mos.*(M.44.417D).

***πρωτοσπαθαρία, ἡ,** *wife of a* πρωτοσπαθάριος, Thdr.Stud.*epp.*1.18(M.99.964D).

***πρωτοσπαθάριος, ὁ,** *chief of imperial ceremonial bodyguard*, Thdr. Stud.*epp.*2.57 tit.(M.99.1269C); Thphn.*chron.*p.206(M.108.529B).

πρωτοστάτης, ὁ, *leader, chief*; of founders of sects and heresies, Hipp.*haer.*1 proem.(p.3.25; M.16.3021A); Bas.*Eun.*1.1(1.208B; M.29.501A); of Judas as τῆς Ἰουδαίων ἀθεότητος π. Cyr.*Jo.*11.12(4.1012C); of S. Peter as chief of apostles, Cyr.H.*catech.*11.3; †Bas.*contub.*1(M.30.816A); Nil.*epp.*2.21(M.79.208D); of Devil before his fall, as π. of angels, Isid.Pel.*epp.*1.283(M.78.349A); †Jo.D.*B.J.*6(M.96.908A); of Diocletian as senior Augustus, Eus.*h.e.*8.13.11(M.20.777A).

***πρωτοστράτηγος, ὁ,** *commander-in-chief*, Thphn.*chron.*p.153 (M.108.416B).

***πρωτοστράτωρ, ὁ,** *chief groom* or *equerry*, an imperial official Ῥοῦφος ὁ π. τοῦ Ὀψικίου Thphn.*chron.*p.321(M.108.776C); βασιλικὸς π. *ib.*p.369(884A).

***πρωτοσύγκελλος, ὁ,** *chief* σύγκελλος: π. τῆς μεγάλης ἐκκλησίας *Lit.Chrys.*(p.355.36).

***πρωτοσύμβουλος, ὁ,** *chief councillor*, †Jo.D.*B.J.*16(M.96.1000C); title of emirs, Jo.Sync.*narr.*(H.4.320D); ὁ τῶν Σαρακηνῶν π. Thphn.*chron.*p.296(M.108.724B); *ib.*p.309(752C); cf. ὁ...τῶν Σαρακηνῶν ἀρχηγὸς τὸν Ἰωάννην [i.e. Jo. D.]...προεχειρίζετο π. Jo.VI H. *v.Jo.D.*13(M.94.449B).

***πρωτοσύστατος,** *primordial, original*, *Hom.Clem.*6.6.

***πρωτοταγῶς,** *as the first rank* or *order*, ref. first order of angels τῷ κρυφίῳ π. πλησιάζουσαν Dion.Ar.*c.h.*9.2(M.3.260A).

πρωτοτοκία, ἡ, *primogeniture*, ref. Christ's status as πρωτότοκος τῆς κτίσεως, Gr.Nyss.*hom.13 in Cant.*(M.44.1053D); id.*Eun.*4(2 p.64.6; M.45.636B); ἐπὶ μὲν γὰρ τῶν ἄλλων ἡ π. ποιεῖ τὴν ἀγάπην· ἐνταῦθα δὲ ἡ ἀγάπη ἐποίησε πρωτότοκον εἶναι Chrys.*fr.in Jer.*2:3(M.64.756D).

πρωτοτόκια, τά, *right of primogeniture, status of firstborn*, ref. Esau Ἰακὼβ φάσκων...ἐγὼ...ὁ πρωτότοκός σου υἱὸς κατὰ μὲν τὸ πνευματικὸν ἠλήθευεν μεταλαβὼν τῶν π. Or.*Jo.*10.5(4; p.175.22; M.14.313C); Thdr.Mops.*Os.*12:1(M.66.196A); Ἐδὼμ τουτέστι γήινος, διὰ τὸ ἀποδόσθαι τὰ π. Cyr.*Abd.*1(3.354B); Ῥουβὴν τῶν π. ἐκπεπτωκέναι Proc.G.*1Par.*proem.(M.87.1201B); ref. Christ's 'fulfilment of righteousness' πληρῶσαι...τὴν περιτομὴν καὶ τὰς ὑπὲρ τῶν π. προσφορὰς Oecum.*1Tim.*3:16(p.458.22); ref. Christ as πρωτότοκος· χωρῶν [sc. Marcell.] τῇ ἀρνήσει...τῶν π. πάσης κτίσεως Acac.Caes.*fr.Marcell.* ap.Epiph.*haer.*72.8(p.262.28; M.42.393A); ref. Nestorian division of Christ ἔνθα οὖν δύο...υἱοί...π. καὶ ὑστεροτόκια λέγεται Leont.H.*Nest.*3.9(M.86.1641B).

πρωτότοκος, *first-born*;
A. in gen., Just.*dial.*84.1(M.6.673B); πρῶτος, ὡς πρωτότοκος τῷ κόσμῳ, ὁ ἀρχιερεύς, εἶτα ὁ νομοθέτης *Hom.Clem.*2.16; of Cain, *ib.*3.25.
B. of first-born of Egypt τὰ π. Just.*dial.*111.3(M.6.732C); τοὺς π. Mel.*pass.*22 p.4.8; Meth.*symp.*9.1(p.115.14; M.18.180B); slaying interpreted as destruction of primary impulse to sin, Gr.Nyss.*v.Mos.*(M.44.353B).
C. of Wisdom ἡ π. πάντων σοφία Meth.*symp.*9.3(p.117.20; M.18.184B); τῶν ὄντων ἁπάντων πρῶτον ὑφίστησιν αὐτοῦ γέννημα τὴν π. σοφίαν Eus.*d.e.*4.2(p.151.31; M.22.253A).
D. of Logos, ref. Lc.1:35 τὸ...οὐδὲν ἄλλο νοῆσαι θέμις ἢ τὸν λόγον, ὃς καὶ π. τῷ θεῷ ἐστι Just.*1apol.*33.6(M.6.381B); ἔργον π. τοῦ θεοῦ Tat.*orat.*5(p.5.23; M.6.816A).
E. of Christ; **1.** as Son μόνος ἰδίως υἱὸς...λόγος αὐτοῦ ὑπάρχων καὶ π. καὶ δύναμις Just.*1apol.*23.2(M.6.364A); *ib.*46.2(397B); *ib.*53.2(405C); υἱὸς...ὃς καὶ λόγος π. ὢν τοῦ θεοῦ, καὶ θεὸς ὑπάρχει *ib.*63.15(425B); Clem.*prot.*9(p.62.29; M.8.193B); ἡ...π. τῆς ἀγενήτου φύσεως εἰκών, ὁ ...μονογενὴς...υἱός Eus.*d.e.*5.1(p.210.31; M.22.349C); **2.** as Son of God and Son of Man π. ἐν πᾶσιν γενόμενον· π. ἐκ θεοῦ, ἵνα δεύτερος μετὰ τὸν πατέρα υἱὸς θεοῦ ὢν ἀποδειχθῇ· π. πρὸ ἀγγέλων ἵνα καὶ ἀγγέλων κύριος φανῇ· π. ἐκ παρθένου, ἵνα τὸν πρωτόπλαστον Ἀδὰμ ἐν ἑαυτῷ ἀναπλάσσων δειχθῇ Hipp.*Dan.*4.11.5(M.10.684B); θεόν τε ὁμοῦ καὶ ἄνθρωπον, μονογενῆ, π. Cyr.*ep.*67(p.38.14; 5^2.195A); **3.** of *homo assumptus* ὁμολογοῦμεν καὶ μονογενῆ καὶ π.· ἀλλὰ μονογενῆ τὸν λόγον, ὃς πάντοτε ἦν καὶ ἔστιν τῷ πατρί· τὸ πρωτότοκος δὲ τῷ ἀνθρώπῳ CSard.*ep.cath.*ap.Thdt.*h.e.*2.8.44(3.846); περὶ τοῦδε τοῦ σπέρματος [sc. τοῦ Δαβίδ] ὑποσχόμενος ὁ θεός, ὡς...πρωτότοκος τοῦ θεοῦ κληθήσεται Thdt.*eran.*1(4.33); μονογενὴς κατὰ τὴν τοῦ λόγου οὐσίαν, καὶ π. κατὰ τὴν ἔνσαρκον οἰκονομίαν Euther.*confut.*16(M.28.1392A); **4.** ref. Col. 1:15; **a.** of Christ as typified by Israel, Just. *dial.*125.3(M.6.768A); by Noah π. πάσης κτίσεως ὤν, καὶ ἀρχὴ πάλιν ἄλλου γένους γέγονε *ib.*138.2(793B); **b.** of Christ as eternal Son διὰ παρθενικῆς μήτρας τὸν π. τῶν πάντων ποιημάτων σαρκοποιηθέντα ἀληθῶς παιδίον γενέσθαι *ib.*84.2(673B); as Logos τὸν λόγον ἐγέννησε προφορικόν, πρωτότοκον πάσης κτίσεως Thphl.Ant.*Autol.*2.22(M.6.1088B); πρωτότοκον δὲ πάσης κτίσεως, ⟨ὅτι⟩ γεννηθεὶς ἀπαθῶς, κτίστης καὶ γενεσιάρχης τῆς ὅλης ἐγένετο κτίσεως Clem.*exc.Thdot.*19(p.113.8; M.9.668A); hence identified with Wisdom, cf.Or.*princ.*1.2.1(p.28.9; M.11.130B); cf. *creaturarum et dei medium, id est mediatorem quaeramus, quem Paulus...primogenitum omnis creaturae*

pronuntiat, *ib*.2.6.1(p.139.16; 209C); πρωτότοκος πάσης τῆς κτίσεως, κτίσμα, σοφία *ib*.4.4.1(p.349.13); υἱὸν δὲ κατὰ τὴν π. αὐτοῦ δύναμιν id. *Jo*.10.6(4; p.176.5; M.14.316A); ζητήσεις δὲ εἰ...δύναται ὁ π. πάσης κτίσεως εἶναι κόσμος, καὶ μάλιστα καθ' ὃ σοφία ἐστὶν ἡ πολυποίκιλος *ib*.19.22(5; p.324.4; 568B); in his divine nature (typified by Solomon) opp. *homo assumptus* (typified by Hiram the widow's son) ὁ μὲν Σαλομὼν εἰς τὸν π. πάσης κτίσεως λαμβάνεσθαι δύναται, ὁ δὲ Χειρὰμ εἰς ὃν ἀνείληφεν οὗτος ἄνθρωπον *ib*.10.41(25; p.218.29; 388B); πρωτότοκον πάσης κτίσεως...οὐ προγνώσει, ἀλλ' οὐσίᾳ καὶ ὑποστάσει θεὸν...ὁμολογοῦμεν Hymen.*ep*.2(p.324.22); τὸν σωτῆρα...τὸν π. πάσης κτίσεως θεοῦ λόγον...τὸ π. καὶ μονογενὲς τοῦ πατρὸς γέννημα Eus. *d.e*.5.3(p.219.1; M.22.361B); in Arian controversy, denied of pre-existent Logos, Marcell.*fr*.6ap.Eus.*Marcell*.2.3(p.45.19; M.24.801A); π. εἰπών, δηλοῖ μὴ εἶναι αὐτὸν κτίσμα, ἀλλὰ γέννημα †Ath.*exp. fid*.3(M.25.205A); εἰ δὲ καὶ π. τῆς κτίσεως λέγεται, ἀλλ' οὐχ ὡς ἐξισούμενος τοῖς κτίσμασι, καὶ πρῶτος αὐτῶν κατὰ χρόνον, π. λέγεται· (πῶς γάρ, ὅπου γε μονογενής ἐστιν αὐτός;) ἀλλὰ διὰ τὴν πρὸς τὰ κτίσματα συγκατάβασιν τοῦ λόγου Ath.*Ar*.2.62(M.26.277C); τὸ λέγεσθαι τὸν υἱὸν π., οὐ διὰ τὸ συναριθμεῖσθαι αὐτὸν τῇ κτίσει, λέγεται π., ἀλλ' εἰς ἀπόδειξιν τῆς τῶν πάντων διὰ τοῦ υἱοῦ δημιουργίας καὶ υἱοποιήσεως *ib*.3.9(340C); ref. Pr.8:22, CAnc.(358)*ep.syn*.ap.Epiph. *haer*.73.7(p.277.12ff.; M.42.416Bff.); Bas.*Eun*.2.23(1.259B; M.29. 624A); Eunomian argument πῶς ἂν π. κτίσεως ὠνομάσθη, εἰ μὴ τοῦτο ἦν ὅπερ ἡ κτίσις ἐστί; πᾶς γὰρ π. οὐ τῶν ἑτεροφυῶν, ἀλλὰ τῶν ὁμογενῶν ἐστι π. Gr.Nyss.*Eun*.4(2 p.61.28; M.45.633A); εἰ πρὸ τῆς κτίσεως ὁ υἱὸς οὐ γέννημά ἐστι, ἀλλὰ κτίσμα· πρωτόκτιστος ἂν ἐλέγετο, καὶ οὐ π. εἰ ἐπειδὴ π. τῆς κτίσεως εἴρηται, πρωτόκτιστός ἐστι, καὶ π. εἰρημένος τῶν νεκρῶν, προτελευτήσας ἂν εἴη τῶν νεκρῶν. εἰ δὲ π. νεκρῶν εἴρηται, διὰ τὸ αἴτιος εἶναι τῆς ἐκ νεκρῶν ἀναστάσεως· οὕτω καὶ π. κτίσεως, διὰ τὸ αἴτιος εἶναι τοῦ ἐξ οὐκ ὄντων εἰς τὸ εἶναι παραγαγεῖν τὴν κτίσιν...εἰ π., φασίν, ὁ υἱός, οὐκέτι μονογενής... καίτοιγε...καὶ ἐκ Μαρίας...μόνος γεννηθείς, π. αὐτῆς εἴρηται...ὥστε οὐκ ἀνάγκη ἀδελφοῦ πρωτότοκον λέγεσθαι Didym.(‡Bas.)*Eun*.4(1. 292Cff.; M.29.701Bff.); reinterpreted as if written πρωτοτόκος: ὁ πρωτότοκος, εἰ μὲν ἡ δευτέρα ὀξύνοιτο συλλαβή, τὸν τεχθέντα πρῶτον· εἰ δ' ἡ παρεσχάτη, τὸν πρώτως τεκόντα μηνύει. καὶ τοῦτ' ἀκριβῶς ἴστε μάλιστα ὑμεῖς οἱ ὁμηρίζοντες· πρωτοτόκος γὰρ ἡ πρώτως τεκοῦσα ἐκείνῳ εἴρηται. εἰκὸς οὖν...ὅτι...τοιαύτῃ τινὶ ἐννοίᾳ ὁ θεσπέσιος ἐχρήσατο Παῦλος, οὐ πρῶτον τῆς κτίσεως αὐτὸν ἐκτίσθαι δογματίζων... ἀλλὰ πρῶτον τετοκέναι, τουτέστι, πεποιηκέναι τὴν κτίσιν Isid.Pel.*epp*. 3.31(M.78.749C); π. ... ἐστὶ τῆς κτίσεως, οὐχ ὡς ἀδελφὴν ἔχων τὴν κτίσιν, ἀλλ' ὡς πρὸ πάσης κτίσεως γεννηθείς Thdt.*Col*.1:15(3.477); π. denotes primacy of honour, not temporal priority, *ib*.; **c.** of Christ incarnate, in contrast with Adam, Meth.*symp*.3.3(p.29.21; M.18. 64C); εἰ π. μέν ἐστιν ἁπάσης κτίσεως...προσήκει εἰδέναι...ὅτι περὶ τῆς κατὰ σάρκα οἰκονομίας αὐτοῦ ὁ ἀπόστολος νυνὶ μέμνηται Marcell.*fr*.4 ap.Eus.*Marcell*.2.3(p.45.11; M.24.800C); π. οὖν ἁπάσης κτίσεως διὰ τὴν κατὰ σάρκα γένεσιν ὠνομάσθη, οὐ διὰ τὴν πρώτην, ὡς αὐτοὶ οἴονται, κτίσιν *ib*.5(p.45.15; 800D); ἐν δὲ τῇ σαρκὶ π. γίνεται πρῶτος καὶ μόνος τὸν ἄγνωστον τῇ φύσει τόκον ἐφ' ἑαυτοῦ διὰ τῆς παρθενίας καινοτομήσας Gr.Nyss.*Eun*.4(2 p.64.28; M.45.636D); ὅτι γὰρ οὐ κατὰ τὴν προαιώνιον ὕπαρξιν ἐφαρμόζεται τῷ υἱῷ τὸ π., ἡ τοῦ μονογενοῦς προσηγορία διαμαρτύρεται *ib*.(p.65.29; 637B); cf. *interrogant, quemadmodum susceptus homo primogenitus potest videri totius creaturae, cum non sit ante omnem creaturam, sed ut esset in novissimis accepit temporibus*;...τὸ πρωτότοκος οὐκ ἐπὶ χρόνου λέγεται μόνον, ἀλλὰ γὰρ καὶ ἐπὶ προτιμήσεως πολλάκις Thdr.Mops.*Col*.1:15(p.264.8; M.66. 928A); π. is as shocking when applied to divine nature as would be π. ἐκ τῶν νεκρῶν, *ib*.1:18(p.274.20ff.; 928C); εὔδηλον ὡς τῆς οἰκονομίας τὸ πρωτότοκος ὄνομα Thdt.*Trin*.10(M.75.1160B); π. ἐκ μητρὸς ὁ μονογενὴς υἱὸς τοῦ θεοῦ Gr.Ant.*mul.ung*.10(M.88.1860D); **d.** as first-born of new creation, Marcell.*fr*.2 ap.Eus.*Marcell*.1.2(p.11.10; M. 24.737A); cf.Gr.Nyss.*Eun*.4(2 p.64.25; 636D); Thdr.Mops.*Col*.1:16 (p.266.15ff.; M.66.928B); Jo.D.*f.o*.4.8(M.94.1116B); **5.** ref. Col.1:18 π. [καὶ] ἐκ νεκρῶν ἵνα ἀπαρχὴ τῆς ἡμετέρας ἀναστάσεως αὐτὸς γενηθῇ Hipp.*Dan*.4.11.5(M.10.684B); compatibility of this title with appearances of Moses and Elijah before Christ's Resurrection discussed, Meth.*res*.3.5(p.394.13ff.; M.18.317Cff.); Col.1:18 proves reality of Christ's human body, Adam.*dial*.5.10(p.192.14; M.11. 1845B); proves that neither here nor in Col.1:15 does π. imply priority in time, Marcell.*fr*.2 ap.Eus.*Marcell*.1.2(p.11.11; M.24. 737A); διαφέρει δὲ τῇ κοινῇ κτίσει, ὅτι καὶ π. ἐκ τῶν νεκρῶν CSard.*ep. syn*.ap.Thdt.*h.e*.2.8.44(3.846); π. λέγεται...ἐκ τῶν νεκρῶν, οὐχ ὅτι πρῶτος ἡμῶν ἀπέθανε· προετεθνήκειμεν γὰρ ἡμεῖς· ἀλλ' ὅτι τὸν ὑπὲρ ἡμῶν ἀναδεξάμενος θάνατον...ἀνέστη πρῶτος, ὡς ἄνθρωπος, ὑπὲρ ἡμῶν ἀναστήσας τὸ ἑαυτοῦ σῶμα Ath.*Ar*.2.61(M.26.277B); Χριστοῦ δὲ κατὰ σάρκα...π. ἐξ ἀναστάσεως νεκρῶν...πῶς τὸ ἄκτιστον παθητὸν λέγετε; ‡Ath.*Apoll*.1.3(M.26.1097B); γεννήσεις ἁπάσας παρ' ἑαυτοῦ τιμήσας...φαίνεται· τὴν μέν, τῷ ἐμφυσήματι τῷ πρώτῳ...τὴν δέ, τῇ σαρκώσει, καὶ τῷ βαπτίσματι...τὴν δέ, τῇ ἀναστάσει...ὡς ἐγένετο π. ἐν πολλοῖς ἀδελφοῖς, οὕτω καὶ π. ἐκ νεκρῶν γενέσθαι καταξιώσας Gr. Naz.*or*.40.2(M.36.361A); π. γὰρ ἐκ νεκρῶν γίνεται ὁ πρῶτος δι' ἑαυτοῦ τὰς ὠδῖνας τοῦ θανάτου λύσας, ἵνα καὶ πᾶσιν ὁδοποιήσῃ τὸν ἐξ ἀναστάσεως τόκον Gr.Nyss.*Eun*.4(2 p.64.12; M.45.636C); εἰ δὲ μὴ ἀνάστασις ἦν, πῶς ἔμελλε π. ἔσεσθαι, μηδενὸς αὐτῷ τῶν νεκρῶν ἑπομένου; Chrys. *hom.45.4 in Jo*.(8.268B); δεῖ τὴν ἀνάστασιν τοιαύτην εἶναι, οἵα γέγονεν ἡ τοῦ Χριστοῦ. ἀπαρχὴ γὰρ ἐκεῖνος, καὶ π. ἀπὸ τῶν νεκρῶν *ib.66.3* (398B); ὥσπερ ἐν τῷ πρωτοπλάστῳ κατεκλίθημεν εἰς θάνατον, οὕτως ἐν τῷ π. ... ἀναβιώσονται σύμπαντες Cyr.*Jo*.4.2(4.354E); **6.** ref. Rom. 8:29 οὐ δύναται γὰρ ὁ αὐτὸς μονογενής τε καὶ π. εἶναι, εἰ μὴ ἄρα πρὸς ἄλλο καὶ ἄλλο· ἵνα μονογενὴς μὲν διὰ τὴν ἐκ πατρὸς γέννησιν...π. δὲ διὰ τὴν εἰς τὴν κτίσιν συγκατάβασιν, καὶ τὴν τῶν πολλῶν ἀδελφοποίησιν Ath.*Ar*.2.62(M.26.280A); also ref.Mt.12:48–50, Bas.*Eun*.2.23(1.259B; M.29.624A); Gr.Naz.*or*.40.2(M.36.361A) cit. s. 5 supra; ἐν ἀδελφοῖς δὲ πάλιν π. γινόμενος ὁ τοῦ καινοῦ τῆς παλιγγενεσίας τόκου προγεννηθεὶς ἐν τῷ ὕδατι...δι' οὗ τοὺς συμμετασχόντας αὐτῷ τῆς ὁμοίας γεννήσεως ἀδελφοὺς ἑαυτοῦ ποιεῖ, καὶ π. γίνεται τῶν μετ' αὐτὸν γεννωμένων ἐκ τοῦ ὕδατός τε καὶ τοῦ πνεύματος Gr.Nyss.*Eun*.4(2 p.64. 15; M.45.636C); καὶ πρὸς τοὺς διὰ υἱοθεσίας τοῦ ἁγίου πνεύματος ἐκ θεοῦ γεννωμένους, ὡς ὁ Παῦλός φησιν· [Rom.8:29] Didym.(‡Bas.) *Eun*.4(1.292E; M.29.704A); γέγονεν ἀδελφὸς καὶ κεχρημάτικεν ἡμῶν π. διὰ τὸ ἀνθρώπινον καίτοι θεὸς ὑπάρχων, καὶ υἱὸς μονογενὴς Cyr.*Is*. 1.5(2.144E); π. μὲν ὡς ἄνθρωπος ἐν πολλοῖς ἀδελφοῖς· μονογενὴς δὲ πάλιν ὡς λόγος ἐκ θεοῦ id.*hom.pasch*.8(5^2.103C); εἰσῆλθεν εἰς τὸν κόσμον ὁ μονογενὴς ὡς π. καὶ ἐν πολλοῖς γέγονεν ἀδελφοῖς ὁ ἀσύντακτος τῇ κτίσει καθὸ νοεῖται θεός id.*ep*.50(p.91.25; 5^2.159E); τὸ δέ γε π. ὄνομα πῶς ἂν ἁρμόσαι μὴ ἐνανθρωπήσαντι τῷ μονογενεῖ; εἰ γάρ ἐστιν ἀληθὲς ὡς ἐν πολλοῖς ἀδελφοῖς νοεῖται π., τότε κατέβη πρὸς ἀδελφότητα ...ὅτε καθ' ἡμᾶς γέγονεν ἄνθρωπος *ib*.(p.93.32f.; 162D); Jo.D.*f.o*.4.8 (M.94.1117A); **7.** ref. Heb.1:6 and Col.1:15,18, Gr.Nyss.*Eun*.2(2 p.327.11; M.45.501B); Cyr.*ep*.50(p.93.32; 5^2.162D) cit. s. 6 supra.

F. Naassene, of Nous, *Ps.Naas*.ap.Hipp.*haer*.5.10(p.102.23; M. 16.3159A).

G. Sethian τῷ τελείῳ νοῒ τῷ γεννωμένῳ...ὑπὸ τοῦ π. ⟨τοῦ⟩ ὕδατος, ὄφεως, ἀνέμου, θηρίου Hipp.*haer*.5.19(p.120.20; M.16.3183C).

H. exeg. Heb.12:23 τῆς βασιλείας τῆς πατρῴας κοινωνήσει τῷ γνησίῳ, τῷ ἠγαπημένῳ· αὕτη γὰρ ἡ π. ἐκκλησία ἡ ἐκ πολλῶν ἀγαθῶν συγκειμένη παιδίων· ταῦτ' ἔστι τὰ π. τὰ ἐναπογεγραμμένα ἐν οὐρανοῖς ...π. δὲ παῖδες ἡμεῖς οἱ τρόφιμοι τοῦ θεοῦ, οἱ τοῦ π. γνήσιοι φίλοι, οἱ πρῶτοι τῶν ἄλλων ἀνθρώπων τὸν θεὸν νενοηκότες Clem.*prot*.9(p.62.25; M.8.193B); Thdr.Mops.*Col*.1:15(p.266.12; M.66.928B); τὴν τῶν π. μητέρα, ἐν ᾗ καὶ αὐτῷ συνεσόμεθα τῷ Χριστῷ Cyr.*Mich*.41(3.430A); Thdt.*eran*.1(4.46); ἐκκλησίαν πρωτοτόκων ἁγίων παραστῆναι τῷ οἴκῳ *Dorm.BMV* 27(p.103); ref. Church as antitype of Eve ἐξ ἧς καὶ οἱ ἀπογεγραμμένοι π. μετέχουσι θείας ζωῆς, Χριστοῦ μὲν ὄντος πατρός, μητρὸς δὲ ταύτης Proc.G.*Gen*.3:20(M.87.220A); Cosm.Ind.*top*.2(M. 88.72C); *Lit.Jac*.(p.198.26).

I. of Israel, *Pss.Sal*.18.4; μὴ λεγέτω καθ' ἑαυτόν· ἐγὼ γέγονα π. ἐν τέκνοις θεοῦ Ath.*fr.Pss.comm*.(M.27.585B); Chrys.*fr.in Jer*.2:3(M. 64.756D); τὸ 'υἱός π. μου Ἰσραήλ'· ἀντὶ τοῦ 'τίμιος ἐμοί' Thdr.Mops. *Col*.1:15(p.266.13; M.66.928B).

J. π. τοῦ σατανᾶ as epithet of heretic, Polyc.*ep*.7.1; Iren.*haer*.3.3. 4(M.7.853B).

K. met., *first, earliest* Ἀνδρέας, ὁ τοῦ χοροῦ τῶν ἀποστόλων π. Hesych.H.*serm*.7(M.93.1477A).

πρωτότυπος, **1.** *first-formed* τῶν δὲ π. στοιχείων μενόντων Gr.Nyss. *res*.3(M.46.673B); ἐκ ποίου π. ὕλης ἐλήφθη ἡ γῆ, ἐξ οὐκ ὄντων γινομένη; Epiph.*haer*.64.66(p.508.14; M.41.1185A); **2.** *first, primary*, Tat.*orat*.9(p.10.19; M.6.828A); λῦσον τὴν π. ἁμαρτίαν [sc. of Adam] τῇ τῆς τροφῆς μεταδόσει Bas.*hom*.8.7(2.70D; M.31.324C); neut. as subst., *the first clause* of a sentence, opp. τὸ παρεπόμενον, *cat.2Cor*. 2:10(p.360.33); *ib*.10:8(p.415.31); **3.** *principal, chief* πρωτότυπος τῶν κοιτώνων τοῦ βασιλέως εὐνοῦχος Socr.*h.e*.2.2.5(M.67.188A); *ib*.3.1.46 (376C); in financial transaction π. ὀφειλέτης Chrys.*hom.15.8 in Mt*. (7.199B); masc. as subst., *principal party* in an action at law, Ath. Scholast.*coll*.4.13(p.57); neut. as subst., *the leading part* in a play, met. ἡ μὲν ὑπόθεσις ἦν Ἀρειανῶν ἀγών· καὶ τὸ π. ἐκείνους κατορθοῦν Ath.*apol.sec*.17(p.99.36; M.25.276B); **4.** *original* πρωτοτύπους αὐτοῖς Ἑβραίων στοιχείοις γραφάς Eus.*h.e*.6.16.1(M.20.553C); εἰ οὕτως εἶχεν ἡ λέξις ἐν τῇ π. γραφῇ Gr.Nyss.*Eun*.1(1 p.109.6; M.45.344A); *ib*.4(2 p.82.17; M.45.657A); Epiph.*haer*.42.12(p.157.7; M.41.776B); hence = Lat. *principalis* ἀξίως μακάριος ἀπεφάνθη [sc. ὁ Πέτρος] παρὰ τοῦ *κυρίου καὶ ἀπὸ τῆς π. πέτρας τὸ στερεὸν ἐπεσπάσατο τῆς τε ἀρετῆς καὶ τῆς προσηγορίας* Leo Mag.*ep*.28(p.16.23; M.*PL*.54.772B); **5.** *prototypal*; of original model from which subsequent models derive, Epiph.*anac*.1(p.162.3; M.41.165C); masc. as subst., Jo.D.*haer*.(M.94.677A); hence neut. as subst., *pattern, model, original ὁ ζωγράφος ...ἀπεῖδεν εἰς τὸ π.* Didym.(‡Bas.)*Eun*.5(1.301E; M.29.724B); *εἰ εἰκόνα βασιλέως τις ὑβρίσει, εἰς τὸ π. τῆς ἀξίας φέρει τὴν ὕβριν* Sever. *sigill*.6(M.63.544); **6.** *archetypal*; masc. and neut. as subst., *archetype*, opp. *παράγωγος* = derivative *οὐκοῦν, ἡ γνωμικὸν καὶ π.· εἰ δὲ παράγωγον, ἡ γνώμη, ὡς π. οὐσία ἔσται* Max.*Pyrr*.(M.91.308B); *μὴ σχιζομένης τῆς δόξης τοῦ π. ἐν τῷ παραγώγῳ* Thdr.Stud.*epp*.2.1(M.99.1117D); of Godhead, opp. *ἀρχέτυπος*, q.v., used of Logos *πρωτότυπος* may be used of Son *προάγων ἐπὶ μακαριότητα οἷον εἰκόνα τοῦ Χριστοῦ ἀντιτίθησιν, ἤτοι μιμουμένην τὸν π., τὸν υἱὸν τοῦ θεοῦ, τὴν εἰκόνα τοῦ θεοῦ* Or.*hom.8 in Lc*.(p.56.27); *ἡ ὁμωνύμως αὐτὸν ποιεῖν, ὡς τὸν π. υἱὸν ὅτι μία ἐστὶν ἡ φυσικὴ υἱότης, ἐξ ἧς κατὰ μεσοχὴν πᾶσα υἱότης* Leont.B.*fr*.(M.86.2008C); contrasted with *ἀρχέτυπος*, in gen. *μιμουμένην* [sc. *τὴν ἑαυτοῦ ψυχήν*] *τὸν π., τὸν υἱὸν τοῦ θεοῦ* Or.*hom.8 in Lc*.(p.56.27; cf.id.*schol.in Lc*.1:46, M.17.321C); *ἡ αὐτοαλήθεια ἡ οὐσιώδης καὶ...π. τῆς ἐν ταῖς λογικαῖς ψυχαῖς ἀληθείας* id.*Jo*.6.6(3; p.114.22; M.14.209D); *ἡ γὰρ τῆς ἀληθείας π. οὐσία ἐν τῷ Ἰησοῦ μόνῳ* id.*comm.in Eph*.4:20(p.418); *τὴν π. τοῦ πατρὸς καὶ μονογενῆ εἰκόνα* Meth.*res*.1.35(p.274.5; M.41.1100B); *ἀπαράλλακτος εἰκὼν τοῦ πατρὸς τυγχάνων, καὶ τοῦ π. ἔκτυπος χαρακτήρ* Alex.Al.*ep.Alex*.9(p.25.26; M.18.561C); *τὸ γὰρ ἀπαύγασμα τῆς δόξης μὴ εἶναι λέγειν, συναιρεῖ καὶ τὸ π. φῶς, οὗ ἐστιν ἀπαύγασμα ib*.7(p.24.4; 557C); *ἡ γὰρ τῆς εἰκόνος τιμὴ ἐπὶ τὸ π. διαβαίνει* Bas.*Spir*.45(3.38C; M.32.149C); *οὕτως καὶ ὁ τὸ τέλειον τῆς ἀγάπης ἐν ἑαυτῷ κατορθώσας πάντα ὅσα συνθεωρεῖται ταύτῃ τῶν ἀγαθῶν εἴδη, μετὰ τοῦ π. κατορθωμάτων* Gr.Nyss.*laud. Bas*.(M.46.800C); *οὐδὲ κατὰ εἶδος καὶ χρῶμα ὡς ἡ τεχνητὴ καὶ μιμητὴ ἄφωνος εἰκών. ταῦτα γὰρ οὐδὲ κατὰ φύσιν, οὐδὲ μὴν εἰς ὅλα τὰ ἄλλα ἐκφαίνουσι τὸν π. καὶ υἱὸς μὲν γὰρ ἀνθρώπου εἰκὼν οὐσίας τοῦ ἑαυτοῦ πατρός ἐστιν* Didym.*Trin*.1.16(M.39.336C); *ὁ γὰρ χαρακτὴρ ἄλλος τίς ἐστι παρὰ τὸ π., ἄλλος δὲ οὐ πάντῃ, ἀλλὰ κατὰ τὸ ἐνυπόστατον εἶναι* Chrys.*hom.2.2 in Heb*.(12.16D); *Ἀδὰμ...τὸ π. κάλλος τῆς εὐσεβείας ἀποδυσάμενος* ‡Chrys.*fid*.1(1.825D); *πᾶν ὅπερ ἂν καθ' ὁμοίωσιν γένοιτό τινος, ἀπολείπεται πάντως τῆς πρὸς τὸ π. ἰσότητος καὶ τῆς ἐκείνου δόξης ἐστὶ δεύτερον* Cyr.*thes*.6(5¹.45D); **7.** neut. as subst., *type, figure πρωτότυπον ὁμολογεῖ ὁ ἀπόστολος τὸν νόμον τοῦ εὐαγγελίου λέγων* Adam.*dial*.2.17(p.94.6; M.11.1788B); *prophecy τὸ π. διὰ Λαζάρου...ἐπεπλήρωτο* Epiph.*haer*.42.12(p.180.5; M.41.809A).

***πρωτοτυπόω**, *prefigure*, Sev.Ant.ap.*cat.Ac*.3:22(p.68.19).

***πρωτοτύπωμα**, **τό**, *prefigurement τὸ δὲ αἷμα...τοῦ ἀληθινοῦ πνεύματος τὸ π.* ‡Chrys.*pasch*.6(p.159.17; 8.269D).

πρωτοτύπως, **1.** *in the first instance ταύτην* [sc. *τὴν εὐχήν*] *δὲ π. ἐπιτελῶν, ἐπιεικείᾳ καὶ καρδίᾳ ταπεινῇ ζωγράφει τὸν οἶκόν σου* ‡Chrys.*hom.suppl*.6(M.64.465B); Max.*schol.c.h*.4.1(M.4.53A); *in the first place*, opp. *ἑπομένως*, Thdr.Mops.*fr.inc*.12(p.303.2; M.66.984D); **2.** *at first hand, immediately εἴδωλον δέ, ὅσα ἀνατυποῦσα ψυχὴ ποιεῖ ἐξ οὐχ ὑπαρχόντων π. οἷον ἀναμεμιγμένον τι ζῷον ἀπὸ ἀνθρώπου καὶ ἵππου* Or.*adnot.in Ex*.20:4(M.17.16C); Cyr.H.*catech*.14.21; **3.** *primarily, chiefly, especially τὰ δέ γε π. αἴτια* Eus.*d.e*.5 proem.(p.206.32); Thdr.Heracl.*Is*.45:16(M.18.1341A); Bas.*hom*.8.5(2.66E; M.31.316B); Epiph.*haer*.47.1(p.216.5; M.41.852B).

***πρωτοτύπωσις**, **ἡ**, *prefiguration ἡ μὲν ἠπιότης ἐν αὐτῷ* [sc. *Χριστῷ*] *σῴζει τοῦ προβάτου τὴν π.* ‡Chrys.*pasch*.5(8.262B).

[*]**πρωτοΰπνιον** ([*]**πρώθυπνον, πρωθύπνιον**), **τό**, *first watch of the night πρωθύπνου δὲ γενομένου A.Xanthipp*.13(p.66.10); *ἡ π. ἡ πρωΐ* Ath.*virg*.23(p.58.23; M.28.280B); Pall.*h.Laus*.22(p.72.19; *πρώτου ὑπνίου* M.34.1082B); ‡Pall.*h.mon*.8.50(p.47.5, v.l. *πρωθυπνίου* M.34.1147C); *Chron.Pasch*.p.308(M.92.784B); plur., of late evening prayers *εὐχόμενος...πρωθύπνια* Call.*v.Hyp*.(p.54).

***πρωτουργία**, **ἡ**, *initiative, first step in action*, Cyr.*Jo*.12(4.1052B).

πρωτουργός, **1.** *primary, primordial*, of God *τοῦ π. ἀγαθοῦ* Didym.*Trin*.1.18(M.39.352A); of divine nature, *ib*.1.15(308C); Dion.Ar.*c.h*.7.1(M.3.205C); *ib*.7.2(208C); *οὐ π. οὖν τὸ σκότος, ἀλλ' ἀνυπάρκτως γινόμενον κατὰ τὴν πρὸς τὸ φῶς παρακολούθησιν* Proc.G.*Gen*.1:5(M.87.57C); **2.** *originating ὁ υἱὸς...πρωτουργὸς κινήσεως δύναμις* Clem.*str*.7.2(p.8.5; M.9.412C); of souls, opp. bodies, as *π. τοῦ καλοῦ καὶ τοῦ χείρονος* Andr.Caes.*therap.fr*.1(p.165.6).

***πρωτοφάνεια**, **ἡ**, *primary revelation ἱεροὺς νόας...τὴν πρωτοφανῆ ...π. ἀνεκπομπεύτως εἰσδεχομένους* Dion.Ar.*c.h*.15.6(M.3.336A).

πρωτοφανής, *appearing first, first manifested π. ἄνθος τοῦ ἔαρος* Gr.Nyss.*ep*.12(M.46.1045A); Nonn.*par.Jo*.2:11(M.43.701C); of immediate illumination, Dion.Ar.*c.h*.10.1(M.3.272D); *ib*.15.6(336A); Synes.*hymn*.4.89(p.29, conj. for *πρωτοφαῆ* M.66.1605).

***πρωτοφανῶς**, *by direct revelation*, Dion.Ar.*c.h*.13.3(M.3.301C); Max.*schol.c.h*.8.1(M.4.80B).

***πρωτοφόνος**, **ὁ**, *first murderer*, ‡Caes.Naz.*dial*.31(M.38.893).

πρωτόχρονος, *first in time*, Geo.Pis.*hex*.1182(M.92.1525A).

πρωτόχυτος, *first-flowing*, Clem.*paed*.1.6(p.115.3; M.8.300A).

πταῖσμα, **τό**, *error, fault*; synon. with *ἁμάρτημα*, Or.*hom.4.1 in Jer*.(p.24.1; M.13.285D); id.*or*.28(p.381.1; M.11.529A); Meth.*symp*.10.1(p.122.6; M.18.193A); Cyr.H.*catech*.1.1.

πταιστός, *liable to err, erring*, Max.*ep*.12(M.91.469C); Thphn.*chron*.p.210(M.108.537C); neut. as subst., Thdr.Stud.*epp*.2.99(M.99.1352C).

πταί-ω, **1.** *stumble, trip, fall*, hence, met., *sin, lapse*, Pall.*h.Laus*.70(p.166.2; M.34.1241D); *αὐτὴ ἡ τῆς φύσεως ἀσθένεια καθεῖλκεν ἐπὶ τὸ ~ειν* Thdr.Mops.*Gal*.1:3–5(p.8.22; M.66.900B); perf. ptcpl. act. as subst., *sinner*, Bas.*hom.in Ps*.14(1.355C; M.29.257C); perf. ptcpl. pass. neut. as subst., *sin*, Nil.*epp*.3 113(M.79.436D); *ib*.3.243(500C); **2.** *fall away* from; c. genit., Meth.*symp*.8.10(p.92.24; M.18.153B); *ib*.11.1(p.131.3; 208A); **3.** pass., *be crushed*, Apoll.ap.*cat.Mt*.27:3 (p.231.18).

πτερνίζ-ω, **1.** *kick*, Thal.CP *Thds*.(p.8.30; M.91.1476A); †Gregent. *leg.Hom*.9(M.86.585C); *spur* a horse, Ath.*Pet.Ar*.1(M.26.820C); **2.** *catch by heel*; of Jacob, Or.*comm.in Gen*.ap.*philoc*.23.19(p.208.16; M.12.81C); **3.** *trip up, overcome in wrestling*, in interprn. of Jacob *υἱοὶ δὲ Ἰακὼβ...οἱ τῆς κακίας πτερνίσαντες τὴν ἐνέργειαν* Clem.*str*.6.7 (p.462.17; M.9.281C); *ὁ βλέπων θεόν...~ει τὰ πάθη τὰ γαστρίμαργα* Isid.Pel.*epp*.1.192(M.78.305B); Cyr.*glaph.Gen*.3(1.97B); *Ἰακὼβ...τὸν ~οντα τὸν σατανᾶν* id.*Is*.4.4(2.685C); *τύπος δ' ἂν εἴη παντὸς τοῦ ~οντος τὰς ἁμαρτίας* id.*Mal*.4(3.821C); id.*Os*.138(3.170E); *γνώσεται δὲ θεὸν Ἰακὼβ ὁ ἔτι...~ων τοὺς δαίμονας θεὸν δὲ Ἰσραὴλ ὁ τὴν τελείαν θεωρίαν δεξάμενος* Proc.G.*Is*.2:1–4(M.87.1873C); **4.** *deceive, cheat, overthrow by stratagem*, of Dan (antichrist) *ὄφις...ὁ...πτερνίσας τὸν Ἀδάμ* Hipp.*antichr*.14(p.11.16; M.10.737B); Thdr.Mops.*Mal*.3:8–10 (M.66.625B); Nil.*Eulog*.25(M.79.1125C); ‡Just.*ep.Zen.et Ser*.5(M.6.1188C); **5.** *supplant*, Gr.Naz.*ep*.153(M.37.260B); id.*carm*.2.1.11.425 (M.37.1058A); of supplanting of old Israel by Church, †Gregent. *disp*.(M.86.629A) cit. s. *πτερνισμός*.

πτερνισμός, **ὁ**, **1.** *striking with the heel, kick*, ref. Ps.40:10 applied to Judas, Cyr.H.*catech*.13.6; **2.** *deception, stratagem*, ‡Ath.*synops*.18 (M.28.328A); Nil.*Eulog*.25(M.79.1125C); **3.** *supplanting*, ref. Jacob *προοίμιον ἦν ὁ π. ἐκεῖνος τοῦ ἡμετέρου π.· ἐκεῖ γὰρ ὁ νεώτερος υἱὸς τὸν πρεσβύτερον ἐπτέρνισεν· ἐνταῦθα γὰρ ὁ νεώτερος ὄχλος τὸν πρεσβύτερον λαὸν ἐπτέρνισεν* †Gregent.*disp*.(M.86.629A).

***πτερνιστήρα**, **ἡ**, *spur*, Gr.Mag.*dial*.(tr.Zach.)1.2(M.*PL*.77.158C).

πτερνιστής, **ὁ**, **1.** *one who trips up, vanquisher* in wrestling; of Jacob as type of Christian who vanquishes sin, passions, etc., Or. *exc.in Ps*.80:2(M.17.149B); *π. γὰρ ὁ Ἰακὼβ ἑρμηνεύεται, ὡς τὸν ἀρετῆς ἐναθλῶν ἀγῶνα* Eus.*p.e*.11.6(519A; M.21.860D); Nil.*epp*.3.112(M.79.436C); Cyr.*glaph.Gen*.3(1.97B); id.*Os*.138(3.170E); id.*Mal*.4(3.821C); **2.** *deceiver, cheat*, of Devil *τὸν παλαιὸν π.* †Gregent.*disp*.(M.86.664B).

***πτεροβολ-έω**, *put forth wings οἱ γὰρ ὑπομένοντες τὸν κύριον... ~ήσουσι* Hesych.S.*temp*.2.45(M.93.1525B), cf.Is.40:31(*πτεροφυήσουσι* LXX).

***πτεροβόλος**, *having wings*; of an angel, Tim.Ant.*nativ.Jo.Bapt*.2(M.28.909B); *flighty, wanton*, of a disreputable woman, *Ep*.ap. CSyr.*act*.(*ACO* 3 p.95.8; H.2.1369B); *ib*.(p.96.17; 1372B).

***πτεροειδής**, *of winged appearance*; of a demon, *T.Sal*.14.4(M.122.1336D).

πτερόεις, *winged*; of man's nature before Fall, Gr.Nyss.*hom.15 in Cant*.(M.44.1101A).

πτεροκοπέω, *clip the wings of*, c. acc., ‡Epiph.*hom*.4(M.43.481C).

πτερόν, **τό**, *wing*; **1.** worn on head of *ἱερογραμματεύς* in Egyptian rites, Clem.*str*.6.4(p.449.7; M.9.253B); **2.** of 'wings' of God *κατ' ἄλλας καὶ ἄλλας αἰτίας τε καὶ δυνάμεις ὀνομάζουσι τὴν ὑπερφαῆ... ἀγαθότητα καὶ...ὀφθαλμοὺς αὐτῆς...καὶ π. ... ὑμνοῦσι* Dion.Ar.*d.n*.1.8 (M.3.597B); of 'sun of righteousness' *τοῖς πνευματικοῖς χαρίσμασιν οἱόν τισι π. συγκαλύψας, ἴασιν ταῖς...παρέσχε ψυχαῖς* Thdt.*Mal*.4:2(2.1693); cf. *πτέρυξ*; **3.** of wings of angels, esp. seraphim and cherubim *οὐδὲν ἄλλο δηλοῖ τὰ π. ἢ τὸ τῆς φύσεως ὕψος* Chrys.*incomprehens*.3.5 (1.468B); id.*hom.6.2 in Is*.6:1(6.140A); *τῆς δὲ τῶν π. ἐξαπλῆς ἱεροπλαστίας τὴν ἐπὶ τὸ θεῖον ἐν πρώταις, ἐν μέσαις, ἐν τελευταίαις νοήσεσιν ἀπόλυτον καὶ ὑπερτάτην ἀνάστασιν, ἀλλὰ καὶ τὸ ἀπειρόπουν αὐτῶν... ὁρῶν ὁ...θεολόγος, καὶ τὸ τοῖς π. ἀποδιαστέλλεσθαι τὴν ὑπὸ τοὺς πόδας καὶ τὴν ὑπὲρ πρόσωπα θεωρίαν, καὶ τὴν ἐν τοῖς μέσοις π. ἀεικινησίαν, πρὸς τὴν νοητὴν τῶν ὁρωμένων ἀνήγετο γνῶσιν, ἐκφαινομένης...τῆς... τῶν θεομιμήτων ἐνεργειῶν...ὑψιπετοῦς ἀεικινησίας* Dion.Ar.*c.h*.13.4 (M.3.304D); *τὸ γὰρ π. ἐμφαίνει τὴν ἀναγωγικὴν ὀξύτητα...ἡ δὲ τῶν π. ἐλαφρία τὸ κατὰ μηδὲν πρόσγειον, ἀλλ' ὅλον ἀμιγῶς...ἐπὶ τὸ ὑψηλὸν* ἀναγόμενον *ib.*15.3(332D); τὴν δὲ τῶν π. ... ἐξαπλῆν θέσιν, οὐκ ἀριθμὸν ἱερὸν ἐμφαίνειν οἶμαι, κατὰ τὸ δόξαν ἑτέροις, ἀλλ' ὅτι...παντελῶς ἐστι... ὑπερκόσμια τὰ πρῶτα, καὶ μέσα, καὶ τελευταῖα τῶν νοερῶν...δυνάμεων id.*e.h.*4.3.7(M.3.481A); *ib.*4.3.8(481B); **4.** of soul, ref. supramundane fall ἐκεῖθεν δὲ διὰ κακίας τῶν π. ἐκπιπτόντων χαμαιπετεῖς πρόσγειοι γίνονται, τῇ παχύτητι τῆς ὑλικῆς καταμιγνύμεναι φύσεως Gr.Nyss. *anim.et res.*(M.46.113C); **5.** ref. spiritual ascent, Clem.*prot.*10(p.76.9; M.8.221C) cit. s. ἁπλότης; ἡ τῶν π. τῆς σωφροσύνης συγκρατεῖται φύσις Meth.*symp.*8.1(p.82.1; M.18.140B); Chrys.*bapt.Chr.*4(2.374C) cit. s. ἀετός; καθαροὶ τοίνυν κἂν τοῖς λογικοῖς, οἱ μὴ τοῖς γηΐνοις προστετηκότες, ἀλλὰ τὰ π. τῆς πίστεως ἔχοντες...ταῦτα δὲ ἡμῖν... περιτίθησι Παῦλος, τὰ π. λέγων τῆς χάριτος καὶ τὰ ὅπλα τοῦ πνεύματος Thdt.*qu.11 in Lev.*(1.190); of breaking of wings of sacrificed birds, as symbol of soul's humility, Cyr.*ador.*16(1.564D); **6.** of prayer, and almsgiving, Chrys.*poenit.*3.1(2.295C,D) cit. s. ἐλεημοσύνη; π. ἐστι τῆς εὐχῆς ἡ ἐλεημοσύνη Jo.Clim.*scal.*28(M.88.1145C); **7.** of Christ as π. οὐράνιον παναγοῦς ποίμνης Clem.*paed.hymn.*21(p.291; M.8.681B); **8.** of wings of H. Ghost raising soul to heavenly sphere, Chrys. *hom.12.2 in Phil.*(11.292A).

πτεροποι-έω, *make winged,* met. ~οῦσι...αἱ θεῖαι γραφαὶ τοὺς πιστούς, τῷ πόθῳ τῶν οὐρανίων Ath.*fr.1 in Cant.*(M.27.1349C); ἐπτεροποιήθης τῇ πίστει Procl.CP *or.*15.3(M.65.801D).

πτερορρο-έω, = πτερορρυέω: ῥοπῇ δέ τινι τῇ πρὸς κακίαν ~ούσας τὰς ψυχὰς ἐν σώματι γίνεσθαι Gr.Nyss.*anim.et res.*(M.46.112C).

πτερορρυ-έω, *moult, lose feathers* of wings, hence *lose power of flight,* Bas.*hex.*8.5(1.75C; M.29.176C); met. κηλούμενοι γὰρ ταῖς ἡδοναῖς...~οῦσι πολλοί Meth.*symp.*8.1(p.81.17; M.18.140A); ψυχὴ διὰ τῆς παρακοῆς τῶν πρωτοπλάστων ~ήσασα Gr.Nyss.*hom.15 in Cant.*(M.44.1101C); id.*Eun.*1(1 p.210.13; M.45.457C); Thdr.Stud.*epp.* 2.208(M.99.1629C).

πτερορρύησις, ἡ, *moulting;* met., of bias to evil which causes soul's fall into body acc. Platonist doctrine, Gr.Nyss.*anim.et res.* (M.46.117A).

***πτεροφορέω,** *be winged,* Cyr.*ador.*14(1.508A).

πτεροφυ-έω, *grow wings,* 1*Clem.*25.3; met. οἱ ~οῦντες μαθηταί Or.*comm.ser.3 in Mt.*(p.98.12; M.13.1669D); of Jo. Bapt. ἀκρίδας ἐσθίοντα καὶ ~ήσαντα τὴν ψυχήν Cyr.H.*catech.*3.6; ~ῆσαι καὶ πρὸς τὰς οὐρανίους ἁψῖδας ἀναδραμεῖν Chrys.*subintr.*13(1.248B); Isid.Pel.*epp.* 1.282(M.78.348C); ὅστις ἐποχεῖται κουφότητι κενῆς δόξης, οὐδέποτε ~ήσει πρὸς τὸν τῆς ἀληθοῦς δόξης ἔρωτα ‡Nil.*vit.cog.*(M.79.1461C); ἐπεφάνη ὁ Χριστὸς ἵνα δι' ὁσιότητος καὶ δικαιοσύνης αὖθις ~ήσωμεν Proc.G.*Cant.*6:4(M.87.1709D).

πτεροφυΐα, ἡ, *growing of wings,* not to be inferred in lit. sense from descriptions of angelic beings, Dion.Ar.*c.h.*2.1(M.3.137A).

πτερ-όω, *give wings to, provide with wings, make to fly;* **1.** ref. spiritual ascent, Clem.*prot.*10(p.76.9; M.8.221C); ἂν εὐξαίμην τὸ πνεῦμα τοῦ Χριστοῦ ~ῶσαί με εἰς τὴν Ἱερουσαλὴμ τὴν ἐμήν id.*str.*4.26 (p.324.24; M.8.1381A); οἱ δ' ἐντραφέντες γνησίως τοῖς τῆς ἀληθείας λόγοις...εἰς οὐρανὸν ~οῦνται *ib.*1.1(p.5.9; 692A); 'τὴν ψυχὴν ἐπτερωμένην' τῷ πόθῳ τῶν κρειττόνων *ib.*7.7(p.30.23; M.9.456B), cf.Plato *Phaedrus* 246B,C; Serap.*ep.mon.*1(M.40.928A); ἡ σὰρξ ἐβάρησεν, ἀλλ' ὁ λογισμὸς ἐπτέρωσεν Gr.Naz.*or.*37.11(M.36.296B); id.*carm.*1.2.10.415 (M.37.710A); Chrys.*hom.43.5 in Mt.*(7.465C); δυνήσῃ κατὰ μικρὸν ~ῶσαί σου τὴν διάνοιαν id.*hom.17.2 in 1Cor.*(10.148B); φιλοσοφία ἀτάραχον δύναται τηρῆσαι ψυχὴν καὶ ~ῶσαι *ib.27.4*(349A); Isid.Pel. *epp.*1.166(M.78.292C); Cyr.*Is.*2.5(2.344A) cit. s. πτέρυξ; Geo.Pis. *carm.*3.13; **2.** ref. 'wings' of prayer νηστείᾳ καὶ σάκκῳ καὶ σποδῷ τὴν προσευχὴν ~ώσας προσέφερεν τῷ θεῷ Thdt.*Dan.*9:3(2.1229); **3.** ref. departed souls ascending to heaven, Ath.*v.Anton.*66(M.26.937A); **4.** of man's nature before Fall ἐπτέρωται κατὰ τὴν...γραφὴν τὸ πρωτότυπον Gr.Nyss.*hom.15 in Cant.*(M.44.1100D); **5.** in bad sense, *make light* or *wanton,* Clem.*paed.*3.11(p.269.17; M.8.632B).

πτερύγιον, τό, **1.** *little wing,* ref. breaking of wings (Lev.1:17) interpreted as symbol of humility, Cyr.*ador.*16(1.564D); **2.** *border* of high-priestly robe, Nil.*serm.*10(M.79.1277D); of Saul's garment (1Reg.24:15) interpreted as τὸ ἦθος τῆς κατὰ τὴν ἠθικὴν φιλοσοφίαν ἀσχημοσύνης, †Cyr.*coll.VT*(6[4].69A; M.77.1277D); of Scribes' robes, Jo.D.*haer.*15(M.94.688A); of entire high-priestly robe, ‡Bas.Sel. *or.*38.4(M.85.413A); **3.** *pointed roof, 'wing'* of Temple, scene of S. James's martyrdom, Heges.ap.Eus.*h.e.*2.23.12(M.20.200B); fell at earthquake at Crucifixion, *Narr.Jos.*3.4(p.467); in vision of Christ and Moses appearing on Temple, †Gregent.*disp.*3(M.86.749B); **4.** medic., *membrane* in brain, Hipp.*haer.*4.51(p.76.13; M.16.3122B); *cartilage* joining nose to cheek, Melet.*nat.hom.*3(M.64.1180C).

πτερυγόω, *furnish with wings,* ref. creation in divine image, Or.*sel.in Gen.*(M.12.93C) cit. s. sq.

πτέρυξ, ἡ, *wing;* **1.** of 'wings' of God ἡμεῖς μὲν οὐκ ἐπτερυγώμεθα, περὶ δὲ θεοῦ λέγει...ὅτι ὑπὸ τὰς π. αὐτοῦ ἐλπιεῖς. εἰ δὲ ἐκεῖνος μὲν π. ἔχει, ἡμεῖς δέ ἐσμεν ζῷον ἄπτερον, οὐ κατ' εἰκόνα θεοῦ γέγονεν ὁ ἄνθρωπος Or.*sel.in Gen.*(M.12.93C); πτέρυγας δὲ νοήσεις τὰς τῆς προνοίας αὐτοῦ δυνάμεις Eus.*Ps.*16:8(M.23.164A); ἔθος τῇ θείᾳ γραφῇ πτέρυγας καλεῖν τὴν ἐπισκοπικὴν δύναμιν τοῦ θεοῦ Ath.*exp.Ps.*56:2(M.27.257D); τῆς γὰρ φρουρητικῆς αὐτοῦ δυνάμεως εἰς π. λαμβανομένης Cyr.H.*catech.*6.8; τὸ πτερύγων ὄνομα διά τινος τροπικῆς θεωρίας εἰς τὸ θεοπρεπὲς μεταληφθήσεται νόημα, δυνάμεώς τε καὶ μακαριότητος καὶ ἀφθαρσίας...διὰ τοῦ ὀνόματος τῶν π. σημαινομένων Gr.Nyss.*hom.15 in Cant.*(M.44.1101A); π., τὸ σκεπαστικόν Didym.(‡Bas.)*Eun.*5(1.316C; M.29.757C); πανταχοῦ...ἡ εἰκὼν αὕτη τῶν π. ... τὴν...σκέπην καὶ πρόνοιαν ἐνδεικνυμένη Chrys.*hom.74.3 in Mt.*(7.718D); misunderstanding refuted that man is not made in God's image because not possessed of wings, Isid.Pel.*epp.*3.95(M.78.800C); 'wings' interpreted of Son and H. Ghost, Cyr.*Ps.*16:8(M.69.817A); πτέρυγας...τὴν ὀξεῖαν καὶ σύντομον τῆς προνοίας ἀσφάλειαν Thdt. *Ps.*16:8(1.698); π. γὰρ τὴν τοῦ θεοῦ κηδεμονίαν καλεῖ id.*Ps.*60:5(1.1009); **2.** of 'sun of righteousness' (Mal.4:2); prophecy applied to Maccabean age, Thdr.Mops.*Mal.*4:2(M.66.629C); referred to gift of H. Ghost, Cyr.*Mal.*64(3.867Eff.); cf. πτερόν; **3.** of angels, esp. cherubim and seraphim δώδεκα πτέρυγας ἄμφω ἔχει καὶ διὰ τοῦ ζῳδιακοῦ κύκλου καὶ τοῦ κατ' αὐτὸν φερομένου χρόνου τὸν αἰσθητὸν κόσμον δηλοῖ Clem.*str.*5.6(p.350.5; M.9.61B); six wings correspond to spiritual senses, Eus.*Is.*6:2(M.24.125A,B); αἱ π. τὸ ὕψος ἐμφαίνουσι τῆς φύσεως...οὐκ ἐπειδὴ πτερὰ περὶ τὸν ἄγγελον, ἀλλ' ἵνα μάθῃς, ὅτι ἐκ τῶν ὑψηλοτάτων χωρίων...πρὸς τὴν ἀνθρωπίνην ἀφίκται φύσιν Chrys.*incomprehens.*3.5(1.468B); αἰνίττονται αἱ π. τὸ ὑψηλὸν καὶ μετάρσιον τῶν δυνάμεων τούτων id.*Is.interp.*6:3(6.66D); αἱ ἓξ π. ἐνδείκνυνται αὗται τὸ ὑψηλὸν καὶ μετάρσιον καὶ κοῦφον καὶ τὸ ταχὺ ἐκείνων τῶν φύσεων id.*hom.6.2 in Is.*6:1(6.140A); veiling of faces with wings symbol of inability to see beginning or end of thought about God, Cyr.*Is.*1.4(2.103A); Thdt.*Ezech.*1:8(2.684); Dion.Ar.*e.h.* 4.3.5(M.3.480B); πτέρυγες...αἵπερ εἰσὶν ἔμφυτοί τινες ἀρεταί, δι' ἃς ὑψοῦνται τοσοῦτον, ὡς πλησίον εἶναι θεοῦ τὸν νοῦν ἔχοντας Proc.G.*Is.* 6:1–5(M.87.1933A); **4.** of man's original nature, which possessed 'wings' of immortality, etc., Gr.Nyss.*hom.15 in Cant.*(M.44.1101A); **5.** exeg. Ps.54:7 τίς δώσει πτέρυγας ὡσεὶ περιστερᾶς;...τίς καταξιώσῃ με τῆς χάριτος τοῦ πνεύματος; Or.*Ps.*54:7(p.56); cf. *hoc dicit prophetes non orans, ut corporales pennas accipiat columbae, sed pennas columbae spiritus sancti,* id.*hom.6.6 in Is.*(p.277.19; M.13.245B); περιστερᾶς γὰρ δίκην ἀκάκου πτέρυγας ἐκφεῦξαι καὶ πετασθῆναι, ὡς ἂν φύγοι τὰ κακά, ἠξίου Eus.*Ps.*54:7(M.23.477B); **6.** of spiritual 'wings', i.e. virtues, etc.; ref. Pr.23:5, cf. *si accipiamus igitur pennas, leviter audiemus; si autem peccaverimus et negligentes fuerimus circa alas et defluxerunt pennae nostrae, gravabimur et graviter audiemus,* Or.*hom.6.6 in Is.*(p.277.22; M.13.245B); id.*comm. ser.47 in Mt.*(p.98.14; cf.M.13.1669D); of learning, cf.id.*hom.2.2 in Ex.*(p.156.26; M.12.306B); τῷ πτέρυγας περιστερᾶς ἀναλαβεῖν διὰ τῶν ἀρετῶν Proc.G.*Cant.*6:4(M.87.1709D); of profane scholarship, cf.Or.*hom.1.1 in Ex.*(p.145.18; M.12.297C); **7.** exeg. Is.24:16 πτέρυγας δὲ τῆς γῆς ἐοίκασιν ὀνομάζειν τοὺς ἁγίους μυσταγωγούς, ὧν τοῖς λόγοις μονονουχὶ...πτερούμενοι τὰ ἄνω φρονοῦμεν Cyr.*Is.*2.5(2.343E); π. τῆς γῆς τὴν πίστιν καὶ τὴν θεογνωσίαν ὠνόμασεν Thdt.*Is.*24:16 (p.99.16; 2.291); π. ... τοὺς τοῖς θείοις λόγοις αὐτοὺς ἀποστόλους ἀναπτερώσαντας Proc.G.*Is.*24:1–23(M.87.2193A); **8.** liturg., ref. consecration of chrism τὸ μύρον...λαβὼν ἐπιτίθησι τῷ...θυσιαστηρίῳ, περικεκαλυμμένον ὑπὸ δυοκαίδεκα πτέρυξιν ἱεραῖς Dion.Ar.*e.h.*4.2(M.3.473A); *ib.*4.3.4(477C); **9.** ref. Is.18:1 πτέρυγας...ὀνομάζει τὰ ἱστία Cyr.*Is.*2.3(2.274D); Proc.G.*Is.*18:1–7(M.87.2137C).

πτερύσσ-ομαι, *flutter, flap the wings;* met., be *stimulated, excited,* Isid.Pel.*epp.*1.151(M.78.605B); ~εσθαι...τὰ πάθη ‡Nil.*perist.*10.3(M.79.892A).

πτέρωμα, τό, *plumage,* hence *power of flight,* ref. soul's ascent παρθενία...ᾗ καὶ τὸ τῆς ψυχῆς καταρδόμενον ἀληθῶς αὔξεταί τε καὶ κουφίζεται π. Meth.*symp.*8.1(p.81.9; M.18.140A).

πτέρωσις, ἡ, *plumage,* hence met., *that which enables* the soul *to fly* π. γὰρ ἡ τῆς ψυχῆς πνεῦμα τέλειον Tat.*orat.*20(p.22.11; M.6.852A).

***πτερωτής, ὁ,** *one who encourages,* Gr.Naz.*or.*21.10(M.35.1093A).

πτερωτικός, *winged;* of S. Mark, in comparison of Evangelists with four beasts τὴν π. εἰκόνα τοῦ εὐαγγελίου δεικνύων Iren.*haer.*3.11.8(M.7.888B); ‡Germ.CP *contempl.*(M.98.396B) cit s. μανδύας.

πτερωτός, *winged;* **1.** of God in popular anthropomorphic misunderstandings of scripture, Cyr.H.*catech.*6.8; **2.** of angelic beings ὁ προφήτης τὴν ὀξύτητα τῶν ἀγγέλων πετεινῷ π. ὡμοίωσεν διὰ τὸ κοῦφον καὶ ἐλαφρὸν τῶν ἀγγέλων Hipp.*Dan*.4.30.1(M.10.685B); τροχοί, π. μὲν ὄντες,...τῆς πορευτικῆς αὐτῶν ἐνεργείας δύναμιν Dion.Ar.*c.h*.15.9(M.3.337C); ἡ τῶν λογίων...σοφία...τὸ καθόλου π. αὐτῶν αἰνισσομένη, καὶ...τῆς ἐπὶ τὸ ὄντως ὂν ἀναγωγικῆς δυνάμεως id.*e.h*.4.3.7(M.3.481A); **3.** of primal ἄνεμος identified with ὄφις in Naassene system, Hipp. *haer*.5.19(p.120.9; πρῶτον οὖν M.16.3183B).

***πτέσις, ἡ,** prob. error for πεῦσις, Ast.Am.*hom*.7(M.40.253B).

***πτηνοπρόσωπος,** *with the face of a bird*; of demons, *T.Sal*.18.1 (M.122.1341A).

πτῆσις, ἡ, *flight*; **1.** of birds as means of divination first practised by Phrygians and Isaurians, Tat.*orat*.1(p.1.6; M.6.804A); ἡ τῶν ὀρνίθων π. σημαίνει τι, οὐχὶ ποιεῖ Clem.*exc.Thdot*.70(p.129.23; M.9.692B); **2.** of seraphim ἡ δὲ π. τὸ μετάρσιον αἰνίττεται τοῦ φρονήματος Thdt.*Is*.6:2(p.31.23; 2.207); **3.** of H. Ghost at Jordan, indicating Christ, Bas.Sel.*or*.34.1(M.85.369B); **4.** of sun's *course*, Cyr. *Ps*.18:6(M.69.829C).

πτήσσω, 1. *cower for fear* π. ἀπὸ προσώπου αὐτοῦ *Pers*.(p.3.22); med., Cyr.H.*catech*.14.19; **2.** *dread, fear*, Or.*engast*.7(p.290.1; M.12.1021C).

πτισμός, ὁ, *pounding*, Gr.Naz.*carm*.1.2.10.688(M.37.730A).

πτίσσω, *pound, belabour* ὑπέροις σιδηροῖς ἐπτίσσετο [sc. Ἀνάξαρχος] Clem.*str*.4.8(p.274.15; M.8.1269A); Gr.Naz.*ep*.32(M.37.72A); Nemes.*nat.hom*.30(M.40.721A).

πτο-έω, 1. *terrify, scare*; pass. c. acc., *be terrified, scared of*, Jo. Mal.*chron*.18 p.432(M.97.637B); τὸ ἐν μέρος ∼ηθὲν τὸν νόμον †Gregent. *leg.Hom*.32(M.86.597D); **2.** met., *flutter, excite*; pass. c. acc., *be excited at, be desirous of* τὴν δόξαν ἐπτοημένοι Nil.*exerc*.1(M.79.720B).

***πτοητέον,** *one must be scared, dismayed*, Thdr.Stud.*epp*.2.6(M.99.1128B).

***πτυκτίον, τό,** *volume, book* (opp. papyrus roll), Gr.Naz.*ep*.31(M.37.69A); π. τῆς Ὠριγένους φιλοκαλίας *ib*.115(212C); *ib*.202(332B); met. τὸν...τῆς γνώσεως νόμον ἐν π. τῆς καρδίας Const.Diac.*laud*.33(M.88.517A).

πτυκτός, *folded*; fem. as subst. = foreg. ταῖς θείαις π. Isid.Pel. *epp*.1.73(M.78.233A).

πτύξ, ἡ, 1. *volume, book* (opp. papyrus roll) τῶν ἱερῶν πτυχῶν Dion.Ar.*e.h*.3.2(M.3.425C); τῶν ἁγιογράφων π. *ib*.3.3.8(437A); **2.** sens. dub., Synes.*hymn*.2.18(p.44; M.66.1592); *ib*.4.161(p.31; M.66.1606).

πτύξις, ἡ, *enfolding*, Ath.*Ar*.1.1(M.26.13B, vv.ll. τάξιν, πτῆξιν); ‡Caes.Naz.*dial*.183(M.38.1160).

***πτῦρμα, τό,** *consternation*, Jo.Mal.*chron*.7 p 184(M.97.293B).

***πτύρσις, ἡ,** *disturbance, commotion*, Epiph.*haer*.42.12(p.168.16; M.41.792D); *ib*.62.2(p.391.11, v.l. πεῦσιν 1053A).

***πτύρτης, ὁ,** *one who scares* or *disturbs* π. τῶν περιστερῶν Epiph. *haer*.77.16(p.429.20; M.42.661D).

πτύρω, *perturb, scare*, *Hom.Clem*.2.39; Epiph.*haer*.70.9(p.241.15; M.42.353B); *ib*.77.15(p.429.10; 661C); *ib*.77.19(p.433.18; 669A).

πτύσμα, τό, *spittle*; **1.** ref. Jo.9:6, cf. *gentium populus, cui salvator reddidit visum, saliva sua unguens oculos ejus...mittebat eos quos spiritu unxit, ut crederent, ad Siloam*, Or.*hom*.6.3 *in Is*.(p.273.31; M.13.242C); cf.Meth.*res*.2.10(p.353.8); anointing with spittle signifies bestowal of Christ's power and that his body imparts φωτισμός through mere contact, Cyr.*Jo*.6.1(4.602D, 603A); signifies manifestation of Godhead in flesh, Thdt.*eran*.1(4.20); **2.** in other healings, ref. Sampsaean women healers συνεπόμενοι οἱ ὄχλοι αὐτῶν, τὸν χοῦν τῶν ποδῶν λαμβάνοντες ἰάσεως...ἕνεκεν, τὸν σίελον τῶν π. ὡσαύτως Epiph.*haer*.53.1(p.315.20; M.41.960C); **3.** ref. a Marcionite's refusal to be indebted to creator for use of water, and consequent employment of spittle for washing face, Thdt.*haer*.1.24(4.317); **4.** ref. sufferings of Christ as proof of humanity, Anast.S.*hod*.13 (M.89.208C); **5.** in abusive language πτύσματα μᾶλλον ῥημάτων ἢ ῥήματα προφερόμενοι Serap.*Man*.28(p.43; M.18.1124C).

πτύσσω, *roll up*, ref. formation of lips for speech, Thdt.*provid*.4 (4.529); of closing the mouth, *Hymn*.(*AS* 1 p.524).

πτύω, *spit*; ref. Jo.1:9ff., cf. *dominus exspuit in terram...ostendens antiquam plasmationem quemadmodum facta est, et manum dei manifestans...per quam e limo plasmatus est homo*, Iren.*haer*.5.15.2(M.7.1165B); action signifies making of 'unction' of scriptural teaching for anointing eyes of spiritually blind, Or.*fr.63 in Jo*. (p.534.8).

πτῶμα, τό, A. *fall*; **1.** of Adam, exeg. Mt.24:28 (where π. = *corpse*) π. δὲ γεγένηται ἐν παραδείσῳ· ἐκεῖ γὰρ Ἀδὰμ...πέπτωκεν Hipp.*antichr*.64(p.44.15; M.10.784C); Meth.*symp*.3.6(p.32.18; M.18.69A); id.*res*.1.23(p.248.2; M.41.1093A); Ἰησοῦς παρῆν...ἵν' ἐγὼ...τοῦ παλαιοῦ π. ἀνακληθῶ Gr.Naz.*or*.44.2(M.36.609A); ἐμβοᾷ...τῇ ἐκκλησίᾳ ὁ λόγος...λέγων· ἀνάστηθι, δηλαδὴ ἐκ τοῦ π. Gr.Nyss.*hom*.5 *in Cant*. (M.44.868A); resulting in clothing with coats of skin, Chrys.*hom*. *18.1 in Gen*.(4.151B); **2.** of sin in gen. χαλεπώτατον δὲ πάντων π. τὴν ἄπτωτον ἀγάπην ἄνωθεν ἐξ οὐρανῶν ἐπὶ τοὺς ζωμοὺς ῥίπτεσθαι χαμαί Clem.*paed*.2.1(p.157.11; M.8.385C); ἀνάστασις ἡ ἐκ τοῦ π. τῆς ἁμαρτίας ἀνόρθωσις Gr.Nyss.*ep.can*.(M.45.221B); *ib*.(224B); προαιρέσεως τὸ π. Chrys.*hom*.5.3 *in Rom*.(9.464C); **3.** *error* ἵνα...μάθωσιν [sc. Arians] ἐν ποίῳ κεῖνται π. Ath.*Ar*.1.9(M.26.29A); of Jews in rejecting Christ, Thdt.*Am*.5:2(2.1429); Thdr.Stud.*epp*.1.38(M.99.1044D); **4.** *collapse, fall by overthrow* ἔρεισμα τῷ π. τῆς αἱρέσεως Ath. *Ar*.2.43(M.26.240A); **5.** *fall, deposition*; from eccl. office, Eus.*h.e*.5.15(M.20.464A).

B. *corpse*; **1.** in gen. ἐστιν...ὁ μεθύων...π. ἀπολογίας ἐστερημένον Chrys.*stat*.1.5(2.7D); Cyr.*Joel*.31(3.223A); **2.** exeg. Mt.24:28, Or. *comm.ser.47 in Mt*.(p.98.9) cit. s. ἀετός; interpreted as destruction of sin ἐπεὶ δὲ π. γέγονεν—ὅπου γὰρ π., ἐκεῖ καὶ οἱ ἀετοί—, καλὸν τοῦτο τὸ π. ἐφ' ὃ ἦλθεν πρῶτος ὁ Ἰησοῦς id.*hom.16 in Lc*.(p.111.3); Chrys. *hom.76.3 in Mt*.(7.735D).

πτωματίζω, 1. *cause to fall*, morally and spiritually οἱ ἐπιχαίροντες ἐπὶ πτώσει ἑτέρων, ἑαυτοὺς πτωματίζουσιν †Cyr.*hom.div*.14(5²·413E); ὀφείλει ὁ μοναχὸς ἀποκλεῖσαι αὐτοῦ πάσας τὰς πύλας τῆς ψυχῆς, καὶ φυλάξαι πάσας τὰς αἰσθήσεις...τοῦ μὴ πτωματισθῆναι αὐτὴν δι' αὐτῶν Esaias *or*.10(p.68); Jo.Carp.*cap*.44(M.85.1845); Dor.*doct*.5.2(M.88.1677B); **2.** *overthrow* ἔπεσεν γὰρ ὁ...Χοσρόης...καὶ ἐπτωματίσθη εἰς τὰ καταχθόνια Heracl.*ep*.ap.*Chron.Pasch*.(M.92.1017C).

***πτωματιστής, ὁ,** *one who causes to fall*, Thdr.Stud.*epp*.1.52(M.99.1100D).

πτῶσις, ἡ, 1. *fall*; **a.** of Satan as Lucifer, Eus.*p.e*.7.16(328C; M.21.556A); **b.** of moral and spiritual lapses in gen. π. δέ ἐστιν ἡ ἁμαρτία Gr.Nyss.*ep.can*.1(M.45.221B); Chrys.*stat*.1.3(2.6A); †Cyr. *hom.div*.14(5²·413D,E); exeg. Lc.2:34, Bas.*ep*.260.7(3.399E; M.32.964C); **c.** of lapse in persecution, Petr.I Al.*ep.can*.1(M.18.468A); **d.** exeg. Pr.24:16 (Naassene) ἑπτάκις πεσεῖται ὁ δίκαιος καὶ ἀναστήσεται· αὗται γὰρ αἱ π., φησίν, αἱ τῶν ἄστρων μεταβολαὶ ὑπὸ τοῦ πάντα κινοῦντος κινούμεναι Hipp.*haer*.5.7(p.84.12; M.16.3134C); **2.** *overthrow*, ref. Devil τὴν π. τοῦ ἑνὸς τῶν ἀρχόντων, τουτέστι τοῦ...ὄφεως, πεσόντος π. μεγάλην διὰ τὸ ἀποπλανῆσαι τὴν Εὔαν Just.*dial*.124.3(M.6.765A); of persecutors, Eus.*v.C*.4.12 tit.(p.114.19; M.20.1145B); of Chosroes, *Chron.Pasch*.p.398(M.92.1617B); **3.** *falling* in battle, hence *casualties* ἑκατέρων δὲ τῶν μερῶν π. οὐ μικρὰ γέγονεν Thphn.*chron*. p.350(M.108.841C); **4.** *humiliation, depression*, Gr.Naz.*carm*.1.2.2.7 (M.37.578A).

πτωχεία, ἡ, *poverty*;

A. distn. between π. and πενία: τῆς γραφῆς ἐν τοῖς ἐπαινουμένοις τιθείσης τὴν π. καὶ τὴν πενίαν, ὡς ἐν τῷ 'μακάριοι οἱ πτωχοί' καὶ ἐν τῷ 'τὴν ἐπιθυμίαν τῶν πενήτων εἰσήκουσε κύριος'...τίς ἐστιν ἡ διαφορὰ π. καὶ πενίας;...λογίζομαι, ὅτι πτωχὸς μέν ἐστιν ὁ ἀπὸ πλούτου κατελθὼν εἰς ἔνδειαν· πένης δέ, ὁ ἐξ ἀρχῆς ἐν ἐνδείᾳ ὢν Bas.*reg.br*.262(2.504D,E; M.31.1260B); cf. distinctive use of both ἐπὶ τῆς πενίας δὲ μὴ τὴν π. μόνον, ἀλλὰ καὶ τὴν ἐντεῦθεν ἡδονὴν ἀναλογίζου Chrys.*hom.38.6 in 1Cor*.(10.359D).

B. in Christian life; **1.** involuntary: attitude to poverty in others καταπικραίνοντες δὲ ταῖς δυσθυμίαις τοὺς τῇ π. κατηχθισμένους, καίτοι χεῖρα μᾶλλον ὀφείλοντες ὀρέγειν αὐτοῖς τὴν φιλάλληλον Cyr.*Am*. 16(3.267A); and oneself Χριστιανοὶ...ἐὰν ἐν πενίᾳ...ἐξετασθῶσιν, οὐκ ὀφείλουσι ξενίζεσθαι, ἀλλὰ μᾶλλον συνηδύνεσθαι τῇ π. Mac.Aeg.*hom*. 15.19(M.34.596B); λόγος γὰρ οὐδεὶς παραστῆσαι δυνήσεται τὴν ὀδύνην, ὅσην ὑπομένουσιν οἱ π. συζῶντες, καὶ φιλοσοφεῖν οὐκ εἰδότες Chrys. *Laz*.1.9(1.720C); both profitable for souls ἀφῆκεν [sc. Christ] εἶναι πολλοὺς ἐν π., διά τε τὸ ἐκείνοις, διά τε τὸ σοὶ συμφέρον id.*eleem*.5 (3.256E); **2.** voluntary; **a.** in gen. οὐδὲν γὰρ αὐθαιρέτου π. εἰς πῆξιν τῶν καλῶν καὶ συντήρησιν ἰσχυρότερον. θεμέλιος γὰρ τῶν ἐν ψυχῇ θείων οἰκοδομημάτων καθέστηκεν ἀρραγής Max.*opusc*.(M.91.69C); **b.** ref. Mt.5:3 ὁ μέν τις πλοῦτος κτητὸς ἂν εἴη καὶ περίβλητος, ὁ δὲ ἄκτητος καὶ ἀπόβλητος· τὸν αὐτὸν δὲ τρόπον καὶ π. μακαριστὴ μὲν ἡ πνευματική Clem.*q.d.s*.17(p.170.32; M.9.621B); οὐκ ἀεὶ ἐπαινετὴ ἡ π., ἀλλ' ἡ ἐκ προαιρέσεως κατὰ τὸν εὐαγγελικὸν σκοπὸν κατορθουμένη. πολλοὶ γὰρ πτωχοὶ μὲν τῇ περιουσίᾳ, πλεονεκτικώτατοι δὲ τῇ προαιρέσει τυγχάνουσιν· οὓς οὐχ ἡ ἔνδεια σώζει, ἀλλ' ἡ προαίρεσις κατακρίνει. οὐ τοίνυν ὁ ἐνδεὴς πάντως μακαριστός, ἀλλ' ὁ κρείττονα ἡγησάμενος τῶν τοῦ κόσμου θησαυρῶν τὴν ἐντολὴν τοῦ Χριστοῦ. τούτους καὶ ὁ κύριος μακαρίζει λέγων, μακάριοι οἱ πτωχοὶ τῷ πνεύματι· οὐχ οἱ πένητες κατὰ τὴν περιουσίαν, ἀλλ' οἱ τὴν π. ἐκ ψυχῆς προελόμενοι Bas. *hom.in Ps*.33(1.147D; M.29.361A,B); variously interpreted, Gr.Nyss. *beat*.1(M.44.1200B) cit. s. ἀκτημοσύνη; δοκεῖ μοι π. πνεύματος τὴν ἑκούσιον ταπεινοφροσύνην ὀνομάζειν ὁ λόγος *ib*.(1200D); compared with Mt.19:21 μὴ ἀποβάλῃς...καὶ τὸν ἕτερον τῆς π. λόγον, ὃς τοῦ κατ' οὐρανὸν πλούτου πρόξενος γίνεται· 'πώλησόν σου' φησί, 'πάντα τὰ ὑπάρχοντα.' καὶ γὰρ ἡ τοιαύτη π. δοκεῖ μοι μὴ ἀπᾴδειν τῆς μακαριζομένης π. *ib.*(1208A).

C. poverty of Christ, Christol., Alex.Al.*ep.Alex.*9(p.25.18; M.18.561B) cit. s. κένωσις; ref. 2Cor.8:9 δι' ἡμᾶς ἐπτώχευσεν, ἵνα ἡμεῖς τῇ ἐκείνου π. πλουτήσωμεν Bas.*hom. in Ps.*33(1.147E; M.29.361C); τὴν τοῦ θεοῦ π. ὁ ἀπόστολος ἡμῖν λέγων προδείκνυσιν, 'ὃς δι' ἡμᾶς ἐπτώχευσε...' Gr.Nyss.*beat.*1(M.44.1200D); ὁ καθαρὸς...διὰ πάσης τῆς π. ἡμῶν διεξελθὼν μέχρι τῆς τοῦ θανάτου πρόεισι πείρας. ὁρᾶτε τῆς ἑκουσίου π. τὸ μέτρον *ib.*(1201C); ἐκεῖνος δόξαν ἐκένωσεν, οὐχ ἵνα ὑμεῖς τῷ πλούτῳ αὐτοῦ, ἀλλὰ τῇ π. πλουτήσητε. εἰ μὴ πιστεύεις, ὅτι ἡ π. πλούτου ἐστὶ ποιητική, ἐννόησόν σου τὸν δεσπότην, καὶ οὐκέτι ἀμφιβαλεῖς...τὸ γὰρ θαυμαστὸν τοῦτο, ὅτι π. ἐπλούτησε πλοῦτον. ... διὰ... ποίας π.; διὰ τοῦ σάρκα ἀναλαβεῖν...καὶ παθεῖν ἅπερ ἔπαθε Chrys. *hom.17.1 in 2Cor.*(10.558E–559A); πλούσιε σωτὴρ...σὺ γὰρ ἐπτώχευσας, ἵνα τῇ σῇ π. πλουτήσωμεν ‡Ath.*pass.*31(M.28.240A); ‡Meth. *Sym.et Ann.*6(M.18.360C).

D. met., *deficiency* in spiritual goods εἰσιν...πτωχοὶ καὶ οὐκ οἴδασιν τὴν π. αὐτῶν *Agraph.*(p.69); παρέμεινα τῇ π. τοῦ κόσμου ἕως ὅτε σὺ ὁ πλοῦτος τῆς ἀληθείας ἀπεκαλύφθης *A.Thom.*A 145(p.202.17); κατηγορεῖ πτωχείας τοῦ νοῦ Or.*hom.6.3 in Jer.*(p.51.8; M.13.328D); exeg. Pr.13:8 πλοῦτος λύτρον ἐστὶν ἀνδρὸς ψυχῆς κατὰ τὸν Σολομῶντα, ἡ δὲ ἐναντία τούτῳ π. ὀλέθριον id.*Cels.*7.21(p.173.2; M.11.1452B); ὅταν τὴν ἀπόρρητον...ὑπόστασιν ἑρμηνεύῃ, διὰ τὸ ἀχώρητον εἶναι τὴν ἀνθρωπίνην π. τῶν ὑπὲρ λόγον...διδαγμάτων Gr.Nyss.*Eun.*8(2 p.188.1; M.45.781C); π. τῶν ἰδίων λόγων *ib.*9(2 p.206.25; 804C); π. τῆς ἀνθρωπίνης φύσεως id.*beat.*3(M.44.1225A); ὦ φύλαξ καὶ πρόμαχε πιστῶν... τῆς ἡμῶν μὴ ἐπιλάθῃ π. καὶ ταπεινώσεως Nect.*Thdr.*23(M.39.1840A).

E. ref. name of Ebionites βιοῦσι γὰρ κατ' αὐτόν, ἐπώνυμοι τῆς κατὰ τὴν ἐκδοχὴν π. τοῦ νόμου γεγενημένοι Or.*Cels.*2.1(p.126.18; M.11.793A).

F. as self-depreciatory style τὴν ἡμετέραν π. διὰ γραμμάτων... παρακαλοῦντας Cyr.*hom.div.*4(p.104.19; 5².358B).

πτωχεῖον, τό, *alms-house, hospital* υἱὸς ἡμῶν...ὁ συμπρεσβύτερος, πτωχείου προέστηκε...πολυανθρώπου Gr.Naz.*ep.*211(M.37.348C); ὁ πρεσβύτερος καὶ ἀφηγούμενος τοῦ π. τῶν λελωβημένων Pall.*h.Laus.*6 (p.23.8; M.34.1018D); οἱ κληρικοὶ τῶν π. καὶ μοναστηρίων καὶ μαρτυρίων ὑπὸ τῶν ἐν ἑκάστῃ πόλει ἐπισκόπων τὴν ἐξουσίαν... διαμενέτωσαν CChalc.*can.*8; τὸν...ἐκ διακόνου τῆς...ἐκκλησίας, καὶ σπουδαῖον ἐπίτροπον πτωχείων Soz.*h.e.*4.20.2(M.67.1173A); Niceph. Ur.*v.Sym.*76(M.86.3057A).

πτωχεύ-ω, A. *be poor, become poor*; **1.** ref. Christ (cf. 2Cor.8:9) αὐτός ἐστιν ὁ ~σας...ἵνα ἡμεῖς πάντες ἐκ τοῦ πληρώματος αὐτοῦ λάβωμεν Bas.*hom.in Ps.*33(1.148A; M.29.361D); cf.‡Ath.*pass.*31(M.28.240A); ὁ ἐνανθρωπήσας δι' ἡμᾶς καὶ ~σας θεός, ἵνα ἀναστήσῃ τὴν σάρκα Gr.Naz.*or.*7.23(M.35.785C); τοῦ δι' ἡμᾶς ~σαντος τὴν σάρκα ταύτην...ἵνα ἡμεῖς πλουτήσωμεν τὴν θεότητα *ib.*14.15(876C); as example οὗτος τοίνυν εἰ ~ει τῷ πνεύματι, πρὸς τὸν δι' ἡμᾶς ~σαντα ἑκουσίως βλέπων...μακαριστὸς ἀληθῶς Gr.Nyss.*beat.*1(M.44.1205D); ὁ τῷ πτωχῷ κοινωνήσας, εἰς τὴν μερίδα τοῦ δι' ἡμᾶς ~σαντος ἑαυτὸν καταστήσει. ἐπτώχευσεν ὁ κύριος, μὴ φοβηθῇς μηδὲ σὺ τὴν πτωχείαν. ἀλλὰ βασιλεύει πάσης τῆς κτίσεως ὁ δι' ἡμᾶς ~σας. οὐκοῦν ἐὰν ~σαντι συμπτωχεύσῃς καὶ βασιλεύοντι συμβασιλεύσεις *ib.*(1208B,C); Ast.Am.*hom.*1(M.40.176D); Cyr.*Jo.*2.1(4.123E); **2.** ref. voluntary poverty of Christians ἐλεῶν ἐλεήσω ὃν ἂν ἐλεῶ, φησὶ κύριος. λέγει δὲ ταῦτα καὶ τοῖς θέλουσι διὰ τὴν δικαιοσύνην ~σαι Clem.*str.*4.6(p.263.11; M.8.1245B); ἡ ψυχὴ...~ουσα ὧν ἄν τις ὑπὸ πλούτου διαφθείρῃ⟨ται⟩ σώζεται id.*q.d.s.*18(p.171.23; M.9.624A); *ib.*16(p.169.32; 620C); ref. Mt.5:3 ἐκ τοῦ ~σαι κατὰ προαίρεσιν, καὶ τὴν τοῦ μακαρισμοῦ κοινωνίαν ἐφελκυσώμεθα Gr.Nyss.*beat.*1(M.44.1201B); βούλει νοῆσαι, τίς ὁ ~ων τῷ πνεύματι; ὁ ἀνταλλαξάμενος τὸν τῆς ψυχῆς πλοῦτον τῆς σωματικῆς εὐπορίας, ὁ διὰ τὸ πνεῦμα ~ων...εἰ οὖν χρὴ τοῖς ἄνω προσβῆναι, τῶν κάτω καθελκόντων ~σωμεν *ib.*(1208A,B); **3.** ref. spiritual things, *be destitute* ὁ μὲν πλούσιος ἔχει χρήματα πολλά, τὰ δὲ πρὸς τὸν κύριον ~ει περισπώμενος περὶ τὸν πλοῦτον αὐτοῦ Herm.*sim.*2.5; *be stupid* μὴ γὰρ ἐπὶ τοσοῦτον ~σαι ὁ νοῦς ἡμῶν, ὡς οἰηθῆναι σωματικοῦ τινος ἄρτου...τοὺς ἀγγέλους ἀεὶ μεταλαμβάνοντας τρέφεσθαι Or.*or.*27.10 (p.370.3; M.11.513B); μηδὲ ~ε...τὴν διάνοιαν Chrys.*hom.17.3 in 1Cor.* (10.149E).

B. *be lacking* in something, *have deficiency* οὐ γὰρ ἐπτώχευσεν ὁ λόγος αὐτῶν ἀληθὴς ὢν Afric.*ep.Or.*2(p.80.8; M.11.48A); εἰς οὐδὲν ~οντος τοῦ θεοῦ Meth.*res.*2.9(p.349.5; M.18.288D); ref. S. Paul τῇ λέξει π. Chrys.*sac.*4.6(p.120.12; 1.412A); *be lacking in food, starving* ἐπτώχευσαν τὰ ἄλογα αὐτῶν Thphn.*chron.*p.381(M.108.912B).

[*]**πτωχέω,** = foreg., Mac.Aeg.*perf.*7(M.34.848A).

πτωχίζω, *make poor*, Gr.Naz.*carm.*1.2.34.165(M.37.957A).

πτωχικά, τά, *alms*, Isid.Pel.*epp.*1.250(M.78.333C).

***πτωχογενής,** *born poor*, ‡Jo.D.*hom.*5(M.96.660C).

***πτωχοδεκάδες, αἱ,** *tithes devoted to poor-relief* in Israel, Hier. *Ezech.*45:13,14(M.*PL.*25.451A).

***πτωχόκομπος,** *wretchedly boasting*, Geo.Pis.*hex.*63(M.92.1432A).

***πτωχόνοια, ἡ,** *poverty of intellect*, Jo.Mon.*hymn.Nic.Myr.*4(M.96.1385A); Steph.Diac.*v.Steph.*(M.100.1153C).

πτωχοποιός, *making poor*, Chrys.*hom.23.6 in 1Cor.*(10.201C).

***πτωχοπρεπής,** *befitting a poor man, beggarly*; of human nature, Or.*Ps.*10:4(p.465); Anast.S.*monoph.*(M.89.1189C); neut. as subst., id.*hod.*13(M.89.237C).

πτωχός, *poor*;

A. ref. Ps.9:18f. π. δὲ λέγεται καὶ ὁ πτωχεύων δι' ἁμαρτίαν, καὶ ὁ μέτριος καὶ ἄτυφος, καὶ ὁ χρῄζων δέξασθαι παρὰ θεοῦ. ἕκαστος δὲ γενητός ἐστι τοιοῦτος. κατὰ πάντας τούτους τοὺς τρόπους ὁ λεγόμενος π., μνημονεύεται θεῷ Didym.*Ps.*9:18(M.39.1197B).

B. of the materially poor; **1.** dist. from πένης: φασὶ δὲ π. τὸν ἐκπεσόντα πλούτου· πένητα δὲ τὸν ἐκ πόνου τὰ πρὸς τὸν βίον περιποιούμενον. λέγει δὲ ἡ γραφή· 'πλούσιοι ἐπτώχευσαν', καὶ τό, 'ἐπτωχεύσαμεν σφόδρα' Or.*sel.in Ps.*11:6(M.12.1201B); Bas.*reg.br.*262(2.504E; M.31.1260C) cit. s. πτωχεία; ἐπῆλθέν τισιν εἰπεῖν π. μὲν εἶναι τοὺς μεταπεσόντας τοῦ πλούτου· πένητας δὲ τοὺς ἐκ πόνου δι' ἐργασίας γινομένου τὸ ζῆν ἔχοντας. καὶ ἔστιν γε κατὰ ταύτην τὴν νόησιν ὁ π. πένης ἐξ ἀνάγκης, οὐκ ἀντιστρέφοντος τὸν πένητα π. εἶναι. καὶ τάχα γε τὰ εἰρημένα περὶ τοῦ π. κατασκευάσεται καὶ ἐκ τῆς γραφῆς· εἴρηται γάρ, 'πλούσιοι ἐπτώχευσαν' Didym.*Ps.*11:6(M.39.1213C); **2.** treatment of poor πᾶσι...π. ἀνοικτέον τὰ σπλάγχνα Gr.Naz.*or.*14.6(M.35.864C); ἂν μέν τινα ἴδῃς σκεύη κατασκευάσαντα ἱερὰ καὶ προσάγοντα... μὴ κέλευε πραθῆναι...ἂν δὲ πρὶν ἢ κατασκευάσαι τις ἔρηται, κέλευε δοθῆναι πτωχοῖς Chrys.*hom.80.2 in Mt.*(7.768A); ὅταν ἴδῃς π. ... μὴ μόνον μὴ ὑβρίσῃς, ἀλλὰ καὶ αἰδέσθητι id.*hom.20.3 in 2Cor.*(10.582B); seeing Christ in them ὁ Χριστὸς ἕστηκε πρὸ τῶν θυρῶν σου ἐν σχήματι πτωχοῦ id.*hom.1.6 in Ps.48*:17(5.514B); θεὸς γὰρ ἦν ὁ διὰ τῶν π. λαμβάνων id.*hom.79.1 in Mt.*(7.759A); μηδέποτε π. παρίδῃς δακρύοντα, ἵνα μὴ παροφθῇ τῆς σῆς προσευχῆς τὰ δάκρυα Nil.*sent.*22 (M.79.1241C); **3.** rewards for assistance to poor στρατόπεδον τὸ τῶν π., καὶ πόλεμος ὃν ὑπὲρ σοῦ πολεμοῦσιν οἱ πένητες. ὅταν γὰρ λάβωσιν, εὐχόμενοι τὸν θεὸν ἵλεω ποιοῦσιν Chrys.*hom.66.4 in Mt.*(7.659B); πόσα παρέχει τότε [sc. in next world] π. εὐκαίρως τραφείς ‡Nil.*perist.* 12.12(M.79.964B); **4.** relations between rich and poor ὁ πλούσιος ἐπιχορηγείτω τῷ π., ὁ δὲ π. εὐχαριστείτω τῷ θεῷ, ὅτι ἔδωκεν αὐτῷ, δι' οὗ ἀναπληρωθῇ αὐτοῦ τὸ ὑστέρημα *1Clem.*38.2; ref. Mc.12:41f. ὡς μόνος δυνάμενος βλέπειν τοὺς πλουσίους εἶδεν εἴ ποτε π. ψυχὴ καὶ ὑστερουμένη βάλλει ὅλῃ δυνάμει ⟨καὶ⟩ διὰ τοῦτο δικαιουμένη παρὰ τοὺς πολλοὺς πλουσίους Or.*Jo.*19.9(2; p.308.15; M.14.541B); ref. metempsychosis εἴ τις...ἐστὶ πλούσιος ἐν τούτῳ τῷ κόσμῳ, καὶ ἐὰν ἐξέλθῃ ἐκ τοῦ σκηνώματος αὐτοῦ, ἀνάγκη αὐτὸν εἰς πτωχοῦ σῶμα μεταγγισθῆναι, ὥστε περιπατοῦντα αὐτὸν ἐπαιτῆσαι καὶ μετὰ ταῦτα ἀνελθεῖν αὐτὸν εἰς κόλασιν αἰώνιον Hegem.*Arch.*10(p.16.4; M.10.1444A).

C. of the spiritually poor; **1.** in gen., as needing grace of God π. γὰρ ἅπαντες, καὶ τῆς θείας χάριτος ἐπιδεεῖς Gr.Naz.*or.*14.1(M.35.857A); **2.** sinners and heretics ὁ μὲν π. καὶ ἄθεος οὐκ οἶδεν τὰ ἀποκείμενα Tat.*orat.*6(p.7.3; M.6.820A); πρὸς Ἰουδαϊκοὺς καὶ γραώδεις μύθους ἐκτραπείς, πτωχὸς...τῶν ἀξίων περὶ θεοῦ νοημάτων Bas.*Eun.* 1.14(1.226D; M.29.544C); οὐδὲν γὰρ πτωχότερον διανοίας ἐκτὸς θεοῦ φιλοσοφούσης τὰ τοῦ θεοῦ Diad.*perf.*7(p.10.1).

D. of the poor in spirit (Mt.5:3) πῶς τις δύναται εἶναι π. τῷ πνεύματι, μάλιστα ὅτε αἰσθηθῇ ἐν ἑαυτῷ, ὅτι μετετέθη καὶ προέκοψε...; ἕως οὗ ταῦτά τις κτᾶται, καὶ προκόπτει, οὐκ ἔστι π. τῷ πνεύματι, ἀλλ' οἴεται περὶ ἑαυτοῦ· ὅταν δὲ ἔλθῃ εἰς ταύτην τὴν σύνεσιν καὶ τὴν προκοπήν, αὕτη ἡ χάρις διδάσκει αὐτὸν εἶναι π. τῷ πνεύματι...μὴ ἡγεῖσθαί τι ἑαυτὸν εἶναι Mac.Aeg.*hom.*12.3(M.34.557C,D); ἀποσκοποῦσα γὰρ ἡ ψυχὴ ἡ πιστὴ καὶ φιλαλήθης...εἰς τὴν ἄρρητον τῆς μελλούσης ἐπιφοιτᾶν θείας χάριτος εὐεργεσίαν, ἀναξίαν ἑαυτήν, καὶ τὴν σπουδὴν αὐτῆς...ἡγεῖται πρὸς τὰς ἀρρήτους ἐπαγγελίας τοῦ πνεύματος. οὗτός ἐστιν ὁ π. τῷ πνεύματι, ὃν ὁ κύριος μακαρίζει *ib.*29.7(720C); οὗτοί εἰσιν οἱ π. τῷ πνεύματι, οἵτινες οὐ δι' ἄλλην τινὰ αἰτίαν ἐπτώχευσαν, ἀλλὰ διὰ τὴν διδασκαλίαν τοῦ κυρίου...ἐὰν δέ τις, καὶ τὴν ὁπωσοῦν συμβᾶσαν πτωχείαν καταδεξάμενος, κυβερνήσῃ πρὸς τὸ θέλημα τοῦ θεοῦ, ὡς ὁ Λάζαρος, οὐδὲ οὗτος τοῦ μακαρισμοῦ ἀλλότριος Bas.*reg.br.*205(2.484A; M.31.1217C); in connexion with Is.14:30 τίς ἐστιν ὁ βόσκων π., ἢ ὁ ποιμὴν τῶν προβάτων; π. δὲ οὐ τοὺς κατὰ χρήματα ἐνδεεῖς λέγει, ἀλλὰ τοὺς τῇ διανοίᾳ ἠλαττωμένους. οὗτοι δὲ οἱ π., οἱ παρ' αὐτοῦ μακαριζόμενοι τοῦ κυρίου †Bas.*Is.*287(1.597D; M.30.624A); τί ἐστιν, οἱ π. τῷ πνεύματι; οἱ ταπεινοὶ καὶ συντετριμμένοι τὴν διάνοιαν. πνεῦμα γὰρ ἐνταῦθα τὴν ψυχὴν καὶ τὴν προαίρεσιν εἴρηκεν.

ἐπειδὴ γάρ εἰσι πολλοὶ ταπεινοί, οὐχ ἑκόντες, ἀλλ' ὑπὸ τῆς τῶν πραγμάτων ἀνάγκης βιαζόμενοι, ἀφεὶς ἐκείνους...τοὺς ἀπὸ προαιρέσεως ἑαυτοὺς ταπεινοῦντας...μακαρίζει πρώτους. καὶ τίνος ἕνεκεν οὐκ εἶπεν, οἱ ταπεινοί, ἀλλ', οἱ π.; ὅτι τοῦτο ἐκείνου πλέον Chrys.*hom.15.1 in Mt.*(7.185D,E); id.*anom.*10.4(1.533E).

E. of the truly poor γνήσιος π. καὶ νόθος ἄλλος π. καὶ ψευδώνυμος, ὁ μὲν κατὰ πνεῦμα π., τὸ ἴδιον, ὁ δὲ κατὰ κόσμον, τὸ ἀλλότριον. τῷ δὴ κατὰ κόσμον ⟨οὐ⟩ π. καὶ πλουσίῳ κατὰ τὰ πάθη ὁ κατὰ πνεῦμα οὐ π. καὶ κατὰ θεὸν πλούσιος 'ἀπόστηθι' ⟨φησί⟩ 'τῶν ὑπαρχόντων ἐν τῇ ψυχῇ σου κτημάτων ἀλλοτρίων...' Clem.*q.d.s.*19(p.172.1ff.; M.9.624B); δύναται γὰρ π. μὲν τοῖς χρήμασιν εἶναι, ἐπιθυμεῖν δὲ ἢ καὶ πράττειν ὃ...οὐ χρὴ *Hom.Clem.*15.10; ref. Ps.33:7 τῇ δεικτικῇ φωνῇ ἐπὶ τὸν πτωχεύοντα κατὰ θεόν...τὴν διάνοιάν σου προκαλεῖται· οὗτος ὁ π., μονονουχὶ δακτύλῳ δεικνύς· οὗτος ὁ μαθητὴς Χριστοῦ Bas.*hom.in Ps.*33(1.147E; M.29.361B); διπλῆ τις ἐστὶν ἡ περὶ τὸν π. σημασία· ἡ μὲν δηλοῦσα τῶν ἀναγκαίων τὴν ἔνδειαν· ἡ δὲ τὴν μετριοφροσύνην καὶ τοῦ ἤθους τὴν ταπεινότητα...οὐ γὰρ ὁ κατ' ἀνάγκην πενόμενος ἐπαινεῖται· ἀλλ' ὁ τὴν γνώμην αὐθαιρέτως μετριάζων θαυμάζεται...μακαρίζει νῦν ἡ γραφὴ τὸν π. ἐκεῖνον τὸν φιλοσόφῳ ψυχῇ τοὺς μόχθους βαστάζοντα... ὃν καὶ σαφέστερον διαγράφει ἐν τῷ πρώτῳ τῶν μακαρισμῶν ὁ κύριος... οὔτε οὖν πᾶς π. δίκαιος, ἀλλ' ἐκεῖνος οἷος ὁ Λάζαρος Ast.Am.*hom.*1(M.40.176A–C).

F. ref. God and Christ οὐ γὰρ οὕτω π. ὁ θεός, ὡς τοιαῦτα ἐργάζεσθαι μόνα, ἃ τῇ τῶν λογισμῶν ἀσθενείᾳ περιληφθῆναι δύναται τῶν σῶν Chrys.*hom.17.3 in 1Cor.*(10.148E); ref. Phil.2:5ff. τί πτωχότερον ἐπὶ θεοῦ τῆς τοῦ δούλου μορφῆς; τί ταπεινότερον ἐπὶ τοῦ βασιλέως τῶν ὄντων, ἢ τὸ εἰς κοινωνίαν τῆς π. ἡμῶν φύσεως ἐλθεῖν; Gr.Nyss.*beat.*1(M.44.1201B).

G. ref. interprn. of name of Ebionites Ἐβίων...ὁ π. παρὰ Ἰουδαίοις καλεῖται Or.*Cels.*2.1(p.126.19; M.11.793A); ὡς οἱ π. τῇ διανοίᾳ Ἐβιωναῖοι, τῆς π. διανοίας ἐπώνυμοι (ἐβίων γὰρ ὁ π. παρ' Ἑβραίοις ὀνομάζεται) id.*princ.*4.3.8(p.334.1f.; M.11.389A); Ἐβιωναίους ὠνόμαζον, Ἑβραϊκῇ φωνῇ π. τὴν διάνοιαν ἀποκαλοῦντες...τὴν δὲ τοῦ υἱοῦ θεότητα μὴ εἰδότας Eus.*e.th.*1.14(p.74.14; M.24.853A).

H. *miserable, inferior,* of things and thoughts μὴ ἐμπεσεῖν εἰς φλυαρίαν π. νοημάτων Meth.*res.*1.22(p.244.15; M.41.1089C); αἱ περὶ τῆς ἐνσάρκου παρουσίας...π. λέξεις Ath.*Dion.*10(p.53.10; M.25.493C).

πτωχότης, ἡ, *destitution,* Herm.*vis.*3.12.2.

πτωχοτροφεῖον, τό, *alms-house, hospital,* used also as *hostel, guest house,* managed by a chorepiscopus, Bas.*ep.*143(3.235D; M.32.593A); accommodating bishop, *ib.*150.3(240D; M.604C); containing chapel, *ib.*176(263D; M.653C); καθιστᾷ τοῦτον πρεσβύτερον τό τε ξενοδοχεῖον αὐτῷ ἐμπιστεύει, ὅπερ ἐν τῷ Πόντῳ καλεῖται π. τοιαῦτα γάρ τινα κατασκευάζουσι κατὰ φιλοξενίαν καὶ τοὺς λελωβημένους... ἐκεῖσε ποιοῦντες καταλύειν ἐπιχορήγουσι...οἱ τῶν ἐκκλησιῶν προστάται Epiph.*haer.*75.1(p.333.24; M.42.504C); †Gregent.*leg.Hom.*proem.(M.86.580B); τῶν πενήτων ἁπάντων καταταγέντων εἰς τὰ π. ... οὐ προστάττομεν...ἀπαιτεῖν ἄρτον ἐπὶ τῆς μέσης *ib.*55(609B); Max.*ep.*44(M.91.648A).

***πτωχοτροφέω,** *support the poor,* Gr.Naz.*or.*26.6(M.35.1236A); id.*ep.*215(M.37.352A); id.*carm.*2.1.11.1219(M.37.1113A).

***πτωχοτροφία, ἡ,** *care of the poor, management of poor-relief,* Bas.*ep.*142(3.235C; M.32.592C); Gr.Naz.*or.*43.9(M.36.505A); id.*ep.*219(M.37.360A); id.*carm.*2.2(poem.)3.24(M.37.1479A).

πτωχοτρόφος, *caring for the poor, responsible for poor-relief* τρεῖς προεστησάμην π. εἶναι Gr.Naz.*test.*(M.37.389A); id.*carm.*2.2(poem.)2.17(M.37.1479A); θεὸς ἀπαγγέλλεται τῶν π. τὰ ὀνόματα βίβλοις ζώσαις ἐγγράφειν Ast.Am.*hom.*4(M.40.224A); Max.*ep.*44(M.91.645D); διάκονος τῆς μεγάλης ἐκκλησίας...καὶ π. *Chron.Pasch.*p.382(M.92.980A).

πυγμή, ἡ, *fist*; dat. ? *thoroughly, with the whole fist, with a fistful* of water, in washing (cf. Mc.7:3) ἔτυχε Ἰουβῖνον νιπτῆρα λαβόντα νίψασθαι τὰς χεῖρας καὶ τοὺς πόδας πυγμῇ ὕδατι ψυχροτάτῳ Pall.*h.Laus.*55(p.48.21; M.34.1244A).

***πυγμικῶς,** *by fighting as boxers,* Hesych.S.*temp.*2.36(M.93.1521D).

***πυθμεύ-ω,** *give the base of a series* στραφεὶς ὁ τρίπους τρίτην στροφήν, φησίν, ὁ προφήτης ~ει (i.e. this third oracle reveals meaning of two previous ones) *Pers.*(p.8.20).

πυθμήν, ὁ, 1. *bottom* π. τοῦ ᾅδου *the abyss, 1Apoc.Jo.*20(p.88); Bas.*ep.*45(3.139C; M.32.380B); Isid.Pel.*epp.*1.247(M.78.332D); **2.** *column* in architecture, Paul.Sil.*Soph.*559(M.86.2141A); **3.** *branch,* ref. Gen.40:9–10 as type of Trin. μίαν ἄμπελον ἐν τρισὶ π., τοῦτον τοῦ ἄλλου π. οὐδαμοῦ προβαθέστερον Didym.*Trin.*1.18(M.39.348B).

πυθόμαντις, ἡ, *prophetess, woman diviner*; of witch of Endor, Eustrat.*stat.anim.*21(p.507).

πύθων, ὁ, 1. *Python*; as adj., *of divination,* cf. *daemonem, quem Pythonem nominant, id est ventriloquum,* Or.*princ.*3.3.5(p.262.1; M.11.318C); ἡ ἐγγαστρίμυθος ὑπὸ τοῦ ἐν αὐτῇ προσφωνοῦντος πνεύματος π. ἐναερίου...τερατεύεται ‡Jo.D.*ep.Thphl.*16(M.95.368A); **2.** plur., *ventriloquists* π. μαντεύονται, ἀλλ' ὑφ' ἡμῶν ὡς δαίμονες ἐκριζούμενοι φυγαδεύονται *Hom.Clem.*9.16; Proc.G.*Is.*8:19–22(M.87.1993B).

***πυθωνικός,** *possessed of spirit of divination* ἐγγαστριμύθους... τοὺς ψευδομάντεις, ἤτοι π. Cyr.*Is.*4.2(2.596D).

πυκάζω, 1. *cover closely*; med., *be clothed* πυκάσαιντο δικαιοσύνην ἱερῆες †Apoll.*met.Ps.*131:9(M.33.1513B); **2.** met., in pass., *be close, cautious* νοῦς...πεπωπασμένος Cyr.*glaph.Num.*(1.406B, prob. error for πεπυκασμένος).

***πυκασμός, ὁ,** *thick covering* of booths at Feast of Tabernacles ἑορτή, διὰ τοῦ π. τῆς σκηνοπηγίας τῆς κάτω κτίσεως πρὸς τὰς... προβεβλημένας περὶ τὸ ἄνω θυσιαστήριον δυνάμεις συνυπηχοῦσα Gr.Nyss.*nativ.*(M.46.1129A).

πυκνάζω, 1. *be a frequent visitor,* Jo.Mosch.*prat.*211(M.87.3104B); **2.** *attend upon,* Cyr.S.*v.Euthym.*40(p.60.28).

***πυκνοκέντητος,** *very prickly,* Geo.Pis.*carm.*1.83.

πυκν-όω, *make close* or *solid*; pass.; **1.** *be packed full* τὸ κατὰ Λοῦκαν [sc. εὐαγγέλιον] πλείοσιν ἱστορίαις ~ούμενον Max.*ambig.*(M.91.1245D); **2.** *be made dense* or *gross,* met. ἡ ~ωθεῖσα ἕξις τῇ... μοχθηρίᾳ ‡Proc.G.*Pr.*30:21(M.87.1529B); Max.*ambig.*(M.91.1121C); **3.** met., *be made firm, be strengthened* ζήλῳ...~ωθέντες Gr.Naz.*carm.*1.2.10.710(M.37.731A).

πύκνωμα, τό, plur., *abundance,* Or.*schol.in Cant.*7:8–9(M.17.284C).

***πυκτεῦμα, τό,** *boxing contest*; met., of ascetic life, *Hymn.*(*AS* 1 p.594).

πυκτεύ-ω, 1. *box, contend,* met. κινδύνῳ ἐπύκτευσα *Mir.Artem.*32(p.46.18); of spiritual combat Λαζάρου τοῦ...πενίᾳ καὶ ἐρημίᾳ... ~οντος Chrys.*stat.*1.10(2.16C); ταῖς ἀσωμάτοις δυνάμεσι ~ει id.*hom.57.4 in Mt.*(7.581B); of the poor as soldiers fighting agst. Devil with prayers in return for maintenance by almsgiving, *ib.66.5*(659C); *ib.76.5*(739D); Pall.*h.Laus.*34(p.98.22; M.34.1106C); ὁ μεθ' ὑποταγῆς καὶ προσευχῆς ~ων τῷ θελήματι, ἀθλητής ἐστιν εὐμέθοδος Marc.Er.*opusc.*2.148(M.65.953B); **2.** *strive* τοῦτον [sc. ποταμόν] παρελθεῖν ἐπύκτευον Gr.Mag.*dial.*(tr.Zach.)3.9(M.*PL.*77.235A).

πυκτίον, τό, *book, volume* (opp. papyrus roll) πυκτία τῶν θείων γραφῶν Ath.*apol.Const.*4(M.25.600C); Gr.Naz.*ep.*234(M.37.377A); Chrys.*hom.32.3 in Jo.*(8.188A).

πυκτίς, ἡ, = foreg., Isid.Pel.*epp.*1.61(M.78.224A); Jo.D.*parall.*(M.95.1045); met. ὃς [sc. swan] τὴν πτερωτὴν ἐξαπλώσας π. τερπνὴν ξενουργεῖ ταῖς πνοαῖς μελῳδίαν Geo.Pis.*hex.*1186(M.92.1526A).

πύλη, ἡ, *gate*; **1.** in gen., ref. righteousness as gate of life, ref. Ps.117:19, *1Clem.*48.2–3; πύλας δικαιοσύνης...αὗται...ἀνοίγονται τῷ μεταδιώκοντι τὰς κατ' ἀρετὴν πράξεις Or.*Cels.*6.36(p.105.24; M.11.1352B); of gate of life to which γνῶσις is key, *Hom.Clem.*3.18; cf.Or.*hom.14.2 in Ezech.*(p.452.27; M.13.765D); opened by Christ to all nations, Eus.*d.e.*4.10(p.167.16; M.22.280A); **2.** of heaven, opened in visions, *T.Lev.*5.1; †Gregent.*disp.*4(M.86.776D); **3.** of hell (Mt.16:18) contrasted with gates of Sion (cf. Ps.9:15) each of former being a sin, of latter a virtue, Or.*comm.in Mt.*12.12f.(pp.91.18,93.9; M.13.1008B,1009B); id.*Cels.*6.36(p.105.21; M.11.1352B); ref. Christ's descent to gates of Hades, Jo.Eub.*concept.BMV* 9(M.96.1473B); **4.** ref. Christ as gate of tower which represents Church, Herm.*sim.*9.12.3; connected with Christ as 'stone', *Pers.*(p.32.2); **5.** Naassene οἱ λογικοί, οἱ ζῶντες ἄνθρωποι, οἱ διὰ τῆς π. εἰσερχόμενοι τῆς τρίτης Hipp.*haer.*5.8(p.95.3; M.16.3147D); gate of heaven being resurrection from 'choic' to 'pneumatic' state, *ib.*(p.93.19; 3146C); οἱ πνευματικοὶ...διὰ τῆς π. ὁδεύοντες ἀληθινῆς, ἥτις ἐστὶν Ἰησοῦς...καὶ ἐσμὲν...ἡμεῖς Χριστιανοὶ μόνοι, ἐν τῇ τρίτῃ π. ἀπαρτίζοντες τὸ μυστήριον καὶ χριόμενοι ἐκεῖ ἀλάλῳ χρίσματι *ib.*5.9(p.102.13; 3159A); **6.** ref. BMV as typified by Ezech.44:2 π. κατὰ ἀνατολὰς βλέπουσα Ephr.3.530B; αὕτη ἡ βλέπουσα κατὰ ἀνατολὰς π. ἡ διὰ τῆς δεσποτικῆς εἰσόδου καὶ ἐξόδου κλειομένη εἰς τὸν αἰῶνα Procl.CP *or.*6.17(M.65.756A); Rom.Mel.(*BZ* 24, p.5); id.(*SBBAW* 1898^{2} p.193); Thdr.Stud.*nativ.BMV* 7(M.96.689D); id.*or.*5.11(M.99.728A); as gate of heaven δι' ἧς μόνος ὁ τῶν οὐρανῶν δεσπότης διώδευσε Andr.Cr.*or.*4(M.97.880D); **7.** ref. senses as gates of soul, Or.*fr.52 in Lam.*(p.257.26; M.13.636B); Esaias *or.*10(p.68).

πυλών, ὁ, A. *gateway*; **1.** *porch* of church, *A.Mt.*16(p.237.5); **2.** met. τῶν πυλών⟨ων⟩ τῆς ἀθανασίας ἤρξατο ἅπτεσθαι Const.ap. Gel.Cyz.*h.e.*2.7.39(πυλῶν codd., M.85.1241B); *ib.*2.7.4(1233A); exeg. Apoc.21:12 π. δώδεκα, τοὺς θείους ἀποστόλους αἰνίττεται Oecum.*Apoc.*21:12(p.238); Andr.Caes.*Apoc.*67(M.106.429D); ἥ τε χρεία τῶν π. ὡς εἰσαγόντων εἰς τὸ τῆς ζωῆς ταμεῖον τοὺς αὐτοῦ ἀποστόλους παριστᾷ, δι' ὧν τὰ ἔθνη τῷ Χριστοῦ ταμείῳ εἰσήχθησαν Areth.*Apoc.*21:12–14(M.106.768B).

B. ? *alcove* in catacomb κιτε π. τρίτῳ, λάνῳ πέμπτῃ *IG* 14.150 (Syracuse).

πυλωρός, ὁ, *door-keeper,* member of minor order in Church ἐξορκιστὰς δὲ καὶ ἀναγνώστας ἅμα π. δύο καὶ πεντήκοντα Corn.ap.Eus. *h.e.*6.43.11(M.20.621A); *Const.App.*2.26.3; *ib.*2.57.7; not permitted to baptize, *ib.*3.11; to be μονογάμος, *ib.*6.17.2; Phot.*nomoc.*1.31 (p.478; M.104.1016A).

πύξινος, *of box-wood, fitted with box-wood* knuckle-dusters ἐπύκτευον πυξίνοις δακτύλοις πυκτικὰς συμβολάς Jo.Mal.*chron.*12 p.288(M.97.436A).

πυξίον, τό, *tablet of box-wood*; any *tablet* π. μὲν λέγεται κυρίως τὸ ἐκ πύξου κατεσκευασμένον, κοινότερον δὲ καὶ καταχρηστικῶς ἀπ' ἐκείνου π. καὶ τὸ ἐκ μολίβου...καὶ ἄλλης τινὸς ὕλης γεγονός CAnc.(358) *ep.syn.*ap.Epiph.*haer.*73.5(p.275.3; M.42.412C); of tables of Law, Pall.*v.Chrys.*12(p.75.26; M.47.43); met. τὸ ἔργον τοῦ νόμου, γραπτὸν ...ἐν τῷ τῆς καρδίας π. Gr.Nyss.*hom.14 in Cant.*(M.44.1076B); ref. Abac.2:2 ἔοικε τὸ ἡγεμονικὸν τῶν ἁγίων πυξίῳ τινί, ἐν ᾧ καταγράφει ὁ θεὸς ἅπερ λεχθῆναι δέον τῷ λαῷ αὐτοῦ Nil.*epp.*1.108(M.79.129A); ‡Caes.Naz.*dial.*194(M.38.1184).

πῦρ, τό, *fire;*

A. as an element; **1.** qualities ἐν δὲ τοῖς τρισὶ στοιχείοις τὸ π. ἐναιωρεῖται...καὶ ὑπὸ τούτων ἐξάπτεται καὶ τούτοις ἐναποθνήσκει, μὴ ἔχον τόπον ἀποτακτὸν ἑαυτοῦ ὡς καὶ τὰ ἄλλα στοιχεῖα, ἐξ ὧν τὰ συγκρίματα δημιουργεῖται Clem.*exc.Thdot.*48(p.122.17; M.9.681C); id.*ecl.*26(p.144.16ff.; M.9.712A) cit. s. διπλόος; τὸ π. αὐτοκίνητόν ἐστι Or.*princ.*3.1.2(p.196.10; M.11.249B); cf. *ignis autem duplicem habet virtutem, unam, qua illuminat, aliam, qua incendit,* id.*hom.13.4 in Ex.*(p.275.16; M.12.392A); **2.** origin and necessity ἐκ λίθων μὲν π. ἐξάλλεται, ἐκ σιδήρου δέ, ὃς καὶ αὐτὸς ἀπὸ γῆς ἔχει τὴν γένεσιν, π. ἄφθονον ἐν ταῖς παρατρίψεσι πέφυκεν ἀπολάμπειν. ὃ καὶ θαυμάσαι ἄξιον, πῶς ἐν μὲν τοῖς σώμασιν ὑπάρχον τὸ π., ἀβλαβῶς ἐμφωλεύει· προκληθὲν δὲ ἐπὶ τὸ ἔξω, δαπανητικόν ἐστι τῶν φυλασσόντων τέως Bas. *hex.*1.7(1.8B; M.29.20Af.); ἀναγκαία τῷ παντὶ τοῦ π. ἡ οὐσία, οὐ μόνον πρὸς τὴν τῶν περιγείων οἰκονομίαν, ἀλλὰ καὶ πρὸς τὴν συμπλήρωσιν τοῦ παντός *ib.*3.5(1.27B; M.64C); created after earth and water, *ib.*2.3 (1.15A; M.36A); **3.** Gnost. π. ἅπασιν αὐτοῖς ἐκπεφυκέναι θάνατον καὶ φθοράν Iren.*haer.*1.5.4(M.7.500A); **4.** ass. demons πνευματικὴ δέ ἐστιν αὐτοῖς [sc. δαίμοσιν] ἡ σύμπηξις ὡς πυρὸς καὶ ἀέρος Tat.*orat.*15(p.16. 28; M.6.840A); ὁ δαίμων ἀφανὴς ἐγένετο, μόνον δὲ ἀποστάντος αὐτοῦ π. καὶ καπνὸς ὤφθη *A.Thom.*A 46(p.163.15).

B. ref. idea of divinity of fire; **1.** pagan assertions, acc. Parmenides and Heraclitus, Clem.*prot.*5(p.49.3,18ff.; M.8.165A,168Aff.); Persian fire worship, *ib.*(p.49.18ff.; 168Aff.); Chrys.*stat.*4.3(2.54B); **2.** Christian refutation οἱ δὲ νομίζοντες τὸ π. εἶναι θεὸν πλανῶνται. τὸ γὰρ π. ἐγένετο εἰς χρῆσιν τῶν ἀνθρώπων καὶ κατακυριεύεται ὑπ' αὐτῶν περιφερόμενον ἐκ τόπου εἰς τόπον...φθείρεται δὲ καὶ κατὰ πολλοὺς τρόπους ὑπὸ τῶν ἀνθρώπων σβεννύμενον. διὸ οὐκ ἐνδέχεται τὸ π. εἶναι θεὸν ἀλλ' ἔργον θεοῦ Arist.*apol.*5.3; Athenag.*leg.*6.4(M.6.904A); εἰ τοίνυν Ζεὺς μὲν τὸ π., Ἥρα δὲ ἡ γῆ...στοιχεῖα δὲ ταῦτα, τὸ π. ... οὐδεὶς αὐτῶν θεός *ib.*22.1(936C); εἰ ὁ περὶ θεοῦ κρατεῖ λόγος, δυνατὸν αὐτὸν εἶναι κατὰ πάντα, καὶ μηδὲν μὲν αὐτοῦ κρατεῖν...πῶς οἱ τὴν κτίσιν θεοποιοῦντες οὐχ ὁρῶσιν αὐτὴν ἐκτὸς οὖσαν τοῦ τοιούτου περὶ θεοῦ ὅρου;...τὸ π. δέ, εἰ γένοιτό τις ὑδάτων πλημμύρα, σβέννυται Ath.*gent.*29(M.25.57B); **3.** pagan idea ridiculed οἱ μέν τινες [sc. τῶν φιλοσόφων] π. ἔφασαν εἶναι τὸν θεόν (οὗ μέλλουσι χωρήσειν αὐτοί, τοῦτο καλοῦσι θεόν) *Diogn.*8.2; προσκυνῶ τὸ π. ὢ τοῦ γέλωτος...τὸ προσκυνούμενον τί σβεννύεις;...εἰ γὰρ θεός ἐστι τὸ π., ἐπινεμέσθω σου τὸ σῶμα Chrys.*hom.12.2 in Eph.*(11.91C,D).

C. fire as man's servant, Clem.*prot.*11(p.81.11; M.8.233B); id. *paed.*3.12(p.290.18ff.; M.8.680A).

D. as means of testing and purifying; **1.** in gen. τὸ π. οὐχ ὑποκρίνεται. ἐλέγχειν καὶ κολάζειν κελεύεται Clem.*prot.*2(p.17.17; M. 8.89A); Jul.Papa *ep.Alex.*ap.Ath.*apol.sec.*53(p.134.7; M.25.345A); **2.** fig., ref. testing of souls ὥσπερ γὰρ τὸ χρυσίον δοκιμάζεται διὰ τοῦ π. καὶ εὔχρηστον γίνεται, οὕτως καὶ ὑμεῖς δοκιμάζεσθε Herm.*vis.*4.3.4; τὸ γοῦν ἐκπορνεῦσαν τῆς ἐπιθυμίας εἰς χρυσίον εἴδωλον γίνεται βασανιζόμενον πυρί Clem.*paed.*2.12(p.232.31; M.8.549C); **3.** met., ref. purging by fire in present life, exeg. Is.9:5 νομίζω ἐν τῷ 'θελήσωσιν εἰ ἐγένοντο πυρίκαυστοι' τοιοῦτόν τι δηλοῦσθαι· οἷον τοῦ π. προσφερομένου τινὶ καὶ μὴ αἰσθανομένου τοῦ καιομένου, θελήσωσιν ἐκεῖνοι, καταλαβόντες σύγκρισιν μὴ αἰσθανομένων ἐπὶ ταῖς ἀλγηδόσιν καὶ αἰσθανομένων, μᾶλλον αἰσθάνεσθαι ἐπὶ τῷ π. ἢ μὴ αἰσθάνεσθαι. καὶ εὔξαιτο ἄν τις προσαγομένου κἀκείνου τοῦ κεκριμένου π. ἐπὶ τοὺς ἁμαρτωλοὺς αἰσθάνεσθαι μᾶλλον ἢ μὴ αἰσθάνεσθαι Or.*hom.6.2 in Jer.* (p.49.24ff.; M.13.325C); cf. *dat et ignem sciens esse spinas et tribulos, quos debeat ignis ille depasci, de quo dicit dominus: 'ignem veni mittere in terram'; per hunc enim incentiva voluptatis et libidinis consumuntur,* id.*hom.4.7 in Ex.*(p.179.13ff.; M.12.322D); **4.** after death; **a.** in gen. διαπεράσω τὰ τοῦ π. ὕδατα καὶ πᾶσαν τὴν ἄβυσσον *A.Phil.*144(p.86.3); τοῦτο τὸ σαρκίον ἀντίδικον...μὴ τρέφοντας...ἵνα ἐν τῇ διαλύσει...διαπνεῦσαν λάθῃ, ἀλλὰ μὴ...τὴν ἰσχὺν ἔχῃ παράμονον ἐν τῇ διὰ πυρὸς διεξόδῳ Clem.*exc.Thdot.*52(p.124.15; M.9.684C); cf.Or. *princ.*2.10.6(p.180.14; M.11.239A); **b.** contrasted with purging by divine fire, cf. *non omnes purgantur eo igni, qui de altari assumitur. Aaron purgatur illo igni et Esaias et si qui sunt similes illis; alii vero, qui non sunt tales, de quibus etiam me ipsum computo, alio igni purgabimur; timeo ne illo, de quo scriptum est: 'fluvius ignis currebat ante ipsum.' iste ignis non est de altari. qui de altari est ignis, ignis est domini; qui autem extra altare est, non est domini, sed proprius est uniuscujusque peccantium, de quo dicitur: 'vermis eorum non morietur, et ignis eorum non exstinguetur.' iste ergo ignis ipsorum est, qui eum accenderunt, sicut et alibi scriptum est: 'ambulate in igni vestro...' Esaiae autem non suus ignis apponitur, sed ignis altaris,* Or.*hom.9.8 in Lev.*(p.432.18ff.; M.12.519A,B); cf.id. *hom.4.5 in Is.*(p.262.8; M.13.234A); **c.** degrees of purifying, cf. *qui salvus fit, per ignem salvus fit, ut, si quid forte de specie plumbi habuerit admixtum, id ignis decoquat et resolvat, ut efficiantur omnes aurum bonum...veniendum est ergo omnibus ad ignem...sed illuc cum venitur, si qui multa opera bona et parum aliquid iniquitatis attulerit, illud parum, tamquam plumbum, igni resolvitur ac purgatur, et totum remanet aurum purum. et si qui plus illuc plumbi detulerit, plus exuritur,* id.*hom.6.4 in Ex.*(p.196.3ff.; M.12.334C,D); **5.** π. φρόνιμον: καταφλεχθῆναι προσέταξε τὸ Σόδομα, ὀλίγον τι τοῦ φρονιμοῦ π. ἐκείνου ἐπὶ τὴν ἀκολασίαν ἐκχέων Clem.*paed.*3.8(p.262. 13; M.8.616B); ἀντέθηκεν...τῷ δὲ ὑλικῷ τὸ π., οὐ πονηρὸν οὐδὲ κακὸν ὑπάρχον, ἀλλ' ἰσχυρὸν καὶ κακοῦ καθαρτικόν· ἀγαθὴ γὰρ δύναμις τὸ π. νοεῖται καὶ ἰσχυρά, φθαρτικὴ τῶν χειρόνων καὶ σωστικὴ τῶν ἀμείνων, διὸ καὶ φρόνιμον λέγεται παρὰ τοῖς προφήταις τοῦτο τὸ π. id.*ecl.*25 (p.144.5ff.; M.9.709C); φαμὲν δ' ἡμεῖς ἁγιάζειν τὸ π. οὐ τὰ κρέα, ἀλλὰ τὰς ἁμαρτωλοὺς ψυχάς, π. οὐ τὸ παμφάγον καὶ βάναυσον, ἀλλὰ τὸ φρόνιμον λέγοντες, τὸ 'διϊκνούμενον διὰ ψυχῆς'· τῆς διερχομένης τὸ π. id.*str.*7.6(p.27.6ff.; M.9.449B); ref. 1Cor.3:13ff., cf. *quis est... ignis iste, qui probat opera nostra? quis est ignis iste sic sapiens, ut custodiat aurum meum...quis est iste ignis? 'ignem veni mittere super terram'...bonus enim est et novit quia si ignis iste fuerit accensus, malitia consummabitur,* Or.*hom.1.3 in Ezech.*(p.324.15ff.; M.13. 670B).

E. hell fire; **1.** in gen. ἡ μάχαιρα τοῦ θεοῦ ἐστι τὸ π., οὗ βορὰ γίνονται οἱ τὰ φαῦλα πράττειν αἱρούμενοι Just.*1apol.*44.5(M.6.396A); Ath.*h.Ar.*70(p.221.20; M.25.776D); **2.** eternal εἰς τὸ π. τὸ ἄσβεστον χωρήσει Ign.*Eph.*16.2; *2Clem.*17.7; πᾶσι τοῖς ἀδίκως ἐχθραίνουσι καὶ μὴ μετατιθεμένοις κόλασιν διὰ πυρὸς αἰωνίαν ἐργάζεται Just.*1apol.*45. 6(M.6.397B); *ib.*54.2(408C); id.*2apol.*2.2(M.6.444A); id.*dial.*45.4(M. 573A); ἐν ἡμέρᾳ συντελείας π. αἰωνίου βορᾷ παραδοθήσεται Tat.*orat.*17 (p.18.18; M.6.841C); Or.*hom.12.5 in Jer.*(p.92.30; M.13.385D); ἀπόκειται...τοῖς δὲ φαῦλα πράξασι π. αἰώνιον Ath.*inc.*56.3(M.25.196B); **3.** intended principally for Satan, secondarily for sinners, Just. *1apol.*28.1(M.6.372B); id.*2apol.*8.4(M.6.457B); cf. *non homini principaliter praeparatus est aeternus ignis, sed ei qui seduxit et offendere fecit hominem,* Iren.*haer.*3.23.3(M.7.962B); cf. *quoniam quidem transgressoribus ignis aeternus praeparatus est, et dominus manifeste dixit, et reliquae demonstrant scripturae, ib.*3.28.7(810B); Clem.*paed.* 1.7(p.126.8; M.8.324B); id.*q.d.s.*37(p.184.15,19; M.9.641D–644A); cf. *mors, quae poenae causa infertur pro peccato, purgatio est peccati ipsius...absolvitur ergo peccatum per poenam mortis nec superest aliquid, quod pro hoc crimine judicii dies et poena aeterni ignis inveniat. ubi vero quis accipit peccatum et...permanet cum ipso nec aliquo supplicio poena, quae diluitur, transit, cum ipso est etiam post mortem...ubi autem non est soluta vindicta, peccatum manet illis aeternis ignibus exstinguendum,* Or.*hom.14.4 in Lev.*(p.485.2ff.; M. 12.557B); Ath.*v.Anton.*24(M.26.881A); **4.** in rel. to ordinary fire μὴ γὰρ ἐπειδὴ π. ἤκουσας, τοιοῦτον εἶναι νομίσῃς τὸ π.· τοῦτο μὲν γάρ, ὅπερ ἂν λάβῃ κατέκαυσε καὶ ἀπήλλαξεν· ἐκεῖνο δὲ τοὺς ἅπαξ κατασχεθέντας καίει διαπαντός, καὶ οὐδέ ποτε παύεται, διὰ τοῦτο καὶ ἄσβεστον εἴρηται...εἰ γάρ ποτε ἐν βαλανείῳ γένοιο σφοδρότερον κατεσκευασμένῳ τοῦ δέοντος, τότε μοι τὸ τῆς γεέννης ἐννόησον π. ... ὥσπερ γὰρ οὐκ ἔστιν ἀναλωτικὸν ἐκεῖνο τὸ π., οὕτως οὐδὲ φωτιστικόν· οὐδὲ γὰρ ἂν σκότος ἦν Chrys.*Thdr.*1.10(1.13E); οἱ ἁμαρτωλοὶ εἰς τὸ π. αἰώνιον· οὐχ ὑλικόν, οἷον τὸ παρ' ἡμῖν· ἀλλ' οἷον ἂν εἰδείη ὁ θεός Jo.D.*f.o.*4.27(M.94.1228A); **5.** lit by sin, which is also its fuel, Clem.*paed.*2.10(pp.219.31–220.5; M.8.521B,C); *ib.*3.11(p.282.13f.; 661C); cf.Or.*princ.*2.10.4(p.177.2ff.; M.11.236C); διὰ τοῦτο καὶ κόλασις ἡμῖν ἡτοίμασται, καὶ ἑαυτοῖς τὸ π.

ἐξάπτομεν· ὅτι καὶ λογικοὶ ὄντες τοῖς ἀλόγοις ζῴοις ἑαυτοὺς εἰκάζομεν Ath.*virg*.3(p.38.16; M.28.256C); τῆς ζωῆς ταύτης τὰ τερπνὰ...ὕλας μόνον κατασκευάζοντα τῷ αἰωνίῳ π. Bas.*ep*.23(3.101C; M.32.293C); **6.** opp. ἀπάθεια: τοὺς ἀδίκους...ἐν αἰωνίῳ π. κολασθήσεσθαι, τοὺς δ' ἐναρέτους...ἐν ἀπαθείᾳ συγγενέσθαι τῷ θεῷ Just.*2apol*.1.2(M.6.441A); **7.** Gnost. ἡ ψυχὴ μὴ γνοῦσα τὴν ἀλήθειαν, παραδίδοται τοῖς δαίμοσιν, ὅπως δαμάσωσιν αὐτὴν ἐν ταῖς γεένναις τοῦ π., καὶ μετὰ τὴν παίδευσιν μεταγγίζεται εἰς σώματα, ἵνα δαμασθῇ, καὶ οὕτω βάλλεται εἰς τὸ μέγα π. ἄχρι τῆς συντελείας Hegem.*Arch*.11(p.18.11ff.; M.10.1445A,B); **8.** belief in punishment by fire taken into pagan philosophy from Judaism, Clem.*str*.5.14(p.385.24; M.9.133A).

F. eschatol., cf.Dan.7:9–11; **1.** pagan idea of end of world in fire Σίβυλλα δὲ καὶ Ὑστάσπης γενήσεσθαι τῶν φθαρτῶν ἀνάλωσιν διὰ πυρὸς ἔφασαν. οἱ...δὲ Στωϊκοὶ φιλόσοφοι καὶ αὐτὸν τὸν θεὸν εἰς π. ἀναλύεσθαι δογματίζουσι Just.*1apol*.20.1,2(M.6.357B,C); Ἐμπεδοκλέα, ὃς φυσικῶς οὕτως τῆς τῶν πάντων ἀναλήψεως μέμνηται, ὡς ἐσομένης ποτὲ εἰς τὴν τοῦ π. οὐσίαν μεταβολῆς Clem.*str*.5.14(p.396.6; M.9.157B); **2.** Christian ἔρχεται ἤδη ἡ ἡμέρα τῆς κρίσεως...καὶ πᾶσα ἡ γῆ ὡς μόλιβος ἐπὶ πυρὶ τηκόμενος *2Clem*.16.3; δεῖ τὸν κόσμον τοῦτον δι' αἵματος καὶ π. ἀπόλλυσθαι Herm.*vis*.4.3.3; Just.*2apol*.7.2(M.6.456A); cf.Or.*Cant*.1 (p.99.19; M.13.92A); Ath.*inc*.57.3(M.25.197A); ref. Dan.7:10 τότε δὴ ποταμός τε μέγας πυρὸς ῥεύσει ἀπ' οὐρανόθεν καὶ πάντα τόπον δαπανήσει...ψυχαὶ δ' ἀνθρώπων πᾶσαι βρύξουσιν ὀδοῦσιν καιόμεναι ποταμῷ καὶ θείῳ καὶ πυρὸς ὁρμῇ ἐν δαπέδῳ μαλερῷ *Orac.Sib*.2. 196,204; *ib*.8.243; ποταμὸς ἐκπορεύεται πυρὸς ὑποκάτω τοῦ θρόνου τοῦ Τόπου, καὶ ῥεῖ εἰς τὸ κενὸν τοῦ ἐκτισμένου, ὅ ἐστιν ἡ γέεννα, ἀπὸ κτίσεως τοῦ π. ῥέοντος μὴ πληρουμένη Clem.*exc.Thdot*.38(p.118.29ff.; M.9.677B); ὁ κύριος ἥξει...καὶ ποταμὸς πλήρης π. Ephr.2.229F; combined with 1Cor.3:12ff. ἔρχεται πρὸς τὸν πατέρα...ὁ υἱὸς τοῦ ἀνθρώπου ἐπὶ τῶν νεφελῶν τοῦ οὐρανοῦ, ποταμοῦ π. ἕλκοντος, δοκιμαστικοῦ τῶν ἀνθρώπων. εἴ τις χρυσίου ἔχει τὰ ἔργα, λαμπρότερος γίνεται· εἴ τις καλαμώδη ἔχει τὴν πρᾶξιν...κατακαίεται ὑπὸ τοῦ π. Cyr.H.*catech*.15. 21; Chrys.*Thdr*.1.10(1.13D); φοβοῦμαι τὸν ποταμὸν τοῦ π., τὸν πρὸ τοῦ βήματος ἐκείνου συρόμενον †Cyr.*hom.div*.14(5^2.404B); properties of this fire τὸ π. καθάρσιον ἐπάγεται τῷ κόσμῳ, εἰκὸς δ' ὅτι καὶ ἑκάστῳ τῶν δεομένων τῆς διὰ τοῦ π. δίκης ἅμα καὶ ἰατρείας· καίοντος μὲν καὶ οὐ κατακαίοντος τοὺς μὴ ἔχοντας ὕλην δεομένην ἀναλοῦσθαι ὑπ' ἐκείνου τοῦ π., καίοντος δὲ καὶ κατακαίοντος τοὺς ἐν τῇ διὰ τῶν πράξεων καὶ λόγων καὶ νοημάτων τροπικῶς λεγομένῃ οἰκοδομῇ 'ξύλα, χόρτον ἢ καλάμην' οἰκοδομήσαντας Or.*Cels*.5.15(p.16.6ff.; M.11.1201C,D); ἐν ταῖς τῶν βεβιωμένων ἡμῖν ἀνταποδόσεσι λόγος...παιδεύει, διαιρεθήσεσθαι τοῦ π. τὴν φύσιν, καὶ τὸ μὲν φῶς, εἰς ἀπόλαυσιν τοῖς δικαίοις, τὸ δὲ τῆς καύσεως ὀδυνηρόν, τοῖς κολαζομένοις ἀποταχθήσεσθαι Bas.*hex*.6.3 (1.52A; M.29.121D); ἐπειδὴ δύο εἰσὶν ἐν τῷ π. δυνάμεις, ἥ τε καυστικὴ καὶ ἡ φωτιστική, τὸ μὲν δριμὺ καὶ κολαστικὸν τοῦ π. τοῖς ἀξίοις τῆς καύσεως προσαπομείνῃ, τὸ δὲ φωτιστικὸν αὐτοῦ...τῇ φαιδρότητι τῶν εὐφραινομένων ἀποκληρωθῇ. φωνὴ οὖν κυρίου διακόπτοντος φλόγα πυρὸς καὶ μερίζοντος, ὡς ἀλαμπὲς μὲν εἶναι τὸ π. τῆς κολάσεως, ἄκαυστον δὲ τὸ φῶς τῆς ἀναπαύσεως ἀπομεῖναι id.*hom.in Ps*.28(1.121A,B; M.29. 297B,C); descriptions εἰσήνεγκάν με εἰς τὸν οὐρανόν...καὶ εἰσῆλθον εἰς τὰς γλώσσας τοῦ π. ... καὶ π. φλεγόμενον κύκλῳ τῶν τοίχων καὶ θύραι πυρὶ καιόμεναι...καὶ ἰδοὺ ἄλλη θύρα...καὶ ὁ οἶκος...ὅλος οἰκοδομημένος ἐν γλώσσαις πυρὸς...τὸ ἔδαφος αὐτοῦ ἦν π. ... καὶ ἡ στέγη αὐτοῦ ἦν π. φλέγον...καὶ ὑποκάτω τοῦ θρόνου ἐξεπορεύοντο ποταμοὶ πυρὸς φλεγόμενοι...καὶ οὐκ ἐδύνατο πᾶς ἄγγελος παρελθεῖν εἰς τὸν οἶκον τοῦτον... καὶ οὐκ ἐδύνατο πᾶσα σὰρξ ἰδεῖν αὐτοῦ τὸ π. φλεγόμενον κύκλῳ. καὶ π. μέγα παρειστήκει αὐτῷ *Apoc.En*.14.10–22; ῥεύσει δὲ π. μαλεροῦ καταράκτης ἀκάματος, φλέξει δὲ γαῖαν *Orac.Sib*.3.84; *ib*.7.120; π. τὸ ἄσβεστον διατρέχει πανταχοῦ πρὸ προσώπου τοῦ Χριστοῦ, καὶ καλύπτει τὰ πάντα Ephr.3.149B; typified by Flood, id.3.149C; **3.** Gnost. τὸ ἐμφωλεῦον τῷ κόσμῳ π. ἐκλάμψαν καὶ ἐξαφθέν, καὶ κατεργασάμενον πᾶσαν ὕλην, συναναλωθήσεσθαι αὐτῇ, καὶ εἰς τὸ μηκέτ' εἶναι χωρήσειν διδάσκουσι Iren.*haer*.1.7.1(M.7.513A); Manich. ἀπολύεται τὸ μέγα π. καὶ ὅλον ἀναλίσκει τὸν κόσμον...τότε δὲ ταῦτα γενήσεται, ὅταν ὁ ἀνδριὰς ἔλθῃ...καὶ τὸ τεῖχος τοῦ μεγάλου π. ... καὶ τοῦ ἔσωθεν π. τοῦ ζῶντος... ἄχρις ἂν τὸ π. καταναλώσῃ τὸν κόσμον ὅλον Hegem.*Arch*.13(11; p.21. 6ff.; M.10.1448C–1449A).

G. baptism of fire; **1.** twofold nature of fire corresponding to twofold baptism τοῦ π. τὸ μὲν σωματικὸν σωμάτων ἅπτεται πάντων, τὸ δὲ καθαρὸν καὶ ἀσώματον ἀσωμάτων φασὶν ἅπτεσθαι, οἷον δαιμόνων ...αὐτοῦ τοῦ διαβόλου. οὕτως ἐστὶ τὸ ἐπουράνιον...π. διssὸν τὴν φύσιν, τὸ μὲν νοητόν, τὸ δὲ αἰσθητόν. καὶ τὸ βάπτισμα οὖν διπλοῦν ἀναλόγως, τὸ μὲν αἰσθητὸν δι' ὕδατος, τοῦ αἰσθητοῦ π. σβεστήριον, τὸ δὲ νοητὸν διὰ πνεύματος, τοῦ νοητοῦ π. ἀλεξητήριον Clem.*exc.Thdot*.81(pp.131.31–132.5; M.9.696B,C); cf.id.*ecl*.8(p.139.1ff.; M.9.701B) cit. s. ἀόρατος; **2.** after death (cf. also F supra); as universally needed, cf. *quando baptizat Jesus spiritu sancto, et rursum, quando igni baptizat? numquid uno atque eodem tempore et spiritu et igni baptizat, an vario...? baptizati sunt apostoli post ascensionem ejus ad caelos spiritu sancto; quod autem igni fuerint baptizati, scriptura non memorat...stabit in igneo flumine dominus...juxta flammeam romphaeam, ut quicunque post exitum vitae hujus ad paradisum transire desiderat et purgatione indiget, hoc eum amne baptizet et ad cupita transmittat, eum vero, qui non habet signum priorum baptismatum, lavacro igneo non baptizet. oportet enim prius aliquem baptizari aqua et spiritu, ut cum ad igneum fluvium venerit, ostendat se et aquae et spiritus lavacra servasse et tunc mereatur etiam ignis accipere baptismum in Christo Jesu*, Or.*hom.24 in Lc*.(p.158.11ff.; M. 13.1864B–1865A); as not needed by all men ὁ Ἰησοῦς βαπτίζει...ἐν πνεύματι [καὶ] ἁγίῳ καὶ π. οὐχ ὅτι τὸν αὐτὸν ἐν πνεύματι ἁγίῳ καὶ π., ἀλλὰ τὸν μὲν ἅγιον ἐν πνεύματι ἁγίῳ, τὸν δὲ μετὰ τὸ πιστεῦσαι...πάλιν ἡμαρτηκότα λούει ἐν π. ... μακάριος οὖν ὁ βαπτιζόμενος ἐν ἁγίῳ πνεύματι καὶ μὴ δεόμενος βαπτίσματος τοῦ ἀπὸ π. τρισάθλιος δὲ ἐκεῖνος, ὅστις χρείαν ἔχει βαπτίσασθαι τῷ π. id.*hom.2.3 in Jer*.(p.19.10ff.; M. 13.280–281D); ὁ δεόμενος βαπτίσματος τοῦ ἀπὸ π., ὅταν ἔλθῃ ἐπὶ τὸ π. ἐκεῖνο, καὶ τὸ π. αὐτὸν δοκιμάζῃ καὶ εὕρῃ τὸ π. ἐκεῖνο ξύλα, χόρτον καὶ καλάμην, ὥστε αὐτὰ κατακαῦσαι *ib*.(p.20.1ff.; 281B); cf.id.*hom.5.1 in Ezech*.(p.372.9; M.13.705A); reconciliation of the two seemingly opposed views, cf. *si vero in hac vita contemnimus commonentis nos divinae scripturae verba...manet nos ignis ille qui praeparatus est peccatoribus, et veniemus ad illum ignem in quo 'uniuscujusque opus quale sit ignis probabit.' et, ut ego arbitror, omnes nos venire necesse est ad illum ignem. etiamsi Paulus sit aliquis vel Petrus, venit tamen ad illum ignem. sed illi tales audiunt: 'etiamsi per ignem transeas, flamma non aduret te.' si vero aliquis similis mei peccator sit, veniet quidem ad ignem illum sicut Petrus et Paulus, sed non sic transiet sicut Petrus et Paulus...si quidem Aegyptii sumus, et sequimur Pharaonem diabolum...demergemur in illum fluvium sive lacum igneum...si autem sumus Hebraei, et sanguine agni immaculati sumus redempti...ingredimur quidem et nos fluvium ignis. sed...ignis erit murus...et sic sequamur columnam ignis et columnam nubis*, id.*sel.in Ps*.36(M.12.1337B,C); **3.** contrasted with baptism of water οἱ μέν, δι' ὕδατος ἀναγεννῶνται καὶ πνεύματος· οἱ δέ, ἐν πνεύματι ἁγίῳ καὶ π. τὸ βάπτισμα δέχονται...τὸ ὕδωρ τε...καὶ τὸ πνεῦμα, καὶ τὸ π., καὶ τὸ πνεῦμα ἅγιον, τὸ ἓν καὶ τὸ αὐτὸ πνεῦμα νοῶ τοῦ θεοῦ. τοῖς μὲν γὰρ ὕδωρ ἐστὶ τὸ πνεῦμα τὸ ἅγιον, ὡς ῥυπτικὸν τῶν ἐκτὸς περὶ τὸ σῶμα μολυσμῶν· τοῖς δὲ πνεῦμα μόνον, ὡς ἐνεργητικὸν τῶν κατ' ἀρετὴν ἀγαθῶν· τοῖς δὲ π., ὡς καθαρτικὸν τῶν ἐντὸς κατὰ τὸ βάθος περὶ ψυχὴν κηλίδων· τοῖς δὲ...πνεῦμα ἅγιον, ὡς σοφίας καὶ γνώσεως χορηγόν Max.*cap.theol*.2.63(M.90.1152C); **4.** at Judgement, exeg. Mt.3:11 τὸ τοῦ π. βάπτισμα τὴν ἐν τῇ κρίσει δοκιμασίαν λέγων Bas. *Spir*.36(3.30B; M.32.132C).

H. fire as an image of God and divine things; **1.** its suitability as such discussed, Dion.Ar.*c.h*.15.2(M.3.329A–C); must be applied in different ways ἄλλως τὴν αὐτὴν τοῦ π. εἰκόνα κατὰ τοῦ ὑπὲρ νόησιν θεοῦ λεγομένην ἐκλαβεῖν· ἄλλως δὲ κατὰ τῶν νοητῶν αὐτοῦ προνοιῶν ἢ λόγων· καὶ ἄλλως ἐπὶ τῶν ἀγγέλων. καὶ τὴν μὲν κατ' αἰτίαν, τὴν δὲ καθ' ὕπαρξιν, τὴν δὲ κατὰ μέθεξιν, καὶ ἄλλα ἄλλως, ὡς ἡ κατ' αὐτὰ θεωρία καὶ ἐπιστημονικὴ διάταξις ὁροθετεῖ id.*ep*.9.2(M.3.1108D); **2.** God as fire: in gen., Dion.Ar.*ep*.9.2(M.3.1108C); Gel.Cyz.*h.e*.2.22. 8(M.85.1292C); exeg. Dt.4:24 cit.ap.Heb.12:29 ὅταν ὁ θεὸς λέγηται π. καταναλίσκον, οὐ κακίας, ἀλλὰ δυνάμεως ὄνομα...ὡς γὰρ τὸ π. ἰσχυρότατον τῶν στοιχείων καὶ πάντων κρατοῦν, οὕτω καὶ ὁ θεὸς παντοδύναμος καὶ παντοκράτωρ...ὡς οὖν τῶν στοιχείων ὑπερέχει τὸ π., οὕτως θεῶν τε καὶ δυνάμεων...ὁ παντοκράτωρ. διπλῆ τε ἡ δύναμις τοῦ π., ἡ μὲν πρὸς δημιουργίαν...καὶ ζῴων γένεσιν...ἧς εἰκὼν ὁ ἥλιος, ἡ δὲ πρὸς ἀνάλωσιν...ὡς τὸ π. τὸ ἐπίγειον. π. οὖν ὅταν λέγηται ὁ θεὸς καταναλίσκον, δύναμις ἰσχυρὰ...ᾗ μηδὲν ἀδύνατον, ἀλλὰ καὶ τὸ ἀπολέσαι δυνατόν. περὶ τοιαύτης δυνάμεως καὶ ὁ σωτὴρ λέγει· 'π. ἦλθον βαλεῖν ...' δηλονότι δύναμιν τῶν μὲν ἁγίων καθαρτικήν, τῶν δὲ ὑλικῶν...ἀφανιστικήν, ὡς δὲ ἡμεῖς ἂν φαίημεν, παιδευτικήν Clem.*ecl*.26 (p.144.10ff.; M.9.709C–712A); Hipp.*haer*.6.32(p.161.11; M.16.3243B); ὡσεὶ καὶ λεγόντων ἡμῶν ὅτι ὁ θεὸς π. ἐστι καταναλίσκον, ἔλεγεν ὅτι οὐδεμία τοιαύτη φύσις ἐστὶ πυρός, ὥστ' ἀεὶ διαμένειν· οὐχ ὁρῶν πῶς λέγομεν εἶναι π. τὸν θεὸν ἡμῶν, καὶ τίνων ἀναλωτικόν, ὅτι ἁμαρτημάτων Or.*Cels*.6.72(p.142.4ff.; M.11.1408A); id.*Jo*.13.23(p.247.9f.; M.14. 437B); π. καταναλίσκον τοῖς ἁμαρτωλοῖς, φῶς τοῖς δικαίοις id.*hom.2.3 in Jer*.(p.19.19f.; M.13.281A); exeg. Mal.3:2 φασὶ δ' οἱ θεῖοι λόγοι τὸν κύριον ὡς π. χωνευτηρίου...ἑκάστῳ τῶν δεομένων ἐπιδημήσειν διὰ τὸ ἀναμεμῖχθαι οἱονεὶ φαυλὴν χυτὴν ὕλην τὴν ἀπὸ τῆς κακίας, δεομένων δὲ λέγω πυρός, οἱονεὶ χωνεύοντος τοὺς ἀναμεμιγμένους χαλκῷ, καὶ κασσιτέρῳ καὶ μολίβδῳ id.*Cels*.5.15(p.16.12ff.; 1204A); exeg. Dt.4:24

combined with 1Cor.3:12f. πρῶτον ἀκολουθεῖ ἀπολαβεῖν δὲ τὰ ξύλα τὸ π. τὸ ἀναλίσκον...τὴν καλάμην· ὁ θεὸς γὰρ ἡμῶν τῇ οὐσίᾳ λέγεται τοῖς συνιέναι δυναμένοις π. εἶναι καταναλίσκον...τί οὖν ἐστι τὸ καταναλισκόμενον; οὐ γὰρ τὸ κατ' εἰκόνα...ἀναλίσκει...ἀλλὰ τὸν ἐποικοδομηθέντα χόρτον id.*hom.16.6 in Jer.*(p.138.16ff.; 445D); with Lc.12:49 'π. ἦλθον βαλεῖν...' ἔστι γὰρ πύρωσις τοῦ πνεύματος ἡ ἀναζωπυροῦσα τὰς καρδίας. διότι τὸ ἄυλον καὶ θεῖον π. φωτίζει μὲν ψυχάς...κακίαν δὲ ἀναλίσκει...τοῦτο τὸ π. ἐνήργησεν ἐν τοῖς ἀποστόλοις, ἡνίκα ἐλάλουν γλώσσαις πυρίναις. τοῦτο τὸ π. διὰ τῆς φωνῆς Παῦλον περιλάμψαν, τὴν μὲν διάνοιαν αὐτοῦ ἐφώτισε, τὴν δὲ αἴσθησιν τῆς ὄψεως αὐτοῦ ἠμαύρωσεν...τοῦτο τὸ π. ὤφθη Μωϋσῇ ἐν τῇ βάτῳ· τοῦτο τὸ π. ἐν εἴδει ὀχήματος Ἠλίαν ἐκ τῆς γῆς ἥρπασε· τούτου τοῦ π. τὴν ἐνέργειαν ζητῶν ὁ...Δαβὶδ ἔλεγε 'δοκίμασόν με, κύριε'...τοῦτο τὸ π. τὴν καρδίαν Κλεόπα καὶ τοὺς σὺν αὐτῷ ἐθέρμανε, λαλοῦντος τοῦ σωτῆρος μετὰ τὴν ἀνάστασιν, ὅθεν καὶ ἄγγελοι...τούτου τοῦ π. τῆς λαμπρότητος μετέχουσι... τοῦτο τὸ π. τὴν ἐν τῷ ἔνδον ὀφθαλμῷ δοκὸν κατακαῖον, καθαρὸν τὸν νοῦν ἀποκαθίστησιν, ἵνα...ὁρᾷ εἰς τὸ διηνεκὲς τὰ τοῦ θεοῦ θαυμάσια... τοῦτο...τὸ π. δαιμόνων ἐστὶ φυγαδευτήριον, καὶ ἁμαρτίας ἀναιρετικόν, ἀναστάσεως δὲ δύναμις...τοῦτο τὸ π. εὐξώμεθα καὶ εἰς ἡμᾶς φθάσαι, ἵνα πάντοτε ἐν φωτὶ περιπατοῦντες...ὡς φωστῆρες ἐν κόσμῳ φαινόμενοι λόγον ζωῆς ἐπέχωμεν ἀιδίου Mac.Aeg.*hom.*25.9,10(M.34.673A–D); **3.** ref. Father (cf. ἀπαύγασμα); **a.** in rel. to Son ἐκ τοῦ ἀπὸ τοῦ πατρὸς θελήσει γεγεννῆσθαι...ὁποῖον ἐπὶ πυρὸς ὁρῶμεν ἄλλο γινόμενον, οὐκ ἐλαττουμένου ἐκείνου ἐξ οὗ ἡ ἄναψις γέγονεν, ἀλλὰ τοῦ αὐτοῦ μένοντος, καὶ τὸ ἐξ αὐτοῦ ἀναφθὲν καὶ αὐτὸ ὂν φαίνεται, οὐκ ἐλαττῶσαν ἐκεῖνο ἐξ οὗ ἀνήφθη Just.*dial.*61.1(M.6.616A); τὴν δύναμιν ταύτην γεγεννῆσθαι ἀπὸ τοῦ πατρός, δυνάμει καὶ βουλῇ αὐτοῦ, ἀλλ' οὐ κατὰ ἀποτομήν, ὡς ἀπομεριζομένης τῆς τοῦ πατρὸς οὐσίας...παραδείγματος χάριν παρειλήφειν ὡς τὰ ἀπὸ π. ἀναπτόμενα πυρὰ ἕτερα ὁρῶμεν, οὐδὲν ἐλαττουμένου ἐκείνου...ἀλλὰ ταὐτοῦ μένοντος *ib.*128.4(776C); Tat.*orat.*5(p.6.1; M.6.817A); π. δὲ καὶ φῶς ἀλληγορεῖται ὁ θεὸς καὶ ὁ λόγος αὐτοῦ πρὸς τῆς γραφῆς Clem.*str.*5.14(p.393.2; M.9.152A); ὡς γὰρ ἀπὸ π. φῶς, οὕτως ἐκ τοῦ θεοῦ λόγος ‡Ath.*Ar.*4.2(p.45.24; M.26.469C); ἔστω δὲ παράδειγμα ἀνθρώπινον, τὸ π. καὶ τὸ ἐξ αὐτοῦ ἀπαύγασμα, δύο μὲν τῷ εἶναι καὶ ὁρᾶσθαι, ἓν δὲ τῷ ἐξ αὐτοῦ καὶ ἀδιαίρετον εἶναι τὸ ἀπαύγασμα αὐτοῦ *ib.*4.10(p.54.11; 480C); **b.** in rel. to H. Ghost θεόν φαμεν... καὶ πνεῦμα ἅγιον...ἀπόρροια ὡς φῶς ἀπὸ π. τὸ πνεῦμα Athenag.*leg.*24.2(M.6.945B); **4.** ref. Son; **a.** fire as symbol of Christ in OT ἐν ἰδέᾳ πυρὸς ἐκ βάτου προσωμίλησεν αὐτῷ [sc. Moses] ὁ ἡμέτερος Χριστός Just.*1apol.*62.3(M.6.421C); *ib.*63.10(424C); υἱόν...ὃν καὶ ἄνθρωπον γεννηθῆναι διὰ τῆς παρθένου βεβούληται, ὃς καὶ π. ποτε γέγονε τῇ πρὸς Μωϋσέα ὁμιλίᾳ τῇ ἀπὸ τῆς βάτου id.*dial.*127.4(M.6.773A); exegesis opposed by Trypho, *ib.*60.1(612B); τὸ π. ἐκεῖνο τὸ ἐοικὸς στύλῳ καὶ π. τὸ διὰ βάτου σύμβολόν ἐστι φωτὸς ἁγίου τοῦ διαβαίνοντος ἐκ γῆς καὶ ἀνατρέχοντος αὖθις εἰς οὐρανὸν διὰ τοῦ ξύλου Clem.*str.*1.24(p.103.4; M.8.912A); **b.** of Christ's divinity; ref. Christ's soul, cf. *illa anima, quae quasi ferrum in igne sic semper in verbo...posita est, omne quod agit, quod sentit, quod intelligit, deus est...ad omnes denique sanctos calor aliquis verbi dei putandus est pervenisse, in hac autem anima ignis ipse divinus substantialiter requievisse credendus est, ex quo ad ceteros calor aliquis venerit,* Or.*princ.*2.6.6(p.145.18ff.; M.11.214A,B); *addit et ligna altari, quo ignis animetur..., is, a quo non solum de corporalibus virtutibus Christi, sed etiam de divinitate ejus sermo miscetur. desursum enim est divinitas Christi, quo ignis iste festinat. convenienter ergo omnia haec, quae in corpore a salvatore gesta sunt, coelestis ignis absumpsit et ad divinitatis ejus naturam cuncta restituit. lignis tamen adhibitis ignis iste succenditur; usque ad lignum enim in carne passio fuit Christi. ubi autem suspensus in ligno est, dispensatio carnis finita est; resurgens enim a mortuis adscendit ad coelum, quo iter ejus natura ignis ostendit,* id.*hom.1.4 in Lev.*(p.286.17ff.; M.12.410A,B); εἰ θαμβεῖ σε τὸ θαῦμα, πῶς τὸ τῆς θεότητος π. σαρκὶ συνεπλάκη ὑλικῇ, ὅρα μοι καὶ πρὶν ἔνδροσον κάμινον, ἀμάχους δύο ἐναντίας ἔχουσαν φύσεις, π. ὁμοῦ καὶ δρόσου. ἔχεις καὶ τὴν βάτον τὴν Σιναΐτιδα, τοῦ μὲν χόρτου ταύτης εἰς τύπον νοουμένου τῆς σαρκὸς τοῦ Χριστοῦ· πᾶσα γάρ, φησί, σὰρξ χόρτος· τοῦ δὲ ἐν αὐτῇ ἀδιαιρέτου π. εἰκόνα ἔχοντος τῆς ἐν σαρκὶ ἀδιαιρέτου τοῦ λόγου θεότητος Eulog.*fr.Trin.*4.1(p.369); ref. Christ's baptism τὸν τῆς δικαιοσύνης ἥλιον ἐν Ἰορδάνῃ λουόμενον, καὶ π. ἐν ὕδατι βαπτιζόμενον Procl.CP *or.*7.2(M.65.760A); Geo.Pis.*carm.*80.2; but cf. οὐ γὰρ κατὰ τὸ ἐξαπτόμενον ἐκ τῆς θέρμης τοῦ ἡλίου π., ὅπερ καὶ σβέννυσθαι πάλιν εἴωθεν, εἰρήκασιν οἱ ἅγιοι εἶναι τὸν λόγον πρὸς τὸν θεόν Ath.*decr.*23(p.19.11; M.25.456D); **c.** in simile of Christ's death, ref. Inc. διὰ τοῦτο ἐνεδύσατο σῶμα, ἵνα τὸν θάνατον ἐν τῷ σώματι εὑρὼν ἀπαλείψῃ. πῶς γὰρ ἂν ὅλως ὁ κύριος ἐδείχθη ζωή, εἰ μὴ τὸ θνητὸν ἐζωοποίησε; καὶ ὥσπερ τῆς καλάμης ὑπὸ πυρὸς φύσει φθειρομένης, εἰ κωλύει τις τὸ π. ἀπὸ τῆς καλάμης, οὐ καίεται μὲν ἡ καλάμη, μένει δὲ ὅλως πάλιν καλάμη ἡ καλάμη ὑποπτεύουσα τὴν τοῦ π. ἀπειλήν· φύσει γὰρ ἀναλωτικόν ἐστιν αὐτῆς τὸ π.· εἰ δέ τις ἐνδιδύσκοι τὴν καλάμην ἀμιάντῳ πολλῷ, ὃ δὴ λέγεται ἀντιπαθὲς εἶναι τοῦ π., οὐκ ἔτι τὸ π. φοβεῖται ἡ καλάμη, ἔχουσα τὴν ἀσφάλειαν ἐκ τοῦ ἐνδύματος τοῦ ἀκαύστου· τὸν αὐτὸν δὴ τρόπον καὶ ἐπὶ τοῦ σώματος καὶ ἐπὶ τοῦ θανάτου ἄν τις εἴποι· ὅτι εἰ προστάξει μόνον κωλυθεὶς ἦν ὁ θάνατος ὑπ' αὐτοῦ, οὐδὲν ἧττον πάλιν ἦν θνητόν...κατὰ τὸν τῶν σωμάτων λόγον. ἀλλ' ἵνα μὴ τοῦτο γένηται, ἐνεδύσατο τὸν ἀσώματον τοῦ θεοῦ λόγον Ath.*inc.*44.7f.(M.25.176B); **5.** ref. H. Ghost, exeg. Ac.2:3 ἡ πνοὴ καθάπερ κολυμβήθρα γέγονεν ὕδατος· τῆς δαψιλείας δὲ τοῦτο τεκμήριον καὶ τῆς σφοδρότητος τὸ π. ... τὸ π. ἐκάθισε. διατί δὲ μὴ ἐφάνη π. τὸν οἶκον πληροῦν; ὅτι ἐξέστησαν ἄν... τοσοῦτον π. μυρίαν ὕλην ἀνάψαι δύναται Chrys.*hom.4.2 in Ac.*(9.34D–35A); ὥσπερ ἐπὶ τοῦ π., ὅσους ἂν τις θέλοι λύχνους ἀνάπτει, τὸ π. οὐδὲν ἐλαττῶν· οὕτω καὶ ἐπὶ τῶν ἀποστόλων συνέβαινε τότε...διὰ τοῦ π. οὐ μόνον τὸ δαψιλὲς τῆς χάριτος ἐδείκνυτο, ἀλλὰ καὶ πηγὴν ἕκαστος ἐλάμβανε πνεύματος *ib.*(35B,C); **6.** ref. eucharist ἀναλογιζέσθω τῆς φρικτῆς ταύτης τραπέζης τὴν ἀπόλαυσιν, καὶ τοῦ ἐντεῦθεν ἐκπηδῶντος π. τὴν φαιδρότητα, καὶ τὴν καυστικὴν δύναμιν Chrys.*hom.24.8 in Gen.*(4.229D); τοῦ θείου ἄνθρακος μεταλάβωμεν, ἵνα τὸ π. τοῦ ἐν ἡμῖν πόθου προσλαβὸν τὴν ἐκ τοῦ ἄνθρακος πύρωσιν...καὶ τῇ μετουσίᾳ τοῦ θείου π. ... θεωθῶμεν Jo.D.*f.o.*4.13(M.94.1149B); **7.** divine fire in human soul; **a.** origin, cf. *vis tibi ostendam, quomodo de verbis spiritus sancti ignis exeat et accendat corda credentium? audi dicentem David in psalmo: eloquium domini ignivit eum...tu ergo unde ardebis?...unde in te ignis accenditur, qui numquam in divinis meditaris eloquiis?* Or.*hom.9.9 in Lev.*(p.437.21ff.; M.12.522C,D); δεῖ καὶ ἡμᾶς εἰς ἑαυτοὺς τὸ θεῖον ἐξάψαι π. μετὰ δακρύων καὶ πόνων *Apophth.Patr.*(M.65.421B); **b.** properties, cf. *ipse est qui et ignis efficitur in cordibus illorum, quibus adaperit scripturas...aliis ille ignis est, qui conflagrat spinas de terra mala, id est qui malignas cogitationes in corde consumit,* Or.*hom.7.8 in Ex.*(p.216.25ff.; M.12.349D–350A); οἱ Χριστιανοὶ τὸ ἐπουράνιον π. ἐκεῖνο ἔχουσι βρῶσιν. ... ἐκεῖνο...ἁγιάζει αὐτῶν τὴν καρδίαν...ἐκεῖνο αὐτοῖς ἐστιν ἀήρ, καὶ ζωή. ἂν δὲ ἐκεῖθεν ἐξέλθωσιν, ἀπόλλυνται ὑπὸ τῶν πονηρῶν πνευμάτων Mac.Aeg.*hom.*14.7(M.34.573D); τοιοῦτον γὰρ τὸ π. τὸ πνευματικόν· οὐδεμίαν ἐπιθυμίαν ἀφίησιν ἔχειν τῶν ἐνταῦθα, ἀλλ' εἰς ἕτερον ἡμᾶς μεθίστησιν ἔρωτα...ἡ γὰρ τοῦ π. ἐκείνου θερμότης εἰς τὴν ψυχὴν εἰσιοῦσα, πᾶσαν ἐκβάλλει νωθείαν Chrys.*hom.6.5 in Mt.*(7.94C); **c.** as symbol of union with God οὐ δύνασαι γενέσθαι μοναχός, ἐὰν μὴ γένῃ ὡς π. φλογιζόμενος ὅλος *Apophth.Patr.*(M.65.229C); ἐδείχθη αὐτῷ στῦλος πυρὸς ἀπὸ τῆς γῆς ἕως τοῦ οὐρανοῦ, καὶ φωνὴ λέγουσα· εἰ δύνασαι γενέσθαι ὡς ὁ στῦλος οὗτος, ὕπαγε, διακόνησον *ib.*(193B); εἶδον ἄγγελον κυρίου...καὶ ἔθηκε τὴν χεῖρα αὐτοῦ εἰς τὴν κεφαλὴν τοῦ κληρικοῦ, καὶ ἐγένετο ὁ κληρικὸς ὡς στῦλος π. *ib.*(304C); τρεῖς μοναχοὶ ἔστηκαν πέραν τῆς θαλάσσης· καὶ ἐγένετο φωνὴ...λέγουσα· λάβετε πτερὰ πυρός, καὶ δεῦτε πρὸς μέ. καὶ οἱ μὲν δύο ἔλαβον, καὶ ἐπετάσθησαν εἰς τὸ ἄλλο πέραν· ὁ δὲ ἄλλος ἔμεινε, καὶ ἔκλαιε. ὕστερον δὲ ἐδόθησαν καὶ αὐτῷ πτερά, οὐ μέντοι π., ἀλλ' ἀσθενῆ...οὕτως καὶ ἡ γενεὰ αὕτη, εἰ καὶ λαμβάνει πτερά, οὐ μέντοι π. *ib.*(208C,D); θεὸν...τῇ πρὸς αὐτὸν ἑνώσει δίκην πυρὸς ἀφομοιῶσαι τὰ ἑνωθέντα, κατὰ τὴν αὐτῶν πρὸς θέωσιν ἐπιτηδειότητα Dion.Ar.*e.h.*2.2.1(M.3.393A); θαρρῶ γάρ, ὅτι τοῖς εἰρημένοις ἐγὼ τοὺς ἐναποκειμένους ἐν σοὶ τοῦ θείου π. ἀνασκαλεύσω σπινθῆρας *ib.*7.3.11(569A); **d.** action after death τὸ π. τὸ οὐράνιον τῆς θεότητος, ὅπερ δέχονται οἱ Χριστιανοὶ ἐντὸς αὐτῶν ἐν τῇ καρδίᾳ νῦν ἐν τῷ αἰῶνι τούτῳ...ὅταν ἀναλυθῇ τὸ σῶμα, ἐξώτερον γίνεται...καὶ ποιεῖ ἀνάστασιν τῶν λελυμένων μελῶν...τὸ πλησίον σῶμα, ὃ μετὰ τὸ λυθῆναι γίνεται βόρβορος, ἐργάζεται τὸ οὐράνιον π. καὶ ἀνακαινίζει, καὶ ἀνιστᾷ τὰ ἐφθαρμένα σώματα. τὸ γὰρ νῦν ἐσώτερον ἐν τῇ καρδίᾳ ἐνοικοῦν π., τότε ἔξωθεν γίγνεται, καὶ ποιεῖ ἀνάστασιν τῶν σωμάτων Mac.Aeg.*hom.*11.1(M.34.544D–545A); **e.** exeg. Dan.3:20ff. ἐπὶ τοῦ Ναβουχοδονόσορ, τὸ π. ἐν τῇ καμίνῳ οὐκ ἦν θεϊκόν, ἀλλ' ἦν κτίσμα· οἱ δὲ τρεῖς παῖδες διὰ τὴν δικαιοσύνην αὐτῶν ἐν τῷ φαινομένῳ π. ὄντες, ἐν ταῖς καρδίαις αὐτῶν εἶχον τὸ θεϊκὸν οὐράνιον π. ... καὶ αὐτὸ ἐκεῖνο ἐφάνη ἐξώτερον αὐτῶν· ἀνὰ μέσον γὰρ αὐτῶν ἔστη, καὶ ἐπεῖχε τὸ φαινόμενον π., τοῦ μὴ καίειν...τοὺς δικαίους...ὥσπερ οὖν οἱ τρεῖς παῖδες...ἐδέξαντο ἐν ἑαυτοῖς τὸ τοῦ θεοῦ π. ... οὕτω καὶ νῦν αἱ πισταὶ ψυχαὶ δέχονται ἐκεῖνο τὸ θεϊκὸν...π., ἐν τῷ αἰῶνι τούτῳ, ἐν τῷ κρυπτῷ· καὶ αὐτὸ ἐκεῖνο μορφοῖ εἰκόνα ἐπουράνιον εἰς τὴν ἀνθρωπότητα *ib.*11.2(545A–C); **8.** ref. angels οἱ μὲν ἄγγελοι νοερὸν π. καὶ πνεύματα νοερά...φῶς δὲ νοερὸν μεγίστη προκοπὴ ἀπὸ τοῦ νοεροῦ π. ἀποκεκαθαρμένου τέλεον Clem.*exc.Thdot.*12(p.110.26ff.; M.9.661C–664A); ref. Ps.103:4 ἐπὶ τῶν οὐρανίων δυνάμεων. ἡ μὲν οὐσία αὐτῶν, ἀέριον πνεῦμα...ἢ π. ἄυλον Bas.*Spir.*38(3.32C; M.32.137A); κύριος ἥξει...προτρεχόντων τῶν ταγμάτων ἐνώπιον τῆς δόξης αὐτοῦ ἀγγέλων, ἀρχαγγέλων, πάντες φλόγες πυρὸς ὄντες Ephr.2.229F; angels as π. ἄυλον Jo.D.*f.o.*2.3(M.94.865A); **9.** miraculous fire, surrounding martyrs, *A.Phil.*126

(p.55.11); *A.Paul.et Thecl.*34(p.261.1ff.); in vision ἀνέστη κατακλυσμὸς π., καὶ σύρας ἀπώλεσε τοὺς λύκους Agath.*v.Gr.Ill.*114(p.58).

I. various forms of fire contrasted; **1.** purging fire of persecution and sufferings contrasted with hell fire τὸ π. ἦν αὐτοῖς ψυχρὸν τὸ τῶν ἀπανθρώπων βασανιστῶν· πρὸ ὀφθαλμῶν γὰρ εἶχον φυγεῖν τὸ αἰώνιον καὶ μηδέποτε σβεννύμενον *M.Polyc.*2.3; *ib.*11.2; *Diogn.*10.7,8; Or. *hom.18.1 in Jer.*(p.151.14ff.; M.13.464B,C); **2.** material and spiritual fire, exeg. Jer.20:9 εἴρηκέ τι εἶναι εἶδος πυρός, π. οὐκ αἰσθητοῦ, κολάζοντος τὸν κολαζόμενον τῷ πόνῳ εἰς τὸ μὴ φέρειν αὐτόν...φοβοῦμαι μὴ τοιοῦτόν ἐστι τὸ ἀποκείμενον ἡμῖν, π. γινόμενον, ὡς ἐν τῇ καρδίᾳ γέγονεν Ἱερεμίου. οὐ πεπόνθαμεν δὲ αὐτό. εἰ ἐπεπόνθειμεν τοῦτο, καὶ προέκειτο τὰ δύο π., τοῦτο τὸ π. καὶ τὸ ἔξωθεν π. ὃ βλέπομεν ἐπὶ τῶν καιομένων ὑπὸ τῶν ἡγουμένων τῶν ἐθνῶν, εἱλόμεθα ἂν ἐκεῖνο μᾶλλον τὸ π. ἢ τοῦτο. ἐκεῖνο μὲν γὰρ καίει τὴν ἐπιφάνειαν, τοῦτο δὲ καίει τὴν καρδίαν, καὶ ἀρξάμενον ἀπὸ τῆς καρδίας διϊκνεῖται ἐπὶ πάντα τὰ ὀστᾶ...καὶ οὕτως ἔρχεται ὡς μὴ δύνασθαι τὸν καιόμενον φέρειν. ...οἶδα καὶ λῃστὰς τοῦτο τὸ π. δυνηθέντας ὑπομεῖναι, τὸν πόνον ⟨τὸν⟩ ἀπὸ τούτου τοῦ π. ἄλλος ἐστὶν ὁ πόνος ὁ ἀπὸ τοῦ π., ὃν διέγραψεν Ἱερεμίας λέγων· 'καὶ ἐγένετο ἐν τῇ καρδίᾳ μου ὡς π. καιόμενον...καὶ οὐ δύναμαι φέρειν.' ἐκεῖνο τὸ π. ἐκκαίει ὁ σωτὴρ ὁ εἰπών· 'π. ἦλθον βαλεῖν ἐπὶ τὴν γῆν.' καὶ ἐπεὶ ἐκεῖνο τὸ π. ἐκκαίει ὁ σωτήρ, διὰ τοῦτο τοῖς ἀρχομένοις ἀκούειν αὐτοῦ ἄρχεται ἀπὸ τοῦ π. καὶ πρῶτον π. βάλλει αὐτῶν ἐπὶ τὴν καρδίαν· ὅπερ ὁμολογοῦσι Σίμων καὶ Κλεόπας λέγοντες ἐπὶ τοῖς λόγοις αὐ⟨τοῦ⟩ τὸ 'οὐχὶ ἡ καρδία καιομένη ἦν ἐν τῇ ὁδῷ...;' ἐνθάδε ἡ καρδία καίεται πυρί Or.*hom.20.8 in Jer.*(pp.190.23–191.14; M.13.520C–521A); *ib.*20.9(p.192.12ff.; 521D); **3.** divine fire and fire of sin, cf. '*offerre debes deo hostiam laudis*'...*sed ut haec digne offeras, indumentis tibi opus est mundis...et ignem divinum necessarium habes, non aliquem alienum a deo, sed illum, qui a deo hominibus datur...si enim non hoc, sed alio et huic contrario igni utamur, illo, qui se transfigurat sicut angelum lucis, eadem sine dubio patiemur, quae Nadab passus est*, Or.*hom.9.1 in Lev.*(p.419.4ff.; M.12.509A,B); **4.** material and immaterial fire λείπεται δεῖξαι, ποῦ τὸ π. ἐγένετο. εἶπεν ὁ θεός· γενηθήτω φῶς, καὶ ἐγένετο ἡ τοῦ π. φύσις· οὐ γὰρ μόνον τοῦτο τὸ π. ἐστιν, ἀλλὰ καὶ αἱ ἄνω δυνάμεις π. εἰσι, καὶ συγγενές ἐστι τὸ ἄνω π. τούτου τοῦ παρ' ἡμῖν. ζητεῖτε δέ, ὅτι τὸ μὲν σβέννυται, τὸ δὲ οὐ σβέννυται...τὸ π. τὸ ἄνω ἄνευ ὕλης, τὸ π. τὸ κάτω μετὰ ὕλης· τὸ γὰρ ἄνω π. συγγενὲς τούτων ἐστίν, ὥσπερ καὶ ἡ ψυχὴ ἡμῶν συγγενὴς ἀγγέλων... οὔτε οὖν ψυχὴ ἄνευ σώματος φαίνεται, οὔτε π. ἄνευ στυππείου...ἢ ἑτέρας ὕλης ἔστιν ἰδεῖν. ἵνα δὲ δειχθῇ ὅτι τὸ π. τοῦτο οὐκ ἔστιν ἀλλότριον, ἡ κτίσις διδάσκει. πολλοὶ γὰρ πολλάκις παρὰ τοῦ ἡλίου δανείζονται π., καὶ ἅπτουσιν· εἰ δὲ ἦν ἀλλότριον, πῶς τὸ ἀλλότριον ἐξ αὐτοῦ ἐλαμβάνετο; ἄλλως δὲ οὕτως ἐν τῷ οὐρανῷ π. ἐστιν ἄυλον μέγα, ὡς καὶ ἐν τῷ ὄρει Σινᾷ π. φανῆναι, ὅπερ οὐ ξύλων ὑποκειμένων, ἀλλ' ἐξ αὐτοῦ τοῦ ἀύλου π. ἤγαγεν ὁ θεὸς εἰς θέαν...πάντα οὖν π. ἐστι, καὶ ἀστραπή, καὶ οἱ ἀστέρες...καὶ τὸ παρ' ἡμῖν π. συγγενές ἐστι Sever.*creat.*1.4(M.56.434); **5.** illuminating and burning fire, cf.Or.*hom.13.4 in Ex.*(pp.275.16–276.4; M.12.392A,B).

J. met.; **1.** of wrath, Eus.*v.C.*1.32(p.23.1; M.20.948C); esp. wrath of God, Or.*hom.5.15 in Jer.*(p.45.7ff.; M.13.320A,B); Chrys.*exp.in Ps.*45:10(5.186C); **2.** of animal desires, passions, and sin π. φιλόυλον Ign.*Rom.*7.2; Just.*dial.*116.2(M.6.744C); Clem.*paed.*2.2(p.168.16f.; M.8.412B); ref. Ezech.1:27 τίνα μὲν τρόπον αὐτοῦ 'τὰ ἀπὸ τῆς ὀσφύος κάτω' ἐστὶν π., 'τὰ δὲ ἀπὸ τῆς ὀσφύος καὶ ἄνω' ἐστὶν ἤλεκτρον, ἐρευνησάτω τὸν λόγον, διὰ τί τὸ κάτω τοῦ θεοῦ π. ἐστιν. τὰ ἀπὸ ὀσφύος καὶ γενέσεως πράγματα, ταῦτα π. ἐστιν...πάντα τὰ ἐν γενέσει χρήζει τῆς κολάσεως. τὰ δὲ ἀνωτέρω τῆς ὀσφύος...ταῦτά ἐστιν ὕλη ὡς ἐν κόσμῳ καθαριωτάτη...λέγεται γὰρ τὸ ἤλεκτρον χρυσοῦ εἶναι τιμαλφέστερον. ἐπεὶ οὖν παραδείγμασιν χρῆται ἡ γραφή...διὰ τοῦτο εἰσήγαγεν τὸν θεὸν ἐκ π. καὶ ἠλέκτρου συνεστηκότα...ἐν γενέσει π. ἐστιν ἕκαστος ἡμῶν, οὐκ ἐσμὲν τὸ ἤλεκτρον, ἐὰν δὲ ἀναβαίνωμεν...ἐσόμεθα διαβάντες τὸ π. ἤλεκτρον τὸ περὶ τὸ σῶμα τοῦ θεοῦ τὸ ὑψηλότερον Or.*hom. 11.5 in Jer.*(p.83.12ff.; M.13.373C–376A); id.*hom.1.3 in Ezech.*(p.323.25ff.; M.13.769D); ref. Num.26:61 cf. *concalescis in equorum contentionibus, in certamine athletarum? atque iste ignis non est de altari domini, sed hic est, qui dicitur ignis alienus,...concalescis et cum te repleverit iracundia et cum te inflammaverit furor, ureris interdum et amore carnali...sed omnis iste ignis alienus est et contrarius deo*, id.*hom.9.9 in Lev.*(p.438.2ff.; M.12.523A); τοῦ διαρρυέντος τοῖς παραπτώμασιν λογικοῦ νοῦ, καὶ ἐμπρησθέντος, ἀλλοτρίῳ π.· ὅπερ ἡμεῖς ἐξεκαύσαμεν, πορευθέντες τῷ φωτὶ τοῦ π. ἡμῶν, καὶ τῇ φλογί, ᾗ ἐξεκαύσαμεν Max.*qu.Thal.*54(M.90.520A); π. μὲν ἡμῶν ὑπάρχει ψεκτόν, ὁ τῆς σαρκὸς νόμος· φῶς δὲ τούτου τοῦ π. ἐστιν, ἡ κατὰ τοῦτον τὸν ψεκτὸν νόμον ἐν ἕξει τῶν παθῶν ἡ κίνησις...ἢ πάλιν, π. μέν ἐστι ψεκτόν, ἡ κακία· φῶς δὲ ψεκτόν, ἡ τῆς κακίας ἕξις...οὐ δεῖ οὖν τούτῳ τὸν νοῦν θερμαίνεσθαι τῷ π. *Schol.*20 *ib.*(532B,C); of concupiscence, †Bas.Anc.*virg.*14(M.30.700A,B); **3.** of heresy, ref. Num.26:61, cf. *cui scripturae haeretici ignem alienum imponentes, hoc est sensum et intelligentiam alienam a deo et veritati contrariam introducentes*, Or.*hom.9.1 in Num.*(p.54.21; M.12.625B); **4.** ref. conscience ὅσον πλείω καίεται ὑπὸ τοῦ τῆς λύπης π., τοσοῦτον μᾶλλον ἐλεεῖται id.*hom.20.9 in Jer.*(p.192.3; M.13.521C); cf.id.*hom.10.5 in Ezech.*(p.423.8; M.13.745A); Ath.*ep.Drac.*6(M.25.529C); and penitence, cf.Or.*hom.4.8 in Ex.*(p.180.23; M.12.323D); **5.** of love; **a.** natural, id.*mart.*27(p.23.24; M.11.596C); **b.** supernatural; for Christ, Just.*dial.*8.1(M.6.492C); cf.Or.*Cant.*proem.(p.67.16; M.13.67C); Ephr.1.294A; **6.** of grace, faith, etc., cf. *quia autem possit interdum divinus ignis exstingui etiam in sanctis...audi apostolum Paulum*...[1Thess.5:19] Or.*hom.15.3 in Gen.*(p.129.20; M.12.241D); cf. *ignis fidei*, id.*hom.4.6 in Lev.*(p.324.3; M.12.440C); cf.*ib.*9.9 (p.437.15; 522C); ref. truth, cf.id.*hom.13.2 in Num.*(p.109.32; M.12.668C); ref. prayer, v. εὐχή; **7.** ref. preachers, exeg. Ex.35:6 and Jer.5:14, cf. *si doctor es, exstruis tabernaculum aedificans ecclesiam dei; dicit ergo et ad te deus, quod ad Jeremiam dixit: ecce, dedi verba mea in os tuum ignem. si ergo docens et aedificans ecclesiam dei increpas tantummodo...nihil autem consolationis proferas de scripturis...obtulisti quidem coccum, sed non duplicatum. ignis enim tuus incendit tantummodo et non illuminat*, Or.*hom.13.4 in Ex.* (p.276.14ff.; M.12.392C).

K. fire leading to true worship by destroying pagan sanctuaries, Clem.*prot.*4(p.41.4ff.; M.8.145C–148A).

L. for opinion that Adam's name means fire, v. Ἀδάμ.

M. fire as creative; idea attributed to Messalians, Jo.D.*haer.*80 (M.94.732A).

N. 'Greek fire' π. θαλάσσιον Thphn.*chron.*p.295(M.108.721A); π. ὑγρὸν *ib.*p.331(800A).

πυρά, ἡ, 1. *funeral pyre*, Just.*1apol.*21.3(M.6.360B); **2.** *fire*, cf. π. *ignis est*, Isid.H.*etym.*10.221; **a.** lit., *M.Polyc.*13.3; Athenag.*leg.*29.1 (M.6.957B); Hipp.*haer.*4.32(p.58.16; M.16.3095A); **b.** of fire of divine love, Thdt.*Cant.*2:7(2.60); of sensual passion, Chrys.*virg.*34(1.292E); Thdt.*provid.*6(4.567); of despair, Chrys.*Laz.*5.4(1.768D); of disease, Thdt.*provid.*6(583); of fiery language, Chrys.*hom.9.2 in 1Cor.*(10.75B); **3.** *conflagration, disturbance* π. χαλεπὴν κατὰ τῆς τῶν Γαλατῶν ἀναφθεῖσαν ἐκκλησίας id.*comm.in Gal.*1:1–3(10.658E).

πυράγρα, ἡ, *forceps*; used for torture, Const.Diac.*laud.*6(M.88.485B).

***πυρακίζω,** *be fiery red, blush*; of roses, *Asen.*18(p.68.10).

πυρακτ-όω, *heat, make red hot* πάντα ~ῶν ὁ αἰθήρ Bas.*hex.*3.7(1.29B; M.29.69B); pass. ~ούμενον καὶ χαλκευόμενον τὸ ἄγαλμα Meth. *res.*1.43(p.290.6; M.18.272A); esp. of iron, in simile μοιρά τίς ἐστιν ἐγκεφάλου, διὰ παντὸς ἑαυτοῦ τὸ ψυχικὸν ἔχον πνεῦμα, ὡς ὁ πεπυρακτωμένος σίδηρος ἔχει τὸ πῦρ Nemes.*nat.hom.*8(M.40.652B); illustrating coinherence of H. Ghost in Trin., Bas.*Spir.*63(3.53A; M.32.184B); illustrating union of natures in Christ, Thdt.*eran.*2(4.116); illustrating potentiality opp. actuality; of perfection, etc., Isid.Pel. *epp.*4.81(M.78.1144C); Max.*ambig.*(M.91.1076A); met. τῷ περὶ τὴν κτίστην ~ούμενοι πόθῳ Didym.*Trin.*1.32(M.39.429C); Ἠλίαν...ζήλῳ ...~ούμενον Bas.Sel.*or.*11.3(M.85.157A); ἀγάπης πυρσῷ ~ούμενοι Sophr.H.*ep.syn.*(M.87.3197A).

***πυράκτωσις, ἡ,** *inflammation*, Eustrat.*v.Eutych.*54(M.86.2336C); met. ἡ...τῆς πορνείας π., πρὸς ἐκείνην βλέπει τὴν κάμινον Isid.Pel.*epp.* 1.433(M.78.421B); of heresy, Sophr.H.*ep.syn.*(M.87.3185A).

πυραμίς, ἡ, a sort of *cake*, Clem.*prot.*2(p.17.6; M.8.88B).

πυράφλεκτος, *unburnt by fire*; of burning bush, ‡Ath.*occurs.*16 (M.28.993C).

πυρβόλος, *casting fire*, Epiph.*haer.*31.1(p.382.16; M.41.473A).

πυργόβαρις, ἡ, 1. *fortified tower*, *Pss.Sal.*8.21; ref. Ps.121:7 οἱ μεγάλοι δὲ πύργοι λέγονται π. ἐν τοῖς τείχεσι κατασκοπῆς χάριν τῶν ἐπιόντων γινόμενοι Didym.*Ps.*121:7(M.39.1581B); οἱ πρόβολοι [i.e. heretics] κατὰ τῶν ἐκκλησιαστικῶν π., Ὀνώριος, Σέργιος, κτλ. ‡Jo.D. *ep.Thphl.*8(M.95.3356B); **2.** *siege tower*, ref. spiritual warfare σοφία ...ἀποσώζει [sc. τὴν ψυχήν] καὶ καταργεῖ τὰς...π. τῶν αἰσθητῶν ἐφέδρων καὶ νοητῶν Gr.Agr.*Eccl.*7.1(M.98.1024C).

***πυργοκάστελλος, ὁ,** *siege tower*, *Chron.Pasch.*p.394(M.92.1009B); *ib.*p.396(1016A).

πυργομαχέω, *assault*; pass., met. ὀργάνοις τιμωρητικοῖς ἐπυργομαχεῖτο τὴν γνώμην Pall.*h.Laus.*3(p.19.2; ἐπυργομαχεῖ τῇ γνώμῃ M. 34.1012B).

***πυργοποιέω,** *build the tower* of Babel, Or.*fr.9 in Jer.*(p.201.22; M.13.556D); Hesych.H.*fr.Ps.*76:12(M.93.1245C).

πυργοποιΐα, ἡ, 1. *building of the tower* of Babel τὰς γλώσσας... διακριθείσας ἐν τῇ π. ‡Hipp.*fr.17 in Pss.*(p.145.8; M.10.720D); Gr.

Nyss.*Eun*.12(2 p.287.3; M.45.996B); ἐν γὰρ βίβλῳ Γενέσεως, ἐν τῇ π. ὁ θεὸς...τὰς μακαρίας ὑποστάσεις ἐξέφηνεν Didym.*Trin*.1.18(M.39.348A); Epiph.*haer*.3(p.178.19; M.41.189B); contrasted with pentecostal unification of tongues, Chrys.*hom.35.1 in 1Cor*.(10.321C); compared with Nestorian confusion of truth by doctrinal subtleties, Leont.H.*Nest*.4.27(M.86.1693A); Cosm.Ind.*top*.3(M.88.136B); Jo.Mal.*chron*.3 p.58(M.97.136A); *Chron.Pasch*.p.22(M.92.105C); met. ἡ κρηπὶς καὶ ἡ ὑποβάθρα τῆς αἱρετικῆς π. Gr.Nyss.*Eun*.1(1 p.195.10; M.45.441A); ἔδει γὰρ τοὺς ἐπὶ τῇ γηΐνῃ π. τὴν ὁμοφωνίαν λύσαντας, ἐπὶ τῇ πνευματικῇ...τῆς ἐκκλησίας οἰκοδομῇ εἰς ὁμοφωνίαν ἐλθεῖν id.*Steph*.1(M.45.705A); τὸ πλῆθος ἡμῖν ἐπισείεις, ὥσπερ ἀπειλῶν τῷ θεῷ π. δευτέραν Euther.*confut*.1(M.28.1340D); **2.** *tower* of Babel κτίζουσι ...τὴν π. καὶ οἰκοδομοῦσι τὴν Βαβυλῶνα Epiph.*haer*.2(p.176.2; M.41.184A); *ib*.3(p.176.20; 185B); **3.** *defence-work* τούτων ὥσπερ ἀπό τινος ὀξυβελοῦς μηχανήματος...τῇ τῶν ἐναντίων π. διαφεθέντων Const.Diac.*laud*.26(M.88.508D); **4.** *building of a stronghold*; met., of hospitality as καλὴ π. in spiritual life, Ephr.3.300D.

***πυργοποιός, ὁ,** plur., *builders of the tower* of Babel, Ephr.3.542B.

πύργος, ὁ, 1. *tower*, representing Church in vision, Herm.*sim*.3.3.3ff.; βάρεις...ἐλεφαντίνας, τὰς ἐκκλησίας ἐν τούτοις φασί. βάρις μὲν γὰρ καλεῖται π. ἅπας· πεπυργῶσθαι δέ φαμεν τὰς ἐκκλησίας τῇ τοῦ Χριστοῦ δυνάμει καὶ χάριτι Cyr.*Ps*.44:9(M.69.1040D); exeg. Cant.4:4 ὡς π. Δαυὶδ τράχηλός σου, π. εἶναι τὴν σοφίαν Or.*schol.in Cant*.4:4(M.17.272B); 'neck' represents S. Paul in rel. to Christ as head; David is God who created man as a tower, equivalent to 'city set on a hill', Gr.Nyss.*hom.7 in Cant*.(M.44.932Bff.); Proc.G.*Cant*.4:4(M.87.1648A); exeg. π. ἐλεφάντινος (Cant.7:4): πύργοι...οἱ τὰ ἀρεστὰ τῷ νυμφίῳ ποιοῦντες, σκοπευτήριον ἔχοντες τὴν θεωρητικὴν ψυχήν Or.*schol.in Cant*.7:4(281C); represents τὸ εὐσεβὲς φρόνημα Nil.ap.Proc.G.*Cant*.7:2–5(M.87.1729B); met. π. ... τῆς εὐσεβείας Thdt.*h.e*.1.25.15(3.813); id.*provid*.10(4.657); ref. hope, Isid.Pel.*epp*.2.17(M.78.469A) cit. s. ἐλπίς; of God, Geo.Pis.*Sev*.692(M.92.1673A); **2.** *dice-box*, astrol. τὸ δὲ ψηφόβολον καὶ τὰ ἐν αὐτῷ ἑπτὰ κοκκία τὰ ἑπτὰ ἄστρα, τὸν δὲ π. τὸ ὕψος τοῦ οὐρανοῦ, ἐξ οὗ ἀνταποδίδοται πᾶσι καλὰ καὶ κακά Jo.Mal.*chron*.5 p.103(M.97.192B).

πυργοφόρος, *bearing a tower*; met., of a woman with an elaborate hair style, Synes.*ep*.3(M.66.1325A).

***πυρεάζω,** *roast*, *A.Pil*.B 1(p.290n.).

πυρεῖον (πύριον), τό, 1. *censer*, *Dial.Tim.et Aquil*.97 r°(p.78); πύριον *Const.Stud*.2(M.99.1704D); **2.** *fire-temple* in Persia, Thdt.*h.e*.5.39.1(3.1082).

πυρέκβολος, 1. *emitting fire*; of flint stone, ‡Ath.*ep.Cast*.2(M.28.893D); ξύλων π. Leont.H.*Nest*.4.25(M.86.1689C); met. λόγων π. Geo.Pis.*bell.Avar*.476(M.92.1291A); **2.** neut. plur. as subst., *fire-throwing machines*, id.*hex*.512(M.92.1475A).

***πυρέκγονος,** *born of fire*; of salamander, Geo.Pis.*hex*.1042(M.92.1514A).

***πυρεκτιάω,** *be fevered*, Max.*ambig*.(M.91.1349B).

***πυρένδροσος,** *bedewed with fire, containing fire from heaven* τὴν π. βάτον Leont.N.*serm*.3 cit.ap.Jo.D.*imag*.1.27(M.94.1273B) for τὴν ἄφλεκτον βάτον (M.93.1608A).

***πυρένθεος,** *containing divine fire* τὸ π. θυσιαστήριον Leont.N.*serm*.3 cit.ap.Jo.D.*imag*.1.27(M.94.1273B) for τὸ θυσιαστήριον (M.93.1608A).

πυρέσσ-ω, *be feverish*; hence, c. acc., *suffer from, be afflicted with* δεισιδαιμονίαν ∼ων Eust.*engast*.27(p.58.29; M.18.669A); πολυθεΐαν ∼ουσιν Caes.Naz.*dial*.108(M.38.976).

πυρεταίν-ω, *be feverish*, met. εἴ πως δυνηθείης τὸ ∼ον τῆς σαρκὸς φρόνημα καταςβέσαι Nil.*Eulog*.23(M.79.1124B).

πυρεύ-ω, *kindle*, met. τοὺς...εἰς εὐσέβειαν ∼σαντες λογισμούς Thdt.*Ps*.61:3(1.1013).

[*]**πυρέω,** *fire up*; met., *become angry*, Dor.*doct*.18(M.88.1805C).

***πυρίβροχος,** *rained upon by fire*; of Sodomites, Ephr.3.542B.

***πυρίγλωσσος,** *fiery-tongued* τοῦ π. ... Ἡσαΐου Jo.Eub.*concept.BMV* 2(M.96.1461B); π. ῥητόρων Dam.*troph*.2.2(p.219.6).

πυρίδιον, τό, *spark, fiery particle*, acc. Xenophanes' theory τὸν ἥλιον ἐκ μικρῶν π. ἀθροιζομένων γίνεσθαι καθ' ἑκάστην ἡμέραν Hipp.*haer*.1.14(p.17.20; M.16.3040A).

***πυρίζ-ω, 1.** *set on fire*, met. τοῦ θείου πνεύματος τοῦ...∼οντος τὸν ἔσω...ἄνθρωπον Ammon.*Ac*.19:5(M.85.1573D); **2.** *be on fire*, Eus.Al.*serm*.1(M.86.317A); **3.** *be red, fiery*, ref. Is.63:1 ἐξ αἵματος δὲ καὶ σαρκὸς συνέστη ἐκεῖνος ὁ δερμάτινος ∼ων χιτών, ὃν πάλιν καὶ ἕτεροί τινες ὁρῶντες εἰς οὐρανοὺς ἀνερχόμενον, σύνθετον καὶ ἔνθεον καὶ ὁμόθεον, Εὐόῳ Χριστῷ λέγοντες 'ἵνα τί σου τὰ ἱμάτια ἐρυθρά;' Anast.S.*hex*.12(M.89.1053D).

πυρικαής, v. πυρρακής.

πυρίκαος, ὁ, ? *one who commits arson*; in pun on πατρίκιος, *Max.invect*.(M.90.204A).

***πυρικαυστέω,** *burn with fire*, Thdr.Stud.*epp*.2.81(M.99.1321A).

***πυρίμορφος,** *with the appearance of fire, fiery*, *Apoc.Bar*.6(p.88.27); Eulog.*palm*.2(M.86.2916C); τῷ π. θρόνῳ τοῦ ὑψίστου αὐτῷ παριστάμενος *Pap.Chr*.(p.436; saec. vi); τοῦ πνεύματος ἡ...πυρίμορφος ἐπιφοίτησις Jo.D.*hom*.9.4(M.96.729C); of tongues of angels, Jo.Mon.*hymn.Geo*.2(M.96.1396A); of BMV θρόνε π. Ephr.3.528C; Jo.Mon.*hymn.Chrys*.7(M.96.1381D); Germ.CP *hymn.BMV*(M.98.453C).

πύρινος, *fiery*; **1.** of divine presence αὐτὸς δὲ ὁ Τόπος π. ἐστι Clem.*exc.Thdot*.38(p.118.31; M.9.677B); **2.** ref. angelic beings ὥρα ιβ' ἐν ᾗ ἀναπαύονται τὰ π. τάγματα *Apoc.Adam*(p.144); χερουβὶν π. *Apoc.En*.14.11; τοὺς θρόνους...π. Dion.Ar.*c.h*.15.2(M.3.329A); id.*d.n*.1.8(M.3.597A); οἱ π. Rom.Mel.(*BZ* 24 p.6); **3.** of pentecostal tongues, Or.*Cels*.8.22(p.240.2; M.11.1552B); **4.** of Gnost. aeons (Naassene) δημιουργῷ Ἠσαλδαίῳ, θεῷ π. Hipp.*haer*.5.7(p.86.10; M.16.3135B); of third deity in Apelles' doctrine, *ib*.7.38(p.224.4; 3346A); who spoke to Moses from burning bush, *ib*.8.9(p.228.28; 3354A); Thdt.*haer*.1.25(4.317); **5.** πύρινος ποταμός at second advent (cf. Dan.7:10), Ephr.2.192F; π. ποταμὸν ἐξερχόμενον ἀπὸ ἀνατολῶν id.2.213D; id.2.251D; ‡Jo.D.*Const*.8(M.95.324D); **6.** ref. punishments in hell π. ποταμός *Orac.Sib*.2.286; ἐν π. ἁλύσεσσιν *ib*.2.288; π. τροχός *ib*.2.295; **7.** of garland worn in heathen rites (which is equivalent to χάραγμα τὸ ἐπὶ τῆς χειρὸς τῆς δεξιᾶς Apoc.13:16) π. καὶ...θανάτου στέφανον Hipp.*antichr*.49(p.33.1; M.10.769A).

πύριος, 1. *of fire* π. λίθων *flint* stones, Clem.*fr*.32(p.217.28); **2.** neut. as subst.; **a.** *flint stone*, Gr.Nyss.*bapt.diff*.(M.46.421B); **b.** = πυρεῖον.

πυρίπλοκος, *wrapped in fire*, ‡Hipp.*fr.22 in Pss*.(p.48.29; M.10.613B); ref. burning bush as type of BMV π. θαῦμα Thdr.Stud.*nativ.BMV* 7(M.96.689B).

***πυρισπείρητος,** *with network of fire*; of candelabrum, Paul.Sil.*Soph*.892(M.86.2153A).

πυρισπόρος, *scattering fire*; of candelabrum, Paul.Sil.*Soph*.879(M.86.2152B).

***πυρίστομος,** *speaking with fire* π. φλόγα Geo.Pis.*hex*.167(M.92.1445A).

***πυριφαγής,** *devouring like fire, consuming*, †Hipp.*narr*.(p.276.10; M.10.873A).

πυριφλεγής, *burning*, met. π. πόθῳ Nil.*epp*.2.183(M.79.296B); π. τῷ πρὸς θεὸν ἔρωτι Jo.Carp.*cap*.92(M.85.1855).

***πυριφλόγιστος,** *scorched by fire*, Tim.Ant.*Sym*.(M.86.237C).

πυρκαϊά, ἡ, *conflagration, fire* τῆς τοῦ διωγμοῦ π. Eus.*h.e*.6.2.3(M.20.524A); id.*m.P*.13(p.950.7; M.20.1517D).

***πυρκαϊάζω,** *make to burn* or *blaze up*; met., †Nil.*tract*.3(M.79.1284C).

πυροβόλος, *fire-darting* τοὺς π. λίθους *flint stones*, Or.*hom.8.5 in Jer*.(p.60.3; M.13.341C); Ant.Mon.*hom*.17(M.89.1480C).

***πυρογόνος,** *producing fire* (cf. foreg.) λίθων π. Or.*sel.in Jer*.10:13(M.13.549A).

***πυρόδροσος,** *of fire falling like dew* from heaven, ref. burning bush πυροδρόσου φλογὸς ἀφλεκτον ‡Cyr.H.*occurs*.12(M.33.1200A).

πυροειδής (πυρωδής), 1. *like fire, fiery in appearance*, Hipp.*haer*.4.32(p.58.17; M.16.3095A); Or.*Cels*.6.33(p.103.4; M.11.1348B); of Zeus as π. οὐσία *Hom.Clem*.6.7; Gr.Nyss.*v.Mos*.44(M.44.316A); τὴν ...ἐσθῆτα...τὴν π. σημαίνειν...τὸ θεοειδὲς κατὰ τὴν πυρὸς εἰκόνα Dion.Ar.*c.h*.15.4(M.3.333A); acc. Apelles and others, of third deity who appeared to Moses in burning bush, Hipp.*haer*.8.10(p.229.8; 3354B); **2.** *fiery, burning*, met. πυρωδέστερος γὰρ αὐτοῦ [sc. τοῦ ἡλίου] ὁ τῆς ἀληθείας...λόγος Just.*dial*.121.2(M.6.757A); τὸ π. ... τοῦ λόγου Hipp.*Dan*.4.37.4(M.10.657C); π. μανίας Const.ap.Gel.Cyz.*h.e*.2.7.26(M.85.1237B); πνεύματος...τὴν καρδίαν...π. ποιοῦντος Gr.Nyss.*hom.7 in Cant*.(M.44.933A); **3.** *hot* to taste, *pungent*, Thdt.Rom.1:16(3.20); **4.** masc. as subst., name of planet *Mars*, Jo.Mal.*chron*.2 p.25(M.97.92A).

πυροειδῶς, *with fiery appearance*, ref. burning bush π. τὸ φέγγος ἐξήπτετο Gr.Nyss.*v.Mos*.20(M.44.305C).

***πυροθετέω,** *heat with fire*, *Hymn*.ap.*Mir.Geo*.(p.149.16).

***πυροϊππεύς,** *with horses of fire*, Mod.*dorm*.1(M.86.3280A).

***πυροκρατήρ, ὁ,** *volcanic crater*, Jo.D.*dialect*.suppl.(M.94.676B).

***πυρολάβον, τό,** *pair of fire-tongs*, Arist.*apol*.10.1.

***πυρότροφος,** *feeding on fire*; of an inflamed wound, Geo.Pis.*hex*.1347(M.92.1538A).

***πυροφανής,** *like fire*, Thphn.*chron*.p.338(M.108.816C, vv.ll. προφ-, προσφ-).

***πυροφεγγής**, *blazing with fire*, *Orac.Sib.*8.434.

***πυροφλόγος**, *shining like fire*, Amph.*fr.*(M.39.109B).

πυροφόρος, *fire-bearing*; of BMV as typified by burning bush, Mod.*dorm.*3(M.86.3285C).

πυρ-όω, *kindle, set on fire*; met.; **1.** *inflame* with love, devotion, etc., Cyr.H.*procatech.*15; Chrys.*stat.*6.5(2.81D); id.*hom.34.1 in Jo.*(8.195A,D); *Παῦλος...ἐπυροῦτο ἐν ἀγάπῃ τῇ θείᾳ* Philox.*ep.*28(p.177); with anger, Ath.*apol.sec.*87(p.166.7; M.25.405A); with desire, Chrys.*hom.19.1 in 1Cor.*(10.160C); **2.** *test by fire*, Just.*dial.*116.2(M.6.744C); *πεπυρωμένος ὑπὸ τῆς ἁμαρτίας* Or.*or.*13(p.328.20; M.11.457B); *πειρασμούς, καθ' οὓς...~ωθέντες...ἐδοκιμάσθησαν* Meth.*res.*1.56(p.316.14); *διὰ...θλίψεων ~ωθέντες* Bas.*ep.*139.2(3.231D; M.32.584C); *ἐναντίως ὁ διάβολος ~οῖ τῷ θεῷ· θεὸς δὲ ~οῖ, εἴτε τὴν προϋπάρχουσαν εὑρίσκῃ ἀδικίαν, ἢ ἐπεὶ οὐ προϋπάρχει, οὐχ εὑρίσκει* Cyr.*Ps.*16:3(M.69.816B); **3.** *purify by fire*, Herm.*vis.*4.3.4; *M.Polyc.*15.2; Thdt.*Ps.*17:31(1.710); **4.** pass., *be fiery* *βέλη...τιτρώσκοντα τὰς...ψυχὰς...τὰ πεπυρωμένα τοῦ θεοῦ λόγια* Cyr.*Ps.*76:19(M.69.1193A); Nil.*epp.*2.167(M.79.281A).

***πυρπνόως**, *so as to breathe fire*, ref. pentecostal descent of H. Ghost, Jo.D.*carm.pent.*80(p.216; M.96.836C).

πυρπολ-έω, **1.** *set on fire, make fiery* *κεραυνοῦ ~ῶν τὴν ἀτμίδα* Geo.Pis.*hex.*952(*πυρσοβολῶν ἀτμίδα* M.92.1507A); **2.** *inflame* with love, zeal, devotion, etc., ‡Chrys.*Abr.*1(2.742D); Thdt.*Ps.*118:165(1.1479); *~ούμεθα...ὑπὸ τῆς περὶ τὸν Χριστὸν ἀγάπης* id.*2Cor.*5:15(3.316); id.*Gal.*4:20(3.385); with evil desire, Nil.*epp.*2.167(M.79.281C); Thdt.*provid.*8(4.613); *φθόνῳ ~οῦνται* id.*Is.*9:5(p.48.30; 2.234); Bas. Sel.*v.Thecl.*1(M.85.508A).

πυρπόλησις, **ἡ**, *destruction by fire*, Eus.*h.e.*1.2.20(M.20.64A); id.*d.e.*8 proem.(p.350.29; M.22.569D); Chrys.*hom.4.3 in Rom.*(9.458B).

πυρρακής, *red-hot*, to the taste; of mustard-seed, Iren.*fr.*29 (*πυρικαές* M.7.1245A).

***πυρραυγής**, *shining as with fire*, Jo.D.*drac.*(M.94.1601C).

***πυρρώδης**, *fiery red*, Meth.*lepr.*5(p.456.11).

***πυρρωπός**, *of fiery-red appearance*, Sophr.H.*mir.Cyr.et Jo.*60(M.87.3636A).

***πύρσευμα**, **τό**, *effulgence*, met. *τῷ εὐαγγελικῷ...π.* Areth.ap.*cat.Apoc.*12:1(p.352.10) for *τῷ εὐαγγελικῷ...πνεύματι* id.*Apoc.*12:1(M.106.660D).

πυρσεύ-ω, **1.** *inflame*, with love, zeal, etc. *λέξις εἰς ἔρωτα θεῖον ~ει τὴν γνώμην* Thdt.*Ps.*83:3(1.1196); id.*Cant.*2:7(2.60); id.*2Cor.*7:6(3.323); id.*h.e.*4.35(3.1012); Proc.G.*Pr.*31:17–18(M.87.1541A); **2.** *kindle, arouse*, met. *σβέσαι τὸν ~όμενον κατ' αὐτοῦ φθόνον* Isid. Pel.*epp.*2.49(M.78.492A); **3.** *signal by beacon fires*, met. *αἱ παρθένοι τῷ κόσμῳ ~ουσαι τὴν ἀφθαρσίαν* Meth.*symp.*6.4(p.68.15; M.18.117D).

πυρσοβολέω, v. *πυρπολέω*.

***πυρσόγλωσσος**, *with burning tongue*; met., Geo.Pis.*hex.*1780(M.92.1572A).

[*]**πυρσοειδής**, *like a beacon*, Jo.VI H.*v.Jo.D.*12(M.94.448C).

***πυρσόκομος**, *with flame-coloured leaves*, Paul.Sil.*Soph.*881(M.86.2152B).

***πυρσοκόρυμβος**, *with flame-coloured flowers*, Paul.Sil.*ambo*.195(M.86.2259A).

***πυρσολάτρης**, **ὁ**, *fire-worshipper* (i.e. devotee of Persian religion), Geo.Pis.*Heracl.*1.14(M.92.1298A); *ib.*1.181(1313A); id.*carm.*50.1.

***πυρσομορφ-όω**, *give fiery form* *~οῖ Χριστὸς εἰς σωτηρίαν, ὅλην πορίζων τὴν χάριν τοῦ πνεύματος* Jo.D.*carm.pent.*49(p.215; M.96.836A).

***πυρσοπόλος**, *fire-bearing*, Gr.Naz.*carm.*1.2.14.88(M.37.762A).

πυρσός, **ὁ**, **1.** *fire*; met.; **a.** of fire of love, zeal, piety, etc., Thdt.*h.rel.*4(3.1156); id.*provid.*8(4.623); *ἀδελφικῆς ἀγάπης πυρσῷ πυρακτούμενοι* Sophr.H.*ep.syn.*(M.87.3197A); id.*v.Anast.*(M.92.1689B) cit. s. *ἐγκρύφιος*; **b.** of conflagration of discord, enmity, etc. *ὁ τῆς διχονοίας...π.* Const.*ep.*(Opitz 3 p.62.4); Ath.*apol.sec.*61(p.141.22; M.25.360D); Socr.*h.e.*1.24.5(M.67.145A); **2.** *torch* *π. δὲ γαμήλιος ἡ τοῦ ἁγίου πνεύματος ἔλλαμψις* Gr.Nyss.*hom.13 in Cant.*(M.44.1053A); **3.** *beacon*, met. *Θέκλα...ὡς π. ἐκ μέσου τοῦ κλύδωνος τῶν παθῶν ἀναφθεῖσα* Isid.Pel.*epp.*1.87(M.78.244A); *ib.*1.208(313D).

***πυρσοφανής**, *shining as a beacon*, ‡Jo.D.*ep.Thphl.*3(M.95.348B).

***πυρσοφεγγής**, *glowing with flame*, Geo.Pis.*hex.*1489(M.92.1549A); id.*carm.*107.15.

πυρσοφόρος, *torch-bearing* in church procession, Paul.Sil.*Soph.*872(M.86.2152A).

πυρφορ-έω, *bear a torch*; fig., of BMV, ref. Ex.3:2 *~οῦσα παρθένος* Jo.D.*carm.theoph.*123(p.213; M.96.832B).

πυρωνία, **ἡ**, *purchase of wheat*, Euthal.Diac.*Ac.*(M.85.653C).

πυρῶπις, *fiery-eyed*, met. *π. ... ὧραι* Nonn.*par.Jo.*11:4(M.43.840B).

***πυρωπόταμος**, **ὁ**, *river of fire*; as torment of hell, Gr.Naz.*carm.*2.1.76.3(M.37.1423A).

πύρωσις, **ἡ**, **1.** *making fiery*; of making iron red hot (in Christol. simile), Jo.D.*f.o.*3.11(M.94.1024C); met. *ὁ...ψυχρὸς καὶ τῆς τοῦ...πνεύματος π. ἄμοιρος* Or.*Apoc.*23(p.31); **2.** *testing by fire*; of heating of metal, met., with play on Stoic notion of conflagration *ἥξει ἡ κτίσις...εἰς τὴν π. τῆς δοκιμασίας* *Did.*16.5; *π. ἡ μὲν ἔξωθεν προσπίπτουσα δοκιμασίαν κατεργάζεται, ἡ δὲ ἔνδοθεν θάνατον διαπράσσεται* Clem.*q.d.s.*25(p.176.16; M.9.629C); Cyr.*Os.*135(3.167C); Thdt.*Ps.*16:4(1.696); **3.** *kindling, setting on fire* by evil desire, *T.Jud.*16.1; ref. S. Paul's permission for second marriage *δι' ἀκρασίαν καὶ π.* Clem.*str.*3.12(p.233.26; M.8.1184A); *ib.*6.7(p.462.7; M.9.281B); *πίπτουσιν εἰς τὸ πῦρ τῶν π.* Or.*schol.in Lc.*9:42(M.17.348A); *ἡ π. τῆς σαρκὸς μήτηρ γενήσεται τοῦ αἰωνίου πυρός* Bas.*hom.*3.7(2.23B; M.31.213C); Chrys.*hom.19.2 in 1Cor.*(10.161B); *τὴν ἄλογον π.* †Nil.*mal.cog.*16(M.79.1217D).

πυρωτικός, *of fire*, ref. Mt.3:11 *οἱ π. ... λόγοι* Eus.*Is.*4:3–6(M.24.1116B).

πωγωνίτης, **ὁ**, = *πωγωνίας*, *comet*, Thdt.*qu.15 in Gen.*(1.18).

πώεον, **τό**, = *πῶυ*, *flock*, Eudoc.*Cypr.*1.304(M.85.844B).

πωλεύω, *break in* a horse; pass., *be under training*; of the soul, Nil.*epp.*1.132(M.79.140A).

πῶλος, **ὁ**, *colt*; **1.** exeg. Mt.21:1–7 in rel. to Gen.49:11 and Zach.9:9 *π. γάρ τις ὄνου εἱστήκει ἔν τινι εἰσόδῳ κώμης πρὸς ἄμπελον δεδεμένος, ὃν ἐκέλευσεν ἀγαγεῖν αὐτῷ* Just.*1apol.*32.6(M.6.380A); story of Bellerophon an invention of demons due to misinterpretation of Gen.49:11, *ib.*54.7(409B); colt signifies gentiles, unaccustomed to yoke of Law, ass represents Israel, id.*dial.*53.1–4(M.6.592Bff.); Clem.*prot.*12(p.85.19; M.8.244A); id.*paed.*1.5(p.99.7; M.8.268A); Hipp.*fr.22 in Gen.*(p.59.18); *τὸν μὲν π. προσδεδέσθαι ἐν τῇ ἀμπέλῳ, τὸν δὲ ἕτερον ἐν τῇ ἕλικι, ὅπερ ὑπολαμβάνομεν, τὴν μὲν ἐξ ἐθνῶν κλῆσιν προσδεδέσθαι τῷ κυρίῳ, τὴν δὲ ἐκ περιτομῆς τῇ τοῦ νόμου παλαιότητι* *ib.23*(p.60.2; M.10.589B); *τὰς δύο κλήσεις πρὸς αὐτὸν ὡς ἄμπελον δεσμευομένας καὶ τῇ αὐτοῦ ἀγάπῃ εἰς ἑνότητα συναγομένας, ὄνον καὶ π. ἐπὶ τῷ αὐτῷ διὰ λόγου καθαιρομένους* id.*ben.Jac.*18(p.34.7); cf. *pullum novellum eos...qui sunt ex gentibus credentes*, Or.*hom.13.8 in Num.*(p.119.22; M.12.676B); *ὁ π. ... ὁ ὕστερον γενόμενος νέος ἀπὸ τῶν ἐθνῶν...λαός* id.*comm.in Mt.*16.15(p.524.2; M.13.1424B); ass and colt represent those loosed from bondage of sin, *ib.*(p.524.20; 1424B); colt represents men's bestial state before conversion (cf. Ps.72:22), *ib.*16.16(p.527.6ff.; 1425C); *π. ... ἐφ' ὃν οὐδεὶς ἀνθρώπων ἐκάθισεν· οὐδὲν γὰρ λογικὸν καὶ κατὰ τρόπον ἀνθρώπινον γινόμενον...ἵδρυτο τῷ ἀπὸ τῶν ἐθνῶν π.* *ib.*16.17(p.534.19; 1433A); *ὅπου οὖν ὑπακοὴ καὶ ἱερὸς τόπος* [i.e. Bethany and Bethphage] *ἐκεῖ ἀποστέλλει ὁ κύριος τοὺς ἀποστόλους λύσοντας π. δεδεμένον ἐν ᾧ οὐδεὶς...ἐκάθισεν ...ἀντὶ τοῦ· οὐδέποτε ἄνθρωπος λογικὸς ἐπεκάθισεν ἢ Μωϋσέως λόγος ἢ...ἄλλου τινὸς τῶν προφητῶν...ἔργον γάρ ἐστι τῶν λυόντων τὸν π. μαθητῶν ἀγαγεῖν λελυμένον πρὸς τὸν Ἰησοῦν καὶ τὰ ἑαυτῶν ἱμάτια...τὰς πράξεις καὶ τοὺς λόγους...ἐπιρρῖψαι τῷ π. καὶ ἐνιδρῦσαι αὐτῷ τὸν Ἰησοῦν* id.*hom.37 in Lc.*(pp.217.21,220.2,7); or New Covenant, id.*Jo.*28(18; p.201.29; M.14.357C); or gentile believers, *ib.*29(18; p.202.23; 360A); *ἀνθρώπων μὲν οὐδείς πω καθίσας ἐπὶ τὸν π. ἦν, θηρίων δὲ ἢ τῶν ἀλλοτρίων τοῦ λόγου δυνάμεών τινες ἐπεκάθισαν* *ib.*32(18; p.206.16; 365B); ref. Gen.49:11 *αἰνίττεσθαι...τὸν μὲν π. ... τὸν τῶν ἀποστόλων...χορόν, τὴν δὲ ἄμπελον...τὴν ἔνθεον...αὐτοῦ δύναμιν...ἕλιξ δὲ...ἡ τοῦ...λόγου διδασκαλία, ἐν ᾗ τὸν π. τῆς ὄνου κατεδήσατο, τὸν νέον ἐξ ἐθνῶν λαόν, γέννημα τυγχάνοντα τῶν ἀποστόλων...εἴποι δ' ἄν τις καὶ πρὸς λέξιν ταῦτα τέλους τετυχηκέναι ὅτε...εἶπεν ὁ κύριος... εὑρήσετε π. δεδεμένον...ὅτι...μελλήσει ὁ προφητευόμενος οὐχ οἷά τις ...βασιλεὺς ἐφ' ἁρμάτων...ὀχήσεσθαι, ἀλλ' ἐπὶ ὄνου καὶ π., οἷά τις... πένης* Eus.*d.e.*8.1(p.365.17; M.22.593A); *τινές φασιν, ἐπειδὴ ὁ κύριος ἀπέστειλε τοὺς μαθητὰς τὸν π. ἀγαγεῖν...προλέγεσθαι ταῦτα παρὰ τοῦ Ἰακώβ· ἕτεροι δέ, ὅπερ καὶ ἀληθέστερον κατὰ τὴν ἀκολουθίαν εἶναι δοκεῖ τοῖς πολλοῖς, ὅτι ἄμπελος ὁ Ἰσραήλ·...ὄνος δὲ καὶ π., οἱ τοῖς κτήνεσι τοῖς ἀνοήτοις ὁμοιωθέντες...ἕτεροι δὲ λέγουσι, τὸ δυνατὸν τῆς τοῦ σωτῆρος διδαχῆς εἰς τὸ ἥμερον ἀγούσης τὸ ἐν ἀνθρώποις ἄγριον προλέγεσθαι...οὐχ οἷόν τε γὰρ π. ἀμπέλῳ προσδεσμευθέντα μὴ λυμήνασθαι τῇ σταφυλῇ. ἀλλ' ὁ σωτὴρ...προσδήσει τῇ ἀμπέλῳ τὸν π., οὕτως ἡμερώσας αὐτοῦ τὰ σκιρτήματα...ὡς μηδὲν βλάπτεσθαι τὴν ἄμπελον...ταῦτα ἡμεῖς οὐ διϊσχυριζόμεθα* Diod.*Gen.*49:11(M.33.1599C); *διὰ τοῦ π. ... τὴν τῶν ἐθνῶν προμηνύων προσαγωγήν...τὰ ἀκάθαρτα ἔθνη μετὰ τοσαύτης εὐκολίας ἐνάξει, ὡς ἄν τις τῇ ἕλικι τῆς ἀμπέλου τὸν π. προσδήσῃ, τῆς ἐξουσίας τὴν ὑπερβολὴν αἰνιττόμενος, καὶ τῶν* ἐθνῶν τὴν πολλὴν ὑπακοήν. ... ἕλικας δὲ ἐκάλεσε τὸ ἁπαλὸν τῶν προσταγμάτων Chrys.*hom.67.2 in Gen.*(4.638C); mode of entry into Jerusalem exhibits ἐπιείκεια of Christ, contrasted with kingly splendour, id.*hom.66.2 in Mt.*(7.656A); ἡ ἐκκλησία δηλοῦται διὰ τοῦ π., καὶ ὁ λαὸς ὁ νέος,...μετὰ...τὸ καθίσαι τὸν Ἰησοῦν καθαρὸς γενόμενος...διὰ τοῦτο φαίνεται ἡ ὄνος ἀκολουθοῦσα τῷ π. μετὰ γὰρ τὸ καθίσαι τὸν Χριστὸν ἐπὶ τὰ ἔθνη, τότε ἥξουσι κἀκεῖνοι παραζηλοῦντες... οὐ κάθηται δὲ ἐπὶ γυμνὸν τὸν π., ἀλλ' ἐπὶ τὰ ἱμάτια τῶν ἀποστόλων. ἐπειδὴ γὰρ τὸν π. ἔλαβον, ἅπαντα λοιπὸν προΐενται, καθὼς καὶ ὁ Παῦλος ἔλεγεν· ἐγὼ δὲ ἥδιστα...ἐκδαπανηθήσομαι ὑπὲρ τῶν ψυχῶν ὑμῶν *ib.*(656B); whole prophecy of Zach.9:9 referred primarily to Zerubbabel, Thdr.Mops.*Zach.*9:8–10(M.66.556Cff.); προσέδησε γὰρ ὥσπερ ἑαυτῷ διὰ πίστεως, ἡ ἄμπελος ἡ ἀληθινή...τὸν ἐξ ἐθνῶν λαόν, ὃν τῷ π. παρεικάζει. προσέδησε δὲ ὅτι τῇ ἕλικι τῆς ἀμπέλου, τουτέστιν, ἀγάπῃ τῇ παρ' ἑαυτοῦ Cyr.*glaph.Gen.*7(1.224A); ἐπανεπαύσατο γὰρ ὁ Χριστὸς τῷ νέῳ λαῷ, τουτέστι τῷ κεκλημένῳ πρὸς ἐπίγνωσιν ἀληθείας τῷ εἰδωλολατροῦντί ποτε. οἷα γάρ τις ἦν π., οὔπω δεδαμασμένος...οὐ γάρ που τῷ θείῳ πεπαιδαγώγητο νόμῳ id.*Zach.*57(3.736C); π. represents gentiles, two disciples the apostles and prophets, 'village' indicates lawless and uncivilized character of gentiles, id.*Lc.*19:35(M.72.876C); π. δὲ λέγει τὸν ὄνον, ἐπειδὴ ὁ ἐξ ἐθνῶν λαὸς ἀγύμναστος ἦν τῆς εἰς εὐσέβειαν ἀγούσης πίστεως id.*Jo.*8(4.698D); π. = gentiles, formerly untamed, uncared for by legislators or prophets: apostles loose it, setting on it garments representing grace; vine = Christ, Thdt.*qu.110 in Gen.*(1.114); Zach.9:9 referred to Gen.49:11 as indicating Christ's dissimilarity to kings and their splendour, id.*Zach.*9:9(2.1634); cf. *vera enim vitis per vitem alligavit...sibi populum novum...vel vineam intelligit Israelem: per pullum vero denotat populum ex gentibus collectum. ... prophetia ostendit illum non instar terreni regis, vehendum esse equis...vehetur asino et pullo ...ceu pauper aliquis*, Proc.G.*Gen.*49:11(M.87.499); Eulog.*palm.*8 (M.86.2925B) cit. s. διπλόος; **2.** in gen., ref. νοῦς as ἡνίοχος of passions (colts), Thdt.*Rom.*7:17(3.77).

πωλοτροφέω, *bring up* as child, Tim.Ant.*nativ.Jo.Bapt.*1(M.28. 908A).

πωρόω, *harden, make callous* or *insensible*; **1.** ref. heart, mind, etc. ἡ καρδία...πεπώρωται ἀπὸ τῶν προτέρων μου πράξεων Herm. *mand.*4.2.1; *ib.*12.4.4; ἐπώρωσαν τὴν καρδίαν...οἱ...δαίμονες *M. Thdot.*3(p.140); Mac.Mgn.*apocr.*3.23(p.106.2); πεπωρωμένοι τὸ συνειδός Nil.*Alb.*(M.79.697D); τὸ μὲν λεῖμμα τὸ κατ' ἐκλογὴν χάριτος ἐσώθη· οἱ δὲ λοιποὶ ἐπωρώθησαν Proc.G.*Is.*1:7–9(M.87.1840A); ref. spiritual blindness of Jews οὐχ ὁ θεὸς ἐπώρωσεν αὐτούς, ἀλλὰ συνεχώρησε ποιεῖν ἃ ἤθελον· ἔσχον δὲ τὴν πώρωσιν ἐκ τῆς ἀπιστίας Ammon.*Jo.*12:40(M.85.1477B); **2.** ref. state of mind, emotion πεπωρωμένον φθόνον ‡Meth.*palm.*3(M.18.388B).

πώρωμα, τό, 1. *callus, hardened part,* met. τῆς ὑπερηφανίας ἐκτεμὼν τὰ π. Max.*ep.*13(M.91.512A); **2.** = πώρωσις, *hardness, insensibility,* †Nil.*mal.cog.*11(M.79.1213B); †Cyr.*coll.VT*(6^4.58B; M.77.1261D).

πώρωσις, ἡ, *hardening, callousness,* of mental and spiritual obtuseness and insensibility π. ἁμαρτίας *T.Lev.*13.7; τὴν τύφλωσιν τῆς ψυχῆς καὶ π. τῆς καρδίας Thphl.Ant.*Autol.*1.7(M.6.1036A); Gr. Naz.*or.*32.15(M.36.192A); διανοῖξαι αὐτῶν τὴν π. Chrys.*hom.18.2 in Rom.*(9.632D); due to man's fault, not divine decree, id.*hom.13.1 in Eph.*(11.95D); ἀλογίας δὲ τέκνον ἡ π. Cyr.*glaph.Gen.*3(1.85C); id.*Os.*33 (3.61C); π. δὲ καρδίας τὴν ἐσχάτην ἀναλγησίαν ἐκάλεσε Thdt.*Eph.* 4:18(3.426); ἄνοιαν καὶ...π. Max.*ambig.*(M.91.1161C); Sophr.H.*ep. syn.*(M.87.3176B); Jo.D.*hom.*3.5(M.96.585A); τὸν ἐν τάφῳ με καθεύδοντα λιθώδους π., διὰ μετάνοιαν ἀνάστησον Jo.Mon.*hymn.Petr.*4(M. 96.1392D).

P

ῥαββί, *my master,* as title of Christian priest μηδὲ...διὰ κενοδοξίαν ...ἢ ἀναισθησίαν. γίνεται γὰρ διὰ τὸ ῥ. καὶ πατέρες καλεῖσθαι, ἀλλοτρίους ἀναδέχεσθαι λογισμούς. μὴ...ἀναισχύντως...τὴν τῶν ἀποστόλων ἀξίαν ἁρπάζωμεν (i.e. in hearing confessions) ‡Jo.D.*conf.*9(p.118.23; M.95.293B).

***ῥαββίς, ὁ,** *rabbi, master,* plur. ῥαββεῖς *Pers.*(p.2.3); ῥαββίδες *ib.* (p.34.2).

ῥαβδισμός, ὁ, *beating, cudgelling,* ref. 2Cor.11:15, Gr.Naz.*or.*2.53 (M.35.461C); Nect.*Thdr.*6(M.39.1828B).

***ῥαβδιωκέω,** s.v.l., *beat with a rod, Ev.Barth.*(Vassiliev p.17; ῥαβδίζουσιν *RB* p.332).

ῥαβδομαντεία, ἡ, *divination by rod,* Cyr.*Os.*44(3.75C).

ῥάβδος, ἡ, *rod*;

A. *rod, stick*; met.; **a.** of God the Father ἡ ῥάβ[δος ἡ βασι]λική *Pap.Chr.*(p.431); of various divine attributes [Ex.12:11] τῆς θείας δυνάμεως τὰ σημεῖα, τῆς λογικῆς ἰσχύος τὰ ἐρείσματα ῥ. ἡ διὰ Μωϋσέως, ῥ. ἡ διὰ Ἀαρών, ῥ. ἡ καρυΐνη, ῥ. ἡ τεμοῦσα βάθη θαλάσσης, ⟨ῥ.⟩ ἡ γλυκάνασα πικρίαν πηγῶν, ῥ. ἐφ' ἣν τὰ ἑπτὰ πνεύματα... ἀνεπαύσατο τοῦ θεοῦ ‡Chrys.*pasch.*6.3(p.159.6; 8.269D); σημαίνει [sc. ἡ ῥ.] τὴν βασιλείαν...τὴν ἰσχὺν...καὶ...ἐπιστήμην τὴν ποιμαντικήν Cyr.*Heb.*1:8(p.376.2n.; M.74.961A); type of Christ as king, as support of weak and strength of just, as Good Shepherd and Judge, id.*Is.*2.1(2.191D–192A); Proc.G.*Is.*11:1(M.87.2040C,D); ref. Cant.5:7, of H. Ghost ἡ θεία ῥ. ἐκείνη...ἡ διὰ τοῦ πατάσσειν ἐνεργοῦσα τὴν ἴασιν, τὸ πνεῦμά ἐστιν Gr.Nyss.*hom.12 in Cant.*(M.44.1033C); **b.** as a weapon; met., of truth, Hipp.*haer.*5.11(p.104.7; M.16.3159C); of faith, Gr.Nyss.*v.Mos.*(M.44.368A); **c.** *staff of office* denoting authority; met., of divine governance αὐτῷ ῥάβδον περιτίθησιν ἡ προφητεία, ῥ. παιδευτικήν, ἀρχικήν, κατεξουσιαστικήν, ἵν'...οὓς...ἡ ἀπειλὴ οὐκ ἰᾶται, ἡ ῥ. ἰάσεται Clem.*paed.*1.7(p.126.5; M.8.324A); Bas. *hom.in Ps.*44(1.165D; M.29.404C); of angels τὰς...ῥ., τὸ βασιλικὸν καὶ ἡγεμονικὸν καὶ εὐθέα τὰ πάντα περαῖνον Dion.Ar.*c.h.*15.5(M.3.333B); under old dispensation δέδωκα τὴν ῥ. μου, τουτέστιν τὸ στήριγμα τῆς ἐμῆς φυλῆς *T.Jud.*15.3; of pastoral office ῥ. ποιμενικὴν πρὸς τὸ διώκειν τοὺς λύκους...καὶ ποδηγεῖν...τὰς τῶν λογικῶν θρεμμάτων ἀγέλας ‡Gr.Nyss.*hom.5.68 in Jo.*(p.195.19); of Roman rule (ref. Ps.2:9) ἐν ῥ. σιδηρᾷ ‡Anast.S.*Jud.disp.*1(M.89.1209B); of Aaron's rod as type of BMV, Cyr.H.*catech.*12.28; ‡Chrys.*BMV* 2(8.239B,C); also of rod of Moses, *ib.*3(241B); Thdr.Stud.*or.*5.2(M.99.721C).

B. *rod, shoot*; of rod of Jesse as a type of Christ, ref. Is.11:1, Cyr.*Is.*2.1(2.191C); and of BMV τὴν ἀειθαλῆ ῥ. Ἰεσσαὶ...ἐν παντὶ μὲν πρέπει χρόνῳ μακαρίζειν Chrysipp.*enc.in BMV* 1(p.336.4); χαῖρε, ῥ., τὸ θεόφυτον ἔρνος...ἐξ ἀσπορίας ἀνθήσασα υἱέα τὸν τῶν ἁπάντων θεόν Thdr.Stud.*nativ.BMV* 7(M.96.689B); *ib.*2(681B).

C. *beam* of Cross, Thdt.*Ps.*22:4(1.749); Dam.*troph.*2.2(p.220.2).

D. *rivet* in a tripod (said to have been invented by Glaucus), Eus.*Marcell.*1.3(p.15.19; M.24.745C).

ῥαβδουχία, ἡ, *power* τοῦ θανάτου τὴν ῥ. συνέθλασεν Mac.Mgn. *apocr.*3.14(p.90.6).

***ῥαγαδαστεύει,** error in ‡Epiph.*phys.*13(M.43.528C) for ῥαγάδα στενήν *Phys.*A 11(p.38.2).

ῥαγδαῖος, *furious, violent,* met. οὐδὲν...οὕτως...μωρὸν καὶ ῥ. [sc. ὡς ἁμαρτία] Chrys.*hom.9.4 in 1Cor.*(10.78C); ῥαγδαιοτέραν...ἐπιφέρει τὴν ἐπίπληξιν [Col.2:20] Cyr.*glaph.Gen.*4(1.139B).

***ῥάγμα, τό,** sens. dub. (ref. Gal.5:3 and the numberless requirements of Jewish law) αὐτὴν τῶν ὑδάτων τὴν φύσιν ἀπέπλυνεν ἐκ τοῦ συνεχῶς ἀντλεῖν καὶ μεταφέρειν τῷ ῥ. Mac.Mgn.*apocr.*3.40(p.139. 28).

ῥαγολόγος, ὁ, *grape-gatherer,* Jo.Clim.*scal.*10(M.88.848D).

ῥάδαμνος, ὁ, *young shoot, scion, Const.App.*5.7.26; Gr.Naz.*carm.* 2.2(epitaph.)129.24(M.38.80A); ‡Chrys.*hom.*11(13.247C).

***ῥαδιόλογος, ὁ,** v. *ῥεόλογος.

ῥαδιουργ-έω, 1. *practise fraud* λήθη...ἐραδιούργησε, τὸ μόνῳ τῷ ὄντως θεῷ πρέπον ὄνομα, ἐπὶ θνητοὺς μεταφέρουσα ‡Just.*monarch.*1 (M.6.313A); **2.** *falsify, tamper with* text of scripture, ref. Jews ὅπερ ...ὑπὸ Ἰουδαίων ῥεραδιούργηται Or.*ep.*1.9(M.11.65B); ref. followers of Artemon and Theodotus the banker, †Hipp.*Artem.*ap.Eus.*h.e.*5.28. 13(M.20.516A); ~ῆσαι τὴν θείαν γραφὴν ἐτόλμησαν, καὶ τὰ μὲν περικόψαι, τὰ δὲ προσθεῖναι· διωρθωκέναι τὰ οὐκ εὖ ἔχοντα λέγοντες Thdt. *haer.*2.5(4.332); esp. of Marcionites τῶν κυριακῶν ~ῆσαί τινες ἐπιβέβληνται γραφῶν Dion.Cor.ap.Eus.*h.e.*4.23.12(M.20.389A); 'μεταχαράξαντας...τὸ εὐαγγέλιον' ἄλλους οὐκ οἶδα ἢ τοὺς ἀπὸ Μαρκίωνος καὶ τοὺς ἀπὸ Οὐαλεντίνου οἶμαι δὲ καὶ τοὺς ἀπὸ Λουκάνου. τοῦτο δὲ λεγόμενον οὐ τοῦ λόγου ἐστὶν ἔγκλημα ἀλλὰ τῶν τολμησάντων ~ῆσαι τὰ εὐαγγέλια Or.*Cels.*2.27(p.156.8; M.11.848A); ὁ.. Μαρκίων, ~ήσας τὰ κατὰ τὸν ἀπόστολον Adam.*dial.*2.18(p.96.6); τὰ ὑπ' αὐτοῦ γεγραμμένα, μᾶλλον δὲ ἐρραδιουργημένα Epiph.*haer.*42.9(p.104.22; M.41.708B); *ib.* 42.11(pp.139.24,145.7; 749A,756D); also by false exegesis ~οῦντες τὰς ἐξηγήσεις Iren.*haer.*1.3.6(M.7.477A); *ib.*proem.(437A); accusation of Celsus against scriptures παραχαράττοντες καὶ ~οῦντες [i.e. in account of flood] τὸν Δευκαλίωνα Cels.ap.Or.*Cels.*4.41(p.314.5; M. 11.1096A).

ῥαδιούργημα, τό, *false story, fabrication,* Iren.*haer.*1.20.1(M.7. 653A).

ῥαδιουργός, ὁ, *forger,* Or.*Jo.*32.32(19; p.479.35; M.14.828C).

***ῥαδιουργῶς,** *craftily, deceitfully,* Epiph.*anc.*81(p.101.26; M.43. 169B).

***ῥαέτων**, ? name of a monastery ἐν τῷ αὐτῷ μοναστηρίῳ τοῦ ῥ. †Anast.S.*relat*.42(*OC* 3 p.62.3).

ῥαθυμ-έω, **1.** *have ease of mind* τὸ ~εῖν...οὐδέποτε ὠνητέον κενοσπουδίᾳ Clem.*paed*.3.11(p.279.10; M.8.656B); **2.** *be careless, indifferent, apathetic* ~ήσας εἰς οἶστρον ὑπεσύρη Meth.*symp*.1.1(p.8.22; M.18.37C); ἐπιπλήττειν ~ούσαις [sc. γυναιξί] Chrys.*sac*.6.8(p.156.17; 1.428C); Thdt.*Dan*.10:2f.(2.1256); *neglect* μαθημάτων ῥ. Clem.*str*.4.5(p.257.17; M.8.1233A); φιλοστοργίας...~εῖν αὐτὰς ἀναγκάζοντος τοῦ λιμοῦ Cyr.*Os*.5(3.24E); οἷς...ἐπικείσεται ποινή, εἰ τούτου ~ήσουσιν Ath.Scholast.*coll*.12.2(p.143); pass., *be neglected* τὴν ἐκκλησίαν...~ηθεῖσάν τε καὶ χερσομανήσασαν ἐξ ἀναρχίας Gr.Naz.*or*.18.16(M.35.1004C); **3.** *be dejected* λυπούμεθα καὶ ἀδημονοῦμεν, καὶ ἀσχάλλομεν, καὶ ῥ. Thdr.Stud.*epp*.1.2(M.99.913A).

ῥαθυμία, ἡ, 1. *apathy, indifference*, Athenag.*res*.17(p.69.5; M.6.1008C); Meth.*Porph*.5(p.507.15; M.18.345B); Chrys.*stat*.10.1(2.106A); **2.** *indolence*, Ephr.2.95F; Bas.*reg.fus*.proem.3(2.329E; M.31.896B); Dor.*doct*.2.2(M.88.1641C); **3.** *laxity, indulgence*, Clem.*paed*.2.8(p.193.33; M.8.465B); *Const.App*.4.11.5; **4.** *desire, lust*, Clem.*paed*.2.8(p.197.28; M.8.473B); Ath.*fr.1 in Cant*.(M.27.1352D); Chrys.*hom.17.2 in Mt*.(7.223D).

***ῥαθυμοτόκος**, *breeding indolence, sloth-inducing* ῥ. μέριμναι Jo.D.*carm.transfig*.(M.96.849C).

***ῥαιδάριος, ὁ**, (Lat. *raedarius*) *coachman*, Areth.*Apoc*.18:12(M.106.732B).

***ῥαῖδος, τό**, (Lat. *raeda*) *chariot*, Areth.*Apoc*.55(M.106.732B).

***ῥαιφερενδάριος, ὁ**, v. *ῥεφερενδάριος.

***ῥακάμφιος**, *in rags, shabby*, ‡Caes.Naz.*dial*.158(M.38.1117).

***ῥακενδυτέω**, *wear rags*, ‡Barth.Edess.*Muham*.(M.104.1448C); Jo.VI H.*v.Jo.D*.26(M.94.468A).

[*]ῥάκκος, τό, = ῥάκος, *strip of cloth, rag*, *Apophth.Patr*.(M.65.105C).

[*]ῥακκώδης, v. ῥακώδης.

***ῥακόδυτ-έω**, *wear rags*, Chrys.*hom.30.4 in Rom*.(9.743E); Pall.*h.Laus*.59(p.153.21; M.34.1236B); ‡Nil.*perist*.9.4(M.79.869D); met. ἐκ γηΐνων νοημάτων ~οῦντες Or.*fr.100 in Lam*.(p.271.9; M.13.652C).

ῥακοδύτης, ὁ, *wearer of rags*, Chrys.*hom.73.4 in Mt*.(7.713D).

***ῥακοφόρος**, *wearing rags*, ‡Caes.Naz.*dial*.111(M.38.989).

ῥακ-όω, *wither*, hence *enfeeble* ~οῖ [sc. λουτρά] τὰ σώματα καὶ προγηράσκειν ἀναγκάζει Clem.*paed*.3.9(p.263.18; M.8.617B); ~οῦται φύσει ῥευστὸν ὄν [sc. τὸ σῶμα] id.*str*.2.20(p.177.8; M.8.1061B); ῥαβδίζουσίν με...καὶ τὴν δύναμίν μου ~οῦσιν *Ev.Barth*.4.29(*RB* p.332).

ῥακώδης, *ragged*, *T.Job* 25 (ῥακκ- p.118.23); Gr.Nyss.*hom.11 in Cant*.(M.44.1005C); Mac.Aeg.*hom*.2.4(M.34.465D).

ῥάκωμα, τό, plur., *small pieces, rags*, ref. veneration of relics καὶ ῥακώματ', ἤ τι καὶ ῥαντισμάτων σημεῖον, ἀρκεῖν εἰς ὅλου τιμήν ποτε Gr.Naz.*carm*.1.2.10.747(M.37.734A).

ῥαντήρ, ὁ, = ῥάντης, *sprinkler* of scents, Gr.Naz.*carm*.1.2.8.145(M.37.659A).

ῥάντης, ὁ, *sprinkler*, in pagan ceremonies ἀντ' ἐπισκόπων καὶ πρεσβυτέρων καὶ διακόνων καταστήσας [sc. Juln. Imp.] ζακόρους καὶ νεωκόρους καὶ ῥ. κτλ. ‡Jo.D.*Artem*.22(p.82.15; M.96.1272C).

ῥαντίζω, 1. *sprinkle*, *A.Phil*.105(p.40.22); *splash*; (trans.), Pall.*h.Laus*.39(p.125.13; M.34.1195D); **2.** *bedew* as with sweat, met. τὴν ψυχὴν φόβῳ ῥαντίζουσι Nil.*Eulog*.28(M.79.1129D); **3.** *purify* by sprinkling, Cyr.H.*catech*.3.1,4; Gr.Naz.*or*.39.3(M.36.336C); Mac.Aeg.*hom*.25.3(M.34.669A); ref. baptism by heretics, Ath.*Ar*.2.43(M.26.237B); ref. Christ's baptism περιετμήθη καὶ ἐρραντίσθη *Const.App*.6.22.5.

ῥάντισμα, τό, *sprinkling*; **1.** of the liquid sprinkled, *splash*, Gr.Naz.*carm*.1.2.10.747(M.37.734A) cit. s. ῥάκωμα; Bas.*renunt*.8(2.209B; M.31.641C); **2.** of the act of sprinkling, Gr.Nyss.*bapt.Chr*.(M.46.589C).

ῥαντισμός, ὁ, *sprinkling*; of purifications under Jewish law, Or.*hom.8.11 in Lev*.(p.412.29); *Const.App*.6.20.9; Cyr.*Ps*.96:14(M.69.833B); of Christian baptism εἰς ῥ., τὸ λουτρὸν τῆς παλιγγενεσίας †Bas.*Is*.26(1.400B; M.30.169B).

***ῥαντιστήριον, τό**, plur., *ceremonies of sprinkling*, Or.*schol.in Lc*.3:10(M.17.328D).

ῥάπισμα, τό, *slap in the face*, *A.Pil*.A 16.7(p.282); Isid.Pel.*epp*.1.54(M.78.217A); in formalities of manumission ῥ., τὴν τελευταίαν τῶν δούλων πληγήν Bas.*hom*.13.3(2.116B; M.31.429B).

ῥάπτης, ὁ, 1. *one who stitches, seamster* or *clothes-mender*, Pall.*h.Laus*.32(p.94.7; M.34.1100D); *ib*.33(p.97.4,7; 1105C,D); *MAMA* 3.581 (Corycus, ? saec. v); **2.** *deviser, plotter*, ‡Gr.Naz.*Chr.pat*.1884(M.38.286A).

***ῥάσος**, (? Lat. *rasus*); **1.** *threadbare*, Leont.N.*v.Jo.Eleem*.21 (p.38.9); **2.** neut. as subst.; **a.** *gown*; of Christ's robe, *A.Pil*. B 10.3(p.305); **b.** *novice's habit*, ῥάσον *Euchol*.(p.379).

ῥαφανέλαιον, τό, *oil of radishes*, *Apophth.Patr*.(M.65.145A).

***ῥαφανοφαγία, ἡ**, *eating of cabbage, cabbage diet*; ref. Montanists, Hipp.*haer*.8.19(p.238.17; M.16.3367A).

ῥαφή, ἡ, 1. = ῥαφίς, *needle*, *A.Petr.et Andr*.16(p.124.18); **2.** *suture* in the skull, Jo.D.*ep*.(M.95.244C).

ῥαφιδευτής, ὁ, *seamster*; *embroiderer*, Or.*comm.in Mt*.15.20(p.408.3; M.13.1312B).

***ῥαφιδευτικός**, *of needlework*, ‡Chrys.*Spir*.4(3.801E).

***ῥαφίδιον, τό**, (dim. of ῥαφίς) *needle*, Zos.*alloquia* 5(M.78.1689B).

ῥάχη, ἡ, (variant of ῥάχις) *spine* τρίχας...εἶχον κατὰ τῆς ῥ. ἐκφυομένας Thphn.*chron*.p.337(M.108.813A).

ῥαχία (ῥαχεία), ἡ, 1. name of a shrub, species of ῥάχος, prob. *thorn*, *Barn*.7.8; **2.** mountain *ridge*, Gr.Nyss.*ep*.20(M.46.1081A); ῥαχεία Thdt.*h.rel*.18(3.1229); **3.** stone *roof* of a cell, *ib*.27(1284).

***Ῥαψακοειδής**, *like* (*that of*) *Rhapsaces* [i.e. the Rabshakeh (4 Reg.18:17 etc.) as a typical barbarian] ἡ Ῥ. χείρ Thdr.Stud.*epp*.2.75(M.99.1312A).

***ῥαψολογ-έω**, *concoct for discussion, trump up* ἀκαίρους ~οῦντας [sc. Jews] ζητήσεις Dam.*troph*.3.5(p.243.12).

***ῥαψολογία, ἡ**, *trumped-up argument*, Leont.H.*Nest*.4.27(M.86.1693A).

***ῥαψῴδημα, τό**, *rigmarole*; *idle declamation*, Cyr.*Is*.1.1(2.22E); id.*Juln*.6(6^2.193B).

***ῥαψῳδοποιΐα, ἡ**, *rhapsodizing, empty declamation*, Epiph.*haer*.66.34(p.73.25; M.42.84A).

***ῥεβοκατορία, ἡ**, (Lat. *revocatoria*) *letter of recall*, Ath.Scholast.*coll*.20.1(p.174).

ῥεγεών, ἡ, (Lat. *regio*) *district, ward*, CChalc.*act*.13(*ACO* 2.1.3 p.418.12; H.2.565D); †Gregent.*leg.Hom*.(M.86.577D); *Chron.Pasch*.p.322(M.92.821B).

ῥεγεωνάριος, (**[*]ῥεγιωνάριος**), *pertaining to a* regio *or district, of the area* νοτάριος ῥ. τῆς ἀποστολικῆς καθέδρας CLater.*act*.1(H.3.704C); *ib*.2(733A); as subst., official in Church ὑποδιάκονον καὶ ῥεγιωνάριον τῆς ἁγίας ἡμῶν ἐκκλησίας Leo II Papa *ep*.(M.*PL*.96.403A).

***ῥέγιστρον, τό**, (Lat. *regesta*) *archives*; **1.** *file*, CCP(681)*act*.13(H.3.1345D,1348E); **2.** *record*, *ib*.12(1324C,D); **3.** of documents, *copy* τὰ...ἴσα, ἤτοι ῥέγιστρα, ἢ καὶ αὐθεντικά *ib*.13(1348D).

[*]ῥεγιωνάριος, v. ῥεγεωνάριος.

ῥέγχω, *snore*; met., of the careless soul, Cyr.*Is*.5.4(2.825A).

ῥέδα, ἡ, (Lat. *raeda*) *chariot*; ref. Apoc.8:13, ῥεδῶν understood as a graecizing, not apparently of *raeda* but of *radium*, and the ending explained as the Greek equivalent of Lat. *-orum* τὸ ῥεδῶν Ῥωμαϊκὴ μὲν λέξις ἐστίν...ῥεδιοὺμ γάρ ἐστι παρὰ Ῥωμαίοις τὸ ὄχημα, γενικὴν δὲ πληθυντικὴν τέθεικε πτῶσιν· καὶ δέον κατὰ Ῥωμαίους ῥεδιορούμ εἰπεῖν, ὡς ἐξελληνίσας αὐτὴν Ἑλληνικὴν γέγραφε κατάληξιν, ῥεδῶν εἰπών Oecum.*Apoc*.18:13(p.197).

ῥεῖθρον, τό, *stream*, met. μία...ἡ τῆς ἀληθείας ὁδός, ἀλλ' εἰς αὐτὴν...ἐκρέουσι τὰ ῥ. ἄλλα ἄλλοθεν Clem.*str*.1.5(p.18.10; M.8.720A); ῥ. σωτηρίας Or.*fr.54 in Jo*.(p.528.24); *streams* of eloquence, Gr.Naz.*carm*.1.2.32.25(M.37.918A) cit. s. γλυκασμός; Geo.Pis.*carm*.94.1; Thdr.Stud.*cant*.15.2(p.369) cit. s. γλυκυσταγής.

***ῥέκαυτον, τό**, plur., (Lat. *recauta*) *quittance, release* ῥ. τῆς...δαπάνης Ath.Scholast.*coll*.4.22 paratit.(p.70); εἰς παραμυθίαν καὶ ῥ. *ib*.20.2(p.174).

***ῥελεγατίων, ἡ**, (Lat. *relegatio*) *banishment*, Ath.Scholast.*coll*.4.1(p.50).

***ῥεμβάζ-ω, 1.** *drive round, whirl, put in a whirl*, met. καὶ ἕλκουσί σε οἱ λογισμοὶ καὶ ~ουσι Mac.Aeg.*hom*.32.9(M.34.740C); **2.** med., met., *sway, be unbalanced* ὅπερ ἄτοπον καὶ...~ομένης ἔργον διανοίας ἐστίν Max.*opusc*.(M.91.25C).

ῥεμβάς, fem. of ῥεμβός, *Const.App*.4.14.3.

ῥεμβασμός, ὁ, 1. *restlessness* [Lc.10:7b] ὅπερ ῥ. δηλοῖ καὶ διαβολῆς ἐστι τεκμήριον Cyr.*Lc*.10:1ff.(M.72.665A); ὁ ῥ. καὶ ὁ μετεωρισμὸς καὶ ἡ λήθη ἀφαιρονται τὸν τοῦ θεοῦ φόβον Esaias *or*.29.6(p.203); plur., *vagaries* of youth, Gr.Agr.*Eccl*.9.15(M.98.1113B); **2.** *distraction* of mind, ‡Bas.*const*.8.1(2.554C; M.31.1368C); Nil.*Magn*.61(M.79.1052A); Jo.VI H.*v.Jo.D*.35(M.94.484A); plur., Mac.Aeg.*hom*.4.4(M.34.473D); ‡Pall.*h.mon*.1.23(p.10.18; M.34.1116B); Marc.Er.*opusc*.7.6(M.65.1080A).

ῥεμβεύω, *wander*, Just.*dial*.123.3(M.6.761B).

ῥεμβός, (fem. ῥεμβάς) *roaming, gad-about*, *Const.App*.1.5.1; Epiph.*anc*.103(p.123.25; paroxytone M.43.201B); id.*haer*.21.1(p.239.22; M.41.288A); Ant.Mon.*hom*.26(M.89.1517A); neut. as subst., met., *distraction*, †Bas.Anc.*virg*.15(1.603E; M.30.701C).

***ῥέμβος**, τό, *distraction*, Evagr.Pont.*rer.mon.*6(M.40.1257C).

ῥέμβ-ω, med.; **1.** *roam, wander*, hence *gad about* ὑπαρχέτω...ἡ παρθένος μὴ...~ομένη κατὰ τὰς τῶν ἀλλοτρίων οἰκίας *Const.App.*3.6.4; τὸ μὲν κάλλος ἐκ φύσεως ἔχουσαν, κακῶς δὲ τούτῳ χρωμένην, ~ομένην τε καὶ ἀσωτευομένην Nil.*epp.*2.213(M.79.312B); of the eyes, *wander, rove*, Ephr.1.325E; id.2.135A; Cyr.H.*procatech.*9 cit. s. βλέμμα; **2.** met., *vacillate, be uncertain* σκοτισθέντες τὴν ψυχὴν ~όμενον ἔχουσι τὸν νοῦν Ath.*gent.*23(M.25.48A); id.*syn.*25(p.250.24; M.26.725B); *wander, be distracted* παρθενευέτω καὶ ἡ διάνοια· μὴ ~έσθω, μὴ πλανάσθω Gr.Naz.*or.*37.10(M.36.296A); Chrys.*hom.suppl.*2(M.64.428C); ~όμεθα τῇ διανοίᾳ Jo.Jej.*poenit.cont.virg.*(M.88.1961A); ~όμεθα τῷ λογισμῷ Ephr.1.326E; ~ομένους αὐτοὺς συνάγειν Mac.Aeg.*hom.*6.3(M.34.520C); ἡ συντριβὴ τῆς καρδίας ἐστί, τὸ μὴ ἐᾶσαι αὐτὴν ~εσθαι μετὰ ἀλλοτρίων λογισμῶν Bars.*resp.*(M.88.1817A); εὔχῃ σου φυσικῶς μετὰ τοῦ ~εσθαι καὶ διαλογίζεσθαι Mac.Aeg.*hom.*26.21(688D); εὐχόμενοι ἀλλαχοῦ ~όμεθα Chrys.*hom.*24.4 *in Ac.*(9.199E).

***ῥέμψις**, ἡ, ? *mishap*, contretemps; ? *aberration* ῥ. γενομένης τινὸς οἷα φιλεῖ πολλάκις συμβαίνειν Sophr.H.*mir.Cyr.et Jo.*11(M.87.3452C).

***ῥεόλογος**, ὁ, *one with a flow of words, babbler*, Synes.*provid.*2.8 conj. for ῥειόλ-, ῥαιόλ- p.131.9; ῥαδιόλ- M.66.1280C).

***ῥέος**, ὁ, (Lat. *reus*) *defendant*, Heracl.*nov.*25.4(p.47).

***ῥεουοκατορία**, ἡ, (Lat. *revocatoria*) *letter of recall*, Ath.Scholast.*coll.*4 paratit.21(p.70).

***ῥεπετιτεύω**, (Lat. *repeto*) *reclaim, demand back*, Ath.Scholast.*coll.*9.1(p.98); Phot.*nomoc.*2.1(p.495; M.104.576B).

***ῥεπουδιατεύω**, (cf. Lat. *repudio*) *divorce*, Ath.Scholast.*coll.*2 paratit.8(p.44); Phot.*nomoc.*13.4(p.614; M.104.909B).

***ῥεπούδιον**, τό, (Lat. *repudium*) *divorce*, Just.*2apol.*2.6(M.6.444B); Cyr.*fr.Mt.*5:31(M.72.380D); Nil.*epp.*2.181(M.79.293C).

ῥεπτικός, neut. as subst., *tendency, inclination* τὸ ἐπὶ τὸ κρεῖττον ῥ. ἡμῶν Or.*or.*7(p.316.14; M.11.440D).

[*]**ῥέσκομαι**, *be said* or *spoken*, Thphn.*chron.*p.394(M.108.940B); ῥίσκ-, Gr.Mag.*dial.*(tr.Zach.)3.37(M.*PL.*77.314A).

ῥεῦμα, τό, *rheum, discharge*, met. τῶν ἁμαρτημάτων τὰ ῥ. Eulog.*fr.Novat.*ap.Phot.*cod.*280(M.104.328B).

***ῥευματόω**, *make flow, cause to stream*, Geo.Pis.*Pers.*2.311(M.92.1231A).

ῥεῦσις, ἡ, (cf. ῥύσις); **1.** *flow, flux*, met. ὁ νοῦς...πάντα ἐφοδεύων τάχει φορᾶς καὶ ῥεύσεως Gr.Naz.*or.*28.22(p.54.14; M.36.56A); **2.** *transience, mutability*; of what pertains to man, Eun.*apol.*17(M.30.852C); τὴν ἐπίρρυτον...καὶ εὐαλλοίωτον στάσιν, μᾶλλον δέ, στάσιμον ῥεῦσιν εἰπεῖν οἰκειότερον...στάσιν ἀεὶ ῥέουσαν...καὶ ῥ. ἀεικίνητον Max.*ambig.*(M.91.1412B); resulting from Fall, Jo.D.*hom.*4.27(M.96.628B); ref. Inc. καὶ τομὴν καὶ ῥεῦσιν ἐδέξατο τὴν ἐμήν id.*volunt.*36(M.95.173D; 176C); not attributable to God Ἄρειος...πάθος καὶ τομὴν καὶ ῥ. προεξεῦρεν ‡Ath.*Apoll.*1.21(M.26.1129B); Gr.Naz.*or.*29.8(p.84.11; M.36.84B); Didym.(‡Bas.)*Eun.*4(1.280E; M.29.676B); Thdt.*Trin.*9(M.75.1157C).

ῥευστός, of words, *fluent, eloquent* πῶς σε ῥευστοῖς εὐλογήσομεν λόγοις Geo.Pis.*carm.*2.17.

***ῥευστῶς**, *by change* οὔτε ὥσπερ Ἀδὰμ γεγέννηκε τὸν Ἄβελ, οὕτως ὁ θεὸς γεγέννηκε υἱὸν ἐκπορευτῶς, καὶ ῥ. Hier.H.*Trin.*(M.40.853A).

***ῥεφερενδάριος** (*ῥαιφερενδάριος), ὁ, (Lat. *referendarius*) **1.** imperial official, serving as intermediary, reporting petitions to emperor and transmitting his decisions to judges and others ὁ περίβλεπτος τριβοῦνος καὶ ῥ. CCP(449)*act.*(*ACO* 2.1.1 p.149.21; H.2.173C); CCP(536)*act.*1(ῥαιφ- *ACO* 3 pp.128.19,130.42; H.2.1189E, 1193A); Jo.Mal.*chron.*13 p.328(M.97.489C); *IGC As.Min.*324 (Sardis, ? saec. vi); **2.** patriarchal official who bore messages from patriarch to emperor χρὴ...διὰ τῶν ῥ. τῆς μεγάλης ἐκκλησίας πρὸς βασιλέα μηνύεσθαι Ath.Scholast.*coll.*1.1(p.2); Phot.*nomoc.*8.2(p.523; ῥαιφ- M.104.664C).

ῥέω, **1.** *flow, spring* from πάντων...τῶν λόγων ἀπὸ διανοίας καὶ ἤθους ῥεόντων Clem.*paed.*2.5(p.185.1; M.8.445C); ἐκεῖθεν ἡ τῆς προνοίας διδασκαλία ἐρρύη id.*str.*5.1(p.332.21; M.9.24B); Or.*Cels.*6.45(p.116.14; M.11.1368C); of Eve τὴν ἐκ πλευρᾶς [sc. of Adam] πρότερον ῥεύσασαν ...θανατηφόρον ‡Chrys.*pasch.*6(p.181.2; 8.272C); **2.** of time, *elapse, pass*, Thdt.*Is.*9:2(2.232); Thphn.*chron.*p.124(M.108.345C).

***ῥήγισσα**, ἡ, (cf. Lat. *regina*) *queen*, Jo.Mal.*chron.*18 pp.430f.(M.97.636A,B).

ῥῆγμα, τό, **1.** *fragment, shred*, Chrys.*hom.*11.5 *in Eph.*(11.88B); **2.** met., *shattering*, *Lit.*ap.*Const.App.*8.7.5; **3.** eccl., *schism, division*, Chrys.*hom.*2.1 *in 2Thess.*(11.516C); id.*hom.*32.7 *in Mt.*(7.375E); τὸ τῶν Μελετιανῶν ἐν Αἰγύπτῳ ῥ. Thdt.*haer.*4.7(4.361).

ῥήγνυμι, *break asunder, rend, shatter*, ref. demoniacal possession, cf.Mc.9:18 ὁ δαίμων...ἔρρηξεν ἑαυτόν *T.Sal.*9.3(v.l. ἔρριψεν M.122.1329B); πνεύματι πονηρῷ πληγείς, παρὰ τὰ ἴχνη αὐτοῦ πεσών, ἐρράγη Gr.Mag.*dial.*(tr.Zach.)3.26(M.*PL.*77.279D); pass. intrans.; metr. gr. 3rd pers. plur. aor. pass. imper. ῥαγήτωσαν πέτραι Rom.Mel.(*AS* 1 p.117); c. genit., *break away* from ἐρράγη [sc. Ναυᾶτος]...τῆς ἐκκλησίας Eulog.*fr.Novat.*ap.Phot.*cod.*280(M.104.353C).

[*]**ῥήδιον**, τό, = ῥαίδιον, *carriage, conveyance*, Pall.*v.Chrys.*5(p.30.6; M.47.19).

ῥῆμα, τό, **1.** that which is said or spoken, *word, saying*; freq. of prophecy and revelation, *2Clem.*15.4; τὰ τῶν βροντῶν ῥ. Or.*Jo.*13.6(p.230.25; M.14.408A); exeg. Rom.10:6ff. ὡς τοῦ αὐτοῦ ὄντος Χριστοῦ καὶ ῥ. τοῦ ζητουμένου *ib.*1.37(42; p.48.4; 97B); and of Christ's utterances τὰ ῥ. τοῦ κυρίου τὰ λεγόμενα διὰ παραβολῶν Herm.*sim.*5.4.3; ὁ...παρακαλύπτων ἀπ' αὐτῶν τὸ ῥ. Or.*fr.26 in Lc.*9:45(p.245); **2.** ῥ. κυρίου and ῥ. θεοῦ; **a.** of prophecy and revelation ἐπὶ διασπορᾷ τοῦ Ἰσραὴλ κατὰ τὸ ῥ. τοῦ θεοῦ *Pss.Sal.*9.2; ἀνάγει τὴν πίστιν δι' ἀκοῆς καὶ τῆς τῶν ἀποστόλων κηρύξεως ἐπὶ τὸ ῥ. κυρίου καὶ τὸν υἱὸν τοῦ θεοῦ· οὐδέπω συνίεμεν ἀπόδειξιν εἶναι τὸ ῥ. κυρίου; Clem.*str.*2.6(p.126.14ff.; M.8.960B); ἡ κυριακὴ φωνὴ λόγος ἀσχημάτιστος· ἡ ⟨γὰρ⟩ τοῦ λόγου δύναμις, ῥ. κυρίου φωτεινόν, ἀλήθεια οὐρανόθεν...ἐπὶ τὴν συναγωγὴν τῆς ἐκκλησίας ἀφιγμένη *ib.*6.3(p.448.16; M.9.252C); ῥ. θεοῦ τὸ ἐν τῷ εὐαγγελίῳ *Const.App.*2.1.1; **b.** opp. λόγος: οὔτε...ῥ. ὁ λόγος, οὔτε ἆσθμα τὸ πνεῦμα...ἀνενέργητά τε καὶ ἀνυπόστατα τὰ παρ' ἡμῖν ῥ. Gr.Nyss.*or.catech.*4(pp.18.11,19.7; M.45.20Bf.); ὥστε...ἀνυπόστατον τὸν ἐκ θεοῦ φασιν [sc. Marcellus and Photinus] εἶναι λόγον, ῥ. δὲ ἁπλῶς τὸ κατὰ μόνην νοούμενον προφορὰν ἐν ἀνθρώπῳ γενέσθαι Cyr.*Thds.*6(p.45.16; 5^2.5A); ἐγὼ ἕνα μόνον λόγον τοῦ θεοῦ ὁμολογῶ...τὴν δὲ...γραφὴν...οὐ λέγω λόγια, ἀλλὰ ῥ. θεοῦ Jo.D.*disp.*2(M.94.1588B); cf. ῥ. δέ, φησίν [sc. Simon Magus], ἐστι κυρίου τὸ ἐν στόματι γεννώμενον ῥ. καὶ λόγος, ἄλλη δὲ χωρίον γενέσεως οὐκ ἔστι Hipp.*haer.*6.10(p.137.25; M.16.3211A); **c.** of divine ἐνέργεια, exeg. Eph.6:17 εἰς παράστασιν τοῦ δυνατοῦ τῆς ἐνεργείας τοῦ πνεύματος. ῥ. γὰρ θεοῦ λέγει ἀντὶ τοῦ θεοῦ ἐνέργεια ὡς τὸ [Ps.32:6]...καὶ παρὰ τοῖς προφήταις... κἀνταῦθα τοίνυν θεοῦ ῥ. τὴν τοῦ πνεύματος ἐκάλεσεν ἐνέργειαν Thdr.Mops.*Eph.*6:17(p.193.15ff.; M.66.920Df.); **d.** of H. Ghost θεοῦ μὲν λόγος ὁ υἱός, ῥ. δὲ υἱοῦ τὸ πνεῦμα...καὶ ἐπειδὴ ῥ. υἱοῦ, διὰ τοῦτο θεοῦ Didym.(‡Bas.)*Eun.*5(1.304E; M.29.732A); ῥ. θεοῦ ἐνταῦθα [sc. 1Petr.1:25] καλεῖ τὸ πνεῦμα τοῦ θεοῦ id.*Trin.*2.6(M.39.516B); *ib.*2.5(505B); *ib.*2.7(568A); **e.** Montanist, of inspiration claimed by Maximilla ῥ. εἰμι καὶ πνεῦμα καὶ δύναμις Anon.ap.Eus.*h.e.*5.16.17(M.20.472A).

***ῥηματίζω**, *express in words*, ‡Hipp.*Ber.Hel.*3(p.323.10; M.10.833C).

ῥημάτιον, τό, **1.** *trifling phrase* τῶν μὲν πολλῶν καλῶν οὐ πεφροντίκατε, τοῦ δὲ μικροῦ ῥ. ἐπιλαμβάνεσθε Just.*dial.*115.6(M.6.744A); Or.*hom.*6 *in Lc.*(p.43.5); τοῖς δὲ δυσὶ ῥ. ἀσυνθέτοις καθάπερ λίθοις... ἐπιχειροῦσίν με βάλλειν Dion.Al.ap.Ath.*Dion.*18(p.60.6; M.25.508A); **2.** *common word, ordinary expression* ψιλοῖς ῥ. καὶ ταῖς τυχούσαις φωναῖς Eus.*v.C.*4.26(p.127.22; M.20.1176A); id.*p.e.*1.4(12D; M.21.40D); **3.** in derogatory sense *cliché, claptrap*, esp. of heresy διὰ πάντων ἑαυτῶν τῶν ῥ. ἐπιχειρήσαντες τὰ εἰς ἀναίρεσιν τῆς τοῦ λόγου θεότητος Alex.Al.*ep.encycl.*6(p.9.24; M.18.576D); Ath.*syn.*36,39(pp.263.15,265.22; M.26.757A,761C); Cyr.*Am.*17(3.267E).

***ῥήξ**, ὁ, (Lat. *rex*) *king* γράμματα τοῦ ῥηγὸς τῶν Γότθων Chrys.*ep.*14.5(3.601A); Ast.Soph.*Ps.*7(M.40.472A); Evagr.*h.e.*3.27(p.124.18; M.86.2653A).

***ῥηξισθενής**, *breaking the strong*; of David, †Apoll.*met.Ps.*121:5(M.33.1508B).

ῥηξίφρων, *who has discarded reason, crackbrained*, Thdr.Stud.*or.*11.6(M.99.808B); id.*epp.*2.54(M.99.1268A).

ῥῆσις, ἡ, **1.** *saying, speech*; of the prophets, Iren.*haer.*2.32.4(M.7.829B); of angels, Meth.*symp.*7.1(p.71.14; M.18.124B); τὴν τοῦ ἀποστασίου ῥ. [i.e. of Christ] Clem.*str.*3.6(p.219.11; M.8.1153A); **2.** *text* of scripture ἐκθέσθαι τὰς εὐαγγελικὰς ῥ. Bas.*ep.*236(3.361D; M.32.877A); τὴν σήμερον ἀναγνωσθεῖσαν ῥ. προχειρισαμένους Chrys.*stat.*2.4(2.25E); Gel.Cyz.*h.e.*2.15.6(M.85.1260A).

ῥητέον, τό, *thing said, word*, Thdr.Stud.*epp.*1.56(M.99.1112C).

***ῥητλιάζω**, s.v.l., *level off* a measure πλήσας δὲ τὸ μέτρον καὶ ῥητλιάσας, ὁμολογεῖ, ὅτι πεπλήρωμαι Epiph.*mens.*24(M.43.281A), v. not. ad loc.

***ῥητολογία**, ἡ, ? *verbiage* τὰ ὅσα μὴ συνίεσαν διά τινος ἐπιπλάστου ῥ. παρακαλύπτοντες, ὡς εἰς μυθολογίαν τὴν ἀλήθειαν παραβραβεύσωσιν Tat.*orat.*40(p.41.9; M.6.884C; perh. for ἀρεταλογίας).

ῥητορεύω, **1.** *speak in public, preach*, *Didasc.Jac.*4.7(p.69.12); **2.** *recount, tell*, Rom.Mel.(*AS* 1 pp.6,131).

ῥητορίζ-ω, *be an orator*, *dicta autem Rhetorica Graeca appellatione* ἀπὸ τοῦ ~ειν, *id est a copia locutionis*, Isid.H.*etym.*2.1.1.

ῥητός, 1. of writings, *canonical* οἱ μὲν καθαροὶ ταῖς ῥ. μόνον γραφαῖς κέχρηνται· οὗτοι δὲ ταῖς λεγομέναις Πράξεσιν Ἀνδρέου τε καὶ Θωμᾶ...ἐπερείδονται Epiph.*haer*.61.1(p.381.1; M.41.1040D); *ib*. 55.2(p.326.1; 973A); id.*mens*.3(M.43.244A); **2.** of meaning, *literal* ῥ. διάνοιαν Eus.*d.e*.7.1(p.321.35; M.22.525C); **3.** neut. as subst.; **a.** = ῥῆμα, *word, saying*, Or.*Jo*.6.24(14; p.134.12; M.14.244A); Chrys. *hom.15.2 in Jo*.(8.87B); Thdt.*Lam*.4:15(2.665); **b.** *passage* or *saying* of scripture, †Hipp.*Artem*.ap.Eus.*h.e*.5.28.13(M.20.516A); of OT, Clem.*str*.1.21(p.91.8; M.8.888B); Or.*Ps*.57:9(p.62); Ath.*decr*. 13(p.11.23; M.25.'445'(437)B); of NT, Or.*or*.2(p.302.12; M.11.421B); Epiph.*haer*.56.2(p.341.23; M.41.992D); Thdt.*Ps*.109:1(1.1393); **c.** *text* of scripture αὐτῷ μᾶλλον τῷ ῥ. προσέχωμεν Just.*dial*.135.3(M.6. 788D); ἑρμηνείαν γραφικῶν ῥ. Phot.*cod*.280(M.104.325A); of liturgy, Jo.D.*trisag*.6(M.95.36B); **d.** *literal meaning* ὅσον ἐπὶ τῷ ῥ., οἱ Ἰουδαῖοι· ὅσον δὲ ἐπὶ τῇ ἀλληγορίᾳ, ἐγὼ ὁ λόγος καὶ οἱ κατ' ἐμὲ μεμορφωμένοι Or.*Jo*.13.17(p.240.32; M.14.424B); Soz.*h.e*.5.22.3(M.67. 1284A); περὶ...τὸ ῥ. ... τὰς ἐξηγήσεις ποιήσασθαι, τὰς θεωρίας ἀποφεύγοντα [i.e. Diodorus of Tarsus] *ib*.8.2.6(1516A); εἴτε...κατὰ τὸ ῥ. ...εἴτε εἰς τὸ βάθος Thdt.*Ezech*.26:21(2.896).

ῥήτρα, ἡ, *oratory* τὸν λόφον τῆς Ἀττικῆς ῥ. Mac.Mgn.*apocr*.3 proem.(p.51.5).

ῥήτωρ, ὁ, 1. *teacher of rhetoric*, Or.*Cels*.1.28(p.79.16; M.11.713A); ἡ χρῆσις...ἣν ἴσασιν οἱ τοῖς τοῦ ῥ. λόγοις καθομιλήσαντες Gr.Nyss. *Eun*.1(1 p.41.14; M.45.269A); **2.** *advocate, barrister*, *Const.App*.4.6. 5; Evagr.*h.e*.3.10(p.109.11; M.86.2616A); *ib*.5.24(p.219.17; 2841A); in gen., *advocate, supporter* οἱ τῆς πλάνης ῥ. Adam.*dial*.5.27(p.234.17; M.11.1869A).

***ῥιγιάζομαι,** *have a rigor, shiver with fever*, Pall.*h.Laus*.11(p.34. 16; M.34.1034D).

[*]**ῥίγμα, τό,** for ῥῆγμα, *crack* κεράμιον οἴνου ῥίγμα πεποιηκὸς... διὰ αὐτοῦ ἀπολέσει τὸν οἶνον Ephr.3.101A.

***ῥιγοπυρετέω,** *have a rigor, shiver with fever*, Leont.N.*v.Jo. Eleem*.27(p.58.3).

ῥίζα, ἡ, 1. *root*; illustrating relation of Father to Son αὐτοῦ τὴν ῥ. καὶ τὴν πηγήν, τὸν πατέρα Or.*fr.69 in Jo*.(p.538.8); πλείονα... ὁμοιώματα· καὶ γὰρ καὶ φυτὸν εἶπον ἀπὸ σπέρματος ἢ ἀπὸ ῥ. ἀνελθὸν ἕτερον εἶναι τοῦ ὅθεν ἐβλάστησε, καὶ πάντως ἐκείνῳ καθέστηκεν ὁμοφυές Dion.Al.ap.Ath.*decr*.25(p.21.26; M.25.461B); ὁ πατὴρ...ἐγέννησε τὸν υἱόν...καὶ οὐκ ἔκτισεν...ὡς βλαστὸν ἀπὸ ῥ. Ath.*exp.fid*.4(M.25.208A); **2.** met., *source, foundation, basic principle*; **a.** in gen. ἡ βεβαία τῆς πίστεως ὑμῶν ῥ. Polyc.*ep*.1.2; ὁμογενῆ σώματα ἔχοντες τῷ σώματι τοῦ κυρίου ἐκ τοῦ πληρώματος αὐτοῦ λαμβάνομεν, κἀκεῖνο ῥ. ἔχομεν εἰς τὴν ἀνάστασιν Ath.*Dion*.10(p.54.1; M.25.496B); ῥ. τις...καὶ ὑπόμνημα ...τῆς τελεωτέρας ἐξεργασίας Gr.Naz.*or*.30.16(p.134.11; M.36.125A); **b.** Trin. γινώσκοντες...μὴ κτίσμα, ἀλλ' ἐκ τῆς οὐσίας γέννημα εἶναι τὸν λόγον καὶ τὴν οὐσίαν τοῦ πατρὸς ἀρχὴν καὶ ῥ. ... εἶναι τοῦ υἱοῦ Ath. *syn*.45(p.270.8; M.26.772D); ὁ πατὴρ τέλειον ἔχων τὸ εἶναι...ῥ. καὶ πηγὴ τοῦ υἱοῦ καὶ τοῦ πνεύματος ‡Ath.*Sabell*.11(M.28.116B); ref. Mt. 16:17 ἐπέγνω [sc. S. Peter]...τὸν συμφυᾶ κλάδον τοῦ θεοῦ· ἐτίμησεν ἐν τούτῳ τὴν...ἄναρχον ῥ. Didym.*Trin*.1.30(M.39.417A); **c.** Gnost. δύο εἰσὶ παραφυάδες τῶν ὅλων αἰώνων...ἀπὸ μιᾶς ῥ., ἥτις ἐστὶ δύναμις σιγὴ ἀόρατος 'Simon' ap.Hipp.*haer*.6.18(p.144.12; M.16.3222A); Hipp.*ib*. 6.12(p.138.13; 3211B); Naassene τῷ οἰκητηρίῳ οὗ ἡ ῥ. τῶν ὅλων τεθεμελίωται *ib*.5.9(p.98.19; 3154B); Valent. ὁ...ἀγέννητος ὑπάρχων ἀρχὴ τῶν ὅλων καὶ ῥ. καὶ βάθος καὶ βυθός *ib*.6.30(p.158.4; 3239B); view of Bardesanes τὸν διάβολον αὐτοφυῆ λογίζομαι...καὶ δύο ῥ. οἶδα, πονηρὰν καὶ ἀγαθήν Adam.*dial*.3.3(p.118.13; M.11.1793D); **3.** *order* of bishops εἰ ἐποίησα τοῦτο...μὴ ἀριθμηθείην εἰς ἐπισκόπων ῥίζαν Chrys.*a.exil*.1.4(3.418A).

***ῥίζικον, τό,** *risk*, *Nomoc*.522.

***ῥιζοδάκτυλος, ὁ,** *knuckle*, Melet.*nat.hom*.26(M.64.1249B).

***ῥιζοσύνετος,** ? *wisely founded* ῥ. σταυρόν ‡Chrys.*ador*.2(11. 824B).

ῥιζοτομικός, *of the herbalist, botanical* ῥ. τέχνη Bas.*hex*.9.3(1.83D; M.29.196B).

ῥίζωμα, τό, 1. *root principle, basis* Σίμων...λέγει...ἀπέραντον εἶναι δύναμιν, ταύτην ῥ. τῶν ὅλων εἶναι Hipp.*haer*.10.12(p.273.1; M.16. 3426B); **2.** *rooting, implanting*, met. ἀκτημοσύνη, φιλαργυρίας ἐκρίζωμα, ἀφιλαργυρίας δὲ ῥ. †Nil.*vit*.3(M.79.1141D).

ῥιζωρυχέω, *dig up roots*, Gr.Nyss.*or.catech*.37(p.146.6; M.45.96A).

***ῥιζωτής, ὁ,** *founder, planter*, Synes.*hymn*.5.18(p.36; M.66.1608).

ῥικνότης, ἡ, *shrivelled state*, Gr.Nyss.*anim.et res*.(M.46.149B); opp. πολυσαρκία, id.*mart*.1(M.46.752C).

***ῥικνόω,** *shrivel* (trans.), Gr.Naz.*carm*.1.2.29.61(M.37.889A); pass. intrans., *become shrunken, grow shrivelled*, Gr.Nyss.*Apoll*.46(M.45. 1237A); Thdt.*h.rel*.18(3.1230); of clothes, *become worn out* πῶς... τεσσαράκοντα ἔτη τοῦ λαοῦ τὰ ἱμάτια οὐκ ἐρικνώθη; Epiph.*anc*.62 (p.75.3; M.43.128C).

[*]**ῥικνύς,** for ῥικνός, *shrivelled*, Gr.Naz.*carm*.2.1.32.25(M.37. 1302A).

***ῥικνῶς,** ῥ. ἔχω *be shrunken, withered*; with age, †Cyr.*hom.div*.10 (5^2.374E).

ῥιναυλέω, *snort, blow through the nose*, Tat.*orat*.22(p.25.8; M.6. 857A).

ῥινηλάτης, ὁ, *one who tracks by scent*, as adj. κύνας ῥ. ‡Chrys. *meretr*.2(10.762D).

ῥινοκοπέω, *cut off the nose*, Thphn.*chron*.p.283(M.108.697B); *ib*. p.308(749D); *ib*.p.372(892C).

***ῥινοκτυπέω,** *snort loudly*, *Pers*.(p.26.13); Sophr.H.*mir.Cyr.et Jo*. 31(M.87.3521B); Thphn.*chron*.p.52(M.108.184B); with anger, *Mir. Artem*.26(p.38.3).

***ῥινοκτυπία, ἡ,** *loud snorting*, Sophr.H.*mir.Cyr.et Jo*.31(M.87. 3521B).

ῥινολαβίς, ἡ, *instrument for taking hold of the nose* for purpose of torture, Synes.*ep*.58(M.66.1400B).

***ῥινότμητος,** *with the nose cut off*, Pall.*h.Laus*.11(p.33.13; M.34. 1034A).

ῥινοτομέω, *cut off the nose*, Thphn.*chron*.p.335(M.108.809A).

ῥιπίδιον, τό, *fan* with which deacon fans the oblation, *Lit*. ap.*Const.App*.8.12.3; *Lit.Chrys*.(p.384.3); *Chron.Pasch*.p.390(M.92. 1001C); in form of a staff with metal disk depicting a seraph's face and wings, ‡Bas.*h.myst*.49,60(pp.390.9,394.11); ‡Sophr.H.*liturg*.21 (M.87.4001A); representing heavenly powers hiding their faces in awe at Passion, ‡Germ.CP *contempl*.(M.98.436A,B).

ῥιπίζ-ω, 1. *fan*, ref. supposed action of the lungs πνεύμονι...κραδίη ∼εται Geo.Pis.*carm.vit*.43; **2.** med., *shake, tremble*, Chrys.*pan.Laz*. (2.647A).

ῥιπίς, ἡ, = ῥιπίδιον, typifying cherubim, ‡Germ.CP *contempl*. (M.98.420D).

ῥιπισμός, ὁ, *movement of wind* caused by fanning; met., *veering* of the mind, Jo.Clim.*scal*.27(M.88.1109B).

***ῥιπιστήρ, ὁ,** *one who fans*, bearer of the ῥιπίδιον, ‡Ath.*annunt*.7 (M.28.953D).

***ῥιπιστήριον, τό,** = ῥιπίδιον, Jo.Disc.*v.Epiph*.38(M.41.73A); Cyr.S.*v.Euthym*.28(p.45.8).

ῥίπτ-ω, 1. *throw*; **a.** *put* or *thrust* ῥῖψον τὸ δακτυλίδιον...εἰς τὸ στῆθος τοῦ δαίμονος *T.Sal*.1.8(M.122.1317C); **b.** *shoot* an arrow, Jo.Mal.*chron*.5 p.110(M.97.201C); **2.** *cast away*; *expose* an infant, *Diogn*.5.6; Jo.Mal.*chron*.2 p.46(M.97.120A); **3.** *cast downwards*; met.; **a.** thoughts, Bas.*hom.in Ps*.28(1.114D; M.29.281D); **b.** *cast down*; *overthrow* arguments, Ath.*Dion*.9(p.52.1; M.25.492B); *annul* ἔρριψεν τὴν...σύνοδον Thphn.*chron*.p.319(M.108.772C); **4.** *cast* upon; met.; **a.** by leaving undone, *cause to devolve* μὴ πᾶν ἐπὶ τοὺς ἱερέας ∼ωμεν Chrys.*hom.18.3 in 2Cor*.(10.568E); **b.** by entrusting, *commit* τὸ πᾶν ἐπὶ τὸν θεὸν ῥ. id.*hom.6.4 in Tit*.(11.770E); *set* one's hopes ἄνω...ῥ. πρὸς θεὸν τὰς ἐλπίδας Geo.Pis.*carm*.3.64; **5.** *throw* at, *bring up* against, met. τὴν ἑαυτῶν ἀμέλειαν ἔρριψαν εἰς ἐμέ Ath.*apol. Const*.26(M.25.628C).

[*]**ῥίσκομαι,** v. ῥέσκομαι.

ῥιψοκίνδυνος, *fearless*, Chrys.*hom.6.3 in Eph*.(11.42E).

ῥιψοκινδύνως, 1. *rashly, recklessly*, *1Clem*.14.2; Eus.*h.e*.4.15.8(M. 20.345B); Thdt.*qu.5 in Dt*.(1.264); **2.** *fearlessly*, Clem.*str*.2.20(p.172. 14; M.8.1053A).

ῥιψόφθαλμος, *casting the eyes about, having a roving eye* οὐδὲ ῥ. οὐδὲ μέθυσος *Const.App*.7.6.4.

ῥόγα, ἡ, 1. *dole, largess*, †Gregent.*leg.Hom*.(M.86.580A); *Chron. Pasch*.p.386(M.92.989B); Thphn.*chron*.p.41(M.108.157C); **2.** *alms* ῥοῦγα Barth.Edess.*Agar*.(M.104.1416A).

***ῥόγατος,** (Lat. *rogatus*) *summoned* μάρτυρες ἀξιόπιστοι ῥ. Ath. Scholast.*coll*.5.5(p.75).

***ῥογεύ-ω, 1.** *distribute* τὰ μὲν ξέων...τὰ δὲ χωνεύων καὶ ῥ. τοῖς ὁμοτρόποις *Supplic*.ap.CCP(536)*act*.5(*ACO* 3 p.60.37; H.2.1320A); in charity ῥ. αὐτὸ [sc. τὸ γέννημα τοῦ σίτου]...τοῖς πτωχοῖς Call.*v.Hyp*. (p.34); *V.Dan*.4(p.63.13); Leont.N.*v.Sym*.32(M.93.1709A); in bribery, *Chron.Pasch*.p.331(M.92.857B); *ib*.p.339(885A); **2.** *give money* or *alms to* ∼εσθαι αὐτοὺς διὰ τῶν ἰδίων ὀπτιώνων Ath.Scholast. *coll*.20.2 (p.174); abs. ὑπὲρ αὐτοῦ (a bishop deceased) προσήκει τῇ ἐκκλησίᾳ ...∼ειν ἐπεὶ καὶ μνήμης ἕνεκα τῶν ἀρχιερέων *Nomoc*.24.

ῥογίον, τό, *vessel* κατέχων ῥ. σεμνά, ἃ καλεῖται ἀνακλαστάρια... εἰπὼν αὐτῷ...τίνι καὶ τίνι ὤφειλεν δοῦναι τὰ ῥ. τοῦ ἐλαίου *Mir.Artem*. 30(p.43.6,12).

ῥόγχος, ὁ, *deep breath*, *Contrad*.1(p.7) cit. s. σύρω; *ib*.2(p.9).

***ῥοδάσταμα, τό,** perh. for ῥοδόσταγμα *rose-water* γράψον ταῦτα εἰς χάρτην ἀγέννητον μετὰ κιν(ν)αβάρεως ἢ κρόκου ἀλείωνε μετὰ ῥ. ἢ δαλὸν ἅπτοντα ἀποσβέσας ὕδατι *Exorc.*(p.343).

ῥοδίζ-ω, 1. *make rose-coloured* τῷ αἵματι τοῦ Ἰησοῦ τὰς καρδίας ῥαντίζειν, μᾶλλον δὲ ∼ειν ‡Chrys.*phar.*(8.112B); **2.** *deck one's grave with roses, Inscr.* W. M. Ramsay, Cities and Bishoprics of Phrygia p.562 bis (saec. iii).

[*]**ῥοδινός, ὁ,** a gem, one of the varieties of hyacinth stone (identified with ligure or tourmaline), so called prob. because of its pink colour, Epiph.*gemm.*7(M.43.300A).

***ῥοδοειδῶς,** *like a rose,* Nil.*epp.*3.171(M.79.464C).

***ῥοδομιγής,** *compounded of roses,* perh. *rose-coloured* βάμμα... ὀμφάκινον καὶ χλωρὸν ἕτερον ῥοδομιγές Clem.*paed.*2.10(p.222.15; M. 8.528A).

[*]**ῥοδονία, ἡ,** v. ῥοδωνία.

***ῥοδοπαράδεισος, ὁ,** *rose-garden,* Eus.Al.*serm.*1(M.86.317C).

***ῥοδόπατος, ὁ,** *path of roses* εὑρέθη ῥ. ἡ φλόξ Rom.Mel.(*AS* 1 p.194).

ῥοδών, ὁ, met., *bed of roses* τοὺς ἄνθρακας ῥ. ἐνόμιζον [sc. martyrs] ‡Chrys.*pent.*1(3.789A).

ῥοδωνία ([*]**ῥοδονία**), **ἡ, 1.** *rose-bed, garden of roses*; met., of Bas. βουνὸς διηνθισμένος μυστικῆς ῥοδονίας Ephr.*enc.Bas.*90(p.147; 2.290B); ὅσα τῶν...πατέρων τοὺς λειμῶνας ἐπελθὼν τῆς ἐκείνων ῥ. συνήγαγον ‡Caes.Naz.*dial.*1(M.38.856); **2.** met., *bed of roses* τῶν ἐπὶ ῥοδωνίας κατακεκλιμένων...μᾶλλον ἔχαιρον [sc. martyrs] Chrys.*hom. 38.4 in Mt.*(7.430B); cf. ῥοδών.

***ῥοθίζας,** s.v.l., from adj. ῥόθιζος *surging* ῥ. κινήσεις ‡Max.*cap.al.* 150(M.90.1436B; conj. ῥοθίας or ῥοθιζούσας).

***ῥοιγδέομαι,** prob. for ῥοιβδέομαι, *roar,* of fire, *M.Pion.*4.21.

ῥοῖζος, ὁ, *rushing sound* or *motion*; met., *rush, gust* of passion or thoughts πολλῷ τῷ ῥ. τοῦ πάθους τῆς ψυχῆς ὑποσυρομένης Chrys. *sac.*3.14(p.71.10; 1.390C); id.*hom.42.1 in Mt.*(7.453A); of recitation of psalms, *with a swing,* con moto, Nil.*Eulog.*9(M.79.1105A).

ῥοιζόω, med., *rush* through the air, ref. Mt.24:24 ῥ. τότε ὁ δόλιος Rom.Mel.(*AS* 1 p.39).

***ῥοϊκός,** ? **ὁ,** *pomegranate,* Anast.S.*hex.*7(M.89.966D).

ῥομβέω, *spin* or *whirl* like a bull-roarer, i.e. to make artificial thunder, Hipp.*haer.*4.32(p.58.10; M.16.3095A).

ῥομφαία, ἡ, 1. *large, broad sword* ἡ...ῥ. βαρβαρικόν ἐστιν ὅπλον, ὡς ἱστορεῖ Φύλαρχος Max.*schol.epp.Dion.Ar.*9(M.4.561A); any sword, symbol of royalty προηγοῦνται...τὰ σκῆπτρα, καὶ αἱ ῥ. ὡς σύμβολα βασιλέως ‡Sophr.H.*liturg.*21(M.87.4001B); **2.** met.; **a.** ref. Gen.3:24 τίς θήσει φλογέην ῥ. ἐμῷ παραδείσῳ; Gr.Naz.*carm.*2.2(epigr.)16.13 (M.38.91A); οὔτε...ἡ φλογίνη ῥ. φύσις ἦν πυρός, ἀλλ' ὄψις τοιαύτη Thdr.Mops.*Gen.*3:24(M.66.641C); ὅτε...κωλύμην ἡ φλογίνη ῥ. οὐκ ἐπαγάγῃ τῇ χάριτι τοῦ σταυροῦ, εἰσίωμεν...τὸν παράδεισον Germ.CP *or.*1(M.98.225D); various interpretations in Proc.G.*Gen.*3:24(M.87. 229B); **b.** ref. Lc.2:35 ῥ. ... ἐστὶ ψεκτὴ πειρασμὸς εἰς ἀπιστίαν θεοῦ προσκαλούμενος τὴν ψυχήν Or.*sel.in Ps.*21:21(M.12.1257C); ῥ. λέγει [sc. ὁ Σιμεών] τὸν λόγον τὸν πειραστικόν, τὸν κριτικὸν τῶν ἐνθυμήσεων ...προφητεύει οὖν...σοῦ οὖν αὐτῆς τῆς ἄνωθεν δεδιδαγμένης τὰ περὶ κυρίου ἅψεταί τις διάκρισις, τοῦτ' ἔστιν ἡ ῥ. id.*hom.17 in Lc.*(pp.116. 15,118.4) = Bas.*ep.*260.9(3.400D,401A; M.32.965C,968A); αὐτῆς τῆς θεοτόκου ψυχῆς ῥ. διελαθῆναι λέγων, σαφῶς τὸ ἐν τῷ σταυρῷ προφητεύει πάθος ‡Gr.Nyss.*occurs.*(M.46.1176A); ῥ. ἐν τούτοις καταδηλοῦσθαί φαμεν, ὡς ἐν εἴδει μαχαίρας τὸν πειρασμόν, ἢ καὶ αὐτὸ τὸ πάθος τὸ ...ἐπενηνεγμένον τῷ Ἐμμανουὴλ Cyr.*Lc.*2:35(M.72.505C); ῥ. ... ἔλεγε τὴν ὀξεῖαν τοῦ πάθους προσβολὴν πρὸς λογισμοὺς ἐκτόπους κατατέμνουσαν τοῦ γυναίου τὸν νοῦν id.*Jo.*12(4.1065B); **c.** Ezech.33:3 interpreted of enemies of soul, Chrys.*sac.*6.1(p.142.5; 1.422A); **d.** of Herodias ἡ ῥ. ἡ δίστομος Chrysipp.*enc.in Jo.Bapt.*11(p.41.20).

***ῥομφαιόμορφος,** *sword-shaped,* Anast.S.*hex.*12(M.89.1076A).

ῥόος, ὁ, *stream* κατὰ ῥόον *down stream, with the current,* hence *swiftly, suddenly* τὰ πράγματα κατὰ ῥ. ἐφέρετο ὥσπερ ἐν κατακλυσμῷ Constantius *ep.*ap.Ath.*apol.Const.*30(M.25.633B); *in line with* or *according to the sense, intelligibly* ἔστ' ἂν ἴοι κατὰ ῥοῦν τὰ πνευματικὰ καὶ τῆς ἀληθείας οἱ χαρακτῆρες...ἐκφαίνοιντο Cyr.*ador.*13(1.467C).

***ῥοπαληφορέω,** *wield a club,* Cyr.*hom.pasch.*7(5^2.87B).

ῥοπή, ἡ, 1. *turn of the scale, weight,* Bas.*hom.in Ps.*28(1.117E; M.29.289C); met. ἀνήρ...τις ἡβῶν...τρυτάνης θεοῦ ἀηττήτου ἀήττητον ἔχων ῥ. *Pers.*(p.8.8); **2.** met., *propensity, inclination*; **a.** n divine nature immutable οὐχ ὡς ἐπὶ θάτερα ῥοπὴν ἔχοντος αὐτοῦ καὶ δεκτικοῦ τοῦ ἐναντίου Ath.*Ar.*1.52(M.26.121A); πάντα δυναμένην τὴν τοῦ λόγου προαίρεσιν πρὸς οὐδὲν τῶν κακῶν τὴν ῥ. ἔχειν Gr.Nyss. *or.catech.*1(p.10.13; M.45.16A); Cyr.*ador.*2(1.56A); **b.** belonging to angelic nature ὁ διάβολος...κωλυόμενος...νῦν ὑπὸ θεοῦ τῆς ῥ. χρήσασθαι ταύτης, καὶ τὴν καθ' ἡμῶν πληρῶσαι...ὀργήν Leont.et Jo.*sacr.*(M. 86.2077B); **c.** an unstable element in human nature, sometimes towards evil ἡ ἀπαιδευσία πολλὴν ἐνδίδωσι ῥ. εἰς ἀδικίαν Clem.*paed.*3. 11(p.269.3; M.8.632A); ref. pre-existent souls ῥ. ... τινι τῇ πρὸς κακίαν πτερορρυούσας τὰς ψυχὰς ἐν σώμασι γίνεσθαι Or.*princ.*1.8.4 (p.103.2) = Gr.Nyss *anim.et res.*(M.46.112C); παραφυλακτέον...ἡμῖν μάλιστα τοῖς ἐν Χριστῷ τὴν εἰς τὰ φαῦλα ῥ. Cyr.*Os.*129(3.162B); sometimes towards good ὥστε ἂν ἐθέλωμεν πολλὴν ἔχομεν...πρὸς ἀρετὴν τὴν ῥ. Chrys.*hom.22.4 in 1Cor.*(10.198A); Cyr.*Jo.*6(4.569D); ῥ. τοῦ ἡγεμονικοῦ Or.*princ.*3.1.4(p.198.15; M.11.253A); τὴν ῥ. τῆς καρδίας Bas.*hom.*13.4(2.117A; M.31.432B); τέθεικεν ὁ...θεὸς ἐν ταῖς τῶν παιδαγωγουμένων ῥ. τὸ ἑλέσθαι μὲν τὸ ἀγαθὸν ἀποφοιτᾶν δὲ τῶν φαύλων Cyr.*Is.*1.1(2.22D); 'τὴν δὲ πρὸς ἐπικουρίαν τῶν δεομένων ῥ.' 'πόδας' καὶ 'βάδισιν' ὀνομάζει [sc. ἡ γραφή] Hadr.*introd.*27(M.98. 1280B); closely connected with and logically prior to the act of the will ἀνάλογον τῇ ῥ. τοῦ αὐτεξουσίου αὐτῶν πρὸς ἀποδοχὴν τοῦ καλοῦ πολλῷ βελτίους ἐγένοντο Or.*Cels.*6.2(p.72.11; M.11.1292A); Gr.Naz. *carm.*1.1.34.35(M.37.948A) cit. s. βούλησις; αὐτεξούσιον τῆς εἰς τὸ καλὸν ἢ εἰς τοὐναντίον...ῥ. Eus.*d.e.*4.6(p.160.10; M.22.265D); πᾶσα θλῖψις ἐλέγχει τὴν ῥ. τοῦ θελήματος, εἴτε τις εἰς δεξιὰ ῥέπει, εἴτε εἰς ἀριστερά Marc.Er.*opusc.*2.191(M.65.960C); τὸ βούλεσθαι καὶ μὴ βούλεσθαι...ἴδιον...λογικῆς ψυχῆς· περὶ ἣν ἡ αὐτεξουσιότης τε καὶ ἡ ἐφ' ἑκάτερα τοῦ θέλειν ῥ. θεωρεῖται Leont.B.*Nest.et Eut.*2(M.86.1332D); preceding appetition κατανοήσας [sc. θεός] ῥ. τοῦ ἐφ' ἡμῖν...καὶ ὁρμὴν μετὰ τὴν ῥ. Or.*comm.in Rom.*1:1(*JTS* 13 p.211); **3.** *motion*; **a.** any slight movement μικρὰ...ἀνέμου ῥ. Chrys.*hom.9.3 in 2Tim.* (11.719D); **b.** *flow* of water, Synes.*ep.*15(M.66.1352A); **c.** of the changes and chances of earthly life, Thdr.Stud.*nativ.BMV* 7(M.96. 689B); **d.** met., *expression, act* ταῦτα μιᾷ ῥ. φύσεως συντελεῖ [sc. a ray of the sun] Eus.*d.e.*4.5(p.157.15; M.22.261D); μιᾷ ῥ. κατὰ πάντων ἀντιστῆναι ὡς ὁ...λόγος Ath.*inc.*53.1(M.25.189C); τὰ πάντα ὑφέστηκε τῇ ῥ. μόνῃ τοῦ θείου βουλήματος Nil.*epp.*1.112(M.79.132B); **4.** *make-weight,* any *weight* placed in the scale, Bas.*hom.in Ps.*61 (1.197D; M.29.480B); id.*hom.*5.9(2.43B; M.31.260C); **5.** met., *casting weight, decisive influence, help* μηδεμιᾶς ἀπολαῦσαι φιλανθρωπίας, μηδὲ ῥ., μηδὲ βοηθείας Chrys.*hom.3.1 in 2Tim.*(11.673B); πλῆθος ὄντες [sc. Arians] ἐκ τῆς Κωνσταντίου καὶ Οὐάλεντος ῥ. Soz.*h.e.*7.6. 1(M.67.1428A); μετὰ τῆς συμμαχίας τῶν ὅπλων καὶ τὴν τῶν χρημάτων αὐτῷ μεγίστην ῥ. ἐχαρίζετο Thphyl.*exc.gent.*8(p.485.30; M.113. 948B); **6.** freq. of divine help θεοῦ ῥ. Chrys.*hom.15.4 in 2Cor.* (10.549B); μετὰ τῆς ἡμετέρας σπουδῆς, καὶ πρὸ τῆς ἡμετέρας τῆς ἄνωθεν δεόμεθα ῥ. id.*catech.*1.4(2.231D); οὐδενὸς ἂν τούτων ἐδεήθης, εἰ τὴν ἐμὴν ἐπεκαλέσω ῥ. Thdt.*Is.*22:11(p.92.12; 2.286); δήλη πᾶσιν ἡ θεία ῥ. id.*qu.16 in Jud.*(1.334); Proc.G.*Is.*9:8ff.(M.87.2016A); esp. *divine help* within the soul, *grace* 'ἐγὼ παρέμεινα ὑμῖν ἐν τοῖς πειρασμοῖς.' ταῦτα δὲ ἔλεγε, δεικνὺς ὅτι παρὰ τῆς αὐτοῦ ῥ. ἐνδυναμοῦνται Chrys.*hom.65.2 in Jo.*(8.390D); οἱ...τῷ σωτῆρι πεπιστευκότες τὴν αὐτοῦ ῥ. ἀναμένουσι Thdt.*Is.*32:4(p.128.37); indispensable for the performance of meritorious works κἂν μυριάκις σπουδάζωμεν, οὐδὲν οὐδέποτε κατορθῶσαι δυνησόμεθα, εἰ μὴ καὶ τῆς ἄνωθεν ῥ. ἀπολαύσαιμεν...οὕτω πάλιν εἰ μὴ τὰ παρ' ἑαυτῶν εἰσενέγκωμεν, οὐ δυνησόμεθα τῆς ἄνωθεν ἀξιοῦσθαι ῥ. Chrys.*hom.59.5 in Gen.*(4.569B); οὐκ ἀρκεῖ προθυμία ἀνθρώπου, ἂν μὴ τῆς ἄνωθέν τις ἀπολαύσῃ ῥ.· καὶ... πάλιν οὐδὲν κερδανοῦμεν ἀπὸ τῆς ἄνωθεν ῥ., προθυμίας οὐκ οὔσης id. *hom.82.4 in Mt.*(7.787B); ἂν γὰρ μὴ τῆς ἄνωθεν τύχῃς ῥ., πάντα εἰκῇ id.*hom.12.3 in Heb.*(12.125C); τῆς θείας ῥ. χρῄζοντας τοὺς πρὸς τοῦτον ἀγωνισαμένους τὸν ἀγῶνα τὸν ὑπερφυῆ Isid.Pel.*epp.*4.165(M.78.1253C); τῆς ἄνωθεν προηγουμένης ῥ., ὁ βουλόμενος καὶ πονῶν...καὶ μανθάνει... καὶ σώζεται *ib.*2.72(516C); **7.** *turning point, critical moment,* Chrys. *hom.50.3 in Ac.*(9.376A); Pall.*v.Chrys.*6(p.36.3; M.47.22); *moment* generally, Mel.*pass.*21 p.4.3; Clem.*exc.Thdot.*69(p.129.18; M.9.692B); Bas.*hex.*2.7(1.19A; M.29.45A).

[*]**ῥοῦγα, ἡ,** v. ῥόγα.

§**ῥοῦγχος, ὁ,** sens. dub., an evil desire τὰ ἐσὰ [sc. τοῦ διαβόλου] ἔργα τὰ ἐσὰ θελήματα ταῦτά εἰσιν· ῥοῦγχοι, πορνεῖαι, ψευδομαρτυρίαις [sic] *Contrad.*2(p.8).

[*]**ῥουσαῖος** ([*]**-σεος**), *red,* -σεος Jo.Mal.*chron.*2 p.33(M.97.101C); ταβλία ῥ. *Chron.Pasch.*p.117(M.92.305A); *ib.*p.332(861B); of the 'red' faction in Circus, *ib.*p.112(296B).

***ῥουσίς, ἡ,** ? = ῥυτίς, *wrinkle,* met. ἀκανθώδεις ῥουσίδες εἰσὶ τὰ πάθη *Apophth.Patr.*(M.65.361A).

***ῥοφή, ἡ,** ? = ῥόφημα, *broth, porridge,* Cyr.S.*v.Jo.Hes.*(p.215.25).

***ῥοφηδόν,** sens. dub., ? *in gulps* ὥστε αὐτὸν...τὴν ἑαυτοῦ πνοὴν μετ' ἤχου τινὸς καὶ συριγμοῦ ῥ. ἀνασπάσαι *Mir.Artem.*26(p.38.14).

ῥόφημα, τό, liturg., *sip* of wine, *Lit.Chrys.*(M.63.920).

***ῥοχή,** s.v.l., sens. dub. δύο...καὶ δέκα μῆνάς που ῥ. συναντώντων πρὸς ἀλλήλους, πῇ μὲν πολεμούντων, πῇ δὲ ἀναπαυομένων Agath.*v.Gr. Ill.*8(p.7.15).

ῥοώδης, *subject to flux, transitory* τὴν ῥ. καὶ σπερματικὴν γένεσιν Eus.*l.C.*11(p.228.10; M.20.1384A); τῆς ὑλικῆς καὶ ῥ. φύσεως Gr.Nyss. *Eun.*12(2 p.285.19; M.45.897B); Nil.*exerc.*14(M.79.736B).

***ῥυάκιον, τό,** *little stream, Ev.Thom.*A 2.3(p.141); Thphn.*chron.* p.394(M.108.937C).

***ῥυγίτης, ὁ,** name of an insect pest, *Euchol.*(p.555).

***ῥυέντης,** ? *streaming* φάος ῥυέντης Hipp.*haer.*5.20(p.122.9; M.16. 3187A).

[*]**ῥυζηδόν,** = ῥοιζηδόν, *with a rush,* Or.*exp.in Pr.*7:20(M.17. 181D); *with a rushing sound* ῥυζιδόν †Anast.S.*relat.*14(*OC* 2 p.68.13).

***ῥύζημα, τό,** ? *snort*; of a horse, Thdr.Mops.*Ps.*54 proem.(p.352. 15; M.66.673C).

***ῥυζιδόν,** v. ῥυζηδόν.

ῥυθμίζ-ω, *bring into harmony,* met. μνημονεύειν τῶν πράξεων τῶν ἁγίων, πρὸς τὸ τῷ ζήλῳ τούτων ~εσθαι τὴν ψυχήν Ath.*v.Anton.*55(M. 26.921B); ἡ...χάρις τοῦ θεοῦ...διὰ τοῦ βαπτίσματος εἰς τὸ ὅπερ ἦν, ὅτε ἐγένετο ὁ ἄνθρωπος, ~ει τὸν κατ' εἰκόνα Diad.*perf.*89(p.124.20); εἰ... λόγῳ ~οιτο Aen.*dial.*(M.85.916B); pass., *be in harmony, of one mind* αἱ συνεταὶ ῥυθμισθεῖσαι προέπεμψαν...τὴν Μαγδαληνὴν Μαρίαν Rom. Mel.(*AS* 1 p.126).

***ῥυθμιστής, ὁ,** *one who restores to order, arbiter,* of Chrys. ὦ δικαστηρίων τηλικοῦτον ῥυθμιστὴν ἐζημιωμένων Thdt.*serm.Chrys.*(5.99).

ῥυΐσκομαι, *be withered,* †Bas.*parad.*2(1.348C; M.30.64C).

ῥυμοτομέω, *cut lines* or *furrows*; of a ploughing ox, Tim.Ant. *nativ.Jo.Bapt.*1(M.28.905C).

ῥυμουλκέω, *draw in, inhale,* Clem.*str.*7.6(p.24.10; M.9.444B).

ῥύομαι, *deliver* τῶν ἐκ...περιστάσεως ῥερυσμένων Didym.*Ps.*30:22f. (M.39.1317C).

ῥυπαρία, ἡ, *filth,* met. τὴν τῆς αἱρέσεως ῥ. Ath.*Ar.*1.10(M.26.32C).

ῥυπαρός, *filthy, foul,* met. ἡμέραι...πονηραὶ καὶ ῥ. *Barn.*8.6; morally διαλογισμοῖς ῥ. *T.Jud.*14.3; τοὺς...ῥ. τὸν βίον...θηρία προσαγορεύει Clem.*str.*6.6(p.457.19; M.9.273A); τὸ συνειδὸς ἔχουσι ῥ. Ath.*decr.*2(p.2.31; M.25.'428'(420)B); of stale or mouldy bread ἄρτος ῥ. καὶ λάχανα Marc.Diac.*v.Porph.*10.

ῥυπαροφορέω, *wear dirty clothes,* Leont.N.*v.Jo.Eleem.*22(p.44. 16).

***ῥυπαροχίτων,** *wearing a dirty garment,* ref. Mt.22:11 γάμου ῥιπτόμενος ῥ. Cosm.Mel.*schol.*(M.38.449) in Gr.Naz.*carm.*1.1.27.49.

***ῥυπαρώδης,** *foul,* morally αἱ ῥ. ἡδοναί ‡Chrys.*pasch.*6.3(p.157.15; 8.269C).

ῥύπασμα, τό, *dirt, filth, pollution,* Or.*fr.54 in Jo.*(p.528.29); of τριγαμίαι, Bas.*ep.*199 *can.*50(3.297C; M.32.732C); Jo.VI H.*v.Jo.D.*30 (M.94.469C).

***ῥυπήμων,** *dirty,* ‡Caes.Naz.*dial.*111(M.38.989); *ib.*158(1117).

ῥύπος, ὁ, 1. *dirt, filth,* removed by and thus transferred to cleansing medium ὁ ἀλγῶν σάρκα διὰ τοῦ ῥ. τοῦ ὑσσώπου ἰᾶται *Barn.* 8.6; ἵνα τὸν ἐν τοῖς ποσὶ τῶν μαθητῶν ῥ. ἀναλάβῃ εἰς τὸ ἑαυτοῦ σῶμα διὰ τοῦ λεντίου Or.*Jo.*32.7(6; p.437.20; M.14.760C); **2.** met., moral and intellectual *pollution* ῥ. ἐπιθυμίας Ath.*gent.*34(M.25.68C); παντὸς ...ῥ. καὶ πάσης ἀσεβείας πεπλήρωται id.*h.Ar.*80(p.228.12; M.25.792A); Synes.*ep.*44(M.66.1369A); of heresy, Eus.*h.e.*4.30.3(M.20.404A); Ath. *h.Ar.*3(p.184.23; 697C); of usury, Chrys.*hom.56.6 in Mt.*(7.574B); removed by baptism, Or.*hom.14 in Lc.*(p.98.16).

ῥυπόω, 1. trans., *defile,* met. τὴν ἀκοήν...ῥυπωθεῖσαν ἀπὸ τῶν βλασφήμων ῥημάτων Ath.*Ar.*3.28(M.26.384A); **2.** intrans., *be filthy*; met., morally, Gr.Naz.*carm.*2.2(poem.)3.252(M.37.1498A); Pamph. Mon.*Soter.*3(p.119.19); Anast.*poenit.*4(p.283).

ῥυπώδης, *foul*; met., morally, Ath.*ep.Amun.*(M.26.1173D).

***ῥύπωσις, ἡ,** *pollution,* Geo.Pis.*hex.*1763(M.92.1570A).

[*]**ῥυσιδόω,** v. ῥυτιδόω.

***ῥυσιπέλαντος,** vox nihili οἰδήσας...ὡς ἀσκὸς ὁ παῖς τοσοῦτον ἐφλέγμανεν ὡς γενέσθαι πᾶς ῥ. Pall.*h.Laus.*18(p.55.3, cj. ἐρυσιπέλατος; πολυτάλαντον τῷ σηκώματι M.34.1059D).

ῥύσις, ἡ, (cf. ῥεῦσις), *flow*; met.; **1.** *flux, instability*; of heathen philosophical speculation, Clem.*prot.*6(p.51.18; M.8.172B); of corporeal existence, Or.*princ.*3.1.2(p.196.7; M.11.249B); Meth.*res.*2.9 (p.347.22; ῥυήσεως M.18.308C); Epiph.*haer.*76.31(p.380.23; M.42.580B); of atoms, Dion.Al.ap.Eus.*p.e.*14.25(776C; M.21.1277B); not ref. divine generation οὐ...μερισμὸν μέν τινα καὶ μετάστασιν καὶ ῥ. τῆς τοῦ γεννῶντος οὐσίας ἐκ τῆς φωνῆς τοῦ γεννᾶν...ἐννοήσει Bas.*Eun.*2.6(1.242B; M. 29.581B); **2.** *dissipation, effluence* ἔδεισα...ῥ. τινὰ θεότητος παραδέξασθαι στάσιν οὐκ ἔχουσαν Gr.Naz.*or.*31.31(p.187.5; M.36.169A); **3.** *dissipation, laxity of living,* Flav.Ant.*anath.*1(M.48.945).

ῥυτιδόω, 1. *wrinkle, crumple,* Gr.Nyss.*hom.1 in Cant.*(M.44.785D); Pall.*h.Laus.*22(p.71.18, v.l. ἐρυσιδωμένους M.34.1081D); **2.** met., *calumniate* τὴν καὶ πάναγνον ῥυτιδοῦσι παρθένον Cyr.*Nest.*1 proem. (p.16.2; 6[1].6A).

ῥυτίς, ἡ, 1. *wrinkle, fold* in dress, Chrys.*hom.8.2 in 1Tim.*(11. 591E); **2.** met., of moral defect ἄνθρακας...[sc. φησί] τὰς τοῦ... πνεύματος δωρεάς, τὰς...καθαιρούσας τὰς τῶν ἀνθρώπων ῥ. Or.*exp.in Pr.*25:21(M.17.236D); ῥ. καὶ σπίλου Serap.*Man.*8(p.32; M.40.905D); *Const.App.*7.40.1.

Ῥωμαϊκός, 1. *Roman,* i.e. *imperial* opp. ecclesiastical ἐγκαταμίσγειν τὴν Ῥ. ἀρχὴν τῇ ἐκκλησίας διαταγῇ Ath.*h.Ar.*34(p.202.9; M. 25.732D); οὐ...Ῥ. ἐστιν ἡ κρίσις...ἀλλὰ περὶ ἐπισκόπου ἐστὶ τὸ κρῖμα *ib.*76(p.225.26; 785B); Ῥ. ἀρχὴν καὶ ἱερατικὴν ἀρχήν *Can.App.*83; of Roman empire and army τῆς Ῥ. πολιτείας...ἐπίβουλος Heracl.*ep.* (M.92.992B); neut. as subst. ὅτε τῆς ἰδικῆς τὸ Ῥ. κατετόλμησε γῆς Thphyl.*exc.gent.*3(p.480.4; M.113.940A); πρὸς τὸ φυλάττεσθαι τὰ Ῥ. καὶ Ἱεροσόλυμα Jo.Mal.*chron.*18 p.426(M.97.628B); **2.** of language; **a.** *Latin* ἐπιγραφὴν Ῥ. Just.*1apol.*26.2(M.6.368A); τὴν Ῥ. γλῶτταν Ath.*h.Ar.*75(p.224.29; M.25.784C); as subst. ἑρμηνεία ἀπὸ Ῥωμαϊκοῦ id.*apol.sec.*58(p.138.1; M.25.353A); perh. τὴν σχολὴν τῶν Ῥ. Mac. Aeg.*hom.*15.42(M.34.604C); **b.** *Greek* μετήνεγκε ταῦτα εἰς τὴν Ῥ. διάλεκτον *A.Pil.*B proem.(p.287).

Ῥωμαΐς, 1. *Latin* τὴν πόλιν Ἄλμα Ῥώμαν ὀνομάσαι, ὃ δηλοῖ τῇ Ῥωμαΐδι γλώττῃ τὴν ἔνδοξον Philost.*h.e.*2.9(M.65.472B); **2.** *Greek, A.Pil.*B tit.(p.287).

***ῥωμαλεότης, ἡ,** *strength* ῥ. φρενῶν *Hymn.*(*AS* 1 p.596).

***Ῥωμανήσιος,** *Roman, Pet.Ar.*1 tit.(M.26.820A).

***Ῥωμανία, ἡ,** *Roman empire, Roman territory,* Ath.*h.Ar.*35(p.202. 30; M.25.733C); Epiph.*haer.*69.2(p.153.12; M.42.204B); *M.Sab.*4.2; Jo.Mal.*chron.*16 p.398(M.97.589A).

***Ῥωμεύς, ὁ,** a *Roman,* Cosm.Ind.*top.*11(M.88.448C).

ῥώννυμι, *strengthen*; perf. pass., *be valid,* Ath.Scholast.*coll.*2.2 (p.32); *ib.*4.22(p.64); Phot.*nomoc.*2.1(p.487; M.104.568C); *be right* ἔρρωται τῷ φρονήματι Thdr.Stud.*epp.*2.65(M.99.1288B); freq. ptcpl., ἐρρωμένος *valid,* Men.*exc.gent.*15(p.459.5; M.113.820A); neut. plur. as adv., *favourably,* id.*exc.Rom.*3(p.186.8; M.113.873D).

ῥῶσις, ἡ, 1. *bodily health and strength,* Or.*sel.in Ps.*4:6 ap.*philoc.* 26.2(p.233.25; M.12.1153A); Chrys.*ep.*5(3.579E); Mac.Mgn.*apocr.*2.8 (p.10.11); **2.** ass. spiritual *strengthening* ῥ. ψυχῶν καὶ σωμάτων *Apoc. Esd.*(p.33); Serap.*euch.*29.1; of soul only, *A.Phil.*39(p.18.28); Gr. Agr.*Eccl.*9.11(M.98.1104B); ψυχῆς...ῥ. ἐστι τοῖς ὑπομένουσιν, ὁ τοῦ σώματος αἰκισμός Max.*cap.*1.17(M.90.1188A); bestowed by men, *support, encouragement* ῥ. προσφιλεστάτην χαρίσασθαι ἀδελφικοῖς... σπουδάσμασι καὶ πατρικαῖς...προθέσεσιν Sophr.H.*ep.syn.*(M.87. 3196C); **3.** *power, sway* Χριστοῦ...τῆς σῆς βασιλείας φρουροῦ καὶ τῆς σῆς ῥ. προστάτου CArim.*ep.Const.*1(p.237.9; M.26.696C).

***ῥωστέω,** = ἔρρωμαι, *be in good health,* Jo.D.*spir.neq.*(M.95.88A).

ῥωχμή, ἡ, plur., *clefts, fissures,* Cyr.*Abd.*4(3.357C).

Σ

σάβανον ([*]σάββανον), **τό,** *linen cloth, towel,* ref. Jo.13:5 σαβάνῳ περιζωσάμενος Clem.*paed.*2.3(p.179.30; M.8.436B); hence, liturg., as worn at foot-washing ceremonies, *Euchol.*(σαββ- p.593); and at dedication of a church αὐτῷ δὲ τῷ μέλλοντι τὴν καθιέρωσιν αὐτουργεῖν, ἐπάνωθεν τῶν ἱερατικῶν ἀμφίων περιτίθεται σάβανον *ib.*(p.656); as worn by an infant, *ib.*(pp.303f.).

***Σαβαώθ,** [Hebr. צְבָאוֹת] *Sabaoth, hosts*; **1.** as title of God οὐδενὶ ὀνόματι κλητέον τὸν πρῶτον θεὸν ἢ...Σ. κτλ. Or.*mart.*46(p.42. 20; M.11.628A); τὸ μὲν Σ. ὄνομα καὶ τὸ Ἀδωναΐ...μετὰ πολλῆς σεμνολογίας παραδιδόμενα...ἐπί τινος θεολογίας ἀπορρήτου id.*Cels.*1. 24(p.75.1; M.11.705A); οἱ...τὴν Ἑβραίων διάλεκτον εἰς τὴν Ἑλλάδα γλῶσσαν μεταβαλόντες, τινῶν ὀνομάτων τῆς ἑρμηνείας οὐ κατετόλμησαν, ἀλλ' αὐτὴν τὴν Ἑβραϊκὴν φωνὴν μετεκόμισαν· ὡς τὸ Σ., καὶ τὸ Ἀδωναΐ, καὶ τὸ Ἐλωΐ Bas.*Eun.*2.7(1.243C; M.29.585A); Σ. ὅπερ ἐστὶ στρατιῶν ἢ τῶν δυνάμεων Gr.Naz.*or.*30.19(p.137.8; M.36.128B); Epiph.*haer.*26. 10(p.288.22; M.41.348B); Thdt.*haer.*5.3(4.393); in invocation, *A.Phil.* 26(pp.63.6,64.6); Serap.*euch.*13.10; **2.** Gnost. ἄλλον δὲ ἕβδομον οὐρανὸν ὑποτίθενται ἐν ᾧ λέγουσιν εἶναι τὸν Σ. ... φασὶ δὲ τὸν Σ. οἱ μὲν ὄνου μορφὴν ἔχειν, οἱ δὲ χοίρου Epiph.*haer.*26.10(p.287.8,15; M.41.345C,D); φασὶ...τὸν διάβολον εἶναι υἱὸν τῆς ἑβδόμης ἐξουσίας τουτέστι τοῦ Σ. εἶναι δὲ τὸν Σ. θεὸν τῶν Ἰουδαίων *ib.*40.5(p.85.15f.; 684C); Manich.

τὸ...τίμιον...ὄνομα Σ. ... εἶναι τὴν φύσιν τοῦ ἀνθρώπου καὶ πατέρα τῆς ἐπιθυμίας· καὶ διὰ τοῦτο...προσκυνοῦσι τὴν ἐπιθυμίαν Hegem.*Arch*.11 (p.19.10; M.10.1445B).

[*]**σάββανον, τό,** v. *σάβανον*.

***Σαββατιανοί, οἱ,** *followers of the heresy of Sabbatius*; said by Sozomen to be an offshoot of Novatianist heresy but not mentioned by Epiph., Thdt., or Socrates, Soz.*h.e*.7.18.1(M.67.1468D); Thphn.*chron*.p.53(M.108.188B).

σαββατίζω, *observe the sabbath*; **1.** of Jewish observance opp. Christian, Ign.*Magn*.9.1; *Const.App*.6.23.3; Gr.Nyss.*Eun*.9(2 p.216. 23; M.45.816A); **2.** of OT observance, Just.*dial*.19.5(M.6.517A); Cosm.Ind.*top*.5(M.88.200B); of sabbatical year, Cyr.*Am*.4(3.333C); **3.** of Christian practice, *keep a day of rest*, *Agraph*.48(p.68); signifying: abstention from sin, Just.*dial*.12.3(M.6.500C); Mac.Aeg.*hom*. 35.1(M.34.748A); Cyr.*ador*.7(1.227D); Proc.G.*Is*.56:1ff.(M.87.2565C); and from worldly affairs, Cyr.*Am*.3(3.315B); practice of piety rather than idleness, Just.*dial*.19.6(M.6.517B); Clem.*str*.1.1(p.9.24; M.8.701A); *Const.App*.7.36.4; the Christian life, Or.*exc.in Ps*.77:30f. (M.17.144D); Cyr.*Jo*.3.6(4.316C); practice of chastity, †Bas.Anc. *virg*.58,59(M.30.785C,788C); Mod.*occurs*.(M.86.3276C); **4.** met., *take rest* *ἐν ταύτῃ γὰρ* [sc. *ἡμέρᾳ* i.e. Easter Eve] *κατέπαυσεν ἀληθῶς ἀπὸ πάντων τῶν ἔργων αὐτοῦ ὁ μονογενὴς θεός, διὰ τῆς κατὰ τὸν θάνατον οἰκονομίας τῇ σαρκὶ σαββατίσας* Gr.Nyss.*res*.1(M.46.601B).

σαββατικός, *pertaining to the sabbath, proper to the sabbath*; of work, Or.*fr.6 in Lc*.5:14(p.235.20); of numbers 7, 70, etc., id.*Jo*.10. 39(23; p.217.5; M.14.384B); of Easter Day *ἠὼς σαββατικῆς μεγάλης* Eudoc.*Cypr*.1.253(M.85.841C).

σαββατισμός, ὁ, *sabbath observance*; **1.** of Jewish observance opp. Christian, *A.(Pass.)Petr.et Paul*.1(p.118.10); Or.*exc.in Ps*. 77:30f.(M.17.144D); Epiph.*haer*.29.8(p.331.14; M.41.404B); Cyr.*Is*.5. 3(2.791C); **2.** of OT observance, Just.*dial*.23.3(M.6.528A); as fulfilled in new dispensation, Or.*Jo*.2.33(27; p.91.2; M.14.172C); Cyr. *ador*.10(1.346C); Proc.G.*Gen*.5:4–22(M.87.264C); Olymp.*Eccl*.11:2 (M.93.605C); signifying different aspects of the Christian life, Cyr. *ador*.7(1.228A); **3.** Christian observance of a day of rest, *Const.App*. 2.36.2; signifying mortification of the will, Cyr.*Is*.5.4(2.825E,826E); **4.** met., *rest*, Or.*or*.27.16(p.374.20; M.11.520C); Cyr.*Is*.5.4(2.826A); Thdt.*Heb*.4:9(3.568); Oecum.*Heb*.4:9f.(p.463.12); a type of the Kingdom, Chrys.*hom.6.3 in Heb*.(12.66B); of repose of the saints, Cyr.*Jo*.4.6(4.425E); **5.** met., *respite*, Ath.*exp.Ps*.37:1(M.27.184A).

σαββατοκυριακή, ἡ** (σαββατοκυριακόν, τό**), *the sabbath and the Lord's Day, Saturday and Sunday*, Jo.Jej.*canonar*.3.3(p.440) cit. s. *γονυκλισία*; †Jo.Jej.*poenit*.(M.88.1913D,1916D); neut., *Nomoc*. 426.

σάββατον, τό, A. seventh day of the Jewish week, *sabbath*; occasionally plur., *Diogn*.4.3; *Agraph*.59(p.72); **1.** etym. *τῇ ἑβδόμῃ κατέπαυσεν...ὡς δηλοῖ ἡ τοῦ σαββάτου προσηγορία 'κατάπαυσιν' Ἑβραϊκῶς σημαίνουσα* Gr.Naz.*or*.41.2(M.36.429D); **2.** observance discussed, Or.*princ*.4.3.2(17; p.326.3ff.; M.11.380B); ‡Ath.*sabb*.1ff.(M. 28.133ff.); Epiph.*haer*.66.82(p.123f.; M.42.157Bf.); **3.** purpose *γνώσεως...οὐκ ἀργίας ἕνεκεν ἐδόθη τὸ σ.* ‡Ath.*sabb*.3(M.28.136C); *σ. ὥρισας εἰς μνήμην τούτου* [sc. Creation], *ὅτι ἐν αὐτῷ κατέπαυσας ἀπὸ τῶν ἔργων εἰς μελέτην τῶν σῶν νόμων, καὶ ἑορτὰς διετάξω εἰς εὐφροσύνην* *Const.App*.7.36.1; *τὸ σ. ἐδόθη αὐτοῖς* [sc. the Jews], *τοῦ καταπαῦσαι τὴν φιλοχρήματον αὐτῶν ἐπιθυμίαν* †Gr.Nyss.*test*.13(M.46.221B); **4.** abrogated in respect of Christians *οὐ τὰ νῦν σ. ἐμοὶ δεκτά, ἀλλὰ ὃ πεποίηκα...διὸ καὶ ἄγομεν τὴν ἡμέραν τὴν ὀγδόην εἰς εὐφροσύνην, ἐν ᾗ καὶ ὁ Ἰησοῦς ἀνέστη ἐκ νεκρῶν* *Barn*.15.8; Or.*Jo*.2.33(27; p.91.4; M.14.173A); ‡Ath.*sem*.1(M.28.144A); CLaod.*can*.29; Cyr.H.*catech*.4. 37; Chrys.*hom.49.3 in Jo*.(8.292B); **5.** of a 'high sabbath' (either coincidence of sabbath with a festival or sabbath preceding a great festival) *σ. μέγα* *M.Polyc*.8.1,21; **6.** of the sabbatical year *τὰ τῶν ἐτῶν σάββατα* Cyr.*Am*.4(3.333C).

B. seventh day of the Christian week, *Saturday*, ‡Pion.*v.Polyc*. 23; Ath.*ep.Aeg.Lib*.19(M.25.581B); †Gregent.*leg.Hom*.64(M.86.616B); (in East) a feast *εἴ τις κληρικὸς εὑρεθῇ τὴν κυριακὴν ἡμέραν ἢ τὸ σ. πλὴν τοῦ ἑνὸς μόνου νηστεύων, καθαιρείσθω* *Can.App*.64; *Const. App*.5.20.19; *ib*.7.23.3; *τῶν ἐντολῶν καὶ τῶν ἁγίων πατέρων κελευόντων κατὰ σ. καὶ κυριακὴν ἑψεῖσθαι λάχανον τοῖς ἀδελφοῖς* *V.Pach.A* 15(p.138.23); also (in Rome) a fast, Socr.*h.e*.5.22.58(M.67.640B); for other provisions and observances, v. CLaod.*cann*.16,49,51; Bas.*ep*. 93(3.186D; M.32.484B); Tim.I Al.*resp*.(M.33.1305A); Pall.*h.Laus*.7 (p.26.8; M.34.1020C); Socr.*h.e*.5.22.42,55(636A,640A); *Nomoc*.56,123; significance for Christians, Cyr.*ador*.7(1.227B); esp. of Easter Eve *τὸ μέγα σ.* Chrys.*hom.in Ps*.145:2(5.525D); †Jo.Jej.*poenit*.(M.88. 1913A); Dor.*doct*.15.1(M.88.1788C); CTrull.*can*.89.

C. gen. weekly *day of rest*; instituted for avoidance of sin and practice of holiness, Just.*dial*.12.3(M.6.500C); Chrys.*Laz*.1.7(1. 717A); Cyr.*Jo*.4.7(4.439C); Christian *Sunday* *τὸ μέγα σ.* opp. Jewish sabbath *τὸ μικρὸν σ.*, Epiph.*exp.fid*.24(p.525.6; M.42.829Cf.); cf.id. *haer*.8.6(p.192.20; M.41.213C); *ἡμέρᾳ πρώτῃ τῆς ἑβδομάδος, τουτέστιν κυριακῇ ἥ ἐστιν ἡμέρα δευτέρα τοῦ σαββάτου· εἴωθεν γὰρ ἡ...γραφὴ ἑκάστην ἡμέραν ἀνάπαυσιν ἔχουσαν σ. ὀνομάζειν* *Chron.Pasch*.p.211 (M.92.516B); for *σ. δευτερόπρωτον* v.s.v.

D. met.; **1.** signifying self-restraint, Clem.*str*.4.3(p.251.17; M.8. 1220C); Cyr.*Is*.5.4(2.826 pass.); **2.** type of Christian life, Or.*sel. in Ex*.16:23(M.12.289A); Mac.Aeg.*hom*.35.1(M.34.748A); active and contemplative, †Cyr.*coll.VT*(6^4.16Eff.; M.77.1200Bff.); kingdom of heaven, Chrys.*hom.6.1 in Heb*.(12.63A); last days, Cyr.*Jo*.2.5(4. 209A); *ib*.6.1(601E); repose of saints, Or.*sel.in Ex*.16:23(M.12.289B); Ph.Carp.*Cant*.proem.(M.40.29B); Cyr.*Jo*.4.6(424E); for mystical exposition of *σάββατον, σάββατα*, and *σάββατα σαββάτων* v. Max.*cap. theol*.1.37ff.(M.90.1097C).

E. *week*; plur., *Did*.8.1; *Const.App*.2.47.1; Sev.Ant.*res*.(p.804. 1; M.46.632A); sing., Eus.*qu.Marin*.2.2(M.22.941C); Pall.*v.Chrys*.8 (p.44.6; M.47.26); Jo.D.*hom*.4.26(M.96.628A).

***σαβέκ,** (Hebr. סְבָךְ), *thicket*; ref. Gen.22:13, etym. *ὥσπερ δὲ φυτὸν σ., τοῦτ' ἔστιν ἀφέσεως, ἐκάλεσε τὸν...σταυρόν* †Mel.*fr*.(p.313; M.5.1220); *Dial.Tim.et Aquil*.109 r°; as prototype of Cross, Mel. *fr.Gen*.(p.312; M.5.1217A); †Gregent.*disp*.(M.86.636D).

***Σαβελλιανίζω,** *think with Sabellius, hold Monarchian (Patripassian) views* *λέγοντες δὲ μίαν οὐσίαν, ἤτοι φύσιν, οὐ λέγομεν μίαν ὑπόστασιν, ἵνα μὴ Σαβελλιανίσωμεν* Anast.Ant.*fid*.(M.89.1404B).

***Σαβελλιανιστής, ὁ,** *follower of Sabellius*, Tim.CP *haer*.(M.86.60B).

***Σαβελλιανός, ὁ,** = foreg., Epiph.*anac*.62(p.213.22; M.42.868A); teaching on Trin., id.*haer*.62.1(pp.389f.; M.41.1052A–C); *Σαβελλιανῶν ἐσχηκὼς* [sc. Marcellus] *τὴν ἐρεσχελίαν* *ib*.72.1(p.255.14; M.42.381D); *ἀσεβὲς...τοῦτο καὶ τῆς τῶν Σαβελλιανῶν καὶ τῶν ἀπὸ Μαρκέλλου μανίας* Chrys.*hom.7.2 in Jo*.(8.46C).

***Σαβελλίζ-ω,** *hold the views of, follow Sabellius* *ταῦτα Μάρκελλος ἔγραφε· τῆς τοῦ ~ειν ὑπονοίας καθαίρων ἑαυτόν* Eus.*e.th*.1.15(p.75.10; M.24.856A); *διελέγχων* [sc. Dion. Al.] *τοὺς ~οντας ὅτι μὴ ὁ πατήρ ἐστιν ὁ γενόμενος σὰρξ ἀλλ' ὁ τούτου λόγος* Ath.*decr*.25(p.21.11; M.25. 461A); *τοὺς μὲν ~οντας ἀπὸ τῆς περὶ υἱοῦ ἐννοίας ἐλεγκτέον, τοὺς δὲ Ἀρειανοὺς ἀπὸ τῆς περὶ πατρός* ‡Ath.*Ar*.4.3(p.47.15; M.26.472C); *ἀναιρεῖν τὸν υἱὸν καὶ ~ειν* *ib*.4.10(p.54.5; 480C).

***Σαβέλλιος, ὁ,** *Sabellius*; also, *one sharing Sabellius' views, Sabellian*; **1.** teaching on relation of Son to Father *τίνα τοίνυν ἐρεῖ τὸν ἐκ τοῦ οὐρανοῦ κατεληλυθότα...εἰ λέγει τὸν πατέρα γυμνῶς ἀνακαλύψας τὸν Σαβέλλιον* Eus.*e.th*.2.7(p.105.16; M.24.912A); *οὔτε γὰρ υἱοπάτορα φρονοῦμεν, ὡς οἱ Σαβέλλιοι λέγοντες μονοούσιον καὶ οὐχ ὁμοούσιον* †Ath.*exp.fid*.2(M.25.204A); ‡Ath.*Ar*.4.17(p.61.20; M.26. 492A); *αὕτη δὲ ἡ φωνὴ* [sc. *τὸ ὁμοούσιον*] *καὶ τὸ τοῦ Σαβελλίου κακὸν ἐπανορθοῦται· ἀναιρεῖ γὰρ τὴν ταυτότητα τῆς ὑποστάσεως καὶ εἰσάγει τελείαν τῶν προσώπων τὴν ἔννοιαν* Bas.*ep*.52.3(3.146A; M.32.393C); Gr.Naz.*or*.30.6(p.118.1; M.36.112B); Gr.Nyss.*Eun*.10(2 p.249.17; M. 45.853B); **2.** teaching on Trin. *ὁ αὐτὸς ἄρα πατὴρ γέγονε καὶ υἱὸς καὶ πνεῦμα κατὰ Σαβέλλιον* ‡Ath.*Ar*.4.13(p.57.13; M.26.485A); *ἐπεὶ τόν γε ἀνυπόστατον τῶν προσώπων ἀναπλασμὸν οὐδὲ ὁ Σαβέλλιος παρῃτήσατο, εἰπὼν τὸν αὐτὸν θεόν, ἕνα τῷ ὑποκειμένῳ ὄντα, πρὸς τὰς ἑκάστοτε παραπιπτούσας χρείας μεταμορφούμενον, νῦν μὲν ὡς πατέρα, νῦν δὲ ὡς υἱόν, νῦν δὲ ὡς πνεῦμα ἅγιον διαλέγεσθαι* Bas.*ep*.210.5 (3.317A; M.32.776C); *ib*.214.3(3.322B; M.788C); Gr.Naz.*or*.20.5(M.35. 1072A); Epiph.*haer*.62.1(pp.389f.; M.41.1052A–C); **3.** in rel. to other heresies: Arian, Ath.*Dion*.13(p.55.18; M.25.500A); Gr.Naz.*or*.31.9 (p.156.10; M.36.144A); Gr.Nyss.*or.catech*.proem.(p.3.1; M.45.12A); *ὃν γὰρ Σαβέλλιος λέγει 'τριώνυμον' τοῦτον Εὐνόμιος ὀνομάζει 'ἀγέννητον'. οὐδέτερος δὲ τούτων ἐν τῇ τριάδι τῶν ὑποστάσεων θεωρεῖ τὴν θεότητα* id.*Eun*.10(2 p.234.27; M.45.836D); Macedonian, Chrys.*hom. 75.1 in Jo*.(8.439A) v. *πρόσωπον, ὁμοούσιος*.

***Σαβελλιόφρων,** *Sabellius-minded*, ‡Gr.Nyss.*Ar.et Sab*.6(M.45. 1289B).

***Σαβελλισμός, ὁ,** *Sabellian heresy, Sabellianism* *ὅθεν καὶ τὴν τοῦ Σαβελλισμοῦ κατηγορίαν ἐδέξατο* [sc. Apoll.] Thdt.*haer*.4.8(4.363).

***Σαβελλίτης, ὁ,** *follower of Sabellius, Sabellian*, †Cyr.*hom.div*.11 (5^2.380A).

***Σαβελλίως,** *in Sabellian fashion*, Gr.Naz.*or*.31.30(p.186.8; M.36. 168D) cit. s. *Ἀρειανῶς*.

***σαβούρα, ἡ,** *ballast*; met., Nil.*epp*.4.60(M.79.577B).

σάβουρος, **1.** *without cargo, in ballast*, Leont.N.*v.Jo.Eleem*.26 (p.55.6); **2.** gen., *empty* *σκεῦος σ.* Gr.Mag.*dial*.(tr.Zach.)3.7(M.*PL*. 77.231B); *ib*.1.7(185A); **3.** of persons, *empty-handed*, *ib*.1.2(160B).

σαγγάριος, ὁ, *shoemaker*, *Nomoc*.102.

σαγηνευτής, ὁ, *fisherman*; met., of a *fisher* of men Μάρκον τῶν κατ' Αἴγυπτον διδάσκαλον καὶ σ. Eus.*theoph.fr*.6(p.20*.19; M.24.628D); *ib*.(p.18*.19; 625B).

σαγηνεύ-ω, met.; **1.** *enmesh*; *ensnare* ∼ειν ἀτεχνῶς οἱ πλεονέκται ...ἐοίκασιν εἰς ἡδυπάθειαν τὸν κόσμον Clem.*paed*.2.1(p.155.18; M.8.381A); διαγελῶσι [sc. οἱ Φαρισαῖοι] τὸν ὄχλον ὡς ἀμαθῆ, διά τε τοῦτο τοῖς τοῦ σωτῆρος ἡμῶν σεσαγηνευμένον θαύμασιν Cyr.*Jo*.5.2(4.481C); ἁλιεῖς καὶ θηρευτὰς μιμούμενοι οἱ πολέμιοι πάντας αὐτοὺς ∼ουσι Thdt.*Jer*.16:16(2.494); **2.** *draw*, *draw together*, *make captive* (in the net of the gospel); of God, Cyr.*Is*.4.1(2.545E); of Christ, Gr.Naz.*or*.37.1(M.36.281A); of apostles, Gr.Nyss.*hom.5 in Cant*.(M.44.881B); Thdt.*Is*.1:20(p.9.23); of others, Chrys.*pan.Phoc*.1(2.704C); id.*hom.33.2 in Jo*.(8.192E).

σαγήνη, ἡ, *net*;

A. various met. uses; **1.** to catch souls, of scriptures or gospel σαγήνης...πλοκῇ ποικίλῃ ὡμοιώθη ἡ βασιλεία τῶν οὐρανῶν κατὰ τὴν πεπλεγμένην ἐκ...ποικίλων νοημάτων παλαιὰν καὶ καινὴν γραφήν... βέβληται δὲ ἡ σ. αὕτη εἰς τὴν θάλασσαν, τὸν πανταχοῦ τῆς οἰκουμένης τῶν ἀνθρώπων κυματούμενον βίον Or.*comm.in Mt*.10.12(pp.13.26,14.11; M.13.861C f.); ἵνα...λαβόντες...τὴν ἀπὸ παντοίων λόγων νομικῶν τε καὶ προφητ⟨ικ⟩ῶν τῶν τε τῆς ἐνθέου διδασκαλίας αὐτοῦ πλακεῖσαν σ. ἐμβαλῶσιν εἰς τὴν τοῦ ἀνθρωπείου βίου θάλατταν Eus.*theoph.fr*.6(p.18*.23; M.24.625B); Isid.Pel.*epp*.2.157(M.78.612A); τὴν τῶν εὐαγγελικῶν κηρυγμάτων σ. χαλάσαντες Cyr.*Lc*.5:2(M.72.553A); of kingdom of heaven, *A.Xanthipp*.8(p.63.21); of S. Paul Παῦλον...τοῦ σκεύους τῆς ἐκλογῆς, τῆς εὐαγγελικῆς σ. Dam.*troph*.proem.2(p.190.7); of H. Ghost Παῦλον...τῇ σ. τοῦ πνεύματος περιέκλεισεν [sc. S. Barnabas] †Leont.N.*laud.Barn*.(p.199.17); **2.** as repository, store-house μέγα τὸ τῆς διακονίας ἔργον...σ. γάρ ἐστι τῶν ἀρετῶν, πάσας τὰς ἐντολὰς τοῦ θεοῦ ἐν ἑαυτῇ φέρουσα Bas.*renunt*.9(2.210D; M.31.645B); of BMV χαῖρε...ἀτρέπτου θεότητος σ. ἀδιάπτωτος ‡Chrys.*nat.Chr*.1(10.791A); of Herodias ἡ σ. τῆς ἀπάτης Chrysipp.*enc.in Jo.Bapt*.11(p.41.21).

B. *snare*, of Arian heresy ὥσπερ σαγήναις χρῶνται ταῖς ἰδίαις κακοτεχνίαις Ath.*apol.fug*.10(p.75.4; M.25.656C); Thdt.*h.e*.5.30.1(3.1070); τῇ τοῦ κατακλυσμοῦ...σ. Bas.Sel.*or*.5.2(M.85.81B); τὴν ναῦν πεσοῦσαν ἐν σ. τῶν λίθων Geo.Pis.*Pers*.220(M.92.1211B).

σαγίον, τό, dim. of σάγος, *cloak*, Ephr.2.2F; *M.Pers*.10.53(p.512.11); *Chron.Pasch*.p.394(M.92.1012A).

***σαγιτεύ-ω**, *shoot* from a bow, met. εἰ...∼σειεν τὴν σὴν διάνοιαν ὁ Χριστὸς ἄνωθεν Pamph.Mon.*Soter*.1(p.114.20, v.l. σαγητ-).

***σαγίττα (*σαγίτα)**, ἡ, (Lat. *sagitta*) *arrow*, Jo.Mal.*chron*.2 p.52 (M.97.125B); σαγιττοβολῶν Thphn.*chron*.p.266(M.108.660C, v.l. σαγιττῶν); σαγίτα Anton.*v.Sym.Styl*.27(p.64.11); †Anast.S.*relat*.44(*OC* 3 p.64.19ff.).

***σαγιττάρις**, ὁ, (Lat. *sagittarius*) *archer*, *JHS* 4 p.401 (saec. v).

***σαγιττοβολή**, ἡ, = σαγιττόβολον, Thphn.*chron*.p.266(M.108.660C, v.l. σαγιττῶν).

***σαγιττόβολον**, τό, (the distance of) *an arrow's flight*, *arrow-shot*, Jo.Mosch.*prat*.80(M.87.2937C); Leont.N.*v.Jo.Eleem*.36(p.74.7); δύο σ. †Anast.S.*relat*.1(*OC* 2 p.60.5).

***σαγματίζω**, *load* with heavy packs, *encumber* κἂν σαγματισθῇ ὥσπερ ὄνος ὁ ἄνθρωπος Nil.*epp*.1.308(M.79.193C).

***σαγματόω**, *saddle* a pack-horse, Thphn.*chron*.p.355(M.108.853B).

Σαδδουκαῖος, ὁ, *Sadducee*, derivation of name ἐπονομάζουσι... οὗτοι ἑαυτοὺς Σ., δῆθεν ἀπὸ δικαιοσύνης...Σεδὲκ γὰρ ἑρμηνεύεται δικαιοσύνη. ἦν δὲ καὶ Σαδδοὺκ τις τοὔνομα κατὰ τὸ παλαιὸν τῶν ἱερέων Epiph.*haer*.14.2(p.207.14; M.41.240A); tenets of sect οἱ Σ. ... οὐ ⟨μόνον⟩ τὴν...ἀνάστασιν σαρκὸς ἠθέτουν, ἀλλὰ καὶ...ἀνῄρουν τὴν τῆς ψυχῆς οὐ μόνον ἀθανασίαν ἀλλὰ καὶ ἐπιδιαμονήν Or.*comm.in Mt*.17.29 (p.665.22f.; M.13.1561C–1564A); ἠθέτησαν μὲν γὰρ οὗτοι νεκρῶν τὴν ἀνάστασιν...οὐ παραδέχονται δὲ ἀγγέλους...πνεῦμα δὲ ἅγιον οὐκ ἴσασιν Epiph.*haer*.14.2(p.208.1ff.; M.41.240B); Σ. ... λέγουσι μὴ εἶναι ἄγγελον, μήτε πνεῦμα. οὐδὲν ἀσώματον ἴσασι Σ., τάχα οὐδὲ τὸν θεόν, παχεῖς τινες ὄντες· ὅθεν οὐδὲ ἀνάστασιν βούλονται εἶναι πιστεύειν Chrys.*hom.49.2 in Ac*.(9.367E).

***σαθροδοξία**, ἡ, *unsound belief* or *opinion*, Nil.*epp*.3.234(M.79.492D).

***σαθροποι-έω**, *weaken*, *enfeeble* πῶς ὁλόκληρον τὸ [sc. σῶμα] δι' ἐγκρατείας...ῥικνούμενον, καὶ διὰ τῆς σκληροτέρας δουλαγωγίας ∼ούμενον; Gr.Nyss.*Apoll*.46(M.45.1237A); met., *invalidate* ∼εῖν τὸν ἀληθῆ τῆς εὐσεβείας λόγον id.*Eun*.2(2 p.320.3; M.45.493A).

σαθρόω, *render unsound*; **1.** of inanimate matter and vegetation, *allow to rot*, Geo.Pis.*hex*.434(M.92.1468A); usu. pass., *become unsound*, *rot*, ‡Anast.S.*Jud.disp*.2(M.89.1236A); ‡Jo.D.*ep.Thphl*.7(M.95.353C); of buildings, *become dilapidated*, Bas.*ep*.242.3(3.372C; M.32.901B); Chrys.*hom.56.2 in Jo*.(8.328A); †Jo.D.*B.J*.11(M.96.957A); **2.** of the body; pass., *be weak* τὰ...σεσαθρωμένα...γόνατα Eus.*h.e*.10.4.34(M.20.864A); of wounds, *fester*, Ephr.1.194B; met., of human nature assumed by Logos εἰ...τοῦτον σαθρωθέντα εἰς ἑαυτὸν λαβόμενος πάλιν ἀνακαινίζει...πρὸς διαμονὴν ἀτελεύτητον ‡Ath.*Ar*.4.33(p.82.11; M.26.520A); of Israel under the Egyptians, Nil.*epp*.3.257(M.79.512C).

σαθρῶς, *weakly*, *without conviction*, Gr.Naz.*or*.31.28(p.181.11; M.36.165A); Cyr.*Os*.33(3.59E); σ. ἔχω *be unsound*, superl. γέφυραν... σαθρότατα ἔχουσαν Men.*exc.Rom*.20(p.220.8; M.113.925B).

σάθρωσις, ἡ, *weakness*, Thdr.Mops.*Am*.9:11f.(M.66.304A).

σαίνω, *disturb* (cf. 1Thess.3:3) τὰ μὲν περὶ πίστεως, ὅσα ἔσηνεν ἡμᾶς, συνεξετάσθη Or.*dial*.8(p.140.5).

σαΐτης, ὁ, also dim. σαΐτιον, τό, a liquid measure = 22 ξέσται, Epiph.*mens*.24(M.43.284B); = 18 ξέσται Ἰταλικαί, Pall.*h.Laus*.19 (p.59.14; M.34.1066A); *Apophth.Patr*.(M.65.317D).

***σάκελλα**, ἡ, *purse*; of the public purse, Leont.N.*v.Jo.Eleem*.12 (p.23.9); Anast.S.*hod*.2(M.89.84C).

***σακελλάριος**, ὁ, **1.** *finance minister*, head of the privy purse; concerned with military supplies, Thphn.*chron*.p.280(M.108.692B); and fortifications, *ib*.p.306(745A); concerned with legal cases involving eccl. affairs, *V.Max*.18(M.90.88C); Anast.Ap.*a.Max*.1.2(M.90.112D,113B); CCP(681)*act*.12(H.3.1317D); **2.** eccl. *treasurer*, *Chron. Pasch*.p.381(M.92.976C); τῆς μεγάλης ἐκκλησίας...τὸν σ. Thphn.*chron*.p.409(M.108.972C); *ib*.p.246(620A); **3.** local *financial official* τὸν...σ. ... τοῦ στρατηγοῦ Anast.Ap.*a.Max*.1.2(M.90.112A).

σακέλλιον, τό, (Lat. *saccellus*) *purse*; of the wallet of Mercury denoting his love of money, Gr.Naz.*or*.4.121(M.35.661A).

***σακέρδωτις**, ἡ, (from Lat. *sacerdos*) *priestess*, Gr.Naz.*ep*.210(M.37.348A).

***σακκελίζω**, *strain*, *filter*, *Euchol*.(p.509).

σακκίζω, *put in a sack*, Thdr.Stud.*epp*.2.14(M.99.1157D).

***σακκομάχη**, ἡ, *coarse cloak*, Jo.Mosch.*prat*.73(M.87.2925C); *ib*.134(2997C).

***σακκομάχιον**, τό, = foreg., Jo.Mosch.*prat*.134(M.87.2997C); Leont.N.*v.Sym*.14(M.93.1688B).

σάκκος, ὁ, *coarse cloth* ὠμόλινον ἐκ σ. γεγονός Herm.*sim*.8.4.1; used for bedding, Thdt.*h.e*.1.24.1(3.806); hence clothing made from σ., *rough clothing* σ. ἠμπίσχετο ταπεινοφροσύνης ἔνδυμα Clem.*paed*.2.10(p.224.22; M.8.532B); Gel.Cyz.*h.e*.3.10.4; worn as mourning by Jews, *T.Jos*.15.2; *Barn*.7.5.

σακκοφορέω, *wear sackcloth*; as a sign of penitence, Just.*dial*.107.2(M.6.725A); Chrys.*hom.suppl*.2(M.64.425A); of a virgin anchoress, in sense of living an ascetic life, Pall.*h.Laus*.28(p.83.12; M.34.1097A).

***σακκοφορία**, ἡ, *wearing of sackcloth*; as a sign of penitence, Just.*dial*.107.2(M.6.725A); of persons making a show of asceticism προβάλλουσι σ. καὶ κομῶσι τὰς κεφαλάς Eus.Al.*serm*.22.6(M.86.460A).

Σακκοφόροι, οἱ, *those wearing sackcloth*; heretics practising an extreme asceticism, to be baptized when seeking admission to Church, Bas.*ep*.199 *can*.47(3.296D; M.32.729C); οἱ καὶ ἀποτακτικοὶ οἷς συνάπτονται οἱ καλούμενοι σ. Epiph.*rescr*.5(p.160.23; M.41.165A); λαοῦ σ. *MAMA* 1.171(Phrygia); σ. καὶ ἀποτακτῆται καὶ ἐγκρατῖται ...οὗτοι ἀντὶ οἴνου ὕδωρ τῷ θεῷ προσφέρουσι...τὸν γάμον πορνείαν προσαγορεύουσι Tim.CP *haer*.(M.86.16C).

σάκρα, ἡ, (Lat. *sacra*) **1.** *imperial rescript* or *letter*, Nil.*epp*.1.44 (M.79.104A); Men.*exc.Rom*.3(p.175.30; M.113.857D); Jo.Mal.*chron*.13 pp.317,344,348(M.97.476B,513A,520A); **2.** *secretariate*, CChalc.*act*.1 (*ACO* 2.1.1 p.76.3; H.2.81C).

σαλάριον, τό, (Lat. *salarium*) *regular payment*, *salary* of eccl. ministers: Montanist, Apollon.ap.Eus.*h.e*.5.18.2(M.20.476B); Artemonite, †Hipp.*Artem.ib*.5.28.10(M.20.513B).

***σαλγαμάριος**, ὁ, (Lat. *salgamarius*) *pickle-seller* (to denote someone picked at random) σαλγαμαρίους χειροτονοῦσι [sc. at CP] CChalc.*act*.11(*ACO* 2.1.3 p.411.30; H.2.557D); *CG–CI* 1.32(prob. saec. vi); for sundry variations in spelling v. *ib*.pp.65ff.

σάλευσις, ἡ, *shaking*, Gr.Mag.*dial*.(tr.Zach.)3.7(M.*PL*.77.234A).

σαλεύ-ω, **A.** trans.; **1.** *shake*; met., *weaken*; **a.** things ἡμῶν...ἡ σκηνὴ...διὰ τὴν παράβασιν ἐσαλεύθη καὶ ἐκλίθη Meth.*symp*.9.2(p.116.12; M.18.181A); doctrines, ‡Just.*qu.Gr*.11.45(M.6.1489B); χαλεπόν ἐστιν...τὰ δι' ἐπιστήμης εἰς ἀπόδειξιν ἐλθόντα δόγματα ∼θῆναι Synes.*ep*.105(M.66.1485B); pass. c. genit., *lose hold of*, *fall from* ταύτης [sc. σωτηρίας] ∼θέντες Or.*princ*.1.8.1(p.97.14); **b.** ref. God ἄτοπον...τὸ λέγειν μεταβλητὴν τὴν τοῦ θεοῦ δύναμιν...ἢ ∼ομένην τὴν οὐσίαν αὐτοῦ ‡Just.*qu.Chr*.2.7(M.6.1425B); **2.** *break* the peace, Thphyl.*exc.Rom*.6 (p.226.25; M.113.936A); **3.** met., *anchor*, *stay* (cf. B.2) μετὰ θεὸν ἐπὶ σοὶ τὰς ἐλπίδας σ. ‡Proc.G.*Pr*.3:29(M.87.1252A).

B. intrans.; **1.** c. genit., *waver* οἱ πρῶτοι τῆς...εὐσεβείας ∼σαντες ...ἀποπεπτώκασιν Eus.*d.e.*4.9(p.162.17; M.22.272A); **2.** *ride at anchor*, Bas.*hom.*16.2(2.136A; M.31.476C); τῶν ἐν λιμένι ∼όντων Chrys.*ep.*11 (3.591B); met., *rest, depend* on τῶν ἐπὶ πρώτοις υἱοῖς ∼σάντων Eus. *qu.Steph.*12(M.22.924C); Chrys.*ep.*2.7(3.543A); ἐν τούτῳ ∼έτω μόνον id.*oppugn.*2.2(1.59B).

***σαλιβάριον, τό,** horse's *bit* τῶν...ἥλων [sc. τοῦ σταυροῦ] τοὺς μὲν εἰς τὴν ἰδίαν περικεφαλαίαν ἐχάλκευσεν [sc. Const.] τοὺς δὲ ἀνέμιξε τῷ σ. τοῦ ἵππου αὐτοῦ Alex.Sal.*cruc.*(M.87.4064B).

σάλος, ὁ, *tossing*; *swell* of the sea; met., Geo.Pis.*carm.vit.*30; *commotion, storm* τὸν νηΐτην...κλόνον καὶ τὸν ἐντεῦθεν σ. Gr.Ant. *exerc.*(p.229.16; M.86.2861A); in the soul ὁ τὸν ἐκ τῶν πειρασμῶν...σ. ἐπανορθούμενος...ἀνθρωπίνως ὁμολογεῖ τὸν σ. Bas.*hom.in Ps.*61(1. 194D; M.29.473A).

σαλός, *imbecile, half-witted*, Pall.*h.Laus.*34(p.99.16ff.; M.34. 1106Df.); Evagr.*h.e.*4.34 tit.(p.149.31; M.86.2764C); Leont.N.*v.Sym.* 31,64(M.93.1709A,1748A); of animals, *mad*, *Apophth.Patr.*(p.407.5; M.65.240C).

***σαλότης, ἡ,** *imbecility, foolishness*, *Apophth.Patr.*(M.65.121C).

***σαλοφακίαλος,** (Syr. ܙܠܘܦܩܝܬܐ) *shaky cap*; as nickname of Tim.III Al., *one whose mitre sits uneasily*, i.e. *weak character*, *'weathercock'*, Evagr.*h.e.*2.11(p.63.5; M.86.2533C); Thphn.*chron.*p.96 (M.108.284C).

***σαλπιγγοφανής,** *trumpet-like*, Ast.Am.*hom.*16.5(M.40.413C).

σάλπιγξ, ἡ, 1. *trumpet, horn*; hence **a.** of Jewish *feast of trumpets* (Lev.23:24) κἂν πάσχα λέγεις ποιεῖν, κἂν σκηνοπηγίαν, κἂν σ. Dam. *troph.*2.2.4(p.220.7); **b.** in monastery, *call* to recitation of office whether by horn or by other means, Pach.*reg.*A(p.10); ἐὰν...τὴν πνευματικὴν καταφρονήσῃ σ. Thdr.Stud.*poen.*1.99(M.99.1745D); id. *iamb.*10(M.99.1784B); **2.** at gen. resurrection and Day of Judgement, *Did.*16.6; Clem.*q.d.s.*3(p.162.5; M.9.608B); *Const.App.*7.32.3; **3.** met., exeg. Num.11:1, †Cyr.*coll.VT*(6⁴.33Bf.; M.77.1224Bff.); of the gospel σ. Χριστοῦ Clem.*prot.*11(p.82.8; M.8.236B); of S. Paul τῆς μεγάλης τοῦ πνεύματος σ. Thdt.*eran.*3(4.206); of S. Barnabas ἡ τοῦ εὐαγγελικοῦ κηρύγματος σ. Alex.Sal.*Barn.*proem.5(437C).

σαλπίζω, *blow* a trumpet, hence *sound* the wooden gong (cf. s.v. σημαίνω) which superseded the horn as call to prayer in monastery σ. καιρῷ τὸ ξύλον Thdr.Stud.*iamb.*10(M.99.1784B).

σαλπισμός, ὁ, *sounding of a trumpet*, Or.*or.*19.2(p.342.23; M.11. 477A).

***σαλσίκιον, τό,** *salted meat* or *fish*, Leont.N.*v.Sym.*52(M.93.1733B).

***σάλτον, τό,** (Lat. *saltus*) *woodland*, Proc.G.*2Par.*14:14(M.87. 1212C).

***σαμαμίθιον, τό,** *lizard*, Sophr.H.*mir.Cyr.et Jo.*44(M.87.3589D, 3592D).

***σαμάρδακος, ὁ,** *buffoon*, Chrys.*hom.17.3 in Eph.*(11.125C; κόρδακας Gaume).

[*]**Σαμαρείτης (Σαμαρίτης), ὁ,** *Samaritan*, origin of name discussed τὴν ἑρμηνείαν τοῦ Σ. ... σημαίνοντος τὸν φύλακα Or.*Jo.*20.35 (28; p.374.35; M.14.656B); Epiph.*haer.*9.1(p.197.17; M.41.224B); ἐκ διαφόρων προφάσεων καλεῖσθαι Σαμαρείτας ἔκ τε τοῦ Σωμὴρ ἔκ τε τοῦ Σομόρων ἔκ τε τοῦ φυλάττειν τὴν γῆν ἔκ τε τοῦ φυλάττειν τὰ παιδεύματα τοῦ νόμου *ib.*(p.198.6; 224C); Chrys.*hom.31.2 in Jo.*(8.177C); Thdt.*qu.48 in 3Reg.*(1.496); their origin, Ammon.*Jo.*4:4f.(M.85. 1417D); Cyr.*Jo.*2.4(4.181E–182A); Thdt.*Is.*22:6(p.91.28; 2.286); tenets Σ., τὸν μέλλοντα αἰῶνα ἀρνουμένων καὶ μηδὲ τὴν τῆς ψυχῆς ἐπιδιαμονὴν προσιεμένων Or.*Jo.*20.35(28; p.373.27; 653A); Epiph. *anac.*9(pp.166.9ff.; M.41.169Cf.); id.*haer.*9 passim(pp.197ff.; 224Bf.); *ib.*14.2(p.208.2ff.; 240B); πόθεν δὲ Σαμαρείταις τὸ προσδοκᾶν τὴν τοῦ Χριστοῦ παρουσίαν, τὸν Μωϋσέα δεξαμένοις μόνον; Ammon.*Jo.*4:25 (1424C); Σ. δὲ ἐκάλουν τὸν κύριον, ὡς ἀδιαφοροῦντα περὶ τὰς νομικὰς ἐντολὰς καὶ λύοντα τὸ σάββατον· οἱ γὰρ Σ. οὐκ ἀκριβῶς Ἰουδαΐζουσι *ib.*8:48(1453C); τὸ πέντε βιβλία Μωϋσέως, ἃ μόνα ἐδέξαντο οἱ Σ. †Chrys.*synops.*(6.338D), Chrys.*hom.31.2 in Jo.*(8.178A); Cyr.*Jo.*2.4 (568D,E).

***Σαμαρειτίζω,** *profess the Samaritan religion*, *Chron.Pasch.*p.336 (M.92.872B).

***Σαμαρειτικός,** *Samaritan*; by race, Just.*1apol.*53.4(M.6.408A); by religion, Epiph.*rescr.*3,5(pp.157.8,159.26; M.41.161A,164C); of the Pentateuch τὸ ἐν πᾶσι κείμενον παρὰ τοῖς Ἑβδομήκοντα κυροῦται ἀπὸ τοῦ Σ. ἀντιγράφου Or.*adnot.in Dt.*27:26(M.17.36A).

***Σαμαρειτικῶς,** *after the manner of Samaritans*, Or.*Jo.*20.35(28; p.373.33; M.14.653B).

Σαμαρεῖτις, ἡ, *Samaritan* woman, Or.*Jo.*1.5(7; p.10.14; M.14. 33B); Ammon.*Jo.*4:25(M.85.1425A); Chrys.*hom.31.4 in Jo.*(8.180C); Cyr.*Jo.*2.4(4.182C); of the fourth Sunday after Easter τῇ κυριακῇ τῆς Σ. Thdr.Stud.*serm.catech.*index(M.99.24A).

***Σαμαρειτισμός, ὁ,** *religion of the Samaritans, 'Samaritanism'*, Epiph.*rescr.*3(p.157.3; M.41.160D).

Σαμαρεύς, ὁ, = Σαμαρείτης, Just.*1apol.*26.3f.(M.6.368Af.); Or. *comm.in Mt.*17.29(p.666.3; M.13.1564A); id.*Jo.*20.35(28; p.375.7; M. 14.656A).

Σαμαρίτης, ὁ, v. Σαμαρείτης.

***Σαμοσατίτης, ὁ,** plur., *followers of Paul of Samosata*, Epiph.*haer.* 65.2,8(pp.4.17,11.26; M.42.13C,25C); title perh. invented by Epiph.

[*]**σαμπφείρινος,** for σαπφείρινος, *like lapis lazuli* λίθοις σ. *A.Thom.*A 112(p.223.20).

***Σαμψαῖοι (Σαμψῖται, Σαμψηνοί), οἱ,** *Sampseans* (Hebr. שֶׁמֶשׁ), followers of Elchezai forming a heretical sect, so named because said to invoke the sun; commonly known as Elchezaites, Epiph. *anac.*30(p.236.13; M.41.284B); *ib.*53(p.212.13; 848C); id.*haer.*20.3 (p.227.7; Σαμψέων M.41.273B); sect described, *ib.*53(pp.314ff.; 900f.); Σαμψῖται *ib.*20.3(p.226.22; 273A); Σαμψηνοί *ib.*30.3(p.336.2; Ἁμψηνοῖς 409A).

σανδάλιον, τό, *sandal*; plur., as monks' footwear, ‡Ath.*ep.Cast.* 1.6(M.28.856D); symbolism, Max.*qu.dub.*67(M.90.841B); ‡Bas.*h. myst.*(p.263.17).

***σάνδαλος, ὁ,** kind of boat, *Didasc.Jac.*5.20(p.89.10); σανδάλιν *Chron.Pasch.*p.395(M.92.1012C); Thphn.*chron.*p.332(M.108.801A).

σανίς, ἡ, 1. *plank, timber*, *T.Neph.*6.6; Chrys.*hom.34.4 in Mt.*(7. 394E); whirled to simulate thunder, Hipp.*haer.*4.32(p.58.11; M.16. 3094D); esp. as raw material for images, Clem.*prot.*4(p.35.20; M.8. 136A); Chrys.*hom.4.10 in Mt.*(65C); **2.** *board* displaying public notices, etc., Isid.Pel.*epp.*1.491(M.78.449C); Ath.Scholast.*coll.*4.3 (p.53); **3.** plur., artist's *panels, tablets* for pictures, Meth.*symp.*1.4 (p.13.5; M.18.45A); *A.Jo.*28(p.166.16); Thdt.*h.e.*1.1.1(3.722).

***σαόβροτος,** *mankind-saving, salutary*, Gr.Naz.*carm.*1.1.9.99(M. 37.464A).

[*]**σαπούνιον (*σωπ-), τό,** (Lat. *sapo*) *soap*, Barth.Edess.*Agar.* (M.104.1413A); *ib.*(σωπ- 1405B).

σαπρία, ἡ, *corruption, decay*; met., moral, *Pss.Sal.*14.4; *ib.*16.14; Diad.*perf.*97(p.144.8); foreign to Christ's conception ἅμα τε ἐπῆλθε τὸ πνεῦμα τῇ παρθένῳ...τὸ...σκήνωμα οὐδὲν τῆς ἀνθρωπίνης σ. συνεπεσπάσατο Gr.Nyss.*ep.*3(M.46.1021C).

***σαπροειδής,** *foul, repulsive*, Diad.*perf.*86(p.118.17).

σαπρός, *rotten, bad*; ? *dangerous* ποταμὸς δύσβατος...καὶ ῥύακες σ. Thphn.*chron.*p.267(M.108.664A).

***σαπφειροειδής,** *like lapis lazuli*, Ammon.*Ac.*7:55(M.85.1529C).

σαράβαρα, τά, 1. *Persian trousers*, ‡Nil.*perist.*10.5(M.79.893C); Thdt.*Dan.*3:20(2.1112); *Chron.Pasch.*pp.132,134(M.92.333C,337B); **2.** musical instrument, a kind of *cymbals*, Pall.*v.Chrys.*12(p.72.1; M.47.40).

***Σαρακηνικός,** *Saracenic, of Saracens*, *M.Pers.*7.6(p.457.14).

***Σαρακηνός, ὁ,** *Saracen, Arab*, Dion.Al.ap.Eus.*h.e.*6.42.4(M.20. 613B); Cyr.H.*catech.*6.22; Jo.D.*haer.*101(M.94.764A).

***σαρακηνόφρων,** *Saracen-minded* (i.e. iconoclastic), Thphn. *chron.*p.339(M.108.817B).

[*]**σαράκοντα,** = τεσσαράκοντα, *forty*, *A.Barth.*5(p.138.19); *Chron. Pasch.*p.185(M.92.456B); *Mir.Geo.*13(p.131.3).

[*]**σαρακοστός,** = τεσσαρακοστός, *fortieth*, *Nomoc.*286.

[*]**σαράντα,** = τεσσαράκοντα, *forty*, *Contrad.*1(p.6).

***σαρκαῖος,** *belonging to flesh, fleshly*; word coined on analogy of Ναζωραῖος to describe Nestorian Christ as being Logos conjoined with flesh but not truly incarnate, somewhat as Christ was called a Nazaraean from his sojourn there, Jo.D.*haer.Nest.* 22(M.95.200B).

***σαρκεία, ἡ,** *fleshiness, excessive fatness*, Isid.H.*etym.*4.7.28.

***σαρκεύς, ὁ,** *worker in flesh* (cf. χαλκεύς, ἱππεύς, ἱερεύς, πορθμεύς etc.) πῶς οὖν μία οὐσία, τοιαύτης οὔσης παραλλαγῆς; εἰ πνεῦμα μόνον, πόθεν σαρκεύς; εἰ σῶμα μόνον, πόθεν δόξα; †Ath.*fr.*(M.26.1237C).

σαρκικός, *fleshly*;

A. without ethical connotation; **1.** pertaining to the body (opp. soul) of man; **a.** *physical, bodily*; of Christ, Ign.*Eph.*7.2 cit. s. ἰατρός; περιτομὴν...σ. Just.*dial.*18.3(M.6.516B); σ. δουλείας ἐξεκόμιζε τὸν Ἰσραὴλ Cyr.*Abac.*50(3.563D); of *blood* relationship δύο υἱοὶ τοῦ βασιλέως, σ. ἀδελφοί *Apophth.Patr.*(M.65.297B); Gr.Mag.*dial.*(tr. Zach.)4.55(M.*PL.*77.422A); **b.** *external, visible*, Ign.*Magn.*13.2; πᾶς ἄνθρωπος σ. ἐπὶ σαρκικοῖς ἔχων τὸ φρόνημα Thdr.Mops.*1Cor.*1:29 (p.174.18f.); **c.** *substantial, material* opp. πνευματικός, of body of Christ until Resurrection ἡ θεότης...ἐν τῷ ἐσταυρωμένῳ αὐτῆς σώματι, μήτε ποιεῖ τοῦτο ἀπὸ φθορᾶς εἰς ἀφθαρσίαν, ἀπὸ θνητοῦ εἰς ἀθανασίαν ἀπὸ σ. εἰς πνευματικόν... Eulog.*fr.Trin.*7.12(p.377); **2.** *in the flesh, having a body* μετὰ δὲ τὴν ἀνάστασιν συνέφαγεν αὐτοῖς καὶ συνέπιεν ὡς σ. Ign.*Smyrn.*3.3; hence *human* opp. divine τὰ μὲν δουλικὰ δεσποτικῶς ἐνέργων, τουτέστι τὰ σ. θεϊκῶς, τὴν ἀπαθῆ...ἐν τοῖς σ. ἐπεδείκνυτο δύναμιν Max.*ambig.*(M.91.1044C).

B. ref. moral qualities; **1.** *carnal*, i.e. *worldly* οἱ σ. τὰ πνευματικὰ πράσσειν οὐ δύνανται οὐδὲ οἱ πνευματικοὶ τὰ σ. ... ἃ δὲ καὶ κατὰ σάρκα πράσσετε, ταῦτα πνευματικά ἐστιν· ἐν γὰρ Χριστῷ πάντα πράσσετε Ign.*Eph.*8.2; Clem.*paed.*1.6(p.111.21; M.8.293A) cit. s. πνευματικός; ψυχικοὶ ὄντες καὶ σ. [sc. Arians], ἀνακρινόμενοι ἀπὸ ἁγίου πνεύματος Epiph.*haer.*69.19(p.168.16; M.42.229D); *ib.*76.24(p.371.14; 564B); Chrys.*hom.34.4 in Mt.*(7.394D); Thdr.Mops.*1Cor.*1:29(p.174.18f.) cit. supra; **2.** *sensual* τοὺς δὲ ἀχαλιναγωγήτους φησί, καὶ καταφερομένους εἰς τὰς ἑαυτῶν ἐπιθυμίας, μηδεμίαν ἔχοντας ἐπιθυμίαν θείου πνεύματος...δικαίως ὁ ἀπόστολος σαρκικοὺς καλεῖ Iren.*haer.*5.8.2(M.7.1142B); Clem.*paed.*1.6(p.108.25; M.8.288B) cit. s. πνευματικός; Meth.*res.*1.58(p.321.20; M.41 om.); σ. λέγει τὸν νοσοῦντα περὶ τὰς σ. ἐπιθυμίας Sever.*1Cor.*2:14f.(p.235.2); Gennad.*fr.Rom.*7:5(p.369.13; M.85.1680B); Max.*ep.*9(M.91.448A); **3.** Gnost. (cf. ψυχικός) denoting lowest grade of mankind; acc. Naassenes may be born again to become πνευματικός, Hipp.*haer.*5.8(p.93.18; M.16.3146C); *ib.*5.21(p.124.2; 3190B); *ib.*5.8(p.96.5; 3150B); acc. Valentinus without hope of salvation, Epiph.*haer.*31.7(p.397.4ff.; M.41.488B).

***σαρκικῶς**, **1.** *in relation to the body*, Ign.*Eph.*10.3 cit. s. πνευματικῶς; Clem.*paed.*2.10(p.221.25; M.8.525B); **2.** *sensually*, Clem.*str.*4.18(p.299.13; M.8.1324B) cit. s. ἁμαρτητικῶς; **3.** *in material terms* σ. νοοῦντες τὰς γραφὰς...τὸ βούλημα τοῦ ἀπαθοῦς θεοῦ ὁμοίως τοῖς ἡμεδαποῖς κινήμασιν ἀπεκδεχόμενοι Clem.*str.*2.16(p.151.11; M.8.1012A); Epiph.*haer.*55.5(p.330.10; M.41.980C) cit. s. πνευματικῶς; **4.** *after a human manner, as man*, Ath.*Ar.*3.46(M.26.420C); σ. πυνθανόμενος ᾔδει θεϊκῶς ἃ ἔμελλε λέγειν ὁ Πέτρος *ib.*(421B); ὁ...υἱὸς ...γεγέννηται σ. διὰ τῆς ἁγίας παρθένου Cyr.*Pulch.*(p.27.12; 5^2.129E); CLater.*can.*4 cit. s. γέννησις; οὔτε τὰ ἀνθρώπινα [sc. δράσας] κατὰ ἄνθρωπον ὅτι μὴ μόνον σ. κεχωρισμένα θεότητος, οὐ γὰρ ἄνθρωπος μόνον Max.*ambig.*(M.91.1056B).

σάρκινος, **1.** *of the body, bodily* σ. ... ὀφθαλμοῖς ἀθεώρητον Bas.*reg.fus.*2.1(2.337C; M.31.909C); Max.*ambig.*(M.91.1244C); Jo.D.*hom.*12.22(M.96.812A); **2.** *material, temporal* opp. spiritual οἱ σ. πτωχοί Clem.*q.d.s.*19(p.172.16; M.9.624C); *Ep.Lugd.*ap.Eus.*h.e.*5.1.18(M.20.416A); σ. ... σοφίαν τὴν περὶ αἰσθητῶν ὠνόμασεν...ἔθος δὲ τῇ γραφῇ τὰ περὶ τῶν κοσμικῶν καὶ ὑλικῶν μαθήματα σ. καλεῖν Didym.*2Cor.*1:12(p.17.4ff.; M.39.1685B,C); **3.** *guilty of venial* (opp. mortal) *sin*, Or.*comm.in 1Cor.*13:3(*JTS* 9 p.242).

***σαρκίνως**, *in a fleshly manner*, hence *superficially, literally* μὴ σ. ἀκροᾶσθαι τῶν λεγομένων ἀλλὰ τὸν ἐν αὐτοῖς κεκρυμμένον νοῦν... ἐρευνᾶν Clem.*q.d.s.*5(p.163.17; M.9.609C); Or.*princ.*4.3.9(p.335.8; M.11.389B).

σαρκίον, τό, **1.** dim. of σάρξ, *bit of flesh*, hence contemptuously of body opp. soul, ref. 1Cor.15:54 πῶς τὸ θνητὸν τοῦτο σ. ἐνδύσεται ἀθανασίαν...διαγγέλλειν Iren.*haer.*1.10.3(M.7.557A); Clem.*exc.Thdot.*52(p.124.6; M.9.684B); Meth.*res.*2.18(p.369.8; M.18.284B); τὸ συγγενὲς σ. ἀπολαβοῦσα [sc. ψυχή] Gr.Naz.*or.*7.21(M.35.781C); ἀπὸ τοῦ νῦν ἄλλην ἀγρυπνίαν οὐ ποιῶ μεθ' ὑμῶν ἐν τῷδε τῷ σ. Cyr.S.*v.Euthym.*39(p.57.26); and perh. in pathos ὡς μηδὲ τὸ σωμάτιον αὐτοῦ ὑφ' ἡμῶν ληφθῆναι, καίπερ πολλῶν ἐπιθυμούντων...κοινωνῆσαι τῷ ἁγίῳ αὐτοῦ σ. *M.Polyc.*17.1; **2.** = σάρξ, Tat.*orat.*15(p.16.27; M.6.840A) cit. s. δαίμων; δερμάτινον χιτῶνα...τὸ αἰσθητὸν σ. εἶναι λέγουσι Iren.*haer.*1.5.5(M.7.501A); θάνατος ἔκρουσεν τὴν τοῦ σ. θύραν Pall.*v.Chrys.*20(p.138.14; M.47.77) etc.; **3.** of Christ's human nature τὸν υἱὸν τοῦ θεοῦ...ἐν μήτρᾳ παρθένου κυοφορηθέντα, καθὸ γεγέννηται τὸ αἰσθητὸν αὐτοῦ σ. Clem.*str.*6.15(p.496.7; M.9.352A); ὑμέτερον σ. εἴληφα Epiph.*haer.*69.55(p.202.27; M.42.289A); Nil.ap.Proc.G.*Cant.*2:3(M.87.1581A); τὸ ὑπάρχειν μέντοι κατ' ἴδιον λόγον τὸ ἀπαύγασμα τοῦ πατρός, ἕτερον δὲ πάλιν τὸ ἀπὸ γῆς σ., ἤτοι τελείως τὸν ἄνθρωπον Cyr.*hom.pasch.*8.5(5^2.102D); and his body προέβαλε...σ. τῷ λόγῳ ἡ Σοφία Clem.*exc.Thdot.*1(p.105.6; M.9.653A); in words ascribed to an Apollinarian τὸ ἐκ Μαρίας σ. ὁμοούσιον ἡμῖν ‡Ath.*dial.Trin.*4.1(M.28.1249D); ἤξει μὲν μετὰ τοῦ σώματος...τοιοῦτος δὲ οἷος ὤφθη τοῖς μαθηταῖς ἐν τῷ ὄρει...ὑπερνικώσης τὸ σ. τῆς θεότητος Gr.Naz.*ep.*101(M.37.181B).

***σαρκοβλέπτης, ὁ**, *person of merely physical vision, materialist* οἱ σ. ὄντες καὶ μόνον εἰ μὴ τοῖς σαρκὸς ὄμμασι θεωρεῖταί τι, οὐκ ὄντως εἶναι τόδε οἴονται Leont.H.*monoph.*testimonia(M.86.1829D).

σαρκοβορέω, *be carnivorous*, Thphl.Ant.*Autol.*2.16(M.6.1080A).

***σαρκοβορία, ἡ**, *eating of meat*, Gr.Nyss.*v.Mos.*(M.44.412C).

σαρκοβόρος, *carnivorous*; of an executioner as murderous or bloodthirsty, Gr.Mag.*dial.*(tr.Zach.)3.37(M.*PL.*77.311B,C).

***σαρκογενής**, *born of flesh*, Gr.Naz.*carm.*1.1.9.79(M.37.462A); σ. καὶ παραδεισογενὴς καὶ οὐρανοπολίτης Anast.S.*hex.*12(M.89.1064A).

***σαρκολάτρης, ὁ**, *worshipper of the flesh*; used against Apollinarians in reply to the charge of being ἀνθρωπολάτρης, Gr.Naz.*ep.*101(M.37.185C); id.*carm.*1.1.10.28(M.37.467A); *ib.*2.1.30.87(1293A).

***σαρκομανέω**, *rave with lust*, Ephr.3.403F.

***σαρκομανία, ἡ**, *lust*, Anast.S.*hod.*14(M.89.252D).

***σαρκομοιόμορφος**, *resembling flesh*; *life-like*, ‡Jo.D.*Const.*17(M.95.336A).

***σαρκοπέδη, ἡ**, the *fetter of the flesh*, Gr.Naz.*carm.*1.2.2.503(M.37.618A).

σαρκοποιέω, *make flesh, cause to become incarnate*, Just.*1apol.*66.2(M.6.428C); id.*dial.*45.4,84.2(M.6.573A,673B).

***σαρκόσαθρος**, *having a disease of the flesh*; of the man sick of the palsy, Geo.Pis.*carm.*54.1(p.57).

***σαρκότητος**, Gr.Nyss.*Eun.*4(M.45.637B; σαρκός τε 2 p.65.22).

***σαρκοτόκος**, *flesh-bearing*, Cyr.*ep.*1(p.15.20; 5^2.8E,9B); *flesh-begetting*, Leont.H.*Nest.*4.16(M.86.1681C).

***σαρκοτροφέω**, *pamper the flesh*, Gr.Naz.*or.*26.14(M.35.1248A).

σαρκοφαγία, ἡ, **1.** *meat-diet*, Clem.*str.*7.6(p.26.4; M.9.448A); **2.** *cannibalism*, Cyr.H.*catech.*22.4.

***σαρκόφιλος**, *loving the flesh, sensual*, Thdr.Stud.*epp.*2.28(M.99.1197A).

***σαρκοφορ-έω**, *wear flesh* ἀναπαύλης δὲ ἡμεῖς οἱ ∼οῦντες δεόμεθα Clem.*str.*6.16(p.501.23; M.9.364A); πρὶν ἢ δουλεῦσαι καὶ ∼ῆσαι τὸν κύριον id.*paed.*3.1(p.237.7; M.8.557A); Eus.Al.*serm.*21.3(M.86.425B).

***σαρκοφόρος**, **1.** in gen., *corporeal* θεὸς...οὐδέποτε θεαθεὶς ὑπὸ τῶν θνητῶν καὶ σ. Agath.*v.Gr.Ill.*104(p.52); **2.** of Christ; **a.** *wearing flesh, incarnate* τὸν...κύριόν μου βλασφημεῖ, μὴ ὁμολογῶν αὐτὸν σ. Ign.*Smyrn.*5.2; Clem.*str.*5.6(p.348.10; M.9.57B); αὐτὸς οὖν ἐστι θεὸς σ. καὶ ἡμεῖς ἄνθρωποι πνευματοφόροι Ath.*inc.et c.Ar.*8(M.26.996C); Mac.Aeg.*hom.*47.15(M.34.805D); of eucharist τὸν ζωοποιὸν...τοῦ μονογενοῦς σου υἱοῦ σ. ἄρτον ἀξίως μεταλαμβάνειν Ath.*virg.*13(p.47.9n.; M.28.266D n.); Procl.CP *hom.*4.19(p.47); **b.** *with (a body of) flesh* ἐνομίσαμεν αὐτὸν σ. ἄνδρα εἶναι, μὴ εἰδότες ὅτι αὐτός ἐστιν ὁ ζωοποιῶν τοὺς ἀνθρώπους *A.Jo.*45(p.162.20); **c.** Apollinarian, exeg. Mt.26:39 ἐπεὶ θεὸς ἦν σ. ὁ τοῦτο λέγων μηδεμίαν ἐν τῷ θέλειν ἔχων διαφοράν Apoll.*fr.*109(p.233.7)ap.Max.*opusc.*(M.91.169D); Val.Apoll.*apol.*2(p.288.20; M.86.1953C).

***σαρκόφρων**, *carnal-minded*, ‡Ath.*serm.fid.*39(p.31; M.26.1289C); Thdr.Stud.*epp.*2.98(M.99.1352A).

***σαρκοχαρής**, *delighting in carnal things*, Gr.Naz.*carm.*2.2(poem.)7.74(M.37.1556A).

***σαρκοχίτων**, *wearing a robe of flesh, incarnate*, Geo.Pis.*carm.vit.*5(p.51).

σαρκ-όω, *make flesh*;

A. in gen.; **1.** *make into flesh* τὸ κατὰ γαστρὸς τὸ μὲν πρῶτον ὑγροῦ ἐστι σύστασις γαλακτοειδής, ἔπειτα ἐξαιματουμένη ∼οῦται ἡ σύστασις αὕτη, πηγνυμένη δὲ...ζωογονεῖται Clem.*paed.*1.6(p.119.10; M.8.308B); Hipp.*haer.*5.7(p.80.3; M.16.3127B); **2.** *endow with flesh* εἰ ἐκ πρεσβυτέρων ἁμαρτημάτων ἐσαρκώθησαν αἱ ψυχαί, καὶ τρόπος αὐταῖς τιμωρίας ἡ τοῦ σώματος ἐπενοήθη φύσις... Cyr.*Jo.*1.9(4.81A).

B. theol.; *endow with human nature* οὗτος [sc. Χριστός]...ἑαυτὸν ἐσάρκωσεν Procl.CP *or.*2.3(M.65.696C); pass., *become incarnate*, of Son ὁ...μονογενὴς υἱὸς κατὰ τὴν τοῦ πατρὸς εὐδοκίαν ∼ωθεὶς ὑπὲρ ἀνθρώπων Iren.*haer.*1.9.3(M.7.541B); Eus.*e.th.*1.4(p.64.17; M.24.833A); as Logos, Iren.*haer.*3.19.1(939B); Or.*Jo.*1.7(9; p.13.9; M.14.37B); ἐσαρκώθη ἐκ τοῦ σώματος ἡμῶν Meth.*res.*2.24(p.380.13; M.18.329D); as πνεῦμα: τὸ ἐν τῇ παρθένῳ ∼ωθὲν πνεῦμα Hipp.*haer.*9.12(p.248.29; M.16.3383C); cf. ὁ λόγος τοῦ θεοῦ, πνεῦμα ∼ούμενον, ἁγιαζομένη σὰρξ οὐράνιος Clem.*paed.*1.6(p.116.3; M.8.301B); πιστεύομεν...εἰς ἕνα κύριον...∼ωθέντα *Symb.Caes.*ap.Eus.*ep.Caes.*3(M.20.1537B); abs. οἰκονομικῶς σεσαρκωμένος θεὸν ἑαυτοῦ τὸν πατέρα καλεῖ Ath.*exp.Ps.*88:27(M.27.389C); as deity incarnate τὸ ἐκ τοῦ σπέρματος Ἀβραμιαίου μέλλειν ∼οῦσθαι τὸν θεόν Diod.*Gen.*24:2(M.33.1575D); ἄγγελος ∼ωθῆναι...οὐκ ἴσχυεν †Ephr.*nativ.*82(p.88); ἡ ∼ωθεῖσα θεότης Isid.Pel.*epp.*1.59(M.78.221A); Procl.CP *or.laud.BMV* 4(p.104.23; M.65.685A) cit. s. ἀποθεόω; ἐκ τοῦ οἰκείου πλάσματος ∼οῦσθαι id.*or.*2.8(M.65.704B); ass. ἐνανθρωπέω: μυστήριον οἰκονομίας, ὅτι, σεσαρκωμένου τοῦ λόγου καὶ ἐνανθρωπήσαντος, ὁ πατὴρ ἦν ἐν τῷ υἱῷ καὶ ὁ υἱὸς ἐν τῷ πατρί, ἐμπολιτευομένου τοῦ υἱοῦ ἐν ἀνθρώποις Hipp.*Noët.*4(p.241.23; M.10.809A); cf. *se ipsum exinaniens homo factus est, incarnatus est, cum deus esset*, Or.*princ.*1 proem.4(p.10.8; M.11.117B); τοῦ...∼ωθέντος...θεοῦ λόγου καὶ ἐνανθρωπήσαντος

Jo.Thess.*dorm.BMV* 1.1(p.375.16); cf. *πῶς ὁ ἄσαρκος ∼οῦται; πῶς θεὸς ἄνθρωπος γίνεται;* Dam.*troph*.1.7.3(p.210.12); in formal statements, *Symb.Nic.*(325)(p.51; M.20.1540B); *Symb.Hier.*(M.33.533A); *∼ωθέντα τουτέστι γεννηθέντα τελείως...ἐνανθρωπήσαντα τουτέστι τέλειον ἄνθρωπον λαβόντα Symb.*ap.Epiph.*anc.*119(p.148.11; M.43.233B); *οὐκ οἰκήσαντα μόνον ἐν τῇ σαρκί, ἀλλὰ ∼ωθέντα φασί... εἰπόντες αὐτὸν ∼ωθέντα, ἐπήγαγον, ἐνανθρωπήσαντα· τούτοις...θεότητός τε καὶ ἀνθρωπότητος ἄκραν ἕνωσιν ὑποτιθέμενοι* Thdot.Anc.*exp. symb.*16(M.77.1337A); in restricted sense (= A.2), Arian *∼ωθέντα, οὐκ ἐνανθρωπήσαντα οὔτε γὰρ ψυχὴν ἀνθρωπίνην ἀνείληφεν* Eudox.*exp. fid.*ap.*Doct.Patr.*9(p.65.4); Apollinarian *τινες παρηνόχλησαν ἡμῖν... οὐ θεὸν ∼ωθέντα ὁμολογοῦντες αὐτὸν ἀλλ' ἄνθρωπον θεῷ συναφθέντα* Apoll.*fid.sec.pt.*30(p.178.10; M.10.1116D); cf. *τοῦτον* [sc. the second Adam] *δέ φησιν ἐξ οὐρανοῦ διὰ τοῦτο καλεῖσθαι, διότι τὸ πνεῦμα τὸ οὐράνιον ἐσαρκώθη. τίς γραφὴ ταῦτα λέγει...ὅτι πνεῦμα ἐσαρκώθη;* Gr.Nyss.*Apoll.*12(M.45.1145C); for formula *μία φύσις τοῦ θεοῦ λόγου σεσαρκωμένη*, v. *φύσις*.

σαρκώδης, **1.** *fleshly*, i.e. *human* *διαβεβαιοῦται* [sc. Apoll.]...*ἐξ ἀρχῆς ἐν τῷ υἱῷ τὴν σ. ἐκείνην φύσιν εἶναι* Gr.Naz.*ep.*202(M.37.332B); Gr.Nyss.*Apoll.*26(M.45.1180B); **2.** met., *meaty* *ὅσον μὲν οὖν σ. τοῦ λόγου καὶ τρόφιμον, μετὰ τῶν ἐντοσθίων καὶ τῶν κρυφίων τοῦ νοῦ... εἰς πέμψιν πνευματικὴν ἀναδοθήσεται* Gr.Naz.*or.*45.16(M.36.645A); **3.** met., of the '*natural*' man (ref. 1Cor.2:14f.) *διαιρεῖ...τάς τε σ. καὶ τὰς πνευματικὰς τῶν ψυχῶν καταστάσεις* Gr.Nyss.*or.catech.*7(p.38.18; M.45.32B).

σάρκωσις, **ἡ**, *taking flesh, incarnation*; **1.** = taking a human body, favourite word of Apollinarius *κεφάλαιον δὲ τῆς σωτηρίας ἡμῶν ἡ τοῦ λόγου σ.* Apoll.*fid.sec.pt.*11(p.171.1; M.10.1109A); *εἷς υἱός, καὶ πρὸ τῆς σ. καὶ μετὰ τὴν σ. ὁ αὐτός ib.*36(p.181.8; 1120A); id.*corp. et div.*11(p.190.12; M.*PL*.8.875A); id.*fid.inc.*4(p.195.23; M.*PL*.8.877A); id.*fr.*74(p.222.8)ap.Gr.Nyss.*Apoll.*38(M.45.1209B); *ib.*124(p.237.30) ap.Thdt.*eran.*1(4.70); id.*ep.Dion.*2(p.257.17; M.*PL*.8.929B); cf. *θείαν τινὰ σ. ἀνατυποῦται τῷ λόγῳ* Gr.Nyss.*Apoll.*2(1128A); with *ἕνωσις*, Apoll.*quod un.Chr.*3(p.296.6; M.28.124C) cit. s. *σύνθεσις*; in this sense requires supplementing to convey orthodox doctrine of Inc. *τὴν ἐκ παρθένου...τελείαν...σ. καὶ ψύχωσιν* Didym.*Trin.*3.4(M.39.829C); **2.** = taking human nature [1Cor.15:12] *τὴν αἰτίαν ἀποδιδοὺς τῆς σ. αὐτοῦ* Iren.*haer.*3.18.3(M.7.933B); *ib.*3.19.1(939A); ‡Ath.*dial. Trin.*1.9(M.28.1132A,C); Didym.(‡Bas.)*Eun.*5(1.311B; M.29.748A); *οὐ γὰρ πρὸ τῆς σ. ὑπὸ νόμον ἦν* Procl.CP *hom.*2.2(M.65.840A); Thdt. *eran.*2(4.101) cit. s. *ἕνωσις*; Leont.H.*Nest.*2.1(M.86.1533B); *οὐ μόνον τῆς αὐτῆς ὄντα οὐσίας καὶ μετὰ σάρκωσιν τῷ πατρὶ...ἀλλὰ καὶ τῆς αὐτῆς ἐνεργείας* Max.*Pyrr.*(M.91.349A); *προσκύνησιν τῷ...Χριστῷ, καὶ πρὸ σαρκός, καὶ μετὰ σάρκωσιν* Thdr.Stud.*epp.*2.212(M.99.1640A); ass. *ἐνανθρώπησις*, Ath.*tom.*7(M.26.805A); *ἡ σ. εἴτ' οὖν ἐνανθρώπησις* Cyr.*Thds.*19(p.54.5; 5².16E); cf. *οὐκ ἄνθρωπος Χριστός, ἀλλὰ θεὸς Χριστός, θεὸς ἐνανθρωπήσας, οὐκ ἄνθρωπος ἀποθεωθείς, ἀλλὰ χρίσας τὴν οἰκείαν καὶ ἑκούσιον σ. τῇ οἰκείᾳ θεότητι* ‡Eus.*Laz.*15(p.39.11); defined *ἡ μὲν ἕνωσις μόνην δηλοῖ τὴν συνάφειαν· πρὸς τί δὲ γέγονεν ἡ συνάφεια, οὐκέτι. ἡ δὲ σ., ταὐτὸν δ' ἐστὶν εἰπεῖν καὶ ἐνανθρώπησις, τὴν πρὸς σάρκα, ἤτοι πρὸς ἄνθρωπον συνάφειαν δηλοῖ* Jo.D.*f.o.*3.11(M.94.1024B); id.*Jacob.*52(M.94.1461B).

σάρξ, **ἡ**, **A.** *flesh*; **1.** fig., of nominal Christians in body of Christ, Clem.*str.*7.14(p.62.18; M.9.521A); **2.** *flesh meat*, usu. plur., *Barn.*10.4; *Αἰγύπτιοι...οὐκ ἐπιτρέπουσι τοῖς ἱερεῦσι σιτεῖσθαι σ., ὀρνιθείοις τε ὡς κουφοτάτοις χρῶνται* Clem.*str.*7.6(p.26.9; M.9.448B); Or.*Cels.*8.30(p.245.27; M.11.1561A); **3.** the *body*; **a.** an integral part of man, *2Clem.*9.1ff.; *τὴν ἀκήρατον τῆς ψυχῆς ἐσθῆτα, τὴν σ.* Clem.*paed.*2.10(p.222.32; M.8.528B); so in definitions of man's nature, whether regarded as trichotomy *εἰς ὃν ἐλπίζουσιν σαρκί, ψυχῇ, πνεύματι* Ign. *Philad.*11.2; cf.Iren.*haer.*5.9.1(M.7.1144B) cit. s. *ἄνθρωπος*; or as dichotomy of *σ.* and *πνεῦμα*, Ign.*Trall.*12.1; id.*Smyrn.*1.1; Apoll. *inc.*2(p.304.20; M.28.92C) cit. s. *ἄνθρωπος*; or *σ.* and *ψυχή*, Bas.*hom.* 3.3(2.18E; M.31.204B); cf.Iren.*haer.*5.8.2(1142B); *ἐψυχωμένης σ. ψυχῇ λογικῇ καὶ νοερᾷ· ὅρος...ἀνθρωπίνης φύσεως οὗτος* Leont.B.*cap.Sev.*18(M.86.1908A); Eulog.*fr.dogm.*(M.86.2953A,D); **b.** not in itself evil *σάρκα ἡμῖν τὸ πνεῦμα τὸ ἅγιον ἀλληγορεῖ· καὶ γὰρ ὑπ' αὐτοῦ δεδημιούργηται ἡ σ.* Clem.*paed.*1.6(p.115.30f.; M.8.301A); Chrys.*hom.13.2 in Rom.*(9.559Bff.); acc. Manicheans created by Devil, Anast.S. *hod.*14(M.89.253A); **c.** its resurrection *οὔτε γὰρ ἂν αὐτὴ* [sc. *ἡ ψυχή*] *φανείη ποτὲ χωρὶς σώματος οὔτε ἀνίσταται* [*ἡ*] *σ. χωρὶς ψυχῆς* Tat. *orat.*15(p.16.9; M.6.837A); *οὐχ ὡς σάρκες κἂν ἔχωμεν, ἀλλ' ὡς οὐράνιον πνεῦμα μένωμεν* Athenag.*leg.*31.3(M.6.964A); *οἱ ἱερεῖς... εὔχονται...περὶ...τῶν κεκοιμημένων οὕτως 'τὴν ψυχὴν τοῦδε ἀνάπαυσον· συνανεγείρων καὶ τὴν σ. αὐτοῦ'* Cosm.Ind.*top.*7(M.88.385C); in early creeds *σαρκὸς ἀνάστασιν* Marcell.*ep.*ap.Epiph.*haer.*72.3(p.258.12; M.42.388A); *Symb.*ap.*Const.App.*7.41.8; *Symb.Hier.*(M.33.533B); *Symb.Ant.*(341)1 ap.Ath.*syn.*22(p.249.8; M.26.721B); denied by Marcion, Hipp.*haer.*10.19(p.280.13; M.16.3438A); Epiph.*haer.*42.3(p.98.7; M.41.700A); Jo.D.*haer.*42(M.94.704A); **d.** in rel. to divine image in man, Tat.*orat.*15(p.16.21f.; M.6.837B) cit. s. *εἰκών*; Eus. *Marcell.*2.3(p.49.7; M.24.805C); **e.** *σ. καὶ αἷμα* as natural opp. spiritual body (ref. 1Cor.15:44), Or.*Cels.*6.29(p.99.26; M.11.1337C); opp. ethereal body, id.*Jo.*1.26(24; p.32.14; M.14.69C); sts. plur., *ib.* 20.36(29; p.377.20; 660C); as unclean, Hegem.*Arch.*5(p.7.11; M.10.1436A); **4.** met., *literal sense* of scripture, Or.*princ.*4.2.4(p.312.9; M.11.364B) cit. s. *γραφή*.

B. *man* (= Hebr. בָּשָׂר) always implying contrast, sts. with divine or angelic, sts. with what is supernatural, holy, or inward *τῆς γραφῆς ἔθος ἐχούσης λέγειν σ. τὸν ἄνθρωπον* Ath.*Ar.*3.30(M.26.388C); '*σαρκὸς*' *δὲ ποτὲ μὲν τῆς φύσεως λεγομένης, ποτὲ δὲ τῆς προσηγορίας...λαμβανομένης...ἐπὶ σημασίᾳ τῆς θνητότητος...ποτὲ δὲ τοῦ προσκαίρου παντός* Thdr.Mops.*Rom.*7:5(p.125.1; M.66.805D); *ib.*13:14(p.164.11; 865C); *σ. πᾶν τὸ πρόσκαιρον λέγει...'κατὰ σάρκα' λέγει 'περιπατεῖν' τὸ κατὰ νόμον ζῆν* id.*2Cor.*10:3f.(p.199.11); *τῷ τῆς σ. ὀνόματι διχῶς ἡ θεία χρῆται γραφή· νῦν μὲν τὴν φύσιν οὕτως...ὀνομάζουσα ...νῦν δὲ...τὸ αὐτῆς ἐμπαθές* Gennad.*Rom.*7:5(p.369.4ff.; M.85.1680A); Eub.*fr.*ap.*Doct.Patr.*22(p.146.3); **1.** corresponding to OT idea, of natural man in his frailty, Ign.*Magn.*3.2; *σάρκες ὄντες καθ' ἑαυτούς, καὶ ἀεὶ ἡττώμενοι τῷ νόμῳ διὰ τὴν ἀσθένειαν τῆς σ.* Ath.*Ar.*2.68(M.26.293A); *οὐχὶ δὲ Μωϋσῆς αὐτὸς σ. ὢν εἰς μέγιστον ἐτράπη φῶς; Hom. Clem.*20.6; *ib.*20.7; as devoid of baptismal grace *ἐν οἷς...γίνεται βεβαία...ἡ εἰς τὸ εὐαγγέλιον πίστις, οὗτοι διὰ τῆς πίστεως μεταβαίνουσιν ἀπὸ τοῦ εἶναι σάρκες, εἰς τὸ γίνεσθαι πνεῦμα* Gr.Nyss.*fid.*(M.45.144C); *σ. ... εἶπεν καὶ οὐ ψυχή, ἐξευτελίζων τὰ ἀνθρώπινα καυχήματα* Sever. *1Cor.*1:29(p.230.33); ref. catechumens *τὰ κατὰ σάρκα βρέφη* Dion. Ar.*e.h.*3.3.6(M.3.433A); collectively, the *human race, mankind* *ἐν τῷ κατακλυσμῷ ἀπώλετο πᾶσα ἁμαρτωλὸς σ.* Clem.*str.*6.6(p.458.3; M.9.273C); *σ. ... τὸ τῶν ἀνθρώπων γένος λέγουσιν* Ath.*Ar.*3.30(388C); by stressing material aspect *σ. καὶ αἷμα* heightens the contrast *οὐ πρὸς τὰ οὐράνια καὶ τὸν τούτων ποιητὴν ἀλλὰ κάτω πρὸς τὰ ἐπίγεια βλέπουσα...ὡς μόνον αἷμα καὶ σ., οὐκέτι πνεῦμα καθαρὸν γιγνομένη* Athenag.*leg.*27(M.6.952D); cf.Iren.*haer.*5.9.1(M.7.1144B); *πόθεν αὐτοκρατορικὴ δύναμις τῷ σ. καὶ αἵματι πεπιλημένῳ;* Eus.*l.C.*4(p.202.28; M.20.1333A); **2.** of non-ethical physical nature of man; **a.** *physical life*, Ign.*Rom.*2.1; *οὐχ ἡγοῦμαι ἔγωγε μυσάττεσθαι τὴν ἐν σ. ζωὴν τὸν ἀπόστολον* Clem.*str.*3.9(p.226.2; M.8.1168B); *διαβάλλεσθαι τὴν σ. καὶ δι' αὐτῆς τὴν γένεσιν ib.*4.26(p.321.5; 1373A); Caius R.ap.Eus.*h.e.*3.28.2(M.20.273D); generic plur., Eus.*l.C.*4(p.202.20; M.20.1332D); also of outward acts, temporal goods *ἑορτάζων κατὰ σάρκα* Or.*Cels.*8.23(p.240.22; M.11.1552C); *οὐκ ἐν σ. δεῖ προσκυνεῖν καὶ σαρκίναις θυσίαις ib.*6.70(p.140.25; 1405A); *κατὰ σάρκα* explained as *ἀπὸ τῶν ἔξωθεν, ἀπὸ εὐγενείας, ἀπὸ πλούτου, ἀπὸ...τῆς τῶν πολλῶν δόξης* Chrys.*hom. 24.2 in 2Cor.*(10.607E); **b.** *κατὰ σάρκα* freq. of physical descent *ἐξ αὐτοῦ* [sc. *τοῦ Ἰακώβ*] *ὁ κύριος Ἰησοῦς τὸ κατὰ σ. 1Clem.*32.2; *τῷ μὴ κατὰ σ. Ἰσραηλίτῃ Κορνηλίῳ* Or.*Cels.*2.1(p.127.20; 796B); **3.** corresponding to Pauline idea (Gal.5:17ff.; Rom.8:7ff.) *flesh*, not co-terminous with the body, but human nature viewed in active opposition alike to God and to the spiritual effects of grace *δουλεύοντας σ. καὶ αἵματι ἢ κέρδους ἢ ἐπιθυμίας ἐλάττους γενομένους ἁμαρτεῖν* Athenag.*leg.*31.2(M.6.961C); *τούτῳ* [sc. *τῷ γνωστικῷ*] *τέθνηκεν ἡ σάρξ* Clem.*str.*4.22(p.309.9; M.8.1348B); *τὸ 'κατὰ σ. περιπατεῖν' καὶ 'σαρκικοὺς εἶναι' κατὰ τὸν ἀπόστολον ἐν ἁμαρτίαις ὄντας ib.*4.26(p.321.14; 1373B); *τὴν ἐν ἀνθρώποις σ. ἐπιθυμοῦσαν 'κατὰ τοῦ πνεύματος'* Or. *Cels.*3.28(p.226.9; M.11.956C); cf. *cum ergo dicitur quia 'caro pugnat adversum spiritum', ita intellegunt isti quia usus vel necessitas vel delectamentum carnis provocans hominem abstrahit et abducit a divinis et spiritualibus rebus...quod vero inter 'carnis opera' descriptae sunt esse etiam 'haereses' et 'invidiae' et 'contentiones' vel cetera, ita accipiunt quod anima...nihil subtile vel spiritale sentiens, caro dicitur effecta*, id.*princ.*3.4.4f.(pp.269.19,270.9; M.11.324B,325A); [Rom.7:5] *οὐ ταύτην ἔλεγεν τὴν σ., ἣν περιβεβλήμεθα, ἀλλὰ τὰς σαρκικὰς πράξεις* Cyr.H.*hom.*17(M.33.1152B); exeg. Gen.6:3 *ἔθος γὰρ ἀεὶ τῇ θείᾳ γραφῇ σ. τοὺς σαρκικοὺς καλεῖν...ὥσπερ οὖν καὶ τοῖσδε διὰ τὸ ὑπερορᾶν τῶν σαρκικῶν ἔλεγεν* [Rom.8:9] Chrys.*hom.22.3 in Gen.*(4.198B); Proc.G.*Gen.*6:3(M.87.268C); plur. *καθηλώσας τῷ θείῳ φόβῳ τὰς σ. αὐτοῦ* Gr.Nyss.*ep.*3(M.46.1016B); on *φρόνημα σαρκός* v. Didym. *2Cor.*1:12(p.17.7; M.39.1685C); Chrys.*hom.5.4 in Eph.*(11.36C); Jo.D. *Rom.*8:7(M.95.500C); Christian view defended against Manichean, *Disp.Phot.*(M.88.545D–548C); partic. of the unregulated and disordered passions of the body *μισεῖ τὴν ψυχὴν ἡ σ. ... διότι ταῖς ἡδοναῖς κωλύεται χρῆσθαι...ἡ ψυχὴ τὴν μισοῦσαν ἀγαπᾷ σ. καὶ τὰ μέλη Diogn.*

6.5f.; τὸν σωτῆρα ἐνστερνίσασθαι, ἵνα καταργήσωμεν τῆς σ. ἡμῶν τὰ πάθη Clem.*paed*.1.6(p.115.29; M.8.301A); ὅσῳ παχυτέραν τὴν σ. σεαυτῷ ποιεῖς, τοσούτῳ βαρύτερον τῇ ψυχῇ κατασκευάζεις τὸ δεσμωτήριον Bas.*hom.in Ps*.29(1.130B; M.29.320C); τῶν...χοϊκῶν καὶ κατὰ σ. ζώντων id.*hom.in Ps*.7(1.100C; M.29.236A); σ. καλεῖ τὴν ἁμαρτίαν, ἧς καὶ τὰ μέλη καταριθμεῖ Sever.*Col*.3:5(p.327.4); Gennad.*fr.Rom*.7:17ff. (p.373.13); as seat and instrument of sin σαρκὶ ἃ ἐπράξαμεν πονηρὰ μετανοήσωμεν *2Clem*.8.2; τῇ...νομοθεσίᾳ τοῦ διαβόλου καὶ τὴν ἐνοικοῦσαν ἐπιθυμίαν ἐν τῇ σ. Meth.*res*.2.6(p.340.12; M.18.304C); Eus. *d.e*.7.1(p.301.23; M.22.493C) cit. s. ἀναμάρτητος; σ. ὀλοὴ παθέων ῥίζα ...κόσμοιο κάτω ῥείοντος ἑταίρη...ζωῆς ἀντίπαλ' οὐρανίης... Gr.Naz. *carm*.2.1.46.2ff.(M.37.1378A); not intrinsically evil καὶ πύματον θεότητι κεράσσατο, ὥς με σαώσῃ πλάσμα φίλον *ib*.infra(1379A); ὥσπερ... ἡ ἐντολὴ οὐκ ἔστι πονηρά, ἐπειδὴ δι' αὐτῆς ἀφορμὴν ἔλαβεν ἡ ἁμαρτία· οὕτως οὐδὲ τῆς σ. ἡ φύσις, εἰ καὶ δι' αὐτῆς ἡμᾶς καταγωνίζεται Chrys. *hom.13.3 in Rom*.(9.561B); in specialized sense of concupiscence, cf. [Rom.8:13] *non conversationem quae est in carne repellens ab eis... sed concupiscentias abscindens carnis, eas quae mortificant hominem*, Iren.*haer*.5.10.2(M.7.1149B); εἰς ἐπιθυμίαν πεσόντες [sc. angels] παρθένων καὶ ἥττους σαρκὸς εὑρεθέντες Athenag.*leg*.24.5(M.6.948B); **4.** (poet.) *wife* καὶ σ. ἱερῆος, καὶ μήτηρ Gr.Naz.*carm*.2.2(epitaph.)91 (M.38.57A); *ib*.1.2.1.604,607(M.37.568A).

C. Christol.; **1.** ref. act of Inc., *man, manhood, human nature* ἐν σ. γενόμενος θεός Ign.*Eph*.7.2(later cited in form ἐν ἀνθρώπῳ); ἦλθεν ἐν σ. *Barn*.5.10; σαρκὶ ἐνδεθείς Clem.*prot*.11(p.79.1; M.8.228C); *ib*.10 (p.78.16; 228A) cit. s. προσωπεῖον; εἴληφε σάρκα ὁ Χριστός Heraclides ap.Or.*dial*.1(p.118.9); τῇ οὐσίᾳ μένων λόγος...οἱονεὶ σ. γίνεται Or.*Cels*. 4.15(p.285.19; M.11.1048A); θεὸς ἐν σ. Ath.*Ar*.2.10(M.26.168C); λόγος ἐν σ. *ib*.3.54(436C); *ib*.2.15(177B); Χριστὸς αἵματός μοι καὶ σ. κοινωνήσας Cyr.H.*catech*.19.4; v. ἀναλαμβάνω; **2.** *human nature* of Christ καθηλωμένον ὑπὲρ ἡμῶν ἐν σ. Ign.*Smyrn*.1.2; ref. Ps.102:14 συμπάθησον ἡμῖν, ὅτι τὴν ἀσθένειαν τῆς σ. αὐτοπαθῶς ἐπείρασας Clem. *paed*.1.8(p.126.29; M.8.325A); Bas.*hom.in Ps*.44(1.165E; M.29.405A) cit. s. ἐπιδημία; Marcellan τὴν μὲν κατὰ σάρκα οἰκονομίαν τῷ ἀνθρώπῳ διαφέρειν γιγνώσκομεν, τὴν δὲ κατὰ πνεῦμα ἀϊδιότητα ἡνῶσθαι τῷ πατρὶ πεπιστεύκαμεν Marcell.*fr*.61 ap.Eus.*Marcell*.2.2 (p.37.18; M.24.785D); Semi-Arian, CAnc.(358)*ep.syn*.ap.Epiph.*haer*. 73.9(p.279.26ff.; M.42.420A) cit. s. ἁμαρτητικῶς; together with Logos one Christ οὔτε γὰρ ἄσαρκος καὶ καθ' ἑαυτὸν ὁ λόγος τέλειος ἦν υἱός, καίτοι τέλειος [λόγος] ὢν μονογενής, οὔθ' ἡ σ. καθ' ἑαυτὴν δίχα τοῦ λόγου ὑποστῆναι ἠδύνατο διὰ τὸ ἐν λόγῳ τὴν σύστασιν ἔχειν Hipp. *Noët*.15(p.259.19; M.10.824C); οὐκοῦν ἄνευ λόγου μόνον τὸ σῶμα στήσεται ἐν ἀθανάτῳ καὶ ἀφθάρτῳ ἀλογίᾳ καὶ ἀκινησίᾳ; πῶς δὲ αὐτὸς ὁ λόγος εἰς τὸν θεὸν χωρήσει καὶ συναφθήσεται αὖθις αὐτῷ μετὰ τὸν τῆς σ. χωρισμόν; ἆρα μὴ ὢν ἐν τῷ θεῷ, ὅτε τῇ σ. συνῆν; ἀλλ' ὢν ἐν αὐτῷ διὰ παντός, συναΐδιός τε ὢν καὶ ἓν καὶ ταὐτὸν τῷ θεῷ. πῶς οὖν ὑπῆρχεν ἐν τῷ σώματι; εἰ μὲν ψυχῆς δίκην οἰκῶν ἐν αὐτῷ, ἔσται ἄρα ἐν ὑποστάσει, τοῦ πατρὸς κεχωρισμένος, ζῶν τε καὶ ὑφεστὼς ἐν ᾗ ἀνείληφεν σ. τί οὖν ἐκώλυεν καὶ πρὸ τῆς τοῦ κόσμου συστάσεως υἱὸν θεοῦ ζῶντα αὐτὸν ὁμολογεῖν; ἀλλ' εἴποι ἂν ἴσως ἐνεργείᾳ μόνῃ οὐχὶ δὲ οὐσίας ὑποστάσει καὶ ἐν σώματι γεγονέναι· δραστικῇ γὰρ ἐνεργείᾳ μόνῃ φησὶ τῇ σ. συνὼν...οὐσίᾳ τῷ θεῷ συνῆπτο...εἰ δὲ ταῦτα λέγοι... ἀποκρινάσθω, ἆρ' ἐπὶ μόνην τὴν σ. ταύτην ἡ τοῦ λόγου ἐνέργεια ἔφθακεν, οὐχὶ δὲ καὶ ἐφ' ἑτέρους ἀνθρώπους; Eus.*Marcell*.2.4(p.57.6ff.; 820C–821A); πιστεύομεν...εἰς ἕνα κύριον Ἰησοῦν Χριστόν, τὸν υἱὸν τοῦ θεοῦ...εἰς ἑαυτὸν σάρκα ἀναπλάσαντα εἰς μίαν ἁγίαν ἑνότητα *Symb*.ap. Epiph.*anc*.119(p.148.16; M.43.233C); ἐν ἐκ δύο τῶν ἐναντίων, σ. καὶ πνεύματος· ὧν, τὸ μὲν ἐθέωσε, τὸ δὲ ἐθεώθη Gr.Naz.*or*.38.13(M.36. 325C); τοῦ τε λόγου, καὶ τῆς σ., ἓν ὑπάρχει πρόσωπον, ὅπερ ἀχωρίστως καὶ ἀδιαιρέτως κοινὰς ἔχει τὰς πράξεις Leo Mag.*ep*.165.6(p.59.15; M.*PL*.54.1164B); **3.** Christ's *body*; **a.** orthodox ἔχοντα τὸν κόκκινον περὶ τὴν σ. *Barn*.7.9; exeg. Gen.49:4 κοίτην...καὶ στρωμνὴν εἴρηκεν τὴν ἁγίαν σ. Χριστοῦ, ἐφ' ἣν οἱ ἅγιοι ὡς ἐπὶ κλίνην ἁγίαν ἀναπαυόμενοι σώζονται· ἣν τότε λαβόντες οἱ ἄνομοι ἐνύβρισαν Hipp.*ben.Jac*.13(p.38. 2); 'τὸ ὑποπόδιον τῶν ποδῶν'...εἶναι τὴν σ. τοῦ Χριστοῦ, ἥτις διὰ τὸν Χριστόν ἐστι προσκυνητή Or.*sel.in Ps*.98:5(M.12.1557B); Eus. *Marcell*.2.4(p.58.2; M.24.821C) cit. s. ἄλογος; as sinless, exeg. 2Cor. 5:16 ἡμῶν τὸ κατὰ σάρκα ἐστὶ τὸ ἐν ἁμαρτίαις...καὶ τοῦ Χριστοῦ τὸ κατὰ σ. τὸ εἴκειν τοῖς φυσικοῖς πάθεσι Clem.*fr*.2(p.195.13; M.9.745A); Chrys.*hom.11.2 in 2Cor*.(10.514D); v. ἀναμάρτητος; of his glorified body, Ign.*Smyrn*.3.1 cit. s. ἀνάστασις; δεῖ με μετὰ σαρκὸς τὴν ἐκ δεξιῶν τοῦ πατρὸς καθέδραν ἀπολαβεῖν Tim.III Al.*fr*.ap.Cosm. Ind.*top*.10(p.317.12; M.88.269B); **b.** ?of some pre-incarnational 'heavenly' manhood τὸ γὰρ προφητικὸν πνεῦμα τὸ σωματεῖόν ἐστιν τῆς προφητικῆς τάξεως ὅ ἐστιν τὸ σῶμα τῆς σ. Ἰησοῦ Χριστοῦ τὸ μιγὲν τῇ ἀνθρωπότητι διὰ Μαρίας *POxy*.5.9 (saec. iii–iv); **c.** Arian σ. ἤτοι σῶμα, τουτέστιν ἄνθρωπον εἰληφέναι ἀπὸ Μαρίας τῆς παρθένου *Symb. Sirm*.2(p.257.19; M.26.741C); [Jo.1:14] ἀντὶ τοῦ· συνετέθη σαρκί, οὐ μὴν ψυχῇ...ἀλλ' ἥνωτο μὲν τῷ σώματι καὶ εἷς γέγονε μετ' αὐτοῦ Luc.Al.*fr.pasch*.(p.65.17); σαρκωθέντα, οὐκ ἐνανθρωπήσαντα, οὔτε γὰρ ψυχὴν ἀνθρωπίνην ἀνείληφεν, ἀλλὰ σ. γέγονεν...οὐ δύο φύσεις, ἐπεὶ μὴ τέλειος ἦν ἄνθρωπος, ἀλλὰ ἀντὶ ψυχῆς θεὸς ἦν ἐν σ. Eudox. *exp.fid*.(p.65.5ff.); Epiph.*haer*.69.19(p.169.5; M.42.232B); **d.** Apollinarian, Apoll.*fr*.2(p.204.11)ap.Anast.S.*monoph*.(M.89.1184A) cit. s. ψυχή; *ib*.10(p.207.12)ap.Justn.*monoph*.(M.86.1124B) cit. s. μίξις; θεὸς ἐν ἀνθρώπῳ κατοικῶν οὐκ ἔστιν ἄνθρωπος· πνεῦμα δὲ σαρκὶ ἡνωμένον ἄνθρωπός ἐστιν· ἄνθρωπος Χριστός...ὁμωνύμως· πνεῦμα ἄρα θεῖόν ἐστιν ἡνωμένον σαρκί id.*anac*.16(p.244.3ff.); οὐσία γὰρ αὐτοῦ κατὰ μὲν τὸ ἀόρατον ἡ θεότης, κατὰ δὲ τὸ ὁρατὸν ἡ σ. id.*fid.inc*.7(p.199.19; M.*PL*.8.877D); purified by union with divinity οὐδὲ ἐξ οὐρανοῦ τὴν σ. τοῦ κυρίου ἡμῶν...λέγομεν, ἀλλ' ἐκ τῆς ἁγίας παρθένου Μαρίας ὁμολογοῦμεν σεσαρκῶσθαι τὸν θεὸν λόγον καὶ οὐ διαιροῦμεν αὐτὸν ἀπὸ τῆς αὐτοῦ σ., ἀλλ' ἔστιν ἓν πρόσωπον, μία ὑπόστασις, ὅλος ἄνθρωπος, ὅλος θεός *ib*.3(p.194.19ff.; 876C); id.*fid.sec.pt*.2(p.168.10f.; M. 10.1105C); divinized ἀχώριστός ἐστι καὶ ἀμέριστος τῆς ἑαυτοῦ σ., καὶ ...τῆς κατὰ τὴν φύσιν ὁμοουσιότητος τοῦ λόγου τῆς πρὸς τὸν πατέρα ἐπικοινωνεῖ τῷ ὀνόματι ἡ σ. αὐτοῦ, οὗ καὶ σ. ἐστιν, εἴγε ἀληθῶς σ. ὁμολογοῦμεν γεγενῆσθαι τοῦ θεοῦ λόγον *fid.inc*.4(p.195.18ff.; 876Df.); τούτῳ [sc. Χριστῷ] τὴν προσκύνησιν ὀφειλόντως προσφέρομεν καὶ οὐκ ἀφορίζεται τῆς προσκυνήσεως ἡ σ. αὐτοῦ...οὐ γάρ τις τὴν σ. οὐ προσκυνεῖ, τοῦτον οὐ προσκυνεῖ *ib*.6(p.197.21ff.; 877B); effects man's redemption ζωοποιεῖ δὲ ἡμᾶς ἡ σ. αὐτοῦ διὰ τὴν συνουσιωμένην αὐτῇ θεότητα· τὸ δὲ ζωοποιὸν θεϊκόν· θεϊκὴ ἄρα ⟨ἡ⟩ σ., ὅτι θεῷ συνήφθη· καὶ αὕτη μὲν σώζει, ἡμεῖς δὲ σωζόμεθα μετέχοντες αὐτῆς ὡσπερεὶ τροφῆς id.*fr*.116(p.235.8f.)ap.Leont.B.*Apoll*.(M.86.1964Df.); id.*fid. sec.pt*.31(p.179.9; M.10.1117B); **4.** in reply: equivalence with *complete manhood*, soul as well as body, is either **a.** expressed αὐτὸς ὁ λόγος σ. ἐγένετο...ἔκ τε τῆς Μαρίας τὸ κατὰ σάρκα γεγένηται ἄνθρωπος δι' ἡμᾶς, καὶ οὕτω τελείως καὶ ὁλοκλήρως τὸ ἀνθρώπινον γένος ἐλευθερούμενον ἀπὸ τῆς ἁμαρτίας ἐν αὐτῷ...οὐ σῶμα ἄψυχον, οὐδ' ἀναίσθητον, οὐδ' ἀνόητον εἶχεν ὁ σωτήρ Ath.*tom*.7(M.26.804B) where, however, ἄψυχον prob. means 'devoid of a life-principle' rather than 'without a human soul'; ὅπου...σαρκὸς τὸ ὄνομα, ἐκεῖ πάσης τῆς συστάσεως ἡ ἁρμονία χωρὶς ἁμαρτίας ‡Ath.*Apoll*.2.18(M.26. 1164B); ref. Jo.4:7 ὁ αἰτῶν οὐχὶ σ. ἦν ἄψυχος, ἀλλὰ θεότης σ. ἐμψύχῳ κεχρημένη Bas.*ep*.236.1(3.361D; M.32.877C); ἄλλα σαρκὸς πάθη, καὶ ἄλλα σ. ἐμψύχου, καὶ ἄλλα ψυχῆς σώματι κεχρημένης. σαρκὸς μὲν οὖν ἴδιον τὸ τέμνεσθαι...καὶ διαλύεσθαι· καὶ πάλιν σαρκὸς ἐμψύχου τὸ κοποῦσθαι...καὶ πεινᾶν...ψυχῆς δὲ σώματι κεχρημένης λῦπαι καὶ... φροντίδες...ὥστε σάρκα μὲν τὴν ἡμετέραν ἀνέλαβε μετὰ τῶν φυσικῶν αὐτῆς παθῶν, ἁμαρτίαν δὲ οὐκ ἐποίησεν *ib*.261.3(3.402D,403A; M. 972Af.); ἥνωσεν ἑαυτῷ τὴν κτιστὴν σ. ἐψυχωμένην ψυχῇ λογικῇ τε καὶ νοερᾷ Didym.*Heb*.1:6(p.45.5); ἰδίωμα...τῆς γραφῆς ἀπὸ τῆς σ. τὸν ὅλον ἄνθρωπον καλεῖν Thdr.Mops.*Jo*.1:14(M.66.753A); ‡Gr.Nyss. *hom.3 in Jo*.(pp.142f.); or **b.** implied πεινᾶν καὶ διψᾶν καὶ κάμνειν καὶ μὴ εἰδέναι...καὶ αἰτεῖν...καὶ ἁπλῶς πάντα τὰ τῆς σ. Ath.*Ar*.3.34 (M.26.396B); *ib*.3.37f.(404Bf.); Gr.Naz.*or*.29.19(p.103.1; M.36.100A) cit. s. συνανακεράννυμι; *ib*.2.23(M.35.432B) cit. s. μίξις; ὅταν μὲν ἀκούωμεν ὅτι φῶς ἐστι, καὶ δύναμις...πάντα ταῦτα...πιστὰ ποιούμεθα εἰς τὸν λόγον τὸν θεὸν ἀναφέροντες. ὅταν δὲ λύπην, καὶ ὕπνον...οὐδὲν ἧττον πιστά τε καὶ ἀληθῆ εἶναι δεχόμεθα πρὸς τὴν σ. βλέποντες, ἣν τῇ πίστει μετὰ τοῦ λόγου παραδεξάμεθα Gr.Nyss.*Eun*.6(2 p.129.9; M. 45.712D); **c.** in later controversies maintained in its full force θεὸς ὢν φύσει γέγονε σ. ἡ γοῦν ἄνθρωπος ἐμψυχωμένος ψυχῇ λογικῇ Cyr. *ep*.17(p.38.17; 5².73C); id.*apol.Thdt*.1(p.111.23; 6¹.205D), Procl.CP *Arm*.5(p.189.30; M.65.860D) citt. s. ἄνθρωπος; τοῦ μὲν ἑτέρου [sc. Nestorius] τὴν τοῦ κυρίου ἡμῶν Ἰησοῦ Χριστοῦ θεότητα ἀπὸ τῆς σ. χωρίζοντος...τοῦ δὲ ἑτέρου [sc. Eutyches] τὴν ἀλήθειαν τῆς σ. ἐν τῷ κυρίῳ ἀπαναινομένου Horm.*ep.Epiph*.(p.58.18f.; M.*PL*.63.520Bf.); Leont.H.*Nest*.5.30(M.86.1749Cf.); σάρκα...ἑνώσαντα ἑαυτῷ καθ' ὑπόστασιν τὴν ἡμῖν ὁμοούσιον, ἐμψυχωμένην ψυχῇ λογικῇ τε καὶ νοερᾷ Max.*ep*.12(M.91.468A); *ib*.15(553D); Anast.S.*hod*.10(M.89.188B) cit. s. ἐπιδημία; Jo.D.*Jacob*.53(M.94.1464B); **5.** in orth. argument its connotation often confined to physical element in man opp. intellectual (ψυχή or νοῦς), this limitation being freq. indicated by a qualifying adj. such as μόνος, ἄψυχος, ἀνόητος: λογικὴ...[sc. ἡ τοῦ Ἰησοῦ ψυχή] καὶ ταῖς ψυχαῖς τῶν ἀνθρώπων ὁμοούσιος, ὥσπερ καὶ ἡ σ. ὁμοούσιος τῇ τῶν ἀνθρώπων σ. τυγχάνει, ἐκ τῆς Μαρίας προελθοῦσα Eust. *fr*.6(p.68; M.18.685D); λυπούμενος καὶ ἀδημονῶν καὶ προσευχόμενος... ταῦτα...οὔτε σ. ἀνοήτου ἂν εἴη οὔτε θεότητος ἀτρέπτου ἀλλὰ ψυχῆς νόησιν ἐχούσης ‡Ath.*Apoll*.1.15(M.26.1121A); Μαρκίων δὲ καὶ Μανιχαῖος...ἰδίαν σ. ἐπιδεδεῖχθαι ἐξ ἑαυτοῦ καθ' ὁμοίωσιν, ὡς ἠθέλησαν ἐξ *οὐρανοῦ ὀφθεῖσαν...Οὐαλεντῖνος δὲ πάλιν...τῆς θεότητος μέρος τὴν σ. φανταζόμενος. Ἄρειος...ἀντὶ δὲ τοῦ ἔσωθεν ἐν ἡμῖν ἀνθρώπου, τουτέστι τῆς ψυχῆς, τὸν λόγον ἐν σ. λέγει γεγονέναι* ib.2.3(1136C); Bas.*ep*.261.3 (3.402D; M.32.972A) cit. s. 4.a supra; *ὁ λόγος σ. γενόμενος, ὅλην μετὰ τῆς σ. τὴν ἀνθρωπίνην ἀνέλαβε φύσιν* Gr.Nyss.*Eun*.2(2 p.368.30f.; M. 45.549A); *ὁ δεσπότης θεὸς λόγος ἄνθρωπον εἴληφε τέλειον...τὴν φύσιν, ἐκ ψυχῆς τε νοερᾶς καὶ σ. συνεστῶτα ἀνθρωπίνης* Thdr.Mops.*symb*. (p.98.17; M.66.1017B).

D. eucharistic; the *flesh* of Christ, his *body* *τὴν εὐχαριστίαν σ. εἶναι τοῦ σωτῆρος ἡμῶν* Ign.*Smyrn*.6.2; Just.*1apol*.66.2(M.6.429A) cit. s. *αἷμα*; plur. *οὐ δωρεὰν ἐν τοῖς ὀπίσω χρόνοις Χριστοῦ σάρκας καταφαγόντας* Pall.*v.Chrys*.20(p.137.6; M.47.76); ref. Cant.1:2 *ἔλαβεν γὰρ ὁ μὲν υἱὸς τοῦ θεοῦ τὸν ἄνθρωπον, ὃν ἐνεδύσατο ἀπὸ τῆς ἐκκλησίας, καὶ ἀνταπέδωκεν αὐτῇ πάλιν εἰς κοινωνίαν αὐτῆς ἁγίαν τὴν σ. εἰς μετάληψιν* Ph.Carp.*Cant*.ap.Cosm.Ind.*top*.10(M.88.433C); *πᾶσι τοῖς πεπιστευκόσι...ἑαυτὸν ἐνσπείρει διὰ τῆς σ. ἧς ἡ σύστασις ἐξ οἴνου τε καὶ ἄρτου ἐστὶ...ὡς ἂν τῇ πρὸς τὸ ἀθάνατον ἑνώσει καὶ ὁ ἄνθρωπος τῆς ἀφθαρσίας μέτοχος γένοιτο* Gr.Nyss.*or.catech*.37(p.152.3; M.45. 97B); *πρόσιμέν τε οὕτω ταῖς μυστικαῖς εὐλογίαις καὶ ἁγιαζόμεθα, μέτοχοι γινόμενοι τῆς τε ἁγίας σ. καὶ τοῦ τιμίου αἵματος...καὶ οὐχ ὡς σ. κοινὴν δεχόμενοι...ἀλλ' ὡς ζωοποιὸν ἀληθῶς καὶ ἰδίαν αὐτοῦ τοῦ λόγου* Cyr.*ep*.17(p.37.26; 5².72D).

E. of Church *εἰ δὲ λέγομεν εἶναι τὴν σ. τὴν ἐκκλησίαν καὶ τὸ πνεῦμα Χριστόν, ἄρα οὖν ὁ ὑβρίσας τὴν σ. ὕβρισεν τὴν ἐκκλησίαν...οὐ μεταλήψεται τοῦ πνεύματος, ὅ ἐστιν ὁ Χριστός* *2Clem*.14.4; ref. Eph.5:31f. *ὅτι ἐκ τῶν σ. αὐτοῦ καὶ τῶν ὀστέων ἐσμέν, διὰ τὸ μετέχειν Χριστοῦ, καὶ συνηνῶσθαι αὐτῷ ἐν πίστει, καὶ γνώσει, καὶ ἀρεταῖς* Nil.*epp*.1.254(M. 79.176D).

σάρος, ὁ, Babylonian number based on the sexagesimal system, the *square of 60, 3600*; construed as a measure of time, Cyr.*Juln*.1 (6².8D); cf.Eus.*Chronicorum liber* 1.1.1(M.19.106B,C and nn.).

***σάρπος, ὁ,** *bin* for flour, Eustrat.*v.Eutych*.62(M.86.2345A).

σάρωσις, ἡ, *sweeping up*, ref. Lc.15:8 *σ. δὲ* [sc. *εἶναι*] *τὴν τῶν ἁμαρτιῶν ἀποκάθαρσιν* *cat.Lc*.15:8(p.117.18).

§**σάσσω,** *dance*, Leont.N.*v.Sym*.43(M.93.1724C).

***σαταναήλ,** *Satanael*, name of Satan *πρῶτον ἐλεγόμην σ., ὃ ἑρμηνεύεται ἄγγελος θεοῦ* *Ev.Barth*.4.25(p.331; Vassiliev p.16).

σατανᾶς (σατᾶν, σατάν), ὁ, *Satan*, the *Devil*; **1.** etym.; **a.** (= apostate) *τὸν διάβολον, ὃν Μωϋσῆς μὲν ὄφιν καλεῖ, ἐν δὲ τῷ Ἰὼβ καὶ τῷ Ζαχαρίᾳ διάβολος κέκληται, καὶ ὑπὸ τοῦ Ἰησοῦ σ. προσηγόρευται, ὄνομα ἀπὸ τῆς πράξεως ἧς ἔπραξε...τὸ γὰρ σατὰν τῇ Ἰουδαίων καὶ Σύρων φωνῇ ἀποστάτης ἐστί, τὸ δὲ νὰς ὄνομα ἐξ οὗ ἡ ἑρμηνεία ὄφις ἐκλήθη* Just.*dial*.103.5(M.6.717B); *τὸν...τούτων* [sc. *δαιμόνων*] *ἄρχοντα σ. ὀνομάζουσι· δηλοῖ δὲ τοὔνομα τὸν ἀποστάτην κατὰ τὴν Ἑβραίων φωνήν. καλεῖ δὲ αὐτὸν ἡ θεία γραφὴ καὶ διάβολον, ὡς τὸν θεὸν παρὰ τοῖς ἀνθρώποις συκοφαντοῦντα, καὶ αὐτοῖς γε τοῖς ἀνθρώποις ἔριν πρὸς ἀλλήλους καὶ διαμάχην ἐμβάλλοντα* Thdt.*affect*.3(p.97.2; 4.789); **b.** (= adversary), Or.*Cels*.6.44(p.115.8; M.11.1365Df.) cit. s. *ἀντίκειμαι*; *σ. ... διὰ τὸ ἀντικεῖσθαι τῷ ἀγαθῷ* Bas.*hom*.9.9(2.82A; M.31.349D); Cyr.H.*catech*.2.4; Chrys.*hom.26.2 in 2Cor*.(10.620E); **c.** both derivations *σατᾶν...τὸν ἀντικείμενον ἢ ἀποστάτην ἡ Ἑβραίων γλῶττα καλεῖ* Thdt.*qu.5 in 2Reg*.(1.450); id.*qu.37 in 3Reg*.(1.482); Proc.G.*2Reg*.22:1(M.87.1144B); list of synonyms, Didym.*Rom*.7 (p.1.11); **2.** nature: originally among the cherubim, Cyr.*glaph.Gen*. 1(1.7E); cf.Ath.*ep.Serap*.1.26(M.26.592B); leader of other powers *ἄγγελοι τοῦ σ.* *Barn*.18.1; *ὁ ἀρχηγέτης τῶν κακῶν δαιμόνων* Just. *1apol*.28.1(M.6.372B); *A.(Pass.)Petr.et Paul*.56(p.166.7); †Jo.D.*B.J*. 6(M.96.908A); fell by his own free will *ὁ...σωτὴρ διδάξαι βουλόμενος* [ref. Lc.10:18] *τὸ μὲν πρότερον ἄγγελον ὑπὸ τοῦ θεοῦ γενόμενον καὶ φωτὸς μετέχοντα, ὕστερον δὲ τῇ αὐτεξουσιότητι τραπέντα...καὶ πεσόντα ἀπὸ στάσεως* Adam.*dial*.3.13(p.134.6,13ff.; M.11.1804Cf.); *ib*.3.9(p.128.8; 1801A); Thdt.*affect* 3(p.97.2,9f.; 4.789); a mere creature, Mac.Aeg.*hom*.16.5(M.34.616D); **3.** relations with mankind; **a.** enemy *τοῦ πάντων ἐχθροῦ...σ.* Cyr.*Abac*.24(3.538D); id.*Ps*. 34:20(M.69.893A); Anast.S.*hod*.4(M.89.93D); Germ.CP *or*.1(M.98. 236C); 1Cor.5:5 and 2Cor.12:7 interpreted of life's difficulties, Sever.*1Cor*.5:1ff.(p.243.28ff.); **b.** author of evil *τοῦ...σ. τὸ ἐπιχαιρησίκακον* Or.*or*.2(p.300.23; M.11.420A); *σ., τῷ πάσης κακίας δημιουργῷ καὶ συνέργῳ* Cyr.H.*catech*.19.4; *ἡ οἰκοῦσα ἐν τοῖς ἁμαρτάνουσιν ἁμαρτία, τοῦτ' ἔστιν ὁ σ.* Didym.*Rom*.7(p.5.28); Marc.Er.*opusc*.4(M.65. 1016A); Cyr.*Jo*.6(4.560Df.); father of heresy, Polyc.*ep*.7.1; Iren.*haer*. 3.3.4(M.7.853B); Eus.*h.e*.7.31.1(M.20.720C); Epiph.*haer*.69.2(p.153.10; M.42.204A); Gel.Cyz.*h.e*.2.31.8(M.85.1320A); woman and marriage said by certain heretics to be his work, Epiph.*haer*.45.2(p.200.16f.; M.41.833Bf.); **c.** deceiver *τοῦ πολυμόρφου σ.* *A.Jo*.70(p.185.10); *ἴσμεν ...τὰ νοήματα τοῦ σ. ... ἵνα μὴ ἀπατώμενοι παγιδευθῶμεν* Didym.*2Cor*. 2:10f.(p.19.19; M.39.1690C); Cyr.*Jo*.9(4.737Eff.,743B); Diad.*perf*.82 (p.108.26); Eus.Al.*serm*.7(M.86.356Cf.); Germ.CP *or*.1(M.98.229A); *ὁ σ. ... ἐν ταῖς νυκτεριναῖς ἡσυχίαις...τὴν ψυχὴν παρακαλεῖ* Diad.*perf*.31 (p.34.19); *ὁ νυκτιλόχος σ.* Germ.CP *or*.1(228C); **d.** tyrant *ὁ μέν* [sc. *θεός*] *ἐστιν κύριος...εἰς τοὺς αἰῶνας, ὁ δὲ* [sc. *σ.*] *ἄρχων καιροῦ τοῦ νῦν τῆς ἀνομίας* *Barn*.18.2; Or.*hom.1.4 in Jer*.(p.3.10; M.13.257B); *ἅπερ ἔδησεν ὁ σ., ἔλυεν αὐτός* [sc. Christ] Ath.*Ar*.3.40(M.26.408C); *ἡ ἀνθρώπου φύσις...ὑπετίθει...τὴν αὐχένα τῷ πλεονεκτήσαντι σ., ὃς καὶ... ἁπάντων...τῶν ἐπὶ τῆς γῆς κατεθρασύνετο* Cyr.*glaph.Gen*.5(1.164A); †Gregent.*disp*.(M.86.636D); **4.** relations with Christ *καλῶς ὁ Ἰουστῖνος ἔφη, ὅτι πρὸ μὲν τῆς τοῦ κυρίου παρουσίας οὐδέποτε ἐτόλμησεν ὁ σ. βλασφημῆσαι τὸν θεόν, ἅτε μηδέπω εἰδὼς αὐτοῦ τὴν κατάκρισιν· διὰ τὸ ἐν παραβολαῖς...κεῖσθαι· μετὰ δὲ τὴν παρουσίαν τοῦ κυρίου ἐκ τῶν λόγων αὐτοῦ...μαθὼν ἀναφανδόν...βλασφημεῖ τὸν τὴν κρίσιν ἐπάγοντα κύριον...καὶ τὴν ἁμαρτίαν τῆς ἰδίας ἀποστασίας τῷ ἐκτικότι αὐτὸν ἀποκαλεῖ, ἀλλ' οὐ τῇ ἰδίᾳ αὐθαιρέτῳ γνώμῃ* Iren.*haer*. 5.26.2(cf.M.7.1194Cff.); *οὐκ εἰδότι...τῷ σ., ὅτι τῆς ἑαυτοῦ καταστρατεύεται κεφαλῆς, ἀγνοήσαντί τε παντελῶς, ὅτι κατὰ κρημνοῦ τρέχει, τὸν ἐπὶ τοῦ σταυροῦ διαπήξας θάνατον ἔφασκεν ὁ σωτὴρ* [ref. Jo.13:28] Cyr.*Jo*.9(4.741C); cf. *μὴ γυμνῇ τῇ θεότητι, ἀλλ' ὑπὸ τῆς ἀνθρωπίνης φύσεως κεκαλυμμένη, ἀγνοηθέντα παρὰ τοῦ ἐχθροῦ, τὸν θεόν* Gr.Nyss.*or.catech*.26(p.96.13ff.; M.45.68A); vanquished by Christ *ἄρτι δὲ ἡμῶν ἀπὸ γῆς εἰς οὐρανὸν περώντων, αὐτὸς ὁ σ. ὡς ἀστραπὴ λοιπὸν ἀπ' οὐρανοῦ καταπίπτει* Ath.*ep.fest*.24(p.295.25; M. 26.1433A); *Χριστοῦ...τοῦ κατισχύοντος παραλῦσαι τὴν δύναμιν* [sc. *τοῦ Φαραώ*] *τουτέστι τοῦ σ.* Cyr.*hom.pasch*.10(5².132C); id.*Is*.3.1(2. 388E); †Gregent.*disp*.(M.86.636D); *οὐκ ἐν ἰσχύϊ ἐνίκησεν ὁ Χριστὸς τὸν σ., ἀλλὰ κρίσει καὶ δικαιοσύνῃ· τοῦτο καὶ Γρηγόριος ὁ Νύσσης ἐν τῷ κατηχητικῷ φησιν* Max.*schol.e.h*.3.10(M.91.149B); this manifested in renunciation by Christians at baptism *τῶν παλινδρομούντων ἐπὶ τὸν σ., ᾧ βαπτιζόμενοι ἀπετάξαντο* Or.*mart*.17(p.16.20; M.11.585A); Cyr.H.*catech*.19.4; *Symb*.ap.*Const.App*.7.41.2; Cosm.Ind.*top*.1(M. 88.60B); henceforth powerless against mankind *πρὸ μὲν γὰρ τῆς τοῦ σωτῆρος ἐπιδημίας κατεκράτησε* [sc. *ὁ σ.*] *τῆς ὑπ' οὐρανόν...πέπτωκεν ἐκεῖνος ὡς ἀστραπή· ὁ γὰρ πάντας ἔχων προσκυνητὰς τοὺς πεπλανημένους ὑπὸ πόδας τέθειται τῶν προσκυνούντων αὐτόν* Cyr.*Lc*.10:17f. (p.104.22; M.72.668B); cf. *φοβούμενος...τὸν κύριον κατακυριεύσεις τοῦ διαβόλου, ὅτι δύναμις ἐν αὐτῷ οὐκ ἔστιν* Herm.*mand*.7.2; Cyr.*Jo*.10.2 (4.922A); *συνήγαγεν ὁ Χριστὸς οὓς διὰ τῆς ἁμαρτίας συντρίψας ὁ σ. παρειμένους ἀπέφηνε...ἀλλ' εἰ καὶ συνέτριψεν ἐκεῖνος, κατέδησεν ὁ Χριστός* id.*Soph*.4(3.623A); his attacks permitted for sake of man's humility, Marc.Er.*opusc*.9.4(M.65.1116B); **5.** Satan and antichrist *δύο...ἀκρότητας...τὴν μὲν τοῦ καλοῦ ἀκρότητα εἶναι ἐν τῷ κατὰ τὸν Ἰησοῦν νοουμένῳ ἀνθρώπῳ...τὴν δὲ τοῦ ἐναντίου ἐν τῷ κατὰ τὸν ὀνομαζόμενον ἀντίχριστον...ἐχρῆν δὲ τὸν μὲν...βέλτιστον υἱὸν ἀναγορεύεσθαι τοῦ θεοῦ...τὸν δὲ...ἐναντίον υἱὸν τοῦ πονηροῦ δαίμονος καὶ σ. καὶ διαβόλου* Or.*Cels*.6.45(p.116.16,22; M.11.1368Df.); *οἱ δὲ ἐπὶ ἀντιχρίστου αὐτῷ τῷ σ. αὐτοπροσώπως πολεμήσουσιν* Cyr.H.*catech*.15. 17; *κατὰ μίμησιν τοῦ σωτῆρος ἔρχεται ὁ σ. ἐν ἀνθρώπῳ ὁλοκλήρῳ* Sever.*2Thess*.2:4(p.334.18); *ἀποφανεῖ τὸν ἀλάστορα...οὗ ἐστιν ἡ παρουσία κατ' ἐνέργειαν τοῦ σ. ... ἐδίδαξε δὲ* [i.e. in 2Thess.2:8], *ὡς καὶ σατᾶν τοῦ διαβόλου τὴν ἐνέργειαν δέξεται. καθάπερ ὁ μονογενὴς... υἱὸς...ἐνανθρωπήσας...οὐ μερικήν τινα τῇ ληφθείσῃ φύσει δέδωκε χάριν, ἀλλὰ πᾶν τὸ πλήρωμα τῆς θεότητος...οὕτως ὁ διάβολος...τούτῳ δὲ ὅλος αὐτὸς συναφθείς, τὰς παντοδαπὰς αὐτοῦ τῆς πονηρίας δι' αὐτοῦ μηχανὰς ἐπιδείξει* Thdt.*haer*.5.23(4.459); *οὐκ αὐτὸς...ὁ διάβολος γίνεται ἄνθρωπος κατὰ τὴν τοῦ κυρίου ἐνανθρώπησιν...ἀλλ' ἄνθρωπος ἐκ πορνείας τίκτεται, καὶ ὑποδέχεται πᾶσαν τὴν ἐνέργειαν τοῦ σ.* Jo.D. *f.o*.4.26(M.94.1217A); *ἄνθρωπος...ἔσται κατ' ἐνέργειαν τοῦ σ.* Areth. *Apoc*.11:7(M.106.652C); **6.** in heresy; **a.** Manichean *πονηρὸς...ὁ σ. καὶ ἦν πονηρὸς καὶ οὔτε ποτὲ οὐκ ἦν·...καὶ οὐκ ἀπό τινος ἦν...δύο γὰρ ἦσαν ῥίζαι* Serap.*Man*.26(p.41; M.18.1120D); **b.** Messalian *εἰσὶ...οἱ λογισμοί τινων ὑπὸ τοῦ σ. ἐφθαρμένοι, καὶ νεκροὶ ἀπὸ τῆς ζωῆς, καὶ κεχωσμένοι εἰς βόρβορον καὶ γῆν· ἀπώλετο γὰρ αὐτῶν ἡ ψυχή* Mac. Aeg.*hom*.11.3(M.34.545D); *οὐ βλάπτεται...τὸ θεῖον συνὸν τῷ σ., οὔτε ῥυποῦται* ib.7.2(524D); *ἄρα αὐτὸς ὁ σ. ἀπὸ γενετῆς συνών σοι οὐκ οἶδε τοὺς λογισμούς σου; ἑξακισχιλίων γὰρ ἤδη ἐστὶν ἐτῶν* ib.26.9(680C); ib. 15.51(609D); *ὁ σ. καὶ οἱ δαίμονες κατέχουσι τὸν νοῦν τῶν ἀνθρώπων, καὶ ἡ φύσις τῶν ἀνθρώπων κοινωνική ἐστι τῶν πνευμάτων τῆς πονηρίας* Jo.D.*haer*.80(M.94.729A); *συνοικοῦσιν ὁ σ. καὶ τὸ πνεῦμα τὸ ἅγιον ἐν τῷ ἀνθρώπῳ* ib.; **c.** of Sataniani (v.s.v.) *ὁ σ. μέγας ἐστί, καὶ ἰσχυρότερος, καὶ πολλὰ ἐπιτελεῖ κακὰ τοῖς ἀνθρώποις. διὰ τί οὐ μᾶλλον πρὸς τοῦτον καταφεύγομεν, καὶ αὐτῷ προσκυνοῦμεν, αὐτόν τε τιμῶμεν ...ἵνα διὰ τῆς κολακευτικῆς θεραπείας μὴ ἐνεργήσῃ ἡμῖν τὰ πονηρά;* Epiph.*haer*.80.3(p.486.24; M.42.760B).

***Σατανιανοί, οἱ,** name of sect propitiating Satan by worship,

Epiph.*rescr*.4(p.159.13; M.41.164A); id.*haer*.80.3(p.486.29; M.42.760C); Jo.D.*haer*.80(M.94.729A).

***σατανικός**, **1.** *of Satan, of the Devil*, Chrys.*hom*.2.5 *in Mt*.(7.29C); ἆρα τὸ σ. στῖφος οὐ κατασείσει τὸ παρθενικὸν τεῖχος; Procl.CP *or*.6.16(M.65.752C); Hyper.*mon*.10(M.79.1473C); ref. Fall πάλαι γὰρ ἐκ σ. βασκανίας κατολισθήσαντας *Lit.Jac*.(*NBP* 10² p.106); **2.** *diabolical, fiendish, inspired by Satan*; finery, Chrys.*hom*.8.3 *in 1Tim*.(11.593A); thoughts, Alex.Al.*ep.Alex*.10(M.18.564B); Chrys.*hom*.4.1 *in Rom*.(9.454E) cit. s. δόγμα; Marc.Diac.*v.Porph*.87; deeds, Ath.*h.Ar*.60(p.216.32; M.25.765B); passions, ‡Nil.*perist*.9.4(M.79.868D); ‡Proc.G.*Pr*.6:27–29(M.87.1277C); Jo.Mosch.*prat*.60(M.87.2912D).

***σατανικῶς**, *like one possessed; diabolically*, Gr.Nyss.*castig*.(M.46.313B); ὑποκριθεὶς σ. Thphn.*chron*.p.305(M.108.741B).

***σατανοδρόμιον, τό**, word coined on // ἱπποδρόμιον, ‡Chrys.*circ*.(8.88A).

***Σατορνιλιανός, ὁ**, *follower of Saturninus*, Heges.ap.Eus.*h.e*.4.22.5(M.20.381A); Just.*dial*.35.6(M.6.552B); Epiph.*rescr*.5(p.160.2; M.41.165A); id.*anac*.23(p.234.14; M.41.281B); tenets of Satornilians described, Iren.*haer*.1.24.1; Epiph.*haer*.22.1(p.247ff.; M.41.297B–300B); *ib*.23.6,7(pp.254f.; 305C–308B).

[*]**Σατουρνάλια, τά**, (Lat.) *Saturnalia*, Epiph.*haer*.51.22(p.284.12; M.41 om.).

***σατυρίζω**, *travesty, parody*, Clem.*prot*.4(p.46.7; M.8.157B).

***Σαφὰρ φωτήμ**, v. **Σφαρφωτίμ*.

σαφήνεια, ἡ, 1. *clarity of expression, lucidity*; in gen., Clem.*str*.1.20(p.63.27; M.8.817A); *ib*.6.7(p.461.28; M.9.281A); Bas.*hex*.6.5(1.54B; M.29.128B); Nil.*serm*.6(M.79.1273A); **2.** *exposition* of scripture and *interpretation* of prophecy, Or.*fr*.27 *in Jo*.(p.504.10); Eus.*p.e*.12.4(576A; M.21.956C); Thdt.*Cant*.proem.(2.20).

σαφηνίζ-ω, 1. *explain, interpret* scripture τὴν ἀλήθειαν διὰ τῆς ἀκολουθίας τῶν διαθηκῶν ~οντες Clem.*str*.7.16(p.70.31; M.9.540A); Or.*Jo*.13.42(41; p.268.16; M.14.473B); id.*Cant*.3(p.193.28; M.17.261D); prophecy, Clem.*str*.6.15(p.493.32; M.9.345C); Gr.Thaum.*pan.Or*.15(p.34.19; M.10.1093B); abs., *elucidate, explain oneself* σαφήνισον... οὐ παρακολούθησα Or.*dial*.2(p.122.16); **2.** pass., of Son as *revealed* in OT, ‡Ath.*Ar*.4.24(p.71.15; M.26.504C).

σαφηνισμός, ὁ, *explanation, interpretation, exegesis of scripture*, Clem.*q.d.s*.26(p.176.28; M.9.632An.); †Bas.*Is*.192(1.522D; M.30.449A).

***σαφηνιστής, ὁ**, *elucidator, interpreter*, Or.*Jo*.1.29(31; p.36.28; M.14.77B); †Bas.*Is*.192(1.522C; M.30.449A); adjectivally τὴν ἑρμήνειαν τοῦ σ. λόγου Or.*sel.in Ps*.50 ap.*philoc*.1.29(p.35.16; M.12.1453D).

***σάχαρ, τό**, *sugar*, Thphn.*chron*.p.268(ζάχαρ M.108.665A).

σβέννυμι, *quench, put out*; perf. ptcpl. pass., *extinguishable* ἐπειδὴ εἶπες ὅτι σὲ ἀσβέστῳ πυρὶ ἐμβαλεῖ ἐγώ σε ἐνταῦθα τῷ ἐσβεσμένῳ πυρὶ κατακαύσω Agath.*v.Gr.Ill*.53(p.29).

σβέσις, ἡ, *quenching, extinction*, met. σ. τῆς ζωῆς Athenag.*res*.20(p.73.6; M.6.1013B); σ. τῶν κακῶν Clem.*str*.4.6(p.260.26; M.8.1240C).

***σβύνω**, later form of σβέννυμι, *extinguish, put out* fire or light; met., *blot out, obliterate* σ. τοὺς χαρακτῆρας τοῦ δίσκου *Exorc*.29(p.341).

***σγαύδαρι**, for γάδαρε, vocative of γάδαρος *donkey*, *Chron.Pasch*.p.338(M.92.881A).

σεβάζω, *reverence, worship*; God, Hipp.*haer*.10.31(p.287.4; M.16.3446A); pass., Gr.Naz.*or*.28.18(p.48.18; M.36.49A); ref. pagan worship, Clem.*prot*.2(p.29.11; M.8.120A); pass., Arist.*apol*.12.2; Clem.*str*.5.5(p.344.13; M.9.49B); Gr.Naz.*or*.28.14(p.44.5; 44C).

σέβας, τό, 1. divine *worship, adoration*, Ath.*h.Ar*.50(p.212.4; M.25.753C); τὸ θεῖον σ. Philost.*h.e*.3.5(M.65.485B); οὐδὲ θεῖον αὐτοῖς [sc. ἀοράτοις δυνάμεσιν] ἀπονέμομεν σ., οὐδὲ μερίζομεν...τὴν θείαν προσκύνησιν Thdt.*affect*.3(p.93.18; 4.785); id.*h.e*.5.39.22(3.1086); abs. ὥστε διὰ πάσης γῆς τὸ σ. αὐτοῦ [sc. τοῦ σωτῆρος] διαπτῆναι Ath.*inc*.49.5(M.25.184D); μὴ μερίσαι τὸ σ. Thdt.*affect*.2(p.51.16; 4.742); in doxology δι' οὗ σοι δόξα, τιμὴ καὶ σ. ἐν ἁγίῳ πνεύματι *Lit*.ap.*Const.App*.8.5.7; ‡Ath.*Ar*.4.36(p.87.1; M.26.525A); hence *religion* μάγιστρον τὴν ἀξίαν, Ἕλληνα δὲ τὸ σ. Philost.*h.e*.11.2(593C); **2.** *worship; reverence* τὸ σ. ἅρμοττον προσφέρουσα Or.*fr*.17 *in Lc*.8:47(p.241); αὐτοὺς...ἐπὶ σέβας ἀγαγὼν τῆς τοῦ Χριστοῦ δυνάμεως Eus.*h.e*.2.1.7(M.20.136C); τὸ προσῆκον σ. ... ἀπονέμειν τῇ...τοῦ Χριστοῦ εἰκόνι *A.Thadd*.5(p.275.18n.); ναῷ τὸ προσῆκον ἀπονέμομεν σ. Thdt.*1Cor*.3:16f.(3.184); id.*Mal*.1:7(2.1674); for martyrs, id.*affect*.9(p.241.2; 4.948); for a prophet, id.*Jon*.proem.(2.1460); **3.** *respect* τὸ σ. αὐτῇ [sc. S. Elisabeth] ὡς παλαιοτέρᾳ...ἀπονέμουσα [sc. BMV] Or.*hom*.7 *in Lc*.(p.45.2).

σέβασμα, τό, 1. *object of worship*, Arist.*apol*.12.1,6; Ath.*inc*.46.5(M.25.180A); Gr.Nyss.*Eun*.10(2 p.245.20; M.45.848D); *idol*, *A.Mt*.21(p.246.1); *Hom.Clem*.9.18; *ib*.10.21f.; Agath.*v.Gr.Ill*.57(p.31); **2.** *form of worship, religious observance*, Epiph.*anac*.14(p.167.7; M.41.172A); CNic.(787)*act*.2(H.4.92D); **3.** *respect, reverence*; for man and his institutions, Clem.*paed*.3.11(p.271.31; M.8.637C); for God and his law, id.*str*.7.1(p.4.8; M.9.404C); Eus.*v.C*.2.42(p.59.15; M.20.1020A); **4.** *worship, adoration*, Didym.(‡Bas.)*Eun*.5(1.317B; M.29.760C); δαιμονικοῦ σ. Euthal.Diac.*epp.cath*.(M.85.688A); ἐπὶ εἰδώλων σεβάσμασι *Chron.Pasch*.p.118(M.92.305C).

σεβασμιάζω, *inspire with reverence*, Jo.D.*carm.pent*.84(p.216; M.96.837A).

σεβάσμιος, 1. *worthy of veneration, to be venerated, revered* (usu. equivalent of *holy*), dist. from what is worshipped σ. παρὰ τούτοις [sc. Μανιχαίοις] τὸ παρ' ἡμῶν προσκυνούμενον ὄνομα [sc. τοῦ Χριστοῦ] Gr.Nyss.*Maced*.15(M.45.1320B); **a.** of God and divine worship (Christian and pagan) ἱερὰ καὶ σ. ... μυστήρια Hipp.*haer*.5.7(p.84.2; M.16.3134B); τῆς πανσέμνου καὶ σ. πεντηκοστῆς Eus.*v.C*.4.64(p.144.11; v.l. παναγίας M.20.1220B); ἡ πανύμνητος καὶ σ. καὶ προσκυνητὴ τριάς Ath.*hom.in Mt*.11:27(M.25.220A); Didym.(‡Bas.)*Eun*.5(1.317C; M.29.760D); **b.** of angels, Thdt.*Ezech*.28:4(2.914); **c.** of men, Or.*sel.in Ps*.54:2(M.12.1464A); σ. διὰ τὸ σεμνὸν τῆς πολιτείας Nil.*Magn*.40(M.79.1017C); Eustrat.*v.Eutych*.2(M.86.2276D); superl., Synes.*ep*.4(M.66.1341B); of pope, *Cod.Afr*.proem.(H.1.864D); **d.** of scriptures, Nil.*epp*.2.144(M.79.265C); Philost.*h.e*.2.5(M.65.469A); ‡Meth.*Sym.et Ann*.12(M.18.377B); **e.** of relics and holy places, e.g. Jerusalem to Jews, Gr.Nyss.*or.catech*.18(p.77.15; M.45.36C); the manger, Isid.Pel.*epp*.1.378(M.78.396C); an apostle's house, *IGC As.Min*.107 (535–6); effigy of Christ on towel, Geo.Pis.*Pers*.1.139(M.92.1207A); head of a martyr, Sophr.H.*v.Anast*.(M.92.1725A); eccl. buildings, Phot.*nomoc*.2.1(p.495; M.104.576B,C); **f.** of first principles of philosophy, Clem.*prot*.5(p.50.8; M.8.168B); **2.** neut. as subst.; **a.** *reverence*, Or.*Jo*.32.8(6; p.438.11; M.14.761A); Gr.Naz.*or*.28.11(p.39.15; M.36.40B); Philost.*h.e*.3.5(M.65.485B); **b.** objectively, the *awful majesty* of God, Gr.Naz.*or*.29.14(p.94.12; 92C).

σεβασμιότης, ἡ, 1. *reverence*; for God, Dion.Ar.*c.h*.4.1(M.3.177C); Max.*qu.Thal*.10(M.90.289B); for image of Cross, etc., ‡Jo.D.*ep.Thphl*.30(M.95.384C); *worship, religion* τῷ εἰδώλῳ τῆς σ. αὐτῶν Thphn.*chron*.p.304(M.108.741A); **2.** *respect*, Philost.*h.e*.5.2(M.65.529B); for creed of Nicaea, Gel.Cyz.*h.e*.2.27.10(M.85.1309B); **3.** objectively, *dignity*, CNeocaes.*cann*.tit.; **4.** as title, *Reverence*; to Pope Celestine (tr. Lat. *venerabilitas*), *Cod.Afr*.138(H.1.949A).

σεβασμίως, *reverently*, Clem.*prot*.4(p.38.5; M.8.140C); Eus.*h.e*.6.2.11(M.20.525A); Eustrat.*stat.anim*.20(p.505).

***σεβασμοσύνη, ἡ**, *holiness*, *Orac.Sib*.7.73.

***σεβαστέος**, *to be revered*, Gr.Mag.*dial*.(tr.Zach.)1.1(M.*PL*.77.158A).

σεβένινος, and variants, *made of palm fibre*, *Apophth.Patr*.(M.65.108B); σεβέννιος *ib*.(M.65.225B); σεβέννινος †Jo.D.*B.J*.18(M.96.1020A); σίβινα κολόβια †Anast.S.*relat*.31(*OC* 2 p.78.23, v.l. σιβίνινα).

***Σεβηριανός, ὁ**, v. **Σευηριανός*.

***Σεβηρίτης, ὁ**, v. **Σευηρίτης*.

***σέβησις, ἡ**, *cult, worship*, Clem.*str*.6.14(p.487.18; M.9.333A).

σέδετον, τό, (cf. Lat. *sedes*) army *station, quarters*, or *settlement*, ref. ownership of Gadarene swine μὴ δ' ὑποτοπάσῃς Ἰουδαϊκὴν εἶναι τὴν ἀγέλην τῶν χοίρων, ἀλλὰ στρατοπέδων Ῥωμαϊκῶν τῶν ὑπὸ τοῦ αὐτοκράτορος πόλεις τῆς ἀνατολῆς λαβόντων, ὡς Ῥωμαῖοι λαλοῦσιν, εἰς σ. Mac.Mgn.*apocr*.3.11(p.77.12).

σειρά, ἡ, A. *cord*; **1.** *rope*; met., of *bands* of sin (ref. Pr.5:22), Or.*Jo*.28.7(6; p.398.7; M.14.696B); Chrys.*hom*.14.4 *in Mt*.(7.183C); Procl.CP *or*.7(M.65.757D); **2.** *plait* of hair or perh. *hair-ribbon*, Clem.*paed*.3.11(p.271.13; M.8.637A); **3.** *line, lineage*, *T.Sal*.D 1.12(p.89.22); Jo.D.*f.o*.4.14(M.94.1156D); †Jo.D.*B.J*.30(M.96.1144A); **4.** σειρὰ χρυσῆ *catena aurea*; met., of union of theoretical and practical virtues πλουτεῖ [sc. Athanasius] μὲν θεωρίαν, πλουτεῖ δὲ βίου λαμπρότητα, καὶ πλέκει θαυμασίως ἀμφότερα τὴν χρυσῆν ὄντως σ. Gr.Naz.*or*.21.6(M.35.1088B); of consequential relationship, Chrys.*hom*.15.6 *in Mt*.(7.193B); id.*hom*.2.7 *in 2Cor*.(10.438A); of logical sequence εἰ μὲν γὰρ οὐδὲ προσκυνητόν, πῶς ἐμὲ θεοῖ διὰ τοῦ βαπτίσματος; εἰ δὲ προσκυνητόν, πῶς οὐ σεπτόν; εἰ δὲ σεπτόν, πῶς οὐ θεός; ἐν ἤρτηται τοῦ ἑνός, ἡ χρυσῆ τις ὄντως σ. καὶ σωτήριος Gr.Naz.*or*.31.28(p.181.14; M.36.165A); **5.** met., of hope, Chrys.*Thdr*.1.2(1.3A) cit. s. ἐλπίς.

B. (Lat. *sera*) *bolt*, Thphn.*chron*.p.120(M.108.336C).

σειρήν, ἡ, 1. *Siren*, Clem.*str*.1.10(p.32.8; M.8.745B); Paul.Sil.*Soph*.205(M.86.2127B); met., *charm* of words, *felicity* in expression, Clem.*q.d.s*.42(p.190.16; v.l. for ῥήσεσι M.9.649C); Synes.*ep*.139(M.66.1529A); **2.** ref. Is.13:21 etc. [tr. Hebr. יַעֲנָה]; **a.** a bird so named from sweetness of its voice, Gr.Nyss.*Eun.*12(1 p.339.3; M.45.1057B); cf.Cyr.*Is.*2.2(2.226D); **b.** *owl*, *ib.*; **c.** identified with *sparrow*, *ib.*4.1(574A) or *nightingale*, id.*Mich.*10(3.399D); **d.** *ostrich*, †Bas.*Is.*274(1.588A; M.30.601A); Thdt.*Is.*13:22(p.69.20; 2.265); id. *Jer.*50:39(2.617); Proc.G.*Is.*13:17–22(M.87.2089A).

§**σειριάζω**, *link, connect*, ref. authorship of epistle to Hebrews which is without superscription *ἵνα μή, σειριάσαντες αὐτοῦ* [sc. *Παύλου*] *τὸ ὄνομα, κλείσωσι τὴν ἀκοήν* ‡Ath.*dial.Trin.*1.5(M.28. 1124D).

σειρομάστης, ὁ, *barbed spear, lance*, Bas.*hom.*10.6(2.89D; M.31. 368C); *συρομ-*, Thdr.Mops.*Joel* 3:10(M.66.236D); Thdt.*qu.58 in 3Reg.*(1.503); ‡Caes.Naz.*dial.*156(M.38.1112); met., ref. Num.25:8, of baptism *ἡ ἁμαρτία τῷ σ. διελαθεῖσα τοῦ βαπτίσματος* Gr.Nyss. *bapt.Chr.*(M.46.597C); of doctrine, Nil.*epp.*2.142(M.79.265A).

***σειρομάστιξ, ἡ,** *knotted whip, scourge*, Geo.Pis.*hex.*958(M.92. 1508A).

§**σειρόω**, *bind*, Melet.*nat.hom.*22(M.64.1229D).

***σεισμοκράτωρ, ὁ,** *lord of the earthquake*, ‡Jo.D.*ep.Thphl.*18(M. 95.369B).

σεισμός, ὁ, *earthquake*, hence *upset, capsizal*; fig., ref. Church as ship *οἱ ἐπιβάται...ἐπὶ τῶν ἰδίων καθεζόμενοι τόπων, ἵνα μὴ τῇ ἀταξίᾳ σ. ἢ ἑτεροκλινίαν παρέχωσιν* *Clem.ep.*15(M.2.49C).

σεῖστρον, τό, 1. baby's *rattle*, Chrys.*hom.4.6 in 1Cor.*(10.32E); **2.** *brothel*; from the ringing of bells, Socr.*h.e.*5.18.11(M.67.612C).

***Σεκουνδιανοί, οἱ,** a sect of Gnostics, Epiph.*rescr.*4(p.158.4; M. 41.161B); id.*anac.*26(p.235.20; M.41.281C); difference from Valentinians described, id.*haer.*32.1(pp.439f.; M.41.544B–545A).

σεκουνδοκήριος, ὁ, (Lat. *secundocerius*) *deputy chief secretary, second notary*, CCP(536)*act.*1(p.136.18; H.2.1201D).

***σεκρετ-**, v. **σηκρητ-*.

σελαγίζω, *flash, shine brightly*, Nonn.*par.Jo.*1:5(M.43.749A); Soz.*h.e.*1.3.1(M.67.865A); med. or pass., Gr.Naz.*carm.*1.1.7.4(M.37. 439A); Areth.*Apoc.*16:17(M.106.712D).

σελάγισμα, τό, *blaze*, Paul.Sil.*Soph.*634(M.86.2143B).

***σελάριον, τό,** *privy*, Esaias *or.*5.3(p.36; M.40.1122D).

***σελαριώτης, ὁ,** ? *officer of cavalry*, Nil.*epp.*3.252 tit.(M.79.505A); cf. *σελλάριος*.

σέλας, τό, *light*, ref. Transfiguration *νεφέλη...φωτὸς ἐπεσκίασε, τὸ σ. ζωγραφοῦσα τοῦ πνεύματος* Jo.D.*hom.*1.4(M.96.552D).

***σελασφορέομαι**, *blaze*, Cosm.Mel.*schol.*proem.(M.38.342).

σελάω, *illuminate*, Gr.Naz.*carm.*1.2.1.72(M.37.527A).

***σελειῆναι**, vox nihili, Men.*exc.gent.*25(M.113.836D; *ἐκλειῆναι* p.469.22).

***σελεντιαρίκιν, τό,** v. **σιλεντιαρίκι(ο)ν*.

[*]**σελεντιάριος, ὁ,** = *σιλεντιάριος*, Tim.II Al.*fr.*(p.165.14; M.86. 273C); Dor.*doct.*23.3(M.88.1836B).

***σελέντιον, τό,** v. **σιλέντιον*.

***σεληναγωγία, ἡ,** *course, orbit of the moon*, *Apoc.En.*8.3(p.26.19).

***σελήνανδρος**, *wedded to the moon*; met., of Christ *ᾧ* [sc. *ἐκκλησίᾳ*] *σύζυγε καὶ σύνδρομε τοῦ σοῦ ἀμφιφώτου σ. ἡλίου Χριστοῦ* Anast.S.*hex.*12(M.89.1076C).

σελήνη, ἡ, *moon*; **A.** as physical phenomenon; **1.** its phases, Gr. Naz.*or.*28.29(p.67.11; M.36.68C); three in number, Thphl.Ant.*Autol.* 1.13(M.6.1044B); seven, Clem.*str.*6.16(p.504.24; M.9.372A); *σ. ... εἰς καιρῶν τροπὴν αὔξουσα καὶ μειουμένη, καὶ νὺξ ὠνομάζετο καὶ ἡμέρα προσηγορεύετο* *Const.App.*7.34.2; **2.** pagan; acc. Anaxagoras, a burning stone below sun, borrowing its light, Hipp.*haer.*1.8(p.14. 1ff.; M.16.3033Af.); 'lowest' of the stars, acc. Democritus, *ib.*1.13 (p.17.8; 3037C); acc. Xenophanes *ἀπείρους ἡλίους εἶναι καὶ σ., τὰ δὲ πάντα εἶναι ἐκ γῆς* *ib.*1.14(p.17.23; 3040A); acc. Heraclitus and Empedocles *μέχρι μὲν τῆς σ. τὰ κακὰ φθάνειν ἐκ τοῦ περὶ γῆν τόπου ταθέντα, περαιτέρω δὲ μὴ χωρεῖν, ἅτε καθαρωτέρου τοῦ ὑπὲρ τὴν σ. ... ὄντος τόπου* *ib.*1.4(p.9.23ff.; 3028Cf.).

B. as object of religious significance; **1.** pagan *τὴν...ψυχὴν αὐτῆς* [sc. *Σιβύλλης*] *εἶναι τὸ ἐν τῇ σ. φαινόμενον πρόσωπον οἴεται* [sc. *Σεραπίων*] Clem.*str.*1.15(p.45.11; M.8.777A); forming line of demarcation bet. heaven and earth cf. *τῶν μὲν...οὐρανίων ἀεὶ τὰ αὐτὰ ...ἐχόντων...αἰτίαν τὴν εἱμαρμένην ὑποτίθησι* [sc. Aristotle], *τῶν δὲ ὑπὸ σελήνην τὴν φύσιν* Atticus ap.Eus.*p.e.*15.12(814B; M.21.1337B); *οἱ τὰ μετὰ σελήνην ἀπρονόητα λέγοντες εἶναι, προσγειότεροι παρὰ τὴν σ. ὑπάρχοντες...προνοοῦσι τῶν ἀπρονοήτων* Tat.*orat.*2(p.3.5f.; M.6. 808B); *θεοῖς μὲν οὐρανὸν καὶ τῆς ἄχρι σ. αἰθέρα φασὶν ὑποτετάχθαι· δαίμοσι δὲ τὰ περὶ σ. καὶ ἀέρα· ψυχαῖς δὲ τὰ περὶ γῆν καὶ ὑπόγεια* Eus.*p.e.*4.5(141C; M.21.248A); *ὁ Ἀριστοτέλης μέχρι σ. στήσας τὸ θεῖον, τὰ λοιπὰ τοῦ κόσμου μέρη περιγράφει τῆς τοῦ θεοῦ διοικήσεως* *ib.*15.5 (798C; M.1309B); *Πυθαγόρας...διώριζεν...τὰ ἀπὸ σ.* [*καὶ*] *ἄνω ἀθάνατα λέγων, τὰ δὲ ὑποκάτω θνητά* Epiph.*anac.*5(p.165.8; M.41.169A); *ὁ δέ γε Νικομάχου μέχρι σ. ὑπείληφε τὸν θεὸν πρυτανεύειν, τῶν δὲ μετὰ ταύτην ἁπάντων ἠμεληκέναι* Thdt.*affect.*6(p.151.10; 4.848); object of worship, Ath.*gent.*9(M.25.17C); Juln.Imp.ap.‡Jo.D.*Artem.*42(p.162. 24; M.96.1289C); Gr.Naz.*or.*28.14(p.43.17; M.36.44C); *Chron.Pasch.* p.247(M.92.593C); **2.** Christian; its creation *τῆς ἐκκλησίας...τῆς πρὸ ἡλίου καὶ σ. ἐκτισμένης* *2Clem.*14.1; *οὐ...πρὸ τῆς σ., τουτέστι πρὶν γενέσθαι τὴν σ.· ἀλλ' ἐνώπιον ὥσπερ καὶ ἔμπροσθεν...τῆς σ.* Eus.*Ps.* 71:5(M.23.800A); created after vegetation lest it should be regarded as its cause, Thphl.Ant.*Autol.*2.15(M.6.1077A); *τῷ κατ' οὐσίαν λόγῳ πάντα κρείττονα τυγχάνει τῆς ἀνθρώπου σαρκός, λέγω δὴ τὸν αἰθέρα, τὸν ἥλιον, τὴν σ. ...* *Hom.Clem.*16.19; credited with a variety of physical effects *τὸ τῶν ὀστρέων γένος...ζῇ καὶ αὔξεται, πρὸς δὲ καὶ τῇ σ. συμπάσχει* Clem.*prot.*4(p.40.3; M.8.144B); ‡Eust.*hex.* (M.18.721Cf.); subject of fables, *ib.*(721Df.); *Apoc.Bar.*9(p.90.29ff.); ‡Caes.Naz.*dial.*117(M.38.1001); fables criticized by Basil, *hex.*6.4(1. 53Cff.; M.29.125B); *ib.*6.11(1.61D; M.145A); moral lessons, *ib.*6.10(1. 60Bf.; M.141B); Cyr.H.*catech.*18.10; acc. Origen, *solem quoque et lunam et astra...animantia*, Or.*princ.*1.7.4(p.90.22); cf. *ea quae animantia...et rationabilia...utrum cum corporibus pariter animata videantur eo in tempore...ego...suspicor extrinsecus insertum esse spiritum*, *ib.*(p.89.12ff.; M.11.173B); Manich., *μηχανὴν συνεστήσατο* [sc. *ὁ υἱός*] *ἔχουσαν δώδεκα κάδους, ἥ...στρεφομένη, ἀνιμᾶται τῶν θνησκόντων τὰς ψυχὰς καὶ ταύτας ὁ μέγας φωστὴρ ταῖς ἀκτῖσι λαβὼν καθαρίζει καὶ μεταδίδωσι τῇ σ., καὶ οὕτως πληροῦται τῆς σ. ὁ δίσκος ...εἶτα ἐὰν γεμισθῇ ἡ σ., μεταπορθμεύει εἰς ἀπηλιώτην,...τῆς οὖν σ. μεταδιδούσης τὸν γόμον τῶν ψυχῶν τοῖς αἰῶσι τοῦ πατρός, παραμένουσιν ἐν τῷ στύλῳ τῆς δόξης, ὃς καλεῖται ἀὴρ ὁ τέλειος* Hegem.*Arch.*8(p.13. 2; M.10.1440B); Epiph.*haer.*66.52(p.88.30; M.42.108A); Thdt.*haer.*1. 26(4.320); **3.** *ἡμέρα σελήνης* *Monday*, *CIG* 9523; perh. also *ib.*9522.

C. met.; as a type of man, Thphl.Ant.*Autol.*2.15(M.6.1077A); of Church, Or.*Jo.*1.25(24; p.31.11; M.14.68C); *ib.*6.55(37; p.164.21; 297A); *σελήνην δὲ οἱ προφῆται τὴν ἐκκλησίαν καλοῦσιν ἐκκύπτουσαν ὡς ὄρθρον* Nil.*epp.*3.212(M.79.480B); of faith of baptized, Meth.*symp.* 8.6(p.88.5; M.18.148A); of Law of Moses, Oecum.*Apoc.*12:1(p.136); of synagogue, Areth.*Apoc.*12:1(M.106.661A); of BMV *κἀκεῖ τετέλεσται τῆς...νοητῆς σ. ὁ ὑπερκόσμιος δρόμος, ἐξ ἧς ἐλήφθη ὁ ἥλιος εἰς ὧν τοῦ τρισηλίου* Mod.*dorm.*3(M.86.3285A); *ἡ νοητὴ καὶ θεοφώτιστος σ. τῷ τῆς δικαιοσύνης ἡλίῳ συνεισβάλλουσα* Thdr.Stud.*or.*5.1(M.99. 721A).

***σεληνηείς**, *moonlike*, Paul.Sil.*ambo.*273(M.86.2262A).

σεληνιάζομαι, *be moonstruck, lunatic, epileptic, possessed*, *A.Thom.*A 12(p.117.9) cit. s. *δαιμόνιον*; Chrys.*hom.57.3 in Mt.*(7. 579E); word discussed, Or.*comm.in Mt.*13.6(p.193ff.; M.13.1105B); met., of those who fall into sin, id.*schol.in Lc.*9:42(M.17.348A); into heresy, Anast.S.*hod.*7(M.89.116A).

[*]**σεληνιαῖος**, = *σεληναῖος*, *of the moon, lunar*, Afric.*chron.*1 (M.10.65A); Gr.Nyss.*infant.*(M.46.165B); Thdr.Stud.*epp.*2.36(M.99. 1220A).

σεληνιακῶς, *by lunar reckoning*, *Chron.Pasch.*p.196(M.92.484B).

σεληνιασμός, ὁ, *epilepsy, demoniacal possession*, Or.*hom.12.12 in Jer.*(p.98.17ff.; M.13.393C); id.*comm.in Mt.*13.6(p.194.29; M.13. 1108C).

σελλάριος, ὁ, 1. *courser, riding-horse*, *Chron.Pasch.*p.400(M.92. 1021B); **2.** *Persian official*, prob. *officer of cavalry*, Sophr.H. *v.Anast.*(M.92.1700B,1709D); of a governor, *ib.*(1701B).

σελλί(ο)ν, τό, dimin. of *σέλλα*, (Lat. *sella*) *chair, seat*, Leont.N. *v.Jo.Eleem.*5(p.11.8).

σεμίδαλις, ἡ, *finest wheaten flour*; offered by Egyptians to sacred animals, cf.Diodorus Siculus ap.Eus.*p.e.*2.1(51B; M.21.104A); diet of holy virgins, Chrys.*hom.13.3 in Eph.*(11.100E); *ἔβαλλε* [sc. *ὁ ἀββᾶς Ἰωάννης*] *σ. τοῖς μικροῖς μυρμηκίοις, σῖτον δὲ τοῖς μεγάλοις* Jo.Mosch.*prat.*184(M.87.3056C); offering prescribed by Jewish law (Lev.2:5, 9:4, Num.15:4, etc.), one of sacrifices which have ceased after Christ's sacrifice, Just.*dial.*112.4(M.6.733C); Cyr.*Ps.*34:28(M. 69.911D); type of eucharist, Just.*dial.*41.1(564B); an aromatic sacrifice, symbolizing odour of the gospel, Gr.Nyss.*hom.9 in Cant.*(M.44.957A).

σεμιδαλῖται, οἱ, alternative name for sect of *Barsanuphites*, akin to Gaianites and Theodosians, Anast.S.*hod.*10(M.89.149D); *σ. ... σεμίδαλιν γὰρ προστιθέασι...καὶ τῷ ἄκρῳ δακτύλῳ ἐφαπτόμενοι γεύονται τοῦ ἀλεύρου, καὶ τοῦτ' ἀντὶ μυστηρίου δέχονται* Jo.D.*haer.*86 (M.94.756B).

σεμνεῖον, τό, 1. *sacred place* or *room*, cf.Philo ap.Eus.*h.e.*2.17.9 (M.20.177C); **2.** *monastery, convent* *γυναικείῳ σ.* Thdr.Stud.*epp.*1.10 (M.99.941C).

***σεμνογαμία, ἡ,** *holy matrimony*, ‡Chrys.*prod.serv.*4(8.246B).

***σεμνοειδής,** *splendid*; **1.** of philosophical arguments, *impressive*, Gr.Thaum.*pan.Or.*7(p.21.3; M.10.1076C); **2.** *resplendent* Ἶρις ἐστὶν ἔμφασις ἡλίου σ. Jo.D.*dialect.*68(M.94.673D).

***σεμνοειδῶς,** *with great seriousness, impressively*, Gr.Thaum.*pan. Or.*2(p.4.10; M.10.1056A).

***σεμνοήθης,** *of serious character*; *grave-mannered*, Jo.VI H.*v. Jo.D.*8(M.94.441A).

***σεμνοληρέω,** *talk high-sounding nonsense*, Cyr.*dial.Trin.*4(5[1]. 544A); id.*Nest.*2.8(p.46.13; 6[1].51A).

σεμνολογ-έω, A. intrans.; **1.** *speak in all seriousness* ἃ ⟨παρὰ⟩ Πυθαγόρου λαβὼν...∼ῶν ἀνατίθησι Χριστῷ Hipp.*haer.*6.22(p.149.23; M.16.3227B); **2.** med., *wax grandiloquent*, ‡Bas.*struct.hom.*2.12(1. 344D; M.30.56B).

B. trans.; **1.** *talk impressively about* τὰ αἰσχρὰ σ. Eus.*p.e.*3.7(98D; M.21.180D); **2.** *speak with reverence of*, *ib.*3.11(111C; M.200C); Pall. *h.Laus.*56(p.150.8; M.34.1250A).

σεμνολόγημα, τό, 1. subjective, that about which one is proud, *source of pride, boast* σύ τε...[sc. Paulinus of Tyre] νεὼ θεοῦ σ. Eus. *h e.*10.4.2(M.20.849A); τὰ...μάλιστα ἐπονείδιστα δοκοῦντα εἶναι, ταῦτά ἐστι τὰ σ. τῶν ἡμετέρων ἀγαθῶν Chrys.*hom.85.3 in Jo.*(8.508C); Cyr. *Arcad.*(p.62.3; 5[2].42B); as mode of address to a friend περιπτυξόμεθα τὸ ἡμέτερον σ. Gr.Naz.*ep.*93(M.37.168B); in bad sense, Cyr.*Os.* 140(3.173D); **2.** objective; plur., subjects for praise, *glories* τὸ ἐν χιτώνιον...καὶ ἡ χαμευνία, καὶ ἡ ἀγρυπνία...τὰ ἐκείνου [sc. Bas.] σ. Gr.Naz.*or.*43.61(M.36.576B); Gr.Nyss.*v.Ephr.*(M.46.824A,845A); Pall.*v.Chrys.*12(p.77.19; M.47.44); Thdr.Stud.*epp.*2.113(M.99.1377B); **3.** *honourable title, proud epithet* τὸ σ. προσέθηκεν [sc. τὸν ἀδελφὸν τοῦ κυρίου] Chrys.*comm.in Gal.*1:19(10.678E).

σεμνολογία, ἡ, 1. *solemn discourse*, Const.*or.s.c.*11(p.166.21; M. 20.1260B); iron., *impressive language, bombast*, Eus.*p.e.*3.3(91D; M. 21.169B); *profound interpretation* σ. τοῖς περὶ θεῶν μύθοις προσεπενόησαν *ib.*2.6(74C; M.141B); **2.** *reverence in word*, Or.*Cels.*1.24(p.75. 3; M.11.705A); Thdr.Mops.*Mal.*1:6(M.66.601B).

***σεμνοπεριπάτητος,** *dignified in gait* τὸ δὲ ἦθος αὐτῆς [sc. Μαρίας] οὕτως εἶχε...ταχυπήκοος, σ. ‡Hipp.Th.*fr.*17(p.50.4).

σεμνοποιέω, *honour, dignify*, Or.*Jo.*13.29(p.253.25; M.14.449B); σ. τὰ κατὰ τοὺς πένητας Chrys.*hom.27.3 in 1Cor.*(10.245A); ‡Nil. *perist.*9.6(M.79.873C).

***σεμνόπους,** *with stately step*, *Chron.Pasch.*p.312(M.92.793D).

σεμνοπρέπεια, ἡ, 1. *serious bearing, gravity, dignity*, Gr.Naz.*or.* 5.35(M.35.709C); Pall.*v.Chrys.*8(p.45.16; M.47.27); met., of BMV, Ephr.(3.530F); **2.** as complimentary style of address; to a widow, Bas.*ep.*1.10(3.92B,C; M.32.273A); Thdt.*ep.*14(4.1072); to a bishop, Gr.Naz.*ep.*202(M.37.332B); Gr.Nyss.*ep.*21(M.46.1088A); to an abbess, Thdr.Stud.*epp.*2.91(M.99.1341B); to senate, Thphn.*chron.* p.284(M.108.697C); to others, Synes.*ep.*17(M.66.1353A).

σεμνοπρεπής, *august*; *honourable, noble*; of scriptures, Meth.*creat.* 1(p.493.9; M.18.332A); †Bas.*Is.*6(1.382D; M.30.128D); *M.Apollon.*5 (p.30); of persons, Isid.Pel.*epp.*2.171(M.78.621D); of women, *seemly, dignified*; superl., Didym.*Trin.*1.20(M.39.373A); Dion.Al.ap.Eus.*h.e.* 6.41.18(M.20.609C; σεμνοτάτη p.606.17).

σεμνοπρεπῶς, *with sobriety*, Isid.Pel.*epp.*2.289(M.78.720B); *with discretion*, superl. σ. ἡσυχάζουσιν Or.*Jo.*6.22(13; p.131.29; M.14. 240A).

σεμνοπροσωπέω, *assume a solemn countenance*, ‡Bas.*struct.hom.* 2.12(1.344D; M.30.56B).

σεμνός, 1. *holy, sacred*; of God, Clem.*str.*3.5(p.214.24; M.8. 1144C); Or.*Cels.*3.36(p.232.9; M.11.965B); of Passion of Christ, Clem.*paed.*2.8(p.202.10; M.8.485A); of teachings and ordinances of religion (pagan) ἀποφθέγγεται [sc. ἡ Πυθία] τὰ νομιζόμενα εἶναι σ. ... μαντεύματα Or.*Cels.*7.3(p.155.16; 1424D); (Christian) τὸν σ. τῆς παραδόσεως ἡμῶν κανόνα *1Clem.*7.2; σεμνότεραι...αἱ ἑορταὶ [sc. αἱ παρ' ἡμῖν] τῶν δημοτελῶν Or.*Cels.*8.23(p.240.12; 1552C); τὸ σεμνότατον κήρυγμα Dion.R.ap.Ath.*decr.*26(p.22.2; M.25.461D); τὴν σ. ... ἱερωσύνην Gr.Nyss.*or.catech.*18(p.75.19; M.45.56A); neut. as subst., *sacredness, solemnity* τήρει τὸ σ. τῆς γραφῆς Or.*mart.*16(p.15.21; M.11.584B); τὰ...σ. τῆς Αἰγυπτίων θεολογίας Eus.*p.e.*2.1(52A; M.21. 104C); τὰ σ. τῆς ἐνθέου διδασκαλίας id.*v.C.*2.61(p.66.15; M.20.1036C); τῶν μυστηρίων τὸ σ. Bas.*Spir.*66(3.55B; M.32.189A); **2.** *godly, religious* σ. καὶ νεανικῶν πόνων [i.e. of S. Anthony] Ath.*v.Anton.*15(M.26. 865C); of the Christian life, Bas.*ep.*45.1(3.133C; M.32.365B); **3.** *ascetic*; of the monastic life, ‡Ath.*doct.Ant.*1(M.28.557B); of persons leading an ascetic life δόξῃ τῇ σ. ἀσκητρίῃ *MAMA* 1.174; as subst. (pagan) οἱ σ. τῶν Ἰνδῶν...σέβουσί τινα πυραμίδα Clem.*str.*3.7(p.224.2; M.8. 1164B); *Const.App.*6.10.2; **4.** *worthy of respect, honourable, noble*; iron., Tat.*orat.*1(p.2.10; M.6.805C); *ib.*34(p.35.19; 876B); neut. as subst., *1Clem.*47.5; plur., *noble matters*, Gr.Thaum.*pan.Or.*2(p.4. 29; M.10.1056B); **5.** *seemly, sober, chaste* σ. ... ἐπιθυμίαν Herm. *mand.*12.1.1; εὐσταθεστάτους καὶ σεμνοτάτους Or.*princ.*3.1.5(p.200. 14; M.11.256A); ἵνα ὁ λαός σου...ἅγιος καὶ σ. ᾖ Serap.*euch.*1.3; *Const.App.*3.7.6; ἐν σ. γάμοις καὶ τεκνογονίαις *Lit.ib.*8.12.44; of a bishop εἴ ἐστι σ. ... εἰ γυναῖκα σ. ... ἔχει *Const.App.*2.2.3; neut. as subst., *purity* τὸ σ. τῶν παρθένων Ath.*h.Ar.*55(p.214.27; M.25.760C); τὸ σ. τῆς ψυχῆς Gel.Cyz.*h.e.*3.17.22; **6.** *serious* ὁ γνωστικὸς...σ. ὢν καὶ ἱλαρὸς Clem.*str.*7.7(p.28.2; M.9.452A); neut. as adv., *gravely* ὑπομειδιάσας σ. Pall.*h.Laus.*2(p.18.7; M.34.1101D); *ib.*22(p.70.3; 1076D); **7.** *little*, whether *small* or *young* ἅμα τῆς ἑαυτοῦ συμβίου καὶ σ. παιδίου Gr.Mag.*dial.*(tr.Zach.)1.10(M.*PL.*77.202D); *ib.*3.33(298C); χοῖρος σ. *ib.*3.21(274A); σκαλίδιον σ. *ib.*3.9(235A); ἐν σεμνοτάτῳ ἀγγείῳ *ib.*1.9(190C).

***σεμνοτέρως,** adv. formed from comp. of σεμνός, *more delicately, somewhat euphemistically*, Chrys.*hom.15.1 in 1Cor.*(10.125D).

σεμνότης, ἡ, A. *sacredness* of things pertaining to God σ. θεολογίας Or.*Cels.*6.18(p.89.15; M.11.1317C); ἀθανάτου...νόμου...τὴν σ. Const.ap.Gel.Cyz.*h.e.*2.7.4(M.85.1233A).

B. on the part of man; **1.** *holiness, piety, reverence*, Herm.*mand.* 4.1.3; Clem.*str.*1.3(p.14.21; M.8.712A); Max.*myst.*24(M.91.716B); *religion*, Const.ap.Eus.*v.C.*2.53(p.63.13; M.20.1029B); **2.** *nobility, dignity*, Clem.*paed.*3.11(p.267.22; M.8.628C); *Const.App.*2.25.1; Jo. VI H.*v.Jo.D.*8(M.94.441A); in music, Clem.*str.*6.17(p.509.20; M.9. 381B); in literature, Chrys.*sac.*4.6(p.120.8; 1.412A); as mode of address; to a bishop, Const.ap.Eus.*v.C.*3.53(p.101.13; M.20.1117A); Alex.Thess.*ep.Ath.*(p.145.8; M.25.368A); **3.** *gravity, propriety, chastity*, *1Clem.*41.1; Clem.*paed.*2.5(p.186.24; M.8.449B); Chrys. *hom.4.1 in 2Tim.*(11.679E).

***σεμνοφανής,** *outwardly impressive* or *splendid, showy*, Or.*Cels.*3. 17(p.215.22; M.11.940D); Eus.*p.e.*2.8(80B; M.21.152B).

***σεμνοφορέω,** *be well dressed*, *Chron.Pasch.*p.397(M.92.1016B).

***σεμνόφωνος,** *grave-toned, with solemn voice*; of Isaiah, Thdt.*h.e.* 1.8.5(3.760).

***σεμνόψαλτος,** neut. as subst., *solemn singing*, Thdr.Stud.*epp.*2. 124(M.99.1405A).

σεμνύν-ω, A. *magnify, honour*; **1.** as divine, Arist.*apol.*13.5; *hallow, revere as sacred* τῆς εἰς οὐρανοὺς ἀναλήψεως τὴν...μνήμην σ. Eus.*v.C.*3.41(p.95.8; M.20.1101A); ἱερατεία...μόνῳ ∼όμενα τῷ αἵματι τοῦ Χριστοῦ CAlex.*ep.*ap.Ath.*apol.sec.*5(p.91.7; M.25.250C); **2.** in gen., *honour*, Clem.*str.*1.15(p.42.26; M.8.769B); Constantius ap. Ath.*apol.Const.*30(M.25.633C); ἔστω ἐπίσκοπος μὴ ἐκ τόπου ∼όμενος, ἀλλὰ τὸν τόπον ∼ων Bas.*ep.*98.2(3.192D; M.32.497A); id.*Spir.*57(3. 48C; M.32.173A).

B. *make vain*; **1.** σ. τοὺς πονηροὺς πᾶν εἶδος ἀκαθαρσίας Cyr.*Os.*21 (3.44C); **2.** med., *pride oneself on*; **a.** in bad sense, *boast (of), set oneself up as*, Tat.*orat.*2(p.2.19; M.6.808A); Hipp.*haer.*8.20(p.239.12; M.16.3367C); Thdt.*h.e.*3.28.2(3.944); **b.** in good sense; abs., *be proud, content with oneself, hold one's head high* εἰ ἀποπλήσω πάνθ', ἅ μοι δυνατόν ἐστι, καὶ ∼οῦμαι Gr.Thaum.*pan.Or.*3(p.7.17; M.10. 1060A); c. dat., *take pride, glory* in τῷ τοῦ πάθους ∼όμενος τροπαίῳ Eus.*v.C.*3.1(p.76.12; M.20.1053A); οὓς [i.e. heresies] ἐκτραπεῖσα ἡ ἐκκλησία...τῷ τῆς ἀληθείας εὐαγγελικῷ κηρύγματι ∼εται id.*e.th.*1.3 (p.64.3; M.24.832D).

***σενᾶτον (σένατον), τό,** (Lat. *senatus*) *senate house*, *Chron.Pasch.* pp.284,307(M.92.709B,781A); σένατον *ib.*p.337(876C); †Hipp.Th.*fr.*7. 2(p.34.7; M.117.1036A).

***σένζος, ὁ,** v. *σέσσος.

***σενίωρ,** (Lat. *senior*) *elder*, *Chron.Pasch.*p.269(M.92.661Af.).

***σέντζος, ὁ,** v. *σέσσος.

***σεπτέος,** *to be reverenced*, Eus.*l.C.*12(p.232.2; σκεπτέον M.20. 1389C); Gr.Naz.*carm.*2.1.11.579(M.37.1069A).

***σεπτόγραφος,** *designed for veneration*, Leont.N.*serm.*3(M.93. 1597B).

***σεπτόμορφος,** *of sacred form*; neut. plur. as subst., *holy images*, ἡ προσκύνησις τῶν σ. [v.l. σ. εἰκόνων] εἰδωλολατρεία ἐστίν ‡Jo.D.*Const.*17(M.95.333C).

***σεπτοπροσκυνητός,** *worthy of devout worship*, ‡Jo.D.*hom.*5(M. 96.657A).

σεπτός, *worshipped, reverenced, sacred, holy*; **1.** of God and divine things: the Father, Clem.*str.*7.1(p.4.9; M.9.404C); name of Christ, Eus.*h.e.*1.3.2(M.20.69A); H. Ghost, Gr.Naz.*or.*31.28(p.181. 13; M.36.165A); id.*carm.*2.1.7.6(M.37.1024A); Holy Communion, Jo.Mosch.*prat.*106(M.87.2965A); neut. as subst., *worship*, Gr.Naz. *or.*23.8(M.35.1160C); **2.** of what pertains to religion: pagan σεπτὸν αὐτοῦ [sc. τοῦ μιερέως] ἡγοῦνται τὸ ὄνομα *Const.App.*2.28.8; Christian; of the altar, Isid.Pel.*epp.*2.205(M.78.648B); of Jewish Law, Thdt.*Heb.*8:4(3.594); **3.** of human qualities and persons, Cyr.*Ps.* 14:3(M.69.805C); id.*Lc.*6:27(M.72.593D); superl., Eudoc.*Cypr.*1.109 (M.85.836D).

***σεπτῶς,** *reverently, M.Tim.fr.*(p.144.2).

***σεραφικός, 1.** *of the nature of a seraph* σ. ὀφθαλμοῖς ἀπερίληπτος Didym.*Trin.*2.1(M.39.449A); τὰς σ. δυνάμεις ‡Bas.*h.myst.*60(p.394.20); *ib.*59(p.394.4); οἱ μὲν πρεσβύτεροι κατὰ μίμησιν τῶν σ. δυνάμεών εἰσι, ταῖς μὲν στολαῖς, δίκην πτερύγων κατακεκαλυμμένοι *ib.*16(p.261.24); **2.** *belonging to the seraphim; of the seraphim,* ref. priest's sedilium in the sanctuary conceived of as possessed and used by seraphim, Gel.Cyz.*h.e.*2.31.3(M.85.1316C); of hymn of Is.6:3 identified with tersanctus of liturgy ὁ δὲ ὑπὸ τοῦ Ἡσαΐου ἐκφωνηθεὶς σ. ὕμνος...τίνα διαφορὰν φέρει τοῦ παρ' ἡμῶν ᾀδομένου τρισαγίου; ‡Sophr.H.*liturg.*15(M.87.3996C); **3.** *like the seraphim,* ref. S. John τὸ σ. μυσταγώγημα ‡Chrys.*Jo.theol.*1.1(8.130C); *bearing the likeness of the seraphim* τῆς τῶν ῥιπιδίων σ. ἀπεικονισμάτων ἱστορίας ‡Bas.*h. myst.*49(p.390.19).

***σεραφικῶς,** *like the seraphim, Lit.Jac.*(p.164.15); Andr.Cr.*or.*9 (M.97.997A).

σεραφίμ (σεραφείμ), τό, *seraphim*; **1.** derivation and meaning ἑρμηνεύεται...τὰ σ. ἀρχὴ στόματος αὐτῶν Eus.*d.e.*7.1(p.299.11; M.22.489C); τὸ σ. ἑρμηνεύεσθαι ἐμπρησμοί *ib.*(p.299.20f.; 489D); cf.Hier.*comm.in Is.*6:2(M.*PL.*24.93C); ἔμπυρα στόματα ἑρμηνεύεται τὰ σ. Chrys.*Is.interp.*6:2(6.66A); id.*incomprehens.*3.5(1.468C); διερμηνεύεται δὲ σ. ἐμπρησταὶ ἤτοι θερμαίνοντες Cyr.*Is.*1.4(2.102E); Dion.Ar.*c.h.*7.1(M.3.205B); id.*e.h.*4.3.10(M.3.481C) cit. s. ἀνακινητικός; cf. *o seraphim...ob incendendi...vim, qua polletis, quaque omnem malitiam...absumere et expiare consuevistis, incensorum et calfactorum nominibus designemini,* Sophr.H.*or.*6(M.87.3315Cf.); **2.** nature ἀσώματοί τινες θεῖαι καὶ ὑπερκόσμιοι δυνάμεις Eus.*Is.*6:2(M.24.125A); Chrys.*hom.1.3 in Is.*6:*1*(6.100B); Dion.Ar.*e.h.*4.3.6(M.3.480D); highest of angelic orders, forming one hierarchy with cherubim and thrones, id.*c.h.*6.2(M.3.201A); cf.Sophr.H.*or.*6(M.87.3315A); Max. *schol.c.h.*7.1(M.4.65A) cit. s. χερουβίμ; equated with δυνάμεις in Col. 1:16 ὁ...ἀπόστολος...μαθὼν ὅτι τὸ αὐτὸ πρᾶγμα παρὰ τῶν δύο προφητῶν...σημαίνεται [sc. Is.6:3, Ps.102:21], τὴν γνωριμωτάτην τῶν φωνῶν ἐκλεξάμενος 'δυνάμεις' τὰ σ. ὠνόμασεν Gr.Nyss.*Eun.*1(1 p.113.20; M. 45.348B); equated with thrones, Didym.*Trin.*2.18(M.39.545A); unable to comprehend God ὅπερ ἐφ' ἡμῶν ἐστιν ὅρασις, τοῦτο ἐπ' ἐκείνων [sc. τῶν ἀσωμάτων δυνάμεων] γνῶσις. ὥστε ὅταν ἀκούσῃς ὅτι θεὸν οὐδεὶς ἑώρακε πώποτε, ἐκεῖνο νόμιζε ἀκούειν, ὅτι τὸν θεὸν οὐδεὶς ἔγνω οὐσιωδῶς μετὰ ἀκριβείας ἁπάσης. καὶ περὶ τῶν σ. δὲ ὅταν ἀκούσῃς ὅτι ἀπέστρεψαν τοὺς ὀφθαλμούς, καὶ τὴν ὄψιν ἐτείχισαν, καὶ τὰ χερουβίμ...διὰ τούτων τὴν γνῶσιν αὐτῶν αἰνίττεσθαι πίστευε τὸν προφήτην Chrys.*incomprehens.*4.3(1.475C); οὐδεὶς ἔγνω ποτὲ τὸν θεόν...οὐκ ἀνθρώπων μόνον, ἀλλ' οὐδὲ τῶν ὑπερκοσμίων δυνάμεων... τῶν χερουβὶμ καὶ σ. Jo.D.*f.o.*1.1(M.94.789A); passage alternatively interpreted as ref. prophets and apostles, Eus.*d.e.*7.1(p.299.9; M.22.489C); **3.** number: two, *Apoc.Bar.rel.*9.3; Serap.*euch.*13.9; a company, Eus.*d.e.*7.1(p.299.9; M.22.489C); δύο μὲν εἶναι τὰ σ. ἐντεῦθεν [sc. Dan.7:10] ἐνόμισαν ἄλλοι· ἐγὼ δέ, ἐπιστήσας τῇ διανοίᾳ τῆς λεγούσης γραφῆς [sc. Is.6:2] ἡγοῦμαι ταῦτα...πανταχόθεν ὥσπερ μέγαν βασιλέα δορυφοροῦντα id.*Is.*6:2(M.24.125A); φωστῆρες δὲ πολλοὶ καὶ θρόνοι καὶ...χερουβὶμ καὶ σ. καὶ ἀρχάγγελοι πολλοί Ath.*ep.Serap.*1.27(M.26.593B); Proc.G.*Is.*6:1ff.(M.87.1932D); **4.** 'appearance' and significance τὰ περὶ τῶν...σ. ... καὶ τὰ περὶ τῶν...χερουβίμ...καὶ τῶν ὡσανεὶ σχημάτων αὐτῶν...κεκρυμμένως εἴρηται διὰ τοὺς ἀναξίους καὶ ἀσέμνους, μὴ δυναμένους παρακολουθῆσαι μεγαλονοίᾳ καὶ σεμνότητι θεολογίας Or.*Cels.*6.18(p.89.9; M.11.1317C); τὰ ἐν τῷ Ἡσαΐᾳ [6:3] δύο σ. ἑξαπτέρυγα κεκραγότα...τὸν μονογενῆ εἶναι τοῦ θεοῦ καὶ τὸ πνεῦμα τὸ ἅγιον. ἡμεῖς δὲ οἰόμεθα ὅτι καὶ τὸ ἐν τῇ ᾠδῇ Ἀμβακοὺμ [3:3] περὶ Χριστοῦ καὶ ἁγίου πνεύματος εἴρηται id.*princ.*1.3.4(p.52.17; M.11.148C); *ib.*4.3.14(p.346.14; 400A); id.*hom.1.2 in Is.*(M.12.221C); idea refuted by Antip.Bost.ap.Jo.D.*parall.*(M.96.505B); cf.Hier.*comm.in Is.*6:2(M.*PL.*24.94C); τὰ...ἐσόμενα μετὰ τὴν...ἐνανθρώπησιν προδεδηλωκότων τῶν σ. ἀναγκαίως μηνύεται καὶ τῶν δύο λαῶν ἡ συνάφεια Thdt.*Is.*6:4(p.32.2; 2.208); αἱ ἓξ πτέρυγες [sc. τῶν σ.] ἐνδείκνυνται ...τὸ ὑψηλὸν καὶ...τὸ ταχὺ ἐκείνων τῶν φύσεων Chrys.*hom.6.2 in Is.* 6:*1*(6.140A); significance of the number six, Dion.Ar.*e.h.*4.3.7(M. 3.481A); τὸ...ἀπειροπρόσωπον αὐτῶν [sc. τῶν σ.] καὶ πολύπουν ἐκφαντορικόν ἐστιν...τῆς πολυθεάμονος...ἰδιότητος, καὶ τῆς...πολυπόρου ...νοήσεως *ib.*; described as τετράμορφος, Ephr.3.523B; **5.** activities interpreted: covering of face and feet, Chrys.*hom.6.2 in Is.*6:*1*(6.140B); id.*incomprehens.*3.3(1.465C); Cyr.*Is.*1.4(2.103A); Dion.Ar.*e.h.* 4.3.8(M.3.481B); their hymn τὰ ἅγια τῶν ἁγίων, ἃ καὶ τοῖς σ. συγκαλύπτεται καὶ δοξάζεται...εἰς μίαν συννιοῦσι κυριότητα καὶ θεότητα Gr.Naz.*or.*45.4(M.36.628D); τὰ...σ. παρ' ὧν...τὸ τῆς τριάδος ἐκηρύχθη μυστήριον Gr.Nyss.*Eun.*1(1 p.113.2; M.45.348A); Sophr.H.*or.*2.3(M. 87.1076A); ἐκέκραγον ἕτερος πρὸς τὸν ἕτερον...δηλοῦν, ὅτι τῶν θεοπτικῶν αὐτῶν νοήσεων ἀλλήλοις ἀφθόνως μεταδιδόασι Dion.Ar.*e.h.*4.3.9(481C); why ceaseless, Chrys.*hom.6.2 in Is.6:1*(6.141A); watching over Church, Anast.S.*hex.*12(M.89.1076A); sleepless eye signifying Christ, ‡Epiph.*hom.*5(M.43.489C); joining worshippers in praise during liturgy, Chrys.*hom.14.4 in Eph.*(11.108B); typified by fans, ‡Bas.*h.myst.*60(p.394.11); at Last Judgement, ‡Hipp.*consumm.*39 (p.305.17; M.10.941B); Ephr.3.309E; operation of heavenly chariot, id.3.523B cit. s. τετράμορφος; *Apoc.BMV* 26(p.124.17) usu. attributed to χερουβίμ; v. χερουβικός; **6.** figures removed from Temple by Titus (? error for cherubim), *Chron.Pasch.*p.247(M.92.593C); **7.** magical formula, *T.Sal.*18.34(M.122.1345C).

***σεσημειωμένως,** *figuratively,* Max.*qu.Thal.*51(M.90.477B).

***σεσιγημένως,** *silently,* Cyr.*Lc.*5:18(M.72.565C); Max.*ambig.*(M. 91.1141B).

***σέσσος (*σένζος, *σέντζος), ὁ,** (Lat. *sessus*) *throne,* CCP(681) *act.*12(H.3.1304B); σένζος Thphn.*chron.*pp.107,313(M.108.309B,760C); σέντζος *ib.*p.249(625B).

***σεσυκοφαντημένως,** *falsely, slanderously,* Epiph.*haer.*55.9(p.337.23; M.41.989A).

***Σευηριανός, A.** *Severian, of Severus* of Antioch σ. λαοπλανία Dam.*troph.*suppl.(p.283.9).

B. plur. as subst.; *followers of Severus*; **1.** the Gnostic, Epiph. *haer.*45.1(p.199.13; M.41.832D); Thdt.*haer.*1.21(4.312); **2.** the monophysite Σεβηρ-, Anast.S.*haer.*(p.263); Thphn.*chron.*p.199(M.108.513C); cf. Σευηρίτης.

***Σευηριοπαράδοτος,** *handed down by, taught by Severus* of Antioch, the monophysite, Anast.S.*hod.*12(M.89.201B).

***Σευηρίτης, ὁ,** *follower of* the monophysite *Severus* of Antioch, Leont.N.*v.Sym.*32(M.93.1709C); Σεβηρ-, Leont.H.*Nest.*2.24(M.86.1585A); various sects of the name enumerated, Tim.CP *haer.*(M. 86.57–65); cf. Σευηριανός.

σευτλίον, τό, *beet,* ‡Ath.*pat.*2(M.26.1300B).

σεύω, act. intrans., *run about* σ. ἐν τῇ ἐκκλησίᾳ κύων ἢ χοῖρος *Nomoc.*71.

***Σηθιανοί, οἱ,** *Sethians, Sethites*; members of Ophite sect who glorified Seth, Iren.*haer.*1.30.1 tit.(M.7.694B); Hipp.*haer.*5.19(pp.116ff.; M.16.3179Aff.); Epiph.*haer.*39.1(pp.71ff.; M.41.665D–677A); *ib.*40.7(p.88.12; 688D); id.*anac.*39(p.2.8; M.41.589A); Thdt. *haer.*1.14(4.306ff.).

σηκός, ὁ, 1. *sheep-fold, pen*; met., of Church, Chrys.*hom.9.7 in Rom.*(9.508B); **2.** *sacred enclosure*; **a.** heathen; *shrine,* Clem.*prot.*4 (p.37.14; M.8.140A); Thdt.*h.e.*3.6.1(3.917); **b.** Christian; properly, *chapel, shrine* of a martyr or other saint, Bas.*hom.in Ps.*114(1.199B; M.29.484A); Chrys.*hom.37.7 in Mt.*(7.424B); rival shrines sts. built for a reputed saint in anticipation of his death, Thdt.*h.rel.* 3(3.1147); in gen., *church,* Synes.*ep.*58(M.66.1401C); Thdt.*h.e.*5.2.3(3.1015); Gr.Agr.*Eccl.*4.4(M.98.932B); met., of womb of BMV, Leont.B.*parasc.*(M.86.1997C); **3.** *burial place, coffin,* 1*Clem.*25.2f; Epiph.*anc.*84(p.104.14; M.43.173B); **4.** *bulk, mass,* Gr.Nyss.*Apoll.*22 (M.45.1168C).

σηκ-όω ([*]σικόω), **1.** *lift,* σικ-, *A.Pil.*B 15(p.321); *Mir.Artem.*22 (p.30.4); *ib.*17(p.19.4, v.l. σικ-); ἐσήκωσεν τὰ ὄ(μ)μάτια...πρὸς τὸν οὐρανόν *Apoc.BMV*(Vassiliev p.126); **2.** *lift* so as to remove ~ωθῆ τὸ σκότος *ib.*; **3.** met., *uplift, exalt* τύφον πεπαίνειν ἀλόγως ~ούμενον Nil.*Magn.*62(M.79.1053A).

***σηκρητάριος (*σεκρετ-), ὁ,** (Lat. *secretarius*) *secretary, clerk,* CChalc.*act.*1(*ACO* 2.1.1 p.66.21; H.2.68D); *ib.*2(*ACO* 2.1.2 p.29.12; H. 2.384C); CCP(536)*act.*2(*ACO* 3 p.160.18; σεκρετ-, H.2.1233E); σεκρετ-, *Mir.Artem.*18(p.22.22).

***σήκρητον (*σέκρετον), τό, 1.** (Lat. *secretarium*) *court, consistory,* of a governor βῆμα μὲν καὶ θρόνον...ἑαυτῷ κατασκευασάμενος [sc. Paul. Sam.], οὐχ ὡς Χριστοῦ μαθητής, σ. τε, ὥσπερ οἱ τοῦ κόσμου ἄρχοντες, ἔχων τε καὶ ὀνομάζων Malch.*ep.*ap.Eus.*h.e.*7.30.9(M.20.713A); *lawcourt* in gen., *Cod.Afr.*97; σέκρετον †Gregent.*leg.Hom.* (M.86.577D); Thphn.*chron.*p.249(M.108.624B); of court or council of patriarch of CP, Sophr.H.*ep.syn.*(M.87.3200A); CCP(681)*act.*8 (H.3.1161C); **2.** *council-chamber*; in palace, Anast.Ap.*a.Max.*1.12 (M.90.125C); Thphn.*chron.*p.193(M.108.501B); of patriarch, Leont.N. *v.Jo.Eleem.*2(p.8.5).

***σήκωσις, ἡ,** *lifting* into the air, *elevation,* ? ref. 1Thess.4:17, *cat.Apoc.*3:13(p.230.13).

***σημαδαρικός,** *for purposes of barter* τοῦ χρυσοκαταλλακτικοῦ καὶ σ. πόρου *Mir.Artem.*38(p.62.1).

***σημαδάριος, ὁ,** *money-lender, broker,* Thphn.*chron.*p.205(M.108.528A) cit. s. σημάδιον.

***σημαδεύω,** *barter, Mir.Artem.*18(p.23.8).

σημάδιον, τό, *pledge, security* τοὺς...σημαδαρίους ἐκέλευσεν ἐνεχθῆναι τὰς ὁμολογίας τῶν χρεωστούντων καὶ τὰ σ. Thphn.*chron.* p.205(M.108.528A).

σημαία, ἡ, = σημεία, *standard, A.Pil.*B 1.5(p.291); Jo.VI H. *v.Jo.D.*5(M.94.437A).

σημαίνω, 1. *give a signal for* ὥραν λειτουργικὴν...σ. Thdr.Stud. *poen.*1.100(M.99.1745D); hence, *sound* the gong (sc. for prayers) σ. ...τὰ ξύλα *Const.Stud.*2(M.99.1704D); **2.** *reproduce, render,* by copying or translation, cf.Aristeas ap.Eus.*p.e.*8.3(351B; M.21.589B); **3.** ptcpl. pass. neut., *meaning;* true or inner meaning, opp. λέξις, Clem.*str.*6.17(p.510.3; M.9.381C); *ib.*7.16(p.68.13; 533B).

σημαιοφόρος, ὁ, v. σημειοφόρος.

σημαντήρ, ὁ, 1. *signet* ring, Clem.*paed.*3.11(pp.269.24,270.6; M.8.632C,633A); *seal,* ‡Nil.*perist.*5.2(M.79.852C); **2.** *one who gives a signal, starter* in stadium, Thdt.*rect.conf.*13(M.6.1232C); **3.** *herald, preacher,* Ph.Carp.*Cant.*78(M.40.80B).

σημαντήριον, τό, *that which summons* to prayer, *gong* τὸ σ. αἰνίττεται τὰς τῶν ἀγγέλων σάλπιγγας ‡Sophr.H.*liturg.*5(M.87.3985B); cf. χάριν μὲν τῶν...ψαλμῶν τοῦ θεοπάτορος...μετακαλοῦνται οἱ μοναχοὶ διὰ σ. μικροῦ...χάριν δὲ τῆς τῶν εὐαγγελίων ἀνακηρύξεως...τὸ μέγα σ. εὕρηται...τετύπωται γοῦν, διὰ σ. χαλκοῦ, περὶ τῆς τελευταίας ἡμέρας... τοὺς χριστωνύμους ὑπομιμνήσκεσθαι Theodorus Balsamon *jus canonicum* (M.119.1224A).

σημαντικός, 1. *significant* of, *denoting,* Just.*1apol.*63.17(M.6.425B); Alex.Al.*ep.Alex.*9(p.25.21; M.18.561B); δυνάμεως δὲ σ. τὸ κέρας Cyr.*Abac.*41(3.556B); ὑπόστασις...καὶ τὸ ταύτης σ. πρόσωπον Leont.H.*Nest.*2.16(M.86.1573A); not adequate description of Logos, ‡Ath.*Ar.*4.1(p.44.18; M.26.468C) cit. s. οὐσιώδης; **2.** mythological, astrol., *portentous, indicative,* cf.Diodorus Siculus ap.Eus.*p.e.*2.2(54C; M.21.108D); of stars οὐκ αἴτια γενέσεως, σ. δὲ τῶν γινομένων Clem.*ecl.*55(p.152.15; M.9.724B); opp. ποιητικός, Or.*comm.in Gen.*ap. Eus.*p.e.*6.11(292D; M.12.73C); Proc.G.*Gen.*1:14(M.87.96A); **3.** neut. as subst., *name, title,* Athenag.*leg.*23.5(M.6.944C).

σήμαντρον, τό, 1. *mark, sign,* Gr.Nyss.*Eun.*12(1 p.262.6; M.45.965C); Jo.Mosch.*prat.*43(M.87.2897C); †Jo.D.*B.J.*22(M.96.1061B); of military distinction, Cyr.*ador.*6(1.176D); of sign of cross, Max. *ambig.*(M.91.1284C); **2.** *seal,* Thdt.*h.e.*3.26.2(3.943); Isid.Pel.*epp.*1.319(M.78.368A); on sepulchre, Jo.D.*carm.pasch.*64(p.220; M.96.841C); met., of seal of baptism, Didym.*Trin.*2.15(M.39.717A); *ib.* 3.2(805A); of perpetual virginity of BMV, Thdt.*ep.*145(4.1254); **3.** *gong* (as signal for prayer), *Nomoc.*409; *Ep.Chr.dom.*(p.26).

σημασία, ἡ, 1. *signal,* Clem.*paed.*2.7(p.193.6; M.8.464B); Bas. *ascet.*2(2.326A; M.31.885D); as a summons, *Pss.Sal.*11.1; Thdr.Mops. *Joel* 2:1(M.66.220A); to battle, Cyr.*ador.*4(1.121A); Thdt.*qu.15 in Num.*(1.230); id.*1Cor.*14:9f.(3.258); to prayer, *Const.Stud.*2(M.99.1704C); **2.** *meaning, signification;* hence *significance* of types and symbols, Ph.Carp.*Cant.*186(M.40.120A); Thdr.Mops.*Rom.*7:5(p.125.2; M.66.805D); Nil.*epp.*1.243(M.79.172B); **3.** *mark, symptom* of disease, Gr.Nyss.*Eun.*1(1 p.53.20; M.45.281C); met., of sin, Meth. *lepr.*6(p.458.21).

***σημειογραφεῖον, τό,** *office, secretariate,* Anast.S.*hod.*10(M.89.188D).

***σημειογραφικός,** *of a writer of shorthand,* †Bas.Anc.*virg.*31(M.30.733A).

σημειογράφος, ὁ, *shorthand writer,* Jo.Mosch.*prat.*197(M.87.3085A).

σημειολύτης, ὁ, *interpreter of portents, Pers.*(p.13.24; M.10.101C).

σημεῖον, τό, 1. *characteristic mark, hall-mark,* defined σ. ... ἐστι τὰ κατὰ διαφορὰν προσαγόμενα τῷ ὅρῳ οἰκείων πραγμάτων· τὴν δὲ φύσιν αὐτῶν πραγμάτων οὐκ ἐνδείκνυται Clem.*str.*8.6(p.93.1; M.9.585C); *landmark, boundary, Apoc.Bar.rel.*5.12; Cyr.*Ps.*36:22(M.69.940B); **2.** measure; **a.** of distance, *mile,* ‡Just.*coh.Gr.*37(M.6.308A); Epiph.*haer.*59.12(p.377.11; M.41.1036B); Socr.*h.e.*6.6.23(M.67.680A); **b.** of position, of degree of celestial bodies, Arist.*apol.*4.2; 6.1,3; point of the compass (astrol.) σ. δ', ἀνατολικόν, δυτικόν, μεσημβρινόν, μεσουράνημα Anat.Laod.*decad.*(p.32); ref. signs of the zodiac, cf.*Clem.recogn.*9.26(M.1.1414A); **3.** mathematical *point* σ. ἀμερές Clem.*str.*6.11(p.477.18; M.9.312B); *ib.*5.11(p.374.9; 109A); ἀδύνατον...χωρὶς σ. καταγραφῆναι κύκλον Meth.*symp.*8.14(p.100.9; M.18.164A); Dion.Ar.*d.n.*5.6(M.3.821A); **4.** *standard, flag,* Eus. *v.C.*3.60(p.108.26; M.20.1133A); Chrys.*hom.3.1 in 1Tim.*(11.562D); *Chron.Pasch.*p.299(M.92.752B); **5.** *sign;* **a.** indicating presence or truth of some other thing, *evidence, indication,* Athenag.*leg.*7.1(M.6.904B); Clem.*ecl.*5(p.138.15; M.9.700D); σ. ... καὶ μέγα γνώρισμα τῆς τοῦ θεοῦ λόγου παρουσίας τὸ μηκέτι μήτε τὴν Ἱερουσαλὴμ ἑστάναι, μήτε προφήτην ἐγερθῆναι Ath.*inc.*40.1(M.25.165A); id.*h.Ar. ep.*3(p.182.19; M.25.693C); οὐκ ἐπειδὴ τὸ ἔργον τῆς περιτομῆς ἀναγκαῖον, ἀλλ' ὅτι ἡ διαθήκη ἀθετεῖται τοῦ σημείου, δι' οὗ ἐγνωρίζετο, μὴ πληρουμένου Diod.*Gen.*17:14(M.33.1573C); *Const.App.*3.2.2; closely related to but dist. from αἴτιον, Clem.*paed.*3.11(p.268.3; M.8.628C); id.*str.*7.4(p.17.7; M.9.429A); ἅμα δὲ καὶ καθολικόν τι μανθάνομεν, ὅτι, εἴπερ τὸ σ. σημαίνει τι, ἕκαστον τῶν ἀναγεγραμμένων σ. (εἴτε ὡς ἐν γενομένῃ ἱστορίᾳ εἴτε ὡς ἐντολῇ) δηλωτικόν τινός ἐστιν ὕστερον πληρουμένου Or.*comm.in Mt.*12.3(p.73.11; M.13.980D); **b.** *letter* of alphabet, Mac.Aeg.*hom.*15.42(M.34.604C); plur., *shorthand outlines, notes,* Epiph.*exp.fid.*25(p.526.5; M.42.832C); Chrys.*homm.in Heb.*tit.(12.1); Marc.Diac.*v.Porph.*88; **c.** symbolic of some other thing, past, present, or future, *symbol;* defined κυρίως σημεῖον ἔγνωμεν παρὰ τῇ γραφῇ τὸν σταυρὸν εἰρημένον...ἢ σημεῖόν ἐστι τὸ παραδόξου τινὸς καὶ ἀφανοῦς πράγματος ἐνδεικτικόν· ὁρώμενον μὲν παρὰ τῶν ἁπλουστέρων, νοούμενον δὲ παρὰ τῶν ἐντρεχῶν τὴν διάνοιαν Bas.*ep.*260.8(3.400C; M.32.965B); in gen., *1Clem.*12.7; *Did.*16.6; Or.*Jo.*1.26(24; p.32.33; M.14.72A); Hegem.*Arch.*7(p.11.2; M.10.1437B); esp. of the Cross, *Barn.*12.4; Just.*dial.*94.1(M.6.700B); τοῦ...κυριακοῦ σ. Clem. *str.*6.11(p.473.25; M.9.305A); Meth.*Porph.*1(p.504.31; M.18.400C); of sign of the cross (gesture), Eus.*v.C.*3.2(p.78.6; M.20.1056C); Ath. *gent.*1(M.25.5A); Cyr.H.*catech.*4.14; Chrys.*hom.87.3 in Mt.*(7.822A); in baptism, Ath.*inc.*29.4(M.25.145D); Eus.*d.e.*6.25(p.295.3; M.22.484D); Serap.*euch.*25.2; cf.Cyr.H.*catech.*12.8; **d.** *wonder, portent, Hom.Clem.*2.34; Juln.Imp.*ep.*12(p.15.10); **6.** *miracle,* esp. ref. its appeal to the intelligence to discern its significance; thus dist. from τέρας; **a.** its nature: attempts to find difference in kind (not merely in point of view) between τέρας and σ.: acc. Origen σ. does not of itself denote anything extraordinary and therefore to evoke faith a σ. must also be a τέρας, *Jo.*13.64(60; pp.296.24, 297.4; M.14.521B,C); other writers understand by σ. an act whose effect is not in itself beyond nature, though means by which it has been brought about are miraculous; by τέρας (or θαῦμα) that which it is altogether beyond powers of nature to accomplish, Didym. *Ac.*9:33(M.39.1673B); Ammon.*Jo.*4:48(M.85.1428C); Thdot.Anc. *hom.*2.4(M.77.1373C,D); present and evident to senses, though its hidden significance may be past, present, or future, †Bas.*Is.*198(1.527A–C; M.30.460B); a marvel outside ordinary experience, *ib.*201(528E; M.464B); Proc.G.*Gen.*9:13(M.87.300C); with beneficent purpose, Or.*hom.29 in Lc.*(p.183.16); **b.** application of term: to OT miracles, Clem.*prot.*1(p.8.18; M.8.64C); to miracles of Christ, Or. *Jo.*28.12(11; p.403.33; M.14.705B); Ath.*inc.*16.4(M.25.124C); and of apostles, Chrys.*hom.1.4 in Ac.*(9.7A); to eccl. miracles, Clem.*exc. Thdot.*24(p.115.5; M.9.672A); Ath.*v.Anton.*57(M.26.925B); Leont.N. *v.Jo.Eleem.*45(p.94.16); **c.** purpose: to lead men to salvation, Clem. *str.*5.3(p.444.12; M.9.244C); of Christ's miracles, to manifest divinity, Mel.*fr.*6(p.310; M.5.1221A); Anast.S.*hod.*14(M.89.249B); in apostolic times, to induce faith among unbelievers and, as such, not necessary for faithful, Chrys.*hom.12.3 in Mt.*(7.163D); id.*pent.*1.4(2.464A); id.*hom.24.1 in Jo.*(8.138B).

***σημειοποιΐα, ἡ,** *doing of wondrous works, working of miracles,* Anast.S.*hod.*14(M.89.249C).

***σημειουργός, ὁ,** *worker of miracles, Hymn.*(*AS* 1 p.610).

σημειοφόρος (σημαιο-), ὁ, 1. *standard-bearer, ensign,* Chrys.*comm. in Gal.*6:17(10.729D); σημαιο-, Synes.*regn.*9(p.27.7; M.66.1073D); met., of David ὁ τῆς παλαιᾶς καὶ νέας διαθήκης σ. *T.Sal.*D 1.2; of Jews τῆς ματαιότητος σημειοφόροι Ephr.3.174D; of Christians, Chrys. *laud.Paul.*7(2.513A); *confessor* for Faith, of fathers of Nicaea ἐν οἷς πλεῖστοι μὲν γεγόνασι Χριστοῦ μάρτυρες, πλεῖστοι δὲ σ. Anast.S.*hod.* 8(M.89.140C); **2.** *worker of miracles,* ‡Ath.*doct.Ant.*89(M.28.653A); ‡Tit.Bost.*palm.*2(M.18.1256D); *Apophth.Patr.*(M.65.160A); Gr.Mag. *dial.*(tr.Zach.)1.3(M.*PL*.77.166A); †Anast.S.*relat.*55(*OC* 3 p.82.2); Thphn.*chron.*p.96(M.108.284C); σιμαιο-, *MAMA* 3.147.

***σημειόχριστος,** *marked with the sign of Christ,* i.e. of the cross; of the crown of the Christian's reward, Agath.*v.Gr.Ill.*163(p.83); of persons in baptism σ. πάντας πεποιηκώς, καὶ πνευματοφόρους *ib.*152(p.77).

σημειόω, [variant pass. ptcpl. σημειόμενος in *T.Sal.*12.3(p.42.2)]; **A.** *mark, seal,* ref. Ex.34:30 ἐσημειώθη...ἐπ' αὐτὸν τὸ φῶς τοῦ προσώπου κυρίου Ath.*inc.et c.Ar.*15(M.26.1009B); Chrys.*exp.in Ps.* 4:7(5.21C); in baptism, Bas.*hom.*13.4(2.117B; M.31.432C); Jo.Ant. *ep.pop.CP*(p.128.33; H.1.1461D); Const.Diac.*laud.*37(M.88.521C);

sign with sign of the cross, Ephr.3.136A; Niceph.Ur.*v.Sym.*24(M.86.3008C).

B. med.; **1.** *record, note down, 1Clem.*43.1; Eus.*h.e.*6.16.3(M.20.556A); Leont.N.*v.Jo.Eleem.*1(p.7.17); *point out* in writing, Or.*Jo.*32.5(p.434.4; M.14.753C); Eus.*d.e.*2.3(p.67.5; M.22.121C); *signify* in writing, Eus.*p.e.*11.6(519D; M.21.861B); **2.** *take note of*, Clem.*str.*6.15(p.497.34; M.9.356A); Ath.*v.Anton.*4,60(M.26.845B,932A).

σημείωσις, ἡ, 1. *sign, indication*; of Lot's wife, *1Clem.*11.2; provided by luminaries, Bas.*hex.*6.4(1.53B; M.29.125A); written *sign*; of the tetragrammaton, Eus.*p.e.*11.12(530A; M.21.880B); of the obelus, Epiph.*mens.*7(M.43.248A); **2.** written *observation, comment*, Or.*Jo.*10.12(10; p.182.31; M.14.328A); Eus.*h.e.*5.20.2(M.20.484B); Gr. II Papa *conf.*(M.91.1024B); **3.** *signature*; *signed rescript*, Eus.*h.e.*5.19.4(M.20.484A); Philost.*h.e.*12.7(M.65.616A); **4.** *observation* of symptoms; *diagnosis*, Bas.*reg.br.*301(2.521D; M.31.1296A); **5.** *ostentation, Pss.Sal.*4.2.

σημειωτικός, *indicative, significant* τὰ σ. τῶν πραγμάτων ὀνόματα Gr.Nyss.*Eun.*12(1 p.296.15; M.45.1005D).

σήμερον, 1. *today*; hence *at the present time, now*, Athenag.*leg.*2.1(M.6.893B); *T.Sal.*5.4; *ib.*24.3(M.122.1356B); Bas.*hom.*13.6(2.119D; M.31.437B); Chrys.*hom.33.2 in Heb.*(12.303D); Cyr.*Heb.*13:8(p.417.19; M.74.997D); Thdt.*Heb.*3:13(3.565); Christol. χθὲς γὰρ καὶ σ. τὴν ἀνθρωπείαν ἐκάλεσε φύσιν· αἰώνιον δὲ τὴν θεότητα προσηγόρευσε *ib.* 13:8(3.633); **2.** *in this present life, this age*, Or.*Jo.*32.32(19; p.480.5; M.14.828C); id.*or.*27.13(p.372.11; M.11.517A); Cyr.ap.*cat.Heb.*suppl. 3:13(p.447.24); **3.** *in eternity, eternally*, ref. Ps.2:7 ὁ ἀεί, ⟨ὁ⟩ σ. υἱὸς λογισθείς ‡*Diogn.*11.5; exeg. Ps.94:8, Clem.*prot.*9(p.64.1ff.; M.8.196Cff.).

σημικίνθιον, τό, v. σιμικίνθιον.

[*]**σημίσ(σ)ι(ο)ν, τό,** = σιμίσιον, (cf. Lat. *semis*) *half a gold solidus, Mir.Artem.*23(p.32.26); Thphn.*chron.*pp.352,374(M.108.845B, 896B); σημισσ-, Cyr.S.*v.Sab.*31(p.116.13f.).

σηπεδών, ἡ, *putrefaction, decay*; met. τῆς ἁμαρτίας ἡ σ. Chrys.*hom.73.3 in Jo.*(8.433B); τῇ Μαρκίωνος σ. Thdt.*ep.*145(4.1246).

***σηπιώδης,** *like the cuttle-fish*, Gr.Naz.*carm.*2.1.11.1199(M.37.1111A).

σήπω, [irreg. aor. v. infra 2; aor. pass. ἐσήφθεν †Apoll.*met.Ps.*37:6(M.33.1364C)]; **1.** trans.; *make rotten* or *putrid*; met., *corrupt*; perf. ptcpl. pass. as abusive epithet, *filthy* γραῶν σαπεισῶν μασώμενοι ῥήματα Mac.Mgn.*apocr.*3.14(p.91.3); **2.** intrans. in pass. and perf. act.; also in aor. act. οὐκ ἐφλέγμανεν, οὐκ ἔσεψεν, οὐκ ἐπυρομάχησε *Exorc.*(p.334).

σήρ, ὁ, plur., *silks* σ. Ἰνδικούς Clem.*paed.*2.10(p.221.15; M.8.525A); ἐκ λίνου καὶ σ. Gr.Naz.*or.*14.16(M.35.877A).

***σηραγγοειδής,** = σηραγγώδης, *cavernous, hollowed out*; of the nostrils, Thdt.*provid.*3(4.528).

σηρικός, 1. *silk, silken*; **2.** ? variant of συρικός; neut., *red pigment* διὰ συρικοῦ γεγραμμέναι Max.*comput.*3f.(M.19.1221C) but cf. *Sericum lana est quam Seres mittunt; Syricum vero pigmentum quod Syrii Phoenices in Rubri maris litoribus colligunt*, Isid.H.*etym.*19.17.6.

σητόβρωτος, *moth-eaten, Orac.Sib.fr.*3.26; Chrys.*hom.27.3 in Jo.*(8.157D); *ib.59.4*(350C).

***σητοτρόφος, ὁ,** *moth-feeder*; of one who collects books without reading them, Isid.Pel.*epp.*1.127(M.78.268B).

***σηφικάριος, ὁ,** f.l. for σηρικάριος, *silk-worker*, Ephr.2.176C.

σῆψις, ἡ, *putrefaction, rottenness*, met. ὁ διάβολος τὴν ἰδίαν ἀπομάσσεται σ. Gr.Nyss.*hom.in 1Cor.6:18*(M.46.493B); s.v.l., colloquial, *rotten job*, i.e. hard, uncongenial, or unpleasant task, Pall. *h.Laus.*22(p.71.16; κόπον M.34.1081C).

σθενόω, *strengthen*, Gr.Naz.*or.*42.10(M.36.469C).

σιαίνω, A. act.; **1.** *annoy, provoke, V.Dan.*(p.50.5); Dor.*doct.*7.1(M.88.1697B); *trouble, bother*, Leont.N.*v.Sym.*53(M.93.1736A); **2.** *destroy* τοὺς οἴκους...ἐσίαναν *Didasc.Jac.*4.7(p.69.6).

B. pass.; **1.** *be troubled, disturbed* in mind, Pall.*h.Laus.*24(p.78.10); Jo.Mosch.*prat.*205(M.87.3096C); †Anast.S.*relat.*28(*OC* 2 p.76.28); **2.** *feel loathing, be disgusted*, Pall.*h.Laus.*35(p.102.16; M.34.1113D); *V.Aberc.*57(p.41.5); **3.** *be weary, tire* ἐσιάνθην ἐκ τῆς ὁδοῦ Gr.Mag.*dial.*(tr.Zach.)1.4(M.*PL.*77.174C).

σιαλίζω, *slaver, foam at the mouth*; met., of the sea, ‡Caes.Naz.*dial.*156(M.38.1112).

σιάλωμα, τό, *setting* of precious stones, Nil.*spir.mal.*19(M.79.1164C).

[*]**σιβίνινος,** v. σεβένινος.

[*]**σίβινον, τό,** = σεβένιον, *palm-fibre*, Ephr.2.176B; ἀπὸ σ. κολόβιον Jo.Mosch.*prat.*123(M.87.2985A); as adj., v. σεβένινος.

***σίβυνος,** *of* or *pertaining to a* σιβύνη, *hunting spear, V.Dan.*(p.55.22).

***σιγαλέως,** *silently*, Eudoc.*Cypr.*1.251(M.85.841B).

σιγγουλάριοι, (Lat. *singulares*) *orderlies* on governor's staff, *M.Con.*1.3.

σιγερός, v. σιγηρός.

σιγή, ἡ, *silence*; **1.** from speech: a virtue in woman, *1Clem.*21.7; Clem.*paed.*2.7(p.192.5; M.8.461B); observed by Christ at trial, Just.*dial.*103.9(M.6.720A); does not preclude prayer, Clem.*str.*7.7(p.30.17; M.9.456B); **2.** ref. adoration and contemplation τὸν πατέρα τῶν ὅλων...σεβάσματι δὲ καὶ σ. ... σεβαστὸν καὶ σεπτὸν κυριώτατα Clem. *paed.*2.7(p.192.5; M.8.461B); Or.*schol.in Cant.*4:3(M.17.272A); τὴν ὑπὲρ ἡμᾶς κρυφιότητα σιγῇ τιμήσαντες Dion.Ar.*c.h.*15.9(M.3.340B); σιγῇ τιμῶσα τὸν λόγον, οὗτινος τῇ φύσει τῶν ὄντων ἐμπέφυκε λόγος οὐδείς Max.*ambig.*(M.91.1057A); cf. εὐχαριστῶ σοι οὐκ ἐν χείλεσι τούτοις...ἀλλ'...τῇ διὰ σιγῆς νοουμένῃ...σιγῇ φωνῆς, ᾗ τὸ ἐν ἐμοὶ πνεῦμα σὲ φιλοῦν καὶ σοὶ λαλοῦν καὶ σὲ ὁρῶν ἐντυγχάνει *A.Petr.c.Sim.* 10(pp.96.17,98.1); **3.** as absence of revelation ὅς ἐστιν αὐτοῦ λόγος ἀπὸ σ. προελθών Ign.*Magn.*8.2; Athenag.*res.*19(p.71.30; M.6.1012C); Just.Gn.ap.Hipp.*haer.*5.24(p.125.29; M.16.3191C); cf.Tert.*adversus Praxeam* 5(M.*PL.*2.160Bf.); **4.** of inexpressible Godhead εἰκών ἐστι τοῦ θεοῦ ὁ ἄγγελος...ἔσοπτρον...ἀμιγῶς ἀναλάμπον ἐν ἑαυτῷ...τὴν ἀγαθότητα τῆς ἐν ἀδύτοις σ. Dion.Ar.*d.n.*4.22(M.3.724B); τῆς θεολογίας μυστήρια, κατὰ τὸν ὑπέρφωτον ἐγκεκάλυπται τῆς κρυφιομύστου σ. γνόφον id.*myst.*1.1(M.3.997B); τὴν ἐν ἀδύτοις πολυύμνητον τῆς ἀφανοῦς καὶ ἀγνώστου μεγαλοφωνίας σιγὴν τῆς θεότητος, δι' ἄλλης λάλου τε καὶ πολυφθόγγου σ. προσκαλούμενον Max.*myst.*4(M.91.672C); **5.** Gnost. aeon δύο εἰσὶ παραφυάδες τῶν ὅλων αἰώνων...ἀπὸ μιᾶς ῥίζης ἥτις ἐστὶ δύναμις Σ. ἀόρατος, ἀκατάληπτος Simon ap.Hipp.*haer.*6.18(p.144.13; M.16.3222A); Valent., counterpart of Βυθός, the primary aeon, Iren. *haer.*1.1.1(M.7.445A,B); cf. *Monogenem ex patre Bytho et matre Sige*, Tert.*de anima* 12(M.*PL.*2.666A); οἱ μὲν γὰρ αὐτῶν μόνον εἶναι [sc. τὴν τοῦ παντὸς ἀρχὴν πατέρα] καὶ γεννητικόν, οἱ δὲ ἀδυνάτως ἔχειν γεννᾶν ἄνευ θηλείας καὶ τούτου σύζυγον προστιθέασι Σιγήν Hipp.*haer.* 10.13(p.273.27ff.; 3427A); *ib.*6.29(p.156.4f.; 3235C); Marcosian, Iren. *haer.*1.13.6(589A); Thdt.*haer.*1.9(4.301); primacy of Βυθός and Σιγή disputed, Iren.*haer.*1.11.5(569A); as mother of all, acc. Heracleon emanating from Βυθός, Epiph.*haer.*36.2(p.45.15; M.41.633D).

σιγηρός (σιγε-), *silent*; of persons, Hipp.*haer.*4.25(p.53.10; M.16 3087C); σιγε-, *Mir.Artem.*37(p.60.2).

***σίγησις, ἡ,** *silence*, Gr.Mag.*dial.*(tr.Zach.)2.38(M.*PL.*66.203C).

***σιγίλλι(ο)ν, τό,** *pact, treaty, Chron.Pasch.*p.394(M.92.1012A); Thphn.*chron.*p.422(M.108.997B).

***σιγιλλιών, ὁ,** (Lat. *singilio*) *plain* or *short garment*, Gr.Naz.*test.*(M.37.393B).

σιγιστροπύλη, ἡ, prob. *portière curtain* hanging by hooks from rings (method by which veil of Temple was suspended), Cosm.Ind. *top.*5(M.88.205A).

σίγλος, v. σίκλος.

[*]**σίγνιφερ, ὁ,** v. σιγνοφόρος.

σίγνον, τό, (Lat. *signum*), **1.** *standard, ensign*, Ath.*exp.Ps.*73:5(M.27.333B); Chrys.*cruc.*1.4(2.408B); Jo.Mal.*chron.*13 p.316(M.97.476A); Jo.Mosch.*prat.*73(M.87.2925C); hence, plur., of that part of the camp where standards were set up, used as guard-room for prisoners, *PLond.*1914.18; αἶρε αὐτόν,...τουτέστιν, ἐκ τῶν ζώντων ποίησον ἀφανῆ. τινὲς δέ, ὃ παρ' ἡμῖν λέγουσι κατὰ τὴν Ῥωμαϊκὴν συνήθειαν, ἐν τοῖς σ. αὐτὸν ἔμβαλε, τοῦτο εἶναι τό, αἶρε αὐτόν Chrys. *hom.46.2 in Ac.*(9.347B); **2.** *signal, M.Apollon.*45; **3.** *insignia*, Jo. Mal.*chron.*18 p.475(M.97.692A); met., of *seal* imprinted on Christian soul, Mac.Aeg.*hom.*30.5(M.34.724D); *ib.*38.1(757D).

σιγνοφόρος, [*]**σίγνιφερ, ὁ,** (Lat. *signifer*) *standard-bearer, A.Pil.* A 1.5(p.220); σίγνιφερ *MAMA* 1.169b.

***σιγνοφύλαξ, ὁ,** *keeper of the colours*, Anast.Ap.*a.Max.*2.31(M.90.168C).

***σιγνόχριστον, τό,** *cross* on gable of a building, *Chron.Pasch.* p.308(M.92.784B).

***σιδηραγωγέω,** *attract iron, be magnetic*, Hipp.*haer.*4.39(p.63.24; M.16.3103A).

***σιδηραῖος,** = σιδήρεος, *made of iron, iron*, Cyr.H.*catech.*16.19.

***σιδηράμφιος,** *iron-clad*, ‡Caes.Naz.*dial.*125(M.38.1020).

σιδήριον, τό, A. iron tool, weapon, or instrument; **1.** surgeon's *knife*, Or.*hom.20.3 in Jer.*(p.180.14; M.13.505A); iron weapon, Synes.*ep.*108(M.66.1489C); sword-*blade*, Thdt.*qu.9 in Jud.*(1.329); **2.** *fetter*, Chrys.*hom.8.3 in Eph.*(11.56C); *ib.*8.7(64B).

B. ? *jamb* of window σ. τῆς...θυρίδος Cyr.S.*v.Sab.*86(p.194.10).

***σιδηροδέσμιος,** *enchained, fettered in irons, A.Petr.et Paul.*80

(p.213.7,10); ‡Ath.*doct.Ant.*20(M.28.585B); Socr.*h.e.*1.28.3(M.67.160A).

σιδηροδέσμος, = foreg., ‡Epiph.*hom.*3(M.43.473D); Socr.*h.e.*2.42.5(M.67.352A).

***σιδηροδεσμώτης, ὁ,** *prisoner in chains*, Soz.*h.e.*2.9.3(M.67.956C).

σιδηροθήκη, ἡ, ? *surgical instrument case* τὸν Ἀσκληπιὸν τὸν ἐν τῷ νάρθηκι πολλὰ καὶ τῇ σ. περινοστήσαντα Ast.Am.*hom.*10(M.40.324C).

σιδηροκατάδικος, (of eunuchs) *condemned to mutilation*, Bas.*ep.*115(3.208B; M.32.532A); Pall.*v.Chrys.*15(p.92.14; M.47.52); Cyr.*hom. div.*19(M.77.1109B).

σιδηροκόπος, ὁ, *iron-forger, smith*, Chrys.*hom.10.4 in 1Cor.*(10.85E).

σιδηροπέδη, ἡ, *iron fetter*, †Jo.D.*B.J.*2(M.96.872A).

σίδηρος, ὁ, *iron*, in simile of iron made red-hot by fire as illustrating **1.** closeness of union of divine and human natures in Christ, Or.*princ.*2.6.6(p.145.9; M.11.213D); **2.** distinction of his σῶμα and his divinity despite their union, Apoll.*fr.*128(p.238.26)ap. Thdt.*eran.*2(4.171); Cyr.*Lc.*22:19(M.72.909B); id.*Chr.un.*(5^1.776B); Thdt.*eran.*2(4.116); Jo.D.*Jacob.*52(M.94.1461C).

***σιδηρόστομος,** *hard-mouthed*; of a horse, Epiph.*haer.*76.37(p.388.12; M.42.593A).

σιδηροφορέω, *wear fetters*, Pall.*h.Laus.*44(p.131.12; M.34.1209C).

***σιδηροφορία, ἡ,** *enchainment*, Pall.*h.Laus.*45(p.133.3; M.34.1217C).

σιδηροφόρος, **1.** *productive of iron*, Bas.*ep.*110(3.203B; M.32.520C); **2.** *covered with iron*; hence *made of iron* σ. ... γόμφων Nonn. *par.Jo.*19:15(M.43.900C).

σιδηρ-όω, A. *put in fetters, fetter*, Ath.*h.Ar.*70(p.221.26; M.25.777A); Chrys.*hom.14.4 in Mt.*(7.183D); Pall.*h.Laus.*25(p.80.12); *ib.* 26(p.81.10; M.34.1091C); Thphn.*chron.*p.134(M.108.368B).

B. *cover with iron*; hence **1.** *cover with mail, clothe in armour*, Leont.H.*Nest.*4.36(M.86.1704D); **2.** *make into iron* ἡ μὲν φύσις τῆς σαρκὸς θεοῦται, οὐ σαρκοῖ δὲ τὴν φύσιν τοῦ λόγου...ὡς...ὁ σίδηρος [i.e. in the fire] μὲν πυροῦται, τὸ δὲ πῦρ οὐ ~οῦται Jo.D.*Jacob.*52(M.94.1461C); **3.** *strengthen* ὁ θεῖος φόβος ~ῶν...τὰς σαρκὰς ἡμῶν Thdr. Stud.*epp.*2.8(M.99.1137B).

σιδήρωσις, ἡ, *enchainment*, Thdr.Stud.*epp.*2.12(M.99.1152D); *ib.* 2.203(1620A).

***σιελίτης,** *salivary*, Melet.*nat.hom.*30(M.64.1276B).

σίελος (σίαλος), ὁ, *spittle, saliva*, Or.*fr.63 in Jo.*(pp.533.32,534.5); Adam.*dial.*5.17(p.210.16; M.11.1857A); Thdt.*haer.*5.1(4.380); σίαλ- *T.Sal.*17.3(p.50.10; στέλους, M.122.1341A).

***σίκαλος,** sens. dub. ? *noose, thong* σικάλοις ἐνεσφιγμένον [sc. lion's prey] Cyr.*Soph.*29(3.606E).

σικάριος, ὁ, (Lat.) *Sicarius*, member of Jewish nationalist party of desperadoes, so called from wearing a short, curved dagger (*sica*), a branch of Zealots; identified with a sect of Essenes, Hipp. *haer.*9.26(p.260.15; M.16.3403B); Chrys.*hom.46.3 in Ac.*(9.348D); with whom were associated religious fanatics, Isid.Pel.*epp.*3.119 (M.78.824A); also of Samaritans punished under Lex Cornelia de sicariis for practising circumcision, Or.*Cels.*2.13(p.142.11; M.11.821A).

σίκερα, τό, (Hebr. שֵׁכָר) *strong drink*, def. σ. γὰρ πᾶς ὁ σκευαστὸς οἶνος καλεῖται καὶ νόθος, κἂν τε ἐκ τῶν φοινίκων καὶ ἐκ τῶν ἄλλων ἀκροδρύων σκευαζόμενος ᾖ Meth.*symp.*5.6(p.60.7; M.18.108A); Thdt. *Is.*5:11(p.26.8f.; 2.200f.) cit. s. πρόπομα; in gen. contexts, *T.Reub.* 1.10; Bardesanes ap.Eus.*p.e.*6.10(274C; M.21.465B); οἴνου καὶ σικέρατος...μακράν Cyr.*ador.*16(1.577E); plur. σίκερα *Can.App.*2; Procl.CP *or.*6.5(M.65.729A).

***σικεροποτέω,** *drink strong liquor*, ‡Caes.Naz.*dial.*109(M.38.984).

***σικεροπότης, ὁ,** *drinker of strong liquor*, ‡Caes.Naz.*dial.*85(M.38.952).

***σικιννίζω,** *dance the* sicinnis (a dance of the satyric drama), Clem.*paed.*1.7(p.122.33; M.8.316A).

***σίκιννος,** sens. dub. ? *outlandish* ὄρνεις Ἰνδικοὺς...ἐκτρέφουσιν... σικίννοις τέρασι γανύμεναι Clem.*paed.*3.4(p.253.22; M.8.597A).

[*]**σίκλα, ἡ,** v. σίτλα.

σίκλος (σίγλος), ὁ, τό, Hebrew weight and coin, *shekel*, *T.Sal.* 10.9(M.122.1332C); *ib.*21.1(1352A); Bas.*hom.in Ps.*32(1.138D; M.29.340C); ἐπὶ δὲ σταθμοῦ ὁ σ. λαμβανόμενος, ἡμιούγκιον εἷλκεν Thdt.*qu.* *29 in 1Reg.*13:19ff.(1.374); neut., ‡Just.*qu.et resp.*86(M.6.1328B); σ. ὃ λέγεται καὶ κοδράντης, τέταρτον μὲν ἔστι τῆς οὐγγίας, ἥμισυ δὲ τοῦ στατῆρος, δύο δραγμὰς ἔχον Epiph.*mens.*24(M.43.285A); cf.Thdt. supra.

[*]**σικόω,** v. σηκόω.

***σικριτάριον, τό,** (Lat. *secretarium*) *court-room*, enclosed, and sometimes private, place of session of a law-court, *M.Eupl.*1.1; cf. σήκρητον.

σικύδι(ο)ν, τό, *cucumber*, *Apophth.Patr.*(M.65.177B).

σικυήλατον (σικυήρ-), τό, *cucumber-bed*, Cyr.H.*catech.*16.18(v.l. σικυήρα-); Epiph.*haer.*52.1(p.311.15); *Apophth.Patr.*(M.65.177B); σικυηράτων ‡Caes.Naz.*dial.*148(M.38.1100).

***σικυηρά,** vox nihili, Epiph.*haer.*52.1(M.41.953D; σικυήλατα p.311.15).

σικυήρατον, τό, v. σικυήλατον.

***σιλεντιακῶς,** *in the manner of an allocution*, Thphn.*chron.*p.421 (M.108.996D).

***σιλεντιαρίκι(ο)ν (*σελ-), τό,** *antechamber* in palace where σιλεντιάριοι were stationed, Cyr.S.*v.Sab.*51(p.142.4); σελεντιαρίκιν Thphn.*chron.*p.201(M.108.517C).

***σιλέντιον (*σελ-), τό,** (Lat. *silentium*) *reception* by emperor, *audience*, σελέντιον †Gregent.*disp.*(M.86.749A); Jo.Mal.*chron.*18 p.494(M.97.713C); Thphn.*chron.*p.208(M.108.533B); met., of Transfiguration, ‡Caes.Naz.*dial.*188(M.38.1149).

σιλίγνιον, τό, *bread* made from fine wheaten flour (*siligo*), Pall.*h. Laus.*13(p.37.6; M.34.1035C); Dor.*doct.*7.3(M.88.1700C); Leont.N.*v. Sym.*39(M.93.1717C).

***σίλιξ, ὁ,** (Lat. *silex*) *flint stone, rock*, *A.Petr.et Paul.*77(p.211.11).

[*]**σιμαιοφόρος, ὁ,** v. σημειοφόρος.

σιμικίνθιον (σημικίνθιον), τό, (Lat. *semicinctium*) *apron*, Chrys. *sac.*4.6(p.118.7; 1.411A); Leont.B.*mesopent.*(M.86.1989C); σημι-, Chrys.*laud.Paul.*7(2.512E); Ammon.*Ac.*19:12(M.85.1576A) cit. s. σουδάριον.

σιμόω, *turn up* the nose; met., *sneer*, Petr.II Al.*encycl.*1(M.33.1277A)ap.Thdt.*h.e.*4.22.4.

***Σιμωνιανός, ὁ,** plur., *followers of Simon Magus*, Epiph.*haer.*42.12(p.174.18; M.41.801A); origin, tenets, and practices described, *ib.*21.1–4(pp.238ff.; M.41.285ff.); id.*anac.*21(p.234.3; M.41.281A); in Origen's day less than thirty in number, Or.*Cels.*1.57(p.109.8; M.11.765C); given as nickname to Nestorians by command of Thds. Imp.*cod.*16.5.66(p.68.13; H.1.1716D); Phot.*nomoc.*12.3(p.604; M.104.872C); hence, sing., *one guilty of simony*, Thdr.Stud.*epp.*1.53(M.99.1105B) cit. s. χρηματολήπτης.

***Σινάιος,** *of Sinai* ὄρει τῷ Σ. Or.*Ps.*10:4(p.465).

[*]**σιναπήζω,** = σιναπίζω, *blister with mustard*, Ephr.2.394D; Pall.*h.Laus.*34(M.34.1107B; σιναπίσασα p.99.23).

σινδόνη, ἡ, = σινδών, *fine linen cloth, winding-sheet* for Christ's body, *A.Thom.*A 158(p.268.12); ‡Sophr.H.*liturg.*5(M.87.3985B); couch *covering, sheet* σ. χρυσόραντοι Eus.Al.*serm.*21.17(M.86.444C).

σινδόνιον, τό, *fine linen cloth*, Hipp.*haer.*4.33(p.60.8; M.16.3098B); worn as *loin-cloth*, Pall.*h.Laus.*37(p.109.4; M.34.1180D); *winding-sheet* for Christ's body, *A.Pil.*A 15.6(p.274).

σινδών, ἡ, **1.** *fine liner .loth*, sts. *muslin*, Clem.*paed.*3.5(p.254.13; M.8.600A); Hipp.*haer.*4.32(p.58.17; M.16.3095A); worn for baptism, *A.Thom.*A 121(p.231.6); *winding-sheet*, ref. Mc.15:46, Ath.*ep.Epict.* 6(p.10.5; M.26.1060B); *A.Pil.*A 15.6(p.273); Epiph.*haer.*77.28(p.441.2; M.42.681C); Germ.CP *or.*2(M.98.269A); **2.** artist's *canvas*, Chrys. *hom.13.3 in 1Cor.*(10.112B); **3.** liturg., *linen cloth* covering the altar, *A.Thom.*A 49(p.166.1); Isid.Pel.*epp.*1.123 bis (M.78.264D,265A); *towel* worn at foot-washing ceremonies, *Euchol.*(p.593).

σινιάζω, **1.** *sift, winnow*, Mac.Aeg.*hom.*5.2(M.34.496B); **2.** met., (Lc.22:31); **a.** *shake, unsettle, disturb*, freq. coupled with σαλεύω, Bas.*ep.*226.1(3.346B; M.32.844A); Mac.Aeg.*hom.*5.1,3,4(M.34.496A, 497A,B); usu. with idea of thereby testing and proving σινιάσαι... τουτέστι, θορυβῆσαι, ταράξαι καὶ πειράσαι Chrys.*hom.82.3 in Mt.*(7.785D); Nil.*epp.*3.153(M.79.456B); Hesych.H.*serm.*6(M.93.1476D); **b.** *sift*, e.g., good from bad, Thdt.*ep.*77(4.1126); ‡Jo.D.*Artem.*35 (M.96.1284B); hence *eliminate*; of removal of a monk from desert by Thphl. Al., Pall.*v.Chrys.*17(p.106.16; M.47.59); **3.** *handle roughly, ill-treat*, *Didasc.Jac.*3.2(p.53.14).

σινίασμα, τό, *chaff*, Pall.*h.Laus.*32(p.95.1; M.34.1105A).

σινίον, τό, *sieve*, Mac.Mgn.*apocr.*4.11(p.171.27); met. ἐοίκασι σίτῳ βεβλημένῳ ἐν σ. τῆς γῆς ταύτης Mac.Aeg.*hom.*5.1(M.34.496A).

***σινωπίδιον, τό,** *piece of* σινωπίς, i.e. red earth from Sinope, Sophr.H.*mir.Cyr.et Jo.*69(M.87.3664A).

[*]**σίντις, ὁ,** = σίντης, *spoiler*, †Apoll.*met.Ps.*104:14(M.33.1469B; σίντην p.216); of Satan, Jo.D.*carm.theoph.*89(p.212; σίντον M.96.829B).

[*]**σίντος, ὁ,** v. σίντις.

σίνω, *injure*, Jo.Mosch.*prat.*133(M.87.2996D).

σισόη, ἡ, mode of dressing the hair, *roll of hair*, Gr.Naz.*carm.*2.1.

11.758(M.37.1081A); ref. Lev.19:27, *Const.App.*1.3.10 cit. s. *σπατάλιον*; Thdt.*qu.28 in Lev.*(1.207).

***σισυροφόρος,** *wearing a goatskin cloak, skin-clad,* i.e. barbarian, Synes.*regn.*20(p.46.5; M.66.1093A).

[*]σιτάκη, ἡ, = *ψιττάκη, ψιττακός, σιττακός, parrot,* Philost.*h.e.*3.11(p.42.17; M.65.500A).

σιταρκέω, *supply for food,* Germ.CP *or.*2(M.98.285B).

σιταρχία (σιταρκία), ἡ, *provision, maintenance,* Gr.Mag.*dial.*(tr.Zach.)3.1(M.*PL.*77.220D); *σιταρκ-,* Mac.Mgn.*apocr.*3.39(p.136.8); ref. Jo.6:54 *οὐ...μόνοις τοῖς μαθηταῖς ἐδίδου τὴν σάρκα φαγεῖν... ἀλλὰ πᾶσιν ὁμοίως ὁσίοις ἀνδράσι...ταύτην ἀλληγορικῶς τὴν σ. ἔδωκεν* *ib.*3.23(p.105.15).

σιτηρέσιον, τό, *allowance of* or *for food, provisions* in kind or in money; **1.** *supply of food,* Dion.Al.ap.Eus.*p.e.*14.26(780A; M.21.1284A); **2.** soldier's *rations* or *provision-money,* Bas.*mor.*10.1(3.527B; M.32.1245D); Hier.*v.Paul.*A 10(p.20.18); Isid.Pel.*epp.*2.146(M.78.600B); Thdt.*Dan.*4:9(2.1144); id.*Rom.*6:23(3.67); **3.** *allowance of food* to pensioners, Chrys.*David* 3.9(4.782E); to slaves, Thdt.*provid.*7(4.597); **4.** *dole* to populace, Dion.Al.ap.Eus.*h.e.*7.21.9(M.20.685C); Philost.*h.e.*2.9(M.65.472B); **5.** annual *grant to the Church* for virgins, widows, and clergy instituted by Const., Thdt.*h.e.*1.11.2(3.774); abrogated by Juln. Imp. and transferred to pagan priesthood, Philost.*h.e.*7.4(M.65.541C); Soz.*h.e.*5.5.2(M.67.1225C); restored by Jovian, Thdt.*h.e.*4.4.2(3.952).

σίτησις (σίτισις), ἡ, 1. *food,* met. *οὐδὲ τὴν ψυχὴν ἀποστερεῖς τῆς ἐκ τῶν λόγων σιτίσεως* ‡Ath.*polit.*(M.28.1396A); **2.** *meal σιτήσεσι ...δεξιωθέντες* Philost.*h.e.*12.4(M.65.612A); **3.** plur., *supplies,* of stipends *ἐάν τινος ἐκκλησίας ἀποστῶσι κληρικοί, ἕτεροι ἀντικαθιστάμενοι τὰς αὐτῶν σ. λαμβάνωσι* Phot.*nomoc.*8.2(p.523; M.104.665A).

***σιτία, ἡ,** *bread, Did.*13.5.

***σιτίδιον, τό,** *victuals, provisions, T.Sal.*1.2.

σιτίζ-ω, *feed*; pass., *be fed* by, hence *live* on *τὸ μὲν βιάζεσθαι καὶ τοῖς ἀλλοτρίοις ∼εσθαι ἄδικόν ἐστιν* Thphn.*chron.*p.162(M.108.436B).

σιτικός, neut. plur. as subst., *corn-supplies,* Arist.*apol.*5(p.103.3).

***σιτικῶς,** *like grain,* Or.*comm.in 1Cor.*15:35ff.(*JTS* 10 p.49).

σίτισις, ἡ, v. *σίτησις.*

σιτισμός, ὁ, s.v.l., *feeding,* Thphyl.*exc.gent.*15(M.113.952A; *ἐπισιτισμόν* p.488.16).

σίτλα, ἡ, (Lat. *situla*); **1.** *pail*; in form *σίκλα,* Thdr.Lect.*fr.*(M.86.224A); Gr.Mag.*dial.*(tr.Zach.)3.16(M.*PL.*77.262C); **2.** liturg., *font* *τὴν σ. τοῦ ἁγίου βαπτίσματος* Sergia *Olymp.*7(p.47.21); *σ. ἢ ἐπιχύτην* *Euchol.*(p.656).

σιτοβολών, ὁ, *granary,* Pall.*h.Laus.*66(p.163.2; M.34.1218D); Philost.*h.e.*12.9(M.65.617C); Jo.Mosch.*prat.*28(M.87.2876B).

σιτοδοσία, ἡ, *free distribution of corn,* ref. Jo.6:33 *Χριστός, ἡ καινὴ τροφή...ἡ μείζων σ. πάσης τῆς ἱστορουμένης* Gr.Naz.*or.*34.1(M.36.241A).

σιτοδότης, ὁ, *provider of corn,* praefectus annonae, Synes.*ep.*87(M.66.1456A); *Asen.*25(p.79.15); Rom.Mel.(*SBBAW* p.147).

σιτοδοχεῖον, τό, *granary,* Bas.*hom.*6.3(2.46B; M.31.268B); Chrys.*hom.39.8 in 1Cor.*(10.375C).

***σιτοδοχία, ἡ,** *receipt of corn,* Thdt.*qu.94 in Gen.*(1.102).

***σιτοκλέπτης, ὁ,** *corn thief,* Geo.Pis.*hex.*1200(M.92.1527A).

***σιτολειψία, ἡ,** *famine,* Gr.Nyss.*v.Macr.*(p.384.14; M.46.972D).

σιτομέτρης, ὁ, *one who deals out corn* or *provisions ὁ σ. ἡμῶν κύριος* Or.*Jo.*28.24(19; p.421.18; M.14.733D).

σιτομέτριον, τό, *measured allowance of corn,* Cyr.*Lc.*12:42(M.72.749A); *Chron.Pasch.*p.287(M.92.717A); granted by Const. to Church for distribution, Thphn.*chron.*p.23(M.108.117B); increased by Constantius, *Chron.Pasch.*p.294(737B).

σιτοποιέω, *yield corn,* Gr.Nyss.*or.catech.*23(p.88.8; M.45.61D).

σιτοποιΐα, ἡ, *bread-making,* Just.*dial.*131.3(M.6.781A); Gr.Nyss.*homm.in Cant.*proem.(M.44.761D).

σιτοπομπία, ἡ, *transport of corn,* Thdt.*h.e.*1.31.5(3.822).

σιτοπώλης, ὁ, *corn-merchant,* Chrys.*hom.85.4 in Mt.*(7.809D).

σιτόχροος, *corn-coloured*; of bread, Chrys.*hom.2.4 in Gen.*(4.11E); of human complexion, Jo.D.*volunt.*6(M.95.136A); of BMV, *Pers.*(p.17.22); of Christ, *Pers.*(p.17.22; M.10.108A); ‡Jo.D.*ep. Thphl.*3(M.95.349C).

σιτώνης, ὁ, *buyer of corn,* Gr.Naz.*or.*43.34(M.36.544A).

σιτωνικός, *for wheat σ. χρήματα* Jo.Mal.*chron.*12 p.294(M.97.444D); neut. as subst., *wheat fund, Chron.Pasch.*p.316(M.92.805A).

***σιτώνιος,** ? *of the nature of wheat* or *corn*; or perh. *subject to corn-tax χίδρα, πάντες οἱ νεαροὶ καρποὶ τῶν ὀσπρίων καὶ τῶν σ. καρπῶν διαφέρονται· ὑπὸ τοὺς σ. δέ, τέλειοι καρποὶ τῶν ὀσπρίων, κρίθη τε καὶ ζειαί Schol.* in *Can.App.*3(*Mon.*2 p.642).

***σιφάριον, τό,** or ***σιφάριος, ὁ,** ? *screen, curtain γρηγόρησον μετ' ἐμοῦ τῇ νυκτὶ ταύτῃ. καὶ ὅτε ἀνεπαύσησαν πᾶσαι αἱ ἀδελφαί...κατέρχεται ὀπίσω τοῦ σ. V.Dan.*(p.70.6).

[*]σιφέριον, τό, *pen,* ‡Ath.*templ.*(p.111.4; M.28.1429D).

σιφνός, *empty, hollow,* met. *ἡ ἡδονὴ τῆς ἁμαρτίας ἡ ἀκάθαρτος καὶ σ.* †Cyr.*hom.div.*14(5^2.407E).

σιφωνίζω, 1. *siphon*; *squirt,* Herm.*mand.*11.18; **2.** met., *diffuse σιφωνίσει ἐκ τοῦ κάλλους αὐτῆς* [sc. *ψυχῆς*]...*καὶ εἰς τὸν ἔξω ἄνθρωπον* Ephr.1.103F; *inject μὴ τῇ ἐκείνου βασκανίᾳ προσέχων δηχθῇς, ἵνα μὴ ἰὸν πικρὸν τῇ ψυχῇ σου σιφωνίσῃς* Nil.*Eulog.*18(M.79.1116C).

***σιφωνοφόρος,** *carrying pipes,* sc. from which Greek fire was discharged, Thphn.*chron.*p.294(M.108.720A).

[*]σιχαντός ([*]συχ-), = *σικχαντός, disgusting, loathsome ποῦ τότε ἡ ἡδονὴ τῆς ἁμαρτίας ἡ ἀκάθαρτος καὶ σιχαντὴ ἀληθῶς* Ephr.3.227A; *διὰ δὲ μικρὰν ἡδονήν, μισητὴν καὶ συχαντήν* †Cyr.*hom.div.*14(5^2.412C); tr. Lat. *tetrior, Cod.Afr.*138(H.1.948D).

***Σιών, ἡ,** (Hebr. צִיּוֹן) *Sion, Zion*;

A. lit.; **1.** derivation *Σ., ὅπερ ἐστὶν 'σκοπευτήριον'* Or.*Jo.*13.13(p.237.6; M.14.417D); †Bas.*Is.*291(1.600B; M.30.629A); ‡Chrys.*hom. in Ps.*77(5.732E); *Σιὼν ἑρμηνεύεται 'διψῶσα'* ‡Tit.Bost.*palm.*4(M.18.1269C); **2.** dist. from Jerusalem, Eus.*onomast.*(p.162.12); *τὸ γὰρ Σ. ὄρος ἐστὶ τῆς Ἱεροσολύμων ἄκρας ὑπερφαινόμενον...τῶν ἀρετῶν τὴν ἀκρόπολιν, ἣν τῷ ὀνόματι Σ. παραδηλοῖ δι' αἰνίγματος* Gr.Nyss.*hom.7 in Eccl.*(M.44.717C); *τὴν Σ. ... ἡ ἄνω πόλις ἐκέκλητο. πᾶσα δὲ νῦν Ἱερουσαλὴμ ὀνομάζεται* Thdt.*qu.6 in 3Reg.*(1.458); id.*qu.16 in 2Reg.*(1.412); cf. *τὴν μὲν Σ. τὴν ἀρχαίαν εἶναι πόλιν, καὶ ὑποδεεστέραν· τὴν δὲ Ἱερουσαλὴμ τὴν βασιλεύουσαν, ἐν ᾗ τὸ ἁγίασμα* †Bas.*Is.*136(1.474C; M.30.340B); **3.** synonymous with Jerusalem, Cyr.H.*catech.*16.18; Chrys.*exp.in Ps.*49:2(5.225A); *Lit.Jac.*(p.206.3); *ὑπὲρ τῆς ἁγίας καὶ ἐνδόξου Σ. τῆς μητρὸς πασῶν τῶν ἐκκλησιῶν ib.*(p.206.27).

B. met. *κατὰ τρόπους τρεῖς προσήκει νοεῖν τὴν Σ. καὶ τὴν Ἱερουσαλήμ· ἢ αἰσθητῶς· ἢ κατὰ τὸ θεοσεβὲς τῶν ἐπὶ γῆς ὄντων πολίτευμα· ἢ κατὰ τὴν ἐν οὐρανοῖς ἀγγελικὴν πολιτείαν* Proc.G.*Is.*49:14–26(M.87.2476C); **1.** of Church, Clem.*prot.*1(p.4.14; M.8.53B); Meth.*symp.*8.7(p.90.1; M.18.149B); Chrys.*exp.in Ps.*9:12(5.102C); ‡Epiph.*hom.*1(M.43.428B); Olymp.*fr.Jer.*4:6(M.93.636B); of Church above, to which earthly churches are as gates, Thdt.*Ps.*9:15(1.662); **2.** of the intellect *τῆς σκοπευτικῆς καὶ θεωρητικῆς δυνάμεως Σ. καλουμένης* Or.*fr.14 in Lam.*(p.241.2; M.13.613A); *τὸν νοῦν...ὃς ὀνομάζεται Σ. ἐπειδὴ ἐκεῖθέν ἐστι τὸ σκοπευτήριον πάσης φύσεως* †Bas.*Is.*291(1.600B; M.30.629A); **3.** of consummate virtue *τοῦ μὲν ὀνόματος Σ. τὸ ὑψηλὸν τῆς πολιτείας ἐνδεικνυμένου* Gr.Nyss.*hom.7 in Eccl.*(M.44.717C); **4.** of OT saints *οὗτοι, ζητοῦντες τὸν Χριστὸν καὶ διψῶντες, ἐκλήθησαν Σ. ...ὅταν δὲ ἐπέτυχον...ἐγένοντο Ἱερουσαλήμ...θυγατέρα δὲ ταύτης Σ. καλεῖ τοὺς διὰ τῆς πίστεως διψῶντας* ‡Tit.Bost.*palm.*4(M.18.1269C,D); **5.** of word of gospel, Proc.G.*Is.*22:1–14(M.87.2173D).

σιωπάω, 1. intrans., *be silent,* ref. divine opp. human silence, ‡Ath.*Ar.*4.11(p.55.2; M.26.481A); also med., *T.Sal.*6.11; **2.** trans., *keep secret, not speak of*; pass., of unspoken prayers, *Const.App.*7.33.2; in phrase *κατὰ τὸ σιωπώμενον, by inference,* Chrys.*hom.8.1 in 1Thess.*(11.478A).

***σιωπητικός,** *inclined to silence,* Ephr.1.240B; *Apophth.Patr.*(M.65.341C).

***σιωπιστικῶς,** ? *quietly θέλε τοὺς παῖδας σ. προβαδίζειν Didasc. patr.*6(p.16.19).

σκάζ-ω, *stumble, halt,* met. *οὐδὲ πίστις ἐστί, ∼ουσα περί τι* Clem.*paed.*1.6(p.107.19; M.8.285A); *ἵνα μὴ σ. ἡ ἀλήθεια* Or.*Jo.*1.27(p.34.28; M.14.73C); *ἀπὸ τοῦ σφάλματος τῆς ἀναγνώσεως ∼ουσιν* Epiph.*anc.*75(p.94.13; M.43.157A); ptcpl. neut. as subst., *unevenness,* Clem.*paed.*2.9(p.205.14; M.8.492B).

σκαιός, 1. *on the left hand λέγεται* [sc. *ἡ ἀριστερά*] *καὶ 'σκαιὰ' παρὰ τὸ σκάζειν περὶ τὰς πράξεις· ἢ ὅτι ἀσθενεστέρα τῆς δεξιᾶς ἐστιν·...ὅθεν καὶ σ. ἄνθρωπος ὁ σκαμβὸς κατὰ γνώμην καὶ οὐκ ὀρθός* Melet.*nat.hom.*27(M.64.1256C); **2.** *dense, stupid* in spiritual apprehension, Gr.Naz.*or.*31.29(p.182.7; M.36.165B); morally *perverse, wicked Μελιτιανῶν... τῶν σκαιοτάτων καὶ ἀθεμίτων* Const.ap.Ath.*apol.sec.*68(p.146.10; M.25.369B); *σ. καὶ πονηροῦ* Serap.*euch.*20.2; *οὐκ ἀπὸ φιλομαθείας ἀλλ' ἀπὸ γνώμης σ. πεύσεις αὐτῷ προσάγοντες* [sc. *οἱ Ἰουδαῖοι*] Chrys.*hom.61.1 in Jo.*(8.362D).

σκαιότης, ἡ, 1. *insensibility τῇ...σωφροσύνῃ ἀκολασίαν κατὰ μείωσιν, σ. καθ' ὑπερβολήν* Hipp.*haer.*1.19(p.22.16; M.16.3044D); **2.** moral *perversity τὴν σ. τῆς τἀνδρὸς* [sc. Nero]...*μανίας* Eus.*h.e.*2.25.2(M.20.208A); *μὴ καθύβριζε τὴν ἀρίστην παίδευσιν τῇ τῆς γνώμης σ.* Isid.Pel.*epp.*3.41(M.78.760B); *τῆς τοῦ διαβόλου σ. ταῦτα αὐτοῖς ἐνσπειράσης* Cyr.*Ps.*7:15(M.69.756A).

σκαιωρέω, *scheme, plot*, Isid.Pel.*epp*.2.127(M.78.565B); Eut.*ep. Thds*.(p.152.24; H.2.177B); Leont.H.*Nest*.1.6(M.86.1420D).

σκαιώρημα, τό, *mischievous fallacy, error*, Bas.*Eun*.1.5(1.215D; M.29.517C); Gr.Nyss.*Apoll*.36(M.45.1204A); Cyr.*apol.Thdt*.1(p.113. 9; 6[1].207A).

σκαιωρία, ἡ, *plotting, treachery*, Bas.*ascet*.2.2(2.326A; M.31.885D); Nil.*epp*.3.99(M.79.432A); Soz.*h.e*.2.25.1(M.67.1000D); c. genit., *plotting* against τὴν σ. ἤτοι ἐκβολὴν τοῦ ὁσίου Eustrat.*v.Eutych*.76(M. 86.2361A).

σκαιῶς, *perversely*, Clem.*q.d.s*.18(p.171.5; M.9.621C).

σκάλα, ἡ, (Lat. *scala*); **1.** *ladder*, Anton.Hag.*v.Sym.Styl*.27(p.64. 5); **2.** *stairs, steps*, Jo.Mal.*chron*.13 p.343(M.97.512A); Thphn.*chron*. p.365(M.108.876B).

***σκαλαβατέω**, *climb by a ladder*, Anton.Hag.*v.Sym.Styl*.14(p.38. 6).

***σκαληνῶς**, *obliquely, crookedly*; of a snake's progress, Epiph. *haer*.51.10(p.261.25; M.41.905D).

***σκαλίδιον, τό**, *spade*, Hier.*v.Paul*.A 16(p.28.14); *Apophth.Patr*. (M.65.281A); Zos.*alloquia* 10(M.78.1693C); Cyr.S.*v.Sab*.11(p.94.29).

σκάλλω, 1. *hoe*; *scrape* with the hoof, Marcell.*fr*.112 ap.Eus. *Marcell*.1.3(p.14.23; M.24.744D); **2.** met., *disturb, trouble*, Chrys.*ep*. 133(3.678B); *stir up, search* the spirit, Gr.Thaum.*pan.Or*.7(p.19.21; M.10.1073D); Hesych.H.*fr.Ps*.76:5(M.93.1245A,B).

σκάλμη, ἡ, *offscourings, rubbish*, met. τοῖς...ἐκείνων νοήμασι καὶ ῥήμασι σ. ἐπιπολάζει Didym.*Trin*.2.4(M.39.517A).

***σκάλωσις, ἡ**, ? *ladder*, ? *scaffolding*, Cyr.S.*v.Sab*.67(p.169.19).

***σκαμβάζω**, *make crooked*, *A.Thom*.A 147(p.255.19).

σκαμβός, 1. *out of line, crooked*, Marc.Diac.*v.Porph*.82; *V.Pach.A* 32(p.157.35); fig. μηδέποτε οὖν πιστεύσῃς ταῖς ὑπονοίαις σου· σ. γὰρ κανών, καὶ τὰ ὀρθὰ σκαμβὰ ποιεῖ Dor.*doct*.9.2(M.88.1717B); **2.** morally *perverse, depraved* καρδίαν σ. ... καὶ διεστραμμένην Cyr.*Jo*.11.12(4. 1005C); Eustrat.*v.Eutych*.90(M.86.2376B); Melet.*nat.hom*.27(M.64. 1256C) cit. s. σκαιός.

***σκαμβότης, ἡ**, *crookedness*, met. τῆς ἀγάπης τὸ εὐθὲς...ἐσκαμβώσαμεν,...πονηροτέραν σ. διὰ ψεύδους ὀρύξαντες ‡Ath.*serm.Ant*.4(M. 28.596A).

σκαμβόω, *twist, distort*, ‡Ath.*serm.Ant*.4(M.28.596A) cit. s. σκαμβότης; Max.*ep*.1(M.91.385D,388A).

***σκάμβωσις, ἡ**, *making crooked, perversion*, ‡Pamph.Abyd.*ep. Petr*.(p.9.22; H.2.849D).

σκάμμα, τό, A. *that which has been dug*; **1.** *trench*; for a grave, *A.Jo*.115(p.215.3); for water, Cyr.S.*v.Sab*.67(p.169.16); as marking boundaries or terminus of a course, Cyr.*Ps*.12:5(M.69.800D); hence *horoscope*, Geo.Pis.*Heracl*.1.61(M.92.1303A); met., *bounds* of nature, Thdt.*affect*.12(p.308.24; 4.1022); of divine decrees, Geo.Pis.*Heracl*. 1.51(1302A); esp. **2.** place dug up and sanded where athletes landed in the long jump, hence *distance, measure*; met., *scope* ἐπετάθη τὰ τῆς θλίψεως ὑμῖν, καὶ πλατύτερα πάλιν ἐτέθη τὰ σ. Chrys.*ep*.5.1(3.577B); of precepts of religion opp. counsels of perfection ὑπερέβαινε τὰ σ. [sc. S. Paul] id.*hom.22.2 in 1Cor*.(10.194E); *ib*.7.7(10.62E); ref. Jo. Bapt., id.*hom.10.4 in Mt*.(7.144D); **3.** place dug up and sanded, *wrestling ground, arena*; fig., Hipp.*Dan*.2.19.8; Chrys.*ep*.107(3. 652A); Bas.Sel.*or*.7.1(M.85.101C); met., of secular life opp. monastic πῶς...δυνήσῃ ἀρνήσασθαι τὴν πρὸς τὸν ἐχθρὸν μάχην, ἐν τῷ σ. τῆς μάχης διάγων; Bas.*renunt*.2(2.203E; M.31.629B); of Christian life, *1Clem*.7.1; Chrys.*hom.4.4 in Ac.9:1*(3.135B); ‡Caes.Naz.*dial*. 131(M.38.1033); esp. in active evangelization, Paul.Em.*hom*.2(p.11. 20; M.77.1437C); ref. temptation of Christ τρίτον παλαίσαντος τῷ πειράζοντι, ἔξω τοῦ σ. αὐτὸν κατηκόντισεν Cosm.Ind.*top*.2(M.88. 121C); *ib*.5(288C) cit. s. ἀντίπαλος; of present life opp. life to come ὁ ἀγὼν ἐτελέσθη καὶ ἐκενώθη τὸ σ. Epiph.*haer*.59.10(p.376.1; M.41. 1033B); Chrys.*hom.43.2 in Gen*.(4.437B); πόθεν ἀπολύεις; ἐκ τοῦ βιωτικοῦ σ. Cyr.*Lc*.2:28f.(M.72.504C); of eremitic life, ‡Pall.*proem*. (p.4.16,21; M.34.995).

B. that which takes place in arena; **1.** *practice, training* ἵνα... ἀρετῆς ἔχωμεν σ. Chrys.*stat*.2.6(2.30C); Bas.Sel.*or*.18.1(M.85.228C); Sophr.H.*v.Anast*.(M.92.1692A); **2.** *contest, trial*; of persecution, Ath.*exp.Ps*.118 arg.(M.27.480C); Bas.*ep*.221(3.334D; M.32.817A); τὰ ἔπαθλα ὁ μέλλων αἰὼν ἐμπιστεύεται, ὡς οὗτος τὰ σ. Isid.Pel.*epp*.4. 195(M.78.1284B); of fasting, ‡Meth.*palm*.1(M.18.384B); of monastic life, Evagr.*h.e*.5.6(p.201.31; M.86.2804A); *ib*.3.33(p.132.3; 2669A); of crucifixion of Chri:t, Epiph.*haer*.69.60(p.211.19; M.42.304B) cit. s. παραδοξοποιΐα; **3.** *design, enterprise* θλάσον τὸ σχῆμά σου νῦν, καὶ τὸ σ. νεκρῶται Rom.Mel.(*AS* 1 p.180).

***σκαμνάλιον, τό**, *covering for seats, cushion*, *Ep*.ap.CSyr.(p.94. 39; H.2.1369A); CSyr.*act*.(p.99.7; H.2.1376C).

***σκαμνίον (σκάμνον), τό**, *bench*; *stool*, Jo.Mosch.*prat*.61,171(M. 87.2913C,3037C); ‡Chrys.*hom*.2(13.207E); Leont.N.*v.Jo.Eleem*.5(p.11. 9); *Euchol*.(p.593).

σκανδαλίζ-ω, met.; **1.** *cause to fall, lead into sin* ὡς, εἰ δυνατόν, σκανδαλίσαι καὶ τοὺς ἐκλεκτούς Dion.Al.ap.Eus.*h.e*.6.41.10(M.20. 608B); ~ει...τις, παρανομῶν λόγῳ ἢ ἔργῳ, καὶ ἕτερον πρὸς παρανομίαν ἐνάγων...ἢ κωλύων ποιῆσαι τὸ θέλημα τοῦ θεοῦ...ἢ οἰκοδομῶν τὸ φρόνημα τοῦ ἀσθενοῦς εἴς τι τῶν ἀπηγορευμένων Bas.*reg.br*.64(2. 436Ef.; M.31.1125A); τῷ τε πλείονας σκανδαλίσαι καὶ τῷ...προσκροῦσαι τῷ...θεῷ Chrys.*sac*.6.10(p.160.5; 1.430A); τὸ ὀξέως ~εσθαι, οὐ φιλοσόφου, μικρᾶς δέ τινος ψυχῆς Nil.*epp*.1.199(M.79.157B); *tempt to* or *lure into sins against purity* ἀπὸ πάσης γυναικὸς πονηρᾶς ~ούσης ἄφρονα *Pss.Sal*.16.7; Clem.*fr*.1(p.195.6; M.9.745A); pass. intrans. c. εἰς *find a source of temptation in* ἐσκανδαλίσθη εἰς ἐμέ Jo.Mosch. *prat*.179(M.87.3049C); pass. intrans., *err* in morals, Herm.*vis*.4.1.3; id.*mand*.8.10; Didym.*Ps*.9:7(M.39.1192A); Proc.G.*Is*.8:19–22(M.87. 1996C); in faith, Or.*fr.375 in Mt*.(p.160.9; M.17.297C); Ath.*Ar*.3. 37(M.26.404A); Chrys.*hom.23.3 in Jo*.(8.136A); **2.** *cause offence to, shock, hurt one's feelings* οὐ μόνον οὐκ ἐπίστευσαν [sc. οἱ Ἰουδαῖοι], ἀλλὰ καὶ ἐσκανδαλίσθησαν Chrys.*hom.32.2 in Jo*.(8.186A); *Apophth. Patr*.(M.65.209D); †Gr.II Papa *ep.Leon*.1(H.4.4A); †Gr.II Papa *ep. Leon*.2(H.4.17C).

***σκανδαλισμός, ὁ, 1.** *stumbling, lapse, fall* into sin, Or.*Jo*.32.5 (p.434.13; M.14.753D); †Bas.*bapt*.2.10.2(2.670C; M.31.1620C); **2.** *shock* μετὰ τὸν σ. τὸν ἐπὶ τῷ σταυρῷ γενόμενον τοῖς μαθηταῖς καὶ τῇ Μαρίᾳ ταχεῖά τις ἴασις ἐπακολουθήσει Or.*hom.17 in Lc*.(p.118.22) = Bas. *ep*.260.9(3.401A; M.32.968A).

σκάνδαλον, τό, 1. *obstacle*; *obstruction* τί...τὰ σ.; τὰ κωλύματα τῆς ὀρθῆς ὁδοῦ Chrys.*hom.59.1 in Mt*.(7.594C); **2.** *acrobat* [sc. σ.] καὶ οἱ ἐπὶ τῆς σκηνῆς τοὺς περὶ ταῦτα δεινοὺς καλοῦσι, τοὺς τὰ σώματα διαστρέφοντας *ib*.; **3.** usu. met.; **a.** *hindrance, difficulty*, Clem.*fr*. 70(p.230.8)ap.Jo.Mal.*chron*.10 p.242(M.97.372B); Ath.*v.Anton*.23(M. 26.877A); οὐ τοίνυν τὸ σ. ἐπιτεῖναι θέλων ἀλλὰ λῦσαι μᾶλλον Chrys. *hom.47.2 in Jo*.(8.277D); **b.** *stop, end* ἠθέλησαν [sc. οἱ Ἰουδαῖοι] τὸ σ. τῇ διδασκαλίᾳ αὐτοῦ προσθεῖναι διὰ τοῦ σταυρῶσαι αὐτόν Or.*hom. 10.2 in Jer*.(p.72.15; M.13.360B); **4.** *offence, snare, occasion of sin*, described σ....ἐστι...πᾶν τὸ ἤτοι εἰς ἀποστασίαν τινὰ τῆς...ἀληθείας ἄγον, ἢ πρόσκλησιν τῆς πλάνης ἐμποιοῦν, ἢ οἰκοδομοῦν εἰς ἀσέβειαν, ἢ καθόλου, πᾶν τὸ κωλύον τῇ ἐντολῇ τοῦ θεοῦ ὑπακούειν †Bas.*bapt*.2.10.1 (2.669B; M.31.1617C); τὰ σ. ... ἄλλα νομίζω εἶναι τῶν ἀνθρώπων δι' ὧν ἔρχεται. τὰ...σ. στρατιά τις ἐστὶ τοῦ διαβόλου...εὑρίσκει πολλάκις μὲν τοὺς πάντῃ ξένους τῆς εὐσεβείας, ἔσθ' ὅτε δὲ καὶ τῶν νομιζομένων τινὰς πιστεύειν τῷ λόγῳ τοῦ θεοῦ, οἷς χεῖρόν ἐστι τὸ οὐαὶ παρὰ τὸ οὐαὶ τῷ σκανδαλιζομένῳ Or.*comm.in Mt*.13.22(p.240.2; M.13.1153B); γίνεται δὲ τὸ σ. κατὰ πλειόνας αἰτίας, ἢ γὰρ παρὰ τὸν σκανδαλίζοντα τὸ σ. γίνεται, ἢ παρὰ τὸν σκανδαλιζόμενον τὸ σκανδαλισθῆναι συμβαίνει Bas. *reg.br*.64(2.437B; M.31.1125B); ref. Jo.6:41 τῆς ἐκείνων ἀνοίας τὸ σ. ἦν, οὐ τῆς ἀπορίας τῶν λεγομένων Chrys.*hom.46.2 in Jo*.(8.271D); in morals, *Pss.Sal*.4.27; Clem.*paed*.2.8(p.203.8; M.8.488A); Chrys. *hom.57.3 in Jo*.(8.336A); in faith, Ign.*Eph*.18.1; τὸ τοῦ σ. ὄνομα... εἰώθαμεν λέγειν περὶ τῶν διαστρεφόντων ἀπὸ τῆς ὑγιοῦς διδασκαλίας τοὺς ἁπλουστέρους καὶ εὐεξαπατήτους Or.*Cels*.5.64(p.67.19; M.11. 1285A); Ath.*syn*.2(p.232.13; M.26.684B); Thdt.*ep*.113(4.1191); **5.** meton., of persons σὺ τοσούτοις γινόμενος σ. Ath.*ep.Drac*.1(M.25. 524A); **6.** *fall into sin, sinful act* σ. ... ἐνταῦθα τὴν ὕβριν καλεῖ Or.*fr. 375 in Mt*.(p.160.14; M.17.297C); ὅταν...τις [sc. τῶν μελῶν, ref. Mt. 5:29 interpreted as one's close friends] σκανδάλου αἴτιος γένηται... ἐκκόπτειν χρὴ τὸν τοιοῦτον Isid.Pel.*epp*.1.83(M.78.240C).

σκάνδαλος, *giving offence, provocative* τῶν ἀπίστων καὶ σ. λόγων †Just.*fr.res*.(p.48; M.6.1589B); as subst. οὐκέτι ἄλλοις γίνεται σκάνδαλος ἀλλὰ σωτηρία ‡Chrys.*hom*.8(13.231E).

***σκανδαλώδης, 1.** *beset with obstructions* or *difficulties*, met. τὴν τραχεῖαν ὁδὸν καὶ σ. Epiph.*haer*.69.23(p.172.33; M.42.237C); ὁ ὕπνος, τὸ βάδισμα, ὅλα σ. ‡Chrys.*admon*.(11.817B); **2.** *scandalous* πᾶν ὅπερ οὐ κατ' ἐντολήν· ἀδόκιμον, ἕωλον, σ. Thdr.Stud.*epp*.2.159(M.99. 1500A).

σκαπανεύω, *dig, cultivate*, Isid.Pel.*epp*.1.260(M.78.340A).

***σκαραμάγγι(ο)ν, τό**, kind of *caftan*, i.e. long under-tunic with waist girdle, Thphn.*chron*.p.266(M.108.661A).

σκαρίζ-ω, *writhe, wriggle* μέρος ἑρπετοῦ ἔτι ~οντος Epiph.*haer*.54.6 (p.323.22; M.41.972A); *ib*.56.3(p.343.8; 993D); esp. ref. Saturninus' speculations on origin of man, Iren.*haer*.1.24.1 ap.Hipp.*haer*.7.28 (M.16.3322B); Adam.*dial*.2.8(p.74.2; M.11.1772B); met., of man's efforts after virtue, Nil.*epp*.4.60(M.79.577B).

σκαριφεύω, *sketch roughly, outline*, Thdt.*Ezech*.43:10–15(2.1030); id.*qu.1 in 1Par*.(1.566).

σκάριφος, ὁ (**σκάριφον**, τό), *plan* for a building ὁ σ. τῆς ἁγίας ἐκκλησίας σταυροειδής Marc.Diac.*v.Porph.*75; Cosm.Ind.*top.*proem. (M.88.53B); neut., Thdt.*qu.28 in 3Reg.*(2.475).

σκατοφαγέω, *eat filth*, Cels.ap.Or.*Cels.*7.13(p.165.2; M.11.1440A).

σκάφη, ἡ, **1.** *ship*, *Hom.Clem.*13.7; **2.** *spade* μόγις ἂν οἶδε τὴν σ. σ. λέγειν Synes.*ep.*159(M.66.1560B); ‡Jo.D.*Artem.*68(p.96.22; M.96. 1316C).

***σκάφησις**, ἡ, *digging*, ‡Chrys.*sicc.*(10.776B).

σκαφίς, ἡ, *spade*, Synes.*calv.*4(p.197.5; M.66.1173C).

***σκαφοκάραβος**, ὁ, *light man-of-war*, *Chron.Pasch.*p.394(M.92. 1009C); *ib.*p.396(cj. for κἂν ὁ' κάραβοι 1013B).

σκάφος, τό, **1.** *ship*, in simile of Son's relation to Father φασὶ... Διονύσιον εἰρηκέναι ποίημα καὶ γενητὸν εἶναι τὸν υἱὸν τοῦ θεοῦ μήτε δὲ φύσει ἴδιον, ἀλλὰ ξένον...ὥσπερ...ὁ ναυπηγὸς πρὸς τὸ σ. Ath.*Dion.* 4(p.48.22; M.25.485A); met., of the body, Meth.*symp.*11(p.139.9; M. 18.217B); of the world, Eus.*l.C.*12(p.231.26; M.20.1389C); of the Church τῶν ἁγίων ἀποστόλων τὸ σ. τοῦτ' ἔστιν, ἡ ἐκκλησία Cyr.*Jo.* 3.4(4.292E); **2.** pig's *trough*, Clem.*paed.*3.4(p.253.5; M.8.596B).

σκεδάννυμι, *scatter, disperse*; perf. pass., met., *be dispersed, dissipated, divided* mentally, esp. ref. polytheism Αἰγύπτιοι...κατὰ τὰς θρησκείας ἐσκέδανται Clem.*prot.*2(p.29.20; M.8.120B); τὸ ἐσκεδασμένον τῆς διανοίας εἰς πλῆθος θεῶν Gr.Nyss.*or.catech.*proem.(p.5.2; M. 45.12C); *ib.*3(p.17.12; 20A).

σκεδαστής, ὁ, *scatterer, dissipater*, Max.*ambig.*(M.91.1300D).

σκελίζ-ω, *trip up*; met., in sphere of faith or morals, Ath.*v. Anton.*6(M.26.849C); εἰ δὲ ~ει μ' ὁ φθορεὺς τῆς εἰκόνος, τίς μοι γένοιτ' ἔρυμα; Gr.Naz.*carm.*2.1.65.6(M.37.1407A); οἱ τὰ ὅπλα τῆς νηστείας ῥίπτοντες ὑπὸ τῆς γαστριμαργίας ~ονται †Cyr.*hom.div.*14(5^2. 414E); hence *outwit*, Geo.Pis.*Pers.*2.273(M.92.1228A).

***σκέλισις**, ἡ, *falling, fall* from virtue, Thdr.Stud.*epp.*2.10(M.99. 1141D).

§**σκέλισμα**, τό, *snare*, Bas.*ep.*45.2(3.134B; M.32.368B); ‡Chrys. *hom.in Lc.15:11*(10.839C).

σκελισμός, ὁ, *snare, trap*, Serap.*Man.*45(p.63; M.18.1232B).

***σκελιστής**, ὁ, *one who trips up, overthrows* οἱ...τῶν δαιμόνων σ. Ephr.3.463D.

***σκελοκοποῦμαι**, pass., *have one's legs broken*, *Ev.Petr.*4(p.240).

σκέλος, τό, *leg*; met., *part* of a proposition τὸ ἕτερον αἱρήσονται σ. τῆς διαιρέσεως Leont.H.*Nest.*1.1(M.86.1405A).

σκέμμα, τό, *plan, purpose*, Gr.Naz.*ep.*68(M.37.133A); of divine purpose, Cyr.*Juln.*3(6^2.78D); id.*Os.*3(3.13C); id.*hom.div.*5(5^2.361B); *scheme, plot*, *Ep.Mareot.*2(p.157.10; M.25.388C); Cyr.*Juln.*8(6^2.278A); id.*Os.*4(3.22E); Jo.Mal.*chron.*2 p.44(M.97.116B).

σκεπάζ-ω, **1.** *shelter, cover, veil* ἰτέαν ~ουσαν πεδία καὶ ὄρη Herm. *sim.*8.1.1; ἐπίνοιαν...ἐν δόλῳ τινὶ σκεπάσασα Ath.*ep.Aeg.Lib.*3(M.25. 544C); ἐσκέπασταί σου τὸ πρόσωπον Cyr.H.*procatech.*9; μόλις εἶδον θεοῦ τὰ ὀπίσθια, καὶ τοῦτο τῇ πέτρᾳ σκεπασθείς, τῷ σαρκωθέντι δι' ἡμᾶς λόγῳ Gr.Naz.*or.*28.3(p.24.13; M.36.29A); esp. with clothes, Clem.*q.d.s.*13(p.168.9; M.9.617A); Or.*hom.23 in Lc.*(p.153.4); Gr. Nyss.*hom.7 in Cant.*(M.44.924A); of burial μηδὲ γῇ ~οντα τὸ σῶμα Adam.*dial.*4.2(p.138.17; M.11.1808B); **2.** *protect, shield*, *M.Ariadn.* (p.125.9); met. ἀπὸ παντὸς πειρασμοῦ ~ει ἡ ταπείνωσις τὴν ψυχήν Dor.*doct.*2.3(M.88.1644B); of divine protection, *1Clem.*28.1; Or.*fr. 50 in Jo.*(p.525.16); ἀοράτῳ χειρὶ ~όμενος *M.Thdot.*3(p.138.13); **3.** *hide, obscure* αὐτὸς ὁ θεῖος λόγος οὐδὲν ἐσκεπασμένοις...τοῖς ποσὶν ...ἀλλὰ γυμνοῖς,...σαφὴς καὶ πρόδηλος...ἐμβατεύων Gr.Thaum.*pan. Or.*2(p.5.18; M.10.1056C); τοῦ ἡλίου ἀνατείλαντος καὶ σ. τῆς σελήνης τὸ σέλας Epiph.*haer.*50.2(p.247.17; M.41.888A); ἡ ψυχὴ...ὅτε...ὑπὸ τοῦ πνεύματος σφοδρῶς τῆς πλάνης ἐμπνέεται, ὑπὸ τῶν νεφελῶν ὅλη τῆς ἁμαρτίας ~εται Diad.*perf.*75(p.94.4); **4.** *spread* as a cover ἐσκέπασαν τὸ ἱμάτιον ἐπάνω τῶν πινακίων †Anast.S.*relat.*51(*OC* 3 p.72.32).

σκεπαστήριον, τό, *covering* for protection σ. ἀτρώτοις Clem.*str.*2. 20(p.179.16; M.8.1068A); παχὺ τοῦ φύλλου τὸ σ. Bas.*hex.*5.8(1.47D; M.29.112D); Gr.Nyss.*hom.10 in Cant.*(M.44.981C).

σκεπαστής, ὁ, *protector*; of God, Or.*Jo.*13.28(p.252.17; M.14.448B); ‡Meth.*Sym.et Ann.*6(M.18.360C); Areth.*Apoc.*2:8ff.(M.106.532C).

σκεπαστικός, *protective, sheltering* σ. τοῦ θεοῦ δυνάμεις Didym.*Ps.* 16:6ff.(M.39.1240A); neut. as subst., *protection*, id.(‡Bas.)*Eun.*5(1. 316D; M.29.757C).

σκέπη, ἡ, *lodging*, Esaias *or.*4.2(p.17; cf.M.40.1113A–B).

σκεπινός, *sheltered, secluded*, *T.Reub.*3.11; *Hom.Clem.*14.1.

σκέπτομαι, **1.** *see*; abs., Hier.*v.Paul.*A 11(p.22.4); **2.** *plot* κατὰ βασιλέως σκεψάμενος Jo.Mal.*chron.*18 p.494(M.97.713B).

***σκεπτούρι(ο)ν**, τό, (Lat. *exceptorium*) filtering and distributing *reservoir* or *cistern*, Cyr.S.*v.Sab.*82(p.187.7ff.).

σκευαγωγ-έω, **A.** *transport*; **1.** of pack animals, †Bas.*Is.*87(1. 439D; M.30.260D); **2.** met., ref. Ascension σήμερον ἡ ἀνθρώπινος φύσις ~εῖται εἰς οὐρανόν Thds.Al.*fr.*(M.86.285A)ap.Cosm.Ind.*top.*10 (p.314.14).

B. *plunder*, Men.*exc.Rom.*9(p.197.30; M.113.892C).

σκεύασμα, τό, medical *prescription*, †Bas.*bapt.*1.2.25(2.647C; M. 31.1568C).

σκευή, ἡ, *conspiracy, plot*, Ath.*apol.sec.*88(p.167.3; M.25.408A).

***σκευοδαίμων**, ὁ, *evil spirit*, *Mir.Artem.*32(p.45.28).

σκεῦος, τό, **1.** *vessel, instrument*; of sacred vessels: Jewish, Just.*dial.*52.3(M.6.592A); τὰ σ. τῆς λειτουργίας *Apoc.Bar.rel.*3.8; *Const.App.*8.21.3; Christian τῶν ἱερῶν σ. τῶν ἐκκλησιαστικῶν Eus. *m.P.*12(p.946.27; M.20.1513A); ὑμεῖς...ὡς τὰ τοῦ κυρίου σ. φέροντες Ath.*ep.Aeg.Lib.*19(M.25.584A); οὐ δεῖ ὑπηρέτας...ἅπτεσθαι δεσποτικῶν σ. CLaod.*can.*21; τὸ ἐπαξίως ἐφάπτεσθαι τῶν λειτουργικῶν σου σ. *Const.App.*8.21.4; σ. τι μυστηρίων Epiph.*haer.*68.7(p.148. 6; M.42.196C); **2.** ? *hive* ὀλίγων μελισσῶν σκεύη Gr.Mag.*dial.*(tr. Zach.)3.26(M.*PL.*77.279C); **3.** *body* (animal) εἰσῆλθον [i.e. Devil] εἰς τὸ σ. τῆς ὄφεως *V.Zos.*19(p.107.15); (human) ἕως ἔτι τὸ καλὸν σ. ἐστιν μεθ' ὑμῶν *Barn.*21.8; *A.Jo.*22(p.163.13); *V.Zos.*14(p.105.18); of BMV, assumed into heaven, Germ.CP *or.*8(M.98.361C); of Christ's body ἔμελλεν τὸ σ. τοῦ πνεύματος προσφέρειν θυσίαν *Barn.*7.3; τοῦ θεοῦ λόγου ἐξ ἀπειρογάμου παρθένου σ. ἀνθρωπεῖον ἀναληψομένου Eus. *d.e.*7.1(p.301.16; σκῆνος M.22.493B); **4.** met., of persons; **a.** in gen. αὐτὰς μὲν ὡς σ. ἐκδιδοῦσαι ἡδονῆς Clem.*paed.*3.4(p.252.33; M.8.596B); τὸ τιμιώτατον σ. τὸν ἔκγονον τοῦ μακαρίου Ἑρμογένους Bas.*ep.* 81(3.174B; M.32.457A); Mac.Aeg.*hom.*15.37(M.34.601B); τὰ πρῶτα σ. τοῦ διαβόλου τοὺς μάγους Thdt.*Is.*8:3(p.42.12; 2.223); τὸ οὐράνιον ἐκεῖνο καὶ χριστοφόρον σ. Nil.*epp.*4.17(M.79.557D); **b.** *wife* 'σ.' τὴν ἰδίαν ἑκάστου γαμέτην ὀνομάζει Thdr.Mops.*1Thess.*4:4(M.66.932D); ἀγαπῆσαι καὶ μιγῆναι εἰς τὸ ἴδιον σ. Jo.D.*Man.*1.60(M.94.1553A); *ib.* 1.84(1581D); **5.** of human nature as a complete entity τὸ πνεῦμα τὸ ἅγιον...εὐφρανθήσεται μετὰ τοῦ σ. ἐν ᾧ κατοικεῖ Herm.*mand.*5.1.2; Mac.Aeg.*hom.*12.1(M.34.557B); ἔθετο...τὸν νοῦν...ἡνίοχον τοῦ παντὸς σ. Epiph.*anc.*76(p.96.7; M.43.160C); id.*exp.fid.*18(p.519.16; M.42. 817C); collectively, *humanity, mankind* καθαρὰν σάρκα...ἔλαβεν ὁ Χριστός, καὶ τὸ οἰκεῖον διώρθωσε σ. Thdt.*eran.*1(4.68); **6.** of Christ's *human nature*, Eus.*d.e.*4.13(p.172.13; M.22.288A); ἀναστάντος αὐτοῦ ...υἱοῦ θεοῦ σὺν ψυχῇ καὶ σώματι καὶ παντὶ τῷ σ., συνενωθέντος λοιπὸν τοῦ σκεύους εἰς πνεῦμα Epiph.*exp.fid.*17(p.518.8; M.42.816A); τὸ δὲ ἱερὸν σ. ὡς θεοῦ οὐσία τιμᾶται, καθὸ καὶ ἡνώθη σκεύει ἡ θεία οὐσία κατὰ τὴν σάρκωσιν Proc.G.*Num.*3:45(M.87.801A).

σκευοφορ-έω, *carry sacred vessels*, ref. Is.52:11f. οἱ...τῆς θείας... φύσεως κοινωνοὶ γεγονότες...~οῦσι θεῷ Cyr.*Is.*5.1(2.737C).

σκευοφόριον, τό, *pyx*, Anast.S.*qu.et resp.*113(M.89.765A); †Anast.S.*relat.*30(*OC* 2 p.78.4).

σκευοφόρος, as subst., *baggage-carrier, porter*, Thdt.*qu.65 in 1Reg.*(1.403); met. τί...ἀτιμότερον σκευοφόρου πορνείας; Gr.Nyss. *hom.in 1Cor.6:18*(M.46.493A); σ. ... καὶ ὅπλον καὶ ἵππος αἰσχρᾶς πράξεως ῥῆμά ἐστιν αἰσχρόν Chrys.*hom.70.4 in Mt.*(7.692E).

σκευοφυλάκιον, τό, *sacristy*, *Mir.Artem.*32(p.48.20); ‡Bas.*h.myst.* 48(p.389.26); *Lit.Bas.*(p.309.5); used as treasury τοῦ σ. τοῦ φουρίου [v.l. φρουρίου] τοῦ ἁγίου οἴκου *Chron.Pasch.*p.337(M.92.880A); *ib.* p.390(1001C); Thphn.*chron.*p.66(M.108.216C).

σκευοφύλαξ, ὁ, *sacristan*, CCP(448)*act.*3(*ACO* 2.1.1 p.129.19; H.2. 148C); Jo.Mosch.*prat.*180(M.87.3052A); *Chron.Pasch.*p.382(M.92. 977B).

***σκεύρι(ο)ν**, τό, *money-box*, Leont.N.*v.Sym.*52(M.93.1733C).

σκευώρημα, τό, **1.** *fraud*, Bas.*Eun.*1.5(1.215D; M.29.517C); Chrys. *hom.58.1 in Jo.*(8.338B); **2.** *plot*, Thdt.*ep.*145(4.1257).

σκευωρία, ἡ, sens. dub. ? = σκευή *church furnishings* or = σκευοφυλάκιον *sacristy* φλὸξ ἀπὸ μέσου τοῦ θρόνου,...φανεῖσα ἐπεζήτει τὸν ὑποφήτην τοῦ λόγου· ὃν οὐχ εὑροῦσα κατεβόσκετο τὴν σ. Pall.*v. Chrys.*10(p.62.9; M.47.35).

σκέψις, ἡ, **1.** *plan, policy* πρὸς τὸ δοκεῖν τῇ πάντων ὑμῶν σ. γεγενῆσθαι *Ep.Mareot.*2(p.157.17,33; M.25.388D,389B); ref. Ex.1:11 περιτρέπεται...πρὸς τὸ ἐναντίον ἡ σ. Cyr.*ador.*4(1.109C); τὴν σ. τῆς ἐπιβουλῆς μελετήσαντες Jo.Mal.*chron.*18 p.493(M.97.713A); **2.** *conspiracy* συνήδει τῇ...ἐπιβουλῇ καὶ...ἐγίνωσκον τὴν σ. Thphn.*chron.* p.201(M.108.520A).

***σκηνάδιον**, τό, *shell* of tortoise, Cosm.Mel.*schol.*(M.38.635) in Gr.Naz.*carm.*1.2.1.535.

σκηνή, ἡ, **A.** *tent*; **1.** met.; **a.** of this life ἐκεῖ γάρ ἐστιν ὄντως ἡ μονή· ἡ...παροῦσα ζωή, σ. ἐστιν εὐτελὴς σύνδρομον ἔχουσα τῇ συμπήξει καὶ τὴν κατάλυσιν Isid.Pel.*epp.*1.65(M.78.225B); ὃς πᾶσαν τὴν τοῦ βίου τούτου σ. ὡς σκύβαλα καὶ κόπρον ἡγεῖσθαι ἡμᾶς ἐκέλευσεν *M.Thdot.*3(p.134.24); **b.** *habitation* in heaven, ref. Lc.16:9, Clem.

*q.d.s.*31(p.180.25; M.9.637A); Chrys.*stat.*2.5(2.28B); id.*hom.3.6 in Ac.princ.*(3.81B); Thdt.*Rom.*8:38f.(3.97); id.*1Cor.*16:22f.(3.286); **2.** *tabernacle* of Moses; **a.** lit., *1Clem.*43.5; Just.*dial.*132.2(M.6.784A); *Const.App.*8.21.3; model of structure of world, Cosm.Ind. *top.*proem.2(M.88.56C); τὴν σ. ποιῆσαι κατὰ μίμησιν τοῦ κόσμου *ib.*3 (141D); **b.** as type of Church ἡ μὲν σ. σύμβολον ἦν τῆς ἐκκλησίας, ἡ δὲ ἐκκλησία τῶν οὐρανῶν. διὰ τούτων οὕτως ἐχόντων καὶ τῆς σ. ἐν τύπῳ τῆς ἐκκλησίας...λαμβανομένης χρὴ καὶ τὰ θυσιαστήρια σύνθημά τι τῶν κατὰ τὴν ἐκκλησίαν πραγμάτων φέρειν Meth.*symp.*5.8(p.62.16ff.; M.18.112A); ἐπίσκοποι...οἱ λειτουργοῦντες τῇ ἱερᾷ σ., τῇ ἁγίᾳ καθολικῇ ἐκκλησίᾳ *Const.App.*2.25.7; Gr.Naz.*or.*19.8(M.35.1052C); **3.** *nest*, ‡Petr.I Al.*phys.*22(p.54); **4.** *covered sedan chair* or *palanquin*, Chrys.*subintr.*9(1.242D); **5.** *monastic dwelling*, Thdt.*h.e.*4.34.1(3.1012); *V.Pach.Σ* 88(p.267.18).

B. theatrical; **1.** *stage*; met., of this life, Clem.*prot.*2(p.11.14; M.8.72A); **2.** *farce*, of heresy τῇ σ. ταύτῃ λείπει ἡ ἀπολύτρωσις Iren. *haer.*1.9.5(M.7.548A); Epiph.*haer.*31.4(p.389.13; M.41.480C); **3.** *representation*; fig., of a description τὴν σ. τῶν κακῶν, ἣν πρὸ ὀφθαλμῶν ἐθήκατε Innoc.*ep.cler.*(M.52.537); **4.** *piece of acting, pretence* ἐλέγχεται δὲ αὐτοῦ ἡ περὶ τὴν ἀπολογίαν σ. Bas.*Eun.*1.2(1.209C; M.29.504B); μηδεὶς...τὴν ἀρετὴν ἄτεχνος καὶ σκηνῆς ἐλεύθερος Gr.Naz.*or.*22.9(M.35.1141C); *ib.*21.24(M.35.1109C); διήλεγξεν αὐτοὺς καὶ τὴν σ. αὐτῶν φανερὰν ἐποίησεν Chrys.*hom.41.1 in Ac.*(9.309D); **5.** *properties, trappings, insignia* τὴν ἀρχικὴν σ. αἴροντες Gr.Naz.*or.*16.19(M.35.961A); τῶν μὲν [sc. Greek philosophers] τὸ σχῆμα καὶ τὴν σ., ἡμῶν δὲ τὴν ἀλήθειαν καὶ τὸ ὕψος φιλοσοφεῖ *ib.*25.5(1204D); Nil.*exerc.*16(M.79.740B).

C. (= σκῆνος) *body*; **1.** τότε γὰρ αἱ σ. πήγνυνται πάντων ἡμῶν, ὁπότε τῶν ὀστῶν συγκολλωμένων καὶ συμπηγνυμένων ταῖς σαρξὶν ἀνίσταται σῶμα...ὁπότε τὰς σ. αἰωνίους ἀποληψόμεθα...ἦν...ἡμῶν καὶ πρόσθεν ἄπτωτος ἡ σ. Meth.*symp.*9.2(p.116.7,11; M.18.181A); id. *Porph.*1(p.503.10; M.18.397C) cit. s. ἀλλοίωσις; τάχα γὰρ σ. μέν ἐστι τὸ σῶμα, ᾧ ἐνοικεῖ τὸ πνεῦμα τὸ ἅγιον †Bas.*Is.*21(1.393E; M.30.156A); **2.** of human nature of Christ ναὸς γὰρ κυρίως ὁ καθαρὸς καὶ ἄχραντος, ἡ κατὰ τὸν ἄνθρωπόν ἐστι περὶ τὸν λόγον σ., ἔνθα προφανῶς σκηνώσας, ᾤκησεν ὁ θεός Eust.*fr.in Pr.8:22*(M.18.677B); τὸ δὲ σκηνοῦν οὐ ταὐτὸν ἂν εἴη τῇ σ. ... διαπαντὸς κατοικεῖ [sc. Christ] τὴν σ.· τὴν γὰρ σάρκα τὴν ἡμετέραν περιεβάλετο, οὐχ ὡς πάλιν αὐτὴν ἀφήσων, ἀλλ' ὡς διαπαντὸς ἕξων μεθ' ἑαυτοῦ Chrys.*hom.11.2 in Jo.*(8.65B); ref. Pr. 9:1 [sc. ἡ σοφία] τὴν ἀληθεστέραν ἔστησε σ., τουτέστι τὸν ἐκ παρθένου ναόν Cyr.*Jo.*4.4(4.384E); ἐν μήτρᾳ παρθενικῇ τὴν ἀνθρωπείαν ἑαυτῷ περιπήξας σ. προῆλθεν ἐκεῖθεν Χριστὸς ἄνθρωπος ὁρώμενος καὶ θεὸς προσκυνούμενος Thdt.*affect.*6(p.176.12; 4.877); id.*eran.suppl.*10(4.267); id.*Ps.*131:6(1.1507); **3.** met., of BMV αὕτη ἡ σ. τῶν πιστῶν, ἡ τὴν ἔμψυχον τῆς οἰκονομίας κιβωτὸν βαστάσασα...αὕτη ἡ σκηνὴ τοῦ μαρτυρίου ἀφ' ἧς θεὸς ὢν ὁ ἀληθινὸς Ἰησοῦς μετὰ τὸν ἐνναμηνιαῖον τοῦ ἐμβρύου χρόνον ἐξεπορεύετο Procl.CP *or.*6.17(M.65.756B); σ. ὑψίστου *Ev.Barth.*2.4(p.322); Anast.S.*hex.*12(M.89.1053B) cit. s. σκηνώδημος; χαῖρε, σ., ὁ θεότητος πόλος, οὐρανοῦ τῶν ἀψίδων προφερεστέρα, ἀφ' ἧς αὐτοπροσώπως ὡμίλησε θεὸς ἀνθρώποις Thdr.Stud.*nativ.BMV* 7 (M.96.689C).

σκηνικός, *of the stage*; fem. as subst., *actress*, Ath.Scholast.*coll.*1 paratit.7(p.26); *ib.*4 paratit.17(p.69).

σκηνοβατ-έω, A. intrans.; **1.** *act a part, act theatrically, show off*, Clem.*paed.*3.11(p.273.33; M.8.644A); συντάττοντας λόγων κεφάλαια... ἄνω τε καὶ κάτω ~οῦντας ‡Just.*ep.Zen.et Ser.*6(M.6.1189C); οὐ γὰρ ~ῶν οὐδὲ τερατουργῶν ὁ θεὸς ἀλλὰ...κατὰ δίκην τὰ θνήτ' ἄγει Synes. *regn.*17(p.40.1; M.66.1085C); **2.** s.v.l., *climb about* ἐν τοῖς κρημνοῖς αἰγῶν ἀγρίων δίκην ἐσκηνοβάτουν Thphn.*chron.*p.256(M.108.640A).

B. trans.; **1.** *put on the stage, enact* ποσὶν ἀθλίοις τὴν ἐπιθανάτιον ὄρχησιν ~ῶν ‡Nil.*narr.*1(M.79.596A); of Christ's Passion ὑπὸ διαβόλου δραματουργούμενον, ὑπὸ Ἰουδαίων ~ούμενον Bas.Sel.*or.*32.1 (M.85.349C); hence **2.** *exhibit, make manifest* τὸ πνεῦμα τοῦ θεοῦ...τὸ τὰς οἰκονομίας πατρός τε καὶ υἱοῦ ~οῦν καθ' ἑκάστην γενεὰν ἐν τοῖς ἀνθρώποις Iren.*haer.*4.33.7(M.7.1077A); ὧν ὁ βίος λοιπὸν ~εῖται, ἀδοξίαν καὶ κωμῳδίαν τῇ ἱερωτάτῃ θρησκείᾳ προστριβόμενος Isid.Pel. *epp.*3.242(M.78.920D).

***σκηνοβάτης**, ὁ, *one who treads the stage, actor*; in good sense of bishops as persons of prominence, Gr.Naz.*carm.*2.1.13.9(M.37.1228A).

σκηνογραφέω, *represent in painting, paint*, Clem.*str.*6.7(p.460.8; M.9.277C).

σκηνοπηγ-έω, 1. pass., *be put together, composed* ἡ δὲ τοῦ μύθου σύνθεσις ἐσχημάτισται ~ουμένη πιθανῶς εἴσω γαστρός Eust.*engast.*26 (p.58.25; M.18.669A); met., ref. man's restoration ὅταν σκηνοπηχθῇ [v.l. σκηνοπαγηθῇ] πάλιν διὰ τῆς ἀναστάσεως ἡμῶν ἡ φύσις Gr.Nyss. *anim.et res.*(M.46.133C); **2.** med., *encamp* ἐσκηνοπηγεῖτό ποτε κατὰ τὴν ἔρημον ὁ Ἰσραήλ Cyr.*Jo.*6.1(4.589D).

σκηνοπηγία, ἡ, **1.** *pitching of tents, encampment*, Meth.*symp.* 9.3(p.116.26; M.18.181B); **2.** sing. or plur., Jewish *feast of Tabernacles*, Ath.*apol.Const.*18(M.25.617C); Gr.Nyss.*or.2 in Gen.1:26*(M.44.285D); Chrys.*hom.65.2 in Jo.*(8.390C); Cyr.*Os.*68(3.102D); foreshadowing the resurrection, Meth.*res.2.21*(p.375.5; M.18.285C); id. *symp.*9.1(pp.114.8,115.1; M.18.177A,179A); Cyr.*glaph.Dt.*(1.432C); **3.** *tabernacle* of Moses, Epiph.*haer.*8.5(p.191.1; M.41.212C); *ib.*42.11 (p.132.9; 737D); **4.** met., *tale-pitching, fabrication* λέλυται ἡ τῆς ὀγδοάδος σ. Iren.*haer.*1.9.3(M.6.544A).

***σκηνοπηγικός**, *of tent-making*, Ammon.*Ac.*18:3(M.85.1568B).

***σκηνοπήγιον**, τό, *tent*, Thphyl.*exc.Rom.*1(p.222.8; M.113.928C); Thphn.*chron.*p.212(M.108.544A); *ib.*p.219(560).

σκηνοποι-έω, 1. med., *pitch tents*; i.e., *dwell in a tent*, Eus.*v.C.*2.14(p.47.3; M.20.992D); **2.** perh. *make conspicuous* οὐ χρυσὸς ἐκείνην ἐκόσμησε τέχνῃ πονηθεὶς...οὐ...βοστρύχων ἕλικες καὶ σοφίσματα ~ούντων τὴν τιμίαν κεφαλὴν ἀτιμότατα Gr.Naz.*or.*8.10(M.35.800B).

σκηνοποιός, ὁ, *tent-maker*, *Const.App.*2.63.1; Chrys.*sac.*2.8(p.45.1; 1.379C); id.*subintr.*9(1.242C); of Aquila, id.*hom.30.3 in Rom.*(9.742B); of S. Paul, Thdt.*Rom.*16:3(3.157).

σκηνορραφεῖον, τό, *workshop of a tent-maker*, Chrys.*hom.20.6 in 1Cor.*(10.178A).

σκηνορράφος, ὁ, *tent-maker*, Chrys.*hom.20.5 in 1Cor.*(10.177B); of S. Paul, Gr.Nyss.*ep.*17(M.46.1061B); Thdt.*affect.*9(p.225.20; 4.931).

σκῆνος, τό, **1.** *tent, temporary habitation*; met. of the body, cf. 2Cor.5:1,4, Clem.*str.*4.25(p.318.28; M.8.1368B); *ib.*4.26(p.321.27; 1376A); τὴν σάρκα τὸ σ. τῆς ψυχῆς Meth.*res.*1.53(p.309.3; M.41.1128C); τὸ ἑκάστου...σ. ἤτοι τὸ σῶμα Cyr.*glaph.Dt.*(1.432C); τῆς μαχῆς [sc. τῶν ψυχῶν] τοῦ μὴ ἀποσπασθῆναι τοῦ σ. ‡Nil.*perist.*5.1 (M.79.849C); freq. with γήινον or similar qualification τὸ σῶμα...ὃ γήινόν φησιν ὁ Πλάτων σ. Clem.*str.*5.14(p.388.10; M.9.140A); ref. Gen.6:2 θυγατέρας ἀνθρώπων τροπικώτερον τὸ γήινον σ. λέγεσθαι Or. *Jo.*6.42(25; p.151.18; M.14.273B); βρίθει τὸ γεῶδες σ. νοῦν πολυφροντίδα Thdt.*rect.conf.*8(M.6.1221A); of Christ's body τὴν ἐκ παρθένου δηλονότι οὗ ἀνείληφεν σκήνους γένεσιν Eus.*d.e.*6.15(p.269.27; M.22.444B); freq. with ἀνθρώπειον *ib.*6.18(p.278.25; 457C); (or perh. of womb of BMV) τὸ καθαρώτατον σ. εἰς ὃ ἐνθρονισθεὶς ὁ κύριος ἡμῶν Ἰησοῦς Χριστὸς εἰσῆλθεν εἰς τὸν βίον Hipp.*fr.in Is.*19:1(p.180.5; M.10.632A); cf.Thdr.Stud.*nativ.BMV* 7(M.96.693D); of a dead body, corpse, Eus.*h.e.*7.16(M.20.677C); id.*v.C.*4.60(p.142.2; M.20.1212A); Gr.Nyss.*Melet.*(M.45.861D); **2.** prob. *stage scenery* σκηνή τίς ἐστιν ὁ βίος...καθάπερ γὰρ ἐπὶ τῆς σκηνῆς τοῦ σ. ἀρθέντος αἱ ποικιλίαι διαλύονται Chrys.*hom.15.3 in 1Tim.*(11.639B).

***σκηνοφόρος**, *wearing a body* ἐπανιόντος ὅθεν ἐξῆλθε τούτου τοῦ συντεθέντος σ. θεοῦ Anast.S.*hex.*12(M.89.1053C).

***σκηνοχαρής**, *rejoicing in the stage*; *theatrical*, Geo.Pis.*carm.vit.*68(p.53).

σκην-όω, *tabernacle, dwell*, ref. Inc. σὰρξ ἐγένετο ἵνα ~ώσῃ ἐν ἡμῖν, οὕτω μόνον πρῶτον αὐτὸν χωρῆσαι δυναμένοις Or.*Jo.*1.18(20; p.23.5; M.14.56A); Apoll.*fr.*2(p.204.6)ap.Anast.S.*monoph.*(M.89.1181D) cit. s. σκήνωσις; τὸ σῶμα...ἡγιάσθη...τῇ ἐπισκηνώσει τοῦ λόγου τοῦ ~ώσαντος ἐν τῇ σαρκί Gr.Nyss.*or.catech.*37(p.149.6; M.45.96D); Cyr.*Jo.*1.9(4.96C) cit. s. σκήνωσις.

***σκηνώδημος**, ? *dwelling in a body*, Christol. ἐν ᾗ [sc. Μαρίᾳ] ὥσπερ τινὶ σκηνῇ λογικῇ...διδυμοφυῶς συνεπλάκη καὶ συνεπλάσθη καθ' ὑπόστασιν, ἀλλ' οὐ προεπλάσθη ὁ τοῦ θεοῦ λόγος, τὴν σ. φύσιν Anast.S. *hex.*12(M.89.1053B).

σκήνωμα, τό, *tabernacle*; **1.** = σκηνή, *tent*; in gen., *dwelling, house* ξένους εἰς τὰ ἑαυτῶν σ. προθύμως ἀποδέξεσθε *Hom.Clem.*3.69; *ib.*12.17; pagan *temple*, *A.Jo.*1(p.151.10); met. σ. (τοῦ) θεοῦ variously interpreted: of Temple, Or.*sel.in Ps.*42:3(M.12.1420D); of those dwelling in Father's house, *ib.*(1421A); of ἅγιαι δυνάμεις, *ib.*(1421B); of heaven, Eus.*Ps.*14:1(M.23.149C); of human body, *ib.*(149A) = Bas.*hom.in Ps.*14(1.352C; M.29.252C); of Christ's body, Eus.*d.e.*7.2(p.334.24f.; M.22.545C); of ark, Ath.*exp.Ps.*77:60(M.27.356C); Chrys.*exp.in Ps.*131:7(5.377C); of Christian churches, Ath. *exp.Ps.*131:7(521B); of the heart of man, Philox.*ep.*29(p.178); of BMV, Jo.Mon.*hymn.Chrys.*6(M.96.1381C); id.*hymn.Blas.*6(M.96.1404D); of a saint, *ib.*3(1401C); also of BMV (as seed of David from whom Son took flesh) τὸ ἐξ Ἀβραὰμ καὶ Δαβὶδ παμμακάριστον σ. Mod.*dorm.*13(M.86.3309B); **2.** = σκῆνος, *body* ἀθάνατος ἡ ψυχὴ ἐν θνητῷ σ. κατοικεῖ *Diogn.*6.8; τοιούτου [sc. ὡς ναός] δὲ μὴ ὄντος τοῦ σ. προὔχει τῶν θηρίων ὁ ἄνθρωπος κατὰ τὴν ἔναρθρον φωνὴν μόνον Tat. *orat.*15(p.16.24; M.6.840A); σὰρξ γὰρ ὅλως...πᾶς ὁ ὄγκος οὗτος τοῦ σ. ἡμῶν...ἀλλά τι μέρος τοῦ ὅλου, καθάπερ ἢ ὀστᾶ ἢ νεῦρα ἢ φλέβες· σῶμα δὲ τὸ ὅλον Meth.*res*.1.62(p.327.6; M.41.1160C); *ib*.2.21(p.375.7; M.18.285C) cit. s. ἄφθαρτος; of body of BMV πῶς οὖν τὸ ἄχραντον ζωαρχικόν τέ σου σ. τῆς τοῦ θανάτου πείρας γέγονας μέτοχος; Jo.D. *carm.dorm.BMV* 87(p.230; M.96.1365A); of Christ's body, Eus.*d.e.* 9.7(p.421.17; M.22.680A); *ib*.10.1(p.450.13; 724D); Hesych.H.*fr.Ps.* 73:6(M.93.1241C); **3.** *dead body, corpse,* Or.*dial*.28(p.174.6); Eus. *m.P*.11(p.944.11; M.20.1509B); Chrys.*res.mort*.6(2.431C); *V.Pach.A* 5(p.128.17); *Chron.Pasch*.p.382(M.92.981A).

***σκηνωματοφόρος,** *bearing the Tabernacle* ἡ τοῦ μαρτυρίου σκηνὴ ...τὴν σ. ταύτην Εὔαν, γυναῖκα Χριστοῦ τοῦ Ἀδάμ, ἐκκλησίαν ἐσήμανε Anast.S.*hex*.12(M.89.1053B).

σκήνωσις, ἡ, *tabernacling, sojourn,* ref. Jo.1:14 ἥρκει καὶ μόνον τὸ αὐτοῦ θέλημα διὰ τοῦ ἐν τῇ σαρκὶ σκηνώσαντος λόγου πρὸς τὸ ταύτην ζωοποιεῖν καὶ κινεῖν· ἀναπληρούσης τῆς θείας ἐνεργείας τὸν τῆς ψυχῆς τόπον καὶ τοῦ ἀνθρώπου νοός· ὅθεν καὶ σκήνωσιν ὁ Ἰωάννης τὴν ἐπιδημίαν αὐτοῦ τὴν ἐξ οὐρανῶν ὀνομάζει Apoll.*fr*.2(p.204.9)ap.Anast.S. *monoph*.(M.89.1181D); Chrys.*hom.11.2 in Jo*.(8.64E); ἵνα δύο νοήσας τὰ σημαινόμενα, τόν τε σκηνοῦντα καὶ τὸ ἐν ᾧ ἡ σ., μὴ εἰς σάρκα παρατετράφθαι νομίσῃς αὐτόν, σκηνῶσαι δὲ μᾶλλον ἐν σαρκί, ὡς ἰδίῳ προσχρησάμενον σώματι τῷ ἐκ τῆς ἁγίας παρθένου ναῷ Cyr.*Jo*.1.9 (4.96C); διὰ τῆς ἐπιφοιτήσεως καὶ ἐνεργείας τοῦ ἁγίου πνεύματος, καὶ τῆς τοῦ θεοῦ λόγου σ. ἔσται ἡ σύλληψις Jo.D.*haer.Nest*.1(M.95.189A).

***Σκηπιάω,** *be a Scipio,* i.e. a member of an illustrious family, Geo.Pis.*Heracl*.1.98(M.92.1306A).

***σκηπίων, ὁ,** (Lat. *scipio*) consular *staff,* consul's *insignia,* Jo. Mal.*chron*.15 p.384(M.97.569B).

σκηπτουχία, ἡ, *bearing of the sceptre, kingship,* Jo.VI H.*v.Jo.D.* 2(M.94.432C); opp. sovereignty βασιλείαν...οὐ τὸ ἀξίωμα τῆς σ. ‡Gr. Nyss.*Ar.et Sab*.7(M.45.1292D).

[*]σκηπτοφορέω, for σκηπτροφορέω, *bear a sceptre,* Geo.Pis.*carm. vit*.63(p.53).

σκῆπτρον, τό, 1. *sceptre,* as symbol of power and authority; **a.** divine ὁ κάλαμος τὸ βασίλειον σ. καὶ τὸν θεῖον νόμον ὑπέφησεν ‡Dion.Al.*fr.in Lc.22:42*(p.240.13; M.10.1600C); **b.** kingly, Thdt. *h.e*.4.6.3(3.953); καὶ τῶν ὑφ' ἕτερα σκῆπτρα τελούντων εἰς δύναμιν προμηθούμενος Gel.Cyz.*h.e*.3.11.12; εἰς ἑτέραν ἔξιν ἐλθὼν ὑπὸ σκῆπτρα τελοῦσαν τῆς ἀντικειμένης δυνάμεως Proc.G.*Gen*.12:10(M.87.328C); plur., Bas.Sel.*or*.17.3(M.85.221A); **c.** met., of Christ τὸ σ. [sc. τῆς μεγαλωσύνης] τοῦ θεοῦ *1Clem*.16.2; of the Cross τὸ μέγα καὶ σεβάσμιον σ., ἐν ᾧ τὰς χεῖράς μου ἥπλωσα *1Apoc.Jo*.13(p.80); *ib*.16(p.83); **2.** (Hebr. שֵׁבֶט) *tribe, T.Jud*.25.1; *T.Dan* 1.9; σ. ... ὠνόμασε τὰς φυλάς Thdt.*Abac*.3:9(2.1553); Jo.Mal.*chron*.6 p.158(M.97.260B); cf. τὸ δωδεκάσκηπτρον τοῦ Ἰσραὴλ *1Clem*.31.4; **3.** *standard, ensign* θάτερον...τῶν σ. ὃ λάβωρον Ῥωμαῖοι καλοῦσι Soz.*h.e*.9.4.6(M.67.1605A).

***σκήπτωρ, τό,** = σκῆπτρον, *sceptre; power* οὐαί σοι γῆ, ὅταν τὸ τῶν ἀγγέλων σ. βασιλεύσει ἐν σοί *Apoc.Dan.C* 4(p.115, v.l. σκῆπτρον); *ib*.31(p.116).

***σκητής, ὁ,** ? for ἀσκητής: ἔχεις σ. καὶ μονὰς καὶ μονύδρια πολλά *Hymn*.ap.*Mir.Geo*.(p.153.23).

***Σκητιώτης, ὁ,** *monk of Scitis, V.Dan*.(p.50.1).

σκιά, ἡ, 1. *shadow* τρία...δεῖ συνδραμεῖν ἐπὶ τῆς σ., τὸ φῶς, τὸ σῶμα, τὸν ἀλαμπῆ τόπον Bas.*hex*.2.5(1.17D; M.29.41B); met. σ. θανάτου ἐστὶν ἡ ἀνθρωπίνη ζωή Max.*carit*.2.96(M.90.1016C); of Christ's advent in the flesh σ. ... τῆς δόξης τοῦ σωτῆρος τῆς παρὰ τῷ πατρὶ ἡ παρουσία ἡ ἐνταῦθα· φωτὸς δὲ σκιὰ οὐ σκότος, ἀλλὰ φωτισμός ἐστιν Clem.*exc.Thdot*.18.2(p.112.25; M.9.665C); πῶς γὰρ ἂν ἐχώρησε θνητὴ...φύσις τῇ ἀκηράτῳ...συζυγίᾳ συναρμοσθῆναι, εἰ μὴ τοῖς ἐν σκότει ζῶσιν ἡμῖν ἡ σ. τοῦ σώματος πρὸς τὸ φῶς ἐμεσίτευσε; Gr.Nyss.*hom.4 in Cant*.(M.44.836C); *reflection* μεταδοὺς...τῆς ἰδίου λόγου δυνάμεως, ἵνα ὥσπερ σ. τινας ἔχοντες τοῦ λόγου...διαμένειν ἐν μακαριότητι δυνηθῶσι Ath.*inc*.3.3(M.25.101B); **2.** *shade, phantom* τῆς κατὰ τὴν παροιμίαν καλουμένης ὄνου σκιᾶς μάχης Cels.ap.Or.*Cels*.3.1 (p.203.13; M.11.921A); πῶς οὖν ἀνέστησε τὸν Χριστὸν ὁ πατὴρ σ. ὄντα καὶ δόκησιν; Cyr.*Thds*.9(p.47.26; 5².8A); of the dead, Or.*Jo*.28.7(6; p.397.29; M.14.696A); met., of sophistry τὰς σ. ... τῶν λόγων διώκοντες Clem.*str*.6.18(p.515.25; M.9.396A); **3.** *foreshadowing; type, symbol* ἄνθρωποι σ. οὐρανίου βίου παραδεικνύντες ἐπὶ γῆς Or.*Cels*.4.31 (p.301.10; M.11.1073D); esp. of old dispensation, Meth.*symp*.9.2 (p.115.27; M.18.180C), *ib*.5.8(p.62.9; 109C) citt. s. ἀλήθεια; Ath.*Ar*. 2.8(M.26.161C); ἡ δὲ [sc. πίστις] εἰς τὸν Μωυσῆν καὶ τὴν νεφέλην, ὡς εἰς σ. καὶ τύπον Bas.*Spir*.31(3.25E; M.32.121B); Chrys.*hom.7.4 in 1Cor*.(10.55D) cit. s. διαπλάσσω; εὐαρεστεῖν τῷ θεῷ διὰ τοῦ πληροῦν ἐθέλειν τὰ ἐν τύποις καὶ σ. Cyr.*Is*.1.1(2.14A); id.*Lc*.9:45(p.87.11); Max.*schol.e.h*.3.3.2(M.4.137D) cit. s. ἀλήθεια; dist. from εἰκών, exeg. Heb.10:1 οὐκ αὐτὴν τὴν εἰκόνα...τουτέστιν οὐκ αὐτὴν τὴν ἀλήθειαν. ἕως μὲν γὰρ ἂν ὡς ἐν γραφῇ περιάγῃ τις τὰ χρώματα, σ. τίς ἐστιν· ὅταν δὲ τὸ ἄνθος ἐπαλείψῃ τις, καὶ ἐπιχρίσῃ τὰ χρώματα, τότε εἰκὼν γίνεται Chrys.*hom.17.2 in Heb*.(12.167A); πράγματα καλεῖ τὸν μέλλοντα βίον· εἰκόνα δὲ τῶν πραγμάτων τὴν εὐαγγελικὴν πολιτείαν· σ. δὲ τῆς τῶν πραγμάτων εἰκόνος τὴν παλαιὰν διαθήκην. ἡ γὰρ εἰκὼν ἐναργέστερον δείκνυσι τὰ ἀρχέτυπα· ἡ δὲ σκιογραφία τῆς εἰκόνος ἀμυδρότερον ταῦτα παραδηλοῖ Thdt.*Heb*.10:1(3.604); σκιὰν φήσας, ὡς ἂν ὅτε τις σκιαγραφήσει ἄνθρωπον, μὴ ποιήσει δὲ τὴν εἰκόνα αὐτοῦ, τουτέστιν ὄψεις καὶ μέλη πάντα...ἀλλὰ μόνον τὸ μέγεθος τοῦ σώματος σκιαγραφήσει· οὕτω καὶ εἰκόνα λέγει αὐτὰς τὰς ὄψεις καὶ τοὺς χαρακτῆρας, τουτέστι τὰ δι' ἡμῶν τῶν Χριστιανῶν ἐκτελούμενα μυστήρια Cosm.Ind.*top*.5(M.88.193C).

σκιαγραφ-έω ([*]σκιογραφέω, [*]σκιογράφω), 1. *make a rough sketch, preliminary drawing* ὁ ζωγράφος τῇ πρώτῃ ἡμέρᾳ ~ήσας αὐτόν *A.Jo*.27(p.165.17); σκιογραφεῖ πρῶτον ‡Chrys.*pasch*.5(8.261A); ἐνὶ δὲ δὴ πρότερον καὶ ἀκαλλεστέρῳ σχήματι [v.l. χρώματι] ~οῦντες...εἶτα ταῖς σκιαῖς ἐπαλείφοντες, τὸ ἑκάστῃ πρέπον...σχῆμα, μεταφέρουσι τοὺς τύπους ἐς εἶδος τὸ ἐμφανές Cyr.*ador*.1(1.5D); mentally, *preconceive* τὸ πρῶτον ὁ νοῦς τὴν ἀρετὴν ἢ τὴν κακίαν ~εῖ Thdt.*eran*.3(4.179); id. *pental*.(5.128); met., *foreshadow, prefigure,* freq. of OT, Ath.*Ar*.2.8 (M.26.161C); ταῖς ἐναίμοις θυσίαις ~ῶν τὴν μέλλουσαν Gr.Naz.*or*.6.4 (M.35.728A); ‡Chrys.*pasch*.1(8.251A); τὸν Ἐνὼχ ἔχεις...καὶ τὸν Ἠλίαν, τὸ τῆς ἀθανασίας ~οῦντας μυστήριον ‡Nil.*fr.ascens*.3(M.79.1501A); Bas.Sel.*or*.4.1(M.85.65A); in gen. ἐν ποταμῷ τὸ τῆς κολυμβήθρας μυστήριον ἐσκιογράφησε Procl.CP *or*.2.2(M.65.693C); ἡ προφητεία...σ. τὴν τῶν μελλόντων ἀπόβασιν Sophr.H.*v.Anast*.(M.92.1693C); **2.** *outline,* met. (usu. implying inadequacy); **a.** *outline* in words, *give a faint impression of,* Gr.Naz.*or*.18.4(M.35.989C); of prophecy τὰ μὲν ἐσκιογράφει, τὰ δὲ διὰ χρωμάτων ἐτράνου Isid.Pel. *epp*.2.63(M.78.508A); **b.** *outline* by gesture, behaviour, etc., *indicate faintly,* Meth.*symp*.6.2(p.66.4; M.18.116B); Gr.Naz.*or*.28.19(p.50.2; M.36.49C); εἰ δακτύλοις ἐμοῖς τὸν κατ' ἐκείνου [sc. Ἀβεσαλώμ] ἐσκιογράφησα θάνατον Ast.Soph.*Ps*.7(M.40.473C); *make the sign of* the cross ἤ...ἄκρα θεολογία παρ' αὐτοῖς ἐστι δύο ταῦτα, συρίττειν τε πρὸς τοὺς δαίμονας καὶ σκιογραφεῖν ἐπὶ τοῦ μετώπου τὸν σταυρόν Juln. Imp.*ep*.79(p.94.3); **c.** *outline* in one's mind, *form a dim idea,* Gr. Naz.*or*.30.17(p.135.8; M.36.125B); in mind of another, *give a dim idea* δι' ἐσόπτρου καὶ δι' αἰνίγματος ἔμφασίν τινα σκιογραφεῖ Gr.Nyss. *hom.3 in Cant*.(M.44.821A); ἐδίδαξεν ὁ θεός, οὐκ ὄναρ ~ήσας, ἀλλ' ὕπαρ ἐπιδείξας Thdt.*h.rel*.21(3.1244); **3.** gen., *depict, represent,* Iren. *haer*.1.17.1(M.7.637B); Mac.Aeg.*hom*.18.12(M.34.632B); Gr.Nyss. *hom.13 in Cant*.(M.44.1060C); esp. in type λέγεται...τῶν...ἀγγέλων ...διάταξιν ⟨κατὰ⟩ τύπον τινὰ ~ῆσαι Eus.*d.e*.4.15(p.180.19; M.22.300C); **4.** *apply cosmetics to, 'paint',* Clem.*paed*.3.2(pp.239.20,242.21; M.8.561C,572A).

***σκιαγράφητος,** ? *painted in light and shade* ζωγραφίας μὲν γὰρ δι' ὁμοιότητα σκιαγραφήταις περιστεραῖς προσέπτησαν πελειάδες Clem. *prot*.4(p.45.7; σκιαγραφίας M.8.156B).

σκιαγραφία ([*]σκιογραφία), ἡ, 1. art of *line drawing* opp. painting σκιαγραφίας μὲν εὑρεθείσης ὑπὸ Σαυρίου...γραφικῆς δὲ ὑπὸ Κράτωνος Athenag.*leg*.17.2(M.6.924A); Chrys.*Thdr*.1.13(1.20C); **2.** *rough drawing, sketch,* Eus.*v.C*.1.10(p.11.27; M.20.921C); Epiph. *anc*.102(p.123.14; M.43.201A); Thdt.*Heb*.10:1(3.604); *outline* in words, Clem.*str*.1.1(p.8.18; M.8.697B); in gen. *reflection, likeness*; of idols, id.*prot*.1(p.4.27; M.8.56B) cit. s. ἀνοικοδομέω; χαρακτὴρ δέ τις τῆς ἀφράστου φύσεως διὰ τῆς τῶν ἀρετῶν σ. τοῖς πρὸς αὐτὸν ὁρῶσιν ἐγγίνεται Gr.Nyss.*Pss.titt*.B 14(M.44.585D); of man ἐξεικονίζων ὥσπερ ἐν ἐσόπτρῳ τινὶ καὶ σ. τυπικῇ, οὐ φυσικῇ, τῆς τρισυποστάτου θεότητος τὸ μυστήριον ‡Gr.Nyss.*imag*.(M.44.1329B); with emphasis on its illusory nature διελέγχει τὴν σκιογραφίαν τοῦ μιαροῦ δόγματος αὐτοῦ Ath.*Ar*.2.33(M.26.217A); verbal *obscurity, sketchiness,* cf. ὑπὸ σκιαγραφίας τῶν λόγων Numenius ap.Eus.*p.e*.14.5(730B; M.21.1200B); **3.** *foreshadowing, prefiguration,* of name Joshua (Jesus) σ. ... ἦν τοῦ κυρίου τὸ ὄνομα Clem.*paed*.1.7(p.125.30; M.8.324A); τὸ μὲν τῇ σ., τὸ δὲ τῇ τελειώσει τοῦ μυστηρίου Gr.Naz.*or*.4.67(M.35.588C); Thdr.Mops. *Ps*.54(M.66.677A); of first creation of man σ. ... καὶ προτύπωσις τούτου [i.e. of his reformation] ‡Nil.*fr.ascens*.3(M.79.1501A); τῶν προφητῶν...ἄλλοι τῆς οἰκονομίας τύποι ἐγένοντο, ὡς ἐν σ. τὴν εἰκόνα προδεικνύντες τοῦ μέλλοντος Bas.Sel.*or*.10.1(M.85.137B).

σκιαγραφικός, *painted*; of an icon of BMV, Thdr.Stud.*or*.5.2(M.99.721B).

σκιαγράφος, ὁ, *scene-painter*; met., *one who imagines, picturer* ἔστιν οὖν γαστριμαργία...σ. ἀρτυμάτων †Nil.*vit*.2(M.79.1141B).

σκιάδιον, τό, = σκιάδειον; **1.** *parasol*; gen., *shade,* met. σκιερὸς γίνεται καὶ δροσώδης ὁ βίος διὰ τῶν τῆς ἀρετῆς σ. Gr.Nyss.*hom.2 in Cant.*(M.44.793D); **2.** *carriage with a hood*, Cyr.*Is.*2.4(2.307A).

σκιάζ-ω, *overshadow*; pass., of an animal, *be startled, shy*, Cyr.S. *v.Sab.*45(p.136.9); ~ομένη ἡ κάμηλος ποτὲ φεύγει Barh.Edess.*Agar.*(M.104.1441D).

***σκιαλογ-έω,** ? *talk vaguely*; *reason confusedly* τὸν ἐκ τοῦ πατρὸς λόγον ἔξωθεν αὐτῷ εἰσάγει, καὶ τὸ φύσει γέννημα ὡς ποίημα ~ῶν λέγει Ath.*Ar.*1.25(M.26.64C).

σκίασμα, τό, 1. *shadow, shade*; of night, Bas.*hex.*6.8(1.57C; M.29.136A); met., of human virtues in rel. to God, Max.*ambig.*(M.91.1108B); **2.** *covering, protection*; of human skin, Epiph.*haer.*51.32(p.306.2; σκιά M.41.945C); **3.** *shade, phantom*, Serap.*euch.*29.2.

σκιασμός, ὁ, *shade, shelter*; of pillar of cloud, *Lit.*ap.*Const.App.*8.12.26; *Const.App.*6.3.1.

σκιαστής, ὁ, *umbrella-bearer*, Gr.Naz.*carm.*1.2.8.146(M.37.659A).

σκιερός, *shady, dark*; met., of blows, *faint*, Gr.Naz.*carm.*2.2(poem.)4.159(M.37.1517A); of life, Gr.Nyss.*hom.2 in Cant.*(M.44.793D) cit. s. σκιάδιον; of the eye, *blind*, Nonn.*par.Jo.*9:11(M.43.825B).

σκιμπόδιον, τό, *low bed*, ? kind of *stretcher* used as bier, Ath.*v.Anton.*90(M.26.969A); Mod.*dorm.*13(M.86.3308D).

***σκιμποδίσκος, ὁ,** = σκίμπους, *low couch*, Synes.*regn.*20(M.66.1093B; p.47.1 om.).

σκινδαλμός, ὁ, = σκινδάλαμος, *splinter*; met.; **1.** *scruple* of conscience, tr. Lat. *scrupulus*, *Cod.Afr.*132; **2.** *discord*, Thdr.Stud.*epp.*2.157(M.99.1493A).

σκιογρ-, see also σκιαγρ-.

[*]σκιογράφημα, τό, = σκιαγράφημα, *foreshadowing*, Bas.Sel.*or.*6.4(M.85.101A).

***σκιοτύπως,** *symbolically*, Ammon.*Ac.*18:18(M.85.1569D).

***σκιριτήριον, τό,** or ***σκιρήντριον, τό,** ? *haunt* τὸ θυμοῦ γέμον στηθήνιον, ὡς ὄχημα δαιμόνων,...ὡς δαιμόνων σκιρήντριον [σκιριτήριον], ὡς ἀσεβείας χαρτοφυλακεῖον *Max.invect.*(M.90.204C).

σκιρ(ρ)όω, intrans., *harden*, met. πρὸ τοῦ τὸ πάθος τῆς ἁμαρτίας σκιρρῶσαι Meth.*lepr.*6(p.458.26); usu. pass., *become hardened*; met., of imagination, *be obdurate*, ‡Just.*ep.Zen.et Ser.*6(M.6.1189B).

σκιρτάω, 1. *leap, jump*; of Jo. Bapt. in the womb, Or.*engast.*7(p.290.33; M.12.1024B); with pain, Chrys.*hom.30.3 in Heb.*(12.284A); fig. σ. τε καὶ πηδᾷ ὑπὲρ τὰ ἐσκαμμένα Clem.*str.*5.13(p.381.18; M.9.124B); **2.** *be restive, unruly*; of one unwillingly consecrated, Chrys.*sac.*1.3(p.11.8; 1.365D); of the passions, ‡Nil.*perist.*2.1(M.79.817B); **3.** *exult, rejoice* ἐκκλησίας χάρις σ. ‡*Diogn.*11.6; Chrys.*hom.38.4 in Mt.*(7.430A); id.*Kal.*1(1.698A); τὸ...παιδίον [sc. Christ] ἐγέλα καὶ ἐσκίρτα τῇ κολακείᾳ *Pers.*(p.18.15; M.10.108B); Max.*ambig.*(M.91.1068A).

σκίρτημα, τό, *bound, leap*; met.; **1.** *unruliness*; **a.** *restiveness, turbulence* of youth, Clem.*q.d.s.*8(p.165.6; M.9.612D); **b.** *surge* of passions τὰ σ. τῆς γαστρός Chrys.*hom.55.5 in Mt.*(7.561D); τῆς σαρκὸς τὸ σ. Nil.*epp.*1.168(M.79.149B); τῶν τοῦ σώματος...σ. Thdt.*h.e.*4.11.7(3.967); **2.** *exultation, joy* τῆς χαρᾶς καὶ τῶν πολλῶν σ. ἀναιρῶν τὴν ὑπόθεσιν Chrys.*oppugn.*1.4(1.50A); ἐνταῦθα καὶ οἱ ποιμένες ἐδωροφόρουν σκιρτήματα, καὶ οἱ μάγοι τοὺς θησαυρούς Chrysipp.*enc.in BMV* 5(p.343.11); τὸ...τῆς ψυχῆς...ἀτρέπτως θεῖον διετηρήσατε σ. Max.*ambig.*(M.91.1292C).

σκίρτησις, ἡ, *bounding, leaping*; of Jo. Bapt. in the womb, ‡Ign.*Phil.*8; Sophr.H.*ep.syn.*(M.87.3176A); met., ref. Ps.113:4, Gr.Naz.*or.*30.2(p.110.2; M.36.105A).

σκιρτητικός, 1. *frisking, bounding*, fig. ἀλληγορῶν...ἡμᾶς πώλους καλεῖ,...τοὺς ἀδαμάστους πονηρίᾳ...πρὸς...τὸν πατέρα σκιρτητικούς Clem.*paed.*1.5(p.98.27; M.8.265C); **2.** *unruly*; neut. as subst., Didym.*Zach.*3.270; τὸ σ. καὶ ἀφηνιαστικὸν ἀποθεμένους, τό τε ἀπειθὲς καὶ σκληρόστομον Cyr.*Ps.*31:9(M.69.868C).

σκίρ(ρ)ωμα, τό, *hardened swelling, induration*, Marc.Diac.*v.Porph.*4; σκιρρ-, Jo.Mon.*hymn.Blas.*9(M.96.1408A).

σκιώδης, 1. *dark, gloomy*; met., Gr.Naz.*carm.*1.1.6.69(M.37.435A); **2.** *shadowy*, i.e. merely symbolical, Eus.*d.e.*4.15(p.180.22; M.22.300D) cit. s. ἀντίμιμος; σ. ... καὶ τυπικὸν Χριστόν *ib.*7.2(p.336.16; 548D); οὐδὲ γὰρ τὰ 'Ιουδαίων ἀλλότρια Χριστοῦ, τυπικὴν δὲ καὶ σ. τὴν πρὸς Χριστὸν εἶχεν οἰκείωσιν ‡Chrys.*pasch.*5(8.261A); οὐ μὲν τὴν οἰκοδομίαν τῆς 'Ιερουσαλὴμ προσμεῖναι δεῖ...καὶ σ. περιρραντήρια μετὰ τὸ πανάγιον βάπτισμα Thdt.*Ps.*105:47(1.1364); Germ.CP *or.*2(M.98.265B); **3.** *shadowy*, i.e. without substance οὐδὲ παριδὼν τὴν τοῦ ἀνθρώπου ὕπαρξιν σ. τὴν δεῖξιν ἐποιεῖτο [sc. Christ] ‡Ath.*Apoll.*1.7(M.26.1105B); τὴν σ. δόξαν τοῦ παρόντος βίου Pall.*h.Laus.*epilog.(M.34.1260); ἡ ἐνταῦθα σύνθλιψις...σ. καὶ ὀνειρώδης Thdr.Stud.*epp.*2.11(M.99.1145C).

σκιωδῶς, *symbolically, in type*; *obscurely* σ. καὶ προφητικῶς Adam.*dial.*5.5(p.182.17; M.11.1837B); τυπικῶς καὶ σ. Anast.S.*hod.*8(M.89.132C).

***σκλάβα, ἡ,** *concubine*, Barth.Edess.*Agar.*(M.104.1388B).

σκληραγωγ-έω, 1. *discipline, train*; esp. in ascetic life, †Chrys.*Jud.et gent.*9(1.571B); ὅσον ἐπὶ πλεῖον ~εῖς σου τὸ σῶμα, τοσοῦτον διερευνᾷς σου τὸ συνειδός Nil.*Eulog.*29(M.79.1132B); πόνοις τε καὶ φόβοις ~εῖσθαι τὸν ἐντριβῆ Cyr.*ador.*5(1.154B); **2.** *treat harshly*, Cyr.*glaph.Ex.*2(1.281B); Thphyl.*exc.Rom.*3(p.223.18; M.113.929D); *ib.*7(p.227.9; 936B); of excessive asceticism πῶς τινες ἐχρήσαντο τῇ ἀποτομίᾳ ~ήσαντες τὸ σῶμα αὐτῶν *Apophth.Patr.*(M.65.368A).

σκληραγωγία, ἡ, 1. *discipline, austerity* of life, *asceticism* ἐν ἐγκρατείᾳ καὶ ἀσκήσει μέχρι νῦν διάγοντα· εἰ καὶ ὅτι τὸ εὔτονον αὐτοῦ τῆς σ. λοιπὸν κατεδαπάνησε τὴν σάρκα Bas.*ep.*81(3.174C; M.32.457B); τρύφης τε καὶ ἀναπαύλης ἀπόθεσις, σ. τε καὶ πόνος, καὶ ζωῆς ἁγιοπρεποῦς...ἐπιτήδευσις Cyr.*Joel.*10(3.209B); μετὰ...σ. καὶ ἡσυχίας ἐκάθισαν ὧδε *Apophth.Patr.*(M.65.233B); of pagans, Chrys.*hom.8.5 in 1Cor.*(10.72E); in which Jo. Bapt. excelled, id.*hom.16.1 in Jo.*(8.90D); Cosm.Ind.*top.*5(M.88.277A); also Elijah, Chrys.*hom.10.4 in Mt.*(7.145A); and James of Jerusalem, *ib.5.3*(78A); pertaining to practical life opp. contemplation, Nil.*serm.*4(M.79.1269C); a means to perfection, Chrys.*hom.11.8 in Mt.*(7.160A); τὸν ἐπὶ τῇ σ. πόνον ἔκλεπτε τὸ θαῦμα τῆς θεωρίας Nil.*exerc.*20(M.79.748A); Pall.*h.Laus.*2(p.16.22; M.34.1011A); an integral part of the Christian life, Chrys.*stat.*6.3(2.77C); οἱ λόγοι τοῦ κυρίου τὰ τέσσαρα ταῦτα περιέχουσι· τὰς ἐντολάς, τὰ δόγματα, τὰς ἀπειλάς, τὰς ἐπαγγελίας· καὶ πᾶσαν σ. διὰ ταῦτα ὑπομένομεν Max.*carit.*2.24(M.90.992B); rendered vain by sin, Chrys.*stat.*3.6(2.44D); imposed as punishment for witchcraft, ‡Jo.Jej.*exc.poenit.*(M.88.1933B); plur., *ascetic practices, austerities*, †Bas.*Is.*213(1.539A; M.30.488A); Isid.Pel.*epp.*3.401(M.78.1037B); *Apophth.Patr.*(M.65.133B); sing. collective for body of ascetic practices, *A.Xanthipp.*16(p.69.21); Chrys.*sac.*3.12(p.68.24; 1.389C); id.*Stag.*1.1(1.155E); **2.** *hardship* πρὸς λιμὸν καὶ πενίαν, καὶ πρὸς σ. ἅπασαν, καὶ πρὸς κινδύνους, καὶ πρὸς αἷμα Chrys.*hom.15.8 in Mt.*(7.198B); τὴν ἀνεθελητὸν...σ. [sc. of Israelites in Egypt] γύμνασμα ποιούμενοι...ὠφέληνται μᾶλλον ἤπερ ἠδίκηνται Cyr.*ador.*4(1.109B).

***σκληραυχενία, ἡ,** *stiff-neckedness, obstinacy* (properly of horses), Epiph.*haer.*30.9(p.344.13).

***σκληραυχέω,** *be stiff-necked, unmanageable* (properly of horses), ‡Nil.*perist.*2.1(M.79.817B).

σκληρία, ἡ, *hardness*; hence **1.** *hard times*, *T.Sal.*18.15(M.122.1344A; p.53.15n.); **2.** *obstinacy*, Eus.*d.e.*1.6(p.34.11; M.22.65D).

***σκληριάζω,** *become hard* τὰ...γόνατα αὐτοῦ [sc. S. James of Jerusalem] ἐσκληρίασαν δίκην καμήλων Epiph.*ep.Arab.*ap.*haer.*78.14 (conj. p.464.27 for ἐσκληκίασαν cod. M.42.721B).

***σκληρισμός, ὁ,** *hardening* (of the heart), Apoll.ap.*cat.Jo.*12:40(p.332.23).

σκληροκαρδία, ἡ, *hardness of heart, obstinacy*, in impenitence ἐὰν ...μὴ ἀναβῇ [sc. τὰ ἔργα τὰ πονηρά] ἐπὶ τὴν καρδίαν αὐτῶν, οὐ σώζονται διὰ τὴν σ. αὐτῶν Herm.*vis.*3.7.6; ref. adulterers stoned to death ὡς ἂν διὰ σκληροκαρδίαν ἀποθανόντες τῷ νόμῳ, ᾧ μὴ ἐπείσθησαν Clem.*str.*2.23(p.194.3; M.8.1097A); in unbelief τὴν ἀμαθίαν...καὶ τὴν σ. τῶν εἰς τὴν ἀλήθειαν λελιθωμένων id.*prot.*1(p.5.15; M.8.57A); πιστεύσατε εἰς τὸν θεὸν...καὶ μὴ ἑαυτοὺς ὁδηγήσητε ἐν τῇ σ. ὑμῶν *A.Thom.*A 166(p.280.16); ref. Marcellus ὥσπερ ἐν ὀχυρώματι ἑαυτὸν τῇ 'Ιουδαϊκῇ περιφράξας σ., τὴν ἄρνησιν προυβάλλετο τοῦ υἱοῦ τοῦ θεοῦ Eus.*e.th.*2.18(p.123.4; M.24.941D); associated with ἀμαθία, Clem.*prot.*1 cit. supra; id.*str.*4.26(p.323.16; M.8.1377B); with φθόνος, *T.Sym.*6.2; as reason why ceremonial law was given to Jews δι' ἣν αἰτίαν καὶ ὑμῖν προσετάγη, τοῦτ' ἔστι διὰ τὰς ἀνομίας ὑμῶν καὶ τὴν σ. Just.*dial.*18.2(M.6.516A); *ib.*46.7(576C); *Const.App.*6.20.11; and a partial revelation πρὸς τὴν σ. τοῦ 'Ιουδαίων λαοῦ ἡ τοιαύτη αὐτοῖς παρείχετο διδασκαλία. οὐδὲ γὰρ οἷόν τε ἦν τὸ πνεῦμα...ἀνθρώποις ἀτελέσι τὰς φρένας ἐντελῆ παραδοῦναι τὸν τῆς θεοσεβείας λόγον ...διὸ πρὸς τὴν σ. αὐτῶν τὴν περὶ ἑνὸς θεοῦ διδασκαλίαν ἐποιοῦντο Eus.*e.th.*2.20(p.127.9ff.; 949B,D).

σκληροκάρδιος, *hard of heart, stubborn, obstinate* Σοδομῖται...οἱ ἄθεοι καὶ οἱ πρὸς τὴν ἀσέβειαν ἐπιστρεφόμενοι σ. τε καὶ ἠλίθιοι Clem.*prot.*10(p.74.27; M.8.220B); μὴ ἔσο αὐθάδης μηδὲ πονηρόφρων μηδὲ σ. μηδὲ θυμώδης μηδὲ μικρόψυχος· πάντα γὰρ ταῦτα ὁδηγεῖ πρὸς βλασφημίαν *Const.App.*7.7.2; associated with folly, ignorance and weakness οὐδὲ ἀπειλοῦντος τοῦ θεοῦ φρίσσετε, ἀλλ' ἢ λαὸς μωρὸς καὶ σ. ἔστε Just.*dial.*123.4(M.6.761B); ὑμεῖς σ. μένοντες ἢ ἀσθενεῖς τὴν γνώμην *ib.*44.1(569B); σ. καὶ ἀσύνετος *ib.*27.4(533B); ἡ...παρουσία τοῦ σωτῆρος οὐ μωροὺς ἐποίησεν καὶ σ. καὶ ἀπίστους, ἀλλὰ συνετοὺς καὶ εὐπειθεῖς καὶ πρὸς ἔτι πιστούς Clem.*str.*1.18(p.57.9; M.8.804B); esp. of Jews εἰ δὲ...

ἀξιῶ ὑμᾶς ἐπιγνῶναι αὐτάς [sc. γραφάς], σ. πρὸς τὸ γνῶναι νοῦν καὶ θέλημα τοῦ θεοῦ γίνεσθε Just.*dial.*68.1(632D); ἡμεῖς οἱ ἁπαλοὶ πρὸς πειθὼ ...ἡ μὲν γὰρ γενεὰ ἡ παλαιὰ σκολιὰ καὶ σ. Clem.*paed.*1.5(p.101.19; M.8.272B); κατεάγασιν αἱ πλάκες τῶν σ., ἵν' αἱ πίστεις τῶν νηπίων ἐν μαλθακαῖς τυπωθῶσιν διανοίαις *ib.*3.12(p.287.26; 673A); manifested in unbelief τούτων ἁπάντων γενομένων [i.e. entry into Jerusalem] καὶ ἀπὸ τῶν γραφῶν ἀποδεικνυμένων, ὑμεῖς ἔτι σ. ἐστε Just.*dial.*53.2 (593A); οἱ σ. προφητείαν οὖσαν σεσοφισμένην οὐ νοοῦσιν Clem.*paed.*2.8 (p.202.20; 485B); οἱ...σ. καὶ ἰδιῶται τῶν ἐκ περιτομῆς εἰς τὸν σωτῆρα ἡμῶν οὐ πεπιστεύκασι Or.*princ.*4.2.1(p.306.2; M.11.357A); antidotes: fear τούτων [sc. τεράτων καὶ σημείων]...τῷ φόβῳ τοὺς σ. προύτρεπεν Clem.*prot.*1(p.8.20; M.8.64B); 'ἀρχὴ σοφίας φόβος' εἴρηται 'κυρίου'... δοθεὶς τοῖς ἀπειθοῦσι καὶ σ.· οὓς γὰρ οὐχ αἱρεῖ λόγος, τιθασεύει τούτους φόβος id.*str.*2.8(p.132.21; M.8.972C); τὸν σ. οὐκ ὠφελεῖ λεπτοτέρας γνώσεως λόγος, διότι ἐκτὸς φόβου, μετανοίας πόνους οὐ καταδέχεται Marc.Er.*opusc.*1.149(M.65.924B); chastening ὁ διδάσκαλος οὗτος ὁ παιδεύων μυστηρίοις μὲν τὸν γνωστικόν, ἐλπίσι δὲ ἀγαθαῖς τὸν πιστόν, καὶ παιδείᾳ τῇ ἐπανορθωτικῇ δι' αἰσθητικῆς ἐνεργείας τὸν σ. Clem.*str.* 7.2(p.6.10; M.9.409A); neut. as subst. διὰ τὸ σ. ὑμῶν καὶ ἀχάριστον εἰς αὐτόν Just.*dial.*27.2(533A); *ib.*44.2(569B); *ib.*47.2(577A).

***σκληροκοιλιάω**, *become costive*, Call.*v.Hyp.*(p.15).

***σκληρόνους**, *stubborn, determined*, Cyr.*hom.pasch.*10(5^{2}.135C).

σκληροποιός, *making hard, hardening*, met. τὸ πάθος...ἢ μαλακτικὸν τῆς ψυχῆς εἰς ἁπαλότητα, ἢ σ. εἰς τραχύτητα ‡Chrys.*pasch.*2(8.255A).

σκληρόστομος, *hard-mouthed*; of horses; met., of persons, *obstinate*; neut. as subst., Cyr.*Ps.*31:9(M.69.868C) cit. s. σκιρτητικός.

σκληρότης, ἡ, *hardness*; of persons; **1.** *harshness*, Herm.*mand.* 5.2.6; Synes.*ep.*73(M.66.1440C); **2.** *obduracy* in impenitence, Or. *princ.*3.1.11(p.214.4; M.11.269A); **3.** *severity* δι' εὐσεβοῦς σ. Proc.G. *Dt.*17:5(M.87.913B).

***σκληροτραχηλία**, ἡ, *obstinacy*, ‡Epiph.*v.proph.Dan.*(M.43.424C; σκληροτράχηλον p.24); *T.Sym.*6.2(v.l. for σκληροκαρδίαν).

σκληροτράχηλος, *stiff-necked, stubborn* ἵππος σκληρόστομος...καὶ ἄνθρωπος σ. Ephr.1.89C; neut. as subst., Hesych.H.*Ps.tit.*80(v.l. for σκληροτραχεῖν M.27.997C).

***σκληρουχέομαι**, *be hardened, endure hardship*, Nil.*Eulog.*13(M. 79.1109C).

σκληρουχία, ἡ, *harsh self-discipline, austerity*, Nil.*epp.*1.232(M. 79.168C); †Nil.*vit.*2(M.79.1141B); ‡Caes.Naz.*dial.*174(M.38.1140).

σκληρόω, v. σκληρύνω.

[*]σκληρυμμός, ὁ, *hardness*; of Pharaoh, Or.*princ.*3.1.11(p.212.5; σκληρυσμόν M.11.268A).

***σκλήρυνσις**, ἡ, *hardening* ἀνάξιον δὲ θεοῦ τὸ...ἐνεργεῖν σκλήρυνσιν ἐπὶ τὸ ἀπειθῆσαι τῷ βουλήματι τοῦ σκληρύνοντος τὸν σκληρυνόμενον Or. *comm.in Ex.*ap.*philoc.*27(p.242.10; M.12.264A); *ib.*(p.243.14; 265C).

σκληρυντικός, *capable of hardening* μήτε εὐποροῦντες ἀποδείξεων πρὸς τὸ τὸν δίκαιον σ. εἶναί τινος Or.*comm.in Ex.*ap.*philoc.*27(p.243. 21; M.12.265C).

σκληρύν-ω, **A.** *harden, make hard*; **1.** act., met. ἡμεῖς ἐσκληρύναμεν τὸν τράχηλον ἡμῶν *Pss.Sal.*8.35; usu. with καρδία or of the person; **a.** in impenitence καλὸν...ἀνθρώπῳ ἐξομολογεῖσθαι...ἢ ~ει τὴν καρδίαν αὐτοῦ *1Clem.*51.3; freq. ref. Pharaoh ἐγὼ...πνεῦμα χαλεπὸν...ἐγὼ παρήμην...~ων αὐτοῦ τὴν καρδίαν *T.Sal.*25.3(M.122.1356C); εἰ γὰρ ὑπὸ θεοῦ ~εται καὶ διὰ τὸ ~εσθαι ἁμαρτάνει, οὐκ αὐτὸς ἑαυτῷ τῆς ἁμαρτίας αἴτιος· εἰ δὲ τοῦτο, οὐδὲ αὐτεξούσιος ὁ Φαραώ Or.*princ.* 3.1.7(p.204.15; M.11.260A); οὐ προτιθέμενος, '~ειν' ἀλλὰ διὰ προθέσεως χρηστῆς ᾗ ἐπακολουθεῖ διὰ τὸ τῆς κακίας ὑποκείμενον τοῦ παρ' ἑαυτοῖς κακοῦ τὸ ~εσθαι, '~ειν' λεγόμενος τὸν ~όμενον *ib.*3.1.10(p.210. 4ff.; 265A); id.*hom.6.3 in Jer.*(p.50.20; ἐσκληρωμένη M.13.328B); **b.** in ignorance εἰ...~ει [sc. God] καρδίας, καὶ τίς σοφίζει; *Hom. Clem.*2.43; **2.** pass., met., *be hardened, obstinate*; Marc.Diac. *v.Porph.*55; **a.** in impenitence, Or.*sel.in Ex.*3:21(M.12.284A) cit. s. ἀντιτυπέω; Ath.*Ar.*3.26(M.26.377A); *Const.App.*2.38.3; Gr.Nyss. *ordin.*(M.46.548D); **b.** against the truth ἐν...τῷ ὑφ' ἡμῶν παραινεῖσθαι οὐκ ἐσκληρύνετο [sc. Sabellius] Hipp.*haer.*9.11(p.245.22; M.16.3379A); ref. Lc.3:8 αἰνισσόμενος ἡμᾶς...ἐσκληρυμμένους πρὸς τὴν ἀλήθειαν Or.*hom.4.5 in Jer.*(p.28.1; ἐσκληρωμένους M.13.292B); Eus.*h.e.*2.17.18(M.20.181A).

B. *make harsh* or *severe* ἐσκλήρυνεν Χοσρόης τὸν ζυγὸν αὐτοῦ ἐπὶ πάντας ἀνθρώπους εἰς αἱμοβορίαν καὶ φορολογίαν Thphn.*chron.*p.253 (M.108.633B).

σκληρυσμός, ὁ, v. [*]σκληρυμμός.

σκληρώδης, *of a hard nature, hard*; as a human characteristic ? *stubborn, mulish* τὸ φλέγμα [sc. τὴν ψυχὴν ἐργάζεται] ἀργωδεστέραν καὶ σκληρωδεστέραν Melet.*nat.hom.*30(M.64.1272A).

σκληρῶς, *hardly, with hardship*, Ath.*apol.fug.*17(p.80.17; M.25. 665D).

[*]σκνιπία (κνιπία), ἡ, *want, scarcity* ἐγένετο...καὶ θανατικὸν καὶ σ. παντὸς εἴδους Thphn.*chron.*p.248(v.l. κνιπία M.108.621C).

[*]σκνιφεύομαι, = κνιπεύω, *be stingy* or *niggardly*, Leont.N.*v.Jo. Eleem.*7(p.14.16).

σκνιφός, *niggardly, stingy*; characteristic of those born under Gemini, Leo, and Aquarius, Hipp.*haer.*4.17,19,25(pp.50.21,51.19, 53.10; M.16.3083D,3086B,3087C); in gen., Jo.Mal.*chron.*12 p.295(M. 97.448A); Leont.N.*v.Jo.Eleem.*21(p.40.10).

***σκνιφότης**, ἡ, *parsimony, stinginess*, Ephr.3.426C; ἡ σ. ἀπὸ μικροψυχίας ἀναβλαστάνει Ant.Mon.*hom.*10(M.89.1461B).

***σκολάκι(ο)ν**, τό, lamp-*wick*, Ephr.2.176C; *Apophth.Patr.*(M.65. 324B,C).

σκολιάζω, **1.** trans., *pervert, turn aside*, *T.Sal.*4.5; **2.** intrans., *deal crookedly, behave unjustly*, Ephr.1.312B; of one who is unorthodox σκολιάσαι ἔχει εἰς τὴν πίστιν Call.*v.Hipp.*(p.67).

***σκολιεύ-ομαι**, **1.** *wriggle, writhe*, Epiph.*haer.*42.11(p.134.16; ~ει M.41.741B); **2.** met., *wriggle in argument, evade logical issues*, Leont.H.*Nest.*4.24(M.86.1689A); **3.** met., *be tortuous* διὰ τῆς πολυτρόπως ~ομένης πλανώμενος ἡδονῆς Max.*qu.Thal.*47(M.90.428A).

***σκολιόγνωμος**, *wrong-headed, perverse*, Thdr.Stud.*epp.*2.77(M. 99.1316B).

***σκολιοδρομ-έω**, *run crookedly*; met., the race of life, Or.*exc.in Ps.*36:23(M.17.133A); ~εῖ [sc. Satan]...ὥσπερ τὸ θηρίον Cyr.*Is.*3.1(2. 371E); of heretics εἰ...τις ἕλοιτο...~εῖν, καὶ τὴν εὐστιβῆ τῶν θεωρημάτων μεταμείψας ὁδόν, παρατρέπεσθαι πρὸς ἑτέραν, ἀκάνθαις περιπεσεῖται id.*dial.Trin.*5(5^{1}.571A).

***σκολιοπορία**, ἡ, *winding passage*, ‡Caes.Naz.*dial.*77(M.38.944).

σκολιότης, ἡ, **1.** *crookedness, sinuousness*, Or.*Jo.*6.18(10; p.127. 26; M.14.232C); **2.** met., *virulence* ὄφιν...τῆς...θυμώδους σ. Gr.Mag. *dial.*(tr.Zach.)3.55(M.*PL.*77.302B); **3.** met., *crookedness, perversity*, of men's dealings ἵνα...ἁγιασθῆτε ἀπὸ...πονηρίας καὶ ἀπὸ...σ. Herm. *vis.*3.9.1; ἄχολοί τε καὶ ἀνεπίμικτοι κακοφροσύνῃ καὶ σ. Clem.*paed.*1.5 (p.101.18; M.8.272B); *ib.*2.8(p.202.17; 485B); αἱ ἀρεταὶ εὐθύτητές εἰσιν, ὡς αἱ κακίαι σ. Or.*fr.in Pr.*1:3(M.17.153C); of heresy, Bas.*Eun.*1.8 (1.219C; M.29.528A).

σκολιόφρων, *of crooked mind, perverse*, Nonn.*par.Jo.*8:44(M.43. 820B).

***σκολιόω**, *make crooked, pervert* τῆς ἀγάπης τὸ εὐθὲς διαστρέψαντες, ἐσκολιώσαμεν τὴν καρδίαν, καὶ...ἐσκαμβώσαμεν Max.*ep.*1(M.91.385D).

σκολόπενδρα, ἡ, *millipede* ἐν ἑτέροις λόγοις ἔφη· 'δίδωμι ὑμῖν ἐξουσίαν καταπατεῖν ἐπάνω ὄφεων, καὶ σκορπίων, καὶ σκολοπενδρῶν, καὶ ἐπάνω πάσης δυνάμεως τοῦ ἐχθροῦ' [cf.Lc.10:19] Just.*dial.*76.6(M. 6.653C); as typical of something ugly and loathsome, Gr.Nyss.*hom. 4 in Cant.*(M.44.833B).

σκόλοψ (σκώλωψ), ὁ, **1.** *pale, stake*; of Cross, Cels.ap.Or.*Cels.*2. 55(p.178.21; M.11.884B); *ib.*2.69(p.191.23; 905A); Eudoc.*Cypr.*1.191 (M.85.840B); ‡Caes.Naz.*dial.*178(M.38.1148); **2.** *thorn*, ref. Os.2:6, Cyr.*Os.*18(3.39E); σκώλωψ Jo.Carp.*cap.*(M.85.1858); met., of sins, Clem.*str.*7.12(p.53.6; M.9.501B); ἀνὴρ δέ τις διεστραμμένης προθέσεως, καὶ τοῖς τοῦ...ἐχθροῦ σκόλοψιν ἐμπεπαρμένος Gr.Mag.*dial.*(tr. Zach.)4.19(M.*PL.*77.351B); of Israel's troubles, Cyr.*Os.*15(3.37C); ref. 2Cor.12:7 ὑπὲρ τοῦ σ. ... ἐν τῷ σαρκί, τουτέστι, ὑπὲρ τῶν κινδύνων Chrys.*hom.14.7 in Rom.*(9.585E); ἐπὶ μὲν τῶν ἐνύλων, ὁ νοῦς συνεργὸν ἔχει τὸν λογισμόν· ἐπὶ δὲ τῶν ἀΰλων...ὡς σκώλωπα ἕξει κολαφίζοντα ‡Max.*cap.al.*154(M.90.1437A); passage discussed, Didym.*2Cor.*12:7(p.42.12ff.; M.39.1729A); Chrys.*hom.26.2 in 2Cor.* (10.620D–621A); Thdt.*2Cor.*12:7(3.349); cf.Bas.*reg.fus.*55.4(2.400B; M.31.1049C); **3.** *spur* on bird's leg τῶν πτηνῶν οἶμαι ὅσα μὲν σκόλοπας ἔχει κατωτέρω τῶν γονάτων ὑπὲρ τὰς βάσεις καθαρὰ εἶναι βούλεται Or.*sel.in Dt.*14:9(M.12.812B); **4.** *peg* of stringed instrument τὰς χορδὰς οἱ μουσικοὶ διαπαύειν εἰώθασι, καὶ χαλῶσι ταύτας, τοὺς σ. περιστρέφοντες Thdt.*eran.*2(4.174).

σκόπελος, ὁ, *cliff*; fig., ref. Nest. τὸ τῆς ἀσεβείας κῦμα προσέρρηξεν τῷ σ. τῆς καθαιρέσεως Xyst.Papa *tract.*4(p.145.18; M.*PL.*50. 586C); met., *misfortune, adversity*, Gr.Naz.*carm.*2.1.2.18(M.37. 1018A).

***σκοπευτήριον**, τό, **1.** *watch-tower*; freq. of Sion, Or.*fr.19 in Lam.*1:6(p.242.29; M.13.616C); Eus.*d.e.*6.24(p.293.23; M.22.481C); Cyr.*Ps.*9:12(M.69.768D); met. ἐν πάσῃ ψυχῇ Σιὼν οὔσῃ καὶ σ. θεὸς κατοικεῖ Or.*exc.in Ps.*9:12(M.17.105C); τὸν νοῦν...κεκαθαρμένον...ὃς ὀνομάζεται Σιών...ἐπειδὴ ἐκεῖθεν ἔστι τὸ σ. πάσης φύσεως †Bas.*Is.* 291(1.600B; M.30.629A); *ib.*92(443C; M.269B); πᾶς...ὁ τὰ ἀλλότρια κατασκευάζων δόγματα, οἰκοδομεῖ τὴν Σιών, τουτέστι τὸ ἑαυτοῦ σ., ἐν αἵμασι *ib.*152(1.487B; M.368C); σ. ἔχοντες τὴν θεωρητικὴν ψυχήν, ἐκ μετεώρου σκοπεύουσαν ἅπαντα Or.*schol.in Cant.*7:4(M.17.281C); Cyr. *Is.*1.1(2.10B); of OT saints οὗτοι, ζητοῦντες τὸν Χριστὸν καὶ διψῶντες, ἐκλήθησαν Σιὼν...ὅταν δὲ ἐπέτυχον...ἐγένοντο Ἱερουσαλήμ, ὁρῶντες θεόν, καὶ σ. πάσης τῆς γνώσεως ‡Tit.Bost.*palm.*4(M.18.1269C); of Inc. τὴν τοῦ κυρίου νομοθεσίαν, ἀπὸ τοῦ σ. γινομένην, ἀπὸ τῆς σαρκὸς τῆς θεοφόρου ἀφ' ἧς ἐπεσκόπει τὰ κατὰ ἀνθρώπους πράγματα †Bas.*Is.* 72(1.430E; M.30.241A); **2.** *end, aim* σ. τῶν περὶ ἀρετῆς πάσης λόγων ἡ τοῦ νοῦ τήρησίς ἐστιν Hesych.S.*temp.*1.76(M.93.1504C); **3.** *mirror* περιέθετο κόρυθα φρόνησιν, τὸ τῶν ἀρετῶν σ. CCP(681)*or.imp.*(H.3. 1424D).

σκοπευτής, ὁ, *watcher; spy,* Bas.*ep.*223.3(3.338B; M.32.825B); Jo. Eub.*innoc.*3(M.96.1504C).

***σκοπευτικός, 1.** *capable of beholding, contemplating* τῆς σ. καὶ θεωρητικῆς δυνάμεως Σιὼν καλουμένης Or.*fr.14 in Lam.*1:4(p.241.1; M.13.613A); τῆς γνώμης τῆς ἐκκλησιαστικῆς σ. οὔσης τῆς ἀληθείας καὶ διὰ τοῦτο Σιὼν καλουμένης περιληπτέον αὐτῆς ἐν διανοίᾳ τὰ δόγματα id.*sel.in Ps.*47:13(M.12.1441A) = Didym.*Ps.*47:13(M.39.1381B); Or. *Ps.*75:3(p.106); **2.** of places, *giving a view of, looking out* upon, met. τῶν οὐρανίων εἶναι σκοπευτικὸς καταξιωθήσεται †Bas.*Is.*138(1.475E; M.30.341C).

***σκοπεύτρια, ἡ,** = σκοπευτήριον, *watch-tower* Σιὼν...σ. ἑρμηνεύεται *Schol.* in ‡Ath.*fr.Ps.*77:68(p.24); *Schol. ib.*47:3(p.29).

σκοπ-έω, 1. *contemplate* spiritually θεωροῦντες τὸν θεόν, καὶ ~οῦντες τὴν πνευματικὴν γνῶσιν ‡Tit.Bost.*palm.*4(M.18.1269D); **2.** *watch over*; of episcopal jurisdiction, Philost.*h.e.*3.15(v.l. διεσκόπει M.65.505B); ~ούσης τῆς τοῦ θεοῦ δεξιᾶς Leo Mag.*ep.*104.3 (M.*PL.*54.994C; σκεπ- p.59.36).

σκοπός, ὁ, A. of persons; *one that looks about* or *looks after things; look-out man*; of bishops σ. γὰρ εἶναι δεῖ ὑμᾶς τῷ λαῷ τοὺς ἐπισκόπους *Const.App.*2.6.7; *ib.*2.6.10f.

B. of things; **1.** *end, aim, object* ἀποβλέποντες εἰς τὸν σ. τῆς ἀληθείας αὐτοῦ καὶ τὴν οἰκονομίαν δοξαζέτωσαν τὸν κύριον Ath.*ep. Pall.*(M.26.1168D); πάσης νομοθεσίας τῆς θεόθεν γεγενημένης ἕνα σ. Gr.Nyss.*hom.7 in Eccl.*(M.44.716A); Thdr.Mops.*Jon.*proem.(M.66. 317C); cf. *scopon...id est, destinationem et telos, hoc est, finem proprium,* Cassianus *collatio* 1.2(M.*PL.*49.483B); as justifying the means ὁ δὲ σ. τῶν γιγνομένων ἐπὶ τὸ κρεῖττον τὴν παραλλαγὴν ἔχει Gr. Nyss.*or.catech.*26(p.98.13; M.45.68D); *immediate object,* opp. τέλος: τοῖς...γεγαμηκόσι σ. ἡ παιδοποιΐα, τέλος δὲ ἡ εὐτεκνία Clem.*paed.*2. 10(p.208.3; M.8.497A); id.*str.*2.22(p.188.21; M.8.1085B); hence one's *intention, idea* ἀμφότεροι γὰρ πρὸς τὸν ἴδιον σ. ὁρῶντες, καλῶς εἰρήκασιν Ath.*syn.*46(p.271.23; M.26.776B); τὸν Ἰουλιανοῦ μεμαθηκότες... σκοπόν Thdt.*h.e.*3.7.6(3.919); **2.** *purport, meaning, significance,* of tradition εἰ...τὸν...σ. τὸν ἐκκλησιαστικὸν ὡς ἄγκυραν τῆς πίστεως ἐπεγίνωσκον Ath.*Ar.*3.58(M.26.445A); ref. Ac.4:34f. τὸν τῆς εὐσεβείας σ. ἐκπληρούντων Bas.*hom.in Ps.*14(1.357A; M.29.264A); freq. in rel. to scripture, Gr.Nyss.*anim.et res.*(M.46.49C) cit. s. γραφή; ἄνευ τῆς εὑρέσεως τοῦ σ. οὐκ ὠφελεῖ ἡ γραφή Chrys.*exp.in Ps.*3(5.2A); Cyr.*Os.* 1(3.6C); προσήκει τὰ τῆς γραφῆς ἰδιώματα εἰδέναι· οὔτε γὰρ δυνατὸν ἑτέρως αὐτῆς τὸν σ. διαγνῶναι Thdt.*Ezech.*16:53(2.792); εἰ δὲ ταὐτά τις ἐθέλει νοεῖν, τοῦ τῆς...γραφῆς οὐκ ἐκπεσεῖται σκοποῦ id.*Abac.*3:7 (2.1552); Cosm.Ind.*top.*2(M.88.73B); and of heresy, Thdt.*haer.*5.2 (4.388); **3.** *test, proof,* ref. Job's trials οὐ δι' ἁμαρτίας ἐστίν, ἀλλὰ δι' ἀγῶνα καὶ σ. ἀνδρείας Didym.*Job* 13:27(M.39.1149D).

***σκοροδοφάγος, ὁ,** *garlic eater,* Ant.Mon.*hom.*16(M.89.1476D).

σκόρπαινα, ἡ, a kind of fish, Epiph.*haer.*37.9(p.62.10; M.41.653C).

σκορπίζω, 1. *scatter, disperse; spread* a disease; pass., Meth.*lepr.* 10(p.464.10); **2.** *dissipate, squander*; met. σ. ἑαυτούς Tat.*orat.*30 (p.30.21; M.6.868B); **3.** *divide*; **a.** *cause disunion among, Clem.ep.*18 (M.2.53B); **b.** *separate* οὐδαμοῦ σ. ἑαυτὸν [sc. Christ] ἢ διαλύσας εἰς σωτῆρας δύο Thphl.Al.*fr.ep.pasch.*2(*ACO* 1.1.5 p.68.20; M.65.56B).

σκορπισμός, ὁ, *scattering; dispersal, distribution* of wealth δέοντι σ. τὸ βάρος κούφιζε τοῦ πλούτου Isid.Pel.*epp.*1.35(M.78.204C); Max.*ep.*3(M.91.409C).

***σκορπιστήριον, τό,** *instrument of dispersion*; met., *dissipater* κενοδοξία ἐστὶ...καμάτων σ., ἱδρώτων ἀπώλεια Jo.Clim.*scal.*22(M.88. 949A).

***σκορπιστός,** *scattered, out of order*; of letters of the alphabet, Chrys.*hom.4.3 in Col.*(11.355F).

σκοτάζω, 1. intrans., *grow dark,* Or.*hom.12.9 in Jer.*(p.96.6; M. 13.392A); **2.** trans., *darken, make dark,* Ath.*ep.Epict.*10(p.16.12; M.26.1068A).

σκοτασμός, ὁ, *darkening, darkness*; in allegorical interpretations; ref. Jerusalem διὰ τὸ μὴ ἐκ λαμπρῶν μηδὲ πεφωτισμένων πατέρων· διὸ καὶ σκοτασμῷ παραβάλλεσθαι Or.*Cant.*1:4(p.liii; M.17. 256B); Κηδὰρ πάγος γενεᾶς δύναται καὶ σ. κατεσκήνωσα...φησί, μετὰ τῶν σκηνωμάτων τοῦ σ., ὅπερ ἐστὶ τοῦ σώματος τοῦ θανάτου Eus. *Ps.*119:5(M.24.10B); Proc.G.*Is.*42:11(M.87.2372B); Αἴγυπτος...σ. ἂν εἴη καὶ νοηθήσεταί πως εἰς τὴν τοῦ παρόντος αἰῶνος κατάστασιν Cyr. *Jo.*3.6(4.313C); Nil.*exerc.*39(M.79.768C); Αἴγυπτός ἐστι νοητή, ὁ σ. τῶν παθῶν Thal.*cent.*2.35(M.91.1441A).

***σκοτεινόλογος,** *abstruse,* i.e. in one's mode of expression, *M. Apollon.*33.

***σκοτεινόμορφος,** *dark in appearance, gloomy*; of death, Sever. *fic.*2(M.59.588).

σκοτεινός, 1. *dark*; of the west, perh. as unenlightened, *Clem.ep.*1 (M.2.33A) cit. s. δύσις; and as Satanic, Cyr.H.*catech.*19.4; v. 3 infra; **2.** of sight, *blind*; neut. as adv., *dimly* σ. ὁρῶν Clem.*fr.*5(p.221.19); met., *blind* to need or suffering, *heartless, T.Benj.*4.2; οἱ πολλοὶ τοὺς ἀνελεήμονας εἰώθασι καλεῖν σ. Chrys.*hom.78.2 in Mt.*(7.753A); **3.** met., *dark, evil,* of paganism σ. δόγματα Clem.*str.*4.22(p.312.4; M.8.1353B); of heresies ἀστέρας...σ. Meth.*symp.*8.10(p.92.18; M.18. 153B); of Devil, *M.Seb.*5(p.175.27) cit. s. βύθιος; of hell-fire πυρὸς σκοτεινοῦ ἄβυσσον Jo.Clim.*scal.*7(M.88.804C).

***σκοτεινοχαρής,** *rejoicing in darkness* or *secrecy,* Bas.*renunt.*6(2. 208B; M.31.640B).

***σκοτένδυτος,** *clad in darkness, 'black',* of a villain or blackguard, Steph.Diac.*v.Steph.*(M.100.1140A).

***σκοτέω,** for σκοτόω; *darken, blind,* met. ὁ κόσμος μὲν ἐσκότηται καὶ πάντα ἀγνοίαις πεπλήρωται Or.*exc.in Ps.*77:31(M.17.141A); ὁ νοῦς διὰ κακόνοιαν ἐσκοτημένος Eun.ap.Gr.Nyss.*Eun.*10(M.45.825; ἐσκοτω- 2 p.226.8); *cat.Mt.*25:24(p.208.30).

***σκοτήρ, ὁ,** *one who shuns the light, trickster, swindler,* Thdr. Stud.*epp.*2.89(M.99.1337C).

σκοτία, ἡ, *darkness*; **1.** lit. τὸ σῶμα...σ.· ἡ δὲ ὄψις...ὅλη λαμπρά *T.Sal.*13.5(M.122.1336B; v.l. for σκότος p.44.6); **2.** met., ref. Jo.1:5, 1Jo.1:5 ὁ Ἰούδας, τῆς σ. πεπληρωμένος Or.*Jo.*32.24(16; p.469.12f.; M.14.812A); signifying wickedness σ. τὴν κακίαν λέγει †Cyr.*1Jo.*1:5 (p.450; M.74.1021B); of two kinds as touching faith and morals μὴ μίαν σ., ἀλλ' ἤτοι διὰ τὸ γενικὸν δύο, ἢ καὶ διὰ τὸ...πολλὰς εἶναι πράξεις μοχθηρὰς καὶ πολλὰ δόγματα ψευδῆ, πολλαί εἰσι σ. Or.*Jo.*2. 25(20; p.82.29ff.; M.14.160A); Didym.*1Jo.*1:5(M.39.1777C,D); another interprn. σ. ἢ τὸν θάνατον, ἢ τὴν πλάνην φησί *cat.1Jo.*1:5(p.108. 18); **3.** *occultation, obscuring, concealment* ἐν σ. φωτὸς ἀληθείας Eus. *theoph.*6(p.19*.6; M.24.625D).

σκοτίζ-ω, *darken*; in colour ἐκ μέλανος καὶ ἐσκοτισμένου... χιονῶδες εἶδος μεταλαμβάνει [sc. the lily] Gr.Nyss.*Pss.titt.*B 4(M.44. 501D); pass., met., *be clouded* ἐσκοτίσθησαν τὸν νοῦν Ath.*gent.*9(M.25. 20A); σ. καρδίαν τὰ παρ' ἐλπίδα...συμβαίνοντα Cyr.*Am.*75(3.336A); *be confused* ἵν'...τοὺς...ἀκεραίους ~ωσιν Ath.*Ar.*3.59(M.26.448B); *be blinded, dazed* εἰκὼν δὲ τὸ σκότος τοῦ ~εσθαι τοὺς ἐπιβαλόντας χεῖρα τῷ φωτί Or.*comm.ser.134 in Mt.*(p.277.22; cf.M.17.308C); ὑποτρέμων καὶ ~όμενος Meth.*res.*1.27(p.254.11; M.41.1132C); *A.Pil.*B 10.2 (p.303).

σκοτισμός, ὁ, *darkness, blindness,* in allegorical interprn. Ῥαιφὰν δὲ ἑρμηνεύεται σ. ἤτοι τύφλωσις Cyr.*Am.*55(3.310C); Αἴγυπτος μὲν γὰρ σ., Βαβυλὼν δὲ σύγχυσις ἑρμηνεύεται id.*Zach.*73(3.753A); met., of spiritual blindness of Jews, Clem.*paed.*2.8(p.202.23; M.8.485B); the result of wickedness, Or.*or.*28.7(p.379.23; M.11.528B); Cyr.*Is.*3.1 (2.386B,389C).

σκοτοδ(ε)ινι-άω, *grow dizzy*; met., *lose one's head,* e.g. in course of argument, Or.*Jo.*10.3(2; p.173.28; M.14.312A); *ib.*5.4(p.102.3; 189B); ~ῶντες περὶ τὴν ἀλήθειαν Ath.*decr.*18(p.15.11; M.25.'453' (445)D); ~άσας καὶ συμπεδηθεὶς Zach.Mit.*opif.*(M.85.1073A).

σκοτοειδής, *dark-looking*; met., *dark, treacherous* τὰς σ. τῆς ἁμαρτίας ἐφόδους *Lit.Marc.*(Brightman p.137.8); Tit.Bost.*fr.Lc.* 10:18ff.(p.192, v.l. for σκοτώδης).

σκοτόμαινα, ἡ, v. σκοτομήνη.

***σκοτοματικῶς,** *dizzily* σ. πληροῦμαι *suffer from vertigo* or *dizziness,* Thphn.*chron.*p.366(M.108.877B).

σκοτομήνη (-μαινα, [*]-μηνα), ἡ, 1. *moonless night; dense darkness*; of sun and moon opp. divine glory, Bas.*reg.fus.*2.1(2.337C; M. 31.909C); fig., of society τῶν ἐκκλησιῶν φωστῆρες [i.e. οἱ τῆς Χριστοῦ μαθητείας τὸν χαρακτῆρα δεικνύντες]...ἐν τῇ σκυθρωπῇ ταύτῃ καταστάσει, οἷον ἐν σ. διαφαινόμενοι id.*ep.*154(3.243D; M.32.609D); λόγῳ... τὴν νῦν σκοτόμηναν λύσας, εἰς φῶς ἅπαντα...ἐπανήγαγεν [sc. ὁ θεός] Gr.Naz.*or.*5.31(M.35.704B); **2.** met., of concealment, secrecy, ref. Ps.10:2, Cyr.H.*catech.*5.4; Cyr.*ep.*50(p.96.14; 5².165E); τὸ...λαθραῖον κεκρυμμένον σ. ἐκάλεσε Thdt.*Ps.*10:4(1.672); **3.** moral *darkness*; of sin, spiritual ignorance, and error, Mac.Aeg.*hom.*25.4(M.34.669B); Thdt.*ep.*11(4.1068); -μαινα, ‡Proc.G.*Pr.*3:15(M.87.1245C); moral *blindness, lack of spiritual perception* τὴν ἡμετέραν σύγχυσιν καὶ σκοτόμαιναν Gr.Naz.*or*.21.12(M.35.1096A); id.*ep*.206(M.37.341A); ref. Judaism ὥσπερ ἐξ ὕπνου μικρὸν ἀνανήψαντες τῆς κατεχούσης σ. Dam. *troph*.proem.(p.190.12); induced by heresy σύγχυσίν τινα καὶ σ. τῇ ...ἐκκλησίᾳ εἰσπνεύσαντες *ib*.suppl.(p.278.15); and by persistent wickedness, Chrys.*hom*.*13.1 in Eph*.(11.96A); **4.** *night* of despair ὦ κακῆς σ. ἀνατολὴν φωστῆρος οὐκ ἐλπιζούσης Gr.Nyss.*Melet*.(M.46. 852C); of trouble, misfortune, †Jo.D.*B.J*.2(M.96.868A); νὺξ ἀθυμίας καὶ κατηφείας σκοτόμαινα Jo.Mon.*hymn.Chrys*.7(M.96.1381C).

***σκοτοποιΐα, ἡ,** *that which makes darkness*, Dion.Ar.*c.h*.7.1(M.3. 205C).

σκότος, τό (rarely ὁ), *darkness*; **1.** lit., *darkness*; poet., for night ὑπὸ δὲ τούτου τοῦ σκότου...προέπεμψαν...τὴν Μαγδαληνὴν...ἐπὶ τὸ μνημεῖον Rom.Mel.(*AS* 1 p.126); its true nature: absence of light χωρισμὸς...τοῦ θεοῦ θάνατος· καὶ χωρισμὸς φωτὸς σκότος Iren.*haer*.5. 27.2(M.7.1196B); οὐ κτισθὲν σ., ἀλλὰ προαιρετικῶς ἀρξάμενον εἶναι σ. τῇ τοῦ φωτὸς στερήσει Meth.*fr*.*17 in Job* 38:4(p.516.12); not a substance τὸ σ. μὴ κατ' οὐσίαν ὑφεστηκέναι, ἀλλὰ πάθος εἶναι περὶ τὸν ἀέρα στερήσει φωτὸς ἐπιγινόμενον...τὸ...ἐγκόσμιον σ. τῇ σκιᾷ τοῦ οὐρανίου σώματος παρυπέστη Bas.*hex*.2.5(1.17B,18A; M.29.40C,41B); Diod.*Gen*.1:2(M.33.1563A); contingent οὐκ οὐσία τίς ἐστιν [sc. τὸ σ.], ἀλλὰ πρᾶγμα συμβεβηκὸς...ὑποχωροῦντος...τοῦ φωτός, οὐρανοῦ καὶ γῆς ἡ σκιὰ τὸ σ. ἀποτελεῖ...οὐ τοίνυν ἀγένητος οὐσία τὸ σ., οὔτε μὴν γενητή τις ὑπόστασις Thdt.*qu*.*7 in Gen*.(1.11,12); **2.** of evil principle in dualistic heresies δύναμιν κακὴν...παρ' ἑαυτοῦ τὴν ἀρχὴν ἔχον, ἀντικείμενον...τῇ ἀγαθότητι τοῦ θεοῦ ἐξηγοῦνται τὸ σ. Bas.*hex*.2.4(1. 15C; M.29.36B); Gnost.; lowest element in universe, acc. Sethians possessed of understanding, Hipp.*haer*.5.19(pp.116.26,117.12; M.16. 3179A,C); acc. Docetists possessed of power, *ib*.8.9(p.228.17; 3351C); and substance, *ib*.(p.229.10; 3354B); in conflict with the middle element where present, *ib*.(p.228.16ff.; 3351C); Epiph.*haer*.25.5 (p.272.20; M.41.328B); Manich. δύο...θεοὺς...ἕνα τῷ ἑνὶ ἀντικείμενον ...φῶς τῷ ἑνὶ ὄνομα θέμενος καὶ τῷ ἑτέρῳ σκότος καὶ τοῦ μὲν φωτὸς εἶναι μέρος τὴν ἐν ἀνθρώποις ψυχήν, τοῦ δὲ σ. τὸ σῶμα καὶ τὸ τῆς ὕλης δημιούργημα Hegem.*Arch*.7(p.9.14ff.; M.10.1437A); **3.** *primeval darkness* τὸ...περὶ αὐτὴν [sc. τὴν ἄβυσσον] σ. ἀκούσας, τὸ μήπω πεφηνέναι τὴν φωστικὴν δύναμιν τὴν ἐγκειμένην τῇ φύσει τῶν ὄντων ἐνόησα Gr.Nyss.*hex*.21(M.44.84A); στοχαζόμεθα τοίνυν ὅτι τὸ πνεῦμα τοῦ θεοῦ τοσοῦτον ἀπέχει τοῦ σ. εἶναι, ὅσον καὶ παντὸς κακοῦ ἀλλοτρίως ἔχει *ib*.19(81B); **4.** myst., of the divine darkness of light inaccessible τὴν ὑπερούσιον τοῦ θείου σ. ἀκτῖνα Dion.Ar.*myst*.1.1(M. 3.1000A); commented ἐνταῦθα σκότος τὴν παντελῆ ἀκαταληψίαν ἔφη Max.*schol.myst*.1.1(M.4.417B); Jo.D.*f.o*.1.4(M.94.800B) cit. s. ἀπόφασις A; but more usu. γνόφος; **5.** met., *night, darkness*; **a.** of ignorance, esp. ignorance of Christian truth ἐκάλεσεν ἡμᾶς ἀπὸ σ. εἰς φῶς, ἀπὸ ἀγνωσίας εἰς ἐπίγνωσιν δόξης ὀνόματος αὐτοῦ *1Clem*.59.2; λόγος μέν ἐστι τὸ τοῦ θεοῦ φῶς, σ. δὲ ἡ ἀνεπιστήμων ψυχή Tat.*orat*. 13(p.14.20; M.6.833B); Clem.*paed*.2.9(p.206.12; M.8.493B); masc., id.*str*.5.3(p.337.5; M.9.33C); Gr.Nyss.*hom*.*11 in Cant*.(M.44.1000D); Didym.*2Cor*.4:5f.(p.24.26ff.; M.39.1700A); Dion.Ar.*d.n*.4.5(M.3. 700D); **b.** of untruth; ref. apostasy, Iren.*haer*.5.28.1(M.7.1198A); of paganism τὸ σ. τῶν ἀσεβῶν δογμάτων Or.*Cels*.6.67(p.137.8; M.11. 1400B); τῶν ναῶν περιῃρῆσθαι τὰ ἔθη καὶ τοῦ σ. τὴν ἐξουσίαν Const. ap.Eus.*v.C*.2.60(p.65.22; M.20.1033C); of atheism, Eus.*theoph.fr*.6 (p.20*.25; M.24.629A); of error σ. ἐνταῦθα οὐ τὸ αἰσθητὸν καλῶν, ἀλλὰ τὴν πλάνην καὶ τὴν ἀσέβειαν Chrys.*hom*.*17.1 in Mt*.(7.178C); **c.** Satanic ὁ ἄρχων τοῦ σ. Meth.*res*.1.38(p.281.9; οὗτος M.41.1105B); ἐκεῖνος δὲ σκότος τυγχάνων ἐν σκότῳ ἔχει καὶ τὸ κράτος Cyr.H.*catech*. 19.4; abode of demons, *Hom.Clem*.20.9; *Const.App*.5.16.6; **d.** of moral evil ἔχων ὁδοῦ δικαιοσύνης γνῶσιν, ἑαυτὸν εἰς ὁδὸν σκότους ἀποσυνέχει *Barn*.5.4; Mac.Aeg.*hom*.2.1,4(M.34.464A,465B); ἄρχει [sc. Satan]...τῶν ἑαυτοὺς παραδιδόντων αὐτῷ. διὰ τοῦτο καὶ ἄρχοντα τοῦ σ. τοῦ αἰῶνος τούτου καλεῖ, σ. ἐνταῦθα πάλιν τὰς πονηρὰς πράξεις καλῶν Chrys.*hom*.*75.4 in Jo*.(8.444B); Cyr.*ador*.1(1.46C); (more properly ἔργα τοῦ σ.) σ. καλεῖ τὴν ἄγνοιαν, ἔργα δὲ τοῦ σ. τὰς παρανόμους πράξεις Thdt.*Rom*.13:12(3.139); esp. of sensuality τῆς τοῦ σ. ἐνεργείας τῶν παθῶν Mac.Aeg.*ep*.(M.34.409C); Nil.*exerc*.55(M.79. 788B); Cyr.*Jo*.3.4(4.291A); Max.*schol.e.h*.2.3.8(M.4.133A); **e.** of misfortune or calamity, Chrys.*exp.in Ps*.138:11f.(5.413A); σ. ποτὲ μὲν τὴν ἄγνοιαν, ποτὲ δὲ τὰς συμφορὰς ὀνομάζει Thdt.*Ps*.111:4(1.1404); id.*Is*.59:9(p.231.20; 2.376); **f.** of punishment (ref. Jo.9:4) ἡμέραν... ὠνόμασε τὸν αἰῶνα τοῦτον, σ. δὲ καὶ νύκτα τὴν συντέλειαν διὰ τὰς κολάσεις Or.*hom*.*12.10 in Jer*.(p.96.13; M.13.392B); φῶς καλεῖ τὴν εὐαγγελικὴν διδασκαλίαν, σ. δὲ τὴν ἄγνοιαν, ἢ τὴν τῶν ἀσεβῶν κατάκρισιν Ammon.*Jo*.12:35(M.85.1477A); hence of hell ἐν τῷ σκότῳ τῷ ἀσβέστῳ...καθειρχθήσεται, δίκας ὧν ἔδρασεν ἀπαιτηθησόμενος Isid. Pel.*epp*.4.161(M.78.1248A).

σκοτ-όω, *darken*; *blind*; hence *stun*, *T.Jud*.2.7; *kill* ἀνάστησον τὴν φοράδα, ἣν ἐσκότωσεν ὁ πατήρ σου Barth.Edess.*Agar*.(M.104.1441A); ἐὰν δύο ταῦροι παλαιοῦντες, ~ωθῇ ὁ εἷς, μεριζέσθωσαν οἱ δύο οἰκοκυροί, καὶ τὸν ζῶντα καὶ τὸν τεθανατωμένον *Nomoc*.274; *ib*.482.

σκοτώδης, 1. *dark*; neut. as subst., *darkness* of complexion, *swarthiness*, Or.*sel.in Gen*.2:13(M.12.100B); **2.** *wicked* ὡς ἀστραπὴ ἦν [sc. Satan] λαμπρὸς τὴν φύσιν, ἀλλὰ σ. τὴν προαίρεσιν Tit.Bost.*fr*. *Lc*.10:18ff.(p.192).

σκότωμα, τό, 1. ? *dark place* [φ]ωστὴρ πάντων σκοτωμ[ά]των *Pap. Chr*.(p.430); **2.** *act of killing*, ref. one unjustly convicted οἱ δὲ αὐτὸν [sc. τὸν βοῦν] παρεκρίνουν χωρὶς σκοτώματος *Nomoc*.483.

σκότωσις, ἡ, *darkening*; met.; **1.** *clouding*; *eclipse* σ. τῶν διανοημάτων Epiph.*haer*.51.6(p.256.1; M.41.900B); Ἡρωδιάς...ἡ σ. τῆς ἀληθείας Chrysipp.*enc.in Jo.Bapt*.11(p.41.18); **2.** *darkness, blindness* οὔτε τὸ φῶς τυφλότητα...οὔτε τὸ πνεῦμα σ. ἐμποιεῖ †Bas.*Is*.5(1.381C; M.30.125C); Chrys.*hom*.*8.1 in Jo*.(8.48C); †Jo.D.*B.J*.7(M.96.909C); *blinding effect* τοσαύτη ἡ τῆς ἁμαρτίας σ. Chrys.*hom*.*3.4 in 1Tim*. (11.567A).

***σκούλκα, ἡ,** *watch, sentry, outpost*, Heracl.*ep*.(M.92.1021A); *Chron.Pasch*.p.396(M.92.1013C).

***σκουρδώμη, ἡ,** ? = σκόρ(ο)δον, *garlic* μικρὰ βρώματα...ἅπερ ἐστὶν λαψάνια μετὰ ὄξους καὶ ἐλαίου καὶ σκουρδώμας καὶ λεπτολάχανον *V.Pach.Λ* 15(p.139.5).

***σκρίβας, ὁ,** (Lat. *scriba*) *scribe* ὁ πραιπόσιτος καὶ ὁ σ. *PLond*. 1914.18.

***σκρίβων, ὁ,** *officer of the imperial guard* τοὺς γενναιοτάτους σ. Eustrat.*v.Eutych*.70(M.86.2353B); Jo.Mosch.*prat*.174 passim(M.87. 3041Df.); ἐκπέμπει σ. ... τὸν ἐπίσκοπον πρὸς αὐτὸν ἀγαγεῖν Thphn. *chron*.p.231(M.108.585A).

σκρινιάριος, ὁ, (Lat. *scriniarius*) *keeper of records, secretary*, Jo. Mal.*chron*.18 pp.429f.(M.97.633B); Niceph.Ur.*v.Sym*.216(M.86. 3184D); ? of church at CP, *IGC As.Min*.225 (Miletus, 602).

σκρίνιον, τό, (Lat. *scrinium*) *dossier, record*; eccl., *register*, Cyr. *ep*.85(5^2.212D).

σκυβαλίζ-ω, 1. *treat as dirt, regard with contempt* ~ων μέν σου τὴν πολυκίνδυνον περιουσίαν Bas.*ep*.45.1(3.133C; M.32.365B); Ephr. 2.417E; **2.** *defile* τὰ τοιαῦτα τοῦ διαβόλου ἐνεργήματα ἐκτελῶν ὡς ἂν κεχειροτονημένος ὑπὸ τοῦ διαβόλου ~ειν τὴν ἐκκλησίαν *Const.App*.2. 43.3.

σκύβαλον, τό, *excrement*; *refuse*, hence *ruins, remains* σ. τῆς μαρμαρώσεως Marc.Diac.*v.Porph*.76.

σκυβαλώδης, *refuse-like, waste*; of excrement, Or.*fr.in Ezech*. 32:6(M.17.288B); Melet.*nat.hom*.synops.(M.64.1128B); of the heavier and baser elements, Epiph.*haer*.8.1(p.187.4; M.41.205D); of material things τὸ σ. τοῦτο τὸ παχὺ τῆς ὕλης μέρος καὶ γεῶδες Max.*schol.d.n*. 4.20(M.4.277D).

[*]σκυθησμός, ὁ, v. *Σκυθισμός*.

Σκυθίζω, *behave like a Scythian*; hence *collaborate with the enemy, play the traitor*, Synes.*provid*.2.2(p.113.6; M.66.1261C).

Σκυθισμός (Σκυθησμός), ὁ, second of the main chronological divisions in Epiph.'s classification of heresies δευτέρα [sc. ὀνομασία] Σ. ἀπὸ τῶν ἡμερῶν τοῦ Νῶε...ἀχρὶ...Βαβυλῶνος...καὶ μετὰ τὸν τοῦ πύργου χρόνον ἐπὶ ὀλίγοις ἔτεσιν Epiph.*anac*.2(p.162.11; M.41.165D); (ref. Cant.6:7) given third place περὶ τῶν παλλακῶν τούτων τῶν ὀγδοήκοντα εἰρηκότες...βαρβαρισμοῦ καὶ Ἑλληνισμοῦ καὶ Σ. id.*haer*. 80.10(p.495.6; M.42.772B); χρὴ δὲ γινώσκειν ὅτι...ἀπὸ βαρβαρισμοῦ ἕως σκυθησμοῦ ἔτη φ'· καὶ ἀπὸ σκυθησμοῦ ἕως Ἑλληνισμοῦ ἔτη χίλια σλζ' †Hipp.Th.*fr*.8b(p.35.20; M.117.1048C).

***Σκυθότροφος,** *fed by the Scythians*; met., *supplied* or *fomented by the Scythians* ἡ Σ. Σκύλλα Geo.Pis.*bell.Avar*.204(M.92.1276B); ἡ χάρυβδις ἡ Σ. id.*Heracl*.2.73(M.92.1322A).

***σκυθρωπ-άω,** = σκυθρωπάζω, *wear a gloomy* or *sullen look*, of world before Inc. ἡ τοῦ κόσμου πρόσοψις ~ῶσα Const.*or.s.c*.11(p.170. 22; M.20.1269A).

σκυθρωπός, of things; **1.** *sad, gloomy*; of prophecies of Jeremiah, Or.*hom*.*20.2 in Jer*.(p.178.27; M.13.504A); of contemporary society, Bas.*ep*.154(3.243D; M.32.609D); of condemnation of Nestorius, CEph.(431)*act*.1(*ACO* 1.1.2 p.54.25; H.1.1422E); neut. as subst., *misfortune, trial, disaster*, ref. Mt.23:35f. παρὰ τὴν αὐτῶν αἰτίαν τὰ σ. αὐτοὺς μετελεύσεται Eus.*theoph.fr*.12(p.27*.11; M.24.644B); τοὺς... περιπεσόντας σκυθρωποῖς νουθετῶν Didym.*Job* 6:21(M.39.1137A); τὴν θείαν οἰκονομίαν τὴν διὰ τῶν σ. κεκρυμμένην Gr.Nyss.*v.Macr*.(p.390. 4; M.46.977B); Cyr.*Is*.4.3(2.644A,645C); **2.** *grievous, severe*, of a miracle resulting in a death εἰ δὲ σ. εἶναι δοκεῖ τὸ τοιοῦτον ἔργον... ξενιζέσθω μηδείς, πρὸς τὸν μέγαν Πέτρον ὁρῶν Gr.Nyss.*v.Gr.Thaum*. (M.46.941A); τῶν σ. ἡ δριμύτης Cyr.*Am*.75(3.336A); of punishment θείᾳ κρίσει αὐτουργεῖται τὰ σκυθρωπότερα ὑπό τινων πονηρῶν ἀγγέλων Or.*Cels*.8.32(p.247.17; M.11.1564B); id.*comm.in Rom*.2: 15f. (*JTS* 13 p.216); σκυθρωπῶν...ἐπανόρθωσις Gr.Nyss.*or.catech*.8(p.47.5; M.45.36D).

σκυθρωπότης, ἡ, 1. *sorrow, grief*, Gr.Naz.*or*.9.2(M.35.820C); Leont.N.*v.Jo.Eleem*.6(p.12.13); of contrition τὸ ἐν σ. ὁμαλόν, μηδέποτε τῆς ἐννοίας ἡμῶν λειπούσης τοῦ...δικαστηρίου τὴν μνήμην Bas.*ep*.173(3.261D; M.32.649B); id.*mor*.8.9(3.521D; M.32.1233C); **2.** *gloom, melancholy* τὴν χειμερινὴν σ. Gr.Nyss.*hom.5 in Cant*.(M.44.865A); μετὰ σκυθρωπότητος κἂν πολλὰ δῷς, ὀλίγα πεποίηκας τὰ πολλά Chrys.*hom.21.2 in Rom*.(9.673D).

***σκυθρωποφανής,** *unpleasant-seeming* ἐν τῇ γραφῇ...τὰ σ., ἵν' οὕτως ὀνομάσω, πρῶτα ὀνομαζόμενα, εἶτα τὰ δοκοῦντα ἱλαρὰ δεύτερα λεγόμενα Or.*hom.1.16 in Jer*.(p.14.25; M.13.273D).

***σκυλακηδόν,** *puppy-like*, Synes.*provid*.1.2(p.66.9; M.66.1213B).

σκύλευσις, ἡ, *spoliation*, as a sign of victory, Epiph.*haer*.55.9 (p.335.16; M.41.988A); τὴν ἑβδόμην [sc. σφραγῖδα] εἰς τὴν τοῦ ᾅδου σ. Andr.Caes.*Apoc*.13(M.106.588B).

σκυλευτής, ὁ, *despoiler* Παῦλος καὶ σ. τῶν ἐκκλησιῶν ἦν ‡Chrys. *Jud*.(1.821D); met. κενοδοξίαν, τὸν γλυκὺν σ. τοῦ πνευματικοῦ πλούτου ‡Bas.*const*.10.2(2.556D; M.31.1373A).

σκυλεύ-ω, 1. *despoil* a slain enemy; pass., Clem.*q.d.s*.34(p.183.1; M.9.640C); reading of Cant.1:7(SM), Or.*schol.in Cant*.7:1(M.17.280C); met. ἐσκυλεύθητε...παρὰ τοῦ διαβόλου πᾶσαν ὑμῶν τὴν ἀρετὴν *V.Pach.A* 1(p.123.19); **2.** of Christ, as disarming pagan world, Ath. *inc*.53.1(M.25.189C); as *despoiling, harrowing* ἡ θεότης ~σασα τὸν ᾅδην Ph.Carp.*Cant*.126(M.40.100B); Cyr.*Jon*.19(3.381C); id.*Arcad*. 52(p.56.22; 5².173A); Oecum.*Apoc*.5:6(p.79); Eulog.*palm*.8(M.86. 2925B); at Judgement, *T.Lev*.4.1.

[*]**σκύλησις, ἡ,** v. σκύλσις.

σκυλί(ο)ν, τό, *dog*, *Exorc*.10(p.335).

σκύλλ-ω, 1. *molest* σ. τὰ ὀστᾶ *CG–CI* 1 15.7(p.31; saec. iv–v); hence *damage* σκυλθεῖσαν τὴν εἰκόνα [sc. νοτίδι] Thdr.Lect.*fr*.(M.86. 224C); **2.** *trouble, annoy*; **a.** reflex., *A.Xanthipp*.3(p.60.5); **b.** med. and pass. intrans., *worry, be troubled*, *A.Phil*.93(p.36.2); Pall.*h.Laus*. 18(p.55.22; M.34.1060B); **c.** med. and pass., *give oneself trouble, labour* οὐκ ὀφείλεις ἐπὶ τὴν Θηβαΐδα ~όμενος ἀπελθεῖν Ath.*narr. fug*.(M.26.981B); ἐν...ἀσθενείᾳ σώματος...οὕτως ~εσθαι Marc.Diac. *v.Porph*.5; σ. ταῖς χερσί Nil.*Magn*.23(M.79.1000A); esp. *take the trouble of a journey, trouble to come* or *go* ἐδεήθην σου σκυλῆναι πρός με *Ep.Abg*.ap.Eus.*h.e*.1.13.8(M.20.121C); ἐσκύλην ἕως Θηβαΐδος Pall. *h.Laus*.35(p.101.12; M.34.1113C); Marc.Diac.*v.Porph*.40; τί ἐσκύλη πρὸς ἡμᾶς ἡ εὐλάβεια ὑμῶν; CCP(448)*act*.4(*ACO* 2.1.1 p.130.9; H.2. 149A); Cyr.S.*v.Sab*.68(p.170.25); Leont.N.*v.Jo.Eleem*.44b(p.91.7); **d.** act. trans., *trouble* one *to come* or *to attend* καταξίωσον...σκῦλαι αὐτόν CCP(448)*act*.7(*ACO* 2.1.1 p.138.36; H.2.160D); *trouble with one's presence* οὐκ ἂν τὴν σύνοδον ἔσκυλα ἐνταῦθα CChalc.*act.Caros*. (p.100.12; H.2.432E).

σκύλμα, τό, *trouble, confusion*, Geo.Pis.*hex*.342(M.92.1460A).

σκυλμός, ὁ, 1. *effort, trouble* ἆρα γράμματα εἰ ἐμάνθανες, οὐχ ὑπέμενες τὸν σ.; Ephr.2.80D; σ. εὐσεβείας Nil.*epp*.2.167(M.79.284A); ὁ ἐν τῇ σωματικῇ εὐχῇ σ. Jo.Clim.*scal*.15(M.88.900C); esp. of a journey τὸν ἐκ τοῦ πλοῦ σ. *Hom.Clem*.2.2; οὐδὲ ζημίαν ἡγοῦντο τὸν κόπον τῆς ὁδοῦ Ath.*v.Anton*.62(M.26.932C); *ib*.84(961B); Gr. Nyss.*v.Ephr*.(M.46.833C); abs. ἀναγκαίαν τὴν τῶν ἁπανταχόθεν... ἐπισκόπων...σύνοδον ἡγησάμεθα, ὀκνηρότεροι δὲ...περὶ τὸν σ. τῆς αὐτῶν θεοσεβείας γεγόναμεν Thds.Imp.*ep.Cyr*.2(p.115.17; H.1. 1344D); Cyr.S.*v.Sab*.51(p.142.27); hence, *journey* ἠρώτα τὴν αἰτίαν τοῦ σ. Marc.Diac.*v.Porph*.35; cf. σκύλλω; **2.** *suffering*; of persecuted Church, Or.*schol.in Cant*.7:1(M.17.281A); τὸν σ. αὐτοῦ [sc. of Christ] διαβάλλοντες *Pers*.(p.19.7); *sign of suffering* οὐ...στεναγμός, οὐ φωνή, οὐ σ. ‡Jo.D.*Artem*.37(M.96.1285B).

σκύλσις (σκύλησις), ἡ, *trouble*; **1.** *fatigue* εὐμαρῶς...τὰς τῶν ὁδῶν φέρομεν σ. *Hom.Clem*.12.6; **2.** *disturbance* ἐκτὸς σ. τῇ πίστει συνθέσθαι Ibas *ep*.(p.34.13; H.2.532B); **3.** *suffering, distress* οὐκ αἰσθητὴν σκύλησιν λέγει ἀλλὰ νοητήν *cat.Mt*.9:36(p.73.2).

***σκυμνάριον, τό,** *cub*; of a lion-cub, *V.Mac*.A(p.158).

***σκύπτω,** *prostrate oneself*, Leont.Abb.*v.Gr.Agr*.41(M.98.621C); σ. τὰ γόνατα *genuflect*, *Apoc.BMV*(Vassiliev p.125).

σκυρωτός, lit., *stone-paved*; hence *compact, solid* πῶς οὐ κατολισθαίνει τῆς σ. πήξεως τοῦ στερεώματος τὰ ὑπεράνω αὐτοῦ ὕδατα; ‡Caes.Naz.*dial*.92(M.38.956).

***σκυτεργάτης, ὁ,** *worker in skins* or *hides*; of S. Paul, Geo.Pis. *res*.27(M.92.1377A).

σκυτίς, ἡ, *amulet of leather* οὐδὲ ὁ μεμηνὼς σκυτίδων ἐξαρτήμασι θεραπεύεται Tat.*orat*.17(p.18.24; M.6.844A).

***σκυτοεργός, ὁ,** *worker in leather*, Gr.Naz.*carm*.2.1.13.100(M.37. 1235A).

***σκυτόμως,** sens. dub. σπεῦσον καὶ φέρε σ. *Asen*.15(p.62.22; perh. f.l. for συντόμως).

σκυφίον, τό, *small can*, *Mir.Artem*.25(p.35.22).

σκυφοειδής, *shaped like a shield*, Olymp.*Job* 38:38(M.93.409C).

σκύφος, τό, *shield*, Jo.Mal.*chron*.2 p.37(M.97.108B); *ib*.p.35(105A).

***σκυφόω,** *hollow out* γλύψας γὰρ εἶχεν ἐσκυφωμένα σκάφη Geo.Pis. *bell.Avar*.411(M.92.1287A).

σκωληκιάω, *be eaten by worms* τὰ μέλη ἡμῶν τὰ λελυμένα βάψωμεν ἐν αὐτῷ [sc. Christ], ἵνα μὴ ὀζέσωσι καὶ σ. Esaias *or*.11(p.70; cf.M. 40.1136A).

σκωληκόβρωτος, *eaten by worms* σ. τὸ σῶμα εἶχον *T.Job* 20(p.115. 32); of persons, Hipp.*antichr*.49(p.33.10; M.10.769B); Jo.Mal.*chron*. 10 p.231(M.97.356D).

***σκωληκοκάμπη, ἡ,** insect pest which attacks the vine, *Euchol*. (p.555).

***σκωληκόμεστος,** *full of worms* or *maggots*, Sophr.H.*mir.Cyr.et Jo*.10(M.87.3449C).

σκώληξ, ὁ, *worm*; of Christ's humanity as bait to catch Devil, Or.*sel.in Ps*.21:7(M.12.1253C); Mac.Mgn.*apocr*.3.9(p.72.16ff.); ref. eternal punishment σκώληκά τις ἀκούσας μὴ διὰ τῆς ὁμωνυμίας πρὸς τὸ ἐπίγειον τοῦτο θηρίον ἀποφερέσθω τῇ διανοίᾳ· ἡ γὰρ προσθήκη τοῦ ἀτελεύτητον εἶναι ἄλλην τινὰ φύσιν παρὰ τὴν γινωσκομένην νοεῖν ὑποτίθεται Gr.Nyss.*or.catech*.40(p.163.15; M.45.105A).

σκῶλον, τό, 1. = σκάνδαλον; **a.** *obstruction*, Cyr.H.*catech*.3.2; met., *obstacle, hindrance* ὀργὴ...εὐχῆς σκῶλον †Nil.*vit*.3(M.79.1144A); **b.** *trap, snare*; met., Is.8:14b(AQ)cit.ap.Thdt.*Is*.8:14(p.45.4; 2. 227); **c.** *cause of offence, temptation* εἰς σκάνδαλον καὶ παγίδα καὶ σ. Meth.*res*.1.38(p.281.1; M.41.1105A); Thdt.*qu.48 in 4Reg*.(1.540); σ. καὶ προσκόμματα Gr.Agr.*Eccl*.2.5(M.98.817C); **2.** = σκῶλος, *thorn*, Jos.23:13 for LXX βολίδας cit.ap.Thdt.*qu.19 in Jos*.(1.317).

[*]**σκώλωψ, ὁ,** v. σκόλοψ.

σκῶμμα, τό, *jest*; plur., *follies* κατορθώματά τε καὶ σ. Isid.Pel.*epp*. 1.156(M.78.288B).

***σκωπτηλῶς,** *mockingly*, Epiph.*haer*.76.54(p.413.19; M.42.636D).

σκώπτης, ὁ, *mocker*, Nil.*Eulog*.18(M.79.1116C).

***σκωπτωδῶς,** *jeeringly, in mockery*, Epiph.*haer*.64.10(p.419.4; M. 41.1085B).

***σκωρεώδης,** *dross-like*, Gr.Nyss.*mort*.(M.46.529C).

σμαράγδινος, *of smaragdus, emerald* τῆς σ. βώλου Gr.Nyss.*hom. 14 in Cant*.(M.44.1072C).

σμῆγμα, τό, *soap*; met., *purifier* ἡ...ἐλεημοσύνη...σ. [sc. ἐστι] τοῦ ῥύπου τῆς ἡμετέρας ψυχῆς Chrys.*hom.6.3 in Tit*.(11.768C).

σμηκτικός, 1. *cleansing*; of an ointment, Clem.*paed*.2.8(p.203.32; M.8.488C); of a herb, Cyr.*Ps*.18:10(M.69.832C); of hyssop, †Cyr.*coll. VT*(6⁴.28C; M.77.1217B); **2.** *possessed of cleansing power, purgative*, of God's word ὁ λόγος...παντὸς τοῦ καθαρίζοντος δύναμίς ἐστι καὶ σμηκτικώτατος Or.*hom.2.2 in Jer*.(p.18.12; M.13.280A); of H. Ghost, Cyr.*Is*.5.2(2.780A); πῦρ δὲ ἡ σ. τοῦ πνεύματος δύναμις πάντα ῥύπον ἐκτήκουσα Proc.G.*Is*.55:7(M.87.2557A); of penance τὴν συνεκτικὴν [v.l. σμικτικὴν] τῆς τοιαύτης πηρώσεως μετάνοιαν Oecum.*Apoc*.3:18 (p.66); cf. τὴν σ. δύναμιν τῆς τοιαύτης τυφλώσεως *cat.Apoc*.3:18 (p.234.12).

***σμήλη, ἡ,** *cleansing ointment*, ref. 2Reg.12:1 ἐγώ σου τὴν τῆς ἰατρείας σ. ἐπιθήξω τοῖς λόγοις Bas.Sel.*or*.17.3(M.85.221B).

***σμηνεύω,** *settle in a swarm*, Epiph.*haer*.13.1(p.206.16; M.41. 237B).

σμήνη, ἡ, *swarm* of bees, Philost.*h.e*.10.9(M.65.589B).

[*]**σμηρίτης, ὁ,** v. σμυρίτης.

σμήχ-ω, *wipe clean, wash away*, lit. and met. σμήξας τὸ ὄμμα τῆς ψυχῆς Or.*comm.in Rom*.1:1(*JTS* 13 p.211); Meth.*symp*.7.2(p.72.22; M.18.128A); ref. S. Paul's blindness ὑπὸ τοῦ φόβου ~όμενος καὶ προπαρασκευαζόμενος Chrys.*hom.1.6 in Ac*.(9.10B); of baptism σ. ἀνδρομέης κραδίης ῥύπον Nonn.*par.Jo*.3:22(M.43.769C).

[*]**σμιγνύω** ([*]**σμίγω**), for μίσγω = μίγνυμι.

σμικρο-, see also μικρο-.

***σμικροκήρυξ,** *acting as a minor herald*; *dimly precursory*; of Law, Cyr.*Jo*.3.2(4.258D).

***σμικροπρεπεύομαι,** *be small-minded, engrossed in trivialities*, Synes.*ep*.138(μικρο- M.66.1528D).

σμικρότης (μικρότης), ἡ, 1. *smallness*; *limitedness* τοῖς μηδέπω χωρεῖν δυναμένοις τὰ τέλεια διαλέγεται ὁ σωτὴρ συγκαταβαίνων αὐτῶν τῇ σ. Thgn.*hypot.fr*.1(p.76; M.10.240C); τὴν τοῦ θεοῦ δύναμιν opp. τῆς τῶν ἀγαλμάτων σ., Ath.*gent*.21(M.26.41C); οὐ κατὰ τὴν τοῦ σώματος σ. συστέλλεται [sc. ἡ ψυχή] *ib*.33(65C); ref. Inc., Meth.

symp.8.11(p.96.2; M.18.157A) cit. s. σμικρύνω; **2.** *brief duration*, *Pss. Sal*.14.4.

***σμικρ-όω**, s.v.l., *lessen*, *diminish* θεότητα τοῦ μονογενοῦς ~οῦντας ἢ ἀποθεοῦντας τὴν ἀνθρωπότητα Nest.ap.Cyr.*ep*.10(5².33B; νεκροῦντας p.110.22) = *fr*.C 10 tit.(v.l. for νεκροῦντας p.265.4).

σμικρύν-ω (μικρύνω), *make small*; hence **1.** *abase*, *humble* αὐτὸς ταπεινοφρονῶν καὶ ~ων ἑαυτὸν καὶ μὴ καυχώμενος Hipp.*Dan*.2.6.7; **2.** senses combined in theol. contexts; **a.** ref. OT theophanies ὁ θεὸς ὤφθη...~ων ἑαυτὸν καὶ σωματοποιῶν...μεταμορφούμενός τε καὶ ὀπτανόμενος...οὐ καθόσον αὐτός ἐστιν (ἀχώρητος γάρ) ἀλλὰ κατὰ τὴν ἐκείνων χώρησίν τε καὶ δύναμιν Mac.Aeg.*elev*.8(M.34.896B); id.*hom*.4.13(M.34.481C); **b.** ref. Inc. ἑαυτὸν ~ει ὁ μέγας καὶ δεδοξασμένος λόγος γενόμενος σάρξ Or.*Jo*.32.4(p.431.31; M.14.749C); κηρύξω...περὶ τῆς μικρότητος καὶ περὶ τῆς ταπεινώσεως, πῶς ἐταπείνωσεν ἑαυτὸν καὶ ἀπέθετο καὶ ἐσμίκρυνεν αὐτοῦ τὴν θεότητα, καὶ ἐσταυρώθη *Ep.Chr*.ap.Eus.*h.e*.1.13.20(M.20.128C); αὐτὸς γὰρ ἐν ἑαυτῷ σμικρυνθείς, καὶ ἐν τοῖς ἑαυτοῦ μέρεσιν ἀναλυθείς, ἐκ τῆς ἑαυτοῦ σμικρότητος καὶ τῶν ἑαυτοῦ μερῶν εἰς τὴν συμπλήρωσιν πάλιν τὴν ἑαυτοῦ καὶ τὸ μέγεθος κατέστη, οὐδέποτε τοῦ τέλειος εἶναι μειωθείς Meth.*symp*.8.11(p.96.1; M.18.157A); τῆς θεότητος ὑποβὰς καὶ τοῦ συμφυοῦς μεγέθους ἑαυτὸν ~ας Eus.*d.e*.6.9(p.259.10; M.22.425C); ~ουσιν [sc. followers of Paul. Sam.] ἄρα ἀκούοντες αὐτὸν σάρκα γεγενῆσθαι ‡Ath.*Ar*.4.31(p.81.3; M.26.517A); ἐσωματοποίησεν ἑαυτὸν ὁ ἄπειρος καὶ ἀπρόσιτος καὶ ἀποίητος θεός...καὶ ὡς εἰπεῖν ὡς ἐσμίκρυνεν αὐτὸν ἐκ τῆς ἀπροσίτου δόξης ἵνα συνενωθῆναι δυνηθῇ τοῖς ὁρατοῖς αὐτοῦ κτίσμασιν Mac.Aeg.*hom*.4.9(M.34.480A); Jo.D.*f.o*.3.7(M.94.1012B) cit. s. συστέλλω; **3.** *diminish*; hence *attenuate*, *weaken* τῇ τῶν ἐκ περιτομῆς συναγωγῇ, πάσῃ πτωχείᾳ λόγου καὶ βίου καὶ...δόξης ἐσμικρυμένῃ Eus.*d.e*.10.8(p.491.14; ἐσμικρυμμένῃ M.22.789A); ἐσμικρύνθησάν μου [i.e. τοῦ διαβόλου] τὰ κέντρα, ἠσθένησέν μου τὸ κράτος Eus.Al.*serm*.11(M.86.376C).

[*]**σμικτικός**, v. σμηκτικός.

§**σμίλαξ, ὁ**, = σμίλη, *knife*, of S. Paul's preaching τοῦ σκυτοτομικοῦ σ. τὴν...πλάνην ἐκτεμόντος Sophr.H.*v.Cyr.et Jo*.15(M.87.3397B).

***σμιλεύομαι**, pass., *be cut with a knife*, *pruned away*, met. σοφοὺς ...ἐσμιλευμένους Gr.Naz.*carm*.2.1.41.29(M.37.1341A).

σμινύη, ἡ, *hoe*, *mattock*; also *ploughshare*, met. μὴ πρὸς τὴν σ. τὴν τοῦ θείου ἀτονήσῃς ἀρότρου Isid.Pel.*epp*.1.260(M.78.337D).

***σμυραινώδης**, *eel-like*, of perils of Ophite heresies ἄπληκτοι... ἀπὸ σ. ἰοῦ Epiph.*haer*.37.9(p.62.9; M.41.653C).

[*]**σμυρίτης (σμηρ-), ὁ**, *emery*, οὗ [sc. Leviathan] χαλκαὶ μὲν αἱ πλευραί...ἔγκατα δὲ αὐτοῦ σ. λίθος Gr.Nyss.*hom*.5 *in Cant*.(M.44.881A); αἱ κακίαι...μία τῆς μιᾶς ἤρτηνται. τοιαύτη δὲ καὶ ἡ τοῦ σμηρίτου λίθου φύσις Olymp.*Job* 41:6(M.93.441A).

[*]**σμυρνηφόρος**, *myrrh-bearing* δένδρον ἣν σμυρνηφόρον ὁ Παῦλος, ὁ καθ' ἡμέραν ἀποθνήσκων Gr.Nyss.*hom*.10 *in Cant*.(M.44.989A).

σμυρνιάζω, 1. *embalm* for burial, Jo.Mal.*chron*.9 p.220(M.97.341C); **2.** *preserve with myrrh*, *ib*.12 p.304(460A).

σμυρνίζω, 1. *embalm* for burial, *A.Petr.c.Sim*.11(p.100.3); Ephr.2.234F; Hier.*v.Paul*.A 8(p.16.12); **2.** *flavour with myrrh*, ref. Mc.15:23, Cyr.H.*catech*.13.39.

σοβαρεύ-ω, *give oneself airs*, *swagger*, ref. Mt.4:3 λέγων [sc. ὁ διάβολος]· υἱὸς θεοῦ ~εις καλούμενος Bas.Sel.*pasch*.2.6(M.28.1088D); usu. med. πατριαρχίας ὄνομα ἑαυτῷ καὶ σχῆμα περιθείς, ἐξαίφνης ἐσοβαρεύσατο Bas.*ep*.169(3.258C; M.32.641D); Cyr.*Jo*.2.5(4.190B); ref. Mt.20:23 τί τοῖς σοῖς κατὰ σοῦ ~εται [sc. ὁ Ἄρειος] ῥήμασι; Bas.Sel.*or*.24(M.85.284D).

***σοβαρότης, ἡ**, *arrogance*, Jo.D.*virt*.(M.95.88B) = Ephr.3.426D.

σόβας, *licentious*, Didym.*Zach*.1.45.

σόβη, ἡ, *mop of hair* like a mane, Synes.*calv*.17(p.220.20; M.66.1196C).

***σοβητής, ὁ**, *one who scares*, of Apollinarians οἱ...σ. τῶν τοῦ Χριστοῦ ἀρνίων Epiph.*haer*.77.16(p.429.21; M.42.661D).

σόβητρον, τό, *that which frightens away*, *means of scaring*, Mac.Mgn.*apocr*.3 proem.(p.51.7).

***Σοδομ-έομαι**, (from Σόδομα) *be lapped in luxury* ἡ...~ουμένη ψυχὴ χορτασθεῖσα τῶν ἄρτων τῆς γνώσεως Nil.*epp*.3.75(M.79.424B).

***Σοδομηνός (*Σοδομινός)**, *belonging to Sodom*, *of Sodom* τῆς Σ. πενταπόλεως *Lit*.ap.*Const.App*.8.12.22; τὴν Σ. ἁμαρτίαν *Apophth. Mac.Aeg*.2(M.34.225A).

***σοκκεύω (*σοκεύω)**, *catch with a lasso*, *rope*, Jo.Mal.*chron*.14 p.364(M.97.541C); σοκεύω *ib*.18 p.438(645C).

[*]**σόκος, ὁ**, *lasso*, *noose*, Jo.Mal.*chron*.18 p.438(M.97.648A).

***σολαία (*σωλεία), ἡ**, (Lat. *soleas*) raised part of church bet. nave and sanctuary ἡ σωλεία εἰς τύπον τοῦ ποταμοῦ τοῦ πυρὸς τοῦ χωρίζοντος τοὺς ἁμαρτωλοὺς ἐκ τῶν δικαίων ‡Sophr.H.*liturg*.4(M.87.3985A); Thphn.*chron*.p.371(M.108.889A).

σολοικία, ἡ, *solecism*, *incorrectness in use of words* or *construction of sentences*, Or.*comm.in Eph*.3:17b–19(p.411).

σολοικίζω, *speak* or *write incorrectly*, *commit a solecism*; more gen., *be mistaken*, †Gregent.*disp*.(M.86.656C); *ib*.(748C).

***σολοίκιον, τό**, s.v.l., *incorrect diction*, *solecism*, Or.ap.*cat.Eph*.3:18f.(p.161.24) for σολοικίᾳ id.*comm.in Eph*.3:17b–19(p.411).

σολοικιστής, ὁ, *one who speaks incorrectly*, *commits solecisms* ὁ τοὺς ῥήτορας πείσας ἰδιώτων ἀνέχεσθαι καὶ τοὺς σοφιστὰς τοῖς σ. παρέχειν τὰ ὦτα προτρεψάμενος [sc. S. Paul] Ephr.3.464F.

***σολοικοειδῶς**, *apparently incorrectly* expressed, *by an apparent solecism*, Or.*comm.in Os*.(p.52.6; M.13.825B).

Σολομωνιακός, *of Solomon*, *Dial.Tim.et Aquil*.96 v°.

***Σολομώνιος**, = foreg., *Orac.Sib*.1.376.

***Σολομώντ(ε)ιον, τό**, *saying of Solomon*, Eus.*p.e*.11.19(524C; M.21.869B); Jo.D.*jej*.1(M.95.65A); Cosm.Mel.*schol*.(M.38.398) in Gr. Naz.*carm*.1.2.2.419; -τιον Eustrat.*stat.anim*.28(p.578).

***Σολυμήϊος**, *of Solyma* or *Jerusalem* Ἰησοῦ Σολυμήϊε Synes.*hymn*.7.4(p.21; M.66.1612).

***Σολυμηΐς**, *of Jerusalem* σέ, μάκαρ, γόνε παρθένου ὑμνῶ Σολυμηΐδος Synes.*hymn*.9.3(p.22; M.66.1613).

***σολυμνιάζω**, (cf. Lat. *sollemnis*) *pay solemn honours to*, Thdr. Stud.*epp*.2.11(M.99.1149B).

σορός, ἡ, 1. *tomb*, ἐξῆλθεν [sc. Lazarus] τῆς σ. Clem.*paed*.1.2(p.93.22; M.8.256B); *CG–CI* 1 28.1(p.54) = *IGC As.Min*.98 [saec. iv]; Leont.N.*v.Jo.Eleem*.46(pp.94.16,97.19,98.8); **2.** *chest* containing sacred relics, *Chron.Pasch*.p.397(M.92.1016C).

[*]**σοτήρ, ὁ**, v. σωτήρ.

***σουβαδιουβᾶ (*σουβαδίουβα), ὁ**, (Lat. *subadjuva*) *subadjutant*, *deputy assistant* (to the *magister officiorum*), Synes.*ep*.145(M.66.1540C); Marc.Diac.*v.Porph*.26; *Chron.Pasch*.p.380(M.92.973B).

***σοῦβλα, ἡ**, (Lat. *subula*) a pointed instrument, *awl*; *spit*, ref. Judas' cock which crowed while roasting, *A.Pil*.B 1.4(p.290 n.3); as instrument of torture εἰς σ. ξυλίνας προσαρτήσαντες ἐπὶ πυρὸς ὤπτησαν Thphn.*chron*.p.316(M.108.765A); ‡Jo.D.*Artem*.49(M.96.1297A).

σουβλίον, τό, dimin. of foreg., *awl*, Thdr.Stud.*poen*.1.50(M.99.1740B).

***σοῦδα, ἡ**, (Lat. *sudis*); **1.** *palisade*, *Chron.Pasch*.p.396(M.92.1016A); **2.** as instrument of torture, *stake* οἱ μὲν τῷ τῆς σ. πυρί, οἱ δὲ τοῖς ξίφεσιν ὤλοντο Thphn.*chron*.p.416(M.108.988A).

σουδάριον, τό, (Lat. *sudarium*); **1.** *napkin*, *towel* worn round head σ. καὶ σιμικίνθια ἀμφότερα νομίζω λινοειδῆ εἶναι· πλὴν τὰ μὲν σ. ἐπὶ τῆς κεφαλῆς ἐπιβάλλεται...πρὸς τὸ ἀπομάττεσθαι τὰς ὑγρότητας τοῦ προσώπου Ammon.*Ac*.19:12(M.85.1576A); freq. of *head-cloth* of shroud; ref. Lazarus, Or.*Jo*.28.7(6; p.398.24; M.14.696D); ref. Christ, *A.Pil*.A 15.6(p.273); Nonn.*par.Jo*.20:7(M.43.909A); **2.** *towel*, *handkerchief* reputed to have been worn at the left side by Jewish priesthood and symbolized by pallium (as precursor of maniple) τὸ ὠμοφόριον ἐστὶ κατὰ τὴν στολὴν Ἀαρών, ὅπερ ἐφόρουν οἱ ἐν νόμῳ ἀρχιερεῖς, σ. μικρὰ ἐν τῷ εὐωνύμῳ μέρει περιτιθέντες ‡Sophr.H.*liturg*.7(M.87.3988C).

***σουδᾶτον, τό**, = σοῦδα, *palisade*, *Chron.Pasch*.p.396(M.92.1016A).

***σουμμάριος, ὁ**, *treasurer* κελεύουσα τοὺς κηπουροὺς πάντων τῶν ἐν αὐτοῖς διατιμωμένων ὑπό τε τῶν κηπουρῶν καὶ τῶν σ. Ath.Scholast.*coll*.21.1(p.180).

***σούχειον, τό**, = σούχινον, *amber*, Clem.*str*.2.6(p.126.28; σούχιον M.8.961A).

σοφία, ἡ, *wisdom*; δύο σ. λέγει θεοῦ, μᾶλλον δὲ τρεῖς...μίαν μὲν σ. ... δι' ἣν λογικοί τε ἐσμὲν καὶ τῶν πρακτέων τὴν διάγνωσιν ἔχομεν, καὶ τέχνας καὶ ἐπιστήμας εὑρήκαμεν, καὶ θεὸν γνῶναι δυνάμεθα. δευτέραν δέ, τὴν ἐν τῇ κτίσει θεωρουμένην...τρίτην δέ, τὴν διὰ...τοῦ σωτῆρος ἡμῶν δεικνυμένην, ἣν οἱ ἀπιστοῦντες μωρίαν προσαγορεύουσιν Thdt.*1Cor*.1:21(3.171).

A. human wisdom; **1.** prop. *skill*, *cunning*, Bas.*hom*.12.4(2.100A; M.31.392B); Thdt.*provid*.5(4.554); also in bad sense, *cunning*, *craftiness*, id.*2Cor*.1:12(3.292); met. ἡ θεοτόκος τηλικαύτην σ. ἐπεδείξατο...ὥστε ἐκ τῶν ἐρίων τοῦ ἐξ αὐτῆς γεννηθέντος ἀρνίου ἐνδῦσαι τοὺς πιστοὺς ἅπαντας Nil.*epp*.1.267(M.79.181A); **2.** moral; *practical wisdom*, *discernment*, *sound judgement* ὁ σοφὸς ἐνδεικνύσθω τὴν σ. αὐτοῦ μὴ ἐν λόγοις ἀλλ' ἐν ἔργοις ἀγαθοῖς *1Clem*.38.2; *ib*.32.4; φιλοσοφία μὲν...ἐπιστήμη ἐστὶ τοῦ ὄντος καὶ τοῦ ἀληθοῦς ἐπίγνωσις· εὐδαιμονία δὲ ταύτης τῆς ἐπιστήμης καὶ τῆς σ. γέρας Just.*dial*.3.4(M.6.481A); τὰς τεσσάρας ἀρετὰς...ἡ παρ' ἡμῖν σ. ... ἀνακηρύσσει Clem.*str*.6.11(p.479.27; M.9.316B); *ib*.1.26(p.105.4; M.8.916B); Meth.*symp*.

1.1(p.9.7; M.18.40A); σ. πρώτη βίος ἐπαινετὸς καὶ θεῷ κεκαθαρμένος Gr.Naz.*or*.16.2(M.35.936B); σ., καὶ τὸ γινώσκειν ἑαυτόν *ib*.32.21(M.36.200A); **3.** intellectual; **a.** *learning, wisdom* in ethical philosophy or Christian teaching ἡ φρόνησις...ὅταν...ἀποδεικτικῷ λόγῳ βεβαιώσηται, γνῶσίς τε καὶ σ. καὶ ἐπιστήμη ὀνομάζεται Clem.*str*.6.17(p.511.29; M.9.388A); dist. from γνῶσις: *ib*.2.5(p.125.24; M.8.957B); *ib*.7.10 (p.40.30ff.; M.9.477C); Olymp.*Eccl*.1:16ff.(M.93.492D); consisting in recognition of one's ignorance τὸ εἰδέναι τινά, ὅτι ἀγνοεῖ τι, σοφίας ἐστί, ὥστε καὶ τὸ εἰδέναι ὅτι ἠδίκησε, δικαιοσύνης Didym.ap. Jo.D.*parall*.(M.96.360D); dist. from φιλοσοφία: σ. φημὶ καὶ φιλοσοφίαν, τὴν μὲν ὡς περιεκτικὴν καὶ πάντας θεοπρεπῶς τοὺς εὐσεβεῖς ἐπ' αὐτῆς λεγομένους ἐπιδεχομένην τρόπους, καὶ τοὺς περὶ τῶν ἄλλων ἐντὸς ἑαυτῆς μυστικούς τε καὶ φυσικοὺς περικλείουσαν λόγους, τὴν δὲ ὡς ἤθους καὶ γνώμης, πράξεώς τε καὶ θεωρίας, καὶ ἀρετῆς καὶ γνώσεως συνεκτικήν, καὶ οἰκειότητι σχετικῇ πρὸς τὴν σ. ὡς αἰτίαν ἀναφερομένην Max.*ambig*.(M.91.1136D); Stoic definition τὴν φιλοσοφίαν φασὶν ἐπιτήδευσιν εἶναι σοφίας, τὴν δὲ σ. ἐπιστήμην θείων τε καὶ ἀνθρωπίνων πραγμάτων adopted by Philo (*cong*.14) alluded to by Clem. ἐστὶ γὰρ φιλοσοφία ἐπιτήδευσις σοφίας, σ. δὲ ἐπιστήμη θείων καὶ ἀνθρωπίνων καὶ τῶν τούτων αἰτίων *str*.1.5(p.19.15; M.8.721B); Or.*Cels*.3.72(p.263.25; M.11.1013C); Eus.*l.C*.proem.(p.195.17; M.20.1317A); Bas.*hom*.12.3(2.99E; M.31.389C); Gr.Naz.*or*.30.20(p.139.13; M.36.129A); ‡Proc.G. *Pr*.31:29(M.87.1544A); Olymp.*Eccl*.1:16(M.93.492D); **b.** sophistic sense, *eloquence*, disapproved, Thdt.*1Cor*.2:5f.(3.175); id.*2Cor*.1:12 (3.292); since when robbed of ethical or spiritual content it becomes vain, spurious, or 'carnal' wisdom τῆς νόθου σ. ἔλεγχε, τῆς ἐν λόγῳ κειμένης Gr.Naz.*or*.25.2(M.35.1200A); *ib*.16.3(937A); Chrys.*hom*.*7.1 in 1Cor*.(10.49E–50C); οὐκ ἐν κακουργίᾳ...ἢ ἐν συμπλοκῇ σοφισμάτων· ταύτην γὰρ λέγει σ. σαρκικήν id.*hom.3.1 in 2Cor*. (10.442B); Olymp.*Eccl*.7:26f.(M.93.572Cf.); Germ.CP *vit.term*.1(M.98.89B); opp. grace οὐ γὰρ...ἐν σ., ἀλλ' ἐν τῇ χάριτι τοῦ θεοῦ ἐστιν ἡ σωτηρία Bas.*hom.in Ps*.33(1.144D; M.29.353C); ref. Gnosticism ἡ παμποίκιλος σ. Πειρατικῆς αἱρέσεως Hipp.*haer*.5.17(p.114.11; M.16.3175B); of idolatry σ. ἄσοφος Clem.*prot*.5(p.49.7; M.8.165A); Gr.Naz. *or*.4.3(M.35.533B); **4.** *wisdom* as spiritual quality, a gift ὁ κύριος ἡμῶν...ὁ σ. καὶ νοῦν θέμενος ἐν ἡμῖν τῶν κρυφίων αὐτοῦ *Barn*.6.10; cf. *ib*.21.5; ἐπὶ τὴν ἀληθῆ σ. ἥτις ἐστὶ δύναμις θεία τῶν ὄντων ὡς ὄντων γνωστική...παντὸς πάθους ἀπηλλαγμένη, οὐκ ἄνευ τοῦ σωτῆρος Clem. *str*.1.28(p.109.19; M.8.924B); classed as a virtue, Or.*Cels*.8.17(p.235.2; M.11.1544A); gift of H. Ghost, id.*sel.in Ps*.118:131(M.12.1616D); *Const.App*.6.27.5; Cosm.Ind.*top*.proem.1(M.88.52A); one of the seven gifts of Is.11:2, Gr.Naz.*or*.31.29(p.183.5; M.36.165C); cf.*ib*.41.9(441C); Didym.*Trin*.2.3(M.39.467A); Cyr.*Is*.2.1(2.193B); cf.Or.*hom. 3.1 in Is*.(M.13.227D); its character and scope τὴν δὲ σ. ἔμπεδον γνῶσιν θείων τε καὶ ἀνθρωπίνων πραγμάτων, κατάληψίν τινα βεβαίαν οὖσαν καὶ ἀμετάπτωτον, συνειληφυῖαν τά τε ὄντα καὶ τὰ παρῳχηκότα καὶ τὰ μέλλοντα, ἣν ἐδιδάξατο ἡμᾶς διά τε τῆς παρουσίας διά τε τῶν προφητῶν ὁ κύριος καὶ ἔστι ἀμετάπτωτος ὑπὸ λόγου, παραδοθεῖσα τῇ αὐτῇ...βουλήσει...ἡ μὲν αἰώνιός ἐστιν, ἡ δὲ χρόνῳ λυσιτελής Clem.*str*.6.7(p.459.8ff.; M.9.277A); means to knowledge of God, Bas.*hom*.12.3(2.99B,C; M.31.389C–392A); not found in soul of evil-doer, Gr.Nyss.*deit*.(M.46.556D); in its highest form following after divine wisdom, id.*hom. 5 in Eccl*.(M.44.681A); its activity twofold διπλῆ ἡ τῆς σ. ἐνέργεια, καὶ ἡ μέν ἐστιν ἐρευνητική τε καὶ ζητητικὴ τῶν συμφερόντων, ἡ δὲ φυλακτικὴ τῶν εὑρεθέντων id.*Pss.titt*.A 8(M.44.481A); a unity with numerous and varied manifestations, ref. Mt.23:37 δίς, διά τε προφητῶν καὶ διὰ τῆς παρουσίας. πολύτροπον μὲν οὖν τὴν σ. ἡ 'ποσάκις' ἐνδείκνυται λέξις, καὶ καθ' ἕνα ἕκαστον τρόπον ποιότητός τε καὶ ποσότητος πάντως σώζει τινὰς ἔν τε τῷ χρόνῳ ἔν τε τῷ αἰῶνι Clem.*str*.1.5(p.18.22; M.8.720B); cf.*ib*.1.4(p.17.16; 717A); ἡ σ. μονάς ἐστι, ταῖς ἐξ αὐτῆς διαφόροις ἀρεταῖς ἀτμήτως ἐνθεωρουμένη Max.*cap*.3.44(M.90.1280A) = id.*qu.Thal*.54(M.90.533C); having its end in unbroken contemplation, Clem.*str*.6.7(p.462.31; M.9.284A); the end of speculative activity of soul as the good is of practical, Max.*qu.Thal*.54(528A,B); itself the bond of union with God, id.*cap*.3.41(M.90.1277C); bestowing the power of edifying others, Hipp.*fr.16 in Pr*.9:12(p.162.18; M.10.620C); Max.*qu.Thal*.54(533A); rel. to philosophy κυρία τοίνυν ἡ σ. τῆς φιλοσοφίας ὡς ἐκείνη τῆς προπαιδείας Clem.*str*.1.5(p.19.17; M.8.721B); rel. to prophecy, Gr.Nyss.*Eun*.3(2 p.15.31f.; M.45.580C); opp. φρόνησις: δύο...μερίδες φιλοσοφίας, θεωρία καὶ πρᾶξις· καὶ δῆτα δύο δυνάμεις. ἑκατέρα παρ' ἑκατέραν μερίδα, σ. καὶ φρόνησις. αὕτη μὲν δεομένη τύχης· σ. δὲ αὐτάρκης, καὶ ἀκώλυτος ἡ κατ' ἐκείνην ἐνέργεια Synes.*ep*.103(M.66.1476D); rel. to gift of fear, Max.*cap*.3.61(1288C) = id.*qu.Thal*.55(576C).

B. Gnost.; *wisdom* as aeon; **a.** implanter of spiritual seed in Adam, Clem.*exc.Thdot*.53.2(p.124.19ff.; M.9.684C–685A); **b.** together with Theletos, last pair of thirty aeons in Valent. pleroma, Iren.*haer*.1.1.2(M.7.449B); Hipp.*haer*.6.30(p.157.22; M.16.3239A); cf. Epiph. who sets out dodecad before decad and pairs with Ecclesiasticus, *haer*.31.2(p.386.4; M.41.477A); her yearning and fall, Iren.*haer*.1.2.2f.(453A–456A); Hipp.*haer*.6.30(p.157.24ff.; 3239A,B); her restoration, Iren.*haer*.1.2.4(460A); Hipp.*haer*.6.31 (p.158.20ff.; 3239C); **c.** name also given to offspring of Sophia, Iren.*haer*.1.4.1(480B); Hipp.*haer*.6.31(p.159.18ff.; 3242B).

C. divine wisdom; **1.** as divine attribute; **a.** in Godhead, Herm. *vis*.1.3.4; οὐ γὰρ εἶ ἡ ἄναρχος γνῶσις...ἡ ἀδίδακτος σ. *Lit*.ap.*Const. App*.8.12.7; εἰ δὲ καὶ ὑπὲρ πάντα τὰ ὄντα ἐστὶν...τἀγαθόν, καὶ τὸ ἀνείδεον εἰδοποιεῖ...καὶ τὸ ἄνουν ὑπερέχουσα σ. Dion.Ar.*d.n*.4.3(M.3.697A); *ib*.7.1(865B); in which all things are known to God ἑαυτὴν οὖν ἡ θεία σ. γινώσκουσα, γνώσεται πάντα *ib*.7.2(869B); **b.** in rel. to creation; source of all created knowledge θεόσδοτος...ἡ σ., δύναμις οὖσα τοῦ πατρός Clem.*str*.5.13(p.381.29; M.9.125A); σ. ἥτις ἐστὶν ἡ μεταδοθεῖσα ἡμῖν ἄνωθεν φρόνησις καὶ νουνεχία, καὶ λόγων ἀρετή Didym.*Trin*.3.2(M.39.809A); ταύτην...τὴν ἄλογον καὶ ἄνουν καὶ μωρὰν σ. ... εἴπωμεν ὅτι παντός ἐστι νοῦ, καὶ λόγου, καὶ πάσης σ., καὶ συνέσεως αἰτία Dion.Ar.*d.n*.7.1(M.3.868A); itself one, taking manifold forms among men, Clem.*str*.6.18(p.517.28f.; M.9.400A); τὴν σ. τοῦ θεοῦ 'πολυμερῶς καὶ πολυτρόπως' διὰ τέχνης, διὰ ἐπιστήμης, διὰ πίστεως, διὰ προφητείας, τὴν ἑαυτῆς ἐνδεικνυμένην δύναμιν εἰς τὴν ἡμετέραν εὐεργεσίαν *ib*.1.4(p.17.16; M.8.717A); from the intellections of angels to sense perception, even Devil's intellect so far as it is not mere defection, Dion.Ar.*d.n*.7.2(M.3.868B,C); how predicated of God, Max.*schol.c.h*.15.4(M.4.109A); **2.** in rel. to H. Ghost; **a.** identified with third Person of Trin. τὸν ἑαυτοῦ λόγον ἐνδιάθετον ...μετὰ τῆς ἑαυτοῦ σ. ἐξερευξάμενος πρὸ τῶν ὅλων Thphl.Ant.*Autol*. 2.10(M.6.1064C); τῆς τριάδος, τοῦ θεοῦ καὶ τοῦ λόγου αὐτοῦ καὶ τῆς σ. αὐτοῦ *ib*.2.15(1077B); cf. *sua progenies et figuratio sua, id est filius et spiritus sanctus, verbum et sapientia*, Iren.*haer*.4.7.4(M.7.993A); **b.** as creator Spirit, Thphl.Ant.*Autol*.1.7(1036A); οὐκ ἄλλῳ δέ τινι εἴρηκε 'ποιήσωμεν' ἀλλ' ἢ τῷ ἑαυτοῦ λόγῳ καὶ τῇ ἑαυτοῦ σ. *ib*.2.18 (1081B); cf. *adest enim ei semper verbum et sapientia, filius et spiritus...ad quos et loquitur dicens: faciamus*, etc., Iren.*haer*.4.20.1 (1032B); Hipp.*Noët*.10(p.251.22; M.10.817B) cit. s. λόγος; cf. *omnia verbo fecit et sapientia adornavit*, Iren.*haer*.4.20.2(1033B); *verbo suo confirmans et sapientia compingens omnia*, *ib*.3.24.2(967B); cf. εἷς ἐστιν ὁ τῇ αὐτοῦ σ. εἰπὼν 'ποιήσωμεν ἄνθρωπον'. ἡ δὲ σ. ᾗ ὥσπερ ἰδίῳ πνεύματι αὐτὸς ἀεὶ συνέχαιρεν ἥνωται μὲν ὡς ψυχὴ τῷ θεῷ ἐκτείνεται δὲ...ὡς χεὶρ δημιουργήσασα τὸ πᾶν *Hom.Clem*.16.12; **c.** Valent., ref. Inc., Hipp.*haer*.6.35(p.164.19; M.16.3247C); **3.** of Son; **a.** title of second Person of Trin., Just.*dial*.61.1(M.6.613C) cit. s. δύναμις; *ib*. 100.4(616A); Clem.*prot*.8(p.61.18; M.8.192A); τὴν σ. ... διασῶς ἐπιλαβεῖν, τὴν ἐκ πνεύματος ἁγίου...δι' ἧς...ἡ ἐπίγνωσις τοῦ θεοῦ τῷ κόσμῳ ἐγνωρίσθη· ὡσαύτως δὲ καὶ τὸν ἐνυπόστατον υἱὸν τοῦ θεοῦ Or.*exp.in Pr*.9:1(M.17.185B); Ath.*Ar*.1.9(M.26.28D); *ib*.3.65(461A); as alone comprehending God, Or.*Jo*.1.34(39; p.43.19,28f.; M.14.89B,C); not relatively but essentially, *ib*.(p.44.8ff.; 92A); υἱὸς...κατ' οὐσίαν τε ὑφεστὼς οἷα θεοῦ δύναμις καὶ θεοῦ σ. ... λόγου καὶ σ. καὶ φωτὸς...ἐκ τοῦ οἰκείου πληρώματος τοῖς πᾶσιν ἐπιλιμνάζων Eus.*l.C*.12(p.230.22ff.; M.20.1388C); id.*d.e*.5.8(p.230.26; M.22.381A), id.*p.e*.7.12(320D; M.21.541B) citt. s. λόγος; τὴν ζωὴν καὶ τὴν σ. μήτε ξένα τῆς οὐσίας τῆς πηγῆς εἶναι, ἀλλ' ἴδια, μήτε ἀνύπαρκτά ποτε εἶναι, ἀλλ' ἀεὶ εἶναι. ἐστὶ δὲ ταῦτα ὁ υἱός Ath.*Ar*.1.19(M.26.52A); *ib*.(53A); rel. to Logos δημιουργὸς δὲ ὁ Χριστὸς ὡς ἀρχή, καθ' ὃ σ. ἐστιν...κατὰ μὲν τὴν σύστασιν τῆς περὶ τῶν ὅλων θεωρίας καὶ νοημάτων, τῆς σ. νοουμένης, κατὰ δὲ τὴν πρὸς τὰ λογικὰ κοινωνίαν τῶν τεθεωρημένων, τοῦ λόγου λαμβανομένου Or.*Jo*.1.19(22; p.23.19ff.; M.14.56B); **b.** himself the wisdom of Father αὕτη...ἦν ⟨ᾗ⟩ σ. 'ᾗ προσέχαιρεν' ὁ παντοκράτωρ θεὸς...λόγος τοῦ πατρός, καὶ σ. αὐτοῦ Clem.*str*.7.2(p.7.12; M.9.412A); Ath.*Ar*.1.28(M.26.69B); τὸ ἀπαύγασμα χωρισθῆναι ἀμήχανον τοῦ φωτός, καὶ τὴν σ. τοῦ σοφοῦ, τουτέστι τὸν υἱὸν ἀπὸ τοῦ πατρός Didym. *Trin*.2.6(M.39.549B); *ib*.3.3(813B); Cyr.*Jo*.1.3(4.21A); more precisely σ. ὅλος ὁ θεός, οὐκοῦν σ. ὁ υἱὸς ἐκ σ. Epiph.*anc*.70(p.88.2; M.43.145D); ‡Caes.Naz.*dial*.20(M.38.876); a favourite argument for his eternity, Or.*princ*.4.4.1(p.350.2; M.11.402B n.44); Dion.R.ap.Ath.*decr*. 26(p.22.22; M.25.464B), Dion.Al.ap.eund.*Dion*.15(p.57.2; M.25.501C) citt. s. δύναμις; Alex.Al.*ep.encycl*.4(p.9.5; M.18.576B); Didym.(‡Bas.) *Eun*.4(1.287A; M.29.689B); Cyr.*dial.Trin*.4(5^1.539B–E); **c.** with hypostatic existence, Just.*dial*.61.3(M.6.616A) cit. s. δύναμις; Athenag. *leg*.24.1(M.6.945B) cit. s. ἑνόω; Thphl.Ant.*Autol*.2.10(M.6.1064C) cit. s. δύναμις; τῶν ὄντων ἁπάντων πρῶτον ὑφίστησιν αὐτοῦ γέννημα τὴν πρωτότοκον σ. ... μᾶλλον δὲ...αὐτοσοφίαν Eus.*d.e*.4.2(p.151.31; M.22.253A); τὴν σ. θεοῦ καὶ τὴν δύναμιν, καὶ τὴν δικαιοσύνην ἐνυπόστατον

Cyr.H.*catech*.4.7; ἡ...σ. τοῦ πατρὸς ὁ ἐνυπόστατος θεὸς λόγος Epiph. *haer*.69.21(p.171.3; M.42.236A); οὐ μόνον ἐστὶν υἱός, ἀλλὰ καὶ δύναμις καὶ σ. ... ἵνα ἀπὸ τοῦ εἶναι υἱός, τὸ ἐνυπόστατον νοηθῇ ‡Ath.*dial.Trin.* 2.2(M.28.1160C); **d.** agent in Creation τὰ σύμπαντα γεγονέναι κατὰ τοὺς ἐν τῇ σ. προτρανωθέντας ὑπὸ θεοῦ τῶν ἐσομένων λόγους...κτίσας ...ἔμψυχον σ. ὁ θεὸς αὐτῇ ἐπέτρεψεν ἀπὸ τῶν ἐν αὐτῇ τύπων τοῖς οὖσι καὶ τῇ ὕλῃ παρασχεῖν τὴν ὕπαρξιν Or.*Jo*.1.19(22; p.24.7ff.; M.14. 56D); πάντα γεννῶσαν τὴν πρωτόγονον σ. τοῦ θεοῦ Meth.*res*.2.9(p.348. 20; M.18.288C); Gr.Nyss.*hom.5 in Eccl*.(M.44.681A); id.*Eun*.2(2 p.323.24; M.45.497B) cit. s. δύναμις; ὁ δὲ ποιήσας τὴν γῆν ἐκ μὴ γῆς...μονογενής ἐστιν υἱὸς λόγος τοῦ θεοῦ...καὶ θεοῦ σ. Didym.*Trin.* 3.3(M.39.809B); **e.** who became incarnate, Meth.*symp*.3.4(p.30.21; M.18.68A) cit. s. ἄνθρωπος; Ath.*Ar*.2.44(M.26.241B); σάββατον ὥρισας...εἰς μνήμην...τῆς ὑπὸ σοῦ κτισθείσης σ.· ὡς δι' ἡμᾶς γένεσιν ὑπέστη τὴν διὰ γυναικός *Const.App*.7.36.1; χαῖρε, σ. θεοῦ δοχεῖον †Serg.*hymn.acath*.204(p.145; M.92.1344C); καὶ ἐπεσκίασεν ἐπ' αὐτὴν ἡ τοῦ θεοῦ...ἐνυπόστατος σ. καὶ δύναμις, ὁ υἱὸς τοῦ θεοῦ Jo.D.*f.o.* 3.2(M.94.985B); also divine agent in normal human conception, *Dial.Ath.et Zacch*.22; **f.** of incarnate Son in his divine nature Χριστός...ἐστιν...τοῦ θεοῦ πατρὸς ἡμῶν ἡ ἀνωτάτω καὶ ἐνυπόστατος σ. καὶ λόγος Or.*adnot.in Dt*.16:19f.(M.17.28B); παρεληλύθει...ἡ γενεὰ ἐκείνη τῶν αὐταῖς ἀκοαῖς τῆς ἐνθέου σ. ἐπακοῦσαι κατηξιωμένων Eus.*h.e*.3.32.8(M.20.284C); εἰ δὲ δὴ καὶ ἀσθενείας εἶδος περιάπτειν αὐτῷ προσῆκον ἦν τῷ ἀνθρώπῳ ταῦτα προσαρτᾶν ἀκόλουθον εἶναι φαίη τις ἄν, οὔτι γε δὴ...τῷ ἀξιώματι τῆς ἀνωτάτω σ. Eust.ap.Thdt. *eran*.3(4.236); τὸ μὲν γὰρ σῶμα μετάρσιον ἐσταυροῦτο, τὸ δὲ θεῖον τῆς σ. πνεῦμα...πάντα ὁμοῦ συνήθως οἷα θεὸς ἔπραττεν *ib.*; *ib.*(237); τί οὖν [sc. ἔφη] ἡ ἄπειρος σ.; Chrys.*hom.30.2 in Mt*.(7.349E); μόνη τοῦ θεοῦ σοφίαν κυήσασα τὴν ἐνυπόστατον...θεοτόκε ‡Sophr.H.*triod*.(M. 87.3880A); ἡ ὄντως κατὰ φύσιν τοῦ θεοῦ...σ. ὁ κύριος ἡμῶν Ἰησοῦς Χριστός Const.VI Imp.*sacr*.(H.4.36C); **g.** acc. Paul. Sam., a divine attribute without hypostasis, Epiph.*haer*.65.3(p.5.15f.; M.42.16A); inspiring the man Christ ὁ λόγος μείζων ἦν τοῦ Χριστοῦ. ὁ Χριστὸς γὰρ διὰ σοφίας μέγας ἐγένετο Paul.Sam.*fr*.4(p.331.4)ap.Justn. *monoph*.(M.86.1117D); in an altogether unique manner yet not so as to make him divine ἵνα μήτε ὁ ἐκ Δαβὶδ χρισθεὶς ἀλλότριος ᾖ τῆς σ., μήτε ἡ σ. ἐν ἄλλῳ οὕτως οἰκῇ. καὶ γὰρ ἐν τοῖς προφηταῖς ἦν, μᾶλλον δὲ ἐν Μωσεῖ...μᾶλλον δὲ ἐν Χριστῷ ὡς ἐν ναῷ *ib*.6(p.331.15ff.) ap.Leont.B.*Nest.et Eut*.3(M.86.1392A); εἰ δὲ υἱὸς ὁ Ἰησοῦς Χριστὸς τοῦ θεοῦ, υἱὸς δὲ καὶ ἡ σ., καὶ ἄλλο μὲν ἡ σ., ἄλλο δὲ Ἰησοῦς Χριστός, δύο ὑφίστανται υἱοί *ib*.10(p.333.2f.)*ib*.(1393B); its nature precluding essential connexion with what is human οὐ γὰρ συγγεγενῆσθαι τῷ ἀνθρωπίνῳ τὴν σ. οὐσιωδῶς, ἀλλὰ κατὰ ποιότητα *ib*.7(p.332.5f.)*ib.* (1393A); **h.** Arian: ποίημα ὁ υἱός, οὔτε δὲ ὅμοιος κατ' οὐσίαν τῷ πατρί ἐστιν...οὔτε ἀληθινὴ σ. αὐτοῦ ἐστιν...καταχρηστικῶς δὲ λέγεται ...σ. Ar.*Thal.fr*.16 ap.Ath.*decr*.6(p.5.28f.; M.25.433B); δύο γοῦν σ. φησὶν [sc. Ἄρειος] εἶναι, μίαν μὲν τὴν ἰδίαν καὶ συνυπάρχουσαν τῷ θεῷ, τὸν δὲ υἱὸν ἐν ταύτῃ τῇ σ. γεγενῆσθαι, καὶ ταύτης μετέχοντα ὠνομάσθαι μόνον σ. καὶ λόγον. ἡ σ. γάρ, φησί, τῇ σ. ὑπῆρξε σοφοῦ θεοῦ θελήσει Ath.*Ar*.1.5(M.26.21B); **i.** Apollinarian: εἰ μὴ νοῦς ἔνσαρκός ἐστιν ὁ κύριος, σ. ἂν εἴη φωτίζουσα νοῦν ἀνθρώπου. αὕτη δὲ καὶ ἐν πᾶσιν ἀνθρώποις Apoll.*fr*.70(p.220.28)ap.Gr.Nyss.*Apoll*.36(M.45.1204C); εἰ μὴ νοῦς ἔνσαρκος γέγονεν ὁ λόγος, ἀλλὰ σ. ἦν ἐν τῷ νῷ, οὐ κατέβη ὁ κύριος οὐδὲ ἐκένωσεν ἑαυτόν Apoll.*fr*.71(p.221.14)*ib*.37 (1205D); ἑνοῦται ἄρα τὰ τοῦ θεοῦ καὶ σώματος, δημιουργὸς προσκυνητὸς σ. καὶ δύναμις ὑπάρχων αἰώνιος· ἀπὸ θεότητος ταῦτα. υἱὸς Μαρίας ἐπ' ἐσχάτου χρόνου τεχθεὶς προσκυνῶν θεὸν σοφίᾳ προσκόπτων δυνάμει κρατιούμενος· ταῦτα ἀπὸ σώματος Apoll.*fr*.125(p.238.2)ap. Thdt.*eran*.2(4.170); from which body of the Word was formed εἰπεῖν...τὸ σῶμα τῆς τοῦ λόγου θεότητος...συναΐδιον αὐτῷ...ἐπειδὴ ἐκ τῆς οὐσίας τῆς σ. συνέστη Ath.*ep.Epict*.2(p.5.10; M.26.1053B); **4.** divine wisdom revealed in scripture: in prophets, Job, and Proverbs, *Const.App*.1.6.4; in Proverbs, Clem.*str*.2.18(p.156.15; M.8.1021A); ‡Chrys.*hom.in Ps.100*(5.639B); CTrull.*can*.100; in Wisdom of Solomon, Meth.*res*.1.36(p.276.5; M.41.1101A); Ath.*gent.* 9(M.25.20D); Didym.*Trin*.2.20,26(M.39.740D,752B); **5.** as literary title (sts. ass. πανάρετος); **a.** of Proverbs, Just.*dial*.129.3(M.6.777A); Mel.*fr*.3(p.309; M.5.1216A); Eus.*h.e*.4.22.9(M.20.384A); *Const.App.* 1.7.1; ὁ...θεῖος Σολομὼν ἐν τῇ παιδαγωγικῇ σ., ταῖς Παροιμίαις λέγω Gr.Naz.*or*.8.9(M.35.797C); **b.** of Ecclesiasticus, Or.*Cels*.6.7(p.77.12; M.11.1300A); Ἰησοῦς ὁ τοῦ Σιρὰχ...ὁ τὴν καλουμένην πανάρετον Σ. συντάξας Eus.*d.e*.8.2(p.380.15; M.22.616C); αἱ...δύο βίβλοι ἥτε τοῦ Σολομῶντος, ἡ πανάρετος λεγομένη, καὶ ἡ τοῦ Ἰησοῦ τοῦ υἱοῦ Σιρὰχ ἐκγόνου δὲ τοῦ Ἰησοῦ καὶ Σ. Ἑβραϊστὶ γράψαντος Epiph.*mens*.4 (M.43.244C); **c.** of Wisdom, Or.*Jo*.20.5(p.332.29; M.14.584B); Meth. *symp*.1.3(p.1..5; M.18.44B); καθὼς φησί που τῆς παναρέτου σ. ὁ λόγος Gr.Nyss.*Eun*.8(2 p.198.22; M.45.793D); **6.** as dedication of churches ὁ βασιλεὺς τὴν μεγάλην ἐκκλησίαν ἔκτιζεν, ἥτις Σ. μὲν προσαγορεύεται νῦν Socr.*h.e*.2.16.16(M.67.217B); ἐνταῦθα πλησίον τοῦ Φάρου, ἀνάμεσον τῆς ἁγίας Σ. καὶ τοῦ ἁγίου Φαύστου Jo.Mosch.*prat*.106(M.87.2965A).

D. liturg., exclamation calling for *devout attention* before scripture lections, *Lit.Chrys*.(p.368.24; M.63.909); †Jo.Jej.*poenit*.(M.88. 1900C); or creed τὰς θύρας, τὰς θύρας ἐν σ. πρόσχωμεν *Lit.Chrys.* (p.383.4; M.63.915); or in other places, ‡Sophr.H.*liturg*.20(M.87. 4000D); *Lit.Chrys*.(pp.375.24,376.22; M.63.912).

σοφίζ-ω, A. act. and pass., *make wise, instruct* Ἰησοῦν Χριστὸν τὸν θεὸν τὸν...ὑμᾶς σοφίσαντα Ign.*Smyrn*.1.1; *T.Sal*.7.4(M.122. 1325C); Serap.*euch*.14.2; also with evil intent παρέβησαν, ὅτι ἄγγελος πονηρὸς ἐσόφιζεν αὐτούς *Barn*.9.4; pass., *be made wise (in)*; *become skilled* ὁ Χριστιανὸς ἐσοφίσθη τὴν ἐντολὴν τοῦ θεοῦ Or.*Ps*.118:98(M. 12.1605D); Gr.Nyss.*hex*.2(M.44.64B).

B. med. and pass.; **1.** *contrive cunningly* (in good sense); a labyrinth, Gr.Thaum.*pan.Or*.14(p.32.23; M.10.1092C); ref. anonymity of Heb. ἐσοφίσατο διὰ τοῦ κρύψαι τὸ ὄνομα τὴν ἀκρόασιν τὴν ἐκείνων Chrys.*hom.1.1 in Rom*.(9.429D); διὰ γραμμάτων ~εσθαι παρουσίας ἡδονήν id.*ep*.143(3.684B); (in bad sense) ὁ τῆς ἀληθείας ὅρος... οὐ Χαλδαίων...περιεργίᾳ σοφισθείς Hipp.*haer*.10.5(p.265.13; M.16. 3414A); ἐσοφίσαντο...κατὰ τοῦ κυρίου βούλευμα Bas.*hom.20.2*(2. 158C; M.31.529A); ἐσοφίσατο [sc. ὁ Ἡρώδης] τοῦ ἀποκτεῖναι αὐτόν *A.Jo.Bapt*.7(p.532.8); **2.** *deal subtly with, deceive*, Just.*1apol*.14.4 (M.6.348C); Or.*fr.33 in Jo*.(p.509.10); *outwit* ὁ κύριος τὸν διάβολον...~εται Clem.*str*.1.9(p.29.29; M.8.741B); *counteract by a device, beguile* (with good intent) ~εσθαι τὸ λυποῦν...παραμυθίας ῥήμασιν Gr.Naz.*or*.21.17(M.35.1101A); διὰ τῶν γραμμάτων ~ομαι τὸ ποθούμενον Thdt.*ep*.127(4.1212); Bas.Sel.*or*.7.2(M.85.109B); *pervert* δόγματα ...ἀμαθῶς σοφισάμενοι Clem.*str*.1.17(p.56.5; M.8.801A); ~εται... τὴν ἀλήθειαν *ib*.3.12(p.233.1; 1181B); *doctor* the hair, Clem.*paed*.3.3 (p.246.5; M.8.577C); *assume an appearance of, counterfeit*, Gr.Nyss. *v.Mos*.18(M.44.305A); Chrys.*Thdr*.1.13(1.20C).

C. med. intrans.; **1.** *show wisdom*, Gr.Naz.*or*.28.21(p.53.5; M.36. 53B); Jo.Eleem.*v.Tych*.10(p.120); *make a display of wisdom* ἃ ~όμενοι οἱ ἄνθρωποι ὡς ἀνθρώπινα γελῶσι Ath.*inc*.1.2(M.25.97B); *teach wisdom* τῆς ἀρετῆς...~ομένης τὸν γνώριμον Nil.*Magn*.58(M.79. 1045B); **2.** *reason falsely*; *practise evasion*; *quibble*, in argument πεπλάνησαι, ὦ Ἰσραήλ, τοιαῦτα ~όμενος ἐπὶ τῇ τοῦ κυρίου σφαγῇ Mel. *pass*.72 p.12.18; Clem.*str*.2.7(p.130.13; M.8.968B); *ib*.6.16(p.508.13; M.9.380B); Meth.*symp*.10.2(p.122.16; M.18.193B); *trifle with*, of usurer giving alms μὴ ~ου τὸν νόμον Chrys.*hom.56.6 in Mt*.(7.574B); (of one deferring baptism) ~όμενος τοῦ θεοῦ τὴν φιλανθρωπίαν Chrys. *hom.1.6 in Ac*.(9.11D).

σοφισμός, ὁ, = σόφισμα; **1.** *sophism, specious argument*, *Hom. Clem*.2.9; **2.** *clever device, artifice*, Isid.Pel.ap.*cat.Mt*.10:16(p.77.2); id.*epp*.1.461(M.78.436C).

σοφιστεία, ἡ, *wisdom* ἐν οἷς [sc. prophets, Job, and Proverbs] πάσης ποιήσεως καὶ σ. πλείονα ἀγχίνοιαν εὑρήσεις *Const.App*.1.6.4.

σοφίστευμα, τό, = σόφισμα, *sophism, specious but fallacious argument*, Hipp.*haer*.7.14(p.191.18; M.16.3295B).

σοφιστήριον, τό, *school of sophistry*, Clem.*prot*.2(p.11.7; M.8. 69B).

σοφιστικός, 1. *rhetorical* (in good sense), Synes.*Dion* 1(p.234.4; M.66.1112D); **2.** *containing wisdom*; of books of prophets, Job, and Proverbs, *Const.App*.1.6.4.

***σοφιστομανέω,** *have a passion for sophistry*, Gr.Naz.*or*.43.15(M. 36.513D); Isid.Pel.*epp*.3.87(M.78.792C).

***σοφιστότακτος,** ? *ordained by wisdom, wisely ordered*, ‡Chrys. *ador*.2(11.824B).

***σοφοδότις,** *giving wisdom* τὴν οὐσιοποιόν, καὶ ζωοποιόν, καὶ σοφοδότιν αἰτίαν Dion.Ar.*d.n*.5.2(M.3.816C).

***σοφόδωρος,** *giving wisdom*; of divine power. Dion.Ar.*d.n*.2.7(M. 3.645A).

***σοφοποιέω,** *make wise*, Dion.Ar.*e.h*.5.1.2(M.3.501B).

***σοφοποίησις, ἡ,** *making wise, bestowal of wisdom*, Dion.Ar.*d.n.* 2.5(M.3.644A).

***σοφοποιΐα, ἡ,** *making wise, bestowal of wisdom* τῆς θεαρχικῆς... σ. Dion.Ar.*c.h*.14(M.3.321A).

***σοφοποιός,** *making wise, imparting wisdom* τῶν χερουβὶμ...τῆς σ. μεταδόσεως ἀναπεπλασμένον Dion.Ar.*c.h*.7.1(M.3.205C); τῆς...σ. θεαρχίας id.*e.h*.7.3.11(M.3.568A).

σοφός, *wise*; **1.** of God, as Wisdom σ. ... ὁ θεὸς μόνος, ἀφ' οὗ ἡ σοφία Clem.*paed*.1.10(p.145.24; M.8.361A); μόνον τὸ θεῖον σ. εἶναι φύσει id.*str*.2.9(p.136.27; M.8.980C); ὁ ἀδιδάκτως σ. Bas.*Spir*.20(3. 17E; M.32.104C); Didym.*Trin*.2.19(M.39.549B); of his acts ὁ σ. ἐν τῷ κτίζειν *1Clem.*60.1; his will, *Diogn.*8.10; his revelation (ref. Proverbs) ἡ σ. βίβλος †Dion.Al.*fr.4 in Job*(p.206.11); **2.** of inspired men; **a.** OT heroes, Daniel, Bas.*Eun.*3.1(1.273A; M.29.657A); Esther, *ib.*2.19(254D; M.612B); Judith, *Const.App.*3.7.6; esp. authors of Wisdom Books: Solomon, Or.*Cels.*3.45(p.241.1; M.11.977C); Cosm. Ind.*top.*2(89C, v.l. θείου Migne); Sirach, Meth.*res.*1.26(p.253.16; M. 41.1132B); Thdt.*provid.*10(4.686); **b.** S. Paul, Meth.*symp.*3.1(p.27. 2; M.18.60D); Cyr.*Lc.*5:27(M.72.569B); **c.** others possessed of Christian wisdom, *Barn.*6.10; πίστις δὲ οὐ σοφῶν τῶν κατὰ κόσμον, ἀλλὰ τῶν κατὰ θεόν ἐστιν τὸ κτῆμα Clem.*paed.*3.11(p.279.17; M.8. 656C); *Dial.Ath.et Zacch.*44; contrasted with those falsely so called ἀνθρώπους φαύλους...οὐ περὶ τῶν νοητῶν...σοφούς, ἀλλὰ περὶ μόνων τῶν αἰσθητῶν πραγματευσαμένους...εἶναι σοφοὺς τοῦ κόσμου Or.*Cels.*3.47 (p.243.17f.; M.11.981B); ref. Mt.11:25 εἰπὼν δὲ σοφούς, οὐ τὴν ἀληθινὴν σοφίαν λέγει...ἀλλὰ ταύτην ἣν ἐδόκουν ἀπὸ δεινότητος ἔχειν Chrys. *hom.38.1 in Mt.*(7.426A); οὔτε τοὺς λεξίθηρας, οὔτε τοὺς ῥήτορας...σ. κλητέον, ἀλλὰ τοὺς ἐπὶ τῇ πρακτικῇ φιλοσοφίᾳ διαλάμποντας Isid.Pel. *epp.*2.201(M.78.645B).

σοφόω, *make wise*, of Father δυναμοῖ...δι' αὐτοῦ [sc. τοῦ υἱοῦ] τὸ ἠσθενηκὸς καὶ σ. τὸ ἀσύνετον Cyr.*Is.*5(2.778E); σ. [sc. Christ]...τὰ σοφίας δεκτικά id.*Jo.*5.5(4.542E); νόμῳ σεσοφωμένους [i.e. Jews] id. *ador.*13(1.468C).

[*]**σοφρονικός**, for σωφρονικός, *temperate*, *cat.Apoc.*14:8(p.391.1).

σπαθαρία, ἡ, *wife of a* σπαθάριος, Thdr.Stud.*epp.*1.18(M.99.965C).

***σπαθαρικός**, *pertaining to the office of* σπαθάριος or *guardsman*, ‡Jo.D.*ep.Thphl.*11(M.95.357C).

σπαθάριος, ὁ, court dignitary, *member of ceremonial bodyguard*, Thphn.*chron.*p.154(M.108.420A).

***σπαθαροκανδιδᾶτος, ὁ**, court dignitary, *member of ceremonial guard*, ranking higher than a σπαθάριος, †Gr.II Papa *ep.Leon.*1(H. 4.2A).

***σπαθαροκουβικουλάριος, ὁ**, *chamberlain of the bodyguard*; honorary title reserved for eunuchs, *Chron.Pasch.*p.336(M.92.873A).

***σπαθέα, ἡ**, *stroke, thrust* with a sword, Thphn.*chron.*p.266(M. 108.660B).

***σπαθητής, ὁ**, *squanderer*, Ast.Am.*hom.*3(M.40.209A).

***σπαθί, τό**, *sword*, Barth.Edess.*Agar.*(M.104.1433A).

σπαθίζω, *beat* ? with the flat of the sword, *M.Thdot.*3(p.139.17).

σπαθίον, τό, 1. dim. of σπάθη, *sword*; equated with ξίφος, Jo. Mal.*chron.*15 p.387(M.97.576A); *Chron.Pasch.*pp.382f.(M.92.981A,B); Thphn.*chron.*p.265(M.108.657C); **2.** of things sword-shaped, *small shoot* (here proparoxytone) οὐ βάλλει...καρπόν, εἰ μὴ δύο ἢ τρία σ. ἀπὸ τριῶν ναργελλίων Cosm.Ind.*top.*11(M.88.445A).

σπαίρω, 1. *gasp*; of a newborn infant, Nonn.*par.Jo.*9:1(M.43. 824A); of one just rescued from water, Max.*qu.Thal.*65(M.90.765C); **2.** *writhe*, ‡Nil.*narr.*5(M.79.648A).

***σπαλαγμός, ὁ**, ? for σταλαγμός: τρυπᾶται τὸ σπήλαιον ἄνωθεν τῆς κεφαλῆς καὶ τῆς ὄψεώς μου καὶ τοῦ σ. κατερχομένου ἐπλάτυνε τὴν τρύπα⟨ν⟩ τοῦ σπηλαίου *V.Mac.*B(p.163).

***σπανανδρία, ἡ**, *scarcity of population*, Cyr.*hom.pasch.*25(5^2.300C).

***σπάνη, ἡ**, *scarcity*, Epiph.*haer.*61.6(p.386.27; M.41.1048C); Gr. Mag.*dial.*(tr.Zach.)2.21(M.*PL*.66.171B); Jo.D.*hom.*10.1(M.96.753B).

***σπανογένειος**, *scanty of beard*; of a demon, *A.Barth.*7(p.146.24).

σπανός, *scanty, sparse*, Jo.Mal.*chron.*4 p.88(M.97.172C); = σπανοπώγων *with scanty beard*, of prophet Daniel ἦν ἀνὴρ ξηρὸς... καὶ σ. τὴν εἰδέαν, ἀλλ' ὡραῖος ἐν χάριτι ‡Epiph.*v.proph.Dan.*(M.43. 424C); of abbot Daniel τὸ εἶδος αὐτοῦ...σ., ἐπὶ τοῦ χείλους μόνου ἔχων τρίχας, καὶ εἰς τὸ ἄκρον τοῦ πώγωνος Pall.*h.Laus.*18(p.58.5; M.34. 1065A).

σπαραγμός, ὁ, *rending, dismemberment*, met. ἥ τε βάρβαρος ἥ τε Ἑλληνικὴ φιλοσοφία τὴν ἀίδιον ἀλήθειαν σπαραγμόν τινα...τῆς ...θεολογίας πεποίηται Clem.*str.*1.13(p.36.30; M.8.756B); ὑπὸ θεοῦ σπαραχθὲν καὶ εἰς πᾶσαν τὴν γῆν ὑπὲρ τὸν Πενθέως σπαραγμὸν διασπαρέν Or.*Cels.*2.34(p.160.30; M.11.856B).

***σπαράκτης, ὁ**, *one who rends in pieces* ἵνα μὴ δοθῇ τὰ ἅγια τοῖς κυσὶ καὶ κακοῖς τοῦ λόγου σπαράκταις Gr.Naz.*or.*45.16(M.36.645C).

***σπαρακτικός**, *able to rend, tearing*, Cosm.Mel.*schol.*(M.38.349) in Gr.Naz.*carm.*2.1.1.5.

σπαράσσ-ω, 1. *tear, rend in pieces*, met. τὸ Ἰουδαίων ἔθνος... καταδεδίκασται ὑπὸ θεοῦ σπαραχθὲν Or.*Cels.*2.34(p.160.29; M.11. 856A); in anger ἀκουέτωσαν οἱ Χριστομάχοι, καὶ ~έτωσαν ἑαυτούς Ath.*Ar.*2.64(M.26.284B); *separate, tear asunder* natures of Christ, Evagr.*h.e.*1.2(p.7.4; M.86.2424A) cit. s. διαιρέω; **2.** pass., *be convulsed*; with grief, Chrys.*hom.29.4 in Rom.*(9.725C); with rage, id. *hom.4.6 in 1Cor.*(10.32E); **3.** *extort, wring from*, c. acc., Chrys.*hom. 13.5 in 1Cor.*(10.115D); *ib.11.6*(95B); id.*hom.4.4 in Tit.*(11.755A).

σπάργανον, τό, plur., *swathing bands*; **1.** *swaddling clothes*, hence ἐκ σπαργάνων, *from the cradle, from infancy*, Or.*hom.14.5 in Jer.*(p.110.5; M.13.409B); Const.*or.s.c.*11(p.168.30; M.20.1265B); **2.** *grave clothes*, *T.Sal.*18.37(M.122.1345C; p.58.11n.); Chrys.*hom. 63.2 in Jo.*(8.378B).

σπαργαν-όω, *wrap* in swaddling clothes; also in grave clothes, Chrys.*hom.75.3 in Jo.*(8.442C); *ib.63.2*(8.378A); met. τὴν ψυχὴν αὐτῶν ἐσπαργανωμένην ἐστὶν ἰδεῖν...ἐπεὶ οὖν ἀναισθήτως αὐτοὶ διάκεινταί πως νεκροὶ γεγενημένοι id.*hom.27.4 in Mt.*(7.332D); *enfold* ἐσπαργάνωσε τὸν τῇ ἑαυτοῦ δυνάμει τὴν κτίσιν ἅπασαν ~ώσαντα Chrysipp.*enc.in BMV* 4(p.342.22).

σπαργάνωσις, ἡ, *swathing*, in infancy, met. τὰς πρώτας σ. τῆς οὐρανίου κυήσεως ‡Bas.*const.*21.4(2.568D; M.31.1400A); of the covering of the brain, Melet.*nat.hom.*1(M.64.1156D).

σπαρτέον, *one must sow*, Clem.*paed.*2.10(p.208.13; M.8.497B).

σπάρτη, ἡ, *plumb-line*, Thdt.*h.rel.*30(3.1295); met. χηραί τε γυναῖκες...οὐ σπάρτην κατέχουσι βίου *Orac.Sib.*3.45.

σπαρτίον, τό, 1. *cord*, met. τῆς...ἀγάπης τὸ ἀρραγὲς σ. ‡Eust.*Laz.* 16(p.40.7); **2.** *line* of a plummet or of a carpenter's rule θήσω κρίμα εἰς σ. καὶ ⟨δικ⟩αιοσύνην εἰς διαβήτην SM ap.Thdt.*Is.*28:17(p.113.34).

[*]**σπάρτουλα, τά**, for σπόρτουλα (Lat. *sportula*), legal *fees* νόμους ...περὶ τῶν παρεχομένων σπαρτούλων Jo.Mal.*chron.*18(M.97.685A, v.l. σπορτούλλων).

σπάσμα, τό, *convulsion*; of cosmic upheaval, Gnost.ap.Hipp. *haer.*5.14(p.108.17; M.16.3167A).

σπαταλ-άω, *live softly* or *in excessive comfort* or *indulgence* ὅταν ~ῶσιν ἐπιλανθάνονται τοῦ κυρίου *Barn.*10.3; ὅσα ~ῶσα ἐπιθυμεῖ ἡ ψυχὴ ἡμῶν οὐκ ἀρκουμένη τοῖς ἀναγκαίοις Clem.*str.*3.7(p.223.6; M.8. 1161C); παραγγέλλωμεν τὰς ~ώσας τῶν χηρῶν ἐκτὸς εἶναι τοῦ καταλόγου τῶν χηρῶν Chrys.*hom.13.4 in 1Tim.*(11.624D); of animals, *be over-pampered* πρόβατα...τρυφῶντα καὶ λίαν ~ῶντα Herm.*sim.*6. 1.6; of luxuriant growth, Cyr.*Os.*163(3.193B).

σπατάλιον, τό, ? *wantonness* οὐκ ἔξεστίν...τρέφειν τὰς τρίχας... καὶ ποιεῖν σισόην, ὅ ἐστιν σ. *Const.App.*1.3.10.

***σπαταλιστής, ὁ**, *profligate*, Ephr.3.151B; Eus.Al.*serm.*21.16(M. 86.444A).

***σπάτιον, τό**, (Lat. *spatium*) *track* in race course τὰ ἑπτὰ σ. [sc. represent] τὸν δρόμον καὶ τὴν κίνησιν τῆς ἀστρονομίας τῶν ἑπτὰ ἀστέρων τῆς μεγάλης ἄρκτου Jo.Mal.*chron.*7 p.175(M.97.281A).

σπάω, 1. *draw*; abs., *draw one's sword*, Malchus *exc.Rom.*4(p.166. 5; M.113.773B); **2.** *draw in* air or liquid; met., *imbibe* οἱ...τρανότερον σπάσαντες...τὴν ἀλήθειαν Meth.*symp.*3.8(p.37.3; M.18.73D); *ib.*4.5 (p.51.10; 93C); πολλὰ τῆς νόσου ταύτης [i.e. Messalian heresy] σπάσαντα...μοναστήρια Thdt.*h.e.*4.11.3(3.965).

***σπεῖρας, τό**, *garment*, ref. Mt.13:46 μέχρις ἐσχάτου χιτῶνος καὶ σπείρατος Cosm.Mel.*schol.*proem.(M.38.345).

σπείρ-ω, *sow* seed; **1.** met.; **a.** of action of God ὁ τῆς ἐν ἀνθρώποις γῆς γεωργὸς ὁ ἄνωθεν ~ων...τὰ θρεπτικὰ σπέρματα Clem.*str.*1.7 (p.24.18; M.8.732B); of Christ, Or.*Cels.*2.13(p.143.1; M.11.824A); ὡς ~όμενοι ἀναστησόμεθα [sc. οἱ ἐν Χριστῷ πιστοί] Ath.*inc.*21.2(M.25. 132C); ἔσπειρε τὸν λόγον εἰς τὰς ἐκκλησίας Proc.G.*Jos.*13:1(M.87. 1024D); cf.Or.*hom.16.3 in Jos.*(p.397.3; M.12.907C); **b.** of action of Devil ὁ πονηρὸς...σπουδάζει πολλῶν θεῶν...~αι τὴν ὑπόληψιν *Hom. Clem.*3.8; **c.** of action of men, in thoughts ~ατε ἐν ταῖς ψυχαῖς ὑμῶν ἀγαθά *T.Lev.*13.6; ἐν ψυχαῖς ~ειν τὴν ἀθανατοποιὸν πρὸς αὐτὸν [sc. θεόν]...στοργήν *Hom.Clem.*3.8; in deeds ~ειν τὰς τοῦ θεοῦ εὐποιΐας Clem.*str.*2.18(p.165.19; M.8.1040A); id.*fr.*53(p.225.27); bad deeds ὅταν τὸν νοῦν μὴ ἐγρήγορον ποιήσωμεν...τότε ~ονται ⟨ἐν ἡμῖν⟩ τὰ ἁμαρτήματα Epiph.*haer.*66.65(p.106.1, v.l. ~όμεθα M.42.132C); of heret. teachers οὓς οὐκ εἰάσατε ~αι εἰς ὑμᾶς Ign.*Eph.*9.1; **2.** Gnost. ὁ σπείρων one of Heracleon's two Sons of Man χαίρει...ὁ ~ων ὅτι ~ει, καὶ ὅτι ἤδη τινὰ τῶν σπερμάτων αὐτοῦ συνάγεται ἐλπίδα ἔχων τὴν αὐτὴν καὶ περὶ τῶν λοιπῶν...ἔδει γὰρ πρῶτον σπαρῆναι, εἶθ' ὕστερον θερισθῆναι...ἀμφότεροι [sc. ὁ μὲν ~ων, ὁ δὲ θερίζων] τὸ ἴδιον ἔργον εὐεργοῦντες ὁμοῦ χαίρουσιν κοινὴν χαρὰν τὴν τῶν σπερμάτων τελειότητα ἡγούμενοι...ὁ μὲν γὰρ ὑπὲρ τὸν τόπον υἱὸς ἀνθρώπου ~ει· ὁ δὲ σωτὴρ ὢν καὶ αὐτὸς υἱὸς ἀνθρώπου, θερίζει Heracleon ap.Or.*Jo.*13.49(48; p.276.19ff.; M.14.488B,C).

σπεῖσις, ἡ, *treaty, agreement*, Pall.*v.Chrys.*12(p.77.33; M.47.44).

σπέκλον, τό, cf. Lat. *lapis specularis*; **1.** *mica*, Bas.*hex.*3.4(1.26A; M.29.61B); **2.** *window* of mica ὥσπερ λύχνος διὰ σπέκλων, οὕτως... δεικνύειν...ἀμαυρότερον, οἷον σκοτεινότερον Dor.*doct.*3.1(M.88.1653B).

σπεκουλάτωρ, ὁ, (Lat. *speculator*) **1.** member of corps of troops on special duty as messengers, orderlies of governors, etc.; in charge of executions πῶς...σύνοδον ὀνομάζειν τολμῶσιν, ἧς κόμης προυκάθητο καὶ παρῆν σ.; Ath.*apol.sec.*8(p.94.11; M.25.261D); ὁ...

γράψας αὐτὰ Ῥοῦφός ἐστιν ὁ νῦν ἐν τῇ Αὐγουσταμνικῇ σ. *ib.*83(p.162.21; 397B); *M.Tarach.*1(p.452); **2.** in gen., *executioner*, *A.Paul.*5(p.115.17); *M.Das.*12.1; *A.Jo.Bapt.*7,9(pp.534,539); σπεκουλάτωρα *Narr.Jo.Bapt.*(p.3).

***σπεκταβίλιος**, (Lat. *spectabilis*) title of high officers under emperor, Ath.Scholast.*coll.*4.4(p.54); *ib.*7.2(p.83).

σπέρμα, τό, *seed*; **1.** *offspring, descendants*; met. ἡ ῥίζα τοῦ σ. σου τοῦ πνευματικοῦ...οὐ μὴ ἐκλείπῃ *V.Pach.Λ* 18(p.142.25); **2.** *race, stock*; met. ἐπιμένει ὁ θεὸς τὴν σύγχυσιν...τοῦ...κόσμου...διὰ τὸ σ. τῶν Χριστιανῶν Just.*2apol.*7.1(M.6.456A); **3.** *root* of a number ὀγδοὰς πρῶτος κύβος...σ. αὐτῆς ὁ πρῶτος ἄρτιος Anat.Laod.*decad.*(p.38); **4.** met., of Christ οἱ πιστεύοντες αὐτῷ...ἐν οἷς οἰκεῖ τὸ παρὰ τοῦ θεοῦ σ., ὁ λόγος Just.*1apol.*32.8(M.6.380B); σ. θεῖόν ἐστιν ὁ Χριστός, ὃς ἐνοικῶν ἐν τοῖς πιστοῖς ποιεῖ αὐτοὺς γενέσθαι υἱοὺς θεοῦ *cat.1Jo.*3:9(p.126.30); as origin of eternal life, Thdt.*eran.*2(4.174); **5.** met.; **a.** *seed* of salvation σωτηρίων καὶ ἁγίων σ. Or.*Jo.*20.5(p.333.18; M.14.584D); [Eph.5:27,26] πρὸς ὑποδοχὴν τοῦ νοητοῦ καὶ μακαρίου σ. Meth.*symp.*3.8(p.35.16; M.18.73A); Thdt.*Ps.*95:9(1.1292); **b.** of Christian doctrine οἱ μὲν τὴν ἀληθῆ...σῴζοντες...παράδοσιν...ἧκον...καὶ εἰς ἡμᾶς τὰ...ἀποστολικὰ καταθησόμενοι σ. Clem.*str.*1.1(p.9.8; M.8.700A); *ib.*1.2(p.14.10; 709C); *ib.*7.12(p.57.10; M.9.512A); τὰ σ. τὰ ἅγια, τὸν περὶ τοῦ πατρὸς λόγον...τὸν λόγον τὸν περὶ τῆς ἀναστάσεως κτλ. Or.*hom.5.13 in Jer.*(p.42.7; M.13.313A); εὔκαιρον τὴν τῶν σ. καταβολὴν ποιούμενος [sc. Origen] Gr.Thaum.*pan.Or.*7(p.20.12; M.10.1076B); ἴσως...ὑποστρέψομεν πρός σε πάλιν, φέροντες ἐκ τῶν σ. καὶ τοὺς καρπούς *ib.*17(p.38.24; 1101A); ὁ μὲν λόγος ὢν προκόσμιος καὶ σωτὴρ τῶν ὅλων λογικὰ καὶ σωτηριώδη σ. τοῖς αὐτοῦ παραδιδοὺς θιασώταις λογικοὺς ἅμα καὶ τῆς τοῦ πατρὸς βασιλείας ἐπιστημονικοὺς ἀπεργάζεται Eus.*l.C.*2(p.199.20; M.20.1325B); of pre-Christian revelation τοῖς προφητικοῖς...λογικοῖς σ. θερισθεῖσιν κατὰ τὴν...κατανόησιν τοῦ κεκρυμμένου μυστηρίου ἀπὸ τῶν αἰώνων Or.*Jo.*13.46(p.273.3; M.14.481B); τῆς θείας διδασκαλίας σπέρματα νομικά, προφητικά, εὐαγγελικά id.*fr.30 in Lc.*9:62(p.247); of all truth, v. ἀλήθεια; **c.** of *seed* of reason, innate power of reason τὸ ἔμφυτον παντὶ γένει ἀνθρώπων σ. τοῦ λόγου Just.*2apol.*8.1(M.6.457A); τὰ λογικὰ καὶ ἥμερα τῆς ἀνθρώπων ψυχῆς σ. Eus.*h.e.*1.2.19(M.20.64A); λόγον εἰώθαμεν καλεῖν καὶ τὸν σπερματικὸν ἢ φυτικόν, καθ' ὃν δυνάμει τὰ μηδέπω φύντα ἐναπόκειται τοῖς σ. id.*e.th.*2.13(p.114.17; M.24.925D); τὸ νοερὸν ἐν ἡμῖν σ. Synes.*insomn.*7(p.158.3; M.66.1293C); ὁ θεὸς οὗ σ. ὁ νοῦς ἐς ἀνθρώπους ἥκει id.*ep.*101(M.66.1469D); **d.** *seed* of virtue, capacity for virtue τοὺς δυνάμει ἔχοντας τὴν ἀρετὴν καὶ τὰ σ. αὐτῆς πάντῃ ἀπολέσαι οὐ δυναμένους Or.*Cels.*4.25(p.294.18; M.11.1064A); τῶν τῆς ἀνδρείας ἐν ἡμῖν σ. *ib.*4.78(p.348.23; 1152A); **6.** diabolic ὁ...ἐχθρὸς ἐν ταῖς πρὸς θεὸν τῆς καρδίας ἐντεύξεσι...φθοροποιὰ ἐπισπείρων σ., τῆς θείας αὐτὴν ἀποσπῶντα ἑνώσεως Andr.Caes.*Apoc.*72(M.106.456C); **7.** Gnost. ὃ προέβαλε...σαρκίον τῷ λόγῳ ἡ Σοφία, τὸ πνευματικὸν σ., τοῦτο στολισάμενος κατῆλθεν ὁ Σωτήρ Clem.*exc.Thdot.*1(p.105.6; M.9.653A); τὸ ὁρατὸν τοῦ Ἰησοῦ ἡ Σοφία καὶ ἡ Ἐκκλησία ἦν τῶν σ. τῶν διαφερόντων, ἣν ἐστολίσατο διὰ τοῦ σαρκίου...ὅταν...αὐτὸς εἰσέρχηται, καὶ τὸ σ. συνεισέρχηται αὐτῷ εἰς τὸ πλήρωμα *ib.*26(p.115.15,20; 672B,C); *ib.*1(p.105.10; 653A) cit. s. ἐκλεκτός; cf.Iren.*haer.*1.6.4(M.7.509A) cit. s. ἐκλογή; of what is innate in the elect τὸ ἐκλεκτὸν σ. φαμὲν...σπινθῆρα ζωοποιούμενον ὑπὸ τοῦ λόγου...οἱ δ' ἀπὸ Οὐαλεντίνου πλασθέντος φασὶ τοῦ ψυχικοῦ σώματος...ἐντεθῆναι ὑπὸ τοῦ λόγου σ. ἀρρενικόν, ὅπερ ἐστὶν ἀπόρροια τοῦ ἀγγελικοῦ Clem.*exc.Thdot.*1–2(pp.105.12,106.1; 653A); *ib.*21(p.113.22; 668C); πρῶτον οὖν σ. πνευματικὸν τὸ ἐν τῷ Ἀδὰμ προέβαλεν ἡ Σοφία, ἵνα ᾖ...ἡ λογικὴ καὶ οὐρανία ψυχή *ib.*53.5(p.124.25; 685A); as primordial element of cosmos (Ophite) λέγουσιν...περὶ τῆς τοῦ σ. οὐσίας, ἥτις ἐστὶ πάντων τῶν γινομένων αἰτία Hipp.*haer.*5.7(p.84.14; M.16.3134C); τὰ ἀπὸ τοῦ ἀχαρακτηρίστου εἰς τὸν κόσμον κατεσπαρμένα σ., δι' ὧν ὁ πᾶς συντελεῖται κόσμος *ib.*5.8(p.94.15; 3147B); κατενηνέχθαι...φησὶν ἀπὸ τῶν ὑπερκειμένων κόσμων δύο...εἰς τοῦτον τὸν κόσμον...παντοίων δυνάμεων σπέρματα *ib.*5.12(p.105.10; 3162B); (Basilides) of form taken by primordial cosmos ⟨ὁ⟩ οὐκ ὢν θεὸς...κόσμον ἠθέλησε ποιῆσαι...ἀθελήτως·...κόσμον δὲ οὐ τὸν κατὰ πλάτος καὶ διαίρεσιν γεγενημένον ὕστερον καὶ διεστῶτα, ἀλλὰ γὰρ σπέρμα κόσμου. τὸ δὲ σ. τοῦ κόσμου πάντα εἶχεν ἐν ἑαυτῷ, ὡς ὁ τοῦ σινάπεως κόκκος *ib.*7.21(p.197.2ff.; 3303B); ἐγεννήθη ἀπὸ τοῦ κοσμικοῦ σ. ... ὁ μέγας ἄρχων *ib.*7.23(p.200.25; 3310B); (Docetae) God likened to σ. συκῆς *ib.*8.8(p.226.7; 3347C); out of which come all things τρία οὖν εἶναι δοκοῦμεν τὰ πρώτως ὑπὸ τοῦ σ. γενόμενα τοῦ συκίνου· πρέμνον, ὅπερ ἐστὶν ἡ συκῆ, φύλλα καὶ καρπός, τὸ σῦκον...οὕτως, φησί, τρεῖς γεγόνασιν αἰῶνες, ἀπὸ τῆς πρώτης ἀρχῆς τῶν ὅλων ἀρχαί...αὐτοὶ πάντα τοῖς γενητοῖς πᾶσιν ἐπήρκεσαν καὶ ἐπαρκοῦσι *ib.*(p.226.19; 3350A); *ib.*8.9(p.228.1; 3351A) cit. s. ἰσοδύναμος.

σπερμαίνω, *fertilize*; of the female, *bear*, Eudoc.*Cypr.*1.165(M.85.837D).

σπερματικός, *of, for* or *from seed, seminal,* whether of plants or mankind; **1.** *in seed-form, germinal* ἐπεὶ δὲ τὰ μὲν ἐξ ἀγεννήτου καὶ ἀφθάρτου γέγονεν, τὰ σ. ζωῆς, ⟨συνάγεται ὡς⟩ ὁ πυρὸς καὶ ἀποτίθεται· τὸ δὲ ὑλικόν, μέχρι σύνεστι τῷ κρείττονι, μένει Clem.*ecl.*25(p.143.31; M.9.709B); θεὸν τὸν χορηγὸν τῶν σ. καὶ τῆς ἐπιδόσεως τῶν αὐξήσεων Epiph.*haer.*76.26(p.374.33; M.42.569B); met., *pregnant* σ. τινα προκαταβάλλεται λόγον ἐνταῦθα, ὃν ὕστερον ἀναπτύσσειν μέλλει Chrys.*hom.11.3 in Rom.*(9.534D); **2.** λόγος σπερματικός, *Seminal Word, Universal Reason, Generative Principle,* power by which, and material from which, all things come into being; also *generative principle* of individual substances (as comprehended in Universal Reason or Generative Principle) according to which they are what they are; almost their *matter and form*; **a.** Stoic εἰ...ὁ...θεὸς πῦρ τεχνικὸν ὁδῷ βαδίζον ἐπὶ γενέσει κόσμου ἐμπεριειληφὸς ἅπαντας τοὺς σ. λόγους καθ' οὓς ἕκαστα καθ' εἱμαρμένην γίγνεται Athenag.*leg.*6.4(M.6.904A); λέγει [sc. Chrysippus]...ὅτι τοὺς σ. λόγους τοῦ θεοῦ ἡ ὕλη παραδεξαμένη ἔχει ἐν ἑαυτῇ εἰς κατακόσμησιν τῶν ὅλων Or.*Cels.*4.48(p.321.9; M.11.1108A); ἀνάγκη τοὺς πρώτους [sc. ἀνθρώπους] γεγονέναι...ἀπὸ γῆς, σ. λόγων συστάντων ἐν τῇ γῇ *ib.*1.37(p.89.4; 732A); **b.** adopted by some Christian writers, with modifications: in physical realm σ. denotes *in the course of nature, natural*; thus λόγος σ. comes to mean *law(s) of nature* and λόγος σ. of an individual, the *law of one's nature,* or *life-force* ὁ σ. λόγος ἐν τῷ κόκκῳ τοῦ σίτου δραξάμενος τῆς παρακειμένης ὕλης καὶ δι' ὅλης αὐτῆς χωρήσας...τοῦ αὐτοῦ εἴδους ὢν ἔχει δυνάμεων ἐπιτίθησι...καὶ νικήσας τὰς ἐκείνων [sc. material elements] ποιότητας μεταβάλλει ἐπὶ ταύτην, ἧς ἐστιν αὐτὸς δημιουργός Meth.*res.*1.24(p.249.13; M.41.1096A); βουληθεὶς ὁ θεὸς θεῖόν τινα διδάσκαλον πέμψαι τῷ γένει τῶν ἀνθρώπων, πεποίηκεν ἀντὶ σ. λόγου τοῦ ἐκ μίξεως τῶν ἀρρένων ταῖς γυναιξί, ἄλλῳ τρόπῳ γενέσθαι τὸν λόγον τοῦ τεχθησομένου Or.*Cels.*1.37(p.88.28; M.11.732A); Eus.*e.th.*2.13(p.114.16; M.24.925D) cit. s. σπέρμα; οἱ σ. λόγοι, οἱ παρὰ τοῦ δημιουργοῦ ἐξαρχῆς ταῖς φύσεσιν ἐντεθέντες, ὑποτυφόμενοι, εἰ ἀναρριπισθεῖεν, σπινθήρων τρόπον...ἐξάπτεσθαι φιλοῦσιν Isid.Pel.*epp.*2.119(M.78.560B); derived by physical heredity κατὰ τὰ σωματικὰ ἀπὸ πολλῶν σπερμάτων προκύπτει μᾶλλον ἐνεργήσει δυνηθὲν ἔσθ' ὅτε ἓν τῶν σπερμάτων...ὅτε μὲν κρατεῖ ὁ αὐτοῦ λόγος καὶ ἀποτίκτεται τὸ γεννώμενον τῷ σπείροντι ὅμοιον, ὅτε δὲ ὁ λόγος τοῦ ἀδελφοῦ τοῦ σπείροντος κτλ. ... κατὰ τοὺς ἐν ταῖς μίξεσι βρασμοὺς ἅμα πάντων σειομένων, ἕως ⟨ἂν⟩ ἐπικρατήσῃ τις τῶν σ. λόγων Or.*Jo.*20.5(p.333.8; M.14.584C); in spiritual sphere, *innate character* or *principle,* in all men λόγον δέ φημι οὐ τὸν ἐν ἑκάστῳ τῶν γενομένων συμπεπλεγμένον καὶ συμπεφυκότα, ὃν δὴ καὶ σ. τινες εἰώθασι καλεῖν, ἄψυχον ὄντα καὶ μηδὲν λογιζόμενον...ἀλλὰ τῇ ἔξωθεν τέχνῃ μόνον ἐνεργοῦντα κατὰ τὴν τοῦ ἐπιβάλλοντος αὐτὸν ἐπιστήμην· οὐδὲ οἷον ἔχει τὸ λογικὸν γένος λόγον τὸν ἐκ συλλαβῶν συγκείμενον...ἀλλὰ τὸν τοῦ ἀγαθοῦ...θεοῦ ζῶντα καὶ ἐνεργῆ θεὸν αὐτολόγον λέγω Ath.*gent.*40(M.25.81A); in virtue of which we love God ἀδίδακτος μὲν ἡ πρὸς τὸν θεὸν ἀγάπη...ὁμοῦ τῇ συστάσει τοῦ...ἀνθρώπου...σ. τις λόγος ἡμῖν ἐγκαταβέβληται, οἴκοθεν ἔχων τὰς ἀφορμὰς τῆς πρὸς τὸ ἀγαπᾶν οἰκειώσεως Bas.*reg.fus.*2.1(2.336C; M.31.908C); acc. Origen not universal and may be acquired from teachers τὴν πεπληρωμένην ψυχὴν νοητῶν σπερμάτων, ἐληλυθότων ἀπό τινων ὀνομαζομένων πατέρων αὐτῆς καὶ...προκυπτέτωσαν οἱονεὶ σπερματικοί τινες τῶν πατέρων λόγοι *Jo.*20.5(p.333.12; M.14.584C); ἐπεὶ...ἀπὸ ἤθους κρίνεται καὶ ἔργων τὰ τέκνα τοῦ Ἀβραάμ, μήποτε ἀπό τινων σ. λόγων, συγκαταβαλλομένων τισὶν...ψυχαῖς, δεῖ χαρακτηρίζειν τοὺς ὄντας σπέρμα τοῦ Ἀβραάμ. καὶ εἴπερ, ὡς κατὰ τὸ σωματικὸν οὐ πάντες ἄνθρωποι σπέρμα εἰσὶν τοῦ Ἀβραάμ, οὕτω...δῆλον ὅτι οὐ πάντες ἄνθρωποι μετὰ πάντη σ. λόγων τῶν [αὐτῶν] ἐγκατασπαρέντων αὐτῶν ταῖς ψυχαῖς τῷ βίῳ τῶν ἀνθρώπων ἐπιδεδημήκασιν *ib.*20.2(p.328.6ff.; 573C); but, once possessed may be cultivated τοῦτο νοητέον περὶ τοῦ σπέρματος τοῦ Σὴμ καὶ Νῶε καὶ τῶν ἀνωτέρω δικαίων, ὧν τὰς ἰδιότητας σπερματικῶς δοκοῦσιν κοινῇ ἀνειληφέναι εἰς γένεσιν ἐρχόμενοι Ἀβραὰμ καὶ Ναχὼρ καὶ Ἀρράμ· ἀλλ' ὁ μὲν Ἀβραὰμ γεγεωργηκέναι οὓς εἶχεν ἐν ἑαυτῷ σ. λόγους πάντων τῶν πρὸ αὐτοῦ δικαίων *ib.*20.3(p.330.6; 577B); **c.** in Justin ὁ λόγος σ. is divine Word of whom all partake in different measure; σπέρμα τοῦ λόγου or σ. λόγου μέρος is therefore *innate right reason, immanent revelation,* though full knowledge comes only with Christian revelation ἕκαστος γάρ τις [sc. of philosophers] ἀπὸ μέρους τοῦ σ. θείου λόγου τὸ συγγενὲς ὁρῶν καλῶς ἐφθέγξατο *2apol.*13.2(M.6.465B); οὐ κατὰ σ. λόγου μέρος ἀλλὰ κατὰ τὴν τοῦ παντὸς λόγου, ὅ ἐστι Χριστοῦ, γνῶσιν *ib.*8.3(457B); cf. διὰ τὸ ἔμφυτον παντὶ γένει ἀνθρώπων σπέρμα τοῦ λόγου *ib.*8.1(457A); διὰ τῆς ἐνούσης ἐμφύτου τοῦ λόγου σπορᾶς *ib.*13.5

(468A); οἱ πιστεύοντες...ἐν οἷς οἰκεῖ τὸ παρὰ τοῦ θεοῦ σπέρμα, ὁ λόγος id.*1apol.*32.8(M.6.380B).

σπερματικῶς, 1. *in seed-form, germinally,* **a.** in gen. τῷ δὲ ἀνθρώπῳ ἐπιδοθέντα τὰ ὑπ' αὐτὸν ὄντα καὶ σὺν αὐτῷ σ. εἰς δεσποτείαν, οὐ τέλεια παρεδόθη Epiph.*haer.*76.26(p.374.10; M.42.568C); παρέδωκεν αὐτῷ σ. τὴν γῆν...ἵνα...τὰ σ. δι' ἑαυτοῦ μετὰ συνέσεως ἐπὶ γῆν καταβαλλόμενα...τὰ τῆς ἐπιδόσεως τοῦ τελείου θεοῦ πρὸς αὔξησιν προσδέχηται *ib.*(p.374.14ff.; 568D,569A); **b.** ref. innate characters, qualities, or faculties κατὰ τὴν τελείωσιν τοῦ σ. ἐγκειμένου κατὰ τὰς ἐννοίας ἡμῖν λόγου Or.*Jo.*13.41(p.267.25; M.14.472D); *ib.*20.3(p.330.4; 577B) cit. s. σπερματικός; *Hom.Clem.*17.18; ὁ νόμος τῶν σ. ἐνυπαρχουσῶν ἡμῖν δυνάμεων γεωργός ἐστι καὶ τροφεύς Bas.*reg.fus.*3.1(2.340B; M.31.916D); ἔδει τὸν σῖτον εἰς τὸν λόγον μεταλαμβάνειν σ. ὑμῶν ἐγκείμενον ταῖς ψυχαῖς †Bas.*Is.*29(1.402B; M.30.176A); **c.** *in seed form; as seed for further thought,* Clem.*paed.*3.12(p.288.3; M.8.673B); id.*str.*7.14 (p.60.2; M.9.516D); εἰ οὐδὲν τῶν ἀοράτων αὐτὸ ἑαυτοῦ σ. προϋπάρχει Aët.ap.Epiph.*haer.*76.48(p.401.24; M.42.616D); **d.** theol. κατὰ τὸ πάθος ἢ ἀπορροὴν...τὸν υἱὸν μὴ σ. καταβεβλημένον...τελειοῦσθαι CAnc. (358)*ep.syn.*ap.Epiph.*haer.*73.4(p.272.20; M.42.409A); εἰ σ. ἦν ἐν τῷ ἀγενήτῳ θεῷ τὸ γέννημα Aët.*ib.*76.26(p.373.7; 565D); **2.** *like seeds* τὰ διὰ τῶν...αἰσθήσεων ἐμπεσόντα σ. ἀκανθῶν δίκην ὑποβλαστάνειν ἄρχεται Nil.*praest.*14(M.79.1077A); **3.** Gnost., *as by a generative principle* Ἰωάννης...ἀρχήν τινα ὑποτίθεται τὸ πρῶτον γεννηθὲν ὑπὸ τοῦ θεοῦ ὃν δὴ καὶ υἱὸν μονογενῆ καὶ θεὸν κέκληκεν, ἐν ᾧ τὰ πάντα ὁ πατὴρ προέβαλε σ. Val.Gn.ap.Iren.*haer.*1.8.5(M.7.532B); cf. οἵτινές εἰσι λόγοι ἄνωθεν κατεσπαρμένοι...εἰς τοῦτον τὸν κόσμον, κατοικοῦντες ἐν ⟨σώμα⟩τι χοϊκῷ μετὰ ψυχῆς Hipp.*haer.*6.34(p.163.16; M.16.3246D); *ib.*6.43(p.175.12; 3263B).

***σπερματίς, ἡ,** ? for σπερματῖτις fem. adj. *seminal, spermatic*; of veins, Clem.*paed.*1.6(p.119.5; M.8.308A).

σπερματισμός, ὁ, *fertilization,* met. οἱ δαίμονες σπεύδουσιν ὑπαγαγεῖν αὐτὴν [sc. ἀγαθὴν σύνεσιν] τοῖς σ. τοῦ ἄρχοντος αὐτῶν †Cyr. *coll.VT*(6[4].2E; M.77.1177C); id.*ador.*1(1.13A).

***σπερματιστής, ὁ,** *fertilizing male,* Cyr.*thes.*15(5[1].148D).

σπερματώδης, *cereal* σ. ... βρώματος ‡Bas.*const.*25(2.575E; M.31. 1413D).

***σπερμοβόρος,** *vegetarian,* ‡Caes.Naz.*dial.*147(M.38.1096).

***σπερμογονία, ἡ,** *generation by seed,* ‡Ath.*doct.Ant.*51(M.28.629C).

***σπερμογονικός,** *reproducing by seed,* Anast.S.*qu.et resp.*96(M.89. 749A).

σπερμογόνος, = foreg., ‡Gr.Naz.*astron.*(M.36.677A).

σπερμολογ-έω, *pick up seeds* like a bird; hence, met., *pick up scraps of knowledge* πολλὰ δ' ἂν ἔτι πρὸς τούτοις ~ήσαις, εἰ βούλοιο συντιθέναι τὸν ὁμώνυμόν σου θεόν Gr.Naz.*or.*29.18(p.101.7; M.36.97B).

***σπερμοσφαγία, ἡ,** *murder of kindred, cat.Jud.*2:11(p.164.5).

***σπερμοφαγία, ἡ,** *vegetarian diet,* Gr.Nyss.*mart.*(M.46.780).

***σπέτλον, τό,** cf. σπέκλον, *window* οὐκ εἴασεν ἐν τῷ μοναστηρίῳ αὐτοῦ, οὐ θύραν, οὐ θυρίδα, οὐ σ. Jo.Mosch.*prat.*184(M.87.3056C).

σπήλαιον, τό, *grotto, cave*; esp. of Nativity at Bethlehem ἐν...σ. τινὶ σύνεγγυς τῆς κώμης κατέλυσε καὶ...ἐτετόκει ἡ Μαρία τὸν Χριστὸν Just.*dial.*78.5(M.6.657D); δείκνυται τὸ ἐν Βηθλεὲμ σ., ἔνθα ἐγεννήθη, καὶ ἡ ἐν τῷ σ. φάτνη, ἔνθα ἐσπαργανώθη Or.*Cels.*1.51(p.102.12f.; M.11. 756A); σ.; ἀλλ' οὐδέποτε τῷ θρόνῳ ἡ τριὰς ἐνέλειψεν Procl.CP *or.*5.2 (M.65.717C); Thdt.*Joel* 2:30f.(2.1400); id.*affect.*8(p.198.4; 4.901); as place of burial ἐν ἑνὶ σπηλέῳ κατάκιντε *MAMA* 1.235; *A.Jo.Bapt.* 10(p.540); met., of an oratory σ. ἄλλο καὶ φάτνην θεηδόχον Geo.Pis. *carm.*41.1(p.54).

[*]σπήλεον, τό, v. σπήλαιον.

***σπηλοδίαιτος, ὁ,** *one who dwells in a cave,* Steph.Diac.*v.Steph.* (M.100.1113C) cit. s. ὀρεόμενος.

σπῆλυγξ, ἡ, *cave,* met. ψυχὴ...φάος σπήλυγγι καλυφθέν Gr.Naz. *carm.*1.1.8.2(M.37.446A); φωλεοὺς καὶ σ. (οὕτω γὰρ εἴποιμι τὰς τῶν αἱρέσεων συνελεύσεις) Epiph.*haer.*52.2(p.312.28; M.41.956C).

***σπῆτι, τό,** v. σπίτι.

***σπιθαμήσιος,** *a span long, measuring a span,* ‡Ath.*Melch.*(M.28. 528D).

***σπιλολογέω,** *stain,* Ast.Soph.*Ps.*6(M.40.457B).

σπῖλος, ὁ, *spot*; met., *stain,* on virginity μὴ προσιεμένης...κηλῖδα καὶ σ. Meth.*symp.*5.8(p.63.7; M.18.112B); of guilt or sin κοινὸς δὲ σ. ἐστιν αὐτοῖς, ὅτι τὴν αἵρεσίν εἰσι Χριστομάχοι Ath.*fug.*27(p.86.9; M. 25.677C); Gr.Nyss.*or.catech.*36(p.139.11; M.45.92D); *Const.App.*7.40. 1; γῆ ἐσείετο [sc. at Crucifixion], δεσποτικῷ περιρραινομένη αἵματι, τῶν εἰδωλικῶν λύθρων ἐκτινασσομένη τὸν σ. Jo.D.*hom.*4.21(M.96. 620A); Pall.*h.Laus.*proem.(p.9.8; M.34.1002).

σπιλ-όω, *mark, stain, soil*; met., the soul by sin ἄλλους καθαίρων αὐτὸς ἐσπιλωμένος Gr.Naz.*carm.*2.1.12.478(M.37.1200A); Cyr.*ador.*6 (1.196A); κἀκείνων αἰτεῖσθαι συγχώρησιν οἷς ἐγκαυχᾶται...~ούμενος Max.*qu.Thal.*57(M.90.592B); cf. τὸ ~ωθὲν μέρος τοῦ τῆς ἐκκλησίας χιτῶνος Gr.Nyss.*hom.7 in Eccl.*(M.44.725D); the image of God ὁ Ἀδάμ...τὸ πρόσωπον τῇ παρακοῇ ἐσπίλωσε Chrys.*exp.in Ps.*3:1(5. 4A); the mind by error, *Hom.Clem.*8.9.

σπίλωμα, τό, *defilement, stain*; met., of sin φόβος θεοῦ, πάντα ἐξελήλαται τὰ τοῦ πάθους σ. ἐκ τῆς διανοίας ἡμῶν ‡Gr.Nyss.*or.2 in Gen.1:26*(M.44.289C).

σπινθήρ, ὁ, 1. *spark,* behaviour likened to that of σπερματικοὶ λόγοι in human souls σπινθήρων τρόπον ἐν ὕλῃ κατὰ τὰς τῶν χρόνων συναυξήσεις ἐξάπτεσθαι φιλοῦσιν Isid.Pel.*epp.*2.119(M.78.560B); as image of power of H. Ghost, Cyr.*Jo.*4.1(4.340D) cit. s. ἐγκαταχώννυμι; met.; **a.** of light or fire, in good sense, of Origen's zeal οἷος οὖν τις σ., ἐνσκήψας μέσῃ τῇ ψυχῇ ἡμῶν, ἀνήπτετό τε καὶ ἐξεκαίετο Gr. Thaum.*pan.Or.*6(p.17.1; M.10.1072A); ὁ Παῦλος...πανταχοῦ ῥίψας τοὺς σ. τῆς πίστεως Ast.Am.*hom.*8(M.40.293A); εὐσεβείας σπινθήρ *Const.App.*8.2.2; ἐν Πτολεμαΐδι τὸν ἐνόντα σμικρὸν ἔτι τῆς ὀρθοδοξίας σ. θάλψαι Synes.*ep.*67(M.66.1417A); Sophr.H.*v.Anast.*(M.92.1689B) cit. s. ἐγκρύφιος; **b.** of fire, in bad sense, of dissension κἀκ τῆς τῶν διαφορῶν συγκρούσεως σ. τε καὶ φλόγες ἐξανίστανται Const.ap.Eus. *v.C.*3.60(p.108.22; M.20.1133A); of jealousy ὄψις μόνη τοῦ διαφθονουμένου οὐ μικρὸν τοῖς βασκαίνουσιν ἐνιέναι σ. Apoll.ap.*cat.Jo.*5:12 (p.231.1); of unredeemed element ἐνέμεινέ τι [sc. in Saul] τοῦ παλαιοῦ τῆς κακίας σ. καὶ τοῦ πονηροῦ σπέρματος Gr.Naz.*or.*9.2(M.35. 821A); of desire μή πού τις σ. τῆς ἐπιθυμίας ἐκείνης ἐντυφόμενος λάθῃ Chrys.*sac.*3.11(p.67.17; 1.388E); of falsehood opp. λαμπηδών of truth, Procl.CP *or.*6.15(M.65.749C); **2.** Gnost.; **a.** of spark of life which acc. Saturninus raised man upright after his creation μὴ δυναμένου [sc. τοῦ ἀνθρώπου] ἀνορθοῦσθαι...ἡ ἄνω δύναμις...ἔπεμψε σπινθῆρα ζωῆς, ὃς διήγειρε τὸν ἄνθρωπον καὶ ζῆν ἐποίησε· τοῦτον οὖν τὸν σ. τῆς ζωῆς μετὰ τὴν τελευτὴν ἀνατρέχειν πρὸς τὰ ὁμόφυλα λέγει Iren. *haer.*1.24.1 ap.Hipp.*haer.*7.28(M.16.3322B); **b.** that which dwelt in Valent. 'elect' τὸ ἐκλεκτὸν σπέρμα φαμὲν καὶ σ. ζωπυρούμενον ὑπὸ τοῦ λόγου Clem.*exc.Thdot.*1(p.105.12; M.9.653A); ὁ Σωτὴρ τὴν ψυχὴν ἐξύπνισεν...καὶ μετὰ τὴν ἀνάστασιν...ἐξῄπτε...τὸν σ. καὶ ἐζωπύρει *ib.* 3(p.106.12; 656A); (Sethian) element belonging to good Principle of Light βιάζεται κατέχειν εἰς ἑαυτὸ...⟨τὸν⟩ σ. τοῦ φωτὸς...ὡς ἀντιποιεῖται τὸ σκότος...ἵνα ἔχῃ τὸν σ. δουλεύοντα καὶ βλέπῃ Hipp. *haer.*5.19(p.117.16,20; M.16.3179C,D); νοῦν· τὸν ἄνωθεν σ. κάτω ἀναμεμιγμένον *ib.*10.11(p.272.3; 3426A); **3.** ? *sparkle, gleam* ἐπὶ χροῒ πέπλα βαλόντες, Σιδονίης στίλβοντα σοφῷ σ. θαλάσσης Nonn.*par.Jo.* 19:2(M.43.897B).

***σπινθηράκιον, τό,** *tiny spark,* Gr.Nyss.*virg.*10(p.289.23; M.46. 361A).

***σπινθηρακώδης,** *like a spark,* Gr.Mag.*dial.*(tr.Zach.)2.8(M.*PL.* 66.151C).

***σπινθηρισμός, ὁ,** *emission of sparks, A.Phil.*102(p.39.30).

***σπινθηροβόλος,** *emitting sparks,* ‡Chrys.*Laz.et div.*1(8.114A).

σπινθηροειδής, *like a spark,* met. παρελθὸν τὸ φῶς ἀπὸ σ. τρόπου προσεθέτο φαιδρότητι λύχνου φανέντος ἐν αὐχμηρῷ τόπῳ Epiph.*haer.* 66.64(p.104.11; M.42.129B); ἐναύσματά τινα σ. δοκεῖν εἶναι τὰ ῥήματα Gr.Nyss.*hom.3 in Cant.*(M.44.821B).

***σπίτι, τό,** (Lat. *hospitium*) *house, dwelling, Apoc.BMV*(Vassiliev p.127); σπῆτι Barth.Edess.*Agar.*(M.104.1425D).

σπλαγχνίζω, med. with aor. pass., *feel pity* for, *have compassion* on σ. [sc. ὁ θεός] ἐπὶ τὴν ποίησιν αὐτοῦ Herm.*mand.*9.3; ἐσπλαγχνίσθη ἐπὶ πᾶσι τοῖς ἐπικαλουμένοις τὸ ὄνομα αὐτοῦ id.*sim.*9.14.3; ἄνθρωπος σ. εἰς τὸν πλησίον αὐτοῦ *T.Zab.*8.3; σ. ἡμῶν Ephr.3.396F; σ. σοι Jo. Mosch.*prat.*186(M.87.3064C); abs., Herm.*sim.*7.4.

σπλαγχνικός, *merciful, compassionate,* v.l. in *1Apoc.Jo.*9(p.77).

σπλαγχνισμός, ὁ, *feeding on the inwards of a sacrifice* ἔγραψε ψήφισμα...ἅπαντας ἐπιθύειν...τοὺς δὲ μὴ βουλομένους ὑποτάσσεσθαι, τούτους μετὰ σ. καὶ ἐτασμῶν καὶ βασάνων ἀναιρεῖσθαι Hipp.*antichr.* 49(p.33.7).

σπλάγχνον, τό, 1. *inward parts*; met., of God in rel. to generation of Son οὐ γὰρ ζημίᾳ τινὶ τῶν πατρῴων σ. συνέστη τὸ γεννηθὲν Const.*or.s.c.*3(p.156.13; M.20.1240A); **2.** plur., *children,* one's *flesh and blood* ὁ πολύπαις [sc. Job] ἐξαίφνης ἄπαις ἐγένετο, καὶ οὐδὲ κατὰ μικρὸν αὐτῷ τὰ σ. ἀνηλίσκετο, ἀλλ' ἀθρόον ἅπας ὁ καρπὸς ἀνηρπάζετο Chrys.*hom.28.3 in 1Cor.*(10.253E); id.*hom.10.4 in 2Cor.*(10.511B); met., ref. children in the faith, spiritual sons, Thdt.*Philm.*12(3. 715); **3.** usu. plur., *seat of the emotions* and *affections*; hence *mercy, compassion*; **a.** divine ἕως ἐπισκέψεται κύριος πάντα τὰ ἔθνη ἐν σπλάγχνοις αὐτοῦ *T.Lev.*4.4; καὶ διασπερεῖ αὐτοὺς κύριος...ἄχρις οὗ ἔλθῃ τὸ σ. κυρίου *T.Neph.*4.5; ὁ...πατὴρ ἔχει σ. ἐπὶ τοὺς φοβουμένους αὐτόν *1Clem.*23.1; 'ὁ μὴ φιλῶν...τὸν ἀδελφὸν ἀνθρωποκτόνος ἐστί'...

θεοῦ σπλάγχνον οὐκ ἔχει Clem.*q.d.s.*37(p.184.17; M.9.644A); in invocations of Christ υἱὸς σπλάγχνων, ὁ κατὰ φιλανθρωπίαν ἀποσταλεὶς ἡμῖν υἱὸς ἀπὸ τῆς ἄνω πατρίδος τῆς τελείας *A.Thom.*A 156(p.265.8); ἐλθὲ τὰ σ. τὰ τέλεια...ἐλθὲ καὶ κοινώνησον ἡμῖν ἐν ταύτῃ τῇ εὐχαριστίᾳ *ib.*50(p.166.7); ὁ...'Ιωάννης...ἐκάλεσε τὰ τέλεια σ. ... εἶπε· κύριε 'Ιησοῦ Χριστέ *A.Jo.*24(p.164.10); **b.** human μητρικὰ σ. ἔχοντες *Ep. Lugd.*ap.Eus.*h.e.*5.2.6(M.20.436B); ὁ τὸν υἱὸν προσδεξάμενος τὸν καταφαγόντα τὸν βίον αὐτοῦ ἀσώτως πατρικοῖς σ. *Lit.*ap.*Const.App.*8.9.9; esp. Christian κατὰ τὰ σ. ἃ ἔχετε ἐν Χριστῷ 'Ιησοῦ Ign.*Philad.*10.1; πάντοτε σ. ἔχοντες ἐπὶ πάντα ἄνθρωπον Herm.*sim.*9.24.2; οὐδαμοῦ σ. Χριστιανόν Bas.*Spir.*78(3.67A; M.32.216C); τῶν ἁγίων τὰ σ. Chrys. *stat.*3.1(2.36B); σπλάγχνα...'Ιησοῦ Χριστοῦ τὴν πνευματικὴν φιλοστοργίαν ἐκάλεσε Thdt.*Phil.*1:8(3.447); ὁ...νόμος...οὐ συγγινώσκων τοῖς ἡμαρτηκόσι, σ. δὲ ἔχει τὸ εὐαγγέλιον, συστέλλον μὲν τὰς πλημμελείας, κηρύττον δὲ τὰς μετανοίας Serap.*Man.*49(p.70; M.18.1244D).

σπλαγχνοσκοπεία, ἡ, *examination of the entrails of a victim* for omens, Thdt.*Ezech.*21:21(2.845).

***σπλαγχνοσκοπ-έομαι,** *inspect entrails* of sacrifice τελετάς τινας συνίστασαν, ὡς καὶ ~ούμενοι παῖδας καταθύειν Socr.*h.e.*3.13.11(M.67.413C).

***σπλαγχνοσκόπος, ὁ,** *examiner of entrails* (at sacrifice), Thphn. *chron.*p.43(M.108.164B).

***σπληνίζομαι,** *suffer from spleen,* ‡Gr.Naz.*astron.*(M.36.677A).

σπογγίζω, *wipe with a sponge*; **1.** *wipe off* τὰς ψίχας σ. τῶν τραπεζῶν Pall.*h.Laus.*34(p.98.11; σπογγολογοῦσα M.34.1106B); **2.** *wipe*; sacred vessels, *Lit.Chrys.*(M.63.915,920).

σπογγοειδής, *in the form of the sponge* (i.e. one used at Crucifixion), Thdr.Stud.*epp.*2.36(M.99.1220B) cit. s. λογχοειδής.

***σπογγολογέω,** v. σπογγίζω.

σπόγγος, ὁ, 1. *sponge*; one used at Crucifixion symbolically interpreted ὁ...σ. ... τὴν ὅλην δι' ὅλου τοῦ ἁγίου πνεύματος ἐν αὐτῷ γενομένην ἀνάκρασιν ἀνέφηνε ‡Dion.Al.*fr.in Lc.22:42*(p.240.11; M.10.1592B); attached to Cross for third elevation at feast of Exaltation of Cross ἐν τῇ τρίτῃ ὑψώσει ἀποδεθεὶς τῷ...σταυρῷ ὁ τίμιος σ. καὶ αὐτὸς συνυψοῦται αὐτῷ ἐν τῇ ἁγιωτάτῃ Μεγάλῃ ἐκκλησίᾳ, πεμφθεὶς παρὰ Νικήτα πατρικίου *Chron.Pasch.*p.385(M.92.988B); liturg. εἶτα διανέμει τοὺς σ. ἐπιχέων τῇ ἁγίᾳ τραπέζῃ ῥοδόσταγμα, καὶ μετὰ τῶν σ. ἐκμάσσουσιν αὐτόν *Euchol.*(p.498); used to sweep crumbs from paten, *Lit.Chrys.*(p.394.28; M.63.921); **2.** ? *drudge* πᾶσαν ἐποίει ὑπηρεσίαν, καὶ ἦν, τὸ δὴ λεγόμενον, σπόγγος τῆς μονῆς, ἔργῳ πληροῦσα τὸ γεγραμμένον [1Cor.3:18] Pall.*h.Laus.*34(p.98.5; M.34.1106B).

***σποδόδερμος,** *ash-skinned, blackamoor* σ., μέλανε *Apophth.Patr.*(M.65.284B); Zos.*alloquia* 5(M.78.1688B); Dor.*doct.*14.3(M.88.1777B).

σποδοειδής, *like ashes*; of what is *burnt to a cinder, T.Job* 7 (p.107.22).

***σποδόεις,** *ashlike, ashen, Orac.Sib.*4.179.

[*]**σπονδηφόρος,** v. σπονδοφόρος.

***σπονδίζομαι, 1.** pass., met., *be poured out as a libation* πλέον μοι μὴ παράσχησθε τοῦ σπονδισθῆναι θεῷ Ign.*Rom.*2.2; **2.** med., *make a treaty with* τῷ διαβόλῳ σ. ‡Jo.D.*ep.Thphl.*18(M.95.369B).

σπονδοφόρος (σπονδηφόρος), *bringing peace proposals, reconciling* σπονδηφόρῳ μεσιτείᾳ ‡Meth.*Sym.et Ann.*6(M.18.361A); as subst. ὁ σ. καὶ διαλλακτὴς καὶ σωτὴρ ἡμῶν λόγος Clem.*prot.*10(p.78.21; M.8.228B).

σπόνδυλος, ὁ, = σφόνδυλος, plur., *vertebrae* of spine; hence of vertebra-like *lumps* or *swellings,* Pall.*h.Laus.*18(p.49.5; M.34.1051D).

***σπόνζα, τά,** (cf. Lat. *sponsalia*) plur., *betrothal,* Thphn.*chron.* p.374(M.108.897A).

σπορά, ἡ, 1. *sowing of seed*; met. ψυχὴ...ψυχῇ καὶ πνεῦμα πνεύματι συναπτόμενα κατὰ τὴν τοῦ λόγου σ. Clem.*str.*1.1(p.3.22; M.8.689A); ἡ τοῦ διαβόλου σ. τῶν λόγων Epiph.*haer.*78.3(p.453.30; M.42.704A); **2.** *procreation, propagation,* met. ἀγγέλων ἐπὶ τῆς σ. τῶν ἀνθρώπων τεταγμένων Or.*Jo.*13.50(49; p.277.17; M.14.489A); τὴν καθαρὰν τῆς διδασκαλίας...καὶ γόνιμον σ. Meth.*symp.*3.8(p.37.8; M.18.76A); **3.** *seed,* met. διὰ τῆς ἐνούσης ἐμφύτου τοῦ λόγου σ. Just.*2apol.*13.5(M.6.468A).

σποράδην, *in no order,* i.e. without reference to chronology, Thdt.*Ezech.*30:20(2.932).

σπορεύς, ὁ, 1. *sower,* met. τὰ μὲν σπέρματα τῶν σωτηρίων λόγων δέδεγμαι σοῦ ὄντος τοῦ σ. *A.Andr.fr.*12(p.43.12); of God γεωργὸς ἀόρατος τῆς τῶν ἀνθρώπων τροφῆς, σ. εὔκαιρος καὶ ὀχετηγὸς ἐπιστημῶν Gr.Nyss.*paup.*1(M.46.461C); of Devil, Ath.*Ar.*1.10(M.26.33A); ὑπὸ τοῦ τῆς κακίας σ. ζιζανιώδεις αἱρέσεις Gr.Nyss.*v.Ephr.*(M.46.825D); ἡδονή ἐστι διὰ τῶν ἑκουσίων παθῶν σ. ὁ διάβολος Anast.S.*qu. et resp.*32(M.89.572A); **2.** *begetter,* met. νυμφὴν...οὐ τοῦ τυχόντος ἀλλὰ μόνου τοῦ σ. τῶν ἀγαθῶν Or.*fr.*45 *in Jo.*(p.519.22); ὕβριν δὲ σαρκὸς ὁ σ. ἐπέβλυσεν Gr.Naz.*carm.*1.2.8.31(M.37.651A).

σπόριος, v. σπούριος.

σπουδάζω, pass., ref. literary works and problems; **1.** *be studied,* Eus.*p.e.*10.12(5C0B; M.21.833A); οὐκ ἐνδιάθηκον [sc. 2Petr.] μὲν εἶναι παρειλήφαμεν, ὅμως δὲ πολλοῖς χρησιμὸς φανεῖσα, μετὰ τῶν ἄλλων ἐσπουδάσθη γραφῶν id.*h.e.*3.3.1(M.20.216C) or perh. *be valued*; of a lie, *be deliberately invented* (cf. Eng. 'studied falsehood'), Athenag. *res.*1(p.48.7; M.6.976A); **2.** *be composed,* Eus.*h.e.*3.9.2(M.20.241A); *ib.*5.13.8(461B).

***σπουδαιογραφέω,** *take pains in writing,* Thdr.Stud.*or.*11.16(M.99.820A) cit. s. συρμαιογραφέω.

σπουδαιολογία, ἡ, *serious discussion,* Eus.*Hierocl.*22(525C; M.22.828C); Tit.Bost.*Man.*2.1(M.18.1132C).

σπουδαῖος, as subst., *scholar* τῶν ἐν 'Ιεροσολύμοις σ. ‡Ath. *synops.*77(M.28.436A).

σπουδάρχης, ὁ, *one who is eager for office, place-hunter* σ. δὲ πολλοὶ αὐτοχειροτόνητοι, τὴν παροῦσαν λαμπρότητα διώκοντες †Bas. *Is.*112(1.457A; M.30.300B).

σπουδαρχίδης, ὁ, = foreg. αὐτοχειροτόνητοι καὶ σ. τῶν ἐκκλησιῶν τὰς προστασίας διαλαγχάνουσι, τὴν οἰκονομίαν τοῦ ἁγίου πνεύματος παρωσάμενοι Bas.*Spir.*77(3.66D; M.32.216A); Didym.*Trin.*2.27(M.39.768B); Isid.Pel.*epp.*3.119(M.78.824A).

σπούδασμα, τό, *serious pursuit*; hence **1.** *duty, office* ὁ νόμος...ὁ διὰ Μωϋσέως, μόνους ἐκέλευσε τῶν ἱερῶν ἅπτεσθαι σπουδασμάτων τοὺς ἐξ αἵματος Λευΐ Cyr.*Lc.*20:2(M.72.884A); **2.** *zeal, energy* ὅλον τῆς ἑαυτῶν διανοίας δαπανῶντας τὸ σ. Cyr.*Jo.*3.4(4.298C); plur., *zealous efforts* τὰ λοιπὰ...τοῦ πιστοτάτου βασιλέως εὐσεβῆ ὑπὲρ τῆς πίστεως σπουδάσματα Gel.Cyz.*h.e.*2.37.30(M.85.1341C).

***σπουθιστήρ, ὁ,** perh. for ⟨σπαθιστήρ⟩ a surgical instrument, ? *spatula* τέχνῃ τινὶ ἰατρικῇ διὰ τοῦ καλουμένου σ. τὴν τῶν μελῶν ὑποδερματίδα ὑποσπαθισθέντες Epiph.*mens.*16(M.43.264C).

σπούριος (σπόριος), (Lat. *spurius*) *false* ἡ μοιχεία τὰ σ. καὶ γεννῶσα καὶ δρῶσα Pall.*v.Chrys.*16(cj. p.96.15; cod. σπόρια M.47.54).

***σπυριδάλιον, τό,** *small basket,* Pall.*h.Laus.*32(M.34.1105B; p.96.4n.).

σπυρίς, ἡ, *basket*; irreg. acc. σπυρίδαν, Marc.Diac.*v.Porph.*81.

***σταβλιστής, ὁ,** (cf. Lat. *stabularius*) *stable-keeper, groom,* Call. *v.Hyp.*(p.77).

[*]**στάβλος, ὁ,** (Lat. *stabulum*); **1.** *stable,* Call.*v.Hyp.*(p.77); **2.** *dwelling,* Chrys.*fr.in Jer.*38:11(M.64.1004A).

σταγετός, ὁ, *dripping*; *shedding* of tears, Nil.*epp.*3.243(M.79.500D).

***σταδιαρχής, ὁ,** *one in charge of the race-course*; fig., of God, Andr.Cr.*or.*17(M.97.1173C).

σταδιεύ-ω, *run* as in the stadium, *run* or *travel round*; of tongues of fire round circle of the apostles, ‡Chrys.*pent.*3(3.795A); of S. Paul, Bas.Sel.*or.*2.4(M.85.44B); of Noah ὁ καθάπερ ἐν ἀκροπόλει τῇ κιβωτῷ ~σας *ib.*5.2(84A); met., of life as a voyage, *ib.*8.1(112C); and as a contest, ‡Nil.*perist.*11.23(M.79.936D); τὸ φῶς...τῆς ἀναστάσεως, εἰς ἣν ἐπείγεσθε καὶ ὑπὲρ ἧς ἐναγωνίως ~ετε Germ.CP *or.*1(M.98.221D).

[*]**σταδιηδρόμος, ὁ,** = σταδιοδρόμος, *runner* in the stadium, one who runs for a prize, Gr.Naz.*carm.*1.2.9.99(M.37.675A).

***σταδιοδρομία, ἡ,** *running* in the stadium, *race,* Gr.Nyss.*v.Mos.*(M.44.405D).

στάδιον, τό, A. measure of length, *stade*; met., *stage* τῆς νυκτὸς πᾶν σ. Chrysipp.*enc.in Jo.Bapt.*(p.34.23).

B. *amphitheatre*; **1.** lit., as scene of martyrdoms, *M.Polyc.*8.3; *M.Xanthipp.*27(p.83.29); Eus.*h.e.*5.1.1(M.20.408C); **2.** met.; **a.** of world ὁ ἐν τῷ μεγάλῳ σ., τῷ καλῷ κόσμῳ, τὴν ἀληθινὴν νίκην κατὰ πάντων στεφανούμενος τῶν παθῶν Clem.*str.*7.3(p.14.23; M.9.424C); **b.** of present life ὁ τὸν παρόντα αἰῶνα σ. δικαιοσύνης ἐνστησάμενος *Const.App.*7.33.3; σ. δὲ ὁ κοινὸς τῶν ἀνθρώπων βίος ἐστίν Gr.Nyss. *Pss.titt.*B 2(M.44.492B); Chrys.*hom.26.3 in Rom.*(9.715B); μετὰ ἔξοδον τοῦ σ. Pall.*v.Chrys.*20(p.143.15; M.47.80); εἰς τὸ σ. τῆς ἀρετῆς ἀναβῶμεν, τὰ περὶ ψυχῆς 'Ολύμπια ἀγωνισάμενοι Isid.Pel.*epp.*2.161 (M.78.616A); **c.** of sufferings preceding martyrdom τὸν...Γρηγόριον ...ἐτίμησαν, κατὰ τὴν ἐνάρετον αὐτοῦ ἄθλησιν καὶ τὸ μαρτυρικὸν σ. Agath.*v.Gr.Ill.*138; **d.** of Church μέγιστόν ἐστι διδασκαλεῖον τὸ τῆς ἐκκλησίας σ. ‡Chrys.*Laz.et div.*1(8.113A); **e.** of episcopal office δόξης μάλιστα δεῖ καταφρονεῖν τὸν εἰς τοῦτο ἐρχόμενον τὸ σ. Chrys.*sac.*6.7 (p.154.11; 1.427B).

***σταθερογνώμων,** *right-thinking, high-principled,* ‡Proc.G.*Pr.* 19:6(M.87.1412D).

***σταθεροποι-έω (*σταθηρ-),** *make strong, establish* θεῶν...προνοίᾳ διοικεῖται καὶ ∼εῖται Maximinus Daia *rescr*.ap.Eus.*h.e*.9.7.3(M.20.809C); φυλάττει καὶ σταθηροποιεῖ Agath.Papa *ep.imp*.(M.*PL*.87.1167D).

σταθερός (σταθηρός), *standing fast, firm, fixed*; of weather, *steady, settled* ἐν ἡμέρᾳ σταθηρᾷ Gel.Cyz.*h.e*.3.10.10; met. γαλήνης λοιπὸν ἀπήλαυνε σταθερᾶς [sc. ἡ ἐκκλησία] Thdt.*h.e*.1.2.1(3.724); of persons τοὺς ἀμυήτους, καὶ οὔπω ὄντας σ. τε καὶ δεκτικοὺς τῆς θεοπτίας Didym.*Trin*.1.18(M.39.348C).

***σταθερόω,** *strengthen* σ. τὰς...ψυχάς Thdr.Stud.*epp*.2.34(M.99.1208B).

σταθηρ-, v. also σταθερ-.

σταθηρότης, ἡ, *stability*; met., *reliability, certainty* δι' ἀπορίαν τοῦ κατ' αὐτοὺς λόγου σταθηρότητος διωκόντων τοὺς εὐσεβεῖς Anast. Ap.*a.Max*.2.21(M.90.157D).

σταθμίζ-ω, *weigh*;

A. trans.; **1.** lit. πῶς δὴ...θεοί εἰσι...χωνευόμενοι, ∼όμενοι; *Hom. Clem*.10.8; Gr.Nyss.*ordin*.(M.46.552B); Epiph.*mens*.24(M.43.288A); **2.** met.; **a.** *weigh, estimate* ∼εται ἡ τιμὴ τῇ τοῦ δικαίου ἐπικρίσει Serap.*Man*.39(p.57; M.18.1221A); τὰς ἑαυτοῦ πράξεις...ἐπὶ ζυγοῦ ∼ομένας Leont.N.*v.Jo.Eleem*.22(p.41.20); ? *balance* τὸ σταθμιεῖν ἑαυτόν τις ἐπὶ τοῖς τοῦ κυρίου καὶ τοῦ διαβόλου ἔργοις, βδέλυγμα κυρίῳ Or.*exp.in Pr*.20:23(M.17.212D); hence **b.** *repay, requite* οἴκτῳ γὰρ οἶκτος καὶ θεῷ ∼εται Gr.Naz.*carm*.1.2.33.160(M.37.939A); **c.** *regulate* ∼οντες πάντα τὰ μέλη ἡμῶν Esaias *or*.2.2(p.6).

B. intrans. τοῦ ταλάντου ἑκατὸν εἰκοσιπέντε λίτρας ∼οντος *cat.Mt*.10:29(p.80.11).

στάθμιον, τό, (or paroxytone); **1.** *weight* of a balance στάθμια δόλου Thdr.Mops.*Mich*.6:11(M.66.388A); met. καθόλου πᾶσαν ὑπερβολὴν καὶ ἔλλειψιν, τοῦτο σ. μέγα καὶ μικρόν ἐστιν Or.*exp.in Pr*.20:10(M.17.212C); ποίησον...κοῦφον τὸ σ., εἴ πω βούλει μὴ πρὸς τὴν κατακρίνουσαν πλάστιγγα καὶ τὰς σὰς πράξεις καθελκυσθῆναι Ast.Am. *hom*.13(M.40.360D); ἁμαρτάνειν...τὸ ὑπερβαίνειν τὰς ἐντολάς· οἱ μὲν γὰρ ἐγκρατεῖς, τῷ ποιῆσαι σ. μέγα, ἀφωρίκασιν ἑαυτοὺς τῆς ἐκκλησίας Proc.G.*Dt*.12:32(M.87.909A); **2.** *standard weight* μέτρα καὶ σ. Παλαμήδης ἐφεῦρε Ath.*gent*.18(M.25.37C); met. σ. καὶ μέτρον καὶ ἀριθμὸν τῶν ὅλων...τὸν θεόν Clem.*prot*.6(p.52.28; M.8.176A); **3.** plur., *scales, balances*; met. τὰ δίκαια τοῦ θεοῦ σ. Gr.Naz.*or*.5.1(M.35.665A).

***σταθμογραφέω,** *divide into periods, Pers*.(p.45.3).

σταθμός, ὁ, 1. *station, stage*; of the *quarter* of the wind, *1Clem*.20.10; met. τοὺς...οὐδὲ τοῖς πρώτοις ἐναυλισθέντας τοῦ βίου σ. Bas. *hom*.21.2(2.164E; M.31.544C); **2.** *balance, weight*; ? *a weighing, judgement* τοὺς σ. ... ὅταν παραδίδως, μνήμην ἔχῃ τῆς ἀναστάσεως, καὶ πράξεων ἀνταπόδοσιν γινομένην ἡμῖν ὑπὸ τοῦ θεοῦ Ephr.2.246C; **3.** *moderation* [sc. Christ] συνεσθίων...ἄρτον καὶ συμπίνει τὸ ὕδωρ, πλὴν ἐν σ. καὶ μέτρῳ Or.*sel.in Ezech*.4:9(M.13.781A); **4.** *sum, total* καὶ πρόσθεττε [? l. πρόσθες τε] καὶ ἕτερα κδ' καὶ ποίησον σ. †Andr.Cr.*cycl*. (M.19.1329B).

στακτή, ἡ, *balsam*, Thdt.*Ezech*.27:16(2.902); met., of BMV, Thdr.Stud.*nativ.BMV* 7(M.96.692D) cit. s. βαλσαμουργία.

στάλσις, ἡ, *checking* εὐθὺς στάλσεις ποιοῦνται μήπως...διαλύσῃ τὸ ζῷον Adam.*dial*.5.17(p.210.11; M.11.1856C).

σταλτέον, *one must get ready* or *equip*, Clem.*paed*.3.7(p.259.10; M.8.609B).

***στάμα, τό,** *stand*; **1.** emperor's place in the circus, Thphn. *chron*.p.372(M.108.889C); *ib*.p.247(στόμα 620B); **2.** *stop, Apoc.Dan*.C (p.117); σ. ἔχω *be stationary, show no progress* ἐν ὅλῃ τῇ ἡμέρᾳ ἔσχε σ. ὁ πόλεμος Thphn.*chron*.p.266(M.108.661A).

***στάματα, τά,** *ribs of a ship*, Epiph.*haer*.61.3(p.383.9).

στάμνος, ἡ, *jar* (ref. Heb.9:4) met., of womb of BMV αὕτη ἡ... κιβωτὸς...ἐν ᾗ...ἡ στάμνος ἡ χρυσῆ ἡ ἔχουσα τὸ μάννα Procl.CP *or*.6.17 (M.65.756A); of BMV, ‡Epiph.*hom*.5(M.43.489D); Germ.CP *hymn. BMV*(M.98.453C); χαῖρε, στάμνε,...ἀφ' ἧς μαννάδοτεῖται ἅπας ὁ κόσμος Thdr.Stud.*nativ.BMV* 7(M.96.689B).

***στάναι,** s.v.l., for στῆναι: ἔγγυς ἐγένετο τοῦ...διαλυθῆναι τῶν ποδῶν τὰς βάσεις, ὡς μηδὲ σ. δύνασθαι τοῦ λοιποῦ Or.*Ps*.72:2(p.93), but prob. l. μηδ' ἑστάναι.

***στασιαστός,** *rebellious, factious*; of Jews, *A.Pil*.A 9.2(p.242).

***στασίδιον, τό,** *sedile, seat* for clergy in sanctuary of church τὸ σ. τοῦ προεστῶτος *Euchol*.(p.3).

στάσιμος, *stationary, idle*, Bas.*hom*.6.5(2.48A; M.31.272B); neut. as subst., *rest, stability*; opp. motion, Gr.Nyss.*Pss.titt*.A 3(M.44.441B).

στασιοποιός, *causing dissension*, Nil.*epp*.1.188(M.79.153C).

στάσις, ἡ, A. *rest* opp. motion; **1.** *standing still*; of mode of life of Stylites, Niceph.Ur.*v.Sym*.28(M.86.3012B); **2.** *stoppage, cessation* ἡ τοῦ κακοῦ σ. ἀρχὴ τῆς κατ' ἀρετὴν ἐστιν ὁρμῆς Or.*princ*.1.8.4(p.104.2); οὐχ εὑρίσκει...στάσιν τῆς ἀναβάσεως Gr.Naz.*or*.28.21(p.53.13; M.36.53C); Philost.*h.e*.3.9(M.65.492B); *pause* κρούει...ποιῶν σ. τρεῖς, καὶ οὕτως συνάγονται πάντες οἱ ἀδελφοί *Euchol*.(p.439); *suspension* from priestly functions, †Jo.Jej.*poenit*.(M.88.1908C); *impediment* to matrimony, *Schol*. in Bas.*ep*.217 *can*.68(*Mon*.2 p.653); **3.** *fixedness, stability* τὴν ἐπιστήμην...ἀπὸ τῆς σ. τὴν ἐπιβολὴν αὐτῆς ληπτέον, ὅτι ἵστησιν ἡμῶν ἐν τοῖς πράγμασι τὴν ψυχὴν...καὶ τὴν πίστιν ἐτυμολογητέον τὴν περὶ τὸ ὂν στάσιν τῆς ψυχῆς ἡμῶν Clem.*str*.4.22(p.311.17, 20; M.8.1353A); of things and persons μόνη μονὰς στάσιν καὶ μονὴν εἴληφε Eus.*l.C*.6(p.210.1; M.20.1348A); ἀπατωμένης καρδίας καὶ μὴ ἐχούσης σ. ἀληθείας Epiph.*haer*.55.9(p.336.19); Proc.G.*Is*.6:13(M.87.1949B); as a virtue δευτέρα δὲ [sc. τῆς ἡλικίας τρίβος] ὁπηνίκα λοιπὸν εἰς ἄνδρα τέλειον ἐλάσας, ἄρχεται σ. καὶ βεβαιότητα τῶν θορύβων ὁ νοῦς προσλαμβάνειν καὶ τῆς οἰήσεως Meth.*symp*.5.2(p.55.13; M.18.100C); cf.id.*res*.1.62(p.328.24; M.41.1161C); ἐπειδὴ...ἀπὸ τῆς κατὰ τὴν πίστιν σ. οὐκ ἐγνωρίζοντο...ἐκ τῆς περιτομῆς ἐβούλετο γινώσκεσθαι Diod.*Gen*.17:14(M.33.1574A).

B. *place* or *position of standing*; **1.** met., *issue* in a cause, *point* in dispute, *status apud rhetores dicitur ea res, in qua causa consistit, id est constitutio. Graeci autem statum a contentione* στάσιν *dicunt*, Isid.H.*etym*.2.5.1; **2.** statio, *station, assembly* of faithful for prayer πάννυχον σ. Gr.Naz.*or*.27.7(p.12.4; M.36.20B); *ib*.42.26(489C); Thdt. *h.rel*.24(3.1259f.); †Gregent.*disp*.(M.86.781C); †Jo.D.*B.J*.30(M.96.1141C); **3.** priestly *rank* πότε τις καθέδρας μὲν ἢ στάσεως ἱερατικῆς μετέχει, οὐκ ἐνεργεῖ δέ τι τῶν λοιπῶν Phot.*nomoc*.9.19(p.550; M.104.1105D); cf.CAnc.(314)*can*.1; **4.** (Lat. *status*) *condition, state* proper to one's being τῆς δὲ τῶν γεγενημένων φυσικῆς γενέσεως τέλος ἡ σ. ἐστὶν...πάσης...γενέσεώς τε καὶ κινήσεως τῶν ὄντων, ἀρχὴ καὶ τέλος ἐστὶν ὁ θεός, ὡς ἐξ αὐτοῦ γεγενημένων καὶ δι' αὐτοῦ κινουμένων, καὶ εἰς αὐτὸν τὴν σ. ποιησομένων Max.*ambig*.(M.91.1217C,D).

C. *faction*; *discord*; hence *storm* ἡ...σ., ἤρξατο μὲν ἀπὸ τῶν ἀρκτικῶν πνευμάτων· καὶ ὗσέ γε πολλά Synes.*ep*.4(M.66.1337A).

στατήρ, ὁ, *standard coin*, in silver τοσούτων σ. ὁ Ἰούδας τὸν δεσπότην ἀπέδοτο Thdt.*Zach*.11:13(2.1647); in value four drachmae, Epiph.*mens*.(M.43.285B); but also said to equal two drachmae, *ib*. (284B); Proc.G.*Gen*.23:15(M.87.393B); in rel. to shekel τὸν...σίκλον στατῆρα ἐκάλεσαν. ἐπὶ δὲ σταθμοῦ ὁ σίκλος λαμβανόμενος, ἡμιόγκιον [v.l. -ούγκιον] εἷλκεν· ἐπὶ δὲ ἀργυρίου, εἴκοσιν ὀβολούς Thdt.*qu.29 in 1Reg*.(1.374).

στατίων, ἡ, (Lat. *statio*) period of fasting when Christians assembled together, of regular occurrence στατίωνα ἔχω. τί...ἐστι στατίων; νηστεύω Herm.*sim*.5.1.1f.; cf. *similiter et de stationum diebus non putant plerique sacrificiorum orationibus interveniendum quod statio solvenda sit accepto corpore domini*, Tert.*de oratione* 19 (M.*PL*.1.1181–2); *stationibus quartam et sextam sabbati dicamus*, id.*de jejuniis* 14(M.*PL*.2.973A); *qui cum in statione...clamoribus turbulentis proruerent*, Cypr.*ep*.41.1(M.*PL*.3.723A); name said to be derived from custom of standing, cf.Ambr.*serm*.21.1(M.*PL*.17.666A).

στατιωνάριος, ὁ, (Lat. *stationarius* [sc. *miles*]) *gendarme* or *soldier on police duties* esp. at a *statio* or police post, *M.Agap*.3.1.

στατιωνίζω, *be on duty*; of soldiers, *M.Agap*.4.3.

***στατοῦτον, τό,** (Lat. *statutum*) *statute*, Ath.Scholast.*coll*.1.10 (p.19); Phot.*nomoc*.1.30(p.478; M.104.556B).

***σταυλάρης, ὁ,** *muleteer*, Gr.Mag.*dial*.(tr.Zach.)3.8(M.*PL*.77.234B).

[*]**σταῦλον, τό,** variant of στάβλον *stable, Mir.Artem*.13(p.13.17).

***σταῦλος, ὁ,** (Lat. *stabulum*) *stable*, Jo.Mal.*chron*.16 p.396(M.97.585B); Thphn.*chron*.p.98(M.108.289B); fig. ἡ αὐλὴ αὐτῶν οὐκ ἔχει θύραν, καὶ ὁ θέλων εἰσέρχεται εἰς τὸν σ., καὶ λύει τὸν ὄνον. τοῦτο δὲ ἔλεγεν, ὅτι τὰ ἐρχόμενα εἰς τὸ στόμα αὐτῶν λαλοῦσιν *Apophth.Patr*. (M.65.81A).

***σταυριαῖος,** *of the cross*, Leont.B.*parasc*.(M.86.1997C).

σταυρικός, *pertaining to the cross*; **1.** *on the cross* ἐν τῷ σ. πάθει Hipp.*antichr*.4(p.6.22; M.10.732B); Areth.*Apoc*.1:7(M.106.512B); τὸν Πέτρον τὸν σταυρικὸν ἀναδεξάμενον θάνατον ‡Gr.Nyss.*hom*.5.75 *in Jo*.(p.197.12); **2.** *representing the Cross* τοῦ σ. σημείου Eus.*v.C*.1.30 tit.(p.5.3; M.20.944D); Amph.*hom*.2.8(M.39.57A,C); Areth.*Apoc*.21:12(M.106.769A); ref. Jo.10:9 εἰσῆλθε διὰ τῆς σ. θύρας εἰς τὴν ἐκκλησιαστικὴν μάνδραν Tim.Ant.*caec*.13(M.28.1020D); ἡμᾶς...ὡς πειθομένους τῇ σ. βακτηρίᾳ *ib*.14(1021C); τὸ τῶν δαιμόνων στῖφος ἡ σ. καταργεῖ φαρέτρα id.*cruc*.(M.86.256A); **3.** *of the Cross* τὰ ξύλα...τὰ σ. Germ.CP *or*.1(M.98.224B); *ib*. cit. s. διατύπωσις; τὸ ὕψος...τὸ σ. *ib*. (237D).

***σταύρινον, τό,** *small cross*, Jo.Mosch.*prat*.200(M.87.3088D).

σταυρίον, τό, *cross* τὰ σ. τῶν πλησίον κωμῶν ἔχοντες Cyr.S.*v.Euthym.*25(p.38.12); in metal, as church furniture, CBeryt.*act.* cap.8(*ACO* 2.1.3 p.25.13; H.2.520A); worn on the person, Leont.N.*v.Jo.Eleem.*1(p.5.9); embroidered, ‡Bas.*h.myst.*24(p.263.7); of marks of the cross ηὑρέθη τὸ περιβόλαιον αὐτοῦ ὅλον σταυρίων γέμον *V.Alex.Acoem.*16(p.670.2); of a cruciform church ἐποίησε τὴν ἐκκλησίαν κατὰ σταυρίον Thphn.*chron.*p.206(M.108.529C).

***σταυρίσκω,** *crucify*, *Ev.Petr.*2(p.210).

***σταυροδόχος, ὁ,** *socket supporting a cross* ἐν τῷ σ. ἵστατο εἰκὼν τοῦ σωτῆρος Gr.Syc.*v.Thdr.Syc.*8(p.368).

σταυροειδής, *in the form of a cross*, Meth.*Porph.*1(p.504.28; M.18.400C) cit. s. βήξιλλον; ἔκφρασις σταυροειδοῦς σημείου, ὅπερ νῦν οἱ Ῥωμαῖοι λάβαρον καλοῦσιν Eus.*v.C.*1.31 tit.(p.5.4; M.20.945A); *ib.*2.7 tit.(p.36.13; 988A); σ. τύπῳ Gr.Nyss.*ep.*25(M.46.1096A); τὰ ἱερογλυφικά...γράμματα ἐπιστάμενοι, διερμηνεύοντες τὸν σ. χαρακτῆρα Socr. *h.e.*5.17.4(M.67.608B); neut. as subst. τὰ...ὄρνεα τὸ σ. κατὰ τὴν ἔκτασιν τῶν πτερύγων αἰνίσσονται Meth.*Porph.*1(p.504.32; 400C); of the sign of the cross, Dion.Ar.*e.h.*5.3.4(M.3.512A) cit. s. ἀναμαρτησία.

σταυροειδῶς, 1. *in the form of a cross, crosswise*, of manner of wearing scapular ὁ δὲ ἀνάλαβος...ὁ σ. τοῖς ὤμοις αὐτῶν περιπλεκόμενος, σύμβολον τῆς εἰς Χριστόν ἐστι πίστεως ἀναλαμβανούσης τοὺς πραεῖς Evagr.Pont.*cap.pract.*A proem.(M.40.1221A); ὁ ἀνάλαβος τίθεται σ. ἐπὶ τοὺς ὤμους ἡμῶν· τοῦτ' ἔστι, τοῦ σταυροῦ τὸ σύμβολον βαστάζομεν Dor.*doct.*1.13(M.88.1633B); of holding arms in prayer ἐπωφελὲς ἂν εἴη ὡς ἐπὶ τὸ πλεῖστον τὸ σ. εὔχεσθαι Nil.*epp.*1.87(M.79.121A); of Moses (ref. Ex.39:43), *ib.*; ref. Ex.17:11, †Gregent.*disp.* (M.86.637B); Jo.D.*f.o.*4.11(M.94.1133A); of holding hands in receiving Holy Communion προσέλθωμεν αὐτῷ...σ. τὰς παλάμας τυπώσαντες *ib.*4.13(1149A); **2.** liturg., *in the form of a cross, with the sign of the cross* λαβὼν...τὴν λόγχην...σ. χαράξας αὐτὴν [sc. τὴν προσφοράν] ‡Bas.*h.myst.*31[b](p.264.20); σ. θυμιῶν *Lit.Praesanct.* (p.345.7); *Lit.Chrys.*(p.361.21; M.63.906); ‡Germ.CP *contempl.*(M.98.449A) cit. s. λογχεύω; **3.** *crosswise, diagonally*; of deacon's manner of wearing stole, *Lit.Chrys.*(p.393.8; M.63.919).

***σταυρόμορφος,** *in the form of a cross*, Geo.Pis.*hex.*1892(M.92.1577B).

***σταυροπαγής,** *fixed to a cross, crucified*, Eudoc.*Cypr.*1.201,282 (M.85.840B,844A).

***σταυροπάτης, ὁ,** *one who tramples on the Cross*, *Ep.Chr.dom.* (p.25).

***σταυροπήγιον, τό,** *fixture of a cross* by bishop on site of a new church ἐπὶ θεμελίου ἐκκλησίας ὅπερ καὶ σταυροπήγιόν τινες ὠνόμασαν *Euchol.*(p.485); *ib.*(p.488).

σταυρός, ὁ, A. in gen.; **1.** *stake, pale* ὅρον ἔχωμεν τὸν σ. τοῦ κυρίου, ᾧ περισταυρούμεθα καὶ περιθριγκούμεθα τῶν προτέρων ἁμαρτιῶν Clem.*paed.*3.12(p.283.8; M.8.664B), prob. ref. Gnost. beliefs, v. G.1 infra; ἐὰν...ἀπολῦσαι καὶ ἀποστῆσαι καὶ ἀφορίσαι (τοῦτο γὰρ ὁ σ. σημαίνει) τὴν ψυχὴν ἐθελήσῃς τῆς...ἡδονῆς id.*str.*2.20(p.172.17; M.8.1053A) prob. met., signifying mortification, v. F.1 infra; **2.** *cross* as instrument of crucifixion θάνατον ἢ τὸν διὰ σταυροῦ ἢ τὸν διὰ λίθων *Const.App.*2.48.2; abolition attributed to Constantine, Soz.*h.e.*1.8.13(M.67.881A).

B. *Cross* of Christ; **1.** in gen. ἔπαθε...σαρκὶ τῷ σ. προσπαγεὶς ὁ λόγος Meth.*Porph.*3(p.506.23; M.18.401B); θεοῦ λόγον...τὸν ἐπὶ τοῦ σ. ἀναβάντα Ath.*gent.*1(M.25.5A); ἐν αὐτῇ τῇ ἡμέρᾳ ἐγένετο διὰ ξύλου σ. ὁ σωτήριος θάνατος Cosm.Ind.*top.*2(M.88.124D); **2.** discovered in Jerusalem, Chrys.*hom.85.1 in Jo.*(8.505B); by Helena, Cyr.H.*ep. Const.*3(M.33.1168B); cf.Ambr.*de obitu Thds.*45(M.*PL.*16.1401A); cf. τὸ...γνώρισμα τοῦ ἁγιωτάτου ἐκείνου πάθους ὑπὸ τῇ γῇ πάλαι κρυπτόμενον...ἀναλάμπειν ἔμελλε Const.ap.Eus.*v.C.*3.30(p.91.24ff.; M.20.1089C); discovery attested by miracle, Socr.*h.e.*1.17.6(M.67.120A); Soz.*h.e.*2.1.5(M.67.932D); Thdt.*h.e.*1.18.4(3.794); **3.** divinely willed to be instrument of Christ's death αὐτὸν ἐπισήμως ἐπὶ τοῦ σ. ἀποτεθνηκέναι, ἵνα μηδεὶς ἔχῃ λέγειν ὅτι...ἔδοξεν ἀποτεθνηκέναι, οὐκ ἀποτέθνηκε δέ Or.*Cels.*2.56(p.180.20; M.11.888A); cf.Just.*dial.*95.2(M.6.701C); τούτου...ἕνεκα...προσηλώθη τῷ σ. οἰκονομούμενος· ὅπως δι' ἧς σαρκὸς οἱ δαίμονες ἀναδεῖξαι θεοὺς ἠλαζονεύσαντο...διὰ ταύτης ἀνατραπέντες κατοπτευθῶσιν οὐκ ὄντες θεοί...διὰ τοῦτο γὰρ μάλιστα εἰσήχθη καὶ ὁ σ., τρόπαιον κατὰ τῆς ἀδικίας καὶ ἔκπληγμα τεθεὶς Meth.*Porph.*1 (pp.503.15,504.11; M.18.397D,400B); reasons, Ath.*inc.*24f.(M.25.137B–140C); Gr.Nyss.*res.*(M.46.621C–625B); id.*or.catech.*32(pp.115.6,117.9ff.; M.45.80A,Cff.); **4.** set up by Devil in ignorance of what he did (cf. 1Cor.2:7f.) ὁ διάβολος...πάντα ταῦτα θεασάμενος...φοβεῖται ...σταυρῷ με προσηλῶσαι καὶ θανάτῳ παραδοῦναι Amph.*hom.in Mt. 26:39*(p.98.13; cf.M.61.753); ‡Dion.Al.*fr.in Lc.22:42*(p.244.3; M.10.1593B); cf. καὶ ἔλαθεν τὸν ἄρχοντα τοῦ αἰῶνος τούτου...ὁ θάνατος τοῦ κυρίου Ign.*Eph.*19.1; *A.Petr.c.Sim.*8(p.90f.); **5.** as an object of veneration, v. D.4 πάνυ γὰρ πολὺ σέβας εἶχε τοῦ θείου σ. ἔκ τε τῶν ὑπαρξάντων αὐτῷ τῇ ἐνθένδε ῥοπῇ...καὶ ἐκ τῆς συμβάσης αὐτῷ περὶ τούτου θεοσημείας Soz.*h.e.*1.8.12(M.67.881A); *ib.*1.4.1(868A); cf.Eus. *l.C.*9(p.220.6; M.20.1368A); subject of pagan taunt against Christians as idolaters, Juln.Imp.ap.Cyr.*Juln.*6(6[2].194C) cit. s. E.2 infra; Christian explanation, cf. *regem adoravit* [sc. *Helena*], *non lignum utique; quia hic gentilis est error...sed adoravit illum qui perpendit in ligno*, Ambr.*Thds.*46(M.*PL.*16.1464B); cf.Hier.*ep.*108.9 (M.*PL.*22.884A); *Dial.Christ.et Jud.*1(p.51.15); Jo.D.*f.o.*4.11(M.94.1129Cf.); its fragments as relics καὶ τοῦ ξύλου τοῦ σ. πᾶσα λοιπὸν ἡ οἰκουμένη κατὰ μέρος ἐπληρώθη Cyr.H.*catech.*4.10; *ib.*10.19; φασὶ γὰρ ὅτι ηὕρηται μὲν κατὰ καιροὺς τὸ τοῦ σ. ξύλον, ἐμπεπαρμένους ἔτι τοὺς ἥλους ἔχον· ὧν ἕνα λαβὼν ὁ εὐσεβὴς Κωνσταντῖνος ἐπὶ χαλινὸν γενέσθαι τῷ ἵππῳ τῷ ἰδίῳ παρεσκεύασεν Cyr.*Zach.*114(3.812E); cf. Socr.*h.e.*1.17.9(M.67.120C); dedication of Constantine's church in Jerusalem, *Chron.Pasch.*p.286(M.92.713A); **6.** liturg.; Feast of Exaltation of Cross, originally celebrated on completion of church built marking site to commemorate discovery of Cross, *Chron. Pasch.*p.286(M.92.713A) cit. s. σταυροφάνεια; cf. *inventio sanctae crucis quando inventa est ab Helena matre Constantini xvii Kal. octobris, et per septem dies in Hierusalem ibi ad sepulchrum Domni missae celebrantur et ipsa crux ostenditur*, Thds.Archidiaconus *itinera Hierosolymitana* 31(*CSEL* 39 p.149.24); the ceremony followed that of the dedication of the church πάλαι μὲν γὰρ τῆς ἀναστάσεως ὁ σ. προηγήσατο, ἄρτι δὲ ἡγεμόνα καὶ πρόδρομον ὁ σ. τὴν ἀνάστασιν κέκτηται Sophr.H.*or.*4(M.87.3305A); took place at CP as well as Jerusalem since a portion of true Cross had been sent thither [Socr.*h.e.*1.17.8(M.67.120B); Thdt.*h.e.*1.18.6(3.795)] at time of its discovery συνέφθασεν...ἡ ἡμέρα κυριακή, μεθ' ἣν καὶ τὴν μνήμην τοῦ ζωοποιοῦ σ. τῇ τεσσαρεσκαιδεκάτῃ τοῦ Σεπτεμβρίου μηνὸς... ἑορτάσαμεν Eustrat.*v.Eutych.*70(M.86.2353C); Sophr.H.*or.*4(M.87.3305C); id.*v.Mar.Aeg.*2.19,3.22(M.87.3712A,D); *Chron.Pasch.*p.385 (M.92.988B); Leont.N.*v.Sym.*5(M.93.1673C); ἐπὶ τὸν ὑπερβάθμιον τόπον τῆς ἐκκλησίας ἀνιόντες, καὶ τὸν ὑπερένδοξον τουτονὶ καὶ πολυπροσκύνητον σ. εἰς ὕψος ἀνέχοντες, ὑψοῦσι...τοῖς λαοῖς ἐπιδείκνυνται Andr.Cr.*or.*11(M.97.1040A); also venerated at Apamea, Evagr.*h.e.* 4.26(p.173.3ff.; M.86.2745A,B); Adoration of Cross in mid-Lent τῶν ἁγίων νηστειῶν ἡ μέση ἑβδομὰς τὸν...ζωοποιὸν τοῦ σωτῆρος...σ. προσκομίζουσα, καὶ τοῦτον προτιθεμένη εἰς προσκύνησιν...σήμερον τοιγαροῦν προσκυνήσιμος ἡμέρα τοῦ τιμίου σ. καθέστηκε ‡Chrys.*ador.* 1.1(3.819B); ἡ μὲν νηστεία τὸ κοῦφον τοῦ σώματος ἀποτελοῦσα, ἡ δὲ τοῦ θείου σ. καθαρωτάτη προσκύνησις τὸν νοῦν...πρὸς τὰ ἄνω βασίλεια ἐπάγουσα Sophr.H.*or.*5(M.87.3312D); Thdr.Stud.*or.*2(M.99.693C); and on Good Friday, cf. *affertur loculus argenteus deauratus in quo lignum sanctum crucis, aperitur et profertur, ponitur in mensa tam lignum crucis quam titulus...unus et unus omnis populus veniens, tam fideles quam catechumini, acclinantes se ad mensam osculentur sanctum lignum et pertranseant...manum autem nemo mittit ad tangendum*, Aetheria(‡Silvia)*itinera Hierosolymitana* 37 (*CSEL* 39 p.88.9ff.); *consecratur condita in passionis loco basilica, quae...arcano positam sacrario crucem servat: quam episcopus urbis ejus quotannis, cum pascha domini agitur, adorandam populo princeps ipse venerantium promit*, Paulinus Nolae *ep.*31.6(M.*PL.*61.329C); ἐν τῷ ἱερατείῳ...ἐν ᾧ εἰς ὕψος αἴρεσθαι κατ' ἔτος ὁ τίμιος εἰώθει σ. Thdr.Pet.*v.Thds.*(p.71.5); **7.** oil of the Cross, name given to oil which had been brought to the true Cross, cf. *et affertur oleum ad benedicendum ampullis onychinis. hora vero qua tetigerit lignum crucis ampullas, mox ebullit foras*, Antonius Placentius *itinerarium* 20(M.*PL.*72.906C); used to effect cures, Cyr.S.*v.Sab.*45(p.136.17); *ib.*63(p.164.15); Eustrat.*v.Eutych.*45(M.86.2328A); *ib.*55(2337A); to expel demons from a site, Cyr.S.*v.Sab.*27(p.110.11).

C. *Crucifixion*; **1.** the act of crucifying Christ τοῖς μὲν τὸν σ. τετολμηκόσιν, εἶτα μεταμεληθεῖσι, συνέγνω Thdt.*Is.*1:28(p.11.21; 2.181); τοῦ σ. τὴν μανίαν *ib.*33:23(p.137.2; 2.314); id.*Dan.*9:24(2.1240); id.*Zach.*12:3(2.1652); τοῦ σ. τὸ τόλμημα Hesych.H.*fr.Ps.* 108:29(M.93.1321B); **2.** the *sacrifice* or *death of Christ upon the Cross* τὸν σ. ... θεραπείαν τῆς κτίσεως γεγονέναι Ath.*gent.*1(M.25.5A); τὴν πρὸ τοῦ σ. ... διαγωγήν ‡Just.*qu.et resp.*48(M.6.1293A); τὸν [sc. S. Thomas] οὕτως ἀσθενῆ πρὸ τοῦ σ. μετὰ τὸν σ. καὶ τὸ πιστεῦσαι τῇ ἀναστάσει θερμότερον πάντων αὐτὸν ὁρῶμεν Chrys.*hom.62.2 in Jo.* (8.370D); ὀλίγων...μετὰ τὸν σ. διελθόντων ἐτῶν, ἀνάστατον ἅπαν τὸ γένος ἐγένετο Thdt.*Ps.*108:9(1.1383); τοῦτο δὲ καὶ κατὰ τὸν καιρὸν γεγένητ(αι) τοῦ σ. id.*Is.*6:4(p.32.15; 2.209); ὁ θάνατος τοῦ Χριστοῦ, ἤτοι ὁ σ. Jo.D.*f.o.*4.11(M.94.1129A); **a.** means of salvation, Ign. *Eph.*9.1 cit. s. μηχανή; ἐκ σ. ... ἡ σωτηρία Cyr.H.*catech.*13.37;

Chrys.*hom.27.2 in Jo.*(8.155C); ὁ σ., ἡ τοῦ κόσμου σωτηρία καὶ ζωή Cyr.*Thds.*(p.47.12; 5^{2}.7D); ἔσωσε τὸν ἄνθρωπον διὰ τοῦ σ. καὶ τῆς ἀναστάσεως Jo.Mal.*chron.*10 p.228(M.97.353B); Germ.CP *or.*1(M.98.237C); means of union with Christ, Ign.*Trall.*11.2; hence τίμιος and ζωοποιός, ‡Chrys.*cruc.*tit.(2.820B); Cyr.*Is.*2.1(2.205C); id. *Nest.*5.5(p.101.17; 6^{1}.135B); id.*Chr.un.*(5^{1}.769B); Thdt.*carit.*(3.1303); Eustrat.*v.Eutych.*70(M.86.2353C); and σωτήριος, Thdt.*Abac.*3:7(2.1553); id.*Ps.*22:4(1.749); *Lit.Jac.*(p.204.4); **b.** victory over the enemy δι' οὗ σταυροῦ διετράπη καὶ ἐθριαμβεύθη σατανᾶς καὶ πᾶσα δύναμις ἀντικειμένη Serap.*euch.*25.2; ref. Is.8:18 σώζονται...ἐν Χριστῷ...οὐχ ὅπλα κινοῦντες ἐπίγεια...ἀλλ' ἐν δυνάμει τοῦ σώζοντος καὶ κατασείοντος μὲν ἀρχὰς καὶ θρόνους, θριαμβεύοντος δὲ τῷ ἰδίῳ σ. τῶν ἀντικειμένων τὰ στίφη Cyr.*Os.*5(3.25B); ref. Rom.8:37 πρὸς τούτοις λογιζόμενοι τὸν ζωοποιὸν σ. κτλ. Thdt.*carit.*(3.1303); hence a trophy τρόπαιον κατὰ πάσης ἀντικειμένης δυνάμεως τὸν σ. στήσαντος Or.*Jo.*20.36(29; p.376.18; M.14.657C); Meth.*Porph.*1(p.504.11; M.18.400B); τρόπαιον ἐξῄει βαστάζων τὸν σ. κατὰ τῆς τοῦ θανάτου τυραννίδος Chrys.*hom.85.1 in Jo.*(8.504B) v. τρόπαιον; also δόξα, *ib. 51.2*(8.301A); id.*cruc.*2.1(2.411C); id.*hom.4.2 in Heb.*(12.41B); and a defence τεῖχος...ἡμῖν ἄρρηκτον ὁ σ. Cyr.*Is.*2.4(2.294E); **c.** where Christ bore man's sins μόνου Ἰησοῦ τὸ πάντων τῆς ἁμαρτίας φορτίον ἐν τῷ ὑπὲρ τῶν ὅλων χωρὶς θεοῦ σταυρῷ ἀναλαβεῖν εἰς ἑαυτὸν... δεδυνημένου Or.*Jo.*28.19(14; p.413.30; M.14.721B); **d.** where redemption was effected οὐ γὰρ δόκησις ὁ σ., ἐπεὶ δόκησις καὶ ἡ λύτρωσις Cyr.H.*catech.*13.4; ἐγήγερται...σημεῖον ἐν ἡμῖν μέγα...ὁ τοῦ σωτῆρος σ. δι' οὗ...ἐκλελυτρώμεθα...οἱ πεπιστευκότες Cyr.*Zach.*72(3.751E); σεσώσμεθα καὶ ἐκλελυτρώμεθα διὰ τοῦ τιμίου σ. id.*Nest.*5.2(p.96.42; 6^{1}.128C); and recapitulation τοῦτο δὲ ἦν [sc. τὸ θέλημα τοῦ πατρός] ἡ διὰ τοῦ τιμίου σ. λύτρωσις καὶ ἀνακεφαλαίωσις τῶν ὅλων id.*Chr.un.*(5^{1}.769B); **e.** a sacrifice made διὰ τὸν σ. ἑορτάζειν κελεύει, ἐν γὰρ τῷ σ. ἐτύθη ὁ Χριστός Chrys.*cruc.*1.1(2.403C); θυσίαν ἐκάλεσε τὸν σ. id. *hom.15.1 in Heb.*(12.150C); **f.** and an example given πρῶτος εἰς τὸν σ. ὁ κύριος ἡμῶν καὶ τῆς ὑπομονῆς ἑαυτοῦ διδάσκαλος ἀνῆλθεν ἐν τῷ ἰδίῳ τυπῶν ὑποδείγματι ἐκείνους οἷς ἔμελλε βοηθεῖν Horm.Papa *ep. cler.*(p.53.36; M.*PL.*63.417A); **g.** power of cross; in universe, cf. *tantam esse vim crucis Christi...asserimus quae ad sanitatem...non solum praesentis et futuri, sed etiam praeteritorum saeculorum, et non solum humano huic nostro ordini, sed etiam celestibus virtutibus ordinibusque sufficiat,* Or.*comm.in Rom.*5.10(M.14.1053A); esp. in human life τὸ δὲ παραδοξότατον τοῦτό ἐστιν, ὅτι τὴν τοῦ σ. πίστιν ἐνδυσάμενος καταφρονεῖ καὶ τῶν κατὰ φύσιν, καὶ τὸν θάνατον οὐ δειλιᾷ διὰ τὸν Χριστόν Ath.*inc.*28.2(M.25.144C); τίς τοὺς παρὰ βαρβάροις... ἔπεισεν ἀνθρώπους ἀποθέσθαι μὲν τὴν μανίαν, εἰρήνην δὲ φρονεῖν, εἰ μὴ ἡ τοῦ Χριστοῦ πίστις καὶ τὸ τοῦ σ. σημεῖον; τίς δὲ ἄλλος περὶ ἀθανασίας οὕτως ἐπιστώσατο τοὺς ἀνθρώπους, ὡς ὁ τοῦ Χριστοῦ σ., καὶ ἡ τοῦ σώματος ἀνάστασις αὐτοῦ; *ib.*50.5(185C); σ. ... τὸ πάθος [i.e. of Christ] ἐστίν· ὥστε τὸν πρὸς αὐτὸν βλέποντα...ὑπὸ τοῦ ἰοῦ τῆς ἐπιθυμίας μὴ βλάπτεσθαι Gr.Nyss.*v.Mos.*(M.44.415D); cf. *est enim tanta vis crucis Christi, ut si ante oculos ponatur...nulla concupiscentia... nulla superare possit invidia,* Or.*comm.in Rom.*6.1(1056C); μάθε πόση τοῦ σ. ἡ ἰσχύς...διὰ τούτου πάντα τελεῖται· βάπτισμα διὰ τοῦ σ.· ...χειροτονία διὰ τοῦ σ. κἂν ἐν ὁδοῖς ὦμεν...κἂν ὅπου ἄν ποτε, μέγα ἀγαθὸν ὁ σ., σωτήριον ὅπλον...τῷ διαβόλῳ ἀντίπαλος Chrys.*hom.13.1 in Phil.*(11.298A); ἐγηγερμένου...τοῦ σημείου, τοῦτ' ἔστι, τοῦ τιμίου σ. ... γέγονεν ἄφεσις τῶν ἐν αἰχμαλωσίᾳ...συνδρομὴ πρὸς ὁμοψυχίαν, σπουδὴ πρὸς ὁμόνοιαν καὶ ὁμοπιστίαν τῶν πάλαι διῃρημένων Cyr.*Is.*2.1(2.205C); Chrys.*cruc.*1.1(2.403A); *ib.*2.1(411Bf.); Jo.D.*f.o.*4.11(M.94.1129A); Thdr.Stud.*or.*2(M.99.697Cf.); **h.** an offence to unbelievers, glory of the faithful (1Cor.1:23) τοῦ σ. ὅ ἐστιν σκάνδαλον τοῖς ἀπιστοῦσιν, ἡμῖν δὲ σωτηρία καὶ ζωὴ αἰώνιος Ign.*Eph.*18.1; τὸν σ. διαβάλλοντες, οὐχ ὁρῶσι τὴν τούτου δύναμιν...καὶ ὅτι δι' αὐτοῦ τὰ τῆς θεογνωσίας ἔργα πᾶσι πεφανέρωται Ath.*gent.*1(M.25.4B); τὸ νομιζόμενον παρὰ ἀνθρώποις μωρὸν τοῦ θεοῦ διὰ τὸν σ. γέγονε πάντων ἐντιμότερον, ἡ μὲν γὰρ ἀνάστασις ἡμῖν ἐν αὐτῷ ἀπόκειται id.*Ar.*1.43(M.26.100C); τὸν τοῦ σωτῆρος σ. τὸν ὑπὲρ τῆς τοῦ κόσμου ζωῆς τε καὶ ἀφθαρσίας ἐγηγερμένον, καύχημα μὲν εἶναι τῆς ἐκκλησίας...διαβεβαιωσόμεθα...πλατὺ γὰρ γελῶσιν οἱ τάλανες, τὴν τοῦ μυστηρίου δύναμιν εἰσάπαν ἠγνοηκότες Cyr.*Soph.*45(3.623B); id.*Nest.*5.5(p.101.17; 6^{1}.135B); ἀνδρείας ὑπόθεσίς ἐστιν ὁ σ. καὶ καυχήσεως, ἀλλ' οὐκ αἰσχύνης Germ.CP *or.*1(M.98.240A); problem of suffering upon Cross, divine nature being impassible μὴ φεισάμενος σ. καὶ θανάτῳ καὶ τάφῃ, συνεχώρησεν παθεῖν τὸν τῇ φύσει ἀπαθῆ...τὸν θεὸν λόγον *Const.App.* 2.24.3; σῇ συγχωρήσει...κριθεὶς ὁ κριτὴς...σταυρῷ προσηλώθη ὁ ἀπαθὴς καὶ ἀπέθανεν ὁ τῇ φύσει ἀθάνατος καὶ ἐτάφη ὁ ζωοποιὸς *Lit. ib.*8.12.33; yet hypostatic union forbidding denial that God was in Christ suffering on Cross, Thdot.Anc.*exp.symb.*21(M.77.1344B,C); οὕτως ἐν τῷ σ. ἡ ἀπαθὴς θεότης οὐκ ἔστιν ἀπὸ τοῦ τῆς σαρκὸς πάθους διῃρημένη Horm.Papa *ep.Epiph.*(p.58.31; M.*PL.*63.520D); **i.** a refutation of docetism, Polyc.*ep.*7.1; ἐάν τις εἴπῃ ὅτι δόκησις ὁ σ., ἀποστράφηθι...εἰ γὰρ κατὰ φαντασίαν ἐσταυρώθη, ἐκ σ. δὲ ἡ σωτηρία, καὶ ἡ σωτηρία φαντασία Cyr.H.*catech.*13.37; **3.** as prefigured in OT, freq. exeg., v. D.1.d; Ps.1:3 τοῦτο...λέγει· μακάριοι οἱ ἐπὶ τὸν σ. ἐλπίσαντες κατέβησαν εἰς τὸ ὕδωρ *Barn.*11.8; 4Esdras 5.9 ἔχεις πάλιν περὶ τοῦ σ. καὶ τοῦ σταυροῦσθαι μέλλοντος *ib.*12.1; *ib.*8.1; Is.9:6 μηνυτικὸν τῆς δυνάμεως τοῦ σ. ᾧ προσέθηκε τοὺς ὤμους σταυρωθείς Just.*1apol.*35.2(M.6.384A); Ps.21:18 ἐξήγησις τῶν ἐν τῷ σ. παγέντων ἐν ταῖς χερσὶ καὶ τοῖς ποσὶν αὐτοῦ ἥλων ἦν *ib.*35.7(384C); Num.21:6ff. λαβεῖν τὸν Μωϋσέα χαλκὸν καὶ ποιῆσαι τύπον σταυροῦ *ib.*60.3(417A); ref. Lc.2:34 σημεῖον ἔγνωμεν παρὰ τῇ γραφῇ τὸν σ. εἰρημένον. ἔθηκε γάρ, φησί, Μωσῆς τὸν ὄφιν ἐπὶ σημείου· τουτέστιν, ἐπὶ σταυροῦ Bas.*ep.*260.8(3.400C; M.32.965B); Jer.15:18, Or.*hom.14.18 in Jer.*(p.124.7; M.13.428A); Dt.28:66 θάνατος...μετέωρος καὶ ἐν ξύλῳ γινόμενος οὐκ ἄλλος ἂν εἴη εἰ μὴ ὁ σ.· καὶ ἐν οὐδενὶ δὲ πάλιν θανάτῳ διορύσσονται πόδες καὶ χεῖρες εἰ μὴ ἐν μόνῳ τῷ σ. Ath.*inc.*35.5(M.25.156B,C); Gen.28:11ff. μόνον...ἐπάγη τὸ ξύλον τοῦ σ. ἐπὶ τῆς γῆς καθ' ὃν τρόπον ἐστήρικτο κλῖμαξ ἐπὶ Ἰακώβ *Dial.Tim.et Aquil.*98 v° (p.79); Amos 9:6 ἦν τὸ ξύλον εἰκὼν καὶ τύπος τοῦ τιμίου σ., δι' οὗ γέγονε γλυκὺς ὁ νόμος Cyr.*Am.*81(3.347B); Zach.3:9 σταυρῷ παραδοὺς τὸ ἴδιον σῶμα, ἐφ' ᾧ καὶ τὸ τῶν Ἰουδαίων προσκέκρουκεν ἔθνος, καὶ τῆς πρὸς αὐτὸν οἰκειότητος ἀποβέβληται...βόθρῳ...παρεικάζει τὸν τοῦ σωτῆρος σ. id.*Zach.*21(3.679A); ῥάβδος...καὶ...βακτηρία...οὐκ ἂν δέ τις ἁμάρτοι τὸν σωτήριον οὕτως ὀνομάζων σ. ... τῇ μὲν ὀρθῇ βακτηρίᾳ ἡμᾶς τοὺς εἰς αὐτὸν πιστεύοντας στηρίζων...τῇ δὲ πλαγίᾳ ὡς ῥάβδῳ κατὰ τῶν δαιμόνων χρώμενος Thdt.*Ps.*22:4(1.749); ὥς τινες ἐφαντάσθησαν ὅτι τῇ ῥάβδῳ προσκυνήσας, ἐν αἰνίγματι τῷ σ. προσεκύνησεν Gennad. *fr. Gen.*47:31(M.85.1656D); τοῦ σωτηρίου σ. τῆς ῥάβδου τὸ κράτος δηλοῖ Thdt.*Ps.*109:2(1394); ἡ ῥάβδος διπλῆν ἐνέργειαν κέκτηται· καὶ γὰρ μαστίζει καὶ χειραγωγεῖ· καὶ ὁ σ. δὲ ἡμᾶς χειραγωγεῖ, καὶ μαστίζει τοὺς δαίμονας Hesych.H.*fr.Ps.*109:2(M.93.1324B); ἀρχὴν...τὸν σ. καλεῖ· ὡς ἐν αὐτῷ τῆς οἰκουμένης ἄρχοντος...ἡττηθέντος· ἡμέραν δὲ δυνάμεως αὐτοῦ τὴν ἡμέραν εἰκότως τοῦ σ. *ib.*109:3(1324C); rod of Joseph, Jo.D.*f.o.*4.13(M.94.1132C) cit. s. εἰκονίζω.

D. *cross,* as emblem; **1.** its form; **a.** shape of **T** (Gen.14:14; 17:23ff.) ὅτι δὲ ὁ σ. ἐν τῷ ταῦ ἤμελλεν ἔχειν τὴν χάριν, λέγει καὶ τοὺς τριακοσίους *Barn.*9.8; cf. εἶναι τοῦ μὲν κυριακοῦ σημείου τύπον κατὰ τὸ σχῆμα τὸ τριακοσιοστὸν στοιχεῖον Clem.*str.*6.11(p.473.24; M.9.305A); τὰ ἀρχαῖα στοιχεῖα ἐμφερὲς ἔχειν τὸ θαῦ, τῷ τοῦ σ. χαρακτῆρι Or.*sel. in Ezech.*9:4(M.13.801A); cf. *de qua Ezechiel...da signum tau in frontibus virorum. ipsa est littera Graecorum tau, nostra autem T. species crucis, quam portendebat futuram in frontibus nostris,* Tert.*adversus Marcionem* 3.22(M.*PL.*2.353A); **b.** shape of **+**; cf. *et ipse habitus crucis, fines et summitates habet quinque, duos in longitudine, et duos in latitudine, et unum in medio, in quo requiescit qui clavis affigitur,* Iren.*haer.*2.24.4(M.7.794B); τοῦ σ. ... τετραχῆ τοῦ κατ' αὐτὸν σχήματος, ὡς ἐκ τοῦ μέσου...τέσσαρας ἀριθμεῖσθαι τὰς προβολὰς Gr.Nyss. *or.catech.*32(p.119.4; M.45.80D); **c.** exemplified in man τὸ δὲ ἀνθρώπειον σχῆμα οὐδενὶ ἄλλῳ τῶν ἀλόγων ζῴων διαφέρει, ἢ τῷ ὀρθόν τε εἶναι καὶ ἔκτασιν χειρῶν ἔχειν...καὶ οὐδὲν ἄλλο δείκνυσιν ἢ τὸ σχῆμα τοῦ σ. Just.*1apol.*55.4(M.6.412B); in nature, cf.Meth.*Porph.*1(pp.504f.; M.18.400C,D); in Roman *vexilla,* cf.*ib.*(p.504.28; 400C) cit. s. βήξιλλον; cf.Tert.*apol.*16(M.*PL.*1.369A); Minucius Felix *apol.*29(M.*PL.*3.346B); **d.** foreshadowed in OT (cf. C.3 supra) μηνύων τὴν ἰσχὺν τοῦ μυστηρίου τοῦ σ. ὁ θεὸς διὰ Μωϋσέως εἶπεν...[Dt.33:17]...μονοκέρωτος γὰρ κέρατα οὐδενὸς ἄλλου...σχήματος ἔχοι ἄν τις εἰπεῖν...εἰ μὴ τοῦ τύπου ὃς τὸν σ. δείκνυσιν Just.*dial.*91.1ff.(M.6.692f.); cf.Tert. *adversus Judaeos* 10(M.*PL.*2.666B); esp. exeg. Ex.17:11 λέγει...ἵνα ποιήσῃ τύπον σταυροῦ...Μωϋσῆς...ἐξέτεινεν τὰς χεῖρας· καὶ οὕτως... ἐνίκα ὁ Ἰσραὴλ *Barn.*12.2; Just.*dial.*90.4(M.6.692A); Gr.Nyss.*v.Mos.*(M.44.348D); id.*res.*1(M.46.601D); Tim.Ant.*cruc.*(M.86.257B); cf.Tert. *adversus Judaeos* 10(667B); Cypr.*adversus Judaeos* 2.21(M.*PL.*4.744B); **e.** as form of a chapel σ. ἐστι τοῦ εὐκτηρίου τὸ σχῆμα τέσσαρσιν ...οἴκοις Gr.Nyss.*ep.*25(M.46.1096A); **f.** a recognized posture for prayer στὰς οὖν εἰς προσευχήν, τὰς χεῖρας ἐπιζεύξας εἰς τύπον σταυροῦ *A.Xanthipp.*28(p.78.16); Ast.Am.*phar.*(p.117.18); δεικνύουσι [sc. Christians]...διὰ τῆς τῶν χειρῶν ἐκτάσεως τὸ...σχῆμα τοῦ...σ. Cyr. *Ps.*27:2(M.69.856A); τὸν τοῦ σ. τύπον...ἐν ἑαυτῇ ἐκτυπώσασα, ἑαυτὴν δὲ μᾶλλον καὶ ὅλην εἰς τὸν τοῦ σ. τύπον ἀπεικάσασα, διὰ τῆς ἐφ' ἑκάτερα τῶν χειρῶν ἐκτάσεως, εὐθὺς ἐφήλατο...τῇ πυρᾷ Bas.Sel.*v.Thecl.*1(M.85.513B); cf. σταυροειδῶς τὰς χεῖρας εἰς οὐρανὸν ἐκτείνας Nil.*epp.* 1.87(M.79.121A); **g.** decreed the correct position for hands in receiving Holy Communion τὰς χεῖρας σχηματίζων εἰς τύπον σταυροῦ, οὕτω προσίτω, καὶ δεχέσθω τὴν κοινωνίαν τῆς χάριτος CTrull.*can.*101;

h. symbolical significance of the form πῶς ἂν ἡμᾶς προσεκαλέσατο, εἰ μὴ ἐσταύρωτο; ἐν μόνῳ γὰρ τῷ σ. ἐκτεταμέναις χερσί τις ἀποθνήσκει ...τὰς χεῖρας ἐκτεῖναι, ἵνα τῇ μὲν τὸν παλαιὸν λαόν, τῇ δὲ τοὺς ἀπὸ τῶν ἐθνῶν ἑλκύσῃ, καὶ ἀμφοτέρους ἐν ἑαυτῷ συνάψῃ Ath.*inc*.25.3(M.25.140A); διὰ τοῦ σ. διδασκόμεθα...ὅτι ὁ ἐπὶ τούτου...διαταθεὶς ὁ τὸ πᾶν πρὸς ἑαυτὸν συνδέων τε καὶ συναρμόζων ἐστί...ὁ...Παῦλος... ἑκάστην...τοῦ σταυροῦ προβολὴν ἰδίῳ ῥήματι κατονομάζει, ὕψος μὲν τὸ ὑπερέχον, βάθος δὲ τὸ ὑποκείμενον, πλάτος τε καὶ μῆκος τὰς πλαγίας ἐκτάσεις λέγων Gr.Nyss.*or.catech*.32(pp.119.4,120.18; M.45.80D,81B); id.*Eun*.5(2 p.115.12ff.; M.45.696B); id.*res*.1(M.46.624A,B); also ref. Ps.138:7ff., *ib*.(624C); Jo.D.*f.o*.4.11(M.94.1129B); διὰ τῶν ἐν σοὶ [i.e. τῷ σ.] ἐξαδικῶν διαστάσεων τὸ παντοκρατορικὸν ὑπέφηνε [sc. Χριστός] παραδόξως, ὅτι κυριεύει τῶν ἄνω καὶ οὐρανίων, τῶν κάτω καὶ ἐπιγείων ...καὶ ὑποχθονίων...τῶν δεξιῶν, τῶν ἀριστερῶν, τῶν δικαίων, καὶ τῶν ἁμαρτωλῶν Germ.CP *or*.1(M.98.244A); **2.** in visions and popular literature ἐφάνη σ. ἐν τῷ ἀνατολικῷ τοίχῳ καὶ εὐθέως εἰσῆλθεν δι' αὐτοῦ νεανίας εὐειδὴς [i.e. Christ] *A.Xanthipp*.15(p.69.18); ὡς ἐκ βάθους τῆς θαλάσσης σταυρὸς ἀνέβαινεν *A.Mt*.26(p.255.5ff.); Cyr.H.*ep.Const*.3(M.33.1169A); Gr.Naz.*or*.5.4(M.35.669A); legend of speaking Cross ὁρῶσιν...τρεῖς ἄνδρας, καὶ τοὺς δύο τὸν ἕνα ὑπορθοῦντας, καὶ σ. ἀκολουθοῦντα αὐτοῖς...καὶ ὑπακοὴ ἠκούετο ἀπὸ τοῦ σ. *Ev.Petr*. 9(pp.298,302); Cross in Hades πάλιν...ὑμᾶς διὰ ξύλου τοῦ σ. πάντας ἐγὼ ἰδοὺ ἀνιστῶν *A.Pil*.B 24(p.330); v. G.2.b infra; esp. vision of Constantine σταυροῦ τρόπαιον Eus.*v.C*.1.28(p.21.16; M.20.944B); **3.** representations of Cross executed in wood or metal, or simply traced; **a.** carried as a standard, *A.Xanthipp*.25(p.76.23f.); as device on labarum, Eus.*v.C*.1.31(p.22.13; M.20.948A); removed by Juln.Imp., Gr.Naz.*or*.4.66(M.35.588A); Soz.*h.e*.5.17.2(M.67.1265B); **b.** traced in place of signature προτάξας τῇ ἰδίᾳ μου χειρὶ τὸν τίμιον σ., καὶ τὸ ὄνομά μου ὑπέγραψα, διὰ Χριστοῦ ἀναγνώστου, διὰ τὸ ἔμε γήρᾳ κρατεῖσθαι *Libell*.ap.CCP(518)*act*.(*ACO* 3 p.68.8; H.2.1329C); ‡Jo.D.*ep.Thphl*.21(M.95.372D); **c.** in church ἀροῦσιν ἀπὸ τῆς γῆς... τὰς σεπτὰς καὶ ἁγίας εἰκόνας, καὶ τοὺς ἐνδόξους καὶ τιμίους σ. *Apoc.Jo*.13(p.80); πέμπει Γρηγορίῳ σταυρὸν χρυσῷ πολλῷ καὶ λίθοις τιμίοις ἐξησκημένον, πρὸς τιμὴν τοῦ...μάρτυρος Σεργίου Evagr.*h.e*.6.21(p.235.11; M.86.2873A); ἥρπαζον τοὺς σ. ἀπὸ τοῦ εὐκτηρίου *Mir.Mich*.5(p.553.7); ὁρίζομεν...παραπλησίως τῷ τύπῳ τοῦ...σ. ἀνατίθεσθαι τὰς σεπτὰς...εἰκόνας *Symb.Nic*.(787)(H.4.456A); at east end of church στερροῦ...καὶ ἀνδρώδους φρονήματος οἰκεῖον, τὸ ἐν τῷ ἱερατείῳ μὲν κατὰ ἀνατολὰς τοῦ θειοτάτου τεμένους ἕνα καὶ μόνον τυπῶσαι σ. δι' ἑνὸς γὰρ σωτηριώδους σ. τὸ τῶν ἀνθρώπων διασώζεται γένος Nil.*epp*.4.61(M.79.577D); fixed to altar, Evagr.*h.e*.6.21(p.238.2; M.86.2876C); carried in procession, *Lit.Jac*.(*NBP* 10[2] p.49); removal of crosses forbidden, *Symb.Nic*.(787)(H.4.456D); on walls and buildings σταυροῦ σημεῖον ἐν παλατίῳ Eus.*v.C*.3.49 tit.(p.74.19; M.20.1109A); Chrys.*Jud.et gent*.9(1.571C); †Jo.D.*B.J*.33(M.96.1176C);

σταυρὸς	....	σταυρὸς	πεσόντων
νίκ[ην]	πι[στ]οῖς	ἀνάστ	ασις

CIG 8922 (Antioch); in private devotions, ‡Ath.*qu.Ant*.41(M.28.624A) cit. s. ἀντίτυπος; worn on the person in metal, Gr.Nyss.*v.Macr*.(p.404.8; M.46.989C); stamped or embroidered; on monks' cowls, Pall.*h.Laus*.32(p.90.2; M.34.1100A); and vestments, *Lit.Chrys*.(p.382.32); stamped on monastery bread, Gr.Mag.*dial*.(tr. Zach.)1.11(M.*PL*.77.211A); its ubiquity, cf.Chrys.*Jud.et gent*.9(1.571B), calling for legislation to save it from profanation, CTrull.*can*.73; cf. *signum salvatoris Christi nemini licere vel in solo vel in silice vel in marmoribus humi positis insculpere vel pingere*, Justn.*Cod*.1.8.1(p.61) cf. καὶ ὧν ἀναισχύντως ἠπίστουν Ἰουδαῖοι καὶ Ἕλληνες, εὑρίσκοντο τὰ ἱμάτια αὐτῶν πεπληρωμένα σταυρῶν· ἔν τισι δὲ καὶ ἐμελάνιζον Thphn.*chron*.p.44(M.108.165B); **4.** veneration of Cross, cf. B.5 supra; **a.** as emblem of Christianity παρὰ τὸν σ. προσκυνοῦσι [sc. Christians] Chrys.*hom.12.7 in 1Cor*.(10.107D); cf. *qui crucis nos religiosos putat, consecraneus noster erit*, Tert.*apol*.16(M.*PL*.2.365A); Chrys.*Jud.et gent*.9(1.571C); τὸ τοῦ σ. σημεῖον τοῖς ἐνοικοῦσι [i.e. in Egypt] προσκυνητόν Cyr.*Is*.2.4(2.294E); Ἕλληνες, καὶ Ῥωμαῖοι, καὶ βάρβαροι, τὸν ἐσταυρωμένον θεολογοῦντες καὶ τοῦ σ. τὸ σημεῖον γεραίροντες Thdt.*affect*.6(p.178.22; 4.880); cf. εὐχομένῃ... ταύτῃ φαίνεται ὑπὲρ κεφαλῆς τὸ σημεῖον, ὃ δὴ Χριστιανοῖς προσκυνεῖσθαί τε πέφυκε καὶ ἐπιγράφεσθαι Ast.Am.*hom*.11(M.40.337B); †Jo.D.*B.J*.19,33,35(M.96.1032C,1176C,1189C); **b.** practice explained and justified, ‡Ath.*qu.Ant*.39(M.28.621A,C); προσκυνοῦμεν...καὶ [i.e. as well as the true Cross] τὸν τύπον τοῦ τιμίου καὶ ζωοποιοῦ σ., εἰ καὶ ἐξ ἑτέρας ὕλης [γε]γένηται, οὐ τὴν ὕλην τιμῶντες...ἀλλὰ τὸν τύπον, ὡς Χριστοῦ σύμβολον Jo.D.*f.o*.4.11(M.94.1132B); instanced as justifying veneration of images, *Symb.Nic*.(787)(H.4.456B).

E. *sign of the cross* made by a gesture (σημεῖον, τύπος, σχῆμα etc. τοῦ σταυροῦ, or abs.); **1.** made on breast, Chrys.*hom.87.2 in Mt*.(7.820B); and other parts of body, *M.Thdot.1* 21(p.74.26); συνεχῶς... ἅπαντες ἐγχαράττουσιν [sc. σταυροῦ τὸ σχῆμα] ἐπὶ τοῦ τῶν μελῶν ἡμῶν ἐπισημοτέρου μέρους, καὶ ὥσπερ ἐν στήλῃ ἐπὶ τοῦ μετώπου καθ' ἑκάστην ἡμέραν διατυπούμενον περιφέρουσιν Chrys.*Jud.et gent*.9(1.571A); Eudoc.*Cypr*.1.63(M.85.836A); **2.** most commonly on forehead, *T.Sal*.17.4; τὰ ἀρχαῖα στοιχεῖα ἐμφερὲς ἔχειν τὸ θαῦ τῷ τοῦ σ. χαρακτῆρι, καὶ προφητεύεσθαι περὶ τοῦ γενομένου ἐν Χριστιανοῖς ἐπὶ τοῦ μετώπου σημείου· ὅπερ ποιοῦσιν οἱ πεπιστευκότες πάντες οὑτινοσοῦν προκαταρχόμενοι πράγματος, καὶ μάλιστα ἢ εὐχῶν ἢ ἁγίων ἀναγνωσμάτων Or.*sel.in Ezech*.9:4(M.13.801A); cf.Tert.*de corona* 3(M.*PL*.2.99B); τὸ τοῦ σ. προσκυνεῖτε ξύλον, εἰκόνας αὐτοῦ σκιαγραφοῦντες ἐν τῷ μετώπῳ καὶ πρὸ τῶν οἰκημάτων ἐγγράφοντες Juln.Imp.ap.Cyr.*Juln*.6(6[2].194C); ἐπὶ μετώπου...δακτύλοις ἡ σφραγὶς...ὁ σ. γινέσθω· ἐπὶ ἄρτων βιβρωσκομένων, καὶ ἐπὶ ποτηρίων πινομένων· ἐν εἰσόδοις, ἐν ἐξόδοις. ... κοιταζομένοις, καὶ διανισταμένοις Cyr.H.*catech*.13.36; Chrys.*Jud.et gent*.9(1.571B); τὸ τοῦ ἁγίου σ. σημεῖον, ᾧ περιφράττεσθαι τοὺς πιστεύοντας ἔθος Cyr.*Is*.2.4(2.294D); Pall.*h.Laus*.2(p.18.11; M.34.1012A); made on infants τῇ χειρὶ παιδεύετε σφραγίζειν τὸ μέτωπον· καὶ πρὶν ἢ δυνηθῆναι τῇ χειρὶ τοῦτο ποιεῖν, αὐτοὶ ἐντυποῦτε αὐτοῖς τὸν σ. Chrys.*hom.12.7 in 1Cor*.(10.108B); *ib*.(107E); before prayer, Zos.*alloquia* 8(M.78.1692D); before martyrdom, Bas.*hom*.18.8(2.148E; M.31.505C); *M.Thdot.1* 17(p.72.24); Bas.Sel.*v.Thecl*.1(M.85.513B) cit. s. D.1; before exile, Petr.II Al.*encycl*.7(M.33.1288B); **3.** a protection, esp. against demons, cf.Hipp.*trad.ap*.37(p.68); Ath.*gent*.1(M.25.5A) cit. s. δαίμων; id.*inc*.47.2(M.25.180C); id.*v.Anton*.35(M.26.893C); ἐπὶ τὸν σ. καταφεύγει, καὶ τὸ παλαιὸν φάρμακον, καὶ τούτῳ σημειοῦται κατὰ τῶν φόβων Gr.Naz.*or*.4.55(M.35.580A); Gr.Nyss.*v.Gr.Thaum*.(M.46.916A); τὴν ἀπὸ τοῦ σ. φυλακήν Chrys.*hom.12.7 in 1Cor*.(10.107B); ὁ δὲ τὸ τοῦ σ. σημεῖον διατυπώσας, ὡσεὶ καπνὸν διασκεδάζει [sc. τὸν ἐχθρόν] Niceph.Ur.*v.Sym*.47(M.86.3029C); †Jo.D.*B.J*.31(M.96.1153B); *ib*.32(1168A); **4.** in popular literature attended with miraculous results; to quieten a dog, *M.Ner.et Ach*.13(p.12.32); to open a door, *A.Andr.et Mt*.19(p.90.5); effecting a cure, *A.Phil*.76(p.29.23); and deliverance, *ib*.105(p.40.23); made by Christ ὁ σωτὴρ...ἐχάραξεν σ. ἐν τῷ ἀέρι καταβαίνοντα ἀπὸ τῶν ἄνω ἕως τῆς ἀβύσσου, καὶ ἐπλήσθη ἡ ἄβυσσος φωτὸς καὶ ἦν ὁ σ. ἐν ὁμοιώματι κλίμακος ἐχούσης βάθμους *ib*.138(p.70.4ff.); **5.** made in baptism (post-baptismal consignation), Serap.*euch*.25.1f. cit. s. χρίω; σπεύσατε...τὰ πρόβατα, πρὸς...τὸ σημεῖον τοῦ σ. τὸ τῶν κακῶν ἀλεξητήριον Gr.Nyss.*bapt.diff*.(M.46.417B); βάπτισμα διὰ τοῦ σ. (δεῖ γὰρ ἀναλαβεῖν τὴν σφραγῖδα) Chrys.*hom.13.1 in Phil*.(11.298A); cf. Didym.*Trin*.2.14(M.39.697A); *Rit.Bapt*.(p.389); cf. ἡ σφραγὶς ἀντὶ τοῦ σ. *Const.App*.3.17.1; *credit autem etiam catechumenus in crucem domini Jesu, qua et ipse signatur*, Ambr.*myst*.20(M.*PL*.16.394C); hence the mark of the Christian, Ath.*inc*.29.4(M.25.145D); Olymp.*fr.Bar*.5:2(M.93.773A); equivalent of circumcision for Jews, Jo.D.*f.o*.4.11(M.94.1129B); its use an unwritten tradition, Bas.*Spir*.66(3.54E; M.32.188B); **6.** in eucharist εἰπὼν ταῦτα διεχάραξεν τῷ ἄρτῳ τὸν σ. καὶ κλάσας ἤρξατο διαδιδόναι *A.Thom*.A 50(p.166.18); ὁ ἀρχιερεὺς...στὰς πρὸς τῷ θυσιαστηρίῳ τὸ τρόπαιον τοῦ σ. κατὰ τοῦ μετώπου τῇ χειρὶ ποιησάμενος εἰπάτω...καὶ...ἄνω τὸν νοῦν *Lit*.ap.*Const.App*.8.12.4; after Communion καὶ ἐπιχαράττει τὸ θεῖον σημεῖον τοῦ τιμίου σ. *Lit.Bas*. = *Lit.Chrys*.(Brightman p.341.30); in creed, *Lit.Marc*.(Brightman p.124.11); before the dismissal, *Lit.Praesanct*.(p.352.3); **7.** at ordination πάντα δι' αὐτοῦ [sc. τοῦ σταυροῦ] τελεῖται τὰ καθ' ἡμᾶς. κἂν ἀναγεννηθῆναι δέῃ, σταυρὸς παραγίνεται· κἂν τραφῆναι τὴν μυστικὴν ἐκείνην τροφήν, κἂν χειροτονηθῆναι, κἂν ὁτιοῦν ἕτερον ποιῆσαι, πανταχοῦ τοῦτο τῆς νίκης ἡμῖν παρίσταται σύμβολον Chrys.*hom.54.4 in Mt*.(7.551B); id.*Jud.et gent*.9(1.571A).

F. as standing for mortification, freq. under simile of carrying one's cross; **1.** life lived under Christian discipline, life marked with the cross ἡμεῖς...ἄραντες τὸν σ., ὡς καὶ Ἰσαὰκ τὰ ξύλα Iren.*haer*.4.5.4(M.7.985C); perh. Clem.*str*.2.20(p.172.17; M.8.1053A) cit. s. A.1 supra; cf.*ib*.(p.170.14; 1049A); τὸ δὲ πρὸς τὸν σ. βλέπειν τοῦτό ἐστι, τὸ πάντα τὸν ἑαυτοῦ βίον ὡς νεκρὸν τῷ κόσμῳ καὶ ἐσταυρωμένον ποιῆσαι... ἧλος δ' ἂν εἴη σαρκῶν καθεκτικός, ἡ ἐγκράτεια Gr.Nyss.*v.Mos*.(M.44.413D); τὸ...λαβεῖν τὸν σ., οὐδὲν οἶμαι σημαίνειν ἕτερον, ἢ τὸ ἀποτάξασθαι μὲν τῷ κόσμῳ διὰ θεόν, δευτέραν δὲ τῶν ἐν ἐλπίσιν ἀγαθῶν καὶ αὐτὴν ποιεῖσθαι τὴν μετὰ σώματος...ζωήν Cyr.*Jo*.12(4.1058A); **2.** partic., monastic life τί τοίνυν καταλιπὼν τὸ ἐρείδεσθαι ἀσφαλῶς ἐπὶ κύριον, καὶ σ. ἔχειν, τὴν ἀκόλουθον ἄσκησιν, τόπον μεταβάλλεις ἐκ τόπου; Isid.Pel.*epp*.1.41(M.78.208C); σ. ... ἡ τελεία νέκρωσις ἥτις κατορθοῦται ἡμῖν διὰ τῆς εἰς Χριστὸν πίστεως Dor.*doct*.1.13(M.88.1633C).

G. Gnost.; **1.** Gnost. aeon δύο ἐνεργείας ἔχειν αὐτὸν [sc. τὸν Ὅρον] ἀποφαινόμενοι, τὴν ἑδραστικὴν καὶ τὴν μεριστικήν· καὶ καθὸ μὲν... στηρίζει, Σ. εἶναι, καθὸ δὲ μερίζει...Ὅρον...[Lc.3:17] διὰ τούτου τὴν ἐνέργειαν τοῦ Ὅρου μεμηνυκέναι· πτύον γὰρ ἐκεῖνον τὸν Σ. ἑρμηνεύουσιν εἶναι, ὃν δὴ καὶ ἀναλίσκειν τὰ ὑλικὰ πάντα...καθαίρειν δὲ τοὺς σωζομένους, ὡς τὸ πτύον τὸν σῖτον Iren.*haer*.1.3.5(M.7.476A,B); ἵνα ἔχοντες καὶ ἡμεῖς τὸ ὄνομα μὴ ἐπισχεθῶμεν κωλυθέντες εἰς τὸ πλήρωμα παρελθεῖν τῷ Ὅρῳ καὶ τῷ Σ. Clem.*exc.Thdot*.22(p.114.8; M.9.669A); ὁ πατὴρ ἐπιπροβάλλει αἰῶνα ἕνα τὸν Σ. ... εἰς φρουρὰν καὶ χαράκωμα τῶν αἰώνων προβεβλημένος, ὅρος γίνεται τοῦ πληρώματος, ἔχων ἐντὸς ἑαυτοῦ πάντας ὁμοῦ τοὺς τριάκοντα αἰῶνας...καλεῖται δὲ Ὅρος μὲν οὗτος...Μετοχεὺς δὲ...σ. δὲ ὅτι πέπηγεν ἀκλινῶς καὶ ἀμετακινήτως Hipp.*haer*.6.31(p.159.8ff.; M.16.3242A); *ib*.6.34(p.163. 25; 3247A); **2.** in popular Gnost. literature; **a.** cross of light ἔδειξέν μοι σταυρὸν φωτὸς *A.Jo*.98(p.199.20); *Tr.Phil*.2,3(p.161. 22ff.); ὁ σ. οὗτος ὁ τοῦ φωτὸς ποτὲ μὲν λόγος καλεῖται...ποτὲ δὲ νοῦς, ποτὲ δὲ Ἰησοῦς...ποτὲ θύρα...ποτὲ ἄρτος...ποτὲ υἱός, ποτὲ πατήρ, ποτὲ πνεῦμα...ὃ δὲ ὄντως ἐστίν...διορισμὸς πάντων ἐστίν *A.Jo*.98 (p.200.5); οὗτος ὁ σ. ὁ διαπηξάμενος τὰ πάντα λόγῳ καὶ διορίσας τὰ ἀπὸ γενέσεως καὶ κατωτέρω...οὐχ οὗτος δέ ἐστιν ὁ σταυρὸς ὃν μέλλεις ὁρᾶν ξύλινον κατελθὼν ἐντεῦθεν· οὔτε ἐγώ εἰμι ὁ ἐπὶ τοῦ σ. ὃν νῦν οὐχ ὁρᾷς ἀλλὰ μόνον φωνῆς ἀκούεις *ib*.99(p.200.17ff.); οἱ ἐν τῷ σ., Gnostics opp. οἱ περὶ τὸν σ., orthodox: καὶ περὶ τὸν σ. ὄχλον πολύν, μίαν μορφὴν μὴ ἔχοντα. καὶ ἐν αὐτῷ ἦν μορφὴ μία καὶ ἰδέα ὁμοία *A.Jo*.98 (p.199.21); cf. ὁ δὲ περὶ τὸν σ. μονοειδὴς ὄχλος ἡ κατωτικὴ φύσις ὑπάρχει. καὶ οὓς ὁρᾷς ἐν τῷ σ., εἰ καὶ μίαν μορφὴν οὐκ ἔχουσιν, οὐδέπω τὸ πᾶν τοῦ κατελθόντος συνελήφθη μέλος *ib*.100(p.201.1f.); **b.** cross in Hades ἰδού, ὁ σ. φωτίζει ἡμᾶς *A.Phil*.133(p.65.1); ἵλεως ἔσομαι ὑμῖν ἐν τῷ φωτεινῷ μου σ. *ib*.(p.65.5); *ib*.138(p.70.6) cit. s. E.4 supra.

σταυρότυπος, *in the form of a cross, crosswise*; of Moses's hands (ref. Ex.17:11), Gr.Naz.*carm*.2.1.1.2(M.37.969A); of a church πλευραῖς σ. τέτραχα τεμνόμενον *ib*.2.1.16.60(1258A).

σταυροτύπως, *in the form of a cross, with the sign of the cross* σ. Μώσης τὸν Ἀμαλὲκ κατέβαλε ‡Rom.Mel.(*AS* 1 p.206); ῥάβδος Μωσαϊκή, σ. τὴν θάλασσαν πλήξασα Jo.D.*f.o*.4.11(M.94.1133A); σ. πετόμενοι [sc. seraphim] Germ.CP *or*.1(M.98.241B).

***σταυροφάν(ε)ια, ἡ, 1.** *feast of the Exaltation of the Cross* γέγονε τὰ ἐγκαίνια τῆς ἐκκλησίας τοῦ ἁγίου σταυροῦ τῆς οἰκοδομηθείσης ὑπὸ Κωνσταντίνου ἐπὶ Μακαρίου ἐπισκόπου, μηνὶ Σεπτεμβρίῳ ιζ΄. ἐντεῦθεν ἤρξατο ἡ σ. *Chron.Pasch*.p.286(M.92.713A); **2.** ? *procession headed by the cross* καὶ ἐξῆλθε μετὰ σταυροφανίας εἰς τὸν τόπον Alex.Cypr.*laud. Barn*.41(p.450E).

***σταυροφανός**, *revealing the Cross*, superl. Δαβὶδ...περιεκτικώτατον καὶ σταυροφανώτατον, συγκαλεῖται τὸ κήρυγμα, ἀπὸ ἀνατολῶν, καὶ δυσμῶν, καὶ βορρᾶ, καὶ θαλάσσης Eulog.*palm*.4(M.86.2920C).

σταυροφόρος, A. lit., as subst.; **1.** of Christ, *bearer of the Cross*, Ephr.1.203E; id.2.61E; **2.** of Christians, *bearer of the standard of the Cross* τῶν σ. ἀνῃρέθη μὲν ὁ φυγών, ὁ δὲ πίστει παραμείνας ἐσώθη Eus. *v.C*.2.9 tit.(p.36.16; M.20.988C).

B. met., *bearing the Cross*; **1.** *self-sacrificing* πλοῦτον...ὅν ῥα πένησι πάντ' ἀπέδωκα φέρων, σ. πόθοις Gr.Naz.*carm*.2.2(poem.)2.20 (M.37.1479A); πρὸς τὸ μεῖζον λοιπὸν ἀνάνευσον, τὴν ἀγάπην. σ. γὰρ τυγχάνεις ‡Ath.*v.Syncl*.74(M.28.1529D); as subst. πᾶς...σ. νικᾷ †Cyr.*coll.VT*(6⁴.14B; M.77.1196B); **2.** esp. of an ascetic life ὁ τῆς ἐγκρατείας σ. ὁπλίτης *A.Barn*.proem.5(p.437C); τῷ σ. βίῳ τῶν μοναχῶν Bas.*renunt*.1(2.202B; M.31.625C); τῷ σ. βίῳ δουλεύειν ἐν ὁσιότητι καὶ δικαιοσύνῃ Thdr.Stud.*epp*.2.125(M.99.1405D); so, of the scapular as signifying monastic life τὸν σ. ἀνάλαβον Steph. Diac.*v.Steph*.(M.100.1104C); **3.** *through the bearing of the Cross* ἡ σ. νικοποιὸς ἐνέργεια ἐν τῷ Μωσαϊκῷ σχηματισμῷ ἐκ πολλῶν χρόνων προανεζωγράφη Tim.Ant.*cruc*.(M.86.257A); **4.** *bearing the standard of the Cross*; fig., of a treatise as flagship of the Cross καταπαύσωμεν τὴν σ. ὁλκάδα τοῦ λόγου ‡Meth.*Sym.et Ann*.13(M.18.377D).

***σταυροφύλαξ, ὁ,** *guardian of the Cross* at Jerusalem, Chrysipp. *enc.in Mich*.(p.88.1); Cyr.S.*v.Euthym*.20(p.33.30); *ib*.22(p.35.7); id. *v.Sab*.19(p.104.3); Jo.Mosch.*prat*.49(M.87.2904C).

***σταυροχαρής**, *rejoicing in the Cross*, Eudoc.*Cypr*.1.204(M.85. 840C).

σταυρ-όω, 1. *crucify*; **a.** act., of those responsible in various ways for Crucifixion of Christ οὐχ οὗτός ἐστιν ὅν ποτε ἡμεῖς ἐσταυρώσαμεν; *Barn*.7.9; τὸν ἱματισμὸν ἐμερίσαντο ἑαυτοῖς οἱ ∼ώσαντες αὐτόν Just. *1apol*.35.8(M.6.384C); ὃν ἐσταύρωσεν [sc. ὁ λαός] ὡς κακοῦργον Clem. *paed*.2.8(p.202.25; M.8.485B); γέγονε βόθρος...τοῖς ∼ώσασιν ὁ ἀπεσταλμένος Cyr.*Zach*.21(3.679C); **b.** pass., of Christ Χριστοῦ...ὃς... ἀληθῶς ἐσταυρώθη καὶ ἀπέθανεν Ign.*Trall*.9.1; πίστιν θεοῦ...ὑπὲρ ἧς Χριστὸς ἐσταυρώθη id.*Eph*.16.2; μετὰ ταῦτα ἐσταυρώθη, ὅπως τὸ λεῖπον τῆς προφητείας συντελεσθῇ Just.*1apol*.32.6(M.6.380A); ἡμᾶς βεβαπτισμένους ταῖς...ἁμαρτίαις...διὰ τοῦ ∼ωθῆναι ἐπὶ τοῦ ξύλου καὶ δι' ὕδατος ἁγνίσαι ὁ Χριστὸς ἡμῶν ἐλυτρώσατο, καὶ οἶκον εὐχῆς καὶ προσκυνήσεως ἐποίησε id.*dial*.86.6(M.6.681C); ὁ χθὲς καὶ πρώην ∼ωθεὶς ἑκὼν τοῦτον τὸν θάνατον ὑπὲρ τοῦ τῶν ἀνθρώπων γένους ἀνεδέξατο Or.*Cels*.1.31(p.82.23; M.11.717D); οὐ...προεῖπον...θεὸν ∼ωθήσεσθαι *ib*.7.16(p.167.14; 1444B); τὸ αἰσθητὸν τοῦ Ἰησοῦ σῶμα ἐσταύρωται id.*Jo*.10.35(20; p.210.1; M.14.372B); ref. Peter Fullo's addition to *trisagion*, v. τρισάγιος; under Pontius Pilate, Just.*dial*.30.3(M.6. 540B); *ib*.85.2(676C); Iren.*haer*.2.32.4(M.7.829C); *Const.App*.6.30.8; in creeds, cf.Hipp.*trad.ap*.21.15; Marcell.*ep*.ap.Epiph.*haer*.72.3 (p.258.9; M.42.385D); *Symb*.ap.Epiph.*anc*.118(p.147.7; M.43.242C); *Symb.Nic.-CP*(p.80.9; H.2.288B); ὁ ἐσταυρωμένος as epithet of Christ, *M.Polyc*.17.2; Just.*dial*.137.1(M.6.792A); *M.Ariadn*.(p.128. 27); *M.Thdot*.3(p.137.17); Chrys.*hom.27.2 in Jo*.(8.155B); **c.** of a 'second crucifixion', Nil.*epp*.1.204(M.79.160A) cit. s. ἀναβαπτίζω; **2.** met.; **a.** *mortify* the senses or passions οἵτινες...τὸ οἰκεῖον σῶμα... ἐσταύρωσαν καὶ οἷον ἐνέκρωσαν ἀπὸ τῶν σωματικῶν παθῶν, καὶ οὐ μόνον τὸ σῶμα, ὅσον ἧκεν εἰς τὰ πάθη, ἐσταύρωσαν Clem.*fr*.7(p.197. 5ff.; M.9.745B); ∼οῦμεν [sc. τὴν σάρκα]...οἱ ἐν τῷ ὕδατι βαπτιζόμενοι †Bas.*bapt*.1.2.15(2.640B; M.31.1552A); τῶν πιστῶν καὶ ἀκριβῶς ἐσταυρωμένων Chrys.*hom.15.2 in Rom*.(9.596B); ἐσταυρωμένος ἦν καὶ πάντα διὰ τὸν θεὸν ἐποίει Call.*v.Hyp*.(p.71); in partic. of ascetic life τὸν ἐσταυρωμένων βίον Chrys.*compunct*.1.10(1.140B); ὁ [sc. βίος] τῶν μοναχῶν...καὶ τῶν ἐσταυρωμένων id.*hom.68.3 in Mt*.(7.673C); ἡ Πρίσκιλλα...ἡ Κλαυδία...ἤδη ἐσταυρωμέναι, ἤδη παρατεταγμέναι id.*hom.10.3 in 2Tim*.(11.724C); γελᾷς...καὶ διαχεῖς τὸ πρόσωπον ὁ μονάζων; ὁ ἐσταυρωμένος, ὁ πενθῶν, γελᾷς; id.*hom.15.4 in Heb*.(12. 155C); μοναχοὶ...οἱ διὰ πάντων ∼ώσαντες ἑαυτοὺς τῷ κόσμῳ id. *Philogon*.6.3(1.496D); **b.** Manich. τότε ⟨τὸ⟩ ζῶν πνεῦμα...ἀνήνεγκε τοὺς ἄρχοντας καὶ ἐσταύρωσεν ἐν τῷ στερεώματι, ὅ ἐστιν αὐτῶν σῶμα ἡ σφαῖρα Hegem.*Arch*.8(p.11.6; ἐστερέωσεν M.10.1437); **3.** *place in the form of a cross, cross* (e.g. the hands) Ἰακὼβ...ἐπὶ τὸ ἄκρον τῆς ῥάβδου αὐτοῦ ἐπιστηριχθεὶς ἥτις ἐδήλου τὸν τίμιον σταυρὸν ἐν τῷ ∼οῦν τὰς χεῖρας αὐτοῦ...εὐλογεῖ αὐτούς †Gregent.*disp*.(M.86.637A); αὐτὸς δὲ τὰς χεῖρας...δι' ὅλης ∼ώσας τῆς νυκτὸς ἔμεινεν ἀκλινής *V.Pach.Σ* 50 (p.219.12).

***σταυρώνω**, *make the sign of the cross upon*, at baptism ὁ δὲ ἀρχιερεὺς σ. τὸ ὕδωρ *Euchol*.(p.225).

σταυρωσιμός, *pertaining to the Crucifixion* σ. ἡμέρα *Nomoc*. 418.

σταύρωσις, ἡ, *crucifixion*, of Christ τὴν ἄρρητον χρηστότητα ἐφ' ἡμᾶς διὰ τῆς σ. ἐπεδείξατο Mac.Aeg.*hom*.4.18(M.34.485C); διὰ τὴν σ. ἡ κατάρα προσετέτακτο Epiph.*haer*.66.79(p.121.20; M.42.153D); ἅπερ δι' ἡμᾶς ὑπέμεινε, τὴν σ., τὸν θάνατον κτλ. Marc.Er.*opusc*.5.9(M.65. 1044C); met., of a martyr's sufferings τὸ ξύλον τοῦ σταυροῦ τοῦ Χριστοῦ λογιζόμενος, καὶ τὴν ἀντίθετον τοῦ Πέτρου διανοούμενος σ., τῷ ξένῳ τρόπῳ τῆς οἰκείας ἐνετρύφα σ. Sophr.H.*v.Anast*.(M.92. 1720B).

***σταυρωτής, ὁ,** *crucifier*, Gr.Naz.*or*.45.16(M.36.645B); Chrys.*ecl*. 46(12.766B); Cyr.*Ps*.41:6(M.69.1004D).

σταφίς, ἡ, *dried grape, raisin*, Pall.*h.Laus*.13(p.37.5; M.34.1035C); ὄξος...καὶ σταφυλὴν καὶ σ. ... παραιτούμενοι [sc. Nazirites] Cyr.*Am*. 22(3.272B).

σταχυοφορέω, *bear corn*; met., of persons, *be fruitful*; ref. BMV, ‡Gr.Thaum.*annunt*.3(M.10.1176B).

στάχυς, ὁ, *ear of corn*; met., ref. Christ ὁ θάνατος τοῦ Ἰησοῦ σ. σίτου γίνεται Or.*hom.10.3 in Jer*.(p.73.14; M.13.360D); ‡Chrys.*nat. Chr*.1(10.791A) cit. s. ἀθέριστος.

[*]στέας, τό, 1. = στέαρ, *dough*, Thdr.Mops.*Os*.7:4(M.66.165C); **2.** s.v.l., *bone* τὰ μὲν κρέη...ἐσθίεσθε, τὰ δὲ σ. φυλάττετε *Mir.Geo*.5 (p.59.7, v.l. ὀστέα).

στεγαν-όω, *make compact* or *impervious, consolidate* καταβαίνων ἥλιος...τὴν...ὑγρότητα τοῦ πηλοῦ ξηραίνων ∼οῖ αὐτὸς ὅλως τὴν αὐγὴν οὐκ ἀποθολούμενος Mac.Mgn.*apocr*.4.28(p.216.10).

στέγη, ἡ, *covered litter*, Chrys.*hom.11.6 in Rom*.(9.539C).

στεγνός, *close, water-tight*; met., *strict* τὸ στεγνότερον μέρος τοῦ βίου Pall.*v.Chrys*.18(p.112.30; M.47.62); *sad* σ. ἡ ἑστία, οἱονεὶ ἡλίου αὐτὴν ἀπολιπόντος Thdr.Stud.*epp*.2.144(M.99.1453A).

στεγονόμιον, τό, *rent*, Ath.Scholast.*coll*.6.3(p.81).

[*]στέγος, ὁ, ? for στέγος, τό, *roof* κατεπήδησεν ὁ Ἰησοῦς ἀπὸ τοῦ στέγου *Ev.Thom*.A 9.3(p.150); *ib*.B 8.1(p.161).

***στεγότης, ἡ,** ? *firmament* τὸν τρισύστατον οὐράνιον ὄροφον ἐτεκτόνησε [sc. Χριστός]...τὴν τρικάτοικον ταύτην στεγότητα λόγῳ πήξας *Pers*.(p.12.20, v.l. στεγοτίδα M.10.101A).

στέγω, *keep*; the peace, Thphn.*chron*.p.232(M.108.585C); abs., *contain oneself*; *endure, hold out* λάλον καὶ ψιθυρὸν...μὴ δυνάμενον σ. Clem.*str*.5.5(p.342.24; M.9.45C); τὸν μετὰ τὸ πτῶμα μὴ δυνάμενον σ. ἀλλὰ κολαζόμενον τὴν συνείδησιν Or.*hom.20.9 in Jer*.(p.191.24; M.13. 521B); *Hom.Clem*.9.19.

***στειβάριος, ὁ**, ? *merchant* (? *maker*) *of stibium* (powdered antimony) σωματοθήκη διαφέρουσα Λέο[ντος...] στειβαρίου *CIG* 9173 (Corycus).

***στειράω**, *be barren*, *T.Abr*.A 8(p.85.18).

στειρεύ-ω, **1.** *be barren* ἡ...'Ραχὴλ...δώδεκα ἔτη ἐστείρευσεν *T.Benj*.1.4; ἡ πάλαι Ἄννα ~ουσα, δι'...ἐπαγγελίας τὸν Σαμουὴλ ἐγέννησεν Jo.D.*f.o*.4.14(M.94.1157B); of BMV τὴν πρὶν ~ουσαν, εἶτα θεόπαιδα γεννήσασαν Thdr.Stud.*nativ.BMV* 2(M.96.681A); **2.** met. ἀνάγκη ~σαι τὴν ἀπρόσεκτον ψυχὴν παντὸς ἀγαθοῦ...νοήματος Hesych.S.*temp*.2.20(M.93.1517C); ψυχὴν ἡδονῶν σαρκικῶν ~ουσαν Max.*ambig*.(M.91.1124D).

[*]**στείρη, ἡ**, = σπεῖρα, *forepart of a ship's keel*, *Orac.Sib*.1.229.

***στειροποιΐα, ἡ**, *barrenness*, Domit.*Jo.Bapt*.2(p.320).

στεῖρος, *barren* ἡ σ. εὐτεκνεῖ καὶ ἡ ἔρημος καρποφορεῖ Clem.*prot*.1 (p.9.24; M.8.65A); of Sarah, here likened to Wisdom, id.*str*.1.5(p.19. 22; M.8.724A); id.*ecl*.50(p.151.6; M.9.721A); met. σ. ... ἦν ἡ ἐκκλησία ἡμῶν πρὸ τοῦ δοθῆναι αὐτῇ τέκνα *2Clem*.2.1.

***στειροφυής**, *of barren stock*, of BMV χαῖρε, μῆλον εὐωδιάζον, ὁ σ. καρπός Thdr.Stud.*nativ.BMV* 7(M.96.692C).

στειρ-όω, *make barren, sterilize*; met., *destroy, nullify*, ref. S. John Baptist στείρωσιν ἔλυσα μητρὸς γεννηθείς, οὐ παρθενίαν ἐστείρωσα †Hipp.*theoph*.3(p.258.26; M.10.853C); opp. ἐκτρέφω, Meth.*res*.1.44 (p.294.3; M.41.1116A); ~ωθέντος τῇ ἀνηκοΐᾳ τῶν δεξαμένων νόμου τοῦ γραπτοῦ Isid.Pel.*epp*.1.131(M.78.269B).

στείρωσις, ἡ, *barrenness, unfruitfulness*, met. ἄγονοι...ψυχαί, ᾐσθημέναι τῆς σ. τῶν ἰδίων ἡγεμονικῶν...ἀπὸ τοῦ ἁγίου πνεύματος διὰ ἐπιμόνου εὐχῆς κυήσασαι, σωτηρίους λόγους θεωρημάτων ἀληθείας πεπληρωμένους γεγεννήκασιν Or.*or*.13(p.327.7; M.11.456A); σ. πρὸς πᾶν ἀγαθὸν ἐχουσῶν ψυχῶν Diod.*Ps*.51:9(M.33.1589D); ref. seventh day of Creation λεγέτωσαν...περὶ τῆς ἑβδομάδος, ὅτι σ. τίς ἐστιν ἐν τῷ ἑβδόμῳ· οὔτε μὲν γὰρ γεννᾷ ἀφ' ἑαυτοῦ, οὔτε παρ' ἑτέρου τίκτεται ὁ τῶν ἑπτὰ ἀριθμός ‡Bas.*struct.hom*.2.6(1.341A; M.30.48B).

στειρωτικός, *barren*, ‡Hipp.Th.*fr*.19(p.51.19).

[*]**στειχηρός**, v. στιχηρός.

[*]**στεῖχος, ὁ**, v. στίχος.

***στεκτός**, *endurable*, neut. as subst. τὸ σ. τῆς δυνάμεως αὐτοῦ... περιστείλαντα [sc. τὸν κύριον] *cat.Apoc*.17:1ff.(p.427.24).

[*]**στελέχειος**, variant of στελεχιαῖος, *forming a trunk*, of the *vena portae* ἡ σ. φλέψ Melet.*nat.hom*.synops.(M.64.1129A).

στέλλω, med., *cease* from συκῆ...τοῦ φύειν σ. Meth.*res*.1.41(p.285. 15; M.18.269A); *withdraw* from, *avoid* σ. ἀπὸ παντὸς ἀτάκτου Bas. *reg.fus*.14(2.355B; M.31.952A); σ. τῆς κοινωνίας τῶν εἰκονομάχων Thdr.Stud.*epp*.2.163(M.99.1517C); *refuse* σ. ἀναφέρειν τὸν αἱρετικόν *ib*.2.40(1240B).

***στέλος**, vox nihili; v. σίελος.

στεναγμώδης, *with* or *like sighing* or *groaning*, Nemes.*nat.hom*.28 (M.40.709A).

***στεναγωγέω**, *bring sparingly, bring in limited measure* ὦ πάσχα θεῖον, θεὸν ἐξ οὐρανῶν οὐ στεναγωγήσαν, καὶ νῦν πνευματικῶς συνάψαν ‡Chrys.*pasch*.6.5(p.191.4; 8.273E).

στενακτικός, *lamentable*, Thdr.Stud.*epp*.2.144(M.99.1453A).

***στεναρός**, *gruff* ἡ ἄρκτος στεναρὰ ἐκδεδυκῶσα καὶ ὕπουλος ‡Caes. Naz.*dial*.140(M.38.1072).

***στενόβουλος**, *narrow-minded*, *Orac.Sib*.5.242.

***στένοδοι, αἱ**, *narrows*, Thphn.*chron*.p.280(M.108.692C).

στενολεσχέω, *talk subtly, quibble*, Cyr.*inc.unigen*.(5^1.680D); in good sense, *discuss closely* δεῖ...περὶ τούτων προθύμως...σ. id.*Jo*.4.4 (4.385E).

στενολεσχία, ἡ, *quibbling*, Cyr.*Am*.57(3.313D); id.*Juln*.2(6^2.46B); *ib*.10(351E).

[*]**στενόπορος, ἡ**, *narrow way*, met. διὰ τῆς σ. τῶν πειρασμῶν καὶ τῶν θλίψεων διελθεῖν Mac.Aeg.*libert.ment*.13(M.34.945A).

[*]**στενορύμη, ἡ**, for στενορρύμη, *narrow alley*, Leont.N.*v.Sym*.42 (M.93.1721B).

στενός, *narrow*; *scanty*; hence *short* of stature, Gr.Mag.*dial*.(tr. Zach.)1.5(M.*PL*.77.179B); met., *self-centred, selfish*, Gr.Naz.*carm*.2. 1.11.308(M.37.1050).

***στενοτεία, ἡ**, *straitened circumstances, poverty*, ‡Ath.*renunt*.7(M. 28.1416D).

στενόφωνος, *weak-voiced*; of Moses, and met., of Jewish Law εἴρηκεν...οὐχ ὁ 'Ιωάννου πατὴρ τῆς μεγάλα...βοώσης φωνῆς, ἀλλ' ὡς τοῦ σ. καὶ βραδυγλώσσου νόμου φέρων τὸ πρόσωπον· σ. γὰρ ὁ Μωϋσῆς καὶ βραδύγλωσσος Sophr.H.*or*.7.8(M.87.3336A).

στενοχωρ-έω, **1.** *straiten, confine*; met. ὑμῖν ἐναποκλείειν τὴν χάριν, καὶ τὸ καθ' ὑμᾶς μόνῳ χωρίῳ ~εῖν Bas.*ep*.227(3.350E; M.32.853B); τί ~εῖς τῆς ἀγάπης τὸ πλάτος; Chrys.*hom.34.4 in 1Cor*.(10.315B); *reduce* to necessity, id.*hom.10.3 in 1Thess*.(11.498B); **2.** pass.; **a.** *be cramped* or *confined*; met., *be cramped, limited* ἐπὶ τῷ θαύματι... ~ηθήσονται, καὶ σκοτωθήσονται τὴν διάνοιαν †Bas.*Is*.222(1.546D; M. 30.504C); ~ηθεῖσα ἡ πονηρία τοῦ σατανᾶ Nil.*epp*.3.40(M.79.408A); *be in straitened circumstances* τοὺς ἀδίκους πλουτοῦντας, καὶ ~ουμένους τοὺς τοῦ θεοῦ δούλους *2Clem*.20.1; δύο...~ηθέντες ἔτη διὰ τὸ τὴν χώραν ὑπάρχειν ἀργόν Proc.G.*Is*.37:30(M.87.2321B); hence **b.** *be oppressed, be distressed*, Or.*or*.30(p.393.18; M.11.545D); Chrys. *stat*.1.9(2.14A); of Adam δεσπότης ἐν μέσῳ τοῦ παραδείσου πλανώμενος ὁμογενοῦς ἐρημίᾳ ~ούμενος Bas.Sel.*or*.2.4(M.85.41C); ὁ νοῦς εἰς ἄκρον καθαρθεὶς ~εῖται τοῖς οὖσι· καὶ ἔξω θέλει γίνεσθαι πάντων τῶν γεγονότων Thal.*cent*.1.55(M.91.1433A); *be irked* αὐτῷ... ~ουμένῳ τὸ συνδιάγειν ἐπὶ πολὺ τοῖς βουλομένοις Pall.*v.Chrys*.19 (p.120.15; M.47.67); **c.** ref. argument, *be cramped, embarrassed, be in difficulties*, Or.*Cels*.5.26(p.27.18; M.11.1220D); Eus.*e.th*.2.9(p.110. 17; M.24.920B); id.*Marcell*.2.3(p.47.22; M.24.804C); Max.*opusc*.(M. 91.116C); **d.** theol., *be limited, circumscribed* ὡς μήτε ἐκβάλλειν τοῦ δόγματος τὴν ἐπὶ τῷ υἱῷ βούλησιν τοῦ γεννήσαντος, οἷον ~ουμένην ἐν τῇ συναφείᾳ τῆς τοῦ υἱοῦ πρὸς τὸν πατέρα ἑνότητος Gr.Nyss.*Eun*.8 (2 p.181.16; M.45.773D); of H. Ghost in soul ἐὰν δὲ ὀξυχολία τις ἐπέλθῃ, εὐθὺς τὸ πνεῦμα τὸ ἅγιον...~εῖται...πνίγεται γὰρ ὑπὸ τοῦ πονηροῦ πνεύματος Herm.*mand*.5.1.3; **3.** *crowd, throng* ψαλμὸς... μελῳδούμενος...~εῖ ἐκκλησίαν Procl.CP *or*.2.1(M.65.692C); **4.** pass., *be crowded together*; met., *be beset* ἀδελφὸν ~ούμενον ὑπὸ πειρασμοῦ Dor.*ep*.1 tit.(M.88.1837C); **5.** met., *press*; *urge* ἐάν τις καὶ εἰς τὰ μικρὰ ἁμαρτήματα ~ῇ τοὺς ἀδελφούς Bas.*reg.br*.4(2.415D; M.31.1084B); τῶν ...ἀπαιτούντων ~ούντων αὐτόν Leont.N.*v.Jo.Eleem*.30(p.62.19).

***στενοχωρητικός**, *oppressed*, Thdr.Stud.*epp*.2.24(M.99.1189C); neut. as subst., *oppression* τὸ τοῦ διωγμοῦ σ. *ib*.2.143(1449D).

στενοχωρία, ἡ, **1.** *want of room*; **a.** *compression* τῶν σπλάγχνων στενοχωρίας Melet.*nat.hom*.synops.(M.64.1136C); *thronging, crowding* σ. ... τῶν...ἀδελφῶν Paul.Em.*hom*.2(p.11.20; M.77.1437C); **b.** met., *confinement, constraint* τὸ...πνεῦμα τοῦ θεοῦ...λύπην οὐχ ὑποφέρει οὐδὲ σ. Herm.*mand*.10.2.6; **2.** *scarcity, want*, Hipp.*haer*.5.26(p.128.26; M.16.3198A); Chrys.*stat*.1.8(2.13A); τροφῶν σ. Leont.N.*v.Jo.Eleem*. 13(p.26.20); *ib*.20(p.37.14); of time, Gr.Ant.*bapt*.1(M.88.1872C); **3.** *meanness, pettiness* οὐχ ἡ πενία ποιεῖ τὴν σ. Chrys.*hom.21.2 in Rom*. (9.673D); **4.** *distress, anguish*, Herm.*vis*.4.3.4; Chrys.*stat*.5.2(2.62E).

στεν-όω, **1.** *straiten, confine, contract*; theol., ref. Persons of Trin. ἃ μήτε οὕτως ἀλλήλων ἀπήρτηται, ὡς φύσει τέμνεσθαι· μήτε οὕτως ἐστένωται, ὡς εἰς ἓν πρόσωπον περιγράφεσθαι· τὸ μὲν γὰρ τῆς Ἀρειανῆς μανίας, τὸ δὲ τῆς Σαβελλιανικῆς ἀθεΐας ἐστίν Gr.Naz.*or*.34.8(M.36. 249A); **2.** *crowd, pack tight* αἱ ἀποθῆκαι τῷ πλήθει τῶν ἀποκειμένων ~οῦνται καὶ τὸν ἐστενωμένον οὐκ ἐλεοῦμεν Bas.*hom*.8.2(2.64B; M.31. 309B); **3.** *reduce, restrict* ὁπηνίκα διαφόρων βρωμάτων ἐφίεται ἡμῶν ἡ ψυχή, τὸ τηνικαῦτα ἐπ' ἄρτῳ ~ούσθω καὶ ὕδατι Evagr.Pont.*cap.pract*. A 7(M.40.1224B); (in argument) *reduce to straits, corner* ἐπὰν ~ώσωμεν δι' ἐρωτήσεως τὸν δι' ἐναντίας Anast.S.*hod*.1(M.89.40D); **4.** *reduce, subdue* ἵνα ~ωθεῖσα ὑπὸ τῆς ἀκηδίας καταπέσῃ εἰς τὴν αἵρεσιν τοῦ γάμου Pall.*v.Chrys*.17(p.109.2; M.47.60); **5.** *impoverish* οὐ ~οῦσι τοὺς...θησαυροὺς τοῦ κυρίου Leont.N.*v.Jo.Eleem*.7(p.15.3); *ib*.12(p.24.22); pass., *be deficient* τῷ ἐστενῶσθαι τὴν 'Ρωμαϊκὴν φωνὴν καὶ μὴ δύνασθαι πρὸς τὴν ἡμετέραν τῶν Γραικῶν φράσιν τρεῖς ὑποστάσεις λέγειν Acac.B.*ep.Cyr*.(p.99.26; M.77.100D); **6.** pass., *be in straits, be in want*, Bas.*hom*.8.2(2.64B; M.31.309B) cit. s. 2 supra; Gr. Nyss.*usur*.(M.46.436C); ~ωθέντες...τῇ τῶν ἀναγκαίων λήψει, μάλιστα ὕδατος Gel.Cyz.*h.e*.3.9.5; Jo.Mosch.*prat*.85(M.87.2941C).

***στένω**, *erect, set up* τοὺς παπυλεῶνας...ἔστενεν Thphn.*chron*.p.268 (M.108.665A).

***στενώνω**, s.v.l., *stint* οὐκ ἀφίει τίποτε ἐξ αὐτῶν ὃ οὐκ εὐθέως μεταδίδωσι τῷ πένητι, σχεδὸν δὲ καὶ στενώνων τὸν οἶκον αὐτοῦ Leont.N. *v.Jo.Eleem*.1(p.6.9).

στένωσις, ἡ, **1.** *narrowness* ἡ ὁδὸς ἐκ τῶν ἀκάνθων εἶχεν σ. Jo.Mosch. *prat*.181(M.87.3053A); Thphn.*chron*.p.262(M.108.652C); **2.** *straits, need* ἀπὸ σ. ... ἔκλεψα Ephr.1.223F; Bas.*hom*.8.5(2.68A; M.31.317C); Cyr.S.*v.Sab*.67(p.167.25); τὸν νοῦν πλατύνας ἐν σ. πραγμάτων Geo. Pis.*Pers*.1.50(M.92.1201A); **3.** *constraint* λυτρώσασθαί με ᾅδου στενώσεως Jo.Mon.*hymn.Nic.Myr*.6(M.96.1388A).

[*]**στεραιός**, v. στερεός.

στέργω, **1.** *feel affection for, love*; hence *favour* τὰ Ἀρείου ἔστεργεν Philost.*h.e*.10.7(M.65.588B); **2.** *accept, agree upon* τὸν στρατηγὸν ἔστεργον Malchus *exc.Rom.*1(p.156.2; M.113.757B); *agree* that ἐστέρχθη δὲ ὥστε τὰς...σάκρας...ἐπικομισθῆναι Men.*exc.Rom.*3(p.175.29; M.113.857D).

***στερεάω**, = στερεόω, *fortify* ἐκείνους ἔθνος ἐκλεκτὸν οἶδα οὐρανίως οὐράνια ἁπτομένους καὶ οὐκ ἄχρι ὀνόματος καυχωμένους ἀλλὰ καυχήματι αἰωνίῳ στερεωμένους *Pers.*(p.41.26, v.l. στερεουμένους); cf. στερεὰ ταῦτα *ib.*(p.32.14, v.l. στερεᾶ).

στερέμνιος, *firm, fast, solid*; met., of faith, Clem.*paed.*1.6(p.112.27; M.8.296A); Ph.Carp.*Cant.*146(M.40.107C); Nil.*epp.*1.104(M.79.128C); of meaning of scripture γλαφυρωτέραν...καὶ στερεμνιωτέραν Gr.Agr.*Eccl.*proem.(M.98.741A); neut. as subst., Meth.*symp.*10.3(p.124.21; M.18.196D).

***στερεοκαρδία**, **ἡ**, *hardness of heart*, Esaias *or.*14.3(p.81; cf.M.40.1140C).

***στερεόμορφος**, *firm, stable* τὴν ψυχὴν...σ. ... καταστήσει *A.Jo.*29(p.167.4).

στερεοποι-έω, *make firm, strengthen, confirm* ~ούμενος ὑπὸ τοῦ ἐν αὐτῷ ἐνοικήσαντος θεοῦ λόγου ‡Ath.*serm.fid.*4(p.6; M.26.1265C); διὰ τοῦ ~εῖν τὴν εὐαγγελικὴν φωνὴν τοῖς πιστεύουσι Gr.Nyss.*fid.*(M.45.144D); of Christian faith λογισμὸν κρείττονα καὶ ~ηθέντα *M.Tar.*4(p.457).

στερεός, **1.** *firm*; *solid, substantial*; of firmament, Or.*Jo.*1.39(42; p.51.2; M.14.101C) cit. s. στερεόω; ἡ σ. *mainland* οἱ...εἰς τὴν στερεὰν βασιλεῖς Cosm.Ind.*top.*11(M.88.449C); met., of divine nature as not liable to chance ὁ πατήρ, σ. ὢν τῇ φύσει Clem.*exc.Thdot.*30(p.116.27; M.9.673C); τὴν θείαν ψυχὴν αἰνίσσεται τὴν ἐγκεκρυμμένην τῇ σαρκὶ καὶ σ. καὶ δυσπαθῆ *ib.*51(p.124.1; 684B); **2.** *hard, stubborn, cruel* ἵνα ἐμπέσῃ εἰς χεῖρας στεραιωτέρ[ας] αὐτοῦ *Pap.Chr.*(p.441); neut. as subst., *severity* τὸ...σ. τοῦ δόγματος ἀποστρέφονται Const.*or.s.c.*10(p.164.27; M.20.1257B).

στερε-όω, **1.** *make firm* or *solid* κύριον τὸν ἐστερεωκότα τοὺς οὐρανούς Iren.*haer.*1.15.5(M.7.625B); γῆν...ἐστερέωσεν Clem.*prot.*1(p.6.2; M.8.57C); οὕτως...λόγῳ θεοῦ τοὺς οὐρανούς, θειοτέρου τυγχάνοντας σώματος καὶ διὰ τοῦτο καλουμένου στερεοῦ, οὐκ ἔχοντος τὸ ...ῥευστὸν...τῶν λοιπῶν καὶ κατωτέρω ἐστερεῶσθαι Or.*Jo.*1.39(42; p.51.3; M.14.101C); **2.** *establish*, ref. Am.4:13 ~οῦσθαι βροντήν, καὶ κτίζεσθαι πνεῦμα, ὧν ἅπαξ μὲν ὁ λόγος ὑπέστη, συνεχὴς δὲ καὶ νῦν ἡ ἐνέργεια Gr.Naz.*or.*30.11(p.125.4; M.36.117B); **3.** *fortify, confirm* τὰ τοιαῦτα...~ωσάτω σε μᾶλλον ἢ ταραξάτω *M.Perp.*21(p.93.17); τρία τοίνυν νοεῖς, τὸν προστάσσοντα κύριον, τὸν δημιουργοῦντα λόγον, τὸν ~οῦντα [v.l. τὸ στερεοῦν τὸ] τὸ πνεῦμα Bas.*Spir.*38(3.32B; M.32.136C); ἐστερεώθησαν αἱ τῶν οὐρανῶν δυνάμεις παρὰ τοῦ πνεύματος *ib.*49(41B; M.157A).

στερ-έω, [irreg. aor. infin. pass. στερεισθῆναι]; *deprive* εὔχεται μὴ ...~εισθῆναι τῆς θείας κηδεμονίας...μηδὲ γυμνωθῆναι τῆς τοῦ παναγίου πνεύματος χάριτος Or.*Ps.*50:13(p.52).

στερέωμα, **τό**, *solid body*; **1.** *cube*, Nemes.*nat.hom.*5(M.40.621B); **2.** *foundation*; fig., of S. Peter τὸ σ. τῆς πίστεως Chrys.*hom.in Mt.* *18:23*(3.4E); met., *firmness, steadfastness* of faith, Bas.*hom.in Ps.*45(1.172A; M.29.420B); Gr.Naz.*or.*21.33(M.35.1121C); Max.*ep.*12(M.91.508C); τὸ αἰσθητὸν σ. τὸ τῆς πίστεως σημαίνει στερέωμα Thal.*cent.*2.30(M.91.1440D); **3.** *firmament*, *T.Neph.*3.4; Hipp.*Dan.*2.29.5; Cyr.*hom.pasch.*5.4(5².50C); etym. Μωσῆς τὸν οὐρανὸν ἐτύμως... στερέωμα προσαγορεύει, παρὰ τὸ πρῶτον εἶναι μετὰ τὴν ἀσώματον... οὐσίαν τοῦδε τοῦ κόσμου στερεὸν καὶ αἰσθητὸν σῶμα Eus.*p.e.*11.6(517C; M.21.857C); in gen. use synonymous with οὐρανός, *ib.*11.23(545D; M.909A); Cyr.*Ps.*18:2(M.69.828B); οἱ μηδὲ ἓν...ἔχοντες, μήτε πίστιν ὀρθήν, μήτε βίον εὐθῆ...οἱ δὲ ἕνα μὲν ἔχοντες, ἕνα δὲ μὴ ἔχοντες, μέσοι τινές εἰσιν, ἔξωθεν μένειν τοῦ νυμφῶνος κατακρινόμενοι, τουτέστιν τοῦ σ. Cosm.Ind.*top.*5(M.88.284C); of the seven heavens, *Apoc.Mos.*35(p.19); cf. ἕτεροι [sc. ἄγγελοι] τῶν περὶ τὸ πρῶτον τοῦτο σ. Athenag.*leg.*24.5(M.6.948B); relationship of σ. to οὐρανός discussed, Gr.Nyss.*Eun.*12(1 p.293.17; M.45.1004A); Thdt.*qu.11 in Gen.*(1.14); cf. οὐ πολὺ δὲ τῆς ἀναστάσεως γενομένης...πάλιν εἰς οὐρανὸν ἀναφερόμενος...ἔσωθεν τοῦ σ. εἰσῆλθεν Cosm.Ind.*top.*2(121D); met. οὗτος... οὐκ ἐλάσσων φωστὴρ τοῦ ἐκκλησιαστικοῦ σ. ἐχρημάτισεν Jo.VI H.*v.Jo.D.*2(M.94.432B); **4.** Gnost.; one of ten works of Creator signifying the aeons (Valent.), Iren.*haer.*1.18.1(M.7.644A); as abode of aeons (Basilidean) τὸ πνεῦμα τὸ ἅγιον...στερέωμα τῶν ὑπερκοσμίων καὶ τοῦ κόσμου μεταξὺ τεταγμένον Hipp.*haer.*7.23(p.200.18; M.16.3310A); ὄντος οὖν τοῦ σ. ... ἐγεννήθη...ὁ μέγας ἄρχων...οὗτος γεννηθεὶς...ἠνέχθη ὅλος ἄνω μέχρι τοῦ σ., τῆς δὲ ἀναδρομῆς καὶ τοῦ ὑψώματος τὸ σ. τέλος εἶναι νομίσας *ib.*(p.200.23ff.; 3310B); Manich. ζῶν πνεῦμα ἔκτισε τὸν κόσμον, καὶ...κατελθὸν ἀνήνεγκε τοὺς ἄρχοντας καὶ ἐσταύρωσεν ἐν τῷ σ., ὅ ἐστιν αὐτῶν σῶμα ἡ σφαῖρα Hegem.*Arch.*8(p.11.6; M.10.1437C); *ib.*9(p.14.1; 1441A).

στερέωσις, **ἡ**, *making firm, establishing* τρία...νοεῖς, τὸν προστάσσοντα κύριον, τὸν δημιουργοῦντα λόγον, τὸν στερεοῦντα [v.l. τὸ στερεοῦν τὸ] τὸ πνεῦμα. τί δ' ἂν ἄλλο εἴη σ., ἢ ἡ κατὰ τὸν ἁγιασμὸν τελείωσις, τὸ ἀνένδοτον καὶ ἄτρεπτον καὶ παγίως ἐρηρεισμένον ἐν ἀγαθῷ τῆς σ. ἐμφαινούσης; Bas.*Spir.*38(3.32B; M.32.136C); τῆς σ. ... ἐπὶ τὸ δυσμετάπτωτον τῆς ἀπὸ τῶν ἀγαθῶν ἕξεως νοουμένης *ib.*49(41B; M.157A); as translating name Amoz, father of Isaiah, †Bas.*Is.*10(1.385C; M.30.136B); of prophet Amos, *Chron.Pasch.*p.147(M.92.364B).

***στέρνη**, f.l. for τερπνή *delightful, pleasant* ἡδὺς ὁ βίος, ἡ πρᾶξις σ. Evagr.Pont.*rer.mon.*2(M.40.1253C).

***στερνοκτυπία**, **ἡ**, *beating of the breast, lamentation*, Pall.*v.Chrys.*20(p.135.11; M.47.75).

στερνόμαντις, **ὁ**, *soothsayer* who delivers oracles by means of ventriloquism, *one who prophesies from his own breast*, Thdt.*Is.*19:3(p.83.26; 2.281); synon. with ἐγγαστρίμυθος, *ib.*8:19(p.46.14; 2.229).

στέρνον, **τό**, *breast, chest*; *trunk* μέρη τοῦ σώματος ζ', κεφαλή, τράχηλος, στέρνα, πόδες β', χεῖρες β' Anat.Laod.*decad.*(p.36).

***στέρξις**, **ἡ**, *affection*, Clem.*str.*2.9(p.135.8; M.8.977A).

***στέρρησις**, **ἡ**, s.v.l., *appetition, desire* ἄγει οὖν τῶν ὄντων τὴν στέρησιν, ἡ τοῦ μὴ προσήκοντος στέρρησις Jo.D.*Man.*1.31(M.94.1537D).

***στερροκάρδιος**, *stout-hearted*, Thdr.Stud.*cant.*16.4(p.372).

στερρός, **1.** *solid, firm, steadfast* σ. ἡ ἐκ λόγου ἀγάπη Clem.*str.*2.19(p.168.19; M.8.1045B); σ. πρὸς τὴν ὁμολογίαν *Ep.Lugd.*ap.Eus.*h.e.*5.1.22(M.20.417A); διὰ σ. ἦθος καὶ γνησίαν ψυχῆς παίδευσιν Eus.*l.C.*5(p.205.8; M.20.1337B); of persons ὥστε...τοὺς μαθητὰς στερροτέρους γενέσθαι, τὴν παρρησίαν ὁρῶντας τοῦ διδασκάλου *cat.Jo.*7:8(p.261.33); ἐν τῇ πίστει σ. καὶ ἀσάλευτος Thphn.*chron.*p.15(M.108.96B); with ἀκλινής, Chrys.*sac.*6.7(p.152.13; 1.426C); Marc.Diac.*v.Porph.*24; of food, *solid*; met., ref. spiritual instruction τὸν Διονύσιον ἀντιπαρακαλεῖ...στερροτέρας...μεταδιδόναι τροφῆς...ὡς μὴ διὰ τέλους τοῖς γαλακτώδεσιν ἐνδιατρίβοντες λόγοις τῇ νηπιώδει ἀγωγῇ λάθοιεν καταγηράσαντες Eus.*h.e.*4.23.8(388A); neut. as subst. τὸ καρτερικὸν καὶ σ. τῆς ψυχῆς id.*v.C.*2.29(p.54.3; M.20.1008B); ‡Chrys.*pasch.*2(8.257C); Chrys.*pan.Macc.*1.2(2.624D); **2.** *hard, severe* τί...οὐ παίδευσιν στερροτέραν ζητῶν; Isid.Pel.*epp.*1.41(M.78.208C); neut. as subst., Eus.*v.C.*2.3(p.41.17; M.20.981A); τὸ σ. ... τῷ πράῳ συγκεκραμένον Gr.Naz.*ep.*10(M.37.40A).

στερρότης, **ἡ**, **1.** of God, *unchangeableness* τὸ μεγαλόψυχον...οὐθ' ὑπὸ ὕβρεως διατρέπεται, οὐθ' ὑπὸ προπηλακισμοῦ τῆς φυσικῆς σ. ἐξίσταται Const.*or.s.c.*11(p.167.2; M.20.1261A); **2.** as human quality; **a.** *fortitude*; *steadfastness*; *uprightness* βίου στερρότητι καὶ καρτερίας ὑπομονῇ Eus.*v.C.*3.9(p.81.7; M.20.1064A); διανοίας σ. Chrys.*hom.15.3 in Rom.*(9.598C); **b.** *obduracy*, Jo.Eleem.*v.Tych.*33(p.143); **3.** in material things, *hardness, strength* implying resistance; of shoes, Gr.Nyss.*v.Mos.*(M.44.357A); of armour, Diad.*perf.*98(p.146.1); of wine, *ib.*50(p.56.10); **4.** as mode of address; to a bishop, Const. ap.Eus.*h.e.*10.5.20(M.20.888B); Constantius Imp.ap.Ath.*apol.sec.*51(p.132.18; M.25.341B); to civil authorities, Bas.*ep.*86(3.178E; M.32.468A); Gr.Naz.*ep.*125(M.37.220B); *V.Aberc.*49(p.109.17).

***στερρόφρων**, *brave*, Thdr.Stud.*cant.*5.8(p.345).

***στερρόω**, *strengthen*, Eus.*d.e.*2.3(p.90.8; M.22.160B).

στερρῶς, *severely* στερρότατα ὁ παιδαγωγὸς ἀπαγορεύει Clem.*paed.*2.2(p.173.3; M.8.421B).

***στεφανεῖν**, for στέφειν, *crown* ποῦ γὰρ εἶπεν ὁ Χριστὸς ἵνα προσκυνῶμεν κατὰ ἀνατολάς;...ἢ στεφανεῖν ἀνδρόγυνα; ‡Jo.D.*Const.*5(M.95.320B).

στεφάνη, **ἡ**, *coping, parapet* of a building opp. θεμέλιος, Or.*Jo.*1.31(34; p.39.33; M.14.84B); of a wall, Thphn.*chron.*p.219(M.108.557C).

στεφανηδόν, *like a crown*, hence *in a ring* or *circle* σ. ἐκυκλώσαντο μαθηταί Nonn.*par.Jo.*6:3(M.43.793A); *ib.*1:52(760B).

***στεφανητικός**, *pertaining to the coronation tribute* (aurum coronarium) ὅτι τὸν σ. κανόνα οἱ ἔξαρχοι αὐτῶν [sc. τῶν Ἰουδαίων] ἰδιοκινδύνως εἰσάγουσι τοῖς λαργιτιόσι Phot.*nomoc.*12.2(p.601; M.104.869D).

στεφανηφορέω (**στεφανοφ-**), *wear a wreath*; met., *triumph* σ. ἐπὶ τῇ τοιαύτῃ ἀγνοίᾳ Cosm.Ind.*top.*7(στεφανοφοροῦντες M.88.377D).

στεφανικός, *of* or *for a crown*, partic. bridal crown, hence *of marriage* or *wedding*, Thdr.Stud.*epp.*1.35(M.99.1029D); ἡ σ. ἐπίκλησις *ib.*1.50(1093A); τῆς σ. ἁρμογῆς equated with τῆς γαμικῆς συναφείας *ib.*(1092D).

στεφάνιον, **τό**, *crowning*, Jo.Mal.*chron.*12 p.289(M.97.437A).

στεφανίτης, **ὁ**, *wearer of a wreath* or *crown*; **1.** victorious athletes, Or.*enarr.in Job* 2:10(M.17.61D); Chrys.*hom.84.4 in Mt.*(7.803B); **2.** *wearer of the crown of martyrdom*, *M.Thdot.*3(p.139.7);

*M.Niceph.*9(p.288); Mac.Mgn.*apocr.*4.14(p.182.9); **3.** of victors in spiritual life; Christ *τῶν φόβων ἀγαθὸς στεφανίτης* ‡Chrys.*hom.*2(13. 208A); at Temptation, Thdt.*provid.*10(4.664); Job, Chrys.*Saturn.* 5(3.408D); Jo. Bapt., id.*hom.10.4 in Mt.*(7.144D); Cypr., Gr.Naz.*or.* 24.16(M.35.1189A); others, Bas.*ep.*140.1(3.233A; M.32.588A); Ast. Am.*hom.*13(M.40.356A); Pall.*v.Chrys.*20(p.137.4; M.47.76); *οἱ πρὸς ἀρετὴν ἀλειφόμενοι καὶ σ. γενόμενοι* Isid.Pel.*epp.*3.197(M.78.881B); an ascetic *ὁ οὐρανὸς αὐτὸν σ. ἐδέξατο* Thdt.*h.rel.*3(3.1136); *χωρὶς αἵματος μαρτυρικοῦ καὶ σ. φανείς* Jo.Mon.*hymn.Bas.*10(M.96.1377A); **4.** *wearer of a bridal crown, married man σ. ἀντὶ μοναχοῦ...γενέσθαι* Thphn.*chron.*p.368(M.108.880C).

στεφανῖτις, ἡ, fem. of *στεφανίτης, wearer of the crown* (sc. of martyrdom), *victor*; of a virgin martyr, Jo.D.*hom.*12.2(M.96.784D).

***στεφανοδότης, ὁ,** *giver of the crown ἐλεύσεται κύριος ὁ σ.* Thdr. Stud.*epp.*2.8(M.99.1137D); cf. *στεφηδότης, στεφοδότης.*

***στεφανοειδής,** *in the form of a crown, circular,* Proc.G.*3Reg.* 7:27(M.87.1157C).

[*]στεφανοπλοκέω, *plait wreaths,* Gr.Nyss.*hom.5 in Cant.*(M.44. 872A).

στέφανος, ὁ, *crown*; **1.** in gen., *wreath, chaplet*; on wearing of such, Clem.*paed.*2.8 passim(pp.193ff.; M.8.465ff.); symbol of freedom from care, *ib.*(p.201.28; 484A); symbolized by tonsure, ‡Bas. *h.myst.*13(p.260.26); met., of the circle of presbyters, Ign.*Magn.*13. 1; *καὶ τότε μετὰ ταῦτα πάντα καὶ τὸν ποικίλον τῶν ἐπιταγμάτων τούτων σ. ἐπάγει* Chrys.*hom.18.6 in Mt.*(7.242A); of S. Peter as prince of the apostles, ‡Bas.*h.myst.*13(p.261.4); of time, as a circle, *cat.Jac.* 3:6(p.21.4); **2.** of Christ's crown of thorns *σ. ἀκάνθινον Ev.Petr.*3 (p.4.5); *ὁ σ. οὗτος ἄνθος ἐστὶ τῶν πεπιστευκότων...αἱμάσσει δὲ...τοὺς ἠπιστηκότας* Clem.*paed.*2.8(p.203.3; M.8.485C); Chrys.*hom.84.1 in Jo.*(8.499B); in vision, *V.Pach.A* 18(p.142.15); symbolic significance *ὁ...τοῦ κυρίου σ. ... τῆς πίστεώς ἐστιν τύπος, ζωῆς μὲν διὰ τὴν οὐσίαν τοῦ ξύλου, εὐφροσύνης δὲ διὰ τὴν προσηγορίαν τοῦ σ., κινδύνου δὲ διὰ τὴν ἄκανθαν* Clem.*paed.*2.8(p.202.11ff.; 485A); *μυστήριον δὲ ἦν καὶ ὁ σ.· λύσις γὰρ ἦν τῶν ἁμαρτιῶν, ἀπόλυσις τῆς ἀποφάσεως* Cyr.H.*catech.* 13.17; *σ. ... ὁ ἐξ ἀκανθῶν ἐπενήνεκται...τῆς ἐπιγείου βασιλείας σύνθημα δηλῶν...ἐπυθόμην δὲ τινῶν...σ. μὲν τὸν ἐξ ἀκανθῶν τὴν τῶν εἰδωλολατρούντων ἔτι κατασημαίνειν πληθύν, ἀναληφθησομένην ὥσπερ εἰς διάδημα τῷ Χριστῷ διὰ πίστεως* Cyr.*Jo.*12(4.1043Ef.); linked with Cant.3:11, *Dial.Christ.et Jud.*12(p.70.27); **3.** *crown of victory* at public games, fig. *τὸν τοῦ θεοῦ λόγον τὴν ἀνθρωπίνην σάρκα διὰ τῆς ἀναστάσεως ἀθάνατον γενέσθαι παρεσκευακέναι καὶ ὥσπερ τινὰ νίκης σ. ἀναδησάμενον ἐν δεξιᾷ τοῦ πατρὸς καθέζεσθαι* Marcell.*fr.*114 ap. Eus.*e.th.*3.10(p.167.9; M.24.1020B); met.; **a.** in Christian life *ἵνα...εἰ μὴ δυνάμεθα πάντες στεφανωθῆναι, κἂν ἐγγὺς τοῦ σ. γενώμεθα 2Clem.* 7.3; *καθάπερ ἐν τοῖς ἀγῶσι τοῖς γυμνικοῖς, οὕτω καὶ κατὰ τὴν ἐκκλησίαν στέφανοι ἀνδρῶν τε καὶ παίδων* Clem.*str.*7.11(p.48.17; M.9.493A); *ὁ...μηδὲν παραλείψας τῶν ὀφειλόντων πεπρᾶχθαι, στεφάνων ἐστὶν εἰκότως ἄξιος* Isid.Pel.*epp.*5.82(M.78.1376A); pertaining to the age to come, Clem.*paed.*2.8(p.202.6; M.8.485A) cit. s. *ἀμάραντος*; *νυμφεύομαι τῷ λόγῳ καὶ τὸν ἀΐδιον τῆς ἀφθαρσίας προῖκα λαμβάνω σ. καὶ πλοῦτον παρὰ τοῦ πατρός* Meth.*symp.*6.5(p.69.18; M.18.120C), cf. 7 infra; *ἤδη τὰ νοητὰ ἄνθη συλλέγετε πρὸς πλοκὴν ἐπουρανίων σ.* Cyr.H. *procatech.*1; id.*catech.*5.4 cit. s. *ἀμάραντος*; *τοὺς μὲν πόνους συνεκλήρωσε τῷ...προσκαίρῳ αἰῶνι, τοὺς δὲ σ. ἐταμιεύσατο τῷ...ἀθανάτῳ* Chrys.*pan.Juln.*1(2.672D); id.*exp.in Ps.*7:10(5.63C); composition of the crown, from virtue *μὴ μόνον τὸ φορτικὸν ἐννοῶμεν τῆς ἀρετῆς ἀλλὰ καὶ τὸν ἐξ αὐτῆς λογιζώμεθα σ.* id.*hom.16.11 in Mt.*(7.220C); Isid.Pel.*epp.*4.163(1253A); from graces, Nil.*epp.*1.195(M.79.156D); full exposition, Chrys.*exp.in Ps.*5:13(5.38C,D); as reward of heaven *ὅπως μετὰ τὸν πολὺν ἀγῶνα...ἐπὶ ⟨τὸν⟩ τῆς βασιλείας σ. ὁρμήσαντες εὐσεβῶς τὰ ἀληθῆ πιστεύοντες μὴ ταρασσώμεθα* Hipp.*haer.*9.17(p.255. 26; M.16.3394C); ref. 2Cor.12:2f. *δείκνυσιν αὐτῷ* [sc. *τῷ Παύλῳ*]... *τῶν ἀγώνων τοὺς σ.* Cosm.Ind.*top.*9(M.88.412B); for those only who have taken part in the contest, Chrys.*stat.*4.1(2.49C); Isid.Pel.*epp.* 5.58(1361C); dist. from immortality, not for those like the stillborn who have never struggled, Cosm.Ind.*top.*7(377D); **b.** esp. as crown of martyrdom v. *μαρτύριον, ἀφθαρσία, ἄφθαρτος*; **4.** *crown* of glory or honour; met., of Christ as crown of Church, Clem.*paed.*2.8(p.200. 20; M.8.480B); of H. Ghost as crown of the just, Didym.*Trin.*2.1 (M.39.453A); of BMV *ὁ σ. τῆς παρθενίας* Cyr.*hom.div.*4(p.102.21; 5[2]. 355E); of faith as crown of Church, Bas.Sel.*or.*20.2(M.85.253B); of Christian profession, Bas.*ep.*221(3.334B; M.32.816C); ref. apostolic order *τῶν εἰληφότων τὸν σ. τοῦ Χριστοῦ ἐν τῇ ἀποστολικῇ τάξει A.Phil.*30(p.16.11); of Cross *ὁ...τοῦ σταυροῦ σ.* Cyr.H.*catech.*13.1; of a panegyric *ἤδη...τριακονταετηρικοὺς αὐτῷ λόγων πλέξαντες σ.* Eus.*v.C.*1.1(p.7.5; M.20.912A); in spiritual life *οὐκ ἐξῆλθεν ἔχων τὸ διάδημα τοῦ Σαούλ, ἀλλ' ἐξῆλθεν ἔχων σ. δικαιοσύνης* Chrys.*David* 2.2 (4.762A); **5.** *crown* as badge of office; of Jewish kings, Clem.*paed.* 2.8(p.195.24; M.8.468C); of high priest, *T.Lev.*8.2,9; of Enoch as prosecutor at Judgement *καὶ εἶχεν ἐπὶ τὴν κεφαλὴν αὐτοῦ τρεῖς σ. ... οἱ δὲ σ. ἐκαλοῦντο σ. μαρτυρίας T.Abr.*B 10(p.114.23ff.); of emperor, Philost.*h.e.*11.2(M.65.593C); of any king, Chrys.*Jud.et gent.*9(1. 570E); **6.** as mode of address *αἰτοῦμεν ὑμέτερον σ.* CEph.(431)*act.* 3(*ACO* 1.1.3 p.59.25; H.1.1476B); **7.** of nuptial crown *ἐκείνων τοὺς σ. ... ἡμῶν τὰς εὐχάς* Gr.Naz.*ep.*231(M.37.373C); *σ. ταῖς κεφαλαῖς ἐπιτίθενται, σύμβολον τῆς νίκης...ὅτι μὴ κατηγωνίσθησαν ὑπὸ τῆς ἡδονῆς* Chrys.*hom.9.2 in 1Tim.*(11.597B); Bas.Sel.*v.Thecl.*1(M.85. 512A); met., cf.Meth.*symp.*6.5(p.69.18; M.18.120C) cit. s. 3.a supra; ref. Church as bride of Christ, Gr.Nyss.*hom.7 in Cant.*(M.44.916C); also neut. plur., Thphn.*chron.*p.374(M.108.897A).

στεφανοφορέω, v. *στεφανηφορέω.*

στεφαν-όω, 1. *surround,* Clem.*paed.*3.2(p.238.1; M.8.560A); *δυοκαίδεκα κίονες ἐστεφάνουν* Eus.*v.C.*3.38(p.94.19; M.20.1097A); **2.** *crown* or *wreathe,* esp. with nuptial wreath, Gr.Naz.*ep.*231(M. 37.373C); Pall.*h.Laus.*8(p.27.2; M.34.1025A); *ὁ...πρῶτος γάμος... εἰκότως ἐστεφάνωται ὑπὸ τῆς ἱερωσύνης ὡς ἀνέπαφος...καὶ διὰ τοῦτο ὡς νικητὴς τῆς ἁμαρτίας κατεστεμμένος* Thdr.Stud.*epp.*1.50(M.99. 1092C); met., med., *be festive*; *be glad ∼οῦσθαι...καὶ χαίρειν καὶ ἀγάλλεσθαι* Chrys.*hom.31.4 in 1Cor.*(10.283E); of S. Paul *διαπαντὸς ἔδραμε ∼ούμενος ib.6.1*(10.44D); **3.** *crown* as victor, met. *ὁ γνήσιος ἀγωνιστὴς ἐπὶ τῷ παντὸς κόσμου θεάτρῳ ∼ούμενος* Clem.*prot.*1(p.4. 16; M.8.53C); ref. Christian contest; of God, *crown,* i.e. bestow Christian reward *τοὺς προαιρέσει* [sc. *τῆς κακίας*]...*ἀπεχομένους ∼οῦντος τοῦ θεοῦ* Chrys.*sac.*2.3(p.33.5; 1.374C); id.*hom.13.1 in Phil.* (11.298D); pass., in this life by graces and blessings *οὕτως ∼οῦται νικήσας τὴν φύσιν, καὶ κτησάμενος τὰς ἀρετάς* Ephr.1.48D; in life to come, *be rewarded with a crown, receive the Christian prize, 2Clem.* 20.2 cit. s. *γυμνάζω*; *σὺ οὖν ∼ωθεὶς κατ' αὐτῆς ἐλθὲ πρὸς τὴν ἐπιθυμίαν τῆς δικαιοσύνης, καὶ παραδοὺς αὐτῇ τὸ νῖκος ὃ ἔλαβες* Herm.*mand.*12. 2.5; *τὴν ἀληθινὴν νίκην κατὰ πάντων ∼ούμενος τῶν παθῶν* Clem.*str.*7.3 (p.14.24; M.9.424C); *ὁ ἀγὼν...συμμέτοχος τῆς ὑπομονῆς...οὐδὲ γὰρ δυνατὸν ἑτέραν χωρὶς θατέρας ∼ωθῆναι* Ant.Mon.*hom.*79(M.89.1668D); *ὁ οὖν φέρων τοὺς πειρασμοὺς γενναίως, ∼οῦται cat.Jac.*1:13(p.5.9); ref. resurrection of body *ἀρνήσεται...θανάτου νόμον τὸ σῶμα, τοῖς τῆς ἀθανασίας ∼ούμενον ἄνθεσι* Bas.Sel.*pasch.*1.2(M.28.1076B); *οὐ γὰρ ἂν...ἄλλου κατορθώσαντος* [sc. *σώματος*], *ἄλλο ἐστεφανοῦτο cat.2Cor.* 5:10(p.382.22); esp. of martyrdom, *M.Polyc.*17.1; Ephr.3.253B; *ταῖς ἀτελευτήτοις ∼οῦσθαι τιμαῖς* Cyr.*Juln.*6(6[2].204A); v. *στέφω*; **4.** *crown* or *honour,* flesh by Inc. *ἕτεροι...κατερυθριᾶν σκηπτόμενοι τὸ δόκειν ἀνθρώπῳ προσκυνεῖν, καὶ τὴν ἀπὸ γῆς σάρκα ταῖς ἀνωτάτω δόξαις ∼οῦν παραιτούμενοι* Cyr.*Thds.*(p.45.8; 5[2].4D) = id.*inc.unigen.* (5[1].679A); **5.** *bedeck, adorn γῆν παντοίοις φύτοις ἐστεφάνωσεν* Eus. *l.C.*6(p.208.16; M.20.1345A); *Lit.*ap.*Const.App.*8.12.12; *ἦν ὁ τόπος... ἀνθοφορῶν, ὅλος ἐστεφανωμένος V.Zos.*3(p.98.9); **6.** *solemnize a marriage for,* by imposing the nuptial crown, *marry εἴ τις ἐπίσκοπος... δίγαμον ∼ώσει, καθαιρείσθω* ‡Ath.*poenit.can.*1(p.457); Thdr.Stud. *epp.*2.201(M.99.1616B).

στεφάνωμα, τό, 1. *crown of victory,* met. *ὑμεῖς συμμαχήσαντος Χριστοῦ...τοῖς κατὰ τοῦ δράκοντος καταvθεμοῦσαι σ.* Meth.*symp.*8.13 (p.98.16; M.18.161A); **2.** *crowning of bride and bridegroom ἀμέτοχον εἶναι στεφανώματος τὴν δευτερογαμίαν* Thdr.Stud.*epp.*1.50(M.99. 1093B); *ib.*(1092A); *Euchol.*(p.314).

***στεφηδότης, ὁ,** *giver of the crown*; of God, *Hymn.*(*AS* 1 p.620); cf. *στεφανοδότης, στεφοδότης.*

***στεφηφορία, ἡ,** = *στεφανηφορία, wearing of a wreath* or *crown,* Germ.CP *or.*2(M.98.265B).

***στεφοδότης, ὁ,** *giver of the crown*; of God, *Mir.Geo.*4 suppl.(p.43. 5); cf. *στεφανοδότης, στεφηδότης.*

στέφ-ω, *encircle, crown, wreathe,* of God *ὁ...φυτοῖς τε διαφόροις στέψας* [sc. *τὴν γῆν*] *Lit.*ap.*Const.App.*8.12.12; ref. crown of martyrdom *τῶν οὖν...τὸν τῆς ὑπομονῆς καρπὸν τρυγησάντων στεψαμένων τε τὸν πάμμαχον ἀγῶνα A.Jo.*4(p.153.6); *νικήσας χάριτι Χριστοῦ...δεξιᾷ νικοποιῷ ∼θησόμενος* Jo.Mon.*hymn.Geo.*9(M.96.1400D).

[*]στηθαῖος, *breast-high,* Thphn.*chron.*p.331(M.108.797C).

στηθάριον, τό, portrait *bust,* Eustrat.*v.Eutych.*66(M.86.2349B); Jo.Mal.*chron.*7 p.172(M.97.276B); *ταβλίον ἐν ᾧ ὑπῆρχεν ἐν μέσῳ σ. ἀληθινόν, ἔχοντα* [l. *ἔχον*] *τὸν χαρακτῆρα τοῦ αὐτοῦ βασιλέως Ἰουστίνου ib.*17 p.413(612B); *Chron.Pasch.*p.309(M.92.785C); on seal of letter, Thphn.*chron.*p.207(M.108.532B).

***στηθήνιον, τό,** dim. of *στῆθος, breast,* of animals *δεῖν...βραχίονα καὶ σ. ἀποτάττεσθαι τῷ ἱερεῖ* Cyr.*ador.*11(1.396D); Thdt.*1Cor.*9:13(3. 221); of men *τὸ θυμοῦ γέμον σ. Max.invect.*(M.90.204C).

***στηθοδρομέω**, *crawl on the breast*; of the serpent, Geo.Pis.*hex.* 795(M.92.1495A, v.l. for στιχοδρομεῖ).

***στηθοκρουστέω**, *beat the breast*, *Hymn.*(*AS* 1 p.616).

***στηθομελής**, *melodious*; of the grasshopper, Gr.Naz.*carm.*1.2. 14.8(M.37.756A).

στῆθος, τό, *breast*; as seat of memory, *heart* τὰ τῆς ἀληθείας καὶ τὰ τῆς πλάνης γέγραπται ἐπὶ τὸ σ. τοῦ ἀνθρώπου *T.Jud.*20.3; *ib.*20.4; ἀπὸ σ. *by heart*, Socr.*h.e.*7.22.6(M.67.785A); *Didasc.Jac.*4.1(p.63.5); also ἐκ σ. Anast.S.*hod.*1(M.89.40A).

στήκω, pres. formed from ἕστηκα (perf. of ἵστημι), *stand*, *T.Sal.*1. 14; *A.Phil.*65(p.27.1); *stand still*, *A.Thom.*A 78(p.193.5); Anast.S. *synax.*(M.89.833B); *stand firm*, Ath.*v.Anton.*35(M.26.893C); Chrys. *hom.*4.2 *in Col.*(11.352E); Nil.*epp.*2.117(M.79.252A).

στήλη, ἡ, 1. *monument*; met., *memorial*, *record*, of deeds etc. ὁ δὲ τῷ πρακτικῷ καὶ θεωρητῷ βίῳ στήσας στήλην Or.*sel.in Ps.*15:1f.(M. 12.1209C); Cyr.H.*catech.*3.4; in writing ἐν στήλῃ γράμματος ἁγίου θρυλλούμενον...τὸν...Ἰώβ Mac.Mgn.*apocr.*3.12(p.82.2); of Tome of Leo κοινήν τινα σ. ὑπάρχουσαν κατὰ τῶν κακοδοξούντων *Symb. Chalc.*(p.129.15; H.2.456A); *Symb.CP*(681)*act.*18(H.3.1400A); of persons στῆλαι...ἔμψυχοι καὶ εἰκόνες τῆς...ἀρετῆς Thdt.*h.rel.*5(3.1164); of Cain ἔμπνους σ. Bas.Sel.*or.*4.3(M.85.73B); **2.** *statue*, *image*, pagan τῶν θεῶν ὑμῶν τὰς εἰκόνας, στήλας ἀναισχυντίας Clem.*prot.*4(p.47.9; M.8.160B); Christian τοῦ μηκέτι πλανᾶσθαι τοὺς σωζομένους εἰς τὰ εἴδωλα, ἀλλ' ἀντεικονίζειν τὴν θεανδρικὴν...χειροποίητον σ. τοῦ... Χριστοῦ Pamph.H.*can.*4(p.144.20).

***στηλητευτικός**, v. *στηλιτευτικός.

στηλίτευμα, τό, *denunciation*, *exposure* οἱ μάρτυρες...τῆς ἀληθείας κηρύγματα, τοῦ ψεύδους στηλιτεύματα Gr.Naz.*or.*24.4(M.35.1173D); Thdr.Stud.*epp.*2.77(M.99.1316C).

***στηλιτευμός, ὁ**, = foreg., ‡Nil.*perist.*9.1(tit.)(M.79.861D).

***στηλίτευσις, ἡ**, *placarding as infamous*; *denunciation*, Chrysipp. *enc.in Thdr.*(p.53.16); Jo.VI H.*v.Jo.D.*15(M.94.453B).

***στηλιτευτικός (*στηλητευτικός), 1.** *defamatory*, *abusive* οἱ... ἡμᾶς διαθρυλλήσαντες ἐπὶ κακοδοξίᾳ, καὶ ταῖς σ. ἐπιστολαῖς, ἃς συνέγραψαν καθ' ἡμῶν Bas.*ep.*223.3(3.339A; M.32.828A); **2.** esp. in titles of invectives, *denunciatory*, Cyr.*hom.div.*19 tit.(M.77.1105C); στηλητ-, Eustrat.*stat.anim.*16(p.467); Jo.V H.*icon.*tit.(M.96.1348C); abs. (sc. λόγος) *invective* κατὰ Ἰουλιανοῦ βασιλέως σ. πρῶτος Gr.Naz. *or.*4 tit.(M.35.532A).

στηλιτεύ-ω, 1. *inscribe on a stele*, *record*; esp. in scripture τὸ... τρόπαιον τοῦ σωτῆρος...γραφαῖς ἄνωθεν ἐστηλιτεύθη προφητικαῖς Or.*exc.in Ps.*15:1(M.17.109A); Eus.*h.e.*9.9.4(M.20.821A); ~ων [sc. S. Paul] αὐτοῦ τοὺς πόνους Pall.*h.Laus.*proem.(p.11.14; M.34.1004); met., *placard*, *publish abroad* ταῦτα...ὑπὲρ ἁγνείας ἐστηλιτεύσθω Meth.*symp.*7.9(p.80.9; M.18.137A); ~ει τὴν ἀνδρείαν ἐν ταῖς ἁπάντων ὄψεσι Gr.Naz.*or.*25.13(M.35.1217A); Nil.*epp.*2.158(M.79.276B); **2.** *expose*, *show up*, *denounce* ἡ ἀστραπὴ τυφλοὺς καὶ πεπωρωμένους ἐστηλίτευσε τοὺς Ἰουδαίους Or.*fr.*94 *in Jo.*(p.557.29); αὐτὸς Ματθαῖος τὸν ἑαυτοῦ ~ων βίον καὶ κατήγορος αὐτὸς ἑαυτοῦ γιγνόμενος Eus.*d.e.*3.5(p.126.1; M.22.213C); Βίκτωρ...~ει...διὰ γραμμάτων ἀκοινωνήτους πάντας...τοὺς ἐκεῖσε ἀνακηρύττων ἀδελφοὺς [sc. Quartodecimans] id.*h.e.*5.24.9(M.20.497B); Procl.CP *or.*10.1(M.65. 777B); freq. ref. heresy ταῦτα...πάντα [sc. passages of scripture] τὴν μὲν Ἀρειανὴν αἵρεσιν ~ει Ath.*Ar.*2.32(M.26.216B); Ἀρειομανῖται, οὓς ἤδη...ἐστηλιτεύσαμεν Epiph.*anc.*116(p.144.20; M.43.228D); Thdt. *ep.*117(4.1199); *convict* of ἑαυτοὺς τῆς ἀνοίας ~οντες Nil.*Magn.*30(M. 79.1005C).

στηλογραφέω, *make a statue of*, Thdr.Stud.*epp.*2.8(M.99.1133D).

στηλογραφία, ἡ, 1. inscribed *monument*, *memorial*, met. χαρακτὴρ καὶ τύπος ἀνδρείας, καθάπερ ἐν σ., ὁ Ἰὼβ τεθεὶς Didym.*Job* 2:6 (M.39.1129A); of see of Peter στήριγμα...ἀσάλευτον καὶ σ. διαφανῆ τῆς πίστεως...ἱδρύσατο...Χριστός Serg.C.*ep.*(H.3.729A); ἡ...εἰκὼν θριαμβός ἐστι, καὶ φανέρωσις, καὶ σ. εἰς μνήμην τῆς νίκης τῶν ἀριστευσάντων Jo.D.*imag.*2.11(M.94.1296B); μὴ...ἡ διὰ λόγου σ., τῆς ἐν πίναξιν ἀξιολογωτέρα; Thdr.Stud.*antirr.*1.17(M.99.348B); hence **2.** *indictment*, *exposure* of heresy ὑπομνήματα...καὶ σ. κατὰ τῆς Ἀρειανῆς αἱρέσεως Ath.*apol.sec.*90(p.168.6; M.25.409C); οὐ γάρ ἐστιν αὐτοῖς σκάνδαλον τὰ ῥήματα· ἀλλὰ λύπη, ὅτι σ. κατὰ τῆς ἀσεβείας αὐτῶν ἐστιν id.*syn.*34(p.261.23; M.26.752D); ἡ ἐν Νικαίᾳ σύνοδος...σ. κατὰ πάσης αἱρέσεώς ἐστιν id.*ep.Afr.*11(M.26.1048A); **3.** *titular inscription* of certain psalms εἰς σ....ἐστι καὶ ὁ παρὼν λόγος, οὐ μὴν κατὰ τοὺς αὐτοὺς εἴρηται χρόνους ταῖς πρὸ αὐτῆς Eus.*Ps.*59(M.23.552C); τὰ ἐκ τῆς ψαλμῳδίας μυστήρια, ἀνάμνησις, καὶ σ., καὶ ἐπιλήνιος Gr.Nyss. *mart.*1(M.46.749B); δηλοῖ...ἡ ἐπιγραφὴ πρὸς τῷ θανάτῳ καὶ τὴν νίκην. στήλη γὰρ οὐ τάφοις ἐπιτίθεται μόνοις, ἀλλὰ καὶ νικῶσιν ἀνίσταται... τοῦτο...σημαίνει ἡ τῆς σ. ἐπιγραφή Thdt.*Ps.*15:1(1.687); **4.** *painting* εἰκονικὴν σ. Steph.Diac.*v.Steph.*(M.100.1157A); μὴ λέγε ταύτας...σ., ἀλλ' εἰδωλογραφίας *ib.*(1157B).

***στηλογραφικός**, *recorded* τὰ προτυπώματα συμβόλοις παρεδίδοντο στηλογραφικοῖς Germ.CP *or.*1(M.98.236A).

στηλόω, 1. *make as a stele*; hence **a.** *make* or *enable to stand motionless* σάκκῳ...καὶ σποδῷ, καὶ δακρύοις...στάσει τε νυκτῶν ἡμερῶν...πίστις γὰρ ἐστήλωσε καὶ φόβος θεοῦ Gr.Naz.*carm.*1.2.10. 669(M.37.728A); τίς...μᾶλλον...ἀγρυπνίαις τὰς σάρκας ὑπέσπασεν, ἢ ψαλμῳδίαις ἑαυτὴν ἐστήλωσε παννύχοις τε καὶ ἡμερησίαις; id.*or.*18.9 (M.35.996B); **b.** *bring to a standstill* ἕκαστον...ἐν ᾧ κατείληφε τόπῳ τὸ σκότος ἐστήλωσε Gel.Cyz.*h.e.*3.10.11 bis; Geo.Pis.*Pers.*3.72(M.92. 1240A); **c.** pass., *be confirmed*, *established*, Eus.*Is.*22:20ff.(M.24. 252C); **d.** perf. ptcpl. pass., *garrison* (exeg. 2Reg.8:14, Hebr. נְצִבִים) ἔθηκεν ἐστηλωμένους, δηλοῖ ὡς ἐν ἑκάστῃ πόλει κατέστησε τοὺς φρουρούς. οὓς γάρ τινες καλοῦσιν ἐγκαθέτους, ἐστηλωμένους ὠνόμασεν Thdt.*qu.*23 *in 2Reg.*8:4ff.(1.421); **2.** pass. intrans., *be as a stele*; **a.** *stand motionless*, ‡Hipp.Th.*fr.*14(p.45.29); **b.** *be plain* or *obvious* πρὸ ὀφθαλμῶν ἐστηλωμένης τῆς ἐπὶ σοὶ ἀτρεκείας ‡Meth. *Sym.et Ann.*10(M.18.372B).

στήριγμα, τό, *support*, *stay*, met. στῦλος δὲ καὶ σ. ἐκκλησίας τὸ εὐαγγέλιον Iren.*haer.*3.11.8(M.7.885A); *T.Jud.*15.3 cit. s. ῥάβδος; σ. πόνων Clem.*paed.hymn.*15(p.291; M.8.681B); ὠφέλειαν κοινὴν καὶ σ. Gel.Cyz.*h.e.*1 proem.24(M.85.1197B); καρδίας σ. Niceph.Ur.*v.Sym.* 249(M.86.3213B).

στηριγμός, ὁ, *support*, *poise* οὐ γὰρ ἔχον τὸ σῶμα [sc. of a drunkard] τὸν ἐκ φύσεως στηριγμόν Bas.*hom.*14.5(2.127A; M.31.456A); *fixedness*, *firmness* εἰς πῆξιν καὶ σ. τοῦ Πληρώματος Iren.*haer.*1.2.5 (M.7.461A); of mind, *resolution*, *steadfastness*, †Bas.*bapt.*2.6.1(2. 659B; M.31.1596B); ἤτω σοι ὁ τοῦ δικαίου διωγμὸς διανοίας στηριγμός Chrys.*exp.in Ps.*3:1(5.1B); abs., *edification* ἵνα γένωνται [sc. ἄρτος καὶ ποτήριον] τοῖς ἐξ αὐτῶν μεταλαμβάνουσιν εἰς...σ. τῆς ἁγίας σου... ἐκκλησίας *Lit.Jac.*(p.206.17); εἰς ἡμέτερον σ. Gr.Mag.*dial.*(tr.Zach.) 1.10(M.*PL.*77.199B).

στηρικτικός, *pronounced*, of sayings Ἀναστασίου μοναχοῦ... διηγήματα ψυχωφελῆ καὶ σ. γενόμενα ἐν διαφόροις τόποις †Anast.S. *relat.*42 tit.(*OC* 3 p.61.2).

στήριξις, ἡ, *determination*, *steadfastness* τὸ ἅγιον πνεῦμα...ἐπλήρωσεν ἡμᾶς...χαρᾶς, καὶ δακρύων καὶ ἀγαλλιάσεως καὶ σ. †Anast.S.*relat.* 51(*OC* 3 p.74.21).

στιβάζ-ω, 1. *set*, *place* ἐὰν...εἰς ἀποθήκην στιβάσῃς οἶνον ἢ ἔλαιον Herm.*mand.*11.15; ~οντες ἐπὶ τραπέζης ἄρτους Epiph.*haer.*37.5 (p.57.13; M.41.648C); **2.** perf. ptcpl. pass., *decked out* in finery, *elaborately dressed* ποικίλως ἐστιβασμένην [sc. Ἐσθήρ] ὁ Ἀρταξέρξης θεασάμενος Cosm.Mel.*schol.*(M.38.521) in Gr.Naz.*carm.*1.2.29.291.

***στιβακός**, s.v.l., *well-trodden*; met., of sin, *habitual*; or poss. l. στιβαρᾶς *sturdy*, as hard to overcome ὦ ἀπὸ τῆς ἁμαρτίας τῆς στιβακῆς, ὅτι πρὸς τὴν φύσιν καὶ τὰς συνουσίας πεποίηκεν Ephr.1.136A.

***στιβαρέω**, sens. dub., ? met., *trample on*, *treat with contempt* or ? *strengthen oneself* against, *resist* μὴ ἀντιτείνῃς, μὴ στιβαρήσῃς ἐν ἐμοὶ τὸ ἀγαθόν Anast.S.*Ps.*6(M.89.1112C).

***στιβαρότης, ἡ**, *strength*; of a fringe, *heaviness*, *thickness*, Thdr. Stud.*poen.*1.110(M.99.1748C).

***στιβαρόω**, *strengthen*, Thdr.Stud.*epp.*1.34(M.99.1021B).

στιβάς, ἡ, *couch* for reclining at meals, Men.*exc.Rom.*8(p.195.1; M.113.888C).

***στιβασμός, ὁ**, *application of* stibium (powdered antimony) or *eye-shadow*, Ephr.1.32A.

***στίβος, τό**, ? *firmness*, of S. Peter ἐπιστήσας τῇ...προτέρᾳ ἑαυτοῦ προπετείᾳ ὠφελήθη...ὡς γενέσθαι στιβαρώτατος καὶ μακροθυμότατος· ὅπερ δηλοῦται [i.e. by the incident in Gal.2:14], τοῦ δὲ μετὰ στίβους σιωπήσαντος Or.*Jo.*32.5(p.434.19; M.14.753D).

***στιβόω**, *afflict*, ref. penance στιβώσας αὐτὸν ἡμέραις νηστειῶν κατὰ τὸ ἁμάρτημα *Const.App.*2.16.2; *ib.*2.17.5.

***στίβωσις, ἡ**, *discipline*, *punishment*, *Const.App.*6.20.6.

στίγμα, τό, *mark*;

A. ref. wounds of Christ, reproduced in Christians; **1.** exeg. Gal. 6:17 τὰ σ. τοῦ Χριστοῦ, δι' ὧν ἐστιν ἡμῖν ἡ σωτηρία, τὸ σῶμα βαστάζει. πῶς οὖν τὸ βαστάζον τὰ τῆς σωτηρίας σ., καὶ τὴν τῆς πίστεως ἔχον ζωήν, κατ' αὐτοὺς οὐ σῴζεται; ἢ γὰρ οὐδὲν ὠφελεῖται ἔχον τὴν τῆς πίστεως ζωὴν καὶ τὰ τοῦ Ἰησοῦ σ., ἤ, εἰ ἔστι διὰ τούτου ἡ σωτηρία, σάρξ ἐστιν ἡ σωζομένη Adam.*dial.*5.22(p.222.19ff.; M.11.1864C); εἰ οὖν ὑπομένει τις τὰ σ. τοῦ δεσπότου, μὴ οἰηθῇ ἔν τινι Mac.Aeg.*hom.*37.9(M.34. 756D); Gr.Nyss.*hom.*12 *in Cant.*(M.44.1033C) cit. s. στιγματίας; cf. ἦσαν δὲ κατ' ἐκεῖνον χρόνον πολλοὶ μὲν ἀποστολικοῖς χαρίσμασι διαπρέποντες, πολλοὶ δὲ τὰ σ. τοῦ κυρίου Ἰησοῦ, κατὰ τὸν θεῖον ἀπόστολον, ἐν τῷ σώματι φέροντες Thdt.*h.e.*1.7.3(3.755); **2.** ref. martyrs ἄλλοι διαφόροις καταξανθέντες αἰκίαις, ἔτι τὰ σ. τοῦ Χριστοῦ...ἐν τῷ σώματι περιφέρουσι CCP(381)*ep.*ap.Thdt.*h.e.*5.9.4(3.1028); Chrys.*hom.div.*10.2(12.389C); τίμια γὰρ τὰ σώματα,...ἐπειδὴ σ. βαστάζουσι διὰ τὸν Χριστόν id.*pan.Macc.*1.1(2.623B); id.*pan.Bern.*7(2.645D); ‡Chrys.*ascens.*1(3.777C); Ph.Carp.*Cant.*23:10(M.40.53B); ὑπὲρ σοῦ καταξιωθεῖσα παθημάτων καὶ σ. Bas.Sel.*v.Thecl.*1(M.85.536A); τοῖς ὑπὲρ Χριστοῦ ἀθλητικοῖς σ. Jo.D.*hom.*12.16(M.96.804B); ref. those who have long withstood persecution, but at last succumbed διὰ τὸ πολλὰ αὐτοὺς ἠθληκέναι καὶ ἐπὶ πολὺ ἀντιμαχέσασθαι (οὐ γὰρ κατὰ προαίρεσιν ἐν τούτῳ ἐληλύθασιν, ἀλλὰ καταπροδοθέντες ὑπὸ τῆς ἀσθενείας τῆς σαρκός), ἐπειδὴ καὶ στίγματα τοῦ Ἰησοῦ ἐνδείκνυνται ἐν τοῖς σώμασιν ἑαυτῶν Petr.I Al.*ep.can.*1(M.18.468B); **3.** ref. Christians in gen. ἡ ψυχὴ ἡ πιστὴ τὸ τῆς ἀληθείας λαβοῦσα σφράγισμα τὰ σ. τοῦ Χριστοῦ περιφέρει Clem.*exc.Thdot.*86(p.133.7; M.9.697B).

B. ref. marks of cross, miraculously imprinted on clothes, Gr. Naz.*or.*5.7(M.35.672B).

C. mark left by sin ἐχέτωσαν δὲ ἡμῶν καὶ Γαβαωνῖται πλέον, οὓς οὐδὲ εἰς ξυλοκόπους καὶ ὑδροφόρους οἶδ' ὅτι τὸ πνεῦμα τὸ ἅγιον παραδέχεται, μέχρις ἂν προσίωσι τοῖς ἱεροῖς μετὰ τοιούτων τοῦ βίου καὶ τοῦ λόγου στιγμάτων Gr.Naz.*or.*36.6(M.36.273A).

D. plur., ?*words of censure, condemnation* σάκραν...πλήρη στιγμάτων Thphn.*chron.*p.77(M.108.237B).

στιγματίας, ὁ, *one who bears (tattoo) marks*, esp. *branded slave*, met. ἡ θεία ῥάβδος...ἡ διὰ τοῦ πατάσσειν ἐνεργοῦσα τὴν ἴασιν, τὸ πνεῦμά ἐστιν...οὕτω γὰρ καὶ Παῦλος ὁ τῶν τοιούτων πληγῶν σ. τοῖς τραύμασι τούτοις ἐπαγαλλόμενος ἔλεγεν· ὅτι τὰ στίγματα τοῦ Χριστοῦ ἐν τῷ σώματί μου περιφέρω. δεικνὺς τὴν ἐν παντὶ κακῷ ἀσθένειαν, δι' ἧς ἡ κατὰ Χριστὸν δύναμις ἐν ἀρετῇ τελειοῦται Gr.Nyss.*hom.12 in Cant.*(M.44.1033C,D); οὐδὲν τοῦ καυχήματος τούτου μεῖζον ...ὡς στιγματίας τοῦ Χριστοῦ Chrys.*hom.1.1 in Phil.*(11.774E).

***στιγματίζω,** *indicate by a mark, mark*, *Chron.Pasch.*p.13(M.92.94).

στίζω, 1. *brand, mark*, esp. as a disgrace; met., *convict* ἐπιστολαὶ σ. ἡμᾶς καὶ στηλιτεύουσαι Bas.*ep.*226.1(3.346B; M.32.844B); τὸν πρότερον βίον ἑαυτοῦ στηλιτεύων, καὶ...ἑαυτὸν σ. Chrys.*hom.20.3 in Ac.*(9.166C); ἐκεῖνον σ. καὶ μεμφόμεθα Cael.*ep.Cyr.*(p.75.13; M.77.89C); Thdr.Stud.*epp.*2.70(M.99.1300C); **2.** *inscribe* ἡ μεμβράνη ἡ καλὴ [i.e. S. Basil] τῆς ἱερᾶς σοφίας ἡ ἄνωθεν στιχθεῖσα τὰ θεῖα χαράγματα Ephr.*enc.Bas.*21(p.146; στοιχειωθεῖσα 2.290B); **3.** *remark, notice*, Chrys.*hom.6.5 in Phil.*(11.241C); **4.** *mark with accents*, Epiph.*mens.*2(M.43.137B); **5.** perf. pass., met., *be spotted, stained* with sin, Bas.*hom.*13.8(2.122A; M.31.44A).

στιλβότης, ἡ, *brightness, brilliance*, Eus.Al.*serm.*21.17(M.86.444C); Andr.Caes.ap.*cat.Apoc.*21:20(p.575.28) for στιλπνότητα id.*Apoc.*67(M.106.436C).

στίλβωσις, ἡ, *making to shine, burnishing* of weapons, Bas.*hom. in Ps.*7(1.105B; M.29.245C).

στίλψις, ἡ, *brightness*, met. τὴν τῶν νοημάτων στίλψιν Or.*comm. in Mt.*12.39(p.157.5; M.13.1072C).

στίξ, ἡ, *row, rank*, or *file*; hence *quantity*, Nonn.*par.Jo.*4:38(M.43.781A); *ib.*2:14f.(764A); *ib.*8:51(821A).

στίξις, ἡ, *punctuation*, Anast.S.*hod.*3(M.89.88D).

[*]**στίφω,** v. στύφω.

στιχάριον ([*]**στοιχ-**), **τό,** dim. of στίχη; **1.** *thin tunic, shirt*, Gr. Naz.*test.*(M.37.393B); Pall.*h.Laus.*63(p.158.12; M.34.1235B); Leont.N.*v.Jo.Eleem.*23(p.48.8); worn by monks and hermits ἐν...τῷ ὑπνεῖν, ἕκαστον...τὸ στιχάριον αὐτοῦ ἔχειν, ἤτοι σακκίον κεκρυμμένον, ἵνα, ἄν που εὐχὴ νυκτός, ἕτοιμοι εὑρεθῶσιν ‡Ath.*syntag.*6.13(p.126; M.28.844A); worn with hair lining, Anton.Hag.*v.Sym.Styl.*5(p.24.17); †Gregent.*leg.Hom.*(M.86.572B); Jo.Mosch.*prat.*51(M.87.2908A); **2.** as eccl. vestment πλάττονται...κατηγορίαν...περὶ στιχαρίων λινῶν, ὡς ἐμοῦ κανόνα τοῖς Αἰγυπτίοις ἐπιβαλόντος Ath.*apol.sec.*60(p.140.17; M.25.357C); liturg., *alb*, ‡Bas.*h.myst.*17f.(p.262.3,7); σ. λέγεται διότι ἔστηκεν ἡ χάρις τοῦ θεοῦ ἐν αὐτῷ· τύπος δέ ἐστι τῆς σαρκὸς τοῦ Χριστοῦ ὡς λευκόν ‡Sophr.H.*liturg.*7(M.87.3988B); στοιχάριον *Lit. Chrys.*(pp.354.39,355.1); τὸ σ. λευκὸν ὄν, τῆς θεότητος τὴν αἴγλην ἐμφαίνει, καὶ τοῦ ἱερέως τὴν λαμπρὰν πολιτείαν ‡Germ.CP *contempl.*(M.98.393C).

***στιχαροφελόνιον (*-ώνιον), τό, 1.** ? *tunic and cloak*, i.e. *suit of clothes* or simply, *cloak* as worn over the στιχάριον, Jo.Mosch.*prat.*171(M.87.3037C); **2.** liturg., ? *alb and chasuble*, i.e. *vestments* or simply *chasuble* as worn over στιχάριον: εἰ ἔστι στιχαροφελώνιον πυροειδὲς...εἰ δὲ λευκά εἰσι, δεικνύουσι τὴν μεταμόρφωσιν ‡Sophr.H.*liturg.*7(M.87.3988B).

στιχηδόν ([*]**στοηχιδόν**), *in rows, in short lines*; of scripture, *in verses* ἔγωγε τὴν ἀποστολικὴν βίβλον στοηχιδὸν ἀναγνούς τε καὶ γράψας Euthal.Diac.*Ac.*(M.85.629A); τοῦτο...ἐγὼ...πεποιηκώς· στιχηδόν τε συνθεὶς τούτων τὸ ὕφος κατὰ τὴν ἐμαυτοῦ συμμετρίαν, πρὸς εὔσημον ἀνάγνωσιν *ib.*(633C).

στιχήρης, *composed in verse, in poetry*, of poetical books of OT τὰ λοιπὰ...σ. δι' ἐπῶν λέγεται τριμέτρων τε καὶ τετραμέτρων Eus.*p.e.*11.5(514B; M.21.853A); πέντε...σ. ...Ἰὼβ...τὸ Ψαλτήριον, Παροιμία Σαλομῶντος, Ἐκκλησιαστής, Ἆσμα ᾀσμάτων Epiph.*mens.*4(M.43.244B); Jo.D.*f.o.*4.17(M.94.1180B); v. στιχηρός.

στιχηρός ([*]**στειχηρός**), **1.** *composed in verse, in poetry*, of poetical books of OT βίβλων...ἱστορικῶν καὶ σ. Eus.*Is.*2:30(M.24.101A); id.*ecl.*proem.(M.22.1120D); Cyr.H.*catech.*4.35; Gr.Naz.*carm.*1.1.12.16(M.37.473A); Amph.*Seleuc.*271(M.37.1594A); οἱ ἱεροψάλται μελῳδήσουσι σ. τροπάριον συμφώνως *Lit.Jac.*(p.178.2); **2.** set out like poetry, *in verses* or *short paragraphs* ἐν εἴδει τῶν σ. Aët.*synt.* ap.Epiph.*haer.*76.11(p.352.10; M.42.536A); ἐν παλαιοτάτῳ βιβλίῳ σ. Pall.*h.Laus.*64(p.160.11; M.34.1251A); **3.** neut. as adv., *in versicles* ἐξεθέμην...στειχηρόν· τόδε τὸ τεῦχος Παύλου τοῦ ἀποστόλου· πρὸς ...εὐκατάληπτον ἀνάγνωσιν Euthal.Diac.*epp.Paul.*colophon(*TS* 3[3] p.3); **4.** neut. as subst., *sticheron, versicle* τῷ σαββάτῳ...τὰ ἀναστάσιμα σ. τρισσεύονται *Const.Stud.*17(M.99.1709C); variable with the season, *ib.*8(1708B); *ib.*5(1708A); τὸ σ. τοῦ στίχου *ib.*15(1709C); or τῶν ἀπὸ στίχου σ. *Euchol.*(p.4).

στιχίζω, 1. *divide into verses*, Euthal.Diac.*epp.Paul.*(M.85.720B); Anast.S.*hod.*proem.(M.89.36A); **2.** perh. = στοιχίζω *arrange systematically*, Max.*qu.Thal.*54(M.90.509A).

στιχισμός, ὁ, 1. *division into verses* or *short sections* for reading or recitation τὸν σ. τῶν βιβλίων...τῷ φίλῳ δῆλον...ἵνα μὴ ἔρψασα λήθη, σοὶ μὲν ζημίαν, αὐτῷ δὲ ψῆφον ἀγνωμοσύνης ἐπαγάγῃ Isid.Pel.*epp.*3.86(M.78.792B); **2.** *orderly arrangement* σύνθεσιν καὶ διαίρεσιν καὶ σ. Max.*qu.Thal.*54(M.90.509A).

***στιχοβαλτίδιον, τό,** ? *chain-belt* χλαμύδα τις φορῶν καὶ σ., δύο με ἀλύσεσιν ἐκρέμασεν *Mir.Artem.*6(p.7.16).

***στιχοδρομέω,** *crawl by successive, regular movements*; of the serpent, ref. Gen.3:14, Geo.Pis.*hex.*795(M.92.1495A).

στιχολογέω, *recite (the Psalms)* ἐστιχολόγει ἐν ἑαυτῷ Δαυιτικοὺς ψαλμοὺς Cyr.S.*v.Sab.*73(p.178.11); ἐστιχολόγουν ὅλον τὸν ἄμωμον id.*v.Cyriac.*8(p.227.6); *M.Seb.*6(p.176.19); Thdr.Stud.*epp.*2.202(M.99.1617A); abs., Jo.Mosch.*prat.*106(M.87.2965A,C).

στιχολογία, ἡ, *recitation (of Psalms)*, Jo.Jej.*doct.*4(p.230); *Const. Stud.*33(M.99.1717A); abs., Jo.Mosch.*prat.*25(M.87.2869D); *Euchol.*(p.2).

***στιχοποιός, ὁ,** *versifier*; of Menander, Tat.*orat.*24(p.26.13; M.6.860A).

στίχος, ὁ, *line* of prose or *poetry*; **1.** *line* followed in writing χρῶ τοῖς σ. ὀρθῶς Bas.*ep.*334(3.452A; M.32.1077A); **2.** *verse*, of Psalter σ. ἐκ τῆς ψαλμῳδίας Gr.Nyss.*Thdr.*(M.46.745B); στεῖχον †Anast.S.*relat.*20(*OC* 2 p.72.6); liturg. σ. τοῦ κοινωνικοῦ *Chron.Pasch.*p.390(M.92.1001C); **3.** *series* of vices, Chrys.*hom.11.8 in Mt.*(7.159A); **4.** *stipulation, arrangement*, *Chron.Pasch.*p.394(M.92.1009B); **5.** *dot* >· *diple* περὶ στίχον. *hanc pri[m]us Leogoras Syracusanus posuit Homericis versibus ad separationem Olympi a caelo*, Isid.H.*etym.*1.21.14.

[*]**στοηχιδόν,** v. στιχηδόν.

στοιβάζ-ω, 1. *heap, pack, stuff* (ref. Cant.2:5), Gr.Nyss.*hom.4 in Cant.*(M.44.848C); *ib.*6(889A); met., *overload* δόγμασι...ἐστοιβασμένης τῆς διανοίας Synes.*Dion* 4(p.244.20; M.66.1124D); **2.** pass. intrans., *crowd, throng* ἰχθύες...~ονται εἰς τὸ στόμα...τοῦ...κήτους ‡Petr.I Al.*phys.*20(p.51).

στοιβή, ἡ (A), 1. *packing, filling*, ref. Cant.2:5 οὐ...χόρτῳ καὶ καλάμῃ...ἀλλὰ στοιβὴ τῆς τοῦ οἴκου στέγης τὰ μῆλα γίνεται Gr.Nyss.*hom.4 in Cant.*(M.44.848D); **2.** *heap, pile* σ. ξύλων Gr.Mag.*dial.*(tr. Zach.)4.31(M.*PL*.77.371A).

[*]**στοίβη, ἡ (B),** for στίβη, *stibium* (powdered antimony); ref. Jer.4:30, Petr.II Al.*encycl.*2(M.33.1277B).

στοΐδιον, τό, *portico, porch*, CAnt.(445)*act.*(*ACO* 2.1.3 p.69.8; H.2.580A).

[*]**στοιχάριον, τό (A),** v. στιχάριον.

***στοιχάριον, τό (B),** dim. of στίχος (στοῖχος) *verse*, Jo.Nic.*nativ.*(M.96.1445C) cit. s. τροπάριον.

[*]**στοιχειόδης,** v. στοιχειώδης.

***στοιχειολάτρης, ὁ,** *worshipper of the elements*, ‡Ath.*synops.*(M.28.376B).

στοιχεῖον, τό, A. ultimate component into which anything is divisible; **1.** *simple sound* from which syllable is built up, then *letter* of alphabet; books of OT as containing the ABC of religious knowledge being same in number, Or.*fr.3 in Lam.*tit.(p.236.9); **2.** *element* of matter; created by God, *Diogn.*8.2; four in number like four feet, ‡Proc.G.*Pr.*23:1f.(M.87.1449A); or four virtues, *ib.*(1449B); same number as gospels and the virtues, Max.*ambig.*(M.91.1245A); denoted by the four beasts, Andr.Caes.*Apoc.*10(M.106.256D); **3.** very freq. in sense 1 but also in sense 2 and as *ultimate principle*, a leading feature of Marcosian heresy, Iren.*haer.*1.14f.(M.7.596A–713A) passim; *Μάρκος...τῶν εἰκοσιτεσσάρων σ. βούλεται τὰ πάντα ἡγεῖσθαι* Epiph.*anac.*34(p.1.7; M.41.577C); cf. *φεύξονται Μαρκίωνος τὸν ἐκ στοιχείων καὶ ἀριθμῶν θεόν* Gr.Naz.*or.*33.16(M.36.233C).

B. more generally, *component part, element, principle*; hence **1.** *rudiments, elements* of education; esp. religious knowledge, Or.*Jo.*13.5(p.230.14; M.14.405C) cit. s. *γνῶσις*; *ταῦτα* [sc. Heb.6:2] *στοιχεῖα ἐκάλεσε τῶν λογίων· καθάπερ...τοῖς μειρακίοις ὁ γραμματιστὴς πρῶτον ὑποδείκνυσι τῶν σ. τοὺς χαρακτῆρας* Thdt.*Heb.*6:1f.(3.577); denoting knowledge of the incarnate life of Christ, Chrys.*hom.8.3 in Heb.*(12.86C); of Jewish law *ἀπὸ τῶν νομικῶν σ. ἐπὶ τὴν εὐαγγελικὴν τελειότητα* Or.*hom.12.13 in Jer.*(p.100.10; M.13.396D); *τὰ σ. ... τουτέστι, νουμηνίας καὶ σάββατα* Chrys.*comm.in Gal.*4:3(10.704E); *σ. τοῦ κόσμου τὰς νομικὰς παρατηρήσεις ἐκάλεσεν* Thdt.*Gal.*4:3(3.381); cf. (exeg. Gal.4:3) *elementa, primas scilicet litteras legis*, Tert.*adversus Marcionem* 5.4(M.*PL.*2.477A); **2.** *heavenly body*, prob. included with the four elements in *Diogn.*7.2; *ἡλίου τε καὶ σελήνης, καὶ τῶν λοιπῶν σ. ἢ φωστήρων* Arist.*apol.*3.2; Just.*dial.*23.3(M.6.525D); *οὐ παραλιπόντες προσκυνεῖν...θεὸν ἐπὶ τὰ πτωχὰ καὶ ἀσθενῆ σ. καταπίπτομεν, τῷ ἀπαθεῖ ἀέρι κατ' αὐτοὺς τὴν παθητὴν ὕλην προσκυνοῦντες· ...οὐδὲ παραλιπὼν τὸν θεὸν τὰ σ. θεραπεύω...εἰ γὰρ καὶ καλὰ ἰδεῖν τῇ τοῦ δημιουργοῦ τέχνῃ* Athenag.*leg.*16.2,3(M.6.921A,B); *στοιχείων τὸν εὔτακτον δρόμον* Thphl.Ant.*Autol.*1.6(M.6.1033A); Epiph.*haer.*66.23(p.51.18; M.42.69A); of sun and moon *ἀνέστρεψεν...σὺν τῷ ἡλίῳ καὶ ἡ σελήνη...ἵνα μὴ ἡ σύγκρουσις τῶν δύο σ. γένηται* Hipp.*Dan.*1.8.5(M.10.629D); Thdt.*Is.*30:26(p.125.1; 1.307); of the moon, Gr.Nyss.*anim.et res.*(M.46.33A); Chrys.*hom.57.3 in Mt.*(7.579Ef.); *συμφθίνειν οἰόμενοι τῷ σ. τὰ καθ' ἡμᾶς* Cyr.*ador.*6(1.207A); of the sky, the heavens *οὐρανοὶ μὲν οὐκ αὐτὸ τὸ σ., ἀλλ' οἱ ταῖς ἄνω μοναῖς ἐνδιαιτώμενοι* id.*Is.*4.4(2.672C); mutable and perishable, Arist.*apol.*2(p.101.19); created by God, Just.*2apol.*5.2(M.6.452B); and serving him, Thphl.Ant.*Autol.*1.4(M.6.1029B); met., *man of distinction, great light* *κατὰ τὴν Ἀσίαν μεγάλα σ. κεκοίμηται* Polycr.ap.Eus.*h.e.*3.31.3(M.20.280B); *ib.*5.24.2(493B); **3.** *demonic principle* or *power* *ἡμεῖς ἐσμεν στοιχεῖα κοσμοκράτορες τοῦ σκότους* *T.Sal.*8.2(M.122.1328B); *ib.*18.1f.(1341B); **4.** *sign* of the cross *ὁ...σωτήρ, οὗ τὸ σ. ἐν τῷ μετώπῳ ...τοῦτο δὲ τὸ σημεῖον σταυρός* *T.Sal.*17.4(M.122.1341A).

στοιχει-όω, **1.** *instruct in the basic principles*; pass., *be grounded* in the elements; **a.** of general education *~ωθῆναι καὶ οὕτως νοῆσαι τὰ ...σημαινόμενα διὰ τῶν στοιχείων* *Dial.Ath.et Zacch.*13(p.10); *τὴν πρώτην τῶν ἄρτι ~ουμένων εἰσαγωγήν* Eus.*h.e.*6.15(M.20.553B); *~οῦται παρ' αὐτοῦ τὴν τῶν γραμμάτων παράδοσιν* Eustrat.*v.Eutych.*8(M.86.2284B); **b.** of religion *~ωθῆναι καὶ εἰσαχθῆναι εἰς θεοσέβειαν* Or.*hom.19.15 in Jer.*(p.173.32; M.13.496C); *φόβῳ ~ουμένους, καὶ καθαιρουμένους, καὶ...λεπτυνομένους, εἰς ὕψος αἴρεσθαι* Gr.Naz.*or.*39.8(M.36.344A); *~ῶν καὶ διδάσκων τὰ ἐκκλησιαστικὰ κηρύγματα* Socr.*h.e.*3.9.9(M.67.405A); Gr.Agr.*Eccl.*6.1(M.98.977D); of pre-baptismal instruction *δύο τάγματα...τὸ μὲν εἰσέτι ~ούμενον, τὸ δὲ ἤδη διὰ τοῦ λουτροῦ πεφωτισμένον* Eus.*d.e.*2.3(p.77.26; M.22.140B); *τοὺς κατηχουμένους ~ώσαντες βαπτίσατε* *Const.App.*6.18.1; *ib.*7.25.7; of the 'practical' Christian as instructed in *σωμάτικα* opp. *πνευματικά*, Or.*Jo.*1.7(9; p.13.2; M.14.37A); *ib.*6.43(26; p.152.26; 276B); exeg. Is.14:1 *τὸ μὲν γὰρ Ἰακὼβ ἐπὶ τοῦ ἔτι ~ουμένου καὶ σωματικοῦ λαμβάνεται, τὸ δὲ Ἰσραὴλ ἐπὶ τοῦ κρείττονος καὶ πνευματικοῦ* †Bas.*Is.*277(1.590E; M.30.605C); *ib.*204(532C; M.472B); **c.** of monastic life, Pall.*h.Laus.*1(p.16.16; M.34.1010B); Jo.Clim.*scal.*27(M.88.1112B); **d.** *instruct*, not nec. limited to first principles *εὐχαῖς...ἡμᾶς ὑποστηρίζειν καὶ συμβουλαῖς ~οῦν* Maxm.*ep.Cyr.*(p.71.20; M.77.149B); Dion.Ar.*d.n.*3.2(M.3.681A); **2.** *reduce to elements* *τῶν ἐστοιχειωμένων κόσμου μερῶν* ‡Eust.*hex.*(M.18.737C); Bas.Sel.*or.*5.2(M.85.81A); **3.** in a magical sense, *transform*, *Apoc.Adam* day 4(p.140); *ib.*night 2(p.142); *mix* elements *τὴν ξηρὰν ὑγρῷ ~ώσεις αἰθάλην* Geo.Pis.*hex.*1572(M.92.1557A); **4.** for *στίζω*, v.s.v.

στοιχειώδης ([*]-όδης), **1.** *elemental, pertaining to the elements, of the nature of an element* *χωρὶς...χολῆς ἄνθρωπον εἶναι οὐ δυνατόν, ταύτης δὴ λέγω τῆς σ.* Chrys.*hom.15.2 in Eph.*(11.111D); *τὸν δ' στοιχειώδη τε καὶ ὑλικὸν ἀριθμόν* Max.*ambig.*(M.91.1397D); *material* *ἀρχὴ... στοιχειώδης* Dion.Ar.*d.n.*4.10(M.3.705D); *literal* *ὁ σ. λόγος* opp. *τοῦ... ἀγράφως ἐν πνεύματι κατὰ νοῦν μηνυομένου...τελεωτέρου λόγου* Max.*ambig.*(M.91.1252D); **2.** in religion; **a.** *elementary, introductory*; of Greek philosophy, Clem.*str.*6.8(p.463.14; M.9.284C); *ib.*6.15(p.490.28; 341A); of Thphl. Ant.'s *Autol.* *σ. συγγράμματα* Eus.*h.e.*4.24(M.20.389B); ref. Ps.33:15 *σ. αἱ παραινέσεις* Bas.*hom.in Ps.*33(1.153B; M.29.376A); of Jewish Law *οἷς ὁ στοιχειόδης νόμος ἐκράτει τὸν ἔτι νήπιον Ἰσραήλ* Gr.Naz.*or.*6.4(M.35.728A); Areth.*Apoc.*11:1(M.106.648A); **b.** *fundamental* *στοιχειωδεστέραν...τὴν πίστιν* Clem.*str.*2.6(p.129.26; M.8.965C).

στοιχειωδῶς, *as elemental*, Gr.Nyss.*hom.opif.*3.1(M.44.133C); id. *anim.et res.*(M.46.44B).

στοιχείωσις, ἡ, 1. *arrangement of letters* in the alphabet *εἰκόσι... καὶ δύο κατὰ τὴν τοῦ ἀλφαβήτου παρ' Ἑβραίοις σ.* Epiph.*mens.*3(M.43.244A); id.*haer.*66.13(p.35.1; M.42.48C); hence, *couplet, verse* in an acrostic psalm or canticle, Or.*fr.65 in Lam.*(p.262.15); *spelling* as the rudiments of education, v. 3 infra (cf. Eng. ABC) *ὡς...τὰ κβ' στοιχεῖα εἰσαγωγὴ δοκεῖ εἶναι εἰς τὴν σοφίαν καὶ τὰ θεῖα διδάγματα τοῖς χαρακτῆρσι τούτοις ἐντυπούμενα τοῖς ἀνθρώποις· οὕτω σ. ἐστιν εἰς τὴν σοφίαν τοῦ θεοῦ, καὶ εἰσαγωγὴ εἰς τὴν γνῶσιν τῶν ὄντων τὰ κβ' θεόπνευστα βιβλία* Or.*sel.in Ps.*1 ap.*philoc.*3(p.41.3; M.12.1084A); **2.** *elemental matter, material* *οὐκ αὐταὶ...δραστικαί τινές εἰσι, στοιχείωσις δέ ἐστι τῆς τῶν δαιμόνων μοχθηρίας* Tat.*orat.*17(p.19.4; M.6.844A); *elementary* or *basic principle* *στοιχείωσις αὐτοῖς* [sc. demons] *ἡ ζώωσις ἦν* *ib.*9(p.9.24; 825A); Dion.Ar.*d.n.*3.2(M.3.681A); **3.** *elementary instruction*, esp. in religion (ref. Heb.6:1) *τὸν τῆς ἀρχῆς τοῦ Χριστοῦ λόγον, τουτέστι τῆς σ.* Or.*princ.*4.1.7(p.304.14; M.11.356B); ref. Pr.8:22 *ἀρχὴν...ὁδῶν λέγει ἐπειδὴ ἡ τοιαύτη σοφία ἀρχή τις καὶ...σ. τῆς ἐπὶ θεὸν γνώσεως γίνεται* Ath.*Ar.*2.80(M.26.316C); ref. Pr.1:7 *ἡ διὰ τοῦ φόβου σ.* Bas.*reg.fus.*4(2.341B; M.31.920A); of Law, Cyr.*ador.*2(1.62D); **4.** *introduction, preparation* *στοιχειώσεως μὲν ἔχειν λόγον τὴν πίστιν, προκοπῆς δὲ τὴν ἐλπίδα, τελειότητος δὲ τὴν ἀγάπην* Or.*comm.in Rom.*4:18(p.361; cf.M.14.981A); freq. of literary works: of Hermas' *Shepherd* *στοιχειώσεως εἰσαγωγικῆς* Eus.*h.e.*3.3.6(M.20.217B); of Eus.*p.e.* in rel. to *d.e.*, id.*p.e.*1.1(4B; M.21.28A); of Ath.*inc.* *πρὸς στοιχείωσιν καὶ χαρακτῆρα τῆς κατὰ Χριστὸν πίστεως* Ath.*inc.*56.1(M.25.196A).

στοιχειωτικός, *elementary*; hence *instructional* *ὁ αἰσθητὸς κόσμος σ. ἐστι κατὰ φύσιν τῶν πέντε αἰσθήσεων* Max.*ambig.*(M.91.1248A).

στοιχ-έω, 1. in action, *fall into line with, conform to* *~οῦντας τῷ κατὰ τὸ εὐαγγέλιον λόγῳ Ἰησοῦ Χριστοῦ* *M.Polyc.*22; *τῷ εὐαγγελικῷ ~ήσαντες κανόνι* Clem.*str.*3.9(p.226.13; M.8.1168C); Bas.*jud.*8(2.223B; M.31.676B); in thought, *agree with, assent to* *~ῶ ταῖς σαῖς ἀποφάσεσιν* Adam.*dial.*1.1(p.2.23; M.11.1717A); ‡Ath.*Apoll.*1.8(M.26.1108A); *ὁμοίως τῷ εὐαγγελίῳ ~είτωσαν αἱ ἐκ νόμου καὶ προφητῶν ἑρμηνεῖαι* *Const.App.*2.5.4; *be consistent* *εἴπερ ἑαυτῷ διέγνω ~εῖν* Max.*ep.*15(M.91.569A); *τούτων οὕτω ~ούντων* *this being so*, Const. ap.Thdt.*h.e.*1.10.11(3.773); cf.Eus.*v.C.*3.20(p.87.9; M.20.1080A); **2.** *satisfy* *συνετὸς μοναχὸς τὴν χρείαν ~ήσει τοῦ σώματος* Ephr.3.478D; *V.Alex.Acoem.*32(p.682.19); **3.** *be satisfied, contented* *~ήσας τῇ πικρότητι τοῦ ὕδατος* Pall.*h.Laus.*39(p.124.9; M.34.1195B); Dor.*doct.*5.1(M.88.1676A); *τῇ αὐταρκείᾳ ~ῆσαι* Max.*carit.*4.49(M.90.1060A); **4.** *stipulate*, Gr.Mag.*dial.*(tr.Zach.)3.37(M.*PL.*77.310C); Thphn.*chron.*p.282(M.108.696A); *negotiate, fix* terms, *ib.*p.154(417A).

στοίχημα, τό, *what has been agreed upon* or *approved*; *agreed statement*, Anast.S.*hod.*10(M.89.149C); *pact*, Thphn.*chron.*p.281(M.108.693A).

στοιχίζω, *drive into a trap* (hunting net), met. *τῶν δὲ Ἰουδαίων συμφυγόντων...ὥσπερ εἰς κοινὴν παγίδα τὴν Ἱερουσαλήμ,...ὑπὸ τοσούτων κακῶν ἐστοιχισμένων αὐτῶν* ‡Chrys.*pasch.*7.4(8.282D).

στολή, ἡ, *clothes*; **1.** *garment, robe*; met., **a.** of *σωφροσύνη*, Clem.*paed.*3.1(p.236.3; M.8.556A); *σ. πνευματικὴ τῆς σωματικῆς ἀφῃρημένης, ἁρμόζει ψυχῇ χωριζομένῃ τοῦ σώματος* Proc.G.*Num.*20:24(M.87.856B); of light *φωτεινὴν σ. ἀντὶ τῆς γυμνότητος ἐξυφαίνει μοι* [sc. the Cross] Germ.CP *or.*1(M.98.229C); **b.** of Christ's human body *διὰ...τῆς ἁγίας αὐτοῦ σ., ἣν ἐκ παρθενικῶν αἱμάτων κατασκευασάμενος, διὰ τοῦ πνεύματος μυστικῶς ἑαυτῷ περιέπηξεν* Andr.Cr.*or.*7(M.97.949A); esp. exeg. Gen.49:11 *αἵματι σταφυλῆς...τὴν σ. αὐτοῦ πλύνειν ἔφη, ὡς τοῦ αἵματος αὐτοῦ οὐκ ἐξ ἀνθρωπείου σπέρματος γεγεννημένου, ἀλλ' ἐκ θελήματος θεοῦ* Just.*dial.*63.2(M.6.620C); *ib.*76.2(653A); **c.** of human nature of Christ *δικάσει δὲ τὴν τῆς ἡμετέρας φύσεως στολὴν περικείμενος· ἀόρατος γὰρ ἡ τῆς θεότητος φύσις* Thdt.*affect.*11(p.293.25; 4.1006); *ὁ ἐμὸς υἱός...στολὴν ἀνθρώποις ὁμοιοπαθῆ περιθήσεται· σάρκα περιβαλεῖται παρὰ ἀνθρώπων ὑπὲρ ἀνθρώπων* Bas.Sel.*or.*13.3(M.85.180C); *πυροειδὴς ἡ σ. τοῦ ἱερέως ...ἐμφαίνοντος τὴν βαφεῖσαν τῆς σαρκὸς τοῦ Χριστοῦ σ. ἐν αἵμασι* ‡Bas.*h.myst.*14(p.261.16); *δεικνύντος τοῦ ἀρχιερέως διὰ τῆς σ. αὐτοῦ τὴν τῆς σαρκὸς τοῦ Χριστοῦ σ. τὴν ἐρυθρὰν καὶ αἱματώδη* *ib.*

33(p.265.16); esp. exeg. Gen.49:11 *τουτέστι διὰ τοῦ ἁγίου πνεύματος καὶ τοῦ λόγου τῆς ἀληθείας καθαριεῖ τὴν σάρκα, ὅπερ ἐμφαίνει, τὴν σ.* Hipp.*fr.24 in Gen.*49:11(p.60.10; M.10.589C); cf.id.*antichr.*11 (p.10.14; M.10.736C); **d.** of Church *σ. ἐκάλεσε τὸ ἅγιον πνεῦμα τοὺς δι' αὐτοῦ ἄφεσιν ἁμαρτιῶν λαβόντας, ἐν οἷς ἀεὶ δυνάμει μὲν πάρεστι, καὶ ἐναργῶς δὲ παρέσται ἐν τῇ δευτέρᾳ...παρουσίᾳ* Just.*dial.*54.1(M. 6.593C); id.*1apol.*32.7f.(p.51.21ff.; M.6.380B); **2.** *vestment*; **a.** of Jewish priest *ἑτοίμασον τὴν σ. τοῦ ἁγιάσματός σου Pss.Sal.*11.8; *T.Lev.*8.2; *ib.*8.5; and high priest, Or.*Cels.*5.50(p.54.23; M.11.1260B); Eus.*h.e.*1.6.10(M.20.89A); Cosm.Ind.*top.*3(M.88.172D); **b.** Christian; of vestment presented by Const. to Macarius of Jerusalem in which to administer baptism, Thdt.*h.e.*2.27.2(3.894); of vestment whether for baptism, *Euchol.*(p.287); or eucharist *ἡ δὲ σ. σημαίνει, ὅ τι ἐξ ἐρίου ἦν, τὸ πλανηθὲν πρόβατον ὃ ἤγαγεν ἐπὶ τῶν ὤμων ὁ Χριστός* Jo.Jej.*liturg.*(p.441); *ἡ σ. τοῦ ἱερέως ἐστὶ κατὰ τὸν ποδήρη Ἀαρών, τουτέστιν ἱμάτιον ὅ ἐστιν ἱερατικὸν τὸ μέχρι τῶν ποδῶν ἔνδυμα τὸ τιμιώτερον...ἐστὶ* [sc. *ἡ σ.*] *πυροειδὴς κατὰ τὸν προφήτην* [Is.63:1f.] ‡Bas.*h.myst.*14(p.261.8ff.); *Lit.Praesanct.*(p.345.2); *Lit.Chrys.*(p.399. 7); **3.** *robe* of baptism, both lit. and met., *A.Barn.*13(p.297.9f.); *παρασκευάσασθε· οὐχ ἱματίων λαμπροτάτας ἐνδυσάμενοι στολάς, ἀλλὰ ψυχῆς εὐσυνείδητον εὐλάβειαν* Cyr.H.*catech.*3.3; *τὴν ἁγίαν...σ. ἣν αὐτὸν ἡ τοῦ ἁγίου βαπτίσματος ἠμφιάσατο χάρις* †Jo.D.*B.J.*30(M.96.1140D).

στολίζω, med., *put on*; met., *clothe oneself in, assume*, ref. Inc. *σῶμα ἔμψυχον ἐκ τῆς...ἀειπαρθένου καὶ ὄντως θεοτόκου Μαρίας, ἀσπόρως ἐστολίσω Lit.Jac.*(*NBP* 10² p.106); Gnost. *σαρκίον τῷ λόγῳ...τὸ πνευματικὸν σπέρμα, τοῦτο στολισάμενος κατῆλθεν ὁ σωτήρ* Clem.*exc.Thdot.*1(p.105.7; M.9.653A).

στολισμός, ὁ, 1. *equipping, dressing; mode of dressing* or *wearing*, Ath.*gent.*18(M.25.37A); Pall.*h.Laus.*proem.(p.14.20; M.34.1010); **2.** *equipment, attire, dress ὃς ἐὰν διαθείη μοι κοσμικὸν σ.* Ephr.2. 234F; Chrys.*hom.2.5 in Ac.princ.*(3.68C); Andr.Cr.*imag.*(M.97. 1304A); met. *ψυχῆς...στολισμός* Nil.*epp.*2.74(M.79.233A).

στόμα, τό, 1. *mouth*, as organ of speech; esp. of Christ as mouth of God, Ign.*Rom.*8.2 cit. s. *ἐν*; of Son *σ. γὰρ τοῦ θεοῦ ὁ υἱός. διὸ καὶ θεὸς ὤν, λόγος προσαγορεύεται* Ph.Carp.*Cant.*1(M.40.36A); of mouth of God as source of what proceeds from him *ἡμεῖς...οὐκ ἐκ γαστρὸς τῆς ὑποστάσεως ἐγεννήθημεν, οὕτω καὶ τὰ ἐκπορευόμενα πνεύματα...οὐκ ἐκ τοῦ σ. τῆς ὑποστάσεως αὐτοῦ εἰσι. τὸ δὲ πνεῦμα τὸ ἅγιον ἐκ τοῦ σ. τῆς ὑποστάσεώς ἐστι πνεῦμα* ‡Ath.*dial.Trin.*1.19(M. 28.1145Cf.); *ὁ υἱὸς...ἐκ τῆς ὑποστάσεως...καὶ ἐκ γαστρὸς εἴρηται· καὶ τὸ πνεῦμα...ἐκ τῆς ὑποστάσεως...καὶ πνεῦμα στόματος εἴρηται· ἵνα ἡ διαφορὰ μὴ κατὰ τὸν ἐκ τῆς ὑποστάσεως λόγον γένηται, ἀλλὰ κατὰ τὸν ἐκ γαστρὸς καὶ σ. ... ἡ ὑπόστασις τὸ εἶναι σημαίνει· ἡ γαστὴρ τὸ γεννητικόν· τὸ σ. τὸ διδακτικόν ib.*1.19f.(1148A); Bas.*hom.in Ps.*32(1. 135E; M.29.333B) cit. s. *ἐκπορεύω*; *ἡμῶν ψυχὴ...διὰ τοῦ θείου σ. γεννηθεῖσα, ἐξελθοῦσα* Anast.Ant.*serm.*3(M.89.1164D); hence *utterance, words*, of vocal prayer *τῇ διὰ στόματος εὐχῇ* Clem.*str.*7.7(p.37.9; M. 9.469B); of lip service *οὐχ ἵνα σαίνωμεν ἀλλήλους ἐν τῷ σ.* id.*paed.* 3.11(p.281.18; M.8.661A); introducing quotations *ἐκ σ. as spoken by ὡς γέγραπται ἐν βίβλῳ Βαρουχ ἐκ στόματος Ἰερεμίου* Gel.Cyz.*h.e.* 2.16.11(M.85.1261D); **2.** *mouthpiece σ. κυρίου τοὺς προφήτας* Or.*fr.38 in Jer.*1:18(p.253.2); of S. Peter in rel. to disciples, Chrys.*hom. in Mt.18*:23(3.4E); *ὁ κορυφαῖος τῶν μαθητῶν, τὸ σ. τῶν ἀποστόλων* Vict.*Mc.*8:29(p.346.9); of deacon in rel. to bishop *ἔστω ὁ διάκονος τοῦ ἐπισκόπου ἀκοὴ καὶ ὀφθαλμὸς καὶ σ. Const.App.*2.44.4; of bishops *σ. θεοῦ εἶναι τοὺς ἐπισκόπους ib.*2.28.9; of Christ *τὰ...ἡμέτερα οἰκειούμενος στόμα τῆς φύσεως γέγονεν* Thdt.*Heb.*2:6(3.556); of H. Ghost *τὸ...σ. κυρίου* Clem.*prot.*9(p.62.8; M.8.192D); **3.** *beak*, Hier.*v.Paul.*B (p.21.16); **4.** fig., of persons *ἀπεκρίθη...τὸ ἀγγελικὸν ἐκεῖνο σ.* Leont.N.*v.Jo.Eleem.*2(p.8.12); *τὸ ἱερὸν ἐκεῖνο σ. ib.*45(p.92.16).

στομαχ-έω (*-άω*), *have a weak stomach, be squeamish*, Bas.*hom. in Ps.*33(1.149B; M.29.365A); met. *~οῦντες καὶ εὐανάτρεπτοι τὰ μυσαρὰ τῶν θεαμάτων ἐκτρέπονται* †Bas.*Is.*82(M.30.253A; v.l. *~ῶντες* 1.436A).

στόμιον, τό, *approach φυλάξαι τὰ σ. τῆς ἐρήμου...ἐπὶ τὴν χώραν Γάζης στομίου οὔσης τῆς ἐρήμου* Thphn.*chron.*pp.278,279(M.108. 689A,B).

***στομίσαντες**, for *νομίσαντες*, Thds.Imp.*ep.Diosc.*(H.2.72B; *νομίσαντες* p.68.13).

[*]στομυλία, ἡ, for *στωμυλία, fluency*, Cosm.Ind.*top.*2(M.88.72D).

[*]στόμυλμα, τό, for *στώμυλμα, eloquence*, Sophr.H.*mir.Cyr.et Jo.* 28(M.87.3501A); *ib.*64(3645B).

[*]στομύλος, for *στωμύλος, fluent, glib*, Leont.et Jo.*sacr.*(M.86. 2084C).

στοργή, ἡ, *affection, love*; **1.** in gen., esp. of family, *Hom.Clem.*3. 19; *ib.*5.24; an element of *φιλία*: *ἡ...φιλία εἰρήνη τίς ἐστι καὶ ὁμόνοια καὶ σ.* Hipp.*haer.*7.29(p.211.12; M.16.3326A); and the essence of *φιλανθρωπία* which is defined as *ἡ ἄνευ τοῦ φυσικῶς πείθοντος ἡ πρὸς οἱονδήποτε σ. καθὸ ἄνθρωπός ἐστιν Hom.Clem.*12.25; **2.** of God for mankind *τὴν τοῦ θεοῦ πρόνοιαν καὶ τὴν πρὸς τοὺς ἀνθρώπους σ.* Const.*or.s.c.*25(p.192.6; M.20.1313A); **3.** of man for God *τὴν πρὸς τὸ θεῖον σ. ἔμφυτον ib.*2(p.155.29; 1237A); *αὐτάρκης...εἰς σωτηρίαν ἡ εἰς θεὸν ἀνθρώπων σ. ... τὴν ἀθανατοποιὸν πρὸς αὐτὸν ἀνθρώπων σ. Hom. Clem.*3.8; *ὁ εἰς τὸν αὐτοῦ ποιητὴν οὐκ ἔχων σ. οὐδ' εἰς ἕτερον ἔχειν ποτὲ δύναται ib.*18.22; *Χριστῷ...συνεκράθης...διαπύρῳ σ.* Jo.Mon.*hymn. Petr.*1(M.96.1389D); of emotion felt by aeon Sophia for Father, Iren.*haer.*1.2.2(M.7.453B); **4.** of Christ as man for the good *πλείστη αὐτῷ τῆς κατὰ πρόθεσιν προσῆν ἡ...τοῦ καλοῦ στοργή* Thdr.Mops.*fr. inc.*14.2(p.308.28; M.66.989D); **5.** for one's bishop, Eus.*h.e.*4.15.11 (M.20.345C); *Clem.ep.*17(M.2.53A).

***στούπρον, τό,** (Lat. *stuprum*) *adultery*, Ath.Scholast.*coll.*9.3 (p.101).

στοχασμός, ὁ, *moral aim, purpose ἔστιν οὖν γαστριμαργία... ἀσκήσεως φίμωτρον, στοχασμοῦ φόβητρον* †Nil.*vit.*2(M.79.1141B).

στοχαστέον, *one must have regard for, one must consider*, Clem. *paed.*2.7(p.193.8; M.8.464B).

στοχαστής, ὁ, 1. *one who guesses, conjecturer*, Gr.Nyss.*Eun.*10(2 p.230.27; M.45.832B); opp. *προγνώστης*, Ath.*v.Anton.*33(M.26.892B); opp. *τῆς ἀληθείας ἐπιστήμονες* (or *διαγνώμονες*) Cyr.*Jo.*2.5(4.187E); id.*Juln.*2(6².47B); *ib.*1(28E); **2.** *diviner of truth*, def. *σ. δὲ εἶναί φαμεν τὸν οἱονεὶ συμβάλλοντα καὶ διατεκμαιρούμενον ὀρθῶς ἕκαστα τῶν πραγμάτων, καὶ ὅποι ποτὲ ἥξει, καὶ εἰς ποῖον καταντήσουσι τέλος, εὖ μάλα διαγινώσκοντα* Cyr.*Is.*1.2(2.55B); *ἀρθῆναι ἀπ' αὐτῶν προφήτην καὶ σ.* †Bas.*Is.*110(1.455C; M.30.296B); ‡Nil.*narr.*7(M.79.681A).

στραβόω** (στραυόω**), *cause to squint*, Leont.N.*v.Sym.*48(M.93. 1729B); *στραυόω ib.*(1728D,1729A).

στραγγαλιά, ἡ, 1. *tight knot*; met., *knotty point, complication*, ‡Ath.*Apoll.*1.12(M.26.1113B); *στραγγαλιὰς βιαίων δογμάτων* Gr.Naz. *or.*29.21(p.107.6; M.36.104A); Anast.S.*haer.*(p.257); **2.** plur., met., *crooked ways τὰς σ. ὁ μὲν Ἀκύλας διαπλοκὰς ἑρμήνευσε, σκολιότητας δὲ ὁ Σύμμαχος, ὁ δὲ Θεοδοτίων διεστραμμένα* Thdt.*Ps.*124:5(1.1492).

στραγγαλιώδης, *involved, complicated*, usu. with implication of deliberate crookedness, Bas.*hom.in Ps.*32(1.132C; M.29.325A); of heresy *ἐπέβητε ταῖς στραγγαλιώδεσι τῶν ὑπὸ θεοῦ ἀπειπαμένων δυσφημιῶν* ‡Felix III Papa *ep.Petr.*2(p.14.21; H.2.825D).

στραγγαλ-όω, 1. *choke, strangle*, Afric.*ep.Or.*2(p.79.19, v.l. *ἀστραγαλωμένοι*; *ἠστραγαλωμένοι* M.11.45A); met. *συγγνωμονεῖτέ μοι, μήποτε οὐ δυνηθέντες χωρῆσαι ~ωθῆτε* Ign.*Trall.*5.1; **2.** *tie* the hands, *handcuff τὼ χεῖρε ~ῶσαι, καὶ ἀπαγαγεῖν εἰς τὸ σκότος τὸ ἐξώτερον* Chrys.*oppugn.*3.1(1.76E); **3.** *make convulsive movements with* or *contort* the hands, id.*hom.81.3 in Mt.*(7.777B).

***στραγγισμός, ὁ,** *stricture*, *T.Sal.*18.27(M.122.1345A; p.57.1n.).

στραγός, *shameless*, Bas.*hom.*14.8(2.130A; M.31.461C).

***στραγών**, ? gender unknown, s.v.l., form of torture *φρικτὰ κολαστήρια...τήγανα καὶ λέβητας πεμπομένας λέβητας οἷον στραγώνας* Ephr.3.249E; poss. for *οἷόν περ ἀγῶνας*, or *σταγόνας*.

***στράτα, ἡ,** (Lat. *strata*) *road, way*, Call.*v.Hyp.*(p.34); Leont.N. *v.Sym.*38(M.93.1717A); *Vaticin.*2(p.53); *Apoc.BMV*(Vassiliev p.133).

στρατεία, ἡ, 1. *military service*; fig., of baptism *στρατείας κλῆσις* Cyr.H.*procatech.*1; of a martyr's service, Chrysipp.*enc.in Thdr.* (p.57.3); **2.** *military appointment*; also *civil appointment ἐπίσκοπον ἢ πρεσβύτερον ἢ διάκονον στρατείαις παραμένοντα...καθαιρεῖν χρὴ Can. App.*83; *τοὺς ἅπαξ ἐν κλήρῳ...μονάσαντας ὡρίσαμεν μήτε ἐπὶ στρατείαν μήτε ἐπὶ ἀξίαν κοσμικὴν ἔρχεσθαι* CChalc.*can.*7; *βασιλεῖ καὶ τοῖς ἀμφ' αὐτὸν ἐπιτήδειον καὶ λαμπρᾶς ἐπειλημμένον στρατείας* Soz.*h.e.*7. 21.8(M.67.1484D); *ποιήσας διάταξιν μὴ εἰσέρχεσθαι εἰς ἀξίας συγκλητικῶν ἢ πατρικίων τοὺς εὐνούχους κουβικουλαρίους μετὰ τὸ πλήρωμα τῆς αὐτῶν στρατείας, τοῦτ' ἔστι τοὺς ἀπὸ πραιποσίτων παλατίου* Jo.Mal. *chron.*14 p.361(M.97.537A); **3.** = *στρατιά, army, host*, Thdt.*Ezech.* 17:20(2.804); id.*Eph.*6:12(3.439).

[*]στρατειλάτης, ὁ, for *στρατηλάτης, army commander, general*, *Exorc.*2(p.334).

στρατεύ-ω, A. med.; **1.** *serve in the army*, ref. profession of certain converts *γεώργει, φαμέν, εἰ γεωργὸς εἶ, ἀλλὰ γνῶθι τὸν θεὸν γεωργῶν...~όμενόν σε κατείληφεν ἡ γνῶσις· τοῦ δίκαια σημαίνοντος ἄκουε στρατηγοῦ* Clem.*prot.*10(p.72.33; M.8.216A); cf. *navigamus et nos vobiscum et militamus*, Tert.*apol.*42(M.*PL.*1.491A); *vestra omnia implevimus...castra ipsa, ib.*37(462Af.); *τοιόσδε...ὁ ἐντελὴς τῆς κατὰ τὸν Χριστιανισμὸν πολιτείας τρόπος· ὁ δ' ὑποβεβηκὼς ἀνθρωπινώτερος, οἷος καὶ γάμοις συγκατιέναι σώφροσιν...τοῖς κατὰ τὸ δίκαιον ~ομένοις* [*τε*] *τὰ πρακτέα ὑποτίθεσθαι* Eus.*d.e.*1.8(p.39.30; M.22.77A); *τῶν ~ομένων...τί τοίνυν οὐχ ἁμαρτάνουσιν οὗτοι καθ' ἑκάστην ἡμέραν,* ὑβρίζοντες, λοιδορούμενοι...τὰς ἀλλοτρίας πραγματευόμενοι συμφοράς; Chrys.*hom.61.2 in Mt.*(7.613A); cf. ἄλλοι τὸν στρατιωτικόν, ἄλλοι δὲ τὸν ἐμπορικὸν βίον Eus.*p.e.*1.5(15C; M.21.45A); to continue after conversion regarded by some as incompatible with profession of Christianity ἡμεῖς...οὐ συστρατευόμεθα μὲν αὐτῷ [sc. τῷ βασιλεῖ], κἂν ἐπείγῃ· ~όμεθα δὲ ὑπὲρ αὐτοῦ, ἴδιον στρατόπεδον εὐσεβείας συγκροτοῦντες διὰ τῶν πρὸς τὸ θεῖον ἐντεύξεων Or.*Cels.*8.73(p.291.14; M.11.1628C); ἐν...τῷ ~εσθαί με, Βίκτωρ ἐκλήθην...διὰ δὲ τὸ Χριστιανόν με εἶναι, νῦν παγανεύειν ᾐρετησάμην *M.Tar.*1(p.452); cf. *plurimi...adducerentur ad fidem domini nostri...derelicto militiae cingulo,* Hegem.*Arch.*1(p.2.8; M.10.1430A); cf.Tert.*de idololatria* 19 (M.*PL.*1.690Af.); id.*de corona* 11(M.*PL.*2.91Bf.); cf. *mihi non licet militare, quia Christianus sum, M.Maximiliani* 1(Ruinart,p.340); *in militia saeculari, in qua adhuc tu teneris...spero enim et te ex eadem via ad viam nostram esse venturum...huic militemus...qui militantibus sibi gloriam vitae aeternae...largitur...commuta in melius militiam ut aeterno regi incipias militare,* Paulinus Nolae *ep.*25.1,4,8(M.*PL.*61.300C,302A,304B); **2.** met., *serve* God ~σώμεθα... ἐν τοῖς ἀμώμοις προστάγμασιν αὐτοῦ. κατανοήσωμεν τοὺς ~ομένους τοῖς ἡγουμένοις ἡμῶν...πῶς ὑποτεταγμένως ἐπιτελοῦσιν τὰ διατασσόμενα *1Clem.*37.1f.; ἀρέσκετε ᾧ ~εσθε Ign.*Polyc.*6.2; οὐ γὰρ ὡς ὑμεῖς ὑπονοεῖτε βασιλεῖ ἀπὸ γῆς ἐρχομένῳ ~όμεθα, ἀλλ' ἀπ' οὐρανοῦ, ζῶντι θεῷ *A.Paul.*4(p.114.7); *ib.*2(p.108.11); ἄνδρες, οἱ εἰς Χριστὸν ~όμενοι *A.Petr.c.Sim.*7(p.90.11); Χριστιανός εἰμι καὶ οὐ ~ομαι ἐπιγείῳ βασιλεῖ ἀλλὰ βασιλεῖ οὐρανίῳ *M.Das.*7.2; οἱ πιστεύσαντες καὶ βουλόμενοι ~εσθαι τῷ Χριστῷ *V.Aberc.*13(p.11.13); and Devil ἀποτάξασθαι ὁμολογήσαντες...τῷ διαβόλῳ...πάλιν ~ονται αὐτῷ ἐν τοῖς ἔργοις τοῖς πονηροῖς *M.Das.*3.3.

B. act.; **1.** *receive into the army, enrol, enlist,* met. ἐστράτευσεν γὰρ [sc. Ἰησοῦς] πλήθη πολλὰ *A.Phil.*15(p.8.19); ~σοι ὑμᾶς ἑαυτῷ Cyr.H.*procatech.*17; ἔξεστιν...ἐν τοῖς οὐρανοῖς αὐτὸν ~σαι Chrys.*hom.6.4 in 1Thess.*(11.471C); ὁ ἑτέρῳ μέλλεις ~ειν σῶμα, τοῦτο ~σον ἐμοί id.*hom.76.4 in Mt.*(7.738B); pass. μηδένα ἀποκλεισθῆναι θέλοντα ~θῆναι τῷ ἐμῷ βασιλεῖ *A.Paul.*3(p.110.14); **2.** met., *put to warlike use* τὴν κοσμοφθόρον ἐκείνην ἐστράτευσε σάλπιγγα Thphyl.*exc.Rom.*8 (p.227.28; M.113.936D); id.*exc.gent.*3(p.479.17; M.113.937B); **3.** *control* σ. ὀργήν id.*exc.Rom.*5(p.225.22; 933B).

στρατηγ-έω, 1. *command, lead an army*; met., *lead* τὸ στρατηγῆσαν ἡμᾶς εἰς ζωὴν Meth.*symp.*4.2(p.46.12; M.18.88B); *lead on* ἀπεκτείνασι γὰρ [sc. τὴν λυτρωτήν]...ἀνημέρῳ θράσει πρὸς τὴν ἀνωτάτω λοιπὸν ἀνοσιότητα ~ούμενοι Cyr.*glaph.Dt.*(1.415E); **2.** *wage war* εἰ δὲ βούλεται ἡμᾶς...~εῖν ⟨ὑπὲρ⟩ πατρίδος, ἴστω ὅτι καὶ ταῦτα ποιοῦμεν...ἐν γὰρ τῷ κρυπτῷ ἡμῶν...εὐχαί εἰσιν, ἀναπεμπόμεναι ὡς ἀπὸ ἱερέων ὑπὲρ τῶν ἐν τῇ πατρίδι ἡμῶν Or.*Cels.*8.74(p.291.17; M.11.1629A); ἰατροὺς ἐπέστησε...καὶ ~εῖν καὶ ἀριστεύειν κατὰ τῶν νοσημάτων ἐκέλευσεν Thdt.*affect.*1(p.5.9; 4.694); **3.** *manœuvre, contrive* ἐστρατήγησαν [sc. τὴν ἐπὶ τῷ θανάτῳ διαφθοράν] αὐτοὶ [sc. οἱ δαίμονες] ταῖς Ἰουδαίων μανίαις Cyr.*Ps.*9:16(M.69.773C); τὴν Ἀθανασίου γνώμην ~ῆσαι τῆς πράξεως Philost.*h.e.*7.2(M.65.537B); of Christ, *accomplish* ὁ κύριος ...ἐστρατήγησε μέγα καὶ θαυμαστὸν ἔργον ‡Ath.*pass.*24(M.28.228B).

στρατηγός, ὁ, 1. *general* in command of the army of a province, Thphn.*chron.*p.75(M.108.233B); **2.** *governor, ib.*p.99(292B); *ib.*p.197 (509C); **3.** of Jewish officials appointed by Romans to keep order in Temple, Chrys.*hom.80.3 in Mt.*(7.769A); **4.** met., in army of Christ ὁ...τοῦ δεσπότου Χριστοῦ στρατηγὸς ἅπασιν ὁμοίως διανέμει τὴν βασιλικὴν πανοπλίαν Thdt.*Eph.*6:11(3.438); of Elijah ὁ τῷ ἀντιχρίστῳ διατηρούμενος στρατηγός Cosm.Ind.*top.*5(M.88.260B); of Jo. Bapt. παρθενίας στρατηγὸς...Ἰωάννης Sophr.H.*or.*7.7(M.87.3332D); of S. Peter as head of Church, Rom.Mel.(*SBBAW* 1901 p.742); of Logos ὁ μέγας ἡμῶν...στρατηγός Clem.*paed.*1.8(p.128.19; M.8.329A); of Christ ὁ σ. ἡμῶν καὶ ποιμὴν Ἰησοῦς Meth.*symp.*4.6 (p.52.7; M.18.96B); *V.Aberc.*13(p.12.7); of God ὦ σ. τῶν σοφῶν βουλευμάτων Geo.Pis.*Pers.*1.35(M.92.1200A).

***στρατηλατία, ἡ,** office of στρατηλάτης, *generalship,* Thphn. *chron.*p.107(M.108.309A).

***στρατηλατιανός, ὁ,** *one serving under the* στρατηλάτης, *commander,* Thdt.*ep.*79(4.1135); Jo.Mal.*chron.*18 p.430(M.97.633B).

στρατιά, ἡ, = στρατός, *army, host, company*; of martyrs, Sophr.H.*mir.Cyr.et Jo.*36(M.87.3556D); of angels, Clem.*str.*7.2(p.6.3; M.9.409A); Or.*or.*17(p.339.19; M.11.472C); Eun.*exp.fid.*2(p.256); *Lit.*ap.*Const.App.*8.12.27; of sun, moon, and stars, Or.*Cels.*8.67 (p.283.22; M.11.1617C); *Const.App.*2.22.5f.; Thdt.*qu.53 in 4Reg.*21:3 (1.548); of demons, *M.Agap.*2.4(p.96.8); rank of celestial hierarchy τὰ χερουβὶμ καὶ σεραφίμ, αἰῶνάς τε καὶ στρατιάς, δυνάμεις τε καὶ ἐξουσίας κτλ. *Lit.*ap.*Const.App.*8.12.8; ἀγγέλων, ἀρχαγγέλων...δυνάμεων, στρατιῶν αἰωνίων *ib.*8.12.27; *court* of king τοῦ...βασιλέως Αἰγύπτου μεταπεμψαμένου αὐτὸν [sc. Ἰωσήφ]...καὶ ἐπὶ πάσης τῆς σ. πυνθανομένου ἐπὶ πράγματι Chrys.*hom.5.2 in Phil.*(11.230B).

***στρατικός,** *military,* opp. civil, Or.*Cels.*1.27(p.79.1, v.l. στρατιωτῶν M.11.712B).

***στρατιώδης,** *military,* Gr.Nyss.*v.Mos.*(M.44.337C).

στρατιώτης, ὁ, 1. *soldier*; **a.** of Christians mentioned as serving in army τοὺς δὲ ἡμετέρους...καὶ στρατιῶται καὶ ἰδιῶται Dion.Al.ap.Eus. *h.e.*7.11.20(M.20.669B); τοὺς...ἐπὶ τῆς Μελιτηνῆς...λεγεῶνος σ. διὰ πίστεως...γόνυ θέντας ἐπὶ γῆν κατὰ τὸ οἰκεῖον ἡμῖν τῶν εὐχῶν ἔθος Eus. *h.e.*5.5.1(M.20.441A); *ib.*8.4.3(749B); παραπεσόντες...καὶ θύσαντες... οἱ μὲν στρατιωτῶν ὄντες, οἱ δὲ ἀπὸ κληρικῶν ὑπάρχοντες Epiph.*haer.* 68.2(p.141.26; M.42.185B); by some considered incompatible with profession of Christianity, cf.Hipp.*trad.ap.*16.17,19; σ. προσιὼν διδασκέσθω...πειθόμενος προσδεχέσθω, ἀντιλέγων δὲ ἀποβαλλέσθω *Const. App.*8.32.10; cf.Paulinus Nolae *ep.*25.3f.,8(M.*PL.*61.301C,302A,304B); **b.** met., of the first disciples of Christ τοὺς...μαθητὰς...νοητοῖς καὶ λογικοῖς ὅπλοις περιφράξας...καὶ τούτους...ὡς οἰκείους σ. ὁπλίτας παρεσκεύασεν Eus.*d.e.*7.1(p.322.13; M.22.525D); of other members of Church militant, Clem.*q.d.s.*35(p.183.4; M.9.640D) cit. s. στρατός; τῇ τῶν θεοφιλῶν τελευτῇ, οὓς σ. τῆς...εὐσεβείας οὐκ ἂν ἁμάρτοις εἰπών Eus.*p.e.*13.11(663B; M.21.1096C); as serving in army of God οὐκ εἰμὶ δραπέτης τοῦ Χριστοῦ ἀλλ' ἔννομος σ. θεοῦ ζῶντος *A.Paul.*4(p.114.14); *ib.*6(p.116.7); οἱ...τοῦ οὐρανίου βασιλέως σ. Isid.Pel.*epp.*3.370 (M.78.1021A); and of Christ, Clem.*prot.*11(p.82.6; M.8.236B); Eus. *h.e.*8.4.3(M.20.749B); πόσον τὸ ἀξίωμα, σ. εἶναι τοῦ Χριστοῦ Chrys. *hom.4.1 in 2Tim.*(11.679C); Thdr.Pet.*v.Thds.*(p.8.12); of monks ἥδιον ἰδεῖν ἐρημίαν σκηνὰς ἔχουσαν μοναχῶν συνεχεῖς, ἢ στρατιώτας ἐν στρατοπέδῳ παραπετάσματα τείνοντας...ἂν γὰρ ἀπέλθωμεν εἰς τὴν ἔρημον, καὶ ἴδωμεν τῶν τοῦ Χριστοῦ σ. τὰς σκηνάς, οὐ παραπετάσματα τεινόμενα ὀψόμεθα Chrys.*hom.59.3 in Mt.*(7.684A,B); **2.** *officer* of imperial civil service, *civil servant* πρῶτα μὲν τῆς οἰκίας τῆς αὐτοῦ πάντα Χριστιανὸν ἀπελαύνει...εἶτα δὲ τοὺς κατὰ πόλιν σ. ἐκκρίνεσθαι καὶ ἀποβάλλεσθαι τοῦ τῆς τιμῆς ἀξιώματος εἰ μὴ τοῖς δαίμοσιν θύειν αἱροῖντο Eus.*h.e.*10.8.10(M.20.897A); id.*v.C.*1.54(p.32.27; M.20.968A); Gr.Mag.*dial.*(tr.Zach.)4.36(M.*PL.*77.383B); profession forbidden to all ranks of clergy, CChalc.*can.*7; but ruling not always observed, ref. return of a priest who had been absent for a long period κἄντε ἱερεύς, κἄντε ἐπίσκοπος, ἤτε ἡγούμενος, ἤτε σ. *Nomoc.*105.

Στρατιωτικοί, οἱ, name of certain Gnostics, Epiph.*haer.*25.2(p.268.20; M.41.321C); id.*anac.*26(p.235.18; M.41.281C).

στρατιῶτις, ἡ, fem. of στρατιώτης; **1.** *soldier's wife,* Thdr.Stud. *epp.*1.7(M.99.932D); **2.** *female soldier* of Christ, *ib.*2.68(1296C).

στρατοκῆρυξ, ὁ, *army* or *camp herald,* Or.*adnot.in Dt.*20:5(M.17.29A); of angel of Apoc.19:17 as herald of heavenly host, Areth. *Apoc.*19:17(M.106.745B).

στρατολογ-έω, *levy an army, enlist soldiers,* met. ~οῦμεν...ἐκ τῆς οἰκουμένης πάσης *A.Paul.*3(p.110.13); μέλλετε ~εῖσθαι τῷ μεγάλῳ βασιλεῖ Cyr.H.*catech.*3.3; διὰ τῆς σφραγῖδος ἐστρατολόγησε τῷ Χριστῷ Bas.Sel.*v.Thecl.*1(M.85.548A).

***στρατολόγημα, τό,** *enlistment,* lit. and met. ἐν μὲν τοῖς σ. τοῖς ἔξωθεν...γέροντες...παρορῶνται...ἐν δὲ...τῷ σ. τῆς εὐσεβείας γέροντες καλοῦνται Nil.*epp.*4.4(M.79.552C).

στρατολογία, ἡ, 1. *raising an army, enlisting soldiers,* met. ἔξεστιν...ἐν τοῖς οὐρανοῖς αὐτὸν στρατεῦσαι, εἰς ἐκείνην καταλέξαι τὴν σ. Chrys.*hom.6.4 in 1Thess.*(11.471C); *terms of enlistment* οὐδὲν οὕτω τῆς ἐπαγγελίας καὶ σ. ἀλλότριον, ὡς τὸ τῷ παρόντι προστετηκέναι βίῳ id.*hom.13.1 in Phil.*(11.297D); **2.** *army, host* ἀγγελικῆς σ. ‡Chrys. *annunt.et Ar.*(11.842A).

***στρατολόγος, ὁ,** ? *recruiting officer,* Philost.*h.e.*11.3(M.65.597A).

***στρατοπεδαρχέω,** *command* troops, *Mir.Geo.*4(p.21.5).

στρατοπεδάρχης, ὁ, *military commander,* -παιδάρχης Jo.Eub. *innoc.*2(M.96.1504A); of leaders of angelic armies, id.*concept.BMV* 17(M.96.1488B); met., of Moses and Elijah at Transfiguration, Tim. Ant.*cruc.*(M.86.261D).

[*]στρατοπεδαρχία, ἡ, 1. *encampment,* Cosm.Ind.*top.*5(M.88.221C); **2.** *military command, Mir.Geo.*4(p.22.15).

στρατοπεδεύω, *encamp*; met., *occupy* ὑπὸ τοιούτου φρονήματος στρατοπεδευθεὶς †Bas.*ep.*41.1(p.285.5; M.32.345B); *encamp against, make war on, Apoc.Dan.*C(p.119).

στρατόπεδον, τό, 1. *encamped army*; **a.** *praetorian guard, Chron. Pasch.*p.287(M.92.717A); **b.** in gen., *army*; met., of Christian army ἐπὶ τῶν σ. ἐστίν [sc. Παῦλος] *A.Paul.*3(p.110.8); στρατευόμεθα... ὑπὲρ αὐτοῦ, ἴδιον σ. εὐσεβείας συγκροτοῦντες Or.*Cels.*8.73(p.291.15; M.11.1628C); **2.** *imperial court,* CSard.*can.*7; Bas.*ep.*74.2(3.168E; M.32.445A); Synes.*ep.*5(M.66.1341C); σ. ἐν ᾧ τόπῳ ὁ βασιλεὺς διατρίβει, εἰώθασιν οἱ παλαιοὶ καλεῖν *Schol.* in CSard.*can.*7(*Mon.*2 p.660).

στρατός, ὁ, *army, host*; met., of Christians σεαυτῷ κατάλεξον σ. ἄοπλον, ἀπόλεμον...χήρας πραότητι ὡπλισμένας, ἄνδρας ἀγάπῃ κεκοσμημένους...οὗτοι πάντες οἱ στρατιῶται...οὐδεὶς ἀργός, οὐδεὶς ἀχρεῖος Clem.*q.d.s.*34(p.182.25; M.9.640C); of heavenly host, *Const. App.*7.35.3.

στράτωρ, ὁ, (Lat. *strator*) *groom*, title of members of an order of dignitaries who formed part of the ceremonial bodyguard σπαθαρίων τινῶν καὶ στρατόρων καὶ ἑτέρων βασιλικῶν ἀνθρώπων Thphn.*chron.*p.380(M.108.909A); *ib.*p.325(785B).

***στραυόω,** v. *στραβόω.

***στρεβλοκαρδιάζω,** *be perverse of heart*, Thdr.Stud.*epp.*2.184(M. 99.1568D).

***στρεβλόρινος,** *having a crooked nose*, Jo.Mal.*chron.*5 p.103(M.97. 192B); *ib.*11 p.282(428A).

***στρεβλόστομος,** *wry-mouthed*, Jo.Mal.*chron.*12 p.298(M.97.452A).

***στρεβλόχειλος,** *perverse of speech, argumentative*, Gr.Naz.*or.*32. 26(M.36.204C).

στρέβλωμα, τό, *racking, torturing*, Gr.Naz.*carm.*1.2.10.716(M.37. 732A).

***στρεβλῶς,** *crookedly*, fig. σ. βαδίζειν [sc. scorpion] Sophr.H.*v. Anast.*(M.92.1684A); met. σ. ὑπὸ τῆς ἐσκοτισμένης αὐτῶν διανοίας Thdr.Stud.*epp.*2.36(M.99.1224B).

στρέβλωσις, ἡ, 1. *twisting* of clothes, *wringing*, Gr.Nyss.*hom. opif.*13.4(M.44.168A); of the hair, *curling*, Chrys.*hom.18.4 in Jo.* (8.110A); of the hands, ? *clenching*, ? *writhing*, id.*Stag.*1.1(1.156D); **2.** met., *perversity, crookedness* τῇ σ. τῆς διανοίας Sophr.H.*v.Anast.* (M.92.1684B).

***στρεβλωτήρ, ὁ,** *rack* (for torture), Const.Diac.*laud.*6(M.88.485B); Thdr.Stud.*epp.*2.28(M.99.1196D).

στρεβλωτήριον, τό, *rack* (for torture), Or.*mart.*15(p.15.16; M.11. 584A); Const.ap.Eus.*v.C.*2.52(p.63.5; M.20.1029A); Eus.*l.C.*17(p.257. 11; M.20.1436B); Bas.*Spir.*27(3.22D; M.32.116A); Chrys.*hom.5.4 in 2Tim.*(11.691A); met. βασανιστήριον καὶ σ. ἡ ἄβυσσος Serap.*Man.*30 (p.46; M.18.1117B).

***στρεβλωτικός,** *for racking, torturing*, Gr.Nyss.*v.Gr.Thaum.*(M. 46.945A); ‡Sophr.H.*v.m.Cyr.et Jo.*11(M.87.3685A).

***στρεγγίζω,** v. *στριγγίζω.

στρέμμα, τό, *turning* of the eyes, i.e. to look at, *notice, attention* μὴ ἅμα πολλοὶ εἰσέρχεσθε...οὐ γὰρ βούλομαι στρέμματα γίνεσθαι εἰς ὑμᾶς τῶν πολιτῶν *Hom.Clem.*12.12.

στρεπτός, *revolving* στρεπτῇσι κελεύθοις Geo.Pis.*carm.vit.*12(p.52, v.l. στρεπτοῖσι).

στρέφ-ω, 1. trans., *recall* a person, Thphn.*chron.*p.280(M.108. 692A); **2.** *turn over*; met., in words, *repeat, harp on* συνεχῶς ~οντες οὐ διαλιμπάνομεν Chrys.*hom.79.1 in Mt.*(7.757E); *ib.29.3*(345D); συνεχῶς ἄνω καὶ κάτω ~ει τὴν ἀνάστασιν id.*hom.45.3 in Jo.*(8.266E); met., *move* one's feelings τὰ σπλάγχνα μου ἐστρέφετο...εἰς συμπάθειαν *T.Zab.*7.4; *disturb* σ. τὸ κοινόβιον *V.Dan.*(p.388.17); **3.** med. and pass. intrans., *move, live* in, ref. life in world opp. life of solitary ἐν μέσῳ ~εσθαι καὶ τοὺς ἄλλους ῥυθμίζειν Chrys.*hom.6.4 in 1Cor.*(10. 48E); τοὺς...ἐν βίῳ ~ομένους Thdt.*h.rel.*10(3.1196).

στρεψαύχην, *turning the neck*, i.e. to look back; hence *back-sliding* ἀπτόλεμον δ' ἅτε τόξον ἔχον στρεψαύχενα λώβην †Apoll.*met.Ps.*77:57 (M.33.1428C).

στρῆνος ([*]**στρῖνος**), **ὁ, τό, 1.** *concupiscence, wantonness*, Chrys. *hom.1.2 in Philm.*(11.776D); masc., Anast.S.*qu.et resp.*98(M.89. 753A); *ib.*123(773B); plur., Thdr.Mops.*1Tim.*5:11(p.163.19); στρῖνος *T.Benj.*9.1; neut., Nil.*epp.*3.83(M.79.425C); †Jo.Jej.*poenit.*(M.88. 1900B); στρῖν-, Nil.*epp.*4.1(M.79.548C); **2.** ? *insolence*, or as above, Epiph.*haer.*66.2(p.17.24; M.42.32C); *ib.*66.3(p.19.6; M.42.33B).

στριγγίζω** (στρεγγίζω**), *cry out*, *V.Aberc.*9(p.8.21) στριγγίσαντα τὰ δαιμόνια καὶ σπαράξαντα τοὺς ἀνθρώπους ἀπῆλθον *ib.*11(p.10.11); ἤρξατο στρεγγίζειν καὶ κόπτεσθαι κοπετὸν μέγαν πενθοῦντες τὰς ἁμαρτίας αὐτῶν Anton.Hag.*v.Sym.Styl.*24(p.58.18); of wild goats, *bleat*, †Anast.S.*relat.*16(*OC* 2 p.69.10).

[*]**στρῖνος, ὁ, τό,** v. στρῆνος.

***στρόβησις, ἡ,** *distraction, bewilderment*, Epiph.*haer.*16.3(p.212. 8; M.41.252B).

στρόβιλος, *whirling*; of winds, Thdt.*Ps.*54:9(1.962).

στρόβιλος, ὁ, *round ball* or any round object; of a dome or cupola ὁ ὀκτάγωνος οἶκος...τὸ δὲ ἀπ' ἐκείνου σ. ἔσται κωνοειδής Gr. Nyss.*ep.*25.6(M.46.1096B).

***στροβλωθέντες,** ? for στροβιλωθέντες, aor. ptcpl. pass. of στροβιλόω; pass. intrans., *go about, go here and there* πολλὰ ἐρευνήσαντες καὶ σ. *Chr.Sac.*A(p.58).

***στρογγύλεος,** *round* ,*Chron.Pasch.*p.382(M.92.980B).

***στρογγυλιστής, ὁ,** *whirling dancer*, Cosm.Mel.*schol.*(M.38.532) in Gr.Naz.*carm.*2.2(epigr.)25.3.

στρογγύλλ-ω, *spin*, met. ~ων λογάρια Synes.*calv.*4(p.197.9; M.66. 1173C); *spin out, prolong*, id.*provid.*1.3(p.70.17; M.66.1217B).

στρογγυλοειδής, *round*, Ammon.*Ac.*19:35(M.85.1577C); of eucharistic host ὁρῶμεν ὅτι οὐκ ἴσον ἐστὶν...οὐ τῇ ἐνσάρκῳ εἰκόνι οὐ τῇ ἀοράτῳ θεότητι οὐ τοῖς χαρακτῆρσι τῶν μελῶν. τὸ μὲν γάρ ἐστι σ. Epiph.*anc.*57(p.67.2; M.43.117A).

***στρογγυλόψις,** *round-faced*, Jo.Mal.*chron.*5 p.100(M.97.187B).

***στρογγυλόω,** *be round*, *Chron.Pasch.*p.382(M.92.980B) cit. s. καστέλλιον.

στρογγύλωσις, ἡ, 1. *rounding*; *roundness*, Epiph.*haer.*45.1(p.200. 10; M.41.833B); **2.** *surrounding, encirclement* τῇ σ. δηλοῖ...τὸ ἐν μέσῳ τοῦ λαοῦ κατακεκλῖσθαι τὸν βασιλέα Thdt.*qu.60 in 1Reg.*26:7 (1.396); Proc.G.*1Reg.*26:7(M.87.1116A).

στρομβέω, = στροβέω, *whirl round*; *agitate*, met. παραγυμνώσας ...τὴν θεότητα Χριστὸς...τοὺς στύλους τῆς ἐκκλησίας ἐστρόμβησε ‡Caes.Naz.*dial.*41(M.38.908).

[*]**στρουθεών, ὁ,** *ostrich*, Thphn.*chron.*p.267(M.108.664B).

[*]**στρουθιοκάμηλος, ὁ,** = foreg., Or.*fr.96 in Lam.*4:3(M.13.652A; στρουθοκάμηλος p.270.8).

***στρούκτωρ, ὁ,** (Lat. *structor*) *waiter*, Eus.Al.*serm.*21.17(M.86. 444C).

***στρούμεντον, τό,** (Lat. *instrumentum*) *instrument*, Ath.Scholast. *coll.*20.1(p.172).

στροφή, ἡ, 1. *turning, revolving*; met., *vicissitude* τὰς σ. τοῦ βίου Gr.Naz.*ep.*178(M.37.292A); **2.** *transposition, inversion* of words, Or. *fr.in Pr.*1:3(M.17.153A); **3.** *twist* as made by wrestlers; met., of phrase, language, etc., *twist, perversion* ὅταν...ἄλλως μὲν φύσεως ἔχῃ τὰ πράγματα, ἄλλως δὲ οἱ λόγοι περὶ αὐτῶν ἀναπείθωσι, σ. τίς ἐστι, μᾶλλον δὲ διαστροφή, ὑπὸ τοῦ λόγου περὶ τὴν ἀλήθειαν γινομένη Bas. *hom.*12.7(1.103E; M.31.401A); **4.** met., *occupation, concern* ἡ πρὸς ἡμᾶς τοὺς ἀνθρώπους ἐπιμέλεια καὶ σ. Proc.G.*Is.*6:6ff.(M.87.1941B).

στρόφος, ὁ, *twirling, whirling* (= στρόβος); hence *whirlwind*, *T.Sal.*7.4(p.29.9); *lathe*, Geo.Pis.*hex.*569(M.92.1479A); ? *giddiness, vertigo* τρίωρον φρίκην καὶ κεφαλαλγίαν, πρότερόν τε καὶ στρόφον ἀκηδίας δαίμων πεποίηκε Jo.Clim.*scal.*13(M.88.860B).

***στρύγγη, ἡ,** a kind of *female vampire* λέγουσί τινες τῶν ἀμαθεστέρων ὅτι γυναῖκές εἰσι σ., αἱ καὶ Γελοῦδες λεγόμεναι Jo.D.*drac.* (M.94.1604A).

στρυφνότης, ἡ, *rough, harsh taste, sourness*; hence *sternness* Χριστός, εἰδὼς τὴν μεγάλην τῶν ἐχθρῶν ἡμῶν ἀνελεημοσύνην, καὶ οἰκτείρων τὸ γένος τῶν ἀνθρώπων ἐνετείλατο ἐν στρυφνότητι καρδίας [Lc.12:39] Esaias *cap.spir.*13(M.40.1209B); ἐὰν εἶ ἀδελφῶν ἐπιστάτης, φρόντισον αὐτῶν ἐν σ. καρδίας καὶ σπλάγχνοις οἰκτιρμοῦ Dor.*doct.*17.1 (M.88.1800C); *austerity* of life τὰ...ἐπὶ τῆς ἱερωσύνης ἠσφαλισμένα περὶ δευτέρου γάμου καὶ τῶν ἄλλων οὗτοι [sc. οἱ Καθαροί] εἰς ἅπαντα τὸν λαὸν νενομίκασι καὶ τὰ δι' ὑπερβολὴν στρυφνότητος ὑπὸ θεοῦ κεκηρυγμένα...αὐτοὶ εἰς ἀπανθρωπίαν θεῷ προσῆψαν Epiph.*haer.*59.11 (p.376.20; M.41.1036A); of the ascetic ἱμάτια στρυφνότητος ἐκδυόμενος Nil.*epp.*3.4(M.79.412B).

στρυφνόω, *make sour*, Gr.Thaum.*pan.Or.*7(p.19.3; M.10.1073B).

στρωματεύς, ὁ, 1. plur., *patchwork*, as title of literary *Miscellanies*, freq. of the work by Clem. περιέξουσι...οἱ Στρωματεῖς ἀναμεμιγμένην τὴν ἀλήθειαν τοῖς φιλοσοφίας δόγμασι Clem.*str.*1.1(p.13. 1; M.8.708A); ἡ τῶν Στρωματέων ἡμῖν ὑποτύπωσις λειμῶνος δίκην πεποίκιλται *ib.*6.1(p.423.5; M.9.209A); of a lost work by Origen, Or. *Jo.*13.45(p.272.1; M.14.480B); derivation of the name ἔστω δὲ ἡμῖν τὰ ὑπομνήματα...ὡς αὐτό που τοὔνομά φησι, διεστρωμένα, ἀπ' ἄλλου εἰς ἄλλο συνεχὲς μετιόντα...συλλαμβάνουσι μὲν οὖν πρός τε ἀνάμνησιν πρός τε ἔμφασιν ἀληθείας...οἱ τῶν ὑπομνημάτων Στρωματεῖς Clem.*str.* 4.2(p.249.29; M.8.1217A); **2.** sing., *book*, i.e. *section of the Miscellanies* ὁ...κατὰ τὴν ἀληθῆ φιλοσοφίαν γνωστικῶν ὑπομνημάτων πρῶτος ἡμῖν Στρωματεύς *ib.*1.29(p.112.6; M.8.929A); *ib.*6.1(p.422.4; M.9. 208A); *ib.*5.1(p.332.14; 24A); of the work as a whole (a source for life of S. Barnabas) ὀλίγα τῶν εἰς ἡμᾶς ἰόντων περὶ τῆς τούτου βιώσεως καὶ τελειώσεως, ἐκ δὲ τοῦ Στρωματέως Alex.Sal.*Barn.*proem. 8(p.438F); **3.** title of Clem. as *author of a Miscellany* σύγγραμμα Κλήμεντος τοῦ Στρωματέως εἰς τὸν προφήτην Ἀμώς Pall.*h.Laus.*60 (p.154.20; M.34.1236D); Jo.Mosch.*prat.*176(M.87.3045C); Max.*ambig.* (M.91.1085A); Anast.S.*hex.*7(M.89.962A).

στρωμνηφόρος, *carrying the bed* or *bedding*; of the paralytic, Geo.Pis.*carm.*54.2(p.57).

***στρώνω,** s.v.l., *spread, diffuse*, *T.Sal.*5.8(p.23.5) cit. s. θηλυμανία.

στρῶσις, ἡ, *bed*, *Apophth.Patr.*(M.65.149A); Dor.*doct.*4.10(M.88. 1672A); plur., *bedclothes*, Sophr.H.*mir.Cyr.et Jo.*67(M.87.3653B).

στυγηρός, *abominated, hateful*, Thdot.Anc.*hom.BMV* 12(p.331.10); ‡Meth.*Sym.et Ann.*5(M.18.360A).

στυγνάζ-ω, **1.** *look gloomy, wear a frown* στυγνάσας ἐπέτρεψεν ὁ ἡγεμών *A.Paul.et Thecl.*35(p.261.10); οὐδεὶς ἀθυμῶν στεφανοῦται· οὐδεὶς ∼ων τρόπαιον ἵστησι Bas.*hom.*1.1(1.2A; M.31.164B); Chrys. *Anna* 5.2(4.741A); **2.** *look grave* or *sad*, ref. Gen.3:17 ∼ειν προσετάχθης, μὴ γὰρ τρυφᾶν Bas.*hom.*1.3(1.3B; M.31.168A); Epiph.*haer.*69.10 (p.160.17; M.42.217C); met., *grow grave*; of sins, v.l. in Leo Mag.*ep.* 106(συχνάζουσιν p.56.32, v.l. στυγνάζουσιν M.*PL.*54.1004A); **3.** *grow gloomy, be overcast*, ‡Bas.*inc.*58(p.247); Mac.Aeg.*hom.*8.2(M.34.529A); †Marc.Er.*temp.*27(M.65.1069A); Thphn.*chron.*p.171(M.108.453D); met., *be heavy* ἄρχεται ∼ειν ἡ ψυχὴ καὶ οἱονεὶ καταβέννυσθαι Or. *fr.*500 *in Mt.*(p.205; M.17.305A); ἔστι καιρὸς ὅτε ὑποστέλλει [sc. ἡ εὐχή], καὶ ∼ει †Marc.Er.*temp.*26(1068A).

***στυγνηγόρος**, *pronouncing doom*; of the Day of Judgement, Gr.Naz.*carm.*2.1.40.3(M.37.1337A).

στυγνία, ἡ, *sadness, gloom*, Jo.Mosch.*prat.*171(M.87.3040B).

***στυγνιάω**, = στυγνάζω, *be gloomy*, Geo.Pis.*carm.*4.75(p.13).

***στυγνοπρόσωπος**, *of sad countenance*, ‡Gr.Naz.*Chr.pat.*638(M.38.187A).

στυγνός, *gloomy*; *grave, serious* σ. καὶ ἀνακόλουθον ἵνα...τοσαῦται ἐκκλησίαι ἄνευ ἐπισκόπων δοκῶσιν εἶναι CArim.*ep.Const.*2 ap.Thdt. *h.e.*2.20.3(3.878).

στυλίζω, ? *hold up to public ridicule, mock* (cf. στηλιτεύω) γυμνοὺς ἡμᾶς δεσμίους...ἐστύλισαν ἐκραββάτισαν καὶ ἐπτέρνισαν Thal.CP *Thds.* 3(p.8.30; M.91.1476A); ὅτε...τοῖς παισὶν ἔνευε καὶ ἐστύλιζον αὐτόν Leont.N.*v.Sym.*38(M.93.1717A).

στυλίτης, ὁ, *one who lives on a pillar*, Cyr.S.*v.Euthym.*30(p.47.23,26); Jo.Mal.*chron.*14 p.369(M.97.549B); Jo.Mosch.*prat.*129(M.87.2993B,C); on Simeon, first to adopt this mode of life, v. Thdt.*h.rel.* 26(3.1265ff.); Evagr.*h.e.*1.13f.(p.20ff.; M.86.2453Bff.).

[*]**στῦλον, τό**, v. στῦλος.

***στυλοπύρ, τό**, *pillar of fire*, ‡Caes.Naz.*dial.*36(M.38.900).

στῦλος, ὁ, *pillar*, **1.** as home of certain ascetics, Nil.*epp.*2.114(M.79.249B); v. κίων; **2.** ref. Ex.13:21 ὁ δὲ πεφωτισμένος σ., πρὸς τῷ τὸ ἀνεικόνιστον σημαίνειν, δηλοῖ τὸ ἑστὸς καὶ μόνιμον τοῦ θεοῦ καὶ τὸ ἄτρεπτον αὐτοῦ φῶς Clem.*str.*1.24(p.102.17f.; M.8.909C); symbolizing Christ as σ. καὶ ἑδραίωμα τῆς ἀληθείας (1Tim.3:15), Or.*Jo.*32.1 (p.425.10; M.14.740B) cit. s. ἐκβιάζω; κἄν τε στῦλος, ἐπειδὴ αὐτός ἐστιν ἑδραίωμα τῆς ἀληθείας...κἄν τε στῦλος, διὰ τὸ φωτεινὸν τοῦ πυρός Epiph.*haer.*69.35(p.183.24f.; M.42.256D); and also apostles by virtue of their conformity to Christ, Cyr.*ador.*3(1.84B,C); cf. Proc.G.*Ex.*13:21(M.87.582B); **3.** ref. Ps.74:3 τὸν σ. τῆς γῆς *Mir.Geo.* 13(p.131.5); **4.** exeg. 1Tim.3:15, Or.*Jo.*32.1(p.425.10; M.14.740B), Epiph.*haer.*69.35(p.183.24f.; M.42.256D) citt. supra; of Church σ. αὐτὴν καὶ ἑδραίωμα τῆς ἀληθείας ἐκάλεσεν, ὡς ἂν ἐν αὐτῇ τῆς ἀληθείας τὴν σύστασιν ἐχούσης Thdr.Mops.*1Tim.*3:15(p.131.19; M.66.941C); ἐκκλησίαν τῶν πεπιστευκότων τὸν σύλλογον προσηγόρευσε. τούτους ἔφη σ. ... τῆς ἀληθείας. ἐπὶ γὰρ τῆς πέτρας ἐρηρεισμένοι... διαμένουσι...διὰ τῶν πραγμάτων κηρύττοντες τὴν τῶν δογμάτων ἀλήθειαν Thdt.*1Tim.*3:15(3.657); of truth as pillar of Church (by inversion of the text) ἡ γὰρ ἀλήθειά ἐστι τῆς ἐκκλησίας...σ. ... σ. ἐστι τῆς οἰκουμένης ἡ ἐκκλησία Chrys.*hom.11.1 in 1Tim.*(11.605E); **5.** met. in gen., of gospel as σ. τῆς ἐκκλησίας Iren.*haer.*3.11.8(M.7.885A) cit. s. στήριγμα; of saints (sts. ref. Gal.2:9, Apoc.3:12, 1Tim.3:15): SS. Peter and Paul οἱ μέγιστοι καὶ δικαιότατοι σ. *1Clem.*5.2; πύργοι καὶ σ. Chrys.*proph.obscurit.*2.5(6.187E); †Chrys. *hom.prec.*2(2.788C); S. Peter, Chrys.*hom.in Mt.18:23*(3.4E); ‡Chrys. *Petr.et El.*1(2.732B); SS. Peter and John as pillars of truth, Thdt. *provid.*10(4.657); John, Paul, Moses οἱ σ. τῆς πίστεως Gr.Nyss.*beat.* 6(M.44.1204D); τοὺς ὑπηρέτας τοῦ θείου μυστηρίου, οὓς καὶ σ. τῆς ἐκκλησίας κατονομάζει...ἀποστόλους τε καὶ διδασκάλους καὶ προφήτας ...οὐ γὰρ μόνον Πέτρος καὶ Ἰωάννης καὶ Ἰάκωβος σ. τῆς ἐκκλησίας εἰσίν...ἀλλὰ πάντες οἱ δι' ἑαυτῶν τὴν ἐκκλησίαν ἐρείδοντες id.*v.Mos.* (M.44.385A); martyrs σ. καὶ ἑδραίωμα *Ep.Lugd.*ap.Eus.*h.e.*5.1.17 (M.20.416A); στερροὶ καὶ μακάριοι σ. τοῦ κυρίου Dion.Al.ap.Eus.*h.e.* 6.41.14(M.20.609A); bishops οἱ στῦλοι καὶ τὸ ἑδραίωμα τῆς ἀληθείας Bas.*ep.*243.4(3.375A; M.32.908C); Athanasius, Gr.Naz.*or.*21.26(M.35.1112A); Basil σ. τῆς ἐκκλησίας καὶ ἔδρασμα Thdr.Stud.*cant.*6.3 (p.347); holy and upright men, Or.*Apoc.*21(p.29); Chrys.*hom.10.2 in Eph.*(11.78B); τὸν νοητὸν σ. ὅς ἐστιν ὁ τοῖς θείοις προστάγμασιν ...κατηρτισμένος Areth.*Apoc.*3:12(M.106.560A); victor over temptations, Oecum.*Apoc.*3:11(p.62); ὁ γὰρ νικητὴς τῶν ἐναντίων δυνάμεων, σ. καὶ ἑδραίωμα τῆς ἐκκλησίας καθίσταται Andr.Caes.*Apoc.*8 (M.106.248B); **6.** Manich. τῷ σ. τῆς δόξης, ὃς καλεῖται ἀὴρ ὁ τέλειος. ὁ δὲ ἀὴρ οὗτος σ. ἐστι φωτός, ἐπειδὴ γέμει ψυχῶν τῶν καθαριζομένων Hegem.*Arch.*8(p.13.11f.; M.10.1440C); **7.** Gnost., in list of aeons τοῦ Ὅρου, καὶ Στύλου [l. Σταυροῦ] Iren.*haer.*1.3.1(M.7.465B).

***στυμών, ὁ**, sens. dub. (? for στήμων *rafter*) τὸ τοῦ ναοῦ ἥμισυ κατέπεσεν, ὡς καὶ τὸν ἱερέα κατερχομένου τοῦ στυμόνος μονόπληγα ἀναιρεθῆναι *A.Jo.*42(p.171.11).

[*]**στυπεῖον, τό**, = στυππεῖον, *hemp*, Chrys.*hom.21.4 in Rom.*(9.662E).

στυπτικός, *astringent*; met., *stringent, severe*, Clem.*paed.*1.9(p.139.1; M.8.349B); στυπτικῶν...λόγων *Const.App.*2.22.1; comp., Max. *ambig.*(M.91.1208B); neut. as subst. τὸ σύντονον καὶ σ. τῶν ἁγίων Sophr.H.*mir.Cyr.et Jo.*29(M.87.3508A); *tonic, bracing* τὸν...δίκην οἴνου στυπτικὸν πρὸς φυγὴν τῆς κακίας θεῖον φόβον ‡Proc.G.*Pr.*21:17 (M.87.1433C).

***στυπτός**, *dyed* (cf. Ex.26:7,14) καὶ τὰς δέρρεις τὰς τριχίνας τὰς ἀπὸ ἐρίων αἰγῶν, ἵνα εἴπῃ στυπτά Cosm.Ind.*top.*5(M.88.201D); τῶν δευτέρων σκεπασμάτων...τῶν ἀπὸ τῶν αἰγείων ὄντων δὲ σ., ἃς καὶ δέρρεις ἐκάλουν *ib.*(205A).

στυράκιον, τό, *turret*, †Hipp.Th.*fr.*7.1(p.33.4; M.117.1033C).

***στυφή, ἡ**, *severity, austerity* ὁ τῆς ἀρετῆς καρπός, τῇ σ. καὶ τῇ τῆς ἐγκρατείας περιβολῇ πεφραγμένος Gr.Nyss.*hom.9 in Cant.*(M.44.969C).

[*]**στυφνότης, ἡ**, ? for στρυφνότης or στυφότης, *severity*, Ephr.2.132B.

στύφος, also oxytone; **1.** *astringent* στυφός Bas.*hex.*5.8(1.48C; M.29.113C); οἱ ὀδόντες...γομφιασμὸν ὑπομενοῦσιν...ὑπὸ ὄμφακος ἤ τινος τῶν στυφοτέρων Thdt.*Am.*4:6(2.1426); *Schol.*12 in Jo.Clim.*scal.*7(M.88.824A); **2.** met., *harsh, hard, austere* τὸν ἐν ἱερωσύνῃ βίον, ἐγκρατῆ τινα, καὶ κατεστυμμένον καὶ περιεσκληκότα τῇ φαινομένῃ ζωῇ· ἔνδοθεν δὲ τὸ ἐδώδιμον...περιέχοντα· ὃ τότε ἀνακαλύπτεται, ὅταν...περιρραγῇ τὸ σ. περιβόλαιον, καὶ περιτριβῇ τὸ ξυλῶδες...τοῦ ἐδωδίμου προκάλυμμα Gr.Nyss.*v.Mos.*(M.44.417C); ὡς...τῆς ῥόας ὁ καρπὸς...οὕτω καὶ ὁ σ. τε καὶ ἐγκρατὴς καὶ κατασκληκὼς βίος φύλαξ γίνεται τῶν τῆς σωφροσύνης καλῶν id.ap.Proc.G.*Cant.*4:3(M.87.1645B) for στύφων Gr.Nyss. *hom.7 in Cant.*(M.44.929B); σ. ἦθος καὶ βλόσυρον καὶ καταπληκτικόν Melet.*nat.hom.*9(M.64.1188A).

στυφότης, ἡ, **1.** *astringency*, Jo.Eleem.*v.Tych.*(p.123); Melet. *nat.hom.*10(M.64.1189D); fig., Synes.*Dion* 11(p.263.8; M.66.1145A); usu. met., *sharpness, bitterness*, as possessing a tonic or bracing character, exeg. Mt.5:13 μή...προδῶτέ, φησι, τὴν προσήκουσαν ὑμῖν σφοδρότητα, καὶ στερρότητα, καὶ σ., τὴν τῷ ἅλατι προσήκουσαν paraphrase of Chrys. ap. *cat.Mt.*5:13(p.33.29) but cf. id.*hom.15.7 in Mt.* (7.194B); of thought of death, ‡Max.*cap.al.*119(M.90.1428B); **2.** *severity, restraint*, whether towards oneself, Pall.*h.Laus.*45(p.133.12; M.34.1218A); Cyr.S.*v.Euthym.*19(p.31.19); or others, *Const.Stud.*18 (M.99.1712A).

στύφ-ω (στίφω), **1.** *contract, draw together*; *draw up*, pass. καὶ ὀργισθεὶς διὰ τὴν ταραχὴν ἐστύφθη τοὺς πόδας αὐτοῦ· καὶ ἐξ αὐτοῦ ἀρρωστήσας...καὶ σαπεὶς ἐτελεύτα Jo.Mal.*chron.*14 p.368(M.97.549A); *ib.*12 p.291(440B); Thphn.*chron.*p.209(M.108.537A); **2.** *be astringent* τοῖς στίφουσι τῶν φαρμάκων Thdt.*2Tim.*4:1f.(3.692); met., *be* or *act as an astringent*; **a.** *sting, brace*, of Lot's wife οὐ μωρὰν καὶ ἄπρακτον εἰκόνα, ἀρτῦσαι δὲ καὶ στῦψαι τὸν πνευματικῶς δυνάμενον διορᾶν Clem. *str.*2.14(p.146.16; M.8.1000B); παρρησιαζομένου καὶ ∼οντος ἅμα καὶ θεραπεύοντος id.*q.d.s.*41(p.187.11; M.9.645C); ὁ λόγος...τὸ στῦφον ἐχέτω, καὶ τὸ μεθ' ἡδονῆς Chrys.*hom.11.2 in Col.*(11.407E); Nil.*epp.* 2.190(M.79.300B); **b.** *be severe, be hard (on)*; *correct* ∼ετε...αὐτὰ [sc. τὰ τέκνα] δαρμοῖς καὶ ποιεῖτε ὑποτακτικά *Const.App.*4.11.4; Pall. *h.Laus.*21(p.68.1; M.34.1075C); τοῦ τῶν ἁγίων ἐμβριθοῦς τε καὶ ∼οντος Sophr.H.*mir.Cyr.et Jo.*49(M.87.3604C); opp. χαλάω, Chrys. *hom.29.1 in Rom.*(9.730C); pass. ὅπως τῷ πολλῷ τρόπῳ ∼θεῖσα ἡ ἐνυπάρχουσα ἡμῶν τῇ ψυχῇ λαγνεία συναφθῇ τῇ ἀφθάρτῳ ἁγνείᾳ Jo. Clim.*scal.*7(M.88.804C); **c.** *harden*; in good sense, *make austere* ὁ ∼ων τε καὶ ἐγκρατὴς καὶ κατασκληκὼς βίος Gr.Nyss.*hom.7 in Cant.* (M.44.929B); in bad sense τὰς...στυφείσας ὑπὸ τῶν ἁμαρτιῶν ἡμῶν συνειδήσεις Proc.G.*Is.*1:20(M.87.1856C); pass., *be austere* ἄνδρας... ἐστυμμένους καὶ νηφαλέους Cyr.S.*v.Sab.*28(p.113.7); Sophr.H.*conf.* (M.87.3365A).

στῦψις, ἡ, *astringency*; met., *practice of austerity, asceticism*, Max.*ep.*8(M.91.441D).

***στωμύλης**, *eloquent*, Gr.Naz.*carm.*1.2.32.25(M.37.918A) cit. s. γλυκασμός; Cyr.*Is.*2.1(2.196A).

***στώου**, vox nihili ἐπὶ στώου Gr.Nyss.*ep.*6.10(M.46.1036A; τοῦ περιστῴου p.33.21).

σύ, *thou*, [nom. sing. ἐσύ Barth.Edess.*Agar.*(M.104.1436C); *Contrad.*2(p.9); acc. ἐσέ *ib.*]; when added to an imper. denoting contempt and, as such, equated with Ῥακά (Mt.5:22) καθάπερ..

ἡμεῖς...οἰκέταις...λέγομεν· ἀπελθέ, εἰπὲ τῷ δεῖνι σύ· οὕτω καὶ οἱ τῇ Σύρων κεχρημένοι γλώττῃ ῥακὰ λέγουσιν, ἀντὶ τοῦ 'σύ' τοῦτο τιθέντες Chrys.*hom.16.7 in Mt.*(7.214C).

συγγάλακτος, as subst., *foster-brother*, Thphn.*chron.*p.270(M.108.669C).

σύγγαμβρος, ὁ, *husband of one's wife's sister, brother-in-law,* Thdr.Lect.*h.e.*1.37(M.86.181C).

***συγγαυριάω**, *rejoice with,* Bas.Sel.*or.*15.3(M.85.200A).

***συγγειτνιάω**, *live near, be neighbour, Mir.Artem.*34(p.51.29).

***συγγεμίζω**, *join in loading, help to load* an animal, *Apophth.Patr.*(M.65.281A).

***συγγεμ-όω, 1.** = foreg., *Apophth.Patr.*(M.65.269C); **2.** intrans., *fill* with water ~ώσαντος τοῦ καράβου Gr.Mag.*dial.*(tr.Zach.)4.57 (M.*PL.*77.423D).

συγγένεια, ἡ, *relationship*; **1.** *kinship*; *family connexion*; of marriage in particular, Thdt.*qu.24 in 4Reg.*(1.528); id.*qu.in 2Par.*18:1 (1.580); **2.** met.; **a.** ref. nature of man as formed of the earth τὴν πρὸς τὰ τέσσαρα τῶν στοιχείων συγγένειαν Or.*Jo.*13.40(p.266.3; M.14.469B); ταύτης [sc. τῆς ψυχῆς] δὲ ἐξιούσης, εἰς τὴν οἰκείαν σ. τὸ σῶμα χωρεῖ Thdt.*Ps.*145:4(1.1566); ref. man as intelligent τῆς πρὸς τὰ ἄνω σ. ... ἣν θνητῶν μόνος ἄνθρωπος ἐπιδείκνυται Eus.*p.e.*7.18(332B; M.21.560D); Nil.*exerc.*15(M.79.737C); of the first-fruits with the lump ἡ...ἀπαρχὴ τὴν πρὸς τὸ ὅλον ἔχει σ., οὐπέρ ἐστιν ἀπαρχή· οὐ τοίνυν ᾗ θεός ἐστιν, ἀπαρχὴ προσηγόρευται. ποία γὰρ σ. θεότητός τε καὶ ἀνθρωπότητος; Thdt.*eran.suppl.*3.6(4.275); of the eye with light, Proc.G.*Is.*62:1ff.(M.87.2661D); **b.** of thought, *connexion*; *idea in common*; *consistency* τὸ...ψηλαφητὸν ἐκεῖνο σκότος...πρὸς τὸ τῆς ἀγνοίας καὶ ἁμαρτίας σκότος πολλὴν ἔν τε τῷ ῥήματι καὶ τῷ νοήματι τὴν σ. ἔχει Gr.Nyss.*v.Mos.*(M.44.349C); id.*Eun.*3(2 p.40.25; M.45.608C); Chrys.*serm.7.4 in Gen.*(4.681A); τῆς παλαιᾶς καὶ νέας διαθήκης τὴν σ. Thdt.*Jon.*proem.(2.1461); id.*Ps.*38:2f.(1.851); τὴν τῶν κηρυγμάτων σ. id.*eran.*1(4.41); **c.** of representation or manner, *affinity*; of rites of baptism with redemptive acts of Christ, Gr.Nyss.*or.catech.*35 (p.131.1; M.45.88A); **d.** of spiritual relationship κρείττων ἡ πνευματικὴ συγγένεια τῆς σωματικῆς Gr.Naz.*ep.*197(M.37.321C); **3.** theol.; **a.** non-existent as bet. divinity and humanity, Thdt.*eran.suppl.*3.6(4.275) cit. supra 2.a; therefore not bet. H. Ghost and creatures, Ath.*ep.Serap.*1.22(M.26.581B); *ib.*1.23(584C); nor bet. Son and angels, Cyr.*Heb.*1:4(p.370.16; M.74.953B); **b.** may be predicated of Persons in Trin. πολλὴ ἡ ἰσότης διὰ τὴν τῆς φύσεως σ. Chrys.*hom.82.1 in Jo.*(8.483C); *cat.Jo.*12:46(p.333.30); τῆς κατὰ τὴν οὐσίαν σ. *ib.*14:9(p.347.8); **c.** of Christ's human nature with mankind οὔτε ἡ ὑπεροχὴ τὴν ὁμοίωσιν καὶ σ. ἐλυμήνατο, οὔτε ἡ πρὸς ἡμᾶς σ. τὴν ὑπεροχὴν ἠμαύρωσεν Chrys.*hom.49.2 in Gen.*(4.494A); αὐτὸς γέγονεν ἄνθρωπος, πολλὴν ἔχει πρὸς ἡμᾶς τὴν σ. διὰ τὴν τῆς σαρκὸς φύσιν Cyr.*thes.*15(5^1.171C); τὴν κάτω σ. Thdt.*eran.*1(4.39).

***συγγενειάζω**, met., *be akin to,* Epiph.*haer.*76.53(p.408.13; M.42.628C).

συγγενεύς, ὁ, *kinsman, relative, Ep.Mareot.*1 ap.Ath.*apol.sec.*74 (M.25.381C; v.l. for συγγενέσιν p.154.2); Cyr.H.*catech.*6.24; Cyr.*Ps.*48:8(M.69.1069C); of spiritual children of the martyrs, Ephr.3.253F.

συγγενής, 1. *of the same family, akin*; as subst., *kinsman, relative*; of those spiritually related to one ὅπως διὰ τῆς ἐμῆς ἐξόδου... ἡ τῶν πολλῶν μου συγγενῶν σύνοδος γένηται *A.Andr.*B 9(p.63.4); *A.(Pass.)Andr.*13(p.30.24; M.2.1241C); συγγενεῖς οὓς ἔχων ψυχῆς ἐμῆς οἰκείους ὕστερον γινώσκειν ἠρξάμην Gr.Thaum.*pan.Or.*16 (p.36.9; M.10.1097A); **2.** met., *akin, cognate, of like kind* οὐδὲ σαρκικοῖς ὀφθαλμοῖς τὸ φῶς ἑωράκεισαν (οὐδὲν γὰρ σ. καὶ οἰκεῖον ἐκείνῳ τῷ φωτὶ καὶ τῇδε τῇ σαρκί) Clem.*exc.Thdot.*5(p.107.6; M.9.656C); of (gnostic) man with the uncreate, *A.Andr.fr.*6(p.40.32); ἄφθαρτον γὰρ φύσιν πεποίηκε τὴν νοερὰν καὶ αὐτῷ συγγενῆ Or.*princ.*3.1.13(p.218.12; M.11.273A); its use in patristic literature discussed ἐπὶ...ὁμοουσίων καὶ ἑτεροουσίων λέλεκται τοῖς ἁγίοις πατράσι τὸ σ. ... διὰ τὴν ἕνωσιν, ἀλλ' οὐ τὴν φύσιν συγγενῆ...καὶ πάλιν...διὰ τὴν φύσιν, ἀλλ' οὐ τὴν ἕνωσιν εἴρηκεν Max.*opusc.*(M.91.104A,B).

συγγενίς, ἡ, fem. of συγγενής, *female relative, kinswoman,* Or.*schol.in Lc.*1:43(M.17.321B); Eus.*qu.Steph.*1.8(M.22.889B); Gr.Naz.*test.*(M.37.392B).

***συγγένισσα, ἡ,** = foreg., of BMV ἐκ μητρὸς Ἄννης καὶ ἐκ πατρὸς Ἰωακείμ, συγγένισσαν...τῆς Ἐλισάβετ Epiph.*ep.Arab.*ap.*haer.*78.17(p.468.15; M.42.728B).

συγγενν-άω, pass., *come into existence at the same time* οὐ σ. τοῖς ἀνθρώποις ἀλλ' ἐπίκτητός ἐστιν ἡ γνῶσις Clem.*str.*6.9(p.470.21; M.9.297C); ψυχὴ...καὶ σῶμα αἱ ~ηθεῖσαι φύσεις κατ' αὐτήν [sc. γέννησιν], διάφοροί εἰσι Leont.H.*Nest.*4.5(M.86.1661C); ~ᾶται, οὐ συσπείρεται Proc.G.*Gen.*2:7(M.87.153B); not applicable to rel. of Persons in Trin. ξυμπρόεισι...τῷ λόγῳ τὸ πνεῦμα, οὐ ~ώμενον ἀλλὰ...ἐκπορευόμενον Thdt.*affect.*2(p.65.18; 4.757); οὐδὲ συγγεγεννημένος ἢ προγεγεννημένος ἢ μεταγεγεννημένος υἱὸς ἕτερος τοῦ θεοῦ τῷ μονογενεῖ υἱῷ Gel.Cyz.*h.e.*2.19.9(M.85.1277A); ref. Inc. διδοῦσαν [sc. BMV] αὐτῷ γέννησιν, ὡς συγχρόνως αὐτῇ τῇ σαρκὶ ἔχοντι τὴν σύνθεσιν ἑαυτοῦ συγγεγεννημένῳ ταύτῃ ἐξ αὐτῆς οὔσης κατὰ τὸ εἶναι ὑποχρόνως Leont.H.*Nest.*4.3(1657C); ref. union with Christ, Gr.Naz.*or.*38.4(M.36.316A) cit. s. συγγί(γ)νομαι.

συγγέρων ὁ, *companion in old age,* Gr.Thaum.*ep.can.*5(M.10.1037B).

συγγηράσκω, *grow old together with*; irreg. perf. med. συνεγγήραμαι, Jo.Mosch.*prat.*45(M.87.2900B).

σύγγηρος, *growing old together*; as fem. subst., *fellow-widow* ἐλεημοσύνη...τῇ συγγήρῳ μου *Const.App.*3.13.1.

***συγγίγας, ὁ,** *fellow giant,* Isid.Pel.*epp.*1.351(M.78.384A).

συγγί(γ)ν-ομαι, 1. *be born with*; Christol. οὐ γὰρ συγγεγενῆσθαι τῷ ἀνθρωπίνῳ τὴν σοφίαν...οὐσιωδῶς, ἀλλὰ κατὰ ποιότητα Paul.Sam.*fr.*B 7(p.332.4)ap.Leont.B.*Nest.et Eut.*3(M.86.1393A); ref. union with Christ συγγεννώμενοι [v.l. συγγενόμενοι], καὶ συσταυρούμενοι ...καὶ συνανιστάμενοι Gr.Naz.*or.*38.4(M.36.316A); **2.** *come into existence together*; of time and creation, Clem.*str.*6.16(p.504.15; M.9.369C); ptcpl., *first, original,* Meth.*res.*3.6(p.397.16; M.18.321B); **3.** *associate, hold converse with,* Christol. ἡσυχάζοντος μὲν τοῦ λόγου ἐν τῷ πειράζεσθαι...~ομένου δὲ τῷ ἀνθρώπῳ ἐν τῷ νικᾶν Iren.*haer.*3.19.3(M.7.941A).

συγγι(γ)νώσκω, [variant aor. ptcpl. συγγνώσας, Thphn.*chron.*p.249(M.108.625A)]; *be aware of*, c. acc. πείθων τὸν μάγιστρον...μὴ συνεγνωκέναι τὸ γεγονὸς *ib.*p.110(316A).

***συγγνωμέομαι**, s.v.l., *beg for pardon,* ‡Ath.*Melch.*(M.28.525B).

συγγνώμη, ἡ, 1. *fellow-feeling, forbearance, leniency, mercy,* Chrys.*stat.*3.6(2.45C); **2.** *excuse* συγγνώμην τῆς πλάνης ἔχει τὴν ἄγνοιαν Clem.*prot.*10(p.72.20; M.8.213C); Bas.*Spir.*13(3.10B; M.32.88A); τῷ μὲν γὰρ ἡ πενία σ. δίδωσιν, εἰ καὶ λόγον οὐκ ἔχουσαν Chrys.*hom.42.5 in Jo.*(8.254A); exeg. Jo.15:21 συγγνώμης αὐτοὺς ἀποστερῶν καὶ τιθεὶς καὶ ἑτέραν παραμυθίαν *ib.77.2*(453C); **3.** *forgiveness, pardon,* from God for sins συγγνώμην μετάνοια πέφυκε γεννᾶν· ἡ σ. δὲ οὐ κατὰ ἄφεσιν, ἀλλὰ κατὰ ἴασιν συνίσταται Clem.*str.*2.15 (p.150.14f.; M.8.1009A); συγγνώμην νέμων id.*paed.*1.10(p.145.8; M.8.360C); σ. αἰτεῖσθαι id.*str.*2.13(p.144.21; M.8.996C); Meth.*lepr.*10 (p.464.8); συγγνώμης τυχεῖν Or.*Jo.*2.11(6; p.66.14; M.14.129C); Chrys.*hom.25.7 in Gen.*(4.242C); συγγνώμην ἕξομεν *Const.App.*2.18.5; Thdt.*affect.*11(p.283.1; 4.994); id.*haer.*5(4.397); eccl., *absolution* εἴ τις...ἐκ τοῦ καταλόγου τοῦ ἱερατικοῦ προσφορᾶς γενομένης μὴ μεταλάβοι, τὴν αἰτίαν εἰπάτω καί, ἐὰν ᾖ εὔλογος, συγγνώμης τυγχανέτω *Can.App.*8; *Const.App.*2.50.3.

***σύγγνωμος**, *united in will,* of Trin. σύσσοφος, σύζωος, σ. Eulog.*fr.Trin.*2.1(p.364).

σύγγνωσις, ἡ, *knowledge,* Clem.*str.*1.2(p.13.19; M.8.709A); περὶ τῆς σ. τῆς ἐκ μέρους εἴρηται...ὅτι καταργηθήσεται *cat.1Cor.*13:10(p.256.1).

συγγνωστός, *deserving leniency*; *in need of pardon* ὁ...ἐλάχιστος σ. ἐστιν ἐλέους Mac.Aeg.*hom.*29.6(M.34.720B); neut. as subst. τὸν ἔλεον τοῦ δεσπότου καὶ τὸ σ. τῆς φύσεως Epiph.*haer.*59.1(p.364.8; M.41.1017B).

***συγγόης, ὁ,** *fellow wizard,* Thphn.*chron.*p.421(M.108.996C).

***συγγονυκλιτέω**, *kneel also* or *at the same time,* Thdr.Stud.*epp.*2.63(M.99.1281D).

***συγγρηγορέω**, *wake* or *watch with,* Rom.Mel.(*AS* 1 p.76).

συγγυμνασία, ἡ, *common exercise*; *experience, training*; esp. *intellectual training* or *discipline* τὴν φιλοσοφίαν...θείαν δωρεὰν Ἕλλησι δεδομένην...συγγυμνασίαν τινὰ πίστεως ἀποδεικτικὴν ἐκπορίζεσθαι Clem.*str.*1.2(p.14.3; M.8.709B); *ib.*6.11(p.477.26; M.9.312C); id.*ecl.*29(p.146.7; M.9.713B); *spiritual exercise, discipline,* of Christian life ἡ...ἀληθὴς...σοφία...ταῖς θείαις ἐντολαῖς συγγυμνασίᾳ τε καὶ συνασκήσει μελετῶσα, δύναμιν θείαν...λαμβάνει id.*str.*2.20 (p.179.17; M.8.1068A); πλείονος...συγγυμνασίας δεόμεθα εἰς τὸ...διακριτικοὺς γενέσθαι Or.*Jo.*13.24(p.248.3; M.14.440A); †Bas.*parad.*3.12 (1.351D; M.30.72B); esp. in corporate life of Church τῇ χρονιωτέρᾳ συνδιαγωγῇ καὶ τῇ ἀφιλονείκῳ σ. Bas.*ep.*113(3.206C; M.32.528A).

***συγκαγχάζω (συγκαχάζω)**, *join in laughter,* Pall.*v.Chrys.*12(p.69.28, v.l. συγκαχ- M.47.39).

***συγκαθαγνίζω**, *purify together* ψυχὴν οὖν ἐπεὶ συγκαθήγνισμαι σώματι, ὡς τὸ ῥῆμά σου, γενέσθω μοι ‡Jo.D.*carm.annunt.*139(p.241; M.96.852C).

συγκαθαίρω, *purify together with* συμπεριτμηθῶμεν Χριστῷ, ἵνα καὶ συγκαθαρθῶμεν αὐτῷ Tim.III Al.*fr.*(M.86.268B)ap.Cosm.Ind.*top.*10(p.316.2).

*συγκαθεδρία, ἡ, right or privilege of sitting by the side of, ref. Mt.20:21 ἀξίους εἶναι...τῆς θεϊκῆς σ. Didym.Trin.3.29(M.39.948A); ‡Caes.Naz.dial.131(M.38.1032).

συγκάθεδρος, ὁ, 1. one who sits down beside, implying equality ἐπὶ μείζονί σου μὴ προπετεύσῃ καθίσαι...μὴ γίνου σ. Bas.renunt.8(2.209B; M.31.644A); hence one who sits in council with ἔφασκον μὴ δεῖν Διόσκορον σ. σφίσι γενέσθαι Evagr.h.e.2.4(p.42.12; M.86.2497A); partner ὁ σ. πατρικῆς δόξης ἄνω Geo.Pis.carm.55.1(p.57); 2. adviser to magistrate, etc., assessor ἄρχων λαμβάνει ἑαυτῷ βοηθὸν τὸν σ. Mac.Aeg.hom.15.42(M.34.604D); Pall.h.Laus.62(p.157.20; M.34.1233C); Socr.h.e.7.20.3(M.67.780B).

συγκαθείργνυ-μι, shut up with; hence marry (trans.), cause to be married τὴν Θάμαρ...τῷ πρωτοτόκῳ ~σι [sc. Ἰούδας] Cyr.glaph.Gen.6(1.194A).

συγκαθέλκω, drag down together; degrade at one and the same time; met., Bas.ascet.1.4(2.322B; M.31.877C); ὁ υἱός...τῷ κοινωνεῖν τῆς κτίσεως εἰς τὸ κοινωνεῖν καὶ τῆς δουλείας συγκαθελκόμενος [i.e. if what Eunomius said was true] Gr.Nyss.Eun.6(2 p.140.27; M.45.725C).

*συγκάθεσις, ἡ, consent, Thdr.Stud.epp.1.43(M.99.1065A).

*συγκαθήκομαι, go down together; met., abate accordingly, Cosm.Mel.schol.(M.38.348) in Gr.Naz.carm.2.1.1.1.

*συγκαθηλ-όω, nail on together; sc. on Cross, pass., be crucified together with ἐγώ φημι, ὁ λόγος ~ώθη, καὶ συνέπαθε τῇ σαρκί ‡Ath.disp.19(M.28.460B).

συγκαθίζω, 1. seat with, sc. as judges τὸ ἀποστολικὸν...ῥητὸν οὐ σ. Χριστῷ κριτὰς τοὺς ἁγίους Eulog.fr.Novat.ap.Phot.cod.280(M.104.352C); 2. intrans., sit with, A.Jo.31(p.167.28); ref. Eph.2:6 ὁ...Παῦλος...συνήγειρεν καὶ συνεκάθισεν Cosm.Ind.top.5(M.88.300A).

*συγκάθισμα, τό, sitting with, companionship, Ephr.1.215C,223B.

*συγκαθοπλίζω, arm simultaneously, Cyr.Nah.1(3.475E).

*συγκαθυβρίζω, insult at one and the same time; pass., be insulted together, Gr.Nyss.Maced.20(M.45.1325D).

συγκαθυφαίνω, pass., be interwoven with, Meth.symp.7.8(p.79.15; M.18.136B).

*συγκαινουργ-έω, renew or refashion with ~εῖσθαι τῇ κτίσει τὸν δι' ὃν ἡ κτίσις Cyr.1Cor.15:51ff.(p.316.6; M.74.912C).

συγκαί-ω, 1. burn up, consume away; of the digestive process, Clem.paed.2.9(p.204.29; M.8.492A); met. τῷ τῆς καρδίας νοσήματι ~όμενον Gr.Mag.dial.(tr.Zach.)1 proem.(M.PL.77.150C); 2. be overheated, Clem.paed.1.6(p.120.9; M.8.309B); Gr.Mag.dial.(tr.Zach.)2.32(M.PL.66.191B).

συγκακοπαθ-έω, 1. share in sufferings στρατιώτας ~ήσοντας Didym.Ps.5:12(M.39.1173C); διδάσκαλος...~ῶν καὶ συνεκπονῶν τῆς ὠφελείας ἕνεκα Mac.Mgn.apocr.3.37(p.132.12); Max.ambig.(M.91.1372D); 2. sympathize ~ῆσαι αὐτὸν διὰ τὴν πολλὴν πονηρίαν A.Phil.95(p.37.9).

*συγκακόσχολος, companion in frivolity, fellow trifler, M.Artem.(v.l. for κακόσχολος p.171.5).

συγκακουχ-έω, inflict hardship; hence do harm, Isid.Pel.epp.1.148(M.78.281C); usu. pass., endure adversity with, Chrys.hom.11.3 in Col.(11.408E); id.hom.3.1 in Philm.(11.787E); Pall.v.Chrys.20(p.126.8; M.47.71); συνοικήσας...καὶ ~ηθεὶς αὐτῷ Marc.Diac.v.Porph.3.

*συγκαλλωπίζω, glorify together with, ‡Nil.fr.ascens.3(M.79.1500D).

συγκάλυμμα, τό, covering, Max.ambig.(M.91.1157D).

*συγκάλυψις, ἡ, covering up, concealment, Max.opusc.(M.91.181A).

συγκάμπτ-ω, bend, bow down (trans.); fig., weigh down, depress, exeg. Ex.12:16 ὅπερ δηλοῖ μὴ συγκάπτεσθαι τὴν ψυχὴν περὶ τὰς πραγματείας τὰς ἐπιγείας ‡Chrys.pasch.3(8.259C, l. -κάμπτεσθαι); οἱ ~οντες εἰς γῆν τὴν ψυχήν μου λογισμοί Hymn.(AS 1 p.502).

*συγκαπηλεύομαι, be corrupted together, Philost.h.e.3.18(M.65.609B).

*συγκάπτομαι, v. συγκάμπτω.

συγκαταβαίν-ω, 1. come or go down with, descend together; a. in gen. συγκαταβάντων καὶ συναναβάντων Iren.haer.1.15.3(M.7.621A); ~ει [sc. into water at baptism] τισὶ καὶ ἀκάθαρτα πνεύματα Clem.exc.Thdot.83(p.132.16; M.9.696D); of those who acquire a knowledge of the mystery of the descent into Hades ~ων τῷ καταβεβηκότι εἰς ᾅδου Or.Jo.6.35(18; p.144.18; M.14.260C); ἐκκλησία...ὡς ἂν...βλέπῃ τοῦτον [sc. Christ] ἐπτερωμένον, καὶ μηκέτι ~οντα δι' αὐτήν meaning εἰ καὶ ἐγνώκαμεν κατὰ σάρκα Χριστόν, ἀλλὰ νῦν οὐκέτι γινώσκομεν id.schol in Cant.6:4(M.17.276D); b. in rel. to Inc. κἂν ὁ θεός...τῇ ἑαυτοῦ δυνάμει ~ῃ τῷ Ἰησοῦ εἰς τὸν τῶν ἀνθρώπων βίον id.Cels.4.5(p.277.26; M.11.1033D); c. consort with μὴ ~ειν...εἰς ταὐτὸν γυναικί Malch.ep.ap.Eus.h.e.7.30.14(M.20.716B); 2. make allowances, show consideration δεῖν τῇ ἀσθενείᾳ ~ειν τῶν ἀσθενεστέρων Or.comm.in 1Cor.7:2(JTS 9 p.500); δι' ὑπερβάλλουσαν φιλανθρωπίαν ἔχοντα [sc. Christ] μὲν διδόναι τοῖς συνετωτέροις θεολογίαν...οὐδὲν ⟨δ'⟩ ἧττον ~οντα καὶ ταῖς ὑποδεεστέραις ἕξεσιν ἰδιωτῶν ἀνδρῶν id.Cels.7.41(p.192.17; M.11.1480C); πείθων τὸ διάπυρον τοῦ προφήτου, συγκαταβῆναι τῷ μετανοοῦντι Cyr.H.catech.2.13; τῇ ἀσθενείᾳ ~οντες τῶν ἐξ Ἰουδαίων πιστευόντων Chrys.comm.in Gal.1:1(10.658D); ὀφείλει ~ειν τῷ σώματι μικρόν Bars.resp.7(M.88.1820C); hence indulge μὴ ~ε τῇ σαρκὶ πρὸς ἡδυπαθείας ‡Proc.G.Pr.22:26(M.87.1448C); 3. stoop, condescend; a. in gen. ~ειν εἰς τὰς ζητήσεις Clem.str.7.15(p.65.18; M.9.528B); ib.7.9(p.39.23; 476A); συγκατέβαινεν ὁ Παῦλος εἰς συναγωγὰς Ἰουδαίων Or.comm.in 1Cor.9:20(JTS 9 p.513); id.Jo.13.13(p.237.13; M.14.417C); to persons, accommodate oneself to, come down to the level of; of teachers to pupils, ref. God's dealings with mankind, id.Cels.4.12(p.282.22; M.11.1041C); ὡς...ἀγαθὸς διδάσκαλος...διὰ τῶν εὐτελεστέρων ~ων αὐτοὺς παιδεύει, οὕτως καὶ ὁ τοῦ θεοῦ λόγος...λαμβάνει ἑαυτῷ σῶμα Ath.inc.15.1(M.25.121C); Chrys.hom.22.3 in 1Cor.(10.196E); of God θεὸς...οὐ τοπικῶς ἀλλὰ προνοητικῶς ~ει τοῖς ἀνθρώποις Or.Cels.5.12(p.13.2; M.11.1197C); οὐ βουλόμενος...συνεχώρησε...ἀλλὰ σ. Chrys.hom.33.2 in Jo.(8.191D); in language of scripture ἡ...θεία φύσις...συγκατέβη τῇ ἰδιωτείᾳ τοῦ πλήθους Or.Cels.7.60(p.210.20; M.11.1508B); of Logos κατ' ἀρχὴν μὲν δημιουργῶν ὁ λόγος τὰ κτίσματα συγκαταβέβηκε τοῖς γεννητοῖς, ἵνα γενέσθαι ταῦτα δυνηθῇ· οὐκ ἂν γὰρ ἤνεγκεν αὐτοῦ τὴν φύσιν ἄκρατον...εἰ μὴ...συγκαταβὰς ἀντελάβετο Ath.Ar.2.64(M.26.284A,B); ref. post-resurrection appearances οὐχ ἑωρᾶτο εἰ μὴ συγκατέβη, διὰ τὸ λοιπὸν ἄφθαρτον εἶναι τὸ σῶμα Chrys.hom.87.2 in Jo.(8.521C); b. esp. in rel. to Inc. where senses of descend and condescend are combined μένων...τῇ οὐσίᾳ ἄτρεπτος ~ει τῇ προνοίᾳ καὶ τῇ οἰκονομίᾳ τοῖς ἀνθρωπίνοις πράγμασιν Or.Cels.4.14(p.284.18; M.11.1045A); ηὐδόκησεν ὁ θεὸς συγκαταβῆναι τὴν ἑαυτοῦ σοφίαν τοῖς κτίσμασιν Ath.Ar.2.78(M.26.312B); ib.2.51(256B); id.inc.8.1(M.25.109A); τῇ φθορᾷ ἡμῶν συγκαταβάς ib.8.2(109B); ὁ τῷ πράγματι συγκαταβὰς...πῶς οὐχὶ καὶ τοῖς ῥήμασι ~ειν ἔμελλεν, ὁ παντὸς λόγου ἀνώτερος; Didym.Trin.3.18(M.39.884D, 885A); ἀνθρώποις συγκατέβη καὶ διὰ τοῦτο γέγονεν ἄνθρωπος Thdot.Anc.exp.symb.(M.77.1316C); ~ει τοῖς ἑαυτοῦ δούλοις Jo.D.f.o.3.1(M.94.984B).

συγκαταβάλλ-ω, throw down along with; overthrow together, destroy along with οὐ γὰρ ὥστε καταβαλεῖν, ἀλλ' ὥστε συγκαταβαλεῖν ἐπείγεται [sc. ὁ διάβολος] Chrys.hom.22.5 in Eph.(11.172E); εἰ μέλλοιτε...κατασφάττειν τοὺς αἱρετικούς, ἀνάγκη πολλοὺς καὶ τῶν ἁγίων ~εσθαι id.hom.46.2 in Mt.(7.482C).

συγκατάβασις, ἡ, 1. descent; of Christ into Hades, Dial.Tim.et Aquil.87 v°; of angels from heaven, ‡Caes.Naz.dial.48(M.38.920); downward step, declension, met. εἰ δ' εἰσί τινες οἳ μηδ' ἀπὸ τῆς σ. βλάπτονται, δύναιντ' ἂν καὶ ἱερᾶσθαι καὶ πόλεων προστατεῖν Synes.ep.57(M.66.1396C); 2. resort to, association with (cf. συγκαταβαίνω) ἡ πρὸς τοὺς πέντε ἄνδρας κοινωνία καὶ μετ' ἐκείνους ἡ πρὸς τὸν ἕκτον οὐ γνήσιον ἄνδρα σ. Or.Jo.13.13(29; p.254.20; M.14.452A); 3. accommodation; a. in respect of laws, customs, leniency, concession, e.g. to human weakness, on part of Old Law δύο...ὁμοῦ γυναῖκας ἔχειν ὁ νόμος ἐπέτρεπε καὶ πολλὴ...καὶ ἐν τοῖς ἄλλοις ἅπασιν ἡ σ. ἦν· μετὰ δὲ τὴν τοῦ Χριστοῦ παρουσίαν πολλῷ στενωτέρα γέγονεν ἡ ὁδός Chrys.virg.44(1.303E); id.stat.19.4(2.196C); of Church opp. Law ἡ...ἱεροσυλία...ἐπὶ...τῆς ἐκκλησιαστικῆς συνηθείας...σ. τις ἐγένετο καὶ συμπεριφορά Gr.Nyss.ep.can.8(M.45.236A); ref. a penance οὐδεὶς ὁ τοῦτον τῆς τοιαύτης ἐπιτιμίας παραιτούμενος, ἢ συγκαταβάσει τολμῶν οἱᾳδήτινι χρήσασθαι ‡Jo.Jej.can.(p.432); laxity, Bas.renunt.3(2.205A; M.31.632D); hence b. in human relationships deference, consideration ἴσθι ἀκριβὴς πρὸς συγκατάβασιν...εἴτε νεωτέρῳ συνδιαιτήσῃ εἴτε πρεσβυτέρῳ Ephr.1.259B; βέλτιον τοῦ τάχους ἡ μακροθυμία καὶ τῆς αὐθαδείας ἡ σ. Gr.Naz.ap.Max.loc.comm.42(M.91.636D); c. in respect of one statement with another, agreement, correspondence ἔχαιρον ἐπὶ...τῇ πρὸς πάντας σ. καὶ συνδιαθέσει Dion.Al.ap.Eus.h.e.7.24.9(M.20.696C); τὸ ἀνερμάτιστον τῆς πίστεως καὶ ἀβέβαιον τῆς πρὸς τὸν λόγον τοῦ θεοῦ σ. Or.comm.in Mt.13.21(p.239.25; M.13.1153B); d. in respect of truth, diplomacy; reserve τῶν ἀποστόλων ἡ σ. ἣν καὶ τὸ πνεῦμα αὐτοῖς ὑπέβαλλε, παρασκευάζον αὐτοὺς τῷ τῆς οἰκονομίας ἐνδιατρίβειν λόγῳ Chrys.hom.1.1 in Ac.(9.2E); οὐχ ὑπόκρισις ἀλλὰ σ. καὶ οἰκονομία id.hom.12.1 in 1Cor.(10.96E); ἄρα ἡ εὐχὴ [sc. of Christ] σ. καὶ οἰκονομίας ἐστίν; id.hom.27.4 in Heb.(12.251A); manœuvre, stratagem οὐ...λέγει τὴν οὖσαν αἰτίαν, οἷον ὅτι σ. ἕνεκεν καὶ οἰκονομίας τοῦτο ἐποίουν οἱ ἀπόστολοι...δεῖ γὰρ τῆς οἰκονομίας ἀγνοεῖν τὴν αἰτίαν τοὺς μέλλοντάς τι καρποῦσθαι παρ' αὐτῆς χρήσιμον id.comm.in Gal.2:5(10.682E); ὁ γὰρ διάβολος...πολλῇ κέχρηται τῇ σ. πρὸς τὴν τῶν ἀνθρώπων ἀπώλειαν, καὶ ἀπὸ τῶν μικροτέρων προσβάλλει id.*hom.86.3 in Mt.*(7.814c); *σκόπει πῶς συνετῶς λέγει* [sc. the Samaritan woman]· *οὐ γὰρ εἶπε, δεῦτε ἴδετε τὸν Χριστόν, ἀλλὰ καὶ αὐτὴ μετὰ συγκαταβάσεως, μεθ᾽ ἧς καὶ ὁ Χριστὸς αὐτὴν ἐσαγήνευσεν, ἐπισπᾶται τοὺς ἄνδρας* id.*hom.34.1 in Jo.*(8.195D); *διὰ τὴν τῶν ἐκκλησιῶν εἰρήνην...αἱ σ. οὐκ ἀκερδεῖς* Cyr.*ep.*43(p.19.24; M.77.222D); **e.** on part of God, *accommodation, concession* to human limitations *διὰ συγκαταβάσεως ὤφθη ὁ ἄγγελος τῷ Ζαχαρίᾳ· οὐδὲ γὰρ φθαρτοῦ σώματος ὀφθαλμοῖς δύναταί τις ἰδεῖν ἄφθαρτον σῶμα* Or.*hom.4 in Lc.*(p.24.5; M.17.317A); ref. Is.6:1 *σ.* [i.e. to the seraphim] *ἦν τὰ ὁρώμενα. τί δέ ἐστι σ.; ὅταν μὴ ὡς ἔστιν ὁ θεὸς φαίνηται, ἀλλ᾽ ὡς ὁ δυνάμενος αὐτὸν θεωρεῖν οἷός τέ ἐστιν, οὕτως ἑαυτὸν δεικνύῃ, ἐπιμετρῶν τῇ τῶν ὁρώντων ἀσθενείᾳ τῆς ὄψεως τὴν ἐπίδειξιν* Chrys. *incomprehens.*3.3(1.465c); id.*hom.15.1 in Jo.*(8.85B); **4.** *condescension* of God; **a.** in gen. *μονογενὴς μὲν* [sc. *λέγεται*] *διὰ τὴν ἐκ πατρὸς γέννησιν...πρωτότοκος δὲ διὰ τὴν εἰς τὴν κτίσιν σ.* Ath.*Ar.*2.62(M.26.280A); of operation of H. Ghost, Didym.(‡Bas.)*Eun.*5(1.297E; M.29.716A) cit. s. *μετάβασις*; of grace of God *τὴν* [sc. *ἀρετὴν*] *ὑμᾶς μὲν θεῷ κατὰ χάριν θεουργοῦσαν...ὑμῖν δὲ τὸν θεὸν κατὰ συγκατάβασιν ἀνθρωπίζουσαν* Max.*ep.*2(M.91.408B); **b.** partic. in rel. to Inc. in which connexion the idea of *descent* is usu. also present, †Hipp. *theoph.*2(p.258.12; M.10.853B) cit. s. *φυσικῶς*; *εὐγενεῖς καὶ βασιλικαὶ ψυχαί, διὰ τὴν εἰς ἡμᾶς σ. εὐγνώμονες οὖσαι* Or.*Ps.*44:9f.(p.42); ‡Ath. *Ar.*4.31(p.80.10; M.26.516c) cit. s. *ἐνανθρώπησις*; *ἡ περὶ τὴν ἐνανθρώπησιν οἰκονομία καὶ ἡ πρὸς τὸ ταπεινὸν...τῆς ἀνθρωπότητος σ.* Bas. *hom.in Ps.*44(1.163D; M.29.400B); *τοῦ τε ἀνθρωπίνου διὰ τῆς ἀναλήψεως δοξαζομένου καὶ τοῦ θείου διὰ τῆς σ. μὴ μολυνομένου* Gr.Nyss. *Eun.*6(2 p.132.14; M.45.716c); *μὴ τοπικῶς λέγων καταβαίνειν τὸ θεῖον πανταχοῦ ὂν...ἀλλὰ τὴν πρὸς τὸ ταπεινὸν τῆς φύσεως ἡμῶν παραδηλῶν σ.* id.*Apoll.*9(M.45.1141c); Didym.*Trin.*3.18(M.39.881B,884D); *ἡ ἐξ οὐρανῶν τοῦ θεοῦ πρὸς ἡμᾶς κατάβασις, μᾶλλον δὲ σ.* ‡Epiph. *hom.*4(M.43.480A); *ib.*(485B); Chrys.*hom.38.3 in Jo.*(8.219E); *οὐχὶ φύσεώς ἐστιν ἀλλὰ χάριτος καὶ σ. καὶ κενώσεως* id.*hom.7.2 in Heb.*(12.75D); Thdot.Anc.*exp.symb.*2(M.77.1317A); *ib.*5(1320c); Cyr.*Ps.* 76:11(M.69.1192B); Thdt.*inc.*23(M.75.1460c); Leont.B.*arg.Sev.*(M. 86.1940A); *δοξάσω σου, Χριστέ, τὴν πιστὴν σ., πῶς ἐνηνθρώπησας* Rom.Mel.(*AS* 1 p.146); Max.*ambig.*(M.91.1041D); id.*ep.*19(M.91. 592D); Jo.D.*f.o.*3.1(M.94.984B).

***συγκαταβάτης, ὁ,** as adj., *compromising, abetting*, Thdr.Stud. *epp.*2.119(M.99.1393A).

***συγκαταβατικός, 1.** in respect of law, *lax, accommodating πρὸς τὰ ἐν σοὶ πάθη συγκαταβατικὸν διδάσκαλον* Bas.*renunt.*3(2.205A; M. 31.633A); **2.** in human relationships, *deferential, considerate μέτριον δέ φημι, οὐ τὸ πρὸς τοὺς μείζους κολακευτικόν, ἀλλὰ τὸ πρὸς τοὺς ἐλάττους σ.* Isid.Pel.*epp.*3.222(M.78.905A); neut. as subst., *Mir. Artem.*35(p.57.22); **3.** in respect of truth, *diplomatic, reserved αἱ τῶν πλουτούντων...ψυχαὶ ἀσθενέστεραι...ὥστε ἐκεῖ σ. εἶναι δεῖ· αἱ τῶν πενήτων...συνετώτεραι· ὥστε ἐνταῦθα καὶ παρρησίᾳ χρὴ μείζονι κεχρῆσθαι, πρὸς ἓν ὁρῶντα, τὴν οἰκοδομήν* Chrys.*hom.11.2 in Col.*(11. 407c); **4.** on the part of God, *condescending τὴν τοῦ θεοῦ...σ. σάρκωσιν* ‡Jo.D.*hom.*6.2(M.96.664B); ref. men, *gracious δοκῶν ὁρᾶν σοῦ τὸ...πρόσωπον...τῇ πρὸς τὸν γραμματηφόρον σ. ὁμιλίᾳ καὶ θεωρίᾳ σου* Thdr.Stud.*epp.*2.56(M.99.1269A).

***συγκαταβατικῶς, 1.** *with reserve; with accommodation* in language, *by adaptation* in terminology *ἔδει συγκαταβατικώτερον ὁμιλεῖν τοὺς προφήτας βαρυτάτοις τὸν νοῦν, ἵνα χωρηθῇ* Or.*sel.in 1Reg.*15:11(M.12.992A); of the woman of Samaria calling her husband *συνετῶς...καὶ σ.* *cat.Jo.*4:28(p.221.27) for *μετὰ συγκαταβάσεως* Chrys.*hom.34.1 in Jo.*(8.195D); *εἰρῆσθαι τὰ τοιαῦτα...τροπικῶς τε καὶ σ.* Cyr.*thes.*24(5^1.235D); **2.** *with condescension, graciously*, *σ. διακύπτει* [sc. God] *ἐπισκοπῶν τοὺς τῆς ὑποδεεστέρας καταστάσεως* Didym.*Ps.*13:2(M.39.1220D); as between man and man, Jo.D.*inst. el.*1(M.95.445B); hence *concerning the Incarnation, with reference to the Incarnation* as supreme act of condescension *εὔδηλον ὅτι σ. κατ᾽ οἰκονομίαν τῷ υἱῷ...ἔφη δεδόσθαι διὰ τὴν σάρκα τὴν ἀποκάλυψιν* Andr. Caes.*Apoc.*69(M.106.445B).

***συγκαταβιάζ-ομαι,** *be forced in accordance with εἰ μὲν γὰρ ἦσαν δύο θεοί...τὸ ἀπεικὸς οὐδὲν ταῖς τῶν ποιησάντων γνώμαις ∼εσθαι τὰ ποιήματα καὶ...στάσιν...εἰσδέχεσθαι* Cyr.*Mal.*25(3.841D; *συγκαταμερίζεσθαι* Aubert).

***συγκαταβρόχω,** [aor. ptcpl. *συγκαταβρώξας*] *gulp down*, Sophr. H.*mir.Cyr.et Jo.*49(M.87.3605c).

***συγκαταγί(γ)νομαι,** *concern oneself along with, take part in together*, Iren.*haer.*1.6.2(M.7.505B).

συγκαταγράφω, *join in writing, record at the same time*, Gr.Nyss. *hex.*14(M.44.76c).

συγκατάγω, 1. *bring down with one*, in doctrine ascribed to Apoll. *σάρκα οὐρανόθεν ἑαυτῷ σ.* [sc. Christ] Max.*ambig.*(M.91. 1048D); **2.** met., *bring down to the level of, reduce to τῇ τῶν νηπίων ὑπολήψει σ. τὸν λόγον* Gr.Nyss.*Eun.*1(1 p.210.20; M.45.457D).

***συγκαταδηιόω,** *lay waste with, include in destruction*, Cyr.*Is.*3.4 (2.488A); id.*Nah.*proem.(3.475D); *ib.*9(485D).

***συγκαταδικάζω,** *condemn with*; pass., *share condemnation*, †Bas. *Is.*245(1.566c; M.30.549B); Cyr.*ador.*7(1.247D); *ib.*12(421E); Max. *ambig.*(M.91.1373B); of Christ with sinners, Cyr.*2Cor.*5:21(p.356.6; M.74.945B).

***συγκατάδικος,** *condemned together, sentenced with*, Jo.Clim.*scal.* 5(M.88.772c).

***συγκαταδιχάζω,** met., *cleave asunder τὴν πίστιν ταῖς διχονοίαις συγκατεδίχαζον* Const.Pogon.*sacr.*3(M.*PL.*96.390A).

συγκατάθεσις, ἡ, A. *approval, assent*; **1.** in gen.; of BMV at annunciation, Thdt.*eran.*2(4.140); *admission συγκαταθέσεις τῶν τέως ἀντιλεγόντων* Synes.*ep.*67(M.66.1421c); **2.** *assent* to propositions *μετὰ ἀποδείξεως καὶ σ.* Just.*dial.*123.7(M.6.764B); *οὐ γάρ ἐστιν ὑπόληψις ἡ ἑκούσιος πρὸ ἀποδείξεως σ. ἀλλὰ σ. ἰσχυρῷ τινι* Clem.*str.*2.6 (p.127.30; M.8.964A); plur., *acts of assent τοῦ διανοητικοῦ εἶναι, ἰδικῶς μὲν τὰς νοήσεις τῶν νοητῶν, τὰς ἀρετάς, τὰς ἐπιστήμας τοὺς τῶν τεχνῶν λόγους...τὸ βουλευτικόν, γενικῶς δὲ τὰς κρίσεις, τὰς σ., τὰς ἀποφυγάς, τὰς ὁρμάς* Max.*ambig.*(M.91.1109A); *τοῦ διανοητικοῦ... εἰσιν αἵ τε κρίσεις καὶ αἱ σ., καὶ ἀποφυγαὶ...καὶ ὁρμαὶ καὶ αἱ νοήσεις τῶν ὄντων καὶ αἱ ἀρεταί, καὶ αἱ ἐπιστῆμαι, καὶ τῶν τεχνῶν οἱ λόγοι, καὶ τὸ βουλευτικόν* Melet.*nat.hom.*synops.(M.64.1104B); *ἡ δόξα...τὰ φαντασθέντα καὶ διανοηθέντα...διὰ τῆς τοῦ λογισμοῦ σ. ἐκπληροῖ ib.* (1104c); an essential element of faith, Clem.*str.*2.2(p.117.9,13; M.8. 940A); *ὁρίζονται...οἱ ἀπὸ Βασιλείδου τὴν πίστιν ψυχῆς συγκατάθεσιν πρός τι τῶν μὴ κινούντων αἴσθησιν διὰ τὸ μὴ παρεῖναι ib.*2.6(p.127. 20; 961c); *ib.*5.1(p.327.24; M.9.12c); *πίστις...ἐστι σ. ἀδιάκριτος τῶν ἀκουσθέντων* Bas.*hom.*15.1(2.224c; M.31.677D); by itself an elementary form of faith, Didym.ap.*cat.Ac.*5:14(p.90.7); exeg. Jo.8:47 *ψιλὴ σ.* opp. *τηρεῖν τὰς ἐντολάς* Or.*Jo.*20.33(27; p.371.17; M.14.649B); cf. *ταῖς τῆς ψυχῆς σ.* opp. *τοῖς αἰσθητικοῖς ὤτοις* Ammon.*Jo.*8:47 (M.85.1453B); **3.** in partic., *conviction*; **a.** objective, i.e. act of convincing *τῶν χαρισμάτων...δοθέντων τοῖς ἀποστόλοις...εἰς τὴν τῶν ἀπίστων σ.* *Const.App.*8.1.2; **b.** usu. subjective, deliberate *assent* to, *assurance* or *conviction* of Christian truth *ἵνα ἡ τῶν πιστευόντων σ. μὴ ᾖ ἐν σοφίᾳ ἀνθρώπων, ἀλλ᾽ ἐν δυνάμει θεοῦ* Or.*Jo.*4.2(p.99.10; M.14.185B); *πείθειν ἐπεχείρουν ἐκ τοῦ Ἑλληνισμοῦ πρὸς τὴν σ. τοῦ καθ᾽ ἡμᾶς δόγματος μετατάξασθαι* Gr.Nyss.*fat.*(M.45.148B); *τὸν κεκληκότα* [sc. God] *πρὸς συγκατάθεσιν* id.*or.catech.*30(p.112.15; *κατάθεσιν* M.45.77A); *εἶδεν* [sc. God] *ἤδη τὴν ἐσομένην σ. πρὸς τὴν διδασκαλίαν* Didym.ap.*cat.Ac.*18:11(p.304.32); *πιστεύσας ὅτι Ἰησοῦς ἐστιν ὁ Χριστός, ὑψηλὴν σ. ἔχων περὶ τῆς τοῦ Χριστοῦ διαλήψεως, γεννᾶται* *cat.1Jo.*5:1(p.138.23); or of orthodoxy opp. heresy *τὸ κρινόμενον τῆς ἡμετέρας ἐξετάσεώς τε καὶ σ. φανερὸν ὑμῖν καθιστῶντες* Eus.*ep.Caes.*11(p.47; M.20.1544B); a necessary preliminary to baptism *σφράγισον τὴν σ. τοῦ δούλου σου* Serap.*euch.*21; *ἐπακολουθεῖ... τὸ βάπτισμα ἐπισφραγίζον ἡμῶν τὴν σ.* Bas.*Spir.*28(3.24A; M.32.117c); *ἔστι...τὸ βάπτισμα σφραγὶς τῆς πίστεως, ἡ δὲ πίστις, θεότητος σ.* id. *Eun.*3.5(1.276E; M.29.665c); *ἀποδεξάμενοι τὸν λόγον...καὶ μετὰ τὴν σ. τότε ἐπὶ τὸ βάπτισμα ἔρχονται* Chrys.*hom.7.2 in Ac.*(9.58A); id.*hom. 40.1 in 1Cor.*(10.378E); **4.** *belief, view τῆς ἀληθοῦς σ. τῶν...γεγενημένων* Antip.Bost.*annunt.*21(M.85.1789B); **5.** in moral sphere, *conscious acquiescence* in, *consent* of the will to a course of action (sts. referred to the intellect) *τὴν εἰκόνα ἔλαθεν περιφέρουσα τοῦ πάθους ἡ ψυχή, τῆς αἰτίας ἀπό τε τοῦ δελέατος καὶ τῆς ἡμῶν σ. γινομένης* Clem. *str.*2.20(p.174.4; M.8.1056B); *εὐδόκησις...καὶ σ. καὶ ῥοπὴ τοῦ ἡγεμονικοῦ ἐπὶ τόδε τι* Or.*princ.*3.1.4(p.198.14; M.11.253A); *ὅπου εἰκόνες λογισμῶν, ἐκεῖ γέγονε σ.* Marc.Er.*opusc.*1.142(M.65.921D); ref. sin *αἱ τοιαίδε σ. τοῖς χεῖροσι καὶ ῥοπαὶ ἐπὶ τὰς σ. προκαλοῦνται τὸν διάβολον εἰσελθεῖν* Or.*comm.in Eph.*4:27(p.554); *τῇ...ἐπὶ τὸ κακὸν σ.* Oecum. *Apoc.*2:13(p.52); *ἡ πάλη, ἢ στεφάνων, ἢ τιμωρίας ἀξία. ἡ σ., αἰτία καὶ ἀρχὴ τῶν ἐπιτιμίων* ‡Jo.Jej.*can.*(p.436); *οἱ δαίμονες...διὰ τούτων* [sc. *ἐμπαθῶν λογισμῶν*] *πολεμοῦντες τὸν νοῦν, ἐκβιάζονται αὐτὸν εἰς σ. ἐλθεῖν τῆς ἁμαρτίας* Thal.ap.*cat.Mt.*24:15(p.197.19); *ὁ νοῦς σκοτιζόμενος κυριεύεται ὑπὸ πάντων τῶν παθῶν ἅτινά εἰσιν ἀσέβεια...διψυχία, αἱ σ. τῶν ἁμαρτημάτων ἐκ τοῦ παθητικοῦ μέρους* Jo.D.*virt.*(M.95. 88c) = Ephr.3.426D; *σ. ἡ ἐγγίζουσα καὶ παρομοιοῦσα τῇ πράξει ib.* (93A) = Ephr.3.429c; *σ. ... ἡ κατάνευσις πρὸς τὸ πάθος τοῦ λογισμοῦ ib.*(93B) = Ephr.3.429E; exeg. Mt.5:28 *τὴν τοῦ πάθους σ. μοιχείαν καλέσας* †Jo.D.*B.J.*11(M.96.953A); as that which makes a sin deliberate *ἁμαρτάνειν...οὐ μετὰ τοῦ καταλαμβάνειν ἢ κατὰ τὴν σ.* Or.*comm.in 1Cor.*4:3(*JTS* 9 p.355); id.*comm.in Eph.*4:26(p.420); *γνώμης...ἐστι τὸ πταῖσμα, αὐθαίρετος σ. καὶ οὐκ ἀγνοίας ἀκούσιον* ἔθος Nil.*Magn*.7(M.79.977D); τὴν [sc. μοιχείαν]...πόθῳ καρωθεὶς ἐξειργάσατο· ὁ δὲ λογισμοῦ σ. ἔχει Proc.G.*2Reg*.12:10(M.87.1133B). **B.** *agreement, concord* μὴ ξενοπαθεῖν τοῖς περὶ τοῦ δόγματος λόγοις, ὅταν εἰς τὸ δυσθεώρητον ἐμπεσόντες, πρὸς τὴν τῶν λεγομένων σ. ἰλιγγιάσωμεν Gr.Nyss.*diff.ess*.5(M.32.336B); σ. ἐποιήσατο παλαιᾶς διαθήκης πρὸς νέαν διαθήκην Epiph.*haer*.66.69(p.110.7; M.42.137D); *conformity* πρὸς τὴν τοῦ ἐκκλησιαστικοῦ δόγματος σ. Gr.Nyss.*Eun*.1(1 p.146.20; M.45.385D); id.*or.catech*.33(p.124.8; M.45.84B); ὀρθοδόξου ...πίστεως καὶ τελείας σ. Epiph.*anc*.(p.5.13; M.43.17A); plur., *points of agreement* περὶ ὧν ἀεὶ συγκαταθέσεις ἡμῖν γεγένηνται Just.*dial*. 67.4(M.6.629C); τὰς ἐρωτήσεις καὶ τὰς ἐπαπορήσεις καὶ τὰς σ. Dion. Al.ap.Eus.*h.e*.7.24.8(M.20.696A).

***συγκαταθήγ-ω,** *sharpen together with*, met. ἀεὶ...πως ὀργιζομένῳ θεῷ ∼εται πρὸς ὀργὰς καὶ ἡ δούλη κτίσις Cyr.*Is*.2.2(2.222D).

***συγκαταθρώσκω,** *leap (down) together*, met. πρὸς ὄλεθρον Cyr. *ador*.15(1.549E).

***συγκαταισχύνομαι,** *be put to shame together*, Gr.Nyss.*hom.in 1Cor.6:18*(M.46.492C).

***συγκαταιχμάζω,** *strike down together*, Max.*ambig*.(M.91.1201B).

***συγκατακάμπτ-ω,** s.v.l., *bow together* ἡ τῶν χερουβὶμ ὀπτικωτάτη φύσις πόδας, πρόσωπα ∼ουσα τρόμῳ Geo.Pis.*carm*.35.2(p.53); perh. συγκαλύπτουσα).

συγκατακεράννυμι, pass., *be mixed with, commingle*, ‡Caes.Naz. *dial*.140(M.38.1053).

***συγκατακλάω,** met., *destroy utterly*, Amph.*Seleuc*.92(M.37. 1583A).

***συγκατακλεί-ω,** *enclose* or *shut up together*, of *contubernales* or 'spiritual companions' εἰς ἔσχατον γῆρας ἑαυτοῖς ∼ουσιν Chrys. *subintr*.1(1.228B); ἄνδρας τινὰς...λαβοῦσαι ∼ουσι καὶ τὸν πάντα συνοικίζουσι χρόνον id.*fem.reg*.2(1.250E); *ib*.3(254D).

***συγκατακληρόω,** *secure* one *an inheritance with* ἡ πίστις...τὴν πόρνην Ῥαὰβ τοῖς ἁγίοις συγκατεκλήρωσε Ephr.3.199A.

συγκατακλίνω, trans., *bow down with*; fig., pass. τῇ κλίσει τῶν γονάτων καὶ ἡ ψυχὴ σ. πρὸς εὐλάβειαν...ὅταν διὰ τῆς εὐχῆς συγκατακλιθεῖσα τῷ σώματι τὸν ἑαυτῆς κύριον ἐκλιπαρῇ τὰ προσήκοντα Ast. Am.*phar*.(pp.116.29,117.5).

***συγκατακρίν-ω,** *condemn with, condemn together* ὅπως μὴ συγκατακριθῶμεν, οὓς ὁ ἀπόστολος αἰτιᾶται Ephr.2.89E; ἐκ...τῶν ἀλαζονευμάτων τίνι συγκατακέκριται [sc. Eun.] διδαχθῶμεν Bas.*Eun*. 1.3(1.211E; M.29.509A); συμπάσχον καὶ ∼όμενον Mac.Mgn.*apocr*.4.16 (p.187.8); ∼ας ἡμῖν ἑαυτὸν ἑκουσίως, ὁ μόνος...ἀναμάρτητος [sc. Christ] Max.*ambig*.(M.91.1348C).

συγκαταλαμβάν-ω, *apprehend together* τὸ ἅγιον πνεῦμα...τοῦ υἱοῦ μὲν ἤρτηται, ᾧ ἀδιαστάτως ∼εται Gr.Nyss.*diff.ess*.4(M.32.329C).

***συγκαταλγύνομαι,** *be grieved together*, Cyr.*Jon*.22(3.384E).

συγκαταλέγ-ω, 1. *appoint to* as well or in company with ψυχὴ [i.e. of a martyr]...ἡ ∼εῖσα τῇ χώρᾳ τῶν ζώντων Eustrat.*stat.anim*. 15(p.444); hence *appoint to the company of*, ref. creation of man ἐν ἀγαθῶν παραδείσῳ χορείαις συγκαταλέξας θείαις Eus.*p.e*.7.18(332C; M.21.561A); **2.** *number together* or *with, reckon among*, Dion.Al.ap. Eus.*h.e*.7.21.9(M.20.685C); ὁ σπουδάζων...τοῖς ἁγίοις συγκαταλεχθῆναι Meth.*symp*.9.4(p.118.19; M.18.185B); Thdt.*provid*.9(4.638); εἰ μὴ πρῶτον ὁμολογήσειέν τις τὴν τῆς ἁγίας τριάδος ὁμολογίαν...οὐ βαπτίζεται, καὶ ∼εται μετὰ Χριστιανῶν Cosm.Ind.*top*.5(M.88.221B).

***συγκατάλεξις, ἡ,** *inclusion*, ‡Caes.Naz.*dial*.140(M.38.1068).

συγκαταλήγ-ω, *finish together*; **1.** intrans., *come to an end together* μὴ...τῆς ψυχῆς...∼ούσης τῇ διαλύσει τοῦ σώματος; Gr.Nyss.*anim.et res*.(M.46.17A); Cyr.*Jo*.2.7(4.225D); **2.** trans., *bring to an end together* τῇ προσευχῇ τὴν ζωὴν συγκατέληξεν Gr.Nyss.*v.Macr*.(p.399.9; M.46.985B); id.*Maced*.9(M.45.1312D).

συγκαταλύ-ω, 1. *dissolve at the same time*; **a.** *bring to an end with, abolish also* τοῦ θανάτου τὴν τυραννίδα ἐκβαλών, συγκατέλυσε καὶ... τοῦ διαβόλου τὴν ἰσχύν Chrys.*hom.4.4 in Heb*.(12.45C); τοῦ...πατρὸς Ἀθάμαντος τῷ μακρῷ βίῳ τὴν ἱερωσύνην συγκαταλύσαντος Synes.*ep*.76 (M.66.1441B); θαυμάζω ὅτι μὴ...καὶ τῶν ἐπιεικῶν ∼ει τὴν ἐξουσίαν Aen.*dial*.(M.85.909B); *break at the same time* a commandment ἐν τῇ λύσει τῆς μιᾶς [sc. ἐντολῆς] καὶ τὰς λοιπὰς ἐξ ἀνάγκης ∼εσθαι Bas. *reg.fus*.proem.2(2.328C; M.31.893A); **b.** pass. intrans., *come to an end together* ἀμφότερα ἀλλήλοις συμπέπλεκται καὶ ∼εται Chrys.*hom. 17.1 in 1Cor*.(10.146A); οὐδὲ...τῷ Παυλίνου θανάτῳ συγκατελύθη τὸ ἔχθος Thdt.*h.e*.5.23.2(3.1060); esp. in phrase τῷ παρόντι ∼εται βίῳ Chrys.*hom.15.5 in Mt*.(7.191A); id.*hom.14.3 in 1Cor*.(10.121D); id. *hom.2.4 in Rom*.(9.435B); Isid.Pel.*epp*.5.186(M.78.1440B); and τῷ παρόντι αἰῶνι σ. Chrys.*hom.4.1 in Eph*.(11.26B); **2.** *halt (for the night) together*, ref. Num.9:15ff. συναπαίρειν καὶ ∼ειν αὐτῇ [sc. τῇ νεφέλῃ] προστέταχε τοὺς ἐξ Ἰσραὴλ Cyr.*ador*.5(1.163E); **3.** *stay, abide*, ref. Ex.40:30f. ἀναπαυομένῳ...καὶ καταλύοντι, συναναπαυόμεθα καὶ ∼ομεν *ib*.10(353E).

***συγκαταμελίζω,** *dismember* Ἡρώδης...τὴν νηπίων πληθὺν...σ. *Hymn*.(*AS* 1 p.460).

***συγκαταμένω,** *stay behind with*, Synes.*insomn*.7(p.157.12; M.66. 1293B); opp. συνεκπλεύω, *ib*.14(p.174.7; 1308B).

***συγκαταμιαίνομαι,** *be defiled with*, Cyr.*ador*.12(1.422A); id.*Mal*. 25(3.841A).

συγκαταμίγνυμι, *mix in with, mingle, blend*, Gr.Nyss.*v.Macr*. (p.407.9; M.46.993A); Philost.*h.e*.7.4(M.65.541A); Const.VI Imp.*sacr*. (H.4.36D).

συγκατανέμομαι, med., *be pastured together*, Cyr.*Mal*.14(3.831D).

***συγκατανο-έω,** *conceive in the mind along with* ἵνα...∼ηθῇ τῇ ἀρχῇ καὶ ὁ λόγος ὁ ἐν ἐκείνῃ ὢν Gr.Nyss.*Eun*.8(2 p.183.24; M.45. 777A).

συγκαταπίπτ-ω, *fall down with*, lit. and met.; in moral sphere, in gen., *degenerate also*, Bas.*renunt*.3(2.205A; M.31.633A); of partic. falls τῷ πτώματι τῶν εἰδωλολατρούντων ∼οντες Gr.Nyss.*Eun*.4(2 p.71.8; M.45.644C); ref. Inc. τῆς θείας δυνάμεως οὐ ∼ούσης τῇ πρὸς τὸ ταπεινὸν συναφείᾳ τῆς φύσεως *ib*.6(2 p.131.18; 716A); ὡς συναλλάξαι... τὸν ἄφθαρτον τῷ φθαρτῷ, ὡς συνανακλιθῆναι τοῖς...ἁμαρτωλοῖς καὶ μὴ συγκαταπεσεῖν, ἀλλὰ συναναστῆναι Mac.Mgn.*apocr*.4.18(p.195.20).

***συγκαταποντίζω,** *sink in the sea together*, Hipp.*haer*.4.5(p.38. 20, v.l. συγκαταποντόω M.16.3067B).

***συγκαταριθμητέον,** *one must reckon also, one must include*, Or. *Cels*.1.9(p.62.14; M.11.673B).

***συγκαταρρήγνυμι,** *break* or *burst out at the same time*; of fire from heaven, Philost.*h.e*.12.8(M.65.617A).

***συγκαταρρωστέω,** *become weak* or *languish together*; of vines, Cyr.*Ag*.5(3.631B).

συγκατάρχ-ω, *rule jointly, share rule over*, of Son as reigning with Father καὶ ἔστιν ὁμόθρονος αὐτῷ καὶ ∼ει τῶν ὅλων Cyr.*hom.pasch*.18. 5(5².246D); id.*Is*.1.5(2.145A); id.*Zach*.101(3.794D).

***συγκατάρχων, ὁ,** *joint ruler*, of Son with Father σ. τῶν ὅλων καὶ συνδεσπότης Cyr.*ador*.11(1.388D).

***συγκατασείομαι,** *be overwhelmed also, be involved in the same fall*, Gr.Nyss.*fat*.(M.45.169A).

***συγκατασημαίνω,** *signify together with, denote at the same time*, Cyr.*Juln*.8(6².264C).

***συγκατασήπω,** *rot away together*, Bas.*hom*.14.6(2.127A; M.31. 456A).

***συγκατασκευή, ἡ,** *accompanying preparation* τὰ σπέρματα... πολλῆς δεῖται τῆς κατασκευῆς Chrys.*hom.3.3 in 2Thess*.(cod. συγκατασκευῆς 11.525E).

***συγκατασμικρύνω,** *make small, lessen at the same time*; *reduce to the level of* 'ἐκένωσε'...τὴν ἄφραστον αὐτοῦ τῆς θεότητος δόξαν καὶ τῇ βραχύτητι ἡμῶν συγκατεσμίκρυνεν Gr.Nyss.*Apoll*.20(M.45.1164C).

συγκατασπ-άω, *drag down with* or *also*; met., in moral sense τὸν μὴ συναμαρτάνοντα μηδὲ ∼ώμενον Clem.*str*.2.20(p.180.11; M.8. 1068C); ∼ᾶν τῇ τῆς ἀκολασίας δουλείᾳ Bas.Sel.*or*.8.2(M.85.120A); object of Devil's efforts, Gr.Nyss.*or.catech*.24(p.93.3; M.45.65A) cit. s. δέλεαρ; πρώτην τὴν γυναῖκα ἠπάτησε, καὶ τότε ἐκείνη τὸν ἄνδρα συγκατέσπασε Chrys.*hom.17.7 in Gen*.(4.144A); ὁ δαίμων...φθονήσας ∼αν [sc. τὸν ἄνθρωπον] ἐπειρᾶτο Cosm.Ind.*top*.2(M.88.120C).

συγκατασπείρω, 1. *sow together*, hence *beget together with*, Iren. *haer*.1.5.6(M.7.501A); id.ap.Hipp.*haer*.6.51(p.183.15; M.16.3282A) cf. Iren.*haer*.1.15.3(M.7.621A συμπαρέντων); **2.** *interweave, interlace*, Gr.Nyss.*v.Mos*.(M.44.389D).

***συγκατασφραγίζω,** *make the sign of the cross together*, *Tr.Phil*.3 (p.162.19).

συγκατατάσσ-ω, *range with* οἱ καθαιροῦντες τὴν τοῦ πνεύματος δόξαν, καὶ τῇ ὑποχειρίῳ φύσει ∼οντες Gr.Nyss.*Maced*.16(M.45.1320D); σὺ δὲ καὶ τῷ περὶ τῆς γεέννης τὸ πνεῦμα τὸ θεῖον ∼εις, διὰ τὸ λέγειν [Mt.3:11] Didym.(‡Bas.)*Eun*.5(1.308B; M.29.740A); ref. Heb.2:10 ἐν τῷ τῆς υἱότητος λόγῳ καὶ ∼ων ὁ ἀπόστολος φαίνεται τὸν ἀναληφθέντα ἄνθρωπον τοῖς πολλοῖς Thdr.Mops.*fr.inc*.12(p.303.12; M.66.985A); εἰ τὸ πρωτότοκος ὄνομα ∼ει τῇ κτίσει τὸν υἱόν, ὑπεξελεῖται...αὐτὸν ἡ τοῦ μονογενοῦς προσηγορία Cyr.*thes*.25(5¹.236B); *reckon along* or *in with* ἵνα...καὶ τὴν ἑτοιμασίαν συγκατατάξωμεν τῷ χρόνῳ τῆς οἰκοδομῆς Or. *Jo*.10.38(22; p.213.30; M.14.377C); med., *range oneself with, agree with* ∼εται...αὐτῷ καὶ Ἐπίκουρος Clem.*str*.2.23(p.189.17; M.8.1088B).

***συγκατατελέω,** *join the number of* ἕως ἂν νεκροὶ ὄντες ταῖς πράξεσι συγκατατελῶσι τοῖς νεκροῖς Olymp.*Eccl*.9:3(M.93.585C).

συγκατατήκομαι, pass., *melt away together*, Gr.Nyss.*anim.et res*. (M.46.100A); met., *pine away over*, Tit.Bost.*Man*.2.8(M.18.1148C).

***συγκαταυγάζω,** *illuminate together*; met., Cyr.*Zach*.23(3.683C).

***συγκαταυλίζομαι**, *lodge* or *settle together*, ref. Num.9:17 καταλυούσης [sc. τῆς νεφέλης], συγκατηυλίζετο [sc. ὁ λαός] Cyr.*ador*.10(1.353E).

***συγκαταυλισμός, ὁ**, *encamping together*, Cyr.*ador*.10(1.372C).

συγκαταφέρω, *carry down with* κειμένῳ...'Εωσφόρῳ μὴ συγκατηνέχθησαν ἀγγέλων χοροί; Gr.Naz.*carm*.1.2.6.21(M.37.645A); met., *depress at the same time* or *with others* ἵνα μὴ συγκατενέγκῃ τὴν ψυχὴν τῶν ἀκουόντων...καὶ διανίστησιν αὐτούς Chrys.*hom.11.2 in Col.*(11.406D).

συγκαταφθείρω, *destroy together*, Mac.Mgn.*apocr*.4.16(p.187.11); Cyr.*ador*.10(1.356D); Geo.Pis.*Heracl*.1.25(M.92.1300A).

***συγκαταφοιτάω**, *come down together*, Cyr.*Juln*.4(6^2.146C).

***συγκαταχράομαι**, **1.** *use both...and, make use of also*, Clem.*str*.4.18(p.298.18; M.8.1324A); **2.** *make full use of*, *ib*.7.4(p.16.16; M.9.428C).

***συγκαταψέγω**, *condemn along with, stigmatize also*, Or.*adnot.in Dt*.14:19(M.17.25C); Cyr.*ep*.40(p.23.17; 5^2.112D).

συγκάτειμι, (*ibo*), **1.** *go down together, descend with* εἰς ᾅδην κατιόντι τῷ λόγῳ...συγκάτεισι Max.*ambig*.(M.91.1384C); **2.** *consort, associate* with γάμοις συγκατιέναι σώφροσιν Eus.*d.e*.1.8(p.39.28; M.22.77A); ἐν βρώματι...καὶ φιλίᾳ σ. τοῖς αἱρετικοῖς Thdr.Stud.*epp*.2.32(M.99.1205A); **3.** *descend*; of Logos, ? in condescension, cf. infra 5; Eus.*d.e*.4.6(p.159.5; M.22.265A) = id.*l.C*.11(p.227.19; M.20.1381B); of beams of his light, *ib*.(p.159.8; 265B); **4.** *make allowances, show consideration*, for weakness συγκατιόντες τῇ τῶν πλειόνων ἀσθενείᾳ Eus.*d.e*.1.8(p.39.9; M.22.76B); ὥσπερ ἰατρὸς...τῷ κάμνοντι...συγκατιών Chrys.*hom.22.3 in 1Cor*.(10.196E; συγκαταβαίνει Gaume); ταῦτα οὐ νομοθετῶν λέγω, ἀλλὰ συγκατιών id.*hom.62.5 in Jo*.(8.374C); Thdt.*eran*.1(4.97); πρὸς τὴν ἐκείνων ἀσθένειαν συγκατιών id.*Dan*.1:2(2.1066); to inferiors, Isid.Pel.*epp*.3.41(M.78.760B); **5.** *stoop, condescend*, Chrys.*hom.62.3 in Jo*.(8.372B); Thdt.*Rom*.14:13(3.143); *accommodate oneself, come down to the level of* ποικίλον αὐτὸν [sc. τὸν ἱερέα] εἶναι δεῖ...εἰδότα...συγκατιέναι χρησίμως, ὅταν ἡ τῶν πραγμάτων ὑπόθεσις τοῦτο ἀπαιτῇ Chrys.*sac*.6.4(p.149.10; 1.425B); of God ἐπειδὴ ἄπιστόν ἐστι τὸ τῶν ἀνθρώπων γένος, συγκάτεισιν εἰς τὰ αὐτὰ ἡμῖν id.*hom.11.2 in Heb*.(12.113B); esp. in Inc. τοῦ υἱοῦ...διὰ τὸ...παρηλλαγμένον πρὸς τὴν τῶν παθημάτων κοινωνίαν συγκατιόντος Gr.Nyss.*Eun*.6(2 p.137.1; M.45.721B); **6.** *agree* τοῖς Ἀρειανοῖς συγκατιέναι Epiph.*haer*.77.24(p.437.32).

συγκατέρχομαι, **1.** *go down with*; *descend together*, Hipp.*haer*.10.30(p.285.12; M.16.3443A); ἂν εἰς ᾅδου κατίῃ [sc. ὁ Χριστός], συγκάτελθε Gr.Naz.*or*.45.24(M.36.657A); οὐρανόθεν ταύτην [sc. τὴν σάρκα] τῷ θεῷ λόγῳ συγκατεληλυθέναι ἔφησεν [sc. Apoll.] Thdt.*h.e*.5.3.6(3.1017); **2.** *descend, come down* ? in condescension ἡμᾶς μὲν γὰρ ἐν χρήσει τὴν χάριν λαμβάνειν λέγουσι...αὐτοὺς δὲ ἰδιόκτητον ἄνωθεν...συγκατεληλυθυῖαν ἔχειν τὴν χάριν Iren.*haer*.1.6.4(M.7.509A); ἀδύνατόν...τινα μέλος καταλεχθῆναι Χριστοῦ, ἐὰν μὴ πρότερον καὶ ἐπὶ τούτου συγκατελθὼν ὁ λόγος Meth.*symp*.3.8(p.36.12; M.18.73C); Geo.Pis.*carm*.102.3(p.66); **3.** *assent, approve*, Thdr.Stud.*epp*.1.17(M.99.964A).

συγκατεσθί-ω, *eat up, devour with* or *together*; met., *consume with* ὥστε αὐτοὺς [sc. Pharisees] εἰς τὸ ἡτοιμασμένον πῦρ...αἰωνίως ~εσθαι μετ' αὐτοῦ [sc. Beelzebub] Ath.*ep.Serap*.4.17(M.26.661C).

***συγκατευνάζομαι**, *lie with*, Cyr.*Joel*.38(3.233A).

***συγκατεύνασις, ἡ**, *carnal intercourse*, ‡Caes.Naz.*dial*.48(M.38.920).

συγκατέχω, *hold* and *keep down*, v.l. for κατεχομένη, Chrys.*hom.74.4 in Mt*.(7.720C).

***συγκατηφής**, = κατηφής, *with downcast eyes*, *Apoc.Dan*.C(p.118).

***συγκατισχνόομαι**, *waste away together with*, Cyr.*ador*.6(1.207D).

συγκατοικίζω, *cause to live with* or *together* προφάσεις αἱ τὰς γυναῖκας σ. τοῖς ἀνδράσι Chrys.*subintr*.1(1.228A).

***συγκάτοικος**, *dwelling with*, Cyr.*glaph.Gen*.7(1.226A).

συγκατολισθάνω, *slip and fall also*; of Adam's fall, Cyr.*glaph.Gen*.1(1.6C).

***συγκατονομάζ-ω**, *name together* ἐν τῇ τελειώσει τοῦ βαπτίσματος ~εται τῷ πατρὶ ὁ υἱός Ath.*Ar*.2.41(M.26.233A); Cyr.*thes*.16(5^1.178E).

συγκατορθ-όω, *accomplish, perfect at the same time*, †Bas.*bapt*.1.2.11(2.637E; M.31.1545A); τοῖς ἐσχάτοις καὶ ἡ τῶν ἐν ἀρχαῖς ~οῦται λύτρωσις Cyr.*ador*.2(1.70B); Thdt.*Ps*.89:17(1.1256); *furnish at the same time*; a need, Gr.Nyss.*or.dom*.4(p.90.24; M.44.1176D).

***σύγκατος**, *mixed, blended* ἐκ δ' στοιχείων...σ. κτίσις Areth.ap.*cat.Apoc*.4:7(p.244.28) for σύγκρατος, id.*Apoc*.4:6(M.106.572C).

***συγκατουσι-όω**, *make to form part of the essence* of τὸ λογικὸν ...εἶναι κοινὸν ἄν τις εἴποι τῆς ἀνθρωπίνης οὐσίας καὶ ἴδιον ἄνωθεν ~ωμένον τῇ φύσει Gr.Nyss.*Eun*.12(1 p.370.24; M.45.1096C).

***συγκάττυσις, ἡ**, *combination, mixture* βρωμάτων σ. Clem.*str*.7.7(p.28.15; M.9.452B).

συγκαττύω, *cobble, patch up* or *together*; met., from fables, etc., Iren.*haer*.1.8.1(M.7.521B); Clem.*str*.3.4(p.213.13; M.8.1141B); Nil.*epp*.1.247(M.79.173C); a letter, Socr.*h.e*.2.35.11(M.67.300B); a creed or system of belief, Hipp.*haer*.5.4(p.77.12; M.16.3123A); Socr.*h.e*.2.18.2(221B); *fabricate* falsehoods, heresies, Clem.*str*.7.16(p.70.7; M.9.537A); Const.ap.Gel.Cyz.*h.e*.3.19.14(M.85.1348C).

***συγκαχάζω**, v. *συγκαγχάζω.

σύγκει-μαι, as pass. of συντίθημι; **1.** *be composite*; theol. λόγος...ὤν, οὐ κατὰ τὴν τῶν ἀνθρώπων ὁμοιότητα...ἐστὶ ~μενος Ath.*gent*.41(M.25.81C); Epiph.*anc*.12(p.20.13; M.43.37C); Jo.D.*f.o*.1.4(M.94.797B); Christol., of incarnate Son as God and man ἐξ ὧν συνέκειτο ⟨ὁ⟩ ἐνανθρωπήσας Ἰησοῦς Or.*Cels*.1.66(p.121.1; M.11.785A); **2.** of writings, *be composed*; of laws, *be framed*; *be codified* or perh. *be composed one with another*, i.e. *be harmonized* οἱ...⟨νόμ⟩οι,...⟨οὔτε⟩ ~μενοι οὔτε καὶ ἐκμανθανόμενοι ἀταλαιπώρως Gr.Thaum.*pan.Or*.1(p.2.25; M.10.1052C); **3.** *be in agreement with* Ἀκάκιον...τὸν καὶ τὰ σύμμικτα συγγραψάμενον, τοῖς δὲ Ἀρειανοῖς λίαν ~μενον Thphn.*chron*.p.28(M.108.128C).

συγκεκροτημένως, *as welded together, unitedly*, ‡Bas.*const*.18.4(2.563A; M.31.1385C).

***σύγκελλος, ὁ**, *associate of a patriarch*, a high eccl. official σ. Κυρίλλου Iren.Tyr.*ep*.(p.136.17; H.1.1549E); Leont.N.*v.Jo.Eleem*.24(p.50.12); esp. *associate* of Patriarch of CP, a high cleric, often succeeding to patriarchate, nominated by emperor, Thal.CP *Thds*.(p.9.24; M.91.1477A); CCP(448)*act*.6(*ACO* 2.1.1 p.135.8; H.2.156B); Jo.Mosch.*prat*.42(M.87.2896D); Thphn.*chron*.p.1(M.108.56A).

συγκερ-άννυμι, **1.** *mix, blend, commingle*; **a.** lit. τὸ ὑλικὸν [sc. in Adam]...ὡς ἂν τῷ σπέρματι συγκεκραμένον Clem.*exc.Thdot*.55(p.125.12; M.9.685B); τῷ γεώδει συγκεκραμένην [sc. ψυχήν] Gr.Nyss.*anim.et res*.(M.46.44C); τῶν ἀλλήλοις συγκεκραμένων ὑγρῶν Cyr.*Nest*.1.3(p.22.9; 6^1.15C); ὅλων [sc. light from many lamps] ἐν ὅλοις ἀμιγῶς συγκεκραμένων Dion.Ar.*d.n*.2.4(M.3.641B); in creation τὰς ...ἀρχὰς πάσης αἰσθητῆς οὐσίας...εἰς ἓν ~αννύων [sc. ὁ λόγος] Ath.*gent*.42(M.25.84C); πάντα πρὸς ἄλληλα ~άννυσι κατὰ τὴν ἀσύγχυτον αὐτῶν ἕνωσιν Dion.Ar.*d.n*.11.2(M.3.949C); **b.** met. καθαρίσαι τὰς καρδίας ὑμῶν καὶ σ. ὑμῶν τὴν φρόνησιν Herm.*vis*.3.9.8; of mingled emotions, *Ep.Lugd*.ap.Eus.*h.e*.5.1.35(M.20.421A); οἱ...πράττοντες ἦσαν κατὰ ἀλήθειαν ἄγγελοι, τὴν οἰκείαν τῷ πράγματι φύσιν οὐ ~άσαντες Mac.Mgn.*apocr*.4.27(p.215.19); ref. man and wife (cf. infra 3) συγκέκραταί πως ὁ ἀνὴρ σαρκικῶς τε καὶ ψυχικῶς τῇ κατὰ νόμον συνηρμοσμένῃ Cyr.*Mal*.28(3.845E); **2.** *temper*; *compose* (cf. 1Cor.12:24) τὰ πολλὰ μέλη τὸ ἓν ἔσται σῶμα...τὴν δὲ κρίσιν ποδὸς καὶ χειρὸς κτλ. ... μόνου θεοῦ ἔστιν ποιήσασθαι, ὃς ~άσει τὸ σῶμα Or.*Jo*.10.36(20; p.211.8; M.14.373B); cf.†Nil.ap.Proc.G.*Cant*.7:2(M.87.1728D); **3.** *be one* with, *be intimately united* to, morally ᾧ συγκέκραται, καὶ συνήνωται ἡ ψυχὴ ἐν τοῖς θελήμασιν Mac.Aeg.*hom*.1.8(M.34.457C); οὐ συνεκράθησαν, τουτέστιν, ἀστασιάστως διέστησαν τῶν πάντων, μίαν καὶ τὴν αὐτὴν γνώμην ἐσχηκότων *cat.Heb*.4:2(p.178.18); ἑαυτὸν καταδουλώσας τῇ ἁμαρτίᾳ καὶ συγκραθεὶς τῇ γηίνῃ ἐπιθυμίᾳ ἐκ προαιρέσεως Jo.D.*hom*.2.1(M.96.576D); mystically ~άσατέ με τῷ σώματι τοῦ Χριστοῦ Or.*schol.in Cant*.2:4(M.17.261C); ὥσπερ γάρ τις αἰσθάνεται τῶν ἐνεργειῶν τῆς κακίας ἐκ τῶν παθῶν...οὕτως αἰσθάνεσθαι ὀφείλει τῆς χάριτος...τοῦ θεοῦ ἐν ταῖς ἀρεταῖς...ἵνα ἐξομοιωθῆναι δυνηθῇ, καὶ ~ασθῆναι τῇ ἀγαθῇ καὶ θείᾳ φύσει Mac.Aeg.*hom*.24.6(665D); ὅταν...ἡ ψυχὴ...καταξιωθῇ πνεῦμα γενέσθαι συγκεκραμένη τῷ πνεύματι *ib*.19.10(641A); Jo.Mon.*hymn.Petr*.1(M.96.1389D); **4.** Christol. in attempts to express union of divinity and humanity ~άσας τὸ θνητὸν ἡμῶν σῶμα τῇ ἑαυτοῦ δυνάμει Hipp.*antichr*.4(p.6.22; M.10.732B); πηλοπλαστῶν τὸν αὐτὸν...ὁ θεός...καὶ συνενώσας καὶ ~άσας τῷ λόγῳ Meth.*symp*.3.5(p.31.20; M.18.68B); τὴν θείαν εἰκόνα δουλικῇ μορφῇ ~άσαντι Gr.Naz.*or*.30.3(p.112.7; M.36.105D); συνανέβαινεν αὐτῷ καὶ ἡ εἰκὼν συγκεκραμένη εἰς τοὺς οὐρανοὺς...ἄνθρωπον συγκεκραμένον θεῷ ‡Chrys.*pasch*.6(p.189.1,7; 8.273C,D); τὸ πνεῦμα τὸ οὐράνιον ἐν τῷ Ἀδὰμ εἰσελθὸν εἰργάσατο, καὶ τοῦτον συνεκέρασε τῇ θεότητι Mac.Aeg.*hom*.11.9(M.34.549D); λέγεται...παρὰ...τοῖς Εὐνομιανοῖς ἡνῶσθαι τὸν θεὸν λόγον τῷ σώματι οὐ κατ' οὐσίαν...ἀλλὰ τὰς δυνάμεις τοῦ σώματος ταῖς δυνάμεσι ταῖς θείαις συγκεκρᾶσθαι Nemes.*nat.hom*.3(M.40.605A); of his glorified body σῶμα πνευματικὸν καὶ οὐχ ὑλικόν...συνενωθὲν καὶ συγκραθὲν τῇ θεότητι...εἰς ἀεὶ διαμένον Epiph.*haer*.64.64(p.504.15; M.41.1181B); term favoured by Apoll. ὁ τοῦ θεοῦ λόγος...πάντα πεπληρωκὼς ἰδίως τε τῇ σαρκὶ συγκεκραμένος Apoll.*fid.sec.pt*.11(p.171.9; M.10.1109B); τῶν συγκιρναμένων αἱ ποιότητες κεράννυνται καὶ οὐκ ἀπόλλυνται· ὥστε τινὰ καὶ διΐστανται ἀπὸ τῶν συγκερασθέντων, καθάπερ οἶνος ἀπὸ ὕδατος id.*fr.*127(p.238.15)ap.Thdt.*eran.*2(4.170); εἰ...οὐ κοινὴ ἡ ἐπωνυμία, οὐδὲν οὕτως ἔσται τὸ συγκεκραμένον Apoll. *fr.*144(p.242.5)ap.Leont.B.*Apoll.*(M.86.1968B); πρὸς οὐδὲν...ἐκείνων [sc. the angels] συγκέκραται ὁ θεός Apoll.*fr.*11(p.207.24)*ib.*(1961D); condemned by Cyr. εἰ συγκεκρᾶσθαι φασὶ τῷ λόγῳ τὴν σάρκα... ἀνάγκη λέγειν ἑκάτερον...ἀποστῆναι μὲν τοῦ εἶναι ὅ ἦν, ἐν δέ τι τὸ ἐξ ἀμφοῖν ἀποτελέσαι...ἑτεροφυές Cyr.*synous.*10(p.486.18; cf.M.76. 1433B).

***συγκέρασμα, τό,** *mixture* κ. τῆς ἁμαρτίας Geo.Pis.*hex.*799 (v.l. συμπέρασμα M.92.1495A).

***συγκεραστικῶς,** *willingly, readily, A.(Pass.)Andr.*A 4(p.9.12).

συγκεραστός, *mixed*; neut. as subst., *wine and water mixed,* Ephr.1.306A; *Apophth.Patr.*(M.65.376C).

συγκεφαλαι-όω, *bring together under one head, sum up, summarize,* theol. τὴν...τριάδα εἰς ἕνα...~οῦσθαί τε καὶ συνάγεσθαι πᾶσα ἀνάγκη Dion.R.ap.Ath.*decr.*26(p.22.11; M.25.464A); τὴν τριάδα ἀμείωτον εἰς τὴν μονάδα ~ούμεθα Dion.Al.ap.eund.*Dion.*17(p.58.25; M.25.505A); τριάδα ὁμοούσιον...εἰς μίαν ~ουμένην θεότητα, καὶ εἰς μίαν συναγομένην κοινὴν κυριότητα Sophr.H.*ep.syn.*(M.87.3152D).

συγκεφαλαίωσις, ἡ, 1. *sum, consummation* πρὸς συγκεφαλαίωσιν ἁγνείας Clem.*paed.*3.11(p.282.6; M.8.661B); of eccl. hierarchy καθολικωτάτη τῶν τῆσδε τυχὸν ἱεραρχίας, ἡ τῆσδε ἱερῶν συγκεφαλαίωσις Dion.Ar.*e.h.*1.3(M.3.373C); of NT in rel. to OT ἔστι τῆς θεολογίας ἡ θεουργία σ. *ib.*3.3.5(432B); **2.** *summing up* οὐ μόνον γὰρ οἱ κατακερματισμοὶ τῶν οἰκονομουμένων καὶ οἱ καθ' ἕνα λόγοι τῶν διοικουμένων εἰσὶν ἐν τῷ τοῦ θεοῦ λόγῳ καὶ τῇ σοφίᾳ αὐτοῦ, ἀλλὰ καὶ ἡ ἀνακεφαλαίωσις καὶ...σ. πάντων Or.*comm.in Eph.*1:10(p.241).

συγκεχυμένως, *confusedly,* Leont.H.*Nest.*3.8(M.86.1625D).

***συγκηρύσσω, 1.** *preach along with, join in preaching* Βαρνάβας ὁ...συγκηρύξας τῷ ἀποστόλῳ...τὸν λόγον Clem.*str.*5.10(p.368.12; M. 9.96C); **2.** *proclaim also, herald...with* ὁμοῦ τῇ ἀρχῇ καὶ τὸν ἐν ἀρχῇ συνεκήρυξε Gr.Nyss.*Eun.*4(2 p.53.25 M.45.624B).

συγκινέω, *go with, Mir.Geo.*11(p.110.29).

συγκίνημα, τό, = συγκίνησις, *movement in the same direction,* Geo.Pis.*hex.*111(M.92.1440A).

συγκιρν-άω, = συγκεράννυμι; **1.** *mix, blend, commingle*; **a.** of liquids ἀδύνατον...σῶμα διὰ σωμάτων διήκειν...ὥσπερ ὅσα τῶν ὑγρῶν μίγνυται καὶ ~ᾶται Jo.D.*f.o.*1.4(M.94.797C); **b.** met. τῇ θεοσεβείᾳ ~ῶντες τὴν πλάνην Meth.*symp.*2.3(p.19.1; M.18.52B); ταῦτα ~ώμενα ἀλλήλοις...τὴν ἀγάπην ἀποτελεῖ ‡Bas.*const.*13(2.558C; M.31.1377A); χρὴ τῇ φιλανθρωπίᾳ ~ᾶν τὸ δίκαιον Thdt.*qu.*65 *in 3Reg.*(1.509); **2.** *temper, mitigate* τῆς ἡλιακῆς αἴγλης ~ῶσαν τὴν φλόγωσιν Jo.D. *hom.*4.5(M.96.608B); *subdue* ~ᾶν δεῖ μετρίως τὸ σῶμα...ἵνα μὴ...ὁ ἀγωνιστὴς ὑπὸ τῶν τῆς σαρκὸς κινημάτων βιάζεται Ephr.3.404B; **3.** med., *be intimate* with; myst., *be intimately united* with γυμνὴ ...ἡ καρδία παντὸς σαρκικοῦ...δύναται τῷ Χριστῷ ~ᾶσθαι πνεύματι ‡Chrys.*pasch.*3(8.258A).

συγκίρν-ημι, = συγκεράννυμι; **1.** *mix, blend, commingle* ἑνουμένων...τῶν τεσσάρων [sc. στοιχείων] καὶ ~αμένων. καὶ τὸ ἀποτελούμενον...ἐκ τούτων παρὰ ταῦτα ἕτερον Jo.D.*Jacob.*24(M.94.1449A); met. ὦ φωνῶν καὶ βοῶν...ταῖς ψαλμῳδίαις ~αμένων Gr.Naz.*or.*18.28 (M.35.1020B); myst. κίρναται ὁ μὲν οἶνος τῷ ὕδατι, τῷ δὲ ἀνθρώπῳ τὸ πνεῦμα...τὸ θεῖον κρᾶμα τὸν ἄνθρωπον τοῦ πατρικοῦ βουλήματος πνεύματι καὶ λόγῳ ~άντος μυστικῶς Clem.*paed.*2.2(p.168.9; M.8. 412A); Christol. τῶν ~αμένων αἱ ποιότητες κεράννυνται καὶ οὐκ ἀπόλλυνται Apoll.*fr.*127(p.238.15)ap.Thdt.*eran.*2(4.170); ταύταις [sc. ταῖς αἰσθήσεσι]...αἱ ῥεῖαι δυνάμεις ~άμεναι τὴν ἕνωσιν ἀπειργάσαντο κατ' αὐτούς [sc. τοὺς Εὐνομιανούς] Nemes.*nat.hom.*3(M.40.605A); **2.** *be intimate* with; *be intimately united* with ἡμῖν ἐδωρήσατο χάριν... δι' ἧς τελειούμεθά τε...καὶ ~άμεθα τῷ φωτὶ τῆς θεότητος Nil.*epp.*2. 314(M.79.353C).

συγκλ-άω, *break*; pass. intrans., *fail* συνεκλάσθη τὰ σπλάγχνα αὐτῆς...καὶ ἐφοβήθη φόβον μέγαν *Asen.*6(p.46.7); *be nonplussed, confounded,* Gr.Mag.*dial.*(tr.Zach.)2.31(M.*PL.*66.191A); of one possessed, *be doubled up, contorted,* Call.*v.Hyp.*(p.79); met., of opinions, *clash* αἱ...αἱρέσεις...εἰς ἑαυτὰς ~ώμεναι Epiph.*haer.*4.2 (p.183.9; M.41.201A).

σύγκλεισις, ἡ, *shutting* or *closing up*; = συγκλεισμός, *confinement, Ep.Lugd.*ap.Eus.*h.e.*5.1.7(M.20.409B).

συγκλεισμός, ὁ, 1. *being shut up, confinement*; **a.** *investment, siege,* Clem.*str.*4.19(p.300.15; M.8.1328B); ‡Epiph.*v.proph.Is.*(p.20; M.43.397B); Cyr.*Abd.*2(3.356C); Thdt.*Is.*30:33(p.126.22); *enclosure* of fish in a net, Isid.Pel.*epp.*1.204(M.78.313A); **b.** met., of soul's condition after death εἰς τὴν φυλακὴν σ. Clem.*str.*3.4(p.210.33; M.8. 1137A); **2.** *conclusion, termination* τῆς κατ' αὐτὸν [sc. τὸν νόμον] ἱερωσύνης τὸν σ. Cyr.*Mal.*11(3.828C); of the end of one's life on earth, Gr.Naz.*or.*40.24(M.36.392C); ὁ...θεὸς...δικαίας ἑκάστῳ... ἀμοιβὰς ἀποδίδωσιν...ἔσχατον πᾶσι τοῖς οὖσι διδοὺς σ. Max.*ep.*1(M.91. 389D); fig., *shutting the door, finality* ὅπου...θεοῦ συγκλεισμός, ποία λοιπὸν ἐκεῖ μετάνοια; Anast.S.*Ps.*6(M.89.1097A); *ib.*(1128D).

***συγκλειστήριον, τό,** *prison,* Chrys.*fr.in Jer.*20:2(M.64.925D).

σύγκλειστος, ὁ, *fellow captive,* Thdr.Stud.*epp.*2.38(M.99.1233A).

συγκλεί-ω, 1. *shut* or *coop up, hem in, enclose*; ref. evil in Antichrist, Iren.*haer.*5.29.2(M.7.1201C) cit. s. ἀνακεφαλαίωσις; ref. incarnate Word τοῦ σώματος...~σθέντος διὰ τοῦ λίθου...οὐχὶ τῆς θεότητος ~σθείσης Epiph.*exp.fid.*17(p.517.28; M.42.813C); ὁ...θεὸς λόγος σαρκωθεὶς οὐ κωλύεται καὶ σαρκὶ ἡνῶσθαι καθ' ὑπόστασιν καὶ μὴ συγκεκλεῖσθαι ἐν αὐτῇ, ἀλλὰ τὰ πάντα πληροῖ Oecum.*Col.*2:9(p.454. 24); in good sense, *surround,* pass. πανταχόθεν σ. ὁ ἄνθρωπος [i.e. by divine revelation] Ath.*inc.*45.6(M.25.177B); **2.** *border, bind* κολόβιον ἄσπρον συγκεκλεισμένον πορφύρᾳ *A.Barth.*2(p.131.22); **3.** *exclude, prevent* ἐρχομένους τινὰς σ. ἡ ἡμέρα Ath.*apol.sec.*25(p.106.11; M.25. 289D); **4.** *conclude, complete* ὁ τὰς ἀγγελικὰς ~ων ἱεραρχίας, ὁ... ἀρχῶν, ἀρχαγγέλων τε καὶ ἀγγέλων διακοσμούμενος Dion.Ar.*c.h.*9.1 (M.3.257B); **5.** *conclude* by reasoning εἰς τοῦτο σ., ὅτι κτλ. Ath.*Ar.*3. 60(M.26.449C); **6.** *connect closely* τὴν δοκιμάζουσαν αὐτὴν σοφίαν ἐξ αὐτῆς τῆς ὕβρεως συλλογίζεται [sc. the Syrophoenician woman], καὶ σ. πρὸς ἔλεον Sev.Ant.ap.*cat.Mt.*15:30(p.125.10); **7.** *shut, close*; *fasten* σταυροῖο συνεκλήισσαν ὀχῆι Nonn.*par.Jo.*19:20(M.43.901C); *ib.*20:19(912A).

συγκληρία, ἡ, *community, participation* χρησώμεθα...τῇ τοῦ δοθέντος ἀγαθοῦ συγκληρίᾳ Const.ap.Eus.*v.C.*2.59(p.65.12; M.20. 1033B).

***συγκληρικός, ὁ,** *fellow cleric, colleague in holy orders, Cod.Afr.* 38; CChalc.*can.*18; Phot.*nomoc.*8.14(p.529; M.104.689B).

συγκληρονομ-έω, *inherit together* with, *be joint heir* τούτῳ ~εῖ [i.e. body with soul] τῆς...δόξης Gr.Naz.*or.*7.21(M.35.784A).

***συγκληρονομία, ἡ,** *joint-inheritance,* Clem.*str.*6.14(p.489.22; M. 9.337C).

συγκληρονόμος, ὁ, *joint-heir* οὗτοι σ. τῶν ἀντικειμένων εἰσίν, οἱ τῆς αὐτῆς αὐτοῖς κακίας μεταλαμβάνοντες Or.*exp.in Pr.*1:14(M.17. 164C); ἔσεσθέ μου ἀδελφοὶ καὶ σ. τῶν ἐμῶν πάντων *Asen.*24(p.77.18); esp. of Christians as joint-heirs with Christ (Rom.8:17), Clem. *prot.*11(pp.80.12,81.25; M.8.232A,236A); *Const.App.*2.33.2; *ib.*3.18.1; Chrys.*hom.in Rom.*5:3(3.145B); in words ascribed to Christ χαίρετε οἱ σ. μου *A.Petr.et Andr.*2(p.117.21).

σύγκληρος, *having part* or *lot in,* Eunomian term οὐ κοινωνὸν ἔχων [sc. the Father]...τῆς θεότητος...οὐ σ. τῆς ἐξουσίας Eun.*exp. fid.*1(p.254)ap.Gr.Nyss.*Eun.*2(2 p.311.3; M.45.484A); criticized by Gr.Nyss.*Eun.*2(2 p.313.1ff.; 485B–D).

συγκληρ-όω, 1. *join in one lot, cast one's lot together,* Bas.*hom.*5.6 (2.38E; M.31.249C); **2.** *embrace in one,* med. θεὸν...πᾶσαν ἀστείαν ἀρετὴν συγκεκληρωμένον Clem.*ecl.*21(p.142.23; M.9.708B); **3.** *assign* or *destine* to ὁ ταύταις [sc. συμφοραῖς] αὐτοὺς ~ώσας Thdt.*Ps.*106:12 (1.1369); τοῖς μὲν πλοῦτον συνέζευξε, τοῖς δὲ πενίαν σ. id.*provid.*6(4. 571); pass. τῶν ἀνθρώπων ἡ φύσις ἄνωθεν...συγκεκληρωμένην ἔχουσα τὴν ἀνωμαλίαν Athenag.*res.*17(p.68.20; M.6.1008B); παντὶ γεννητῷ αἰτία συγκεκλήρωται Aët.*synt.*ap.Epiph.*haer.*76.44(p.398.4; M.42. 609C); of fallen man ἄνευ τῆς συγκεκληρωμένης τῷ χοϊκῷ ἀνδριάντι θείας μορφῆς ‡Nil.*perist.*10.3(M.79.892B); Messalian ἡ...προσευχὴ... τὸν ἐξ ἀρχῆς ~ωθέντα πονηρὸν δαίμονα τῆς ψυχῆς ἐξελαύνει Thdt.*haer.* 4.11(4.366); **4.** pass., *be bound up with, belong* to τῇ...τοῦ ἑνὸς φύσει ~οῦται ἐκκλησία ἡ μία, ἣν εἰς πολλὰς κατατέμνειν βιάζονται αἱρέσεις Clem.*str.*7.17(p.76.9; M.9.552A); τοῦτο...ἴδιον θεοῦ...καὶ τῇ φύσει συγκεκληρωμένον Chrys.*hom.1.3 in 2Cor.*(10.421B); id.*hom.31.1 in 1Cor.*(10.279B); id.*hom.7.1 in Phil.*(11.245C); **5.** pass., *be made an inheritor with* Βηθλεὲμ...τοῖς ἀνθρώποις συγκεκληρωμένη Amph.*hom.* 1.4(M.39.41A).

συγκλήρωσις, ἡ, *community, fellowship* οὐ μόνον τῇ ἐν Καρχηδόνι ἐκκλησίᾳ ἀλλὰ καὶ πάσῃ τῇ ἱερατικῇ σ. *Cod.Afr.*53(tr. Lat. *consortium*).

συγκλητικός, ὁ, *senator*; by analogy, of highly-placed officials in foreign countries σ. Περσῶν *Chron.Pasch.*p.299(M.92.752A).

***συγκλητίς, ἡ,** *woman of senatorial rank* or *wife of senator A.Petr.et Paul.*84(p.219.4).

σύγκλητος, 1. *called together, summoned*; as fem. subst., *summoned council,* esp. Roman *Senate,* also of Byzantine senate, Thphn.*chron.*p.69(M.108.221B); *ib.*p.322(780A); **2.** s.v.l., *casually assembled, forgathered* τῶν συγκλήτων καὶ μιγάδων ἀνθρώπων Nil. *exerc.*7(M.79.728A); ? f.l. for συγκλύδων; cf. μιγάδων καὶ συγκλύδων ὄχλος ἀνθρώπων Philo *de decalogo* 2(Cohn–Wendland 4 p.271.2);

συγκλύδων καὶ μιγάδων ἠθῶν id.*de specialibus legibus* 3.14(*ib*.5 p.171.21).

***συγκλίδων**, v. σύγκλυς.

σύγκλινος, *sleeping beside, sharing one's room* or *bed*, Sophr.H.*v.Anast.*(M.92.1708C).

***συγκλόνησις, ἡ**, *commotion*, Gr.Naz.*or*.43.80(M.36.601C).

***συγκλονίζ-ω**, *dash together* ἡ θάλασσα ξηραίνεται, ὁ ἀὴρ ∼εται, τὰ ἄστρα πίπτουσι Ephr.3.145D.

σύγκλυς, *washed together*, hence, met., of a crowd, *promiscuous, casual* μιγάδων λογισμῶν καὶ σ. ‡Eust.*Laz*.24(p.46.12); συγκλίδων Nil.*Magn*.6(M.79.977B); Bas.Sel.*v.Thecl*.1(M.85.497B); of a sound, *confused*, Clem.*str*.6.3(p.447.28; M.9.252B).

συγκλώθ-ω, **1.** *weave together*, met. εἰ συγκλώσαιμεν εἰς ἓν σωματοποιοῦντες τὰ ἐν τοῖς εὐαγγελίοις γεγραμμένα Or.*Jo*.6.22(13; p.132.8; M.14.240B); pass., *be of one piece with, be of the warp and woof of* οὐ ∼εται, οὐδὲ συντάττεται [sc. the good which is found in the creature] τῷ δημιουργῷ ἑνὶ καὶ πρωτουργῷ ἀγαθῷ Didym.*Trin*.2.6(M.39.529B); **2.** *combine* δεινὸν ἡ κολακεία...μετὰ δυστροπίας συγκεκλωσμένη Pall.*v.Chrys*.16(p.94.11; M.47.53); pass., of persons, *be in league with*, *ib*.5(p.32.6; M.47.20).

συγκοιμάομαι, *go to bed at the same time*, Ign.*Polyc*.6.1.

συγκοινων-έω, **1.** *share* with, *go shares* with ∼ήσεις...πάντα τῷ ἀδελφῷ σου *Did*.4.8; ∼ήσατε ἡμῖν τῆς εὐωχίας ‡Meth.*palm*.2(M.18.385C); **2.** *have fellowship* with, *associate* with, (ref. Eph.5:11) †Bas.*bapt*.2.9.2f.(2.666E,668B; M.31.1612D,1616B); **3.** *join in making one's communion, in communicating* φωνὴ ἐγένετο· Πλάτων ἐπίσκοπε...∼ήσατέ μοι ὡς ὁ κύριος Ἰησοῦς ὑπέδειξεν *A.Mt*.25(p.253.2); **4.** *communicate with, be in communion with*, in the sense of *admit to communion* διὰ τὸ μὴ ∼εῖν τοῖς ἐν τῷ διωγμῷ παραπεσοῦσι Epiph.*haer*.59.13(p.378.29; M.41.1037B); ∼ῶ ὑμῖν Anast.S.*hod*.10(M.89.188B).

***συγκοινωνητέον**, *one must share* with μεταδοτέον καὶ σ. αὐτῷ Thdr.Stud.*epp*.2.219(M.99.1664C).

***συγκοινωνία, ἡ**, *state of being in communion with, communion* αἱρετικὴ σ. *communion with heretics*, Thdr.Stud.*epp*.1.39(M.99.1049D).

***συγκολαφίζομαι**, *be buffeted together with*; met. πάσχοντι [sc. ἑτέρῳ τινί] συγκολαφισθήσεται [sc. ἡ ψυχή] Leont.H.*Nest*.1.1(M.86.1405A).

συγκολλ-άω, *glue, cement, solder together*, Chrys.*hom.5.4 in Eph.*(11.37E); pass., met., *form a close friendship with*, *A.Petr.et Paul*.84(p.218.9); met., of unity of members of Christ ∼ήσας τὰ μέλη μετὰ ἀκριβείας Chrys.*hom.22.1 in Rom.*(9.679C); the work of charity, id.*hom.19.7 in Mt.*(7.255B); of union with God ∼ᾷ καὶ ἑνοῖ τῷ θεῷ...τὰ ...δάκρυα *ib*.6.5(95A).

συγκομιδή, ἡ, **1.** *bringing in, supply* κατασκεύασται [sc. ἡ τῶν ἀνέμων πνοή]...πρὸς μεταγωγὴν πλοίων καὶ συγκομιδὰς τῶν σιτικῶν Arist.*apol*.5(p.103.3); **2.** *burial* ἡμεῖς ἐπὶ τὴν σ. ἐξήλθομεν τῶν σωμάτων ‡Nil.*narr*.6(M.79.664A).

συγκομίζω, **1.** *collect, bring together* συνεκόμισε μὲν γὰρ εἰς ἑαυτὸν [sc. Satan] πάντα τὰ ἔθνη Cyr.*Abac*.23(3.537B); **2.** *bring in* the harvest, met. ἡμᾶς ὁ Χριστός, συνεκόμισε διὰ τῆς πίστεως εἰς ἁγιασμόν Cyr.*Nah*.13(3.491D; ἀνεκόμισε Aubert).

συγκομιστός, *brought together*; *gathered in* περὶ τοῦ θερισμοῦ, ὅστις ἐστὶν ἡ συντέλεια τῶν σ. τῆς ἀληθείας ἔργων Or.*Jo*.13.40(p.266.5; M.14.469B).

συγκονίομαι, med., *roll in the dust together*, i.e. *wrestle* or *struggle alongside*, Dion.Al.*fr*.ap.Leont.et Jo.*sacr*.2(cj. p.225.6 for συγκομισάμενον M.86.2073A).

συγκοπή, ἡ, **1.** *amputation* συγκοπαὶ μελῶν Ign.*Rom*.5.3; **2.** *slaughter* πολλὴν σ. αὐτοῖς ἐποίουν Thphn.*chron*.p.262(M.108.652B).

συγκοπι-άω, **1.** *be a fellow labourer, toil together* ∼ᾶτε ἀλλήλοις συναθλεῖτε Ign.*Polyc*.6.1; ∼άσασαν [sc. τὴν σάρκα] τῷ πνεύματι καὶ συνεργήσασαν...εἵλατο [sc. ὁ θεός] Herm.*sim*.5.6.6; Ephr.2.89E; Leont.N.*v.Sym*.26(M.93.1701C); **2.** *help* with money or other assistance πόσον...ἰσχύεις μοι ∼άσαι; †Jo.D.*B.J*.13(M.96.977D).

συγκόπτω, **1.** *chop up*; *cut off* χεῖρα [i.e. of Arsenius]...ὡς συγκοπέντος αὐτοῦ Ath.*apol.sec*.63(p.143.9; M.25.364B); met., *strike a blow at* σ. τοῦ διαβόλου τὴν δύναμιν Chrys.*hom.43.3 in 1Cor.*(10.404C); **2.** pass., *be afflicted, suffer* παθαίνομαι τῇ ψυχῇ καὶ τὰ σπλάγχνα σ. *Ep.Tib*.(p.79.1).

***συγκορυφεύς, ὁ**, *fellow head* or *chief* προτρέπεται Πέτρος τὸν σ. ...Παῦλον Germ.CP *or*.8(M.98.368C).

***συγκοσμίζω**, *adorn at the same time*, met. κοσμουμένης σου συνεκοσμίσθη σοι [sc. ἡ παρθενεία] *M.Ner.et Ach*.8(p.6.30).

***συγκουστουδιάζω**, (cf. Lat. *custodia*) *watch together*, ‡Chrys.*poenit*.1.2(9.764B).

συγκουφίζ-ω, *help to lift* or *lighten*; abs., met., *lighten the load* Χριστὸς ὁ ∼ων, ὁ συναντιλαμβανόμενος, ὡς συναθλῶν καὶ συντυπτόμενος Thdr.Stud.*epp*.2.55(M.99.1268C).

συγκραδαίνω, pass., *be shaken* τὸ ὅλον τῷ μέρει σ. ‡Caes.Naz.*dial*.140(M.38.1065).

***συγκραιφνής**, prob. from συγκεραιοφανής (cf. ἀκραιφνής), *intermingled, combined*; neut. as subst., †Nil.ap.Proc.G.*Cant*.2:3(M.87.1581A).

σύγκραμα, τό, *mixture, compound product*; esp. *physical constitution* of creatures τῶν...σ. οὐχ ὡσαύτως ἀεὶ διαμενόντων *Hom.Clem*.20.5; τροφὴν...ἐξαιματοῖ ἧπαρ, καὶ διὰ φλεβῶν ὅλον ἄρδει τοῦ ζῴου τὸ σ. ‡Nil.*perist*.4.12(M.79.837D); human *system* εἰ...πᾶν τὸ ἀνθρώπινον σ. ἐν αὐτῷ ἦν [i.e. in incarnate Son] Gr.Nyss.*Eun*.3(M.45.597C; v.l. for σύγκριμα 2 p.32.9); ref. constitution of Apollinarian Christ κατασκευάζει...τὴν θεότητα τοῦ μονογενοῦς, τὴν τοῦ νοῦ φύσιν ἀναπληρώσασαν, μέρος γενέσθαι τοῦ ἀνθρωπείου συγκράματος τὸ τριτημόριον, ψυχῆς τε καὶ σώματος κατὰ τὸ ἀνθρώπινον περὶ αὐτὸν ὄντων, νοῦ δὲ μὴ ὄντος Gr.Naz.*ep*.202(M.37.333A).

σύγκρασις, ἡ, **1.** *admixture, blending* οἱ μεγάλοι δίχα τῶν μικρῶν οὐ δύνανται εἶναι, οὔτε οἱ μικροὶ δίχα τῶν μεγάλων· σ. τίς ἐστιν ἐν πᾶσιν, καὶ ἐν τούτοις χρῆσις *1Clem*.37.4; εἴ τι δοκεῖ ἀληθὲς δι' αὐτῶν [sc. pagan writers] ἐκπεφωνῆσθαι, σ. ἔχει τῇ πλάνῃ Thphl.Ant.*Autol*.2.12(M.6.1069C); τῶν ζώντων σωμάτων...οἷς ἡ ὑπόστασις ἐκ τῆς τῶν στοιχείων ἐστὶ σ. Gr.Nyss.*anim.et res.*(M.46.44B); πυρὸς πρὸς ἀέρα σ. καὶ ἀέρος πρὸς ὕδωρ Leont.B.*Nest.et Eut*.1(M.86.1304C); opp. διάκρισις, Hipp.*haer*.5.21(p.123.27; M.16.3190A); *absorption, assimilation* τὴν πρὸς τὸ τρεφόμενον σῶμα δέχεται [sc. τροφή] σ. Athenag.*res*.6(p.54.27; M.6.985B); **2.** ref. creation, *constitution* εἰ δὲ φρονήσει τὰ πάντα τὴν σ. καὶ διακόσμησιν εἴληφεν *Hom.Clem*.6.19; αἱ ἐν τῷ παντὶ σ. Dion.Ar.*d.n*.4.8(M.3.704C); id.*c.h*.1.2(M.3.121B); esp. of constitution of man as body and soul τοῦ μὲν φωτὸς εἶναι μέρος τὴν ἐν ἀνθρώποις ψυχήν, τοῦ δὲ σκότους τὸ σῶμα,...μῖξιν δὲ ἤτοι σ. τοῦτον λέγει γεγονέναι τὸν τρόπον Hegem.*Arch*.7(p.9.16; M.10.1437A); ἡ...κατὰ σύνθεσιν ἕνωσις...ὡς ἐπὶ ψυχῆς καὶ σώματος, ἥντινα ἕνωσίν τινες σ. ἐκάλεσαν, ἤγουν συμφυΐαν Jo.D.*dialect*.65(M.94.664A); **3.** that which is constituted; **a.** *blend, combination* τῇ τῶν σ. ἐπιμιξίᾳ Eus.*d.e*.4.5(p.155.32; M.22.260C); *ib*.(p.155.18; 260B); **b.** a partic. blend, *temperament, characteristic* τῇ φυσικῇ ταύτῃ σ. χρώμενοι Clem.*str*.3.1(p.195.10; M.8.1100A); **4.** *union* with God, in Holy Communion (cf. συγκεράννυμι) ἀμετάληπτον γὰρ καθίσταται [sc. τὸ θεῖον σῶμα] τοῖς ἀργῶς αὐτὸ μεταχειριζομένοις, καὶ μὴ δὲ ἔργων ἀγαθῶν τῆς πρὸς αὐτὸ σ. ἀντιποιουμένοις ‡Chrys.*pasch*.2(8.255D); μὴ διαρρήξῃς τὴν ἕνωσιν ἀλλ' εὐδόκησον τελείαν γενέσθαι τὴν σ.· ἐνταῦθα μὲν διὰ βίου καὶ θεωρίας καὶ ἀρίστης πολιτείας· ἐκεῖ δὲ...τῇ αὐτοπτοθείᾳ τῆς δόξης σου *Lit.Jac.*(*NBP* 10[2] p.109); **5.** theol. οἷον ἐν ἡλίοις τρισὶν...ἀδιαστάτοις ...μία τοῦ φωτὸς σ. τε καὶ συνάφεια ‡Cyr.*Trin*.10(6[3].16B; M.77.1144C); **6.** Christol. τὰ...ἀμφότερα ἐν τῇ σ. θεοῦ μὲν ἐνανθρωπήσαντος, ἀνθρώπου δὲ θεωθέντος Gr.Naz.*ep*.101(M.37.180A); δύο φύσεις εἰς ἓν συνδραμοῦσαι, οὐχ υἱοὶ δύο, μὴ καταψευδέσθω ἡ σ. id.*or*.37.2(M.36.285A); *ib*.30.8(p.120.6; 113B); τῆς ἱερᾶς αὐτοῦ σ. ‡Chrys.*pasch*.6.3(p.161.10; 8.269E); rarely in later orthodox writings, Pamph.H.*panopl*.6.5(p.618) cit. s. ἐπίνοια; an Apollinarian term οὐδὲ ἐπὶ τοῦ Χριστοῦ τὸ σῶμα ἡ σ. μήτε μετέβαλεν ὡς μὴ εἶναι σῶμα Apoll.*fr*.134(p.240.2)ap.Thdt.*eran*.2(4.172); id.*corp.et div*.5(p.187.7; M.*PL*.8.873C) cit. s. ἄκτιστος; cf.id. *fid.inc*.7(p.199.27) cit. s. ἕνωσις; cf.Ath.*Apoll*.2.16(M.26.1157D); *ib*.(1160C); with σύγχυσις condemned as Apollinarian and charged against Cyr. by Easterns, Cyr.*ep*.44(p.35.19; 5[2].133C); *ib*.45(p.152.2; 136E); *ib*.46(p.160.8; 143C); rejected by Cyr. εἰ εὐποροῦσι...ἀναπεῖσαι...ὡς ἐν σ. καὶ μίξει τῶν ὠνομασμένων τὸ ἑκατέρῳ προσὸν ἰδίωμα τῆς ἑτέρου ποιότητος ἀμέτοχον ἔσται παντελῶς, ...ἀδικῆσαι...τοῦτό φαμεν τὸ σύμπαν οὐδὲν τῆς ἀληθείας τὴν δύναμιν τὸ τῆς σ. ὄνομα. εἰ δὲ ὡς ἐν τάξει τῶν ὑγρῶν ἀναμεμίχθαι φασὶν ἀλλήλοις σάρκα τε καὶ λόγον, πῶς ἠγνόησαν ὅτι τὰ ἀλλήλοις ἀνακιρνάμενα τῶν ὑγρῶν...μεθίσταται; Cyr.*synous*.10(p.486.9ff.; cf.M.76.1433A,B); παραιτητέον οὖν ἄρα τὴν σ., παρελάσομεν γὰρ οὕτω καὶ τὰ ἐντεῦθεν βλάβη *ib*.11(p.487.20; cf.1434A); ἡ...σ. ἀφανισμὸν τῶν φύσεων ἐργάζεται id.*hom.div*.21(p.538.9; M.77.1112C); rejected also in argt. against Eutyches ἐὰν μὴ δύο φύσεις μετὰ τὴν ἕνωσιν εἴπῃς, σύγχυσιν λέγεις καὶ σ. Bas.Sel.ap.CCP(448)*act*.7(*ACO* 2.1.1 p.93.31; H.2.168A); περιπίπτει τῷ τῆς συγχύσεως σκότῳ καὶ τῆς σ. Anast.S.*haer*.(p.260); **7.** Valent. aeon Ἀκίνητος καὶ Σύγκρασις Iren.*haer*.1.1.2(M.7.449A).

***συγκράτεια, ἡ**, *continence*, Euthal.Diac.*epp.Paul.*(M.85.752D).

συγκρατ-έω, **1.** *hold together*; *keep alive, hold in being, sustain* πέντε ἰσχᾶσι καθ' ἑκάστην ἡμέραν ∼εῖται Hier.*v.Paul*.A 6(p.10); τῶν ἀνθρώπων ∼εῖται ζωή Thdt.*pental.*(5.125); esp. of God as preserver as well as creator ὑφ' οὗ γεγένηται τὸ πᾶν...καὶ διακεκόσμηται καὶ ∼εῖται Athenag.*leg.*10.1(M.6.908B); τοῦ πατρὸς τοῦ ἀφ' ἑαυτοῦ δημιουργήσαντος καὶ ἐν ἑαυτῷ ∼οῦντος τὸ πᾶν Meth.*symp.*8.11 (p.94.13; M.18.156B); Chrys.*hom.5.3 in Jo.*(8.39A); id.*hom.38.3 in Ac.*(9.289E); **2.** *strengthen, support* καθέζεται...ἵνα συγκρατηθῇ ἡ ἀσθένεια τοῦ σώματος Herm.*vis.*3.11.4; **3.** *hold in, control*; of God, exeg. Heb.1:3 τουτέστι, κυβερνῶν τὰ διαπίπτοντα ∼ῶν. τοῦ γὰρ ποιῆσαι τὸν κόσμον οὐχ ἧττόν ἐστι τὸ ∼εῖν Chrys.*hom.2.3 in Heb.*(12. 17D) but in sequel to this quotation it approximates to 1 supra; πάντα...προνοίᾳ σοφῇ ∼εῖ τῶν οἰκείων ἔργων ὡς θεὸς προϊστάμενος Sophr.H.*ep.syn.*(M.87.3180D); pass., *be subject* to ἐπεὶ συνεκρατήθη [sc. ἡ σάρξ] ὑπὸ τῆς φθορᾶς Meth.*res.*2.18(p.368.16); ἐκρατήθη M.18. 284A).

συγκράτησις, ἡ, *holding together*, with a view to coherence or unity πρὸς τὴν τοῦ ἔθνους σ. ἦν Thdr.Mops.*Zach.*2:13(M.66.521C,D); exeg. Col.3:14 κορυφὴ μὲν γὰρ ἐπίτασις τελειότητος, σύνδεσμος δὲ σ. τῶν τὴν τελειότητα ποιούντων, ὡσανεὶ ἡ ῥίζα Chrys.*hom.8.2 in Col.* (11.383A); with a view to preservation, *conservation* τὴν πρόνοιαν αὐτοῦ...καὶ τὴν σ., τὸ εἶναι παρ' αὐτοῦ, τὸ ἐνεργεῖν, τὸ μὴ ἀπολέσθαι id. *hom.38.3 in Ac.*(9.290C).

§**συγκρατικός (A)** (συγκρατέω), *strengthening*, Anast.S.*qu.et resp.* 127(M.89.780C).

συγκρατικός (B) (συγκεράννυμι), *blending together* (trans.) τὸν ἔρωτα...ἑνωτικήν τινα καὶ σ. ἐννοήσωμεν δύναμιν Dion.Ar.*d.n.*4.15(M. 3.713A); *ib.*4.12(709D).

***συγκρέμαμαι,** *hang* or *be crucified together*, Vict.*Mc.*15:24(p.437. 9); Cyr.*Ps.*48:16(M.69.1072D); τοῖς ἁμαρτωλοῖς συγκατεδικάσθη καὶ συγκεκρέμαται δι' ἡμᾶς id.*2Cor.*5:21(p.356.6; M.74.945B).

σύγκριμα, τό, 1. *body formed by combination, compound structure*; shown to be inappropriate to divine nature, Athenag.*leg.*22.2f.(M. 6.937A,B); acc. Gnostics that into which passions of Sophia were ultimately transformed, Iren.*haer.*1.4.5(M.7.488B); Clem.*exc.Thdot.* 46(p.121.14; M.9.681A); *constitution* of human body, Nil.*epp.*1.220 (M.79.164B); and (myst.) of soul ἐκκλησία ἐν δυσὶ προσώποις νοεῖται, τῷ συστήματι τῶν πιστῶν, καὶ τῷ σ. τῆς ψυχῆς, ὅταν οὖν πνευματικῶς εἰς τὸν ἄνθρωπον λαμβάνεται, ἐκκλησία ἐστὶν ὅλον αὐτοῦ τὸ σ. Mac. Aeg.*hom.*37.8(M.34.756A); freq. of *union* of soul and body in man, Gr.Nyss.*hom.opif.*27.5ff.(M.44.228A,C,229A); id.*or.catech.*16(p.70.12; M.45.52B); id.*Apoll.*35(M.45.1201C); Mac.Aeg.*cust.cor.*8(M.34.825C); enlightened by Christ ὁ ἐλλάμψας τῇ ἐσκοτισμένῃ φύσει, διὰ παντὸς τοῦ σ. ἡμῶν τῆς θεότητος τὴν ἀκτῖνα διαγαγών, διὰ ψυχῆς λέγω καὶ σώματος Gr.Nyss.*ep.*3(M.46.1020C); since assumed by him in its entirety τὸ τὰς ἀρχὰς ἔχειν ἐκ τῆς θεοτόκου...πάσης κοινωνούσης τῆς ἰδιότητος τοῦ ἀνθρωπείου σ. Leont.B.*Nest.et Eut.*2(M.86.1325C); Hesych.H.*qu.ev.*9(M.93.1401B) cit. s. ἀνθρώπινος; ref. monothelitism τοῦ δεσπότου Χριστοῦ ὅλον τὸ ἀνθρώπινον αὐτοῦ σ. ... θεοκίνητον ἦν Serg.*ep.*3 ap.CCP(681)*act.*12(H.3.1316E); of *union* of natures in Christ σῴζον ἑκάστου τὸν φυσικὸν λόγον διὰ τῆς τῶν ἰδιωμάτων ἀντιδόσεως ἐν τῷ ἑνὶ σ. Leont.H.*monoph.*25(M.86.1785C); **2.** *judgement, sentence*, Hipp.*Dan.*3.7.5; *decision, answer* to a problem, *Apophth. Patr.*(M.65.348B); *interpretation, explanation* of dreams, Mart.Ant. *pan.*6(M.47.xlvii); cf. σύγκρισις.

συγκρίν-ω, 1. *bring into combination*; **a.** *link, combine* τὴν προσευχὴν ∼ε τῇ μελέτῃ· τοὺς ἀσθενεῖς θεράπευε Dor.*doct.*18(M.88. 1805B); **b.** mentally, *class with* τῶν εἰς ζῷα συγκεκριμένων σχημάτων Meth.*res.*3.15(p.411.22; M.18.316C); Petr.II Al.*encycl.*ap.Thdt.*h.e.*4. 22.32(M.33.1290A); **c.** for purposes of comparison, *compare* συγκρῖναι τὰ πρότερον...τοῖς ὕστερον...ἐπιδιαστραφεῖσιν †Hipp.*Artem.* ap.Eus.*h.e.*5.28.17(M.20.517A); Or.*Jo.*13.50(49; p.279.8; M.14.492C); ∼όμενος [sc. Jo. Bapt.]...πρὸς τοὺς ἤδη πρὸς θεὸν ἐκδημήσαντας... μέγας ἐστίν *cat.Lc.*7:24ff.(p.59.24); as bet. Father and Son, declared impious by Eun.*apol.*20(M.30.856A); **d.** exeg. 1Cor.2:13 τῷ συνεξετάζειν τήνδε τὴν λέξιν τῇδε τῇ λέξει καὶ τὰ ὅμοια συνάγειν, ἀνακαλύπτεται ὡσπερεὶ ὁ νοῦς τῆς γραφῆς Or.*comm.in 1Cor.*2:13(*JTS* 9 p.240); ὅταν...ἡ δευτέρα ἀποκάλυψις ἑρμηνεία ᾖ τοῦ προτέρου... ∼οντες οἱ δεχόμενοι τὰς ἀποκαλύψεις τὰ δεύτερα τοῖς πρώτοις, καὶ τὰ αὐτὰ εὑρίσκοντες πληροφορίαν μείζονα ἐλάμβανον τῆς ἀποκαλυφθείσης ἀληθείας Sever.*1Cor.*2:13(p.234.28); ὅταν πνευματικὸν καὶ ἄπορον ᾖ, ἀπὸ τῶν πνευματικῶν τὰς μαρτυρίας ἄγομεν...καὶ οὐδαμοῦ χρείαν ἔχω τῆς ἔξωθεν σοφίας Chrys.*hom.7.4 in 1Cor.*(10.55cf.); in sense of *establish, demonstrate* τὸ γὰρ 'συγκρίνοντες' οὐκ ἀντὶ τοῦ, παρεξετάζοντες, λέγει, ἀλλ' ἀντὶ τοῦ, ἀποδεικνύντες, ∼ειν τὸ ἀποδεικνύναι εἰρηκὼς ἐπὶ τοῦ παρόντος ἐκ μεταφορᾶς τῶν τῇ συγκρίσει μείζονα τοῦ δοκιμωτέρου τὴν ἀπόδειξιν ποιουμένων Thdr.Mops.*1Cor.* 13(M.66.880B); cf.Thdt.*1Cor.*2:13(3.178); **e.** pass., *be comparable* οὐ ∼εται [sc. the Son] κατ' οὐδὲν τῷ πατρὶ Heracleon ap.Or.*Jo.*13. 25(p.249.28; M.14.444A); Didym.*Trin.*1.27(M.39.400A) cit. s. ἀθεέω; **2.** *interpret*, †Gregent.*disp.*(M.86.752D); **3.** med., *give judgement* ὁ... δεσπότης...∼εται πρὸς τὸν...πονηρὸν δοῦλον *cat.Mt.*18:32ff.(p.149.30); **4.** *approve* ἡ συνείδησις οὐ ∼ει τοὺς...λογισμοὺς τοὺς ὑπακούοντας τῇ ἁμαρτίᾳ, ἀλλ'...ἐλέγχει Mac.Aeg.*hom.*15.34(M.34.597D); ταύτην [sc. τὴν ὁδόν] σ. πάντες, εἰ καὶ ἀποτομωτέρα...ὑπῆρχεν Thphn.*chron.* p.261(M.108.649C).

σύγκρισις, ἡ, 1. *comparison*; **a.** in gen., Tat.*orat.*31(p.31.9; M.6. 869A); Clem.*exc.Thdot.*11(p.110.17; M.9.661B); Or.*Jo.*6.22(17; p.142. 2; M.14.256B); confined to things of like nature, Clem.*str.*4.26(p.322. 15f.; M.8.1376C); ἐν...τοῖς ὁμογενέσιν...φιλεῖ τὰ τῆς σ. γίνεσθαι Ath. *Ar.*1.57(M.26.132A); Cyr.H.*catech.*3.6 cit. s. ἀσύγκριτος; **b.** as t.t. in rhetoric, *comparison* 'κατὰ σύγκρισιν', (ὅταν) τὰ παρόντα τοῖς παλαιοῖς ἐκ τῶν ὁμοίων ἐθέλει εἰκάζειν Hadr.*introd.*110(M.98.1304A); **c.** theol., may be made between Persons in Trin., not as differing in degree οὐ...σύγκρισίν τινα ποιούμενος [sc. Son] τῆς εἰς ἑαυτὸν καὶ τῆς εἰς τὸ πνεῦμα τὸ ἅγιον βλασφημίας...ὡς μείζονος ὄντος τοῦ πνεύματος Ath.*ep.Serap.*4.17(M.26.661C); but as one in essence εἰ δὲ μὴ σ. ἐστι τῷ υἱῷ πρὸς τὸν πατέρα, μηδὲ κοινωνία...ψευδεῖς...οἱ ἀπόστολοι ...τὸν γὰρ μήτε σύγκρισιν ἐπιδεχόμενον, μήτε κοινωνίαν...πῶς ἂν ἔδειξεν ἐν ἑαυτῷ ὁ υἱός; Bas.*Eun.*1.17(1.229C,D; M.29.552B); this had been denied by Eunomius ἀγέννητος...ὢν...ἐκφύγοι...πᾶσαν σ. καὶ κοινωνίαν τὴν πρὸς τὸ γεννητόν Eun.*apol.*9(M.30.844B); *ib.*11(845D); impossible bet. the divine and the created πάντων μὲν τῶν γενητῶν ὑπερέχειν οὐ συγκρίσει ἀλλ' ὑπερβαλλούσῃ ὑπεροχῇ φαμεν τὸν σωτῆρα καὶ τὸ πνεῦμα τὸ ἅγιον Or.*Jo.*13.25(p.249.19; M.14.441B); and so bet. the natures of Christ θεὸν ἄπειρον ὁμοῦ καὶ περίγραπτον ἄνθρωπον ὄντα τε καὶ νοούμενον...ἀλλ' οὐχ, ὥς τινές φασι, κατὰ σύγκρισιν... ὁμοφυῶν γάρ, οὐχ ἑτεροφυῶν, αἱ σ. ‡Hipp.*Ber.et Hel.*1(p.322.4ff.; M. 10.832B); Max.*Pyrr.*(M.91.349C); **2.** *interpretation* τῆς σ. τῶν ὀνειράτων Chrys.*hom.63.3 in Gen.*(4.604B); Procl.CP *annunt.*4(M.85. 441A); cf. σύγκριμα.

συγκριτέον, *one must compare*, Or.*Jo.*13.28(p.251.33; M.14.445D).

συγκριτικός, 1. *combining, uniting*, met. σ. τινα ἀγάπην νοῶν [i.e. φιλότητα] Clem.*str.*5.2(p.335.21; M.9.32A); **2.** *pertaining to comparison*; neut. as subst. σ. ἐστι πρότασις διὰ τοῦ μᾶλλον καὶ ἧττον προσαγομένη *Doct.Patr.*33(p.264.27); **3.** *comparable*, Didym.*Trin.* 2.5(M.39.500B).

συγκροτ-έω, 1. *strike together* sc. the hands; **a.** in anger; met., *disapprove, reject* τῆς 'Ιουδαίας μητρὸς...κλαιούσης ὡς παρεωραμένης παρὰ τοῦ ∼οῦντος θεοῦ Cyr.*Is.*4.4(2.673E); **b.** *applaud*; met., *approve, support the cause of* τοὺς ∼οῦντας τὸν πεπορνευκότα Chrys.*hom.14.2 in 1Cor.*(10.119A); τὸ ∼εῖν καὶ αὔξειν τὸν φιλοῦντα id.*hom.27.3 in 2Cor.*(10.630C); καὶ τὸν Ἀέτιον ∼εῖν ἐπειρᾶτο Socr.*h.e.*2.37.10(M.67. 304A); *help* ἵνα κατὰ δύναμιν τὴν ἑαυτῶν τοὺς τῶν ἐκκλησιῶν προεστῶτας ∼ῶσιν Chrys.*Philogon.*6.3(1.496D); id.*hom.14.1 in 1Cor.*(10. 117D); with money, Leont.N.*v.Jo.Eleem.*2,16(pp.8.15,34.24); ὑμᾶς προαναβιβάσαι ἔχω καὶ σ. Thphn.*chron.*p.271(M.108.672A); *ib.*p.118 (333A); of God in regard to men πόσα με συνεκρότησας· κἀγώ σε ἠγνωμόνηκα Anast.S.*Ps.*6(M.89.1084C); *support, maintain* servants, Leont.N.*v.Jo.Eleem.*33(p.65.9); **2.** *join* battle, *wage* war πόλεμον συνεκρότησε χαλεπόν Chrys.*hom.42.3 in Mt.*(7.455B); Cyr.*Is.*1.6(2. 161B); id.*ador.*4(1.119B); Geo.Pis.*Heracl.*1.223(M.92.1315B); fig. ὁ ∼ούμενος πόλεμος μεταξὺ ἡμῶν τε καὶ τῶν ἀκαθάρτων πνευμάτων Evagr.Pont.*or.*49(M.79.1177A); met., of contention in argument ἅπας ἡμῖν ὁ περὶ τῆς πίστεως ἀγὼν συγκεκρότηται Cyr.*ep.*39(p.18.4; 5².106E); **3.** trans.; **a.** *gather together, assemble*, Chrys.*hom.51.1 in Jo.*(8.299C); id.*hom.30.2 in Heb.*(12.281D); Or.*mart.*18(p.16.24; M. 11.585A); βουλόμενος [sc. ὁ 'Ιησοῦς] μετὰ ἀκριβείας ∼ῆσαι τὸ θέατρον Chrys.*hom.44.2 in Mt.*(7.470A); cf. οἱ τὸ ὠμὸν τοῦτο...∼οῦντες θέατρον [i.e. by standing around watching] id.*hom.21.6 in 1Cor.* (10.188C); of Jews τὴν τῶν 'Ιουδαίων λέγει συναγωγήν, ὡς τῷ ψεύδει ∼ουμένην Areth.*Apoc.*3:9ff.(M.106.557A); of Christians, Dion.Al.ap. Eus.*h.e.*7.11.12(M.20.665C); for instruction ὁ Γολγοθᾶς ἐν ᾧ νῦν... συγκεκροτήμεθα Cyr.H.*catech.*4.10; for eucharist, Anast.S.*synax.*(M. 89.829C); **b.** more formally, *summon, convene*, Clem.*prot.*1(p.3.10; M.8.52A); Bas.*hom.*17.2(2.139C; M.31.484C); persons for an eccl. council, Eus.*h.e.*5.23.3(M.20.492B); Ath.*syn.*1(p.231.11; M.26.681B); δικαστήριον Or.*Cels.*1.65(p.118.14; M.11.781B); Alex.Al.*ep.Alex.*5 (p.20.14; M.18.549B); Bas.*Eun.*1.2(1.209E; M.29.504C); ἐκκλησίαν Thphyl.*exc.gent.*6(p.484.13; M.113.945B); **c.** *proclaim* a feast ἑορτὴ ∼εῖται τῷ κυρίῳ Meth.*symp.*9.1(p.115.1; M.18.180A); ‡Meth.*Sym.et Ann.*8(M.18.368C); **d.** eccl., *convoke* a synod or council συνόδους ...συνεκρότει Eus.*v.C.*1.44(p.28.21; M.20.957D); Ath.*ep.Afr.*2(M.26. 1032C); Pall.*v.Chrys.*7(p.38.10; M.47.23); **4.** *collect, gather* so as to *form, establish,* or *organize*; **a.** τούτους ἀναλαβὼν καὶ λῃστήριον ∼ήσας Clem.*q.d.s.*42(p.189.6; M.9.648D); Χριστομάχον συνεκρότησαν ἐργαστήριον Alex.Al.*ep.Alex.*1(p.20.7; M.18.549A); μοναστήριον Pall. *v.Chrys.*20(p.128.2; M.47.72); ‡Pall.*h.mon.*2.2(p.25.1; M.34.1027A); **b.** esp. *collect, levy* troops; hence *train* διὰ τῆς πανούργως συγκεκροτημένης πιθανότητος Iren.*haer.*proem.1(M.7.437A); intellectually, Or.*princ.*4.2.2(p.310.2f.; M.11.361A); in Christian life, id.*or.* 29(p.392.29; M.11.545B); ὁ τῇ πνευματικῇ ∼ούμενος αἰσθήσει *cat. Apoc.*2:11(p.206.29); fig., of Christian army στρατευόμεθα...ὑπὲρ αὐτοῦ [sc. τοῦ βασιλέως] ἴδιον στρατόπεδον εὐσεβείας ∼οῦντες διὰ τῶν πρὸς τὸ θεῖον ἐντεύξεων Or.*Cels.*8.73(p.291.15; M.11.1627C); Chrys. *pan.Rom.*1.2(2.613E); **5. a.** *weld together, fuse, unite* εἰ χρὴ...πλείονας ἀδελφότητας ∼εῖσθαι Bas.*reg.fus.*35(2.378D; M.31.1004A); οὐδὲν οὕτω φίλους ποιεῖ καὶ ∼εῖ ὡς θλῖψις Chrys.*hom.42.3 in Ac.*(9.321D); ψάλλων μοναχὸς συνετῶς, ∼ῆσαι φιλίαν πνευματικήν Hyper.*mon.*152(M. 79.1488D); soul and body, Max.*myst.*7(M.91.685A); of Christ forming Church ὁ διὰ Χριστοῦ ∼ηθεὶς λαός Eus.*d.e.*10.3(p.459.22; M. 22.740B); ἐν αὐτοῖς γενόμενος καὶ τὸν πατέρα ἔχων μεθ' ἑαυτοῦ, ὥστε αὐτοὺς ∼εῖν Chrys.*hom.82.2 in Jo.*(8.485C); Cyr.*Ps.*76:19(M.69. 1193A); of consummation of Christ's marriage with Church ∼εῖται ὁ γάμος ἐν ἡμέρᾳ τῇ τρίτῃ Cyr.*Jo.*2.1(4.137A); **b.** *consolidate*; *establish, assure* κεκρότηται κρηπὶς ἀληθείας Clem.*paed.*1.1(p.89.25, v.l. συγκεκρότηται; M. om.); τριῶν...δι' ὧν τὸ ἔθνος [i.e. the Hebrew nation] συνεκροτεῖτο, ἑνὸς μὲν τοῦ βασιλικοῦ, ἑτέρου δὲ τοῦ προφητικοῦ, καὶ ἐπὶ τούτοις τοῦ ἀρχιερατικοῦ Eus.*d.e.*8 proem.(p.349.12; M. 22.568B); of Satan and his kingdom τὰ γὰρ ἑαυτοῦ ∼εῖν εἴωθεν, οὐ καταλύειν ἐκεῖνος Chrys.*hom.32.3 in Mt.*(7.366C); ∼οῦν τὴν ἀρετήν id.*hom.77.1 in Jo.*(8.452A); ∼εῖ [sc. love for God] τὴν σωτηρίαν id.*hom.30.3 in 2Cor.*(10.652E); id.*hom.7.2 in 2Tim.*(11.701D); **c.** persons, *fortify, rally, brace* ψυχρᾷ ταύτῃ...∼ούμενος [sc. ὁ διάβολος] παραμυθίᾳ †Just.*fr.*(M.6.1593A); νεανικῆς ἐστι ψυχῆς δυναμένης ∼ῆσαι τὴν ἑαυτῆς...ζωὴν ἀναμέσον τῶν σκανδάλων Ephr.3.`34F; διαχεῖ [sc. οἶνος] τὸ τῆς ψυχῆς εὔτονον, διαλύει τὸ συγκεκροτημένον Chrys. *hom.11.1 in 1Tim.*(11.606D); id.*hom.31.2 in Heb.*(12.287B); of a child in the womb, *form part of* ἐγέννησεν Ἐλισάβετ τὸν ἐξ ἀπροσδοκήτου ∼ήσαντα τὴν μήτραν Chrysipp.*enc.in Jo.Bapt.*3(p.33.3); **d.** *establish, confirm* a truth or an opinion, Chrys.*hom.61.2 in Jo.* (8.364A); ἡ ἀλήθεια...ὑπὸ τῶν ἐχθρῶν μειζόνως συνεκροτεῖτο id.*hom. 7.1 in Mt.*(7.102C); οἱ ἀμφὶ Βασίλειον...πανταχοῦ φοιτῶντες, τὸ ὁμοούσιον συνεκρότουν Philost.*h.e.*4.9(M.65.521D); ὥστε τὴν ἀληθῆ πίστιν ∼ηθῆναι CChalc.*act.2*(*ACO* 2.1.2 p.78.6; H.2.284E); ref. Law and the gospel τῶν προφητῶν ἐδημηγόρει τοὺς λόγους, οὐ νόμου κρατύνων, ἀλλ' ἀπ' ἐκείνου τὸν Χριστὸν ∼ῶν Ast.Am.*hom.*8(M.40.289B); οὐ μόνον οὐκ ἐναντιουμένου ἦν, ἀλλὰ καὶ ∼οῦντος αὐτήν Chrys.*hom.16.2 in Mt.*(7.205D); **e.** *pass* judgement or sentence συνεκροτεῖτο ψῆφος *Dial.*ap.Thdt.*h.e.*2.16.11(3.866); παρ' οἷς ἂν τὰ ἀμφότερα μέρη βούληται, τὰ τῆς δίκης ∼είσθω CChalc.*can.*9; **f.** intrans. *become strong, consolidate* συγκεκρότηκε [sc. ἡ Τύρος]...πάλιν, καὶ ἀναπεφοίτηκεν εἰς τὸ ἐν ἀρχαῖς Cyr.*Is.*2.5(2.334A); **6.** *go to make up, compose* διαδήματος ἁλουργίδος ἢ τῶν ἄλλων τῶν τὴν βασιλείαν ∼ούντων Chrys.*Jud.* 7.2(1.663E); διττὸν πεφηνέναι τὸ γένος τῶν δαιμόνων, ∼ούμενον ἔκ τε ψυχῶν ἀνθρωπίνων καὶ ἐκ κρειττόνων...πνευμάτων CCP(543)*anath.*6; of Church ἡ ἐκκλησία...∼εῖταί τε καὶ συμπήγνυται ἐξ ἀμφοῖν σώματος μὲν τῆς πίστεως, ψυχῆς δὲ τῆς ἐλπίδος Clem.*paed.*1.6(p.113.4; M.8.296B); ἡ ἐκκλησία...ἐκ παντὸς γένους ἀνθρώπων συγκεκροτημένη Eus.*d.e.*10.8(p.491.10; M.22.788D); id.*h.e.*4.6.4(M.20.316A); Isid.Pel.*epp.*2.246(M.78.685A) cit. s. ἐκκλησία; Areth.*Apoc.*2:5(M. 106.529B); Eunomians accused of introducing idea of composition into their theology, Gr.Nyss.*Eun.*1(1 p.213.2; M.45.461A) cit. s. ἀντίκειμαι; Christol. εἰ...τοῦ λόγου τὴν μίαν φύσιν ἐκ δύο λέγειν τολμῶσιν, ἔσται...τριπλῆ...ἀντὶ διπλῆς ἐκ δύο σαρκῶν καὶ μιᾶς θεότητος συγκεκροτημένη Leont.H.*monoph.*60(M.86.1801D); διπλοῦς... ὢν τὴν φύσιν ὁ κύριος...κατὰ ταυτὸν ἀσυγχύτως συγκεκροτημένον Max.*ambig.*(M.91.1057D); **7.** = συγκρατέω (and in following senses textual confusion between the two verbs is frequent), *conserve, preserve* τὸ ἅλας...καὶ ἑαυτὸ ∼εῖ καὶ τὰ ἄλλα διακρατεῖ σώματα Chrys. *hom.18.3 in Mt.*(7.237B); of God in rel. to creation αὐτὸς ἐποίησεν, αὐτὸς ∼εῖ id.*hom.19.7 in Rom.*(9.653D); id.*hom.4.3 in Jo.*(8.31A); οὐκ ἀναλυθήσεται...∼εῖται γὰρ θείᾳ δυνάμει *Disp.Phot.*(M.88. 533A); *sustain* ζωήν or βίον, Chrys.*hom.15.5 in 2Cor.*(10.550B); id. *hom.21.1 in Eph.*(11.143C); *maintain* ἵνα...τὸ γένος ἡμῖν ∼ῆται ταῖς τοιαύταις διαδοχαῖς id.*hom.17.1 in Mt.*(7.223C; συγκρατῆται Gaume); cf. τὴν ἐπιθυμίαν τῶν σωμάτων ἐνέθηκε ταῖς παιδοποιΐαις, συγκρατῶν ἡμῶν τὰς διαδοχὰς ὁ θεός id.*hom.85.2 in Jo.*(8.506B); φαίην ἂν ἐγὼ βασιλέα τοῦτον...τὰ εἰς εἰρήνην συγκεκροτῆσθαι, ὅστις οὐκ ἐθέλων ἀδικεῖν τοῦ μὴ ἀδικεῖσθαι πεπόρισται δύναμιν Synes.*regn.* 22(p.52.6; M.66.1100A); ἡ ἐξ εὐχῆς ∼ουμένη κατάστασις Evagr.Pont. *or.*47(M.79.1177A); **8.** *contain,* fig. θησαυρὸν...δι' ὀστρακίνων σκευῶν ∼ούμενον *cat.Apoc.*9:3(p.314.2); met., *keep in, hold in control* πεποίηκε...τοσαῦτα ὧν ἐδύνατο περιδράξασθαι...καὶ ∼εῖν ὑπὸ τὴν αὐτοῦ πρόνοιαν Or.*princ.*2.9.1(M.11.225C, v.l. for συγκρατεῖν p.164.8); πάντα ∼ῶν αἰωνίῳ κράτει Meth.*symp.*11(p.136.28; συγκρατῶν M.18. 213A); Chrys.*hom.23.6 in Mt.*(7.292D); pass., *be composed* τὸ φεύγειν τοὺς πονηρούς, καὶ πρὸς ἑαυτὸν συγκεκροτημένον καὶ συνηγμένον εἶναι ἅπαντα τὸν βίον id.*exp.in Ps.*140:10(5.442C).

συγκρότημα, τό, 1. *thing adapted for a purpose, device, organization* ἡμῶν τῆς σωτηρίας σ. Chrys.*hom.5.1 in Phil.*(11.229B); **2.** *combination* μηδεὶς...ὑπονοείτω τρεῖς συγκεκροτῆσθαι ψυχὰς ἐν τῷ ἀνθρωπίνῳ συγκρίματι...ὥστε σ. τι πολλῶν ψυχῶν τὴν ἀνθρωπίνην φύσιν εἶναι νομίζειν Gr.Nyss.*hom.opif.*14.2(M.44.176B); **3.** *organized body, company* or *band*, Eus.*h.e.*2.14.3(M.20.169C); τὸ σ. τῶν δαιμόνων, ἢ λεγεών Gr.Nyss.*v.Mos.*(M.44.421B); Cyr.*Am.*31(3. 284A); of a monastery τὸ ἱερὸν σ. τῆς ἀδελφότητος Ephr.3.338F; of Church ὁ μακάριος Παῦλος τὸ πλῆθος τῶν πιστῶν καὶ τὸ σ. τῆς ἐκκλησίας σώματι ἀπείκασεν Procl.CP *ep.*13(p.67.25; M.65.881B).

συγκρότησις, ἡ, 1. *joining* γωνία ἐστὶ σ. δύο τοίχων Or.*fr.428 in Mt.*(p.178); **2.** *assembly* σύνοδοι...καὶ σ. ἐπισκόπων Eus.*h.e.*5.23.2(M. 20.492A); τὰς...σ. τῶν λαῶν ποιεῖσθαι id.*v.C.*1.53(p.32.23; M.20.968); **3.** *support* of one's cause τὸ εὐλαβὲς αὐτοῦ καὶ...σπουδαῖον περὶ τὴν τοῦ ἐπισκόπου σ. Socr.*h.e.*6.23.5(M.67.733A); θέλων διὰ σ. καὶ προστασίαν οἰκειωθῆναι τῷ Τιβερίῳ Eustrat.*v.Eutych.*67(M.86.2349D); *confirmation* σ. τῆς...πίστεως Hesych.H.*fr.Ps.*55:6(M.93.1224D); **4.** *promotion,* ? *Service commission* οἱ μετασχόντες στρατείας ἢ ἀξίας συνηγορίας, ἢ δημοσίας φιλοτιμίας, ἢ συγκροτήσεως Phot.*nomoc.*10. 8(p.584; M.104.832C, v.l. -σεων).

***συγκροτητικός,** *tending to combine, making for union* ὥσπερ γὰρ ἡ ἔρις διαλυτικόν, οὕτως ἡ συμφωνία συγκροτητικόν Chrys.*hom. 82.2 in Jo.*(8.485C); συγκροτικός *ib.*ap.*cat.Jo.*13:23(p.375.3).

***συγκροτικός,** v. *συγκροτητικός.

***σύγκρουσμα, τό,** *collision*, Geo.Pis.*Pers.*2.140(M.92.1221A); Thphn.*chron.*p.255(M.108.636C).

συγκρουσμός, ὁ, *collision*; hence *gnashing* of teeth, Meth.*res.*1.24 (p.248.21; M.41.1093C).

***συγκρουστής, ὁ,** *one who is contentious, 'permanent member of the opposition'*, Ephr.3.503C.

[*]σύγκρουτον, τό, for σύγκρουστον, *tomb-chamber, vault* κατ[ε]σκεύασεν τὸ ἡρῷον σὺν τῷ σ[υ]νκρού[σ]τῳ καὶ τῷ γράδῳ *CIG* 3. 3900; σύνκρου[σ]τον καὶ γράδον *ib.*3902 i.

συγκρού-ω, 1. *bring into collision, oppose, contrast*; lit. and met., persons ἀδελφὸν ἀδελφῷ ∼εσθαι Ath.*apol.Const.*5(M.25.601C); with πόλεμον, *join* battle, Thphn.*chron.*p.197(M.108.512A); words or written records οὐκ ἀπιθάνως τις συγκρούσει τὸ [Mt.10:5] τῷ ῥητῷ τούτῳ Or.*Jo.*13.52(51; p.280.8; M.14.493B); id.*or.*27(p.374.1; M.11.520B); παραθείς τε καὶ συγκρούσας τὰ διαφόρως σημαινόμενα Eus.*d.e.*9.17 (p.440.28; M.22.709B); Thdr.Stud.*epp.*2.170(M.99.1536D); *bandy* words μηδὲ...σ. λόγους ἡδονικούς Ephr.1.219D; *conflict* or *clash with* ὁ βρασμὸς ἐκταράττει καὶ σ. τὴν ἁρμονίαν τοῦ σώματος Clem.*paed.* 2.10(p.214.17; M.8.509B); **2.** = συγκροτέω, *try to reconcile* or *harmonize*, Eus.*p.e.*10.9(487C; M.21.812A).

***συγκτησία, ἡ,** *possession as an integral whole*, *Cod.Afr.*56(tr. Lat. *massa*).

σύγκτησις, ἡ, *joint possession*, Nil.*Magn.*32(M.79.1008C).

***συγκτητορία, ἡ,** *joint ownership*, Didym.*Trin.*3.20(M.39.897A).

συγκτίζ-ω, 1. *create along with* or *at the same time*; pass., Or.*Cels.* 4.74(p.344.4; M.11.1145A); ref. Son οὐχ ἅμα τὸ εἶναι τὴν χρίσιν συνυπάρχουσαν καὶ συγκτισθεῖσαν λαβών...ὁ μὲν ἄνθρωπος αὐτοῦ Χριστὸς ὤν, κατὰ τὴν ψυχήν...ὁ δὲ βασιλεὺς κατὰ τὸ θεῖον id.*Jo.*1.28 (30; p.35.20; M.14.76B); μὴ κατ' οὐσίαν συνεκτίσθη τοῖς ἔργοις Ath. *Ar.*2.80(M.26.317A); **2.** *join in creating* ἡ τριὰς...∼ουσα καὶ συνδημιουργοῦσα Epiph.*haer.*76.44(p.398.32; M.42.612B); Gel.Cyz.*h.e.*2. 21.1(M.85.1284A).

***συγκυβερνάω,** *assist in guiding* or *ruling*, Chrysipp.*enc.in Thdr.* (p.62.13).

συγκυλινδέομαι, *wallow together*; met., Chrys.*hom.4.6 in 1Cor.* (10.32E); Nil.*epp.*4.1(M.79.548C).

συγκυλίω, 1. *set rolling together* σ. τοὺς τροχούς Cyr.*Am.*23(3. 273B); **2.** pass., met., *wallow together*, Ath.*Ar.*3.16(M.26.356B).

συγκύπτ-ω, 1. *be bent double*; **a.** as a symbol of baseness, abjectness τὸ διορατικὸν κάτω που κείμενον καὶ ∼ον Or.*Jo.*13.42(p.267.32; M.14.473A); *ib.*2.5(4; p.60.2; 117C); συγκεκυφὼς τῇ ψυχῇ Gr.Nyss. *virg.*4(p.272.15; M.46.344A); by sin, Chrys.*hom.37.5 in Gen.*(4.381A); **b.** as a symbol of hard work, Isid.Pel.*epp.*1.275(M.78.345A);

including brain work *φιλοσοφίαν ἐκείνην περὶ ἧς πολλὰ συγκεκύφαμεν* Synes.*ep*.137(M.66.1525B); **2.** *lie down also* or *at the same time τούτου ...μετακύπτοντος, ὁμοίως αὐτῷ πάλιν συνέκυπτε* [sc. *ὁ ὄφις*] Gr.Mag. *dial.*(tr.Zach.)3.16(M.*PL*.77.258C); ptcpl., *fellow patient οἱ σ. καὶ αἱ τούτους ὑποδεχόμεναι ἑστίαι* Thdr.Stud.*epp*.2.162(M.99.1509A).

συγκυρέω, 1. *happen upon, meet*; c. dat., Gr.Thaum.*pan.Or*.2 (p.4.21; M.10.1056A); **2.** *coincide* in resemblance, Synes.*ep*.61(M.66. 1405B).

***συγκυριολογ-έομαι,** *be called Lord together with συμπροσκυνεῖται καὶ ~εῖται* [sc. *τὸ πνεῦμα*] *τῷ υἱῷ* ‡Ath.*dial.Trin*.3.13(M.28.1221B).

σύγκυρσις, ἡ, *coincidence*, Synes.*insomn*.2(M.66.1284D; *συγκυρήσεις* p.146.11).

***συγκωμήτης, ὁ,** *fellow villager*, Marc.Diac.*v.Porph*.22.

συγξενιτεύω, *live abroad along with, exile oneself also*; ref. monastic solitude, Chrys.*hom.14.3 in 1Tim*.(11.628E).

συγχαλ-άω, *relax with* or *at the same time τῷ ἦρι ~ώμενον...τὸ πνεῦμα* Clem.*paed*.2.10(p.209.17; M.8.500B).

***συγχαριεντίζομαι,** *yoke together*, Nil.*epp*.2.167(M.79.280D).

***συγχαρίκιον, τό,** plur., *congratulatory presents*, Thphn.*chron*. p.278(v.l. *συγχαρίκεια* M.108.688B).

***συγχαρίσονται,** for *συγχαρήσονται* (*συγχαίρω*) *rejoice with*, v.l. for *χαρίσονται T.Benj*.10.7.

συγχαριτικός, *rejoicing with another*, ‡Nil.*narr*.6(M.79.676C).

συγχειροτονέω, 1. *appoint at the same time*; *accord to* one with another *πρῶτα ἡμῖν συνεχειροτονήθη ἡ τοῦ ἄρχειν δύναμις* Gr.Nyss.*or. 1 in Gen.1:26*(M.44.264D); **2.** *join in ordaining, officiate together at an ordination τῶν σ. ἀρχιερέων εἰς Euchol*.p.250.

***συγχειρουργός, ὁ,** *fellow workman*, Didym.*Trin*.2.7(M.39. 565A).

συγχέ-ω, *confound*;

A. in gen.; **1.** *pour together, commingle*, lit. and met. *~ομένων τοῖς θρήνοις* Gr.Nyss.*v.Mos*.29(M.44.309A); *τῶν...κατ' οὐσίαν ἑνουμένων, τὰ μὲν...σώζει τὸν ἴδιον τῆς ὑπάρξεως λόγον, τὰ δὲ συγχεῖται* Leont.B.*Nest.et Eut*.1(M.86.1304B); **2.** *confuse, blur*, lit. and met. *συγκεχύσθαι τὰ πλείονα τῶν γραμμάτων* Synes.*ep*.133(M.66.1517C); *τῆς θείας εἰκόνος τὴν ὁμοιότητα...ἐζοφώσαμέν τε καὶ σ.* Jo.D.*hom*.1. 4(M.96.552C); **3.** *confuse* ideas, *fail to distinguish*; *confound, fuse ~οντος τὸν μισθὸν καὶ τὴν συναγωγὴν τοῦ καρποῦ εἰς ἕν, ἄντικρυς τῆς γραφῆς δύο πράγματα παριστάσης* Or.*Jo*.13.46(p.272.13; M.14.480C); *οὐ συγχεῖται ἡ δικαιοσύνη τοῦ θεοῦ καὶ τὸ κατ' ἀξίαν ἕκαστον οἰκονομεῖσθαι ib*.32.3(p.429.24; 748A); *οὐ γὰρ οὕτως ἄθλιός εἰμι, ὡς ὁμοῦ πάντα φύρειν καὶ συγχεῖν* Chrys.*fem.reg*.2(1.250D); **4.** *throw into confusion*, ref. orderly succession of high priesthood, Eus.*h.e*.1.6.8(M. 20.88C); *χάριν ἀποστολῆς οὐ διαιροῦσαν...αὐτῶν τὸ ἀξίωμα, οὔτε τὴν τάξιν ~ουσαν* Sophr.H.*or*.8.2(M.87.3356C); pass., of the mind, *be disturbed*; *troubled*; *confused*, Herm.*vis*.5.4; id.*mand*.12.4.1f.; *ὑπὸ τῶν λυπηρῶν συγχεθησομένου* Clem.*str*.6.9(p.468.12; M.9.293C); Gr.Thaum.*pan.Or*.9(p.23.12; M.10.1080A); *δακρύοις...συγχεῖσθαι* Const.ap.Eus.*v.C*.2.72(p.71.8; M.20.1048A); †Bas.*Is*.3(1.379D; M.30. 121C); Gr.Naz.*or*.27.3(p.5.4; M.36.16A); over doctrinal questions *οἱ ~όμενοι ἐν τῷ περὶ πατρὸς καὶ υἱοῦ τόπῳ* Or.*Jo*.10.37(21; p.212.8; M. 14.376A); of Eutychians *πάντα ~ουσι, τοῖς θεολογικοῖς τὰ οἰκονομικὰ καταμίσγοντες* Sophr.H.*or*.2.6(M.87.3224C); *move* to compassion *σ. ... τοῖς δάκρυσιν τὴν εὔσπλαγχνον ἐκκλησίαν* †Hipp.*Artem*.ap. Eus.*h.e*.5.28.12(M.20.513D); pass., *be moved* with sorrow, of Christ at death of Lazarus *δακρύει...καὶ συγχεῖται* Chrys.*hom.63.1 in Jo*. (8.376E); **5.** *confound, destroy ἃ χωρὶς τῆς φιλίας οὐ δύναται μένειν ὑπὸ τοῦ νείκους ~όμενα* Athenag.*leg*.22.2(M.6.937A); *put to confusion, vanquish in argument οὐ δύνασαι ~ειν Ἰουδαίους διὰ τῆς φωνῆς; ποίησον αὐτοὺς συγχυθῆναι διὰ τῆς πολιτείας* Chrys.*hom.1.5 in Ac. princ*.(3.59E).

B. theol., *confound* Persons in Trin. *διὰ τοὺς ~οντας πατέρα καὶ υἱὸν τὸ μὲν 'κύριος' τέτακται ἐπὶ τοῦ υἱοῦ τὸ δὲ 'εἷς θεὸς' ἐπὶ τοῦ πατρὸς* Or.*comm.in Eph*.4:5f.(p.412); *~οντες πατρὸς καὶ υἱοῦ ἔννοιαν καὶ τῇ ὑποστάσει ἕνα διδόντες εἶναι τὸν πατέρα καὶ τὸν υἱόν* id.*comm.in Mt*. 17.14(p.624.12; M.13.1520B); *οὔτε τὰ ἡνωμένα διαιρεῖν θέμις, οὔτε τὰ διακεκριμένα συγχεῖν* Ant.Mon.*hom*.1(M.89.1436C); Jo.D.*hom*.11.3 (M.96.765A) cit. s. *ἅμπαξ*; *οὐ ~ομένων τῶν προσώπων* Jo.V H.*icon*. 4(M.96.1353A); freq. ref. Sabellius *ὁ μὲν προσώπων ~ων ὑπόστασιν* Amph.*Seleuc*.206(M.37.1590A); cf.*ib*.196(1590A); *τὴν Σαβελλίου νόσον ...~ομένων τῶν ὑποστάσεων* CCP(381)*ep*.ap.Thdt.*h.e*.5.9.11(3.1031); Thdt.*eran*.2(4.78); id.*Heb*.1:9(3.553); *οὔτε τὰ ἡνωμένα διαιρεῖν...οὔτε τὰ διακεκριμένα συγχεῖν* Dion.Ar.*d.n*.2.2(M.3.640A); *ib*.2.4(641A); *ὡς Σαβέλλιος συναλείφων καὶ ~ων, υἱοπατορίαν...παιδεύων* ‡Caes.Naz. *dial*.3(M.38.861).

C. Christol. *confound, confuse τοὺς φαντασίᾳ δοξολογίας τῆς περὶ τοῦ Χριστοῦ συγχέαντας τὰ περὶ τοῦ πρωτοτόκου πάσης κτίσεως τοῖς περὶ ψυχῆς καὶ σώματος Ἰησοῦ, τάχα δὲ καὶ τοῦ πνεύματος αὐτοῦ καὶ ἐν πάντῃ ἀσύνθετον οἰομένους εἶναι τὸ ὀφθὲν καὶ ἐπιδημῆσαν τῷ βίῳ* Or. *comm.in Mt*.16.8(p.500.4; M.13.1400A); esp. the divine with the human nature *ὡς...τραπεῖσαν τὴν θεότητα εἰς σάρκα ἢ συγχυθεῖσαν* Apoll.*ep.Jov*.(p.253.9; M.28.29A); *τοὺς δὲ λέγοντας...τὰς δύο οὐσίας τοῦ Χριστοῦ κατὰ ἀνάκρασιν συγχυθείσας μίαν γεγενῆσθαι οὐσίαν... τούτους ἀναθεματίζει ἡ καθολικὴ...ἐκκλησία* Ambr.*fr*.ap.*Doct.Patr*. 2(p.15.18)ap.Jo.D.*Jacob*.88(M.94.1496A); *ἐπιτιμᾶν τοῖς εἰς μίαν κατακιρνῶσιν οὐσίαν τήν τε τῆς σαρκὸς καὶ τὴν τῆς θεότητος φύσιν, καίτοι μηδενός...ταυτὶ ~οντος* Cyr.*Nest*.4.6(p.90.23; 6^{1}.118B); *ib*.2.6 (p.42.36; 45E); id.*apol.Thdt*.3(p.118.25; 6^{1}.212C); *οὐ συνεχύθησαν αἱ φύσεις, ἀλλ' ἔμειναν ἀκραιφνεῖς* Thdt.*eran*.2(4.105); Leont.B.*cap.Sev*. 15(M.86.1905B); *εἰ...θεότης καὶ ἀνθρωπότης κατ' οὐσίαν ἑνωθεῖσαι μὴ φυλάττουσι...τὴν ἑαυτῶν φυσικὴν ἰδιότητα, συγκέχυνται* id.*Nest.et Eut*.1(M.86.1305B); Sophr.H.*or*.2.47(M.87.3281A); in accusation against Cyr. by Eastern bishops *οὐδὲν αὐτῷ ἐξαρκεῖ εἰς τὸ τῆς ἑνώσεως ἄκρον, μὴ τὰς φύσεις ~οντι* Cyr.*apol.orient*.11(p.58.9; 6^{1}.191C).

***συγχήρα, ἡ,** *fellow widow*, *Const.App*.3.12.4; *ib*.3.13.1.

***σύγχθονος,** ? = *κατάχθονος*, *nourishing πνεύμονι γὰρ κραδίη ῥιπίζεται, ὄφρα φυλάξῃ σύγχθονα σαρκὸς ἄλευρα* Geo.Pis.*carm.vit*.44 (p.53).

***συγχλευάζω,** *join in mockery* or *jeering*, Chrys.*hom.87.3 in Mt*. (7.820D).

συγχόνδρωσις, ἡ, *joining by cartilege*; of bones, Melet.*nat.hom*. synops.(M.64.1120A); *οὐ μόνον συνάρθρωσις καὶ διάρθρωσις, ἀλλὰ καὶ συννεύρωσις καὶ σ. ib*.28f.(1265C).

συγχορευτής, ὁ, 1. *fellow chorister σ. ἀγγέλων* Clem.*paed*.1.6 (p.117.4; M.8.304B); Chrys.*hom.19.3 in Mt*.(7.248C); Cyr.*Ps*.46:6 (M.69.1053B); **2.** *fellow worshipper σ. τῶν Ἑλλήνων* Bas.Sel.*or*.27.2 (M.85.313B).

συγχορεύτρια, ἡ, fem. of *συγχορευτής*, *companion in the choir*, met. *ἡ ἔνδοξος κορυφὴ τοῦ βαπτιστοῦ...ἡ τῶν ἀγγέλων σ.* Chrysipp. *enc.in Jo.Bapt*.15(p.47.11).

συγχορεύ-ω, *(dance and) sing in chorus with*; met., *rejoice with σ. βραβεύοντι τῷ Χριστῷ* Meth.*symp*.6.5(p.69.20; M.18.120C); *οἷς καὶ ~ων τῷ πνεύματι καὶ συνευωχούμενος* ‡Meth.*palm*.2(M.18.385B); *σ. τοῖς σεραφίμ* Chrys.*hom.27.5 in 1Cor*.(10.249B); Isid.Pel.*epp*.2.151 (M.78.604D); *join in worshipping τοῖς ἐχθροῖς τῆς χάριτος ~ουσι δαίμοσι* Bas.Sel.*or*.27.2(M.85.313B).

***συγχραίνομαι,** *become soiled, get dirty*, Mac.Mgn.*apocr*.3.24 (p.109.2).

συγχρ-άομαι, 1. *make use of, avail oneself of ~ησαμένου τοῦ πνεύματος* [sc. *τοῖς προφήταις*] *ὡς εἰ καὶ αὐλητὴς αὐλὸν ἐμπνεύσαι* Athenag.*leg*.9.1(M.6.908A); **2.** *take advantage of, abuse μὴ σ. τῇ ἡλικίᾳ τοῦ ἐπισκόπου* Ign.*Magn*.3.1; *κακῶς τῷ ῥητῷ ~ησάμενοι* Cyr.H. *catech*.8.2; **3.** *use as synonymous*, Leont.B.*arg.Sev*.(M.86.1924D).

συγχρηματίζ-ω, *be called by the same name*, theol. *ἔπρεπε...τὸν μηδέποτε κεχωρισμένον τοῦ μονογενοῦς συγχρηματίσαι τῷ μονογενεῖ* Or.*princ*.2.6.4(p.143.22; M.11.212C); Christol. *ὁ ληφθεὶς ὡς τῷ λαβόντι συναφθεὶς ~ει θεός* Nest.*fr*.C 9(p.262.12)ap.Cyr.*Nest*.2.13 (p.51.8; 6^{1}.58B); condemned by Cyr. *ὁ...ταῦτα λέγων...ἀρνεῖται... τὴν ἕνωσιν, καθ' ἣν οὐχ ὡς ἕτερος ἑτέρῳ συμπροσκυνεῖταί τις, οὔτε μὴν ~ει θεός* Cyr.*ep*.17(p.37.5; 5^{2}.71E); id.*apol.Thdt*.8(p.131.22; 6^{1}. 225E); id.*apol.orient*.8(p.50.16,26f.; 6^{1}.180B,E).

σύγχρησις, ἡ, 1. *use in combination*, Clem.*str*.1.20(p.62.29; M.8. 816A); Max.*qu.Thal*.49(M.90.453D); **2.** *use* of words *as synonymous*, Leont.B.*arg.Sev*.(M.86.1924D).

***συγχρηστέον,** *one must use*, Clem.*str*.7.7(p.30.13; M.9.456A); ‡Just.*ep.Zen.et Ser*.11(M.6.1196C).

***συγχρηστός, 1.** s.v.l., *thoroughly good* or *worthy τοῦτο...ποιοῦντες συγχρηστοὶ κληθησόμεθα PLond*.1919.32; **2.** ? for *συγχρηστιανοί fellow Christian*, *ib*.17; or ? for *συγχριστοί fellow workers with Christ* or *anointed together*.

συγχρονίζω, 1. *be contemporary with*, Clem.*str*.1.21(pp.69.2,80.14; M.8.832B,861B); Eus.*h.e*.4.7.9(M.20.317B); id.*proph*.3(M.22.1264B); **2.** *spend time, stay with* or *at*, Or.*sel.in Ps*.25:4(M.12.1273C); *μηδὲ... αὐτοῖς συγκαθέζεσθαι μηδ' ἐπὶ πολὺ σ.* Eus.*Ps*.25:4f.(M.23.236A); Pall. *h.Laus*.15(p.39.21; M.34.1041A); *continue some time κἂν...φιλήδονος εἴη, συγχρονίσει πάντως καὶ ἐμπαθῶς προσομιλήσει ταῖς προσβολαῖς* Marc.Er.*opusc*.2.140(M.65.952C); **3.** *synchronize, assign to the same date*, Afric.*chron*.ap.Eus.*p.e*.10.10(488B; *συνεχρόνησεν* M.10.73B, cj. *συνεχρόνισεν*).

σύγχρονος, *contemporaneous*; philos. and theol., *coexistent*, predicated of God and matter by various pagan schools, Hipp.*haer*.1. 19(p.20.2; M.16.3041B); *τὸν θεὸν ἐξ ὕλης σ. καὶ ἀγενήτου πάντα* πεποιηκέναι *ib*.8.17(p.236.17; 3363B); and Manicheans, Tit.Bost. *Man*.1.7(M.18.1077D); δύο...ἐπὶ τὸ αὐτὸ εἶναι σ. τε καὶ ἀΐδια Epiph. *haer*.66.14(p.36.13; M.42.49A); denied by Jews τὸν...θεὸν...ποιήσαντα πάντα...οὐδὲ ἔκ τινος ὑποκειμένης σ. οὐσίας, ἀλλὰ θελήσαντα καὶ κτίσαντα Hipp.*haer*.9.30(p.263.10; M.16.3410B); and Christians οὐκ ἦν σ. τι τῷ θεῷ Meth.*arbitr*.22(p.206.9); 'ἐν τῷ κόσμῳ ἦν' ἀλλ' οὐχ ὡς τοῦ κόσμου σ. Chrys.*hom.8.1 in Jo*.(8.48D); ref. eternal life ζωὴν... σύγχρονον αἰῶνος παλιναυξέος Nonn.*par.Jo*.3:36(M.43.773A); predicated of Father and Son, ‡Gr.Nyss.*Ar.et Sab*.4(M.45.1284B); of hypostatic union and Christ's human nature (i.e. as not pre-existent), Sophr.H.*ep.syn*.(M.87.3161B).

***συγχρώννυμι**, ? *paint in one colour*; pass. ptcpl. ? *of one colour, self-coloured*, met. τῷ τοῦ θεοῦ ἀγαθῷ, ὃ κατὰ συμβεβηκός ἐστιν αὐτῷ καὶ συνυπάρχον ὡς χρόα σώματι...(οὐχ ὡς μέρους ὄντος, ἀλλ' ὡς κατ' ἀνάγκην συνόντος παρακολουθήματος, ἡνωμένου καὶ συγκεχρωσμένου ὡς τῷ πυρὶ ξανθῷ εἶναι καὶ τῷ αἰθέρι κυανῷ) Athenag.*leg*.24.2(M.6.945B).

συγχρωτίζ-ω, **1.** met., *colour, give a complexion to*, i.e. a certain aspect ἦσαν κατὰ ἀλήθειαν ἄγγελοι, τὴν οἰκείαν τῷ πράγματι φύσιν οὐ συγκεράσαντες, ἀλλὰ τὴν μὲν ὄψιν πρὸς τὴν οἰκείαν τοῦ Ἀβραὰμ θέαν συνεχρώτισαν κτλ. Mac.Mgn.*apocr*.4.27(p.215.20); *colour, infect*, i.e. make like εἰ πλησιάζοντες αὐτῷ...τῷ τῆς θειότητος λόγῳ ~ονται *ib*.4.26(p.212.2); in bad sense, med., *infect, stain* οὐδὲ πλάνη ~εται ‡*Diogn*.12.8; **2.** more gen.; med., *come into contact* with σ. τινι μοναχῷ *Mir.Artem*.39(p.63.27).

συγχύνω (συγχύννω), **1.** *confound* in argument, Chrys.*hom.1.5 in Ac.princ*.(3.59E); **2.** *disturb, trouble* the mind τὰ ῥεύματα τῆς ἡδυπαθείας...τὰ σ. καὶ ταράσσοντα τὴν ψυχήν Meth.*symp*.4.4(p.49.14; M.18.92A); pass., *be agitated, troubled* μὴ συγχύννου, ἀλλὰ ἰσχυροποιοῦ Herm.*vis*.5.5.

σύγχυσις, ἡ, *confusion*;

A. in gen.; **1.** *mixing up, disorder*, as characteristic of matter, Tat.*orat*.5(p.6.12; M.6.817A); of elements in primordial chaos τῆς ἀνέκαθεν σ. *Hom.Clem*.6.3; Gr.Naz.*or*.14.33(M.35.904A); of general anarchy, *Hom.Clem*.5.5; in a partic. instance εἰ τὸν αὐτὸν ἅπαντες ἔσωζον ἀπαραλλάκτως χαρακτῆρα, πόση σ. Melet.*nat.hom*.30(M.64.1277D); **2.** linguistic ὁ δὲ σχηματισμὸς τῆς ἡμετέρας γλωττῆς μὴ συμβαίνων τῷ σχηματισμῷ τῆς Ἑβραϊκῆς εὐγλωττίας, σ. τινα... ἀπεργάζεται Gr.Nyss.*hom.2 in Cant*.(M.44.796B); ref. tower of Babel (Gen.11:9) τῆς διαλέκτων σ. Or.*Cels*.4.21(p.290.13; M.11.1053C); πρὸ τῆς σ. τῶν γλωσσῶν Cyr.*Ps*.48:1(M.69.1068B); **3.** mental *confusion, failure to distinguish*, in matters of doctrine οὐ σ. ... εἰσάγομεν Dion.Ar.*c.h*.11.2(M.3.284D); id.*d.n*.2.2(M.3.637D); Εὐτυχοῦς ...νενοσηκότες τὴν σ. ... τοῖς θεολογικοῖς τὰ οἰκονομικὰ καταμίσγοντες Sophr.H.*or*.2.6(M.87.3224C); v. s. B.2; **4.** *blurring* σ. ἐστι τοῦ χαρακτῆρος καὶ τῆς κατὰ φύσιν μορφῆς ἀλλοτρίωσις...ὅταν μὴ συμπαραληφθῇ τῇ πίστει τὸ πνεῦμα τὸ ἅγιον Gr.Nyss.*Maced*.15(M.46.1320C); **5.** *tumult, disturbance*; **a.** lit., of weeping, *A.Paul.et Thecl*.10(p.243.3); of waves or sea, Cyr.*Jon*.13(3.378A); Geo.Pis.*carm*.4.95(p.14); of a mob or others, Ath.*fug*.24(p.84.15; M.25.676A); Chrys.*hom.83.3 in Jo*.(8.493C); Isid.Pel.*epp*.1.462(M.78.436C); **b.** of the mind, *trouble, disturbance*, Bas.*hom*.8.2(2.63E; M.31.309A); ref. Jo.11:33, of Christ ἐπιτιμήσας τῷ πάθει...ἐπέσχε τὴν σ. Chrys.*hom.63.1 in Jo*.(8.377A); as coming upon Church corporately ἀγράφοις χρῆσθαι φωναῖς διὸ σχεδὸν ἡ πᾶσα γέγονε σ. καὶ ἀκαταστασία τῆς ἐκκλησίας Eus.*ep.Caes*.(p.46.11; M.20.1544A); caused by the passions, Max.*ep*.4(M.91.413A); characteristic of worldly life ἐν σ. γάρ, καὶ θορύβοις ἐσόμεθα τοῖς εἰκαίοις τοῦ παρόντος βίου περισπασμοῖς. σ. ἡ Βαβυλὼν ἑρμηνεύεται Cyr.*Mich*.43(3.432C); Βαβυλῶνα οἶμαι λέγειν αὐτὸν τὴν τοῦ παρόντος βίου σ. καὶ τὸν εἰκαῖον πειρασμόν· σ. γὰρ ἡ Βαβυλὼν ἑρμηνεύεται Oecum.*Apoc*.14:8(p.162); *ib*.17:5(p.185); **6.** *destruction* τὴν σ. καὶ κατάλυσιν τοῦ παντὸς κόσμου Just.*2apol*.7.1(M.6.456A).

B. theol., *confusion, mixture*; **1.** of Persons in Trin., usu. with ὑπόστασις or allied words, ref. Jo.1:1 οὐκ εἶπεν 'ἐν τῷ θεῷ' ἵνα μὴ πρόφασιν δῷ τῇ σ. τῆς ὑποστάσεως Bas.*hom*.16.4(2.137D; M.31.480C); αἱ...τρεῖς ὑποστάσεις, μηδεμιᾶς ἐπινοουμένης συναλοιφῆς...ἢ σ. Gr.Naz.*or*.20.7(M.35.1073A); ὡς ἂν μή τις σ. περὶ τὸ ὑποκείμενον θεωρηθείη Gr.Nyss.*or.dom*.3(p.64.9; M.46.1109B); ref. 1Cor.8:6 οὕτως εἴρηνται, τοῦτο μὲν διὰ τὸ μὴ σ. νοῆσαι τῶν θείων ὑποστάσεων...τοῦτο δὲ διὰ τὸ ἐκβάλλεσθαι...τὴν πολυθεΐαν Didym.*Trin*.3.23(M.39.924C); μονάδα μὲν κατὰ τὸν τῆς οὐσίας...λόγον...ἀλλ' οὐ κατὰ...τὴν οἱανοῦν σ. Max.*myst*.23(M.91.701A); with πρόσωπον: οἱ μὲν γὰρ ἐπὶ Ἰουδαϊσμὸν διὰ τῆς σ. τῶν προσώπων Bas.*Spir*.77(3.66C; M.32.213C); τῇ δυάδι τῶν προσώπων ἐξήλασε τοῦ Σαβελλίου τὴν σ. Thdt.*Heb*.1:9(3.553); freq. specifically ref. Sabellius τὸ [sc. φρόνημα] τῆς σ. τῶν ὑποστάσεων, ἐν ᾧ ἡ ἀσεβεστάτη αἵρεσις τοῦ Σαβελλίου ἀνενεώθη Bas.*ep*.224.2(3.343C; M.32.837B); Gr.Naz.*or*.33.16(M.36.233D) cit. s. κατάπαυσις; opp. ἕνωσις: οὐ συγχύσει τῶν τριῶν ὑποστάσεων, ἀλλὰ τῇ ἑνώσει Marc.Er. *opusc*.4(M.65.1009A); opp. διαίρεσις as opposite error δεῖ...τὴν ἀσεβῆ σ. ἐκείνου [sc. Σαβελλίου] καὶ τὴν μανιώδη τούτου [sc. Ἀρείου] διαίρεσιν ἀποστρέφεσθαι καὶ φεύγειν Chrys.*sac*.4.4(p.115.15; 1.410A); **2.** ref. union of natures in Christ, rejected αὐτὸς...μορφὴν δούλου ἔλαβε, προσφάτως προσφάτῳ ἐπικοινωνήσας τῶν ἀρχαϊζόντων μενόντων ἐν ταυτότητι, καὶ μὴ εἰς σ. μεταβαινόντων Epiph.*haer*.76.34(p.383.23; M.42.585B); τέλειον θεόν, τέλειον τὸν αὐτὸν ἄνθρωπον...συνενωθέντα οὐκ εἰς σ. οὐδ' εἰς ἀνυπαρξίαν id.*ep.Arab.ib*.78.24(p.475.15; 740A); ἕτερον μέν τι ἕτερον θεότης τε καὶ ἀνθρωπότης...ἀλλ' ἦν ἐν Χριστῷ... εἰς ἑνότητα συνδεδραμηκότα, σ. δίχα καὶ τροπῆς Cyr.*Chr.un*.(5^1.736A); id.*ep*.46(p.159.16; 5^2.143A); ἕνα...ἐξ ἑκατέρας φύσεως...σύνθετον τὸν κύριον ἡμῶν Ἰησοῦν Χριστὸν ὁμολογοῦντες, σ. τῇ ἑνώσει οὐκ ἐπεισάγομεν Just.Imp.*edict*.ap.Evagr.*h.e*.5.4(p.199.26; M.86.2797B); in accusation against Eutychians, Isid.Pel.*epp*.1.496(M.78.452C) cit. s. ἀνάκρασις; οἱ τὰ τῆς κράσεως καὶ σ. ... πραγματευόμενοι Thdt.*rect. conf*.15(M.6.1233B); οἱ δὲ σ. καὶ κρᾶσιν εἰσάγοντες...παθητὴν τοῦ μονογενοῦς τὴν θείαν φύσιν τῇ σ. τερατευόμενοι *Symb.Chalc*.(p.128.31; H.2.453D); *ib*.(p.129.19; 456B); Anast.S.*haer*.(p.260); and monophysites εἰ ἐκ δύο φύσεων ἀσυγχύτως μίαν ποιεῖν ἔστιν, ἐκ δύο φύσεων ἡνωμένων κατὰ σ. τί ἕτερον γίνεται; †Leont.H.*monoph*.8(M.86.1773B); λέγοντες τὴν...σάρκα γενέσθαι ταὐτουργὸν τῇ θεότητι διὰ τὴν πρόσληψιν, τὴν θεότητα δὲ γενέσθαι ταὐτοπαθῆ ⟨τῇ σαρκὶ⟩ διὰ ⟨τὴν⟩ κένωσιν· τροπὴν ὁμοῦ, καὶ...σ. ‡Hipp.*Ber.Hel*.5(p.324.15; M.10.836D); also monothelites μέχρι...τότε σαφῶς ἕνωσις πραγμάτων ἐστίν, ἕως ἂν ἡ τούτων σώζηται φυσικὴ διαφορά· ἐπεὶ ταύτης πανσαμένης, παύεται πάντως κακείνη, τῇ σ. τελείως ἀφανισθεῖσα Max. *opusc*.(M.91.97A); θεανδρικὴν ἐνέργειαν ὁ εἰπών, οὐ σ. ταῖς φυσικαῖς ἐνεργείαις εἰσήγαγεν ‡Cyr.*Trin*.19(6^3.25A; M.77.1157C); freq. in association with τροπή and allied words ἀναθεματισθῆναι χρὴ τοὺς... κατὰ σ. ἢ τροπὴν νοοῦντας τὴν...ἕνωσιν Amph.*fr*.(M.39.113C); ἔμεινεν ἄτρεπτος...καὶ σ. πάσης ἐλεύθερος Sophr.H.*or*.2.47(M.87.3281A); ἀληθῶς φύσει γέγονεν ἄνθρωπος, δίχα πάσης τροπῆς καὶ σ. Jo.D. *hom*.4.11(M.96.612B); with κρᾶσις: συνάφειαν κηρύττομεν καὶ οὐ σ., ἕνωσιν, οὐ κρᾶσιν Jo.Ant.*hom*.(p.84.20); τοὺς δὲ λέγοντας ὅτι κρᾶσις ἢ σ. ... ἐγένετο τοῦ θεοῦ λόγου πρὸς τὴν σάρκα...ἐπιστομίζειν Cyr. *ep*.39(p.19.2; 5^2.107E); τὴν πολυθρύλλητον κρᾶσιν καὶ σ. Thdt.*eran.2*(4.113); *Symb.Chalc*.(p.128.21; H.2.453D); Leont.H.*Nest*.3.4(M.86.1612A); and σύγκρασις: φαντάζεσθαι...ὅτι σ. ἤτοι σύγκρασις...ἐγένετο τοῦ λόγου πρὸς τὸ σῶμα Cyr.*ep*.45(p.152.27; 5^2.136E); ἐὰν μὴ μετὰ τὴν ἕνωσιν ἀχωρίστους καὶ ἀσυγχύτους εἴπῃς δύο φύσεις, σ. λέγεις καὶ σύγκρασιν Bas.Sel.ap.CCP(448)*act*.7(p.93.21; H.2.168B); in accusation against Cyril by Eastern bishops νομίζουσιν ἡμᾶς τοὺς ὀρθοδόξους...φρονεῖν ὅτι σύγκρασις ἐγένετο ἢ σ. Cyr.*ep*.44(p.35.20; 5^2.133C); τὴν καθ' ὑπόστασιν ἕνωσιν εἰσάγει, καὶ σύνοδον καθ' ἕνωσιν φυσικήν, κρᾶσίν τινα καὶ σ. διὰ τούτων τῶν ὀνομάτων γεγενῆσθαι διδάσκων τῆς τε θείας φύσεως καὶ τῆς τοῦ δούλου μορφῆς Thdt.*ep*.151(4.1292); opp. ἕνωσις: οὔτε χωρίζομεν τοῦ θεοῦ λόγου τὴν σάρκα, οὔτε σ. ποιοῦμεν τὴν ἕνωσιν id.*eran.2*(4.102); τῆς δὲ κατ' οὐσίαν ἑνώσεως...κηρυττέσθω ἡ ἀλήθεια...κίνδυνος γὰρ...παρατραπέντας αὐτῆς εἰς τὸ ἐναντίον μέν, ἴσον δὲ κακόν, τὴν σ. φαμεν, ἐμπεσεῖν Leont.B.*Nest.et Eut*.1(M.86.1301C); ἡ κατὰ σύνθεσιν ἕνωσις τὴν σ. καὶ διαίρεσιν ἀποβάλλεται Justn. *conf*.(p.76.33; M.86.999C); and διαίρεσις as opposite error ἐγὼ δὲ ἑκάτερον διαφυγεῖν σπουδάζω κρημνόν, καὶ τὸν τῆς δυσσεβοῦς σ., καὶ τὸν τῆς δυσσεβοῦς διαιρέσεως Thdt.*eran.2*(4.109); εἰς οὖν Νεστορίῳ τε καὶ Σευήρῳ...ὑπάρχει σκοπός...ὁ μὲν γὰρ διὰ τὴν σ. φεύγων τὴν καθ' ὑπόστασιν ἕνωσιν τὴν οὐσιώδη διαφορὰν προσωπικὴν ποιεῖται διαίρεσιν· ὁ δὲ διὰ τὴν διαίρεσιν...τὴν καθ' ὑπόστασιν ἕνωσιν φυσικὴν ἐργάζεται σ. Max.*opusc*.(M.91.56C); id.*myst*.23(M.91.701A); δύο δὲ φύσεις λέγοντες, οὐ διαιροῦμεν τὴν ἕνωσιν, τὴν δὲ τροπὴν καὶ τὴν σ. φεύγομεν Jo.D.*Jacob*.81(M.94.1477C); **3.** of Valent. aeons οὔτε ἀρχαῖς ...οὔτε πάσῃ σ. περινοηθῆναι δυναμένων Val.Gn.ap.Epiph.*haer*.31.5(p.390.9; M.41.481A).

***συγχυταί, οἱ**, *those who confound* or *confuse* the natures of Christ, Andr.Cr.*Agath*.109(M.97.1441D).

συγχυτικός, **1.** *confounding, confusing*; fem. as subst., of Babel καὶ μισθὸν ἔλαβον τῆς ἀσεβείας τὴν σ. τῆς γλώσσης Jo.D.*hom*.11.4(M.96.765D); **2.** *able to confound* in argument λογισμόν...σ. Or.*fr.26 in Jer*.27:16(p.212.1); **3.** *confusing, disturbing* the mind δύναμιν σ.... διανοίας †Bas.*Is*.5(1.381C; M.30.125C); *ib*.276(589B; M.604A); Proc.G. *Is*.13:19(M.87.2092A); **4.** theol., *confounding, commingling*; **a.** of those heresies which confounded Persons in Trin. Βαβυλῶνος...τὰς ἀρχὰς τῶν σ. ἁμαρτημάτων...εἰπών Eus.*Ps*.136:8(M.24.37B); **b.** of a heret. interprn. of mode of union of natures in Christ πενταχῶς...

λέγεται ἡ ἕνωσις, συγχυτική, διαιρετική κτλ. ‡Ath.*def*.5(M.28.544D); ἄμφω [sc. Juln. Hal. and Sev. Ant.]...τῆς σ. προεμάχουν ἑνώσεως Thdr.Raith.*praep*.(p.196.26; M.91.1497D).

***συγχωλεύω**, *be disabled, defective*; met., of power of reason, Bas.*hom*.17.2(2.139D; M.31.485A).

συγχώννυμι, **1.** *heap with earth; bury*, met. τὴν βασιλικὴν εἰκόνα συγκεχωσμένην τοῖς πάθεσι Gr.Naz.*or*.38.14(M.36.328B); ἀνακαθᾶραι τὰ τῆς εὐσεβείας δόγματα τῷ χρόνῳ συγκεχωσμένα Phot.*cod*.40(M.103.72D); *overrule* τούτους...εἰς ἓν συμφωνοῦσα ἡ ψῆφος...συνέχωσεν CEph.(431)*act*.1(p.53.20; H.1.1421A); **2.** *shore up* ᾧ ῥινὸς ἐκτύπωμα συγκεχωσμένης τοῖς τῶν παρειῶν σαρκικοῖς προπυργίοις Geo.Pis.*carm*.1.64(p.3).

συγχωρ-έω, **1.** *accede, allow, accept* ἡ θεία φύσις...παρῆν μὲν τῇ ἀνθρωπείᾳ φύσει, σ. δὲ πάσχειν...πραγματευομένη τὴν σωτηρίαν Thdt.*Ps*.108:31(1.1390); *ib*.21:2(733); τοὺς συγχυτὰς ἕλοιο ~εῖν ὅλως Andr.Cr.*Agath*.109(M.97.1441D); of God's permissive will ὁ θεὸς συνεχώρει ἄγεσθαι αὐτοὺς εἰς δικαστήριον Chrys.*hom.13.2 in Ac*.(9.104D); οὐκ ἐνεργήσας εἰς τοῦτο, ἄπαγε, ἀλλ' ἀφεὶς καὶ ~ήσας id.*hom.8.2 in 2Cor*.(10.494A); ποικίλοις περιπεσεῖν συνεχωρήθησαν πειρασμοῖς Thdt.*Ps*.118:52(1.1451); Proc.G.*Gen*.3:24(M.87.232C); *bear with* οὐκ ἤλεγξε δὲ φανερῶς ἀλλὰ συνεχώρησεν [sc. τὸν Ἰούδαν], ἀνακαλέσασθαι αὐτὸν θέλων Chrys.*hom.65.2 in Jo*.(8.391D); **2.** *allow of, admit of* μήτε τὸν τῆς ἀρχῆς λόγον ~εῖν προεπινοεῖν τι πρεσβύτερον Gr.Nyss.*hex*.proem.3(M.44.64D); **3.** *ascribe, accord* σφίσιν αὐτοῖς τὰ μέγιστα τῶν ὄντων ἐγνωκέναι ~οῦντες Clem.*str*.7.16(p.72.31; M.9.541C); Synes.*ep*.122(M.66.1501D); *grant, provide* ~ήσεις ἑκάστῳ...καὶ φαγεῖν καὶ πιεῖν Pall.*h.Laus*.32(p.88.10; M.34.1099C); **4.** *excuse, waive* σ. αὐτῷ τὴν ἐνόχλησιν Bas.*ep*.281(3.424A; M.32.1017C); *remit* sin's penalty μηδὲ αὐτοῦ Μωϋσέως ἱκετεύοντος ~ηθῆναι αὐτῇ τῆς ἁμαρτίας τὸ ἐπιτίμιον id.*jud*.5(2.217E; M.31.664A); *remit* taxes, Cyr.S.*v.Sab*.73(p.177.1); **5.** *forgive*; **a.** sins and offences as bet. man and man, *make allowances, excuse* χαρίζεσθαί τε καὶ ~εῖν ὅσα ἀνθρώπινα Eus.*v.C*.3.21(p.88.5; M.20.1081A); Chrys.*hom.40.4 in Jo*.(8.241E); **b.** *condone* μήτε...συναίνεσις λυέτω γάμον, ἢ ~είτωσαν ἀλλήλοις...τὰ ἁμαρτήματα Ath.Scholast.*coll*.4.22(p.64); **c.** of God's forgiveness, Or.*fr.in 1Reg*.3:14(M.17.40C); *A.Andr.et Mt*.18(p.88.1); Ath.*v.Anton*.18(M.26.869C); ~ησον ψάλλοντος Anast.*poenit*.8(p.284); ref. original sin τόν τε ἡμέτερον ἀποσμῆξαι ῥύπον, καὶ τὴν παλαιὰν ~ῆσαι ἁμαρτίαν Didym.*Trin*.2.12(M.39.684B); its forgiveness in baptism compared with forgiveness of post-baptismal sin εἰς τὸ βάπτισμα δωρεὰν ~εῖ ...ἐν τῇ μετανοίᾳ δὲ τῶν ἁμαρτιῶν τῇ μετὰ βάπτισμα οὐχὶ δωρεὰν ~εῖ, ἀλλὰ ζητεῖ κόπους καὶ θλίψεις...καὶ οὕτως ~εῖ Philox.*ep*.41(p.187); **d.** pass., *be forgiven* (sins), Or.*comm.in Mt*.14.6(p.286.17,21; M.13.1196A); ἡ ἐν τῇ ἀγνοίᾳ ἁμαρτία ~εῖται Cyr.H.*catech*.3.8; ἐὰν ~ήσῃς ~ηθήσεται Gr.Nyss.*or.dom*.5(p.108.32; M.44.1188D); Chrys.*prod.Jud*.1.1(2.377E); Cyr.*Ps*.50:10(M.69.1097B); man for sins παρακαλοῦντα καὶ μὴ ~ούμενον Bas.*jud*.5(2.218A; M.31.664B); ~ήσωμεν ἵνα ~ηθῶμεν Gr.Naz.*or*.17.11(M.35.977C); ~ῆσαι ἵνα μείζονα ὑπὸ θεοῦ ~ηθῇς Dor.*doct*.17.1(M.88.1801A); **e.** *obtain* or *effect forgiveness* ἡ ἀξία μετάνοια πάντα ~εῖ τὰ...ἁμαρτήματα *cat.Mt*.12:22(p.95.7) cf. Chrys.*hom.41.3 in Mt*.(7.449C) into which context this passage has been interpolated; ἡ ταπείνωσις ~εῖ ἁμαρτίαν Esaias *cap.spir*.8(M.40.1208B); πᾶσαν ἁμαρτίαν ~εῖ βάπτισμα Dor.*doct*.1.4(M.88.1621C); **f.** *forgive* on behalf of God, *grant absolution for* ~οῦντες [sc. apostles] τὰς ἁμαρτίας τῶν πιστευόντων *A.Petr.et Andr*.11; τίς...παρ' ὑμῖν μετὰ τὸν Δανιὴλ ἅγιος ἁγίων ~ῶν ἁμαρτίας; Dam.*troph*.4.4(p.267.8); ref. persons arrogating powers to themselves αὐχοῦσιν...καὶ εἰδωλολατρείας ~εῖν Or.*or*.28(p.381.14; M.11.529B).

συγχώρησις, ἡ, **1.** *agreement, assent*; **a.** *permission, will* of God, of such things as are allowed without being in his absolute will, Or.*fr.57 in Lc*.12:6(p.261) cit. s. *βούλησις*; Πέτρος...συνεχωρήθη ἁμαρτῆσαι, ἵνα ἡ σ. τούτου ὑπόθεσις φιλανθρωπίας τοῖς ἄλλοις γένηται ‡Chrys.*Petr.et Hel*.1(2.732B); Pall.*v.Chrys*.20(p.132.21; M.47.74); Proc.G.*Gen*.4:15(M.87.245B); τὴν πάνσοφον δείκνυσι τοῦ θεοῦ σ., τοὺς πιστοὺς δούλους διὰ πειρασμῶν δοκιμάζουσαν Areth.*Apoc*.6:4(M.106.589B); v. *εὐδοκία*; opp. God's absolute will πώρωσιν δὲ καρδίας ἐπαγόμενον ὑπὸ θεοῦ, μὴ τῆς ἁγίας δυνάμεως ἐνέργημα εἶναι νομίσωμεν, ἀλλὰ σ. μὲν τῆς θείας κρίσεως, ἐνέργημα δὲ τῆς...ἀντικειμένης δυνάμεως Apoll.ap.*cat.Jo*.12:41(p.332.25); τὸ...'ἔδωκεν', ἐνταῦθα μὴ ἐνέργειαν νόμιζε εἶναι, ἀλλὰ σ. Chrys.*hom.19.1 in Rom*.(9.643A); θέλημα θεοῦ, ἢ σ. καὶ ἀνοχὴν καὶ μακροθυμίαν; Jo.D.*disp*.(M.96.1341B); freq. ref. sufferings of Christ Ἰουδαῖοι...τοῦτο πεπράχασι· πλὴν κατὰ συγχώρησιν τοῦ θεοῦ Ath.*exp.Ps*.88:39(M.27.392B); ἔπαθεν δι' ἡμᾶς σῇ σ. ... καὶ ἀνέστη σῷ κράτει *Const.App*.7.36.2; δεικνὺς [sc. ὁ Ἰησοῦς] ὅτι οὐ τῆς ἐκείνων δυνάμεως τὸ γινόμενον, ἀλλὰ τῆς αὐτοῦ σ. Chrys.*hom.83.2 in Jo*.(8.491C); in phrase κατὰ θείαν σ., ‡Just.*qu.et resp*.24(M.6.1269D); Thdr.Mops.*Abd*.proem.(M.66.305A); and κατὰ σ. θεοῦ: ἐγὼ...ἡ κατὰ σ. θεοῦ μήτηρ ὑμῶν προσαγορευομένη Sergia *Olymp*.2.11(p.49.25); *ib*.2.4(p.46.7); κατὰ σ. θεοῦ αὐτός με ποιεῖ πρεσβύτερον καὶ οἰκονόμον τῆς ἁγιωτάτης ἐκκλησίας Leont.N.*v.Jo.Eleem*.1(p.7.2); *ib*.45(p.92.23); ὅτε κατὰ σ. θεοῦ, μᾶλλον δὲ διὰ τὰς ἁμαρτίας ἡμῶν, ἔμελλεν Ἀλεξάνδρεια τοῖς ἀθέοις Πέρσαις παραδίδοσθαι *ib*.44b(p.90.25); and simply κατὰ σ.: οἶδεν ὅτι κατὰ σ. ἀφίεται δοκιμασθῆναι Mac.Aeg.*hom*.16.3(M.34.616A); **b.** ? *compliance, submission* συγχωρήσεως καιρὸς καὶ ἡ ἐξουσία τοῦ σκότους Apoll.ap.*cat.Lc*.22:53(p.161.3); but more prob. in sense a (supra) as season when Devil is allowed to work his will; **2.** *concession, indulgence* ἡ ...διγαμία...οὐ μὴν νόμος...ἀλλὰ σ. Thdr.Stud.*epp*.1.50(M.99.1092B); **3.** *remission, forgiveness*; **a.** of taxes, Eus.*v.C*.4.2 tit.(p.114.3; M.20.1152A); Cyr.S.*v.Sab*.54,75(pp.146.3,181.21); Ath.Scholast.*coll*.20.6(p.177); of a debt, Chrys.*hom.61.3 in Mt*.(7.615C); id.*hom.in Mt.18:23*(3.12C); of a penalty, Pall.*v.Chrys*.14(p.85.5; M.47.48); ἐπηγγείλατο αὐτοῖς μετανοοῦσι ἄφεσιν ἁμαρτιῶν, σ. ὀφλημάτων Eus.Al.*serm*.15(M.86.396B); **b.** official *pardon*, *M.Scill*.1(p.22.18); Eus.*v.C*.2.37(p.57.14; 1016A); **4. a.** *forgiveness* of sin by God, Or.*fr.in 1Reg*.3:14(M.17.40C); ἡ παρὰ τῆς σ. χάρις †Bas.*Is*.34(1.407E; M.30.188B); ἡ δὲ ἄφατος αὐτοῦ ἀγαθότης καὶ ἡ χάρις τὴν σ. ἐχαρίσατο Chrys.*hom.31.2 in Gen*.(4.307D); σ. ἁμαρτημάτων *ib.34.2*(4.342D); id.*hom.21.5 in Rom*.(9.678E); *ib.30.4*(744A); rarely with ἐκ: λαμβάνει σ. ἐκ τῶν ἀνομιῶν αὐτοῦ *Contrad*.1(p.6); plur. ἐν ταῖς τοιαύταις σ. Chrys.*hom.7.4 in Heb*.(12.137A); **b.** dist. from justification and sanctification οὐδὲ γὰρ δὴ μόνον ἁμαρτημάτων σ. ἡμῖν ἐδόθη· ἀλλὰ καὶ δικαιοσύνη, καὶ ἁγιασμός id.*hom.14.2 in Jo*.(8.81A); as means of justification θεοῦ δὲ δικαιοσύνη τὸ μὴ ἐξ ἔργων, ἀλλὰ διὰ συγχωρήσεως δικαιωθῆναι ἐν αὐτῷ δι' αὐτοῦ *cat.2Cor*.5:21(p.387.19); freedom from passions a mark of forgiveness γνῶναι εἰ γέγονεν ἐν σοὶ σ. τῶν ἁμαρτιῶν σου, τοῦτο σημεῖόν ἐστιν—ἐὰν μηδὲν κινηθῇ ἐν τῇ καρδίᾳ σου ὧν ἥμαρτες Esaias *or*.8.14(p.57); σ. ἁμαρτιῶν, παθῶν ἐστιν ἐλευθερία, ὧν ὁ μήπω ἀπαλλαγεὶς χάριτι, τῆς σ. οὔπω ἔτυχεν Thal.*cent*.1.100(M.91.1437A); **c.** means; **i.** baptism τῶν γὰρ ἡμαρτημένων, οὐ τῶν ἁμαρτανομένων τὸ λουτρὸν ἔχει σ. Gr.Naz.*or*.40.32(M.36.405A); διὰ τοῦ βαπτίσματος ὁλόκληρον τῶν ἁμαρτημάτων τὴν σ. ἐδωρήσατο Chrys.*hom.27.1 in Jo*.(8.155A); **ii.** repentance τοῖς...γνησίαν πρότερον κακῶν μετάνοιαν ἐνδειξαμένοις ἡ σωτήριος χάρις τὴν σ. τῶν πεπραγμένων ἐδωρήσατο Eus.*theoph.fr*.9(p.24*.4; M.24.633B); τῷ παρόντι τῆς μετανοίας καιρῷ κατάλληλον τὴν σ. δωρούμενος Cyr.H.*catech*.2.13; τὴν σ. διὰ μετανοίας ἀπολαμβάνει *M.Ner.et Ach*.5(p.4.23); κύριε...ὁ τῷ Πέτρῳ, καὶ πόρνῃ διὰ δακρύων τὴν σ. παρασχόμενος †Jo.Jej.*poenit*.(M.88.1889B); Sophr.H.*mir.Cyr.et Jo*.37(M.87.3564C); ἐμοῦ τὰ μικρὰ πρόσδεξαι δάκρυα, καθαίρων με...ἐν αὐτοῖς· ἐνθανάτιον σ. ὡς βάπτισμα, μὴ ἀπαιτῶν μέ τι πλέον Anast.S.*Ps.6*(M.89.1112C); **iii.** confession ὅταν γὰρ...διὰ τῆς ἐξομολογήσεως ἀπονίψασθαι τὰ πεπλημμελημένα δυνηθῶμεν, καὶ τὴν σ. εὑρέσθαι παρὰ τοῦ δεσπότου, ἄπιμεν ἐκεῖ καθαροὶ τῶν ἁμαρτημάτων Chrys.*hom.5.2 in Gen*.(4.33D); by forgiveness of others, id.*prod.Jud*.1.1(2.378A); by sufferings, id.*paralyt*.6(3.43A); **d.** *pardon*; *absolution* for apostasy, Epiph.*haer*.68.2(p.142.4; M.42.185C); under the old dispensation δοὺς τὴν χάριν τῷ θεράποντι αὐτοῦ ὑπὲρ τῆς σ. τοῦ ἁμαρτήματος τοῦ λαοῦ ὁ θεός †Bas.*Is*.187(1.517D; M.30.437B); for other sins καὶ πόρνοις κτλ. ... σ. ἁμαρτημάτων ὑπισχνούμενοι [sc. Anomoeans] *ib*.232(555D; M.525B); πρὸς τῶν ἁγίων ᾔτει σ. Sophr.H.*mir.Cyr.et Jo*.36(M.87.3552A); from a martyr in heaven διανέμων ἡμῖν...πταισμάτων σ. *Mir.Geo*.epilog.(p.41.16).

***συγχωρητής, ὁ**, **1.** *one who is complaisant, accommodating*, Hipp.*haer*.4.24(p.53.2; M.16.3087C); **2.** *one who pardons, forgiver*; of Christ, Ephr.3.393A; id.3.387B; Cyr.H.*hom*.19(M.33.1153A).

συγχωρητικός, **1.** *making a concession* νόμῳ ὁρμᾶται συγχωρητικῷ ἡ διγαμία Thdr.Stud.*epp*.1.50(M.99.1093C); **2.** *forgiving* διδάσκειν...σ. εἶναι τῶν εἰς ἡμᾶς ἡμαρτημένων τοῖς ἀδικήσασιν ἡμᾶς Or.*comm.in Mt*.14.6(p.286.13; M.13.1193C); ἡ βασιλεία...τοὺς μὴ σ. ... οὐ παραδέχεται Eus.*fr.Lc*.17:3(M.24.581B); τὸ...πνεῦμα...λυτικὸν καὶ σ. ἦν πάσης ἁμαρτίας id.*qu.Marin.suppl*.2.9(M.22.1013B); denied of angels τιμωροὶ μὲν τῶν ἁμαρτανομένων ἄγγελοι, συγχωρητικοὶ δὲ τῶν πλημμελουμένων οὐκέτι †Bas.*Is*.187(1.517E; M.30.437B); neut. as subst. διὰ τὸ...ἀνεξίκακον ἐλεημονικόν τε καὶ σ. τοῦ θεοῦ Eus.*fr.Lc*.17:3(M.24.581B).

***συγχωρητικῶς**, *by way of concession*, Or.*Cels*.5.53(p.57.3; M.11.1264B).

συγχωρίζω, *forgive*, Philox.*ep*.41(p.187).

***συγχωρισμός, ὁ**, *permission* τῆς φαύλης...συνόδου, τῆς γενομένης κατὰ θεοῦ συγχωρισμὸν ἐν Κωνσταντινουπόλει Jo.V H.*icon*.3(M.96.1352A); cf. συγχώρησις.

σύγχωσμα, τό, *heap*, *Orac.Sib.fr.*3.30.

***συγχωσμός, ὁ,** *engulfing*, *overwhelming*, Germ.CP *vit.term.*15 (M.98.116D).

***συδοροκέφαλον, τό,** *head scarf*, *veil*, *Nomoc.*251.

συζάω, 1. *live with*, *live in company with*; lit. and met., as husband and wife, Herm.*mand.*4.1.4f.,9; with Christ *συναποθάνοντα αὐτὸν* [sc. *τὸν βαπτιζόμενον*] *συναναστῆναι καὶ σ. αὐτῷ* *Const.App.*7.44.2; **2.** *pass one's life in*, *live in a state of*; hence *be invariably associated with*, *possess as a characteristic* *τῶν δὲ ζώντων, τὰ μὲν αἰσθήσει συζῇ, τὰ ἀμοιρεῖ ταύτης* Gr.Nyss.*anim.et res.*(M.46.60B).

συζεύγνυ-μι, 1. *join together in pairs*, *couple* *ὁ Σαοὺλ...ἐγυμνώθη μὲν τῆς τοῦ πνεύματος χάριτος, πονηρῷ δὲ πνεύματι συνεζύγη* Thdt.*Ps.*118:8(1.1440); of Gnost. aeons, Iren.*haer.*1.29.1(M.7.692D not.74); **2.** *unite closely*, ref. Inc. *τὴν σάρκα ἣν ἑαυτῷ...ὁ λόγος συνέζευξεν* Euther.*confut.*15(M.28.1385C); usu. pass., *be closely united*; *be bound up with*; of soul and body, Or.*Jo.*6.52(p.161.17; M.14.292B) cit. s. *βαρέω*; ref. Phil.2:13 *συνεζευγμένης τῆς...ἐνεργείας...τῷ καλῷ θέλειν* *ib.*20.23(20; p.357.13; M.14.625A); *τὸ ὕδωρ* [sc. in baptism]... *ἀρετῇ ἠθικῇ τε καὶ διανοητικῇ* ~*μενον* id.*fr.36 in Jo.*(p.512.23); *συνέζευκται...τῷ νόμῳ καὶ φυλακὴ καὶ παράβασις* Thdt.*Rom.*4:15 (3.50); theol., of Son and H. Ghost *τῷ...πατρὶ πανταχοῦ συνέζευκται* id.*rect.conf.*7(M.6.1220A); of the two wills in Christ, ‡Cyr.*Trin.*19 (6³.25A; M.77.1157C); **3.** *assign*, *give* *τίνος χάριν...τοῖς μὲν πλοῦτον συνέζευξε τοῖς δὲ πενίαν συνεκλήρωσε;* Thdt.*provid.*6(4.571); id.*Rom.*3:27(3.45); **4.** pass., *be in a state of* *ὁ ἀσθενείᾳ συνεζευγμένος* id.*Jer.*14:9(2.485); *ἐσχάτῃ πενίᾳ συνεζευγμένοι* id.*Phil.*4:18(3.469).

[*]**συζευτικός,** for *συζευκτικός*, *uniting*, Dion.Ar.*c.h.*15.9(M.3.337C).

***συζηλ-όω,** s.v.l., *be zealous together*, *emulate together* ~*οῦντες ἕσθ' ὅτε τῶν πολεμουμένων ἐκκλησιῶν* Cyr.*ador.*5(M.68.405B; but cf. not. ad loc. and 1.170D *συζητοῦντες*).

***συζηλωτής, ὁ,** *fellow emulator*, Cyr.*ador.*4(1.140B).

σύζησις, ἡ, *living together*; *living in communion with* the saints, Ath.*inc.*57.3(M.25.197A); id.*gent.*2(M.25.5D).

συζητέω, 1. *discuss* or *dispute* with *ὁ συνεζήτει μετὰ τῆς γυναικός* Heracleon ap.Or.*Jo.*13.38(p.263.17; M.14.465A); *πρὸς Ἀρχέλαον... συζητήσας* Epiph.*mens.*20(M.43.269B); **2.** abs., *debate*, *ponder*, Herm.*sim.*2.1; *ib.*6.1.1.

συζητητής, ὁ, *joint inquirer*, *disputant*, Jo.Clim.*scal.*26(M.88.1057C).

συζυγής, *yoked together*, *united*; lit. and met., Gr.Nyss.*Eun.*12(2 p.294.27; M.45.908C); *ψυχὰς...καὶ τὰ σ. σώματα* Dion.Ar.*d.n.*6.2(M.3.856D); of Persons of Trin. *συζυγέα...θεότητα* Gr.Naz.*carm.*2.2(poem.) 3.241(M.37.1497A).

συζυγία, ἡ, 1. *yoke* of animals; gen., *pair*; met., of *union* of soul and body *οὐδὲ ψυχὴ καὶ σῶμα, λυθέντα τῆς σ., καθ' ἑαυτὰ ποιῆσαί τι δύναται* †Just.*fr.res.*(p.45; M.6.1584D); Gr.Naz.*or.*4.78(M.35.604B); *ib.*21.2(1084C); of union of forces against which man has to contend *διττὸς ὁ ἀγὼν...διττοὶ δὲ καὶ ἡμεῖς, καὶ πρὸς συζυγίαν ἐχθίστην παρατταττόμεθα· ἥ τε γὰρ μάχη κατὰ νοῦν τε καὶ αἴσθησιν* Const. Diac.*laud.*30(M.88.513A); **2.** *wedlock*, *married state*, Just.*2apol.*2.4(M.6.444B); Eus.*h.e.*3.30.1(M.20.277C); Bas.*reg.fus.*12(2.354B; M.31.948C); freq. with such words as *παιδοποιΐα*, Clem.*str.*3.12 (p.237.16; M.8.1189C); *τεκνογονία*, *Lit.*ap.*Const.App.*8.10.10; Gr.Nyss.*v.Mos.*(M.44.336D); *τεκνοτροφία*, Bas.*renunt.*1(2.203A; M.31.628C); opp. *παρθενία*, *ib.*(203A; M.628B); of *συνείσακτοι* or *contubernales* *ἐν ταῖς ἀμφιβόλοις ζήσατε σ.* Gr.Naz.*carm.*2.2(epigr.) 15.16(M.38.90A); †Bas.*contub.*5(M.30.820D); Chrys.*fem.reg.*3(1.254B); *ib.*6(259E); myst. *νυμφοστολεῖται...ἡ ψυχὴ πρὸς τὴν...πνευματικὴν...τοῦ θεοῦ σ.* Gr.Nyss.*hom.1 in Cant.*(M.44.765B); **3.** *conjunction*; *association* of words or things in pairs, *syzygy* *κατὰ τὸν λόγον τῆς σ.* *Hom.Clem.*2.23; *διακεκριμένην τούτων* [sc. unrelated terms]...*τὴν πρὸς τὸ κατάλληλον σ. ἐπιγινώσκομεν* Gr.Nyss.*Eun.*4(2 p.82.26; M.45.657B); *τὰς...περὶ τὴν ψυχὴν νοουμένας πέντε σ. περὶ τὴν μίαν τὴν τοῦ θεοῦ σημαντικὴν σ. ... καταγίνεσθαι* (enumerated), Max.*myst.*5(M.91.676A); *correlation* *τὴν σχετικὴν σ.* Gr.Nyss.*Eun.*4 (2 p.82.14; 657A); of syllables too many to be contained in a foot, *syzygiae...sunt pentasyllabi et hexasyllabi pedes; et dictae apud Graecos συζυγίαι quasi quaedam declinationes. sed hi non sunt pedes, sed appellantur pentasyllabi et hexasyllabi, quia ultra quinque et sex syllabas non procedunt*, Isid.H.*etym.*1.17.20; **4.** *that which is associated*; *correlative*, Eus.*e.th.*1.16(p.76.23; M.24.857B); Gr.Naz.*or.*31.23(p.174.8; M.36.160A); Leont.B.*Nest.et Eut.*1(M.86.1288C); *δεδομένης...γενέσεως, ἀλλοιώσεως...τῷ σώματι τοῦ κυρίου, τί τὸ κωλῦον μὴ οὐχὶ καὶ τὴν λοιπὴν αὐτῷ σ. διδόναι;* *ib.*2(1345D); **5.** theol., of union of Father and Son, Nonn.*par.Jo.*14:11(M.43.868C); Christol., of union of natures in Christ *ὡς ἐπὶ συζυγίᾳ τοῦ λόγου καὶ τῆς σαρκὸς ἐπιθαλάμιον ᾄδει τὸ Ἆσμα τῶν ᾀσμάτων* ‡Ath.*synops.*24(M.28.352B); *τὴν σ. τῶν φύσεων* Procl.CP *or.laud.BMV* 2(p.104.5; M.65.684A); *πρὸ τῆς συνδρομῆς καὶ σ. τῶν ἑκατέρων...μετὰ τὴν σ.*‡Gr.Nyss.*hom.3.30 in Jo.*(p.143.28); **6.** Gnost., *pairing* of aeons, *syzygy* *τὸν προπάτορα ἡνῶσθαι κατὰ συζυγίαν τῇ ἑαυτοῦ Ἐννοίᾳ* Iren.*haer.*1.1.1 (M.7.448B); *τοὺς Αἰῶνας...βουληθέντας καὶ αὐτοὺς...προβαλεῖν προβολὰς ἐν σ.* *ib.*1.1.2(449A); *φασὶ κεκαθάρθαι Σοφίαν...καὶ ἀποκατασταθῆναι τῇ σ.* *ib.*1.2.4(460A); *ἕκαστος τῶν αἰώνων ἴδιον ἔχει πλήρωμα, τὴν σ.* Clem.*exc.Thdot.*32(p.117.14; M.9.676A); *τοὺς νοεροὺς καὶ αἰωνίους γάμους τῆς σ.* *ib.*64(p.128.19; 689C); *καλεῖ τὴν πρώτην σ. νοῦν καὶ ἐπίνοιαν* Hipp.*haer.*6.13(p.138.26; M.16.3211D); *ἀγέννητος ὢν μόνος* [sc. *ὁ πατήρ*] *διὰ πρώτης τῆς μιᾶς σ. τοῦ Νοῦ καὶ τῆς Ἀληθείας πάσας τὰς τῶν γενομένων προβαλεῖν εὐπόρησε ῥίζας* *ib.*6.29 (p.157.1; 3238B); *οἱ...ἄλλοι πάντες αἰῶνες γεννητοὶ ὑπάρχοντες κατὰ συζυγίαν γεννῶσιν* *ib.*6.30(p.158.1; 3239A); instanced as characteristic of Gnosticism *τοὺς τὴν περὶ αἰώνων ἀναπλάσαντας ἐν συζυγίαις μυθολογίαν* Or.*Jo.*2.24(19; p.81.2; M.14.156C); Epiph.*haer.*31.1(p.383.1; M.41.473B).

σύζυγος, 1. *yoked together*, *paired*, *united*, ref. list of apostles *ὁ Ματθαῖος...τοῦ σ. δεύτερον ἑαυτὸν κατέλεγεν, συνεζευγμένος γοῦν τῷ Θωμᾷ* Eus.*d.e.*3.5(p.126.16; M.22.216A); met. *σ. ... ἡ προφήτεια προφήτῃ* Or.*Apoc.*3(p.22); *αὐτὰς* [sc. *τὰς ψυχάς*] *καὶ πρὸ τῆς τῶν σ. σωμάτων ἐγέρσεως* Andr.Caes.*therap.fr.*1(p.165.6); theol. (adj. and subst.), of Son in rel. to Father *σ. εἰμὶ τοκῆος* Nonn.*par.Jo.*14:9(M.43.868C); of H. Ghost in rel. to Logos *τὸ σ. αὐτῷ ἅγιον πνεῦμα* Eus.*p.e.*7.16(328B; M.21.553C); *ib.*7.15(327B; M.552D); **2.** *united in marriage*; **a.** as subst., *consort*, ref. Gnost. syzygies of aeons *ὃ γέγονεν ἐν αὐτῷ ζωὴ ἦν, ἡ σ.* Clem.*exc.Thdot.*6(p.107.25; M.9.657A); Or.*Jo.*2.24(19; p.81.4; M.14.156C); *τὸν ἀπὸ τοῦ πληρώματος σ.* Heracleon *ib.*13.11(p.235.27; 416B); cf. *μητροπάτωρ...ἀφορμὰς τοῖς τὰς προβολὰς εἰσάγουσι τάχα καὶ σύζυγον νοῆσαι τοῦ θεοῦ* Clem.*str.*5.14 (p.411.18; M.9.185C); **b.** fem. as subst., *wife*; ref. Phil.4:3 *καὶ ὅ γε Παῦλος οὐκ ὀκνεῖ ἔν τινι ἐπιστολῇ τὴν αὑτοῦ προσαγορεύειν σ. ἣν οὐ περιεκόμιζεν διὰ τὸ τῆς ὑπηρεσίας εὐσταλές* *ib.*3.6(p.220.17; M.8.1157A); cf. *Paulus ergo, sicut quidam tradunt, cum uxore vocatus est; de qua dicit ad Philippenses scribens: rogo etiam te, germane compar...: qui quoniam ab ipsa ex consensu liber effectus est, servum se nominat Christi*, Or.*comm.in Rom.*1.1(M.14.839B); *σ. γνήσιε..., τινὲς τὴν γυναῖκα αὐτοῦ παρακαλεῖν ἐνταῦθά φασιν· ἀλλ' οὐκ ἔστιν, ἀλλά τινα γυναῖκα, ἢ καὶ ἄνδρα μιᾶς αὐτῶν* [sc. Euodia and Syntyche]... *παρατίθεται αὐτὰς ἀνδρὶ ἴσως θαυμαστῷ, ὃν καὶ σ. καλεῖ...ᾧ ἴσως εἰώθει παρατίθεσθαι, ὡς συνεργῷ καὶ συστρατιώτῃ...τινὲς δέ φασιν ὄνομα ἐκεῖνο κύριον εἶναι τὸ Σύζυγε* Chrys.*hom.13.2–3 in Phil.*(11.300F–301D); *τὸν δὲ σ. τινες ἀνοήτως ὑπέλαβον γυναῖκα εἶναι τοῦ ἀποστόλου, οὐ προσεσχηκότες τοῖς ἐν τῇ πρὸς Κορινθίους γεγραμμένοις ...σ. οὖν αὐτὸν καλεῖ, ὡς τὸν αὐτὸν ἕλκοντα τῆς εὐσεβείας ζυγόν* Thdt.*Phil.*4:3(3.466); in gen. *ἑαυτὸν* [sc. Simon Magus] *εἶναι δύναμιν θεοῦ λέγων τὴν μεγάλην, τὴν δὲ σ. πορνάδα πνεῦμα ἅγιον* Epiph.*haer.*21.2 (p.240.1; M.41.288B); met. *ἡ...φιλοσοφία γένοιτο ἄν ποτε τῷ ὑψηλοτέρῳ βίῳ σ. τε καὶ φίλη καὶ κοινωνὸς τῆς ζωῆς* Gr.Nyss.*v.Mos.*(M.44.337A); **3.** as subst., *associated term*, *correlative*, ref. Phil.2:13 *ἑπομένου πάντως τῷ καλὸν θέλειν τοῦ σ. αὐτῷ* ⟨*τοῦ*⟩ *ἐνεργεῖν* Or.*Jo.*20.23(20; p.357.10; M.14.625A); *Disp.Phot.*(M.88.556D).

***συζυγοστατέω,** *act as* libripens or *paymaster*, Thdr.Stud.*or.*11.5(M.99.808B).

συζυμόω, *leaven*; met., Germ.CP *or.*1(M.98.240B).

σύζυξ, *united*, of Father and Son *σύζυγες ἓν μόνον ἐσμὲν ἐν ἀλλήλοισιν ἐόντες* Nonn.*par.Jo.*17:22(M.43.888B); *ib.*17:21(888A); ref. Inc. *λόγος...ξυνώσας ζαθέην βροτοειδέϊ σύζυγα μορφήν* *ib.*1:14(752B).

συζωοποι-έω, *make alive together*, pass. *χθὲς συνενεκρούμην* [sc. *Χριστῷ*], ~*οῦμαι σήμερον* Gr.Naz.*or.*1.4(M.35.397B).

***σύζωος,** *living one life*, of Trin., Eulog.*fr.Trin.*2.1(p.364) cit. s. *σύγγνωμος*.

συκαλίς, ἡ, a kind of wheat *διάφορος...ἡ ζειά...τὸ γυμνόκριθον ὀνομάζεται καὶ ἡ σ.* *Schol.* in *Can.App.*3(*Mon.*2 p.642).

συκαμινέα, ἡ, *ulcer*, *Mir. Artem.*20(p.25.7).

συκῆ, ἡ, *fig-tree*, exeg. Jud.9:10f., Meth.*symp.*10.2f.(p.123.19ff.; M.18.196Aff.); *ib.*10.5(p.126.22ff.; 200Bff.); exeg. Mt.21:19ff. // Mc.11:13ff., Or.*comm.in Mt.*16.26(pp.561f.; M.13.1457Cf.); Chrys.*hom.67.1f.in Mt.*(7.662Bff.); Sever.*fic.*(M.59.585f.); Isid.Pel.*epp.*1.51(M.78.213B,C); Vict.*Mc.*11:12f.(pp.391f.); exeg. Mt.24:32 // Mc.13:28 // Lc.21:29, Or.*comm.ser.53 in Mt.*(p.118.16; cf.M.13.1682D); Eus.*fr.Lc.*21:29(M.24.601B); Chrys.*hom.77.1 in Mt.*(740Bf.); Cyr.*Lc.*21:29 (M.72.900C); Vict.*Mc.*13:28(p.414.6ff.).

***συκήλατον, ? τό,** ? *fig-orchard*, Ephr.1.313E.

σῦκον, τό, *fig*, ref. Gen.3:7 ἅμα ἔφαγον, πάντων τῶν φυτῶν... κατέρρεον τὰ φύλλα παρὲξ τοῦ σύκου μόνου *Apoc.Mos.*20(p.11).

***συκότια, τά,** *entrails*, Jo.Mal.*chron.*16 p.397(M.97.588C).

***συκοτόκυλα, τά,** prob. compound of συκωτός *fattened on figs* and κοιλία, a species of *foie gras* σ. ... ὀρνιθίων ἔφαγεν Eustrat. *v.Eutych.*38(M.86.2320B).

συκοφαντ-έω, *calumniate* persons; also things, *misrepresent*; *explain away* τὴν ἀλήθειαν Clem.*prot.*4(p.35.28; M.8.136A); μήτε βαπτίσματι μήτε εὐχαριστίᾳ χρώμενοι, ∼οῦντες τὰς γραφὰς ὡς...οὐ βουλομένας Or.*or.*5(p.308.20; M.11.429B); οὐδαμῶς ∼ῆσαι τὴν ἑρμηνείαν ἡμῶν δυνήσονται Thdr.Mops.*Col.*1:18(p.274.21; M.66.928C); τὸ ...τῆς ἀναστάσεως ∼ῆσαι μυστήριον Cyr.*Is.*5.1(2.749E); id.*Abac.*10 (3.525E).

***συκοφάντησις, ἡ,** *false accusation, misrepresentation*, Epiph. *haer.*73.1(p.268.27; M.42.401C).

συκοφαντητός, *exposed to slander* or *misrepresentation*, Just.*dial.* 94.4(M.6.701A).

συκοφαντία, ἡ, 1. ref. persons, *vexatious* or *dishonest prosecution*; *slander, calumny* γράφει πρὸς τὸν ὁμώνυμον αὐτῷ Διονύσιον... Ῥώμης, ἀπολογούμενος σ. εἶναι ταύτην Ath.*decr.*25(p.21.14; M.25. 461A); Chrys.*hom.61.1 in Jo.*(8.361E); Isid.Pel.*epp.*1.275(M.78. 345A); **2.** ref. things, *misrepresentation*, ref. paganism ἀσέβειαν καὶ σ. Ath.*gent.*22(M.25.44C); κατὰ τῶν Δωνατιανῶν συκοφαντίας Hier. *vir.ill.*(tr. Sophr.Pal.)110(p.56.18; M.*PL.*23.706B); ref. Ananias and Sapphira ἡ τῶν παρανόμων σ. *cat.Ac.*5:5(p.86.34).

συκοφαντικῶς, *slanderously*, Gr.Nyss.*anim.et res.*(M.46.57C).

***συκοφύλαξ, ὁ,** *guardian of fig-trees*, of the cherubim in paradise θυρωροὶ καὶ σ. Anast.S.*hex.*12(M.89.1061C).

συλαγωγ-έω, 1. *carry off captive*; met. τὸν ὄφιν...∼ῆσαί σε θέλοντα Bas.*renunt.*8(2.209A; M.31.641B); οἱ συλλαγωγηθέντες Or.*exp. in Pr.*31:11(M.17.249D); *carry away, lead astray*, Tat.*orat.*22(p.25.4; M.6.856B); μέγιστον...κτῆμά ἐστι, τὸ τῶν δογμάτων μάθημα· καὶ χρεία νηφαλίου ψυχῆς, ἐπειδὴ πολλοί εἰσιν οἱ ∼οῦντες, διὰ τῆς φιλοσοφίας καὶ κενῆς ἀπάτης Cyr.H.*catech.*4.2; **2.** *rob*; met. λεγέσθωσαν ...ἱερόσυλοι οὗτοι, οἱ ∼ήσαντες τὴν ἀποστολικὴν ἐκκλησίαν, τοιούτων στερήσαντες διδασκάλων Pall.*v.Chrys.*20(p.147.6; M.47.82); *appropriate* words, etc., of another οὐκ αὐτὸν διασπῶν μόνον τὸν νόμον Μωσέως, ἀλλὰ καὶ τὸν σκοτεινὸν Ἡράκλειτον ∼ῶν Hipp.*haer.*6.9 (p.136.14; M.16.3210A); *ib.*7.30(p.215.18; 3334A).

***συλαγωγία, ἡ,** *spoliation, robbery, pillage*, Epiph.*haer.*21.2 (p.240.14; M.41.288C); τὴν ψυχὴν ἀφίημι...ἀρκοῦμαι...τῇ...σ. τοῦ σώματος Chrysipp.*enc.in Mich.*(p.92.27).

συλ-άω, 1. *strip off* arms of a slain enemy; in gen., *strip off*; met. εἰ μὴ...∼ήσωσι τὰ τῶν ἀρετῶν περιβόλαια *cat.Lc.*10:30(p.87.28); **2.** *pillage, rob*; met., *deprive of* ὑφ' ἧς τὸν τῆς σωτηρίας ἐσυλήθη καιρόν Bas.*hom.*21.6(2.168A; M.31.552A); of pagan deities who *usurp* title of god θεοὶ ἐκαλοῦντο τὴν θείαν προσηγορίαν ∼ήσαντες Thdt.*Jer.*3:3(2.423); id.*Ps.*85:8(1.1212); **3.** *rob, take away* things τὸ κλέος...ὑπὸ τῆς λήθης ∼ώμενον Thdt.*h.e.*1.1.2(3.723); in good sense, *remove*; *relieve* ∼ῶσι τῇ ψυχαγωγίᾳ τὴν τῶν πόνων βαρύτητα id.*Ps.* 1:4(1.613); id.*qu.1 in 1Par.*(1.562); id.*provid.*6(4.582); met. ? *cast aside, dismiss* ὡς ἀπλήρωτον τοῦτο ∼ῶν καὶ ἀτέκμαρτον Mac.Mgn. *apocr.*3.40(p.138.16); **4.** Manich. παρθένος τις...∼ᾶν ἐπιχειρεῖ τοὺς ἄρχοντας Hegem.*Arch.*9(p.13.15; M.10.1441A); ὁ θερισμὸς ἄρχων ἐὰν ∼ηθῇ ὑπὸ τῆς παρθένου, καταχέει λοιμὸν ἐφ' ὅλης τῆς γῆς *ib.*(p.14.11; 1441B); τὸν...θεὸν...μηδὲ χαίρειν ἐπ' αὐτῷ [sc. τῷ κόσμῳ], διὰ τὸ ἐξ ἀρχῆς σεσυλῆσθαι αὐτὸν ὑπὸ τῶν ἀρχόντων *ib.*12(p.20.9; 1448A); ἐσύλησε καὶ ἥρπαξε, φησίν, ἡ κακία μέρος ἀπὸ τοῦ θεοῦ, καὶ διὰ τοῦτο πέμπει ὁ θεός, καὶ ∼ᾷ καὶ ἁρπάζει τὸ μέρος τὸ ∼ηθὲν ἀπ' αὐτοῦ Jo.D. *Man.*1.67(M.94.1561D); cf.Epiph.*haer.*21.2(p.240.14; M.41.288C).

συλεύ-ω, variant of συλάω, *despoil* τοῦ Χριστοῦ παθόντος καὶ ἔτι ἐν τῷ μνημείῳ κειμένου τοῦ σώματος, αὐτοῦ τε ∼οντος τὸν ᾅδην Diod. *Ps.*67:2(M.33.1602B).

συλ-έω, = συλάω, *rob*; ‖ κλέπτω, *Orac.Sib.fr.*3.24; met. ὁρῶ...σε φθονούμενον ὑπὸ τοῦ ἐχθροῦ, καὶ τὸν κάματόν σου...∼ούμενον *V.Pach.* Σ 54(p.224.19).

συλητής, ὁ, *robber*, ‡Caes.Naz.*dial.*109(M.38.980); of Marcion suppressing portions of scripture, Epiph.*haer.*42.11(p.140.20; M.41. 749C); referred by Judas to Christ παραδώσω...τῶν προφητῶν συλητήν *Narr.Jos.*2.3(p.463).

***συλήτρια, ἡ,** *plunderer, robber*, met., of ῥαθυμία, ‡Chrys.*poenit.* 1.1(9.763E).

συλλαβή, ἡ, A. act.; mental *conception, idea* προσπταίουσι [sc. the heretics]...καὶ περὶ τὰς ἀναιτίους καὶ μείζονας σ. τοῦ τὰ κακυνθέντα ἡμῶν ἰωμένου Didym.*Trin.*3.25(M.39.940B).

B. pass., *that which is held together*; **1.** *combination, compound*, cf. μήτε στοιχεῖα ὑπάρχοντα, μήτε συλλαβάς Numenius ap.Eus.*p.e.*15.17 (819B; M.21.1345A); **2.** esp. of several letters taken together, *syllable*; not applicable to divine Word συνεχῶς χρῶνται τὸ [Ps. 44:2] οἰόμενοι προφορὰν πατρικὴν οἱονεὶ ἐν συλλαβαῖς κειμένην εἶναι τὸν υἱόν Or.*Jo.*1.24(23; p.29.23; M.14.65B); Eus.*e.th.*2.17(p.121.11; M.24.940A); of words of God, Isid.Pel.*epp.*3.95(M.78.801C); of writing against Belshazzar, Thdt.*Dan.*5:31(2.1173); **3.** *epistle, letter*; plur., Cyr.*ep.*48(p.31.9; 5².155B); Leo Mag.*ep.*104.4(p.60.23; M.*PL.*54.998A); sing., Sophr.H.*ep.syn.*(M.87.3189A); Max.*ep.*45(M. 91.649A,C); Thdr.Stud.*epp.*2.41(M.99.1240D); **4.** plur., *letters* of the alphabet, denoting elementary stage of education ἔτι ἐν ταῖς σ. ὄντα [sc. τὰ παιδία] ‡Ath.*v.Syncl.*14(M.28.1493C).

***συλλάβιον, τό,** *element, rudiment* ἡμεῖς...οἱ ἀπὸ Ἰουδαίων ἀκμὴν οὐδὲ τὰ σ. τῆς πίστεως τοῦ Χριστοῦ ἐμάθομεν *Didasc.Jac.*2.5(p.48.12).

συλλαγχάνω, [irreg. perf. ptcpl. συνειλοχώς]; **1.** *be joined by lot*; ptcpl., *colleague*, of fellow clergy, colleagues in ministry βουλοίμην ἂν...ὄφελος εἶναι τοῖς σ. Synes.*ep.*91(M.66.1457A); **2.** of a see, *be allotted*, *ib.*66(1409A); **3.** *become possessed of* ὁ...πλοῦτον συνειλοχώς, ὡς ἐσχάτῃ πενίᾳ συζῶν Thdt.*h.rel.*21(3.1251); *ib.*proem.(3.1105); *ib.*5 (1166); **4.** intrans., *fall to one's lot, come into one's possession*, c. dat., Melet.*nat.hom.*30(M.64.1280C).

[*]συλλαγωγέω, v. συλαγωγέω.

***συλλαϊκός, ὁ,** *fellow layman*, *Const.App.*2.36.9.

συλλαλ-έω, *speak with*; *talk together, converse*, *M.Perp.*19(p.89. 22); Geo.Pis.*Pers.*1.82(M.92.1203A); Max.*ambig.*(M.91.1168D); pass., *be spoken of* ἡμεῖς...συνακουόμενοί τε ἀλλήλοις καὶ ∼ούμενοι Gr.Naz. *or.*43.22(M.36.525A).

συλλαλιά, ἡ, *conversation*, Niceph.Ur.*v.Sym.*120(M.86.3097C); Jo. Clim.*scal.*4(M.88.685B).

***συλλαμπρύν-ω,** pass., *join in being bright, splendid, distinguished* ἡ...πανήγυρις ∼εται *Rit.Epiph.*(p.426).

***συλλάμπ-ω,** *shine together*, fig. τὸ ἐνυπάρχον φῶς τῷ Μωσέως νόμῳ, 'καλύμματι' ἐναποκεκρυμμένον, συνέλαμψε τῇ Ἰησοῦ ἐπιδημίᾳ Or.*princ.*4.1.6(p.302.8; M.11.353A); met., Gr.Naz.*carm.*1.1.8.96(M. 37.454A); of Logos οὗτος...ἀενάῳ συνέλαμπε θεῷ Nonn.*par.Jo.*1:2(M. 43.749A); of natures of Christ ἀμερίστως ἑτερότητι ∼οντα Sophr.H. *ep.syn.*(M.87.3165D).

συλλατρεύ-ω, pass., *be worshipped together* or *at the same time* ὁ υἱὸς ὁμοούσιος ὁμολογεῖται τῷ πατρί, καὶ τὸ πνεῦμα τὸ ἅγιον...∼εται Bas.*ep.*90.2(3.182C; M.32.473C); ἐπειδὴ τῆς τριάδος τὸ λατρεύεσθαι, ∼εται ἐν τῇ εἰκόνι καὶ ὁ πατὴρ καὶ τὸ πνεῦμα Thdr.Stud.*epp.*2.151(M. 99.1472C).

συλλέγ-ω, A. *bring together*; **1.** *contract*, Geo.Pis.*carm.*1.57(p.3); **2.** *collect* for consideration ταῦτα οὖν ἅπαντα ∼οντες, ἐχώμεθα σφοδρῶς τῆς σωτηρίας Chrys.*hom.18.6 in Rom.*(9.640A); pass., ζήτημα...παρὰ πολλῶν ζητούμενον, καὶ πολλαχόθεν ∼όμενον id.*hom. 4.1 in 1Thess.*(11.451B); *acquire* knowledge, Cyr.*Ps.*35:4(M.69.916C); Thdt.*h.e.*4.28.1(3.1007); met., *collect, compose*, e.g. one's thoughts τοῖς...προσευχομένοις ἀναχωρεῖν καὶ ∼ειν τὴν διάνοιαν Diod.*Gen.* 25:22(M.33.1576A); **3.** *muster, rally*, met. ὁ ἑαυτῷ τὴν ἐπιθυμίαν ∼ων, ὁ...τὸ θηρίον ἐπεισάγων ἠρεμοῦντι τῷ λογισμῷ Chrys.*hom.17.2 in Mt.*(7.223D); **4.** *find, provide* ἄμφια ∼ειν Cyr.*ador.*7(M.68.513A); perh. also ἂν δὲ μικρὸν ἀργύριον πένητι δῶμεν, ἄνω καὶ κάτω τοῦτο στρέφομεν· ὅπερ ἐσχάτης ἐστὶν ἀνοίας, καὶ μεγίστη τοῦ ∼οντος ζημία Chrys.*hom.3.5 in Mt.*(7.41A).

B. *speak with* ἰδὼν ὅτι συνέλεγέν μοι, εἶπον αὐτῷ *A.Pil.*A 15.6 (p.273).

συλλειτουργ-έω, *minister with* or *together*; *be fellow ministers* CSard.*ep.cath.*ap.Ath.*apol.sec.*47(p.123.1; M.25.333C); ∼ούντων τῷ Χριστῷ Cyr.*ador.*13(1.454A); ∼ούντων αὐτῷ καὶ ἁγίων ἀγγέλων id. *Zach.*19(3.676A,B); Jo.Thess.*dorm.BMV* 2.13(p.433.20); *Lit.Bas.* (p.312.22); as bet. men, Jo.Ant.*ep.Ruf.*(p.40.33; M.83.1477C).

***συλλειτούργησις, ἡ,** *ministering together, joint ministry*, Thdr. Stud.*epp.*1.53(M.99.1105C).

***συλλειτουργός, ὁ,** *fellow minister, colleague in the sacred ministry*, Dion.Al.*ep.can.*(p.94.2; M.10.1272B); CAnt.(341)*can.*19; ‡Pion.*v.Polyc.*17; Λέων πρεσβύτερος τοῖς κατὰ τόπον συ`ν'λιτουργοῖ[ς] πρεσβυτ[έ]ροις *Pap.Chr.*(p.397, saec. iv); ὁ ἀδελφὸς ἡμῶν καὶ σ. Ἰωάννης Innoc.*ep.cler.*(M.52.537); of earthly hierarchy with the heavenly συλλειτουργὸν αὐτῶν τελοῦσα τὴν καθ' ἡμᾶς ἱεραρχίαν Dion. Ar.*c.h.*1.3(M.3.124A); met., σ. αὐτοὺς [sc. Πρίσκιλλαν καὶ Ἀκύλαν] καλεῖ, τῶν...πόνων...δεικνὺς αὐτοὺς κοινωνούς Chrys.*hom.30.2 in Rom.*(9.741A); *ib.*(742C); of Jo. Bapt. ἀγγέλων σ. Chrysipp.*enc.in Jo.Bapt.*2(p.31.16); of his head, *ib.*15(p.47.11).

***συλλεπρόομαι,** *be stricken by leprosy along with*, Cyr.*glaph.Ex.* (1.385A).

συλλεπτύν-ω, pass., *be attenuated, reduced* εἴτ' οὖν μία [sc. εἱμαρμένη]...εἴτ' οὖν πολλαὶ αἱ ἐπὶ τοῖς τοῦ χρόνου τμήμασι ~όμεναι Gr.Nyss.*fat.*(M.45.160D).

***συλλευθήσεται**, vox nihili διαρραγήσεται ὁ ναὸς οὗτος καὶ σ. πᾶσα Ἱερουσαλὴμ ἀπὸ βασιλέως Περσῶν κτλ. ... καὶ τὰ σκεύη τούτου τοῦ ναοῦ...δουλεύσουσι θεοῖς *T.Sal.*15.8(p.47.9; M.122.1337C; edd. συνλευσθήσεται, (συν)λυθήσεται, or poss. συλληστευθήσεται; prob. l. συλευθήσεται).

***συλλήπτειρα**, ἡ, fem. ? *helper*; of Ἀρετή personified, Meth. *symp.*5.1(p.53.4; συλλήπτρια M.18.97A).

συλληπτικός, *promoting conception* τὸ σ. [sc. φάρμακον] Phot. *nomoc.*9.25(p.556; M.104.768C).

συλλήπτωρ, ὁ, *helper*; of God, Clem.*str.*4.20(p.304.22; M.8.1337C); of Son, Cyr.*Os.*29(3.53D); Didym.*Trin.*3.17(M.39.876B).

***συλληρωδέω**, *trifle, talk foolishly*, Leont.H.*Nest.*4.17(M.86.1684A).

σύλληψις, ἡ, **1.** *taking together*; *inclusion, comprehension*; hence what is so comprehended, *mass, generality* ἐν πολυανθρώπῳ συλλήψει...ἄλογον τοῦ λαοῦ καταμαθὼν ῥαθυμίαν Bas.*ep.*213.1(3.320A; M.32.784A); **2.** a rhetorical figure, cf. *syllempsis est in dissimilibus clausulis aut pluralis dictio singulari verbo finita...aut singularis dictio plurali verbo expleta...ubi et pro multis unus et pro uno multi ponuntur, syllempsis est*, Isid.H.*etym.*1.36.5f.; **3.** *seizing, laying hold of, arrest*; met., mental *apprehension* τὴν διάνοιαν πλατυνθῆναι πρὸς σύλληψιν θεωρημάτων θείων Diad.*perf.*92(p.132.18); **4.** *taking, assumption* of flesh (Christol.) ἅμα ἡ σ. καὶ ἡ ὕπαρξις τεθαυματούργηται· ἡ μὲν σ. τοῦ λόγου, τῆς δὲ σαρκὸς ἡ ἐν αὐτῷ τῷ λόγῳ ὕπαρξις Jo.D.*Jacob.*83(M.94.1481D); *cat.Apoc.*5:14(p.261.21); **5.** *conception, pregnancy*; ref. regeneration (Jo.1:13) χωρὶς μήτρας σ., χωρὶς γαστρὸς γέννησις Chrys.*hom.3.6 in Ac.princ.*(3.80D); of conception of Christ τῆς παραδόξου ἀπὸ ἁγίου πνεύματος σ. Or.*Cels.*1.32(p.84.1; M.11.721A); Epiph.*haer.*42.9(p.104.24; M.41.708B); Cosm.Ind.*top.*5 (M.88.193B); as beginning of Inc. περὶ τοῦ πρὶν σ. εὐαγγελισθέντος Or.*hom.1.8 in Jer.*(p.7.4; M.13.264C); **6.** mental *conception* ἐπὰν... τὸ παρ' ἡμῶν εὐεπίφορον ὁ τῶν ἀγαθῶν λάβῃ δοτήρ, ἀθρόα πάντα τῇ σ. αὐτῇ ἕπεται τὰ ἀγαθά Clem.*str.*7.7(p.32.21; M.9.460B).

***συλλιθόω**, *petrify*, Geo.Pis.*Pers.*3.36(M.92.1238A).

***συλλιμενίζω**, *bring to harbour together*; met., Cyrus Al.*ep.*1(H.3.804B).

***συλλιμώσσω**, *be famished* or *hungry together* with, Bas.Sel.*or.*11.2(M.85.153B).

***συλλιτανεύ-ω**, *join in supplications* with, *pray together* with τοῦ βασιλέως ~οντος τῷ λαῷ Thphn.*chron.*p.184(M.108.480A).

συλλογή, ἡ, *gathering, collecting*; *accumulation*; hence, *recollection* μίαν τῆς ἑβδομάδος ἡμέραν ταύτην ὅλην ἀνατιθέναι τῇ ἀκροάσει καὶ τῶν ἀκουσθέντων τῇ σ. Chrys.*hom.5.1 in Mt.*(7.73A); *ib.*(72A,B).

***συλλογῆσαι**, v. συνευλογέω.

συλλογίζ-ομαι, **A.** intrans., *debate* in syllogisms, *reason*, Epiph. *haer.*70.3(p.235.7f.; M.42.341D,344A); Thdt.*h.rel.*8(3.1181).

B. trans.; **1.** *reason about, discuss* ἀποκαλύπτει...δι' ἁγίου πνεύματος οὐ τοῖς αὐτὸν ~ομένοις, ἀλλὰ τοῖς εἰς αὐτὸν πεπιστευκόσι Epiph. *haer.*76.24(p.371.21; M.42.564C); ~εσθαι τοὺς νόμους Chrys.*hom.16.4 in Mt.*(7.208C); *throw into syllogistic form*, id.*hom.6.3 in Heb.*(12.68A); **2.** *reason* or *debate with* ~εται αὐτοὺς διὰ τοῦ παραδείγματος τούτου Chrys.*hom.40.1 in Mt.*(7.437E); id.*hom.49.2 in Jo.*(8.291D); ἵνα...καυχήσηται ὡς συλλογισάμενος τὸν βασιλέα Thdt.*h.e.*2.16.12(3.867); **3.** *overcome* in argument, *out-reason* συνελογίσαντο τὴν εὐμένειάν σου καὶ συνέδησάν σε *A.Petr.et Paul.*67(p.206.11) = *A.(Pass.) Petr.et Paul.*46(p.158.14); οἱ...λόγοι ἀληθεῖς ὄντες συνελογίσαντό με συνθέσθαι σοι *Clem.recogn.suppl.*5 ap.Or.*philoc.*23.22(p.211.1); νικώμενον...καὶ ~όμενον· οὐκ εἴ τις δὲ συλλογισθείη, συναρπασθεὶς τὴν ἐν αὐτῷ ἀλήθειαν νενικημένην ἔχει *Hom.Clem.*18.9; ἐξ αὐτῶν...ὧν ἐδίδαξε τὸν κόσμον συλλογισμῶν καὶ αὐτὸς συλλογισθήσεται Epiph. *haer.*76.27(p.375.25; M.42.572A); *forestall* in argument, Chrys.*hom.6.1 in Ac.*(9.48C).

***συλλογιστία**, ἡ, *syllogistic argument*, διαλεκτικῆς ἐφευρετὴς [sc. Aëtius]...συλλογιστίας Epiph.*haer.*76.45(p.399.3; M.42.612C).

σύλλογος, ὁ, *assembly*, esp. for worship, *congregation* τὸν κοινὸν... σ. Or.*Cels.*3.51(p.247.15; M.11.988B); οὐκέτι σ. Χριστιανῶν Bas.*ep.*243.2(3.374A; M.32.905B); ὁ σ. ἡμῖν ἐλάττων γέγονε Chrys.*anom.*7.1 (1.501B); σύναψον ἡμᾶς τῷ παμμακαρίστῳ τῶν εὐαρεστησάντων σοι σ. *Lit.Marc.*(Brightman p.142.22); of heretics, Thdt.*Ps.*67:17(1.1064).

***συλλογχεύομαι**, *be pierced with a spear together* with, Thdr. Stud.*epp.*2.11(M.99.1148A).

***συλλουκιανιστής**, ὁ, *fellow-pupil of Lucian* of Antioch, *fellow Lucianist*, Ar.*ep.Eus.*(p.3; cj. for σὺν Λουκιανιστᾷ M.42.212B).

***συλλυτρωτής**, ὁ, *fellow liberator, co-redeemer* τὸν..."Ορον τοῦτον ...Συλλυτρωτὴν...καλοῦσι Iren.*haer.*1.2.4(M.7.460A); ‡Epiph.*epit. haer.*31(p.361.17).

***συλοχρηματέω**, *rob of money*, Bas.*ep.*44.1(3.131D; M.32.361B).

***συλωτής**, ὁ, *plunderer, robber*, †Ath.*fr.Mt.*(M.27.1377C); paroxytone in †Caes.Naz.*dial.*148(M.38.1100), cf. συλητής.

***συμβαδισμός**, ὁ, *walking together*; met., *going the way* of, *association* ἵνα...τῇ συνηθείᾳ καὶ τῷ σ. ἐφελκύσηται αὐτοὺς εἰς τελειοτέραν ἐπίγνωσιν Pall.*v.Chrys.*19(p.124.23; M.47.70).

συμβαίν-ω, **1.** *come together* ἐν ταῖς γωνίαις τῶν οἰκοδομημάτων δύο ~ουσι τοῖχοι, καὶ ἀλλήλοις συναρμολογούμενοι κατασφίγγονται πρὸς ἑνότητα Cyr.*Is.*3.2(2.398A); of union of natures in Christ συμβῆναι δὲ φαμὲν καθ' ἕνωσιν ἀδιάσπαστον...τῇ ἰδίᾳ σαρκὶ τὸν ἐκ θεοῦ λόγον id.*Nest.*1.3(p.22.11; 6^1.15C); pass. τὰς συμβαθείσας [sc. wills of Christ] εἰς ἑνώσεως λόγον ἀλλ' οὐ τραπείσας εἰς ἑαυτὰς οὐσίας Andr. Cr.*Agath.*121(M.97.1444A); **2.** aor. ptcpl. neut. as adv., // τυχόν *perchance, perhaps* τυχὸν μὲν γονεῖς, τυχὸν δὲ παῖδας, ξυμβὰν δὲ τοὺς φιλτάτους Men.*exc.Rom.*3(p.173.9; M.113.856A).

συμβαλλομάχος, ὁ, *prone to fighting*; *contentious*, †Cyr.*hom.div.*14(5^2.412E).

συμβάλλω, **1.** *throw, dash together*; simply *throw, hurl* σ. τὸν διάβολον κάτω *Contrad.*1(p.7); **2.** *bring together, join* ἴχνη ἴχνεσι σ. Cyr.H.*catech.*19.2; Thdt.*Is.*41:7(p.161.22; 2.331); *close* fetters τῶν ἁλύσεων ταῖς χερσὶ...συμβεβλημένων Chrys.*hom.9.1 in Mt.*(7.131A); *close* the mouth of the dead τὸ παρακαθῆσθαι νοσοῦντι, τὸ σ. στόμα, τὸ μύσαι ὀφθαλμοὺς id.*hom.8.3 in Phil.*(11.259F); **3.** med., *be of service, avail* οὔτε...νὺξ σ. ἡμῖν *Ep.Lugd.*ap.Eus.*h.e.*5.1.61(M.20.432B); πρὸς τοὺς Ἀρειομανίτας ἡμῖν σ. Ath.*fr.Job*(M.27.1344A); τοῦτο πρὸς τὰς θλίψεις σ., τὸ συμπεπράχθαι Chrys.*hom.2.1 in 2Thess.*(11.515F); πόσον ταῖς ψυχαῖς σ. ἡ τῆς ἱερᾶς θυσίας προσφορά Gr.Mag.*dial.* (tr.Zach.)4.55(M.*PL.*77.419); **4.** *bring together* in hostile sense; *set against, incite* σ. αὐτὸν πρὸς τὸν κύριον αὐτοῦ *T.Gad* 4.4; σ. τὴν μητέρα κατὰ τοῦ υἱοῦ Thphn.*chron.*p.391(M.108.933A).

συμβαπτίζω, **1.** *baptize together* ἡ ἀξίωσις αὐτῆς τοῦ συμβαπτισθῆναι αὐτῇ τὴν ξενοδόχον *Hom.Clem.*13.10; μὴ ἀπαξιώσῃς συμβαπτισθῆναι πένητι Gr.Naz.*or.*40.27(M.36.396D); *ib.*40.42(420B); **2.** *baptize so as to unite* with or *incorporate* into τὴν καλὴν παρακαταθήκην...τὴν εἰς πατέρα καὶ υἱὸν καὶ ἅγιον πνεῦμα ὁμολογίαν. ταύτην πιστεύω σοι...ταύτῃ καὶ συμβαπτίσω καὶ συνανάξω σε *ib.*40.41(417A).

***συμβάπτω**, *dye together*; pass., met., *be tinged with*, ref. Son's 'tincture' of humanity οὐδὲ ὁ πατὴρ καὶ τὸ ἅγιον πνεῦμα καθ' ὑπόστασιν συνεβάφη, καὶ συναιματώθη τῷ υἱῷ Anast.S.*hod.*17(M.89.265A), v. συμπορφυροβαφέω.

***συμβαρβαρίζω**, *behave* or *speak like a barbarian together* with συνεβαρβάριζεν ὁ τρόπος τῷ τῆς γλώττης ὀργάνῳ Bas.*hom.*17.2(2.139C; M.31.485A).

***συμβασιλεύς**, ὁ, **1.** *fellow king, joint emperor*, *T.Job* 29(p.121.19); *ib.*31,39(pp.122.11,128.8); of Licinius and Constantine, Eus. *h.e.*10.8.4(M.20.896B); of Arcadius and Honorius, Pall.*v.Chrys.*3 (p.21.5; M.47.11); **2.** theol., of Son with Father σύνθρονον αὐτὸν ἑαυτῷ καὶ σ. ἀποδείξας Eus.*fr.Lc.*9:28ff.(M.24.549C).

συμβασιλεύω, *rule, reign together*; theol., of Logos with Father, Marcell.*fr.*104 ap.Eus.*Marcell.*2.4(p.54.8; M.24.816A), Thdt.*Ps.*109:1(1.1393) citt. s. βασιλεία; of H. Ghost with other Persons of Trin., *Lit.Jac.*(p.204.26); met., of Christians with Christ or God, ref. 2Tim.2:12, Polyc.*ep.*5.2; Just.*1apol.*10.2(M.6.341A) cit. s. ἄφθαρτος; Didym.*Ps.*20:2f.(M.39.1273B); of BMV δεῦρο, συμβασίλευσον τῷ ἐκ σοῦ σὺν σοὶ πτωχεύσαντι Jo.D.*hom.*10.4(M.96.760B).

σύμβασις, ἡ, **1.** *agreement* ἡ τῶν ἐν Χαλκηδόνι...σύμβασις Sophr.H. *ep.syn.*(M.87.3188B); **2.** *coming together*; **a.** *association* of ideas etc., Leont.H.*Nest.*4.41(M.86.1716B); **b.** of persons; **i.** sexually οἶδα ὡς ἀνδρὸς ἄνευ συμβάσεως οὐδέποτε τέτοκε γύναιον Sophr.H.*or.*2.35(M.87.3264A); **ii.** *fellowship, communion* διὰ τῆς τοῦ πνεύματος δυνάμεως τε καὶ σ. Epiph.*haer.*62.1(p.390.12; M.41.1052C); **c.** *reconciliation* ἐν Χριστῷ ἡ πρὸς τὸν θεὸν σ. ἐστὶ τοῦ κόσμου Didym.*Trin.*1.7(M.39.273A); **d.** Christol. σ. οἰκονομικὴν...πεπρᾶχθαι φαμὲν ἀνομοίων πραγμάτων Cyr.*ep.*40(p.26.2; 5^2.115C); id.*inc.unigen.*(5^1.700B); φυσικῶς σύγχρονον ἔχοντα τῇ ὑπάρξει τὴν ἕνωσιν καὶ οὐ πρὸ τῆς πρὸς τὸν λόγον ἀληθεστάτης σ. καθ' ἑαυτὰ γενόμενα πώποτε, ἤ τινος ἀνθρώπου τῶν καθ' ἡμᾶς ἑτέρου τὸ παράπαν ὑπάρξαντα, ἀλλὰ σύνδρομον ἔχοντα τῇ φυσικῇ τοῦ λόγου σ. τὴν ὕπαρξιν Sophr.H.*ep.syn.*(M.87.3161Bf.); τὴν ἔννουν καὶ ἔμψυχον κηρύττομεν σ. *ib.*(3164C); rejected in sense 2.b.ii ἑνοῦσθαι λέγονται κατὰ σ. φιλικήν Cyr.*schol.inc.*8(5^1.782A); **3.** *happening*; hence *untoward happening, calamity*, Thdr.Stud.*epp.*1.18(M.99.964B).

συμβαστάζ-ω, **1.** *join in bearing, help to carry*, Or.*Jo.*10.39(23:

p.216.13; M.14.381C); **2.** met., *bear with, tolerate* οὐκ ἐπαινῶν, φησί, γάμον...ἀλλὰ ~ων, ἵνα μὴ εἰς περιττὸν ὄλεθρον ἐμπέσωσιν Epiph. *haer*.67.2(p.134.19; M.42.173D); **3.** *support mutually*, Cosm.Ind.*top*. 2(M.88.80D) cit. s. ἀντιπεριςπάω.

συμβατικός, *fortuitous, chance* οὐκ ἐκ τῶν προαιρετικῶν πόνων μόνον, ἀλλὰ καὶ ἐκ τῶν σ. θλίψεων κρατύνεται Marc.Er.*opusc*.7.3(M. 65.1073D); *ib*.2.191(960C); Thdr.Stud.*epp*.2.206(M.99.1624D).

συμβατικῶς, 1. *in agreement* or *friendship, on good terms with* ἐκ τούτου [sc. τοῦ οὐρανοῦ] σ. ἐπισκοπεῖ τοὺς τῆς ὑποδεεστέρας καταστάσεως Or.*exc.in Ps*.13:2(M.17.108C); σ. ἔχω *be inclined to agree*, Gr.Naz.*ep*.19(M.38.53A); **2.** *accidentally, by chance*, Dion.Al.ap. Eus.*p.e*.14.24(773D; M.21.1273A).

συμβατός, *accidental, contingent*, Max.*schol.d.n*.4.1(M.4.240A).

συμβεβαιόω, *confirm*, Clem.*str*.4.4(p.254.16; M.8.1228A); ‡Meth. *Sym.et Ann*.12(M.18.377B).

συμβιβάζ-ω, *bring* or *put together*; *order* σ. ὡς θέμις τὰ πράγματα Andr.Cr.*Agath*.39(M.97.1440A); *bring to the point of* ἐξ ὧν συμβιβάσομεν αὐτοὺς...ἐπὶ τὸ πάντα ἡγεῖσθαι ἑνὸς εἶναι γράμματα θεοῦ Or. *princ*.3.1.16(p.225.11; M.11.281C); εἰς ἀνάγκην ~όμενος τοῦ διηγεῖσθαι τὴν θαυμαστὴν...οἰκονομίαν Dion.Al.ap.Eus.*h.e*.7.11.2(M.20. 664A).

συμβίβασις, ἡ, *bringing together*; **1.** *reconciliation* τὴν πρὸς τοὺς Ἀνατολικοὺς σ. Thdr.Lect.*h.e*.2.39(M.86.205A); **2.** *offer of conciliation, overture* τὰς εἰς εἰρήνην σ. ἐποίει Cyr.*glaph.Gen*.5(1.156C).

συμβιβασμός, ὁ, *reconciliation*, effected by presbyters in lawsuits bet. Christians, *Hom.Clem*.3.67; εἰς σ. εἰρήνης Epiph.*haer*.66.14 (p.38.11; M.42.52A); σ. ... τῶν σχισμάτων Geo.Pis.*hex*.1394(M.92. 1541A); *coming together, union* ὁ...σ. κοινωνία γνώμης ἐστί Jo.D. *Man*.1.22(M.94.1525D).

σύμβιος, ὁ, ἡ, *companion*; hence *spouse*; *husband*, *A.Jo*.23 (p.164.3); Or.*hom.14 in Lc*.(p.100.10; M.17.324C); *wife*, *M.Ner.et Ach*.15,16(pp.14.28,15.11); Chrys.*hom.1.1 in Philm*.(11.775A); Pall. *h.Laus*.8(p.28.17; M.34.1025D); met., of soul in Christ, Jo.Clim. *scal*.25(M.88.992B) cit. s. ἀνεπίδεκτος.

συμβίωσις, ἡ, 1. *living with, companionship*; **a.** as husband and wife, myst. γάμος, ἡ τῆς σοφίας σ. Gr.Nyss.*res*.1(M.46.604D); τῆς θείας...μετ' αὐτοῦ σ. id.*hom.6 in Cant*.(M.44.897D); **b.** of monastic life, Bas.*reg.fus*.7.2(2.346E; M.31.932B); **c.** of celibates of opposite sexes living as 'spiritual companions' τῇ ὁμοσκήνῳ σ. †Bas.*contub*. 5(M.30.820D); ἀδελφότητα τὴν τοιαύτην σ. ὀνομάζοντες Gr.Nyss.*virg*. 23(p.338.7; M.46.409B); **2.** *marriage*, *A.Andr.fr*.4(p.39.12); **3.** *wedded couple*, *A.Phil*.37(p.18.16).

συμβιωτέον, *one must live with*, Clem.*paed*.3.8(p.260.18; M.8. 612C).

συμβιωτής, ὁ, *companion*, of one living in the same monastery ὁ συμβιωτὴς ἀδελφὸς Nil.*Eulog*.30(M.79.1133B).

***συμβιωτικός**, *of living together*; myst., of soul with God, Gr. Nyss.*virg*.14(p.310.3; M.46.381C).

***συμβλητικός**, ? *of intellection* or *understanding*; or ? *of putting together* or *comparing* σύνεσις ἐπιστήμη συμβλητοῦ...ἡ συμβλητικὴ δύναμις ὧν φρόνησίς ἐστι καὶ ἐπιστήμη Clem.*str*.2.17(p.153.6; M.8. 1013C).

συμβλύω, *flow together*, of sap, or *grow together*, ref. a graft on a plant βλαστὸν ἥμερον ἐμφυτεύσαι, μέσον σχίσας, εἶτα συμβαλὼν καὶ συνδήσας, ἄχρις ἂν συμβλύσαντα ὡς ἐν ἄμφω τρέφηται Gr.Thaum. *pan.Or*.7(p.19.7; M.10.1073C).

συμβολαιογράφος, ὁ, *writer of contracts, notary*, Gr.Nyss.*usur*. (M.46.440A); Ast.Am.*hom*.4(M.40.224A); Isid.Pel.*epp*.3.176(M.78. 868B).

συμβόλαιον, τό, 1. *contract*, Chrys.*hom.9.6 in Ac*.(9.79A); gen., *business transactions, commerce*, id.*hom.in Rom.12*:*20*(3.161B); Thdt.*Dan*.3:87(2.1127); fig. τῶν...σ. πνευματικῶν ὑπόθεσίς ἐστι...τὸ ἀργύριον τοῦτο τὸ πνευματικόν Chrys.*hom.4.2 in Ac.princ*.(3.83C); in rel. to civic rights, Const.*or.s.c*.25(p.192.4; M.20.1513A); **2.** plur., *treaty, pact*, Chrys.*hom.81.2 in Mt*.(7.775C, v.l. συμβούλια); τοῖς τῆς εἰρήνης σ. Men.*exc.Rom*.3(p.179.4, v.l. συμβουλ- M.113.864B); **3.** *official document* or *record* ἔστεψε Θεοδόσιον...εἰς βασιλέα. οὐ μέντοι ἐτάγη εἰς σ. *Chron.Pasch*.p.377(M.92.965A); *ib*.p.379(972A); **4.** *pledge* τὰ σ. διδόμενα οὐ ποιεῖ πλουσίους Chrys.*hom.2.4 in Eph*. (11.14F).

***συμβολέτης, ὁ**, *feaster*, Gr.Naz.*carm*.2.2(epigr.)48.7(M.38.108A).

συμβολικός, *symbolical*; **1.** ref. three kinds of Egyptian hieroglyphs; pictorial, representations; by conventional association, mere emblems; and by allegory or analogy, types or symbols, Clem.*str*.5.4(p.339.16; M.9.40B); **2.** *prefigurative, typical* of something yet to be realized, of worship and teaching under Law τῆς... σ. λατρείας Eus.*h.e*.1.3.4(M.20.69B); τὸ εὐαγγέλιον ἐν ᾧ ὁ γενόμενος τῆς σκιώδους διδασκαλίας διὰ τῶν τυπικῶν τε καὶ σ. νοημάτων οὐκέτι προσδέεται Gr.Nyss.*hom.5 in Cant*.(M.44.877A); **3.** *representative, typical* of some present reality; **a.** indicative of heavenly realities in this world σ. τίς ἐστιν...ἡ καθ' ἡμᾶς ἱεραρχία Dion.Ar.*e.h*.1.5(M.3. 377A); *ib*.4.3.10(481C); ἐν μιᾷ τῶν μυστικῶν τῆς σ. θεοφανείας ὁράσεων id.*d.n*.1.6(M.3.596A); hence *mystical* διττὴν...τὴν τῶν θεολόγων παράδοσιν...τὴν μὲν σ. καὶ τελεστικήν, τὴν δὲ φιλόσοφον καὶ ἀποδεικτικήν id.*ep*.9.1(M.3.1105D); **b.** indicative of spiritual realities in the world of sense, ref. scriptural miracles as signs εἴπερ ἦν τεράστιόν τι γινόμενον οὐ συμβολικὸν ἑτέρου, ἐγέγραπτο ἂν Or.*Jo*.13.64(60; p.296.32; M.14.521C); ἡ τοῦ μύρου συμβολικὴ σύνθεσις Dion.Ar.*e.h*. 4.3.4(480A); ἡ σ. διδασκαλία μυσταγωγεῖ ταῖς ἐν ὕδατι τρισὶ καταδύσεσι...Ἰησοῦ...μιμεῖσθαι θάνατον *ib*.2.3.7(404B); *ib*.2.3.1(397B); ὅλος ὁ νοητὸς κόσμος ὅλῳ τῷ αἰσθητῷ μυστικῶς τοῖς σ. εἴδεσι τυπούμενος φαίνεται Max.*myst*.2(M.91.669C); hence *sacramental*, ref. eucharist ὑμνήσας...τὴν σεβασμίαν...θεωρίαν ἐν νοεροῖς ὀφθαλμοῖς ἐποπτεύσας, ἐπὶ τὴν σ. αὐτῶν ἱερουργίαν ἔρχεται Dion.Ar.*e.h*.3.3.12(441D); **c.** *parabolic* προτίθησι τὸ σ. ὃν τῆς ἱστορικῆς διηγήσεως ἐν τῇ αὐτοῦ ὑποθέσει Or.*adnot.in Num*.23:7(M.17.21B); Vict.*Mc*.11:13(p.392.16); **4.** *allegorical, figurative*, opp. literal, of scriptures σ. ... καὶ αἰνιγματῶδες εἶδος Clem.*str*.2.1(p.113.14; M.8.932A); *ib*.4.1(p.248.7; 1216A); τὰ παντοδαπὰ μορφώματα τῆς περὶ θεοῦ σ. ἱεροπλαστίας Dion.Ar.*ep*.9. 1(M.3.1104C); and Christian tradition, *ib*.9.6(1113C); of certain prescriptions of Law ὁ...νόμος διαιρεῖται...εἴς τε τὴν καθαρὰν νομοθεσίαν...καὶ εἰς τὸν συμπεπλεγμένον τῷ χείρονι...καὶ εἰς τὸ τυπικὸν καὶ σ. τὸ κατ' εἰκόνα τῶν πνευματικῶν καὶ διαφερόντων νομοθετηθέν Ptol.*ep*.ap.Epiph.*haer*.33.5(p.454.4; M.41.561B); *ib*.33.6(p.456.3; 565B); neut. as subst., *symbolism, imagery* τὸ σ. τῶν γραφῶν Clem. *paed*.2.12(p.228.18; M.8.541A); of NT, Or.*Jo*.32.20(13; p.461.26; M. 14.800A); **5.** *symbolic*, opp. actual, real ἔθος...τὰς ἀγάμους κόρας... θρηνεῖν διὰ τῶν σ. γάμων Cyr.*fr.Mt*.9:23(M.72.393C); **6.** *pertaining to divination* οὐ σ. ταῦτα ἦν, ἀλλὰ πίστεως καὶ εὐσεβείας δηλωτικά Thdt.*qu.74 in Gen*.24:14(1.87); as subst., *soothsayer* τὸν ἐπίτροπον τῆς οἰκίας εἶχε σ. Juln.Imp.ap.Cyr.*Juln*.10(6^2.356C); *ib*.(360D,361C); Proc.G.*Gen*.24:63ff.(M.87.404B).

συμβολικῶς, 1. *symbolically, by means of symbols* denoting or representing some reality, freq. one which is supra-sensible τῶν ἐν τοῖς προφήταις αἰνιγμάτων καὶ τῶν ἐν τοῖς εὐαγγελίοις παραβολῶν καὶ ἄλλων μυρίων σ. γεγενημένων ἢ νενομοθετημένων Or.*Cels*.1.9(p.61.26; M.11.673A); **a.** *in type, under a figure*, foreshadowing a future realization, freq. of OT pointing forward to NT λίθος Χριστὸς...σ. ἐκηρύσσετο Just.*dial*.86.3(M.6.681A); βασιλεῖς δὲ οἱ Ἰουδαίων... ποικίλῳ χρώμενοι στεφάνῳ, οἱ χριστοί, τὸν Χριστὸν ἐπὶ τῆς κεφαλῆς σ. ἐπιφερόμενοι Clem.*paed*.2.8(p.195.25; M.8.468C); ref. Jos.5:2ff. τοῦτο οὐκ ἀργῶς ἀλλὰ σ.· ἡ γὰρ πέτρα ἐστὶν ὁ Χριστός· ἐν ᾧ περιτεμνώμεθα *Dial.Ath.et Zacch*.125(p.62); διὰ τοῦ νόμου μυστικῶς τὸ τοῦ πάσχα μυστήριον ἐπετελεῖτο ἐν Αἰγύπτῳ, σ. δὲ διὰ τῆς τοῦ ἀμνοῦ σφαγῆς ἐδηλοῦτο Procl.CP *or*.14(M.65.796C); **b.** *with symbolic significance* denoting some present but usu. supra-sensible reality σ. τῷ μηνὶ ἑβδόμῳ...ἑορτάζειν προστασσόμεθα τῷ κυρίῳ Meth.*symp*.9. 1(p.114.15; M.18.177B); σ. πρὸς δυσμὰς ἀποβλέποντες Cyr.H.*catech*. 19.4; οἱ περὶ τὸ θεῖον σ. ἀεὶ παρεστηκότες θυσιαστήριον Dion.Ar.*ep*.8 (M.3.1089A); καὶ τὸν ἐκ γεννητῆς δὲ τυφλὸν σ. ὁ σωτὴρ εἰς τὸν Σιλωὰμ ἐξαπέστειλεν Proc.G.*Is*.8:5ff.(M.87.1980B); of Christ's acts σ. πάντα ὁ κύριος ἐπραγματεύσατο καὶ οἰκονομικῶς εἰς ἀνθρώπους...σωτηρίαν *A.Jo*.102(p.202.7); ὁ κύριος σ. ἐπιτιμᾷ διὰ τῆς συκῆς Proc.G.*Gen*. 3:7(M.87.192C); cf. παραδεῖξαι ἐξ ἑαυτοῦ σ. ἑαυτόν Max.*ambig*.(M. 91.1165D); **c.** *in symbolic language, figuratively*, opp. literally, freq. of scriptures τὰς ὑπ' αὐτῶν σ. ἡμῖν καὶ ἀναγωγικῶς ἐκφανθείσας τῶν οὐρανίων νοῶν ἱεραρχίας...ἐποπτεύσωμεν Dion.Ar.*c.h*.1.2(M.3. 121A); πλεῖστα περὶ θεοῦ σωματικώτερον ἐν τῇ θείᾳ γραφῇ σ. εἰρημένα εὑρίσκομεν Jo.D.*f.o*.1.11(M.94.841A); of OT οὐ γὰρ ἐνοεῖτο αὐτοῖς, σ. ...τῶν εἰς τοῦτο εἰρημένων πάντων λελεγμένων Just.*1apol*.55.1(M.6. 412A); βορέαν...σ. τὸν πονηρὸν καλεῖ Hipp.*fr.8 in Pr*.4:27(p.159.18; M.10.617C); ἀναθεὶς ἐμοὶ καὶ τὴν ψυχὴν καὶ τὴν αἴσθησιν καὶ τὸν νοῦν· ἃ σ. δάμαλιν ἔφη καὶ αἶγα καὶ κριόν Meth.*symp*.5.2(p.54.13; M.18. 100A); τὴν τοῦ αἵματος...φύσιν σ. ἐνδεικνύμενος διὰ τοῦ ἐρυθήματος Gr.Nyss.*hom.13 in Cant*.(M.44.1052C); and of NT σ. τούτοις [sc. precious stones] εἰκότως τειχίζεται τῶν ἁγίων ἡ πόλις πνευματικῶς οἰκοδομουμένη Clem.*paed*.2.12(p.228.14; M.8.541A); σ. τότε ἡ αἰσθητὴ νὺξ ἦν Or.*Jo*.32.24(16; p.468.26; M.14.809C); of certain injunctions of Law εἰς τύπους σ. τινα ἐν τῷ νόμῳ γέγραπται Ptol.*ep*.ap.Epiph. *haer*.33.11(p.463.13); σ. ἀργίαν ἐπὶ τοῦ σαββάτου προσέταττεν Vict. *Mc*.3:4(p.294.26); comp. τῇ...Ἄγαρ...συμβολικώτερον...ἀσκὸν δίδωσιν ὕδατος Epiph.*exp.fid*.7(p.503.13; M.42.785B); superl., ref. Ex.

12:3 λαμβάνεται δὲ τῇ δεκάτῃ τοῦ μηνός, καὶ πάνυ συμβολικώτατα ‡Chrys.*pasch*.6(p.151.4; 8.268D); **d.** *by means of* σύμβολα (v. σύμβολον), *sacramentally* τῆς Ἰησοῦ μετουσίας [sc. εἰκόνα], τὴν τῆς θειοτάτης εὐχαριστίας μετάληψιν· καὶ ὅσα ἄλλα ταῖς οὐρανίαις μὲν οὐσίαις ὑπερκοσμίως, ἡμῖν δὲ σ. παραδέδοται Dion.Ar.*c.h*.1.3(M.3.124A); ὦ θειοτάτη...τελετή, τὰ περικείμενά σοι σ. ἀμφιέσματα τῶν αἰνιγμάτων ἀποκαλυψαμένη, τηλαυγῶς ἡμῖν ἀναδείχθητι id.*e.h*.3.3.2(M.3.428C) ∞ *Lit.Jac*.(p.196.6); οἱ πιστοὶ σ. τῶν μυστηρίων μεταλαμβάνοντες τοῦ σώματος τοῦ δεσπότου Χριστοῦ μετὰ τὸ βάπτισμα Cosm.Ind.*top*.5(M.88.305D); **2.** *by means of divination* καὶ οὐ ταύτης ἕνεκα τῆς αἰτίας σ. μαντεύεσθαι φαίη τις ἂν ἡμᾶς Cyr.*Juln*.10(6^2.361D); Thdt.*qu.74 in Gen*.24:5ff.(1.87).

***συμβολογράφημα, τό,** *type* ὁ νόμος δὲ πολλοῖς καὶ ποικίλοις σ. ταύτην προϋπεσκίασε Germ.CP *or*.2(M.98.277C).

***συμβολογραφία, ἡ,** *metaphor*; *allegory*, Areth.*Apoc*.19:19(M.106.748A); cf.*cat.Apoc*.19:19(συμβουλογραφία p.466.24).

***συμβολογράφ-ω,** *symbolize, represent* βαστάζων τὰς ἡμῶν ἁμαρτίας, ταῖς ἀκανθηραῖς ὀξύτησι ~ομένας Germ.CP *or*.2(M.98.265B).

***συμβολοδείκτης, ὁ,** *interpreter of oracles, portents*, etc., *Const. App*.8.32.11.

***συμβολομαντεία, ἡ,** *divination from portents*, Gr.Nyss.*engast*.(p.65.8; M.45.109C).

***συμβολομαχία, ἡ,** s.v.l., *divination from portents*, ‡Jo.D.*ep. Thphl*.9(M.95.356C, ? συμβολομαντεία).

σύμβολον, τό, *symbol* representing a reality (freq. suprasensible) other than itself οὐκ ἔστι τι παράδοξον γινόμενον ἐν τῇ γραφῇ ὁ μὴ ἐστι σημεῖον καὶ σ. ἑτέρου παρὰ τὸ αἰσθητῶς γεγενημένον Or.*Jo*.13.64(60; p.296.30; M.14.521C); Dion.Ar.*d.n*.1.4(M.3.592C) cit. s. ἀλήθεια.

A. in gen.; **1.** *standard* τὰ πολεμικὰ σ. Men.*exc.Rom*.14(p.204.20; M.113.901C); *emblem, figure*, Just.*dial*.88.8(M.6.688B) cit. s. δικαιοσύνη; πένθους ἦν σ. τὸ ἔνδυμα Ἰωάννου Chrys.*hom.10.4 in Mt*.(7.1448B); αἷμα καὶ ὕδωρ, τὸ μὲν τῆς ἀναγεννήσεως σ., τὸ δὲ τῆς μυστικῆς μεταλήψεως Thdr.Mops.*fr.136 in Jo*.19:32ff.(p.413.19); πῶς οὐκ... ἔρριψεν [sc. ὁ Ἀβραάμ]...τῆς θυσίας τὰ σ.; Bas.Sel.*or*.7.2(M.85.109C); **2.** *portent*, Chrys.*hom.53.5 in Ac*.(9.403D); id.*hom.10.3 in 1Tim*.(11.603B); **3.** OT *type* foreshadowing reality of new dispensation, Just.*dial*.42.1,4(M.6.565A,C); Or.*hom.1.6 in Jer*.(p.4.29; M.13.260D); Chrys.*hom.23.2 in 1Cor*.(10.203B); ἔστι τοίνυν τὸ μὲν πρόβατον, κατὰ τὸν Ἡσαΐαν, ἠπιότητος τῆς τοῦ Χριστοῦ σ. ... ἔριφος δὲ κατὰ τὸν νόμον, ὑπὲρ ἁμαρτίας θῦμα id.*pasch*.1(8.253E); **4.** *mark, token, indication* σ. δὲ μνήμης γράμματα Bas.*ep*.73.1(3.166E; M.32.440D); τὸ τοὺς ἐν Ἱεροσολύμοις τόπους ἰδεῖν ἐν οἷς τὰ σ. τῆς διὰ σαρκὸς ἐπιδημίας τοῦ κυρίου ὁρᾶται Gr.Nyss.*ep*.2(M.46.1009B); ὁ σταυρὸς...τῆς βασιλείας ἐστὶ σ. Chrys.*cruc*.1.3(2.407C); τὸ σ. τῶν αὐτοῦ μαθητῶν...ἐὰν ἀγάπην ἔχητε ἐν ἀλλήλοις Nil.*Magn*.66(M.79.1059B); ref. Is.62:10 τὸ ἀκουστὸν σύσσημον...τὸ ῥῆμα τῆς πίστεως...ἢ τάχα που καὶ τοῦ σωτηρίου πάθους τὸ σ. Cyr.*Is*.5.5(2.875C); ἐπηγγείλου μοι καὶ ἐκ τοῦ νόμου διδόναι σύμβολα *Dial.Tim.et Aquil*.94 v°; of prodigal son τὰ σ. τῆς υἱότητος ἀνακτᾶται πάλιν Job.Mon.*inc*.5(M.86.3320A); *credential*, Bas.*ep*.191(3.284E; M.32.704A); *ib*.203.3(301D; M.741C); *handwriting*, *ib*.223.6(341B; M.832B); **5.** ? *indication* of the meaning of a word, *etymologia est origo vocabulorum, cum vis verbi vel nominis per interpretationem colligitur. hanc Aristoteles* σύμβολον, *Cicero adnotationem nominavit, quia nomina et verba rerum nota facit exemplo posito; utputa 'flumen', quia fluendo crevit, a fluendo dictum*, Isid.H.*etym*.1.29.1; **6.** *significance* of liturgical acts τὸ διὰ τοῦ ὕδατος λουτρὸν σ. τυγχάνον καθαρσίου ψυχῆς Or.*Jo*.6.33(17; p.142.28; M.14.257A); Cyr.H.*catech*.19.9; *ib*.20.1; ref. Rom.8:26 οὐ...σ. ἐστι ὁ διάκονος ὁ ὑπὲρ τοῦ δήμου ἀναφέρων εὐχάς Chrys.*hom.14.7 in Rom*.(9.586C); of rites of baptism, ‡Just.*qu.et resp*.137(M.6.1389C); Chrys.*hom.25.2 in Jo*.(8.146C); θανάτου καὶ ἀναστάσεως σ. ... εἶναι τὸ βάπτισμα Thdr.Mops.*fr.21 in Jo*.3:4ff.(p.321.15); σ. τοῦ μεταλαχεῖν ἁγίου πνεύματος τὸ χρῖσμα ποιούμενοι Cyr.*Is*.3.1(2.353E); Proc.G.*Gen*.1:9f.(M.87.77C); the *sign* of the cross, Chrys.*hom.54.4 in Mt*.(7.551B); σταῦρον... νικοφόρον Χριστοῦ σ. ἀθάνατον *IGC* 104(Ephesus, c. 435); in baptism, Chrys.*hom.25.1 in Jo*.(8.143E); Bas.Sel.*or*.27.2(M.85.313B); **7.** *type, image* of celestial realities τῆς τῶν οὐρανίων τύπων διὰ συμβόλων ναοῦ κατασκευῆς Eus.*h.e*.10.4.25(M.20.860A); Dion.Ar.*c.h*.1.2(M.3.121B); id.*d.n*.4.9(M.3.705B); id.*ep*.9(M.3.1004B); Jo.V H.*icon*.13(M.96.1360A); **8.** *symbol*, opp. reality; of idols, Or.*Cels*.3.40(p.236.17; M.11.972C); of OT sacrifices, Eus.*d.e*.1.10(p.46.16; M.22.88C); of observances of Law, Thdr.Mops.*Tit*.1:15f.(M.66.949A); of water in baptism τὸ μὲν πνεῦμα μετὰ πατρὸς καὶ υἱοῦ ὀνομάζομεν, τοῦ δὲ ὕδατος οὐ μεμνήμεθα, ὡς φαίνεσθαι ὅτι τὸ μὲν συμβόλου...ἕνεκεν παραλαμβάνεται, τὸ δὲ ⟨πνεῦμα⟩ ὡς ἐνεργοῦν μετὰ πατρὸς καὶ υἱοῦ ἐπικαλούμεθα id.*fr.21 in Jo*.(p.321.7); *ib*.(p.322.6); mere *external rite* ἡμεῖς δὲ τὰ μὲν σ. τῶν πραγμάτων κατέχομεν, τῆς δὲ ἀληθείας αὐτῆς ἐκπεπτώκαμεν Chrys.*compunct*.1.3(1.127B).

B. partic. ref. cultus; **1.** pagan *cult formula*, Clem.*prot*.2(p.13.10; M.8.76B); *cult object*, *ib*.(pp.14.14,17.10; 80A,89A); Cels.ap. Or.*Cels*.6.22(p.92.3; M.11.1324A); Bas.*ep*.276(3.421B; M.32.1012B); **2.** Christian *rite*, esp. *sacramental rite* πεπραγμένα σ. μυστηρίων θεοσεβείας ἁγίων Or.*Jo*.6.6(3; p.113.21; M.14.209A); †Bas.*Is*.28(1.401D; M.30.173B); πεπείσμεθα τῇ ὁμολογίᾳ τῶν θείων ὀνομάτων... κυροῦσθαι τὸ τῆς εὐσεβείας μυστήριον καὶ τῇ τῶν μυστικῶν ἐθῶν τε καὶ συμβόλων κοινωνίᾳ τὴν σωτηρίαν κρατύνεσθαι Gr.Nyss.*Eun*.11 (2 p.270.13; M.45.880B); περιορᾷ δὲ τὴν τῶν μυστικῶν σ. τε καὶ ἐθῶν κοινωνίαν ἐν οἷς ὁ Χριστιανισμὸς τὴν ἰσχὺν ἔχει...λέγει μηδὲ τὰ μυστικὰ σ. φυλακτήρια...τῶν περὶ τὴν ψυχὴν ἀγαθῶν *ib*.(2 pp.270.22,271.7; 880B,D); σύμβολα ἢ θεσμούς Chrys.*hom.15.1 in Heb*.(12.149A); Dion.Ar.*e.h*.5.1.5(M.3.505B); *sacrament* τὰ σ. τῆς σωτηρίας ἡμῶν Chrys.*hom.86.4 in Jo*.(8.519A); πρὸς τῶν ἱερέων τελοῦνταί τινα τῶν σεβασμίων σ. Dion.Ar.*e.h*.5.1.5(505B); Max.*schol.e.h*.1.2(M.4.117B); **3.** partic. of sacrament of baptism, Or.*Cels*.3.51(p.247.11; M.11.988A) cit. s. ἄρχω; τὰ σωτηριώδη σ. Isid.Pel.*epp*.2.37(M.78.480C); *ib*.5.569(1644A,D); of baptismal water (or perh. oil for post-baptismal anointing) χωρήσας δ' ἔνδον τῶν μακαρίων ὑδάτων ἐπὶ κωλύσει τῶν μυουμένων τὴν ἀνάστασιν τοῦ σωτῆρος, καὶ τῷ μὲν διακόνῳ θρασέως ἐντιναχθείς, τὰ σ. ἐκχέει Pall.*v.Chrys*.9(p.57.24; M.47.33); **4.** of service of eucharist, Cyr.H.*catech*.19.11; Chrys.*hom.82.1 in Mt*.(7.783C); Thdr.Mops.*1Cor*.11:34(M.66.889D); Mod.*dorm*.11(M.86.3305C); **5.** of eucharistic elements both before and after consecration, as a symbol in some sense united with that which it signifies τούτου...τοῦ θύματος τὴν μνήμην ἐπὶ τραπέζης ἐκτελεῖν διὰ συμβόλων τοῦ τε σώματος αὐτοῦ καὶ τοῦ σωτηρίου αἵματος Eus.*d.e*.1.10 (p.47.33; M.22.89D); αὐτὸς τὰ σ. τῆς ἐνθέου οἰκονομίας τοῖς αὐτοῦ παρεδίδου μαθηταῖς, τὴν εἰκόνα τοῦ ἰδίου σώματος ποιεῖσθαι παρακελευόμενος *ib*.8.1(p.366.22; 596A); id.*h.e*.10.3.3(M.20.848B); *Const. App*.6.23.5; ἡ θυσία, ἡ προσφορά, τὰ σ. Chrys.*hom.29.2 in Rom*.(9.732B); ἵνα μὴ ἀκουσίως...συνεκπτύσωσί τι τοῦ σ. Pall.*v.Chrys*.8(p.45.10; M.47.27); κοινωνήσας τῶν δεσποτικῶν σ. *ib*.11(p.68.9; M.47.38); Thdt.*1Cor*.11:26(3.238); id.*eran*.1(4.26); τῶν σεβασμίων σ. δι' ὧν ὁ Χριστὸς σημαίνεται καὶ μετέχεται Dion.Ar.*e.h*.3.3.9(M.3.437C); διὰ τῶν ἐνταῦθα αἰσθητῶν σ. ἡμῖν ἀρχέτυπα χαριζομένου μυστήρια Max. *myst*.24(M.91.705A); ἁγιάζειν καὶ χειρίζειν τὰ σ. τῶν ἁγίων μυστηρίων †Gr.II Papa *ep.Leon*.2(H.4.16C); this usage rejected as insufficiently realistic οὐκ εἶπε· τοῦτό ἐστι τὸ σ. τοῦ σώματός μου...ἀλλά· τοῦτό ἐστι τὸ σῶμά μου Thdr.Mops.*Mt*.26:26(M.66.713B); Petr.Laod. *fr.Mt*.26:26(M.86.3325A); cf.Jo.D.*f.o*.4.13(M.94.1148A); **6.** ritual *formula*, ref. Mt.28:19 συνηρίθμησεν αὐτὸ [sc. H. Ghost] ὁ υἱὸς τοῦ θεοῦ ἐν τῷ σ. τοῦ ἁγιασμοῦ ‡Ath.*disp*.38(M.28.489B); ‡Ath.*ep.cath*.(M.28.84B); hence *creed*, CLaod.*can*.7; Gel.Cyz.*h.e*.2.26.4(M.85.1308B) cit. s. ἐγγράφως; Cyr.*ep*.39(p.19.21; 5^2.108C); Leo Mag.*ep*.28.1(p.11.13; M.*PL*.54.758A); Basilisc.*encycl*.(p.50; M.86.2600ff.); Πέτρον φησὶ τὸν Κναφέα ἐπινοῆσαι...ἐν πάσῃ συνάξει τὸ σ. λέγεσθαι Thdr.Lect.*h.e*.2.48(M.86.209A); Justn.*conf*.(p.90.2; M.86.1013B); ‡Bas.*h.myst*.57(p.392.16); of an heret. creed, Philost.*h.e*.2.7(M.65.469C).

σύμβολος, ὁ, *throwing together*, hence *chance* φασὶ γὰρ...κατά τινα σ. ἐκεῖ καταπαῦσαι τὸν πόλεμον, καὶ ἐξ ἐκείνου καλεῖσθαι τὸν τόπον Εἰρήνην Marc.Diac.*v.Porph*.18.

***συμβόμβοις,** vox nihili, Hipp.*haer*.5.9(M.16.3155A; σὺν βόμβοις p.100.2).

***συμβόσκ-ω, 1.** act. trans., *join in feeding* ὅπως...τὸ Χριστοῦ μοι τοῦτο ~οιτε ποίμνιον Sophr.H.*ep.syn*.(M.87.3197B); **2.** med. intrans., *feed together* οἱ νοητοὶ λύκοι ~ονται μετὰ ἀρνῶν Cyr.H.*catech*.17.10.

[*]συμβούλαιον, τό, v. συμβόλαιον.

συμβουλευτικός, 1. *advisory, hortatory*; neut. as subst., of *hortatory ways* of God as rejecting compulsion of man's free will, Iren. *haer*.4.37.3(M.7.1101C); **2.** *imperative* mood τὸ ὀργίζεσθε [Ps.4:5] δύναται...εἶναι καὶ ὁριστικόν, καὶ σ.· οἷον· ὀργίζεσθε, καὶ διὰ τί ὀργίζεσθε...καὶ...ὀργίζεσθε τῷ ἐνοχλοῦντι ὑμῶν πάθει Isid.Pel.*epp*.2.239(M.78.676D).

συμβουλεύω, 1. *counsel, advise*; med., *agree*, Thphn.*chron*.p.259 (M.108.645A); **2.** med., c. dupl. acc., *consult* one *about* τίνα σ. τὸ μυστήριόν μου; *Mir.Geo*.8(p.95.4).

συμβουλία, ἡ, 1. *advice, counsel*; of indwelling spirit, Or.*Jo*.2.11 (6; p.66.17; M.14.129C); of serpent in Eden, Meth.*res*.2.2(p.333.3; M.18.300B); Ath.*gent*.3(M.25.8D); of evil counsel οὐδὲ κοινωνὸς τῆς τούτων [sc. Jewish leaders] πονηρίας ἢ σ. γίνεσθαι θέλει Hipp.*ben*.

*Jac.*13(p.28.11); **2.** eccl. *council* εἰς ἐκκλησιαστικὴν σ. Ath.*h.Ar.*38 (p.204.31; M.25.737C); †Gr.II Papa *ep.Leon.*1(H.4.9C).

συμβούλιον, τό, 1. *counsel, advice,* Const.ap.Eus.*v.C.*3.61(p.109. 22; M.20.1136B); ref. 3Reg.22:20ff. τὸ σ. ἐκεῖνο τὸ κατ' οὐρανὸν ἐπὶ δόλῳ...τοῦ Ἀχαὰβ σκευαζόμενον Dion.Ar.*ep.*9(M.3.1105B); σ. ποιέω *consult, take counsel, A.Paul.et Thecl.*22(p.249.3); *A.Pil.*A 15.2 (p.266); *ib.*1.1(p.214); **2.** *evil counsel* ὅσῳ τις ἐγγίζει τῷ Ἰησοῦ, σ. οὐ λαμβάνει Or.*schol.in Mt.*12:14(M.17.293C); **3.** *consultation* ποιοῦνται αὐτοῦ τὴν ἐξέτασιν μετὰ σ. πολλοῦ *Const.App.*2.52.1.

***συμβουλογραφία, ἡ,** v. *συμβολογραφία.

***συμβουλοκοπ-έω,** ? *discuss* περὶ τοῦ μὴ συνεδριάζειν τοῦ ~εῖν μετ' ἀλλήλων τὰ φθάνοντα Thdr.Stud.*catech.*index 151(M.99.40A).

***συμβράζομαι,** *boil, foam*; of the abyss, ‡Ath.*serm.Ant.*2(M.28. 592A).

συμβρέχω, *moisten together*; **1.** *wet, T.Job* 20(p.115.23); **2.** *smear* with oil, *A.Mt.*18(p.240.8).

***συμβροντ-άω,** *thunder together* with, met. ὁ...νόμος καὶ οἱ προφῆται...τῷ εὐαγγελικῷ...~ῶντες κηρύγματι Sophr.H.*or.*7.17(M. 87.3349A).

***συμβροχθίζω,** *drink together, soak, tipple with,* Pall.*v.Chrys.*12 (p.69.28; συμβροχθήσῃ M.47.39); Nil.*epp.*3.150(M.79.453A).

***συμμάθημα, τό,** *summary of doctrine, creed,* Max.*schol.e.h.*3.2 (M.4.136D).

***συμμαθήτρια, ἡ,** *fellow* (woman) *disciple,* Gr.Mag.*dial.*(tr.Zach.) 4.15(M.*PL.*77.343C).

συμμαλάσσω, *soften together*; met., *be melted, softened* by strong emotion κατεκλάσθη [sc. Joseph], συνεμαλάχθη, συνετρίβη, καὶ ἔκλαυσε Chrys.*hom.*4.5 *in 1Thess.*(11.458A).

συμμαραίνομαι, *fade, wither together* with, met. αὐτῷ [sc. τῷ ἀνθρώπῳ] συμμαρανθεῖσα [sc. ἡ ἁμαρτία] καὶ συμφθινήσασα Meth. *res.*1.42(p.288.9; M.41.1112B).

συμμαρτυρ-έω, *bear joint witness, bear witness in support of one another*; of Marcellus with a Jew, Eus.*e.th.*2.2(p.100.25; M.24. 901B); καὶ ἑτέρων δὲ θεοφόρων προφητῶν καὶ ἀποστόλων ~ούντων αὐτῷ [sc. Μωϋσῇ] Cosm.Ind.*top.*5(M.88.164A).

σύμμαρτυς, ὁ, ἡ, *fellow-witness*; hence *fellow-martyr, M.Perp.* 15(p.85.4); *M.Areth.*(p.28); Κοσμᾶν καὶ Δαμιανὸν τοὺς...συνιατροὺς καὶ σ. Sophr.H.*mir.Cyr.et Jo.*30(M.87.3520C).

***συμμασσάομαι,** for ⟨συμμασάομαι⟩, *chew together,* Amph.*Seleuc.* 136(M.37.1586A).

συμμαχ-έω, *be* or *fight as an ally, help*; apptly. also *fight against,* of Devil ~ήσας [i.e. with archangel Michael] ἀφείλετο Chrysipp. *enc.in Mich.*(p.93.14).

συμμαχία, ἡ, 1. *alliance,* offensive or defensive; met., *help, assistance* πότε σου τῆς ξυμμαχίας χρείαν ἔχει ὁ Χριστός; *Clem.ep.*4(M.2. 37B); freq. of divine assistance ἕλκεται...οὐκ ἄκων, ἀλλὰ ἀπολαύων συμμαχίας Ammon.*Jo.*6:44(M.85.1437A); οἱ ἀπόστολοι...τῇ θείᾳ σ. θωρακισθέντες Isid.Pel.*epp.*2.54(M.78.497C); τὴν ἐσομένην ἀντίληψιν παρ' αὐτοῦ, καὶ σ. ἐπὶ τῇ τῶν ἀγαθῶν ἐργασίᾳ Thdt.*Ezech.*11:19(2. 748); τί ταύτης τῆς σ. ἴσον; ὁ ἐχθρός, ὁ μεμισημένος οὗτος ἐξαίφνης ἄνω γέγονεν Chrys.ap.Cosm.Ind.*top.*10(p.310.16) for εὐμηχανίας id. *hom.1.4 in Eph.*(11.7D); **2.** *allied* or *auxiliary force*; hence gen., *ally, friend* ἐπὶ συμμαχίαν ἐλθὼν πολέμιον εὗρεν Bas.*hom.in Ps.*14(1. 108B; M.29.268A).

συμμεθίστ-ημι, 1. trans., *change at the same time* ~ησι ταῖς ὀργαῖς καὶ τὰ ἐξ αὐτῶν συμβαίνοντα Cyr.*Zach.*45(3.721C); **2.** pass. intrans., *change along with* ~αται γὰρ οἱονεὶ πως ὁ...θεὸς τοῖς μετανοεῖν ᾑρημένοις Cyr.*Ag.*9(3.636E); **3.** *help in changing* τῇ ἑαυτῆς ἀλλοιώσει ~ᾶν Bas.*hex.*6.10(1.61A; M.29.144B).

***συμμελανειμονέω,** *wear black* (i.e. mourning) *also,* Bas.*hom.*5. 8(2.41E; M.31.257A).

***συμμελανόομαι,** = συμμελαίνομαι, *be stained black together* with; met., Or.*hom.19.14 in Jer.*(p.170.22; M.13.492A).

συμμελετ-άω, *exercise* or *practise together* with ἔχει...αὐτὴν τὴν χάριν τότε καὶ ~ῶσαν αὐτῇ ἡ ψυχὴ καὶ συγκράζουσαν τὸ κύριε Ἰησοῦ, καθὼς ἂν μήτηρ διδάσκοι καὶ...~ᾷ ἑαυτῆς κνωδάλῳ τὸ πατὴρ ὄνομα Diad.*perf.*61(p.70.3).

***συμμελῳδ-έω,** *chant, sing together* with εὔκαιρον...~εῖν ἡμᾶς τῷ Δαβίδ ‡Caes.Naz.*dial.*140(M.38.1073).

συμμένω, *live with,* c. dat., Thphn.*chron.*p.67(M.108.217B).

***σύμμεπτος,** vox nihili ? for συνάμεμπτος *likewise perfect* ὁ δὲ Πέτρος (λέγει) τῷ Ἰωάννῳ. σὺ ὡς παρθένος καὶ σ. κέχρησαι ἐρώτησαι αὐτήν *Ev.Barth.*(Vassiliev p.11; καὶ ἄμεμπτος *RB* p.321).

συμμερίζω, 1. act. and med., *distribute, share out* ἣν [sc. ζωήν] καὶ συνεμερίσαντο τοῖς πλησίον *Ep.Lugd.*ap.Eus.*h.e.*5.2.7(M.20.436B); **2.** med., *take a share of, have a share in* τὸν τοῦ θεοῦ υἱόν...οὐχὶ τῷ μερίσαντι συμμερισάμενον τὴν ἀξίαν, οὐκ ἄλλῳ τινὶ τὴν πατρικὴν οὐσίαν, οὐ τὴν βασιλείαν Eun.*exp.fid.*2(p.255); ἡ μήτηρ...ζητοῦσα δύναμιν ἵνα συμμερίσηται τὸν πόνον [sc. for her sick child] ‡Chrys.*Abr.*2(2. 744C); ref. BMV μόνη συμμερίσασθαι θεῷ τὰ τοῦ θεοῦ κατηξίωσαι ‡Meth.*Sym.et Ann.*10(M.18.373C); †Jo.D.*B.J.*23(M.96.1065C); ref. 1Cor.9:13, Or.*sel.in Num.*18:21(M.12.577A); Eus.*Is.*23:18(M.24. 257A); **3.** pass., *be separated from one another, be mutually divided,* Nemes.*nat.hom.*2(M.40.577A).

***συμμεριστέον,** *one must share* with, Gr.Naz.*or.*14.18(M.35.880D).

συμμεριστής, ὁ, *sharer*; of material things, Bas.*hom.*6.6(2.49D; M.31.276B); Nect.*Thdr.*20(M.39.1837A); Isid.Pel.*epp.*4.18(M.78. 1068C); of Devil ὁ κακὸς σ. ἡμῶν Bas.*hom.*13.6(2.119E; M.31.437C); συμμερισταὶ τῷ συκοφάντῃ παρὰ θεοῦ εὑρεθήσεσθε *Const.App.*2.51.1; τὸν ἐμὸν ἑταῖρον καὶ συνεργόν, τὸν σ. τῆς ψυχῆς Gr.Naz.*or.*18.35(M.35. 1032C).

συμμεταβάλλ-ω, med., *change along with* or *at the same time*; **1.** trans. ~ονται τοῖς τόποις καὶ τὰ σχήματα Clem.*paed.*3.11(p.280. 19; M.8.657C); ὁ θεὸς παραδέχεται αὐτὴν κατὰ μικρὸν ~όμενος αὐτήν Mac.Aeg.*hom.*47.17(M.34.808B); **2.** intrans., οὐδὲ συμμετεβάλλετο [sc. ἡ ψυχή] ἀλγοῦντι καὶ πάσχοντι τῷ σώματι Meth.*res.*3.18(p.415. 7; M.18.325B); Isid.Pel.*epp.*5.408(M.78.1569C); Max.*ambig.*(M.91. 1193A).

συμμετάγω, *carry along with,* Thdr.Mops.*Nah.*3:4ff.(M.66.417B).

***συμμεταίρω,** *remove* or *migrate with,* Isid.Pel.*epp.*1.430(M.78. 420C) = *ib.*4.197(1285B).

***συμμετακεράννυμι (συμμετακίρνημι),** *blend together* with; *mix up together* with, c. dat., Gr.Nyss.*fat.*(M.45.153B); Max.*ambig.*(M. 91.1104B).

συμμεταλαμβάν-ω, *partake in together* with, hence *communicate* with πάντως καὶ πᾶσι τοῖς ~ουσιν ἡμῖν κατὰ προαίρεσιν ἑνούμεθα Jo.D.*f.o.*4.13(M.94.1153B).

συμμεταμορφόω, *transform completely,* ‡Meth.*Sym.et Ann.*12(M. 18.377A).

***συμμετανίστημι,** intrans., *remove, migrate with,* Gr.Nyss.*v.Mos.* 36(M.44.312C).

***συμμετανοέω,** *repent along with,* Gr.Nyss.*Eun.*12(1 p.335.14; M. 45.1053A).

***συμμεταπλέκω,** *wind round together, intertwine,* Geo.Pis.*Heracl.* 2.185(M.92.1329A).

συμμεταποιέω, pass., *be changed along with,* Gr.Nyss.*Apoll.*42(M. 45.1224A); id.*Maced.*4(M.45.1305B).

***συμμεταστέλλομαι,** s.v.l., *summon together,* Const.ap.Eus.*v.C.* 3.12(M.20.1068C, v.l. μετεστειλάμην p.83.1).

***συμμεταστρέφω,** *turn round in concert* with, Geo.Pis.*Pers.*2.162 (M.92.1222A).

συμμετατίθημι, *move, remove along with* or *at the same time,* Gr. Nyss.*hex.*21(M.44.84B); Chrys.*hom.14.11 in Rom.*(9.593A).

***συμμέτειμι** (*ibo*), *pursue together*; met., *collaborate* τοῦ συμμετιόντος τὸ ἔργον Nil.*Magn.*58(M.79.1045D).

***συμμετέρχομαι,** *transfer,* Gr.Nyss.*Eun.*6(2 p.132.24; M.45.716D); Sophr.H.*mir.Cyr.et Jo.*67(M.87.3653C).

συμμετέχω, [aor. infin. συμμεθέξαι] *participate in together,* Thdr. Stud.*epp.*1.50(M.99.1096B).

συμμετεωροπολ-έω, *walk aloft together* with διὰ...τὴν πρὸς τὰς ἄνω δυνάμεις τῆς ψυχῆς συγγένειαν, τὰ πολλὰ ~εῖν ἐκείναις Nil.*exerc.*15(M. 79.737C).

***συμμετεωροπορέω,** *walk on high* with τῷ θεῷ Ephr.3.118F; Gr. Nyss.*hom.8 in Cant.*(M.44.945B); with Christ, id.*ep.*3(p.18.19; M. 46.1016C); ταῖς οὐρανίαις δυνάμεσι id.*v.Macr.*(p.383.5; M.46.972A); id.*laud.Bas.*(M.46.813D); id.*ordin.*(M.46.549C).

***συμμετοχή, ἡ, 1.** *sharing, participation,* Epiph.*haer.*76.18(p.363. 28; M.42.552A); *ib.*76.19(p.365.23; 553C); *ib.*77.35(p.447.13; 693B); id.*exp.fid.*8(p.504.1; M.42.788A); **2.** *fellowship* τῶν ἀγγέλων...ἡ σ. Gr.Mag.*dial.*(tr.Zach.)3.34(M.*PL.*77.299B).

συμμέτοχος, 1. *sharing jointly,* and subst., *joint partaker, fellow sharer*; Origen tries to distinguish from μέτοχος: μήποτε ὁ μὲν μέτοχος ἐπὶ κρείττονος εἴρηται, ὁ δὲ σ. ἐπὶ χείρονος...οὐ μέμνημαι δὲ ἀλλαχοῦ παρὰ τὴν ἐνεστηκυῖαν λέξιν τὸν σ. εἰρῆσθαι Or.*comm.in Eph.* 5:7(p.561); c. genit., of thing shared ἄνθρωπος γέγονεν, ὅπως καὶ τῶν παθῶν τῶν ἡμετέρων σ. γενόμενος καὶ ἴασιν ποιήσηται Just. *2apol.*13.4(M.6.468A); τῆς...μανίας...δειχθῆναι συμμέτοχοι *M.Scill.*9 (p.24.21); ref. Phil.1:7 σ. τῆς χάριτος καλῶν Clem.*str.*4.13(p.289.7; M.8.1300C); and dat. of person shared with, *ib.*3.4(p.208.26; 1133A); οἱ συκοφάνται...σ. καὶ συγκληρονόμοι γίνονται τοῖς προδώκασιν καὶ σταυρώσασιν τὴν ἀλήθειαν Ant.Mon.*hom.*40(M.89.1557C); Jo.VI H. *v.Jo.D.*10(M.94.445A); genit. of person shared with τὰ...ἔθνη...

συμμέτοχα τῶν ἁγίων Iren.*haer*.1.10.3(M.7.557A); συμμέτοχοι τοῦ... παιδὸς αὐτοῦ [sc. θεοῦ] *Const.App*.1 proem.; **2.** *allied*, and subst., *associate* θεὸν ἔχειν ἀντίμαχον, καὶ τὸν ἀρχαῖον ἀντάρτην σ. Isid.Pel. *epp*.1.64(M.78.292B); *ib*.1.420(417A).

συμμετρ-έω, *measure by* comparison with, *number among* μὴ ταῖς ἀσυνέτοις ~ήσῃς ἑαυτήν, πάνσοφε κόρη Rom.Mel.(*AS* 1 p.103).

***συμμετρημένως,** *in due measure* or *proportion*, Chrys.ap.*cat. Phil*.4:19(p.288.29) for συμμεμετρημένως id.*hom.15.4 in Phil*.(11. 315E).

συμμετρία, ἡ, 1. *due proportion*; opp. ἀμετρία, Ath.*gent*.38(M.25. 76A); **2.** *moderation* οὐ κηδεύειν κωλύων, ἀλλὰ μετὰ συμμετρίας τοῦτο ποιεῖν Chrys.*hom.86.5 in Jo*.(8.511C); in speech, Euthal.Diac.*epp. cath*.(M.85.677B); *temperance* οἶνος...φάρμακόν ἐστιν ἄριστον, ὅταν τὴν σ. ἔχῃ ἀρίστην Chrys.*stat*.1.4(2.7B); Isid.Pel.*epp*.1.277(M.78.345B); **3.** *limit* ἵνα μὴ τὴν σ. ἐκβαίνω τῶν λόγων Meth.*res*.1.58(p.320.3; M.41. 1153C); Eus.*Marcell*.1.4(p.31.10; M.24.773D); Dion.Ar.*c.h*.15.9(M.3. 340B); *limitation* τῇ τῆς ἐπιστολῆς λόγισαι σ. Firm.*ep*.33(M.77. 1505A); **4.** *arrangement, system* τὴν ἀσθενῆ καὶ συνεσταλμένην ὑπερβεβηκυῖαι τῶν καθ' ἡμᾶς ὑλαίων ἀριθμῶν συμμετρίαν Dion.Ar.*c.h*.14 (M.3.321A); στοιχηδόν τε συνθεὶς τούτων [sc. of scripture] τὸ ὕφος, κατὰ τὴν ἐμαυτοῦ σ. Euthal.Diac.*Ac*.(M.85.633C); **5.** *competency, adequate amount* ὁ μὲν πλείω τῆς χρείας εἶχεν, ὁ δὲ οὐδὲ τῆς σ. ἀπέλαυεν Chrys.*ecl*.11(12.502A).

***συμμετριάζω,** *keep to the same measure*; *observe moderation together*, Gr.Naz.*or*.19.2(M.35.1045B); Cyr.*Jo*.5.5(4.532A); συμμετριάσωμεν Χριστῷ Eulog.*palm*.13(M.86.2937A).

σύμμετρος, *commensurate* with, *corresponding* to; hence **1.** *in proportion*; abs., *in due measure, right-sized* ἔστω σ. ὁ θυρεός Chrys. *hom.24.2 in Eph*.(11.182B); **2.** *moderate*; opp. ἄμετρος, Isid.Pel. *epp*.2.45(M.78.488A); esp. exeg. 1Cor.10:13, v. s. ἀνθρώπινος; neut. as subst., *moderation* 'πολλοὺς' καὶ οὐ πάντας, διὰ τὸ σ. Eus.Em.*fr. Gal*.1:14(p.48.12); opp. ἀμετρία, Chrys.*incomprehens*.5.1(1.480E); opp. τὸ ἄμετρον, id.*hom.16.4 in Ac*.(9.134A); plur. σύμμετρα τῇ ἀσθενείᾳ νομοθετεῖ Thdt.*Rom*.6:12(3.64); id.*1Tim*.3:3(3.654); **3.** *limited*; of temporal rewards, Chrys.*hom.14.2 in Rom*.(9.578A); theol. τὸ παγκρατὲς ἅγιον πνεῦμα...πρόεισιν ἐξ αὐτοῦ οὐ συμμετρότερον Didym.*Trin*.2.27(M.39.753A).

***συμμηρυσμός, ὁ,** met., *concatenation, interweaving*; of thoughts and emotions, Dor.*doct*.8.2(M.88.1709A).

***συμμιγή, ἡ,** *mixture*, *Apophth.Patr*.(M.65.101A).

***συμμιγία, ἡ,** *commixture* σ. τινὰ καὶ συμφωνίαν τοῦ θείου πρὸς τὰ κτίσματα ἐργάζονται [sc. Arians] Didym.*Trin*.2.11(M.39.661C).

συμμίγνυμι, med., *be mixed together, mingle*; not applicable to essence of H. Ghost as if a demi-god, Gr.Nyss.*Maced*.17(M.45. 1324A).

σύμμικτος, 1. *commingled*; eucharistic ὁ οἶνος...καὶ τὸ ὕδωρ... σύμ[μικτα] *Lit.Marc*.(*P.Dêr-Baliz*.2 v° 8); **2.** *miscellaneous*; neut. as subst., plur., of work by Acac. Caes. ἀπέθανεν [sc. Εὐσέβιος] Ἀκάκιον μαθητὴν καὶ διάδοχον τοῦ θρόνου Καισαρείας ἐάσας...τὸν καὶ τὰ σ. συγγραψάμενον Thphn.*chron*.p.28(M.108.128C); **3.** *compounded, composite*; of nature of man, Dion.Ar.*d.n*.6.2(M.3.856D); and his activities, *ib*.4.9(705B).

συμμισέω, pass., *be hated together*, cf. *nescio quem* συνταλαίπωρον ...*et* συμμισούμενον Tert.*adversus Marcionem* 4.9(M.*PL*.2.374C).

συμμνημονεύω, *mention at the same time, refer to in the same breath*; Persons of Trin., Didym.*Trin*.2.6(M.39.545A); *ib*.2.8(616A); *ib*.2.12(677C).

συμμοιχεύομαι, *join in committing adultery*, Thdr.Stud.*epp*.1.49 (M.99.1088C).

***συμμονάζω,** *be a fellow monk*, Soz.*h.e*.6.28.5(M.67.1372B).

συμμορία, ἡ, 1. *district* of a chorepiscopus, Bas.*epp*.142,290(3. 235C,428E; M.32.592C,1029A); **2.** *company* in general; of the prophets, Thdt.*Dan*.proem.(2.1057); of the Twelve, Chrys.*prod.Jud*.1.2(2. 378E); *company* of monks, id.*hom.13.7 in Rom*.(9.567E); Jo.D.*haer*. 80(M.736D); *fellowship* ἡμεῖς αὐτῷ συμμορίαν ἀδελφῶν παρεσχόμεθα Synes.*ep*.53(M.66.1380D); within Church, *sodality* ἐπειδὴ καθ' αὐτὸν ἕκαστος οὐκ ἂν εὐκόλως αὐτὸ κατορθώσειεν, ποιησώμεθα φρατρίας καὶ σ. Chrys.*stat*.11.5(2.121D); **3.** *party, faction*, esp. of a heretic's following τοῦτον δή φασιν...ἀποσχίσαι μὲν τῆς ἄλλης Εὐνομιανῶν μοίρας, ἰδίας δὲ σ. ἀρχηγὸν ἑαυτὸν ἀναδεῖξαι Philost.*h.e*. 12.11(M.65.620C); πρὸς τὴν ἐναντίαν...σ. μεταβέβηκας Thdt.*eran*. 1(4.31); τῆς Ἀπολιναρίου σ. *ib*.2(4.112); τῆς τῶν τοῦ αἱρετικοῦ Εὐτυχοῦς ὁμοφρόνων συμμορίας Gel.Cyz.*h.e*.1 proem.(p.3.22; M.85. 1193D).

***συμμορφία, ἡ,** *conformity, likeness*, esp. ref. Rom.8:29 ὕδατος τὴν ἰσχὺν...ἁμαρτιῶν ἀπόθεσιν, ἀναγέννησιν πνευματικὴν εἰς σ. τὴν εἰς αὐτὸν Χριστόν Eus.*Is*.3:1f.(M.24.109C) = Cyr.*Is*.1.2(2.53C); τὴν πρὸς τὸν υἱὸν σ. ἀναλαμβάνοντες Cyr.*Jo*.3.5(4.302D); id.*glaph.Ex*.2 (1.276D,280A).

σύμμορφος, 1. *of similar form* or *shape, like* εἰ κατ' εἰκόνα θεοῦ γεγόναμεν, φησί, σ. ἡμῖν ἐστιν ὁ θεός ‡Gr.Nyss.*or.1 in Gen.1:26*(M. 44.261A) = ‡Bas.*struct.hom*.1.4(1.326A; M.30.16A); ref. Ac.6:15 τῶν ἀγγέλων σ. ὤφθης ἐν βίῳ Geo.Pis.*carm*.16.1(p.17); met. τὰ εὐαγγέλια τούτοις [sc. τοῖς τετραπροσώποις ζῴοις] σ. εἰσιν ‡Bas.*h.myst*.44(p.389. 3); **2.** *possessing one form*, of Trin. τρία ἔμμορφα τρία σ. Epiph. *anc*.67(p.82.3; M.43.137C) ∞ Caes.Naz.*dial*.3(M.38.861); of H. Ghost πατροσθενὲς σ. Jo.D.*carm.pent*.60(p.215, conj. for πατρόθεν ὀξύμορφον M.96.836B); **3.** *conformed*; c. dat.; also c. genit. of that which one comes to possess (cf. Phil.3:21, Rom.8:29); **a.** of Christ in Inc. σ. τοῖς δούλοις ὁ δεσπότης γέγονεν, ἵνα οἱ δοῦλοι γένωνται σ. πάλιν θεοῦ Amph.*hom*.1.4(M.39.41A); σ. γενόμενος τῷ σώματι τῆς ταπεινώσεως ἡμῶν ἵνα ἡμᾶς σ. ποιήσῃ τῆς εἰκόνος τῆς δόξης αὐτοῦ *Lit.Bas*.(p.404.2); **b.** of men to Christ, his image, glory etc. σ. γεγονότας αὐτῷ νοητῶς Cyr.*Abac*.51(3.565C); id.*Zeph*.41(3.619E); id.*Mich*.35(3.422A); σ. ἡμᾶς πεποίηκε καὶ τῆς αὐτοῦ ἀναστάσεως Or.*schol.in Lc*.9:43f.(M.17. 349B); ref. Rom.8:29, Cyr.H.*catech*.21.1; ἵνα σε σ. τῆς οἰκείας δόξης ἐργάσηται Acac.Mel.*hom*.ap.CEph.(431)(p.90.32; M.77.1469B); οἱ πιστεύοντες...τῆς ὁμοφυοῦς ἀνθρωπότητος...εἰσι...σ. Thdt.*Trin*.10(M. 75.1160B); Amph.*hom*.1.4(M.39.41A), *Lit.Bas*.(p.404.2) citt. supra; **4.** *congenial, agreeable* μὴ...ἐκλέγου [sc. τῶν ἐδεσμάτων] σ. τῇ σῇ κοιλίᾳ †Jo.Jej.*paraen*.(p.235).

συμμορφ-όω, 1. s.v.l., act., *make like* ~ῶν [sc. τὸ σῶμά μου] τῇ μορφῇ τῆς ἁγίας δόξης σου *A.Phil*.B 144(p.87.19); **2.** pass., *be conformed*, to Christ κατὰ τὸ μέτρον τῆς ἐνανθρωπήσεως ~ούμενοι τὸν ἔσω ἄνθρωπον †Bas.*bapt*.1.2.15(2.640D; M.31.1552C); ~ωθέντες αὐτῷ πρὸς τὸ ἀπαθές τε καὶ θειότερον Gr.Nyss.*hom.1 in Cant*.(M.44.764D); ref. Inc. ὁ...λόγος...γεγονὼς ἄνθρωπος...ἡμῖν τοῖς ὑπὸ ζυγὰ δουλείας ~ούμενος Cyr.*apol.Thdt*.6(p.129.15; v.l. for συμμετρούμενος 6^1.223C); ὁ τέλειος ἄνθρωπος, ὃν ἐφόρησεν, οὗτος ὡραιώθη, τῇ τῆς θεότητος ὡραιότητι ~ωθείς Ph.Carp.*Cant*.204(M.40.129A).

***συμμόρφωσις, ἡ,** *unity of form*, ref. incarnate Word in both natures ὅταν...ἐξ ἀμφοῖν ἅμα, ἕνωσιν, κοινωνίαν, χρῖσιν, συμφυΐαν, σ. ...φάσκομεν ‡Cyr.*Trin*.24(6^3.29E; M.77.1165B).

***συμμουσουργέω,** *sing together*, ‡Meth.*palm*.2(M.18.385B).

συμμύστης, ὁ, 1. *one who is initiated with others, fellow initiate*; **a.** of one of the same faith, ref. Daniel and his companions σ. καὶ θεοσεβεῖς ἄνδρες Hipp.*Dan*.2.10.2(M.10.677A); of fellow Christians ἔδωκε...μείζονα τράπεζαν,...ἴσασιν οἱ σ. τὸ λεγόμενον Chrys.*hom. 15.3 in Jo*.(8.89B); of the Twelve, Rom.Mel.(*AS* 1 p.174); **b.** myst. οὗτοι καταξιοῦνται ἐλθεῖν εἰς μέτρα τῆς τελειότητος...συμμύσται τοῦ ἐπουρανίου βασιλέως Mac.Aeg.*hom*.17.2(M.34.624D); **c.** Gnost., into esoteric doctrines ὁ ἀπόστολος τοῦ ὑψίστου καὶ σ. τοῦ λόγου τοῦ Χριστοῦ τοῦ ἀποκρύφου *A.Thom*.A 39(p.156.13); **2.** more gen., of one sharing the same opinions or way of life; **a.** *companion* δεῖ...εἶναι τοὺς πρεσβυτέρους...σ. τοῦ ἐπισκόπου *Sent.App*.(p.83); Εὐσέβιος...ὁ τῆς τυραννικῆς ὠμότητος σ. Thdt.*h.e*.1.20.1(3.797); τὸν κατ' ἐκεῖνο καιροῦ σ., τὸν...Γαβάλων ἐπίσκοπον Σευηριανόν Cosm.Ind.*top*.10(M. 88.417C); Jo.VI H.*v.Jo.D*.11(M.94.445B); ‡Jo.D.*ep.Thphl*.16(M.95. 368B); **b.** freq. in bad sense, *confederate* τοὺς συμβούλους σου καὶ συμμύστας *Ep.Tib*.(p.79.17); of followers of Arius, Epiph.*haer*. 69.9(p.159.16; M.42.216C); and other heretics σ. καὶ συναιρετικόν Thphn.*chron*.p.319(M.108.772C); of fallen man γέγονας διαβόλου συμμύστης Bas.Sel.*ascens*.2(M.28.1096A).

συμμύω, *shut up, close*; met., *close the eyes to, close oneself against* κακίας ἔρωτι συμμύσασα τὰς φυσικῶς ἐνεσπαρμένας αὐτῇ πρὸς τὸ φωτίζεσθαι δυναμεῖς Dion.Ar.*e.h*.2.3.3(M.3.400A); τοὺς νοεροὺς αὐτῶν ὀφθαλμοὺς ἀνακαθαίρειν τῆς...ἀχλύος, καὶ ἀνακινεῖν...τῷ πολλῷ βάρει τοῦ σκότους συμμεμυκότας id.*d.n*.4.5(M.3.700D).

συμπάθεια, ἡ, 1. *sharing of* or *readiness to share another's feelings, fellow-feeling, sympathy* ἡ...σ. πάθος τινὸς διὰ πάθος ἑτέρου Clem. *exc.Thdot*.30(p.117.1; M.9.673C); **a.** its character; in pleasure, id. *paed*.2.5(p.186.14; M.8.449A); in sorrow, Chrys.*hom.3.4 in Phil*.(11. 217B); pre-eminently a feminine endowment, Clem.*str*.2.23(p.190. 21; M.8.1089B); but dist. from effeminacy, Cyr.*Jo*.7(4.686A); a virtue, Jo.D.*hom*.2.6(M.96.585D); an expression of charity, Gr.Naz. *or*.14.5(M.35.864B); **b.** as between man and man τὸ ἐλεεῖν τινα σ. τις πρὸς τὸ οἰκεῖόν ἐστι γινομένη Adam.*dial*.1.3(p.6.19; M.11.1720C); ἐλεεινοὶ τῆς ἀρρωστίας, τῆς σ. ἐλεεινότεροι Gr.Naz.*or*.14.13(M.35. 873C); Synes.*ep*.139(M.66.1529A); Dor.*doct*.4.7(M.88.1668B); πλέον σου τοῦ τυπτομένου, ἤλγουν τὴν ψυχήν, τῷ τῆς σ. θεσμῷ *V.Pach.Α* 2 (p.125.3); of Moses, Gr.Nyss.*v.Mos*.46(M.44.317A); of Job, Chrys. *hom.28.3 in 1Cor*.(10.254C); of S. Paul, id.*hom.15.5 in Phil*.(11.

319D); pre-eminently of BMV *πηγὴ συμπαθείας* *Lit.Chrys.*(p.354.23); **c.** simulated by Devil, Bas.Sel.*or.*3.3(M.85.56A); **d.** *being sympathetically affected*, of persons *τῶν παίδων...ἐκ τῆς πρὸς τὴν μητέρα σ. βραυκανομένων* Philost.*h.e.*11.6(M.65.600B); for interaction between soul and body v. 2.b; **e.** *instance of sympathy, act of compassion*, Chrysipp.*enc.in Thdr.*(p.68.4); **f.** of God for man, *compassion*, Didym.*Trin.*3.21(M.39.909A); Jo.D.*Man.*1.75(M.94.1753B); **g.** of Christ for man *ἐν μὲν τῷ υἱὸς εἶναι, τὸ ἀπαράλλακτον σώζων πρὸς τὸν πατέρα...ἐν δὲ τῷ φιλοικτίρμων, τὸ εἰς σ. ἀνυπέρβλητον ἐδημοσίευσεν* Procl.CP *or.laud.BMV* 6(p.105.20; M.65.688A); Euthal. Diac.*epp.cath.*(M.85.681A) cit. s. *ἀνεξικακία*; **2.** *affinity*; **a.** *σ.* and *ἀντιπάθεια*, in Democritus, Tat.*orat.*17(p.18.12; M.6.841B); in Apollonius, ‡Just.*qu.et resp.*24(M.6.1272A); **b.** *sympathetic affection, interaction*; of all things in universe, Gr.Nyss.*fat.*(M.45.152C); of soul and body, Athenag.*res.*15(p.66.6,9; M.6.1004B,C); *τὸ σῶμα...τὴν ψυχὴν ἕλκει πρὸς σ. καὶ κοινωνίαν τῶν ἐφ' ἃ κινεῖται πράξεων* *ib.*21(p.74.17; 1016B); *ψυχῆς...ἀπερισπάστου...οὔσης περὶ τὰς τοῦ σώματος σ.* Clem.*paed.*2.9(p.207.25; M.8.496C); *κόσμου ἀναχώρησις...τῆς πρὸς τὸ σῶμα σ. τὴν ψυχὴν ἀπορρῆξαι* Bas.*ep.*2.2(3.71E; M.32.225B); ‡Caes.Naz.*dial.*140(M.38.1056) cit. s. *ἀνακλάω*; **c.** of man with higher things *τοὺς ἀνθρώπους...κατὰ τὸν τῆς ὕλης λόγον καὶ τῆς πρὸς τὰ θεῖα σ. ... κινοῦσαι* Athenag.*leg.*25.3(M.6.949C); *ποιηταὶ...καὶ φιλόσοφοι...κινηθέντες...κατὰ συμπάθειαν τῆς παρὰ τοῦ θεοῦ πνοῆς* *ib.* 7.1(904B); *οὐ γὰρ ἔχουσιν* [sc. those who deify elements] *σ. εἰς τὸν οὐράνιον τόπον* *ib.*22(940B); Dion.Ar.*d.n.*2.9(M.3.648B); with Christ *Χριστῷ προσῳκειώμεθα, καὶ εἰς συγγένειαν διὰ τὸ αἷμα αὐτοῦ...καὶ εἰς σ. διὰ τὴν ἀνατροφὴν τὴν ἐκ τοῦ λόγου* Clem.*paed.*1.6(p.119.23; M.8.308C); **3.** *strong emotion, feeling strongly*, of grief (ref. Mt.15:22) *γυναῖκα...βοῶσαν μετὰ σ. τοσαύτης* Chrys.*hom.52.1 in Mt.*(7.530B); of affection *ὁ μακάριος Ἰὼβ...ἔστη τὰ παλαίσματα...πρὸς παίδων ἀποβολήν, πρὸς γυναικὸς σ. πρὸς σώματος μάστιγας* *ib.33.6*(7.385D); of indignation *οἱ ἀδικούμενοι οὐκ ἂν δύναιντο εἰπεῖν ὑπὲρ ἑαυτῶν ζέοντες τῇ ὀργῇ, καίτοι γε οὐκ ἔστιν ἔγκλημα ἡ σ. αὕτη* id.*hom.44.3 in 1Cor.*(10.411E); Jo.D.*spir.neq.*7(M.95.81B); **4.** *inordinate affection* for, *attachment* to *πᾶσαν ὑπερέκπτωσιν καὶ σ. παραιτουμένους* Clem.*str.*4.13(p.290.4; M.8.1301B); *ἐξορίσαι τῆς ψυχῆς τὴν πρὸς αὐτὰ* [sc. *χρήματα*] *σ.* id.*q.d.s.*11(p.166.27; M.9 om.); *αἱ θλίψεις ἀποσχίζουσιν ἡμᾶς τῆς σ. τῆς πρὸς τὸν παρόντα κόσμον* Chrys.*hom.42.3 in Ac.*(9.322A); id.*hom. 22.3 in Mt.*(7.278B); abs., Mac.Mgn.*apocr.*2.7(p.5.14).

συμπαθ-έω, 1. *be sympathetically affected* *τοῦ πατρὸς...ἐμφύτως καὶ ἀδιδάκτως ἀντιλαμβάνεται πάντα πρὸς πάντων, τὰ μὲν ἄψυχα ~οῦντα τῷ ζῴῳ* Clem.*str.*5.14(p.416.18; M.9.196B); between persons, *have sympathy, sympathize* *εἰ ὡς θεὸν οὐκ ἐδέξασθε, κἂν ὡς ἰατρῷ τούτῳ συνεπαθήσατε* *Ep.Tib.*(p.79.10); *οἱ ζῶντες νῦν δίκαιοι τῶν τελευτησάντων ἀδίκων οὐδαμῶς ~οῦσι* Gr.Mag.*dial.*(tr.Zach.)4.44(M.*PL.*77.406A); *show compassion*, ref. Mt.18:27 *ὁ πονηρὸς δοῦλος, ~ηθεὶς παρὰ τοῦ δεσπότου* Eus.Al.*serm.*21.10(M.86.436B); *Mir.Geo.*5(p.51.3); Jo.Mal.*chron.*5 p.116(M.97.209C); of God with man, Adam. *dial.*1.3(p.6.20ff.; M.11.1720C); *τοῦ θεοῦ...συγγνόντος καὶ ~ήσαντος* Didym.*Trin.*3.3(M.39.808A); of Christ with man [Ps.102:14b] *τουτέστι ~ησον ἡμῖν, ὅτι τὴν ἀσθένειαν τῆς σαρκὸς αὐτοπαθῶς ἐπείρασας* Clem.*paed.*1 8(p.126.28; M.8.325A); Cyr.*Pulch.*37(p.46.30; 5^2.158C); Gnost., of God with aeons, *share the πάθος of* *ὁ γὰρ συνεπάθησεν ὁ πατήρ...ἐνδόσιμον ἑαυτὸν παρασχών...πάθος ἐστίν* Clem.*exc. Thdot.*30(p.116.27; M.9.673C); ref. other heretics *~οῦσαν τῇ τοῦ σωτῆρος σαρκὶ καὶ τὴν αὐτοῦ θεότητα ὁρίζοντες* Dam.*troph.*suppl.(p.280.6); **2.** *have an attachment to* *αἱ περὶ αὐτὸν* [sc. *Πλοῦτον*] *ἐπτοημέναι καὶ ~οῦσαι* Clem.*paed.*3.2(p.242.7; M.8.569C); **3.** pass., *be suffered, be allowed to* *οὐδαμινὸν ἱμάτιον αὐτοῦ μόνον συνεπαθήθη ἆραι* Eus.Al.*serm.*21.12(M.86.437D).

συμπαθής, *ready to share another's feelings, sympathetic; compassionate*; **1.** as between men *ὁ σύμπνους, καὶ σ.· τὸ δὲ σ., καὶ γνήσιον* Gr.Naz.*ep.*216(M.37.352C); *τοὺς οὕτω πενθοῦντας μακαρίζει ὁ κύριος, τοὺς συμπαθεῖς* Chrys.*hom.15.5 in Heb.*(11.319D); of bishop *ὡς ἔμπειρος καὶ σ. ἰατρὸς πάντας ἰώμενος τοὺς ἐν ἁμαρτίαις πεπληγμένους* *Const.App.*2.20.10; *ib.*2.41.5; *τὴν ἐκκλησίαν ἔγνω γινομένην αὐτῷ συμπαθῆ* Synes.*ep.*58(M.66.1401B); neut. as subst., Cyr.*Am.*62(3.319A); id.*Abac.*4(3.519D); **2.** of the image of God in man *οἱ τὴν εἰκόνα τοῦ θεοῦ περιφέροντες...σύνοικον εἰκόνα...σ., ὑπερπαθῆ* Clem. *prot.*4(p.46.18; M.8.157C); **3.** of God, Clem.*paed.*3.1(p.237.7; M.8.557A); *τὸ μὲν ἄρρητον αὐτοῦ πατήρ, τὸ δὲ εἰς ἡμᾶς συμπαθὲς γέγονε μήτηρ* id.*q.d.s.*37(p.184.2; M.9.641C); *ὁ σ. μάλιστα περὶ τὸ πλάσμα τὸ σόν* *Lit.Jac.*(p.200.14); **4.** of Christ *γέγονε δὲ σ. οὐκ ἀπό γε τοῦ πεπειρᾶσθαι, πόθεν· ἦν γὰρ ἐλεήμων φύσει καί ἐστιν ὡς θεός· ἐπειδὴ δὲ μετὰ τοῦ εἶναι ὅ ἐστι, καὶ γέγονε καθ' ἡμᾶς, ἀνθρωποπρεπῶς καὶ ταῦτα λέγεται περὶ αὐτοῦ* Cyr.*Pulch.*37(p.47.7; 5^2.159B).

***συμπαθητέον,** *one must sympathize*, Thdr.Stud.*epp.*2.22(M.99.1188A).

***συμπαθητικός, 1.** *sympathetic, compassionate*, a mark of holiness *φιλόστοργοι ἦσαν οἱ ἅγιοι, καὶ σ.* Chrys.*hom.4.4 in 1Thess.*(11.457A); Marc.Diac.*v.Porph.*8; of S. Paul, Chrys.*hom.13.1 in Phil.*(11.298D); of Christ, Cyr.*Ps.*21:15(M.69.837D); neut. as subst. *τὴν ἀγάπην...καὶ τὸ σ. καὶ τὸ φιλάνθρωπον* Meth.*symp.*11(p.130.10; M.18.205B om.); *τὸ...κηδεμονικόν, τὸ σ., τὸ προστατικόν, τὸ μὴ τὰ ἑαυτοῦ ζητεῖν...πολιτείας ἐστίν, οὐχὶ θαυμάτων* Chrys.*hom.2.4 in Ac.princ.*(3.66D); *τὸ...συνετὸν καὶ σ. καὶ ἐντελὲς τῆς σῆς ἱερωσύνης* Acac.B.*ep. Cyr.*(p.100.9; M.77.101B); *Mir.Artem.*35(p.57.21); **2.** of a mode of death, *merciful* *σ. θανάτῳ τὴν ζωὴν αὐτοῦ ἀπαλλάξωσι* Gr.Mag.*dial.*(tr.Zach.)3.37(M.*PL.*77.311A).

***συμπαθητικῶς,** *with compassion*, ‡Bas.Sel.*or.*38.5(M.85.424C); Thdr.Stud.*epp.*2.109(M.99.1369C).

***συμπαθοπρεπῶς,** *as becomes a sympathizer*, Thdr.Stud.*epp.*2.121(M.99.1396D).

συμπαθῶς, 1. *sympathetically; in sympathy*, Clem.*q.d.s.*35(p.183.5; M.9.640D); **2.** *in pity*, Petr.II Al.*encycl.*1 ap.Thdt.*h.e.*4.22.5(M.33.1277A).

συμπαίκτης, ὁ, 1. *companion*, Pall.*h.Laus.*37(p.109.11; M.34.1180D); **2.** *fellow deceiver, accomplice* in magic, Hipp.*haer.*4.35(p.61.17,25; M.16.3099C).

συμπαίκτρια, ἡ, fem. of *συμπαίκτης*, *fellow deceiver, confederate* in making sport of, Ephr.2.155A.

***συμπαλαμάομαι,** *plan together*; *suggest* or *provide* *μηχανάς*, Synes.*insomn.*14(p.175.11; M.66.1308C).

συμπανηγυρίζ-ω, 1. *celebrate, keep festival with* or *together* *μυριάσιν ἀγγέλων σ.* Clem.*prot.*9(p.62.28; M.8.193B); *σ. τῷ θεῷ* id.*paed.*1.5(p.103.9; M.8.276B); *οἱ δὲ κάτω τῇ ἐπουρανίῳ...~οντες ἔκραζον* ‡Meth.*palm.*2(M.18.388B); **2.** *celebrate, extol* *συμπανηγυρίσατέ μοι περὶ τὸν λόγον κάμνοντι* Gr.Naz.*or.*21.10(M.35.1092C); *Σαββάτιος...Ἰουδαίοις...τὴν τοῦ φόνου ~ει συναίνεσιν* Tim.CP *haer.*(M.86.37B).

***συμπάντιμος,** *alike solemn* *ἡ τῶν κυριοτήτων σ. δοξολογία* Chrysipp.*enc.in Jo.Bapt.*15(p.47.11).

***συμπαραβαίνω,** *join in transgressing* *τοῦ...ἀνθρώπου παραβάντος, καὶ αὐτὰ* [sc. *τὰ θηρία*] *συμπαρέβη* Thphl.Ant.*Autol.*2.17(M.6.1080C).

***συμπαραβάλλω,** fig., *place alongside, range with*, Ephr.3.318A.

συμπαραγί(γ)νομαι, *arrive* or *be present at the same time*, Meth. *symp.*11(p.137.10; M.18.213B).

***συμπαραγράφ-ω, 1.** *write alongside* (either in space or time) *Μωϋσῆς...τῇ Γενέσει συμπαραγράψας τὴν Ἔξοδον* Gr.Nyss.*hom.6 in Eccl.*(M.44.701B); **2.** *express at the same time* *οἱ τὰς εἰκόνας τῶν κρατούντων κατασκευάζοντες...τῇ περιβολῇ τῆς πορφυρίδος τὴν βασιλικὴν ἀξίαν ~ουσι* Gr.Nyss.*hom.opif.*4(M.44.136C); **3.** *record with, register together* *κοινωνὸς τῆς προφητείας ~εται ὁ Ἀμώς* [i.e. father of Isaiah] †Bas.*Is.*255(1.574C; M.30.568D); **4.** *subjoin, add* *ταῖς εἰκόσι ~ων τοὺς δαίμονας* Gr.Naz.*or.*4.81(M.35.608A).

***συμπαραδέχ-ομαι,** *accept, include at the same time* *ὅ τε γὰρ θεὸν ἀκούσας, ὅσα περὶ θεοῦ πρέπει νοεῖν, διὰ τῆς προσηγορίας ταύτης συμπαρεδέξατο* Gr.Nyss.*Apoll.*50(M.45.1244D); id.*Eun.*3(2 p.23.31; M.45.589A); *πατρὶ καὶ υἱῷ ~εσθαι τὸ πνεῦμα τὸ ἅγιον* Max.*ambig.*(M.91.1261A).

συμπαραδίδω-μι, *join in betraying* *ὁ...ταύτας* [sc. *τὰς καθολικὰς νηστείας*] *λύων ~σι τὸν σωτῆρα καὶ συνσταυροῖ* ‡Pall.*h.mon.*8.58(p.48.23; M.34.1148B).

***συμπαραζεύγνυμι,** *yoke together*; met., *associate, join* *διὰ τί τὰ φαῦλα τῇ ἡμετέρᾳ ζωῇ συμπαρέζευκται*; ‡Just.*qu.et resp.*46(M.6.1292B,C); Gr.Nyss.*deit.*(M.46.560A); *συμπαρέζευκται τῇ περὶ τοῦ πατρὸς γνώσει καὶ ἡ περὶ τοῦ υἱοῦ* Cyr.*hom.div.*1(p.96.5; 5^2.350C).

***συμπαραίτιος,** *being in part the cause*, Cyr.*Juln.*4(6^2.147D).

***συμπαρακάθημαι,** *sit beside*, Mac.Mgn.*apocr.*3.12(p.82.14).

συμπαρακαλ-έω, *plead together* *εὐχόμενος* [sc. *ὁ υἱός*] *ὑπὲρ τῶν εὐχομένων καὶ ~ῶν τοῖς παρακαλοῦσιν* Or.*or.*10(p.320.22; M.11.445D); Petr.I Al.*ep.can.*11(M.18.496C); *Hom.Clem.*13.9.

***συμπαράκλητος, ὁ,** *co-advocate* *αὐτοῦ τοῦ κυρίου παρακλήτου ὄντος καὶ τοῦ πνεύματος τοῦ ἁγίου σ. ὄντος ὁμοίως* Epiph.*haer.*74.13(p.331.9; M.42.500B).

***συμπαραληπτός,** *acceptable*, Or.*Cels.*7.42(p.193.15; M.11.1481B).

συμπαράληψις, ἡ, 1. *calling in*; met., *inclusion*, Evagr.Pont.*ep.*3(M.32.252B); *Const.App.*3.17.2; **2.** *combination* *αἱ ὑποστάσεις συνθέσει φύσεων καὶ ἰδιωμάτων συμπαραλήψει ὑφίστανται* Leont.H. *monoph.*61(M.86.1804B).

***συμπαραμαρτυρέω,** *bear witness together* with *εἰ ὁ ἀγαθὸς βίος σ. τῇ πίστει* Thdr.Stud.*catech.parv.*29(p.71).

***συμπαραμετρέω,** *take relative measurements*; **1.** *measure* one *by* another, Or.*princ*.1.6.2(p.81.2; M.11.167A); **2.** pass., *become a standard of measurement*, Bas.*Spir*.71(3.60C; M.32.200C).

συμπαραναλίσκω, *destroy at the same time*, Bas.*ep*.227(3.350C; M. 32.853A).

συμπαρανήχομαι, *swim together alongside* in the air, i.e. *fly together alongside*, Bas.Sel.*or*.22.1(M.85.264C).

συμπαραπέμπω, *hand on* or *transmit along with*, Bas.Sel.*v.Thecl*. 1(M.85.524C).

***συμπαραπολαύ-ω,** *enjoy, experience together, share* ἵνα μὴ ∼σῃ τῆς ὀργῆς τοῦ θεοῦ Bas.*reg.br*.164(2.470C; M.31.1192A).

***συμπαρασπείρω,** *intersperse* τῇ ἱστορίᾳ τὸ δόγμα τῆς θεολογίας μυστικῶς συμπαρέσπαρται Bas.*hex*.6.2(1.51B; M.29.120D).

συμπαρατείν-ω, 1. act.; **a.** trans., *stretch out alongside*, met. (ref. Jo.1:1) ∼ει τῷ ἀπείρῳ τὸ ἄπειρον Gr.Nyss.*Eun*.4(2 p.54.16; M.45. 624D); **b.** intrans., *extend, reach out as far as* ἡ τοῦ μετέχοντος ἐπιθυμία τῷ ἀορίστῳ ∼ουσα id.*v.Mos*.7(M.44.301B) ∾ ‡Caes.Naz.*dial*. 171(M.38.1136) cit. s. συμπαρεκτείνω; **2.** act., *fit, conform* ἐπιχειρήσας ∼ειν τὸν λόγον τοῖς φάσμασιν Synes.*insomn*.18(p.184.6; M.66.1316C); *ib*.17(p.180.14; 1313A); **3.** pass. intrans.; **a.** *be co-extensive* with, *extend concurrently* with, †Bas.*Is*.226(1.550C; M.30.513B); *ib*.31 (404C; M.180B); Bas.*hom.in Ps*.14(1.354A; M.29.256A); esp. of time in rel. to change, Gr.Nyss.*hom.6 in Eccl*.(M.44.700C); id.*Eun*.9(2 p.214.8; M.45.812D); *ib*.8(2 p.198.24; 793D); **b.** *extend, reach out* καὶ ἀρχὴν αὐτοῦ τινα τῆς συστάσεως βλέπειν καὶ πρὸς τὸ μέσον ὁρᾶν καὶ πρὸς τὸ πέρας ταῖς ἐλπίσι ∼εσθαι *ib*.(2 p.198.28; 793D); **4.** med., *stretch* (i.e. exert) oneself, *strain* along with οὕτω γὰρ ἂν καὶ πασχούσης τῆς σαρκός, τὸν λόγον ὀδυνᾶσθαι...καὶ ταῖς ἐνεργείαις αὐτῇ ∼εσθαι Leont.H.*Nest*.1.14(M.86.1456C).

συμπαρατρέχ-ω, *run alongside* with; met., *be concurrent* with τῷ χρόνῳ σ. Bas.*hex*.9.2(1.81C; M.29.189C); ἡ...εὐχὴ πασῶν τῶν ἐντολῶν ἀφετηρία τις ὑπάρχει, ∼ειν τῷ οἰκείῳ κόσμῳ πάσας καταναγκάζουσα ‡Chrys.*hom.suppl*.6.2(M.64.461C).

συμπαρεδρεύ-ω, *pertain* to τὸ...ἁμαρτάνειν τῷ φθαρτῷ κόσμῳ... ∼ει *cat.Apoc*.9:6(p.315.30).

***συμπαρεισάγ-ω,** *introduce together* with τῇ τῶν προσηγοριῶν οἰκειότητι·καὶ τὸ κατ' οὐσίαν οἰκεῖον ∼εται Gr.Nyss.*Eun*.3(2 p.30.20; M.45.596C).

συμπαρεισέρχομαι, *enter along with, find one's way in with*; met., of notions, Gr.Nyss.*Eun*.9(2 p.213.28; M.45.812C); *ib*.8(2 p.203.2; 800B).

***συμπαρεισκρίνω,** *supply* words to a text, Gr.Agr.*Eccl*.1.16(M.98. 793A).

συμπαρεκτείν-ω, A. act.; **1.** trans., *extend as far as, extend at the same time* to ὥστε ὅλῃ σχεδὸν ἀνθρώπου γενεᾷ τὴν ἐκ τοῦ μίσους ὀργὴν συμπαρεκτεῖναι Bas.*ep*.204.1(3.303A; M.32.745A); τῇ...ἀπειρίᾳ ∼ων σου τοῦ ποθοῦντος τὴν κίνησιν Max.*opusc*.(M.91.9A); *unfold, put forth at the same time* τῇ τοῦ σώματος ἡλικίᾳ ∼ειν τὰ ἑαυτοῦ Cyr.*schol.inc*. 13(5^{1}.789A); ∼εται ἀνθρώποις ὁ βίος ἐν ἐνιαυτοῖς, ἐν μησίν...τούτοις ἄρα ἐχρῆν καὶ ἡμᾶς ∼ειν τὰς ἐναρέτους ἐργασίας Hesych.S.*temp*.2.58(M.93. 1529Df.); **2.** intrans., of time, *stretch out, endure as long as*, ref. Ps. 2:7 ὁ ∼ων τῇ...ἀϊδίῳ αὐτοῦ ζωῇ...χρόνος ἡμέρα ἐστὶν αὐτῷ σήμερον Or.*Jo*.1.29(32; p.37.9; M.14.77D).

B. pass.; **1.** be stretched alongside in order to *be compared* τί καινὸν τοῦ μονογενοῦς ἐνοήσατε ἢ πρᾶγμα ἢ νόημα, ὃ τῷ πατρὶ ∼όμενον περισσοτέραν αὐτοῦ τὴν ζωὴν τοῦ μονογενοῦς ἀποδείκνυσι; Gr.Nyss. *Eun*.1(1 p.199.18; M.45.445C); **2.** *be coextensive with, extend alike to* τοσοῦτοι [sc. φωστῆρες]...ὡς...πᾶσι τοῖς οὖσι ∼εσθαι Proc.G.*Gen*. 1:16(M.87.100A); met. τῷ μέτρῳ τῆς πολιτείας ἡ γνῶσις συμπαρεκταθήσεται Andr.Caes.*Apoc*.39(M.106.341C); of the mind's action ἐν τῷ χωρισμῷ αὐτῶν ∼ομένη οὐ διακόπτεται Gr.Nyss.*anim.et res*.(M. 46.48B); ἀκάθαρτοι λογισμοὶ ∼ονται πολλοῖς πράγμασι †Nil.*mal.cog*.26 (M.79.1232A); ἡ τοῦ μετέχοντος ἐπιθυμία τῷ ἀορίστῳ συμπαραθέουσα καὶ ∼ομένη ‡Caes.Naz.*dial*.171(M.38.1136) ∾ Gr.Nyss.*v.Mos*.7(M. 44.301B) cit. s. συμπαρατείνω; with stress on limitation, *extend (only) as far as, be extended within* διαστηματικῇ τινι παρατάσει ∼εται [sc. ἡ κτιστὴ οὐσία] Gr.Nyss.*Eun*.12(1 p.235.31; M.45.933A); **c.** theol. τὰ...θεῖα θελήματα...τῇ θείᾳ ἀπειρίᾳ ∼όμενα ‡Proc.G.*Pr*. 4:12(M.87.1256D); of divine presence in creation παντὶ...καὶ ὅλῳ τῷ κόσμῳ ∼όμενος [sc. Christ as God] Or.*Jo*.6.30(15; p.140.12; M. 14.252D); ἴδιόν ἐστι τῆς θεότητος τὸ διὰ πάντων ἥκειν καὶ τῇ φύσει τῶν ὄντων κατὰ πᾶν μέρος ∼εσθαι Gr.Nyss.*or.catech*.32(p.118.12; M.45. 80D); Christol. οὐ ∼ομένης τῆς σαρκὸς αὐτοῦ τῇ ἀπεριγράπτῳ αὐτοῦ θεότητι Jo.D.*f.o*.3.7(M.94.1012B); **3.** freq. in rel. to time; **a.** *endure as long as, extend concurrently with*, ref. 1Cor.8:13 τὸ...∼όμενον τῇ συστάσει τῆς ζωῆς αὐτοῦ, αἰῶνα ὠνόμασεν Or.*exp.in Pr*.10:30(M.17. 189A); ὅπερ ἡμῖν ὁ χρόνος...τοῦτο τοῖς ἀϊδίοις, αἰών, τὸ ∼όμενον τοῖς οὖσιν, οἷόν τι χρονικὸν κίνημα Gr.Naz.*or*.38.8(M.36.320B); *ib*.45.4 (628C); τῷ παντὶ αἰῶνι ∼ομένην...τὴν τιμωρίαν Chrys.*hom.27.10 in Gen*.(4.149A); **b.** *persist for as long* ὁ θεὸς τοῦ χρόνου τῆς ζωῆς αὐτῶν ὑπετέμετο· ἵνα μὴ εἰς χρόνον μακρὸν παραμένοντες, ∼ωνται τῇ κακίᾳ Thdt.*Is*.26:14(2.296); theol. τῇ ἑαυτοῦ ἀϊδιότητι ∼ομένην ἔχει τὴν... πατρότητα Bas.*Eun*.2.12(1.247B; M.29.593B); *ib*.2.13(248B; M.596B).

C. med., *stretch* (i.e. exert) *oneself, strain* ἀντιφιλοτιμούμενον καὶ ∼όμενον κατὰ τὸ δυνατόν Or.*comm.in Eph*.1:8(p.239).

***συμπαρενύλησις, ἡ,** *equation with the material* (as result of Fall) τῆς σὺν θεῷ...τιμῆς τὴν μετὰ τῶν ἀνοήτων κτηνῶν ἄτιμον ἀντιλαβεῖν σ. Max.*ambig*.(M.91.1348A).

συμπαρέρχ-ομαι, 1. intrans.; **a.** *pass (through) together* with εἰ τέτοκεν ἄνθρωπον συμπαρελθόντος αὐτῷ τοῦ θεοῦ λόγου, ἀλλ' οὐ διὰ τοῦτο θεοτόκος Nest.*fr*.D 1(p.352.12)ap.Cyr.*Nest*.1.4(p.24.25; 6^{1}.18E); cf.id.*fr*.C 11(p.277.25)*ib*.(p.18.26; 10B); **b.** *pass away together* with, ref. 1Cor.7:31 ἐπειδὰν...τοῦτο παρέλθοι τὸ σχῆμα, συμπαρελεύσεται αὐτῷ καὶ ὁ ἥλιος Eus.*fr.Lc*.21:28(M.24.600B); **2.** trans., *pass by as well, leave on one side also* ὁ ὑπερβὰς τὸν υἱὸν τῇ πολυπραγμοσύνῃ καὶ τὴν περὶ τοῦ πατρὸς ἔννοιαν ∼εται Gr.Nyss.*Eun*.9(2 p.222.3; M.45. 821A).

***συμπαρθενεύειν,** *practise celibacy together*, ‡Pall.*h.mon*.29.1(p.90. 14).

συμπαρίπταμαι, *fly alongside*, Gr.Naz.*or*.12.5(M.35.849A).

συμπαρίστ-ημι, intrans., stand beside so as to *assist* θεοῦ ∼αμένου ταῦτα ἀνύεται Or.*princ*.3.1.19(p.232.4; M.11.289B); ἐπεύχεται ὁ ἱερεὺς τοῖς ∼αμένοις *Lit.Jac*.(p.184.25).

συμπαροδεύ-ω, *travel together with*, Gr.Nyss.*hom.opif*.30.12(M.44. 245A); met., *accompany in one's course* ἡ...μακαρία ζωὴ ἅτε μηδενὸς ∼οντος αὐτῇ διαστήματος τὸ διαμετροῦν καὶ διαλαμβάνον οὐκ ἔχει id. *Eun*.1(1 p.128.27; M.45.365B).

***συμπαροικέω,** *live as an alien together* with βαρβάρῳ Geo.Pis. *carm*.2.32(p.5).

συμπαρομαρτ-έω, *go along with, accompany*; of statements, *follow*, Cyr.*ador*.7(1.235A); theol., of H. Ghost ᾧ [sc. Χριστῷ] παρῆν, οὐχ ὡς ἐνεργοῦν, ἀλλ' ὡς ὁμοτίμῳ ∼οῦν Gr.Naz.*or*.41.11(M.36.444B); πνεῦμα...θεοῦ, τὸ ∼οῦν τῷ λόγῳ Jo.D.*f.o*.1.7(M.94.805A,B); cf.Thdt. *qu.20 in Gen*.(1.28).

***συμπαρομαρτυρέω,** ? error for συμπαρομαρτέω, Cyr.*glaph.Gen*.3 (1.84D).

συμπαρορμάω, *press forward together*, Eus.*Ps*.24:10(M.23.228C).

***συμπαρυφίστημι,** *exist alongside*, c. dat., Gr.Agr.*Eccl*.1.5(M.98. 769C); Thdr.Stud.*antirr*.3.4.12(M.99.433B).

συμπάσχ-ω, 1. *undergo the same suffering*, Ign.*Polyc*.6.1; **2.** *suffer with* ∼ομεν...τοῖς πάσχουσιν ἀδελφοῖς ἡμῶν, καὶ τὰ ἐκείνων παθήματα ἴδια ἡγούμεθα CSard.*ep.Alex*.ap.Ath.*apol.sec*.38(p.117.21; M.25.316B); of martyrs τῷ κυρίῳ, ᾧ καὶ συνέπαθον Polyc.*ep*.9.2; theol. ὡς καλεῖσθαι [sc. Callistus] πατέρα καὶ υἱὸν ἕνα θεόν...καὶ οὕτως τὸν πατέρα συμπεπονθέναι τῷ υἱῷ Hipp.*haer*.9.12(p.249.8; M. 16.3386A); not directly applicable to the divine nature of Christ, Eus.Em.*fr.dogm*.1(M.86.540Ef.); ∼ει δὲ τῇ σαρκί, ἵνα τὸ πάθος εἰς τὴν θεότητα λογισθῇ, μὴ πασχούσης τῆς θεότητος Epiph.*haer*.69.24 (p.174.24; M.42.241A); id.*inc*.1(p.227.25; M.41.273C) cit. s. ἀπαθής; συμμένοντα, ἀλλ' οὐχὶ συμπαθόντα τὸν λόγον λέγω Eulog.*palm*.8(M. 86.2925A).

συμπαταγέω, *strike together, collide*; of clouds, ‡Nil.*narr*.6(M.79. 656C).

***συμπατήρ, ὁ,** *fellow Father, another Father* (i.e. of Church) οὐ... τοῖς σ. ὁ πατὴρ μάχεται Jo.D.*imag*.2.18(M.94.1305A).

συμπαχύν-ω, pass., *become materialized in* τὴν...ἀλήθειαν... ἀσωμάτως ἐμφαίνουσα, μὴ ∼ομένην ταῖς φωναῖς ἢ τοῖς σώμασιν Max. *ambig*.(M.91.1244B).

***συμπεινάω,** *share hunger* with, *Hom.Clem*.13.18; of Christ with mankind, Or.*sel.in Ezech*.4:9(M.13.781A).

συμπείρω, *pierce through together*, perf. ptcpl. pass. συμπεπαρμένος, τὸ σῶμα *weak, debilitated, ruined in health*, Isch.*libell*.(p.18. 30; H.2.328D); Marc.Diac.*v.Porph*.100.

***συμπελάζω,** *come next* to, c. dat.; of letters in a word, Cyr.*syn. def*.1(M.76.1421B).

***συμπελεκάω,** *hew*, Or.*Jo*.10.39(23; p.217.13; M.14.384B).

***συμπελτάζομαι,** *serve as a targeteer together* with, Synes.*regn*.13 (p.25.11; M.66.1073A).

***συμπένης,** *companion in poverty*, Gr.Naz.*or*.14.1(M.35.857).

***συμπενθερά, ἡ,** *the husband's mother in relation to the wife's mother* or vice versa, ‡Jo.Jej.*poenit*.(M.88.1893D).

συμπεραίνω, *conclude, finish* τῆς ἐπιστολῆς τὴν προγραφὴν σ. Thdr.Mops.*Eph*.1:1f.(p.118.24); ὁ...προφήτης ἐνταῦθα τὴν πρώτην σ.

ὅρασιν Thdt.*Is.*1:31(p.12.16); med. σ. λόγον Clem.*str.*4.1(p.248.8; M.8.1216A); Ast.Am.*hom.*8(M.40.293C).

συμπεραίωσις, ἡ, *conclusion, sum* τοῦ βίου Clem.*str.*4.21(p.306.2; M.8.1341A); πίστις μήτηρ καὶ στεφάνη καὶ σ. τῶν ἀρετῶν ὑπάρχει †Max.*loc.comm.*51(M.91.952A).

***συμπέρανσις**, ἡ, *accomplishment*, Eus.*d.e.*9.1(p.405.27; M.22.653C).

συμπέρασμα, τό, **1.** *completion, accomplishment, realization* πάσης ἀγαθῆς ἡ καταρχὴ πράξεως ἐν τῇ ἡμετέρᾳ βουλῇ τὴν ὑπόστασιν κέκτηται, τὸ δὲ σ. ἐν τῷ θεῷ Meth.*fr.mart.*2(p.520.7); πᾶν...ἁμάρτημα ...τὸ σ. κτᾶται διὰ τῆς σαρκός id.*res.*2.4(p.336.9; M.41.1169A); v. συγκέρασμα; of new in rel. to old dispensation σ. ... προφητείας τῷ Δαβὶδ κεχρησμένης...πεπληρωμένης...ἐπὶ τοῦ σωτῆρος Eus.*qu.Steph.*15.4(M.22.932B); τὸ σ. τῆς...συμβολικῆς λατρείας id.*h.e.*1.3.4(M.20.69B); of BMV χαίροις, τὸ τῆς παλαιᾶς καὶ καινῆς διαθήκης σ. ‡Jo.D.*hom.*5(M.96.649B); **2.** *accomplished work, achievement* τὸ τῆς τελειοτάτης ἑνώσεως παρακολουθήσειν σ. Thds.Imp.*ep.Jo.Ant.*(p.3.13; M.77.1460A); τῶν...δημιουργῶν ἐπὶ τῆς ἴσης ἐπιστήμης τὸ ἰσοσχέδιον τοῦ σ. φανεροῦσθαι πέφυκεν ἐπὶ τὸ τοῦ ἀνθρώπου πρόσωπον Gel.Cyz.*h.e.*2.21.5(M.85.1284C); **3.** *consummation* ἐν αὐτῷ πάσας ἀρχάς, πάντα σ. Dion.Ar.*d.n.*5.8(M.3.824B); of the age, Gr.Naz.*carm.*1.2.34.252(M.37.963A); ἐπὶ...τοῦ σταυροῦ, ὅπου τὸ σ. τῆς πάσης οἰκονομίας Mac.Mgn.*apocr.*3.14(p.92.13); ὁ δὲ καλῶν τοῦδε σ. τῆς δικαιοσύνης ἐν τῷ Κύρῳ μὴ ἱσταμένου ἐπὶ τὴν αὐτοδικαιοσύνην Χριστὸν ὁ λόγος ἀνάγεται Proc.G.*Is.*41:1ff.(M.87.2349A, v.l. συγκέρασμα).

***συμπεραστικός**, *syllogistic*, Gr.Nyss.*Eun.*11(2 p.258.25; M.45.865C).

συμπεριάγω, *carry about along with* or *together*; intrans., *go about together*, Chrys.*hom.14.8 in Rom.*(9.587E).

***συμπεριαιρέω**, *remove, do away with at the same time*, Thdr.Stud.*epp.*2.8(M.99.1133C); *ib.*2.17(1169D).

***συμπεριακολουθέω**, *follow about*, Chrys.*hom.14.8 in Rom.*(conj. Gaume for -παρακολουθῶν 9.587E).

συμπεριγράφ-ω, **1.** *include*; *embrace*, Clem.*str.*6.15(p.491.31; M.9.344A); *ib.*8.7(p.93.26; 588B); Meth.*symp.*3.2(p.28.24; M.18.61D); Thdr.Stud.*epp.*2.67(M.99.1296B); **2.** med., *limit oneself to*, ‡Proc.G.*Pr.*5:20(M.87.1268A); pass., *be limited to, coincide with* ~ομένων, φησί, τοῖς ἔργοις τῶν ἐνεργειῶν...ἡ δὲ τοῦ ~εσθαι λέξις δηλοῖ τὸ ἰσοστάσιον τῆς ἀποτελεσθείσης οὐσίας πρὸς τὴν ὑποστήσασαν δύναμιν Gr.Nyss.*Eun.*1(1 p.92.22ff.; M.45.325A); *ib.*(1 p.125.27; 361C); Bas.Sel.*or.*14.1(M.85.181C); ref. the Word with human nature συγκλειόμενον ἀλλ' οὐ ~όμενον Eulog.*palm.*8(M.86.2925B).

***συμπεριειλημμένως**, *comprehensively, inclusively*, Epiph.*haer.*76.53(p.409.6; M.42.629B).

συμπεριέρχ-ομαι, *go round with*; met., *associate oneself* with; *be connected* with [Rom.12:16] τουτέστιν, εἰς τὴν ἐκείνων εὐτέλειαν κατάβηθι, συμπεριφέρου, ~ου Chrys.*hom.22.2 in Rom.*(9.681C); τὴν ἰδίαν τῆς ψυχῆς κατασκευὴν...πῶς ~εται μετὰ τοῦ σώματος; Hier.H.*Trin.*(M.40.856A).

συμπεριέχω, **1.** *include* or *embrace jointly in common with another* οὔτε ὁ γεννητὸς οὐ σ. τῷ πατρὶ τὸ ἀΐδιον Epiph.*haer.*76.49(p.404.2; M.42.620D); **2.** pass., *be embraced* or *contained*, e.g. in a definition where not expressly mentioned διὰ τὸ συμπεριέχεσθαι αὐτὸ τῷ θεῷ, οὗ πνεῦμα τυγχάνει ὄν Didym.*Trin.*1.36(M.39.440B); Dion.Ar.*d.n.*7.2(M.3.868B); τῷ ὀνόματι τῆς ἐμῆς φαμιλίας καὶ ἡ νύμφη μου σ. Ath. Scholast.*coll.*9.11(p.106).

συμπεριΐπταμαι, *fly, rush around with* συμπεριϊπτάμενος [sc. Τιμόθεος] Παύλῳ τὴν οἰκουμένην Chrys.*ep.*4.3(3.574E).

συμπερικλεί-ω, pass., *be limited together, share one's limitations* τὸν νοῦν...τὸν μηδαμῶς τοῖς σώμασιν ἀλλήλων διαιρουμένοις τοπικῶς, συνδιαιρούμενον ἢ ~όμενον Max.*ep.*8(M.91.440C).

σαμπεριλαμβάνω, **1.** *gather, embrace*; of Christ on Cross ἵνα... συμπεριλάβῃ...τὰ τῆς οἰκουμένης πέρατα πρὸς ἑαυτόν Or.*fr.552 in Mt.*(p.226); **2.** ref. Inc., *assume*, Epiph.*anc.*75(p.95.7; M.43.157C) cit. s. ἄνθρωπος; id.*exp.fid.*15(p.516.6; M.42.812A) cit. s. ἐνανθρωπέω; εὐδόκησεν ὁ θεός, ὅτι κατελθὼν...συμπεριέλαβε τὴν φύσιν σου τὴν λογικήν, τὴν σάρκα τὴν ἐκ τῆς γῆς, καὶ συνεκέρασε τῷ θείῳ αὐτοῦ πνεύματι Mac.Aeg.*hom.*32.6(M.34.737B); **3.** *include, imply* what is not explicitly stated ὠνόμασας υἱόν, συμπεριείληφας τῇ διανοίᾳ τὴν τριάδα Epiph.*anc.*10(p.18.12; M.43.36A); αὐτὸ οὐδαμοῦ τέθεικε...συμπεριέλαβε δὲ αὐτό, καὶ...φανερῶς αὐτὸ οὐκ εἶπεν Chrys.*hom.7.2 in Heb.*(12.74A); **4.** ? in pass. sense, *be understood* οἱ ποιμένες εὐθέως ἐν ἐκείνῃ τῇ νυκτὶ...ἀπήεσαν...οἱ δὲ μάγοι συμπεριλαβόντος ἔτους δευτέρου Or.*fr.23 in Mt.*(p.25.9)

***συμπεριληπτικός**, *comprehensive, inclusive*, Epiph.*haer.*69.56(p.203.30; M.42.289D).

***συμπερίλυπος**, *sad together* or *very sad* πάντες σ. γεγονότες *A.*(*Pass.*)*Andr.*B 3(p.7.26; cf.M.2.1221B).

***συμπερινήχ-ομαι**, *swim* or *float around together*; met., *go with* ἀνθρωπίνας τέχνας...ὧν ἡ χρῆσις...τῷ παντὶ ~εται βίῳ Bas.Sel.*or.*14.1 M.85.181C).

***συμπεριορίζω**, *fix the same limit for*; pass., *be limited to*, ‡Gr. Nyss.*Ar.et Sab.*4(M.45.1285D).

συμπεριπλέκω, pass., *be connected with*, Tat.*orat.*13(p.14.31; M.6.836A); Eus.*d.e.*7.1(p.310.22; M.22.508C); Epiph.*haer.*21.2(p.239.24; M.41.288A).

συμπεριπολ-έω, *go round together with*; hence *converse with, associate with* ἄλλους μετὰ ἄλλων θεῶν ~οῦντας τῶν ἀγαθῶν ἀνδρῶν Hipp.*haer.*1.19(p.21.20; M.16.3044B); Nil.*spir.mal.*7(M.79.1152C); Aen.*dial.*(M.85.880A); ψυχαὶ ἐν σώματι...μηκέτι δυνάμεναι ~εῖν τῇ ὑπερκοσμίῳ τελευτῇ ‡Caes.Naz.*dial.*149(M.38.1100).

συμπερισπάω, *distract also* or *at the same time*, Thal.*cent.*2.42(M.91.1441B).

συμπεριστρέφω, *turn round, convert*; ? *silence* an uproar, Geo.Pis. *carm.*106.2(p.66).

***συμπερισύρω**, *drag about* with, Gr.Nyss.*Eun.*1(1 p.191.10; M.45.436D).

***συμπεριτέμνω**, pass., *be circumcised together* with, Tim.III Al. *fr.*(p.316.2; M.86.268B).

***συμπεριτορνέω**, *turn* as in a lathe; met., *turn into*, c. dat., ‡Caes.Naz.*dial.*140(M.38.1053).

συμπεριφέρ-ω, *carry round with* or *together*; pass.; **1.** *revolve with*; met., *be carried away* ἀνοήτως ~όμεθα μὲν τοῖς ἀσεβέσι, μᾶλλον δὲ καὶ ἀντιπεριφερόμεθα παντὶ ἀνέμῳ τῆς διδασκαλίας Leont.H. *monoph.*(M.86.1812C); **2.** *have intercourse, converse with one* παρακαλῶ...πρὸς ἑαυτοὺς συμπεριενεχθῆναι *Pers.*(p.29.10); **3.** *accommodate* or *adapt oneself* to, *agree* τούτῳ [sc. Heracleon] κατὰ τὴν ἐκδοχὴν ταύτην ~όμενός τις καὶ ἐκκλησιαστικός Or.*Jo.*13.44(p.270.28; M.14.477B); **4.** *show indulgence, make allowances* ~όμενοι τῇ ἀκεραιότητι αὐτῶν Meth.*res.*1.20(p.242.9; M.41.1088C); freq. with τῇ ἀσθενείᾳ etc., Clem.*str.*2.16(p.151.17; M.8.1012A); Or.*comm.in Mt.*14.23(p.339.13; M.13.1244C); Bas.*ep.*113(3.206B; M.32.525D); Nil.*epp.*3.243(M.79.501A); Gr.Ant.*bapt.*2.11(M.88.1864B); abs., Clem.*paed.*2.10(p.221.12; M.8.525A).

συμπεριφορά, ἡ, *accommodation* in human relationships, *consideration* τῆς ἀνδρῶν πρὸς γυναῖκας σ. Euthal.Diac.*epp.cath.*(M.85.681A); in Christian teaching and practice, *diplomacy* (ref. 1Cor. 9:22) τοῖς πᾶσι...πάντα γίγνεσθαι ὁμολογεῖ, κατὰ συμπεριφορὰν σώζων τὰ κύρια τῶν δογμάτων, ἵνα πάντας κερδήσῃ Clem.*str.*6.15(p.494.15; M.9.348B); τί ἄτοπον τοὺς ἀποστόλους ἐν Ἰουδαίοις ποιουμένους τὰς διατριβάς, κἂν τὰ πνευματικὰ νοῶσι τοῦ νόμου, χρῆσθαι τῇ σ., ὡς καὶ Παῦλος Τιμόθεον περιτεμών Or.*comm.in Mt.*11.8(p.46.32; M.13.925D); ref. Inc. διὰ τοῦ χρέω προκυροῖ ἑαυτῷ πᾶσαν τὴν νομὴν τῶν ἐπιγείων, καὶ διὰ βραχείας συμπεριφορᾶς, κύριος πάντων γίνεται, οὐ μόνον ὡς δημιουργός, ἀλλὰ καὶ ὡς λυτρωτής Ephr.2.271E; cf. συγκατάβασις.

***συμπεριφορικῶς**, *complaisantly, courteously*, Max.*ep.*7(M.91.436A); id.*ambig.*(M.91.1265D).

***συμπεριχέω**, pass., *be poured over* (*one*) *together with* συμπεριεχεῖτο τῷ ἐλαίῳ τὸ πνεῦμα τῆς χάριτος Bas.Sel.*or.*26.1(M.85.301B).

***συμπεριψηφίζομαι**, *forbear* with μακροθυμοῦντες...συμπεριεψηφίσθημεν αὐτοῖς CCP(360)*ep.*ap.Thdt.*h.e.*2.28.5(3.900).

συμπήγνυμι, **1.** *put together, compact, frame*; pass., of Christ's body, Bas.*Spir.*12(3.9E; M.32.85C) cit. s. θεοφόρος; **2.** *make solid, condense*; hence **a.** *establish, set up* μοναχικὰ συμπήγνυσθαι παλαιστήρια Isid.Pel.*epp.*1.262(M.78.340B); met., in health πάρετον ἐπὶ κλίνης...ἄνθρωπον λόγῳ συμπήξας Mac.Mgn.*apocr.*2.8(p.10.5); **b.** *establish, fix fast* συμπεπῆχθαι τὸν ἥλιον...ἐν τῷ οὐρανῷ Diod. *Gen.*1:17(M.33.1564A).

σύμπηξις, ἡ, **1.** *putting together, framing*, esp. of the body, ref. resurrection of body τῆς σκηνοπηγίας...τουτέστι τῆς τῶν σωμάτων σ. ...λελυμένης...τῆς φθορᾶς Cyr.*Jo.*3.4(4.270B); id.*ador.*17(1.619E); ref. Inc. (ref. Ex.40:2) ἡ ἀνισταμένη σκηνὴ τὸ ἅγιον σῶμα σημαίνει Χριστοῦ καὶ...τὴν σ. τοῦ τιμίου σκήνους αὐτοῦ id.*Jo.*4.4(386A); ἡ τοῦ σώματος σ. ἐκ πανάγνων αἱμάτων παρθενικῶν ‡Cyr.*Trin.*14(6^3.20D; M.77.1152A); **2.** met., *solidarity, unity* τῆς τοῦ λαοῦ...σ. Gr.Naz.*or.*42.25(M.36.488C).

συμπιλέω, *condense* συνεπίλησεν τὸν οὐρανὸν ἄνωθεν ἀπείροις ὕδασιν, ἵνα ἡ αὐγὴ στενουμένη κάτω πέμπηται Sever.*creat.*2.4 ap. Cosm.Ind.*top.*10(M.88.421C; ἐπίλησε M.56.443); *solidify*, ref. Mt. 14:25 θεοῦ...συμπιλῆσαι ὕδωρ Max.*schol.ep.*4(M.4.533C).

συμπίλησις, ἡ, *compression*; **a.** *condensation*, Gr.Nyss.*hex.*34(M.

44.93D); id.*Eun*.3(2 p.15.2; M.45.577D); **b.** *solidification, becoming concrete*, *ib*.8(2 p.186.11; 780C).

συμπίνω, perf. pass.; met., *be swallowed up, absorbed* πάθει ἐπιθυμίας συμπέποται Serap.*Man*.8(p.32; M.18.905D).

συμπίπτω, **1.** *fall in, collapse*; met., *lapse, fall into error*, Gr. Nyss.*Apoll*.4(M.45.1129C); Chrys.*hom.54.1 in Mt*.(7.546D, v.l. συνεμπεσεῖν); into sin, Thdr.Stud.*epp*.2.50(M.99.1260C); also pass., Gr. Agr.*Eccl*.4.1(M.98.916C); **2.** cf.Gen.4:5, *be downcast, dejected* μὴ λυπεῖσθε...μηδὲ συμπέσητε ὅτι ἀπολήγω *T.Zab*.10.1; *T.Jos*.7.1; τὸ πρόσωπον αὐτοῦ χάριτος ἐπληροῦτο, ὥστε οὐ μόνον μὴ συμπεσεῖν ταραχθέντα ὑπὸ τῶν λεγομένων πρὸς αὐτόν *M.Polyc*.12.1; **3.** *have sexual intercourse* with, *T.Jos*.9.5; ἐρασθεὶς αὐτῆς συνέπεσα εἰς αὐτήν *T.Jud*.13.7; v. συνεμπίπτω.

συμπιστεύω, pass., *be believed to be one* with, *be reckoned together* with, ‡Ath.*dial.Trin*.5.4(M.28.1268B).

συμπλανάομαι, *wander with*; met., *err together* in heresy, Hipp. *Noët*.1(p.235.14; M.10.804B).

συμπλάσσω, med.; **1.** *mould, conform* to, Cyr.*Ps*.15:8(M.69. 812C); id.*Jo*.5.5(4.520D); ref. Inc., Anast.S.*hex*.12(M.89.1053B) cit. s. σκηνώδημος; **2.** *pretend* κληρικοὺς...σ. ἐξ οἱουδήποτε τάγματος ἱερατικοῦ ἢ βαθμοῦ εἶναι Heracl.*nov*.24(p.41).

***συμπλάστουργος**, *fashioning jointly, creating together*; of H. Ghost, Jo.D.*carm.pent*.119(M.96.837C; ἀκτιστοσυμπλαστουργοσύνθρονον p.217).

***συμπλατύν-ω**, *extend concurrently* with or *in proportion* to ἐν ταῖς διαδοχαῖς ἡ κακία συνεπλατύνετο Gr.Nyss.*res*.(M.46.608D); ~ω τῇ...κακίᾳ τῆς ἐμῆς φιλανθρωπίας τὰ διαστήματα Bas.Sel.*or*.5.2(M.85. 77B); *ib*.4.3(73C).

σύμπλεγμα, τό, *synthesis, combined* or *complex whole* ἔσφιγγε τὸ σ. τοῦ πυκνοῦ...ταρτάρου Hipp.*haer*.5.14(p.108.24; M.16.3167A); of Christ ἔρεισμα τῆς ὅλης οἰκουμένης, σ. κοσμικόν, τῆς ποικίλης καὶ ἀνθρωπίνης οὐσίας συνεκτικόν ‡Chrys.*pasch*.6.5(p.179.4; 8.272B); Christol. τοῦ διπλοῦ τῶν συμπλακέντων καὶ ἑνιαίου τοῦ σ. Leont.H. *monoph*.testimonia (M.86.1809B).

συμπλεκής, *closed, folded* σ. παλάμης Nonn.*par.Jo*.6:11(M.43. 796A).

συμπλέκ-ω, **A.** trans.; **1.** *twine together*; *interweave with*, met. τὸ συμπεπλεγμένον *what is bound up with oneself, one's own interests and concerns* πρὸς μὲν τὸ διεζευγμένον μεγάλην ἔχε ἀξίαν, πρὸς τὸ σ. δὲ ἀπαξίαν ‡Nil.*Epict*.55(M.79.1305D); met., *combine, blend* τῇ χαρᾷ ~εται φόβος Clem.*exc.Thdot*.83(p.132.18; M.9.696D); Ath.*gent*.40(M. 25.81A) cit. s. σπερματικός; εἰ...ἐν τῷ σώματι συνεπλάκη ὁ θάνατος... ἀνάγκη καὶ τὴν ζωὴν συμπλακῆναι τῷ σώματι...διὰ τοῦτο...ἐνεδύσατο σῶμα ὁ σωτήρ, ἵνα συμπλακέντος τοῦ σώματος τῇ ζωῇ, μηκέτι... ἀπομείνῃ ἐν τῷ θανάτῳ id.*inc*.44.5f.(M.25.176A); θάρσει...συμπεπλεγμένην δειλίαν Cyr.*Lc*.8:26f.(M.72.633C); id.*Ps*.36:7(M.69. 928B); **2.** *combine*; **a.** numbers, *multiply, combine with multiples of*, Iren.*haer*.1.15.2(M.7.617A); **b.** words so as to form a proposition; so, τὸ συμπεπλεγμένον *proposition*, ‡Nil.*Epict*.61(M.79.1308C); **3.** *unite* τὸν ἀμνὸν τοῦ θεοῦ...τὸ πῦρ τῆς θείας οὐσίας σαρκὶ...~οντα Isid.Pel.*epp*.1.219(M.78.321A); v. B.3 infra.

B. pass. intrans.; **1.** *become entangled, get caught* in; met., *be implicated, involved*; perf. ptcpl. pass., *intricacy, subtlety* διακρουσάμενος...τὸ σ. τῆς ἐρωτήσεως...πρὸς τὴν τῶν ἀκουόντων ὠφέλειαν εἶπον Dam.*troph*.2.1(p.216.7); **2.** *combine, mix* πνεύματα ἀκάθαρτα συμπεπλεγμένα τῇ ψυχῇ Clem.*ecl*.7(p.138.31; M.9.701B); σύνθετον εἴποιεν [sc. Arians in maintaining eternity of Wisdom] τὸν θεόν, ἔχοντα συμπεπλεγμένην ἢ συμπληρωτικὴν τῆς οὐσίας ἑαυτοῦ σοφίαν Ath.*Ar*.2.38(M.26.228C); of persons, *consort* with συμπεπλεγμένοι τοῖς πατράσι, καὶ τὴν ἐκείνων πορείαν ὁδεύουσι Thdt.*Jer*.11:9f.(2.469); of two categories, *merge into, overlap*, Dion.Ar.*ep*.9.1(M.3.1105D); **3.** *be joined*; **a.** of flesh to soul, Clem.*exc.Thdot*.5(p.107.9; M.9.656C); **b.** ref. Inc. ἡ θεία φύσις πρὸς τὴν ἡμετέραν ~εται Gr.Nyss.*or.catech*. 19(p.78.5; M.45.56C); *ib*.24(p.92.15; 64D); term later suspect κἂν τε δέ, 'συμπέπλεκται', θέλῃς λέγειν, κἂν τε, ὡς ἡ γραφὴ εἶπεν, 'ἔλαβεν', κἂν τε, 'ἐγένετο' ‡Ath.*dial.Trin*.5.6(M.28.1277D); of natures in Christ, Leont.H.*monoph*.testimonia(M.86.1809B); ‡Gr.Nyss.*hom. 9.21 in Jo*.(p.288.27) cit. s. ἑνωθέω; **c.** ref. eucharistic union, Chrys. *hom.15.4 in 1Tim*.(11.641D) cit. s. ἀνάκρασις.

σύμπλευρος, *lying side by side*, of Abishag with David τὴν σύσσωμον καὶ σ. Epiph.*haer*.69.46(p.193.23; M.42.273C); id.*anc*.20(p.29. 18; M.43.53C).

***συμπλημμυρέω**, for ⟨συμπλημυρέω⟩, *abound with*, c. dat., Gr. Nyss.*anim.et res*.(M.46.105C).

συμπληρ-όω, *complete*; of Logos enlightening humankind, Or. *Jo*.1.37(42; p.48.8,10; M.14.97B); of Christ as God and man κοινὴν... σαρκὸς καὶ θεότητος...γεγενῆσθαί φαμεν τὴν...~ωθεῖσαν τοῦ Χριστοῦ μίαν ὑπόστασιν Max.*ep*.15(M.91.556C); myst. Ἰησοῦν...~ωθέντα δι' ἐμοῦ σωζομένου id.*myst*.5(M.91.676B); pass., *be composed of* δευτέραν [sc. ἱεραρχίαν]...τὴν ὑπὸ τῶν ἐξουσιῶν, καὶ κυριοτήτων, καὶ δυνάμεων ~ουμένην Dion.Ar.*c.h*.6.2(M.3.201A); *ib*.9.2(260A).

συμπλήρωμα, τό, **1.** *completion, fulfilment* ἐπὶ συμπληρώματος τῶν προειρημένων κατορθωμάτων παρέλαβεν ὁ λόγος τὴν ἁγνείαν Meth. *symp*.9.4(p.119.13; M.18.188A); τὸ εὐαγγέλιον τὸ τούτων [sc. νόμου, βασιλείων, προφητῶν] σ. *Const.App*.3.5.2; τέλος νόμου Χριστός, τουτέστι, τὸ σ. Chrys.*hom.2.1 in 1Tim*.(11.555D); **2.** *complement* σ. [sc. τὸ πνεῦμα] τῆς ἁγίας ὑπάρχον τριάδος Cyr.*thes*.34(5[1].358B).

***συμπληρωματικός**, *constituent* αἱ σ. τοῦ σώματος ποιότητες Gr. Nyss.*anim.et res*.(M.46.123D); Sever.*1Cor*.2:11ff.(p.233.27); θεὸς λόγος δυνατὸς ὡς ὁ πατήρ, οὐ δύναμις μέρος σ. τῆς οὐσίας τῆς πατρικῆς id.*1Cor*.1:25(p.230.8).

συμπλήρωσις, ἡ, **1.** *filling up, repletion* δυσαποσπάστως ἔχεις πρὸς τὴν τράπεζαν πρὸ τῆς κατὰ χρείαν σ. Bas.*renunt*.8(2.210A; M.31. 644C); **2.** *completion*; freq. in rel. to creation τῆς τῶν γενητῶν ἁπάντων σ. Eus.*e.th*.3.3(p.156.6; M.24.1000C); ἔσται τὸ κακὸν εἰς τὴν τοῦ παντὸς σ. συντελοῦν Dion.Ar.*d.n*.4.19(M.3.717B); *ib*.4.28(729A); Jo.D.*f.o*.1.3(M.94.796C); not function of Son in rel. to Father ὁ... πατὴρ...οὐδὲν εἰς σ. τῆς ἑαυτοῦ θεότητος παρὰ τοῦ υἱοῦ λαμβάνων Eus. *d.e*.4.3(p.153.9; M.22.256B); nor in rel. to universe εἰς σ. τῆς...ὁλότητος γινώσκεται πεποιημένη [sc. πᾶσα σύνθετος φύσις]...περὶ τοῦ...λόγου ...εἰς διόρθωσιν καὶ ἀνακαινισμόν, ἀλλ' οὐκ εἰς σ. τοῦ παντός, ἐνανθρωπήσαντος Max.*ep*.13(M.91.517A,B); **3.** *perfecting*; of faculty of reason, Or.*comm.in Rom*.7:7(*JTS* 14 p.12; M.14.1077D); id.*fr.79 in Lc*.19:22(p.272); πρὸς συμπλήρωσιν διαγωγῆς κρείττονος Meth.*res*.1. 25(p.250.15; M.41.1096B); **4.** *fulfilment, accomplishment, consummation* τὴν σ. τῆς ἀμοιβῆς εἰς τὴν τοῦ βίου σ. ἡμῶν ὑπερτίθεται Const. *or.s.c*.23(p.189.25f.; M.20.1308A); id.ap.Eus.*v.C*.3.18(p.85.14; M.20. 1076A); Eus.*d.e*.1.1(p.6.3; M.22.20D); ‡Ath.*Apoll*.1.3(M.26.1096D); of martyrdom, Gr.Naz.*or*.15.9(M.35.925C); ἐκ μεταμελείας ἐλθοῦσα εἰς σ. τελειότητος *ib*.41.9(M.36.441B); **5.** *end* (of Law) ἀρχὴν τῆς ὁδοῦ ...οὐ συμπλήρωσιν Vict.*Mc*.10:24(p.379.4); μετὰ...τὴν τούτων σ. *Lit. Praesanct*.(p.346.12); μετὰ τὴν σ. τοῦ τρισαγίου *Lit.Chrys*.(p.370.35); *death* δεδήλωται...ἡμῖν...ἡ ἡμέρα τῆς σ. ἡμῶν *V.Zos*.14(p.105.13); πρὸς τὸ τέλος ὁρᾶν τῆς αὐτοῦ σ. Euthal.Diac.*epp.Paul*.(M.85.705B).

συμπληρωτικός, **1.** *forming an essential part* ἡ...αὐγὴ συνυπάρχει τῷ φωτί, σ. τις οὖσα αὐτοῦ Eus.*d.e*.4.3(p.153.5; M.22.256A); τῇ...κτίσει ἑτέρωθεν ἐπεισήχθη ὁ ἁγιασμός· τῷ δὲ πνεύματι συμπληρωτικὴ τῆς φύσεώς ἐστιν ἡ ἁγιότης Bas.*Spir*.48(3.40D; M.32. 156B); μὴ δύνασθαί, τινος τῶν σ. τῆς φύσεως λείποντος, ἄνθρωπος λέγεσθαι Gr.Nyss.*Apoll*.47(M.45.1240B); **2.** *forming a part of, going to make up*, ref. essence, as implication of Arian refusal to identify Wisdom with Son σύνθετον...τὸν θεόν, ἔχοντα...σ. τῆς οὐσίας ἑαυτοῦ σοφίαν Ath.*Ar*.2.38(M.26.228C); cf. πατέρα τὸν γεννήσαντα καὶ σ. τῆς οὐσίας αὐτοῦ [sc. τοῦ υἱοῦ] *cat.Ac*.2:22(p.42.6); οὐκ ἔσται σ. τὰ ποιήματα τῆς θείας οὐσίας Proc.G.*Gen*.proem.(M.87.29D); τὰς τῆς ψυχῆς δυνάμεις...σ. τῆς οὐσίας αὐτῆς Max.*ambig*.(M.91.1261C); more gen. χεὶρ καὶ ὀφθαλμὸς καὶ ποὺς περὶ ἓν σῶμά εἰσιν σ. μέρη Athenag.*leg*.8.1 (συμπληροῦντες τά M.6.905A); μέρη...σ. τοῦ ὅλου Clem.*str*.2.16(p.152. 14; M.8.1013A); Mac.Mgn.*apocr*.2.20(p.39.17); πάντων [τῶν] τοῦ κόσμου σ. μετέχων [sc. ὁ ἄνθρωπος] στοιχείων Isid.Pel.*epp*.1.259(M. 78.337C); **3.** Trin. τὸ πνεῦμα τὸ ἅγιον...οὐ σ. ... τῆς ἁγίας τριάδος [sc. in Arian view], οὐδὲ κοινωνὸν τῆς θείας...φύσεως Bas.*ep*.243(3.375C; M.32.909A); orthodox πνεῦμα θεοῦ...τῆς τριάδος σ. id.*hex*.2.6(1. 18B; M.29.44A); Isid.Pel.*epp*.1.109(M.78.256B); Cyr.*thes*.34(5[1].358E); Thdt.*Jer*.4:12(2.432); id.*Trin*.20(M.75.1176D); **4.** *complementary* to δευτέραν [sc. ἐντολήν]...ὁμοίαν ἐκείνῃ, μᾶλλον δὲ σ. τῆς προτέρας Bas. *reg.fus*.1(2.336A; M.31.908A); τὴν...τετάρτην γέννησιν...σ. τῆς ἐκ σωμάτων...γεννήσεως Max.*ambig*.(M.91.1316C); **5.** *mutually complementary* κοινωνοῦντα τοῦ εἶναι, οὐχ ὡς σ. τῆς ἀλλήλων οὐσίας Leont.B. *Nest.et Eut*.1(M.86.1280B); οὐ...σ. ἡ τοῦ πατρὸς καὶ υἱοῦ καὶ ἁγίου πνεύματος φύσις *ib*.(1288B); Christol. ἐκ δύο οὖν φύσεων, οὐ δύο φύσεις, ἀλλὰ μίαν ὑπόστασιν λέγομεν Χριστὸν σύνθετον· τούτων ὡς ἰδίων μερῶν περιεκτικὴν τῶν φύσεων, καὶ ταύτας ὡς ἴδια καὶ σ. μέρη περιέχουσαν Max.*ep*.11(M.91.493A).

***συμπληρωτικῶς**, *complementally, by making up the complement* or *completing* τάξιν ἀγγελικὴν...τὴν σ. ἀποπερατοῦσαν τὰ...οὐράνια τάγματα Dion.Ar.*c.h*.5(M.3.196B); *ib*.9.2(257D).

συμπλήσσομαι, s.v.l., *be terror-struck* συμπεπληγμένην δειλίαν Cyr.ap.*cat.Lc*.8:27(p.69.6) for θάρσει...συμπεπλεγμένην δειλίαν Cyr. *Lc*.8:26f.(M.72.633C).

συμπλοκή, ἡ, **1.** *interweaving*; met., of the thread binding together all creation, *connexion*, Dion.Ar.*d.n*.11.2(M.3.949D) cit. s.

ἀσυγχύτως; **2.** *combination* τὴν εὐχαριστίαν καὶ τὴν εὐλογίαν ἀγαλλίασίν τε καὶ εὐφροσύνην, ἔτι τε ὑπομονὴν συνεργοῦσαν, καὶ τὴν τούτων σ., τὴν ἐκκλησίαν Clem.*paed*.1.5(p.103.21; M.8.277A); **3.** between persons, *association, close connexion*, Gr.Thaum.*pan.Or*.5(p.13.13; M.10.1065D); σ. τὴν πρὸς ὑμᾶς ἐμπορεύσομαι, ἣν ἡ πίστις συνδεῖ τοὺς ὁμόφρονας Sophr.H.*ep.syn*.(M.87.3149C); denied of Son's relation to Father ὁ υἱὸς ἁπλῶς καὶ χωρὶς σ. τινός ἐστιν ἐν τῷ πατρί· φύσει γὰρ ὑπάρχει τοῦτ' αὐτῷ Ath.*Ar*.3.23(M.26.372A); **4.** *union* of soul and body in man, †Just.*fr.res*.(p.45; M.6.1585B); τὸ διττὸν καὶ ἑτερογενὲς τῆς ἐν ἡμῖν σ. ... καὶ ψυχῆς καὶ σώματος Eus.*p.e*.6.6(247A; M.21.420C); **5.** Christol., *union* of natures in Christ, Cyr.*hom.pasch*. 17.2(5^2.226E); τὴν δευτέραν ἑαυτοῦ...ἐνεργῆσαι γέννησιν ἐν τῇ σ. τοῦ καθ' ἡμᾶς ἀνθρώπου ὁμολογοῦμεν Leont.H.*Nest*.4.9(M.86.1669B); *ib*. 6.8(1757A); οὐσιώδους σ. *ib*.1.19(1476D); id.*monoph*.testimonia(M. 86.1809D); πρὸς τὴν ἀνθρωπίνην φύσιν ἕνωσιν τοῦ λόγου καὶ σ. καὶ συνάφειαν ἀληθεστάτην ‡Gr.Nyss.*hom.3.44 in Jo*.(p.147.6); **6.** *embrace* (of sexual intercourse); met., of death, Eus.*theoph*.3(p.6.13); Ath. *inc*.26.1(M.25.141A).

σύμπλοκος, *combined*; of a multitude of people, Nonn.*par.Jo*. 6:10(M.43.793C); *fixed* to σταυρῷ σύμπλοκος οὗτος...ἔστω *ib*.19:6 (897C).

***συμπλουτέω,** *be rich together*, Sophr.H.*or*.4(M.87.3308A).

***συμπλωτήρ, ὁ,** *fellow sailor*, Sophr.H.*v.Mar.Aeg*.2.20(M.87. 3712C); *fellow voyager*, Gr.Mag.*dial*.(tr.Zach.)2.17(M.*PL*.66.167C).

σύμπνευσις, ἡ, 1. *inspiration* by God, Eus.*v.C*.1.20(p.18.6; συννεύσει M.20.936C); **2.** *agreement* ὁμοψυχίαν καὶ σ. ‡Ath.*ep.cath*.(M. 28.81C).

συμπνέ-ω, 1. *be in accordance, agree*; **a.** of things σ. αἱ πᾶσαι ἑρμηνεῖαι Clem.*str*.1.22(p.92.19; M.8.893A); Or.*Cels*.1.28(p.80.2; M. 11.713C); τοῦ κόσμου...ἑνὸς ὄντος...καὶ σ. αὐτοῦ ὅλῳ ἑαυτῷ *ib*.1.23 (p.73.25; 701A); **b.** of persons πάντας πρὸς τὴν κατὰ Νίκαιαν πίστιν συμπεπνευκέναι Liber.*ep.Maced*.ap.Socr.*h.e*.4.12.35(M.67.493B); οὐχ ὑπετάγη Θεοδοσίῳ· εἶχε δὲ σ. αὐτῷ καὶ συντρέχοντα Ἀρταύασδον Thphn.*chron*.p.323(M.108.781C); **2.** *help forward, cooperate towards* things ὁ βοῦς...σ. εἰς γεωργίαν Or.*enarr.in Job* 21:10(M.17.77C); ἵνα σ. [sc. the angels] οἷς ὁ εὐχόμενος ἠξίωσεν id.*or*.11(p.324.7; M. 11.452B); ἀγγέλων τρεφομένων...καὶ ἑτοιμοτέρων γινομένων πρὸς τὸ ...συνεργῆσαι καὶ πρὸς τὸ ἑξῆς συμπνεῦσαι τῇ...καταλήψει τοῦ... ἀναθρέψαντος αὐτούς *ib*.27(p.370.20; 513D); **3.** *inspire, help* persons ~οντος ὑμῖν τοῦ θεοῦ Leo Mag.*ep*.45.1(p.47.14; M.*PL*.54.834A); ~ούσης αὐτῷ τῆς τύχης Men.*exc.Rom*.3(p.177.14; M.113.861A); abs. συναγωνιζομένης σου καὶ σ. Meth.*symp*.8.13(p.99.10; M.18.161B).

συμπνίγ-ω, *suffocate*, Meth.*symp*.2.6(p.23.8; M.18.56D); met., *choke, throttle* (ref. Mt.13:22 and parallels) τὰς ἀκάνθας τοῦ βίου, αἳ τὸ σπέρμα τῆς ζωῆς σ. Clem.*q.d.s*.11(p.166.29; M.9.616A); id.*str*. 6.7(p.461.25; M.9.281A) cit. s. γῆ; τὰ ἐκ τοῦ χείρονος ἐκφυόμενα... συστέλλοντα καὶ ~οντα [sc. ἡμᾶς] ὑπὸ ταπεινότητος Gr.Thaum.*pan. Or*.9(p.23.19; M.10.1080A); καλῶς τὴν ὕλην ὡς ~ουσαν φεύγεις Isid. Pel.*epp*.1.101(M.78.252B); *harass, annoy* υἱοὶ ἢ θυγατέρες ὑμᾶς οὐ σ., διαφόρους αἰτήσεις ὑμῖν προσφέροντες Serap.*ep.mon*.5(M.40.932A).

***σύμπνιξις, ἡ,** *press, crush*; of a crowd, Steph.Diac.*v.Steph*.(M. 100.1077A).

σύμπνοια, ἡ, *taking breath together*; hence **1.** *acquiescence, concurrence* τὴν σ. τῶν ὁρμητικῶν παθῶν Or.*Ps*.19:8(p.475); **2.** *unanimity, agreement* μίαν...ὁδὸν βοηθείας ταῖς καθ' ἡμᾶς ἐκκλησίαις, τὴν παρὰ τῶν δυτικῶν ἐπισκόπων σ. Bas.*ep*.66.1(3.159A; M. 32.424B); between husband and wife, *Const.App*.7.2.9; theol. μοναρχία...ἣν φύσεως ὁμοτιμία συνίστησι, καὶ γνώμης σ. Gr.Naz.*or*. 29.2(p.75.4; M.36.76B); **3.** *consent* ἐμοῦ [sc. God] δίχα καὶ σ. τὴν ἐμὴν οὐκ ἔχων Cyr.*Os*.90(3.122A); **4.** *concord, union*; **a.** between things, the elements, Gr.Naz.*or*.28.16(p.46.14; M.36.48A) cit. s. συμφυΐα; in universe τὴν μίαν τοῦ παντὸς σ. καὶ ἁρμονίαν καλλιεργοῦσα [sc. ἡ σοφία] Dion.Ar.*d.n*.7.3(M.3.872B); the parts of a body, Gr.Nyss. *fat*.(M.45.152C); id.*Eun*.1(1 p.23.17; M.45.252B); **b.** moral, between persons τὸ τῆς φιλίας, εἴτουν σ. καὶ συμφυΐας Gr.Naz.*or*.43.14(M.36. 513B); esp. in Church ἡ σ. ... ἐπὶ τῆς ἐκκλησίας λέγεται κυρίως Clem. *str*.7.6(p.24.12; M.9.444C); Or.*schol. in Cant*.8:8(M.17.285C); ὦ σ. τῶν φίλων καὶ θεραπόντων γνησίων Χριστοῦ Ἰησοῦ ‡Eust.*Laz*.16(p.40. 4); Gr.Naz.*ep*.216(M.37.353B); μία γὰρ τῶν αὐτήν [sc. τὴν ἐκκλησίαν] πληρούντων ἡ διὰ τῆς πρὸς ἀλλήλους σ. ψυχή Proc.G.*Is*.61:10(M.87. 2652C); stemming from charity, Bas.*reg.fus*.34(2.377D; M.31.1000C); id.*Spir*.78(3.67A; M.32.216B); οὐδὲν ὡς ἀγάπη...μίαν αὐτῶν [sc. τῶν ἐσκορπισμένων] δημιουργεῖ τὴν γνώμην συμπνοίᾳ κρατουμένην *Schol*. 5 in Max.*qu.Thal*.(M.90.460C); **5.** *cooperation, help* οὐδὲν...ὁρῶ ἄνευ τῆς τῶν ὁμοφύλων σ. ἐπιτελούμενον Bas.*ep*.97(3.191B; M.32.493B); of Christ οὐ χωρὶς σ. καὶ ἐνεργείας κρείττονος αὐτῶν περιεσόμεθα Or. *Rom*.8:38f.(*JTS* 14 p.20); of H. Ghost μετὰ τηλικαύτης...σ. τῆς εἰς τὸ καλὸν ἔτι ἀποπίπτοντας id.*Jo*.2.11(6; p.66.15; M.14.129C); **6.** *inspiration* of scripture by H. Ghost τὴν ἑνοειδῆ καὶ μίαν σ., ὡς ὑφ' ἑνὸς...πνεύματος κεκινημένην Dion.Ar.*e.h*.3.3.5(M.3.432B); μίαν ἔμπνευσίν φησι, τουτέστι μίαν σ. Max.*schol.e.h*.3.3.4(M.4.140B).

συμποδίζω, 1. *tie the feet together, bind hand and foot*; met., *hamper, impede*, ref. Ps.77:9 σ. τοὺς ἐκλεκτοὺς...ἵνα μὴ ζῶντες πάλιν ἑτέρας ἐπιθυμήσωσι τροφῆς Marc.Er.*opusc*.9.2(M.65.1113A); ἐμὲ... τὸν συμποδίσαντα, καὶ τῆς ἀτάκτου φορᾶς ἀπαλλάξαντα, καὶ πατρικὴν περὶ αὐτὸν φιλοστοργίαν ἐπιδειξάμενον Thdt.*Os*.11:3f.(2.1361); **2.** med., *stagger, reel* ἀνθρώπῳ μεθυσθέντι...καὶ ἐπὶ τῆς ἀγορᾶς διοδεύοντι, καὶ σ., τοίχῳ τε πρὸς τοίχῳ συντρίβοντι †Gregent.*leg.Hom*.25 (M.86.596B).

***συμποδιστής, ὁ,** *one who binds hand and foot, fetterer* οἱ τοῦ διαβόλου σ. καὶ τῶν δαιμόνων σκελισταί Ephr.3.463D.

***συμποιητής, ὁ,** *fellow maker*; of Father and H. Ghost τοῦ υἱοῦ κτίσαντος συμποιητὴς ὁ πατήρ ἐστιν τῇ εὐδοκήσει, οὕτω καὶ τὸ πνεῦμα αὐτοῦ Didym.*Trin*.2.7(M.39.573C).

συμποιμαίνω, 1. *help in shepherding*; of dogs, Thdt.*provid*.5(4. 558); **2.** met., *be a shepherd together* with; of angels of churches with human pastors, Or.*hom.13 in Lc*.(p.91.15); of divine Shepherd, Gr. Naz.*or*.11.7(M.35.841A).

***συμποίμην, ὁ,** *fellow pastor* (sc. of Christ's flock), Gr.Naz.*or*.9.4 (M.35.824B); *ib*.42.1(M.36.457A); id.*carm*.2.1.12.136(M.37.1176A); Thdr.Stud.*epp*.1.25(M.99.988D).

***συμποιόω,** *make of a certain quality*, Germ.CP *or*.1(M.98.240B).

συμπολίτευσις, ἡ, *fellow citizenship*; of Christ's dwelling with man and sharing his life, Leont.B.*Nest.et Eut*.2(M.86.1329B).

συμπολιτεύω, usu. med.; **1.** *be a fellow citizen, live with*; **a.** of God with man in Inc., Eus.*d.e*.6.17(p.273.15; M.22.449B); ‡Ath. *disp*.21(M.28.464A); Gnost. ὁ λόγος ἡμῖν ἀπὸ τοῦ βάτου, τουτέστιν ἀέρος, νομοθετεῖ καὶ σ. Hipp.*haer*.8.9(p.229.6; M.16.3354A); **b.** of man with God in a life of holiness, ‡Pall.*h.mon*.1.63(p.23.19; M.34. 1130B); in the life to come, *A.(Pass.)Andr*.B 13(p.30.14; M.2. 1241B); **2.** *associate* with; of God with man, Clem.*prot*.11(p.82.20; M.8.236C); ὁ Σαοὺλ ὁ σ. τῷ πονηρῷ δαίμονι τῆς σαρκικῆς ἐπιθυμίας Hipp.*haer*.5.9(p.102.17; M.16.3159); συμπολιτεύου [sc. Elias] μετὰ σαρκὸς τοῖς ἀγγέλοις Bas.Sel.*or*.11.3(M.85.157B).

συμπολίτης, ὁ, *fellow citizen*; in kingdom of God κληρονόμον... γενόμενον τῆς βασιλείας σ. ... καὶ τῶν πάλαι δικαίων Clem.*str*.2.19 (p.196.17; M.8.1044A); with Christ εἴ τις...ἀγαπᾷ σ. γενέσθαι τοῦ βασιλέως, ὀξυποδισάτω Ephr.1.44E; of man with angels through Christ, ‡Epiph.*hom*.6(M.43.504B); τὸν ἄνθρωπον...σ. τῶν οὐρανίων γινόμενον Cosm.Ind.*top*.3(M.88.153B); through death ὃς καὶ αὐτὸς σ. γέγονεν τῶν ἀγγελικῶν δυνάμεων Marc.Diac.*v.Porph*.11; ὅσοι...τοῦ μέλλοντος αἰῶνος σ. τῶν ἁγίων σπεύδουσιν εἶναι Cosm.Ind.*top*.1 (57B).

συμπολῖτις, ἡ, fem. of foreg. νύμφη Χριστοῦ χρηματίζεις...σ. τῶν δικαίων καὶ ἁγίων Thdr.Stud.*epp*.2.68(M.99.1297A).

σύμπονος, ὁ, 1. *assessor, assistant of magistrate*, Nil.*epp*.2.236(M. 79.321A); Ath.Scholast.*coll*.4.2(p.51); **2.** *fellow worker*, Thdr.Stud. *epp*.2.38,215(M.99.1233A,1653C).

***συμπόρευσις, ἡ,** *company* on a journey; met. ὅπως...τὴν...σ. [sc. of the cross] ἔχοιεν, ἐν ὁδοιπορίαις συνθέουσαν Sophr.H.*or*.4(M. 87.3305B).

***συμπορθμεύω,** *carry over* a river, etc., *in company with*; met., of assumption of BMV σὲ συνεπόρθμευσαν σὺν ἀρχαγγέλοις ἄγγελοι Jo.D.*hom*.8.11(M.96.716D).

συμπορνεύω, 1. *join in committing fornication*; of pagan deities, Clem.*prot*.4(p.47.2; M.8.160B); **2.** *commit fornication with* ἡ διάκονος ἡ τῷ Ἕλληνι σ., δεκτή ἐστιν εἰς μετάνοιαν Bas.*ep*.199 *can*.44(3.296B; M.32.729B).

***συμπορφυροβαφέω,** *dye purple together*, in analogy of Son's 'tincture' of humanity in rel. to other Persons of Trin. οὔτε γὰρ ἐὰν τὸν...ὄνυχά τις πορφυροβαφήσῃ, ἤδη καὶ τὴν σάρκα καὶ τὸ ὀστοῦν τοῦ δακτύλου συνεπορφυροβάφησε Anast.S.*hod*.17(M.89.265A).

συμποσιάζω, *drink together*; fig., of souls in Elysium, Aen.*dial*. (M.85.956B).

συμποσιαρχία, ἡ, *office of toastmaster, being toastmaster*, Pall. *v.Chrys*.12(p.75.16; M.47.42).

***συμποσιασμός, ὁ,** *drinking bout*, Thphn.*chron*.p.373(M.108. 892C).

συμπόσιον, τό, *drinking-party*, freq. in sense of carousal; *banquet, feast*, met. τὰ ἐν τῇ βασιλείᾳ τοῦ θεοῦ τῶν ὁσίων σ. Dion.Ar. *ep*.9.5(M.3.1112D); *meal*, Eus.*h.e*.2.16.2(M.20.173B); of the Last Supper τῷ τοῦ πάσχα σ. id.*d.e*.10.3(p.458.3; M.22.737A).

***συμποτνιάζω**, *lament also, join in lamenting*, Thdr.Stud.*epp*.2.6 (M.99.1128B); fut. dep., *ib*.1.18(964C).

συμπραγματεύομαι, *do business with* or *together*, Just.1*apol*.16.4 (M.6.352D); Or.*comm.in Mt*.14.8(p.293.23; M.13.1201B).

***συμπράκτης, ὁ**, *one who acts together with another, fellow agent*; of evil, *accomplice* τὸν σ. αὐτοῦ τῶν κακῶν Pall.*h.Laus*.19(p.59.19; M.34.1066B); of Persons of Trin. τρία σ. ‡Caes.Naz.*dial*.3(M.38. 861).

συμπρακτικός, *acting together in union*, of Persons of Trin. τὸ σ. καὶ ἀπαράλλακτον τῆς τε οὐσίας αὐτῶν Didym.*Trin*.2.1(M.39.452A).

***συμπρεπόντως**, *as befits, agreeably to* ποιεῖ ὁ βούλεται σ. τῇ αὐτοῦ θεότητι Epiph.*haer*.76.31(p.381.8; M.42.580D); σ. ... πατρὶ τὸ ἀεὶ ἔχειν...τὸ...ἀνέκλειπτον *ib*.76.53(p.408.35; 629A); abs., *fittingly, properly* ἐκ τοῦ ὄντος, σ. ἅμα θεωρεῖται *ib*.76.49(p.403.25; 620C); σ. πατὴρ γεννήσας υἱὸν καὶ οὐ κτίσας *ib*.76.50(p.405.3; 621D).

συμπρέπω, *befit, beseem*; hence *go well with, agree with* τὴν περιτομὴν τῷ νόμῳ σ. ἀπέδειξε Epiph.*haer*.42.12(p.176.24; M.41. 804C); ὁ γεννηθεὶς...σ. τῷ γεννήτορι *ib*.76.28(p.377.21; M.42.573C); *ib*. 76.46(p.400.2; 613B).

συμπρεσβευτής, ὁ, *fellow ambassador*; met., *intercessor* Συμεὼν... σ. ἡμῶν γενοῦ πρὸς τὸν σωτῆρα θεόν ‡Meth.*Sym.et Ann*.14(M.18. 381C).

συμπρεσβεύω, *be a fellow ambassador*; met., *join in intercession* τοὺς ἐν τῷ νεῷ σ. Sophr.H.*mir.Cyr.et Jo*.31(M.87.3524B).

συμπρεσβύτερος, ὁ, *fellow presbyter, fellow priest*, Anon.ap.Eus. *h.e*.5.16.5(M.20.465B); Ephr.2.200C,219F; specifically of companions in priest's orders παρακαλοῦμεν...καὶ ὑπὲρ τῶν σ. Serap.*euch*.11.2; *Const.App*.8.28.3 cit. s. ἐπιδίδωμι; Synes.*ep*.67(M.66.1425A); τῷ σ. Τιμοθέῳ Διονύσιος ὁ πρεσβύτερος Dion.Ar.*c.h*.1 inscr.(M.3.120A); freq. used by bishops in addressing, or referring to, priests (cf. 1Petr.5:1) σ. ... μου Μάξιμος Dion.Al.ap.Eus.*h.e*.7.11.3(M.20.664A); Ursac.*ep.Ath*.(p.138.23; M.25.356A); Bas.*ep*.205(3.308A; M.32.756C); Gr.Naz.*epp*.211,216(M.37.348C,353A); Epiph.*rescr*.(p.155.4; M.41. 157C); exeg. Phil.1:1 τὸ 'σὺν ἐπισκόποις' λέγει, οὐχ ὥς τινες ἐνόμισαν, ὥσπερ ἡμεῖς συμπρεσβυτέροις γράφειν εἰώθαμεν· οὐ γὰρ πρὸς τὸ ἑαυτοῦ πρόσωπον εἶπεν τὸ 'σύν' Thdr.Mops.*Phil*.1:1(p.200.14; M.66.921B); explained οἱ πρεσβύτεροι τὸ παλαιὸν ἐκαλοῦντο ἐπίσκοποι καὶ διάκονοι..., καὶ οἱ ἐπίσκοποι πρεσβύτεροι· ὅθεν καὶ νῦν πολλοὶ συμπρεσβυτέρῳ ἐπίσκοποι γράφουσι καὶ συνδιακόνῳ Chrys.*hom.1.1 in Phil*.(11. 195B).

συμπροβάλλω, *project, produce together*; pass., of Valentinian emanations συμπροβεβλῆσθαι...αὐτῷ [sc. τῷ Νῷ] Ἀλήθειαν Iren. *haer*.1.1.1(M.7.448A); *ib*.1.11.1(564A); *ib*.1.2.6(465A) ∞ ‡Epiph.*epit. haer*.31(p.362.4).

συμπροδίδωμι, *join in betraying*, Gr.Naz.*ep*.58(M.37.116A).

***συμπροεληλυθότως**, *as proceeding together* [Jo.15:26] ἡ ἀπὸ τοῦ ἑνὸς πατρὸς...ἐκπόρευσις...συνυφεστώτως καὶ σ. Didym.*Trin*.2.2(M. 39.460B).

συμπροέρχομαι, 1. *go forward together*, Bas.*hom*.21.5(2.167C; M. 31.549B); met. τῷ καθαρισμῷ τὸ καθαροποιὸν σ. Job.Mon.*inc*.2(M.86. 3316C); **2.** *come forth at the same time, proceed together*, Leont.H. *Nest*.4.37(M.86.1712A); ἐκ πνοῆς θεοῦ...σ. πάντα τὰ τῆς ψυχῆς... ἰδιώματα Anast.S.*serm.imag*.3(M.89.1165C).

***συμπροθυμοποιέομαι**, *join in encouraging*, Thdr.Stud.*epp*.2.46 (M.99.1249C).

***συμπροκύπτω**, *extend, advance along with*, c. dat., Synes.*regn*. 16(p.35.15; M.66.1081C).

συμπροπέμπω, *join in sending in advance* τοῦ πατρὸς...ἀποστέλλοντος τὸν υἱὸν συναποστέλλει καὶ σ. τὸ ἅγιον πνεῦμα αὐτόν, ἐν καιρῷ ὑπισχνούμενον καταβῆναι πρὸς τὸν υἱόν Or.*Jo*.2.11(6; p.67.1; M.14. 132B).

***συμπροσαγορεύομαι**, pass., *be called also*; *share the same title* αἱ αὐτοτελεῖς ὑποστάσεις ἃς ἐσήμανε τὸ ἓν ὄνομα ᾧ καὶ τὸ πνεῦμα σ. Didym.*Trin*.2.6(M.39.525B).

***συμπροσδοκάω**, *look for, expect*; pass. ptcpl., *expected together* with, †Bas.*Is*.66(1.427A; M.30.232C).

συμπρόσειμι, (*sum*) *be present together*; *correspond*, *cat.Lc*.2:51 (p.27.28).

συμπροσέρχομαι, *come into, enter upon together* with σ. αὐτῷ εἰς τὸ εἶναι Leont.H.*Nest*.1.27(M.86.1493B).

***συμπροσεύχ-ομαι**, *pray together, pray with* σ. τε καὶ μυστικῆς ἀπολαύσας τροφῆς Eus.*Ps*.54:15(M.23.481B); εὐσεβὴς μετὰ αἱρετικοῦ, μήτε κατ' οἶκον ∼έσθω *Const.App*.8.34.12; Anast.S.*qu.et resp*.63(M. 89.653B); of guardian angel ὁ...φύλαξ ἡμῶν...ὁ σ. Jo.Clim.*scal*.28 (M.88.1132B).

***συμπροσκυν-έω**, *worship together* with, *worship equally* with; **1.** Trin.; **a.** Son with Father ἵνα...τῷ πατρὶ ὁμοτίμως ∼ηθῇ ‡Meth. *palm*.7(M.18.397B); ‡Eust.*alloc*.(M.18.673D) cit. s. δοξολογέω; υἱὸν... συνυμνούμενόν τε καὶ σ. Cyr.*Abac*.39(3.555A); ἀεὶ συνυπάρχοντα...καὶ ∼ούμενον υἱόν *Juln*.8(6^2.255E); an argument for his divinity οὐ ∼εῖται αὐτῷ [sc. τῷ πατρί] τι τῶν ἐξ οὐκ ὄντων γεγονότων Epiph. *haer*.76.46(p.400.14; M.42.613C); with Father and H. Ghost, Justn. *cod*.1.1.6.7(p.8); **b.** H. Ghost with Father and Son, Didym.*Trin*. 2.5(M.39.493A); *ib*.2.21(741B); πνεῦμα ἅγιον...τὸ τῷ πατρὶ καὶ υἱῷ σ. καὶ συνδοξαζόμενον Jo.D.*f.o*.1.8(M.94.821B); in credal statements, *Symb*.ap.Epiph.*anc*.118(p.147.13; M.43.232D) cit. s. συνδοξάζω; *Symb.Nic.-CP*(p.80.13; H.2.288B); **c.** Trinity συνυπουργεῖ [sc. ὁ υἱός]...τῷ πατρὶ καὶ ∼εῖται...τὸ ἅγιον πνεῦμα...στερεοῖ...τὴν δύναμιν τῶν ἀπάντων καὶ ∼εῖται Epiph.*haer*.76.52(p.407.4f.; M.42.625C); σ. ... τριάδα τελείαν μονάδι τελείᾳ Max.*ambig*.(M.91.1261A); προσκυνῶν γὰρ αὐτόν [sc. Χριστόν], σ. τὸν πατέρα καὶ τὸ ἅγιον πνεῦμα Thdr.Stud. *epp*.2.85(M.99.1328D); **2.** Christol.; **a.** Apollinarian: Christ's flesh with his divinity οὐδὲ...ὁ λόγος διὰ τὴν σάρκα προσκυνεῖται, ἀλλ' ἡ σὰρξ τῷ λόγῳ σ. Val.Apoll.*apol*.9(p.291.24)ap.Leont.B.*Apoll*.(M.86. 1960A); *ib*.2(p.288.4)ap.*eund*.(1953B) cit. s. συνδοξάζω; on account of nature of the union εἰ ∼εῖς τὸν ἄνθρωπον τῷ θεῷ λόγῳ κατὰ τὴν ἐνοίκησιν,∼ει καὶ τοὺς ἁγίους Apoll.*inc*.3(p.305.16; M.28.93A); **b.** used by Nestorius σέβωμεν τὸν τῇ θείᾳ συναφείᾳ τῷ...θεῷ ∼ούμενον ἄνθρωπον Nest.*fr*.C 8(p.249.4)ap.Cyr.*Nest*.2.14(p.52.29; 6^1.60C); ἕνα Χριστὸν...τέμνων εἰς δύο προσκυνεῖς, μᾶλλον δὲ σ. Cyr.*Nest*.2.10(p.47. 28; 53A); id.*expl.xii cap*.5(p.21.4; 6^1.152A) cit. s. συνδοξάζω; so fell into disfavour Χριστὸν...οὐχ ὡς ἄνθρωπον ∼οῦντες τῷ λόγῳ, ἵνα μὴ τομῆς φαντασία παρεισκρίνηται διὰ τὸ λέγειν τὸ 'σύν', ἀλλ' ὡς ἕνα ...προσκυνοῦντες id.*ep*.4(p.28.3; 5^2.24B); προσκυνεῖν...ὁμολογεῖ σὺν τῇ θεότητι τοῦτον'...διΐστησιν ἐναργῶς...τὸ γὰρ ἑτέρῳ ∼ούμενον, ἕτερόν που πάντως ἐστὶ παρ' ἐκεῖνο μεθ' οὗ προσκυνεῖσθαι λέγεται id. *Nest*.2.10(p.47.28; 53A); εἴ τις τολμᾷ λέγειν τὸν ἀναληφθέντα ἄνθρωπον σ. δεῖν τῷ θεῷ λόγῳ καὶ συνδοξάζεσθαι...ὡς ἕτερον ἑτέρῳ...ἀ. ἔ. id. *ep*.17 *anath*.8(p.41.13; 5^2.76E); οὐ δέον τι λέγειν ἕτερον ἑτέρῳ ∼εῖσθαι ἐν Χριστῷ, ἀλλὰ μιᾶς ὑποστάσεως προσκυνήσει τιμᾶσθαι τὸ τοῦ λόγου πρόσωπον ἕν Leont.H.*Nest*.1.44(M.86.1504B); flesh of Christ only to be worshipped in Person of incarnate Word σὰρξ τῆδε οὐ συμπεριέχεται ἵνα καὶ ὡς τῆσδε οὖσα τῆς μονάδος ∼ῆται *ib*.(1504C); deliberately readopted by Jo. D. τί...τὸ κτίσμα σ. τῷ κτίστῃ εἰ οὐδὲ μιᾶς φύσεως οὐδὲ μιᾶς ὑποστάσεως; Jo.D.*fid.Nest*.35(p.575); **c.** rehabilitated in orthodox use, id.*imag*.1.4(M.94.1236B) cit. s. ἀλουργίς; **3.** in iconoclastic controversy τῇ...προσκυνήσει τοῦ τύπου, ∼εῖται τὸ ζωοποιὸν ξύλον Thdr.Stud.*epp*.2.1(M.99.1117D).

***συμπροσκύνησις, ἡ, 1.** *worshipping in concert* with ἡ τῶν ἀρχῶν καὶ ἐξουσιῶν σ. Chrysipp.*enc.in Jo.Bapt*.15(p.47.12); **2.** *joint-worship*; of manhood of Christ with divinity, Leont.H.*Nest*.1.44 (M.86.1504B).

***συμπροσκυνητέον**, *one must worship together* or *equally* δέον... τρισὶ μὲν ὁμοτίμοις προσκυνήσεσι τὰς τρεῖς ὑποστάσεις...προσκυνεῖν... τῇ θείᾳ δὲ σαρκὶ...σ. κατὰ τὸν ἕνα υἱόν Leont.H.*Nest*.1.44(M.86. 1504C).

***συμπροσκυνητής, ὁ**, *fellow worshipper* with τὸν τῶν ἄνω δυνάμεων σ. Chrysipp.*enc.in Jo.Bapt*.3(p.33.14).

***συμπροσκυνητός**, (also proparoxytone), *to be worshipped together* or *with* ὡς γέννημα...ὁμοούσιον τῷ πατρὶ καὶ σ. ... τὸ ἅγιον πνεῦμα ἐξ αὐτοῦ...διὸ καὶ σ. Epiph.*haer*.76.53(p.408.17ff.; M.42.628D); of Christ's humanity together with divinity τὸν ἅγιον καὶ σ. αὐτοῦ ναόν ‡Eust.*Laz*.26(p.48.6).

συμπροστάτης, ὁ, *one who stands in front with others and protects*, *fellow champion*; met., of one's writings, Gr.Naz.*carm*.2.1.39.21 (M.37.1331A).

***συμπροσφέρω**, *offer together with* τῆς γνώμης τὴν ἀρετὴν συνάπτων τοῖς δώροις, καὶ αὐτὴν ψυχὴν σ. τῷ δεχομένῳ Bas.Sel.*or*.4.3(M.85. 69A).

***συμπροϋπάρχω**, *pre-exist with*, Gel.Cyz.*h.e*.2.16.1(M.85.1260C).

συμπροφητεύω, *prophesy along with*, Or.*hom.8.3 in Jer*.(p.59.14; M.13.341A).

***συμπροφήτης, ὁ**, *fellow prophet*, ‡Chrys.*hom*.2(13.207E); of parents of Jo. Bapt., Cosm.Ind.*top*.5(M.88.277B).

***σύμπτημα, τό**, *flock* of pigeons, ‡Caes.Naz.*dial*.140(M.38.1072).

***συμπτυκτικός**, *folding together, embracing*, Dion.Ar.*d.n*.11.1(M.3. 949A).

συμπτύσσ-ω, 1. *fold together*; of ranges of hills, ?*overlap*, Philost.*h.e*.3.24(M.65.512B); **2.** *embrace, enfold*, met. τῶν μεριστῶν ἡμῶν ἑτεροτήτων ὑπερκοσμίως ∼ομένων Dion.Ar.*d.n*.1.4(M.3.589D); **3.** *unify* σ. τὰς...ἑτερότητας...εἰς ἑνοειδῆ...ζωήν id.*e.h*.1.1(M.3. 372B); perf. ptcpl. pass., *unified, single* ἡ θεία τῆς συνάξεως τελετή...

ἐνιαίαν καὶ ἁπλῆν ἔχουσα κα σ. ἀρχήν *ib*.3.3.3(429A); *ib*.1.5(376D); id. *d.n*.4.16(M.3.713C).

σύμπτωμα, τό, 1. *falling together*; *conjunction* of heavenly bodies, Eus.*p.e*.6.6(252B; M.21.429A); **2.** *falling together, collapse*; of buildings in an earthquake, *ruins* ἐκ τοῦ κινδύνου περισώζεται, καὶ σωτηρίαν ἀπιστουμένην αὐτῷ σκεπασθεὶς τῷ σ. Gr.Naz.*or*.7.15(M.35.773A); πολλοὶ ἀπέθανον ἐν τοῖς σ. Jo.Mal.*chron*.18 p.489(M.97.708A); fig. ὃς ἐξ ἀρχῆς τὸν ἄνθρωπον κατεσκεύασε πύργον εἶναι καὶ οὐχὶ σ. Gr.Nyss. *hom.7 in Cant*.(M.44.933D); **3.** met., *fall* into sin, of *Fall* of Adam, ‡Ath.*Apoll*.1.7(M.26.1104C); other lapses, Gr.Nyss.*or.dom*.1(p.20.15; M.44.1132B).

σύμπτωσις, ἡ, *falling together*; **1.** *calamity, disaster* ἡ...τῶν ἀναγκαίων ἔνδεια γυμνάζει τὸν νοῦν...καὶ πᾶσαι σ. Proc.G.*Is*.proem.(M.87.1820C); ὦ καρδίας σ. ἠθλιωμένη Geo.Pis.*Pers*.1.27(M.92.1200A); **2.** *fall* into sin, *lapse* τὸ σῶμα...ἐκ τῷ πολλῷ πρότερον συμπτωθείσης ψυχῆς ταῖς πρὸς τὸ χεῖρον ἐπιθυμίαις, τὴν τοιαύτην πέπονθε σ. Gr.Agr. *Eccl*.4.1(M.98.916D).

***συμπτώσσω,** *shrink, cower* τῷ φόβῳ σ. Mac.Mgn.*apocr*.2.7(p.6.10).

***συμπτωχεύ-ω,** *be poor along with, share poverty with*; **1.** of men with Christ ἐὰν πτωχεύσαντι ∼σῃς, καὶ βασιλεύοντι συμβασιλεύσεις Gr.Nyss.*beat*.1(M.44.1208C); **2.** of Christ with men in Inc. τὸ σάρκα γενέσθαι τὸν...λόγον...καὶ σ. τοῖς ἐπὶ τῆς γῆς Cyr.*Is*.5.1(2.738D); id. *hom.pasch*.27.4(5².323D); εὐδοκία ἦν αὐτοῦ τοῦ λόγου σ. ἐν πάσῃ τῇ διαβιώσει τῆς σαρκὸς τὴν φυσικὴν αὐτοῦ μεγαλειότητα Leont.H.*Nest*.5.1(M.86.1724C).

***σύμπτωχος, 1.** *equally poverty-stricken* τῶν παρ' Ἕλλησι συμπτωχοτάτων αὐτοῖς θεῶν Didym.*Trin*.3.24(M.39.937C); **2.** *poor along with*; as subst., *companion in poverty, fellow pauper*, Ast.Am.*hom*.1 (M.40.173A); Synes.*ep*.67(M.66.1424C).

***σύμπυρος,** *akin to fire*, ref. Dan.3:25 ὁ ἐν τῷ καμίνῳ εἰς τύπον Χριστοῦ ὀφθεὶς...ὅλος ἦν...ἐν σχήματι ἀνθρώπου, ἔμπυρος, καὶ σ. καὶ ὁλόπυρος Anast.S.*hod*.21(M.89.281B).

συμπυρόω, *kindle, set on fire*; met., pass., of the mind, Dor.*doct*. 22.1(M.88.1821B).

συμπωλέω, *sell*, Bas.*ep*.108(3.202A; M.32.517B).

[*]**συμπωνέω,** for συμπονέω, *toil* or *suffer with*; *labour together*, *PLond*.1919.7.

***συμφαής,** *shining together*; met., of Son with H. Ghost, Gr. Naz.*carm*.2.1.38.8(M.37.1326A).

***συμφαιδρύνω,** *make bright, cause to rejoice at the same time* or *together* with, Max.*ep*.2(M.91.393B); Areth.*Apoc*.7:3(M.106.604D).

συμφαίνομαι, *appear along with* or *together*, ref. Gen.6:4 μετεσχηματίζοντο [sc. οἱ Ἐγρήγοροι]...εἰς ἄνδρα καὶ ἐν τῇ συνουσίᾳ τῶν ἀνδρῶν αὐτῶν συνεφαίνοντο αὐτοῖς *T.Reub*.5.6.

***συμφάμιλος,** [Lat. *familia*] *being with one's family*, †Anast.S. *relat*.suppl.(*OC* 2 p.87.20); Thphn.*chron*.p.316(M.108.765An.); *ib*. p.360(865A).

***συμφατνιάζω,** *lie with in a manger* ὁ θεὸς λόγος ὁ ἡμῖν ἀλόγοις συμφατνιάσας ‡Epiph.*hom*.6(M.43.504C).

***συμφατριάζω,** for ⟨συμφρατριάζω⟩, *conspire* with ὁ Μελίτιος... κατὰ τοῦ ἐπισκόπου σ. αὐτῷ [sc. τῷ Ἀρείῳ] Socr.*h.e*.1.6.39(M.67.53B); ἐκβληθεὶς διὰ τὴν αἵρεσιν σ. μετὰ Ἰωάννου...καὶ ἄλλων Cyr.S.*v.Sab*.84 (p.189.26).

***συμφέναξ, ὁ,** *fellow impostor*, Pall.*v.Chrys*.8(p.44.23; M.47.26).

***συμφερομένως,** *in agreement, harmoniously*, Didym.*Ps*.2:9(M. 39.1161A).

συμφθάνω, 1. of things, *come to pass, be accomplished* τὰ ἔτη τῶν χρόνων συνέφθασε...καὶ πάντα σ. τὰ προφητευθέντα *Dial.Ath.et Zacch*. 120(p.58f.); *ib*.121(p.60); τὰ πράγματα σ. Socr.*h.e*.1.32.2(M.67.164B); Bas.Sel.*v.Thecl*.1(M.85.500B); **2.** of persons, *be present*, Bas.*reg.br*. 136(2.461C; M.31.1172D); **3.** *attain* or *manage to, succeed in* μὴ συμφθάσας ἆραί τι πρὸς βραχὺ ἔχον ἐφόδιον Eus.Al.*serm*.21.12(M.86.437D).

***σύμφθασις, ἡ,** *arrival*, Thdr.Stud.*epp*.2.107(M.99.1368B).

συμφθέγγομαι, 1. *say the same things* as, *speak with one voice* συνήργουν, τάχα δὲ καὶ συνεφθέγγοντο τοῖς νεωτέροις Ath.*h.Ar*.55 (p.214.32; M.25.760D); **2.** *combine to express* χρυσῷ...ὁ περικείμενος πέπλος...τοῖς παραγεγυμνωμένοις καὶ ἀχρύσοις τοῦ σώματος εἰς ἄφραστόν τι σ. κάλλος ‡Jo.D.*Artem*.52(p.87.23; M.96.1300B); **3.** *agree* with οὗτος τοῖς ἄλλοις ⟨συμ⟩φθεγγόμενος Philost.*h.e*.1.6 (φθεγγόμενος M.65.464B); *assent to, acknowledge* τὴν...ἰσχὺν [sc. τοῦ βασιλείου τοῦ μεγάλου] καὶ τὸ κάλλος...ἐβιάσθη [sc. Philost.] σ. Phot.*cod*.40(M.103.73B).

συμφθίνω, *wane*; of the day, Rom.Mel.(*AS* 1 p.183).

***συμφιλιάζ-ω, 1.** intrans., *make friends with* μὴ συμφιλιάξῃς μετὰ αἱρετικοῦ Ephr.3.369F; *ib*.3.370A; ‡Proc.G.*Pr*.17:9(M.87.1396C); **2.** trans., *make* one *friends* with ∼ει [sc. ἀρετή] τῷ θεῷ τοὺς ἑπομένους αὐτῇ Or.*exp.in Pr*.15:19(M.17.176C).

***συμφιλιόω,** c. dat., *make a friend* of, Hesych.S.*temp*.1.33(M.93.1492B); pass., *become friends* with, Ephr.1.121E.

***συμφιλοπονέω,** *work together*, Or.*Cels*.1.14(p.66.27; M.11.681A).

συμφιλοσοφέω, 1. *live* a well-regulated *life together with*; *follow a way of life together* τὸ συγγενὲς σαρκίον ἀπολαβοῦσα [sc. ἡ ψυχή] ᾧ τὰ ἐκεῖθεν συνεφιλοσόφησε Gr.Naz.*or*.7.21(M.35.781C); of fellow religious τοὺς σ. σοι †Jo.D.*B.J*.17(M.96.1016A); **2.** *join in philosophizing, discussing*, or *studying* σ. σοι...τὰ σά Gr.Naz.*ep*.222(M. 37.361C).

συμφιλοτιμέομαι, *associate oneself* ἐρωτᾷ [sc. Christ] μὲν ὑπὲρ ἡμῶν ὡς ἄνθρωπος, σ. δὲ ὡς θεὸς τῷ...πατρί, διανέμοντι...τὰ ἀγαθά Cyr.*Jo*.11.8(4.966E).

συμφλέγ-ω, *scorch* θάλατταν ὁ ἥλιος...∼ει Philost.*h.e*.3.10(M.65.493A).

***συμφοινίσσομαι,** *be red as well* as, Cyr.*Zach*.95(3.784E).

συμφοιτάω, *frequent together*; hence *be a companion* οἱ...τοῖς ἀποστόλοις σ. Iren.*ep.Flor*.ap.Eus.*h.e*.5.20.4(M.20.483A).

συμφοίτησις, ἡ, *acquaintance, friendship*, Proc.G.*ep*.108(M.87.2757A).

συμφοιτητής, ὁ, *fellow disciple*, ref. Jo.13:8 οὐ μόνον τοῦ Ἰησοῦ κατηγορεῖ [sc. ὁ Πέτρος]...ἀλλὰ καὶ τῶν σ. Or.*Jo*.32.6(5; p.435.9; M.14.756B); *ib*.32.21(13; p.463.23; 801C).

συμφόρησις, ἡ, 1. *bringing together*; *conjoining* of soul and body in man, Leont.H.*Nest*.2.20(M.86.1581B); **2.** ? *admixture* τοὺς καρποὺς ζιζανίων ἀμιγεῖς καὶ πάσης ἀχυρώδους ἄχνης καὶ σ. καθαρούς Max. *ambig*.(M.91.1357B).

σύμφρασις, ἡ, 1. *connexion*, Or.*Jo*.6.6(3; p.113.33; M.14.209B); Gr. Nyss.*hom.2 in Cant*.(M.44.796A); **2.** *context* ἐκ τῆς σ. κατανοητέον... Or.*Jo*.19.2(1; p.299.23; M.14.525C); id.*comm.in Rom*.7:7a(*JTS* 14 p.13); Eus.*e.th*.3.3(p.153.24; M.24.996B); Gr.Nyss.*Eun*.3(2 p.14.1; M.45.577C).

συμφράσσ-ω, 1. *press closely together*; met., med., *unite, conspire*, Thdt.*ep*.152(4.1314); εἰς...τὸν τούτου [sc. τοῦ Ἀθανασίου] διωγμὸν πᾶσα ἡ οἰκουμένη σ. Jo.Mosch.*prat*.197(M.87.3085B); **2.** *bring into close union, stick together* ∼ωμεν...ἀλλήλους Chrys.*hom.4.4 in 2Thess*.(11.535B); τὸ συμπεφράχθαι, τὸ ἀλλήλων ἔχεσθαι *ib*.2.1 (515F); τὸν θεὸν τοῦτο δοξάζει, τὸ σ. id.*hom.27.3 in Rom*.(9.722A).

***συμφρονίζομαι,** pass., *be brought to one's senses, be restored to one's right mind*, ‡Jo.Jej.*exc.poenit*.(M.88.1936A).

***συμφρονικός,** s.v.l., ? *agreeable to prudence* ὃς ἐξιστῶν τῶν σ. ... ἐπὶ πᾶν βοσκηματῶδες...πάθος ἐλαύνει *cat.Apoc*.14:11(p.393.6) perh. for σωφρονικῶν.

συμφροντίζω, *deliberate, confer*, Synes.*regn*.20(p.46.8; M.66.1093A).

***συμφρουρέω,** *guard* or *watch together*, i.e. one with another; ptcpl. pass., *fellow captive*, Thdr.Stud.*epp*.1.39(M.99.1049D).

συμφρύγω, pass., *be quite burnt up*; of a martyr's bones, Chrys. *pan.Dros*.4(2.693E); of persons by famine, *be dried up, shrivelled*, Thdt.*Ezech*.24:9ff.(2.878).

σύμφρων, *of one mind, agreeing*; as subst. masc. or fem., *one likeminded, sympathizer, partisan* Μοντανὸν...καὶ Μανιχαῖον τὸν σ. αὐτοῦ Isid.Pel.*epp*.1.245(M.78.332C); Dam.*troph*.proem.2(p.190.9).

συμφυής, A. in gen.; **1.** *born with one, congenital, natural*, opp. ἐπιγενητός: ἆρ' οὖν ἐπιγενητή ἐστιν ἡ τοῦ υἱοῦ τοῦ θεοῦ βασιλεία καὶ οὐ σ. αὐτῷ; Or.*Jo*.1.28(30; p.35.22; M.14.76B); ὁ ἐν ἀνθρώπῳ σ. λόγος Eus.*e.th*.1.20(p.91.23; M.24.884C); *ib*.2.16(p.119.35; 936D); οἰκείας αὐτῷ [sc. human mind] καὶ σ. ἀναγωγῆς Dion.Ar.*c.h*.2.1f.(M.3.137B, 140A); also of what is *proper* to God τὸν ἐν θεῷ σ. λόγον Eus.*e.th*.2.7 (p.105.23; 912D); id.*Marcell*.2.1(p.31.30; M.24.777A); **2.** *natural, in accordance with nature*, ref. birth of Christ ὑπερφυᾶ τε καὶ σ. καρπὸν ἐβλάστησε [sc. ἡ γαστήρ] ‡Meth.*Sym.et Ann*.4(M.18.356C); **3.** *grown together, united*; esp. of parts of the body, *attached, adhering, forming one organ*; of matrix from which particular stone is hewed, Gr.Nyss.*hom.opif*.30(M.44.253C); Gnost. ζιζάνιον σ. τῇ ψυχῇ, τῷ χρηστῷ σπέρματι Clem.*exc.Thdot*.53(p.124.16; M.9.684C); met., *attached, following* τὸ νικᾶν σ. τοῖς σοῖς πόνοις Paul.Sil.*Soph*.10(M. 86.2119A); *like* ὦ πλάσμα γαστρὸς συμφυὲς τοῖς βατράχοις Geo.Pis. *carm*.1.66(p.3).

B. theol.; **1.** Trin., *organically one, naturally united*, ref. Mt. 16:16f. ἐπέγνω...τὸν σ. καὶ συναΐδιον κλάδον τοῦ θεοῦ Didym.*Trin*.1. 30(M.39.417A); *integral* οἰκεία καὶ σ. καὶ ἀχώριστος ἡ κοινωνία Bas. *Spir*.63(3.53B; M.32.184B); *united by nature, of one nature*, of Son with Father τὴν ἐξ ἀϊδίου ὕπαρξιν, τὴν ἀπαθῆ γέννησιν, τὸ σ. τῷ πατρί id.*Eun*.2.15(1.250D; M.29.601C); τὸ προσεχὲς καὶ...σ. τοῦ μονογενοῦς πρὸς τὸν πατέρα Gr.Nyss.*diff.ess.*7(M.32.337D); Nonn.*par.Jo.*14:9 (M.43.868B); Sophr.H.*or.*2.30(M.87.3253C); οὗτος σ. γόνος πέλων Jo.D.*carm.theoph.*68(p.211; M.96.828C); of the three Persons σ. καὶ συναΐδια Anast.*fid.*(p.272); πλέκει ἐκ τριῶν ἰσοσθενῶν καὶ σ. καὶ συναϊδίων προσώπων συνιόντων εἰς μίαν οὐσίαν καὶ δύναμιν καὶ βούλησιν καὶ...κυριότητα Gr.Agr.*Eccl.*4.1(M.98.920A); superl., Jo.D. *carm.pent.*42(p.214; M.96.836A); **2.** Christol.; **a.** of Christ's human nature, *made one* with σ. ἑαυτῷ τὴν ἀνθρωπότητα καὶ ἡνωμένην κατακτησάμενος, καὶ διὰ τῆς συγγενοῦς ἡμῶν σαρκὸς αὐτοῦ πρὸς ἑαυτὸν ἐπανάγων πᾶσαν τὴν ἀνθρωπότητα †Bas.*Chr.generat.*2(2. 596D; M.31.1460B); **b.** of Christ in rel. to mankind, *of like nature* τῷ πατρὶ ὁμοούσιος καὶ ἡμῖν σ. καὶ ὁμόφυλος Jo.D.*hom.*1.12(M.96.564B); **c.** (Apollinarian) of Christ's flesh with his divinity ζῶν...Χριστὸς σῶμα θεόπνουν καὶ πνεῦμα ἐν σαρκὶ θεϊκόν, νοῦς οὐράνιος..., σὰρξ ἁγία θεότητι σ. Apoll.*fr.*155(p.249.5)ap.Leont.B.*Apoll.*(M.86.1964B); cf. τίς δέ ἐστιν ὁ ἔνσαρκος ἐκεῖνος νοῦς, ὁ σ. τῆς σαρκὸς καὶ ἀχώριστος; Gr.Nyss.*Apoll.*35(M.45.1201C); but not of divinity with common flesh ὁ μὴ σώματι σ. θεὸς ἀμεταβλήτως ἑνοῦται πρὸς σῶμα Apoll.*fr.* 134(p.239.30)ap.Thdt.*eran.*2(4.172).

***συμφύησις**, ἡ, *a sharing of the same nature, being of like nature,* of Christ's relation to mankind οὐ προϋποστάσης τῆς πρὸς τὸν λόγον ἑνώσεως τῆς...αὐτοῦ σαρκός, ἀλλ' ἅμα τε φύσις καὶ σ. τῷ ὑπερφυεῖ Leont.H.*Nest.*1.14(M.86.1457C).

συμφυΐα (συμφυεία), ἡ, *growing together, union;*

A. in gen.; **1.** *affinity, kinship,* in spiritual life ἀμπελών ἐστιν ἡ ἀθανασία...ἡ ἀπάθεια καὶ ἡ πρὸς τὸ θεῖον ὁμοίωσις, καὶ ἡ παντὸς κακοῦ ἀλλοτρίωσις...ἕλιξ δὲ τοῦ ἀμπελῶνος, ἡ πρὸς τὴν ἀΐδιον ζωὴν περιπλοκή τε καὶ σ. Gr.Nyss.*hom.2 in Cant.*(M.44.800C); between persons, of bond of common humanity νενοσηκότας ἡμᾶς οὐ περιόψεσθε, οὐδὲ τῆς ἑαυτῶν σ. ἡμᾶς ἀποπέμψοισθε Jo.V CP *ep.*(M.96. 1417B); **2.** *cohesion, unity* τίς ἡ κοινωνία τούτων πρὸς ἄλληλα [sc. τῶν οὐρανίων καὶ τῶν ἐπιγείων], καὶ σ., καὶ σύμπνοια; Gr.Naz.*or.*28.16 (p.46.14; M.36.48A); τῆς ἁπάντων ὁμονοίας τε καὶ σ. ... ἀπεργαστική [sc. ἡ θεία εἰρήνη] Dion.Ar.*d.n.*11.1(M.3.948D); *ib.*11.2(949D); of members in human body καθάπερ καὶ ἐν ἡμῖν γίνεται διὰ τῆς πρὸς τὰ μέλη σ. ... τὸ πᾶν τῷ πεπονθότι συνδιατίθεται Gr.Nyss.*Apoll.*21(M.45. 1165A); of a work of art, *coherent whole, unity* πανθαυμάστη...τέχνη πρὸς μιᾶς σ. ἰδέαν συναρμοσθέν ‡Jo.D.*Artem.*52(p.87.21; M.96.1300A); **3.** *coming together into one, union;* of relation between soul and body, Gr.Nyss.*or.catech.*11(p.57.8; M.45.44A); id.*Apoll.*44(M.45. 1229A); id.*anim.et res.*(M.46.44D,48C); ὡς ἐπὶ ψυχῆς καὶ σώματος, ἥντινα ἕνωσίν τινες σύγκρασιν ἐκάλεσαν, ἤγουν σ. Jo.D.*dialect.*65(M.94. 664A); in spiritual world, ref. 1Jo.4:18 εἰ...μεταποιηθεὶς ὁ φόβος, ἀγάπη γένοιτο· τότε εὑρίσκεται μονὰς τὸ σωζόμενόν, ἐν τῇ πρὸς τὸ μόνον ἀγαθὸν σ., πάντων ἀλλήλοις ἑνωθέντων Gr.Nyss.*hom.15 in Cant.* (M.44.1116C); **4.** logical *continuity, connexion* δοκεῖ μὴ ἀκολουθεῖν ...ἔστι δὲ πολλὴ μᾶλλον ἡ σ. Cyr.*Ps.*18:8(M.69.832A); δεικνυμένης... τῆς περὶ τὸν ὀρθὸν λόγον τοῦ ἡμετέρου φρονήματος ὑγείας τε καὶ σ. Jo.V CP *ep.*(M.96.1433B); **5.** moral *union* τῆς πρὸς τὸ κακὸν σ. ἑαυτὴν ἀποστήσασα Gr.Nyss.*hom.11 in Cant.*(M.44.1001A); exeg. Mt.26:39 οὐκ ἀντιπτώσεως, οὔτε δειλίας, σ. δὲ μᾶλλον ἐντελοῦς καὶ συννεύσεως Max.*opusc.*(M.91.65B).

B. theol.; **1.** Trin., *oneness of nature, unity* ἄρνησίς ἐστιν...θεοῦ... μὴ σέβειν σ. Gr.Naz.*carm.*1.2.34.154(M.37.956A); νῷ καὶ λόγῳ καὶ πνεύματι, τῇ μιᾷ σ. τε καὶ θεότητι id.*or.*12.1(M.35.844A); ὧν [sc. πατρὸς καὶ υἱοῦ καὶ ἁγίου πνεύματος] πλοῦτός ἐστιν ἡ σ., καὶ τὸ ἓν ἔξαλμα τῆς λαμπρότητος *ib.*40.5(M.36.364B); τριῶν ἀπείρων ἄπειρον σ., θεὸν ἕκαστον καθ' ἑαυτὸ θεωρούμενον *ib.*40.41(417B); τῆς πρὸς τὸ ἕτερον σ. τε καὶ σχέσεως οὐσιώδους Cyr.*Jo.*1.5(4.46D); denied by Eunomius γεγεννῆσθαι παρὰ τοῦ πατρὸς τοῦ υἱοῦ τὴν οὐσίαν...οὐ κατὰ ῥεῦσιν ἢ διαίρεσιν τῆς τοῦ γεννήσαντος σ. ἀποσπασθεῖσαν Eun.ap.Gr. Nyss.*Eun.*4(2 p.57.3; M.45.628B); μηδεμίαν...τῆς ἀληθείας μήτε τῷ θεῷ συμφυΐαν προσμαρτυρούσης *ib.*12(1 p.385.25; 1113D); **2.** Christol.; *coming together into one;* **a.** of union of natures [1Cor.15:47f.] νομιστέον λέγεσθαι...οὐ κατὰ τὸ φαινόμενον τοῦ θεοῦ, ἀλλὰ κατὰ τὸ νοούμενον, κιρναμένων ὥσπερ τῶν φύσεων, οὕτω δὴ καὶ τῶν κλήσεων, καὶ περιχωρουσῶν εἰς ἀλλήλας τῷ λόγῳ τῆς σ. Gr.Naz.*ep.*101(M.37. 181C); ὡς διὰ τὴν συνάφειάν τε καὶ σ. κοινὰ γίνεσθαι τὰ ἑκατέρας ἀμφότερα Gr.Nyss.*Eun.*5(2 p.124.16; M.45.705D); τὴν πρὸς τὴν σάρκα τοῦ λόγου σ. ἀχώριστον εἶναι Leont.B.*Nest.et Eut.*2(M.86.1332A); περὶ...τῆς πρὸς ἄλληλα...ἑνώσεώς τε καὶ σ., ἣν οἱ πατέρες οὐσιωδῶς γεγενῆσθαι ἐφρόνησαν, Νεστόριος δὲ σχετικήν τε καὶ γνωμικὴν ταύτην εἰσάγει id.*fr.*(M.86.2009C); Leont.H.*Nest.*1.18(M.86.1468C) cit. s. ἐκθέωσις; τῆς σαρκικῆς σ. *ib.*5.23(1745B); κιρναμένων...τῶν...φύσεων, καὶ περιχωρουσῶν εἰς ἀλλήλας τῷ λόγῳ τῆς σ. καὶ τῆς ἑνώσεως Thdr. Raith.*inc.*(p.194.15; M.91.1496A); τὰ φυσικὰ ἰδιώματα τῇ πρὸς ἄλληλα σ. ... ἐνίζουσα [sc. the hypostatic union] Max.*opusc.*(M.91. 96D); ὅταν [sc. λέγωμεν]...ἐξ ἀμφοῖν ἅμα, ἕνωσιν, κοινωνίαν...σ. ... φάσκομεν ‡Cyr.*Trin.*24(6^3.29D; M.77.1165B); **b.** of union of wills διὰ τὴν ἕνωσιν καὶ τὴν πρὸς ἀλλήλας διόλου τῶν φυσικῶν ἐνεργειῶν σ. Max. *opusc.*(M.91.100C); *ib.*(101A); εἰ...τεθέωτο, τῇ τοῦ θεοῦντος...σ. τεθέωτο *ib.*(48B).

συμφυλέτης, ὁ, *member of the same tribe,* Hermias *irris.*8(M.6. 1177A).

***συμφυλέτις**, ἡ, fem. of συμφυλέτης, Isid.Pel.*epp.*1.7(M.78.184C).

σύμφυλος, *of the same stock; of the same class* with, *cognate* φησὶ γὰρ ἡμᾶς εἰ μὴ ἐκεῖνο λέγομεν μήτε...πρὸ πάντων εἶναι [sc. the Son] λέγειν μήτε 'σ. εἶναι θεοῦ'...τὸ δὲ σ. εἶναι θεοῦ ἄπαγε. μηδεὶς οὕτως ἐν Χριστιανοῖς ταπεινὰ...ὀνοματοποιήσειε ῥήματα, ὥστε τὸν ὄντως ὄντα θεὸν σ. θεοῦ καὶ μὴ ἀληθινὸν ἀνακηρύσσειν θεόν...εἴποι γὰρ ἂν καὶ ἐκεῖνος [sc. Εὐνόμιος]...τὸ σ. αὐτὸν εἶναι θεοῦ Apoll.*fr.*55(p.217. 10)ap.Gr.Nyss.*Apoll.*28(M.45.1184B,C); εἰρῆσθαι τὸ σ. ὅπερ ἐστὶ συμφυῆ τε καὶ ὁμοούσιον Gr.Nyss.*Apoll.*19(M.45.1161B).

συμφύρδην, *confusedly,* Tat.*orat.*1(p.2.8; M.6.805B).

***συμφυρμός**, ὁ, *mingling;* met., *involvement* σ. πονηρίας Herm. *vis.*2.2.2.

σύμφυρσις, ἡ, **1.** *admixture* with evil etc., Dion.Ar.*c.h.*3.3(M.3. 165D); Max.*schol.c.h.*3.2(M.4.52A); Thdr.Stud.*epp.*2.219(M.99.1664A); **2.** theol., *mixture, confusion,* Trin. ἑνοῦται...ὥστε ἔχεσθαι ἀλλήλων· καὶ τὴν ἐν ἀλλήλαις περιχώρησιν ἔχουσι [sc. hypostases of Son and H. Ghost] δίχα πάσης συναλοιφῆς καὶ σ. ‡Cyr.*Trin.*10(6^3.16A; M. 77.1144B); ἀσύγχυτον ἔχουσαι τὴν ἐν ἀλλήλαις περιχώρησιν...ὥστε ἔχεσθαι ἀλλήλων...μηδεμίας γινομένης συναλοιφῆς, ἢ σ. ἢ συγχύσεως Jo.D.*f.o.*1.14(M.94.860B); Christol. τὰ φυσικῶς ἑκατέρῳ μέρει τοῦ Χριστοῦ προσόντα θατέρῳ πεποιημένον, χωρὶς τῆς ἑκατέρου μέρους πρὸς θάτερον κατὰ τὸν φύσει λόγον μεταβολῆς καὶ σ. Max.*ambig.*(M. 91.1060A).

συμφύρω, **1.** *mix,* usu. pass.; in the mind, *confuse* σ. τὰ ἄμικτα Ath.*Ar.*1.18(M.26.49A); **2.** with persons socially, *associate, converse,* Pall.*h.Laus.*28(p.83.17; M.34.1097A); sexually, Isid.Pel.*epp.* 1.464(M.78.437B); **3.** *mix up, confound;* pass., *be mixed up* with, *involved* in, Dion.Al.ap.Eus.*h.e.*7.7.2(M.20.648B); Alex.Al.*ep.Alex.*6 (p.23.17; M.18.556C); ‡Ath.*doct.Ant.*16(M.28.580B).

***συμφυσιόομαι**, **1.** *be imparted as a second nature* συμπεφυσιωμένον τι ἔχω *possess* something *as second nature* αἱ ἅγιαι δυνάμεις ἐκ τῆς πρὸς τὸ φύσει ἅγιον κοινωνίας...συμπεφυσιωμένον τὸν ἁγιασμὸν ἔχουσι Bas.*Eun.*3.2(1.274B; M.29.660B); **2.** *become a second nature, coalesce with the nature of* ὁ ὑετὸς δένδρεσι καὶ φυτοῖς σ. Epiph.*anc.*66 (p.79.19; M.43.136A).

σύμφυσις, ἡ, *growing together;* hence *union* of soul and body μετὰ τὴν εἰς τὸ σῶμα σ. τῆς ψυχῆς γίγνεται τὸ παράπτωμα, ὅτι τὸ συναμφότερον ὁ ἄνθρωπος Meth.*res.*1.55(p.314.16; M.41.1149A).

σύμφυτος, **1.** *born in, innate* τοῦ...σ. νόμου σωτῆρος οἷα καὶ ἰατροῦ Eus.*p.e.*6.6(250D; M.21.425C); ὅτε τὸν Ἀδὰμ...ἔπλασε ὁ θεός, μήτιγε σ. αὐτῷ δέδωκε τὴν ἁμαρτίαν; ‡Ath.*Apoll.*1.15(M.26.1120B); **2.** *natural; cognate, kindred* τὸν οὐράνιον διψῶσαι καὶ σ. τόπον Meth. *symp.*4.5(p.51.2; M.18.93B); **3.** *grown together, united,* ref. Rom.6:5 σ. ἐγένου τῷ ὁμοιώματι τοῦ θανάτου τοῦ σωτῆρος Cyr.H.*catech.*3.12; γενόμενοι σ. τῷ ὁμοιώματι τοῦ θανάτου τοῦ...υἱοῦ διὰ τοῦ βαπτίσματος *Rit.Bapt.*(p.401); *Euchol.*(p.287).

συμφύω, **1.** *unite* (intrans.), [irreg. perf. συμπεφυῶτες ἐμῷ...θάμνῳ ...συμπεφυῶτες ἐμοί Nonn.*par.Jo.*15:4(M.43.873A)]; of union by grace τοῦ θεοῦ τοῦ...ἐν πᾶσι πληρουμένου, μελῶν δίκην, κατὰ τὴν ἀναλογίαν τῆς ἐν ἑκάστῳ πίστεως αὐτῷ συμφυεῖσιν Max.*opusc.*(M.91. 25B); Christol. ἡ σὰρξ γενομένη τῇ φύσει θεότητος σάρξ...ὅπερ ἦν καὶ θεότητι συμφυεῖσα μεμένηκε τὴν φύσιν τὴν ἐνέργειαν ‡Hipp. *Ber.Hel.*2(p.322.24; M.10.833A); **2.** perf.; **a.** *be with one from birth;* ptcpl., *natural* ὀμνύομεν κατὰ τῆς σ. εὐδαιμονίας τοῦ...βασιλέως *M.Scill.*3; ref. Ezech.1:6 ἑτέρας...ἐν ἑαυτῷ σ. κεφαλὰς ἔχειν Meth. *res.*2.10(p.352.4); of reason in man τὸν σ. λόγον Or.*Jo.*10.24(16; p.196.21; M.14.349B); Ath.*gent.*40(M.25.81A); **b.** *be united* διακεῖσθαι κατὰ τὸν λόγον καὶ συμπεφυκέναι αὐτῷ Or.*Jo.*8.23(6; p.325.10; M.14. 569C); ὥσπερ ἡ σκιὰ τῷ σώματι ἕπεται οὕτω καὶ ἡ ἁμαρτία τῇ ψυχῇ σ. ‡Bas.*Lac.*5(2.590E; M.31.1445C).

συμφυῶς, **1.** *naturally;* σ. ἔχω *bear a relationship* to, *have an affinity* with τὴν νοερὰν...φύσιν ἣν καλοῦμεν ψυχήν, ἀκόλουθον σ. πρὸς τὸ ἡνωμένον ἔχειν Gr.Nyss.*anim.et res.*(M.46.45B); **2.** *in accordance with one's nature* τὴν θεαρχικὴν ἀκτῖνα...τοῖς καθ' ἡμᾶς...σ. καὶ οἰκείως διεσκευασμένην Dion.Ar.*c.h.*1.2(M.3.121C); id.*d.n.*4.16(M.3. 713C); id.*ep.*9.1(M.3.1108A); **3.** theol., *connaturally,* of mode of existence of each Person of Trin. in rel. to the others πατέρα...ἐν υἱῷ, ὡς ἐν ὁμοουσίῳ γεννήματι, σ. ... μένει...ὁ πατὴρ τοῦθ' ὅπερ ἐστί, κἂν ὑπάρχῃ σ. υἱῷ...καὶ πάλιν ὁ υἱὸς οὐχ ἕτερόν τι...κἂν ὑπάρχῃ σ. ἐν πατρί Cyr.*Jo*.1.5(4.46B,C).

[*]**συμφώδης**, for σομφώδης, *porous, spongy* αἱ σ. τῶν ἠπείρων καὶ ὕπαντροι Bas.*hex*.4.6(M.29.92C; σομφώδεις 1.38E); ref. tongue δέον... αὐτὴν δέρμα σ. γ' ἔχειν πρὸς τὰς ἀνακλάσεις τε τῶν ἐδεσμάτων Geo.Pis. *hex*.703(M.92.1489A; σομφῶδες φέρειν p.625).

συμφων-έω, **1.** *be in harmony with*; lit. and met.; of stones, *fit together* ἡρμοσμένοι ἦσαν καὶ συνεφώνουν τῇ ἁρμογῇ μετὰ τῶν ἑτέρων λίθων Herm.*vis*.3.2.6; of statements, *agree*, ref. scriptures ταύτῃ τῶν ἡμερῶν τῇ ἀκριβείᾳ αἱ γραφαὶ σ. Clem.*fr*.28(p.217.7; M.9.757B); τοῖς διδάγμασι τοῖς παρὰ τοῦ πνεύματος ἡμῖν δεδομένοις τὸν λόγον συγκρίνοντας, ὃ μὲν ἂν ἐκείνοις σ. εὕρωμεν καταδέχεσθαι Bas.*Eun*.2.1 (1.239A; M.29.573C); ταύτην τὴν μαρτυρίαν τῇ δεσποτικῇ σ. διδασκαλίᾳ Thdt.*Heb*.2:5ff.(3.556); theol., of the Persons in the Trinity, by Asterius made the basis of union ἓν...εἶναι καὶ ταὐτὸν Ἀστέριος κατὰ τοῦτο ἀπεφήνατο μόνον τὸν πατέρα καὶ τὸν υἱόν, καθ' ὃ ἐν πᾶσιν σ. Marcell.*fr*.63 ap.Eus.*Marcell*.1.4(p.29.10; M.24.772A); criticized by the orthodox οὐκοῦν εἰ διὰ τὴν συμφωνίαν ἕν ἐστιν ὁ πατὴρ καὶ ὁ υἱός, εἴη ἂν καὶ τῶν γενητῶν τὰ σ. οὕτω πρὸς τὸν θεόν Ath.*syn*.48(p.273.4; M.26.780A); v. συμφωνία; **2.** *fix by agreement* τὸν καιρὸν ὃν συνεφώνησε μετὰ τῶν Μελιτιανῶν προφέρων [sc. Eus. Nic.] Ath. *apol.sec*.60(p.140.12; M.25.357C); **3.** *conspire* εἰς τὴν καθ' ἡμῶν συμφωνήσαντα βλάβην Bas.*hom*.8.2(1.63E; M.31.308D); **4.** *make the subject of a transaction* οἱ ἐξωνούμενοι τὸν ἐξωνούμενον τῷ ζωοποιῷ αὐτοῦ αἵματι τὸν κόσμον σ. τριάκοντα ἀργυρίοις ‡Meth.*palm*.7(M.18.397A); Chrys.*hom.15.2 in Phil*.(11.313D); Χριστὸς ∼εῖταί τε καὶ πιπράσκεται Evagr.*h.e*.1.2(p.7.3; M.86.2424A).

***συμφωνητής**, **ὁ**, *companion, friend*, *Apophth.Patr*.(M.65.377B).

συμφωνία, **ἡ**, **1.** *concord, unison*; met., *harmony, agreement*; **a.** ref. Christian revelation ἡ σ. νόμου τε καὶ προφητῶν τῇ κατὰ τὴν τοῦ κυρίου παρουσίαν παραδιδομένῃ διαθήκῃ Clem.*str*.6.15(p.495.6; M.9.349A); *ib*.6.11(p.476.10; 309B); of prophets with apostles, Meth. *arbitr*.1(p.146.19; M.18.241A); between evangelists, Eus.*h.e*.6.31.3 (M.20.592A); its ground in H. Ghost τῆς σ. τοῦ ἁγίου πνεύματος, διὰ πολλῶν καὶ διαφόρων προσώπων...μαρτυρούσης Marcell.*fr*.48 ap. Eus.*Marcell*.2.2(p.35.8; M.24.784A); H. Ghost also the ground of mutual unity between Christians ἡμεῖς...καθὼς ὁ πατὴρ καὶ ὁ υἱός, οὕτω γινόμεθα ἐν τῷ φρονήματι καὶ τῇ τοῦ πνεύματος σ. Ath.*Ar*.3.23 (M.26.372A); **b.** theol., ref. Trin. οἰκονομία συμφωνίας συνάγεται εἰς ἕνα θεόν Hipp.*Noët*.14(M.10.821A; cj. συμφώνως p.257.4); τοῦτό εἰμι ἐγώ [sc. Χριστός], τοῦτο βούλεται ὁ θεός, τοῦτο συμφωνία ἐστί, τοῦτο ἁρμονία πατρός, τοῦτο υἱός Clem.*prot*.12(p.85.5; M.8.241B); Or.*Cels*. 8.12(p.230.1; M.11.1533C) cit. s. βούλημα; accepted by those with Arian tendencies as ground of union between Persons οὕτω...ἔφη [sc. Ἀστέριος]· καὶ διὰ τὴν ἐν πᾶσιν λόγοις τε καὶ ἔργοις ἀκριβῆ σ., ἐγὼ καὶ ὁ πατὴρ ἕν ἐσμεν Marcell.*fr*.63 ap.Eus.*Marcell*.1.4(p.29.11; M. 24.772A); τῇ μὲν ὑποστάσει τρία, τῇ δὲ σ. ἓν *Symb.Ant*.(341)2(p.249.33; M.26.724B); rejected as such by Marcellus οὐ διὰ τὴν ἐν ἅπασιν οὖν λόγοις τε καὶ ἔργοις ἀκριβῆ σ., ὡς Ἀστέριος ἔφη, ὁ σωτὴρ λέγει [Jo.10:30], ἀλλὰ διότι ἀδύνατόν ἐστιν ἢ λόγον θεοῦ ἢ θεὸν τοῦ ἑαυτοῦ μερίζεσθαι λόγου...ποία γὰρ ἐν καιρῷ τοῦ πάθους σ. τοῦτο λέγοντος [Mt.26:39] Marcell.*fr*.64 ap.Eus.*Marcell*.2.2(pp.37.29,38.4; 788A,B); πῶς σ. ἔχειν πρὸς τὸν πατέρα ὁ υἱὸς δύναται ἢ ὁ πατὴρ πρὸς τὸν υἱόν; τοῦ υἱοῦ [Jo.16:15] λέγοντος; id.*fr*.65 *ib*.(p.38.18; 788C); ὁρᾷς ὅτι οὐδ' ἐνταῦθα ἀφίσταται τῆς σ. id.*fr*.66 ap.eund.*e.th*.2.19(p.123.28; M.24. 944C); and by homoousians in gen. εἰρηκέναι αὐτὸν φιλονεικοῦσιν... ἐγὼ καὶ ὁ πατὴρ ἕν ἐσμεν, διὰ τὴν σ. καὶ τὴν ὁμόνοιαν CSard.*ep.cath*. ap.Thdt.*h.e*.2.8.45(3.846); τὸ ἓν εἶναι τὸν πατέρα καὶ τὸν υἱόν· εἰ μὲν οὖν τῇ σ. τῶν δογμάτων...ὡς οἱ Ἀρειανοὶ λέγουσι, φαῦλος ὁ τοιοῦτος νοῦς· καὶ γὰρ καὶ οἱ ἅγιοι καὶ μᾶλλόν γε ἄγγελοι...τὴν τοιαύτην ἔχουσι πρὸς τὸν θεὸν συμφωνίαν Ath.*syn*.48(pp.272.32,273.2; M.26.780A); τὴν σ. κατὰ σε [sc. the Arian] ἢ τὴν θεότητα κατὰ τὸν ὀρθὸν λόγον ‡Ath. *disp*.9(M.28.448A); used in conjunction with other definitions of divine unity ἓν ὁμολογοῦμεν τῆς θεότητος ἀξίωμα, καὶ μίαν ἀκριβῆ τῆς βασιλείας τὴν σ. *Symb.Ant*.(345)9(p.254.2; M.26.733C); τριὰς αὕτη ἁγία καλεῖται, τρία ὄντα μία σ. μία θεότης Epiph.*anc*.67(p.82.5; M. 43.137C); τοῦ μὲν πατρὸς βουληθέντος, τοῦ δὲ υἱοῦ σαρκωθέντος, τοῦ δὲ πνεύματος συνεργήσαντος...πᾶσι συμφωνίᾳ τε καὶ ἑνότητι καὶ ταυτότητι τῆς μιᾶς βουλῆς τε καὶ αὐθεντίας καὶ βασιλείας τῆς ἐν τριάδι ‡Caes.Naz.*dial*.167(M.38.1129); **2.** in concrete sense, *agreement, pact* εἰ βούλοιντο τὴν προτέραν σ. ὅρκοις βεβαιῶσαι Thphn.*chron*.p.281(M. 108.693B); **3.** *concourse* ἔτους πρώτου βασιλεύοντος τοῦ Ἀντωνίνου... ἦν σ. πολλὴ τῶν Χριστιανῶν *M.Glyc*.1(p.12*); **4.** title of Gnost. book or books τὸ μὲν γὰρ Συμφωνίαν μικρὸν δῆθεν βιβλίον καλοῦσι, τὸ δὲ μέγα Συμφωνίαν Epiph.*haer*.40.2(p.82.9f.; M.41.680B).

σύμφωνος, *harmonious*; **1.** *concordant, consistent*, of scriptures παραστῆσαι τὴν δοκοῦσαν διαφωνίαν σ. ὑπάρχειν Or.*Jo*.10.22(15; p.194.21; M.14.345D); ref. Is.9:6f. τούτοις...σ. ἦν καὶ ἅπερ ὁ Γαβριὴλ τὴν παρθένον εὐηγγελίζατο Eus.*Marcell*.2.1(p.33.5; M.24.780A); ὅτι...ἡ θεία γραφὴ καὶ σ. ... ἑαυτῇ καὶ καθ' ἑαυτὴν διηγουμένη Cosm.Ind. *top*.3 tit.(M.88.136A); **2.** of the self, *integrated* αὕτη [sc. the peace of Christ]...οὐ μόνον...πάντας κοινῇ πρὸς ἀλλήλους συνάπτει, ἀλλὰ καὶ ἰδίᾳ ἕκαστον ἑαυτῷ σ. ἀποτελεῖ Thdr.Heracl.ap.*cat.Jo*.14:27(p.352.27); **3.** of relations bet. persons, *friendly*; neut. plur. as subst., *harmony*, Hipp.*Dan*.4.47.6; **4.** pass., *agreed upon, fixed*; in concrete sense, neut. plur., *agreement* σ. ... πρὸς ἐμὲ πεποιήκασιν *A.Thom*.A 108(p.220.4); δωρεὰν ἦλθεν ὁ Χριστὸς ἐκχέαι τὸ αἷμα... ὑπὲρ οὗ σ. σὺ ποιεῖς Chrys.*prod.Jud*.1.3(2.381E); τῶν γαμικῶν σ. Ath. Scholast.*coll*.9.12(p.110); **5.** = *pactum, way, kind* ἐν οἵῳ δή ποτε συμφώνῳ, ἢ ἔκοντα ἢ μὴ ἔκοντα, ὅμως δὲ τῷ σταυρῷ ὁμολογεῖς προσηλῶσθαι *A.(Pass.)Andr*.A 4(p.8.15); *ib*.B 4(p.8.25; M.2.1224A); ὥσπερ εἰσὶ κύρια καὶ γνήσια τέκνα...οὕτω καὶ ἀναδόχων πλεῖστα τὰ σ. γνωρίζονται Jo.Clim.*past*.12(M.88.1189B); **6.** Trin., *in harmony, in agreement* φασὶ [sc. Arius]...ἐπεὶ...ἐν πᾶσίν ἐστι [sc. ὁ υἱός] σ. αὐτῷ [sc. τῷ πατρί]...διὰ τοῦτο αὐτὸς καὶ ὁ πατὴρ ἕν εἰσι Ath.*Ar*.3. 10(M.26.341A).

***συμφωνότης**, **ἡ**, *harmony, agreement*, opp. διαφωνία, Or.*comm. in Mt*.2(p.5.14; M.13.832B).

συμφώνως, **1.** *with one voice, in accord*; **a.** *in concert* οἱ χοροὶ μαρτύρων, εἷς μὲν τῆς διαθήκης τῆς καινῆς, θάτερος δὲ τῆς παλαιᾶς, ἀντίφθογγον ὕμνον σ. τῷ ... θεῷ...ἀναπέμποντες Meth.*res*.1.56(p.316. 10); πάντες σ. λεγέτωσαν καὶ μετὰ τοῦ πνεύματός σου *Lit*.ap.*Const. App*.8.12.4; met. οὔτε ὀφθαλμὸς ὑγιῶς ἴδοι μὴ κοινωνὸν ἔχων τὸν ἕτερον, καὶ μετ' αὐτοῦ σ. προσβάλλων τοῖς ὁρατοῖς Bas.*ep*.97(3.191A; M.32.493B); **b.** met., *unanimously* τὰς δυνάμεις [sc. τοῦ Ἰησοῦ] σ. πρὸς ἁπάντων μαρτυρουμένας Eus.*h.e*.1.13.2(M.20.120B); πάντες σ. ἔγραψαν τὰ δόξαντα Ath.*syn*.11(p.239.9; M.26.701A); παρὰ πάντων σ. ... θρυλλεῖται Bas.*ep*.48(3.142A; M.32.385A); **2.** *in accordance with, corresponding to* τροφή...τῇ...παρὰ τοῦ διδόντος...χορηγίᾳ σ. ἅπασι... παροῦσα Clem.*str*.3.2(p.198.19; M.8.1108B); πήχεις δώδεκα σ. τῷ... ἑλιγμῷ τῶν μηνῶν ιβ' *ib*.6.11(p.475.20; M.9.309A); σ. τῇ προαιρέσει τὴν ζωὴν διεξάγειν Bas.*ep*.293(3.431E; M.32.1036A); **3.** *concordantly, in agreement*, Or.*Jo*.6.43(26; p.152.23; M.14.276B); τὸ ὁμοούσιον σ. τοῖς ἐκ τῶν γραφῶν περὶ τοῦ σωτῆρος εἰρημένοις ἔγραψαν Ath.*decr*.28 (p.25.3; M.25.468C); Bas.*fid*.6(2.229E; M.31.692B).

συμφωτίζομαι, pass., *be baptized together* ὁ Ἰσραὴλ...συνεφωτίζετο ὑπὸ τοῦ χυθέντος αἵματος Mel.*pass*.30 p.5.22.

***συμψάλλω**, *sing [psalms] with* or *together* σ. τῷ πλήθει *A.Mt*. 23(p.250.3); Gr.Naz.*or*.5.25(M.35.693B); Gr.Nyss.*ep*.2(M.46.1013B); γυναιξὶ δὲ παραγγέλλεσθαι ἐν ἐκκλησίαις μὴ λαλεῖν...μήτε σ. *Didasc. Patr*.8(p.18.2); other than psalms, Pall.*h.Laus*.43(p.130.17; M.34. 1210D) cit. s. ἀντίφωνος; met., *A.Jo*.95(p.198.5) cit. s. ὀγδοάς.

σύμψαλμα, **τό**, *a sounding in concert, ut quemadmodum synpsalma dicitur vocis copulatio in cantando, ita diapsalma disjunctio earum*, Isid.H.*etym*.6.19.15.

***συμψαλτέον**, *one must sing psalms together*, Thdr.Stud.*epp*.1.40 (M.99.1056A).

συμψάω, *obliterate, erase*; met., *dispose of* τὸ θνητὸν...ἀπωλείᾳ σ. Eus.*l.C*.15(p.244.24; συμψήσας M.20.1413C); *clean by erasing* συμψήσας τὸν χάρτην Hipp.*haer*.4.28(p.54.7; cj. συμπτύξας M.16. 3090B).

συμψέλιον, **τό**, v. συμψέλλιον.

συμψελλίζω, *stammer with*, e.g. children, beginners ὡς διδάσκαλος σ. παιδίοις Or.*adnot.in Dt*.1:31(M.17.24A); Gr.Nyss.*comm.not*.(M.45. 181A); Chrys.*hom.3.2 in Tit*.(11.745F); συψ-, Nil.*epp*.1.127(M.79. 137A).

συμψέλ(λ)ιον, **τό**, (Lat. *subsellia*) *bench*; seen in Hermas' vision, Herm.*vis*.3.1.4; *ib*.3.2.4; *ib*.3.10.1; its four legs symbolizing perfection, *ib*.3.10.5; *ib*.3.13.3; symbol of truth, opp. καθέδρα (? tripod) of false prophet, id.*mand*.11.1; used for an altar παρέθηκαν...σ. ὃ εὗρον ἐκεῖ, καὶ...ἐπέθηκεν ἄρτον τῆς εὐλογίας *A.Thom*.A 49(p.165.19); article of church furniture τὰ σ. καὶ τὸν θρόνον καὶ τὴν τράπεζαν Ath.*h.Ar*.56(p.214.35; M.25.760D); ἁρπάζουσι...τοὺς τοιούτους...ἐπὶ συμψελίοις δήσαντες Epiph.*haer*.58.1(p.358.23; M.41.1012B).

συμψεύδομαι, *lie, tell a lie together with*, fig. τοιαῦτα ψευδομένης τῆς ἐπιστολῆς, σ. τοῖς γεγραμμένοις καὶ ὁ κονιορτός Men.*exc.Rom*.19 (p.218.28; M.113.924A).

***συμψηλαφάω**, *grope also, join in feeling*, Leont.N.*v.Sym*.29(M. 93.1705B).

συμψηφίζω, **1.** *reckon*; *count up* συμψηφίσας τὴν ποσότητα τῆς δαπάνης Herm.*sim*.5.3.7; id.*vis*.3.1.4; accounts, Or.*comm.in Eph*. 1:10(p.241); ‡Ath.*doct.Ant*.16(M.28.580C); v. συμψάω; **2.** med.;

vote with, agree, approve οὐ σ. ταῖς ἡμετέραις γνώμαις, οὐδὲ συνυπογράψαι ταῖς περὶ αὐτοῦ ψήφοις ἐξενεχθείσαις ἠβουλήθησαν CCP (360)*ep*.ap.Thdt.*h.e*.2.28.3(3.900); Thdt.*eran*.1(4.6); of God παραλήψομαι συνεργοῦντά τε καὶ συμψηφιούμενον τοῖς ἐμοῖς πλεονεκτήμασιν ...πατέρα Cyr.*Jo*.5.2(4.492E); and Christ ἀπόστολόν με προεβάλετο, φησίν, ὁ δεσπότης θεὸς συμψηφισαμένου καὶ τοῦ υἱοῦ Thdt.*2Tim*.1:1(3.676); **3.** pass., *be a candidate along with* προεβλήθη ἐπίσκοπος Παλλάδιος...συνεψηφίσθη δὲ Παλλαδίῳ καὶ Ἰωάννης Thphn.*chron*.p.116 (M.108.329A).

σύμψηφος, **1.** *voting with* or *together*; hence *ratifying* σ. ἔχει [sc. bishop] καὶ συνίστορα τῆς δίκης τὸν Χριστόν *Const.App*.2.47.2; **2.** *of the same opinion*, Phil.2:2 cit. as σ., τὸ ἓν φρονοῦντες *cat.Phil*.2:2 (p.245.33) for σύμψυχοι Chrys.*hom*.5.*1 in Phil*.(11.228D); **3.** in bad sense, *confederate* σ. γεγόνασι [sc. Pharisees and Herodians] Chrys. *hom*.70.*1 in Mt*.(7.687E).

***συμψυχία, ἡ,** *unanimity, harmony*, Gr.Naz.*carm*.1.2.34.160(M.37.957A); *V.Chrys*.59(p.325.7); Thdr.Stud.*epp*.2.134,140,177(M.99.1432C,1445A,1549D).

σύμψυχος, **1.** *of one mind*, Eus.Nic.*libell*.(p.65.14; v.l. for συμψήφους M.67.113A); neut. as subst., *unity* τὸ σ. τῷ ἑτεροδόξῳ λύσαντες Gr.Naz.*or*.33.2(M.36.216B); **2.** in bad sense *confederate*, v. σύμψηφος; **3.** *with all inhabitants, with all on board*, etc. σεισθήσεται ἡ Ἑπτάλοφος καὶ καταποντισθήσεται σ. ἐν βυθῷ *Apoc.Dan*.C(p.119); τὰ... σκάφη ἐνέπρησε καὶ σ. κατέκαυσεν Thphn.*chron*.p.295(M.108.721A).

σύν, **1.** *with, together with*; theol.; **a.** in early doxologies linking Persons of Trin. indifferently Ἰησοῦς Χριστός...ᾧ ἡ δόξα σὺν τῷ πατρὶ καὶ ἁγίῳ πνεύματι *M.Polyc*.22.3; *ib*.14.3 cit. s. διά; εὐχάριστον αἶνον τῷ μόνῳ πατρὶ καὶ υἱῷ, υἱῷ καὶ πατρί...σὺν τῷ ἁγίῳ πνεύματι Clem.*paed*.3.12(p.291.9; M.8.681A); εὐχαριστοῦμεν τῷ πατρὶ τῷ παρασχομένῳ τοῖς ἰδίοις ἡμῖν τὸν τῶν ὅλων σωτῆρα...ᾧ ἡ δόξα...σὺν ἁγίῳ πνεύματι Afric.ap.Bas.*Spir*.73(3.62A; M.32.204C); τῷ...θεῷ πατρὶ καὶ υἱῷ...σὺν τῷ ἁγίῳ πνεύματι δόξα καὶ κράτος Dion.Al.*ib*.72 (60E; M.201B); τὸν τῶν προφητῶν ἅγιον θεὸν φωταγωγὸν διὰ τοῦ σωτῆρος ἡμῶν Ἰησοῦ Χριστοῦ σ. ἁγίῳ πνεύματι καλέσαντες Eus.*ib*. (61C; M.204A); ἐν Χριστῷ...δι' οὗ καὶ μεθ' οὗ αὐτῷ τῷ πατρὶ σ. αὐτῷ τῷ υἱῷ ἐν ἁγίῳ πνεύματι...δόξα Ath.*inc*.57.3(M.25.197A); Bas.*Spir*.17 (15A; M.97B) cit. s. μετά; ἐν Χριστῷ Ἰησοῦ...ᾧ ἡ δόξα καὶ τὸ κράτος...σὺν τῷ πατρὶ καὶ τῷ ἁγίῳ πνεύματι Gr.Naz.*or*.17.13(M.35.981A); Gr.Nyss.*res*.1(M.46.628B); **b.** gradually tending to be appropriated for third Person ἐν Χριστῷ...δι' οὗ καὶ μεθ' οὗ τῷ πατρὶ ἡ δόξα...σὺν τῷ ἁγίῳ πνεύματι Ath.*ep.Serap*.4.7(M.26.648B); ἤδη... Ὠριγένην ἐν πολλαῖς τῶν εἰς τοὺς ψαλμοὺς διαλέξεων εὕρομεν 'σ. τῷ ἁγίῳ πνεύματι' τὴν δόξαν ἀποδιδόντα Bas.*Spir*.73(3.61C; M.32.204B); μοι...ἀμφοτέρως τὴν δοξολογίαν ἀποπληροῦντι τῷ θεῷ καὶ πατρί, νῦν μὲν 'μετὰ τοῦ υἱοῦ σ. τῷ πνεύματι τῷ ἁγίῳ', νῦν δὲ 'διὰ τοῦ υἱοῦ ἐν τῷ ἁγίῳ πνεύματι' *ib*.3(3D; M.72C); ὁ...ἐπισυνάξας καὶ χαρισάμενος τοῦ μέλλοντος τὴν ἐνέργειαν, διαφυλάξειεν ἡμᾶς ἐν αὐτῷ ἀβλαβεῖς... αὐτῷ ἡ δόξα καὶ τὸ κράτος σ. τῷ ἁγίῳ πνεύματι id.*hom*.23.4(2.189C; M.31.600A); cf. ἡ πατρὸς καὶ υἱοῦ σὺν ἁγίῳ πνεύματι δοξολογία Cyr.H. *catech*.6.1; Χριστῷ Ἰησοῦ...ᾧ πᾶσα δόξα, τιμὴ καὶ κράτος σὺν ἁγίῳ πνεύματι εἰς δόξαν θεοῦ πατρός Gr.Naz.*or*.44.12(M.36.621A); Epiph. *haer*.76.53(p.409.10; M.42.629B) cit. s. ἐν; id.*ep.Arab*.ap.*haer*.78.24 (p.475.2; M.42.737D); **c.** objected to by Arians as implying equality οὔτε μὴν 'σ. τῷ πατρί', φασί, 'καὶ τῷ υἱῷ' τὸ πνεῦμα τακτέον, ἀλλ' 'ὑπὸ τὸν υἱὸν καὶ τὸν πατέρα' Bas.*Spir*.13(3.10C; M.32.88B); their reasons for preferring ἐν refuted πῶς οὖν, φησίν, ἡ γραφὴ οὐδαμοῦ συνδοξαζόμενον πατρὶ καὶ υἱῷ τὸ πνεῦμα παρέδωκεν, ἀλλὰ...ἐξέκλινε τὸ 'σ. τῷ πνεύματι' εἰπεῖν, πανταχοῦ δὲ τὸ 'ἐν αὐτῷ' δοξάζειν ὡς ἁρμοδιώτερον προετίμησεν; ἐγὼ δὲ οὐδ' ἂν αὐτὸς φαίην ἀτιμοτέρας εἶναι διανοίας παραστατικὴν τὴν 'ἐν' συλλαβήν,...καὶ ἀντὶ τῆς 'σ.' πολλαχοῦ κειμένην αὐτὴν τετηρήκαμεν *ib*.58(49A,B; M.173C,D); **d.** comparison with ἐν: ἡ μὲν 'σ.' τὴν πρὸς ἀλλήλους συνάφειαν τῶν κοινωνούντων παρίστησιν...ἡ δὲ 'ἐν' τὴν σχέσιν τὴν πρὸς τὸ ἐν ᾧ τυγχάνουσιν ἐνεργοῦντες δηλοῖ...εἴ τῳ φίλον ἐν δοξολογίαις τῇ καὶ συλλαβῇ συνδεῖν τὰ ὀνόματα καὶ δοξάζειν ὡς ἐν εὐαγγελίοις ἐπὶ τοῦ βαπτίσματος μεμαθήκαμεν...οὐδεὶς ἀντερεῖ... 'ἐν τῷ πνεύματι', φησί, 'τῷ ἁγίῳ τὴν δοξολογίαν ἀποδοτέον τῷ θεῷ, οὐχὶ δὲ καὶ πνεύματι', καὶ ἐκθυμότατα τῆς φωνῆς ταύτης ὡς ταπεινωτικῆς τοῦ πνεύματος περιέχονται *ib*.60(50Df.; M.177Cf.); ὥστε ὅπου μὲν οἰκεία καὶ συμφυὴς...ἡ κοινωνία, σημαντικωτέρα φωνὴ ἡ 'σ.'...ὅπου δὲ προσγίνεσθαι ἡ ἀπ' αὐτοῦ χάρις καὶ πάλιν ἀπογίνεσθαι πέφυκεν, οἰκείως...τὸ ἐνυπάρχειν λέγεται *ib*.63(53B; M.184B); ἡ μὲν γὰρ 'ἐν' τὰ πρὸς ἡμᾶς παρίστησι μᾶλλον, ἡ δὲ 'σ.' τὴν πρὸς θεὸν κοινωνίαν τοῦ πνεύματος ἐξαγγέλλει. διόπερ ἀμφοτέραις κεχρήμεθα ταῖς φωναῖς... οὕτω καὶ 'ἐν τῷ πνεύματι' τὴν δόξαν προσάγομεν τῷ θεῷ καὶ 'σ. τῷ πνεύματι' *ib*.68(57Bf.; M.193Bf.); **e.** comparison with καί, *ib*.59 (50A,C,D; M.176C,177B) cit. s. καί; *ib*.68(57D; M.196A); **2.** in compounds, *together with*, to be avoided (e.g. in συμπροσκυνέω) ref. Christ's two natures as possibly implying two persons, Cyr.*ep*.4 (p.28.4; 5^2.24C) cit. s. συμπροσκυνέω = Pamph.H.*panopl*.4(p.611); Cyr.*apol.orient*.8(p.50.7ff.; 6^1.180A); Andr.Samos.*fr*.ap.Cyr.*apol. orient*.8(p.48.13; 177D).

***συνααρών, ὁ,** *fellow Aaron*, i.e. coadjutor ἔστην σ. Γρηγορίῳ γενέτῃ Gr.Naz.*carm*.2.1.98.4(M.37.1451A).

***συναγαλλιάομαι,** = συναγάλλομαι, *M.Ner.et Ach*.8(p.7.31).

***συναγαλλίασις, ἡ,** *rejoicing together*, Thdr.Stud.*epp*.2.145(M.99.1457B).

συναγάλλομαι, *rejoice with* σ. μετὰ τῆς...σοφίας ‡Proc.G.*Pr*.5:18 (M.87.1265B); abs., *rejoice together* τῇ ἐπιστροφῇ [sc. τῶν αἱρετικῶν] χαίρων καὶ σ. Max.*ep*.12(M.91.465C); in spirit Χριστῷ σ. Bas.*renunt*. 10(2.211E; M.31.648C); ταῖς ἄνω δυνάμεσι σ. Sophr.H.*or*.5(M.87.3312B).

***συνάγαμαι,** *share one's wonder*, Dion.Ar.*ep*.7.3(M.3.1081C).

συναγελάζ-ω, **1.** *herd with, cause to be herded together*, met. μήποτέ με...ταῖς ἀλλοτρίαις τῶν σῶν ποιμνίων ἀγέλαις ἡ τῆς ἀληθείας ἄγνοια σ. Gr.Nyss.*hom.2 in Cant*.(M.44.801C); with flock of Christ, the Church τοὺς πεπλανημένους...σ. ... οὕτω τοῖς ἁγίοις προσκυνηταῖς, παρατιθεὶς ἑαυτὸν ὡς ἄρτον ἐξ οὐρανοῦ Cyr.*ador*.12(1.427A); ref. head of Jo. Bapt. τὸ ῥεῦν σου αἷμα...σ. λαὸν...δοξάζειν θεόν Thdr.Stud. *cant*.14.3(p.368); **2.** met.; **a.** in Church, *join to the flock, unite* καθαρίζων αὐτὰ [sc. τὰ πρόβατα]...διὰ τῆς μετανοίας, καὶ πάλιν σ. αὐτὰ ἐν τῇ ἐκκλησίᾳ *Didasc.Patr*.8(p.17.19); pass. σ. τοῖς προβάτοις Cyr.H.*catech*.6.36; in the assembly, ref. Helena τὴν θαυμασίαν...τῷ πλήθει σ. Eus.*v.C*.3.45(p.96.30; M.20.1105B); ref. body of Const. τὸ... σκῆνος...τῷ λαῷ τοῦ θεοῦ σ. *ib*.4.71(p.147.13; 1225C); τοῖς ἁγίοις σ. Isid.Pel.*epp*.5.469(M.78.1600A); **b.** *join oneself* to a religious community μοναχοῖς σ. Evagr.*h.e*.3.26(p.123.22; M.86.2652A); **c.** in life to come ἀπέθανε...δι' ἡμᾶς...ἵνα...τοῖς οὐρανίοις ~εσθαι παρασκευάσῃ χοροῖς Cyr.*Jo*.6.1(4.648A).

***συναγένητος,** *uncreated together with, alike increate*; **1.** of matter, held by Greeks and Manicheans to be uncreated along with the demiurge, ‡Just.*confut*.52(M.6.1545C); Jo.D.*Man*.2(M.96.1333C); **2.** of universe, the uncreatedness of which is held to be implied in Origen's teaching on its eternity, Meth.*creat*.7(p.498.18; M.18.340B); and in Manich. doctrine, Tit.Bost.*Man*.1.18(M.18.1093A); **3.** of Logos σ. ὢν τῷ θεῷ Eus.*e.th*.3.3(p.154.1; συναγέννητος M.24.996C).

***συναγέννητος,** *unbegotten together with, alike ingenerate*; **1.** of Son with Father Φιλογονίου καὶ Ἑλλανικοῦ καὶ Μακαρίου, ἀνθρώπων αἱρετικῶν ἀκατηχήτων, τὸν υἱὸν λεγόντων οἱ μὲν ἐρυγήν, οἱ δὲ προβολήν, οἱ δὲ συναγέννητον Ar.*ep.Eus*.(p.2.7, v.l. ἀγέννητον M.42.212A); οὐδὲ γάρ ἐστιν...σ. τῷ πατρί id.*ep.Alex*.(p.13.11, v.l. συναγένητος M.26.709C); ἡνῶσθαι τῷ θεῷ καὶ σ. εἶναι αὐτῷ τὸν λόγον ἔφασκεν [sc. Marcellus] Eus.*e.th*.2.3(p.102.14; M.24.904C); οὔτε μὴν συνάναρχον καὶ σ. τῷ πατρὶ τὸν υἱὸν εἶναι νομιστέον *Symb.Ant*.(345)3(p.252.16; M.26.729A); **2.** of the universe and matter with the creator; in pagan philosophy δημιούργημα σ. ἐστι τῷ ἀγεννήτῳ δημιουργῷ ‡Just.*qu. Chr*.4.3(M.6.1452A): in heresy of Hermogenes ἐξ ὑποκειμένης ὕλης καὶ σ. τὸν θεὸν ἔφη δημιουργῆσαι τὰ πάντα Thdt.*haer*.1.19(4.311).

***συναγερτικός,** *collected within the sphere of, arranged under the principle of* θέλημά ἐστι φυσικόν...θέλημα δὲ γνωμικόν, ἡ τῶν καθ' ἡδονὴν συναγερτικῶν ποιὰ καὶ διάφορος κίνησίς τε καὶ ὄρεξις Max. *opusc*.(M.91.280A).

συναγιάζω, *sanctify together, make holy with*, cf. Rom.11:16 ἵνα ...ὅλον διὰ τῆς ἐν ἑαυτῷ ἀπαρχῆς σ. τὸ φύραμα Gr.Nyss.*Eun*.4(2 p.65.27; M.45.637B); *ib*.12(2 p.279.10; 889C); Cyr.ap.*cat.Heb*.suppl.2:11 (p.403.28); Cyr.S.*v.Cyriac*.(p.222.26).

***συνάγιος,** *of equal* or *of one holiness*, ref. Trin. τρία ἅγια τρία σ. Epiph.*anc*.67(p.82.2; M.43.137C); ‡Caes.Naz.*dial*.3(M.38.861).

συναγνοέω, *share the ignorance of, be in ignorance together with* συνηγνόηκε [sc. ὁ σατανᾶς]...τοῖς ἐσταυρωκόσιν, ὅτι πέπονθεν ἑκών Cyr.*hom pasch*.17.4(5^2.234C).

συναγόρευσις, ἡ, *joint advocacy* συναγόρευσιν...ὑπὲρ...τῶν ἱερῶν δογμάτων...ἀναλαβών Cyr.*Chr.un*.(5^1.768C).

συναγορεύω, **1.** *advocate jointly*; *plead the cause of* σ. [sc. Nestorius]...τῷ ἁγίῳ πνεύματι, περιυβρίζει δὲ τὸν υἱόν Cyr.*Nest*.4.2 (p.80.43; 6^1.103D); *ib*.2.10(p.47.34,40; 53B,C); **2.** *join in pleading, make joint supplication* with ἐν τῇ προσευχῇ σ. τῷ Δανιὴλ πρὸς τὸν θεόν Hipp.*Dan*.2.10.2(M.10.677A); **3.** *agree, tally* with τῇ λέξει σ. ἡ ἱστορία Or.*Jo*.5.2(p.101.13; M.14.188B); **4.** *harmonize* with πῶς ταύτῃ δυνήσεται σ. τῇ διηγήσει τὸ 'ἀπεθάνομεν σὺν Χριστῷ'; Or.*comm.in Rom*.6:8ff.(*JTS* 13 p.364); **5.** *comply with, observe* τοὺς φαρισαίους ...σ. τῷ νόμῳ προσποιουμένους Cyr.*Jo*.3.4(4.270C).

συναγραυλέω, *live* out of doors *together*; met., *live with, be a constant companion* αὗται [sc. prayer, fasting, and psalmody] σ. σοι Bas.*hom*.13.7(2.121A; M.31.440D).

συναγρυπνέω, *keep vigil with, watch together*, *V.Pach.Σ* 50(p.219.26).

***συνάγχω**, *constrict, synanchis a continentia spiritus et praefocatione dicta. Graeci enim συνάγχειν continere dicunt. qui enim hoc vitio laborant, dolore faucium praefocantur*, Isid.H.*etym*.4.6.6.

συνάγ-ω, **A.** *bring* persons *together*; **1.** *bring* or *gather together* persons esp. for deliberation or festivity; pass., of an eccl. council, *be gathered, meet*, Ath.*apol.sec*.1(p.87.14; M.25.248B); eschatol. ἵνα κἀμὲ σ. ὁ κύριος...μετὰ τῶν ἐκλεκτῶν αὐτοῦ *M.Polyc*.22.4; *Did*. 9.4 cit. s. B.1; συναχθήσεσθαι τὸν λαὸν...καὶ εὐφρανθῆναι σὺν τῷ Χριστῷ ἅμα τοῖς πατριάρχαις Just.*dial*.80.1(M.6.664B); Gnost., ref. Jo.10:7 ὅταν αὐτὸς εἰσέρχηται, καὶ τὸ σπέρμα συνεισέρχηται αὐτῷ εἰς τὸ πλήρωμα διὰ τῆς θύρας συναχθὲν καὶ εἰσαχθέν Clem.*exc.Thdot*.26(p.115.21; M.9.672C); cf. μέχρις ἂν ἐνταῦθα τὸ σπέρμα μένῃ, συνέχεται, καὶ συναχθέντος αὐτοῦ πάντα τάχιστα λυθήσεται id.*q.d.s*.36(p.183.29; M.9.641B); **2.** *assemble a congregation* for worship; *hold a service* esp. of celebrating eucharist; **a.** act., trans. and intrans. Αἰμιλιανὸς...οὐκ εἶπέν μοι...μὴ σύναγε...οὐ γὰρ περὶ τοῦ μὴ σ. ἑτέρους ὁ λόγος ἦν αὐτῷ Dion.Al.ap.Eus.*h.e*.7.11.4(M.20.664B); ~όντων ἡμῶν συνήθως ἐν εἰρήνῃ, τῶν τε λαῶν εὐφραινομένων ἐπὶ ταῖς συνάξεσι Ath.*ep.encycl*.2(p.170.24; M.25.225B); ἐλθεῖν τὸν πρεσβύτερον σ. αὐτάς Ephr.2. 115C; of heretics and schismatics μή τις...~ειν...τολμήσῃ Eus.*v.C*.3. 65(p.112.11; M.20.1141A); συγχωρεῖται τοῖς Μελετιανοῖς ἔκτοτε καθ' ἑαυτοὺς σ. Epiph.*haer*.68.6(p.146.8; M.42.193A); *ib*.68.5(p.145.12,18; 192B); ὁ...κλῆρος ὁ Ἀντιοχέων...κεκρυμμένως σ. ... πλῆθος ἀπέστη τῆς ἐκκλησίας σ. ἐν τῷ ὑπαίθρῳ Pall.*v.Chrys*.16(p.98.11,15; M.47.55); for a baptism, Dion.Ar.*e.h*.2.2.4(M.3.393C); hence *organize* a festival ἡ μήτηρ ἡ ἐμή...ἦν ἡ τῷ θεῷ ~ουσα καὶ κοσμοῦσα τὴν ἑορτήν Gr.Nyss.*mart*.2(M.46.785A); παῦσαι τὴν ἑορτὴν τοῦ σ. Pall.*v.Chrys*.9(p.57.14; M.47.33); *call together*, i.e. by being the occasion of an assembly ὁ μακάριος Παῦλος, ὁ τήμερον ἡμᾶς σ. Chrys.*laud.Paul*.4.1(2.490E); **b.** pass. intrans., *gather, assemble* for worship τὰ ...ὀστᾶ αὐτοῦ ἀπεθέμεθα...ἔνθα ὡς δυνατὸν ἡμῖν ~ομένοις ἐν ἀγαλλιάσει καὶ χαρᾷ *M.Polyc*.18.3; κατὰ κυριακὴν δὲ κυρίου σ. κλάσατε ἄρτον καὶ εὐχαριστήσατε *Did*.14.1; πυκνῶς...σ. ζητοῦντες τὰ ἀνήκοντα ταῖς ψυχαῖς ὑμῶν *ib*.16.2; ἔνθα σ. εἰσί [sc. οἱ ἀδελφοί], κοινὰς εὐχὰς ποιησόμενοι Just.*1apol*.65.1(M.6.428A); τῶν...λαῶν...ἐν ταῖς ἐκκλησίαις συναχθέντων Ath.*ep.encycl*.3(p.171.24; M.25.228B); *join in corporate worship, be present at eucharist* εἰδότες ὅτι καὶ αὐτοὶ ἁμαρτωλοί εἰσι τῷ ἁμαρτωλὸν εἶναι τὸν σ. μετ' αὐτῶν Or.*comm.in 1Cor*.5:2(*JTS* 9 p.363); οὐκ ἔστιν λαϊκὸς οὐδὲ σ. id.*dial*.5(p.130); Epiph.*haer*.69.10(p.160.8,10; M.42.217B); of heret. gatherings τινες γυναῖκες...σ. ἐπὶ τὸ αὐτὸ καὶ εἰς ὄνομα τῆς ἁγίας παρθένου...ἱερουργεῖν διὰ γυναικῶν id.*ep.Arab*.ap.*haer*.78.23(p.473.11; 736B); διατάξεις πανταχοῦ ἔπεμψεν μὴ ἔχειν αὐτοὺς [i.e. Arians] ἐκκλησίας ἢ ὅλως ~εσθαι *Chron.Pasch*.p.323(M.92.828A); **3.** *admit to the σύναξις* or *eucharist* μὴ ~ειν τοὺς διγάμους μηδὲ κοινωνεῖν αὐτοῖς ὡς παραβεβηκόσιν Or.*comm.in 1Cor*.7:8(*JTS* 9 p.503); σ. αὐτούς, οὐ δεηθεὶς ἐπ' αὐτῶν ἑτέρου βαπτίσματος Dion.Al.ap.Eus.*h.e*.7.7.4(M.20.646A); καθῃρέθη [sc. Ischyras] καὶ λαϊκὸς σ. *Ep.Mareot*.1 ap.Ath.*apol.sec*.74(p.154.4; M.25.381C); Epiph.*haer*.42.1(p.95.3; M.41.696D); ἀναγκαζομένου Ἀλεξάνδρου...σ. τὸν Ἄρειον *ib*.68.6(p.146.24,27; M.42.193C); μετὰ χρόνου διάστημα σ. ἐν τῇ ἐκκλησίᾳ καὶ ἐν τῇ κοινωνίᾳ *ib*.68.2(p.142.14; M.42.188A); pass., *be a member of the congregation, be in communion with* οὐδὲ ἀποστάντας, ἀλλὰ ~εσθαι μὲν δοκοῦντας... προσφοιτῶντάς τινι τῶν ἑτεροδιδασκαλούντων Dion.Al.ap.Eus.*h.e*.7.7.4(649A); τῶν...σ. ἀδελφῶν id.*ib*.7.9.2(653A); θελήσαντα...αὐτὸν σ. ... μετὰ Μελιτιανῶν...οὐκ ἐδέξαντο αὐτόν *Ep.Mareot*.1 ap.Ath.*apol.sec*.74(p.154.17; M.25.384A); ἐπίσκοπον...μετὰ Ἀλεξάνδρου σ. Soz.*h.e*.2.25.4(M.67.1001A); **4.** *take* one *in, show hospitality* ὄντινα...ἐν ἐσχάτῳ κινδύνῳ...λαβὼν σ. Marc.Diac.*v.Porph*.14; **5.** moral, *bring together, reconcile*; *conciliate*, Hipp.*Noët*.14(p.257.4; M.10.821A) cit. s. συμφωνία; Chrys.*hom.7.2 in Col*.(11.373A); *rally, get together, unite*, id.*hom.27.4 in 2Cor*.(10.632D); id.*hom.19.2 in Heb*.(11.183D); myst., man with God εἰς θεοειδῆ μονάδα ~όμεθα πρὸς τὸ ἓν ~εσθαι Dion.Ar.*e.h*.3.3.8(M.3.437A); of monks in particular, *ib*.6.3.2(533D); of an individual, *collect* oneself τὸ φεύγειν τοὺς πονηρούς, καὶ πρὸς ἑαυτὸν συγκεκροτημένον καὶ συνηγμένον εἶναι ἅπαντα τὸν βίον Chrys.*exp.in Ps*.140:10(5.442C); cf. C.2.

B. *bring together*; **1.** in gen., ref. eucharistic bread ὥσπερ ἦν τοῦτο ⟨τὸ⟩ κλάσμα διεσκορπισμένον ἐπάνω τῶν ὀρέων καὶ συναχθὲν ἐγένετο ἕν, οὕτω συναχθήτω σου ἡ ἐκκλησία...εἰς τὴν σὴν βασιλείαν *Did*.9.4; ref. knowledge αἱ νοηταὶ...τῶν ἀγγέλων δυνάμεις τὰς ἁπλᾶς...ἔχουσι νοήσεις, οὐκ...ἀπὸ...αἰσθήσεων, ἢ λόγων διεξοδικῶν ~ουσαι τὴν θείαν γνῶσιν Dion.Ar.*d.n*.7.2(M.3.868B); ref. gift of tongues ἐν τῇ ἡμέρᾳ τῆς ν' διὰ πνεύματος ἁγίου συνάξας ἃς ποτε διεῖλεν γλώσσας, οὐρανόθεν τοῖς ἀποστόλοις δίδωσι Cosm.Ind.*top*.3(M.88.137B); *retrieve*, *Nomoc*.426 cit. s. ἅλς; **2.** *unite*, Trin. τριάδα ὁμοούσιον...εἰς μίαν σ. κοινὴν κυριότητα ἄνευ προσωπικῆς ἀναχύσεως Sophr.H.*ep.syn*.(M.87.3152D); Christol. αὐτὸς ἑκὼν...τὸ μέγεθος πᾶν τῆς θεότητος εἰς ἑαυτὸν συναθροίσας καὶ ~αγών, τοσοῦτος ἦλθεν ὅσος ἠθέλησεν ‡Chrys.*pasch*.6.4(p.165.14; 8.270C); τὸ ἱδρυμένον καὶ ἐν ταυτότητι πεπηγὸς ὑποδηλούσης τῆς οὐσίας αὐτοῦ μετὰ τοῦ ~εσθαι Cyr.*Jo*.5.5(4.542B); **3.** of a writer, *collect*, e.g. material; *put together* different passages, Or.*Jo*.6.37(21; p.146.2; M.14.264B); *compile* a work, Eus.*h.e*.5.21.5(M.20.489A); Dion.Ar.*d.n*.2.9(M.3.648B); **4.** abs., *make a collection* sc. of alms, Chrys.*hom.43.2 in 1Cor*.(10.402C; συλλέγειν Gaume); *collect, amass* wealth, Marc.Diac.*v.Porph*.13; τοὺς ...μισθοὺς ἡμῖν σ. [sc. ὁ Χριστός] Chrys.*hom.20.1 in Mt*.(7.260D); **5.** *concoct, devise* a plot τὰς κατὰ τοῦ σωτῆρος ἡμῶν ~ων ἐπιβολάς Cyr.*Ps*.11:3(M.69.796D).

C. *bring in*; **1.** *concentrate*, ref. Mt.14:25 ὁ...Ἰησοῦς...τῶν ὑδάτων τὴν ῥέουσαν οὐσίαν σ. ἐπύκνωσε Mac.Mgn.*apocr*.3.13(p.86.13); **2.** *recall* the mind; with διάνοια etc., *recollect oneself* ὁ δὲ φαιδροῖς ὄμμασι τοὺς πάντας...ἐμβλέψας κἄπειτα σ. αὐτὸς πρὸς ἑαυτὸν τὴν διάνοιαν Eus.*v.C*.3.11(p.82.14; M.20.1068A); τὸν σώφρονα σ. λογισμόν *ib*.2.3(p.41.17; 981A); ὅτε...συναγήοχεν αὐτῶν τὴν διάνοιαν ἀπὸ πολυθεΐας Epiph.*haer*.66.71(p.112.20; M.42.141C); Dion.Ar.*d.n*.4.9(M.3.705A); *Didasc.Jac*.3.4(p.55.1); εἴ τις σ. τὸν νοῦν ἀπὸ παντὸς μετεωρισμοῦ ἐξωτέρου Philox.*ep*.27(p.176); *concentrate* τῶν πολεμούντων... καρδίαν διεγηγερμένην...συνηγμένον νοῦν Chrys.*hom.17.2 in Eph*.(11.124A); cf. A.5; **3.** *sum up*, an argument μετὰ ἀποδείξεως καὶ συγκαταθέσεως καὶ τοῦτο συνηγάγομεν τὸ ζήτημα Just.*dial*.123.7(M.6.764B); *amount to* αἱ σ. χρόνον ἐτῶν φμη' Eus.*p.e*.10.9(483D; M.21.805A); id.*d.e*.8.2(p.368.25; M.22.600A); met., of statements τὸ εἰρημένον...εἰς τοῦτο σ. Just.*dial*.81.3(669A); **4.** *bring in, introduce* σ. τὸ τῶν ἱερέων εἰς τὸ αὐτό Chrys.*hom.39.2 in Mt*.(7.434C); **5.** *conclude, infer*; pass., *be involved, follow* from ἥξουσι...οἱ Χαλδαῖοι, ἔσονται δὲ καὶ τοιοίδε, καὶ τόδε τι δράσουσι...καὶ τὸ σ. ἐκ τούτων, τὸ ἄρδην...ἀπολέσθαι τοὺς ἠσεβηκότας Cyr.*Abac*.10(3.525D); συνῆκται... ἡμῖν Dion.Ar.*c.h*.10.1(M.3.272D); id.*e.h*.6.3.5(M.3.536D).

D. *bring about*; **1.** *realize* [sc. in Inc.] ὁ Μελχισεδὲκ ~εται· ὁ ἀμήτωρ, ἀπάτωρ γίνεται Gr.Naz.*or*.38.2(M.36.313A); **2.** *bring down upon, be the cause of* to another δυνατὸν...συγγνώμην αὐτοῖς σ. ἀπὸ τῶν εὐχῶν Chrys.*hom.41.5 in 1Cor*.(10.393B,C); oneself μυρίας ἑαυτῷ σ. νόσους, ἀνεῳγμένων αὐτοῦ τῶν ὀφθαλμῶν id.*hom.27.4 in Mt*.(7.331C); *ib*.42.2(454A).

συναγωγή, ἡ, *assembly*;

A. of persons; **1.** act of *gathering together, assembling* τὰ ἀγαθὰ Ἰσραὴλ ἐν σ. φυλῶν, ἃ ποιήσει ὁ θεός *Pss.Sal*.17.50; **2.** *assemblage, concourse, crowd* πεπλήθασι...πολλῆς ἀταξίας...αἱ σ. αὗται [sc. ἐπὶ τὰς θέας] Clem.*paed*.3.11(p.278.25; M.8.653B); *A.Jo*.26(p.165.4); of a social *gathering* ταῖς...ἐπὶ τῇ εὐφροσύνῃ σ. Clem.*paed*.2.1(p.156.18; 385A); *multitude* of nations, ref. Gen.35:11 ὁ Χριστὸς...πολλὰς σ. ἐθνῶν...συνεκρότησε Eus.*d.e*.2.1(p.54.22; M.22.101A); **3.** *union* with God 'εἷς ἅγιος' καὶ τῶν ἑξῆς...τὴν...πρὸς τὸ ἓν τῆς θείας ἁπλότητος κρυφίαν γενησομένην τῶν μυστικῶς...τετελεσμένων, σ. τε καὶ ἕνωσιν δηλοῖ Max.*myst*.21(M.91.696D).

B. of things; **1.** *bringing* or *drawing together* προσευχὴ...ἐστιν... εἰρήνης ἀσφάλεια, τῶν διεστώτων σ., τῶν συνεστώτων διαμονή Gr.Nyss.*or.dom*.1(p.8.8; M.44.1124B); **2.** *collection*; of thoughts, i.e. recollection ταῖς σ. τῶν λογισμῶν τὸν ὄγκον τῆς σαρκὸς ἐπαποδύῃ Nil.*Eulog*.1(M.79.1096A); Dion.Ar.*e.h*.3.3.8(M.3.437A); *combination* σ. ἀρετῶν Or.*schol.in Cant*.7:2(M.17.281B); τῶν αἰσθητηρίων σ. Chrys.*ep*.2.12(3.550E); ἡ τοῦ μύρου σύνθεσις σ. τίς ἐστιν εὐπνόων ὑλῶν Dion.Ar.*e.h*.4.3.4(M.3.477C); **3.** ? *content* ἵνα...μὴ ἄπρακτοι μείνωμεν... ἐπισυνάπτει πᾶσαν τοῦ βίου τὴν σ. [Is.1:16] †Bas.*Is*.39(1.410D; M.30.193C) or poss. *scheme*; **4.** *conclusion, summary* ἐπανάληψις καὶ σ. Dion.Ar.*c.h*.10 tit.(M.3.272C).

C. in connexion with public worship; **1.** Jewish; **a.** act of *assembling for worship* οὐδέποτε παραφιόντες...τῆς σ. αὐτῶν *Const.App*.2.60.3; **b.** *assembly* of persons for worship, *congregation* οἱ ἀγαπῶντες σ. ὁσίων *Pss.Sal*.17.18; τῶν...σ. μὴ ἀπολειπόμενος Or.*or*.2(p.302.20; M.11.421C); οἱ ἀπόστολοι κηρύξαντες ταῖς τῶν Ἰουδαίων σ. id.*hom.4.2 in Jer*.(p.24.6; M.13.288A); ἐπεί εἰσίν τινες συνάγοντες σ. ἐξ αἱμάτων variously explained, Didym.*Ps*.15:4(M.39.1228C); **c.** the *congregation* of Israel (= קָהָל) καὶ σ. Ἰσραὴλ δοξάσουσι τὸ ὄνομα κυρίου *Pss.Sal*.10.8; ἐν σ. διακρινεῖ λαοὺς *ib*.17.48; ἵστατο μέσων τῆς σ. *T.Lev*.11.5; τῆς Ἰσραὴλ σ. ... τῆς σ. τοῦ Ἰούδα Or.*hom.4.1 in Jer*.

(p.23.22f.; M.13.285C); ἦλθε γὰρ ὁ υἱὸς τοῦ θεοῦ...πρὸς τὴν τοῦ ἀρχισυναγώγου θυγατέρα, τὴν τῶν Ἰουδαίων σ. id.*fr.15 in Lc.*8:41(p.240); δύναται...Μάρθα μὲν εἶναι καὶ ἡ ἐκ περιτομῆς σ. *ib.39 in* 10:38(p.252); τῆς Ἰουδαίων σ. οἱ καθηγεῖσθαι λαχόντες Cyr.*Is.*1.1(2.20D); as forebear of Church, v. ἐκκλησία; opp. ἐκκλησία, Or.*fr.12 in Lc.*8:16(p.238); ταῖς Ἰουδαίων προσομιλεῖν σ. opp. ἐκ προσώπου τῆς ἐκκλησίας βοᾷ Eus.*e.th.*1.4(p.64.12; M.24.833A); τὴν πολύπαιδα ἐνίκησε [sc. ἡ ἐκκλησία] σ. Chrys.*comm.in Gal.*4:31(10.712C); id.*hom.3.4 in Mt.*(7.38B); exeg. Cant.3:11 ὡς εἶδεν ἡ ἐκκλησία στεφανώσασαν αὐτὸν ταῖς ἀκάνθαις τὴν σ. Procl.CP *or.laud.BMV* 9(p.107.7; M.65.689C); τουτέστιν ἡ σ. τῶν Ἰουδαίων, μήτηρ γὰρ Χριστοῦ αὕτη κατὰ σάρκα νοεῖται *Dial.Christ.et Jud.*12(p.70.30); as representing Jewish religion τὴν ἐξ ἐθνῶν ἐκκλησίαν...θυγατέρα τῆς ἐπουρανίου Σιὼν ἢ καὶ τῆς προτέρας σ. ἀποκαλεῖ, διὰ τὸ πάντας ἡμᾶς τοὺς ἐξ ἐθνῶν...πεπιστευκότας γεννήματα εἶναι...Χριστοῦ...οἷα ἐκ μητρὸς τῆς τῶν Ἰουδαίων σ. προελθόντας Eus.*d.e.*9.17(p.441.18; M.22.712A); Ast.Soph.*hom.3 in Ps.*5(M.40.417B) cit. s. ἀντίζηλος; τοῦ ἐν ᾅδου δεσμωτηρίου τύπον τὸ τοῦ Ἰωσὴφ δεσμωτήριον ἔνθα αὐτὸν ἡ μοίχαλις σ. κατέκλεισεν ‡Epiph.*hom.*3(M.43.469D); τῇ ἀπιστίᾳ τῆς Ἰουδαίων σ. Cyr.*glaph.Gen.*3(1.92D); opp. τὸ εὐαγγέλιον: ἠμαυρώθη ἡ Ἰουδαϊκὴ σ., κατηύγασε δὲ τὸ εὐαγγέλιον Epiph.*haer.*50.2(p.247.20; M.41.888A); **d.** the Jewish *community* Σαλώ[μη] θυγάτηρ Γαδία...συναγωγῆς Αἰβρέων *CG–CI* 1 p.18 (= *CIG* 9909, saec. ii or iii); **e.** *place of worship, synagogue* [Pr.9:18] τόπον τὴν σ., οὐχὶ δὲ ἐκκλησίαν ὁμωνύμως προσεῖπεν Clem.*str.*1.19(p.62.2; M.8.813A); [συν]αγωγὴ Ἑβρ[αίων] (*CG–CI* 1.6 = *Corinth* 8.111) (building inscription saec. ii or iii); Or.*or.*20(p.344.3; M.11.480A); οὐκ εἰσῆλθεν εἰς τὴν τῶν Ἰουδαίων σ. id.*hom.12 in Lc.*(p.83.12); *A.Andr.et Mt.*14(p.81.8); οἱ τὰς κατ' αὐτοῦ [sc. Christ] ἀρὰς ἐν ταῖς ἑαυτῶν σ. ποιούμενοι Eus.*d.e.*10.3(p.460.27; M.22.741B); *Can.App.*65; *ib.*71; as representing the Jews τὰ ἐκ τῆς σ. δόγματα Gr.Nyss.*Eun.*11(2 p.263.7; M.45.872A); **f.** *synagogue* of the Samaritans, Justn.*cod.*1.5.17(p.56); *Chron.Pasch.*p.327(M.92.841A); **2.** Christian; **a.** *coming together, meeting for worship* πυκνότερον σ. γινέσθωσαν Ign.*Polyc.*4.2; οὐδὲ τῆς αἰσθητῆς ἡμεῖς μετὰ τοῦ κυρίου σ. ἀπέστημεν Dion.Al.ap.Eus.*h.e.*7.11.12(M.20.665C); κατὰ μέρος ἔσονται σ. Dion.Al.*ib.*7.11.17(668B); οὐχ...ἁπλῶς τὴν σ. βούλομαι γίνεσθαι, ἀλλ' ἵνα αἱ καρδίαι αὐτῶν παρακληθῶσι Chrys.*hom.5.2 in Col.*(11.360D); **b.** *assembly* of persons for worship, Christian *congregation* ὅταν...ἔλθῃ εἰς σ. ἀνδρῶν δικαίων Herm.*mand.*11.9; εἰ δέ τις ἐν τῷ ὅλῳ σώματι τῶν σ. τῆς ἐκκλησίας Or.*comm.in Mt.*13.24(p.245.22; M.13.1157A); οὐ γὰρ ἐπὶ τὸ κοινὸν τῆς σ. ἀνάπαυμα ἐν τῇ κυριακῇ καταντῶσιν *Const.App.*3.6.5; ἐκκλησία καὶ ἡ κατ' οἶκον σ. τῶν εὐσεβούντων λέγεται Hesych.H.*Ps.*67:27(M.93.1228D); as representing Church καθάπερ ἐν θαλάσσῃ νῆσοί εἰσιν...ἔχουσαι...λιμένας πρὸς τὸ...ἔχειν...καταφυγάς· οὕτω δέδωκεν ὁ θεὸς τῷ κόσμῳ...τὰς σ., λεγομένας δὲ ἐκκλησίας ἁγίας Thphl.Ant.*Autol.*2.14(M.6.1076B); ἀλήθεια οὐρανόθεν...ἐπὶ τὴν σ. τῆς ἐκκλησίας ἀφιγμένη Clem.*str.*6.3(p.448.17; M.9.252C); ἀξίως ἀπετμήθη τῆς τοῦ κυρίου σ. *Const.App.*2.43.4; **c.** the whole Christian body, *Church* τοῖς εἰς αὐτὸν πιστεύουσιν ὡς οὖσι μιᾷ ψυχῇ, καὶ μιᾷ σ., καὶ μιᾷ ἐκκλησίᾳ...τῇ ἐξ ὀνόματος αὐτοῦ γενομένῃ Just.*dial.*63.5(M.6.621B); plur., of Jewish and Christian communities, Iren.*haer.*4.31.1(M.6.1068C); τὸ σῶμα αὐτοῦ...ὅπερ ἐστὶν ἡ ἐκκλησία...σ. εὐλογημένη Clem.*exc.Thdot.*13(p.111.12; M.9.664B); δαιμόνων...σπουδαζόντων...τὴν σ. αὐτοῦ [sc. τοῦ θεοῦ] σκορπίζειν Vict.*Mc.*9:40(p.366.9); **d.** = σύναξις, *public worship* τὸ...τῆς σ. ἔνθεον...ἀποθέμενοι Clem.*paed.*3.11(p.280.22; M.8.657C); καταργεῖ...τὴν καλὴν γῆν...ὁ ἐρχόμενος εἰς σ. καὶ μὴ καρποφορῶν Or.*hom.18.5 in Jer.*(p.157.11; M.13.473A); **e.** *place of worship,* Christian *church* ἀπὸ τῶν κοιμητηρίων...ἠρχόμεθα ἐπὶ τὰς σ. Or.*hom.4.3 in Jer.*(p.25.30; M.13.288D); ποιήσω αὐτὴν [sc. τὴν οἰκίαν μου] σ. Χριστιανῶν *A.Phil.*50(p.22.3); οἰκοδομήσωμεν σ. καὶ ἐπισκοπεῖον ἐπὶ τῷ ὀνόματι τοῦ Χριστοῦ *ib.*88(p.34.18); **3.** as term of contempt; **a.** heret. *congregation, Const.App.*6.5.2; ἵνα καὶ ἑαυτῷ σ. ποιήσηται τῶν ἠπατημένων Epiph.*haer.*36.1(p.44.17; M.41.633B); ὃς τῆς ἐν Κωνσταντινουπόλει Εὐνομιανῆς σ. ἐπῆρχεν Philost.*h.e.*12.11(M.65.620B); **b.** *party, sect,* of followers of Aëtius τὴν ὁμόδοξαν σ. *ib.*3.14(M.65.501B); **c.** *meeting-house, conventicle* ἐπὶ τοῖς Μοντανισταῖς καὶ Τασκοδρούγοις καὶ Ὀφίταις θεσπίζομεν...ὥστε μήτε σ. τινα τολμᾶν αὐτοὺς ἔχειν Justn.*cod.*1.5.18(p.56).

***συναγωγικός**, *adhering to the synagogue,* Or.*or.*21(p.345.8; M.11.480C).

συναγωγός, **1.** *bringing together, uniting*; of God, Dion.Ar.*c.h.*1.1(M.3.120B); **2.** *of recollection* or *concentration,* Dion.Ar.*c.h.*15.4(333A); **3.** as subst., *one who embraces* or *enfolds*; of Simeon, Rom.Mel.(*SBBAW* 1898² p.184).

συναγωνιάω, *contend along with, take the side of* πάντα...αὐτοῖσιν σ. ἠδὲ βοηθεῖ *Orac.Sib.*3.712; δυνάμεις ἱεραὶ συμπαρέχουσαι τῷ ἐπικήρῳ ἡμῶν γένει καὶ...σ. Or.*Cels.*8.64(p.280.14; M.11.1613A).

συναγωνίζομαι, *fight for, further the cause of, help*; ἀμφότεροι τῷ θείῳ σ. Isid.Pel.*epp.*2.85(M.78.529A); τῷ Βενιαμὶν συκοφαντουμένῳ σ. Thdt.*qu.106 in Gen.*(1.108); esp. *join in supplication and prayer* σ. μοι ἐν τῇ πρὸς τὸν θεὸν δεήσει Hipp.*antichr.*2(p.5.21; M.10.729B); μετὰ βίον σ. τοῖς πιστοῖς Proc.G.*Jos.*1:16(M.87.997C); σ. μοι ἐν ταῖς προσευχαῖς Alex.Sal.*Barn.*proem.3(p.437B).

***συναγωνισμός, ὁ**, *help, support* εἰς σ. ἦλθε τῆς ἀληθείας †Jo.D.*B.J.*26(M.96.1101C).

συναγωνιστής, ὁ, *one who shares with* another *in a contest*; with Christ σοὶ τῷ σ. αὐτοῦ Or.*mart.*36(p.33.18; M.11.609D); in a wordy battle, Meth.*res.*1.27(p.255.2; M.41.1132D); in spiritual contest of monastic life, *V.Dan.*(p.384.4); *one who cooperates in the cause of, fellow worker* σὺ ὁ ἐκείνων σ. καὶ συγκληρονόμος Isid.Pel.*epp.*1.454(M.78.432C); ἀρετῇ σ. *ib.*5.13(1332D); παρῆν...σ. τοῦ γυναίου [sc. Potiphar's wife] διάβολος ὁ τῆς μοιχείας ἀγωνοθέτης Bas.Sel.*or.*8.2(M.85.124A).

συνάδελφος, ὁ, **1.** *brother with oneself*; of fellow Christians, *A.Andr.*B 10(p.63.12); of the poor ῥογεύσας ὑπῆρχεν συναδέλφοις Jo.Mosch.*prat.*185(M.87.3060C); met., *doublet* or *duplicate* in a text ἐστὶν αὐτὸ συναμφότερον ἢ σ. τῇ λέξει ᾗ ἐπίκειται Epiph.*mens.*8(M.43.249B); **2.** theol., *brother to*; as adj., *sharing brotherhood with,* Trin. υἱὸς...ἀεὶ οὐ συναλοιφὴ ὢν τῷ πατρί, οὐ σ. Epiph.*anc.*6(p.12.12; M.43.25B); as against Sabellius υἱὸς...οὐ σ. ὢν πατρὶ...τὸ πνεῦμα...οὐ συνάδελφον πατρί id.*haer.*62.3,4(p.392.13,19; M.41.1053C,D); agst. Arians εἰ κατ' αὐτοὺς ἦν ἡ τῆς ἀληθείας διάνοια...οὐκέτι υἱὸς ὁ υἱὸς ἦν, ἀλλ' ἀδελφός, σ. συνόντος *ib.*69.54(p.201.4; M.42.285C); τὸ ἅγιον πνεῦμα...οὐ σ., οὐ προπάτορον *ib.*76.39(p.394.5; 604A); agst. Pneumatomachoi, *ib.*74.12(p.330.12f.,20; 497C,D); *Didasc.Patr.*proem.(p.8.18).

***συναδολέσχης, ὁ**, *one trained in the same school* of thought σ. τῆς νομικῆς παιδείας ‡Caes.Naz.*dial.*170(M.38.1133).

***συνᾳδόντως**, *in harmony* with, *consistently* πάνυ σ. ... εἴρηται Or.*fr.12 in Jo.*(p.494.15); id.*Cels.*4.79(p.349.17; M.11.1152B); σ. τούτῳ...φησὶν Epiph.*haer.*21.6(p.245.8; M.41.293D); *ib.*66.44(p.81.22; M.42.96C).

συναδοξέω, *share in humiliation,* Bas.*hom.*20.6(2.161D; M.31.537A).

***συναδρύνω**, *mature, grow together* with, Cyr.ap.*cat.Lc.*2:44(p.26.4).

συνᾴδ-ω, **1.** *sing together* with ψαλλούσῃ ~οντες προφητείᾳ Clem.*paed.*1.1(p.90.6; M.8.249A); τούτοις...~ειν Meth.*arbitr.*1(p.147.3; M.18.241B); Dion.Ar.*e.h.*3.2(M.3.425B); **2.** *celebrate together* in song ~όντων τὰ θεῖα μυστήρια Meth.*arbitr.*1(p.147.11; M.18.241B); **3.** *be in accord, agree* with ὁ νόμος ~ει...αὐτῷ [sc. τῷ νόμῳ] Clem.*str.*2.23(p.193.23; M.8.1096D).

***συναέξομαι**, *rise, mount together with,* Paul.Sil.*ambo*.75(M.86.2255A).

***συναθάνατος**, *likewise immortal* τοῦ ἀθανάτου λόγου καὶ τῆς σ. αὐτοῦ ψυχῆς Anast.S.*hod.*12(M.89.204A).

συναθετέω, *set at naught together with,* ‡Nil.*fr.pasch.*1(M.79.1492A).

συναθλ-έω, *share a contest, contend* or *labour along with* συγκοπιᾶτε ἀλλήλοις, ~εῖτε Ign.*Polyc.*6.1; ὥστε σ. μοι καὶ ὑπουργῆσαι ‡Pion.*v.Polyc.*23; οἱ...μαθηταὶ καὶ οἱ σ. αὐτοῖς...ἐν τῷ εὐαγγελίῳ Cyr.*Mich.*50(3.441A); σύνταγμα...ἐν Χαλκηδόνι...~οῦσαν εἶχεν Εὐφημίαν τὴν μάρτυρα Sophr.H.*ep.syn.*(M.87.3185B); of soul and body μετὰ τῆς ὁσίας ψυχῆς καὶ τὸ σ. αὐτῇ σῶμα Dion.Ar.*e.h.*7.3.9(M.3.565B); *ib.*7.1.1(553A); of Christ, Thdr.Stud.*epp.*2.55(M.99.1268D) cit. s. συγκουφίζω; met., *second, support* a statement ἐπαγωνιεῖται...καὶ σ. τῷ λόγῳ καὶ ὁ σοφὸς Ἰωάννης Cyr.*inc.unigen.*(5¹.711E).

***συνάθλησις, ἡ**, *joint contest, common struggle,* Bas.*reg.fus.*35.3(2.380B; M.31.1005C).

***συναθλητής, ὁ**, *one who shares the contest*; hence *fellow labourer* ὁ Κλήμης...Παύλου συνεργὸς καὶ σ. Eus.*h.e.*3.4.9(M.20.221A); *fellow martyr, Mir.Geo.*4(p.43.8); Thdr.Stud.*epp.*2.38(M.99.1233A).

[*]**σύναθλος, ὁ**, = συνάεθλος, *companion in the struggle* ὁμολογητῶν σ. καὶ συμμέτοχος Jo.Eleem.*v.Tych.*29(p.140); Thdr.Stud.*epp.*2.11(M.99.1145B).

συναθροίζω, **1.** *gather together, assemble*; pass. intrans., of Christians for worship οὐκ εὐσυνείδητοι...διὰ τὸ μὴ βεβαίως κατ' ἐντολὴν σ. Ign.*Magn.*4.1; ἐπὶ τὸ αὐτὸ ἐν τῇ ἐκκλησίᾳ σ. *Const.App.*5.19.3; σ. ἐν τοῖς κοιμητηρίοις...καὶ τὴν...εὐχαριστίαν προσφέρετε *ib.*6.30.2; εἰ μήτε ἐν οἴκῳ μήτε ἐν ἐκκλησίᾳ σ. δυνατόν, ἕκαστος παρ' ἑαυτῷ ψαλλέτω *ib.*8.34.10; **2.** *unite, draw* into one αὐτὸς [sc. Χριστὸς] ἑκὼν...τὸ μέγεθος πᾶν τῆς θεότητος εἰς ἑαυτὸν σ. καὶ συναγαγών, τοσοῦτος ἦλθεν ὅσος ἠθέλησεν ‡Chrys.*pasch.*6.4(p.165.14; 8.270C); **3.** of things, *gather into one mass*; met., *heap upon* one τῆς εἱμαρμένης αὐτῷ σ. τὰ χρήματα Bas.*hex*.6.7(1.57A; M.29.133C).

συνάθροισις, ἡ, **1.** of things, *mass*, *M.Seb.test*.1.3; **2.** of persons, *gathering*, for eucharist ἵνα συνίδῃς τῶν μυστηρίων τὴν ἔκβασιν, καὶ μάθῃς τίς καὶ ποταπὴ ἡμῶν ἡ σ. ‡Meth.*Sym.et Ann*.2(M.18.352A).

συνάθροισμα, τό, *collection, collected mass*; **1.** of things τὸ πάντων ὑδάτων σύστημα καὶ σ. Mac.Mgn.*apocr*.3.13(p.85.1); **2.** of persons for worship τῶν πιστῶν τὸ σ. opp. συναγωγὴν Χριστοκτόνων *Const.App*. 2.61.2; τὸ τῶν Ἰουδαίων σ. Leont.B.*mesopent*.(M.86.1980A); of body of the faithful λέγων ὡς ἀπὸ κοινοῦ τοῦ τῶν πιστῶν σ. ... 'πάτερ ἡμῶν' κτλ. *Const.App*.3.18.1; ἐξ ἀλλήλων [sc. clergy and laity]...ἡ σύστασις τοῦ σ. *Const.App.epit*.1.20; of saints in heaven, ‡Just.*qu. et resp*.76(M.6.1317B).

***συναθροιστέος**, *that must be assembled* ἀναγκαία ἐστὶ διάγνωσις συνοδική, ἣν καὶ πάλαι ἔφημεν σ. Innoc.*ep.cler*.(M.52.538).

***συναθυμέω**, *be despondent in sympathy* with, ‡Bas.*const*.20.2(2.565D; M.31.1392B) cit. s. ἀστοχία.

συναθύρ-ω, *play with*, Philost.*h.e*.10.11(M.65.592B); τῶν ~όντων αὐτοῖς δαιμονίων Cyr.*ador*.6(1.211C).

***συναϊδιάζω**, *make coeternal*, Gr.Nyss.*Eun*.4(2 p.53.21; M.45.624B).

συναΐδιος, *coeternal*; **1.** of Trin. ὁμοτίμου τε τῆς ἀξίας καὶ σ. βασιλείας ἐν τρισὶ τελειοτάταις ὑποστάσεσιν CCP(381)*ep*.ap.Thdt.*h.e*. 5.9.11(3.1031); τρία πρόσωπα...σ. Epiph.*haer*.72.11(p.266.5; M.42.397B); μία ἐστὶ θεότης, ἴση δόξα, σ. μεγαλειότης ‡Ath.*symb*.2(M.28.1585A); Jo.D.*hom*.1.1(M.96.545A); **2.** of attributes of God ἡ δύναμις, καὶ σοφία, καὶ πᾶν θεοπρεπὲς ὄνομα, συναΐδιόν ἐστι τῇ θεότητι Gr.Nyss.*Apoll*.52(M.45.1249B); συνάναρχον καὶ σ. τῇ μακαρίᾳ φύσει τὴν περὶ τῶν εὐεργετησομένων καὶ δημιουργεῖσθαι μελλόντων ἐκέκτητο βούλησιν Zach.Mit.*opif*.(M.85.1097A); **3.** of Son, denied by Arius οὐδὲ γάρ ἐστιν ἀΐδιος ἢ σ. ἢ συναγέννητος τῷ πατρί Ar.*ep.Alex*.(p.13.11; M.26.709C); affirmed by orthodox, Tit.Bost.*fr.Lc*.8:5(p.172); ‡Eust.*Laz*.15(p.39.3); ἄκτιστος καὶ σ. Χριστὸς θεῷ Didym.(‡Bas.)*Eun*.4(1.287A; M.29.689B); ref. Mt.16:16 ἐπέγνω δὲ [sc. Πέτρος] τὸν συμφυᾶ καὶ σ. κλάδον τοῦ θεοῦ id.*Trin*.1.30(M.39.417A); σ. ἐστι γέννημα ὡς ἀπαύγασμα φωτὸς ἀϊδίου ‡Ath.*dial.Trin*.2.16(M.28.1184A); Chrys.*hom.4.2 in Jo*.(8.28D); Cyr.*Chr.un*.(5^{1}.717B) cit. s. γεννάω; opinion ascribed to Eunomius refuted συναΐδιον, φησί, καὶ αὐτοὶ τῷ πατρὶ τὸν υἱὸν ὁμολογοῦμεν εἶναι, καθὸ τὴν τοῦ δύνασθαι τεκεῖν αὐτὸν ἐξουσίαν εἶχεν ἐν ἑαυτῷ καὶ πρὶν αὐτὸν τέκῃ, εἰ τὸ δύνασθαι γεννᾶν τὸν πατέρα σ. αὐτῷ τὸν υἱὸν εἶναι ποιεῖ, καὶ οὐχ ὅτι συνῆν αὐτῷ γεννητῶς, τί κωλύσει λέγειν ὅτιπερ ἐπειδὴ τὸ δύνασθαι κτίζειν ἦν ἐν θεῷ, ἔσται πάντως αὐτῷ καὶ τὰ ποίηματα σ.; id.*thes*.5(5^{1}.40E); ἀΐδιον ἀποφαίνει [sc. τὸν υἱόν], καὶ τοῦ πατρὸς σ., καὶ τῶν ἁπάντων δημιουργόν Thdt.*Heb*.proem.(3.544); ἱκανὴ γὰρ ἡ εἰκὼν [sc. ὡς φῶς ἐκ φωτός] παραστῆσαι τό τε σ. τό τε τῆς οὐσίας ταὐτὸν τό τε τῆς γεννήσεως ἀπαθές id.*rect.conf*.9(M.6.1221C); of generation of Logos ἄχρονός τε καὶ τῷ πατρὶ συναΐδιος Jo.D.*hom*.9.15(M.96.744A); assertion of coeternity of Christ's human nature charged against Apoll. νῦν μέν φησι θείαν εἶναι τὴν σάρκα τοῦ λόγου καὶ σ. Gr.Nyss.*Apoll*.41(M.45.1217A); denied by orthodox εἰ δὲ ὁμοούσιος τοῦ λόγου ἡ σάρξ καὶ σ. ἐκ τούτου ἐρεῖτε καὶ τὰ πάντα κτίσματα σ. τῷ τὰ πάντα κτίσαντι θεῷ ‡Ath.*Apoll*.1.12(M.26.1113B); τὴν γὰρ ποιηθεῖσαν τῆς ἀνθρωπότητος φύσιν, μὴ τῇ ἑνώσει τοῦ λόγου εἶναι ἰδίαν, ἀλλὰ σ., καὶ τῇ τοῦ θεοῦ φύσει ἐξισουμένην τῇ ταυτότητι τῆς φύσεως ἐννοεῖν, ἀσεβὲς *ib*.1.5(1100C); **4.** of created things, ‡Just.*confut*.6(M.6.1508A); πῶς ὁ οὐρανός, ὁ ὢν ἐκ τῆς ὕλης καὶ τοῦ εἴδους, συναΐδιος ἀμφοτέροις; *ib*.52(M.6.1545C); ὁ Ὠριγένης...ἔλεγε σ. εἶναι τῷ μόνῳ...θεῷ τὸ πᾶν Meth.*creat*.2(p.494.16; M.18.333B); τῶν Ἑλλήνων παῖδες σ. τῷ θεῷ τὴν κτίσιν εἶναί φασιν· ὕλην γάρ τινα τῷ θεῷ σ. ὑποτίθενται Proc.G.*Gen*.proem.(M.87.29A); εἰ σ. ὁ κόσμος τῷ θεῷ... ἐκ θεοῦ ἔχειν αἰτίαν οὐ δύναται ποιητικὴν Zach.Mit.*opif*.(M.85.1112D); ἡ δὲ κτίσις ἐπὶ θεοῦ θελήσεως ἔργον οὖσα, οὐ σ. ἐστι τῷ θεῷ· ἐπεὶ οὐ πέφυκε τὸ ἐκ μὴ ὄντος εἰς τὸ εἶναι παραγόμενον, σ. εἶναι τῷ ἀνάρχῳ καὶ ἀεὶ ὄντι ‡Cyr.*Trin*.7(6^{3}.10A; M.77.1133C); of angels τὰ δὲ ἑπτὰ πνεύματα εἰσὶν ἄγγελοι ἑπτά· οὐχ ὡς ἰσότιμα δέ, ἢ σ. ... τῇ ἁγίᾳ τριάδι Oecum.*Apoc*.1:4(p.34); dist. from αἰώνιος: χρὴ...οὐχ ἁπλῶς συναΐδια θεῷ τῷ πρὸ αἰώνος οἴεσθαι τὰ αἰώνια λεγόμενα Dion.Ar.*d.n*.10.3(M.3.940A).

***συναϊδιότης, ἡ**, *coeternity* εἷς θεὸς λέγεται διὰ τὸ ἓν καὶ τὸ ταὐτὸν ...τῆς συναϊδιότητος Jo.V H.*icon*.4(M.96.1353B); τῆς τοῦ ἁγίου πνεύματος τῷ πατρὶ καὶ τῷ υἱῷ συναϊδιότητος τὸ ἀκατάληπτον *Chron. Pasch*.p.304(M.92.772A).

***συναϊδίως**, *coeternally*, ref. generation ref. Son κύριον πρὸ αἰώνων σ. τε καὶ συναnάρχως...γεννηθέντα ‡Eust.*Laz*.29(p.50.9); ὁ υἱὸς ἀπαύγασμα τυγχάνων, οὐ ποτὲ ἔσται, ἀλλὰ σ. Didym.(‡Bas.)*Eun*.4(1.281A; M.29.676B); ‡Ath.*dial.Trin*.1.6(M.28.1125A); of divine Wisdom σ. ὑπῆρχον ὁμοουσιότητι παρ' αὐτῷ ‡Proc.G.*Pr*.8:30(M.87.1297C); of H. Ghost ἐκ τῆς μιᾶς καὶ ἀνωτάτω θεϊκῆς φύσεως ἐξεφάνη συναϊδίως τὸ ἅγιον πνεῦμα Didym.*Trin*.2.25(M.39.748A).

***συναιματόομαι**, *be stained with blood together* with; ref. Son's assumption of human flesh and blood, Anast.S.*hod*.17(M.89.265A) cit s. συμβάπτω.

***συναινέτης, ὁ**, *one who assents* or *approves*, Jo.D.*trisag*.1(M.95.24C).

συναινέω, *advise*; c. dat., *Mir.Artem*.32(p.46.23); error in Nest. ap.Cyr.*Nest*.2.8(6^{1}.47E) v. σύνειμι.

σύναινος, *of the same opinion* οἷς ἐγὼ οὐ σ. εἰμι Just.*dial*.47.2(M.6.577A).

συναίρεσις, ἡ, **1.** *contraction*, (theol.) implied in Sabellian and Marcellan expositions of doctrine of Trin. καὶ ἡ Σαβελλίου σ., καὶ ἡ Ἀρείου διαίρεσις Gr.Naz.*or*.22.12(M.35.1145A); τὴν...Σαβελλίου σ. ἀσεβεστέρᾳ διαιρέσει...λύοντες *ib*.43.30(M.36.537A); *ib*.42.16(476C); οὐ γὰρ ἓν λέγομεν τριώνυμον κατὰ τὴν τοῦ Σαβελλίου καὶ Φωτεινοῦ καὶ Μαρκέλλου σ. τε καὶ σύγχυσιν Thdt.*Trin*.28(M.75.1188C); Mac.Ant.*symb*.(H.3.1169C); ‡Cyr.*Trin*.10(6^{3}.16A; M.77.1144B); and Eutychian Christology τὴν Εὐτυχοῦς μετὰ τὴν ἕνωσιν εἰς μίαν οὐσίαν τῶν ἑνωθέντων...σ. Max.*opusc*.(M.91.40C); having no place in orth. statements τριάδα ὁμοούσιον...εἰς μίαν συναγομένην κοινὴν κυριότητα ἄνευ προσωπικῆς ἀναχύσεως, καὶ ὑποστατικῆς ἐκτὸς σ. Sophr.H.*ep. syn*.(M.87.3152D); μονάδα μὲν κατὰ τὸν τῆς οὐσίας...λόγον· ἀλλ' οὐ κατὰ σύνθεσιν ἢ σ. Max.*myst*.23(M.91.701A); id.*opusc*.(M.91.88B); **2.** *postponement* in rhetoric, *synaeresis est, cum differimus aliquid, petentes ut aliud interim nos permittant dicere*, Isid.H.*etym*.2.21.48.

συναιρεσιώτης, ὁ, *fellow in the sect, fellow heretic* μηδὲν ἀποκρύπτειν τοὺς σ., ἑτέρῳ δὲ μηδὲν ἐξειπεῖν Hipp.*haer*.9.23(p.259.3; M.16.3402A); Philost.*h.e*.2.8(M.65.472A); *ib*.4.4(520B).

συναιρέτης, ὁ, **1.** *one who contracts* or *maintains a contraction* in οἱ τῆς ἀρεύστου τριάδος σ. Gr.Naz.*carm*.2.1.11.1176(M.37.1109A); **2.** *companion in heresy, heretical follower* ἡ...σύνοδος τὸν...Μακάριον σὺν τοῖς αὐτοῦ σ. τοῦ μὲν ἱερατικοῦ σχήματος ἀπεγύμνωσε Const. Pogon.*sacr*.3(M.*PL*.96.391C).

***συναιρετίζω**, *join in heresy, be a fellow heretic*, Thdr.Stud.*epp*. 1.36(M.99.1032D).

συναιρετικός, ὁ, *fellow member of a sect, co-heretic*, Thphn.*chron*. p.319(M.108.772C).

συναιρέω, **1.** *bring together*; *close* the mouth of a corpse τοὺς ὀφθαλμοὺς καθηρημένους, καὶ τὸ στόμα συνῃρημένον Chrys.*hom.1.6 in 2Cor*.(10.426C); Εὐνομίου τὸ...στόμα [sc. τοῦ Ἀετίου] συνελόντος καὶ τοὺς ὀφθαλμοὺς...περιστείλαντος Philost.*h.e*.9.6(M.65.573B); **2.** *bring into small compass, shorten*; *reduce* a number εἰς δύο σ....τὰς... δυνάμεις Dion.Ar.*d.n*.4.16(M.3.713C); id.*ep*.7.2(M.3.1080D); **3.** *comprise* in οὐκ εἰς τὸ εἶναι σ. τὸ δειχθὲν ἀκολουθεῖν...τὸ μὲν 'συναιροῦντες' ἴσως ἄν τινες τῶν αἰνιγματιστῶν εἴποιεν ἀντὶ τοῦ 'συνάπτοντες' αὐτῷ νενοῆσθαι Eun.ap.Gr.Nyss.*Eun*.1(1 p.207.8,16; M.45.453D,456A); **4.** med., *agree to* ἀπειθοῦσι τοὺς ἀπὸ Σικίμων τὴν...αὐτοῖς...συνειλέσθαι περιτομὴν...ἀπεκτόνασι τοὺς συνελομένους τὰ ἴσα φρονεῖν αὐτοῖς Cyr.*glaph.Gen*.5(1.174D,E); **5.** *remove all trace of*; *clear away* a meal, ref. Lc.14:21ff. οὐ συνεῖλε τὰ προκείμενα, ἀλλ' ἑτέρους ἐκάλεσεν Chrys.*comm.in Gal*.2:20(10.694A); preparations for a sacrifice, id. *hom.16.9 in Mt*.(7.216D).

συναίρ-ω, **1.** *take up together, raise together* from death Χριστῷ συνθανέειν γὰρ ἐέλδομαι, ὡς συναερθῶ Gr.Naz.*carm*.1.2.2.566(M.37.623A); **2.** σ. λόγον *cast up* accounts; also *hold* a debate, *conduct* an argument ᾧ πᾶν στόμα σ. λόγον οὐκ ἠδύνατο *Pers*.(p.3.18); πεισθῆναι θέλομεν, ~όντων ἡμῶν λόγους μετ' αὐτῶν *ib*.(p.28.17); **3.** med., *take part* in, *combine, cooperate* in and with ~εται...πρὸς τὸ...συνιέναι ὑμᾶς τὸν Ἰησοῦν Just.*dial*.132.1(M.6.781C); τὸ πᾶν σ. πρὸς τὴν τελειοτάτην σωτηρίαν Clem.*str*.7.7(p.36.23; cod. συναιρεῖται M.9.469A); οὐδ' ἂν συνήρατο πρὸς τὴν Χριστοκτονίαν ὁ λαὸς Vict.*Mc*.10:46(p.387.33); abs. τοῦτον...συστρατιώτην καλεῖ, ὥστε παντὶ τρόπῳ συνάρασθαι Chrys.*hom.1.1 in Philm*.(11.775C); **4.** *support* one *in an opinion*, Didym.*Trin*.3.3(M.39.824B); **5.** *have fellowship* with, *join*, Or.*or*.31(p.399.8; M.11.556A).

συναισθάν-ομαι (συναίσθ-ομαι), *perceive*; **1.** by the senses; **a.** *have sense perception* πῶς...αἱ κολαζόμεναι ψυχαὶ σ. μὴ σώματα οὖσαι; Clem.*exc.Thdot*.14(p.111.20; M.9.664C); **b.** *be sensible along with, share in perception* κινεῖται...εἰς ὀρέξεις τὸ σῶμα φυσικάς, καὶ ~εται...ἡ ἐνοῦσα ψυχή, συμμετέχει δὲ κατ' οὐδένα τρόπον Cyr.*schol. inc*.8(p.220.29; 5^{1}.782D); **2.** of mental or spiritual perception; **a.** *perceive at the same time* σ. τῆς ἑαυτοῦ παρρησίας καὶ τῆς τῶν ἀκουόντων ἀσθενείας Clem.*paed*.1.9(p.138.19; M.8.349A); simply, *perceive* τοῖς μηδέπω...συνηθημένοις τὴν πολυποίκιλον σοφίαν τοῦ θεοῦ

Meth.*symp*.8.9(p.91.15; M.18.152B); **b.** *share the sentiments of, be of the same mind* ~εται...τοῦ λέγοντος Clem.*str*.2.11(p.141.23; M.8.989B); *ib*.2.20(p.174.22; 1057A); Or.*hom.19.15 in Jer*.(p.173.33; M.13.496C); id.*Cels*.1.13(p.66.20; M.11.680C); **c.** *be aware* or *conscious of, realize in oneself* σ. ὅτι ἁμαρτάνουσι Clem.*str*.2.13(p.144.2; M.8.996B); κολάζων τὸ ὁρατικόν, ὅταν ἡδομένου ἑαυτοῦ κατὰ τὴν προσβολὴν τῆς ὄψεως σ. *ib*.7.12(p.54.24; M.9.505A); Or.*Cels*.2.76(p.197.18, v.l. συνησθημένως M.11.913B); *ib*.3.64(p.258.4; 1004C); Μάρκελλος...σ. ἑαυτοῦ εἰς ἄτοπον ἐκπεπτωκότος προστίθησιν Eus.*Marcell*.2.4(p.55.9, 19; M.24.817A,B); τῆς ἐκ θεοῦ συνησθημένος βοηθείας id.*h.e*.9.9.10(M.20.824A); Dion.Ar.*d.n*.3.3(M.3.684B); **d.** pass., *be perceived*, Olymp.*Job* 4:13ff.(M.93.76A).

συναίσθησις, ἡ, *perception*; **1.** *sense perception* τὴν κατὰ συναίσθησιν ζωήν Athenag.*res*.16(p.68.3; M.6.1005D); *power of sensation* ὁ... Ἰουλιανὸς...βληθεὶς νόσῳ ἐπὶ τεσσαράκοντα τὰς ὅλας ἡμέρας ἀποτάδην ἔκειτο, μήτε φθεγγόμενος μήτε τινὰ σ. ἔχων Philost.*h.e*.7.10(M.65.548C); **2.** *particular feeling, sensation*; *sentiment* δι' ἀκοῆς ἐγγίγνεσθαι τῆς ἀγάπης τὴν σ. Clem.*str*.5.1(p.334.17; προαίσθησιν M.9.28B); **3.** *perception, apprehension, sense*; **a.** aesthetic or intellectual οἱ δὲ ἀμφὶ τὴν παιδείαν διατρίβοντες τὴν σ. χορηγοῦνται, καθ' ἣν τῶν μέτρων οἱ ποιηταὶ καὶ τῆς λέξεως οἱ σοφισταὶ καὶ τῶν συλλογισμῶν οἱ διαλεκτικοὶ καὶ οἱ φιλόσοφοι τῆς...θεωρίας ἀντιλαμβάνονται. εὑρετικὸν γὰρ καὶ ἐπινοητικὸν ἡ σ. *ib*.1.4(p.17.11,14; M.8.717A); οἱ...φιλόσοφοι οἱ εἰς τὴν οἰκείαν σ. πνεύματι αἰσθητικῷ συνασκηθέντες *ib*.6.17(p.511.4; M.9.385A); **b.** moral and spiritual; **i.** objective ἡ ὀξυτάτη σ. τῶν ἀγγέλων *ib*.7.7(p.29.2; 453A); ἀντέθηκεν...αὐτῇ [sc. τῇ κατὰ φιλοσοφίαν αἰσθήσει] τὴν ἐν θεοσεβείᾳ αἴσθησιν...τοῖς γὰρ ὑπὸ φιλοσοφίας δεδικαιωμένοις βοήθεια θησαυρίζεται καὶ ἡ εἰς θεοσέβειαν σ. *ib*.1.4(p.17.30; M.8.717C); Or.*Jo*.13.9(p.233.26; M.14.412C); προσθήκην δὲ [sc. λέγει] θλίψεως τὴν σ. τῶν αἰτίων, δι' ἃς καὶ τὰ κακὰ αὐτοῖς ἐπενήνεκται Thdr.Heracl.*Is*.28:10(M.18.1317B); τῆς σωτηρίου θεότητος σ. ... εἰληφὼς Eus.*l.C*.18(p.259.4; M.20.1437C); ὑπορραΐσας [sc. Julian] πολλὰ μὲν κατεγίνωσκεν ἑαυτὸν τῆς ἀθεμίτου τόλμης, καὶ τὴν δίκην ἐκεῖθεν αὐτῷ σ. ἔλαβε καταρραγῆναι Philost.*h.e*.7.10(M.65.548C); πεπωρωμένη ψυχή, μαστιζομένη οὐκ αἰσθάνεται, καὶ εἰς σ. ἐλθεῖν τοῦ εὐεργέτου οὐκ ἀνέχεται Thal.*cent*.2.61(M.91.1444B); a divine gift ἡ [sc. θεία] δύναμις καὶ ἐντίθησι ταῖς φρεσὶν ἰσχύν τε καὶ σ. ἀκριβεστέραν Clem.*str*.6.17(p.515.3; M.9.393B); opp. ἐπίγνωσις, of consciousness of God among heathen ἡ σ. εἰς τὸν παντοκράτορα ἐπιβαλλόντων τὸν νοῦν ἐθνῶν opp. τῷ κατ' ἐπίγνωσιν εἰδότι *ib*.5.14(p.417.31; 200A); **ii.** subjective *consciousness, awareness*, ref. Apoc.10:9f. βίβλον μίαν, ἡδίστην κατὰ τὰς ἀρχὰς νοουμένην...πικρὰν δὲ τῇ ἑκάστου τῶν ἐγνωκότων σ. τῇ περὶ ἑαυτοῦ ἀναφαινομένην Or.*Jo*.5.7(4; p.104.22; M.14.193C); μετὰ πάσης φιλοτιμίας καὶ σ. τῆς ἀνθρωπίνης ἀσθενείας id.*fr.1 in Jer*.(p.195.11); ref. Jo.13:8 εἰς σ. ἐλθὼν τῆς ἰδίας ἀναξιότητος Bas.*jud*.7(2.221C; M.31.672B); esp. *conviction, sense* of sin, ref. Ps.128:5 εὔχεται...τοὺς ἀναισθήτους ⟨τῶν⟩ τῆς αἰσχύνης ἔργων εἰς σ. ἔρχεσθαι Or.*hom.5.5 in Jer*.(p.36.11; M.13.303C); *ib.20.6*(p.186.22; 513C); τὸν ἀναισθητοῦντα τῶν ἰδίων πταισμάτων εἰς τὴν σ. ἄγων καὶ μεταμέλειαν ἀληθινὴν †Bas.*Is*.73(1.431C; M.30.241C); ὁ Δαβὶδ ὑπὸ σ. ὑγιοὺς Cyr.*Ps*.37:6(M.69.960A); οὐκ ἀρκεῖ...στεναγμός, ἀλλὰ καὶ τρόπων ἐπιστροφή, ὅτε τις ἑαυτοῦ λαμβάνει σ. Proc.G.*Is*.30:15(M.87.2265B); attained through suffering τοσούτοις παλαίων κακοῖς...συναίσθησιν τῶν...τετολμημένων αὐτῷ λαμβάνει Eus.*v.C*.1.57(p.34.19; M.20.972B); λιμοῦ κατατήκοντος... ἐκαλοῦντό τινες εἰς σ. μόλις τῶν...τολμημάτων, ᾔδεσαν τε λοιπόν, τοῦ κακοῦσθαι τὰς αἰτίας Cyr.*Zach*.94(3.783E); γενναίως δ' ὑπομείνας τὰ ἀλγεινά, ὁ ἐντεῦθεν ἐν σ. γενόμενος τῶν οἰκείων πλημμελημάτων ‡Proc.G.*Pr*.16:14(M.87.1385A); **c.** *coming to oneself, self-possession, recollection* ἡ δ' εἰς σ. ἐλθοῦσα Eus.*qu.Marin*.3.1(M.22.949B); Pall.*h.Laus*.33(M.34.1105D; p.97.13n.); of aeon Sophia ἐν σ. γεγονυῖαν ‡Epiph.*epit.haer*.31(p.361.12); **4.** *fellow-feeling* μετὰ πολλῆς τῆς σ. καὶ συμπαθείας Acac.B.*ep.Cyr*.(p.100.18; M.77.101C); **5.** *agreement, unity* εἰς σ. ἦλθον Anast.S.*serm.imag*.3(M.89.1156C).

***συναισθήτως**, error in Or.*fr.*138^{1} *in Mt*.(M.17.292B; συναισθήσει p.69).

συναίσθομαι, v. συναισθάνομαι.

***συναιχμαλωτεύω**, *take captive along with*, Thphn.*chron*.p.244 (M.108.828C).

***συναιώθης**, vox nihili in Thdr.Stud.*epp*.2.213(M.99.1641C; error for συνηνώθης).

***συνακέφαλος**, ὁ, *fellow Acephalite* (lit., *equally without head*) τοὺς τῶν Ἀκεφάλων σ. Thdr.Stud.*test*.(M.99.1816B)ap.*Proem*.in Dor.*doct*.(M.88.1612B).

συνακμάζω, **1.** *flourish at the same time*; of plants, persons, institutions etc.; met., *ripen* or *mature with* φρόνησις κτλ. σ. τῷ χρόνῳ Clem.*paed*.3.3(p.247.12; M.8.581A); **2.** *be as old as* τὸ ἔνδυμα σ. αὐτοῦ τῷ ἐκεῖ βίῳ Nil.*Alb*.(M.79.708B).

***συνακμαστής**, ὁ, *one who flourishes at the same time*, Epiph.*haer*.68.1(p.140.23; M.42.184C).

συνακόλουθος, as subst., *companion* οἱ διάκονοι οἱ σ. μου ‡Ign.*Ant*.13.

***συνακουμβίζω**, (cf. Lat. *accumbo*) *recline at table* or *be sitting together with*, Nil.*epp*.3.92(M.79.428D).

συνακρο-άομαι, *join in hearing* a case παρὰ τῷ ἰδίῳ καταδικαζέσθωσαν μητροπολίτῃ, ~ωμένων δύο ἐπισκόπων τῆς συνόδου Ath.Scholast.*coll*.1.2(p.10).

***συνακροατής**, ὁ, *ellow student, fellow disciple*, M.*Ign.Ant*.3.

συνακτέον, *one must bring together*; hence *one must combine* or *reconcile* statements σ. ἀμφότερα καὶ ἕνα λόγον ἀποδοτέον Or.*princ*.3.1.24(p.243.9; M.11.301B).

συνακτήριον, τό, **1.** *place of meeting*; met., of BMV in rel. to Inc., Thdr.Stud.*nativ.BMV* 1(M.96.681A); **2.** *meeting-house, conventicle* of heretics, Tim.CP *haer*.(M.86.60B); οἱ αἱρετικοὶ σ. ποιεῖν οὐ δύνανται Justn.*cod*.1.5.4(p.55); Thphn.*chron*.p.204(M.108.524C); τὰ σ. αὐτῶν ἡ ὀρθόδοξος ἐκκλησία λαμβάνει Phot.*nomoc*.12.2(M.104.869B); **3.** met., *bond, that which holds fast* σὺ [sc. BMV] πτωχῶν εὐθυμία...ἀστατούντων σ. *Hymn*.(*AS* 1 p.537).

συνακτικός, *pertaining to the* σύναξις; of a garment, *worn for the eucharist* λεβιτῶνα τὸν σ. *Apophth.Patr*.(M.65.196B).

***συνάκτιστος**, *also uncreated*; *uncreated like* another σ. τῷ πατρὶ ...τὸν υἱόν Gel.Cyz.*h.e*.2.16.22(M.85.1265A); ὁ σωτήρ, ὡς θεός, τῷ σ. αὐτοῦ ἐχρίσατο...πνεύματι Didym.*Trin*.2.6(M.39.556C).

συναλγέω, *share in suffering*; *sympathize*, also c. genit. rei ἐλεῆσαι...καὶ σ. τῆς ἀπροσεξίας τοὺς ὀλιγώρους τῆς εὐπαιδευσίας ἐξεταστάς Max.*schol.Dion.Ar*.proem.(M.4.17D).

***συνάλγησις**, ἡ, *sympathy*, Thdr.Stud.*epp*.2.38(M.99.1232B).

[*]**συναλειφή**, ἡ, v. συναλοιφή.

συναλείφ-ω (-αλοίφω), **1.** *anoint thoroughly*, met. γυνὴ...τῷ σωφροσύνης ἀμβροσίῳ χρίσματι ~έσθω...καὶ αὐτὸς ὁ κύριος σ. τῷ μύρῳ Clem.*paed*.2.8(p.197.1,4; M.8.472B); **2.** *fuse together*; pass., *coalesce*, freq. in Trin. controversy; **a.** *combine* οὐκ εἰς μίαν ὑπόστασιν τὴν περὶ αὐτῶν ἔννοιαν σ., ἀλλὰ φυλάσσοντες μὲν διῃρημένην τὴν τῶν ὑποστάσεων ἰδιότητα Gr.Nyss.*Eun*.1(1 p.164.4; M.45.405B); **b.** *confound, confuse* in thought, *regard as one and the same* πῶς οὖν ὁ Ἰωάννης περὶ τοῦ υἱοῦ λέγει, ὁ δὲ Παῦλος περὶ τοῦ πνεύματος; οὐχ ὡς σ. τὰς ὑποστάσεις, ἀλλὰ μίαν ἀξίαν δηλοῦντες εἶναι Chrys.*hom.68.2 in Jo*.(8.407A); id.*hom.29.3 in 1Cor*.(10.262D); οὐ ~ων τὰς ὑποστάσεις...ἀλλὰ εἰδὼς καὶ τὸ τούτων ἰδιάζον καὶ διῃρημένον, καὶ τῆς οὐσίας τὴν ἑνότητα id.*hom.30.2 in 2Cor*.(10.652C); error ass. Sabellius οὐδὲ εἰς ἓν τὰ τρία σ. ἵνα μὴ τοῦ Σαβελλίου νόσον νοσήσωμεν Pamph.H.*panopl*.16.1 (p.642); ὡς Σαβέλλιος σ. καὶ συγχέων ‡Caes.Naz.*dial*.3(M.38.861); **c.** pass., *coalesce* εἰς ἓν αἴτιον καὶ υἱοῦ καὶ πνεύματος ἀναφερομένων, οὐ συντιθεμένων, οὐδὲ σ. Gr.Naz.*or*.20.7(M.35.1073A) = Jo.D.*f.o*.1.8 (M.94.829A) = ‡Cyr.*Trin*.10(6^{3}.16A; συναλοιφομένων M.77.1144B); ἐν ἀλλήλοις φῶτα [sc. three Persons]· μήτε ~όμενοι...καὶ οὔτε...ἡ μία οὐσία εἰς ἓν πρόσωπον...συνηλείφθη ‡Caes.Naz.*dial*.3(M.38.860); Jo.D.*Jacob*.78(M.94.1476A); [sc. αἱ ὑποστάσεις] ἀσύγχυτον ἔχουσαι τὴν ἐν ἀλλήλαις περιχώρησιν· οὐχ ὥστε σ. ἢ συγχεῖσθαι id.*f.o*.1.14(M.94.860B); **d.** pass., *be conceived as coalescing* καὶ βασιλικῆς τριάδος τὴν θεότητα τεμνομένην, ἔστι δὲ ὑφ' ὧν καὶ ~ομένην Gr.Naz.*or*.24.13(M.35.1185A); ὑπὸ μὲν τῶν, ὡς θεός, τιμᾶται καὶ σ. [sc. incarnate Word], ὑπὸ δὲ τῶν, ὡς σάρξ, ἀτιμάζεται καὶ χωρίζεται *ib*.38.15(M.36.329A) = *ib*.45.27(660C).

συναληθεύ-ω, **1.** *join* or *agree in speaking the truth* Ἰώσηπον... ταῖς θείαις ~οντα γραφαῖς Eus.*h.e*.2.10.10(M.20.161B); **2.** *be true also, be equally true*, Leont.B.*arg.Sev*.(M.86.1936B); τὰ...ἐναντία, οὐ σ. ποτε Leont.H.*Nest*.4.35(M.86.1701D); τὴν ἀντίφασιν δείξας σ. Max.*ambig*.(M.91.1052D).

[*]**συναληφή**, ἡ, v. συναλοιφή.

συναλίζομαι, *eat salt with*, ref. Ac.1:4 (v. συναυλίζομαι), Chrys.*hom.2.11 in Ac.princ*.(3.768A); ‡Chrys.*hom*.12(13.247E); Leo Mag.*ep*.28.5(p.17.3; M.*PL*.54.774A).

συναλιφή, ἡ, v. συναλοιφή.

συναλλαγματικός, **1.** *contractual* σ. ποιήσασθαι τὴν...λύτρωσιν Gr.Nyss.*or.catech*.23(p.90.11; M.45.64A); σ. τινα τῆς βασιλείας τὴν ἐμπορίαν τοῖς ἀξιουμένοις προσγίνεσθαι λέγει id.*infant*.(M.46.169A); **2.** *commercial, bargaining* πραγματευτικῇ τινι καὶ σ. διαθέσει κατεμπορευομένους τῆς ἐναρέτου ζωῆς id.*v.Mos*.(M.44.429C).

συναλλακτής, ὁ, (also paroxytone); **1.** *one with whom one does business, business associate* λογοθετήσω τοὺς σ. ‡Chrys.*hom*.13(13.255C); met. γαστὴρ σ. ἐστιν ἀπιστότατος Bas.*hom*.2.7(2.15B; M.31.

196B); *party to a contract* or *negotiation* κυρωθήτω τοῖς σ. ἡ ἄφεσις Gr.Nyss.*or.dom.*5(p.96.25; M.44.1180C); **2.** *one engaged in commerce* μηδὲ κακοὶ σ. γίνεσθε †Bas.*hom.in Ps.*115(1.375B; M.30.112C); Χριστὸς ἀποδίδωσιν ἑκάστῳ, οὐχ ὡς σ. πραγμάτων Marc.Er.*opusc.* 2.21(M.65.933B).

συναλλάσσω, 1. intrans., *have intercourse, associate with*; of sexual intercourse, CCP(381)*can.*14; **2.** *make a contract with*, hence *marry* σ. ὁ δεῖνα τῇ δεῖνι, τουτέστιν, ἔγημε Chrys.*hom.73.4 in Mt.*(7. 713A); **3.** *change at the same time* δεῖ τούτου [sc. τοῦ ἀνθρώπου] λαμβάνοντος ἀλλαγὴν..., συναλλαγῆναι τὸ πᾶν Mac.Mgn.*apocr.*4.30(p.222. 30).

***συναλληγορ-έομαι,** *be interpreted entirely allegorically, be treated as a complete allegory* ~ουμένοις τοῖς ὅσον...μὴ γεγενημένοις Or.*princ.*4.5(p.331.12; M.11.385B).

συναλλοι-όω, *change at the same time* or *together with*; pass. intrans., Meth.*res.*3.6(p.397.23; M.18.321C); τῇ συνεχείᾳ τῆς κατὰ τὴν κίνησιν ἑτερότητος ~οῦται Gr.Nyss.*fat.*(M.45.153B); ref. Inc. τὸ... φύσει...ἀναλλοίωτον ἀεὶ τοιοῦτόν ἐστιν, οὐ ~ούμενον τῇ ταπεινῇ φύσει ὅταν ἐν ἐκείνῃ κατ᾽ οἰκονομίαν γένηται id.*ep.*3(M.46.1020B); εἰς...ἐφ᾽ ἑκατέρων τῆς οὐσίας ὁ λόγος, οὐδὲν τῇ παρόδῳ τοῦ χρόνου σ. id.*Eun.* 1(1 p.74.2; M.45.304B).

***συναλλοτριόω,** *alienate together*; pass., *be foreign also to* ὁ τῆς ἀγαθῆς οὐσίας ἀμέτοχος καὶ τῆς τοῦ ἀγαθοῦ...ἐπωνυμίας σ. Gr.Nyss. *Eun.*11(2 p.252.11; M.45.857D); acc. Eunomius' argument τὸ τοῦ πάθους ἀλλότριον σ. ... καὶ τῆς γεννήσεως *ib.*4(2 p.51.30; 621B).

***συνάλογος,** vox nihili θάτερον τῶν ἰχθύων τὴν ἐγκύκλιον, τὸν λοιπὸν δὲ...τὴν ἐπαναβεβηκυῖαν μηνύειν φιλοσοφίαν, αἳ δὴ τὰ συνάλογοι λόγου τοῦ κυριακοῦ Clem.*str.*6.11(p.479.14, conj. εἰσιν ἄλογοι, συνανάλογοι; M.9.316A).

συναλοιφή ([*]**συναλ(ε)ιφή,** [*]**συναληφή**), **ἡ,** *coalescing, identification*; **1.** in gen. σ. ... καὶ σύγχυσιν...τῶν ὅλων Eus.*e.th.*3.15(p.172. 12; M.24.1028D); of individual persons πῶς...ἠδύνατο...εἶναι ἓν ὡς κατὰ συναλοιφήν; Epiph.*haer.*57.10(p.356.14, v.l. συναλειφήν M.41. 1009B); ref. Christian unity ποιῶν ἡμᾶς ἓν...οὐ κατὰ σ. μιᾶς οὐσίας κατὰ δὲ τελείωσιν τῆς εἰς ἄκρον ἀρετῆς Eus.*e.th.*3.18(p.179.29; 1041C); **2.** Trin.; **a.** denied by orthodox εἷς ἐστιν οὐ συναλοιφῇ τῶν τριῶν, ἀλλ᾽ οὐσίᾳ μιᾷ †Or.*fr.in Mt.*28:18(p.235; M.17.309D); αἱ δὲ τρεῖς ὑποστάσεις, μηδεμιᾶς ἐπινοουμένης σ., ἢ ἀναλύσεως, ἢ συγχύσεως Gr. Naz.*or.*20.7(M.35.1073A); ἵνα μὴ σ. ἡ τριὰς νομισθείη Epiph.*exp.fid.* 16(p.517.3; M.42.813A); *ib.*18(p.520.6; 820B); οὐ σ. τις ὢν ὁ υἱὸς τῷ πατρί, οὐδὲ τὸ ἅγιον πνεῦμα, ἀλλ᾽ ὁ πατὴρ πατὴρ καὶ ὁ υἱὸς υἱὸς καὶ ἅγιον πνεῦμα ἅγιον πνεῦμα id.*haer.*76.6(p.346.20; M.42.525B); ὁ υἱὸς ...ἐξ αὐτοῦ γεννηθείς, οὐ σ. ὢν τῷ πατρί ‡Caes.Naz.*dial.*10(M.38.868); μηδεμιᾶς γινομένης σ. ἢ συμφύρσεως ἢ συγχύσεως Jo.D.*f.o.*1.14(M.94. 860B); assertion being one of two opposing errors μήτε χωρίζωμεν, μήτε σ. ἐργαζώμεθα Cyr.H.*catech.*11.18; ἢ κατὰ σ., ἢ κατὰ υἱοθεσίαν Epiph.*haer.*69.54(p.201.5; 285C); τριὰς τελεία οὖσα καὶ μία θεότης... οὔτε σ. τις οὖσα οὔτε ὑποβεβηκυῖα *ib.*72.1(p.255.23; 384A); **b.** denial chiefly directed agst. Sabellian heresy μήτε ἀπαλλοτριώσωμεν, μήτε σ. υἱοπατορίας ἐργασώμεθα Cyr.H.*catech.*11.16; *ib.*4.8; οὐ σ. ἡ τριάς, ὡς ὁ Σαβέλλιος ἐνόμισεν Epiph.*haer.*62.3(p.392.3; M.41.1053B); τὸν Σαβέλλιον...τὴν σ. παρεισφέροντα *ib.*62.4(p.393.7, v.l. συναλειφήν 1056B); Σαβέλλιον...τὸν νομίζοντα τὸν υἱὸν καὶ τὸν πατέρα σ. εἶναι *ib.*69.69 (p.217.32; M.42.313C); σ. τῶν ὑποστάσεων εἰσάγεται, καὶ ὀνόματα ψιλὰ ...ἐπὶ τῆς...τριάδος, κατὰ τὴν Σαβελλίου...κενοφωνίαν Pamph.H. *panopl.*7.2(p.624); οὐ...κατὰ τὴν Σαβελλίου συναίρεσιν...τὴν ἐν ἀλλήλαις περιχώρησιν ἔχουσι δίχα πάσης σ. καὶ συμφύρσεως Jo.D.*f.o.*1.8 (M.94.829A) = ‡Cyr.*Trin.*10(6^{3}.16A; M.77.1144B); ἡ κατὰ συναλοιφὴν ἕνωσις, ἐπὶ τῶν ἀποσπωμένων, καὶ αὖθις ἀποκαθισταμένων· οἷον λαμπάδος ἐκ πυρός *Schol.* in Max.*opusc.*(M.91.213C); **c.** also against Noëtus διὰ τὸ μὴ νομίζεσθαι σ. εἶναι πρὸς τὸν υἱόν, τὸ ἅγιον πνεῦμα σχηματίζεται ἐν εἴδει περιστερᾶς Epiph.*haer.*57.4(p.348.25, v.l. συναληφήν M.41.1000C); and Paul. Sam. οὐ πατρὸς ἅμα λόγῳ συναλοιφῇ πεφηνότος, ὡς ἄνθρωπος ἅμα τῷ ἑαυτοῦ λόγῳ φαινόμενος *ib.*65.5(p.8.7, cod. συναλιφῇ M.42.20C); **d.** agst. Pneumatomachci τὸ...πνεῦμα... οὐκ ἀλλότριον πατρὸς καὶ υἱοῦ. οὐ σ. δέ ἐστι πατρὶ καὶ υἱῷ *ib.*74.11 (p.329.14; 496D); οὔτε συνάδελφος υἱὸς πατρὶ οὔτε σ., καὶ τὸ πνεῦμα οὔτε σ. οὔτε συνάδελφον πατρὶ καὶ υἱῷ *ib.*74.12(p.330.12f.; 497C).

[*]**συναλοίφω,** v. συναλείφω.

συναλύω, *be distraught along with*, Bas.*hom.*5.8(2.41D; M.31. 256D).

***συναμαθαίνω,** *be as ignorant* or *as senseless as* τοῖς ἀγνοήσασι σ. Cyr.*Jo.*5.2(4.483A); id.*ep.*50(p.96.11; 5^{2}.165D); id.*Chr.un.*(5^{1}.751E).

***συναμαρτήμων, ὁ,** *fellow sinner*, Leont.H.*Nest.*7.1(M.86.1760B).

συναμείβω, pass., *be changed along with*, Gr.Nyss.*hom.opif.*22.5 (M.44.205C).

συναμιλλ-άομαι, 1. *struggle together* against, *come to grips* with ἀγγέλων...σχῆμα φοροῦντες, τῷ διαβόλῳ ~ώμεθα Ephr.1.112A; τοῦ προσέχειν καὶ μὴ σ. τοῖς δηλητηρίοις Epiph.*haer.*proem.2.3(p.171.18; M.41.177B); **2.** *vie with, rival* (sc. in worship) τοῖς ἀθροιζομένοις συμψάλλων καὶ σ. *Mir.Geo.*4(p.31.11); **3.** abs., *contend together* συναγωνιστὰς κέκτημαι τοὺς πρὸς τὸν δρόμον τῆς ἄνω πορείας συμπονοῦντας καὶ σ. †Jo.D.*B.J.*18(M.96.1016A).

συνάμιλλος, *rival*, Cyr.*thes.*17(5^{1}.181B).

***συναμφιέννυμαι,** *be clothed in as well* or *at the same time*, Anast.S. *hod.*17(M.89.265B).

συναμφότερος, sg. (collective) and plur., *both together*, of Persons in Trin. συνεργάζεσθαι [sc. τὸν πατέρα]...τῷ υἱῷ, οὐχ ὡς δύο νοοῦντες διῃρημένως...οὐδ᾽ ὡς ἓν τὸ σ. Cyr.*Jo.*1.5(4.48B); of more than two, *all together* ἢ εἶδος, ἢ γνώμην, ἢ δύναμιν, ἢ ἀξίαν, ἢ τὰ σ. Didym. *Trin.*1.16(M.39.336C); neut. freq. as subst.; **1.** *combination*, esp. of man as a combination of body and soul λέγω...σ. τὸν ἐκ ψυχῆς καὶ σώματος ἄνθρωπον Athenag.*res.*18(p.70.25; M.6.1009C); μετὰ θάνατον οὐδὲ...ἔστιν ἔτι τὸ σ. χωριζομένης...τῆς ψυχῆς ἀπὸ τοῦ σώματος *ib.*(p.71. 11; 1012A); *ib.*25(p.78.12; 1021B); τοῦ ἀνθρώπου ἤτοι ἐν ψυχῇ ἢ ἐν σώματι ἢ ἐν συναμφοτέροις Or.*Jo.*2.21(15; p.78.4; M.14.149D); hence of Christ's manhood τοῦ κατὰ τὴν ἀνθρωπότητα σ. τοῦ...Χριστοῦ, ψυχῆς λέγω καὶ σώματος Max.*ambig.*(M.91.1325A); Christol. of divine and human natures united in Person of Christ τὸ σ. ἔχων ἐν ἑαυτῷ τήν τε τοῦ θεοῦ οὐσίαν καὶ τὴν ἐξ ἀνθρώπων Hipp.*Bal.*(p.82.3; M.10.605B); φασὶ...τὸ σ., τόν τε λόγον καὶ τὸν ἄνθρωπον, εἶναι υἱόν ‡Ath.*Ar.*4.21(p.68.4; M.26.500B); τὸ σ. ἕν...οὐ τῇ φύσει, τῇ δὲ συνόδῳ Gr.Naz.*or.*30.8(p.120.10; M.36.113B); ποτὲ μὲν...ἀνθρώπῳ...ποτὲ δὲ ...θεότητι...ἵνα νοῆται τὸ σ. Cyr.*thes.*24(5^{1}.231B); ὁ τῆς μιᾶς ὑποστάσεως δηλωτικός, καὶ τοῦ σ. παραστατικός ‡Cyr.*Trin.*25(6^{3}.30D; M.77. 1168A); ποτὲ μὲν ἐκ τοῦ σ. Χριστὸν ὀνομάζομεν...ποτὲ δὲ ἐξ ἑνὸς τῶν μερῶν *ib.*27(33B; M.1172C); **2.** literary *parallel*, Epiph.*mens.*8(M.43. 248D).

***συναμφοτέρως,** *in more than one way, in two ways at once* τὸ αὐτὸ μὲν ὑπάρχον, διαφόρως τε ὀνομαζόμενον...σ. ἐκφωνοῦνται Epiph. *mens.*8(M.43.249A); *ib.*17(265C).

συναναβαίνω, 1. *go up with, ascend together*, with Moses up Sinai, Clem.*str.*5.12(p.377.30; M.9.116B); with Christ up the Mount of Transfiguration, Or.*Jo.*13.47(46; p.273.31; M.14.484A); Max. *ambig.*(M.91.1125D); fig., from the waters of baptism σ. μετ᾽ αὐτῶν καὶ συνηρμόσθησαν εἰς τὴν οἰκοδομὴν τοῦ πύργου Herm.*sim.*9.16.7; of the spirits seen ascending with Samuel, Or.*engast.*7(p.290.9; M. 12.1021C); **2.** *rise*, i.e. raise the mind to higher things, *ascend* in spirit *together with* ὁπόταν τις...σ. αὐτῷ [sc. τῷ κυρίῳ] ἔνθα ἐστὶν ὁ... θεός Clem.*str.*7.9(p.41.10; M.9.480A); εἰ καὶ ἐγνώκαμεν κατὰ σάρκα Χριστόν, ἀλλὰ νῦν οὐκέτι γινώσκομεν· τῇ σῇ τοίνυν συνανέβη προκοπῇ... χωρησάσης σου ἐνορᾶν Or.*schol.in Cant.*6:4(M.17.277A); ὅση δύναμις, ὑψοῦν μὲν τῷ λόγῳ τὸ πνεῦμα, ὑψοῦν δὲ καὶ πρὸ τοῦ λόγου κατὰ διάνοιαν· οὐ γὰρ δυνατόν ἐστι σ. τῇ διανοίᾳ τὸν λόγον Gr.Nyss.*Maced.* 20(M.45.1328A); **3.** met.; **a.** *rise to the level of* τοῖς τῶν μειζόνων ἀκροαταῖς σ. πως αὐτοῦ τὴν ἐξήγησιν id.*hex.*4(M.44.65B); **b.** *mount* or *rise to correspond* with τῷ ἀναβαίνοντι ἐναρέτῳ συναναβήσεται ἡ δόξα αὐτοῦ Or.*sel.in Ps.*48:17(M.12.1448C); ὁ λόγος οὐ σ. τοῖς θαύμασιν Anast.Ant.*serm.*3.4(M.89.1388D).

***συνανάβασις, ἡ,** *ascent together* πρὸς τὸν ἐπὶ τὰ ὑψηλότερα χειραγωγεῖν ἐθέλοντα λόγον· οὐ προσιζομένη τὴν σ., λέγουσα [sc. ἡ ψυχὴ ἐθισμοῖς ἀκολουθοῦσα] Nil.*exerc.*54(M.79.785C).

συναναβλαστάνω, *grow up with*; of a person with an organic defect, Bas.Sel.*or.*35.1(M.85.373C).

***συναναβλύζω,** *gush forth together* τὸ τίμιον αἷμα σ. ὕδατι Cyr.*inc. unigen.*(5^{1}.681D); id.*1Cor.*10:1(p.280.2; M.74.880C).

***συναναβράσσω,** *boil* or *foam together*; of the abyss, Max.*ep.*1(M. 91.381C).

***συναναγεννάομαι,** *be regenerated together* with, of Christian brethren τοὺς...ἐν Χριστῷ ἡμῖν συναναγεγεννημένους Or.*or.*28.2 (p.376.8; M.11.521C).

συναναγινώσκω, *read together*, hence *study together* Θεοδόσιος... ἀνεγίνωσκε...καὶ σ. αὐτῷ ἄλλος νεώτερος Jo.Mal.*chron.*14 p.352(M.97. 525B); ptcpl. as subst., *fellow student*, *ib.*5 p.134(229B).

συναναγκάζω, *necessitate at the same time*; of man's resurrection as implied by Christ's, Chrys.*hom.39.1 in 1Cor.*(10.363C).

***συναναγορεύω,** *call* (i.e. *name*) *in addition*, Thphn.*chron.*p.402 (M.108.957C).

συνανάγω, *take* or *lead aloft with* (*one*), i.e. to heaven ταύτην [sc. τὴν καλὴν παρακαταθήκην] πιστεύω σοι σήμερον· ταύτῃ καὶ συμβαπτίσω καὶ σ. σε Gr.Naz.*or.*40.41(M.36.417B); συνανήγαγε...ἡμᾶς εἰς οὐρανοὺς ἀνερχόμενος †Jo.D.*B.J.*34(M.96.1189A).

συναναδείκνυμι, *show at the same time*; pass., *be shown to be involved* or *inherent in* συνημμένως...σ. τῇ βουλῇ καὶ τὸ ἔργον Gr.Nyss.*hex*.7(M.44.69A); id.*Eun*.8(2 p.197.2; M.45.792D); πάλιν σκοπήσωμεν τὴν σ. ἀτοπίαν τῷ λόγῳ *ib*.1(1 p.211.19; 460B).

*__συναναζυμόομαι__, *be leavened together*, Phot.*1Cor*.5:6ff.(Staab p.553.20)ap.*cat.1Cor*.5:6ff.(p.96.27).

*__συναναθάλλ-ω__, *put forth new shoots together*, Gr.Nyss.*v.Mos*.20 (M.44.305C); fig., *spring up together*; of vain thoughts, Clem.*str*.2.18 (p.165.9; M.8.1037B); ὁ πολυειδὴς τῶν θείων ἀρετῶν κόσμος ἐστί, τῶν ∼όντων τῷ πνεύματι Gr.Nyss.*hom.2 in Cant*.(M.44.800C).

*__συναναθέω__, *go up together*; to Jerusalem, Cyr.*Jo*.8(4.699E).

*__συναναθρώσκω__, **1.** *go up together, ascend with* σ. εἰς τὸ ὄρος Μωσεῖ Cyr.*glaph.Ex*.3(1.329A); σ. ... ἐπὶ τὸ ὄρος id.*ador*.10(1.328C); **2.** *go up* or *rise together* σ. τῷ μέσῳ καυλῷ καὶ εἰς ὕψος αἴρεσθαι...τὸ ἰσοστατοῦν *ib*.9(298E).

*__συνανακαινίζομαι__, *be renewed together*; of spiritual renewal effected by Christ, Cyr.*hom.pasch*.9.2(5^{2}.109E).

συνανάκειμαι, pass., *recline together* at table, Ephr.2.95D.

συνανακεράννυμαι ([*]-**κίρναμαι**, [*]-**κιρνάομαι**), **1.** *be mingled together, blended*, ref. Heb.4:2 ἄρα γὰρ ἔμελλον...συνανακιρνᾶσθαί τε ἀλλήλοις, καθάπερ ἀμέλει καὶ οἶνος ὕδατι, καὶ ἀνάχυσίν τινα τῶν ὑποστάσεων τὴν εἰς ἀλλήλας παθεῖν...ἢ μᾶλλον ἑνοῦσθαι κατὰ ψυχήν Cyr.*Nest*.1.3(p.22.16; 6^{1}.15D); not to be applied to H. Ghost as if a semi-divine being οὐδὲ γὰρ ἐνδέχεται μίξιν τινὰ τῶν ἐναντίων καὶ συμπλοκὴν ἐννοῆσαι τοῦ κτιστοῦ πρὸς τὸ ἄκτιστον συνανακιρναμένων Gr.Nyss.*Maced*.17(M.45.1324A); **2.** *be intimately united*, ref. Inc. τὴν σὴν παχύτητα κατεδέξατο διὰ μέσου νοὸς ὁμιλήσας σαρκί, καὶ γενόμενος ἄνθρωπος ὁ κάτω θεός· ἐπειδὴ συνανεκράθη θεῷ, καὶ γέγονεν εἷς Gr.Naz.*or*.29.19(p.103.2; M.36.100A) cit. Max.*ambig*.(M.91.1040C); Gr.Nyss.*or.catech*.37(p.148.4; M.45.96C); δουλείας συνανακιρναμένης τῇ κυριότητι id.*Eun*.10(2 p.244.25; -κιρνωμένης M.45.848B); of Christ with soul, Meth.*symp*.7.4(p.75.18; M.18.129C); of eucharistic union γίνεται...ἐν ἡμῖν ὁ υἱός, σωματικῶς...ὡς ἄνθρωπος, συνανακιρνάμενός τε καὶ συνενούμενος δι᾽ εὐλογίας τῆς μυστικῆς Cyr.*Jo*.11.12(4.1001E); ἔδει...αὐτὸν...συνανακιρνᾶσθαι...ὥσπερ τοῖς ἡμετέροις σώμασιν διὰ τῆς ἁγίας αὐτοῦ σαρκός Vict.*Mc*.14:22ff.(p.423.19) = Petr.Laod.*fr. in Mc*.14:22(M.86.3328A); of individuals mutually in Church συνανακιρνᾶσθαι...ἡμᾶς ἀλλήλοις βούλεται...ὡς ἓν νοεῖσθαι τὸ σύμπαν τῆς ἐκκλησίας σῶμα Cyr.*Jo*.11.11(4.997B).

συνανακλίνομαι, *recline with*, Clem.*paed*.3.4(p.253.22; M.8.597A); at table, Eus.*v.C*.3.15(p.84.8; M.20.1072B); ‡Eust.*Laz*.10(p.35.8).

*__συνανάκλισις__, **ἡ**, *a reclining together*, ‡Eust.*Laz*.20(p.43.4).

συνανακομίζομαι, pass., *be offered up together* or *in addition to* σεμίδαλις...συνανεκομίζετο τῷ μόσχῳ Cyr.*ador*.11(1.409B); *ib*.17(1.612A); τί τὸ κωλύον ἐστὶ ταῖς ὑπὲρ αὐτῶν προσευχαῖς σ. τὴν θυσίαν; id.*defunct*.(p.542.17; M.76.1424D).

*__συνανακουφίζω__, *raise together* or *at the same time*; one's thoughts, Nil.*exerc*.15(M.79.737B).

*__συνανακράζω__, *lift up the voice, cry out together with*, Cyr.*hom.pasch*.15.1(5^{2}.198E).

*__συνανάκρασις__, **ἡ**, **1.** *blending, commingling*; of the sensible and intelligible in man πρὸς τὴν αἰσθητὴν κτίσιν γίνεταί τις τοῦ νοητοῦ σ. Gr.Nyss.*or.catech*.6(p.31.1; M.45.25D); of iron in the fire as an image of Inc. ὥσπερ οὐδὲ τῆς οἰκείας τὸν σίδηρον [sc. ἐξίστησιν] ἡ ἄκρα καὶ δι᾽ ὅλου πρὸς τὸ πῦρ σ. τε καὶ ἕνωσις Max.*opusc*.(M.91.189C); of those in beatitude ἑκάστου τοσοῦτον...μεθέξοντος, ὅσον ἐπόθησε· καὶ πρὸς αὐτὸ τὸ φύσει ποθούμενον ἄμεσος σ. *ib*.(24D); **2.** of persons, *association, intercourse*, Thdr.Stud.*epp*.2.142(M.99.1448C); **3.** *union* of natures in Christ ὅταν ἐπιφανῇ τὸ φῶς...τοῖς ἐν σκότει...καθημένοις, διὰ τῆς πρὸς τὴν φύσιν ἡμῶν σ. Gr.Nyss.*hom.5 in Cant*.(M.44.864D); id.*or.catech*.16(p.70.13; M.45.52B); τὸν πρὸς τὴν φύσιν ἡμῶν ἀνακιρνάμενον διὰ πάντων δέξασθαι τῶν ἰδιωμάτων αὐτῆς [sc. τῆς φύσεως ἡμῶν] τὴν πρὸς ἡμᾶς σ. *ib*.27(p.101.12; 69C); **4.** eucharistic *union* τῶν δύο φύσεων μετέχωμεν...κατὰ συνανάκρασιν τοῦ σώματος καὶ αἵματος Jo.D.*imag*.3.26(M.94.1348B).

*__συνανακρατικός__, *serving to fuse together, unitive*; of the hypostatic union, Leont.H.*Nest*.1.18(M.86.1468C).

συνανακρίνω, *examine together*, Dion.Ar.*ep*.7.3(M.3.1081C).

*__συνανακτίζ-ω__, *restore likewise* ἔδει...τῆς ἰδίας εἰκόνος καινουργουμένης, καὶ αὐτὸν τὸν τῆς εἰκόνος οἶκον ∼εσθαι Bas.Sel.*pasch*.1.2(M.28.1076B).

συναναλαμβάν-ω, **1.** *take up along with*, ref. Inc., *assume together with* or *at the same time as* ὥσπερ...ἀνείληφε σῶμα...οὕτως σ. τῷ σώματι καὶ τὰ ἀλγεινὰ αὐτοῦ Or.*Cels*.2.23(p.152.24; M.11.841C); **2.** *incorporate, include* τὴν καρτερίαν...σ. ταῖς ἄλλαις [sc. ἀρεταῖς] *ib*.8.65(p.281.2; 1613B); ∼ομένου τοῦ αὐτῶν ἀριθμοῦ Epiph.*haer*.70.12 (p.245.27; M.42.365A); ἅμα Παύλῳ συνανειλημμένους *Chron.Pasch*. p.214(M.92.524B); med., *consider included in, associate with* τὸ ἅγιον πνεῦμα θεολογήσαντες τῇ ὁμοουσίῳ τριάδι συνανελαμβάνοντο Socr.*h.e*.3.7.2(M.67.392A).

συναναλάμπ-ω, **1.** *shine together* with, met. ἡ τῷ ἀληθινῷ φωτὶ τὰ πρῶτα ∼ουσα Gr.Nyss.*hom.2 in Cant*.(M.44.800C); Cyr.*ep*.55(p.49.17; 5^{2}.174E); **2.** *shine forth in proportion* to, *brighten along with* τῇ τοῦ ὀργάνου τελειώσει ∼ουσαν [sc. τὴν τῆς ψυχῆς δύναμιν] Gr.Nyss.*hom.opif*.29(M.44.253C).

*__συνανάλογος__, v. συνάλογος.

*__συναναμετρ-έω__, *measure out in accordance with* ∼οῦντος...τοῦ... θεοῦ τοῖς τῶν πταισμάτων ἐγκλήμασι τὰς ἐφ᾽ ἑκάστῳ δίκας Cyr.*Zach*.30(3.698C).

συναναμίγνυμαι, **1.** of persons; **a.** with other persons; **i.** *mix, associate* with καλὸν...μὴ σ. τοῖς ἀτάκτοις Clem.*paed*.2.1(p.160.17; M.8.393B); Bas.*reg.fus*.14(2.355B; M.31.952A); *Dial.Tim.et Aquil*. 114 v°; **ii.** *join up* with κελεύει καταλιπόντας [sc. τοὺς στρατιώτας] τὸ ἄστυ τῇ Ῥωμαϊκῇ πληθύϊ σ. Thphn.*chron*.p.231(M.108.585A); **b.** with things, *be mixed up with, involved in* σ. καὶ συναπογραφόμενος τῶν οὐκ ἀστείων τὰ πταίσματα Mac.Mgn.*apocr*.3.30(p.125.22); **2.** of things, *be fused* or *blended* χωρήσας αὐτοῦ [sc. the baptized] τὰ ἐπισκοτοῦντα καὶ συναναμεμιγμένα αὐτῷ πάθη Clem.*exc.Thdot*.4 (p.119.29; M.9.677D); properties of divine Persons, Gr.Nyss.*diff. ess*.7(M.32.340A) cit. s. ἐπιμορφάζω.

*__συνανανεύ-ω__, *agree in refusing* or *denying* μετέθετο πάλιν πρὸς τοὐναντίον τὸν λόγον καὶ ἀρνεῖται τοῦ υἱοῦ τὴν πρὸς τὸν γεγεννηκότα σχέσιν· πάλιν...καὶ τούτῳ ∼ουσιν, ὥσπερ αἱ τῶν σωμάτων σκιαὶ τῇ αὐτομάτῳ μιμήσει Gr.Nyss.*Eun*.4(2 p.72.22, v.l. συννεύουσιν M.45.645B).

*__συναναπαίρω__, *take away, remove with one*, Cyr.*ador*.1(1.33A).

συναναπαύ-ομαι, **1.** pass., *lie down with*; of waves, *subside at the same time as*, Synes.*ep*.4(M.66.1332C); **2.** med. and pass., *refresh oneself together* with, *be refreshed also* ἐπέσχον αὐτὸν...∼όμενοι αὐτῷ *A.Jo*.18(p.161.2); συνδιέτριψα τοῖς Κορινθίοις ἡμέρας ἱκανάς, ἐν αἷς συνανεπάημεν τῷ ὀρθῷ λόγῳ Heges.ap.Eus.*h.e*.4.22.2(M.20.377D); abs. τὸν ἔνθα συναναπαύσεται τόπον Or.*Cant*.3(p.201.19; M.13.165D); as a state of soul, *be refreshed with* Christ νύμφη σ. ἐν κοινωνίᾳ τῷ νυμφίῳ αὐτῆς ἀναπαύσει θεϊκῇ Mac.Aeg.*hom*.18.7(M.34.640B); ζῇς τὴν αἰώνιον τέως ζωήν, ἐκ τοῦ παρόντος ἤδη τῷ Χριστῷ σ. id.*elev*.12(M.34.900C); ἀναπαυομένῳ...καὶ καταλύοντι, ∼όμεθα καὶ συγκαταλύομεν Cyr.*ador*.10(1.353E); *ib*.5(163A); **3.** *stop, cease together with* συνεμετρήθη τῷ βίῳ τοῦ δωρουμένου βασιλέως καὶ σ. τούτου τῇ τελευτῇ τὸ δωρούμενον Men.*exc.Rom*.5(p.190.33; M.113.881B).

συναναπέμπ-ω, *admit* to succession or inheritance *together* with εἰ μὴ οἱ ἀδελφοὶ τοῦ τελευτήσαντος μετὰ τῶν γονέων ∼ονται εἰς τὴν ἐκείνου διαδοχήν Ath.Scholast.*coll*.9.10(p.105).

*__συναναπέτομαι__, *fly up together*, met. σ. κατὰ διάνοιαν Gr.Nyss.*or.dom*.2(p.32.6; M.44.1140B).

συναναπηδ-άω, *develop alongside* ∼ώσης...τοῖς τοῦ σώματος μέτροις καὶ τῆς...συνέσεως Cyr.*Chr.un*.(5^{1}.760A).

συναναπίπτω, *recline together*; **1.** *lie down beside* ἡ...ἄρκτος...σ. τῷ ἁγίῳ *M.Tar*.10(p.474); **2.** *recline* or *sit together at table*; of Christ with men, Ephr.3.169E; Chrys.*hom.21.1 in Jo*.(8.121C); of apostles with Christ, Epiph.*haer*.42.11(p.149.20; M.41.764C).

συναναπλάσσομαι, **1.** *be fashioned* or *formed along with* τὰς θείας ἐντολὰς ἔχων...καὶ ὡς σ. καὶ πεποιημένος αὐταῖς, καὶ οἷον ἡνωμένος Olymp.*Job* 23:12(M.93.252D); **2.** of divine and human elements in Christ, *be put together, composed* κατ᾽ οὐσίαν συνῆφθαι καὶ σ. Gr.Naz.*ep*.101 ap.CEph.*act*.1(*ACO* 1.1.2 p.44.2; H.1.1408A) also ap.Leont.H.*monoph*.(M.86.1820B) for κατ᾽ οὐσίαν συνῆφθαι καὶ συνάπτεσθαι Gr.Naz.*ep*.101(M.37.180B).

συναναπλέκω, *entwine also*; met., *combine, join* τὴν μυστικὴν μετάληψιν λέγει...συναναπλέξας τῷ θεοπρεπεῖ τὸ ἀνθρώπινον Ammon.*Jo*.6:27(M.85.1433B).

*__συναναπτερόομαι__, met., *be set on the wing also, be given wings together* with ἡ σὰρξ...τῇ ψυχῇ σ. Chrys.*hom.13.8 in Rom*.(9.569B).

συναναρτάομαι, *be hung up*, hence *be crucified together*, Cyr.*Jo*.5.1(4.466D).

*__συνάναρχος__, **A.** *also without beginning, likewise unoriginate*, i.e. in rel. to Godhead; **1.** of Son in rel. to Father τῷ...πατρὶ πρέπει δόξα...σὺν τῷ σ. αὐτοῦ υἱῷ Ath.*decr*.32(p.28.25; M.25.476C); ὁμολογοῦντες...υἱὸν εἶναι αὐτὸν σ. τοῦ θεοῦ Didym.*Trin*.1.15(M.39.304B); υἱὸς θεοῦ ἐστι...σ. τῷ πατρὶ *cat.Jo*.7:38(p.269.16); τὴν πρὸς ἑαυτὸν [sc. πατέρα] τοῦ υἱοῦ σ. σχέσιν Nil.*Magn*.63(M.79.1053C); σ. ἔχει τὴν ὕπαρξιν τῷ ἰδίῳ γεννήτορι Cyr.*resp*.(p.580.26; 6^{2}.388A); denied by

Arians οὔτε...σ. καὶ συναγέννητον τῷ πατρὶ τὸν υἱὸν εἶναι νομιστέον· σ. γὰρ καὶ συναγεννήτου οὐδεὶς κυρίως πατὴρ ἢ υἱὸς λεχθήσεται *Symb. Ant.*(345)3(p.252.16; M.26.729A); freq. with συναΐδιος, Gel.Cyz.*h.e.* 2.15.3(M.85.1257C); *ib.*2.16.16(1264C); υἱὸν τοῦ πατρὸς συναΐδιον, καὶ κλάδον τῆς ῥίζης σ. ‡Bas.*inc.*(p.235.13); ἔστι σ. [sc. ὁ υἱός] κατὰ χρόνον, καὶ συναΐδιος τῷ ἰδίῳ γεννήτορι Cyr.*Arcad.*3(p.63.11; 5². 44A); †Jo.D.*B.J.*2(M.96.873B); with ὁμοούσιος specified as principal attributes of Second Person, ‡Ath.*templ.*(p.111.13; M.28.1429D) cit. s. προκηρύσσω; Didym.*Trin.*1.15(M.39.308A); ἡ δὲ ἁγία σύνοδος ὁμοούσιον καὶ σ. ὥρισε τὸν υἱὸν τῷ πατρὶ Anast.S.*hod.*5(M.89.100A); τοῦ δὲ υἱοῦ...τὸ σ. καὶ ὁμοούσιον καὶ γεννητόν ‡Bas.*h.myst.*59(p.393. 31); with συνύπαρκτος, Anast.S.*hod.*1(M.89.49D); liturg. Ἰησοῦ Χριστὲ...ὁ σ. λόγος τοῦ ἀνάρχου πατρὸς *Lit.Marc.*(Brightman p.124. 22); **2.** of H. Ghost θεὸν σ. καὶ ὁμοούσιον τῷ πατρὶ Didym.*Trin.*3. 2(M.39.800C); σ. πνεύματος γνώρισμα Dam.*troph.*suppl.(p.282.2); **3.** of Trin., Cosm.Ind.*top.*6(M.88.333C); Jo.D.*fr.*(M.95.229A); ‡Caes. Naz.*dial.*3(M.38.861); ἄναρχον τὸν πατέρα, σ. τὸν υἱόν, καὶ τὸ πνεῦμα ἐκήρυξας Jo.Mon.*hymn.Bas.*3(M.96.1372C); **4.** of divine attributes σ. καὶ συναΐδιον τῇ μακαρίᾳ φύσει τὴν περὶ τῶν...δημιουργεῖσθαι μελλόντων ἐκέκτητο βούλησιν Zach.Mit.*opif.*(M.85.1097A); **5.** in controversies with pagans and heretics, denied of **a.** matter εἷς θεὸς· ὕλη...καὶ εἴδεα...Ἑλλήνων πινυτοῖσι νοούμενα ὡς σ. Gr.Naz.*carm.*1.1. 4.4(M.37.416A); οὐ...σ. καὶ συναΐδιον τῷ θεῷ...νοεῖσθαι τὴν ὕλην Cyr. *Juln.*2(6².54A); **b.** evil τινὰς μὲν σ. τῷ θεῷ τὴν κακίαν λέγειν ἐδίδαξε Jo.D.*imag.*2.2(M.94.1285B).

B. *likewise without source* or *origin*, in this sense dist. from συναΐδιος and denied of Son and H. Ghost in rel. to Father συναΐδια ...λέγουσι τῷ πατρὶ τὸν υἱόν, καὶ τὸ πνεῦμα τὸ ἅγιον, οὐ σ. δέ· συναΐδια μέν, ὡς ἐξ ἀπείρου τῷ πατρὶ συνυπάρχοντα· οὐ σ. δέ, ὡς οὐκ ἀναίτια Thal.*cent.*4.100(M.91.1469B,C).

***συνανάρχως**, *also without beginning* κύριον...συναϊδίως τε καὶ σ. ... ἐκ πατρὸς...γεννηθέντα ‡Eust.*Laz.*29(p.50.10).

συνανασκάπτω, *join in digging up*; met., *join in overthrowing* a ruler, Thphn.*chron.*p.342(M.108.824B).

συναναστρέφ-ω, **1.** *live together, associate with*, rarely act. ~οντός μου πᾶσιν ὑμῖν *A.Andr.fr.*16(p.44.21); med. and pass., of apostles with Christ after Resurrection, *Const.App.*5.7.30; of Christ with apostles ἐνδιέτριψεν ὁ κύριος...ἕτερα γ' ἔτη σ. τοῖς μαθηταῖς αὐτοῦ *Chron.Pasch.*p.215(M.92.524D); **2.** ? *live in*, e.g. partic. circumstances θλίψει σ. *T.Neph.*4.2; or perh. *wrestle with* (cf. Gen.30:8); **3.** *behave* ἐδίδαξα τοὺς δεσπότας ἐπιεικῶς σ. τοῖς δούλοις *M.Petr.et Paul.*37(p.150.15); **4.** *live in accordance with* οἷς συνανεστράφη Chrys. *hom.*5.2 *in Mt.*(7.74A; cj. Gaume συνανετράφη); ἐν τοῖς αὐτοῖς ~ονται id.*hom.*20.9 *in Eph.*(Gaume; ἀναστρέφονται 11.158A, v.l. ~ουσιν); **5.** *live with* or *among*, ref. Christ's sojourn upon earth: accompanied by words signifying, or itself denoting, not only association but life as man among men διὰ τῆς θείας οἰκονομίας τοῖς ἀνθρώποις σ. *A.Petr.et Paul.*43(p.198.5); τοῖς ἀνθρώποις σ. κατὰ τὰς ἡμετέρας εἰδέας, ὁ υἱὸς τοῦ θεοῦ *Ascens.Is.*B 2.11(p.344); ἀνθρώποις σ. ὡς ἄνθρωπον, θεὸν ὄντα λόγον καὶ ἄνθρωπον *Const.App.*7.26.3; σ. ἀνθρωπίνως ἡμῖν Sophr.H.*ep.syn.*(M.87.3177D); *Lit.Jac.*(p.200.24); ref. Bar.3:38 σαφῶς θεὸν ἐπὶ γῆς ὤφθαί φησι, συναναστραφῆναί τε τοῖς ἐν αὐτῇ Cyr.*Juln.*8(6².282C); Thdt.*Trin.*7(M.75.1156B); *Dial.Christ.et Jud.*8(p.57.21); other prob. references τοῖς ἀνθρώποις σ. *T.Dan* 5. 13; οὗτος ὁ ὤν, καὶ ὁρώμενος ἄνθρωπος...ὁ ταπεινὸς ἡμῖν σ. Jo.D.*hom.* 1.18(M.96.572C); κατῆλθεν ἐπὶ τῆς γῆς...οὐκ...ὤφθη μόνον, ἀλλὰ καὶ σ. τοῖς ἀνθρώποις· τοῦτο γὰρ ἴδιον ἰατρῶν γνησίων...τὸ σ. τοῖς ἀρρωστοῦσι *cat.Lc.*10:35(p.88.19); specifically referred to his humanity ἵνα μή τις ὑπολάβῃ ἕτερον εἶναι τὸν ἀόρατον...παρὰ τὸν ἐνανθρωπήσαντα καὶ ἐπὶ τῆς γῆς ὀφθέντα καὶ τοῖς ἀνθρώποις σ. Or.*Jo.*6.30(15; p.140. 20; M.14.253A); τὸ κατὰ σάρκα βλεπόμενον, καὶ τοῖς ἀνθρώποις σ., εἶχέ τι ἐν ἑαυτῷ ἑαυτοῦ τιμιώτερον Gr.Nyss.*Apoll.*27(M.45.1181D); id.*hom.*13 *in Cant.*(M.44.1048A) cit. s. προσωπεῖον; ὁ αὐτὸς...ὡς θεὸς ἰσοσθενὴς τῷ πατρί, ὁ αὐτὸς καὶ...κατὰ τὸ ἀνθρώπινον τοῖς ἀνθρώποις σ. Nil.*epp.*3.92(M.79.428D); ἡ θεότης ἔπλασεν ἑαυτῇ ἀνθρωπότητα, γυμνῇ τῇ οὐσίᾳ τοῖς ἀνθρώποις σ. οὐκ ἐβούλετο †Gregent.*disp.*(M.86. 709C); in a Gnost. writing put into mouth of Satan who is conceived to be ignorant of his divinity τοῖς βροτοῖς σ. *A.Pil.*B 20 (p.326).

συναναστροφή, ἡ, **1.** *living with, familiar intercourse* Ἰακώβου... ἀδελφοῦ τοῦ κυρίου κληθέντος διὰ τὴν σ. Epiph.*haer.*29.3(M.41.393B; cod. p.324.13, ed. συναναστροφήν); ὁ κύριος ἡμῶν...υἱὸς...τοῦ Ἰωσὴφ λέγεται, ἐπειδὴ τῶν υἱῶν αὐτοῦ...ἀδελφὸς ἐστιν ἐκ τῆς σ. Hipp.Th.*fr.* 1.6(p.10.5, v.l. συναναστροφῆς M.117.1041B); ἀντὶ τῆς πρὸς τὴν γῆν ἐπιστροφῆς τὴν μετ' ἀγγέλων ἐν οὐρανοῖς σ. Germ.CP *or.*1(M.98.229C); **2.** *manner of life* χηροσύνη μετὰ...ἀχράντου σ. Epiph.*exp.fid.*21 (p.522.3; M.42.824A); **3.** of Christ's sojourn upon earth τῆς εἰς ἡμᾶς αὐτοῦ σ. ‡Jo.D.*ep.Thphl.*12(M.95.360C).

***συνανάστροφος**, *sharing one's mode of life* σε [sc. θεοτόκε] μεθ' ἡμῶν σ. ἔχειν ὁμολογοῦμεν Germ.CP *or.*7(M.98.357A).

συνανατείνω, *extend to cover also* τὴν μαρτυρίαν εἰς ἑαυτὸν σ., ψευδῶς...λέγων Epiph.*haer.*42.12(p.169.14; M.41.793B).

***συνανατελ-έω**, *be fulfilled also* πεφηνότος ἤδη Χριστοῦ ~εῖ...τῆς ἐν πνεύματι περιτομῆς ὁ καιρός Cyr.*glaph.Gen.*3(1.80A).

συνανατίθημι, *offer one up with another, dedicate together* αὐτοὺς σ., φησί, καὶ ποιῶ προσφοράν Chrys.ap.*cat.Jo.*17:19(p.374.2) for αὐτοὺς σοι ἀνατίθημι id.*hom.*82.1 *in Jo.*(8.484C).

***συνανατολεύς**, *rising at the same time* or *together* ὁ...τῆς δικαιοσύνης ἥλιος...Στέφανον...τὸν πρωτομάρτυρα συνανατολέα τῶν ἀθανάτων ἀκτίνων πεποίηται Proc.CP *or.*17.1(M.65.809A).

συνανατρέπω, *refute together with* something else ἀνατραπεῖσι... τοῖς προειρημένοις συνανετράπη καὶ τὸ συμπέρασμα Or.*Cels.*2.19(p.148. 1; M.11.833D).

συνανατρέφω, **1.** persons, *rear along with, bring up together*, Ephr. 3.XXXD; Ἰάκωβον τὸν ἀδελφὸν τοῦ κυρίου καλούμενον διὰ τὸ συνανατραφῆναι αὐτῷ Epiph.*anc.*60(p.70.20; M.43.124A); **2.** things, *rear in, bring up among* σ. αὐτοῖς ἀθεότητα Clem.*prot.*6(p.51.15; M.8.172B).

***συνανατροφή, ἡ**, v. συναναστροφή.

***συναναφανίζομαι**, s.v.l., *disappear* or *perish together with*, Sever. ap.Thdt.*eran.*3(4.254) cit. s. ἔνδυμα, perh. error for συναφανίζομαι.

συναναφέρ-ω, **1.** *carry along with* τῇ τοῦ κόσμου κινήσει ~όμενον Clem.*exc.Thdot.*69(p.129.18; M.9.692B); **2.** pass., *be raised to the level of*, of humanity of Christ ὁ...ληφθεὶς...σ. τῇ τε ὀνομασίᾳ καὶ τῇ τίμῃ τοῦ...υἱοῦ Thdr.Mops.*symb.*(p.99.3; M.66.1017D); **3.** pass., *be offered together* σ. δεῖν τῷ προβάτῳ φησὶ τὴν σεμίδαλιν Cyr.*ador.*17(1.612B); *ib.*11(395C).

συναναφλέγω, *join in setting fire to*; met., *join in enraging* or *setting one against* τὸν Κωνστάντιον...σ. κατὰ τοῦ Γάλλου Philost.*h.e.*4.1 (M.65.517A).

***συνανάφυρσις, ἡ**, *mixing up, jumble*, Leont.H.*Nest.*1.18(M.86. 1469D).

συναναφύρω, pass.; **1.** *be mixed up*, with things ταῖς πραγματείαις σου σ. ταῖς πονηραῖς Herm.*vis.*2.3.1; fig., *wallow* in mire, Thdr. Mops.*Nah.*3:13ff.(M.66.421D); *associate*; with persons, Cyr.*ador.*12 (1.422E); **2.** *be combined, incorporated*, *Apophth.Patr.*(M.65.84A).

***συναναφύω**, intrans. and pass., *grow up together*; of weeds, Clem.*str.*7.15(p.65.5; M.9.528A); met., of heresies, *ib.*6.8(p.465.27; 289A).

***συναναφώνησις, ἡ**, *general chorus of sound*, Cyr.*Is.*1.3(2.87E).

συναναχ-έω, pass.; **1.** *be mingled, merged*, ref. Gnost. aeon Theletus, Iren.*haer.*1.11.1(M.7.564A); **2.** Trin., *be confounded* οὔτε κατὰ τὸ ἀγέννητον τῷ πατρί, οὔτε κατὰ τὸ μονογενὲς τῷ υἱῷ ~όμενον [sc. τὸ πνεῦμα] Gr.Nyss.*Maced.*2(M.45.1304B).

***συνανεγείρω**, *raise up together*; from the dead, *Lit.Marc.*ap. *PRyl.*v° 43.

συνάνειμι, (*ibo*) **1.** *go up with*, Moses to Sinai, Cyr.*ador.*10(1. 328E); Proc.G.*Ex.*34:3(M.87.688A); Christ to heaven, Gr.Naz.*or.*38. 17(M.36.332B); αἱ τάξεις τῶν ἀγγέλων...βροτείαν φύσιν θεασάμεναι συνανιοῦσάν σοι...ἀνυμνοῦν σε Jo.D.*carm.assumpt.Chr.*23(p.226; M. 96.844C); myst. εἰς οὐρανοὺς ἀπὸ γῆς ἀνιόντι τῷ λόγῳ συνάνεισι Max. *ambig.*(M.91.1384D,1385A); **2.** met., *rise to, be equal to* τίς ἂν εὑρεθείη δύναμις λόγων συνανιοῦσα τῷ μεγέθει τοῦ θαύματος Gr.Nyss.*virg.*2 (p.255.14; M.46.324C).

***συνανελίττομαι**, med., *follow one back, reverse together with* ταυτολογίαις σ. καταδεξόμεθα Leont.H.*Nest.*4.31(M.86.1696D).

συνανέρχομαι, *go up with*, Jesus up Mount of Transfiguration, Or.*Cels.*6.77(p.146.25; M.11.1416A); to a monastery τούτοις διὰ τῆς Ἀρμενίων σ. γῆς Sophr.H.*v.Anast.*(M.92.1729A); *ascend with* σ. αὐτῷ εἰς τὸ ὕψος *T.Neph.*5.7; οὐδεὶς ἀναβέβηκεν [sc. εἰς τὸν οὐρανόν] ἕως ὅτε αὐτῷ συνανῆλθον Epiph.*haer.*75.7(p.339.20; M.42.513D).

***συνανθρωπιστικός**, *domesticated*; of birds, Bas.*hex.*8.3(1.73C; M. 29.172B).

συνανιάομαι, pass., *suffer affliction together*, Synes.*ep.*46(M.66. 1376A).

***συνανίπταμαι**, *fly away together*, Gr.Naz.*or.*21.25(M.35.1112A); met., Thdr.Stud.*epp.*2.208(M.99.1629D).

συνανίστημι (συνανιστάω), **1.** trans. in pres. and aor. 1; *cause to rise together*; esp. *raise* from the dead *with* oneself, of Christ τοὺς ...δεσμίους ὄντας...συνανέστησεν ἑαυτῷ Cyr.*Ps.*67:7(M.69.1145D); ἔμελλε Χριστὸς...ψυχὰς συνανιστᾶν ἑαυτῷ Proc.G.*1Reg.*2:6(M.87. 1084B); **2.** intrans. in fut. and aor. 2; **a.** *rise, get up at the same time*, met. ἀνισταμένης σου συνανέστη [sc. ἡ παρθενεία] σοι *M.Ner.*

*et Ach.*8(p.6.29); **b.** *rise* from the dead *with* 'συνετάφημεν' τῷ Χριστῷ ...καὶ συνανέστημεν αὐτῷ Or.*hom.1.16 in Jer.*(p.15.7; M.13.276A); Gr.Nyss.*Apoll.*30(M.45.1189B); ἅπασα ἡμῶν ἡ...φύσις...αὐτῷ συνανέστη Thdr.Mops.*Rom.*6:6(M.66.801B); συναναστήσεταί μοι, φησίν, ἡ πεσοῦσα τοῦ ἀνθρώπου φύσις Cyr.*Jo.*4.2(4.353A).

συνανίσχω, 1. *sustain, uphold mutually*; of love of God and neighbour, Cyr.*ador.*7(1.218C); **2.** med., *rise at the same time*; of stars, Philost.*h.e.*10.9(M.65.589C).

***συνανομολογέομαι,** pass., *be generally agreed* or *accepted* σ. παρὰ πάντων Dion.Al.ap.Eus.*h.e.*7.23.1(M.20.692A).

***συναντάρτης, ὁ,** *fellow rebel*, Thphn.*chron.*p.243(M.108.612B).

συνάντημα, τό, 1. *chance happening, coincidence* opp. θεοῦ γνώμη, Proc.G.*Num.*16:21(M.87.840B); Thdr.Stud.*epp.*2.214(M.99.1644C); **2.** *visitation of, encounter with* a demon, Bas.*ep.*6.1(3.79A; M.32.241C); Eustrat.*v.Eutych.*51(M.86.2332D); Niceph.Ur.*v.Sym.*166(M.86.3140B).

συνάντησις, ἡ, *meeting* ἐξῆλθεν...εἰς σ. Παύλου *A.Paul.et Thecl.*2 (p.236.7); Or.*Jo.*13.30(29; p.254.1; M.14.449C); *A.Mt.*13(p.232.12).

συναντιβάλλ-ω, *compare* ~όντων ἑκάστου τὴν ἑαυτοῦ ἑρμηνείαν Iren.*haer.*3.21.2(M.7.948A); Clem.*str.*1.22(p.92.19; M.8.893A); *Hom. Clem.*14.8.

***συναντικός,** *visiting with hostile intent, molesting*; of the Devil, ‡Chrys.*prec.*6(*Euchol.*p.583; M.64.1065D).

συναντιλαμβάν-ομαι, *aid, help*, by prayers ὑμῶν ἐν ταῖς προσευχαῖς ~ομένων ἡμῖν Bas.*reg.fus.*2(2.336C; M.31.908C); *M.Thdot.1* 3(p.63.10); and in other ways, Chrys.*hom.44.2 in 1Cor.*(10.409A); οὐδένα ἔχω τὸν ~όμενόν μοι τοῦ εὐαγγελίου id.*hom.10.1 in 2Tim.*(11.720C); of God κούφην τὴν ἀρετὴν ἐποίησεν ὁ θεός, συνεφαπτόμενος ἡμῖν...καὶ σ. id.*hom.16.11 in Mt.*(7.220E); of Christ, Thdr.Stud.*epp.*2.55(M.99.1268C) cit. s. συγκουφίζω.

***συναντιλήπτωρ, ὁ,** *fellow supporter* of a cause σ. ... καὶ συναγωνιστήν Meth.*res.*1.27(p.255.2; M.41.1132D).

***συναντινεύω,** *join in disapproving, show a like sign of disapproval*, Geo.Pis.*carm.*2.89(p.7).

***συνανυμν-έω, 1.** *join in singing praises* πῶς ~ησαν πηλίνοις οἱ πύρινοι; Rom.Mel.(*BZ* 24(1923)p.6); **2.** *praise* or *celebrate* one *with* another in a hymn, *at the same time sing of* κἂν τις ὑμνῶν τὸν Πέτρον οὐκ αὐτὸν μόνον...ἀλλὰ ~ήσοι σὺν αὐτῷ ἅπαντα τὸν ἀποστόλων χορόν Jo.D.*trisag.*14(M.95.48C).

***συνανυψ-όω,** *exalt together* ἵνα...~ώσῃ [sc. Christ] τὸ κάτω νεῦον ὑπὸ τῆς ἁμαρτίας Gr.Naz.*or.*38.14(M.36.328B); in Ascension σ. αὐτοῦ τῇ θεότητι ὁ πλαστουργὸς τὸ πλαστούργημα ‡Nil.*fr.ascens.*3(M.79.1501C); τούτου τοῦ ὁρατοῦ [sc. Christ's body] ὑψουμένου, ~οῦται τὸ ἀφανές μου Rom.Mel.(*AS* 1 p.153).

***συνανωθοῦμαι,** *be pushed up together with*; met., *be uplifted, raised* ἡ...σὰρξ...ἀπὸ τῆς φθορᾶς συνανωσθεῖσα ἐπὶ τὸ ἄφθαρτον Gr. Nyss.*Eun.*5(2 p.125.7; M.45.708A).

συνάξιμος, *of assembly, when the eucharist is offered* δευτέρᾳ... ὥρᾳ οὐ σ. ἡμέρας ὁ σεισμὸς ἐνέσκηψεν Soz.*h.e.*4.16.4(M.67.1156A).

συναξιόω, *join in supplicating*; God, Or.*Cels.*8.64(p.280.11; M.11.1613A).

σύναξις, ἡ, A. *a bringing together, combination, sum, Chron. Pasch.*p.13(M.92.93).

B. *gathering, assembly* for public worship and instruction, *religious service*; **1.** in gen., incl. eucharist ἡμεῖς...ὅσον ἐπὶ τὸ αὐτὸ συναγόμεθα, τηροῦμεν τότε ποίμνης μυστήριον· ὅτε δὲ ἀμελοῦμεν τῶν σ., μιμούμεθα τὰ ἀποσκιρτῶντα...πρόβατα, καὶ δύνανται καθ' ἡμῶν... οἱ ἐχθροί Or.*Ps.*77:52(p.129); πράγματα οὐκ ὀλίγα ἔχει...δυνάμενα ἀσχολῆσαι ὥρας οὐ μιᾶς σ., ἀλλὰ καὶ πλειόνων id.*engast.*1(p.283.21; M.12.1013B); συναγόντων ἡμῶν συνήθως...τῶν τε λαῶν εὐφραινομένων ἐπὶ ταῖς σ. Ath.*ep.encycl.*2(p.170.24; M.25.225B); id.*h.Ar.*25(p.196.25; M.25.721C); Cyr.H.*catech.*1.6; *ib.*18.33; σπουδάζοντος περὶ τὰς σ. ἀπαντᾶν ὁσημέραι *Const.App.*2.39.6; ἀχώριστον εἶναι...τῶν ἐκκλησιαστικῶν σ. Didym.*Trin.*2.27(M.39.768A); οὐ καθ' ἑκάστην σ. ... ἀλλ' ἐν ἑορτῇ μόνον Chrys.*bapt.Chr.*1(2.367A); ὅταν μὲν καιρὸς συνάξεως πρὸς τὴν ἐκκλησίαν καλῇ id.*Jud.*2.3(1.605A); ὁ μὴ ἀπολιμπανόμενος τῶν ἐκκλησιαστικῶν συλλόγων ἤγουν τῶν κοινῶν σ. καὶ εὐχῶν id.*ecl.*48(12.775B); καὶ εἰσελθόντες μετὰ ψαλμῶν, γέγονε ἡ σ. ἐν τῇ...ἐκκλησίᾳ Cyr.S.*v.Sab.*61(p.163.1); for public baptisms, Pall. *v.Chrys.*9(p.56.26; M.47.33); *ib.*(p.58.8; M.47.34); ass. λιταί, *Supplic.* ap.Evagr.*h.e.*2.8(p.57.30; M.86.2524D); τὸν ἔπαρχον ἐν ταῖς σ. καὶ ἐν ταῖς λιταῖς τότε ἐπενόησεν ἀκολουθεῖν ὁ βασιλεὺς Thphn.*chron.*p.128 (M.108.353A); **2.** ἐν τῇ σ. *during a service*, cf. English '*in church*' ἐάν τις λαλήσῃ ἐν τῇ σ. Pach.*reg.*B 3(M.40.948A); οἱ ἀδελφοὶ ἐν τῇ σ. ἑστῶτες εὐλογοῦσι τὸν θεόν Ephr.1.104C; id.2.117A; id. 2. 171B; *Chron. Pasch.*p.292(M.92.729A); **3.** σ. ποιέω *conduct a service* (or *celebrate the eucharist*) ἰδίᾳ σ. ποιούμενοι CGangr.*ep.*(H.1.530E); οὐ δεῖ Χριστιανοὺς ἐγκαταλείπειν τὴν ἐκκλησίαν τοῦ θεοῦ...καὶ σ. ποιεῖν CLaod.*can.*35; εὔχεσθαι ἐκτενῶς...ὡς ἀδιαλείπτως σ. ποιῶν Ammonas *opusc.*2.5(p.463.5); Jo.Mosch.*prat.*27(M.87.2873B); also σ. τελέω: εἰ τελεῖται σ. ἐν ἐκκλησίᾳ, παράβαλε Nil.*paraen.*105(M.79.1260A); cf. περὶ τῶν ἐν τῇ σ. τελουμένων Dion.Ar.*e.h.*3.1 tit.(M.3.424B); and σ. ἐπιτελέω, *M.Sab.*8.3(p.123.32); Epiph.*exp.fid.*22(pp.522.26,523.9, 15; M.42.825B,828A,B); Thdt.*ep.*160(4.1330); Leont.N.*v.Sym.*12(M.93.1685A); also, rarely, *be present at eucharist, go to, attend a service* πάντας μετὰ...ἐμμελείας τὰς σ. ἐπιτελοῦντας Chrys.*scand.*19(3.506E); usu. παραβάλλω τῇ σ.: ὁ μὲν ὄκνῳ, ὁ δὲ δειλίᾳ, οὐ παραβάλλουσι [sc. two priests] τῇ σ. id.*ep.*210(3.717A); also βάλλω τὴν σ., Ephr.2.115A, but perh. in sense, *recite the office*; **4.** ἀπολύει ἡ σ. *the eucharist is over, the meeting is dispersing, breaking up*, Ephr.2.94B; *Apophth. Patr.*(M.65.241A); εὐχαὶ ἀπολυτικαὶ τῆς σ. *Lit.Jac.*(*NBP* 10[2] p.105); **5.** occasions; in commemoration of martyrs ἐπιτελοῦντες...ἐν ᾗ τὸν στέφανον...[sc. ὁ μάρτυς] ἀπείληφεν ἡμέρᾳ σ. πνευματικήν *M.Sab.*8.3 (p.123.32); τὰς σ. ... τῶν ἁγίων ἐκκλησιῶν καὶ μαρτυρίων Didym. *Trin.*2.16(M.39.721A); for the dead σ. ἐν τῷ καλουμένῳ μαρτυρίῳ τῶν ἀποστόλων ἐπὶ τῇ Κωνσταντίνου τελευτῇ Eus.*v.C.*4.71 tit.(p.117.25; M.20.1225A); οὐκ αἰσθάνονταί τινος εὐεργεσίας καὶ αἱ τῶν ἁμαρτωλῶν ψυχαί, γινομένων ὑπὲρ αὐτῶν σ. καὶ εὐποιῶν καὶ προσφορῶν ‡Ath.*qu. Ant.*34(M.28.617A); **6.** times: following a vigil τοῦ λαοῦ τινες ἐπαννύχιζον προσδοκωμένης σ. Ath.*fug.*24(p.84.11; M.25.673D); ἐπὰν οὖν ἐγρηγορότες ὦμεν νυκτὸς μὴ τὴν σ. τῇ ἀκηδίᾳ ἀνακλίνωμεν...πρὸ συνάξεως διυπνισθέντες λογισμοὺς φωτὸς...προγυμνάζωμεν Nil.*eulog.*8(M.79.1104D); early in morning ἔξυπνος γινόμενος μὴ δυσόκνει τοῦ ἐγερθῆναι εἰς σ. Ephr.2.94B; μετὰ τὴν σ. πρωΐ *V.Pach.Φ* 88(p.59.21); or upon breaking of fast νηστεύσαντες ἐν τῇ ἡμέρᾳ ἐκείνῃ... ἑσπέρας ἐπετέλεσαν τὴν ἁγίαν σ. Marc.Diac.*v.Porph.*66; on Wednesdays and Fridays at ninth hour when fast ended, except in pentecostal season when there was no fast and Sunday rule of an early morning hour prevailed, Epiph.*exp.fid.*22 passim(p.522.26ff.; M.42.825Bff.); in some places also on Saturdays, *ib.*24(p.525.18; 832A); hence complaint of a congregation when custom was not observed ἔρχεται...κυριακή, καὶ ποιεῖ τὴν σ. ὥραν ἐνάτην, καὶ οὐ φυλάττει τὴν νενομισμένην τάξιν τῆς ἁγίας σ. Jo.Mosch.*prat.*27(M.87.2873B); **7.** at which a sermon or instruction was given τῶν ἐπισκόπων ἐν συνάξεσι προσομιλίαι Eus.*v.C.*4.45 tit.(p.116.16; M.20.1196A); καθὼς ἤκουσας ἐν τῇ κυριακῇ διαλεγομένων ἡμῶν ἐπὶ τῆς σ. Cyr.H.*catech.*10.14; *ib.*14.26; *ib.*23.1; κατὰ τὴν εἰθισμένην σ. τὸν...λαὸν διδάσκων Epiph.*haer.*69.2(p.154.3; M.42.205B); cf.Or.*engast.*1(p.283.21; M.12.1013B); and creed recited ἐν πάσῃ σ. ἐπενόησε τὸ σύμβολον λέγεσθαι Thdr.Lect. *h.e.*2.48(M.86.209A); **8.** due reverence to be shown in matters of dress, *Apophth.Patr.*(M.65.249A,B); **9.** of gatherings of schismatics or heretics, Eus.*v.C.*3.65 tit.(p.75.18; M.20.1141A); CGangr.*ep.*(H.1.530E), CLaod.*can.*35 citt. s. 3 supra; παρασυναγωγὰς δὲ τὰς σ. τὰς...παρὰ τῶν ἀνυποτάκτων πρεσβυτέρων ἢ ἐπισκόπων καὶ παρὰ τῶν ἀπαιδεύτων λαῶν γινομένας Bas.*ep.*188 *can.*1(3.268E; M.32.665A); ἐκ τῆς Μαρκέλλου σ. εἰς τὴν ἐκκλησιαστικὴν κοινωνίαν Gr.Nyss.*ep.*5(M.46.1029C); of Gnostics αὐτὴν...τὴν σ. αὐτῶν ἐν αἰσχρότητι... φύρουσιν Epiph.*haer.*26.3(p.279.4; M.41.336B); of Meletians ἔχων ἰδίαν τὴν σ. σὺν τοῖς ἰδίοις *ib.*68.4(p.144.2; M.42.189B); Messalians ψαλμῳδιῶν τε καὶ σ. *ib.*80.6(p.491.17; 765C); **10.** partic. the *eucharist*: while σ. often signifies 'eucharist' its meaning not always determinable in a particular passage; in the following however the identification may reasonably be inferred from context: Ephr. 2.242A; πάσχα...οὐ νηστεία ἐστίν, ἀλλὰ ἡ προσφορά, καὶ ἡ θυσία, ἡ καθ' ἑκάστην γινομένη σ. Chrys.*Jud.*3.4(1.611B); εἰρήνη ὑμῖν ...ἐν ταῖς ἁγίαις...συνόδοις ἤτοι σ. παρ' αὐτὰς τοῦ μυστηρίου τὰς ἀρχάς, τοῦτο καὶ ἡμεῖς ἀλλήλοις φαμὲν Cyr.*Jo.*12.1(4.1093C); Bas.Sel. *v.Thecl.*2.18(M.85.596C); Dion.Ar.*e.h.*3.1 tit.(M.3.424B); *ib.*4.2(473A); *Apophth.Patr.*(M.65.241B); ἕως ἂν ἴδω τὸ πνεῦμα οὐκ ἄρχομαι τῆς σ. ὅταν δὲ θεάσωμαι τὴν ἐπιφοίτησιν τοῦ...πνεύματος, τότε καὶ τὴν λειτουργίαν ἐπιτελῶ Jo.Mosch.*prat.*27(M.87.2873C); Max.*myst.*8(M.91.688B); τοῦ ἀχράντου σώματος μετασχεῖν ἐν τῷ τῆς σ. ... καιρῷ CTrull.*can.*101; Anast.S.*synax.*(M.89.829B); Gr.Mag.*dial.*(tr.Zach.) 2.23(M.*PL.*66.177C); εὐχὴ τοῦ θυμιάματος τῆς εἰσόδου τῆς σ. *Lit. Jac.*(*NBP* 10[2] p.42); ass. κοινωνία: ἐκσπόνδους εἶναι καὶ ἀκοινωνήτους τῶν ἐκκλησιαστικῶν σ. Liber.*ep.Maced.*ap.Socr.*h.e.*4.12.37(M.67.493C); οὐκέτι...τὸ μακάριον ἐκεῖνο τῶν ψυχῶν ἀγαλλίαμα, τὸ ἐπὶ ταῖς σ. καὶ τῇ κοινωνίᾳ τῶν πνευματικῶν χαρισμάτων ταῖς ψυχαῖς ἐγγινόμενον τῶν πιστευόντων εἰς κύριον Bas.*ep.*243.2(3.374A; M.32.905B); τῆς σ. ἀπαρτισθείσης μετὰ τὴν τῶν μυστηρίων κοινωνίαν Chrys.*hom.27.1 in 1Cor.*(10.240E); ἐνιαίως ἀνηγόρευται κοινωνία τε καὶ σ. Dion.Ar.*e.h.*3.1(M.3.424C); *ib.*3.2 tit.(425B); *ib.*4.1.1(472D);

παρατηρεῖ...εἰς τὴν ὥραν τῆς σ. ἰδεῖν τί ποιεῖ ὁ ἀδελφὸς εἰς τὴν κοινωνίαν Dor.*doct.*9.2(M.88.1717C); called φρικώδης, Chrys.*stat.*5.7(2.71A); cf. τὰ φρικώδη μυστήρια...τὰ καθ' ἑκάστην τελούμενα σ. id.*hom.25.3 in Mt.*(7.310D); requiring episcopal licence τοὺς...κανόνας πατήσαντες οἱ μὲν καθαιρεθέντες, οἱ δὲ ἀκοινώνητοι γενόμενοι, ἐν τοῖς εὐκτηρίοις ἑορτάζουσιν οἴκοις σ. ἐπιτελοῦντες Thdt.*ep.*158(4.1327); *ib.*160(1330); χειροτονίας καὶ σ. παρὰ τὴν Ἰωάννου γνώμην ἐποίησεν Thphn.*chron.* p.67(M.108.217B); **11.** identified with *Holy Communion* ὁ δεῖνά με... ἐπείγει, καὶ οὐκ ἀναμένω τὴν σ.· καὶ...πρὸ τῆς τῶν πιστῶν εὐχῆς ὑπεξῆλθεν †Bas.*Is.*19(1.392B; M.30.152B); τὴν πρὸς τὸ ἓν ἡμῶν... ἱερουργοῦντα κοινωνίαν καὶ σ. Dion.Ar.*e.h.*4.1.1(M.3.472D); *ib.*3.3.3 (425A); and with the elements themselves ὤκνησας μετασχεῖν αὐτῷ τῆς σ. Bas.*ep.*156(3.246C; M.32.617A); Dion.Ar.*e.h.*3.3.3(M.3.429A) cit. s. ἁπλοῦς.

C. of the day on which a σύναξις was held, *feast day, festival* σ. ... οὔσης τοῦ ἁγίου Τιμοθέου Eustrat.*v.Eutych.*37(M.86.2317B); τῇ ἡμέρᾳ τῆς σ. τῶν...ἀποστόλων Πέτρου καὶ Παύλου, κατέλαβε πρόκουρσον τοῦ...Χαγάνου *Chron.Pasch.*p.392(M.92.1005B); *ib.*p.322(821B).

D. those assembled for a service, *congregation* κἂν ἀχώριστος τῶν αἰσθητῶν σ. εἶναι δοκῇ †Bas.*hom.in Ps.*28(1.358C; M.30.73B); καταλείψαντες τὴν σ. τῶν ἀδελφῶν *V.Pach.Λ* 1(p.123.5); ἀπέλυσε...τὰς σ. Jo.Mosch.*prat.*127(M.87.2989A); as representing the church πᾶσαν τῶν πιστευόντων...τὴν σ. Mac.Mgn.*apocr.*3.28(p.120.17).

E. form of worship or prayer obligatory upon monks and nuns, perh. sometimes referring to eucharist but also to an *office* μετὰ τὴν ἐκπλήρωσιν τοῦ κανόνος τῆς συνήθους σ. Ephr.2.96A; ἰδοὺ περισπῶμαι πάντοθεν, καὶ οὐδὲ τὴν μικράν μου σ. εὑρίσκω βαλεῖν...ὅτε δὲ ἤμην ἐν τῷ κοινοβίῳ...ἡ...μεριμνά μου ἦν εἰς τὴν σ. μου id.2.105C; ὅτε ἤμην νεώτερος, καὶ ἐκαθήμην εἰς τὸ κελλίον μου, μέτρον συνάξεως οὐκ εἶχον· ἡ νύξ μοι καὶ ἡμέρα, σ. ἦν *Apophth.Patr.*(M.65.220C,D); κατὰ δύναμίν μου ποιῶ τὴν μικράν μου σ., καὶ...νηστείαν...καὶ εὐχήν, καὶ...μελέτην, καὶ...ἡσυχίαν *ib.*(229C); needful for the soul ὥσπερ ὑετὸς αὔξει σπόρον, οὕτως καὶ ἡ σ. πρὸς ἀρετὴν ψυχάς Ephr.2.113D; to deter from which is ambition of Devil, id.101B; Nil.*Eulog.*8(M.79.1104C); Ant. Mon.*hom.*26(M.89.1516C); including reading of scripture ἤρξατο ὁ γέρων τῆς σ. αὐτοῦ...ἐτέλεσεν...ὅλον τὸ ψαλτήριον...ἀρξάμενος τοῦ ἀποστόλου...οὕτως ἐπλήρωσε τὴν σ. *Apophth.Patr.*(416A,B); τὰς ἐν ταῖς σ. ῥαθυμίας, ὅτε αὐτὸς μὲν ὁ θεὸς διὰ τῶν γραφῶν διαλέγεται Jo.Jej.*poenit.cont.virg.*(M.88.1961B); said in common, Ath.*virg.*16 (p.51.9; M.28.272A); Ephr.1.326D; id.2.171B; μετὰ...τὴν καθολικὴν τῶν ἀδελφῶν λειτουργίαν τῆς ἐπὶ τὸ αὐτὸ σ. *V.Pach.Σ* 50(p.220.3); or privately ἐπιτελέσεις τὴν σ. μετὰ τῶν ὁμοψύχων σου παρθένων· ἐὰν δὲ μὴ ἔχῃς ὁμόψυχον, μόνη ἐπιτέλει τοῦ θεοῦ συνόντος Ath.*virg.*16(p.51. 9; 272A); *Apophth.Patr.*(201C,D); *ib.*(416A,B); recited several times daily at fixed hours μετὰ τρίτην ὥραν συνάξεις ἐπιτέλει...καὶ μετὰ τὴν σ. τῆς ἐνάτης ἔσθιε τὸν ἄρτον σου Ath.*virg.*12(p.46.9,16; M.28.265A,B); ὅταν κρούσῃ εἰς τὴν σ. Ephr.2.101B; incl. the night κρούουσιν... εἰς τὴν νυκτερινὴν σ. *V.Pach.Λ* 19(p.143.13); *ib.*29(p.156.28); or privately at a variable hour, *Apophth.Patr.*(96A); ἐγερθῶ...πρὶν ἀποθάνω, καὶ βάλω τὴν σ. ... καὶ πάλιν τούτῳ τῷ λογισμῷ... ἀνθέστηκε· καὶ ἔβαλε τὴν σ., καὶ ἐνίκησε τὸν λογισμόν *ib.*(201C,D).

F. *shrine*; **1.** of the martyrs τὰς σ. τῶν μαρτύρων ἢ τὰς ἐν αὐτοῖς γινομένας λειτουργίας CGangr.*can.*20; **2.** monastery *chapel* or *church* αἱ ἀδελφαὶ...προσέλαβον αὐτὸν...καὶ...ἐπέκλεισαν ἐν τῇ σ. τοῦ μοναστηρίου Ephr.2.115D; πόρευσον μελετῶν ἀχρὶ τῆς θύρας τῆς σ. Pach.*reg.*B 1(M.40.948A); τῆς σ. ἀπολυόμενοι *ib.*6(948A); μηδεὶς ἐξείτω τῆς σ., τῶν ἀδελφῶν εὐχομένων *ib.*5(948A); κατέβη εἰς τὴν σ. εὔξασθαι *V.Pach.Φ* 88(p.59.17); ἐν ταῖς σ. ἀπερχόμενος, τοὺς σεπτοὺς οἴκους ἀναθεωρεῖσθαι κελεύων Thdr.Lect.ap.Jo.D.*imag.*3(M.94.1397D); cf. Ath.*fug.*4(p.70.20; M.25.649A); cf. B.2 supra, some of which references may bear this sense.

***συναξογράφι(ο)ν, τό,** *ecclesiastical calendar* ψηλαφήσαντες τὸ σ. ηὗρον, ὅτι ἡμέρα τῆς ἀθλήσεως τοῦ ἁγίου Ἀρτεμίου, εἰκὰς τοῦ Ὀκτωβρίου μηνὸς ἦν *Mir.Artem.*40(p.67.22).

συναπάγ-ω, 1. pass.; **a.** *be led away together*, Clem.*fr.*14(p.200. 8)ap.Eus.*h.e.*2.9.3(M.20.157A); **b.** met. ὁ δικαστὴς...προλήψει...σ. ... κενῇ Clem.*str.*4.11(p.283.18; M.8.1288C); Or.*fr.63 in Jer.*(p.229.18); id.*fr.76 in Lam.*(p.265.10); by error, *be led astray* τῇ γνώμῃ σ. Eus. *e.th.*1.7(p.65.23; M.24.836C); *ib.*2.21(p.131.17; 957A); Εὐσέβιον δὲ καὶ Μάριν καὶ Θέογνιν σ. μὲν τῇ κατὰ Νίκαιαν συνόδῳ, ἀνενεχθῆναι δὲ τῆς μεταβολῆς Philost.*h.e.*2.15(M.65.477A); by passions, *be carried away*, Clem.*str.*1.17(p.54.22; M.8.800A); Ephr.2.101B; Ant.Mon.*hom.*81(M. 89.1677B); **2.** med., *consort with* τοῦ μὲν ἐπιεικοῦς...ὑπερορᾶν ἠθισμένος, ἥκιστα δὲ ἀγαπῶν τὸ τοῖς ταπεινοῖς σ. Or.*adnot.in Dt.*14:19 (M.17.25C); ἵνα...μάθωμεν τοῖς ταπεινοῖς ∼εσθαι Cyr.*Lc.*4:38(M.72. 549B).

***συναπαγωγή, ἡ,** *going off together, consorting*, Thdr.Stud.*epp.*2. 142(M.99.1448C).

***συναπαθανατίζομαι,** *become immortal, attain to immortality along with* τὸ φθαρτὸν...ἡμῶν ἀφθαρσίαν ἐνδυσάμενον σ. τῷ μὴ ἑωρακότι διαφθορὰν ὁσίῳ τοῦ θεοῦ Didym.*Ps.*15:9(M.39.1233C).

***συναπαθίζω,** *free likewise from subjection to the influence of the passions* or, *render likewise immune from sinful emotions* σ. [sc. θεός] αὐτὴν [sc. τὴν σάρκα] ἑαυτῷ, καὶ τρεπτὸν φύσει...εἰς τὴν ἰδίαν αὐτοῦ ἀτρεψίαν Leont.H.*Nest.*1.6(M.86.1425C).

συναπαίρ-ω, 1. *go away also, leave together* σ. ... ἡμῖν...τὰ ἔργα τὰ ἀστεῖα καὶ συνίπταται τῷ τῆς ἀληθείας πτερῷ Clem.*prot.*10(p.68. 25; M.8.205C); ᾧ [sc. κυρίῳ]...ἀπαίροντι μὲν τοῦ κόσμου...∼ομεν κατ' ἴχνος ἰόντες τὸ δεσποτικόν Cyr.*ador.*10(1.353D); Thdt.*qu.8 in Jos.*(1. 309); id.*Bar.*1(2.630); *set out together* with σ. καὶ συγκαταλύειν αὐτῇ [sc. τῇ νεφέλῃ] τοὺς ἐξ Ἰσραὴλ Cyr.*ador.*5(1.163E); *ib.*(165C); *ib.*10 (353E); **2.** *go away at the same time* τῇ τύχῃ συνέμεινας. ἔπειτα σ. αὐτῇ Synes.*ep.*46(M.66.1376A).

***συναπαιωρέομαι,** *be hung* from or on *together with* or, *be uplifted* on *together with* τῷ ἐπὶ ξύλου συναπῃωρημένῳ λῃστῇ ‡Caes. Naz.*dial.*143(M.38.1093).

***συναπαλλάσσομαι,** *depart from this life with* σ. ἐκείνοις ἀσμενέστατα Dion.Al.ap.Eus.*h.e.*7.22.7(M.20.688C).

***συναπαμφιάζω,** *take off one* garment *with another*, met. τὴν αἰσχύνην τοῖς λοιποῖς σ. πάθεσιν Jo.D.*hom.*12.16(M.96.804A).

***συναπάντημα, τό,** ? *conspiracy* δῆσον πᾶσαν ἀρχὴν...τὴν κατ' ἐμοῦ φθεγγομένην...τὴν καταλαλιάν, τὸ ψεῦδος καὶ τὸ σ. *Exorc.*(p.344).

***συναπαριθμ-έομαι,** *be reckoned up together*; *reckoned with, included* τοὺς προφήταις ∼ουμένους Hier.*vir.ill.*(tr.Sophr.Pal.)21(p.22. 2; M.*PL.*23.640B).

***συναπαρν-έομαι,** *deny at the same time* διὰ τῶν εἰκόνων ἀριδήλως ∼ούμενοι τὰ πρωτότυπα Thdr.Stud.*epp.*2.41(M.99.1241A).

***συναπαρτάω,** pass., **1.** *be hung together*, †Bas.*Is.*125(1.466D; M. 30.321B); **2.** *be likewise dependent* on, ‡Caes.Naz.*dial.*156(M.38.116).

συναπαρτίζ-ω, 1. *finish off, complete, accomplish, perfect together* or *at the same time*, Clem.*exc.Thdot.*41(p.119.18; M.9.677C); ὁ... κατὰ πρόθεσιν ἁμαρτάνων τῷ τάχει τῶν νοημάτων ∼ομένην ἔχει τὴν ἁμαρτίαν Bas.*hom.*3.1(2.17D; M.31.201A); τὸ τοῦ σώματος κάλλος ∼εται Gr.Nyss.*hom.13 in Cant.*(M.44.1052B); δι' ἑκατέρων σ. *complete in both respects*, id.*Eun.*1(1 p.211.18; M.45.460B); **2.** *join in completing* or *perfecting* συντελεῖ...καὶ ἡ τῶν χειλῶν ὑπουργία ἐν διαφόρῳ τῷ τῆς κινήσεως τρόπῳ ποικίλως συνεφαπτομένη τοῦ φθόγγου καὶ τὸν τῶν ῥημάτων τύπον σ. Gr.Nyss.*Eun.*12(1 p.271.23; M.45.977B); pass., *be perfected also* by συντελειοῦται τῷ πιστῷ καὶ ∼εται αὖ τῇ ἐκ μαθήσεως περιγινομένῃ [sc. πίστει] Clem.*str.*5.1(p.327.13; M.9. 12B); **3.** *correspond with*; pass., *be made to correspond with* σ. ... τῷ φθαρτῷ τούτῳ κόσμῳ καὶ ἡ τοῦ χρόνου φύσις τοῦ παραρρέοντος †Bas. *Is.*66(1.427A; M.30.232C); ἑτέρῳ τινὶ πέρατι...ᾧ ∼όμενον τὸ διάστημα ἑαυτὸ περιγράφει Gr.Nyss.*Eun.*1(1 p.125.15; M.45.361B).

***συναπαυγάζομαι,** *shine out simultaneously*, Gr.Nyss.*diff.ess.*7 (M.32.337C).

συνάπειμι, (*ibo*) *go away, depart together*; met., *go the way of, follow* (sc. in a course of conduct), Thphn.*chron.*p.291(M.108.713A).

***συναπείργ-ομαι,** *be shut out, be excluded together with* ὥστε τοῖς πᾶσι καὶ τὸν μονογενῆ θεὸν τοῦ ἀγαθοῦ ∼εσθαι Gr.Nyss.*Eun.*11(2 p.251.31; M.45.857C).

***συνάπειρος,** *likewise infinite*, of Father in rel. to Son and H. Ghost τὸν πατέρα...τοῦ μὲν υἱοῦ καὶ τοῦ πνεύματος, ὡς γεννήτορα, καὶ ὡς πηγὴν ἀΐδιον καὶ σ. Thal.*cent.*4.99(M.91.1469B).

***συναπεκδύομαι,** *despoil together*; met., with Christ (cf. Col. 2:15), Or.*mart.*42(p.39.23; M.11.617C).

***συναπελέγχω,** *confute together* or *at the same time*, Bas.*Eun.* 1.1(1.208C; M.29.501A); Gr.Nyss.*Apoll.*35(M.45.1200D); id.*Eun.*8(2 p.175.7; M.45.768A); Thdr.Mops.*Rom.*9:14(p.144.35; M.66.836C); *convict together*, Gr.Nyss.*Eun.*1(1 p.67.6; M.45.296C).

συναπεμπολάω, *sell with*, Chrys.*hom.11.3 in 1Thess.*(11.505D); hence, *part with, lose also* καταληφθήσεται...τῷ τῆς ζωῆς τέλει, καὶ ὁμοῦ τῇ σαρκὶ σ. ταῦτα Cyr.*Ps.*36:10(M.69.929C).

***συναπέραντος,** *likewise infinite* ἀδύνατον...τὸ γενέσεως ἀρχῇ περιορισθὲν σ. εἶναι τῷ ἀπεράντῳ Meth.*creat.*5(p.497.5; M.18.337A); *ib.*7(p.498.16; 340B).

συναπεργάζομαι, *embellish* τὴν τῆς μορφῆς ὥραν σ. Gr.Nyss.*ep.*19 (M.46.1072C).

συναπέρχ-ομαι, *go away together*; hence **1.** *disappear also* ἀπελθόντων τῶν ὀδυνώντων ἡμᾶς, ∼εται καὶ ἡ μνήμη Chrys.*paralyt.*2(3.36C); **2.** *go with, follow* τοῖς σ. αὐτῷ ὄχλοις Or.*Cels.*2.64(p.186.19; M.11. 897B); met. φύεται ἐν Περσίδι τύραννος...καὶ σ. αὐτῷ πολλοί Thphn.

*chron.*p.336(M.108.809B); **3.** *depart* (sc. this life) *with* πλοῦτος...οὔτε συμπροῆλθε πρὸς τὸν βίον ἡμῖν, οὔτε σ. τισιν Bas.*hom*.21.5(2.167C; M. 31.549B).

***συναπιστέομαι**, *be disbelieved in* or *doubted as well* εἰ...πνεῦμα ἀπιστεῖται, καὶ λόγος σ. Didym.(‡Bas.)*Eun*.5(1.307E; M.29.737B).

συναπλόω, *stretch out together*, Max.*ep*.21(M.91.604C).

συναποβάλλω, *reject also* or *at the same time* ἀποβαλόντα τὸν λόγον σ. καὶ τὸ δόγμα Or.*Cels*.8.51(p.266.15; M.11.1592C); τὴν διαστηματικὴν ἔννοιαν ἐπὶ τῆς θείας σ. γεννήσεως Gr.Nyss.*Eun*.3(2 p.28.7; M.45.593B); *ib*.6(2 p.146.18; 732D); Cyr.*Jo*.2.4(4.177D).

***συναπόβλητος**, *equally to be cast away* or *rejected*, ‡Ath.*ep. Cast*.2.3(M.28.880C).

συναπογενν-άω, *generate* or *produce at the same time* παραπλησίως τοῖς ἀλόγοις ~ηθῆναι πάντα ὁ δημιουργὸς ἡμῶν οὐ συνεχώρησεν †Bas. *Is*.6(M.30.128B; -γενηθῆναι 1.382B); pass., (theol.) *be begotten while being coexistent with* υἱὸν...ὡς συναπεγεννήθη ἐκ τοῦ πατρὸς ἀϊδίως ἡ ὅμοια δόξα καὶ δύναμις Ath.*exp.fid*.2(M.25.204C); ~ηθείσης ἄνωθεν αὐτῷ [sc. τῷ υἱῷ] τῆς δημιουργικῆς δυνάμεως Eun.*apol*.15(M.30. 849D); ὁ υἱὸς...~ηθεὶς ἔμφυτον ἔχει τὴν ἀγαθότητα Didym.*Trin*.2.3 (M.39.477C).

συναπογίγνομαι, **1.** *be taken away* or *destroyed together* or *at the same time* οὔτε...εἰ ὑποθώμεθα τὰ ἐκ τοῦ θεοῦ γενόμενα...ἀπογενέσθαι, τούτοις καὶ τὸ...οὐσιῶδες αὐτοῦ...θέλημα συναπογενήσεται Max.*Pyrr*. (M.91.293B); **2.** s.v.l., *be produced, come into being at the same time as*, v. foreg.

συναπογράφομαι, *enlist with, be a supporter of*, met. τὰ καθαρὰ τῶν ...ψυχῶν...σώματα σ. καὶ συναθλήσαντα Dion.Ar.*e.h*.7.1(M.3.553A); *subscribe to*, Mac.Mgn.*apocr*.3.30(p.125.22) cit. s. συναναμίγνυμαι.

συναπογυμνόομαι, *be stripped naked along with*; met., *be despoiled together with* ἔδει...σ. τῷ ᾅδῃ τὸν τάφον Bas.Sel.*pasch*.2.2(M. 28.1084B).

συναποδέχομαι, *receive at the same time*, Thdr.Stud.*epp*.2.41(M. 99.1240D).

συναποδημέω, *go abroad, travel with*; met., to the next world πρὸς τὴν μέλλουσάν σοι ζωὴν σ. Chrys.*hom.52.4 in Mt*.(7.535C); id. *hom.1.4 in Rom*.(9.435C); σ. πρὸς τὸν οὐρανὸν ἡμῖν id.*hom.8.2 in Jo*. (8.52A); with συμμεθίστημι, id.*paralyt*.1(3.33B); id.*hom.17.1 in 1Tim*. (11.648F); μεθ' ἡμῶν πρὸς τὴν μέλλουσαν σ. ζωήν id.*hom.38.5 in Jo*. (8.224D).

συναπόδημος, ὁ, *fellow traveller, travelling companion*; of fellow martyrs, Eus.*m.P*.9(p.929.7; M.20.1493A); *ib*.11(p.942.9; 1508B); συνέμπορον ἔχων [sc. S. Ignatius on the road to martyrdom] Ἰησοῦν καὶ σ. τῆς...ὁδοιπορίας Chrys.*pan.Ign*.4(2.598B).

συναποθε-όω, *deify together*; by Christ's glorification, Eus.*d.e*.4. 14(p.173.14; M.22.289A) cit. s. ἄνθρωπος; by Inc. ὁ...θεὸς...κατέμιξεν ἑαυτὸν τῇ ἐπικήρῳ φύσει, ἵνα τῇ τῆς θεότητος κοινωνίᾳ ~ωθῇ τὸ ἀνθρώπινον Gr.Nyss.*or.catech*.37(p.152.1; M.45.97B); *ib*.35(p.130.4; 88A); id.*Apoll*.15(M.45.1152C).

συναποθνήσκ-ω, *die together* with πρὸς τὴν ὕλην νεύει [sc. the soul devoid of truth] κάτω, σ. τῇ σαρκί Tat.*orat*.13(p.14.22; M.6. 833B); εἶτα...οὔτε σ. οὔτε ὑπεραπέθανον αὐτοῦ...νῦν δὲ ὑμεῖς σ. Cels. ap.Or.*Cels*.2.45(p.167.19f.; M.11.868B); οὐδέποτε σ. τοῖς τελευτῶσιν αἱ ἀρεταί Marcian.Imp.*const.Flav*.(p.121.17; H.2.676A); ref. death of Christ εἰ...θεότης τέθνηκε, πῶς συναποτεθνηξόμεθα οἱ ἐν σαρκί, τῇ θεότητι; σαρκὶ σὰρξ σ., καὶ συνεγείρεται Gr.Nyss.*Apoll*.30(M.45. 1189B); εἰ γὰρ αὐτὴ τέθνηκε τοῦ μονογενοῦς ἡ θεότης, σ. ταύτῃ πάντως καὶ ἡ ζωή, καὶ ἡ ἀλήθεια κτλ. *ib*.5(1132C); Sever.ap.Thdt.*eran*.3(4. 254) cit. s. ἔνδυμα; myst., in baptism (cf. 2Tim.2:11) σ. Χριστῷ...τῇ ἁμαρτίᾳ κατὰ τὸ βάπτισμα Dion.Ar.*e.h*.2.3.6(M.3.404A); with BMV σοὶ...θνησκούσῃ ~ειν μακάριον Jo.D.*hom*.9.8(M.96.736A).

***συναποθρηνέω**, *lament* or *mourn at the same time*, Bas.*hom*.4.3(2. 28A; M.31.225A).

***συναποθρώσκω**, *break away, secede together*, Cyr.*ador*.10(1.341A).

***συναποκείρομαι**, *be shorn of at the same time*; met., Philost.*h.e*. 9.17(M.65.581B).

***συναποκεντέω**, *pierce through together* with τὸν μαθητὴν τῷ διδασκάλῳ συναπεκέντησεν Petr.Seb.*ep*.(p.87.18; M.45.241B).

συναποκλείω, *shut up, store away*, Gr.Nyss.*or.dom*.4(p.90.2; M. 44.1176C); *shut up with*; pass., met., *be shut up* or *confined to* μὴ συνδιατεμνομένη [sc. ἡ ψυχή] ᾖ σ. αὐτῷ [sc. τῷ σώματι] Max.*ambig*. (M.91.1100A).

συναποκληρόω, **1.** *assign at the same time* ἡ...δημιουργὸς...τόπους ἁρμόζοντας τοῖς γινομένοις σ. Mac.Mgn.*apocr*.4.2(p.159.16); **2.** pass., *be assigned to the lot of*, Jo.VI H.*v.Jo.D*.8(M.94.440D).

***συναποκυέομαι**, *be born together*, Gr.Nyss.*Eun*.12(1 p.297.13; M. 45.1008B).

συναπολαμβάνω, *receive in common*, esp. that which is due τὰ ...τῶν ἱερῶν ψυχῶν ὁμόζυγα...σώματα...συναπολήψεται τὴν οἰκείαν ἀνάστασιν Dion.Ar.*e.h*.7.1.1(M.3.553A).

συναπόλαυσις, ἡ, *enjoyment in common, joint happiness*, Tit. Bost.*Man. fr*.(M.18.1260C).

***συναπολεπτύνομαι**, *refine in accordance with*, Cyr.*Jo*.4.3(4. 373D).

συναπολήγω, *leave off, cease along with*, Isid.Pel.*epp*.1.430(M.78. 420C) = *ib*.4.197(1285B); intrans., *come to an end with* or *together* ὁ... ἀριθμὸς [sc. of chapters]...σ. ... τῇ ἐπιστολῇ Euthal.Diac.*epp.cath*. (M.85.672A); abs. αἱ [sc. πηγαί]...σ. τε καὶ συναύξονται Gr.Nyss.*hex*.5 (M.44.68A); Eust.Mon.*ep*.(M.86.908A).

***συναπολούω**, *wash away at the same time*, Niceph.Ur.*v.Sym*. 216(M.86.3185B).

συναπομειόω, *diminish together*, pass. intrans. εἰ τοῦτο...συναύξοιτο καὶ σ. ... τῷ σώματι Leont.H.*Nest*.1.1(M.86.1405B).

***συναπονεκρόω**, **1.** *kill together* with ἐπὶ τοῦ ὄφεως ὁ τὴν κεφαλὴν πλήξας, ὅλον σ. τὸν κατόπιν ὁλκὸν Gr.Nyss.*v.Mos*.(M.44.353B); of Apoll. τὸν...θεὸν...θνητὸν εἶναι κατασκευάζει...καὶ ἐν τῇ...νεκρώσει τοῦ σώματος, καὶ τὴν θεότητα συναπονεκρωθῆναι τῷ σώματι Gr.Naz. *ep*.203(M.37.333A); **2.** met., *destroy*, through heresy, Martin.*ep*.12 (M.*PL*.87.186A).

***συναποξενόομαι**, *be in exile together*, Eus.*Ps*.4:3(M.23.113D).

***συναποπέτομαι**, **1.** *fly away together*, Bas.*hom*.13.7(2.120B; M.31. 440A); **2.** met., *disappear*, Gr.Nyss.*Eun*.1(1 p.195.14; M.45.441B); Niceph.Ur.*v.Sym*.59(M.86.3041A); act. aor. ptcpl. συναποπτάσας αὐτῷ [sc. τῷ ὀνείρῳ]...τὰς οἰδήσεις ἐπεγίγνωσκεν Sophr.H.*mir.Cyr.et Jo*.16(M.87.3473A); hence *die*, Thdr.Stud.*epp*.2.197(M.99.1597A).

συναπορέω, *be in doubt also*, Thdr.Stud.*epp*.2.168(M.99.1532B).

***συναποριζόω**, *root out completely* or *all together*; met., vices from the soul, Max.*ep*.2(M.91.397D).

συναπορρήγνυμι, pass., *be torn asunder at the same time*, met. σ. ταῖς συλλαβαῖς τὰ πέρατα Gr.Naz.*or*.21.35(M.35.1125A).

***συναποσιωπ-άομαι**, *be passed over in silence together* τὴν ἔκθεσιν ...καὶ...ἀσεβέστατον τύπον [i.e. of Constans], οἷα τὰς...ἐπ' αὐτοῦ Χριστοῦ...δύο φυσικὰς θελήσεις...τῇ...μιᾷ θελήσει...συνεξαρνηθῆναι καὶ ~ηθῆναι CLater.*can*.18(Hard.3.923E).

***συναποσμήχομαι**, *wipe clean, wipe off completely*, Mac.Mgn. *apocr*.4.16(p.187.9); *ib*.4.30(p.222.31).

συναποσπάω, *tear off together with*; met., pass., *break away, withdraw at the same time* or *together* σ. ... καὶ ἠκολούθησεν αὐτῷ [sc. Devil], καὶ συνέπεσε πλῆθος...τῶν ὑπ' αὐτῷ τεταγμένων ἀγγέλων Jo.D.*f.o*.2.4(M.94.876B); †Jo.D.*B.J*.7(M.96.908A).

***συναποστατ-έω**, *fall away, apostatize together* with τινὰς τῶν τῷ Νεστορίῳ ~ησάντων CEph.(431)*ep*.(*ACO* 1.1.3 p.7.21; H.1.1508B); *rebel likewise* πλείστων ἀγγέλων μοῖραν σ. πείσασα ἀπὸ θεοῦ Areth. *Apoc*.12:4(M.106.664B).

συναποστάτης, ὁ, *fellow rebel* or *apostate*, Synes.*ep*.66(M.66. 1409A); of Juln.Imp., Gr.Naz.*or*.21.32(M.35.1120B); of associates of Thphl. Al. agst. Chrys., Isid.Pel.*epp*.1.152(M.78.285A); of the evil angels, Areth.*Apoc*.12:4(M.106.664A).

συναποστέλλω, *join in sending*, of Son σ. ... τὸν ἅγιον πνεῦμα Or. *Jo*.2.11(6; p.66.34; M.14.132B).

***συναπόστολος, ὁ**, *fellow apostle* Πέτρῳ τῷ σ. ἡμῶν *A.Thom*.A 86 (p.202.13); Eus.*d.e*.3.5(pp.125.28,126.19; M.22.213C,216A); Chrys. *hom.33.3 in Jo*.(8.193D); of S. Paul, *Const.App*.2.24.4; Chrys.*hom. in Gal.2:11*(3.377C); of the Twelve in relation to S. Paul, id.*comm. in Gal*.1:9(10.671A); and to S. Barnabas, Alex.Sal.*Barn*.proem.5 (437C); applied to Philip the Deacon, *Const.App*.6.7.2; as mode of address, *brother apostle* λέγει [sc. ὁ Ἰωάννης] τῷ Φιλίππῳ· ἀδελφέ μου καὶ σ. *A.Phil*.32(p.16.22).

***συναποστυγέω**, *hate as well*, Cyr.*Jo*.10.2(4.910A).

***συναποσχίζ-ομαι**, *be severed completely together* with; met., *be torn in two* of a mother yearning over her child τὸ τὴν καρδίαν αὐτῆς τῷ τεχθέντι ~εσθαι Gr.Nyss.*virg*.3(p.262.6; M.46.332B).

***συναποτελεστικός**, *helping to complete, complementary* τὸ σῶμα ...σ. τῆς ὑποστάσεως τοῦ ἑνὸς ἀνθρώπου Cyr.*ep*.50(p.92.19; 5^2.160E).

συναποτελέω, pass., *be completed at the same time*, ‡Bas.*struct. hom*.1.20(1.333D; M.30.32A); hence *grow up with*, e.g. a disability, Gr.Nyss.*anim.et res*.(M.46.140A).

συναποτέμν-ω, *cut off at the same time*, met. τὸν...υἱὸν τῆς τοῦ πατρὸς φύσεως ἀλλοτριοῦντες ~ουσι καὶ τῆς αἰωνίου ζωῆς Gr.Nyss. *Eun*.10(2 p.232.29; M.45.833C); Const.Pogon.*edict*.(H.3.1456D).

συναποτίθεμαι, med., *put off in company with* αὐτῷ...σ. τὸ σῶμα Or.*fr*.79 *in Jo*.(p.546.18); pass. πᾶσα δυσμένεια...τῷ βίῳ τούτῳ σ. Synes.*ep*.66(M.66.1408D).

συναποτίλλ-ω, *pluck out together* with, med., met. τῇ...φιλαυτίᾳ ὡς ἀρχῇ...πάντα τὰ ἐξ αὐτῆς...~εσθαι Max.*ep.*2(M.91.397D).

***συναποτρέχω**, *run off together* πρόβατα...καὶ βόας σ. Cyr.*ador.*1 (1.43E).

συναποφέρ-ω, 1. *bring about together* with σ. τῇ ἀρχῇ τὸ τέλος Thdr.Stud.*epp.*2.77(M.99.1316D); 2. med., *carry along with oneself*; met., *bear in itself* τὰς κηλῖδας τῶν ἁμαρτιῶν σ. [sc. ὁ πλοῦτος] *A.Thom.*A 66(p.183.15); *take* or *lead away with* τὸ μὲν γὰρ πρὸς Ἰουδαϊσμὸν εὐθὺς ἀποφέρεται, καὶ ἑαυτῷ σ. τὸν λέγοντα Sophr.H.*ep. syn.*(M.87.3153C); pass., *be borne away also* ὅταν δύσῃ [sc. ὁ ἥλιος], σ. τὸ φῶς Just.*dial.*128.3(M.6.776A); 3. pass., met., *be carried away* τῇ κοινῇ καὶ ἀλόγῳ φήμῃ σ. Athenag.*leg.*2.4(M.6.896B); *ib.*11.1 (912A); ἡ λογικὴ...δύναμις...ὀφείλει...διακρίνειν τὰς φαντασίας καὶ μὴ σ. αὐταῖς Clem.*str.*2.20(p.173.24; M.8.1056A); *ib.*7.11(p.45.7; M.9. 488A); Cyr.*ador.*6(1.211C); *be carried away like* or *with* τί δακρύεις, μῆτερ; τί ταῖς ἄλλαις γυναιξὶ ~ῃ; Rom.Mel.(*AS* 1 p.102).

***συναποφθέγγομαι**, *say with one voice* or *with one consent*, *M.Scill.*13.

***συναποφοιτ-άω**, *desert*; *go far* from κύων...πόρρω τοῦ θηρολέκτου σ. ‡Caes.Naz.*dial.*140(M.38.1072); met., *diverge* εἰ χωρίζεις τὰς φύσεις, ~ήσειεν ἂν αὐταῖς καὶ τὰ ἑκατέρας ἴδια φυσικῶς Cyr.*Nest.*2.12 (p.50.35; 6^1.57E).

συναποχρ-άομαι, *join in exploiting* ταῖς γραφικαῖς οἱ αἱρετικοὶ κατὰ τὸ αὐτοῖς δοκοῦν συναποκέχρηνται Leont.B.*arg.Sev.*(M.86. 1929A); τῇ τοῦ καιροῦ ~ώμενοι ταραχῇ...ἐπλάνησαν Steph.Dor.*ep.*(H. 3.717B).

***συναπτήριον, τό**, *instrument of union, link*, met. χαῖρε, θεοτόκε, ...τὸ πρὸς θεὸν ἀνθρώποις φρικτὸν σ. Thdr.Stud.*nativ.BMV* 7(M.96. 696B); σταυρός, οὐρανοῦ καὶ γῆς εἰρηνοβράβευτον σ. id.*or.*2(M.99. 697D).

***συνάπτης, ὁ**, *compounder, contriver*, Thdr.Stud.*epp.*1.22(M.99. 976C).

συναπτικός, 1. *compacting, unitive* πάντων μὲν οὖσα περιληπτικὴ καὶ σ. Dion.Ar.*d.n.*1.5(M.3.593A); ἀγάπη γάρ ἐστιν...ἑνωτικὴ καὶ σ. τῆς ψυχῆς διάθεσις πρὸς τὸ ποθούμενον id.ap.Anast.S.*serm.imag.*3 (M.89.1177A); 2. of moral union, *serving to unite, conciliatory* σ. καὶ συνδετικὴν...φωνήν,...'εἰρήνη πᾶσιν' Eustrat.*v.Eutych.*25(M. 86.2304A); τό τε ἁπλοῦν τοῦ ἤθους καὶ χαρίεν πρὸς τοὺς φίλους καὶ σ. τοῦ γένους Thdr.Stud.*epp.*2.144(M.99.1452C).

συναπτικῶς, *conjointly* ἐπὶ μὲν γὰρ τοῦ κυριακοῦ σώματος τῇ φυσικῇ συναφείᾳ ἡ θεότης σ. καὶ προσκυνεῖται καὶ δοξάζεται Thdr. Stud.*antirr.*1(M.99.344A).

συναπτός, 1. *joined together, united*; in contrast bet. soul of Adam and soul of Christ τότε μὲν χωριστὰς θεοῦ τὰς ἑαυτῆς δυνάμεις...ἔσχε, νῦν δὲ σ. θεοῦ...τῇ καθ' ὑπόστασιν ἑνώσει Anast.S.*serm.imag.*3(M.89. 1172B); 2. of time; a. *continuous, prolonged* ὧν ἀπέσχετο βρωμάτων, καὶ σ. ἀσιτιῶν Nil.*Eulog.*33(M.79.1137C); b. *successive* νηστεύειν ἑβδομάδας σ. *V.Dan.*(p.256.26); 3. liturg., of a prayer consisting of a number of suffrages with responses or litany by which psalms or prayers were linked together; freq. abs. συναπτή [sc. εὐχή] *litany*; a. ἡ μεγάλη σ. in liturgy καὶ ἡ σ. σὺν τῇ ἐκφωνήσει *Lit.Bas.*(p.310. 14); λέγει ὁ ἀρχιδιάκονος σ. *Lit.Jac.*(p.166.14); ὁ διάκονος τὴν σ. *Lit. Marc.*(Brightman p.119.16); during office of vespers ὁ ἱερεὺς τὰς εὐχὰς ἐπιλέγει τοῦ λυχνικοῦ· τέλος δὲ κἀκείνων...τὴν σ. σὺν τῇ ἐκφωνήσει ἐπιτελεῖ Thdr.Stud.*praesanct.*(M.99.1688C); in vespers of vigils μετὰ τὴν συμπλήρωσιν [sc. τῶν εὐχῶν τοῦ λυχνικοῦ] λέγει τὴν μεγάλην σ.· ὁ δὲ διάκονος...λέγει τὴν μικρὰν σ.· εἰ δ' οὐκ ἔστι στιχολογία...λέγει τὴν μεγάλην σ. *Euchol.*(pp.2f.; p.24 not.24); b. ἡ μικρὰ σ. in daily offices, after Psalms καὶ μετὰ τὸ κάθισμα, λέγει τὴν μικρὰν σ. *Euchol.*(p.30; p.38 not.3); c. on other occasions γίνεται πρὸς τοῦ διακόνου εὐχὴ σ. *Const.Stud.*37(M.99.1717D); 4. of any prayer linking together other prayers, *Lit.Jac.*(p.192.13).

συνάπτ-ω, force of the word explained τοῦ συνῆφθαι λέγειν, τὸ τῆς κολλήσεως ὄνομα, μείζονά που πάντως καὶ ἀξιολογωτέραν τὴν ἔμφασιν ἔχει· εἴπερ ἐστὶν ἀληθὲς εἰπεῖν, ὡς τό τισι κολλώμενον, ἐν ἐπιτάσει πολλῇ τὴν συνάφειαν ἔχει Cyr.*Chr.un.*(5^1.733A);

I. in gen.; A. *join*; 1. material things, *fasten, attach* σταυροῦ τρόπαιον ἐκ φωτὸς συνιστάμενον, γραφήν τε αὐτῷ συνῆφθαι λέγουσαν· τούτῳ νίκα Eus.*v.C.*1.28(p.21.17; M.20.944B); ἐκ τοῦ μέσου, καθ' ὃ πρὸς ἑαυτὸν ~εται [sc. σταυρός] Gr.Nyss.*or.catech.*32(p.119.6; M.45.80D); of streams, *unite*, ‡Chrys.*Jord.*(10.778A); 2. met. συνῆψεν ἐν ἑαυτῷ τοὺς δύο λαοὺς...ὥσπερ...ὁ γωνιαῖος λίθος ἀμφοτέρους συνδεῖ τοὺς τοίχους Meth.*fr.*19 *in Job* (p.516.23); 3. abstracts ἡ...μίμησις...σ. πρὸς ὃ μιμεῖται τὸ μιμούμενον Synes.*ep.*31(M.66.1360A); *ib.*57(1396B); *ib.* 159(1560A); αὕτη γὰρ [sc. σοφία]...ἀεὶ τὰ τέλη τῶν προτέρων ~ουσα ταῖς ἀρχαῖς τῶν δευτέρων Dion.Ar.*d.n.*7.3(M.3.872B); 4. *unite* sexually ἐτόλμησέ τις εἰπεῖν κατὰ τῆς Μαρίας, ὡς ἄρα ὁ σωτὴρ αὐτὴν ἠρνήσατο, ἐπεί, φησίν, συνήφθη μετὰ τὴν ἀπότεξιν τὴν τοῦ σωτῆρος τῷ Ἰωσήφ Or.*hom.*7 *in Lc.*(p.49.10); Epiph.*anc.*13(p.22.8; M.43.44A); id.*haer.*30.18(p.357.22; M.41.436A); τὴν δορυάλωτον...θρήνῳ τοὺς οἰκείους τιμῆσαι, εἶτα...συναφθῆναι Thdt.*haer.*5.16(4.438); *come together*; of those who have had their marriage dissolved, Ath. Scholast.*coll.*4.22(p.64); *be related to* ὃς [sc. Δομετιανός] πρὸς γένος συνῆπται τῷ βασιλεῖ Thphyl.*exc.gent.*6(p.485.2; M.113.945D); 5. *add*, Synes.*ep.*79(M.66.1445A); αὖθις δὲ ~ει τούτοις, λέγων... Eus.*Marcell.* 1.4(p.20.11; M.24.756C); words, *subjoin*, Just.*dial.*65.2(M.6.625B); Clem.*str.*2.22(p.186.6; M.8.1081A); Or.*Jo.*6.30(15; p.140.20; M.14. 253A); ἵν' οἱ πολλοὶ...ἐκ τῆς προτεταγμένης ἡμῶν κατηγορίας ἡμέτερα εἶναι νομίσωσι τὰ συνημμένα Bas.*ep.*224.1(3.342D; M.32.836B); 6. *continue* πάντα τὸν βίον τοῦ ἁγίου μίαν ~ομένην μεγάλην εἴποιμεν εὐχήν Or.*or.*12(p.325.3; M.11.452D); 7. mentally, *link, associate, connect* Ἑρμῆς ὁ Τρισμέγιστος ἐπικαλούμενος ~ων τὸ ἴδιον αὐτοῖς [sc. θεοῖς] γένος Athenag.*leg.*28.4(M.6.956B); οἱ δὲ ἐπιστάται, ⟨τρισχίλιοι καὶ⟩ ἑξακόσιοι τυγχάνοντες, τῷ τοῦ ἐξ τελείῳ ἀριθμῷ οἱονεὶ ἐφ' ἑαυτὸν πολυπλασιαζομένῳ ~ονται Or.*Jo.*10.39(23; p.216.29; M.14.384A); οἱ Ἀρειανοὶ...ποτὲ μὲν τῇ κάμπῃ ~ουσι τὴν σοφίαν, ποτὲ δὲ συνυπάρχειν τῷ πατρὶ...λέγουσι Ath.*Ar.*2.40(M.26.232B); Σεκουνδιανοί, οἷς ~εται Ἐπιφάνης Epiph.*anc.*13(p.21.20; M.43.40B); οἱ τῆς οὐσίας τοῦ θεοῦ λόγου τολμῶντες κατηγορεῖν, καὶ τὸν υἱὸν τοῖς γενητοῖς ~ειν σπουδάζοντες Cyr.*thes.*20(5^1.199B); in logic; perf. ptcpl. pass., of a syllogism, *containing hypothetical proposition* as premiss, *conjunctive*, opp. διεζευγμένον, †Hipp.*Artem.*ap.Eus.*h.e.*5.28.13(M.20. 516A); *string together* in series καὶ πλείονας συνάψουσι θεοὺς Ath. *Ar.*3.16(M.26.356A); perf. ptcpl. pass., *consecutive* τρεῖς πρὸ τοῦ πάσχα ἑβδομάδας...συνημμένας νηστεύουσιν Socr.*h.e.*5.22.32(M.67. 632B); 8. morally, *attach, bind* τὴν προαίρεσιν τῇ σωτηρίᾳ συνάψαντες Clem.*prot.*10(p.75.15; M.8.221A); μὴ ἀπάγου...ἀλόγοις ὁρμαῖς μηδὲ μὴν τοῖς πολιτικοῖς ἔθεσι συνάπτου id.*str.*3.15(p.240.28; M.8.1197A); Ath.*gent.*2(M.25.8A); ἐμὲ πολλὰ μὲν ἦν...τὰ ~οντά σου τῇ τιμιότητι Bas.*ep.*64(3.157C; M.32.420C).

B. *compound, compact, combine*; 1. in gen. ~ων...ὡς ἕνα τῷ περὶ τοῦ ἱεροῦ ἐκείνου τὸν περὶ τοῦ ἰδίου σώματος λόγον Or.*Jo.*10.35(20; p.209.10; M.14.369C); ἐκ πάντων συνεστῶσά τε καὶ συνημμένη [sc. ἡ ἐκκλησία] τῶν ἀποστόλων Meth.*symp.*7.7(p.78.3, v.l. συνηνωμένη M. 18.133B); τίς ὁρῶν τὰ ἐναντία τῇ φύσει συνημμένα καὶ σύμφωνον ἔχοντα τὴν ἁρμονίαν, οἷον...ξηρὸν ὑγρῷ κεκραμένον...οὐκ ἂν ἐνθυμηθείη ἔξωθεν εἶναι τούτων τὸν ταῦτα συνάψαντα; Ath.*gent.*36(M.25.72B); pass., of words, *go together, be associated*, Or.*Cels.*4.33(p.303.31; M.11.1080A); *join forces* Θεοδόσιος...τῷ Οὐαλεντινιανῷ συναφθεὶς στρατεύει κατὰ Μαξίμου Philost.*h.e.*10.8(M.65.589A); 2. of moral union; a. *combine, unite* τῆς...κατ' εὐχὴν ἐπανόδου εἰς εὐφροσύνην ...χαρᾶς ~ούσης τοὺς πάντας Jul.Papa *ep.Alex.*ap.Ath.*apol.sec.*53.4 (p.134.20; M.25.345C); Synes.*ep.*19(M.66.1353B); σ. ... ὑμᾶς ἀλλήλοις διὰ τῆς ἐπιστολῆς *ib.*131(1513C); hence *reconcile* τὴν...κακῶς γεγενημένην ~ει διαίρεσιν Thdt.*1Cor.*1:2(3.165); b. *incorporate* politically πρὶν ἢ τὴν Ἰουδαίαν τελείως συναφθῆναι Ῥωμαίοις Epiph.*haer.*51.22 (p.288.22; M.41.928B); c. *join in communion* ἵνα...παύσωνται τῆς πρὸς ἐκεῖνον μυσαρᾶς κοινωνίας καὶ λοιπὸν ἑαυτοὺς συνάψωσι τῇ καθολικῇ ἐκκλησίᾳ CSard.*ep.Alex.*ap.Ath.*apol.sec.*39.3(p.118.7; M.25.316C); med., *be in communion with*, Bas.*ep.*265.3(3.410E; M.32.989A).

C. intrans.; 1. *join on* ἡ τετρὰς τῶν ἀρετῶν καθιεροῦται τῷ θεῷ, τῆς τρίτης ἤδη μονῆς ~ούσης ἐπὶ τὴν τοῦ κυρίου τετάρτην ὑπόστασιν Clem.*str.*2.18(p.165.13; M.8.1037B); αἱ ἀρτηρίαι ἃς ἔφημεν...πρὸς τὴν μεγάλην ~ουσιν ἀρτηρίαν Hipp.*haer.*6.14(p.140.24; M.16.3215B); 2. *continue in, adhere to* a way of life πολὺν χρόνον...σ. ἀσκούμενος Ath.*v.Anton.*12(M.26.861B).

II. theol.;

A. Trin.; 1. pass., *be united* Μάρκελλος...θεὸν...ἕνα ὀρθῶς ὁριζόμενος, τοῦτον αὐτὸν λόγον ἔχειν ἐν ἑαυτῷ ἡνωμένον καὶ συνημμένον αὐτῷ φησιν Eus.*e.th.*1.5(p.64.23; M.24.833B); *ib.*1.20(p.87.31; 877A); συνῆπται μὲν ὁ υἱὸς τῷ πατρὶ ἀδιαστάτως· συνῆπται δὲ τῷ υἱῷ τὸ πνεῦμα Bas.*hom.*24.4(2.193E; M.31.609B); ὁ υἱός...ἐκ τῆς οὐσίας ἐξέλαμψεν τοῦ πατρὸς ἀδιαστάτως, ἀχρόνως πατρὶ συνημμένος Nil.*epp.*2.323(M.79. 357C); Cyr.*Pulch.*(p.49.32; 5^2.163B); ~εται διῃρημένως Just.Imp. *edict.*(p.198.23; M.86.2796B); perf. ptcpl. neut. as subst., *unity* ἀπαύγασμα εἴρηται ἵνα τὸ συνημμένον νοήσωμεν Bas.*Eun.*1.20(1. 231D; M.29.556C); 2. *unite* in thought, Trin. πρὶν συνάψαι διαιροῦντες, καὶ πρὶν διαιρεῖν ~οντες Gr.Naz.*or.*6.22(M.35.749C); Father and Son in Trin. τῆς διανοίας ἡμῶν ἀπὸ τοῦ υἱοῦ δι' οὐδενὸς κενοῦ πρὸς τὸν πατέρα χωρούσης, ἀλλ' ἀδιαστάτως τὸν υἱὸν τῷ πατρὶ ~ούσης Bas. *Eun.*2.12(1.247C; M.29.593C); cf. (ref. Jo.1:2) τῇ προσθήκῃ τοῦ 'ἦν' τῇ ἀϊδιότητι τοῦ πατρὸς τοῦ μονογενοῦς ~ων τὴν γέννησιν *ib.*2.15(250E;

M.601C); ἀπαθῶς...~ων τὸν υἱὸν τῷ γεννήσαντι Gr.Nyss.*Eun*.4(2 p.99.17; M.45.676D); H. Ghost (exeg. 1Cor.1:12) τῆς μὲν κτίσεως αὐτὸ ἀποχωρίσας ἁπάσης, θεῷ δὲ συνάψας Thdr.Mops.*symb*.(p.98.6; M.66.1017A).

B. Christol., *join*; **1.** act., of assumption of human nature τὸν ἀγαπηθέντα ὑπ' αὐτοῦ ἄνθρωπον τῷ ἑαυτοῦ συνῆψεν λόγῳ Marcell.*fr*.1 ap.Eus.*Marcell*.1.2(p.9.30; M.24.732C); τοιαύτη γέγονεν ἡ συναφὴ ἵνα τῷ κατὰ φύσιν τῆς θεότητος συνάψῃ τὸν φύσει ἄνθρωπον Ath.*Ar*.2.70(M.26.296B); ὁ δι' ἑαυτοῦ ~ων τῷ θεῷ τὸ ἀνθρώπινον Gr.Nyss.*perf*.(p.204.18; M.46.277C); term suspect after adoption by Thdr. Mops. and Nest. ἄνθρωπον...γενόμενον ἐκ γυναικὸς...ἀπορρήτως συνῆψεν ἑαυτῷ Thdr.Mops.*symb*.(p.98.21; M.66.1017B); Cyr.*hom.pasch*.27(5^2.323B) cit. s. ἄνθρωπος; οἱ...τολμῶντες λέγειν ὅτι τὸν ἐκ σπέρματος τοῦ Δαυὶδ ἄνθρωπον ἑαυτῷ συνῆψεν ὁ θεὸς λόγος καὶ μετέδωκεν αὐτῷ τῆς ἀξίας id.*ep*.50(p.54.39; 5^2.182A); returned later to orthodox meaning μορφῇ τε σῇ συνῆψας ἀνέρος φύσιν ‡Gr.Naz.*Chr.pat*.1536 (M.38.259A); **2.** pass.; **a.** of God joined to man ἵν' ὁ πρωτότοκος λόγος θεοῦ πρωτοτόκῳ ἀνθρώπῳ ~όμενος δειχθῇ Hipp.*fr.2 in 1Reg*.(p.121.12; M.10.864B); εὐδόκησεν θεοῦ λόγος ὢν...τῷ κοινῷ πάντων ἡμῶν σκηνώματι συναφθῆναι Eus.*d.e*.10.1(p.450.14; M.22.724D); τὸν ...τοῦ θεοῦ λόγον...~εσθαι τῇ σαρκί Bas.*hom.in Ps*.44(1.163C; M.29.400A); εἴ τις...λέγοι...μὴ κατ' οὐσίαν συνῆφθαί τε καὶ ~εσθαι...ἀ. ἔ. Gr.Naz.*ep*.101(M.37.180B); Apoll.*fr*.81(p.224.14)ap.Gr.Nyss.*Apoll*.39(M.45.1212C) cit. s. ἄνθρωπος; καὶ τῆς συναφθείσης τῷ ναῷ θεότητος ‡Bas.Sel.*or*.38.2(M.85.405C); τῇ ἀφοριστικῇ ἰδιότητι τῇ ἀπὸ τοῦ πατρὸς ~εται πρὸς τὴν σάρκα ὥσπερ ἀμέλει τῇ ~ούσῃ αὐτὸν φυσικῇ ἰδιότητι τῷ πατρί, τὸ διάφορον ἔχει πρὸς τὴν σάρκα Leont.B.*cap.Sev*.25(M.86.1909D); in Nestorius' teaching ἐγέννησε τὴν ἀνθρωπότητα, ἥτις ἐστὶν υἱὸς διὰ τὸ συνημμένον υἱόν...ἐπειδήπερ ἐκείνῳ συνῆπται τῷ ἐν ἀρχῇ ὄντι υἱῷ τῷ πρὸς αὐτὸν συναφθέντι, οὐ δύναται κατὰ τὸ ἀξίωμα τῆς υἱότητος διαίρεσιν δέξασθαι Nest.*fr*.C 10(p.274.17ff.)ap.Cyr.*Nest*.2.2,8(pp.36.32,44.11f.; 6^1.36E,47E); Nest.*fr*.C 11(p.278.3)*ib*.1.2(p.20.2; 12B) cit. s. ἄνθρωπος; **b.** of man joined to God ἠξίωσεν τὸν πεσόντα διὰ τῆς παρακοῆς ἄνθρωπον τῷ ἑαυτοῦ διὰ τῆς παρθένου συναφθῆναι λόγῳ Marcell.*fr*.96 ap.Eus.*Marcell*.2.3(p.50.33; M.24.809A); Ath.*Ar*.2.70(M.26.296A) cit. s. ἄνθρωπος; *ib*.2.67(289C); τὸ... ἀχωρίστως θεῷ συναφθὲν καὶ ταὐτὸν ἐκείνῳ...γενόμενον Apoll.*fr*.12 (p.208.5)ap.Leont.B.*Apoll*.(M.86.1964A); πῶς εἰς ἡμᾶς διέβη ἡ τῆς ἐνανθρωπήσεως ὠφέλεια, εἰ μὴ τὸ ἡμέτερον σῶμα, τῇ θεότητι συναφθέν, κρεῖττον ἐγένετο τῆς τοῦ θανάτου ἐπικρατείας; Bas.*ep*.262.2(3.404B; M.32.973C); ἀνθρωπεία φύσις θεότητι ~εται, μενούσης ἐφ' ἑαυτῆς ἑκατέρας τῆς φύσεως Flav.Ant.*fr*.6(p.107)ap.Thdt.*eran*.2(4.160); in teaching of Paul. Sam., and 'Nestorian' doctrine of 'Jesus Christ' συναφθεὶς τῇ σοφίᾳ Paul.Sam.*fr*.(p.337.18); ‡Paul.Sam.*fr*.5(p.339.29) cit. s. ἐνέργεια; ‡Paul.Sam.*fr*.3(p.339.14) cit. s. προκοπή; ἐπειδή τινες παρηνόχλησαν ἡμῖν...οὐ θεὸν σαρκωθέντα ὁμολογοῦντες...ἀλλὰ ἄνθρωπον θεῷ συναφθέντα...ὁμολογίαν ποιούμεθα Apoll.*fid.sec.pt*.30(p.178.11; M.10.1116D); ἄνθρωπον...γενόμενον ἐκ γυναικὸς...ἀπορρήτως συνῆψεν ἑαυτῷ Thdr.Mops.*symb*.(p.98.21; M.66.1017B); ᾧπερ οὗτος [sc. ὁ θεὸς λόγος] συνημμένος τε καὶ μετέχων θεότητος κοινωνεῖ τῆς υἱοῦ προσηγορίας τε καὶ τιμῆς *ib*.(p.98.29; 1017C); κατὰ...τὸν τῆς εὐδοκίας τρόπον τῷ θεῷ λόγῳ συναφθεὶς...ἐξ αὐτῆς τῆς μήτρας ὁ...ναὸς μεμένηκεν ἀδιαίρετος, τὴν ἐν πᾶσιν αὐτοῦ ταυτοβουλίαν καὶ ταυτουργίαν ἐσχηκώς, ὧν οὐδέν ἐστιν συναφέστερον id.*ep.Domn*.(p.339.7; M.66.1013A); ἐπειδήπερ ἐν τῷ ληφθέντι θεός, ἐκ τοῦ λαβόντος ὁ ληφθείς, ὡς τῷ λαβόντι συναφθείς, συγχρηματίζει θεὸς Nest.*fr*.C 9(p.262.12)ap.Cyr.*Nest*.2.13(p.51.8; 6^1.58B); τὴν συνημμένην τῇ φύσει τῆς θεότητος σάρκα [sc. πάθους δεκτικὴν εἶναι] Nest.*ep.Cyr*.2(p.31.20; M.77.53D); οὐκ ἐπὶ ψιλὸν...βρέφος ἀλλ' ἐπί τι σῶμα συνημμένον ἀρρήτως θεῷ id.*fr*.D 5(p.354.25)ap.Cyr.*Nest*.2.9(p.46.40; 52A); such views condemned by Cyril, *ep*.17(p.37.27; 5^2.72D); *ib*.anath.11(p.41.29; 77C); *ib*.18 (p.114.6; 79C); *ib*.50(p.92.4; 160B); *ib*.55(p.59.11; 188A); **c.** of two natures τόν τε λόγον καὶ τὸν ἄνθρωπον...συνημμένα...ἀμφότερα υἱός... ὀνομάζεται ‡Ath.*Ar*.4.21(p.68.5; M.26.500B); ἀσυγχύτους φυλάττομεν τὰς φύσεις, οὐ κατ' οὐσίαν, γνώμην δὲ συνημμένας· διὸ καὶ μίαν αὐτῶν τὴν θέλησιν, ἐνέργειάν τε καὶ δεσποτείαν ὁρῶμεν Nest.*fr*.B 9(p.224.6) ap.CLater.*act*.5(H.3.896C); Nest.'s use criticized by Cyr. οὐχ ἕν τι νοεῖται πρὸς ἡμῶν τὸ ἑτέρῳ τινὶ σχετικῶς συνῆφθαι λεγόμενον; δύο γὰρ πάντως τὰ ἀλλήλοις συμβαίνοντα καὶ οὐχ ἓν αὐτό τι τὸ ἑαυτῷ ~όμενον νοοῖτ' ἂν εἰκότως Cyr.*Nest*.2.8(p.46.4; 6^1.50D); ἐκ δύο φύσεων νοεῖται συνημμένος ὁ Ἐμμανουὴλ Oecum.*Apoc*.1:1f.(p.32); **3.** act., *unite* in human thought, ref. Jo.10:36 τῷ ἁγιαζομένῳ συνάψας τὸ ἁγιάζον Apoll.*corp.et div*.12(p.191.9; M.*PL*.8.875A); τὰ τῶν φύσεων χωρίζοντες ἴδια, τὴν τῆς ἑνώσεως ἀξίαν συνάπτομεν Nest.*hom.in Heb*.3:1 (p.242.15; M.64.492B); Cyr.*ep*.17 *anath*.3(p.40.30; 5^2.76B) cit. s. συνάφεια.

III. spiritual, *unite*, of Christ's work in reuniting creatures to God οὐ γὰρ κτίσμα συνῆπτε τὰ κτίσματα τῷ θεῷ, ζητοῦν καὶ αὐτὸ τὸν ~οντα Ath.*Ar*.2.69(M.26.293A); αὕτη [sc. the peace of Christ] ~ει ...τοὺς ἐν ἕξει αὐτῆς γινομένους τῷ πατρί Thdr.Heracl.ap.*cat.Jo*.14:27(p.352.24); ἵνα τῇ πρὸς ἑκάτερον κοινωνίᾳ δι' ἑαυτοῦ συνάψῃ τὰ διεστῶτα τῇ φύσει Gr.Nyss.*Eun*.3(2 p.32.5; M.45.597C); Cyr.*Os*.28 (3.52D) cit. s. ἕνωσις; pass.; of H. Ghost united to man's body, ‡Chrys.*pasch*.6(p.173.2; 8.271B); of souls united to God in Christ τέλειοι κατεργασθέντες τῷ πατρικῆς θεότητος ἀλέκτῳ φωτὶ συναφθησόμεθα, φῶτα καὶ αὐτοὶ ἐκ τῆς πρὸς αὐτὸν συναφείας γενησόμενοι Eus.*e.th*.3.18(p.179.33; M.24.1041C); οὐ συναφθήσονται τῷ πατρὶ μὴ ἔχοντες τὸν...ἐξ αὐτοῦ φύσει υἱόν Ath.*Ar*.2.43(M.26.240B); ἄνθρωπός τις ὤν, υἱὸς θεοῦ γίνεται, διὰ τῆς πνευματικῆς γεννήσεως Χριστῷ ~όμενος Gr.Nyss.*Eun*.3(2 p.41.18; M.45.609A); κατὰ φύσιν αὐτῷ ~όμεθα Cyr.*thes*.15(5^1.171D); πῶς ἂν εἴη ποίημα, τὸ [sc. πνεῦμα] δι' οὗ τῷ θεῷ...~όμεθα; *ib*.34(360D); myst. (exeg. Is.61:10) βασιλίδα ὡς συναφθεῖσαν τῇ θεότητι τῆς δόξης τοῦ μονογενοῦς Mac.Aeg.*ep*.(M.34.417A); Diad.*perf*.9(p.10.22) cit. s. γνῶσις; τὴν διὰ τῶν ἀποφάσεων ἄνοδον...αὐτῷ ~ουσαν, καθ' ὅσον καὶ ἡμῖν ἐκείνῳ συνάπτεσθαι δυνατόν Dion.Ar.*d.n*.13.3(M.3.981B); τὴν δύναμιν εἰς τὸ νοεῖν...δι' ἧς ~εται πρὸς τὰ ἐπέκεινα ἑαυτοῦ *ib*.7.1(865C); *ib*.1.1(585B).

συναπωθ-έω, *push away together*; met., *expel together* with τὴν ἀλλόφυλον ἡδονὴν τῷ ἐμπαθεῖ λογισμῷ...~εῖσθαι χρὴν παντάπασι τῆς ψυχῆς Max.*ambig*.(M.91.1201B).

***συνάρθρως**, *using the definite article, with the definite article*, Cyr.*Jo*.12.1(4.1109C).

συναριθμ-έω, **1.** *take into account, include*, Ign.*Philad*.5.2; pass., *be numbered with, included among* ~ουμένην [sc. the Samaritan woman] τοῖς κατὰ ἀλήθειαν προσκυνηταῖς Heracleon ap.Or.*Jo*.13.16 (p.240.7; M.14.421D); Serap.*euch*.12.5; **2.** *put on a level with, place in the same category as*; theol.; **a.** ref. Son πῶς μονογενὴς ὁ τοῖς πᾶσι κατ' ἐκείνους ~ούμενος; Alex.Al.*ep.encycl*.4(p.9.1; M.18.576A); Eus.*e.th*.1.10(p.68.31; M.24.841C); οὐκ ἄρα μετὰ τὴν σάρκωσιν, καθ' ὑμᾶς, συνθεολογεῖται ὁ υἱὸς τῷ πατρί. εἰ δὲ οὐ συνθεολογεῖται, οὐδὲ ~εῖται κατὰ τὴν ἐπίκλησιν τοῦ βαπτίσματος Max.*Pyrr*.(M.91.348D); **b.** of H. Ghost as no creature οὐδαμῶς...ὡς ~ουμένου τοῖς πᾶσι τοῦ πνεύματος Bas.*Eun*.3.7(1.278C; M.29.669C); τίς ἡ ἀνάγκη...τῇ δουλευούσῃ κτίσει ~ούμενον; Gr.Nyss.*Maced*.17(M.45.1321C); but the equal of Father and Son εἰ...ἀλλότριον ἦν τῇ φύσει, πῶς συνηριθμεῖτο τὸ πνεῦμα; Bas.*hom*.24.5(2.194A; M.31.609D); τὸν ~οῦντα αὐτὸ καὶ συντάσσοντα πατρὶ καὶ υἱῷ id.*Spir*.69(3.59A; M.32.197B); Gr.Naz.*or*.41.9(M.36.441B); as implied in baptismal formula, Bas.*Spir*.68(57C; M.193C); to which Anomoeans objected τὸν παράκλητον...οὔτε τῷ πατρὶ ~ούμενον· εἷς γάρ ἐστι καὶ μόνος πατὴρ ὁ ἐπὶ πάντων θεὸς Eun.*exp.fid*.3(p.258); οὔτε μὴν σὺν τῷ πατρί, φασί, καὶ τῷ υἱῷ τὸ πνεῦμα τακτέον, ἀλλ' ὑπὸ τὸν υἱὸν καὶ τὸν πατέρα, οὐ...σ. ἀλλ' ὑπαριθμούμενον Bas.*Spir*.13(10C; M.88B); **c.** of all three Persons, ref. Gen.3:22, 11:7, Didym.(‡Bas.)*Eun*.5(1.315D; M.29.756C).

συναρίθμησις, ἡ, *connumeration*; **1.** *being numbered among*, Thdr. Stud.*epp*.1.18(M.99.965C); **2.** *ranking with*, implying equality, ref. Persons of Trin. ἡμεῖς [i.e. Anomoeans] τοῖς...ὁμοτίμοις φαμὲν τὴν σ. πρέπειν Bas.*Spir*.42(3.36A; M.32.145A); εἰ ἕν τι...ἀπὸ τῆς κτίσεως προσαφθείη, πᾶσα ἡ κτίσις συνεισελεύσεται εἰς τὴν τοῦ πατρὸς καὶ υἱοῦ σ. id.*hom*.24.5(2.194B; M.31.612A); τῆς...τριάδος τὴν θεότητα... εἰς τὸ ἀρχαῖον ἐπανήγαγεν, ἐν ὅροις μείνας εὐσεβοῦς ἑνώσεώς τε καὶ σ. (ref. S. Cyprian) Gr.Naz.*or*.24.13(M.35.1185A).

συναρίθμιος, *numbered along with, counted in with* αἷς συναρίθμια ...τῶν ἀνατολικῶν προέδρων τὰ γράμματα λέγομεν Sophr.H.*ep.syn*.(M.87.3188C); *counted among*, i.e. classed as τοῦτον...σ. ἀγγέλοις... τάσσων Epiph.*haer*.24.2(p.258.13; M.41.309D); θνητός...τοῖς θνητοῖς σ. ἐστι Leont.H.*Nest*.7.2(M.86.1761C); ὅπως σ. σε τῶν ὑπ' αὐτοῦ καταστήσειεν Steph.Diac.*v.Steph*.(M.100.1133A).

***συναριστ-έω**, = συναριστάω, *take breakfast* or *luncheon with*, ref. the wedding breakfast *be an invited guest* ὡς φίλον αὐτοῦ καὶ μεσάσαντα τῷ γάμῳ καὶ ~οῦντα αὐτοῖς *Chron.Pasch*.p.313(M.92.796C).

συναρμόζω, *join, unite* persons, Bas.*Spir*.38(3.33B; M.32.140A); Geo.Pis.*carm*.2.30(p.5); pass. συναρμοσθῆναι [sc. disciples of Jo. Bapt.] τῷ τελείῳ διδασκάλῳ Or.*fr.45 in Jo*.(p.520.5).

συναρμολογ-έω, (cf.Eph.2:21,4:16); **1.** *fit together* ἀνάγκη...τὸν θεμέλιον τοιοῦτον εἶναι, οἷα καὶ τὰ ἐποικοδομούμενά ἐστιν, ἵνα καὶ ~εῖσθαι δυνηθῇ Ath.*Ar*.2.74(M.26.304B); ἀεί...πως ἐν ταῖς γωνίαις τῶν οἰκοδομημάτων δύο συμβαίνουσι τοῖχοι, καὶ ἀλλήλοις ~ούμενοι κατασφίγγονται πρὸς ἑνότητα Cyr.*Is*.3.2(2.398A); Melet.*nat.hom*.30 (M.64.1280C); pass., *be put together, formed*, Isid.Pel.*epp*.1.199(M.78.309C); med., gram., *agree* τῷ ὑπαρκτικῷ ~ούμενον ῥήματι *cat.Apoc.*

11:8(p.333.17); **2.** of man with Christ, *join closely* to, *unite* to λόγος μὲν οὖν...οὐκ ἔχει...τοὺς ~ουμένους αὐτῷ· μονογενὴς γάρ ἐστιν·... [Pr.8:23] δι' ἡμᾶς θεμελιοῦται...ἵνα ἡμεῖς, ὡς σύσσωμοι ~ούμενοι καὶ συνδεθέντες ἐν αὐτῷ...ἄφθαρτοι διαμείνωμεν Ath.*Ar.*2.74(M.26.304B, 305A); Dion.Ar.*e.h.*3.3.12(M.3.444B); ψυχῆς τρόπον πρὸς σῶμα ἐν πνεύματι ~οῦντος ἑαυτῷ καὶ συμβιβάζοντος Max.*ambig.*(M.91.1097B); in Church μὴ ἔχοντες τὸν ~οῦντα αὐτοὺς καὶ συμβιβάζοντα, λελυμένοι εἰσὶ καὶ ἐσχισμένοι ἀπ' ἀλλήλων †Bas.*Is.*107(1.453B; M.30. 292A).

συναρμοστής, ὁ, *one who joins* in matrimony ἐγὼ τούτου σ., ἐγὼ νυμφοστόλος Gr.Naz.*or.*40.18(M.36.381B).

συναρπαγή, ἡ, 1. *robbery, plunder*; met., of soul by body, Athenag.*res.*21(p.74.4; M.6.1016A); **2.** *fraud, deception* μηδένα τῶν ξένων...ἄνευ συστατικῶν προσδέχεσθε...πολλὰ γὰρ κατὰ συναρπαγὴν γίνεται *Can.App.*33; ἀπὸ σ. ... πεποιηκότες Chrys.*hom.in Phil.*proem. (11.191E); τὰ ἐν Τύρῳ πάλαι πραχθέντα, ἐκ σ. ἐγεγόνει Socr.*h.e.*2.17.8 (M.67.220A); **3.** as acting upon man from without, *beguilement*; **a.** of mind by false teachers τοὺς κατὰ σ. καὶ διαστροφὴν τῶν διδασκάλων ἠπατημένους Eus.*Is.*3:13f.(M.24.113A); ὑπὸ τῶν δοξασάντων τότε κατὰ συναρπαγὴν παραβεβλάφθαι Liber.*ep.Maced.*ap.Socr.*h.e.*4.12.35(M. 67.493B); κατὰ συναρπαγὴν περιπεπαρμένους τῇ ἀσεβείᾳ Nil.*epp.*2.190 (M.79.300B); **b.** of soul by Devil εἰ...κατὰ συναρπαγὴν τοῦ ἐχθροῦ ἐδέξω τῇ ψυχῇ βουλεύματα Bas.*hom.in Ps.*1(1.96B; M.29.225A); Cyr. *Ps.*37:5(M.69.957B); Nil.*epp.*3.262(M.79.516A); **c.** of senses τὸ σανδάλιον τῆς Ἰουδὶθ ἥρπασε τὸν ὀφθαλμὸν τοῦ Ὀλοφέρνου, καὶ ἡ σ. τοῦ ὄμματος εἰς θάνατον ἐτελεύτησεν id.*praest.*22(M.79.1088A); **4.** a source of action within oneself; a *being carried away*; κατὰ συναρπαγὴν *on an impulse* τὰ [sc. πταίσματά μου] ἐκ σ. καὶ ἀπροσεξίας Ephr.3.484D; τῷ κυρίῳ ἀπελογησάμεθα ἐφ' οἷς κατὰ συναρπαγὴν ἡ ψυχὴ ἡμῶν διετέθη πρὸς τὸ συμβάν Bas.*ep.*300(3.436C; M.32.1045A); ῥοπή τίς ἐστι καὶ σ. τὸ πρᾶγμα· καρτερήσωμεν μικρὸν καὶ τὸ πᾶν ἠνύσαμεν Chrys.*hom. 50.3 in Ac.*(9.376A); ἐκ σ. τινος ἀνεπαισθήτος ῥυπωθεῖσαν τὴν ψυχήν Diad.*perf.*38(p.44.16); esp. of the passions τῆς τοῦ πάθους σ. Chrys. *hom.15.2 in Eph.*(11.112D); ἵνα...μὴ νομίσῃς θυμοῦ τὰ ῥήματα εἶναι ...ἢ κατὰ σ. τινα id.*comm.in Gal.*1:8(10.670C); opp. premeditated actions οὐ γὰρ ἀπὸ σ. διαπράττονται τὸ κακόν, ἀλλ' ὥσπερ τι ἀναγκαῖον Thdr.Mops.*Ps.*30:7(p.138.17; M.66.668B); Chrys.*hom.22.5 in Gen.* (4.200A); ἀπὸ περιστάσεώς τινος καὶ σ., οὐκ ἀπὸ μελέτης id.*hom.16.7 in Rom.*(9.613D; π. τινος συναρπαγείς cj. Gaume); *ib.5.1*(9.460C).

συναρπάζ-ω, 1. *snatch and carry away with one, seize*, Just.*1apol.* 58.2(M.6.416B); Iren.*haer.*proem.(M.7.441A); **2.** met.; **a.** rarely in good sense, *carry* one's audience *with one, carry conviction*, of the spoken word ἀκωλύτως...φέρεται ῥεῦμα τοῦ λέγοντος, καί που τάχα καὶ συναρπάσαι δυνάμενον Clem.*ecl.*27(p.144.32; M.9.712B); usu. by specious arguments, *carry away, mislead* σ. καὶ σοφίζεσθαι Or.*Jo.* 20.24(20; p.358.30; M.14.628B); *ib.*13.3(p.228.21; 404A); Philost.*h.e.* 2.4(M.65.468A); of heretics, Or.*Jo.*20.33(27; p.370.8; 648B); ~ειν οἴεται τοὺς ἀκούοντας...τὸ...τὴν τρίτην ὡσαύτως οἴεσθαι Gr.Nyss.*Eun.* 4(2 p.85.3; M.45.660D); σ. τοὺς πλείστους τῶν μοναχῶν, ἀνθρώπους ἀκεραίους...ὄντας Socr.*h.e.*6.7.21(M.67.685C); Cyr.*ep.*23(p.67.28; 5[2]. 86A); *ib.*44(p.35.6; 132E); pass., *be carried away* by the subject of the argument μὴ ~όμενον ὑπὸ τῶν δυνάμεων, τίς μὲν ἀπὸ κρείττονος τίς δὲ ἀπὸ χείρονος τὰ τοιαῦτα ἐπιτελεῖ, ἵνα ἢ μὴ πάντα κακολογῶμεν ἢ μὴ πάντα ὡς θεῖα θαυμάζωμεν Or.*Cels.*2.51(p.174.23; M.11.877C); **b.** pass., *be a prey* to; *be seized, carried away* or *swept off one's feet* by passions, Just.*1apol.*5.2(M.6.336B); Chrys.*hom.16.3 in Eph.*(11. 120D); id.*hom.13.1 in Rom.*(9.558C); μὴ συναρπαγῇς· μόνον κράτησον σαυτοῦ, καὶ κρατήσεις τῆς τοῦ διαβόλου ἐπιβουλῆς id.*hom.3.6 in 1 Thess.* (11.450B); Nil.*epp.*2.140(M.79.261C); δύο πώλοις εὑρεθῇς δυσηνίοις ~όμενος Isid.Pel.*epp.*1.423(M.78.417C); Cyr.*ador.*7(1.241D); opp. deliberate sin, Chrys.*hom.5.1 in Rom.*(9.460E); **c.** pass., *be a prey* to, *be caught up, entangled* in bad habits ὥστε γενέσθαι ἡμῶν τοὺς ὅρκους ἔθει μᾶλλον ἢ κρίσει. ~όμεθα γοῦν Or.*hom.5.12 in Jer.*(p.40. 33; M.13.312A); **d.** pass., *be rapt, ravished* ὁ δὲ ἐν ἁγίοις συναρπαγεὶς εἶπεν Marc.Diac.*v.Porph.*101; **3.** *catch one unawares, trap, beguile* εἰώθαμεν λέγειν, οὐκ οἶδα πῶς ὁ δεῖνα ἐλθὼν σ., οὐκ ἄγνοιαν προβαλλόμενοι ἀλλὰ ἀπάτην τινὰ...καὶ ἐπιβουλὴν ἐμφαίνοντες Chrys.*hom.13.1 in Rom.*(9.558D); Socr.*h.e.*2.8.3(M.67.196B); ἕνα τῶν μαθητῶν αὐτοῦ εἰς προδοσίαν συναρπάσαντες †Jo.D.*B.J.*7(M.96.913D); **4.** *beg the question* σ. τὸν λόγον Or.*Cels.*2.51(p.173.22; M.11.876D); abs. ἵνα μὴ σ. δοκῶ *ib.*1.32(p.84.23; 724A); **5.** pass., *be hasty in judgements, form rash judgements* ἐν χρόνῳ μακρῷ, ὥστε μὴ εἰπεῖν, ὅτι συνηρπάγη τὸ δικαστήριον Chrys.*hom.51.1 in Ac.*(9.379B).

***συναρπακτικός,** *specious, beguiling*, Gr.Naz.*or.*26.3(M.35.1229D).

***συναρπακτικῶς,** *speciously*, Didym.*Trin.*2.3(M.39.476A); *ib.*2.6 (545B).

συναρρωστέω, *suffer from* one thing *as well as* another σ. τε τῇ πορνείᾳ τὴν ἀπόστασιν Cyr.*ador.*4(1.119C).

σύναρσις, ἡ, *support, assistance, help* μυρίας φωνὰς...ἐκ τοῦ νόμου πρὸς σύναρσιν ἔλαβε Mac.Mgn.*apocr.*3.34(p.129.2); τῆς παρ' ἀλλήλων βοηθείας καὶ σ. Ant.Mon.*hom.*79(M.89.1668D); from God διὰ τῆς ἐκ θεοῦ δοθείσης αὐτῷ σ. Gel.Cyz.*h.e.*2.1.1(M.85.1224C); not appropriate to cooperation of Persons in Trin. οὐκ εἰς τὴν οὐχ ὁμοίων ἐξέτασιν, τῶν συνάρσεως τῆς ἀλλήλων καὶ τῆς ἀπὸ τοῦ χρόνου δεομένων Didym.*Trin.*2.7(M.39.573C).

***συναρχάριος, ὁ,** *fellow novice*, Ephr.1.305A.

σύναρχος, *of one and the same source*, not applicable to creation in rel. to God πῶς οὖν σ. λέγουσιν Ἕλληνες τά τε ζῷα καὶ τὰ φυτὰ τῷ θεῷ; ‡Just.*confut.*1(M.6.1496B); ταύτης [sc. θείας προόδου] ἀρχὴ μὲν ἄναρχος ὁ πατὴρ...μεσότης δὲ σ. ὁ υἱὸς...τέλος δὲ...τὸ πνεῦμα τὸ ἅγιον Proc.G.*Procl.*(M.87.2792[h]A); πῶς...ὁ τοῦ θεοῦ λόγος ἡνώθη τῷ χαρτίῳ...ἵνα ὑπάρχει τὸ Κουράνιόν σου λόγος σ. τοῦ θεοῦ; Barth.Edess. *Agar.*(M.104.1396B).

συνάρχω, med., *begin with* or *at the same time as* τὴν σύντροφον καὶ συναρξαμένην Αὐγούστῳ φιλοσοφίαν Mel.*fr.*1(p.308; M.5.1212A); Epiph.*haer.*66.11(p.32.21; M.42.45C); *Chron.Pasch.*pp.12,14(M.92. 89C,93A).

συνασελγαίνω, *be a companion in debauchery*, Bas.*hom.*14.7(2. 128D; M.31.460A); *Const.App.*2.8.1.

συνασθεν-έω, *be ill together, suffer with* ἀσθενοῦντι ~εῖν καὶ ἰσχύοντι συνευφραίνεσθαι Gr.Naz.*or.*6.6(M.35.729A); ref. conclusion of Arian arguments about nature of Son ἀνάγκη...σ. καὶ αὐτὸν ὡς κτιστῆς ὄντα φύσεως Cyr.*thes.*15(5[1].150C); of man with Christ ὅτι... ἡμεῖς ζήσομεν σὺν αὐτῷ, συνησθενηκότες αὐτῷ κατά γε τὸ ἀποθνήσκειν τέως id.*Pulch.*(p.58.11; 5[2].175C).

συνασκ-έω, 1. *practise, train*, esp. in spiritual life ἡ δὲ ἡμετέρα φύσις...ἐγκρατείας δεῖται, δι' ἧς πρὸς τὸ ὀλιγοδεὲς ~ουμένη συνεγγίζειν πειρᾶται...τῇ θείᾳ φύσει Clem.*str.*2.18(p.155.16; M.8.1020B); σοφίαν συνασκηθῆναι χρὴ εἰς ἕξιν θεωρίας ἀΐδιον *ib.*6.7(p.462.31; M.9.284A); ref. scripture, Eus.*h.e.*5.11.1(M.20.456B); ἱεροῖς μαθήμασι ~ούμενος Philost.*h.e.*3.20(M.65.509C); **2.** *live as an ascetic with* ἀπετάξαντο τῷ βίῳ καὶ συνήσκουν αὐτῇ *A.Paul.et Thecl.*(p.271n.).

συνάσκησις, ἡ, 1. *practice, training* ἡ εἰς ἐπιστήμην σ. Clem.*str.*1.4 (p.17.15; M.8.717A); ἡ...γνῶσις σ. ... ἐργάζεται *ib.*6.9(p.468.28; M.9. 296A); σ. γνωστικὴ *ib.*7.18(p.77.10; 556A); ἐπὶ τὴν πίστιν ἐκ σ. κοινῆς εἰς σύνεσιν ἰδίαν ἄγονται *ib.*6.17(p.511.11; 385B); ἐδεῖτο χρόνου καὶ σ. ἵν' οὕτως ἴδῃ τὸν Ἰησοῦν Or.*fr.93 in Jo.*(p.556.20); Eus.*p.e.*9.1(403D; M.21.681A); **2.** *study* of scripture, id.*h.e.*9.6.2(M.20.808C); **3.** *ascetical discipline*, *ib.*7.32.31(736A).

***συνασκητής, ὁ,** *fellow ascetic, fellow monk*, Ath.*v.Anton.*55(M. 26.924C); †Jo.D.*B.J.*18(M.96.1025A); *ib.*21(1049C).

***συνασκήτρια, ἡ,** *fellow nun*, Pall.*h.Laus.*61(p.157.3; M.34.1228D).

συνασμενισμός, ὁ, *taking pleasure together, enjoying oneself in company* φεύγοντες τὰς πόλεις, μήποτε τῷ σ. σπάσωσί τι τῶν πολιτικῶν θορύβων ἐκπίπτοντες τῆς προθέσεως Pall.*h.Laus.*66(p.163.7; M. 34.1218D); συμπαίζειν...τῷ...Ἰσαὰκ ἀπαξιοῖ, μή πως τῷ σ. ὑποσύρῃ τοῖς αὐτοῦ ἐπιτηδεύμασι id.*v.Chrys.*19(p.123.19; M.47.69).

συνασπάζομαι, *embrace together* a way of life τὸν αὐτὸν βίον αὐτῷ σ. *Apophth.Patr.*(M.65.152A).

συνασπίζ-ω, 1. *support, second, ally oneself with*, med. τῷ διαβόλῳ τῇ ἡδυπαθείᾳ ~ομένους Bas.*renunt.*6(2.208B; M.31.640C); act., persons in a controversy, Philost.*h.e.*4.12(M.65.525A,B); persons in a course of action, Isid.Pel.*epp.*3.153(M.78.845A); an opinion οἱ παρ' Ἕλλησι σοφοί, σ. τῇ πλάνῃ Cyr.*Ps.*9:15(M.69.773A); a practice οὐχ ὅπως...παραλύουσαν...τὸν ἐπὶ τῷ σαββάτῳ νόμον τὴν περιτομὴν εὑρήσομεν, ἀλλ' ἤδη καὶ ~ουσαν id.*Jo.*4.7(4.439A); *reinforce* acts of will τὴν...~ουσαν αὐτοῦ τοῖς θελήμασιν ἐνέργειαν *ib.*5.1(458C); **2.** *fight shoulder to shoulder, close the ranks* ἐκεῖνοι ἑαυτοῖς σ., καὶ ἡμεῖς τὸν ἡμέτερον συνασπισμὸν διαλύομεν Gr.Nyss.*ordin.*(M.46. 548B); ἀσθενεῖς...ὅτι...οὐ σ. ἀλλήλοις Chrys.*hom.59.5 in Mt.*(7. 602A); of God προεστηκότα τε καὶ ~οντα τὸν τῶν ὅλων ἔχοντες θεόν Cyr.*glaph.Num.*(1.387C); ἴσασι...ὅτι σ. θεὸς id.*Ps.*32:20(M.69.881D).

συνασπισμός, ὁ, 1. *fighting together, joint combat* σ. καὶ... ἐπιμαχίας Bas.*hex.*8.5(1.75B; M.29.176B); **2.** *close formation, closed ranks*; met., of Christians τὸν ἡμέτερον σ. διαλύομεν Gr.Nyss.*ordin.* (M.46.548B); Const.Diac.*laud.*28(M.88.512A); συγκροτήσατε, καὶ συσφίγξατε, καὶ οἷόν τινα σ. ποιησάμενοι Olymp.*Job* 17:11(M.93. 193A); fig., of remains of a martyr ἐγεγόνει...τις, ὡς εἰπεῖν, σ. τῶν μελῶν πρὸς τὴν κίνησιν, μὴ τολμῶντος ἑνὸς προπηδῆσαι τοῦ σώματος Sophr.*H.v.Anast.*(M 92.1709A); **3.** in gen., *ranks*; met., of the martyrs νηπίων...πλῆθος...τὸν σ. ἀνεπλήρωσεν Const.Diac.*laud.*4(M. 88.484B).

***συνασπιστής, ὁ,** *supporter, aider and abettor,* Bas.*Spir.*77(3.65E; M.32.213A); Thphn.*chron.*p.336(M.108.812B).

***συναστατ-έω,** *be likewise unsettled* or *uncertain* τῆς καρδίας... ἀστάτως κινουμένης ~ούσας εἶχε καὶ τὰς ἐλπίδας Geo.Pis.*Pers.*3.162 (M.92.1244A).

***συναστείτης, ὁ,** *fellow citizen,* ‡Caes.Naz.*dial.*140(M.38.1065).

***συνάστερος,** *born under the same star,* Gr.Naz.*carm.*1.1.5.19(M.37.425A).

συναστράπτ-ω, *flash like lightning together, shine likewise,* ref. Num.22:23 ~ούσῃ ῥομφαίᾳ Cyr.*ador.*6(1.192D); theol., of Son with Father ~οντα τοκῆϊ...ἀνθρώπου πάλιν υἷα Nonn.*par.Jo.*6:62(M.43.801B); *ib.*13:1(860B); of Godhead and manhood in Christ μετεφυτεύθη...ἡ βάτος τῆς θεότητος...συναστράψαι ἐν φωτὶ προσώπου Χριστοῦ...ἐν αὐτῇ...κυοφορηθέντος, καὶ ὑπ' αὐτοῦ φυλαχθεῖσα ἄφλεκτος, ἡ...παρθενομήτωρ Mod.*dorm.*3(M.86.3285C).

συναστρέω, *coincide with a star;* hence *be favourable, prosper* καλῷ ἄστρῳ ἐγεννήθη, διὸ καὶ σ. αὐτῷ τὰ πάντα Eus.Al.*serm.*22.2(M.86.453C).

συναστρία, ἡ, *conjunction* of the stars οἴεσθαι τὰς τῶν πόλεων εἱμαρμένας, ἐν τοῖς τῶν σεισμῶν καταπτώμασι τὰς σ. ποιεῖν Gr.Nyss.*fat.*(M.45.168B).

***συναστρός,** *born under the same star, T.Sal.*4.6(M.122.1321A).

***συνασωματόω,** *make incorporeal likewise,* i.e. *regard as incorporeal like,* Nest.*hom.in Heb.*3:1(p.242.13; M.64.492B).

***συνασωτεύομαι,** *be a companion in profligacy,* Or.*Cels.*3.67(p.260.7; M.11.1008B).

συνατιμάζω, *degrade to the same level* ἢ καὶ ταύτην [sc. τὴν γῆν]... θεοποιήσει ἢ καὶ ἐκεῖνον [sc. τὸν κύριον] ταύτῃ σ. Gr.Nyss.*Eun.*11(2 p.268.30; M.45.877B).

συναυλία (A), ἡ, *concert,* i.e. *piece of concerted music; chorus* of voices τίς οὐ κατακλᾶται τούτων τοῖς ὀδυρμοῖς, οἰκτρὰν ξυναυλίαν ἁρμοζομένων; Gr.Naz.*or.*14.13(M.35.873B); ταῦτα δακρύων ἄξια καὶ θρηνητικῆς σ. Gr.Nyss.*Eun.*11(2 p.259.6; M.45.865D); Synes.*ep.*4(M.66.1328C).

συναυλία (B) (συναυλεία), ἡ, *dwelling together;* **1.** ref. emperor, *being at court* with πολλοὶ λέουσι συνοικεῖν...ᾑρετίσαντο, ἢ τὴν σ. ποιεῖσθαι μετ' ἐκείνου Jo.VI H.*v.Jo.D.*2(M.94.432C); **2.** *close association, intimacy,* ref. Ps.83:11 τὸ παραλελογισμένον τῆς συναυλείας ἐπίπροσθεν ἄγων τῆς τῶν ἁμαρτωλῶν ἀστενοχωρήτου καὶ ἐλευθέρας διαίτης *cat.Apoc.*3:9ff.(p.227.20); **3.** *congregation* of Israel ἀπρακτούσης...τῆς ἐν νόμῳ λατρείας...καιρὸς ἦν ἤδη, τὴν τῶν Ἰουδαίων ἀποπέμπεσθαι σ. καὶ συναγωγήν Cyr.*glaph.Gen.*3(1.81A).

συναυλίζομαι, 1. *dwell together; live side by side, Clem.ep.*15(M.2.52A); of troops, *be encamped side by side,* Thphyl.*exc.gent.*15(M.113.951B; συνηλίζοντο p.488.27); **2.** *associate with* τοῖς...ἀφορισθεῖσιν... καὶ συναναστρέφεσθε καὶ σ. *Const.App.*2.40.2; ἀνόμημα...τὸ τοῖς... αἱρετικοῖς σ. φιλεῖν Cyr.*glaph.Lev.*(1.351C); of Christ in his earthly life τοῖς οὔπω κεκαθαρμένοις οἰκονομικῶς σ. id.*Lc.*5:30(M.72.569D); ref. Ac.1:4 (v. συναλίζομαι) δι' ἡμερῶν τεσσαράκοντα ὀπτανόμενος αὐτοῖς καὶ σ. Eus.*qu.Marin.suppl.*1.11(M.22.1005D); Epiph.*exp.fid.*17 (p.518.17; M.42.817A); Gel.Cyz.*h.e.*2.24.29(M.85.1305A).

***συναυλισμός, ὁ,** *camping together, encampment,* Cyr.*ador.*10(1.354A).

συναυξάνω (-ξω), 1. *increase in size, grow along with,* ref. Dt.29:5 οὐδὲ αὐτὰ τὰ ὑποδήματα ἐπαλαιώθη οὐδὲ τὰ ἐνδύματα κατετρίβη ἀλλὰ καὶ τὰ τῶν νεωτέρων συνηύξανε Just.*dial.*131.6(M.6.781C); *grow with, increase likewise* αἱ...ἐκ παίδων μαθήσεις σ. τῇ ψυχῇ Iren.*ep.Flor.*ap. Eus.*h.e.*5.20.6(M.20.483A); οἰκονομεῖ ὁ θεὸς μὴ εἶναι μετ' ἀλλήλων τοὺς φαύλους...ἵνα μὴ σ. αὐτῶν ἡ κακία Or.*hom.12.4 in Jer.*(p.91.15; M.13.384D); ἀναλόγως...τῆς τοῦ σώματος...τελειώσεως, καὶ τὰς τῆς ψυχῆς ἐνεργείας τῷ ὑποκειμένῳ σ. Gr.Nyss.*hom.opif.*29.6(M.44.237B); Synes.*ep.*9(M.66.1348A); **2.** *help to increase* αἱ...διαπορήσεις...τὴν θεωρίαν συναύξουσι Clem.*str.*8.6(p.90.20; M.9.581C).

συναύξησις, ἡ, *growth, increase,* Clem.*str.*6.12(p.482.4; M.9.321A); plur., *common growth, growing together with* κατὰ τὰς τῶν χρόνων σ. Isid.Pel.*epp.*2.119(M.78.560B).

συναφαιρέω, v. *συνυφαιρέω.

***συναφαμαρτάνω,** *join in sinning against,* Cyr.*ador.*15(1.527A).

***συναφαυαίνομαι,** *wither together with,* Meth.*symp.*7.2(p.73.12; M.18.128B).

συνάφεια, ἡ, *union;*

A. in gen.; **1.** *combination, conjunction;* **a.** *assembly* of parts, ref. resurrection of διαλυθέντα σώματα: τῆς ἑκάστου τούτων...πρὸς ἄλληλα σ. εἴ γε δεῖ καὶ σ. εἰπεῖν ὡς ἑτερότητί τινι κεχωρισμένων Athenag.*res.*11(p.59.17; M.6.993A); *harmony* ὁ Τατιανὸς σ. τινα καὶ συναγωγὴν...τῶν εὐαγγελίων συνθεὶς Eus.*h.e.*4.29.6(M.20.401A); personal *presence* or *contact* ἐπεὶ δὲ τὴν σωματικὴν σ. πολλὰ τὰ διακωλύοντα, λειπόμενον ἦν διὰ τοῦ γράμματος κοινωνεῖν ὑμῖν τῶν παρόντων Bas.*ep.*28.1(3.106C; M.32.304D); met. γωνίᾳ δὲ παρεικάζει τὸ γράμμα τὸ ἱερόν, τὴν σ. τῶν δύο λαῶν ‡Ammon.*Mt.*23:42 (M.85.1385A); Thdt.*Is.*6:4(p.32.3; 2.208); **b.** sexual *union,* Diod. *Gen.*5:4(M.33.1569D); Epiph.*haer.*21.2(p.239.23; M.41.288B); ref. Mt. 1:18ff. μήπως ἐντεῦθεν μετὰ τὸν θεῖον τόκον νομίζεσθαι...τὸν...Ἰωσὴφ ἔχεσθαι τῆς γαμικῆς σ. Procl.CP *or.*6.7(M.65.732D); Thdt.*Cant.* proem.(2.13A); of marriage πρὸς τὴν γυναῖκα...ἐνομοθέτησαν...κολληθῆναι...καὶ ἑτέραν μείζονα σ. ἐπεζήτησαν Chrys.*hom.62.1 in Mt.*(7.621A); τὴν νόμιμον σ. Thdr.Mops.*1Tim.*3:2(M.66.941B); **c.** *union* of human body and soul τῆς ἀποδύσεως τῶν φυσικῶν παθημάτων διὰ τῆς πρὸς τὸ πνεῦμα σ. Euthal.Diac.*epp.Paul.*(M.85.752A); τῆς σ. ψυχῆς πρὸς σῶμα Thdt.*rect.conf.*11(M.6.1228B); οὐδὲ τῆς ἀνθρωπίνης ψυχῆς τὴν πρὸς τὸ ἑαυτῆς σῶμα σ. φυσικῶς πάσχειν ἄνευ τῆς θείας δυνάμεως Leont.B.*arg.Sev.*(M.86.1940B); **d.** *unity* τὰ δὲ κλάσματα αὖθις οὐκ εἰς σ. ἄρτων ὡς ἦσαν ἐποίησε Epiph.*anc.*48(p.57.25; M.43.101B); ὁ ἄρτος ἐκ πολλῶν συγκείμενος κόκκων ἥνωται...ἄδηλον δὲ αὐτῶν εἶναι τὴν διαφορὰν τῇ σ. Chrys.*hom.24.2 in 1Cor.*(10.213E); ἡ ὑπεροχὴ δόξης οὐ ποιεῖ τῆς πρὸς τὰ λοιπὰ μέρη συναφείας ἀλλοτρίωσιν id.*pan.Rom.*1.1(2.611B); met. πόλις...οὕτως ἦν ᾠκοδομημένη ὡς δοκεῖν ἕνα εἶναι οἶκον διὰ τὴν σ. καὶ ἁρμονίαν τῶν ἐν αὐτῇ οἰκοδομημάτων Eus.*Ps.*121:1(M.24.13A); **e.** *fusion* τὸν σίδηρον ἀψηλάφητον ποιεῖ τοῦ πυρὸς ἡ σ. Nil.*epp.*3.155(M.79.457B); **2.** *relationship;* **a.** *kinship, connexion* διὰ τὴν πρὸς τὸ σωτήριον γένος σ. Afric.*ep.Arist.*5(p.61.21; M.10.61A); **b.** spiritual relationship, religious *community* ἀποπηδῶντα τῆς τῶν οἰκείων ἀδελφῶν σ. Thdr.Stud.*epp.*1.14(M.99.956C); **c.** philos., exeg. 1Cor.15:28 σ. τινα πάντων καὶ ἕνωσιν σημαίνειν Eus. *e.th.*3.15(p.172.4; M.24.1028C); ἡ μὲν τῶν ὑποστάσεων διαίρεσις πράγματι θεωρεῖται...ἡ δὲ κοινότης καὶ ἡ σ. καὶ τὸ ἕν, λόγῳ καὶ ἐπινοίᾳ θεωρεῖται ‡Cyr.*Trin.*10(6^{3}.14E; M.77.1141C); effected in Son εὐδοκίᾳ πατρὸς ἐν τῷ μονογενεῖ υἱῷ τὴν τῶν ἁπάντων σ. συνεκρότησεν Jo.D. *hom.*1.18(M.96.573A); **d.** logical *relation* υἱὸς δὲ ἢ δοῦλος ἢ φίλος μόνης τῆς πρὸς τὸ συνεζευγμένον ὄνομα συναφείας ἐστὶ δηλωτικὰ Bas. *Eun.*2.9(1.245A; M.29.588C); **e.** *logical connexion, context* λόγους... τοὺς ἐν σ. τῶν εἰρημένων...καὶ τοὺς ὁμοίως συνημμένους κατ' ἐπακολούθησιν Just.*dial.*65.3(M.6.625C); ἑξῆς καὶ κατὰ τὸ αὐτὸ ὑπὸ μίαν σ. διανοίας Eus.*d.e.*6.13(p.265.23; M.22.436D); ref. Jo.3:14 τοῦτο δοκεῖ ἀπηρτῆσθαι τῶν ἔμπροσθεν, πολλὴν δὲ καὶ αὐτὸ τὴν σ. ἔχει Chrys.*hom.27.1 in Jo.*(8.154E); ταῦτα τῆς τῶν ῥημάτων ὄντα συναφείας τὰ μέλη διασπῶντες Nest.*hom.in Heb.*3:1(p.234.1; M.64.484A); **f.** κατὰ συνάφειαν *consecutively* οὐ γὰρ ὥσπερ ἡμεῖς ἀθρόως συνάπτοντες τὸ πᾶν ἀνάγνωσμα διερχόμεθα, οὕτω καὶ ὁ προφήτης κατὰ σ. πάντα λόγον τῆς προφητείας τροχάδην ἐξηνέγκατο Eus.*Is.*16:13f.(M.24.205A); **3.** moral *association;* **a.** *social intercourse* πόσων κακῶν μοι αἰτία ἡ σ. αὐτοῦ Ephr.1.206B; τῇ σ. κατευφραίνειν τὸν ἅγιον Sophr.H. *v.Anast.*(M.92.1716A); *bond* of affection, *friendship* οὐκ ἐπὶ τῷ χωρισμῷ δυσφόρως ἔχειν, ἀλλ' ἐπὶ τῇ ἐξ ἀρχῆς σ. χάριν ἔχειν Bas.*hom.* 5.6(2.38E; M.31.249C); *attachment* τῆς ἐπὶ τὸ κακὸν σ. ἀπαλλαγῆναι id.*hom.in Ps.*33(1.153D; M.29.376B); **b.** political *incorporation* τῆς Αὐγούστου πρὸς Ἰουδαίους συναφείας Epiph.*haer.*51.22(p.288.21; M.41.928B); **c.** *concord, unity* in Church ἃς [sc. ἐπιστολάς] ἐπὶ συναφείᾳ καὶ εἰρήνῃ τῶν λαῶν...συνέγραψε Eus.*v.C.*3.59(p.106.14; M.20.1128B); ὅπως ταῖς ἐκκλησίαις...ἡ θεῷ ἀρεστὴ γένοιτο σ. Jo.Ant.*ep.Cyr.*4(p.155.6; M.77.248A); τηρεῖσθαι...ἐν τῇ καθ' ὁμόνοιαν...ἑνώσει βούλεται τοὺς μαθητὰς...ὡς μέχρι τοσούτου προελθεῖν τὴν ἕνωσιν, ὥστε καὶ εἰκόνα τῆς φυσικῆς ἑνότητος, τῆς ἐν πατρὶ καὶ υἱῷ νοουμένης, τὴν προαιρετικὴν γενέσθαι σ. ... ὃ καὶ γενέσθαι συμβέβηκεν Cyr.*Jo.*11.9(4.972B); hence *communion* ἀσπάσασθαι τὴν πρὸς τὰ οἰκεῖα μέλη σ. τε καὶ εἰρήνην CHier.(335)*ep.*(p.248.15; M.26.720B); μετατίθεσθαι πρὸς τὴν τῶν ὀρθῶν σ. βουλομένους Bas.*ep.*125.1(3.214E; M.32.545B); cf. σεαυτὸν τῆς τῶν οὐρανίων ἀγαθῶν σ. ἀλλότριον κατεσκεύασας †Jo.D.*B.J.*2(M.96.873D).

B. theol.; **1.** Trin.; **a.** in gen. οὐκ ἴσασιν ὅτι μήτε ἀπηλλοτρίωται πατὴρ υἱοῦ ἢ πατήρ, προκαταρκτικὸν γάρ ἐστι τῆς σ. τὸ ὄνομα Dion. Al.ap.Ath.*Dion.*17.1(p.58.20; M.26.504D); *Symb.Ant.*(345)9(p.253.36; M.26.733B) cit. s. διάστημα; οὐκ ἐν τῷ αὐτὸ εἶναι ἐκεῖνο, πρὸς ὃ ἕν ἐστιν εἰπεῖν, ἀλλ' ἐν τῷ αὐτὸν ἐν τῷ πατρὶ καὶ τὸν πατέρα ἐν τῷ υἱῷ, τὴν σ. καὶ τὸ ἀχώριστον ‡Ath.*Ar.*4.17(p.62.7; M.26.492B); συνῆπται μὲν ὁ υἱὸς τῷ πατρὶ ἀδιαστάτως· συνῆπται δὲ τῷ υἱῷ τὸ πνεῦμα. τὸ γὰρ διορίζον οὐκ ἔστιν...τὴν ἐξ ἀϊδίου σ. Bas.*hom.*24.4(2.193E; M.31.609B); id.*Spir.*14(3.10D; M.32.88C) cit. s. διάστημα; τῆς κατὰ τὴν ἁγίαν τριάδα σ. καὶ συνθείας Gr.Naz.*or.*43.68(M.36.585D); καινὴν καὶ παράδοξον διάκρισίν τε συνημμένην καὶ διακεκριμένην σ. Gr.Nyss.*diff.ess.*4 (M.32.333A); τοῦ θεοῦ πάντως υἱὸς νοεῖται διὰ τὴν τῆς οὐσίας αὐτοῦ πρὸς τὴν ἐξ ἧς ὑπέστη συνάφειαν id.*Eun.*3(2 p.31.29; M.45.597B);

ib.8(2 p.181.11; 773D) cit. s. ἄμεσος; ἡ...[sc. τριάς] ἀδιαίρετον ἔχει διαίρεσιν, καὶ ἀσύγχυτον φέρει σ. Sophr.H.ep.syn.(M.87.3153A); οἷον ἐν ἡλίοις τρισὶν ἐχομένοις ἀλλήλων καὶ ἀδιαστάτοις οὖσι, μία τοῦ φωτὸς σύγκρασίς τε καὶ σ. ‡Cyr.Trin.10(6^{3}.16B; M.77.1144C); μήτε τῆς οὐσιώδους ἑνώσεως καὶ σ. τε καὶ ταυτότητος διαιρουμένης τὸ σύνολον ‡Gr.Nyss.hom.1.15 in Jo.(p.98.13); **b.** in teaching of Paul. Sam. τὴν δὲ σ. ἑτέρως πρὸς τὴν σοφίαν νοεῖ κατὰ μάθησιν καὶ μετουσίαν, οὐχὶ κατ' οὐσίαν, οὐσιωμένην ἐν σώματι Paul.Sam.fr.(p.333.26; M.86.1393B); and Ebionites τὸν...Χριστὸν προφήτην λέγουσι τῆς ἀληθείας καὶ Χριστόν, υἱὸν ⟨δὲ⟩ θεοῦ κατὰ προκοπὴν καὶ κατὰ σ. ἀναγωγῆς τῆς ἄνωθεν πρὸς αὐτὸν γεγεννημένης Epiph.haer.30.18(p.358.5; M.41.436B); **2.** Christol.; **a.** in early writers without hint of heterodoxy πολλὰ...περὶ τῆς πρὸς τὸν ἄνθρωπον σ. εἰρημένα εἰς τὸν περὶ τῆς θεότητος ἀναφέρουσι λόγον Bas.ep.210.5(3.316E; M.32.776B); ἡ σὰρξ...τοῦ κυρίου...διὰ τῆς σ. τῆς πρὸς θεὸν ἀνυψώθη †Bas.Is.66(1.427C; M.30.233B) = Proc.G.Is.2:1ff.(M.87.1872A); θεὸς ὤν, ἄνθρωπος γέγονεν, ἵνα καὶ ἄνθρωπος γένηται θεός, τῇ σ. ταύτῃ πρὸς θεϊκὴν δόξαν ἀναγόμενος Thdot.Anc.hom.1.5(p.83.35; M.77.1356C); τὴν σ. μὴ μέριζε, ἵνα μὴ μερισθῇς ἀπὸ τοῦ θεοῦ Procl.CP or.laud.BMV 8(M.65.689A; ἕνωσιν p.106.25); denoting close degree of union δοῦλος ὁ κύριος καλεῖται καὶ...πλαστὸς ὁ ἄκτιστος ὀνομάζεται τῇ σ. Apoll.corp.et div.4(p.187.4; M.PL.8.873C); οὕτω γὰρ ἔζησεν τὸ σῶμα θεότητος ἁγιασμῷ καὶ οὐκ ἀνθρωπίνης ψυχῆς κατασκευῇ, καὶ ὅλως τὸ ὅλον ἐν σ. ib.12(p.190.19; 875A); id.fr.138(p.240.23)ap.Thdt.eran.3(4.255); αἱ μὲν πληγαὶ τοῦ δούλου ἐν ᾧ ὁ δεσπότης, αἱ δὲ τιμαὶ τοῦ δεσπότου περὶ ὃν ὁ δοῦλος· ὡς διὰ τὴν σ. τε καὶ συμφυΐαν κοινὰ γίνεσθαι τὰ ἑκατέρας ἀμφότερα Gr.Nyss.Eun.5(2 p.124.16; M.45.705C); τῇ γὰρ ἑνώσει καὶ τῇ σ. ἕν ἐστιν ὁ θεὸς λόγος καὶ ἡ σάρξ Chrys.hom.11.2 in Jo.(8.65A); Isid.Pel.epp.1.199(M.78.309C); τῆς πρὸς σάρκα συνδρομῆς καὶ τῆς καθ' ἕνωσιν σ. Cyr.dial.Trin.6(5^{1}.605D); **b.** use by Thdr. Mops. and Nest., Thdr. Mops.fr.inc.8(p.299.25; M.66.981B) cit. s. ὑπόστασις; ὁ δὲ ἄνθρωπος [sc. λέγεται] πολλῷ γε μείζονος οὔσης ἢ κατ' αὐτὸν τοῦ υἱοῦ τῆς ἀξίας ἀπολαύειν διὰ τὴν πρὸς ἐκεῖνον σ. ib.12(p.306.18; 988C); ὥστε καὶ κύριον αὐτὸν ἀποφῆναι τῶν ἁπάντων διὰ τῆς πρὸς ἑαυτὸν σ. id.fr.Apoll.(p.321.9; M.66.1001B); λέγει [sc. ἡ γραφή] πολλάκις καθ' ἕνωσιν τὰ ἑκάτερα τῶν φύσεων ἰδιαζόντως προσόντα, ὡς ἂν τὴν πρὸς τὸν λαβόντα ἕνωσιν τοῦ ληφθέντος ἡμῖν παραδηλώσειεν, ὅσα τε τούτῳ ἐκ τῆς πρὸς ἐκεῖνον γέγονεν σ. ib.(p.321.19); id.symb.(p.98.26; M.66.1017C) cit. s. ἀχώριστος; οὐχ ὥσπερ ἡμῶν ἕκαστος καὶ καθ' ἑαυτὸν ὑπάρχων υἱός...ἀλλὰ μόνος ἐξαίρετον ἔχων τοῦτο ἐν τῇ πρὸς τὸν θεὸν λόγον σ. ... ἀναιρεῖ μὲν πᾶσαν ἔννοιαν δυάδος υἱῶν τε καὶ κυρίων ib.(p.99.6; 1017D); παρέχει δὲ ἡμῖν ἐν τῇ πρὸς τὸν θεὸν λόγον σ. πᾶσαν ἔχειν αὐτοῦ τὴν πίστιν ib.(p.99.8; 1017D); ἕνα...κύριον Ἰησοῦν Χριστόν...πρωτοτύπως μὲν τὸν θεὸν λόγον νοοῦντες τὸν κατ' οὐσίαν υἱὸν θεοῦ...συνεπινοοῦντες δὲ τὸ ληφθέν, Ἰησοῦν τὸν ἀπὸ Ναζαρέτ, ὃν ἔχρισεν ὁ θεὸς...ὡς ἐν τῇ πρὸς τὸν θεὸν λόγον σ. υἱότητός τε μετέχοντα ib.(p.99.13; 1020A); τὴν μὲν τῶν φύσεων ἐπῄνουν διαίρεσιν κατὰ τὸν τῆς ἀνθρωπότητος καὶ θεότητος λόγον καὶ τὴν τούτων εἰς ἑνὸς προσώπου σ. Nest.ep.Cyr.2 (p.30.19; M.77.52C); εἶναι μὲν οὖν τῆς τοῦ υἱοῦ θεότητος τὸ σῶμα ναόν, καὶ ναὸν κατὰ ἄκραν τινὰ καὶ θείαν ἡνωμένον σ., ὡς οἰκειοῦσθαι τὰ τούτου τὴν τῆς θεότητος φύσιν ib.(p.31.26; 56A); ὁ...ἐκ σπέρματος γεγεννημένος Δαυείδ, παντοκράτωρ τῇ σ. θεός id.fr.C 8(p.248.10); ὁμολογεῖ τὸν ἄνθρωπον πρότερον καὶ τότε τῇ τοῦ θεοῦ σ. θεολογεῖ τὸ φαινόμενον, ἵνα μηδεὶς ἀνθρωπολατρεῖν τὸν Χριστιανισμὸν ὑποπτεύῃ· ἀσύγχυτον τοίνυν τὴν τῶν φύσεων τηρῶμεν σ., ὁμολογῶμεν τὸν ἐν ἀνθρώπῳ θεόν, σέβωμεν τὸν τῇ θείᾳ σ. τῷ παντοκράτορι θεῷ συμπροσκυνούμενον ἄνθρωπον ib.(p.248.20)ap.Cyr.Nest.2.13(p.52.26ff.; 6^{1}.60C); Χριστὸς ὁ θεὸς λόγος ὀνομάζεται, ἐπείπερ ἔχει τὴν σ. τὴν πρὸς τὸν χριστὸν διηνεκῆ· καὶ οὐκ ἔστι τὸν θεὸν λόγον ἄνευ τῆς ἀνθρωπότητος πρᾶξαί τι, ἀπηκρίβωται γὰρ εἰς ἄκραν σ., οὐκ εἰς ἀποθέωσιν ib.C 10 (p.275.10); διαίρεσις οὐκ ἔστι τῆς σ. ... καὶ αὐτοῦ τοῦ εἶναι Χριστός·... τῆς δὲ θεότητος καὶ ἀνθρωπότητος ἔστι διαίρεσις ib.C 12(p.280.18)ap. Cyr.Nest.2.6(p.42.1; 44D); σφόδρα τις τῆς θεότητος ὑπῆρχε σ. καὶ ἐν βρέφει τῆς δεσποτικῆς καθορωμένης σαρκός· ἦν γὰρ ὁ αὐτὸς καὶ βρέφος καὶ τοῦ βρέφους δεσπότης ib.C 15(p.292.2); σ. κηρύττομεν καὶ οὐ σύγχυσιν, ἕνωσιν, οὐ κρᾶσιν Jo.Ant.hom.(p.84.20); **c.** apparently first criticized by Cyr. τοῦ συνῆφθαι λέγειν, τὸ τῆς κολλήσεως ὄνομα, μείζονά που πάντως καὶ ἀξιολογωτέραν τὴν ἔμφασιν ἔχει· εἴπερ ἐστὶν ἀληθὲς εἰπεῖν, ὡς τό τισι κολλώμενον, ἐν ἐπιτάσει πολλῇ τὴν σ. ἔχει Cyr.Chr.un.(5^{1}.733A); σ. ὀνομάζων, τάχα που τὴν κατ' ἐγγύτητα μόνην καὶ κατὰ παράθεσιν ἢ γοῦν σχετικὴν νοουμένην id.Nest.2.5(p.41.38; 6^{1}.44C); ib.2.8(p.46.12ff.; 50Ef.); and rejected as an innovation, id. Chr.un.(5^{1}.733A) cit. s. ἕνωσις; and as weak in meaning παραιτοῦνται μὲν τὴν ἕνωσιν, σ. δὲ ὀνομάζουσιν, ἣν ἂν ἔχοι τυχὸν καὶ ἕτερός τις πρὸς θεόν, ὡς ἐξ ἀρετῆς καὶ ἁγιασμοῦ μονονουχὶ συνδούμενος...συνάπτοιτο δ' ἂν καὶ μαθητὴς διδασκάλῳ ib.(733B); τὸ τῆς σ. ὄνομα παραιτούμεθα, ὡς οὐκ ἔχον ἱκανῶς σημῆναι τὴν ἕνωσιν id.ep.17(p.36.19; 5^{2}.71B); οὐ σ. ψιλῇ καὶ ὡς ἐν ἰσότητι μόνῃ τῶν ἀξιωμάτων συνημμένον ἄνθρωπον θεῷ ib.18(p.114.5; 79C); κατὰ μόνην τῆς υἱότητος τὴν ὁμωνυμίαν καὶ κατὰ μόνην τὴν ἰσότητα τῶν ἀξιωμάτων, εἴπερ τις ὅλως συναφείας οὑτοσὶ νοεῖται τρόπος id.apol.Thdt.1(p.113.24; 6^{1}.207D); γέγονεν ἄνθρωπος καὶ οὐχ, ὡς σὺ φῄς, ἀνέλαβεν ἄνθρωπον, σχετικὴν αὐτῷ δωρούμενος τὴν σ., καὶ τῇ τῆς υἱότητος χάριτι στεφανῶν καθάπερ ἡμᾶς ib.3(p.119.24; 213C); οὐ κατὰ σ. σχετικὴν ἐν ὁμοιώματι ἀνθρώπων γενόμενος id.Chr.un.(769E); as leading to further errors τὸ γὰρ λέγειν ὅτι διὰ τοῦτο ὁ θεὸς λόγος Χριστὸς ὀνομάζεται ὅτι ἔχει τὴν σ. τὴν πρὸς τὸν Χριστὸν πῶς οὐκ ἐναργές ἐστι δύο λέγειν Χριστούς, εἰ Χριστὸς πρὸς Χριστὸν ἔχει σ., ὡς ἄλλος πρὸς ἄλλον; id.ep.44(p.36.21; 5^{2}.134C); οἱ διαιροῦντες...τὰς ὑποστάσεις μετὰ τὴν ἕνωσιν...ἐπινοοῦντες δὲ συνάφειαν αὐτοῖς τὴν κατά γε μόνην τὴν ἀξίαν, δύο που πάντως ἱστῶσιν υἱούς id.expl.xii cap.(p.19.6; 6^{1}.149D); as favoured by Nest. ὥσπερ συνῆν τοῖς προφήταις, οὕτω, φησὶ [sc. Νεστόριος] καὶ τούτῳ, κατὰ μείζονα σ. ... φεύγει πανταχοῦ τὸ λέγειν τὴν ἕνωσιν, ἀλλ' ὀνομάζει σ. id.ep.11a(p.171.16; M.77.85C); contrasted with orthodox terminology θεὸς ὢν φύσει γέγονεν ἄνθρωπος...οὐ κατὰ συνάφειαν ἁπλῶς...τὴν θύραθεν ἐπινοουμένην ἤτοι σχετικήν· ἀλλὰ καθ' ἕνωσιν ἀληθῆ id.Nest.2 proem.(p.33.5; 31B); οὐκοῦν ἀναγκαῖον εἶναί φαμεν τὴν καθ' ὑπόστασιν ἕνωσιν τοῦ λόγου πρὸς τὴν σάρκα, καὶ οὐχὶ δὴ μόνην τὴν ἐν προσώποις καὶ κατὰ θέλησιν ἤτοι σ. ἁπλῆν id.Arcad.(p.103.9; 5^{2}.103E); οὐκ ἄρα ψιλῇ σ. τῇ πρὸς θεὸν λόγον τετιμημένος ἄνθρωπος ὁ Χριστός, συνόδῳ δὲ μᾶλλον τῇ πρὸς τὸ ἀνθρώπινον καθ' ἕνωσιν οἰκονομικὴν υἱὸς εἷς καὶ κύριος id.Pulch.33 (p.44.1; 5^{2}.154C); hence σ. became test word εἴ τις ἐπὶ τοῦ ἑνὸς Χριστοῦ διαιρεῖ τὰς ὑποστάσεις μετὰ τὴν ἕνωσιν, μόνῃ συνάπτων αὐτὰς σ. τῇ κατὰ τὴν ἀξίαν...καὶ οὐχὶ δὴ μᾶλλον συνόδῳ τῇ καθ' ἕνωσιν φυσικήν, ἀ. ἔ. id.ep.17 anath.3(p.40.30; 5^{2}.76B); cf. ἀδιαίρετος; **d.** used, however, by Leo Mag. (ref. 1Jo.5:4–8) τὰ τρία ἕν ἐστιν καὶ ἀμέριστα μένει καὶ οὐδὲν αὐτῶν ἀπὸ τῆς ἑαυτῶν χωρίζεται σ., ἐπειδήπερ ἡ καθολικὴ ἐκκλησία ἐν ταύτῃ ζῇ καὶ προκόπτει τῇ πίστει, ἵνα μήτε δίχα τῆς ἀληθοῦς θεότητος ἡ ἀνθρωπότης μήτε δίχα τῆς ἀληθοῦς ἀνθρωπότητος ἡ θεότης πιστεύηται Leo Mag.ep.28(p.18.21; M.PL.54.778A); and occasionally by later orthodox writers ἐν...τῷ λόγῳ τοῦ μεγαλείου τῆς θείας φύσεως, ἀκοινώνητον τὸ τῆς ἑνώσεως...ἐπεὶ οὐκ ἔσται φιλανθρωπίας συγκατάβασις ἀλλὰ φυσικὴ τοῦ ὑψηλοῦ πρὸς τὸ ταπεινὸν ἡ σ. Leont.B.arg.Sev.(M.86.1940A); πρὸς τὴν ἀνθρωπίνην φύσιν ἕνωσιν τοῦ λόγου καὶ συμπλοκὴν καὶ σ. ἀληθεστάτην ‡Gr.Nyss.hom.3.44 in Jo.(p.147.6); ib.7.154(p.279.11); ib.10.33(p.305.20); τί δὲ καὶ τῆς ἐνανθρωπήσεως ἀπωνάμεθα, τοῦ πρωτοπαθήσαντος μὴ σεσωσμένου, μηδὲ τῇ σ. τῆς θεότητος ἀνακεκαινισμένου; Jo.D.f.o.3.18 (M.94.1072C); **e.** of Christ's human will in rel. to the divine, ref. Jo.5:30 οὐκ ἄλλο μὲν τοῦ πατρὸς τὸ θέλημα, ἄλλο δὲ τὸ αὐτοῦ· ἀλλ' ὥσπερ μιᾶς διανοίας ἓν θέλημα, οὕτως ἐμοῦ καὶ τοῦ πατρός. καὶ μὴ θαυμάσῃς, εἰ τοσαύτην εἶπε σ. Chrys.hom.39.4 in Jo.(8.232C).

C. spiritual; **1.** of union of believers with one another ἀναγκαζόμεθα γὰρ πάλιν τὰ αὐτὰ ὀδύρασθαι...οὕτω σφόδρα ἀπ' ἀλλήλων ἐσμὲν ἀπερρηγμένοι, δέον ἑνὸς σώματος μιμεῖσθαι σ. Chrys.hom.18.3 in 2Cor.(10.569B); **2.** and of believers with God and Christ.; **a.** in gen. ὅτι ἡ πρὸς θεὸν σ., καὶ τὰ τοῦ νόμου περιέχει πνευματικῶς εἰς τὸ συζῆν Χριστῷ Euthal.Diac.epp.Paul.(M.85.768C); Chrys.hom.9.3 in Eph.(11.71F); οὐ κατὰ τὴν οἰκείαν φύσιν πάλιν διαδοχῇ τινι σωματικῶς τικτόμενοι, ἀλλὰ θείᾳ δυνάμει διὰ τῆς πρὸς αὐτὸν...σ. τὴν γένεσιν δεχόμενοι Thdr.Mops.Jo.1:13(M.66.732B); κεκλήμεθα δὲ δι' αὐτὸ καὶ θεοί, ἅτε δὴ τῇ θείᾳ τε καὶ ἀπορρήτῳ φύσει, τῇ πρὸς αὐτὸ σ. κεκοινωνηκότες Cyr.dial.Trin.7(5^{1}.639E); id.Os.28(3.52D) cit. s. ἕνωσις; Thdt. Rom.7:4(3.69); effected through Inc. ἄνθρωπος...γέγονεν ὁ δημιουργὸς...ὅπως διὰ τῆς αὐτοῦ πρὸς ἡμᾶς κοινωνίας, καὶ ἡμῶν πρὸς αὐτὸν συναφείας ὑπολωφήσῃ τῆς ἐν ἡμῖν ἁμαρτίας ἡ εἴσδυσις ‡Meth.Sym.et Ann.13(M.18.380C); through baptism, Chrys.comm.in Gal.3:28(10.704C); mediated by 'gnostic' μᾶλλον ἐπιτείνει τὸ γνωστικὸν ἀξίωμα ὁ τὴν προστασίαν τῆς τῶν ἑτέρων διδασκαλίας ἀναλαβὼν...δι' ἧς πρὸς τὸ θεῖον συνάφειάν τε καὶ κοινωνίαν ἐμμεσιτεύει Clem.str.7.9(p.38.31; M.9.473B); gained by following Christ, †Ath.fr.(M.26.1244C) cit. s. ἕνωσις; **b.** eucharistic ἡ μυστικὴ μετάληψις, ὥσπερ τινὰ φυσικὴν σ. ποιεῖ Ammon.Jo.6:57(M.85.1440B); exeg. 1Cor.10:16 on the use of term κοινωνία: ἠβουλήθη, καὶ πολλὴν ἐνδείξασθαι τὴν σ. Chrys.hom.24.2 in 1Cor.(10.213C).

D. myst.; **1.** of Church with Christ τὴν σ. τῶν μελῶν τοῦ σώματος τοῦ Χριστοῦ Bas.ep.156.1(3.245C; M.32.613D); μέλη Χριστοῦ πάντες ὑμεῖς, οἱ διὰ τοῦ πνεύματος ἀναγεννήσεως τὴν πρὸς αὐτὸν δεξάμενοι σ. Thdr.Mops.1Cor.6:15(p.181.2; M.66.884D); τῆς σ., ἣν ἡ ἐκκλησία συνῆπται Χριστῷ νυμφικῶς ἅμα καὶ μυστικῶς Sev.Ant.ap.cat.1Petr.3:7(p.60.22); ἦλθεν οὖν ὁ γάμος τοῦ ἀρνίου καὶ ἡ γυνὴ αὐτοῦ ἡ ἐκκλησία ἑτοίμη πάρεστιν τῶν ἀμυθήτων ἐκείνων τυχεῖν ἀγαθῶν τῇ πρὸς

Χριστὸν σ. Oecum.*Apoc*.19:7(p.202); γάμον δὲ ἀρνίου τὴν τῆς ἐκκλησίας πρὸς Χριστὸν λέγει σ.· ἧς ἁρμοσταὶ οἱ θεῖοι γεγόνασιν ἀπόστολοι· δι' ὧν αὐτῇ ὁ ἀρραβὼν ἐδόθη τοῦ πνεύματος, ὡς ἀποληψομένῃ τότε τὴν πρόσωπον κατὰ πρόσωπον εἰλικρινῆ σ. Andr.Caes.*Apoc*.56 (M.106.397C); **2.** of individual souls with God and Christ ἐπιποθῶν τὴν περί σε τὸν ἅγιον σ. Ath.*exp.Ps*.62:3(M.27.277D); τῆς σῆς ἀντεχόμην, ὦ δέσποτα, σ. *ib*.72:28(332D); ἵνα κερδάνωμεν τὴν σ. ἡμῶν τὴν πρὸς θεὸν ἐν Χριστῷ γενομένην †Ath.*fr*.(M.26.1244B); ψυχὴ... τετρωμένη γὰρ τῇ εἰς αὐτὸν [sc. Χριστόν] ἀγάπῃ ἐπιποθεῖ...τὴν πρὸς αὐτὸν...μυστικὴν συνουσίαν κατὰ τὴν ἄφθαρτον σ. Mac.Aeg.*ep*.2(M.34.416D); Bas.*ep*.46.2(3.135E; M.32.372A); Gr.Nyss.*hom.8 in Cant.* (M.44.948B); *ib*.1(776B); Sophr.H.*or*.4(M.87.3309A); προαγωγικὸν καὶ κινητικὸν πρὸς ἐρωτικὴν σ. τὴν ἐν πνεύματι, τὸν θεὸν εἶναί μοι νόει Max.*cap*.5.88(M.90.1385B) = id.*schol.d.n*.4.14(M.4.265D); ἐκολλήθη γὰρ ὄντως ἡ ψυχὴ αὐτοῦ ὀπίσω τοῦ Χριστοῦ, συναρμοσθεῖσα αὐτῷ ἀρραγεῖ σ. †Jo.D.*B.J*.40(M.96.1236D); consummated in next world ὑπ' αὐτοῦ [sc. Christ] σοφίᾳ...καὶ ἀρετῇ πάσῃ τέλειοι κατεργασθέντες τῷ πατρικῆς θεότητος ἀλέκτῳ φωτὶ συναφθησόμεθα φῶτα καὶ αὐτοὶ ἐκ τῆς πρὸς αὐτὸν σ. γενησόμενοι, καὶ υἱοὶ θεοῦ κατὰ μετοχὴν τῆς τοῦ μονογενοῦς αὐτοῦ κοινωνίας ἀποτελεσθέντες Eus.*e.th*.3.18(p.179.34; M.24.1041C); ὁ θάνατος οὐ χωρισμόν, ἀλλὰ σ. τοῦ ποθουμένου [sc. Christ] ποιεῖ Gr.Nyss.*virg*.(p.264.16; M.46.333C).

συνάφεσις, ἡ, *joint abstention*, Gr.Agr.*Eccl*.3.7(M.94.856A).

συναφή, ἡ, *connexion*; **1.** *combination*; ref. Christian and Hellenic thought ἡ σ. τῶν δογμάτων διὰ τῆς ἀντιπαραθέσεως τὴν ἀλήθειαν μνηστεύεται Clem.*str*.1.2(p.14.4; M.8.709B); **2.** *continuity* διὰ τὴν σ. τῆς καινῆς [sc. διαθήκης] πρὸς τὴν παλαιάν Or.*Jo*.1.13(14; p.18.17; M.14.48A); Eus.*d.e*.8.2(p.378.33; M.22.613B); **3.** *affinity, relation* εἰ γάρ τις καθ' ἑαυτὰ τὰ μέρη τῆς κτίσεως λάβοι...οἷον...ξηρὰν καὶ ὑγρὰν οὐσίαν διέλων ἀπὸ τῆς πρὸς ἄλληλα σ. Ath.*gent*.27(M.25.53B); Dion.Ar.*d.n*.11.2(M.3.949C); **4.** moral *attachment* εἰ δέ τις... φαντασία...ἀπιστεῖ, μήτοι καὶ κατ' αὐτήν ποτε πορισθῆναι τὴν εὐδαίμονα σ. [i.e. συνάψαι τῷ νοητῷ τὸν...πεπλανημένον] Synes.*insomn*.4 (p.151.12; M.66.1288D); **5.** Christol., of *union* of natures τοιαύτη γέγονεν ἡ σ. ἵνα τῷ κατὰ φύσιν τῆς θεότητος συνάψῃ τὸν φύσει ἄνθρωπον Ath.*Ar*.2.70(M.26.296B).

συναφής, *united, connected*; theol., of relation of Logos to Father λόγος δέ, ὅτι οὕτως ἔχει πρὸς τὸν πατέρα, ὡς πρὸς νοῦν λόγος· οὐ μόνον διὰ τὸ ἀπαθὲς τῆς γεννήσεως, ἀλλὰ καὶ τὸ σ. Gr.Naz.*or*.30.20 (p.139.5; M.36.129A); τὸ σ. τῆς οὐσίας *ib*.34.13(253B); Gr.Nyss.*Eun*.8 (2 p.180.21; M.45.773B); *ib*.9(2 p.208.20; 805C); *ib*.(2 p.217.19; 816C); Christol. τῷ θεῷ λόγῳ συναφθεὶς...ὁ τεχθεὶς ἐκ τῆς παρθένου ναὸς μεμένηκεν ἀδιαίρετος, τὴν...ταυτοβουλίαν καὶ ταυτουργίαν ἐσχηκώς· ὧν οὐδέν ἐστιν συναφέστερον Thdr.Mops.*ep.Domn*.(p.339.9; M.66.1013A).

***συναφθαρσία,** ἡ, *like incorruptibility*; of BMV, Germ.CP *or*.6(M.98.345C).

***συναφθαρτίζω,** *make immortal also* σῶμα Χριστοῦ...σ. ... ἡμᾶς ‡Jo.D.*corp*.(M.95.404B,409C).

[*]**συναφιστάνω,** *transport together, take away with* σ. τῷ λόγῳ τὸ σῶμα τῆς γῆς Clem.*str*.7.7(p.30.22; M.9.456B).

συναφομοιόω, med., *become like*, c. dat., Evagr.*h.e*.1.21(p.30.25; M.86.2480B).

συναφορίζω, **1.** *banish with* εἶναι σὺν κυρίῳ πάντοτε, καὶ μὴ τοῖς ἀκοῖς...συναφορισθῆναι Dion.Ar.*ep*.8.5(M.3.1097B); **2.** *excommunicate together* with, ‡Bas.*poen.mon*.3(2.527A; M.31.1305C).

***συναφραίνω,** *be a companion in folly, join in folly* with, Cyr.*Jo*.5.2(4.484D).

***συνάφραστος,** *likewise indescribable* or *ineffable*, Geo.Pis.*hex*. 1751(M.92.1569A).

***συναφυπνίζομαι,** *awake together from sleep*, Gr.Nyss.*Eun*.12(1 p.335.20; M.45.1053A).

***συναχρειόω,** pass., *be made worthless at the same time, be tainted* or *corrupted together* τῷ φθοροποιῷ πρὸς τὸ ὑγιαῖνον ἀναμιχθέντι ἅπαν τὸ ἀνακραθὲν συνηχρείωται Gr.Nyss.*or.catech*.37(p.143.6; M.45.93C).

σύναψις, ἡ, *contact*; sexual *intercourse*, ‡Ath.*Ar*.4.22(p.69.11; M.26.501B); τὴν γαμικὴν σ. Procl.CP *or*.6.7(M.65.733A).

***συνδαίμων,** ὁ, *fellow demon*; of the followers of Nestorius, †Cyr. *hom.div*.11(5^2.383E).

***σύνδακρυς,** **1.** *in tears*, *Hom.Clem*.12.7; σ. ἐγένετο Socr.*h.e*.4.23. 27(M.67.513B); †Jo.D.*B.J*.10(M.96.940B); **2.** *prone to tears of sympathy* οἱ περὶ τὸ φιλήδονον ῥέποντες, συμπαθεῖς καὶ ἐλεήμονες, καὶ σ., καὶ κόλακες Jo.Clim.*scal*.15(M.88.889A).

συνδαπαν-άω, *consume together* or *along with*, Gr.Naz.*or*.43.40(M.36.549C); πῶς ὁ...νοῦς...τῇ ἀφαιρέσει τῶν σωματικῶν ἰδιωμάτων ∼ώμενος; Gr.Nyss.*anim.et res*.(M.46.41B); Cyr.*ador*.7(1.250D).

συνδείκνυμι, *demonstrate at the same time*, Gr.Nyss.*Eun*.4(M.45.621D, v.l. συνενδ- 2 p.52.20).

συνδειπνέω, *dine* or *sup together with*, Tat.*orat*.18(p.20.3; M.6.845B); Clem.*paed*.2.7(p.190.12; M.8.457B); ‡Eust.*Laz*.3,8(pp.28.3, 33.10); in eucharist ἀποκληροῖ...τὸν οὐχ ὁσίως αὐτῷ...σ. Dion.Ar. *e.h*.3.3.1(M.3.428B).

***συνδεισιδαίμων,** *likewise superstitious, involved in superstition together with* τὸν ὁμόφρονά τε καὶ σ. αὐτῷ Cyr.*Juln*.4(6^2.125B).

***συνδέρ-ομαι,** *be beaten together* with εἶχες τὸν βασιλεύοντα [i.e. Christ]...ἐν τῷ δέρεσθαι ∼όμενόν σοι τῇ διαθέσει Thdr.Stud.*epp*.2.55 (M.99.1268D).

συνδέσμιος, ὁ, *fellow prisoner*, *M.Seb.test*.3.4.

σύνδεσμος, ὁ, **1.** *bond* of union, of man in universe σ. ἁπάντων τὸν ἄνθρωπον κατεσκεύασεν Thdt.*qu.20 in Gen*.(1.30); Cosm.Ind.*top*.2 (M.88.120B); σ. [sc. ὁ ἄνθρωπος]...ἐστιν ὁρατῆς καὶ ἀοράτου, ἤτοι αἰσθητῆς τε καὶ νοητῆς κτίσεως Jo.D.*volunt*.15(M.95.144B); ‡Caes. Naz.*dial*.160(M.38.1120); moral τῷ σ. τῆς ἀγάπης τῆς πρὸς αὐτὸν καὶ ἡμᾶς ἡνῶσθαι CHier.(350)*ep*.(p.137.10; M.25.352C); Ath.*Ar*.3.21(M.26.368B); Chrys.*hom.88.2 in Jo*.(8.527C); theol., of H. Ghost σ. τῆς τριάδος Epiph.*haer*.62.4(p.392.27; M.41.1056A); *ib*.74.11(p.329.23; M.42.497A); *ib*.76.46(p.400.5; 613B); **2.** *fixing* of date of Easter ἐκ τριῶν...συνέστηκεν ὁ τοῦ πάσχα σ. Epiph.*haer*.70.11(p.243.24; M.42.360A); **3.** that which is bound together; **a.** *band, college* τοὺς... πρεσβυτέρους...συνέδριον θεοῦ καὶ...σ. ἀποστόλων Ign.*Trall*.3.1; **b.** fig., *knot, snare, difficulty* πλέκων συνδέσμους, καὶ διαλύων κρατούμενα Gr.Naz.*or*.28.11(p.39.4; M.36.40A); **4.** *banding together, conspiracy*, Or.*hom.9.4 in Jer*.(p.69.3ff.; M.13.353Df.); ἡ Ἰεζάβελ... ἐβόησε 'σ., σ.', τουτέστιν ἀποστασία καὶ τυραννίς Thdt.*qu.45 in 3Reg*.(1.491); id.*qu.38 in 4Reg*.(1.535).

***συνδεσμόω,** *bind together*, morally ἡ πίστις συνδεῖ τοὺς ὁμόφρονας, καὶ ἡ ἐλπὶς συνενοῖ τοὺς εὐθύφρονας, καὶ ἡ ἀγάπη σ. τοὺς θεόφρονας Sophr.H.*ep.syn*.(M.87.3149C).

***συνδεσπόζ-ω,** *rule together* with πνεῦμα...σ. τῷ...πατρὶ καὶ υἱῷ Didym.*Trin*.2.8(M.39.621A); Χριστὸν...τὸν ἀϊδίως αὐτῷ [sc. τῷ πατρὶ] συνεδρεύοντα καὶ τῆς οὐκ ἀϊδίου ∼οντα κτίσεως Sophr.H.*v.Cyr. et Jo*.15(M.87.3396D).

***συνδεσποτεία,** ἡ, *joint rule* or *authority*, ref. Jo.14:16 'ἄλλος'... τοῦτο δὲ σ., ἀλλ' οὐκ ἀτιμίας ὄνομα Gr.Naz.*or*.41.12(M.36.445A).

συνδεσποτεύω, *rule together* with; of Son with Father, Didym. *Trin*.3.2(M.39.797A).

***συνδέσποτος,** *of like authority* κοινωνόν σε τοῦ οἴκου μου τίθημι, καὶ σ., κατ' ἐμέ Jo.VI H.*v.Jo.D*.10(M.94.445A).

συνδετικός, *binding together, serving to unite* φθέγγεται καὶ αὐτὸς τὴν συναπτικὴν καὶ σ. ... φωνήν, λέγων παντὶ τῷ λαῷ 'εἰρήνη πᾶσιν' Eustrat.*v.Eutych*.25(M.86.2304A); neut. as subst., *bond of union*, of H. Ghost as bringing about unity of Christians τὸ...σ. τῆς ἑνότητος ταύτης, ἡ δόξα ἐστί· δόξαν δὲ...τὸ πνεῦμα τὸ ἅγιον Gr.Nyss.*hom.15 in Cant*.(M.44.1117A).

συνδέ-ω, **1.** *bind together, bind to*; **a.** fig. ἡ συνδοῦσα ζώνη καὶ συσφίγγουσα τὴν πρόθεσιν τῆς ψυχῆς εἰς ἁγνείαν Meth.*symp*.4.6(p.52.5; M.18.96B); ∼ουσα [sc. peace] τὰ ἄκρα διὰ τῶν μέσων τοῖς ἄκροις Dion.Ar.*d.n*.11.2(M.3.952A); **b.** met. τὴν ψυχὴν σ. τῷ σώματι πρὸς κόλασιν Or.*princ*.1.8.1(p.96.11); Ath.*gent*.33(M.25.65C,68A); οὐ δὴ τοιοῦτος ἦν ὁ τοῦ θεοῦ λόγος ἐν τῷ ἀνθρώπῳ· οὐ γὰρ συνεδέδετο τῷ σώματι id.*inc*.17.4(M.25.125C); συνδουμένης ἐν αὐτῷ [sc. τῷ ἀνθρώπῳ] πάσης τῆς κτίσεως Cosm.Ind.*top*.2 (v.l. συνδονουμένης M.88.121A); **2.** moral; pass., *be in union* with, Dion.Ar.*e.h*.3.3.7(M.3.436A); of the individual with God συνάφειαν...ἣν ἂν ἔχοι...τις πρὸς θεόν, ὡς ἐξ ἀρετῆς καὶ ἁγιασμοῦ μονονουχὶ συνδούμενος Cyr.*Chr.un*.(5^1.733B); **3.** *bind to, unite with* παρ' ἡμῖν γίνεται συμπάσχων ἡμῖν, καὶ συνδέδεται ἡμῖν Or.*sel.in Ezech*.4:9(M.13.781A); in the mind or thought of man φύσει τῇ καθ' ἡμᾶς τὸν...λόγον συνδοῦντες εἰς ἕνωσιν Cyr.*hom. pasch*.17.2(5^2.226D); *bind together, associate* in union ἀνάγκη σ. εἰς ἕνα κύριον καὶ Χριστόν id.*Nest*.3.5(p.72.29; 6^1.90D); διπλῆν θέλησιν δογματίζεις, ∼ων ἀλλ' οὐ διϊστῶν ἢ μερίζων ἰδίως Andr.Cr.*Agath*.116 (cf.M.97.1444B); creation to Christ ὁ τὸ πᾶν πρὸς ἑαυτὸν σ. τε καὶ συναρμόζων Gr.Nyss.*or.catech*.32(p.119.8; M.45.80D); **4.** abs.; **a.** *bind at the same time* δέδεσαι γάμῳ; καὶ τῇ σφραγῖδι συνδέθητι Gr.Naz.*or*. 40.18(M.36.381B); **b.** *bind fast, confirm*, opp. λύω: ἐπικουρίᾳ γὰρ εὔνοια μὲν συνδεῖται, λύεται δὲ ἔχθρα Clem.*str*.2.19(p.169.11; M.8.1048A); Gr.Naz.*or*.38.11(M.36.324A); **c.** *hamper* ἃ...ἡ ἄγνοια σ. κακῶς, ταῦτα διὰ τῆς ἐπιγνώσεως ἀναλύεται καλῶς Clem.*paed*.1.6(p.107.32; M.8.285B); τοὺς τρυφῶντας...καρηβαροῦντας, διατεινομένους, συνδεδεμένους, κλίνης δεομένους Chrys.*hom.39.9 in 1Cor*.(10.377D); **5.** pass. met., *be bound up* or *associated with* ὥσπερ τάφον τὸ σῶμα περιφέρει μυρίοις συνδεδεμένον κακοῖς Chrys.*hom.39.9 in 1Cor*.(10.376D); ἡ κτίσις τῇ τοῦ ἀνθρώπου χρείᾳ...συνδουμένη Thdt.*qu.20 in Gen.*(1.30); perf. ptcpl. pass., of a literary work, *compendious*, Melet.*nat. hom.*epit.(M.64.1077A).

συνδημιουργ-έω, **1.** *join in creating, participate in the Creation*; of Son with Father, Epiph.*anc.*15(p.24.11; M.43.44D); id.*haer.*23.5(p.253.15; M.41.304C); ἡ τριὰς...συγκτίζουσα καὶ σ. *ib.*76.44(p.398.33; M.42.612B); Eunomian ἔμαθεν...ὅτι καὶ υἱὸς αὐτοῦ ἔσται, καὶ ~ήσει τὰ πάντα Cyr.*thes.*7(5^1.58D); **2.** *create with* or *at the same time* ἀνάγκη ...ἢ συστολήν τινα τοῦ θεοῦ λέγειν...ἢ καὶ ἑαυτὸν τῇ ὕλῃ σ. [sc. if God is in all matter] Meth.*arbitr.*6(p.160.9; M.18.252B); Leont.B.*Nest.et Eut.*3(M.86.1369C); Paul.Sil.*ambo.*6(M.86.2251C); of soul and body, Thdt.*eran.*3(4.180); Justn.*ep.CP*(M.86.993B); **3.** *create in the same way* ἀγαθὸς...ἐκτίσθη [sc. ὁ ὄφις], καὶ τοῖς ἀσωμάτοις σ. Thdt.*qu.34 in Gen.*(1.46).

συνδημιουργός, **ὁ**, *joint creator, fellow creator*; of Son with Father, Epiph.*haer.*23.5(p.253.11; M.41.304C); *ib.*69.55(p.202.14; M.42.288C); ‡Chrys.*Trin.*(1.832C); Gel.Cyz.*h.e.*2.14.5(M.85.1256D); φύσις...ὑπουργὸς μὴ σ. ... τοῦ προστάττοντος Bas.Sel.*or.*21.2(M.85.257A).

συνδιαβαπτίζω, *immerse, drench*, met. τῇ ἰλύϊ τῶν...αὐτοῦ ῥημάτων σ. τὸν λόγον Gr.Nyss.*Apoll.*39(M.45.1212B); id.*Eun.*10(2 p.235.7; M.45.837A); med., *plunge into, immerse oneself in* τοὺς μὴ σ. ... ταῖς...ἀπάταις id.*v.Mos.*(M.44.329B).

συνδιαβαστάζω, *help to carry*, ‡Jo.D.*Artem.*18(p.157.17; M.96.1268C).

***συνδιαγράφ-ω**, *cancel together, cancel along with* ὥστε ἑνὸς ὄντος, πάντα ἐν αὐτῷ νοεῖσθαι, καὶ μὴ ὄντος, τὰ πάντα ~εσθαι Gr.Nyss.*Apoll.*5(M.45.1132C); τῷ...ἐλλείποντι τῶν ἰδιωμάτων ὅλος ὁ τῆς οὐσίας αὐτῷ ~εται λόγος id.*Eun.*1(1 p.76.11; M.45.305D).

συνδιάγω, *go through together*; **1.** *pass, spend time together*, Gr.Nyss.*ep.*1(M.46.1001C); **2.** *observe also* a festival τὴν μνήμην τοῦ μακαριωτάτου Πέτρου παρὰ Σεβαστηνοῖς πρώτως ἀγομένην ἐπιτελέσας, καὶ...τῶν ἁγίων μαρτύρων μνήμας κατὰ τὸν αὐτὸν χρόνον συνδιαγαγὼν ἐκείνοις...ὑπέστρεφον *ib.*(v.l. συνδιαγαγόντων ἐκείνῃ 1001A).

συνδιαγωγή, **ἡ**, **1.** *living together, association with* ἀξιοῦσθαι τῆς ἐν οὐρανοῖς τῶν ἀγγέλων σ. Justn.*Or.*(p.195.24; M.86.957D); **2.** *sharing of the same way of life, common life* κοινωνεῖν αὐτοῖς τῆς τοιαύτης σ. Just.*dial.*47.3(M.6.577B); συνασκήσας...αὐτῷ τὸν μονήρη βίον ἐν...τῷ αὐτῷ μοναστηρίῳ τῆς ἐκεῖσε σ. ἀναμιμνήσκει αὐτόν Justn.*conf.*(p.108.17; M.86.1031D); of Christ's earthly life with men τὴν μετὰ πορνῶν καὶ τελωνῶν ἀδιάφορον σ. Max.*schol.d.n.*3.2(M.4.236D); 'μίαν τῶν ἡμερῶν τοῦ υἱοῦ τοῦ ἀνθρώπου...' τουτέστιν ἐπὶ γῆς συνδιαγωγῆς αὐτοῦ *cat.Lc.*17:22(p.130.1).

***συνδιαγωγός**, **ὁ, ἡ**, *companion*; of BMV νυκτοπορούντων συνοδοιπόρος καὶ σ. ‡Jo.D.*hom.*5(M.96.660B).

***συνδιαζάω**, *spend one's life with, live among* μὴ σ. κακοῖς Ephr.1.192A; †Bas.*ep.*42.4(3.128C; M.32.353D).

[*]**συνδιάζω**, v. συνδυάζω.

***συνδιάθεσις**, **ἡ**, **1.** *disposition to, sympathetic affection, inclination* καλοῦ καὶ κακοῦ γνῶσις ὑπὸ τῆς γραφῆς ὠνομάσθη, σ. τινα καὶ ἀνάκρασιν ἑρμηνευούσης τῆς γνώσεως Gr.Nyss.*hom.opif.*20.3(M.44.200B); θεοῦ...ἴδιον ἡ τῶν ἀγαθῶν ποίησις· ἀνθρώπου δέ, ἡ πρὸς αὐτὰ σ. Max.*ep.*14(M.91.533B); ἡ πρὸς ἀλλήλους τῶν ἀνθρώπων...σ. *ib.*13(512A); id.*myst.*(M.91.713A); φευκτὴ...ἡ μετὰ τῶν παραπικραινόντων τὸν θεὸν σ. Andr.Caes.ap.*cat.Apoc.*18:4(p.558.9) for καὶ διαίτησις id.*Apoc.*55(M.106.388B); Thdr.Stud.*epp.*2.176(M.99.1548D); **2.** *readiness to agree, spirit of conciliation* ἔχαιρον ἐπὶ τῇ...πρὸς πάντας συγκαταβάσει καὶ σ. Dion.Al.ap.Eus.*h.e.*7.24.9(M.20.696C).

συνδιαθέω, *go about with, accompany*; c. dat., Cyr.*glaph.Ex.*3(1.324E).

***συνδιαίρεσις**, **ἡ**, *division* τέλειος...ἐστὶ θεός...τέλειος ἄνθρωπος...εἷς...ἄνευ τῆς οἱασοῦν σ. γνωριζόμενος Jo.D.*hom.*4.12(M.96.612C).

συνδιαιρ-έω, *divide together*; **1.** pass., *be divided like* or *along with*, met. μίαν...αἴσθησιν εἶναι φυσικὴν τῆς ψυχῆς...σ. δὲ αὐτῇ διὰ τὸν ἐκ τῆς παρακοῆς...ὄλισθον ὁ τόνος ταῖς αὐτῆς τῆς ψυχῆς κινήσεσιν Diad.*perf.*29(p.32.10); Trin. ἡ...φύσις μία ἐστίν...τοῖς μετέχουσιν αὐτῆς τοῖς καθ' ἕκαστον οὐ ~ουμένη Gr.Nyss.*tres dii*(M.45.120B); *ib.*(133A); φυλάσσοντες μὲν διῃρημένην τὴν τῶν ὑποστάσεων ἰδιότητα, οὐ ~οῦντες δὲ τοῖς προσώποις τὴν τῆς οὐσίας ἑνότητα id.*Eun.*1(1 p.164.5; M.45.405B); ταῖς προσηγορίαις ὁμοῦ καὶ τὴν οὐσίαν παχυμερῶς σ. δοξάζοντες †Gr.Thaum.*ep.Philagr.*(M.46.1104C); **2.** med., *divide with, claim a share of* ὁ...ὕπνος ὥσπερ τελώνης τὸν ἥμισυν ἡμῖν τοῦ βίου σ. χρόνον Clem.*paed.*2.9(p.207.16; M.8.496B); **3.** pass.; *be differentiated likewise, vary with* τῇ διαφορᾷ τῶν τῇ φύσει διαφερόντων ζῴων ἡ κατὰ φύσιν σ. τροφή Athenag.*res.*6(p.54.24; M.6.985A); †Proc.G.*Procl.*(M.87.2792^h); theol., of names by which are known Persons of Trin., Gr.Naz.*or.*29.13(p.93.1; M.36.92A) cit. s. ἐπίνοια; and natures of Christ ἡνίκα αἱ φύσεις διΐστανται, ταῖς ἐπινοίαις σ. καὶ τὰ ὀνόματα *ib.*30.8(p.120.7; 113B).

συνδιαιτάομαι, *live, dwell together*; **1.** of animals, Thdt.*1 Tim.*6:5(3.669); usu. of persons; of Christ's sojourn upon earth, Cyr.*Joel.*34(3.226B); of *contubernales* or spiritual companions γυναιξὶ...σ. Epiph.*haer.*47.3(p.218.17; M.41.853C); **2.** met., of Christ's humanity with the divinity ζῇ...ἐκ δυνάμεως θεοῦ τῷ θείῳ πνεύματι...σ. ὁ ἄνθρωπος Eust.*fr.in Pr.*8:22(M.18.684A); σ. κυρίως ἡ ψυχὴ τοῦ Χριστοῦ τῷ λόγῳ καὶ θεῷ id.*fr.*(p.91; M.18.689D).

συνδιαιωνίζ-ω, **A.** *remain for ever with*; **1.** all one's life σ. αὐτῷ τὴν βασιλείαν εἰσαεὶ δοκοῦντος †Jo.D.*B.J.*14(M.96.981B); **2.** for all eternity; **a.** of divine gifts, etc., with man, Thdr.Heracl.*Is.*51:6(M.18.1352C); Gr.Naz.*or.*41.13(M.36.448A); σὺ ὦ ψυχή...εἴ σοι μέλει τοῦ σ. σοι τῆς εὐμορφίας τὴν χάριν Gr.Nyss.*hom.2 in Cant.*(M.44.805B); τὰ παρὰ θεοῦ, τοῖς λαβοῦσι ~οντα Cyr.*hom.pasch.*24.4(5^2.295B); **b.** of angels with God, Mac.Mgn.*apocr.*4.18(p.194.20); **c.** of man, *live for ever with* or *amongst* τοῖς δὲ...λογικῆς κρίσεως μεμοιραμένοις τὴν εἰς ἀεὶ διαμονὴν ἀπεκλήρωσεν ὁ ποιήσας, ἵνα...τούτοις σ. ἀπόνως, οἷς τὴν προλαβοῦσαν ἐκράτυναν ζωήν Athenag.*res.*12(p.62.19; M.6.997B); *ib.*25(p.78.31; 1021D); Bas.*inst.ascet.*3(2.201B; M.31.624C); of the soul σ. λοιπὸν...τῇ μακαριότητι, καὶ τῇ ἀναμαρτησίᾳ Nil.*epp.*2.82(M.79.237C); and body δεῖ...τῷ τῆς ψυχῆς ἀτελευτήτῳ σ. τὴν τοῦ σώματος διαμονὴν κατὰ τὴν οἰκείαν φύσιν Athenag.*res.*15(p.67.7; 1005B); cf. ἀνάξιον εἶναί φασι [i.e. Platonists and others] τὸ ὑλικὸν σ. ψυχῇ Max.*schol.e.h.*7.1.2(M.4.176A); **d.** in hell: of man, *remain for ever with* or *in* ἡ αἰσχύνη...ᾗ μέλλουσι σ. οἱ ἁμαρτωλοί Bas.*hom.in Ps.*33(1.147C; M.29.361A); Oecum.*Apoc.*9:6(p.113); of eternal punishment σκώληξ...ὁ τῷ πυρὶ σ. Chrys.*hom.23.3 in Eph.*(11.178D); ~ούσης αὐτοῖς τῆς τιμωρίας †Jo.D.*B.J.*8(M.96.928B); **e.** ref. Mt.13:45f. ἔχει [sc. ὁ Χριστός] τὴν ἐξουσίαν τῶν ζώντων ἐν τῷ ἀγρῷ. ἔχει τὴν δεσποτείαν τῶν νεκρῶν ἐν τῷ θησαυρῷ. ἔχει τὴν πρόσληψιν, ἐν τῷ μαργαρίτῃ ~ουσαν Ephr.2.274A.

B. *be coeternal with* αἱ τρεῖς ὑποστάσεις σ. ἑαυταῖς εἰσι ‡Ath.*symb.*1(M.28.1584A); ~οντος...τῇ ἀληθείᾳ τοῦ κραταιωθέντος ἐφ' ἡμᾶς ἐλέους Hesych.H.*fr.Ps.*116:2(M.93.1336A).

συνδιάκει-μαι, **1.** *be sympathetically affected* σ. ... τῇ γῇ καὶ οἱ κάτοικοι Cyr.*Os.*36(3.66D); **2.** *be drawn to* λέγεις μοι, κατὰ τίνα τρόπον εἰς τὴν ἔρημον ~σαι καὶ ποθεῖς ἐμμένων...οὕτως; Chrysipp.*enc.in Jo.Bapt.*5(p.35.3); *ib.*4(p.34.2).

συνδιακονέω, *join in ministering* or *serving, minister also*; (ref. Rom.15:8) of H. Ghost with Christ, Epiph.*anc.*68(p.82.24; M.43.140B); of manual work, Dor.*doct.*4.10(M.88.1672C).

συνδιάκονος, **ὁ**, **1.** *fellow minister, fellow deacon*; term employed, sts. by bishops, ref. those in other orders of ministry, not necessarily always deacons, Alex.Thess.*ep.Ath.*(p.145.10; M.25.368B); Bas.*ep.*67(3.160C; M.32.428A); *ib.*265.1(409A; M.985A); Epiph.*exp.fid.*25(p.526.8; M.42.832C); οἱ πρεσβύτεροι τὸ παλαιὸν ἐκαλοῦντο...διάκονοι τοῦ Χριστοῦ...ὅθεν καὶ νῦν πολλοὶ συμπρεσβυτέρῳ ἐπίσκοποι γράφουσι καὶ συνδιακόνῳ Chrys.*hom.1.1 in Phil.*(11.195B); **2.** *fellow deacon*, Ephr.2.200C,219F,3.157F); ὁ ἅγιος ἡμῶν σ. Στέφανος *Const.App.*5.8.1; fem.; of apostles' wives who supposedly acted as their deaconesses, ref. 1Cor.9:5 ὡς ἀδελφὰς περιῆγον τὰς γυναῖκας σ. ἐσομένας πρὸς τὰς οἰκουροὺς γυναῖκας Clem.*str.*3.6(p.220.22; M.8.1157A).

συνδιακοσμέω, met., *adorn, honour*, Philost.*h.e.*11.2(M.65.596A).

***συνδιακρατέω**, pass., met., *be bound* by a law, Cyr.*Jo.*4.1(4.337E).

***συνδιακριβόω**, *examine together with care and precision* σ. τοῦ Χριστιανισμοῦ τὴν ἔννοιαν *Symb.Sirm.*1 *anath.*27(p.256.19; M.26.740C).

***συνδιαλάμπω**, *shine through* or *forth together*, Gr.Nyss.*hom.1 in Cant.*(M.44.768D).

***συνδιαλοιδορέω**, *rail equally at*, Max.*opusc.*(M.91.260C).

συνδιαλύω, trans., *dissolve together with* or *at the same time*, Max.*opusc.*(M.91.109C).

συνδιαμένω, *remain* or *endure together, continue to exist with*, of Son ἴδιον...τὸ ἀεὶ εἶναι, καὶ σ. σὺν τῷ πατρί Ath.*Ar.*1.58(M.26.133A).

συνδιανέμω, *assign also* εἰσὶ γὰρ συνδιανενεμημένοι...ἄγγελοι κατὰ ἔθνη Clem.*str.*7.2(p.6.18; M.9.409B).

συνδιανήχ-ομαι, *swim about with*, met. τῆς ψυχῆς τὴν διάθεσιν, ~ομένην ἀστάτως τοῖς ῥέουσιν Max.*qu.Thal.*proem.(M.90.260C).

***συνδιανίστ-ημι**, ***συνδιανιστ-άω**, **1.** *help to raise up, restore* φίλων ψυχὰς ~άναι Chrys.*hom.15.9 in Mt.*(7.201A; v.l. ~ῆσαι Gaume); ὁ...καταπίπτων τῇ ψυχῇ, πολλοὺς ἔχει τοὺς...~ῶντας αὐτὸν ‡Bas.*const.*18.2(2.561B; M.31.1384A); **2.** med., *rise up together with* θυμοῦσθαι λέγεται [sc. τὸν οὐρανόν] καὶ ~ασθαι τῇ ὀργῇ τοῦ θεοῦ †Bas.*Is*.269(1.584B; M.30.592B).

***συνδιανυκτερεύω**, *spend the night with*, Eus.*v.C*.4.57(p.141.7; M.20.1209A); *ib*.tit.(p.117.2; 1208C); σ. αὐταῖς ἐν ταῖς προσευχαῖς Bas.*ep*.223.5(3.340A; M.32.829A); οὐδὲ ὀφείλει...σ. ταῖς γυναιξί Nil.*epp*.3.150(M.79.453A).

συνδιαπίπτω, *perish together* with, Gr.Nyss.*Apoll*.51(M.45.1248B).

συνδιαπλέκ-ω, pass. intrans., *blend with* ἑνοῦσθαι [sc. τροφήν] τῷ τρεφομένῳ σώματι ~ομένην τε καὶ περιπλαττομένην πᾶσι τοῖς τούτου μέρεσιν Athenag.*res*.6(p.54.11; συμπλεκομένην M.6.984D).

***συνδιαπληκτίζομαι**, *spar, wrangle with* σ. τοῖς ἀγνωμονοῦσιν Bas.*reg.fus*.9.2(2.351D; M.31.941C).

***συνδιαπορεύ-ομαι**, *accompany on one's journey*, pass. σταυρὲ... ὁ ἐν τῇ δευτέρᾳ...αὐτοῦ ἐλεύσει μέλλων ~θῆναι ταῖς οὐρανίαις δυνάμεσι Sophr.H.*or*.5(M.87.3313D).

συνδιαπορέω, **1.** *start by doubting together* σ. αὐτοῖς περὶ ὧν δοξάζουσιν Athenag.*res*.19(p.71.27; M.6.1012C); **2.** *start an inquiry together*, *Hom.Clem*.2.50.

συνδιαρρήγνυμι** (συνδιαρρήσσω**), **1.** *join in breaking*, fig. τὰ δεσμὰ τῆς ὑλικῆς προσπαθείας τῶν ψυχῶν, ἀνδρικῶς τῷ λόγῳ συνδιαρρήσσων Max.*ambig*.(M.91.1384C); **2.** pass., *be broken, shattered, torn in pieces also*, met. παντοδαποῖς ἕλκεσι τὴν γαστέρα σπασθείς, συνδιερράγη καὶ τὴν ψυχήν Philost.*h.e*.7.10(M.65.548C).

συνδιασείω, met., *shake, disturb together*, Gr.Nyss.*virg*.14(p.311.2; M.46.384A).

συνδιασκέπτομαι, *investigate together*, Athenag.*res*.19(p.71.28; M.6.1012C); Gr.Naz.*carm*.1.2.28.297(M.37.878A).

[*]**συνδιασμός, ὁ**, v. συνδυασμός.

συνδιαστέλλω, pass. intrans., *expand with* ὁ θεός, μήτε...σ. ταῖς τῶν ὄντων οἷς ἔνεστιν ὡς ὧν ἀπείροις διαφοραῖς, μήτε...συστελλόμενος κατὰ τὴν τοῦ ἑνὸς ἰδιάζουσαν ὕπαρξιν Max.*ambig*.(M.91.1257B).

***συνδιαστρεβλόομαι**, *be contorted, distorted also*, Gr.Nyss.*Eun*.8(2 p.194.16; M.45.789B).

***συνδιασχηματίζω**, *mould, shape together*, Gr.Nyss.*hom.opif*.8.8(M.44.149A).

***συνδιασχίζ-ω**, *split up, divide also* or *at the same time* οὐ τὸ ὑποκείμενον ταῖς ἐννοίαις ταύταις ~οντες Gr.Nyss.*Eun*.12(1 p.349.19; M.45.1069C); *ib*.7(2 p.170.3; 760D); ἡ ψυχὴ τῇ διακρίσει τῶν στοιχείων συνδιασχισθῆναι τὴν φύσιν οὐκ ἔχουσα id.*anim.et res*.(M.46.45B,48A); οὐ μὴν ~εται τῷ χωρισμῷ τούτων [i.e. soul and body at Christ's death] ὁ ἁπλοῦς καὶ ἀσύνθετος, ἀλλὰ...ἓν ἐργάζεται id.*Apoll*.17(M.45.1156B); συντέμνει [sc. like the Arians, so Apollinarius] τῇ φύσει τὴν βούλησιν...τῷ ὑποβεβηκότι πρὸς τὸ προέχον σ. τὸν τῆς θεότητος λόγον *ib*.31(1192C).

συνδιασῴζω, **1.** *join in saving, help to save* προνοήσατε τῆς ἑαυτῶν ψυχῆς, καὶ ἀλλήλους σ. Chrys.*hom.4.2 in Ac*.9:1(3.131D); **2.** *save as well* or *at the same time* ὥστε...δεῖν...ἀκοινώνητον ταύτῃ [sc. τῇ προσηγορίᾳ] σ. καὶ τὴν οὐσίαν Eun.*apol*.9(M.30.844C); from loss at sea, Mac.Aeg.*pat*.26(M.34.888A); of salvation effected by Christ ἵνα διὰ τῆς ἀναληφθείσης παρ' αὐτοῦ...σαρκὸς ἅπαν συνδιασωθῇ τὸ συγγενὲς αὐτῇ Gr.Nyss.*or.catech*.35(p.130.5; M.45.88A).

συνδιαταλαιπωρέω, med., *endure hardship with* or *together*, Chrys.*Stag*.1.1(1.154).

***συνδιατέμν-ω**, *cut in two also, divide at the same time*, Gr.Nyss.*anim.et res*.(M.46.48B); οὐδὲ τὸ ἀΐδιον τῆς θείας ζωῆς διπλοῖς ὀνόμασι ...γνωριζόμενον...τῇ διαφορᾷ τῶν ὀνομάτων ~εται id.*Eun*.12(1 p.350.1; M.45.1069D); ἡ ψυχὴ...μὴ ~ομένη ἢ συναποκλειομένη αὐτῷ [sc. τῷ σώματι] Max.*ambig*.(M.91.1100A); τὸν κατὰ σάρκα ἡμῖν ἐπιφανέντα ...θεὸν...ἑαυτὸν ἐπιμερίζοντα καὶ τοῖς μετέχουσιν οὐδ' ὁπωσοῦν ~όμενον *ib*.(1172C).

συνδιατίθ-ημι, **1.** *arrange according to* μὴ γὰρ ὅτι προεπινοεῖται τοῦ υἱοῦ ὁ πατὴρ...διὰ τοῦτο καὶ τὴν τῶν ὀνομάτων τάξιν ἀξιούτω τις τῇ τῶν ὑποκειμένων αὐτοῖς προσώπων ἀξίᾳ καὶ τάξει ~εσθαι Gr.Nyss.*Eun*.1(1 p.203.21; M.45.452A); **2.** pass., *be disposed* or *prone to* μετασχεῖν ὁμολογοῦμεν κύριον γεννήσεως κτλ. ... καὶ ὅσα πρὸς τὰς σωματικὰς ἀχθηδόνας ἡ ψυχὴ...~εσθαι πέφυκε Gr.Nyss.*Eun*.6(2 p.137.24; M.45.721D); **3.** pass., *experience, undergo* τότε, βαπτισθέντα εἰς τὸν θάνατον τοῦ κυρίου, συνδιατεθῆναι τῷ θανάτῳ, ὅπερ ἐστὶ νεκρωθῆναι τῇ ἁμαρτίᾳ †Bas.*bapt*.1.2.10(2.636D; M.31.1541D).

***συνδιατμήγω**, *cut in two*; met., *sever*, Thphn.*chron*.p.284(M.108.697C).

***συνδιατρέχ-ω**, *run through, range*, of angels οἱ ~οντες τὰ ἐπουράνια καὶ τὰ ἐπίγεια *Ev.Barth*.(Vassiliev p.19); hence *reach* or *penetrate* to, met. τὸ...φῶς...τῷ πέρατι τῶν ἀτοπημάτων σ. ‡Bas.*const*.5(2.547D; M.31.1353B).

συνδιατριβή, ἡ, *spending time with, association* τεχνίτης ἐκ τῆς ἐκ πολλοῦ τοῖς λόγοις σ. Gr.Thaum.*pan.Or*.14(p.33.7; M.10.1093A); τὴν μετὰ τῶν θνητῶν σ. τοῦ θανάτου ‡Eust.*Laz*.21(p.44.3); *association one with another* ἐν προσώπων ἐνδόξων σ. καὶ συνεστιάσεσι *ib*.2(p.27.9); συγγενικῶν σ. Diad.*perf*.55(p.60.22); of Christ with men τῆς μετὰ τῶν ἀποστόλων αὐτοῦ σ. Eus.*d.e*.8.2(p.387.23; M.22.625C); Apoll.*fr*.114(p.234.26)ap.Leont.B.*Apoll*.(M.86.1964C); τῆς...αὐτοῖς σ. καὶ διδασκαλίας Epiph.*haer*.30.32(p.377.25; M.41.464A).

συνδιατρίβω, **1.** *pass* or *spend* time *with* or *together*, ref. Jo.1:39 τὴν ἡμέραν ἐκείνην συνδιατρίψαι τῷ υἱῷ τοῦ θεοῦ Or.*Jo*.2.36(29; p.95.14; M.14.180C); **2.** intrans., *live constantly with*, esp. of disciples with their master; of Christ σ. τοῖς μαθηταῖς Or.*Jo*.13.64(60; p.297.22; M.14.524A); Eus.*d.e*.10.8(p.490.32; M.22.788C); mystically τοῦ θεωρήσαντος τὸν θεὸν καὶ ὁμιλήσαντος αὐτῷ καὶ σ. τοιαύτῃ θέᾳ Or.*Jo*.32.27(17; p.472.32; 817A); Trin. υἱὸν θεοῦ καὶ Χριστόν...συνόντα καὶ σ. πρὸ αἰώνων τῷ...πατρί *Symb.Ant*.(345)6(p.253.6; M.26.732B).

***συνδιατριπτέον**, *one must associate* with, τίσι σ. Clem.*paed*.3.4 tit.(p.251.15; M.8.592B).

συνδιαφεύγω, *escape* one thing *as well as* another, Cyr.*ador*.5(1.160A); *ib*.6(195C).

συνδιαχέω, pass., *be dissolved into* δοκεῖν μὲν συνδιακέχυται, κατ' ἀλήθειαν δ' εὑρήσεις ἕτερον μὲν τὸν ἀέρα, ἄλλο δὲ τὴν ὀδωδήν ‡Gr.Nyss.*Ar.et Sab*.12(M.45.1297D).

***συνδιαχωρίζ-ω**, *separate likewise* or *at the same time* τῇ τῶν φύσεων διαφορᾷ ~ονται ἀπ' ἀλλήλων καὶ αἱ παρὰ τούτων ἐνέργειαι Gr.Nyss.*Trin*.6(p.78.4; M.32.693A); id.*Eun*.4(2 p.95.18; M.45.672C).

***συνδιαψελλίζομαι**, *talk inarticulately, talk baby language with* μήτηρ εὔσπλαγχνος τοῖς ἀσήμοις τῶν νηπίων κνυζήμασι σ. Gr.Nyss.*Eun*.12(1 p.333.20; M.45.1049D).

***συνδιδασκαλίτης, ὁ**, *one who teaches together* with others ἀρχὴν ἔχω τοῦ μαθητεύεσθαι καὶ προσλαλῶ ὑμῖν ὡς σ. μου Ign.*Eph*.3.1.

***συνδιδάσκαλος, ὁ**, *fellow teacher* παρακαλοῦμεν ὡς ἀδελφοὺς καὶ σ. Cyr.*ep*.67(p.39.18; 5[2].196C).

συνδιδάσκω, *teach concurrently* (i.e. one thing simultaneously with another) πατέρα...μαθόντες, τῇ αὐτῇ φωνῇ καὶ τὴν εἰς τὸν υἱὸν πίστιν συνεδιδάχθημεν Gr.Nyss.*Eun*.2(2 p.299.7; M.45.469B).

συνδιεγείρω, *raise together*, Chrys.*fr.in Pr*.12:10(M.64.962C).

συνδιέξειμι, (*ibo*) **1.** *go through together* συνεῖναί [sc. ἀπορίαν] σοι διαπαντός, καὶ σ. τὴν παροῦσαν ζωήν ‡Proc.G.*Pr*.6:11(M.87.1272D); met., *unite to pervade* τὸ πᾶν περιέχων...τῆς μεγάλης δυνάμεως τῷ ἀγαθῷ θελήματι συνδιεξιούσης Gr.Nyss.*ep*.4(M.46.1028A); **2.** *go out in company with*; met., *issue forth with and pervade* τὴν συνδιεξιοῦσαν ταῖς ἀνθρωπίναις γενεαῖς...κακίαν id.*laud.Bas*.(M.46.792B).

συνδιεξέρχομαι, **1.** *come out with* τὸ τοῖς ῥήμασι σ. πνεῦμα Gr.Nyss.*or.catech*.4(p.19.7; M.45.20C); **2.** met., *go through, pervade* ἡ ἀρχὴ τοῦ θανάτου ἐν ἑνὶ γενομένη πάσῃ σ. τῇ ἀνθρωπίνῃ φύσει *ib*.16(p.71.11; 52C); τῇ πρώτῃ...τῶν πρωτοπλάστων φωνῇ συνεβλάστησε καὶ τῇ διαδοχῇ τῶν ἐπιγινομένων σ. id.*Eun*.2(1 p.369.33; M.45.1096A).

συνδιέπω, *manage together, share* an office or responsibility *with* σοι σ. τὴν ἱερωσύνην ὁ...θεός Gr.Naz.*ep*.91(M.37.165B).

συνδιΐστημι, **1.** *change* one thing *with* another συνδιέστησας...τῷ τόπῳ τὴν γνώμην Synes.*ep*.138(M.66.1528C); **2.** pass., *differ also* or *at the same time* εἰ...διέστηκε...ἐν τῷ λόγῳ τῆς φύσεως πρὸς τὴν γεννητὴν ἡ ἀγέννητος συνδιαστήσεται πάντως καὶ τοῦ ἀγεννήτου τὸ ἴδιον ἀπὸ τοῦ κατὰ τὸ γεννητὸν ἰδιάζοντος Gr.Nyss.*Eun*.1(p.168.13; M.45.412A).

συνδικαζω, **1.** *have a share in judging*; pass., *be judged along with*, Meth.*fr.1 in Job* (p.511.5); **2.** *pass the same judgement, confirm* ὅσον σοφοὶ νοοῦσιν, ὅσον φύσις παιδεύει, καὶ πεῖρα σ. ‡Paul.Sil.*therm.Pyth*.11(M.86.2263).

συνδικαστής, ὁ, **1.** *fellow judge*, ref. Mt.19:28 οὗτοι [sc. οἱ ἀπόστολοι]...σ. καὶ σύνθρονοι κατηξιώθησαν γενέσθαι Mac.Aeg.*hom*.28.6(M.34.713C); εἴ τις ἐν δίκῃ ὑποπτεύων [sc. ἐστί] τὸν ἄρχοντα, σ. λαμβανέτω τὸν ἐπίσκοπον Ath.Scholast.*coll*.(p.15); **2.** *assessor* τῶν δικαστῶν ἢ σ. Justn.*cod*.1.15.2(p.69).

συνδιογκόομαι, *swell* or *rise high*; of waves, Gr.Nyss.*hom.11 in Cant*.(M.44.996B).

συνδιοικέω, *join in administering*; abs., *share the government* with, of Son with Father σ. τῷ γεννήσαντι Bas.Sel.*or*.24(M.85.285A).

***συνδιοικονομέω**, *share in regulating, help to manage* πᾶσαν αὐτῇ [sc. her mother] σ. τὴν ἐπικειμένην φροντίδα Gr.Nyss.*v.Macr*.(p.376.17; M.46.965A).

***συνδιολισθάνω**, *slip away with*, c. dat., Didym.*Trin*.1.15(M.39.308B).

***συνδιομολογέομαι**, pass., *be agreed, conceded as well*, Max.*ep*.6(M.91.428B).

***συνδιορθρίζω,** *rise early with*, Bas.*hex*.8.7(1.77E; M.29.181B).

συνδιπλόω, *multiply by two*, *double*; hence pass., *be bent double*, *be turned back on itself* κατὰ μικρὸν συνεδιπλοῦτο ὄπισθεν αὐτοῦ καὶ ἡ νεφέλη, μέχρις οὗ ἔνδον ἐχώρησε τῶν οὐρανίων †Gregent.*disp*.(M.86.777C).

***συνδιυλίζω,** *filter*, *refine together*, Clem.*exc.Thdot*.41(p.119.21; M.9.677C).

συνδιψάω, *feel thirst along with* or *like*, of Christ συμπεινῶν ἡμῖν καὶ σ. Or.*sel.in Ezech*.4:9(M.13.781A).

***συνδιωκομένως,** *hastily* οὐδὲ τροχαλῶς καὶ σ. ὁμιλητέον Clem.*paed*.2.7(p.192.21; M.8.461C).

[*]συνδοιάζω, v. συνδυάζω.

[*]συνδοιασμός, ὁ, v. συνδυασμός.

συνδοκτικός, *agreed*, *approved*, Anast.S.*hod*.10(M.89.149C).

***συνδολιχεύω,** *last as long as* τῷ παντὶ αἰῶνι σ. Jo.D.*hom*.12.21 (M.96.809D).

συνδοξάζ-ω, *glorify together*; **1.** in gen. ἵνα συνδοξάσῃ τὴν κατὰ θεὸν αὐτοῖς γενομένην εὐδίαν Ign.*Smyrn*.11.3; τὸ μὲν τῆς τρισμακαρίας ψυχῆς σκῆνος [sc. of Const.] τῷ τῶν ἀποστόλων προσρήματι ~όμενον Eus.*v.C*.4.71(p.147.13; M.20.1225B); οἱ γὰρ νυνὶ συμπάσχοντες, συνέσονταί τε διαπαντὸς καὶ συνδοξασθήσονται καὶ συμβασιλεύσουσι Cyr.*Mich*.40(3.429A); **2.** theol.; **a.** Trin., of Son in rel. to Father and H. Ghost ἡ εἰς τὸν ἀεὶ ~όμενον τῷ πατρὶ καὶ τῷ ἁγίῳ πνεύματι... πίστις ‡Eust.*Laz*.5(p.30.5); Just.Imp.*edict*.(p.200.17; M.86.2796C); to H. Ghost οὐ γὰρ ὁμοδούλου δημιουργός, ἀλλ' ὁμοτίμῳ ~όμενος Gr.Naz.*or*.31.12(p.160.19; M.36.148A); ὁ Δαβὶδ λόγον καὶ πνεῦμα ~ων Didym.(‡Bas.)*Eun*.5(1.307D; M.29.737B); ref. implications of Arianism τό ποτε μὴ ὂν τῷ ἀεὶ ὄντι συνθεολογεῖται καὶ ~εται Ath.*Ar*.1.17(M.26.48B); of H. Ghost in rel. to Father and Son, id.*ep.Jov*.4 (M.26.820A); Bas.*Spir*.58(3.49A; M.32.173C); Didym.*Trin*.2.1(M.39.452B); id.(‡Bas.)*Eun*.5(306A; M.733B); Epiph.*haer*.76.9(p.350.5; M.42.532B); Thdot.Anc.*exp.symb*.24(M.77.1348C); Jo.D.*f.o*.1.8(M.94.821B); in credal statement τὸ πνεῦμα τὸ...σὺν πατρὶ καὶ υἱῷ συμπροσκυνούμενον καὶ ~όμενον *Symb*.ap.Epiph.*anc*.118(p.147.13; M.43.232D); *Symb.Nic.–CP*(p.80.14; H.2.288B); **b.** Christol., of Christ's humanity ἔπρεπε δὲ τὸν μηδέποτε κεχωρισμένον τοῦ μονογενοῦς συγχρηματίσαι τῷ μονογενεῖ καὶ συνδοξασθῆναι αὐτῷ Or.*princ*.2.6.4 (p.143.23; M.11.212C); πιστεύομεν ὅτι τῷ λόγῳ τοῦ θεοῦ συμπροσκυνεῖται καὶ συνθεολογεῖται καὶ ~εται ἡ τοῦ κυρίου σάρξ Val.Apoll.*apol*.2(p.288.4)ap.Leont.B.*Apoll*.(M.86.1953B); πῶς οὖν συνδοξασθήσεται ὁ τῆς παρθένου υἱὸς τῷ θεῷ, εἰ ἄλλης φύσεως καὶ ἄλλης ὑποστάσεως; Jo.D.*fid.Nest*.45(p.578); use condemned by Cyr. as denoting division of Person, *ep*.27(p.41.13; 5^2.76E); ἵνα μηκέτι Χριστὸς εἷς ὁμολογῆται καὶ υἱός...ἀλλ' ὡς ἄνθρωπος ἰδικῶς καὶ κατὰ μόνας νοούμενος, μόνῃ συναφείᾳ τῇ κατὰ τὴν ἑνότητα τῆς ἀξίας τετιμημένος συμπροσκυνῆται καὶ σ. id.*expl.xii cap*.5(p.21.4; 6^1.152A); **c.** ref. angels οὐδὲ ~ομεν ἀγγέλους θεῷ Didym.(‡Bas.) *Eun*.5(1.304D; M.29.729C).

***συνδοξολογ-έω, 1.** *join in glorifying* ἡ [sc. κεφαλὴ] τῶν χερουβὶμ ἰσότιμος, ἡ τῶν σεραφὶμ ~οῦσα τὴν ἁγίαν τριάδα Chrysipp.*enc.in Jo.Bapt*.15(p.47.13); *Lit.Bas*.(p.312.23); **2.** *glorify likewise* or *together* with δοξολογίας...τοῦ θεοῦ διὰ Χριστοῦ ~ουμένου ἐν τῷ ἁγίῳ πνεύματι συνυμνουμένῳ Or.*or*.33(p.401.15; M.11.557B); ~οῦμεν...τῷ πατρὶ τὸν υἱόν Cyr.*glaph.Gen*.3(1.104D); Jo.D.*trisag*.10(M.95.44A).

σύνδορπος, ὁ, *companion at table* Χριστὸς...κλητὸς ἔην σ. Nonn.*par.Jo*.2:2(M.43.760C); of Judas ἀνὴρ...ἡμετέρῃ σύνδορπος ἐπεσκίρτησε τραπέζῃ *ib*.13:18(864A).

***συνδοτήρ,** ὁ, *fellow giver*, *partner in bestowing* τὰ ἡτοιμασμένα παρὰ τοῦ θεοῦ ἀγαθὰ εἶπεν, ὅτι τὸ πνεῦμα ἀπεκάλυψεν ὡς σ. Didym.*Trin*.2.2(M.39.457A); of Christ ἅπασιν ἁγιασμοῦ χορηγὸς καὶ σ., ὡς θεός Cyr.*ador*.10(1.352C); id.*Nest*.3.4(p.70.12; 6^1.87A).

σύνδουλος, ὁ, and adj., *(who is) a fellow slave*, *slave of the same master*; used by a bishop in addressing deacons, cf.Col.1:7; 4:7 διὰ ...τοῦ ἀξιοθέου ὑμῶν ἐπισκόπου καὶ πρεσβυτέρων ἀξίων...καὶ τοῦ σ. που διακόνου Ign.*Magn*.2.1; ἀσπάζομαι τὸν ἀξιόθεον ἐπίσκοπον καὶ θεοπρεπὲς πρεσβυτέριον, [καὶ] τοὺς σ. μου διακόνους id.*Smyrn*.12.2; id.*Philad*.4.1; id.*Eph*.2.1; elsewhere between Christians in gen., not limited to deacons ἀδελφοὶ καὶ σ. *Clem.contest*.5(M.2.32B); *Clem.ep*.17(M.2.53A); *Const.App*.5.10.1; of Devil as subject to God like other creatures ὁ εὐεργέτης οὐκ ἐπιστεύθη, ὁ δὲ σ. προεπιστεύθη [i.e. in paradise] ‡Ath.*diab*.5(p.6.39).

***συνδραματουργ-έω,** *play a part in the villainy* or *wickedness of* μεταπεμφθῆναι Ἰωάννην καὶ τοὺς ~ήσαντας αὐτῷ Cyr.*libell*.(p.17.6; H.1.1488C).

συνδρομή, ἡ, **1.** of persons; **a.** Gnost., *concourse* of powers γίνεται τῶν δυνάμεων ἡ σ. οἱονεί τις τύπος σφραγῖδος κατὰ συνδρομὴν ἀπὸ πληγῆς, παραπλησίως πρὸς τὸν ἐκτυποῦντα τὰς ἀναφερομένας οὐσίας Hipp.*haer*.5.19(p.118.5f.; M.16.3182A); γέγονεν...ἐκ πρώτης τῶν τριῶν ἀρχῶν σ. μεγάλης μεγάλη τις ἰδέα σφραγῖδος, οὐρανοῦ καὶ γῆς *ib*.(p.118.11; 3182B); **b.** *association*, *coming together* τῶν ἀνομοίων τὴν σ. οὐκ οἶδε τιμᾶν Cyr.*hom.pasch*.17.2(5^2.225D); **c.** *intermingling*, in sexual intercourse πορνείαν...οὐ μόνον οἶδεν ἡ γραφὴ τὴν πρὸς τὸ θῆλυ τοῦ ἄρρενος ἀσελγῆ σ., ἀλλὰ καὶ πᾶσαν ἀπὸ τοῦ ἀγαθοῦ ἔκκλισιν Areth.*Apoc*.14:8(M.106.688B); **d.** *onslaught*, *attack* τῇ καθ' ἡμῶν...σ. Cyr.*Ps*.41:8(M.69.1008B); met. τῇ τῶν πειρασμῶν σ. Chrys.*hom.18.6 in Rom*.(9.639A); **2.** of things; **a.** *collection*, *combination* μῖξις τῶν ἐναντίων καὶ σ. Gr.Nyss.*or.catech*.1(p.10.9; M.45.16A); σ. πανταχόθεν ἀστέρων...ἐγίνετο Philost.*h.e*.10.9(M.65.589B); of man τὸ σῶμά ἐστιν ...σ. τῶν στοιχείων Gr.Nyss.*anim.et res*.(M.46.24B); *ib*.(48A,B); id.*or.catech*.16(p.68.4; M.45.49C); *ib*.(p.69.16; 52A); ἡ...σ. τούτων τῶν δύο [sc. ψυχῆς νοερᾶς καὶ σώματος] ἄνθρωπος καὶ ἔστι, καὶ λέγεται id.*Apoll*.2(M.45.1128B); **b.** *concurrence*, *combination*, of circumstances or events σύμβολον τίθεμαι τῆς...περὶ ἐμὲ προνοίας, τὴν σ. ταύτην οὕτως τοῖς ἔτεσι διηριθμημένην Gr.Thaum.*pan.Or*.5(p.11.11; M.10.1064C); Cyr.*ador*.6(1.211C); of qualities, etc. ἀκούσαντες Παῦλον, ἑτέρων ἰδιωμάτων σ. ἐνοήσαμεν Bas.*Eun*.2.4(1.240E; M.29.580A); εἶδεν τοσούτων ἀγαθῶν σ. περὶ μίαν ψυχήν Gr.Nyss.*Melet*.(M.46.857C); τῆς πνευματικῆς λατρείας ἡ δύναμις...σ. ... δέχεσθαι φιλεῖ καὶ τὴν ἐξ ἔργων ἀγαθῶν εὐοσμίαν Cyr.*Ps*.50:19(M.69.1101C); **c.** theol., ref. Trin. ὑπόστασιν εἶναι τὴν σ. τῶν περὶ ἕκαστον ἰδιωμάτων Gr.Nyss.*diff.ess*.6 (M.32.336C); **3.** *concurrence*, *agreement* τῶν παρ' Ἕλλησιν εὐδοκίμων φιλοσόφων πρὸς τὰς Ἑβραίων δόξας σ. Eus.*p.e*.15.1(789B; M.21.1293D); πίστις δὲ διττή· ἡ μὲν ἐκ λόγου βίας...ἡ δ' ἕτοιμος σ. Gr.Naz.*carm*.1.2.34.156(M.37.956A); Cyr.*Os*.72(3.107D); *compliance*, *concession* ἐπλημμέλησε [sc. ἡ ψυχή] ποτὲ μὲν...ἄλλοτε δὲ κατὰ συνδρομὴν ἐν χάριτος μέρει καὶ θεραπείας τῆς τούτου [sc. τοῦ σώματος] συστάσεως Athenag.*res*.21(p.74.5; M.6.1016A); of the will, Gr.Naz.*carm*.1.2.34.35(948A) cit. s. βούλησις; as bet. Persons of Trin. μόνη...θέλησις θεία καὶ πατρική, δι' υἱοῦ μονογενοῦς αὐτουργοῦντος τὴν οἰκείαν σάρκωσιν, καὶ πνεύματος ἁγίου συνδρομῇ, ταύτην εἰργάσατο Max.*opusc*.(M.91.237D); **4.** *support*, *assistance* ἐκβληθῆναι μὲν κελεύει τῶν βασιλείων τὸν Ἀέτιον· ὕστερον δέ, τῇ σ. Ἀκακίου, καὶ καθαιρέσεως ὑποβληθῆναι ψήφοις...καὶ πάλιν ἐνταῦθα συνδρομῇ τοῦ Ἀκακίου...ὑπογράφουσι πάντες Philost.*h.e*.4.12(M.65.528A,B); ταῖς ἐξ ἀνθρώπων σ. ἐπικουρούμενοι Cyr.*Nah*.31(3.508E); Jo.Mosch.*prat*.43(M.87.2897C); Gr.Mag.*dial*.(tr.Zach.)1.4(M.*PL*.77.167B); *ib*.2.1(M.*PL*.66.129A); ἐκαλησυργήθη τὸ ἔργον τοῦτο διὰ συνδρομῆς Λέοντος προτοπρ[εσβ]υτέρου *CIG* 4.8837 (? post 800); *ib*.8839; or poss. sub 3, *concession*, *permission*; **5.** *effort*, *zeal*, ref. Eus. Nic. μεθ' ὅσης νομίζεται σ. ἅτε δὴ ὑπὸ τῆς συνειδήσεως αὐτῆς ἡττώμενος, μεθ' ὅσης δὲ αἰσχύνης τῇ πανταχόθεν ἐληλεγμένῃ ψευδολογίᾳ συνίστατο Const.ap.Thdt.*h.e*.1.20.6(3.799); βρῶσιν αὐτοῦ τὴν ἡμετέραν καλεῖ πρὸς ὃ βούλεται συνδρομήν Hadr.*introd*.22(p.80; M.98.1280A); **6.** Christol., *union* of natures in Christ σ. οὐσιώδης stigmatized as Apollinarian συνδρομὴν οὐσιώδη καὶ μῖξιν θεσπεσίαν...θεότητός τε καὶ σαρκός, μίαν τε ἐντεῦθεν ἀποτελεσθῆναι φύσιν...τοῦτο...τοῦ...Ἀπολιναρίου τὸ ἀτόπημα ‡Chrys.*ep.Caes*.(3.743A); but standing alone σ. was adopted into orthodox vocabulary as synonym of ἕνωσις or as denoting its mode δύο... φύσεων τελείων σ., θεότητος φημὶ καὶ ἀνθρωπότητος, τὸν ἕνα ἡμῖν ἀπετέλεσεν υἱόν, τὸν ἕνα Χριστόν, τὸν ἕνα κύριον Paul.Em.*hom*.1(p.10.20; M.77.1436B); Cyr.*ep*.4.3(p.27.5; 5^2.23C) cit. s. ἀνθρωπότης; *ib*.45 (p.153.21; 5^2.137D); σύνοδον μέν τινα καὶ τὴν...σ. εἰς ἕνωσιν...ἀνομοίων πεπρᾶχθαι φύσεων id.*inc.unigen*.(5^1.688D); id.*Jo*.4.2(4.361B); πρὸ σ. τῆς εἰς σάρκα *ib*.4.3(375E); Leont.B.*Nest.et Eut*.1(M.86.1293B) cit. s. ἀνακεφαλαιόω; Leont.H.*Nest*.5.5(M.86.1729B); Sophr.H.*or*.2.42(M.87.3273B); *ib*.2.48(3284B); Anast.S.*hod*.2(M.89.69C) ∞ ‡Ath.*def*.5(M.28.544D) cit. s. ἕνωσις; ‡Gr.Nyss.*hom.3.30 in Jo*.(p.143.27); *ib.7.154* (p.279.19); *cat.Heb*.1:7(p.322.4); *union* of wills ἡ τῶν ἐνεργειῶν σ. τὸ ἑνιαῖον εἰσφέρει ταύταις, οὐ κατὰ φύσιν, ἀλλὰ καθ' ἕνωσιν ‡Cyr.*Trin*.19 (6^3.25B; M.77.1157D); **7.** of indwelling of the H. Ghost συντρέχειν... δεῖ τῇ κατ' ἀρχὴν καινότητι τὴν νῦν ἀνακαίνωσιν καὶ τὴν σ. Didym.(‡Bas.)*Eun*.5(1.303E; M.29.729A).

σύνδρομος, A. *running together*, i.e. *meeting*; in time, *coincident* ἡ...παροῦσα ζωή, σκηνή ἐστιν εὐτελής, σ. ἔχουσα τῇ συμπήξει καὶ τὴν κατάλυσιν Isid.Pel.*epp*.1.65(M.78.225B); σύγχρονον ἔχοντα [sc. Christ's body and soul] τῇ ὑπάρξει τὴν ἕνωσιν...σ. ἔχοντα τῇ φυσικῇ τοῦ λόγου συμβάσει τὴν ὕπαρξιν Sophr.H.*ep.syn*.(M.87.3161B).

B. *running alongside*; **1.** as subst., *fellow runner* ὁ ταχυδρόμος καὶ ὁ σ. αὐτοῦ *Ep.Abg*.5(p.282.21); *ib*.7(p.283.6); Jo.Eleem.*v.Tych*.(p.123); *companion* τὸν βαπτιστήν...τὸν τῶν ἀγγέλων σ. Chrysipp.*enc.in Jo.Bapt*.3(p.33.13); **2.** *accompanying* Χριστῷ σ. ἦλθεν ἔσω...αὐλῆς Nonn.*par.Jo*.18:15(M.43.892B); fig. ὃς...διαστείχει...σ. ὄρφνῃ *ib*.

11:10(840C); abs. σ. ἄλλον ἔχων κορυνηφόρον ἐσμὸν ὁδίτην *ib.*18:3 (889A); met. σ. ... ἔχω παλιναυξέα τιμήν *ib.*17:10(885A); **3.** in time, *concurrent, contemporaneous* μήτε μὴν παντὶ τοῦ βίου μήκει σ. ἔχοιμι τὴν πληγήν Cyr.*Ps.*38:6(M.69.976A); τοὺς σύνδρομον τῇ ζωῇ τὸν δι' ἀπιστίας ὑπομένοντας θάνατον Andr.Caes.*Apoc.*33(M.106.321A); ref. generation of Son ἐνταῦθα...σ. τῷ εἶναι τὸ γεγεννῆσθαι Gr.Naz.*or.*29. 9(p.85.6; M.36.85A); of God in rel. to mankind σ. πάντα θεῷ...ὢν γὰρ θεός, γίνεται ἄνθρωπος, οὐκ ἐκστὰς τοῦ εἶναι θεός †Chrys.*nativ.*2(6. 392B); **4.** mentally; **a.** *agreeing, in agreement with* σ. ... ἀλλήλοις εἰσὶ περὶ τὴν τῶν θείων δογμάτων ἐξήγησιν Cyr.*Jo.*1(4.8B); σ. ἔχω σε τοῦ μίσους μου Areth.*Apoc.*2:6(M.106.529B); **b.** in bad sense, *consenting* ταῖς τῶν Ἰουδαίων ἀπονοίαις σ. ἦν ὁ Πιλᾶτος Cyr.*Is.*5.1(2. 746E); as subst., *aider and abettor* ἄλλων...δημευθέντων ὡς σ. Ὑπατίου Thphn.*chron.*p.158(M.108.428A); **5.** *corresponding; commensurate; befitting; appropriate*; **a.** of things πότερον ἀπᾴδει τῆς οὐσίας ἢ σ. ἐστι κατὰ τὴν ἔννοιαν; Gr.Nyss.*Eun.*1(1 p.207.21; M.45. 456A); τότε σ. τῇ κατὰ σάρκα γεννήσει δέχεται τὴν κλῆσιν [sc. τοῦ Χριστοῦ] Cyr.*Is.*4.4(2.656E); id.*Os.*111(3.143B); abs. ἡ ψυχὴ...τῆς αἰωνίου σωτηρίας σὺν πᾶσι τοῖς ἁγίοις καταξιοῦται ἅτε δὴ κοινωνὸς καὶ σ. κατὰ μίμησιν αὐτῶν...διαστραφεῖσα Mac.Aeg.*hom.*4.27(M.34.494C); λέγε Χριστὸν παθόντα, καὶ σ. εὑρήσεις τὸ ὄνομα τῆς σαρκός Euther. *confut.*10(M.28.1368A); χρὴ...ἑνὸς ὄντα ποιήματα τοῦ φιλαρέτου θεοῦ, σ. ἔχειν τὴν ἀποκάθαρσιν Cyr.*Lc.*11:39(M.72.713A); **b.** theol., of various divine attributes, exeg. Jo.14:9 τὸ ἀγαθὸν τοῦ θελήματος, ὅπερ σ. ὂν τῇ οὐσίᾳ ὅμοιον καὶ ἴσον, μᾶλλον δὲ ταὐτὸν ἐν πατρὶ καὶ υἱῷ θεωρεῖται Bas.*Spir.*21(3.18B; M.32.105B); ὁ...υἱὸς σ. ἔχει τῇ γεννήσει τὴν τελειότητα Thdt.*Heb.*7:28(3.593); σ. ἔχει θεὸς τῇ φύσει τὴν θέλησιν ‡Just.*fr.*ap.Max.*opusc.*(M.91.280B); esp. of God's power in rel. to his will ἡ βούλησις, σ. ἔχουσα τὴν δύναμιν, ὑπεστήσατο ὅσα ἠθέλησεν ‡Ath.*dial.Trin.*1.8(M.28.1129A); *ib.*1.4(1121C); ἐπὶ τῆς θείας φύσεως σ. ἐστι τῇ βουλήσει ἡ δύναμις Gr.Nyss.*hex.*7(M.44.69A); id.*or.catech.*8(p.50.24; M.45.40A); Thdt.*Ps.*88:9(1.1233); id.*Dan.* 3:42f.(2.1120); Jo.D.*f.o.*1.7(M.94.805B); exeg. Ps.32:6 (ref. argument ascribed to Macedonians that Word of God here = impersonal λόγος προφορικός) οὐ γὰρ ἔσχεν ὁ λόγος σ. τὴν δύναμιν, ἀλλ' ἐνέμεινεν τὴν τοῦ υἱοῦ ἐνέργειαν ‡Ath.*dial.Trin.*3.24(M.28.1240B); of H. Ghost as δύναμις οὐσιώδης: πρὸς πᾶσαν πρόθεσιν σ. ἔχουσαν τῇ βουλήσει τὴν δύναμιν Gr.Nyss.*or.catech.*2(p.15.8; M.45.17C).

συνδυάζ-ω ([*]**συνδιάζω**, [*]**συνδοιάζω**), **1.** *join oneself* with, *combine, associate oneself* with πλησίον γινομένους καὶ ~οντας Chrys. *hom.*6.3 *in Tit.*(11.769D); μὴ ἀνασχόμενος συνδιάσαι τῷ μιαρορρήμονι Nil.*epp.*1.147(M.79.144B); οἱ Ἰουδαῖοι σ. μετὰ Ἑλλήνων Ammon.*Ac.* 14:2(M.85.1544C, v.l. συνδιάζουσι); **2.** *harbour, entertain* thoughts σ. λογισμοῖς ἀκαθάρτοις Nil.*epp.*3.81(M.79.425A); Marc.Er.*opusc.*4(M. 65.997A); Cyr.S.*v.Euthym.*50(p.73.1); **3.** med., *be in collusion with*; also act. εἰς τὸ μὴ συνδοιάσαι μετ' ἀλλήλων, ἀλλ' ἀνοθεύτως ἑρμηνεῦσαι Epiph.*mens.*3(M.43.241C); ἄνευ τοῦ πρὸς ἀλλήλους σ. *ib.*17(265A); ὥστε τὴν ἁγίαν σύνοδον...εἰς συνδυάσαι σοι ἀναγκασθῆναι Leo Mag. *ep.*106.2(p.57.3; M.*PL.*54.1004B); abs. ἐμοῦ, ὅπερ ἀπείη, ~οντος *ib.* 104.3(p.60.9; 996B); **4.** *conspire* σ. μετὰ τοῦ...δαίμονος τὰς κατὰ τῆς...ἐκκλησίας ἐπιβουλὰς κατεσκεύασεν Jo.Mosch.*prat.*43(M.87. 2897C).

***συνδύασμα, τό,** *act of fornication*, †Gregent.*disp.*(M.86.720A).

συνδυασμός, ([*]**συνδιασμός,** [*]**συνδοιασμός**), **ὁ,** *combination of one and one, coupling*; **1.** *copulation, coition*, ref. Adam's creation μὴ ἐκ σ. ἀνδρὸς καὶ γυναικὸς ἀλλ' ἐκ τῆς θείας χειρὸς διαπλασθῆναι Bas. *Eun.*1.15(1.227D; M.29.548A); Didym.(‡Bas.)*Eun.*4(1.282B,283C; M. 29.680A,681B); ref. Son's generation θαυμάζω...ὅτι μὴ καὶ τοῦτο τολμᾷς, σ. τινας ἐννοεῖν Gr.Naz.*or.*29.4(p.78.4; M.36.77C); λόγος...καὶ ἀπαύγασμα λέγεται διὰ τὸ ἄνευ σ. ... γεγεννῆσθαι ἐκ τοῦ πατρός ‡Cyr. *Trin.*8(6^{3}.11C; M.77.1136C); Jo.D.*f.o.*1.8(M.94.813C); ἡ Μαριάμ...ἐξ αὐτῆς, οὐκ ἐκ σ. συλλαβοῦσα (mystically interpreted ref. scripture) Clem.*str.*7.16(p.66.26; M.9.532A); οὐχ ὁμοίως ἀνθρώποις ἐγεννήθη (οὐ γὰρ ἐκ σπορᾶς καὶ σ.) CAnc.(358)*ep.syn.*ap.Epiph.*haer.*73.9 (p.279.20; M.42.420A); cf.Gr.Nyss.*or.catech.*13(p.61.5; M.45.45B); οὐκ ἀπὸ σπέρματος ἀνδρὸς συνελήφθη ἵνα μὴ σ. καὶ παραπλοκὴ ἐν τῇ ἐνσάρκῳ γεννήσει γένηται Epiph.*haer.*69.25(p.175.24; M.42.244A); οὐδὲ ...ἐτέτεκτο ἐκ σ. ... ἀλλ' ὑπὸ τῆς θείας τοῦ πνεύματος ἐνεργείας διέπλαστο Thdr.Mops.*fr.inc.*7(p.296.30; M.66.977A); ‡Cyr.*Trin.*14 (6^{3}.20C; M.77.1152A); **2.** plur., *social intercourse, companionship* τῶν πονηρῶν ἀνθρώπων σ. καὶ κοινωνίαι Mac.Aeg.*hom.*9.11(M.34. 540A); Nil.*epp.*3.328(M.79.540C); **3.** *harbouring* in the mind φυλάττεις ἑαυτὸν ἀπὸ σ. αἰσχρῶν λογισμῶν Cyr.S.*v.Euthym.*50(p.74.6); ἐνέστηκε...ἡ πάλη, διὰ τὸ ὑμᾶς καταφρονῆσαι εἰσελθεῖν καὶ τὴν προσβολὴν καὶ τὸν σ. Jo.Jej.*doct.*1(p.229); ἄλλο δέ ἐστι προσβολή, καὶ ἄλλο συνδοιασμός...σ. δέ ἐστιν ἡ παραδοχὴ τοῦ ὑποβαλλομένου λογισμοῦ παρὰ τοῦ ἐχθροῦ, καὶ οἷον μετ' αὐτοῦ μελέτη καὶ ἐνήδονος ὁμιλία ἢ παρὰ τῆς προαιρέσεως ἡμῶν Jo.D.*spir.neq.*(M.95.93A) = Ephr.3.429C,D (συνδιασμός) = ‡Ath.*polit.*(συνδυασμός M.28.1400A).

***συνδυαστέον,** *one must act in collusion* with ἀδελφῷ περί τινος φαύλου πράγματος μὴ σ. Niceph.Ur.*v.Sym.*36(M.86.3017D).

***συνδυναμόω,** *give the same power to* one as another, *infuse with equal power*, Christol. σ. σῶμα γήινον τῇ θεότητι εἰς μίαν δύναμιν ἥνωσεν Epiph.*anc.*80(p.100.26; M.43.168C).

***συνδυσχεραίνω,** *be thoroughly annoyed* σ. ἐπὶ τῇ ἀμελείᾳ Gr. Nyss.*v.Macr.*(p.412.15; M.46.997C).

***συνδύω,** *dress at the same time*, met. ἐνδιδυσκομένης σου συνεδύθη [sc. ἡ παρθενεία] σοι *M.Ner.et Ach.*8(p.6.29).

συνεγγράφω, *paint one* thing *with another*; pass., *be painted* or *depicted likewise* ὁ σταυρὸς ἐγγέγραπταί σοι, ὁ δὲ σταυρωθεὶς οὐ συνεγγέγραπται Thdr.Stud.*ref.*(M.99.456C).

σύνεγγυς, 1. of place, *near, close to*, met. τὸν γνωστικὸν τὴν ὑπέκβασιν παντὸς τοῦ κόσμου...ἑκουσίως ποιούμενον, ἐνδεικνύμενον... ὅτι μάλιστα σ. ἔσοιτο τοῦ θεοῦ Clem.*str.*7.7(p.30.28; M.9.456B); **2.** of time, *lately* ἐκ τοῦ σ. Acac.B.*ep.Cyr.*(p.99.8; M.77.100B).

συνεγείρ-ω, 1. *join in raising*; s.v.l., of raising money, *earn* τῷδε τῷ βίῳ προσμεῖναι πονοῦντα...καὶ τὸν ἐντεῦθεν ~οντα πλοῦτον Thdt. *h.rel.*13(3.1207) but prob. f.l. for συναγείροντα; **2.** *raise together*, i.e. one with another; med. and pass., *rise, get up together*, Ign.*Polyc.* 6.1; from the dead ~όμεθα ἐν Χριστῷ †Bas.*bapt.*1.2.15(2.640D; M. 31.1552C); Gr.Nyss.*Apoll.*30(M.45.1189B); with Christ ὁ συνεγερθεὶς τῷ Χριστῷ †Bas.*Is.*69(1.429B; M.30.237B); *ib.*284(595B; M.617A); *Const.App.*7.45.1; Cyr.*Arcad.*(p.112.29; 5^{2}.118A).

***συνεδιαζόμενος,** vox nihili ὁ ὄνυξ...μαρμάρῳ ἐστὶ σ., σὺν τῇ τοῦ αἵματος ἰδέᾳ Epiph.*gemm.*12(M.43.301B, conj. συνδιαζόμενος).

συνεδρεία (συνεδρία), ἡ, 1. *seat in, membership of, the Sanhedrin* οἱ...πρεσβύτεροι καὶ ἱερεῖς...ἱερώτεροι κατὰ τὸν νόμον, καὶ τῇ σ. τετίμηντο Cyr.*Zach.*20(3.677D); **2.** theol., *consession* of Son with Father ἐπανῆλθε...εἰς ἰδίαν τὴν ἐκ δεξιῶν τοῦ...πατρὸς σ. Didym. *Trin.*3.10(M.39.856D); ἡ...σ. οὐδὲν ἕτερον δείκνυσιν, ἢ τὸ ὁμότιμον Chrys.*hom.*2.3 *in Heb.*(12.19C).

***συνέδρευσις, ἡ,** *sitting together*; *consession* of Son with Father, Cyr.*apol.orient.*8(p.50.21; 6^{1}.180D).

***συνεδρευτής, ὁ,** *one who sits with*, e.g. as *assessor* πρεβυτέριον... σύμβουλοι καὶ σ. τοῦ ἐπισκόπου ‡Ign.*Trall.*7.

συνεδρεύ-ω, 1. *sit together*; hence, theol., of Son as sitting at right hand of Father αὐτῷ σ. τῷ πατρί, καὶ τοῦτο ἐκ δεξιῶν Cyr.*Jo.*3.5(4. 304E); implying equality ἀπό τε τοῦ σ. αὐτὸν τῷ πατρί, καὶ ἀπὸ τοῦ κεκλῆσθαι κατὰ φύσιν υἱόν, εἰς ἀκριβεστάτην ἐρχόμενος τοῦ μυστηρίου κατάληψιν...[Heb.1: 5] *ib.*5.4(505A); *ib.*9(721D); therefore never of men or angels ἆρ' οὖν...ἀντ' ἐκείνου τῷ πατρὶ ~σομεν, καὶ ὑπόθεσιν ἀσεβείας τὴν τοῦ τιμῶντος ποιησόμεθα χάριν; *ib.*1.9(74E); id. *dial.Trin.*4(5^{1}.536A); except in Christ ~οντος τοῦ...Χριστοῦ, ἐφ' ὅλην δραμεῖται τὸ καύχημα τὴν ἀνθρώπου φύσιν id.*Heb.*1:9(p.384.22); controv. Nestorius μὴ ἀλλότριον τοῦ λόγου τὸ σῶμα αὐτοῦ, μεθ' οὗ καὶ αὐτῷ σ. τῷ πατρί, οὐχ ὡς δύο πάλιν ~όντων υἱῶν, ἀλλ' ὡς ἑνὸς καθ' ἕνωσιν μετὰ τῆς ἰδίας σαρκός id.*ep.*4(p.28.6; 5^{2}.24C); id.*apol.orient.*8 (p.50.2,20; 6^{1}.179E,180C); **2.** *assemble, congregate*, for worship; of Christ with Jewish multitude in Temple, Eus.*d.e.*8.2(p.388.14; M. 22.628B); of Christian congregations ὁ...Ἰωάννης μετὰ τὴν ὁμιλίαν τὴν πρὸς τοὺς ἀδελφοὺς καὶ τὴν εὐχὴν καὶ τὴν εὐχαριστίαν καὶ μετὰ τὴν χειροθεσίαν τὴν ἐφ' ἑκάστου τῶν σ. ποιησάμενος *A.Jo.*46(p.173.22); *ib.*(p.173.17); μήτε...ἀπολειπέσθω τις τοῦ ~ειν *Hom.Clem.*3.69; *ib.* 9.23; *ib.*11.18; πολλοὶ τῶν σ. ... ἡμῖν ἐγκαλέσουσιν Chrys.*hom.*43.1 *in* 1*Cor.*(10.401B); *sit in church* ὅταν...μήτε ἀγρυπνῇ, μήτε φροντίζῃ, ἀλλὰ ἁπλῶς σ. ἐν ἀδείᾳ id.*hom.*15.2 *in* 1*Tim.*(11.636E).

συνεδριάζω, 1. *sit with* or *beside*, as a mark of honour σ. αὐτῷ τὸν υἱὸν ἐκέλευσεν. ὁ δέ, τῇ πρὸς τὸν πατέρα εὐλαβείᾳ...τοῦτο μὴ θελήσας ποιῆσαι †Jo.D.*B.J.*26(M.96.1101C); *ib.*(1105B); *ib.*29(1133A); theol., of consession of Son with Father τὴν κάτω φύσιν...ἐν τοῖς οὐρανοῖς συναγαγών, σ. τῷ θεῷ καὶ πατρὶ πεποίηκε †Gregent.*disp.*(M.86.772A); **2.** *meet in council* οἱ δὲ...σ. ... πέμπουσι...τὴν κοινωνίαν αὐτῶν ἐπιζητοῦντες Philost.*h.e.*10.1(M.65.584B); *ib.*4.10f.(524B,C).

συνέδριον, τό, A. *council*; **1.** prob. of Jewish *sanhedrin*, *Pss.Sal.* 4.1; **2.** of college of presbyters as bishop's council τῶν πρεσβυτέρων εἰς τύπον συνεδρίου τῶν ἀποστόλων Ign.*Magn.*6.1; τοὺς...πρεσβυτέρους ὡς σ. θεοῦ id.*Trall.*3.1; ἐὰν μετανοήσωμεν εἰς ἑνότητα θεοῦ καὶ σ. τοῦ ἐπισκόπου id.*Philad.*8.1; ὁ καθεζόμενος ἐν πρεσβυτερίῳ συνειδότι μεμιασμένος...τὸ Χριστοῦ μολύνων σ. Or.*fr.*50 *in Jer.*36:21(p.223. 23; M.13.580A); *Const.App.*2.28.4 cit. s. βουλή; **3.** σ. ἐπισκόπων *council, synod* ὅτι δ' ἂν ἐν τοῖς ἁγίοις τῶν ἐπισκόπων σ. πράττηται, τοῦτο πρὸς τὴν θείαν βούλησιν ἔχει τὴν ἀναφοράν Const.ap.Eus.*v.C.*

3.20(p.87.11; M.20.1080A); Jo.Ant.*ep.pop.CP*(p.129.9; M.83.1449B); cf. τοῦ ἀρχιερατικοῦ σ. Thdt.*ep*.42(4.1100); abs. ποία...σύνοδος ἐπισκόπων ἦν τότε; ποῖον σ. ἀληθείας ἐχόμενον; CAlex.*ep*.ap.Ath.*apol.sec.* 8(p.94.5; M.25.261C); Ath.*syn*.1(p.231.9; M.26.681A); Pall.*v.Chrys*.3 (p.16.10; M.47.12); Philost.*h.e*.2.7,11(M.65.472A,473B); σ. ποιέω, Gr.Naz.*or*.27.9(p.16.5; M.36.24A); σ. συγκροτέω, Pall.*v.Chrys*.7(p.38.11; M.47.23); σ. καθίζω Philost.*h.e*.8.4(M.65.560A); of a council lacking proper eccl. authority τῷ τῆς ἀποστασίας σ. CEph.(431)*can*. 1,2; hence **a.** *session, meeting* of a council τὸ σ. τῆς συνόδου συνεκροτεῖτο CArim.*ep.Const*.1 ap.Ath.*syn*.10(p.237.23,35; M.26.697A,B); Acac.Mel.*hom*.(p.90.9; M.77.1468A); **b.** *council-chamber* ἵν'...αὐθαίρετος εἰσέλθῃ εἰς τὸ σ. Pall.*v.Chrys*.4(p.22.20; M.47.15); *ib*.8(pp.45.24, 46.12,15; M.47.27); Thdt.*haer*.4.2(4.353).

B. of non-legislative assemblies; **1.** any *public gathering, concourse*, Clem.*paed*.3.11(p.278.27; M.8.656A); **2.** *assembly, congregation*; **a.** as signifying whole body of Jews or Christians καταλέλοιπε ...ὁ λόγος τοῦ θεοῦ τὸ Ἰουδαίων σ. καὶ ἄλλο σ. καὶ ἐκκλησίαν ἑαυτῷ πεποίηκε τὴν ἀπὸ τῶν ἐθνῶν Or.*hom.14.15 in Jer*.(p.122.1; M.13.423C); ἀπηλλάγη τοῦ σ. τοῦ λοιμικοῦ, καὶ περιέτυχε τῇ σωτηρίῳ πηγῇ Chrys.*hom.59.1 in Jo*.(8.344D); ἐξεβάλλετο...τοῦ κοινοῦ σ. id.*hom.5.2 in 1Tim*.(11.576F); **b.** local assembly or congregation ἄνδρες οἱ ἐλθόντες εἰς τὸ σ. τοῦ Χριστοῦ καὶ θέλοντες εἰς τὸν Ἰησοῦν πιστεῦσαι *A.Thom*.A 37(p.154.19); of gatherings of Ophites, Or.*Cels*.6.28(p.98.19; M.11.1336B); of other heretics οἴκους, ἐν οἷς τὰ σ. ταῦτα πληροῦτε Const.ap.Eus.*v.C*.3.65(p.112.12; M.20.1141A); **c.** of the building, whether *church* ὅπως ἁγίων ἀνθρώπων ἄξιον σ. ἀποδειχθῇ Const.*ib*. 3.53(p.100.27; 1116A); or *conventicle* τὰ τῆς δεισιδαιμονίας ὑμῶν σ. Const.*ib*.3.65(p.112.28; 1141C).

σύνεδρος, 1. *seated with*; theol., of Son with Father implying equality σ. ἔχων τὸν ἴδιον υἱόν Cyr.*Jo*.5.4(4.505D); id.*dial.Trin*.4(5^{1}.536A); ἀνεφέρετο εἰς τὸν οὐρανὸν ἵνα σ. εἴη τῷ πατρί id.*Lc*.24:45ff.(M.72.949B); of incarnate Lord as God θεὸς...ὢν κατὰ φύσιν καὶ σ. τῷ θεῷ καὶ πατρί id.*Heb*.2:14(p.393.5); ὡς θεὸς...σ. ἦν τῷ γεγεννηκότι id. *ep*.17(p.35.25; 5^{2}.70B); **2.** *sitting with* or *together in council* ἐπισκόπους...τῶν σ. ἀνίστασαν μάρτυρας Synes.*ep*.67(M.66.1417B).

συνεζευγμένως, *in conjunction, conjointly*, in anon. accusation against Bas. of following Apoll. in Sabellian teaching σ., μᾶλλον δὲ ἡνωμένως Bas.*ep*.129.1(3.220C; M.32.557C); τὸν ἔλεον καὶ σ. αὐτῷ τὴν ἀνάστασιν...ἡμῖν αἰτεῖ Cyr.*Ps*.40:11(M.69.997B); νοεῖται σ. Ammon. *Jo*.21:11(M.85.1521A).

***συνεθέλησις, ἡ,** *a willing the same, consensus of will*, as bet. Father and Son, Cyr.*Jo*.4.5(4.414B).

***συνεθελητής, ὁ,** *one who wills the same as another*; in gen., *like-minded person*, Cyr.*ador*.14(1.482E); id.*Jo*.4.5(4.401B); theol., of Son as consentient with Father ἰδιογνώμων οὐδαμῶς, σ. δὲ...τῷ... πατρί *ib*.5.5(521C); ἰσογνώμων...καὶ σ. ... τῷ γεννήσαντι πρὸς πᾶν ὁτιοῦν *ib*.(530B); *ib*.2.9(239C).

συνεθέλω, *will the same* as another, ref. Son as consentient with Father, Cyr.*Jo*.5.5(4.521E).

***σύνεθνος, ὁ,** *member of the same race* or *nation, fellow countryman* καθὰ καὶ...λέγουσιν οἱ σ. ὑμῶν *A.Pil*.A 2.4(p.225); Jo.Disc.*v. Epiph*.2(M.41.25C); Cyr.S.*v.Sab*.70(p.172.8).

συνείδησις, ἡ, συνειδός, τό, I. *consciousness, mind*;

A. in gen. ἐν ὁμονοίᾳ ἐπὶ τὸ αὐτὸ συναχθέντες τῇ σ. *1Clem*.34.7; ἥ τε τοῦ σ. ... τῆς ψυχῆς δύναμις Clem.*str*.7.7(p.29.3; M.9.453A); γυμνὴ δὲ ἡ ψυχὴ ἐν δυνάμει τοῦ σ. id.*exc.Thdot*.27(p.116.2; M.9.673A); μετὰ τοῦ λόγου εἰσελθόντας εἰς τὴν παντὸς οὑτινοσοῦν σ. Or.*Cels*.5.1(p.1.7; M.11.1181A); †Bas.*bapt*.2.8.6(2.664B; M.31.1605D); *disposition* τὴν αὐτὴν σ. τῇ...ἐκκλησίᾳ...φυλάττων Gr.Naz.*test*.(M.37.389B).

B. as private and secret αὗται καταγελῶσιν ὑμῶν αἱ συνοικοῦσαι, εἰ καὶ μὴ φανερῶς, ἀλλ' ἐν τῷ συνειδότι Chrys.*subintr*.11(1.245C); id.*Jud*. 8.8(1.687C); οὐ μόνον τὴν ἐπιφάνειαν τοῦ φαινομένου σώματος ἀλλὰ καὶ τοῦ σ. αὐτὸ τὸ ἀπόκρυφον Mac.Mgn.*apocr*.4.25(p.209.2); καλαὶ μὲν αἱ πράξεις· ἐὰν δὲ φυλάξῃς τὴν σ. ἀπὸ τοῦ πλησίον σου, οὕτως σώζῃ *Apophth.Patr*.(M.65.369A); *ib*.(372A).

C. esp. ref. Christians πεπεισμένος οὖν πάντῃ τὸν θεὸν εἶναι πάντοτε καὶ αἰδούμενος μὴ ἀληθεύειν ἀνάξιόν τε αὑτοῦ τὸ ψεύδεσθαι γινώσκων, τῇ σ. τῇ θείᾳ καὶ τῇ ἑαυτοῦ ἀρκεῖται μόναις Clem.*str*.7.8(p.38.24; M.9.473A); μόνη δὲ σ. πίστεως ἀνύπουλος διαμένει διὰ μέσων οὐρανῶν μετὰ ἀληθείας ἀνερχομένη *Const.App*.7.33.3; Chrys.*hom.1.4 in 2Cor*.(10.423C); τῶν ἀποστόλων...ὁ λόγος ἐξέλαμπε τοῦ σ. αὐτοῦ φωτίζων τὰ ἀπόκρυφα Mac.Mgn.*apocr*.3.28(p.119.26).

II. *knowledge shared with others* Εὐσέβιος...ὑπὸ τῆς σ. ὧν οἶδε πληττόμενος CAlex.*ep*.ap.Ath.*apol.sec*.6(p.92.10; M.25.257C).

III. *observation, evidence* μαθηταῖς...τεθεαμένοις τὰ τεράστια τοῦ Ἰησοῦ καὶ παριστᾶσιν ἐναργῶς τὸ εὔγνωμον τῆς ἑαυτῶν σ. συγκαταθώμεθα, ὁρῶντες τὸ ἀπάνουργον αὐτῶν, ὅσον ἔστιν ἰδεῖν συνείδησιν ἀπὸ γραμμάτων Or.*Cels*.3.24(p.220.20f.; M.11.948B).

IV. *conscience*;

A. nature and functions; **1.** natural endowment of man, Meth. *fr.10 in Job* (p.513.9; M.18.408A); δύο...διδάσκαλοι γεγόνασιν ἡμῖν ἐξ ἀρχῆς, ἡ κτίσις, καὶ τὸ σ.· καὶ οὐδέτερος αὐτῶν φωνὴν ἀφιείς, σιγῇ τοὺς ἀνθρώπους ἐπαίδευον. ἥ τε γὰρ κτίσις διὰ τῆς ὄψεως ἐκπλήττουσα τὸν θεατήν, εἰς τὸ τοῦ ποιήσαντος αὐτὴν θαῦμα παραπέμπει τὸν ὁρῶντα ἅπαντα· τὸ δὲ σ. ἔνδον ἐνηχοῦν, ἅπαντα ὑποβάλλει τὰ πρακτέα Chrys.*Anna* 1.3(4.703C); ὁμοῦ γὰρ πλάττων τὸν ἄνθρωπον ὁ θεός, τοῦτο αὐτῷ ἐνέθηκε δικαστήριον ἀδέκαστον, τὴν ἐν ἑκάστῳ τοῦ σ. ψῆφον id.*exp.in Ps*.147:9(5.486D); φυσικὴ βίβλος ἐστὶ σ. ὁ ἐμπράκτως ἀναγινώσκων αὐτήν, λαμβάνει πεῖραν θείας ἀντιλήψεως Marc.Er.*opusc*. 1.187(M.65.928C); ὅτε ἐποίησεν ὁ θεὸς τὸν ἄνθρωπον, ἐνέσπειρεν αὐτῷ τί ποτε θεῖον, ὥσπερ λογισμόν τινα θερμότερον...φωτίζοντα τὸν νοῦν καὶ δεικνύοντα αὐτῷ τὸ καλὸν ἀπὸ τοῦ κακοῦ. τοῦτο κατακαλεῖται συνείδησις ὅς ἐστιν ὁ φυσικὸς νόμος Dor.*doct*.3.1(M.88.1652D); **2.** sufficient for leading a moral life ἀρίστη γὰρ πρὸς τὴν ἀκριβῆ αἵρεσίν τε καὶ φυγὴν ἡ σ., θεμέλιος δὲ αὐτῆς βέβαιος ὀρθὸς βίος Clem.*str*.1.1(p.5.21; M.8.692B); ἡ σ. οὐ συγκρίνει τοὺς...λογισμοὺς τοὺς ὑπακούοντας τῇ ἁμαρτίᾳ, ἀλλ' εὐθὺς ἐλέγχει. οὐ ψεύδεται γάρ, ἐπεὶ τί εἴποι ἐνώπιον τοῦ θεοῦ ἐν τῇ ἡμέρᾳ τῆς κρίσεως μαρτύρεται, ὡς πάντοτε ἐλέγχουσα Mac.Aeg.*hom*.35.34(M.34.597D); ἀρκοῦντα γὰρ ἔχομεν διδάσκαλον τὸ σ., καὶ οὐχ οἷόν τέ τινα ἀπεστερῆσθαι τῆς ἐκεῖθεν βοηθείας Chrys.*hom. 54.1 in Gen*.(4.522B); τοῖς δὲ Ἰουδαίοις ἐξαίρετόν τι ἐπραγματεύσατο, τὸ καὶ διὰ γραμμάτων δηλῶσαι τὰ νόμιμα...ἡ μέντοι πᾶσα φύσις ἡ ἀνθρωπίνη ἀρκοῦντα εἶχε τὸν ἀπὸ τοῦ σ. νόμον id.*exp.in Ps*.147:9(5.486E); id.*Laz*.4.5(1.759A); ζητῶν θεραπείαν, ἐπιμέλησαι τῆς σ.· καὶ ὅσα λέγει, ποίησον...τὰ κρυπτὰ ἑκάστου ὁ θεὸς οἶδε, καὶ ἡ σ.· καὶ τούτων αὐτῶν λαμβανέτω διόρθωσιν Marc.Er.*opusc*.1.69f.(M.65.913C); τῇ σ. εἴξαντες οἱ πατριάρχαι, καὶ πάντες οἱ ἅγιοι πρὸ τοῦ γραπτοῦ νόμου, εὐηρέστησαν τῷ θεῷ Dor.*doct*.3.1(M.88.1652D); λόγος δὲ θεοῦ τὴν ψυχὴν πρὸς ἀρετὴν...διεγείρει, καὶ μάλιστα τῶν ῥαθυμοτέρων περὶ τὴν ἐργασίαν τῶν θείων παραγγελμάτων...τοῖς μὲν γὰρ σπουδαίοις...ἱκανὴ καὶ ἡ σ. πρὸς διδασκαλίας ὑπόθεσιν, πάντα τὰ ἀγαθὰ συμβουλεύουσα, καὶ πάντων τῶν πονηρῶν ἀποστρέφουσα Leont.N.*v.Sym*.2(M.93.1669C); **3.** as judge τὸ σ. λέγω...οὐκ ἔστιν οὐδεὶς δικαστὴς οὕτως ἄγρυπνος ἐν ἀνθρώποις, οἷον τὸ ἡμέτερον σ. οἱ μὲν γὰρ ἔξωθεν δικασταὶ καὶ ὑπὸ χρημάτων διαφθείρονται...καὶ πολλὰ ἕτερά ἐστι τὰ λυμαινόμενα τὴν ὀρθὴν ἐκείνων ψῆφον· τὸ δὲ τοῦ σ. δικαστήριον οὐδενὶ τούτων εἴκειν οἶδεν Chrys.*Laz*.4.4(1.745A); id.*hom.17.1 in Gen*.(4.134C); id. *hom.42.3 in Mt*.(7.455C); ἄνοιξόν σου τὰς θύρας τοῦ σ., καὶ βλέπε τὸν ἐν τῇ διανοίᾳ σου καθήμενον δικαστήν id.*hom.9.3 in 2Cor*.(10.502E); but without power to absolve τότε ἐρχόμεθα ἐπὶ δέησιν, ὅταν ὁ δικαστὴς ἡμῖν μὴ ἀφῇ ὁ ἔνδον, τὸ σ. λέγω τὸ ἡμῖν ἐγκαθήμενον. οὐδὲ γὰρ ἐξουσίαν ἔχει τοῦ ἀφιέναι id.*exp.in Ps*.142:1(5.448C); εἶχε γὰρ ἕκαστος κριτὴν ἀδέκαστον τὴν ἰδίαν σ. Nil.*exerc*.5(M.79.724B); **4.** as teacher τὸ σ. διδάσκει Gr.Naz.*or*.16.5(M.35.941A); ἀπὸ τοῦ τῇ φύσει τῇ ἀνθρωπίνῃ ἐγκειμένου τῷ σ. διδασκάλου ὁδηγούμενος Chrys.*hom.52.4 in Gen*.(4.512D); εἶχε γὰρ τὸν κατὰ φύσιν διδάσκαλον ἐρρωμένον, τὸ ἴδιον σ. Pall.*h.Laus*.4(p.19.25; M.34.1017A); **5.** as accusing and condemning μὴ τὰ αὐτὰ παθεῖν βουλομένους ἅπερ αὐτοὶ τοὺς ἄλλους διατιθέασι, καὶ ἐν σ. ἐχθραῖς ταῦτα ὀνειδίζοντας ἀλλήλοις ἅπερ ἐργάζονται Just.*dial*.93.2(M.6.697B); ἡ δυσωπία ἡ πρὸς ἑαυτὴν τῆς ψυχῆς ἐκ συνειδήσεως Clem.*str*.4.6(p.265.9; M.8.1249A); ὁ...δεσπότης...διαπλάττων τὸν ἄνθρωπον, τὸ σ. αὐτῷ ἐνέθετο κατήγορον ἀδιάλειπτον Chrys. *hom.17.1 in Gen*.(4.134C); ἐννόει μοι...τοῦ σ. τὴν κατηγορίαν, καὶ ὅπως ὠθούμενος...ὑπὸ τῆς σ. οὐκ ἔστη μέχρι τοῦ εἰπεῖν 'οὐ γινώσκω' *ib*. 19.2(164D); γυμνὸς δὲ ἕστηκε...ὁ κατήγορος, τοῦ σ. δημίου τάξιν ἐπέχοντος id.*ep*.7.2(3.585E); Rom.Mel.(*AS* 1 p.147); βλέπε μὴ πρὸ καιροῦ κατακρίνῃ σε ἡ σ. σου Jo.Jej.*poenit.cont.virg*.(M.88.1969C); **6.** other functions διὰ τί δὲ καλεῖ τὴν σ. ἀντίδικον;...ἐπειδὴ αὐτὴ ἀντίκειται πάντοτε τῷ θελήματι ἡμῶν τῷ κακῷ Dor.*doct*.3.1(M.88.1653C); θέλει γάρ τις φυλάξαι συνείδησιν πρὸς τὸν θεὸν καὶ τὸν πλησίον, καὶ πρὸς τὰς ὕλας. καὶ πρὸς μὲν τὸν θεόν, ἵνα μὴ καταφρονῇ τῶν ἐντολῶν αὐτοῦ...ἡ δὲ πρὸς τὸν πλησίον ἐστίν, ἵνα μὴ ποιῇ τις τίποτε... εἰς ὃ οἶδεν ὅτι θλίβει ἢ πλήσσει τὸν πλησίον...τὸ δὲ πρὸς τὰς ὕλας φυλάξαι ἐστίν, ἵνα μὴ κακῶς κέχρηταί τις πράγματι *ib*.3.3(1656B,C); τὸ σ. σοι ἔσοπτρον τῆς ὑποταγῆς ἔστω Jo.Clim.*scal*.4(M.88.712B); **7.** functions varying acc. circumstances ἀεὶ...ἡμᾶς κεντεῖ τῶν ἁμαρτημάτων τὸ σ., μάλιστα δὲ κατ' ἐκείνην τὴν ὥραν, ὅταν μέλλωμεν ἐντεῦθεν ἀπάγεσθαι πρὸς...τὸ φοβερὸν δικαστήριον Chrys.*Laz*.2.2(1.729D); ὅρα σοφίαν θεοῦ. οὔτε διηνεκῆ τὴν κατηγορίαν ἐποίησεν εἶναι τοῦ σ. (οὐ γὰρ ἂν ἠνέγκαμεν τὸ φορτίον, συνεχῶς ἐγκαλούμενοι) οὔτε οὕτως ἀσθενῆ, ὡς ἐκ πρώτης καὶ δευτέρας ἀπαγορεῦσαι παραινέσεως. εἰ μὲν γὰρ καθ' ἑκάστην ἡμέραν καὶ ὥραν ἔμελλεν ἡμᾶς κεντεῖν, κἂν ἀπεπνίγημεν ἀπὸ τῆς ἀθυμίας· εἰ δὲ ἅπαξ καὶ δεύτερον ὑπομνῆσαν ἀπέστη τῆς ἐπιτιμήσεως, οὐκ ἂν πολλὴν ἐκαρπωσάμεθα τὴν ὠφέλειαν *ib*.4.5(758B); ἀεὶ...κεντεῖται τὸ σ., μάλιστα δὲ ὅταν περὶ τῆς κρίσεως διαλεγώμεθα Jo.Jej.*poenit.cont. virg*.(M.88.1968D); **8.** in rel. to conscience of others, exeg. 1Cor. 10:25–29 'διὰ τὴν σ.' οὖν ἀφεκτέον ὧν ἀφεκτέον. 'σ. δὲ λέγω οὐχὶ τὴν ἑαυτοῦ', γνωστικὴ γάρ, 'ἀλλὰ τὴν τοῦ ἑτέρου', ἵνα μὴ κακῶς οἰκοδομηθῇ ἀμαθίᾳ μιμούμενος ὃ μὴ γινώσκει, καταφρονητὴς ἀντὶ μεγαλόφρονος γινόμενος Clem.*str*.4.15(p.291.26ff.; M.8.1305A); cf.*ib*.4.7(p.273.12; 1265B); ref. scandal given to Nestorians by term θεοτόκος: μάτην ἡμεῖς...δῆθεν ἀκριβείας περιττῆς ἕνεκα πρὸς αἱρετικὴν κακοδοξίαν μόνον βλεπούσης τὰς σ. τῶν ἀδελφῶν εἰς οὐδὲν δέον πληττομένας περιορῶμεν Jo.Ant.*ep.Nest*.4(p.95.22; M.77.1456A).

B. of bad conscience; **1.** causes; **a.** sin in gen. ἐπὶ τῷ καθικέσθαι διανοίας τοῦ τὴν σ. μεμολυσμένου ἐπί τινι ἁμαρτίᾳ Or.*hom.6.2 in Jer.*(p.49.2; M.13.325A); Chrys.*hom.18.1 in 1Cor.*(10.151E); **b.** specific sins ἡ σ. μου συνέχει με περὶ τῆς ἀσεβείας μου *T.Reub*.4.3; ὁ χωρὶς ἐπισκόπου καὶ πρεσβυτερίου καὶ διακόνων πράσσων τι, οὗτος οὐ καθαρός ἐστιν τῇ σ. Ign.*Trall*.7.2; τὴν θεόθεν ἤκουσαν σ. ἀπιστίᾳ κατεμίαναν Clem.*str*.2.6(p.129.1; M.8.965A); (Sabellian) heresy οὗ τῷ ὅρῳ ἀρεσκόμενοι πολλοὶ συνείδησιν πεπληγότες Hipp.*haer*.9.12(p.249.18; M.16.3386B); μηδὲ συνείδησιν ἐπὶ ἀνόμῳ κέρδει μολύνειν *ib*.9.23(p.259.2; 3402A); **c.** sin of Adam and Eve, Thdt.*qu.26 in Gen.*(1.41); *ib.* *33*(1.46); **2.** its torments ψυχὴν...περιφέροντα σ. βαρούμενον ὑπὲρ 'φορτίον βαρὺ' καὶ βαρούμενον ὑπὸ τοῦ τῆς ἀρνήσεως πτώματος Or.*mart*.39(p.37.8; M.11.616A); ἁμαρτίαν δ' οὐ δεδοίκαμεν, ὅπερ ἐστὶν ἀληθῶς φοβερόν, καὶ πυρὸς κατεσθίει τὸ σ. Chrys.*stat*.5.3(2.64C); οὐδὲ ἡνίκα καθεύδωσι, ταύτης ἀπαλλάττονται τῆς ἀγωνίας, τοῦ πονηροῦ σ. ὀνείρατα πολλῶν γέμοντα φόβων ἀναπλάττοντος αὐτοῖς id.*hom.12.7 in Rom.*(9.553B); id.*hom.5.3 in 2Tim.*(11.689D); **3.** its effects; **a.** unbelief τὸ μὴ πιστεύειν ἀπὸ πονηρᾶς γίνεσθαι σ. Chrys.*hom.18.3 in Jo.*(8.163B); πολλῶν γὰρ πεπληρωμένον τὸ σ. πονηριῶν, δεδοικὸς...τὴν μέλλουσαν ἀντίδοσιν, ἐπειδὴ μὴ βούλεται ἀπὸ τῆς μεταβολῆς τῆς ἐπὶ τὰ κάλλιστα τὴν παραμυθίαν πορίζεσθαι, ἀπὸ τῆς ἀπιστίας ἀναπαύεσθαι βούλεται id.*hom.17.3 in 1Cor.*(10.149C); id.*hom.9.3 in Rom.*(9.514B); **b.** fear of death, id.*stat*.6.3(2.77C); ‡Pall.*h.mon*.11.15(p.57.22; M.65.452D); **c.** other consequences βαρύτητα τὴν τῆς σ. εἰς ἀπόγνωσιν ὤθησιν μετ' ἐπιτάσεώς φησιν Ath.*exp.Ps*.37:5(M.27.184C); οὐ τολμήσει καταφρονήσας εἰς ἐκκλησίαν θεοῦ εἰσελθεῖν, πλησσόμενος τῇ σ. αὐτοῦ *Const.App*.2.10.3; **d.** its external expression εἰ μὴ τῷ χρώματι τοῦ προσώπου δείξουσι τὴν συκοφαντίαν· τοῦτο γὰρ τοῦ σ. ἔλεγχός ἐστι... οὕτω τοὺς μὲν ἐπιβουλεύσαντας τῷ Ἰωσὴφ ἡ σ. ἤλεγξε Ath.*apol.Const.*12(M.25.609B,C); κατηφὲς...ἀεὶ τῶν δυσσεβῶν τὸ πρόσωπον...τοῖς τοῦ σ. ἐλέγχοις ἀχθοφοροῦντος τοῦ νοῦ Cyr.*Is*.4.3(2.654E).

C. the hardened conscience, cf.1Tim.4:2 εἴ τις ἐπίσκοπος...ἐν ταῖς ἡμέραις τῶν ἑορτῶν οὐ μεταλαμβάνει κρεῶν καὶ οἴνου, καθαιρείσθω ὡς κεκαυτηριασμένος τῆς σ. *Can.App*.53; τὸ δὲ σ. κεκαυτηριασμένοι, τουτέστι, πονηροῦ ὄντες βίου Chrys.*hom.12.1 in 1Tim.*(11.610C); ὅταν γὰρ ἡ σ. λέγει ἡμῖν, ποιῆσαι τόδε ἔτι, καὶ καταφρονῶμεν, καὶ πάλιν λέγει, καὶ οὐ ποιῶμεν, ἀλλὰ μένωμεν καταπατοῦντες αὐτήν, λοιπὸν καταχωννύομεν αὐτήν, καὶ οὐκ ἔτι δύναται τρανῶς λαλεῖν ἡμῖν...οὕτως εὑρισκόμεθα μὴ αἰσθανόμενοι ὧν λέγει ἡμῖν ἡ σ. ἡμῶν, ὡς νομίζειν ἡμᾶς σχεδὸν μὴ ἔχειν αὐτήν. οὐδεὶς δέ ἐστιν ὁ μὴ ἔχων αὐτήν Dor.*doct*.3.1(M.88.1653A,B); πρόσχωμεν, μήπως οὐκ ἐκ καθαρότητος, ἀλλὰ περικακήσαν ὥσπερ, τοῦ ἐλέγχειν τὸ σ. ἐπαύσατο Jo.Clim.*scal*.5(M.88.780B).

D. the purification of conscience; **1.** by baptism συνείδησις δέ ἐστι λόγος καὶ ἔλεγχος τοῦ ἡμετέρου φύλακος τοῦ ἐκ βαπτίσματος παραδοθέντος ἡμῖν. διόπερ οὐδὲ τοσοῦτον τοὺς ἀφωτίστους εὑρίσκομεν τυπτομένους ἐπὶ ταῖς κακαῖς πράξεσιν ἐν τῇ ἑαυτῶν ψυχῇ· ἀλλ' ἀμυδρῶς πως Jo.Clim.*scal*.26(M.88.1092A); τὸ μυστικὸν ὕδωρ ἐποιεῖτο τῆς σ. κάθαρσιν Max.*qu.Thal*.6(M.90.281B); **2.** through confession δεῖ...καὶ περὶ τῶν ἀκουσίων πταισμάτων ἐξομολόγησιν σύντονον προσφέρειν τῷ δεσπότῃ...ἄχρις οὗ πληροφορηθῇ ἡ σ. ἡμῶν ἐν δακρύῳ ἀγάπης...προσέχειν δὲ δεῖ ἀδιαλείπτως τῇ αἰσθήσει τῆς ἐξομολογήσεως, μήπου ἄρα ἡ σ. ἡμῶν ψεύσηται ἑαυτήν...ὅτι πολὺ κρείττων ἐστὶν ἡ τοῦ θεοῦ κρίσις τῆς ἡμετέρας σ. Diad.*perf*.100(p.148.15ff.); and repentance, Chrys.*stat*.18.3(2.186B).

E. contrast bet. good and bad conscience καθάπερ γὰρ τὸ πονηρὸν σ. ῥυπαροὺς ἡμᾶς ἐργάζεται, καὶ εἰς ἀπόγνωσιν ἡμᾶς ἐμβάλλει· οὕτως ἂν ἐδαφίσωμεν ἡμῶν τὰς ἁμαρτίας, ἂν ἐκκαθάρωμεν τὴν πονηρίαν, δυνησόμεθα διαβλέψαι εἰς τὸν πνευματικὸν πόθον, καὶ μετὰ πολλῆς τῆς προθυμίας καλεῖν τὸν θεόν Chrys.*exp.in Ps*.41:2(5.138A); οὐδὲν γὰρ οὕτω βαρεῖ ψυχήν...καὶ πιέζει κάτω, ὡς ἁμαρτίας συνειδός· οὐδὲν οὕτω πτεροῖ καὶ μετέωρον ποιεῖ, ὡς δικαιοσύνης κτῆσις id.*hom.38.3 in Mt.*(7.429C); οὐδὲν γὰρ σ. κεντουμένης μνήμῃ πράξεως πονηρᾶς ἀσθενέστερον, πάντα ἡγουμένη ἐχθρὰ...καὶ πρὸς ἄμυναν ἐπιτήδεια, δι' ἣν ἔνδον ἔχει κολάσεως ἀεὶ προσδοκίαν ἐπὶ τοῖς πεπραγμένοις κακοῖς, κἂν μηδεὶς ἐλέγχειν δύνηται...ἀλλ' οὐχ ἡ καθαρεύουσα πονηρίας οὕτω· πολὺ γὰρ αὕτη τὸ πεποιθὸς ἔχει οὐδαμόθεν ὁρῶσα καταγνώσεως εὔλογον αἰτίαν...τὸ ἀνυπαίτιον ἔχουσα παρρησίας ἐφόδιον ‡Nil.*perist*.12.8(M.79.953C).

F. pure conscience of Christians; **1.** in gen., *1Clem*.1.3; ἕκαστος ὑμῶν...ἐν ἀγαθῇ σ. ὑπάρχων *ib*.41.1; Polyc.*ep*.5.3; **2.** cause ἡ δὲ ἀγαθὴ σ. ἀπὸ βίου καὶ πράξεων ὀρθῶν Chrys.*hom.1 in 2Cor.4:13*(3.269A); **3.** effects; **a.** removal of fear of death, Clem.*str*.7.12(p.56.25; M.9.509B); Hipp.*haer*.9.26(p.260.24; M.16.3403C); **b.** joy and consolation, Ath.*exp.Ps*.36:8(M.27.180A); οὐδὲν γὰρ ἡμᾶς οὕτως εὐφραίνειν εἴωθεν, ὡς σ. χρηστόν Chrys.*subintr*.11(1.245D); εὐθυμίαν γὰρ καὶ χαρὰν οὐκ ἀρχῆς μέγεθος, οὐ χρημάτων πλῆθος...οὐκ ἄλλο τι τῶν ἀνθρωπίνων ποιεῖν εἴωθεν, ἀλλ' ἢ κατόρθωμα...πνευματικόν, καὶ σ. ἀγαθόν id.*hom.1.4 in Rom.*(9.435D); εἰ γὰρ ἀπὸ τοῦ σ. γένοιτο χαρά... οὐδὲν λείπει εἰς εὐθυμίαν ὑμῖν καὶ παράκλησιν· οὐδὲν γὰρ οὕτω ποιεῖ παράκλησιν, ὡς καθαρὸν σ. id.*hom.30.1 in 2Cor.*(10.649Ef.); exeg. 2Cor.1:12 'ἡ γὰρ καύχησις ἡμῶν...τὸ μαρτύριον τῆς σ. ἡμῶν'· τουτέστιν, ἡ σ. ἡμῶν, οὐκ ἔχουσα ἡμᾶς καταδικάζειν...κἂν γὰρ μυρία πάσχωμεν δεινά,...ἀρκεῖ εἰς παραμυθίαν ἡμῖν, μᾶλλον δὲ οὐ μόνον εἰς παραμυθίαν, ἀλλὰ καὶ εἰς τὸ στεφανοῦσθαι, τὸ σ. καθαρὸν ὄν, καὶ μαρτυροῦν ἡμῖν, ὅτι δι' οὐδὲν πονηρόν, ἀλλὰ διὰ τὸ τῷ θεῷ δοκοῦν, ταῦτα πάσχομεν *ib.3.1*(441Ef.); **c.** confidence and hope, Or.*Jo*.20.31(25; p.368.25; M.14.645A); οὐδὲν γὰρ οὕτω χρηστὰ ἐλπίζειν παρασκευάζει, ὡς ἀγαθὸν σ. Chrys.*hom.9.2 in Rom.*(9.514A); ὥστε μὴ πλέον δυνηθῆναι τὴν ὕβριν ἐν τῷ συντρίβειν, ἢ τὸ ἀγαθὸν σ. ἐν τῷ ἐλπίζειν...καὶ ἔστιν ὡς ἀληθῶς βέβαιον πρᾶγμα τὸ σ. εἰς πάντα τὰ ἀδίκως συμπίπτοντα...παραμυθείτω τὴν ἀγάπην σου αὐτὸ τὸ σ., ἄδελφε τιμιώτατε, ὅπερ ἐν ταῖς θλίψεσιν ἔχει τὴν παραμυθίαν τῆς ἀρετῆς Innoc.*ep.Chrys.*(M.52.537); **d.** also risk of pride οὐδὲν γὰρ οὕτως ἀπόνοιαν τίκτειν εἴωθεν, ὡς σ. ἀγαθόν, ἐὰν μὴ προσέχωμεν Chrys.*hom.3.1 in Is.6:1*(6.112D).

G. God and conscience; **1.** in gen. οὐχὶ καὶ αἱ προαιρέσεις φθάνουσι πρὸς τὸν θεὸν προϊεῖσαι τὴν φωνὴν τὴν ἑαυτῶν; οὐχὶ δὲ καὶ ὑπὸ τῆς σ. πορθμεύονται; Clem.*str*.7.7(p.29.10; M.9.453B); θεὸς μάρτυς τοῦ ἡμετέρου σ. Or.*Cels*.1.46(p.96.16; M.11.745B); τῶν ἀμέμπτων πατὴρ ...διὰ συνειδήσεως ἐρευνᾷς ἑκάστου τὴν γνώμην *Const.App*.7.33.2; μετὰ ἀσφαλείας...τὸ μαρτύριον τῆς σ. ἡμῶν κατεργάζεσθαι ἐνώπιον τοῦ θεοῦ Diad.*perf*.94(p.138.26); ref. grace ἡ μὲν χάρις...πρῶτον μὲν θεοπρεπῶς διεγείρει τὴν σ. Marc.Er.*opusc*.2.56(M.65.937D); **2.** pure conscience needed for worship in gen. μετὰ καθαροῦ σ. ἐπιτελεῖν τὴν ἡμέραν τῆς...ἀναστάσεως Gr.Ant.*mul.ung*.12(M.88.1865A); esp. for Communion ἁγίασον...διακόνους, ἵνα...δυνηθῶσιν καθαρᾷ σ. λειτουργεῖν καὶ παραστῆναι τῷ ἁγίῳ σώματι καὶ τῷ ἁγίῳ αἵματι Serap.*euch*.11.3; cf.*ib*.27.2; exeg. 1Cor.11:28 σφόδρα φοβερῶς περὶ αὐτῆς διελέχθη, τὸ κεφάλαιον τῶν ἀγαθῶν κατασκευάζων, τὸ μετὰ καθαροῦ προσιέναι σ. αὐτοῖς...οὐ γὰρ ὅπως παρασκευασμένοι καὶ τὰ κακὰ ἑαυτῶν ἐκκαθάραντες...προσέλθοιμεν σκοποῦμεν, ἀλλ' ὅπως ἐν ἑορταῖς, καὶ ἡνίκα ἂν ἅπαντες. ἀλλ' οὐχ οὕτως ὁ Παῦλος ἐκέλευσεν, ἀλλ' ἕνα καιρὸν οἶδε προσόδου καὶ κοινωνίας, τοῦ σ. τὴν καθαρότητα Chrys.*hom.28.1 in 1Cor.*(10.250C,D); χρόνος προσόδου ἔστω ἡμῖν τὸ καθαρὸν σ. id.*hom.6.3 in 1Tim.*(11.577D); id.*hom.89.3 in Mt.*(7.835B); συγχωρῆσαι δὲ ἕκαστον τῷ ἰδίῳ σ. τῶν μυστηρίων μετέχειν Socr.*h.e*.5.19.9(M.67.617A); cf.*Lit.Chrys.*(p.390.25); in prayer before Communion ὁ θεὸς...ἀνάκρινον τὰς σ. καὶ ἔκβαλον ἀφ' ἡμῶν πᾶσαν ἔννοιαν πονηράν *Lit.Jac.*(p.224.7); ποίῳ γὰρ σ. ... προσέρχῃ τοῖς μυστηρίοις;...ἔχων ἔνδον τὸ σὸν σ. κατήγορον Anast.S.*synax.*(M.89.832C).

H. in spiritual life; **1.** examination of conscience; **a.** prescribed ἕκαστος ἡμῶν ἐξετασάτω τὴν σ. ἑαυτοῦ Or.*hom.20.9 in Jer.*(p.192.10; M.13.521D); for monks τῆς ἡμέρας παρελθούσης...πρὸ τῆς ἀναπαύσεως ἀνακρίνεσθαι προσήκει τὸ σ. ἑκάστου ὑπὸ τῆς ἰδίας καρδίας Bas.*ascet*.1.5(2.323C; M.31.881A); for catechumens ὧδε οὖν ζητεῖται...ἵνα τις ἐξ ὑμῶν πιστὸς ἐκ συνειδήσεως εὑρεθῇ. ἄνδρα γὰρ πιστὸν ἔργον ἐστὶν εὑρεῖν...οὐχ ἵνα ἐμοὶ δείξῃς σου τὴν σ. ... ἀλλ' ἵνα τῷ θεῷ δείξῃς τῆς πίστεως τὸ ἄδολον Cyr.H.*catech*.5.2; εἰς τὸ σ. εἰσελθὼν τὸ σεαυτοῦ, ἀναλογίσαι τὰ πεπραγμένα σοι παρὰ πᾶσαν τὴν ζωήν Chrys.*hom.in Mt.18:23*(3.6D); ἕκαστος...εἰς τὸ ἑαυτοῦ συνεισελθών, καὶ ἀναλογιζόμενος τὰ πεπλημμελημένα ἀπαιτείτω τὰς εὐθύνας ἑαυτὸν ἀκριβεῖς id.*hom.5.6 in Rom.*(9.469B); **b.** its method τὸ σ. τὸ ἡμέτερον καλέσαντες ποιήσωμεν αὐτῷ λόγον τῶν ῥημάτων, τῶν πραγμάτων, τῶν ἐνθυμήσεων· ἐξετάσωμεν, τί μὲν εἰς δέον ἀνήλωται, τί δὲ ἐπὶ βλάβῃ τῇ ἡμετέρᾳ· ποῖος λόγος ἐδαπανήθη κακῶς, εἰς λοιδορίας, εἰς αἰσχρολογίας, εἰς ὕβρεις· ποῖον ἐνθύμημα τὸν ὀφθαλμὸν εἰς ἀκολασίαν ἐκίνησε· τίς λογισμὸς ἐπὶ βλάβῃ τῇ ἡμετέρᾳ εἰς ἔργον ἐξηνέχθη, ἢ διὰ χειρῶν, ἢ διὰ γλώττης, ἢ διὰ τῶν ὀμμάτων αὐτῶν id.*grat*.4(2.665A); ἐν τῷ καιρῷ τῷ μετὰ τὰ δεῖπνα...ἡνίκα ἂν μέλλητε κατακλίνεσθαι, καὶ μηδενὸς παρόντος πολλὴ ἡ ἡσυχία...τὸ δικαστήριον ἔγειρον τοῦ σ., εὐθύνας ἀπαίτησον αὐτό, καὶ ἃ μεθ' ἡμέραν ἐβουλεύσω πονηρά, ἢ δόλους ῥάπτων, ἢ τὸν πλησίον ὑποσκελίζων...ταῦτα ἐν τῷ καιρῷ τῆς ἡσυχίας ἐκείνης εἰς μέσον ἀγαγών, καὶ τὸ σ. ἐπιστήσας τοῖς ἀτόποις τούτοις λογισμοῖς, κατάξαινε αὐτούς, καὶ δίκην ἀπαίτει id.*exp.in Ps.*4:5(5.18D); to be done daily, *ib.*(19A); esp. in Lent ἡμᾶς δίκαιον...μὴ ἁπλῶς τὰς ἑβδομάδας τῶν νηστειῶν παρατρέχειν, ἀλλὰ διερευνᾶσθαι τὴν ἑαυτῶν σ., καὶ τὸν λογισμὸν βασανίζειν, καὶ σκοπεῖν τί μὲν ἐν ταύτῃ τῇ ἑβδομάδι ἡμῖν κατώρθωται, τί δὲ ἐν τῇ ἑτέρᾳ, καὶ τίνα προσθήκην ἐδεξάμεθα εἰς τὴν ἐπιοῦσαν, καὶ ποῖον τῶν ἐν ἡμῖν παθῶν διωρθώσαμεν id.*hom.11.2 in Gen.*(4.84E); id.*hom.42.3 in Mt.*(7.455C); **2.** purity of conscience necessary for prayer προσευχὴ δὲ ἐκ καλῆς σ. ἐκ θανάτου ῥύεται *2Clem.*16.4; οὐ προσήξεις ἐπὶ προσευχὴν ἐν σ. πονηρᾷ *Did.*4.14; ποῖον γὰρ θεῷ δῶρον ἀπὸ τοῦ λογικοῦ μεῖζον ἀναπέμπεσθαι δύναται εὐώδους λόγου εὐχῆς, προσφερομένης ἀπὸ συνειδότος μὴ ἔχοντος δυσώδες ἀπὸ τῆς ἁμαρτίας; Or.*or.*2.2(p.300.14; M.11.420A); προσευχαὶ ἀπὸ σ. καθαρᾶς id.*Cels.*8.17(p.234.20; M.11.1544A); Cyr.H.*catech.*22.9; σ. ἀγαθὴ διὰ προσευχῆς εὑρίσκεται, καὶ προσευχὴ καθαρὰ διὰ σ.· θάτερον γὰρ θατέρου κατὰ φύσιν προσδέεται Marc.Er.*opusc.*1.199(M.65.929B); ὅταν γὰρ ἡ σ. ἡμῶν ἑαυτὴν τοῖς ἐλέγχοις ταράττοι, οὐκέτι τῆς ὀσμῆς ὁ νοῦς τῶν ὑπερκοσμίων ἀγαθῶν παραχωρεῖται αἰσθάνεσθαι, ἀλλ' εὐθὺς εἰς ἀμφιβολίας μερίζεται, θερμῇ μὲν κινήσει διὰ τὴν προλαβοῦσαν πεῖραν τῆς πίστεως ὀρεγόμενος, μηκέτι δὲ αὐτῆς ἐπιλαβέσθαι ἐν αἰσθήσει τῆς καρδίας διὰ τῆς ἀγάπης δυνάμενος διὰ τοὺς νυγμοὺς...τῆς ἐλεγχούσης σ. Diad.*perf.*23(p.24.20,27); ἡ μεσότης τῆς ἐνεργείας τῆς ἁγίας γνώσεως οὐ μικρῶς ἡμᾶς λυπεῖσθαι παρασκευάζει, ὅταν ἐκ παροξυσμοῦ τινος ὑβρίσαντές τινα ἐχθρὸν αὐτὸν ἑαυτῶν κατασκευάσωμεν. διόπερ οὐδέποτε ἐνδίδωσι νύττουσα τὴν σ. ἡμῶν, ἕως ὅτε...εἰς τὴν πάλαι ἐπαναγάγωμεν τὸν ὑβρισθέντα διάθεσιν *ib.*92(p.132.10).

I. ref. eternal punishment, exeg. Is.66:24 τὸ κριτήριον τῆς οἰκείας αὐτῶν σ., ὃ δίκην σκώληκος ἀτελευτήτου ἐν αὐτοῖς ἐνειλεῖται Thdr.Heracl.*Is.*66:24(M.18.1377D); σκώληξ ἐκεῖθεν ἐσθίων ἀϊδίως· μέσον συνειδός, ἄγραφος κατήγορος Gr.Naz.*carm.*1.2.8.196(M.37.663A); ὅτε ἡ σ. ἐπιστρέφειν εἰωθυῖα πρὸς πεπλημμελημένα τρέμει τὴν ...κόλασιν ‡Nil.*perist.*7.1(M.79.860B); Dor.*doct.*12.3(M.88.1753A); σκώληκα δέ φησιν ἀτελεύτητον τὴν ἐν τῷ μετανοεῖν τῶν ἰδίων ἁμαρτημάτων σ. Proc.G.*Is.*66:24(M.87.2716D); διὰ τὴν τῶν ἔργων ἀτοπίαν τὸ σκότος ὑποδέξεται...καὶ ὁ ἀκοίμητος σκώληξ...καὶ τὸ πάντων βαρύτατον, ἡ ἐν τῷ σ. αἰσχύνη πέρας οὐκ ἔχουσα Max.*ep.*4(M.91.641B).

J. divinized in Stoicism θεὸν εἶναι μόνον φασὶ τὴν ἑκάστου σ. Thphl.Ant.*Autol.*2.4(M.6.1052A).

συνειλ-έω, *crowd together*; *bind together*; pass., met., *be bound up with* τὴν οἰκείαν ἐν τῇ τοῦ ἀγαθοῦ θεοῦ μονῇ ταυτότητα ∼ουμένην διὰ παντός Max.*schol.c.h.*15.4(M.4.109D).

***συνειλημμένως,** *in combination* ἐν αὐτῇ [sc. τῇ αὐτοϋπεραγαθότητι] ...τὰ ὄντα πάντα...καὶ τοῦτο ἀσχέτως, καὶ σ., καὶ ἑνιαίως Dion.Ar.*d.n.*5.6(M.3.820D).

***συνειλοχώς,** v. συλλαγχάνω.

σύνειμι, (*sum*), **1.** *exist with* or *alongside, coexist*; **a.** in gen. συνυπάρχον ὡς χρόα σώματι οὗ ἄνευ οὐκ ἔστιν (οὐχ ὡς μέρους ὄντος, ἀλλ' ὡς κατ' ἀνάγκην συνόντος παρακολουθήματος) Athenag.*leg.*24.2(M.6.945B); τὸ δὲ ὑλικόν, μέχρι σύνεστι τῷ κρείττονι, μένει Clem.*ecl.*25(p.143.32; M.9.709C); of constituent parts of man ἄνθρωπος...οὐ μέρει μέρος, ἀλλὰ ὅλῳ ὅλος σ. id.*exc.Thdot.*51(p.123.18; M.9.684A); of soul and body in man οὐδὲ σ. ἀεὶ τῇ ψυχῇ τὸ σῶμα Just.*dial.*6.2(M.6.489B); συνῆν...ἐξ ἀρχῆς αὐταῖς καὶ τὸ σῶμα Meth.*res.*1.54(p.311.5; M.41.1145B); in the life to come τὸ σῶμα ἐν τῇ κατὰ τοὺς αἰῶνας διαγωγῇ...συνέσεσθαι τῇ ψυχῇ *ib.*1.32(p.269.12; M.18.268B); **b.** in eternity with God; **i.** ref. Creation πότερον ἔκ τινος συνόντος ἀεὶ τῷ θεῷ, ἢ ἐξ αὐτοῦ καὶ μόνου id.*arbitr.*2(p.149.24; M.18.244D); τὰ πάντα ...κεκτίσθαι...οὔτε σ. τῷ θεῷ, οὔτε προϋπάρξαντα Epiph.*exp.fid.*14(p.514.23; M.42.809A); **ii.** Trin., ref. Gen.3:12 ἀριθμὸν τῶν ἀλλήλοις συνόντων, καὶ τὸ ἐλάχιστον δύο, μεμήνυκεν Just.*dial.*62.3(M.6.617B); of Son's pre-existence with Father, *ib.*62.4(617C); ὁ...υἱὸς...καὶ σ. καὶ γεννώμενος id.*2apol.*6.3(M.6.453A); acc. Marcellus μόνον εἶναι λόγον φάσκων...τῷ θεῷ...σ. καὶ ἡνωμένον, οἷος ἂν εἴη καὶ ὁ ἐν ἀνθρώπῳ λόγος Eus.*Marcell.*2.1(p.31.31; M.24.777A); acc. Eus. οὐ τὸν αὐτὸν ὄντα τῷ πατρί, καθ' ἑαυτὸν δὲ ὄντα...καὶ ἀληθῶς υἱὸν σ. id.*e.th.*1.8(p.66.20; M.24.837B); ὁ...υἱὸς ἦν πρὸς...τὸν θεὸν σ. καὶ συμπαρὼν αὐτῷ ἀεὶ καὶ πάντοτε *ib.*2.14(p.116.35; 932A); σ. ... καὶ παρῆν ⟨αὐ⟩τῷ πρὶν καὶ γενέσθαι τὸν οὐρανόν *ib.*3.3(p.154.23; 997B); and Ath. εἰ...οὐκ ἀϊδίως σ. ὁ λόγος τῷ πατρί, οὐκ ἔστιν ἡ τριὰς ἀΐδιος Ath.*Ar.*1.17(M.26.48A); in creeds πιστεύειν...εἰς ἕνα υἱόν...συνόντα τῷ γεγεννηκότι αὐτὸν πατρί *Symb.Ant.*(341)1 ap.Ath.*syn.*22(p.249.2; M.26.721A); in later writings ὁ θεὸς λόγος...υἱὸς καὶ θεὸς καὶ συνὼν τῷ πατρὶ Nest.*fr.* C 10(p.275.2)ap.Cyr.*Nest.*2.8(p.44.8; συναινῶν 6^1.47E); ἐκ τῆς ἡμετέρας οὐσίας σε ἐξεγέννησα, συνόντα καὶ συνυπάρχοντα Cosm.Ind.*top.*5(M.88.256B); **iii.** Christol. ἡ σοφία...ἀπαθὴς...κἂν τεμνομένῳ συνῆν... σώματι Meth.*Porph.*2(p.506.4; M.18.404B); ὁ...τὸ πάθος ὑπομείνας... ἐν τῇ σαρκὶ...συνούσης αὐτῷ τῆς θεότητος Epiph.*exp.fid.*17(p.517.19; M.42.813C); of the divinity with the glorified body τῆς θεότητος συνούσης τῷ...σώματι *ib.*(p.518.13, v.l. συνηνωμένης 816B); denied by Marcellus πῶς ἔτι τὴν τοῦ δούλου μορφήν...σ. τῷ λόγῳ δυνατὸν γένοιτ' ἄν; Marcell.*fr.*104 ap.Eus.*Marcell.*2.4(p.54.26; M.24.816C); or explained away ἆρα μὴ ὢν [sc. ὁ λόγος] ἐν τῷ θεῷ, ὅτε τῇ σαρκὶ συνῆν;... δραστικῇ γὰρ ἐνεργείᾳ μόνῃ φησὶ τῇ σαρκὶ σ. Eus.*Marcell.*2.4(p.57.7,14; 820C,821A); Christol., usage condemned εἴ τις...τὸν θεὸν λόγον σ. τῷ Χριστῷ λέγει γενομένῳ ἐκ γυναικός...ἀ. ἔ. Justn.*conf.anath.*3(p.90.25; M.86.1015A) = CCP(553)*anath.*3(p.168); **2.** *be with*; *be joined with*; ref. Christian unity τοῖς λειπομένοις πᾶσιν ἐπικουροῦμεν καὶ σ. ἀλλήλοις ἀεί Just.*1apol.*67.1(M.6.429B); ref. union with God πολλοὺς...καταγηράσκοντας ἀγάμους ἐλπίδι τοῦ μᾶλλον συνέσεσθαι τῷ θεῷ Athenag.*leg.*33.1(M.6.965A); ὁ γνωστικὸς...δι' εὐχῆς σ. σπεύδων τῷ θεῷ Clem.*str.*7.7(p.30.30; M.9.456C); ἵν' ἢ σ. [sc. the angels] αὐτῷ καὶ ἀπολαύσωσι μακαριότητος, ἢ...κρίνωνται Meth.*res.*1.37(p.278.15; M.41.1104B); μαθὼν καὶ σ. ... καὶ ἕπεσθαι θεῷ Gr.Thaum.*pan.Or.*15(p.34.11; M.10.1093D); of God with man ἐν πᾶσι μένειν καὶ ἑκάστῳ σ. Gr.Nyss.*or.catech.*34(p.127.8; M.45.85B); of baptismal grace, *ib.*(p.129.4; 85D); **3.** *be* or *become acquainted with* things τῶν νῦν ἀκουόντων...καὶ τοὺς ὕστερόν ποτε συνεσομένους τῷ λόγῳ Bas.*Eun.*1.3(1.211B; M.29.508B); *experience, find* εἰς ἀρρενωπότερον ἀνακτήσομαι, καὶ τοῦ λοιποῦ...ἀκλινεστέρῳ [sc. μοι] συνέσεσθε Synes.*ep.*56(M.66.1381D); **4.** *live with* or *together* οἱ δὲ ἐν...ἀθανασίᾳ σ. Just.*dial.*45.4(M.6.573A); Eus.*Marcell.*2.1(p.33.24; M.24.780C); of a man with his wife, Synes.*ep.*105(M.66.1485A); **5.** ref. states, *be in, live in* συνέσο γλυκείαις ἐλπίσιν *ib.*31(1360A).

συνείρω, 1. *combine* τά τε ὄντα τά τε μὴ ὄντα ἑαυτῷ σ. [sc. Marcellus] Eus.*Marcell.*1.4(p.27.33; M.24.769A); Christol., of union of natures μεσιτεύει...καταλλάττων ἡμᾶς τῷ θεῷ...καὶ σ. ὥσπερ εἰς ἕνωσιν τὰ...διενηνεγμένα Cyr.*synous.*5(p.483.5); **2.** ? for συναίρω *cast up* or *keep* accounts τὸν τελώνην...τῶν ἐκ τῆς πλεονεξίας χρημάτων τοὺς λόγους σ. Vict.*Mc.*2:14(p.288.11).

συνεισάγ-ω, *bring in together*; **1.** *introduce at the same time* or *together*, e.g. into a discourse συνεισήγετο...τὸ περὶ πνεύματος...ὅτι ἐστὶν ἐν τῇ αὐτῇ θεότητι †Apoll.*ep.Bas.*2(M.32.1108A); λανθανόντως ἑαυτὸν σ. Chrys.*hom.24.1 in Mt.*(7.299D); id.*hom.5.2 in Rom.*(9.463B); οὐσίας...οὐδὲ ὀνόματι μνήμη τοῖς ἄλλοις λόγοις συνεισήγετο Philost.*h.e.*4.8(M.65.521B); πῶς...∼ετε πρώτῳ καὶ μόνῳ...θεῷ καὶ πατρὶ τὸν υἱόν; Cyr.*thes.*27(5^1.247B); **2.** *include*; hence *imply, involve at the same time* or *together* with τὴν ἐπέκεινα...ζωήν, ἥτις ἑαυτῇ σ. τὴν ἀνάστασιν Athenag.*res.*16(p.68.17; M.6.1008A); ἡ τοῦ ἑτέρου γνῶσις...σ. τὸ ἕτερον Gr.Naz.*or.*30.15(p.132.9; M.36.124B); τῆς...τῶν φύσεων δυάδος οὔσης νοερᾶς ἐξ ἀνάγκης καὶ θελημάτων αὐτῇ συνεισαχθήσεται δυάς Polem.*fr.*(Lietzmann p.276.17); ‡Ath.*dial. Trin.*2.22(M.28.1192A); of correlative terms συνεισάγεσθαι...ἀλλήλοις τὰ τοιαῦτα πέφυκε Max.*ep.*12(M.91.473A); ref. father and son as correlative terms, Bas.*Eun.*1.5(1.215A; M.29.517A); σ. [sc. πατήρ] τὸν υἱόν, οὐκ ἀλλοτριώσει, κατὰ...τὴν τῶν κλήσεων τούτων δύναμιν Gr.Naz.*or.*29.16(p.98.12; M.36.96A); ἡ τοῦ υἱοῦ προσηγορία σ. ... τὴν τοῦ πατρὸς ὕπαρξιν Cyr.*thes.*12(5^1.112A); **3.** *contribute* ἐὰν μὴ ἡμεῖς εἰς τὸ ἀγαθόν τι σ. Or.*princ.*3.1.24(p.243.12; M.11.301B); μηδὲν διὰ δωρεᾶς ...τούτοις [sc. non-Catholics] σ. (tr. Lat. *conferant*) *Cod.Afr.*22; **4.** *bring* or *display* a quality τῶν προσιόντων...σ. τὴν πρόνοιαν Philost.*h.e.*9.4(M.65.569B); cf. συνεισακτέον; **5.** *bring in, introduce as spiritual companion* of the opposite sex (v. s. συνείσακτος) ὅσοι ὑπὸ τοῦ ∼ειν ἑαυτοῖς γυναῖκας ἐξέπεσον, οἱ δ' ὑπωπτεύθησαν Malch.*ep.*ap. Eus.*h.e.*7.30.13(M.20.716A); μηδὲ ∼άγῃς ἀρσένα κηδεμόνα Gr.Naz.*carm.*2.2(epigr.)18.2(M.38.92A).

***συνεισαγωγικός,** *each involving the other, correlative*, Max.*ep.*12(M.91.472D).

***συνεισακτέον,** *one must bring* or *display*, e.g. a quality πολλὴν προσοχὴν σ. τῷ εὐλαβῶς ἐντυγχάνοντι...ταῖς θείαις βίβλοις Or.*princ.*4.3.5(p.331.15; M.11.385B).

συνείσακτος, *brought in, introduced together*; applied to a virgin companion of a celibate man or conversely; freq. as subst., of a man ἄρσενα πάντ' ἀλέεινε, σ. δὲ μάλιστα Gr.Naz.*carm.*1.2.2.96(M.37.586A) = *ib.*2.2(epigr.)14.1(M.38.88A); of women σ. καὶ ἀγαπητὰς ἐπικαλουμένας Epiph.*haer.*78.11(p.461.31; M.42.716A); τοὺς ἔχοντας παρθένους σ. Chrys.*subintr.*tit.(1.228A); **1.** def., cf. σ. δέ φησι, τὰς ἑλομένας συνοικεῖν ἱερεῦσιν ἀζύγοις, τὰς πρὸς τὰς ἀναγκαίας χρείας αὐτοῖς διακονουμένας Matthaeus Monachus *schol.*CNic.(325)*can.*3(M.119.1296C); εἰπόν τινες ἐπείσακτον ἢ σ. εἶναι τὴν ἀντὶ νομίμου γυναικὸς συναχθεῖσαν, καὶ συνοικοῦσάν τινι πορνικῶς· ἄλλοι δὲ εἶπον εἶναι πᾶσαν γυναῖκα συνοικοῦσάν τινι ἀλλοτρίαν πάντως, κἂν ἀνύποπτός ἐστι Thdr.Bals.*schol.*CNic.(325)*can.*3(M.137.232B); **2.** earliest use of term appears to be at Antioch ref. Paul. Sam. τὰς...σ. αὐτοῦ γυναῖκας, ὡς Ἀντιοχεῖς ὀνομάζουσιν, καὶ τῶν περὶ αὐτὸν πρεσβυτέρων καὶ διακόνων, οἷς καὶ τοῦτο καὶ τὰ ἄλλα ἁμαρτήματα ἀνίατα ὄντα συγκρύπτει Malch.*ep.*ap.Eus.*h.e.*7.30.12(M.20.713C); **3.** subject of legislation μήτε ἐπισκόπῳ...μήτε ὅλως τινὶ τῶν ἐν τῷ κλήρῳ ἐξεῖναι σ. ἔχειν, πλὴν εἰ μὴ ἄρα μητέρα ἢ ἀδελφὴν ἢ θείαν, ἢ ἃ μόνα πρόσωπα πᾶσαν ὑποψίαν διαπέφευγε CNic.(325)*can.*3; περὶ τοῦ μὴ ἔχειν σ. κληρικὸν οἱονδήποτε Jo.Scholast.*coll.cap.*71; περὶ ἐπισκόπων καὶ κληρικῶν συνόντων γυναιξὶ σ. Phot.*nomoc.*8.14(p.529; M.104.1092C); cf. *episcopus vel quilibet alius clericus aut sororem aut filiam virginem dicatam Deo tantum secum habeat; extraneam nequaquam habere placuit,* CEliberitanum(306)*can.*27; τὰς...συνερχομένας παρθένους τισὶν ὡς ἀδελφὰς ἐκωλύσαμεν CAnc.(314)*can.*19; **4.** in the following sections the word συνείσακτος, where not found in the immediate context, may be understood as subject of author's remarks, e.g. †Bas.*contub.*tit.(M.30.812B); perh. the term to which such opprobrium was attached that Chrys. was unwilling to employ it, Chrys.*fem.reg.*3(1.254C); **a.** opp. both married and truly celibate τοὺς...σ. ... οὐκ οἶδ' εἴτε γάμῳ δώσομεν, εἴτ' ἀγάμους θήσομεν Gr.Naz.*carm.*2.2(epigr.)15.3(M.38.89A); ὁ μὲν γάμος οὐδὲν ὄνειδος τῶν δὲ σ. φείδεται οὐδὲ λίθος *ib.*14.6(89A); Chrys.*subintr.*1(1.228B); *ib.*6(236D,E); cf.id.*fem.reg.*1(1.248E,249A); πολλῷ...βέλτιον γαμεῖν ἐκείνως, ἢ παρθενεύειν οὕτως *ib.*3(254A); **b.** status of σ. defended on ground that it provided protection for weaker sex ἐρεῖς, ὅτι διὰ Χριστὸν αὐτὸ πράττεις προνοούμενος τοῦ ἀσθενοῦς σκεύους †Bas.*contub.*9(M.30.824B); παρθένε...μηδὲ συνεισαγάγῃς ἀρσένα κηδεμόνα Gr.Naz.*carm.*2.2(epigr.)18.2(M.38.92A); cf. παρθένε, μὴ συνοίκει προστάτῃ *ib.*1.2.3.67(M.37.638A); Chrys.*subintr.*6(1.235E); cf.id.*fem.reg.*4(1.255A); and supplied men's practical needs, †Bas.*contub.*9(824B); ἐπισκόπου...ἐσχηκότος...τοιαύτας γυναῖκας ἐξυπηρετουμένας αὐτῷ, φημὶ δὲ σ. Epiph.*haer.*63.2(p.400.10; M.41.1065A); σ. γυναῖκας, [δι'] ἃς εἰώθαν [sc. Hieracites] φιλοτιμεῖσθαι ἔχειν εἰς ὑπηρεσίαν *ib.*67.8(p.140.10; M.42.184A); cf. διὰ τὴν αὐτῶν διακονίαν ὑμᾶς κατέχουσι Chrys.*fem.reg.*4(255A); **c.** motives: basic motive alleged to be voluptuous pleasure, conscious or unconscious, on part of man, Chrys.*subintr.*1(1.228C–229B); and vainglory on part of woman, cf.id.*fem.reg.*6(1.259A); οὐδὲ γὰρ ἡ δουλουμένη τοὺς ἄνδρας γυνή, ἀλλ' ἡ αἰδουμένη, αὕτη...ἐστιν αἰδέσιμός τε καὶ ἐπίδοξος *ib.*(259D); regarded by some writers as no more than a cloak for immorality, †Bas.*contub.*9(M.30.824C); *ib.*10(824D); τῆς ἐπιπλάστου ἀδελφοζωΐας, τὸ δ' ἀληθές,...τῆς ἀσχήμου κακοζωΐας περὶ τῶν καλουμένων σ. Pall.*v.Chrys.*5(p.31.19; M.47.20); but gross sin not usu. alleged οὔτε...τὸν ἑβδομηκονταετῆ γεγονότα πείθομαι ἐμπαθῶς συνοικεῖν γυναικί Bas.*ep.*55(3.149D; M.32.404A); ἐγὼ δὲ τοῦτο μὲν οὐκ ἂν εἴποιμι, ὅτι τὰς συνοικούσας φιλοῦσιν ἢ ἐπαφῶνται Chrys.*subintr.*2(230B); cf.id.*fem.reg.*3(253C); *ib.*5(258D); **d.** relationship of σ. condemned as cause of offence τὸ παρά τινων ὑγιῶς γινόμενον ἄλλοις ἀφορμὴ πρὸς ἁμαρτίαν ὑπάρχει Bas.*ep.*55(3.149D; M.32.404A); Chrys.*subintr.*3(1.231D); cf.id.*fem.reg.*5(1.257Af.); and occasion of impurity in thought if not in act ἂν πάλιν γυνὴ τῶν ἰδίων ἀποστᾶσα συγγενῶν ξένῳ ἀνδρὶ συνοικεῖν ἐπιχειρῇ τῆς ἐπιπλάστου ἀγάπης ἕνεκεν, τοῦτο μῖξις λοιπὸν συζυγίας ἀθεμίτου πυρκαϊὰν ἐργαζομένης †Bas.*contub.*5(M.30.820D) et passim; Chrys.*subintr.*5(235Af.); cf.id.*fem.reg.*1,3(249D,253B); κάκιστον μοναχὸς σ., ὡς πῦρ εἰς καλάμην Hyper.*mon.*55(M.79.1480A) ∞ Ephr.2.359A; as a grave distraction in itself, †Bas.*contub.*11(M.30.825f.); and in virtue of business responsibilities undertaken on behalf of the virgins, Chrys.*subintr.*6(1.236A); those in such relationship would live to regret it, †Bas.*contub.*9(824B); μὴ ἔχειν γυναῖκα σ., καθάπερ τινὲς ἀγαπητὰς ἐπέθεντο αὐταῖς ὀνόματα· τάχα δὲ ἐναντίως μισηταὶ αὐτοῖς εὑρεθήσονται ‡Ath.*syntag.*2.7(p.123; M.28.837C); and faced a terrible judgement, †Bas.*contub.*11(828A); *ib.*8(824A); but condemnation chiefly on grounds of scandal, Bas.*ep.*55(3.149D,150A; M.32.404A,B); μὴ σκανδαλίζετε τὸν κόσμον, οἱ τὰς σ. ἔχοντες, μὴ γὰρ γῆμαί σε ἡ γραφὴ οὐκ ἐπέτρεψε; †Bas.*contub.*4(M.30.820B); μηδὲ συνεισάκτῳ σὸν βίον ἐξυβρίσῃς Gr.Naz.*carm.*2.2(epigr.)17.4(M.38.91A); τὴν τοῦ θεοῦ δόξαν ὑβριζομένην...διὰ τὴν ἡδονὴν ταύτην Chrys.*subintr.*1(1.228D); *ib.*8(240C,D); cf.id.*fem.reg.*3(1.253B,E); ἡ...παρθενία αὕτη ἡ μετὰ ἀνδρῶν πορνείας χαλεπώτερον παρὰ πᾶσι διαβέβληται *ib.*(254A).

***συνεισάλλομαι,** *rush in also,* Synes.*ep.*35(M.66.1361C); Cyr.*Ps.*40:11(M.69.997C).

συνεισβαίν-ω, **1.** *go in together, enter with* μέχριπερ ἂν...τρανῶς ἐποπτεύσῃ Χριστῷ συνεισβᾶσα [sc. the Church] Meth.*symp.*8.11(p.94.11; M.18.156A); **2.** *be included,* of Persons in Trin. ἅμα τε θεὸς νοεῖται ὁ πατήρ, καὶ συνεισβέβηκεν εὐθὺς ἡ ὕπαρξις τοῦ δι' ὅν ἐστι πατήρ, καὶ...τὸ...ἅγιον πνεῦμα Cyr.*Abac.*35(3.549E); πατρὸς μὲν .. νοουμένου τε καὶ ὄντος...τοῦ πατρός, υἱοῦ δὲ...νοουμένου τοῦ υἱοῦ, ∼οντος...τοῦ ἁγίου πνεύματος id.*Jo.*1.5(4.46D).

συνεισβάλλω, *interject* ἐπίτριπτον λόγον σ. Thdr.Stud.*epp.*2.162(M.99.1512B).

***συνεισδέχομαι,** **1.** *receive* one *together with* another, *take in at the same time,* ref. image and likeness of God συνεισδεξόμεθα τῷ υἱῷ τὸν πατέρα Cyr.*dial.Trin.*3(5^1.491C); **2.** *admit, allow* τὰ...καθ' ὑπόστασιν...ἑνούμενα, οὔτε τροπὴν σ., οὔτε γνωρίζει διαίρεσιν Sophr.H.*ep.syn.*(M.87.3164B).

συνεισδύομαι, *enter together,* Cyr.*ador.*3(1.99C).

συνεισέρχομαι, *enter along with,* of persons τοῦ χρόνου τύπος ἂν εἴη Μωϋσῆς...ὡς μὴ σ. ἐκείνοις σωματικῶς εἰς τὴν κατάπαυσιν Max.*ambig.*(M.91.1164B); αὐτῷ...ὥσπερ εἰς νυμφῶνα, τὴν ἀνάπαυσιν τῶν καινῶν αἰώνων...συνεισελεύσεσθαι Meth.*symp.*7.3(p.74.7; M.18.128D); Andr.Caes.*Apoc.*57(M.106.397D); Gnost. τὸ σπέρμα σ. αὐτῷ εἰς τὸ πλήρωμα διὰ τῆς θύρας Clem.*exc.Thdot.*26(p.115.20; M.9.672C); *ib.*35(p.118.16; 676D); *ib.*86(p.133.9; 697B); myst., ref. indwelling of Trin. σ. τὸ πνεῦμα Ath.*ep.Serap.*1.31(M.26.601B); of soul into divine mysteries τῷ Μωϋσῇ σ. εἰς τὸν γνόφον τῆς...θεωρίας Gr.Nyss.*hex.*5(M.44.65C); of things εἰ ἕν τι...ἀπὸ τῆς κτίσεως προσαφθείη, πᾶσα ἡ κτίσις συνεισελεύσεται εἰς τὴν τοῦ πατρὸς καὶ υἱοῦ συναρίθμησιν Bas.*hom.*24.5(2.194B; M.31.612A); of conceptions τῇ τοῦ πατρὸς ἐννοίᾳ ἡ υἱοῦ σ. id.*Eun.*2.12(1.247B; M.29.593C); τῇ...τῆς θεότητος ἐννοίᾳ πάντα τὰ τοιαῦτα νοήματα σ. Gr.Nyss.*Maced.*6(M.45.1309A).

συνεισηγέομαι, *bring in, introduce together* or *at the same time,* perf. in pass. sense αὕτη [sc. ἡ παράκλησις]...παρ' αὐτῶν...συνεισήγητο Chrys.*hom.3.1 in 2Cor.*(10.442A, v.l. συνεισήγετο Gaume).

***συνεισθέ-ω,** *run into*; **1.** *enter with* οἱ τῷ Νῶε σ. εἰς τὴν κιβωτόν Cyr.*glaph.Gen.*2(1.38A); **2.** *accompany, be associated* with μετάπεμπτον...Μωσέα, ∼οντος Ἀαρών id.*ador.*1(1.44D); met., of things γινώσκομεν...δι' αὐτοῦ [sc. τοῦ υἱοῦ] τέ καὶ σὺν αὐτῷ τὸν πατέρα, ∼οντος...τῇ τοιᾷδε γνώσει καὶ τοῦ ἐλεεῖσθαι *ib.*11(405D); τῆς ἀγαθουργίας οἱ τρόποι τῇ τῆς φαυλότητος ἀνατροπῇ ∼οντες id.*Mich.*20(3.409C); of the H. Ghost in Trin. συνθεολογουμένου τε καὶ ∼οντος id.*hom.pasch.*15.3(5^2.204D).

***συνεισκομίζω,** **1.** *carry* or *take in along with*; into the ark, Cyr.*glaph.Gen.*2(1.38A); **2.** *introduce also* or *at the same point* in a discussion, *include* τῇ τοῦ μυστηρίου παραδόσει καὶ ὁ περὶ τῆς ἀναστάσεως τῶν νεκρῶν συνεισκεκόμισται λόγος Cyr.*Is.*3.1(2.354B); id.*Juln.*9(6^2.291C); Max.*ambig.*(M.91.1072D).

***συνεισκομιστέον,** *one must include,* Cyr.*ador.*2(1.80B).

συνεισκρίνω, *include, imply,* Thdr.Stud.*epp.*2.204(M.99.1621B); *ib.*2.212(1640C); pass. σ. ... ἐπ' ἀμφοῖν ἡ ἑκατέρου γνῶσις Cyr.*ador.*7(1.235B); Thdr.Stud.*epp.*2.212 loc. cit.

***συνείσοδος, ἡ,** *entry together*; of Law with Israel into Promised Land, Max.*ambig.*(M.91.1164B).

συνεισπέμπω, *send in along with*; met., *introduce, instil together* thoughts, Isid.Pel.*epp.*3.91(M.78.796C).

συνειστρέχ-ω, **1.** *run in together with* ∼οντας τῷ κηρύγματι τοὺς ἀγῶνας Cyr.*hom.pasch.*9.1(5^2.107B); **2.** *go with, be associated with* εἰσφέρεται...δι' ἀμφοῖν ἡ θατέρου περίνοια, καὶ σ. ... συνεπινοηθέντι τῷ πατρὶ καὶ ἡ τοῦ γεννήματος μνήμη id.*Jo.*5.2(4.495D); συνεπινοουμένου καὶ σ. *ib.*1.2(19A); **3.** in time, *coincide* Χριστὸς Ἰησοῦς ὠνόμασται... τῆς...κλήσεως ὁ καιρὸς ∼ουσαν ἔχει τὴν γέννησιν id.*Nest.*1.7(p.28.10; 6^1.24A).

συνεισφέρ-ω, **1.** *join in paying*; intrans., *make a contribution* in money (ref. Mc.12:44) ἡ δὲ ἐκ τῆς ὑστερήσεως συνεισήνεγκεν Clem.*str.*4.6(p.264.7; M.8.1248A); Or.*Jo.*19.8f.(2; pp.307f.; M.14.540Bf.); †Bas.*bapt.*1.2.1(2.629C; M.31.1525B); **2.** in gen.; **a.** *contribute, make one's contribution* βούλομαι...σ. τι καρποφορίᾳ αὐτῶν Iren.*haer.*1.4.4(M.7.484B); ταῦτα...ὑπὲρ ἁγνείας...σ. Meth.*symp.*3.14(p.45.6; M.18.85C); προθυμίαν ἄφατον αὐτῷ σ. Eus.*h.e.*6.23.2(M.20.576B); ἵνα ἔχῃς τι...σ. εἰς τὴν σωτηρίαν Chrys.*hom.14.6 in Rom.*(9.585A); ὁ δὲ...τῷ θεῷ θαρρῶν, καὶ τὰ παρ' αὐτοῦ σ. Thdt.*qu.in 2Par.*(1.597); τὰ τοιαῦτα τοῖς κάμνουσι σ. Olymp.*Job* 30:25f.(M.93.317A); ἡ...ἑβδομὰς τῶν μαρτύρων νόμῳ θανοῦσα τὴν χάριν ∼ει Geo.Pis.*carm.*21.2(p.51); med. οὔτε τὸ ἀγέννητον τοῦ γεννητοῦ δέεται εἰς τὸ ∼εσθαι ἑαυτοῦ τῇ οὐσίᾳ Epiph.*haer.*76.38(p.391.7; M.42.597C); τῷ βίῳ συνεισενεγκάμενοι *ib.*77.1(p.416.21; 641B); τὰ παρ' ἑαυτῆς συνεισενεγκαμένη Chrys.*hom.12.5 in Col.*(11.420B); **b.** *supply, furnish* σ. εἴ τι... παραλέλειπται Or.*ep.*1.1(M.11.49A); αὐτὸς ὑφάνας τοὺς λόγους τῆς συκοφαντίας, τούτων μόνον συνεισενεγκάντων τὸ ὑπογράψαι Pall.*v.Chrys.*7(p.39.2; M.47.24); **c.** *help to bring about*; *go to make up* τὰ εὐαγγέλια καὶ...τὰ ἐν νόμῳ, τὴν ἐν Χριστῷ γνῶσιν ἡμῖν...~οντα Cyr. ador.8(1.286C); τὰ μέρη σ. τοῦ ἑνὸς κάλλους τὸ ἀποτέλεσμα id.Ps. 29:8(M.69.856B); ῥοπὴν ~ουσαν...τὸ κατ' ἐνέργειαν ἐν πράγματι τέλος Max.ambig.(M.91.1261C); 3. introduce the notion of, imply (at the same time) τὸ γέννημα σ. τῇ ἑαυτοῦ οὐσίᾳ τὸν αἴτιον Aët.ap.Epiph. haer.76.38(p.390.7; M.42.596D) ∞ τὸ γέννημα σ. τῆς ἑαυτοῦ οὐσίας τὸ αἴτιον ‡Ath.dial.Trin.2.22(M.28.1192A); οὔτε τὸ γέννημα σ. τὴν ἑαυτοῦ οὐσίαν· εἰ γὰρ ἄν, πάντα τὰ γεννητὰ τὴν αὐτὴν συνεισέφερον οὐσίαν ib. (1192B); σ. ... ἐξ ἀνάγκης τὸν ἀριθμὸν ἡ διαφορά Jo.D.Jacob.21(M.94. 1448B); associate, connect, med. τοὺς ἀποστόλους...τῇ ~ομένῃ τὸν λόγον [sc. τοῦ κυρίου] δυνάμει πρὸς ἐργασίαν ἀποχρησαμένους Marc. Er.opusc.3.1(M.65.965D); pass. ἐν τῇ τοῦ πνεύματος χάριτι πυρὸς δήλωσις ~εται Cyr.Ps.49:3(M.69.1076D); 4. in textual confusion with συμφέρω; a. bring, take μέριμναν συνεισενεγκάμενος Epiph.haer. 69.11(M.42.217D; συνενεγκ- p.160.25); b. bring together, v.l. for συνενεγκὼν Cyr.expl.xii cap.8(p.23.12; 6[1].154C).

συνεισφορά, ἡ, 1. joint contribution, of money, ref. Mt.17:24ff. τὴν τοῦ διδράχμου σ. ἐποιήσατο, καίτοι κατὰ φύσιν ἐλεύθερος ὁ υἱός Cyr.glaph.Ex.2(1.306C); id.Chr.un.(5[1].734C); ? gain ὡς σφόδρ' ἄπληστον, καὶ ξένης σ. Gr.Naz.carm.1.1.6.49(M.37.433A); 2. in gen., any contribution τῆς ἀπὸ τόπου ἢ χρόνου σ. Bas.Spir.4(3.4D; M.32. 73C); ἀλλήλοις διάδοτε, ἃ οἶδεν ἕκαστος, τῷ μὴ εἰδότι...καὶ οὕτως ἐκ σ. ἀλλήλους συνεστιάσαντες id.hom.23.1(2.185D; M.31.589D); ἡ τοῦ ὑψίστου δύναμις...τὴν ἐκ τοῦ παρθενικοῦ σώματος πρὸς τὸ πλασσόμενον σ. παρεδέξατο Gr.Nyss.Apoll.54(M.45.1256B); οὐδὲ γὰρ ἕπεται...τῇ θελήσει τὸ θεληθὲν...χωρὶς τῆς τοῦ ταύταις ὑποκειμένου ἐν ᾧ καὶ εἰσὶ συνεισφορᾶς Max.ambig.(M.91.1261D); esp. to virtue, etc. πρὸς τὸν κατ' ἀρετὴν βίον σ. Gr.Nyss.v.Mos.(M.44.326C); πρὸς τὸ καλὸν...σ. id.v.Gr.Thaum.(M.46.893B); ἡ...τῶν πλειόνων κατορθωμάτων σ. τῆς τελείας ἀρετῆς τὴν εὐοσμίαν ἐργάζεται Thdt.Ps.132:2(1.1512); 3. offering, ref. Is.1:11 τοῦ προφήτου βδελυσσομένου τὴν ἀπὸ τῶν τοιούτων σ. Gr.Nyss.or.dom.4(p.86.32; M.44.1173D); 4. a bringing together, relation, association, of divine power with human response τοὺς μὴ χρησαμένους τοιαύτῃ σ. ... κατέκρινεν, εἰπών [Jo. 8:40] Marc.Er.opusc.3.1(M.65.965D).

συνεισφρέω, enter together, Cyr.Soph.22(3.603E).

συνεκβάλλω, cast out along with, reject one with another, Gr.Nyss. Apoll.27(M.45.1181C); Chrys.hom.33.2 in Jo.(8.191C).

συνεκβιβάζω, carry out, execute sentence, decree, etc., Sophr.Al. libell.(p.23.31; H.2.336E).

*συνεκδείκνυμι, indicate at the same time, Gr.Nyss.tres dii(M.45. 133D).

συνεκδέχομαι, await σ. ... τὴν ἀνάλυσιν τῆς ψυχῆς καθ' ἡμέραν Pall.h.Laus.proem.(p.10.18; M.34.1002).

συνεκδημ-έω, go abroad together; met.; 1. of departing from this world for the next οὐκ ἐθέλει [sc. χρυσός] τοῖς κτησαμένοις σ. Bas. hom.21.3(2.165E; M.31.545C); ~εῖν ἐκδημούσῃ τοῦ θεοῦ τῇ μητρὶ ἐφιέμενοι Jo.D.hom.9.9(M.96.736B); σ. ... διὰ θανάτου ὁ τοῦ Ἰωάννου πατήρ Jo.VI H.v.Jo.D.13(M.94.449B); 2. of living apart from this world τοῖς Χριστιανοῖς...ἀναγκαιότατον...ζωῆς τῆς παρούσης σ. ‡Cyr. Trin.1(6[3].1A; M.77.1120A).

συνεκδημία, ἡ, going together on a journey abroad, of the death to sin τὸ φώτισμα...σ. Χριστοῦ Gr.Naz.or.40.3(M.36.361B).

συνέκδημος, ὁ, companion in travel, fellow traveller; 1. of persons; met., of companion in death δέξαι με οὖν σ. σου A.Andr.A 7 (p.50.14); σ. κἀμὲ τοῦ βίου λαβεῖν †Jo.D.B.J.39(M.96.1228B); 2. met., of things φύλασσέ μοι τὴν καλὴν παρακαταθήκην ᾗ ζῶ καὶ πολιτεύομαι, ἣν καὶ σ. λάβοιμι Gr.Naz.or.40.41(M.36.417A) ∞ Justn.conf.(p.78.3; M.86.999D); τὴν ταῖς ἡμετέραις σ. ἀρετὴν...πρὸς...ἅπαν εἶδος ἀγαθουργόν Cyr.hom.pasch.11.3(5[2].147D).

συνεκδίδ-ωμι, impart alike to κατὰ τὸ συνεχὲς...τῆς φύσεως ἐκ τοῦ μέρους ἐπὶ τὸ ὅλον ~ομένη [sc. ἡ ἀνάστασις] Gr.Nyss.or.catech.(p.117. 7; συνδιδομένη M.45.80C).

*συνέκδοσις, ἡ, joint publication, Phot.cod.280(M.104.356A).

συνεκδοχή, ἡ, way of understanding σ. ... πλείονας...λαμβάνειν Clem.str.5.9(p.364.20; M.9.88B).

συνεκδοχικός, of synecdoche σ. τρόπῳ...ὁ καπνὸς παρείληπται· οὔτε γὰρ καπνὸς ἄνευ πυρὸς ὑφίσταται cat.Apoc.15:8(p.408.26).

συνεκδοχικῶς, 1. by way of synecdoche, a figure in which the part is made to stand for the whole or vice versa; exeg. scripture Ἠλίας, σ. οὐχ εἷς μόνος ἀλλὰ πάντες οἱ προφῆται Or.comm.in Mt.12.38 (p.155.15; M.13.1072A); Bas.hex.1.7(1.8C; M.29.20C); ref. Lc.22:19b συγκεφαλαίωσις...τῆς ὅλης οἰκονομίας τόδε τὸ μυστήριον· ἐκ τοῦ κυριωτέρου μέρους σ. τὸ ὅλον ἐπισημαινόμενος Thdr.Stud.antirr.1. 10(M.99.340C); 2. in a measure, partially τὴν ἀληθῆ τῶν ὄντων...σ. ὑποδέξασθαι γνῶσιν Max.ambig.(M.91.1152D).

*συνεκθεόω, make divine along with, Christol. τὸ τῆς θείας φύσεως ἄτρεπτον κατεκράτησε τοῦ τῆς ἀνθρωπίνης φύσεως τρεπτοῦ καὶ... συνεξεθέωσεν αὐτὴν ἑαυτῷ Leont.H.Nest.4.21(M.86.1685D).

συνεκκεντέω, pierce or stab one with another, Gr.Naz.or.14.3(M.35. 861A).

συνεκκλησιάζω, 1. be fellow members of the Church, Clem.paed.2. 8(p.203.2; M.8.485C); Pamph.Mon.Soter.2(p.115.22); 2. act. and pass. intrans., gather in church together with, Didym.Trin.1.27 (M.39.397A); Leont.H.monoph.(M.86.1900C); ib.(1876D); ἀπέβη τοῦ στύλου...καὶ τῷ λαῷ...σ. Thdr.Lect.h.e.1.32(M.86.181A).

συνεκκόπτω, cut off at the same time or together with; met., children with parents, Isid.Pel.epp.1.195(M.78.308B).

*συνεκκυλί-ω, roll out or away together; met., cause to decline with τὸ δὲ πρὸς Ἑλληνισμὸν ἐκκυλίεται, καὶ ἑαυτῷ ~ει τὸν φάσκοντα Sophr.H.ep.syn.(M.87.3153C).

συνεκλαμβάνω, receive from; met., pass., be produced, formed τὸ ἐκ τῆς...συνηθείας συνεκλελημμένον ἦθος Alex.Lyc.Man.1(M.18. 412D).

*συνεκλαμπρύνομαι, shine forth together, †Sophr.H.orat.(M.87. 4004A).

συνεκλάμπω, shine forth together with; fig., of saints with Christ οἱ λύχνοι...σ. τῷ λαμπαδίῳ Cyr.Zach.24(3.685D); met. τῷ καθαρῷ... τῆς γεννήσεως αὐτοῦ [sc. of the Son] συνεκλάμψασα [sc. παρθενία] Gr. Nyss.virg.2(p.253.15; M.46.321C); of Son ὁ τῇ δόξῃ τοῦ πατρὸς σ. id. Eun.2(2 p.313.21; M.45.485C); cf.id.fid.(M.45.140B).

συνεκλεκτός, chosen together by God; of Church in Rome, cat. 1Petr.5:13(p.82.31).

*συνεκνήχομαι, swim away with, c. dat., met., Bas.leg.lib.gent.4 (p.48; M.31.572C).

*συνεκπίμπλημι, fulfil, accomplish one thing with another, Athenag.res.7(p.56.11; M.6.988B).

συνεκπίπτω, fall out together; 1. fall away together with ὅπως δὴ καὶ αὐτοὶ [sc. men] συνεκπέσοιεν αὐτῷ [the Devil] Clem.str.2.13 (p.143.25; M.8.996A); δύναμίς τις...τῷ ἀποστάτῃ σατανᾷ συνεκπεπτωκυῖα Areth.Apoc.13:1f.(M.106.672A); 2. fall away also or at the same time from ἡ...ζωὴ...τῆς τῶν ἀγαθῶν μετουσίας ἐκπεπτωκυῖα, συνεκπέπτωκεν καὶ τοῦ θείου βουλήματος Gr.Nyss.or.dom.4(p.76.30; M.44. 1168B); 3. come forth together τῶν...ἀπ' Αἰγύπτου συνεκπεσόντων ἐπιμίκτων Afric.ep.Arist.5(p.61.11; M.10.61A).

συνεκπληρόω, accomplish to the full, Symb.Ant.(341)1 ap.Ath. syn.22(p.249.5; M.26.721A).

συνεκπολεμ-όω, excite to join in war against ~ῶσαί γε αὐτὸν Πέρσαις Men.exc.gent.16(p.459.18; M.113.820C).

*συνεκπονητέον, one must work out thoroughly or to completion, Clem.str.2.9(p.137.10; M.8.981A).

συνεκπορεύ-ομαι, go forth together; theol., of H. Ghost, proceed from while being coexistent with ὁ υἱὸς...συναπογεννηθεὶς...καὶ τὸ ἅγιον πνεῦμα ~θέν, κατὰ φύσιν ἐστὶν ἀγαθόν Didym.Trin.2.3(M.39.477C).

*συνεκπορνεύω, commit fornication together with ὁ...ἁλοὺς τῇ αἱρετικῇ κοινωνίᾳ, οὗτός ἐστι ὁ ἐκπορνεύσας εἰς θεόν, καὶ σ. δυνάμει καὶ τῷ σώματι Thdr.Stud.catech.parv.3(p.6).

*συνεκπτύω, spit out or vomit at the same time, i.e. one thing with another, Gr.Nyss.hom.5 in Eccl.(M.44.689D); Pall.v.Chrys.8 (p.45.10; M.47.27).

*συνεκριζ-όω, root out together; met., Gr.Nyss.anim.et res.(M.46. 65A); οὐχί, τοῦ πνεύματος...ἐρχομένου, καὶ ἡ...ἐπιθυμία ~οῦται μετὰ τῆς ἁμαρτίας; Mac.Aeg.hom.26.2(M.34.676B).

*συνεκριπίζ-ω, winnow out together ὡς ἄχυρον τῷ τῆς ῥαθυμίας ἀνέμῳ τοῖς κατηχουμένοις ~ονται Nest.hom.in Heb.3:1(p.241.24; M. 64.489D).

συνεκτείν-ω, extend together or along with, trans. and intrans.; 1. in space; a. extend as far as, pass. intrans. παραστάδες τῷ μήκει τοῦ νεὼ συνεξετείνοντο Eus.v.C.3.37(p.94.12; M.20.1097A); spread, stretch, fig. τούτου [sc. φυτοῦ signifying Christ] ταῖς μὲν ῥίζαις ὑπορριζοῦμαι, τοῖς δὲ κλάδοις ~ομαι ‡Chrys.pasch.6(p.177.9; 8. 272A); b. stretch out on a cross; pass., be crucified ~ονται αὐτῷ δύο λῃσταί ib.; myst. ὁ Χριστῷ...συνεσταυρωμένος καὶ ~όμενος αὐτῷ καταλαμβάνει τὸ πλάτος κτλ. Or.comm.in Eph.3:18f.(p.412); 2. in time, endure, last for, cover a period of time, ref. Ps.94:8 σήμερον ἡ ἀνελλιπὴς τοῦ θεοῦ ἡμέρα τοῖς αἰῶσι ~εται Clem.prot.9(p.64.4; M.8. 196C); κατὰ τρεῖς βασιλεῖς ἡ προφητεία...συνεξέτεινε Or.hom.1.2 in Jer.(p.2.17; M.13.257A); in eternity, endure throughout or as long as ἀνακαινισμὸς...διαιωνιζούσῃ παρατάσει ~όμενος cat.Apoc.14:8(p.391. 14); theol., of Son as coeternal with Father συντρέχων τῇ τοῦ πατρὸς ἀϊδιότητι καὶ ~όμενος Cyr.thes.5(5[1].41C); 3. in gen.; a. extend as far as, stretch out along with, pass. intrans. τὸ ~εσθαι...τοῖς μεγάλοις καὶ συνεξισάζεσθαι...τὸ δὲ βραχύνεσθαι ἐν τοῖς μικροῖς καὶ συστέλλεσθαι Meth.*Porph*.2(p.505.12; M.18.401D); τὴν πρόνοιαν...τῇ τῶν πεπληθυσμένων ἀκαταληψίᾳ ~ομένην Max.*ambig*.(M.91.1193A); **b.** *make commensurate with*, ref. Inc. τοῦ θεοῦ λόγου τῇ τοῦ σώματος ἡλικίᾳ ~οντος κατὰ βραχὺ τῆς σοφίας τὴν ἔκφανσιν Cyr.*Lc*.2:40(M.72.508B); **c.** *make equal with* οὐ χρὴ...~ειν ἑαυτοὺς τῷ υἱῷ κατὰ τὴν φύσιν Ath.*decr*.31(p.27.27; M.25.473C); pass. intrans. οὐδὲν ἔστι ὃ τοῖς ἐνοῦσι αὐτῷ [sc. τῷ θεῷ] πλεονεκτήμασι ~εται Cyr.*Is*.5.2(2.780D).

συνεκτέμνω, *excise together*; met., *cut off*, *exterminate together*, i.e., one with another, Isid.Pel.*epp*.1.195(M.78.308B).

συνεκτικός, *apt for holding together*; **1.** *astringent* τὴν...ὕσσωπον πόαν...σ. ἔχουσαν τὴν ἐνέργειαν Cyr.*Ps*.50:9(M.69.1096C); **2.** of a kind of cause, approximating to the *efficient* cause τὰ μὲν [sc. αἴτια] προκαταρκτικά, τὰ δὲ σ., τὰ δὲ συναίτια, τὰ δὲ συνεργά Clem.*str*.8.9(p.101.13; M.9.600C); cf. τῶν αἰτίων τὰ μὲν προκαταρκτικά, τὰ δὲ σ., τὰ δὲ συνεργά, τὰ δὲ ὧν οὐκ ἄνευ *ib*.(p.95.27; 592C); described σ. δὲ ἅπερ συνωνύμως καὶ αὐτοτελῆ καλεῖται, ἐπειδήπερ αὐτάρκως δι' αὐτῶν ποιητικά ἐστι τοῦ ἀποτελέσματος. ἑξῆς δὲ πάντα τὰ αἴτια ἐπὶ τοῦ μανθάνοντος δεικτέον. ὁ μὲν πατὴρ αἴτιόν ἐστι προκαταρκτικὸν τῆς μαθήσεως, ὁ διδάσκαλος δὲ σ., ἡ δὲ τοῦ μανθάνοντος φύσις συνεργὸν αἴτιον, ὁ δὲ χρόνος τῶν ὧν οὐκ ἄνευ λόγον ἐπέχει *ib*.(p.95.31ff.; 592C); προκαταρκτικὰ μὲν αἴτια ἑνὸς γίνεται πλείονα κατὰ γένος καὶ κατ' εἶδος...τὰ δὲ σ. αἴτια κατὰ γένος μόνον, οὐκέτι δὲ καὶ κατ' εἶδος. τοῦ γὰρ εὐωδιάζεσθαι κατὰ γένος ἑνὸς ὄντος πολλὰ τὰ αἴτια κατ' εἶδος *ib*.(p.100.16; 600A); τῶν μὲν οὖν προκαταρκτικῶν αἰρομένων μένει τὸ ἀποτέλεσμα, σ. δέ ἐστιν αἴτιον, οὗ παρόντος μένει τὸ ἀποτέλεσμα καὶ αἰρομένου αἴρεται. τὸ δὲ σ. συνωνύμως καὶ αὐτοτελὲς καλοῦσιν, ἐπειδὴ αὐτάρκως δι' αὐτοῦ ποιητικόν ἐστι τοῦ ἀποτελέσματος *ib*.(p.101.18f.; 600C,D); τὸ σ. αἴτιον οὐ δεῖται χρόνου *ib*.(p.98.19; 596C); οὐδὲν τῶν ἐκ τοῦ σ. αἰτίου τοῖς αἰτιατοῖς παραμένειν πέφυκεν, μὴ τοῦ αἰτίου παρόντος Leont.B.*Nest.et Eut*.2(M.86.1329D); with ποιητικός, of God as creator and preserver θεὸν...τὴν πάντων ποιητικήν τε καὶ σ. αἰτίαν Gr.Naz.*or*.28.6(p.29.4; M.36.32C); id.*carm*.1.1.6.4(M.37.430A); Jo.D.*hom*.10.4(M.96.760C), cf. 3; **3.** *holding together*; *maintaining*, *conserving*; **a.** freq. with ποιητικός: ἡ τοῦ θεοῦ δύναμις, ἡ ποιητικὴ τῶν ὄντων...ἡ σ. τῶν γεγονότων Gr.Nyss.*or.catech*.5(p.22.3; M.45.21B); Max.*ambig*.(M.91.1081C); ‡Cyr.*Trin*.7(6³.8B; M.77.1132A); of Christ's human will προσηγόρευσαν αὐτὴν [sc. τὴν ἀνθρωπίνην κίνησιν] δύναμιν ...ὡς...σ. ἀναλλοίωτον Max.*Pyrr*.(M.91.352A); **b.** with περιεκτικός: σ. δυνάμεως, καὶ περιεκτικῆς ἀποπερατώσεως Dion.Ar.*c.h*.14(M.3.321A); τὴν περιεκτικὴν καὶ σ. τοῦ...κόσμου...δεσποτείαν Melet.*nat.hom*.1(M.64.1152A); **4.** *essential*, *cardinal*, *important*, *leading* οὐ πάσας ἀναλέξομαι...τὰς φωνάς, μόναις δὲ ταῖς σ. χρήσομαι Eus.*Marcell*.1.1(p.8.29; M.24.728C); freq. superl. σ. δόγμα id.*p.e*.7.10(317A; M.21.536B); ἃ δὴ καὶ σ. γένοιτ' ἂν τῶν ἐν φιλοσοφίᾳ λόγων...παρὰ μόνων Ἑβραίων πεπορισμένοι [sc. Gentiles] *ib*.10.1(460D; M.768A); ἕν τι τῶν μάλιστα σ. τῇ προκειμένῃ πραγματείᾳ *ib*.10.8(482D; M.804B); Synes.*ep*.67(M.66.1424A); τῶν ἀστέρων...τοὺς σ. Geo.Pis.*hex*.368(M.92.1462A); neut. as subst., *cardinal point*, *important principle*, *essence* of a matter τὰ σ. τῶν πρὸς γνῶσιν φερόντων Clem.*str*.6.11(p.477.29; M.9.312C); εἰς τὸ σ. κατερχόμενοι Epiph.*haer*.69.45(p.193.4; M.42.292D); τὰ...ἀναγκαῖα καὶ σ. ... τοῦ νόμου Cyr.*Lc*.11:42(M.72.716A); superl. plur. τὴν ...γνῶσιν...τῶν σ. τῆς κατὰ τὸν σωτῆρα...οἰκονομίας Eus.*p.e*.1.1(4C; τῆς σ. M.21.28A); **5.** = περιεκτικός, *embracing*, *comprehending*, Max.*ambig*.(M.91.1136D); of man as a microcosm ὁ ἐπὶ πᾶσιν, ὥσπερ τι τῶν ὅλων συνεκτικώτατον ἐργαστήριον...ἄνθρωπος *ib*.(1305A); of Christ σύμπλεγμα κοσμικόν, τῆς ποικίλης καὶ ἀνθρωπίνης οὐσίας σ. ‡Chrys.*pasch*.6(p.179.5; 8.272B); of God ἀρχηγική, τελειωτικὴ καὶ σ. φρουρά Dion.Ar.*d.n*.1.7(M.3.596C); πρόνοιαν...σ. τοῦ παντός Max.*ambig*.(M.91.1133D); neut. as subst., *assembly point*, *point of collection* τὰ...νῶτα [sc. ἐμφαίνειν] τὸ σ. τῶν ζωογόνων ἁπασῶν δυνάμεων Dion.Ar.*c.h*.15.3(M.3.332C).

συνεκτικῶς, **1.** *by way of maintaining* or *preserving*, Dion.Ar.*d.n*.4.10(M.3.708A); **2.** *effectively*, *conclusively* συνεκτικώτατα ἀνθυπήνεγκας...εἰ...ἠνείχοντο...συναριστεῖν Pall.*v.Chrys*.13(p.79.14; M.47.45); Max.*ambig*.(M.91.1265A).

***συνεκτίλλω**, *pluck up together*; met., *cut off* persons, Isid.Pel.*epp*.1.195(M.78.308B).

***συνεκτιμάω**, pass., *be honoured together* or *at the same time*, Bas.Sel.*enc.in Andr*.1(M.28.1101B).

***συνεκτίστης, ὁ**, *one who joins in repaying*, ‡Nil.*narr*.7(M.79.689C).

συνεκτρέπομαι, *be turned aside*, Geo.Pis.*Heracl*.2.35(M.92.1319A).

συνεκτρέφω, ptcpl. pass., *brought up to*, *habituated* φόνοις καὶ ἁρπαγαῖς συνεκτραφείσαις χώραις Mart.Ant.*pan*.2(M.47.xliii).

***συνεκτυπ-όω**, *impress*, *imprint* τοῖς ἤθεσιν...~οῦσθαι τὸ ὑπήκοον ὡς σημάντρῳ κηρόν Isid.Pel.*epp*.1.319(M.78.368A).

***συνεκτυφλόομαι**, *be blinded together* with; c. dat., Thdr.Stud.*epp*.2.66(M.99.1289D).

***συνεκφανίζ-ομαι**, *shine out together*, *appear plainly with* πάντων ἑαυτῷ...τοὺς ἀληθεῖς βούλεται ~εσθαι λόγους Max.*ambig*.(M.91.1156B).

***συνέκφρασις, ἡ**, *use of synonyms*, *two-fold descriptions*, ‡Ath.*annunt*.10(M.28.932B).

***συνεκφροντίζω**, *think out together* Εὐαγρίῳ τῷ...πολλά μοι συγκαμόντι καὶ σ. Gr.Naz.*test*.(M.37.393B).

συνεκφων-έω, **1.** *join in singing*, Chrysipp.*enc.in Thdr*.(p.54.7); **2.** pass., *be pronounced together* or *simultaneously*, Athenag.*leg*.22.2(M.6.937A); τοῦ ἰῶτα στοιχείου ἢ προστεθέντος ἢ συγγραφομένου μέν, μὴ ~ουμένου δέ Isid.Pel.*epp*.4.112(M.78.1181A); **3.** pass., *be mentioned in the same breath*; of nouns, *be used together* σ. τῷ κυρίῳ τὸ πνεῦμα Bas.*Spir*.43(3.36E; M.32.148A); Gr.Naz.*or*.31.19(p.167.16; M.36.153B); cf.Max.*ambig*.(M.91.1269C); Trin., ref. Son as γέννημα: διὸ οὐδὲ τὸ ~εῖσθαι τῷ θεῷ καὶ πατρὶ αὐτοῦ ἀνέχεται Aët.*synt*.37 ap. Epiph.*haer*.76.53(p.407.21; M.42.628A); ἑτέρῳ δὲ τῶν κεκτισμένων τὸ θεὸς ὄνομα οὐ ~εῖται Epiph.*haer*.76.53(p.408.19; 628D); *ib*.(p.409.6; 629B).

συνεκφώνησις, ἡ, **1.** *simultaneous utterance*, *saying together* τὴν... τῆς εὐχῆς σ. Clem.*str*.7.7(p.30.21; M.9.456B); **2.** *corresponding utterance* ἂν γὰρ προαναφώνησίν τις εἴπῃ καὶ σ. αἰτιάσηται, προφητείας εἴδη λέγει *ib*.1.19(p.60.20; M.8.809B); **3.** *common expression*, *expression in each case* ἡ...τῶν ὀνομάτων σ. ἐπ' ἀμφοῖν Gr.Naz.*or*.31.19(p.169.10; M.36.156A).

***συνεκχαλάω**, *become loose* or *slack at the same time*; perh. *become weak* or *relaxed also* καθ' ἣν [sc. βάσανον] ἔξω γεγόνασιν αὐτοῦ τῶν φυσικῶν θαλάμων οἱ ὀφθαλμοί· δῆλον γάρ, ὅτι καὶ τὰ λοιπὰ τῶν κρυφίων συνεξεχάλασαν μόρια *Mir.Artem*.24(p.35.6).

συνελαύν-ω, **1.** *drive together*; met., *harry*, *persecute* τοὺς τῆς ἐκκλησίας διακρινομένους συνήλαυνεν...καὶ Ναυατιανοὺς...συνηλαύνοντο οὖν καὶ οὗτοι Socr.*h.e*.2.38.5(M.67.324C); **2.** *drive*, *force*, *compel* μηδενὸς ~οντος Eus.*Marcell*.2.4(p.58.27; M.24.824B); τὸ πῦρ... πρὸς μὲν τὸ πᾶν φέρεσθαι ὑπὸ τῆς ἐγκειμένης τῇ φύσει δυνάμεως ~όμενον Gr.Nyss.*hex*.14(M.44.77A); τοῦ πυρετοῦ...πρὸς τὸν θάνατον ~οντος id.*v.Macr*.(p.390.18; M.46.977C); *reduce* εἰς ἀφωνίαν συνελάσας...τὸν Ἀφθόνιον Philost.*h.e*.3.15(M.65.508A); ref. pagan oracles τὸ ἀσθενὲς αὐτῶν καὶ πεπλανημένον διελέγχειν τῇ θείᾳ προνοίᾳ συνηλαύνοντο *ib*.7.12(549C); **3.** *draw*, *induce*, *constrain* persons; to good αὐτοὺς σ. ... τὰς ἐλπίδας...ἔχειν Chrys.*hom*.65.3 *in Mt*.(7.647E); *ib*.17.7(7.232C); σ. ... πρὸς μετάγνωσιν Cyr.*Abac*.9(3.524E); id.*ador*.8(1.253B); to evil ὁ πονηρὸς...πρὸς ἀδικίαν ἡμᾶς...σ. Meth.*res*.2.7(p.342.4; M.18.305A); pass., *be drawn* into εἰς μάχας καὶ...εἰδωλολατρείας σ. id.*symp*.10.1(p.122.10; M.18.193A); *ib*.10.4(p.126.10; 200A); **4.** pass., of things, *be brought about*, *ordered* σκόπει πῶς συνηλάθη τὸ πρᾶγμα, ὥστε ἐν ἑορτῇ γενέσθαι Chrys.*hom*.85.2 *in Mt*.(7.805D); **5.** *draw* or *come* (*to an end*) τῆς...εἰς Βαβυλῶνα...αἰχμαλωσίας εἰς πέρας... ~ούσης Eus.*d.e*.8.2(p.367.28; M.22.597B); abs. ~οντος τοῦ καιροῦ *ib*.10.8(p.492.13; 789D).

***συνελαφρίζ-ω**, *join in lightening* or *relieving*; *lighten* by cooperation αὐτῷ...συμπονοῦντα...~ειν τοὺς πόνους Gr.Naz.*carm*.2.1.11.499(M.37.1063A); ἔσχεν ~ουσας...τὰς δύο πτέρυγας τοῦ ἀετοῦ *cat.Apoc*.12:14(p.365.22).

συνελέγχω, **1.** *convict also of*, *expose at the same time* τὴν ἀκρασίαν τοῦ Ἀπόλλωνος νικήσασα σ. αὐτοῦ τὴν μαντικήν Tat.*orat*.8(p.9.18; ἤλεγξας M.6.825A); **2.** *confute* κηρύττων τὴν ἀλήθειαν λίχνους τοὺς φιλοσόφους...σ. *ib*.19(p.21.6; 849A); *ib*.3(p.3.18; διήλεγξεν 809A); pass., *ib*.35(p.37.17; 877C).

συνέλευσις, ἡ, *coming together*; **1.** of persons, *assembly*, *gathering*, *congregation* αἱ πρωτοκαθεδρίαι...ἐν ταῖς σ. Bas.*renunt*.8(2.209D; M.31.644B); τὴν γὰρ βουλὴν [Hebr. עֵדָה] ὁ μὲν Ἀκύλας καὶ ὁ Θεοδοτίων συναγωγὴν ἡρμηνεύκασι, σ. δὲ ὁ Σύμμαχος Thdt.*Ps*.1:6(1.615); exeg. Pr.26:26 συνέδριον [Hebr. קָהָל]: ἀνακαλύπτει...τὰ ἑαυτοῦ παραπτώματα ὁ ἐν σ. ... εὐδιάγνωστος ‡Proc.G.*Pr*.26:26(M.87.1489A); **a.** for social purposes, Clem.*paed*.2.7(p.189.28; M.8.456C); Meth.*symp*.proem.(p.4.12; M.18.29B); **b.** for worship ἐπὶ τὸ αὐτὸ σ. γίνεται Just.*1apol*.67.3(M.6.429B); κοινῇ πάντες τὴν σ. ποιούμεθα *ib*.67.8(429C); ἐπὶ τῆς τῶν ἁγίων...ἐπὶ τὸ αὐτὸ τῇ ἐκκλησίᾳ γινομένων συνελεύσεως Or.*or*.31(p.400.20; M.11.555C); τὰς σ. τὰς...τεταγμένας Epiph.*haer*.80.4(p.489.22; M.42.764A); σ. τῆς ἑορτῆς ‡Ath.*annunt*.1(M.28.917A); ὑπὲρ τῆς ἁγίας ἐκκλησίας ἡμῶν καὶ τῶν σ. ἡμῶν *Lit.Marc*.(Brightman p.121.24); heret. οὐ γὰρ ἀγάπην εἴποιμ' ἂν τὴν σ. αὐτῶν [sc. Carpocratians]

Clem.*str*.3.2(p.200.7; M.8.1112A); *τῆς πανδήμου τῶν πεπλανημένων σ.* Epiph.*exp.fid*.11(p.511.12; M.42.801B); hence *conventicle* *τὰς αὐτῶν ἐκκλησίας ἤτοι φωλεοὺς καὶ σπήλυγγας* (*οὕτω γὰρ εἴποιμι τὰς τῶν αἱρέσεων σ.*) id.*haer*.52.2(p.312.28; M.41.956C); **c.** for eccl. council *Ἄρειος ἡμῖν ὁ τῆς μανίας ἐπώνυμος...καὶ τῆς σ. αἴτιος* ‡Eust. *alloc*.(M.18.676A); Ath.*syn*.1(p.231.12; M.26.681B); *σ. τῶν ἐπισκόπων* Socr.*h.e*.1.8.14(M.67.64A); *ἐν Χαλκηδόνι τὴν θείαν ποιεῖται θεόθεν σ.* Sophr.H.*ep.syn*.(M.87.3185B); **d.** *chorus* of angels *ἀγγελικὴν σ.* ‡Meth.*Sym.et Ann*.4(M.18.357A); **2.** *meeting, encounter*, †Jo.D.*B.J*. 38(M.96.1220B); **3.** *coming together, rapprochement*, ref. Lc.23:12 *τὴν γεγενημένην Ἡρώδου...καὶ Πιλάτου...κατὰ τοῦ Χριστοῦ σ.* Just. *1apol*.40.6(M.6.389A); **4.** ref. time *τῇ σ. over a period of τῇ τοῦ τοσούτου χρόνου σ. συνέστη αὐτοὺς μηδενὶ τρόπῳ πεπεῖσθαι δεδυνῆσθαι* Sabinus ap.Eus.*h.e*.9.1.5(M.20.800C); **5.** theol., *union*; **a.** Christol. *ὁ θεανδρικὴν φήσας ἐνέργειαν...τὸ τὰς δύο ἐνεργείας ἓν εἶναι τῇ σ. ... δεδήλωκεν* ‡Cyr.*Trin*.19(6^3.25B; M.77.1157D); *ἡ τῶν δύο φύσεων ἐν μιᾷ ὑποστάσει σ.* †Jo.D.*B.J*.19(M.96.1029A); **b.** of individual with God *τῆς...γνωμικῆς σ.* Leont.H.*Nest*.2.20(M.86.1581B); **6.** (Gnost.), *coming together, union* of aeons, Val.Gn.ap.Epiph.*haer*.31.5(p.391. 9; M.41.481C); **7.** = *ἔλευσις*, messianic *coming*, *Apoc.Bar.rel*.3.8.

***συνέλιξις, ἡ,** *rolling up* or *together*; **1.** *concentration* in one area; of stars, Philost.*h.e*.10.9(cj. for *συνέλιψις*; M.65.589B cj. *σύνθλιψις*); **2.** met., ref. activity of spiritual beings, *introversion*, signifying *concentration* of spiritual faculties *ὁ θεῖος ἔρως...διὰ τἀγαθὸν... καὶ εἰς τἀγαθόν, ἐν ἀπλανεῖ σ.* Dion.Ar.*d.n*.4.14(M.3.712D); *αἱ* [sc. *τῶν νοητῶν οὐσιῶν*] *περὶ ἑαυτὰς ἀμετάπτωτοι σ. ib*.4.2(696B); *ψυχῆς ...κίνησίς ἐστι, κυκλικὴ...ἡ εἰς ἑαυτὴν εἴσοδος ἀπὸ τῶν ἔξω, καὶ τῶν νοερῶν αὐτῆς δυνάμεων ἡ ἑνοειδὴς σ. ib*.4.9(705A); *ib*.7.2(868C); what is turned over in the mind and made the subject of concentration, *fruit of meditation, reflection* *διακρίναι...τὰς συνοπτικὰς καὶ ἐνιαίας...σ. ib*.3.2(681B).

συνελίσσ-ω, *roll up together*; met.; **1.** *bind up with, connect* *κυβερνήτης...τὸν πελάγιον δρόμον τῷ κατ' οὐρανὸν φέγγει σ.* Bas.Sel. *or*.8.1(M.85.112C); **2.** *turn inwards, concentrate* *ἀναλαβόντες ἅπαντας εἰς τὸν ἕνα...ἔρωτα, καὶ πάντων αὐτῶν πατέρα συνελίξωμεν ἅμα* Dion. Ar.*d.n*.4.16(M.3.713C); pass., *be recollected* *τῇ ἀμεταπτώτῳ ταυτότητι περὶ ἑαυτὴν ∼εσθαι* id.*c.h*.15.4(M.3.333B).

***συνέλιψις,** vox nihili, v. *συνέλιξις*.

συνελπίζω, *hope for along with*, †Bas.*Is*.66(1.427A; M.30.232C).

συνεμβαίνω, *embark*; met., *embark on, enter into*, Clem.*str*.1.2 (p.13.19; M.8.709A).

συνεμπίπτω, 1. *fall into at the same time*; met., errors, Clem.*str*. 6.12(p.481.24; M.9.320C); *ταῖς τῶν Ἑλλήνων ἢ τῶν Ἰουδαίων σ. δόξαις* Gr.Nyss.*Apoll*.4(M.45.1129C); **2.** *fall in with, concur in* opinions *ἐννοήσαντες ὅτι οὐ χρὴ εἰς τὴν αὐτῶν ταπεινότητα αὐτοὺς σ. ... ἐγκαλούμενος* [sc. Christ] *αὐτοὺς...εἰς τὸ...μὴ σ. τοῖς πολλοῖς* Vict.*Mc*. 8:29(p.346.1,8); pass. *οὐδενὶ τῶν ταπεινῶν νοημάτων σ.* Gr.Nyss. *Eun*.1(1 p.198.10; M.45.444D); **3.** *befall* or *occur together, coincide* *μετ' αὐτοῦ...τὸν λιμὸν εἰς τὰς πόλεις σ.* Chrys.*hom.4.1 in Mt*.(7.47B); *οὐκ ἔνι ταῦτα πάντα εἰς γυναῖκα μίαν σ. ib*.30.5(7.354A; *συμπεσεῖν* Gaume); *ὁ συνεμπεσών one whom one chances to meet, chance visitor*, Bas.*reg.fus*.32.2(2.375E; M.31.996C); **4.** *fall under the same heading* *πάντα...ἀλλήλοις σ. καθ' ὁτιοῦν πάντως, εἰ καὶ μὴ πάντῃ* Max.*ambig*. (M.91.1312B).

***συνεμπορεύομαι,** *join in business, trade in company with*; met., Synes.*insomn*.14(p.174.7; M.66.1308B).

***συνεναπόκειμαι,** *be stored up with* or *together*; met., *reside in* or *coexist with*, Leont.H.*Nest*.5.20(M.86.1741C).

συνενδείκνυμι, med., *show, point to at the same time*, Gr.Nyss.*hex*. 9(M.44.72B); id.*Eun*.7(2 p.165.28; M.45.756B); Didym.*Trin*.2.14(M. 39.693A); in Trin. controversy, Gr.Nyss.*Eun*.12(1 p.319.16; M.45. 1033C); *τὴν τοῦ πατρὸς κλῆσιν...ἥτις καὶ τὸν υἱὸν μεθ' ἑαυτῆς σ. ib*.2(2 p.300.15; 472A); v. *συνδείκνυμι*.

***συνένδειξις, ἡ,** *joint indication* *ἡ λαμπρὰ τῶν ἐσθημάτων τῷ φωτὶ τοῦ προσώπου αὐτοῦ γενομένη σ.* Max.*ambig*.(M.91.1156B).

***συνένδημος,** met., *at home with, living naturally in accordance with* *ὡς ἄνθρωπον τὸν θεὸν...τελείῳ τῷ κατὰ φύσιν διὰ φιλανθρωπίας λόγῳ συνένδημον* Max.*ep*.2(M.91.400C).

***συνενδιάω,** *stay in a place with* *ἑτέρῳ...σ. μαθητῇ* Nonn.*par.Jo*. 20:2(M.43.908C).

συνενδίδωμι, *give way*; *concede* *εἰ...συνενδῴη τις αὐτοῖς ἄλλο τι εἶναι* Clem.*paed*.1.6(p.116.14; M.8.301C).

συνενδύομαι, *put on in company with*, fig. *συνεκδυσάμενος αὐτῷ τὸ κακοπαθοῦν ἔνδυμα καὶ σ. ... τῆς ἀπαθείας τὸ πέπλον* Mac.Mgn. *apocr*.4.16(p.187.12).

***συνενθυμέομαι,** *ponder along with*; c. dat., *Clem.ep*.4(M.2.37B).

συνεν-όω, 1. *unite*; *join*; perf. pass., *be joined* or *united*; of a literary work, *be connected, cohere* *πᾶσα πραγματεία ἐξ ὑπαρχῆς σ. ... καὶ...διηρθρωμένη* Melet.*nat.hom*.epit.(M.64.1077A); of words, etc., *be next, following* *τῶν σ. αὐτῷ στίχων Lit.Praesanct*.(p.346.15); **2.** *come together into, unite to form* *τέσσαρα μέρη γενόμενος τέσσαρας σίλικας συνήνωσεν A.Petr.et Paul*.77(p.211.11); pass., *be put together* *τοσαῦτα...περὶ τοῦ σώματος ἡμῶν καὶ τῆς τούτου...συνθέσεως συνήνωται* Melet.*nat.hom*.30(M.64.1280B); s.v.l., of an instrument *χαλκευθῆναι* [sc. *ὑδροσκόπιον*] *καὶ σ.* Synes.*ep*.15(M.66.1352A); v. *συνάπτω*; **3.** *unite* morally *ᾧ συγκέκραται, καὶ συνήνωται ἡ ψυχὴ ἐν τοῖς θελήμασιν* Mac.Aeg.*hom*.1.8(M.34.457C); *ἡ ἐλπὶς σ. τοὺς εὐθύφρονας* Sophr.H. *ep.syn*.(M.87.3149C); **4.** theol.; **a.** *unite* mankind with God *εἰ μὴ συνηνώθη ὁ ἄνθρωπος τῷ θεῷ οὐκ ἂν ἠδυνήθη μετασχεῖν τῆς ἀφθαρσίας* Iren.*haer*.3.18.7(M.7.937B); God with created things *∼ωθῆναι...τοῖς ὁρατοῖς αὐτοῦ κτίσμασιν* Mac.Aeg.*hom*.4.9(M.34.480A); **b.** Christol., *unite, join* manhood to Godhead *ὁ θεὸς...σ. καὶ συγκεράσας* [sc. human nature] *τῷ λόγῳ* Meth.*symp*.3.5(p.31.20; M.18.68B); *λόγον... πᾶν εἴ τι ἐστιν ἄνθρωπος...εἰς ἑαυτὸν τῇ ἑαυτοῦ θεότητι ∼ώσαντα* Epiph.*inc*.1 ap.*haer*.20(p.228.5; M.41.273D); pass. *ὁ ἀπροσδεὴς τῇ προσδεομένῃ συνῆλθε καὶ συνηνώθη σαρκί* Apoll.*quod un.Chr*.9(p.300. 22; M.28.129B); pass., of Christ's human nature, Epiph.*haer*.69.64 (p.213.11; M.42.305D) cit. s. *ἐνανθρώπησις*; *τὸν ∼ωθέντα τῷ λόγῳ ναόν* Cyr.*inc.unigen*.(5^1.689B); of Christ's glorified body *τοῦ σωτῆρος τὸ σῶμα...συνήνωται...τῇ τοῦ λόγου...ἀφθαρσίᾳ* Epiph.*anc*.61(p.73.25; M.43.128A); *τὸ σῶμα...εἰς θεότητα σ.* id.*haer*.44.6(p.197.33; M.41. 829D); v. *σύνειμι*; **c.** with *ἕνωσις*, *form* a union *τὴν...ἕνωσιν κατὰ δύναμιν πατρὸς συνηνωμένην ib*.57.8(p.354.13; M.41.1008B); **5.** *unite* individuals to Christ *τὸ ∼ῶσαν ἡμᾶς τῷ σωτῆρι...τὸ ἅγιον πνεῦμα αὐτοῦ ἐστιν* Cyr.*Jo*.10.2(4.857B); of men, usu. pass. *συνηνῶσθαι αὐτῷ* [sc. *Χριστῷ*] *ἐν πίστει καὶ γνώσει, καὶ ἀρεταῖς* Nil.*epp*.1.254(M.79. 176D); *τοῖς ἁγίοις...∼ωθεῖσιν αὐτῷ διά τε τῆς πίστεως καὶ τῆς...ὁσιότητος* Cyr.*Jo*.10.2(4.858B); *ib*.(866E); in Church, ref. newly baptized *συνδεθῆναι καὶ ∼ωθῆναι τῇ ποίμνῃ* Serap.*euch*.22.2.

***συνεντίθημι,** *put in at the same time, insert also* *οὐχ οἷόν τε ἦν... μή τινος φυσικῆς δυνάμεως συνεντεθείσης* Gr.Nyss.*hom.opif*.30.11(M. 44.240B).

***συνεντρέπω,** *put to shame together with* *σ. τοῖς ἤδη παρ' αὐτοῦ... ἐντραπεῖσι καὶ τούτους ὁ μακάριος Κύριλλος* CLater.*act*.5(H.3.908D).

***συνεντρυφάω,** *delight in together with*, Gr.Naz.*ep*.6(M.37.29C).

***συνενυπόστατος,** *having independent existence together in one hypostasis*; Christol., *subsisting in one Person with* *τοῦ δὲ ἀνθρώπου, σ. ἐστιν ἡ θεότης· καινισθέντος...καθ' ὑπόστασιν· ἀντὶ γὰρ ἰδικῆς, κοινήν· καὶ ἀντὶ ἀνθρωπείας, θείαν κτησαμένου ὑπόστασιν* Leont.H. *Nest*.5.30(M.86.1749D).

***συνένωσις, ἡ, 1.** *unity* of Church, Epiph.*haer*.69.11(p.161.22; M. 42.220C); **2.** *union* of natures in Christ *τὴν...δόξαν...ἡ σὰρξ... λαβοῦσα ἐν τῇ σ. τοῦ θεοῦ λόγου ib*.69.80(p.228.16; 332D); *περὶ τῆς ἐνσάρκου παρουσίας τὴν σ. δηλῶν ib*.69.77(p.225.15; 328B); *μίαν ἑνότητα σημαίνων τῆς τοῦ λόγου σ. καὶ τῆς ἐνανθρωπήσεως ib*.57.8 (p.354.7; M.41.1008A).

***συνεξαγμένως,** s.v.l., *in such a way as to be brought out together* or *at the same time* *νοεῖται σ.* Ammon.ap.*cat.Jo*.21:12(p.408.19) for *συνεζευγμένως* Ammon.*Jo*.21:11(M.85.1521A).

συνεξαιθερόω, *change into air together*, Synes.*insomn*.9(p.162.16; M.66.1297C).

***συνεξαιτέω,** *join in asking for*, Chrysipp.*enc.in Thdr*.(p.71.2).

***συνεξακουστέον,** *one must understand also as implied in* *σ. δὲ τούτοις τὸ ἄρθρον εἰς ἐντέλειαν τοῦ νοήματος* Areth.*Apoc*.1:12(M.106. 516C).

συνεξαλείφω, *blot out, abolish together* or *at the same time*, Gr.Nyss. *hom.13 in Cant*.(M.44.1040A); pass., id.*anim.et res*.(M.46.40C).

συνεξαλλάσσω, *vary* or *change with* *ὁ ἀγεώργητος ἄρτος...τῷ πολυειδεῖ τῆς ποιότητος κατὰ τὰς τῶν ἐσθιόντων ἐπιτηδειότητας σ. τὴν δύναμιν* Gr.Nyss.*v.Mos*.(M.44.368C); *ib*.25(308C); *σ. τῷ χρόνῳ τὸ εἶδος, ἀνθῶν, κυπρίζων...πεπαινόμενος* id.*hom.3 in Cant*.(M.44.828D); id.*fat*.(M.45.153B); pass. *τῆς...τροφῆς...τῷ τρεφομένῳ σώματι συνεξαλλασσομένης* Athenag.*res*.6(p.53.28; M.6.984B).

συνεξαλλοιόω, *change together with* *σ. τοῖς σκεδαστοῖς τῆς ψυχῆς τὴν διάθεσιν* Max.*qu.Thal*.(M.90.260C); pass., id.*ambig*.(M.91.1109D).

συνεξάλλ-ομαι, 1. *leap out also*, met. *ἐξωθείσης...τῆς ἁμαρτίας, συνεξήλατο καὶ ὁ θάνατος* Cyr.*Ps*.40:11(M.69.997C); **2.** *leap up with* *τοῖς ὑπὸ δαιμονίας νόσου παραπεπληγόσι συνδιαστρεβλοῦσθαι καὶ ∼εσθαι καὶ συγκαταπίπτειν τῷ σώματι* Gr.Nyss.*Eun*.8(2 p.194.16; M. 45.789C).

***συνεξαλμυρόομαι,** *become briny*; *be made salt*, *A.Jo*.39(p.170. 10).

συνεξανύ-ω, *run together with; complete together,* met. τὸν εὐαγγελικὸν δρόμον τῆς μητρὸς τοῦ δεσπότου ~ούσης τῷ υἱῷ Mod.*mul. ung.*(M.86.3276B).

***συνεξαρνέομαι,** *deny along with* or *at the same time as* εἴ τις...τὰς δύο θελήσεις...σ. καὶ συναποβάλλεται, εἴη κατάκριτος CLater.*can.*14; *ib.*18 cit. s. συναποσιωπάομαι; pass. σ. ... μετὰ τοῦ υἱοῦ καὶ τὸ πνεῦμα τὸ ἅγιον ‡Ath.*Sabell.*10(M.28.112C).

***συνεξαστράπτ-ω,** *flash like lightning with* or *around* ~ούσης αὐτῇ [sc. ψυχῇ]...δυνάμεως Eustrat.*stat.anim.*14(p.429).

***συνεξαφανίζω, 1.** *cause to disappear together; do away with also* οἰόμενος...σ. τούτοις [sc. written records] τῆς ἀληθείας τὸν λόγον Jo. VI CP *ep.*(M.96.1428B); **2.** pass., *disappear together,* ‡Ath.*haer.*17(M. 28.516B).

***συνεξελληνίζ-ω,** *turn into Greek, put in a Greek form* ἀστέρων διαμνημονεύει ~ουσα τῇ φωνῇ Πλείαδα καὶ Ἀρκτοῦρον καὶ Ὠρίωνα τινὰς αὐτῶν καλοῦσα Hypat.*fr.*(p.128.17).

***συνεξεπαίρω,** *lift off also* or *at the same time* θελόντων...ἀποτυλίξαι τὴν σινδόνα...σ. πάσας τὰς σάρκας αὐτοῦ Thdr.Lect.*fr.*(M.86.224A).

συνεξεργάζομαι, *join in working out* or *accomplishing* ἐμοὶ...συγγράμματα [sc. divination by dreams] συνεξείργασται Synes.*insomn.* 14(p.175.2; M.66.1308C).

***συνεξερεύγομαι,** *utter at the same time; refer, ascribe at the same time* μετὰ τῶν ἄλλων μαθητῶν διδασκόμενος ὁ Πέτρος, σ. τῷ διδασκάλῳ τὴν δόξαν Bas.Sel.*or.*25.4(M.85.297A).

συνεξετάζ-ω, 1. *search out and examine together,* i.e. one thing with another; hence *compare* 'πνευματικοῖς...πνευματικὰ συγκρίνοντες', τῷ ~ειν τήνδε τὴν λέξιν τῇδε τῇ λέξει Or.*comm.in 1Cor.* 2:13(*JTS* 9 p.240); id.*Jo.*10.27(17; p.199.36; M.14.356A); τὸν... Χριστιανῶν βίον...σ. τῷ τρόπῳ τῶν ἀμφὶ τοῦ Ἀβραάμ Eus.*d.e.*1.5 (p.20.29; M.22.44D); **2.** pass., *be reckoned among* or *associated with* ὁ πρὸ ἐμοῦ διέπων τὸν τόπον τῆς ἐπισκοπῆς...καὶ νῦν ~όμενός μοι διὰ τῶν εὐχῶν Alex.H.*fr.*ap.Eus.*h.e.*6.11.3(M.10.205A).

***συνεξέτασις, ἡ, 1.** *close scrutiny* or *examination* of statements, Gr.Nyss.*Eun.*12(1 p.302.23; M.45.1013C); Thdr.Mops.*1Cor.*1:22ff. (p.174.8; M.66.880A); *inquiry, discussion* τὴν περὶ τοῦ υἱοῦ...σ. ‡Ath. *disp.*42(M.28.496C); **2.** *searching out* θεοῦ τὴν σοφίαν τὴν ὑπερβαίνουσαν σ. Epiph.*haer.*76.35(M.42.589A; πᾶσαν ἐξέτασιν p.385.26).

***συνεξεταστέον,** *one must compare* σ. ὕδωρ πηγῆς τοῦ Ἰακώβ... ὕδατι τοῦ Ἰησοῦ Or.*comm.in Mt.*12.8(p.79.14; M.13.992D); id.*Jo.*1.25 (24; p.30.18; M.14.68A).

***συνεξηχέω,** *sound forth together, join in singing,* Eus.*h.e.*2.17.22 (M.20.184A).

***σύνεξις, ἡ,** *union* τῇ διαιρέσει καὶ τῇ σ. τοῦ θεορρύτου λόγου Geo. Pis.*hex.*184(M.92.1447A).

συνεξισ-όω, 1. *equate* σ. τῶν πάντῃ διεστηκότων τὰς δυνάμεις Athenag.*res.*9(p.58.1; M.6.989C); *ib.*16(p.67.26ff.; 1005C); τὸ κτίσμα ~οῦτε τῷ θεῷ Ath.*ep.Serap.*1.29(M.26.597A); id.*ep.Epict.*9(p.15.1; M.26.1065A); pass. τῷ ἀνενδεεῖ κατὰ τὴν φύσιν, τὸ...μέτριον κατὰ τὸν τῆς ἀπαθείας λόγον ~οῦται Gr.Nyss.*or.dom.*4(p.78.15; M.44.1168D); **2.** pass. intrans., *be equal, rank with,* Athenag.*res.*16(p.67.16; M.6. 1005B); καίπερ ὄντα νέον ~οῦσθαι τῇ τοῦ πρεσβυτέρου Ζαχαρίου μαρτυρίᾳ *Ep.Lugd.*ap.Eus.*h.e.*5.1.9(M.20.412A); τὸν παράκλητον... οὔτε τῷ υἱῷ ~ούμενον· μονογενὴς γάρ ἐστιν, οὐδένα ἔχων ἀδελφὸν ὁμογενῆ Eun.*exp.fid.*3(p.258).

***συνεξόδιος,** *coming* or *going out together,* Anast.S.*hex.*12(M.89. 1060C).

***συνεξόλλυμαι,** med., *perish utterly together* with σ. ... τοῖς παροξύνουσιν ὁ παρωξυμ[μ]ένος Cyr.*hom.pasch.*11.6(5^2.155B).

συνεξομοιόω, *treat as similar, equate* μήτε...τοῖς ὀνόμασιν σ. πειρᾶσθαι τὰς σημασίας Eun.*apol.*18(M.30.853A).

***συνεξοπλίζομαι,** med., *arm oneself thoroughly,* Cyr.*hom.pasch.* 8.2(5^2.96A).

συνεξορίζω, pass., *be banished together,* Cyr.*ep.*27(p.45.30; 5^2. 91C).

συνεξορμάω, 1. *start out along with,* Or.*princ.*3.1.11(p.212.7; M.11. 268A); **2.** *yield to the impulse of* συνενδιδόντες...καὶ σ. αὐτοῖς [sc. unbroken colts] Bas.*hom.*5.8(2.42B; M.31.257C).

***συνεξορχέομαι,** *dance away* with, *join in dances* with, Synes. *calv.*6(p.201.7; M.66.1177B).

***συνεξυβρίζομαι,** *be treated with insolence, insulted at the same time,* Eulog.*fr.Novat.*ap.Phot.*cod.*280(M.104.328C).

***συνεξυφαίν-ω, 1.** *weave together, weave in one piece,* Cosm.Ind. *top.*5(M.88.213B); **2.** *put together, compose, form together* σ. ῥήματα Melet.*nat.hom.*30(M.64.1281B); ἡ...ψυχὴ ἀρχῆθεν σὺν τῇ σπορᾷ τῷ σώματι ~εται *ib.*synops.(1088C).

συνεορτάζω, 1. *feast together;* of Lazarus with Christ, ‡Eust.*Laz.*8 (p.33.12); *join in a* marriage *feast, A.Thom.*B 65(p.44.17); Gr.Naz. *ep.*232(M.37.376A); **2.** *join in celebrating a feast, join in a festival;* **a.** with pagans οὐ δεῖ τοῖς ἔθνεσι σ. CLaod.*can.*39; ἵνα σ. ἡμῖν καὶ θύσῃς τοῖς θεοῖς *V.Alex.Acoem.*12(p.666.14); **b.** with Jews, CLaod. *can.*37; of Christ σ. πονηροῖς τὸν ἀγαθόν Apoll.ap.*cat.Jo.*7:6(p.261. 17); ἡ τοῦ Χριστοῦ ἐκκλησία τὴν ἁγίαν ἀνάστασιν αὐτοῦ ἑορτάζει...καὶ οὐκέτι Ἰουδαίοις σ. Eutych.*pasch.*4(M.86.2396D); ref. Essenes τοῖς... παρατυγχάνουσι σ. Jo.D.*haer.*12(M.94.685B); **c.** ref. feasts of Church σ. ταῖς φιλεόρτοις ψυχαῖς Gr.Naz.*or.*39.11(M.36.345B); of Christ, angels, and the Church triumphant with Church on earth, Chrys. *res.Chr.*3(2.441B); id.*pasch.*3(3.753A); χορὸς ἁγίων ἐκκλησιάζει ἡμῖν· καὶ ἄγγελοι μετὰ ἀνθρώπων σ. †Sophr.H.*orat.*(M.87.4001D) ∾ *Rit. Arm.*(p.425); τὰ ἄνω τοῖς κάτω σ. †Sophr.H.*orat.*(4004B) = *Rit. Arm.*(p.426); Jo.D.*hom.*1.1(M.96.545A); τῷ πνεύματι συμπαρόντες, καὶ σ. τοῖς ἐκεῖσε τιμιωτάτοις πατράσι καὶ ἀδελφοῖς ‡Meth.*Sym.et Ann.*13(M.18.380A); **3.** in gen., *keep festival;* **a.** met., ref. those who embrace celibate life, Gr.Nyss.*virg.*20(p.327.25; M.46.400C); **b.** in life to come σ. τῷ Χριστῷ τὴν χιλιονταετηρίδα τῆς ἀναπαύσεως Meth. *symp.*9.5(p.120.14; M.18.189A); *ib.*9.3(p.117.18; 184A); in heaven σ. καὶ συμβασιλεύσοντας Isid.Pel.*epp.*2.111(M.78.552D).

***συνεόρτασις, ἡ,** *joint celebration, sharing in festal joy* ἐπὶ συνεργίᾳ...καὶ σ. τῆς τἀνδρὸς σωτηρίας Dion.Ar.*e.h.*2.2.4(M.3.393C).

συνεπάγ-ω, *lead together* or *bring in against;* **1.** ? *perpetrate, apply* measures ἄλλα...τῆς αὐτῆς κακοτεχνίας σ. Philost.*h.e.*7.4(M. 65.541C); **2.** med.; **a.** *take* or *carry with one* αὐτὸν...ἐπὶ λωποδυσίαν ἐξιόντες ~ονται Clem.*q.d.s.*42(p.188.21; M.9.648C); κατιόντος...τοῦ Μωσέως...καὶ σ. τὴν γαμετήν Gr.Nyss.*v.Mos.*22(M.44.308A); ἑαυτῷ κεκηλιδωμένην σ. συνείδησιν Max.*ep.*4(M.91.416A); **b.** *bring in, introduce together; adduce;* in argument, Ath.*ep. Serap.*1.14(M.26.565B); Bas.*Eun.*2.27(1.263E; M.29.633C); **c.** *lead (astray) with oneself* ἑαυτόν τε κατακρημνίζων, καὶ τοὺς ἑπομένους ~όμενος Bas.*reg.fus.*25(2.370D; M.31.985B); **d.** s.v.l., *consort with* τοῖς ταπεινοῖς ~εσθαι Cyr.ap.*cat. Lc.*4:38(p.40.8) for συναπάγεσθαι Cyr.*Lc.*4:38(M.72.549B).

συνεπαίρ-ω, *raise* or *lift with* or *to the level of;* **1.** pass., *be lifted with* or *to the height of* 'ἡ ἀρχὴ ἐπὶ τοῦ ὤμου αὐτοῦ' (τῷ γὰρ σταυρῷ σ.) Gr.Naz.*or.*38.2(M.36.313B); **2.** of mental or emotional exaltation ἀμήχανον ταῖς ὑπερβολαῖς τῆς ὑποθέσεως σ. τὸν λόγον Gr.Nyss.*virg.*2 (p.254.9; M.46.321D); σ. τοῖς ἰδίοις λογισμοῖς τὴν μητέρα id.*v.Macr.* (p.381.8; M.46.969B); pass. τὴν ψυχὴν...τῆς ἀνθρωπίνης φύσεως... συνεπαρθεῖσαν τοῖς λεγομένοις *ib.*(p.390.8; 977B); id.*infant.*(M.46. 161A); **3.** theol., *exalt along with, raise by union with,* ref. creation of man, soul as well as body ὡς ἂν συνεπαρθείη τῷ θείῳ τὸ γήινον Gr. Nyss.*or.catech.*6(p.31.8; M.45.28A); ref. Inc. σ. ἑαυτῷ τὴν φύσιν [sc. of man] Max.*ambig.*(M.91.1048D); ref. glorification of Christ, in Resurrection ὁ διὰ τῆς ἀναστάσεως συνεπαρθεὶς τῇ θεότητι Gr.Nyss. *or.catech.*32(p.117.1; ἡ...συνεπαρθεῖσα 80B); id.*Apoll.*55(M.45.1257C); in Ascension ἑνωθεῖσα...τῷ κυρίῳ ἡ ἀνθρωπίνη φύσις ~εται τῇ θεότητι *ib.*21(1165C); *ib.*(1168A); **4.** myst., ref. disciples on mount of Transfiguration συναναβῆναί τε καὶ συνεπαρθῆναι αὐτῷ Max.*ambig.* (M.91.1125D).

***συνέπαρσις, ἡ,** *arrogance, pride,* Thdr.Stud.*epp.*2.124(M.99. 1404B).

***συνεπαρτίζ-ω,** *prepare together;* pass. intrans., *be ready with* or *as soon as* ὁ...κατὰ πρόθεσιν ἁμαρτάνων τῷ τάχει τῶν νοημάτων ~ομένην ἔχει τὴν ἁμαρτίαν Nil.*epp.*4.1(M.79.549A).

***συνεπεγείρω,** *help to rouse against, Orac.Sib.*1.220.

συνεπέρχομαι, *come upon, come against together, M.Polyc.*7.1.

***συνεπερωτάω,** *ask also* or *at the same time,* Didym.(‡Bas.)*Eun.*5 (1.313E; M.29.752C).

συνεπιβοηθ-έω, *co-operate, assist* ἄνδρα...ἤγαγεν ἐνταῦθα, ~ήσοντα καὶ κοινωνήσοντα τῶν...πόνων Gr.Thaum.*pan.Or.*5(p.13.18; M.10. 1068A).

***συνεπιγνώμων, ὁ,** *joint adjudicator, judge along with,* Just. *1apol.*56.3(M.6.413B).

***συνεπιδαψιλεύομαι,** pass., *be lavished, freely bestowed also,* ‡Bas.*struct.hom.*1.8(1.328B; M.30.20B).

συνεπιδημ-έω, 1. *sojourn,* Dion.Al.ap.Eus.*h.e.*7.11.12(M.20.665C); **2.** met., *stay, remain* τῆς θείας φύσεως ἀπαύγασμα...ἐνανθρωποῦσῃ ψυχῇ...τοῦ Ἰησοῦ ~ήσει Or.*Cels.*7.17(p.168.16; M.11.1445A); σ. ... ταύτῃ καὶ φῶς...ἔδει γὰρ τοὺς φωτὸς ὑπηρέτας σὺν φωτὶ παραγενέσθαι Sophr.H.*v.Anast.*(M.92.1708B).

συνεπιδίδωμι, 1. *give up wholly* or *willingly;* hence *offer, lend,* or *contribute willingly* ἀξιωσάντων τῶν Σαμαρειτῶν σ. βοήθειαν Ἰουδαίοις Epiph.*haer.*10(p.204.12; M.41.233A); τῶν Μελετιανῶν...συκοφαντησάντων αὐτόν...Ἀρειανῶν δὲ...συνεπιδόντων ἑαυτούς *ib.*68.7(p.148.1; M.42.196B); **2.** *increase along with* or *at the same time,* ref. Lc.2:52

αὐξάνοντος ἐν ἡλικίᾳ τοῦ σώματος, συνεπεδίδοτο ἐν αὐτῷ καὶ ἡ τῆς θεότητος φανέρωσις Ath.*Ar*.3.53(M.26.433C); Synes.*provid*.3(p.69. 11; M.66.1216C); *σ. καὶ συναύξεται* Melet.*nat.hom*.synops.(M.64. 1088D).

συνεπιθεωρ-έω, pass., *be envisaged together*, ref. Eunomius *ὥστε... νομίζειν τοῦ θεοῦ τὴν οὐσίαν, ἀχώριστον ἔχουσαν καὶ ∼ουμένην ἑαυτῇ τὴν ἐνέργειαν, ὥς τι συμβεβηκός* Gr.Nyss.*Eun*.1(1 p.82.14; M.45. 313B); ‡Ath.*dial.Trin*.2.26(M.28.1197A); *τοῦ θείου...μηδὲν...κατ' οὐσίαν διάφορον συνθεωρούμενον ἢ σ. ἔχοντος* Max.*ep*.1(M.91.364B); id.*ambig*.(M.91.1184D); *οὐδὲ γάρ ἐστι τὸ...γενητὸν κυρίως ἁπλοῦν... ἀλλ' ὡς ἐν ὑποκειμένῳ τῇ οὐσίᾳ ἔχει τὴν συστατικήν τε καὶ ἀφοριστικὴν διαφορὰν ∼ουμένην* *ib*.(1400C); *ib*.(1401B).

συνεπικαλέομαι, *join in invoking*, Cyr.*ador*.7(1.241D).

[*]**συνεπικεράννυμι,** *mix with* *τῇ πειθοῖ σ. τὴν βίαν* Philost.*h.e*. 4.9(M.65.524A).

***συνεπικερδαίνω,** *gain together*, ‡Ath.*occurs*.3(M.28.977A).

***συνεπικομίζομαι,** med., *bring with one, bear about with one*, Max. *ambig*.(M.91.1153C).

***συνεπίκουρος, ὁ,** *ally, helper*, ‡Jo.D.*Artem*.1(p.151.15; M.96. 1252A).

***συνεπιμαρτύρομαι,** = *συνεπιμαρτυρέω*, *join in attesting*, Philost. *h.e*.1.2(M.65.461C).

***συνεπιμαχέω,** *stand by; defend*, met. *σ. τῷ ἐπισκόπῳ* *Const.App*. 2.17.2.

***συνεπίμαχος, ὁ,** *supporter* *δεῖ...εἶναι τοὺς πρεσβυτέρους...συμμύστας τοῦ ἐπισκόπου καὶ σ.* *Sent.App*.(p.83).

***συνεπιμοχθέω,** *labour together, toil alongside*, Mac.Mgn.*apocr*.3. 39(p.136.14).

συνεπινο-έω, *include in the idea of; understand also* or *in connexion with; think of together*, Eun.*apol*.17(1.624B; M.30.852C); *ἅπερ πάντα τῷ...τῆς ἀφθαρσίας ∼οῦσι ὀνόματι* Leont.B.*Nest.et Eut*.2(M. 86.1321A); ref. Persons in Trin. *πῶς ὁμολογήσει Χριστόν, ὁ μὴ σ. τῷ χρισθέντι τὸ χρῖσμα;* Gr.Nyss.*Maced*.15(M.45.1320C); ref. Person of Christ *σ. τῷ ἐν ἀρχῇ ὄντι λόγῳ τὸν φανέντα ἄνθρωπον* id.*Apoll*.13(M. 45.1148A); *τὸν θεὸν λόγον νοοῦντες...σ. δὲ τὸ ληφθέν, Ἰησοῦν* Thdr. Mops.*symb*.(p.99.11; M.66.1020A); monophysite, Sev.Ant.*fr*.ap. Eust.Mon.*ep*.(M.86.908A) cit. s. *ἐπίνοια*.

***συνεπιπάρειμι,** *be present in addition*, Eus.*d.e*.3.4(p.114.19; M. 22.196C).

συνεπιπλέκω, 1. *interweave with*; met., *blend*, Cyr.*Jo*.2.5(4.214A); Max.*ambig*.(M.91.1361A); pass., *be involved*, Afric.*ep.Arist*.(M.10. 56A; v.l. *ἐπεπλάκη* p.58.17); **2.** *implicate with* *σ. αὐτὸν τῷ...ὑγιασθέντι βουλευόμενοι* Cyr.*Jo*.2.5(4.210B).

***συνεπιπνέω,** *assist with a fair wind*, met. *βουλομέναις...ταῖς ψυχαῖς ὁ θεὸς σ.* Clem.*q.d.s*.21(p.173.19; M.9.625B).

***συνεπιπολάζω,** *float together on the surface* (*of the water*), Bas.Sel. *or*.5.2(M.85.81C).

***συνεπιπρεσβεύω,** *join in interceding*, Thdr.Stud.*epp*.2.35(M.99. 1209D).

συνεπιρρέω, *flow together*; met., *contribute* *ἐξ ἧς αἰτίας καὶ ἑτέρων συνεπιρρευέντων* Philost.*h.e*.3.28(M.65.516A).

***συνεπίσκοπος, ὁ, 1.** *fellow bishop*, Ephr.2.200C,219F; id.3.157F; *πρὸς τὸν σ. ἡμῶν Ἀθανάσιον γράφων* CAlex.*ep*.ap.Ath.*apol.sec*.8(p.94. 20; M.25.264B); *Cod.Afr*.proem.(H.1.865E); *ὁ σ. αὐτοῦ* Jo.Mosch. *prat*.210(M.87.3101B); Phot.*nomoc*.9.7(p.545; M.104.1104A); in reference by pope to other bishops *περὶ...τοῦ...ἡμᾶς ὑποδεδέχθαι εἰς κοινωνίαν τοὺς σ. ἡμῶν* Jul.Papa *ep.Dian*.ap.Ath.*apol.sec*.27(p.107.1; 292D); Innoc.*ep.cler*.(M.52.538); Gr.Mag.*dial*.(tr.Zach.)1.5(M.*PL*.77. 178B); in reference by other bishops to pope *τῷ...ἀδελφῷ ἡμῶν καὶ σ. Ἰουλίῳ τὰς δεήσεις...παρέχειν* CSard.*can*.9; **2.** exeg. Phil.1:1 (reading *συνεπισκόποις καὶ διακόνοις*) '*συνεπισκόποις*'...*τοὺς πρεσβυτέρους οὕτως ἐκάλεσε* Chrys.*hom.1 in Phil*.(11.194F); *οὐχ...ὥσπερ ἡμεῖς 'συμπρεσβυτέροις' γράφειν εἰώθαμεν· οὐ γὰρ πρὸς τὸ ἑαυτοῦ πρόσωπον εἶπεν τὸ 'σύν'...ἀλλὰ πρὸς τὸ 'πᾶσιν'* Thdr.Mops.*Phil*.1:1 (p.200.13; M.66.921B).

συνεπισπάω, *draw on together*; med.; **1.** *draw on along with one*; of things, *involve, bring on*; also, *take away* (*with one*) *οὐδέν τι τῶν ἑτέρων φώτων ἐν ἑαυτῷ* [sc. a lamp which has been removed] *συνεπισπώμενον* Dion.Ar.*d.n*.2.4(M.3.641B); **2.** *bring up*, i.e. *vomit together*, Synes.*ep*.120(M.66.1500A).

συνεπίσταμαι, *be fully conscious of, know perfectly well*; hence *οὐ σ. ἑαυτόν be baffled, be at a loss, not to know where one is*, *A.(Pass.) Petr.et Paul*.25(p.140.17).

***συνεπισυνάπτω,** *subjoin, add* *τούτοις εὐθὺς σ.* Thdt.*eran*.2(4. 171).

συνεπισφραγίζ-ω, med., *seal* or *approve* one *with* another *τοῦ ...πατρὸς αὐτῶν* [sc. of the aeons] *∼ομένου* Iren.*haer*.1.2.6(M.7. 465A).

συνεπιτείνω, *extend* or *increase also* or *along with* *τῷ κατὰ φύσιν ἐντεῦθεν τὸ ὀπτικὸν τῆς ψυχῆς σ. λόγῳ* Max.*ambig*.(M.91.1116C).

συνεπιτελέω, *celebrate as well*, i.e. one thing with another *τὴν τῶν φώτων...ἡμέραν θεοφανείας προσηγορίᾳ τιμῶντες, οὐκ ἔλαττον, καὶ αὐτῷ σωματοειδῶς ἐπιφανέντι σ. τῷ πνεύματι* Job.Mon.*inc*.2(M. 86.3316C).

***συνεπιτηδεύω,** *practise at the same time* *τῇ εἰς θεὸν ἀγάπῃ σ.... τὴν εἰς ἀδελφούς* Cyr.*ador*.7(1.218B); id.*Nah*.16(3.495A); id.*hom.pasch*.18 (5^2.240E).

συνεπιτίθημι, med.; **1.** *join in attacking* *σ. τοῖς ἀδικοῦσιν* Socr. *h.e*.3.3.2(M.67.384A); *κατὰ τῶν ἀνδρῶν σ.* Dion.Ar.*ep*.8.6(M.3.1100B); **2.** *set about, apply oneself to* *σ. τοῦτο δρᾶν* Chrys.*hom.62.2 in Mt*.(7. 621C).

συνεπιφθέγγομαι, 1. *utter together, join in pronouncing* *σ. τὸ ἀμήν* Dion.Al.*fr*.ap.Eus.*h.e*.7.9.4(M.20.656A); **2.** *utter at the same time* *ταῖς τοῦ μύρου...ἐπιβολαῖς ἰσαρίθμως τὸ ἱερὸν...μελῴδημα σ.* Dion.Ar.*e.h*.2.2.7(M.3.396C); **3.** *speak of together, speak of* one thing *with* another *ταῖς εἰς Χριστὸν ὁμολογίαις σ. τῆς σαρκὸς τὴν ἀνάστασιν* Cyr.*Jo*.1.9(4.80D).

συνεπιφύομαι, *press upon*, met., of enemies of Church, Cyr.*Zach*. 54(3.733A).

***συνεπιχωριάζ-ω,** *be in the same place* *τὰ ἀλλήλοις ἀντικείμενα τῷ αὐτῷ μετ' ἀλλήλων ∼ειν φύσιν οὐκ ἔχει* Gr.Nyss.*hom.10 in Cant*.(M. 44.981B).

συνεπιψηφίζω, act. and med., *join in ratifying* or *approving* *τῇ συνόδῳ ἡμῶν...σ. δι' ὑπογραφῆς ὑμετέρας* CSard.*ep.cath*.ap.Ath.*apol. sec*.47(p.123.22; M.25.336C); Philost.*h.e*.3.28(M.65.516B).

συνέπομαι, s.v.l., *associate with, live with* *γαμικαῖς ὁμιλίαις τῇ Πλακιδίᾳ συνήπτετο* Philost.*h.e*.12.4(M.65.612A, cod. *συνήπετο*).

συνεποτρύνω, *join in urging on*, Malch.*exc.gent*.3(p.571.25; M. 113.785A).

συνεπτυγμένως, 1. *together in one, inclusively* *τὸ ἐνιαίως τε καὶ σ. δωρηθέν* Dion.Ar.*e.h*.1.4(M.3.376B); **2.** *implicitly* *τὰ σ. ... ῥηθέντα ...ἐξαπλοῦντες* Max.*ambig*.(M.91.1356D).

***συνεπώνυμος,** *known by the same name as* *ὁ σ. τούτῳ* [sc. *τῷ Ἰωάννῃ Θεολόγῳ*] *Γρηγόριος* Areth.*Apoc*.1:1(M.106.500A).

συνερανίζω, *join in contributing, contribute jointly*; literary contributions *ἐκ τῶν ἰδίων πόνων σ. αὐτῷ τὰ λεξείδια* Gr.Nyss.*Eun*.7 (2 p.159.10, v.l. *συντρανίζων* M.45.748C); pass., Christol. *ἐκ...τῆς ἀμιάντου παρθένου ἡ τῆς σαρκὸς μοῖρα σ.* id.*Apoll*.6(M.45.1136C).

συνεραστής, ὁ, *fellow lover* *ὦ...τῆς ἀληθείας σ.* Gr.Naz.*or*.28.3 (p.24.9; M.36.29A).

συνεργάζομαι, 1. *work alongside*, Just.*1apol*.9.4(M.6.340B); **2.** *work with, co-operate*; of Father with Son *συνθαυματουργεῖ...μοι ...καὶ σ.* Cyr.*Jo*.5.2(4.493A); **3.** *contribute* to *ὁ γάμος σ. τι τῇ κτίσει* Clem.*str*.3.9(p.226.18; M.8.1168C).

συνεργάτης, ὁ, *fellow worker*; of Father with Son, Cyr.*Jo*.5.2(4. 493A).

συνεργάτις, ἡ, fem. of *συνεργάτης*, *fellow worker*, of Christ's human nature *σ. ὥσπερ τινὰ...τὴν ἁγίαν αὐτοῦ σάρκα λαμβάνειν...καὶ ζωοποιεῖν καὶ θεραπεύειν δι' αὐτῆς καὶ τῆς κατ' αὐτὴν ἀφῆς καὶ φωνῆς* Max.*opusc*.(M.91.101B); *ib*.(101C).

συνέργεια (συνεργία), ἡ, 1. *working with, co-operation*; theol.; **a.** of H. Ghost with Father *'ποιήσωμεν' εἶπεν, ἵνα τὴν σ. εἴπῃ* ‡Ath. *dial.Trin*.3.16(M.28.1228C); *μετὰ τῆς τοῦ πνεύματος σ.* *ib*.3.17(1228D); *ἵνα ἐκ τῆς σ. τὸ ταὐτὸν τῆς φύσεως δείξῃ* *ib*.3.18(1232B); **b.** of God with man *τῇ ἐκ θεοῦ χάριτι καὶ σ.* Eus.*h.e*.3.37.3(M.20.293B); *ὑπὸ θείας σ. ... μετεφερόμην* Thdt.*Ezech*.3:12(2.703); of Logos, Or.*Jo*.28. 10(9; p.400.18; M.14.700B); id.*or*.30(p.393.23; M.11.548A); of Christ, Thdt.*Phil*.4:3(3.470); **c.** angelic *τὰς ἀγγελικὰς σ., τινὰς μὲν εὐτρεπιζούσας αὐτῷ τὴν ὁδὸν ἐν ταῖς ψυχαῖς* Or.*Jo*.10.28(18; p.202.9; M.14 357D); ref. celestial hierarchy *ἀνάγεται πρὸς τὴν θείαν σ.* Dion.Ar. *c.h*.3.3(M.3.168A); *ἡ πρώτη τῶν οὐρανίων οὐσιῶν διακόσμησις...κοινωνίας θεοῦ καὶ σ. ἠξιωμένη* *ib*.7.4(212A); of Devil *διαβόλου ἐνέργειαν, μᾶλλον δὲ σ.* Clem.*str*.7.11(p.47.16; M.9.492A); Or.*Cels*.6.45(p.116. 25,28f.; M.11.1369A); *ib*.3.31(p.228.14; 960B); **2.** *assistance, help* *πάντας ἀναστήσει* [sc. *ὁ Χριστός*] *θελήματι, συνεργείας μὴ δεόμενος* *Const.App*.5.7.18; Gr.Nyss.*v.Mos*.(M.44.322A); *ib*.(340C); *σ. πρὸς τὴν...σαφήνειαν* id.*tres dii*(M.45.120D).

συνεργ-έω, 1. *co-operate, work also*; **a.** in gen. *αὐτὴν* [sc. *τὴν σάρκα, ἐν ᾗ κατῴκησε τὸ πνεῦμα τὸ ἅγιον*] *συγκοπιάσασαν τῷ πνεύματι, καὶ σ. ἐν παντὶ πράγματι* Herm.*sim*.5.6.6; *εἰς γένεσιν ἀνθρώπου ἄνθρωπος σ.* Clem.*paed*.2.10(p.208.11; M.8.497B); *ὁ γνωστικὸς...εὔχεται, ∼ῶν ἅμα καὶ αὐτὸς εἰς ἕξιν ἀγαθότητος ἐλθεῖν* id.*str*.7.7(p.30.1; M.9.453C);

τὸ...σῶμα...πρὸς τὸ δίκαιον καὶ ἄδικον σ. Meth.*res*.1.54(p.311.12; M.41.1145B); *co-operate in* τῶν σ. ταῦτα δαιμόνων Or.*Cant*.2(p.130.30; M.13.114D); Dion.Ar.*d.n*.11.5(M.3.953A); **b.** theol., of Father with Christ, ref. Jo.8:18 σ. τε καὶ συμψηφιούμενον τοῖς ἐμοῖς πλεονεκτήμασι τὸν θεὸν καὶ πατέρα Cyr.*Jo*.5.2(4.492E); of Son with Father, ‡Gr.Nyss.*Ar.et Sab*.5(M.45.1288C); of H. Ghost with Father σ. εἰς τὴν δημιουργίαν τῶν ἀνθρώπων τὸ πνεῦμα ‡Ath.*dial. Trin*.3(M.28.1228D); **c.** of Devil, Or.*Cant*.2 cit. supra; σ. τοῖς οἰκείοις ὁ τῶν ἀνθρώπων ἀλάστωρ Thdt.*2Tim*.3:13(3.690); **2.** *work concurrently* or *together* but not in co-operation σ. ... τὸ κακὸν τῷ ἀγαθῷ, προαιρέσει οὐ καλῇ Mac.Aeg.*cust.cor*.12(M.34.833A); id.*pat*.6(M.34.869C); **3.** med., *come into operation* οὐκ ἄνευ...αἰτίας μεγάλης ἡ τοιαύτη ~εῖται οἰκονομία Gr.Nyss.*Eun*.3(2 p.18.16; M.45.584A); **4.** *co-operate, assist*, of divine assistance to man θεὸν αἰτώμεθα σ. διὰ Χριστοῦ ἡμῖν ἐν ἁγίῳ πνεύματι πρὸς ἀνάπτυξιν Or.*Jo*.1.15(p.19.33; M.14.49B); ὁ...θεὸς σ. τοῖς τῆς ἀρετῆς ἐρασταῖς Thdt.*Ps*.89:17(1.1256); κύριε εὐλόγησον καὶ σ. *Lit.Jac*.(*NBP* p.39); of Son τὸν μὲν [sc. πατέρα] εὐδοκεῖν, τὸν δὲ σ., τὸ δὲ ἐμπνεῖν Gr.Naz.*or*.28.1(p.22.2; M.36.25D); of H. Ghost, Bas.*Spir*.55(3.47D; M.32.172B); Thdt.*Gal*.5:22f.(3.392); pass., *be helped*, Or.*princ*.3.1.13(p.217.7; M.11.273A); Bas.*Spir*.55(l.c.); Mac.Aeg.*cust.cor*.8(M.34.825D); **5.** *work for, assist, further* the end to be obtained πρὸς τὴν ὑγείαν σ. ἡ κρᾶσις Clem.*paed*.2.2(p.170.13; M.8.416B); σ. αὐτοῦ τῇ σωτηρίᾳ Or.*or*.6(p.314.17; M.11.437C); id.*Jo*.2.11(6; p.67.2; M.14.132B); σ. πρὸς τὸ χωρῆσαι ἡμᾶς τὸ...χάρισμα *ib*.20.32(26; p.369.23; 645D); *lend a hand* πλῆθος...~οῦν κατὰ τοῦ Ἰησοῦ *ib*.10.25(16; p.197.24; 352A).

***συνέργητος**, ? *worked, effected* ἡ ὀφεοδαίμονος συνέργητος παραδοχή ‡Gr.Thaum.*annunt*.2(M.10.1157B).

συνέργιον, τό, *guild, company of fellow workmen, trade association* τῶν σ. ἤτοι συστημάτων Jo.Mal.*chron*.10 p.246(M.97.376C).

συνεργός, *working together, joining* or *helping in work*; **1.** in gen., *helping, conducive* πάντα...σ. πρὸς ἀρετὴν ἐποίησεν [sc. ὁ κύριος] Clem.*str*.7.2(p.9.23; M.9.416A); ὁ...τοῦ θεοῦ φόβος τῆς ἀρετῆς σ. Thdt.*Is*.33:18(p.135.7; 2.313); δόλῳ χρώμενοι συνεργῷ εἰς ὄλεθρον id.*1Thess*.2:3(3.507); **2.** of a kind of cause, *co-operative, contributory* τῶν αἰτίων τὰ μὲν προκαταρκτικά, τὰ δὲ συνεκτικά, τὰ δὲ σ., τὰ δὲ ὧν οὐκ ἄνευ Clem.*str*.8.9(p.95.28; M.9.592C); ὃ δὲ μεθ' ἑτέρου ποιεῖ, ἀτελὲς ὂν καθ' αὑτὸ ἐνεργεῖν, σ. φαμεν καὶ συναίτιον...ἀπὸ τοῦ ἑτέρῳ συνελθὸν αἴτιον γίγνεσθαι ὠνομασμένον *ib*.1.20(p.63.16; M.8.816C); τὸ σ. ὑπηρεσίαν σημαίνει καὶ τὴν σὺν ἑτέρῳ λειτουργίαν...τὸ...σ. αἴτιον τῷ συνεκτικῷ...βοηθεῖ *ib*.8.9(pp.101.22,102.1; M.9.601A); οὐκ...ἔστι συνεκτικὸν τὸ οὗ μὴ ἄνευ, σ. δέ *ib*.(p.98.9; 596B); ἡ...τοῦ μανθάνοντος φύσις σ. αἴτιον [sc. τῆς μαθήσεως] *ib*.(p.96.4; 593A); ref. place of philosophy in knowledge συναίτιον ⟨τὴν⟩ φιλοσοφίαν καὶ σ. λέγοντες τῆς ἀληθοῦς καταλήψεως *ib*.1.20(p.63.8; M.8.816C); **3.** as subst., *helper*; of the body in rel. to soul, Meth.*res*.1.31f.(pp.267.17–269.1; M.41.1144A–C); νοήσει...φίλον πως καὶ σ. ἐστι σιωπή Gr.Thaum.*pan.Or*.1(p.2.17; M.10.1052B); of ἡσυχία: πάσης ἀρετῆς σ. Ephr.3.103A; of God τὸν θεὸν σ. ἕξομεν, καὶ αὐτοὶ αὐτοῦ συνεργοὶ ἐσόμεθα Chrys.*hom.14.11 in Rom*.(9.592D); of grace ἔχοντες σ. τὴν χάριν τοῦ πνεύματος Thdt.*Gal*.5:17(3.391); in evil, *abettor, accomplice* ὁ σ. γινόμενος τῇ...πονηρίᾳ Clem.*str*.4.10(p.282.25; M.8.1285C); σατανᾷ τῷ...κακίας...σ. Cyr.H.*catech*.19.4; **4.** *sharing the same work* τοὺς σ. σου [sc. of the bishop] τῆς ζωῆς καὶ τῆς δικαιοσύνης ἐργάτας διακόνους *Const.App*.3.16.1; as subst., *fellow worker, colleague, worker in the same cause*, of Barnabas σ. τοῦ Παύλου Clem.*str*.2.20(p.176.7; M.8.1060B); of man with God σ. αὐτοῦ γινόμενος πρὸς τὸ πλεονάσαι αὐτῷ τοὺς σωζομένους *Const.App*.2.54.4; οἱ...ἀπόστολοι εἰς τὴν σωτηρίαν τῶν ἀνθρώπων σ. ἐπειδὴ τοῦ πνεύματος ἦσαν...ναός ‡Ath.*dial.Trin*.3.17(M.28.1228D); Chrys.*hom.14.11 in Rom*.(9.592D) cit. s. 3 supra; of angels ὡς τὰ λόγιά φησι, θεοῦ σ. γενέσθαι, καὶ δεῖξαι τὴν θείαν ἐνέργειαν ἐν ἑαυτῷ Dion.Ar.*c.h*.3.2(M.3.165B); theol., of Son with Father, *jointly active, sharing the same activity* τὸν θεὸν υἱὸν...σύμβουλον καὶ σ. Didym.(‡Bas.)*Eun*.5(1.317A; M.29.760B); τῷ θεῷ ὃς τὰ πάντα πεποίηκε σ. χρησάμενος τῷ υἱῷ Thdt.*Eph*.3:9(3.419); id.*1Thess*.5:10(3.523); ὃν [sc. Christ]...ὠνόμαζεν [sc. Νεστόριος]...τῆς θείας συνηγορον ἤτοι σ. αὐθεντίας Cyr.*Nest*.2.11(p.48.39; 6[1].54E); ταῦτα βουλευόμενος σύμψηφον ἔσχε τόν...Χριστόν, καὶ ἐπιτελῶν σ. Thdt.*2Tim*.1:10(3.678); of H. Ghost τὸ πνεῦμα τὸ ἅγιον σ. ... πατρὸς καὶ υἱοῦ ‡Ath.*dial.Trin*.3.17(M.28.1228C); ‡Ath.*Maced.dial*.1.17(M.28.1317D); of H. Ghost with Christ in ministering grace to man, Or.*or*.1(p.297.5; M.11.416A); of the three Persons τρία ἐνεργὰ τρία σ. ... ἀλλήλοις συνόντα Epiph.*anc*.67(p.82.3; M.43.137C) = id.*haer*.74.4(p.318.17; M.42.481A); in this sense not to be predicated of angels in rel. to God οἱ ἄγγελοι γενόμενοι, σ. μὲν οὐκ ἦσαν τοῦ θεοῦ, ἀλλὰ λειτουργοί Sever.*creat*.4.6(M.56.465B).

***συνερέτης, ὁ,** *fellow oarsman*, Acac.Mel.*hom*.(p.90.19; M.77.1468B).

***συνερμηνεύω,** *interpret alongside* or *in the same way*, c. dat., Gr.Nyss.*Eun*.4(2 p.85.9; M.45.660D).

συνέρχ-ομαι, 1. *come together, assemble, meet*; of Christian assembly σ. εἰς εὐχαριστίαν θεοῦ καὶ εἰς δόξαν Ign.*Eph*.13.1; *ib*.20.2; ἐπὶ τὸ αὐτὸ ~όμενοι συζητεῖτε περὶ τοῦ κοινῇ συμφέροντος *Barn*.4.10; μὴ συνελθέτω ὑμῖν ἕως οὗ διαλλαγῶσιν *Did*.14.2; τοῖς μὴ οὕτω φρονοῦσι οὐ σ. ἀλλὰ καὶ ἀναθεματίζω *Lit.Jac*.(*NBP* p.38); **2.** *live with* as συνείσακτος or spiritual companion τὰς...σ. παρθένους τισὶν ὡς ἀδελφὰς ἐκωλύσαμεν CAnc.(314)*can*.19; cf. κωλύει ὁ κανὼν τὰς παρθενίαν ἐπαγγελλομένας ~εσθαι ἀνδράσιν, ἀντὶ τοῦ συζῆν συνοικεῖν Zonaras in CAnc.(314)*can*.19(M.137.1181C); **3.** of things, *be joined in one, united*; of the two natures in Person of Christ, *A.Petr.et Paul*.22(p.128.8) cit. s. δόξα; ἐν ἑνὶ...προσώπῳ ἀμφοῖν τῶν φύσεων συνελθουσῶν Leont.H.*Nest*.3.1(M.86.1604B); id.*monoph*.25(M.86.1785B); ἡ...κατὰ σύνθεσιν ἕνωσις...ἀσύγχυτα τὰ συνελθόντα διαφυλάττει CCP(553)*anath*.4(Hahn p.169; H.3.196C); ἐκ θεότητος αὐτὸν ἴσμεν καὶ ἀνθρωπότητος συγκείμενον, καὶ ἑτεροφυῆ τὰ σ. γνωρίζομεν Eulog.*fr.dogm*.(M.86.2957A); **4.** (= Lat. *subvenio*) *help*, *Cod.Afr*.55; Chrysipp.*enc.in Thdr*.(p.68.11).

συνεσθί-ω, 1. *eat together* Πέτρος...μετὰ τῶν ἐθνῶν σ. Or.*Cels*.2.1(p.127.24; M.11.796B); πολλοὶ...ἦσαν...Ἀρειανοί, τούτοις τε σ. Ath.*apol.Const*.25(M.25.625B); abs., *be a table companion* πάντας τοὺς σ. παραδραμών ‡Eust.*Laz*.2(p.27.7); med. or pass. for act. δορυφόροι καὶ οἱ ~όμενοι ἄρχοντες Thdt.*qu.16 in 3Reg*.5:22ff.(1.464); of Christ on earth συμπεινῶν ἡμῖν καὶ συνδιψῶν, καὶ ~ων καθαρὸν ἐσθίουσιν ἄρτον, καὶ συμπίνει τὸ ὕδωρ Or.*sel.in Ezech*.4:9(M.13.781A); after Resurrection σ. αὐτοῖς καὶ συνέπιεν ὡς σαρκικός Ign.*Smyrn*.3.3; *Const.App*.5.7.30; *ib*.6.30.9; Chiliastic πάλιν παραγενήσεσθαι ἐν Ἰερουσαλήμ, καὶ τότε τοῖς μαθηταῖς αὐτοῦ συμπιεῖν πάλιν καὶ σ. Just.*dial*.51.2(M.6.589A); **2.** *eat* one thing *with* another πικρίδας σ. τοῖς ἄρτοις τοῖς οὐκ ἐζυμωμένοις Cyr.*ador*.2(1.80B).

σύνεσις, ἡ, 1. *intelligence, understanding* οὐ δι' ἑαυτῶν δικαιούμεθα οὐδὲ διὰ τῆς ἡμετέρας σοφίας ἢ σ. ἢ εὐσεβείας *1Clem*.32.4; of God in Creation τῇ ἀκαταλήπτῳ αὐτοῦ σ. διεκόσμησεν αὐτούς *ib*.33.3; Herm.*vis*.1.3.4; as gift of God αἰτοῦ σύνεσιν πλείονα ἧς ἔχεις Ign.*Polyc*.1.3; exercised in testing claims of prophets δοκιμάσαντες αὐτὸν γνώσεσθε. σ. γὰρ ἕξετε δεξιὰν καὶ ἀριστεράν *Did*.12.1; and in providing for prophet κατὰ τὴν σ. ὑμῶν προνοήσατε, πῶς μὴ ἀργὸς μεθ' ὑμῶν ζήσεται Χριστιανός *ib*.12.4; exhibited in repentance ἐγώ, φησίν, ἐπὶ τῆς μετανοίας εἰμὶ καὶ πᾶσιν τοῖς μετανοοῦσιν σύνεσιν δίδωμι. ἢ οὐ δοκεῖ σοι...αὐτὸ τοῦτο τὸ μετανοῆσαι σ. εἶναι; τὸ μετανοῆσαι, φησί, σ. ἐστι μεγάλη. συνίει γὰρ...ὁ ἁμαρτήσας ὅτι πεποίηκεν τὸ πονηρὸν...καὶ ἀναβαίνει ἐπὶ τὴν καρδίαν αὐτοῦ ἡ πρᾶξις ἣν ἔπραξεν, καὶ μετανοεῖ... βλέπεις οὖν ὅτι ἡ μετάνοια σ. ἐστι μεγάλη Herm.*mand*.4.2.2; in interpretation of revelations ὃς ἂν...δοῦλος ᾖ τοῦ θεοῦ...αἰτεῖται παρ' αὐτοῦ σ. καὶ λαμβάνει...καὶ γνωστὰ αὐτῷ γίνονται τὰ ῥήματα τοῦ κυρίου τὰ λεγόμενα διὰ παραβολῶν id.*sim*.5.4.3; *ib*.9.2.6; opp. αὐθάδεια, *ib*.9.22.2–3; as personified virtue, *ib*.9.15.2; as spiritual gift, cf.Is.11:2 ὁ μὲν γὰρ λαμβάνει συνέσεως πνεῦμα, ὁ δὲ βουλῆς, ὁ δὲ ἰσχύος Just.*dial*.39.2(M.6.560B); σοφίας μὲν γὰρ πνεῦμα Σολομῶν ἔσχε, συνέσεως δὲ καὶ βουλῆς Δανιήλ *ib*.87.4(684B); of political wisdom of emperor ἡ σύμπασα οἰκουμένη τῇ ὑμετέρᾳ σ. βαθείας εἰρήνης ἀπολαύουσιν Athenag.*leg*.1.3(M.6.892B); *ib*.6.2(901A); ἡ σ. ὄψις ἐστὶ ψυχῆς Clem.*paed*.1.9(p.135.8; M.8.341C); ὁρᾷς τίνα τρόπον ἡ σ. μέγα βοήθημα ἡμῖν δέδοται καὶ παντὸς ὅπλου κρεῖττον, οὐ δοκεῖ ἔχειν τὰ θηρία Or.*Cels*.4.78(p.348.8; M.11.1149C); οὐ γὰρ ὑπέβαλε τοὺς ἀνθρώπους τοῖς θηρίοις ὁ θεός, ἀλλὰ τῇ σ. τῶν ἀνθρώπων ἁλωτὰ δέδωκεν εἶναι τὰ θηρία καὶ ταῖς ἀπὸ συνέσεως ὑφισταμέναις κατ' ἐκείνων τέχναις *ib*.4.80(p.350.15; 1153A); ref. capacity to understand gospel ὀστᾶ γὰρ καὶ σάρκα σοφίας ὁ λέγων εἶναι σύνεσιν καὶ ἀρετὴν ὀρθότατα λέγει, πλευρὰν δὲ τὸ πνεῦμα τῆς ἀληθείας τὸ παράκλητον Meth.*symp*.3.8(p.36.8; M.18.73C); οὐ γὰρ ἄν πώποτε δικαιοσύνης αὐτῆς ἢ συνέσεως ἢ εἰρήνης ὀφθαλμοῖς ἐθεάσατό τις μέγεθος ἢ σχῆμα ἢ κάλλος· ἐκεῖ δὲ ἐν τῷ ὄντι, ὡς εἰσίν, ὁλοτελῆ βλέπονται καὶ σαφῆ *ib*.8.3(p.84.4; 141B); εἰ δὲ καὶ αἴσθοιντο καὶ οὗτοι τῆς χάριτος τὸ μυστήριον, τότε δὴ καὶ αὐτοῖς, ὁπότε ἐπέστρεψαν καὶ ἐπίστευσαν, κατὰ τὴν γνῶσιν καὶ τὴν σ. γεννᾶται [sc. ὁ Χριστός] *ib*.8.9(p.91.19; 152B); ξύλον παρὰ τὰς διεξόδους πεφυτευμένον [Ps.1:3]...διδασκαλία καὶ ἀγάπη καὶ σ. ἐστιν, ἐν καιρῷ προσήκοντι τοῖς ἐπὶ τὰ ὕδατα τῆς ἀπολυτρώσεως ἀφικνουμένοις διδομένη *ib*.9.3(p.117.24; 184B); ἡ περὶ τὰ θεῖα σ. Eus.*h.e*.4.23.8(M.20.388A); δώῃ σοι ὁ θεὸς σ., ἵνα ἐπιγνῷς περὶ ὧν κατηχήθης λόγων ‡Ath.*dial.Trin*.3.29(M.28.1249B); ref. divine wisdom τὴν ἀγαθὴν καὶ αἰωνίαν ζωὴν...ὑπὲρ πᾶσαν σοφίαν καὶ σ. ὑπεροῦσαν. οὐ γὰρ μόνον ὁ θεὸς ὑπερπλήρης ἐστὶ σοφίας, καὶ τῆς σ. αὐτοῦ οὐκ ἔστιν ἀριθμός, ἀλλὰ καὶ παντὸς λόγου...καὶ σοφίας ὑπερίδρυται Dion.Ar.d.n.7.1(M.3.865B); πάσης σοφίας καὶ σ. αἰτία· καὶ αὐτῆς ἐστι πᾶσα βουλή, καὶ παρ' αὐτῆς πᾶσα γνῶσις καὶ σ. ib.(868A); as Valent. aeon paired with Ἀείνους, Iren.haer.1.1.2(M.7.449B); Epiph.haer.31.2(p.386.11; M.41.477A); 2. instinct κατανόησον...τὴν ἐν αὐτοῖς τοῖς ζώοις δεδομένην σ. πρὸς τὸ γεννᾶν καὶ ἐκτρέφειν Thphl.Ant.Autol.1.6(M.6.1033A); 3. skill γενναῖος παλαιστής, μέγας ὢν τῇ συνέσει καὶ τῇ ἀνδρίᾳ Ath.inc.24.3(M.25.137B); 4. meaning, significance ἐπὶ τῷ γνῶναι καὶ ὑμᾶς τοῦ μυστηρίου τὴν σ. Thdr.Mops.Eph.3:5(p.155.22); 5. decision, judgement κατά γε τὴν τοῦ λαοῦ καὶ τῆς ὑμετέρας προαιρέσεως σ. τε καὶ βούλησιν Const.ap.Eus.v.C.3.62(p.110.10; M.20.1137A); 6. consent ὅπως τὴν τῆς Δομετίλλας φθάσει σ. M.Ner.et Ach.19(p.18.12); 7. as style of address, intelligence, wisdom τὰ γραφέντα παρὰ τῆς ὑμετέρας σ. Const.ap.Eus.v.C.3.62(p.109.30; M.20.1136C); id.ap.Ath.apol.sec.68(p.146.33; M.25.372A); Mac.Aeg.ep.(M.34.409C); δεῖ δὲ τὴν σὴν ἱεραρχικὴν σ. μὴ χαλεπαίνειν ἐπὶ τοῖς πεπλανημένοις Dion.Ar.e.h.7.3.11(M.3.568A); 8. gramm., coordination, conjunction of sentences, ref. Jo.5:20 ἀναγνωσόμεθα...οὐ πάντως προστακτικῶς, ἀλλ' ὡς ἐν σ. μᾶλλον καὶ ὑποστιγμῇ Cyr.Jo.3.2(4.260C).

*συνεσκιασμένης, v. *συνεσκιασμένως.

*συνεσκιασμένως, 1. of expression, obscurely, enigmatically, ref. scripture τῶν ἱερῶν λογίων, τὰ πολλὰ σ. προενηνεγμένων Eus.p.e.6.10(280D; M.21.476D); id.d.e.7.1(p.313.6; M.22.512C); προφητεία ἦν...σ. ἀπαγγεῖλαι ἔδει Chrys.ecl.34(12.697E); βλέπει δὲ αὐτὸν ἡ νύμφη ὀπίσω ἑστῶτα τοῦ νόμου...διὰ τὸ σαφῶς ἐν τούτῳ τὰ περὶ αὐτοῦ, καὶ συνεσκιασμένης εἰρῆσθαι Nil.ap.Proc.G.Cant.2:9(M.87.1600C; prob. l. συνεσκιασμένως); τὰ σ. ἐν τοῖς ψαλμοῖς λεγόμενα Max.schol.e.h.3.3.5(M.4.141A); ref. Christ's words ἐν...προοιμίοις σ. ...προϊὼν δὲ σαφέστερον Chrys.hom.28.3 in Jo.(8.163B); τὸ...πάθος οὐ...γυμνῶς τίθησιν, ἀλλὰ σ. ib.27.2(8.156C); σ. ... αἰνίττεται αὐτό id.hom.41.2 in Mt.(7.446E); ref. S. Paul ἐπειδὴ...περὶ τῆς Ῥωμαϊκῆς ἀρχῆς τοῦτό φησιν, εἰκότως ἠνίξατο, καὶ τέως φησὶ σ. id.hom.4.1 in 2Thess.(11.529D); indirectly, allusively ἐν τῇ πρὸς Ῥωμαίους ἐπιστολῇ κινεῖ μὲν αὐτό, σ. δὲ καὶ ἐν βραχεῖ id.hom.29.1 in 1Cor.(10.258C); in liturgy ἐν...ταῖς ἄλλαις ἱερουργίαις ἀνακεκαλυμμένως καὶ ἀνενδοιάστως ἡ ἱερουργία ἐπιτελεῖται· ἐν δέ γε ταύτῃ σ. καὶ πενθηρῶς Thdr.Stud.praesanct.(M.99.1688B); 2. confusedly, not clearly ἀσαφῶς καὶ ἀπαιδεύτως καὶ σ. γράφεις ‡Ath.dial.Trin.2.29(M.28.1200C); 3. of actions or events, in a hidden manner συνῴκει...τῷ μνηστῆρι ἡ Μαριάμ, διὰ τὸ σ. γενέσθαι τὴν γέννησιν Chrys.ap.cat.Mt.1:18(p.10.13); of Christ's first coming οὐχ ὡς τὸ πρῶτον ἐν παραβύστῳ καὶ σ. ... ἀλλὰ παρρησίᾳ καὶ φανερῶς Areth.Apoc.1:7(M.106.509C).

συνεσταλμένως, 1. briefly, concisely σ. μὲν...ἐμφαντικώτερον δέ Chrys.hom.27.2 in Jo.(8.156B); id.hom.22.1 in 2Cor.(10.590B); Cyr.Lc.16:1(M.72.809C); 2. humbly σ. χεῖρας ἐπαίρομεν Cyr.Ps.27:2(M.69.856A).

συνεστίασις, ἡ, feasting together, entertaining, ‡Eust.Laz.2(p.27.10); Isid.Pel.epp.2.146(M.78.592C); CNic.(787)can.22.

συνεστιάτωρ, ὁ, table companion, guest, Ast.Am.hom.9(M.40.312A).

συνεστι-άω, 1. help to entertain, met. ἐκ συνεισφορᾶς [sc. of knowledge] ἀλλήλους σ. Bas.hom.23.1(2.185D; M.31.589D); 2. pass., live or feast with; of Lazarus with Christ τῷ ἐγείροντι κυρίῳ σ. ‡Eust.Laz.8(p.34.3); met. τούτῳ [sc. φυτῷ signifying Christ] ~ῶμαι ‡Chrys.pasch.6.5(p.177.8; 8.272A).

συνέστιος, 1. sharing the table of or with, being a fellow guest σ. δαιμόνων Cels.ap.Or.Cels.8.28(p.243.28; M.11.1557B); τοῖς ἀγγέλοις... σ. ... γινομένων Or.or.27(p.370.2; M.11.513B); of the apostles σ. καὶ ὁμοτράπεζοι τοῦ...δεσπότου γεγένηνται Isid.Pel.epp.2.5(M.78.461B); as subst., table companion, guest, of the disciples τοὺς ἑαυτοῦ [sc. τοῦ θεοῦ] σ. Cels.ap.Or.Cels.2.20(p.148.14; 836A); 2. in gen.; a. being at home; intimate τοῖς οἰκοῦσι τὴν Καπαρναοὺμ σ. ἦν [sc. the centurion] cat.Lc.7:1f.(p.55.22); met. σ. τρυφῇ Clem.paed.3.3(p.249.6; M.8.584C); b. as subst., intimate companion, of S. Peter in rel. to Christ ὁ κλητὸς καὶ ἐκλεκτὸς καὶ σ. καὶ συνοδοίπορος Clem.ep.1(M.2.33A); met. ὁ γνωστικὸς...σύνοικος ὢν τῷ κυρίῳ ὀαριστής τε καὶ σ. κατὰ τὸ πνεῦμα διαμενεῖ Clem.str.2.20(p.170.12; M.8.1049A); of divine image in man σύνοικον εἰκόνα, σύμβουλον, συνόμιλον, σ. id.prot.4(p.46.18; M.8.157C).

*συνεστραμμενόθριξ, curly-haired, of Christ οὖλος τοὺς βοστρύχους ἦγουν σ. ‡Hipp.Th.fr.21(p.55.14; συνεστραμμένος θρίξ M.117.1056A).

*συνετάω, give understanding to, Dor.doct.7.6(M.88.1708A).

*συνετής, ὁ, one who understands, v. συνήγορος.

συνετίζ-ω, 1. give understanding, make wise; of God ἀπόστολοι ~ονται Diogn.12.9; ἵνα ὁ ἀγαθὸς...φωτίσῃ αὐτοὺς καὶ σ. Lit.ap.Const.App.8.6.1; Pall.h.Laus.18(p.58.2); ὁ ὑπὸ θεοῦ συνετισθεὶς ἄνθρωπος Olymp.Job 28:9(M.93.292A); of H. Ghost οἱ...προφῆται ὑπὸ τοῦ ἁγίου πνεύματος ἀεὶ ~όμενοι Hipp.Dan.3.2.3; Ephr.1.226E; Cyr.Jo.10.2(4.925E); of Christ, Ephr.1.161A; of an angel, Herm.mand.4.2.1; ref. Dan.9:22 ὅπως αὐτὸν σ. πρὸς τὰ ὑπ' αὐτοῦ ζητούμενα Hipp.Dan.4.29.2; ‡Bas.Sel.or.38.2(M.85.404A); Anast.Ant.serm.3.1(M.89.1385D); ‡Anast.S.Jud.disp.3(M.89.1240B); of other sources of understanding μνήμη [sc. τοῦ θεοῦ] σ. τοὺς ἔχοντας αὐτήν †Cyr.coll.VT(6⁴.59B; M.77.1264B); τὰ ἔθνη συνετισθέντα τῷ διδασκαλικῷ λόγῳ Areth.Apoc.20:4(M.106.749D); 2. cause to understand, instruct δέδοταί σοι...σύνεσις τοῦ συνετίσαι τοὺς υἱούς σου περὶ τούτου T.Lev.4.5; καὶ ἐδίδασκέ με...καὶ ἦν καθ' ἑκάστην ἡμέραν ~ων με ib.9.8; καὶ δοθήσεται αὐτοῖς καρδία ~ομένη τὸ ἀγαθὸν καὶ λατρεύειν θεῷ μόνῳ Apoc.Mos.13(p.7); Gr.Naz.or.43.66(M.36.585A); Areth.Apoc.1:20(M.106.524D); ref. Lc.2:52 τὸ ~εσθαι κατὰ τὴν ἀνθρωπίνην φύσιν τὸν Χριστόν Thdt.Ps.15:7(1.692).

συνετῶς, intelligently, wisely; irreg. comp. συνετωτέρως, Chrys.hom.58.1 in Jo.(8.337A).

*συνευαγγελιολυτέω, join in undoing, denying the gospel τῷ εὐαγγελιολύτῃ σ. Thdr.Stud.epp.1.49(M.99.1088C).

συνευδοκ-έω, 1. join in approving, give one's consent; hence agree to, approve of things οὐδὲ τῷ...τῆς ἀδικίας καιρῷ σ. Diogn.9.1; σ. τῇ ἐπιστολῇ Polycr.ap.Eus.h.e.5.24.8(M.20.497A); 2. agree or sympathize with persons οὐ μόνον οἱ πράσσοντες...ἀλλὰ καὶ οἱ σ. αὐτοῖς 1Clem.35.6; 3. participate, share in, by sympathy or consent οὐ μόνον τοὺς ποιοῦντας...ἀλλὰ καὶ τοὺς σ. αὐτοῖς εἰς ταῦτα [sc. τὰ ἄτοπα] Meth.res.2.4(p.336.7; M.41.1168D); ὁ ἄγγελος ὁ σ. μοι ἐπὶ τῆς τραπέζης V.Zos.20(p.108.1); Christol. τῆς θεότητος ~ούσης εἰς τὰ εὔλογα Epiph.inc.3(p.230.22; M.41.277A); ἔλαβε...σῶμα...ἵνα ἐν αὐτῷ ~ήσῃ τοῦ παθεῖν id.haer.69.24(p.174.21; M.42.241A).

*συνευδοκητής, ὁ, one who agrees, Cyr.Jo.5.5(4.525A).

*συνευδοκία, ἡ, s.v.l., joint consent or approval, Epiph.haer.69.59(M.42.296D; σὺν εὐδοκίᾳ p.207.13).

*συνευδοκιμέω, be esteemed equally with, share commendation σ. τοῖς ἄγαν ἐξειλεγμένοις Cyr.ador.4(1.126C).

συνευεργετέω, be beneficent also or together with; of Father with Son and H. Ghost, Didym.Trin.2.12(M.39.677C).

συνευθύν-ω, direct, govern together with θεῷ...τῷ τὴν ἐπίγειον ~οντί σοι βασιλείαν ‡Eust.alloc.(M.18.673D).

*συνευλογέω, bless one with another, bless at the same time, Just.dial.139.1(M.6.793C); Proc.G.Dt.33:7(M.87.981B); Geo.Pis.Pers.3.428(M.92.1257A); Thdr.Stud.epp.1.50(συλλογῆσαι M.99.1096B).

*συνεύνεια, ἡ, sleeping together; sexual intercourse, ‡Caes.Naz.dial.139(M.38.1045).

*συνευοδιάζ-ω, put in the right way; hence commend τῆς τῶν ἔργων φαιδρότητος, ~ούσης παρὰ θεῷ Cyr.Ps.36:7(M.69.928B).

*συνευπαθέω, share a feeling of well-being, be at ease also, Or.Jo.10.36(20; p.211.11; M.14.373B).

συνευρίσκω, pass., be found with; be present with, Max.Pyrr.tit.(M.91.288A).

*συνευρυθμίζω, pass., met., be attuned to, Ign.Philad.1.2.

[*]συνευσις, ἡ, v. σύννευσις.

*συνευτελίζ-ω, depreciate along with ὡς καὶ τὰς ὑψηλὰς ἐνεργείας αὐτοῦ τῇ πρὸς τὸ ταπεινὸν ἐπιμιξίᾳ ~εσθαι Gr.Nyss.or.catech.14(p.62.15; M.45.48A); cat.2Cor.10:1(p.412.11).

συνευφημ-έω, 1. join in praise with, of Const. ~ήσει τῇ θεολογίᾳ Eus.l.C.1(p.196.18; M.20.1320A); 2. pass., be blessed together with σ. τοῦτον [sc. τὸν υἱόν] τῷ πατρὶ καὶ τῷ πνεύματι Jo.D.trisag.14(M.95.48B).

*συνευφημίζ-ω, acclaim simultaneously ~εται [sc. εἰρήνη] σὺν αὐτῷ [sc. Κωνσταντίνῳ] Thphn.chron.p.394(M.108.940A).

συνευφραίν-ομαι, rejoice together; usu. with dat. σ. μετ' αὐτοῦ ἐν πᾶσιν T.Abr.A 4(p.81.24); M.Ner.et Ach.9(p.8.30); ἡ...παρθενεία ἀγγέλων συνευφρανθείη καὶ συναγαλλιασθείη σοι ib.8(p.7.31); of S. Basil in heaven εἰσελήλυθας τὸν ἀνείδεον γνόφον...ὁμιλεῖν...καὶ ~εσθαι Jo.Mon.hymn.Bas.10(M.96.1377B).

*συνευχαριστέω, join in thanksgiving, ‡Ath.diab.7(p.7.40).

συνεύχ-ομαι, A. pray with, pray together; 1. act., Synes.ep.101(M.66.1469D); ib.130(1513B); 2. med.; a. as between Christians ὁ γνωστικὸς...σ. τοῖς κοινότερον πεπιστευκόσι Clem.str.7.7(p.37.1; M.9.469B); σ. ὅπως ὁ...θεὸς...προθυμίαν ἐμποιήσῃ Bas.ep.221(3.334D; M.32.817A); νῦν τε ὑπερευξόμεθά σου τῆς ἁμαρτίας, καὶ τοῦ λοιποῦ σ. Synes.ep.72(M.66.1436B); of corporate prayer ἡμῶν ~ομένων καὶ συννηστευόντων αὐτοῖς [sc. candidates for baptism] Just.1apol.61.2(M.6.420C); οὐδὲ ἐν τοῖς μετάλλοις ἀλλήλοις ἐκοινώνουν ἢ σ. Epiph.haer.68.3(p.143.27; M.42.189B); of a misguided ascetic οὐδενὶ ὅλως σ. id.exp.fid.13(p.513.13; M.42.805A); as a sign of unity οὐ δεῖ *αἱρετικοῖς ἢ σχισματικοῖς σ.* CLaod.*can.*33; *Μελετιανοὶ...σχίσμα ὄντες...μὴ σ. τοῖς ἐν τῷ διωγμῷ παραπεπτωκόσι* Epiph.*anac.*68(p.2. 4; M.42.12B); *οὗτοι* [sc. *Αὐδιανοί*]...*οὐ σ. ... ἡμῖν ib.*70(p.230.7; 336B); **b.** of angels with men *ἀνθρώποις...εὐχομένοις τῷ θεῷ μυρίαι... σ. δυνάμεις ἱεραί* Or.*Cels.*8.64(p.280.13; M.11.1613A); *ib.*8.36(p.252. 3; 1572C); id.*or.*11(p.324.11; M.11.452B); **c.** of Christ with man *τοῦ ...λόγου θεοῦ...σ. πρὸς τὸν πατέρα τῷ ὑπ' αὐτοῦ μεσιτευομένῳ ib.*10 (p.320.19; 445D); *ὁ ἀρχιερεὺς τοῖς γνησίως εὐχομένοις σ. ib.*11(p.321. 15; 448B); **d.** of man with Christ *εὐχομένῳ αὐτῷ καὶ δεομένῳ τοῦ πατρὸς...διδασκόμεθα σ.* Eus.*d.e.*4.16(p.185.30; M.22.309B).

B. *wish one well τὸν δὲ γυμνὸν...τῶν ὑποπιπτόντων τῷ τέλει... ~όμενοι παραπέμπουσι* Clem.*str.*4.18(p.299.27; M.8.1325B); *ἐκείνῳ... ἐπαρῶνται...τούτῳ σ.* Chrys.*hom.22.5 in 1Cor.*(10.199B).

[*]**συνεύω**, v. *συννεύω*.

***συνεφαπλόω**, *spread coextensively* with, *display as widely as ταῖς ἀκτῖσι τοῦ ἡλίου σ. ... αὐτῶν...λαμπηδόνος τὸ φαιδρόν* Bas.*ep.*221 (3.334C; M.32.817A).

συνεφάπτ-ω, *take part along with, join* in a course of action, act. *θείας ἄνωθεν ~ούσης χειρός* Mac.Aeg.*perf.*1(M.34.841C); med., ref. action of Trin. *ὁ υἱὸς τῆς δημιουργίας τῷ πατρὶ σ.* Bas.*Eun.*2.21 (1.257A; M.29.617B); *οὐχ...ὁ πατὴρ ποιεῖ τι καθ' ἑαυτόν, οὗ μὴ σ. ὁ υἱός* Gr.Nyss.*tres dii*(M.45.125C); of divine grace *βοηθείας ~ομένης* Mac.Aeg.*perf.*11(M.34.849A).

συνεφαρμόζω, *fit along with*; met., *apply* or *ascribe also τὴν... ἀκολουθίαν τῷ περὶ τοῦ υἱοῦ λόγῳ συνεφαρμόσει* Gr.Nyss.*Eun.*8(2 p.199.16; M.45.796A).

συνεφέλκ-ω, **1.** *draw after* or *along with one*; act. and med., hence *bring over* to an opinion *ἡ δὲ πεισθεῖσα τοὺς ἀδελφοὺς ~εται* Philost.*h.e.*9.9(M.65.576B); **2.** med., *absorb* into oneself *τῇ τροφῇ καταμεμιγμένον σ. τι φαρμακῶδες* Athenag.*res.*6(p.54.20; M.6.985A); *ὁ Εὐφράτης...πλείστους...ποταμοὺς εἰς τὴν ἑαυτοῦ προσηγορίαν σ.* Philost.*h.e.*3.8(M.65.489C); **3.** *draw* or *drag in, include*, Synes.*ep.*154 (M.66.1556A).

***συνεφευρίσκω**, *discover* one thing *alongside* or *accompanying* another, Gr.Nyss.*fat.*(M.45.164A).

συνεφίστημι, pass. with aor. 2 act., *stand over*; met., *join in insisting* or *putting pressure upon σ. τῷ βασιλεῖ* Chrys.*hom.43.4 in Mt.*(7.464D).

συνέχεια, ἡ, **1.** *continuity, continuous succession*, ref. baptism *οὐ μὴν τελείως ἀφανισμόν, ἀλλά τινα διακοπὴν τῆς τοῦ κακοῦ σ.* Gr. Nyss.*or.catech.*35(p.134.13; M.45.89B); *conjunction αἱ φωναὶ ἐπετελοῦντο ἐκ τῆς τῶν ὁρωμένων σ. δημιουργούμεναι στοιχείων* Or.*sel.in Dt.*4:12(M.12.808A); of a period of time, *length, duration ἡμέρα κατὰ συνέχειαν σχεδὸν τριπλασιάζηται* Dion.Ar.*ep.*7.2(M.3.1080C); **2.** *sequence, connexion*, in rel. of human reason with Christ *τῆς τοῦ λόγου χάριν πρὸς ἑαυτὸν οἰκειώσεώς τε καὶ σ.* Eus.*d.e.*4.6(p.160.4; M. 22.265D); in thought or expression *ἵνα ᾖ κατὰ συνέχειαν* Phot.*Rom.* 7:8ff.(Staab p.504.27; M.101.1237B)ap.*cat.Rom.*7:8(p.96.21); opp. *κατὰ πλάτος: κατὰ σ. μὲν οὖν εἴρηται, οἷά ἐστι τὰ τοῦ νόμου καὶ τῶν προφητῶν, καὶ τὰ ἱστορούμενα πάντα μετὰ τῆς καινῆς διαθήκης· κατὰ πλάτος δὲ λέγεται, οἷά ἐστι τὰ τῶν ψαλμῶν καὶ ᾠδῶν καὶ ᾀσμάτων ῥήματα* Ath.*ep.Marcell.*27(M.27.40A); of a continuous narrative *μίαν σ. φυλάττειν* Proc.G.*1Par.*proem.(M.87.1201A); **3.** *continuance* of, *persistence* in an act, ‡Bas.*Lac.*5(2.590E; M.31.1448A); esp. *continual repetition τῇ σ. τῆς διαλέξεως κόρον...λήψεσθαι* Chrys.*diab.*1.1 (2.246A); *τοὺς...λόγους ἀνακυκλοῖ, ἵνα τῇ σ. παγίαν τὴν μνήμην ἐργάσηται* Thdt.*qu.1 in Dt.*4:35(1.261); id.*qu.28 in Num.*15:1ff.(1. 239).

συνεχής, **1.** of space, *continuous*; of a path, *endless*, Gr.Thaum. *pan.Or.*14(p.32.11,23; M.10.1092B,C); of a continuous substance *τὸ σ. σῶμα διατέμνει* [sc. *ὁ τοῦ κηρύγματος λόγος*] Nil.*serm.*5(M.79. 1272C); neut. as subst., *sequence* or *continuity τὸ σ. τοῦ λόγου* Clem. *str.*7.1(p.3.15; M.9.404A); *ἡ...ἀνάστασις...κατὰ τὸ σ. τε καὶ ἡνωμένον τῆς φύσεως ἐκ τοῦ μέρους ἐπὶ τὸ ὅλον συνεκδιδομένη* Gr.Nyss.*or. catech.*32(p.117.6; M.45.80C); **2.** *contiguous*; *successive*; neut. plur. as subst., *what follows* or *comes next τὰ...σ. τούτοις* Meth. *res.*1.46(p.296.14; M.41.1117B); Thdt.*Ps.*68:26(1.1084); id.*Rom.*1:25 (3.26); **3.** *conjoined*, of Persons of Trin. *ἔχει ἐξ ἑαυτοῦ ἀνάρχως... ἡνωμένως καὶ σ. τὰς ὑποστάσεις* Didym.*Trin.*2.6(M.39.520D); **4.** of time; **a.** *continuous, incessant, unremitting διηνεκῆ μὲν ταύτην* [sc. *τὴν κατηγορίαν τοῦ συνειδότος*] *ἐποίησεν εἶναι...οὐ μὴν σ.· διηνεκῆ μέν, ἵνα...ἀεὶ καὶ μέχρι τελευτῆς ὑπομιμνησκόμενοι νήφωμεν· οὐ σ. δὲ οὐδὲ ἐπάλληλον, ἵνα μὴ καταπίπτωμεν ἀλλὰ ἀνέσεις τινὰς λαμβάνοντες ...ἀναπνέωμεν* Chrys.*Laz.*4.5(1.758C); **b.** *frequent, constantly occurring*, of a word *εὑρήσει...σ. τὴν ἀλήθειαν τὴν χάριν κτλ.* Dion.Al.ap. Eus.*h.e.*7.25.21(M.20.701B).

συνέχ-ω, **A.** trans.; **1.** *keep together, keep from dispersing*; hence *maintain*; **a.** of God, *sustain* (*in existence*) *ὑφ' οὗ λόγῳ δεδημιούργηται καὶ τῷ παρ' αὐτῷ πνεύματι ~εται τὰ πάντα* Athenag.*leg.*6.3(M.6. 901C); *ib.*13.2(916B); Or.*princ.*1.3.5(p.56.1; M.11.150B); Gr.Nyss.*or. catech.*25(p.96.3; M.45.65D); *ὁ...τὰς πρώτας οὐσίας καὶ πρὸς τὸ εἶναι παραγαγών, καὶ...σ.* Dion.Ar.*c.h.*13.4(M.3.308A); *θεὸν...δύναμιν... περιέχουσαν τὰ σύμπαντα, καὶ σ., καὶ προέχουσαν* Jo.D.*f.o.*1.8(M.94. 808C); in Gnost. view of divine action in Creation *θεία τις...δύναμις ...ἡ σ. τὰ ὅλα, ἣν καὶ θεὸν δικαίως ἂν εἴποιμεν* Meth.*arbitr.*2(p.149. 19; M.18.244C); ref. Christ's body *ἔφαγεν...οὐ διὰ τὸ σῶμα, δυνάμει ~όμενον ἁγίᾳ* Clem.*str.*6.9(p.467.11; M.9.292C); met. *αἷμα τῆς πίστεως ἡ ἐλπίς, ὑφ' ἧς ~εται* id.*paed.*1.6(p.113.6; M.8.296D); **b.** *maintain* life, of the bodily organs and functions *τὴν παροῦσαν σ. τῶν ἀνθρώπων ζωήν* Gr.Nyss.*or.catech.*28(p.107.1; M.45.73C); **c.** *σ. ἑαυτόν maintain oneself, keep going ἡ τοῦ σώματος ἡμῶν φύσις ...διὰ τῆς ἐπιρρεούσης αὐτῇ δυνάμεως σ. ... ἑαυτήν ib.*37(p.145.6; 93D); **d.** *maintain* social and political order, of angels as appointed to particular spheres *δύναμις...ἡ τὸν περίγειον τόπον σ. τε καὶ περικρατεῖν τεταγμένη ib.*6(p.32.13; M.45.28A); **2.** *contain, restrain, keep in ἡ πηγή, ἐὰν σ. τὰ νάματα παρ' ἑαυτῇ, σήπεται* Chrys.*hom.47.4 in Mt.*(7.492B; *ἐὰν μὴ ἔχῃ συνεχῇ* Gaume); moral *ἑαυτὸν σ. καὶ ἐκόσμει ἀρετῇ* Just.*1apol.*12.2(M.6.341C); *ὀργὴν ~έτω* Clem.*paed.*3.12(p.290.18; M.8.680A); met., of man's resurrection body *οὐ τοιούτοις ἔτι δεσμοῖς οἷς καὶ τὸ πρῶτον συνέσχετο* Meth.*res.*2.21(p.375.12); *ἐλευθερίαν καὶ ἄνεσιν τῶν σ. ἐκήρυττεν* Eus.*d.e.*9.10(p.427.21; M.22.689A); persons, *detain, keep in*, esp. in prison *σ. τὸν αἰχμάλωτον...παῖδα ἐν δεσμοῖς T.Jos.*14.3; *ἐν οἰκήματι ~ομένῳ* Thphl.Ant.*Autol.*2.13(M.6.1073A); *τοῖς ἐν φυλακῇ... ~ομένοις* Clem.*str.*6.6(p.454.16; M.9.268A); *arrest εὐθέως δὲ σύνεσχεν τοὺς...πρωτεύοντας* Marc.Diac.*v.Porph.*27; **3.** *compel, constrain, subject ἀβύσσων...κρίματα τοῖς αὐτοῖς ~εται προστάγμασιν 1Clem.* 20.5; *συμπαθεῖτέ μοι εἰδὼς τὰ σ. με* Ign.*Rom.*6.3; *τῇ ἀπληστίᾳ ~ομένων* Clem.*paed.*2.1(p.162.8; M.8.397A); *τὸ σ. ... καὶ ἐλαῦνον αὐτούς* Eus.*d.e.*6.13(p.263.35; M.22.433C); physically *ἐν λεπτῷ...καὶ ~ομένῳ τῷ ἄσθματι* Gr.Nyss.*v.Macr.*(p.395.14; M.46.981C); **4.** *cause pain, afflict ἡ συνείδησίς μου σ. με περὶ τῆς ἀσεβείας μου T.Reub.*4.3; Eus.*v.C.*1.41(p.27.6; M.20.956B); id.*d.e.*10.8(p.482.23; M.22.776C); Cyr.*Ps.*38:1(M.69.952C).

B. intrans.; **1.** ptcpl., *important, essential περὶ τὰ ἀναγκαιότατα καὶ σ. τὴν πίστιν καταγίνεσθαι* Clem.*str.*1.1(p.13.6; M.8.708B); *ἐπὶ τὰ σ. τὸν λόγον τρέψωμεν* Bas.*Spir.*42(3.36D; M.32.145C); *ἐν τοῖς κεφαλαίοις καὶ σ. ἡμῶν τὴν ζωήν* Chrys.*hom.1.2 in Mt.*(7.6A); *τὰ κατεπείγοντα ἑρμηνεύει καὶ σ. μάλιστα, καὶ δι' ἃ ἡ παραβολὴ εἴρηται ib.47.1*(7.488A); Vict.*Mc.*14:66(p.432.7); neut. as subst., the *main thing, essence of the matter τὸ δὲ νῦν σ. ῥητέον κτλ.* Tat.*orat.*15(p.16. 17; M.6.837B); *ib.*41(p.41.15; 885A); *τὸ ~ον ἀκουέτω* Meth.*arbitr.*6 (p.159.8; M.18.252A); **2.** s.v.l., *be suitable for οὐδὲ...σ.* [sc. feather beds] *ἐπιστρεφομένοις τοῖς εὐναζομένοις ἐν αὐτοῖς* Clem.*paed.*2.9 (p.204.27; M.8.489C); **3.** *τῶν ~όντων ὑπὸ τὸν πόλον* ‡Just.*monarch.*1 (M.6.313A, perh. for *συνεχομένων*).

συνεχῶς, **1.** *perpetually, unremittingly*; hence *still ἀκούων ταῦτα σ. ἐταράττετο* Chrys.*hom.26.2 in Jo.*(8.149B); **2.** *without leaving an interval, at once, immediately ἐὰν συμβῇ σε ἀσθενείᾳ περιπεσεῖν, μὴ σ. γράφε τοῖς...γονεῦσι...ἀλλὰ μᾶλλον μακροθυμήσωμεν* Ephr.1.314E; Gr.Nyss.*Eun.*4(2 p.55.9; M.45.625B); Chrys.*hom.16.3 in Jo.*(8.94A); **3.** *always*, i.e. *frequently, repeatedly οὐδὲ σ. καὶ πολλάκις* ⟨*τῆς*⟩ *ἡμέρας λούεσθαι καθάπερ εἰς ἀγορὰν θαμίζοντες* Clem.*paed.*3.9(p.263.27; M. 8.620A); *ὑφ' οὗ* [sc. *τοῦ πατρός*] *καὶ αὐτὸς ἀπεστάλθαι σ. ὁμολογεῖ* Eus.*e.th.*1.6(p.65.3; M.24.836A); *σ. ἐκπίπτων τῆς πίστεως* Chrys.*hom. 24.3 in Jo.*(8.141A); **4.** *consecutively, in order* opp. *διεσπαρμένως: σ. τὰ στοιχεῖα μανθάνοντα* Chrys.*hom.29.6 in 1Cor.*(10.267D).

***συνηγεμονικός**, *equally authoritative, of equal authority*, Gr. Naz.*ep.*101(M.37.185B).

***συνηγόρευσις**, ἡ, *advocacy* or *pleading* on another's behalf, Cyr. *Nest.*2.10(p.48.14; 6[1].54A).

συνηγορ-έω, **1.** *plead in court μισθοῦ σ.* Clem.*str.*1.16(p.51.15; M. 8.792C); met. *ἡμεῖς οὐ σ. ὑπὲρ θεοῦ* Epiph.*anc.*7(p.14.8; M.43.28C); **2.** in gen.; **a.** *advocate, hold a brief for, defend ἡ μὲν ἡδονὴ σ. τῇ πορνείᾳ* Bas.*hom.*12.9(2.106B; M.31.405C); Mac.Aeg.*ep.*(M.34.413C); Thdt.*Pss.proem.*(1.603); also med. *ὁ* [sc. *Χριστός*]...*τοῖς τῆς φύσεως νόμοις...~ούμενος* Cyr.*ador.*7(1.237E); **b.** *support, second ~ῆσαι Εὐσεβίῳ...βουλόμενος Ἀστέριος* Marcell.*fr.*30ap.Eus.*Marcell.*1.4(p.19. 23; M.24.756A); Marcell. *fr.*77 *ib.*(p.20.32; 757A); *τῆς...συνηθείας ~ούσης τῷ πράγματι* Sev.Ant.*res.*(p.806.6; M.46.632C); **c.** pass., *be defended, find support* in *νομίζων ὑπὸ τοῦ ῥητοῦ ~εῖσθαι* Hipp. *haer.*8.17(p.237.10; M.16.3366A); **d.** pass., *be appealed to, invoked* ἄνθρωποι ἦσαν οἱ πρὸς αὐτῶν ~ούμενοι...καὶ οὐ θεοί Epiph.*haer*.77.17 (p.430.21; M.42.664C); **3.** acc. Cyr., might be forced into serving as equivalent of ἰσηγορέω *speak as an equal* though this would be a deviation from its proper meaning ἀλλ' ἴσως τὸ σ....τάχα που ὑπεμφήνειεν ἂν τὸ ἰσηγορεῖν...συνηγορίαν δὲ λέγων...οὐχ ἕτερόν τι πάλιν ἑτέρῳ ~εῖν Cyr.*Nest*.2.10(p.48.5,14; 6^1.53D,54A).

συνηγορητέον, *one must plead for, speak in defence of* τῇ νηπιότητι ἡμῶν σ. Clem.*paed*.1.6(p.110.26; M.8.292A).

συνηγορία, ἡ, 1. *advocacy of* another's *cause*, ref. abstracts τῇ σ. τῆς ἀληθείας Bas.*ep*.7(3.80B; M.32.245A); Gr.Naz.*ep*.202(M.37.332B); acc. Cyr. necessarily implies another person συνηγορίαν δὲ λέγων ...οὐχ ἕτερόν τι πάλιν ἑτέρῳ συνηγορεῖν Cyr.*Nest*.2.10(p.48.14; 6^1.54A), but cf. 2.b; **2.** *defence, apology, plea*; **a.** on behalf of another οὐ...μοι πρόκειται, τό, σ. τινὰ τοῖς...ἐναντιώμασιν ἐπινοῆσαι Gr.Nyss. *hex*.1.6(M.44.68D); ἡ ἐπὶ μικροῖς...κατηγορία, μεγάλην σ. τῆς δεξιότητος τοῦ κατηγορουμένου παρίστησιν id.*Eun*.1(p.54.11; M.45.284A); προσθήσει...τὴν ἀπὸ τοῦ καιροῦ σ. Chrys.*stat*.3.1(2.36B); προβάλλεται ...εἰς σ. τοῦ πάθους τὸν ἀποστολικὸν ῥητόν ‡Nil.*vit.cog*.(M.79.1452B); **b.** on one's own behalf βίᾳ νόμον εἰς σ. προβαλλομένη Chrys.*dimiss. Chan*.2(3.434C); id.*hom.52.2 in Mt*.(7.531D); ἐρανίζεσθαι τὰς ἑαυτῶν σ. Isid.Pel.*epp*.1.447(M.78.428C); **3.** *support* in controversy ἡ κατασκευὴ...τοῦ παρόντος λόγου σ. γίνεται Gr.Nyss.*or.catech*.34(p.126.10; M.45.85A); σ. τοῦ Ἰουδαϊκοῦ δόγματος id.*Eun*.1(1 p.74.21; M.45.304D); τοῦ χρυσίου πείθοντος πάντας...εἰς τὴν ὑπὲρ αὐτοῦ σ. Alex. Sal.*Barn*.34(p.447C).

συνηγορικός, *supporting, corresponding* τὴν πολιτείαν καὶ τὴν σ. ἐπιστήμην ‡Cyr.*obit*.(M.77.1117A).

συνήγορος, 1. *speaking with*; *in harmony with*; *in agreement with* τὸν βίον σ. τῆς φωνῆς ταύτης προστήσασθαι Gr.Nyss.*or.dom*.5(p.112.26; M.44.1192A); of persons τὸν ἀπόστολον...σ. τῆς...κατηγορίας προστήσασθαι id.*or.catech*.7(p.38.16; M.45.32B); neut. as subst., *unity* τὸ...τῆς Τριάδος σ. καταλύσασα Gr.Naz.*or*.21.22(M.35.1108A); as subst., *one who sides with, supporter* ἵνα τούτους [sc. τοὺς θεοὺς] σ. ἔχοντες τῆς κακίας μοιχεύωσιν Arist.*apol*.8.4; τοῦ σ. τῆς αἱρέσεως Ath.*Ar*.3.2(M.26.324C); Ἰουδαϊκῆς μανίας κοινωνοὶ καὶ σ. Mac.Mgn. *apocr*.3.14(p.91.6); **2.** *pleading, suppliant* τὸν σ. λόγον Geo.Pis.*Pers*. 1.152(M.92.1208A); as subst., *one who speaks for*, i.e. on behalf of *another, advocate* σ. τῆς ἀληθείας Gr.Nyss.*Eun*.2(2 p.320.5, v.l. συνετής M.45.493B); Cyr.*Nest*.2.10(p.47.31; 6^1.53A); of Severus ὁ σ. καὶ ἀντίδικος Eust.Mon.*ep*.(M.86.905B); before God, of Christ τὸν σωτῆρα...τὸν τῆς σῆς σ. καὶ παράκλητον ψυχῆς Clem.*q.d.s*.25(p.176.23; M.9.629D); ἔστιν...ὁ κύριος σ. καὶ ὄφελος πάντων *V.Zos*.22(p.108.23); in heaven ὁ πολλοὺς εὐποιῶν πένητας πολλοὺς...εὑρήσει σ. κρινόμενος Ephr.1.38E; ὁ...πνευματικὸς πλοῦτος...σ. γίνεται...οἷς ἂν ἐκεῖ συναπέλθῃ Chrys.*paralyt*.1(3.33B); **3.** *speaking with the voice of, speaking as*, i.e. with equal authority προσκυνῶ δὲ σὺν τῇ θεότητι τοῦτον ὡς τῆς θείας σ. αὐθεντίας Nest.*fr*.C 9(p.260.6)ap.Cyr.*Nest*.2.10 (p.47.12; 6^1.52C); ὃν...ὠνόμαζεν...τῆς θείας σ. ἤτοι συνεργὸν αὐθεντίας Cyr.*Nest*.2.11(p.48.39; 54E); *ib*.2.10(p.48.21; 54B).

συνηδύνω, *please thoroughly, charm*, Mac.Aeg.*hom*.3.3(M.34.469C); *ib*.15.28(593D).

συνήδω, 1. *rejoice in* τοῖς...καρποῖς...σ. ‡Chrys.*pasch*.6.5(p.177.14; 8.272A); usu. med., *find pleasure in, relish*, abs. μὴ σ. διὰ συμπάθειαν δοκῶμεν Clem.*paed*.2.5(p.186.13; M.8.449A); οἱ...γαργαλιζόμενοι καὶ σ. Mac.Aeg.*hom*.15.50(M.34.609C); **2.** *felicitate* τῇ...πόλει ὅτι κτλ. Proc.G.*ep*.70(M.87.2773D).

συνήθεια, ἡ, 1. *habit, custom, practice*, *Hom.Clem*.5.25 cit. s. δεύτερος; also of bad habits; ref. idolatry, Clem.*prot*.4(pp.35.13, 48.5; M.8.133B,161B); ref. pagan life in gen., *ib*.12(p.83.8; 237B); ref. Jewish traditions, *Const.App*.6.19.1; **2.** *habit of mind* τὴν ἀπατῶσάν σε σ. ἀποσκευασάμενος *Diogn*.2.1; οὐχὶ τῇ κοσμικῇ ἐνέχεται σ. Clem. *str*.1.1(p.7.31; M.8.696B); Evagr.*h.e*.2.5(p.53.17; M.86.2516B); **3.** *custom, tradition*; **a.** of Church τὸ...ἅπαξ σ. ἐσχηκὸς ἐν τῇ ἐκκλησίᾳ καὶ ὑπὸ συνόδων βεβαιωθέν Jul.Papa *ep.Dian*.ap.Ath.*apol.sec*.22(p.103.29; M.25.284D); ἐκ τῶν ἀποστολικῶν...χρόνων ἡ τοιαύτη σ. [i.e. standing instead of kneeling in paschal time] ἔλαβε τὴν ἀρχήν ‡Just.*qu.et resp*.115(M.6.1364B); οὐκ ἔχομεν τοῦτο ἐν σ. ἐκκλησιαστικῇ τὸ παρατήρημα Bas.*ep*.188 *can*.9(3.274A; M.32.677C); διὰ μακρᾶς τῆς σ. ταῖς ἐκκλησίαις ἐγκατερρίζωσαν id.*Spir*.71(3.60A; M.32.200C); ref. Origen τῆς σ. τὸ ἰσχυρὸν δυσωπούμενος *ib*.73(61C; M.204B); **b.** of heretics οὐ...δίκαιον...τὴν παρ' αὐτοῖς [sc. τοῖς αἱρετικοῖς] ἐπικρατοῦσαν σ. νόμον καὶ κανόνα τοῦ ὀρθοῦ ποιεῖσθαι λόγου Gr.Nyss.*Trin*.3 (p.73.12; M.32.688A); **4.** *customary usage* of language; *ordinary, everyday language* or *signification* of words ἀπὸ τῆς σ. Or.*princ*.3.1.11 (p.213.4; M.11.268B); ἐπὶ τῆς σ. id.*Jo*.13.43(p.270.2; M.14.476C); ἐν τῇ σ. *ib*.(p.270.5; 476D); Chrys.*hom.1.4 in Eph*.(11.8D); id.*hom.4.2 in 1Tim*.(11.569D); **5.** *usage* of language, *mode of expression* μαθόντες τὴν σ. τῆς θείας γραφῆς Ath.*Ar*.2.17(M.26.181C); κατά τινα σ. τῆς γραφῆς ἰδιάζουσαν τὸ 'ἕως' παραλαμβάνεσθαι εἴωθεν Eus.*e.th*. 3.14(p.170.29; M.24.1025C); παρὰ τῇ σ. τῆς θείας γραφῆς Oecum.*Apoc*. 21:17(p.241); of an individual οὐ μόνον τὸ τοῦ δόγματος βλάσφημον, ἀλλὰ καὶ τὸ τῆς σ. ἄτονον Gr.Nyss.*Eun*.12(1 p.353.31; M.45.1076A); **6.** *formulary* σ. σαφὴς καὶ σύντομος...τῆς πίστεως ἡμῶν ‡Ath.*polit*. (M.28.1401D); **7.** plur., *customs, dues*, *IGC As.Min*.4.17 (491–518).

συνηθέω, s.v.l., *sift* or *filter together* or *thoroughly*; met., *be mixed up* in συνήθησα ἐν πάσῃ ἁμαρτίᾳ Anast.S.*Ps*.6(M.89.1100C, conj. συνείθισα).

συνήθης, 1. *sociable* παιδερασταί, σ., ψυχῇ μεγάλῃ Hipp.*haer*.4.20 (p.52.1; M.16.3086C); *ib*.4.21(p.52.10; 3087A); **2.** *habituated, accustomed*; sts. c. genit. σ. τῆς...φωνῆς Clem.*exc.Thdot*.5(p.107.3; M.9.656C).

***συνηθίζω,** [coined from συνήθης rather than a variant of συνεθίζω: aor. infin. συνηθίσαι, perf. σεσυνήθικα, ptcpl. σεσυνηθηκώς, σεσυνηθικώς], intrans., *grow accustomed, become used*, Jo.Clim. *scal*.15(M.88.889A); *ib*.(900D); *ib*.4(697A); *ib*.26(1025D).

συνηλικιώτης, ὁ, *one of like age, companion* τοὺς πρεσβυτέρους... τιμᾶν...καὶ...ἀγαπᾶν σ. *Ev.Thom*.A 6.2(p.145); Pall.*h.Laus*.15(p.39.12; συνηλίκων M.34.1041A).

***συνηλικιῶτις, ἡ,** fem. of συνηλικιώτης, *one as old as*, as adj. σ. ἐστι [sc. ἡ νηστεία] τῆς ἀνθρωπότητος Bas.*hom*.1.3(2.3A; M.31.168A).

***συνήλικος,** *of one's own age, of the same age*, *A.Phil*.40(p.18.36).

σύνηλυς, 1. *going together with, being with* ἐγγύθι...σταυροῖο σ. ἦσαν ἑταῖροι Nonn.*par.Jo*.19:25(M.43.904B); *ib*.2:12(761C); *ib*.17:22 (888B); **2.** *assembled, gathered together* Πιλᾶτον λίσσαντο σ. *ib*.19:31 (905A); ἐν οἷς ἦν ἐπίσκοπος Ἀθανάσιος καὶ σ. ἄλλοι πρεσβύτεροι καὶ διάκονοι Gel.Cyz.*h.e*.3.15.11.

***συνήλυσις, ἡ,** *gathering, assembly*; social, Clem.*paed*.2.1(p.156.19; M.8.385A); *ib*.3.11(p.278.25; 653B); religious τὰς διατριβὰς καὶ τὰς σ. [sc. of Christians] Eus.*h.e*.2.16.2(M.20.173B); ἐπισκόπων ἐπὶ ταὐτὸν σ. [i.e. for dedication of churches] *ib*.10.3.1(848A); of heretics μεταγενεστέρας τῆς καθολικῆς ἐκκλησίας τὰς ἀνθρωπίνας σ. πεποιήκασιν Clem.*str*.7.17(p.75.8; M.9.548A); met., of Church ἁγίαν σ. ἀγάπης, οὐράνιον ἐκκλησίαν id.*paed*.2.1(p.157.25; 388A).

συνημμένως, 1. *connectedly, in close connexion* σ. μεθ' ἑαυτοῦ συνήγαγε Gr.Nyss.*virg*.13(p.307.23; M.46.380B); id.*res*.1(M.46.604A); *by implication* or *association* τὴν περὶ τοῦ υἱοῦ ἔννοιαν σ. αὐτῇ... συνεισάγειν [sc. word πατήρ] Bas.*Eun*.1.5(1.215A; M.29.517A); Gr. Nyss.*Eun*.1(1 p.179.4; M.45.424A); *in connexion with, in this connexion* τὰ εἰς τὴν αὐτὴν ὑπόθεσιν τοῦ βαπτίσματος σ. εἰρημένα †Bas. *bapt*.1.2.9(2.635D; M.31.1540C); *ib*.1.2.10(636D; M.1544A); *in conjunction, together* διεσπασμένως μὲν...ἕκαστόν ἐστιν εὑρεῖν, σ. δὲ...οὐδαμοῦ δεικνύειν ἔξουσιν Bas.*Spir*.58(3.49C; M.32.176A); κἂν λόγῳ διακρίνῃς τὸ σχῆμα τοῦ σώματος, ἡ φύσις οὐ παραδέχεται τὴν διάκρισιν, ἀλλὰ σ. νοεῖται μετὰ τοῦ ἑτέρου τὸ ἕτερον Gr.Nyss.*diff.ess*.7(M.32.337D); ref. Creation by God σ. καὶ ἀδιαστάτως συναναδείκνυται τῇ βουλῇ καὶ τὸ ἔργον id.*hex*.7(M.44.69A); τὰ τρία σ. ἡμῖν συνεισάγει πρόσωπα Thdt.*rect.conf*.5(M.6.1216B); *ib*.(1216D,1217C); *continuously, without a break* εἶτα σ. καὶ ἐφεξῆς Cyr.*ador*.2(1.56E); **2.** theol.; **a.** of Persons in Trin., *as conjoined, in unity* τοῦτο μὲν [sc. τὸ πνεῦμα] τοῦ ἀποστόλου σ. ἡμῖν παραδιδόντος, καὶ νῦν μὲν Χριστοῦ λέγοντος, νῦν δὲ τοῦ θεοῦ Bas.*Eun*.2.34(1.271B; M.29.652B); πῶς οὐχ ὅσιον, ὡς ἔχει φύσεως, οὕτω καὶ τὴν ὁμολογίαν σ. ἀποδιδόναι; id.*Spir*.69(3.58B; M.32.196C); ἓν ὄντα διῃρημένως, καὶ διαιρούμενα σ. Gr.Naz.*or*.23.8(M.35.1160C); σ. ἔχεται τοῦ ἑτέρου τὸ ἕτερον Gr.Nyss.*Eun*.8(2 p.192.27; M.45.788C); ᾧ [sc. God] σ. καὶ ἡ τοῦ υἱοῦ ὁμολογία συναναδείκνυται *ib*. (2 p.197.2; 792D); ἀκολούθως τε καὶ σ. ὁ πατὴρ καὶ ὁ υἱὸς καὶ τὸ πνεῦμα...ἐν...τῇ τριάδι γνωρίζονται id.*Maced*.12(M.45.1316B); in the Macedonian view κατὰ καιρούς τινας ποτὲ μὲν ἐφ' ἑαυτοῦ θεωρεῖσθαι [sc. τὸ πνεῦμα], ποτὲ δὲ σ. καταλαμβάνεσθαι *ib*.11(1313D); κατὰ τὸ [Lev.26:11f.] τὰ τρία σ. ἡμῖν συνεισάγει πρόσωπα Thdt.*rect.conf*.5 (M.6.1216B); [Gal.4:6] σ. ἡμῖν τὴν περὶ τοῦ πατρὸς καὶ υἱοῦ καὶ πνεύματος ἔννοιαν παραδιδοὺς *ib*.(1216D); **b.** Christol., of activity of Christ in two natures, *jointly, in union* ἐγίνετο...ταῦτα οὐ διῃρημένως...ὥστε τὰ μὲν τοῦ σώματος χωρὶς τῆς θεότητος...δείκνυσθαι· σ. δὲ πάντα ἐγίνετο, καὶ εἷς ἦν ὁ ταῦτα ποιῶν κύριος Ath.*ep.Serap*.4.14 (M.26.657A).

συνηνιοχέω, *join in directing* or *guiding*, met. σ. [sc. ἡ ταπεινοφροσύνη] τῷ...βασιλεῖ τὴν...ἀρχὴν Gr.Nyss.*Placill*.(M.46.892A).

συνηνωμένως, *by union in one, unitedly*; of Son as begotten by Father τῇ...προκριτέου ὁμοουσιότητι ἐκ τοῦ τετέχθαι σ. ἔχων τὸ ἀξίωμα Epiph.*haer*.76.19(p.364.32; M.42.552D).

συνηρεμ-έω, 1. *remain still* or *stationary with* τῇ νεφέλῃ...

ἠρεμούσῃ σ. Cyr.*ador*.5(1.165C); **2.** met., *be at peace with* σ. ... αὐτῇ ὁ κολάζων νόμος Cyr.*Ps*.4:5(M.69.737B); μηδὲ τῷ σώματι ~οῦντος τοῦ νοῦ Sophr.H.*v.Anast*.(M.92.1708D).

***συνησθημένως,** v.l. for *συνησθημένος* v. *συναισθάνομαι*.

συνηχ-έω, *sound together* or *in accord*; met., of persons in agreement, *chime in* ὁ...Παῦλος ~είτω βοῶν Cyr.*ador*.14(1.492A).

συνθάπτω, *bury together*; met., pass., of Christian with Christ (Rom.6:4) ζῶν...ὁ λόγος καὶ ⟨ὁ⟩ συνταφεὶς Χριστῷ συνυψοῦται θεῷ Clem.*prot*.2(p.20.10; M.8.97A); Or.*hom.19.14 in Jer*.(p.172.23ff.; M.13.493C); *Const.App*.7.22.6; *ib*.7.43.5; of patriarchs καὶ αὐτοὶ συνταφέντες τῷ Χριστῷ συνανέστησαν αὐτῷ Or.*Jo*.20.12(p.342.19; M.14.600C).

***συνθαυματουργ-έω,** *work wonders along with, join in working miracles*, of man with God ~εῖν αὐτῷ, χάριν παρ' αὐτοῦ ἐκομίσαντο Isid.Pel.*epp*.1.16(M.78.189C); of the Father with Christ ~οῦντος αὐτῷ τοῦ θεοῦ Cyr.*Jo*.10.2(4.914D); *ib*.5.2(492E).

***συνθεΐα, ἡ,** *coequal divinity* τῆς κατὰ τὴν...τριάδα συναφείας καὶ συνθεΐας Gr.Naz.*or*.43.68(M.36.585D).

***συνθέλησις, ἡ,** *consent, giving consent* σ. τὴν εἰς ἁμαρτίαν Cyr.*ador*.7(1.248A).

***συνθελητής, ὁ,** *one who is united* with another *in will*; **1.** of Adam before Fall as σ. with God, CCP(681)*act*.8(H.3.1181D); **2.** of Christ as σ. with Father ὥσπερ γάρ ἐστιν ὁμοούσιος, οὕτω καὶ σ. τῷ ἰδίῳ γεννήτορι Cyr.*Jo*.10(4.828A); Max.*opusc*.(M.91.77C); σ. αὐτῷ πεφυκώς Jo.D.*hom*.4.23(M.96.621C).

σύνθεμα, τό, 1. = σύνθημα, any *agreed signal*; *password*, Bas.ap. Jo.D.*parall*.(M.95.1273B) for σύνθημα Bas.*hom*.13.4(2.117A; M.31.432B); **2.** *theme* of discourse or literary composition τὰ τῶν ποιητῶν ὑμῶν σ. ... ἀκρασίας ἐστὶ μνημεῖα ‡Just.*or.Gr*.1(M.6.229A); ὁ...πατὴρ ...ἐπεμψέν μοι τοῦ λόγου τὸ σ. Gr.Ant.*bapt*.2.1(M.88.1872B); **3.** *composition*, of Person of Christ as God and man σ. σὸν νοέοντα λαλεῖ σιγώμενον ὕμνον Gr.Naz.*carm*.1.1.29.10(M.37.508A).

***συνθεματίζω,** *pledge oneself mutually*, Ephr.2.345C.

***συνθεοκατηγορέω,** *join in speaking against* or *accusing God*, Thdr.Stud.*epp*.1.49(M.99.1088C).

συνθεολογ-έω, A. *regard as equally divine, account* as *God also*; **1.** Trin., ref. implications of Arianism τό ποτε μὴ ὂν τῷ ἀεὶ ὄντι ~εῖται καὶ συνδοξάζεται Ath.*Ar*.1.17(M.26.48B); of Son with Father υἱός, ἔχων τε αὖ πάλιν ἐν ἑαυτῷ τὸν πατέρα, ~εῖται καὶ συνδοξάζεται Cyr.*thes*.32(5[1].282C); of H. Ghost with other Persons, *ib*.1,34(12E, 349A); ὁ πατὴρ ἐν ἰδίᾳ ἐστὶν ὑποστάσει καὶ ὁ υἱὸς ὡσαύτως, ~ουμένου... τοῦ ἁγίου πνεύματος id.*Jo*.1.2(4.15E); τοῦ...πνεύματος...~ουμένου τε καὶ συνεισθέοντος id.*hom.pasch*.15.3(5[2].204D); **2.** Christol.; **a.** Apoll., of Christ's flesh with divinity, Val.Apoll.*apol*.2(p.288.4)ap.Leont. B.*Apoll*.(M.86.1953B) cit. s. συνδοξάζω; **b.** of Christ's human nature, Nest.*fr*.C 9(p.263.12); τὴν θεοδόχον τῷ θεῷ λόγῳ ~ῶμεν μορφήν, τὴν θεοδόχον τῷ θεῷ μὴ σ. παρθένον id.*fr*.C 10(p.276.4f.); cf. Cyr.*ep*.10(p.112.2; 5[2].35C); **c.** applicable to incarnate Word equally with Godhead or pre-incarnate Word, Max.*Pyrr*.(M.91.348D) cit.s. συναριθμέω; *ib*.(349B).

B. *hold the same theological views, agree in theological matters* παρῆτε...καὶ ὑμεῖς σὺν τῷ οἰκουμενικῷ ἀρχιποίμενι ~οῦντες Const. Pogon.*sacr*.4(M.*PL*.96.398A).

***σύνθεος,** *alike God, divine* ἀλλ' οὔτε αὐτὴ [sc. BMV] ψιλὸν τέτοκεν ἄνθρωπον, οὔτε ἐκεῖναι [sc. the rest of women] σ. [sc. ἄνθρωπον] πώποτε γεγενήκασι Leont.H.*Nest*.4.36(M.86.1708C); ref. Dan.3:25 ὥσπερ ἐκεῖνος ὁ ἐν τῇ καμίνῳ εἰς τύπον Χριστοῦ ὀφθεὶς...ἔμπυρος, καὶ σύμπυρος...οὕτως...ἡ τοῦ Χριστοῦ ἀνθρωπότης...ἔνθεος, καὶ σ. Anast.S.*hod*.21(M.89.281B).

***συνθεότης, ἡ,** *co-divinity with, union with the Godhead of* ἀλλότριον τῆς τοῦ πατρὸς σ. Didym.*Trin*.1.15(M.39.321B).

***συνθε-όω,** *make divine together with*, of hypostatic union τῇ θείᾳ...σαρκὶ ὡς ~ωθείσῃ αὐταῖς [sc. three Persons] καθ' ὑπόστασιν φύσει...συμπροσκυνητέον κατὰ τὸν ἕνα υἱόν Leont.H.*Nest*.1.44(M.86.1504C); ὥσπερ...ἐν Χριστῷ...ἡ ἀνθρωπίνη τεθέωτο φύσις· οὕτω δὴ καὶ ἡ θέλησις συντεθέωτο, καὶ ἡ ἐνέργεια ‡Cyr.*Trin*.19(6[3].25A; M.77.1157C).

***συνθεραπαινίδα,** vox nihili, Clem.*str*.1.5(M.8.725B; σὴν θεραπαινίδα p.21.10).

***συνθεράπων, ὁ, 1.** *fellow servant*, term used by Const. of himself in rel. to Christians ὁ σ. ὑμῶν Const.ap.Eus.*v.C*.2.69(p.68.27; M.20.1041B); τῶν...τοῦ θεοῦ λαῶν, τῶν σ. λέγω τῶν ἐμῶν *ib*.2.72(p.71.9; 1048A); **2.** *fellow minister* οὗτος...καὶ οὓς φησιν ἔχειν σὺν αὐτῷ συνιερεῖς τε καὶ σ. ‡Pion.*v.Polyc*.30.

συνθερίζω, *reap together* or *at the same time*; fig., Leont.B. *parasc*.(M.86.1996C).

σύνθεσις, ἡ, A. 1. *putting together, composition, combination*; what is put together, *complex whole* τὰς ἐν τῇ ἁρμονίᾳ τῆς πάσης σ. αὐτῆς [sc. τῆς γραφῆς]...συνοχὰς οὐ συντριπτέον Or.*Jo*.10.18(13; p.189.11; M.14.337B); ἐκ λίθων οἰκίαν γεγονέναι...οὐκέτι λίθοι μένουσι τῇ οὐσίᾳ γενόμενοι οἱ λίθοι—τῇ γὰρ ποιότητι τῆς σ. τὴν οἰκίαν γεγονέναι Meth.*arbitr*.10(p.171.12; M.18.257C); esp. of *composition* or *constitution* of man as body and soul, Clem.*str*.4.26(p.321.20; M.8.1376A); Cyr.*ep*.45(p.154.4; 5[2].137E) cit. s. 7 infra; ἅμα...γένεσις, ἅμα σ., ἅμα καὶ ἡ κατὰ σύνθεσιν ἐξ αὐτῶν τοῦ εἴδους συμπλήρωσις Max.*ep*.15 (M.91.552D); abs. δεσμῶν ἔκλυσις [sc. baptism], σ. μεταποίησις Gr. Naz.*or*.40.3(M.36.361B); τῆς κάτω σ. *ib*.40.7(365C); also of members of body, Andr.Cr.*or*.7(M.97.937C); **2.** *construction* τὰ εἰς τὴν σ. παραλαμβανόμενα τῆς σκηνῆς Meth.*symp*.9.3(p.116.26; M.18.181B); in concrete sense, *construction, building* Σαλομὼν...ἐποίησε σκολιὰν σ. ‡Epiph.*v.proph.Is*.7(p.20; M.43.397D); **3.** *compounding*; of chrism, Just.*dial*.86.3(M.6.681A); Dion.Ar.*e.h*.4.4(M.3.477C); *ib*.(480A); of incense τὸ θυμίαμα ἐκ (or τῆς) σ. (cf.Ex.31:11, etc.): ὀσμὴ...θυμιάματος ἐκ σ. κατεσκευασμένου Hipp.*haer*.5.19(p.117.1; M.16.3179B); Gr.Nyss.*hom.9 in Cant*.(M.44.957A,C); Jo.Mon.*hymn.Nic.Myr*.8(M.96.1388D); met., of the ministry ἐοικότας φιάλαις τοῦ ἀρώματος· διὰ τὸ ἐρριζωμένον ἐν αὐταῖς ποικίλον ἐν πάσῃ σ. γραφῆς λόγον Or.*schol. in Cant*.5:13(M.17.276B); **4.** literary; **a.** *composition* σ. λόγου καὶ προφορὰ φωνῶν καὶ ἠσκημένη καλλιλεξία Or.*Jo*.1.8(10; p.13.28; M.14.40A); cf. μύθου σ. Eust.*engast*.26(p.58.25; M.18.669A); πλάσματος αὐτοσχεδίου σ. ἐστιν ἡ μυθοποιΐα *ib*.27(p.59.3; 669B); **b.** *haphazard combination* of words; *synthesis* [sc. *est*], *ubi ex omni parte confusa sunt verba*, Isid.H.*etym*.1.37.20; **5.** in various specialized senses; **a.** as an intellectual operation; in gen., *synthesis, combination* τὴν ...κρᾶσιν τῶν ὄντων ἤτοι σ. τῆς ἡμετέρας γνώμης εἶναι σύμβολον Max.*ambig*.(M.91.1136A); **b.** math., *addition*; hence *sum, total*, Or. *Jo*.28.1(p.389.10; M.14.680B); **c.** philos., *composition*; *complexity* opp. simplicity, e.g. of the monad σ. ... ἀρχὴ μάχης Gr.Naz.*or*.28.7(p.32.1; M.36.33C); σ. ... ἀρχὴ διαστάσεως *ib*.40.7(365C); οὐ γὰρ ἐπὶ μόνων τῶν ἁπλῶν κατὰ φύσιν τὸ ἓν ἀληθῶς λέγεται, ἀλλὰ καὶ ἐπὶ τῶν κατὰ σύνθεσιν συνηγμένων, ὁποῖόν τι χρῆμά ἐστιν ὁ ἄνθρωπος, ὁ ἐκ ψυχῆς καὶ σώματος Cyr.*ep*.46(p.160.3; 5[2].143B); δυὰς...ὕπαρξιν ἔχουσα τῶν μονάδων τὴν σ. Max.*ambig*.(M.91.1184C); **d.** in Dion. Ar. of the manifold and complex system of symbols by which celestial realities, simple and unknowable in themselves, are expressed, Dion.Ar.*c.h*.2.2(M.3.137B,C); ἐν ταῖς ἱερογραφικαῖς τῶν λογίων σ. *ib*.1.3(124A); ἁπάσης...ἱερᾶς θεοφανείας καὶ θεουργίας ἐν τῇ ποικίλῃ σ. τῶν ἱεραρχικῶν συμβόλων ἱερογραφουμένης id.*e.h*.4.3.12(M.3.485B); *ib*.3.3.1(428A); **6.** theol., not applicable to divine nature, Gr.Nyss.*or.catech*.1(p.9.11; M.45.13C) cit. s. διπλόη; not to God as Trinity θεὸν ἕνα φαμὲν τὴν τριάδα, ἀλλ' οὐχ ὡς ἐκ σ. ...(μέρος γὰρ ἅπαν ἀτελὲς τὸ ἐκ σ. ὑφιστάμενον) Apoll.*fid.sec.pt*.18(p.173.14f.; M.10.1112B); πῶς ὁ θεὸς ἀσύνθετος λέγεται...ἐκ...πατρὸς...καὶ υἱοῦ καὶ... πνεύματος...τὴν σ. ἔχων;...ἐπὶ μὲν τοῦ θεοῦ τὴν ἀΐδιον λέγομεν συνύπαρξιν, οὐκέτι δὲ καὶ σ. ‡Just.*qu.et resp*.129(M.6.1380B,C); δέος... μὴ σ. τις ἐπινοῆται τῆς ἀσυνθέτου φύσεως [sc. in likening Trin. to the sun, the ray, and the light] Gr.Naz.*or*.31.32(p.187.11; M.36.169B); *ib*.31.33(p.189.10; 172A); μονάδα μὲν κατὰ τὸν τῆς οὐσίας...λόγον ...ἀλλ' οὐ κατὰ σ. ἢ συναίρεσιν, ἢ...σύγχυσιν Max.*myst*.23(M.91.701A); **7.** Christol., *union* of natures in Christ; **a.** as parallel or equivalent of ἕνωσις: κατὰ τὴν ἕνωσιν καὶ τὴν σύνοδον καὶ τὴν σ. τὴν ἀνθρωποειδῆ Apoll.*ep.Dion*.1.9(p.260.1; M.*PL*.8.934B); ἐνοίκησιν ἀντὶ σαρκώσεως κατεσκεύασαν, καὶ ἀντὶ ἑνώσεως καὶ σ. ἐνέργειαν ἀνθρωπίνην id.*quod un.Chr*.3(p.296.6; M.28.124C); τὸ κατὰ σύνθεσιν ἓν λέγει ὁ διὰ τὴν πρὸς σάρκα ἕνωσιν λέγων [Jo.1:14] id.*fr*.123(p.237.22)ap.Thdt.*eran*.1(4.70); μετὰ τὴν σ., ἤγουν ἕνωσιν Eust.Mon.*ep*.(M.86.908B); ὅπου...ἕνωσις φυσικὴ μὴ προέρχεται, μηδ' ἡ καθ' ὑπόστασιν γίνεται σ. Sophr.H. *or*.2.46(M.87.3280A); cf. κατὰ σ., ἤγουν συμπλοκήν, ἢ κρᾶσιν, ἢ ἕνωσιν...τὰς οὐσιώδεις...σχέσεις Leont.B.*Nest.et Eut*.1(M.86.1304A); cf. δύο τὰς φύσεις εἶναι φαμὲν τὰς ἑνωθείσας, ἕνα δὲ Χριστὸν...δεξώμεθα πρὸς παράδειγμα τὴν καθ' ἡμᾶς αὐτοὺς σ. καθ' ἥν ἐσμεν ἄνθρωποι Cyr.*ep*.45(p.154.4; 5[2].137E); and, like ἕνωσις, used of Inc. συγχρόνως αὐτῇ τῇ σαρκὶ ἔχοντι τὴν σ. αὐτοῦ Leont.H.*Nest*.4.3(M.86.1657C); σάρκα προσλαβὼν...οὐ προϋποστᾶσαν δὲ τῆς πρὸς αὐτὸν...σ. Sophr.H. *or*.2.46(M.87.3277C); **b.** a favourite expression among Severians (v. s. σύνθετος) who believed that by this means they were avoiding confusion of Godhead and manhood τῶν ἐξ ὧν ἡ ἕνωσις...ἐν σ. ὑφεστώτων, καὶ οὐκ ἐν μονάσιν ἰδιοσυστάτοις...τὰ ἐξ ὧν εἷς ὁ Χριστὸς ἐν τῇ σ., τελείως καὶ ἀμειώτως ὑφέστηκεν Sev.Ant.ap.Leont.H.*monoph*. (M.86.1848A); πῶς καὶ σ. ὀνομάζεις [sc. Sergius Grammaticus] τὴν σάρκωσιν; ἔστιν ὅπου...λέγεις, μιᾶς γεγεννημένης καθάπαξ οὐσίας ἢ ποιότητος· ἄρα γὰρ ἤρχθη μὲν ἡ ἕνωσις ἐκ συγχύσεως, καὶ πέπαυται δὲ ἢ σ., καὶ εἰς μίαν οὐσίαν μετεχώρησεν; ib.(1848B); οἷς γὰρ ἂν λόγοις, τὰς ὑποστάσεις εἰς ὑπόστασιν συναγαγόντες, ἀτρέπτους ταύτας ἀποδείξητε, τούτοις καὶ ἡμεῖς ἀρκούμεθα εἰς τὸ τὰς φύσεις εἰς φύσιν συντιθέναι καὶ ἄτρεπτα ἐν τῇ τοιαύτῃ σ. τὰ ἑνωθέντα φυλάττειν Leont.B. (voicing argument of his opponents)*arg.Sev.*(M.86.1932A); but in the σύνθεσις two φύσεις (equated with ὑποστάσεις) were distinguishable only in idea ἐν τῇ ἐπινοίᾳ διαιρουμέναις ταῖς φύσεσιν ἤγουν ὑποστάσεσιν, συνεπινοεῖται τὰ πρόσωπα...ἐν σ. δὲ ὑφισταμέναις ταῖς φύσεσιν ἐξ ὧν ὁ εἷς Χριστός, καὶ μίαν ἀποτελούσαις ὑπόστασιν καὶ φύσιν Sev.Ant.ap.Eust.Mon.*ep.*(M.86.908A); **c.** among orthodox σ. preserved its original force as something composite opp. the simple, the monad ἐν τῷ Χριστῷ δύο φύσεις, καὶ ταύτας ὑφισταμένας ἐν τῇ σ. Eust.Mon.*ep.*(M.86.912C); ἡμᾶς τοὺς εἰς μιᾶς ὑποστάσεως ἕνωσιν μόνον πιστεύοντας εἶναι τὴν σ. τῶν φύσεων Leont.H.*Nest.*1.8(M.86.1433A); *ib.*1.14(1457B) cit. s. ἄνθρωπος; *ib.*1.18(1465Df.); ἡ μὲν τεκοῦσα τὸ σύνθετον, πάντως καὶ τὸ ἁπλοῦν τέτοκεν...ὁ δὲ τὸ ἁπλοῦν τεκών, οὐ τέτοκε καὶ τὸ σύνθετον...μητέρα ἀληθῶς καὶ τοῦ ἁπλοῦ· διὰ μέντοι συνθέσεως γενομένην ἴσμεν τὴν ἀμίαντον *ib.*4.3(1657C); τί οὖν ἐποίησεν ἡ σ. ἐπὶ Χριστοῦ; οὐδὲν ἕτερον ἀλλ' ἢ τὰ πρώην ἀσύνθετα ἀλλήλοις, σύνθετα εἶναι κατὰ μίαν τὴν θατέρου τῶν συγκειμένων ὑπόστασιν *ib.*1.49(1512B); σ. ... ὁμολογουμένης καὶ τὰ μέρη ἐν τῷ ὅλῳ ὑπάρχει, καὶ τὸ ὅλον ἐν τοῖς μέρεσι γινώσκεται Justn.*conf.*(p.74.20; M.86.997A); αἱ σ. τῶν ἐν τῇ ὑποστάσει ὄντων, καὶ οὐ τῶν ἐν ἑτέρῳ, καὶ οὐκ ἰδίῳ λόγῳ θεωρουμένων, εἰσί...εἰ...τῶν θελημάτων σ. λέγετε, καὶ τῶν ἄλλων φυσικῶν τὴν σ. λέγειν ἐκβιασθήσεσθε Max.*Pyrr.*(M.91.296B); denoting a particular form of ἕνωσις as shown by the phrase ἡ κατὰ σύνθεσιν ἕνωσις: ἡ κατὰ σ. ἕνωσις τὴν σύγχυσιν καὶ διαίρεσιν ἀποβάλλεται Justn.*conf.*(p.76.32; M.86.999C) = CLater.*act.*3(H.3.793D); εἴ τις...οὐχ ὁμολογεῖ τὴν ἕνωσιν...κατὰ σ. ἤγουν καθ' ὑπόστασιν γεγενῆσθαι...ἀ. ἔ. CCP(553)*anath.*4; τὴν κατὰ σ. ἤτοι καθ' ὑπόστασιν τῶν φύσεων ἕνωσιν CLater.*can.*8; ἡ...κατὰ σύνθεσιν ἕνωσίς ἐστιν ἡ εἰς ἄλληλα τῶν μερῶν χωρὶς ἀφανισμοῦ περιχώρησις...τινὲς τῶν πατέρων τὸ τῆς κράσεως ὄνομα ἐπὶ τοῦ κατὰ Χριστὸν μυστηρίου οὐκ ἐδέξαντο, τὴν κατὰ σ. ἅπαντες· αὕτη δέ ἐστιν ἡ καθ' ὑπόστασιν ἕνωσις, ἡ κατὰ σ. Jo.D.*dialect.*65(M.94.661Bf.); γεγενῆσθαι τὴν ἕνωσιν· οὐ κατὰ...σύγκρασιν ἢ ἀνάκρασιν...οὐδὲ προσωπικήν, ἢ σχετικήν...ἀλλὰ κατὰ σ. ἤγουν καθ' ὑπόστασιν id.*f.o.*3.3(M.94.993B).

B. *agreement*; **1.** *concord* τῇ κατὰ τοὺς δικαίους σ. τε καὶ ἁρμονίᾳ Clem.*fr.*36(p.218.32; M.9.769A); **2.** *assent* ἤρκεσε τούτοις πρὸς τελείαν ἀποτροπὴν τοῦ ἐγκλήματος ἡ τῆς ὑγιοῦς ὁμολογίας σ. Jo.VI CP *ep.*(M.96.1429D).

C. *set*; **1.** *suit* of clothes νεανίσκον ἐνδεδυμένον σ. ἱματίων τῷ χρώματι κροκώδη Herm.*sim.*6.1.5; cf.‡Ath.*doct.Ant.*18(M.28.581B); **2.** single *game* in a match; at dice, ? *throw* οἱ μὲν σφόδρα πλούσιοι, ἑνὸς νομίσματος ἑκάστην σ. παίζουσιν Phot.*nomoc.*13.29(p.630; M.104.964A); cf.Justn.*cod.*3.43.4(p.147).

συνθέτης, ὁ, *author, contriver* ὡς ἂν σοφιστὴς τῶν κακῶν καὶ σ. Gr.Naz.*carm.*2.1.11.786(M.37.1083A).

συνθετικός, *complex* ἀναλυτικὴ [sc. μέθοδος], ἡ τὸ συνθετικώτερον ἀναλύουσα εἰς τὰ ἁπλούστερα Jo.D.*dialect.*68(M.94.672C).

σύνθετος, masc. and fem., fem. also συνθετή;

I. *put together, compounded, composite*;

A. philos., opp. ἁπλοῦς, Clem.*str.*8.3,6(pp.83.28,91.15; M.9.568A, 584B); Hipp.*haer.*7.21(p.196.16; M.16.3303A); Gr.Naz.*or.*45.3(M.36.628B); τὸ...σ. ἁπλῶν τινων μῖξιν μηνύει Meth.*arbitr.*12(p.176.3; M.18.260C); associated with the material οἰόμενοι χεῖρας...ἔχειν ὡς σ. ζῷον τὸν πατέρα τῶν ὅλων Just.*dial.*114.3(M.6.740B); πνεῦμα...ὁ θεός ...κρεῖττον παντὸς αἰσθητοῦ καὶ σ. σώματος Eus.*Marcell.*1.1(p.5.15; M.24.721A); id.*e.th.*3.3(p.157.7; M.24.1001B) cit. s. C.1; σ. ... τὸν ἁπλοῦν, καὶ σωματικῶς αὐτὸν ἐπινοοῦντες Ath.*syn.*34(p.261.37; M.26.753B); φύσιν τοῦ σώματος σ. οὖσαν καὶ εἰς διάλυσιν ῥέουσαν Gr.Nyss.*or.catech.*7(p.39.10; M.45.32C); ἐμμένειν...πρὸς τὸν ἔσω ἡμῶν ἄνθρωπον, ὅπου οὐκ ἔστιν...θεωρία τῶν σ. Philox.(‡Isaac)*ep.*22(p.174); οὕτως...τὰ σ. γέγονεν Jo.D.*Man.*2(M.96.1320B); characteristic of the world σῶμα οὕτω στερεὸν...καὶ σ. καὶ ἀλλοιούμενον Just.*dial.*5.2(M.6.488A); and of the human soul ψυχὴ...ἡ τῶν ἀνθρώπων πολυμερής ἐστι...συνθετὴ γάρ ἐστιν, ὡς εἶναι φανερὰν αὐτὴν διὰ σώματος Tat.*orat.*15(p.16.7; M.6.837A); as an epithet of human nature τὸν πάντων ἄρχοντα δημιουργῶν ἐκ πασῶν σ. οὐσιῶν ἐσκεύασεν...ἄνθρωπον Hipp.*haer.*10.33(p.290.2; M.16.3450A); σ. εἶναι τὸν ἄνθρωπον μεμαθήκαμεν ἀπὸ τῶν ἱερῶν γραφῶν [1Thess.5:23] Or.*dial.*6(p.136.5); σ. ... ζῷον...ἐκ πολλῶν συμπαγὲν ὁ ἄνθρωπος Meth.*lepr.*9(p.463.9); ἡμῶν... τοῦ σ. καὶ ταπεινοῦ καὶ κάτω βρίθοντος κράματος Gr.Naz.*or.*28.3(p.26.10; M.36.29B); ἡμεῖς...οὐ σ. μόνον, ἀλλὰ καὶ ἀντίθετοι καὶ ἀλλήλοις καὶ ἡμῖν αὐτοῖς *ib.*31.15(p.164.3; 149B); Thdt.*eran.*2(4.75); σ. οἱ ἄνθρωποί εἰσιν...πρῶτον μὲν ἐκ σώματος καὶ ψυχῆς· δεύτερον δὲ αἱ ψυχαὶ ἐκ τῶν οἰκείων μερῶν, εἰ δεῖ λέγειν ἐπὶ ψυχῶν τὰ μέρη· τὸ δὲ σῶμα ἐκ τῶν δ' στοιχείων καθέστηκεν *Disp.Phot.*(M.88.541B); Pamph.H.*panopl.*6.1(p.614) cit. s. ἄνθρωπος; its denial chosen as an instance of what is not said and is not true ἡ σφαῖρα τετράγωνος...οὐ σ. ὁ ἄνθρωπος Gr.Naz.*or.*31.23(p.174.11; M.36.160A).

B. partic. applications; **1.** of things composed of different materials, Eun.*apol.*19(M.30.853C) cit. s. C.3 infra; *ornamented, variegated* βασιλεῖς...οἱ Ἰουδαίων...σ. καὶ ποικίλῳ χρώμενοι στεφάνῳ Clem.*paed.*2.8(p.195.23; M.8.468C); *Chron.Pasch.*p.382(M.92.977B); **2.** of things composed of different ingredients, *compounded, mixed*, of incense (ref. Ex.30:34) τὸ θυμίαμα...τὸ σ. Clem.*str.*7.6(p.26.18; M.9.449A); so, ref. Ps.140:2, met., of prayer, Or.*hom.18.10 in Jer.*(p.164.7; M.13.484A); of a syllogism as composed of three simple statements, Clem.*str.*8.3(p.83.14; 565B); of a dish, e.g. salad, *mixed* ἄρτους, λαψάνας, συνθετὰς ἐλαίας, τυροὺς βοῶν Pall.*h.Laus.*32(p.95.9; M.34.1105B); ‡Pall.*h.mon.*2.5(p.25.18; M.34.1027B); *ib.*8.40(p.44.4; 1146A); s.v.l., of a *complex* or *complicated* structure σκολιάν, σ., ἀνυπονόητον ‡Epiph.ap.*Chron.Pasch.*p.155(M.92.381B) for σύνθεσιν ‡Epiph.*v.proph.Is.*7(p.20; M.43.397D); **3.** as subst., *sum* of numbers, Or.*Jo.*28.1(p.389.7; M.14.680B).

C. theol., *composite*, charge against Aristotelians οἱονεὶ ζῷον σ., ἐκ ψυχῆς καὶ σώματος συνεστηκότα λέγουσι τὸν θεόν Athenag.*leg.*6.3(M.6.901C); not implicit in Christian doctrine of Logos, Ath.*gent.*41(M.25.81C) cit. s. εἰμί; εἰ...τὸν θεὸν ἡγεῖταί τις εἶναι σ. ὡς ἐν τῇ οὐσίᾳ τὸ συμβεβηκὸς ἢ...εἶναί τινα περὶ αὐτὸν τὰ συμπληροῦντα τὴν οὐσίαν αὐτοῦ...μεμφέσθωσαν...τὴν σύνοδον γράψασαν ἐκ τῆς οὐσίας εἶναι τοῦ θεοῦ τὸν υἱόν id.*decr.*22(p.18.21; M.25.453C); nor of Trin. οὐδὲ ἄνθρωπον ἐκ τριῶν ὑπονοῶν σ. ... οὕτω καὶ θεόν...τὰ γὰρ τοῦ σ. μέρη...πρὸς τὴν ἀσύνθετον...φύσιν οὐδεμίαν ἔχει κοινωνίαν ‡Ath.*Sabell.*13(M.28.117B); nor is it to be predicated of H. Ghost, Gr.Naz.*or.*31.6(p.152.8; M.36.140B); Evagr.Pont.*ep.*10(M.32.264B); as notion was rejected alike by orthodox and heretics it was used by both sides in *reductio ad absurdum* arguments; **1.** against Marcellus σ. τοῦ ἑνὸς θεοῦ τὸ μέν τι πατέρα καλεῖ, τὸ δὲ υἱόν, ὡς διπλῆν τινα καὶ σ. οὐσίαν ἐν αὐτῷ εἶναι Eus.*e.th.*1.5(p.64.24; M.24.833B); *ib.*2.14(p.115.7; 928C); τὸ λέγειν εἶναί τι ἐντὸς καὶ ἐκτὸς τοῦ θεοῦ σ. τι ὑποτίθεται καὶ σωματικὸν πάθος *ib.*3.3(p.157.7; 1001B); **2.** against Sabellius εἰ μὴ οὐσιώδης σοφία καὶ ἐνούσιος λόγος, καὶ ὢν υἱός...εἴη ἂν αὐτὸς ὁ πατὴρ σ. ἐκ σοφίας καὶ λόγου ‡Ath.*Ar.*4.2(p.45.7; M.26.469A); **3.** by Arius and Eunomius against orthodox, ref. Rom.11:36 et al. ὡς μέρος αὐτοῦ ὁμοουσίου καὶ ὡς προβολὴ ὑπό τινων νοεῖται, σ. ἔσται ὁ πατὴρ καὶ... σῶμα κατ' αὐτοὺς...ὁ ἀσώματος θεός Ar.*ep.Alex.*(p.13.18; M.26.712A); Ath.*decr.*22(p.18.21; M.25.453C); σ. τὸ ἐξ ἑτέρου καὶ ἑτέρου συγκείμενον. τὸ δὲ σ. οὐκ ἀγέννητον Eun.*apol.*19(M.30.853C); ἡμᾶς μορμολυττόμενος...ὅτι εἴπερ ἕτερόν τι εἴη τὸ φῶς παρὰ τὸ ἀγέννητον, ἀναγκαίως ἡμῖν σ. ὁ θεὸς ἀποδειχθήσεται Bas.*Eun.*2.28(1.265E; M.29.640A); **4.** against Arians εἰ μὴ ἄρα σ. ... τὸν θεόν Ath.*Ar.*2.38(M.26.228C); id.*ep.Aeg.Lib.*16(M.25.573B); id.*ep.Afr.*8(M.26.1044B) cit. s. βελτίωσις; and Eunomians πολλαὶ οὐσίαι θεοῦ...ἢ σ. ἐκ τούτων [sc. τὸ ἀθάνατον, ἄκακον, ἀναλλοίωτον] τὸ θεῖον Gr.Naz.*or.*29.10(p.88.11; M.36.88B); οὐκ ἂν αὐτὸν οἶμαι τοῦτο εἰπεῖν, ὥστε ποικίλον τι χρῆμα καὶ σ. νομίζειν τοῦ θεοῦ τὴν οὐσίαν Gr.Nyss.*Eun.*1(1 p.82.12; M.45.313B); *ib.*(1 p.213.2; 461A) cit. s. ἀντίκειμαι.

D. Christol.; **1.** of Christ as divine and human; **a.** in early authors δῶρα ἃ...σ. τινι ἐκ θεοῦ καὶ ἀνθρώπου θνητοῦ προσήνεγκαν [sc. the Magi] Or.*Cels.*1.60(p.111.21; M.11.772A); περὶ μὲν τῆς ἐν αὐτῷ θειότητος λέγοντι [Jo.14:6]...περὶ δὲ τοῦ, ὅτι ἐν ἀνθρωπίνῳ σώματι ἦν [Jo.8:40] σ. τι χρῆμά φαμεν αὐτὸν γεγονέναι *ib.*1.66(p.119.21; 784B); *ib.*(p.121.1; 785A); ἓν πρόσωπον σ. ἐκ θεότητος οὐρανίου καὶ ἀνθρωπείας σαρκός ‡*Symb.Ant.*(269)2(p.6.12; Hahn p.182); opp. τῇ θεότητι: οὐδ' ὁ πρὸ τοῦ νεκροῦ Ἰησοῦς ὁ σ. ἀθάνατος ἦν Or.*Cels.*2.16(p.146.11; 832B); τὰ μὲν ὑψηλότερα πρόσαγε τῇ θεότητι...τὰ δὲ ταπεινότερα τῷ σ., καὶ τῷ διὰ σὲ κενωθέντι καὶ σαρκωθέντι...καὶ ἀνθρωπισθέντι, εἶτα καὶ ὑψωθέντι...ὃ μὲν ἦν, διέμεινεν· ὃ δὲ οὐκ ἦν, προσέλαβεν Gr.Naz.*or.*29.18f.(p.101.15; M.36.97B); **b.** by Marcellus τοῦ ἑνὸς θεοῦ τὸ μέν τι πατέρα καλεῖ [sc. Marcellus], τὸ δὲ υἱόν, ὡς διπλῆν τινα καὶ σ. οὐσίαν ἐν αὐτῷ εἶναι Eus.*e.th.*1.5(p.64.24; M.24.833B); **c.** in Arian doctrine πῶς Χριστός, εἰ μὴ ἓν πρόσωπον, μία σ. φύσις; Luc.Al.*fr.pasch.*ap.*Doct.Patr.*9(p.65.20); **d.** in Apollinarian writings Apoll. appears to reject notion in rel. to Christ τὸ ἁπλοῦν ἕν ἐστι, τὸ δὲ σ. οὐ δύναται ἓν εἶναι...εἰ δὲ καὶ τὸ σ. ἕν ἐστιν ὥσπερ ἄνθρωπος, τὸ κατὰ σύνθεσιν ἓν λέγει ὁ διὰ τὴν πρὸς σάρκα ἕνωσιν λέγων [Jo.1:14a] Apoll.*fr.*123(p.237.19ff.)ap.Thdt.*eran.*1(4.70); cf. μὴ οὖν τοῖς διατέμνουσι πρόφασιν διδότωσαν οἱ δύο λέγοντες φύσεις· οὔτε γὰρ τὸ σῶμα καθ' ἑαυτὸ φύσις... οὔτε ὁ λόγος...ἐπειδὴ ἐν σαρκὶ ὁ κύριος...ἐπεδήμησε τῷ κόσμῳ...εἰ δὲ ἓν ἑκάτερόν ἐστι κατὰ τὴν ἕνωσιν...καὶ τὴν σύνθεσιν τὴν ἀνθρωποειδῆ, ἓν καὶ τὸ ὄνομα τῷ σ. προσεφαρμόζεται id.*ep.Dion*.1.9(p.260.2; M.*PL*.8.934B); but describes nature resulting from union as φύσεως σ. μεταξὺ οὔσης θεοῦ καὶ ἀνθρώπων id.*fr*.111(p.233.28)ap.Justn.*monoph*.(p.16.39; M.86.1121D); so also his followers οὐ γέγονε διφυὴς ἢ διθελὴς σαρκωθεὶς ὁ λόγος...ἀλλὰ σ. οὐ γὰρ ποσότητι φύσεων ἐπηυξήθη σαρκωθείς, ⟨ἀλλ'⟩ ἐξ ἁπλοῦ γέγονε σ. Eun.Berrh.*fr*.(p.276.25f.)ap.*Doct.Patr*.41(p.309.9f.); τὸν Χριστὸν εἶναι μίαν οὐσίαν καὶ φύσιν σ. Juln.Apoll.*ep*.(p.277.10)ap.*Doct.Patr*.41(p.308.4); but Polemon writes of Tim. Beryt. οὐκ αἰσχύνονται μίαν φύσιν τοῦ λόγου σεσαρκωμένην καθάπερ μίαν σ. ὁμολογοῦντες· εἰ γὰρ θεὸς τέλειος καὶ ἄνθρωπος τέλειος· ὁ αὐτός, δύο φύσεις ἄρα ὁ αὐτός, καθάπερ ἡ τῶν Καππαδοκῶν εἰσηγεῖται καινοτομία Polem.*fr*.(p.274.19)ap.Leont.H.*monoph*.(M.86.1864C); and Jobius ὑπόστασιν μίαν σ. καὶ πρόσωπον ἓν ἀδιαίρετον Job.Ep.*symb*.(p.286.22)ap.Leont.B.*Apoll*.(M.86.1952C); **e.** used against Nestorians κατὰ τὴν ὑπόστασιν οὖν ταῖς φύσεσιν ἡ σύνθεσις...οὔτε δὲ φύσις σ. ἐκ τῶνδε γέγονεν, οὐ γὰρ κατὰ σύγχυσιν συνετέθησαν [as against Eutychians], οὔτε ὑπόστασις σ. ὅτι [sc. in this sense that] οὐκ ἐξ ὑποστάσεων Leont.H.*Nest*.1.20(M.86.1485D); *ib*.1.49(1512B) cit. s. σύνθεσις; σ. δὲ γενομένου τοῦ φυσικοῦ αὐτῆς [sc. τῆς τοῦ θεοῦ λόγου ὑποστάσεως] λόγου *ib*.2.40(1596D); μετὰ προσλήμματος γάρ τινος πρόσφατος γινώσκεται, καὶ οὐχ ἁπλῶς λόγος λοιπὸν ἀλλὰ σ. Χριστὸς ὀνομάζεται *ib*.4.3(1657B); **f.** Severians and monophysites adopted μία φύσις σ. as their watchword εἰ δὲ ἡ ἁπλῆ καὶ ἡ σ. μίαν κατ' αὐτοὺς φύσιν δηλοῖ, λεγέτωσαν τὴν διαφορὰν τῆς σ. κατ' αὐτοὺς Χριστοῦ φύσεως καὶ τῆς ἁπλῆς τοῦ λόγου φύσεως Leont.B.*cap.Sev*.14(M.86.1904Df.); τὴν μίαν, ὡς αὐτοί φασι, σ. τοῦ Χριστοῦ φύσιν...τῆς δὲ Ἀπολιναρίου ἀσεβείας καὶ τῆς Ἀρείου ἀρνεῖσθαι τὸ τέλειον τῆς θεότητος τοῦ Χριστοῦ καὶ τῆς κατ' αὐτὸν ἀνθρωπότητος *ib*.19(1908B); τὰς φύσεις μόνῃ τῇ ἐπινοίᾳ καὶ ἡμεῖς θεωροῦμεν· ἑνώσαντες μὲν οὖν ταύτας, λοιπὸν μίαν ἄμφω φύσιν καὶ ταύτην σ. εἶναι... φαμεν [i.e. presentation of his opponent's argument] id.*arg.Sev*.(M.86.1929D); εἰ μία φύσις...ἡ...ἀρχὴ τοῦ εἶναι ταύτης τῆς σ. φύσεως, πότε τε καὶ ὅπως; Leont.H.*monoph*.5(M.86.1772B); εἰ μία σ. φύσις τοῦ Χριστοῦ, μία δὲ ἁπλῆ φύσις τοῦ πατρός, πῶς τῷ πατρὶ ὁ υἱὸς ὁμοούσιος; *ib*.36(1792B); ταῦτα τερατείαν ἐπιφημίζων ἑαυτῷ τὴν Ἀκέφαλον καὶ φύσιν μίαν αὐτοῦ τοῦ σωτῆρος ἡμῶν Χριστοῦ φανταζόμενος σ. Sophr.H.*ep.syn*.(M.87.3193A); also ref. ἐνέργεια of Christ τὴν φωνὴν τοῦ... Διονυσίου...τὴν λέγουσαν...τὴν θεανδρικὴν ἐνέργειαν..., μίαν ἐνοήσαμεν σ. ... ἑτέρως ἡμῖν νοηθῆναι μὴ δυναμένην Sev.Ant.ap.*Doct.Patr*.41(p.309.21); cf. monothelite assertion μίαν ὑπόστασιν σ. ἐν δύο καὶ μετὰ τὴν ἕνωσιν κηρύττοντες φύσεσι...καὶ ἓν θέλημα...νοοῦμεν Paul.CP *ep.Thdr*.(M.*PL*.87.95A); **g.** in reply orthodox defined its meaning with greater precision ἐν...τῷ σ. ὄνομα τὸ ποῖόν φατε προσαρμόζεσθαι; εἰ μὲν τὸ ὑποστατικόν, ἀναντίρρητος ὁ λόγος· εἰ δὲ φυσικόν, τίς αὐτῷ ἡ ὑποκειμένη φύσις; Leont.H.*monoph*.(M.86.1872D); ἐξ ἑκατέρας φύσεως...ἕνα Χριστὸν σ. λέγοντες, σύγχυσιν τῇ ἑνώσει οὐκ ἐπεισάγομεν Justn.*conf*.(p.74.15; M.86.997A); *ib*.(p.76.31; 999C); εἰ δὲ φήσωσί τινες, ὅτι ὥσπερ μία ὑπόστασις σ. εἴρηται ἐπὶ Χριστοῦ, οὕτω δεῖ καὶ μίαν φύσιν σ. λέγειν, ἀποδείξομεν καὶ τοῦτο ἀλλότριον εἶναι τῆς εὐσεβείας *ib*.(p.86.21f.; 1009C,D); εἴ τις λέγει κατ' εὐδοκίαν τὴν ἕνωσιν γεγενῆσθαι...οὐχὶ καθ' ὑπόστασιν...καὶ διὰ τοῦτο μίαν αὐτοῦ τὴν ὑπόστασιν σ. ... ἀ. ἔ. *ib.anath*.4(p.90.36; M.86.1015B); τὸν αὐτὸν... ὁμολογοῦντες ἐν θεότητι...καὶ ἐν ἀνθρωπότητι, ἐξ ὧν καὶ συνετέθη, διαίρεσιν μὲν...οὐκ ἐπιφέρομεν τῇ μιᾷ αὐτοῦ σ. ὑποστάσει, τὴν δὲ διαφορὰν τῶν φύσεων σημαίνομεν Just.Imp.*edict*.(p.200.2; M.86.2797B); πρεσβεύομεν...ἐπὶ Χριστοῦ μίαν ὑπόστασιν σ., ἐκ δύο συντεθειμένην φύσεων ‡Cyr.*Trin*.18(6³.24B; M.77.1157A); *ib*.27(33B; M.77.1172B) = Jo.D.*f.o*.3.4(M.94.997B); σ. ... τὸν Χριστὸν δοξάζομεν, τῇ τῶν ἁγίων πατρῶν ἀκολουθοῦντες διδασκαλίᾳ Heracl.*ecth*.(H.3.793D); καὶ γίνεται σ. ὁ ἁπλούστατος ‡Gr.Nyss.*hom.3.8 in Jo*.(p.137.18); τὸ... σ. φύσεως ὑπάρχον, καὶ σ. κατὰ φύσιν δηλονότι ἐστί· τὸ δὲ κατὰ φύσιν σ., τῷ κατὰ φύσιν ἁπλῷ οὐκ ἂν εἴη ποτὲ ὁμοφυὲς καὶ ὁμοούσιον. οὐ θέμις οὖν μίαν τὸν Χριστὸν λέγειν σ. φύσιν τοὺς εὐσεβεῖς...ὑπόστασιν δὲ μᾶλλον Χριστοῦ σ. μίαν ὁμολογεῖν, καὶ δύο φύσεις Max.*ep*.12(M.91.489B,C); *ib*.13(516D–517C,525D–529A); ὑπόστασιν μίαν παρεῖχεν ὁρᾶν ἐκ τῆς ἑνώσεως σύνθετον, τῇ κατὰ φύσιν τῶν ἐξ ὧν συνετέθη μερῶν ὑπάρξει συντηρουμένην *ib*.15(556C); ἐκ δύο φύσεων, τουτέστι θεότητός τε καὶ ἀνθρωπότητος ἕνα Χριστὸν...μίαν...φύσιν σεσαρκωμένην...ἤγουν μίαν ὑπόστασιν σ. Cyrus Al.*cap*.6(H.3.1341B); εἰ...μιᾶς φύσεως σ. ὢν ὁ Χριστός, ὁμοούσιός ἐστι τῷ πατρί, ἔσται ἄρα καὶ ὁ πατὴρ σ. Jo.D.*f.o*.3.3(989B); οὐχ ὡς τῶν δύο φύσεων μεταβληθεισῶν εἰς μίαν φύσιν σ. ἀδύνατον γὰρ ἐν μιᾷ φύσει ἅμα τὰ ἐναντία φυσικὰ γενέσθαι *ib*.4.18(1184C); μία φύσις σ. ἐκ διαφόρων φύσεων γίνεται, ὅταν ἑνουμένων φύσεων ἕτερόν τι παρὰ τὰς ἑνωθείσας φύσεις ἀποτελεσθῇ...ὁ δὲ... Χριστός, ἐκ θεότητος ὢν καὶ ἀνθρωπότητος, καὶ ἐν θεότητι καὶ ἀνθρωπότητι...ὅπερ ἐπὶ τῆς σ. φύσεως οὐκ ἔστιν εἰπεῖν...οὐ μία ἐστὶ σ. φύσις, ἀλλὰ μία ὑπόστασις...καὶ δύο φύσεις ἐν μιᾷ σ. ὑποστάσει id.*nat*.1(M.95.112C–113B); **h.** as against monothelite heresy πῶς...τὸ ἐκ τῶν θελημάτων, θέλημα προσαγορευθήσεται; οὐ γὰρ δυνατὸν τὸ σ. τῇ τῶν συντεθειμένων ὀνομάζεσθαι προσηγορίᾳ. ἢ οὕτω γε καὶ τὸ ἐκ τῶν φύσεων, φύσις Max.*Pyrr*.(M.91.296C); πάλιν αὐτὸν θελήμασι τοῦ πατρὸς χωρίζετε, σ. θελήματι σύνθετον καὶ μόνην χαρακτηρίσαντες φύσιν *ib*.; εἰ δὲ ὡς ὅλου σ. ... πάλιν αὐτὸν τοῦ πατρὸς ἠλλοτριώσας, σ. θελήματι μόνην χαρακτηρίσας ὑπόστασιν σ. id.*opusc*.(M.91.56A); **2.** of Christ's human nature opp. the divine ἀσύνθετος: τὰ μὲν ὑψηλότερα πρόσαγε τῇ θεότητι...τὰ δὲ ταπεινότερα τῷ σ. καὶ τῷ διὰ σὲ... ἀνθρωπισθέντι Gr.Naz.*or*.29.18(p.101.15; M.36.97B); τὸ μὲν γὰρ σ. μερίζεται, τὸ δὲ ἀσύνθετον λύσιν οὐκ ἐπιδέχεται· ἀλλὰ παραμένει μὲν τῷ μερισμῷ τοῦ σ. ἡ ἀσύνθετος φύσις, καὶ τῆς ψυχῆς τοῦ σώματος ἀποχωρούσης οὔθ' ἑτέρου χωρίζεται Gr.Nyss.*Apoll*.17(M.45.1156B); Dion.Ar.*e.h*.3.3.12(M.3.444A) cit. s. ἁπλοῦς.

E. ref. formation of a Gnost. aeon by whole Pleroma ἡ τοῦ δευτέρου Χριστοῦ, ὃν καὶ Σωτῆρα λέγουσιν, ἐξ ἐράνου σύνθετος κατασκευή Iren.*haer*.1.3.1(M.7.468A).

II. *forming a composite whole* (with);

A. Trin., exeg. 1Cor.2:11, ref. 11b οὐκ ἔτι τὸ ἐν αὐτῷ [as in 11a] ἵνα μή τις σ. τὸ πνεῦμα νομίσῃ ‡Chrys.*Trin*.(1.838E).

B. Christol., ref. 1Cor.6:17 πῶς οὐ πολλῷ μᾶλλον θειοτέρως...ἕν ἐστι τό ποτε σ. πρὸς τὸν λόγον τοῦ θεοῦ; Or.*Cels*.2.9(p.137.3; M.11.812A).

συνθέτως, *by composition*; **1.** Trin., excluded from concepts of Trin. μήτε ὁ σοφὸς θεὸς μεθέξει σοφίας σ. σοφὸς ἡμῖν νοεῖται, ἀλλ' ἀσυνθέτως αὐτός ἐστι σοφός CAnc.(358)*ep.syn*.ap.Epiph.*haer*.73.6(p.276.18; M.42.413C); of Son ἐπεὶ μὴ ἀγεννήτως ἔχει μηδὲ σ. *ib*.ap. eund.73.8(p.279.6; 417C); τὸ ἓν καὶ τὸ τρεῖς πρόσεστι τῷ πνί καὶ τῷ θεῷ· ἀλλὰ τῷ μὲν πνί γενητῶς καὶ σ., τῷ δὲ θεῷ ἀγενήτως τε καὶ ἀσυνθέτως ‡Just.*qu.et resp*.129(M.6.1380C); **2.** Christol.; acc. Severians, applicable to union only conceptually ὥστε τὰ δύο τὰ ἐξ ὧν ἡ ἕνωσις, ἐν τῷ συντεθεῖσθαι τῷ νῷ μόνον ἀπ' ἀλλήλων σ. διακρινόμενα Sev.Ant.ap. Eust.Mon.*ep*.(M.86.936D); acc. orthodox, also ontologically καθ' ἑτέραν μὲν αὐτοῦ [sc. Logos] γέννησιν, ἀΐδιόν τε ὑπάρχειν αὐτὸν...καθ' ἑτέραν δὲ ἀρχόμενον τοῦ σ. εἶναι Leont.H.*Nest*.4.3(M.86.1657B).

συνθεωρ-έω, **1.** *see, observe together*, i.e. one thing with another ἐν ᾧ [sc. φωτί] τὰ πάντα ~εῖται Clem.*str*.6.16(p.502.2; M.9.364B); with the mind's eye, *see at the same time* τὸ ποιητικὸν αἴτιον... ~οῦντες [sc. as the reflection in the mirror] *ib*.1.19(p.60.25; M.8.809C); pass., *be seen* or *envisaged together*, Gr.Nyss.*tres dii*(M.45.128D); ὅλῳ...τῷ θεῷ ὅλως σ. ὁ λόγος id.*fid*.(M.45.141A); id.*Eun*.2(2 pp.300.10,305.4; M.45.472A,476D); τὸ πνεῦμα...αὐτῷ σ. *ib*.(2 p.301.9; 472C); Max.*ambig*.(M.91.1296D); οὐδεὶς...εἴποι ἂν ἄπειρον εἶναι ᾧ ἐξ ἀϊδίου σ. τι ἢ συνεπιθεωρεῖται κατ' οὐσίαν διάφορον *ib*.(1184D); id.*ep*.1(M.91.364B).

***συνθεωρία, ἡ,** a *like envisaging, simultaneous consideration* μὴ ...θατέραν τελείαν υἱότητα, ἄνευ τῆς σ. τῆς ἑτέρας φύσεως εἰδέναι Leont.H.*Nest*.3.1(M.86.1604B).

***συνθηκάρι(ο)ς, ὁ,** *schemer* ἔξω βάλε τὸν σ. καὶ Μανιχαῖον...μετὰ σοῦ ἐστι, καὶ συνθηκίζει τοὺς ἐπισκόπους CCP(536)*act*.5(p.86.12; H.2.1356B).

συνθήκη, ἡ, **1.** in gen., *putting together, composition, association* διὰ τῆς σωματικῆς τῶν ποιοτήτων σ. Gr.Nyss.*Eun*.12(1 p.377.34; M.45.1104D); *combination* of different substances ἐν εἰκόνι [sc. of Nebuchadnezzar] τῶν ὑλῶν...τὴν σ. Thdt.*Dan*.2:31ff.(2.1091); *composition, constitution* of the body, Mac.Mgn.*apocr*.3.12(p.81.21); *ib*.3.13(p.88.8); *fabric* of a house, *ib*.4.16(p.187.27); **2.** literary *composition*; **a.** gramm., *construction* πολὺ δὲ ταύτης κἀκείνης τῆς σ. τὸ μέσον [ref. insertion or omission of article with predicate] Chrys.*hom.7.4 in 2Cor*.(10.486A); **b.** more gen., *structure* of sentences, *mode of expression, style* δυσερμήνευτος...ὁ νοῦς διά τοι τάς τε τῶν προσώπων εἰς πρόσωπα μεταβάσεις, καὶ τὸ τῆς σ. τραχὺ καὶ οὐ βάσιμον νῷ παντί Cyr.*Is*.2.3(2.254B); *ib*.(279B); id.*Os*.129(3.161C); παραμείβοντες τὴν ἐν τῇ λέξει σ. id.*Jo*.4.6(4.420C); τῇ διανοίᾳ καὶ τάξει τῶν τότε λεχθέντων...ἀκολουθήσαντες, δι' ἑτέρας μόνον...σ. καὶ λέξεως τὸν ἄλλοις προπονηθέντα πόνον ᾠκειωσάμεθα Bas.Sel.*v.Thecl*.1(M.85.480B); ῥημάτων κομψείαις καὶ Ἀττικῶν ὀνομάτων ἁρμονίᾳ τε καὶ σ. Zach.Mit.*disp*.(M.85.1037A); opp. content, subject-matter ἀπ' αὐτῆς τῆς ἀπαγγελίας καὶ τῆς σ. τὴν παρρησίαν δηλοῖ Chrys.*hom.10.3 in Ac*.(9.85B); οὐ φράσεως δεῖ, ἀλλὰ νοημάτων...οὐδὲ σ., ἀλλὰ φρενῶν id.*hom.15.2 in 1Tim*.(11.637B); ἡ δύναμις...τοιάδε ὑπῆρχεν. εἴποιμι δὲ αὐτὴν γε δήπου τῶν λόγων τὴν σ. Men.*exc.Rom*.3(p.176.19; M.113.860B); **c.** in concrete sense, a *composition* γέγονε...λιγυρὸν ἀπήχημα τῇ εὐρύθμῳ γλυκερᾷ σ. Jo.Mon.*hymn.Chrys*.6(M.96.1381B); **d.** κατὰ συνθήκην ? *in literary form* or ? periphrasis for ptcpl. of συντίθημι:

γραμματικοὶ καὶ ποιηταὶ...τὰς κατὰ σ. ἱστορίας ἐγράψαντο Mac.Aeg. *hom.*45.2(M.34.788A); **3.** *gathering* of people διαβαλεῖν Χριστιανισμόν, ὡς συνθήκας κρύβδην πρὸς ἀλλήλους ποιουμένων Χριστιανῶν παρὰ τὰ νενομισμένα Or.*Cels.*1.1(p.56.2; M.11.652A); id.*mart.*17(p.16.15; M. 11.585A); **4.** *pact, agreement*; dist. from διαθήκη, Isid.Pel.*epp.*2.196 (M.78.641D) cit. s. διαθήκη; **a.** of marriage vows, Hipp.*haer.*5.26 (p.130.3; M.16.3199A); also of a promise of marriage εἰμὶ σός· καὶ εἰ μηδέπω τῷ γάμῳ, τῷ νόμῳ λοιπὸν καὶ ταῖς ἐπὶ σοί μοι γεγενημέναις σ. Bas.Sel.*v.Thecl.*1(M.85.489B); **b.** with God; **i.** *covenant*, of Law τὴν ἀπ' οὐρανοῦ μέχρι γῆς...σ. Clem.*str.*5.6(p.347.7; M.9.56C); Ἰουδαίοις ...τοῖς τὰς ἐπαγγελίας ἐπὶ συνθήκαις εἰληφόσιν Or.*Cels.*8.69(p.286.28; M.11.1621B); τῆς μὲν γνώσεως αὐτοῦ [sc. Ἀβραάμ] προώδευσεν ἡ πίστις, τῆς δὲ πίστεως ἀκόλουθος ἦν ἡ σ. *Const.App.*7.33.4; **ii.** *pledge, commitment* involved in Christian profession εἰ...τὰς ψυχὰς ὀφείλομεν τοῖς ἀδελφοῖς, καὶ τοιαύτην τὴν σ. πρὸς τὸν σωτῆρα ἀνθωμολογήμεθα Clem.*q.d.s.*37(p.184.12; M.9.641D); Or.*Jo.*5.2(p.101.12; M.14. 188B); μία τις ἐν ὑμῖν ἔστω πίστις, μία σύνεσις, μία σ. τοῦ κρείττονος Const.ap.Eus.*v.C.*2.71(p.70.27; M.20.1045B); of baptismal promises τὰς καλουμένας τοῦ θεοῦ διαθήκας ἐπὶ συνθήκαις παρεδεξάμεθα αἷς πρὸς αὐτὸν ἐποιησάμεθα ἀναδεχόμενοι τὸ κατὰ Χριστιανισμὸν βιοῦν. καὶ ἐν ταῖς πρὸς θεὸν σ. ἡμῶν ἦν πᾶσα ἡ κατὰ τὸ εὐαγγέλιον πολιτεία Or. *mart.*12(p.11.24; M.11.577C); εἰ τοίνυν ὁ παραβὰς τὰς πρὸς ἀνθρώπους σ. ἄσπονδός τίς ἐστι καὶ σωτηρίας ἀλλότριος, τί λεκτέον περὶ τῶν... ἀθετούντων ἃς ἔθεντο πρὸς θεὸν σ.; *ib.*17(p.16.17ff.; 585A); τῆς ὁμολογίας τῆς πίστεως, καὶ τοῦ βαπτίσματος τὰς σ. Ephr.2.378D; ἵνα... ᾖ τὸ...μύρον σφραγὶς τῶν σ. *Const.App.*7.22.2; σ. πρὸς θεὸν δευτέρου βίου καὶ πολιτείας καθαρωτέρας ὑποληπτέον τὴν τοῦ βαπτίσματος δύναμιν Gr.Naz.*or.*40.8(M.36.368B); **iii.** monastic *vows* παραδεχθέντα ...εἰς τὴν ἀδελφότητα...εἶτα τὴν ὁμολογίαν ἀθετήσαντα, οὕτω χρὴ ὁρᾶσθαι, ὡς εἰς θεὸν ἐξαμαρτόντα, ἐφ' οὗ καὶ εἰς ὃν τὴν ὁμολογίαν τῶν σ. κατέθετο Bas.*reg.fus.*14(2.355B; M.31.949C); βλέπε, ἀδελφε, οἵας σ. δίδως τῷ Χριστῷ *Euchol.*(p.379); **c.** *league* with evil ἔστι ποτὲ συνθήκας θέσθαι κακῶς...ἀθετεῖν μέλλω τὰς σ. τὰς πρὸς τὸν κόσμον... ἵνα ἀναλάβω οὐρανίους σ. Or.*hom.20.7 in Jer.*(p.187.8ff.; M.13.516A,B); λύσας τὰς...πρὸς ᾅδην σ. Cyr.H.*catech.*19.9.

***συνθηκίζω**, *intrigue with*, CCP(536)*act.*5(p.86.14; H.2.1356B) cit. s. συνθηκάριος.

***συνθηλάζω**, *be suckled*, hence *brought up, together*, *M.Ner.et Ach.*15,21(pp.15.3,20.18).

σύνθημα, τό, A. anything agreed upon; **1.** *preconcerted signal, agreed sign*; supposedly among Christians τὸ πιστὸν ἡμῖν ἀφανοῦς καὶ ἀπορρήτου κοινωνίας οἴεται εἶναι σ. [i.e. absence of altars, images, and shrine] Or.*Cels.*8.17(p.234.17; M.11.1541A); **2.** *watchword, password*; at gates of paradise εἰρήνης σ. ποιεῖται τὴν πίστιν Cyr. *Jo.*5.1(4.466A); translates שִׁבֹּלֶת [LXX codd.], Thdt.*qu.19 in Jud.*12:6(1.336); to angel at tomb of Christ συμβάδιζε φέρων ἐπὶ τοῦ στόματος τῆς βασιλείας τὸ σ. Gr.Ant.*mul.ung.*7(M.98.1856D); **3.** *formulary* τριὰς ἡμῖν καταγγέλλεται καὶ πιστεύεται...⟨ἐκ⟩ συνθημάτων ἀκοῆς Epiph.*anc.*67(p.81.22; M.43.137B); **4.** = Lat. *evectio, permit, warrant* to travel by imperial post, cf.*Cod.Thds.*8.5.12; δημοσίοις σ. ἀπεστάλησαν Pall.*v.Chrys.*4(p.22.14; M.47.15); *letter of introduction*, Gr.Naz.*or.*4.111(M.35.648C); **5.** any *token* or *sign*; περιμενέτω τῆς συγγνώμης τὸ σ. Synes.*ep.*67(M.66.1425B); of OT type χρὴ...τὰ θυσιαστήρια σ. τι τῶν κατὰ τὴν ἐκκλησίαν πραγμάτων φέρειν Meth.*symp.*5.8(p.62.19; M.18.112A); of an acted parable, *symbol* ἐφιζήσας...σποδῷ σ. τοῖς ἄλλοις ἐδίδου τὸ χρῆναι καὶ ἀσιτεῖν, καὶ...ἐξαιτεῖν τὸν ἔλεον Cyr.*Jon.*22(3.384A); in Dion. Ar. of symbolic language in which transcendent realities have to be expressed ἡ τῶν...θεολόγων...σοφία...διανιστῶσα...τὸ ἀνωφερὲς τῆς ψυχῆς...τῇ δυσμορφίᾳ τῶν σ. [i.e. compelling realization of their inadequacy] *c.h.*2.3(M.3.141B); τῆς...θεοπλαστίας ἱερὰ σ. φαινόμενα τῶν κρυφίων id.*ep.*9.1(M.3.1105B); τὰ ἱερὰ σύμβολα...ταῖς αἰτίαις... ἀναπτύσσειν ὧν...ἐστιν ἐκφαντορικὰ σ. *ib.*9.2(1109A); in a particular instance τὴν...στερεὰν τροφήν, σ. φέρειν οἴομαι τῆς... *ib.*9.4(1112A); *sign* of the cross, Jo.D.*hom.*3.1(M.96.589C); **6.** *standard*, of the labarum μεταποιεῖν ἔγνωκεν [sc. Juln. Imp.] εἰς τὸ πρότερον σχῆμα, τὸ κορυφαῖον τῶν Ῥωμαϊκῶν σ., ὅπερ Κωνσταντῖνος...εἰς σταυροῦ σύμβολον μετετύπωσεν Soz.*h.e.*5.17.2(M.67.1265B); **7.** *pledge* εἰσεδέξατο ὁ πατὴρ τοὺς ἐξ ἐθνῶν σ. δοὺς αὐτοῖς εἰρήνης, τὴν σωτηρίαν τὴν διὰ τῆς ...πίστεως Or.*hom.15 in Lc.*(p.106.6); of eucharist τὰ τῆς σωτηρίας σ. Isid.Pel.*epp.*2.37(M.78.480D).

B. *agreement, covenant*; **1.** *agreement, accord*, as between Christians, Or.*Cels.*3.14(p.213.19; M.11.937A); ἐξ ἑνὸς σ. ἐπιδημεῖν [sc. angels] ἐπ' εὐεργεσίᾳ καὶ σωτηρίᾳ τῶν εὐχομένων θεῷ *ib.*8.34(p.249. 25; 1568A); οἱ πλεῖστοι τῶν ἀφελεστέρων πρὸς τὸ τούτων ἔξων σ. Constantius Imp.ap.Ath.*apol.Const.*30(M.25.633B); **2.** *agreement, assent* to ordination, *Const.App.*8.4.5; ἐκθέσμως μὲν οὖν [sc. the ordination]...εἰ μήτε ἐν Ἀλεξανδρείᾳ κατέστη, μήτε παρὰ τριῶν ἐνθάδε, καὶ εἰ τὸ σ. τῆς χειροτονίας ἐκεῖθεν ἐδέδοτο Synes.*ep.*67(M.66. 1416A).

***συνθήμων, ὁ,** *plotter*, Eudoc.*Cypr.*1.92(M.85.836C).

[*]συνθιασωτεύω, = συνθιασιτεύω, *be a fellow member of a θίασος*; in gen., *associate* with ξυνέπεσθαι...τῷ κυρίῳ καὶ σ. Meth.*symp.*6.5 (p.69.25; M.18.121A).

συνθιασώτης, ὁ, *partner in the θίασος*; in gen., *comrade, associate*; of the prophets with Moses, Clem.*prot.*8(p.60.23; M.8.189A).

[*]συνθλαύω, v. συνθραύω.

συνθλά-ω, 1. *crush together, crush*; met. ὅτε...τοῦ θανάτου τὴν ῥαβδουχίαν σ. Mac.Mgn.*apocr.*3.14(p.90.7); σκῆπτρα ~σασα Περσικοῦ κράτους...Παρθένε Geo.Pis.*carm.*63.3(*WS* 14 p.60); pass., of the wicked, Didym.*Ps.*109:5(M.39.1541A); **2.** *break* σ. αὐτῶν τὰ σκέλη *A.Pil.*B 11.2(p.311); *break up, shatter* so as to *destroy*, †Bas.*bapt.* 1.2.7(2.634B; M.31.1537A); τὴν δάμαλιν [sc. τὴν χρυσῆν]...σ. Cyr. *Os.*114(3.146A); cf.Ps.106:16 αἱ χαλκαῖ πυλαὶ συνετρίβησαν καὶ οἱ σιδηροῖ μοχλοὶ σ. [i.e. at descent into Hades] *A.Pil.*B 21.3(p.328); Or.*princ.*4.3.11(p.340.11; M.11.396A); Jo.D.*hom.*4.22(M.96.620C).

συνθλίβω, 1. *press together, compress*; hence *crowd* ἵνα μὴ σ. τὴν χεῖρα τῶν πρεσβυτέρων Or.*Jo.*32.22(14; p.465.30; M.14.805B); **2.** met.; **a.** *oppress, afflict* ἐπιμένει [sc. ὁ πειρασμός] καὶ σ. Jo.Jej. *doct.*1(p.229); pass., *suffer tribulation with*, Chrys.*hom.5.1 in 2Tim.* (11.686A); **b.** pass., *be pressed* or *forced* in argument πρὸς μιᾶς θεότητος ὁμολογίαν σ. Gr.Nyss.*or.catech.*proem.(p.6.3; M.45.12D); **c.** pass., *be depressed, downcast* σ. δι' ὧν ἔπασχον Chrys.*hom.14.1 in Phil.*(11.304D).

***σύνθλιψις, ἡ,** *affliction*, Thdr.Stud.*epp.*2.11(M.99.1145C); v. συνέλιξις.

συνθολόω, 1. *make turbid, confuse*, Geo.Pis.*hex.*12(συνθολεῖ M.92. 1427A); and, since this is done by stirring, **2.** pass., *be whirled, be sent spinning*, *ib.*1728(1568A).

***σύνθραυσμα, τό,** *fragment* ὀστράκινον εἰς λεπτὰ συνθραύοιτο, ὡς τῶν σ. ἕκαστον ἀχρεῖον εἶναι Cyr.*Is.*3.2(2.424D).

συνθραύ-ω, *break in pieces, shiver*; met. κωφοῦται...καὶ ὅλως ~εται, μηδὲν δυνάμενος λαλῆσαι Herm.*mand.*11.14; ὅλον μου τὸ σῶμα συνθλαύεται ἐκ (sic) ἀθυμίας καὶ γυμνότητος Eus.Al.*serm.*21.14 (M.86.441A); with contrition ἀπέλυσε τῶν τῆς ἁμαρτίας δεσμῶν τοὺς συντεθραυσμένην ἔχοντας καρδίαν Cyr.*Lc.*4:18ff.(M.72.541C); *impair* τὰς ἐνεργείας...συντεθραυσμένας id.*Ps.*33:21(M.69.893A).

***συνθρηνέω,** *join in lamentation* σ. τῷ πεπονθότι Bas.*hom.*5.8(2. 41E; M.31.257A); Gr.Naz.*or.*6.18(M.35.745B); *Mir.Artem.*34(p.52. 19); abs. οἱ συγγενεῖς συνέκλαιον καὶ σ. *Mir.Geo.*4(p.30.13); met. ὁ οὐρανὸς σ. αὐτῷ *Apophth.Mac.Aeg.*(M.34.221A).

συνθριαμβεύω, *share in a triumph* οἱ...ἐν Χριστῷ μάρτυρες...σ. ὡς κοινωνοὶ τῶν παθημάτων αὐτοῦ Or.*mart.*42(p.39.24; M.11.620A).

σύνθρονος, *sharing a throne, reigning with*; adj. and subst.; **1.** in gen. ὁ σ. ὑμῶν *Pers.*(p.28.18); fig. πᾶς ὃς ἂν διδάσκει καλὰ καὶ πράττει σ. ἔσται βασιλέων *T.Lev.*13.9; *seated beside* ἐφαντάζετο σ. αὐτὸν τῶν ἀποστόλων γινόμενον ‡Pall.*h.mon.*8.17(p.37.14; M.34.1139B); ἐν τῷ ὀχήματι σ. τῷ ἐπάρχῳ Socr.*h.e.*2.16.8(M.67.216C); met., *of equal worth* or *dignity, ranked together* τὴν εἰς τὸν θεὸν...εὐσέβειαν καὶ τὰς σ. ταύτης ἀρετάς Or.*Cels.*3.50(p.246.19; M.11.985C); θεὸν...ᾧ οὐχ ὕλη σ. Adam.*dial.*5.28(M.11.1884A, v.l. σύγχρονος p.240.9); Heracl. *nov.*22(p.34); ref. bishops, *sharing a throne*, i.e. a see σ. γενέσθαι Παυλίνῳ τὸν Μελέτιον Socr.*h.e.*5.5.3(M.67.569D); of a successor in a see ὁ...σ. τοῦ ἁγίου Γρηγορίου [i.e. Gr. Ill.] Jo.Nic.*nativ.*(M.96. 1436A); **2.** theol.; **a.** of Son as coequal with Father, Eus.*Lc.*9:28 (M.24.549C); ἱερεὺς ὢν τοῦ...θεοῦ καὶ τῆς ἀγενήτου δυνάμεως σ. id.*d.e.* 4.15(p.179.19; M.22.297D); Gr.Naz.*or.*4.78(M.35.604B); Germ.CP *or.* 2(M.98.253C); abs. τὸ...εὔχεσθαι, οὐ κατὰ θεόν, οὐδὲ κατὰ σ. Chrys. *hom.64.3 in Jo.*(8.386C); id.*hom.39.6 in 1Cor.*(10.371D); σ. τὸν υἱὸν ἐκήρυξεν, οὐ λειτουργὸν τὸν ὁμοούσιον ἐστηλίτευσε Procl.CP *or.*2.1(M. 65.692C); and with H. Ghost ἄτρεπτος...ἡ θεότης, συναΐδιος τῷ πατρὶ καὶ σ. τῷ ἁγίῳ πνεύματι Jo.Nic.*nativ.*(M.96.1449C); **b.** of H. Ghost τὸν σ. καὶ ὁμότιμον Bas.*Spir.*15(3.12E; M.32.93A); ‡Ath. *templ.*(p.111.13; M.28.1432A) cit. s. προκηρύσσω; **c.** of creatures, by grace of God, ref. Ps.81:6 θεοὶ τὴν προσηγορίαν κέκληνται, [οἱ] σ. τῶν ἄλλων θεῶν Clem.*str.*7.10(p.41.24; M.9.480C); cf.Eph.1:6 ὁ λόγος...ἔμελλεν...τὴν ἀνθρωπίνην ἀναλήψεσθαι σάρκα...ἵνα...μὴ μόνον ἄφθαρτον αὐτὸν...γενέσθαι παρασκευάσῃ, ἀλλὰ καὶ σ. ἐν οὐρανοῖς τῷ θεῷ Marcell.*fr.*98 ap.Eus.*Marcell.*2.3(p.51.19; M.24.809C); ἀπόστολοι ...καθεζόμενοι σ. τῷ κριτῇ Ephr.3.523A; οἱ σ. αὐτοῦ πάντες οἱ ἅγιοι Epiph.*haer.*66.19(p.44.11; M.42.57D); Chrys.*hom.5.1 in Col.*(11. 358E); **3.** neut. as subst., *raised seats of bishop and presbyters* in the apse of a church, also of one such *seat* ἐὰν μὴ διαλλαγῇς τῷ πλησίον σου...μὴ ἀνέλθῃς ἐν τῷ σ. ‡Chrys.*de scientia*(10.841D); cf.Eus.Al. *serm*.5(M.86.345C); τὸ ἀνελθεῖν ἐν τῷ σ. τὸν ἀρχιερέα...ἐστιν ὅτι ὁ υἱὸς τοῦ θεοῦ μέλλων πληροῦν τὴν...οἰκονομίαν ‡Bas.*h.myst*.36(p.266. 19); τὸ σ. ἐστι τύπος τοῦ δεσποτικοῦ θρόνου...σ. δὲ λέγεται...διὰ τὸ συγκαθέζεσθαι τὸν υἱὸν μετὰ τοῦ πατρός· τὰ λοιπὰ σ. δηλοῦσι τὴν τιμὴν ἣν μετὰ τὴν ἀνάστασιν ὀφείλουσιν ἀπολαβεῖν οἱ δίκαιοι ‡Sophr.H. *liturg*.2(M.87.3984A); μετὰ δὲ τὸ Τρισάγιον ἀνέρχεται ὁ ἀρχιερεὺς ἐν τῷ σ. βασταζόμενος ὑπὸ τῶν διακόνων *ib*.16(3996C); τοῦ πατριάρχου...ἐν τῷ σ. καθεζομένου Thphn.*chron*.p.371(M.108.889B).

συνθρύπτω, *break in pieces*; met., ref. Ac.21:13, Bas.*hom*.18.7(2. 147C; M.31.504B); Didym.ap.*cat.Ac*.21:13(p.347.11).

***σύνθρυψις, ἡ**, *breaking in pieces, crushing*; **1.** of a crowd, *crushing, thronging* τὴν τοῦ λαοῦ...σύμπνιξιν καὶ σ. ἀλλήλων Steph. Diac.*v.Steph*.(M.100.1077A); **2.** met., of the heart, *breaking*, Didym. ap.*cat.Ac*.21:13(p.347.19).

***συνθυμι-άω**, *burn at the same time* ~ωμένης αὐτῷ [sc. ὁλοκαυτώματι] σεμιδάλεως Cyr.*ador*.11(1.409A); *ib*.17(622E).

***συνθυραυλέω**, *live together under canvas, camp out together*, Synes.*regn*.14(p.31.10; M.66.1077C).

***σύνθυρος**, *dwelling with, akin to* δειλίαν τὴν ἀπῳκισμένην καὶ σ. αὐτῇ [sc. ἀμαθίᾳ] Evagr.*h.e*.5.19(p.215.7; M.86.2832B).

συνθύτης, ὁ, *fellow offerer of sacrifice*; of fellow priests, Gr.Naz. *carm*.2.1.7.1(M.37.1024A); *ib*.2.1.33.16(1306A).

συνιαίνω, *delight in together*, Gr.Naz.*carm*.1.2.1.7(M.37.522C).

***συνιατρός, ὁ**, *fellow physician* Κοσμᾶν καὶ Δαμιανὸν...σ. καὶ συμμάρτυρας Sophr.H.*mir.Cyr.et Jo*.30(M.87.3520C).

συνιδρύ-ω, pass., *be seated with* or med., *take one's station with*; of H. Ghost οὐκ ἐξιστάμενος...τοῦ ~σθαι...τῷ πατρί Didym.*Trin*.2.4 (M.39.484B).

συνιερατεύ-ω, *exercise the priestly office together with* ὁ ~ων *fellow priest* οἱ τῷ Ἀαρὼν ~οντες Cyr.*ador*.13(1.454A); σ. καὶ συλλειτουργοῦντας ἀγγέλους id.*Zach*.19(3.676B); in Church τοὺς ὁμοπίστους...καὶ σ. αὐτοῖς CEph.(431)*ep*.(*ACO* 1.1.3 p.66.26; H.1.1613D); μετὰ ἀρχαγγέλων δοξάζοντα, καὶ θεῷ ~σαντα Eustrat.*v.Eutych*.82(M. 86.2368B).

συνιερεύς, ὁ, *fellow priest*; of Christian priests, ‡Pion.*v.Polyc*.30; *Cod.Afr*.47.

***συνιερεύ-ω**, = συνιερατεύω, *exercise one's priesthood together* with ἐπὶ τὸ ἄνω θυσιαστήριον ἀναπέμψοντα τὰς θυσίας, καὶ Χριστῷ ~σοντα Gr.Naz.*or*.2.73(M.35.481B).

***συνιερουργία, ἡ**, *joining in offering* (sc. the Christian sacrifice) ἐν τῇ τοῦ μοιχοζεύκτου παραδοχῇ καὶ σ. Thdr.Stud.*epp*.1.33(M.99. 1017C).

***συνιερουργός, ὁ**, *fellow offerer of sacrifice, fellow priest*, Thdr. Stud.*epp*.1.48(M.99.1076A).

συνιζάν-ω, **1.** *sink* or *settle down*; hence *diminish* μιμεῖσθαι τῶν σκιῶν τὰς μεσημβρινάς, ἢ τῶν γραμμῶν τὰς κατὰ πρόσωπον ἀπαντώσας, ὧν ~ει τὰ μήκη Gr.Naz.*ep*.51(M.37.105A); **2.** = συνίζω, *sit together* in council, Eus.*v.C*.1.44(p.28.22; M.20.960A).

συνίζω, *sit together*; hence *hold a session, sit to consider*; met., Rom.Mel.(*AS* 1 p.126).

συνί-ημι, [pres. ptcpl. συνέων †Apoll.*met.Pss*.17:26(M.33.1333A)] *perceive, understand*; **1.** esp. spiritual truth by rational processes σ. τὸν κινοῦντα [sc. τὸν κόσμον]...εἶναι θεόν Arist.*apol*.1.2 as well as by spiritual faculties, ref. Jo.10:27 σ. γνωστικῶς τὰς ἐντολάς Clem.*str*. 6.14(p.486.12; M.9.329B); σ. τοῖς ἔνδοθεν ὠσίν Or.*fr.287 in Mt*. (p.128); Clem. would make such perception dependent on trained intellect, *str*.1.6(p.23.7; M.8.729B); children not yet possessed of the necessary powers, Dion.Ar.*e.h*.7.3.11(M.3.565D); such perception may be impeded by the will καλεῖ...ἀνόητον τὸν καλούμενον σοφόν, ὡς συνιέναι τὸ δέον οὐκ ἐθελήσαντα Thdt.*Ps*.48:10f.(1.919); ἀβούλητον...τὸ σ. τοῦ ἀγαθῦναι Dion.Ar.*d.n*.4.3.35(M.3.736A); and is a gift of God, Just.*dial*.7.3(M.6.492C); χάρις παρὰ θεοῦ...εἰς τὸ σ. τὰς γραφὰς αὐτοῦ ἐδόθη μοι *ib*.58.1(608A); *ib*.121.4(757C); Tat.*orat*.29 (p.30.12; M.6.868A); as more than beholding or hearing ἡμῖν...ἐδόθη καὶ ἀκοῦσαι καὶ σ. καὶ σωθῆναι διὰ...Χριστοῦ Just.*dial*.121.4(757C); σ. μετὰ πάσης ἀκριβείας Tat.*orat*.39(p.39.25; M.6.881B); τὸ...σ. γινώσκειν λέγεται...οὔτε γὰρ ἐκ τοῦ θεωρεῖν ἤδη καὶ τὸ σ. παράκειται Adam.*dial*.1.23(p.44.18,20; M.11.1752A); **2.** some objects of spiritual understanding; **a.** significance of events ἐκ τῶν ἔργων καὶ ἐκ τῆς παρακολουθούσης δυνάμεως σ. πᾶσι δυνατόν, ὅτι οὗτός ἐστιν ὁ καινὸς νόμος Just.*dial*.11.4(M.6.500A); *ib*.12.2(500C); Clem.*prot*.2(p.20.1; M.8.97A); **b.** spiritual exegesis of OT, *Barn*.4.6; *ib*.10.12; τοῦτο σὺ οὐ ζητεῖς...τοιγαροῦν λέληθέ σε ὁ Χριστός· καὶ ἀναγινώσκων, οὐ ~ῃς Just.*dial*.113.1(736B); *ib*.34.1(548A); καθάπερ...ἡ μαγνῆτις λίθος ...τὰ βιβλία...τοὺς οἵους τε ~εναι...ἐπισπᾶται Clem.*ecl*.27(p.145.7; M. 9.712C); id.*paed*.2.12(p.228.18; M.8.541A); τοῖς ἀναγινώσκειν νομίζουσι τὸν νόμον καὶ μὴ σ. αὐτόν, μὴ ~έναι κρίνων ἐκείνους, ὅσοι μὴ ἀλληγορίας εἶναι ἐν τοῖς γεγραμμένοις νομίζουσι Or.*princ*.4.2.6(p.316. 13; M.11.369A); **c.** Christ's parables οὐκ ἐβούλετο τοὺς μὴ ἐσομένους ...ἀγαθοὺς ~έναι τῶν μυστικωτέρων ὁ σωτὴρ καὶ διὰ τοῦτο ἐλάλει αὐτοῖς ἐν παραβολαῖς Or.*princ*.3.1.16(p.224.7; M.11.281A); Eus.*Ps*. 48:4(M.23.429C); μυστηριωδῶς...ὑπὸ τοῦ σωτῆρος διὰ παραβολῶν μεμηνύσθαι τοῖς ~εῖν δυναμένοις Iren.*haer*.1.3.1(M.7.468A); **d.** mysteries of the Faith Σολομῶν...τὴν τοῦ ἀληθινοῦ νεὼ κατασκευὴν σ. οὐ μόνον ἐπουράνιον εἶναι...ἤδη δὲ καὶ εἰς τὴν σάρκα διαφέρειν, ἣν ἔμελλεν οἰκοδομεῖν ὁ...κύριος εἴς τε τὴν αὐτοῦ παρουσίαν Clem.*fr*.36 (p.218.25; M.9.768D); **e.** *know* Christ πρὸς τὸ...σ. ὑμᾶς τὸν Ἰησοῦν Just.*dial*.132.1(M.6.781D); but not God in himself εἴ τις ἰδὼν θεόν, σ. ὃ εἶδεν, οὐκ αὐτὸν ἑώρακεν, ἀλλά τι τῶν αὐτοῦ τῶν...γινωσκομένων Dion.Ar.*ep*.1(M.3.1065A); **3.** *perceive dimly, have an inkling* of σ. ... μὴ δ' ἀκριβοῦντα Or.*Jo*.20.2(corr.p.328.23; συνθέντα M.14.576A); cf. Tat.*orat*.39(p.39.25; M.6.881B) cit. supra.

***συνικέτης, ὁ**, *fellow suppliant, intercessor on one's behalf* ἐπί τινα τῶν ὁσίων ἀνδρῶν...γενέσθαι συλλήπτορα, καὶ σ. Dion.Ar.*e.h*.7.3.6 (M.3.561B); Jo.Mal.*chron*.5 p.124(M.97.217C).

συνιππάζ-ω, *ride with*; met., *accompany* λόγοι...πνευματικοὶ βίον σεμνὸν...μὴ ἔχοντες ~οντα στάχυές εἰσιν ἀνεμόφθοροι Pall.*h.Laus*.47 (p.140.10; M.34.1202A).

συνίπταμαι, *fly together with*, fig. ἡμῖν σ. τῷ τῆς ἀληθείας πτερῷ Clem.*prot*.10(p.68.26; M.8.205C); Geo.Pis.*carm.vit*.86(p.54).

***συνισοπροσήγορος, ὁ**, *one simultaneously and equally addressed*, ref. Gen.1:26 ἡ...τοῦ 'ποιήσωμεν' σημασία τὸ εἶναι πρόσωπον συνδημιουργὸν σημαίνει καὶ σ. εἰσάγει Gel.Cyz.*h.e*.2.14.5(M.85.1256D).

συνιστάνω, v. συνίστημι.

συνιστάω, = συνίστημι, Adam.*dial*.5.7(p.188.20; M.11.1844A); Mac.Aeg.*hom*.4.24(M.34.492A); Didym.*Trin*.2.12(M.39.673C).

συνίστ-ημι, **I.** trans.; **A.** *set together*; **1.** *combine, associate* Ἱέρωνα τῇ διαδοχῇ τοῦ χρόνου συνέστησε [i.e. ensured his fame] Synes.*ep*. 49(M.66.1377A); *form, start*, a dance, Thdt.*Jon*.proem.(2.1460); **2.** pass., *be made* or *allowed to stand with* (sc. the faithful) v. II.A.6 infra, Bas.*ep*.217 *can*.57(3.326C; M.32.797B).

B. *put together* so as to form a whole; **1.** *build* a city, Chrys.*hom*. *31.1 in Jo*.(8.174D); **2.** *frame, constitute*; **a.** freq. of God creating universe, *1Clem*.27.4; Arist.*apol*.1.5; Ath.*Dion*.25(p.65.10; M.25. 517B); λόγος...ἐδημιούργησε τὸ πᾶν καὶ ~η καὶ διεκόσμει id.*gent*.46(M 25.93B); ἐκ τοῦ μὴ ὄντος αὐτὰ ~η id.*inc*.44.1(M.25.173B); Jo.D.*f.o*.1.3 (M.94.796C); // κτίζω, Ath.*Ar*.2.29(M.26.208C); pass., *be brought into being*, *ib*.2.11(169A); εἰ...κτίσμα...ὁ υἱός, οὐχ ὑπάρχων πατρί, εἰς τὸ εἶναι συστήσεται καὶ ὁ πατήρ Petr.II Al.*encycl*.ap.Thdt.*h.e*.4. 22.18(M.33.1284A); **b.** of God in rel. to Logos αὐτὸς ὁ πατὴρ προνοίᾳ τῶν ὅλων πρὸ τῶν ἄλλων ἁπάντων συνεστήσατο [sc. τὸν λόγον] Eus. *d.e*.4.6(p.159.23; M.22.265C); **c.** ref. Inc., *form* ἐκ παρθένου μόνης ἑαυτῷ συνεστήσατο σῶμα Ath.*inc*.49.1(M.25.184B); τὸ ἅγιον ἐκ τῆς παρθένου ~αται βρέφος Apoll.*corp.et div*.13(p.191.9; M.*PL*.8. 875B); ἐπουράνιος...ἄνθρωπος ὁ κύριος, οὐχὶ ἐξ οὐρανοῦ τὴν σάρκα ἐπιδειξάμενος, ἀλλὰ τὴν ἐκ γῆς ἐπουράνιον συστησάμενος ‡Ath.*Apoll*. 2.16(M.26.1160A); τὴν ψυχήν, Χριστὸς ἀναμάρτητον...συνεστήσατο ἐν ἑαυτῷ *ib*.1.19(1125C); of union of divinity with flesh only ἓν ζῷον ἐκ κινουμένου καὶ κινητικοῦ ~ατο καὶ οὐκ...ἐκ δύο τελείων ἢ αὐτοκινήτων Apoll.*fr*.107(p.232.17)ap.Justn.*monoph*.(p.17.5; M.86.1124A); id.*corp.et div*.5(p.187.8; M.*PL*.8.873C); **d.** *frame, concoct* αἱρέσεις ...σ. Hipp.*haer*.4.13(p.45.9; M.16.3075C); *ib*.8.4(p.225.14; 3347A); **e.** συνίσταμαι ἐκ *be formed from, take one's rise in*, Herm.*mand*. 5.2.4; ἡ ἀρετὴ...ἐν ἡμῖν ἐστι, καὶ ἐξ ἡμῶν ~αται Ath.*v.Anton*.20 (M.26.873A); *ib*.(872C); Trin. εἰ...ὁ υἱὸς...ἐξ οὐκ ὄντων γέγονεν, ἐξ οὐκ ὄντων ~αται τριάς id.*Ar*.1.17(M.26.48B); id.*ep.Serap*.1.28(M.26. 596A); ἐκ μεταβολῆς καὶ προκοπῆς λέγουσι [i.e. Pneumatomachoi] ~ασθαι τὴν τριάδα *ib*.3.6(636B); **3.** *establish, found, organize*, Church ὁ Πέτρος τὰς ἐκκλησίας συστησάμενος μνημονεύεται Eus.*theoph.fr*.6 (p.20*.14; M.24.628C); id.*d.e*.2.3(p.77.24; M.22.140B); οἱ τελῶναι [sc. προσελθόντες μοι] κατέλιπον τὰ τελώνια, καὶ συνεστήσαντο τὰς ἐκκλησίας Ephr.2.208D; Eus.*d.e*.1.1(p.5.8; M.22.20A) cit. s. ἐκκλησία; Proc.G.*Is*.66:5ff.(M.87.2701D); other things ῥητορικὴν...ἐπ' ἀδικίᾳ καὶ συκοφαντίᾳ συνεστήσασθε Tat.*orat*.1(p.2.14; M.6.805B); ἀρχὴν ἔχοντος τότε καὶ ~αμένου τοῦ βίου Eus.*d.e*.1.9(p.40.15; M.22.77C); ὁ θεὸς...δύο αἰῶνας συνεστήσατο *Hom.Clem*.20.2; μοναστήριον...ὃ συνεστήσατο...Ἀβράμιος Jo.Mosch.*prat*.187(M.87.3064D); **4.** *put, place in, ascribe* to ἡ βάρβαρος φιλοσοφία...ἐν μὲν τῇ μονάδι ~ᾶσιν οὐρανὸν ἀόρατον Clem.*str*.5.14(p.388.1; M.9.137B).

C. bring and keep together, *maintain*; **1.** *preserve* τὰς ἀναλογίας ἑκάστου ~άνουσιν Dion.Ar.*d.n.*8.9(M.3.897A); **2.** *maintain, support, recommend* a line of action or a point of view, Clem.*str.*6.12(p.481.1; M.9.320A); ~άνουσι δεῖν τὸ πάσχα τῇ τεσσαρακαιδεκάτῃ τοῦ πρώτου μηνὸς φυλάσσειν Hipp.*haer.*8.18(p.237.16; M.16.3366B); CAlex.*ep.*ap.Ath.*apol.sec.*19(p.101.17; M.25.280A); τὴν ζωὴν ~ησι τὴν ἡμετέραν... πολιτείας...ἀκρίβεια Chrys.*hom.46.3 in Mt.*(7.485B); one's own case or point of view τὰ ἴδια σ. βουλόμενος, τὰ τῶν ἄλλων ἀτίμως ἐκβάλλει Or.*exp.in Pr.*22:10(M.17.220A); τὸ συστῆσαι τὰ οἰκεῖα ‡Max.*cap.al.*35(M.90.1409A); **3.** *exhibit*; **a.** subjectively, *evince* ~η...ὁ λόγος τοῦ σωτῆρος...τὸ ἐμβριθὲς καὶ αὐστηρὸν τοῦ τρόπου Eus.*d.e.*3.6(p.132.28; M.22.224C); **b.** objectively, *present* φοβερὸν καὶ δίκαιον ~ησι θεόν *Hom.Clem.*17.5; **4.** *commend* oneself to others οὐ γὰρ ἡ λέξις ἀλλ' ἡ διάνοια καὶ ἡ...ἀγωγὴ ~ησι τὸν πιστόν Ath.*ep.Aeg.Lib.*9(M.25.557C); *praise*, Eus.*h.e.*6.19.3(M.20.561C); ~άνειν ὡς καλῶς φρονοῦντας Ath.*Ar.*1.2(M.26.16A); Chrys.*hom.34.1 in Heb.*(12.312C); **5.** *present* petitions, etc., *Dial.*ap.Thdt.*h.e.*2.16.10f.(3.866); **6.** *stand for, signify* ἡ ῥάμνος τὴν ἁγνείαν ~ησι Meth.*symp.*10.3(p.124.17).

D. *make solid* or *firm*; hence *substantiate, confirm, attest*, Iren.*haer.*1.9.1(M.7.537A); οἱ δὲ διὰ τῆς τῶν ἄστρων ἱστορίας αἱρετικοὶ θέλοντες τὰ ἑαυτῶν δόγματα σ. Hipp.*haer.*4.47(p.70.6; M.16.3111D); ~άνειν τὴν Ἰησοῦ θείαν διδασκαλίαν Or.*Cels.*1.46(p.96.17; M.11.745B); σ. τὸν διὰ Ἰησοῦ ὡς σωτήριον τοῖς ἀνθρώποις λόγον *ib.*3.28(p.225.11; 956A); Eus.*d.e.*3.7(p.142.1; M.22.240A); σ. ... τὴν...ἑρμηνείαν Ἰωάννης *ib.*7.1(p.298.31; 489B); οἱ ἑτερόδοξοι σ. ἀπὸ γραφῶν τὰ τῆς θρησκείας αὐτῶν ἀποροῦντες Didym.*Trin.*1.9(M.39.280A); Adam.*dial.*1.22(p.42.25; M.11.1749B); opp. καταργέω, Ath.*inc.*48.5(M.25.181C); pass., Eus.*d.e.*3.5(p.129.8; 220A); Chrys.*hom.1.5 in Mt.*(7.155B); *show, demonstrate*; pass., Eus.*d.e.*7.3(p.340.20; 556A); *ib.*8.4(p.397.2; 641A); *ib.*6.20(p.287.4; 472B).

E. *bring together in opposition, oppose*, Afric.*ep.Arist.*(p.54.24; M.10.53A).

II. intrans.; **A.** *stand together*; **1.** of individuals, Dion.Ar.*ep.*7.2(M.3.1081A); **2.** *stand with, act in support, ally oneself* κἂν μόνος εὔχηται, τὸν τῶν ἁγίων χορὸν ~άμενον ἔχει Clem.*str.*7.12(p.56.8; M.9.508C); γέγραφεν ~άμενος τοῖς...ὑπὸ Εὐσεβίου γραφεῖσιν Marcell.*fr.*29 ap.Eus.*Marcell.*1.4(p.19.11; M.24.753C); τοῦ Χριστοῦ...τὴν θεότητα ...ἀθετοῦσιν ἐπὶ προφάσει τοῦ ~ασθαι δοκεῖν τῇ μοναρχίᾳ *Symb.Ant.*(345)6(p.253.3; M.26.732A); ὁ...φόβος τοῦ θεοῦ τῇ σωφροσύνῃ ~αται Bas.*hom.*12.9(2.106B; M.31.405C); ~αμένους...τοῖς τῆς ἀληθείας δόγμασιν Chrys.*hom.3.1 in Rom.*(9.448C); Εὐσέβιος ~αται τούτῳ Germ.CP *syn.haer.*9(M.98.48A); **3.** *confirm* a statement, *assent* to an accusation μετ' αἰσχύνης τῇ...ἐληλεγμένῃ ψευδολογίᾳ ~ατο Const.ap.Thdt.*h.e.*1.20.6(3.799); **4.** *come together, assemble*, *Ep.Lugd.*ap.Eus.*h.e.*5.1.47(M.20.425B); ὄχλον...συνεστῶτα εἶδεν *Hom.Clem.*16.1; **5.** *take one's stand, stand firm*; **a.** of persons οἱ...θαρροῦντες οἷς λέγουσι τούτοις καὶ εἰς πρόσωπον συστῆναι δύναται CSard.*ep.cath.*ap.Ath.*apol.sec.*42(p.120.12; M.25.328A); **b.** *stand* in a comparison ἡ γὰρ ἡμετέρα βιοτὴ οὐδὲ συνεστάναι δοκεῖ τῇ σῇ παραβαλλομένη ζωῇ Thdt.*Ps.*38:6(1.852); **c.** *stand, hold good, remain valid* μηκέτι τὸν Μωσέως νόμον μανθάνειν, τῷ μηκέτι συνεστάναι αὐτόν Eus.*d.e.*9.14(p.434.30; M.22.701A); ἴδωμεν εἰ τοιοῖσδε οὖσιν αὐτοῖς συστῆναι οἷόν τε ἦν τὸ ἐπιχείρημα *ib.*3.4(p.117.23; 201A); *Hom.Clem.*19.19; of words in a context, Chrys.*hom.24.1 in Mt.*(7.300B); **d.** in law, *stand by* a charge or plea ἀπαντήσαντα καὶ συστάντα τοῖς ἑαυτοῦ δικαίοις Pall.*v.Chrys.*14(p.87.13; M.47.49); σ. ἑαυτοῖς ἐπί *prove one's case with regard to, substantiate* συστῆναι ἑαυτοῖς ἐπὶ τοῖς ἐγκλήμασιν *ib.*8(p.43.17; M.47.26); **6.** of fourth grade of penitents as allowed to *stand with* the faithful during offering of eucharist although still debarred from Communion ὁ δὲ...μόλις παρακαλούμενος συνεστάναι ταῖς προσευχαῖς ἀνέχεται (of one not under penitential discipline) Dion.Al.ap.Eus.*h.e.*7.9.5(M.20.656B); ἡ σύστασις, ἵνα ~αται τοῖς πιστοῖς, καὶ μὴ ἐξέρχηται μετὰ τῶν κατηχουμένων Gr.Thaum.*ep.can.*11(M.10.1048B); οἱ συνειδότες ἐκελεύσθησαν...δεχθῆναι εἰς τοὺς συνεστῶτας CAnc.(314)*can.*25; συστήσεται μόνον τοῖς πιστοῖς, προσφορᾶς δὲ οὐ μεταλήψεται Bas.*ep.*217 *can.*56(3.326B; M.32.797A); συνεστὼς ἄνευ κοινωνίας *ib.can.*58f.(326D; M.l.c.); δύο ἔτη συστὰς...τοῖς πιστοῖς, οὕτω λοιπὸν καταξιούσθω τῆς τοῦ ἁγίου κοινωνίας *ib.can.*75(328E; M.804C); CTrull.*can.*87; also of the faithful with the penitents εἰσεδέξαντο καὶ συνήγαγον καὶ συνέστησαν καὶ προσευχῶν αὐτοῖς... ἐκοινώνησαν Dion.Al.ap.Eus.*h.e.*6.42.5(613C).

B. *come together*; **1.** ref. states of existence; **a.** *be put together, be formed, come into being* δι' αὐτοῦ...τὰ πάντα συνέστηκεν Arist.*apol.*1.5; πάντα δι' αὐτοῦ οὐ μόνον ἐν ἀρχαῖς τῶν ὅλων συνέστη, ἀλλὰ καὶ εἰς ἀεὶ γέγονέν τε καὶ γίνεται Eus.*d.e.*4.5(p.155.14; M.22.260B); Ath.*gent.*40(M.25.80D); Gr.Nyss.*ep.*24(M.46.1093B) cit. s. ἐν; τέσσαρες... ἀρεταί, ἐξ ὧν ὁ κατὰ διάνοιαν πνευματικὸς συνέστηκε κόσμος Max.*ambig.*(M.91.1245A); Καμπανῶν ἔθνος ἐν Ἰταλίᾳ συνέστη *Chron.Pasch.*p.168(M.92.413A); of body of Christ, ‡Chrys.*pasch.*2(8.257C) cit. s. ἀσύντριπτος; **b.** perf. ptcpl. neut., in concrete sense, *formation, structure* ἐξαίρει πᾶν τὸ συνεστηκὸς τοῦτο *Pers.*(p.30.9); **c.** συνέστηκα ἐκ *consist of*, Arist.*apol.*4.2; ὁ...θεὸς...οὐ...σ. ἐκ μερῶν Athenag.*leg.*8.2(M.6.905A); *ib.*6.3(901C); ἡ ἐκκλησία.. ἐκ πολλῶν συνεστηκυῖα μελῶν Clem.*paed.*1.6(p.113.3; M.8.296B); Or.*princ.*4.2.4(p.313.2; M.11.365A) cit. s. ἄνθρωπος; Eus.*h.e.*4.5.2(M.20.309A); Ath.*gent.*43(M.25.85B); τῶν τεσσάρων στοιχείων, ἐξ ὧν καὶ συνέστηκεν ἡ τῶν σωμάτων φύσις *ib.*27(56A); Trin. οὐκ ἐκ διαφορῶν...συνέστηκεν ἡ...τριάς id.*ep.Serap.*3.6(M.26.636A); **d.** συνέστην ἐκ *have one's origin in, take one's rise from*, of David and Solomon συστάντες ἐκ φυλῆς Ἰούδα Eus.*d.e.*7.3(p.347.26; M.22.565B); ἐξ ἐκείνου [sc. Ἀβραάμ]...τὸ Ἰουδαίων συνέστη γένος Thdt.*Ps.*118:160(1.1478); of Christ's human body ὁ...λόγος ἐπιπαρὼν...ἐν τῇ συστάσῃ αὐτοῦ ἐξ ἁγίας παρθένου σαρκί Eus.*d.e.*6.20(p.286.18; συστάσει 469D); τὸ...σῶμα συνέστη ἐκ παρθένου μόνης Ath.*inc.*20.4(M.25.132B); τὸ σῶμα τῆς τοῦ λόγου θεότητος...ἐκ τῆς οὐσίας τῆς σοφίας συνέστη id.*ep.Epict.*2(p.5.10; M.26.1053B); ἐσαρκώθη μίαν λοιπὸν...φύσιν ἔχων, κἂν ἐκ δύο συνέστη τῶν ἐναντίων Oecum.*Col.*2:9(p.455.5); **e.** *be based* or *founded* upon ἀληθινὴ παιδεία ἐπιθυμία τίς ἐστι γνώσεως, ἄσκησις δὲ παιδείας ~αται δι' ἀγάπην γνώσεως Clem.*str.*6.15(p.492.29; M.9.344D); αἱ...κρίσεις οὕτω ~ανται κατὰ τὰς...γραφάς *Ep.Alex.*ap.Ath.*apol.sec.*73(p.152.14; M.25.380B); τὴν καθ' ὅλης τῆς οἰκουμένης τῷ Χριστῷ ὀνομαστὶ συστᾶσαν ἐκκλησίαν Eus.*d.e.*4.16(p.192.28; M.22.321A); **f.** *be conserved* ἔμενε...αὐτοῦ συνεστὼς ὁ ὀφθαλμός Epiph.*haer.*67.3(p.136.18; M.42.177A); hence *exist* οἱ μὲν ἄνθρωποι, οὐ δυνάμενοι καθ' ἑαυτοὺς εἶναι...καὶ συνεστῶτες ἐν τῷ...λόγῳ Ath.*decr.*11(p.10.2; M.25.'441'(433)D); ἐν ᾧ [sc. τῷ λόγῳ] τὰ κτίσματα γέγονε καὶ συνέστηκεν id.*Dion.*2(p.47.8; M.25.481B); ὥσπερ τὰ δι' αὐτοῦ γενόμενα συνέστη id.*Ar.*3.61(M.26.452A); also med., *ib.*2.2(152B); *remain*, id.*gent.*27(M.25.53C); id.*decr.*8(p.8.13; '437'(429)C); διὰ τοῦτο Ἱερουσαλὴμ ἐπὶ τοσοῦτον συνειστήκει id.*inc.*40.2(M.25.165A); **2.** *be commended* or *introduced* παρ' ἑτέρων αὐτοῖς συνέστησαν Thdt.*2Cor.*3:1(3.301); **3.** *be reconciled* τῷ θεῷ συστάντας Dion.Al.*fr.*(p.61.1); **4.** *be associated with, indicative of* ἐκ τῆς τοῦ ὀνόματος ἑρμηνείας ἀεὶ ~αμένης τῆς...βασιλείας Eus.*d.e.*7.1(p.310.24; M.22.508C).

C. *be compact, concentrated, solid*; **1.** met., *be concentrated, preoccupied*, ref. rich opp. poor καταγελῶμεν αὐτῶν ἀγρυπνούντων, αὐτοὶ καθεύδοντες· καὶ συνεστώτων ἀεὶ καὶ φροντιζόντων, αὐτοὶ ἀφροντιστοῦντες καὶ ἀνειμένοι Bas.*hom.in Ps.*14(1.110C; M.29.273A); **2.** *be consistent, be applicable*, Eus.*d.e.*4.16(p.184.29; M.22.308C); μόνως δ' ἂν συσταίη...εἰ...περὶ τῆς φυλῆς ἁπάσης λέγεσθαι ταῦτα νοήσαιμεν *ib.*8.1(p.357.27; 581B); οὐ συνέστηκεν ὁ λόγος αὐτῷ *ib.*7.3(p.344.32; 561C); **3.** *be established, made clear*; **a.** ὃ...συνέστη διὰ τοῦ [Ps.67:12] Eus.*d.e.*3.1(p.95.32; M.22.168A); συνέστηκεν ἀψευδὴς ἡ πρόρρησις *ib.*7.3(p.345.8; 561D); ἐρρήθη...οὕτω...διὰ τὸ συστῆναι θεομισεῖς τὰς μὴ κατὰ...λόγον εἰσπροεδρίας Didym.*Trin.*3.29(M.39.948A); **b.** impers. συνέστηκε *it is well known, it is clear* or *evident that*; also συνίσταται: ἀνατρέχουσιν εἰς μίαν ἀρχὴν..., σ. ἡμῖν, τὰ τῆς εὐσεβοῦς θεολογίας Eus.*d.e.*5.8(p.230.29; 381A); σ. φανερῶς ὅτι Ath.*Ar.*2.60(M.26.276C).

***συνιστόρησις, ἡ,** *connivance* at or *complicity* in; c. genit., Ephr.1.121D.

συνίστωρ, 1. *knowing as well* as another, of a witness σύμψηφον ἔχει [sc. ἐπίσκοπος] καὶ σ. τῆς δίκης τὸν Χριστόν *Const.App.*2.47.2; **2.** as subst., *exponent of one's views, sympathizer, advocate* Ἐλισάβετ ...τῆς νηστείας τὸν σ. Chrysipp.*enc.in Jo.Bapt.*3(p.33.9); τούτων οἱ σ. καὶ βεβαιωταὶ καὶ ὑπέρμαχοι Jo.D.*haer.*85(M.94.744A).

***συνισχύω,** *be strong also* or *at the same time*, e.g., in another respect ἐπειδὴ...ζωὴ ἦν, καὶ θεοῦ λόγος...διὰ τοῦτο ὡς μὲν ζωὴ καὶ δύναμις ὢν σ. ἐν αὐτῷ τὸ σῶμα Ath.*inc.*21.5(M.25.133B).

σύνκρουστον, v. σύγκρουτον.

***συνλιτουργός,** v. *συλλειτουργός.

σύνναος, *having the same temple* φιλοσοφίας, καὶ τῆς σ. ταύτῃ ποιητικῆς Synes.*ep.*1(M.66.1321A).

***συνναυτίλλομαι,** *navigate, sail on together* τὴν αὐτὴν ἀλλήλοις σ. θάλατταν ‡Chrys.*hom.suppl.*5(M.64.460C).

συννεάζω, *be young with*; hence *remain new along with*, ref. Dt.29:5 σ. τῇ ἐσθῆτι τῶν ὑποδημάτων ἡ χρεία Bas.Sel.*or.*31.1(M.85.340C).

συννεκρ-όω, 1. *put to death with* ἐπὶ τοῦ ὄφεως, εἰ κατὰ κεφαλῆς τὴν καιρίαν λάβοι, οὐκ εὐθὺς ~οῦται τῇ κεφαλῇ καὶ ὁ κατόπιν ὁλκός Gr.Nyss.*or.catech.*30(p.110.4; M.45.76C) = id.*nativ.*(M.46.1133A); **2.** met. (ref. Col.3:5) *mortify with* Χριστῷ σ. τὴν γλῶσσαν ἡνίκα ἐνήστευον Gr.Naz.*ep.*119(M.37.213B); ‡Caes.Naz.*dial.*140(M.38.1048)· Χριστῷ συσταυροῦσθαι καὶ ~οῦσθαι τῷ κόσμῳ Germ.CP *or.*1(M.98.237D).

***συννέκρωσις, ἡ,** *dying with,* of fasting ἡμῖν...τὴν σ. Χριστοῦ τοῦτο δύναται, καὶ καθαρσίς ἐστι προεόρτιος Gr.Naz.*or*.40.30(M.36.401B).

συννεύρωσις, ἡ, *union by sinews,* Melet.*nat.hom*.synops.(M.64.1120A); οὐ μόνον συνάρθρωσις καὶ διάρθρωσις, ἀλλὰ καὶ σ. καὶ συγχόνδρωσις *ib*.28f.(1265C).

σύννευσις, ἡ, 1. *convergence; inclination, tendency* πρὸς τὸ ἕν Dion.Ar.*e.h*.2.3.5(M.3.401B); *ib*.2.3.8(404C); πρὸς τὰ θεῖα *ib*.3.3.7 (436B); τὴν πρὸς τὸ ἓν τῆς ὅλης κτίσεως...σ. δείξας ἐν ἑαυτῷ [i.e. Christ by assumption of human nature] Max.*ambig*.(M.91.1309C); πρὸς φόνους σ. αἱμάτων δίχα Geo.Pis.*Pers*.2.144(M.92.1221A); ref. speed, ? *approximation,* ? *equality* ἡ τοῦ τάχους σ. ἀντωθουμένη id. *hex*.114(σύνευσις M.92.1440A); **2.** *agreement, union* of will in Godhead μοναρχία δὲ...ἣν φύσεως ὁμοτιμία συνίστησι...καὶ πρὸς τὸ ἓν τῶν ἐξ αὐτοῦ σύννευσις Gr.Naz.*or*.29.2(p.75.5; M.36.76B); of Christ with Father, ref. Mt.26:39 τί σοι δοκεῖ; συστολῆς ὑπάρχειν ἢ ἀνδρείας; σ. ἄκρας, ἢ διαστάσεως;...συμφυΐας...ἐντελοῦς καὶ σ. Max.*opusc*.(M.91.65A); of creatures with God πάντα εἰς ἓν ἀγούσας [sc. angels] πρὸς μίαν σ. τοῦ τὰ πάντα δημιουργήσαντος Gr.Naz.*or*.28.31(p.71.11; M.36.72C); of a man τῆς πρὸς αὐτὸ [sc. τὸ πνεῦμα] τελείας σ. Max. *opusc*.(M.91.89D); s.v.l., *agreement, consent,* v. s. σύμπνευσις; *consent, yielding* τῷ...δελεασμῷ κάμπτειν εἰωθότι πρὸς σύννευσιν Nil. *Magn*.2(M.79.972A).

συννεύω, 1. *contract, narrow;* hence *converge* μεμηχάνηται...ἅπαντα συννεύειν εἰς ἓν Synes.*ep*.154(συνεύειν M.66.1556B); *concentrate* τηνικάδε [sc. at night] ἡ ψυχὴ πεπαυμένη τῶν αἰσθήσεων σ. πρὸς αὐτὴν καὶ μᾶλλον μετέχει τῆς φρονήσεως Clem.*str*.4.22(p.310.11; M.8.1349B); Gr.Naz.*or*.42.24(M.36.488B); Gr.Nyss.*laud.Bas*. (M.46.793A); **2.** *consent, agree* οἷς ἂν λέγοι Χριστὸς...σ. Cyr.*Is*.3.2 (2.396B); **3.** *beckon* σ. ... ἡ Σάρρα τὸν Ἀβραὰμ...ἐλθεῖν *T.Abr*.A 6 (p.83.5).

συννέφεια, ἡ, *cloudy sky,* met. ἵνα φωτίζωνται τῆς αἱρετικῆς φαυλότητος αἱ σ. Leo II Papa *ep*.(M.*PL*.96.403A).

***συννεώτερος, ὁ,** *young man of the same age* τὸν φίλον ὄντα καὶ σ. τοῦ υἱοῦ αὐτοῦ Jo.Mal.*chron*.7 p.181(M.97.289B).

***συννηπιάζω,** *become an infant with* σ. υἱὸς τοῦ θεοῦ...τῷ ἀνθρώπῳ Iren.*haer*.4.38.2(M.7.1107A); σ. καὶ συνηύξησε, καὶ συνέφαγε Ath.*inc. et c.Ar*.22(M.26.1024C); ὁ τέλειος τῶν νηπίων διδάσκαλος σ. τοῖς νηπίοις Cyr.H.*catech*.12.1; met., *come down to the level of a child* ἐπειδὴ...ἦσαν οὕτω δυσμαθεῖς...οἰκονομικῶς ὁ σωτὴρ σ. ... αὐτοῖς Cyr. *Jo*.2.9(4.237C).

***συννηστεύ-ω, 1.** *fast with* or *together* συνευχομένων καὶ σ. αὐτοῖς [sc. candidates for baptism] Just.*1apol*.61.2(M.6.420C); Νινευΐταις ...τὰ ἄλογα σ. Bas.*hom*.1.9(2.8C; M.31.180B); ἵενται...ὀκνηρῶς ἐπὶ τὸ ...βάπτισμα...μετριώτερον σ. Cyr.*ador*.5(1.170D); of the tempter τοῖς νηστεύουσι ~ειν, αὐτοὺς οἰήσει φενακίσαι βουλόμενος Mac.Aeg.*libert. ment*.7(M.34.940C); **2.** *observe the same fasts as, share the fasts of* συσσαββατίζων...καὶ σ. ... εὑρίσκετο [sc. ὁ ἀπόστολος]...ἵνα τῇ συνηθείᾳ...ἐφελκύσηται αὐτούς Pall.*v.Chrys*.19(p.124.22; M.47.70); περὶ ὀρθοδόξων...~όντων Ἰουδαίοις Phot.*nomoc*.13.15(p.622; M.104.1201B).

***συννοητός,** *understandable* οὐ γὰρ συνοπτὰ οὐδὲ σ. πᾶσιν...εἰ μή τῳ θεὸς δῷ συνιέναι Just.*dial*.7.3(M.6.492C); Adam.*dial*.3.13(p.136.1; M.11.1805A).

συννόμως, *in compliance with the (Christian) law* μηδεὶς...κρινέτω τὸν ἱερουργὸν...καὶ εἰ τὸ ῥάθυμον ἔχοι πρός γε τὸ βιοῦν ἑλέσθαι σ. Cyr. *ador*.13(1.477A).

***συννυμφεύομαι,** *be married to;* met., of Sion's marriage to true faith, †Bas.*Is*.46(1.416B; M.30.208A).

συνοδεύ-ω, *journey with, go with;* ref. συνεισακτοί (*contubernales*) *associate* with γυναιξὶ...σ. καὶ συνδιαιτώμενοι Epiph.*haer*.47.3(p.218.17; M.41.853C); met. ~σόν μοι ταῖς προσευχαῖς σου Pall.*h.Laus*.60 (p.154.17; ~σάτωσάν μ. αἱ πρεσβεῖαί σου M.34.1236D); of God with man ἐμοὶ σ. ἐν ὁδῷ δικαιοσύνης κύριος *Barn*.1.4; ἵνα σ. ταῖς ψυχαῖς ὑμῶν Or.*hom.21 in Lc*.(p.140.17); Ἰησοῦ ~οντος ὑμῖν id.*mart*.36 (p.34.4; M.11.612A); of peace of God, *A.Thom*.A 67(p.185.3); of angels; with Christ, Hipp.*fr.20 in Pss*.(p.147.8; M.10.609C); docetic ἄγγελος ~σας αὐτῷ ἄνωθεν τὴν Μαριὰμ εὐηγγελίσατο id.*haer*.8.10 (p.230.13; M.16.3355A); with men, Or.*or*.31(p.399.16; M.11.556A); of Satan, Clem.*str*.4.14(p.290.12; M.8.1301C).

συνοδία, ἡ, 1. *journey in company; orbit* of heavenly body, Dion. Al.ap.Eus.*p.e*.14.25(778A; M.21.1280B); **2.** Christian *fellowship, company* of the faithful, local *congregation* ἀφιστάμενος τῆς τῶν ἀδελφῶν σ. Iren.*haer*.3.4.3(M.7.857A); ἐρρῶσθαί σε ἅμα τῇ σ. εὔχομαι Afric.*ep.Or*.(p.80.15; M.11.48A); μνήσθητι...τῶν κατὰ τόπον ὀρθοδόξων σ. καὶ τῆς ἐνθάδε ἐν Χριστῷ σ. ἡμῶν *Lit.Jac*.(p.210.17); **3.** *gathering, assembly* for worship μήτε εἰς σ. βουλόμενος εἰσελθεῖν Pall.*h. Laus*.21(p.64.13; M.34.1073B); **4.** *community* of religious προσήκει... τῷ προεστῶτι...ὑποχείριον εἶναι τὴν σ. Bas.*ascet*.1.3(2.321A; M.31.876B); ἓν γενέσθαι σῶμα...πᾶν τὸ πλήρωμα τῆς σ. *ib*.2.1(324B; M.881C); τῶν ἐν τῇ σ. ζώντων *ib*.2.2(325B; M.885A); ἀνδρῶν...εἰσὶν αἱ σ. ... καὶ παρθένων *ib*.(326B; M.888A); μηδαμῶς ἀλλαχόσε ἀποβαίνειν τῆς ἑαυτοῦ σ. CCP(448)*act*.(*ACO* 2.1.1 p.161.3; H.2.188D); Call.*v.Hyp*. (p.106); ὑπὸ ζυγὸν συνοδίας Cyr.S.*v.Jo.Hes*.20(p.217.3); id.*v.Euthym*. 9(p.18.1,5); Gr.Mag.*dial*.(tr.Zach.)4.13(M.*PL*.77.342B); v. s. συνῳδία.

***συνοδικάριος, ὁ,** ? *bishop's secretary, bishop's chaplain* ἀπορία Θεοδώρου διακόνου Βυζαντίου ῥήτορος καὶ σ. Παύλου ἀρχιεπισκόπου Κωνσταντινουπόλεως Thdr.CP *qu.Max*.tit.(M.91.216B); σάκρας... σταλείσης διὰ τῶν ἐκεῖθεν ἀποσταλέντων σ. παρὰ...Ἀγάθωνος Const. Pogon.*sacr*.3 inscr.(M.*PL*.96.387C).

συνοδικός, 1. *of a synod* or *council* τόμου σ. Gr.Naz.*ep*.101(M.37.177A); τὰς συνήθεις ἔγραφον ἐπιστολάς, ἃς σ. καλοῦσι Soz.*h.e*.7.11.3 (M.67.1441C); τῶν σ. συλλαβῶν τὸ ἐπίτομον Sophr.H.*ep.syn*.(M.87.3160B); *of synodical origin, of conciliar authority* τὰς παραδόσεις... δέχομαι· τάς τε δεσποτικὰς ἀποστολικάς τε καὶ πατρικὰς καὶ σ. *Lit. Jac*.(*NBP* p.38); esp. τὸ σ. (with or without γράμμα), Bas.*ep*.92.3(3.186C; M.32.484A); CChalc.*act*.11(*ACO* 2.1.3 p.47.3; H.2.549C); Jo.Mal.*chron*.18 p.491(M.97.712A); Thphn.*chron*.pp.116,388(M.108.328C,928A); ἡ σ. (with or without ἐπιστολή), *Cod.Afr*.90; Justn.*ep. Thdr.Mops*.(p.63.39; M.86.1081A); τὰ σ. [sc. βιβλία] *acts of council* καθὰ ὁ Σαβῖνος ἐν τῇ συναγωγῇ τῶν σ. φησι Socr.*h.e*.3.10.11(M.67.409A); cf. ἐν τῷ Συνοδικῷ Ἀθανασίου *ib*.1.13.12(108C); Thphn.*chron*. p.274(M.108.680B); **2.** *who subscribes to the Chalcedonian definition, orthodox* (cf. συνοδίτης) τῆς ἁγίας ἐκκλησίας τῶν ὀρθοδόξων τῶν σ. *Apophth.Patr*.(M.65.433A); **3.** astron., *of a new moon;* hence *moonless* τὴν σ. νύκτα Synes.*ep*.4(M.66.1337A).

***συνοδικῶς, 1.** *by the pronouncement of a synod, with conciliar authority* ἄδειαν διδοὺς πράττειν ἅπερ ἐν Ἀντιοχείᾳ ὑπὲρ τῶν αὐτῶν σ. διεπράξατο Philost.*h.e*.9.3(M.65.569A); τὰ ἐν Χαλκηδόνι δογματισθέντα σ. κυρώσαντα Cyr.S.*v.Sab*.50(p.140.14); ὅπως ἄν...ἡ μὲν βέβηλος σ. ἀποσταίη, ἡ δὲ ἀληθὴς ἀντισταίη πίστις Anast.S.*haer*. (p.269); τὰς ἤδη σ. ὁρισθείσας φωνάς Jo.VI CP *ep*.(M.96.1424B); *by a council* τὰ κατὰ σφᾶς ἱκετεύοντες σ. κριθῆναι Evagr.*h.e*.2.2(p.39.1; M.86.2489C); Thdr.Stud.*epp*.1.34(M.99.1024B); **2.** astron., *by conjunction,* i.e. of sun and moon γίνεται...ἔκλειψις ἡλίου σ. ὑποδραμούσης αὐτὸν σελήνης Or.*schol.in Mt*.27:45(M.17.309B) for συνόδῳ Or. *fr.556 in Mt*.(p.228).

συνοδίτης, ὁ, 1. *fellow traveller, companion on a journey,* met. ἐπέρχεταί...σοι...τις βλαπτικὸς σ. ἢ...ἀπορία ‡Proc.G.*Pr*.6:11(M.87.1272D); πόσοις...ὁδοιποροῦσι τῇ εὐχῇ γέγονεν σ.; Steph.Diac.*v.Steph*. (M.100.1153C); **2.** *one who subscribes to the Chalcedonian formula* τούτου [sc. Ἰουστινιανοῦ]...τῶν σ. ὄντος †Leont.B.*sect*.5(M.86.1229C); πεῖσαι γενέσθαι σ. *ib*.(1232A); *ib*.7(1248C).

συνοδοιπορ-έω, 1. *travel together,* met. ἡ πλάνη...ῥυθμίζουσα τὴν ψυχὴν τοῦ ~οῦντος αὐτῇ ‡Ath.*disp*.45(M.28.500B); **2.** *be* or *take place on a journey* τὴν...~ήσασαν συνεξέτασιν *ib*.42(496C).

συνοδοιπόρος, ὁ, ἡ, *companion in travel, fellow traveller;* met., of a fellow martyr ὡσεὶ σ. ἐν ὁδῷ τῆς αὐτῆς ἐλπίδος *M.Perp*.15(p.85.5); of S. Peter with Christ, *Clem.ep*.1(M.2.33A); τὴν σὴν βοηθείαν σ. ἔχων Jo.Mosch.*prat*.180(M.87.3052C); of BMV μόνη τῶν νυκτοποροὐντων σ. καὶ συνδιαγωγός ‡Jo.D.*hom*.5(M.96.660B); of God σύμπλους καὶ σ. αὐτῶν [sc. of travellers] γενέσθαι καταξίωσον *Lit.Marc*.(Brightman, p.127.14).

σύνοδος, ἡ, A. = συνοδοιπόρος, *companion on a journey, fellow traveller* ἐστὲ...σ. πάντες Ign.*Eph*.9.2; *A.Paul.et Thecl*.1(p.235.3); of Christ, *A.Thom*.A 103(p.216.6); met. πανταχοῦ τὴν ψαλμῳδίαν εἶχεν, οἷόν τινα σ. ἀγαθήν Gr.Nyss.*v.Macr*.(p.374.5; M.46.964A); of things that go together, *equivalent* ἑκάτερον...θατέρου σ. τε καὶ ἰσοδύναμον [sc. recollection and portrayal of the Passion] Thdr.Stud.*epp*.2.36 (M.99.1212D).

B. of persons, *coming together, meeting;* **1.** for purposes of deliberation, eccl. *synod, council* δὶς τοῦ ἔτους σ. γίνεσθαι CNic.(325) *can*.5; cf. δεύτερον τοῦ ἔτους σ. γινέσθω τῶν ἐπισκόπων *Can.App*.37; ἐπισκόπων τε καὶ σ. ἐπιστολαῖς Eus.*Marcell*.1.4(p.19.4; M.24.753B); *ib*.2.4(p.56.33; 820C); Apoll.*inc*.4(p.306.21; M.28.93D); Θεόδωρος... μαχόμενος τῇ τε ἐκκλησιαστικῇ παραδόσει καὶ πάσαις ταῖς σ. *cat.1Tim*. 3:2(p.26.2); of particular synods and councils: ref. Quartodeciman controversy σ. δὴ καὶ συγκροτήσεις ἐπισκόπων ἐπὶ ταὐτὸν ἐγίνοντο Eus.*h.e*.5.23.2(M.20.492A); ref. Montanism ταῖς σ. τῶν ἀδελφῶν ἐν Ἰκονίῳ καὶ Συνάδοις Dion.Al.*ib*.7.7.5(649A); ἐν ταῖς μεγίσταις τῶν ἐπισκόπων σ. *ib*.7.5.5(645A); ref. Beryllus τῆς δι' αὐτὸν γενομένης σ., ὁμοῦ τὰς Ὠριγένους πρὸς αὐτὸν ζητήσεις Eus.*ib*.6.33.3(593B); again in Arabia *τότε συγκροτηθείσης οὐ σμικρᾶς σ. πάλιν Ὠριγένης παρακληθεὶς ib.*6.37(597B); ref. Novatian *σ. μεγίστης ἐπὶ Ῥώμης συγκροτηθείσης ib.*6.43.2(616B); at Antioch, *ib.*6.46.3(636A); and ref. Paul. Sam., *ib.*7.27.2(795B); of CAnc.(314) *τῆς σ. ταύτης* CAnc.(314)*can.* 6; of CNic.(325) *τῇ κατὰ Νίκαιαν σ.* Marcell.*ep.*ap.Epiph.*haer.* 72.2(p.256.16; M.42.384C); CAlex.*ep.*ap.Ath.*apol.sec.*6(p.92.6; M.25.257C); *ἡ οἰκουμενικὴ σ.* Ath.*Ar.*1.7(M.26.25B); of CCP(336) *τὴν ἁγίαν σ. ἐν τῇ βασιλικῇ συνελθοῦσαν πόλει ἐξ ἐπαρχιῶν διαφόρων...στηλιτεύειν τὸν ἄνδρα* [i.e. Marcellus] Eus.*Marcell.*2.4(p.58.7; M.24.821D); ref. condemnation of Apoll. by CRom.(379) *ὑπὸ τῆς δυτικῆς σ.* Gr.Naz.*ep.*101(M.37.177A); **2.** for Christian worship, *assembly, gathering, meeting*; **a.** *οὐδαμῶς...ἔξεσται...σ. ποιεῖσθαι ἢ εἰς τὰ καλούμενα κοιμητήρια εἰσιέναι* Dion.Al.ap.Eus.*h.e.*7.11.10(M.20.665B); *τὴν ἐν ταῖς ἐκκλησιαστικαῖς σ. τερατείαν ἣν μηχανᾶται* [sc. Paul. Sam.] Malch.*ep.*ap.Eus.*h.e.*7.30.9(712C); *ἀναγινώσκειν, οἷα δὴ ἔθος ἐν ταῖς σ.* Eus.*m.P.*13.8(p.948.28; M.20.1516C); *τοὺς οἴκους τοῦ θεοῦ τιμῶμεν καὶ τὰς σ. τὰς ἐπ' αὐτοῖς ὡς ἁγίας καὶ ἐπωφελεῖς ἀποδεχόμεθα* CGangr.*can.*21; *πᾶν...σάββατον ἄνευ τοῦ ἑνὸς καὶ πᾶσαν κυριακὴν ἐπιτελοῦντες σ. εὐφραίνεσθε Const.App.*5.20.19; *οἱ πατέρες...ἐτύπωσαν ἡμέρας τεσσεράκοντα νηστείας, εὐχῶν ἀκροάσεως, σ.* Chrys.*Jud.*3.4 (1.611D); in commemoration of the departed *τῆς ἐν τοῖς κοιμητηρίοις σ.* Eus.*h.e.*9.2(804A); esp. martyrs *τόπον ἐπίσημον μαρτύρων περιφανείᾳ, καὶ πολυανθρωπίᾳ συνόδου τῆς κατὰ ἔτος ἕκαστον...τελουμένης* Bas.*ep.*95(3.189C; M.32.489C); *συνήγαγον πάντες ἐν τῇ σ. τοῦ μακαρίου μάρτυρος Εὐψυχίου...τοὺς χωρεπισκόπους ib.*142(235B; M.592B); of eucharist *ἡ ὑμετέρα σ. τῶν ἅμα τε καὶ ἀκουόντων καὶ συνᾳδόντων τὰ θεῖα μυστήρια* Meth.*arbitr.*1(p.147.10; M.18.241B); *ἐν ταῖς ἁγίαις...σ. ἤτοι συνάξεσι* Cyr.*Jo.*12.1(4.1093C); *ib.*(1104D); **b.** of gathering of heretics, Hipp.*haer.*9.23(p.258.11; M.16.3399B); **3.** as equivalent of *ἐκκλησία*, Chrys.*exp.in Ps.*149:1(5.498C) cit. s. *σύστημα*; *τὸ...αὐτοὺς καλέσαι...ἀπὸ τῆς σ. μόνης* id.*comm.in Gal.*1:2 (10.662B); **a.** the persons assembled, *company* (sc. of the elect) *ὅπως διὰ τῆς ἐμῆς ἐξόδου...ἡ τῶν πολλῶν μου συγγενῶν σ. γένηται A.Andr.* B 9(p.63.4) ∾ *A.(Pass.)Andr.*B 14(p.32.27; M.2.1245A); *congregation*, representing the Church locally *ταῦτα πάντα* [sc. places of worship corporately owned] *τοῖς αὐτοῖς Χριστιανοῖς, τοῦτ' ἔστιν τῷ σώματι* [*αὐτῶν*] *καὶ τῇ σ.* [*ἑκάστῳ*] *αὐτῶν ἀποκατασταθῆναι κελεύσεις* Licinius Imp.ap.Eus.*h.e.*10.5.11(M.20.884C); *τὰς σ. διατέμνουσι* [i.e. by absenting themselves] Chrys.*hom.19.1 in Heb.*(12.183A); by not observing festivals with Church but at other times, id.*Jud.*3.5(1.613B); **b.** building in which gatherings took place, *church οἱ τὸν περίβολον τῆς σ. τειχίζοντες* Gr.Naz.*ep.*57(M.37.112B); cf.Bas.*ep.*286 (3.425D; M.32.1021B); **4.** *intercourse τῆς ἐν ὑμῖν διχονοίας ἐγερθείσης ἡ μὲν σ. ἠρνήθη, ὁ δὲ...λαὸς...σχισθεὶς* Const.ap.Eus.*v.C.*2.69(p.68.25; M.20.1041B).

C. of things, *coming together*; **1.** *combination, union ἡ εἱμαρμένη ἐστὶ σ. πολλῶν ἐναντίων δυνάμεων* Clem.*exc.Thdot.*69(p.129.15; M.9.692A); *εἰ πολλὰ* [sc. *αἴτια*] *κατὰ σύνοδον ἑνὸς αἴτια γίνεται πολλά* id. *str.*8.9(p.100.4; M.9.597C); *τὴν ἐν καιρῷ μητέρα καὶ παρθένον. ἐπέραστος ἡ σ.* Procl.CP *or.laud.BMV* 1(p.103.7; M.65.680C); opp. *διάστασις*, Gr.Naz.*or.*31.32(p.189.4; M.36.169C); // *ἕνωσις*: *ὅπου γὰρ ἕνωσις ὀνομάζεται, οὐχ ἑνὸς πράγματος σημαίνεται σ., ἀλλ' ἢ δύο, ἢ πλειόνων* Cyr.*ep.*44(p.36.8; 5^2.133E); *unity τὴν κατὰ σύνοδον πίστεως ἐγειρομένην ἐκκλησίαν* Clem.*fr.*36(p.218.29; M.9.769A); **2.** Christol.; *union* of natures in Christ *εἰ...καὶ τὸ συναμφότερον ἕν, ἀλλ' οὐ τῇ φύσει, τῇ δὲ σ. τούτων* Gr.Naz.*or.*30.8(p.120.11; M.36.113B); Gr.Nyss.*Eun.*6(2 p.150.20; M.45.737A) cit. s. *μίξις*; Cyr.*ep.*17 *anath.*3(p.40.30; 5^2.76B) cit. s. *συνάφεια*; *σ. ... ἀληθῆ γενέσθαι φαμέν, ἑνώσαντος μὲν ἑαυτῷ τοῦ λόγου τὸ σῶμα, μεμενηκότος δὲ ὅπερ ἦν* id.*Nest.*2.1(p.34.35; 6^1.33E); *ib.*2.12(p.50.12; 57A); *δύο φύσεων σ., καὶ ἑνὸς υἱοῦ τόκος* Procl.CP *or.*3.3(M.65.708A); // *συνδρομή*: *οὐ γὰρ ὁμοούσιον τῷ...λόγῳ τὸ σῶμα· ἐν δὲ τῇ σ. καὶ τῇ...συνδρομῇ* Cyr.*Jo.*4.2(4.361B); *διϊσχυριζόμεθα δέ, σ. μέν τινα καὶ...συνδρομὴν εἰς ἕνωσιν, ἀνίσων τε καὶ ἀνομοίων πεπρᾶχθαι φύσεων* id.*inc.unigen.*(5^1.688D); // *ἕνωσις*: *ἀναμιγνὺς ὥσπερ ἑαυτὸν τῇ ἡμετέρᾳ φύσει διὰ τῆς...σ. τε καὶ ἑνώσεως* id.*Jo.*11.11(998B); *ἕνα καὶ τὸν αὐτὸν καὶ πρὸ τῆς πρὸς σάρκα σ. καὶ ἑνώσεως ἀληθοῦς καὶ μετὰ τοῦτο ἔτι* id.*Pulch.*(p.27.10; 5^2.129E); objection of Thdt. *σ. καθ' ἕνωσιν φυσικήν, κρᾶσίν τινα καὶ σύγχυσιν...γεγενῆσθαι διδάσκων τῆς τε θείας φύσεως καὶ τῆς τοῦ δούλου μορφῆς ep.*151(4.1292); adopted by monophysites but with modified signification *θεωρημάτων ἄθροισμα ἀλλ' οὐ φύσεων σ., τὸν Χριστὸν εἶναι ὁρίσῃ* Leont.B.*arg. Sev.*(M.86.1932B); *τῶν φύσεων...τὴν σ. ἴστε, καὶ...τὸ ἀσύγχυτον ὁμολογεῖτε τῶν συνελθόντων* Leont.H.*monoph.*25(M.86.1785B); in later authors, Sophr.H.*ep.syn.*(M.87.3165B) cit. s. *φυσικός*; *μὴ τὴν πρὸς τὴν σάρκα τοῦ λόγου σ. ἀκούσιον ποιώμεθα* Max.*ep.*13(M.91.517A); *ib.*15(556C); *τὸ...ἔκ τινων ἀσυγχύτως ἑνώσει τῇ κατὰ σ. φυσικὴν ἀποτελούμενον, καὶ τὰς φύσεις...ἀτρέπτους διατηρεῖ, καὶ τὰς...συστατικὰς ἀμειώτως διασώζει δυνάμεις...κατὰ τὴν εἰκόνα τοῦ...παραδείγματος τῆς ἐκπυρωθείσης μαχαίρας, ἧς τὴν τομὴν ἐπιστάμεθα καυστικήν, καὶ τὴν καῦσιν οἴδαμεν τμητικήν. πυρὸς γὰρ καὶ σιδήρου καθ' ὑπόστασιν γέγονε σ. ib.*19(593B); *ib.*12(484A) cit. s. *ἕνωσις*; *ὁ μὲν τὴν φύσιν, ὁ δὲ τὴν οἰκονομίαν...ὧν ἡ σ. τὸ μέγα τῆς ὑπερφυοῦς Ἰησοῦ φυσιολογίας ποιησαμένη μυστήριον* id.*ambig.*(M.91.1052B); *ἀληθῆ τῶν πραγμάτων κατ' οὐσίαν γεγενῆσθαι τὴν σ. λέγειν οὐκ ἀνεχόμενος* [sc. Nestorius] id.*opusc.*(M.91.41D); ‡Meth.*Sym.et Ann.*11(M.18.376C).

συνοδυνάομαι, *suffer pain in union* (*with*) *τῆς καρδίας ὀδυνωμένης, σ. τὸ σῶμα* †Jo.D.*B.J.*22(M.96.1057C).

***συνοζένω**, *smell, stink*, met. *γηΐνης πράξεως τῷ κονιορτῷ σ.* [sc. *ἡ ψυχή μου*] Gr.Mag.*dial.*(tr.Zach.)1 proem.(M.*PL.*77.151A).

***συνοικεσία, ἡ,** *living with* or *together*, of celibates as 'spiritual companions' *ἡ...σ. τὴν νόσον ἐγγὺς ἔχει* Gr.Naz.*carm.*2.2(epigr.)18.8 (M.38.92A); of life of professed virginity *τὴν μετὰ Χριστοῦ σ.* ‡Chrys.*hom.*10(13.239D).

συνοικέσιον, τό, 1. *marriage ἵστασθαι τὸ σ.* Bas.*ep.*199 *can.*22(3.293B; M.32.721B); *νόμιμον ποιεῖ σ. ... τὸ...μετὰ σωφροσύνης καὶ σεμνότητος τὴν συνέλευσιν γίνεσθαι* Chrys.*hom.66.2 in Gen.*(4.541A); *τοὺς ἁρπάζοντας γυναῖκας ἐπ' ὀνόματι σ.* CChalc.*can.*27; *wedlock τὰ τέκνα τῶν κληρικῶν ἐν σ.* (tr. Lat. *matrimonio*) *Cod.Afr.*21; **2.** *married couple εἰρήνην καὶ ὁμόνοιαν τοῦ σ. ποιῆσαι A.Thom.*A 127 (p.235.22); *ἔξεστιν τοῖς σ. ... ὡς βούλονται, διατίθεσθαι* Ath.Scholast. *coll.*9 paratit.12(p.110); *συνοικησ-, ib.*10.2(p.113); **3.** *cohabitation, living together*; **a.** of husband and wife *πολλοὺς μὲν γεγαμηκότας τοῦ σ. ἐχώριζε* Socr.*h.e.*2.43.3(M.67.353A); **b.** in concubinage, †Jo.Jej. *poenit.*(M.88.1904D); **c.** *union ἤδη...αὐτῷ τὸ πονηρὸν ἐλέλυτο σ.* Sophr.H.*v.Anast.*(M.92.1693A).

συνοικέτης, ὁ, *member of the same household*, Dion.Ar.*ep.*8.4(M.3.1096A).

συνοικ-έω, *dwell, live together*; **1.** in gen.; **a.** met., *be associated*, Clem.*str.*2.12(p.141.26; M.8.989B); *ib.*5.5(p.342.26; M.9.48A); Ath. *apol.Const.*34(M.25.641A); **b.** *live in wedlock*; met., of the soul, Or. *Jo.*13.9(p.233.25; M.14.412C); **c.** *live together* as brother and sister, of spiritual companions (v. *συνείσακτος*), of men *ἄλλοι...ὡς μετ' ἀδελφῶν προσποιούμενοι σ. ... ἠλέγχθησαν* Iren.*haer.*1.6.3(M.7.509A); *γυναιξὶ κατὰ τὸ φανερὸν ~οῦντες καὶ ἀδελφότητα τὴν τοιαύτην συμβίωσιν ὀνομάζοντες* Gr.Nyss.*virg.*23(p.338.6; M.46.409B); *ὑμῖν αὐταῖς καὶ τοῖς ~οῦσιν* Chrys.*fem.reg.*3(1.253B); abs. *ἔστω ὁ σ. ... μὴ τῶν εὐτελῶν τις ib.*6(259A); of women, †Bas.*contub.*5(M.30.820D); *περὶ τοῦ μὴ τὰς κανονικὰς σ. ἀνδράσιν* Chrys.*fem.reg.*tit.(1.248D); practice tantamount to a denial of vow of virginity *ὡς ἐὰν ἐπαγγελλόμενός τις τῷ ὀνόματι, ἔργῳ τὰ τῶν γυναιξὶ ~ούντων ποιῇ* Bas.*ep.*55(3.149C; M.32.401C); its power of attachment illustrated *ὁ...Λεόντιος...κωλυόμενος σ. αὐτῇ, δι' αὐτὴν ἑαυτὸν ἀπέκοψεν, ἵν' ἐπ' ἀδείας ἔχῃ διατρίβειν μετ' αὐτῆς* Ath.*fug.*26(p.85.28; M.25.677B); cf.id.*h.Ar.*28(p.198.2f.; M.25.725A); *οὔτε πρῶτοι, οὔτε μόνοι...ἐνομοθετήσαμεν γυναῖκας ἀνδράσι μὴ σ.* Bas.*ep.*55(3.149C; M.32.401C); *~οῦντα...παρθένοις, καὶ προσδεδεμένον...καὶ τὴν ψυχὴν προϊέμενον μᾶλλον ἢ τὴν σύνοικον, καὶ πάντα καὶ παθεῖν, καὶ ποιῆσαι αἱρούμενον, ἢ χωρισθῆναι τῆς ποθουμένης* Chrys.*subintr.*5(1.234E); **2.** Christol. *εἶχε* [sc. *τὸ σῶμα*]...*τῆς ἀφθαρσίας τὴν φύσιν ἐκ τοῦ ~ήσαντος αὐτῷ λόγου* ‡Ath.*serm.fid.*7 (p.7; M.26.1268C).

[*]**συνοικήσιον, τό,** v. *συνοικέσιον*.

συνοίκησις, ἡ, *living together*; **1.** in gen. *οὐ γὰρ ἡ σ. κατακρίνει τοὺς δικαίους σὺν τοῖς ἀδίκοις, ἀλλ' ἡ τῆς γνώμης ὁμόνοια Const.App.* 2.14.9; **2.** ref. celibate persons living together as 'spiritual brother and sister', of life of *συνείσακτοι*: *μισῶ καὶ τὴν προσηγορίαν αὐτὴν ...καὶ προσίσταταί μοι καὶ ἡ ἐπωνυμία τῆς σ.* Chrys.*fem.reg.*3(1.254C); *ἡ ψυχρὰ αὕτη σ. ib.*5(258B); *ἡ ἡδίστη αὕτη σ.* id.*subintr.*1(1.229C); a cause of scandal *οὐκ ἄρα δόξαν ὑμῖν χρηστὴν προστίθησιν αὕτη ἡ κοινωνία τῆς σ.* id.*fem.reg.*6(259C); and fraught with moral dangers *οὔτε γὰρ εὐσχήμων οὔτε ἀκίνδυνος ἡ τοιαύτη σ.* id.*sac.*3.17(p.91.1; 1.399A); *σφοδρά τις...καὶ τυραννικὴ τῆς σ. ταύτης ἡ ἡδονή* id.*subintr* 1(1.228D); *ἡ σ. αὕτη...δι' ἔρωτα καὶ πόθον ib.*5(235C); **3.** met., *harbouring* of evil thoughts *οἱ...τοῖς ῥυπαροῖς...λογισμοῖς συζῶντες... ἀπαλλάσσονται τῆς πονηρᾶς αὐτῶν σ.* Gr.Nyss.*v.Mos.*(M.44.348D).

συνοικία, ἡ, 1. a *living together, common life ὁ Χριστὸς...εἰς φιλίαν καὶ εὐλογίαν καὶ μετάνοιαν καὶ σ. καλῶν, τὴν ἐν τῇ αὐτῇ γῇ τῶν ἁγίων ...μέλλουσαν γίνεσθαι* Just.*dial.*139.4(M.6.796C); met. *τὸν...τοῦ παντὸς πόλεμον ἐνούσης* [sc. *τῆς θείας εἰρήνης*] *εἰς ὁμοειδῆ σ.* Dion.Ar.*d.n.* 11.1(M.3.949A); **2.** *body of people living together, community*, of religious *Παχώμιον φασι...συνοικιῶν ἡγούμενον ὠφελεῖν πολλοὺς* Soz. *h.e.*3.14.9(M.67.1072A); *καθάπερ μητέρα τὴν ἐν Ταβέννῃ νήσῳ σ. ἡγοῦντο ib.*3.14.17(1073B); *μοναχικῶν σ. ἀνδρῶν τε καὶ γυναικῶν ib.*4.

20.2(1173A); μοναστικὰς σ. *ib.*9.1.10(1596C); **3.** *common life* of such a community τὰ χαλεπώτερα τῶν ἔργων πονεῖν, καὶ οὕτω μετέχειν τῆς αὐτῶν σ. *ib.*3.14.12(1072B); **4.** ? *out-building* οἰκίας καὶ σ. Synes.*calv.* 9(p.207.6; M.66.1184B).

συνοικίζ-ω, 1. *make to live with* or *together*; perf. ptcpl. pass., *wife*, Mac.Aeg.*elev.*9(M.34.897A); cf.id.*hom.*4.15(M.34.484B); in 'spiritual companionship' ἄνδρας τινὰς...τὸν πάντα ∼ουσι χρόνον Chrys.*fem. reg.*2(1.250E); **2.** myst., *unite* ὁ...νοῦς...σ. ἑαυτῷ πᾶσαν τὴν ψυχὴν πρὸς ἐκεῖνον [sc. τὸν θεόν] Gr.Nyss.*instit.*(p.75.9; M.34.429B).

συνοικοδομ-έω, 1. *join in building, help to build*, met. δύναμις...σ. τῷ μὴ δυναμένῳ Or.*sel.in Ps.*4:6(M.12.1161A); ∼οῦντος τῷ προθεμένῳ ...τοῦ θεοῦ Or.*Jo.*6.1(p.106.9; M.14.197A); **2.** *build together*; pass., fig., of righteous dead before Christ ἀλατόμητοι συνῳκοδομήθησαν Herm.*sim.*9.16.7.

σύνοικος, 1. *living* or *dwelling with* in the same house, of virgins living with clergy as 'spiritual companions' (cf. συνείσακτος) σ. ... καὶ συνέστιον καὶ συμπότην ἔχοντες CAlex.*ep.*ap.Ath.*apol.sec.*14(p.98. 5; M.25.272B); οἱ τὰς σ. ἔχοντες παρθένους Chrys.*hom.17.2 in Mt.*(7. 224A); met. δαίμονα ἔχειν σ. Clem.*paed.*2.1(p.165.12; M.8.404A); as subst. ὁ γνωστικὸς...σ. ὢν τῷ κυρίῳ id.*str.*2.20(p.170.11; M.8.1049A); ἐκεῖ δι' ὅλων αἰώνων σύνοικόν σε ποιήσεται id.*q.d.s.*32(p.181.15; M.9. 638C); **2.** as subst.; **a.** masc., *husband*, Chrys.*hom.17.4 in Mt.*(7. 227D); **b.** fem., *wife* νυμφὴ καὶ σ. αὐτοῦ Mac.Aeg.*hom.*15.1(M.34. 576B); *ib.*4.15(484B); cf.id.*elev.*9(M.34.897A); met., *life partner* τὴν ἀληθινὴν σοφίαν σ. τε καὶ βίου κοινωνὸν ἑαυτῷ λαμβάνειν Gr.Nyss. *virg.*20(p.327.21; M.46.400B); **c.** *'spiritual companion'*, Chrys. *subintr.*5(1.234E).

συνοιμώζω, *lament together*, Cyr.*Os.*36(3.66D).

συνοκλάζω, 1. of an elephant, *kneel down*, Bas.*hex.*9.5(1.85E; M.29.201A); **2.** met., *come down to, sink to the level of*, Gr.Nyss.*v. Mos.*(M.44.324B).

συνολισθαίνω, *slip down* the throat *with* διὰ τὴν πολλὴν λειότητα σ. τῷ πινομένῳ ὕδατι ‡Eust.*hex.*(M.18.748D).

συνολκή, ἡ, *drawing back* παραπετασμάτων σ. Andr.Caes.*Apoc.* 58(M.106.401A).

***συνολομαραίνω,** *quench* or *destroy completely together* τὴν φιλαυτίαν...σ. τῇ ῥίζῃ *Ep.Dor.*2(M.88.1616A).

σύνολος, neut. as adv. τὸ σ., *on the whole, in general*; freq. after a neg., *at all, whatsoever* οὐ καίει τὸ σ. Hipp.*haer.*4.31(p.58.3; M.16. 3094D); μηδὲ ὑποχωρήσητε τὸ σ. Meth.*symp.*8.13(p.97.15; M.18. 160A); τὸ σ. οὐ παρορᾷ Ath.*inc.*10.1(M.25.112C); also τὸ σ. ὅλως: οὐδὲ ἔστιν [sc. ὁ θεός] τὸ σ. ὅλως...αἴτιος κακοῦ Meth.*res.*1.38(p.281.2; M.18.265D); *ib.*1.41(p.287.4; 269C).

συνομαρτέω, *follow along with, attend on*; met., *be consequent upon, follow* ἕπεται...καὶ...σ. ταῖς ἀποστροφαῖς ἡ ὀργή Cyr.*Am.*15(3. 265E); Max.*ep.*28(M.91.621A).

[*]**συνομελέω,** v. συνομιλέω.

[*]**συνομελία, ἡ,** v. συνομιλία.

***συνομήγυρος, ὁ,** *companion*; of fellow Christians, *V.Aberc.*77 (p.53.17) = Aberc.*epitaph.*11(ΣΥΝC...).

συνομιλέω, *converse with*, *Hom.Clem.*20.15; of Dives with Abraham, Adam.*dial.*2.11(p.78.13; M.11.1777A); ref. Gen.1:26 ἔστι τις δύναμις, ᾗ συνήθως σ. ὁ θεός *Dial.Ath.et Zacch.*13(p.9); *hold converse* or *commune with, have intercourse with* σ. τοῖς σώμασιν ὁ νοῦς Ath.*gent.*2(M.25.8A); myst. μεγάλην...ἐσχήκασιν οὗτοι τιμήν, ἀγγέλοις ὁμιλήσαντες καὶ τὸν θεὸν...θεασάμενοι Meth.*symp.*7.5(p.76. 20; M.18.132B); *ib.*3.4(p.31.4; 68A); of David with the Church, Ph. Carp.*Cant.*1:1(M.40.32D); of man with God ἵνα...ἔχων...χάριν...καὶ ...δύναμιν...σ. τῷ θείῳ Ath.*gent.*2(M.25.5D); σὺ δὲ καυχοῦσαι σ. τῷ ἁγίῳ πνεύματι διὰ τῶν...γραφῶν Ephr.3.231C; συνομελ-, id.3.99E.

συνομιλία, ἡ, *conversing*, Ephr.3.231C; συνομελ-, id.3.99E.

συνόμιλος, 1. *consorting, associating*, Ἠλίας...οὐδὲ μετὰ γυναικῶν σ. ἐγίνετο Epiph.*haer.*63.4(p.402.13; M.41.1068B); **2.** as subst., *constant companion, associate*; **a.** lit., *A.Thom.*A 109(p.221.1); *ib.*135 (p.241.15); μεχρὶ τούτων τῶν ὑπάτων οἱ σ. τῶν...ἀποστόλων ἐπίσκοποι γεγονότες ἐγνωρίζοντο *Chron.Pasch.*p.253(M.92.612B); of one's husband ὁ σύζυγος καὶ σ. μου Jo.Eub.*concept.BMV* 8(M.96.1472C); **b.** met., of virtues σύνοικον ἔχειν καὶ σ. παντότε τὴν σωφροσύνην Gr. Naz.*ep.*244(M.37.385D); of divine image in man σύνοικον εἰκόνα, σύμβουλον, σ. Clem.*prot.*4(p.46.17; M.8.157C); of light of H. Ghost διαφυλάσσοντα ὡς γνησίαν κοινωνὸν καὶ σ. Gr.Naz.*or.*31.33(p.190.8; M.36.172B); of Christ, ref. 1Tim.5:5 οὐκ ἔχεις σ. τὸν ὁμόδουλον, ἀλλ' ἔχεις τὸν δεσπότην Chrys.*hom.6.4 in 1Thess.*(11.471F); of Samson with God, Procl.CP *or.*5.2(M.65.717B).

***συνομογνωμονέω,** *hold the same opinion* as, *agree* with; c. dat., Thdr.Stud.*epp.*2.190(M.99.1580D).

***συνομόδουλος, ὁ,** *one likewise a slave, fellow slave* οἰκέταις ὡς οἰκέτης καὶ σ. προσελάλει Μωσῆς τοῖς ἀρχαιοτέροις Cyr.*ador.*8(1. 280E).

***συνόμοιος,** *like, similar* οἱ σ. σου *T.Abr.*B 9(p.113.21).

***συνομοκέρωτος,** *having the same number of horns* τοῦ λεγομένου δεκακεράτου συνομοκερώτους Thdr.Stud.*test.*(M.99.1816B).

συνομολογ-έω, 1. in discussion, *acknowledge* ὅτι...τὸν Χριστὸν τοιοῦτον εἶναι δεῖ...ὑμεῖς ∼ήσετε Ath.*Ar.*2.16(M.26.180A); σ. ὡς *ib.*3.44(416B); pass. impers. συνωμολόγηται...ἐκείνους μόνους εἰς τὸ διηνεκὲς ἀποθνήσκειν ὧν ἥ τε ζωὴ καὶ ὁ θάνατος σεσιώπηται Marcian.Imp.*const.Flav.*(p.121.22; H.2.676B); **2.** in making profession of faith, *acknowledge, confess also* or *at the same time* Χριστὸν υἱὸν εἶναι ὁμολογεῖ τοῦ...θεοῦ, καὶ...ἐκ παρθένου γεγενῆσθαι καὶ πνεύματος σ. Hipp.*haer.*8.17(p.237.6; M.16.3366A); τὸν μὲν... θεὸν Ἰουδαίων...εἰδέναι διϊσχυρίζοντο, καὶ δεύτερον, τὴν σάρκα τὴν ἐκ τῆς ἁγίας παρθένου, συνωμολογήκασιν [sc. Sabellius and Marcellus] Eus.*e.th.*1.7(p.65.25; M.24.836C); ἀπὸ τοῦ πατέρα ὁμολογεῖν ἀρχομένου, καὶ εἰς τὸ υἱὸν ∼εῖν πατρὶ προβαίνοντος Max. *ambig.*(M.91.1261A); **3.** *confess* sin, Phot.*nomoc.*9.20(p.550; M.104. 1108A); **4.** *agree with, be proportionate to* τῶν ποδῶν αὐτοῦ πρὸς τὸ ἄλλο τοῦ σώματος μὴ ∼ούντων τὸ ὕψος Philost.*h.e.*10.11(M.65.592B); **5.** *be a fellow confessor* ἱερόν σου τὸ πάθος, στήριγμα τῶν ∼ούντων Thdr.Stud.*epp.*2.47(M.99.1252B).

***συνομολογητέος,** *that must be acknowledged*, Eust.*engast.*17 (p.44.1; M.18.649B).

***συνομολογητής, ὁ,** *fellow confessor*, Thdr.Stud.*epp.*2.71(M.99. 1301D).

***συνομόλογος,** *in agreement with* σ. τῆς τοιᾶσδε δόξης Clem.*str.*5.8 (p.357.21; M.9.76A).

***συνομολογουμένως,** v. *συνωμολογημένως.

***συνόμορος,** *bordering on*, as subst. σ. καὶ γείτονας Andr.Cr.*or.* 19(M.97.1217B).

[*]**συνομότης, ὁ,** = συνωμότης, *fellow conspirator, confederate*, Ath.*ep.mort.Ar.*4(M.25.688D; συνωμότης p.179.30).

***συνομοφρονέω,** *agree* with; c. dat., Thdr.Stud.*epp.*2.72(M.99. 1304C).

***συνονομάζ-ω, 1.** *name together in the same breath*, Son with Father in baptismal formula, Ath.*Ar.*2.41(M.26.233C); H. Ghost with Son τὸ μὲν ∼εσθαι τῷ Χριστῷ τὸ πνεῦμα τὸ ἅγιον...ἄτοπόν ἐστι τὰ ἀνόμοια τῇ φύσει σ. καὶ συνδοξάζειν id.*ep.Serap.*1.9(M.26.552B); **2.** *include in a name, call by the same name*, Gr.Nyss.*virg.*1(p.251.18; M.46.320C); ὀνομάτων κατάλογος οἷς ἀπαραλλάκτως ὁ μονογενὴς τῷ πατρὶ ∼εται id.*Eun.*7(2 p.162.24; M.45.752C); ref. Eunomian view of Christ οὐκ ἐκεῖνο ὄντες, ὅπερ ἐστὶ κύριος, ἀλλ' ἐκείνου μετέχοντες, καὶ τῷ μετεχομένῳ ∼όμενοι id.*Apoll.*28(M.45.1184C); of Son by correlation with Father ὁ υἱὸς...κατὰ τὸ σιωπώμενον ἀεὶ τῷ πατρὶ ∼όμενος id.*Eun.*1(1 p.199.9; 445C); ἐν συζυγίᾳ τινὶ σχετικῇ τῷ πατρὶ πάντως ∼όμενος λέγεται *ib.*3(2 p.44.18; 612D).

συνοπαδός, *following along with, accompanying*; as subst.; **1.** *companion*, Clem.*paed.*3.7(p.259.7; M.8.609B); Dion.Ar.*d.n.*13.4 (M.3.981C); **2.** *follower* ἐραστὴν ἀληθῆ καὶ σ. ἡγεμόνος ἐνθέου Dion.Ar. *e.h.*2.3.4(M.3.401A).

συνοπλίζομαι, pass., *be a companion in arms*, met. ᾗ [sc. πόλει] καὶ θάλασσα σ. Cyr.*Soph.*24(3.605C).

***συνοπλιτεύω,** *serve as a soldier with* σ. τῷ ὁπλίτῃ Synes.*regn.*13 (p.25.10; M.66.1073A).

σύνοπλος, *allied*; as subst. ὁ σ. τὴν κτίσιν λαβών Or.*fr.82 in Lc.* 23:44(p.273); Cyr.*Juln.*proem.(6².3C).

***συνόπορος,** s.v.l., *accompanying* or, as subst., *companion in travel* εὐχὰς ἡμῖν συνοπόρους πέμψατε Gr.Nyss.*hom.in 1Cor.*6:18(M. 46.1109A) prob. for συνοδοιπόρους (cj. Zacagnius), συνοπαδούς, or συμπόρους.

συνοπτικός, 1. of language or style, *condensed, compressed* σ. ... ὅρους Dion.Ar.*d.n.*3.2(M.3.681B); ἀναπτύξαι...τὰς σ. καὶ ἑνιαίας... συνελίξεις *ib.*; τὴν αὐτοπτικὴν...θέαν καὶ τὴν σ. ... διδασκαλίαν *ib.* (681C); Max.*ambig.*(M.91.1053D); **2.** *apprehending instantly*, of the angelic intellect σ. τῶν θείων νοήσεων ἀμερείᾳ Dion.Ar.*d.n.*7.2(M.3. 868B); **3.** as subst., *interview* ἵνα...ἡμεῖς οἱ εὐτελεῖς τύχωμεν τοῦ πρὸς τὸν ἀρχιερέα σ. Thdr.Stud.*epp.*1.32(M.99.1016A).

συνοπτικῶς, *in a condensed* or *compressed style* τὰ σ. εἰρημένα... διακρίνοντες καὶ ἐκφαίνοντες Dion.Ar.*d.n.*3.3(M.3.684D); μυστικῶς... σ., ὡς ἔθος αὐτῷ [sc. Isaiah] Max.*ambig.*(M.91.1281C).

σύνοπτος, *intelligible*, Just.*dial.*7.3(M.6.492C).

***συνόρασις, ἡ,** *seeing the whole together, taking in the whole at a glance* τὴν ἐνόρασίν τε καὶ περιόρασιν καὶ σ. Clem.*str.*6.17(p.512.24; M.9.388C).

συνορ-άω, **1.** *see, comprehend*, sts. c. genit. σ. ... τούτων ἁπάντων ...ὡς ἐν...σώματι κεφαλῆς δεησομένων Eus.*d.e.*4.1(p.151.2; M.22. 252B); and c. acc. and infin. σ. ... μισεῖσθαι τὴν αἵρεσιν Ath.*h.Ar.* 32(p.201.2; M.25.729B); ἔστι ~ᾶν, ἥρκει σ. etc., *one can see, it is evident* εἰ...ἐπὶ τεχνῶν ἐστιν ἀληθὲς...πόσῳ πλέον ἐπὶ τῆς τέχνης τῶν τεχνῶν...ἔστι συνιδεῖν Or.*Jo.*13.46(p.272.28; M.14.481A); ~ᾶν ἔστι καθαρὰς ὑμᾶς...ἀεὶ τὰς εὐχὰς ἀνενηνοχέναι πρὸς τὸν θεόν Jul.Papa *ep. Alex.*ap.Ath.*apol.sec.*52(p.133.23; M.25.344C); ἥρκει...αὐτοὺς συνιδεῖν...μὴ εἶναι ἐξ οὐκ ὄντων...τὸν υἱόν Ath.*Ar.*2.1(M.26.148A); **2.** *determine*; **a.** *see one's way* ἐὰν ~ᾷς, κύριε· καὶ οὐ συνεχώρησέ μοι Dor.*doct.*4.9(M.88.1669D); **b.** *decide* σ. τὰ κατὰ μέρος...εἰρημένα... συναγαγεῖν Vict.*Mc.*proem.(p.263.8); σ. μὴ καταλιπεῖν αὐτὸν τὴν ἑαυτοῦ λαῦραν Cyr.S.*v.Sab.*35(p.122.3); ὡς ἂν σ. οἱ ἱερεῖς, ποιήσωσιν *Pers.*(p.38.8); **c.** officially, *decree* σ. τὰ ὀφείλοντα δοθῆναι εἰς ἀνανέωσιν ἑκάστου σεβασμίου τόπου Cyr.S.*v.Sab.*73(p.177.4); Heracl.*ep.*(M. 92.1021C,1025A,C); CCP(681)*act.*13(H.3.1332C); **d.** with neg., *refuse* οὐ σ. ἀπολῦσαι αὐτὸν λέγων· μηδαμοῦ ἀπέλθῃς Cyr.S.*v.Euthym.*20 (p.33.15).

συνοργιάζω, *join in celebrating mysteries* or *rites* σ. σοι τὰ φιλοσοφίας Synes.*ep.*151(συνεργ- M.66.1552B).

συνουλ-όω, **1.** *cause to cicatrize completely*; fig., Pall.*v.Chrys.*7 (p.40.20; M.47.24); pass., *be completely healed*; met., of Church emerged from persecution τῆς παλαιᾶς ὑγιείας, τάχιστα τοῦ διεστῶτος ~ωθέντος Gr.Naz.*or.*21.32(M.35.1120B); Nil.*epp.*1.104(M.79.128C); **2.** intrans., *cicatrize, heal over completely*, med., Thphn.*chron.*p.10 (M.108.80B); met. οἶδεν [sc. secular literature] ἀναστομοῦν τοὺς τῶν τραυμάτων ~ώσαντας μώλωπας Isid.Pel.*epp.*1.63(M.78.224C).

συνούλωσις, **ἡ**, *complete cicatrization*; met., *complete healing* of wound of sin εἰ...θεραπεύσοις τὴν ἁμαρτίαν, τάχα ἄν τις ὑμῖν ἔλθοι σ. Gr.Naz.*ep.*217(M.37.353C); νῦν δ' οὐδὲν οἶδα φάρμακον, πλὴν δακρύων, ἐξ ὧν σ. μὲν ἔρχεται μόγις id.*carm.*2.1.12.498(M.37.1202A); ἡ σ. τὴν τελείαν ἴασιν δηλοῖ Thdt.*Jer.*40:6(2.556); CTrull.*can.*102; of wound of suffering in BMV caused by Crucifixion τὸ τῆς ἀναστάσεως θαῦμα σ. παντελῆ τῆς τομῆς ἀπειργάσατο ‡Gr.Nyss.*occurs.*(M.46.1176B).

συνουλωτικός, *able to heal completely*, met. [Os.13:9] τί φάρμακον εὕρωμαι σ.; Gr.Naz.*or.*26.18(M.35.1252B).

συνουσία, **ἡ**, **1.** *habitual association, living with*, with God ἀφθαρσίας καὶ σ. καταξιωθῆναι Just.*1apol.*10.3(M.6.341A); μεταβᾶσα δὲ τῆς οὐρανίου σ. τῶν ἐλαττόνων μετουσίαν ἐπεπόθησεν Tat.*orat.*20 (p.22.14; M.6.852A); πρὸς ὀλίγον ἔσται ὁ χωρισμός [sc. by Ascension], καὶ διηνεκὴς ἡ μετ' αὐτῶν σ. Chrys.*hom.79.1 in Jo.*(8.465C); **2.** freq. *sexual intercourse*; unknown to BMV either before birth of Christ, Just.*dial.*84.1(M.6.673B); *ib.*78.3(657C); τὸ ἐκ τῆς παρθένου Μαρίας τεχθὲν ἄνευ σ. κυριακὸν σῶμα †Ath.*exp.fid.*3(M.25.205B); or after οὐδὲ ἔχουσιν αὐτὴν ἀποδεῖξαι, ὅτι σ. ἐχρήσατο μετὰ τὴν ἀπότεξιν τοῦ σωτῆρος Or.*hom.7 in Lc.*(p.49.23); **3.** *community of essence, consubstantiality*, of Persons of Trin. τριῶν ἀσωμάτων τελείων ἀχώριστον δέχου τὴν σ. Bas.*hom.*24.5(2.193E; M.31.609C); ἀδιαίρετον δεχώμεθα σ. συνόντων ἀλλήλοις ἀδιαστάτως ‡Ath.*Sabell.*12(M.28. 116C); v. s. συνουσίωσις.

συνουσιαστής, **ὁ**, *one who asserts* Christ's flesh *to be of the same essence* as his divinity; name applied to Apollinarians, Diod. *synous.*1 tit.(M.33.1560A)ap.Leont.B.*Nest.et Eut.*3(M.86.1385D); Cyr. *synous.*tit.(p.476.4); Eust.Mon.*ep.*(M.86.940A); Πολέμων ὁ σ. Leont. H.*monoph.*(M.86.1864B).

***συνουσιάω**, v. συνουσιόω.

***συνούσιος**, *sharing an essence*; **1.** (Arian) as having been *given a share of* or *taken into partnership with an essence* υἱός...ὁμοούσιος τῷ πατρί, οὐ σ. ... τουτέστιν οὐκ ἔξωθεν τοῦ πατρὸς γεννηθείς Epiph. *anc.*6(p.12.14; M.43.25B); **2.** (ref. Sabellian confusion of Persons) as *having a portion of an essence* inasmuch as there was no eternal distinction in Godhead πίστευε...ὁμοούσιον τῷ πατρὶ τὸν υἱόν, μὴ σ. κατὰ τὴν τοῦ Σαβελλίου παροινίαν ‡Caes.Naz.*dial.*10(M. 38.868).

συνουσι-όω, **A.** act., ? *make real* ἔρως ~ώσας τὴν φιλάλληλον σχέσιν Geo.Pis.*carm.*4.37.

B. pass.; **1.** *belong essentially to, be inherent in* or *intrinsic to* τῶν ἐλάφων φύσιν, οἷς ἀφανιστικὴ τῶν ἑρπετῶν ~ωται δύναμις Gr.Nyss. *Pss.titt.*B 12(M.44.553A); χρώματα οὐκ ἐξίτηλα, ἀλλὰ σχεδὸν σ. τοῖς ὑποκειμένοις Chrys.*hom.12.4 in Heb.*(12.127B); ~ᾶσθαι τὸν ἁγιασμὸν τοῖς οὐρανοῖς ‡Ath.*dial.Trin.*3.24(M.28.1240C); opp. what is grafted, ref. Rom.11:21 τοῦτ' ἔστι τῶν κατὰ ἀλήθειαν σ. ἐν τῇ ῥίζῃ Anast.S. *hod.*8(M.89.125B); ref. human nature τὸ ἐπιθυμητικὸν καὶ τὸ θυμοειδές, εἴτε ~ωμένα τῇ ψυχῇ...εἴτε τι ἄλλο παρ' αὐτὴν ὄντα καὶ ὕστερον ἡμῖν ἐπιγινόμενα Gr.Nyss.*anim.et res.*(M.46.49B); *ib.*(52B); ὁ ἄνθρωπος οὐ κατὰ φύσιν οὐδὲ ~ωμένον ἔσχεν ἐν ἑαυτῷ παρὰ τὴν πρώτην γένεσιν τὸ παθητικόν τε καὶ ἐπίκηρον id.*virg.*12(p.298.4; M.46.369B); of θυμός as an appetite indifferent in itself ἄνθρωπος δέ τις ὢν καὶ θυμὸν σ. ἔχων τῇ φύσει id.*Pss.titt.*B 15(M.44.589C); εὑρήσει...σ. τε καὶ συμπεφυκυῖαν τῷ ἀνθρώπῳ τὴν ἐπὶ τὸ καλὸν...ὁρμήν, καὶ τῆς νοητῆς... εἰκόνος...ἔρωτα συνημμένον τῇ φύσει id.*instit.*(p.40.7; M.46.288A); πᾶσα ἡ λογικὴ διῄρηται φύσις, ἡ μὲν ἀσώματος...ἡ δὲ διὰ σαρκὸς εἰς γῆν ἐπιστρεφομένη...ἡ μέν τοι τοῦ καλοῦ...ἐπιθυμία, ὁμοτίμως ἑκατέρᾳ ~ώθη τῇ φύσει id.*or.dom.*4(p.76.6; M.44.1165D); τὴν παρρησίαν...τὴν ἐξ ἀρχῆς ~ωμένην τῇ φύσει *ib.*5(p.94.26; 1180A); of divine image opp. likeness ὃ μὲν παρὰ τοῦ κτίζοντος ἐδίδοτο τῇ φύσει ἡμῶν οἱονεὶ ~ωμένον ‡Bas.*struct.hom.*1.20(1.333D; M.30.32A); thus term has reference to man's nature as created by God τοῦτο ...λέγει, διὰ τὸ ἠσθενηκέναι τὴν φύσιν ἐκ τῆς ἐν Ἀδὰμ παραβάσεως... οὐ μὴν ὡς ~ωμένης ἡμῖν τῆς ἁμαρτίας Olymp.*Job* 14:4f.(M.93.165D); but Marcionites could speak of τοῦ δαίμονος τούτου τοῦ ~ωμένου τοῖς ἀνθρώποις Tim.CP *haer.*(M.86.49B); which acc. their theory was consequence of Adam's condemnation οὐδὲ γάρ ἐστιν ἱκανὸν τὸ ἅγιον βάπτισμα τὰς ῥίζας τῶν ἁμαρτιῶν τὰς ~ωμένας ἀρχῆθεν τοῖς ἀνθρώποις ἐκτεμεῖν *ib.*(48B); **2.** met., *be associated* or *united with* τοῦ σταυροῦ...ᾧ σπουδάζει [sc. Παῦλος] ~ωθῆναι Chrys.*hom.13.1 in Phil.*(11.298B); σ. [sc. βασιλεύς] τοῖς φίλοις τὴν δύναμιν ἑαυτῷ πολυπλασιάζων Synes.*regn.*11(p.24.9; M.66.1072C); *be essentially connected with* ἡ...τῶν ψαλμῶν ἱερολογία ~ωμένη πᾶσι σχεδὸν τοῖς ἱεραρχικοῖς μυστηρίοις Dion.Ar.*e.h.*3.3.4(M.3.429C); **3.** theol. (mostly in heret. statements); **a.** ref. Inc.; **i.** ref. divinity, a true incarnation denied τὸ δὲ ἀνώτατον φῶς τοῖς ἑαυτοῦ ~ωμένον ἔδειξεν ἑαυτὸν ἐν τοῖς ὑλικοῖς σώμασιν σῶμα Man.*ep.Add.*ap.Eust.Mon.*ep.*(M.86. 904A); **ii.** of Christ's humanity ἐπλάσθη προηγουμένως ὡς ἄνθρωπος ἐν γαστρὶ ~ωμένος τῷ ἀνθρωπίνῳ Paul.Sam.*fr.*B 14(p.334.2)ap. Leont.B.*Nest.et Eut.*3(M.86.1393C); ref. teaching of Eunomius τῇ τοῦ υἱοῦ φύσει ~ῶσθαι τὰ πάθη Gr.Nyss.*Eun.*12(2 p.286.16; συνοικειοῦσθαι M.45.897D); as against Nestorius οὐ...ψιλὸς ἄνθρωπος ὁ Χριστός, ἵνα τὸ ὅμοιον τῷ ὁμοίῳ ἀνελλιπῶς ~ωθῇ Thdot.Anc.*hom.*4.8 (M.77.1401A); **iii.** freq. in Apollinarian statements of essential unity of Christ's flesh with divinity ζωοποιεῖ...ἡμᾶς ἡ σὰρξ αὐτοῦ διὰ τὴν σ. αὐτῇ θεότητα Apoll.*fr.*116(p.235.8)ap.Leont.B.*Apoll.*(M. 86.1964D); ὡς καὶ πρὶν τοῦ κατελθεῖν αὐτὸν υἱὸν ἀνθρώπου εἶναι, καὶ κατελθεῖν ἰδίαν ἐπαγόμενον σάρκα ἐκείνην...προαιώνιόν τινα καὶ σ. id. *fr.*165(p.263.28)ap.Gr.Naz.*ep.*202(M.37.332C); cf.Tim.CP *haer.*(M.86. 40B); καθὼς ἐκεῖνός φησιν, οὐχὶ ἐπικτητὸς ἐπὶ τῇ εὐεργεσίᾳ γίνεται ἡ σὰρξ τῇ θεότητι, ἀλλὰ σ. καὶ θεότητι, ἀλλὰ σ. καὶ σύμφυτος Apoll.*fr.* 36(p.212.25)ap.Gr.Nyss.*Apoll.*17(M.45.1157A); κατὰ μηδένα λόγον ~ῶσθαι αὐτὴν [sc. τὴν σάρκα] τῇ θεότητι γράψας Tim.Beryt.*ep. Homon.*(p.278.10)ap.Leont.B.*Apoll.*(1960C); Apollinarian usage condemned τοὺς δὲ λέγοντας...~ωμένον ἐσχηκέναι τὸ σῶμα ἢ οὐρανόθεν τοῦτο κεκομικέναι...ἀναθεματίζει ἡ...ἐκκλησία Ambr.*fr.symb.* ap.Thdt.*eran.*2(4.141); οὐ...σάρκα σ. οὐρανόθεν ἑαυτῷ συγκατήγαγε κατὰ τοὺς Ἀπολιναρίου μύθους Max.*ambig.*(M.91.1048C); οὐδὲ λαβών, ἀλλ' ἄνωθεν καὶ ἀπ' ἀρχῆς ~ωμένην αὐτῷ κατενέγκας, ἥνωσεν ἑαυτῷ· καὶ τὴν...οἰκονομίαν ἐφάντασεν id.*opusc.*(M.91.93B); **iv.** but that it is context rather than word itself which is heret. is shown by ὁ ~ούμενος τῷ κατ' ἄνδρα θεοῦ λόγος καὶ θεὸς καὶ πρὸς μίαν ὑπόστασιν τοῦ Ἰησοῦ Χριστοῦ συντελῶν κατὰ τὴν θείαν φύσιν *cat.Apoc.*12:7ff. (p.359.2); **b.** ref. H. Ghost τὸ πνεῦμα φυσικὴν ἔχει τὴν ἁγιότητα, οὐ κατὰ χάριν λαβὸν ἀλλὰ ~ωμένην αὐτῷ Bas.*ep.*159.2(3.248C; M.32. 621B); as equivalent of ὁμοούσιος: ὁμοσθενοῦς...καὶ ~ωμένου [sc. τῷ θεῷ λόγῳ]...πνεύματος Jo.D.*carm.pent.*64(p.215; M.96.836B); **4.** *coexist* ἑνὶ καὶ τῷ αὐτῷ συνυπάρχουσι καὶ ~ωνται τὰ ἐναντία Jo.D. *Man.*1.23(M.94.1528B).

***συνουσιωμένως**, *essentially*, i.e. *as an essential attribute* τὸ πνεῦμα τὸ ἅγιον...πάντα ἔχον καὶ αὐτὸ σ. κατὰ τὴν φύσιν, τὴν ἀγαθότητα... Bas.*hom.*15.3(2.132D; M.31.468C).

συνουσίωσις, **ἡ**, **1.** *fusion of essences*, a word implying Apollinarian or Eutychian confusion οὔτε μὴν φυρμὸν ἢ σύγκρασιν ἢ τὴν θρυλουμένην παρά τισι σ. ὑπομείνας Cyr.*ep.*55(p.54.27; 5².181D); περιττολογοῦσι...οἱ...κατὰ σύγκρασιν ἤγουν σ. ἐν τῇ φύσει τῆς... τριάδος χωρῆσαι τὸ σῶμα λέγοντες id.*resp.*(6².391E; συνουσίαν Aubert); Πολέμιός...τις...σ. λέγει γεγενῆσθαι, καὶ κρᾶσιν τῆς θεότητος καὶ τοῦ σώματος Thdt.*haer.*4.9(4.363); εἰ κατὰ τὴν σ. θεότητος καὶ σαρκὸς εἷς υἱὸς ὁ υἱός, δῆλον ὅτι πρὸ τῆς σ., οὐκ ἦν εἷς ὁ λόγος, οὔτε θεός, οὔτε υἱός. ἀλλὰ καὶ πρὸ τῆς σ. θεὸς καὶ υἱὸς ὁ λόγος· καὶ ἐπὶ τῇσδε ὁμοίως... προσκτήσει τῶν οὐκ ἐνόντων, γέγονε Χριστὸς...ὁ...υἱός Leont.H.*Nest.* 1.40(M.86.1500D–1501A); of which Cyr. was accused by Nestorians τὸ δὲ τῆς σ. ὄνομα οὐδὲ ὅ τί ποτέ ἐστιν, ἴσμεν ὅλως. εἰκὸς δὲ τοὺς τοιαῦτα γράφοντας ἐκεῖσε ἀπολογουμένους περὶ τῆς προπετείας τῆς ἐν τῇ Ἐφέσῳ καθ' ἡμῶν γενομένης εὑρησιλογεῖν τοιαῦτά τινα Cyr.*ep.*54

(p.165.14; M.77.289C); in orthodox charge against monophysites τοὺς οὐχὶ ἕνωσιν καθ' ὑπόστασιν...ὁμολογοῦντες, ἀλλὰ σύμφυρσιν καὶ σύγχυσιν καὶ σ. ἀσεβῶς τερατευομένους, οἵτινές φασι τήν τε τῆς θεότητος φύσιν καὶ τὴν τῆς σαρκὸς μίαν ἀποτελεσθῆναι φύσιν Cyr.S. *v.Euthym.*27(p.43.17); ἀναιροῦντες [sc. the orthodox] τὴν Εὐτυχοῦς σ. Justn.*monoph.*(p.8.33; M.86.1108D); εἰ ὁμοούσιος ἡ τοῦ...λόγου σὰρξ τῇ ἀκτίστῳ αὐτοῦ θεότητι καθ' ὑμᾶς, σ. νοσεῖτε Jo.D.*Jacob.*20(M.94.1448A); *ib.*44(1456D); and monothelites, Max.*opusc.*(M.91.28B); *ib.*(49C); ἵνα μὴ σ. δογματίσωσι, καὶ οὕτω κατὰ τῶν τὰς δύο [sc. ἐνεργείας] πρεσβευόντων...πολεμήσωσιν *ib.*(208D); **2.** rarely in orthodox use, *coexistence* τὴν μὲν τῶν αὐτοῦ φύσεων ἀρχὴν οὐ τῆς οὐσιώσεως ἀλλὰ τῆς σ. μόνον ἐν τῇ ἁγίᾳ παρθένῳ λαβεῖν, τουτέστι τὴν τοῦ λόγου· τὴν δὲ ἑτέραν...ἤγουν τὴν τῆς σαρκός, ἀρχὴν τῆς τε οὐσιώσεως καὶ σ. ἐν αὐτῇ λαβεῖν Leont.H.*Nest.*4.17(M.86.1684B); 'θεοῦ μου' οὐχ οὕτω τῆς...θείας φύσεως...ἀναιρετικόν, ὅσον τῆς σ. παραστατικόν Areth. *Apoc.*3:12(M.106.557D).

συνόφρυς, *with meeting eyebrows*; of S. Paul, *A.Paul.et Thecl.*3 (p.237.8).

συνοχέομαι, *ride in a chariot with*; c. dat., Soz.*h.e.*3.9.3(M.67.1056C).

συνοχεύς, ὁ, *that which holds together* (trans. sense); **1.** *hinge* ξυνοχῆας ἀνακλίνουσι θυρέτρων διζυγέων Paul.Sil.*Soph.*572(M.86.2141A); of anything which holds together, *ib.*540(p.242; συνοχῆρας 2140A in error); *ib.*696(2146A); **2.** esp. of God as *upholder* of creation τὸν τοῦ εἶναι αὐτὴν [sc. τάξιν] σ. καὶ αἴτιον Dion.Ar.*ep.*7.2(M.3.1080C); εἷς...ἐστὶ θεὸς...τοῦ παντὸς ποιητής, σ. τε καὶ κυβερνήτης Jo.D.*f.o.* 1.5(M.94.801B) = ‡Cyr.*Trin.*4(6^3.5E; M.77.1128B); τῆς...κτίσεως τὸν σ. χερσὶ συνέχεις [sc. BMV] Jo.Mon.*hymn.Nic.Myr.*6(M.96.1388A); Areth.*Apoc.*4:10(M.106.576B); by mere exercise of will, Chrys.ap. Max.*opusc.*(M.91.281B); **3.** ref. Inc., *agent of union* ἡλίθιον αὐτοῦ παρόντος, ἕτερον ζητεῖν σ. ἐπὶ τῆς αὐτοῦ συνθέσεως Leont.H.*Nest.*1.13 (M.86.1452B).

συνοχή, ἡ, A. (συνέχω) *holding together*; **1.** *conservation, preservation*, of God πᾶσα ἀρχή, πᾶσα σ., πᾶν πέρας Dion.Ar.*d.n.*4.10 (M.3.705D); *ib.*4.4(700A); *ib.*1.7(596D); ἡ ταύτης [sc. τῆς κτίσεως] σ. τε καὶ κυβέρνησις Jo.D.*f.o.*1.1(M.94.789B); ἡ τῆς κτίσεως σ., καὶ συντήρησις *ib.*1.3(796C); **2.** that which holds together; **a.** *fastening* of a belt; of one of the zones of the terrestrial sphere, Mac.Mgn. *apocr.*2.20(p.39.11); **b.** *means* or *ground of union, bond* ὃν ἀνείληφεν οὗτος [sc. God the Son] ἄνθρωπον, ἀπὸ τῆς τῶν ἀνθρώπων σ. ... τῇ φύσει τὸ γένος ἔχοντα Or.*Jo.*10.41(25; p.218.30; M.14.388B); Synes. *hymn.*4.196(p.31; M.66.1606); πάσης οὐσίας...ἀρχὴ καὶ αἰτία, καὶ πάντων...ἀσχέτῳ σ. περιδεδραγμένη Dion.Ar.*c.h.*7.4(M.3.212D); αἱ ἀδιάλυτοι σ. τῶν ὄντων id.*d.n.*4.7(M.3.704C); of God ὑποβέβληταί σοι τὰ πάντα...ὡς συνοχῇ καὶ φρουρᾷ τῶν παρενηνεγμένων ‡Meth.*Sym. et Ann.*6(M.18.361B).

B. (συνέχομαι) *a being held together*; **1.** *confinement*; of embryo in womb, Meth.*symp.*2.6(p.23.8; M.18.57A); id.*res.*2.20(p.373.8; M.18.285A); *detention, imprisonment, Did.*1.5; **2.** *crush* of people, *crowd* πῶς ἦν βέλτιον μετὰ μέρος καὶ διῃρημένως τὸν λαὸν μετ' ἐπικινδύνου σ. ἢ ὄντος ἤδη τόπου τοῦ δυναμένου δέξασθαι πάντας... συνελθεῖν; Ath.*apol.Const.*16(M.25.616A); **3.** met., *distress, affliction*, ‡Eust.*hex.*(M.18.793C); Bas.*ep.*46.5(3.139A; M.32.377C); *ib.*207(311B; M.764A); Jo.Mon.*hymn.Nic.Myr.*6(M.96.1388A); **4.** *struggle, difficulty* τὴν σ. τοῦ ἄσθματος Gr.Nyss.*v.Macr.*(p.389.16; M.46.977A); cf.*ib.* (p.395.14; 981C); **5.** *coherence* τὰς...εὐτονωτάτας καὶ στερροτάτας σ. οὐ συντριπτέον οὐδὲ διακοπτέον Or.*Jo.*10.18(13; p.189.11; M.14.337C); **6.** *union* of natures in Christ τὴν διάκρισιν τοῦ λόγου ἀπὸ τοῦ συγκειμένου αὐτῷ παρεχωρήσατε, τὴν δὲ σ. ὑπὸ κρείττονος εἶναι συνεισάγετε Leont.H.*Nest.*1.13(M.86.1452D); **7.** that which is kept together, *combination, whole* τὰ συνεχόμενα πάντα κατὰ μίαν...σ. ἀσφαλιζομένην [sc. by God] Dion.Ar.*d.n.*10.1(M.3.937A); διασώζουσαν πάντα ἐν ἀσυγχύτῳ πάντων σ. καὶ ἀμιγῆ καὶ συγκεκραμένα *ib.*11.2(949C).

συνοχικός, *conserving, preserving*, of God τὴν...εἰς τὸ εἶναι τὰ ὄντα παρακτικὴν καὶ σ. ἀγαθότητα Dion.Ar.*d.n.*1.3(M.3.589C); *ib.*4.10 (705C); τῆς ζωοποιοῦ...καὶ σ. αἰτίας *ib.*6.1(856B).

συνοψίζω, 1. *bring into a general view, sum up*; hence *epitomize* σ. ... τὴν ἐν τῇ...τριάδι πίστιν ‡Ath.*polit.*1(M.28.1396B); *ib.*(1396A); **2.** *estimate* οἱ προθέμενοι οἰκοδομίαν ποιήσασθαι, συνοψίσαντες πρότερον τὰς ἁρμοζούσας ὕλας ἀποτίθενται Didym.*Trin.*3.1(M.39.781C); **3.** pass., *meet* σ. τῷ...Μαξίμῳ Thphn.*chron.*p.275(τὸν...Μάξιμον M.108.681A); *be granted, have an interview with* ἀπέστειλε Παγανὸς... πρὸς τὸν βασιλέα αἰτούμενος σ. αὐτῷ *ib.*p.367(877C); *ib.*p.311(756C); Thdr.Stud.*epp.*1.48(M.99.1069C).

σύνοψις, ἡ, 1. a *seeing all together, synoptic* or *general view* ὅσῳ πρὸς τὸ ἄναντες ἀνανεύομεν, τοσοῦτον οἱ λόγοι ταῖς σ. τῶν νοητῶν περιστέλλονται Dion.Ar.*myst.*3(M.3.1033B); *survey* φρόντισον...ἐν τάχει τὴν σ. ποιησάμενος, εἰς τὴν τάξιν ἀνενεγκεῖν, ἵνα τὰ θειωδῶς προσταχθέντα ἐπὶ πέρας ἀχθῆναι δυνηθῇ Flavius *ep.*ap.Ath.*apol.sec.*85 (p.164.10; M.25.401B); *estimate* σ. γενομένης πρὸς ἡμᾶς γράψαι σπούδασον, ἵν' ὅσων τ' ἂν καὶ ὁποίων χρείαν εἶναι...ἐπιγνῶμεν Const. ap.Eus.*v.C.*3.31(p.92.23; M.20.1092C); **2.** a particular *aspect* ἣν ὁτὲ μὲν Ἱερουσαλὴμ οἱ προφῆται κατὰ τὴν σ. τῶν ἐπιφερομένων, ὁτὲ δὲ νύμφην, ὁτὲ δὲ Σιὼν ὄρος...κεκλήκασιν Meth.*symp.*8.5(p.87.2; M.18.145B); ἡ ἐκκλησία κατὰ τὴν τῆς σελήνης σ. *ib.*8.6(p.88.9; 148B); **3.** *brief but comprehensive statement, conspectus* Λέων...μιᾷ κυρώσει καὶ σ. πάντα τὰ...εἰρημένα...ἐπισφραγίζεται Leont.H.*monoph.*(M.86.1844C).

***συνόψισις, ἡ,** *sight of, meeting with* a person κἀνταῦθα...καταξιῶσαι τῆς τε τοῦ υἱοῦ σου σ. καὶ συναγαλλιάσεως αἰωνίου Thdr.Stud.*epp.* 2.145(M.99.1457B).

***συνοψισμός, ὁ,** = foreg., Thdr.Stud.*epp.*2.28(M.99.1196D).

συνταγή, ἡ, 1. *promise, undertaking, A.Petr.et Andr.*22(p.126.27); Marc.Diac.*v.Porph.*37; of promises or vows to God; of virginity by BMV, *A.Barth.*4(p.135.23); καὶ ψεύστης πρός σε τῆς σ. ἐγενόμην Anast.S.*Ps.*6(M.89.1084B); esp. at baptism ὁμολογίαν τῆς πίστεως καὶ τὴν σ. τοῦ βαπτίσματος Ephr.2.195C; μανθανέτω τὰ περὶ τῆς ἀποταγῆς τοῦ διαβόλου καὶ τὰ περὶ τῆς σ. τοῦ Χριστοῦ *Const.App.* 7.40.1; τὴν ἀποταγὴν τοῦ διαβόλου καὶ τὴν σ. τὴν πρὸς τὸν Χριστόν Chrys.*catech.*4.7(p.173.13); μνησθῶμεν τῆς ἀποταγῆς, καὶ σ. τῆς γενομένης ἐν τῷ βαπτίσματι Jo.D.*hom.*2.6(M.96.585C); **2.** *covenant, agreement*, ref. betrayal of Christ τὴν σ. περὶ τῶν ἀργυρίων Eus.*d.e.* 10.1(p.452.9; M.22.728A); plur. σ. ἔχουσι κατ' ἐμοῦ Hesych.H.*Ps.tit.* 70(M.27.933D); **3.** *assignation* ἐν ὀφθαλμοῖς αὐτοῦ λαλεῖ πάσῃ γυναικὶ ἐν σ. κακίας *Pss.Sal.*4.5.

σύνταγμα, τό, *that which is put together in order*; **1.** of persons; **a.** *band* of soldiers, Dion.Al.ap.Eus.*h.e.*6.41.22(M.20.612B); **b.** any organized *band* or *company* μονὴ δέ...σ. πρὸς σωτηρίαν Gr.Naz.*carm.* 1.2.34.178(M.37.958A); *ib.*1.2.34.224(961A); of sects opp. body of Church πρὸς πᾶν ὁμοῦ τὸ σ. τὸ...ὥσπερ τι μέλος νενοσηκὸς τοῦ ὑγιαίνοντος σώματος τῆς ἐκκλησίας ἀπορραγέν Bas.*Eun.*1.2(1.209E; M.29.504D); καθαροὺς μὲν τοὺς ὅσοι αὐτῷ ἐπλήρουν τὸ κατὰ τῆς ἐκκλησίας ὀνομάσας σ. Eulog.*fr.Novat.*ap.Phot.*cod.*280(M.104.353C); **c.** eccl. *council* τέταρτον ἀθροίζεται σ. ... ὅπερ ἐν Χαλκηδόνι...ποιεῖται ...συνέλευσιν Sophr.H.*ep.syn.*(M.87.3185A); οἱ προφάσει τοῦ ἐν Χαλκηδόνι σ. τοῦ τόμου ἀποσχίσαντες τῆς...ἐκκλησίας Jo.D.*haer.*83 (M.94.741A); **2.** *treatise, work, book*; of scriptures, Just.*1apol.*63.11 (M.6.424C); Clem.*prot.*9(p.65.7; M.8.200A); Meth.*res.*2.5(p.338.17); of commentaries thereon πολλὰ πολλῶν σ. ... εἴς γε τὴν Παλαιὰν καὶ τὴν Καινὴν γραψάντων Ath.*Ar.*1.4(M.26.20A); of Christian polemical and other works ἔστιν δὲ ἡμῖν καὶ σ. κατὰ πασῶν τῶν...αἱρέσεων συντεταγμένον Just.*1apol.*26.8(M.6.369A); καλῶς Ἰουστῖνος ἐν τῷ πρὸς Μαρκίωνα σ. φησίν Iren.*haer.*4.6.2(M.7.987B); τῆς συμμετρίας τοῦ σ. [sc. the *Paedagogus*] Clem.*paed.*2.1(p.154.1; M.8.377B); Bas. *ep.*223.4(3.339C; M.32.828C); of heret. works κατὰ τοῦ νόμου καὶ τῶν προφητῶν σ. ἐποίησε [sc. Apelles] Hipp.*haer.*10.20(p.281.1; M.16.3438C); of anti-Christian polemics τὸν Κέλσου ἄλλο σ. μετὰ τοῦτο ποιήσειν Or.*Cels.*8.76(p.293.8; M.11.1632B); of a compilation τὸ παρόν σοι προσενήνοχα σ., ἐκ διαφόρων μὲν πατέρων...ἀπανθισθέν ‡Ath.*polit.*1(M.28.1396A); **3.** *pronouncement, definition* ἐπιχειροῦσιν ἀνατρέπειν πᾶν ἀληθείας σ. CArim.*ep.Const.*1(p.237.34; M.26.697B).

συνταγμάτιον, τό, dimin. of σύνταγμα, *little treatise, little work* αἰτῶ...τὸ ἐν ἰάμβοις ἐκεῖνο σ. Synes.*ep.*141(M.66.1533A); of commentaries on scriptures τούτων [sc. of Origen and Theognostus]... τοῖς περὶ τούτων σ. Ath.*ep.Serap.*4.9(M.26.649B); freq. of heret. works Ἀστέριος...ἐν τῷ ἰδίῳ σ. Ath.*Ar.*1.30(M.26.76A); *ib.*1.32(77B); id.*syn.*18(p.245.23; M.26.713B); σ. τι ... ὃ εὐαγγέλιον τοῦ Ἰούδα καλοῦσι [sc. Cainites] Epiph.*haer.*38.1(p.63.13; M.41.656A); by Aëtius, *ib.*76.10(p.351.16; M.42.533C); *ib.*76.13(p.360.11; 545B).

συντακτήριος, *farewell, valedictory* γέγραπται...αὐτῷ καὶ σ. πρὸς τοὺς Ἀντιοχέας λόγος Evagr.*h.e.*4.40(p.191.26; M.86.2784D); Γρηγόριος...τὸν σ. αὐτοῖς προσφωνήσας λόγον...εἰς τὴν ἰδίαν παραγίνεται χώραν, τὴν ἡσυχίαν ἀσπαζόμενος Germ.CP *syn.haer.*22(M.98.61A); Thphn.*chron.*p.59(M.108.200B); sc. λόγος, Gr.Naz.*or.*42.25(M.36. 489A); neut. as subst. ὅτι βλέπουσι τοὺς γνωρίμους [sc. at the Last Day]...οἱ ἄθλιοι...ἀποχωριζόμενοι, θρηνοῦσι τὸ σ. Ephr.ap.‡Jo.D. *fid.dorm.*31(M.95.276D); Thdr.Stud.*epp.*2.71(M.99.1300D).

***συντάκτης, ὁ,** *writer, composer*; of Origen, Epiph.*haer.*63.1 (p.398.17; M.41.1061D); id.*anac.*64(p.214.1; M.41.849C).

συντακτικός, 1. *written, in writing* opp. διδασκαλικός, Clem.*ecl.*27 (p.144.30; M.9.712B); as subst., *composer, writer* Ὠριγένους τοῦ... σ. Epiph.*anac.*(M.42.868B) but συντάκτου *anac.*64(p.214.1; M.41.

849C); **2.** = συντακτήριος, *farewell, valedictory* σ. ... ὁμιλίαν Eus. *v.C.*3.21(p.87.25; M.20.1080B); **3.** of statements, *co-ordinate*, ‡Nil. *Epict.*63(M.79.1308D).

***συνταλαίπωρος,** masc. or fem., *companion in misfortune*, cf. σ., *id est commiseronem*, Tert.*adversus Marcionem* 4.9(M.*PL*.2.403C); τῇ σ. εἰς τροφὰς κομίζω *Hom.Clem.*12.18.

***συνταλανίζω,** *join in calling* or *deeming unhappy* ὁ υἱὸς τῆς ἀπωλείας...ὃν...τῷ προφήτῃ σ. Const.Pogon.*edict.*(H.3.1468A).

***συνταξιαρχ-έομαι,** *be enrolled with* Ζαχαρίας...ὁ τοῖς ἁγίοις ~ούμενος Chrysipp.*enc.in Jo.Bapt.*2(p.32.5).

σύνταξις, ἡ, 1. *putting together* συντάττεται τῷ πατρὶ ὁ υἱὸς καὶ τὸ πνεῦμα...οὐ γὰρ ἄλλο τι τῆς σ. ὁ λόγος παρίστησι, ἀλλ' ἢ πατρός, καὶ υἱοῦ καὶ ἁγίου πνεύματος τὸ τῆς οὐσίας ταὐτόν Thdt.*rect.conf.*7(M.6.1217C); **2.** *putting in order*; hence **a.** *order, arrangement* διὰ τῆς παναρμονίου ταύτης [sc. τῆς κτίσεως] σ. γινώσκειν τὸν δημιουργόν Ath.*gent.*4(M.25.9D); **b.** a *ranging oneself* with τὴν ἀπόταξιν τοῦ σατανᾶ καὶ τὴν πρὸς τὸν Χριστὸν σ. Cyr.H.*catech.*19.8; **c.** *ascription, reference* πρὸς τὰ γενόμενα τὴν σ. ἔχειν Ath.*Ar.*1.21(M.26.56B); **d.** *sequel, continuation* τῶν προτέρων λόγων ἀποδοῦναι τὴν σ. ἣν βούλεσθε Gr.Ant.*bapt.*2.1(M.88.1872B); **e.** in music = σύνταγμα, *arrangement* of notes, *mode, scale* ἡ ἁρμονία...δείκνυται καὶ ἡ σ. ὀρθή, ὅταν ὁ κατέχων τὴν λύραν πλήξῃ τὰς νευράς Ath.*gent.*31(M.25.64A); **3.** esp. in writing; **a.** *composition, writing* of a book τὴν...τῶν λόγων σ. ποιήσασθαι Just.*2apol.*1.1(M.6.441A); Or.*Jo.*5.2(p.101.5; M.14.188B); ὁ δὲ Λουκᾶς ἀρχόμενος...τὴν αἰτίαν προύθηκεν δι' ἣν πεποίηται τὴν σ. [sc. the gospel] Eus.*h.e.*3.24.15(M.20.268B); **b.** *ordered collection, compilation* ὃς [sc. Πέτρος] πρὸς τὰς χρείας ἐποιεῖτο τὰς διδασκαλίας, ἀλλ' οὐχ ὥσπερ σ. τῶν κυριακῶν ποιούμενος λογίων Papias ap.Eus.*h.e.*3.39.15(M.20.300C); τῶν γεγενημένων ἡμῖν λόγων...σ. ποιήσομαι Just.*dial.*80.3(M.6.665A); **c.** systematic *treatise*, of various Christian writings οὐδενὸς τῶν ἁγίων ἐκδεδωκότος σ. πλείονας Or.*Jo.*5.2(p.101.14; M.14.188B); θειοτέρως διηγήσαιτο...ἐν προηγουμένῃ σ. id.*Cels.*2.69(p.191.21; M.11.905A); τὰς τῶν διδασκάλων σ. Ath.*gent.*1(M.25.4B); Cyr.*ep.*72(p.18.10; 5².200A); *book* of Bible ἀρχόμενος τῆς κατ' αὐτὸν σ. γράφει [Jo.1:1] Or.*fr.1 in Jo.*(p.484.8); Dion.Ar.*e.h.*3.3.5(M.3.432B); **d.** more gen., *book, writing* opp. speech διὰ τῆς σ. παραπεμπομένης τῆς φωνῆς Clem.*ecl.*27(p.145.2; M.9.712C); **4.** *construction*; *arrangement of words* or *clauses*, Tat.*orat.*12(p.13.32; M.6.832C); ἀπὸ τῶν νοημάτων δὲ καὶ ἀπὸ τῶν ῥημάτων καὶ τῆς σ. αὐτῶν εἰκότως ἕτερος οὗτος παρ' ἐκεῖνον ὑποληφθήσεται [i.e. author of S. John's Gospel and Epistles from author of Apocalypse] Dion.Al.ap.Eus.*h.e.*7.25.17(M.20.701A); ταῖς σ. τῆς ἑρμηνείας *ib.*7.25.25(704A); τολμῆσαί [sc. Τατιανόν] τινας...μεταφράσαι φωνάς, ὡς ἐπιδιορθούμενον αὐτῶν τὴν τῆς φράσεως σ. [sc. in the Diatessaron] Eus.*h.e.*4.29.6(M.20.401A); ἐναλλάξασα τὴν τοῦ λόγου σ., τὴν διάνοιαν ἐσώσατο id.*d.e.*6.14(p.268.15; M.22.441A); μὴ λίαν ἀκριβολογεῖσθαι πρὸς τὴν τῆς λέξεως σ. ἀλλὰ πρὸς τὸν εἱρμὸν τοῦ νοήματος βλέπειν Gr.Nyss.*hom.2 in Cant.*(M.44.796A); τὰς σολοικοφανεῖς τοῦ λόγου σ. ἐκ τῆς γραφῆς καταλέγειν id.*tres dii*(M.45.132C); of an elliptical expression, Cyr.*Ps.*38:9(M.69.977B); **5.** *form* of words, ref. invocation of Trin. at baptism τὴν...παραδεδομένην τοῦ λόγου σ. Bas.*Spir.*43(3.36E; M.32.148A); **6.** *passage* in a book τὰ Παύλῳ Κορινθίοις γραφέντα, σ. ἔχοντα τοιαύτην Or.*fr.45 in Jo.*(p.520.14); **7.** a prescribing or ordering; **a.** *discipline, rule of life* ἐν τῇ Χριστιανῇ σ. γεγυμνασμένος *Ep.Lugd.*ap.Eus.*h.e.*5.1.43(M.20.425A); **b.** *assignment* ἐπαγγέλλειν τὸ μάθημα τὸ ἐπιτεταγμένον, καὶ ἀποδοῦναι τοῦ ἐργοχείρου τὴν σ. τῷ προεστῶτι Ephr.1.238D; **8.** ? *contest, match* παρορᾶται...ὁ ἀθλητὴς...ἀλλ' εἰς τὴν σ. συμβαλλόμενος Clem.*str.*1.9(p.29.13; M.8.740C).

συνταπειν-όω, 1. *abase* or *humble together with* ταπεινούμενος [sc. ὁ Ἄρειος], ~οῦν ἑτόλμησεν ἑαυτῷ καὶ φύσιν θεότητος Gr.Naz.*or.*43.30(M.36.537B); τοῦ σώματος ταπεινουμένου, ~οῦται καὶ ἡ ψυχή Dor.*doct.*2.9(M.88.1652B); Anast.S.*qu.et resp.*64(M.89.661B); **2.** *lower, reduce to the level* or *measure of* ~ῶσαι ἑαυτῷ θεότητος μορφήν Jo.Mon.*hymn.Bas.*10(M.96.1377A); simply, *lower, reduce* πρὸς τὸ τῆς φύσεως τῆς ἡμετέρας μέτρον ~οῦνται καὶ αἱ τῶν...ὀνομάτων ἐμφάσεις Gr.Nyss.*or.catech.*1(p.8.8; M.45.13B); **3.** pass., *be lowered* or *depressed together with* ~ουμένη [sc. ψυχή] τῇ κακοπαθείᾳ τοῦ σώματος Bas.*ascet.*1.3(2.321D; M.31.877A); τῷ ἡμετέρῳ ~ωθῆναι πάθει Gr.Nyss.*v.Macr.*(M.46.977B).

***συνταρταρόω,** *cast into hell with*, Cyr.*Ps.*30:18(M.69.864B).

συντάσσ-ω, A. *put in order together* οὐδ' ἐναλλάξαι θέμις ἢ ὡς συντέτακται [sc. names of Persons in Trin. in Mt.28:19] Ath.*ep.Serap.*4.5(M.26.644C); hence **1.** *bring into line*; *associate* τὰ ἕτερα τοῖς ἑτέροις σ. Dion.Ar.*d.n.*9.4(M.3.912C); φίλα τἀγαθὰ...καὶ μιᾶς ζωῆς ἔκγονα, καὶ πρὸς ἓν ἀγαθὸν συντεταγμένα *ib.*4.21(724A); ὑφ' ἧς [sc. divine unity], καὶ ἐν ᾗ, καὶ εἰς ἣν πάντα ἐστί, καὶ συντέτακται *ib.*13.3(980B); of Christ with mankind in Inc. πῶς...Ἰησοῦς...ἀνθρώποις οὐσιωδῶς συντεταγμένος; id.*ep.*4(M.3.1072A); **2.** mentally, *rank with, place in the same category, regard as co-ordinate*; **a.** in gen. τὸν βασιλέα...τοῖς ὑπηκόοις σ. Ath.*Ar.*1.18(M.26.49A); med. σ. ... τούτοις καὶ ἐπαριθμοῖτο ἄν Cyr.*ador.*6(1.197E); **b.** Trin.; **i.** act. οὐ γὰρ ~ομεν υἱὸν τῷ πατρί, ἀλλ' ὑποτεταγμένον *Symb.Sirm.*1 *anath.*18; Ath.*ep.Serap.*1.11(M.26.560B); *ib.*1.2(533B); συναριθμοῦντα αὐτὸ καὶ σ. πατρὶ καὶ υἱῷ Bas.*Spir.*69(3.59A; M.32.197B); *ib.*24(3.21A; M.112A); πατρὶ καὶ υἱῷ αὐτὸ διατελεῖ ~ων, τῇ κτίσει δὲ οὐ συνέταξε πώποτε Thdt.*haer.*3(4.389); abs. πολλοὺς υἱοὺς σ. Ath.*Ar.*2.19(M.26.188A); pass., Bas.*Spir.*24(20E; M.109D); αἱ τὴν αὐτὴν τιμὴν καὶ ἐνέργειαν ἔχουσαι ὑποστάσεις...μόναι...συμφύεσθαι, καὶ σ., καὶ πανταχοῦ συνεπινοεῖσθαι δύνανται τῷ ἑνί Didym.*Trin.*2.6(M.39.520D); Thdt.*rect.conf.*7(M.6.1217C); **ii.** pass., *be in the same category, be associated*, i.e. as being coequal εἰπάτωσαν τίς ἐκ πάντων τούτων ἐστὶν ὁ τῇ τριάδι ~όμενος; Ath.*ep.Serap.*1.11(M.26.560A); κτίσμα δὲ εἰ ἦν τὸ πνεῦμα, οὐκ ἂν συνέταξεν αὐτὸ τῷ πατρί· ἵνα μὴ ᾖ ἀνόμοιος ἑαυτῇ ἡ τριάς, ξένου τινὸς...~ομένου αὐτῇ *ib.*3.6(635D,636A); ἵνα μετὰ πατρὸς καὶ υἱοῦ συνταχθῇ [sc. τὸ πνεῦμα] καὶ γένηται ἡ τριάς [acc. Pneumatomachoi] *ib.*3.7(636C); τὸ...πνεῦμα...διὰ τὴν ἐκ φύσεως κοινωνίαν συντέτακται τῷ θεῷ Bas.*Spir.*30(3.25C; M.32.121A); *ib.*43(3.36E; M.148E); Eunomian view οὔτε μὴν σὺν τῷ πατρί, φασί, καὶ τῷ υἱῷ τὸ πνεῦμα τακτέον, οὐ συντεταγμένον, ἀλλ' ὑποτεταγμένον, οὐδὲ συναριθμούμενον, ἀλλ' ὑπαριθμούμενον *ib.*13(10C; M.88B); Gr.Nyss.*Eun.*1(1 p.67.26; M.45.297A); *be associated in* an action πνεῦμα γὰρ τῷ ζῶντι λόγῳ συντεταγμένον εἰς τὸ δημιουργεῖν Didym.(‡Bas.)*Eun.*5(1.303E; M.29.728D); **iii.** σ. εἰς or ἐν *include (in the category of)* ἐν τούτοις [sc. τοῖς γενητοῖς]...αὐτὸν [sc. τὸν υἱόν] σ. οἱ περὶ Ἄρειον Ath.*Ar.*1.22(M.26.57B); τὸν...λόγον εἰς ἕκαστον τῶν ποιημάτων σ. *ib.*2.11(169C); τὸ πνεῦμα κατάγοντες εἰς τοὺς ἀγγέλους εἰς τὴν τριάδα σ. id.*ep.Serap.*1.10(M.26.557A); ἐν ἀγγέλοις τὸ πνεῦμα σ. *ib.*1.13(564A); pass. ἔδει...καθ' ὑμᾶς, ἅπαξ ἀγγέλου...ὄντος τοῦ πνεύματος, καὶ ~ομένου εἰς τριάδα, μὴ ἕνα, ἀλλὰ καὶ πάντας τοὺς κτισθέντας ἀγγέλους ~εσθαι ταύτῃ *ib.*1.29(597B); **3.** *write, compose, compile* a written work σ. βιβλία πολλά Or.*Jo.*5.2(p.100.16; M.14.188A); τὴν ἐπιστολὴν σ. Marcell.*fr.*77 ap.Eus.*Marcell.*1.4(p.20.34; M.24.757B); ref. OT ἐν βιβλίοις ὑπ' αὐτῶν τῶν προφητῶν συντεταγμένας Just.*1apol.*31.1(M.6.376A); ref. NT, id.*dial.*103.8(M.6.717C); Eus.*l.C.*17(p.256.29; M.20.1433D); id.*h.e.*1.12.4(M.20.120A); of various early Christian writings, Just.*1apol.*26.8(369A); πολλοὶ τῶν μακαρίων ἡμῶν διδασκάλων εἰς ταῦτα συνταχθέντες λόγοι Ath.*gent.*1(M.25.4A); of the works in hand, Just.*2apol.*15.2(M.6.468C); Tat.*orat.*42(p.43.10; M.6.888A); *write*, i.e. *use* a particular word (ref. Lc.22:43) τοῦτο [sc. ἐνισχύω]...σ. καὶ Μωϋσῆς ᾄσας ᾠδήν [Dt.32:43] Didym.*Trin.*3.21(M.39.913A).

B. *arrange, settle, prescribe*; hence **1.** *enact, issue* an edict, Const. ap.Eus.*v.C.*2.51(p.62.30; M.20.1028C); med., Eus.*ib.*1.11(p.12.28; 924C); **2.** med., *give orders*, Ephr.2.186D; **3.** *arrange, settle*, affairs generally; med., *settle one's affairs* before death, Eus.*v.C.*3.46(p.97.1; M.20.1105C); **4.** *constitute, maintain* οἱ...φωστῆρες...μίαν συνταξάμενοι μελῳδίαν id.*l.C.*1(p.198.8; M.20.1321C).

C. med.; **1.** *promise* πάντως...ἔχουσι πολλά σοι συντάξασθαι Marc.Diac.*v.Porph.*29; Anast.S.*defunct.*(M.89.1200A); id.*Ps.*6(M.89.1084B); pass. μακάριος ὅστις ἐφύλαξε καθὼς καὶ συνετάχθη Ephr.2.217A; **2.** *swear allegiance to*, *A.Barn.*12(p.296.24); εἰς ἃ βεβαπτίσμεθα, εἰς ἃ πεπιστεύκαμεν, καὶ οἷς συντετάγμεθα Justn.*conf.*(p.72.15; M.86.995A); in a formula recited by candidate for baptism μετὰ...τὴν ἀποταγὴν...λεγέτω...~ομαι τῷ Χριστῷ *Const.App.*7.41.3; μετὰ τὸ εἰπεῖν 'ἀποτάσσομαί σοι, σατανᾶ, καὶ σ. σοί, Χριστέ' Chrys.*hom.6.4 in Col.*(11.369C); Nil.*epp.*3.287(M.79.525C); cf. πάντες ὁμοίως τῷ διαβόλῳ ἀπεταξάμεθα, ἐμφυσήσαντες αὐτόν· καὶ πάντες ὁμοίως τῷ Χριστῷ σ. προσκυνήσαντες αὐτῷ Ephr.2.195E; Chrys.*hom.1.3 in Eph.*(11.6E) cit. s. ἀποτάσσω; ὑπὲρ...τῶν ἐσχάτῃ νόσῳ κατειλημμένων, μελλόντων τε διὰ τοῦτο βαπτίζεσθαι, καὶ ἀποτάττονταί τινες καὶ σ., τὴν οἰκείαν...κιχρῶντες φωνὴν τοῖς νόσῳ πεπεδημένοις Cyr.*Jo.*7(4.683E); οὐδὲ γὰρ...ὡς ὑπὲρ τοῦ παιδὸς ἐγὼ τὰς ἀποταγάς, ἢ τὰς...ὁμολογίας ποιοῦμαι· ἀλλ' ὅτι ὁ παῖς ἀποτάσσεται καὶ σ. Dion.Ar.*e.h.*7.3.11(M.3.568C); *ib.*2.2.6(396B).

D. med. = ἀποτάσσομαι; *take one's leave, bid* one *farewell* ἐγὼ ἀνῆλθον εἰς τὴν Ῥώμην σ. τῇ ἐκκλησίᾳ καὶ τῷ ἐπισκόπῳ Ath.*apol.sec.*52(p.133.14; M.25.344A); Marc.Diac.*v.Porph.*36; Eus.Al.*serm.*15(M.86.393B); abs. συνταξαμένη ἔσπευδεν...ἀπελθεῖν *A.Xanthipp.*37(p.84.6); μετὰ δακρύων...σ. Pall.*v.Chrys.*10(p.60.26; M.47.35); CCP(448) *act.*3(*ACO* 2.1.1 p.128.31; H.2.148A); *bid a last farewell* to υἱοῖς... καὶ θυγατράσι σ. ... διανεπαύσατο [sc. Constantius] Eus.*v.C.*1.21(p.18.

18; M.20.937B); Ath.*v.Anton*.91(M.26.969B); as variant of ἀποτάσσομαι in Lc.9:61 ἐπίτρεψόν μοι πρῶτον...συντάξασθαι τοῖς εἰς τὸν οἰκόν μου †Bas.*bapt*.1.1.4(2.627B; M.31.1521A); Chrys.*hom.68.5 in Mt*.(7.677C).

E. s.v.l., *disturb, rouse*, prob. for συνταράσσω: Δημήτριος...πᾶσαν κατ' αὐτοῦ τὴν Ἔφεσον σ. Thdt.*2Tim*.4:14f.(3.695).

συντείν-ω, 1. *strain, draw tight, brace up*; lit. and met.; pass., *be distended*; of veins, Clem.*paed*.1.6(p.116.20; M.8.304A); **2.** *strain into* τὸ ἐγγὺς σ. αὐλίας Max.*schol.c.h*.1.3(M.4.36A); **3.** c. εἰς, of time, *extend* (*over* a period); of numbers, *make up, amount to* a sum ἑξακισχιλιοστὸν...ἔτος...ἀπὸ Ἀδὰμ εἰς δεῦρο σ. Meth.*creat*.12(p.499.29; M.18.344B); εἰς ἔτη ἐννέα καὶ τεσσαράκοντα σ. Eus.*d.e*.8.2(p.379.15; M.22.613C); *ib*.(p.381.32; 617C); ~όντων εἰς εἰκοσιδύο ἐπισκόπους Pall.*v.Chrys*.13(p.83.14; M.47.47); *ib*.14(p.89.9; M.47.50); **4.** *be concerned* or *connected with, relate* or *refer to* τὸ ῥητὸν καὶ εἰς τὸν Χριστὸν...σ. καὶ εἰς τὴν ἐκκλησίαν ἀποφηναμένου [sc. S. Paul] Meth.*symp*.3.2(p.29.16; M.18.64B); id.*res*.2.25(p.380.18); τὰ πρὸς τὸν θεοφιλῆ ~οντα βίον Eus.*v.C*.1.11(p.12.31; M.20.924C); τοὺς χρόνους καὶ τὰ τούτοις ~οντα id.*d.e*.8.2(p.375.1; M.22.608D); τὰ σ. κεφάλαια τῶν δέκα λόγων id.*h.e*.2.18.5(M.20.185B); Ath.*Ar*.1.34(M.26.81C).

***συντέκνη, ἡ,** v. σύντεκνος.

***συντεκνία, ἡ,** *co-parentage*, spiritual relationship between two families, e.g. between parents and godparents or sponsors of a candidate for baptism or confirmation; or between best man and bridesmaids on the one hand and bride and groom on the other; religious being forbidden to act as sponsors σὺ σχοίης μετὰ κοσμικῶν ἀδελφοποιΐας ἢ σ., ὁ φυγὰς τοῦ κόσμου καὶ τοῦ γάμου Thdr.Stud.*test*.8 (M.99.1820B); id.*epp*.1.10(M.99.941B); precluded marriage, though one bond of spiritual relationship might be fortified by another γαμβρὸς...μὴ βαπτίσει...τὸ δὲ κατὰ ἀδελφοποιητοῦ...γαμβρὸς...βαπτισάτω. ἐν τούτῳ γὰρ στερεώτερόν ἐστιν ἡ συγγένεια, καὶ ἡ σ., καὶ ἡ φιλία αὐτῷ ἡ καθαρὴ καὶ ἀγαθή *Nomoc*.277; abuse of the relationship regarded with especial horror like incest οἱ τὸν ἅγιον βάπτισμα ἀρνησάμενοι, καὶ οἱ πορνεύοντες περὶ ἄφλεκτον μύρον τῆς σ., καὶ ὁ πορνεύων εἰς μητέρα καὶ θυγατέρα *Apoc.BMV* 23(p.123.20).

***συντέκνισσα, ἡ,** *fellow mother*; of godmother in rel. to mother, Jo.Jej.*canonar*.1(107C).

σύντεκνος ὁ, ἡ, (also **συντέκνη, ἡ**), **1.** in connexion with baptism, *fellow parent* (in respect of mutual relationship of parents and godparents) τίς ἡ εὐδοξία...σου, ὅτι τηλικοῦτον...σ. προσεκτήσω [sc. icon of martyr brought to baptism as sponsor] Thdr.Stud.*epp*.1.17 (M.99.961C); *CIG* 2.2015; marriage bet. those so related regarded as incestuous, †Gregent.*leg.Hom*.(M.86.608B); Jo.Jej.*canonar*.1(107C); τῶν ὑψηλῶν αἱμομιξιῶν...σ. ἢ θυγατρὸς ἧς ἐδέξατο [i.e. god-daughter], ἢ μητρός †Jo.Jej.*serm*.(M.88.1929A); †Jo.Jej.*poenit*.(M.88.1896A); marriage with god-children being forbidden, cf.Justn.*cod*.5.4.26 (p.197); as also marriage between σύντεκνοι, cf.CTrull.*can*.53; conversely a priest must not baptize his own child and so become σ. with his wife, *Nomoc*.54; prohibition of marriage extended to direct descendants, *ib*.189; some authorities included collaterals and contended for identity of treatment between such spiritual affinity and consanguinity, *ib*.159; *ib*.184; **2.** in connexion with marriage (= παράνυμφος) *best man* or *bridesmaid* in relation to groom and bride, *Euchol*.(p.311); *ib*.(p.319); this relationship also constituting a bar to marriage, *Nomoc*.197.

συντεκνόω, *bear children* to, *A.Andr.fr*.4(p.39.20).

συντέλεια, ἡ, A. *joint contribution to public funds* in money or kind; *quota* of contribution ὁ εἰς χρῆσιν λαμβάνων ἀκίνητον πρᾶγμα ...διδότω...ἕτερον ὁμοίας προσόδου τε καὶ σ. Ath.Scholast.*coll*.2.2 (p.30).

B. *end*; **1.** in gen.; **a.** *end* of the day, fig. πρὸ τῆς σ. τῆς ἐν τῷ βίῳ τούτῳ ἡμέρας πνευματικῆς Or.*Jo*.32.2(p.426.12; M.14.741B); of one's life οὐχὶ ἑκάστῳ ἡ σ. τὸ τῆς αὐτοῦ ζωῆς πέρας ἐστί; Chrys.*hom.9.1 in 1Thess*.(11.486A); of other things τὸ 'συντελῶν' δηλοῖ ὅτι πέρας ἔχουσι πάντες λόγοι...πίστεως θεοῦ...οὐχ ὥσπερ ἦν τὰ Ἰουδαίων καὶ μετέπεσεν εἰς τὰ νῦν, ἀλλ' ἐπὶ συντελείᾳ πάσης πίστεως...δέδοται ὁ νῦν τῆς πίστεως λόγος Oecum.*Rom*.9:28(p.429.6); **b.** *completion, fullness* ὁ...θεὸς δίδωσι τόπον μετανοίας καὶ οὐχ ἅμα τῷ ἁμαρτῆσαι κολάζων φέρει τὴν σ. τῆς κολάσεως ἐπὶ τὸν ἡμαρτηκότα Or.*hom.7.1 in Jer*.(p.51.19; M.13.329A); ὀλίγα πρὸς ἱερωσύνης τελείωσιν συνεισφέροντες, πλείω πρὸς φιλοσοφίας σ. ἀντελάμβανον Gr.Naz.*or*.21.20(M.35.1104C); Gr.Nyss.*Eun*.1(1 p.26.1; M.45.253B); **c.** *end, destruction, extermination* εἰς μετάνοιαν καλεῖ, συντελοῦντα βέλη πρὸς συντέλειαν τῶν ἀσεβῶν...ἀποκείμενα ἔχων *Hom.Clem*.16.20; ταῦτα...αὐτοῖς τῆς σ. ἔσται καὶ τοῦ θανάτου τὰ αἴτια Thdr.Mops.*Ps*.58:14(p.388.21; M.66.684A); ἐὰν ἀποθάνῃς, γενικὴ γίνεται σ.; Olymp.*Job* 18 proem.(M.93.196C);

2. *consummation, end* of an age or period μετ' ἐμὲ προφήτης οὐκέτι ἔσται, ἀλλὰ σ. Maximilla ap.Epiph.*haer*.48.2(p.222.2; M.41.857B); ‡Chrys.*pasch*.5(8.263A) cit. s. διάστημα; esp. ref. Heb.9:26 σ. τῶν αἰώνων and Mt.13:39 σ. τοῦ αἰῶνος; meaning discussed ὥσπερ σ. τοῦ ἐνιαυτοῦ ὁ τελευταῖός ἐστι μήν, μεθ' ὃν ἀρχὴ μηνὸς ἑτέρου ἐνίσταται· οὕτω μή ποτε, πλειόνων αἰώνων...συμπληρούντων, σ. ἐστιν ὁ ἐνεστὼς αἰών, μεθ' ὃν μέλλοντές τινες αἰῶνες ἐνστήσονται, ὧν ἀρχή ἐστιν ὁ μέλλων Or.*or*.27(p.374.10ff.; M.11.520C); σ. ... ἐπὶ τὴν Ἱερουσαλήμ, ὅτε ἡ αἰχμαλωσία ἐστὶν ἡ Ναβουχοδονόσορ. καίτοιγε ἐρεῖ τις ὅτι...σ. τῷ λαῷ ἐπὶ τῆς τοῦ...Χριστοῦ παρουσίας id.*hom.7.1 in Jer*.(p.52.16ff.; M.13.329C); **a.** ref. Heb.9:26 ἐπ' ἐσχάτων τῶν ἡμερῶν τῆς σ. φανερὸς ἐγένετο Herm.*sim*.9.12.3; ἡμεῖς οἱ ἐπὶ συντελείᾳ τῶν αἰώνων ἐληλυθότες Or.*engast*.10(p.294.12; M.12.1028D); τοῦτον πιστευόμεν ἐπὶ σ. τῶν αἰώνων εἰς ἀθέτησιν τῆς ἁμαρτίας σάρκα ἀνειληφέναι *Symb.Sel*.(p.258.11; M.26.745A); ὁ υἱός...ἐπὶ σ. τῶν αἰώνων κατελθὼν...τὸν ἡμέτερον ἀνείληφεν ἄνθρωπον †Ath.*exp.fid*.1(M.25.201B); Ath.*Dion*.9(p.52.14; M.25.493A); τὸν ἑαυτοῦ λόγον οὐκ ἀπέστειλεν εἰ μὴ ἐπὶ σ. τῶν αἰώνων id.*Ar*.1.29(M.26.72C); ἐπὶ σ. τῶν αἰώνων γενομένην ἐπιδημίαν...τοῦ μονογενοῦς Cyr.*Ps*.8:1(M.69.757A); **b.** ref. Mt.13:39 al.; **i.** σ. τοῦ αἰῶνος or τῶν αἰώνων alternative expressions, Cyr.*Juln*.10(6^2.329C); Oecum.*Apoc*.10:11(p.125); σ. τῶν ὅλων *Hom.Clem*.9.9; σ. τοῦ παντός Hipp.*haer*.9.30(p.264.16; M.16.3411B); σ. τοῦ κόσμου Tat.*orat*.13(p.14.13; M.6.833A); σ. τοῦ βίου, v. s. βίος; abs., Herm.*vis*.3.8.9; Ath.*ep.Serap*.1.11(M.26.560A); *Const.App*.6.18.9; **ii.** in rel. to time μεχρὶ σ.: ὑπεράνω μὲν τοῦ δημιουργοῦ, ὑποκάτω δὲ ἢ ἔξω τοῦ πληρώματος μεχρὶ σ. Iren.*haer*.1.5.3(M.7.497A); cf. ἐν δεξιᾷ τοῦ δημιουργοῦ...κάθηται... μεχρὶ σ. Clem.*exc.Thdot*.62(p.128.3; M.9.689A); μετέχει...ἡ βασιλεία τῶν Ῥωμαίων τῶν ἀξιωμάτων τῆς βασιλείας τοῦ...Χριστοῦ...ἀήττητος διαμένουσα μεχρὶ τῆς σ. Cosm.Ind.*top*.2(M.88.125A); τῶν ἁγίων αἱ ψυχαὶ τὸ αὐτὸ ποιεῖν οὐ παύσονται μεχρὶ τῆς σ. Eustrat.*stat.anim*.26 (p.535); ἀχρὶ τῆς σ. Clem.*exc.Thdot*.63(p.128.11; 689B); ἡ ψυχὴ μὴ γνοῦσα τὴν ἀλήθειαν...βάλλεται εἰς τὸ μέγα πῦρ ἀχρὶ τῆς σ. Hegem. *Arch*.11(p.18.13; M.10.1445B); ἕως σ.: ἕως σ., ὁ 'ἀνταναίρεσις' ὠνόμασται 'σελήνης' [Ps.71:7] Or.*princ*.4.1.5(p.299.12; M.11.349B); ref. Dan.9:27, *Dial.Christ.et Jud*.17(p.82.13); ἐν τῇ σ. Or.*schol.in Mt*.13:47(M.17.297A); οἱ ἄνθρωποι...υἱοὶ θεοῦ καθιστάμενοι ἐν τῇ σ. τοῦ κόσμου Cosm.Ind.*top*.2(M.88.125A); ἐν ἡμέρᾳ συντελείας Tat.*orat*.17(p.18.18; M.6.841C); ἐπὶ τῇ σ. Or.*Jo*.6.13(7; p.122.24; M.14.224C); μετὰ τὴν σ. Or.*hom.12.10 in Jer*.(p.96.16; M.13.392B); ref. Mt.28:20 οὐκ ἀναιρῶν τὸ συνέσεσθαι αὐτοῖς καὶ μετὰ τὴν σ. Eus.*e.th*.3.14(p.170.33; M.24.1025C); **iii.** its character; a mystery, Eus.*d.e*.6.18(p.278.28; M.22.457C); ἐπείγεται μανθάνειν...ἡμῶν ἡ διάνοια...τὸν περὶ τῆς σ. καιρόν Chrys.*hom.9.1 in 1Thess*.(11.485D); μόνος...οἶδεν ὁ θεὸς...τὴν τῆς σ. ἡμέραν Cyr.*Zach*.105(3.800D); associated with an apocalypse, *A.Jo*.14(p.159.15); with second coming of Christ in glory, Meth.*res*.3.17(p.414.14; M.18.325A); Eus.*d.e*.1.1(p.4.11; M.22.17B); Thdr.Mops.*Gal*.1:4f.(p.6.14; M.66.900A); Chrys.*bapt*.2(2.369C); with judgement and wrath of God, Or.*hom.12.10 in Jer*.(p.96.13; M.13.392B); Eus.*Lc*.27:28ff.(M.24.585A); in credal formulae τὸν ...υἱόν...ἐρχόμενον ἐπὶ συντελείᾳ τοῦ αἰῶνος κρῖναι ζῶντας καὶ νεκρούς *Symb.Ant*.(341)4(p.251.9; M.26.725C); *Symb.Sirm*.1(p.254.25; M.26.736B); with a return to chaos, Const.*or.s.c*.11(p.170.17; M.20.1268C); passing away of all things, Proc.G.*Is*.24:21(M.87.2203C); but not complete destruction οὐ πάντως δὲ ἡ σ. τοῦ παντελοῦς ἀφανισμοῦ ἐστι σημαντική· ἀλλὰ τῆς κατὰ τόδε ἐνεργείας...κωλυτική †Bas.*Is*.60 (1.423D; M.30.224C); rather a transformation σ. καὶ μεταβολὴν τὴν ἐπὶ τὰ κρείττω τοῦδε τοῦ παντός Eus.*d.e*.3.3(p.112.19; M.22.193A); κατὰ τὸν τῆς σ. καιρὸν ἑτέρα τις ἔσται τῆς ὁρωμένης κτίσεως ἡ κατάστασις Cyr.*Zach*.105(3.800A); marked by resurrection of body, Tat.*orat*.6(p.6.16; M.6.817B); Bas.*fid*.4(2.227C; M.31.685B); Chrys.*serm.7.4 in Gen*.(4.680D); establishment of new Jerusalem, Proc.G.*Is*.66:20(M.87.2713A); the kingdom of Christ ἐπουράνιος...καὶ ἀγγελική [sc. ἡ τοῦ Χριστοῦ βασιλεία], ἐπὶ συντελείᾳ τοῦ αἰῶνος γενησομένη Heges.ap.Eus.*h.e*.3.20.4(M.20.253C); ἀρξαμένου τούτων ἁπάντων [i.e. incl. Christ's kingdom] ἐκ τοῦ δηλωθέντος χρόνου, ἔπειτα καιρῷ τῆς σ. τούτων ἁπάντων ἀθρόως παυθήσεται Eus.*Marcell*.2.4(p.56.31; M.24.820B); constituted an article of faith ἀναθεματίζομεν...τούς...Χριστὸν...μὴ εἶναι πρὸ αἰώνων θέλοντας, ἀλλ'...ἐκτότε [i.e. Inc.]...τὸν Χριστὸν ἀρχὴν βασιλείας ἐσχηκέναι ἐθέλουσι, καὶ τέλος ἕξειν αὐτὴν μετὰ τὴν σ. καὶ τὴν κρίσιν *Symb.Ant*.(345)5(p.252.40; M.26.732A); **iv.** ref. eternity of God the Son εἰ...ἐπὶ συντελείᾳ τοῦ παντὸς ἔσται ὁ λόγος ἐν τῷ θεῷ...πῶς ἔσται ὁ λόγος ὁ προελθὼν τοῦ θεοῦ ὥσπερ καὶ πρότερον ἦν πρὸ τοῦ καιροῦ τῆς σ.; Eus.*e.th*.2.9(p.108.13ff.; M.24.916C); *ib*.3.8(p.165.21; 1017A); εἰ...διὰ τὴν κτίσιν ἐπλατύνθη...ἔσται μετὰ τὴν σ. μονὰς ἀπὸ πλατυσμοῦ ‡Ath.*Ar*.4.14(p.59.11; M.26.488B).

C. perh. for συγγενείας: τῶν...τριῶν υἱῶν τοῦ Νῶε, καὶ τῆς σ.

αὐτῶν, καὶ γενεαλογίας, ἐγένετο ἡμῖν ὁ κατάλογος ἐν ἐπιτομῇ ἐν ᾗ προειρήκαμεν βίβλῳ Thphl.Ant.*Autol.*2.31(M.6.1101A).

συντελειόω, pass., *be made perfect* ὑπὸ τοῦ κυρίου σ. Clem.*str.*3.6 (p.221.27; M.8.1160B); ἡ δὲ [sc. πίστις]...σ. τῷ πιστῷ *ib.*5.1(p.327.13; M.9.12A); Pall.*h.Laus.*48(p.143.7; M.34.1211C); Cyr.*ador.*4(1.126D).

συντελείωσις, ἡ, 1. *completion* γαμητέον...καὶ τῆς πατρίδος ἕνεκα καὶ...τῆς τοῦ κόσμου...σ. Clem.*str.*2.23(p.190.16; M.8.1089B); **2.** *perfection* τοὺς σπευδόντας εἰς σ. *ib.*4.21(p.306.11; 1341B).

***συντελεσμός, ὁ,** = συντέλεια, *end, consummation* μεχρὶ ἡμέρας κρίσεως αὐτῶν καὶ σ. *Apoc.En.*10.12.

συντελεστής, ὁ, 1. member of a body responsible for collection and payment of its taxes, Socr.*h.e.*4.34.5(M.67.556A); *tributary*, of one ruler to another ἐγένετο αὐτοῦ...δοῦλος, τουτέστιν σ. *Chron. Pasch.*p.107(M.92.285B); **2.** *accomplisher, perfecter* ἡ σοφία...ὁ σ. καὶ μεταποιητής Gr.Naz.*or.*30.15(p.131.15; M.36.124A); τῷ σ. τῶν ἀμηχάνων Geo.Pis.*hex.*1028(M.92.1513A); τὸν...τοῦ θεοῦ λόγον...σ. τοῦ αἰῶνος Max.*ambig.*(M.91.1120B); *ib.*(1357B).

συντελεστικός, 1. *completing, perfecting*, Melet.*nat.hom.*synops. (M.64.1104C); **2.** of the συντέλεια τοῦ αἰῶνος, ref. Mc.13:32 οὐδεὶς οἶδε τὴν σ. ἡμέραν καὶ τὴν ὥραν ‡Gr.Nyss.*Ar.et Sab.*6(M.45.1289A).

συντελ-έω, 1. *bring to an end, complete, finish* ἐν ἑξακισχιλίοις ἔτεσιν ~εσθήσεται τὰ σύμπαντα *Barn.*15.4; μετὰ τὸ σ. αὐτὸν τὰς ἐπιλύσεις Herm.*sim.*8.11.1; ἐπὶ...τοῦ σωτῆρος...τά τε παραπτώματα παλαιοῦται καὶ αἱ ἁμαρτίαι σ. Afric.*chron.*16.2(M.10.80B); ref. Creation χρονικοῖς ἐξ διαστήμασι σ. τὸν κόσμον *Hom.Clem.*17.9; τὴν οἰκουμένην σ. [i.e. Wisdom] Ath.*Ar.*2.82(M.26.320C); pass., of a harvest, *be gathered in*, Meth.*symp.*9.1(p.114.9; M.18.177A); **2.** pass. intrans., *finish in* εἰς πῆχυν ἄνωθεν σ. Clem.*str.*6.11(p.475.6; M.9.308B); **3.** *accomplish, carry out, execute*, Herm.*sim.*5.3.7; τὰ...νόμιμα σ. Eus.*d.e.*1.6(p.28.29; M.22.57B); *ib.*1.7(p.38.20; 73D); *go through* temptation, ‡Ath.*Apoll.*2.9(M.26.1148A); pass., *be brought about*, Clem.*str.*6.15(p.497.8; M.9.353A); of prophecy, *be fulfilled*, Just.*1apol.*32.6(M.6.380A); **4.** ?med. or pass., *bear upon, be concerned with* τὸ...κεφάλαιον τῆς προφητείας...ἐπὶ μεγάλοις συνετελεῖτο Eus.*d.e.*5 proem.(p.206.22; M.22.344A); **5.** *make an end of, destroy* σ. ... τοὺς υἱοὺς Ἐμμώρ *T.Lev.*5.4; Adam.*dial.*1.13(p.28.21; M.11.1737C); Thdr.Mops.*Ps.*58:14(p.388.20; M.66.684A); **6.** *put to death*, *A.Petr.et Paul.*79(p.212.13); **7.** *pay towards common expenses, pay taxes*; *provide* recruits τὸν...~ούμενον ἐκ τῶν ἐπαρχιῶν κατὰ κώμας στρατιώτην ἐξηργύρισεν Socr.*h.e.*4.34.5(M.67.553C); gen., of persons, *provide, give*, Herm.*mand.*12.3.2; Eus.*d.e.*1.1(p.3.11; M.22.16C); of things, *contribute*; with neg., *guard against, spare...from* σ. ... πρὸς τὸ μηδὲ...ἡμᾶς ἐναπομεῖναι ταῖς...φαντασίαις Dion.Ar.*c.h.*15.9(M.3.340B); dat., *be profitable, help*; abs., Proc.G.*Gen.*3:24(M.87.228D); **8.** *belong* to a class τοὺς ἐς τὸ σῶμα ~οῦντας τῆς ἐκκλησίας Gr.Nyss. *hom.14 in Cant.*(M.44.1064A); id.*Eun.*1(1 p.202.23; M.45.449C); τῶν εἰς τὴν ἐκκλησίαν δοκούντων ~εῖν Chrys.*virg.*14(1.278E).

συντέμν-ω, 1. *cut down, cut short*; met., *curb* ἄφεσιν βούλει λαβεῖν; ...τὰ...πάθη σύντεμε Clem.*q.d.s.*40(p.187.3; ~ε M.9.645C); **2.** of verbal expression, *cut (the matter) short, make an end, state briefly*; freq. of the gospel (cf. Is.10:23 cit. Rom.9:28; Is.28:22) ὁ Παῦλος... ὁ τοῦ συντετμημένου λόγου κῆρυξ Gr.Naz.*or.*27.1(p.2.2; M.36.12A); τὸν σ. τοῦ εὐαγγελίου λόγον Gr.Nyss.*hom.14 in Cant.*(M.44.1077C); Leont.B.*Nest.et Eut.*1(M.86.1297B); τὸ εὐαγγέλιον πλατὺ καὶ μέγα, καὶ αὖθις συντετμημένον Dion.Ar.*myst.*1.3(M.3.1000B); Χριστὸς συντετμημένη πίστει δικαιῶν Proc.G.*Is.*28:22(M.87.2249A).

συντηρ-έω, 1. *keep, maintain closely* σ. τῷ λόγῳ, καθ' ὃν ἐγένετο Gr.Naz.*or.*28.31(p.70.7; M.36.72A); *maintain, preserve* in being θεοῦ τὸ σ. διὰ προνοίας τὰ ὄντα Gr.Nyss.*or.catech.*12(p.59.4; M.45.44D); Max.*ambig.*(M.91.1156D); τὴν τὸ φῶς ~οῦσαν τῆς γνώσεως θεωρίαν *ib.*(1125C); ref. hypostatic union ὑπόστασιν μίαν...τῇ κατὰ φύσιν τῶν ἐξ ὧν συνετέθη μερῶν ὑπάρξει ~ουμένην id.*ep.*15(M.91.556C); fig., ref. Mt.5:13 τὸ ἁλίζον καὶ σ. τὴν γῆν Or.*Jo.*6.59(38; p.168.12; M.14.304A); in safety μετ' αὐτῶν ἔσομαι καὶ σ. αὐτούς Herm. *mand.*5.1.7; ὁ υἱὸς κατέστησε τοὺς ἀγγέλους ἐπ' αὐτοὺς τοῦ ~εῖν αὐτούς id.*sim.*5.6.2; Just.*dial.*30.2f.(M.6.540A); *Pap.Chr.*(p.401); **2.** *observe, practise* ἀδελφότητα σ. Herm.*mand.*8.10.

συντήρησις, ἡ, 1. *preservation, maintenance* τὴν ζῴων ψύχωσιν, μᾶλλον δὲ τῆς ψυχῆς πρὸς τὸ σῶμα Gr.Naz.*or.*28.28(p.65.6; M.36.65B); ἡ ψυχὴ...ὅλη παροῦσα τὰ...μέλη...πρὸς τὴν τοῦ ἓν εἶναι σῶμα σ. ἐπισφίγγει Max.*ambig.*(M.91.1100B); in being τὴν σ. ... τῆς σωματικῆς οὐσίας Gr.Nyss.*or.dom.*4(p.78.28; M.44.1169A); of eucharist αὐτὸ τὸ σῶμα καὶ αὐτὸ τὸ αἷμα εἰς σύστασιν τῆς ἡμετέρας ψυχῆς τε καὶ σώματος χωροῦν...οὐκ εἰς ἀφεδρῶνα...ἀλλ' εἰς τὴν ἡμῶν οὐσίαν τε καὶ σ. Jo.D.*fr.Mt.*(M.96.1409C); esp. *conservation* of creation τὴν ὧν πεποιήκασιν οἰκονομίαν καὶ σ. Gr.Naz.*or.*30.11(p.125.1; M.36.117B); ἡ τῆς κτίσεως συνοχή, καὶ σ. Jo.D.*f.o.*1.3(M.94.796C); τὴν...κατασκευὴν καὶ σ. τῆς κτίσεως †Jo.D.*B.J.*17(M.96.1012A); πάντα...διὰ τὴν σὴν πρόνοιαν καὶ σ. γεγονότα Melet.*nat.hom.*30(M.64.1277C); **2.** *observance, keeping* σ. τῶν ἐντολῶν...Χριστοῦ *Mir.Geo.*4 epilog.(p.44.2); **3.** *keeping, holding in one's possession* τὸ...πατρῷον ὁ παῖς οὐ παρεδέξατο μίασμα, ἀλλὰ τοῦ κλήρου τῆς δυσσεβείας ἀποστάσιον ἐποιήσατο...συντηρήσει μεμφόμενος Sophr.H.*v.Anast.*(M.92.1684B).

***συντηρητής, ὁ,** *upholder, preserver*, Areth.*Apoc.*4:10(M.106.576B).

συντηρητικός, 1. *conserving, preserving* in being, of God ὑπερκεῖσθαί τινα δύναμιν ποιητικὴν τῶν γινομένων καὶ σ. τῶν ὄντων καταλαμβάνομεν Gr.Nyss.*or.catech.*12(p.58.16; M.45.44D); id.*deit.*(M.46.564C); Sophr.H.*ep.syn.*(M.87.3157A); Max.*ambig.*(M.91.1133D); Jo.D.*f.o.*1.8(M.94.808C); of Son, Gr.Naz.*or.*30.20(p.139.16; M.36.129B); of whole Trin., Gr.Nyss.*tres dii*(M.45.128D); **2.** *protective* σ. φωνὴν [i.e. εἰρήνη πᾶσιν] Eustrat.*v.Eutych.*25(M.86.2304A).

συντίθ-ημι, I. act. and pass.; **A.** *place* or *put together*; pass., of various physical features, *be close together* ὀφρύσι συντεθειμένοις Hipp.*haer.*4.17(p.50.20; M.16.3083D); ὀφθαλμοῖς...σ. *ib.*4.20(p.51.22; cf.3086C); hence, of ears, *be close to the head*, *ib.*4.22(p.52.15; 3087A); of hair, *lie close to the head, be smooth* τριχὶ καλῶς συντεθειμένῃ *ib.*4.20(p.51.23; 3086C).

B. *put together constructively* so as to make a whole; **1.** *compound* medicines, Bas.*hom.*14.4(2.125E; M.31.452B); fig. Χριστὸς...ἐκ τῶν οὐρανίων ~εὶς ἀρωμάτων τὸ μύρον Clem.*paed.*2.8(p.197.3; M.8.472B); *frame* laws, Arist.*apol.*13.7; ref. Creation οὐ...σύνθετος ὁ θεὸς ὁ τὰ πάντα εἰς τὸ εἶναι συντεθεικώς Ath.*ep.Afr.*8(M.26.1044B); **2.** pass. with ἐκ, *be composed of, consist of*, Clem.*str.*1.24(p.100.30; M.8.908B); τὴν ὕλην...ἐξ ἁπλῶν τινων συντεθεῖσθαι Meth.*arbitr.*12(p.176.5f.; M.18.260C); ref. man; of body and soul, id.*res.*1.34(p.272.9; M.41.1097D) cit. s. ἄνθρωπος; *ib.*1.50(p.304.10; M.18.280C); Cyr.*ep.*45 (p.154.7; 5².138A); Leont.H.*Nest.*1.16(M.86.1460D); **3.** *compose* or *comport oneself* ἐὰν...ἀνεπιτηδεύτως συνθεῖσα ἑαυτὴν εἰσέλθῃ Chrys. *hom.28.5 in Heb.*(12.265A); **4.** in writing, *narrate*; *compose* music, ref. Rom.1:25 ὡς εἴ τις τὸ μὲν μουσικὸν ὄργανον ἐπαινοίη, τὸν δὲ συνθέντα καὶ ἁρμοσάμενον ἐκβάλλοι...πῶς γὰρ ἂν ἔγνωσαν ἄλλως οἰκοδομὴν...ἢ λύραν, μὴ οὐχὶ...τοῦ ἀρχιτέκτονος οἰκοδομήσαντος, καὶ τοῦ μουσικοῦ σ.; Ath.*gent.*47(M.25.96A,B); **5.** *join, unite* τὰ διὰ τῶν μέσων συσφιγγόμενα ἢ διακρινόμενα τῇ αὐτοῦ διαταγῇ τε καὶ συνοχῇ, καὶ διατηρεῖσθαί τε καὶ ~εσθαι Leont.H.*Nest.*1.13(M.86.1452B); φύσις πυρὸς...συνετέθη τῇ φύσει τοῦ σιδηροῦ *ib.*1.49(1512B); Jews with gentiles in Church Ἰσραὴλ...περιμένων δέ, ὥσπερ ἐκ τῆς τῶν ἐθνῶν κλήσεως ὑποστρέφοντα Χριστὸν...τῷ τῆς ἀγάπης νόμῳ μονονουχὶ καὶ συνθῆσαι [sic] τοῖς ἄλλοις Cyr.*glaph.Gen.*5(1.163B).

C. *piece together, concoct, devise*, in disparaging sense ἐκ τῆς... μετανοίας κατεμάνθανον τὴν κατὰ Ἀθανασίου συντεθεῖσαν συκοφαντίαν Ath.*h.Ar.*79(p.227.33; M.25.789C); οἱ τὰ πρῶτα πλάσαντες αὐτοὶ καὶ ταῦτα συνέθηκαν id.*apol.Const.*2(p.280.6; M.25.597A); ἐμελέτων καὶ συνετίθουν id.*ep.encycl.*6(p.175.19; M.25.236B); σ. τὸν ὁμώνυμόν σου θεόν Gr.Naz.*or.*29.18(p.101.7; M.36.97B); οὔτε...συνέθηκαν [sc. οἱ μάγοι] ἀπὸ τῆς τῶν ἄστρων κινήσεως τὰ μέλλοντα ἔσεσθαι Chrys.*hom.* *6.1 in Mt.*(7.85A); κατά τινων σ. συντριβάς Cyr.*Mich.*16(p.625.16; Aubert om.); a creed: of Theophronius of Tyana, Ath.*syn.*24 (p.250.5; M.26.724C); of CSirm.(357) συνέθηκαν αὖθις πίστιν *ib.*27 (p.254.14; 736A).

D. Christol. (pass.); **1.** Arian [Jo.1:14] ἀντὶ τοῦ συνετέθη σαρκί, οὐ μὴν ψυχῇ Luc.Al.*fr.pasch.*ap.*Doct.Patr.*9(p.65.17); **2.** Apoll., *become one with, be identified with*; **a.** of the flesh, Apoll.*fr.*107(p.232.13,21)ap.Justn.*monoph.*(M.86.1124A) cit. s. αὐτοκίνητος; **b.** of the divinity τὸ ἀόρατον καὶ συντεθὲν πρὸς σῶμα ὁρατὸν...μένει καὶ ἀόρατον *ib.*133(p.239.21)ap.Thdt.*eran.*2(4.172); δεῖ...τῇ πάντων ἐπέκεινα... φύσει σῴζεσθαι καθαρῶς τὸ ἁπλοῦν καὶ ἀσυμμιγὲς ἑτέρῳ, καὶ τὸ μὴ συντεθεῖσθαι δοκεῖν ἔν γε τοῖς καθ' ἑαυτήν Cyr.*synous.*3(p.480.11); Leont.H.*Nest.*1.16(M.86.1461B) cit. s. ἄνθρωπος; **3.** of both natures, *be conjoined* or *united* μίαν τὴν θατέρου τῶν συγκειμένων ὑπόστασιν *ib.*1.49(1512B); οὐ...δυνατὸν τὸ σύνθετον τῇ τῶν συντεθειμένων ὀνομάζεσθαι προσηγορίᾳ Max.*Pyrr.*(M.91.296C); id.*ambig.*(M.91.1060B); **4.** *be made* or *become composite*, Gr.Naz.*carm.*1.1.10.25(M.37.467A) cit. s. ἀνθρωπολάτρης; τοῖς καθ' ἡμᾶς...ἐν μιᾷ τῶν αὐτῆς ὑποστάσεων ἐκοινώνησεν [sc. ἡ θεαρχία], ἀνακαλουμένη πρὸς ἑαυτὴν καὶ ἀνατιθεῖσα τὴν ἀνθρωπίνην ἐσχατίαν, ἐξ ἧς ἀρρήτως ὁ ἁπλοῦς Ἰησοῦς συνετέθη Dion.Ar.*d.n.*1.4(M.3.592A); Mod.*dorm.*13(M.86.3309A) cit. s. ἁπλοῦς; **5.** with ἐκ, of Christ as God and man in one Person περὶ τοῦ συνθέτου, καὶ ἐξ ὧν συνέκειτο ⟨ὁ⟩ ἐνανθρωπήσας Ἰησοῦς Or.*Cels.*1.66 (p.121.1; M.11.785A); οὔτε συγκέχυται τὰ ἐξ ὧν συντεθεῖται φυσικῶς

Sever.*1Tim.*2:5f.(p.337.1); τῶν φύσεων, ἐξ ὧν καὶ συνετέθη Justn.*conf.*(p.74.19; M.86.997A); τὸν αὐτὸν...ὁμολογοῦντες ἐν θεότητι...καὶ ἐν ἀνθρωπότητι, ἐξ ὧν καὶ συνετέθη Just.Imp.*edict.*ap.Evagr.*h.e.*5.4 (p.199.34; M.86.2797B); Χριστὸν...ἐκ δύο συντεθέντα τῶν φύσεων CLater.*can.*1; πρεσβεύομεν...ἐπὶ Χριστοῦ μίαν ὑπόστασιν σύνθετον, ἐκ δύο συντεθειμένην φύσεων ‡Cyr.*Trin.*18(6^{3}.24B; M.77.1157A); *ib.* 27(33B; 1172B); ὑπόστασιν μίαν...σύνθετον, τῇ κατὰ φύσιν τῶν ἐξ ὧν συνετέθη μερῶν ὑπάρξει συντηρουμένην Max.*ep.*15(M.91.556C).

II. med.; **A.** *excogitate, devise for oneself* ἅπερ ἔκρυψαν αὐτοὶ πράξαντες, καὶ καθ' ἑαυτοὺς ἐν γωνίᾳ συνέθεντο Ath.*apol.sec.*2(p.88.18; M.25.249C).

B. *agree* with persons ὁ...Χριστός, εἰ μὴ ἦν ἀνάστασις σαρκός... συνέθετο ἂν αὐτοῖς [sc. τοῖς Σαδδουκαίοις] Meth.*res.*1.51(p.305.5; M.18.281A); μή με βιάζου ἀκρίτως συνθέσθαι σοι *Hom.Clem.*16.4; σ. τοῖς Ἀρειανοῖς Ath.*ep.Serap.*1.10(M.26.556B); *agree* that ὅτι...εὐσέβεια καλόν, κἀγὼ σ. Just.*dial.*4.7(M.6.485C); *Hom.Clem.*20.6; μαρτυροῦντες οἰκείᾳ φωνῇ [i.e. in the 'Amen'] καὶ ~έμενοι ὡς ἀληθές ἐστι [sc. body and blood of Christ in eucharist] Sophr.H.*mir.Cyr.et Jo.*38 (M.87.3568A); *agree* on or about πάντων...ἐπὶ τούτῳ συνθεμένων Ath.*syn.*9(p.236.18; M.26.693C); ἀλλήλοις σ. περὶ τῶν ὑποστάσεων id.*tom.*10(M.26.808C); abs., *be agreed* συντεθεμένων πάντων Just.*dial.*130.1(M.6.777B); ἠναγκάσθησαν συνθέσθαι *Hom.Clem.*12.3; Ath.*ep.Afr.*5 (M.26.1037B).

C. *assent to* ἀντειπὼν πολλάκις οἷς συνετέθης Just.*dial.*67.11(M.6.632C); τῷ ἀληθεῖ σ. *ib.*44.1(569B); Bas.*hom.*13.1(2.114C; M.31.425B); τῇ...αἱρέσει σ. Hipp.*haer.*8.19(p.238.19; M.16.3367A); Ath.*apol.fug.*4 (p.71.5; M.25.649B).

D. *grant, concede, allow* that ἐγὼ φαιδόμενος ὑμῶν, ὦ οὗτοι, ταῦτα συνεθέμην Meth.*symp.*3.13(p.42.23; M.18.84A); Ath.*Ar.*2.4(M.26.153C); σ. ... ὅτι...ἐνεδήμησεν id.*tom.*7(M.26.804B); σ. ... βελτίονα... εἶναι *ib.*6(804A); Jo.D.*f.o.*1.3(M.94.796B); abs. οὔτε σ. οὔτε ἀποτάσσομαι Epiph.*anc.*43(p.53.19; M.43.93C).

E. *covenant* or *agree* to do; of soldiers as bound by the *sacramentum* τοὺς ~εμένους καὶ καταλεγομένους στρατιώτας Just.*1apol.*39.5 (M.6.388C); *consent* to temptation ταῖς...κακαῖς...ἐπινοίαις...σ. *Hom.Clem.*9.12; σ. ταῖς κακαῖς...ἐπιθυμίαις *ib.*11.3; *promise* to do σ., ὀμόσας μηκέτι ἱερατεύειν Pall.*h.Laus.*18(p.54.13; M.34.1059B); προσπεσόντες σ. αὐτῷ μηκέτι προσεγγίζειν τινί Cyr.S.*v.Sab.*59(p.160.24); *ib.*56(p.150.8); σ. τῷ ἁγίῳ οὕτως ποιεῖν id.*v.Euthym.*43(p.63.28); πληροῖς ὅσα συνέθου τῷ θεῷ *ib.*10(p.20.11); σ. τῷ θεῷ μηκέτι ἀδικῆσαι ἄνθρωπον id.*v.Sab.*34(p.120.1).

συντίκτ-ω, **1.** *procreate together*, ptcpl., of parents μονογενὴς...ἐάν γε κράτῃ τὰ ὑμέτερα, μὴ μονώσεως ἀδελφῶν, ἀλλ' ἐρημίας τῶν ~όντων δηλωτικὸν εἶναι Bas.*Eun.*2.21(1.257A; M.29.617B); **2.** *confound, confuse* οὐκέτ' ἂν ἐν τῷ κοινῷ τῆς φύσεως τὸν τῶν ὑποστάσεων λόγον ~ειν αἰτιαθείημεν. ἐπειδὴ τοίνυν τὰς μὲν ὑποστάσεις...ὁ τοῦ αἰτίου διακρίνει λόγος Gr.Nyss.*tres dii*(M.45.133D).

***συντολμητής**, ὁ, *fellow adventurer*; of Barabbas as *accomplice* of the Jews, Isid.Pel.*epp.*1.292(M.78.353B).

συντομία, ἡ, **1.** *brevity, conciseness*; in concrete sense, *epitome, compendium*, ref. Jon.3:4f., τῇ σ. τοῦ κηρύγματος ἕπεσθαι, ἧς ὑπακούσαντες οἱ Νινευεῖται...τὴν καλὴν ἀντικατηλλάξαντο σωτηρίαν Clem.*prot.*10(p.72.14; M.8.213B); τὴν ἐπὶ ταῖς ἀρεταῖς πρακτικὴν σ. Max.*ambig.*(M.91.1125C); *curtness, abruptness* μεγάλη...σ. τοῦτό ἐστιν, εἰπεῖν ὅτι τὸν κόσμον ἔξελθε *T.Abr.*B 4(p.109.5); *suddenness* τῆς τοῦ θαύματος σ. Gr.Mag.*dial.*(tr.Zach.)2.31(M.*PL.*66.192A); ἐν σ. *in a short while, soon* ἀποδώσει τὴν ψυχὴν ἐν σ. Andr.Cr.*or.*19(M.97.1245B); **2.** *division*, ref. schism ὥστε μηδεμίαν...τῆς ἑνότητος συντομίαν περιεργάζεσθαι (tr. Lat. *concisio*) *Cod.Afr.*68.

συντόμιον, τό, *tessera, tally, token*, Jo.Mal.*chron.*13 p.322(M.97.484A); Jo.Mosch.*prat.*184(M.87.3057B).

***συντομολογία**, ἡ, = συντομία, *brevity*, ‡Ath.*def.*1.3(M.28.533C).

σύντομος, *cut short, abridged*; esp. of a road, *short* cut; **1.** of language; **a.** *concise, brief*; ἐν σ. *in brief*, Hipp.*haer.*7.14(p.191.15; M.16.3295B); Chrys.*hom.12.1 in Heb.*(12.121B); of the gospel (cf. Is.10:23 = Rom.9:28) ὁ σ. τοῦ εὐαγγελίου λόγος Eus.*d.e.*2.3 (p.80.8; M.22.144B); διδάσκει τοῦ κηρύγματος τὸ σ. Thdt.*Is.*10:22f. (p.57.18; 1.246); **b.** *curt, terse, clean-cut* βραχεῖς...καὶ σ. παρ' αὐτοῦ λόγοι γεγόνασιν· οὐ γὰρ σοφιστὴς ὑπῆρχεν Just.*1apol.*14.5(M.6.349A); τοῦ κελεύσματος τοῦ σ. *Hom.Clem.*7.10; Cyr.ap.*cat.Lc.*14:23 (p.115.3); cf.Cyr.*Lc.*14:23(συντονωτέρας M.72.792D); **2.** ref. time, *prompt, quick, sudden* σ. μοι [sc. τὰ θηρία] Ign.*Rom.*5.2; σ. ... θάνατον Or.*Ps.*54:21(p.59); Chrys.*hom.22.3 in Eph.*(11.168F); τὸν σ. πρὸς βοήθειαν...Ἀρτέμιον *Mir.Artem.*33(p.51.2); neut. as subst., ref. Ps.75:7 νυσταγμὸν...ἐκάλεσε τοῦ θανάτου τὸ σ. Thdt.*Is.*10:26 (p.58.17).

***συντομουργός**, *working quickly* τὴν σ. τοῦ θεοῦ λεπτουργίαν Geo.Pis.*hex.*1505(M.92.1550A).

συντονία, ἡ, **1.** physical *tension*; *straining* of the eye; fig., of the eye of the soul, Dion.Ar.*c.h.*15.1(M.3.328A); **2.** *zeal* in the way of Christian perfection, Isid.Pel.*epp.*1.283(M.78.349A); *ib.*1.202(312C); **3.** *intensity* of powers or activities ἐν σ. τοῦ θείου...ἔρωτος Dion.Ar.*c.h.*4.2(M.3.180A); τῇ πρὸς τὸ ἓν ἐν σ. συννεύσει id.*e.h.*2.3.8(M.3.404C); τὴν αἰώνιον αὐτῶν [sc. the seraphim]...ἐν σ. πάσῃ καὶ εὐχαριστίᾳ τῶν θείων ἐπιστήμην *ib.*4.3.5(480C).

σύντονος, **1.** *strained tight, taut*; of a road, *straight*, Clem.*paed.*1.3 (p.95.23; M.8.260B); **2.** *intense, eager, vehement*; of powers, esp. desires, and actions προστάγμασι σ. Clem.*q.d.s.*34(p.183.2; M.9.640D); neut. as adv., *intently* σ. βλέπειν Bas.*leg.lib.gent.*4(p.49; M.31.573B); neut. as subst., *zeal, eagerness* in the way of Christian perfection τὸ σ. τῆς ἀληθείας Ign.*Polyc.*7.3; τὸ πρὸς τὰς εὐχὰς σ. Ath.*v.Anton.*4(M.26.845A); *strain* τὸ...σ. τῆς...πορείας Gr.Nyss.*v.Mos.*34(M.44.312B).

συντοξεύω, *shoot together*, i.e. from the same side in a war, Isid.Pel.*epp.*3.3(M.78.729A).

***συντρανίζω**, v. συνερανίζω.

***συντραυλίζω**, *lisp together* with σ. τοῖς νηπίοις Clem.*paed.*1.6 (p.109.11; M.8.288C).

συντρέχεια, ἡ, *compliance* ἄλλων...μετὰ...πανουργίας καὶ σ. ἀπατώντων Or.ap.*cat.Eph.*4:14(p.172.5) for ἐντρεχ-, id.*comm.in Eph.* 4:14ff.(p.415).

συντρέχ-ω, **A.** *run together* so as to meet; **1.** *assemble, gather*, for synod ὥστε...ἐπισκόπους...σ. κατά τινα σκέψιν πολιτικήν Synes.*ep.*67(M.66.1421A); προσέταξεν ἐκεῖ σ. παρεγγυήσας τὴν σύνοδον Thdt.*h.e.*2.26.1(3.892); ὥρισε...δὶς τοῦ ἐνιαυτοῦ ἐπὶ τὸ αὐτὸ σ. ... τοὺς ἐπισκόπους CChalc.*can.*19; of parts, *be assembled*, Amph.*hom.*3.5(M.39.65A); **2.** of events, *concur, coincide* πολλὰ...ἐφ' ἓν ἀποτέλεσμα σ. Clem.*str.*8.9(p.97.16; M.9.593D); esp. *synchronize* συνδραμούσης τῇ τοῦ σωτῆρος...διδασκαλίᾳ...τῆς τῶν ἐθνῶν πάντων ὁμονοίας Eus.*l.C.*17 (p.257.20; M.20.1436C); of times and seasons, Afric.*chron.*16.2(M.10.81B); κατὰ τὸ αὐτὸ ~όντων τῶν χρόνων τῆς γεννήσεως αὐτοῦ καὶ τῆς συμπληρώσεως τῶν παρὰ τῷ Δανιὴλ...ἑβδομάδων Eus.*d.e.*8.2(p.383.14; M.22.620D); astrol., of conjunction of stars, Synes.*ep.*4(M.66.1337A); **3.** of liquids, *mingle*; met., *coalesce, coincide* δεῖ...ἀμφοτέρων τὴν πίστιν σ. καὶ τοῦ ὑγιαζομένου καὶ τοῦ ὑπερευχομένου Ammon.*Ac.* 3:16(M.85.1525B); of persons, *mix* or *associate with* τῷ ἀγαπῶντι τὸν θεὸν σ. *T.Benj.*4.5; μετὰ ἁμαρτωλῶν καὶ πονηρῶν σ. *Barn.*4.2; *join together, be united* πάντες ὡς εἰς ἕνα ναὸν ~ετε Ign.*Magn.*7.2; ref. Jo.14:27 οὐκ ἄλλο δὲ τοῦτό ἐστιν ἢ τοὺς πιστεύοντας εἰς αὐτὸν εἰς μίαν καὶ τὴν αὐτὴν ἐκκλησίαν σ. Just.Imp.*edict.*ap.Evagr.*h.e.*5.4 (p.198.5; M.86.2796A); *ib.*(p.200.32; 2800B); of body and soul in man, Cyr.*Heb.*2:14(p.463.21; M.74.964D); Anast.S.*hod.*2(M.89.69D); **4.** Christol.; **a.** of natures united in Christ δύο φύσεις εἰς ἓν σ. Gr.Naz.*or.*37.2(M.36.285A); Cyr.*hom.pasch.*17.2(5^{2}.226E); id.*synous.*5 (p.483.7); id.*ep.*1(p.15.32; 5^{2}.9B) cit. s. ἀνακίρνημι; σωζομένης...τῆς ἰδιότητος ἑκατέρας φύσεως καὶ εἰς ἓν πρόσωπον...~ούσης *Symb.Chalc.* (p.129.33; H.2.456C); εἰ δὲ δύο φύσεις ὑποθώμεθα ἔχειν τὸν Χριστόν, οὐδὲν τούτων ἀναιροῦμεν τῶν ἀρχῶν, ἀλλὰ πάντα ~οντα εὑρίσκομεν Leont.B.*fr.*(M.86.2016A); οὔτε τινὸς ἑτέρου σὰρξ τῶν καθ' ἡμᾶς ἀνθρώπων γέγονε πώποτε. καὶ τότε τῷ θεῷ λόγῳ σ. καὶ τὴν πρὸς αὐτὸν ἐποιήσατο σύνθεσιν Sophr.H.*or.*2.46(M.87.3277C); ὁ...τῆς ἑνώσεως λόγος τῆς φυσικῆς...τηρεῖ συνδραμόντα πρὸς ἕνωσιν ἄτρεπτα id.*ep.syn.*(M.87.3165B); Andr.Cr.*Agath.*87(M.97.1441A); **b.** of the two wills δύο φυσικὰ θελήματά τε καὶ ἐνεργείας...πρὸς σωτηρίαν τοῦ ἀνθρωπίνου γένους καταλλήλως ~οντα *Symb.CP*(681)(H.3.1401B).

B. *run alongside, run parallel with*; **1.** met. ἅμα τῷ βουληθῆναι γνησίως τὸ σωθῆναι σ., ὁμοζυγούντων...προαιρέσεως καὶ ζωῆς Clem.*prot.*11(p.82.26; M.8.236D); **2.** *run a race with, race in company*; met., of Christian race σ. συμπάσχετε Ign.*Polyc.*6.1; **3.** *concur, agree*; *concede* a point in argument συνέδραμε τῷ λόγῳ Chrys.*hom.6.4 in Rom.*(9.477E); *agree, conform to, comply with* σ. τῇ γνώμῃ τοῦ θεοῦ Ign.*Eph.*3.2; σ. τῇ τοῦ ἐπισκόπου γνώμῃ *ib.*4.1; μελετήσαντες σ. τῷ θελήματι τοῦ θεοῦ Clem.*str.*4.21(p.307.7; M.8.1344B); οὐκ ἤλλαξαν [sc. Jews in time of Christ]...ἀλλὰ συνέτρεχε τῷ χρόνῳ τῶν προγόνων ἡ γνώμη Bas.Sel.*or.*31.2(M.85.341B); *side with, take the part of, abet* σ. τοῖς κατ' αὐτοῦ συκοφάνταις Eus.*d.e.*3.5(p.129.28; M.22.220C); παραδοθέντες εἰς κρίσιν θανάτου, μετὰ τοῦ συνδραμόντος αὐτοῖς... δαίμονος Valent.Imp.*ep.episc.*ap.Thdt.*h.e.*4.8.6(3.958); **4.** *be contemporaneous with, endure for* or *as long as* τὴν τοῖς ἀπεράντοις αἰῶσι ~ουσαν εὐημερίαν ἀποληψόμεθα Cyr.*glaph.Dt.*(1.429A); theol., of Son as coeternal with Father σ. τῇ τοῦ πατρὸς ἀϊδιότητι id.*thes.*5 (5^{1}.41C).

συντριβή, ἡ, **1.** *friction* εἰργάζετο ψίαθον τοσαύτην ὑπομένων σ., ὡς ...τὰς χεῖρας κεντωμένας αἵματος ἀφιέναι *V.Pach.Σ* 87(p.265.20); **2.** *breaking, shattering*; **a.** in gen., lit. and fig. ἐπιδέχεται [sc. τὸ σκεῦος] μετὰ τὴν σ. ἐπανόρθωσιν Or.*hom.18.1 in Jer.*(p.150.24; M.13.464A); cf. σ. ... ἀδιόρθωτον Cyr.*Ps.*2:9(M.69.724C); *ib.*33:21(893B); as an act of divine justice τὴν ἐπενεχθεῖσαν αὐτοῖς [sc. τοῖς Ἰουδαίοις] ἐρήμωσιν καὶ τὴν ὁλοτελῆ σ. καὶ ἀπώλειαν id.*Nah.*6(3.483A); by Christ ὡς λίθος ἰσχυρὸς ἐτέθη εἰς σ. *Barn.*6.2; ἁπάντων ἔσται σ. καὶ πτῶσις Eus.*Is.*11:1(M.24.169A); *demolition* εἰκονοκλάσται...τὰς ...σεπτὰς εἰκόνας...συντριβῇ, καὶ πυρὶ παραδεδώκασιν Jo.D.*haer.*102 (M.94.773A); **b.** met., *suppression*; of Christ's word, ref. Jo.8:37, Or.*Jo.*20.6(p.334.6; M.14.585B); *oppression* κατὰ τῶν ἀσθενεστέρων σ. Cyr.*Zach.*36(3.712D); *weight, strain* ἄνδρα...τεταλαιπωρημένον ἐκ τῆς σ. τοῦ κόπου τοῦ πολλοῦ Jo.Mosch.*prat.*37(M.87.2888A); **3.** *distress, trouble*; **a.** in gen. ἵνα...πᾶσα σ. ἀποστῇ ἀπὸ τῶν ψυχῶν ἡμῶν Or.*hom.12.13 in Jer.*(p.101.21; M.13.398D); 'ἡ κακία αὐτῆς'· τουτέστιν, ἡ ταλαιπωρία αὐτῆς, ἡ σ. Chrys.*hom.22.3 in Mt.*(7.279B); ἡ σ. σημαίνει ποτὲ μὲν τὴν ἁμαρτίαν, πῇ δὲ τὴν τιμωρίαν id.*fr.in Pr.*16:18 (M.64.709A); Cyr.*Mich.*16(p.625.16; Aubert om.); **b.** *contrition* τῆς κατὰ διάνοιαν σ. Chrys.*hom.19.3 in Mt.*(7.248A); τὴν σ. ψυχῆς [sc. of David] *ib.*3.5(43B); σ. καρδίας id.*hom.9.4 in Heb.*(12.99A); Thdr. Mops.*1Cor.*5:5(p.178.18; M.66.881B); τὴν τῆς διανοίας...σ. Thdt.*Dan.* 6:10(2.1181); a means of propitiation τὴν ἐξ ἀμυθήτων πταισμάτων σ. Anast.S.*Ps.*6(M.89.1080A); cf.†Jo.D.*B.J.*34(M.96.1185C); element in fruit of Spirit, *ib.*11(949B).

συντρίβ-ω, **1.** *shatter, shiver, crush*, fig. βραχίονές εἰσι Φαραώ, ἡ κακία...καὶ...τὸ φρόνημα σαρκός, οὓς βραχίονας ὁ θεὸς σ. Or.*fr.in Ezech.*30:25(p.550; M.17.288A,B); ἥτις ῥάβδος, πάντας τοὺς ὑψηλοὺς συντρίψασα, ταπεινώσει Eus.*Is.*11:1(M.24.169B); Bas.*hom.in Ps.*44 (1.165D; M.29.404D); met., *crush, destroy* οὗτοι...ἀποκτεῖναι θέλουσιν τὸν λόγον καὶ...σ. αὐτόν, τὸ μέγεθος μὴ χωροῦντες αὐτοῦ Or.*Jo.*20.6 (p.334.2; M.14.585B); *ib.*10.18(13; p.189.13; 337C); Const.ap.Ath. *apol.sec.*86(p.165.33; M.25.406); εἰς τέλος συνέτριψαν σατανᾶν ὑπὸ τοὺς πόδας αὐτῶν Ephr.1.178A; σ. τὸ σῶμα τῷ βάρει τῶν ἐσθιομένων Bas.*hom.*1.4(2.3D; M.31.168C); βούλεσθαι τῷ τε χρόνῳ καὶ τῇ περιουσίᾳ καὶ τῇ δυναστείᾳ σ. αὐτούς [i.e. in litigation] Thdr.Mops. *1Cor.*6:1ff.(p.179.10; M.66.881C); **2.** *hit, strike*, Chrys.*stat.*1.12(2.18D); ἄρας λίθον ἵνα κρούσῃ ἕνα τῶν ἁγίων, κατὰ τῆς ὄψεως τοῦ ἡγεμόνος ἤνεγκεν τὸν λίθον καὶ σ. αὐτοῦ τὴν ὄψιν *M.Seb.*5; *wound, damage* by striking πατάξας συνέτριψε, τουτέστιν ἐτραυμάτισεν Thdt. *qu.66 in 3Reg.*21:37(1.509); **3.** *afflict, oppress*; **a.** of anxiety or grief τὴν τῆς μιᾶς ἡμέρας φροντίδα ἀρκεῖν εἰς τὸ κακοῦν ἡμᾶς καὶ σ. Chrys. *hom.22.4 in Mt.*(7.280C); *break*, ref. Ac.21:13 ἐκείνην τὴν ἀδαμαντίνην ψυχὴν σ. δάκρυον ἴσχυσε id.*hom.4.4 in 1Thess.*(11.457C); pass. ἡ τῶν συντετριμμένων φροντὶς Pall.*v.Chrys.*13(p.80.4; M.47.45); τοῖς...φιληδόνοις καὶ ταῖς τοῦ παρόντος βίου τύρβαις...συντετριμμένοις Cyr.*Ps.* 33:21(M.69.893A); **b.** pass. intrans., *break down* κατεκλάσθη [sc. Joseph], συνεμαλάχθη, σ., καὶ ἔκλαυσε Chrys.*hom.4.5 in 1Thess.*(11.458A); **c.** oneself with contrition σ. τὴν διάνοιαν πλημμελοῦντες id.*hom.4.5 in 1Cor.*(10.462C); σ. αὐτοῦ τὴν ψυχήν, καὶ ἁμαρτωλὸν ἑαυτὸν ἐκάλεσε id.*hom.in Phil.1:18*(3.300B); ἵνα...μεταμελείᾳ τινὶ κατὰ τὸν παρόντα βίον συντρίψας ἑαυτόν, δυνηθῇ τῆς μελλούσης σωτηρίας ἄξιον ἑαυτὸν καταστῆσαι Thdr.Mops.*1Cor.*5:5(p.178.16; M.66.881B); Jo.Mosch.*prat.*97(M.87.2956C); pass. ἡμεῖς...τῶν συντετριμμένων τὴν καρδίαν, οὐ τῶν ~όντων Chrys.*hom.12.2 in Col.*(11.415B); perf. pass., *be contrite* καρδίας καθαρᾶς καὶ πνεύματος συντετριμμένου Ephr.1.279E; ‡Nil.*perist.*11.4(M.79.909B); ‡Procl.CP *tract.*(M.65.849D); εἶδον αὐτὸν πάνυ συντετριμμένον Jo.Mosch.*prat.*78(M.87.2932D); perf. ptcpl. pass. neut. as subst., *contrition* τὸ ταπεινὸν καὶ σ. καὶ εὐμετάδοτον τοῦ ἐξαγορεύοντος Jo.Jej.*canonar.*2(p.438); **d.** *mortify* σ. τὰ σώματα αὐτῶν κατὰ τοῦ διαβόλου *V.Dan.*(p.53.20).

σύντριμμα, τό, **1.** *breaking to pieces, smash*; of vehicles, Gr.Naz. *or.*8.15(M.35.808A); Amph.*Seleuc.*164(M.37.1588A); met., *ruin, destruction* τοῦ πολέμου τὸ σ. Cyr.*Mich.*22(3.411A); of a cause of offence τὸ θέλειν αὐτὸν [sc. τὸν πλησίον] ἀναγαγεῖν ἐν καλῇ φύσει, μέγα σ. ἐστι τῆς ψυχῆς Es.*or.*8.16(p.59); of eternal ruin, *perdition* τοῦ κατὰ τὸν Ἀπολινάριον...τοῦ κατὰ τὸν Ἄρειον πτώματος, ἴσον...τοῖς καταπίπτουσίν ἐστι τὸ σ. Gr.Nyss.*Apoll.*26(M.45.1180A); Dion.Ar.*ep.*8(M.3.1093C); **2.** *crushing*; abs., of masturbation, †Jo.Jej.*serm.*(M.88.1921D); met., *oppression* σ. ... φησι τὴν πλεονεξίαν τὴν κατά γε τῶν ἐν ὑφέσει καὶ ἀσθενείᾳ Cyr.*Is.*5.5(2.853C).

συντριμμός, ὁ, **1.** *ruin*, †Bas.*Is.*18(1.389E; M.30.145B); **2.** *contrition*, as a breaking of the heart, Bas.*hom.in Ps.*44(1.165D; M.29.404D); τὸ ἰσχυρὸν τοῦ σ. καὶ τῆς ταραχῆς παρίστησιν Thdr.Mops.*Ps.* 6:3b(p.32.19; M.66.649D); ἔστι σ. καρδίας ὁμαλὸς καὶ ἐπωφελής, εἰς κατάνυξιν αὐτῆς...ἀγρυπνία, καὶ προσευχὴ...σ. ἐστιν ἀνεπηρέαστος Marc.Er.*opusc.*1.15f.(M.65.908B); *ib.*2.197(961A); freq. with ταπείνωσις or cognate words καρδίας σ. ἢ ταπείνωσις φρονήματος Bas.*reg. fus.*8.3(2.350D; M.31.940C); ὁ...σάκκος σ. καὶ ταπεινώσεώς ἐστιν ἐφόδιον †Bas.*Is.*131(1.470E; M.30.332B); Mac.Aeg.*hom.*41.3(M.34.769B); Philox.(‡Isaac)*ep.*18(p.170).

***συντριπτέον**, *one must smash* or *destroy*, Or.*Jo.*10.18(13; p.189.12; M.14.337C).

***συντρομάζω**, *shake, tremble*, *Asen.*6(p.46.8); Gr.Mag.*dial.*(tr. Zach.)3.1(M.*PL.*77.222A).

***σύντρομος**, *trembling*; with emotion, *Hom.Clem.*12.7; with fear δαίμονες...σ. *A.Thom.*A 43(p.161.7); Call.*v.Hyp.*(p.94); with awe; of BMV at Annunciation, *Protev.*11.1(p.22); ὡς...τὸ ὅραμα εἶδον, σ. γενόμενος ἀπῆλθον *A.Barn.*4(p.293.7); τὰς δεσποτικὰς δυνάμεις ἐθεάσατο, καὶ πάντες σ. γενόμενοι Anast.S.*defunct.*(M.89.1200B); ὡς ἦλθεν ἡ ὥρα τῆς προκομιδῆς, σ. ὅλος καὶ σύνδακρυς γέγονε †Anast.S.*relat.* 51(*OC* 3 p.72.3).

σύντροφος, **1.** of persons; **a.** *brought up together with*; as subst., *foster-brother*; also fem., *foster-sister* μήτηρ...καὶ...ὁ ἀδελφός...καὶ... ἡ σ. μου *CG–C1* 1 p.125; **b.** *living with*; as subst., *companion* of man as created ἀγγέλων ἐποίησε σ. Jo.D.*hom.*1.4(M.96.552C); *mate* δότω τῷ οἰκέτῃ αὐτοῦ σ., καὶ ὁ ἐλεύθερος αὐτοῦ σχήτω γυναῖκα †Gregent.*leg.Hom.*59(M.86.613A); met. γνῶσις καὶ πίστις, αἱ τῆς φύσεως ἡμῶν σ. Marc.Er.*opusc.*1.105(M.65.917C); **2.** of things, *habitual, familiar*; *natural*; of Christ's human body, exeg. Jo. 1:14b διὰ τοῦ σ. σώματος ἡμῖν ὤφθη Chrys.*hom.12.1 in Jo.*(8.66C).

συντρώγω, *eat with* or *together* σ. αὐτοῖς *T.Zab.*4.2; abs., Nil.*epp.*2.167(M.79.280D).

συντυγχάνω, *meet, meet with*; hence *speak* ὁ σωτὴρ τοῖς μαθηταῖς σ. πεποίηται τοὺς προειρημένους λόγους Or.*Jo.*13.51(50; p.279.17; M.14.492D); τοῖς ἁγίοις [i.e. the prophets] δυνατὸν ἦν αὐτοὺς σ. Ath. *inc.*12.4(M.25.117B); *Hom.Clem.*14.12; *V.Dan.*(p.68.17); *talk, carry on a conversation*, Leont.N.*v.Jo.Eleem.*5(p.11.9); Gr.Mag.*dial.*(tr. Zach.)4.30(M.*PL.*77.370A); abs. καθεζομένων...αὐτῶν, καὶ σ. Anast.S. ap.Jo.D.*imag.*3(M.96.1393A); med., Mac.Mgn.*apocr.*3.14(p.92.18); *tell* about σ. αὐτῷ περὶ πάντων τῶν συμβεβηκότων αὐτῇ Barth. Edess.*Agar.*(M.104.1425D); as subject of ascetic discipline οὐ σ. τινί· ἡσυχάζει γάρ Cyr.S.*v.Euthym.*10(p.19.19); στιχολογῶν, καὶ μὴ σ. τινί Jo.Mosch.*prat.*106(M.87.2965A); and of canonical legislation εἴ τις σ. ἐν τῇ ἐκκλησίᾳ...ἐπικατάρατος ἔστω *Poen.App.*1.14; ὁ σ. ἀπὸ τῶν ἀποδείπνων, βαλλέτω ἀνὰ μετανοίας ν′ Thdr.Stud.*poen.*1.20 (M.99.1736B).

συντυπόω, *impress* one thing *along with* another; pass., *be stamped along with* or *at the same time*, Soz.*h.e.*1.8.13(M.67.881A).

***συντύπτομαι**, *be smitten together*, Thdr.Stud.*epp.*2.55(M.99.1268D) cit. s. συγκουφίζω.

συντυραννέω, *share in absolute power with*; ptcpl., *fellow tyrant*, Eus.*h.e.*8.14.11(M.20.784D).

συντυφλόομαι, *be blind as regards* one thing *and* another, *be doubly blind* σ. τοῖς σωματικοῖς ὀφθαλμοῖς, καὶ τὸ ψυχικὸν βλέμμα οὐκ ὀξυδόρκουν Amph.*mesopent.*(M.39.125C).

συντυχία, ἡ, **1.** of things, *chance meeting, concourse* σ. τις ἀτόμων τὰς τοσαύτας ποιότητας πεποίηκε, καὶ κατὰ τοσαῦτα εἴδη Or.*Cels.*4.75 (p.345.9; M.11.1145C); **2.** of persons; **a.** *association, relationship*; of Moses and Aaron (ref. Ex.32:27), Gr.Nyss.*v.Mos.*(M.44.396A,B); **b.** in gen., social *contact, association, conversation* τὴν σ. ... ἐπωφελῆ...γεγενῆσθαι τὴν πρὸς τοὺς εὐσεβεῖς *Const.App.*4.10.4; θέλω ...τὴν ἄκαιρον σ. κόψαι...ἀφελεῖν γλῶτταν αὐτοῦ Rom.Mel.(*AS* 1 p.180); *M.Ner.et Ach.*7(p.6.1); opp. ἀπουσία, Isid.Pel.*epp.*1.281(M.78.348B); plur. αἱ...συνεχεῖς σ. ... αὐταῖς...ἐστι νόσος *T.Reub.*6.3; ἔστω [sc. ἡ παρθένος] μὴ ῥεμβὰς...φεύγουσα τὰς τῶν πολλῶν σ. *Const. App.*4.14.3; ἐν...ταῖς σ. ἀλαζονικὸς τοῖς ἀγνοοῦσιν αὐτὸν ἐνομίζετο Socr.*h.e.*6.3.14(M.67.669B); a subject of ascetic discipline, Bas.*reg. fus.*33(2.376B; M.31.997B); τὰς σ. ἐξετράποντο τῶν πολλῶν Nil.*exerc.* 60(M.79.792D); Thal.*cent.*1.68f.(M.91.1433C); **c.** in concrete, *society* ὕποπτος ἦν ὁ βίος, ὕπουλος ἡ κατάστασις, αὐτὸ τῆς σ. τὸ πρᾶγμα τεθόλωτο Mac.Mgn.*apocr.*3.42(p.146.19); **d.** single *interview, meeting, conversation* πρώην...σ. πεποιηκὼς...πρὸς αὐτὸν *A.Barn.*17(p.298.10); Ast.Am.*prod.*(p.113.8); οὐ καὶ σ. ἔσχηκα τέσσαρας Pall.*h.Laus.*4 (p.19.20; M.34.1012D); σ. ποιήσασθαι πρὸς αὐτὸν καὶ διαλεχθῆναι αὐτῷ περὶ τῆς ὀρθῆς πίστεως CCP(448)*act.*1(*ACO* 2.1.1 p.102.3; H.2.112D); τοῦ λοιποῦ οὐκέτι εἰς σ. τὸν Σεβηριανὸν Ἰωάννης ἐδέξατο Socr. *h.e.*6.23 suppl.16(M.67.733D); **e.** *conversation, talk* ἡσυχάζειν...μήτε... τινὰ δέξασθαι εἰς σ. παρεκτὸς μόνου τοῦ ὑπηρετοῦντος αὐτῷ Cyr.S.*v. Sab.*41(p.132.5); εἰς πλάτος ἐλθεῖν συντυχίας id.*v.Jo.Hesych.*15(p.213.22); σ. ὠφελεῖ μόνη ἡ πνευματική Thal.*cent.*1.68(1433C); εἰ μὲν διὰ τὸ εὔξασθαι παρεγένου ἐνταῦθα, εἰς τοῦτο...τὸ στόμα σου ἀπασχόλησον·

εἰ δὲ σ. ἕνεκεν, γέγραπται [Mt.21:13] Leont.N.*v.Jo.Eleem.*42(p.84.11); plur. συντυχίας τινὰς ποιήσαντας ἐσημειώσατο Jo.Clim.*scal.*4(M.88.701B); id.*past.*14(M.88.1200C); Thdr.Stud.*epp.*1.38(M.99.1041B); of the *converse* of holy men or on holy things τῶν λαῶν...γλυκαινομένων αὐτοῦ τῇ σ. Pall.*v.Chrys.*5(p.29.11; M.47.19); περὶ κῆπον ἀσχολούμενος καὶ περὶ σεμνὰς σ. id.*h.Laus.*61(121; p.157.10; M.34.1233A); τῶν εὐχῶν σου καὶ τῆς ἀγαθῆς σου σ. Cyr.S.*v.Cyriac.*18(p.233.21); Gr.Mag.*dial.*(tr.Zach.)4.28(M.*PL.*77.366C).

συντυχικός, *accidental, fortuitous* ἀπρονοήτῳ καὶ σ. Meth.*res.*2.10(p.349.16); οὐ...σ. ὁ κλῆρος...ὅτε λέγει κλῆρον θεοῦ Proc.G.*Jos.*18:1(M.87.1036C); in discussions on Creation or divine providence σ. ... καὶ αὐτόματον εἰσηγησάμενος τὴν τοῦ παντὸς διακόσμησιν Eus.*p.e.*1.7(21D; M.21.56B); ἄλογόν τι καὶ σ. καὶ αὐτόματον ἐν τοῖς θεόθεν ὑφεστῶσι νοεῖται οὐδέν Gr.Nyss.*hex.*(M.44.73A); id.*fat.*(M.45.164A).

***συντυχικῶς**, *accidentally, fortuitously, at random* ἀλόγως καὶ σ. καὶ οὐκ ἐξητασμένως ἀκούσαντα Or.*comm.in 1Cor.*15:1(*JTS* 10 p.43); id.*hom.8.2 in Jer.*(p.57.1; M.13.337B); Gr.Nyss.*Eun.*1(1 p.170.18; M.45.413B); Proc.G.*Jos.*18:1(M.87.1036C); freq. ref. Creation φησιν [sc. Celsus]...σ. ... καὶ οὐ κατὰ πρόνοιαν...ταῦτα συμβαίνειν Or.*Cels.*4.75(p.344.21; M.11.1145B); τῶν...φασκόντων...τὸν κόσμον...αὐτομάτως...καὶ σ. ὑφεστάναι Eus.*p.e.*7.11(320A; M.21.541A); *ib.*7.17(330C; M.557B); ref. providence οὐδέ...-ι σ. οἴομαι συμβαίνειν Didym.*Ps.*30:16(M.39.1316B,C).

συνυβρίζω, pass., *be insulted as well* or *at the same time*, Or.*Jo.*10.25(16; p.197.24; M.14.352A); Chrys.*hom.39.2 in Jo.*(8.227D).

συνυμν-έω, **1.** *join in praise with* ∼οῦντος ἡμῖν τοῦ θεοῦ λόγου Clem.*prot.*12(p.84.29; M.8.241A); abs., Sophr.H.*mir.Cyr.et Jo.*35(M.87.3548B); **2.** pass., of Persons of Trin., *be praised together* with, *share equal praise* with δοξολογίας...τοῦ θεοῦ διὰ Χριστοῦ συνδοξολογουμένου ἐν τῷ ἁγίῳ πνεύματι σ. Or.*or.*33(p.401.16; M.11.557B); Didym.*Trin.*2.6(M.39.545C); σύνεδρον ἔχει [sc. ὁ θεὸς τὸν υἱόν] ∼ούμενόν τε καὶ συμπροσκυνούμενον Cyr.*Abac.*39(3.555A); τὸν υἱὸν ...συμβασιλεύοντα τῷ πατρί, μεθ' οὗ καὶ συγκαθέζεται καὶ σ. Eut.ap.CCP (448)*act.*7(*ACO* 2.1.1 p.142.31; H.2.165A).

***συνυμνολογέω**, *sing canticles with*, Niceph.Ur.*v.Sym.*127(M.86.3104D).

συνυπακούω, *join in the responses* γυναιξὶ δὲ παραγγέλλεσθαι ἐν ἐκκλησίαις μὴ λαλεῖν...μήτε συμψάλλειν, μήτε σ., εἰ μὴ μόνον σιγᾶν καὶ εὔχεσθαι θεῷ δι' ἐντεύξεως καὶ σεμνῆς πολιτείας *Didasc.Patr.*8(p.18.3).

***συνύπαρκτος**, *coexistent*; of Persons of Trin., Epiph.*haer.*74.4(p.318.17; M.42.481A) cit. s. συνυπόστατος; of Son with Father, Anast.S.*hod.*1(M.89.49D).

συνύπαρξις, ἡ, **1.** *coexistence*; **a.** of soul and body, Max.*ambig.*(M.91.1325B,1341B); **b.** theol. εἷς ἐστιν ὁ θεὸς τῇ σ. τῶν τριῶν θείων ὑποστάσεων ‡Just.*qu.et resp.*139(M.6.1392C); ἐπὶ μὲν τοῦ θεοῦ τὴν ἀΐδιον λέγομεν σ., οὐκέτι...σύνθεσιν *ib.*129(1380C); ὥσπερ...ἐν τούτοις [i.e. fire and heat] τὸ ἐνυπάρχειν τὰ ἐξ αὐτῶν οὐκ ἀναιρεῖ τὴν σ. ... οὕτω καὶ ἐφ' υἱοῦ Cyr.*Jo.*1.1(4.12C); **c.** Christol. ἕνωσιν ἀληθῆ πιστεύομεν, καὶ σ. αὐτῶν [sc. τῶν φύσεων]...φυσικὴν δι' ὑποστατικῆς ἑνώσεως Leont.H.*Nest.*2.12(M.86.1557D); τοῦ λόγου...ἐξ αὐτῆς [sc. BMV] ἀρξαμένου τῆς μετὰ σαρκὸς...σ., δι' ὑποστατικῆς ἑνώσεως *ib.*3.2(1609A); **2.** *coming into existence with* ἡ τῶν ψυχῶν μυθευομένη σ. ἐν τῇ ἀπαφρίσει τοῦ ἄρρενος ‡Caes.Naz.*dial.*140(M.38.1049); *ib.*(1048).

συνυπάρχ-ω, *coexist*; opp. ἐνυπάρχω: τὸ...κυρίως καὶ ἀληθῶς ∼ειν ἐπὶ τῶν ἀχωρίστως ἀλλήλοις συνόντων λέγεται. τὴν γὰρ θερμότητα τῷ μὲν πυρακτωθέντι σιδήρῳ ἐνυπάρχειν φαμέν, αὐτῷ δὲ τῷ πυρὶ σ., καὶ τὴν μὲν ὑγίειαν τῷ σώματι ἐνυπάρχειν, τὴν δὲ ζωὴν τῇ ψυχῇ σ. Bas.*Spir.*63(3.53A; M.32.184B); opp. μεθυπάρχω, Leont.H.*Nest.*4.3(M.86.1656B); **1.** *originate together and exist alongside, coexist* γλῶσσαν καὶ δάκτυλον...ἱστοροῦνται ἔχειν, οὐχ ὡς σώματος ἑτέρου ∼οντος αὐταῖς... ἀλλ' ὅτι αὐταὶ φύσει αἱ ψυχαί...τοιαῦται κατὰ τὴν οὐσίαν ὑπάρχουσιν Meth.*res.*3.18(p.415.18; M.18.328A); τὸ...σ. οὐχ ἑαυτῷ ἀλλ' ἑτέρῳ σ. Ath.*Ar.*1.32(M.26.77B); *ib.*2.38(228C); κἂν ὁ γονεὺς τῷ χρόνῳ διαφέρῃ...ἀλλ' ἔσχεν ἂν καὶ αὐτὸς ἀεὶ ∼ον τὸ τέκνον *ib.*1.26(68A); ὡς ἂν μὴ ἅμα τῷ γενέσθαι τὴν γῆν, τῶν ὀρῶν συνυπαρξάντων αὐτῇ Diod.*Ps.*89:1(M.33.1624C); impossible for things mutually opposed ἀμήχανον σ. ἀλλήλοις φῶς καὶ σκότος Or.*Jo.*19.21(5; p.323.4; M.14.565C); of good and evil, id.ap.*cat.Jac.*4:4(p.26.17); τὰ μηδέπω σ. ἀλλήλοις δυνάμενα, χαράν τέ φημι καὶ πένθος Max.*ambig.*(M.91.1212D); excluded by nature of infinity δύο...ἄπειρα σ. οὐ δύνανται *Hom.Clem.*16.17; εἰ...ἄπειρόν τι εἶναι οὐ δύναται ᾧ ἐξ ἀϊδίου ∼ει ἕτερόν τι κατ' οὐσίαν διάφορον, ἄπειρον εἶναι οὐδαμῶς ἐνδέχεται δυάδα Max.*ambig.*(M.91.1185A); **2.** in gen., *be contemporaneous* σημεῖον δ' εἶναί φασι τὸ προηγούμενον ἢ σ. ἢ ἑπόμενον...σημεῖον δὲ τοῦ εἶναι τὸν σωτῆρα ἡμῶν αὐτὸν ἐκεῖνον τὸν υἱὸν τοῦ θεοῦ αἵ τε προηγούμεναι τῆς παρουσίας αὐτοῦ προφητεῖαι...αἵ τε σ. τῇ γενέσει αὐτοῦ τῇ αἰσθητῇ περὶ αὐτοῦ μαρτυρίαι, πρὸς δὲ καὶ ⟨αἱ⟩ μετὰ τὴν ἀνάληψιν...ἐμφανῶς δεικνύμεναι δυνάμεις αὐτοῦ Clem.*str.*6.15(p.493.5ff.; M.9.345A); **3.** *be intrinsic* or *belong essentially to from the beginning* τοῖς...σώμασιν ...∼ει καὶ τὸ σκιὰν ἔχειν †Just.*fr.*(p.50; M.6.1597A); τῷ τοῦ θεοῦ ἀγαθῷ ὃ κατὰ συμβεβηκός ἐστιν αὐτῷ, καὶ σ. ὡς χρόα σώματι Athenag.*leg.*24.2(M.6.945B); τὸ...πνεῦμα τὸ ἅγιον...ἔχον τὴν ἀγαθότητα...ἐκ φύσεως αὐτῷ ∼ουσαν Bas.*Eun.*3.3(1.274E; M.32.661B); οὐδὲ εὐσεβὲς ...ἐπὶ τοῦ πνεύματος μεθεκτὴν λέγειν αὐτοῦ τὴν θεότητα...καὶ οὐχὶ φύσει αὐτῷ ∼ειν *ib.*3.5(276E; M.665C); ἀντὶ τοῦ ∼ειν αὐταῖς ἔξωθεν παρεπόμεναι Gr.Nyss.*Eun.*1(1 p.82.6; M.45.313B); τὸ ἐπιθυμητικὸν καὶ τὸ θυμοειδές, εἴτε συνουσιωμένα τῇ ψυχῇ, καὶ παρὰ τὴν αὐτὴν εὐθὺς τῇ κατασκευῇ ∼οντα, εἴτε τι ἄλλο παρ' αὐτὴν ὄντα καὶ ὕστερον ἡμῖν ἐπιγινόμενα id.*anim.et res.*(M.46.49B); εὐγνωμόνως...τοῦ πάθους ἀκουστέον...τὸ φύσει σ. τοῖς οὖσι Max.*ambig.*(M.91.1073B); **4.** *be with, remain with* ὁ Χριστὸς ∼ετω σοι φίλος Or.*exp.in Pr.*17:17(M.17.200D); ? *be in the same category with* or ? *share in with* τοῖς ἐσομένοις ἀγαθοῖς ἀνδράσιν οὐδὲν ∼ουσιν [sc. those thought to have committed injustice] *Hom.Clem.*15.8; **5.** *have the same origin* πόθεν ...σ. τῷ Ἀδὰμ τὴν ψυχὴν νοήσωμεν, ἄνευ...σπορᾶς δημιουργηθέντι;... πῶς γὰρ ἡ ἄφθαρτος...τῷ φθαρτῷ...σ.; ‡Caes.Naz.*dial.*140(M.38.1048f.); **6.** theol., *coexist, be coexistent* with God (implying coeternity); **a.** of matter, Valent. πότερον ἔκ τινος συνόντος ἀεὶ τῷ θεῷ, ἢ ἐξ αὐτοῦ καὶ μόνου, ∼οντος αὐτῷ οὐδενός...ἔδοξέν μοι σ. τι αὐτῷ, ᾧ τοὔνομα ὕλη Meth.*arbitr.*2f.(pp.149.24,153.14; M.18.244D, 248B); *ib.*7(p.162.6; 253A); οὔτε ἀνάγκη σ. αὐτῷ τὸ πᾶν δεῖν λέγειν διὰ τὸ μὴ ἀναγκάζεσθαι λέγειν ἠλλοιῶσθαι id.*creat.*4(p.496.29; M.18.336C); **b.** of an opposing principle τὰ...οὐκ ὄντα...πῶς ἠδύνατο σ. τῷ ἀεὶ ὄντι θεῷ; Ath.*Ar.*1.29(M.26.72C); τὸ κακὸν...ἐπάγει [sc. the Manichean] ὡς ἀΐδιον καὶ σ. θεῷ *Disp.Phot.*(M.88.556B); **c.** of Son with Father, maintained against Arians οὐ συμφωνοῦμεν αὐτῷ ...λέγοντι...∼ει ὁ υἱὸς ἀγεννήτως τῷ θεῷ Ar.*ep.Eus.*(p.2; M.42.212A); λέγειν τολμῶσι 'πῶς...δύναται ὁ υἱὸς ἀϊδίως σ. τῷ πατρί;' Ath.*Ar.*2.34(M.26.220C); who were followed by Eunomius in denying Son's coexistence καταγέλαστον, τοὺς ἓν μόνον παραδεξαμένους ἀγέννητον, ἢ προϋπάρχειν τι τούτου φάσκειν, ἢ σ. ἕτερον...εἴτε ∼οι [sc. τι], τῇ πρὸς θάτερον κοινωνίᾳ τοῦ ∼ειν ἑκάτερον, ἀφαιρεθήσεται τὸ ἓν μόνον εἶναι Eun.*apol.*10(M.30.845C); or allowing coexistence of God's wisdom and power but denying their identity with Christ, Ast.Soph.*fr.*1 ap.Ath.*syn.*18(p.246.4; M.26.713C); δύο ...σοφίας φησὶν εἶναι, μίαν μὲν τὴν ἰδίαν καὶ σ. τῷ θεῷ, τὸν δὲ υἱὸν ἐν ταύτῃ τῇ σοφίᾳ γεγενῆσθαι Ath.*Ar.*1.5(M.26.21B); ποτὲ μὲν τῇ κάμπῃ συνάπτουσι τὴν σοφίαν, ποτὲ δὲ σ. τῷ πατρὶ...λέγουσι *ib.*2.40(232B); λέγειν μὲν σοφίαν σ. τῷ πατρί, μὴ λέγειν δὲ ταύτην εἶναι τὸν Χριστόν... τὸ...∼ον οὐχ ἑαυτῷ, τινὶ δὲ ∼ει *ib.*2.38(228B,C); Eusebius of Caesarea also denying it ἡ μὲν αὐγὴ σ. τῷ φωτί, συμπληρωτική τις οὖσα αὐτοῦ... ὁ δὲ πατὴρ προϋπάρχει τοῦ υἱοῦ καὶ τῆς γενέσεως αὐτοῦ προϋφέστηκεν, ᾗ μόνος ἀγέννητος ἦν Eus.*d.e.*4.3(p.153.4; M.22.256A); ἡ...αὐγή... οὐσιωδῶς σ. τῷ φωτί, οὐκ ἂν δύναιτο ἐκτὸς ὑφεστάναι τοῦ ἐν ᾧ ἐστιν· ὁ δέ γε τοῦ θεοῦ λόγος καθ' ἑαυτὸν οὐσίωταί τε καὶ ὑφέστηκεν, καὶ οὐκ ἀγενήτως σ. τῷ πατρί *ib.*5.1(p.213.18,20; 353C,D); coexistence admitted by Marcellus εἷς θεὸς καὶ ὁ τούτου μονογενὴς υἱὸς λόγος, ὁ ἀεὶ σ. τῷ πατρί Marcell.*ep.*ap.Epiph.*haer.*72.2(p.257.22; M.42.385B); and consistently asserted by orthodox, ref. Heb.1:3 ἀδιαίρετόν ἐστι τὸ ἀπαύγασμα πρὸς τὸ φῶς, καὶ ἴδιον αὐτοῦ ∼ον τούτῳ φύσει, καὶ οὐκ ἐπιγέγονεν ὕστερον Ath.*ep.Aeg.Lib.*13(M.25.568C); ὥσπερ λόγος ὢν...τοῦ πατρός, ἔχει...τὸ μὴ πρότερον καὶ ὕστερον, ἀλλὰ τὸ ∼ειν τῷ πατρὶ *ib.*17(577A); id.*Ar.*1.27(M.26.68C); *ib.*3.26(380B); id.*v.Anton.*69(M.26.941A); εἰκόνα τοῦ θεοῦ...σ. καὶ παρυφεστηκυῖαν τῷ πρωτοτύπῳ ὑποστήσαντι Bas.*Eun.*2.16(1.251D; M.29.605A); ἵνα ἐκ πηγῆς ἀεὶ οὔσης ἀΐδιος πηγὴ σ. Epiph.*haer.*76.35(p.385.17; M.42.588D); εἰ λέγοιτο χαρακτὴρ τῆς ὑποστάσεως τοῦ πατρός, ἀχωρίστως τε ἅμα καὶ προσπεφυκότως ∼οντα νοεῖ Cyr.*dial.Trin.*5(5¹.558D); id.*Jo.*1.1(4.12B); Thdt.*Heb.*1:3(3.547); εἰ μὴ ἐξ ἀρχῆς δῶμεν τὸν υἱὸν σ. τῷ πατρὶ...τροπὴν τῆς τοῦ πατρὸς ὑποστάσεως παρεισάγομεν ‡Cyr.*Trin.*7(6³.9D; M.77.1133A); **d.** Christol. ὁ ποιητὴς τῶν ὅλων...μόνῳ πατρὶ καὶ πνεύματι ∼ων ἀθάνατος,...ἐκ παρθένου γεννώμενος Amph.*fr.*3(M.39.100C); εἰ...προϋπάρχει μὲν ἡ θεότης, ἡ δέ γε ἀνθρωπότης οὐ σ. Thdt.*eran.*2(4.99); **7.** Gnost., of one aeon as originating and coexisting with another as a pair ∼ειν δ' αὐτῷ [sc. Βυθῷ] καὶ Ἔννοιαν Iren.*haer.*1.1.1(M.7.445A,B); acc. a different theory first tetrad was otherwise composed τῇ μονότητι σ. δύναμις, ἣν...ὀνομάζω ἑνότητα...ταύτῃ τῇ μονάδι σ. δύναμις ὁμοούσιος αὐτῇ ἦν...ὀνομάζω τὸ ἓν *ib.*1.11.3(565A); *ib.*1.15.1(613A) = Hipp.*haer.*6.49(p.181.6; M.16.3275B); ὁ Πτολεμαῖος...δύο συζυγίας τῷ Βυθῷ...ἐπενόησεν...τὴν μὲν Ἔννοιαν ἀεὶ σ. αὐτῷ φήσας...τὸ δὲ Θέλημα ἐπιγίνεσθαι ‡Epiph.*epit.haer.*33(p.363.14).

***συνυπηχέω**, *echo, answer*; met., Gr.Nyss.*nativ.*(M.46.1129A).

***συνυπνόω**, *sleep with*, Epiph.*haer.*49.1(p.242.3; M.41.880C).

συνυποβάλλ-ω, intrans., *form a foundation together* or *join in contributing*, met. πρὸς...τὴν τούτων θεωρίαν ἥ τῶν καθ' ἕκαστα γνῶσις καὶ ἡ τῶν καθόλου ~ει Clem.*str.*8.6(p.90.15; M.9.581B).

συνυπογράφω, *subscribe along with* or *together* to a statement, Alex.Al.*ep.Alex.*14(p.29.15; M.18.569C); ἅμα τοῖς πολλοῖς...σ. Socr. *h.e.*1.8.34(M.67.69B); Anast.S.*hod.*10(M.89.149C).

συνυπόκειμαι, *be subject* or *liable to* σ. ταῖς ποιναῖς Cyr.*ador.*17(1.601C); id.*Heb.*1:3(p.367.28).

***συνυποκουφίζω**, *help to lighten* or *relieve*, Gr.Naz.*or.*18.9(M.35.996B).

συνυποκρίνομαι, *play a part along with, join in dissimulation*, Chrys.*comm.in Gal.*2:13(10.688D); id.*hom.15.7 in Mt.*(7.194D).

συνυπολαμβάνω, *conceive of one thing as with another, envisage together* οὐ μὴν παρατάσει τινὶ διαστηματικῇ τῆς τοῦ πατρὸς ὑπάρξεως τὸν μονογενῆ διορίζεσθαι, ἀλλ' ἀεὶ τῷ αἰτίῳ τὸ ἐξ αὐτοῦ σ. Gr.Nyss.*diff. ess.*7(M.32.337C).

***συνυπομέν-ω**, *endure together, be partaker in sufferings*, ref. 2Tim.2:12 ~οντες συμβασιλεύσομεν Chrys.*hom.11.2 in Phil.*(11.286A).

***συνυποσπάω**, *drag along with, draw in the wake of*; met., Gr. Nyss.*Eun.*1(1 p.198.25; M.45.445A).

συνυπόστασις, ἡ, *common hypostasis*, of Person of Christ as both divine and human χωρὶς...τῆς...σ. ἑτέρας οὐσίας [i.e. the humanity] Leont.H.*Nest.*5.23(M.86.1745B).

***συνυπόστατος, 1.** *of one essence, consubstantial* τρία ὑπαρκτὰ τρία συνύπαρκτα...τρία ἐνυπόστατα τρία σ. ἀλλήλοις συνόντα Epiph.*haer.* 74.4(p.318.18; M.42.481A); **2.** *forming one hypostasis with* or *together* ἐν τῇ τοῦ σιδήρου ὑποστάσει, φύσις πυρὸς ἀνυπόστατος καθ' αὑτὴν οὖσα, συνετέθη τῇ φύσει τοῦ σιδήρου, σ. αὐτῇ γενομένη Leont.H.*Nest.* 1.49(M.86.1512B); τί δὲ ἆρά ἐστιν αὐτοῖς [sc. Godhead and manhood] ἢ μόνον σ. διὰ τῆς ἑνώσεως τῆς καθ' ὑπόστασιν; *ib.*5.31(1752A).

***συνυποστηρίζ-ω**, *sustain jointly, join in giving support* οὔτε γὰρ ἂν ποὺς ἀσφαλῶς βαδίσειε, μὴ ~οντος τοῦ ἑτέρου Bas.*ep.*97(3.191A; M.32.493B).

συνυπουργέω, *cooperate, work with* ἐποίησε...πάντα ὁ θεὸς δι' υἱοῦ, ἀλλ' οὐχὶ τὸν υἱόν· οὐ γάρ ἐστι σὺν πᾶσι· σ. γὰρ τῷ πατρὶ καὶ συμπροσκυνεῖται Epiph.*haer.*76.52(p.407.3; M.42.625C).

***συνυπουργός, ὁ**, *assistant*, *Euchol.*(p.226).

συνυποφέρω, pass., *be carried away together with*; c. dat., Cyr. *Lc.*12:4(M.72.725C); Thdr.Stud.*epp.*2.119(M.99.1392D).

συνυφαίν-ω, *weave together*; met., *interweave, associate*, Eus.*d.e.*4.2(p.152.16; M.22.253C); Gr.Naz.*or.*28.24(p.58.19; M.36.60A); Melet. *nat.hom.*30(M.64.1280C); *weave* into a narrative σ. ἡ γραφὴ τῇ ἱστορίᾳ τὸ μὴ γενόμενον Or.*princ.*4.2.9(p.322.1; M.11.376A); *ib.*4.3.1 (p.325.3; 377B); Sophr.H.*mir.Cyr.et Jo.*37(M.87.3561A); theol., of union of natures in Christ ἀπ' ἐκείνου ἤρξατο θεία καὶ ἀνθρωπίνη ~εσθαι φύσις Or.*Cels.*3.28(p.226.14; M.11.956D); Aët.*synt.*29 ap. Epiph.*haer.*76.46(M.42.613A; συνεμφ- p.399.24).

***συνυφαιρ-έω**, *take away, remove together*; met., pass., *disappear with* or *together* πάσης...διαφορᾶς ὑφαιρουμένης ~εῖται...τὸ τῶν θεῶν πλῆθος Gr.Nyss.*or.catech.*proem.(p.6.9; συναφαιρεῖται M.45.12D); id. *Eun.*1(1 p.198.24; M.45.445A).

***συνυφεστώτως**, *as coexistent* ὁ κύριος...ὡς...ἀΐδιον φῶς σ. καὶ ὁμοουσίως ἐκ τοῦ πατρικοῦ φωτὸς ἐκλάμψαν Didym.*Trin.*3.3(M.39.808B); *ib.*(821B); ἐπὶ μὲν τῶν κτισμάτων ἡγεῖται [sc. H. Ghost] τῷ χρόνῳ ὁ πρωτότυπος· ἐπὶ δὲ τοῦ θεοῦ...σ. καὶ συμπροεληλυθότως *ib.*2.2 (460B).

συνυφής, *woven together*; met., *interwoven, connected* τὰ ὀνόματα λεγόμενα μετά τινος τοῦ σ. αὐτοῖς εἱρμοῦ Or.*Cels.*1.24(p.75.6, v.l. συμφυοῦς M.11.705A).

συνυφίστ-ημι, A. trans.; **1.** *bring into existence simultaneously* or *along with* τὸ τέλειον ἐν πᾶσι τῷ ἐξ αὐτοῦ συνυποστῆσαι Gr.Nyss. *Eun.*1(1 p.141.15; M.45.380D); **2.** *cause to share with oneself* υἱόν... κτισθέντα καὶ τὸ ζῆν καὶ τὸ εἶναι παρὰ τοῦ πατρὸς εἰληφότα, καὶ τὰς δόξας συνυποστήσαντος αὐτῷ τοῦ πατρός Ar.*ep.Alex.*(p.13; M.26.709B); med., *share, undergo together* τὴν περιπόνησιν ὑμῶν ~άμενοι Thdr.Stud.*epp.*1.56(M.99.1109C).

B. intrans.; **1.** *come into existence together* or *simultaneously with* ἡ ψυχὴ τῶν ἀλόγων...τῷ προστάγματι συνυπέστη Bas.*hex.*9.3(1.82A; M.29.192B); τῇ βουλήσει τοῦ θεοῦ ἀχρόνως συνυφεστάναι τὸν κόσμον *ib.* 1.6(1.7B; M.17A); *ib.*2.3(1.14E; M.33C); id.*Eun.*2.21(1.257B; M.29.617C); ὁποία τῶν νοημάτων ἡ φύσις τοῖς τοῦ νοῦ κινήμασιν ἀχρόνως ~αμένη *ib.*2.16(1.252A; M.605A); συναπερχόμενος [sc. ὁ χρόνος] μὲν τοῖς φθειρομένοις ~άμενος δὲ τοῖς γινομένοις...συνελπιζόμενος δὲ τοῖς ἔτι μέλλουσιν †Bas.*Is.*66(1.427A; M.30.232C); δύο μὲν οὐρανοὺς λέγει γεγενῆσθαι, ἕνα μὲν τοῦ ὁρωμένου ἀνώτερον, ὃν καὶ συνυφεστάναι τῇ γῇ, θάτερον δὲ τὸν ὁρώμενον Diod.*fat.*ap.Phot.*cod.*223(M.103.872B); οὕτινος γὰρ τῷ χωρισμῷ διαλύεσθαι πέφυκε τὸ σῶμα, τούτου δηλαδὴ τῇ ὑπάρξει κατὰ τὴν γένεσιν...καὶ συνυφέστηκεν Max.*ambig.*(M.91.1337B); **2.** *co-exist, subsist in a unity* ἡ μὲν αὐγὴ συνυπάρχει τῷ φωτί, συμπληρωτική τις οὖσα αὐτοῦ...ὁμοῦ τε καὶ καθ' ἑαυτὸ συνυφέστηκεν Eus.*d.e.* 4.3(p.153.6; M.22.256A); Gr.Nyss.*Eun.*1(1 p.172.12; M.45.416B); ἐν κέντρῳ πᾶσαι αἱ τοῦ κύκλου γραμμαὶ κατὰ μίαν ἕνωσιν συνυφεστήκασι Dion.Ar.*d.n.*5.6(M.3.821A); **3.** *be linked essentially with, belong intrinsically to* ὄγκῳ...~αται τόπος Or.*exp.in Pr.*41:11(M.17.136D); Nemes.*nat.hom.*3(M.40.600B); Didym.*Trin.*1.9(M.39.284A); in gen., *be associated with, linked with* πάντα...λογικὰ σὺν ἀλόγοις, θνητὰ σὺν ἀθανάτοις, καὶ εἴ τι τούτοις ἕτερον συνυφέστηκεν τε καὶ συνύφανται Eus.*d.e.*4.2(p.152.15; M.22.253C); **4.** theol., *coexist* from eternity with God; **a.** denied of matter, ‡Just.*qu.Chr.*3.3(M.6.1436C,D); opp. γίνομαι, *ib.*2.8(1428A,B); **b.** ref. Son, Eus.*d.e.*5.1(p.213.27; M.22.353D) cit. s. ἀνάρχως; Didym.*Trin.*3.3(M.39.813B); ὁ υἱὸς συνυφεστηκὼς τῷ ἰδίῳ γεννήτορι Cyr.*Heb.*1:8(p.376.1; M.74.961A); πᾶσά πως ἀνάγκη συνυφεστάναι νοεῖν τὸν υἱόν, ἵνα καὶ ἀληθῶς ὑπάρχῃ πατὴρ ὁ θεὸς *ib.*(p.375.13; 960C); id.*Juln.*8(6^2.264D); συνομολογεῖ...τὸν...ἴδιον αὐτοῦ θεὸν λόγον, ἀεὶ συνυπάρχοντα, καὶ ἀχρόνως συνυφεστηκότα, καὶ συμπροσκυνούμενον υἱόν *ib.*(255D); **5.** Christol., *subsist in a unity, form one hypostasis with* ὁ τρόπος...τῆς ἑνώσεως...ὡς εἶναι ἐν τῇ τελείᾳ ἀνθρωπότητι τὸν λόγον, ὅπερ ἐν ἡμῖν ὁ ἔσω ἄνθρωπος... συνυφεστὼς καὶ εἰς τὸν τοῦ ὅλου ὅρον συντελῶν μετὰ τὴν ἕνωσιν Leont.B.*Nest.et Eut.*3(M.86.1380C) = id.*fr.*(M.86.2009B); τὸ δὲ ληφθέν, οὐχ ὑπόστασις...ἀλλὰ φύσις, τῇ φύσει τοῦ λόγου ἐν τῇ ἰδίᾳ αὐτοῦ ὑποστάσει συνυποστᾶσα Leont.H.*Nest.*7.2(M.86.1761B); *ib.*5.31(1752B); συγκείμενόν τε καὶ ~άμενον, καὶ οὐδαμῶς καθ' αὑτὸ γνωριζόμενον Max.*opusc.*(M.91.149C); διὰ...τῆς ἑνώσεως δηλοῦται, τί ἔσχεν ἑκάτερον ἐκ τῆς τοῦ συνυφεστῶτος αὐτῷ...περιχωρήσεως ‡Cyr.*Trin.* 24(6^3.29E; M.77.1165C); Jo.D.*Jacob.*79(M.94.1476D); of the ἐνέργειαι: μηδετέρας τῆς φυσικῆς ἑκατέρας ἐνεργείας διὰ τὴν ἕνωσιν, μήτε μὴν ἄσχετον αὐτὴν κεκτημένης μετὰ τὴν ἕνωσιν, καὶ τῆς συγκειμένης καὶ συνυφεστώσης διακεκριμένην Max.*ambig.*(M.91.1060B).

***συνυψ-όω, 1.** *exalt* with Christ (cf. Rom.6:4, Col. 2:12) ⟨ὁ⟩ συνταφεὶς Χριστῷ ~οῦται θεῷ Clem.*prot.*2(p.20.11; M.8.97A); Gr. Naz.*carm.*1.2.10.573(M.37.721A); human nature by hypostatic union ἵνα ὁ...λόγος...~ώσῃ τὴν ἑνωθεῖσαν αὐτῷ ἀνθρωπότητα Leont.H. *Nest.*5.1(M.86.1724C); θεοῦ μὲν συγκαταβαίνοντος τῇ τῆς σαρκὸς κοινωνίᾳ, ταύτης δὲ ~ουμένης ἑνώσει τῇ πρὸς αὐτόν Proc.G.*Is.*2:3(M.87.1873B); **2.** *raise, elevate* in mind ἐκ...τῆς ἀστρονομίας γῆθεν αἰωρούμενος...τῷ νῷ ~ωθήσεται οὐρανῷ Clem.*str.*6.10(p.471.28; M.9.301A); myst., with the Logos, Max.*ambig.*(M.91.1385B); **3.** eccl., *elevate, hold up to view* ἀποδεθεὶς τῷ ζωοποιῷ σταυρῷ ὁ τίμιος σπόγγος καὶ αὐτὸς ~οῦται αὐτῷ *Chron.Pasch.*p.385(M.92.988B).

***συνχρηστός**, v. *συγχρηστός.

συνῳδία, ἡ, *concord*; met., *agreement, accord*; of different parts of scripture, Clem.*str.*6.11(p.476.13; M.9.309C); κανὼν...ἐκκλησιαστικὸς ἡ σ. καὶ ἡ συμφωνία νόμου τε καὶ προφητῶν τῇ κατὰ τὴν τοῦ κυρίου παρουσίαν παραδιδομένῃ διαθήκῃ *ib.*6.15(p.495.5; 349A); of Father and Son in Trin. ὁ...υἱὸς...ἀναγορεύεται καὶ θεὸς ὁμοδόξῳ σ. Eust. *engast.*19(p.46.19, v.l. συνοδίᾳ M.18.653A).

συνωδίν-ω, met., *bring forth, bring* οὐ μετρίαν...τοῖς ἀρτίως... εἰρημένοις ~ον τὴν ὄνησιν Cyr.*ador.*1(1.18D).

συνῳδός, lit. and met., *in unison* with, of a fellow Christian ταῦτα ὁ νοῶν εὔξαι ὑπὲρ Ἀβερκίου πᾶς ὁ σ. *V.Aberc.*77(p.54.5, v.l. σύνοδος); neut. plur. as adv. τούτοις σ. σαφῶς τοῖς λόγοις...ἀναφθέγγεται Meth.*res.*1.56(p.315.13; M.41.1149B); εὐθὺς...Δαυὶδ...λέγει καὶ Πέτρος τῷ Δαυὶδ σ. Epiph.*anc.*34(p.43.6; M.43.77C); Cyr.*Lc.*9:27 (p.80.15; M.72.653C).

συνωθ-έω, 1. *drive together, compress by force*, ref. Ex.14:21f. τὴν ...'Ερυθρὰν θάλασσαν...νότῳ βιαίῳ...~ήσας οὕτω διέστησεν Philost. *h.e.*12.10(συνωθίσας M.65.620B); met. οἱ...ἑνὶ πνεύματι ~ούμενοι Hipp.*haer.*5.23(p.125.21; M.16.3191C); **2.** *crowd, throng* τῷ πλήθει ~εῖσθαι Eus.*l.C.*proem.(p.195.6; M.20.1317A); τὸ ~οῦντας ἀλλήλους τὸν ἐνδοτέρω τόπον ἐπείγεσθαι καταλαβεῖν Chrys.*hom.3.1 in Jo.*(8.16B); **3.** *help to drive along*; fig., ‡Gr.Nyss.*Ar.et Sab.*14(M.45.1300C); met., *drive, compel* ἑτέρους σ. καὶ ἄκοντας πρὸς τὰ ἁμαρτήματα Diod. *fat.*ap.Phot.*cod.*223(M.103.865B); Gr.Nyss.*or.catech.*35(p.138.1; M.45.92A); ~ούμεθα πρὸς τὸν τῆς βασιλείας πόθον Chrys.*hom.3.2 in 2Tim.*(11.675B); πανταχόθεν αὐτοὺς ἐπὶ τὸν δεσπότην ~ῶν id.*hom.17.5 in Mt.*(7.228E); τῷ τοῦ κολάζεσθαι δέει ~ούμενοι πρὸς τὸ ἄμεινον Cyr.*Ps.*36:9(M.69.929A); ~ήθη...τὴν ὀρθὴν πίστιν ὁμολογῆσαι Justn. *conf.*(p.94.23; M.86.1019A); ἠτήσατο ἵνα...ἐξελθεῖν αὐτὸν μὴ ~ήσωσιν

Gr.Mag.*dial.*(tr.Zach.)3.14(M.*PL*.77.243C); **4.** *urge, exhort* πρὸς τὸ ὑπερβάλλειν τὴν Φαρισαίων πολιτείαν τοὺς μαθητὰς αὐτοῦ σ. Just.*dial.* 105.6(M.6.721C); ~ούμενός τε καὶ συνελαυνόμενος Chrys.*hom.17.7 in Mt.*(7.232C); κατεπείγων αὐτοὺς καὶ σ. εἰς τὸ διαναστῆναι id.*hom.12.1 in 2Cor.*(10.521D); ~ηθήσεται...ἕνα...σοι δαψιλεύσασθαι (Lat. *persuadebitur Cod.Afr.*55).

***συνωθίζω**, *drive, compel*, met. ὑπὸ τοῦ φόβου συνωθισθεὶς Chrys. *ep.*14.3(3.598B); v. συνωθέω.

συνωθισμός, ὁ, *attack* τοὺς σ., οὓς κατὰ τῶν...ἀρχιερέων εἰργάσαντο *Libell.*ap.CCP(536)*act.*5(p.39.21; H.2.1285B).

***συνωμολογημένως**, *confessedly*, Eust.*engast.*27(p.59.1; συνομολογουμένως M.18.669B).

συνωνέομαι, *buy*, Clem.*paed.*3.4(pp.251.20,252.18; M.8.592B,596A); *ib.*2.1(p.155.14; 381A).

συνωνή, ἡ, 1. a *buying up, deal*, or *bargain*, met. ὦ τῆς ἐξουσίας ἐν ἐμοὶ...τῆς ἁμαρτίας...ἄγω πρὸς τὴν φύσιν, καὶ τὰς σ. πραγματεύεται, καὶ τοὺς ἀρραβῶνας δίδωσιν, ἵνα πωλήσῃ αὐτῇ τῇ ἁμαρτίᾳ τὴν διάνοιαν Ephr.3.509B; id.3.446A; **2.** *purchase* εἰς σ. ... σίτου ‡Nil.*perist.*11.16 (M.79.928A).

συνωνυμ-έω, *have the same name as* κατὰ μετουσίαν...ἐκείνων [i.e. good things to come] τὰ [i.e. good things of this life] τῇδε ~εῖ Clem. *paed.*3.12(p.283.29; M.8.665A) ∞ Isid.Pel.*epp.*1.469(M.78.440B).

συνωνυμία, ἡ, 1. *sameness of name*, Clem.*prot.*2(p.20.28; M.8. 100A); **2.** *synonymity* opp. equivocation (ref. OT and NT) ἐκεῖνα μὲν ὡς τύποι, ταῦτα δὲ ὡς ἀλήθεια, ὁμωνυμίαν τινά, ἀλλ' οὐχὶ σ. φυλάττοντα Chrys.*hom.14.1 in Jo.*(8.79C); οὐθ' ἡ ὁμωνυμία συνωνυμίαν ἐκ παντὸς τρόπου ἐμφαίνει Isid.Pel.*epp.*3.31(M.78.752D).

συνώνυμος, *having the same name as*; philos., *having the same name and nature and included in one definition*, opp. ἑτερώνυμος, Clem.*str.*8.8(p.95.6f.; M.9.589C,592A); opp. ὁμώνυμος, Athenag.*leg.* 11.2(M.6.912B); Clem.*str.*8.6(p.90.11; 581B); εἰμὶ τοῦ μακαρίου μὲν ἐκείνου ὁμώνυμος, οὐ μὴν σ.· οὐκ εἰμὶ Ἰωάννης, ἀλλὰ καλοῦμαι Chrys.*hom.52.5 in Ac.*(9.395D).

συνωνύμως, 1. *synonymously, by one and the same name*, i.e. one term for more than one entity σ. κόσμον τε καὶ οὐρανὸν ἀποκαλῶν [sc. ὁ Πλάτων ἐν τῷ Τιμαίῳ] Clem.*str.*5.12(p.378.25; ἀνωνύμως M.9. 117B); ref. Rom.8:39 κτίσις δὲ σ. καὶ ἐνέργεια λέγεται *ib.*4.14(p.290. 24; M.8.1304A); σ. τῷ ἐλαιοτριβείῳ καλούμενον βίθ Epiph.*mens.*21(M. 43.273A); **2.** *by the synonym* or *alternative name*, i.e. two terms for one entity συνεκτικὰ...σ. καὶ αὐτοτελῆ καλεῖται Clem.*str.*8.9(pp.95. 31,101.19; M.9.592C,600D).

συνωρίς, ἡ, *pair* or *couple*; met., *band, company* of persons μετὰ τὴν ἀνάστασιν...εἰσερχόμενον πρὸς πᾶσαν τῶν ἀποστόλων τὴν ξυνωρίδα ‡Ath.*Ar.*4.35(p.84.21; M.26.521C); Cyr.*Jo.*4.2(4.357A); cf.Thdt.*Is.* 1:20(p.9.23); *community* of nuns, Thdr.Stud.*epp.*2.60(M.99.1276B).

συνωφελέω, *join in helping*; simply, *help*, Clem.*str.*6.17(p.514.25; M.9.393A); abs., *be of use*, id.*q.d.s.*15(p.169.25; M.9.620B).

***συοθρέμμων**, *for the feeding of pigs*, Gr.Naz.*carm.*2.2(poem.) 5.199(M.37.1536A).

***σuόμορφος**, *in the form of swine*, Jo.Mal.*chron.*5 p.120(M.97. 213B).

***Συριάζω**, *speak Syriac*, Or.*Cels.*7.60(p.210.14; M.11.1508A).

***Συριακός**, *Syrian, from Syria* τὸ σῶμά μου...ἐνταφίασον...ἐν χάρταις σ. ... ἐν ταῖς χάρταις σφίγξον αὐτὸ παπύροις *A.Phil.*143(p.83. 5,23); cf. '*Syriaca*' [sc. *vitis*] *vel quia de Syria adlata vel quia nigra est*, Isid.H.*etym.*17.5.28 (for latter interpretation cf. συρικός).

Συριάρχης, ὁ, *president of the provincial council of Syria*, *A.Paul. et Thecl.*26(p.253.12); *M.Tar.*10(p.474).

***Συριατικός, 1.** *Syrian*, *A.Phil.*143(p.83.18); **2.** *Syriac* Σαβιθά... Συριατικόν ἐστι τὸ ὄνομα, ὃ ἑρμηνεύεται 'ληιαῖον ἄντλημα' Epiph. *mens.*24(M.43.284C).

***συριγγόφωνος**, *with a piping note* τέττιξ σ. ‡Caes.Naz.*dial.*140 (M.38.1072).

συριγγώδης, *like a pipe, perforated*; of an abscess, etc., *fistular*, Eus.*v.C.*1.57(p.34.13; M.20.972B) = id.*h.e.*8.16.4(M.20.789B).

συριγμός (συρισμός), ὁ, 1. *hissing*, as of serpents, συρισμός, Anton.Hag.*v.Sym.Styl.*19(p.46.12); **2.** *crackling* of fire, Ephr.3. 250B.

σύριγξ, ἡ, 1. *shepherd's pipe*; hence any *hollow stalk*, Epiph. *haer.*64.68(p.513.15; M.41.1189D); **2.** anything like a pipe; hence bee's *cell* ἵνα...τὰ κηρία πλέκηται...δι' ἑξαγώνων σ. καὶ ἀντιστρόφων Gr.Naz.*or.*28.25(p.59.18; M.36.60C); Chrys.*hom.68.5 in Mt.*(7. 676E).

Συρικός, *red* or *purple*, *Apoc.Mos.*40(p.21); ‡Jo.D.*Const.*3(M.95. 316D); cf. *Syricum rubri coloris pigmentum...quod Syrii Phoenices in Rubri maris litoribus colligunt*, Isid.H.*etym.*19.17.6.

σύρισμα, τό, later form of σύριγμα; **1.** *whistling* χειλέων σ. †Bas. *contub.*3(M.30.817B); **2.** *hissing* Εὔα...δρακοντιαίων σ. ἀγαπήτρια ‡Chrys.*hom.in Ps.92:3*(5.622E).

συρισμός, ὁ, v. συριγμός.

συρίττω, 1. *hiss* like a serpent; of demons, Ath.*v.Anton.*26(M.26. 884A); *ib.*39(901A); **2.** *hiss* as a sign of derision, acc. Juln. Imp. the practice of Christians at baptism οὐδὲ ἐσύριττεν [sc. an ex-Christian priest] ὥσπερ ἐκεῖνοι, αὐτὸς καθ' ἑαυτόν· ἡ γὰρ ἄκρα θεολογία παρ' αὐτοῖς ἐστι...σ. τε πρὸς τοὺς δαίμονας καὶ σκιογραφεῖν ἐπὶ τοῦ μετώπου τὸν σταυρόν Juln.Imp.*ep.*79(Bidez p.86.14,16).

σύρμα, τό, *anything dragged* or *trailed*; *trail*; *efflux* of air, Geo. Pis.*hex.*211(M.92.1449A).

***συρμαιογραφέω**, ? *draw* or *trace letters* ποία...χεὶρ τῆς ἐκείνου [sc. S. Paul] δεξιᾶς μουσικώτερον ἐσυρμαιογράφησεν, ἢ τίς ἐπιπονώτερον τῆς ἐκείνου προθυμίας ἐσπουδαιογράφησεν; Thdr.Stud.*or.*11.16(M.99. 820A).

συρμός, ὁ, 1. any *sweeping motion*; *surge, wave*; met., *spread* of original sin to whole race ἐπὶ πολὺ προσεχύθη καὶ φερόμενον...σ. ἐξαισίοις οὐ μόνον ἔξωθεν...ἀλλ'...εἴσω κατέκλυζε τὰς ψυχάς Meth. *symp.*4.2(p.47.1; M.18.88C); **2.** met., *violence* πληγὰς καὶ συρμοὺς καὶ διαρπαγάς *Ep.Lugd.*ap.Eus.*h.e.*5.1.7(M.20.409B).

***Συρομακεδόνες, οἱ,** *people inhabiting that part of Syria near to Egypt who kept the Macedonian year* of months of exactly thirty days with intercalary days at the end of the year, Euthal.Diac. *epp.Paul.*(M.85.713B).

[*]**συρομάστης, ὁ,** v. σειρομάστης.

***συρομένως**, *by being drawn* or *dragged along* τὰ...τῷ κινουμένῳ ἐνδεδεμένα σ. κινεῖται ‡Just.*confut.*56(M.6.1557A).

Σύρος, ὁ, *Syrian*; used by non-Christians to denote a Christian παρ' ἡμῶν ἀπῆρες ποικίλης σοφίας σεαυτὸν γεμίσας τοῖς Σ. Aen.*dial.* (M.85.873A); cf.Epictetus 2.9.20; Lucian *Philops.*1.16.

***συρράμων, ὁ,** *one who sews together*; met., *fellow contriver* συμμύστην καὶ σ. τῆς αὐτοῦ ἀνομίας ‡Jo.D.*Const.*19(M.95.337A).

συρράπτω, 1. *sew* or *stitch together*; fig., ref. Gen.3:7 τὰ πρόσκαιρα φύλλα τῆς ὑλικῆς ταύτης ζωῆς, ἅπερ...κακῶς ἑαυτοῖς συνερράψαμεν Gr.Nyss.*or.dom.*5(p.100.37; M.44.1184B); **2.** ref. dilapidated buildings, *patch* or *piece together, make repairs* οὐδεὶς ὑποστήριγμα τίθησιν, οὐδὲ σ. ταῖς παλαιαῖς οἰκοδομαῖς Chrys.*hom.5.3 in Tit.*(11. 761B); met. πῶς, μετὰ τὸ σχισθῆναι τὴν εἰρήνην, σ. ταύτην δυνήσῃ; Ath.*ep.Drac.*2(M.25.525A); **3.** met., *concoct, devise* μηχανὴν θανάτου [sc. Κωνσταντίνῳ] σ. Eus.*v.C.*1.47(p.29.22; M.20.961B) = id.*h.e.*8.13. 15(M.20.780C); διαβολὰς...σ. Philost.*h.e.*3.27(M.65.513B).

συρρήγνυμι, *dash together*; pass. intrans.; **1.** of fighting and quarrels, *break out* ἄρξαι τῆς αἰτίας ἐξ ἧς ἡ διαφορὰ Ἀλεξάνδρῳ τῷ ἐπισκόπῳ καὶ Ἀρείῳ συνερράγη Philost.*h.e.*1.4(M.65.464A); **2.** of men, *come into collision, be at variance* with καὶ ἑαυτοῖς καὶ ἀλλήλοις συνερράγησαν Chrys.*hom.5.2 in 1Cor.*(10.35E); *ib.39.5*(369B); **3.** pass., *break treaty with* μεταπεῖσαι ξυρραγῆναι ἐκείνῳ Malchus *ex.gent.*6 (p.574.16; M.113.789B).

σύρρηξις, ἡ, *clash, fight*, Gr.Naz.*carm.*2.1.14.16(M.37.1246A); *collision* νεφῶν...σ. id.*or.*28.28(p.66.10; M.36.68A).

συρριζόω, *cause to take root, plant*; met., psalmody of Church as teaching worshipper various aspects of truth, Dion.Ar.*e.h.*3.3.4(M. 3.429D) cit. s. ᾆσμα; *strengthen, encourage* ὡς συνερρίζωσας ἡμᾶς... μὴ ἐκκακεῖν Thdr.Stud.*epp.*2.79(M.99.1317D).

***συρρίζ-ω**, *plant*; met., *establish* εἰς προῦπτον αὐτὴν ἐξελέγχει τὴν πλάνην καὶ τὴν νέαν ~ειν ὡς λαοπλάνον Andr.Cr.*Agath.*49(M.97. 1440C; συρίζειν *BZ*).

***συρριπτ-έω**, *throw together*, pass., met. καιροῖς...~ούμενον κακοῖς Gr.Naz.*carm.*2.1.68.57(M.37.1413A).

συρρίπτω, *throw* ? in wrestling τὰ πνεύματα τῶν γιγάντων... ἐμπίπτοντα καὶ συμπαλαίοντα καὶ σ. ἐπὶ τῆς γῆς *Apoc.En.*15.11.

σύρροια, ἡ, *conflux*; *confluence*; met.; **1.** *accumulation* κακῶν σ. Socr.*h.e.*2.26.1(M.67.265B); **2.** *flux* τὴν τοῦ πάθους σ. Geo.Pis.*carm.*4. 110(p.14).

σύρσις, ἡ, *drawing* or *dragging*, Steph.Diac.*v.Steph.*(M.100. 1140B).

***συρτικός**, *crawling* μετὰ τὸν νηπιώδη σ. ἐπὶ τοῦ ἐδάφους περίπατον χειροκρατούμενος Anast.S.*hod.*13(M.89.220C).

***συρφετής**, *promiscuous*, *cat.Apoc.*19:14(p.461.9).

***συρφετία, ἡ,** *vulgarity*, Nil.*epp.*2.286(M.79.341D).

***συρφετολογία, ἡ,** *jumble of arguments*, Didym.*Trin.*1.18(M.39. 341C); Leont.H.*Nest.*1.19(M.86.1473A).

συρφετός, ὁ, *sweeping, refuse, litter*; met.; **1.** denoting a collection of rubbish or nonsense, *sweepings, scrap-heap, pile* τῶν περὶ Ἄρειον ἐξ ἀγράφων ἐπινοησάντων τοσούτων ῥηματίων συρφετόν Ath.

syn.36(p.263.15; M.26.757A); τὴν ὀρθὴν...ἐκπολιορκοῦσι πίστιν, συρφετοὺς εἰκαίων συναγείροντες ἐννοιῶν Cyr.*ep*.50(p.97.2; 5².166C); id. *Mich*.60(3.453B); also of persons πολὺν πεπορνευμένων γυναικῶν σ. Chrys.*Jud*.1.2(1.590B); **2.** of things, denoting moral worthlessness; **a.** *refuse, garbage* κρότου καὶ μέθης καὶ παντὸς...σ. Clem.*paed*.3.11 (p.280.28; M.8.660A); σ. ἀσεβείας Chrys.*hom.2.5 in Ac*.(9.21D); τῆς ἁμαρτίας...σ. Cyr.*Ps*.49:3(M.69.1077A); *trash* τῆς...κενοδοξίας τὸν σ. Ast.Am.*hom*.1(M.40.165A); **b.** as adj., *filthy* τῆς συρφετῆς τοῦδε τοῦ βίου κόπρου Steph.Diac.*v.Steph*.(M.100.1107A); **3.** of persons; **a.** *one of the mob, common fellow*, Gr.Nyss.*v.Gr.Thaum*.(M.46.936A); **b.** of the morally worthless, *scum, sweepings* ἡμᾶς...ἀπεσκυβάλισε ...ὡσανεὶ σ. τινα Gr.Naz.*ep*.88(M.37.161C); id.*or*.27.9(p.17.2; M.36. 24A); of the frivolous, *froth* ἄτακτοι καὶ σ. Nil.*epp*.2.49(M.79.221A).

συρφετώδης, 1. *vulgar, commonplace, undistinguished* τὴν ἀνεπιστημόνα καὶ...σ. διάνοιαν Epiph.*haer*.80.9(p.494.4; M.42.769B); *ib*.80. 8(p.493.7; 768C); τὰ σ. ... ἤθη Nil.*epp*.2.96(M.79.244B); **2.** *worthless*, Cyr.H.*catech*.13.11; **3.** morally *worthless, base* καθάρωμεν...ἑαυτοὺς ...παντὸς...σ. μολύσματος Nect.*Thdr*.15(M.39.1833B); σ. διδασκαλίας Epiph.*haer*.19.6(p.223.16; M.41.268D); τῆς τῶν παθῶν σ. ἰλύος ‡Proc.G. *Pr*.2:20(M.87.1240C).

***συρφετωδῶς, 1.** *vulgarly* σ. βοῶντες Chrys.*hom.19.3 in Mt*.(7. 247E); **2.** *through stupidity* ἄπιστοι μὲν γὰρ ἀρνοῦνται τὸ πᾶν τῆς ἀναστάσεως, κακόπιστοι δὲ σ. καὶ ἀνοήτως τῆς...ἐλπίδος ἐκπεπτώκασι Epiph.*anc*.83(p.103.8; M.43.172C).

σύρ-ω, 1. *drag, draw, trail along*; **a.** abs., opp. ὠθέω: κοντοῖς ὠθοῦντες, μακέλλαις σ. Chrys.*hom.13.4 in 1Tim*.(11.623E); **b.** *draw* a sword, Jo.Mal.*chron*.18 p.492(M.97.712B); **c.** *draw, take* breath ὁ διάβολος ~ει ῥόγχον ἐν τῷ στόματι αὐτοῦ καὶ ἐπειρᾶτο πιάσαι τὸν Ἰησοῦν *Contrad*.1(p.7) cf. βάλας ῥόγχον *ib*.2(p.9); **d.** met., pass., *be dragged at the heel, trailed in the wake* τὸν...νοῦν ἀφεὶς ~εσθαι δεδεμένον ὀπίσω τῶν ἀλόγων παθῶν Chrys.*hom.69.2 in Mt*.(7.682D); id.*hom.13.7 in Rom*.(9.568C); **2.** pass., *crawl, swarm*; of reptiles and insects, and of persons; met. ἐν τῇ πλάνῃ διάγοντες χαμαὶ ἐσύρεσθε Chrys.*comm.in Gal*.4:8(10.705D); id.*hom.23.2 in Eph*.(11. 176A); id.*hom.68.5 in Mt*.(7.677A); perf. ptcpl. pass., *grovelling, low, common* γνώμη...ταπεινὴ καὶ σεσυρμένη *ib*.66.3(7.657A); ἀγοραίων...καὶ σεσυρμένων ἀνθρώπων id.*hom.27.4 in Rom*.(9.724A); **3.** *drag by force, hale* ~ωμεν τὸν υἱὸν τοῦ θεοῦ *Ev.Petr*.3(p.222); οὐδέποτε ἐφόνευσα ἄνθρωπον, εἰ μὴ τὸν Βόνοσον ὃν ἔσυρα μετὰ τῶν Χριστιανῶν *Didasc.Jac*.1.54(p.777.25); *draw to oneself, take* without force ἀπαθὴς...ἡ θεία φύσις, τὸ δὲ σῶμα τὸ πάθος ἐδέξατο· ~οντος μὲν αὐτὸ τοῦ ἑνωθέντος θεοῦ λόγου, πάθος δὲ ἐκεῖθεν οὐχ ἑλκύσαντος Thdt.*Cant*.5:10ff.(2.116).

***συσθένεια, ἡ,** *conjoined might* or *power* μία οὐσία, μία σ. ‡Caes. Naz.*dial*.3(M.38.860).

συσκέπτομαι, 1. *consider* σ. ... ἀλλήλοις...ἀπελθεῖν *Ev.Petr*.10 (p.302); Just.*dial*.46.2(M.6.573B); **2.** *plan, intrigue* ὁ κτίστης τοῖς κτίσμασι συνανεστρέφετο, καὶ ὁ λῃστὴς τοῖς δαίμοσι σ. Procl.CP *or*.6. 15(M.65.749B).

συσκευάζ-ω, A. act., *put together, prepare* οὐ γὰρ ὑπ' ἐμοῦ συνεσκευασμένοι εἰσὶν οἱ λόγοι Just.*dial*.29.2(M.6.537A); τὴν παιδείαν... χρὴ συνεσκευάσθαι Clem.*str*.6.11(p.477.28; M.9.312C).

B. med.; **1.** *pack one's baggage, prepare; be provided* with ἧκε [sc. the good Samaritan] συνεσκευασμένος ὢν ὁ κινδυνεύων ἐδεῖτο Clem. *q.d.s*.28(p.178.28; M.9.633C); **2.** in bad sense; **a.** trans., *devise, concoct* συσκευασάμενοι τὴν...παραβολὴν ἵνα τὸν περὶ ἀναστάσεως... λόγον ἀπορήσωσι Meth.*res*.1.51(p.304.19; M.18.281A); *Ep.Mareot*.1 ap.Ath.*apol.sec*.75(p.154.35; M.25.384C); ἀπολογήσασθαι περὶ ὧν συνεσκευάσαντο αὐτῷ οἱ περὶ Εὐσέβιον CAlex.*ep.ib*.3(p.89.6; 252B); ἐπιβουλὴν σ. Eus.*h.e*.4.18.7(M.20.376A); id.*d.e*.1.6(p.35.2; M.22.68C); **b.** intrans., *intrigue, devise a plot*, *Ep.Mareot*.1 ap.Ath.*apol.sec*.75 (p.154.29; M.25.384B); κατὰ πάντων ἐπιφύονται, καὶ πᾶσι σ. *Ep.Aeg*. *ib*.77(p.156.31; 388A); ἐπεβούλευον καὶ σ. τῷ ἀνδρί CAlex.*ep.ib*.6(p.92. 11; 257C); Epiph.*haer*.68.7(p.148.1; M.42.196B); Jo.Mal.*chron*.4 p.87 (M.97.169C); also with κατά: κατὰ δὴ τοῦ Ἀετίου...σ. Philost.*h.e*. 8.4(M.65.560A); **c.** trans., *plan to overthrow, plot against*, Eus.*h.e*. 10.8.14(M.20.900B); ref. Num.22:1ff. ~ονται τὸν Ἰσραὴλ id.*onomast*. (p.78.2); τίνα φρονοῦντα κατ' αὐτῶν οὐ συνεσκευάσαντο; Ath.*apol. fug*.3(p.69.29; M.25.648B); Pall.*h.Laus*.63(p.158.5; M.34.1235B); Jo. Mal.*chron*.2 p.40(M.97.112B); **d.** pass., *suffer intrigue, be plotted against* or *betrayed* ἅμα τῷ συσκευασθῆναι τὸν...Ἀθανάσιον CAlex. *ep*.ap.Ath.*apol.sec*.3(p.89.4; M.25.252B); Pall.*v.Chrys*.18(p.113.6; M. 47.62); συσκευασθεὶς ὑπὸ τῶν ἰδίων ἐσφάγη Jo.Mal.*chron*.2 p.25(M. 97.92A).

συσκευαστής, ὁ, 1. *one who prepares* οἱ τῶν πεμμάτων...σ. Clem. *paed*.3.4(p.251.24; M.8.592B); **2.** in bad sense, *one who plots, schemer* Εὐσέβιος...τῆς Νικομηδείας, ὁ...σ. τῆς κατὰ τὴν ἐκκλησίαν.. βλάβης Epiph.*haer*.68.7(p.148.4; M.42.196C).

συσκευή, ἡ, 1. *compilation* γράφει...ἐν τῷ τετάρτῳ τῆς καθ' ἡμῶν σ. ὁ Πορφύριος Eus.*p.e*.10.9(485A; M.21.808A); **2.** *fabrication*, Gr. Nyss.*Eun*.1(1 p.52.24; σκηνή M.45.281A); **3.** *intrigue, plot* τῆς τῶν ἀρχιερέων σ. [i.e. against Christ]...μνημονεύων Or.*Ps*.58:13(p.66); σ. καὶ ἐπιβουλή *Ep.Alex*.ap.Ath.*apol.sec*.73(p.152.20; M.25.380C); σ. καὶ συκοφαντίαν CAlex.*ep.ib*.8(p.94.28; 264B); ὀψόμενον τῆς σ. τὴν ἀποκάλυψιν Pall.*v.Chrys*.1(p.7.26; M.47.8); usu. with κατά: τὴν μέλλουσαν ἔσεσθαι κατ' αὐτοῦ [sc. Christ] σ. Eus.*h.e*.1.3.6(M.20.69C); τῆς κατ' ἐμοῦ...σ. Ath.*apol.Const*.1(p.279.6; M.25.596A); id.*apol.sec*. 88(p.167.4; 408A); plur. αἱ κατ' αὐτοῦ τῶν Ἰουδαίων σ. Cyr.*Ps*.40:8 (M.69.996B); also with εἰς: τῆς εἰς τὴν...ψυχὴν ἐπιχειρουμένης ὑπὸ ...τοῦ...διαβόλου σ. Epiph.*haer*.26.18(p.299.1; M.41.361B); or genit. simply ἔσωθεν...εἰργάζετο τὴν σ. τῆς ἐκκλησίας *ib*.69.9(p.159.18; M. 42.216C); Innoc.*fr.ep*.ap.Pall.*v.Chrys*.3(p.21.15; M.47.14); **4.** *device, subterfuge* ἐροῦσι...οὐκ ἔστιν ἀνάστασις, ἀλλὰ χλεύη τὰ τῶν Χριστιανῶν, ἀπάτη καὶ σ. Chrys.*hom.62.4 in Jo*.(8.373B); Mac.Mgn.*apocr*.2.19 (p.33.13).

συσκευωρέομαι, *contrive*, Eus.*d.e*.10 proem.(p.445.6; M.22.716B).

συσκηνία, ἡ, *company* ἡ καλὴ σ. τῶν τεσσαράκοντα [sc. μαρτύρων] Gr.Nyss.*mart*.1(M.46.756C); τῆς...ἀποστολικῆς σ. id.*Melet*.(M.46. 852A).

συσκίασμα, τό, *shadow, obscurity*, met. ἀθόλωτον...καὶ παντὸς ἐλευθέραν σ. τὴν...γνῶσιν Cyr.*Jo*.12(4.1072A).

σύσκιος, *thickly shaded*; of 'groves' of OT pagan sacrifice (cf. 3Reg.14:23, Ezech.6:13) τῇ Βάαλ [sc. ἔθυον]...ἐν σ. ἢ μετεώροις τόποις Just.*dial*.136.3(M.6.789C); met., exeg. Cant.1:16 σ. ... φησι τὸν νυμφίον διὰ τὴν πυκνότητα τῶν ἐν τῷ λόγῳ καὶ τῇ σοφίᾳ θεωρημάτων Or.*Cant*.3(p.175.27; M.13.147D); of Logos by Inc. ἔγνω σε, ἤτοι γνώσεται ἡ ἀνθρωπίνη φύσις, σύσκιον τῇ οἰκονομίᾳ γενόμενον Gr.Nyss. *hom.4 in Cant*.(M.44.836C).

***συσκοτασμός, ὁ,** *darkness*, Or.*hom.12.9 in Jer*.(p.96.2,5f.; M.13. 392A).

***συσκοτίζω,** *darken*, met. τῷ μεμελανωμένῳ καὶ συνεσκοτισμένῳ φῶς ἀνέτειλεν ἄσβεστον Rom.Mel.(*AS* 1 p.24).

***συσκώπτω,** *join in mockery* or *scoffing*, Chrys.*hom.87.3 in Mt*. (7.820D).

συσμικρύνομαι, med., *be small together with*, Mac.Aeg.*hom*.32.7 (M.34.737C).

συσπ-άω, *contract; clench, close the hand*, ref. Ecclus.4:31 μὴ γίνου πρὸς...τὸ δοῦναι ~ῶν *Did*.4.5 = *Barn*.19.9.

συσπείρ-ω, 1. *sow together with*; pass., ref. question whether soul originates with body, Or.*Jo*.2.30(24; p.87.12; M.14.165C); *ib*.6.14 (7; p.124.9; 228A); ψυχὴ...συγγεννᾶται, οὐ συσπείρεται. ἡ φύσις ἐστὶν ὁ δεσμὸς ἡ καὶ ~ομένη τῷ σώματι...κτίζεται ἡ ψυχὴ ὅτε καὶ τὸ σῶμα εἰκονίσθη Proc.G.*Gen*.2:7(M.87.153B); met., of Gnost. aeons τούτων τῶν συσπαρέντων αὐτῷ Iren.*haer*.1.15.3(M.7.621A; συμπαρέντων Harvey); **2.** pass., *be innate*, ‡Nil.*perist*.9.6(M.79.876B); σ. ἡμῖν ἡ πρὸς ἀγαθὸν ἔφεσις...καὶ γνῶσις Proc.G.*Gen*.2:2(M.87.144D).

***συσσαββατίζω,** *observe the sabbath with*, of S. Paul σ. ... καὶ συννηστεύων [sc. with Jews] πολλάκις εὑρίσκετο Pall.*v.Chrys*.19(p.124. 21; M.47.70).

***συσσαλεύω,** *shake together with* or *at the same time* τὸ πρόσωπον ...σειόμενον...σ. πᾶσαν ὁμοῦ τὴν κεφαλὴν καὶ τὸν τράχηλον Sophr.H. *mir.Cyr.et Jo*.63(M.87.3644A).

***συσσαρκία, ἡ,** *marriage union*, Gr.Naz.*carm*.1.2.6.2(M.37.643A).

συσσαρκόω, *cause to take flesh together with, clothe with flesh also* σαρκωθεῖσα ἡ τοῦ υἱοῦ ὑπόστασις, οὐ σ. ἑαυτῇ τὴν ἀγεννησίαν τοῦ πατρός Anast.S.*hod*.17(M.89.264C); pass., *become flesh together with* ὁμολογεῖν [sc. Nestorius]...ὅτιπερ καὶ ἡ τοῦ πατρὸς καὶ ἡ τοῦ ἁγίου πνεύματος θεότης συνεσαρκώθη τῷ λόγῳ Acac.Mel.ap.CEph.(431)*act*.1 (*ACO* 1.1.2 p.38.25; H.1.1400A).

συσσάρκωσις, ἡ, *union by flesh*, opp. συγχόνδρωσις and συννεύρωσις, Melet.*nat.hom*.synops.(M.64.1120A).

***συσσέβω,** *worship* one object *together with* another οὐ σ. τῷ θεῷ τὸν οὐρανόν Or.*Cels*.5.6(p.6.18; M.11.1188D).

σύσσεισις, ἡ, *shaking, convulsion* ἐνταῦθα...τὴν μεταβολὴν τὴν ἐπὶ τῆς γῆς πραγμάτων σ. ὠνόμασεν Or.*Ps*.59:4(p.68).

συσσεισμός, ὁ, 1. *whirlwind, hurricane*, ref. 4Reg.2:1,11, Or.*Jo*. 6.46(27; p.155.10; M.14.280B); 'ἥξει ὁ κύριος...' ἐν σ. 'ἐπάνω τῶν νεφελῶν' *Const.App*.7.32.4; συναθροίσθητε εἰς τὴν ἁγίαν Βηθλεὲμ...ἐν σ. *Dorm.BMV* 12(p.99); **2.** *earthquake*, ref. 3Reg.19:11f., Gr.Naz. *or*.28.19(p.49.16; M.36.49C); **3.** met., *disquiet* of mind, *turmoil* ἐπιβλαβὲς τὸ ὑλικοῖς ἐνέχεσθαι...τάραχον καὶ σ. σχοίη Thdr.Mops.*Ps*. 59:4(M.66.684D); f.l. for σύσσημον, Thdr.Stud.*epp*.1.7(M.99.929C).

συσσεί-ω, **1.** *whirl* βοῦν...εὗρον...καὶ κρατήσας τῶν κεράτων καὶ κύκλῳ σ. *T.Jud.*3.1; **2.** *make to tremble, shake* ~ει [i.e. by the flight into Egypt]...τὰ χειροποίητα Αἰγύπτου Thdt.*ep.*151(4.1300); **3.** met., *disturb, agitate*, Thdr.Mops.*Ps.*59:4(M.66.684D).

συσσεύομαι, *come together quickly, hasten together*, Nonn.*par.Jo.* 6:2(M.43.793A).

***σύσσημα, τό**, = σύσσημον, *mark of identity*, Jo.Mal.*chron.*8 p.195 (M.97.308A).

συσσημαίν-ω, *signify along with* or *at the same time, connote* ὁ τοῦ ἐνεργοῦντος μνησθεὶς καὶ τὴν ἐνέργειαν...σ. Gr.Nyss.*Eun.*1(1 p.82.26; M.45.313C); *ib.*4(2 p.94.20; 672A); id.*Apoll.*27(M.45.1184A); ptcpl. pass., *correlate* συνέζευκται τῷ μὲν γεννήματι ὁ γεννήσας, ὁ δὲ κτίσας τῷ κτίσματι, καὶ δεῖ πάντως...σώζειν ἑκάστῳ τῶν πρός τι λεγομένων τὸ οἰκείως ~όμενον id.*Eun.*4(2 p.83.2; 657C).

***σύσσοφος**, *one in wisdom*; of Trin., Eulog.*fr.Trin.*2.1(p.364) cit. s. σύγγνωμος.

[*]**σύσστεμα, τό**, v. σύστημα.

συσσώζω, **1.** *join in saving* ὁ υἱὸς ἢ τὸ πνεῦμα συμπάρεστιν καὶ...σ. ἅμα τῷ...πατρί Didym.*Trin.*2.12(M.39.677C); **2.** pass., *be saved together* with συνσωθῆναι τοῖς ἀγγέλοις Or.*hom.13 in Lc.*(p.92.10).

σύσσωμος, **A.** *body to body, in bodily contact*; of David and Abishag, Epiph.*anc.*20(p.29.18; M.43.53C); id.*haer.*69.46(p.193.23; M.42.273C).

B. ref. Eph.3:6, *one body with*; **1.** ref. union with Christ through Inc. τοὺς σ. ἐκείνου πάντας ἡμᾶς Ath.*Ar.*1.42(M.26.100B); τὰ ἡμῶν ἀναδεχόμενος, ἵνα ἡμεῖς, ὡς σ. συναρμολογούμενοι καὶ συνδεθέντες ἐν αὐτῷ διὰ τῆς ὁμοιώσεως τῆς σαρκός...ἀθάνατοι καὶ ἄφθαρτοι διαμείνωμεν *ib.*2.74(305A); *ib.*2.61(277B); and of Christ with man ἵνα θεμέλιος γένωμαι...τῶν ἐποικοδομουμένων εἰς ἐμὲ...καὶ σ. τούτοις Cyr.*thes.*15(5[1].172C) and in special sense with BMV ὁ σύνθρονος τοῦ πατρός, σ. [sc. γίνεται] γυναικός Procl.CP *or.*6.11(M.65.740D); **2.** of union of members of Church as Christ's body; **a.** with Christ ὁ...λόγος θεὸς...ἄνθρωπος ὤφθη...τῆς ἀνθρωπότητος καινοποίησιν ἐργασάμενος...ὥστε εἶναι τὰ ἔθνη σ. καὶ συμμέτοχα τοῦ Χριστοῦ ‡Ath. *Apoll.*1.5(M.26.1140B); εἶναι τὰ ἔθνη συγκληρονόμα καὶ σ. αὐτοῦ γὰρ τούτου, οὗ ἡ ἀρχὴ ἐστιν ἐπὶ τοῦ ὤμου αὐτοῦ †Bas.*Is.*226(1.550A; M.30.512C); σ. τοῦ Χριστοῦ καὶ συμμέτοχοι, οἱ τὴν...πίστιν παραδεξάμενοι, γίνονται Gr.Nyss.*Apoll.*28(M.45.1184C); τῷ...τελειότητα...ἐπιδείξαντι σ. τε καὶ συμμέτοχοι γενησόμεθα †Gr.Nyss.*occurs.*(M.46.1152C); οἰκεῖοι τοῦ θεοῦ, σ. τε τοῦ Χριστοῦ Cyr.*Mich.*19(3.408B); **b.** with each other τὰ...ἔθνη συγκληρονόμα καὶ σ. καὶ συμμέτοχα τῶν ἁγίων πεποίηκεν ὁ θεός Iren.*haer.*1.10.3(M.7.557A); τῶν ἐν πίστει...οἱ ἐξ ἁπάσης...χώρας συνειλεγμένοι, σ. γεγόνασιν ἐν Χριστῷ Cyr.*glaph. Gen.*3(1.67D); ἐπειδὴ ἓν σῶμα προσηγόρευσε τοὺς πιστούς, σ. τὰ ἔθνη γεγενῆσθαί φησι Thdt.*Eph.*3:6(3.417); **3.** of BMV with Christ in glory χαίροις...θεοτόκε, ὅτι ὁ βασιλεὺς...Ἰησοῦς ὁ...διὰ σοῦ δωρησάμενος ἡμῖν τὴν ἐπουράνιον αὐτοῦ βασιλείαν, ἐν ταύτῃ σε εἶναι σ. ἐν ἀφθαρσίᾳ...προσέταξεν Mod.*dorm.*10(M.86.3301B); *ib.*5(3289C); *ib.* 6,14(3293A,3312B); **4.** of eucharistic union σ. ... ἀξιωθέντα γὰρ μετασχεῖν τῆς εὐλογίας τῆς μυστικῆς, ἓν πρὸς αὐτὸν γέγονε σῶμα Cyr. *Jo.*10.2(4.862E); *ib.*11.11(1000A) cit. s. δύναμις; ἐπειδὴ...ἐξ ἑνὸς ἄρτου μεταλαμβάνομεν πάντες...ἀλλήλων μέλη γινόμεθα, σ. Χριστοῦ χρηματίζοντες Jo.D.*fr.Mt.*26:27(M.96.1409D); **5.** myst., of soul with Christ τῆς κατὰ τὴν νυμφὴν σημασίας σ. αὐτὴν...ποιούσης τῷ ἀφθάρτῳ νυμφίῳ Gr.Nyss.*hom.9 in Cant.*(M.44.968A); αἱ ψυχαὶ...σ. τῷ λόγῳ...αἱ μὲν ἐρωτικῇ τινι διαθέσει...αἱ δὲ φόβῳ κολάσεως *ib.15*(1112C); τὴν δύναμιν ἔχουσαν...τῆς...ἀναστάσεως, κατὰ...τὴν εἰς ὕψος τῆς διανοίας...ἔγερσιν, ἵνα γένωμαι σ. αὐτοῦ καὶ σύμψυχος Max.*ep.*25(M.91.613C).

συστάδην, v. κατασυστάδην.

σύστασις, ἡ, **I.** from trans. tenses of συνίστημι;

A. a *setting together*; **1.** *disposition, arrangement*, Clem.*str.*6.17 (p.512.3; M.9.388A); *system* of reckoning, Epiph.*haer.*70.13(p.247.1; M.42.369A); **2.** *ordering, government* μοναρχία...τῆς πάντων ὑπερκεῖται σ. τε καὶ διοικήσεως Eus.*l.C.*3(p.201.24; M.20.1332A); οἰκετῶν ἀρετὴ συντελεῖ εἰς σ. καὶ προστασίαν οἰκίας Chrys.*hom.22.1 in Eph.* (11.165B); by God πατήρ, τῆς τῶν ὅλων σ. τε καὶ διοικήσεως μόνῳ [sc. τῷ υἱῷ] τοὺς οἴακας ἐγχειρίσας Eus.*e.th.*1.13(p.73.13; M.24.852A); αὐτὸς μὲν ἀκίνητος μένων παρὰ τῷ πατρί, πάντα δὲ κινῶν τῇ ἑαυτοῦ σ. Ath.*gent.*42(M.25.85A); Eustrat.*v.Eutych.*10(M.86.2285C).

B. a *setting together* so as to form a whole, *formation* νέου ἔθνους ...σ. ποιήσασθαι Eus.*d.e.*3.6(p.137.29; M.22.232D); τίς...δύναμις... τηλικαύτη ὡς ἐξαρκεῖν πρὸς οὐρανῶν σ.; Gr.Nyss.*or.catech.*4(p.19.2; M.45.20C); ref. Person of Christ ἀτρέπτῳ νῷ τρεπτὸς οὐ μίγνυται νοῦς εἰς ἑνὸς ὑποκειμένου σύστασιν Apoll.*fr.*151(p.248.3); τὰ...κατὰ σύνθεσιν πρὸς ἑνὸς τελείου σ. συνδεδραμηκότα Cyr.*Thds.*(p.53.2; 5[2].15C) = id. *inc.unigen.*(5[1].689A).

C. a *keeping together, support, maintenance*; **1.** *conservation, preservation* in being ἐπαύσατο...τοῦ εἶναι, λυθείσης αὐτοῦ τῇ τοῦ θεοῦ δυνάμει...τῆς σ. Athenag.*leg.*24.2(M.6.945B) = Meth.*res.*1.36(p.277.11; M.41.1101D); ἵνα...τὴν σ. ἔχωμεν τῆς ζωῆς καὶ τὴν ἀσθένειαν διακρατῶμεν τοῦ σώματος Chrys.*Laz.*7.5(1.797D); Jo.D.*f.o.*1.7(M.94.805A); *continuance* of the race by propagation, Gr.Nyss.*or.catech.*28 (p.106.15; M.45.73B); **2.** *sustenance, nourishment* τὸ πρὸς σύστασιν δικαίως μεταλαμβανόμενον ἄριστον *Const.App.*6.11.5; τὸ σῶμα ᾧ ἐκ τοῦ ἄρτου ἡ σ. ἦν Gr.Nyss.*or.catech.*37(p.149.11; M.45.97A); τοῖς πεπιστευκόσι...ἑαυτὸν ἐνσπείρει διὰ τῆς σαρκός [i.e. in eucharist], ἧς ἡ σ. ἐξ οἴνου τε καὶ ἄρτου ἐστί *ib.*(p.152.3; 97B); met., of meditations, Cyr.*Ps.* 21:15(M.69.840A); **3.** *repair* of fabric διὰ τὴν σ. ... τῶν...ἐκκλησιῶν... καὶ ἀνοικοδομὴν τῶν...καέντων σεβασμίων οἴκων Cyr.S.*v.Sab.*72(p.175.8); **4.** in concrete sense, *support, mainstay* τὸ...κεφάλαιον τῆς τῶν γενητῶν ἁπάντων...σ. τε καὶ σωτηρίας αὐτὸς ἦν, ὃν ἐγέννα...ὁ πατὴρ υἱὸν μονογενῆ Eus.*e.th.*3.2(p.142.6; M.24.976D); met. τὴν...Ὀλυμπιάδα γενέσθαι ἀρχηγὸν καὶ σ. καὶ σωτηρίαν τοῦ...μοναστηρίου *V.Olymp.* 2.2(p.45.14); *ib.*2.15(p.50.23); **5.** *commendation* of, *testimony* to, persons πλεῖον...τῷ ὄντι εἰς πρεσβυτέρου σ. τῆς ἐν θριξὶ λευκότητος, τὸ ἐν φρονήσει πρεσβυτικόν †Bas.*Is.*104(1.451B; M.30.285C); ref. 1Cor.8:6 εἴωθε...ἀεὶ τὸ...πνεῦμα οὐ σ. ἑαυτοῦ ποιούμενον, ἵνα μὴ ἡμῖν ὑπογραμμὸν δώσει τοῦ περὶ ἑαυτῶν καὶ ἡμᾶς τὴν σ. ... ποιήσασθαι Epiph.*haer.*57.5(p.350.29f.; M.41.1004B); μὴ εὐγενείᾳ καὶ πλούτῳ καὶ τῇ τοῦ δήμου σ. ... θαρρ͜οῦντες Chrys.*hom.44.1 in 1Cor.*(10.407A); to Christ from Father θεόθεν ἦν αὐτῷ δοθεῖσα σ. Or.*Cels.*3.36(p.233.10; M.11.968A); id.*mart.*35(p.33.5; M.11.609B); Chrys.*bapt.Chr.*3(2.372B); from scripture τὸ μέγιστον περὶ τῆς σ. τοῦ Ἰησοῦ κεφάλαιον, ὡς ὅτι ἐπροφητεύθη ὑπὸ τῶν...προφητῶν Or.*Cels.*1.49(p.100.12; 752C); and from other sources αὕτη παρ' ἐμοὶ σ. ἀρίστη, ἡ ἀπὸ τῶν ἔργων ἐπίδειξις Chrys.*anom.*8.5(1.521E); ἔχω τὴν ἀπὸ τοῦ χρόνου σ. μαρτυροῦσάν μοι id.*Jud.*5.4(1.633E); **6.** *letter of introduction* or *recommendation* εἰ...τις ἀπὸ παροικίας ἀδελφὸς ἢ ἀδελφὴ ἐπέλθοι σύστασιν ἐπικομιζόμενοι *Const.App.*2.58.1; Euthal.Diac.*epp.Paul.* (M.85.789A); Chrys.*hom.6.1 in 2Cor.*(10.474C,D); plur., Epiph.*haer.* 68.9(p.149.25; M.42.197D); **7.** *confirmation, establishment, support* of statements, etc.; of Faith αὐταρκής ἐστι [sc. faith of Nicaea]... πρὸς σύστασιν...τῆς...ἐν Χριστῷ πίστεως Ath.*ep.Epict.*1(p.3.5; M.26.1052A); πρὸς σύστασιν τῆς τῶν σωμάτων ἀναστάσεως ‡Just.*qu.et resp.* 111(M.6.1360A); of authority of eccl. canons, Pall.*v.Chrys.*9(p.53.27; M.47.31); of heresy σ. τῷ δόγματι Hipp.*Noët.*2(p.237.4; M.10.805A); ἡ δοκοῦσα σ. τῆς κακοδοξίας Ath.*decr.*2(p.2.17; M.25.'425' (417)D); id.*Dion.*1(p 46.15; M.25.480B); Gr.Nyss.*or.catech.*7(p.37.16; M.45.29D); from scripture εἴρηται...μόνον εἰς σ. τοῦ γεννηθησομένου Afric.*ep.Arist.*(p.57.14; M.10.53C); Meth.*symp.*3.8(p.35.3; M.18.72C); Eus.*d.e.*1.5(p.22.30; M.22.48C); πρὸς σύστασιν...τούτου [i.e. Montanist teaching] Didym.*Trin.*3.41(M.39.984B); of persons νομοθεσίας... εἰς τὴν αὐτῶν σ. Eus.*d.e.*1.6(p.30.25; 60D); or practices ἀπ' αὐτοῦ τοῦ Χριστοῦ τὴν σ. ταύτης [i.e. circumcision] βούλονται φέρειν Epiph. *haer.*30.26(p.368.11; M.41.449C); in law, *establishment, proof* of charges, Phot.*nomoc.*9.30(p.568; M.104.788C); *ib.*9.39(p.578; 816B); *final settlement*; *determination* of a question περὶ...τοῦ χρόνου τοῦ... ποιητοῦ...συστάσεως Tat.*orat.*31(M.6.872A; στάσεως p.32.16); Eus. *p.e.*11 proem.(508B; M.21.844C); **8.** *restoration, reconstitution*, of general resurrection διὰ μόνων τῶν ἀνθρώπων τὴν σ. χάριν κρίσεως Tat.*orat.*6(p.6.20; M.6.817B); of restoration of human nature through redemption, *A.(Pass.)Andr.*3(p.5.18); of restoration of all things, Bas.*ep.*164.2(3.255D; M.32.637A).

II. from intrans. tenses of συνίστημι;

A. *standing together*; **1.** eccl., [sc. with the faithful] the fourth grade of penitential discipline ἡ σ., ἵνα συνίσταται τοῖς πιστοῖς, καὶ μὴ ἐξέρχηται μετὰ τῶν κατηχουμένων †Gr.Thaum.*ep.can.*11(M.10.1048B); τῷ τετάρτῳ [sc. ἔτει] εἰς σ. μετὰ τοῦ λαοῦ, ἀπεχομένους τῆς προσφορᾶς Bas.*ep.*199 *can.*22(3.293C; M.32.724A); μερισθήσεται...αὐτῷ ὁ χρόνος εἰς ὑπόπτωσιν καὶ σ.· καὶ τότε ἀξιούσθω τῆς κοινωνίας *ib.*217 *can.*61(327A; M.800A); **2.** *congregation, company* of angelic beings, Ign.*Trall.*5.2; μὴ τάγμα ἓν καὶ μία σ. ... τῶν ἀθανάτων Meth.*res.*1.49 (p.302.15; M.18.277B); of apostles, Eus.*d.e.*2.3(p.90.19; M.22.160C); of an Arian synod τὴν ἑαυτῶν ἄδικον σ. ὀνομάζειν σύνοδον ἐπιχειροῦσι CAlex.*ep.*ap.Ath.*apol.sec.*7(p.93.21; M.25.261A); **3.** *conspiracy* ἀεὶ ...συστάσεις ποιήσουσι κατὰ τῆς ἀληθείας Ath.*syn.*32(p.260.8; M.26.749B); ref. trial of Christ οὐχὶ δικαστήριον ἀλλὰ σ. καὶ τυραννὶς τὰ γινόμενα Chrys.*hom.73.3 in Jo.*(8.493D).

B. *coming together into one*; **1.** *coming into existence*; *origin* ἡ τῶν ἀγγέλων σ. τῷ θεῷ ἐπὶ προνοίᾳ γέγονε τοῖς ὑπ' αὐτοῦ διακεκοσμημένοις Athenag.*leg.*24.2(M.6.948A) = Meth.*res.*1.37(p.278.4); Valent. ἐκ...τοῦ φόβου...τὰ ψυχικὰ τὴν σ. εἰληφέναι Iren.*haer.*1.5.4

(M.7.497A); ὑπὸ τῆς θείας τέχνης...ἐπιτελουμένοις...γενέσεσι καὶ σ. καὶ τροφαῖς καὶ αὐξήσεσι Or.*mart*.4(p.6.7; M.11.568C); τῆς ἀρχῆθεν Χριστιανῶν σ. id.*Cels*.8.47(p.262.16; M.11.1588A); ἅμα τῇ πρώτῃ σ. τοῦ βίου Eus.*d.e*.1.10(p.43.27; M.22.84B); οὐδὲ ἐξ αὐτοῦ [sc. θεοῦ] τὴν ὑπόστασιν ἔχειν [sc. evil], οὐδὲ τὴν τοῦ εἶναι σ. Adam.*dial*.4.2(p.140.6; M.11.1808C); *source* τὴν θεοτόκον...ἀποκυήσασαν τὴν τῆς ἀφθαρσίας σ. ‡Meth.*Sym.et Ann*.9(M.18.369C); of human conception and birth τὴν σ. ... ἐκ συνουσίας εἰληφότες Clem.*str*.3.6(p.217.24; M.8.1149C); Or.*schol.in Cant*.3:1ff.(M.17.269C); Ath.*inc*.35.7(M.25.156D); denied in regard to God θεὸς ὁ καθ' ἡμᾶς οὐκ ἔχει σ. ἐν χρόνῳ Tat.*orat*.4(p.5.1; M.6.813A); common to all creatures πᾶσιν τὸ εἶναι αὐτὸς [sc. God] παρέσχεν...οὐδὲ τὴν σ. ἀνάρχως ἔχουσιν Meth.*arbitr*.21(p.206.6); Ath.*Ar*.2.24(M.26.197B); τὴν σ. ἔχω ἐκ *originate in, spring* or *derive from* ἡ...Μαρκίωνος αἵρεσις, ἐξ ἀγαθοῦ καὶ κακοῦ τὴν σ. ἔχουσα Hipp.*haer*.7.31(p.216.15; M.16.3334B); τοῖς ὑπ' αὐτῶν λεγομένοις τὴν σ. ἔχειν ἐκ γεωμετρικῆς τέχνης καὶ ἀριθμητικῆς *ib*.8.15(p.235.24; 3363A); esp. of creation τὴν τοῦ...κόσμου σ. Athenag.*leg*.25.3(p.34.13; M.6.949C); Meth.*symp*.7.5(p.76.12; M.18.132A); ἐκ πρώτης αἰῶνος σ. Eus.*v.C*.4.66(p.145.7; M.20.1221A); ὢν [sc. ὁ υἱός] καὶ πρὸ τῆς τῶν γενητῶν ἁπάντων σ. id.*e.th*.3.3(p.154.21; M.24.997A); ἄλλοι ὑπό τινων ἀγγέλων λέγουσιν εἶναι τὴν τῶν πάντων σ. Ath.*decr*.19(p.16.13; M.25.449B); ἀρκεῖ τὸ βούλημα αὐτοῦ πρὸς σ. τῶν γινομένων id.*Ar*.2.2(M.26.152A); οὐκ...ἐπιδεῖται τινος πρὸς τὴν ὧν βούλεται σ., ἀλλ' ἅμα τε βούλεται, καὶ γέγονεν ὅπερ ἠθέλησεν Eun.*apol*.23(1.627A; M.30.860B); Sever.*Eph*.2:2f.(p.307.27) cit. s. δημιουργικός; heret. of Trin., εἰπεῖν ...γενητὴν τὴν τῆς τριάδος σ. Ath.*Ar*.1.17(M.26.48B); ἐκ προσθήκης ἔσχε τὴν σ. *ib*.(48C); of Son πρὸ τῆς πρωτοτόκου σ. Eun.*apol*.24 (M.30.860C); αὐτῆς...τῆς σ., καὶ παντός, ὅπερ ἐστί, τὸν πατέρα φαμὲν αἴτιον *ib*.21(857A); **2.** *existence*; **a.** in eternity πατὴρ...τῆς τοῦ υἱοῦ σ. αἴτιος Eus.*d.e*.4.3(p.153.9; M.22.256B); *ib*.4.15(p.182.2; 304B); **b.** in time ἐπ' ἐσχάτου τῆς σ. τοῦ Ἰουδαίων ἔθνους *ib*.8.1(p.361.3; 585D); ὁ...ὅριον θέμενος τῇ κτίσει, καὶ τὸ ποσὸν τῶν ἡμερῶν παγιώσας τῆς σ. αὐτῆς Didym.*Trin*.3.22(M.39.917C); τὰ...πάντα... ἐκτισμένα καὶ εἰς σ. ὑπ' αὐτοῦ...προεληλυθότα Epiph.*haer*.32.1(p.440.9; M.41.545A); τῶν τεχνῶν ἑκάστη δεῖται τῆς ἑτέρας πρὸς σ. Thdt.*affect*.4(4.808); ref. God in rel. to creatures ὕλην ὥσπερ τινὰ καὶ οὐσίαν τῆς τῶν ὅλων γενέσεώς τε καὶ σ. τὴν ἑαυτοῦ βουλὴν καὶ δύναμιν προβεβλημένος Eus.*d.e*.4.1(p.151.20; 252D); ζῴων σ. Lit.ap.*Const.App*.8.12.15; of Son τοῦτον ἀποκαλύπτει τοῖς πᾶσι διὰ τῆς τῶν πάντων δι' αὐτοῦ σ. καὶ ζωῆς Ath.*gent*.47(M.25.93D); ζωὴ δέ, ὅτι φῶς, καὶ πάσης λογικῆς φύσεως σ. καὶ οὐσίωσις Gr.Naz.*or*.30.20(p.140.12; M.36.129C); υἱόν, τὴν τῶν ὅλων σ., δεδόσθαι φησὶν τῇ ἐκκλησίᾳ κεφαλήν Cyr.*Pulch*.(p.37.7; 5².144B); ref. council holding its *session* ἡ σύνοδος ἐν Σελευκείᾳ τὴν σ. λαμβάνει Philost.*h.e*.4.11(M.65.524C); **c.** *actual existence* opp. potential ἑκάστη...τῶν τεχνῶν διὰ τῆς ἐνεργείας... λαμβάνει τὴν τοῦ εἶναι σ. Meth.*arbitr*.21(p.203.13); **d.** *substantive, independent existence* τὸ λογιστικὸν...αἴτιον εἶναί φαμεν τῆς σ. τῷ ζῴῳ Clem.*str*.6.16(p.500.15; M.9.360B); ref. human nature of Christ οὔθ' ἡ σὰρξ καθ' ἑαυτὴν δίχα τοῦ λόγου ὑποστᾶναι ἠδύνατο, διὰ τὸ ἐν λόγῳ τὴν σ. ἔχειν Hipp.*Noët*.15(p.259.20; M.10.825A); ὑπέλαβον 'οὐδὲν' τυγχάνειν πᾶν τὸ οὐχ ὑπὸ θεοῦ...τὴν δοκοῦσαν σ. εἰληφὸς Or.*Jo*.2.13 (7; p.68.31; M.14.136A); τὸ...γένος εἴπαμεν τὴν σ. ἐν τοῖς εἴδεσιν ἔχειν, μὴ εἶναι δέ τι ἕτερον καθ' ἑαυτό Meth.*arbitr*.13(p.179.8); denied to actions opp. the agent, *ib*.8(p.168.6; 256C) = Adam.*dial*.4.9 (p.160.18; M.11.1824B); **3.** *state* of existence, Clem.*exc.Thdot*.22 (p.114.2; M.9.669A); ποῖον...σῶμα...διαφθαρὲν οἷόν τε ἐπανελθεῖν εἰς ...τὴν πρώτην σ.; Cels.ap.Or.*Cels*.5.14(p.15.12; M.11.1201B); ref. Ps.21:15f. τί γὰρ ἂν ἄλλο...σημαίνοι ἢ νεκροῦ σώματος σ.; Eus.*d.e*.10.8(p.485.31; M.22.780D); τοῦ ζῆν τὴν σ. *Hom.Clem*.3.35; *frame* of mind τὴν ἁπάντων...περὶ τὸ θεῖον διάθεσιν πρὸς μίαν ἕξεως σ. ἑνῶσαι Const.ap.Eus.*v.C*.2.65(p.67.10; M.20.1037B); **4.** *composition, structure, constitution* ἄνθρωπος...ἀληθέστατα λέγεται κατὰ φύσιν...τὸ ἐκ σ. ψυχῆς καὶ σώματος συντεθὲν Meth.*res*.1.34(p.272.8); of Christian congregation ἐξ ἀλλήλων [i.e. clergy and laity]...ἐστιν ἡ σ. τοῦ συναθροίσματος *Const.App*.8.1.20; Christol. ἡμῶν ἐνί...διαφέρειν αὐτοῦ τὴν σ. ἀξιούντων τῷ τὸν θεὸν λόγον ἐν αὐτῷ εἶναι, ὅπερ ἐν ἡμῖν ὁ ἔσω ἄνθρωπος Paul.Sam.*fr*.(p.332.10)ap.Leont.B.*Nest.et Eut*.3(M.86.1393A); of human nature of Christ πάντα λαβὼν ἐκ παρθένου, ὅσα ἀρχῆθεν ὁ θεὸς εἰς σ. ἀνθρώπου ἔπλασε...χωρὶς ἁμαρτίας ‡Ath.*Apoll*.2.5(M.26.1140A); ὅ γε θεὸς...τῷ μὲν ἐκ τῆς παρθένου γεννηθέντι...καὶ ὑπὸ τοῦ ἁγίου πνεύματος...διαπλασθέντι...καὶ τήν γε σ. ἐπὶ τῆς γυναικείας δεξαμένῳ γαστρὸς ἐνῆν Thdr.Mops.ap.Justn.*ep.Thdr.Mops*.(p.53.13; M.86.1057B); τὴν...σ. καὶ τὴν ἰδιότητα τοῦ σώματος, ἐκ τῆς ἐνεργείας γενέσθαι τοῦ πνεύματος Leont.B.*Nest.et Eut*.2(M.86.1353A); *ib*.(1325C); s.v.l. ὁ...λόγος ἐπιπαρὼν...ἐν τῇ σ. αὐτοῦ ἐξ ἁγίας παρθένου, σαρκί Eus.*d.e*.6.20(M.22.469D; συστάσῃ p.286.18); τὴν σ. ἔχω ἐκ *be composed of* τί...τῆς ὕλης κρείττους οἱ θεοί, τὴν σ. ἐξ ὕδατος ἔχοντες; Athenag.*leg*.19.2(M.6.929B); Meth.*arbitr*.12(p.176.1; συνεστὼς ἐστιν M.18.260C); Eus.*d.e*.1.10(p.45.6; 85C); **5.** *nature, essence* τὸ...τοιοῦτον τῆς σ. εἶδος εἰ μὲν ὡς ναὸς εἴη, κατοικεῖν ἐν αὐτῷ θεὸς βούλεται Tat.*orat*.15(p.16.22; M.6.837B); τὴν...τῆς πονηρίας σ. ἐοικυῖαν τῇ τῶν βραχυτάτων σπερμάτων ἴσμεν *ib*.30(p.30.18; 868B); ἡ τοῦ κόσμου γένεσις καὶ φθορὰ καὶ σ. ἐξ ἀγαθοῦ καὶ κακοῦ συνεστῶσα φιλοσοφεῖται Hipp.*haer*.7.29(p.214.31; M.16.3331A); τὸ...βάπτισμα, ἐν ᾧ πάσης πίστεως ἡμῶν ἡ σ. ὁρμεῖ †Ath.*Ar*.4.21(p.67.17; M.26.500A); ref. Ecclus.10:12 ἡ...ἀρχὴ ἢ τὴν πρώτην ὁρμὴν δηλοῖ τὴν ἐπὶ τὸ κακόν, ἢ τὴν σ. Chrys.*hom.1.2 in 2Thess*.(11.512B); **6.** particular modes of existence; **a.** *concentration*; *solid knot* or *lump*; hence *coagulation*, Clem.*paed*.1.6(p.119.10f.; M.8.308B); **b.** *consistence, coherence, firmness* ἐν τῷ τρεπομένῳ τὸ ἄτρεπτον ἀδύνατον λαβεῖν πῆξιν καὶ σ. id.*str*.6.9(p.470.16; M.9.297B); opp. ἀσύστατος, Ath.*gent*.37(M.25.73C); *firmness* of character, *M.Ner.et Ach*.6(p.5.3); **c.** logical *consistency, coherence* οὐδεμίαν σ. ὁ λόγος ἔχει Gr.Nyss.*Eun*.1(1 p.143.17; M.45.384A); *consistency between two, agreement* τοιαῦτα...ὑπ' αὐτοῦ τοῦ κυρίου λεγόμενα τὴν σ. ποιεῖται νόμου...πρὸς τὴν καινὴν διαθήκην Epiph.*haer*.23.6(p.255.1; M.41.305C); **7.** a *substance* ἅλες...εἰσὶ τηρητικοὶ τῶν ἐπὶ γῆς σ. τοῦ κόσμου οἱ τοῦ θεοῦ ἄνθρωποι Or.*Cels*.8.70 (p.287.3; M.11.1621C); κατὰ μὲν τὴν σ. τῆς περὶ τῶν ὅλων θεωρίας ...τῆς σοφίας νοουμένης, κατὰ δὲ τὴν πρὸς τὰ λογικὰ κοινωνίαν τῶν τεθεωρημένων τοῦ λόγου λαμβανομένου id.*Jo*.1.19(22; p.23.22; M.14.56B); δοκεῖ σοι τὴν οὐσίαν σωματικήν τινα σ. εἶναι Meth.*arbitr*.8(p.166.4); ἥτις λέγεται μορφὴ δούλου, νοερά τις σ. νοουμένη ‡Ath.*Apoll*.2.1 (M.26.1133A); *ib*.2.2(1136A); ὅπου...σαρκὸς τὸ ὄνομα, ἐκεῖ πάσης τῆς σ. ἡ ἁρμονία χωρὶς ἁμαρτίας *ib*.2.18(1164B).

συστατ-έω, ? *establish, settle* ~εῖν μὲν περὶ σεαυτὸν τοὺς ὁμοψύχους, δηλῶσαι δὲ καὶ χρόνον καὶ τόπον τῆς συντυχίας Bas.*ep*.191(3.284D; M.32.701C).

συστατικός, 1. *which goes to make up* the whole, *component, constituent* τὰ σ. κεφάλαια τῆς θείας γραφῆς Marc.Er.*opusc*.10.1(M.65.1117C); τὸν ὁρισμὸν ἐκ γένους καὶ συστατικῶν διαφορῶν συγκεῖσθαι, τὴν δὲ ὑπογραφὴν τῶν ἐπουσιωδῶν Jo.D.*dialect*.8(M.94.557B); of soul and body in Adam, Leont.H.*Nest*.4.7(M.86.1665B); ref. Christ's natures, Eust.Mon.*ep*.(M.86.937B); and wills, Max.*opusc*.(M.91.36C,221D); **2.** *conserving* μίαν ἴσμεν θεότητα...εἴτε τῶν...ἁπάντων δημιουργικήν, εἴτε προνοητικήν, εἴτε σ. καὶ συντηρητικήν Sophr.H.*ep.syn*.(M.87.3157A); ? as imperial title νικᾷ ἡ τύχη Κωνσταντίνου μεγάλου βασιλέως τοῦ συστατηκοῦ νικητοῦ *CIG* 4.8788; **3.** *commendatory* σ. λόγος Γρηγορίου εἰς Ὠριγένην Socr.*h.e*.4.27.6(M.67.536C); freq. (with or without ἐπιστολή or γράμμα) of letters of introduction or letters of communion εἴ τις κληρικὸς ἢ λαϊκὸς...ἀπελθὼν ἐν ἑτέρᾳ πόλει δεχθῇ ἄνευ γραμμάτων σ., ἀφοριζέσθωσαν οἱ δεξάμενοι καὶ ὁ δεχθεὶς *Can.App*.12; σ. ἐφωδιάσθησαν γράμμασι Thdt.*2Cor*.3:1(3.301); σ., τουτέστι παραθετικῶν, ἐπιστολῶν *cat.2Cor*.3:1(p.364.23); esp. as carried by clergy or religious travelling to other dioceses or places where they were not known, Eugen.*exp.fid*.1(M.18.1301A); CSard.*can*.9; *Can.App*.33; τοὺς...κοινωνικοὺς τῆς ἐκκλησίας, μετὰ σ. ἐλθόντας γραμμάτων CQuerc.(M.103.112B); Call.*v.Hyp*.(p.104); ξένους κληρικοὺς καὶ ἀναγνώστας ἐν ἑτέρᾳ πόλει δίχα σ. γραμμάτων τοῦ ἰδίου ἐπισκόπου μηδ' ὅλως μηδαμοῦ λειτουργεῖν CChalc.*can*.13; opp. ἐπιστόλιον: πάντας τοὺς...δεομένους ἐπικουρίας μετὰ δοκιμασίας ἐπιστολίοις εἴτουν εἰρηνικοῖς ἐκκλησιαστικοῖς μόνοις ὡρίσαμεν ὁδεύειν καὶ μὴ συστατικοῖς, διὰ τὸ τὰς σ. ἐπιστολὰς προσήκειν τοῖς οὖσι μόνοις ἐν ὑπολήψει παρέχεσθαι προσώποις CChalc.*can*.11; **4.** *testifying* to; *confirmatory* ταῦτα πάντα τῆς ἰσότητός ἐστι σ. [i.e. of Son with Father] Chrys.*hom*.49.2 *in Jo*.(8.290E).

συσταυρ-όω, 1. *take part in crucifying* ὁ...ταύτας [sc. τὰς καθολικὰς νηστείας] λύων συμπαραδίδωσι τὸν σωτῆρα καὶ ~οῖ ‡Pall.*h.mon*.8.58(p.48.23; M.34.1148B); **2.** pass., *be crucified with*; **a.** of the two malefactors, Or.*Jo*.19.16(4; p.316.24; M.14.556C); *A.Pil*.A 9.5 (p.245); Gr.Naz.*or*.29.20(p.105.15; M.36.101B); **b.** of Christian with Christ (Gal.2:20, Rom.6:4ff.) in baptism πρῶτον ~οῦται, ἵνα... παιδευθῶμεν, ὅτι...ὁ...συσταυρωθεὶς τῷ Χριστῷ ἀπαλλοτριοῦται παντάπασι τῶν κατὰ τὸν παλαιὸν ἄνθρωπον ζώντων †Bas.*bapt*.1.2.14 (2.639E; M.31.1549C); ὥστε τὸν βαπτιζόμενον...αὐτῷ συσταυρωθῆναι *Const.App*.7.43.5; συννεκρούμενοι προθύμως Χριστῷ, καὶ σ. καὶ συνθαπτόμενοι ἐν τῇ ἀπεκδύσει τοῦ σώματος τῶν ἁμαρτιῶν τῆς σαρκὸς ἐν τῇ περιτομῇ τοῦ Χριστοῦ ἐν τῷ βαπτίσματι ‡Amph.*circ*.1.9(p.21B); τὸ βάπτισμα σταυρός ἐστι, καὶ συνεσταυρώθη ὁ παλαιὸς ἡμῶν ἄνθρωπος...καὶ πάλιν [Rom.6:4] Chrys.*hom.9.3 in Heb*.(12.96C); by mortification ὁ καταξιωθεὶς συσταυρωθῆναι Χριστῷ διὰ τῆς...τῶν παθῶν ἐκκρούσεως καὶ δεξιῶς αὐτῷ ~ούμενος, τουτέστι μετὰ λόγου καὶ γνώσεως πᾶσαν διεξιὼν ἀρετὴν Max.*ambig*.(M.91.1173B,C) commenting on Gr.Naz.*or*.45.24(M.36.656C); τῆς τῷ Χριστῷ συνεσταυρωμένης τοῦ ἀποστόλου σαρκός Germ.CP *or*.1(M.98.236A); in Church as his body ὥσπερ τὸ αἰσθητὸν τοῦ Ἰησοῦ σῶμα ἐσταύρωται...οὕτως τὸ ὅλον τῶν ἁγίων Χριστοῦ σῶμα Χριστῷ σ. Or.*Jo*.10.35(20; p.210.3; M.14.372B); in liturg. act of Church συνεγείρομαι σήμερον ἀναστάντι σοι, συνεσταυρούμην σοι χθές Jo.D.*carm.pasch*.26(p.218; M.96.840D).

***συσταύρωσις**, ἡ, *crucifying together* ἡ σ. τῶν δύο λῃστῶν Cyr.*Jo*.12(4.1059D).

συστέλλ-ω, A. *draw together*; 1. *brace, gird* ~ειν χρὴ τὰς γυναῖκας κοσμίως καὶ περισφίγγειν αἰδοῖ σώφρονι, μὴ παραρρυῶσι τῆς ἀληθείας διὰ χαυνότητα Clem.*paed*.3.11(p.269.18; M.8.632B); or perh. simply *dress*, cf.1Tim.2:9; pass., met., *be braced up, pull oneself together* παρόντες μὲν καὶ τῆς ἀκροάσεως ἀπολαύοντες, ~όμεθα· ἐξελθόντες δὲ...τὸ πῦρ τῆς προθυμίας σβεννύντες Chrys.*hom.5.1 in Mt*.(7.71); ἐν ταῖς τρυφαῖς ἀναπίπτομεν, ἐν ταῖς συμφοραῖς μᾶλλον ~όμεθα *ib*.77.4(746D); *ib*.40.5(444B); 2. *gather together* τὰ...ἀρρενικὰ μετὰ τοῦ λόγου συνεστάλη, τὰ θηλυκὰ δὲ...ἑνοῦται τοῖς ἀγγέλοις Clem.*exc.Thdot*.21(p.113.25; M.9.668C); ‡Nil.*perist*.10.1(M.79.888A); liturg. λαβὼν τὴν Μοῦσαν σ. τὰς ἐν τῷ δίσκῳ μερίδας ὑποκάτω τοῦ ἁγίου ἄρτου ὥστε...μὴ ἐκπεσεῖν τι *Lit.Chrys*.(p.359.26); at end of liturgy εὐχὴ ἐν τῷ σ. τὰ ἅγια μυστικῶς *Lit.Bas*.(p.411.23); s.v.l., *blend* λέγουσι αὐτὸν...ἐν αὐτῷ [sc. τῷ φυράματι] συνεσταλκέναι ἐπειδὴ ἦν αὐτὸς ζύμη Iren.*haer*.1.8.3(M.7.529A; συνεστηκέναι Harvey); 3. *draw* τῆς πίστεως ἡ κοινωνία...πρὸς τὸν παθητὸν ἄνθρωπον, τὰς σαρκικὰς ἐπιθυμίας ἐξορροῦσα, εἰς ἀιδιότητα σ. τὸν ἄνθρωπον Clem.*paed*.1.6(p.120.30; M.8.312A); 4. *restrict*; a. *restrain* τῶν δεσμῶν μὴ ἐώντων ἐλευθεριάζοντα χρῆσθαι ταῖς ἡδοναῖς, ἀλλὰ ~όντων καὶ τὸ δίκαιον διδασκόντων τιμᾶν Meth.*res*.1.31(p.266.9; M.41.1141C); ~εσθαι...καὶ κατευνάζεσθαι τῇ πίστει τὴν ἁμαρτίαν εἰς τὸ μὴ οἴσαι καρποὺς βλαβοποιοὺς...τὰς βλάστας αὐτῆς...~ομεν *ib*.1.41(p.287.5,8; M.18.269C); μὴ τοῖς πτεροῖς ᾄδειν τὸν κύκνον ἡ ἀλογία συνέστειλεν; Diod.*fat*.ap.Phot.*cod*.223(M.103.857C); φιλαργυρίαν...σ. ἀκτημοσύνη ...πλανώμενον νοῦν σ. ἀνάγνωσις λογίων θεοῦ Nil.*inst*.(M.79.1236A); ref. God refraining from exercise of his will οὐδὲ...ὅταν σ. τὴν ἐνέργειαν κατὰ μεταβολὴν σ. τῆς δυνάμεως ‡Just.*qu.Chr*.2.7(M.6.1425A,B); εἰ μὲν γὰρ ~ομένης τῆς ἐνεργείας, οὐκέτι ἠδύνετο ὁ θεὸς τῇ παυσαμένῃ ἐνεργείᾳ κεχρῆσθαι, δικαίως ἂν ἐλέγετο φθορὰ ἐνεργείας· εἰ δὲ ἀεὶ δύναται τὴν αὐτὴν ἐνέργειαν ὅτε βούλεται προβάλλεσθαι, οὐκ ἄρα φθείρεται ἡ ἐνέργεια τοῦ θεοῦ ~ομένη *ib*.(1425C); b. *confine, limit* οὐκ εἰς πολλοὺς ἐρχομένη, ἀλλ' ἑαυτὴν εἰς τοὺς ὀλίγους σ. *M.Thdot*.18 (p.66.21); Chrys.*oppugn*.2.9(1.72D); expression τὸ...τραχὺ βραχέσι συστεῖλαι ῥήμασι...ἐπὶ τὰ ἡδύτερα μεταπηδῆσαι id.*virg*.29(1.289E); σ. τὸ μῆκος τῆς ἐπιστολῆς Synes.*ep*.142(M.66.1533C); pass. οὐ κατὰ τὴν τοῦ σώματος σμικρότητα ~εται καὶ συμμετρεῖται [sc. ἡ ψυχή] Ath.*gent*.33(M.25.65C); Chrys.*hom.80.1 in Jo*.(8.473C); συνεσταλμένη μὲν γὰρ ἡ διὰ Μωσέως χάρις...μακρὰ δὲ...ἡ διὰ Χριστοῦ Cyr.*Is*.4.3(2.622E); τὴν ἀσθενῆ καὶ συνεσταλμένην...τῶν καθ' ἡμᾶς ὑλαίων ἀριθμῶν συμμετρίαν Dion.Ar.*c.h*.14(M.3.321A); of words, *be limited, become few* κἀκεῖ μὲν...κατιὼν ὁ λόγος, κατὰ τὸ ποσὸν τῆς καθόδου, πρὸς ἀνάλογον πλῆθος ηὐρύνετο· νῦν δὲ...ἀνιών, κατὰ τὸ μέτρον τῆς ἀνόδου ~εται id.*myst*.3(M.3.1033C); *keep* to oneself οὐδένα τῶν παραδοθέντων ἡμῖν...λόγων εἰς ἑαυτοὺς συνεστείλαμεν id.*d.n*.13.4(M.3.984A); c. *reduce, subdue*, Clem.*str*.7.3(p.10.24; M.9.417A); Chrys.*hom.22.1 in 2Cor*.(10.589D); Aen.*dial*.(M.85.896A); *relieve* pain αἱ...τῶν ῥόδων...ἀποφοραὶ ἡσυχῇ οὖσαι ψυχραὶ σ. καὶ ἐπιστύφουσι τὰς καρηβαρίας Clem.*paed*.2.8(p.201.4; M.8.481A); 5. pass., *contract*; perf. pass., of a withered hand, Chrys.*hom.88.3 in Mt*.(7.829B); fig., of the parsimonious ἡ χεὶρ...ἐστὶ συνεσταλμένη πρὸς διάδοσιν *ib*.88.4(829E); φαμὲν...περὶ τῶν ἀποσειομένων αἰσχροκερδείαις, ὅτι συνεσταλμένην ἔχει τὴν χεῖρα Cyr.*Is*.5.4(2.820B); of light σ. ἑαυτὸν ...ὡς φῶς ὄψεως ὑπὸ τοῖς βλεφάροις συνεσταλμένον Hipp.*haer*.8.10 (p.229.27f.; M.16.3354C); τὸ φῶς...~όμενον τῇ νυκτὶ τὴν πάροδον ἐδίδου opp. τὸ φῶς...περικεχυμένον, Thdt.*rect.conf*.12(M.6.1229C); of the soul ἐκτείνεται...ἡ ψυχὴ ἡμῶν πρότερον συνεσταλμένη, ἵνα δυνηθῇ χωρῆσαι τὴν σοφίαν τοῦ θεοῦ Or.*hom.8.2 in Jer*.(p.57.27; M.13.340A); οὐ κατὰ τὴν τοῦ σώματος σμικρότητα ~εται καὶ συμμετρεῖται Ath.*gent*.33(M.25.65C); cf. οὔτε ~εται, οὔτε διαχεῖται τὸ νοητόν Gr.Nyss.*anim.et res*.(M.46.45C); theol. (non-Christian) εἰ...τὸ συνεκτείνεσθαι μὲν τοῖς μεγάλοις...τὸ δὲ βραχύνεσθαι ἐν τοῖς μικροῖς καὶ σ. ἀδύνατον, οὐκ ἦν δύναμις Meth.*Porph*.2(p.505.14; M.18.401D); Trin., ref. teaching of Sabellius ἀπὸ τῶν Στοϊκῶν...διαβεβαιουμένων σ. καὶ πάλιν ἐκτείνεσθαι τὸν θεόν ‡Ath.*Ar*.4.13(p.57.4; M.26.484C); τὸ μὲν εἰς ἀριθμὸν ἕνα τὰ τρία ~ειν...τῆς Σαβελλίου [sc. ὂν] καινοτομίας Gr.Naz.*or*.21.13(M.35.1096B); and Marcellus τῆς...ἀναλλοιώτου οὐσίας, ἐφ' ἧς τὸ εἶναι μόνον ἐπιτρέπει νοεῖν...μὴ σ., μὴ ἐκτεινομένην Eus.*e.th*.2.9(p.108.34; M.24.917A); v. πλατύνω; cf.Cyr.*Jo*.1.2(4.17A); in orthodox use never of divine nature οὐχ οὕτως αὐτὸν [sc. τὸν λόγον] ἐν τῷ πατρὶ λέγομεν, ὡς ἐν τοῖς λοιποῖς εἶναι, οὐ διὰ τὸ τὴν οὐσίαν ἐν τοῖς ἄλλοις...~εσθαι, ἀλλὰ διὰ τὸ τῶν δεχομένων μέτρον, ἀτονούντων τὴν εἰσδοχὴν τὴν θείαν Thdt.*rect.conf*.17(1237C); μίαν... φύσιν τοῦ θεοῦ λόγου σεσαρκωμένην ὁμολογοῦμεν...σμικρύνεται σωματικῶς καὶ ~εται, καὶ θεϊκῶς ἐστιν ἀπερίγραπτος Jo.D.*f.o*.3.7(M.94.1012B); 6. pass.; a. *be sobered, subdued, restrained*, Clem.*str*.7.12 (p.54.1; M.9.504A); †Bas.*Is*.146(1.482B; M.30.357A) cit. s. ἄμπελος; κατεσοφίσθημεν, συνεστάλημεν Gr.Naz.*ep*.203(M.37.336B); Chrys.*hom.31.3 in Jo*.(8.179E); ref. Herod οὐκ ἐχρῆν θυμωθῆναι, ἀλλὰ φοβηθῆναι καὶ συσταλῆναι id.*hom.9.1 in Mt*.(7.130A); as result of an earthquake, id.*hom.7.2 in Ac*.(9.59A); τοὺς τετραυματισμένους συνεχῶς θεραπεύων ἰατρὸς ~εται ῥᾳδίως, ἐν ταῖς ἑτέρων συμφοραῖς τὴν ἀνθρωπίνην καθορῶν φύσιν id.*hom.81.3 in Jo*.(8.482C); in church ἐνταῦθα μὲν ἡμῖν ἡ καρδία ~εται, ἐξελθόντες δὲ πάντα ῥίπτομεν *ib*.79.5 (471C); ὁ ἐν τῷ οἴκῳ τοῦ θεοῦ διακονούμενος...σ. τότε καὶ σεμνότερος γίνεται id.*hom.20.2 in Rom*.(9.658B); Cyr.*Ps*.34:10(M.69.901A); with ταπεινός and cognates: ἄρχεται ἀπὸ ταπεινῶν καὶ συνεσταλμένων, καὶ καταφεύγει εἰς τὸν πατέρα Chrys.*hom.68.1 in Jo*.(8.405E); id.*hom.22.1 in 2Cor*.(10.590B); id.*hom.13.4 in Ac*.(9.109C); b. *be cast down, dispirited*, Ath.*v.Anton*.14(M.25.865A); κἂν ὑβρίσῃ τις, δακρύομεν καὶ ~όμεθα Chrys.*hom.79.5 in Mt*.(7.765A); *ib*.80.4(771A); ἂν τὸν δικαστὴν...[sc. ἴδωσιν] οἱ στασιάζοντες, συνεσταλμένοι γίνονται, οὐχὶ διαχέονται id.*hom.5.3 in Ac*.(9.45B).

B. *draw in* or *back, withdraw*; 1. trans. ἥλιος ἐπαφιεὶς τὰς ἀκτῖνας πολλαῖς κηλῖσι, πάλιν αὐτὰς σ. καθαράς Chrys.*hom.25.1 in 1Cor*.(10.221D); Thdt.*qu.36 in Gen*.(1.103); Valent., of aeon Christ after formation of Enthymesis ἀναδραμεῖν [sc. to Pleroma] συστείλαντα αὐτοῦ τὴν δύναμιν Iren.*haer*.1.4.1(M.7.480A); 2. pass. *retire* τοῦ καταβάντος ἐπ' αὐτῷ...πνεύματος...συσταλέντος, ἵνα καὶ εὐεργετήσῃ ὁ θάνατος Clem.*exc.Thdot*.61(p.127.17; M.9.688C); Χριστοῦ...συσταλέντος εἰς τὸ πλήρωμα *ib*.33(p.117.25; 676B); τὸ κέντρον...προπηδᾷ καὶ πάλιν ~εται Geo.Pis.*Pers*.1.94(M.92.1204A); 3. reflex. and pass., *withdraw* into solitude σ. ἐμαυτὸν ἐν τῇ ἐρήμῳ *Protev*.25.1(p.49); οὐ δύναται ἡ ψυχὴ...τὸν θεὸν ἐπιγνῶναι ἐὰν μὴ σ. ἑαυτὴν ἀπὸ τῶν ἀνθρώπων Ammonas *ep*.1(p.432.6); *ib*.(p.433.1); 4. *remove, take away*, *M.Ner.et Ach*.18(p.18.3); Dion.Ar.*ep*.8(M.3.1088B); pass. ἀπὸ τοῦ συσταλέντος ἀπὸ τῆς μητρὸς Iren.*haer*.1.11.1(M.7.564A); τῆς σκιᾶς συνεσταλμένης Cyr.*Ps*.44:17(M.69.1044D); εἰ...ἀποσταίεν τῆς προθυμίας, καὶ τὸ δοθὲν...πνεῦμα συνεστάλη id.*q.d.s*.21(p.173.20; M.9.625C); ref. Christ on the Cross οὐ γὰρ αὐτὸς ἐγκαταλέλειπται, ἢ ὑπὸ τοῦ πατρός, ἢ ὑπὸ τῆς ἑαυτοῦ θεότητος...ὡς ἂν φοβουμένης τὸ πάθος, καὶ διὰ τοῦτο συνεσταλμένης ἀπὸ τοῦ πάσχοντος Gr.Naz.*or*.30.5(p.115.4; M.36.109A); 5. *withhold, refuse* ὁ λόγος σιωπᾷ...ὁ ἰατρὸς τὰ φάρμακα σ. Chrys.*dimiss.Chan*.5(3.436E); πρὸς αὐτοὺς [sc. catechumens and others] ἡ τῶν πανιέρων θέα καὶ κοινωνία ~εται Dion.Ar.*e.h*.3.3.7 (M.3.433C); 6. *cut off, put an end to* τῆς φιλανθρωπίας τὸν κύριον ὅτι μὴ ἄρδην τὸ ὅλον συνέστειλεν Petr.II Al.*encycl*.2 ap.Thdt.*h.e*.4.22.6 (M.33.1277B); Chrys.*hom.5.3 in Ac*.(9.45C); of time, pass., *be cut short* (cf. 1Cor.7:29), *M.Seb*.2.3(p.117.35); ὡς τοῦ καιροῦ πάντων παρόντος, συνεστάλη τὰ ἔτη Ath.*fug*.14(p.78.10; M.25.661C); ἡ ἐμὴ ὑπόστασις συνεσταλμένη ἐστὶ Cyr.*Ps*.38:6(M.69.976A); *cut short, break off* speech or writing, Chrys.*hom.58.5 in Jo*.(8.343E); id.*hom.8.8 in Rom*.(9.508D).

συστενοχωρέω, pass., *be straitened with, suffer difficulties with*, *M.Ner.et Ach*.8(p.6.27).

συστεφανόω, *crown* one *with* another, Cyr.*ador*.12(1.446D).

***συστήκ-ω**, pres. from συνέστηκα (perf. of συνίστημι); 1. *stand with* [sc. the faithful], of the fourth grade of penitents (v. συνίστημι) καὶ μετὰ ταῦτα ἐπιτρέπειν σ. μέν, τῆς δὲ κοινωνίας...ἀπέχεσθαι Bas.*ep*.188 *can*.4(3.272A; M.32.673B); 2. *consist, subsist*, Ath.*gent*.28(M.25.56B); 3. *exist together, side by side* ἐκ...τοῦ πάσας τὰς βασιλείας ~ειν δείκνυνται μήπω ἐληλυθὼς ὁ...Χριστός Adam.*dial*.1.25(p.48.8; M.11.1753A).

σύστημα, τό, 1. *composite* and *orderly whole, system* ὁ βίος ὁ Χριστιανῶν...σ. τί ἐστι λογικῶν πράξεων Clem.*paed*.1.13(p.151.25; M.8.376A); ἕκαστον...εὐαγγέλιον, σ. ἀπαγγελλομένων ὠφελίμων τῷ πιστεύοντι Or.*Jo*.1.5(7; p.10.2; M.14.33A); *ib*.2.18(12; p.75.19; 145D); freq. of heaven and earth οὐ μόνον τῷ περιγείῳ τόπῳ ἀλλὰ καὶ παντὶ τῷ σ. τῷ ἐξ οὐρανοῦ καὶ γῆς *ib*.1.15(p.19.22; 49A); id. *Cels*.6.59(p.129.29; M.11.1389A); Bas.*Spir*.53(3.45E; M.32.168A); Gr.Naz.*or*.38.10(M.36.321B); τὸ σύμπαν σ. τῆς νοητῆς καὶ αἰσθητῆς κτίσεως Proc.G.*Is*.6:1ff.(M.87.1937C); τῶν ὁρωμένων ἁπάντων τὸ σ. Jo.D.*hom*.1.8(M.96.560A); of human body, fig. αὐτὸς...ἀντὶ χειρὸς ὢν τῷ σ. Gr.Naz.*or*.21.21(M.35.1105B); met., *body* of Church, *Clem.ep*.7(M.2.41B); μὴ ἐκβαίνειν τοῦ σ. τῆς ἐκκλησίας, καὶ καθ' ἑαυτὸν κατάρχειν...σχισμάτων †Bas.*hom.in Ps*.28(1.358A; M.30.73A); **2.** *composition, constitution* οὐδὲ πῶς τῶν...ξύλων ἡ φύσις, καὶ τῶν ὑδάτων τὰ σ. ... γινώσκεται Ath.*ep.Serap*.1.18(M.26.572D); **3.** = σύστασις, *formation; creation* οὐδὲν τῆς ἀνθρωπίνης σαρκίας συνεσπάσατο [sc. human nature of Christ] ἀλλ' ὅπερ ἦν ἐν τῷ σ. Gr.Nyss.*ep*.3(p.23.14; M.46.1021C); **4.** *constituent part* ἀρχὴ σωφροσύνης νηστεία, τουτέστι, θεμέλιος καὶ σ. Chrys.*hom.1.2 in 2Thess*.(11.512B); *group* within a larger body χορῶν συστήματα καὶ στρατῶν τάγματα Gr.Naz.*or*.22.3(M.35.1133C); *member* τὰ...μέλη τῆς νύμφης συστήματα τυγχάνοντα πλείονα, χοροὶ μέν εἰσι Or.*schol.in Cant*.7:1(M.17.280Df.); **5.** *organized government, constitution*, of Church νομίσας δυνατὸν εἶναι...καταλῦσαι...τῶν ἐκκλησιῶν τὰ σ. Gr.Nyss.*v.Gr.Thaum*.(M.46.944C); *state* περὶ τοῦ πεσόντος αὐτῶν οἴκου...καὶ κατὰ παντὸς αὐτῶν τοῦ σ., ὡς μηκέτ' ἀναστησομένων Eus.*d.e*.4.16(p.190.7; M.22.317A); **6.** *organized community, society*; **a.** in gen. ὁ δῆμος ἀστεῖόν τι σ. καὶ πλῆθος ἀνθρώπων ὑπὸ νόμου διοικούμενον Clem.*str*.4.26(p.324.28; M.8.1381A); πόλις ἐστὶ σ. ἀνθρώπων...ἐπὶ κοινωνίᾳ βίου συγκεκροτημένον †Bas.*Is*.19(1.391C; M.30.149B); ὠφέλησε Χριστὸς τὰ ἐν κόσμῳ τῶν ἐθνῶν σ. Cyr.*glaph.Ex*.1(1.258E); Sever.*Eph*.2:2f.(p.307.28) cit. s. δημιουργικός; **b.** *company, guild* θήκη διαφέρουσα τῷ σ. τῶν λημενητῶν λινοπωλῶν τῆς Κωρυκαιωτῶν *MAMA* 3.770; τοῦ συσστέματος τὸν εὐγενεστάτον τραπεζιτὸν *ib*.3.771 = *CG-CI* I p.121; **c.** *body of soldiers, corps* ἕκαστον ἱππικόν τε καὶ πεζικὸν σ. Synes.*regn*.13 (9; p.27.9; M.66.1073D); **d.** *band* of demons ἄρχων τοῦ τῶν δαιμόνων σ. *T.Sal*.7.2 MS D; Or.*Cels*.7.70(p.219.13; M.11.1520B); of brigands, Thdt.*qu.65 in 1Reg*.(1.403); *league* σ. πονηρῶν ἀνθρώπων... ἐπ' ὀλέθρῳ...τῶν ἐκκλησιῶν συγκροτούμενον id.*h.e*.2.27.1(3.894); **7.** eccl. *community, society*; **a.** in gen., Iren.*haer*.4.33.8(M.7.1077B); ὃν ἔκβαλε ἐκ σ. πνευματικοῦ Or.*exp.in Pr*.22:10(M.17.220A); τοῦ σ. Χριστιανῶν id.*Cels*.3.18(p.216.14; M.11.941B); Nil.*epp*.1.267 (M.79.181A); τῶν εὐσεβῶν τὸ σ. Thdt.*Cant*.6:10f.(1.134); Sophr.H.*ep.syn*.(M.87.3185A); opp. civil society ἡμεῖς...ἐν ἑκάστῃ πόλει ἄλλο σ. πατρίδος κτισθὲν λόγῳ θεοῦ ἐπιστάμενοι Or.*Cels*.8.75(p.292.3; 1629C); opp. blood relationship πατριὰ μὲν γὰρ ἡ συγγένεια λέγεται, φρατρία δὲ τὸ σ.· ἐν δὲ τοῖς οὐρανοῖς συγγένεια μὲν οὐδεμία, σ. δὲ καὶ πολλά Thdr.Mops.*Eph*.3:14f.(p.159.14; M.66.917A); in definitions of ἐκκλησία: τὴν ἐκκλησίαν...πόλιν μέν, διὰ τὸ σ. εἶναι νομίμως οἰκούμενον Bas.*hom.in Ps*.59(1.192C; M.29.468B); τὸ τῆς ἐκκλησίας ὄνομα καὶ σ. ἤδη συγκεκροτημένου Chrys.*hom.1.1 in 1Thess*.(11.426A); ἐκκλησία...σ. καὶ συνόδου ἐστὶν ὄνομα id.*exp.in Ps*.149:1(5.498C); τὸ ἐξ αὐτῶν [sc. πιστῶν ἄνδρων] σ., ἐκκλησία καλεῖται Ammon.*Ac*.12:1(M.85.1540A); ἔστιν...ἡ...ἐκκλησία, τὸ σ. τῶν ἀπ' αἰῶνος ἁγίων πατέρων, πατριαρχῶν κτλ. Jo.V H.*icon*.11(M.96.1357C); of saints in paradise, †Bas.*parad*.12(1.351D; M.30.72B); of local congregation or community τῆς τῶν Κεγχρεῶν ἐκκλησίας τὸ σ. Thdt.*Rom*.16:1ff.(3.156); **b.** *assembly, meeting, congregation* συνάξεων συστήματα Ephr.2.242A; Gr.Naz.*or*.41.8(M.36.440C); Cyr.*hom.div*.4(p.102.14; 5².355D); δεῦτε πανηγυρίσωμεν σήμερον, ὦ φιλόθεον σ. Jo.D.*hom*.1.1(M.96.545A); ‡Meth.*Sym.et Ann*.3(M.18.353A); of *groups* of inquirers συστήματα κατὰ τόπους ἐγίνετο βουλῆς καὶ σκέψεως, τὸ τίς ἂν εἴη ὁ φανείς *Hom.Clem*.1.6; and of heretics οἱ τὰς αἱρέσεις διὰ τῶν οἰκείων πληροῦντες σ. Const.ap.Eus.*v.C*.3.64(p.111.20; M.20.1140B); *ib*.3.65(pp.112.16,113.2; 1141B,C); μηδαμοῦ γῆς αἱρετικοῦ σ. μηδὲ σχισματικοῦ λειπομένου Eus.*ib*.3.66(p.113.26; 1144B); Cyr.H.*catech*.18.26 cit. s. ἐκκλησία; Chrys.*hom.46.1 in Mt*.(7.480D); for antiphonal singing, Soz.*h.e*.8.8.1(M.67.1536B) cit. s. ἀντίφωνος; **c.** *religious congregation, community* of monks or nuns σ. ἀνδρῶν ἀσκητῶν Ephr.1.275D; μηδὲ ἐξουθένη...ἀδελφούς, ὡς ἐξ οἰκτροῦ σ. ὑπαρχόντων id.1.307B; ἦμεν...τοῦ αὐτοῦ σ. ἀμφότεροι id.3.256A; ἦν δὲ σὺν ταῖς ἀδελφαῖς αὐτοῦ σ. παρθένων ἑβδομήκοντα Pall.*h.Laus*.1(p.16.14; M.34.1010B); Thdt.*h.rel*.27(3.1283); *V.Alex.Acoem*.6(p.661.15); collective, of monasticism as an institution 'πόλις πιστὴ'...οἷον ἀποικίας τινὰς στέλλουσα τῶν μοναζόντων τὸ σ. Proc.G.*Is*.1:24ff.(M.87.1864B); **d.** *college, body, order* νομοθέταις...προφήταις...διδασκάλοις καὶ παντὶ πνευματικῷ πληρώματι καὶ σ. Gr.Naz.*or*.21.3(M.35.1085A); θρέψον διάκονον καὶ ἱερατικὸν σ. Chrys.*hom.18.4 in Ac*.(9.150A); τῶν μαθητῶν...τὸ σ. Bas.Sel.*or*.25.2(M.85.289A); **e.** *sect* or *party* τῷ τόμῳ τῷ παρὰ τοῦ σ. Εὐδοξίου συντεταγμένῳ Bas.*ep*.244.5(3.379E; M.32.920A); τῶν Ἰουδαίων ἅπαντα τὰ σ. Chrys.*anom*.11.1(1.542C); Bas.Sel.*or*.34.2(M.85.372B); **8.** unorganized but all together, *large quantity, mass, collection*, of water τῶν φρεάτων ἐν σ. τὸ ὕδωρ ἐχόντων Gr.Nyss.*hom.9 in Cant*.(M.44.977C); Philost.*h.e*.9.14(M.65.580B); Procl.CP *or*.8.1(M.65.764C); of fish in a net, Bas.Sel.*or*.29.2 (M.85.332A); of thoughts and desires, *complex, network* τὰ τῆς ψυχῆς αἰσθητήρια ἐν οἷς συστήματα πονηρῶν διαλογισμῶν καὶ πλῆθος ἐπιθυμιῶν †Bas.*Is*.290(1.599C; M.30.628A); s.v.l. ἐξάρατε τὸ πονηρὸν σ. ἀφ' ἑαυτῶν, τοῦτ' ἔστιν τὰς κακίας ἐπιθυμίας *A.Phil*.A 111(p.43.11).

[*]συστοιχεία, ἡ, v. συστοιχία.

***συστοιχειόομαι,** *be combined*; of elements, Eus.*d.e*.4.5(p.156.6; M.22.260D).

συστοιχ-έω, 1. *rank with* ὁ ἀφαιρούμενος τῆς δεσποτείας τὸ ἀξίωμα, καὶ εἰς τὸ τῆς δουλείας ταπεινὸν καταβάλλων, οὐχὶ δῆλός ἐστι καὶ διὰ τοῦτο ~οῦντα αὐτὸν τῇ πάσῃ κτίσει δεικνύς; Bas.*Eun*.2.31(1.268A; M.29.644C); **2.** *correspond to* τὰ μηδεμίαν ἔχοντα κοινωνίαν ὡς ~οῦντα τοῖς εἰρημένοις προστίθησι Gr.Nyss.*Eun*.4(2 p.88.20; M.45.664D).

συστοιχία, ἡ, *coordinate series, class* φάσκουσιν...τῆς...αὐτῶν [sc. τῶν ἀγγέλων] εἶναι σ. καὶ αὐτό [sc. τὸ πνεῦμα] Ath.*ep.Serap*.1.10(M.26.556C); ζωὴ...καὶ φῶς...τῆς ἀγαθῆς σ. ἐστί τε καὶ νομίζεται Synes.*calv*.11(p.211.7; M.66.1188B); *respect* ἡ περὶ τῶν θείων διάληψις...δύο συστοιχείαις...προτεροῦσα φαίνεται Gel.Caes.*fr*.1(p.44.9); ref. Trin. τοιαύτης σ. καὶ ἑνότητος τῆς ἐν τῇ...τριάδι Ath.*ep.Serap*.1.20(576D); ἐν μιᾷ καὶ τῇ αὐτῇ σ. κατατεταγμένων τῶν ὀνομάτων [i.e. of Trin.] Bas.*Spir*.43(3.37A; M.32.148A); οὐ πεποιηκότος ἐνέργειαν, ἀλλὰ γεννήσαντος φύσιν ἐν τῇ τοῦ υἱοῦ θεωρεῖ σ. Gr.Nyss.*Eun*.4(2 p.88.25; M.45.664D).

συστολή, ἡ, *drawing together, drawing up, contraction*; **1.** met., *shrinking, dread, pusillanimity* εἴ...ποτε αἰσθάνοισθε συστολῆς περὶ τὴν ψυχὴν ὑμῶν Or.*mart*.4(p.5.17; M.11.568A); πᾶσα ἡ κτίσις ἐν τρόμῳ καὶ σ. ‡Bas.*struct.hom*.2.9(1.342F; M.30.52C); τὴν...σ. πρὸς ἀνδρείαν μετάγων καὶ δύναμιν Max.*opusc*.(M.91.72A); ἵνα τῆς ἡμῶν φύσεως πᾶσαν θανάτου σ. ἀπελάσῃ *ib*.(84C); ref. Christ καὶ κατὰ φύσιν μὲν δειλία ἐστί, δύναμις κατὰ συστολὴν τοῦ ὄντος ἀνθεκτική· παρὰ φύσιν δέ, παράλογος σ. τὴν οὖν παρὰ φύσιν ὁ κύριος,...οὐ προσήκατο· τὴν δὲ κατὰ φύσιν...ἐδέξατο id.*Pyrr*.(M.91.297D); τὴν...ἀφορμὴν ἐν τῷ καιρῷ τοῦ πάθους, ἑκουσίως τὴν πρὸς τὸν θάνατον σ. ποιήσασθαι *ib*.(297C); ref. Mt.26:39 συστολῆς ὑπάρχειν, ἢ ἀνδρείας; συννεύσεως ἄκρας, ἢ διαστάσεως; id.*opusc*.(M.91.65B); **2.** theol., *contraction* τὸν θεὸν...εἰ δὲ ἐν πᾶσι εἶναι λέγοι...ἀνάγκη ἢ σ. τινα τοῦ θεοῦ λέγειν...ἢ καὶ ἑαυτὸν τῇ ὕλῃ συνδημιουργεῖν Meth.*arbitr*.6(p.160.7; M.18.252B) = Adam.*dial*.4.5(p.148.12; M.11.1813B); esp. ref. teaching of Sabellius τὸ μὲν εἰς ἀριθμὸν ἕνα τὰ τρία συστέλλειν...τῆς Σαβελλίου [sc. ὂν] καινοτομίας, ὃς πρῶτος θεότητος σ. ἐπενόησε Gr.Naz.*or*.21.13(M.35.1096B); and of Marcellus, Dam.Papa *anath*.ap.Thdt.*h.e*.5.11.5(3.1037) cit. s. ἔκτασις; denied, Photinus et al.*ep*.ap.Epiph.*haer*.72.12 (p.266.6; M.42.397C) cit. s. πλατυσμός; involved in human generation, Epiph.*haer*.76.31(p.380.24; M.42.580B); but not in divine, *ib*.76.6(p.346.33; 525C) cit. s. πλατυσμός; **3.** gramm., *shortening of a long syllable*, opp. ἔκτασις, Or.*mart*.46(p.42.15; M.11.628A); **4.** *withdrawal, removal*; **a.** trans. σὺ...εἶ...ὁ ἐξαγαγὼν φῶς...καὶ τῇ τούτου σ. ἐπαγαγὼν τὸ σκότος *Lit*.ap.*Const.App*.8.12.9; τῆς μὲν φυσικῆς ἀπεχόμενος θεωρίας, τῆς δὲ προσευχῆς κατὰ τὴν ἐκ πάντων πρὸς ἑαυτόν τε καὶ τὸν θεὸν τοῦ νοῦ συστολὴν ἀντεχόμενος Max.*qu.Thal*.49(M.90.457B); **b.** intrans. ἡ ἐν νυκτὶ τῆς ψυχῆς σ. ἀπὸ τοῦ σώματος Clem.*str*.4.22(p.310.14; M.8.1349B); ἡλιακῆς ἀκτῖνος κατάδυσις, καὶ φωτὸς σ. Cyr.*Mich*.32(3.419B); **5.** *failure to exercise, not putting forth* ἡ τῆς ἐνεργείας σ. ‡Just.*qu.Chr*.2.7(M.6.1425A); **6.** ? a *becoming invisible*, Epiph.*haer*.26.12(p.291.20; M.41.352B); **7.** *limitation, cutting short*, ref. 1Cor.7:29 αἴτιον εἶναι τῆς τῶν γάμων σ. Eus.*d.e*.1.9(p.40.32; M.22.77D); διὰ τὴν τοῦ καιροῦ σ. Gr.Nyss.*virg*.8(p.285.12; M.46.356D); *end* πρὸ μὲν τῆς τῶν αἰώνων σ. Cyr.*Jo*.4.6(4.426E).

συστομόομαι, perf. pass., *be joined mouth to mouth*, Gr.Nyss.*hom.opif*.30.22(M.44.249B); Melet.*nat.hom*.synops.(M.64.1125C); of seas τὴν Ἐρυθρὰν...τῇ μεγάλῃ συνεστομῶσθαί φασιν Proc.G.*Gen*.1:9 (M.87.76B); ‡Caes.Naz.*dial*.81(M.38.948).

***συστρεβλ-όω,** *behave cunningly, deal craftily together with* ἐν μὲν τοῖς ὁσίοις ὅσιός ἐστιν ὁ θεός...ἐν δὲ τοῖς στρεβλοῖς οὐ στρεβλός, ἀλλὰ ~ούμενος αὐτοῖς διὰ τὸ εὔφημον Or.*sel.in Ps*.17:26f.(M.12.1233C).

σύστρεμμα, τό, 1. *troop, company*, ref. 1Reg.30:8,15,23 τὸ δὲ σ. γαδδοὺρ ὁ Ἑβραῖος καλεῖ Thdt.*qu.65 in 1Reg*.(1.403); **2.** ? *league* σ. καὶ ἐπιβουλὴν ἐπ' αὐτόν τινα ποιησαμένου Cyr.*Os*.1(3.8D); **3.** *swarm* of bees, Gennad.*fr.Gen*.3:8(M.85.1637A).

συστρέφω, 1. *roll up*; hence *form into an organized whole, unite*; perf. ptcpl. pass. ἡνοῦτο...τὰ τοῦ κοινοῦ σώματος μέλη...μόνη τε ἡ καθολικὴ...ἐκκλησία εἰς ἑαυτὴν συνεστραμμένη διέλαμπεν Eus.*v.C*.3.66(p.113.25; M.20.1144B); of man *in his entirety* ἄνδρα ὀνομάζειν ἔθος τὸν εὐσεβῆ καὶ σ. Cyr.*ador*.12(1.419A); **2.** pass., *conspire*, Pall.*v.Chrys*.8(p.45.12; M.47.27); **3.** *collect, gather*; met.; **a.** *brace* ἐκλυθέντας τῷ φόβῳ...σ. λέγων Chrys.*hom.75.3 in Mt*.(7.728A); reflex., *pull oneself together* συστρέψαντας ἑαυτούς, διεγείρωμεν πρὸς ἀρετὴν id.*hom.2.6 in Col.*(11.342E); id.*hom.18.2 in 1 Tim.*(11.657C); **b.** pass., *be concentrated, earnest, alert* ἑστὼς συνεστραμμένῳ προσώπῳ κατεσταλμένῃ τε φωνῇ Eus.*v.C.*4.29(p.128.24; M.20.1177B); Chrys.*hom.* *17.2 in 1 Tim.*(11.650C); id.*hom.3.4 in 2 Thess.*(11.527F); σ. εἰς ἑαυτόν *be recollected,* Gr.Naz.*or.*28.3(p.24.12; M.36.29A); Dion.Ar.*c.h.*15.4 (M.3.333A); **4.** *oppress, subdue* τῇ ἡμέρᾳ τῇ τελευταίᾳ...σ. ψυχὴν ἁμαρτήματα Chrys.*hom.53.5 in Mt.*(7.545B); τὸ...συνειδὸς αὐτὴν [sc. τὴν ψυχήν] σ., κατεστάλθαι ποιεῖ id.*hom.9.4 in Heb.*(12.99A).

συστροφή, ἡ, A. *twisting together*; **1.** *converse, familiarity* διὰ τὴν περὶ μόνα τὰ σαλευόμενα τοῦ νοῦ σ. Max.*ambig.*(M.91.1352C); **2.** *turning round,* i.e. to look back, Thphyl.*exc.Rom.*5(p.225.9; M. 113.932D).

B. that which is rolled into one mass; **1.** *concentration, mass*; of persons, *gathering, concourse*; met., of the *essence* of a quality, of Christ οὔτε τανότητι τῶν τριχῶν ἐπασπασμένος, ἀλλὰ συστροφῇ κοσμιότητος σεμνυνόμενος ‡Hipp.Th.*fr.*21(p.55.19); **2.** σ. πνεύματος *whirlwind*; also σ. ὑδάτων *whirlpool, M.Thdot.1* 10(p.67.15).

συστυγνάζω, *mourn together* τοῖς λυπουμένοις σ. Socr.*h.e.*7.2.4(M. 67.741A).

***συσφαιρόω,** *make round, round,* Athenag.*leg.*13.1(M.6.916B).

συσφίγγ-ω, 1. *fasten* or *bind together, hold together*; **a.** in gen.; the hair, *M.Perp.*20(p.91.19); τὰ τέσσαρα ἄκρα τοῦ σταυροῦ διὰ τοῦ μέσου κέντρου κρατοῦνται καὶ ∼ονται Jo.D.*f.o.*4.11(M.94.1129B); of corner-stones of a building, Dor.*doct.*14.2(M.88.1776A); fig., ref. Eph.2:20ff. ὅπως...ὁ ἀκρογωνιαῖος Χριστὸς...συσφίγξῃ ἡμῶν ἀμώμων εἰς ἅπαν τὸ πᾶν οἰκοδόμημα Anast.S.*hod.*1(M.89.48D); τοῦ τὰ κατερραγμένα ἀνορθοῦντος καὶ τὰ συντετριμμένα σ. Areth.*Apoc.*5:3 (M.106.577B); **b.** pass., of fruit, *set* φασι...τὰς τῶν καρπῶν ἀπορρεούσας ἡμέρους συκᾶς, διὰ τῶν ὀλύνθων τῶν ἀγρίων ∼εσθαι Isid.Pel. *epp.*3.84(M.78.789D), cf.Pliny *nat.h.*15.81; **c.** medic., *bind, make costive, M.Ner.et Ach.*4(p.3.18); **d.** the universe λόγος...θεοῦ... συνήγαγεν τόδε τὸ πᾶν καὶ σ. Eus.*l.C.*11(p.228.21; M.20.1384B); ἀνάγκη λογίζεσθαι...ἔννοιαν τοῦ ταῦτα συναγαγόντος καὶ σ. Ath.*gent.* 38(M.25.76A); τὰ...πάντα εἰς ἑαυτὸν συνέχει καὶ σ. *ib.*42(84B); λέγει [sc. Πλάτων]...μίαν...εἶναι τοῦ παντὸς τὴν ψυχὴν...τὴν συνέχουσαν καὶ σ. τὸ σωματοειδὲς τοῦ κόσμου Nemes.*nat.hom.*2(M.40.580A); τὰ σώματα...δεῖται τοῦ συντιθέντος καὶ συνάγοντος καὶ ὥσπερ σ. καὶ συγκρατοῦντος αὐτά, ὅπερ ψυχὴν λέγομεν *ib.*(540A); διακρατῆσαι καὶ σ. Chrys.*hom.3.2 in Col.*(11.344F); **e.** more generally, *bind together, combine, unite* συνεσφιγμένων ἐν τῷ συγκρίματι τῶν στοιχείων Gr.Nyss.*anim.et res.*(M.46.45C); πάντα ἐκεῖνα αὕτη [sc. ἡ ἀγάπη] σ. Chrys.*hom.8.2 in Col.*(11.382F); Leont.H.*Nest.*1.13(M.86.1452B); **f.** in moral sense τῇ ὁμονοίᾳ ∼εσθε Thdt.*2Cor.*13:11(3.356); in depravity, Cyr.*Jo.*4.5(4.401B); φιλόχριστος ὄχλος...οὕτω συνεσφιγμένοι τυγχάνετε Gr.Ant.*mul.ung.*1(M.88.1848B); **2.** *bind* to; **a.** σ. καὶ συγκρατῶν τὸ ὑπόδημα περὶ τοὺς πόδας αὐτοῦ Or.*fr.18 in Jo.*(p.498. 20); **b.** met. ἡ συνδοῦσα ζώνη καὶ σ. τὴν πρόθεσιν τῆς ψυχῆς εἰς ἁγνείας, ἐστὶν ἡ πρὸς θεὸν ἀγάπη Meth.*symp.*4.6(p.52.5; M.18.96B); to God τὸ...πάσχειν με ∼ει θεῷ Gr.Naz.*carm.*1.2.8.201(M.37.663A); ὁ...βασιλεὺς...πίστει πρὸς τὸν θεὸν συνεσφιγμένος Gel.Cyz.*h.e.*3.9. 1; οἱ...πειρασμοὶ σ. καὶ ἑνοῦσιν αὐτὴν [sc. τὴν ψυχὴν] τῷ θεῷ Dor. *doct.*13.9(M.88.1772C); **3.** *hold in*; **a.** *gird* ἡ ὀσφὺς...οὐκ ἔζωσται... οὐδὲ συνέσφιγκται Or.*enarr.in Job* 40:3(M.17.97B); Gr.Nyss.*v.Mos.* (M.44.356C); **b.** *control, govern* τὴν ἄσκησιν τῆς ἁγνείας...τὰ αἰσθητήρια τηρεῖν ἑαυτοῦ καθαρὰ καὶ συνεσφιγμένα Meth.*symp.*11(p.130.23; M.18.208A); ‡Chrys.*hom.*2(13.206F); σ. σωφροσύνῃ τοὺς οἰκείους λογισμοὺς Nil.*epp.*1.271(M.79.181C); τὴν τὰς μερίζουσας τὸν νοῦν ∼ουσαν αἰσθήσεις...πίστιν Proc.G.*Cant.*8:9(M.87.1776B); ὅστις ἑαυτὸν ἐν τῷ τῆς ἁγίας ἀναστροφῆς κανόνι δυνάμει σ. Gr.Mag.*dial.*(tr. Zach.)3.18(M.*PL.*77.267A); **c.** *bind up* so as to close or limit the mind ἀρότρου δίκην διατέμνειν εἰδὼς τὰς συνεσφιγμένας αὐτῶν καρδίας, καὶ νοῦν τὸν κεχερσωμένον Cyr.*Is.*3.2(2.404A); so as to shorten or limit the time τῶν μελλόντων σ. τὸν χρόνον Ammon.*Ac.*17:30(M.85. 1565B); **d.** reflex., *be crowded together* διὰ...τὴν τοῦ τόπου στενοχωρίαν τὸ τοῦ λαοῦ πλῆθος ἑαυτοὺς σ. Gr.Mag.*dial.*(tr.Zach.)3.30(M. *PL.*77.287B); **e.** ? *condense,* of action of sun τὰ ῥυπαρὰ...καὶ σεσηπότα ξηραίνει καὶ ∼ει †Jo.D.*B.J.*31(M.96.1161A); **4.** *bind to oneself, lay fast hold of, A.Phil.*24(p.13.3); exeg. Os.11:4 ἐξέσπασα...αὐτοὺς...τῇ ἀγάπῃ συσφίγξας τῇ ἐμῇ Thdr.Mops.*Os.*11:4(M.66.189D); τουτέστι, σ. καὶ συνέσχον ὡς ἐν δεσμοῖς ἀγάπης Cyr.*Os.*126(3.159B); **5.** *brace, strengthen*; **a.** the paralytic, Chrys.*hom.37.1 in Jo.*(8.212B); Bas. Sel.*or.*23.1(M.85.273C); Leont.B.*mesopent.*(M.86.1985A); **b.** spiritually σ. ἑαυτὸν ὁ Ἀντώνιος, ἀπήρχετο εἰς τὰ...μνήματα Ath.*v.Anton.* 8(M.26.853C); Chrys.*hom.81.5 in Mt.*(7.781B, v.l. σφίγξαντες); τὴν ...ἀρχὴν [v.l. ψυχὴν] ἡμῶν σ., ζωννύων την οσφὺν id.*hom.23.1 in Eph.*(11.175B).

σύσφιγξις, ἡ, *bracing, strengthening* τῶν παραλύτων ἡ σ. Sophr.H. *ep.syn.*(M.87.3176B); ‡Jo.D.*Const.*3(M.95.316A).

σύσχεσις, ἡ, 1. *constraint* τῇ σ. τοῦ φόβου Chrysipp.*enc.in Jo. Bapt.*(p.40.18); **2.** *happening,* v. σχέσις.

συσχηματίζ-ω, med. and pass.; **1.** *conform*; **a.** in gen., Just.*dial.* 91.2(M.6.693A); ∼ονται αἱ περικοπαὶ πρὸς διαφόρους ποιότητας προσώπων Or.*comm.in Rom.*7:14(*JTS* 14 p.15); ἡ τῶν σωμάτων σκιὰ τῷ τύπῳ τῶν προηγουμένων ∼εται Gr.Nyss.*nativ.*(M.46.1141B); **b.** theol. ὁ δὲ λόγος οὗτος [sc. τοῦ κυρίου] συναρμόζεται καὶ ∼εται καιροῖς, προσώποις, τόποις Clem.*paed.*2.4(p.183.21; M.8.444B); δύναμιν...συγκατιοῦσαν καὶ...∼ομένην τοῖς τῆς ἄκρας ἀπολιμπανομένοις Eus.*l.C.*11 (p.227.20; M.20.1381B) ∞ id.*d.e.*4.5(p.159.5 M.22.265A); τοῦ Χριστοῦ... κτιστὸν...τὸ κατὰ τὴν ὑπὲρ ἡμῶν οἰκονομίαν συσχηματισθὲν τῷ σώματι τῆς ταπεινώσεως ἡμῶν Gr.Nyss.*hom.13 in Cant.*(M.44.1045C); id.*or. catech.*27(p.104.2; M.45.72B); ταῖς ἡμετέραις ὀλιγοτιμίαις ∼εται κύριος Cyr.*Jo.*2.4(4.172E); **2.** *make gestures* συνεσχηματίζοντο τοῖς σώμασιν Dion.Al.ap.Eus.*h.e.*6.41.22(M.20.612B).

συσχηματισμός, ὁ, 1. *configuration*; of stars, Hipp.*haer.*4.7(p.39. 22; M.16.3070A); **2.** *conformation,* of Christ οὐ γὰρ ἐσμίκρυνεν ἐν ὀφθαλμοῖς αὐτῶν τοῦ ἀοράτου θεοῦ τὴν δόξαν ὁ πρὸς ἡμᾶς σ. αὐτοῦ ‡Eust.*Laz.*20(p.43.2).

***σύσχημος,** *wearing the same dress,* i.e. *companion,* Steph.Diac. *v.Steph.*(M.100.1133A).

***συσχιδής,** *divided,* Gr.Naz.*carm.*2.1.14.10(M.37.1245A).

συφεών, ὁ, *pigsty,* Chrys.*hom.88.4 in Mt.*(7.830C); met., Sophr.H. *mir.Cyr.et Jo.*1(M.87.3424C).

συχαντός, v. σιχαντός.

συχνάζ-ω, *be, go,* or *do frequently* εἰς τὴν ἐκκλησίαν σ. Nil.*paraen.* 65(M.79.1253D); Thal.*cent.*1.69(M.91.1433C); ∼ων ἐν ταῖς προόδοις †Jo.D.*B.J.*5(M.96.892C); οὐ διέλιπε σ. πρὸς αὐτόν *ib.*19(1025C).

***συχνότης, ἡ,** *frequency,* Thdr.Stud.*epp.*2.139(M.99.1441D).

[*]συψελλίζω, v. συμψελλίζω.

σφαγή, ἡ, 1. *slaughter* δέχομαι τὴν σ. *be slain,* Thdt.*Ps.*77:64(1. 1163); id.*Os.*proem.(2.1311); id.*h.e.*3.24.2(3.941); in sacrifice θυσίας ...ζῴων ἀλόγων καὶ ἀνθρώπων σφαγάς Ath.*inc.*11.5(M.25.116C); of death of Christ ὁ μόσχος ὁ Ἰησοῦς ἐστιν, οἱ φέροντες ἄνδρες ἁμαρτωλοὶ οἱ προσενέγκαντες αὐτὸν ἐπὶ τὴν σ. *Barn.*8.2; Mel.*pass.*3 p.1.12 cit. s. ἄφθαρτος; ὁ ἀμνὸς...κατὰ τὴν τοῦ πατρὸς φιλανθρωπίαν καὶ τὴν σ. ἀνεδέξατο Or.*Jo.*6.53(35; p.162.7; M.14.292D); *ib.*6.58(37; p.167.3; 301A); of martyrdom σφαγὴν νίκην ἐργαζομένην Chrys.*Is.interp.*2. 3(6.21D); **2.** met., *persecution, vexation* τὴν ἄδικον...σ. ὑπεμείναμεν Thdt.*ep.*117(4.1199); τὴν καθ' ἡμῶν...γεγενημένην...σ. *ib.*118(1200); αἱ τῶν ἐπισκόπων σ. id.*h.e.*1.20.1(3.797); cf. τῶν...ἐπισκόπων ἡ παραπλησία σ. id.*ep.*113(1189).

σφαγιάζω, *slay, cause the death of, M.Ner.et Ach.*4(p.3.27).

σφάγιον, τό, *victim, offering,* of sacrifice of Christ οὐδέπω τὸ κρεῖττον...καὶ θεοπρεπὲς σ. παρῆν ἀνθρώποις Eus.*d.e.*1.10(p.45.15; M.22.85D); Gr.Naz.*or.*45.13(M.36.640C) cit. s. ἀφθαρσία.

σφαδαϊσμός, ὁ, v. sq.

σφαδασμός, ὁ, 1. *galling, exasperation,* Meth.*Porph.*1(p.504.3; σφαδαϊσμόν M.18.400A); **2.** ? *impulse* σ. τε καὶ λογισμῶν ἀνοικείων ἐπληρώθημεν id.*res.*2.6(p.339.14; M.18.304B).

σφάζ-ω (σφάττω), 1. *slaughter* a victim for sacrifice, of Isaac τοῦ κυρίου τὴν θειότητα αἰνίττεται μὴ σφαγείς Clem.*paed.*1.5(p.104.3; M. 8.277B); of S. Paul ὁ μέν, ὡς πρὸς τοὺς ἰδίους σπεύδων, ἐγάννυτο ∼όμενος Ath.*fug.*18(p.81.8; M.25.668C); of any killing πάντων πιστῶν...ἀναιρουμένων καὶ...∼ομένων Hipp.*Dan.*4.51.1; **2.** met.; **a.** *torment, persecute* ὅπως παυσώμεθά ποτε ὑπὸ τῶν συκοφαντῶν σφαττόμενοι Athenag.*leg.*1.3(M.6.893A); Thdt.*ep.*141(4.1235); **b.** pass., apptly., *be ready* or *willing to be slain*; of S. Paul before his conversion τὸν...ὑπὲρ...τῆς περιτομῆς σφαττόμενον καὶ ἑτέρους ἀποσφάττοντα Chrys.*comm.in Gal.*6:15f.(10.729A) or, poss., *be worn out* with one's labours.

σφαῖρα, ἡ, *ball*; **1.** *button* fixed on the point of a foil, etc., Clem. *str.*2.14(p.145.19; M.8.1000A); **2.** an instrument of torture ταῖς μολυβδίναις σ....δερόμενος...πρὸς κύριον ἐξεδήμησεν *M.Ner.et Ach.* 17(p.16.18).

***σφαιρητικός,** *of* or *for playing ball,* Clem.*str.*2.6(M.8.960B; v.l. for -ριστικούς p.126.18).

σφαιρίζω, *play at ball with,* i.e., *play with as a ball,* of demons τοῦτον [sc. ἅγιόν τινα εὐχόμενον] ἐσφαίριζον Evagr.Pont.*or.*111(M.79. 1192C); *V.Zos.*20(p.107.27).

σφαιρίον, τό, dim. of σφαῖρα; **1.** of celestial *sphere* ὄψει τὸ τοῦ ἀστρονόμου σ. μικρόν Gr.Nyss.*res.*3(M.46.668A); Mac.Mgn.*apocr.*4.17 (p.191.18); **2.** comestible in the form of balls, Leont.N.*v.Sym.*55 (M.93.1737B).

σφαιρισμός, ὁ, s.v.l., ? *hustling* ὠθισμοῖς καὶ σ. *V.Max.*2.27(M.90.164C).

σφαιροειδής, *globular, spherical*; of the heavens, Meth.*symp.*8.14 (p.101.13; M.18.164C); denied, Chrys.*hom.14.1 in Heb.*(12.140B); of celestial bodies, Or.*or.*31(p.397.5; M.11.552B); of the resurrection body in a theory attributed to Origen εἴ τις λέγει...ἐν τῇ ἀναστάσει σ. τὰ τῶν ἀνθρώπων ἐγείρεσθαι σώματα...ἀ. ἔ. Justn.*Or.anath.*5(p.213.25; M.86.989B); εἴ τις λέγει ὡς τὸ τοῦ κυρίου ἐξ ἀναστάσεως σῶμα... σ. τῷ σχήματι, καὶ ὅτι τὰ τοιαῦτα καὶ τὰ τῶν λοιπῶν ἐξ ἀναστάσεως ἔσται σώματα...ἀ. ἔ. CCP(543)*anath.*10.

***σφαιροκύλιστος,** *revolving on a circular course*, ‡Caes.Naz.*dial.* 98(M.38.964).

***σφαιρόμορφος,** *spherical*; of the vault of heaven, Geo.Pis.*hex.* 86(M.92.1436A).

***σφαιροσύνθετος,** *built in the form of a sphere*, Geo.Pis.*hex.*1410 (M.92.1542A).

σφαιρόω, 1. *make into a round*; hence *allow* the stomach *to protrude*, Geo.Pis.*carm.*1.81(p.3); **2.** pass., *form globules*; of manna, Gr.Nyss.*v.Mos.*39(M.44.312D); **3.** met., pass., *circle round, swarm* μελιττῶν περὶ τὸν ἡγούμενον σφαιρουμένων Philost.*h.e.*10.9(M.65.589B).

σφαίρωμα, τό, anything globular; *sphere, star*, *Orac.Sib.*3.88; *ib.*13.69.

σφαιρωτήρ, ὁ, *strap, thong*, of a sandal σ. φησι τὸ παρὰ τοῖς πολλοῖς λεγόμενον λωρίον, σ. δὲ λέγεσθαι διὰ τὸ πολλάκις κυκλοειδὲς ἀπεργάζεσθαι τὸ δέρμα τὸν τεχνίτην, καὶ οὕτω τέμνειν. τινὲς δέ φασι τὴν κλῆσιν λαβεῖν ἀπὸ τοῦ σφυρὰ τηρεῖν Chrys.ap.Phot.*cod.*274(M.104.237C); ἱμάντα φησὶ τὸν σ. τοῦ ὑποδήματος Vict.*Mc.*1:7(p.269.27); ἀπὸ σπαρτίου ἕως σ. ὑποδήματος Leont.H.*monoph.*(M.86.1889C).

***σφαιρωτής, ὁ,** *maker of spheres*, of Christ κόσμου κτίστας... σφαιρωτὰς ἄστρων Synes.*hymn.*5.17(M.66.1608).

[*]**σφακελλισμός, ὁ,** = σφακελισμός, *gangrene*; *rot*; met., *convulsion, spasm* σ. ἐστι ζέσις καὶ κίνησις θυμοῦ Evagr.Pont.*cap.*3(M.40.1265A).

[*]**σφαλάκρωμα, τό,** = φαλάκρωμα, *baldness*, *Apoc.Dan.*B(p.41).

σφαλίζω, *lock up, close* doors, *Chron.Pasch.*p.339(M.92.884C); a building, *ib.*p.338(881B); Thphn.*chron.*p.203(M.108.521C); Thdr. Stud.*epp.*2.219(M.99.1665B).

σφάλλω, 1. pass., of persons, *err, be mistaken*, c. ptcpl. ἐσφάλη παραγνοὺς τὸ τοῦ Δανιήλ Ath.*apol.Const.*17(M.25.617A); id.*Ar.*1.15(M.26.44A); perf. ptcpl. pass., of teaching, *erroneous*, Cels.ap. Or.*Cels.*4.11(p.281.22; M.11.1040D); opp. ὑγιής, Or.*ib.*7.63(p.213.3; 1509C); Vict.*Mc.*8:14ff.(p.343.26); **2.** pass., in the moral sphere, *do wrong, fall* ἐλευθέρᾳ προαιρέσει καὶ κατορθοῖ καὶ σ. Just.*1apol.*43.4 (M.6.393A); ὡς μὴ σ. περὶ ἃ μὴ προσῆκεν Clem.*paed.*2.7(p.190.5; M.8.457A); Esaias *or.*3.2(p.9; cf.M.40.1109D).

σφάλμα, τό, false step; met.; **1.** *mistake, error* ἀκούσιά...φησιν [sc. Plato] εἶναι τὰ ἁμαρτήματα...κατὰ ἄγνοιαν...καὶ σ. τοῦ ἀγαθοῦ Hipp.*haer.*1.19(p.23.8; M.16.3045B); τὸ...περὶ τὰ ὀνόματα σ. Or.*Jo.*6.41 (24; p.150.21; M.14.272A); τοῖς πλημμεληθεῖσιν εἴτ' οὖν κατὰ σφάλμα συμβεβηκόσι Const.ap.Eus.*v.C.*4.42(p.135.7; M.20.1192C); κατά τι σ. γραφικόν Eus.*h.e.*2.10.10(M.20.161B); Bas.*Spir.*12(3.9E; M.32.85C); in doctrine τὰ τοσαῦτα παρ' ἀνθρώποις ἐστὶ περὶ θεοῦ σ. Or.*Cels.*7.44 (p.195.5; M.11.1484C); Eus.*Marcell.*1.2(p.12.19; M.24.740A); περὶ τὸ σῶμα σ. ἔχουσι, λέγοντες μὴ ἐκ Μαρίας Ath.*Ar.*2.43(M.26.237C); **2.** *fault, sin* θέλει...διὰ καινοτέρας διορθώσεως...ὁ θεὸς τὰ σ. ἀναλαμβάνειν Or.*Cels.*4.69(p.339.5; M.11.1137C); βάλε μετάνοιαν...καὶ τὸ σ. παρέρχεται Esaias *or.*3.2(p.9; cf.M.40.1109D); ἥμαρτον...καὶ τὸ σ. μου ἐπιγινώσκω *V.Pach.A* 36(p.160.36); *ib.*1,2(pp.124.9,125.5); λύω ...Πέτρῳ σ. ‡Gr.Naz.*Chr.pat.*821(M.38.202A); of sin of Adam ἀνώρθωσεν τὰ τοῦ Ἀδὰμ σ. Hipp.*ben.Jac.*22(p.37.11); ταπεινοῦται... ἀπὸ σ. τὸ ἔνδοξον [sc. ἡμῶν τὸ σῶμα] Meth.*res.*3.14(p.411.3).

***σφαλτός,** *mistaken*, Barth.Edess.*Agar*(M.104.1445B).

***Σφαρφωτίμ (*Σαφὰρ φωτήμ),** (Hebr. סֵפֶר שׁוֹפְטִים) *the book of Judges*, ‡Epiph.*v.proph.Mal.*3(p.30; *divisim* M.43.419C; prob. for *Σφαρσωφτίμ*).

σφάττω, v. σφάζω.

σφεδανός, *vehement, violent*; of the Cross, *powerful*, Eudoc.*Cypr.* 1.212(M.85.840C).

***σφενδοβόλον, τό,** *sling*, Jo.Mal.*chron.*5 p.127(M.97.221C); *ib.*12 p.296(448B).

σφενδονάω, *bind* the hair *in a σφενδόνη* or *headband* in the shape of a sling, Gr.Naz.*carm.*2.1.11.771(M.37.1082A).

σφενδόνη, ἡ, 1. *sling*; anything so shaped: **a.** *ring* μὴ σ. τοῖς δακτύλοις σου περιθῇς *Const.App.*1.3.9; more properly the *bezel* ὄρνιν...ἀποτυποῦσι ταῖς σ. Clem.*prot.*4(p.46.33; M.8.160B); Gr.Nyss. *Eun.*4(2 p.94.5; M.45.669D); Chrys.*pan.Melet.*(2.519C); **b.** *far end* of the circus, Jo.Mal.*chron.*7 p.175(M.97.281A); *ib.*12 p.307(464A); *Chron.Pasch.*p.339(M.92.885B); Thphn.*chron.*p.308(M.108.749D); **2.** *stone* of the sling; of hailstones χαλάζης σφενδόναι Thdt.*Is.*24:6 (p.98.17; 2.290).

σφενδονίζω, 1. *strike by slinging*, *T.Jud.*7.5; **2.** ? *wind round*; a turban, Jo.Mal.*chron.*18 p.457(M.97.669B) or poss., *ornament with a tassel.*

***σφενδονίτης, ὁ,** s.v.l., *missile* from a sling δέχου ὁ Ἰακωβίτης... παρὰ Ἰακὼβ λίθον σ. Anast.S.*hod.*8(M.89.129A; perh. l. σφενδονίτου, σ. being a variant form of σφενδονήτης, *slinger*).

***σφενδών, ἡ,** *far end* of the circus, so named apparently from its shape οὐκ ἀπὸ λευκῆς ἐπὶ σφενδόνα μιλιοδρομῶν [sc. ὁ Ἠλίας] ἀλλ' ἀπὸ γῆς εἰς οὐρανόν ‡Chrys.*circ.*(8.88A); τὸ...πέλμα τοῦ Ἱππικοῦ τὴν γῆν πᾶσαν εἶναι, τὸν δὲ Εὔριπον τὴν θάλασσαν...τὸν δὲ ἐπὶ τὰς θύρας καμπτὸν τὴν ἀνατολήν, καὶ τὸν ἐπὶ τὴν σ. τὴν δύσιν *Chron.Pasch.* p.112(M.92.296A); *ib.*p.302(757B,760A).

Σφερτελλείμ, (Hebr. סֵפֶר תְּהִלִּים) *the book of Psalms*, ‡Epiph. *v.proph.Mal.*A 3 ap.*Chron.Pasch.*p.153(M.92.376C), an error for *the book of Judges* (*Σφαρφωτίμ* p.30).

σφετερίζ-ω, 1. *appropriate* ~οντες μὲν τοὺς λόγους, διαλεγόμενοι δὲ καθάπερ τυφλὸς κωφῷ Tat.*orat.*26(p.28.7; M.6.861C); **2.** usu. med., *attach to oneself* or *to one's point of view, win over* πλείους...ἐπὶ τὴν πλάνην σ. Eus.*h.e.*2.13.1(M.20.168A); τὸν νοῦν τῶν γεγραμμένων κλέπτοντες τοὺς πολλοὺς ~ονται Gr.Naz.*or.*30.1(p.108.5; M.36.104C); **3.** med., *hand over, transfer* τὸ κράτος εἰς τὸν ἴδιον ἀδελφὸν σ. Thphn. *chron.*p.402(M.108.957B).

***σφετέρισμα, τό,** *appropriation, borrowing*; of ideas, Hipp.*haer.* 7.20(p.196.9; M.16.3302D).

σφετερισμός, ὁ, *appropriation, assuming*, Chrys.*hom.56.1 in Mt.* (7.566D).

σφηκίον, τό, *wasp*, Epiph.*haer.*29.9(p.333.1; M.41.405A); *ib.*44.7 (p.198.16,20,27; 832B,C).

***σφηκιώδης,** *waspish*; of a heresy, Epiph.*haer.*44.7(p.199.3; M.41.832C).

σφηκόω, *bind tightly*; of nailing of Christ to Cross σφηκώσατε τοῦτον ὀλέθρῳ Nonn.*par.Jo.*19:6(M.43.900A).

σφήν, ὁ, *keystone*, Geo.Pis.*hex.*1410(M.92.1542A); ὁ τὸ πᾶν τῆς οἰκοδομῆς συνέχων εἰς ὑπάρχει κορυφαῖος λίθος...ὃν σ. οἱ οἰκοδόμοι προσαγορεύουσιν ‡Caes.Naz.*dial.*140(M.38.1057); met., of soul in rel. to God ἐκβαλὼν τὸν σ. τὸν ψυχοκράτην, ὡς...ἔσφιγξε καὶ λύει μόνος Geo.Pis.*hex.*1416(1542A).

σφιγγία, ἡ, *rapacity*, †Nil.*vit.*3(M.79.1141D).

***σφιγγοπρόσωπος,** *with the face of a sphinx* δαίμονα...σ. *T.Sal.* 18.1.

σφίγγ-ω, 1. *bind fast* σειραῖς τῶν ἰδίων ἁμαρτημάτων δεδεμένος καὶ ἐσφιγμένος Or.*Jo.*28.7(6; p.398.8; M.14.696B); **2.** *bind* or *hold together* ὕδωρ...σωλῆνι ~όμενον Gr.Naz.*or.*29.1(p.74.10; M.36.76A); of God joining soul and body to make man, Geo.Pis.*hex.*1417(M.92.1542A); met. εἰ...ἐσμὲν...ἅλας...δεῖ σ., οὐ παραλύειν Chrys.*hom.25.2 in 1Cor.*(10.222D); σ. [sc. sound doctrine], καὶ οὐκ ἀφίησι διαρρεῦσαι id.*hom.15.7 in Mt.*(7.195A); **3.** *hold* or *press together* and so *close*, *T.Sal.*22.14; σ. τὸ στόμα σου Bas.*renunt.*8(2.209C; M.31.644A); of shells μὴ δυνάμενοι διὰ τὸ ἐσφίχθαι αὐτὰς ἀνελεῖν ‡Eust.*hex.* (M.18.729A); **4.** *heal* one of paralysis, *strengthen* physically σ. τὸ σῶμα τοῦ παραλελυμένου Chrys.*hom.29.2 in Mt.*(7.344C); Isid.Pel. *epp.*2.5(M.78.461A); Rom.Mel.14.8(*AS* 1 p.103); morally and spiritually δείκνυσιν ὁδὸν...τίκτουσαν ἀγάπην καὶ ~ομένην ὑπὸ τῆς ἀγάπης Chrys.*comm.in Gal.*5:16(10.719D); δῆμος ἀγάπῃ ἐσφιγμένος id.*a. exil.*1.2(3.416C); στῦλοι [i.e. of Church]...οὐ σιδήρῳ δεδεμένοι, ἀλλὰ πίστει ἐσφιγμένοι *ib.*(416B); σ. [sc. ἡ τοῦ πνεύματος περιβολή] τὴν ἀνθρωπίνην ἀσθένειαν Anon.ap.Proc.G.*Cant.*8:9(M.87.1745D); reflex., *brace, be firm with oneself*, Dor.*doct.*3.3(M.88.1656B); v. συσφίγγω; **5.** met., *strengthen, reinforce*, Epiph.*haer.*42.12(p.162.14; M.41.784A); ἡ φιλία ~εται Chrys.*hom.48.7 in Mt.*(7.502E); **6.** *make firm* θέρμη...~ουσα [sc. τὰς ὀπώρας] Geo.Pis.*hex.*326(M.92.1459A).

σφίγμα, τό, *nexus* παρακρατεῖ τὸ σ. τῶν κυλισμάτων Geo.Pis.*hex.* 115(M.92.1440A); of a dome, *ib.*1411(1542A).

σφίγξις, ἡ, *binding tight, constriction*; **1.** *wringing* of the hands ἡ σ. χεροῖν Gr.Naz.*carm.*2.1.11.1458(M.37.1130A); **2.** *bracing, strengthening* of a paralytic τῆς μὲν τῶν ἁμαρτημάτων ἀφέσεως τεκμήριον, τὴν τοῦ σώματος σ. ποιεῖται Chrys.*hom.29.2 in Mt.*(7.344E); id.*hom.39.3 in Jo.*(8.231B); σφίξις Jo.D.*disp.*1(M.94.1597B).

[*]**σφίκωμα, τό,** = σφήκωμα, *cord*, *Euchol.*p.490.

[*]**σφίξις, ἡ,** = σφίγξις, Jo.D.*disp.*1(M.94.1597B).

***σφογγᾶτον, τό,** ? comestible of light, spongy texture, ? *sponge cake*, *Mir.Geo.*10(pp.104.8,106.2).

[*]σφογγίζω, variant of *σπογγίζω*, *sponge, wipe away, wipe out* σ. *τὸ δάκρυον* Nil.*epp.*2.270(M.79.337B); Jo.Mosch.*prat.*92(M.87.2949B).

σφόδρα, neut. plur. of *σφοδρός* as adv., *very much, exceedingly*, with superl. *ὡραιότατον σ.* Clem.*prot.*4(p.38.7; M.8.140C); also preceding the adj., id.*paed.*3.11(p.276.7; M.8.649A); Chrys.*hom.9.1 in 1Cor.*(10.75C); repeated *κατίσχυον σ. σ.* Or.*Jo.*2.27(22; p.84.20; M.14.161B); *οὐ σ. not very much*; also *very much not, far from οὐ σ. ἄτοπον* Dion.Ar.*c.h.*13.3(M.3.300C).

σφοδρός, 1. of things; *strong κημὸν...σ.* Chrys.*hom.4.4 in Jo.*(8.32A); **2.** of persons, *violent, impetuous*; of a judge, *harsh, severe*, Chrys.*hom.60.5 in Jo.*(8.358D).

***σφοδροτάτως,** superl. adv., formed from *σφόδρα*, *most vehemently*, Gr.Mag.*dial.*(tr.Zach.)2.1(M.*PL*.66.127B).

σφοδρότης, ἡ, 1. *severity τοῦ κρίματος τὴν σ.* Bas.*jud.*6(2.219C; M.31.665D); **2.** *zeal, ardour μετὰ πολλῆς τῆς σ. ... ἐσπούδασαν τὴν ἀκρόασιν* Chrys.*hom.1.2 in Jo.*(8.3C); id.*hom.64.4 in Mt.*(7.639D).

[*]σφουγγίζω, = *σπογγίζω*, *wipe with a sponge, sponge off τὰς ψίχας σ. τῶν τραπεζῶν* Ephr.2.393E ∾ Pall.*h.Laus.*34 cit. s. *σπογγίζω*.

σφραγίζ-ω, A. in gen.; **1.** *set as a seal ἐν τῇ πέτρᾳ ἐσφράγισε* [sc. Jeremiah] *τῷ δακτύλῳ τὸ ὄνομα τοῦ θεοῦ καὶ γέγονεν ὁ τύπος ὡς γλυφὴ σιδήρου, καὶ νεφέλη ἐσκέπαζε τὸ ὄνομα* ‡Epiph.*v.proph.Jer.*13(p.22; M.43.400C); **2.** *seal*; *fasten* or *close with a seal*; of Temple door (ref. Ezech.44:1–3) entered by Christ at Presentation, Germ. CP *or.*3.2(M.98.293C); *οἱ πατρίκιοι...ἔφυγον...καὶ ἐσφραγίσθησαν οἱ οἶκοι αὐτῶν* [i.e. for confiscation] *Chron.Pasch.*p.340(M.92.888B); exeg. *πηγὴ ἐσφραγισμένη* (Cant.4:12): *δεύτερον ὁ κῆπος κεκλεισμένος ἐρρέθη, τὸ μὲν ἐπὶ προκόπτοντος, τὸ δὲ ἐπὶ τελείου, ὅτε τὸ ἡγεμονικὸν αὐτοῦ καθοραθέν, τῇ τῆς θεολογίας σφραγῖδι τετύπωται· ἢ καὶ νῦν μὲν ἡ νύμφη κῆπός ἐστιν κεκλεισμένος μόνον, ἐν τῷ μέλλοντι αἰῶνι διὰ τὴν τελειότητα καὶ τὸ βέβαιον, καὶ πηγή ἐστιν ἐσφραγισμένη* Or.*schol.in Cant.*4:12(M.17.273A); cf.*ib.*8:6(285B); *τὴν ἀκρότητα ἔοικεν ἀρετὴν μαρτυρεῖν τῇ νύμφῃ ἐνταῦθα ὁ ἔπαινος, ὅτι ἀνέπαφος αὐτῆς μένει τοῖς ἐχθροῖς ἡ διάνοια, ἐν καθαρότητι καὶ ἀπαθείᾳ φυλασσομένη. τῷ ἰδίῳ δεσπότῃ ∼εται τὴν πηγὴν ταύτην ἡ καθαρότης μηδεμιᾷ νοημάτων ἰλύι τὸ διαυγὲς...τῆς καρδίας ἐπιθολώσασα* Gr.Nyss.*hom.9 in Cant.*(M.44.965A); *πηγὴ δέ ἐστιν ἐσφραγισμένη, ἵνα μὴ πρόχειρος ᾖ τοῖς ἀναξίοις ἀντλεῖν ἐπιχειροῦσιν· αἱρετικῶν γὰρ ὀφθαλμοῖς...ἄψαυστον εἶναι θέλων τὴν νύμφην, πηγὴν αὐτὴν καλεῖ ἐσφραγισμένην, τῇ σφραγῖδι τὸ ἀνεπιβούλευτον σημαίνων* Nil.ap.Proc.G.*Cant.*4:12(M.87.1664B); *ἡ δὲ πηγὴ τῷ ἁγίῳ πνεύματι ἐσφράγισται, ᾧ χριόμεθα μετὰ τὸ βάπτισμα* Cyr.*fr.Cant.*4:12(M.69.1289A); *εἰκότως τοίνυν αὐτὴν πηγὴν ἐσφραγισμένην καλεῖ* [ref. Jo.4:14], *ὡς μὴ πᾶσιν, ἀλλὰ τοῖς ἀξίοις προκειμένην. οὐ γὰρ τοῖς ἀμυήτοις, ἀλλὰ τοῖς μεμυημένοις πρόκειται τὰ θεῖα μυστήρια· οὐ τοῖς ἐν ἀνομίαις μετὰ τὴν μύησιν κυλινδουμένοις, ἀλλὰ τοῖς ἀκριβείᾳ συζῶσιν, ἢ διὰ μετανοίας καθαιρομένοις* Thdt.*Cant.*4:12(2.103); *πηγὴ ἐσφραγισμένη· τῇ τοῦ Χριστοῦ σφραγῖδι, τῇ ὑπὸ τοῦ λουτροῦ τῆς παλιγγενεσίας* Ph.Carp.*Cant.*114(M.40.96D–97A); Cant.4:12 as allusion to BMV *περὶ ταύτης τῆς πύλης* [ref. Ezech.44:2] *καὶ ἐν τοῖς Ἄσμασι...ὁ προφήτης...καταλέγεται κεκραγὼς...πηγὴ ἐσφραγισμένη· ἔμεινεν ἐν τῇ παρθενίᾳ ἡ ἁγία...κόρη...ἔνδον ἔχουσα τὸν θεὸν λόγον* ‡Epiph.*hom.*5(M.43.492C); cf.Ephr.3.529F; Andr.Cr.*or.*4(M.97.872B); *χαίροις...ἐσφραγισμένη πηγὴ τοῦ ἀθανάτου ῥείθρου* ‡Sophr.H.*triod.*(M.87.3860A); *χαῖρε πηγὴ ἐσφραγισμένη, ὁ βρυτὴρ τῆς ἀφθαρσίας, ἡ τὸ ῥεῖθρον τῆς ζωῆς Χριστὸν ἐκβλύσασα τῶν σημάντρων μηδαμῶς τῆς παρθενίας λυμανθέντων* Thdr.Stud.*nativ.BMV* 7(M.96.692B); **3.** *seal down, suppress δαίμονας σφραγίσας* [sc. Solomon] *κατέχωσεν* †Gregent.*disp.*(M.86.644A); *∼ει τὴν ὄσφρησιν δράκοντος* Hyper.*mon.*(M.79.1489A); **4.** *seal up, put away*, ref. Dan.9:24 *ἐπειδὴ γὰρ πλήρωμα νόμου καὶ προφητῶν αὐτὸς παρῆν,...ἔδει τὰ ὑπ' ἐκείνων λαλούμενα ∼εσθαι, ἵνα ἐν τῇ τοῦ κυρίου παρουσίᾳ πάντα λυθέντα φωτισθῇ καὶ τὰ ἐσφραγισμένα* Hipp.*Dan.*4.33.2(M.10.653C); *κεκλεῖσθαι καὶ ἐσφραγίσθαι τὰς θείας γραφὰς οἱ θεῖοί φασι λόγοι, τῇ κλειδὶ τοῦ Δαυίδ, τάχα δὲ καὶ σφραγῖδι, περὶ ἧς εἴρηται τό, ἐκτύπωμα σφραγῖδος ἁγίασμα κυρίῳ· τουτέστι τῇ δυνάμει τοῦ δεδωκότος αὐτὰς θεοῦ, τῇ ὑπὸ τῆς σφραγῖδος δηλουμένῃ* Or.*comm.in Ps.*1(M.12.1076C); *οὐ γὰρ ἀποκλεῖσαι καὶ ὥσπερ σφραγίσαι τὰς προφητικὰς ὁράσεις ἐπιδεδήμηκεν ὁ σωτὴρ...ὅς γε καὶ πάλαι οὔσας ἀσαφεῖς καὶ κατεσφραγισμένας, ὥσπερ ἐπικειμένας περιελὼν σφραγῖδας, ἀνέῳξέν τε καὶ ἀνήπλωσεν...οὐκ ἄρα ἀποκλεῖσαι ὅρασιν καὶ προφήτην ἐλήλυθεν ὁ Χριστὸς...μᾶλλον δὲ ἀναπετάσαι...ὅθεν δοκεῖ μοι κυριώτερον ὁ Ἀκύλας φάναι τοῦ τελέσαι ὁραματισμὸν καὶ προφήτην. ... δύναται δὲ καὶ κατὰ τὴν τῶν ἑβδομήκοντα ἑρμηνείαν τοιαύτην ἔχειν διάνοιαν τὸ τοῦ σφραγίσαι ὅρασιν καὶ προφήτην· ἐπεὶ ὁ νόμος καὶ οἱ προφῆται μέχρις Ἰωάννου διήρκεσαν, ἐξ ἐκείνου τε διαλελοίπασιν οἱ πάλαι παρὰ τῷ Ἰουδαίων ἔθνει πνευματοφορούμενοι* Eus.*d.e.*8.2(p.372.8; M.22.604D); *ἐσφραγίσθη γὰρ ὅρασις καὶ προφητεία μετὰ τὸν τοῦ σωτῆρος σταυρόν* Cyr.*Is.*1.2(2.37D); in gen. *τὸ σφραγίσαι* [sc. *ἐστί*] *τὸ καταπαῦσαι ἁμαρτίας* ‡Bas.Sel.*or.*38.2(M.85.408A); **5.** *seal up, preserve intact ὅσοι δὲ ἠπίστουν αὐτῷ, ...τούτων αἱ ἁμαρτίαι ὡς ἀναφαίρετοι ἐσφραγίζοντο* Hipp.*Dan.*4.32.5(M.10.653B); *οἱ ἐν ἀπιστίᾳ διαμείναντες, ἀναφαίρετον καὶ ὥσπερ ἐσφραγισμένην ἔσχον τὴν ἁμαρτίαν* Thdr.Heracl.ap.*cat.Jo.*16:11(p.362.30); of virginity, ref. BMV *ἐγκαταλείψας αὐτὴν...ἐσφραγισμένην παρθένον ἀμόλυντον* ‡Ath.*qu.al.*18(M.28.789A); *τὴν παρθενίαν ἐσφραγισμένην διαφυλάξαι* Jo.VI H.*icon.*7(M.96.1356C); in gen., *M.Ner.et Ach.*7(p.5.22); **6.** *preserve for, seal as belonging to θεῷ τὸ κάλλος ἐσφραγισμένον τηρεῖν θέλουσα* Gr.Naz.*carm.*1.2.10.917(M.37.746A); **7.** *set a seal upon, complete τὸ σφραγίσαι καὶ τελειῶσαι τὴν πᾶσαν ἡμῶν...πραγματείαν* Epiph.*haer.*80.10(p.494.26; M.42.772A); Nil.*Eulog.*32(M.79.1136C); *σπουδὴ σφραγισθεῖσα θεοῦ δωρεαῖς* id.*exerc.*19(M.79.745B); **8.** *set limits to, define τὰ τοῦ εὐαγγελίου ∼ει* [sc. S. Paul] Cyr.ap.*cat.Heb.* suppl.7:1(p.545.2); **9.** *shut in, imprison ὁ σφραγίσας σε* [sc. the deep] *ἐν ἑπτὰ σφραγῖσιν* *Apoc.Bar.rel.*3.8; **10.** *attest, confirm*; of presbyters' part in ordination, opp. bishop's prerogative of ordaining, cf.Hipp.*trad.ap.*9.8; in gen., Cyr.*Jo.*3.5(4.300C); *ὁ ἱερεὺς...∼ει τὴν πίστιν τῆς τριάδος* ‡Bas.*h.myst.*58(p.392.27); **11.** *set a distinguishing mark* (of ownership) *upon, brand*, prisoners and convicts, †Gregent.*leg.Hom.*5(M.86.584B) cit. s. *σφραγίς*; *σφραγίσας, ὡς ἔθος Πέρσαις, τὸν ἅγιον πρὸς τὴν...φρουρὰν προσέταττεν ἀποφέρεσθαι* Sophr.H.*v.Anast.*(M.92.1712B); soldiers, v. *σφραγίς*; met., of catechumens *σφραγισθέντων νεολέκτων στρατιωτῶν Χριστοῦ* *Rit. Bapt.*(p.392); in Carpocratian initiation *πυρὶ τὰ ὦτα τῶν ∼ομένων κατεσημήναντο* Heracleon ap.Clem.*ecl.*25(p.143.22; M.9.709B); in circumcision, as type of baptism, Epiph.*haer.*42.12(p.159.9; M.41.777D); met., of Christ sealing or marking souls with H. Ghost, Mel.*pass.*36 p.11.8; of face of Moses as marked with divine glory *τὸ πρόσωπον ἐσφραγίσθη τῷ ἁγίῳ πνεύματι* Ath.*inc.et c.Ar.*15(M.26.1009B); of Son as 'sealed' by Father, and of men as 'sealed' with divine image, v. *σφραγίς*; **12.** *seal against* evil, etc., *protect*; of Moses sealing doors of Israelites' houses (by Passover anointing), Mel.*pass.*15 p.3.4; met. (ref. Passover anointing) *αἱ κατησφαλισμέναι τῷ αἵματι* [sc. *τοῦ Χριστοῦ*] *καὶ σφραγισθεῖσαι ψυχαί* Meth.*symp.*9.1(p.115.18; M.18.180B); **13.** *give authority to*, hence *appoint* to office *ὃν καὶ ἐσφράγισε...εἰς ἐπίσκοπον* *A.Barn.*20(p.299.15).

B. *sign* with cross; intrans., *make the sign* (*of the cross*) (cf. A.11 supra), *A.Jo.*115(p.215.1); *πολλὰ σφραγίσας ἑαυτόν* *A.Mt.*11(p.228.4); *σφραγίσας ἑαυτὸν εἰσῄει εἰς τὴν πόλιν* *A.Xanthipp.*7(p.62.14); *αὐτὸς ἐσφράγισεν* *ib.*10(p.64.35); *συνήθως ἡμῖν τὰ πρόσωπα ∼ομένους τῇ τοῦ Χριστοῦ σφραγῖδι* Eus.*d.e.*7.14(p.434.29; M.22.701A); *ὑμεῖς σφραγίσατε ἑαυτούς* Ath.*v.Anton.*13(M.26.864A); *ib.*35(893B); *τῷ δακτύλῳ ὑμῶν σφραγίσατε τὰ πρόσωπα ὑμῶν* *A.Barn.*7(p.146.21); *σφραγίσας τὸ ὕδωρ* [i.e. for use in exorcism] Epiph.*haer.*30.10(p.345.19; M.41.421C); *ἐν βαλανείοις εἰσιόντες ἅμα τῷ τὰς θύρας ὑπερβῆναι ∼ονται* Chrys.*hom.10.5 in Ac.*(9.87C); as prophylactic against demons, id.*Jud.*8.8(1.687A); *πιστὴ εἶ; σφράγισον* id.*hom.13.5 in Col.*(11.387A); *μὴ ἁπλῶς ∼όμενος, ἀλλὰ τὰ τοῦ σταυροῦ πάσχων* id.*hom.13.1 in Phil.*(11.298B); *∼ων...μέτωπον καὶ στῆθος σημείῳ σταυροῦ* Nil.*epp.*3.278(M.79.521B); *σφραγίσας τὸν τόπον* *Apophth.Patr.*(M.65.257A); *σφραγίσας ἐμαυτὸν ἀπῆλθον* Dor.*doct.*7.1(M.88.1697C); *σφραγίσαντος τὸ πάθος* Jo.Mosch.*prat.*56(M.87.2912A); ref. mark of antichrist *δίδωσιν...ἐπὶ μέτωπον τὸν δυσσεβῆ χαρακτῆρα, ἵνα ἐξουσίαν μὴ ἔχῃ ὁ ἄνθρωπος σφραγίσασθαι τῇ δεξιᾷ τὸ σημεῖον Χριστοῦ* Ephr.3.136A; *χάριν τούτου ∼ει τὴν δεξιὰν τοῦ ἀνθρώπου, αὕτη γάρ ἐστι ἡ ∼ουσα ἅπαντα τὰ μέλη ἡμῶν* *ib.*136B; at grace at table *σφράγισον, εὐχαρίστησον* Chrys.*hom.12.1 in 1Tim.*(11.611B); *∼ω εὐχαριστίᾳ* Nil.*Eulog.*32(M.79.1136C); cf.Ath.*virg.*13(p.47.2; M.28.265C); in blessing *ἀπέλυσεν αὐτοὺς...μετ' εἰρήνης σφραγίσας τῇ τοῦ σταυροῦ σφραγῖδι* Marc.Diac.*v.Porph.*21; *σφραγίσας αὐτῶν τὰ μέτωπα καὶ στήθη ἀπέλυσεν αὐτούς* Leont.N.*v.Sym.*20(M.93.1696A); *σ. ὁ ἱερεὺς τὸν λαόν* *Lit.Marc.*(Brightman p.118.13); *τὸ δὲ ∼ειν ὁ ἱερεύς, κατὰ μίμησιν τῆς τοῦ Χριστοῦ ἀναλήψεως, ᾗ καὶ τοὺς ἀποστόλους ἐσφράγιζεν* Jo.Jej.*liturg.*(p.441); ‡Bas.*h.myst.*36(p.266.19); in ordination, cf.Chrys.*Jud.et gent.*9(1.571A); in eucharistic action, of signing the elements, cf.*A.Thom.*A 50(p.166.18); *∼ει* [sc. *ὁ ἱερεύς*] *τὰ δῶρα* *Lit. Jac.*(p.200.7); *σ. τὸν δίσκον* *Lit.Marc.*(Brightman p.124.8); *ἐσφράγισε τὰ δῶρα* Leont.H.*monoph.*(M.86.1900B); *∼εσθαι τὴν προσφοράν* ‡Sophr.H.*liturg.*(M.87.3989A); v. *σφραγίς*; in baptismal consignation, v. infra C; perh. of visible mark of Cross *ὁρᾶτε...ποίῳ τύπῳ* ἐν τῷ μετώπῳ ἐσφραγίσθημεν...καὶ εἰποῦσα ταῦτα, ἔδειξε τὸν σταυρόν *M.Glyc.*2.3(p.13*.3A).

C. ref. baptism as conferring stamp of God's ownership on believers; **1.** by virtue of it being sacrament of inward gift of H. Ghost, cf.Mel.*pass.*36 p.11.8; μέλλει τὸ πνεῦμα τὸ ἅγιον ∼ειν ὑμῶν τὰς ψυχάς Cyr.H.*catech.*3.3; τῇ βασιλικῇ αὐτοῦ δυνάμει ἀναγεννώμεθα καὶ ∼όμεθα...τοῦ ἀναγεννήσαντος καὶ σφραγίσαντος ἡμᾶς ἁγίου πνεύματος Didym.*Trin.*2.12(M.39.680A); v. βάπτισμα, σφραγίς; **2.** of baptism in gen. as conferring seal on believers ἱεροφαντεῖ δὲ ὁ κύριος καὶ τὸν μύστην ∼εται φωταγωγῶν Clem.*prot.*12(p.84.25; M.8.241A); ∼ει διὰ λουτροῦ παλιγγενεσίας *A.Xanthipp.*28(p.78.34); τάχυνον τοῦ σφραγίσαι με, ἵνα καὶ εἰ καὶ φθάσῃ ἐπ' ἐμὲ θάνατος ἀπέλθω πρὸς ἐκεῖνον τὸν εὔσπλαγχνον *ib.*13(p.67.2); τῶν ἐσφραγισμένων Χριστιανῶν *A.Barn.*1(p.292.6); σὺ γίνῃ...προφήτης ἐν τῷ λουτρῷ ...ἔνθους γινόμενος καὶ σφραγισάμενος Chrys.*hom.3.7 in 2Cor.*(10.454B); πῶς δὲ ἐνδύσῃ [sc. Χριστόν] ὁ μὴ σφραγισάμενος; πῶς ἐνδύσῃ ὁ μήπω τὸ βάπτισμα εἰληφώς; ‡Bas.*struct.hom.*(1.334E; M.30.33B); πολλοὺς κατηχήσασα [sc. Thecla] καὶ σφραγισαμένη Bas.Sel.*v.Thecl.*1 (M.85.557C); **3.** sealing associated esp. with power of threefold Name in baptism διὰ...πατρὸς καὶ υἱοῦ καὶ ἁγίου πνεύματος σφραγισθεὶς ἀνεπίληπτός ἐστι πάσῃ τῇ ἄλλῃ δυνάμει Clem.*exc.Thdot.*86 (p.133.5; M.9.697B); εἰς πατέρα καὶ υἱὸν διὰ τῆς ἐν τῷ βαπτίσματι χάριτος ἐσφραγίσθημεν Bas.*Eun.*2.22(1.258B; M.29.620D); **4.** and esp. with post-baptismal consignation with chrism τοῦ σφραγισθῆναι ὑπὸ τοῦ ἐπισκόπου Corn.ap.Eus.*h.e.*6.43.15(M.20.624A); χρίσεις πρῶτον ἐλαίῳ ἁγίῳ, ἔπειτα βαπτίσεις ὕδατι, καὶ τελευταῖον σφραγίσεις μύρῳ *Const.App.*7.22.2; ὁ ἐπίσκοπος δι' οὗ ἐσφραγίσθητε ἐλαίῳ ἀγαλλιάσεως *ib.*2.32.3; τῷ μύρῳ ∼όμεθα ὕστερον [i.e. after baptism] ‡Just.*qu.et resp.*137(M.6.1389C); cf.Dion.Ar.*e.h.*2.2.7(M.3.396C); CCP(381)‡*can.*7; CTrull.*can.*95; Thdr.Stud.*epp.*2.219 *qu.*14(M.99.1665A); perh. cf. ref. Jo.6:27 ἢ τὸ ἐσφραγίσθαι πάλιν, ἀντὶ τοῦ κεχρίσθαι τεθεικώς· κατασφραγίζεται γὰρ ὁ χριόμενος Cyr.*Jo.*3.5(4.300C); **5.** of baptism as covenant seal (i.e. attestation, cf. A.10 supra) σφράγισον τὴν συγκατάθεσιν τοῦ δούλου σου Serap.*euch.*21.1.

σφραγίς (σφρηγίς), ἡ, *seal* [acc. σφραγῖδαν metr. gr., Aberc. *epitaph.*9];

A. in gen.; **1.** *seal, signet*; of eucharistic body of Christ, likened to seal from which many impressions are taken while it remains intact, Eutych.*pasch.*2(M.86.2393C); **2.** *design on a seal*; of pagan mythological designs, Clem.*prot.*4(p.46.33; M.8.160B); of designs suitable for Christians αἱ δὲ σ. ἡμῖν ἔστων πελειὰς ἢ ἰχθὺς ἢ ναῦς οὐριοδρομοῦσα ἢ λύρα μουσική...ἢ ἄγκυρα ναυτική...οὐ γὰρ εἰδώλων πρόσωπα ἐναποτυπωτέον...οὐδὲ μὴν ξίφος ἢ τόξον τοῖς εἰρήνην διώκουσιν ἢ κύπελλα τοῖς σωφρονοῦσιν id.*paed.*3.11(p.270.7; M.8.633A); of Christ's seals on letter to Abgar, bearing design +ΨΧΕΥΡΑ, and explanation of design, *Ep.Abg.*2(p.281.17); of Solomon's magic seal, *T.Sal.*passim; binding demons, *ib.*5.11(M.122.1324B); cf.*ib.*7.8(1328A); *ib.*14.2(1336D); **3.** *impression of a seal*; **a.** authenticating a document, fig. τὴν συνήθη εὐλογίαν οἷόν τινα σ. τοῖς γράμμασιν ἐπιτέθεικε Thdt.*Gal.*6:18(3.397); hence **i.** *attestation, proof* τῇ δικαίᾳ ψυχῇ θεία τις ἀγαθωσύνης δύναμις...οἷον ἀπαυγάσματος νοεροῦ καθάπερ ἡλιακῆς ἀλέας ἐναποσημαίνεταί τι, δικαιοσύνης σ. ἐπιφανῆ, φῶς ἡνωμένον ψυχῇ δι' ἀγάπης Clem.*str.*6.12(p.484.18; M.9.325B); of baptismal renunciation of Devil and profession of faith as seal set on conversion, cf.Or.*hom.12.4 in Num.*(p.105.25; M.12.665C); of circumcision as attestation of covenant, id.*hom.3.3 in Gen.*(p.42.2; M.12.177A); and as attestation of Abraham's righteousness οὐχ ὡς δικαιοσύνης ποιητικὴ ἐδόθη, ἀλλὰ σ. καὶ σημεῖον τῆς ἐκ πίστεως δικαιοσύνης τοῦ Ἀβραάμ Sever.*Rom.*4:11(Staab p.217.11); cf.Chrys.*hom.9.3 in Rom.*(9.500D); of prophecies attesting gospel record τὰς εὐαγγελικὰς...παραθήσομαι λέξεις, εἶθ' ὥσπερ ἁρμονίους σφραγῖδας τὰς προφητικὰς αὐταῖς ἐπιθήσω μαρτυρίας Eus.*d.e.*7.2 (p.337.13; M.22.549C); εἰ δὲ χρὴ ταῦτα ἐπισφραγίσασθαι προφητικῇ σ. id.*e.th.*3.17(p.176.1; M.24.1036B); of virgin birth as sign of Christ's divinity, Eulog.*palm.*10(M.86.2933A); **ii.** *confirmation, ratification*; of episcopal anointing as seal of covenant, *Const.App.*7.22.2; of baptism as ratification of orthodox belief, ‡Hipp.*consumm.*42(p.306.29; M.10.945A); ἔστι γὰρ τὸ βάπτισμα σ. τῆς πίστεως, ἡ δὲ πίστις, θεότητος συγκατάθεσις Bas.*Eun.*3.5(1.276E; M.29.665C); of prayer said behind ambo as ratification of all prayers of the faithful, ‡Germ.CP *contempl.*(M.98.452C); **b.** setting a seal upon; hence *completion, perfection* βίῳ μὲν ὁδηγῷ θεωρίας, θεωρίᾳ δὲ σφραγῖδι βίου χρησάμενος Gr.Naz.*or.*21.6(M.35.1088B); of Cyril as σ. τῶν πατέρων Anast.S.*hod.*7(M.89.113D); of knowledge κυρίαν εἶναι τὴν σ. τῆς γνώσεως, ἐκ φύσεως, καὶ μαθήσεως, καὶ ἀσκήσεως συνεστῶσαν Clem.*str.*1.5(p.20.17; M.8.725A); **c.** sealing up a letter, book, etc. σφραγῖδας λύοντες ἐσφραγισμένα τὰ γράμματα αὐταῖς ταῖς σφραγῖσιν ἀποδιδόασι· πίσσαν καὶ ῥητίνην καὶ θεῖον, ἔτι δὲ ἄσφαλτον ἴσα τήξαντες κολλυρίων σχήματι πλάσαντες φυλάττουσι· καιρὸς δὲ ὅταν ᾖ λύειν γραμματίδιον, τὴν γλῶσσαν ἐλαίῳ δεύσαντες, εἶτα ἐξ αὐτῆς τὴν σ. χρίσαντες, πυρὶ συμμέτρῳ τὸ φάρμακον θερμάναντες ἐπιφέρουσι τῇ σ. καὶ μέχρι ἂν παγῇ παντελῶς ἐῶσι, καὶ τούτῳ δίκην σημάντρου χρῶνται...οὕτως μὲν οὖν καὶ τὰς σ. λύειν ἐπιχείρουσι τὰ ἔνδον γεγραμμένα μανθάνειν πειρώμενοι Hipp.*haer.*4.34(p.60.16; M.16.3093C); on valuables, cf. Clem.*paed.*3.11(pp.268–9; M.8.632C); Jo.Mosch.*prat.*198(M.87.3085A); on prison doors, cf.*A.Thom.*A 151(p.260.17); on Christ's tomb, ‡Sophr.H.*triod.*(M.87.3940B); of seals set by God on the abyss ἄκουε, γῆ, τῆς φωνῆς τοῦ κτίσαντός σε ἐν τῇ περιουσίᾳ τῶν ὑδάτων, ὁ σφραγίσας σε ἐν ἑπτὰ σφραγῖσιν, ἐν ἑπτὰ καιροῖς *Apoc.Bar.rel.*3.8; met. τὸν θησαυρὸν τὸν ἐν τῇ σ. τοῦ Χριστοῦ ὑπουργήσαντα καλῶς Jo.Thess.*dorm.BMV* 2.12(p.427.5); hence, in gen. of a protective seal or safeguard; of an amulet, *BCH* 17.638; met., of prayer as seal of virginity, Gr.Nyss.*or.dom.*1(p.8.10; M.44.1124B); Christ as seal of virginity of BMV, Max.*ambig.*(M.91.1025D); hence **d.** of 'seal' of silence αἴκε φυλάξῃς χείλεσιν ὑμετέροισι σοφὴν σφρηγῖδα σιωπῆς Nonn.*par.Jo.*11:40(M.43.845B); ref. *disciplina arcani* τἆλλα δὲ εἴσω μαθήσῃ τῆς τριάδος χαριζομένης, ἃ καὶ κρύψεις παρὰ σεαυτῷ σφραγῖδι κρατούμενα Gr.Naz.*or.*40.45(M.36.425A); **e.** as mark or brand of ownership: on cattle καὶ τὰ ἄλογα ζῷα διὰ σφραγῖδος δείκνυσι τίνος ἐστὶν ἕκαστον· καὶ ἐκ τῆς σ. ἐκδικεῖται Clem.*exc.Thdot.*86(p.133.4; M.9.697B); cf. ref. baptism (v. infra) ὁ θεὸς...διὰ τῆς αὐτοῦ σ. ἐπιγινώσκει τὰ ἴδια πρόβατα *A.Thom.*A 26(p.141.18); on convicts σημείῳ τινί, ἤγουν σφραγῖδι σιδηρᾷ σφραγίσαντες πεπυρακτωμένῃ ἐπὶ τοῦ μετώπου †Gregent.*leg.Hom.*5(M.86.584B); on captives υἱοὶ καὶ θυγατέρες ἐν αἰχμαλωσίᾳ πονηρᾷ, ἐν σφραγῖδι ὁ τράχηλος αὐτῶν *Pss.Sal.*2.6; cf.Sophr.H.*v.Anast.*(M.92.1712B); on soldiers, Chrys. *hom.3.7 in 2Cor.*(10.454A,B); cf. (ref. circumcision of Abraham) οὐχ ὑστέρα δὲ μόνον τῆς πίστεως, ἀλλὰ καὶ σφόδρα αὐτῆς καταδεεστέρα, καὶ τοσοῦτον, ὅσον σημεῖον τοῦ πράγματος οὗπέρ ἐστι σημεῖον· οἷον ὅσον ἡ σ. τοῦ στρατιώτου id.*hom.9.3 in Rom.*(9.500D); cf.Vegetius *de re militari* 1.8,2.5; **f.** of image or impression of seal; met., of Son in rel. to Father ἡ μὴ κινουμένη σ., ἡ ἀπαράλλακτος εἰκών Gr.Naz.*or.*38.13(M.36.325B); ὅμοιον τῷ γεννήσαντι...ὡς εἰκόνα καὶ ὡς σ. πάσης τῆς τοῦ παντοκράτορος ἐνεργείας καὶ δυνάμεως, σ. τῶν τοῦ πατρὸς ἔργων καὶ λόγων καὶ βουλευμάτων Eun.*exp.fid.*2(p.257); ref. Jo.6:27 ὥσπερ...ἐν κηρῷ τις ἐμπήξει σφραγῖδα χρυσῆν...ὅλην ἐξ ὅλης τὴν αὐτῆς ἐμφέρειαν ἐνσημαίνεται· οὕτω καὶ ὁ...πατὴρ τοὺς τῆς ἑαυτοῦ φύσεως χαρακτῆρας οὐσιωδῶς ἐμπρέποντας ἔχει τῷ υἱῷ καὶ τοῦτό ἐστι τὸ ἐσφραγίσθαι λέγειν αὐτὸν παρὰ τοῦ πατρός Cyr.*Arcad.*(p.98.23; 5^{2}.97A); σ. γὰρ τοῦ θεοῦ...ὁ υἱὸς ὅλην αὐτοῦ...ὁμοίωσιν ἔχων, καὶ ἐν ἰδίῳ κάλλει τὴν τοῦ γεννήσαντος ἀναστράπτων φύσιν id.*Ag.*20(3.650E); id.*Jo.*3.5(4.302Cff.); σοφία...ἡ ἀπαράλλακτος τοῦ πατρὸς εἰκών, ἡ ζῶσα σ. ... ὁ ἀκριβὴς χαρακτήρ Jo.Mon.*hymn.Chrys.*8(M.96.1384B); of image of God imprinted on man at Creation τῇ γὰρ αὐτοῦ μορφῇ ὡς ἐν μεγίστῃ σ. τὸν ἄνθρωπον διετυπώσατο *Hom.Clem.*17.7; cf.*ib.*16.19; καθάπερ τινὰ σ. τῆς ἑαυτοῦ φύσεως ἐνέπηξεν ὁ δημιουργὸς τὸ πνεῦμα ἅγιον, τουτέστιν τὴν πνοὴν τῆς ζωῆς, δι' ἧς πρὸς τὸ ἀρχέτυπον διεπλάττετο κάλλος, ἀπετελεῖτο δὲ κατ' εἰκόνα τοῦ κτίσαντος...δυνάμει τοῦ ἐνοικισθέντος αὐτῷ...πνεύματος Cyr.*Jo.*9.1(4.822D); of H. Ghost as seal by which character of Logos is impressed on creation εἰ δὲ τὸ πνεῦμα...σ. ἐστιν, ἐν ᾧ...σφραγίζει πάντα ὁ λόγος· ποία ὁμοιότης ἢ ἰδιότης...τῆς σ. πρὸς τὰ...σφραγιζόμενα; οὐκοῦν καὶ κατὰ τοῦτο οὐκ ἂν εἴη τῶν πάντων αὐτό· οὐ γὰρ ἂν εἴη ἡ σ. ἐκ τῶν σφραγιζομένων,...ἀλλ' ἴδιόν ἐστι τοῦτο τοῦ...σφραγίζοντος λόγου Ath.*ep.Serap.*1.23(M.26.585A); of divine image imprinted on Christian believers through conformation to Christ; combined with concept of 'sealing up' human thoughts, etc. προτρέπεται αὐτὴν ὁ νυμφίος πᾶν νόημα καὶ πρᾶξιν μορφῶσαι τῷ ἑαυτοῦ χαρακτῆρι...ἢ τοῦτο λέγει ὁ νυμφίος πρὸς αὐτήν, θές με ὡς σ. πρὸς τὸ σφραγίζειν τὰς ἐνθυμήσεις σου Or.*schol. in Cant.*8:6(M.17.285B); conformation to the image being effected through believers' possession of H. Ghost, cf.Cyr.*Jo.*3.5(4.302E); τῷ ἁγίῳ πνεύματι σφραγιζόμενοι πρὸς θεὸν ἀναμορφούμεθα...οὐ γὰρ δήπου τὸ πνεῦμα ἐν ἡμῖν σκιαγράφου δίκην τὴν θείαν οὐσίαν ζωγραφεῖ...ἀλλ' αὐτὸ θεός τε ὑπάρχον καὶ ἐκ θεοῦ προελθόν, ὥσπερ ἔν τινι κηρῷ ταῖς τῶν δεχομένων αὐτὸ καρδίαις ἀοράτως δίκην σφραγῖδος ἐνθλίβεται...καὶ κατ' εἰκόνα θεοῦ δεικνύον αὖθις τὸν ἄνθρωπον id.*thes.*34(5^{1}.360Aff.); cf. Mac.Aeg.*hom.*30.5(M.34.724C); hence of H. Ghost as mark of Christ's ownership for recognition at Judgement μέλλει...ἐκ τῶν οὐρανῶν κατέρχεσθαι...καὶ εἰς δύο μέρη στήσει πάντας, καὶ τοὺς ἔχοντας τὸ ἴδιον σημεῖον, τουτέστι τὴν σ. τοῦ πνεύματος, τούτους ὡς ἰδίους προσφωνήσας ἐκ δεξιῶν στήσει...καὶ τότε δόξῃ θείᾳ τὰ σώματα τούτων περιβληθήσονται...καὶ δόξης πνεύματος ἔσονται πλήρεις, ἧς ἀπὸ τοῦ νῦν εἶχον ἐν ταῖς ψυχαῖς *ib.*5.12(517A); ζητήσωμεν...τὸν καυτῆρα τοῦ κυρίου καὶ τὴν σ. ἐν ἑαυτοῖς ἔχειν· ὅτι ἐν τῷ καιρῷ τῆς κρίσεως, γινομένης τῆς ἀποτομίας τοῦ θεοῦ...ὅταν καλέσῃ ὁ ποιμὴν τὴν ἰδίαν ποίμνην, ὅσοι ἔχουσι τὸν καυτῆρα ἐπιγινώσκουσι τὸν ἴδιον ποιμένα, καὶ ὁ ποιμὴν τοὺς ἔχοντας τὴν ἰδίαν σ. γνωρίζει. ... εἰς δύο γὰρ μέρη ἵσταται ὁ κόσμος, καὶ γίνεται μία ποίμνη σκοτεινή,...καὶ μία πλήρης φωτός,...αὐτὸ οὖν ὃ νῦν κτώμεθα ἐν ταῖς ψυχαῖς, αὐτὸ ἐκεῖνο λάμπει καὶ φανεροῦται, καὶ τὰ σώματα ἐνδύει δόξαν *ib.*12.13(564D); seal impressed on the faithful being inward presence of H. Ghost, cf.Or.*comm.in Eph.*1:13(p.243); H. Ghost as σφραγίς and χρῖσμα, Didym.*Trin.*2.1(M.39.452C); divine glory being revealed by H. Ghost as seal or imprint of God διὰ τοῦ φωτισμοῦ τοῦ πνεύματος, τὸ ἀπαύγασμα τῆς δόξης τοῦ θεοῦ καθορῶμεν· διὰ δὲ τοῦ χαρακτῆρος, ἐπὶ τὴν οὗ ἐστιν ὁ χαρακτὴρ καὶ ἡ ἰσότυπος σ. ἀναγόμεθα Bas.*Spir.*64 (3.54A; M.32.185C); distinguishing mark of Christian a protection against demons ἤδη φερέτω σφραγῖδα πατρὸς [i.e. wisdom] ἱκέτις ψυχά, δεῖμα μὲν ἐχθροῖς δαίμοσιν...σύνθημα δὲ σοῖς ἁγνοῖς προπόλοις Synes.*hymn.*3.621(p.24; M.66.1602); and, as borne by Gnost. redeemer, against hostile cosmic powers τούτου με χάριν πέμψον, πάτερ· σφραγῖδας ἔχων καταβήσομαι, αἰῶνας ὅλους διοδεύσω *Ps.Naas.* ap.Hipp.*haer.*5.10(p.103.18; M.16.3159B); cf.*A.Phil.*144(p.86.6); of BMV as seal impressing stamp of human nature on Son, Thdr. Stud.*nativ.BMV* 7(M.96.692B).

B. of sign of cross as distinguishing mark of Christians and safeguard against demons σῆμα δέ τοι τότε πᾶσι βροτοῖς, σφρηγὶς ἐπίσημος τὸ ξύλον ἐν πιστοῖς *Orac.Sib.*8.244; cf.*A.Jo.*115(p.215.1); ὥπλισεν τὸ μέτωπον αὐτοῦ τῇ σ. τοῦ τιμίου σταυροῦ *M.Das.*11.2(p.94. 31); τίς θεώμενος τῷ σωτηριώδει σημείῳ πάντας τοὺς εἰς Χριστὸν πεπιστευκότας σφραγῖδι χρωμένους, οὐκ ἂν εὐλόγως καταπλαγείη ἀκούων πρόπαλαι τοῦ κυρίου εἰρηκότος· '...καταλείψω ἐπ' αὐτῶν σημεῖον' Eus.*d.e.*6.25(p.295.4; M.22.484D); συνήθως ἡμῖν τὰ πρόσωπα σφραγιζομένους τῇ τοῦ Χριστοῦ σ. *ib.*7.14(p.434.29; 701A); Χριστὸν ἀπειπεῖν μετὰ τῆς σ. ἄνω βλέψαντας Gr.Naz.*or.*4.84(M.35.612A); as part of regular Christian practice ἡ σ., ἡ προσευχή, τὸ βάπτισμα Gr.Nyss.*Eun.*11(2 p.271.1; M.45.880C); esp. effective as prophylactic against demons when used in conjunction with name of Christ, id. *v.Gr.Thaum.*(M.46.952B,C); ἐπετίθει τὴν σ. τοῖς ὀφθαλμοῖς καὶ τῷ στόματι καὶ τῇ καρδίᾳ id.*v.Macr.*3(p.398.18; M.46.985A); τὴν σ. ἐπιθῶμεν τῷ στήθει καθάπερ τινὰ χαλινόν Chrys.*hom.17.4 in Ac.*(9. 141C); children to be taught to make sign of cross, id.*hom.12.7 in 1Cor.*(10.108A); seal likened to military mark of identity, id. *catech.*2.5(2.244Aff.); warding off attacks of demons, Evagr.Pont. *cap.pract.*A 66(M.40.1240D); χρήσασθε...τῇ σ. τοῦ σταυροῦ Nil.*epp.* 3.98(M.79.429D); ποιήσας τὴν ἐν Χριστῷ σ., τοῦτ' ἔστιν τὸ σημεῖον τοῦ σταυροῦ ἐπὶ τῷ μετώπῳ καὶ τῇ καρδίᾳ αὐτοῦ *Dial.Tim.et Aquil.*76 v°; contrasted with mark of antichrist, Hipp.*antichr.*6(p.8.10; M.10. 733B); Ephr.3.135F–136B; τὴν ἑαυτοῦ [sc. τοῦ δράκοντος] σ. ἀντὶ τοῦ σταυροῦ id.2.225D; cf. φασὶ δὲ καὶ διδόναι χάραγμα καὶ σ. τὸν ἀντίχριστον τοῦ οἰκείου ὀνόματος Oecum.*Apoc.*13:15(p.157); in reception of catechumens, cf.Hipp.*trad.ap.*20.8; Marc.Diac.*v.Porph.*21; Dion. Ar.*e.h.*2.3.4(M.3.400D); in baptismal consignation, v. infra C.4.b; in ordination ἡ σταυροειδὴς δὲ πάλιν σ., τὴν ἀνενεργησίαν δηλοῖ τῶν σαρκικῶν ὀρέξεων Dion.Ar.*e.h.*6.3.3(548C); in signing of eucharistic elements, ‡Germ.CP *contempl.*(M.98.440A); v. σφραγίζω; in episcopal blessing, position of bishop's fingers denoting 6500 (number of years to Parousia), *ib.*(417A); seal of cross guarantees reality of sacramental grace, ‡Chrys.*ador.*1.2(3.822A); sign of cross poss. marked visibly on persons of some Christians παρθένος...εἶδεν... τὸν τράχηλον αὐτοῦ λαμπρὸν ὡς χιόνα καὶ σ. ἐπάνω ‡Pion.*v.Polyc.* 21; cf.*A.Andr.et Mt.*27(p.105.8); Chrys.*exp.in Ps.*109:3(5.259B); *M.Glyc.*2,3(p.13*.3A); σφραγῖδες σταυροῦ indelibly painted by miraculous means on garments of Jews concerned in Julian's attempt to rebuild Temple, Socr.*h.e.*3.20.14(M.67.432A); sign of cross engraved on image of Kore borne in Egyptian procession at Epiphany season, Epiph.*haer.*51.22(p.285.18).

C. of seal given to Christians in baptism, considered as distinguishing mark of Christ's flock and also as protection against evil, demonic powers, etc.; **1.** of inward possession of H. Ghost received in baptism (cf. A.3.f supra), Clem.*exc.Thdot.*86(p.133.5; M. 9.697B); cf.Hipp.*antichr.*59(p.40.1; M.10.780A); as sign by which believers will be recognized at Last Day πῶς ἀντιποιηθῇ σου ὁ ἄγγελος; πῶς δὲ ἀφέληται τῶν ἐχθρῶν, ἐὰν μὴ ἐπιγνῷ τὴν σ.; Bas. *hom.*13.4(2.117B; M.31.432C); σ., ὡς συντήρησις καὶ τῆς δεσποτείας σημείωσις Gr.Naz.*or.*40.4(M.36.364A); Didym.*Trin.*2.15(M.39.717A); Christians' possession of H. Ghost, received in baptism, corresponds to OT seal of circumcision and is likened to σφραγίς of soldier, Chrys.*hom.3.7 in 2Cor.*(10.454A,B); Eus.Al.*serm.*5(M.86. 349A); seal received at baptism is rescued from Devil through repentance and restoration of sinner, Eulog.*fr.Novat.*3(M.104. 342Dff.); εἴ τις οὐκ ἐνεσημάνθη τῇ σ. τοῦ πνεύματος, σημειωθήτω φωτὶ τοῦ βαπτίσματος, καὶ τῷ ἀχράντῳ αἵματι τὰς νοερὰς ἐπιχρίσει φλιάς... οὐ γὰρ ἄλλως τὸν ὀλοθρευτὴν διαφεύξεται Const.Diac.*laud.*37(M.88. 521C); H. Ghost received through baptism is royal seal with which Christ brands his sheep, ‡Jo.D.*conf.*3(M.95.285B); hence **2.** baptism itself is a sealing, and σφραγίς = βάπτισμα; as seal to be preserved unbroken ἐὰν μὴ τηρήσωμεν τὸ βάπτισμα ἁγνὸν..., ποίᾳ πεποιθήσει εἰσελευσόμεθα εἰς τὸ βασίλειον τοῦ θεοῦ;...τῶν γὰρ μὴ τηρησάντων...τὴν σ. ὁ σκώληξ αὐτῶν οὐ τελευτήσει *2Clem.*6.9,7.6; ἄρα οὖν τοῦτο λέγει· τηρήσατε τὴν σάρκα ἁγνὴν καὶ τὴν σ. ἄσπιλον, ἵνα τὴν ζωὴν ἀπολάβωμεν *ib.*8.6; λαὸν...λαμπρὰν σ. ἔχοντα Aberc.*epitaph.*9; Clem.*str.*2.3(p.118.32; M.8.941C); εἶεν δ' ἂν αἱ τρεῖς ἡμέραι [ref. Resurrection] τῆς σ. μυστήριον, δι' ἧς ὁ τῷ ὄντι πιστεύεται θεός *ib.*5.11 (p.375.17; M.9.112A); id.*q.d.s.*42(p.188.18; M.9.648C); as seal which safeguards believer as God's possession πληρωθέντων γὰρ τῶν κενῶν, τότε ἡ σ. ἐπακολουθεῖ, ἵνα φυλάσσηται τῷ θεῷ τὸ ἅγιον id.*ecl.* 12(p.140.19; M.9.704C); but which seals up the evil spirits in the soul unless they are previously exorcized, id.*exc.Thdot.*83(p.132. 17; M.9.696D); τῶν ἀδελφῶν τῆς ἐν κυρίῳ σφραγῖδος μεταδόντων αὐτῷ Eus.*h.e.*6.5.6(M.20.533C); τῆς ἀθανατοποιοῦ σ. Const.ap.eund.*v.C.*4. 62(p.143.8; M.20.1216A); σ. ἁγία, ἀκατάλυτος Cyr.H.*procatech.*16; προσέλθετε εἰς τὴν μυστικὴν σ., ἵνα εὔγνωστοι ἦτε τῷ δεσπότῃ id. *catech.*1.2; τὴν σ. τῆς ζωῆς Ephr.2.6C; *Const.App.*2.14.7; associated with φωτισμός, Chrys.*hom.3.4 in Phil.*(11.217C); τὴν δεσποτικὴν ἐπιθεῖναι...σ. Thdt.*h.e.*4.18.11(3.979); administered by Thecla to many converts ἡ μάρτυς διὰ τῆς σ. ἐστρατολόγησε τῷ Χριστῷ Bas.Sel.*v. Thecl.*1(M.85.548A); cf.*ib.*(557C); προσῆλθον τῷ ἁγίῳ βαπτίσματι, καὶ λαβόντες τὴν ἐν Χριστῷ σ. ... †Gregent.*disp.*(M.85.780C); τὴν σ. ... τοῦ σωτηρίου βαπτίσματος †Jo.D.*B.J.*18(M.96.1021B); cf. τοὺς πιστεύσαντας καὶ τὴν σ. τοῦ βαπτίσματος δεξαμένους *V.Aberc.*8 where idea of baptism as proof or token of faith may be implicit; **3.** baptismal sealing as antitype of anointing of door-posts at Passover, cf.Mel.*pass.*5 p.3.4ff.; *ib.*36 p.11.4ff.; Gr.Naz.*or.*1.3(M.35. 397A); id.*carm.*1.1.9.91(M.37.464A); ‡Chrys.*pasch.*1(8.254E–255B); Const.Diac.*laud.*37(M.88.521C); **4.** sealing referred to particular part of baptismal rite; **a.** baptism in water ἡ σ. οὖν τὸ ὕδωρ ἐστίν Herm.*sim.*9.16.4; *A.Paul.et Thecl.*25(p.253.7–9); cf. δοκιμάσεις δὲ αὐτοὺς ἐκ τοῦ ὕδατος τοῦ Ἰορδάνου...τοῦτο τὸ σημεῖόν ἐστι τῆς μεγάλης σ. *Apoc.Bar.rel.*6.23; prob. implied: Const.ap.Eus.*v.C.*4.62 (p.143.8; M.20.1216A); seal being associated with λουτρόν, Cyr.H. *catech.*5.6; τὸ λουτρὸν ἐστι δευτέρου βίου σ. Gr.Naz.*carm.*1.2.34.237 (M.37.962A); Epiph.*haer.*30.4(p.339.10; M.41.412B); and with κολυμβήθρα, Didym.*Trin.*2.12(M.39.680A); seal is conferred in clinical baptism, Chrys.*hom.7.4 in Heb.*(12.135C); **b.** with post-baptismal chrismation and esp. with consignation by bishop with sign of cross (cf. B supra); cf.Hipp.*trad.ap.*22.1–3; as ἐπισφράγισμα τῆς σ. *A.Thom.*26(p.141.18); cf.Corn.ap.Eus.*h.e.*6.42.15(M.20.624A); Eus.*d.e.*9.14(p.434.28; M.22.701A); Serap.*euch.*25.2; ἐλαίῳ ἐλίπανέ σου τὴν κεφαλὴν ἐπὶ μετώπου διὰ τὴν σ. ἣν ἔχεις τοῦ θεοῦ, ἵνα γένῃ ἐκτύπωμα σφραγῖδος, ἁγίασμα θεοῦ Cyr.H.*catech.*22.7; cf. βάπτισμα διὰ τοῦ σταυροῦ· δεῖ γὰρ ἀναλαβεῖν τὴν σ. Chrys.*hom.14.1 in Phil.*(11. 298A); Dion.Ar.*e.h.*2.3.4(M.3.400D); chrismation, with formula σ. δωρεᾶς πνεύματος ἁγίου *Rit.Bapt.*(p.405); used as rite of reconciling certain heretics and dist. from baptism, CCP(381)‡*can.*7; CTrull. *can.*95; **c.** with emphasis on chrismation itself rather than on sign of cross, *Disp.Phot.*45(M.88.572C); Didym.*Trin.*2.1(M.39.452C); Thdt.*Cant.*1:2(2.30); **d.** ass. Trinitarian profession of faith, which is 'holy and royal seal', Epiph.*inc.*3(p.231.12; M.41.277C); θεότητος...ἐν μιᾷ σ. ὀνομάτων πατρὸς καὶ υἱοῦ καὶ ἁγίου πνεύματος τοῖς φωτιζομένοις κηρυττομένης id.*haer.*76.20(p.367.14; M.42.557A); cf. διὰ...πατρὸς καὶ υἱοῦ καὶ ἁγίου πνεύματος σφραγισθείς Clem.*exc. Thdot.*80(p.131.28; M.9.696B); cf. ἔχων τὸ κεφάλαιον τῆς πίστεως ἐν τῷ βαπτίσματι, καὶ ἐν ταῖς τρισὶν ἁγίαις σ., δι' ὧν εἰς σωτηρίαν ἀναγεγέννηται ‡Ath.*Sabell.*8(M.28.109C); **5.** seal equated with divine image imprinted on soul in baptism, cf.Clem.*exc.Thdot.*86(p.133.5; M.9.697B); Meth.*symp.*8.8(p.91.2; M.18.152A); Didym.*Trin.*2.15(M. 39.717A), v. B. supra; **6.** baptism as a seal which must not be broken by subsequent sin, *2Clem.*7.6, *ib.*8.6 citt. s. C.2 supra; οἱ πιστεύσαντες καὶ εἰληφότες τὴν σ. καὶ τεθλακότες αὐτὴν καὶ μὴ τηρήσαντες ὑγιῆ Herm.*sim.*8.6.3; μέγα, τὸ προκείμενον βάπτισμα·... σ. ἁγία, ἀκατάλυτος Cyr.H.*procatech.*16; σ. ἀνεπιχείρητος Bas.*hom.* 13.5(2.117D; M.31.433A); ‡Germ.CP *contempl.*(M.98.388B); likened to seal on a money-bag, Jo.Mosch.*prat.*198(M.87.3085D); **7.** penance as renewal of baptismal seal, Herm.*sim*.8.6.3; **8.** of circumcision as distinguishing seal of old covenant, *Barn*.9.6; as type of baptism *μετὰ τὴν πίστιν ὁμοίως ἐκείνῳ* [sc. Abraham] *τὴν πνευματικὴν λαμβάνομεν σ.· ἁγίῳ πνεύματι διὰ τοῦ λουτροῦ περιτεμνόμενοι... τὴν καρδίαν* Cyr.H.*catech*.5.6; Chrys.*hom.2.2 in Eph*.(11.11Aff.).

D. of Christian doctrine as seal imprinted on the faithful (cf. baptismal profession of faith, C.4.d. supra) *Θωμᾶς ὁ ἀπόστολος...σε διδάξει τὴν σ. τοῦ σώματος καὶ τοῦ αἵματός μου, ὅτι θεὸς ὢν ἐνηνθρώπησα δι' ὑμᾶς A.Thom*.B 52(p.40.34).

E. perh. of eucharist as Christian covenant-sign and assurance of salvation; in repudiation of idea that reception of sacramental pledges can dispense Christians from obligation of charity to the poor (ref. Mt.25:44) *οὐ σ. τοῦ σώματός σου ἔχομεν;* Eus.Al.*serm*.21.14 (M.86.440D), or perh. of baptism as seal of membership of body of Christ.

σφράγισμα, τό, *impression of a seal, seal*; hence **1.** *conclusion ἵνα ἐπὶ τῷ τέλει τοῦ σφραγίσματος μάθωμεν ἀναγνόντες τὰ παρὰ σοί* Epiph.*haer*.42.12(M.41.812B; v.l. for *συντάγματος* p.182.17); **2.** *inscription, marking out*; of figure of circle marked out on the ground, Gr.Mag.*dial*.(tr.Zach.)3.12(M.*PL*.77.242A); met., in comparison of Christian with piece of money stamped with royal image and name (ref. baptismal seal) *ἡ ψυχὴ...τὸ τῆς ἀληθείας λαβοῦσα σ.* Clem.*exc.Thdot*.86(p.133.7; M.9.697B); hence *seal* of baptism *ὥρα καὶ ἡμᾶς ἀπολαῦσαι τῆς ἀθανατοποιοῦ σφραγῖδος, ὥρα τοῦ σωτηρίου σ. μετασχεῖν* Eus.*v.C*.4.62(p.143.8; M.20.1216A).

σφραγιστής, ὁ, *sealer*; of one who ordains *ἱερέων οἱ σφραγισταί* [sc. the apostles] Ephr.3.462F.

[*]σφραδάζ-ω, variant of *σφαδάζω, chafe, be strangely moved* or *excited τὸν θυμὸν ~οντα καὶ κυκώμενον* [sc. the elder brother] Ast.Am.*prod*.(p.115.13).

[*]σφράττω, = *φράσσω, fence in; put up as a fence,* Jo.D.*hom*. 11.13(M.96.776B).

σφριγάω, 1. *be vigorous, in full health and strength,* whether of persons, animals, or vegetation; met. *σφριγήσασαν ἔχων εἰς τὸ ἀγαθὸν τὴν γνώμην* Cyr.*Joel*.35(3.229D); Thphyl.*exc.gent*.3(p.480.25; M.113.940C); **2.** met., *swell* with anger or desire (in form *σφρίγω*) *ἤδη τὰ θηρία ἐσφρῖχθαι καὶ μέλλειν ἐξορμᾶν* Alex.Thess.*ep.Dion*.ap. Ath.*apol.sec*.80(p.160.26; M.25.393C).

σφριγώδης, *swollen, swelling*; of passions *τὸ...σ. ἀνέχειν* Cyr. *glaph.Ex*.2(1.278C).

***σφυγμή, ἡ,** = *σφυγμός, unhealthy excitement,* Ephr.2.365F.

σφύζ-ω, *throb, beat violently*; of the passions Areth.*Apoc*.16:2 (M.106.704B); *rage τὴν ~ουσαν τῶν διωκτῶν μανίαν* Thdr.Stud.*epp*. 2.22(M.99.1185C); met., *be very eager, long σ. ... αὐτῷ προσλαλῆσαι* Geo.Pis.*hex*.216(M.92.1450A); id.*carm*.1.36(p.2).

σφῦρα, ἡ, *hammer,* signifying reproof *οἱ μὲν οὖν δυσίατοι...πρὸς τοῦ πυρὸς καὶ σ. καὶ ἄκμονος, τουτέστιν ἀπειλῆς, ἐλέγχου, ἐπιτιμήσεως ἐλαύνονται* Clem.*paed*.1.10(p.145.29; M.8.361B); or the Devil, Or.*fr. 30 in Jer*.27:23(p.214.9).

σφυρηλατέω, *hammer, beat*; as a form of torture, Sophr.H. *v.Anast*.(M.92.1721A).

σφυροκοπ-έω, *beat with a hammer,* Herm.*vis*.1.3.2; Chrys.*hom. 20.6 in 1Cor*.(10.177E); met. *~είσθω τὸ σκληρὸν τῆς ἀπιστίας* Cyr.H.*procatech*.15.

σφυροκοπία, ἡ, *hammering,* Jo.Mal.*chron*.1 p.4(M.97.68A).

σχάδιον, τό, = *ἰσχάδιον, dried fig,* Cyr.S.*v.Jo.Hes*.(p.220.10).

σχάς, ἡ, = *ἰσχάς, dried fig,* acc. *σχάδαν,* Cyr.S.*v.Jo.Hes*.(p.220.15).

σχάστης, ὁ, term of abuse *σχάστα...ἀλλότρια χρήματα ἔκλεψας* Pall.*h.Laus*.21(p.65.8; *σχάτα* M.34.1073D).

***σχάτα,** voc. of *σχάτης,* for *σχάστης.*

σχεδάριον, τό, 1. *memorandum συναγαγεῖν τὰ σ. τὰ πρὸς Εὐνόμιον ...ὑπηγορευμένα* Gr.Nyss.*ep*.29(M.45.237A; *σχιδάρια* p.84.5); *διὰ... σημείων καὶ σ. τὰ κατὰ τῶν αἱρέσεων...γράψαι καὶ διορθώσασθαι* Epiph.*exp.fid*.25(p.526.5,8; M.42.832C); ‡Ath.*Maced.dial*.1(M.28. 1292A); **2.** any short *document τὸ...σ. τῆς δεήσεως τὸ παρ' ὑμῶν ἀποσταλέν* Cyr.*ep*.10(p.112.6,12; 5².38Df.); *ὁ...σηκρητάριος ἀπὸ σ. πραχθέντος ἐν ὑπατείᾳ τοῦ...Μαρκιανοῦ...ἀνέγνω* CChalc.*act*.4(*ACO* 2.1.2 p.92.12; H.2.384C); *ib*.(p.93.3; 385A); *εὗρον...αὐτοῦ* [sc. *τὸ μαρτύριον*] *ἐν σ. ἐν τῇ βιβλιοθήκῃ* ‡Hesych.H.*m.Long*.16(M.93.1560A).

***σχέδη, ἡ,** *draft*; hence *document ἀνέγνω σεκρετάριος ἀπὸ σ. ἐπὶ λέξεως ταῦτα* Evagr.*h.e*.2.18(p.86.17, v.l. *σχέδους* M.86.2577B).

σχεδία, v. **σχεδιαστής.*

σχεδιάζ-ω, A. *do* something *offhand* or *on the spur of the moment*; *improvise*; **1.** perf. pass., *be ready made, ready to hand ἐσχεδιασμένον παρέχων τὸν πλοῦτον* Chrys.*laud.Max*.1(3.211B); **2.** *act with insufficient care*; hence *make, constitute hastily* or *rashly,* ref. consecration of a bishop *παρὰ κανόνας ἑαυτοῖς ἀνεπλάσαντο ψευδώνυμον Ἀντιοχείας ἐπίσκοπον οἱ...αἱρετικοί, καθάπερ οὖν καὶ Πέτρον τῆς Ἀλεξανδρέων ἐσχεδίασαν* Martin.*ep*.11(M.*PL*.87.178D); *οἱ...~οντες τοὺς ἱεροὺς βαθμοὺς Schol*. in CSard.*can*.10(*Mon*.2 p.660); **3.** *bring about unwittingly, be the occasion of τοῦ σιτευτοῦ ἀπήλαυσε μόσχου, καὶ ἑορτὴν μεγίστην ἐσχεδίασε τῷ πατρί* Thdt.*haer*.5.28(4. 478); **4.** *speak* or *write at random,* Or.*Jo*.13.15(p.239.19; M.14.421B); *ἄνευ θείας ἐπινοίας ἐσχεδίασται* Eus.*d.e*.8.2(p.377.21; M.22.612B).

B. without the idea of improvisation or carelessness; **1.** *constitute, form δύο...φύσεις...συναφθεῖσαι μίαν υἱότητα...οὐ ~ουσιν;* †Ath. *fr*.(M.26.1236D); Anast.S.*qu.et resp*.96(M.89.737D); Thphn.*chron*. p.11(M.108.81A); *create κἀκ μὴ ὄντων εἰς τὸ εἶναι παρήγαγε, καὶ οὐκ ὄντα πρὶν ἐσχεδίασε* Sophr.H.*ep.syn*.(M.87.3180D); ref. Christ's human will *εἰ...εἶχε τότε, καὶ ἀπ' ἀρχῆς εἶχεν ἐξ οὗ γέγονεν ἄνθρωπος, ἀλλ' οὐχ ὕστερον ἐσχεδίασεν* Max.*opusc*.(M.91.196C); **2.** *bring forward, assert,* Serap.*Man*.46(p.64; M.18.1233C); *ὅσα σ. ἡμῖν νῦν ἡ μνήμη ὡς γνωριμώτερα* Gr.Naz.*or*.21.5(M.35.1088A); *ξένον εἶναι τοῦ νόμου τὸν Χριστὸν σχεδιάσαντες* Isid.Pel.*epp*.1.371(M.78.393A); **3.** *pass* judgement or sentence *τὴν κρίσιν σ. cat.Apoc*.19:11(p.458.17).

σχεδίασμα, τό, *whim, caprice σ. καρδίας* Hipp.*haer*.10.33(p.291.9; M.16.3451A).

***σχεδιαστής, ὁ,** *inventor, improviser ἐρωτικῆς σ. ἀδημονίας, ὁ κῶμος* Clem.*paed*.2.4(p.181.17, conj. edd. for *σχεδίας τῆς* M.8.440B).

σχέδος, τό, 1. ? *papyrus sheet ἀντὶ σχέδους τὴν τετράδα κατέχοντες οὕτως ἐξεθέμεθα* Anast.S.*hod*.proem.(M.89.36A); v. *σχέδη*; **2.** *book τῷ δὲ περὶ οὐσίας καὶ φύσεως, ὑποστάσεώς τε δὴ καὶ προσώπου... ἐνέτυχον σχέδει Θεοδώρου τοῦ τῆς Φαράν* Max.*opusc*.(M.91.136C).

σχέσις, ἡ, 1. *possession οὐχ ἡ σ. ... ἀλλ' ἡ ἀναίρεσις...φθορά* Dion. Ar.*d.n*.4.23(M.3.725B); **2.** *participation ὁ πάσης ἀρχῆς ὑπεράρχιος... καθ' ὅσον ἀμίμητος καὶ ἄσχετος, ὑπερέχει τῶν μιμήσεων καὶ σχέσεων, καὶ τῶν μιμουμένων καὶ μετεχόντων* id.*ep*.2(M.3.1069A); *θεοῦ...τὸ πάσης ἐλεύθερον σ.* Zach.Mit.*opif*.(M.85.1100C); **3.** *happening τὴν ἐν ἑνὶ καιρῷ σ. πάντων* Epiph.*haer*.31.1(p.383.17, v.l. *σύσχ-* M.41.473C); **4.** *kind, category τὰς ἀμφοτέρας σ. τῶν αἱρέσεων ἐλέγξας ib*.28.6 (p.319.7; 385B); *ib*.42.12(p.180.19; 809B); **5.** name of a rhetorical figure, *schesis onomaton multitudo nominum conjunctorum quodam ambitu copulata, ut: nubila, nix, grando, procellae, fulmina, venti,* Isid.H.*etym*.1.36.13; **6.** *condition*; **a.** *posture ἡ σ. καὶ εἰς τὸ εὔχεσθαι παρασκευή* Or.*or*.9.2(p.318.23; M.11.444C); **b.** *nature, quality σχέσει λογισμῶν, δωρεῶν ὑποσχέσει* Geo.Pis.*bell.Avar*.99(M.92.1271A); **c.** *arrangement τὸ πολύπειρον τῆς σ. ἠφάνισαν* Epiph.*haer*.8.8(p.195.5; M.41.220B); **d.** intellectual *position,* Ath.*gent*.3(M.25.9A); *τῆς πρὸς τοὺς Ἀρειομανίτας σχέσεως ἀποστάντες* id.*tom*.1(M.26.796B); **7.** *relationship*; **a.** in gen., Clem.*str*.2.16(p.152.7; M.8.1012C) cit. s. *ὁμοούσιος*; *ὁ θεὸς λέγεται εἶναι ἐν τῷ οὐρανῷ...τῇ σ. καὶ τῇ οἰκειώσει τῇ πρὸς τοὺς ἀγγέλους* Chrys.*hom.16.3 in Heb*.(12.161A); *πῶς ἐξῆλθεν; οὐ τόπῳ, ἀλλὰ σχέσει καὶ οἰκονομίᾳ τῇ πρὸς ἡμᾶς, ἐγγύτερος ἡμῖν γενόμενος διὰ τῆς κατὰ σάρκα περιβολῆς* id.*hom.44.3 in Mt*.(7.470C); *οὐ σχέσεσι τοπικαῖς...παραστήματι δὲ διανοίας* Cyr.*Zach*.64(3.744B); *οὔτε γὰρ μέρος, ἢ ὅλον ἢ σ. ἐστιν ἡ μονάς* Max.*ambig*.(M.91.1185B); *ἐπειδὴ ἡ ἕνωσις σ. ἐστί, καὶ οὐ πρᾶγμα, σ. ἄρα, καὶ οὐ πρᾶγμα ἡ τοῦ Χριστοῦ ἐνέργεια* id.*Pyrr*.(M.91.340D–341A); *κατὰ σχέσιν* opp. *καθ' ὑπόστασιν,* Jo.D.*hom*.1.4(M.96.552D); **b.** astrol. *τὸ αὐτὸ σχῆμα τῆς σ. τῶν ἀστέρων* Or.*Cels*.5.21(p.22.25,27; M.11.1213A); **c.** theol.; **i.** within Trin. *τῆς πρὸς ἄλληλα σ.* Gr.Naz.*or*.23.8(M.35.1160C); of Father and Son *ἐξ αὐτῆς τῆς προσηγορίας* [i.e. of Marcellus] *ὁ υἱὸς τὴν πρὸς τὸν πατέρα φυσικὴν σ. παρίστησιν* Eus.*e.th*.1.10(p.69.1; M.24. 841C); *τὸ θεὸς τὴν φύσιν δηλοῖ· τὸ δὲ πατὴρ τὴν σ. τὴν πρὸς τὸν υἱόν* ‡Ath.*dial.Trin*.1.25(M.28.1153D); *οὔτε οὐσίας ὄνομα ὁ πατήρ...οὔτε ἐνεργείας, σχέσεως δέ* Gr.Naz.*or*.29.16(p.98.7; M.36.96A) al.; *ἡ τοῦ πατρὸς κλῆσις οὐκ οὐσίας ἐστὶ παραστατική, ἀλλὰ τὴν πρὸς τὸν υἱὸν σ. ἀποσημαίνει* Gr.Nyss.*Eun*.2(2 p.302.25; M.45.473B); **ii.** Christol., opp. *οὐσία,* Thdr.Mops.*Zach*.1:7–10(M.66.504C); *ἀνοήτως ἔτι ζωὴν εἶναι δώσετε, καὶ οὐχὶ μᾶλλον ζωῆς τῆς παρ' ἑτέρου μέτοχον, σχέσει δὲ μᾶλλον καὶ οὐκ οὐσιωδῶς εἰς τὸ τοῦ χορηγοῦντος ἀνακεκλημένον ἀξίωμα* Cyr.*Jo*.4.3(4.369C); *οἱ τὴν ἕνωσιν μὴ κατ' οὐσίαν ἀλλὰ κατ' ἐνέργειαν, ἢ εὐδοκίαν ἢ ἄλλην τινὰ τοιαύτην σ. δογματίσαντες, κατ' οὐδὲν μὲν τῇ ἀληθείᾳ ἐγγίζουσι* Leont.B.*Nest.et Eut*.1(M.86.1300B); opp. *φύσις*: *ἀνθρωποτόκος μὲν γὰρ τῇ φύσει...θεοτόκος δέ, ἐπείπερ θεὸς ἦν ἐν τῷ τεχθέντι ἀνθρώπῳ, οὐκ ἐν αὐτῷ περιγραφόμενος κατὰ τὴν φύσιν, ἐν αὐτῷ δὲ ὢν κατὰ τὴν σ. τῆς γνώμης* Thdr.Mops.*fr.inc*.15(p.310.20; M.66.992C); *δύο δὴ πάλιν ἀναμφιλόγως υἱοί, εἴπερ ἐστὶν ἀληθές, ὡς ἕτερόν τι καὶ ἔλαττον κατὰ φύσιν ἐστὶ τοῦ τὴν μέθεξιν ἐμποιοῦντος αὐτῷ, τὸ σχέσει τῇ πρὸς αὐτὸν τιμώμενον* Cyr.*Nest*.2.2(p.36.5; 6¹.35E); opp. *ἕνωσις, moral relationship* (v. 8 infra); acc. Nest. *ἄνθρωπον συνάπτει θεῷ κατά γε τὴν ἔξωθεν σ. ib*.2.11(p.49.18; 56D); *ὁ...Νεστόριος ἔλεγε* δύο φύσεις, οὐκ ἔλεγε δὲ αὐτὰς δέξασθαι ἕνωσιν. ἀλλὰ σχέσιν πολλὴν ἔχειν τὸν ἄνθρωπον ἐκεῖνον πρὸς τὸν υἱόν, ὥστε καὶ δι' αὐτοῦ ἐνεργεῖν ὅσα βούλεται †Leont.B.*sect.*1.4(M.86.1200A); τοσαύτη ἦν ἡ φιλία καὶ ἡ σ. τοῦ θεοῦ λόγου πρὸς τὸν ἄνθρωπον ὅτι οἱ δύο εἷς υἱὸς ἐλέγοντο *ib.* (1200B); εἰ δὲ καὶ ἄνθρωπον, καὶ θεὸν ἀπεκάλει τὸν Χριστόν· ἀλλ' οὐκέτι ὡς ἡμεῖς, ἀλλὰ τῇ σχέσει καὶ τῇ οἰκειώσει. ὥσπερ λέγομεν περὶ δύο τινῶν φίλων πάνυ ἀλλήλους ἀγαπώντων· ὅτι οἱ δύο οὗτοι μίαν ψυχὴν ἔχουσι *ib.*4.4(1221C); εἴ τις λέγει...κατ'...ἀναφορὰν ἢ σ. ... τὴν ἕνωσιν τοῦ θεοῦ λόγου πρὸς ἄνθρωπον γεγενῆσθαι...ἀνάθεμα ἔστω Justn.*conf.* (p.90.30; M.86.1016A) = CCP(553)*anath.*4; ἡ κατὰ σ. ἕνωσις, ἐπὶ τῶν γνωμῶν εἰς ἓν θέλημα Max.*opusc.*(M.91.213B); ἡ δὲ τοῦ κυρίου ψυχὴ παντελῶς πρὸς τὸ κακὸν ἀκίνητος ἦν, αὐτὸν ἔχουσα τὸν θεὸν λόγον ἐν ἑαυτῇ· οὐ κατὰ σ., ἀλλὰ καθ' ἕνωσιν ‡Cyr.*Trin.*16(6^{3}.22E; M.77.1153D); Jo.D.*hom.*1.4(M.96.552D) = id.*fr.Mt.*17:2(M.96.1408D); opp. σωματικῶς, cf. *inhabitavit namque in eo omnis plenitudo divinitatis corporaliter; id est non per participatum vel schesim simpliciter, quasi lumine inlucente,* Cyr.*schol.inc.*27(Pusey 6 p.550.9; M.75.1398B); **iii.** of H. Ghost to Son τί οὖν ἐστί...ὃ λείπει τῷ πνεύματι πρὸς τὸ εἶναι υἱόν;...τὸ δὲ τῆς ἐκφάνσεως, ἵν' οὕτως εἴπω, ἢ τῆς πρὸς ἄλληλα σ. διάφορον, διάφορον αὐτῶν καὶ τὴν κλῆσιν πεποίηκεν Gr.Naz.*or.*31.9(p.155.15; M.36.141C); **d.** by grace, between man and God 'ἀναλαμβάνων πραεῖς ὁ κύριος', κατὰ σχέσιν δηλονότι...ἀλλ' οὐχὶ τοῦτό ἐστι τὸ ἐνανθρωπῆσαι θεόν Cyr.*apol.Thdt.*10(p.138.10; 6^{1}.232D); οἰκεῖοι πάντες ἐσμὲν Χριστῷ κατὰ σ. μυστικήν id.*Jo.*7(4.665D); of S. Paul δοῦλον ἑαυτοῦ καλεῖ ὁ θεὸς οὐχὶ ὡς σχέσει ὄντα δοῦλον καὶ διαθέσει, ἀλλ' ὡς φύσει δοῦλον· τοῦ γὰρ ποιητοῦ δοῦλον τὸ ποίημα Thdt.*Jer.* 43:13(2.579); ὁ Ναβουχοδονόσωρ δοῦλος ὁ δυσσεβής. ἀλλ' ἐκεῖνος μὲν φύσει· Ἀβραὰμ δέ, καὶ Δαβίδ...καὶ οἱ κατὰ τούτους καὶ σχέσει id. *1Tim.*6:11(3.670); σχέσει δὲ καὶ χάριτι καὶ οἱ δίκαιοι λέγονται θεοί Anast.S.*hod.*2(M.89.53C); **8.** *relationship, attachment* bet. persons and things, esp. of soul to earthly or heavenly things πρὸς ἕτερον κόσμον διὰ τῆς σ. μεταβαίνοντες Bas.*reg.fus.*5.2(2.342B; M.31.921A); τὸν προσιόντα τὴν οἷον προτέραν ζωὴν ἀπεκδύσασα καὶ μεχρὶ τῶν κατ' ἐκείνην ἐσχάτων σ. ἀπολύσασα Dion.Ar.*e.h.*2.5(M.3.401A); κόπτε τῶν πολλῶν τὰς σ., μή σου ὁ πόλεμος πρὸς τὸν νοῦν περιστατικὸς γένηται *Apophth.Patr.*(M.65.161C); νῷ πάσης ἐλευθέρῳ τῆς πρὸς ὁτιοῦν πάρεξ θεοῦ σ. Max.*ambig.*(M.91.1117B); ἀδύνατον τὸν νοῦν σχολάσαι τοῖς νοητοῖς, εἰ μὴ τὴν σ. τὴν πρὸς τὴν αἴσθησιν καὶ τὰ αἰσθητὰ ἀποκόψῃ Thal.*cent.*2.41(M.91.1441B); πολλοὶ...ἔγραψαν εἰκόνας τῶν ἀνθρώπων εἴτε [οἱ] γονεῖς τῶν τέκνων...διὰ τὸν πόθον καὶ τὴν σ., ἣν εἶχον πρὸς ἀλλήλους ‡Jo.D.*Const.*2(M.95.313A); between an icon and its object, v. εἰκών; τῆς πρὸς ἄλληλα κοινωνίας τε καὶ σ. ἀμέτοχα Thdr.Stud. *antirr.*3.4.1(M.99.428C); ἡ σ. κατὰ τὸ εἶναι ἐν τῷ πρωτοτύπῳ τὸ παράγωγον εἴρηται *ib.*3.3.10(424D); οὐδὲ αὐτῆς τῆς ἀναστηλωθείσης σαρκὸς ἡ φύσις πάρεστιν, ἀλλ' ἢ μόνον ἡ σ. *ib.*1.12(344B); πῶς οὖν ἔσται μία προσκύνησις τῆς εἰκόνος πρὸς Χριστόν; εἴπερ ἡ μὲν σχέσει, ὁ δὲ φύσει προσκυνεῖσθαι ὡμολόγηται. οὐκοῦν δύο προσκυνήσεις ἐν τῷ ἑνὶ Χριστῷ διὰ τῆς εἰκονικῆς προσκυνήσεως· ὅπερ ἀσεβὲς *ib.*3.3.9(424C); bet. persons τίς ἡ τῆς φύσεως ὁλκὴ καὶ πρὸς ἄλληλα σ. τοῖς γεννῶσι καὶ τοῖς γεννωμένοις; Gr.Naz.*or.*28.22(p.55.7; M.36.56B); ὑπὸ τῆς ἐρωμένης δεδέσθαι τὸν ἐραστήν, οὐ σωματικῶς, οὐδὲ τοπικῶς, ἀλλὰ κατὰ σ. Nemes.*nat.hom.*3(M.40.600B); εἰώθαμεν δὲ καὶ ἡμεῖς τοῖς προσκρούουσι λέγειν τὸ 'οὐκ οἶδά σε' οὐχ ὡς ἀγνοοῦντες πάντως, ἀλλ' ὡς τῆς πρὸς ἡμᾶς ἀγάπης καὶ σ. ἀλλοτριοῦν ἐθέλοντες Cyr.*Ps.*36:18(M.69.93A); ἡ τῶν γονέων σ. καὶ φιλία πρὸς αὐτόν †Jo.D.*B.J.*25(M.96.1093D); plur. τὰς δὲ σ. ἀποσεισώμεθα Thdr.Stud.*epp.*2.66(M.99.1292B).

σχετικός, 1. *containing* δεσμὸς δὲ τῆς σαρκὸς ψυχή, σ. δὲ τῆς ψυχῆς ἡ σάρξ Tat.*orat.*15(p.16.21; M.6.837B); **2.** ? *of habits* χελιδών *Phys.* B 18(p.228.7); **3.** *of relationship*; **a.** in gen. ἄσχετον μὲν τὸ αὐτὸ εἶναι, σ. δὲ τὸ ἄλλου εἶναι ‡Just.*qu.et resp.*113(M.6.1361C); τὸ γὰρ 'θεὸς' ὄνομα φύσεως ἐστὶ θεωρουμένης...τὸ δὲ 'πατὴρ' σχετικὸν καὶ τὸ 'υἱὸς' ὁμοίως ‡Ath.*Maced.dial.*1.1(M.28.1292B); πατέρα ἡμῶν τὸν πατέρα τὸν ἐν τοῖς οὐρανοῖς καλεῖν προσετάχθημεν, αὕτη πάλιν ἡ σ. σημασία Gr.Nyss.*Eun.*1(1 p.183.6; M.45.428B); 'Τιμοθέῳ γνησίῳ τέκνῳ'...τῷ σ. ὀνόματι Thdt.*1Tim.*1:2(3.639); Proc.G.*Is.*57:15(M.87.2581C); Leont.H.*Nest.*5.24(M.86.1745C); **b.** Christol., *relative, incidental,* i.e. *non-essential*; of union of natures acc. Nestorius and other Antiochenes εἰ...σ. ἐν ἀνθρώπῳ τὴν ἐνοίκησιν ἐποιήσατο Cyr. *Nest.*1.2(p.20.20; 6^{1}.13A); σ. λέγει [sc. Theodoret] τὴν ἕνωσιν τοῦ θεοῦ λόγου πρός τόν τινα ἄνθρωπον Justn.*conf.*(p.94.16; M.86.1017D); Max.*Pyrr.*(M.91.337A); id.*ep.*12(M.91.481B); Leont.B.*Nest.et Eut.*3 (M.86.1380D); cf. examples of σ. ἕνωσις: σ. ἕνωσίς ἐστιν, ἡ τὰς διαφόρους γνώμας εἰς ἓν συνάγουσα θέλημα· σ. δὲ διαφορά ἐστιν, ἡ τὸ ἓν θέλημα γνώμης ἑτερότητι διατέμνουσα κίνησις Max.*opusc.*(M.91.152C); id.*ep.*12(M.91.484A); πενταχῶς δὲ λέγεται ἡ ἕνωσις· συγχυτική ...διαιρετική...σ. ὡς τὰ ἔθνη ἐν τῇ πίστει· θετική...καθ' ὑπόστασιν Anast.S.*hod.*2(M.89.69C) = ‡Ath.*def.*5(M.28.544C,D); ἕνωσις σ., ὡς φίλου πρὸς φίλον Jo.D.*dialect.*65(M.94.661B–664B); esp. of συνάφεια σ. (v. συνάφεια): οὐκ ἄνθρωπός τις ἀνὰ μέρος τε καὶ ἰδικῶς νοούμενος, καὶ σ. ἔχων συνάφειαν πρὸς θεόν Cyr.*apol.orient.*8(p.49.18; 6^{1}.179B); ἐθελοντὴς ὁ μονογενὴς γέγονεν ἄνθρωπος καὶ οὐχ ὡς σὺ [sc. Nestorius] φής, ἀνέλαβεν ἄνθρωπον, σ. αὐτῷ δωρούμενος τὴν συνάφειαν id.*apol.Thdt.*3(p.119.23; 6^{1}.213C); acc. Theodore and Nestorius ψιλὸν ἄνθρωπον...κατὰ σ. συνάφειαν Justn.*conf.*(p.98.1; 1021B); κατὰ μόνην τὴν σ. συνάφειαν τὴν ἕνωσιν γεγενῆσθαι Max.*ep.*12(M.91.484A); orthodox objections to ἕνωσις σ.: κατοικῆσαι δέ φησιν ὁ θεσπέσιος Παῦλος ἐν τῷ Χριστῷ πᾶν τὸ πλήρωμα τῆς θεότητος σωματικῶς, ἵνα μὴ ἁπλῆν ἢ γοῦν σ. τὴν κατοίκησιν ὑποτοπήσειέ τις, ἀλλ' ὥσπερ ἔφην ἀρτίως, ἀληθινήν τε καὶ καθ' ὑπόστασιν Cyr.*Nest.*1.8(p.30.37; 28A); cf. Leont.B.*arg.Sev.*(M.86.1940D) cit. s. ἀντιδίδωμι; εἰ...τις...λέγων ὅτι ...χρὴ καὶ τὴν ἀνθρωπίνην φύσιν τοῦ Χριστοῦ ἰδίαν ὑπόστασιν, ἤτοι πρόσωπον ἴδιον ἔχειν, πρόδηλός ἐστιν ὁ τοιοῦτος ὅτι προϋποστάντι ἀνθρώπῳ ἑνωθῆναι λέγει τὸν λόγον, καὶ σ. γεγενῆσθαι τὴν ἕνωσιν Justn.*conf.*(p.88.6; 1011B); Thdr.Raith.*inc.*(p.191.18; M.91.1492B); Jo.D.*Jacob.*81(M.94.1480A); **c.** of union with God by grace, cf. *igitur in Christo unitatem summam veramque credimus factam: sin autem in nobis inhabitare dicatur, scheticam ipse faciet inhabitationem,* Cyr.*schol.inc.*27(Pusey 6 p.550.7; M.75.1398A); κατὰ μέθεξιν σ., ὡς καὶ ἡμεῖς κολλώμενοι τῷ κυρίῳ κατὰ τὸ γεγραμμένον ἓν πνεῦμά ἐσμεν πρὸς αὐτόν id.*ep.*17.5(p.36.19; 5^{2}.71B); ὅταν ἀκούσωμεν ἕνωσιν πατρὸς καὶ υἱοῦ, τὴν φυσικὴν νοοῦμεν· ὅταν δὲ ἕνωσιν θεοῦ καὶ ἀνθρώπων, σ. νοοῦμεν τὴν ἐκ πίστεως γινομένην τοῖς ἁγίοις Ammon. *Jo.*14:23(M.85.1492C); Max.*ambig.*(M.91.1192B); **d.** of union of an icon with its object ἐπεὶ καὶ ἐπὶ τύπου σταυροῦ τῶν τε ἄλλων θείων ἀναθημάτων, ἀλλ' οὐ φυσικῇ ἑνώσει...σ. δὲ μεταλήψει, ὅτι χάριτι καὶ τιμῇ τὰ μετέχοντα Thdr.Stud.*antirr.*1.12(M.99.344C); **e.** of *relative* veneration due to icons ἐπ' αὐτοῦ δὴ Χριστοῦ λατρευτικὴ ἡ προσκύνησις...ἐπὶ δὲ τῆς εἰκόνος, ἡ αὐτὴ μὲν...σ. δὲ ὅμως, ἤγουν ὁμωνυμική· προσκυνῶν γὰρ αὐτήν...προσεκύνησα Χριστόν, οὐ διαιρούμενον καθ' ὑπόστασιν, ἀλλὰ διαφορούμενον κατὰ τὸν τῆς οὐσίας λόγον ὅπερ ἐστὶ σ., ἀλλ' οὐ λατρευτική id.*ep.*2.85(M.99.1329A); εἴ τις τὴν κατὰ τὴν εἰκόνα σ. προσκύνησιν τοῦ Χριστοῦ, εἰδώλων προσκύνησιν...ἀποφαίνοι, καὶ οὐκ αὐτοῦ Χριστοῦ...αἱρετικός ἐστιν id.*antirr.*1.20(M.99.349C); ταύτας [sc. εἰκόνας] σ. πόθῳ προσκυνοῦμεν Taras.ap.CNic.(781)*act.*2 (H.4.104C); τὴν σ. τῶν σεπτῶν εἰκόνων...προσκύνησιν...τὸν περὶ τῆς σ. προσκυνήσεως λόγον Thphn.*chron.*p.340(M.108.820B,821A), v. προσκύνησις.

σχετικῶς, 1. *by relationship* σ. τῆς προσηγορίας ταύτης [sc. υἱός] καὶ τὸν πατέρα συνεμφαινούσης Gr.Nyss.*diff.ess.*7(M.32.340A); **2.** *by an external relationship, in an incidental way*; **a.** Christol., ref. relationship between the natures, opp. φυσικῶς, οὐσιωδῶς etc.; **i.** acc. Nest. συναφθέντα θεῷ σ., κατὰ μόνον τὴν ἰσοτιμίαν, ἤγουν, αὐθεντίαν Cyr.*ep.*40(p.27.8; 5^{2}.116E); τὴν ἕνωσιν τῆς θεότητος μετὰ τὸν τόκον τῆς ἀνθρωπότητος...γενέσθαι πρὸς αὐτὴν σ. Leont.H. *monoph.*(M.86.1785A); *ib.*(1809D); σ. ... ἓν πρόσωπον τοῦ θεοῦ λόγου καὶ τῆς σαρκός †Leont.B.*sect.*1.4(M.86.1152B); **ii.** orthodox denial 'ἐν αὐτῷ' φησι 'κατοικῆσαι πᾶν τὸ πλήρωμα τῆς θεότητος', οὐ μεθεκτῶς μᾶλλον ἢ σ. ἢ γοῦν ὡς ἐν δόσει χάριτος, ἀλλὰ σωματικῶς, ὅ ἐστιν οὐσιωδῶς Cyr.*Pulch.*19(p.37.18; 5^{2}.144D); οὔτε μὴν κοινὸν ἄνθρωπον ἰσότητι μόνῃ τῶν ἀξιωμάτων τετιμημένον σ. συνῆφθαι τῷ λόγῳ διοριζόμεθα id.*apol.Thdt.*2(p.115.19; 6^{1}.209C); θεός ἐστιν ὁ υἱὸς προαιώνιος, οὐ σ. ... ἀλλὰ φυσικῶς Hier.H.*Trin.*(M.40.853A); ὁ τρόπος ...τῆς ἑνώσεως οὐσιωδῶς, ἀλλ' οὐ σ. γεγονώς Leont.B.*Nest.et Eut.* 3(M.86.1380C); **b.** of union of believers with God ἐν ἡμῖν ἐστι θεός, καὶ ἡμεῖς αὐτῷ συναπτόμεθα σ., καὶ κοινωνοὶ τῆς θείας αὐτοῦ γεγόναμεν φύσεως Cyr.*Nest.*2.13(p.52.5; 6^{1}.59D); ὁ ἀληθὴς μεσίτης Χριστὸς ᾧ κεκολλήμεθα σ. id.*glaph.Ex.*(1.316C); ὁ πατὴρ ἐν τῷ υἱῷ ἐστι φυσικῶς, ἐν ἡμῖν δὲ σ. Ammon.*Jo.*14:20(M.85.1492C); **c.** *relatively,* ref. relationship bet. icon and its object, Thdr.Stud.*antirr.*1.8(M.99.337B); ref. relative veneration due to an icon προσκυνῶν τὴν εἰκόνα Χριστοῦ...προσκυνῶ...αὐτὸν Χριστὸν σ. id.*ep.*2.85(M.99.1329B); †Gr.II Papa *ep.Leon.*1(H.4.5C) cit. s. προσκύνησις; Taras.*praesent.BMV* (M.98.1496C); προσκυνητής εἰμι σ. ἀλλ' οὐ λατρευτικῶς *Euchol.*(p.255).

*σχέτλη, ἡ, *woe* τὸ 'οὐαί' ἐπίρρημά ἐστι σχετλιαστικόν· σ. δὲ τὸ ὀδύνην ἐπιφέρον καλεῖται Areth.*Apoc.*9:12(M.106.629A).

*σχετλιαστικῶς, *with bitter complaint,* †Bas.*Is.*83(1.436D; M.30.253C); Max.*opusc.*(M.91.52A); Anast.S.*qu.et resp.*17(M.89.485D).

σχῆμα, τό, 1. *shape, form* defined σ. ... τὸ ἐκ τριῶν γραμμῶν τοὐλάχιστον συνιστάμενον Thdr.Stud.*antirr.*3.1.30(M.99.404B); dist. from μορφή: ἐδίδασκε δὲ καὶ ὅσον πρὸς τὰ παρόντα τῆς ἀρετῆς τὸ διάφορον. ταῦτα γὰρ ἐκάλεσε σ., τὴν ἀρετὴν δὲ μορφήν· ἡ μορφὴ δὲ ἀληθῶν πραγμάτων σημαντική, τὸ δὲ σ. εὐδιάλυτον χρῆμα Thdt.

*Rom.*12:2(3.130); of man 'κατ' εἰκόνα θεοῦ' γεγονέναι ὁ ἄνθρωπος εἴρηται, οὐ κατὰ τῆς κατασκευῆς τὸ σ. Clem.*str.*6.16(p.500.33; M.9.361A); met., of the world τοῦ πρόσθεν σ. ἀπολλυμένου Meth.*res.*1.48 (p.300.11; M.41.1120D); *ib.*(p.300.15; M.41.1121A); **2.** *dimension* τὰ τριττὰ τῶν σωμάτων σ. ... πλάτος...μῆκος...βάθος Dion.Ar.*d.n.*9.5(M.3.913A); **3.** *frame, form,* ref. Christ's humanity (cf. Phil.2:7) τὸ αὐτὸ σ. ⟨τοῦ σώματος καὶ⟩ τῶν μελῶν καὶ εἰκόνα καὶ σάρκα τὴν αὐτὴν τῇ ἡμετέρᾳ φορέσας ἐφάνη Meth.*res.*2.18(p.369.17); Gr.Nyss.*Apoll.*57 (M.45.1264D) cit. s. ἀνθρώπινος; καλῶς ὅπερ ἀνείληφε σ. λόγῳ τε καὶ ἔργῳ φυλάττων Cyr.*thes.*9(5^1.71B); ὁ ἀσχημάτιστος ἐν σ. ἀνθρώπου ὡράθη Thdr.Stud.*antirr.*3.1.13(M.99.396B); δούλου μορφὴν μορφωσάμενος καὶ φύσει καὶ σ. γενόμενος ἄνθρωπος Jo.D.*hom.*1.4(M.96.552B); in opinion of Paul. Sam. ὁ φαινόμενος οὐκ ἦν σοφία· οὐ γὰρ ἠδύνατο ἐν σ. εὑρίσκεσθαι, οὐδὲ ἐν θέᾳ ἀνδρός Paul.Sam.*fr.*(p.337.14)ap.Leont.B. *Nest.et Eut.*3(M.86.1392C); as mere outward appearance; in opinion of Valentinus, Bas.*ep.*261.2(3.402D; M.32.969C) cit. s. ἄνθρωπος; ref. Marcion's Christology τὸ...σχήματι εἶναι ἄνθρωπον, οὐκ ἔστι φύσει ἄνθρωπον εἶναι Chrys.*hom.8.2 in Phil.*(11.246C); τῶν τολμώντων λέγειν ὅτι σχήματι ἐνεδύσατο σῶμα ὁ κύριος, καὶ σχήματι ἀπέθανεν ‡Chrys.*ascens.Ac.*5(3.763B); acc. Apoll. ἀντὶ τοῦ ἔσωθεν ἐν ἡμῖν ἀνθρώπου νοῦς ἐπουράνιος ἐν Χριστῷ· ὡς γὰρ ὀργανικῷ χρῆται σ. τῷ περιέχοντι, οὐ γὰρ οἷόν τε ἦν τέλειον ἄνθρωπον αὐτὸν γενέσθαι ‡Ath. *Apoll.*1.2(M.26.1096B); cf.Apoll.*quod un.Chr.*11(p.302.14; M.28.132A) cit. s. βάπτισμα; σχήματι εὑρῆσθαι ὡς ἄνθρωπον, ὡς οὐχὶ τοῦ ἀνθρωπίνου εἴδους ἐν τούτοις δηλουμένου, φαντασίας δέ τινος ἀπατηλῆς καὶ δοκήσεως Gr.Naz.*ep.*102(M.37.197C); in Nestorian controversy, cf. *Sophronius: il a voulu être chair, et il a été chair, non pas l'apparence de la chair, mais la nature de la chair, c'est à dire chair en vérité,* Nest.*Heracl.*1.1.15(p.11); **4.** astrol., *sign* of zodiac, Meth.*symp.*8.15 (p.104.1; M.18.168A); **5.** *attitude* of body τὼ χεῖρε δ' ἐκτεταμένος εὐχομένου σχήματι Eus.*v.C.*4.15(p.123.26; M.20.1164B); of man's upright stance, Bas.*hom.*3.8(2.24B; M.31.216C); of kneeling, Dion.Ar. *e.h.*5.3.7(M.3.516A); **6.** *position* τοὺς μὲν γὰρ τῶν εἰδώλων κατέλυον τόπ(ους), τοὺς δὲ τῷ θεῷ ἀνακειμένους κατελίμπανον ἐπὶ σχήματος Thdt.*Is.*36:7(p.143.26; 2.318); **7.** *action, act* γνώσῃ καὶ τοῖς σ. καὶ τοῖς ῥήμασι ὡς ὅλην ἀποπέμπῃ τὴν ἀθεΐαν Gr.Naz.*or.*40.45(M.36.424A); ἀποβιοῦντα ἐκκλησίας σ. Philost.*h.e.*2.13(M.65.476C); in phrase τὸ αὐτὸ σ. *the same thing* ἅπαξ οὖν καὶ δεύτερον ποιήσας τὸ αὐτὸ σ. ...μὴ πάλιν τὸ αὐτὸ σ. ποιήσῃ Leont.N.*v.Jo.Eleem.*42(p.84.4,6); ἐν ἄλλοις χρόνοις ἐγένετο τὸ αὐτὸ σ. Jo.Mal.*chron.*17 p.418(M.97.620A); **8.** *clothing, habit;* **a.** secular ἀνὴρ...σχήματι ποιμενικῷ Herm.*vis.* 5.1; Or.*fr.ep.*2 ap.Eus.*h.e.*6.19.14(M.20.569A); Thdt.*h.e.*3.14.10(3.929); **b.** Jewish and eccl. τὸν Ἰουδαίων ἀρχιερέα ἐνδύντα τὴν ἱερατικὴν στολήν...ὤφθαι αὐτῷ τούτῳ τῷ σ. Or.*Cels.*5.50(p.54.24; M.11.1260B); τὸ κανονικὸν σ. Marc.Diac.*v.Porph.*102; baptismal, *ib.*101; episcopal τινὰ ἐν σ. ἐπισκόπου Dor.*doct.*5.5(M.88.1681D); of deaconesses κἂν εἰ ...συνοικοίη τινὶ μετὰ τοῦ ῥηθέντος ὀνόματος ἢ σχήματος Justn.*nov.* 6.6(p.44); **c.** monastic; **i.** in gen. τὸ ἅγιον καὶ ἱερὸν ὑμῶν σ. Serap. *ep.mon.*8(M.40.933B); τὸ συμβολικὸν σ. τῶν ἐν Αἰγύπτῳ μοναχῶν Evagr.Pont.*cap.pract.*A proem.(M.40.1220C); **ii.** in various phrases, *monastic life* or *order* ἐνεδύθην τὸ σ. *V.Pach.A* 18(p.142.4); λαμβάνειν τὸ σ. *Apophth.Patr.*(M.65.164C); φορεῖν τὸ σ. *ib.*(161B); εἰς τὸ σ., ἐν τῷ σ. *ib.*(188B); τοῦ τῶν μοναχῶν σ. ... ἀξιωθείς Cyr.S.*v.Euthym.*49 (p.71.15); **iii.** of a novice τὸ σ. τὸ ἀποτακτικόν Pach.*reg.*B 16(p.14.3; M.40.949A); **iv.** distinction between μέγα (also called ἀγγελικόν) and μικρόν: ἀββᾶ Ὥρ...σ. ... ἔχοντα ἀγγελικόν ‡Pall.*h.mon.*2.1(p.24.15; M.34.1026D); Leont.N.*v.Sym.*12(M.93.1685C); τὸ ἰσάγγελον τοῦ μοναχικοῦ βίου σ. id.*v.Jo.Eleem.*24(p.49.22); this distinction disapproved of οὐ δοίης ὅπερ λέγουσι μικρὸν σ., ἔπειτα ὡς μέγα· ἐν γὰρ τὸ σ., ὥσπερ καὶ τὸ βάπτισμα, καθὼς οἱ ἅγιοι πατέρες ἐχρήσαντο Thdr.Stud.*epp.*1.10(M.99.941C); but kept in rite of clothing a monk, *Euchol.*(pp.382,407,411); **d.** met. εἰ φιλάργυρον ἔχεις τὸ σ. τῆς ψυχῆς Cyr.H.*procatech.*4; **9.** used of *sex* σ. μὲν τὸ τῆς σαρκὸς ἕτερον καὶ ἕτερον ὁρῶμεν γεγενημένον ἄρρενος καὶ θηλείας Just.*dial.*23.5(M.6.528B); τοῦδε τοῦ σ., ᾧ διακρίνεται τὸ ἄρρεν καὶ τὸ θῆλυ Clem.*str.*3.13 (p.239.4; M.8.1193B); *ib.*6.12(p.482.12; M.9.321B); ἐπ' αὐξήσει γὰρ τοῦ γένους τῶν ἀνθρώπων διαφορὰ σχημάτων διεπλάσθη ἐν τῷ Ἀδὰμ καὶ τῇ Εὔᾳ *Const.App.*6.11.6; *ib.*7.2.8; Thdt.*provid.*7(4.589); **10.** *rank, position* ἐν...τῷ τοῦ Καίσαρος σ. πέντε ἐνιαυτούς Philost.*h.e.*7.15(M.65.553C); οἱ εὑρισκόμενοι ἐν τῷ κλήρῳ ἔσονται ἐν τῷ αὐτῷ σ. CNic. (325)*can.*8; *ib.*19; παρέλαβε τὸ σ. τῆς ἐπισκοπῆς Ἱεροσολύμων Συμέων Jo.Mal.*chron.*10 p.259(M.97.392C), cf. 6 supra; **11.** *figure* in rhetoric καὶ τὸ ψαλμικὸν μεμίμηται σ.· καὶ γὰρ ἐκεῖ ὁμοίως ἐρωτῶσί τινες· τίς ἐστιν οὗτος ὁ βασιλεὺς τῆς δόξης; Thdt.*Is.*63:1(p.245.14; 2.388); cf. *schema, id est perfectam sermonum conexionem,* Isid.H.*etym.*1.35.7; *schemata ex Graeco in Latinum eloquium figurae interpretantur, quae fiunt in verbis vel sententiis per varias dictionum formas propter eloquii ornamentum, ib.*1.36.1; **12.** *phraseology* σ. πολεμικόν Or. *schol.in Cant.*7:1(M.17.280D); Oecum.*Apoc.*1:2(p.33); **13.** *kind, sort* ἐναλλάττει τὸ σ. τοῦ χρόνου· τὰ γὰρ ἤδη γεγενημένα ὡς μέλλοντα λέγει Thdt.*Zach.*7:13(2.1624); ἐπηρημένου...τῆς συναγωγῆς τοῦ ἄνω σ. id.*Is.*6:4(2.209); Jo.D.*haer.*83(M.94.741A, v.l. σχίσματος); **14.** *appearance* opp. reality; **a.** *semblance* πιστεύειν τῷ σ. τῶν Χριστιανῶν εἶναι νομιζομένων Eus.*v.C.*4.54(p.139.32; M.20.1205A); Alex.Al.*ep.Alex.*2(p.20.21; M.18.549C); Bas.*hom.*1.2(2.2C; M.31.165B); σ. ἅπας ὁ παρὼν βίος, καὶ ἀπάτη, καὶ ὀνειράτων οὐδὲν διενήνοχε Chrys.*hom.35.7 in Gen.*(4.360C); **b.** *appearance* ἡ ἀντικειμένη δύναμις ἀεὶ μιμεῖται τῆς ἀρετῆς καὶ τῆς δικαιοσύνης τὰ σ. Meth.*symp.*10.5 (p.127.1; M.18.200C); 'διέρρηξε τὰ ἱμάτια' τῷ μὲν σ. πρὸς τὸ πάθος ἀποσυρόμενος, τῷ δὲ πράγματι πρὸς τὴν ἀρετὴν ἀποδυόμενος ‡Chrys. *hom.3.4 in Job*(6.591C); **c.** plur., of vanities of this world, Meth. *symp.*8.1(p.81.15; M.18.140A); Dion.Ar.*e.h.*6.3(M.3.536A); σχήματα μὲν καλεῖ τὰ τοῦ παρόντος αἰῶνος, οἷον πλοῦτον καὶ δυναστείαν καὶ τὴν ἄλλην περιφάνειαν· πράγματα δὲ τὰ μέλλοντα Thdt.*Rom.*12:2(3.129); **15.** *figure, type* σ. πληρῶν μόνον ἕστηκεν ὁ ἱερεύς...ἡ δὲ χάρις...ἐστιν ἡ τοῦ θεοῦ Chrys.*prod.Jud.*2.6(2.394A); διὰ πολλῶν σ. τοῦ πανσόφου Μωυσέως τὸ ἐπὶ Χριστῷ προανατυποῦντος μυστήριον Cyr.*Jo.*3.2(4.264E); ὁ Χριστὸς ...αὐτὴν ἡμῖν...ὑπέδειξε τὴν ἀλήθειαν, οὐκ ἐν τύποις ἔτι καὶ σχήματι τὸ τῆς ἀρετῆς καταγράφων εἶδος *ib.*10(835C); *ib.*5.1 (469A); hence *meaning, interpretation* ἐν ἱστορίας σχήματι Or.*Cels.* 5.31(p.32.20; M.11.1228B); σ. ... τῷ λόγῳ περιτέθειται βαθύ Cyr.*Jo.* 5(4.442A); *ib.*5.1(469B); id.*thes.*32(5^1.309A); **16.** *form of thought* τὴν ἑτερότητα τῶν ποικίλων τοῦ θεοῦ κατὰ τὰς πολυειδεῖς ὁράσεις σχημάτων Dion.Ar.*d.n.*9.5(M.3.912D); Jo.D.*haer.*83(M.94.741A); **17.** *scheme, plot,* Rom.Mel.(*AS* 1 p.180) cit. s. σκάμμα; **18.** error for ὄχημα: γῇ δὲ ποσὶ μὲν ὑποβέβηκε σ. Bas.Sel.*or.*9.1(M.85.128A).

***σχηματάριος**, ὁ, *deceiver,* Jo.D.*parall.*(M.96.464).

σχηματίζ-ω, **1.** *form, fashion* τὸ ἄρρεν ⟨μὲν⟩ μορφώσας, τὸ δὲ θῆλυ σχηματίσας Eus.*l.C.*11(p.228.9; M.20.1384A); fig. ὁ παιδοτρίβης ~ων τὸν παῖδα Clem.*str.*6.17(p.514.23; M.9.393A); *ib.*7.7(p.27.20; 449C); Chrys.*hom.22.4 in Mt.*(7.280A); Cyr.*Jo.*3.5(4.305C); **2.** *endue with form* or *substance* εἰπὼν 'ἐν δεξιᾷ', οὐκ ἐσχημάτισεν αὐτόν, ἀλλὰ τὸ ὁμότιμον ἔδειξε τὸ πρὸς τὸν πατέρα Chrys.*hom.2.3 in Heb.* (12.19C); μὴ ~ῃς τὸ θεῖον ἐν ἑαυτῷ προσευχόμενος Evagr.Pont.*or.*66 (M.79.1181A); of Inc. μετὰ τὸ σχηματισθῆναι ἤτοι σωματωθῆναι Nil. *epp.*2.40(M.79.213D); **3.** *give form to, represent* τὸ πνεῦμα...ἐν εἴδει περιστερᾶς ~εται Epiph.*haer.*62.6(p.394.27; M.41.1057B); τὸ πνεῦμα ...ἐν τῷ πραοτάτῳ ~όμενον ζῴῳ Cyr.*Jo.*2.1(4.127A); *ib.*6(564C); ἄγγελος δέ, καὶ ψυχή, καὶ δαίμων, εἰ μὴ σωματικῶς καὶ παχέως, ἀλλὰ κατὰ τὴν ἑαυτῶν φύσιν, καὶ ~ονται καὶ περιγράφονται Jo.D.*imag.*3.24 (M.94.1344Bf.); **4.** *represent, describe* οὐ γὰρ ταὐτὰ νομίζω σημαίνεσθαι ἐν τῷ 'ἐμαρτύρησεν' ὅτε δηλοῦται τὸ ῥῆμα, παρ' ὃ ὁ μάρτυς ἐσχημάτισται τοῦ θεοῦ Or.*Jo.*32.18(11; p.456.29; M.14.792A); ~ει δὲ αὐτὸν [sc. τὸν λόγον] διεξοδικῶς ἡ γραφή Bas.*hex.*3.2(1.23B; M.29.56A); Gr.Nyss. *Apoll.*5(M.45.1132B); λόγον προφορικὸν αὐτὸν σχηματίσας Epiph. *anac.*65(p.1.6; M.42.9A); τὸ φιλάργυρον οὕτως ἐσχηματίσαμεν Chrys. *hom.28.5 in Mt.*(7.340B); ἡ θεολογία τοὺς οὐρανίους ἐσχημάτισε νόας Dion.Ar.*c.h.*2.3(M.3.141B); **5.** *typify, symbolize* τίνος οὖν ἕνεκεν...τὸ βιβλίον ῥαντίζεται...ἢ τοῦ τιμίου αἵματος ἄνωθεν ~ομένου; Chrys. *hom.16.2 in Heb.*(12.159B); ‡Sophr.H.*liturg.*11(M.87.3992A); **6.** *express* ἕν τι γένος ἐκάλει Σαβαὶ ⟨ὁ⟩ Ἑβραῖος, παρ' ὃ ἐσχηματίσθαι τὸν Σαβαώθ Or.*Jo.*1.31(34; p.38.23; M.14.81A); Bas.*hom.in Ps.*44(1.164B; M.29.401A); τῇ εὐχαριστίᾳ ~ει τὴν εὐφημίαν Thdt.*2 Thess.* 1:3(3.528); **7.** *mean* λέγει μὲν γὰρ ὅτι..., ἐσχημάτισε δὲ οὕτως... Thdr.Mops.*Rom.*8:26(p.140.5; M.66.828D); *ib.*8:27(p.141.7; 829C); **8.** med., *make a show of;* hence *feign, counterfeit,* ‡Just.*coh.Gr.*20 (M.6.276C); οὐ πρὸς ἡμᾶς ἔχουσιν τὴν μάχην οἱ Ἀρειανοὶ περὶ τῆς αἱρέσεως, ἀλλὰ ~ονται μὲν πρὸς ἡμᾶς, πρὸς αὐτὴν δὲ τὴν θεότητα μάχονται Ath.*Ar.*2.32(M.26.213C); ~όμενοι τὴν εὐσέβειαν Thdt.*Ps.* 30:9(1.795); of Christ ἅπερ οἶδεν ὡς θεός, ἀγνοεῖν ὡς ἄνθρωπος ~εται Cyr.*Jo.*5.5(4.529C); ἀσθένειαν ὁ λόγος ~εται, ἔχει δὲ οὐχ οὕτως κατ' ἀλήθειαν, ἐπείπερ ἴσος ἐστὶ τῷ πατρί Ammon.*Jo.*5:30(M.85.1429D); of God προνοητικῶς δὲ ἐσχηματίζετο οἰκονομῶν τὴν σωτηρίαν ἡμῶν, ἵνα δείξῃ πόσον δύναται μετάνοια Jo.D.*Man.*80(M.94.1580A); **9.** astrol., *be in configuration* τοὺς ἀστέρας, οὓς νομίζουσιν ἑαυτοῖς ἐσχηματικέναι κατὰ τὸν καιρὸν τῆς τοῦ δεῖνος γενέσεως ἐσχηματισμένους οὑτωσί Or. *comm.in Gen.*ap.Eus.*p.e.*6.11(291Af.; M.12.72A); *ib.*(295B; M.80C); **10.** ? *examine* ἐνέγκαντες μαίας πιστὰς πρὸς τὸ σχηματίσαι αὐτήν, καὶ σχηματίσαντες εὗρον αὐτὴν τοῦ καθαροῦ καθαρωτέραν *Chr.Sac.*A(p.59).

σχηματικός, ? *one who believes that* Christ's humanity *is only in appearance,* not in reality Αἴγυπτοι, οἱ καὶ σ. καὶ μονοφυσῖται Jo.D. *haer.*83(M.94.741A, prob. f.l. for σχισματικοί).

σχημάτισμα, τό, *pretence* κενοδοξία...σ. φιλοπονίας †Nil.*vit.*4(M.79.1144C).

σχηματισμός, ὁ, 1. *form*; **a.** *shape, similitude*, of devils ἀλλάττοντες τὰς μορφάς, καὶ τοὺς παῖδας ἐκφοβοῦντες, τῇ τῶν ὄχλων φαντασίᾳ καὶ τοῖς σ. Ath.*v.Anton.*28(M.26.888A); of incorporeal beings as depicted ὡς δυνατὸν συγγενέσιν ἀναπλάττειν τε καὶ ἐκφαίνειν σχηματισμοῖς Dion.Ar.*c.h.*2.2(M.3.137C); ἐμπυρίοις σ. id.*ep.*9.2(M.3.1108D); τοῖς...μὴ ἔχουσι σ. σωματικῶς Jo.D.*imag.*3.24(M.94.1344D); **b.** external *form* or *appearance*, Meth.*symp.*10.5(p.127.3; M.18.200C); τὸν ἔνδον καρπὸν...οὐ τὸν ἐκ φύλλων ἐπικείμενον σ. Mac.Aeg.*ep.*2(M.34.413C); τοὺς ἔξωθεν σ. οἷς τὰ πάθη ἡμῶν ἐπισκιάζομεν †Bas.*Is.*62(1.424E; M.30.228B); Cyr.*fr.Mt.*23:26(M.72.440B); of BMV, Andr.Cr.*imag.*(M.97.1304C); hence **c.** *pretence* ὄργανον ἀπάτης καὶ τέχνη σχηματισμοῦ Bas.*Eun.*1.4(1.213C; M.29.513A); **2.** *style* of dressing hair, Clem.*paed.*3.2(p.242.23; M.8.572B); **3.** astrol., *configuration* οἱ ἀστέρες κατὰ τοὺς διαφόρους σ. Or.*comm. in Gen.*ap.Eus.*p.e.*6.11(281C; M.12.52A); *ib.*(286C; M.61A); id.*Cels.*5.21(p.22.23; M.11.1213A); Diod.*fat.*ap.Phot.*cod.*223(M.103.860D); **4.** in language; **a.** *figure of speech*, Clem.*str.*6.15(p.497.16; M.9.353B); Thdr.Mops.*Rom.*8:26(p.140.1; M.66.828C); *ib.*(p.140.22; 829B); id.*Ps.*17:10(p.114.1; M.66.664A); Isid.Pel.*epp.*2.177(M.78.629A); **b.** *grammatical construction* ὁ δὲ σ. τῆς ἡμετέρας γλώττης μὴ συμβαίνων τῷ σ. τῆς Ἑβραϊκῆς εὐγλωττίας Gr.Nyss.*hom.2 in Cant.*(M.44.796B).

***σχηματόγραπτος,** *circumscribed in a form* τὸ σῶμα [i.e. Christ's] σ. πέλει Thdr.Stud.*iamb.*31(M.99.1792C).

***σχηματολογία, ἡ,** *transference of application*, Cyr.*Rom.*7:13 (Pusey 5 p.201 not.).

***σχηματολόγιον, τό,** *complete monastic habit* τίθησιν ὁ ἱερεὺς ἐπάνω αὐτοῦ τὸ σ. *Euchol.*(p.385).

σχηματοποι-έω, *give a representation of, represent*, Just.*dial.*30.2 (M.6.540A); τὰ τῆς κωμῳδίας αἰσχρὰ...διηγεῖσθαι...~οῦντες τῶν παλαιῶν τοὺς μύθους Epiph.*haer.*73.1(p.268.2; M.42.401A); id.*exp. fid.*16(p.517.4; M.42.813A); Thdr.Mops.*Ps.*49 proem.(p.324.16).

σχηματοποιΐα, ἡ, *figurative representation* συνθέσεις φησὶ τὰς εἰρημένας πλάσεις καὶ σ. Max.*schol.c.h.*2.2(M.3.37A).

σχηματουργέω, *fashion, make*, Geo.Pis.*hex.*1071(M.92.1516A); id. *Heracl.*2.139(M.92.1326A); *ib.*2.205(1331A).

σχηματουργία, ἡ, 1. *configuration*; of stars, Tat.*orat.*9(p.10.22; M.6.928A); **2.** *symbolism* διὰ τῆς παραπεποιημένης αὐτῶν [sc. Adamites] σ. Epiph.*haer.*52.3(p.314.11; M.41.957C).

***σχιαστή, ἡ,** a kind of *tunic*, Jo.Mal.*chron.*18 p.457(M.97.669B).

***σχιδακίζω,** *cleave, splinter*, Epiph.*anc.*103(p.124.16; M.43.204A).

σχιδανόπους, *with parted toes*, Clem.*str.*7.18(p.78.2; M.9.556B).

[*]σχιδάριον, τό, v. σχεδάριον.

σχίζα, ἡ, *cleavage*; hence *fork* of a road, Synes.*provid.*3(p.69.4; M.66.1216C).

σχιζίον, τό, *small piece*, Cyr.S.*v.Sab.*24(p.107.25).

σχιζόπτερος, *with cloven*, i.e. *feathered, wings*; of birds, Bas.*hex.* 8.3(1.72E; M.29.169C).

σχίζ-ω, 1. trans., *divide*; **a.** in gen. ~οντας τὴν τῶν προσεχόντων αὐτοῖς ψυχήν Or.*Cels.*5.3(p.4.4; M.11.1185A); τὸν βίον αὐτῷ ~όμενον πρὸς ἀρετὴν καὶ κακίαν Bas.*hom.in Ps.*1(1.95C; M.29.224A); **b.** theol. μιᾷ θεότητος...ἐν τριάδι·...καὶ ~ειν αὐτὴν εἰς διαφόρους φύσεις τολμᾶτε Ath.*Ar.*1.18(M.26.48C); μὴ ~ων τὴν προσκύνησιν, ἀλλ' ἑνῶν τὴν θεότητα ‡Bas.*struct.hom.*1.2(1.325C; M.30.13B); μήτε τὸ τῆς μοναρχίας ~εσθαι κράτος εἰς θεότητας διαφόρους κατατεμνόμενον Gr.Nyss.*or. catech.*3(p.16.8; M.45.17D); ἐν υἱῷ γνῶθι πατέρα, ἐν πατρὶ δόξασον υἱόν...μὴ ~ε τὰ ἄσχιστα. κἂν γὰρ θέλῃς, οὐ ~εται Didym.(‡Bas.) *Eun.*5(1.317C; M.29.760D); **2.** *divide, separate, be in schism*, act. εἴ τις ~οντι ἀκολουθεῖ Ign.*Philad.*3.3; ἕνεκεν τοῦ μὴ σχίσαι Dion.Al. ap.Eus.*h.e.*6.45(M.20.633B); Arsen.Hyps.*ep.*(p.147.16; M.25.372C); τούς...Ἡμιαρείους...καὶ τοὺς ἀπ' αὐτῶν σχίσαντας Epiph.*haer.*73.37 (p.311.25; M.42.472A); pass. τέμνονται καὶ ~ονται καὶ στάσεις ἰδίας ἔχειν ἕκαστοι θέλουσιν Cels.ap.Or.*Cels.*3.9(p.210.16; M.11.392C); μετὰ τοῦ ~εσθαι καὶ ἀποπίπτειν τοῦ θεοῦ Or.*Cels.*8.62(p.278.22; 1609D); id. *Jo.*13.13(p.237.29; M.14.420A); Const.ap.Eus.*v.C.*2.69(p.68.25; M.20.1041B); μὴ ~εσθαι τὰς ἐκκλησίας Jul.Papa ap.Ath.*apol.sec.*32(p.111.7; M.25.301C); **3.** *cut off, separate* μὴ δέξησθε...τὰ γράμματα αὐτοῦ, ἀλλὰ σχίσατε καὶ δυσωπήσατε τοὺς κομίζοντας Ath.*ep.encycl.*7(p.176.26; M.25.237B); **4.** *make a schism in* τοῖς ~ουσι τὴν ἐκκλησίαν Chrys.*hom.11.5 in Eph.*(11.86F); τοῦ εἰς αἵρεσιν ἐμπεσεῖν τὸ τὴν ἐκκλησίαν σχίσαι οὐκ ἔλαττόν ἐστι κακόν *ib.*(88A).

σχίσις, ἡ, *cleavage, parting*; of rivers, Hipp.*haer.*6.15(p.141.15; M.16.3215C); of the heavens at Christ's baptism, Or. *fr.20 in Jo.* (p.500.29).

σχίσμα, τό, 1. *division, cleavage*, within Godhead ἢ τοίνυν δὸς ἐκεῖ σχίσματα, ἵνα εἴπωμεν τρεῖς θεούς...ἤ, εἰ οὐκ ἔνι σ., εἷς θεὸς πατὴρ καὶ υἱὸς καὶ ἅγιον πνεῦμα ‡Ath.*dial.Trin.*1.2(M.28.1120C); **2.** *division, schism*, dist. from heresy, Bas.*ep.*188 *can.*1(3.268D; M.32.665A) cit. s. αἵρεσις; Μελιτιανοί, οἱ ἐν Αἰγύπτῳ, σ. ὄντες ἀλλ' οὐχ αἵρεσις Epiph. *anac.*68(p.2.3; M.42.12A); Thdr.Stud.*epp.*1.40(M.99.1052D); but cf. αἱρέσεις ἐνταῦθα, οὐ ταύτας λέγων τὰς τῶν δογμάτων, ἀλλὰ τὰς τῶν σ. τούτων Chrys.*hom.27.2 in 1Cor.*(10.242B); σ. οὐ δογματικὰ λέγει, ἀλλ' ἐκεῖνα τὰ τῆς φιλαρχίας Thdt.*1Cor.*11:18(3.236); to be avoided, *Barn.*19.12; ἡμᾶς ὡς αἰτίους σχίσματος μέμψιν ὑπομεῖναι Ath.*apol. sec.*32(p.111.8; M.25.301C); ἀκμάζοντος...τοῦ σ. ἐν Ἀλεξανδρείᾳ Evagr.*h.e.*3.22(p.120.9; M.86.2641B); παῦσον τὰ σ. τῶν ἐκκλησιῶν *Lit.Jac.*(p.210.23).

***σχισματάριος,** *schismatic*, Pall.*v.Chrys.*16(p.99.20; M.47.56).

***σχισματικός,** *schismatic*; **1.** σ. κακόν Eus.*v.C.*3.4(p.78.29; M.20.1057C); *ib.*3.66(p.113.26; 1144B); ἀνδρῶν *ib.*(p.113.19; 1144B); Μελιτιανοί οἱ ἀεὶ σ. CAlex.*ep.*ap.Ath.*apol.sec.*19(p.101.30; M.25.280C); Ath.*v.Anton.*68(M.26.940B); **2.** as subst. ἡ τῶν αἱρετικῶν καὶ σ. διχόνοια Const.ap.Eus.*v.C.*3.65(p.112.21; M.20.1141B); οὐ δεῖ αἱρετικοῖς ἢ σ. συνεύχεσθαι CLaod.*can.*33; μηδεμία ἔστω ὑμῖν κοινωνία πρὸς τοὺς σ., μήθ' ὅλως πρὸς τοὺς αἱρετικοὺς Ἀρειανούς Ath.*v.Anton.* 91(M.26.969C).

***σχισματοποιός,** *making a schism* τοῦ σ. Μαρκίωνος Adam.*dial.* 1.8(p.18.2; M.11.1729B); τὰ περὶ Ἱεροβοὰμ καὶ Ῥοβοὰμ τῶν σ. ‡Ath. *synops.*(M.28.384B); masc. as subst. αἱρεσιαρχῶν καὶ σ. Epiph.*exp. fid.*12(p.512.17; M.42.804B).

σχισμή, ἡ, *crack*; in a stone, Herm.*vis.*3.6.3; Ephr.3.219C; in a stick, Herm.*sim.*8.10.1; *cleft*; in a mountain, *ib.*9.1.7.

***σχοινίζομαι,** *rope* δεθέντας αὐτοὺς καὶ σχοινισθέντας εἰς τοὺς τραχήλους *M.Seb.*7(p.177.2); ‡Chrys.*eleem.*1(1.819A).

σχοινίον, τό, 1. *rope*, in icons of angels τινὰ τὰ γεωμετρικὰ σ. Dion.Ar.*c.h.*15 tit.(M.3.325D); described later as τὰ δὲ γεωμετρικὰ καὶ τεκτονικὰ σκεύη *ib.*15.5(333B); fig. ἀναφερόμενοι εἰς τὰ ὕψη...σ. χρώμενοι τῷ πνεύματι τῷ ἁγίῳ Ign.*Eph.*9.1; exeg. Ps.15:6 σχοινία γὰρ τὰς ἐπιβουλὰς ὀνομάζει Thdt.*Ps.*15:6(1.691); σ. μέτρον ἐστίν Cyr. *Ps.*15:6(M.69.812A); **2. a.** a measure, equal to four miles, Hipp.*haer.* 9.13(p.251.14ff.; σχοίνων M.16.3387C); hence **b.** what is measured, a *lot, portion*; used for σχοίνισμα (Ps.104:11), Jo.D.*hom.*2.4(M.96. 584B).

σχοίνισμα, τό, 1. *portion, allotment*, freq. in biblical phrase σ. κληρονομίας Meth.*symp.*10.6(p.128.27; M.18.204A); Eus.*d.e.*2.3(p.66. 31; M.22.121B); Cyr.*Is.*4.1(2.579C); ὑμεῖς κλητοὶ ἅγιοι..., σ. κυρίου τὸ κράτιστον Gr.Naz.*or.*42.9(M.36.469B); πλάτυνόν σου ἐν ἐμοὶ τὰ σ., τὰς ἐνεργείας τοῦ παναγίου πνεύματος Jo.D.*hom.*2.7(M.96.588C); **2.** = σχοινίον, *mooring rope*, Ephr.1.214C.

σχοινοειδής, *like a rope* or *cord*, Gr.Nyss.*res.*3(M.46.669B).

***σχοῖνον, τό,** *rope*, Jo.Mal.*chron.*11 p.279(M.97.421B).

***σχοινοπλοκ-έω,** *make a rope*, fig. μὴ λάθῃς...~ῶν κατὰ σαυτοῦ τῇ συνηθείᾳ τῆς ἁμαρτίας Chrys.*fr.in Pr.*5:22(M.64.669C).

σχοῖνος, ὁ, ἡ, 1. *a reed pen*, Clem.*str.*6.3(p.449.9; M.9.253B); **2.** = σχοίνισμα 1, Apoll.*met.Ps.*15:6(M.33.1328D).

σχοινοστρόφος, ὁ, *rope-maker*, Chrys.*catech.*2.4(2.242B).

***σχοινωτός,** *twisted like a rope*; of a pillar, Cosm.Ind.*top.*2(M.88. 101B).

σχολάζ-ω, 1. *have leisure*; **a.** *do nothing* οὐ δεῖ Χριστιανοὺς Ἰουδαΐζειν καὶ ἐν τῷ σαββάτῳ σ. ... τὴν δὲ κυριακὴν προτιμῶντας εἴγε δύναιντο σ. ὡς Χριστιανοί CLaod.*can.*29; of a newly-clothed monk ὀφείλει προσκαρτερεῖν ἐν τῇ ἐκκλησίᾳ ἡμέρας πέντε, ~ων ἀπὸ παντὸς ἔργου, ἄνευ ἀναγνώσεως, εἰ ἐπίσταται *Euchol.*(p.388); **b.** *be unoccupied*, ἐπίσκοπος ~ων ἐπὶ ~ουσαν ἐκκλησίαν ἑαυτὸν ἐπιρρίψας CAnt.(341)*can.* 16; σ. ἀπὸ τοῦ ἱερατικοῦ ἀξιώματος Dam.Papa ap.Thdt.*h.e.*5.11.6(3. 1038); **2.** *be at leisure*; **a.** *be still*, cf.Ps.45:11 ὅντινα γνῶναι οὐκ ἔστιν μὴ σχολάσαντα καὶ ἐκκαθάραντα τὸν νοῦν Or.*Jo.*19.3(p.301.22; M.14.529B); ἴδιόν ἐστι τοῦ ~οντος ἐκζητεῖν τὸν θεόν Bas.*hom.in Ps.* 45(1.175E; M.29.429A); σχόλασόν μοι, τέκνον Marc.Diac.*v.Porph.*26; Jo.Clim.*scal.*29(M.88.1152B); **b.** *be free* from, esp. from things of this world σχολασάτω ἀπὸ τοῦ κόσμου †Didym.ap.Jo.D.*parall.*(M. 96.483A); καρδίαν ἀνθρώπου ~ουσαν ἀπὸ πάσης ἀκαθαρσίας Cyr.*Lc.* 11:25(M.72.705D); ‡Pall.*h.mon.*1.27(p.11.21; M.34.1116D); **c.** *be free* to, *have the opportunity* διὰ τὴν εἰρήνην ~ει τὸν διαβόητον οἰκοδομῆσαι ναόν Or.*Jo.*6.1(p.107.7; M.14.200A); abs., *be free*; of a woman, *be unbetrothed*, Bas.*ep.*199 *can.*22(3.293B; M.32.721A); **d.** *have rest* or *respite*; **i.** *cease* πάντα τὰ πρὸ τούτου...νῦν ἀμνηστίᾳ παραδοθῆναι, πᾶσάν τε ὑποψίαν σχολάσαι τοῦ λοιποῦ Const.ap.Ath.*apol.sec.*54(p.135. 9; M.25.348B); ἐὰν...ἐάσαι τὸ πῦρ σχολάσαι Diad.*perf.*97(p.144.11); ἐὰν...μὴ σχολάσῃ...τοῦ μεμνῆσθαι τοῦ θεοῦ *ib.*100(p.148.9); πάσης ἀπάτης ∼ούσης Procl.CP *Arm.*12(p.193.10; M.65.868C); hence **ii.** *be useless, antiquated* τὰ...ἐν Νικαίᾳ πραχθέντα σ. ποιήσωμεν Ath.*syn.*7 (p.235.1; M.26.689C); ἐκελεύθη τῆς προτέρας ἐκδόσεως ∼ούσης [sc. of Justinian Code] αὐθεντεῖσθαι *Chron.Pasch.*p.344(M.92.896B); **iii.** *be of no avail*, Nil.*Magn.*12(M.79.984D); τὸ ἐν τῷ ᾅδῃ ∼ειν μετάνοιαν *cat.Apoc.*14:10(p.392.21); **iv.** pass., of Devil at Christ's temptation, ? *be unsuccessful* οὔτε εἰς ὁδὸν αὐτὸν ἔδωκεν [sc. Χριστός], ἀλλ' ἀφῆκεν αὐτὸν οὕτω ∼εσθαι Eus.Al.*serm.*11(M.86.377B); **3.** *have leisure* or *time* for a thing, *devote one's time* to a thing, *be intent* on a thing, esp. ref. prayer (cf. 1Cor.7:5) or fasting ἐσχόλαζον ταῖς εὐχαῖς Or. *hom.19.13 in Jer.*(p.169.13; M.13.489A); ἐσχόλαζον ταῖς συνάξεσι Ath. *apol.Const.*4(M.25.600C); σ. ταῖς προσευχαῖς CLaod.*can.*1; σ. θεωρίᾳ *Apophth.Patr.*(M.65.208B); c. acc. τὰς νηστείας σ. Const.ap.Eus.*v.C.* 3.18(p.86.12; M.20.1077A); *bend* the mind σ. τὴν διάνοιαν εἰς τὸ μαθεῖν Cyr.H.*procatech.*16; also in gen. ἀμφὶ τὴν Ἰταλίαν καὶ πάντα τὰ ἀμφὶ ταύτην ἔθνη ἐσχόλαζεν Eus.*theoph.fr.*6(p.20*.17; M.24.628C); *ib.*16 (p.34*.7; 656B); περὶ τὸ ἐξωθεῖν μόνον ἐσχόλαζον Socr.*h.e.*2.27.4(M. 67.269C); **4.** *spend time* in a place, *frequent, be* τῷ ὄρει μὲν τῷ Ἀμανῷ σ. Thdt.*h.rel.*9(3.1192); ἐν εἱρκτῇ διατρίψαντα id.*ep.*83(p.48.26, v.l. σχολάσαντα 4.1145); σ. τῇ ἁγίᾳ ἐκκλησίᾳ Marc.Diac.*v.Porph.*31; **5.** of a place, *be vacant* ἐπὶ ἐρεμίζοντα τόπον καὶ ἀνδρῶν ἐσχοληκότα παριόντες Eus.*qu.Marin.suppl.*1(M.22.988B); *ib.*(981B); of a see, CAnt.(341)*can.*16; ∼ουσαν καὶ ἐκδεχομένην αὐτὸν τὴν ἐκκλησίαν εὗρεν Jul.Papa *ep.Dian.*(p.109.4; M.25.297B); ἐπὶ ἔτη ὀκτὼ λέγεται τὸν ἐν Ἀντιοχείᾳ θρόνον τῆς ἐκκλησίας σχολάσαι Socr.*h.e.*1.24.8(M.67.145B); hence *be reserved* for ἔδει γὰρ ⟨αὐτῷ⟩ μόνῳ ∼ειν [sc. Christ's tomb] τῷ μόνῳ παραδόξῳ νεκρῷ Eus.*theoph.fr.*3(p.14*.12; M.24.620A).

σχολαῖος, 1. of a bishop, *without a see*, Socr.*h.e.*4.7.11(M.67. 473B); **2.** *at leisure, unoccupied* πῶς...ἐγχωρεῖ, τὸν μὲν ἄρχειν, τὸν δέ, ὡς ἐν ἀνθρώποις, σχολαῖον εἶναι, ὅταν ὁ πατὴρ ἐν τῷ υἱῷ καὶ ὁ υἱὸς ἐν τῷ πατρὶ μένει; Didym.*Trin.*1.31(M.39.425A).

***σχόλασις, ἡ,** *being at leisure*, ὦ ἡσυχία, σ. προσευχῆς καὶ ἀναγνώσεως ‡Chrys.*pat.et consumm.*(12.819E).

σχολαστής, ὁ, *one who has leisure*; for contemplation, Jo.Clim. *scal.*29(M.88.1152B).

σχολαστικός, masc. as subst.; **1.** *one who has passed through the* σχολὴ τῶν γραμμάτων, *one with a general education* ἀπέρχεται πρὸς τὴν σχολὴν τῶν γραμμάτων...εἶτα ὅταν γένηται σ. ὅλων τῶν δικολόγων ἀρχάριος καὶ ἔσχατός ἐστι Mac.Aeg.*hom.*15.42(M.34.604D); σ., ὁ μετρίως μαθὼν γράμματα *ib.*26.17(685B); **2.** *advocate, lawyer* ἐάν τις πλούσιος ἢ σ. ἀπὸ τῆς ἀγορᾶς ἀξιοῖτο ἐπίσκοπος γίνεσθαι, μὴ πρότερον καθίστασθαι, ἐὰν μὴ καὶ ἀναγνώστου καὶ διακόνου καὶ πρεσβυτέρου ὑπηρεσίαν ἐκτελέσῃ CSard.*can.*10; τοῦ σ. Εὐσεβίου Socr.*h.e.*6.6.36(M. 67.681A); σ. Ἰωάννης ὁ τοῦ ἐκσπελλευτοῦ Cyr.S.*v.Sab.*61(p.163.3); Jo.Mosch.*prat.*131(M.87.2996B); Ἀναστάσιος πατριάρχης γενόμενος Ἀντιοχείαις ὁ ἀπὸ σ. *Chron.Pasch.*p.382(M.92.980A); for church affairs, *Cod.Afr.*97.

***σχολαστικῶς,** *in the fashion of the schools*, Gr.Nyss.*hex.*6(v.l. στοχαστικῶς; M.44.68C).

σχολή, ἡ, 1. *leisure, rest*; **a.** on the sabbath διὰ τὴν πρὸς τὸ ἀκούειν τῶν θείων νόμων σ. τὰ καλούμενα σάββατα Or.*Cels.*4.31(p.302. 4; M.11.1076C); Eus.*p.e.*7.6(304D; M.21.516D); **b.** on Sunday τοῖς ὑπὸ τῇ Ῥωμαίων ἀρχῇ πολιτευομένοις ἅπασι σ. ἄγειν ταῖς ἐπωνύμοις τοῦ σωτῆρος ἡμέραις ἐνομοθέτει Eus.*v.C.*4.18f.(p.124.15f.; M.20. 1165Bf.); τὴν δὲ κυριακὴν καλουμένην ἡμέραν...ἐνομοθέτησε [sc. Κωνσταντῖνος] δικαστηρίων καὶ τῶν ἄλλων πραγμάτων σ. ἄγειν πάντας, καὶ ἐν εὐχαῖς καὶ λιταῖς τὸ θεῖον θεραπεύειν Soz.*h.e.*1.8.11(M. 67.881A); **c.** its employment, in philosophy ὁ γνωστικὸς...εἰ δέ που σχολὴ καὶ ἀνέσεως καιρὸς ἀπὸ τῶν προηγουμένων, ἀντὶ τῆς ἄλλης ῥαθυμίας καὶ τῆς Ἑλληνικῆς ἐφάπτεται φιλοσοφίας Clem.*str.*6.18 (p.515.18; M.9.396A); Christian use of leisure dist. from pagan αὕτη μὲν οὖν ἡ σ. ἀγαθὴ τῷ σχολάζοντι καὶ ὠφέλιμος, ἡσυχίαν ἐμποιοῦσα πρὸς τὴν τῶν σωτηρίων διδαγμάτων ἀνάληψιν. πονηρὰ δὲ σ. ἡ τῶν Ἀθηναίων, οἳ 'εἰς οὐδὲν ἄλλο εὐκαίρουν, ἢ λέγειν τι καὶ ἀκούειν καινότερον' ἣν καὶ νῦν τινες μιμοῦνται, τῇ τοῦ βίου σ. πρὸς τὴν ἀεί τινος καινοτέρου δόγματος εὕρεσιν ἀποχρώμενοι Bas.*hom.in Ps.*45(1. 175Ef.; M.29.429A); cf. σχολῆς χρεία πρὸς τὸ γνῶναι τὸν κύριον Or. *sel.in Ps.*45:11(M.12.1436B) = Ath.*exp.Ps.*45:11(M.27.216D); 'σχολάσατε καὶ γνῶτε, ὅτι ἐγώ εἰμι ὁ θεός'· ὥστε πολλῆς σ. χρεία τῷ μέλλοντι ταύτης ἀπολαύσεσθαι τῆς φιλοσοφίας Chrys.*bapt.*1(2.369A); to be spent in prayer, CArim.*ep.Const.*1 ap.Ath.*syn.*10(p.238.29; M. 26.700B); hence **2.** *study, attention* ἀνεξικάκως ἐπηκροᾶτο βασιλεὺς τῶν πάντων σχολῇ τε εὐτόνῳ τὰς προτάσεις ὑπεδέχετο Eus.*v.C.*3.13 (p.83.18; M.20.1069B); χρῆναι τὴν πᾶσαν σ. διδόναι τῇ ψυχῇ μᾶλλον ἢ τῷ σώματι Ath.*v.Anton.*45(M.26.909A); esp. of divine things τῆς περὶ τὸ θεῖον σ. Eus.*d.e.*1.9(p.40.27; M.22.77D); id.*h.e.*6.15(M.20. 553B); **3.** *vacancy*; **a.** *vacant space* or *place, room* σ. οὔσης ἐν τῇ Βηθλεέμ, κατὰ τὸν Ματθαῖον εὐπόρουν καταγωγίου id.*qu.Steph.*16.3 (M.22.936C); **b.** *free access* σ. αὐτοῖς εὐτρεπῆ διὰ τῆς τῶν φρουρῶν ἀπελάσεως id.*qu.Marin.suppl.*1(M.22.985B); **4.** *deprivation* τὸ τῆς γνώμης ἡμῶν ἀκόλαστον τῇ σ. τῆς παρακλήσεως κολάζων Diad.*perf.*87 (p.120.13); **5.** *relaxation* of a rule σ. τῇ συνήθει διαίτῃ *ib.*46(p.52.12); **6.** *school, party*; **a.** of a theological school or group Ἡρακλέων ὁ τῆς Οὐαλεντίνου σ. δοκιμώτατος Clem.*str.*4.19(p.280.11; M.8.1281B); Οὐαλεντῖνος...καὶ Ἡρακλέων καὶ Πτολεμαῖος καὶ πᾶσα ἡ τούτων σ. Hipp.*haer.*6.29(p.155.20; M.16.3235B); Σαβέλλιον καὶ τὴν αὐτοῦ σ. Epiph.*haer.*69.69(p.217.31; M.42.313C); **b.** of catechumens and newly baptized persons, Eus.*h.e.*6.4.3(M.20.532B); **c.** of secular groups: imperial guard and civil bureaux στρατιώτης τῶν περὶ τὸν βασιλέα σχολῶν Pall.*v.Chrys.*20(p.129.1; M.47.72); ἀπὸ τῆς πρώτης τῶν σχολαρίων σ. εἰς τὸν μοναδικὸν μεταστάντα βίον Cyr.S.*v.Sab.*38 (p.128.18); *Chron.Pasch.*p.391(M.92.1004B); of *silentiarii*, Evagr.*h.e.* 3.29(p.125.13; M.86.2653C); **7.** *idleness, waste of time* ὁπότε γὰρ τοῦ εὐαγγελίου ἀποτροπάδην ἦλθον, σ. περὶ αὐτῶν [sc. κανόνων] φροντίζειν Thdr.Stud.*epp.*1.34(M.99.1025C).

***σχολιογραφέω,** *make notes on* εἴποιμ' ὅτι τὰ μὲν νοήματα τοῦ ἀποστόλου ἐστίν, ἡ δὲ φράσις καὶ ἡ σύνθεσις ἀπομνημονεύσαντός τινος τὰ ἀποστολικὰ καὶ ὥσπερ σχολιογραφήσαντός τινος τὰ εἰρημένα ὑπὸ τοῦ διδασκάλου Or.*fr.in Heb.*ap.Eus.*h.e.*6.25.13(M.14.1309A).

σχόλιον, τό, 1. *interpretation, comment, short note*, ‡Ath.*dial. Trin.*2.5(M.28.1164D); Justn.*conf.*(p.80.5; M.86.1001D, referring to Cyr.*schol.inc.*13); Anast.S.*hod.*proem.(M.89.36B); **2.** *extract, passage quoted* (interpretation being called ἔλεγχος) σ. ἀπὸ τοῦ εὐαγγελίου τοῦ παρ' αὐτῷ τῷ Μαρκίωνι Epiph.*haer.*42.11 tit.(p.125.1; M.41. 728B); *ib.*(p.125.19; 728D).

***σχολίον, τό,** = σχολεῖον, *school* σ. τῶν παιδίων Leont.N.*v.Sym.* 31(M.93.1703C).

***σχολιοποι-έω,** *make with explanatory notes* ἡ ∼ηθεῖσα σύντομος Epiph.*haer.*42.11(p.124.22; M.41.728A).

σῴζ-ω, *save, preserve*;

A. in gen.; **1.** from sickness or afflictions, *1Clem.*59.4; Just.*dial.* 112.1(M.6.733B); δι' οὗ σημείου ἐσῴζοντο οἱ ὀφιόδηκτοι *ib.*94.1(700B); *Ev.Thom.*A 18.2(p.149); τίς οὖν ἡ διαφορὰ τοῦ ∼εσθαι καὶ τοῦ ῥύεσθαι; ὅτι τῆς σωτηρίας μὲν κυρίως οἱ ἀσθενοῦντες χρῄζουσι, τοῦ ῥυσθῆναι δὲ οἱ ἐν τῇ αἰχμαλωσίᾳ κατεχόμενοι Bas.*hom.in Ps.*7(1.99A; M.29.232B); **2.** in health, esp. as a salutation ∼εσθε *Barn.*21.9; σωθείης *Apophth. Mac.Aeg.*3.3(M.34.240C); *Apophth.Patr.*(M.65.240A); **3.** ? *come safely*; hence simply *come* ἄρχεται τὸ λυχνικόν· καὶ ὅπου σῴσει ἡ ἀπόλυσις, ἐσθίομεν *Const.Stud.*30(M.99.1716C).

B. ref. salvation; **1.** by God τοῦτο γὰρ τὸ μέγιστον καὶ βασιλικώτατον ἔργον τοῦ θεοῦ, ∼ειν τὴν ἀνθρωπότητα Clem.*paed.*1.12(p.150. 4; M.8.369C); Or.*princ.*3.1.7(p.206.8; M.11.260C); Ath.*inc.*44.1(M. 25.173B); Father, Clem.*prot.*10(p.68.30; M.8.208A); by Christ, Or. *hom.17.5 in Jer.*(p.149.6,7; M.13.461A); *Lit.*ap.*Const.App.*8.10.19,21; Χριστὸς...∼ει τοὺς πιστεύοντας ἐν ἀνθρώπου μορφῇ ‡Ath.*Apoll.*2.7(M. 26.1144B); τὸ ∼ειν τὸν κόσμον οὐκέτι διὰ τοῦ λόγου ἐλέχθη, ἀλλὰ διὰ τοῦ μονογενοῦς υἱοῦ ‡Ath.*Ar.*4.20(p.67.5; M.26.497C); Christ's body ἦλθεν ἐπὶ ταύτην [sc. τὴν γῆν] φορέσας σῶμα τὸ σῶσαν Or.*hom.7.3 in Jer.*(p.54.26; 333D); through men μὴ μόνον ἑαυτὸν θέλειν ∼εσθαι, ἀλλὰ καὶ πάντας τοὺς ἀδελφούς *M.Polyc.*1.2; πολὺν μισθὸν λήψῃ, ἐὰν σωθῇ διὰ σοῦ ψυχή Ath.*virg.*9(p.43.13; M.28.261C); οὐδὲ γὰρ αὐτὸς τοῦτο πιστεύειν ἔχω, ὅτι ∼εσθαι ἔνεστι τὸν οὐδὲν εἰς τὴν τοῦ πλησίον κάμνοντα σωτηρίαν Chrys.*sac.*6.10(p.159.17; 1.429E); Law unable to save, Meth.*symp.*10.3(p.152.2,3; M.18.197A); although intended to do so μὴ ἐπὶ τῷ βλάψαι ἀλλ' ἐπὶ τῷ σῶσαι ἐδόθη Meth.*res.*2.2(p.332. 6; M.18.300A); ὁ νόμος...οὐ ∼ει Chrys.*hom.17.3 in Rom.*(9.624D); **2.** objects: God's will to save all men μιμοῦ τὸν θεόν· εἰ πάντας θέλει σωθῆναι, εἰκότως ὑπὲρ ἁπάντων δεῖ εὔχεσθαι· εἰ πάντας αὐτὸς ἠθέλησε σωθῆναι, θέλε καὶ σύ id.*hom.7.2 in 1Tim.*(11.585B); *ib.4.1*(568A); few saved πόσους οἴεσθε ἐν τῇ πόλει τῇ ἡμετέρᾳ εἶναι τοὺς ∼ομένους;... οὐκ ἔστιν ἐν τοσαύταις μυριάσιν ἑκατὸν εὑρεῖν τοὺς ∼ομένους· ἀλλὰ καὶ ὑπὲρ τούτων ἀμφισβητῶ id.*hom.24.4 in Ac.*(9.198B); ὀδύρομαι, ἐννοῶν ὅσον πλῆθος ἀπόλλυται τῶν ∼ομένων id.*hom.in Rom.12:20*(3. 158E); including simpler people ∼εσθαι χρὴ καὶ τοὺς ἁπλουστέρους προσιόντας κατὰ δύναμιν τῇ θεοσεβείᾳ Or.*Cels.*6.13(p.83.31; M.11. 1309C); not the powerful but the willing, Gr.Naz.*or.*32.22(M.36. 200B); the soul ψυχὴ γὰρ οὐκ αὐτὴ τὸ πνεῦμα ἔσωσεν, ἐσώθη δὲ ὑπ' αὐτοῦ Tat.*orat.*13(p.14.9; M.6.833B); the flesh, Meth.*res.*1.51(p.305. 5; M.18.281A); τί καὶ περισσῶς σάρκα ἐφόρει, ἣν οὔτε σῶσαι οὔτε ἀναστῆσαι προῄρητο; *ib.*2.18(p.370.4; 284C); the body οὐχ ὡς ταύτης [sc. ψυχῆς] ∼ομένης μόνης, ἀλλὰ...καὶ τὸ σῶμα κοινωνήσει τῆς σωτηρίας Chrys.*hom.15.2 in 1Cor.*(10.127D); flesh assumed by Christ πρώτη τῶν ἄλλων ἐσώθη καὶ ἐλευθερώθη ἡ ἐκείνου σάρξ, ὡς αὐτοῦ τοῦ λόγου σῶμα γενομένη, καὶ λοιπὸν ἡμεῖς, ὡς σύσσωμοι τυγχάνοντες, κατ' ἐκεῖνο ~όμεθα Ath.*Ar*.2.61(M.26.277B); saints of OT οἱ πρὸ Μωϋσέως γενόμενοι δίκαιοι καὶ πατριάρχαι...~ονται ἐν τῇ τῶν μακαρίων κληρονομίᾳ Just.*dial*.67.7(M.6.632A); ἐνῆν γὰρ καὶ μὴ ὁμολογήσαντας τὸν Χριστὸν τότε σωθῆναι. οὐ γὰρ τοῦτο ἀπῃτεῖτο παρ' αὐτῶν, ἀλλὰ τὸ μὴ εἰδωλολατρεῖν, καὶ τὸ τὸν ἀληθινὸν θεὸν εἰδέναι Chrys.*hom*.*36.3 in Mt*.(7.411A); **3.** means of salvation: Christ's Inc. and suffering ταῦτα γὰρ πάντα ἔπαθεν δι' ἡμᾶς ἵνα σωθῶμεν Ign.*Smyrn*.2; εἰ γὰρ μὴ ἦλθεν ἐν σαρκί, πῶς ἂν ἐσώθησαν οἱ ἄνθρωποι βλέποντες αὐτόν; *Barn*. 5.10; *M.Polyc*.17.2; cf. Χριστὸς...ἦν θεὸς καὶ ἔπασχεν δι' ἡμᾶς αὐτὸς ὢν πατήρ, ἵνα καὶ σῶσαι ἡμᾶς δυνηθῇ Hipp.*Noët*.2(p.237.29; M.10.805C); Ath.*hom.in Mt.11*:27(M.25.213A); κτίσμα δὲ ὑπὸ κτίσματος οὐκ ἄν ποτε ἐσώθη id.*ep.Adelph*.8(M.26.1081D); μέρος δὲ κόσμου κόσμον σῶσαι οὐ δύναται ‡Ath.*Apoll*.2.7(M.26.1144A); through faith διὰ τῆς ἐν τούτῳ πίστεως πάντες...οἱ πιστεύοντες ~εσθαι δύνωνται Ath.*Ar*. 2.81(M.26.320A); Gr.Naz.*carm*.2.1.11.1229(M.37.1113A); Chrys.*hom*. *8.1 in Rom*.(9.497A); by grace ἡ χάρις ~ει id.*hom*.*45.1 in Ac*. (9.337C); with man's co-operation ἡ θεία χάρις τῇ ἀνθρωπίνῃ κιρνωμένη προθυμίᾳ ~ει τὸν ἄνθρωπον Isid.Pel.*epp*.4.51(M.78.1101A); cf. δεῖ γὰρ τὸ ἐφ' ἡμῖν εἶναι καὶ τὸ ἐκ θεοῦ ~εσθαι Gr.Naz.*or*.37.13(M.36.297D); ἐν τῇ γνώμῃ κεῖται τῇ ἡμετέρᾳ, τὸ σωθῆναι καὶ ἀπολέσθαι Chrys.*hom*.*47.4 in Jo*.(8.281C); Anast.S.*qu.et resp*.55(M.89.617Df.); orthodox belief εἴ τις θέλει σωθῆναι, πρὸ πάντων χρὴ αὐτῷ τὴν καθολικὴν κρατῆσαι πίστιν ‡Ath.*symb*.1(M.28.1581A); through faith and works οὐ γὰρ τοὺς μόνον λέγοντας, ἀλλὰ τοὺς καὶ τὰ ἔργα πράττοντας σωθήσεσθαι Just.*1apol*.16.8(M.6.353B); οὐχὶ ἔχοντας ἔργα ἀπώσατο, ἀλλὰ προδεδομένους ἀπὸ τῶν ἔργων χάριτι ἔσωσεν, ὥστε μηδένα λοιπὸν ἔχειν καυχᾶσθαι Chrys.*hom*.*4.2 in Eph*.(11.28C); οὐκ ἐνὸν ἀπὸ πίστεως μόνον σωθῆναι· χρὴ γὰρ τῇ πίστει κρίνεσθαι τὰς πράξεις Isid.Pel.*epp*.4.65(M.78.1121C); σεσώσμεθα γὰρ 'οὐκ ἐξ ἔργων δικαιοσύνης...' ἀλλ' ἐξ ἡμερότητος τοῦ θεοῦ καὶ πατρός Cyr.*Abac*.42(3.557C); in view ascribed to Apoll. ἀλλὰ λέγετε, τῇ ὁμοιώσει καὶ τῇ μιμήσει ~εσθαι τοὺς πιστεύοντας, καὶ οὐ τῇ ἀνακαινίσει καὶ τῇ ἀπαρχῇ ‡Ath.*Apoll*.2.11(M.26.1149C); by mediation of BMV οὐδεὶς γὰρ ὁ ~όμενος εἰ μὴ διὰ σοῦ, πανάμωμε Germ.CP *or*.9(M.98.380B); **4.** salvation being from spiritual death, Just.*dial*.105.6(M.6.721C); Or.*hom*. *16.5 in Jer*.(p.137.29; M.13.445B); and physical death, Meth.*symp*. 9.2(p.116.20; M.18.181B); Ath.*inc.et c.Ar*.5(M.26.992A); sin, Just. *dial*.111.4(M.6.733A); **5.** Gnost. doctrine of those naturally predisposed to salvation φύσει ~ομένου, ὡς Οὐαλεντῖνος βούλεται, τινὸς καὶ φύσει πιστοῦ καὶ ἐκλεκτοῦ ὄντος, ὡς Βασιλείδης νομίζει Clem.*str*. 5.1(p.327.26; M.9.12C); τὸ...πνευματικὸν φύσει ~όμενον Clem.*exc. Thdot*.56(p.125.18; M.9.685C); **6.** perf. ptcpl. pass., of priests who have not lapsed into heresy, Thdr.Stud.*epp*.2.103(M.99.1617C); *ib*. 2.211(1637C); *ib*.2.215(1649A).

[*]**σωκάρην, τό,** = σωκάριον, dimin. of σόκος, *lasso*, Jo.Mal. *chron*.14 p.364(M.97.541B).

***σωκίζω,** *catch with a lasso, noose*, Thphn.*chron*.p.184(M.108. 480C).

§**σῶκος, ὁ,** = [*]σόκος, *lasso, noose*, Thphn.*chron*.p.184(M.108. 480C).

***Σωκρατίτης, ὁ,** *disciple of Socrates*, name sometimes given to certain Gnostics οἱ καὶ Στρατιωτικοὶ καὶ Φιβιωνῖται, παρὰ δέ τισι Σεκουνδιανῖται, παρ' ἄλλοις δὲ Σ. Epiph.*anc*.13(p.21.17; M.43.40B); Jo.D.*haer*.26(M.94.693A).

***σωλεία, ἡ,** v. *σολαία.

σωλήν, ὁ, *channel*, in Valent. image of Inc. τὸν διὰ Μαρίας διοδεύσαντα, καθάπερ ὕδωρ διὰ σωλῆνος ὁδεύει Iren.*haer*.1.7.2(M.7. 513A); Adam.*dial*.5.9(p.190.25; M.11.1845A); Cyr.H.*catech*.4.9; Chrys.*hom*.*4.3 in Mt*.(7.51A); Thdt.*ep*.145(4.1248) cit. s. πάροδος; Martin.ap.CLater.*act*.3(H.3.772B).

***σωληνοδοχεῖον, τό,** *pipe container*; part of a musical instrument, Sever.*Abr*.4(M.56.558).

σωληνοειδῶς, *like a pipe*, Gr.Nyss.*hom.opif*.30.25(M.44.249C).

σῶμα, τό, *body*;

I. of man; **A.** earthly; **1.** in rel. to soul; **a.** together with soul constituting man, Eus.*p.e*.6.6(246A; M.21.417D); σ. τέλειον τουτέστιν ἄνθρωπον τέλειον ψυχῇ καὶ σ. Epiph.*anc*.117(p.145.7; M.43. 229B); Nemes.*nat.hom*.1(M.40.504A); Cyr.*inc.unigen*.(5^1.697C); this the scriptural view, Thdt.*eran*.2(4.73); **b.** their connexion ἔσπαρται κατὰ πάντων τῶν τοῦ σ. μελῶν ἡ ψυχή...οἰκεῖ μὲν ἐν τῷ σ. ψυχή, οὐκ ἔστι δὲ ἐκ τοῦ σ. *Diogn*.6.2,3; ἐν τῷ σ. ἐστιν ἡ ψυχή Just. *dial*.4.4(M.6.485A); δέμας κέκληται τὸ σ. διὰ τὸ δεδέσθαι τὴν ψυχὴν ἐν τῷ σ. Or.*princ*.1.8.1(p.97.3); ἐπὰν...ἐν σ. λέγηται [sc. ἡ ψυχή] εἶναι, οὐχ ὡς ἐν τόπῳ, τῷ σ. ... ἀλλ' ὡς ἐν σχέσει Nemes.*nat.hom*.3 (M.40.600A); ἡ δὲ ψυχὴ συνδέδεται τῷ σ. ὅλη ὅλῳ, καὶ οὐ μέρος μέρει· καὶ οὐ περιέχεται ὑπ' αὐτοῦ, ἀλλὰ περιέχει αὐτό, ὥσπερ πῦρ σίδηρον Jo.D.*f.o*.1.3(M.94.853A); created simultaneously μήτε ψυχὴν πρὸ τοῦ σ. μήτε χωρὶς ψυχῆς τὸ σ. ... ἀλλὰ μίαν ἀμφοτέρων ἀρχήν Gr.Nyss. *hom.opif*.29.3(M.44.236B); οὐδὲ προϋπάρχουσιν αἱ ψυχαὶ τῶν σ., ὡς οἱ Μανιχαῖοι δογματίζουσι ‡Ath.*qu.Ant*.16(M.28.608A); ἅμα δὲ τὸ σ. καὶ ἡ ψυχὴ πέπλασται· οὐ τὸ μὲν πρότερον, τὸ δὲ ὕστερον, κατὰ τὰ Ὠριγένους ληρήματα Jo.D.*f.o*.2.12(M.94.921A); φάσκοντες [sc. Origenists] τὴν μὲν ψυχὴν προϋπάρχειν τοῦ σ., τὸ δὲ σ. τοὺς δερματίνους εἶναι χιτῶνας *Schol*. in Leont.et Jo.*sacr*.2(M.86.2036A); **c.** in tripartite constitution of man ὁ ἄνθρωπος συνέστηκεν ἐκ σ. καὶ ψυχῆς καὶ πνεύματος Or.*princ*.4.2.4(p.313.2; M.11.365A); ἐκ τριῶν εἶναι τὸν ἄνθρωπον...πνεύματος καὶ ψυχῆς καὶ σ. Apoll.*fr*.88(p.226. 25)ap.Gr.Nyss.*Apoll*.46(M.45.1233C); **2.** in rel. to flesh οὐκ ἔστι τὸ αὐτὸ [sc. σ. καὶ σάρξ]. μὴ δυνάμεθα τὸν οὐρανὸν σάρκα ὀνομάσαι, σ. δὲ ὀνομάζομεν Adam.*dial*.5.2(p.176.19; M.11.1833A); ἕως...ἐστι τὸ σ. τὸ ἀνθρώπινον σὰρξ καὶ αἷμα Cyr.*1Cor*.15:50(p.315.18; M.74.912B); τὴν δὲ σάρκα [i.e. of Christ] τί νοοῦμεν; σ. μόνον, ὡς Ἀρείῳ καὶ Εὐνομίῳ δοκεῖ, ἢ σ. καὶ ψυχήν; σ. καὶ ψυχήν Thdt.*eran*.2(4.73); **3.** its mortality ἔστι δὲ τὸ σ. φύσει θνητόν...οὐ γὰρ ἡ ψυχή ἐστιν ἡ ἀποθνήσκουσα· ἀλλὰ διὰ τὴν ταύτης ἀναχώρησιν ἀποθνήσκει τὸ σ. Ath.*gent*.33(M.25.65B,C); τὸ μὲν σ. θνητόν ἐστι καὶ ἐπίκηρον Chrys. *hom.in Mt.7*:14(3.25D); θνητὸν μέν σου τὸ σ., ἀθάνατος δὲ ἡ ψυχή Nil. *epp*.4.1(M.79.548D); overcame death by virtue of Inc. τὸ ἡμέτερον σ., τῇ θεότητι συναφθέν, κρεῖττον ἐγένετο τῆς τοῦ θανάτου ἐπικρατείας Bas.*ep*.262.2(3.404B; M.32.973C); can be translated and ascend οὐδὲν ἐνεπόδισεν αὐτοῖς [sc. Enoch and Elijah] τὸ σ. πρὸς τὴν μετάθεσιν καὶ ἀνάληψιν Iren.*haer*.5.5.1(M.7.1134C); Ἠλίας ὅλος ἀνελήφθη ἐν σ. καὶ οὐκ εἶδεν ἄχρι τῆς δεῦρο θάνατον Epiph.*anc*.98(p.119.9; M. 43.193D); ref. Adam's Fall τὸ σ. αὐτοῦ γέγονεν οὐ μόνον θνητὸν ἀλλὰ καὶ παθητόν Isid.Pel.*epp*.4.204(M.78.1292B); cf. οὐχ ὅμοιον δὲ μορφὴν καὶ σ. ἔχουσι τοῖς ἐν τῷδε τῷ κόσμῳ σ. Clem.*exc.Thdot*.10(p.109. 22; M.9.660C); **4.** its moral nature; **a.** evil acc. Manich. theory τοῦ μὲν φωτὸς εἶναι μέρος τὴν ἐν ἀνθρώποις ψυχήν, τοῦ δὲ σκότους τὸ σ. καὶ τὸ τῆς ὕλης δημιούργημα Hegem.*Arch*.7(p.9.16; M.10. 1437A); thought by some to be given to man as punishment for sin, Meth.*res*.1.32(p.267.27); this incorrect, because sins are committed not by, but through, body, Ath.*inc*.56.3(M.25.196B); Cyr.H. *catech*.4.23; ‡Bas.*const*.2.2(2.542B,C; M.31.1341B); ὅτι δὲ οὐδὲ κακίας αἴτιον τῇ ψυχῇ τὸ σ., δῆλον ἐκ τοῦ δυνατὸν εἶναι καὶ ἄνευ σ. παρυφίστασθαι κακίαν, ὥσπερ ἐν δαίμοσι Dion.Ar.*d.n*.4.27(M.3.728D); and because of his body man can repent ἀνεπίδεκτος μετανοίας ὅτι καὶ ἀσώματος [sc. ἄγγελος]. ὁ γὰρ ἄθρωπος διὰ τὴν τοῦ σ. ἀσθένειαν μετανοίας ἔτυχεν Jo.D.*f.o*.2.3(M.94.868B); **b.** morally indifferent ἐν τούτῳ ἡ ἀρετὴ τοῦ σ., ἐν τῷ εἴκειν τῇ ψυχῇ, ἐπεὶ καθ' ἑαυτὴν οὔτε κακὴ οὔτε καλή Chrys.*hom*.*5.4 in Eph*.(11.37D); **5.** its sanctity μὴ νομίσῃς ὅτι ...τὸ σ. γέγονε διὰ συνουσιασμόν. ... ἵνα ναὸς ᾖ τῷ κυρίῳ Or.*comm. in 1Cor*.6:13(*JTS* 9 p.370); ἵνα ὦσιν ἅγιοι σ. καὶ ψυχῇ *Lit*.ap.*Const. App*.8.11.4; after death in case of saints' bodies τὰ σ. τῶν ἁγίων ὡς τιμηθῆναι καὶ μήτε κενὰ γενέσθαι ἐνεργείας μήτε δυνάμεως θείας Serap. *Man*.11(p.34; M.40.909A); Cyr.H.*catech*.18.16; *Const.App*.6.30.5; τὰ τῶν ἁγίων σ. καὶ πηγὰς καὶ ῥίζας καὶ μύρα καλῶ πνευματικά Chrys. *pan.Eust.Ant*.2(2.605C); κἂν τοῖς μαρτυρίοις δὲ ἡ ἐφεδρεύουσα τοῖς σ. τῶν ἁγίων χάρις τούτους [sc. δαίμονας] βασανίζει Isid.Pel.*epp*.2.85(M. 78.528B); εἰ γὰρ ἐν ψυχῇ καὶ σ. τὴν θεοφιλῆ ζωὴν ὁ κεκοιμημένος ἐβίω, τίμιον ἔσται μετὰ τῆς ὁσίας ψυχῆς καὶ τὸ συναθλῆσαν αὐτῇ σ. κατὰ τοὺς ἱεροὺς ἱδρῶτας Dion.Ar.*e.h*.7.3.9(M.3.565B); οἱ γὰρ ἅγιοι καὶ ζῶντες πεπληρωμένοι ἦσαν πνεύματος ἁγίου, καὶ τελευτησάντων αὐτῶν ἡ χάρις τοῦ ἁγίου πνεύματος ἀνεκφοιτήτως ἔνεστι καὶ ταῖς ψυχαῖς καὶ τοῖς σ. ἐν τοῖς τάφοις Jo.D.*imag*.1.19(M.94.1249D); **6.** ref. effect of sacraments δεῦρο δὴ ἐπιφοιτήσας ὁ Χριστός, κουφότερον ἡμῖν τὸ σ. διὰ τοῦ βαπτίσματος πεποίηκε, τῷ πτερῷ τοῦ πνεύματος διεγείρων Isid.Pel. *epp*.4.204(M.78.1292B); μὴ εἶναι δυνατὸν ἐν ἀθανασίᾳ γενέσθαι τὸ ἡμέτερον σ., εἰ μὴ διὰ τῆς πρὸς τὸ ἀθάνατον κοινωνίας ἐν μετουσίᾳ τῆς ἀφθαρσίας γενόμενον Gr.Nyss.*or.catech*.37(p.144.6; M.45.93C); τὸ παχὺ τοῦτο καὶ γεῶδες σ. διὰ παχυτέρας, καὶ συγγενοῦς ἁγιάζεσθαι μεταλήψεως καὶ καλεῖσθαι πρὸς ἀφθαρσίαν Cyr.*Jo*.4.2(4.362B); εἰς φυλακτήριον ψυχῆς καὶ σ. Jo.D.*f.o*.4.13(M.94.1148A); **7.** final destiny; **a.** Origenist view ἡ ψυχὴ...τάχα κατ' ἀξίαν τῆς ἐπὶ πλεῖον ἀποπτώσεως τῆς κακίας ἐνδύεται σ. ⟨τοι⟩οὔδε ἢ τοιοῦδε ἀλόγου ζῴου Or.*princ*. 1.8.4(p.104.13; M.11.180B); εἰ δὲ τὰ ὑποτεταγμένα τῷ Χριστῷ ὑποταγήσεται ἐπὶ τέλει καὶ τῷ θεῷ, πάντες ἀποθήσονται τὰ σ.· καὶ οἶμαι ὅτι τότε εἰς τὸ μὴ ὂν ἔσται ἀνάλυσις τῆς τῶν σωμάτων φύσεως, ὑποστησομένης δεύτερον, ἐὰν πάλιν λογικὰ ὑποκαταβῇ *ib*.2.3.3(p.118.5,6); ὅτι τῶν λογικῶν τὰ ἁμαρτήσαντα καὶ διὰ τοῦτο ἐκπεσόντα τῆς ἐν ᾗ ἦσαν καταστάσεως κατὰ τὴν ἀναλογίαν τῶν οἰκείων ἁμαρτημάτων τιμωρίας χάριν σώμασιν ἐνεβλήθη καὶ καθαιρόμενα πάλιν ἀνάγονται ἐν ᾗ πρότερον ἦσαν καταστάσει παντελῶς ἀποτιθέμενα τὰ σ. καὶ πάλιν ἐκ δευτέρου καὶ τρίτου καὶ πλεονάκις διαφόροις ἐμβάλλονται σώμασι πρὸς τιμωρίας Justn.*Or*.(p.190.20ff.; M.86.949A); condemned εἴ τις λέγει, τὰ λογικὰ τὰ τῆς θείας ἀγάπης ἀποψυγέντα σώμασι παχυτέροις τοῖς καθ' ἡμᾶς ἐνδυθῆναι καὶ ἀνθρώπους ὀνομασθῆναι· τὰ δὲ ἐπὶ τὸ ἄκρον τῆς κακίας ἐληλακότα ψυχροῖς καὶ ζοφεροῖς ἐνδυθῆναι σ. καὶ δαίμονας ἢ πνευματικὰ τῆς πονηρίας εἶναί τε καὶ καλεῖσθαι, ἀνάθεμα ἔστω CCP(543)*anath*.4; εἴ τις λέγει ὅτι ἡ μέλλουσα κρίσις ἀναίρεσιν παντελῆ τῶν σ. σημαίνει,...ἀνάθεμα ἔστω *ib*.11; **b.** resurrection κέκληκε δὲ ὁ θεὸς εἰς ζωὴν καὶ ἀνάστασιν τὸν ἄνθρωπον, οὐ τὸ μέρος ἀλλὰ τὸ ὅλον κέκληκεν, ὅπερ ἐστὶ τὴν ψυχὴν καὶ τὸ σ. †Just.*fr.res.* (p.46; M.6.1585C); οὐ γὰρ ψυχῶν ἀνάστασίς ἐστι τῶν μὴ πεσουσῶν, ἀλλὰ σ. τῶν τεθαμμένων Epiph.*haer*.64.63(p.502.16; M.41.1180A); εἰ γὰρ μὴ ἀνίσταται σ., οὐκ ἀνίσταται ὁ ἄνθρωπος· ὁ γὰρ ἄνθρωπος οὐκ ἔστι ψυχὴ μόνον, ἀλλὰ ψυχὴ καὶ σ. Chrys.*res.mort*.7(2.434C); μή μοι λέγε, πῶς δύναται ἀναστῆναι τὸ σ. πάλιν καὶ γενέσθαι ἄφθαρτον; ὅταν γὰρ ἡ τοῦ θεοῦ δύναμις ἐργάζηται, τὸ πῶς μὴ προσκείσθω *ib*.(433D); πάντες ἄνθρωποι ἀναστήσονται σὺν τοῖς ἑαυτῶν σ. ‡Ath.*symb*.1(M.28.1584C); ref. future punishment τοῖς αὐτοῖς σ. μετὰ τῶν ψυχῶν γινομένων καὶ αἰωνίαν κόλασιν κολασθησομένων Just.*1apol*.8.4(M.6.337C); ἡ ψυχὴ...ἀνίσταται...σὺν τῷ σ. θάνατον διὰ τιμωρίας ἐν ἀθανασίᾳ λαμβάνουσα Tat.*orat*.13(p.14.14; M.6.833A); μήτε τὴν ψυχὴν μόνην δεῖ κομίσασθαι τὰ ἐπίχειρα τῶν μετὰ τοῦ σ. εἰργασμένων...μήτε τὸ σ. μόνον Athenag.*res*.18(pp.70.30,71.1; M.6.1009D); *ib*.21(p.74.16; 1016B); εἰς ἀνάστασιν νεκρῶν καὶ κρίσιν δικαίαν ψυχῶν καὶ σ. *Symb*.ap.Epiph. *anc*.119(p.149.3; M.43.236B); εἰς ἀνάστασιν νεκρῶν, εἰς κρίσιν αἰώνιον ψυχῶν τε καὶ σ. ‡Ath.*interpr*.(p.66.27; M.26.1232B).

B. of resurrection body; **1.** identical with earthly τὰ νεκρούμενα καὶ εἰς γῆν βαλλόμενα πάλιν ἀπολήψεσθαι ἑαυτῶν σ. προσδοκῶμεν Just.*1apol*.18.6(M.6.356B); τῶν μὲν ἀνισταμένων σ. ἐκ τῶν οἰκείων μερῶν πάλιν συνισταμένων Athenag.*res*.7(p.55.14; M.6.985C); ὡς ἑκάστῳ σ. ἡ ἰδία ψυχὴ ἀποδοθήσεται Iren.*fr*.12(M.7.1236A); ἅπερ ποτὲ ἐχαρακτηρίζετο ἐν τῇ σαρκί, τοῦτο χαρακτηρισθήσεται ἐν τῷ πνευματικῷ σ. Or.*sel.in Ps*.1:5(M.12.1096B); cf. κἂν ῥευστὴ ἦν ἡ φύσις τοῦ σ., τῷ τὸ εἶδος τὸ χαρακτηρίζον τὸ σῶμα ταυτὸν εἶναι *ib*. (1093B); οἱ αἱρετικοὶ...λέγουσιν ὅτι ἕτερον σ. πίπτει καὶ ἕτερον σῶμα ἀνίσταται Chrys.*hom.41.2 in 1Cor*.(10.387E); ποῖον δὲ τὸ σ. τῆς ταπεινώσεως ἡμῶν; τουτὶ τὸ ἐκ γῆς...ἔσται δὲ ὁ μετασχηματισμὸς οὐκ εἰς ἑτέραν τινὰ φύσιν ἀποκομίζων ἡμᾶς, ἐσόμεθα γὰρ ὅπερ ἐσμέν, τουτέστιν ἄνθρωποι, πλὴν ἀμείνους ἀσυγκρίτως· ἄφθαρτοι γὰρ καὶ ἀνώλεθροι, καὶ πρός γε τούτῳ δεδοξασμένοι Cyr.*1Cor*.15:51(p.316.29; M.74.913A); Thdt.*eran*.2(4.121); **2.** but changed to become incorruptible τὸ γὰρ σ. τοῦτο ἐγείρεται, οὐ τοιοῦτον μένον ἀσθενές, ἀλλ' αὐτὸ τοῦτο ἐγείρεται· ἐνδυσάμενον δὲ τὴν ἀφθαρσίαν μεταποιεῖται, ὥσπερ σίδηρος πυρὶ προσομιλήσας γίνεται πῦρ...ἐγείρεται μὲν οὖν τοῦτο τὸ σ., ἀλλ' οὐ μένει τοιοῦτον, ἀλλὰ μένει αἰώνιον, οὐκέτι τροφῶν τοιούτων χρείαν ἔχει πρὸς ζωήν, οὐδὲ κλιμάκων πρὸς ἀνάβασιν· γίνεται γὰρ πνευματικόν, θαυμάσιόν τι, καὶ οἷον εἰπεῖν κατ' ἀξίαν οὐκ ἔχομεν Cyr.H.*catech*.18.18; ἐγειρόμεθα τοίνυν αἰώνια μὲν πάντες ἔχοντες τὰ σ., οὐ πάντες δὲ ὅμοια. ἀλλ' εἰ μέν τίς ἐστι δίκαιος, λαμβάνει σ. ἐπουράνιον, ἵνα δύνηται μετὰ ἀγγέλων ἀναστρέφειν ἐπαξίως. εἰ δέ τις ἁμαρτωλός ἐστι, λαμβάνει σ. αἰώνιον, ὑπομονητικὸν τιμωρίας ἁμαρτιῶν ...οὐδὲν γὰρ χωρὶς σ. ἡμῖν πέπρακται *ib*.18.19; cf.*ib*.4.31; ὅμοια τῇ τῶν φωστήρων καὶ ἀστέρων δόξῃ οὐ πάντων τῶν ἀνισταμένων τὰ σ., ἀλλ' ἢ μόνον τῶν εὖ βεβιωκότων καὶ σωφρονησάντων· κἂν γὰρ τὰ τῶν φαύλων σ. ἄφθαρτα ἐγείρονται, ἀλλ' οὖν στεροῦνται τῆς τῶν ἐπουρανίων δόξης Didym.*1Cor*.15:41(p.9.27f.); Chrys.*res.mort*.6(2.431D); οὐ τὴν σάρκα ἀποθέσθαι βουλόμεθα, φησίν, ἀλλὰ τὴν φθοράν, οὐ τὸ σ. ἀλλὰ τὸν θάνατον *ib*.(432B); τὰ σ. τῶν ἁμαρτωλῶν ἄφθαρτα ἀνίστανται καὶ ἀθάνατα· ἀλλ' ἡ τιμὴ αὕτη ἐφόδιον αὐτοῖς κολάσεως γίνεται καὶ τιμωρίας· ἄφθαρτα γὰρ ἀνίσταται, ἵνα διαπαντὸς καίηται. ἐπειδὴ γὰρ τὸ πῦρ ἄσβεστόν ἐστι ἐκεῖνο, τοιούτων αὐτῷ δεῖ καὶ σ. μηδέποτε δαπανωμένων *ib*.8(435A); ἐκείνῳ, τῷ καθημένῳ ἐν δεξιᾷ τοῦ πατρός, σύμμορφον τοῦτο τὸ σ. γίνεται id.*hom.13.2 in Phil*.(11.300B); cf.id.*delic*.6(3.343D,E); αὐτὸ...τὸ σ. τὸ φθειρόμενον καὶ διαλυόμενον, αὐτὸ ἀναστήσεται ἄφθαρτον Jo.D.*f.o*.4.27(M.94.1220A); ref. view ascribed to Or. οὐχὶ ἐναλλαγὴ τοῦ σ. εἰς σφαιροειδὲς σ., καθώς τισι πλανηθεῖσιν ἔδοξεν Andr.Caes.*therap.fr*.2(p.166.10f.); **3.** meaning of σ. πνευματικόν (cf. ἀερώδης): ἀναγκαῖον χρῆσθαι σ. πνευματικοῖς, οὐχὶ τοῦ εἴδους τοῦ προτέρου ἀφανιζομένου, κἂν ἐπὶ τὸ ἐνδοξότερον γένηται αὐτοῦ ἡ τροπή Or.*sel.in Ps*.1:5(M.12.1093D); ὅτι δὲ ἔστι σ. ψυχικὸν καὶ ἔστι σ. πνευματικόν, οὐκ ἄλλο σῶμα πνευματικὸν καὶ ἄλλο ψυχικόν, ἀλλ' αὐτὸ ψυχικὸν αὐτὸ πνευματικόν Epiph.*haer*.64.63(p.502.20ff.; M.41.1180B); ἐπειδὴ δὲ ἡ τοῖς πάθεσιν ἐμμένουσα ψυχή, εἰκότως καὶ τὸ τῆς τοιαύτης ψυχῆς σ. ψυχικὸν καλεῖται. ἐὰν δὲ ὑπεραναβῇ τὴν παθητικὴν ἕξιν ἡ ψυχή, γίνεται πνευματική, καὶ λέγεται τὸ σ. τῆς τοιαύτης ψυχῆς τῆς συμπλεκομένης αὐτὸ πνευματικόν Didym.*1Cor*.15:44–46(p.10.21f.); δεδιψήκαμεν γὰρ οὐ τὴν τῶν σ. ἀπόθεσιν, οὔτε μὴν ταύτην εἶναί φαμεν τὴν λύτρωσιν· ἔσεσθαι δὲ προσδοκῶμεν τὸ σ. πνευματικόν, τουτέστιν ἀποβεβληκὸς εἰσάπαν φρόνημα τὸ σαρκικὸν καὶ γεῶδες, καὶ τῆς ἁμαρτίας τὸ κέντρον Cyr.*Rom*.8:23(p.217.26f.; M.74.824B); **4.** called mystical ἀετούς...τοὺς ὑψιπετεῖς καὶ τοῦ μυστικοῦ σ. ἐφιεμένους, ἐν τοῖς...εὐαγγελίοις ὠνόμασε Thdt.*provid*.5(4.550).

C. body of Moses identified with Israel ὅταν γὰρ περὶ τοῦ Μωϋσέως ἀκούσῃς σώματος ἐν τῷ νόμῳ, γραφῇ νόμιζέ σοι χαρακτηρίζεσθαι τὸν ὅλον Ἰσραηλίτην λαὸν Chrysipp.*enc.in Mich*.(p.93.9).

D. body of BMV οὐ μὴ ἴδῃ διαφθορὰν τὸ ὅσιον καὶ τίμιόν σου σ. *Dorm.BMV* 10(p.98); ἀμφοτέρων [sc. of Christ and BMV] σ. μὲν ἀφαντάστως ὑποδεξαμένων, διαφθορὰν δὲ μηδαμῶς ἐνεργησάντων Germ.CP *or*.6(M.98.345D); ἔσται τὸ τίμιόν σου σ. μετατιθέμενον ἐν τῷ παραδείσῳ, ἡ δὲ ἁγία σου ψυχὴ ἐν τοῖς οὐρανοῖς *Dorm.BMV* 39 (p.108); μετετέθη τὸ ἄμωμον καὶ τίμιον αὐτῆς σ. ἐν παραδείσῳ *ib*.48 (p.111); τὸ τίμιον σ. ... ἀπέθεντο ἐν μνημείῳ καινῷ...μετὰ δὲ τρίτην ἡμέραν ἀνοίξαντες τὴν σορὸν...ηὕραμεν μόνας τὰς σίνδονας, διότι μετετέθη [γὰρ] ὑπὸ τοῦ ἐξ αὐτῆς σαρκωθέντος Χριστοῦ τοῦ θεοῦ εἰς ἀέναον λῆξιν Jo.Thess.*dorm.BMV* A 14(p.401.28); εὗρον τὸ τάφον κενὸν καὶ οὐκ ἦν ἐν αὐτῷ τὸ σ. τῆς θεομήτορος *ib*.B 38(p.405.9); ὧν [sc. SS. Paul and Peter] ἐκ χειρῶν πάντων ἀποσκοπούντων τὸ ἄχραντον ἀφηρπάγη τῆς παρθένου σ. καὶ ὁ μὲν ἁρπάσας αὐτό, πᾶσιν ἄβλεπτος· θεὸς γὰρ ἦν ἀθεώρητος Germ.CP *or*.8(M.98.369C).

II. of Christ σ. γὰρ πιστεύομεν εἶναι τήν τε ἐκκλησίαν, καὶ τὸν ἅγιον ἄρτον, καὶ τὸ σταυρωθέν...διὰ γὰρ τὸ τοῦ αὐτοῦ πνεύματος μετασχεῖν τούτων ἕκαστον, τοῦ χρίσαντός τε τὸ σταυρωθὲν ἐκεῖνο, καὶ ἁγιάζοντος τοῦτον τὸν ἄρτον, καὶ τὴν ἐκκλησίαν πάλιν διὰ τῆς μεταλήψεως αὐτοῦ πᾶσαν ἁγιοποιοῦντος, σ. Χριστοῦ νοοῦνται πάντα· ὡς Χριστοῦ οὖν, ἕν· εἰ μέντοι ἁπλῶς τάδε ὡς σώματα κρίνομεν, τρία εἰσί, τό τε Χριστοῦ ἰδικόν, καὶ ὁ ἄρτος, καὶ ἡ ἐκκλησία Leont.H.*Nest*.3.12 (M.86.1648Af.).

A. his human body; **1.** ref. various opinions οὐ παύονται ζυγομαχοῦντες περὶ τῆς ἐνανθρωπήσεως τοῦ κυρίου· οἱ μὲν ἀνειληφέναι σ., οἱ δὲ ἀσώματον αὐτοῦ τὴν ἐπιδημίαν γεγενῆσθαι διοριζόμενοι· καὶ οἱ μὲν παθητὸν ἐσχηκέναι τὸ σ., οἱ δὲ φαντασίᾳ τινὶ τὴν διὰ σώματος οἰκονομίαν πληροῦν· καὶ ἄλλοι χοϊκόν, ἄλλοι δὲ ἐπουράνιον σ. Bas.*ep*. 260.8(3.400C,D; M.32.965B); **2.** as real ἀληθινὸν ἦν τὸ σ. ... ἐπειδὴ ταυτὸν ἦν τῷ ἡμετέρῳ Ath.*ep.Epict*.7(p.11.14; M.26.1061B); τὸ...σ. ...κοινὸν ἔχει τοῖς πᾶσι τὴν οὐσίαν (σ. γὰρ ἦν ἀνθρώπινον) id.*inc*.20. 4(M.25.132A); **a.** created εἴ τις λέγει ἄκτιστον τὸ σ. τοῦ Χριστοῦ, καὶ ὁμολογεῖ αὐτὸν τὸν ἄκτιστον τὸν θεὸν λόγον ἐκ τῆς κτιστῆς ἀνθρωπότητος τὴν σάρκωσιν καὶ τὴν ἐνανθρώπησιν ἐπιδειξάμενον, καθὼς γέγραπται, ἀνάθεμα ἔστω Gr.Thaum.*fid.cap*.12(p.147.19; M.10.1128A); τίς γάρ, ἄκτιστον ἀκούων τὸ τοῦ κυρίου σ., ἑαυτὸν δὲ ποιηθέντα καὶ κτισθέντα εἰδώς, οὐκ ἐννοηθήσεται ψευδεῖς μὲν εἶναι τὰς ἁγίας γραφάς, ἑαυτὸν δὲ μὴ ἔχειν πρὸς Χριστὸν κοινωνίαν; ‡Ath.*Apoll*.1.4(M.26.1100B); Didym.(‡Bas.)*Eun*.5(1.298B; M.29.716B); but Γαϊανῖται, ἤτοι Ἰουλιανισταὶ ἄλλοι, οἵτινες καλοῦνται καὶ Ἀκτιστῆται· λέγουσι γὰρ ὅτι οὐ μόνον ἄφθαρτον ἐξ αὐτῆς τῆς ἑνώσεως, ἀλλὰ καὶ ἄκτιστον γεγονέναι τὸ τοῦ κυρίου σ. Tim.CP *haer*.(M.86.44C); **b.** hungering εἰ μηδὲν εἰλήφει παρὰ τῆς Μαρίας...οὐδ' ἂν εἰς τεσσαράκοντα ἡμέρας...νηστεύσας ἐπείνησε, τοῦ σ. ἐπιζητοῦντος τὴν ἰδίαν τροφήν Iren.*haer*.3.22.2(M.7.957A); τὸ ἐσθίειν καὶ τοῦ σ. ἡ ὄψις ἐδείκνυεν αὐτὸν καὶ ἄνθρωπον Ath. *ep.Serap*.4.18(M.26.665A); but cf. ἔφαγεν...οὐ διὰ τὸ σ., δυνάμει συνεχόμενον ἁγίᾳ, ἀλλ' ὡς μὴ τοὺς συνόντας ἄλλως περὶ αὐτοῦ φρονεῖν ὑπεισέλθοι, ὥσπερ ἀμέλει ὕστερον δοκήσει τινὲς αὐτὸν πεφανερῶσθαι ὑπέλαβον Clem.*str*.6.9(p.467.11; M.9.292C); ταῖς τοῦ σ. ἀνάγκαις ὁμοίως ἡμῖν οὐδαμῶς καταδεσμούμενος, οὐδέ τι χεῖρον ἢ μεῖζον αὐτὸς ἑαυτοῦ τῆς θεότητος ὑπομένων, οὐδ' οὕτως οἷα ἀνθρώπου ψυχὴ τῷ σ. πεδούμενος Eus.*d.e*.7.1(p.302.6,9; M.22.496A); **c.** suffering, in contradistinction to the divinity μανθανέτω ὅτι ὁ λόγος τῇ οὐσίᾳ μένων λόγος οὐδὲν μὲν πάσχει ὧν πάσχει τὸ σ. ἢ ἡ ψυχή Or.*Cels*.4.15(p.285.14; M.11.1048A); Ath.*ep.Epict*.6(p.10.17,19; M.26.1060C) cit. infra 3.b; ἐνεργεῖ γὰρ ὡς ἀληθῶς ἡ θεότης διὰ τοῦ περὶ αὐτὴν σ. σωτηρίαν, ὡς εἶναι τῆς μὲν σαρκὸς τὸ πάθος, τοῦ δὲ θεοῦ τὴν ἐνέργειαν Gr.Nyss.*Eun*.6(2 p.129.23; M.45.713A); ἐπειδὴ δὲ τὸ γεγονὸς αὐτοῦ ἴδιον σ. πέπονθε, ταῦτα πάλιν αὐτὸς λέγεται παθεῖν ὑπὲρ ἡμῶν· ἦν γὰρ ὁ ἀπαθὴς ἐν τῷ πάσχοντι σ. Cyr.*ep*.4(p.27.17f.; 5[2].24Af.); τὰ ἱμάτιά μου, τουτέστι τὸ σ. μου· ἀπαθὴς γὰρ ἡ θεία φύσις, τὸ δὲ σ. τὸ πάθος ἐδέξατο Thdt.*Cant*.5:10 (2.115f.); τοῦ παθητοῦ σ. τὸ πάθος εἶναι φαμέν, τὴν ἀπαθῆ δὲ φύσιν ἐλευθέραν μεμενηκέναι τοῦ πάθους ὁμολογοῦμεν id.*eran*.3(4.190); ὑπὲρ μὲν τῶν σ. τὸ σ. δέδωκεν id.*eran.suppl*.4(4.274); **d.** dying τὸ γὰρ γεγεννημένον ἀπὸ τῆς παρθένου σ. ἦν ἀπὸ τῆς ἀνθρωπίνης ὕλης συνεστηκός, δεκτικὸν τῶν ἀνθρωπίνων τραυμάτων καὶ θανάτου Or.*Cels*.3.25(p.222.

4; M.11.952A); εἰ δὲ λέγεται Χριστὸς τεθνάναι καὶ τεθάφθαι, περὶ τοῦ σ. αὐτοῦ τοῦτο ἐκληπτέον, οὐ τῆς ψυχῆς Didym.*1Cor.*15:3–4(p.6.19); **e.** corruptible, denied by Aphthartodocetae ἴδικτον γράφει [sc. ὁ Ἰουστινιανός], ἐν ᾧ ἄφθαρτον τὸ σ. τοῦ κυρίου κέκληκε Evagr.*h.e.*4.39 (p.190.17; M.86.2781B); ὁ μὲν γὰρ Ἰουλιανός...ἔλεγεν ὅτι ἄφθαρτόν ἐστι τὸ σ. τοῦ Χριστοῦ· εἰ μὴ γὰρ εἴπωμεν αὐτὸ ἄφθαρτον, ἀλλὰ φθαρτόν, διαφορὰν εἰσάγομεν πρὸς τὸν λόγον τοῦ θεοῦ. διαφορᾶς δὲ εἰσαγομένης, δύο φύσεις εὑρίσκονται ἐν τῷ Χριστῷ...πρὸς ταῦτα ἔλεγεν ὁ Σεβῆρος ὅτι δύναται καὶ ἄφθαρτον εἰπεῖν τὸ σ. τοῦ Χριστοῦ καὶ διαφορὰν εἰσαγαγεῖν καὶ μίαν φύσιν εἰπεῖν †Leont.B.*sect.*5.3(M.86. 1229Df.); Γαϊανῖται, ἤτοι Ἰουλιανισταί· οἵτινες λέγουσιν, ἐξ αὐτῆς τῆς ἑνώσεως τὸ τοῦ κυρίου σ. κατὰ πάντα τρόπον ἄφθαρτον εἶναι Tim.CP *haer.*(M.86.44B); incorruptible only in special sense πρὸς ταύτην οὖν τὴν φθορὰν τῆς ἁμαρτίας, ἄφθαρτον, τοῦτ' ἔστιν, ἀναμάρτητον λέγομεν τὸ πανάγιον καὶ πανάμωμον σ. τοῦ Χριστοῦ Anast.S.*hod.*23(M.89. 300A); **f.** not a mere appearance, as in docetic view, Ath.*Ar.*2.43 (M.26.237C); εἰ γὰρ θέσει ἦν ἐν τῷ σ. ὁ λόγος κατ' ἐκείνους, τὸ δὲ θέσει λεγόμενον φαντασία ἐστίν, εὑρίσκεται δοκήσει καὶ ἡ σωτηρία καὶ ἡ ἀνάστασις τῶν ἀνθρώπων λεγομένη, κατὰ τὸν ἀσεβέστατον Μανιχαῖον. ἀλλὰ μὴν οὐ φαντασία ἡ σωτηρία ἡμῶν οὐδὲ σώματος μόνου, ἀλλ' ὅλου ἀνθρώπου ψυχῆς καὶ σ. ἀληθῶς ἡ σωτηρία γέγονεν ἐν αὐτῷ τῷ λόγῳ Ath.*ep.Epict.*7(p.11.8,12; M.26.1061B); ἐνανθρωπήσαντα...σῶμα καὶ ψυχὴν καὶ νοῦν καὶ πάντα ὅσα ἐστὶν ἀνθρώποις, χωρὶς ἁμαρτίας, ἀληθινῶς καὶ οὐ δοκήσει ἐσχηκότα ‡Ath.*interpr.*(p.66.17; M.26.1232A); cf. ἀνθρωπίνου μὲν σώματος εἰκόνα ἔχειν αὐτόν, ἀνθρωπίνης δὲ σαρκὸς μὴ ἀνειληφέναι ἀλήθειαν Leo Mag.*ep.*35.1(p.40.31; *M.PL.*54.806A); **g.** united with human soul εἴ τις λέγει ἄψυχον ἢ ἀνόητον τὸ σ. τοῦ Χριστοῦ καὶ μὴ ὁμολογεῖ αὐτὸν τέλειον κατὰ πάντα, ἕνα καὶ τὸν αὐτόν, καθὼς γέγραπται, ἀναθεματιζέσθω Gr.Thaum.*fid.cap.*2(p.146.12; M.10.1133A); 'πάτερ, εἰς χεῖράς σου παρατίθημι τὸ πνεῦμά μου.' τοῦτο δὲ τὸ πνεῦμα, οἱ μὲν Ἀρείου καὶ Εὐνομίου τὴν θεότητα τοῦ μονογενοῦς εἶναι φασίν· ἄψυχον γὰρ ἀνειλῆφθαι τὸ σ. νομίζουσι Thdt.*eran. suppl.*12(4.277); Apollinarian view ψυχὴν οὐκ ἀνέλαβεν, ἀλλὰ σ. μόνον, ἡ δὲ θεότης ἀντὶ ψυχῆς ἑνωθεῖσα τῷ σ. πάντα τὰ τῆς ψυχῆς ἀνεδέξατο *ib.*2(111); **h.** possession of νοῦς denied by Apoll. ὥσπερ ὑμεῖς λέγετε νοῦν ἐπουράνιον ἐν σ. ἐμψύχῳ ‡Ath.*Apoll.*1.20(M.26. 1128B); Gr.Naz.*ep.*203(M.37.333A); Thdt.*ep.*104(4.1174) cit. s. νοῦς; **i.** similar to all men's bodies εἰ καὶ σ. μοι ὅμοιον ἀνθρώποις ἦν, ἀλλ' οὐ καὶ τὴν δύναμιν οὐδὲ τὴν οὐσίαν τοῖς πολλοῖς ὢν ἐμφερής Eus.*d.e.* 10.8(p.481.27; M.22.773D); εἴποι ἂν ἴσως ἐνεργείᾳ μόνῃ οὐχὶ δὲ οὐσίας ὑποστάσει καὶ ἐν τῷ σ. γεγονέναι· δραστικῇ γὰρ ἐνεργείᾳ μόνῃ φησὶ [sc. Marcellus] τῇ σαρκὶ συνών id.*Marcell.*2.4(p.57.13; M.24. 821A); not homoousios acc. Eutyches ἕως σήμερον οὐκ εἶπον τὸ σ. τοῦ κυρίου καὶ θεοῦ ἡμῶν ὁμοούσιον ἡμῖν, τὴν δὲ ἁγίαν παρθένον ὁμολογῶ εἶναι ἡμῖν ὁμοούσιον καὶ ὅτι ἐξ αὐτῆς ἐσαρκώθη ὁ θεὸς ἡμῶν Eut.ap. CCP(448)*act.*(p.142.13; H.2.164E); cf. ἀρκέσει τῷ ἐξ ἡμῶν σώματι, τὸ τῆς κατὰ χάριν υἱότητος Diod.*synous.*(M.33.1560C); μὴ τῆς Μαρίας υἱὸς ὁ θεὸς λόγος ὑποπτευέσθω· θνητὸς γὰρ θνητὸν γεννᾷ κατὰ φύσιν, καὶ σ. τὸ ὁμοούσιον *ib.*; cf. αὐτοόμοούσιον, αὐτοετεροούσιον σ. τῇ θεότητι διὰ τὴν ἕνωσιν λέγοντες [sc. Apollinarians] Val.Apoll.*apol.*3 (p.288.23; M.86.1953D); **j.** as πνευματικόν: ὁ δὲ Χριστὸς πνευματικὸν ἔσχε σ., ὅλην δεξάμενον τοῦ ἁγίου πνεύματος τὴν παρουσίαν καὶ δηλοῖ μείνασα ἐπ' αὐτὸν ἡ περιστερά Oecum.*1Cor.*15:44(p.443); **k.** as ψυχικόν, acc. Valentinus ἀσώματον...τὸν Χριστὸν...σ. ψυχικὸν παρὰ τοῦ δημιουργοῦ κομισάμενον, ὅπερ ἅπτον καὶ ὁρατὸν μὴ ὂν πρότερον γέγονεν ὕστερον Tim.CP *haer.*(M.86.17B); **3.** relationship to Logos; **a.** not converted into divine nature οὐδὲ ἡ τοῦ θεοῦ πρὸς τὸ σῶμα ἕνωσις μεταβολὴ σώματός ἐστιν, καίτοι τοῦ σ. τὰς θείας ἐνεργείας παρεχομένου τοῖς ἐφάψασθαι δυναμένοις Apoll.*fr.*128(p.238.28f.) ap.Thdt.*eran.*2(4.171); *ib.*147(p.246.23ff.)ap.Leont.B.*Apoll.*(M.86. 1965Af.); θεῖον μὲν εἶναι φαμὲν τὸ σ. τοῦ Χριστοῦ, ἐπειδὴ καὶ θεοῦ σ. ἐστι...ὅτι δὲ εἰς θεότητος φύσιν μετεβλήθη, οὔτε τῶν πατέρων τις τῶν ἁγίων ἢ πεφρόνηκεν, ἢ εἴρηκεν, οὔτε ἡμεῖς οὕτω διακείμεθα Cyr.*ep.*45 (p.156.16f.; 5².140B); nor divine nature into it οὔτε οὖν ὁ λόγος εἰς σ., ὡς εἴπομεν, οὔτε εἰς λόγον τὸ σ. ἠλλοίωται Leo Mag.*ep.*35.2(p.41. 25; *M.PL.*54.808A); Apollinarian view σ. ἀνθρώπινον [οὐκ] ἔσχεν ὁ Χριστὸς...ἀλλὰ...θεϊκόν...ἔμψυχον ἦν τὸ σ. ... θεία ἦν ἐμψυχία ψυχωθέν ‡Ath.*dial.Trin.*4.1(M.28.1249Df.); answered τὸ σ. φύσει μέν ἐστιν ἀνθρώπινον, τῇ δὲ ἑνώσει τῆς οἰκονομίας θεϊκὸν *ib.*4.2(1253A); πῶς ὑμεῖς πάλιν λέγετε ἐξ οὐρανοῦ τὸ σ.; ‡Ath.*Apoll.*1.7(M.26.1104B); οὐκ εἶπεν δὲ σῶμα, ἵνα μὴ εἴπωσί τινες, ὅτι οὐράνιον σῶμα ἐφόρεσεν Ammon.*Jo.*1:14(M.85.1397C); τοῦ Εὐτυχοῦς...λέγοντος...οὐρανόθεν κατελθὸν τὸ σ. αὐτοῦ Anast.S.*hod.*7(M.89.113A); σῶμα λεγόντων ἔχοντα τὸν κύριον...οὐράνιον Thdr.Stud.*ref.*4(M.99.445C); **b.** indwelt by Logos ἐν τῷ περιτμηθέντι σ., καὶ βασταχθέντι...ἦν ὁ ἀπαθὴς καὶ ἀσώματος τοῦ θεοῦ λόγος Ath.*ep.Epict.*5(p.9.19; M.26. 1060A); ἦν παράδοξον, ὅτι αὐτὸς ἦν ὁ πάσχων καὶ μὴ πάσχων, πάσχων μέν, ὅτι ἴδιον αὐτοῦ ἔπασχε σ., καὶ ἐν αὐτῷ τῷ πάσχοντι ἦν· μὴ πάσχων δέ, ὅτι τῇ φύσει θεὸς ὢν ὁ λόγος ἀπαθής ἐστι. καὶ αὐτὸς μὲν ὁ ἀσώματος ἦν ἐν τῷ παθητῷ σ. *ib.*6(p.10.17,19; 1060C); not of the οὐσία of the Logos, *ib.*2(p.5.2; 1053A); οὐ τὸ σ. ἀλλ' αὐτὸν τὸν υἱὸν ὁμοούσιον...τοῦ πατρός, καὶ τοῦτον μὲν ἐκ τῆς οὐσίας τοῦ πατρός, τὸ δὲ σ. ἐκ Μαρίας... εἶναι πάλιν κατὰ τὰς γραφάς *ib.*4(p.7.8,10; 1056B,cf.); *ib.*8(p.14.2f.; 1064Bf.); Logos not identical with it οὔτε ὃ ἀνείληφεν σῶμα ταὐτὸν ἦν τῷ ἀνειληφότι υἱῷ τοῦ θεοῦ Eus.*e.th.*1.6(p.65.7; M.24.836A); μὴ τὸ σ. ἦν ὁ λόγος, ἀλλὰ σ. ἦν τοῦ λόγου Ath.*ep.Epict.*6(p.10.5,6; 1060B); **c.** united with Logos ...ἵνα καὶ τολμῶσι λέγειν· οὐ προσκυνοῦμεν ἡμεῖς τὸν κύριον μετὰ τῆς σαρκός· ἀλλὰ διαιροῦμεν τὸ σ. καὶ μόνῳ τούτῳ λατρεύομεν Ath.*ep.Adelph.*5(M.26.1077D); οὐ γὰρ ὁμοούσιον τῷ ἐκ θεοῦ λόγῳ τὸ σ.· ἓν δὲ τῇ συνόδῳ καὶ τῇ ἀπερινοήτῳ συνδρομῇ Cyr. *Jo.*4.2(4.361B); μιᾷ προσκυνήσει τιμᾶν εἰθίσμεθα τὸν Ἐμμανουήλ, οὐ διϊστάντες τοῦ λόγου τὸ ἐνωθὲν αὐτῷ καθ' ὑπόστασιν σ. id.*Nest.*2. 10(p.47.30; 6¹.53A); id.*apol.orient.*11(p.58.55; 6¹.192C); adoptionist view αὐτὴν δὲ τὴν σοφίαν δι' ἑαυτῆς ἐπιδεδημηκέναι οὐσιωδῶς ἐν τῷ ἐκ Μαρίας σ. Paul.Sam.*fr.*(p.332.24)ap.Leont.B.*Nest.et Eut.*3(M.86. 1393B); *ib.*(p.333.27; M.l.c.); διὰ τοῦ σ., ὡς δι' ὀστρακίνου σκεύους, ἐνοικήσασα ἐν αὐτῷ ἡ θεία δύναμις Eus.*d.e.*4.16(p.189.15; M.22.316B); **d.** in rel. to deity οὐδ' ἡμεῖς ὑπολαμβάνομεν τὸ βλεπόμενον τότε καὶ αἰσθητὸν τοῦ Ἰησοῦ σ. εἶναι θεόν Or.*Cels.*2.9(p.135.15; M.11.808B); ὅλον θεὸν καὶ μετὰ τοῦ σ., ἀλλ' οὐχὶ κατὰ τὸ σ. θεόν ‡*Symb.Ant.*(269) (p.6.13); οὐ γὰρ ἀνθρώπου τινὸς ἦν τὸ βλεπόμενον σ., ἀλλὰ θεοῦ Ath.*ep.Max.*2(M.26.1088B); in iconoclastic argument ἢ τὸ θεῖον περιγραπτὸν καὶ τῇ σαρκὶ συγχυθέν, ἢ τὸ σ. τοῦ Χριστοῦ ἀθέωτον καὶ διῃρημένον CCP(754)*decr.*(H.4.365A); **e.** Logos not sullied by contact with body, Eus.*d.e.*4.13(p.170.29; M.22.285A); μηδὲ ἐκ τῆς σαρκὸς ὁ ἀμίαντος ἐμιαίνετο μηδὲ συνεφθείρετο τῇ τοῦ σ. οἰκείᾳ φύσει ὁ ἀπαθὴς τοῦ θεοῦ λόγος *ib.*7.1(p.302.18; 496A); **f.** Logos separated from body by death ὁ λόγος...τῷ πατρὶ παρατιθεὶς τὸ πνεῦμα...οὕτως ἄφετος καὶ ἐλεύθερος αὐτὸς ἀφ' ἑαυτοῦ τὴν ἐκ τοῦ σ. ἀναχώρησιν ἐποιεῖτο *ib.*3.4(p.115.4; 197A); this denied εἰ δὲ ὁ θεὸς ἐχωρίσθη τοῦ σ., καὶ οὕτως ἡ νέκρωσις ἐδείκνυτο, πῶς τὸ σ., χωρισθὲν τοῦ ἀφθάρτου θεοῦ, τὴν ἀφθαρσίαν ἐπεδείκνυτο; ‡Ath.*Apoll.*2.15(M.26. 1157A); τούτου τοῦ πνεύματος ἡ ἀποχώρησις γέγονεν ἀπὸ τοῦ σ. ἐπὶ τοῦ σταυροῦ. καὶ οὕτω ἐνεκροῦτο τὸ σ. καὶ αὐτοῦ γέγονεν ἡ λύσις, θεοῦ τοῦ λόγου ἀμεταθέτως ἔχοντος πρός τε τὸ σ., πρός τε τὴν ψυχήν, πρός τε ἑαυτὸν ὄντα εἰς τὸν κόλπον τοῦ πατρὸς ἐν ἐπιδείξει ἀτρεπτότητος *ib.*2.16(1161B).

B. Christ's resurrection body, v. ἀνάστασις; **1.** identical with crucified body ἐκεῖνο τὸ αἰσθητὸν τοῦ Ἰησοῦ σ. ἐσταύρωται καὶ τέθαπται καὶ μετὰ τοῦτο ἐγήγερται Or.*Jo.*10.36(20; p.210.1; M.14. 372B); Ath.*ep.Epict.*7(p.12.2; M.26.1061B); ἐκεῖνο τὸ σ. τὸ μὲν πρότερον εἶδος ἔχει, καὶ σχῆμα καὶ περιγραφήν, καὶ ἁπαξαπλῶς εἰπεῖν, τὴν τοῦ σ. οὐσίαν Thdt.*eran.*2(4.126); οὐ μετεβλήθη οὖν εἰς πνεῦμα τὸ σ. ... μετὰ τὴν ἀνάστασιν σ. τὸ σ. μεμένηκεν id.*eran.suppl.*10(4.272); but exalted πρῶτον οὖν τὸ ἴδιον σ. ἤγειρεν ὁ κύριος ἐκ νεκρῶν, καὶ ὕψωσεν ἐν ἑαυτῷ Ath.*inc.et c.Ar.*12(M.26.1004B); Chrys.*hom.41.2 in 1Cor.*(10.388Af.); not subject to human frailty but incorruptible, Ath.*ep.Epict.*10(p.16.12; 1068A); οὐ σ. παθητὸν ἔχων, ἀλλ' ἀθάνατον λοιπὸν καὶ ἄφθαρτον, καὶ οὐ δεόμενον τροφῆς. οὐ τοίνυν διὰ χρείαν μετὰ τὴν ἀνάστασιν ἔφαγέ τε καὶ ἔπιεν· οὐδὲ γὰρ ἐδεῖτο λοιπὸν τὸ σ. τούτων Chrys.*hom.82.2 in Mt.*(7.784A); μετὰ...τὴν ἀνάστασιν ἦν μὲν αὐτὸ τὸ σ. τὸ πεπονθός, πλὴν οὐκέτι τὰς ἀνθρωπίνας ἀσθενείας ἔχον ἐν ἑαυτῷ. οὐ γὰρ ἔτι πείνης, ἢ κόπου, ἢ ἑτέρου τινὸς τῶν τοιούτων δεκτικὸν εἶναί φαμεν αὐτό, ἀλλὰ λοιπὸν ἄφθαρτον Cyr.*ep.*45(p.156.1; 5².139C); πρὸ μὲν τοῦ πάθους, φθαρτὸν ἦν τὸ τοῦ Χριστοῦ...σ. μετὰ δὲ τὴν...ἔγερσιν ἄφθαρτον Anast.S.*hod.*23(M.89.300B); solid, Or.*Cels.*2. 61(p.183.25; M.11.893A); εἴ τις λέγει ὡς τὸ τοῦ κυρίου ἐξ ἀναστάσεως σ. αἰθέριόν τε καὶ σφαιροειδὲς τῷ σχήματι, καὶ ὅτι τὰ τοιαῦτα καὶ τὰ τῶν λοιπῶν ἐξ ἀναστάσεως ἔσται σ., καὶ ὅτι αὐτοῦ τοῦ κυρίου πρῶτον ἀποτιθεμένου τὸ ἴδιον αὐτοῦ σ. καὶ πάντων ὁμοίως εἰς τὸ ἀνύπαρκτον χωρήσει ἡ τῶν σ. φύσις, ἀνάθεμα ἔστω CCP(543)*anath.*10; **2.** retained after Ascension: denied by Hermogenes ἀνερχόμενον εἰς τοὺς οὐρανοὺς ἐν τῷ ἡλίῳ τὸ σ. καταλελοιπέναι, αὐτὸν δὲ πρὸς τὸν πατέρα πεπορεῦσθαι Hipp.*haer.*8.17(p.237.9; M.16.3366A); asserted by orthodox καὶ μετὰ τὴν ἀνάληψιν σ. καλούμενον τοῦ δεσπότου τὸ σ. Thdt.*eran.*2(4.124); εἰ τοίνυν τοῦ ὄντως σ. ἀντίτυπά ἐστι τὰ θεῖα μυστήρια, σ. ἄρα ἐστὶ καὶ νῦν τοῦ δεσπότου τὸ σ., οὐκ εἰς θεότητος φύσιν μεταβληθέν, ἀλλὰ θείας δόξης ἀναπλησθὲν *ib.*(125); ἀνελθόντα εἰς οὐρανοὺς ἐν αὐτῷ τῷ σ. ἐνδόξως καθίσαντα ἐν δεξιᾷ τοῦ πατρός, ἐρχόμενον ἐν αὐτῷ τῷ σ. ἐν δόξῃ κρῖναι ζῶντας καὶ νεκρούς ‡Ath.*interpr.*(p.66. 20f.; M.26.1232B); **3.** considered as intermediate between fleshly body and soul, Or.*Cels.*2.62(p.184.13; M.11.893C) cit. s. ἀνάστασις;

οὐκ ἔτι μὲν σάρκα, οὐκ ἀσώματον δέ, οἷς αὐτὸς οἶδε λόγοις θεοειδεστέρου σ., ἵνα καὶ ὀφθῇ ὑπὸ τῶν ἐκκεντησάντων, καὶ μείνῃ θεὸς ἔξω παχύτητος Gr.Naz.*or*.40.46(M.36.424C).

C. eucharistic, v. ἀντίτυπος, τύπος, σύμβολον, ὁμοίωμα, μυστικός; **1.** in gen.; words of institution cited, *Lit*.ap.*Const.App*.8.12.36; *Lit.Chrys*.(p.328.6); *Lit.Bas*.(p.328.6); ἐκεῖνος τὸ σ. ἐξίσης ἔδωκε... καὶ γὰρ ὑπὲρ ἁπάντων ὁμοίως ἐκλάσθη, καὶ σ. γέγονεν ὑπὲρ ἁπάντων Chrys.*hom.27.4 in 1Cor*.(10.246D); **2.** thought by iconoclasts to be only true image of Christ ἰδοὺ οὖν ἡ εἰκὼν τοῦ ζωοποιοῦ σ. αὐτοῦ, ἡ ἐντίμως καὶ τετιμημένως πραττομένη CCP(754)*decr*.(H.4.368D); theory denied οὐκ εἶπε· λάβετε, φάγετε τὴν εἰκόνα τοῦ σ. μου CNic.(787)*refut*.(H.4.369C); οὐδαμοῦ οὔτε ὁ κύριος οὔτε οἱ ἀπόστολοι ἢ πατέρες εἰκόνα εἶπον τὴν διὰ τοῦ ἱερέως προσφερομένην ἀναίμακτον θυσίαν, ἀλλ' αὐτὸ σ. καὶ αὐτὸ αἷμα *ib*.(H.4.369D); **3.** in relation to Christ's earthly body; **a.** essential identity, Chrys.*hom.24.4 in 1Cor*.(10.217Af.); ἐνταῦθα κείσεται τὸ σ. τὸ δεσποτικόν, οὐχὶ ἐσπαργανωμένον, καθάπερ τότε, ἀλλὰ πνεύματι πανταχόθεν ἁγίῳ περιεστελλόμενον id.*Philogon*.3(1.498A); οὐ μόνον τοῖς ἕνδεκα ἀποστόλοις, ἀλλὰ καὶ τῷ προδότῃ, τοῦ τιμίου μετέδωκε σ. τε καὶ αἵματος Thdt.*1Cor*.11:25(3.238); ἐν ἀληθείᾳ σ. καὶ αἷμα ὁρατὸν καὶ κτιστὸν καὶ γηγενὲς Χριστοῦ εἶναι Anast.S.*hod*.13(M.89.208D); **b.** dist. θέα τὴν πᾶσαν τοῦ σωτῆρος ἡμῶν διδασκαλίαν ὅπως οὐ περὶ ἧς ἀνείληφεν σαρκὸς διελέγετο, περὶ δὲ τοῦ μυστικοῦ σ. τε καὶ αἵματος Eus.*e.th*.3.12(p.168.3; M.24.1021B); μετὰ...τὴν αὐτοῦ παρουσίαν, οὐκέτι χρεία τῶν συμβόλων τοῦ σ., αὐτοῦ φαινομένου τοῦ σ. Thdt.*1Cor*.11:26(3.238); **4.** in rel. to bread; **a.** in liturgical texts: in epiclesis παρακαλοῦμεν τὸν φιλάνθρωπον θεὸν τὸ ἅγιον πνεῦμα ἐξαποστεῖλαι ἐπὶ τὰ προκείμενα, ἵνα ποιήσῃ τὸν μὲν ἄρτον σ. Χριστοῦ, τὸν δὲ οἶνον αἷμα Χριστοῦ. πάντως γὰρ οὗ ἂν ἐφάψηται τὸ ἅγιον πνεῦμα, τοῦτο ἡγίασται καὶ μεταβέβληται Cyr.H.*catech*.23.7; ἐπιδημησάτω...ὁ ἅγιός σου λόγος ἐπὶ τὸν ἄρτον τοῦτον, ἵνα γένηται ὁ ἄρτος σ. τοῦ λόγου Serap.*Euch*.13.15; ἀξιοῦμέν σε, ὅπως ...καταπέμψῃς τὸ ἅγιόν σου πνεῦμα ἐπὶ τὴν θυσίαν ταύτην...ὅπως ἀποφήνῃ τὸν ἄρτον τοῦτον σ. τοῦ Χριστοῦ σου *Lit*.ap.*Const.App*.8.12.39; προθέντες τὰ ἀντίτυπα τοῦ ἁγίου σ. καὶ αἵματος τοῦ Χριστοῦ ...σε παρακαλοῦμεν...ἐλθεῖν τὸ πνεῦμά σου τὸ πανάγιον ἐφ' ἡμᾶς καὶ ἐπὶ τὰ προκείμενα δῶρα ταῦτα καὶ εὐλογῆσαι αὐτὰ καὶ ἁγιάσαι καὶ ἀναδεῖξαι τὸν μὲν ἄρτον τοῦτον αὐτὸ τὸ τίμιον σ. τοῦ...Χριστοῦ *Lit. Bas*.(pp.329f.); ἱκετεύομεν κατάπεμψον τὸ πνεῦμά σου τὸ ἅγιον ἐφ' ἡμᾶς καὶ ἐπὶ τὰ προκείμενα δῶρα ταῦτα καὶ ποίησον τὸν μὲν ἄρτον τοῦτον τίμιον σ. τοῦ Χριστοῦ σου, μεταβαλὼν τῷ πνεύματί σου τῷ ἁγίῳ *Lit.Chrys*.(p.330); *Lit.Marc*.(Brightman p.134); αὐτὸ τὸ πνεῦμά σου τὸ πανάγιον κατάπεμψον, δέσποτα, ἐφ' ἡμᾶς καὶ ἐπὶ τὰ προκείμενα ἅμα δῶρα ταῦτα, ἵνα ἐπιφοιτῆσαν τῇ ἁγίᾳ...αὐτοῦ παρουσίᾳ ἁγιάσῃ καὶ ποιήσῃ τὸν μὲν ἄρτον τοῦτον σ. ἅγιον Χριστοῦ *Lit.Jac*.(p.206.10); in words of administration σῶμα Χριστοῦ *Lit*.ap.*Const.App*.8.13.15; σ. ἅγιον τοῦ κυρίου καὶ θεοῦ καὶ σωτῆρος ἡμῶν Ἰησοῦ Χριστοῦ τοῖς πιστοῖς μεταδιδόμενον εἰς ἄφεσιν ἁμαρτιῶν καὶ εἰς ζωὴν αἰώνιον *Lit. Jac*.(p.234.8); σ. ἅγιον τοῦ κυρίου καὶ θεοῦ καὶ σωτῆρος ἡμῶν Ἰησοῦ Χριστοῦ *Lit.Marc*.(Brightman p.140); σ. καὶ αἷμα τοῦ κυρίου καὶ θεοῦ καὶ σωτῆρος ἡμῶν Ἰησοῦ Χριστοῦ Anast.S.*hod*.13(M.89.208D); **b.** relationship discussed μὴ πρόσεχε οὖν, ὡς ψιλοῖς τῷ ἄρτῳ καὶ τῷ οἴνῳ· σ. γὰρ καὶ αἷμα Χριστοῦ κατὰ τὴν δεσποτικὴν τυγχάνει ἀπόφασιν...μὴ ἀπὸ τῆς γεύσεως κρίνῃς τὸ πρᾶγμα, ἀλλ' ὑπὸ τῆς πίστεως πληροφοροῦ ἀνενδοιάστως σ. καὶ αἵματος Χριστοῦ καταξιωθείς Cyr.H.*catech*.22.6; ὁ φαινόμενος ἄρτος οὐκ ἄρτος ἐστίν, εἰ καὶ τῇ γεύσει αἰσθητός, ἀλλὰ σ. Χριστοῦ *ib*.22.9; Chrys.*poenit*.9(2.350A) cit. s. ἀπουσιάζω; σ. ἐστι καὶ αἷμα Χριστοῦ εἰς σύστασιν τῆς ἡμετέρας ψυχῆς τε καὶ σ. χωροῦν, οὐ δαπανώμενον, οὐ φθειρόμενον, οὐκ εἰς ἀφεδρῶνα χωροῦν...ἀλλ' εἰς τὴν ἡμῶν οὐσίαν καὶ συντήρησιν Jo.D.*f.o*.4.13(M.94.1152A); ὥσπερ φυσικῶς διὰ τῆς βρώσεως ὁ ἄρτος, καὶ ὁ οἶνος καὶ τὸ ὕδωρ διὰ τῆς πόσεως εἰς σῶμα καὶ αἷμα τοῦ ἐσθίοντος καὶ πίνοντος μεταβάλλονται, καὶ οὐ γίνονται ἕτερον σ. παρὰ τὸ πρότερον αὐτοῦ σ.· οὕτως ὁ τῆς προθέσεως ἄρτος, οἶνός τε, καὶ ὕδωρ, διὰ τῆς ἐπικλήσεως καὶ ἐπιφοιτήσεως τοῦ ἁγίου πνεύματος, ὑπερφυῶς μεταποιοῦνται εἰς τὸ σ. τοῦ Χριστοῦ καὶ τὸ αἷμα, καὶ οὐκ εἰσὶ δύο, ἀλλ' ἓν καὶ τὸ αὐτό *ib*.(1145A); cf. *antequam sanctificetur panis, panem nominamus: divina autem illum sanctificante gratia, mediante sacerdote, liberatus est quidem ab appellatione panis, dignus autem habitus dominici corporis appellatione, etiamsi natura panis in ipso permansit, et non duo corpora, sed unum corpus filii praedicamus*, ‡Chrys.*ep.Caes*.(3.744C); τὸ φύσει σ. σῖτον καὶ ἄρτον προσαγορεύσας, καὶ αὖ πάλιν ἑαυτὸν ἄμπελον ὀνομάσας, οὗτος τὰ ὁρώμενα σύμβολα τῇ τοῦ σ. καὶ αἵματος προσηγορίᾳ τετίμηκεν, οὐ τὴν φύσιν μεταβαλών, ἀλλὰ τὴν χάριν τῇ φύσει προστεθεικώς Thdt.*eran*.1(4.26); cf.*ib*.2 126); οὐκ ἄρτος λιτός ἐστιν, ἀλλ' ἡνωμένος θεότητι· σ. δὲ ἡνώμενον θεότητι, οὐ μία φύσις ἐστίν, ἀλλὰ μία μὲν τοῦ σ., τῆς δὲ ἡνωμένης αὐτῷ θεότητος ἑτέρα· ὥστε τὸ συναμφότερον, οὐ μία φύσις, ἀλλὰ δύο Jo.D.*f.o*.4.13(1149B); δύο φύσεις ἐν τῷ μεταλαμβανομένῳ ὑφ' ἡμῶν σ. τοῦ Χριστοῦ, ἡνωμέναι καθ' ὑπόστασίν εἰσιν ἀδιασπάστως. καὶ τῶν δύο φύσεων μετέχομεν, τοῦ σ. σωματικῶς, τῆς θεότητος πνευματικῶς id.*imag*.3.26(M.94.1348B); **c.** relationship effected **i.** through prayers of liturgy ἡμεῖς δὲ τῷ τοῦ παντὸς δημιουργῷ εὐχαριστοῦντες καὶ τοὺς μετ' εὐχαριστίας καὶ εὐχῆς τῆς ἐπὶ τοῖς δοθεῖσι προσαγομένους ἄρτους ἐσθίομεν, σ. γενομένους διὰ τὴν εὐχὴν ἅγιόν τι καὶ ἁγιάζον τοὺς μετὰ ὑγιοῦς προθέσεως αὐτῷ χρωμένους Or.*Cels*.8.33(p.249.7; M.11.1565C); ὅταν αὐτὸν [sc. ἄρτον] τὸ μυστήριον ἱερουργήσῃ, σ. Χριστοῦ λέγεταί τε καὶ γίνεται Gr.Nyss.*bapt.Chr*.(M.46.581C); calling down word of God, Ath.ap.Eutych.*pasch*.8(M.86.2401B) cit. s. μυστήριον; τὸν τῷ λόγῳ τοῦ θεοῦ ἁγιαζόμενον ἄρτον εἰς σ. τοῦ θεοῦ λόγου μεταποιεῖσθαι πιστεύομεν· καὶ γὰρ ἐκεῖνο τὸ σ., ἄρτος τῇ δυνάμει ἦν, ἡγιάσθη δὲ τῇ ἐπισκηνώσει τοῦ λόγου τοῦ σκηνώσαντος ἐν τῇ σαρκί Gr.Nyss.*or. catech*.37(p.149.3; M.45.96D); **ii.** through epiclesis in partic., Cyr.H.*catech*.19.7 cit. s. ἐπίκλησις; ἐν τῇ ἐπικλήσει τοῦ ἁγίου βαπτίσματος ...καὶ ἐπὶ τῆς τραπέζης τῆς μυστικῆς τὸν ἄρτον τὸν κοινόν, σ. ἰδικὸν τῆς αὐτοῦ σαρκώσεως ἀποφαίνον Isid.Pel.*epp*.1.109(M.78.256C); διὰ τοιούτων τοίνυν εὐχῶν τὴν ἐπιφοίτησιν τοῦ ἁγίου πνεύματος προσεδόκων, ὅπως τῇ αὐτοῦ θείᾳ παρουσίᾳ τὸν προκείμενον εἰς ἱερουργίαν ἄρτον, καὶ οἶνον ὕδατι μεμιγμένον, αὐτὸ ἐκεῖνο τὸ σ. καὶ αἷμα τοῦ σωτῆρος ἡμῶν Ἰησοῦ Χριστοῦ ἀποφήνῃ τε καὶ ἀναδείξῃ ‡Procl.CP *tract*.(M.65.852A); ἐρωτᾷς, πῶς ὁ ἄρτος γίνεται σ. Χριστοῦ...λέγω σοι κἀγώ· πνεῦμα ἅγιον ἐπιφοιτᾷ, καὶ ταῦτα ποιεῖ τὰ ὑπὲρ λόγον καὶ ἔννοιαν Jo.D.*f.o*.4.13(M.94.1141A); *ib*.(1145A); **iii.** by words of institution ὁ ἄρτος...οὐ διὰ βρώσεως προϊὼν εἰς τὸ σ. γενέσθαι τοῦ λόγου, ἀλλ' εὐθὺς πρὸς τὸ σ. διὰ τοῦ λόγου μεταποιούμενος, καθὼς εἴρηται ὑπὸ τοῦ λόγου ὅτι τοῦτό ἐστι τὸ σ. μου Gr.Nyss.*or.catech*.37 (p.150.2,3; M.45.97A); τοῦτό μού ἐστι τὸ σ., φησί· τοῦτο τὸ ῥῆμα τὰ προκείμενα μεταρρυθμίζει Chrys.*prod.Jud*.2.6(2.394A); **5.** to be received with great reverence, Cyr.H.*catech*.23.21; τοῦ καθαρᾷ τῇ συνειδήσει τὸ ἅγιον ὑποδέχεσθαι σ. Gr.Nyss.*perf*.(M.46.268D); Thdt.*1Cor*.11:27(3.238); Anast.S.*synax*.(M.89.832B); **6.** sustaining bodies of recipients and uniting them with Christ γίνεται ἡ εὐχαριστία σ. Χριστοῦ, ἐκ τούτων [sc. ποτήριου, ἄρτου] δὲ αὔξει καὶ συνίσταται ἡ τῆς σαρκὸς ἡμῶν ὑπόστασις Iren.*haer*.5.2.3(M.7.1125B); ἵνα γένῃ μεταλαβὼν σ. καὶ αἵματος Χριστοῦ σύσσωμος καὶ σύναιμος αὐτοῦ. οὕτω γὰρ καὶ Χριστοφόροι γινόμεθα, τοῦ σ. αὐτοῦ καὶ τοῦ αἵματος εἰς τὰ ἡμέτερα ἀναδιδομένου μέλη Cyr.H.*catech*.22.3; Gr.Nyss.*or.catech*.37(p.142.2f.; M.45.93Af.); τὸ ἀθανατισθὲν ὑπὸ τοῦ θεοῦ σ. ἐν τῷ ἡμετέρῳ γενόμενον ὅλον πρὸς ἑαυτὸ μεταποιεῖ καὶ μετατίθησιν *ib*.(p.143.4; 93B); **7.** forming recipients into one body τί γάρ ἐστιν ὁ ἄρτος; σ. Χριστοῦ. τί δὲ γίνονται οἱ μεταλαμβάνοντες; σῶμα Χριστοῦ. οὐχὶ σώματα πολλά, ἀλλὰ σ. ἕν Chrys.*hom.24.2 in 1Cor*.(10.213E); γεγόναμεν ἡμεῖς Χριστοῦ σ. ἓν καὶ σὰρξ μία id.*hom.82.5 in Mt*.(7.788C); thus a means of unity 'εἷς ἄρτος, ἓν σῶμα οἱ πολλοί ἐσμεν, οἱ γὰρ πάντες ἐκ τοῦ ἑνὸς ἄρτου μετέχομεν.' συνδεῖ γὰρ ἡμᾶς εἰς ἑνότητα τὸ ἐν ἡμῖν σ. Χριστοῦ, μεμέρισται δὲ κατ' οὐδένα τρόπον...διὰ τοῦ σ. τοῦ Χριστοῦ πρὸς ἑνότητα τὴν πρὸς αὐτόν, καὶ πρός γε τὴν εἰς ἀλλήλους συνενηνέγμεθα Cyr.*Nest*.4.5(p.85.39f.; 6¹.111B); **8.** not reverting to mere bread if not consumed ἀκούω δὲ ὅτι φασὶν ἀπρακτεῖν εἰς ἁγιασμὸν τὴν μυστικὴν εὐλογίαν, εἰ ἀπομείνοι λείψανον αὐτῆς εἰς ἑτέραν ἡμέραν. μαίνονται δὲ ταῦτα λέγοντες· οὐ γὰρ ἀλλοιοῦται Χριστός, οὐδὲ τὸ ἅγιον αὐτοῦ σ. μεταβληθήσεται, ἀλλ' ἡ τῆς εὐλογίας δύναμις, καὶ ἡ ζωοποιὸς χάρις διηνεκής ἐστιν ἐν αὐτῷ Cyr.*ep.Calos*.(p.606.1; 6².365B); **9.** whole body is received ὅλον...ἅπας τὸ ἅγιον σ. καὶ τὸ τίμιον αἷμα τοῦ κυρίου δέχεται, κἂν εἰ μέρος τούτων δέξηται· μερίζεται γὰρ ἀμερίστως ἐν ἅπασι, διὰ τὴν ἔμμιξιν Eutych.*pasch*.2(M.86.2393C).

D. Church as Christ's body, v. ἐκκλησία; **1.** in gen., Ign.*Smyrn*. 1.2; Clem.*str*.7.14(p.62.19; M.9.521B); σ. τὴν ἐκκλησίαν καὶ οἶκον θεοῦ ἐκ λίθων ζώντων οἰκοδομούμενον Or.*Jo*.10.39(23; p.215.30; M.14.381B); id.*Cels*.6.79(p.151.2; M.11.1417D); τοῦ σ. τοῦ ἐκκλησιαστικοῦ Chrys.*hom.10.1 in Eph*.(11.86B); Thdr.Mops.*Eph*.5:23(p.184.22; M.66.920B); also of a single Christian ἓν σ. εἶ τοῦ Χριστοῦ, φέρε τὸν σταυρόν· καὶ γὰρ ἐκεῖνος ἤνεγκε...τοιοῦτον ἐκεῖνο τὸ σ. ἦν Chrys.*hom.3.3 in Eph*.(11.21B,C); **2.** its composition; **a.** Christ the head, v. κεφαλή; **b.** Christians its members ἡμῖν τῷ κοινῷ Χριστοῦ σ. Gr.Naz.*or*.32.10(M.36.185B); v. μέλος; **c.** relation between body and head discussed σ. Χριστοῦ εὑρίσκοντες λεγομένην τὴν ἐκκλησίαν, ζητοῦμεν πότερόν ποτε, ὡς παρὰ τὴν κεφαλὴν τὸ λοιπὸν σ., ὄργανον τῆς κεφαλῆς δεῖ αὐτὴν νοεῖν, ἢ ὥσπερ τοῦ ἀνθρώπου σ., οὗ σ. μέρος ἐστὶν ἡ κεφαλή, οὕτως Χριστοῦ σ. ἐστι ψυχούμενον ὑπὸ τῆς θεότητος αὐτοῦ καὶ πληρούμενον ὑπὸ τοῦ πνεύματος αὐτοῦ ἡ πᾶσα ἐκκλησία Χριστοῦ, ἢ ἄλλως πως δεῖ ταῦτα ἐκλαμβάνειν. ἐὰν μέντοιγε τὸ δεύτερον ᾖ, ἔσται τὸ μὲν ἀνθρωπικώτερον αὐτοῦ καὶ αὐτὸ μέρος τυγχάνον τοῦ ὅλου σ., τὸ δὲ θεῖον καὶ ζωοποιο[ῦ]ν πᾶσαν τὴν ἐκκλησίαν ἡ ὥσπερεὶ ψυχοῦσα αὐτὴν δύναμις θεία Or.*comm.in Eph.*1:23(p.401); ref. 1Cor.12:12 οὕτω καὶ τοῦ Χριστοῦ τὸ σῶμα, ὅπερ ἐστὶν ἡ ἐκκλησία. καθάπερ γὰρ καὶ σ. καὶ κεφαλὴ εἷς ἐστιν ἄνθρωπος, οὕτω τὴν ἐκκλησίαν καὶ τὸν Χριστὸν ἓν ἔφησεν εἶναι. διὸ καὶ τὸν Χριστὸν ἀντὶ τῆς ἐκκλησίας τέθεικε, τὸ σ. αὐτοῦ οὕτως ὀνομάζων. ὥσπερ οὖν, φησίν, ἕν τι ἐστὶ τὸ ἡμέτερον σ., εἰ καὶ ἐκ πολλῶν σύγκειται· οὕτω καὶ ἐν τῇ ἐκκλησίᾳ ἕν τι πάντες ἐσμέν Chrys.*hom.30.1 in 1Cor.*(10.270A); **d.** qualification for membership τί δέ ἐστιν 'ἓν σ.'; οἱ πανταχοῦ τῆς οἰκουμένης πιστοί, καὶ ὄντες καὶ γενόμενοι καὶ ἐσόμενοι· πάλιν καὶ οἱ πρὸ τῆς τοῦ Χριστοῦ παρουσίας εὐηρεστηκότες, ἕν σ. εἰσι id.*hom.10.1 in Eph.*(11.75B); σ. καὶ μέλη λέγει Χριστοῦ, τὸ σ. τῶν πιστευσάντων καὶ βαπτισθέντων Sever. *1Cor.*6:15(p.247.17); cf. ἡ τοῦ ἁγίου πνεύματος ἐν πάσῃ τῇ καθολικῇ ἐκκλησίᾳ μία ἐστὶ μάθησις καὶ ἡ αὐτὴ διδασκαλία, ἣν εἴ τις μὴ δέχεται, οὐκ ἔστι μέλος τοῦ σ. τοῦ Χριστοῦ Leo Mag.*ep.*35(p.40.24; M.*PL.*54.806A); **3.** its resurrection τὴν γενομένην ἀνάστασιν τοῦ Χριστοῦ ἀπὸ τοῦ κατὰ τὸν σταυρὸν πάθους περιέχειν μυστήριον τῆς ἀναστάσεως τοῦ παντὸς Χριστοῦ σ. Or.*Jo.*10.35(20; p.209.32; M.14.372B); ὅτε δὲ γίνεται αὕτη ἡ ἀνάστασις τοῦ ἀληθινοῦ καὶ τελειοτέρου Χριστοῦ σ., τότε τὰ μέλη τοῦ Χριστοῦ τὰ νῦν, ὡς πρὸς τὸ μέλλον, ξηρὰ ὀστᾶ συναχθήσεται *ib.*10.36(20; p.210.32; 373A); ἐγερεῖ καὶ τὰ μέλη τοῦ σ. αὐτοῦ, ἵνα χαρίσηται αὐτοῖς τὰ πάντα, ὡς θεός, ὅσα αὐτὸς ὡς ἄνθρωπος ἔλαβεν Ath.*inc.et c.Ar.*12(M.26.1004B); **4.** exeg. Eph.1:23 ἂν γὰρ μὴ ὦμεν πολλοί, καὶ ὁ μὲν χείρ, ὁ δὲ ποῦς, ὁ δὲ ἄλλο τι μέρος, οὐ πληροῦται ὅλον τὸ σ. διὰ πάντων οὖν πληροῦται τὸ σ. αὐτοῦ. τότε πληροῦται ἡ κεφαλή, τότε τέλειον σ. γίνεται, ὅταν ὁμοῦ πάντες ὦμεν συνημμένοι καὶ συγκεκολλημένοι Chrys.*hom.3.2 in Eph.*(11.20A,B); ὥσπερ γάρ, φησίν, 'ἐν πᾶσι τὰ πάντα πληροῖ', οὕτως καὶ ἐν τῇ ἐκκλησίᾳ πληροῦται κατὰ τὸ εἶναι σ. τοῦ Χριστοῦ. Χριστοῦ οὖν σ., πλήρωμα δὲ θεοῦ ἡ ἐκκλησία Sever.*Eph.*1:23(p.307).

III. of God: said by Arius to be a consequence of homoousian doctrine, Ar.*ep.Alex.*(p.13; M.26.709C–712A) cit. s. ὁμοούσιος.

IV. of angels τὰ δαιμόνια 'ἀσώματα' εἴρηται, οὐχ ὡς σ. μὴ ἔχοντα (ἔχει γὰρ καὶ σχῆμα· διὸ καὶ συναίσθησιν κολάσεως ἔχει), ἀλλ' ὡς πρὸς σύγκρισιν τῶν σῳζομένων σ. πνευματικῶν σκιὰ ὄντα ἀσώματα εἴρηται. καὶ οἱ ἄγγελοι σ. εἰσιν· ὁρῶνται γοῦν Clem.*exc.Thdot.*14(p.111.15f.; M.9.664B); ἄγγελος δέ, καὶ ψυχή, καὶ δαίμων, πρὸς μὲν θεὸν συγκρινόμενοι, τὸν μόνον ἀσύγκριτον, σώματά εἰσι· πρὸς δὲ τὰ ὑλικὰ σ., ἀσώματοι Jo.D.*imag.*3.25(M.94.1345A); τῷ ὄντι...ὡς πρὸς ἡμᾶς ἀόρατοί εἰσιν· ὡς ὁραθέντες δὲ παρὰ πλειόνων αἰσθητῶς πλεονάκις τῷ εἴδει τῶν οἰκείων αὐτῶν σ. Jo.Thess.*fr.*ap.CNic.(787)*act.*5(H.4.293C).

V. *figure of three dimensions, solid* τὰ τριττὰ τῶν σ. σχήματα Dion. Ar.*d.n.*9.5(M.3.913A); σ. δέ ἐστι, τὸ τριχῇ διαστατόν, ἤγουν τὸ ἔχον μῆκος, καὶ πλάτος, καὶ βάθος, ἤτοι πάχος Jo.D.*f.o.*2.12(M.94.925A).

VI. *book, volume,* opp. papyrus roll ἓν...σ. τῆς γραφῆς ὡς ἑνὸς καὶ μόνου τὰς ἁπάντων ἡμῖν ἐκθεμένου φωνάς Proc.G.*Gen.*proem.(M.87.21A); βιβλίον ἔχον ὅλην τὴν νέαν διαθήκην...ἐν σώματι πολὺ καλῷ Jo. Mosch.*prat.*134(M.87.2997A); βιβλίον...ἐν σώμασι ἀργυρένδετον CCP (681)*act.*10(H.3.1201E); *ib.*(1208D).

VII. *corporate body, corporation* τῷ προειρημένῳ σ. τῶν Χριστιανῶν Const.ap.Eus.*h.e.*10.5.12(M.20.885A).

VIII. *body, unit* τοῦ τὸ ἓν σ. τῆς ἀληθείας μετὰ σοφίας συναχθῆναι Or.*Jo.*13.46(p.272.31; M.14.481A); ποῦ νῦν εἰσιν οἱ τὴν παλαιὰν διαβάλλοντες, οἱ τὸ σ. τῆς γραφῆς διασπῶντες; Chrys.*hom.2.2 in 2Cor.4:13*(3.270D); id.*hom.in Jer.10:23*(6.160C) cit. s. γραφή.

IX. *reality*, *POxy.*5.9 (saec. iii–iv) cit. s. πνεῦμα.

X. *kernel, essential part* of a book ὡς τὸ σ. καὶ τὸ ὕφος τῆς προφητείας ὑπαγορεύει Clem.*str.*7.16(p.68.9; M.9.533B); τὸ σ. τοῦ ὅλου λόγου Or.*Jo.*6.3(1; p.108.14; M.14.201A); ὡς ἂν μὴ τὸ σ. τῆς παρούσης ἡμῖν διακόπτοιτο ἱστορίας Eus.*v.C.*3.24(p.89.10; M.20.1085A).

XI. *bodily aspect* or *form*; hence of literal sense of scripture, v. γραφή; οἱ μὲν τὸ σ. τῶν γραφῶν, τὰς λέξεις καὶ τὰ ὀνόματα, καθάπερ τὸ σ. τὸ Μωϋσέως, προσβλέπουσιν, οἱ δὲ τὰς διανοίας καὶ τὰ ὑπὸ τῶν ὀνομάτων δηλούμενα διορῶσι Clem.*str.*6.15(p.498.29,30; M.9.357A); μὴ τὸ σ. τῆς ἐπιστολῆς ἀναγινώσκειν μόνον, ἀλλὰ καὶ τὴν κάτω κειμένην πρόσρησιν Chrys.*hom.1.1 in Rom.16:3*(3.172B); Thdt.*eran.*proem.(4.3C).

XII. *personal service* κελεύει δὲ ἐκ τούτων ὀκτακόσια μὲν ἐν σώμασι λειτουργεῖν, τὰ δὲ λοιπὰ ἐν ἀπαργυρισμῷ Ath.Scholast.*coll.*2.11(p.41).

σωματεῖον, τό, *corporate body* ἀπεκατεστάθη αὐτοῖς τὸ ἴδιον σ. Ign.*Smyrn.*11.2; met. τὸ γὰρ προφητικὸν πνεῦμα τὸ σ. ἐστιν τῆς προφητικῆς τάξεως *POxy.*1.5.9.

***σωματέμψυχος,** *having both soul and body* ὁ λόγος...ἑαυτῷ ἥνωσε τὴν ἡμετέραν σ. φύσιν, οὐκ ἄψυχον Eulog.*fr.Trin.*3.1(p.368).

σωματικός, 1. *bodily, of the body, corporeal*; in gen. οὐ σ. γὰρ τὸ ἐκείνου [sc. Christ] βάπτισμα, τὸν μετανοοῦντα πληροῦντος ἁγίου πνεύματος καὶ θειοτέρου πυρὸς πᾶν ὑλικὸν ἀφανίζοντος καὶ πᾶν γεῶδες ἐξαναλίσκοντος Or.*Jo.*6.32(17; p.141.27; M.14.256A); τῆς σ. ἐπιφανείας [i.e. of Christ] Ath.*inc.*20.1(M.25.129C); σάρκα γεγονότα... ἄνευ μεταβολῆς καὶ μειώσεως, ἄνευ σ. ἀλλοιώσεως Sophr.H.*or.*2.36(M.87.3265A); used only met. of God ἐὰν ἐκ γαστρὸς ἡ γραφὴ λέγῃ, οὐ σ. δεῖ ταύτην ἐκδέχεσθαι ‡Ath.*Ar.*4.27(p.75.17; M.26.509C); μηδὲ στόμα θεοῦ σ. Didym.(‡Bas.)*Eun.*5(1.306E; M.29.736B); of communion with God τῆς πρὸς αὐτὸν ἐχόμενοι κοινωνίας, οὐχὶ μόνον πνευματικῆς ἀλλὰ καὶ σ. Cyr.*Jo.*10.2(4.864A); neut. as subst., *bodily nature* ἐκ τούτου μὲν γὰρ τὸ σ. τοῦ κυρίου σημαίνεται, ἐξ ἐκείνων δὲ τὸ ἀΐδιον τῆς θεότητος αὐτοῦ Ath.*Dion.*20(p.61.12; M.25.209A); plur. οἱ μὲν τὰ σ. βλέποντες τοῦ σωτῆρος id.*ep.Serap.*4.15(M.26.657B); **2.** *having a body* σ. ... ἐστιν οἰκήτωρ κόσμου Tit.Bost.*Man.*2.2(M.18.1137A); **3.** *corporal* σ. ὅρκον ὑποτελῶν ἐν τῇ παρ' αὐτοῦ γενομένῃ διαθήκῃ Ath. Scholast.*coll.*9.4(p.101); τὸν σ. ἐπὶ τῶν προκειμένων ἀχράντων τοῦ θεοῦ εὐαγγελίων καταβαλλόμενοι ὅρκον CCP(681)*act.*10(H.3.1248E); *ib.*13 (1352A); **4.** *bodily, fleshly, sexual* σαρκικῶν καὶ σ. ἐπιθυμιῶν *Did.*1.4; ὁ Αὔγουστος...σωφρονήσας ἀπὸ σ. ἁμαρτίας Jo.Mal.*chron.*10 p.232 (M.97.357B); neut. as subst. κακῶς βιοῦντες πρὸς τὰ σ. *ib.*18 p.436 (644A); **5.** *concerned with corporeal* or *earthly things*; **a.** of things and abstracts, usu. opp. πνευματικός: οὐ τὰς σ. ... πράξεις...ἀλλὰ... τὰς πνευματικάς Or.*Cels.*4.44(p.317.19; M.11.1101A); σ. περιτομῆς καὶ σ. σαββάτου καὶ σ. ἑορτῶν καὶ σ. νουμηνιῶν *ib.*2.7(p.133.13; 805A); ὑπεράνω μὲν τῶν αἰσθητῶν καὶ πάσης σ. φαντασίας γινόμενος, πρὸς δὲ τὰ ἐν οὐρανοῖς θεῖα καὶ νοητὰ τῇ δυνάμει τοῦ νοῦ συναπτόμενος Ath.*gent.*2(M.25.8A); εἰς γάμον σ. κληθεὶς [i.e. at Cana] Cyr.H.*catech.*22.2; τὸ δὲ πλῆθος τῆς σ. δυνάμεως ἐμπόδιόν ἐστι πρὸς τὴν σωτηρίαν τοῦ πνεύματος Bas.*hom.in Ps.*32(1.141B; M.29.343C); 'ὁ λόγος ὁ σὸς ἀλήθειά ἐστι'· τουτέστι, οὐδὲν ψεῦδος ἐν αὐτῷ...καὶ ὅτι οὐδὲν τυπικὸν δηλοῖ πάλιν, οὐδὲ σ. Chrys.*hom.82.1 in Jo.*(8.484A); οὐκ ἔστι [sc. fasting] σ. γυμνασία, ἀλλὰ πνευματική id.*hom.12.2 in 1Tim.*(11.612A); σ. ἔννοιαι Cyr.*Jo.*3.6(4.320C); **b.** of persons, *earthly-minded* ὁ σ. θεολόγος Gr.Nyss.*Eun.*10(2 p.190.16; M.45.785A); τοῖς σ. Ἰουδαίοις ‡Chrys.*pasch.*4(8.260B); **c.** neut. plur. as subst., *earthly things*, Clem.*ecl.*11(p.139.26; M.9.704A); ἐλθὼν οὐκ εἰρήνην ἐπὶ τὴν γῆν, τοῦτ' ἔστιν ἐπὶ τὰ σ. καὶ αἰσθητά, βαλεῖν ἀλλὰ μάχαιραν Or.*Jo.*1.32 (36; p.40.32; M.14.85A); οἱ ἐν σ. νοοῦντες εἶναι τὸν θεόν Ath.*inc.*15.2 (M.25.121D); οὐκ ἀργήσεις σωματικῶν, ἵνα ἄρῃς πνευματικά; Cyr.H.*procatech.*6; διὰ τῶν σ. αὐτοὺς ἐπὶ τὰ πνευματικὰ ποδηγεῖ Thdt.*qu.36 in Ex.*(1.148); **6.** *concrete, physical*; **a.** in gen. ἐὰν λάβῃς τὰς φυλὰς ταύτας σωματικάς...ποῦ ιβ' χιλιάδας εὕροις; Or.*Apoc.*32(*JTS* 25 p.10); ποῖος γὰρ σ. δράκων ἐν τῷ σ. τῆς Αἰγύπτου ποταμῷ ὀφθεὶς ἱστόρηται ποτε; id.*Jo.*6.48(29; p.157.12; M.14.284B); διὰ τοῦτο ζῶντές εἰσιν Ἀβραὰμ καὶ Ἰσαὰκ καὶ Ἰακώβ, ἐπεὶ καὶ αὐτοὶ συνταφέντες τῷ Χριστῷ συνανέστησαν αὐτῷ, οὐ πάντως κατὰ τὴν σ. τοῦ Ἰησοῦ ταφὴν ἢ σ. ἀνάστασιν αὐτοῦ *ib.*20.12(p.342.20f.; 600C); εἰ ὁ εὐαγγελιζόμενος 'ἀγαθὰ εὐαγγελίζεται', πάντες δὲ οἱ πρὸ τῆς σ. Χριστοῦ ἐπιδημίας Χριστὸν εὐαγγελίζονται ὄντα 'τὰ ἀγαθά' *ib.*1.15(p.19.18; 49A); ταῦτα τροπικῶς λέγεται εἰς παράστασιν τὴν ἀπὸ τῶν συνήθων καὶ σ. ὀνομάτων τῆς νοητῆς φύσεως id.*Cels.*6.70(p.140.3; M.11.1404C); **b.** *external*, of Jewish worship 'μόδιον' δὲ συμβολικῶς κέκληκε τὴν συναγωγὴν τῶν Ἰουδαίων καὶ τὴν σ. τοῦ νόμου λατρείαν τὴν πάλαι ἐν τῷ γράμματι συμβόλων id.*fr.12 in Lc.*(p.238); τῆς ἐν τῷ τόπῳ σ. λευϊτικῆς καὶ ἱερατικῆς λατρείας id.*Jo.*28.12(11; p.402.22; M.14.704B); τὴν παραίτησιν τῆς κατὰ τὸν Μωσέως νόμον σωματικωτέρας λατρείας διδάσκει Eus.*d.e.*6.3 (p.255.5; M.22.420A); of words opp. writing ἐκ νοὸς εἰς νοῦν, διὰ μέσου λόγου, σωματικοῦ μέν, ἀυλοτέρου δὲ ὅμως, γραφῆς ἐκτός Dion. Ar.*e.h.*1.4(M.3.376C); **c.** *literal, actual*; **i.** ref. interpretation of scriptures ἢ προϊέμενος τὰ τέσσαρα εἶναι ⟨ἐρεῖ τ'⟩ ἀληθὲς αὐτῶν οὐκ ἐν τοῖς σ. χαρακτῆρσιν Or.*Jo.*10.2(2; p.173.31; M.14.312B); προέκειτο... αὐτοῖς [sc. the evangelists] ὅπου μὲν ἐνεχώρει ἀληθεύειν πνευματικῶς ἅμα καὶ σωματικῶς, ὅπου δὲ μὴ ἐνεδέχετο ἀμφοτέρως, προκρίνειν τὸ πνευματικὸν τοῦ σ., σῳζομένου πολλάκις τοῦ ἀληθοῦς πνευματικοῦ ἐν τῷ σ., ὡς ἂν εἴποι τις, ψεύδει *ib.*10.5(4; p.175.19; 313C); οἱ Ἰουδαῖοι τὰ βάθη τῶν γραφῶν μὴ συνησθημένοι καὶ πάντα σ. τὸν νόμον ἡγούμενοι καὶ τοὺς προφήτας εἰρηκέναι Meth.*symp.*9.1(p.115.6; M.18.180A); ὅταν ἀκούω 'ἄμπελον ἐξ Αἰγύπτου μετῆρας', οὐκ ἄμπελον σ. περιβλέπομαι, ἀλλὰ τὸν λαὸν νοῶ ‡Ath.*dial.Trin.*3.27(M.28.1245A); τῆς σ. τῶν ὀνομάτων ἐμφάσεως Gr.Nyss.*Eun.*8(2 p.187.12; M.45.781B); Cyr.*Am.*5(3.258D); **ii.** *literal-minded*; of the Jews, Or.*comm.in Mt.*11.12(p.52.30; M.13.940C); id.*Jo.*10.15(12; p.185.25; M.14.332C); οἱ σ. καὶ τοῖς αἰσθητοῖς φίλοι δοκοῦσίν μοι νῦν διὰ τῶν Ἰουδαίων δηλοῦσθαι *ib.*10.38(20; p.209.5; 369C); **iii.** neut. as subst., *literal sense* of scripture, v. γραφή, ἔνδυμα; κατὰ τὸ σ. *literally* ἐκ τῆς 'διψῆν' φωνῆς καὶ ἐκ τῆς 'πεινῆν' κατὰ τὸ σ. δύο σημαινόμενα *ib.*13.2(p.227.15; M.14.401A); κατὰ τὸ σ. οὐ πάντες ἄνθρωποι σπέρμα εἰσὶν τοῦ Ἀβραάμ *ib.*20.2(p.328.13; 573C); opp. κατὰ τὴν ἀναγωγήν, *ib.* 32.27(17; p.472.24; 816D); τὸ σ. ἐκβαλών, τὸ πνευματικὸν πληροῦν ἐπαγγέλλεται Proc.G.*Is.*1: 11–15(M.87.1485D); **d.** ?*factual* ἀναγκαῖον πνευματικῶς καὶ σωματικῶς Χριστιανίζειν· καὶ ὅπου μὲν χρὴ τὸ σ. κηρύσσειν εὐαγγέλιον, φάσκοντα 'μηδὲν εἰδέναι' ⟨ἐν⟩ τοῖς σαρκίνοις 'ἢ Ἰησοῦν Χριστὸν καὶ τοῦτον ἐσταυρωμένον', τοῦτο ποιητέον Or.*Jo.* 1.7(9; p.13.4; M.14.37B); **e.** *solid* τὰ σ. τοῦ κόσμου στοιχεῖα Iren. *haer.*1.4.2(M.7.484A); **f.** *material* εἰκονίζονται μὲν οὖν σωματικῶς, ὡς εἰκόνισε Μωϋσῆς τὰ χερουβίμ, καὶ ὡς ἑωράθησαν τοῖς ἀξίοις, ἀλλ' ἀσώματον καὶ νοητήν τινα θεωρίαν δηλούσης τῆς σ. εἰκόνος Jo.D. *imag.*3.24(M.94.1344B).

σωματικῶς, **1.** *in bodily form*; **a.** in gen. ἐκθεοῦνται τοῖς ἀνθρώποις καὶ σ. ἀναπλάττονται, Δίκη τις καὶ Κλωθὼ κτλ. Clem.*prot.*2(p.19. 27; M.8.96B); Ἀβραὰμ εἶπεν...· σ. ἤθελον ἀναληφθῆναι *T.Abr.*B 7 (p.112.7); **b.** ref. Christ, at Transfiguration σ. ἐπεδείκνυτο πρὸς τὸ καὶ τοῖς θνητοῖς αὐτῶν εἰς θέαν ὑποπεσεῖν ὀφθαλμοῖς Or.*fr.22 in Lc.* (p.243) = Cyr.*Lc.*9:29(M.72.656B); in Inc. σ. παρών Ath.*inc.*18.2 (M.25.128A); Ἰησοῦς Χριστός, χθὲς καὶ σήμερον σ., ὁ αὐτὸς πνευματικῶς, καὶ εἰς τοὺς αἰῶνας Gr.Naz.*or.*30.21(p.144.2; M.36.133A); παρέδειξε σ., ὡς καὶ αὐτοῖς ὄμμασι καταθεᾶσθαι παρόν Cyr.*inc.unigen.* (5^1.703E); in glory ἐν δεξιᾷ τοῦ πατρὸς κεκάθικε σ. Jo.D.*f.o.*4.23(M.94. 1205B); **c.** ref. H. Ghost at Pentecost ἔπρεπε...καὶ αὐτὸ φανῆναι σ. Gr.Naz.*or.*41.11(M.36.444C); **2.** *when in the body* κατὰ τὸν σ. ὑπὸ τοῦ κυρίου διδαχθέντα τύπον Didym.(‡Bas.)*Eun.*5(1.303E; M.29.729A); **3.** *through the body* μὴ ἐνεργούσης ἔτι σ. τῆς ψυχῆς [i.e. in sleep] Clem.*paed.*2.9(p.207.22; M.8.496C); **4.** *by using bodily terms* μὴ τοίνυν διὰ τὰ σ. περὶ τοῦ θεοῦ λεγόμενα, ὡς ἐχώρουν οἱ παλαιοί, σῶμα τὸν θεὸν νομίζωμεν Or.*fr.4 in 1Reg.*(p.296.23; M.17.44D); Thdr.Mops. *Ps.*37:4(p.223.25); περὶ γὰρ τοῦ θεοῦ...σωματικώτερον ἔθος τῇ θείᾳ γραφῇ λαλεῖν Thdt.*Ps.*6:2(1.635); ὅσα τοίνυν περὶ θεοῦ σωματικώτερον εἴρηται, συμβολικῶς μὲν λέγονται· ἔχει δέ τινα ὑψηλοτέραν διάνοιαν ‡Cyr.*Trin.*12(6^2.28A; M.77.1148A); **5.** *in respect of humanity*, opp. θεϊκῶς; of Christ, Cyr.*Jo.*11.12(4.1001E) cit. s. ἐν; **6.** *bodily*, exeg. Col.2:9 τὸ γὰρ σ. κατοικεῖν τὸν πατέρα καὶ τὸ πνεῦμα ἐν Χριστῷ, ἐπειδὴ σὰρξ γέγονεν ὁ λόγος ‡Dion.Al.*ep.Paul.Sam.*(p.32); '...σ.', ἐν τῇ σαρκὶ αὐτοῦ κατοικεῖν πᾶν τὸ πλήρωμα τῆς θεότητος νοητέον Ath.*inc.et c.Ar.*4(M.26.989C); 'σ.'· τουτέστιν οὐσιωδῶς Didym.*Trin.* 1.27(M.39.401B); φασὶν ὅτι τὴν ἐκκλησίαν λέγει πεπληρωμένην ὑπὸ τῆς θεότητος αὐτοῦ...τὸ δὲ σ. ὡς ἐν κεφαλῇ σῶμα Chrys.*hom.6.1 in Col.*(11.366E); ἡ ἐκκλησία πλήρης ἐστίν, ἐν τῷ Χριστῷ δὲ κατοικεῖ σ., τοῦτ' ἔστιν ὡς σῶμα ἡνωμένον κεφαλῇ Sever.*Col.*2:9(p.322.8); but cf. τινὲς τῶν διδασκάλων ἐνταῦθα Χριστὸν τὴν ἐκκλησίαν ἔφησαν ὠνομᾶσθαι...οὐκ οἶδα δέ, εἰ καὶ σ. ἁρμόττει τῇ τοιαύτῃ τοῦ νοήματος θεωρίᾳ...σ., τουτέστιν ὡς ἐν ἰδίῳ σώματι Thdt.*Col.*2:9(3.485f.); 'σ.'· ἐγὼ δ' οἶμαι εἰρῆσθαι ἀντὶ τοῦ οὐσιωδῶς Isid.Pel.*epp.*4.160 (M.78.1256A); σ., ἵνα μὴ ἁπλῆν ἢ γοῦν σχετικὴν τὴν κατοίκησιν ὑποτοπήσειέ τις, ἀλλ'...ἀληθινήν τε καὶ καθ' ὑπόστασιν Cyr.*Nest.*1.8 (p.30.37; 6^1.28A); ἐν αὐτῷ φησι κατοικῆσαι πᾶν τὸ πλήρωμα τῆς θεότητος, οὐ μεθεκτῶς μᾶλλον ἢ σχετικῶς ἤγουν ὡς ἐν δόσει χάριτος, ἀλλὰ σ., ὅ ἐστιν οὐσιωδῶς, ὡς ἂν εἰ καὶ ἐν ἀνθρώπῳ λέγοιτο κατοικεῖν τὸ πνεῦμα αὐτοῦ, οὐχ ἕτερον ὂν παρ' αὐτόν id.*Pulch.*(p.37.19; 5^2. 144D); σ., ὅ ἐστιν οὐσιωδῶς Eutych.*pasch.*3(M.86.2396A); ἢ σ. νόει οἷον σεσαρκωμένος Oecum.*Col.*2:9(p.455.3); ἵνα μή τις νομίσῃ σχετικὴν εἶναι τὴν κατοίκησιν, ἢ συναπτικὴν ἁπλῶς, τούτου χάριν εἶπε 'σ.' ἀντὶ τοῦ οὐσιωδῶς Jo.D.*Col.*2:9(M.95.893B); 'σ.', τουτέστιν, ἐν τῇ σαρκὶ αὐτοῦ id.*f.o.*3.7(M.94.1004B); **7.** *in a corporeal* or *physical way*; **a.** Christ ἀληθῶς σ. ἀνέστη †Just.*fr.res.*(p.46; M.6.1589A); ἀναστρεφόμενος σ. *Ev.Thom.*B 1(p.158); παρθένος οὖσα ἐν γαστρὶ σ. παρὰ τὴν κοινὴν συνελάμβανε φύσιν, σ. μὲν ὡς ἐν σώματι, πνευματικῶς δὲ ὅτι ἄνευ κοινωνίας Or.*hom.7 in Lc.*(p.54.9,11); οὐδὲ...χωρίζομεν αὐτὸν τοῦ πατρός, τόπους καὶ διαστήματά τινα μεταξὺ τῆς συναφείας αὐτῶν σ. ἐπινοοῦντες *Symb.Ant.*(345)9 ap.Ath.*syn.*26(p.253.36; M.26. 733B); οἱ...τὸν Σαμοσατέα καθελόντες σ. ἐκλαμβάνοντες τὸ ὁμοούσιον Ath.*syn.*45(p.269.37; M.26.772C); οὐχὶ παρὼν τοῖς μαθηταῖς ὁ Χριστὸς σ. μόνον Chrys.*hom.43.1 in Jo.*(8.254D); τὸ...ἐν Βηθλεὲμ σ. γεννηθῆναι ‡Meth.*Sym.et Ann.*3(M.18.353A); **b.** ref. baptism τῇ δὲ ὕδατος φυσικῇ καθάρσει, σωματικώτερον αὐτῷ διαγγέλλουσα Dion.Ar.*e.h.*2.3. 1(M.3.397B); **c.** ref. man's union with Christ, esp. at eucharist γίνεται μὲν γὰρ ἐν ἡμῖν ὁ υἱός, σ. μὲν ὡς ἄνθρωπος, συνανακιρνάμενός τε καὶ συνενούμενος δι' εὐλογίας τῆς μυστικῆς Cyr.*Jo.*11.12(4.1001E); τὸν γὰρ φύσει τε καὶ ἀληθῶς υἱόν, οὐσιώδη πρὸς αὐτὸν ἔχοντα τὴν ἕνωσιν, λαβόντες ἐν ἑαυτοῖς καὶ σ. καὶ πνευματικῶς...τῆς ὑπὲρ πάντα φύσεως μέτοχοι καὶ κοινωνοὶ γεγονότες δεδοξάσμεθα *ib.*(1002B); διδασκέτω... τῆς μυστικῆς εὐλογίας τὴν δύναμιν. γίνεται γὰρ ἐν ἡμῖν διατί; ἆρ' οὐχὶ καὶ σ. ἡμῖν ἐνοικίζουσα τὸν Χριστὸν τῇ μεθέξει καὶ κοινωνίᾳ τῆς ἁγίας αὐτοῦ σαρκός; *ib.*10.2(862D); οὐ γὰρ ἦν ἑτέρως ζωοποιηθῆναι δύνασθαι τὸ φθείρεσθαι πεφυκός, εἰ μὴ συνεπλάκη σ. τῷ σώματι τῆς κατὰ φύσιν ζωῆς τουτέστι, τοῦ μονογενοῦς *ib.*(863B); τί μάτην ἡμῶν καταφλυαρεῖ, λέγων ὡς ἐπείπερ οὐ σ. τῆς πρὸς αὐτὸν κοινωνίας ἐξήμμεθα, πίστει δὲ μᾶλλον καὶ διαθέσει τῆς κατὰ τὸν νόμον ἀγάπης, οὐ τὴν σάρκα, φησί, τὴν ἰδίαν ἄμπελον ὠνόμασε, μᾶλλον δὲ τὴν θεότητα *ib.*(864A); ταῦτά φαμεν, οὐκ ἐπιχειροῦντες ἀναιρεῖν τὸ συνενοῦσθαι δύνασθαι τῷ Χριστῷ, διά τε πίστεως ὀρθῆς καὶ ἀγάπης εἰλικρινοῦς, ἀποδεικνύντες δὲ μᾶλλον ὅτι καὶ πνευματικῶς καὶ σ. ἄμπελος μὲν ὁ Χριστός, κλήματα δὲ ἡμεῖς *ib.*(864B); ζωοποιούμεθα καὶ εὐλογούμεθα καὶ σ. καὶ πνευματικῶς id. *Lc.*22:19(M.72.903C); **8.** *corporeally, physically*, Eus.*h.e.*1.3.15(M.20. 73B); σ. ... χρισθέντα *ib.*1.3.18(73C); χιλιάδα τινά φησιν ἐτῶν ἔσεσθαι μετὰ τὴν ἐκ νεκρῶν ἀνάστασιν, σ. τῆς Χριστοῦ βασιλείας ἐπὶ ταυτησὶ τῆς γῆς ὑποστησομένης *ib.*3.39.12(300A); **9.** *in a material way* εἰκονίζονται [sc. incorporeal beings]...σ., ὡς εἰκόνισε Μωϋσῆς τὰ χερουβίμ, καὶ ὡς ἑωράθησαν τοῖς ἀξίοις Jo.D.*imag.*3.24(M.94.1344B); **10.** *literally, in a literal sense*, usu. opp. πνευματικῶς, ref. scriptural exegesis ἀναγκαῖον πνευματικῶς καὶ σ. Χριστιανίζειν Or.*Jo.*1.7(9; p.13.4; M.14.37B); ἀληθεύειν πνευματικῶς ἅμα καὶ σ. *ib.*10.5(4; p.175.17; 313C); οἱ...ἁπλούστεροι καὶ ἀκεραιότεροι θαυμαζέτωσαν τὰ μεγαλεῖα τοῦ θεοῦ κατὰ ταῦτα· οἰκοδομεῖ γὰρ καὶ σ. νοούμενα id.*fr.15 in Lc.*8:41(p.239); ἡ Μάρθα σωματικώτερον ὑπεδέξατο τὸν λόγον..., ἡ δὲ Μαρία πνευματικῶς ἤκουεν αὐτοῦ *ib.*40(p.252); οὐδὲ περὶ τοῦ θρόνου τοῦ σωματικώτερον νοουμένου αἱ πρὸς Δαβὶδ ἦσαν ἐπαγγελίαι Eus.*qu. Steph.*15.3(M.22.929D); μηκέτι σ. ... ἀλλὰ πνευματικῶς διανοεῖσθαι περὶ τοῦ θεοῦ Ath.*ep.Serap.*4.10(M.26.668A); τῶν...σωματικώτερον τοῖς γεγραμμένοις ἐντυγχανόντων Gr.Nyss.*Eun.*7(2 p.154.28; M.45. 744A); τηρῆσαι σ. τὸ σάββατον †Bas.*Is.*23(1.397D; M.30.164B); οὐδὲ ...τὴν γῆν ὑποπόδιον τῶν ποδῶν αὐτοῦ πατουμένην σ. θέλει λέγειν περὶ θεοῦ, ἀλλ' ὡς ὑποκειμένην τῇ θεϊκῇ ἐξουσίᾳ Didym.(‡Bas.)*Eun.*5(3. 316C; M.29.757C); Epiph.*haer.*8.7(p.193.15; M.41.216B); Cyr.*Is.*2.4 (2.298B).

σωμάτιον, τό, 1. *body* (with no dim. sense), *M.Polyc.*17.1; Clem. *str.*7.7(p.36.15; M.9.468D); Pall.*h.Laus.*19(p.60.23; M.34.1067A); **2.** *slave* σ. πρίασθαι *Const.App.*2.62.4; **3.** *whole body*, met. προσαρμόσας τῷ τῆς ἀληθείας σ. Iren.*haer.*1.9.4(σωματείῳ M.7.548A); **4.** *book, volume* of parchment (opp. papyrus roll) πεντήκοντα σ. ἐν διφθέραις Const.ap.Eus.*v.C.*4.36(p.131.24; M.20.1185A); Bas.*ep.*261 (3.354E; M.32.861C); Mac.Aeg.*hom.*26.6(M.34.677B).

***σωματοβόρος**, *man-eating*, *Ep.Dor.*(M.88.1613C).

***σωματογραφέω**, *depict as having a body*, Thdr.Stud.*epp.*2.74(M. 99.1309C).

σωματοειδής (σωματώδης), *corporeal*; **1.** *in bodily form* σ. τὸ θεῖον ὑπολαμβάνουσιν Ath.*gent.*22(M.25.44C); **2.** *material*, -τώδης, Gr.Nyss.*Eun.*12(1 p.286.10; M.45.993D); -τώδης, id.*infant.*(M.46. 173A,B); **3.** *bodily* προσκυνήσεως Dion.Ar.*e.h.*2.2.3(M.3.393C); *ib.* 2.8.7(404B).

σωματοειδῶς (-τωδῶς), *in bodily form* εἰ τὴν ψυχὴν αὐτὴν σ. ὁ λόγος διέπλαττε Dion.Ar.*d.n.*9.5(M.3.913A); σ. τὰς ἀσωμάτους διαπλάττει Eustrat.*stat.anim.*19(p.496); *V.Chrys.*59(p.325.8); σὴν σωματωδῶς... ἐνδημίαν Jo.D.*carm.pent.*117(p.217; M.96.837C).

***σωματοκάπηλος, ὁ,** *slave-dealer*, Chrys.*hom.*40.5 *in 1Cor.*(10. 385B).

σωματοκτόνος, ὁ, *one who kills* or *mortifies the body* ἡμεῖς οὐκ ἐδιδάχθημεν σ., ἀλλὰ παθοκτόνοι *Apophth.Patr.*(M.65.368A); ref. Mt.20:28 μὴ φοβηθῶμεν τοὺς σ. Thdr.Stud.*epp.*2.28(M.99.1197A).

σωματόμορφος, *in bodily shape* οἱ...σωματόμορφον τὸν θεὸν... δογματίσαντες Anast.S.*hex.*7(M.89.963C).

σωματοποι-έω, 1. *provide with a body*; **a.** in gen. συνέστηκεν...πρὸ τῶν δερματίνων σεσωματοποιῆσθαι χιτώνων τὸν ἄνθρωπον Meth.*res.*1. 39(p.283.6; M.41.1108A); πνεῦμα σεσωματοποιημένον *T.Sal.*4.4(σεβωμάτω (?) πεποιημένον M.122.1321A); **b.** *make into a body* ὁ τὸ εὐτελέστατον οὕτω σ. [sc. God] Cyr.H.*catech.*18.9; intrans. ἐξ ἀσωμάτων σ. Iren.*haer.*1.5.2(M.7.493A); **c.** *embody* ὁ δὲ σωτὴρ ἐπιδημήσας καὶ τὸ εὐαγγέλιον σωματοποιηθῆναι θελήσας τῷ εὐαγγελίῳ πάντα εὐαγγέλιον πεποίηκεν Or.*Jo.*1.6(8; p.11.5; M.14.33D); met., of words embodied in writing, of the writing on the wall τὸν λόγον...~εῖσθαι καὶ σχῆμα ἀνθρώπου ἀναλαμβάνειν Hipp.*Dan.*3.14.6; ὁ τῷ πνεύματι σωματοποιηθεὶς ἄνθρωπος χαρακτὴρ Eust.*fr.in Pr.*8:22(M.18.677D); **d.** *consolidate, materialize* οὐδέ ἐστιν [sc. ἡ ξηρὰ ψυχή] κάθυγρος ταῖς ἐκ τοῦ οἴνου ἀναθυμιάσεσιν νεφέλης δίκην ~ουμένη Clem.*paed.*2.2(p.174. 16; M.8.425A); πίστις...βρώματι ἐπεικάζεται, ἐν αὐτῇ ~ουμένη τῇ ψυχῇ *ib.*1.6(p.112.28; 296A); οἱ Στρωματεῖς τῇ πολυμαθίᾳ ~ούμενοι id.*str.*1.2(p.14.9; M.8.709C); **e.** *depict in bodily form, represent in art* τὴν ἀσώματον ψυχὴν ~εῖ Eustrat.*stat.anim.*19(p.496); μὴ γὰρ εἶναι θεμιτὸν ἔλεγεν ὁ Ξεναίας ἀσωμάτους ὄντας ἀγγέλους ~εῖν Jo. Diacr.*fr.h.e.*ap.CNic.(787)*act.*5(H.4.305D); **2.** *make into bodily form*, *incarnate* πατρικὸς χαρακτὴρ ἄνωθεν μετενηνεγμένος ἐνθάδε σωματοποιηθείς Hipp.*haer*.5.17(p.115.2; M.16.3178A); ἐσωματοποίησεν ἑαυτὸν ὁ...θεός Mac.Aeg.*hom*.4.9(M.34.480A); sacramentally ~εῖ... ἑαυτὸν καὶ εἰς βρῶσιν καὶ πόσιν ὁ κύριος *ib*.4.12(481B); σ. ... ἑαυτὸν ὥσπερ εἰς βρῶσιν πνευματικήν id.*elev*.7(M.34.1896A); med. εἰς ἀνάμνησιν τοῦ τε σ. αὐτόν Just.*dial*.70.4(M.6.641A); **3.** *embark on the body* or *main part of, construct*, of a written work πρότερον μὲν... ὑποσημειώσασθαι τὰ κεφάλαια...εἶτα μετὰ τοῦτο ~ῆσαι τὸν λόγον Or. *Cels*.proem.6(p.55.2; M.11.649B); βραχέσι αὐτὸ μόνον παρασημειώσεσιν χρήσομαι, εἱρμῷ καὶ τάξει ~ῶν τὸν λόγον Eus.*Marcell*.1.1(p.2.26; M. 24.713C); **4.** met., *make into one body* or *whole, collect together* ἀπὸ τῶν ἐσχάτων ἀνάγει ὁ θεὸς καὶ σ. τὰς νεφέλας Or.*hom.8.4 in Jer*.(p.59. 28; M.13.341B); εἰ συγκλώσαιμεν εἰς ἓν ~οῦντες τὰ ἐν τοῖς εὐαγγελίοις γεγραμμένα id.*Jo*.6.22(13; p.132.8; M.14.240B); ἡ δρόσος ἐκείνη ἡ ἐκ πολλῶν συναγομένη σταγόνων, ὑφ' ἓν ~εῖται καὶ συμπήγνυται Eus. *Ps*.132:3(M.24.28D); ὅσα...λυσιτελεῖν ἡγούμεθα...ἀναλεξάμενοι...δι' ὑφηγήσεως ἱστορικῆς πειρασόμεθα σ. id.*h.e*.1.1.4(M.20.52A); **5.** *give material existence to, represent as material* (cf. σωματοποίησις), ref. employment in scripture of metaphors concerning bodily or material things to express truth about spiritual things, sometimes to be translated *personify* οὐδὲ γὰρ ἀνόητος οὕτως τις ἦν ἵνα σ. δάκρυα παραπλήσια τοῖς τῶν ἀνθρώπων ἐν τοῖς καταβεβηκόσιν ἐξ οὐρανῶν ἀγγέλοις Or.*Cels*.5.55(p.59.12; M.11.1269A); ἀναγινώσκων τὸν Ἰεζεκιὴλ καὶ ὁρῶν τὸν θεὸν τῷ λόγῳ οἱονεὶ ~ούμενον id.*hom.11.5 in Jer*.(p.83.11; M.13.373C); σ. ... τὴν ἐκκλησίαν ὁ λόγος εἰς τὸ τῆς νύμφης εἶδος Gr.Nyss.*hom.7 in Cant*.(M.44.929A); *ib*.*14*(1080B); τὸ δὲ 'ἀπὸ προσώπου' ~ήσας περὶ τῆς ὀργῆς ἔφησεν Thdr.Mops.*Ps*.37:4 (p.223.17); σ. ... τὸ πρόσωπον τοῦ σατανᾶ ἡ γραφή Olymp.*Job* 40:11 (M.93.425B).

σωματοποίησις, ἡ, *physical representation*, used of employment in scripture of metaphors concerning bodily or material things to express truth about divine things (cf. σωματοποιέω) 'ὁ θεὸς κάθηται ἐπὶ θρόνου ἁγίου αὐτοῦ'. τῇ σ. τὸ γενόμενον διηγούμενος Thdr.Mops. *Ps*.46:9(p.309.15); ἠκολούθησεν τῇ οἰκείᾳ σ. ὡς γὰρ στρατηγοῦντος αὐτοῖς τοῦ θεοῦ καὶ προηγουμένου καὶ οὕτω διάγοντος αὐτοὺς τὴν θάλασσαν, ἐφάνης φησὶ προοδεύσας ἡμῶν ἐν τῇ θαλάσσῃ *ib*.86:20(p.516. 13); *ib*.17:8(p.113.8; M.66.661D).

σωματοποιΐα, ἡ, *bodily representation* τοὺς θεολόγους ἐπὶ σωματοποιΐαν ὅλως τῶν ἀσωμάτων ἐληλυθότας Dion.Ar.*c.h*.2.2(M.3.137C); τοῦ...δαίμονος διαγράψαι ὡς ἐν σ. τήν τε κακίαν καὶ ἰταμότητα Olymp. *Job* 40 proem.(M.93.421B); *ib*.41:25(449B).

***σωματοπράτης**, ὁ, *slave-dealer*, Barth.Edess.*Agar*.(M.104. 1425A).

***σωματοπρεπής**, *suited to corporeal things*, Dion.Ar.*d.n*.4.12(M.3. 709B).

***σωματοπρεπῶς**, *in corporeal form*, Dion.Ar.*ep*.9.1(M.3.1105A).

***σωματοτροφέω**, *nourish the body*, Gr.Thaum.*pan.Or*.15(p.35.6; M.10.1096B).

σωματουργέω, *endow with solid substance*, Geo.Pis.*hex*.1591(M.92. 1558A).

σωματουργία, ἡ, *whole work of Creation*, Geo.Pis.*hex*.138(M.92. 1443A).

σωματουργός, *creative of bodies* τέχναι καὶ χειρουργίαι τούτων ὑπ' ἀνθρώπων εὕρηνται σωματουργοί Dion.Al.ap.Eus.*p.e*.14.26(780C; σωματουργῶν M.21.1284B).

***σωματοφθόρος**, *destroying the body*, Cyr.*hom.div*.19(M.77.1109A).

σωματοφόρος, *wearing a body*; of Christ, Jo.Mon.*hymn.Bas*.(M. 96.1376D); id.*hymn.Chrys*.(M.96.1380C).

***σωματοφυλάκισσα**, ἡ, *bodyguard*, *Pers*.(p.20.2).

***σωματοφυῶς**, *according to the nature of the body* οὔτε τρεῖς ὑποστάσεις μεμερισμένας καθ' ἑαυτάς, ὥσπερ σ. ἐπ' ἀνθρώπων ἐστὶ λογίσασθαι, ἵνα μὴ πολυθεΐαν...φρονήσωμεν †Ath.*exp.fid*.2(M.25.204A).

***σωματοψύχως**, *with a body and a soul*, Anast.S.*serm.imag*.3(M. 89.1161C) cit. s. εἰκών.

σωματ-όω, *embody*; **1.** of Logos ἑαυτὸν ἐσωμάτωσε ‡Caes.Naz.*dial*. 183(M.38.1160); pass., *be embodied, take bodily form* σωματωθεὶς ὁ υἱὸς τοῦ θεοῦ ‡Ath.*synops*.59(M.28.416A); πῶς σαρκοῦται θεός, πῶς ~οῦται; Apoll.*quod un.Chr*.3(p.95.22; M.28.124B); μετὰ τὸ σχηματισθῆναι ἢ σ. Nil.*epp*.2.40(M.79.213D); σεσωματωμένος ἐξ ἀσωμάτου Leont.H.*Nest*.4.16(M.86.1681D); μίαν...ὑπόστασιν...ἐκ τῆς ἁγίας ἀειπαρθένου ~ωθεῖσαν Jo.D.*nat*.9(M.95.125A); **2.** *make into a body* σ. τὰ ποικίλα εἰς σάρκας Geo.Pis.*hex*.1229(M.92.1529A); med. ὁ σπόρος... ~οῦται τῇ κυήσει τὸ βρέφος *ib*.1336(1537A); pass., *be embodied, be made into a body* τότε δὲ ἄνθρωπος λέγεται, ὅτε ἡ λογικὴ ψυχὴ ~οῦται καὶ τὸ σῶμα ψυχοῦται ‡Ath.*dial.Trin*.5.9(M.28.1264B); Cyr.*Jo*.1.9 (4.81D); εἰ ἐπὶ γῆς διάγουσι αἱ ψυχαὶ πρὸ τοῦ ἐν μήτρᾳ σωματωθῆναι Antip.Bost.*fr*.ap.Leont.et Jo.*sacr*.2(M.86.2052D); of spiritual beings εἰς διάφορα τάγματα ~ωθέντες Or.*princ*.1.8.1(p.97.6); of an angel, Cyr.*Mal*.1(3.817A); met. ψυχουμένης τῆς ἀρετῆς κατὰ γνῶσιν, καὶ τῆς γνώσεως...~ουμένης κατ' ἀρετήν ‡Proc.G.*Pr*.9:1(M.87.1300D); ἐν σεαυτῷ δεικνὺς τὸν θεὸν ταῖς ἀρεταῖς ~ούμενον Max.*ambig*.(M.91. 1032B); met., of words embodied in writing ὁ λόγος οὗτος ὁ προφορικὸς κατὰ τὴν οἰκείαν φύσιν ἀναφής ἐστι καὶ ἀόρατος· ὅταν δὲ ἐν βιβλίῳ γραφῇ, καὶ οἱονεὶ ~ωθῇ, τότε καὶ ὁρᾶται καὶ ψηλαφᾶται Or. *schol.in Mt*.1:18(M.17.289A); ~οῦται...ὁ λόγος διὰ τοῦ γράμματος Sever.*sigill*.6(M.63.542); Max.*ambig*.(M.91.1285D); Melet.*nat.hom*. synops.(M.64.1104D).

σωματώδης, v. σωματοειδής.

[*]**σωματωδῶς**, v. σωματοειδῶς.

σωμάτωσις, ἡ, **1.** *embodying*, of Christ τῷ μυστηρίῳ τῆς αὐτοῦ σ. ‡Hipp.*Ber.Hel*.2(p.322.33; M.10.833B); τῆς...τοῦ θεοῦ σ. *ib*.3(p.323. 20; 836A); ἡ πρὸς τὸ σῶμα συνάφεια οὐ κατὰ περιγραφὴν τοῦ λόγου, ὥστε μηδὲν ἔχειν πλέον τῆς σ. Apoll.*fr*.138(p.240.25)ap.Thdt.*eran*.3 (4.255); ἡ τοῦ λόγου σ. Proc.G.*Gen*.1:26(M.87.120C); Max.*opusc*. (M.91.237B); **2.** *corporeality* τῆς σ. τούτου τοῦ κόσμου Philox.*ep*.21 (p.172); **3.** *stuff* of which bodies are made πῇ δὲ προβάλλει σωματώσεις ἀρρένων; Geo.Pis.*hex*.656(M.92.1486A).

***σωμαφορέω**, *have a body* (perh. for σῶμα φορέω), Isaac *cog*.(M. 86.885C).

***σωμεραστής**, ὁ, *lover of the body*, i.e. one *sexually passionate* Ast.Am.*hom*.5(M.40.240B).

***σωμεραστία**, ἡ, *love of the body*, i.e. *sexual passion*, Ast.Am.*hom*. 13(M.40.360A).

***σωπούνιον**, τό, v. *σαπούνιον.

σωρεία, ἡ, **1.** a *heaping up* ψάμμου Gr.Nyss.*Eun*.10(2 p.236.30; M.45.837D); met. τοῦ κακοῦ id.*res*.1(M.46.609A); Chrys.*hom.44.5 in Mt*.(7.474A); τῶν χρημάτων *ib*.*63.4*(633E); **2.** as a figure of speech, Gr.Nyss.*Eun*.1(1 p.24.12; M.45.252C); ὁ μὲν λόγος πολλῶν ῥημάτων σ. τίς ἐστιν καὶ σύνοψις Ast.Soph.*hom.1 in Ps*.5(M.40.400A); **3.** as a logical figure, *sorites*, Tat.*orat*.27(p.29.14; M.6.865B); **4.** *combination* οὐ κατὰ σωρείαν συντιθεμένων αὐτῶν ἀλλὰ...ἀνακιρναμένων Nemes. *nat.hom*.5(M.40.620B); σ. μονάδων ἢ χύσιν μονάδων Jo.D.*Jacob*.50 (M.94.1457C); *ib*.81(1480A); **5.** *heap, quantity*, Gr.Nyss.*anim.et res*. (M.46.136B); id.*v.Mos*.(M.44.345D); id.*Eun*.1(1 p.142.18; M.45.381C).

σώρευμα, τό, *gathering, meeting*, Thphn.*chron*.p.296(M.108.721C).

σωρεύ-ω, **1.** *gather, pluck* τοῦ ~σαι ἐκ τῶν δένδρων τὰς ἐλαίας Gr. Mag.*dial*.(tr.Zach.)1.7(M.*PL*.77.183C); **2.** *collect* ~σαι πνοὴν τοῦ λαλῆσαι Gr.Mag.*dial*.(tr.Zach.)4.11(M.*PL*.77.338A); pass., *be gathered, collected together*; of persons, Thphn.*chron*.p.249(v.l. σορ-; πορευθέντες M.108.624B); Barth.Edess.*Agar*.(M.104.1429A).

σωρηδόν, *by heaps, in quantities, cumulatively*, *Ep.Lugd*.ap.Eus. *h.e*.5.1.7(M.20.409B); Eus.*h.e*.8.6.6(M.20.753A); Cyr.*Is*.1.4(2.97D).

σωσικόσμιος, *saving the world* ἡ σ. ἐκ παρθένου γένεσις Jo.Eub. *concept.BMV* 10(M.96.1476A).

***σῶσμα**, τό, *recovery*; from sickness, Sophr.H.*carm*.6.18(M.87. 3761A); *deliverance* ἐνέγκαι μετὰ σώσματος τὸ πλοῖον Leont.N.*v.Jo. Eleem*.26(p.54.22); *salvation*; from heresy, Thdr.Stud.*epp*.2.158(M. 99.1493C).

***σωστικῶς**, *in a saving manner*, Dion.Ar.*d.n*.4.24(M.3.725D); Max.*myst*.5(M.91.681B).

Σωτάδειος, *like Sotades*, i.e. scurrilous ὁ κίβδηλος καὶ σ. Ἄρειος Ath.*Ar*.1.4(M.26.20C); neut. plur. as subst. *scurrilous songs* like those by Sotades, Just.*2apol*.15.3(M.6.469A); Gr.Nyss.*Eun*.1(1 p.25. 11; M.45.253A).

σωτήρ, ὁ, *saviour*; **1.** of God τὸν θεόν...τόν...σ. εἴς τε τὸ παρὸν εἴς τε τὸ μέλλον Clem.*str*.4.20(p.304.23; M.8.1337C); σύ...εἶ ὁ σ. Serap. *Euch*.5.11; σ. γὰρ καλοῦμεν τὸν θεόν, οὐκ ἀνὰ μέρος μὲν τῷ πατρί, ἀνὰ μέρος δὲ αὐτῷ τῷ υἱῷ, ἤτοι τῷ ἁγίῳ πνεύματι τὰ ἐφ' οἷς ἠλεήμεθα ἀποκομίζοντες χαριστήρια, ἀλλ' ὄντως τῆς μιᾶς θεότητος κατόρθωμα λέγοντες τὴν ἑαυτῶν σωτηρίαν Cyr.*Jo*.10.2(4.858C); id.*Arcad*.(p.83.37, 39; 5².75A,B); **2.** of Christ; translation of 'Jesus', Just.*1apol*.33.7 (M.6.381B); ‡Ath.*Ar*.4.36(p.86.5; M.26.524B); freq. in place of name Jesus or Christ, Just.*dial*.8.2(M.6.492D); Or.*Cels*.6.43(p.114.8; M.11. 1365A); Ath.*Ar*.2.8(M.26.161C); as physician ἦλθε σ. ὁ κύριος ἡμῖν μᾶλλον ὡς ἰατρὸς ἀγαθὸς τοῖς ἁμαρτιῶν μεστοῖς ἢ τοῖς δικαίοις Or. *Cels*.2.57(p.189.17; 901B); Eus.*d.e*.4.10(p.168.12; M.22.280C); two senses dist. ἐπικαλεῖται σ. διὰ τὸ σώζειν τοὺς αἰχμαλώτους· ἰατρὸς ἐπικέκληται ἐπειδὴ οὐράνιον καὶ θεϊκὸν φάρμακον δίδωσι Mac.Aeg. *hom*.26.23(M.34.689D); as saviour of all πῶς δὲ ἂν εἴη σ. καὶ κύριος, εἰ μὴ πάντων σ. καὶ κύριος; Clem.*str*.7.2(p.7.17; M.9.412A); ὅλῳ τῷ γένει τῶν ἀνθρώπων σ. Or.*Cels*.4.99(p.373.16; 1180B); ἁπάντων σ. Eus.*Marcell*.2.4(p.57.34; M.24.821C); ὁ πάντων δεσπότης καὶ σ. Ath.

*inc.*9.4(M.25.112C); Gnost. τοῦ δευτέρου Χριστοῦ, ὃν καὶ Σ. λέγουσιν Iren.*haer.*1.3.1(M.7.468A); εἰς τοῦτον ἐπὶ τοῦ βαπτίσματος κατελθεῖν ἐκεῖνον τὸν ἀπὸ τοῦ Πληρώματος ἐκ πάντων Σωτῆρα ἐν εἴδει περιστερᾶς *ib.*1.7.2(513A); ἐληλυθέναι τὸν σ. ἐπὶ καταλύσει τῶν φαύλων ἀνθρώπων καὶ δαιμόνων, ἐπὶ σωτηρίᾳ δὲ τῶν ἀγαθῶν Hipp.*haer.*7.28 (p.209.12; M.16.3323A); Thdt.*haer.*1.7(4.298); v. *Χριστός*; **3.** of men: of Const. οἷα λυτρωτὴν σ. τε καὶ εὐεργέτην Eus.*h.e.*9.9.9(M.20.824A); of apostles ἐκπέμπει...ἀποστόλους, σωτῆρας τῶν ἀνθρώπων Clem.*ecl.*16(p.141.14; M.9.705B); Thdt.*affect.*8(p.197.2; 4.900A); of S. George, Jo.Mon.*hymn.Geo.*5(M.96.1396D); of S. Stephen, *BCH* 13 p.294 (saec. v).

σωτηρία, ἡ, A. *preservation*; **1.** in sickness, i.e. *recovery* θάνατος... προεκηρύσσετο τῷ ὄφει, σ. δὲ τοῖς καταδακνομένοις ὑπ' αὐτοῦ Just.*dial.*91.4(M.6.693B); Bas.Sel.*v.Thecl.*2.25(M.85.609C); Niceph.Ur. *v.Sym.*89(M.86.3069D); **2.** in health, i.e. *well-being, welfare*, esp. of emperor, in prayers and oaths ὑπὲρ τῆς σ. εὐχόμενος Ath.*apol.Const.*10(M.25.608A); τὴν σ. τῶν βασιλέων, ἀπολύσατε ἡμᾶς CChalc.*act.*17 (*ACO* 2.1.3 p.99.13; H.2.644B); in a letter τῷ ἀδελφῷ ἡμῶν...σ. αἰώνιος *M.Ner.et Ach.*11(p.10.17).

B. *salvation*; **1.** as purpose; **a.** of Inc. ἄνθρωπος γενόμενος...ὑπὲρ σωτηρίας τῶν πιστευσόντων αὐτῷ Just.*1apol.*63.16(M.6.425B); ἀπ' οὐρανοῦ καταβὰς διὰ τὴν σ. τῶν ἀνθρώπων Arist.*apol.*15.1; τὸν σαρκωθέντα ὑπὲρ τῆς ἡμετέρας σ. Iren.*haer.*1.10.1(M.7.549A); Or.*fr.* *1 in Jo.*(p.483.10); Ath.*inc.*1.3(M.25.97C); Chrys.*hom.in Jo.5:19*(6.259D); in credal statements τὸν διὰ τὴν ἡμετέραν σ. σαρκωθέντα *Symb.Caes.*(p.43; M.20.1537B); τὸν δι' ἡμᾶς τοὺς ἀνθρώπους καὶ διὰ τὴν ἡμετέραν σ. κατελθόντα καὶ σαρκωθέντα *Symb.Nic.*(325)(p.51; M.20.1540B); *Symb.Nic.-CP*(p.80.7; H.2.288B), etc.; **b.** of Christ's passion and Crucifixion, *1Clem.*7.4 cit. s. αἷμα; τοῦ σταυροῦ, ὅ ἐστιν σκάνδαλον τοῖς ἀπιστοῦσιν, ἡμῖν δὲ σωτηρία καὶ ζωὴ αἰώνιος Ign.*Eph.*18.1; πάσχει...ὑπὲρ τὴν τῶν ἀνθρώπων σ. Or.*Cels.*4.73(p.343.3; M.11.1144B); διὰ τοῦ σταυροῦ...τὴν σ. Ath.*inc.*26.1(M.25.140D); εἰ γὰρ κατὰ φαντασίαν ἐσταυρώθη, ἐκ σταυροῦ δὲ ἡ σ., καὶ ἡ σ. φαντασία Cyr.H.*catech.*13.37; Chrys.*hom.27.2 in Jo.*(8.155C); Thdt.*qu.37 in Gen.*(1.49); of Christ's passion, death, and Resurrection, ‡Ath.*Apoll.*2.5 (M.26.1140C); **2.** as meaning of the name 'Jesus' Ἰησοῦς..., ὃς ἑρμηνεύεται πῇ μὲν σ., πῇ δὲ σωτήρ †Ath.*exp.fid.*3(M.25.205A); **3.** perfected in Christ because of his relationship both to Father and to men σοῦ γάρ εἰμι λόγος, καὶ ἐπειδὴ σὺ μὲν ἐν ἐμοί, ὅτι σοῦ λόγος εἰμί, ἐγὼ δὲ ἐν αὐτοῖς διὰ τὸ σῶμα, καὶ διὰ σὲ τετελείωται ἐν ἐμοὶ τῶν ἀνθρώπων ἡ σωτηρία, ἐρωτῶ ἵνα καὶ αὐτοὶ γένωνται ἕν, κατὰ τὸ ἐν ἐμοὶ σῶμα καὶ τὴν αὐτοῦ τελείωσιν Ath.*Ar.*3.22(M.26.369A); work of Son ἐν τῇ τοῦ πνεύματος χάριτι Gr.Nyss.*tres dii*(M.45.129B); of whole Trin. (full discussion of theol. problem), *ib.*(129B,C); **4.** acquired from God παρ' ἐκείνου μόνου σ. καὶ βοήθειαν ζητεῖν Just.*dial.*102.6(M.6.713D); ἐπὶ τῆς ἡμετέρας γοῦν σ. πολλαπλάσιόν ἐστιν εἰς ὑπερβολὴν τὸ ἀπὸ τοῦ θεοῦ τοῦ ἀπὸ τοῦ ἐφ' ἡμῖν Or.*princ.*3.1.19(p.233.6; M.11.292B); οὐ γὰρ ἐν δυνάμει ἀνθρώπου, οὐδὲ ἐν σοφίᾳ, ἀλλ' ἐν τῇ χάριτι τοῦ θεοῦ ἐστι ἡ σ. Bas.*hom.in Ps.*33(1.144D; M.29.353C); Chrys.*hom.* *1.1 in 1Cor.*(10.3E); Thdt.*Soph.*3:19(2.1579); through scriptures ἡ οἰκονομηθεῖσα ὑπὸ θεοῦ εἰς ἀνθρώπων σ. δοθῆναι γραφή Or.*princ.*4.2.4 (p.313.4; 365A); ἡμῶν ὡς ἐχόντων πρὸς σωτηρίαν τὰς θείας γραφάς Ath.*ep.fest.*39(M.26.1436B); ἡ σ. ... ἐξ ἀποδείξεως τῶν θείων ἐστὶ γραφῶν Cyr.H.*catech.*4.17; in many ways, Gr.Naz.*or.*32.25(M.36.204A); οὐχ εἷς σωτηρίας τρόπος, ἀλλὰ πολλοὶ καὶ διάφοροι Chrys.*oppugn.*3.5(1.83D); id.*hom.45.2 in Mt.*(7.478C); by baptism, τὸ πρὸς σωτηρίαν βάπτισμα *Hom.Clem.*3.29; Cyr.H.*catech.*3.10; Bas.*Spir.*26(3.21E; M.32.113A); πίστις δὲ καὶ βάπτισμα δύο τρόποι τῆς σ. *ib.*28(23E; M.117B); Gr.Naz.*or.*40.14(M.36.376C); eucharist πιστὸν εἰς σ. Clem.*paed.*1.5 (p.99.12; M.8.268B); cf. ὑπόμνησιν ποιεῖτε τῆς σωτηρίας τῆς ὑπὲρ ὑμῶν Chrys.*hom.1.4 in Eph.*(11.22C); exorcisms before baptism τοὺς ἐπορκισμοὺς δέχου μετὰ σπουδῆς· κἂν ἐμφυσηθῇς, κἂν ἐπορκισθῇς, σ. σοι τὸ πρᾶγμα Cyr.H.*procatech.*9; unction of dead τὴν ὁλικὴν αὐτοῦ σ. ἱερουργοῦσα Dion.Ar.*e.h.*7.9(M.3.565B); by faith, Just.*dial.*47.4 (M.6.577C); by right belief, Clem.*paed.*1.6(p.108.11; M.8.285C); Chrys.*hom.33.1 in Jo.*(8.189D); by orthodox profession, Gr.Naz.*or.*32.25(M.36.204A); Isid.Pel.*epp.*4.51(M.78.1101B); Just.Imp.*edict.*ap. Evagr.*h.e.*5.4(p.198.8; M.86.2796A); by γνῶσις and good works, Clem.*str.*6.15(p.493.26; M.9.345C); cf.*ib.*7.7(p.36.11; 468C); ἡ σ. τῆς λογικῆς φύσεως ἡ γνῶσίς ἐστιν ἡ τοῦ θεοῦ Or.*Ps.*53:3(p.55); by faith and an upright life, Chrys.*hom.31.1 in Jo.*(8.175cf.); not by Law, Meth.*symp.*10.1(p.122.11; M.18.193A); dependent on free will, Or. *princ.*3.1.16(p.224.4; M.11.281A); **5.** scope of salvation; some not saved οὗτοί εἰσιν οἱ υἱοὶ τῆς ἀνομίας· ἐπίστευσαν δὲ ἐν ὑποκρίσει, καὶ πᾶσα πονηρία οὐκ ἀπέστη ἀπ' αὐτῶν· διὰ τοῦτο οὐκ ἔχουσιν σ. Herm. *vis.*3.6.1; id.*mand.*12.3.6; εἰς ὀλίγους τὰ τῆς σ. περιΐσταται Chrys.*hom.* *in Rom.12:20*(3.158E); but salvation offered to all, Ath.*inc.*31.3(M.25.149C); ‡Ath.*Apoll.*1.5(M.26.1101A); προθέντος ἅπασι τοῦ θεοῦ καὶ πατρὸς τὴν διὰ Χριστὸν σ. Cyr.*Rom.*11:2(p.238.26; M.74.845C); embracing body as well as soul, Or.*fr.36 in Jo.*(p.512.9); Ath.*tom.*7(M.26.804B); ἵνα τελείαν τὴν σ. κατεργάσηται ὅλου τοῦ ἀνθρώπου, ψυχῆς λογικῆς καὶ σώματος, ἵνα τελεία ᾖ καὶ ἀνάστασις ‡Ath.*Apoll.*1.15(M.26.1121A); grades of salvation μετέχει μὲν σ. τινὸς καὶ ἡ δίγαμος, οὐ μὴν τοσαύτης μακαριότητος, ὅσης παρὸν διγαμεῖν καθαρεύσασα Or.*hom.20.4 in Jer.*(p.182.29; M.13.508C); cf.id.*hom.17 in Lc.* (p.121.11); **6.** agents of man's salvation: BMV σωτὴρ γάρ μου ἐστὶν ὁ θεὸς σ. ἐξ ἐμοῦ χαριζόμενος τῷ κόσμῳ *ib.8*(p.58.16); τὴν σ. δι' αὐτῆς ἀπεκδεχόμενοι Jo.Eub.*concept.BMV* 11(M.96.1476C); χαῖρε, ἀφορμὴ τῆς πάντων σ. Taras.*praesent.BMV* 15(M.98.1500B); ἡ Ἄννα μετὰ τὸ γεννῆσαι τὴν παντὸς τοῦ κόσμου σ. ‡Hipp.Th.*fr.*16(p.49.1); angels τὸ εἶναί τινας ἀγγέλους καὶ δυνάμεις κρείττονας, λειτουργικὰς τῆς σ. τῶν ἀνθρώπων Or.*princ.*proem.10(p.16.2; cf.M.11.1200C); apostles, Thdt.*Ps.*48:2(1.914); id.*Rom.*1:5(3.16); salvation promoted also by fellow men συμφέρει ἡμῖν ἐάν γε σωτηρίας ἄξιοι γενώμεθα δι' ἄλλων κολαζομένων, ἢ ἄλλων κόλασις. καὶ ὡς συνήνεγκεν τὸ παράπτωμα τοῦ Ἰσραὴλ τῇ σ. τῶν ἐθνῶν, οὕτως συνοίσει ἡ κόλασίς ⟨τινων⟩ τῇ ἑτέρων σ. Or.*hom.12.6 in Jer.*(p.93.12ff.; M.13.388Af.); τοῦτο γὰρ ἡμῶν καὶ σωτηρίας ὑπόθεσις γενήσεται, ὅταν μὴ ὑπὲρ ἑαυτῶν μόνον σπουδάζωμεν, ἀλλ' ὅταν καὶ τὸν πλησίον ὠφελῶμεν καὶ πρὸς τὴν τῆς ἀληθείας ὁδὸν χειραγωγῶμεν Chrys.*hom.3.4 in Gen.*(4.19B); *ib.9.2*(69C); **7.** final salvation ἕκαστον ἐπ' αἰωνίαν κόλασιν ἢ σ. κατ' ἀξίαν τῶν πράξεων πορεύεσθαι Just.*1apol.*12.1(M.6.341C); id.*dial.*131.2(M.6.780C); 'σ.' καλεῖ τὴν παντελῆ τῶν κακῶν ἀπαλλαγήν, ἥτις αὐτοῖς ἐπὶ τοῦ μέλλοντος αἰῶνος προσγίνεσθαι ἔμελλεν Thdr.Mops.*Rom.*8:24(p.139.20; M.66.828B); θέλημα μέν ἐστιν ἡ λογικὴ σ. καθ' ἡμᾶς τε καὶ ὑπὲρ ἡμᾶς οὐσιῶν· ἡ δὲ οὐχ ἑτέρως γενέσθαι δύναται, μὴ θεουμένων τῶν σωζομένων Dion.Ar.*e.h.*1.3(M.3.373D); **8.** in Gnostic theory μὴ γὰρ εἶναι τὴν ὕλην δεκτικὴν σωτηρίας Iren.*haer.*1.6.1(M.7.505A); Hipp.*haer.*7.28(p.209.13; M.16.3323A) cit. s. σωτήρ; τὸν δὲ Χριστὸν...κατεληλυθέναι ἐπὶ σωτηρίᾳ τοῦ ἀποπλανηθέντος πνεύματος, ὃ κατοικεῖ ἐν τῷ ἔσω ἡμῶν ἀνθρώπῳ *ib.*10.13(p.274.11; 3427B); *ib.*10.19(p.280.10; 3438A).

***σωτηριοποιός**, *safeguarding*, Thdr.Stud.*epp.*1.2(M.99.909B).

σωτήριος, 1. *saving, of salvation, bringing salvation* σ., εἰ καὶ πικρός, ὁ φόβος Clem.*paed.*1.9(p.139.2; M.8.349B); cf.*Lit.*ap.*Const. App.*8.6.5; οὐδὲ ἐλήλυθέν τις κενὸς σωτηρίων καὶ ἁγίων σπερμάτων Or. *Jo.*20.5(p.333.18; M.14.584D); *ib.*13.43(p.270.22; 477B); τὰ σ. σπέρματα τῆς τῶν οὐρανῶν βασιλείας Eus.*h.e.*3.37.1(M.20.293A); of Cross ξύλον σ. Thdt.*Ps.*50:9(1.939); of sign of cross σ. ... σφραγῖδα id.*h.e.*3.17.1(3.933); of the labarum σ. ... σημεῖον Eus.*v.C.*2.16(p.47.31; M.20.993C); σ. τροπαίῳ *ib.*(p.47.22; 993B); of Easter festival, *ib.*3.14 (p.83.26; 1069C); Thdt.*ep.*37(4.1097); *ib.*38(1098); of Sunday τὴν σ. καὶ κυριακὴν ἡμέραν Eus.*v.C.*4.18(p.124.11; 1165B); of baptism and baptismal water, Or.*Jo.*13.29(p.253.31; M.14.449C); σ. ... λουτρῷ Eus.*v.C.*4.61(p.143.29; 1212C); ἐν τῷ σ. ὕδατι ἀφανίζεται [sc. Devil] Cyr.H.*catech.*19.3; τοῦ σ. βαπτίσματος Bas.*Eun.*3.2(1.273D; M.29.657C); Cyr.*Juln.*7(6^2.248A); of eucharistic elements τοῦ σ. σώματος καὶ τοῦ τιμίου αἵματος *Const.App.*2.33.2; βρῶμα σ. Sever.*creat.*6.4 ap.Cosm.Ind.*top.*10(M.88.425A; θυσιαστήριον M.56.488); of prayer, Chrys.*hom.3.2 in Philm.*(11.788B); of doctrines, Or.*princ.*4.1.1 (p.293.7; M.11.344A); of a creed, CChalc.*act.*5(*ACO* 2.1.2 p.128.16; H.2.453D); of churches, *Pers.capt.*(M.86.3236A); **2.** *of the saviour* τοὔνομα...τὸ σ. Clem.*str.*6.11(p.473.26; M.9.305A); τὸ σ. γένος Afric. *ep.Arist.*5(p.61.21; M.10.61A); τοῦ σ. πάθους Or.*fr.25 in Jer.*(p.216.21); τῆς ἐν τῷ σ. σταυρῷ γεγονυίας ἐκλείψεως Dion.Ar.*ep.*7.2(M.3.1081A); ref. Church of Holy Sepulchre τὸ σ. μνῆμα Eus.*v.C.*4.45 (p.136.13; M.20.1196A); CHier.*ep.*ap.Ath.*apol.sec.*84(p.162.33; M.25.397C); τὸν σ. ... τάφον Thdt.*h.e.*1.16.5(3.790); **3.** *saving, preserving* τὸ ἀσθενὲς τῆς μνήμης τῆς ἐμῆς ἐπικουφίζων, κεφαλαίων συστηματικὴν ἔκθεσιν μνήμης ὑπόμνημα σ. πορίζων ἐμαυτῷ Clem.*str.*1.1(p.10.26; M.8.704A); **4.** *healing*, Bas.*hom.in Ps.*61(1.196E; M.29.477B); *Const. App.*6.28.7; Mac.Mgn.*apocr.*1.6(p.1.5); Thdt.*h.e.*1.18.4(3.794); *healthful*, Cyr.*Jo.*7(4.679B); **5.** neut. as subst.; **a.** *salvation*; **i.** in gen., Just.*dial.*13.1(M.6.501A); Clem.*str.*3.18(p.244.21; M.8.1208C); τὸ διὰ τοῦ σταυροῦ σ. Ath.*ep.fest.*22(p.295.19; M.26.1433A); **ii.** of Christ τὸ σ. ἡμῶν Ἰησοῦν Χριστόν *1Clem.*36.1; Συμεὼν...λαβὼν τὸ σ. τοῦ θεοῦ Or.*Jo.*10.43(27; p.222.9; M.14.393A); Cyr.*glaph.Gen.*4(1.109D); **b.** *peace-offering* νόμον σωτηρίου *T.Lev.*9.7(v.l. -ων); interpreted of recovery or rescue τὰς δὲ θυσίας σωτηρίου· δηλοῖ δὲ καὶ τοὔνομα ἀρρωστίας, ἢ χαλεπῶν τινων ἑτέρων ἀπαλλαγήν Thdt.*qu.1 in Lev.*(1.177); of Christian thank-offerings, *Const.App.*2.26.1.

***σωτηριοτόκος**, *bearing the Saviour, who is mother of the Saviour* ἐγὼ δὲ λέγω καὶ Χριστοτόκον, καὶ κυριοτόκον, καὶ σωτηριοτόκον, καὶ θεοτόκον τὴν ἁγίαν παρθένον κατὰ τὴν φωνὴν τοῦ ἀγγέλου ‡Ath.*nativ. Chr.*4(M.28.965C).

σωτηριώδης, *saving, of salvation* τῷ σ. σημείῳ Eus.*d.e.*6.25(p.295.3; M.22.484D); τοῦ σ. σταυροῦ Ath.*ep.Serap.*1.20(M.26.577B); αἱ σ. ...τελεταί Dion.Ar.*e.h.*3.3.7(M.3.436C); ἡ σ. οἰκονομία τοῦ...σωτῆρος Taras.*ep.*2(M.98.1436D); neut. as subst., *salvation*, Epiph.*haer.*42.16 (p.185.5; M.41.816B).

σωτηριωδῶς, *in a saving way*, Gr.Thaum.*pan.Or.*5(p.14.15; M.10.1068C); Epiph.*haer.*8.7(p.193.12; M.41.216A); Andr.Cr.*or.*6(M.97.916C).

σωτηρίως, 1. *in a way that brings salvation*, Clem.*paed.*1.8(p.133.16; M.8.340A); Or.*Cels.*3.17(p.216.3; M.11.941A); Dion.Ar.*c.h.*4.4(M.3.181B); ‡Meth.*Sym.et Ann.*11(M.18.373D); **2.** *in a way conducive to health* σ. τὸ σῶμα διοικοῦσα Clem.*paed.*2.1(p.158.9; M.8.388C); **3.** *in a way conducive to well-being* τῶν ἐν οὐρανῷ σ. τῷ παντὶ χορευόντων ἀστέρων Or.*or.*7(p.316.11; M.11.440D); Ath.*gent.*40(M.25.80C); Dion. Ar.*e.h.*3.3.6(M.3.432C,433A).

σωφρον-έω, 1. *be moderate in sensual desires*; hence *be chaste*, Just.*2apol.*2.2(M.6.444A); εἰ...μὴ δύνασθε...παντάπασι ~εῖν...ἐπέτρεψα...ταῖς σφῶν αὐτῶν κοινωνεῖν γαμεταῖς Meth.*symp.*3.11(p.39.17; M.18.77B); Chrys.*hom.37.3 in 1Cor.*(10.348A); of youths before marriage, id.*Anna* 1.6(4.710D); **2.** = σωφρονίζω, *chasten, make to learn self-control* ἐπὶ σωτηρίαν παρακαλέσαιμι ~οῦσαν Clem.*prot.*12 (p.84.3; M.8.240B); πόρνην γυναῖκα, ἣν καὶ λαβὼν ἐσωφρόνησεν Eus. *proph.*1(M.22.1264B, unless for ἐσωφρόνισεν).

σωφρόνισμα, τό, *chastisement*, Gr.Naz.*or.*45.28(M.36.661B).

σωφρονισμός, ὁ, *chastisement*, Meth.*symp.*1.1(p.8.22; M.18.37C); Cyr.*Ps.*7:15(M.69.750B); Jo.Clim.*past.*12(M.88.1189C).

σωφρονιστήριον, τό, *house of correction*, Eus.*d.e.*4.1(p.151.1; M.22.252B); *V.Const.*18(p.555.22).

***σωφρονολογ-έω,** *speak with moderation* or *speak with chastisement* τὸν ἀρχάγγελον Μιχαὴλ ἐπὶ τοῦ Μωϋσέως σώματος ~οῦντα *cat. Apoc.*19:10(p.456.23).

σωφροσύνη, ἡ, A. *discretion, moderation*; **1.** def. and properties ὁρίζονται...τὴν δὲ σ. ἕξιν ἐν αἱρέσει καὶ φυγῇ σώζουσαν τὰ τῆς φρονήσεως κρίματα Clem.*str.*2.18(p.154.18; M.8.1017B); opp. φρόνησις, *ib.*6.15(p.495.8; M.9.349A) cit. s. φρόνησις; as gift of God, *ib.*2.20(p.181.19; M.8.1072A); water its φάρμακον, id.*paed.*2.2(p.168.12; M.8.412A); σωφροσύνης ἴδιον, κοσμίαν ἑαυτῷ διὰ πάντων ἄγειν Constantius Imp. ap.Ath.*apol.Const.*30(M.25.632D); σ. ... τὴν τῶν παθῶν ἐλευθερίαν Thdt.*provid.*6(4.566); **2.** effects ἡ δὲ δι' αὑτὴν αἱρετὴ σ., κατὰ τὴν γνῶσιν τελειουμένη...κύριον καὶ αὐτοκράτορα τὸν ἄνδρα κατασκευάζει Clem.*str.*7.11(p.49.2; M.9.493C); likeness to God, *ib.*4.23(p.316.2; M.8.1361A); **3.** in rel. to other virtues, coupled with δικαιοσύνη, ἀνδρεία, εὐσέβεια, φρόνησις, Clem.*paed.*2.12(p.230.13; M.8.544C); *ib.*3.11(p.272.5; 640A); also with κοσμιότης and ἁρμονία, id.*str.*1.25 (p.103.22; M.8.912C); σ. ... οὐκ ἄνευ ἀνδρείας *ib.*2.18(p.155.7; 1020A); Or.*hom.12.11 in Jer.*(p.97.16; M.13.393A); with παιδεία, Meth.*res.*1.31(p.264.9; M.41.1141A); περιβεβλημένοι σ. καὶ δικαιοσύνην Ath.*ep. fest.*40(p.296.31; M.26.1440B); **4.** opp. vices: ἐπιθυμία, Clem.*str.*4.23 (p.315.16; 1360C); ἀκολασία, *ib.*4.19(p.303.16; 1336A); id.*paed.*2.1 (p.164.2; 400C); ἀπαιδευσία, *ib.*3.4(p.254.4; 597B); ἡ σ. φύσει ἀγαθόν, ἀκολασία δὲ ἐναντίον σ. Meth.*symp.*8.16(p.106.4f.; M.18.169A); **5.** common to men and women, Clem.*str.*4.8(p.275.8ff.; 1272A); cf.id.*paed.*1.4(p.96.3; 260C); **6.** taught by Christ, opp. μέθη taught by Dionysus, Ath.*inc.*49.3(M.25.184C); **7.** = *honesty, probity* λῃσταί τινες,...τοὺς σώφρονας συναριθμοῦσιν ἑαυτοῖς καταψευδόμενοι τῆς ἐκείνων σ. id.*Dion.*1(p.46.18; M.25.480B).

B. esp. sexually; hence *chastity*; **1.** coupled with other virtues, ἐγκράτεια, etc., *1Clem.*62.2; *ib.*64; Ign.*Eph.*10.3; Just.*1apol.*6.1(M.6.336C); id.*dial.*8.3(M.6.493A); Clem.*str.*3.12(p.235.21; M.8.1188A); *ib.*3.1(p.197.8; 1104B) cit. s. ἐγκράτεια; Meth.*symp.*1.3(p.12.6; M.18.44B); Nil.*spir.mal.*4(M.79.1148C); **2.** opp. πορνεία, Just.*1apol.*14.2 (M.6.348B); adultery, ref. Mt.5:28, *ib.*15.1(349A); Clem.*paed.*3.8 (p.261.1; M.8.613A); Christian σ. opp. pagan ἀκρασία, id.*prot.*4(p.47.18; M.8.161A); opp. πορνεία, Bas.*ep.*260.7(3.400B; M.32.965A); **3.** *conjugal* τὴν γαμήλιον σ. ἑταιρικαὶ καθυβρίσωσιν ἡδοναί Clem.*paed.*2.10(p.215.25; M.8.513A); *ib.*3.12(p.282.23; 664A); id.*str.*2.23(p.192.7; M.8.1093B); dist. from παρθενία which is above it, Meth.*symp.*1.2(p.10.22f.; M.18.41B); but cf.*ib.*1.3(p.11.21; 44A); τῆς μετ' αἰδοῦς καὶ σ. παιδοποιήσεως *ib.*8.2(p.82.10; 140C); dist. from παρθενία, Ath.*v.Anton.*79 (M.26.953A); τὴν ἐν γάμῳ κατορθοῖ σ. Thdt.*1Cor.*7:5f.(3.203); acc. Christian (opp. pagan) teaching, same standard for both sexes, *ib.*7:3(201); Susanna its OT example, Or.*Jo.*28.5(4; p.394.22; M.14.688C); of widows, Clem.*str.*7.12(p.52.3; M.9.500C); of perfect continence in marriage, Thdt.*h.e.*4.13.3(3.969); **4.** of youths before marriage, Chrys.*Anna* 1.6(4.710C); Joseph its OT example, Or.*fr. in Lam.*(p.279.7; M.13.613D); Bas.*ep.*2.3(3.73A; M.32.228C); **5.** virginal διαδέχεται τὴν ἐπὶ μιᾷ γυναικὶ συναλλαγὴν ἡ σ., μέχρις ἂν τελείως τὴν ἐκ τοῦ ἔθους ἐπὶ τὴν συνουσίαν καταφορὰν Meth.*symp.*1.3 (p.11.21; M.18.44A); παρθένοι, σ. ἀχράντου θυγατέρες *ib.*8.4(144B); Ath.*inc.*48.2(M.25.181B); **6.** endangered by pride, Ath.*virg.*22(p.57.20; M.28.277C); **7.** willow its symbol (exeg. Ps.136:2), Meth.*symp.*4.4(p.49.15; M.18.92A).

T

τ, v. ταῦ.

ταβελλάριος, ὁ, v. [*]ταβουλάριος.

***Ταβεννησιῶται, οἱ,** name of an order of monks in the Thebaid, ‡Pall.*h.mon.*3.1(p.27.9; M.34.1131C); Soz.*h.e.*6.28.3(M.67.1372A).

τάβλα, ἡ, (Lat. *tabula*) **1.** *tablet*, *Chron.Pasch.*p.9(M.92.85D); *label*, *A.Andr.et Mt.*3(p.68.6); **2.** *dice-board*, Apollon.ap.Eus.*h.e.*5.18.11 M.20.480B).

ταβλίζω, v. ταυλίζω.

ταβλί(ο)ν, τό, 1. *stripe* (*clavus*) on border of garment, denoting senatorial rank, Jo.Mal.*chron.*2 p.33(M.97.104A); *ib.*17 p.413(612B); *Chron.Pasch.*p.117(M.92.305A); *ib.*p.332(861B); **2.** *table*, Leont.N.*v. Sym.*31(M.93.1709A).

***ταβλοπαρόχιον, τό,** *room for dice-tables*, Jo.Mal.*chron.*13 p.345 (M.97.516A).

[*]ταβουλάριος, ὁ, = ταβελλάριος, (Lat. *tabularius*) *registrar, recorder*, Eus.*m.P.*9.2(p.928.10; M.20.1492A); Pall.*v.Chrys.*3(p.19.19; ταβελλάριος M.47.14); Nil.*epp.*2.214 tit.(M.79.312C); as commissioner for affidavit, CEph.(431)*act.*4(*ACO* 1.1.3 p.19.19; H.1.1492B).

ταγή, ἡ, 1. *command, direction*; of God, Meth.*symp.*11(p.136.16; M.18.213A); plur., *1Clem.*20.8; Meth.*symp.*10.1(p.122.8; 193A); id. *Porph.*1(p.503.1; M.18.397C); **2.** *prescribed allowance*; of food, *Chron.Pasch.*p.138(M.92.344C); *ib.*254(613B).

***ταγίζω,** poss. for ⟨φαγίζω⟩ ? *appoint portion of food to, feed* ἐπότισαν καὶ ἐτάγισαν τὰ ἄλογα Thphn.*chron.*p.266(M.108.660C, v.l. for ἐπότισαν τὰ ἄ. de Boor).

τάγμα, τό, something ordered or arranged; **1.** *fixed* or *estimated payment*, of a vow εὐχὴν καλεῖ τὴν ὑπόσχεσιν, ὃ πολλοὶ τ. προσαγορεύουσι Thdt.*qu.38 in Lev.*(1.215); *votive offering* λαβόντες...τῶν γυναίων τὰ τ. ... Κύρῳ μηδὲν καὶ Ἰωάννῃ τοῖς μάρτυσι...προσκομίσαντες Sophr.H.*mir.Cyr.et Jo.*49(M.87.3605B); **2.** *assigned portion*; of land, Or.*hom.25.3 in Jos.*(p.456.22; M.87.1040D); **3.** *regular body, formation*; of troops, Ign.*Rom.*5.1; Eus.*v.C.*2.3(p.41.28; M.20.981B); Synes.*ep.*4(M.66.1333A); plur., Soz.*h.e.*1.8.11(M.67.880C); *Chron.Pasch.*p.299(M.92.749B); of officers, *staff*, Eus.*v.C.*4.67(p.145.13; 1221B); met. κατὰ πόλιν καὶ κώμην...πολλὰ τῶν πιστευόντων τὰ τ. Chrys.*hom.2.4 in Rom.*(9.441A); of Jews, Cyr.*Ps.*34:12(M.69.904A); Thdt.*serm.Chrys.*(5.100); **4.** *order, rank, position*; **a.** military, Eus.*v.C.*1.54(p.32.27; M.20.968C); **b.** civil; of status of cities, Or. *hom.20.5 in Jos.*(p.423.16; M.87.1029D); of ranks in civil service, Eus.*v.C.*4.1(p.118.13; 1152A); met., ref. heavenly city ὅσα τῶν δήμων ἐκείνων τὰ τ. Chrys.*hom.1.8 in Mt.*(7.18A); **c.** of various classes or orders in Christian body ἕκαστος ὑμῶν...ἐν τῷ ἰδίῳ τ. εὐχαριστείτω θεῷ...μὴ παρεκβαίνων τὸν ὡρισμένον τῆς λειτουργίας αὐτοῦ κανόνα *1Clem.*41.1; of baptized and catechumens, Or.*Cels.*3.51(p.247.9; M.11.988A); δύο τ. ... τὸ μὲν εἰσέτι στοιχειούμενον, τὸ δ' ἤδη διὰ τοῦ λουτροῦ πεφωτισμένον Eus.*d.e.*2.3(p.77.25; M.22.140B); of clergy, faithful, and catechumens, *ib.*7.1(p.311.17; 509B); δύο τ. ...ἐν μὲν τῶν ἐν γνώσει καὶ...τοῖς...τοῦ...πνεύματος χαρίσμασιν τελειουμένων, θάτερον δὲ τῶν διὰ βίου κατορθούντων *ib.*6.18(p.279.31; 460C); **d.** of laity εἴτε τῶν ἐν κλήρῳ, εἴτε ἐν λαϊκῷ τ. CNic.(325)*can.*5; CCP(381)*can.*6; ἐν τῷ τ. ⟨δὲ τῶν λαϊκῶν⟩ καὶ ἐν κλήροις Epiph. *haer.*68.2(p.142.14; M.42.188A); of monks and laity, Eus.Al.*serm.*1 (M.86.316A); **e.** of orders of ministry, CSard.*can.*10; Epiph.*haer.*68.3(p.143.8; M.42.188C); Thdt.*1Tim.*proem.(3.638); Sophr.H.*v.Cyr. et Jo.*51(M.87.3613C); Areth.*Apoc.*4:5(M.106.569C); of clerical order as a whole μὴ δεῖν πρόσφατον φωτισθέντας προσάγεσθαι ἐν τ. ἱερατικῷ CLaod.*can.*3; Epiph.*haer.*75.7(p.339.8; M.42.513C); τελεῖν ἐν τῷ ἱερατικῷ τ. ‡Nil.*narr.*6(M.79.676B); τοῦ ἐκκλησιαστικοῦ τυγχάνοντες τ. Socr.*h.e.*4.16.1(M.67.500C); μηδένα δὲ ἀπολελυμένως χειροτονεῖσθαι μήτε πρεσβύτερον μήτε διάκονον μήτε ὅλως τινὰ τῶν ἐν τῷ ἐκκλησιαστικῷ τ. CChalc.*can.*6; μνήσθητι, κύριε, πάσης ἐπισκοπῆς ὀρθοδόξων...παντὸς τοῦ πρεσβυτερίου...καὶ παντὸς ἱερατικοῦ τ. *Lit.*

Chrys.(p.332.12); dist. from monks οὔτε ἐπίσκοποι, οὔτε κληρικοί, οὔτε ὅλως ἐκ τοῦ ἱερατικοῦ τ. ὄντες, ἀλλ' ὡσανεὶ μονάζοντες Tim.CP *haer.*(M.86.33A); ἄλλος ὁ τρόπος τοῦ ἐκκλησιαστικοῦ τ. καὶ ἄλλος τῶν μοναζόντων Sophr.H.*conf.*(M.87.3365A); of staff of a church τὸ τ. τῆς δεσποίνης...Μαρίας τῆς νέας Jo.Mosch.*prat.*61(M.87.2913B); partic., of bishops τὸ πάντων ἁγιώτατον τ. Gr.Naz.*or.*43.26(M.36.532C); priests τὸ τῶν πρεσβυτέρων τ. Chrys.*hom.11.1 in 1Tim.*(11.604D); Thdt.*h.e.*2.24.12(3.890); τοῦ σεμνοῦ τῶν ἱερέων τ. Dion.Ar.*e.h.* 3.3.10(M.3.440A); deacons, *Const.App.*8.46.16; deaconesses διακονισσῶν τ. ἐστὶν εἰς τὴν ἐκκλησίαν Epiph.*haer.*79.3(p.478.16; M.42.744D); virgins, Meth.*symp.*7.3(p.75.2; M.18.129B); *ib.*(p.74.6; 128D); ἐν τῷ τῆς παρθενίας τ. καθιέρωσεν αὐτήν *M.Ner.et Ach.*9(p.9.11); widows, Pall.*v.Chrys.*5(p.32.19; M.47.20); monks οὐ δεῖ ἱερατικοὺς ἀπὸ...τοῦ τ. τῶν ἀσκητῶν εἰς καπηλεῖον εἰσιέναι CLaod.*can.*24; Epiph.*haer.*70.1(p.232.17; M.42.340A); τ. τῶν μοναζόντων Bas.*ep.*199 *can.*19(3.292C; M.32.720C); τ. τῶν μοναχῶν Pall.*v.Chrys.*6(p.37.13; M.47.23); τῷ μοναδικῷ τ. Nil.*epp.*2.63(M.79.228D); Eus.Al.*serm.*1 (M.86.316A); abs., Leont.B.*Nest.et Eut.*3(M.86.1361C); ref. division of monks into groups ἐκέλευσε...εἰκοσιτέσσαρα τ. εἶναι καὶ ἑκάστῳ τ. ... στοιχεῖον ἑλληνικόν Pall.*h.Laus.*32(p.90.3f.; M.34.1100A); **f.** of angelic orders, Or.*princ.*1.8(p.97.6); ἄλλο...γένος τὸ τῶν ἀγγέλων καὶ ἄλλο τὸ τῶν ἀρχῶν...ὅτι μὴ τ. ἓν καὶ μία σύστασις...τῶν ἀθανάτων, ἀλλὰ γένη...καὶ διαφοραί Meth.*res.*1.49(p.302.15; M.18.277B); Eus. *e.th.*2.20(p.128.14; M.24.952B); θεὸν...ἑνὸς παρακλήτου διὰ Χριστοῦ, καὶ τῶν ἄλλων τ. ποιητήν *Const.App.*6.11.2; ἀρχιερέα [sc. Christ] πάντων τῶν λογικῶν τ. *ib.*6.30.10; τὰ ἕτερα τῶν τ. πλήθη, ἀρχάγγελοι, θρόνοι *ib.*7.35.3; ἕκαστον τ. τῶν οὐρανίων δυνάμεων CCP(543) *anath.*5(p.228); τὸ ἀγγελικὸν τ. μετὰ τῶν ἀνθρώπων τὰς ἱκεσίας τῷ θεῷ προσάγουσιν Eustrat.*stat.anim.*11(p.395); **g.** of demons τὰ διάφορα τῶν δαιμόνων τ. Thdt.*Ezech.*34:28(2.974); **h.** of various grades in future life κατὰ τάγματα τῶν ἀνισταμένων ἔσονται ἀναπαύσεις Or.*hom.8.6 in Jer.*(p.61.1; M.13.344B); τὰ διάφορα...τ. τῶν ἐν Χριστῷ ζωοποιηθησομένων id.*Jo.*32.3(p.429.27; M.14.748A); **5.** *class, division*; **a.** *party* ὑπάγεσθαι τούτους τῷ ἑαυτοῦ τ. βουλόμενος [sc. Devil] Clem.*str.*3.15(p.240.19; M.8.1196C); ὅτε μεσίτης γίνεται θεοῦ καὶ ἀνθρώπου, μέσος ὢν ἑκατέρου τ. Eus.*Marcell.*1.1(p.8.9; M.24.728A); of pagans τὸ τῶν ἐναντίων τ. id.*v.C.*4.55(p.140.14; M.20.1205C); id.*l.C.*proem.(p.196.11; M.20.1317C); Christians and pagans, *ib.*9(p.221.31; 1372A); Jews τὸ...τ. τῶν ἐκ περιτομῆς Cyr.*Ps.* 74:5(M.69.1188C); **b.** religious *system* ἣν [sc. Χριστιανισμός] τὸ μεταξὺ Ἰουδαϊσμοῦ καὶ Ἑλληνισμοῦ τρίτον ἡμῖν ἀποδεδειγμένον τ. Eus.*d.e.*1.2(p.8.31; M.22.25A); **c.** *division* of a subject, Or.*Jo.*2.3 (p.57.9; πράγματα M.14.113B); **d.** in gen., *group, division,* Herm. *sim.*8.5.2; εἰς δύο διελόντες τ. ἁπάσας τὰς αἱρέσεις Clem.*str.*3.5(p.214.10; cod. πράγματα M.8.1144B); Or.*hom.20.4 in Jer.*(p.183.2; M.13.508D); Eus.*d.e.*3.5(p.131.23; 221D); id.*theoph.fr.*14(p.33*.6; M.24.680A); **6.** *order* of succession (= τάξις), Herm.*sim.*8.4.2; *ib.*8.2.8.

τάγχαρας, ὁ, foreign word for *gold*, Cosm.Ind.*top.*2(M.88.100C).

ταινία, ἡ, *headband*; in architecture, *cornice*, Cyr.*ador.*8(1.248E).

ταινιάζω, *crown*; met., *adorn* εὐφημίαις τοὺς ἡμετέρους ἐταινίασας λόγους Thdt.*ep.*2(4.1061).

***ταινιάω,** *wear a crown* ἐν οἷς εἱστήκει κατὰ τοὺς ταινιῶντας καὶ τῶν ἐπάθλων ἐφιεμένους ἀγωνιστάς ‡Nil.*perist.*10.7(M.79.900C; perh. f.l. for ταινιοῦντας).

τακερός, *soft, weak* τακερὰν...τὴν σάρκα φαρμάκοις Clem.*paed.*3.2 (p.239.20; M.8.561C).

***τακτέος,** *to be placed*, Synes.*Dion* 1(p.234.7; M.66.1113A).

τακτικός, as subst.; masc., ref. Dan.6:2, of high-ranking Babylonian official with authority over satraps, *president, minister*, Hipp.*Dan.*3.19.5; Ath.*h.Ar.*45(p.209.8; M.25.748C); neut., *that which marshals* or *orders*, Clem.*str.*1.24(p.100.14; M.8.908A).

***ταλαιπωροποιός,** *making miserable* ἡ ἁμαρτία τ. ἐστι Dor.*doct.*7.3 (M.88.1700D).

ταλανίζ-ω, 1. *call, pronounce unhappy, miserable*, Or.*sel.in Ps.*70 proem.(M.12.1520A); of Christ γέλωτι...μηδαμοῦ χρησάμενος...ἀλλὰ καὶ ~ων τοὺς κατεχομένους ὑπ' αὐτοῦ Bas.*reg.fus.*17.1(2.360B; M.31.961C); Epiph.*haer.*30.8(p.343.16; M.41.420A); in moral sense οὐ μικρὸν τὸ κέρδος ~ειν ἑαυτόν Chrys.*hom.53.3 in Jo.*(8.313D); ταπεινώσεώς ἐστι τὸ ἑαυτὸν ~ειν Dor.*doct.*9.4(M.88.1721D); **2.** *denounce* ~ει τοὺς ἄφρονας τοὺς ἐξ ἀπαιδευσίας κλέψαι τοῦ μονογενοῦς τὴν ἀξίαν τολμήσαντας Mac.Mgn.*apocr.*2.8(p.9.8); τὰ παρὰ τῷ προφήτῃ ~όμενα σάββατα †Bas.*Is.*30(1.403D; M.30.177C); Chrys. *hom.17.4 in Rom.*(9.627A); Nil.*epp.*1.316(M.79.196D); **3.** *deplore*, Jo. Eub.*concept.BMV* 1(M.96.1461A); **4.** *attack, accuse, blame*, †Jo.D. *B.J.*13(M.96.980B); **5.** *depreciate* ~ουσα τὸ σῶμα αὐτῆς Jo.Mosch. *prat.*205(M.87.3096C); **6.** *commiserate* τὸ κύριον ὄνομα τιθείς, ὃ μᾶλλον ~οντος ἦν καὶ ἀνακαλοῦντος ἢ ὀργιζομένου ‡Dion.Al.*fr.in Lc.22:48* (p.248.13; M.10.1596B); **7.** *vex, torture* ἀφ' οὗ...ἐθεασάμην σε [sc. θάνατον]...τὸ πνεῦμά μου ἐπὶ πολὺ ~εται *T.Abr.*A 20(p.103.8); Chrys. *dimiss.Chan.*2(3.434A).

ταλανισμός, ὁ, 1. *woe* pronounced on one ἐν τῷ κατὰ Ματθαῖον ὁ πρὸς τοὺς γραμματεῖς καὶ Φαρισαίους δεύτερος τ. Or.*Jo.*20.34(p.372.3; M.14.649D); εἰς ἑαυτοὺς ἀναστρέφειν τὸν τ. Eus.*Is.*24:16(M.24.261D); †Bas.*Is.*178(1.509D; M.30.420A); Chrys.*hom.90.3 in Mt.*(7.842C); διατί...τὸν τ. τοῦ προφήτου ἐφέλκεις; Nil.*epp.*2.177(M.79.292A); Ant. Mon.*hom.*50(M.89.1588B); opp. μακαρισμός, Ephr.2.334B(tit.); Euthal.Diac.*Ac.*(M.85.633A); **2.** *misery, woe* μεμνημένοι...τῶν πολλῶν αὐτῶν καμάτων ὧν προϋπήνεγκαν ἐν ὀνόματι Χριστοῦ καὶ τῶν τ. Petr.I Al.*ep.can.*11(M.18.496C; cod. ταντaλισμῶν).

ταλαντεύ-ω, A. intrans., *swing to and fro*; met., *hang in the balance* ~ούσῃ ἐκβάσει Gel.Cyz.*h.e.*3.18.18; *swing* in a particular direction ἡ ἕξις τῆς ἀρετῆς...εὐκόλως...~ουσα ἐπὶ τὰ ἐναντία Nil.*epp.* 2.224(M.79.317B); ‡Nil.*perist.*12.5(M.79.948D); *waver* ἐν ταύταις μου ταῖς διανοίαις Anast.Ant.*redit.*(p.254).

B. trans.; **1.** *weigh, appraise* παρὰ θεῷ ~εται καὶ νόημα πᾶν, καὶ λόγος, καὶ πρᾶξις Gr.Naz.*or.*32.14(M.36.189B); Cyr.*Is.*2.5(2.341E); οὐ τρία [sc. in Trin]...ἀνόμοια, ἀλλήλων ὑπερκείμενα, νῷ καὶ γλώττῃ μετρούμενά τε καὶ ~όμενα, κατὰ τὴν τοῦ Ἀρείου διαίρεσιν Thdt.*Trin.* 28(M.75.1188C); **2.** *weigh down* τὸ ~ον αὐτὴν [sc. τὴν ψυχήν] εἰς τὸ φθορὰν κάτω...σῶμα Meth.*res.*1.29(p.259.6; M.41.1137A).

***ταλάντιον, τό,** *little talent* φόλης, ὃ καὶ τ. καλεῖται Epiph.*mens.* (M.43.292A).

τάλαντον, τό, *weight*, in gen. φεῦ τοῦ τ. τῶν ἐκεῖθεν μαστίγων Gr. Naz.*carm.*1.2.10.151(M.37.691A); exeg. Mt.25:15ff. ψιλὸν ἄνθρωπον ὁμολογοῦσι πεφηνέναι τὸν Χριστὸν εἰς τὸν βίον, τῆς θεότητος αὐτοῦ τὸ τ. ἀρνούμενοι Hipp.*fr.in Mt.25:24*(p.209.6; M.10.868A); τὴν παραβολὴν πρὸς πᾶσαν θεοῦ δωρεὰν εἰρῆσθαι Bas.*reg.br.*253(2.500D; M.31.1252B); τάλαντα γὰρ ἐνταῦθά ἐστιν ἡ ἑκάστου δύναμις Chrys.*hom.78.3 in Mt.*(7.754E); id.*Jud.*4.7(1.626E); id.*hom.30.2 in Heb.*(12.282A); κατορύξας τῇ σιωπῇ τὸ πνευματικὸν τ. Nil.*epp.*2.30(M.79.212C).

ταλαντόομαι, *sink in the scale*; met., *outweigh*, Meth.*symp.*4.4 (p.49.16; M.18.92A).

ταλάντωσις, ἡ, *oscillation*; *ebb and flow*, Bas.*hex.*6.11(1.61B; M. 29.144C).

τάλας, irreg. superl. ταλανώτατος, *extremely miserable*, †Bas.*Is.* 160(1.492D; M.30.380D).

***ταμβούρα, ἡ,** a disease of the eye, *Exorc.*14(p.337).

[*]ταμεῖον, τό, v. ταμιεῖον.

***ταμειοφάγος, ὁ,** *one who preys upon the treasury, peculator*, Ath. *h.Ar.*51(p.212.11; M.25.753D).

ταμιακός (ταμειακός), 1. *belonging to the* fiscus, Pall.*v.Chrys.*3 (p.20.16; M.47.14); Thdt.*ep.*42(4.1101); *Chron.Pasch.*p.256(M.92.624A); neut. plur. as subst., *money due to the* fiscus, Ath.*h.Ar.*75 (p.225.1; M.25.784C); **2.** *belonging to a steward* (ταμίας) or *a housekeeper* (ταμία), Chrys.*vid.*(1.343C).

ταμιεῖον ([*]ταμεῖον), τό, 1. *treasury*, *T.Jos.*9.2; Eus.*v.C.*1.16 (p.16.11; M.20.932B); Chrys.*sac.*1.5(p.20.3; 1.369B); of imperial *fiscus*, Eus.*h.e.*6.2.13(M.20.525B); id.*v.C.*2.21(p.50.3; 1000B); Thdt. *h.e.*3.12.1(3.925); met. τὰ τ. τῆς εὐλογίας τὰ ὄντα ἐν τῷ οὐρανῷ *Apoc. En.*11.1; κἂν ἐν ποταμοῖς ἐκδαπανηθῶ...ταμείοις ἐναπόκειμαι πλουσίου δεσπότου Tat.*orat.*6(p.7.2; M.6.820A); Meth.*symp.*11(p.133.21; M.18.209B); of the soul τὸν κλέπτην διαφυλάττειν μὴ λαθὼν διορύξειε τὸ τῆς ψυχῆς τ. Eus.*fr.Lc.*12:42(M.24.564C); Chrys.*pent.*1.2(2.460D); τ. ... κακίας καὶ θησαυρὸν ἀναισχυντίας Isid.Pel.*epp.*2.108(M.78.549A); **2.** *storehouse*, Clem.*paed.*3.10(p.264.28; M.8.621A); Tit.Bost.*fr.Lc.* 8:5(p.173.18); Bas.*hom.*8.6(2.68D; M.31.320B); for coffins of dead in Egypt, *T.Sym.*8.3(v.l. μνήμασι); **3.** *receptacle*, Bas.*hom.*1.10(2.9E; M.31.184A); met., Clem.*paed.*1.12(p.149.12; M.8.368C); ἀεὶ ἦν οὐσία οὖσα, οὐχ ὕλη ὡς θεοῦ τ. *Hom.Clem.*19.17; Gr.Nyss.*or.catech.*23(p.88.9; M.45.61D); of the mind τοῖς τ. ἐναποθέσθαι τῆς διανοίας Chrys. *hom.25.1 in Jo.*(8.143B); γαστέρα...τὸ τῶν λογισμῶν τ. ἐκάλεσεν Thdt.*Ps.*30:10(1.795); **4.** *inner chamber*, *T.Jos.*3.3; Clem.*str.*1.6 (p.22.16; M.8.728C); ἐν τῷ τ. προσεύχεσθαι μετὰ τῆς ἡσυχίας Chrys. *hom.61.3 in Jo.*(8.365C); Bas.*reg.br.*277(2.513A; M.31.1277A); *private apartment*: of women, Eus.*v.C.*1.34(p.23.19; M.20.949B); of emperor, *ib.*4.22(p.125.21; 1169A); id.*l.C.*9(p.218.5; M.20.1361C); met., of source of a river νάματα...ἐκ τῶν οἰκείων ἀνεφαίνετο τ. Thdt.*h.rel.* 1(3.1110); ref. God βασιλεὺς δ' οἷα ἐν ἀπορρήτοις εἴσω τοῖς αὐτοῦ τ. ἱδρυμένος τὰ πρακτέα βουλεύεται Eus.*e.th.*2.17(p.121.4; M.24.937D); of BMV ἔτι...ἔνδον ἐν τῷ τ. τῆς κυοφορούσης με φερόμενός [sc. Christ] σε, τὸν θεόν μου, ἑώρων id.*d.e.*10.8(p.481.33; M.22.776A); of heart, mind, and soul τ. καρδίας ἐπίσταται [sc. God] *Pss.Sal.*14.5;

εὔχεται κἂν ἐν αὐτῷ τῷ τ. τῆς ψυχῆς ἐννοηθῇ μόνον Clem.*str*.7.7(p.37.14; M.9.469C); Diad.*perf*.28(p.30.24); ἐν τῷ νοερῷ τ. τῆς ψυχῆς, τοῦτ' ἔστι τῷ νῷ, ἔχειν διὰ τῶν ἀρετῶν τὸ κατ' εἰκόνα αὐτοῦ καὶ ὁμοίωσιν Gel. Cyz.*h.e.*2.15.9(M.85.1260B); of heaven τὴν ψυχήν, τὸ πνεῦμα αὐτοῦ ἀνάπαυσον ἐν τόποις χλόης, ἐν ταμιείοις ἀναπαύσεως Serap.*euch*.30.2.

***ταμιεύσιμος**, neut. as subst., *worthiness to be garnered*, Areth. *Apoc*.9:14(M.106.632A).

***ταμιεύτρια**, ἡ, *dispenser, stewardess*, fig. ἀρετὴν...τὴν τῶν ἀγαθῶν...δωρεῶν τ. Andr.Cr.*or*.19(M.97.1213A).

ταμιεύ-ω, **1.** *manage, control*; med., of God τὴν...ποιητικὴν ἐξουσίαν μέχρι τοῦ προσήκοντος ἐταμιεύσω Const.*or.s.c.*20(p.185.14; M.20.1297B); **2.** med., *keep in reserve*; hence *postpone*, Bas.*mor*.8.6 (3.518D; M.32.1228B); σώματα μὲν προκαθαίρειν, ψυχῆς δὲ κάθαρσιν ~εσθαι Gr.Naz.*or*.40.13(M.36.376A); Chrys.*stat*.7.5(2.90A); **3.** med., *leave unexpressed, suppress*, Hadr.*introd*.128(M.98.1308D); esp., *exercise reserve* in religious teaching εἰς καιρὸν εὔκαιρον τὸν περὶ αὐτοῦ ~όμενοι λόγον Eus.*e.th*.2.20(p.129.16; M.24.953B); μυστικῶς πρότερον οἱ τοῦ θεοῦ προφῆται διαφόροις αὐτὸν ἐδόξαζον ἐπηγορίαις, τὸ ἀπόρρητον ἀποκρύπτοντες καὶ...τὴν εἰς πάντας ἀποκάλυψιν αὐτοῦ ~όμενοι *ib*.1.20(p.98.4; 896B); ἐπειδὴ νῦν πρὸς Ἕλληνας ὁ λόγος ἦν αὐτῷ...διὰ τοῦτο ~εται τέως Chrys.*hom.20.4 in 1Cor.*(10.173E); abs., *be reserved, keep one's counsel* ἐταμιεύσατο λέγων οὐδέν Jo. Mosch.*prat*.203(M.87.3093A); **4.** pass., *be stored* or *saved up*; hence be *reserved, set apart* θρόνος τῆς βασιλείας...παισὶ...ἐταμιεύετο Eus. *v.C.*1.9(p.11.19; M.20.921B); Gr.Naz.*or*.8.23(M.35.816C); *be apart*, of God as transcendent πάντῃ καὶ πάντων ἐκτὸς ἐν ἀπορρήτῳ βυθῷ γνώσεως τεταμιευομένου Eus.*l.C.*12(p.229.25; M.20.1385B); **5.** pass., *be proscribed, banished* περὶ κληρονομίας οὐσιῶν τῶν μαρτύρων καὶ ὁμολογητῶν καὶ μετοικισθέντων καὶ ~θέντων Eus.*v.C.*2.35 tit.(p.37.22; M.20.1012B).

[*]**ταμιουλκέω**, v. τιμιουλκέω.

ταμιοῦχος (ταμειοῦχος), ὁ, *keeper of the wardrobe*, *A.Thom.*A 112 (p.223.13); *steward*, *cat.Apoc.*16:7(p.413.19); Jo.Mon.*hymn.Petr.*5 (M.96.1393A).

ταμιόω, = ταμιεύω, *dispense*, Pamph.Mon.*Soter*.1(p.115.4).

***τάνη (*τάνυς)**, ἡ, a kind of tree like a vine with white branches, *Phys.*B 2(p.155); τάνυς, ‡Epiph.*phys*.3(M.43.520C).

***τανότης**, ἡ, *length*, ‡Hipp.Th.*fr*.21(p.55.18) cit. s. συστροφή.

***τανταλισμός**, ὁ, v. ταλανισμός.

***Ταντλιστής**, ὁ, *one as rich as Tantalus* τὴν δὲ δημώδη παροιμίαν ...τὴν λέγουσαν· τὰ Ταντλιστῶν φάγονται κροταλισταί Nil.*epp*.2.153 (M.79.272D).

τανύθριξ, *long-haired*; of persons, Nonn.*par.Jo*.18:23(M.43.893B).

***τανύμετρος**, *long*, Paul.Sil.*ambo*.78(M.86.2255A).

τανυμήκης, *stretched lengthwise, tall*, *Orac.Sib*.1.262.

τανύπλευρος, *stretched broadways, wide*; of a porch, Nonn.*par. Jo*.5:2(M.43.784C).

τανυπλόκαμος, *with long locks of hair* τ. Γαλιλαίων Nonn.*par.Jo.* 1:44(M.43.757B).

***τάνυς**, ἡ, v. *τάνη.

***τανυσκόπελος**, *with high cliffs*, Nonn.*par.Jo*.4:21(M.43.777B).

***τανυσμός**, ὁ, *stretching, wracking*, *Hymn*.ap.*Mir.Geo.*(p.148.22).

***τανυστέον**, *one must stretch, extend* χεῖρας πρὸς οὐρανὸν τ. συχνῶς Nil.*epp*.4.41(M.79.569B).

τανύ-ω, *stretch*; hence *spread* a liquid, Geo.Pis.*carm.vit*.34(p.52); *extend* abstracts ἐξ ἑτέρης ἑτέρην δὲ κράτος ~σειε θαλάσσης †Apoll. *Ps*.71:8(M.33.1413B); σὴν ἐλεημοσύνην, βασιλεῦ, ποθέουσι ~σσαις *ib.* 35:11(1360C); *turn* the eye ἱκεσίαις τεὸν ὄμμα, μάκαρ, ~σειας ἐμῇσι *ib*.16:1(1329B).

***ταξατίων**, ἡ, (Lat. *taxatio*) *taxation*, Ath.Scholast.*coll*.5.4(p.73).

***ταξατιών**, ὁ, (Lat. *taxatio*) *garrison*, Thphn.*chron*.p.309(M.108.752B).

ταξᾶτος, ὁ, (Lat. *taxatus*) *regular soldier*, CNic.(787)*act*.4(H.4.221D); Thphn.*chron*.p.271(M.108.672B).

ταξείδιον ([*]**ταξίδιον**), τό, **1.** *military expedition, foreign service* ἐπὶ ταξειδίων...ἁμαρτάνοντες καὶ ἐξομολογούμενοι Jo.Jej.*canonar*.1 (111D); τάξει †Jo.Jej.*poenit*.(M.88.1912A); ταξιδ-, Barth.Edess. *Agar*.(M.104.1405A); **2.** *foreign travel* ὅταν μέλλει ἀποδημῆσαί τις ἐν τ. *Euchol*.(p.680); *Nomoc*.340.

ταξεώτης (ταξιώτης), ὁ, *magistrate's officer, sergeant, commissary*; member of the *militia palatina*, *Ep.Pil.*(p.67.18); Serap.*ep.mon*.7 (M.40.933A); ‡Pall.*h.mon*.16.5(p.72.7; M.34.1164D); Mac.Aeg.*hom.* 15.48(M.34.609A); guard of a prefect, Socr.*h.e.*7.14.6(M.67.765C); †Gregent.*leg.Hom.*(M.86.580A): ὁ τ. τοῦ ἐπάρχου τῆς πόλεως *Chron. Pasch*.p.383(M.92.981B).

ταξιαρχ-έω, **1.** *be a* ταξίαρχος, *M.Acac*.2(p.762B); **2.** *command*, of Christ ὅτε...ἀγγέλοις ~ῶν ἐπιστατεῖ, μεγάλης βουλῆς ἄγγελος ἀναγορεύεται Eus.*d.e.*4.10(p.168.6; M.22.280C); of God ~ήσας τὸ ἔθνος Cosm.Ind.*top*.5(M.88.221A); **3.** *be a leader of a chorus*, met. εἰ...τὸ μὲν κορυφαῖον [i.e. right doctrine] ~οίη, αἱ δὲ [sc. the virtues] χορεύοιεν ...ὁ χορὸς στεφθήσεται Isid.Pel.*epp*.5.240(M.78.1477B); **4.** *hold the office of* ταξιάρχης in a monastery, Thdr.Stud.*iamb*.11(M.99.1784C).

ταξιαρχία, ἡ, **1.** *command*, Geo.Pis.*Pers*.2.20(M.92.1214A); **2.** *principle of order*, i.e. God τοῦτο...ἐστι...τῇ θείᾳ τ. θεοπρεπῶς νενομοθετημένον, τὸ διὰ τῶν πρώτων τὰ δεύτερα τῶν θεαρχικῶν μετέχειν ἐλλάμψεων Dion.Ar.*c.h.*8.2(M.3.240D); τὴν ὑπερούσιον...τ. *ib*.9.1(257B); ἡ πάσης εὐκοσμίας ὁρατῆς καὶ ἀοράτου τ. *ib*.13.3(301C); ἡ τῶν ἱερῶν ἁγία τ. id.*ep*.8.1(M.3.1089A); **3.** *order* τὰς τῶν οὐρανίων ταγμάτων τ. ... ἀρχῆθεν ἐκ θεοῦ κεκτίσθαι κωλύοντες Sophr.H.*ep.syn.*(M.87.3181D).

ταξίαρχος (ταξιάρχης), ὁ, *commander of a detachment*, Eus.*v.C.* 4.51(p.138.19; M.20.1201A); *ib*.4.68(p.145.32; 1224A); -χης, Bas.*hom. in Pr.6*:4(2.620A; M.31.1504C); Synes.*ep*.62(M.66.1405D); met., of God as creator of order (τάξις): ἐκ τῆς τῶν γεγονότων εὐρυθμίας τὸν τ. καὶ ἡγεμόνα καὶ δημιουργὸν τοῦδε τοῦ παντὸς ἐννοεῖν Cyr.*ador*.6(1.181C); τί...τῶν ὄντων οὐχὶ τὴν ἰδίαν τετήρηκε τάξιν καὶ μονονουχὶ τὸν τ. ἀναφωνεῖ *ib*.(200C); of archangels as commanders of angels, *Pap.Chr.*(p.436); *Mir.Geo.*11(p.108.18); οἱ ταξιάρχας τοὺς τέσσαρας ἐκλαβόμενοι, Μιχαήλ, Γαβριήλ, Οὐριήλ, Ῥαφαήλ, οὐκ ἀδοκίμως ἠνέχθησαν. φιλεῖ γάρ πως τῷ τ. τὸ στῖφος ἕπεσθαι Areth.*Apoc*.9:16(M.106.632B); of S. Paul, -χης, Cosm.Ind.*top*.5(M.88.297D); of S. Peter, Geo.Pis.*carm*.82.3(p.62); of bishop πειρᾶσθε κατὰ πάσας συνόδους ἔρχεσθαι, ἵνα μὴ ὡς λειποτάκται ὑπὸ τῆς τοῦ τ. ἀδυναμίας ἁμαρτίας ἔγκλημα λάβητε *Clem.ep.*17(M.2.53A); following are all in form -χης: of head of a coenobium κοινοβιακὸν μετέρχονται βίον...ὑφ' ἑνὶ τ. καὶ προεστῶτι...ἑαυτοὺς ἔταξαν †Jo.D.*B.J.*12(M.96.969A); of a monastic official, a steward seeing to order, esp. in choir and refectory, *Const.Stud.*28(M.99.1713C); placing brethren in choir according to age, learning, voice, etc., keeping registers, bringing back any who ran away and acting as sacristan, Thdr.Stud.*poen*.1.105–107(M.99.1748A,B); id.*iamb*.11(M.99.1784C).

***ταξιδεύω**, *travel*, Barth.Edess.*Agar*.(M.104.1425D).

[*]**ταξίδιον**, τό, v. ταξείδιον.

τάξις, ἡ, **1.** *body of troops*; of angelic hosts, Meth.*symp*.3.6(p.32.20; M.18.69A); Cosm.Ind.*top*.5(M.88.301C); in gen., *band, company* ἐν τ. ἁγίων Or.*Jo*.2.17(11; p.74.5; M.14.144C); *Const.App*.2.57.21; **2.** *post* or *place in the line of battle* καθάπερ...οὐ λειπτέον τὴν τ. ἣν ὁ στρατηγὸς ἔταξεν τῷ στρατιώτῃ, οὕτως οὐδὲ ἣν ἔδωκεν ὁ λόγος... γνώσεώς τε καὶ βίου λειπτέον τ. Clem.*str*.7.16(p.70.16; M.9.537B); *position, place* κατηχούμενος ἐὰν εἰσέρχεται εἰς κυριακὸν ἐν τῇ τῶν κατηχουμένων τ. στήκῃ CNeocaes.*can*.5; **3.** *order*; **a.** chronological, *Hom.Clem.*2.16; Chrys.*hom.2.6 in Rom.*(9.445C); Proc.G.*Gen*.4:2 (M.87.237C); **b.** plur., *successions*, *Lit*.ap.*Const.App*.8.12.15; **c.** plur., *degrees* τ. παραπτωμάτων Eus.*h.e.*6.46.1(M.20.633C); **d.** ref. position τὸ ποσόν...περιΐσταται...καὶ ἀπὸ τῆς τ., οἷον πρὸ τοῦδε, καὶ μετ' ἐκεῖνο, καὶ ἐπ' ἀρχῆς, καὶ ὕστερον Leont.B.*cap.Sev.*29(M.86.1912D); of books in OT ὁποῖα τὴν τ. εἶεν Mel.*fr*.3(p.309; M.5.1213); of words in a book, *text* of a book καθ' ἣν ἔχομεν τ. τῆς γραφῆς Or. *Cels*.2.46(p.168.24; M.11.869A); *ib*.6.30(p.100.3; 1340A); **e.** *arrangement, system* in orderly composition of books, sentences, etc. Μάρκος...ὅσα ἐμνημόνευσεν...ἔγραψεν, οὐ μέντοι τάξει, τὰ ὑπὸ Χριστοῦ ἢ λεχθέντα ἢ πραχθέντα Papias *fr*.2.15; Clem.*str*.6.1(p.423.4; M.9.209A); Or.*Jo*.1.31(34; p.39.30; M.14.84A); *ib*.2.19(13; p.76.17; 148C); Chrys. *hom.3.2 in Eph.*(11.20A); in affairs of life, Dion.Al.ap.Eus.*h.e.* 6.42.6(616A); in created universe, *T.Neph*.3.2; Clem.*str*.5.1(p.331.7; M.9.20A); *ib*.6.16(p.504.5; 369B); νοεῖν ἀπὸ τῆς τ. τοῦ κόσμου τὸν πεποιηκότα Or.*Cels*.8.38(p.253.18; M.11.1573C); *Hom.Clem.*6.19; *Const.App*.7.39.2; Aen.*dial*.(M.85.916C); in man's nature, *T.Neph.* 3.4,5; of natural and artificial order τ., ἡ μὲν φυσική τίς ἐστιν· ἡ δέ, κατ' ἐπιτήδευσιν· φυσικὴ...ὡς ἡ τῶν κτισμάτων κατὰ τοὺς δημιουργικοὺς λόγους διαταχθεῖσα...ἀριθμητῶν θέσις...τῶν αὐτῶν πρὸς τὰ αἰτιατὰ σχέσεις...ἐπιτετηδευμένη...καὶ τεχνική, ὡς ἡ ἐν τοῖς κατασκευάσμασι...καὶ μαθήμασι...ἔστι τι τάξεως εἶδος οὐκ ἐκ τῆς παρ' ἡμῶν θέσεως συνιστάμενον, ἀλλ' αὐτῇ τῇ κατὰ φύσιν ἀκολουθίᾳ συμβαῖνον Bas.*Eun*.1.20(1.231E; M.29.556C); **4.** *orderliness, regularity* of the stars, Arist.*apol*.4.2; **5.** *order, discipline* in Church πάντα τάξει ποιεῖν ὀφείλομεν ὅσα ὁ δεσπότης ἐπιτελεῖν ἐκέλευσεν *1Clem*.40.1; *Hom.Clem.*3.67; Cyr.H.*procatech*.4; οὐκ ἐπιτρέπομεν...πρεσβυτέρους χειροτονεῖν...ἀλλὰ μόνοις τοῖς ἐπισκόποις· αὕτη γάρ ἐστι τ. ἐκκλησιαστικὴ καὶ ἁρμονία *Const.App*.3.11.3; οὔτε διάκονον προσφέρειν θυσίαν θεμιτόν...οὐ γὰρ ὅσιον ἀνεστράφθαι τὴν τ. *ib*.8.46.11; τάξεως...ἐστι στρατιωτικῆς ἁρμοδιωτέρα αὕτη ἡ τ. τῆς ἐκκλησίας Chrys.*hom.10.2 in 1Thess.*(11.496E); **6.** monastic *rule* ἀφιέναι τὴν τ. τῆς ἀποταγῆς καὶ τὸ μοναστήριον Eus.Al.*serm*.22.7(M.86.460C); Cosm.Ind.*top*.2(M. 88.73A); **7.** *order, ordinance*, Papias *fr*.4; Or.*Jo*.32.3(p.430.24; M.14. 748D); τῆς...ἁγιωτάτης καὶ σωτηρίου...θεοῦ τάξεως Const.ap.Gel. Cyz.*h.e*.2.7.22(M.85.1236D); Chrys.*hom.39.1 in Ac*.(9.295C); **8.** *rank, position*, of junior status πρέπει μὴ συγχρᾶσθαι τῇ ἡλικίᾳ τοῦ ἐπισκόπου, ἀλλὰ...πᾶσαν ἐντροπὴν αὐτῷ ἀπονέμειν, καθὼς ἔγνων καὶ τοὺς ἁγίους πρεσβυτέρους οὐ προσειληφότας τὴν φαινομένην νεωτερικὴν τ., ἀλλ' ὡς φρονίμους ἐν θεῷ συγχωροῦντας αὐτῷ Ign.*Magn*.3.1; in gen. εἰς τοσαύτην αὐτοὺς [sc. Christians] τ. ἔθετο ὁ θεός, ἣν οὐ θεμιτὸν αὐτοῖς παραιτήσασθαι *Diogn*.6.10; τὴν τ. τῆς ζωῆς Clem.*q.d.s*.20(p.172. 22; M.9.624D); ἡ τ. ἡ μετὰ τῶν ἁγίων δυνάμεων Or.*hom.10.7 in Jer*. (p.77.16; M.13.365C); ὁ διάβολος...τῆς προτέρας τ. ἐκπεσών Thdt. *haer*.5.8(4.407); Proc.G.*Gen*.4:2(M.87.237A); of things, Clem.*q.d.s*.29 (p.179.1; 633C); ταῦτα ἐλάττονα ἔχει τ. ... τῶν γεγεννῆσθαι λεγομένων ἐκ τοῦ θεοῦ Or.*Jo*.20.15(13; p.345.36; M.14.605B); Cyr.*Jo*.3(4.27C); of order of Persons of Trin. υἱὸν αὐτοῦ τοῦ ὄντως θεοῦ μαθόντες καὶ ἐν δευτέρᾳ χώρᾳ ἔχοντες, πνεῦμα δὲ προφητικὸν ἐν τρίτῃ τ. Just.*1apol*. 13.3(M.6.348A); τὴν ἐν τῇ ἑνώσει δύναμιν καὶ τὴν ἐν τῇ τ. διαίρεσιν Athenag.*leg*.10.3(M.6.909B); τὸ ἅγιον πνεῦμα...εἶναι...τάξει ⟨πρῶτον⟩ πάντων τῶν ὑπὸ τοῦ πατρὸς διὰ Χριστοῦ γεγενημένων Or.*Jo*.2.10(6; p.65.20; 128B); τοῦτο μὲν [sc. τὸ πνεῦμα] τρίτην ἐπέχον τὴν τ. Eus. *p.e*.7.15(325C; M.21.549C); Arian view τρίτον ὂν τὸ πνεῦμα...τὴν τ., οὐκ ἂν πρῶτον εἴη τὴν φύσιν Eun.*apol*.25(M.30.861B); τρίτον αὐτὸ ἀξιώματι καὶ τ. μαθόντες, τρίτον εἶναι καὶ τῇ φύσει πεπιστεύκαμεν *ib*. (861B); orthodox view τίς...ἀνάγκη, εἰ...τῇ τ. τρίτον ὑπάρχει τὸ πνεῦμα, τρίτον εἶναι αὐτὸ καὶ τῇ φύσει; Bas.*Eun*.3.1(1.272B; M.29. 653B); τίνος...ἕνεκεν ἀθετεῖ τὴν τ. ἐπὶ θεοῦ λαμβάνεσθαι;...ἡμεῖς...κατὰ μὲν τὴν τῶν αἰτίων πρὸς τὰ ἐξ αὐτῶν σχέσιν προτετάχθαι τοῦ υἱοῦ τὸν πατέρα φαμέν· κατὰ δὲ τὴν τῆς φύσεως διαφορὰν οὐκέτι, οὐδὲ κατὰ τὴν τοῦ χρόνου ὑπεροχήν *ib*.1.20(232B; M.557B); τὸ μετὰ τὸν πατέρα πῶς τὸν υἱὸν λέγουσιν; ὡς χρόνῳ νεώτερον ἢ ὡς τάξει; id.*Spir*.14(3.10D; M.32.88C); ἀκολούθως μὲν κατὰ τὴν τ., συνημμένως δὲ κατὰ τὴν φύσιν τῶν τριῶν Gr.Nyss.*diff.ess*.4(M.32.332C); φαμεν...μηδεμίαν τῆς οὐσίας ἐπὶ τῆς...τριάδος διαφορὰν ἐξευρίσκειν ἐκτὸς τῆς τ. τῶν προσώπων...τ. γάρ ἐστιν ἐν τῷ εὐαγγελίῳ παραδοθεῖσα, καθ' ἣν ἐκ πατρὸς ἡ πίστις ἀρχομένη διὰ μέσου τοῦ υἱοῦ εἰς τὸ πνεῦμα...καταλήγει id.*ep*.24(M.46.1092A); ἣν ἀνάγκη συνομολογεῖν...ὑποκεῖσθαι...τῷ πατρὶ τὸν υἱὸν ὡς οἰκετικὴν ἔχοντα τ.,...εἴπερ ἐστὶ κατ' ἐκείνους ὀψιγενής Cyr.*Jo*.1.1(4.13E); προτέταχε τὸν Χριστὸν τοῦ πατρὸς οὐ τὴν τ. ἀνατρέπων, ἀλλὰ διδάσκων ὡς ἡ τ. τῶν ὀνομάτων, οὐκ ἀξιωμάτων καὶ φύσεων διδάσκει διαφοράν Thdt.*ep*.146(4.1259); **9.** *role, office*, Clem. *str*.6.16(p.502.6; M.9.364B); ὁ μὲν προεστὼς ὑστερεῖ..., πρεσβύτεροι δ' αὐτοῦ παρόντες τὴν αὐτοῦ τ. ἐπλήρουν Eus.*v.C*.3.7(p.80.21; M.20. 1061B); Cyr.H.*procatech*.4; τοῦ δεσπότου τὴν τ. ἁρπάζεις Chrys.*hom. 11.2 in 1Cor*.(10.89B); ἣν ἐπέχει τ. ὁ Χριστὸς τῇ ἐκκλησίᾳ...ταύτην ἐπέχει τὴν τ. ὁ ἀνὴρ τῇ γυναικί Thdr.Mops.*Eph*.5:23(p.183.29; M.66. 920B); εἰ ἦν...ἐλάττων τοῦ πατρὸς ὁ υἱός, οὐ ταπεινοφρονῶν ὑπήκουσεν, ἀλλὰ τ. ἐπλήρωσεν Thdt.*Phil*.2:11(3.456); ὦ τάξις μεσίτου ὑπερφυής Cosm.Ind.*top*.5(M.88.245B); in administration, *department, section* Εὐπ[ρά]κτου κανκελλαρίου τάξεως καθολικοῦ *IGC As.Min*.13 (Cyzicus, saec. v); *ib*.220 (Miletus, saec. vi); **10.** *principle*, Athenag.*leg*.2.3(M. 6.896A); **11.** *class, group, order*; in gen., Or.*Cels*.6.61(p.131.29; M.11. 1392B); of clerical order in gen. εἰ δύνανται οἱ λαϊκοὶ...προάγεσθαι εἰς τ. CAnc.(314)*can*.3; *ib*.12; CNeocaes.*can*.1; CLaod.*can*.24; of the several orders of ministry ὁ...κανόνας τῇ ἐκκλησίᾳ καὶ τάξεις δεδωκὼς εἰς ὠφέλειαν καὶ σωτηρίαν τῶν ποιμνίων Serap.*euch*.26.1; μεταλαμβανέτω ἑκάστη τ. καθ' ἑαυτὴν τοῦ κυριακοῦ σώματος *Const.App*.2.57. 21; *ib*.8.46.3; partic. of apostles, Or.*Jo*.32.18(11; p.456.32; M.14. 792B); *A.Phil*.30(p.16.11); Chrys.*prod.Jud*.1.2(2.379A); prophets, Heracleon ap.Or.*Jo*.6.20(12; p.129.3; 236A); bishops, Epiph.*haer*. 75.4(p.336.5; M.42.508D); priests, Iren.*haer*.3.11.8(M.7.886B); Philost.*h.e*.10.12(M.65.592C); monks, Ephr.2.412B; Gr.II Papa *conf*. (M.91.1024C); †Jo.D.*B.J*.38(M.96.1221D); of OT high-priesthood, Eus.*d.e*.7.3(p.345.2; M.22.561C); of angels, Heracleon ap.Or.*Jo*.13. 60(59; p.292.33; 516A); Or.*princ*.1.6.2(p.81.4; M.11.167A); Oecum. *Apoc*.4:3(p.69); cf.*Lit.Chrys*.(p.379.7); of human order of being τότε ὁ Ἰησοῦς μετῆλθεν εἰς τὴν ἀνθρωπίνην τ. καθὼς ἐγεννήθη δι' ἡμᾶς *Contrad*.1(p.7); of a class of things, Serap.*Man*.41(p.60; M. 18.1225C); **12.** plur., *records, acts*, Ath.*apol.sec*.56(p.136.9; M.25. 349C); αἱ τῶν ἐπισκοπικῶν ὑπομνημάτων τ. δηλοῦσι Leo Mag.*ep*.29.1 (p.45.7; M.*PL*.54.782B); *ib*.28.1(p.11.1; 756A); **13.** *form, order*; of ritual or ceremonial, Or.*hom.1.4 in Jos*.(p.291.26; M.87.1004B); Jul.Papa *ep.Dian*.ap.Ath.*apol.sec*.30(p.109.24; M.25.300A); *Lit.Jac*. tit.(p.160.1); *Euchol*.(p.208); *ib*.(p.238); **14.** phrases: κατὰ τάξιν, *in order*, *Diogn*.8.7; *Lit*.ap.*Const.App*.8.13.14; Thdt.*h.e*.5.40.3(3. 1088); *step by step*, id.*qu.37 in Lev*.(1.215); πρὸς τάξιν, *in due order*, Thphl.Ant.*Autol*.2.13(M.6.1072B); *ib*.2.25(1092B); μετὰ τάξεως, *in an orderly way*, Clem.*paed*.2.1(p.163.7; M.8.397C); εἰς τ. ἄγω, *bring into order*, Bas.*hex*.2.2(1.13B; M.29.32A); ἐν τ., *in due order*, *T.Neph*. 2.8; Clem.*str*.7.3(p.13.26; M.9.424A); Dion.Al.ap.Eus.*h.e*.7.24.8(M. 20.696A); *in the position* of ὁ γνωστικὸς...ἐν υἱοῦ καταλεγεὶς τ. Clem. *str*.7.11(p.49.14; M.9.496A); ἐν τ. τοῦ πνεύματος ὁ νόμος ἦν Chrys. *comm.in Gal*.5:18(10.721C); Cyr.*Os*.129(3.162A); *in the character* of, Chrys.*hom.4.6 in Heb*.(12.49C); id.*hom.6.1 in Ac*.(9.55C); Cyr.*Os*. 127(3.159D); of things, *in the way* of, *by way* of, Chrys.*hom.8.4 in Mt*.(7.125A); Cyr.ap.*cat.Heb*.suppl.1:8(p.360.13); Παῦλος, οὗ ὁ ἀσπασμὸς ἐν πάσαις ταῖς ἐπιστολαῖς αὐτοῦ ὡς ἐν τ. σημείου Cosm. Ind.*top*.5(M.88.297D); *in the form* of, *under the form* of ἑαυτὸν...ἐν τ. θυμιάματος νοητοῦ τῷ ἰδίῳ πατρὶ προσαγαγών Didym.*Trin*.3.27 (M.39.944A); ἐν τ. μακαρισμοῦ Chrys.*hom.15.2 in Mt*.(187A); id. *hom.24.3 in 2Cor*.(10.609D); Cyr.*Am*.66(3.323C).

***ταπεινολογέω**, *speak humbly*, Ephr.1.26A; Nil.*epp*.2.322(M.79. 357B); cf.Isid.Pel.*epp*.1.342(M.78.377D); Bars.*resp*.(M.88.1816D).

***ταπεινόλογος**, *humble in speech*, Hesych.H.*Ps.tit*.33(M.27.773B).

***ταπεινόνοος**, (**-νους**), *humble-minded*, Jo.Clim.*scal*.25(M.88. 1000B).

***ταπεινοποιός**, *humiliating, dispiriting*, †Bas.*Is*.256(1.575B; M. 30.569C).

***ταπεινορρημοσύνη**, **ἡ**, *humble speech*, Chrys.*hom.3.1 in 1Tim*. (11.561D).

ταπεινός, **1.** *low*, *Apoc.En*.26.4(p.56.30); **2.** *depressed, faint-hearted* ἔδει ἀποθανεῖν· οὐκ ἐγένετο τ. Chrys.*hom.12.4 in Phil*.(11. 296A); id.*hom.1.1 in 2Thess*.(11.511A); **3.** of persons, *mean, poor*, *Pss.Sal*.5.14; τοὺς ἐν θλίψει σῶσον, τοὺς τ. ἐλέησον *1Clem*.59.4; *Hom. Clem*.19.23; of Christ τ. ἐπὶ γῆς καὶ ἔνδοξος ἐν οὐρανῷ *T.Benj*.9.5; not applicable to pre-existent Son, Cyr.*thes*.20(5^1.194E); of BMV τ. ... ἤμην καὶ ἀπερριμμένη καὶ νῦν ἀπὸ γῆς εἰς οὐρανὸν μεταβαίνω Or.*hom. 8 in Lc*.(p.59.23; cf.M.13.1821B); in polite self-depreciation, Max. *ep*.13(M.91.509C); *ib*.15(544C); Leont.N.*v.Jo.Eleem*.21(p.38.16); as designation of abbot of monastery, *IGC As.Min*.238 (Marmarica, saec. vi–vii); **4.** of language, *suited to the humble* στοιχεῖα...τοὺς ταπεινοτέρους περὶ τοῦ Χριστοῦ λόγους ἐκάλεσε Thdt.*Heb*.5:12(3.576); **5.** of things, *mean, low*, Marcell.*fr*.55 ap.Eus.*e.th*.2.15(p.118.26; M.24. 933C); Thdt.*h.rel*.2(3.1122); neut. as subst., *poverty, weakness* τὸ τ. τῆς ψυχῆς Gr.Thaum.*pan.Or*.8(p.22.1; M.10.1077B); **6.** *base, degraded* τ. ... ἐννοίας Clem.*str*.7.7(p.29.18; M.9.453B); τ. ... οἱ νομίζοντες περὶ σωματικοῦ ἄρτου λέγειν τὸν διδάσκοντα μὴ μεριμνᾶν περὶ τῆς αὔριον Or. *fr.88 in Lc*.11:3(p.275); μικρολόγῳ φύσει καὶ τ. ... οὐ χρὴ μαθημάτων θείων κοινωνεῖν Meth.*symp*.1.1(p.9.15; M.18.40B); ἔστι...τ. ... ὁ κατὰ τὴν ἁμαρτίαν πορευόμενος Bas.*hom.in Ps*.33(1.155D; M.29. 380D); Chrys.*hom.66.3 in Mt*.(7.656E); *ib.71.1*(695C); **7.** *humble, lowly*, in good sense ὁ δίκαιος καὶ τ. αἰδεῖται ποιῆσαι ἄδικον *T.Gad* 5.3; *Barn*.19.6; ὁ μηδὲν ἔχων ἔπαρμα, μηδὲ φρονῶν ἐπί τινι τῶν ἀνθρωπίνων, οὗτος...τ. τῷ πνεύματι Bas.*hom.in Ps*.33(1.155D; M.29. 380D); τ. ἄνθρωπος ἢ ὁ τῇ συγκρίσει τῆς τοῦ θεοῦ μεγαλοπρεπείας τὸ μηδὲν ἑαυτὸν λογιζόμενος· ἢ ὁ διὰ μετριοπάθειαν τὸ ἀλαζονικὸν ἀποθέμενος φρόνημα· ἢ ὁ διὰ τῆς ἁμαρτίας ἐκ τοῦ πρώτου ὕψους ἑαυτὸν καταρρίψας †Bas.*Is*.86(1.620D; M.30.260A); λόγος ταπεινοῦ μάλαγμα ψυχῆς Nil.*spir.mal*.19(M.79.1164C); προσευχὴ ταπεινοῦ ἐπικάμπτει θεόν *ib*.; of one who ascribes nothing to himself, Thdt.*Rom*.1:11(3. 18); ὁ τ. ... οὐ παύεται ἀδιαλείπτως δεόμενος τοῦ θεοῦ Dor.*doct*.2.8 (M.88.1649D); σκόλοψ καὶ βάρος τῷ τ. τὸ οἰκειόπιστον· ὥσπερ τῷ ὑπερηφάνῳ τὸ ἑτερόλεκτον Jo.Clim.*scal*.25(M.88.1000C); of humble mind as distinguishing characteristic of Christian, Hesych.S.*temp*. 1.82(M.93.1505B); neut. as subst., *humility* τὸ τ. τῆς ψυχῆς *1Clem*.55. 5; Gr.Naz.*or*.32.19(M.36.196B,C); **8.** vocative ταπεινέ, *poor fellow*, Leont.N.*v.Sym*.36(M.93.1716A).

***ταπεινοστρεφής**, *revolving in low orbits* or *spheres*; of stars, Meth.*symp*.8.10(p.92.18; M.18.153B).

***ταπεινόσχημος**, *humble in appearance* only, Hesych.H.*Ps.tit*. 33(M.27.773B).

***ταπεινόσωμος**, *humble, mean in body*, Geo.Pis.*hex*.1035(M.92. 1514A).

ταπεινότης, **ἡ**, **1.** *lowness, low situation* geographically, Or.*Jo*.6. 49(30; p.158.31; M.14.288A); *lowering* of hills, Philost.*h.e*.3.9(M.65. 493A); **2.** *baseness, earthliness*, Gr.Thaum.*pan.Or*.9(p.23.20; M.10. 1080A); κατὰ Ἰουδαϊκὴν τ. Chrys.*hom.51.4 in Mt*.(7.525E); id.*hom. 22.3 in 1Cor*.(10.195C); εἰς τὰς χαμαιζήλους ἐμπαθῶς ἐμπαγῆναι τῶν εἰκόνων ταπεινότητας Dion.Ar.*c.h*.2.2(M.3.140A); καθαιρεῖται πρὸς ταπεινότητα τὸ μεγαλεῖον τῆς θείας φύσεως, εἰ καθ' ὁμοιότητα τοῦ ἡμετέρου πνεύματος...τὸ ἐν αὐτῷ πνεῦμα ὑπονοοῖτο Jo.D.*f.o*.1.7(M. 94.805B); **3.** *humility* of God in condescension to men πόση τ. τῶν λόγων κέχρηται Chrys.*hom.28.3 in Gen.*(4.272D); of Christ in Inc. τῆς δουλικῆς τ. ἣν ὑπῆλθεν κατ' οἰκονομίαν ὁ κύριος Gr.Nyss.*Eun.*11 (2 p.264.15; M.45.872D); of his humanity opp. divinity, Chrys. *hom.2.2 in Heb.*(12.15D); **4.** as self-depreciatory style esp. used by bishops τῇ ἡμῶν τ. Epiph.*haer.*78.1(p.452.4; M.42.700B); *ib.*49.3 (p.244.10; M.41.881C); τὰ γράμματα τῆς ἡμετέρας τ. CArim.*ep.Const.* 2 ap.Thdt.*h.e.*2.20.2(3.878).

ταπεινοφρον-έω, 1. *be humble-minded, lowly in heart,* of Christ οὐκ ἦλθεν ἐν κόμπῳ...ὑπερηφανίας, καίπερ δυνάμενος, ἀλλὰ ∼ῶν *1Clem.*16.2; as example to men, *ib.*16.17; Epiph.*haer.*69.29(p.178. 26; M.42.248D); Chrys.*hom.70.2 in Jo.*(8.415D); ref. expressions denoting inferiority to Father of incarnate Christ τί...οὐκ ἔδει ∼οῦντα ἥττονα τοῦ πατρὸς ἑαυτὸν ἀποδεικνύναι; ‡Gr.Nyss.*Ar.et Sab.*11(M. 45.1296C); *ib.*14(1300D); of Jo. Bapt., †Or.*fr.220ᵇ in Mt.*(p.105); Cyr.*Jo.*1.10(4.111A); of men in gen. οἱ πατέρες ἡμῶν εὐηρέστησαν τ. πρὸς τὸν θεόν *1Clem.*62.2; Herm.*sim.*5.3.7; ἐν κραδίῃ τε ∼εῖν *Orac.Sib.*8.480; Hipp.*Dan.*4.2.9(M.10.681A); τοῖς ∼οῦσι πρὸς τοὺς ὁμοιοπαθεῖς Meth.*lepr.*12(p.466.16); ref. humility required in prophets, *Const.App.*8.2.10; ref. humility as source of wisdom, Marc.Er.*opusc.*1.81(M.65.916A); ἄλλο ∼εῖν, καὶ ἄλλο ἀγωνίζεσθαι ∼εῖν...τὸ μὲν πρῶτον τελείων· τὸ δὲ δεύτερον ὑποτακτικῶν ἀληθινῶς Jo.Clim.*scal.*25(M.88.995A); ref. temptations as school of humility, Thal.*cent.*4.37(M.91.1461C); **2.** *be depressed, abased,* Chrys.*hom.8.5 in 2Tim.*(11.712F).

***ταπεινοφρόνημα, τό, 1.** *act of humility,* Ath.*exp.Ps.*85:1(M.27. 373C); **2.** *lowliness of heart,* Jo.D.*spir.neq.*7(M.95.81B).

***ταπεινοφρόνησις, ἡ,** = ταπεινοφροσύνη, *humility,* Herm.*sim.*8.7. 6; Tertullian *jej.*12(M.*PL.*2.1020C); *ib.*13(1023B); *ib.*16(1828A).

***ταπεινοφρόνως,** *humbly,* Bas.*ep.*219.2(3.332D; M.32.813A); *Const. App.*1.3.8; Epiph.*anc.*23(p.32.18; M.43.60C).

ταπεινοφροσύνη, ἡ, A. *humility;* **1.** def. and descriptions ἡ τ. πραότης ἐστίν, οὐχὶ κακουχία σώματος Clem.*str.*3.6(p.218.18; M.8. 1152B); τ., μὴ φρονεῖν ἐπάξιον Gr.Naz.*carm.*1.2.34.86(M.37.951A); τί οὖν ἐστι τ.; τὸ ταπεινὰ φρονεῖν· ταπεινὰ δὲ φρονεῖ οὐχ ὁ ἀπὸ ἀνάγκης ταπεινός, ἀλλ' ὁ ἑαυτὸν ταπεινῶν Chrys.*hom.6.2 in Phil.*(11.236D); τοῦτο οὔτε τ. ἐστὶ τὸ ὄντα ἁμαρτωλὸν νομίζειν εἶναι ἁμαρτωλόν. τ. γάρ ἐστιν, ὅταν τις πολλὰ καὶ μεγάλα συνειδὼς ἑαυτῷ, μηδὲν μέγα περὶ ἑαυτοῦ φαντάζηται id.*incomprehens.*5.6(1.489C); dist. from εὐγνωμοσύνη, which acknowledges sinfulness, id.*hom.4.6 in Ac.9:1*(3.139C); consists in bearing injuries patiently, id.*hom.27.5 in Heb.*(12. 253A); Esaias *or.*25.2(p.183); τὴν ὄντως τ., οὐ τὴν ἐν λόγῳ μόνῳ καὶ σχήματι ταπείνωσιν, ἀλλὰ διάθεσιν εἰδικῶς ταπεινὴν γενομένην ἐν αὐτῇ τῇ καρδίᾳ Dor.*doct.*1.6(M.88.1625A); τ. ἐστὶ πύργος ἰσχύος ἀπὸ προσώπου ἐχθροῦ Jo.Clim.*scal.*25(M.88.993D); *ib.*(1004A); τ. ἐστὶν ἄβυσσος εὐτελείας πᾶσι κλέπταις οὖσα ἀνεπιχείρητος *ib.*(993D); τ. ἐστὶ προσευχὴ συνεχὴς μετὰ δακρύων καὶ πόνων Max.*carit.*3.87(M.90. 1044B); **2.** fundamental virtue πᾶσα ἐρώτησις τ. χρῄζει Herm.*vis.*3. 10.6; τῶν μακαρισμῶν ἐντεῦθεν ἤρξατο ὁ Χριστός. ὥσπερ...θεμέλιον... μεγίστης οἰκοδομῆς καταβάλλεσθαι μέλλων οὕτω τὴν τ. πρώτην ἔθηκεν. οὐ γάρ ἐστιν...ταύτης σωθῆναι χωρὶς Chrys.*hom.33.3 in Jo.*(8.194A); πάντα ἀκάθαρτα...τ. ἀπούσης id.*hom.in Phil.1:18*(3.302A); preferred by scripture, Gr.Nyss.*Placill.*(M.46.892A); 'mother' of all others, Chrys.*hom.70.1 in Jo.*(8.414C); id.*hom.30.3 in Ac.*(9.237E); *V.Pach.Φ* 135(p.85.13); οὐκ ἄσκησις, οὔτε ἀγρυπνία, οὔτε παντοῖος πόνος σῴζει, εἰ μὴ γνησία τ. *Apophth.Patr.*(M.65.204A); *ib.*(333B); πρὸ παντὸς χρῄζομεν τῆς τ. Esaias *or.*3.1(p.7); *ib.*16.5(p.93); Dor.*doct.*2.1 (M.88.1640D); μὴ παρούσης τ. πάντα ἡμῶν ἕωλα Jo.Clim.*scal.*25(M.88. 993A); not to be found in heretics, *ib.*(996B); **3.** origin; **a.** natural; ascetic effort, Mac.Aeg.*hom.*19.8(M.34.648D); remembrance of past sins, Evagr.Pont.*cap.pract.*A 22(M.40.1228B); Marc.Er.*opusc.*3.12 (M.65.984A); τ. ... μετὰ πολλῶν ἀγώνων κατορθοῦται Diad.*perf.*95 (p.138.30); obedience, *ib.*41(p.46.23); ὁ σωματικὸς κόπος ὁδηγεῖ εἰς τὸν τῆς τ. τρόπον *Apophth.Patr.*(M.65.396B); τὸ μὴ πλῆξαι τὴν συνείδησιν τοῦ πλησίον τίκτει τὴν τ. Esaias *or.*16.4(p.92); to be learned, Dor.*doct.*1.6(1625A); **b.** supernatural; gift of H. Ghost, Mac.Aeg. *cust.cor.*14(M.34.840D); id.*hom.*18.8(M.34.640C); τὴν θεοδώρητον ταύτην ἀρετὴν τῆς τ. Ant.Mon.*hom.*70(M.89.1640B); Hesych.S.*temp.*1.64 (M.93.1501A); τ. ἐστὶ σκέπη θεία, ἐπὶ ἀβλεψίᾳ τῶν οἰκείων κατορθωμάτων Jo.Clim.*scal.*25(993D); **4.** various manifestations πολλάκις...σάκκον ἠμπίσχετο ταπεινοφροσύνης ἔνδυμα Clem.*paed.*2.10(p.224.22; M.8. 532B); in assuming blame, Bas.*ep.*128.2(3.219D; M.32.556C); τεκμήριον βαθυτάτης τ. καθέστηκε τὸ τὰς μὴ παρούσας ἡμῖν αἰτίας... εὐτελείας χάριν σχηματίζεσθαι Jo.Clim.*scal.*25(M.88.997C); in asking counsel of others, †Bas.*Is.*57(1.422C; M.30.221B); Chrys.*hom.33.4 in Gen.*(4.338E); yielding to inferiors, *ib.*(339A); Thdt.*Heb.*2:13(3. 559); Max.*carit.*3.90(M.90.1045A); not judging others, ‡Ath.*qu. Ant.*93(M.28.656A); bearing insults, Ant.Mon.*hom.*70(M.89.1637A); **5.** degrees; **a.** as virtue of beginners ἦν ὡς νεόφυτος, χθὲς γενόμενος μοναχός, τ. πολλῇ...κεκοσμημένος *V.Pach.Φ* 109(p.71.35); **b.** more often of the advanced, dist. from a. ἔχει ἐκείνη μὲν ἡ τ. τὰ πολλὰ καὶ ἀθυμίαν, αὕτη δὲ χαρὰν μετὰ αἰδοῦς πανσόφου Diad.*perf.*95(p.140. 12); τελείαν τ. κτησάμενος Jo.Clim.*scal.*25(1001A); οὐχὶ πᾶς ὁ κατὰ φύσιν ἐπιεικὴς καὶ...πρᾶος οὗτος ἔφθασε εἰς τὸν βαθμὸν τῆς τ. Isaac *serm.*20(p.79); **c.** highest stage ὅρος τῆς τ. λήθη τῶν κατορθουμένων προσεχής Diad.*perf.*proem.(p.5.7); ὅτε...ἐν αἰσθήσει πολλῇ καὶ πληροφορίᾳ ὁ νοῦς ὑπὸ τῆς ἁγίας χάριτος καταυγασθῇ, τότε ὑπερφυσικὴν ἔχει τὴν τ. ἡ ψυχή *ib.*95(p.140.7); τῶν ἁμαρτωλῶν ἁπάντων πρῶτον ἑαυτὸν φάναι καὶ αὐτὸν ὑπερβαίνει τῆς τ. ὅρον Thdt.*1Tim.*1:15(3. 643); τῶν ἁγίων οἱ κορυφαῖοι, ὅτε τῶν ὑπὲρ φύσιν ἀξιωθῶσι, τότε μάλιστα πρὸς τ. ὁρῶσιν Bas.Sel.*or.*28.1(M.85.317B); Dor.*doct.*2.2(M. 88.1641C); **6.** effects; **a.** forgiveness of sins and mercy of God, *1Clem.*58.2; θεωρῶν ὁ κύριος...πῶς βιάζει ἑαυτὸν...εἰς τὴν τ. ... ποιεῖ μετ' αὐτοῦ τὸ ἔλεος αὐτοῦ Mac.Aeg.*cust.cor.*13(M.34.837B); διὰ τῆς τ. ἐπισπᾶται τοῦ θεοῦ τὴν εὔνοιαν Chrys.*grat.*4(2.664C); ὁ τὴν τ. κτησάμενος ἀποκαλύπτει αὐτῷ ὁ θεὸς τὰς ἁμαρτίας αὐτοῦ Esaias *or.*17.2 (p.103); *ib.*26.3(p.184); καθάπερ...ἀκολουθεῖ ἡ σκιὰ τῷ σώματι, οὕτω καὶ τῇ τ. τὸ ἔλεος Isaac *serm.*19(p.71); **b.** patience and contempt of self ἡ τ. δίδωσι τὸ φέρειν ἐξουδένωσιν Esaias *or.*17.6(p.108); *ib.*21.1 (p.120); Dor.*doct.*1.6(1624C); τῆς τ. τέκνα εἰσὶ τὸ ἑαυτὸν μέμφεσθαι, τὸ μὴ πιστεύειν τῇ ἰδίᾳ συνέσει, τὸ μισεῖν τὸ ἴδιον θέλημα *ib.*1.9(1628B); **c.** victory over demons τ. πολλῆς ἐπιμέλησαι καὶ οὐ μή σου δαιμόνων ἐπήρεια καθάψηται τῆς ψυχῆς Evagr.Pont.*or.*96(M.79. 1188D); *Apophth.Patr.*(M.65.204B); διὰ...τῆς τ. πάντα τοῦ ἀντικειμένου διαφθείρεται Esaias *or.*3.1(p.7; cf.M.40.1108D); Dor.*doct.*2.1 (M.88.1640D); Jo.Clim.*scal.*4(688B); **d.** spiritual advancement μέγα ...ἐφόδιον πρὸς τὸ εὐχόμενον ἐπακούεσθαι ἡ τ. Ath.*exp.Ps.*85:1(M. 27.373C); ἐὰν...ἀναλάβῃ τ. καὶ ἐπιγνῷ ἑαυτοῦ τὰ μέτρα,...ἐπανέρχεται ...εἰς αὐτὸν ἡ ἐμμάρτυρος γνῶσις Pall.*h.Laus.*95(p.140.7; M.34.1202A); ἡ τ. ὑψιπετεῖ καὶ ἀεροπόρον ἀποτελεῖ τὸν ἄνθρωπον Ant.Mon.*hom.*70 (M.89.1637A); πόσην τιμὴν κέκτηται ἡ τ. καὶ πόσον ἀνώτερός ἐστιν ὁ βαθμὸς αὐτῆς Isaac *serm.*20(p.76); **7.** combined with other virtues ἐπιείκεια and πραότης, *1Clem.*30.6; *ib.*56.1; μακροθυμία, Herm.*sim.* 8.7.6; κατάνυξις, Evagr.Pont.*cap.pract.*B 57(M.40.1248B); μεγαλοψυχία, Chrys.*hom.71.2 in Jo.*(8.418E); παρρησία, *V.Pach.Φ* 112(p.73. 30); ὑποταγή, *ib.*144(p.90.19); ἀγάπη and ἁγνεία, Jo.Clim.*scal.*25(M. 88.993C); **8.** of Christ ὁ Ἰωάννης θεασάμενος τὴν τοσαύτην τ. ... ἤρξατο διακωλύειν αὐτόν †Hipp.*theoph.*4(p.259.17; M.10.856B); in Inc. ὁ κύριος διὰ πολλὴν τ. οὐχ ὡς ἄγγελος ὤφθη, ἀλλ' ὡς ἄνθρωπος Clem.*exc.Thdot.*4(p.106.13; M.9.656A); exeg. Ps.21:7 εἰς τὸν Χριστὸν ἐκλαμβάνει...σκώληκα λέγει οὐ διὰ κακίαν, ἀλλὰ διὰ τὴν τ. Meth.*fr. 8 in Job*(p.512.18); example of humility to Christians, Bas.*reg.fus.* 10.2(2.353B; M.31.945C); σκεπάσαντα τὴν ἑαυτοῦ δόξαν ἐν τ. Isaac *serm.*20(p.76).

B. *humiliation,* in sense of *voluntary privation* ἐκ τῆς τ. σου ὁ εἰληφὼς ἐμπλήσῃ τὴν ἑαυτοῦ ψυχήν Herm.*sim.*5.3.7; so perh. also εὐχαῖς...καὶ ἐλεημοσύναις διαρκεῖν καὶ ταπεινοφροσύναις Nil.*epp.*4.61 (M.79.580A).

C. self-depreciatory style of personal reference used by bishops, Hadr.Papa *ep.Const.*(M.96.1222D).

ταπεινόφρων, 1. *base, abject,* Clem.*paed.*2.1(p.159.2; M.8.389B); **2.** *humble-minded, lowly in heart,* Ign.*Eph.*10.2; *Barn.*19.3; τοὺς τ. ἡ δόξα, ἣν ἐδόξαζον τὸν θεὸν...δοξάσει αὐτοὺς Or.*exp.in Pr.*29:23(M. 17.248D); ref. greatness of the humble, Chrys.*hom.65.5 in Mt.*(7. 650C); comp., id.*hom.2.2 in 2Cor.*(10.429E); ὁ διδάσκαλος ὀφείλει εἶναι...πάσῃ δυνάμει τ. *Apophth.Patr.*(M.65.204A); character of truly humble, Isaac *serm.*20(p.79); *ib.*56(p.224); τὰ μυστήρια τοῖς τ. ἀποκαλύπτονται *ib.*20(p.80); τοῦ πνεύματος τῶν ἀποκαλύψεων καὶ δεικνύοντος τὰ μυστήρια ἀξιοῦνται οἱ τ. *ib.*; quietude of the humble, *ib.*81(p.312); ὁ τ. ὅταν ποτὲ μόνος γένηται αἰδεῖται ἐξ ἑαυτοῦ *ib.*; τ. τέλειός ἐστιν ὁ μὴ χρῄζων μηχανᾶσθαι αἰτίας τῷ ἑαυτοῦ φρονήματι τοῦ ταπεινοφρονεῖν...καὶ...χωρὶς βίας οὕτως ἐστὶν ἐν τῇ καρδίᾳ ἑαυτοῦ *ib.*20 (p.79); ὁ ἀληθινὸς τ. οὐχὶ μόνον οὐ θέλει βλέπεσθαι...ὑπὸ τῶν ἀνθρώπων...ἀλλὰ...εἰ δυνατὸν...γενέσθαι ὥς τινα οὐκ ὄντα ἐν τῇ κτίσει καὶ οὐκ ἐλθόντα εἰς τὸ εἶναι *ib.*81(p.311); προσεγγίζει ὁ τ. τοῖς...θηρίοις καὶ...ἡμεροῦται ἡ ἀγριότης αὐτῶν...διότι τὴν ὀσμὴν...τοῦ Ἀδὰμ πρὸ τῆς παραβάσεως...ὠσφράνθησαν *ib.*20(p.78); prayers of humble are heard, *ib.*56(p.228); of truly humble opp. those who are humble in word only, Bars.*resp.*5(M.88.1816D); διακριτικοί τε καὶ τ. Jo.Clim. *scal.*4(M.88.688A); μοναχὸς τ. οὐ πολυπραγμονήσει ἄρρητα *ib.*25 (992C); humble bear all temptations, Thal.*cent.*3.15(M.91.1449B); neut. as subst., *humility* of Christ, ‡Dion.Al.*fr.in Lc.22:42*(p.235. 6; M.10.1598C).

ταπειν-όω, **1.** *lower, depress*; lit., *Pss.Sal.*11.5; *Apoc.En.*1.6(p.18. 17); **2.** *abase, bring low, oppress*, *T.Benj.*5.5; Or.*Jo.*1.12(13; p.18. 5; M.14.45C); οὗτος...ὁ σωτὴρ ∼ώσας συκοφάντην διὰ τοῦ ἑαυτὸν τεταπεινωκέναι *ib.*6.55(37; p.164.19; 297A); τόπος κακώσεώς ἐστι τῆς ψυχῆς τὸ χωρίον τοῦτο ἐν ᾧ τεταπεινώμεθα id.*mart.*20(p.19.3; M.11. 589A); ὅσῳ αὐτοὺς [sc. Christians] ἐταπείνουν βασιλεῖς...καὶ δῆμοι... τοσούτῳ πλείους ἐγίνοντο id.*Cels.*7.26(p.177.28; M.11.1457D); of man's body after Fall, Meth.*res.*3.14(p.411.3); Thdt.*Dan.*11:30(2.1283); **3.** pass.; *be depressed, dejected*, Const.ap.Gel.Cyz.*h.e.*3.18.5; Chrys. *sac.*5.4(p.131.12; 1.417A); id.*hom.13.4 in Mt.*(7.172C); *be humiliated, abased*, Apoll.*fr.*3(p.205.18)ap.Thdt.*eran.*2(4.173); **4.** *humble, make lowly* ὁ ἁμαρτήσας...μετανοεῖ...καὶ ∼οῖ τὴν ἑαυτοῦ ψυχήν Herm. *mand.*4.2.2; ὑπὸ τοῦ σωτῆρος προσκληθὲν τὸ ∼ῶσαν ἑαυτὸ πνεῦμα ἅγιον Or.*comm.in Mt.*13.18(p.226.24; M.13.1141B); ἔστι...τὸ ∼ῶσαι ἑαυτὸν ὡς τὸ παιδίον...τὸ μιμήσασθαι τὸ ὑπὲρ τῆς σωτηρίας ἀνθρώπων ∼ῶσαν ἑαυτὸ τὸ πνεῦμα ἅγιον *ib.*(p.227.27; 1144A); οὐ διδάσκομεν... ὅτι αὔταρκες...τὸ διὰ τὴν μοχθηρίαν ἑαυτὸν ∼οῦν πρὸς τὸ δεχθῆναι ὑπὸ τοῦ θεοῦ id.*Cels.*3.62(p.256.28; M.11.1001C); οὐκ ἐταπείνωσε...ὁ εἰς ἑαυτὸν ὀπίσω τοῦ ἑτέρου...διὰ τοῦτο ἔμειναν ἔξω τῆς πύλης *Apophth. Patr.*(M.65.100D); οὐδὲν οὕτως πτωχὴ κατάστασις καὶ προσαιτῶν δίαιτα ψυχὴν ∼ῶσαι δεδύνηται πώποτε Jo.Clim.*scal.*25(M.88.1001C); med. ἑαυτὸν δι' εὐλαβείας τῷ θεῷ ἐταπεινοῦτο Gel.Cyz.*h.e.*3.9.1; pass., *humble oneself* οὐ πάντως ὁ ταπεινοφρονῶν ἀσχημόνως καὶ ἀπαισίως ∼οῦται, χαμαιπετὴς ἐπὶ τῶν γονάτων καὶ πρηνὴς ἐρριμμένος Or.*Cels.* 6.15(p.85.20; 1312D); through afflictions, †Bas.*Is.*146(1.482B; M.30. 351A); τοσοῦτον ∼οῦνται ὑποκάτω παντὸς ἀνθρώπου...ὡς ἑαυτοὺς πάντων ἐσχατωτέρους καὶ ἐλάττους νομίζειν Mac.Aeg.*hom.*18.8(M.34. 640C); οὐκ ἐταπεινώθησαν τοῦ διορθώσασθαι ἑαυτοὺς καὶ πορευθῆναι τῇ ταπεινῇ ὁδῷ τοῦ Χριστοῦ *Apophth.Patr.*(M.65.101A); δεῖ...λυπεῖσθαι...ἡμᾶς συμμέτρως ὡς ἐγκαταλειφθέντας, ἵνα πλέον ∼ωθῶμεν καὶ ὑποταγῶμεν τῇ δόξῃ τοῦ κυρίου Diad.*perf.*69(p.84.24); ἐξ ἀρχῆς... εἰ ἐταπεινώθη [sc. Adam]...οὐκ εἶχεν ἐκπεσεῖν Dor.*doct.*1.8(M.88. 1625B); ἵνα ∼ωθῇ ἡ ψυχή σου καὶ ἐλεηθῇς *ib.*(1628A); ἔστιν...ὅτε ∼οῦταί τις διὰ δόξαν *ib.*2.5(1645B); ἡ ψυχὴ ὅταν ∼οῦται, τότε καρπὸν φέρει καὶ ὅσον ποιεῖ καρπόν, τοσοῦτον ∼οῦται *ib.*2.6(1645B); ὁ τὰ ἔσω τεταπεινωκὼς ὑπὸ χειλέων οὐ κλέπτεται Jo.Clim.*scal.*25(993B); c. dat., Jo.D.*Man.*1.83(M.94.1581B); πῶς ∼ωθῶ τῷ δικαίῳ μου πατρί; Thdr. Stud.*epp.*1.3(M.99.913B).

ταπεινῶς, **1.** *in an earthly, unspiritual fashion*, ref. Jewish exegesis of OT prophecies of Christ, Just.*dial.*112.1(M.6.733A); Meth.*symp.*4.5(p.50.25; M.18.93B); ref. Christ's utterances as adapted to his hearers, Chrys.*hom.84.1 in Mt.*(7.798D); **2.** *humbly*; ref. obedience to spiritual father, Jo.Clim.*ep.*(M.88.625D).

ταπείνωσις, ἡ, **A.** *abasement, humiliation, low estate*; **1.** in gen. δύο γὰρ ταπεινώσεις· ἡ μὲν κενή, ἡ δὲ πλήρης· ἡ μὲν ἐπαινετὴ περὶ ἧς φησιν ὁ σωτήρ...ἡ δὲ ψεκτὴ ἣν ταπεινοῦται ὁ ἁμαρτωλός Or.*hom.20.5 in Jos.*(p.423.22; M.87.1032A); of body; produced by penitential exercises, Eus.*d.e.*3.5(p.124.16; M.22.212E); *V.Pach.Φ* 14(p.9.19); through poverty, *Hom.Clem.*19.23; in self-depreciation ἐπαισθανόμενος τῆς ἐμαυτοῦ τ. Bas.*fid.*1(2.223D; M.31.676C); τὴν εἰδώλων τ. Bas.Sel.*or.*3.3(M.85.57B); **2.** condition of men as creatures, as opp. God, Cyr.*thes.*23(5^1.229B); τὸ 'ἐξ οὗ' τῶν ποιημάτων κατηγορούμενον οὐ κατοίσει πρὸς τὴν οἰκείαν τ. ... τὸ τοῦ πνεύματος...θεϊκόν *ib.*33 (335B); **3.** consequence of sin; **a.** original τοῦτο...ἡμῶν τὸ σῶμα... μετὰ τὴν παράβασιν σῶμα ταπεινώσεως λέγεται· οὐ γὰρ ἂν εἰ μὴ ἔνδοξον ἦν, ταπεινώσεως νῦν ἐκλήθη Meth.*res.*3.14(p.411.2); *ib.*3.16 (p.412.19; M.18.317A); **b.** actual ἡ κυρίως τ. οὐκ ἄλλη τίς ἐστιν τῆς ἁμαρτίας, ὥσπερ ὕψωσις ἡ κατόρθωσις Or.*fr.20 in Lam.*(p.243.26; M. 13.617B); Ath.*exp.Ps.*12:3(M.27.96D); μεγάλη τ. ἡ ὑψηλοφροσύνη Mac.Aeg.*hom.*19.18(M.34.648D); **c.** as corrective remedy παιδείᾳ παραδοθεὶς...ὡς ἂν γνῶ ὅτι ἡ τ. ἡ γενομένη μοι κατὰ χρηστότητα καὶ παιδείαν ἐγένετο Ath.*exp.Ps.*118:67(492B); **4.** of Christ in Inc., Alex.Al.*ep.Alex.*9(p.25.18; M.18.561B); τῆς μετὰ σαρκὸς οἰκονομίας ὁ λόγος καὶ ἡ διὰ τοῦτο λεγομένη τ. Cyr.*Jo.*1.3(4.22C); id.*thes.*20(5^1. 195A); τὸν ἀνθρώπινον χαρακτῆρα...Χριστοῦ τοῦ θεοῦ...ἀναστηλοῦσθαι ὁρίζομεν δι' αὐτοῦ τὸ τῆς τ. ὕψος τοῦ θεοῦ λόγου κατανοοῦντες Hadr. Papa *ep.Taras.*(M.*PL.*96.1235C); **5.** of soul, = *dejection* ἣν εἶχες πρότερον συντριβὴν καὶ τ. διὰ γὰρ τῶν πολέμων προκόπτει ἡ ψυχή *Apophth.Patr.*(M.65.208C); Thdt.*Ps.*34:14(1.823).

B. *humility*; **1.** necessary; as sign of Christianity, Mac.Aeg. *hom.*15.37(M.34.601B); δίχα...τ. οὐ δύναται ὑποταγῆναι ταῖς ἐντολαῖς, οὐδὲ ἐλθεῖν εἴς τί ποτε ἀγαθόν Dor.*doct.*1.9(M.88.1628C); Ant.Mon. *hom.*19(M.89.1488C); Hesych.S.*temp.*1.98(M.93.1509C); **2.** caused by **a.** self-knowledge ἡ ἀπὸ τοῦ ἐπάρματος καὶ ὕψους ἀλαζονικοῦ... πρὸς τὴν οἰκείαν ἀξίαν ἐπάνοδος τ. ἐστιν †Bas.*Is.*86(1.438E; M.30. 260A); ὁ μὴ γινώσκων τὴν ἑαυτοῦ ἀσθένειαν, ἐλλείπει ἐκ τῆς τ. Isaac *serm.*21(p.85); cf. Jo.Clim.*scal.*25(M.88.993A); **b.** knowledge of God ἐπίγνωσις θεοσεβείας, ἐπίγνωσις τ. Bas.*renunt.*10(2.211C; M.31. 648B); Max.*ep.*13(M.91.512A); whose gift it is, *ib.*12(505C); Isaac *serm.*20(p.80); **3.** developed; **a.** through ascetic training; by external acts, of which Christ's washing of disciples' feet was an example, Jo.Clim.*scal.*25(M.88.1000D); ἐμποιεῖ...τ. ἀληθῆ...τὸ ἵνα τις τῶν πέλας τὰ κατορθώματα...περιστρέφει Hesych.S.*temp.*1.64(M. 93.1501A); τ. ... οὐ δύναταί τις κτήσασθαι ἀλλ' ἢ διὰ τῶν τρόπων αὐτῆς δι' ὧν πέφυκε γίνεσθαι ἡ καρδία συντετριμμένη Isaac *serm.*21(p.85); **b.** through imitation of Christ, Bas.*renunt.*10(2.211C; M.31.648B); Mac.Aeg.*cust.cor.*13(M.34.837A); ὅνπερ [sc. Χριστόν] μιμούμενος... ἐνδιαθέτως καὶ αὐτὸς ἐκτήσατο...τὴν τ. Max.*ep.*13(M.91.509D); **4.** degrees δύο...εἰσὶ ταπεινώσεις...ἡ πρώτη τ. ἐστι...τὸ εἶναι ὑποκάτω πάντων. ἡ δὲ δευτέρα τ. ἐστι τὸ ἐπιγράφειν τῷ θεῷ τὰ κατορθώματα. αὕτη ἐστὶν ἡ τελεία τ. τῶν ἁγίων Dor.*doct.*2.4,6(M.88.1644C–1645C); ἄλλη ἡ τῶν μετανοούντων σκυθρωπὴ τ. ... καὶ ἄλλη ἡ τοῖς τελείοις δι' ἐνεργείας θεοῦ προσγινομένη μακαρία πλουτοταπείνωσις Jo.Clim. *scal.*5(777B); **5.** as myst. state ταύτην τὴν τ. οὐδεὶς δύναται λόγῳ φράσαι πῶς ἐστιν...ἢ πῶς ἐγγίνεται τῇ ψυχῇ ἐὰν μὴ ἀπὸ πείρας μάθῃ αὐτὴν ἄνθρωπος· λόγῳ δὲ οὐδεὶς δύναται μαθεῖν αὐτήν Dor.*doct.*2.7 (1648C); *ib.*2.8(1649C); taught by Christ, Jo.Clim.*scal.*25(M.88. 997B); τ. ἐστι δύναμίς τις μυστική, ἣν μετὰ τὴν τελείωσιν τῆς πολιτείας ὑποδέχονται οἱ τέλειοι ἅγιοι Isaac *serm.*20(p.79); **6.** effects: liberation from sin and passions, *T.Gad* 5.3; Esaias *or.*9.2(p.66); Dor.*doct.*2.3 (M.88.1644B); ἐκ τ. ἀπάθεια Jo.Clim.*scal.*4(M.88.709D); *ib.*25(1001B); ὁδὸς ἐπὶ τὴν γνῶσιν, ἀπάθεια καὶ τ. Hesych.S.*temp.*1.67(M.93.1501D); *ib.*1.75(1504C); discernment, Jo.Clim.*scal.*25(1004A); union with God, Diad.*perf.*12(p.14.13); Dor.*doct.*2.2(1644A); **7.** as self-depreciatory style of personal reference, used esp. by bishops, Bas.*ep.*79(3.172E; M.32.453C); Chrys.*ep.*23(3.608E); CIllyr.*ep.*ap.Thdt.*h.e.*4.9.3(3.961); †Gr.II Papa *ep.Leon.*1(H.4.12E).

C. *exhaustion* τὴν τῶν ἵππων τ. Thphn.*chron.*p.240(M.108.605B).

***ταπεινωτής**, ὁ, *abaser* εἰπών· ἔλαιον ἅγιον εἰς ἁγιασμὸν ἡμῖν δοθέν,...σὺ εἶ ὁ τ. τῶν σκληρῶν ἔργων *A.Thom.*A 121(p.231.1).

***ταπεινωτικός**, **1.** *humiliating, abasing* δυσπρόσιτος...ἐστι τοῖς τ. πάθεσι Bas.*hom.in Ps.*28(1.119B; M.29.293B); τ. μάλιστα πάντων ἡ ἁμαρτία *ib.*33(155D; M.380D); τ. τῶν ματαίων φυσιώσεων λόγος †Bas. *Is.*18(1.390E; M.30.148C); **2.** *indicative of inferiority, subordination*, in relation of Son to Father πότερον ταπεινωτικὰς [sc. μαρτυρίας] εἶναί φαμεν ἢ...τὸ μεγαλοπρεπὲς τοῦ μονογενοῦς...ἀνακηρύττειν Bas. *Spir.*15(3.12A; M.32.92A).

***ταραξανδρία**, ἡ, (a woman who is a) *plague of men*, Pall.*v.Chrys.* 4(p.25.11; M.47.16); in form ταραξάνδρα name applied to one of the Sibyls because she disturbed men's minds, Clem.*str.*1.21(p.82.18; M.8.868A); *Orac.Sib.*proem.45.

***ταραξάρχης**, ὁ, *leader in disorder*, Pall.*v.Chrys.*4(p.27.14; M.47. 18).

ταραξίας, ὁ, *mischief-maker*, Evagr.*h.e.*5.18(p.213.9; M.86.2828B).

ταραχοποιός, **1.** of persons, *mischievous, mischief-making*, †Cyr. *hom.div.*14(5^2.412E); Leont.B.*fr.*(M.86.2030B); **2.** of things, *producing trouble, turbulent*, Cyr.S.*v.Sab.*86(p.193.9); Cosm.Mel.*schol.* (M.38.442) in Gr.Naz.*carm.*2.1.46.50.

ταρίχευσις, ἡ, met., *wasting*, Nil.*epp.*2.268(M.79.336D).

[*]ταρταραῖος (-ρειος, -ρεος), *of* or *belonging to Tartarus, hellish*; of demons, *M.Pion.*14.11; incl. pagan gods, Bas.Sel.*v.Thecl.*1(M. 85.497B); ὁ σατὰν τοῦ ἄνω φωτὸς...ἐξέπεσεν καὶ εἰς τοὺς ζοφωδεστάτους τ. μυχοὺς κατωλίσθησεν Didym.*Trin.*2.27(M.39.768A); ταρτάρειος: τ. Χάρυβδιν...μόνας τὰς ἁμαρτίας εἶναι νομίζετε *Clem.ep.*14(M. 2.49B); φιλήδονος καὶ φιλενδείκτης ὑπάρχων οὐ μακρὰν ἀφέστηκας τῆς τ. Χαρύβδεως Nil.ap.Jo.D.*parall.*(M.95.1340C); ταρτάρεος: of Rome, *Orac.Sib.*5.178; of demons, Gr.Naz.*carm.*1.1.7.79(M.37.444A); *ib.*1.1. 35.9(517A).

***ταρταρηφόρος**, *that brings to hell* μέθη μύωψ, κρημνηστά, ταρταρηφόρε Gr.Naz.*carm.*1.2.25.531(M.37.850A).

***ταρτάρινος** (-τάριος), *hellish* ὦ φθόνε, πλοῖον πισσοειδές, τ., ναυαγιοφόρον· σὸς ναύκληρός ἐστιν ὁ διάβολος ‡Chrys.*hom.in Mt. 12:14*(10.759E); of demonic powers who seek to oppose passage of souls to heaven ἐν τῷ καιρῷ τῆς ἐξόδου...ὁ...ἐν φόβῳ εὑρισκόμενος...ἐλευθερίῳ τρόπῳ τοὺς τ. οὐ παρελεύσεται ἄρχοντας Diad.*perf.* 100(p.150.8); of demons κόλασις ἀτελεύτητος...σκώληξ ἀκοίμητος καὶ τ. δαίμονες Jo.D.*haer.*101(M.94.772D); met., *horrible*, †Apoll. *met.Ps.*17:6(M.33.1332A); ταρτάριος, of hell, *Orac.Sib.*1.101; *ib.*2.291.

τάρταρος, ὁ, **1.** *Hades, the nether world*, *Orac.Sib.*1.10; plur., *Apoc.Esd.*(p.27); **2.** *hell*, as place of torment and abode of Devil; **a.** pagan, Arist.*apol.*9(*TS* p.104.27); Hipp.*haer.*5.14(p.108.25; M.16. 3167A); *Hom.Clem.*1.4; **b.** Jewish, *Orac.Sib.*1.119; Οὐριήλ, ὁ εἷς τῶν ἁγίων ἀγγέλων, ὁ ἐπὶ τοῦ κόσμου καὶ τοῦ τ. *Apoc.En.*20.2(p.48.21); τὰ κατώτερα μέρη τοῦ τ. *Apoc.Esd.*(p.28); **c.** Christian; as abode of Devil, *T.Sal.*6.3(M.122.1324C); *Hom.Clem.*20.9; as the dragon, *A.Thom.*A 32(p.149.18); *A.Phil.*110(p.43.6); as place of eternal darkness, Hipp.*fr.21 in Pr.*(p.164.11; M.10.621B); id.*haer.*10.34(p.292.15; M.16.3454A); as place of cold, opp. gehenna, †Cyr.*hom.div.*14(5^2.404A); place of punishment, *Apophth.Patr.*(M.65.173B); ταύτην [sc. obedience] ἀθετήσας ὁ Ἀδὰμ εἰς τὸν βύθιον ἀπωλίσθησεν τ. Diad.*perf.*41(p.48.1); Max.*ep.*1(M.91.381C); *ib.*(385B); dist. from Hades as being reserved for worst offenders, e.g. Jewish murderers of Christ, opp. idolaters, *1 Apoc.Jo.*22(p.89); as quailing at glance of Christ, *M.Artem.*(p.169.10); **3.** met., of this world, opp. heaven ψυχὰς...ἀγαθὰς...καταλιπούσας τὸν ὑπερουράνιον τόπον ὑπομεῖναι ἐλθεῖν εἰς τόνδε τὸν τ. καὶ σῶμα ἀναλαβούσας τῶν ἐν γενέσει κακῶν Clem.*str.*1.15(p.42.16; M.8.769A); **4.** synon. with *Devil*, Cyr.S.*v.Euthym.*24(p.37.13).

***ταρταρότης, ἡ,** *hellishness*, Jo.Carp.*cap.*96(M.85.1856).

ταρταροῦχος, *controlling hell* καταχθόνια...πνεύματα ταρταρούχων ἀγγέλων Hipp.*Dan.*2.29.11(M.10.868A); ἐκφεύξεσθε...τ. ἀγγέλων κολαστῶν ὄμμα ἀεὶ μένον ἐν ἀπειλῇ id.*haer.*10.34(p.292.17; M.16.3454A); παραδοθήτω ἡ ψυχὴ αὕτη τ. ἀγγέλῳ καὶ φυλαττέσθω ἕως τῆς μεγάλης ἡμέρας τῆς κρίσεως *Apoc.Paul.*18(p.48).

***Τασκοδοῦργοι, οἱ,** for τασκόδρουγοι, nickname of Montanist sect, Sophr.H.*ep.syn.*(M.87.3193C) = τασκοδρουγῖται.

***Τασκοδρουγῖται, οἱ,** nickname of adherents of Cataphrygian heresy, a variety of Montanism κατὰ Φρύγας, οἱ καὶ Μοντανισταὶ καὶ Τ. Epiph.*anac.*48(p.211.7; M.41.845D); ἡ [sc. αἵρεσις] Πεπουζιανῶν, ἡ Ἀρτοτυριτῶν, ἡ Τασκοδούργων Sophr.H.ap.CCP(681)*act.*11(H.3.1292B); cf. *quis unquam Passalorynchitas et Ascadrobos, et Artotyritas...in aliqua parte Romani orbis audivit?* Hier.*comm.in Gal.*2(M.*PL.*26.382C); cf. *alii sunt Ascodrogitae in Galatia, qui utrem inflatum ponunt et cooperiunt in sua ecclesia, et circumeunt eum insanientes potibus*, Philastrius *haer.*75(M.*PL.*12.1187A); meaning of name καλοῦνται δὲ διὰ τοιαύτην αἰτίαν Τ. τασκὸς παρ' αὐτοῖς πάσσαλος καλεῖται, δροῦγγος δὲ μυκτὴρ...καλεῖται, καὶ ἀπὸ τοῦ τιθέναι ἑαυτῶν τὸν δάκτυλον τὸν λεγόμενον λιχανὸν ἐπὶ τὸν μυκτῆρα ἐν τῷ εὔχεσθαι...ἐκλήθησαν ὑπό τινων Τ. τουτέστιν πασσαλορυγχῖται Epiph.*haer.*48.14(p.239.12ff.; M.41.877B); cf.Tim.CP *haer.*(M.86.13B,16A); opp. Passalorinchitae, *qui digitum imponentes in nares...et in labia, quasi silentium semper exercent*, Philastrius *haer.*76(1188A); tenets Τ. οἵτινες παλαιὰν καὶ νέαν διαθήκην δέχονται, ἑτέρους δὲ προφήτας παρεισφέρουσι μετὰ τοὺς προφήτας, Μοντανόν τινα αὐχοῦντες καὶ Πρίσκιλλαν Epiph.*anac.*48(p.211.7; M.41.845D); v. Ἀσκοδρουγῆται, Ἀσκοδρουπῖται, Ἀσκοδρούται, Πασσαλορυγχῖται.

***Τασκόδρουγοι, οἱ,** = foreg., Justn.*cod.*1.5.18(p.56); also oxytone, Tim.CP *haer.*(M.86.13B,16A).

τάσσω, *vow* τ. τῷ θεῷ...μηδένα ἀμύνεσθαι τῶν ἐχθρῶν σου Thphn.*chron.*p.312(M.108.757B).

***Τατιανοί, οἱ,** followers of Tatian τοῦ Τατιανοῦ καὶ τῶν ἀπ' αὐτοῦ Τ. καλουμένων Epiph.*haer.*46.4(p.207.26; M.41.844A); *ib.*61.1(p.380.14; 1040C); cf. οὗτος [sc. Tatian] συνήκμασεν Ἰουστίνῳ τῷ μάρτυρι. ... μετὰ δὲ τὴν τοῦ...Ἰουστίνου τελευτὴν προσεφθάρη τοῖς τοῦ Μαρκίωνος δόγμασιν...ἕτερα προσθεὶς παρ' ἐκεῖνον id.*anac.*46(p.4.5; M.41.581B).

τ (ταῦ), τό, the letter *T*; as numeral τ′, *300*, ref. Gen.14:14, 17:26–27 μάθετε...ὅτι Ἀβραὰμ...ἐν πνεύματι προβλέψας εἰς τὸν Ἰησοῦν περιέτεμεν, λαβὼν τριῶν γραμμάτων δόγματα· λέγει γάρ· καὶ περιέτεμεν Ἀβραὰμ ἐκ τοῦ οἴκου αὐτοῦ ἄνδρας δεκαοκτὼ καὶ τριακοσίους. ... τὸ δεκαοκτὼ ἰῶτα δέκα, ἦτα ὀκτώ· ἔχεις Ἰησοῦν. ὅτι δὲ ὁ σταυρὸς ἐν τῷ ταῦ ἤμελλεν ἔχειν τὴν χάριν, λέγει καὶ τοὺς τριακοσίους. δηλοῖ οὖν τὸν μὲν Ἰησοῦν ἐν τοῖς δυσὶν γράμμασιν, καὶ ἐν τῷ ἑνὶ τὸν σταυρόν *Barn.*9.8; cf. *Marcus quidam et Colorbasus novam haeresim ex Graecorum alphabeto componentes...propter hanc enim causam Christum dixisse: ego sum A et Ω. denique ⟨in⟩ Jesum Christum descendisse, id est, columbam in Jesum venisse, quae Graeco nomine cum* περιστερὰ *pronuntietur habere secum hunc numerum DCCCI* (i.e. Christus = α+ω = 801; περιστερά = 80+5+100+10+200+300+5+100+1 = 801 = α+ω; therefore Christ = περιστερά = H. Ghost), Tertullian *haer.*50(M.*PL.*2.88A).

ταυλίζω, = ταβλίζω, *play at dice*, Ephr.2.379C; ταβλ-, Justn.*nov.*123.10(p.603.2); Leont.N.*v.Sym.*57(M.93.1740C).

[*]**ταυρέα, ἡ,** = ταυρεία, **1.** *ox-hide whip*, Ath.*h.Ar.*60(p.216.24; M.25.765A); Pall.*h.Laus.*16(p.41.2; M.34.1041D); **2.** *drum*, Jo.Mal.*chron.*11 p.272(M.97.412C).

[*]**ταυρελέφας, ὁ,** = ταυρέλαφος, '*bull-elephant*'; a huge ox with the hide of an elephant, prob. *rhinoceros*, Philost.*h.e.*3.11(p.40.4; M.65.496B).

***ταυριανός,** *born under Taurus*, Bas.*hex.*6.6(1.55C; M.29.129C) = ‡Caes.Naz.*dial.*111(M.38.988).

ταυροειδής, *bull-like*; of Suriel (Uriel) in Ophite diagram, Or.*Cels.*6.30(p.100.10; M.11.1340A).

***ταυροπολέω,** *be drawn by a yoke of bulls*; of Artemis, ‡Jo.D.*Artem.*42(p.162.24; M.96.1289B).

ταυροπρόσωπος, *bull-faced*, Geo.Pis.*van.*59(M.92.1586A).

***ταὐταληθής,** *absolutely true*; of Christ, Gr.Agr.*Eccl.*3.5(M.98.852D).

***ταὐτεμφερής,** *of the same form, exactly like*, Thdr.Stud.*antirr.*3.3(M.99.425B); *ib.*3.2(420A,C).

ταὐτίζ-ω, *identify, make identical* ὑπόστασις σύνθετος, τὴν φυσικὴν τῶν ἄκρων διαίρεσιν ἐν ἑαυτῇ...∼ουσα Max.*opusc.*(M.91.204A); pass., Christol ἐν οἷς διακρίνεται τοῦ πατρὸς ὁ λόγος...τούτοις...καὶ πρὸς τὴν σάρκα ∼εται Eulog.*fr.dogm.*(M.86.2948A); ἡ σὰρξ λόγος γέγονεν, οὐκ ἀπολέσασα τοῦθ' ὅπερ ἐστί, ∼ομένη δὲ μᾶλλον πρὸς τὸν λόγον καθ' ὑπόστασιν Jo.D.*imag.*3.6(M.94.1325B); εἷς οὖν καθ' ὑπόστασιν πρὸς ἑαυτὸν ∼όμενος, τῶν δ' ἄκρων τοῖς χαρακτηριστικοῖς ἀφοριζόμενος ἰδιώμασιν id.*Jacob.*80(M.94.1477B); λάμπει...τὸ πρόσωπον αὐτοῦ ὡς ὁ ἥλιος· φωτὶ γὰρ ἀΰλῳ ∼εται καθ' ὑπόστασιν id.*hom.*1.4(M.96.552C); ref. union of saints with God ᾧ [sc. θελήματι] πεφύκασι πρὸς τὸ θεῖον ∼εσθαι Max.*opusc.*(M.91.25C); ref. identity of images with originals τῇ ὁμοιώσει ∼ομένη [sc. εἰκών], ἠλλοτρίωται τῆς οὐσίας τοῦ ἀρχετύπου ὡς εἰκὼν τοῦ Χριστοῦ πρὸς...Χριστόν Thdr.Stud.*antirr.*3.2(M.99.417B); τοῦτο...φύσις εἰκόνος, ∼εσθαι μὲν κατὰ τὴν ὁμοίωσιν τοῦ πρωτοτύπου, διαφορεῖσθαι δὲ κατὰ τὸν τῆς οὐσίας λόγον *ib.*3.4(432A); id.*epp.*2.65(M.99.1288B); *ib.*2.171(1537C).

***ταὐτισμός, ὁ,** *identity*, Thdr.Stud.*epp.*2.84(M.99.1328B).

***ταὐτοβούλητος,** *having the same will*, ‡Jo.D.*Const.*2(M.95.312B).

***ταὐτοβουλία, ἡ,** *identity of will*; **1.** Trin. κατὰ τὴν...τ. τοῦ πατρός Cyr.*Jo.*4.5(4.414B); κἀκεῖνο κατὰ Ἀρειανῶν σημειωτέον, ὅτι ἐν τῷ εἰπεῖν 'ἐγὼ καὶ ὁ πατὴρ ἕν ἐσμεν' οὐ τῆς τ. ἡ δήλωσις, ἀλλ' ἡ τῆς οὐσίας ἑνότης σημαίνεται *ib.*7(Pusey p.254:24; Aubert om.); *ib.*5.5(526D) cit. s. ταὐτολογία; Hesych.H.*fr.Ps.*40:11(M.93.1193D); ἐν τ. καὶ ταυτουργίᾳ τοῦ πατρὸς καὶ τοῦ υἱοῦ καὶ τοῦ ἁγίου πνεύματος ‡Gr.Nyss.*hom.2.24 in Jo.*(p.119.21); πατρός, υἱοῦ καὶ ἁγίου πνεύματος...ἐν συμφυΐᾳ καὶ τ. Melet.*nat.hom.*1(M.64.1149D); **2.** Christol. τῷ θεῷ λόγῳ συναφθείς...ὁ τεχθεὶς ἐκ τῆς παρθένου ναὸς μεμένηκεν ἀδιαίρετος, τὴν ἐν πᾶσιν αὐτοῦ τ. καὶ ταυτουργίαν ἐσχηκώς Thdr.Mops.*ep.Domn.*(p.339.8; M.66.1013A); objections to Nestorian use φασὶ...ὅτι τῇ ἰσοτιμίᾳ, τῇ τ., τῇ αὐθεντίᾳ ἀδιαίρετός ἐστι τοῦ λόγου ὁ ἐν ᾧ κατῴκηκεν, ἄνθρωπος Cyr.*ep.*46(p.162.20; 5^2.145E); id.*Heb.*(p.420.12; M.74.1004B); φασὶ τὴν ὑπόστασιν ἀντὶ τοῦ ταυτοβουλίαν καὶ ὁμογνωμοσύνην σημαίνειν τῶν φύσεων Leont.H.*Nest.*2.1(M.86.1525C); μήτε ὡς ὁ...Νεστόριος σχετικὴν τὴν ἕνωσιν λέγομεν ἢ ἰσοτιμίᾳ καὶ τ. καὶ θελημάτων...ταυτότητι παραληροῦμεν τὴν σύμβασιν Sophr.H.*ep.syn.*(M.87.3165A); ἡ γὰρ τ. βουλῶν ἐστιν ἕνωσις φυλάττουσα τὴν τῶν κατ' αὐτὴν ἡνωμένων διαφοράν Max.*opusc.*(M.91.45B); τὴν ἕνωσιν ποιησάμενος ἐξ ἧς καὶ τὴν τ. συνίστησιν ἢ πολυβουλίαν εἰπεῖν οἰκειότερον *ib.*(192C); ὁ δὲ Νεστόριος ἄλλας ἐπενόει ἑνώσεις κατὰ τὴν ἀξίαν...καὶ ὁμοτιμίαν καὶ τ. Jo.D.*dialect.*65(M.94.664B); εἰ γὰρ κατὰ χάριν καὶ τ. καὶ σχέσιν καὶ ἀγάπην εἴπωμεν τὴν ἐνανθρώπησιν, καὶ τοῦ πατρὸς καὶ τοῦ πνεύματος λέξομεν τὴν ἐνανθρώπησιν id.*fr.Nest.*42(p.577); in sense of *unity, singleness of will* Νεστόριος ταυτοβουλίαν ἤγουν ἓν θέλημα τῶν πλαττομένων αὐτῷ δύο προσώπων ἐδόξασεν CLater.*act.*4(H.3.852B); *ib.*5(904C); monophysite, Anast.S.*hod.*1(M.89.48B) cit. s. ταὐτοπραξία; **3.** of moral identity of will between men, Cyr.*ador.*7(1.247E); id.*Jo.*11.9(4.972A) cit. s. ἕνωσις; Eulog.*fr.dogm.*(M.86.2949B).

***ταὐτογενής,** *of the same genus*, Leont.H.*Nest.*1.10(M.86.1440A).

***ταὐτόγνωμος,** s.v.l., *concordant* τὴν ἰσόρροπον καὶ τ. τὴν περὶ τῶν θείων συμφωνίαν Thdr.Stud.*epp.*1.26(M.99.992B; poss. for ταυτογνώμονα).

***ταὐτόγνωστος,** *having the same knowledge*, ‡Jo.D.*Const.*2(M.95.312B).

***ταὐτόδοξος,** *of the same glory*, ‡Caes.Naz.*dial.*128(M.38.1025).

***ταὐτοδύναμος,** *having the same force* or *meaning*, Dion.Ar.*e.h.*7.3.2(M.3.556C); Trin., *having the same power*, Jo.D.*hom.*4.4(M.96.605A) cit. s. ταὐτοτελής; †Jo.D.*B.J.*19(M.96.1028B) cit. s. ταὐτοθελής.

***ταὐτοεθνής,** *of the same race* τοὺς κατὰ πίστιν ἡμῖν ἰδίους καὶ τ. Cyr.*ador.*4(1.111B).

ταὐτοειδής, *of identical form* μίαν...θεότητος φύσιν τὴν ἐν τρισὶν ὑποστάσεσιν ἰδικαῖς, αἱ σύμμορφοι καὶ τ. ἀλλήλαις Cyr.*dial.Trin.*3(5^1.491D); ὅτι δέ ἐστιν ἐν ταὐτότητι τῇ κατὰ πάντα τῷ... πατρί, διὰ τὴν φυσικὴν ἐμφέρειαν καὶ τὸ τῆς οὐσίας ταὐτοειδές, διεσάφει *ib.*5(553E);

ἡνίκα τινὸς ταὐτογενοῦς ἢ ταὐτοειδοῦς...ὁ λόγος ζητεῖται Leont.H. *Nest*.1.10(M.86.1440A).

***ταὐτοειδῶς**, *as identical in form* ὑφ' ἑαυτοῦ μονοειδῶς καὶ τ. ἀφοριζόμενον [sc. God] Dion.Ar.*d.n*.9.4(M.3.912C).

***ταὐτοενεργ-έω**, *work in the same way, operate in unity* ∼εῖ...ἡ... τριὰς καὶ ἅπερ ἂν δρῴη καὶ βούλοιτο ὁ πατήρ, ταῦτα καὶ ὁ υἱὸς κατὰ τὸν ἴσον τρόπον, ὁμοίως δὲ καὶ τὸ πνεῦμα Cyr.*Nest*.4.2(p.80.30; ταὐτοεργεῖ 6¹.103A).

ταὐτοέπεια, ἡ, *identity of speech*, Cyr.*Ps*.46:10(M.69.1057B).

ταὐτοεπέω, **1.** *repeat oneself, be tautologous*, Didym.*Trin*.3.1(M. 39.781C); Cyr.*Mich*.35(3.421C); **2.** *say the same thing, speak with one voice, in identical terms*, Cyr.*Is*.3.5(2.522B).

***ταὐτοεπής**, *tautologous*; neut. as subst., *tautology*, Cyr.*ador*.1(1. 334A).

ταὐτοεργία** (ταὐτουργία**), ἡ, a *doing of the same thing*, Cyr. *Ps*.36 proem.(M.69.924B); id.*ador*.12(1.430A); *ib*.14(510D); Trin., *identity of operation* θεὸς ἐκ θεοῦ κατὰ φύσιν εἰς ταυτοβουλίαν καί, ἵν' οὕτως εἴπω, τ. ἀναβαίνει τῷ φύσαντι id.*Jo*.5.5(4.531E); ἐνδέχεται... κατὰ μόνην τὴν τ. εἰς ὁμοίωσιν ἀναβαίνοντα τῷ πατρὶ τὸν υἱόν, καὶ ὑποβάθρᾳ...οὐκ ἐρηρεισμένον φυσικῇ...ὑπομεῖναι...τροπὴν *ib*.3.5(304C); Christol. ὁ γὰρ ἑτεροφυῶν εἰδὼς ταυτουργίαν σύγχυσιν ὁμοῦ φυσικὴν καὶ διαίρεσιν αὐτῶν εἰσηγεῖται προσωπικήν ‡Hipp.*Ber.Hel*.6(p.325.6; M.10.837C).

***ταὐτοθελής**, *having the same will* πνεῦμα ἅγιον, τὸ ἐκ τοῦ πατρὸς ἐκπορευόμενον...τ., ταὐτοδύναμον, συναΐδιον, ἐνυπόστατον †Jo.D.*B.J*. 19(M.96.1028B).

***ταὐτόθρους**, *declaring the same thing, of the same import*, Cyr. *Jo*.6.1(4.624C).

***ταὐτοκίνητος**, *moved uniformly*; Apollinarian, of divine opp. human mind of Christ, Apoll.*fr*.151(p.247.30) ap.*Doct.Patr*.41(p.307. 12) cit. s. αὐτοκίνητος; of angelic beings τῆς οἰκείας αὐτοκινήτου καὶ τ. ... τάξεως ἀρρεπῶς ἀντεχομένας Dion.Ar.*c.h*.7.2(M.3.208B); cf. Max.*schol.c.h*.7.2(M.4.68C); of fire, Dion.Ar.*c.h*.15.2(329B); of particular objects ἕως ἂν...ποιήσειεν [sc. God] ἀλλήλοις τε καὶ τῷ ὅλῳ σύμφωνα καὶ τ. Max.*qu.Thal*.2(M.90.272B).

***ταὐτόλεκτος**, *expressing the same thing*, Sophr.H.*or*.7.13(M.87. 3344A); Thdr.Stud.*probl*.10(M.99.481D).

***ταὐτολεξία**, ἡ, *identity of meaning*, Leont.H.*monoph*.(M.86. 1816D).

ταὐτολογ-έω, **1.** *say the same thing, agree in speech* ∼ῶ τῷ πέμψαντί με πατρί Cyr.*Jo*.5.4(4.514C); ὁ παράκλητος...ἐπείπερ ἐστὶ πνεῦμα ἐμόν, ταυτολογήσει...πάντως καὶ τὰ ἐκ τῶν ἐμῶν ἀναγγελεῖ θελημάτων *ib*.11.1(930C); **2.** *repeat oneself*, Just.*dial*.85.5(M.6.677A); Or.*Cels*.2.32(p.159.8; M.11.852B); δόξει ∼εῖν ὁ εὐαγγελιστής, οὐδὲν πλέον λέγων ἐν τῷ, 'οὗτος ἦν ἐν ἀρχῇ πρὸς τὸν θεόν', παρὰ τό, 'καὶ ὁ λόγος ἦν πρὸς τὸν θεόν' id.*Jo*.2.9(5; p.63.9; M.14.124B).

ταὐτολογία, ἡ, **1.** *needless repetition*, Or.*Cels*.7.54(p.204.8; M.11. 1497C); Ath.*inc*.20.3(M.25.132A); Chrys.*hom*.*35.5 in 1Cor*.(10.328B); plur., Cyr.*Zach*.1(3.653D); **2.** *identity of utterance*, of the Son ἀδίδακτόν τινα μάθησιν...ἐκ τῆς τοῦ γεννήσαντος ἰδιότητος ἔχων...εἰς ταυτοβουλίαν τὴν ἐφ' ἅπασι καὶ τ. ἀναβαίνων τῷ θεῷ καὶ πατρί Cyr. *Jo*.5.5(4.526E).

***ταὐτόματον**, τό, *chance, hap*, in phrase ἀπὸ τ. *by chance*, Chrys. *hom.51.1 in Mt*.(7.520E); also ἐκ τ., Ath.*decr*.19(p.16.10; M.25.449A).

***ταὐτονόητος**, *expressing the same thought*, Thdr.Stud.*probl*.10 (M.99.481D).

***ταυτονομία**, ἡ, *general tenet*, Eun.Berrh.*fr*.(Lietzmann p.276. 24).

ταὐτοούσιος** (ταυτούσιος**), *of the same substance, identical in essence*; Trin.; **1.** dist. from ὁμοούσιος and rejected by orthodox οὐ δύναται δὲ εἶναι ἑτεροούσιος τῷ γεγεννηκότι οὐδὲ τ., ἀλλὰ ὁμοούσιος Epiph.*haer*.65.8(p.11.10; M.42.25A); οὐ λέγομεν...τ. ἵνα μὴ ἡ λέξις... Σαβελλίῳ ἀπεικασθῇ...ὁμοούσιόν τε φαμεν *ib*.76.7(p.348.13; 528C); **2.** identified with ὁμοούσιος and rejected by 'Semi-Arians' εἴ τις... ὁμοούσιον...ἢ τ. λέγοι τὸν υἱὸν τῷ πατρί, ἀ. ἔ. CAnc.(358)*anath*.19; accepted by orthodox τὸ γὰρ ὁμοούσιόν ἐστι τὸ τ. ‡Ath.*Maced.dial*. 2(M.28.1336C); πιστεύω εἰς...τριάδα...τ. καὶ ὁμοούσιον ‡Jo.D.*Const*. 2(M.95.312B); ταυτούσιος: neut. as subst. κατὰ τὸ σύμμορφον καὶ τ. ... ἀπαύγασμα εἶναι δόξης Didym.*Trin*.1.16(M.39.337B).

ταὐτοπάθεια, ἡ, **1.** *identical suffering*, Thdr.Stud.*epp*.1.2(M.99. 912A); *ib*.1.56(1109B); **2.** *corresponding suffering*; of punishment acc. *lex talionis*, CNic.(787)*can*.4; Phot.*nomoc*.1.14(p.470; M.104. 504A).

***ταὐτοπαθέω**, *suffer the same*, Thdr.Stud.*epp*.2.89(M.99.1337B); *ib*.2.154(1480B).

***ταὐτοπαθής**, *undergoing the same experience, experiencing the same suffering* λέγοντες τὴν μὲν προσληφθεῖσαν τῷ λόγῳ σάρκα γενέσθαι ταὐτουργὸν τῇ θεότητι διὰ τὴν πρόσληψιν, τὴν θεότητα δὲ γενέσθαι τ. ⟨τῇ σαρκὶ⟩ διὰ ⟨τὴν⟩ κένωσιν ‡Hipp.*Ber.Hel*.5(p.324.14; M.10.836D).

ταὐτοποιέω, *make to be the same, unify*; med., Max.*myst*.1(M.91. 668C).

***ταὐτοπραγέω**, *perform the same actions*, Thdr.Stud.*epp*.2.196 (M.99.1593C).

***ταὐτοπραξία**, ἡ, *identity in act* μονοφυσῖται ταὐτοβουλίαν καὶ τ. ἐφαντάσθησαν Anast.S.*hod*.1(M.89.48B).

***ταὐτοσθενής**, *of same force* or *power*, Cyr.*dial.Trin*.3(5¹.469B).

***ταὐτοτελής**, *having the same end in view*, of Christ ὡς μὲν θεὸς τ. ὢν τῷ πατρί Jo.D.*f.o*.3.24(M.94.1092B); of H. Ghost τοῦ πατρὸς ἐκπορεύεται ὁμοσθενές, τ., ταὐτουργόν, ταὐτοδύναμον id.*hom*.4.4(M. 96.605A).

ταὐτότης, ἡ, **A.** *identity*; **1.** def. τ. ἐστὶν ἀπαραλλαξία, καθ' ἣν ὁ τοῦ σημαινομένου λόγος τὸ πάντη κέκτηται μοναδικόν, μηδενὶ τρόπῳ διαφορᾶς γνωριζόμενον Max.*opusc*.(M.91.153B); as generic identity, Clem.*str*.8.6(p.92.8; M.9.585A); Max.*ambig*.(M.91.1312D); **2.** in gen. πάντων τῶν λογικῶν τὴν παραγωγὴν νόας ἀσωμάτους...γεγονέναι δίχα παντὸς ἀριθμοῦ καὶ ὀνόματος, ὡς ἑνάδα πάντων τούτων γενέσθαι τῇ τ. τῆς οὐσίας καὶ δυνάμεως καὶ ἐνεργείας καὶ τῇ πρὸς τὸν θεὸν λόγον ἑνώσει CCP(543)*anath*.2; of natural identity of mankind, Ath.*ep. Serap*.2.3(M.26.612B); of identity of name, Thdt.*h.e*.2.26.3(3.892); τ. ἔσται τῆς γνώσεως καθάπερ καὶ τῶν ὑποστάσεων CCP(543)*anath*. 14; *exact correspondence, identity of content*, Cyr.*Jo*.4.5(4.401B); **3.** Trin., of identity of Son as God with Father τὸν ἐν τ. λόγον θεὸν ἐν θεῷ φαμεν Clem.*exc.Thdot*.8(p.108.20; M.9.657C); ἐν ἀρχῇ ὁ ἐν τ. λόγος, κατὰ περιγραφὴν καὶ οὐ κατ' οὐσίαν γενόμενος [ὁ] υἱὸς *ib*.19(p.112.28; 665D); ὁ...ἐν τ. μονογενής, οὗ κατὰ δύναμιν ἀδιάστατον ὁ σωτὴρ ἐνεργεῖ *ib*.8(p.108.27; 660A); ἀνάγκη γὰρ καὶ ἐν τούτῳ τὴν τ. πρὸς τὸν ἑαυτοῦ πατέρα σώζειν Ath.*decr*.23(p.19.17; M. 25.456D); ἐν τούτῳ γὰρ μᾶλλον χαρακτὴρ ὢν καὶ εἰκὼν τοῦ πατρὸς δείκνυται, μένων ὅ ἐστι καὶ οὐκ ἀλλασσόμενος, ἀλλ' ἔχων ἐκ τοῦ πατρὸς τὴν τ. id.*Ar*.1.22(M.26.57A); ἤκουσας υἱόν; νόησον τὴν πρὸς τὸν πατέρα ὁμοιότητα...ταυτότητα λέγω, φυλάσσων υἱοῦ καὶ πατρὸς ἰδιότητα...οὐκ οὐσιῶν σύγχυσιν, ἀλλὰ χαρακτήρων ταυτότητα Bas. *hom*.23.4(2.188E; M.31.597C); ὄντος τε καὶ ὑφεστηκότος ἑκατέρου, καὶ ἰδίαν ἔχειν λεγομένου τὴν ὕπαρξιν ἡ τῆς οὐσίας τ. βραβεύει τὴν ἕνωσιν Cyr.*dial.Trin*.1(5¹.408C); οὐχ ἕτερος ἂν νοοῖτο παρ' αὐτὸν ὑπάρχειν, ὅσον τ. φυσικὴν *ib*.3(498C); ὥσπερ ἡ σύνεσις ἡ ἐν ἡμῖν...καὶ ἡ σοφία τοῦ θεοῦ καὶ πατρός, τουτέστιν ὁ υἱός, οὐχ ἕτερόν τι παρ' αὐτόν ἐστιν ὅσον εἰς οὐσίας ταυτότητα λέγω, καὶ φύσεως ἀπαράλλακτον ὁμοιότητα id. *Jo*.5.5(4.525D); ὁ υἱὸς μίαν ἔχων ὡς πρὸς αὐτὸν τὴν οὐσίαν, καὶ τῇ τ. τῆς φύσεως ὥσπερ ἐνυπάρχων πρὸς τὸν γεννήσαντα id.*thes*.32(5¹. 284E); αὐτὸ τῆς πατρικῆς οὐσίας τὸ ἴδιον ὑπάρχων ὁ υἱός, ὅλον ἐν ἑαυτῷ φορεῖ τὸν πατέρα καὶ ὅλος ἐστὶν ἐν πατρὶ κατὰ τὴν τ. τῆς οὐσίας *ib*.12(111E); υἱὸς...δευτερότης ὑποστάσεως ἐν τ. φύσεως Anast.S.*hod*.2 (M.89.56A); of identity of essence of the three Persons αὕτη γὰρ τῶν ἰδιωμάτων ἡ φύσις, ἐν τῇ τῆς οὐσίας τ. δεικνύναι τὴν ἑτερότητα Bas. *Eun*.2.28(1.265C; M.29.637C); ἡνωμένως τῇ ἑτερότητι νοεῖν ἀναγκαῖον τὴν πρώτην τ. καὶ δευτέραν καὶ τρίτην...τὴν αὐτήν. ὅπερ γάρ ἐστι πρώτως ὁ πατήρ, τοῦτό ἐστι δευτέρως ὁ υἱός, καὶ τρίτως τὸ πνεῦμα id. *ep*.129.1(3.220C; M.32.557C); εἷς θεός ἐστί τε καὶ εἶναι πιστεύεται, οὐχ ἧττον διὰ τὴν ὁμόνοιαν ἢ τὴν τῆς οὐσίας τ. Gr.Naz.*or*.6.13(M.35.740A); οὐ συναλοιφὴ οὖσα ἡ τριὰς οὐδὲ διῃρημένη τῆς ἑαυτῆς τ. Epiph.*haer*. 62.7(p.395.28; M.41.1060A); id.*anc*.10(p.18.17; M.43.36B); μὴ τρεῖς... οὐσίας...νομίζειν, ἀλλὰ μίαν τῇ τ. τῆς θεότητος γνωριζομένην Thdr. Mops.*symb*.(p.98.11; M.66.1017A); τῆς...τριάδος διὰ τὴν τ. τῆς οὐσίας εἰς μίαν θεότητα δι' ἑαυτῆς ἀναπλεκομένης ὡς εἶναι μόνην τὴν θείαν οὐσίαν τὸ κυρίως ἀγαθόν Cyr.*thes*.32(5¹.311A); τὸ κοινὸν δὲ τῶν ὀνομάτων τὴν τ. τῆς οὐσίας δηλοῖ Thdt.*Ps*.109:1(1.1392); οὐδὲ γὰρ ἐξίστησιν ὅλως τῆς ἀρχῆς τὰ ἐξ αὐτῆς, ἀλλ' ἀνεκφοίτητα πάντη ταύτης τηρεῖ, διὰ τὴν τῆς οὐσίας τ., εἰ καὶ ὡς ἴδια πρόσωπα πρόεισι †Proc.G. *Procl*.(M.87.2792ʰB); 'Semi-Arian' doctrine οὐδὲ ὁ υἱὸς ὅμοιος κατ' οὐσίαν γενόμενος τῷ...πατρὶ εἰς τ. ἄξει τοῦ πατρὸς τὴν ἑαυτοῦ οὐσίαν, ἀλλ' ἐπὶ τὴν ὁμοιότητα CAnc.(358)*ep.syn*.ap.Epiph.*haer*.73.9(p.280. 19; M.42.420C); οἱ μὲν...τὴν οὐσίαν ἐν οὐδεμιᾷ τ. παραδεξάμενοι, τὴν ὁμοίωσιν ἔξωθεν φέροντες τῷ υἱῷ προστιθέασιν...οἱ δὲ τὴν ὁμοίωσιν τοῖς ποιήμασι πρέπουσαν εἰδότες, ἐν τ. μὲν τὸν υἱὸν συνάπτουσι πατρί, ὑφειμένη δὲ τῇ τ.· ἵνα μὴ αὐτὸς ὁ πατὴρ ἢ μέρος πατρὸς...οὕτω θεός, οὐχ ὡς ἐκεῖνος, ἀλλ' ὡς ἐξ ἐκείνου †Apoll.*ep.Bas*.1(M.32.1104C); in doctrine of 'tritheists' μίαν θεότητα ἤγουν θεὸν...ὁμολογοῦσιν, οὐκ ἀριθμῷ, ἀλλὰ τῇ ἀπαραλλάκτῳ τῆς θεότητος τ. Tim.CP *haer*.(M.86. 61A); ref. meaning of 'ὁμοούσιος': τὴν λέξιν τοῦ ὁμοουσίου ἀκούοντες ...ὡς ἐπὶ ἀσωμάτων διανοούμενοι τὴν ἑνότητα τῆς φύσεως καὶ τὴν τ.

τοῦ φωτὸς μὴ διαιρῶμεν Ath.*decr*.24(p.20.5; M.25.457C); τὸ ὅμοιον οὐκ ἐπὶ τῶν οὐσιῶν, ἀλλ' ἐπὶ σχημάτων καὶ ποιοτήτων λέγεται ὅμοιον· ἐπὶ γὰρ τῶν οὐσιῶν οὐχ ὁμοιότης, ἀλλὰ τ. ἂν λεχθείη id.*syn*.53(p.276.26; M.26.788C); τὸ ὁμοιούσιον ἔδει λέγεσθαι...ἐπὶ τῶν σωμάτων, ἐφ' ὧν καὶ ὁμοιότης, τὸ δὲ ὁμοούσιον ἐπὶ τῶν ἀσωμάτων, ἐφ' ὧν ἡ τ. ‡Ath.*Maced.dial*.2(M.28.1336C); αὕτη δὲ ἡ φωνὴ [sc. ὁμοούσιος] καὶ τὸ τοῦ Σαβελλίου κακὸν ἐπανορθοῦται· ἀναιρεῖ γὰρ τὴν τ. τῆς ὑποστάσεως καὶ εἰσάγει τελείαν τῶν προσώπων τὴν ἔννοιαν Bas.*ep*.52.3(3.146A; M.32.393C); ὅμοιον γὰρ καὶ ἀνόμοιον κατὰ τὰς ποιότητας λέγεται· ποιότητος δὲ τὸ θεῖον ἐλεύθερον· ταυτότητα δὲ τῆς φύσεως ὁμολογοῦντες, καὶ τὸ ὁμοούσιον ἐκδεχόμεθα καὶ τὸ σύνθετον φεύγομεν Evagr.Pont.*ep*.3(M.32.249C); ref. indwelling of Trin. εἰ δὲ ναοὶ χρηματίζομεν, ἑνὸς...καὶ οὐ δύο θεῶν, ὅταν ἡμῖν ὁ πατὴρ καὶ ὁ υἱὸς ἐναυλίζωνται, ποῖος...λόγος συστέλλει πρὸς ἑνότητα τοὺς δύο, τῆς κατ' οὐσίας τ. οὐκ ἐχούσης τόπον; Cyr.*Jo*.10(4.832C); of second and third Persons Χριστὸν... τὸ πνεῦμα καλεῖ...οὐκ ἀλλότριον αὐτὸ δεικνύων τῆς τοῦ λόγου φύσεως, ἀλλ' οὕτως ἡνωμένον, εἰ καὶ ἔστιν ἰδιοσύστατον, ὡς αὐτό τε ὑπάρχειν ἐν υἱῷ, καὶ υἱὸν ἐν αὐτῷ διὰ τὴν τῆς οὐσίας τ. id.*thes*.33(5[1].334E); of identity of will between Father and Son, v. βούλημα; of operation ἡ τῆς ἐνεργείας τ. ἐπὶ πατρός τε καὶ υἱοῦ καὶ πνεύματος ἁγίου δείκνυσι... τὸ τῆς φύσεως ἀπαράλλακτον Gr.Nyss.*Trin*.7(p.80.4; M.32.693C); ἐπειδὴ...τὴν οὐσίαν αὐτοῦ ἰδεῖν ἀμήχανον ἦν, ἀπὸ τῆς τῶν ἔργων...τ. τὴν ἀπόδειξιν τῆς κατὰ τὴν δύναμιν ἀπαραλλαξίας παρέχεται Chrys.*hom.61.2 in Jo*.(8.364C); τὸ ταυτὸν τῆς οὐσίας καὶ τῆς ἐνεργείας... τήν τε τῆς ἐξουσίας καὶ τῆς δυνάμεως...τ.· οὐκ εἶπον ὁμοιότητα, ἀλλὰ τ.· καὶ τὸ ἓν ἔξαλμα τῆς κινήσεως Jo.D.*f.o*.1.8(M.94.828C); **4.** Christol. τὴν γὰρ ποιηθεῖσαν τῆς ἀνθρωπότητος φύσιν μὴ τῇ ἑνώσει τοῦ λόγου εἶναι ἰδίαν, ἀλλὰ...τῇ τοῦ θεοῦ φύσει ἐξισουμένην τῇ τ. τῆς φύσεως ἐννοεῖν, ἀσεβὲς ‡Ath.*Apoll*.1.5(M.26.1100D); ταυτότητι ὑπάρξεως καὶ φύσεως κοινότητι ὤφθη ὁ κύριος *ib*.2.11(1149B); ὁ τεχθεὶς ἐκ τῆς παρθένου...ἄνθρωπος...ταυτότητι γνώμης αὐτῷ [sc. λόγῳ] συνημμένος Thdr.Mops.*fr.inc*.14(p.311.27; H.3.896B; cf.M.66.994A); πιστεύειν... εἰς τὸν...ἐγηγερμένον ἐκ νεκρῶν, οὐχ ὡς ἕτερον ὄντα παρὰ τὸν... λόγον, οὐχ ὅσον εἰς οὐσίας ταυτότητά φημι...ἀλλ' ὅσον εἰς τὸ τῆς ἀληθοῦς υἱότητος χρῆμα Cyr.*Jo*.9(4.763A); ἡ ἄκρα ἕνωσις καὶ τ. ἔχει καὶ ἑτερότητα· ἡ τ. οὐσιῶν καὶ ἑτερότητα προσώπων καὶ τὸ ἔμπαλιν. ...ἐπὶ τῆς...τριάδος τ. μέν ἐστιν οὐσίας· ἑτερότης δὲ προσώπων...ἐπὶ ...τοῦ ἀνθρώπου τ. μέν ἐστι προσώπου, ἑτερότης δὲ οὐσιῶν...ὁμοίως... ἐπὶ...Χριστοῦ τ. μέν ἐστι προσώπου, ἑτερότης δὲ οὐσιῶν· ἑνὸς γὰρ ὄντος προσώπου ἤτοι ὑποστάσεως, ἑτέρας οὐσίας ἐστὶν ἡ θεότης καὶ ἑτέρας ἡ ἀνθρωπότης Max.*opusc*.(M.91.145B); ὑποστατικῇ τ. ... αὐτὴν [sc. σάρκα] τοῦ προσλαβόντος λόγου θεώσαντος id.*ambig*.(M.91.1040C); ref. Transfiguration μένων...αὐτὸς ἐν τ. παρ' ὃ τὸ πρὶν ἐφαίνετο νῦν τοῖς μαθηταῖς ἑωρᾶτο φαινόμενος Jo.D.*hom*.1.12(M.96.564C).

B. *consistency, fixity, immutability*, in gen. τὰς γνωστικὰς ψυχὰς... ταυτότητι τῆς ὑπεροχῆς...τετιμημένας διαμένειν Clem.*str*.7.3(p.10.15; M.9.416C); Eus.*d.e*.4.3(p.154.6; M.22.257A); τῆς γνώμης ταυτότητι Max.*ambig*.(M.91.1044A); theol. ἐν τ. ... ἀγεννήτῳ ὁ ὢν αὐτὸς μόνος Clem.*str*.6.16(p.501.19; 364A); τὸν ὄντως θεὸν τὸν ἐν τ. τῆς δικαίας ἀγαθωσύνης ὄντα *ib*.7.3(p.12.2; 420B); τὸ θεῖον ἐν τ. ὑπάρχει καὶ οὐκ ἐπιδέεται προσθήκης οὐ δόξης οὐ προκοπῆς Epiph.*anc*.6(p.12.7; M.43.25A); κάθηται...ἡ πάντων...δημιουργὸς σοφία τοῦτ' ἔστιν ἀκλόνητον ἔχει τὴν ἐν τ. διαμονήν Cyr.*Is*.1.4(2.102D); ἁπάντων ἐπέκεινα τῆς ἐπέκεινα πάντων ὅλης ἰδιότητος ταυτότητος Dion.Ar.*d.n*.2.4(M.3.641A); οἱ θεῖοι νόες...ἀνεκφοιτήτως μένουσιν ἐν τ. περὶ τὸ τῆς ταυτότητος αἴτιον καλὸν καὶ ἀγαθὸν ἀκαταλήκτως περιχορεύοντες *ib*.4.8(705A); ref. BMV ἡ...ταύτης γαστὴρ...ἐν ταυτότητι διαμείνασα τῆς παρθενίας ‡Meth.*Sym.et Ann*.4(M.18.356C).

C. *unity, harmony* τὴν τῶν δογμάτων τ. Or.*Cels*.7.59(p.208.25; M.11.1505A); in created order, Didym.*Trin*.2.1(M.39.452B); Max.*ambig*.(M.91.1189A); among Christians, Clem.*str*.2.9(p.135.11; M.8.977B); in OT, *ib*.3.2(p.199.20; 1109A); *interdependence* of knowledge of God and eternal salvation, *ib*.4.22(p.308.30; 1348A).

D. plur., *repetitions* ἀνέπλασαν κατὰ περιόδους ταυτότητας Or.*Cels*.4.12(p.282.13; M.11.1041B).

***ταὐτοτρόπως**, *in the same manner* as τ. ... τοῦ διδασκάλου Geo.Pis.*carm*.24.3(p.52).

***ταυτουργείς**, ὡς τῷ θεῷ καὶ πατρὶ τ., εἶπε Hesych.H.*fr.Ps*.40:11(M.93.1193C); prob. error for ταυτουργός.

***ταὐτουργία**, ἡ, v. *ταὐτοεργία.

***ταὐτουργός**, *performing the same work*, ‡Hipp.*Ber.Hel*.3(p.323.28; M.10.836B); *ib*.5(p.324.13; 836D) cit. s. ταὐτοπαθής; ταύτην [sc. blessing of chrism] οἱ θεῖοι καθηγεμόνες...ὡς ὁμοταγῆ καὶ τ. τῷ συνάξεως ἱερῷ τελεστηρίῳ...διετάξαντο Dion.Ar.*e.h*.4.3.3(M.3.476C); of H. Ghost in rel. to Father, Jo.D.*hom*.4.4(M.96.605A) cit. s. ταὐτοτελής.

***ταὐτούσιος**, v. *ταὐτοούσιος.

***ταὐτοφυής**, *of the same nature* ποῖον ἴστε ἱερέα τ. τῷ ἱερατευομένῳ ποτέ; Leont.H.*Nest*.5.4(M.86.1728D).

***ταυτωνυμία**, ἡ, *identity of name* ἕνωσιν γεγενῆσθαι λέγοντες οὐ κατὰ...σύγχυσιν...φάσκομεν· οὐδ' αὖ πάλιν...κατ' ἀξίαν ἢ...τ., ὡς ὁ Νεστόριος...ἔφη Jo.D.*Jacob*.81(M.94.1480A).

ταὐτώνυμος, *called by the same name*, ‡Caes.Naz.*dial*.128(M.38.1025).

ταφεών, ὁ, *burial-place*, met. τ. ψυχῶν Eus.*v.C*.3.26(p.89.32; M.20.1085C).

ταφή, ἡ, *burial*, of Christ κατὰ τὴν σωματικὴν τοῦ Ἰησοῦ τ. ἢ σωματικὴν ἀνάστασιν αὐτοῦ Or.*Jo*.20.12(p.342.21; M.14.600C); οὗ [sc. the sinner] χάριν μὴ φεισάμενος σταυρῷ καὶ θανάτῳ καὶ ταφῇ συνεχώρησεν παθεῖν...τὸν υἱὸν τὸν ἀγαπητόν *Const.App*.2.24.3; τῆς τριημερονύκτου τ. Leont.B.*Nest.et Eut*.2(M.86.1336B); ref. observance of Holy Saturday ἓν...μόνον σάββατον ὑμῖν φυλακτέον ἐν ὅλῳ τῷ ἐνιαυτῷ, τὸ τῆς τοῦ κυρίου τ., ὅπερ νηστεύειν προσῆκεν *Const.App*.7.23.4; ref. baptism τίς οὖν ὁ τρόπος τῆς τ.; καὶ τί ἐκ τῆς μιμήσεως χρήσιμον; Bas.*Spir*.35(3.28E; M.32.129A); μιμούμενοι τὴν τ. τοῦ Χριστοῦ διὰ τοῦ βαπτίσματος *ib*.(29A; M.129B); τὸ...ὕδωρ τοῦ θανάτου τὴν εἰκόνα παρέχει, ὥσπερ ἐν τ. τὸ σῶμα παραδεχόμενον *ib*.(29C; M.129D); τὸν...βαπτιζόμενον ἡ συμβολικὴ διδασκαλία μυσταγωγεῖ ταῖς ἐν τῷ ὕδατι τρισὶ καταδύσεσι τὸν θεαρχικὸν τῆς τριημερονύκτου τ. Ἰησοῦ...μιμεῖσθαι θάνατον Dion.Ar.*e.h*.2.3.7(M.3.404B).

τάφιος, *for burial* τ. ὀθόναις Nonn.*par.Jo*.20:7(M.43.909A).

τάφος, ὁ, *tomb*; **1.** lit., ref. martyr cults πάντα ἐπληρώσατε τ. καὶ μνημάτων Juln.Imp.ap.Cyr.*Juln*.10(6[2].335C); of Christ's tomb προσκυνοῦμεν...τὸν τ. τὸν ἅγιον, τὴν πηγὴν τῆς ἡμῶν ἀναστάσεως Jo.D.*imag*.3.34(M.94.1353B); of a living tomb κολακεύσατε τὰ θηρία, ἵνα μοι τ. γένωνται Ign.*Rom*.4.2; τίς ἂν...ἀνάστασιν πεπιστευκὼς [ἐπὶ] σώμασιν ἀναστησομένοις ἑαυτὸν παράσχοι τ.; Athenag.*leg*.36.1(M.6.969B); ἢν Ἰωνᾶς...ἐν ζῶντι τ. φερόμενος Bas.Sel.*or*.12.2(M.85.164A); as synon. with death μετὰ τὸν τ. ... ὁ μέλλων...βίος Thdt.*1Cor*.6:13(3.197); **2.** of the womb ἀναλογισώμεθα...ἐκ ποίου τ. καὶ σκότους ὁ πλάσας ἡμᾶς...εἰσήγαγεν εἰς τὸν κόσμον αὐτοῦ *1Clem*.38.3; Clem.*str*.2.18(p.163.23; M.8.1036A); **3.** met. ἐὰν...περὶ...Χριστοῦ μὴ λαλῶσιν, οὗτοι ἐμοὶ στῆλαί εἰσιν καὶ τ. νεκρῶν Ign.*Philad*.6.1; of temples of pagan gods, Clem.*prot*.3(p.34.6; M.8.132A); of body as tomb of soul, id.*str*.3.11(p.230.25; M.8.1177A); of sinful life, Or.*Jo*.20.37(29; p.378.6; M.14.631A).

ταχινός, *swift*; **1.** adverbially τ. ... ἱκάνω Nonn.*par.Jo*.14:18(M.43.869B); comp., *ib*.13:27(864C); **2.** neut. as subst., Chrys.*hom.54.5 in Mt*.(7.554C).

***ταχύγουνος**, *swift-footed*, Nonn.*par.Jo*.6:20(M.43.796C); *ib*.11:31(844B).

ταχυγράφος, ὁ, *shorthand-writer*, *Orac.Sib*.proem.; Or.*Jo*.6.2(p.108.5; M.14.200C); Eus.*h.e*.6.23.2(M.20.576B); Bas.*ep*.134(3.226A; M.32.572A); τ. βασιλικός ‡Jo.D.*Artem*.2(p.152.22; M.96.1253B).

ταχυδινής, *whirling quickly*, Nonn.*par.Jo*.5:35(M.43.792A).

ταχυδρομέω, *run fast*, ptcpl. as subst., *courier*, Thphyl.*exc.gent*.5(p.481.34; M.113.941B).

ταχυδρόμος, *quickly running*, *A.Jo*.5(p.153.23); Ath.*v.Anton*.31(M.26.889C); of ships, Geo.Pis.*Pers*.1.200(M.92.1211A); as subst., *courier*, *A.Thadd*.2(p.274.3); *Ep.Abg*.3(p.281.31); Epiph.*haer*.66.7(p.28.13; M.42.40D); met., *swift messenger*, ‡Chrys.*concept.Jo.Bapt*.(2.795E).

ταχύμητις, *swift* or *hasty in counsel*, Nonn.*par.Jo*.1:47(M.43.757C); *ib*.19:4(897C).

ταχυπετής, *quickly flying*; neut. as subst., *speed in flight*, Dion.Ar.*c.h*.15.8(M.3.337A).

***ταχυπήκοος**, *quick to obey*; of BMV, ‡Hipp.Th.*fr*.17(p.50.3).

ταχυπλοέω, *sail fast*, Cosm.Ind.*top*.2(M.88.89A).

ταχύποτμος, *bringing death soon* τ. ἑὴν [sc. of Christ] αὐτάγρετον ὥρην Nonn.*par.Jo*.7:33(M.43.809C).

***ταχύρεμβος**, *quickly-moving*, Eudoc.*Cypr*.2.147(M.85.852A).

ταχύς, neut. as subst., *fleetingness, quickness to perish*, Alex.Lyc.*Man*.25(p.37.23).

***ταχυσυγχώρητος**, *quickly forgiven*, Jo.Jej.*canonar*.2(p.438); †Jo.Jej.*poenit*.(M.88.1904D).

***ταχυτέρως**, adv. formed from comp. of ταχύς, *more quickly*, Hipp.*haer*.1.9(p.15.28; M.16.3036C).

***ταχυφάρμακον**, τό, *speedy cure* τούτων οἱ μώλωπες τῷ τῆς μετανοίας τ. καθαίρονται Chrysipp.*enc.in Mich*.(p.92.32).

[*]**τεάφιον**, τό, = θειάφιον, *sulphur* ἐξῆλθεν ὁ δαίμων...καὶ ἐπλήρωσε...τὸν τόπον δυσωδίας ὡς καιομένου τ. Cyr.S.*v.Euthym*.24(p.37.27); *Contrad*.2(p.9).

***τεθεωρημένως, 1.** *with circumspection, carefully*, Or.*Cels*.1.26 (p.78.9; M.11.709B); id.*Jo*.20.36(29; p.377.8; M.14.660B); Meth.*symp*. 3.12(p.40.14; M.18.77D); **2.** *deliberately, of set purpose* τ. παλλακὰς προσηγόρευσε τὰς ψυχὰς τὰς προφητικὰς ὁ λόγος *ib*.7.4(p.75.22; 129D); id.*lepr*.9(p.463.12); **3.** *spiritually* ὁ...λόγος...τ. ἐκλαμβανόμενος Bas.*hex*.3.9(1.31E; M.29.76B); τ. προφέρειν...τὰ ἀρετῆς...ἐπίχειρα Didym.*Trin*.1.20(M.39.369C).

***τεθήμερος**, v. τετραήμερος.

***τεῖσις, ἡ,** *stretching*, noun formed from verb τείνω (fut. τενῶ) and introduced to justify spelling Τιτάν with diphthong Τειτάν, Oecum.*Apoc*.13:18(p.158).

τειχίζω, *build a wall (around)*; met., *fortify* τῇ πίστει καὶ ταῖς εὐχαῖς καὶ νηστείαις ἐτείχιζε τὸ σῶμα Ath.*v.Anton*.5(M.26.848B); perf. pass. τετειχισμένοι τῷ σημείῳ τοῦ σταυροῦ *ib*.13(864A); τὸν νόμον ᾧ τετειχίσμεθα Gr.Naz.*or*.15.5(M.35.920B); *Didasc.Jac*.5.20(p.91.9).

τεῖχος, τό, *wall*; fig., of the teeth, Geo.Pis.*carm.vit*.46(p.53); met. τῷ τ. τῆς ὑπομονῆς Innoc.*ep.cler*.(M.52.538); τ. δὲ ὁ κύριος, ὡς πολλάκις εἴρηται Oecum.*Apoc*.21:19(p.242).

***τεκνάδελφος, ὁ,** *brother's son, nephew*, *Apophth.Patr*.(M.65.101B); Ath.Scholast.*coll*.9.10(p.104).

***τεκνάρπαξ,** *snatching children*, Geo.Pis.*Sev*.372(M.92.1649A).

***τεκνοβόρος,** *devouring one's own children*; of Cronos, *Hom. Clem*.5.23.

τεκνογον-έω, *bear children* γαμοῦσιν [sc. Christians] ὡς πάντες, ∼οῦσιν, ἀλλ' οὐ ῥίπτουσι τὰ γεννώμενα *Diogn*.5.6; τὸ μὲν γὰρ εἰς παρθενίαν...προκόψαι τὸν ἄνθρωπον...δοκεῖ μοι καλῶς διελέσθαι, τὸ δὲ μηκέτι χρῆναι λέγειν τοὐντεῦθεν ∼εῖν οὐ καλῶς Meth.*symp*.2.1(p.15.8; M.18.48B); as aim of marriage, Cyr.H.*catech*.4.25.

***τεκνογονικόν, τό,** *faculty of begetting children* κατ' εἰκόνα... λέγεται πᾶς ἄνθρωπος κατὰ τὸ τοῦ νοὸς ἀξίωμα...ἤτοι τὸ ἀκατάληπτον ...νὰ μὴν καὶ τὸ ἀρχηγὸν καὶ τ. καὶ οἰκοδομικόν Jo.D.*spir.neq*.(M.95.97A); Ephr.3.433B.

***τεκνοθυσία, ἡ,** *sacrifice of children*, Ath.*gent*.25(M.25.49C); Dam. *troph*.1.1(p.193.5).

***τεκνοθύτης, ὁ,** *sacrificer of children*, Leont.N.ap.Jo.D.*imag*.3(M.94.1388A).

τεκνοκτονέω, *murder children*, Clem.*str*.8.9(p.97.17; M.9.596A).

***τεκνοκυΐσκ-ω,** *beget, procreate children* μετὰ γὰρ τὸ προφητεῦσαι Μωϋσῆν...οὐκέτι ∼ει Epiph.*ep.Arab*.ap.*haer*.78.16(M.42.724D; τέκνα κυΐσκει p.466.21).

***τεκνολογία, ἡ,** *list of children*, Cyr.*glaph.Gen*.1(1.22A).

τεκνοποι-έω, 1. act., *beget children*; of Son (Arian) ἀρχὴν δὲ τὸν υἱὸν ἔθηκε τῶν γενητῶν ὁ ἄναρχος καὶ ἤνεγκεν εἰς υἱόν, ἑαυτῷ τόνδε τεκνοποιήσας Ar.*Thal.fr*.2.7(p.217)ap.Ath.*syn*.15(p.242.15; M.26.705D); **2.** *adopt as a child*; med., Pall.*h.Laus*.5(p.22.10; M.34.1018B); Jo.Mal.*chron*.16 p.401(M.97.593B); of Church θυγατέρα αὐτὴν προσαγορεύων, οἱονεὶ ∼ούμενος αὐτὴν διὰ τῆς ἀγάπης Bas.*hom.in Ps*.44 (1.167C; M.29.403A); pass. ἦσαν...καὶ ἐν τῇ παλαιᾷ υἱοὶ...διὰ τοῦ υἱοῦ ∼ούμενοι ‡Ath.*Ar*.4.29(p.77.24; M.26.513A); pass. αὐτῆς [sc. Creation] μετὰ πάντων τῶν τεκνοποιηθέντων πρωτότοκος ὁ κύριος Ath. *Ar*.2.63(M.26.281C).

***τεκνοσφαγία, ἡ,** *child-slaughter*, Cyr.*ador*.1(1.15B).

***τεκνοτρεφής,** *bringing up children*; neut. as subst., Thdr.Stud. *epp*.2.144(M.99.1452C).

***τεκνοτρόφος,** *bringing up children*, ‡Chrys.*hom.3.4 in Gen*.(6. 551D).

***τεκνοφαγέω,** *eat children*; of Cronos, ‡Just.*or.Gr*.2(M.6.232B).

τεκνοφαγία, ἡ, *eating of children*, Athenag.*res*.4(p.52.19; M.6. 981C); Gr.Nyss.*virg*.3(p.266.5; M.46.336C); Cyr.*Jo*.5.4(4.517C).

τεκνοφάγος, *eating children*; of Cronos, Thphl.Ant.*Autol*.3.3(M. 6.1125A).

***τεκνοφόρος,** *child-bearing*, of BMV ἡ μόνη πασῶν παρθένων τ. Thdr.Stud.*nativ.BMV* 7(M.96.689B).

***τεκτονάρχης, ὁ,** *chief carpenter, craftsman*, of God οὗτος γὰρ ὁ γεννώμενος τέκτων, ὁ τοῦ τ. παῖς, τὸν τρισύστατον οὐράνιον ὄροφον ἐτεκτόνησε πανσόφοις τέχναις *Pers*.(p.12.18; M.10.101A).

τεκτονεύω, *forge* a shield, Geo.Pis.*carm*.1.40.

***τεκτόνημα, τό,** *fabrication* τὴν ὕλην...κακίστην καλεῖ [sc. Marcion] καὶ τὸν κόσμον τοῦ πονηροῦ τεκτόνημα Tim.CP *haer*.(M.86.16A).

τεκτονική, ἡ, [sc. τέχνη], *joiner's work, carpentry*, met. τ. ἐστι κατὰ πνεῦμα ἡ πρακτικὴ τῶν ἀγαθῶν ἀρετῶν ἐργασία Or.*exp.in Pr*. 11:27(M.17.192C).

τέκτων, ὁ, *craftsman*; met., *worker, agent* τ. αὐτῷ καὶ θιάσωτας... προχειρισάμενος [sc. ὁ δαίμων] Anast.S.*haer*.(p.259).

***τελειοδύναμος,** *of perfect power*, Dion.Ar.*d.n*.8.7(M.3.896A).

τελειοποιέω, *make perfect*, Max.*schol.c.h*.3.1(M.4.49A).

***τελειοποιός, 1.** *perfecting* τὰ...τ. τῆς εἰς Χριστὸν πίστεως διδάγματα Meth.*creat*.1(p.494.8; M.18.332A); πνεῦμα ἅγιον...τὴν πηγὴν τῆς ἁγιότητος,...χάριν τ., δι' οὗ υἱοθετεῖται ἄνθρωπος Bas.*ep*.105 (3.200B; M.32.513B); χωρὶς ἀγάπης καὶ ἡ τῶν...χαρισμάτων...ἐνέργεια καὶ ἡ τ. ἐντολὴ ἀνωφελής †Bas.*bapt*.1.2.24(2.646E; M.31.1565D); καλεῖται...θεὸς καὶ ἐν τρισὶ τοῖς μεγίστοις ἵσταται, αἰτίῳ καὶ δημιουργῷ καὶ τ.· τῷ πατρί, λέγω, καὶ τῷ υἱῷ καὶ τῷ...πνεύματι Gr.Naz.*or*.34.8 (M.36.249A); τελειότατον...καὶ τ., ὃν [sc. νόμον] αὐτὸς θεσμοθετεῖ, ἀγαπᾶν...διδάσκων Arsen.*tent*.(M.66.1624D); of spiritual joy, Diad. *perf*.60(p.66.24); of wisdom, ‡Proc.G.*Pr*.2:6(M.87.1236B); ἡ τῆς ψυχῆς...ἐκθεωτικὴ καὶ τ. ... κατάστασις Max.*myst*.22(M.91.697B); of eucharist τοῦ τελειοτάτου καὶ τ. τῶν θυσιῶν δώρου id.*schol.epp.Dion. Ar*.8.6(M.4.556A); **2.** partic., *consecrating, sanctifying*, Gr.Naz.*or*.40. 26(M.36.396C).

***τελειοπρόσωπον, τό,** *perfection* or *completeness of person*, ref. Christ ἐν τῷδε οὐδὲ τὸ ὁμοούσιον τῶν ὑποστάσεων τοῦδε, οὔτε τὸ τ. τῶν ἰδικῶν δυνάμεων ὅμοιον ἡμῖν Leont.H.*Nest*.1.52(M.86.1521B).

***τελειοπώγων,** *having a perfect beard*, Jo.Mal.*chron*.12 p.311(M. 97.468B).

τέλειος, I. *perfect*;

A. ref. God; **1.** in gen. οἱ...ἐφιέμενοι τῆς τοῦ τ. θεοῦ γνώσεως τελειοτέραν διὰ τῶν ἀγώνων ἐν ἡμέρᾳ κρίσεως τὴν μαρτυρίαν λάβωσιν Tat.*orat*.12(p.13.27; M.6.832C); ὁ τ. θεός *ib*.15(p.16.20; 837B); *ib*.17 (p.19.18; 844C); πάντα γὰρ ὁ θεός ἐστιν αὐτὸς αὑτῷ...κόσμος τ. Athenag.*leg*.16.2(M.6.920D); τ. δὲ ὢν [sc. θεός] τέλεια χαριεῖται Clem. *paed*.1.6(p.105.29; M.8.281A); ὁ θεὸς...τ. μόνος *ib*.1.10(p.145.25; 361A); **2.** ref. Creation οὐχὶ τ. πάντῃ δι' ἑαυτὸν καὶ ἀπροσδεής...τὸ γὰρ αὐτὸ δι' ἑαυτὸ ἑαυτοῦ πλήρωμα ὂν καὶ αὐτὸ ἐν ἑαυτῷ μένον, τ. εἶναι τοῦτο μόνον δοξαστέον;...οὐκ ἄρα τ. φατέον...διὰ κόσμον τὸν θεόν; οὐ. ὅπως δι' ἑαυτόν, ἀλλὰ μὴ διὰ κόσμον...αὐτὸς καθ' ἑαυτὸν τ. εὑρίσκοιτο Meth.*creat*.3(p.495.1–25; M.18.333C–336A); cf.*ib*.7(p.497.31ff.; 340A); εἰ τ. τότε νοοῦμεν τὸ τ. ὅτε πάντα κέκτηται τέλεια, τ. δὲ ἄκρως τὸ καθ' ὁτιοῦν προσθήκην ἢ αὔξησιν μὴ δεχόμενον, πῶς ὁ θεὸς μὲν προϋπάρχων τῆς κτίσεως, ὕστερον δὲ τὴν κτίσιν ποιησάμενος, οὕτω θεὸς τὸ δημιουργὸς ὄνομά τε καὶ πρᾶγμα προσέλαβε, καὶ ἐκ τοῦ θεὸς εἰς τὸ καὶ δημιουργὸς εἶναι τὴν αὔξησίν τε καὶ τὴν γένεσιν δέδεκται;...ἐπειδὴ οὖν τὸ τ. τοῦ θεοῦ ἐν τῷ αὐτὸ εἶναι, διὰ τοῦτο οὐκ αὔξει αὐτὸν τὸ ἄλλου εἶναι. καὶ καθάπερ τὸ ἀρχὴν εἶναι ἀριθμοῦ οὐδὲν συντελεῖ τῷ ἑνὶ πρὸς τὴν αὐτοῦ τελειότητα (καὶ γὰρ μὴ ὄντος αὐτοῦ ἀρχῆς ἀριθμοῦ, τ. ἦν...) οὕτως καὶ ὁ θεὸς πρὸ τῆς κτίσεως ἦν τ., καὶ μετὰ τὴν κτίσιν οὐκ ηὐξήθη ‡Just.*qu.et resp*.113(M.6.1361B,C); τ. ... ἐστιν οὐ μόνον ὡς αὐτοτελές, καὶ καθ' ἑαυτὸ ὑφ' ἑαυτοῦ μονοειδῶς ἀφοριζόμενον, καὶ ὅλον δι' ὅλου τελειότατον, ἀλλὰ καὶ ὡς ὑπερτελὲς κατὰ τὸ πάντων ὑπερέχον ...τ. δ' αὖ λέγεται καὶ ὡς ἀναυξὲς καὶ ἀεὶ τ., καὶ ὡς ἀμείωτον, ὡς πάντα ἐν ἑαυτῷ προέχον, καὶ ὑπερβλύζον κατὰ μίαν τὴν ἄπαυστον... καὶ ἀνελάττωτον χορηγίαν, καθ' ἣν τὰ τ. πάντα τελεσιουργεῖ Dion.Ar. *d.n*.13.1(M.3.977B,C); **3.** as Father, Alex.Al.*ep.Alex*.7(p.23.30; M. 18.557B) cit. s. ἀνελλιπής; εἰ τ., φησίν [sc. heretic], ἐστιν ὁ πατὴρ ἐν τῇ οἰκείᾳ μεγαλειότητι καὶ οὐδὲν ἐλλείπει πρὸς τοῦτο τῇ αὐτοῦ φύσει, περιττῶς ὡς πλήρωμα τῆς θεότητος αὐτοῦ ὁ υἱὸς ἐπεισφέρεται. τ. μὲν ὁ πατὴρ ἐν τῇ ἑαυτοῦ μεγαλειότητι·...τ. δέ, οὐχ ὅτι μόνον ἐστὶ θεός, ἀλλ' ὅτι καὶ πατήρ. εἰ γὰρ ἀφέλοις τοῦ θεοῦ τὸ εἶναι πατέρα, ἀναιρήσεις τῆς θείας φύσεως τὸ καρπογόνον...φυσικὸν οὖν τῷ πατρὶ τὸ καρπογόνον, καὶ διὰ τοῦτο τ. Cyr.*thes*.5(5.37C–38A); **4.** perfection of Logos; **a.** perfection as creature only κτίσμα τοῦ θεοῦ τέλειον Ar. *ep.Alex*.(p.12; M.26.709A); **b.** divine perfection admitted without assertion of *homoousion* πιστεύομεν...εἰς ἕνα κύριον Ἰησοῦν Χριστὸν ...τ. ἐκ τ. *Symb.Ant*.(341)2 ap.Ath.*syn*.23(p.249.15; M.26.721C); *Symb.Ant*.(341)3 *ib*.24(p.250.11; 724C); εἰ καὶ ὑποτέτακται τῷ πατρὶ ...ἀλλ' ὅμως πρὸ αἰώνων γεννηθέντα ἐκ τοῦ θεοῦ θεὸν κατὰ φύσιν τ. εἶναι *Symb.Ant*.(345)4 *ib*.26(p.252.31; 729C); **c.** full perfection of divinity upheld εἷς ὁ λόγος, ἵνα τ. μόνος αὐτὸς Ath.*decr*.17(p.14.10; M.25.'452'(444)C); γέννημα τ. ἐκ τ. id.*Ar*.2.35(M.26.221C); †Ath.*exp. fid*.3(M.25.204C); ἐρέσθαι γὰρ αὐτοὺς δίκαιον, εἰ ὁ λόγος, ἐν τῷ θεῷ ὢν τ. ἦν, ὥστε καὶ ποιεῖν δύνασθαι. εἰ μὲν οὖν ἀτελὴς ἦν ἐν θεῷ ὤν, γεννηθεὶς δὲ τ. γέγονεν, ἡμεῖς αἴτιοι τῆς τελειότητος αὐτοῦ...εἰ δὲ τ. ἦν ἐν θεῷ, ὥστε καὶ ποιεῖν δύνασθαι, περιττὴ ἡ γέννησις αὐτοῦ· ἠδύνατο γὰρ καὶ ἐν πατρὶ ὢν δημιουργεῖν· ὥστε ἢ οὐ γεγέννηται, ἢ γεγέννηται οὐ δι' ἡμᾶς, ἀλλ' ὅτι ἀεὶ ἐκ τοῦ πατρός ἐστιν ‡Ath.*Ar*.4.11(p.55.5ff.; M.26. 481B); ὁμοούσιον τὸν υἱὸν τῷ πατρί...καὶ τ. ἐκ τ. ‡Ath.*Apoll*.1.2 (M.26.1096A); τ. δὲ ὁ πατὴρ διὰ τὸ πάντα ἔχειν ἐν ἑαυτῷ τελείως· τ. ... καὶ ὁ υἱός Cyr.*Jo*.1.3(4.21A); ὁ δὲ θεὸς...τ. ὤν, καὶ τ. καὶ ἐνυπόστατον ἕξει τὸν ἑαυτοῦ λόγον Jo.D.*f.o*.1.6(M.94.804A); **5.** of H. Ghost πτέρωσις γὰρ ἡ τῆς ψυχῆς πνεῦμα τὸ τ. Tat.*orat*.20(p.22. 12; M.6.852A); πιστεύομεν εἰς τὸ πνεῦμα τὸ ἅγιον...τὸ τ. ‡Ath.*interpr*. (p.66.23; M.26.1232B); **6.** of Trin. ὄντα καὶ ὑφεστῶτα πατέρα τ. καὶ ὑφεστῶτα υἱὸν τ. καὶ ὑφεστὼς τὸ πνεῦμα τὸ ἅγιον τ. Paulin.T.*symb.* (p.434.34f.; M.42.672B); ἡ πίστις ἄτρεπτον καὶ τ. ... οἶδε τριάδα Ath. *Ar.*1.18(M.26.49B); δείκνυται τ. εἶναι ἐν τούτῳ [sc. πνεύματι] τὴν τριάδα id.*ep.Serap.*1.25(M.26.589B); *ib.*1.28(596A); *ib.*4.12(652C); ἅγιος, ἅγιος, ἅγιος λέγοντα, τὰς τρεῖς ὑποστάσεις τ. δεικνύντα id.*hom. in Mt.11:27*(M.25.220A); ἡ...τριάς, καὶ λαβόντος ἐκ Μαρίας σῶμα τοῦ λόγου, τριάς ἐστιν οὐ δεχομένη προσθήκην οὐδὲ ἀφαίρεσιν· ἀλλ' ἀεὶ τ. ἐστίν id.*ep.Epict.*9(p.15.12; M.26.1065B); ὥσπερ γὰρ ὁ υἱός, ὁμοούσιος πρὸς τὸν πατέρα ὁμολογούμενος, τ. πρὸς τέλειον ὁμολογεῖται, καθὰ καὶ τὸ ἅγιον πνεῦμα· ὁμοούσιος γὰρ ἡ τριάς ‡Ath.*Apoll.*1.9(M.26.1109A); perfection of Trinitarian number, Ath.*syn.*28(p.257.25; M.26.744A); theology, id.*Ar.*1.18(M.26.49A); faith, id.*ep.Afr.*11(M.26.1048B).

B. of Christ; **1.** in Godhead σήμερον ἀναγεννηθεὶς ὁ Χριστὸς ἤδη τ. ἐστιν...μή τι οὖν ὁμολογήσουσιν ἄκοντες τὸν λόγον, τ. ἐκ τ. φύντα τοῦ πατρός, κατὰ τὴν οἰκονομικὴν προδιατύπωσιν ἀναγεννηθῆναι τελείως; καὶ εἰ τ. ἦν, τί ἐβαπτίζετο ὁ τ.; ἔδει, φασί, πληρῶσαι τὸ ἐπάγγελμα τὸ ἀνθρώπινον Clem.*paed.*1.6(p.105.7ff.; M.8.280C); τοῦ Ἰησοῦ θεότης ...τ. μὲν ἔστιν ἐν τοῖς ἀτελέσιν, ὡς τελετάρχις· ἀτελὴς δὲ ἐν τοῖς τ., ὡς ὑπερτελής Dion.Ar.*d.n.*2.10(M.3.648C); **2.** in manhood ἐν τῷ ὀνόματι Ἰησοῦ Χριστοῦ...αὐτοῦ με ἐνδυναμοῦντος τοῦ τ. ἀνθρώπου Ign.*Smyrn.*4.2; πάντα δὲ ὁμοῦ τ. οὐκ οἶδ' εἴ τις ἀνθρώπων, ἔτι ἄνθρωπος ὤν, πλὴν μόνον ὁ δι' ἡμᾶς ἄνθρωπον ἐνδυσάμενος Clem.*str.*4.21(p.305.21; M.8.1340B); καθὸ δὲ ἄνθρωπος ἦν...ὑπέμεινεν ὡς...τ. ἅπερ ἐχρῆν ὑπομεῖναι Or.*Cels.*7.17(p.168.28; M.11.1445B); ὁ λόγος... ἄνθρωπος τ. Ath.*inc.et c.Ar.*8(M.26.996C); ἐν τῇ τ. ἐνανθρωπήσει Epiph.*exp.fid.*17(p.517.19; M.42.813B); Cosm.Ind.*top.*2(M.88.128B); **3.** in both natures οὕτως ἂν λέγοιτο τ. θεὸς καὶ τ. ἄνθρωπος ὁ Χριστός· οὐχ ὡς τῆς θεϊκῆς τελειότητος εἰς ἀνθρωπίνην τελειότητα μεταποιηθείσης, ὅ ἐστιν ἀσεβές· οὔτε μὴν ὡς δύο τελειοτήτων κατὰ διαίρεσιν ὁμολογουμένων...ἀλλὰ καθ' ὕπαρξιν ἀνελλιπῆ· ἵνα εἷς ᾖ τὰ ἑκάτερα, τ. κατὰ πάντα, θεὸς καὶ ἄνθρωπος ὁ αὐτός ‡Ath.*Apoll.*1.16(M.26.1121C–1124A); τ. ἔχει τὴν διπλῆν φύσιν ὁ Χριστός, ἵνα μὴ ἀπολέσαι τὰς δύο Ephr.2.263F; ἐκ τ. τέλειος, ἐξ ἀνθρώπου ἄνθρωπος, ἐκ θεοῦ θεός, ἐκ παρθένου Χριστός id.263E; ὁμολογεῖν...Χριστὸν...τ. τὸν αὐτὸν ἐν θεότητι καὶ τ. τὸν αὐτὸν ἐν ἀνθρωπότητι *Symb.Chalc.*(p.129.24; H.2.456C); Just.Imp.*edict.*(p.199.34; M.86.2797B); ὁ τῶν πατέρων χορός, τ. τὸν Χριστὸν πρεσβεύει ὥσπερ ἐν θεότητι, οὕτω καὶ ἐν ἀνθρωπότητι Ephr.Ant.*fr.*(M.86.2108A); ὁ μονογενὴς υἱός...ἐκ...Μαρίας γεγέννηται ...καὶ ἄνθρωπος τ. ἐξ αὐτῆς γέγονε·...θεὸς τ. ἐστιν ὁμοῦ καὶ ἄνθρωπος τ., ἐκ δύο φύσεων Jo.D.*f.o.*1.2(M.94.793A); cf. Θεοδόσιον, τὸν μικρὸν ἀληθῶς βασιλέα, τὸν οὐδὲν τ. ἐπὶ Χριστοῦ φρονήσαντα Anast.S.*haer.*(p.261); **4.** but with manhood imposing limitations on Godhead ὁ ἄρτος ὁ τ. τοῦ πατρός, γάλα ἡμῖν ἑαυτὸν παρέσχεν Iren.*haer.*4.38.1(M.7.1106A); καὶ τὴν ἀρχὴν ὁ μὲν θεὸς δυνατὸς ἦν διδόναι τὸ τ. τῷ ἀνθρώπῳ, ἐκεῖνος δὲ ἄρτι γεγονώς, ἀδύνατος ἦν λαβεῖν αὐτό...καὶ διὰ τοῦτο συνενηπίαζεν υἱὸς τοῦ θεοῦ, τ. ὤν, τῷ ἀνθρώπῳ, οὐ δι' ἑαυτόν, ἀλλὰ διὰ τοῦ ἀνθρώπου νήπιον οὕτω χωρούμενος, ὡς ἄνθρωπος αὐτὸν χωρεῖν ἠδύνατο *ib.*4.38.2(1107A); exeg. Ps.5:7, Eph.4:13–15 ἡ προφητεία τὸ τ. τῇ τοῦ ἀνδρὸς τετίμηκεν προσηγορίᾳ καὶ διά γε τοῦ Δαβὶδ ἐπὶ μὲν τοῦ διαβόλου 'ἄνδρα αἱμάτων', φησί, 'βδελύσσεται κύριος'. ἄνδρα αὐτὸν ὡς τ. ἐν κακίᾳ καλεῖ. λέγεται δὲ καὶ ὁ κύριος ἀνὴρ διὰ τὸ εἶναι αὐτὸν τ. ἐν δικαιοσύνῃ...σαφέστατα δὲ...ἀπεκάλυψεν [sc. S. Paul] τὸ ζητούμενον...λέγων, 'μέχρι καταντήσωμεν...εἰς ἄνδρα τ. ...' ταῦτα λέγων εἰς οἰκοδομὴν τοῦ σώματος τοῦ Χριστοῦ, ὅς ἐστι...ἀνὴρ ὁ μόνος ἐν δικαιοσύνῃ τ., ἡμεῖς δὲ οἱ νήπιοι...τελειούμεθα τότε, ὅτε ἐσμὲν ἐκκλησία τὴν κεφαλὴν τὸν Χριστὸν ἀπειληφότες Clem.*paed.*1.5(p.100.16ff.; M.8.269B); Χριστοῦ ἐπιδημίαν καὶ πρὸ τῆς κατὰ σῶμα ἐπιδημίας τὴν νοητὴν γεγονέναι τοῖς τελειοτέροις καὶ οὐ νηπίοις...ὥσπερ δὲ πρὸ τῆς ἐμφανοῦς...ἐπιδημίας ἐπεδήμησε τοῖς τ., οὕτω καὶ μετὰ τὴν κεκηρυγμένην παρουσίαν τοῖς ἔτι νηπίοις Or.*Jo.*1.7(9; pp.11.27–12.2; M.14.36B,C); ὁ δὲ τοῦ θεοῦ υἱός, ἐπεὶ προκόπτειν οὐκ εἶχε, τ. ὢν ἐν τῷ πατρί, ἐταπείνωσεν ἑαυτὸν ὑπὲρ ἡμῶν...οὐκ ἄρα ὁ λόγος ἦν, ᾗ λόγος ἐστίν, ὁ προκόπτων, ὁ τ. ἐκ τ. ὢν τοῦ πατρός...ἀλλὰ ἀνθρωπίνως εἴρηται καὶ ἐνταῦθα τὸ προκόπτειν Ath.*Ar.*3.52(M.26.432B,C); διὰ τοῦτο ὁ τ. τοῦ θεοῦ λόγος τὸ ἀτελὲς περιτίθεται σῶμα,...ἵνα, ἀνθ' ἡμῶν τὴν ὀφειλὴν ἀποδιδούς, τὰ λείποντα τῷ ἀνθρώπῳ δι' ἑαυτοῦ τελειώσῃ *ib.*2.66(288B); τὴν ἄγνοιαν τῶν ἀνθρώπων ἐν τῷ σώματι ἔχων ...τ. καὶ ἁγίαν παραστήσῃ τῷ πατρὶ τὴν ἀνθρωπότητα id.*ep.Serap.*2.9 (M.26.624A); **5.** ref. controversy with Apollinarians; heret. propositions: perfect manhood involves sin, ‡Ath.*Apoll.*1.2(M.26.1096B) cit. s. ἁμαρτία; εἰ γὰρ ἕτερός ἐστιν ὁ Χριστὸς παρὰ τὸν ἐπουράνιον νοῦν τὸν ἐν αὐτῷ γενόμενον, τ. δὲ καὶ ὁ νοῦς, δύο ἄρα καθ' ὑμᾶς *ib.*1.13(1116C); orthodox replies: τ. τὴν καινότητα ἐπιδειξαμένου τοῦ Χριστοῦ, ἵνα τ. τὴν σωτηρίαν κατεργάσηται ὅλου τοῦ ἀνθρώπου, ψυχῆς λογικῆς καὶ σώματος, ἵνα τ. ᾖ καὶ ἀνάστασις *ib.*1.15(1121A); σῶμα ἀντὶ σώματος, καὶ ψυχὴν ἀντὶ ψυχῆς δέδωκε, καὶ τ. ὕπαρξιν ὑπὲρ ὅλου ἀνθρώπου *ib.*1.17(1125A); **6.** of incarnate Son's knowledge of Father τῷ γινώσκειν αὐτόν...ἐπὶ τ. γνῶσιν, ἣν γινώσκει ὁ υἱὸς τὸν πατέρα, ἐδοξάσθη...καὶ ἑαυτὸν γινώσκων, ὅπερ καὶ αὐτὸ οὐ μακρὰν ἀποδεῖ τοῦ προτέρου, ἐδοξάσθη ἐκ τοῦ αὐτὸν ἐγνωκέναι Or.*Jo.*32.28(18; p.473.14; M.14.817B); **7.** of things relating to Christ υἱὸς ἐν πατρί, καὶ πατὴρ ἐν υἱῷ· καὶ πῶς οὐ τ. ἡ παιδεία τοῦ παιδίου ἐκείνου; Clem. *paed.*1.5(p.104.14; M.8.277C); μέχρι τοῦ...Ἰησοῦ ὁ τ. ἐβλάστησε λόγος Or.*Jo.*1.2(4; p.6.14; M.14.28A); ἡ ἀνάστασις τοῦ...τελειοτέρου Χριστοῦ σώματος *ib.*10.36(20; p.210.32; 373A).

C. of man; **1.** relativity of human perfection, ref. Phil.3:12–14 ἐμοὶ...θαυμάζειν ἔπεισιν ὅπως σφᾶς τ. τινὲς τολμῶσι καλεῖν καὶ γνωστικούς, ὑπὲρ τὸν ἀπόστολον φρονοῦντες...καὶ τ. μὲν ἑαυτὸν ἡγεῖται, ὅτι ἀπήλλακται τοῦ προτέρου βίου, ἔχεται δὲ τοῦ κρείττονος, οὐχ ὡς ἐν γνώσει τ., ἀλλ' ὡς τοῦ τ. ἐφιέμενος· διὸ καὶ ἐπιφέρει 'ὅσοι οὖν τ., τοῦτο φρονοῦμεν', τελείωσιν δηλονότι λέγων τὸ ἀποτετάχθαι ταῖς ἁμαρτίαις καὶ εἰς πίστιν τοῦ μόνου τ. ἀναγεννῆσθαι Clem.*paed.*1.6(p.121.9ff.; M.8.312B,C); ὡς γὰρ τ. φαμεν ἰατρὸν καὶ τ. φιλόσοφον, οὕτως...καὶ τ. γνωστικόν· ἀλλ' οὐδὲν τούτων, καίτοι μέγιστον ὄν, εἰς ὁμοιότητα θεοῦ παραλαμβάνεται. ... μή τι οὖν τ. γίγνεσθαι ὀφείλομεν ὡς ὁ πατὴρ βούλεται; ἀδύνατον γὰρ...ὡς ὁ θεός ἐστι γενέσθαι τινὰ τ.· βούλεται δὲ ὁ πατὴρ ζῶντας ἡμᾶς κατὰ τὴν τοῦ εὐαγγελίου ὑπακοὴν...τ. γίγνεσθαι id.*str.*7.14(p.63.7ff.; M.9.521C–524A); **2.** reached by progress ὁ γεννητὸς...ἄνθρωπος κατ' εἰκόνα...τοῦ ἀγεννήτου γίνεται θεοῦ· τοῦ μὲν πατρὸς εὐδοκοῦντος...τοῦ δὲ υἱοῦ...δημιουργοῦντος, τοῦ δὲ πνεύματος τρέφοντος...τοῦ δὲ ἀνθρώπου ἠρέμα προκόπτοντος, καὶ πρὸς τέλειον ἀνερχομένου, τουτέστι, πλησίον τοῦ ἀγεννήτου γινομένου· τ. γὰρ ὁ ἀγέννητος· οὗτος δέ ἐστι θεός Iren.*haer.*4.38.3(M.7.1108B); καθάπερ τὸ ἔμβρυον...κατὰ μέρος γίγνεται εἰκὼν καὶ γεννᾶται, οὐκ ἤδη δέ ἐστι τ. ἄνθρωπος, ἀλλ' αὐξάνει ἐν ἔτεσι πολλοῖς...ὡσαύτως κἂν τοῖς πνευματικοῖς...κατὰ μικρὸν ὁ ἄνθρωπος αὐξάνει καὶ γίνεται εἰς ἄνδρα τ. Mac.Aeg.*hom.*15.41(M.34.604B,C); **3.** Christian in gen. called τ.: τ., ζῶμεν δὲ ἤδη οἱ θανάτου κεχωρισμένοι Clem.*paed.*1.6(p.106.3; M.8.281B); Or.*Cels.*3.61(p.255.20; M.11.1000D); exeg. 1Cor.2:6 τ. δὲ τοὺς πεπιστευκότας Chrys.*hom.*7.1 *in 1Cor.*(10.50C,D); opp. Jews, id.*hom.*1.1 *in Heb.*(12.5B); of baptized opp. catechumens εἰ δὲ μή εἰσι τ. Χριστιανοὶ οἱ κατηχούμενοι πρὶν ἢ βαπτισθῶσι, βαπτισθέντες δὲ τελειοῦνται ‡Ath.*Maced.dial.*1.6(M.28.1297B); cf.Dion.Ar.*e.h.*3.3.6(M.3.432C); in prayer for catechumens κύριε...αὐτοῦ τὸ ἦθος... διαφύλαξον, ἵνα...σοι τῷ τῶν πάντων ποιητῇ δουλεύῃ πρὸς τὸ τ. αὐτὸν ...ἀποδειχθῆναι Serap.*euch.*21; **4.** of the 'perfect' as dist. from other Christians; **a.** def. κατὰ νόμον...τις ἂν εἴη τ., ὃς ἀποχὴν κακῶν ἐπαγγέλλεται Clem.*str.*4.21(p.305.23; M.8.1340C); τ. γὰρ ἐκεῖνον καλοῦμεν τὸν μετὰ τῆς πίστεως βίον ἔχοντα ὀρθόν Chrys.*hom.*6.2 *in Heb.*(12.94C); **b.** characterized by union with God σπευστέον ἀπανδροῦσθαι γνωστικῶς καὶ τελειοῦσθαι ὡς ὅτι μάλιστα ἔτι ἐν σαρκὶ καταμένοντας, ἐκ τῆς τ. ἐνθένδε ὁμοφροσύνης μελετήσαντας συνδραμεῖν τῷ θελήματι τοῦ θεοῦ εἰς τὴν ἀποκατάστασιν τῆς τῷ ὄντι τ. εὐγενείας τε καὶ συγγενείας εἰς τὸ πλήρωμα τοῦ Χριστοῦ τὸ ἐκ καταρτισμοῦ τελείως ἀπηρτισμένον. ἤδη συνορῶμεν ὅπῃ καὶ ὅπως...ὁ θεῖος ἀπόστολος τὸν τ. λέγει καὶ ὡς τελείων ἐμφαίνει διαφοράς Clem.*str.*4.21(p.307.6ff.; M.8.1344B); περὶ δὲ τοῦ τ. καὶ κολλωμένου τῷ...κυρίῳ Or.*Cels.*6.47 (p.119.9; M.11.1372D); ὁ μὲν τ., ἀεὶ ἐν τοῖς λόγοις ὢν καὶ τοῖς ἔργοις καὶ τοῖς διανοήμασι τοῦ τῇ φύσει κυρίου λόγου θεοῦ, ἀεί ἐστιν αὐτοῦ ἐν ταῖς ἡμέραις καὶ ἀεὶ ἄγει κυριακὰς ἡμέρας. ἀλλὰ καὶ ἀεὶ παρασκευάζων ἑαυτὸν πρὸς τὸ ἀληθινῶς ζῆν *ib.*8.22(p.239.13; 1549D); ὅταν ἡ ψυχή σου κοινωνήσῃ τῷ πνεύματι...τότε εἶ τ. ἄνθρωπος ἐν θεῷ Mac.Aeg.*hom.*32.6(M.34.737C); and with Cross of Christ, *ib.*17.1 (624B); **c.** by humility ἴδιον τῶν τ. τὸ μὴ ἑαυτοὺς ὑπεραίρειν Bas. *ep.*204.4(3.304E; M.32.749A); Chrys.*hom.*12.2 *in Phil.*(11.293A); *ib.* (293C); **d.** by charity ὁ γνωστικὸς...μάρτυς τε ἐπὶ τοῖσδε ὀρθότατα ὁμολογήσας δι' ἀγάπην γένοιτο...οὐδ' οὕτως φθάσει τ. ἐν σαρκὶ κληθείς, ἐπεὶ τὴν προσηγορίαν ταύτην προείληφεν ἡ συμπεραίωσις τοῦ βίου, φθάσαντος ἤδη τοῦ γνωστικοῦ μάρτυρος τὸ τ. ἔργον ἐνδείξασθαι Clem. *str.*4.21(p.306.1ff.; M.8.1341A); οἱ γὰρ τ., τῆς θεωρητικῆς ἤδη μυστικῶς ἀξιωθέντες θεολογίας, καὶ πάσης φαντασίας ὑλικῆς τὸν νοῦν καθαρὸν καταστήσαντες...τὴν θείαν ἀγάπην ἐν ἑαυτοῖς ἐνστερνισάμενοι φαίνονται Max.*cap.*1.68(M.90.1208A); **e.** by knowledge τοὺς δὲ τῶν ἐντολῶν λόγους, ἐν οἷς ἡ τῶν τ. ὑπάρχει γνῶσις, τῷ θεῷ παραχωρεῖ διὰ τῆς πίστεως...ὁ τ., οὐ μόνον τὴν τῶν εἰσαγομένων τάξιν, ἀλλὰ καὶ τὴν τῶν προκοπτόντων διαδραμών, οὐκ ἀγνοεῖ τῶν ὑπ' αὐτοῦ κατ' ἐντολὴν γινομένων τοὺς λόγους *ib.*2.14f.(M.90.1225C); **f.** by combination of contemplative and active life, Ath.*fr.Ps.64 comm.*(M.27.576B; p.17); **g.** of martyrs, *Ep.Lugd.*ap.Eus.*h.e.*5.2.5(M.20.436A); Dion.Al. ap.Eus.*h.e.*7.11.24(M.20.672B); Dion.Al.*ib.*7.22.4(688B); **h.** of monks πρὸς ζῆλον μὲν...τῶν τ., πρὸς οἰκοδομὴν δὲ...τῶν ἀρχομένων ἀσκεῖν ‡Pall.*h.mon.*proem.(p.4.7; M.65.445B); τὴν τελειοτάτην αὐτῷ [sc.

newly professed monk] ζωὴν ὑφηγεῖται, μαρτυρούμενος, ὅτι χρὴ τῆς μέσης αὐτὸν ὑπερανεστηκέναι Dion.Ar.*e.h.*6.2(M.3.533B); τελειοτάτην ἐμφαίνει τῶν μοναχῶν φιλοσοφίαν *ib.*6.3.2(533D); οἱ μὲν ἀρχάριοι πληροῦσι τὸ ψαλτήριον...οἱ δὲ τ. μόνον εὔχονται Jo.Jej.*doct.*5(p.230); their 'perfect' way of life signified by habit, Dion.Ar.*e.h.*6.3.4 (536B); **i.** of perfect opp. beginners and those still progressing τοῖς τ. opp. τοῖς πιστεύουσι, Or.*comm.in Mt.*12.30(p.133.20; M.13.1049Af.); οἱ δὲ προκόπτοντες, καὶ μᾶλλον ἔτι οἱ τ., ῥᾳδίως ἃ μετίασι κατορθοῦντες γάννυνται Dion.Al.ap.Eus.*p.e.*14.27(781D; M.21.1285B); ἡ θεία γραφή, τοὺς μὲν εἰσαγομένους...τῆς θείας αὐλῆς τῶν ἀρετῶν, φοβουμένους καλεῖ· τοὺς δὲ κτησαμένους σύμμετρον ἕξιν τῶν κατ' ἀρετὴν λόγων... οἶδεν ὀνομάζειν προκόπτοντας· τοὺς δὲ κατ' αὐτὴν γνωστικῶς ἤδη γεγενημένους τῆς τῶν ἀρετῶν ἐκφαντικῆς ἀληθείας τὴν κορυφήν, προσαγορεύει τ. Max.*qu.Thal.*10(M.90.288B) = id.*cap.*1.68(M.90.1205C).

D. of Christian virtues and doctrines: faith οὐδὲν δὲ ἐνδεῖ τῇ πίστει τ. οὔσῃ ἐξ ἑαυτῆς Clem.*paed.*1.6(p.107.17; M.8.285A); love, Or.*Jo.*20.34(27; p.372.31; M.14.652C); Max.*qu.Thal.*29(M.90.365B); combined with fear τὴν ἀληθινὴν ἀγάπην, ἥν λέγει ὁ ἅγιος τ., καὶ αὕτη ἡ ἀγάπη φέρει αὐτὸν εἰς τὸν τ. φόβον Dor.*doct.*4.1(M.88.1657D); φθάσαι τὴν τ. ἀπάθειαν Marc.Diac.*v.Porph.*8; wisdom and knowledge τ. γὰρ ἡ σοφία θείων οὖσα καὶ ἀνθρωπίνων πραγμάτων ἐπιστήμη ἐμπεριλαβοῦσα τὰ ὅλα Clem.*paed.*2.2(p.171.16; 420A); prayer and worship εὐχαὶ καὶ εὐχαριστίαι...τ. μόναι...θυσίαι Just.*dial.*117.2(M. 6.745C); θεωρία, Clem.*str.*7.3(p.12.22; M.9.421A); θεοσέβεια, Or.*Jo.* 13.13(p.238.12; 420B); εὐχαριστία, Marc.Diac.*v.Porph.*21; union with God, Dion.Ar.*e.h.*2.3.4(M.3.400C); joy, Clem.*paed.*1.6(p.111. 30; 293B); id.*str.*1.24(p.99.23; M.8.905B); divine adoption ἡ...εἰς τὴν τ. υἱοθεσίαν διὰ τοῦ υἱοῦ ἀποκατάστασις *ib.*2.22(p.187.8; 1084A); martyrdom τὸ μαρτύριον...τ. ἔργον ἀγάπης *ib.*4.4(p.255.3; 1228B); *ib.*4.21(p.306.3; 1341A); Christian unity, exeg. Jo.17:22f. μεῖζόν τι καὶ τελειότερον περὶ ἡμῶν ὁ κύριος αἰτεῖ...ἵνα καὶ αὐτοὶ γένωνται τ., ἔχοντες πρὸς τοῦτο τὴν ἑνότητα, καὶ εἰς αὐτὸ ἓν γενόμενοι· ἵνα...πάντες ὦσιν ἓν σῶμα καὶ ἓν πνεῦμα, καὶ εἰς ἄνδρα τ. καταντήσωσιν Ath.*Ar.* 3.22(M.26.368C–369A); partial knowledge on earth opp. perfect knowledge in heaven, Or.*hom.8.7 in Jer.*(p.61.28; M.13.344D); resurrection, id.*Jo.*10.35(20; p.210.10; M.14.372C); Dion.Ar.*e.h.*7.3. 9(M.3.565B); second Advent, Anon.ap.Eus.*h.e.*5.17.4(M.20.473B); eschatol. τ. ἡμέρα Clem.*paed.*3.12(p.291.7; 680C).

E. ref. Adam; **1.** as created perfect τ. ὢν πως ἀτελὴς διὰ τὴν παρακοὴν γέγονεν...ὁ ἄνθρωπος ἐξέπεσεν ἐκ τ. ἐπὶ τὸ ἀτελές Or.*Jo.* 13.37(p.262.20,32; M.14.464B,C); Ath.*Ar.*2.66(M.26.288B) cit. s. ἐλλιπής; **2.** as created immature εἰ δὲ λέγει τις· οὐκ ἠδύνατο ὁ θεὸς ἀπ' ἀρχῆς τ. ἀναδεῖξαι τὸν ἄνθρωπον; γνώτω, ὅτι τῷ μὲν θεῷ...πάντα δυνατά· τὰ δὲ γεγονότα, καθὸ μετέπειτα γενέσεως ἀρχὴν ἰδίαν ἔσχε, κατὰ τοῦτο καὶ ὑστερεῖσθαι δεῖ αὐτὰ τοῦ πεποιηκότος...κατὰ τοῦτο καὶ ὑστεροῦνται τοῦ τ. καθὸ δὲ νεώτερα...καὶ ἀγύμναστα πρὸς τὴν τ. ἀγωγήν. ὡς οὖν ἡ μὲν μήτηρ δύναται τ. παρασχεῖν τῷ βρέφει τὸ ἔμβρωμα, τὸ δὲ ἔτι ἀδύνατεῖ τὴν...δέξασθαι τροφήν· οὕτως καὶ ὁ θεὸς αὐτὸς μὲν οἷός τε ἦν παρασχεῖν ἀπ' ἀρχῆς τῷ ἀνθρώπῳ τὸ τ., ὁ δὲ ἄνθρωπος ἀδύνατος λαβεῖν αὐτό· νήπιος γὰρ ἦν Iren.*haer.*4.38.1(M.7. 1105A–C); v. Ἀδάμ.

F. *fully instructed*, iron. σοὶ ἔξεστι τελείῳ κατὰ τὴν γνῶσιν εἶναι, μὴ πιστεύοντι τῷ μονογενεῖ θεῷ Gr.Nyss.*Eun.*12(1 p.234.5; M.45. 932A); τ. γίνομαι *be initiated*, i.e. *baptized* ἐπιγνόντι σοὶ τὸν Χριστὸν τοῦ θεοῦ καὶ τ. γινομένῳ εὐδαιμονεῖν Just.*dial.*8.2(M.6.493A); Gnost. οὐ δύναται...σωθῆναι ὁ τ. ἄνθρωπος, ἐὰν μὴ ἀναγεννηθῇ διὰ ταύτης εἰσελθὼν τῆς πύλης Hipp.*haer.*5.8(p.93.4; M.16.3146B); οὐδεὶς τούτων τῶν μυστηρίων ἀκροατὴς γέγονεν εἰ μὴ μόνοι ⟨οἱ⟩ γνωστικοὶ τ. *ib.* (p.94.24; 3147C).

G. of numbers ἐπὶ τὸν τ. ἀριθμὸν τὸν ὑπεράνω τῶν ἐννέα Clem.*str.*2. 11(p.140.6; M.8.988A); οἱ φύσεις ἀριθμῶν ἐρευνήσαντες πρῶτον μὲν τ. τὸν ἓξ εἰρήκασιν...δεύτερον δὲ τ. φασιν εἶναι τὸν εἴκοσι καὶ ὀκτώ Or.*Jo.* 28.1(p.389.1ff.; M.14.680B); id.*sel.in Ps.*66:2(M.12.1504B) cit. s. ἕξ; πρῶτος γὰρ ὁ ἓξ τ. ἐστι· τ. δὲ τοὺς ἐκ τῶν ἑαυτῶν μερῶν ἀπαρτιζομένους φασί...οἱ δὲ παρὰ τοὺς τ. ἀριθμοὺς συντιθέμενοι, ἢ λείπουσιν ἢ ὑπερβάλλουσι...ἔδει οὖν τὸν κόσμον τ. ὄντα ἐν τῷ πρώτῳ τ. γενέσθαι τῶν ἀριθμῶν Proc.G.*Gen.*2:2(M.87.140B,C).

H. of evil things: ἁμαρτία, *Barn.*8.1; Herm.*vis.*1.2.1; Olymp.*fr. Lam.*2:22(M.93.741D); ὁ τ. κακοποιός, Mac.Aeg.*hom.*43.3(M.34.773C).

I. *full* stop στίξας τ. στιγμὴν Anast.S.*hex.*9 int. opp. Clem. (*GCS* 3 p.224.32; cf.M.89.1004D).

II. neut. as subst.;

A. *perfection*, def. τὸ τ. εὑρίσκω πολλαχῶς ἐκλαμβανόμενον κατὰ τὸν ἐν ἑκάστῃ κατορθοῦντα ἀρετῇ Clem.*str.*4.21(p.305.18; M.8.1340B); of God ἀναγεννηθέντες γοῦν εὐθέως τὸ τ. ἀπειλήφαμεν, οὗ ἕνεκεν ἐσπεύδομεν. ἐφωτίσθημεν γάρ· τὸ δὲ ἔστιν ἐπιγνῶναι τὸν θεόν. οὔκουν ἀτελὴς ὁ ἐγνωκὼς τὸ τ. id.*paed.*1.6(p.105.1f.; M.8.280B); τὸ τ. ... τῆς τοῦ πατρὸς οὐσίας Ath.*Ar.*1.20(M.26.53B); of Christ ἐπὶ δὲ τῆς θείας σαρκώσεως οὐχ ἅμα, ἀλλὰ κατ' αὔξησιν τὸ τ. δογματίζεται ‡Ath. *annunt.*6(M.28.925A); τοῦ ἀναληφθέντος ἀνθρώπου τὸ τ. Thdt.ap. *cat.Heb.*2:9 suppl.(p.395.34); of angels, Clem.*exc.Thdot.*10(p.109. 30; M.9.661A); v. ἄγγελος; eschatol. τὸ τ. μετὰ τὸν βίον ἐστίν Or. *engast.*9(p.292.25; M.12.1025C); of Christian perfection; consisting in true wisdom, Clem.*str.*1.28(p.109.21; M.8.924C); the same for men and women, *ib.*4.20(p.305.9; 1340A); in Christ, Chrys.*hom.5.2 in Col.*(11.360A); of prayer, Diad.*perf.*61(p.70.13); of charity, *ib.*90 (p.128.15ff.); of wisdom, Gr.Nyss.*Apoll.*28(M.45.1185B).

B. *completion, consummation* τὸ τ. τῶν ἁμαρτιῶν *Barn.*5.11; τῆς γνώσεως *ib.*13.7; τῆς πίστεως Or.*Jo.*10.43(27; p.222.15; M.14.393B); τὸ δὲ τ. τῆς ἀναστάσεως ἦν, ὅτε γίνεται πρὸς τὸν πατέρα *ib.*10.37(21; p.212.7; 376A); μεμαρτύρηται...ὁ Δαβὶδ ἐπὶ τὸ τ. τῆς προφητείας id. *engast.*9(p.292.27; M.12.1025C); πάντα τὰ διὰ γενέσεως ἐν χρόνῳ ἔχει τὸ τ. Dion.Ar.*d.n.*4.25(M.3.728B).

C. liturg. and sacramental; of baptism καλεῖται...τὸ ἔργον τοῦτο ...φώτισμα καὶ τ. Clem.*paed.*1.6(p.105.23; M.8.281A); of Communion εὐχῆς δὲ μόνης κοινωνῆσαι ἔτη δύο, καὶ τότε ἐλθεῖν ἐπὶ τὸ τ. CAnc.(314) *can.*4; ἵνα τὸ τ. τῇ τετραετίᾳ λάβωσι *ib.*5; *ib.*6; *ib.*9; plur., liturgy of the faithful ὡς ἀτελέστων ἀποδιαστέλλει τὰ τ. Dion.Ar.*e.h.*3.3.6(M. 3.433B).

D. plur., *sublime things* ἡ δὲ [sc. ψυχή]...διὰ τὸν χωρισμὸν τὰ τ. καθορᾶν μὴ δυναμένη Tat.*orat.*13(p.14.29; M.6.836A); τὰ τελειώτερα opp. στοιχεῖα, Clem.*str.*5.8(p.360.5; M.9.80A); ὥσπερ τοῖς μηδέπω χωρεῖν δυναμένοις τὰ τ. διαλέγεται ὁ σωτήρ Ath.*ep.Serap.*4.11(M.26.652B).

τελειότης, ἡ, *perfection*;

A. def. and characteristics ὅταν γὰρ ἡ ψυχὴ πρὸς τὴν τ. τοῦ πνεύματος καταντήσῃ, τελείως πάντων τῶν παθῶν ἀποκαθαρισθεῖσα, καὶ τῷ παρακλήτῳ πνεύματι διὰ τῆς ἀρρήτου κοινωνίας ἑνωθεῖσα...καὶ καταξιωθῇ πνεῦμα γενέσθαι συγκεκραμένη τῷ πνεύματι Mac.Aeg.*hom.* 18.10(M.34.641A); id.*perf.*7(M.34.848A); Gr.Nyss.*Eun.*4(2 p.76.27; M.45.649C); its marks enumerated, Thdt.*1Cor.*6:7(3.196); τὴν τ. μὲν ὁ δεσπότης ὁρίζεται τῇ παντελεῖ τῶν χρημάτων ὑπεροψίᾳ, καὶ τῇ αὐθαιρέτῳ πενίᾳ id.*2Cor.*8:13ff.(3.330); αὕτη οὖν ἡ τελεία τῶν τελείων ἀτέλεστος τ. καθὰ μοί τις αὐτῆς γευσάμενος ὑφηγήσατο, οὕτω λοιπὸν τὸν νοῦν ἁγιάζει, καὶ τῶν ὑλῶν ἀφαρπάζει, ὡς τὸ πολὺ τῆς ἐν σαρκὶ ζωῆς, μετὰ τὴν κατάληψιν μέντοι τοῦ οὐρανίου λιμένος, ἐν οὐρανῷ ἐξεστηκότα αὐτὸν πρὸς θεωρίαν ἀνυψοῖ Jo.Clim.*scal.*29(M.88.1148C); τί ἐστιν ἡ τ.; μισθὸς ταπεινώσεως· ὅπερ ἐστὶν ἡ κατάληψις [perh. l. κατάλειψις] πάντων τῶν ὁρατῶν τε καὶ ἀοράτων Isaac *schol.*1 in Jo. Clim.*scal.*26(M.88.1036D).

B. of divine perfection; **1.** in gen. ἡ θεία μακαριότης...ἀνενδεὴς ἁπάσης τ. Dion.Ar.*c.h.*3.2(M.3.165C); ἔστι γὰρ οὐδὲν...ἀπροσδεὲς καθόλου τ., εἰ μὴ τὸ ὄντως αὐτοτελὲς καὶ προτέλειον *ib.*10.3(273C); τέλειον δ' αὖ λέγεται...ὡς...ὑπερβλύζον κατὰ μίαν...χορηγίαν, καθ' ἣν τὰ τέλεια πάντα τελεσιουργεῖ καὶ τῆς οἰκείας ἀποπληροῖ τ. id.*d.n.*13.1 (M.3.977C); ref. Heb.5:14 τὴν...στερεὰν τροφήν, σύνθημα φέρειν οἴομαι τῆς νοερᾶς καὶ μονίμου τ. καὶ ταυτότητος id.*ep.*9.4(M.3.1112A); **2.** ref. Father and Son τὸ δὲ ἑνὶ κεχρῆσθαι λόγῳ τὸν θεόν,...δεικνυσι καὶ τοῦ ἐξ αὐτοῦ λόγου τὴν τ. Ath.*decr.*16(p.14.1; M.25.'452'(444)A); τὸ δὲ γέννημα, ἐὰν μὴ ἀεὶ συνῇ τῷ πατρί, ἐλάττωμα τῆς τ. τῆς οὐσίας αὐτοῦ ἐστιν id.*Ar.*1.29(M.26.73A); ὁ δὲ τὴν ἐν τῷ οἰκείῳ γεννήτορι τ. πληρῶν, πῶς ἂν ἐλάττων νοοῖτο; Cyr.*Jo.*1.3(4.21B); ὁ μονογενὴς υἱὸς σύνδρομον ἔχει τῇ γεννήσει τὴν τ. Thdt.*Heb.*7:28(3.593).

C. in man; **1.** God as man's guide to perfection τῆς προνοίας τῆς ἐπὶ τ. ἡμᾶς ἑλκούσης Or.*hom.*6.2 *in Jer.*(p.50.9; M.13.328A); εἰς δὲ τὰ περὶ τῶν ψυχῶν, οὐκ ἄλλως δυναμένων τῆς τ. τυχεῖν χωρὶς τῆς πλουσίας καὶ σοφῆς περὶ θεοῦ ἀληθείας id.*princ.*4.2.7(p.319.4; M.11. 372B); διὰ ποίας δεῖ γνώσεως εἰς τὴν προδεδηλωμένην τοῦ κυρίου ἡμᾶς ὁδηγοῦντος καταφθάσαι τ. Diad.*perf.*proem.(p.5.16); ἀγαπῶ [sc. Christ] γάρ σου τὴν...ἐν ἀρετῇ τ. ... ὡς τὴν ὑπ' ἐμοῦ νομοθετηθεῖσαν τ. τελοῦσαν Thdt.*Cant.*5:2(2.109); **2.** Christ its pattern ἀκολουθεῖν... τῷ σωτῆρι, ἀναμαρτησίαν καὶ τ. τὴν ἐκείνου μετερχόμενον καὶ πρὸς ἐκεῖνον ὥσπερ κάτοπτρον κοσμοῦντα...τὴν ψυχὴν Clem.*q.d.s.*21(p.174. 8; M.9.625D); τῆς λογικῆς φύσεώς φαμεν ὅλης κρατῆσαί ποτε τὸν λόγον καὶ μεταποιῆσαι πᾶσαν ψυχὴν εἰς τὴν ἑαυτοῦ τ. Or.*Cels.*8.72 (p.288.25; M.11.1624D); ref. Christ's pre-existing human soul τάχα γὰρ ἡ μὲν τοῦ Ἰησοῦ ψυχὴ ἐν τῇ ἑαυτῆς τυγχάνουσα τ. ἐν θεῷ καὶ τῷ πληρώματι ἦν, καὶ ἐκεῖθεν ἐξεληλυθυῖα...ἀνέλαβεν τὸ ἐκ τῆς Μαρίας σῶμα id.*Jo.*20.19(17; p.351.26; M.14.616A); **3.** growth in perfection χρὴ δώδεκα βαθμοὺς παρελθεῖν τινα, καὶ φθάσαι εἰς τὴν τ., ἐν καιρῷ τις ἔφθασε καταλαβεῖν ἐκεῖνο τὸ μέτρον, καὶ εἰσῆλθεν εἰς τὴν τ. Mac. Aeg.*hom.*8.4(M.34.529C); through education τ. δὲ κατ' ἀρετὴν οὐδ' ἡντινοῦν τῶν ἄμεινον φύντων κατηγορεῖ, ὁπότε καὶ οἱ κακῶς πεφυκότες πρὸς ἀρετὴν τῆς προσηκούσης παιδείας τυχόντες ὡς ἐπίπαν καλοκαγαθίας ἤνυσαν Clem.*str.*1.6(p.22.26; M.8.729A); through various virtues πᾶς ὁ περικαλλὴς τῶν ἀρετῶν στέφανος, διὰ τῆς πρὸς θεὸν ἀγάπης τὴν τ. δέχεται Mac.Aeg.*perf.*13(M.34.849D); πρὸς τὴν τ. ἀφορῶντας συμβαίνει δύο τὰ κάλλιστα γίνεσθαι, σύντονόν τε καὶ ἀδιάπαυστον τὸν ἀγῶνα ἔχοντας εἰς τὸ πέρας διώκειν...τύφῳ τε μὴ ἁλίσκεσθαι, ἀλλὰ μετριοφρονεῖν, καὶ μικροὺς ἑαυτοὺς ἡγεῖσθαι διὰ τὴν μήπω τοῦ τελείου κατάληψιν id.*or.*11(M.34.861B); ἵνα ἡ τ. τῇ καθαρότητι πιστευθῇ Gr. Naz.*or.*18.13(M.35.1001A); ἡ ἀγάπη τὸ πλήρωμα τοῦ νόμου τῆς ἐν Χριστῷ τ. Diad.*perf.*17(p.22.11); ἐν ἐγκρατείᾳ καὶ τὴν τ. ὑπέδειξε Thdt. *1Cor.*7:6f.(3.202); ref. temptations ἡ κακία ἔνδον ὑποκαθημένη...τὸν ἄνθρωπον...ἐξάγει πρὸς οἴησιν τελειότητος...ἡ κακία τοσαύτας χιλιάδας ἐτῶν γεγενημένη...ἐνέδρας οἶδε τοιαύτας ἐν ἀποκρύφῳ τῆς καρδίας ἐπινοεῖν...ὥστε τὴν ψυχὴν ἑλκύσαι πρὸς οἴησιν τελειότητος; ὁ μέντοι θεμέλιος τοῦ Χριστιανισμοῦ, κἂν πάσας τις μετέλθῃ δικαιοσύνας, μὴ ἐπαναπαύεσθαι τούτων Mac.Aeg.*carit.*30(M.34.933A); ref. Cross οἱ τέλειοι Χριστιανοὶ οἱ καταξιωθέντες ἐλθεῖν εἰς μέτρα τελειότητος...τῷ σταυρῷ τοῦ Χριστοῦ πάντοτε ἀφιερωμένοι εἰσίν id.*hom.*17.1(M.34.624B); *ib.*17.2(624D); descriptions of process of growth ἐὰν οὖν ἀρξώμεθα θερμῷ ζήλῳ τὰς ἐντολὰς τοῦ θεοῦ διαπράττεσθαι, ἅπαντα ἡμῶν λοιπὸν τὰ αἰσθητήρια ἐν βαθείᾳ τινὶ αἰσθήσει φωτίζουσα ἡ χάρις τὰ μὲν ἡμέτερα ὥσπερ καταφλέγει ἐνθυμήματα, ἡδύνουσα δὲ ἡμῶν τὴν καρδίαν ἐν εἰρήνῃ τινὶ φιλίας ἀνενδότου πνευματικά τινα καὶ οὐκέτι σαρκικὰ λογίζεσθαι ἡμᾶς παρασκευάζει. τοῦτο δὲ τοῖς ἐγγίζουσι τῇ τ. συνεχῶς ἄγαν συμβαίνει, οἵτινες ἄπαυστον ἔχουσιν ἐν τῇ καρδίᾳ τὴν μνήμην τοῦ κυρίου Ἰησοῦ Diad.*perf.*88(p.124.1); ref. Rom.14:17 ἅτινά ἐστιν ὁ καρπὸς τῆς τελείας ἀγάπης. ὥστε οὖν γενέσθαι μὲν αὐτῆς ἐντεῦθεν συνεχῶς οἱ εἰς τ. προκόπτοντες δύνανται, τελείως δὲ αὐτὴν οὐδεὶς δύναται κτήσασθαι, εἰ μὴ [ἂν] ὅταν τελείως καταποθῇ τὸ θνητὸν ὑπὸ τῆς ζωῆς *ib.*90(p.128.27); **4.** perfection dist. from ordinary Christian life; **a.** ref. faith τ. πρὸς τὴν κοινὴν διαστέλλεται πίστιν Clem.*str.*4.16(p.293.2; M.8.1308B); ref. 1Cor.3:2,10 ὁ ἀπόστολος πρὸς ἀντιδιαστολὴν γνωστικῆς τ. τὴν κοινὴν πίστιν πῇ μὲν θεμέλιον λέγει, πῇ δὲ γάλα *ib.*5.4(p.342.2; M.9.45A); **b.** ref. morals μακάριοί γε ὅσοι δεόμενοι τοῦ υἱοῦ τοῦ θεοῦ τοιοῦτοι γεγόνασιν, ὡς μηκέτι αὐτοῦ χρῄζειν ἰατροῦ τοὺς κακῶς ἔχοντας θεραπεύοντος μηδὲ ποιμένος μηδὲ ἀπολυτρώσεως, ἀλλὰ σοφίας καὶ λόγου καὶ δικαιοσύνης, ἢ εἴ τι ἄλλο τοῖς διὰ τελειότητα χωρεῖν αὐτοῦ τὰ κάλλιστα δυναμένοις Or.*Jo.*1.20(22; p.25.19; M.14.60A); ὁ δεσπότης...ἐδίδαξε...ὡς καὶ δίχα τῆς τ. δυνατὸν τυχεῖν τῆς αἰωνίου ζωῆς. ἐρωτηθεὶς γὰρ ὑπὸ τοῦ νεανίσκου, 'τί ποιήσας ζωὴν αἰώνιον κληρονομήσω;' οὐκ εὐθὺς αὐτῷ τὴν περὶ τελειότητος διδασκαλίαν προσήνεγκεν, ἀλλὰ τῶν ἄλλων ἀνέμνησεν ἐντολῶν Thdt. *2Cor.*8:13ff.(3.330); δόγματα δέ, τὴν εὐαγγελικὴν διδασκαλίαν ἐκάλεσεν· ἐπειδὴ ἐν τῇ αἱρέσει τῆς γνώμης κεῖται τῆς τ. ἡ κατόρθωσις...ταῦτα γὰρ οὐ νομοθεσία, ἀλλ' αὐθαιρέτου γνώμης id.*Eph.*2:14f.(3.414); **5.** ref. perfection of gospel opp. Law νηστεύει...καὶ κατὰ τὸν νόμον ἀπὸ τῶν πράξεων τῶν φαύλων καὶ κατὰ τὴν τοῦ εὐαγγελίου τ. ἀπὸ τῶν ἐννοιῶν τῶν πονηρῶν Clem.*str.*7.12(p.54.12; M.9.504B); Χριστοῦ...τοῦ τελειοῦντος ἡμᾶς...ἀπὸ τῶν νομικῶν στοιχείων ἐπὶ τὴν εὐαγγελικὴν τ. Or.*hom. 12.13 in Jer.*(p.100.11; M.13.396D); οἶνος μὲν οὖν εὐφραίνων νεανίδας, τὰ νομικά. ἡ δὲ τ., τοῦ νυμφίου μαστοί id.*Cant.*1(p.111.30; M.13.99D); ἄρτος ἦν ἐκείνου ζωτικώτερος, τοῖς τὴν πατρῴαν κληρονομίαν διὰ τὴν τ. [δεῖ] ἀπολαβεῖν δυναμένοις ἀποδιδόμενος id.*Jo.*6.45(26; p.155.2; M.14.280B); cf.*ib.*10.15(12; p.185.27; 332C); καὶ τῇ τῶν Ἰουδαίων ἀσθενείᾳ τὸν...νόμον ἁρμόδιον· καὶ τῇ εὐαγγελικῇ τ. τὴν τοιαύτην νομοθεσίαν οὐ περιττήν Thdt.*qu.1 in Lev.*(1.179); Δαβὶδ...τὴν εὐαγγελικὴν πόρρωθεν ὁρῶν τ. id.*Ps.*54:5f.(1.960); **6.** perfection and baptism πῶς δὲ οὐ θέλεις προσκυνεῖσθαι τὸ πνεῦμα τὸ ἅγιον, εἰς ὃ ἐβαπτίσθης;...πῶς δὲ οὐχ ὁμολογούμενόν ἐστιν, ὅτι τῆς προσκυνήσεως τὸ βάπτισμα μεῖζον, ὅπου γε καὶ κατηχούμενοι προσκυνοῦσι πατέρα καὶ υἱόν, οὐκ ἔχουσι δὲ τ., ἐὰν μὴ βαπτισθῶσιν εἰς τὸ ὄνομα τοῦ πατρός, καὶ τοῦ υἱοῦ, καὶ τοῦ ἁγίου πνεύματος; εἰ δὲ μή εἰσι τέλειοι Χριστιανοὶ οἱ κατηχούμενοι πρὶν ἢ βαπτισθῶσι, βαπτισθέντες δὲ τελειοῦνται· τὸ βάπτισμα ἄρα μεῖζόν ἐστι τῆς προσκυνήσεως, ὃ τὴν τ. παρέχει ‡Ath.*Maced.dial.*1.6(M.28.1297B); ἐν τῇ σφραγῖδι τῆς μυστικῆς τ. ‡Caes.Naz.*dial.*12(M.38.869); **7.** as state of future life, ref. Mt.18:10 τῶν ἐσομένων ἐν τῇ αὐτῇ κληρονομίᾳ καὶ τ. Clem.*exc.Thdot.*23(p.114.29; M.9.672A); ref. Jo. 4:21,23 οἶμαί γε τὸ μὲν πρότερον δηλοῦν τὴν ἔξω σωμάτων προσκύνησιν ἐνστησομένην καὶ τὴν τ.· τὸ δὲ δεύτερον τὴν τῶν ἐν βίῳ τούτῳ Or.*Jo.*13.14(p.238.21; M.14.420C); τοῖς ἐπὶ τελειότητα φθάσασιν ἐν τῷ μέλλοντι αἰῶνι id.*fr.38 in Jo.*(p.514.22); **8.** possibility of reaching perfection τῆς τ. ἔξεστιν ἐπ' ἴσης μὲν ἀνδρί, ἐπ' ἴσης δὲ καὶ γυναικὶ μεταλαβεῖν Clem.*str.*4.19(p.300.5; M.8.1328A); proved from Mt.5:48, Col.1:28, etc. πρὸς τοὺς λέγοντας ἀδύνατον εἶναι τῆς τ. ἐφικέσθαι, καὶ τῆς εἰσάπαξ ἀπαλλαγῆς τῶν παθῶν...ἀναγκαῖον τὴν ἀπὸ τῶν θείων γραφῶν μαρτυρίαν ἐπενεγκεῖν, καὶ δεῖξαι κακῶς εἰδότας αὐτοὺς Mac.Aeg.*or.*11(M.34. 861A); **9.** evil as lack of perfection κακὸν...ἐρημία τῆς τῶν οἰκείων ἀγαθῶν τ. Dion.Ar.*d.n.*4.24(M.3.728A); κακὸν αὐτοῖς [sc. δαίμοσιν] ἐκ τῆς τῶν οἰκείων ἀγαθῶν ἀποπτώσεως, καὶ ἀλλοίωσις ἡ...ἀσθένεια τῆς προσηκούσης αὐτοῖς ἀγγελοπρεποῦς τ. *ib.*4.34(733C); **10.** ref. counsels and precepts εἴ τινι ὁ ἀπόστολος δι' ἀκρασίαν...δευτέρου μεταδίδωσι γάμου...οὐχ ἁμαρτάνει...οὐ πληροῖ δὲ τῆς κατὰ τὸ εὐαγγέλιον πολιτείας τὴν...τ. Clem.*str.*3.12(p.233.29; M.8.1184A); **11.** exeg. Ps.118:66 τὸ ἔξοχον τῆς γνώσεως ὁ προφήτης ὧδε παραστάς· χρηστότητα καὶ παιδείαν καὶ γνῶσιν δίδαξόν με· κατ' ἐπανάβασιν αὐξήσας τὸ ἡγεμονικὸν τῆς τ. Clem.*str.*7.7(p.28.7; M.9.452B); 1Cor.6:7 τοῦ γνωστικοῦ τὴν τ. ὑπογράφει. οὐ γὰρ ἐπὶ τοῦ ἀδικεῖσθαι μᾶλλον ἢ ἀδικεῖν ἵστησι τὸν γνωστικὸν μόνον, ἀλλὰ καὶ ἀμνησίκακον εἶναι διδάσκει, μηδὲ εὔχεσθαι κατὰ τοῦ ἀδικήσαντος ἐπιτρέπων *ib.*7.14(p.60.20; 517B); Col. 3:14 οὐκ εἶπεν, ὅτι κορυφή ἐστιν, ἀλλ' ὃ μεῖζόν ἐστι, σύνδεσμος·...κορυφὴ μὲν γὰρ ἐπίτασις τελειότητος, σύνδεσμος δὲ συγκράτησις τῶν τὴν τ. ποιούντων, ὡσανεὶ ἡ ῥίζα Chrys.*hom.8.2 in Col.*(11.383A); **12.** Gnost. τὰς φωνὰς...τῶν μὴ βιούντων ὀρθῶς Βασιλειδιανῶν, ὡς ἤτοι ἐχόντων ἐξουσίαν καὶ τοῦ ἁμαρτεῖν διὰ τὴν τ. Clem.*str.*3.1(p.196.19; M.8.1104A); **13.** Pythagorean Πυθαγόραν...Ἡρακλείδης ἱστορεῖ τὴν ἐπιστήμην τῆς τ. τῶν ἀριθμῶν τῆς ψυχῆς εὐδαιμονίαν εἶναι παραδεδωκέναι Clem.*str.*2.21(p.184.9; M.8.1077A ἀρετῶν for ἀριθμῶν); **14.** polite style of address, esp. for bishops and monks παρακαλῶ τὴν ἀσύγκριτον ὑμῶν ἐν Χριστῷ τ. Bas.*ep.*23(3.102A; M.32.296A); Gr.Naz.*ep.*64(M.37.125C); Gr.Nyss.*ep.*25(M.46.1093C); ἡ κατὰ θεὸν σοῦ τ. Thdt.*ep.*83(p.49.8; 4.1146).

***τελειούμνητος**, *perfectly hymned*, ‡Chrys.*ador.*(11.824B).

τελει-όω, **1.** *fulfil, perform* ἐὰν...ἁγνῶς τελειώσωσι τὴν διακονίαν αὐτῶν, δυνήσονται ζῆσαι Herm.*sim.*9.26.2; ἐπέμφθη ὁ σωτὴρ...ἵνα τελειώσῃ τὸ ἔργον τοῦ θεοῦ καὶ ἕκαστος τετελειωμένος οἰκειωθῇ τῇ...στερεᾷ τροφῇ καὶ τῇ σοφίᾳ συνῇ Or.*Jo.*13.37(p.262.24; M.14.464B); ὡς δὲ ὀφείλοντος γενέσθαι τοῦ θανάτου, οὐχ ἑαυτῷ, ἀλλὰ παρ' ἑτέρων ἐλάμβανε [sc. Christ] τὴν πρόφασιν τοῦ τελειῶσαι τὴν θυσίαν Ath.*inc.* 21.6(M.25.133B); σοῦ γάρ εἰμι λόγος...καὶ διὰ σὲ τετελείωται ἐν ἐμοὶ τῶν ἀνθρώπων ἡ σωτηρία id.*Ar.*3.22(M.26.369A); οὐ βασιλικῷ προστάγματι τὰ τῆς συνόδου ~οῦται id.*h.Ar.*11(p.188.35; M.25.705C); ὁ...ἱεράρχης...ὑμνεῖ τὰς θεουργίας Ἰησοῦ...ἃς ἐπὶ σωτηρίᾳ τοῦ γένους ἡμῶν...ἐτελείωσεν Dion.Ar.*e.h.*3.3.12(M.3.441D); esp. of performing God's will ταχὺ καὶ ἐξαίφνης τελειωθήσεται τὸ βούλημα αὐτοῦ *1Clem.* 23.5; οὐδὲν ἐν τῷ πατρὶ πρὸ τοῦ λόγου, ἀλλ' ἐν τῷ λόγῳ καὶ ἡ βούλησις καὶ δι' αὐτοῦ τὰ τοῦ βουλήματος εἰς ἔργον ~οῦται Ath.*Ar.*3.67(M.26. 465A); **2.** *fulfil* prophecies or visions, Herm.*vis.*4.1.3; πᾶν...ῥῆμα, ὃ ἀφῆκεν ἐκ τοῦ στόματος αὐτοῦ [sc. Polycarp] καὶ ἐτελειώθη καὶ τελειωθήσεται *M.Polyc.*16.2; τὴν μίαν τὴν ἐκ προφητείας εἰς εὐαγγέλιον τετελειωμένην δι' ἑνὸς καὶ τοῦ αὐτοῦ κυρίου διδάσκων σωτηρίαν Clem.*str.*2.6(p.128.28; M.8.964D); τὸν ἐγχειρήσαντα εὐλαβούμενος τετελείωκε τὴν προφητείαν Ath.*ep.Drac.*5(M.25.529B); **3.** *finish, accomplish* ταῦτα...πάντα τελειώσας, ἐπῄνεσεν αὐτὰ καὶ ηὐλόγησεν *1Clem.*33.6; προσέχειν...τῷ εὐαγγελίῳ, ἐν ᾧ τὸ πάθος ἡμῖν δεδήλωται καὶ ἡ ἀνάστασις τετελείωται Ign.*Smyrn.*7.2; ἡ ἕκτη ὥρα τῆς...οἰκονομίας..., καθ' ἣν ἐτελειώθη ὁ ἄνθρωπος Clem.*str.*6.16(p.503.27; M.9. 369A); ἡ μὲν...τοῦ κυρίου...διδασκαλία ἀπὸ Αὐγούστου καὶ Τιβερίου Καίσαρος ἀρξαμένη μεσούντων τῶν Αὐγούστου χρόνων ~οῦται, ἡ δὲ τῶν ἀποστόλων αὐτοῦ μέχρι γε τῆς Παύλου λειτουργίας ἐπὶ Νέρωνος ~οῦται *ib.*7.17(p.75.11; 548B); ἡ τοῦ λόγου ἐπιδημία τετελείωκε τὸ ἔργον τοῦ πατρός Ath.*Ar.*1.59(M.26.136C); ἔπρεπε...αὐτὸν...ἐλθόντα τελειῶσαι τὸ ἔργον καὶ δούλου λαβόντα μορφήν, κύριον ὀνομάζειν τὸν πατέρα *ib.*2.50(233A); ταύτην...τὴν πρόθεσιν...ὁ θεὸς τελειώσειεν id.*v. Anton.*proem.(M.26.837A); of end of life ἐτελειώθη...ὁ δρόμος τῶν ἁγίων ἀποστόλων...μηνὶ Ἰουνίῳ κθ' *A.Petr.et Paul.*88(p.221.11); **4.** *complete, perfect*, in gen. μνήσθητι, κύριε, τῆς ἐκκλησίας σου, τοῦ ῥύσασθαι αὐτὴν ἀπὸ παντὸς πονηροῦ καὶ τελειῶσαι αὐτὴν ἐν τῇ ἀγάπῃ σου *Did.*10.5; οὐ γὰρ ὠφελήσει ὑμᾶς ὁ πᾶς χρόνος τῆς πίστεως ὑμῶν, ἐὰν μὴ ἐν τῷ ἐσχάτῳ καιρῷ τελειωθῆτε *ib.*16.2; οἱ ἐν ἀγάπῃ ἐτελειώθησαν πάντες οἱ ἐκλεκτοὶ τοῦ θεοῦ *1Clem.*49.5; οἱ ἐν ἀγάπῃ τελειωθέντες ...ἔχουσι χῶρον εὐσεβῶν *ib.*50.3; cf. ὁ μὲν...πρῶτος βαθμὸς τῆς σωτηρίας ἡ μετὰ φόβου διδασκαλία..., δεύτερος δὲ ἡ ἐλπίς,...~οῖ δὲ ἡ ἀγάπη...γνωστικῶς ἤδη παιδεύουσα Clem.*str.*4.7(p.272.22; M.8. 1265A); πίστις πάντα...~οῖ Herm.*mand.*9.10; cf. οὗτοι δ' ἂν εἶεν οἱ ἑλόμενοι οἰκεῖοι εἶναι αὐτῷ, οἱ διὰ πίστεως ~ούμενοι Clem.*str.*7.2(p.8. 3; M.9.412C); ref. γνῶσις: διὰ ταύτης ~οῦται ἡ πίστις, ὡς τελείου τοῦ πιστοῦ ταύτῃ μόνως γιγνομένου *ib.*7.10(p.40.24; 477C); ~οῦται γοῦν τις καὶ ὡς εὐλαβής, καὶ ὡς ὑπομνηστικὸς...καὶ ὡς μάρτυς καὶ ὡς γνωστικός *ib.*4.21(p.305.19; M.8.1340B); ἡ...σωφροσύνη, κατὰ τὴν γνῶσιν ~ουμένη..., κύριον καὶ αὐτοκράτορα τὸν ἄνδρα παρασκευάζει *ib.* 7.11(p.49.2; M.9.493C); αὕτη...ἡ ἐνέργεια τοῦ τελειωθέντος γνωστικοῦ, προσομιλεῖν τῷ θεῷ διὰ τοῦ μεγάλου ἀρχιερέως *ib.*7.3(p.10.17; 417A);

γνῶσιν...ἔργῳ τε καὶ λόγῳ ~οῦσθαι διδάσκων ib.4.17(p.296.17; M.8.1317A); cf.Dion.Ar.c.h.7.3(M.3.209D); ὅταν...τελειωθῶμεν κληρονόμοι τῆς διαθήκης κυρίου γενέσθαι Barn.6.19; connected with virginity as supreme virtue, Meth.symp.1.2(p.10.19; M.18.41A); through profession of faith τοὺς δι' ὁμολογίας τελειωθέντας Const.or.s.c.12(p.152.7; M.20.1269B); in rel. to spiritual progress, Clem.exc.Thdot.15(p.111.27; M.9.665A); εὐσεβούντων...ἡμῶν οὐκ ἰσχύει [sc. spiritual enemy], ἀσθενεῖ γὰρ προκοπτόντων καὶ νεκροῦται ~ουμένων Or.fr.35 in Lam.(p.251.31; M.13.628C); ἡδὺς...ἐστι καὶ τίμιος ἅπασι τοῖς θεοειδέσιν ὁ κατὰ θείαν ζωὴν τετελειωμένος Dion.Ar.e.h.7.3.8(M.3.565A); τὸ ἐπιχεόμενον ἔλαιον ἐμφαίνει κατὰ τοὺς...ἱεροὺς ἀγῶνας ἀθλήσαντα καὶ τελειωθέντα τὸν κεκοιμημένον ib.; οὐ συνίσταται διάδημα βασιλέως ἐξ ἑνὸς λίθου καὶ οὐ ~οῦται ἀπάθεια, ἂν μιᾶς ἀρετῆς καὶ τυχούσης ἀμελήσωμεν Jo.Clim.scal.29(M.88.1149D); as act of God, Dion.Ar.d.n.2.11(M.3.649C); αὐτὸς ὁ πάντων αἴτιος δι' ἀγαθότητος ὑπερβολὴν πάντων ἐρᾷ, πάντα ποιεῖ, πάντα ~οῖ ib.4.10(708B); ib.13.3(980C); as work of divine πρόνοια, Or.hom.6.2 in Jer.(p.50.8; M.13.328A); ref. attainment of perfection in and through Christ, Clem.paed.1.5(p.103.23; M.8.277A); ἡμεῖς...οἱ νήπιοι...~ούμεθα τότε, ὅτε ἐσμὲν ἐκκλησία, τὴν κεφαλὴν τὸν Χριστὸν ἀπειληφότες ib.(p.101.3; 272A); ἡ φιλοσοφία, προοδοποιοῦσα τὸν ὑπὸ Χριστοῦ ~ούμενον id.str.1.5(p.18.5; M.8.720A); τὸ οἰκητήριον τοῦτο...πνεύματος ἁγίου...καταξιοῦται, τῷ τοῦ σωτῆρος καταρτισμῷ ~ούμενον ib.4.26(p.320.28; 1373A); οὐκ ἀποχῇ κακῶν μόνον δικαιωθείς, πρὸς δὲ καὶ τῇ κυριακῇ τελειωθεὶς εὐποιΐᾳ ib.4.6(p.261.7; 1241A); πᾶς ὁ τετελειωμένος ζῇ οὐκέτι, ἀλλ' ἐν αὐτῷ ζῇ Χριστός Or.Jo.1.4(6; p.9.1; M.14.32A); προσέχωμεν ἑαυτοῖς πάντα πράττοντες...ἵνα ἐν Χριστῷ...τελειωθῶμεν id.hom.12.13 in Jer.(p.101.21; 397D); ib.(p.100.10; 396D); Christ perfecting both men and angels, id.Jo.1.31(34; p.38.31; 81A); perfecting creation through Inc., Ath.Ar.2.67(M.26.289A,B); ὡς...γέγονε ἄνθρωπος εὐθὺς διωρθώθη καὶ ἐτελειώθη τὰ ὅλα id.hom.2 in Mt.11:27(M.25.212A); through his sacrifice, id.Ar.1.9(165B); and redemption of mankind τετελείωται τὸ ἔργον, ὅτι λυτρωθέντες ἀπὸ τῆς ἁμαρτίας οἱ ἄνθρωποι οὐκέτι μένουσι νεκροί ib.3.23(372C); in rel. to work of H. Ghost πνεῦμα, ἐν ᾧ τὰ πάντα ὁ πατὴρ διὰ τοῦ λόγου ~οῖ id.ep.Serap.1.9(M.26.553B); Bas.Spir.38(3.31E; M.32.136B) cit. s. δημιουργέω; ib. cit. s. δημιουργία; τὰ λειτουργικὰ πνεύματα...παρουσίᾳ...τοῦ πνεύματος ~οῦσθαι ib.; θέλει [sc. ὁ πατὴρ] διὰ τοῦ πνεύματος ~οῦν ib.(32A; M.136C); Gr.Naz.or.40.43(M.36.420C); ἦν οὖν ἀεὶ...~οῦν, οὐ ~ούμενον ib.41.9(441B); as work of angelic hierarchy, Dion.Ar.e.h.6.3.3(M.3.537C); of men attaining to perfection of angels, Clem.ecl.57(p.154.7; M.9.725C); Or.Cels.4.29(p.298.13; M.11.1069C); ref. OT saints εἰ γὰρ ἦν προφητῶν διαφορά, οἱ τετελειωμένοι καὶ διαφέροντες οὐκ ἐπεθύμησαν ἰδεῖν, ἃ εἶδον οἱ ἀπόστολοι· τεθεωρήκασι γὰρ αὐτά id.Jo.6.3(2; p.109.26; M.14.204A); οἵ τε ἄλλοι ἅγιοι...οὐχ αἵματος ἐκχυθέντος ἐτελειώθησαν, ἀλλὰ διὰ πίστεως ἐδικαιώθησαν Ath.ep.Aeg.Lib.21(M.25.588B); of apostles opp. ordinary believers, Or.hom.16.5 in Jer.(p.137.25; M.13.445B); ref. Christ as man ἀνὴρ γενόμενος...προέκοπτεν. οὐδεὶς γὰρ προκόπτει τετελειωμένος ib.1.7(p.6.23; 264B); Gnost. ἡμεῖς οἱ πνευματικοί, ἐνθάδε καταλελειμμένοι διακοσμῆσαι...καὶ τελειῶσαι τὰς ψυχὰς κατὰ φύσιν ἐχούσας μένειν ἐν τούτῳ τῷ διαστήματι Hipp.haer.7.25(p.203.2; M.16.3314A); 5. pass., *come to completion* ὁ κύριος...ἐφανερώθη...ἵνα κἀκεῖνοι τελειωθῶσιν τοῖς ἁμαρτήμασιν Barn.14.5; *come to maturity*, Clem.str.2.18(p.165.10; M.8.1037B); Meth.symp.1.2(p.9.24; M.18.40C); 6. pass., *be completed*; of periods of time τρία διαστήματα μυστικὰ ἐξ ἑβδομάσι ~ούμενα Clem.str.1.21(p.92.3; M.8.889C); 7. *perfect through sacramental agency, initiate*, ref. Gnost. initiations ἐπὶ τὸν ἀγαθὸν ἄγει, ~ῶν τοὺς μύστας τὰ ἄλαλα μυστήρια Hipp.haer.5.24(p.126.1; M.16.3191D); ref. orthodox baptism ~οῦται δὲ τῷ λουτρῷ μόνῳ καὶ τοῦ πνεύματος τῇ καθόδῳ ἁγιάζεται Clem.paed.1.6(p.105.16; M.8.280C); βαπτιζόμενοι φωτιζόμεθα, φωτιζόμενοι υἱοποιούμεθα, υἱοποιούμενοι ~ούμεθα, ~ούμενοι ἀπαθανατιζόμεθα ib.(p.105.21; 281A); τοῖς...~ουμένοις συγγίνεται τὸ πνεῦμα τὸ ἅγιον Thgn.hypot.fr.1(p.76.12; M.10.240C); τὸ...πνεῦμα σφραγίς ἐστι τῶν ~ουμένων...ἐπὶ...τοῖς...τελειωθεῖσιν οὐδεμία περιλείπεται συγγνώμης ἀπολογία ib.(p.76.20; M.l.c.); Κωνσταντῖνος Χριστοῦ μυστηρίοις ἀναγεννώμενος ἐτελειοῦτο Eus.v.C.4.62(p.143.20; M.20.1216B); ἐκέλευσε...ἡμᾶς βαπτίζεσθαι...εἰς ὄνομα πατρὸς καὶ υἱοῦ καὶ ἁγίου πνεύματος· οὕτως γὰρ ~ούμενοι υἱοποιούμεθα Ath.decr.31(p.27.25; M.25.473C); ὃν ὁ υἱὸς βαπτίζει, οὗτος ἐν πνεύματι ἁγίῳ ~οῦται id.Ar.2.41(M.26.236A); τὸ ἅγιον...λουτρὸν...εἰς πατέρα καὶ υἱὸν καὶ ἅγιον πνεῦμα δίδοται, καὶ οὕτω ~οῦται τῶν βαπτιζομένων ἕκαστος id.ep.Serap.4.12(M.26.653A); Gr.Naz.or.40.43(M.36.420C); ref. catechumens ἀνακεκαλυμμένοι...εἰσὶν οἱ τῶν συμβόλων λόγοι τοῖς...ἱεροτελεσταῖς, οὓς οὐ θεμιτὸν ἐξάγειν εἰς τοὺς ἔτι ~ουμένους Dion.Ar.e.h.1.5(M.3.377A); *ordain*: OT priests, Gr.Naz.or.41.4(433C); Christian priests, Dion.Ar.e.h.5.2(509B); ib.2.3.3(400C); *consecrate*: baptismal water, ib.2.2(396C); chrism, ib.4.1(472C); a church, Ath.apol.Const.14(M.25.612B); ib.18(617D); 8. pass., *be perfected by death, die*; of apostles, A.Andr.B 11(p.64.4); A.Phil.137(p.69.3); A.Barn.9(p.295.21); of martyrs, Anon.ap.Eus.h.e.5.16.22(M.20.472C); Ep.Lugd.ib.5.2.3(436A); Phil.Thm.ep.ib.8.10.9(765C); Eus.h.e.6.2.12(525B); ib.6.3.13(529B); Ath.v.Anton.46(M.26.909C); id.ep.Jov.1(M.26.816A); τοὺς ἐν τῇ φυγῇ τελειωθέντας μὴ ἀκλεῶς ἀποθνήσκειν, ἀλλ' ἔχειν καὶ αὐτοὺς τοῦ μαρτυρίου τὸ καύχημα id.fug.17(p.80.11; M.25.665C); of Moses and prophets, id.ep.Drac.5(M.25.529A); id.Ar.3.52(M.26.432B); of Christians in gen., Eus.v.C.3.47(p.97.15; M.20.1108A); Ath.v.Anton.90(968C); id.virg.8(p.42.19; M.28.261A); Pall.h.Laus.4(p.19.17; M.34.1012D); Dion.Ar.e.h.7.1.3(M.3.556C); ref. Christ's death μόνος γὰρ ἐν τῷ ἀέρι τις ἀποθνήσκει, ὁ σταυρῷ ~ούμενος Ath.inc.25.5(M.25.140C); τίς...τῶν ἐν τῇ γραφῇ μαρτυρουμένων...σταυρῷ τετελείωται ὑπὲρ τῆς πάντων σωτηρίας; ib.37.1(160A).

τελείωσις, ἡ, *completion, consummation, perfection; sanctification, consecration*;

A. of moral and spiritual *perfection*; 1. def. and descriptions; a. in baptismal context τὸ πιστεῦσαι...καὶ ἀναγεννηθῆναι τ. ἐστιν ἐν ζωῇ Clem.paed.1.6(p.106.8; M.8.281B); τ. ... λέγων τὸ ἀποτετάχθαι ταῖς ἁμαρτίαις καὶ εἰς πίστιν τοῦ μόνου τελείου ἀναγεγεννῆσθαι ib.(p.121.19; 312C); b. in gen. ἐνταῦθα...τῆς γνωστικῆς ψυχῆς ἡ τ. πάσης καθάρσεώς τε καὶ λειτουργίας ὑπεκβᾶσαν σὺν τῷ κυρίῳ γίγνεσθαι id.str.7.10(p.42.1; M.9.481A); οὐ γὰρ ἡ ἀποχὴ τῶν κακῶν αὕτη ἐστὶν ἡ τ., ἀλλ' εἰ εἰσῆλθες εἰς τὸν νοῦν...καὶ ἀπέκτεινας τὸν ὄφιν τὸν κατώτερον τοῦ νοῦ...καὶ πᾶσαν τὴν ἐν σοὶ ἀκαθαρσίαν ἐξέβαλες Mac.Aeg.hom.18.15(M.34.633B); τοῦτο γὰρ ἡ τ., μηδὲν τὸ παράπαν ἐν ἡμῖν αὐτοῖς τοῦ αἰῶνος τούτου γνώρισμα φέροντες Max.ep.1(M.91.376B); c. ref. angelic hierarchies ἔστι γὰρ ἑκάστῳ τῶν ἱεραρχίαν κεκληρωμένων ἡ τ., τὸ κατ' οἰκείαν ἀναλογίαν ἐπὶ τὸ θεομίμητον ἀναχθῆναι Dion.Ar.c.h.3.2(M.3.165B); 2. means of its attainment; a. purification τοὺς Χριστιανοὺς ἡ ἐν τοῖς πειρασμοῖς δοκιμασία πρὸς τὴν τ. ἄγει Bas.ep.101(3.197A; M.32.505C); προστεθήτω δὲ καὶ ὕσσωπον τῷ σπόγγῳ τῆς ὕβρεως, ὅπως ἂν τελείως ἐμφέροιτο τῷ ὑποδείγματι τὸ σχῆμα τῆς ἡμῶν καθάρσεως. τὸ μὲν γὰρ δριμὺ τῶν ἀγώνων ἴδιον, τὸ δὲ καθαριστικὸν πάντως τῆς τ. Diad.perf.51(p.56.22); ἅγιά τε τῶν ἁγίων εἶναί φαμεν τοὺς τῆς μυστικῆς τ. τρόπους. οἷς οὐκ ἄν τις ἐμβάλοι...μὴ οὐχὶ πρότερον πάντα ῥύπον τὸν ἐξ ἁμαρτίας...διανιψάμενος Cyr.hom.pasch.26(5².304D); b. faith εἰ δέ τις Ἑλλήνων ὑπερβὰς τὸ προηγούμενον τῆς φιλοσοφίας τῆς Ἑλληνικῆς εὐθέως ὥρμησεν ἐπὶ τὴν ἀληθῆ διδασκαλίαν, ὑπερεδίσκευσεν οὗτος, κἂν ἰδιώτης ᾖ, τὴν ἐπίτομον τῆς σωτηρίας διὰ πίστεως εἰς τ. ἑλόμενος Clem.str.7.2(p.9.21; M.9.416A); διὰ πίστεως περιπατῶν, οὐ διὰ εἴδους, εἰς τοσοῦτον ἐπήρθη τῇ μεγαλοφυΐᾳ τῆς γνώσεως, ὥστε ὅρος νομισθῆναι τῆς ἀνθρωπίνης τ. Gr.Nyss.Eun.12(1 p.241.12; M.45.940C); c. hope and charity πρόκειται δὲ τοῖς εἰς τ. σπεύδουσιν ἡ γνῶσις ἡ λογική, ἧς θεμέλιος ἡ ἁγία τριάς, πίστις, ἐλπίς, ἀγάπη Clem.str.4.7(p.273.5; M.8.1205B); τὴν τ. ἀπειληφὼς τοῦ κατὰ ἀγάπην δρωμένου ib.7.7(p.30.32; M.9.456C); ib.7.12(p.55.17; 508A); ib.7.14(p.60.6; 517A); d. other virtues οὐ γὰρ ἡ σκέπη μόνη τῆς παντευχίας καὶ ἡ τῶν ἁμαρτημάτων ἀποχὴ ἱκανὴ πρὸς τελείωσιν, εἰ μὴ προσλάβοι τὸ ἔργον τῆς δικαιοσύνης, τὴν εἰς εὐποιΐαν ἐνέργειαν ib.6.12(p.484.2; 324C); ἀφορμὴν εἰς τ. τὴν διάπρασιν τῶν ὑπαρχόντων Bas.ep.223.2(3.337C; M.32.824B); τὴν τοῦ νέου τ. ἐν τῷ τὰ ὄντα δοῦναι πτωχοῖς ὁρισθεῖσαν Gr.Naz.or.14.39(M.35.909A); ἡ τ. τῆς ἀρετῆς χρήζει τῆς ταπεινώσεως Dor.doct.14.2(M.88.1776C); e. co-operation and union with God ἡ ἡμετέρα τ. οὐχὶ μηδὲν ἡμῶν πραξάντων γίνεται, οὐ μὴν ἀφ' ἡμῶν ἀπαρτίζεται, ἀλλὰ θεὸς τὸ πολὺ ταύτης ἐνεργεῖ Or.princ.3.1.19(18; p.232.11; M.11.292A); ἡ τῆς ἑνοειδοῦς τ. ἔνθεος μέθεξις, αὐτοῦ τοῦ ἑνὸς ὡς ἐφικτόν Dion.Ar.e.h.1.3(M.3.376A); f. monastic life ἡ τῶν μοναχῶν...διακόσμησις...εἰς τελειοτάτην ἀναγομένη τ. ib.6.1.3(532D); g. philosophy a preparation for it, designed by God for Greeks, Clem.str.6.14(p.487.11; M.9.333A); ib.6.17(p.510.23; 384C); ib.7.2(p.9.18; 413C); 3. guides towards it: members of eccl. hierarchy, Dion.Ar.e.h.5.1.3(M.3.504B); ib.5.1.4(505A); angelic agencies πρὸς τὴν...τ. ἡγεμόνας, τὰς περὶ θεοῦ πρωτίστας οὐσίας ib.5.1.2(501A); cf. ib.6.3.5(536C); 4. degrees of perfection ἡ ἀποχὴ τῶν κακῶν, ἥν τινες τ. ἡγοῦνται, καὶ ἔστιν ἁπλῶς τοῦ κοινοῦ πιστοῦ.. ἡ τ. αὕτη· τοῦ δὲ γνωστικοῦ μετὰ τὴν ἄλλοις νομιζομένην τ. ἡ δικαιοσύνη εἰς ἐνέργειαν εὐποιΐας προβαίνει· καὶ ὅτῳ δὴ ἡ ἐπίτασις τῆς δικαιοσύνης εἰς ἀγαθοποιΐαν ἐπιδέδωκεν, τούτῳ ἡ τ. ἐν ἀμεταβόλῳ ἕξει εὐποιΐας καθ' ὁμοίωσιν τοῦ θεοῦ διαμένει Clem.str.6.7(p.462.10ff.; M.9.281B,C); ib.6.12(p.483.20; 324B); τὰ δὲ [sc. commandments] προκοπὴν ἐμποιοῦντα πρὸς τελείωσιν ἄγουσαν τῆς πρὸς θεὸν εὐαρεστήσεως †Bas.bapt.2.4.2(2.656C; M.31.1589A); as lost stage on threefold way αἱ μὲν ἅγιαι τελεταὶ *κάθαρσίς εἰσι καὶ φωτισμὸς καὶ τ.* Dion.Ar.*e.h.*6.3.5(M.3.536D); angelic *πρόοδον ἀμυδρουμένης εἰς δευτέρωσιν τελειώσεως* id.*c.h.*8.2(M.3.240C); Gnost. *ἀρχὴ τελειώσεως γνῶσις ἀ(νθρώπου, θεοῦ δὲ) γνῶσις ἀπηρτισμένη τ.* Hipp.*haer.*5.6(p.78.14f.; M.16.3126B) = *ib.*5.8(p.96.7f.; 3150B); **5.** of gospel as perfection of Law, ref. 1Cor.13:11 *ἡ δὲ ἐν Χριστῷ νηπιότης τ. ἐστιν, ὡς πρὸς τὸν νόμον* Clem.*paed.*1.6(p.110.25; M.8.292A); *νομικοῦ μὲν τ. γνωστικὴ εὐαγγελίου πρόσληψις, ἵνα γένηται ὁ κατὰ νόμον τέλειος* id.*str.*4.21(p.305.25; M.8.1340C); **6.** ref. Adam *Ἀδὰμ...ἐν τῷ γίνεσθαι τὴν τ. ἐλάμβανεν καὶ δι' ὑπακοῆς ἐδικαιοῦτο* Clem.*str.*4.23(p.315.9; M.8.1360B); but this perfection only a tendency, frustrated by Fall *ἐπειδὴ δὲ οὐ συνέφερεν αὐτῷ πρὸ τῆς τ. γνῶναι τὴν φύσιν ἑαυτοῦ, ἀπηγόρευσεν αὐτῷ μὴ γεύσασθαι τοῦ ξύλου τῆς γνώσεως...οὐκ ἐβούλετο δὲ αὐτὸν ὁ θεὸς πρὸ τῆς τ. γνῶναι τὴν οἰκείαν φύσιν, ἵνα μή...τῆς σωματικῆς ἐπιμεληθῇ χρείας, καταλιπὼν τὴν τῆς ψυχῆς πρόνοιαν...παρακούσας δὲ καὶ γνοὺς ἑαυτόν, τῆς μὲν τ. ἐξέπεσε, τῆς δὲ σωματικῆς χρείας ἐγένετο* Nemes.*nat.hom.*1(M.40.516A,B); cf. *τὸ μὲν κατ' εἰκόνα εὐθέως κατὰ τὴν γένεσιν εἰληφέναι τὸν ἄνθρωπον, τὸ καθ' ὁμοίωσιν δὲ ὕστερον κατὰ τὴν τ. μέλλειν ἀπολαμβάνειν ἐκδέχονται* Clem.*str.*2.22(p.185.27; 1080C); **7.** Christ and perfection *Χριστῷ μὲν ἡ τροφὴ τῆς πατρικῆς βουλῆς ἡ τ. ἦν* Clem.*paed.*1.6(p.117.19; M.8.304C); id.*str.*2.7(p.131.16; M.8.969B); of his glory, *Const.App.*2.26.2; *τὸν ἄνωθεν ἥκοντα ἄνω ἀνιέναι ἐν τ. θεότητος* Epiph.*haer.*58.8(p.354.8; M.41.1008A); *τὴν πασῶν ἱεραρχιῶν ἀρχήν τε καὶ τ., Ἰησοῦν* Dion.Ar.*e.h.*1.2(M.3.373B); denied by Arians *εὑρεῖν δυνηθέντες, πόσον ἐνδεῖ τῷ μεγέθει τοῦ μονογενοῦς θεοῦ πρὸς τὴν τ.* Gr.Nyss.*Eun.*1(1 p.99.13; M.45.332D); **8.** ref. H. Ghost as author of perfection *ὁ...ἁγιασμὸς ἔξωθεν ὢν τῆς οὐσίας, τὴν τ. αὐτοῖς ἐπάγει διὰ τῆς κοινωνίας τοῦ πνεύματος* Bas.*Spir.*38(3.31E; M.32.136B); *τ. διὰ τοῦ πνεύματος* id. *Eun.*3.5(1.276D; M.29.665B).

B. sacramental uses; **1.** baptismal; **a.** usu. *initiation εἰς ὄνομα πατρὸς καὶ υἱοῦ δίδοται ἡ τ.* Ath.*Ar.*2.42(M.26.236C); *ἡ τοῦ βαπτίσματος τ.* *ib.*(237B); *τὸ τῆς καθάρσεως καὶ τ. ... ἀγαθόν* Gr.Naz.*or.*8.20(M.35.812C); Epiph.*exp.fid.*16(p.516.31; M.42.812D); **b.** ref. baptismal chrismation as consummation of baptism *ἢ τῆς κατηχήσεως τὸ χρῖσμα λαβεῖν, ἤτοι τὸ τῆς τ. ἐπὶ τῷ ἁγίῳ βαπτίσματι* Cyr.*Jo.*7(4.683E); *ἡ γὰρ ἱερὰ τῆς θεογενεσίας τ. ἑνοῖ τὰ τελεσθέντα τῷ θεαρχικῷ πνεύματι* Dion.Ar.*e.h.*2.8(M.3.404C); **c.** ref. baptism of martyrdom *ἐνήλατο τῷ ὕδατι τούτῳ, τῆς διὰ τοῦ θανάτου λοιπὸν ἐρῶσα τ.* Bas.Sel. *v.Thecl.*1(M.85.536B); **d.** perfecting of man by baptism *τῇ δι' ὕδατος ἀναγεννήσει...δι' ἧς ὁμολογοῦμεν θεῷ τὴν τοῦ κατὰ Χριστὸν ἀνθρώπου μόρφωσιν καὶ τ.* Gr.Naz.*or.*18.13(M.35.1001A); **2.** eucharistic; **a.** *consecration* of elements, as consummation of rite *μέχρι τῆς τ. τοῦ φρικτοῦ μυστηρίου* Nil.*epp.*2.294(M.79.345D); *ἔλθωμεν ἐπὶ τὴν τ. τῶν μυστηρίων· οὗτος ὁ ἄρτος καὶ τοῦτο τὸ ποτήριον, ὅσον οὔπω εὐχαὶ ...γεγόνασι, ψιλά εἰσιν· ἐπὰν δὲ αἱ μεγάλαι εὐχαὶ...ἀναπεμφθῶσι, καταβαίνει ὁ λόγος εἰς τὸν ἄρτον καὶ τὸ ποτήριον, καὶ γίνεται αὐτοῦ σῶμα* Eutych.*pasch.*8(M.86.2401B); **b.** eucharist as consummation of other sacraments *ταῖς τῶν ἄλλων ἱεραρχικῶν συμβόλων μεθέξεσιν, ἡ τ. ἐκ τῶν ταύτης* [sc. *συνάξεως*] *θεαρχικῶν καὶ τελειωτικῶν ἐστι δωρεῶν* Dion.Ar.*e.h.*3.1(M.3.424D); *τῆς τοῦ ἁγιασμοῦ τ.* CNic.(787) *refut.*(H.4.369D); **3.** of consecration of persons to service of God: OT priests, Dion.Ar.*e.h.*5.3.5(512B); apostles, *ib.*(512D); priests of Church, Cyr.*ador.*12(1.411A); Dion.Ar.*e.h.*5.2(509A); bishops, Eustrat.*v.Eutych.*25(M.86.2304A); of religious profession *μυστήριον μοναχικῆς τ.* Dion.Ar.*e.h.*6.2 tit.(533A); **4.** of consecration of objects: holy oils, *ib.*4.3.4(477C); *ib.*4.3.10(484B); altar, *ib.*4.3.12(484D).

C. of death as consummation of life; **1.** as synonym of martyrdom *τ. τὸ μαρτύριον καλοῦμεν οὐχ ὅτι τέλος τοῦ βίου ὁ ἄνθρωπος ἔλαβεν ὡς οἱ λοιποί, ἀλλ' ὅτι τέλειον ἔργον ἀγάπης ἐνεδείξατο* Clem.*str.*4.4(p.255.1; M.8.1228B); *οὕτως ἔσται ἡ τ. μου* *A.Phil.*140(p.73.12); *A.Thom.*A 167(p.282.3); as title *ἡ τ. Θωμᾶ* *A.Thom.(consumm.)* tit.(p.289.1); Eus.*h.e.*6.2.15(M.20.525C); id.*m.P.*13(p.949.6; M.20.1517A); Epiph.*haer.*42.12(p.172.1; M.41.787B); ‡Jo.D.*Artem.*39(M.96.1288C); **2.** of death of other saints, Eustrat.*v.Eutych.*84(M.86.2372A); †Jo.D.*B.J.*40(M.96.1237B).

D. of eschatol. *consummation οἱ καθαροὶ δὲ τῇ καρδίᾳ τὸν θεὸν ὄψονται, ἐπὰν εἰς τὴν ἐσχάτην ἀφίκωνται τ.* Clem.*str.*5.1(p.330.16; M.9.17B); ref. union of faithful in heaven *κατὰ δὲ τελείωσιν τῆς εἰς ἄκρον ἀρετῆς* Eus.*e.th.*3.18(p.179.30; M.24.1041C); *τὸ πεποιημένον συναριθμεῖται τῷ ποιήσαντι εἰς τὴν τῶν πάντων τ.* Ath.*Ar.*2.41(M.26.233B); of angels *τ. δὲ ἀγγέλων, ἁγιασμός, καὶ ἡ ἐν τούτῳ διαμονή* Bas.*Spir.*38(3.31E; M.32.136B).

E. of sabbath as consummation of Creation *τ. κόσμου* *Const.App.*7.36.5.

τελειωτής, ὁ, *accomplisher, finisher,* of God *ὁ τῶν τελουμένων τ.* ‡Meth.*Sym.et Ann.*5(M.18.360B).

τελειωτικός, 1. *consummating, perfecting τὴν τ. ἀγάπην* Clem.*str.*6.15(p.492.22; M.9.344C); *τὸ ξύλον, τὸ ὕδωρ, τὰ τ. τῶν μαρτύρων* Bas.*ep.*164.2(3.255C; M.32.637A); ref. Christian baptism opp. that of John *ἐκεῖνο εἰσαγωγικόν,...τοῦτο τ.* id.*hom.*13.1(2.114B; M.31.425A); *τὸ...θεοπρεπὲς κάλλος...ἐστι...τ. ἐν τελετῇ θειοτάτῃ* Dion.Ar.*c.h.*3.1(M.3.164D); of First Cause *ἀρχηγικὴ καὶ τ. καὶ συνεκτικὴ* id.*d.n.*1.7(M.3.596A); *ἡ τοῦ νοητοῦ φωτὸς παρουσία...ἐστὶ...τ. καὶ ἔτι ἐπιστρεπτικὴ πρὸς τὸ ὄντως ὄν* *ib.*4.6(701B); *τῆς τῶν ἐποπτευθέντων ἱερῶν τ. ἐπιστήμης* id.*c.h.*3.3(165D); *ὁ...θεῖος ἀνὴρ...ὁ πρὸς τὸ τοῦ...θεοειδοῦς ἄκρον ἐν...τ. θεώσεσιν ἀνηγμένος* id.*e.h.*3.3.7(M.3.433C); **2.** partic., *perfecting through consecration* or *sanctification τὴν ἱερατικὴν διακόσμησιν...εἰς καθαρτικὴν καὶ φωτιστικὴν καὶ τ. εὐταξίαν διαιρουμένην* *ib.*5.1.3(504C); *ἡ...τάξις τῶν μοναχῶν...ταῖς τῶν ἱεραρχῶν τ. δυνάμεσιν ἐγχειριζομένη* *ib.*6.1.3(532D); *ὁ τ. ἀσπασμός* [i.e. in ordination] *ib.*5.3.1(509C); *ἡ...τοῦ μύρου τ. χρῖσις* [sc. in post-baptismal chrismation] *εὐώδη ποιεῖ τὸν τετελεσμένον* *ib.*2.3.8(404C); cf.*ib.*4.3.1(473B); of eucharist, *ib.*3.1(424D); *τῶν τ. μυστηρίων* *ib.*; *ἡ ἱεραρχικὴ τάξις ἡ τῆς τ. δυνάμεως ἀναπεπλησμένη* *ib.*5.1.6(505C); cf. *ib.*4.3.3(476C); *ἡ τ. τῆς πάσης ἱερατείας δύναμις* *ib.*5.3.7(513C); *ταῖς τῶν λειτουργῶν τ. ἐπικλήσεσιν* *ib.*5.2(509B).

τελειωτικῶς, *so as to consecrate,* Dion.Ar.*e.h.*3.3.3(M.3.429A).

τελέσιος, *completely trained, ready for,* Sophr.H.*v.Anast.*(M.92.1696C).

τελεσιουργ-έω, 1. *bring* their young *to perfection*; of viviparous animals; met. *οὐκ ᾠοτοκοῦσι* [sc. *αἱ νυκτερίδες*]...*ἀλλ' εὐθὺς ζῷα τίκτουσι. τοιοῦτοι...καὶ οἱ δαίμονες, εὐθὺς καὶ σὺν πολλῷ τῷ τάχει ~οῦντες τὴν πονηρίαν* †Bas.*Is.*97(1.447C; M.30.271B); **2.** *fulfil,* ref. prophecies and types, Meth.*symp.*4.5(p.51.15; M.18.93C); *ἐπεὶ...προώριστο ἐκ τῆς ὀφιώδους τῶν Ἰουδαίων φυλῆς τὸν κύριον ἀνατεταλκέναι...καὶ διὰ θανάτου...ζωῆς αἰωνίου γενέσθαι παρεκτικόν..., ἡ ἐπὶ τοῦ ξύλου ἀνάρτησις ὄφεως τοῦ χαλκοῦ τελεσιουργηθῆναι προώρισται* Germ.CP *or.*1(M.98.233A); **3.** *accomplish ἔχρῃζε κατ' εἰκόνα θεοῦ γεγονώς, καὶ τὸ καθ' ὁμοίωσιν ἀπολαβεῖν, ὅπερ τελεσιουργῆσαι καταπεμφθεὶς ὁ λόγος εἰς τὸν κόσμον, τὴν ἡμετέραν μορφὴν...ἀνέλαβε* Meth.*symp.*1.4(p.12.23; M.18.44D); *οὐ μετεδόθη τῷ σώματι εἰς τὸ τελεσιουργηθῆναι ἡ ἐπιθυμία* id.*lepr.*6(p.459.3); *τίς...πιστεύων εἶναι πανταχοῦ τὸν θεὸν...ἢ τὴν ἔννοιαν τὴν πονηρὰν παραδέχεται ἢ ~εῖ τὸ κακόν;* †Bas.*Is.*46(1.416A; M.30.208A) = Cyr.*Ps.*72:27(M.69.1185C); *τὰ παράδοξα τοῦ θεοῦ σημεῖα ἐτελεσιουργεῖτο σὺν τῷ πνεύματι* Didym.(‡Bas.)*Eun.*5(1.298D; M.29.716C); *ἀπάθειαν ἄσκησον...ἐγχωρεῖ γὰρ τοῦτο καὶ ἐν μέσῳ τοῦ κόσμου τελεσιουργηθῆναι* Nil.*epp.*2.182(M.79.296A); *πρῶτον τελεσιούργησον πᾶσαν ἀγαθὴν πρᾶξιν καὶ...τότε...παίδευε τοὺς ἄλλους* *ib.*3.156(457C); *τῆς θειοτάτης εὐχαριστίας...~ούσης...τὴν πρὸς θεὸν κοινωνίαν* Dion.Ar.*e.h.*3.1(M.3.425A); *τῆς συνάξεως...καὶ τῆς τοῦ μύρου τελετῆς τελειωτικῆς τῶν θεουργιῶν γνώσεως...δι' ἧς...ἡ πρὸς τὴν θεαρχίαν...ἀναγωγὴ καὶ...κοινωνία ~εῖται* *ib.*5.1.3(504C); *τῆς διὰ...θανάτου τοῦ Χριστοῦ ~ουμένης αὐτοῦ οἰκονομίας* ‡Bas.*h.myst.*49(p.391.3); *ἡ πόλις τοῦ μεγάλου βασιλέως, ἐν ᾗ τῆς σωτηρίας ἡμῶν ἐτελεσιουργήθη μυστήρια* ‡Meth.*Sym.et Ann.*13(M.18.380A); **4.** *complete, bring to perfection τὰ πάντα ἐξ ἀκοσμίας κοσμῶν* [sc. the Word], *αὔξων τε καὶ ~ῶν* Eus.*d.e.*4.13(p.171.12; M.22.285B); *ὅροι φύσεως...δι' ὧν τόδε τὸ πᾶν μηχάνημά τε καὶ ἀρχιτεκτόνημα τοῦ παντὸς κόσμου ~εῖται* id.*Hierocl.*6(515A; M.22.805A); *μιᾶς κοσμοποιΐας διὰ πατρὸς καὶ υἱοῦ ~ουμένης* ‡Ath.*sem.*3(M.28.148A); *κἂν πᾶς μὲν ὁ ἐκκλησιαστικὸς κανὼν ἐπιτεθείη, ἡ μυστικὴ δὲ...εὐχαριστία καὶ κοινωνία τοῦ σώματος τοῦ Χριστοῦ μὴ γένηται, οὔτε ὁ ἐκκλησιαστικὸς ἐτελεσιουργήθη θεσμὸς καὶ ἐλλειπὴς ἐστιν ἡ λατρεία τοῦ μυστηρίου* Mac. Aeg.*carit.*29(M.34.932C); *ἡ τῆς πάντων ἐπέκεινα θεότητος ἀγαθότης...φωτίζει τὰ δυνάμενα πάντα καὶ δημιουργεῖ καὶ...~εῖ* Dion.Ar.*d.n.*4.4(M.3.697C); *χορηγίαν, καθ' ἣν τὰ τέλεια πάντα ~εῖ καὶ τῆς οἰκείας ἀποπληροῖ τελειότητος* *ib.*13.1(977C); *ἡ θεία μακαριότης...φωτίζουσα καὶ ~οῦσα* id.*c.h.*3.2(M.3.165C); *τάξις ἱεραρχίας ἐστὶ...τοὺς μὲν τελεῖσθαι, τοὺς δὲ ~εῖν* *ib.*(165B); *ib.*7.3(209C); *ib.*8.1(240B); *τῇ τοῦ πατρὸς εὐδοκίᾳ καὶ ὁ υἱὸς τὰ πάντα ἐποίησε καὶ τὸ πνεῦμα τὸ ἅγιον ἐτελεσιούργησεν* Jo.V H.*icon.*4(M.96.1353A); **5.** *perform a sacred rite Μωσῆς...τὴν ἱερατικὴν τελείωσιν ἱεραρχικῶς ἐτελεσιούργησεν* Dion. Ar.*e.h.*5.3.5(M.3.512C); *τὸν...ἱεράρχην...χρὴ...ὑπὸ θεῷ κινοῦντι ταύτας* [sc. sacraments] *ἱεραρχικῶς καὶ οὐρανίως ~εῖν* *ib.*(513A); *ὁ...τύπος τῆς παραδόσεως τῶν μυστηρίων παρὰ πάντων ἀπαραλλάκτως ὁ αὐτὸς ἐτελεσιουργεῖτο, καθὼς καὶ ὁ κύριος...τοῦτο παρέδωκε* ‡Sophr.H. *liturg.*1(M.87.3981C); **6.** *consecrate,* Dion.Ar.*e.h.*5.1(M.3.508C); *ib.*6.1(532B).

τελεσιουργία, ἡ, 1. *completion of work,* Const.ap.Eus.*v.C.*4.35(p.130.33; M.20.1184A); Ath.*apol.Const.*18(M.25.617D); *ἐκκλησιάζων ἐπὶ τῇ τ. τῆς μεγάλης ἐκκλησίας* Soz.*h.e.*4.26.1(M.67.1197B); **2.** *realization, fulfilment ἡ τῆς κακίας τ. θάνατον ἀπεργάζεται* Chrys.*fr.Job*

15:34(M.64.617C); ἡ οὖν τ. τοῦ πνεύματος ἐν τῷ θελήματι τοῦ ἀνθρώπου κεῖται Mac.Aeg.*hom*.38.10(M.34.757A); of fulfilment of OT in NT, Dion.Ar.*e.h*.3.3.5(M.3.432B); **3.** *completion, perfection* μετὰ τὴν τῶν πάντων τ. Ath.*Ar*.2.57(M.26.269A); ὁ τὸ πνεῦμα περιαιρῶν, τὴν τ. τῶν ποιουμένων ἀπέκοψεν Didym.(‡Bas.)*Eun*.5(1.307B; M.29.736D); Dion.Ar.*c.h*.7.3(M.3.209C); id.*e.h*.5.1.7(M.3.508D); **4.** *consecration*, *ib*.5.3.5(512C); *ib*.5.3.6(513B); **5.** *performance of sacramental rite* ἔστι ταύτης [sc. eucharist] ὁμοταγὴς ἑτέρα τ. [sc. μύρου τελετή] *ib*.4.1(472D); *ib*.4.2(473A); τῷ...μύρῳ χρῆται πρὸς παντὸς ἱεροῦ τελεσιουργίαν *ib*.4.3.10(484A).

***τελεσιουργικός**, *perfecting* τῶν ἱερῶν ἡ...ἐπιστήμη...ἐνδίδωσι... αὐτοῖς [sc. catechumens]...τὴν πρὸς τὰ φωτοειδῆ καὶ τ. κοινωνίαν Dion.Ar.*e.h*.3.3.6(M.3.433A); τὸ πνεῦμα τὸ ἅγιον τ. τῆς τῶν πάντων ποιήσεως Jo.D.*f.o*.1.12(M.94.849A).

***τελεσιουργικῶς**, *perfectly, in a manner bringing perfection* οἱ θεολόγοι...ἐπισκοποῦσι...τὰ μὲν ἀνθρωπικῶς καὶ μέσως, τὰ δὲ ὑπερκοσμίως καὶ τ. Dion.Ar.*ep*.9.2(M.3.1108B).

τελεσιουργός, 1. *perfecting* αἱ τ. τῆς θεαρχικῆς δυνάμεως εἰκόνες ἀποτελοῦσαι πάντα τὰ...σύμβολα Dion.Ar.*e.h*.5.1(M.3.505B); ἡ...τῶν ἱεραρχῶν τάξις τελειωτικὴ καὶ τ. *ib*.(508C); of divine wisdom, id.*ep*.9.4(M.3.1112B); of Christ ὁ...τ. πάσης κτίσεως *Chron.Pasch*.p.199(M.92.489B); of regeneration through chrismation, Dion.Ar.*e.h*.4.3.10(M.3.484A); of ἐπιφοίτησις of H. Ghost in consecration of chrism, *ib*.2.3.8(404C); masc. as subst., of celestial hierarchy, id.*c.h*.3.3(M.3.168A); of eccl. hierarchy, id.*e.h*.1.1(372B); of faithful opp. catechumens, *ib*.3.3.6(432C); **2.** neut. as subst., *power of perfecting*, id.*d.n*.4.2(M.3.696B); **3.** *consecrating*, Dion.Ar.*e.h*.5.1.4(M.3.505A); *ib*.(505C); **4.** neut. plur. as subst., *sacred rites*, *ib*.5.1.5(505C).

τέλεσμα, τό, 1. *money paid, payment*; of rent, Chrys.*hom.61.3 in Mt*.(7.614A); id.*hom.17.3 in 2Cor*.(10.562A); of eccl. dues, id. *hom.9.4 in Phil*.(11.269C); of taxes, fig. ἕνα [sc. κύριον]...οἱ πάντες κεκτήμεθα τῇ τῶν τ. καταθήκῃ πρὸς δουλείαν καταγραφόμενοι Cyr.*Jo*.2.5(4.189A); **2.** sacred *rite*; of Eleusinian mysteries, Clem.*prot*.2(p.16.21; M.8.88A); of Christ's offering as mediator, Gr.Naz.*carm*.2.1.1.130(M.37.979A); of miracles performed by demons, Cyr.*Soph*.38(3.615E); through magic, Nil.*epp*.2.148(M.79.269A); by Apollonius of Tyana εἰ θεός ἐστι δημιουργὸς...τῆς κτίσεως, πῶς τὰ Ἀπολλωνίου τ. ἐν τοῖς μέρεσιν τῆς κτίσεως δύνανται; ‡Just.*qu.et resp*.24(M.6.1269C); ὁ ...Ἀπολλώνιος...κατὰ...τὴν ἐπιστήμην τὰ τ. ἐποιεῖτο, οὐ κατὰ τὴν θείαν αὐθεντίαν *ib*.(1272A); ἔδει...αὐτὸν...λόγῳ μόνῳ ποιεῖν...καὶ μὴ τ. τισιν ἐπιτρέπειν τὰ παρ' αὐτοῦ πραττόμενα Anast.S.*qu.et resp*.20(M.97.525C); **3.** *talisman*, against scorpions, Jo.Mal.*chron*.10 p.264(M.97.401A); mosquitoes, *ib*.(401B); floods, *ib*.p.233(360B).

τελεστήριον, τό, 1. *place of initiation* (pagan), Clem.*prot*.1(p.3.27; M.8.53A); **2.** *sacred rite, sacrament* ἀμύητοι [sc. catechumens] παντὸς ἱεραρχικοῦ τ. Dion.Ar.*e.h*.3.3.6(M.3.432D); of eucharist, *ib*.4.3.3(476C).

τελεστής (τελετής), ὁ, *one who initiates into mysteries*; pagan, Or.*Cels*.7.48(p.263.10; M.11.1588C); *ib*.(p.263.17; M.l.c.); *magician*, Jo.Mal.*chron*.10 p.233(M.97.360B); Christian; of a priest, Proc.G.*Cant*.8:1(M.87.1777A); τοῖς τῶν ἱερῶν τελεταῖς [l. τελεσταῖς] Dion.Ar.*c.h*.3.2(M.3.165A); met. Βασιλειδιανοί, τῆς αὐτῆς αἰσχρουργείας τ. Epiph.*anac*.24(p.235.5; M.41.281B); cf.Jo.D.*haer*.24(M.94.632A).

τελεστικός, 1. *of* or *belonging to the mysteries* αἱ...τοῖς ἄνθεσιν ἐοικυῖαι ἐσθῆτες βακχικοῖς καὶ τ. καταλειπτέαι λήροις Clem.*paed*.2.10(p.222.11; M.8.525C); **2.** *mystical* διττὴν εἶναι τὴν τῶν θεολόγων παράδοσιν...τὴν μὲν συμβολικήν καὶ τ., τὴν δὲ φιλόσοφον καὶ ἀποδεικτικήν Dion.Ar.*ep*.9.1(M.3.1105D); **3.** *consecrating* ὁ λειτουργὸς...τελειούμενος...ταῖς τῶν λειτουργῶν τ. ἐπικλήσεσιν id.*e.h*.5.2(M.3.509B); τὰς δὲ τ. ἐπικλήσεις οὐ θεμιτὸν ἐν γραφαῖς ἀφερμηνεύειν *ib*.7.3.10(565C); τὰ τῆς ὅλης ἱεραρχίας τελεστικώτατα *ib*.5.3.7(516A); **4.** *perfecting* τελεσιουργούς, ὡς ἐπιστημονικοὺς τῆς τ. μεταδόσεως τελεῖν τοὺς τελουμένους id.*c.h*.3.3(M.3.168A); *ib*.7.2(208A); τ. ... δυνάμεις οἱ πρῶτοι νόες ὀνομάζονται *ib*.8.2(240C); οἱ...λειτουργοὶ καθαρτικὴ τάξις, οἱ δὲ ἱερεῖς φωτιστική, τ. δὲ οἱ θεοειδεῖς ἱεράρχαι id.*e.h*.6.3.5(536D); ὁ ἱεράρχης ἐπὶ τὴν ἱερωτάτην εὐχαριστίαν καλεῖ τὸν τετελεσμένον καὶ τῆς τῶν τ. μυστηρίων αὐτῷ μεταδίδωσι κοινωνίας *ib*.2.3.8(404D); τ. αὐτοῖς [sc. monks] ἐδωρήσατο χάριν ἡ ἱερὰ θεσμοθεσία *ib*.6.1.3(533A).

τελεσφορ-έω, *bring to perfection* or *full growth*; of God's action in blessing fruits of the earth, cf.Hipp.*trad.ap*.28.3; *Euchol*.p.522; ἀδύνατον ἀνθρώπου τελεσφορηθῆναι γονήν, μὴ μορφώσαντος αὐτὴν καὶ ἐμψυχώσαντος τοῦ κυρίου Meth.*symp*.2.3(p.19.3; M.18.52B); ref. creation of man by angels (acc. Saturninus) γενομένου...τοῦ ἀνθρώπου διὰ τὸ αὐτῶν ἀδρανὲς μὴ δύνασθαι αὐτὸν τελεσφορῆσαι, κεῖσθαι δὲ...χαμαὶ...ἕως ἡ ἄνω δύναμις...ἀπέστειλε σπινθῆρα Epiph.*haer*.23.1(p.249.7; M.41.300B); ref. spiritual development δὸς αὐτοῖς, ἵνα...ἀνθήσουσιν ἐν τῇ σῇ διακονίᾳ καὶ τελεσφορήσουσιν ἐν τῷ πατρί σου *A.Thom*.A 25(p.141.9); μήτρας δίκην ἐν τῷ δοχείῳ τῆς ψυχῆς τὸ θέλημα ~ήσαντες ἀλώβητον τοῦ λόγου Meth.*symp*.3.8(p.37.15; M.18.76A); ref. catechumens τῶν ἱερῶν ἡ...ἐπιστήμη πρῶτα μὲν αὐτοὺς τῇ...τῶν...λογίων εἰσαγωγικῇ τροφῇ μαιεύεται, ~ήσασα δὲ τὴν πρὸς θεογενεσίαν αὐτῶν ὑπόστασιν, ἐνδίδωσι...αὐτοῖς...τὴν πρὸς τὰ φωτοειδῆ...κοινωνίαν Dion.Ar.*e.h*.3.3.6(M.3.433A); of growth of evil in soul, *Hom.Clem*.4.18; Gr.Nyss.*v.Mos*.(M.44.353A).

τελεσφόρησις, ἡ, *perfection, full growth* θεωρῆσαι ἄξιον, εἰ καματηρά ἐστιν ἡ τῶν ἀγγέλων πρὸς τὸ ἐνσπείρεσθαι ψυχὰς σώμασιν λειτουργία...ἐν καιρῷ τῷ τεταγμένῳ ἀρχομένων τε τὴν περὶ ἑκάστου ποιεῖν οἰκονομίαν καὶ εἰς τ. προαγόντων τὸν προπεπλασμένον Or.*Jo*.13.50(49; p.277.25; M.14.489A); ὁ θεὸς...ποικίλαι τοὺς τρόπους ἀξιώσας πρὸς τελεσφόρησιν ὧν τοῖς οὖσιν οἰκείων κατέσπειρεν ἀγαθῶν μέχρι τῆς πάντων ἀποπερατώσεως τῶν αἰώνων Max.*ambig*.(M.91.1357B).

τελετάρχης, ὁ, *author of consecration*; of God, Dion.Ar.*e.h*.5.3.2(M.3.509D); *ib*.5.3.5(512C); *ib*.7.3.7(564A); of Christ, *ib*.5.3.5(512C).

***τελεταρχία, ἡ,** *source* or *principle of consecration*, of God ἕνεκα τῆς ἡμῶν...θεώσεως ἡ φιλάνθρωπος τ. ... ταῖς αἰσθηταῖς εἰκόσι τοὺς ὑπερουρανίους ἀνεγράψατο νόας Dion.Ar.*c.h*.1.3(M.3.124A); *ib*.3.2(165A); *ib*.6.1(200C); *ib*.7.3(209C); id.*d.n*.1.3(M.3.589C).

τελεταρχικός, 1. *being the source of perfection* τὸ...θεοπρεπὲς κάλλος...ὡς τ., ἀμιγὲς μέν ἐστι...πάσης ἀνομοιότητος Dion.Ar.*c.h*.3.1(M.3.164D); *ib*.4.1(177C); *ib*.8.2(240C); τ. ἤγουν τελειοποιοῦν Max.*schol.c.h*.3.1(M.4.49A); **2.** *being the source* or *principle of consecration*, Dion.Ar.*e.h*.5.3.3(M.3.512A); *ib*.5.3.5(512C); *ib*.5.3.7(513C); *ib*.7.3.7(564B).

***τελετάρχις, 1.** *making perfect* ἡ...τοῦ Ἰησοῦ θεότης...τελεία... ἐστιν ἐν τοῖς ἀτελέσιν ὡς τ. Dion.Ar.*d.n*.2.10(M.3.648C); id.*e.h*.7.3.7(M.3.564C); **2.** *consecrating* ἡ τ. ἱεροθεσία id.*c.h*.1.3(M.3.121C).

τελετή, ἡ, I. *rite*, esp. of initiation in mysteries and of sacramental rites;

A. pagan; **1.** in gen. ἄρτος καὶ ποτήριον ὕδατος τίθεται ἐν ταῖς τοῦ μυουμένου τ. μετ' ἐπιλόγων τινῶν [Mithraic] Just.*1apol*.66.4(M.6.429A); τελετὰς καὶ μυστήρια ἄγουσι Athenag.*leg*.1.1(M.6.892A); ἀφραίνοντες ἐκτόπως τελετῇ βακχικῇ Clem.*prot*.1(p.4.5; M.8.53B); Αἰγύπτιοι...πᾶσι τοῖς ἄλλοις ἀνθρώποις...τελετὰς καὶ ὄργια θεῶν... κατηγγελκότες, ἱερὰ καὶ...ἀνεξαγόρευτα τοῖς μὴ τετελεσμένοις τὰ Ἴσιδος ἔχουσι μυστήρια Hipp.*haer*.5.7(p.84.1; M.16.3134B); Orphic, *ib*.5.20(p.121.22; 3186B); Eleusinian, *ib*.(p.121.27; 3186C); of rite concerned with Nile, ‡Pall.*h.mon*.8.25(p.40.4; M.34.1140B); of Persian rites, *Chron.Pasch*.p.40(M.92.156A); **2.** Christian attitude ὑπόληψις κενὴ τὰ μυστήρια καὶ τοῦ δράκοντος ἀπάτη..., τὰς ἀμυήτους ὄντως μυήσεις καὶ τὰς ἀνοργιάστους τ. εὐσεβείᾳ νόθῳ προστρεπομένων Clem.*prot*.2(p.17.3; M.8.88A); τὸ τῆς ἀτελέστου τ. πέρας...ἀλλότριον τῆς Χριστιανῶν...εὐσεβείας Or.*Cels*.6.33(p.103.9; M.11.1348B); comparison with Christian rites rejected ἐπαγγέλλεται ὁ Κέλσος τ. τινα Χριστιανῶν τελετῇ...Περσῶν συνεξετάσαι *ib*.6.24(p.94.15; 1328B); μετὰ τῶν ἀτελέστων τ. καὶ τῶν καλουσῶν δαίμονας μαγγανειῶν *ib*.5.38(p.42.29; 1241A); *ib*.3.34(p.231.3; 964B); their secrecy, Clem.*prot*.2(p.11.13; 72A); Eus.*v.C*.4.25(p.126.16; M.20.1172B); symbolism παρ' οἷς [sc. Πέρσαις] εἰσὶ τελεταί, πρεσβευόμεναι μὲν λογικῶς ὑπὸ τῶν... λογίων, συμβολικῶς δὲ γινόμεναι ὑπὸ τῶν...πολλῶν καὶ ἐπιπολαιοτέρων Or.*Cels*.1.12(p.65.12; 677C); acc. philosophers οὐκ ἄλλως...αὐτὸν τὸν ἀόρατον δύνασθαι γνῶναι ἢ διὰ...ἀγαλμάτων καὶ τ. Ath.*gent*.19(M.25.40C).

B. Gnost. Χριστιανοὺς ἑαυτοὺς λέγουσιν...καὶ ἀνόμοις καὶ ἀθέοις τ. κοινωνοῦσι Just.*dial*.35.6(M.6.552B); Naassene μόνῳ τῷ νάας ἀνακεῖσθαι πᾶν ἱερὸν καὶ πᾶσαν τ. καὶ πᾶν μυστήριον καὶ καθόλου μὴ δύνασθαι τ. εὑρεθῆναι ὑπὸ τὸν οὐρανόν, ἐν ᾗ ὁ ναὸς οὐκ ἔστι καὶ ὁ νάας ἐν αὐτῷ Hipp.*haer*.5.9(p.100.21; M.16.3155C); Marcosian τὰς ἀτελέστους αὐτῶν τ. μυσεράς τε μυσταγωγίας Eus.*h.e*.4.11.4(M.20.329A).

C. in OT; typical and symbolical, Clem.*str*.2.20(p.171.3; M.8.1049B); ὁ...νόμος...μυστηρίων τελετὰς δι' εἰκόνων καὶ σκιογραφιῶν παρεδίδου, χειραγωγῶν...πρὸς τὴν τοῦ Χριστοῦ διδασκαλίαν Or.*fr.9 in Jo*.(p.491.11); τῇ κατὰ νόμον ἱεραρχίᾳ, τ. ... ἡ πρὸς τὴν πνευματικὴν λατρείαν ἀναγωγή Dion.Ar.*e.h*.5.1.2(M.3.501C).

D. Christian; **1.** of sacramental rites in gen. αἱ τ. γίνονται νυκτὸς μάλιστα, σημαίνουσαι τὴν ἐν νυκτὶ τῆς ψυχῆς συστολὴν ἀπὸ τοῦ σώματος Clem.*str*.4.22(p.310.13; M.8.1349B); αἱ τ. τοῖς ἐντυγχάνουσιν ἀνέδην οὐ δείκνυνται, ἀλλὰ μετά τινων καθαρμῶν καὶ προρρήσεων *ib*.5.3(p.339.6; M.9.37C); Eus.*l.C*.proem.(p.196.8; M.20.1317C); οἷς δὴ τὰς θεοπρεπεῖς τ. ἱεροφαντούμενοι ὧδέ πη θείων ὀργίων ἐφαψόμεθα *ib*.(p.196.12; M.l.c.); Dion.Ar.*ep*.9.1(M.3.1108A); οἱ μὲν ἀπερισάλπιγκτοι καθόλου τῶν ἱερῶν τ. id.*e.h*.3.3.6(M.3.432C); οὐδὲ γὰρ ἴσον...τοῦ παντελῶς ἀμυήτου καὶ τῶν θείων τ. ἄκρως ἀκοινωνήτου τὸ μετουσίαν τινὰ τῶν ἱερωτάτων ἐσχηκὸς τελευτηρίων, ἔτι δὲ ταῖς ἐναντίαις...ἐνεσχημένον, ἀλλὰ καὶ πρὸς αὐτοὺς ἡ τῶν πανιέρων θέα καὶ κοινωνία συστέλλεται *ib*. 3.3.7(433B); οἱ τῶν τ. ἀμύητοι καὶ ἀτέλεστοι *ib*.(436B); αὕτη μὲν [sc. catechumens' τάξις] ἀμύητός ἐστι καθόλου πάσης ἱερᾶς τ. καὶ πρὸς οὐδὲν...τῶν ἱερῶς τελουμένων ἐποπτεύειν αὐτῇ θεμιτόν *ib*.7.3.3(557C); **2.** of baptism, cf.Or.*Cels*.3.59(p.254.14; M.11.1009A); τῆς ἱερᾶς τῶν μυστηρίων τ. ἀξιωθείς Chrys.*Thdr*.1.17(1.28D); ἡ τῆς ἱερᾶς τ. θεογενεσίας Dion.Ar.*e.h*.2.3.1(M.3.397A); τὴν ἱερὰν τῆς θεογενεσίας τ., ἐπειδὴ πρώτου φωτὸς μεταδίδωσι καὶ πασῶν ἐστιν ἀρχὴ τῶν θείων φωταγωγιῶν ἐκ τοῦ τελουμένου τὴν ἀληθῆ τοῦ φωτίσματος ἐπωνυμίαν ὑμνοῦμεν *ib*.3.1(425A); αὐτῷ τῷ τελεσθέντι τὴν ἱερωτάτην τῆς θεογενεσίας τ. τὴν τοῦ ...πνεύματος ἐπιφοίτησιν ἡ τοῦ μύρου δωρεῖται τελειωτικὴ χρίσις *ib*. 4.3.11(484C); and post-baptismal chrismation, *ib*.4.1(472D); *ib*.4.2(473A); *ib*.4.3.12(485A); *ib*.5.1.3(504B); **3.** of eucharist ταύτης...τῆς φρικωδεστάτης τ. Chrys.*sac*.3.4(p.53.18; 1.383A); κοινωνῆσαι τῆς ἀπορρήτου τ. Synes.*ep*.58(M.66.1404A); οἱ ἀπόστολοι...ἦσαν προσκαρτεροῦντες τῇ τοιαύτῃ θείᾳ τ., ἀεὶ τοῦ κυριακοῦ μεμνημένοι λόγου ‡Procl.CP *tract*.(M.65.849C); τῆς ἱερᾶς μυσταγωγίας τὴν τ. Dion.Ar.*e.h*.1.1(M.3.372A); ἔστι...τελετῶν τελετή *ib*.3.1(424C); ὅτου...ἕνεκα τὸ κοινὸν καὶ ταῖς ἄλλαις ἱεραρχικαῖς τ. ἐκκρίτως αὐτῇ...ἀνατέθειται καὶ...ἀνηγόρευται κοινωνία τε καὶ σύναξις *ib*.; *ib*.(425A); τῆς ἁγιωτάτης τ. ἱερουργίαν καὶ θεωρίαν *ib*.3.2(425B); *ib*.3.3.3(429A) cit. s. ἁπλοῦς; *ib*.3.3.4(429C); id.*ep*.8.6(M.3.1097B); τάξις...καὶ ἀκολουθία τῆς κατὰ τὴν ἁγίαν σύναξιν ἱερομύστου τ. *Lit.Jac*.(p.160.3); *ib*.(p.196.6); ἐπιστάμεθα μίαν προνήστιμον ἑβδομάδα, ἐν ᾗ...ἀποχὴ...ἐπετελεῖτο, μηδαμῶς...τῆς τῶν ἁγίων προηγιασμένων τ. γενομένης. ἐξ δὲ ἐν αἷς αἱ...προηγιασμέναι ἐπιτελοῦνται...τῇ δὲ τοῦ πάθους ἑβδομάδι ξηροφαγία νενομοθέτητο, οὐ μέντοι προηγιασμένων τ. εἶτα τῇ ἁγίᾳ πέμπτῃ ἡ τῶν μυστηρίων τ., ἐν ᾗ καὶ ἀπήρξατο Jo.D.*jej*.5(M.95.69D); ἐν τῇ ἱερᾷ προσκομιδῇ τῆς τ. τῶν θείων μυστηρίων μετὰ τὸ εἰπεῖν τὸν λαὸν τὸν τρισάγιον ὕμνον id.*trisag*. 27(M.95.57C); **4.** of ordination, Dion.Ar.*e.h*.5.1.2(M.3.501A); *ib*.(501D); **5.** ref. purgation, illumination, perfection as triple effect of sacraments ἡ...ἁγιωτάτη τῶν τ. ἱερουργία πρώτην μὲν ἔχει... δύναμιν...τῶν ἀτελέστων κάθαρσιν, μέσην δὲ τὴν τῶν καθαρθέντων φωτιστικὴν μύησιν, ἐσχάτην δὲ τὴν τῶν μυηθέντων...τελείωσιν *ib*.5.1.3(504A); τῆς ἁγίας τῶν τ. ἱερουργίας ἡ τρισσὴ δύναμις *ib*.(504B); *ib*.6.3.5(536D); *ib*.5.3.8(516A).

E. met. παρθεία...ἡ παρθενία...καλεῖται..., ὡς δὴ μόνη τὸν ἔχοντα καὶ τετελεσμένον αὐτῆς τὰς ἀφθόρους τ. θεῷ παρεικάζουσα Meth.*symp*. 8.1(p.81.6; M.18.137C); of marriage οἱ τετελεσμένοι τὴν γαμήλιον...τ. *ib*.2.2(p.16.19; 49A).

II. *mystery*, ref. union of virgins with Christ ταῦτα τῶν ἡμετέρων ...τὰ ὄργια μυστηρίων· αὗται τῶν ἐν παρθενίᾳ μυσταγωγηθέντων αἱ τ. Meth.*symp*.6.5(p.69.16; M.18.120C); ἠπίστατο [sc. Vergil]...τὴν μακαρίαν καὶ ἐπώνυμον τοῦ σωτῆρος τ. Const.*or.s.c*.19(p.182.23; M. 20.1293A); σιγὴ δὲ βαθεῖα καὶ τ. τις ὁ θάνατος Gr.Naz.*or*.8.22(M.35. 813D); κοίμησις τῆς...θεοτόκου, περὶ ἧς...φοιτῶσι...ἀπόστολοι, ὡς μόνος ἐπίσταται θεός, ὁ...συναθροίσας αὐτοὺς εἰς πανίερον τ. θεομητρικῆς αὐτοῦ κοιμήσεως Mod.*dorm*.7(M.86.3296C).

τελετής, ὁ, v. τελεστής.

***τελετηφορία, ἡ,** *rite*, Synes.*hymn*.3.45(p.8; M.66.1594); *ib*.1.451(p.20; 1600).

***τελετουργ-έω,** *minister sacramentally*, Dion.Ar.*c.h*.13.4(M.3. 305B); ὁ τὴν κάθαρσιν τῷ θεολόγῳ ∼ῶν ἄγγελος *ib*.(305D); ἔστιν οὖν ἡ ἱεραρχικὴ τάξις ἡ...τὰ τελεσιουργὰ τῆς ἱεραρχίας ἐκκρίτως ∼οῦσα id. *e.h*.5.1.6(M.3.505D); *ib*.4.3.12(484C).

***τελετουργία, ἡ,** *performance of a sacred rite*; of sacramental rites in gen., Dion.Ar.*e.h*.6.1.1(M.3.532A); of blessing of chrism, *ib*. 4.3.3(476B); *ib*.4.3.12(485A); *ib*.5.1.1(500D); of consecration of altar, *ib*.5.1.5(505C); of ordination, *ib*.6.1.3(533A).

τελ-έω, 1. *accomplish, execute, perform* νηστείαν τ. Herm.*sim*.5.1. 5; διακονία...∼εσθεῖσα id.*mand*.2.6; ἐντολὴν τοῦ κυρίου τ. *ib*.5.2.4; ∼έσειν δὲ αὐτὸν [sc. demiurge] τὴν κατὰ τὸν κόσμον οἰκονομίαν μέχρι τοῦ δέοντος καιροῦ Iren.*haer*.1.7.4(M.7.517B); οἱ ἁμαρτάνοντες...τὸ θέλημα τῶν πνευματικῶν ∼οῦντες τῆς πονηρίας Meth.*symp*.4.4(p.50. 3; M.18.92C); τοιαῦτα ∼ῶν ἔργα...ἃ...θεὸν λόγον αὐτὸν ἐγνώριζον Ath.*inc*.16.4(M.25.124D); ἑκάστη...τάξις...ἐκεῖνα ∼οῦσα χάριτι...τὰ τῇ θεαρχίᾳ φυσικῶς...ἐνόντα Dion.Ar.*c.h*.3.3(M.3.168A); **2.** *fulfil, bring to fulfilment* κύριος...ὑπὲρ...ἁμαρτιῶν ἔμελλεν...προσφέρειν θυσίαν ἵνα καὶ ὁ τύπος ὁ γενόμενος ἐπὶ Ἰσαὰκ...∼εσθῇ *Barn*.7.3; τὸ τοῦ πάσχα μυστήριον τετέλεσται ἐν τῷ τοῦ κυρίου σώματι Mel.*pass*.34 p.9.27; τὸ τοῦ κυρίου πάθος ἐκ μακροῦ προδηλωθὲν...σήμερον οὕτως τυγχάνει τετελεσμένον *ib*.p.9.38; ἡ μὲν [sc. OT] ἔφη τὰς ἐσομένας Ἰησοῦ θεουργίας, ἡ δὲ [sc. NT] ἐτέλεσε Dion.Ar.*e.h*.3.3.5(M.3.432B); of Christ's prophecies ταῦτα ὄψει καὶ ἐνεργείᾳ ὁρῶμεν ∼ούμενα Just. *dial*.35.2(M.6.549C); **3.** *demonstrate by action* ἐπεχείρει [sc. Aëtius]... διὰ γεωμετρίας...καὶ...σχημάτων περὶ θεοῦ λέγειν..., διδάσκων τε καὶ ∼ῶν Epiph.*haer*.76.2(p.342.4; M.42.517C); **4.** *finish, bring to an end* μετὰ...τὸ ∼εσθῆναι τὸν πύργον Herm.*vis*.3.9.5; λέγειν τὸν πεντηκοστὸν ψαλμόν, ἕως ἂν ∼έσῃς Ath.*virg*.20(p.55.19; M.28.276C); τ. τὸν βίον *come to one's end*, Or.*hom.15 in Lc*.(p.105.4); **5.** *belong to, be reckoned among*, of clergy ὅσοι τε εἰς τὸ βῆμα τοῦτο ∼εῖτε Gr.Naz. *or*.5.33(M.35.705C); οὐκ ἐν ποιήμασι ∼εῖ [sc. Son] Didym.*Trin*.1.7(M. 39.272A); μαθητὰς...καλεῖ καὶ τοὺς μὴ ∼οῦντας εἰς τὸν χορὸν τῶν δώδεκα Chrys.*hom.21.3 in Ac*.(9.172B); ὁ εἰς τὸ σῶμα τοῦ Χριστοῦ ∼ῶν id.*hom.25.2 in Jo*.(8.145C); εἰς τὴν σάρκα αὐτοῦ ∼οῦμεν, καὶ ὥσπερ σῶμα κεφαλῇ, οὕτως ἡνώμεθα id.*hom.10.2 in Rom*.(9.522B); εἰς ναὸν τοῦ θεοῦ ∼οῦμεν Thdr.Mops.*Eph*.2:21(p.153.23; M.66.916D); τῶν δοκούντων ∼εῖν εἰς Χριστιανούς Cyr.*Jo*.6.1(4.588C); οἱ ἐξ ἐθνῶν πιστεύσαντες...εἰς μίαν ∼οῦντες ἀγέλην id.*Ps*.22:1(M.69.840C); ὑπερθρώσκοντος τὸ ∼οῦν ἐν γενητοῖς id.*glaph.Gen*.2(1.53E); ἐτέλει...ἐν τοῖς γεγονόσιν ὁ δράκων ὁ ἀποστάτης *ib*.1(7D); οἱ εἰς τὸν ἱερὸν κλῆρον ∼οῦντες Thdt.*h.rel*.2(3.1130); κληρικοὺς εἰς ἐκκλησίαν ∼οῦντας...μὴ ἐξεῖναι εἰς ἄλλης πόλεως τάττεσθαι ἐκκλησίαν CChalc.*can*.20; πρὸ... τῆς...σαρκώσεως, μιᾶς φύσεως ἁπλῆς ἤτοι τῆς θείας, μία ∼ῶν ὑπόστασις, οὐδὲ Χριστὸς ἦν Jo.D.*Jacob*.78(M.94.1473C); *be included, exist* in ἐν τῇ οὐσίᾳ ∼οῦσι [sc. αἱ ὑποστάσεις] τῆς ἁγίας θεότητος *ib*.12(1441D); ἐπὶ τῆς...τοῦ κυρίου οἰκονομίας ἐνούσιον...φαμὲν τὴν ὑπόστασιν, ὡς ἐν ταῖς οὐσίαις ∼οῦσαν *ib*.; *come to belong to, join* ὁ παῖς ἐκ τοῦ Καίσαρος εἰς τοὺς ἐν Βλαχέρναις ἀναγνώστας ἐτέλεσεν Phot.*cod*.79 (M.103.253A); **6.** *serve* under, *come under the jurisdiction* of, *be subject* to ἡ...γυνὴ ὡς ὑπὸ τὴν τοῦ ἀνδρὸς ἐξουσίαν ∼οῦσα Thdt.*1Cor*.11:7 (3.234); Βοσπορίου ἐπισκόπου ὑπὸ τὸν αὐτὸν ∼οῦντος Κολωνίας...καὶ ἑτέρων ἐπισκόπων καὶ χωρεπισκόπων καὶ μοναστηρίων ὑπὸ τὸν αὐτὸν ∼ούντων Θεόδωρον Justn.*conf*.(p.108.9; M.86.1013C); τοὺς...γονέας παραδιδόναι τὸν παῖδά τινι μεμυημένων ἀγαθῷ τὰ θεῖα παιδαγωγῷ καὶ τὸ λοιπὸν ὑπ' αὐτῷ τὸν παῖδα ∼εῖν, ὡς ὑπὸ θείῳ πατρὶ Dion.Ar.*e.h*. 7.3.11(M.3.568B); **7.** *count* as, *be reckoned* as, *amount* to ἀξιοῦμεν, μὴ ὅτι Χριστιανοὶ λεγόμεθα...κολάζεσθαι (τί γὰρ ἡμῖν τὸ ὄνομα πρὸς κακίαν ∼εῖ;) Athenag.*leg*.2.3(M.6.896A); ‡Just.*confut*.57(M.6.1557B); Chrys.*hom.85.4 in Mt*.(7.810A); Cyr.*Os*.18(3.39E); **8.** *serve* as, *be*, Just.*dial*.139.1(M.6.793C); ἡ δ' [sc. Jephthah's daughter] εὐγενῶς σου τὸν τύπον τῆς σαρκὸς...∼οῦσα, ἔκραζε Meth.*symp*.11(p.134.22; M.18.212A); **9.** *celebrate, solemnize*; **a.** feasts γενεσίων ἡμέρας ∼ουμένης Just.*dial*.49.4(M.6.584C); ὁπότε τὸ πρόβατον σφάζεται καὶ τὸ πάσχα βιβρώσκεται καὶ τὸ μυστήριον ∼εῖται Mel.*pass*.28 p.3.8; ἄνεισιν...εἰς Ἱερουσαλήμ, τὴν ἑορτὴν τοῦ πάσχα ∼εσόμενος Or.*hom. 19 in Lc*.(p.126.16); Ath.*exp.Ps*.73:9(M.27.336A); ref. baptism τῶν ἱλαρίων ἡμερῶν ∼ουμένων Dion.Ar.*ep*.8.1(M.3.1097C); **b.** rites, esp. of initiation and sacraments; **i.** ref. pagan mysteries Κρόνου ...μυστήρια ∼εῖν ἐν τῷ ἀνδροφονεῖν Just.*2apol*.12.5(M.6.464C); ὁ ἱεροφάντης...∼ῶν τὰ μεγάλα καὶ ἄρρητα μυστήρια [of Eleusis] Hipp. *haer*.5.8(p.96.17; M.16.3150C); Mithraic, Dion.Ar.*ep*.7.2(M.3.1081A); **ii.** of OT rites; as typical and symbolical, Meth.*symp*.9.1(p.115. 11; M.18.180B); ὅσα...Μωϋσῆς...ἐν συμβόλοις ∼εῖσθαι παραδέδωκεν Eus.*h.e*.1.4.8(M.20.77C); δεδωκὼς...τοῦ ἀμνοῦ τὸ μυστήριον, διέξοδον δέδωκε τῇ ὀργῇ, ὅπως...μὴ ἅψηται τῶν αὐτοῦ ∼ούντων τὸ μυστήριον Ath.*exp.Ps*.77:50(M.27.356A); Cyr.*Ps*.93:12(M.69.1233C); **iii.** of Christian sacraments, in gen. τίνα λέγει...ἐπουράνια; τὰ πνευματικά. εἰ γὰρ καὶ ἐπὶ γῆς ∼εῖται, ἀλλ' ὅμως τῶν οὐρανῶν εἰσιν ἄξια Chrys. *hom.14.1 in Heb*.(12.141A); of baptism περὶ τῶν ἐν τῷ φωτισμῷ ∼ουμένων Dion.Ar.*e.h*.2.1 tit.(M.3.392A); *ib*.2.2.8(397A); *ib*.3.1(425A); of post-baptismal chrismation οἱ δὲ ἱερεῖς...∼οῦσι τὴν τῆς χρίσεως ἱερουργίαν *ib*.2.3.6(401C); of eucharist τῆς ψυχῆς...τὴν θείαν ∼ουμένης μυσταγωγίαν Chrys.*Philog*.1(1.494E); τὰ μυστήρια...τὰς θύρας κλείσαντες ἐπιτελοῦμεν...οὐκ ἐπειδὴ ἀσθένειαν κατέγνωμεν τῶν ∼ουμένων, ἀλλ' ἐπειδὴ ἀτελέστερον οἱ πολλοὶ πρὸς αὐτὰ ἔτι διάκεινται id.*hom.23.3 in Mt*.(7.288C); id.*sac*.3.5(p.54.4; 1.383B); τὴν φρικτὴν θυσίαν τελεσάμενον Philost.*h.e*.2.13(M.65.476C); θυσιαστήριον ἐφ' οὗ τοῦ Χριστοῦ ∼εῖται μυστήριον Cyr.*glaph.Gen*.3(1.331E); ‡Procl.CP *tract*.(M.65.852B); Dion.Ar.*e.h*.3.1(424D); *ib*.3.3.12(444A); τὰ τῆς θείας κοινωνίας τελέσει μυστήρια *ib*.5.2.5(505B); τῆς...∼ουμένης ἁγίας συνάξεως Max.*myst*.24(M.91.701D); τὸ δηλούμενον διὰ τῶν ∼ουμένων μυστηρίων *ib*.(704A); *Lit.Bas*.(p.344.22); Chrys.*sac*.3.4(p.51.1; 1.382B); Philost.*h.e*.8.4(560B); of consecration of chrism, Dion.Ar. *e.h*.4.1 tit.(472C); of burial rites, Philost.*h.e*.9.6(573B); Dion.Ar.*e.h*. 7.1 tit.(552C); τὰ...ἐπὶ τοῖς ὁσίως κεκοιμημένοις ∼ούμενα *ib*.7.1.3(556B); *ib*.7.3.1(556D); **iv.** of Christian spiritual sacrifices θεοῦ γὰρ εἰσιν [sc. widows] ἔμψυχος βωμός, εἰς ὃν ἀνακομίζοντες...τὰ ἑκούσια θυσίας ∼οῦμεν κυρίῳ Meth.*symp*.5.8(p.62.23; M.18.112B); **v.** pass. ptcpl. neut. plur. as subst., *sacraments, sacred rites*; of baptism, Dion.Ar.*e.h*.2.3.1(397B); *ib*.2.3.2(397C); of eucharist, Chrys.*hom.*

14.2 *in Heb.*(12.141A); Dion.Ar.*e.h.*3.2(428A); *ib.*3.3.3(429B); τοῖς ~ουμένοις παρεῖναι Evagr.*h.e.*2.3(p.40.25; M.86.2493B); Dion.Ar.*e.h.* 7.3.3(557C); of funeral rites, *ib.*7.3.1(557A); *ib.*7.3.9(565B); **10.** *initiate* a person; **a.** Gnost. ταῦτα μὲν ἐπιλέγουσιν οἱ αὐτὸν ~οῦντες· ὁ δὲ τετελεσμένος ἀποκρίνεται Iren.*haer.*1.21.3(M.7.664A); μυρίζουσι τὸν τετελεσμένον τῷ ὀπῷ τῷ ἀπὸ βαλσάμου *ib.*(664B); Hipp.*haer.*5.24 (p.125.29; M.16.3191C); ὁρκίζουσι τοὺς κατακούειν μέλλοντας τούτων τῶν μυστηρίων καὶ ~εῖσθαι παρὰ τῷ ἀγαθῷ *ib.*5.27(p.132.26; 3203A); **b.** in orthodox baptism τοιούτους...ἐχρῆν παρ' ὅλον τὸν βίον φαίνεσθαι ...τοὺς Χριστῷ ~ουμένους, οἵους σφᾶς ἐν ἐκκλησίαις ἐπὶ τὸ σεμνότερον σχηματίζουσιν Clem.*paed.*3.11(p.280.16; M.8.657B); cf.id.*prot.*12(p.83. 28; M.8.240A); Gr.Naz.*ep.*77(M.37.141C); Dion.Ar.*e.h.*5.2.6(M.3.505D); ὁ...ἱεράρχης...ἀναβοησάντων πάλιν...τὸ ὄνομα τοῦ ~ουμένου τῶν ἱερέων, τρὶς...αὐτὸν βαπτίζει *ib.*2.2.7(396D); *ib.*2.3.6(401D); φωτοειδεῖς ἐσθῆτας ἐπιβάλλουσι τῷ ~ουμένῳ *ib.*2.3.8(404C); ref. pre-baptismal unction πρὸ τοῦ...βαπτίσματος πρώτη μέθεξις ἱεροῦ συμβόλου δωρεῖται τῷ ~ουμένῳ *ib.*7.3.8(565A); ref. post-baptismal chrismation ἡ...τοῦ μύρου τελειωτικὴ χρῖσις εὐώδη ποιεῖ τὸν τετελεσμένον· ἡ γὰρ ἱερὰ τῆς θεογενεσίας τελείωσις ἑνοῖ τὰ τελεσθέντα τῷ θεαρχικῷ πνεύματι *ib.*2.3.8 (404C); τῷ ~εσθέντι τὴν...τῆς θεογενεσίας τελετήν, τὴν τοῦ...πνεύματος ἐπιφοίτησιν ἡ τοῦ μύρου δωρεῖται τελειωτικὴ χρῖσις *ib.*4.3.11 (484C); ὁ ἱεράρχης ἐπὶ τὴν...εὐχαριστίαν καλεῖ τὸν τετελεσμένον *ib.*2.3.8 (404D); τέλος...ἡ τῶν θεαρχικῶν μυστηρίων τῷ ~ουμένῳ μετάδοσις *ib.* 3.1(425D); τὸ πνεῦμα τῆς ἀληθείας...τὸ χρῖσμα καὶ χάρισμα τῶν ~ουμένων Geo.Pis.*hex.*1774(M.92.1571A); **c.** ref. OT initiation ~ούμενοι...οἱ πρὸς τῶν νομικῶν συμβόλων ἀναλόγως ἐπὶ τελειωτέραν μύησιν ἀναγόμενοι Dion.Ar.*e.h.*5.2(M.3.501C); **d.** of initiation into mysteries of doctrine ~εῖται [sc. Dionysius] ἅπαντα τῆς σωτηρίας τὰ δόγματα διὰ Παύλου Max.*prol.Dion.*(M.4.17C); **11.** *consecrate*; **a.** in gen.; pass., *be dedicated, consecrated* ὁ...τῷ Βεελφεγὸρ ~ούμενος Chrys.*hom.8.3 in Mt.*(7.125A); τῶν τῷ διαβόλῳ ~ουμένων *ib.*6.7 (99B); οἱ [sc. Manicheans] τὴν κακίαν ἀκίνητον εἶναί φασι, τῷ διαβόλῳ ~ούμενοι *ib.26.5*(321B); ἡ Ἔφεσος...ἐτελεῖτο...τῇ Ἀρτέμιδι id.*hom.1 in Eph.*proem.(11.1A); **b.** of ordination ὁ...ἱεράρχης ~ούμενος Dion.Ar.*e.h.*1.3(M.3.373C); ἡ...τῆς ἱεραρχικῆς χειρὸς ἐπίθεσις...διδάσκει...ἅμα καὶ πάσας ~εῖν τὰς ἱερατικὰς ἐνεργείας, ὡς ὑπὸ θεῷ πράττοντας τοὺς ~εσθέντας *ib.*5.3.3(512A); οὐκ αὐτὸς ἰδίᾳ χάριτι τοὺς ~ουμένους ἐπὶ τὴν ἱερατικὴν ἄγων τελείωσιν, ἀλλ' ὑπὸ θεοῦ κινούμενος *ib.*5.3.5(512B); πάντες καὶ αὐτὸς ὁ τελέσας ἱεράρχης ἀσπάζονται τὸν τετελεσμένον *ib.*5.3.6(513B); ὁ δὲ λειτουργός...ἐπὶ κεφαλῆς ἔχει τὴν τοῦ ~οῦντος αὐτὸν ἱεράρχου δεξιάν, τελειούμενος ὑπ' αὐτοῦ *ib.* 5.2(509B); **c.** of monastic profession, *ib.*6.2(533A); *ib.*6.3.4(536B); *ib.*6.3.5(536D); **d.** of consecration of altar, *ib.*4.3.7(485A); **12.** *perfect, make perfect*, Dion.Ar.*c.h.*3.1(M.3.164D); *ib.*3.2(165A); τάξις ἱεραρχίας ἐστὶ τὸ τοὺς μὲν καθαίρεσθαι, τοὺς δὲ καθαίρειν· καὶ τοὺς μὲν φωτίζεσθαι, τοὺς δὲ φωτίζειν· καὶ τοὺς μὲν ~εῖσθαι, τοὺς δὲ τελεσιουργεῖν *ib.*(165B); *ib.*3.3(165D); *ib.*6.1(200C); *ib.*7.2(208C); ἐξ ἱεραρχικῶν μυστηρίων καὶ παραδόσεων τετελεσμένους id.*e.h.*1.1 (M.3.372A); *ib.*1.3(373C); *ib.*5.1.1(501A); ref. deification ~εσθῆναι κατὰ τὰ θεῖα, καὶ θεωθῆναι *ib.*1.2(372D); σωτηριώδεις...τελεταὶ τῶν ~ουμένων θέωσιν ἱερουργοῦσαι *ib.*3.3.7(436C); id.*d.n.*1.3(M.3.589C); **13.** pass. ptcpl. neut. sing. as subst., *the matter in hand* γνῶσις γὰρ ἦν τὸ ~ούμενον καὶ γνῶσις τελεία Chrys.*hom.20.1 in 1Cor.*(10.169C).

***τελεωτικός**, *consummating, perfecting*, of wisdom in Basilides' doctrine Ἄρχοντα...ἐκπλαγῆναι...καὶ τὴν ἔκπληξιν αὐτοῦ φόβον κληθῆναι ἀρχὴν γενόμενον σοφίας φυλοκρινητικῆς τε καὶ διακριτικῆς καὶ τ. καὶ ἀποκαταστατικῆς Clem.*str.*2.8(p.132.4; M.8.972A).

τελικός, *final*; **1.** in sense of *supreme, perfect*, Clem.*str.*2.21(p.182. 12; M.8.1072C); ὅρος κυρίου τὸ τ. ἀγαθόν Or.*exc.in Ps.*23:3(M.17. 113C); **2.** of final causes ἀρχὴ πάντων τὸ καλόν, ὡς ποιητικὸν αἴτιον... καὶ πέρας πάντων καὶ ἀγαπητόν, ὡς τ. αἴτιον Dion.Ar.*d.n.*4.7(M.3. 704A); *ib.*4.10(705D); of Adam in rel. to Eve αἴτιον δὲ οὐ ποιητικόν, ὡς θεός...ἀλλ' ὡς τ. Proc.G.*Gen.*2:18(M.87.169C).

***τελικῶς**, *with reference to an end* ἐγὼ...ἐβουλόμην καταχρήσασθαί σε τ. μὲν εἰς Χριστιανισμόν, ποιητικῶς δὲ Or.*ep.*2.1(p.64.20; M.11. 88A).

τελίσκω, **1.** *fulfil, accomplish* τ. τὰ λεγόμενα *A.Thom.*A 82(p.198. 3n.); **2.** *finish*, *ib.*17(p.125.8); *ib.*18(p.126.9); Pall.*h.Laus.*2(M.34. 1011B; v.l. for τελειῶν p.17.4); **3.** *perform a sacred rite* (pagan), Clem.*prot.*2(p.11.6; M.8.72A); *ib.*(p.13.6; 76A); pass., *be consecrated*; hence *initiated*, *ib.*(p.15.20; 81B); Epiph.*exp.fid.*12(p.512.13; M.42. 804B); *ib.*11(p.511.7; 801A); **4.** pass., *be a harlot*, *T.Jud.*12.9; Proc.G. *Dt.*23:17(M.87.933C).

***τελματήσιος**, *belonging to marshes*, ‡Caes.Naz.*dial.*102(M.38. 969).

***τελμιστή**, ἡ, *mud, swamp*, ‡Eust.*hex.*(M.18.745B).

τελωνάρχης, ὁ, *controller of customs, chief publican*, met. παραγίνονται...ἐφ' ἡμᾶς...δυνάμεις οὐράνιοι καὶ τῶν ἐναντίων δυνάμεων οἱ τοῦ σκότους ἄρχοντες...οἱ τ. καὶ λογοθέται καὶ πρακτοψηφισταὶ τοῦ ἀέρος καὶ σὺν αὐτοῖς ὁ...διάβολος †Cyr.*hom.div.*14(5^2.405B; cf.M.65. 200B).

τελωνεία (**τελωνία**), ἡ, **1.** *tax-collecting*, Ast.Am.*hom.*13(M.40. 357C); **2.** *state of being a tax-collector*, Chrys.*hom.30.1 in Mt.*(7. 348C); met., *extortion* εἰ μὴ ἀνέλαβε σάρκα [sc. Christ]...πῶς Ζακχαῖος ἠδύνατο...τὸ πάθος τῆς τ. καὶ ἁρπαγῆς καταπαῦσαι Eus.Al. *serm.*3(M.86.329B).

τελων-έω, **1.** *be a tax-collector*, Ast.Am.*hom.*13(M.40.357C); **2.** *take toll of* τὸ τῶν σοφιστῶν γένος, οἷς τέχνη τὸ ~εῖν τοὺς λόγους ἐστί Gr.Nyss.*ep.*27(p.82.2; M.32.1092C); Bas.Sel.*or.*35.3(M.85.381B); Anast.S.*Ps.6*(M.89.1081A); **3.** *exact, extort*, ‡Proc.G.*Pr.*11:24(M.87. 1332B); **4.** med., *be a harlot*, *T.Jud.*12.9n.

τελώνης, ὁ, **1.** *tax-collector, publican*; κυριακὴ τοῦ τ. καὶ Φαρισαίου, name given to fourth Sunday before beginning of Lent when parable of Pharisee and publican is read, cf. *Triodion* (Rome 1879, pp.1–2); met., of evil spirits who stop and examine souls in their ascent to heaven οἶδα καὶ ἄλλους τ., οἳ μετὰ τὴν ἐντεῦθεν ἡμῶν ἀπαλλαγὴν ἐπὶ τοῖς τέρμασι τοῦ κόσμου καθεζόμενοι, οἱονεὶ τελωνοῦσι καὶ κατέχουσι, μήτι αὐτῶν ἐν ἡμῖν ἐστιν Or.*hom.23 in Lc.*(p.154.25; M. 13.1861D); ποῖα...μέλλομεν πράγματα ἔχειν ὑπ' ἐκείνων τῶν τ. τῶν ἐρευνόντων τὰ πάντα ὅταν τις αὐτὸς ὅλος λαμβάνηται ἀντὶ τέλους; *ib.* (p.155.17; M.l.c.); *A.Thom.*A 148(p.257.11); *ib.*167(p.281.10); ἕκαστον πάθος ψυχῆς καὶ πᾶν ἁμάρτημα ἰδίους τ. ἔχει καὶ φορολόγους †Cyr.*hom.div.*14(5^2.406C); **2.** comp. adj., *more extortionate* οἱ τελωνῶν τελωνότεροι ‡Sophr.*H.v.m.Cyr.et Jo.*(M.87.3677B).

τελωνικός, *proper to a publican*; met., of sighing in prayer στεναγμοὺς προσοίσωμεν τ. τῷ κυρίῳ *Triodion* (Rome 1879, p.6).

***τελωνικῶς**, *like the publican* μὴ Φαρισαϊκῶς, ἀλλὰ τ. προσεύχου..., ἵνα καὶ σὺ δικαιωθῇς ὑπὸ κυρίου Evagr.Pont.*or.*102(M.79.1189B); ταπεινωθῶμεν ἐναντίον τοῦ θεοῦ, τ. διὰ νηστείας κράζοντες *Triodion* (Rome 1879, p.1).

τελώνιον, τό, *place of toll, customs-house*; met. ref. stopping and examination of souls on their ascent to heaven ἡ ψυχὴ διὰ τοῦ ἀέρος ...ὑψουμένη, εὑρίσκει τὰ τ. φυλάττοντα τὴν ἄνοδον καὶ κρατοῦντα τὰς ἀναβαινούσας ψυχάς †Cyr.*hom.div.*14(5^2.405D); one such place being assigned to sins of each of the five senses, *ib.*(405E–406B); δύο ἄγγελοι εἰς τὸν οὐρανὸν ψυχὴν ἀνθρώπου φέροντες, ὡς οὖν προσέγγισαν τῷ τ. τῆς πορνείας καὶ τῆς μοιχείας...ταῦτα γάρ εἰσι πάντων τῶν τ. αἰσχρότερα, ἤρξατο ὁ ἄρχων τοῦ τ. ταράττεσθαι *V.Mac.Aeg.*7.2(M.34. 224C,D).

τέμπλον** (τέμβλον**), τό, (Lat. *templum*) **1.** *temple*, *A.Barth.*1 (p.130.14); **2.** *screen* or partition, separating altar from main body of church and covered with icons, τέμβλον, Thdr.Stud.*iamb.*43(M. 99.1796A).

***τεραστικός**, *marvellous*, †Bas.*Chr.generat.*4(2.599C; M.31.1465D).

τεράστιος, **1.** *marvellous, extraordinary*, in gen. οἶμαι...τὰς παραδόξους καὶ τ. δυνάμεις κατ' αὐτὸ τὸ παράδοξον καὶ ἐκβεβηκὸς τὴν συνήθειαν θαυμάσιόν τε καὶ ὑπὲρ ἄνθρωπον γινόμενον τέρατα ὀνομάζεσθαι Or.*Jo.*13.64(60; p.296.21; M.14.521B); of divine signs and works ὁ...θεὸς τοὺς μὲν ἐντολαῖς, τοὺς δὲ ἀπειλαῖς, ἔστιν δ' οὓς σημαίοις τ. ... ἐπιστρέφει πρὸς σωτηρίαν Clem.*str.*6.3(p.444.12; M.9.244C); ἴδετε τὰ ἔργα κυρίου τ. ὄντα καὶ παράδοξα Bas.*hom.in Ps.*45(1.175B; M.29.428A); of OT miracles τὰς...διὰ Μωϋσέως τ. δυνάμεις Or. *Cels.*3.5(p.207.4; M.11.928A); id.*fr.75 in Jo.*(p.542.18); of Christ's miracles, id.*Cels.*1.50(p.101.16; 753B); αἱ...τ. δυνάμεις τοὺς κατὰ τὸν χρόνον τοῦ κυρίου γενομένους προκαλεῖσθαι ἐπὶ τὸ πιστεύειν ἐδύναντο id.*Jo.*2.34(28; p.92.8; M.14.173D); *ib.*13.59(58; p.291.7; 512C); Eus. *l.C.*14(p.244.8; M.20.1413A); Mac.Mgn.*apocr.*2.11(p.19.9); ref. works of apostles ὁ Παῦλος...τὸν λόγον προετίμα τῶν τ. ἐνεργειῶν Or.*Cels.*3. 46(p.242.25; 980C); *ib.*8.47(p.262.22; 1588A); of wonderful spectacles, Hipp.*Dan.*3.29.5; of S. Paul's vision διὰ τῆς τ. ἐπιφανείας πεπίστευκεν; εἰ δ' οὐκ ἄλλως ἐδύνατο πιστεύειν ἢ διὰ τῆς τ. ἐπιφανείας, ἀκολουθεῖ κατ' αὐτοὺς καὶ αὐτὸν εἶναι ψυχικόν Or.*Jo.*13.61(59; p.293. 27; 516D); of properties of Christ's divine nature, Sophr.H.*ep. syn.*(M.87.3176A); **2.** neut. as subst.; **a.** *wonder, marvellous deed, miracle*; of works of God in gen., Or.*princ.*3.1.17(p.228.4; M.11. 285B); *ib.*3.1.10(p.211.10; 265B); †Chrys.*pan.Bab.*2.23(2.575E); in OT, Or.*Cels.*2.48(p.170.9; M.11.872A); *ib.*3.2(p.204.11; 921C); id. *princ.*3.1.11(p.212.11; 268A); †Bas.*Is.*248(1.568D; M.30.556B); Chrys. *hom.14.3 in Mt.*(7.181B); of Christ's miracles, Or.*Cels.*2.49(p.171. 16; 873A); id.*Jo.*13.52(51; p.280.33; M.14.496A); εἴπερ ἦν τ. τι γενόμενον οὐ συμβολικὸν ἑτέρου, ἐγέγραπτο ἂν αὐτὸ τὸ τέρας πεποιηκέναι τὸν Ἰησοῦν *ib.*13.64(60; p.296.31; 521C); ἐπίστευον μὲν αὐτῷ κατὰ τὸ ὁρατὸν διὰ τὰ τ., οὐκ ἐπίστευον δὲ τοῖς βαθύτερον ὑπ' αὐτοῦ λεγομένοις *ib.*20.30(24; p.367.33; 644B); τῶν...σημείων καὶ τ., ἅπερ οὐκέτι ἄνθρωπον, ἀλλὰ θεὸν δείκνυσι τὸν Χριστόν Ath.*v.Anton.*75(M.26.949A); ὁ λαὸς...βλέπων τὰ ὑπ' αὐτοῦ γενόμενα τ. οὐχ ἑώρα †Bas.*Is.*188(1.518E; M.30.440C); Ἰησοῦς...οἷα θεὸς τὸ τ. πεποίηκεν Didym.*Ac.*9:33 (M.39.1073B); θεοῦ γάρ ἐστι λόγου τεράστια...ἰσχὺν...τοῦ δημιουργήσαντος παριστῶντα Procl.CP *or.*1.1(M.65.693A); of apostles, *A.Jo.* 39(p.170.13); Or.*princ.*4.1.5(p.301.5; M.11.352A); Chrys.*sac.*2.5(p.40.18; 1.377D); as work of H. Ghost τὰ ἄλλα τ., ἅπερ ἅπαντα εἰργάζετο τὸ πνεῦμα τὸ ἅγιον ἐν ἡμῖν Chrys.*hom.29.2 in Rom.*(9.732A); Thdr. Heracl.ap.*cat.Jo.*10:5(p.297.28); in Church ἐκκλησία...ὀνομάζεται... περιοχή, ὥσπερ ἔχουσα τὰ τοῦ θεοῦ τ. ‡Sophr.H.*liturg.*2(M.87.3984A); in rel. to preaching, Chrys.*sac.*4.7(p.121.3; 1.412B); θαυματουργεῖν καὶ διὰ τῶν τ. τὰ τῶν ἀναισχύντων ἐμφράττειν στόματα *ib.*4.3(p.110.15; 408B); ascribed to martyrs, Sophr.H.*mir.Cyr.et Jo.*29(M.87.3509C); and others ἐξαίρει δὲ...ἐν τεραστίοις καὶ βίῳ Εὐσέβιον τὸν Νικομηδείας, ὃν καὶ μέγαν ἀποκαλεῖ Phot.*cod.*40(M.103.72D); **b.** in bad sense, of magic tricks and false miracles ὁ...Ἰησοῦς ἐπιστρέφων...ἀπὸ τοῦ... προσέχειν...τοῖς ἐπαγγελλομένοις...ποιεῖν τεράστια Or.*Cels.*2.49(p.171.1; M.11.872C); *ib.*2.77(p.199.32; 917A); *cat.Lc.*23:7(p.164.17).

τεραστίως, *miraculously, marvellously, as a marvel* πῶς...ἄπιστα αὐτοῖς καταφαίνεται τὰ διὰ Μωσέως...τ. ἐπιδεδειγμένα; Clem.*str.*6.3 (p.444.10; M.9.244C); Or.*Cels.*7.57(p.206.22; M.11.1501C); ref. Christ αὐτὸς ὁ τῶν ὅλων δημιουργὸς ἀκολούθως τῇ ἐν τῷ λέγειν τ. πιστικῇ δυνάμει συνέστησεν αὐτόν *ib.*3.36(p.233.5; 968A).

τερατεία, ἡ, 1. *fabulous, portentous nonsense*; of pagan identification of God with elements ταῦτα...τ. καὶ πλάνη τῶν γοήτων ἐστίν *Diogn.*8.4; ref. mysteries ὄργια...τερατείας ἔμπλεα Clem.*prot.*2(p.12.19; M.8.73B); τὴν ἐν ταῖς...συνόδοις τ., ἣν μηχανᾶται, δοξοκοπῶν καὶ φαντασιοκοπῶν Malch.*ep.*ap.Eus.*h.e.*7.30.9(M.20.712C); Ἑλληνικῆς τε πλάνης καὶ νομικῆς τ. Gr.Naz.*or.*18.5(M.35.989D); of heresies, id. *ep.*101(M.37.192C); of scriptural anthropomorphisms understood literally, Dion.Ar.*ep.*9.1(M.3.1104C); **2.** *miracle*; of Christ, Eus.*l.C.* 14(p.243.1; τεραστείας M.20.1409D).

τερατεύ-ομαι, 1. *devise fabulous stories*; of pagans who imitate OT miracle-stories, Clem.*str.*6.3(p.444.5; M.9.244B); of Gnostics, Or.*Cels.*5.62(p.65.18; M.11.1281A); **2.** *tell fabulous tales about*, Epiph.*haer.*19.4(p.221.9; M.41.265B); Gennad.*fr.Gen.*1:1(M.85.1625A); **3.** *maintain fantastic theory* that, Diod.*fat.*ap.Phot.*cod.*223 (M.103.861B); τὸ...Εὐτυχοῦς...δόγμα τὸ καὶ τὴν παρθένον ἑτερούσιον ἡμῖν ~όμενον Oecum.*Apoc.*12:1(p.136); Χριστὸν...σὺν διαβόλῳ βασιλευθησόμενον...~ονται [sc. Origenists] Jo.D.*haer.*64(M.94.716A); ~ονται [sc. Messalians]...ὡς χρὴ...ἐπὶ τοσοῦτον προσεύχεσθαι...ἕως ἂν...τοῦ πνεύματος...τοῦ ἁγίου...τὴν εἴσοδον αἰσθητῶς ὑποδέξωνται *ib.* 80(732D); **4.** *announce in a marvellous way* ὁ...ἀστὴρ οὐράνιόν ἐστι μήνυμα ἐπὶ γῆς ~όμενον *Pers.*(p.14.6; τερατουργούμενον M.10.104A); **5.** *perform as a bogus miracle* Ἰησοῦν...ἐπὶ τοῦ σταυροῦ ἀποτεθνηκέναι, ἵνα μηδεὶς ἔχῃ λέγειν ὅτι...οὐκ ἀποτέθνηκε...⟨ἀλλ'⟩...ἐτερατεύσατο τὴν...ἀνάστασιν Or.*Cels.*2.56(p.180.23; M.11.888B); τὰ πρὸ τῆς δευτέρας τοῦ Χριστοῦ παρουσίας ὑπὸ τῇ πλανώδει τοῦ ἀντιχρίστου ἐπιδημίᾳ τερατευθέντα *cat.Apoc.*9:1(p.311.30).

τερατολογέω, *tell fantastic tales*; of Gnostics, Hipp.*haer.*4.8(p.40.12; M.16.3070B); *ib.*4.51(p.75.31; 3122A); *ib.*9.13(p.251.21; 3387C).

τερατολόγημα, τό, *absurd story*, of Gnostics παυσάσθων...οἱ τῶν αἱρεσιαρχῶν δογματισταί, οἱ δυνάμεις καὶ αἰῶνας καὶ προβολὰς ὀνομάζοντες κενὰ τ. ἐφευρίσκουσιν Hipp.*Dan.*2.30.5.

τερατολογία, ἡ, *marvellous tale, absurd and fantastic story* ἐνεργῆσαι [sc. demons] τ. ἡγήσασθαι τοὺς ἀνθρώπους τὰ περὶ τὸν Χριστόν Just.*1apol.*54.2(M.6.408C); Κήρινθος...τερατολογίας ἡμῖν ὡς δι' ἀγγέλων αὐτῷ δεδειγμένας ψευδῶς ἐπεισάγει Caius R.ap.Eus.*h.e.* 3.28.2(M.20.273C); μείζοσιν ἐπιδαψιλεύεται [sc. Menander] τ., ἑαυτὸν μὲν ὡς ἄρα εἴη, λέγων, σωτήρ Eus.*h.e.*3.26.1(272B); πῶς...οὐ τ. αὐτῶν [sc. Arians] ταῦτα, λέγειν μὲν σοφίαν συνυπάρχουσαν τῷ πατρί, μὴ λέγειν δὲ ταύτην εἶναι τὸν Χριστόν; Ath.*Ar.*2.38(M.26.228B); τῶν Γαλιλαίων ἡ σκευωρία...ἀποχρησαμένη...τῷ φιλομύθῳ...τῆς ψυχῆς μορίῳ, τὴν τ. εἰς πίστιν ἤγαγεν ἀληθείας Juln.Imp.ap.Cyr.*Juln.*2(6^{2}.39B); ἐοικέναι...τερατολογίᾳ...τὸ λέγειν τὸν αὐτὸν καὶ παθεῖν καὶ μὴ παθεῖν Cyr.*Chr.un.*(5^{1}.766B); v. τραγικολογία; ref. Jewish food laws φυλαττομένοις τὴν Ἰουδαϊκὴν τ. Gennad.*fr.Rom.*16:17(p.417.19; M.85.1728A).

***τερατομυθία, ἡ,** *marvellous, monstrous fiction* τὸν ἀνθρωπολάτρην Νεστόριον...Διόδωρόν τε καὶ Θεόδωρον καὶ τοὺς τὴν αὐτῶν τ. πρεσβεύσαντας, ὡς νοήσαντας ἐπὶ Χριστοῦ προσωπικὴν δυάδα...ἐκδιώκω Taras.*ep.*5(M.98.1464C).

τερατοποιέω, *do wonders*, Cyr.*Jo.*2.5(4.203B).

τερατοποιΐα, ἡ, *miracle-mongering* τὰς ἐνθέους...δυνάμεις οἱ φαῦλοι δαίμονες καθυπεκρίνοντο διὰ πολλῆς τῆς τ. Eus.*p.e.*5.2(182A; M.21.316B); Cyr.*Chr.un.*(5^{1}.760B); *jugglery*, id.*ep.*41(p.47.27; 5^{2}.131A).

τερατουργ-έω, 1. *perform wonders, work miracles*, in OT οὐ πάντα τῇ ῥάβδῳ ~εῖ Μωϋσῆς...ἵνα μὴ τὴν ῥάβδον μαγικαῖς ἀπάταις τελεῖσθαι...νομίσωσι Or.*sel.in Ex.*9:29(M.12.284A); ‡Eust.*hex.*(M.18.788A); Jo.D.*carm.pasch.*17(p.218; M.96.840C); Jo.Mon.*hymn.Blas.* 7(M.96.1405A); of apostles ψιλοὶ ἦσαν ἄνθρωποι διὰ πνεύματος ~οῦντες Ammon.*Ac.*14:10(M.85.1545B); of Christ τοιαῦτα διὰ τῶν δούλων αὐτοῦ ~οῦντι Gr.Nyss.*v.Gr.Thaum.*(M.46.957D); ‡Jo.D. *Artem.*59(M.96.1305D); of God, Philost.*h.e.*7.13(M.65.552A); ~ήσει ...καὶ ἐφ' ἡμῖν ὁ τῶν ὅλων θεός, εἰ καὶ μὴ ἐμφανῶς...ἀλλ' οὖν νοητῶς Cyr.*Zach.*91(3.780A); v. τερατεύομαι; **2.** *invent fables*; of Valentinians, Hipp.*haer.*6.55(p.189.7; M.16.3291A).

τερατούργημα, τό, 1. *miracle, wonder*, of Christ τοῖς...ὑπὲρ λόγον τ. θεὸν ὄντα κατὰ φύσιν ἑαυτὸν ἐπιδεικνύς Cyr.*hom.pasch.*11(5^{2}.160A); οἱ τῶν ἐμῶν τ. μάρτυρες id.*Lc.*9:18(M.72.648B); *M.Artem.*(p.161.18; M.96.1278D); of apostles, ‡Jo.D.*ep.Thphl.*3(M.95.349A); of saints, Gr.Nyss.*v.Ephr.*(M.46.845C); in OT, ref. plagues of Egypt, Cyr.*Is.* 4.1(2.568C); **2.** *story of miracles* τοῖς τῶν ἁγίων κατὰ πᾶσαν γενεὰν πνευματικοῖς διηγήμασι καὶ τ. ‡Meth.*Sym.et Ann.*10(M.18.372C).

τερατουργία, ἡ, 1. *working of miracles*, in OT μετὰ μυρίους ὅσους τοὺς περὶ πίστεως λόγους καὶ τερατουργίας ἐπίδειξιν, τετηρήκασι τὸ δυσήκοον Cyr.*ador.*2(1.73E); τοιαύταις...τ. εἰσήγαγεν αὐτοὺς εἰς ἀγαθήν τινα γῆν †Jo.D.*B.J.*7(M.96.912B); of Christ καταπεφρονήκασι τοῦ πάντων...σωτῆρος Χριστοῦ, καίτοι ταῖς διδασκαλίαις προσεπάγοντος καὶ τ. Cyr.*Jon.*2(3.368A); Χριστὸς δι' ἀρρήτου τ. καταπλήττων ἐθαυμάζετο *ib.*(369A); id.*Lc.*4:38(M.72.552C); of saints, Thdt.*h.e.*1.23.9(3.805); id.*h.rel.*3(3.1142); of creation as marvellous work of God, Cyr.*Ps.*45:9(M.69.1049D); **2.** *wonder-working*; in bad sense, of magic, etc., Cyr.*ador.*6(1.211C); of false wonders περὶ τῆς τῶν εὐαγγελίων τ. καὶ σκευωρίας Juln.Imp.ap.Cyr.*Juln.*7(6^{2}.218A).

τερατουργός, ὁ, *wonder-worker*, of God as creator τῷ τ. θεῷ τὴν προσκύνησιν νέμοντες Jo.D.*imag.*1.17(M.94.1248A).

[*]τερεβίνθη (τερέβινθος, [*]τερεμίνθη), ἡ, 1. *terebinth, turpentine tree*, τερέβινθος, *A.Petr.et Paul.*84(p.216.15); cf.*A.(Pass.)Petr.et Paul.*63(p.172.13); Eus.*onomast.*(p.76.2); **2.** *resin* as ingredient of chrism, *Euchol.*(p.508); τερεμίνθη, *ib.*(p.509).

τερετίζω, 1. *chirp*; of the cicada, Clem.*prot.*1(p.3.17; M.8.52A); **2.** *hum*, Pall.*h.Laus.*18(p.57.2; M.34.1065D); **3.** *sing* (trans.), Sophr. H.*v.Cyr.et Jo.*4(M.87.3385B); †Jo.D.*B.J.*35(M.96.1192A); **4.** *whistle at, mock at*, Anast.S.*hod.*12(M.89.201B).

τερετισμός, ὁ, 1. *note* of a stringed instrument, Nil.*Magn.*64(M.79.1056D); **2.** *twittering, prattle, babble*, Meth.*res.*1.55(p.314.9); Cyr.*ador.*11(1.397A).

τερθρεία, ἡ, 1. *subtlety, sophistry*, Clem.*str.*1.3(p.15.2; M.8.712B); Cyr.*hom.pasch.*14(5^{2}.196B); Thdt.*ep.*16(4.1078); πάλιν τ. λόγων, πάλιν μάχη δογμάτων Leont.H.*Nest.*2.14(M.86.1565A); οἱ τῆς Ὠριγενιανῆς τ. μυστηριάρχαι παμμίαροι Sophr.H.*ep.syn.*(M.87.3192B); **2.** *imposture, claptrap*, Constantius Imp.ap.Ath.*apol.Const.*30(M.25.633A); Mac.Mgn.*apocr.*2.15(p.24.1); Cyr.*ador.*5(1.151D); of paganism, Eus. *p.e.*3 proem.(82C; M.21.153C); Chrys.*sac.*4.6(p.119.25; 1.411E); προβάντας...τῷ ὄρει τῆς κατὰ Χριστὸν ὑψηλῆς φιλοσοφίας, μετὰ τὸ διαπτύσαι τὴν Ἑλληνικὴν τ. Nil.*epp.*2.49(M.79.220C); Judaism, Cyr. *Nest.*3.3(p.65.9; 6^{1}.79D); heresy, id.*Jo.*9.10(4.785E); Thdt.*eran.*1(4.44); of OT acc. pagans, *M.Artem.*(p.162.15; M.96.1281D); **3.** of things, *flummery*, *cat.Apoc.*6:15(p.281.10).

***τέρθρευμα, τό,** *piece of folly*, Clem.*paed.*3.11(p.272.2; M.8.640A).

***τερπνοειδῶς,** *with delight*, Thdr.Stud.*iamb.*106(M.99.1805C).

τερπνότης, ἡ, *delight, pleasantness*; of or in God, *T.Job* 44(p.132.29); ἡ...πρὸς...τὸν θεὸν σχέσις...ὅλης τοῦ θεοῦ...μετέχουσα τῆς τ. Max.*myst.*5(M.91.680C); of Christ ὁ υἱὸς ὡραῖος τερπνότητα τῆς σαρκὸς αὐτοῦ ὃς τὴν ἄμορφον...φύσιν ὑψώσας ἐν δεξιᾷ τοῦ πατρὸς θεώσει...ἐκάθισεν Cyr.*Ps.*15:11(M.69.813C); of eternal life, †Jo.D. *B.J.*25(M.96.1096C).

***τερπωλός,** *delightsome, glad*, †Apoll.*met.Ps.*41:5(M.33.1369C); neut. as subst., *charm, delight* τὸν θεωρητικὸν...ἀγαπήσας...βίον καὶ τὸ ἐν αὐτῷ τ. προκρίνας Or.*comm.in Mt.*12.41(p.163.23; M.13.1080A).

τερψίνοος, *gladdening the heart*, Nonn.*par.Jo.*12:25(M.43.853C).

τεσσαρακονθήμερος ([*]τεσσαρακονταήμερος, τεσσαρανθήμερος), 1. *of forty days*, Cyr.*ador.*8(1.277C); **2.** *lasting forty days*; of Christ's fast in wilderness, -ταήμερος, Eus.*h.e.*3.24.9(M.20.265B); Cyr.*Ps.*68:10 (M.66.1164C); as ground of Lenten observance, Cosm.Ind.*top.*5(M.88.197B); Thdr.Stud.*antirr.*1.10(M.99.340C); of Lent, Eus.*pasch.*4 (M.24.697C); *ib.*5(700B); Sophr.H.*or.*5(M.87.3312A); fem. as subst.; of fast of Moses, Epiph.*haer.*77.16(p.429.22; M.42.662A); of period between Resurrection and Ascension, *ib.*77.35(p.448.12; 696A); of

Advent fast from Nov. 15 (day after feast of S. Philip) to Christmas, *Nomoc.*433; τεσσαρανθήμερον, *Euchol.*(p.175); **3.** *forty days old*; of Christ at Presentation, *A.Phil.*B 11.5(p.314); παιδίον θεὸν τ. καὶ προαιώνιον ‡Cyr.H.*occurs.*4(M.33.1192A).

τεσσαράκοντα [σαράκοντα *Chron.Pasch.*p.185(M.92.456B), etc.] *forty*; of days of Moses' fast, *1Clem.*53.2; εἰς καθαίρεσιν τῶν τῇ φύσει τοῦ σώματος ἀκολουθησάντων ἁμαρτημάτων τ. νηστεύει Μωσῆς ἡμέρας, ὁμοίας δὲ καὶ Ἡλίας καὶ ὑπὲρ τῶν ἡμετέρων ἁμαρτημάτων ὁ σωτήρ Or.*fr.79 in Jo.*(p.546.29); of forty-hour fast before Easter in some Asiatic churches, Iren.*ep.Vict.*ap.Eus.*h.e.*5.24.12(M.20.501A); of the forty martyrs of Sebaste, Bas.*hom.*19.1(2.149B; M.31.508A); †Bas.*ep.*365(3.466E; M.32.1108C); of their relics, Soz.*h.e.*9.2.1(M.67. 1597B); ὁρκίζω σε, κάμπα, κατὰ τοὺς σαράκοντα μάρτυρας *Exorc.*2 (p.334); τὰ τ. (perh. for τεσσαρακοστά) *memorial* of the dead on fortieth day after death, ‡Jo.D.*fid.dorm.*15(M.95.261C).

***τεσσαρακονταετηρίς**, ἡ, *period of forty years*, in interprn. of life of Moses as allegory of stages of spiritual life ἐπὶ...τῇ δευτέρᾳ τ. ... τῇ θεωρίᾳ τῶν ὄντων ἀπεσχόλασε †Bas.*Is.*proem.6(1.382E; M.30.129A).

[*]**τεσσαρακονταήμερος**, v. τεσσαρακονθήμερος.

τεσσαρακοντάκις, *forty times*, in doctrine of Alcibiades, the Syrian Elchezaite, on baptism of sick and possessed διδάσκων καὶ βαπτίζεσθαι ἐν ψυχρῷ τ. ἐπὶ ἡμέρας ἑπτά Hipp.*haer.*9.16(p.254.17; M.16.3391C).

***τεσσαρακονταοκτώ**, *forty-eight*, Clem.*str.*1.21(p.85.26; M.8.873B); σαράντα ὀκτώ *Contrad.*(p.6).

τεσσαρακοντάπηχυς, *forty cubits in height*; of pillar of Symeon Stylites the elder, Evagr.*h.e.*1.13(p.22.27; M.86.2456C); as personal nickname, Jo.Sync.*narr.*(H.4.320D).

τεσσαρακοντάς, ἡ, *period of forty days*; of Lent, Gr.Nyss.*mart.*2 (M.46.765C); between Christ's birth and presentation in Temple, ‡Meth.*Sym.et Ann.*4(M.18.356A).

***τεσσαρακοντοῦτις**, fem. adj. (lit., *of forty years*), *of forty days* ἡ ἄλιμος αὐτοῦ τ. νηστεία Leont.H.*Nest.*2.20(M.86.1580D).

τεσσαρακοστά, τά, *commemoration of the dead on the fortieth day after death*; custom in accordance with Mosaic law, *Const.App.*8.42. 3; observed in monasteries, Pall.*h.Laus.*21(p.68.15; M.34.1076A); Thdr.Pet.*v.Thds.*(p.22.25); liturgy celebrated on this day for departed, ‡Jo.D.*fid.dorm.*23–24(M.95.269D).

τεσσαρακοσταῖος, *of forty years*, Diod.*Ps.*94:8(M.33.1628B).

τεσσαρακοστή, ἡ, [sc. ἡμέρα] [in form σαρακοστή, Chrysipp.*enc. in Jo.Bapt.*(p.48.1)];

A. *fortieth day* before Easter; hence usual term for *Lent*; **1.** in gen. σύνοδοι γινέσθωσαν, μία μὲν πρὸ τῆς τ. CNic.(325)*can.*5 (but perh. more prob. in sense C infra: v. S. Salaville, *Échos d'Orient*, Paris 1910,pp.65ff.); CLaod.*can.*45; ἐν αὐτῇ τῇ ἁγίᾳ τ. περὶ τὸ πάσχα Ath.*ep.encycl.*4(p.172.12; M.25.232A); τῶν ἁγίων καὶ θείων τῆς ἁγίας τ. ἡμερῶν Nect.*Thdr.*8(M.39.1828D); Socr.*h.e.*5.22.35(M.67.633A); τὴν...καλουμένην τ., ἐν ᾗ νηστεύει τὸ πλῆθος, οἱ μὲν εἰς ἓξ ἑβδομάδας ἡμερῶν λογίζονται...οἱ δὲ ἑπτὰ...ἄλλοι δὲ τρεῖς Soz.*h.e.*7.19. 7(M.67.1477A); ἀρχόμενοι μὲν τῆς ἁγίας τ. ἀπὸ πεντεκαιδεκάτης τοῦ Μεχὲρ μηνός, τῆς ἑβδομάδος δὲ τοῦ σωτηριώδους πάθους ἀπὸ εἰκάδος τοῦ Φαρμενὼθ μηνός, περιλύοντες δὲ τὰς νηστείας τῇ πέμπτῃ καὶ εἰκάδι τοῦ αὐτοῦ μηνός Cyr.*hom.pasch.*7(5^2.16C); ἐν ταῖς τῆς ἁγίας τ. ἡμέραις Cyr.S.*v.Euthym.*37(p.56.13); **2.** dist. from Holy Week fast, *Const.App.*5.13.3; τὴν τ., τὴν πρὸ τῶν ἑπτὰ ἡμερῶν τοῦ...πάσχα ...φυλάττειν εἴωθεν ἡ αὐτὴ ἐκκλησία ἐν νηστείαις Epiph.*exp.fid.*22 (p.523.16; M.42.828B); ἐν τῇ τ. τῶν νηστείων τὰς πάσας ἡμέρας διὰ δύο ἤσθιεν...τὴν δὲ ἁγίαν πασχαλίαν πᾶσαν εἶλεν τὴν ἑβδομάδα μηδενὸς μεταλαμβάνουσα Marc.Diac.*v.Porph.*102; **3.** objects: commemoration of Christ's πολιτεία and νομοθεσία, *Const.App.*5.13.3; penitence, Chrys.*hom.1.7 in Ac.*(9.12E); release from 'slough' of sin, Ast.Am.*hom.*14(M.40.380B); spiritual health, *ib.*(381A); preparation of catechumens for baptism, Cyr.H.*catech.*4.3; preparation for Communion, Chrys.*hom.3.4 in Eph.*(11.22B); id.*Jud.*3.2(1.608D); offering to God of a tenth of days of year (i.e. 7 weeks, deducting Saturdays and Sundays, or 36 days) as ordered by apostles, an eighth week being later added in honour of 40 days of Christ's fast, Dor.*doct.*15.1(M.88.1788Aff.); but οὐ γάρ...δεκάτας τῶν τοῦ ἐνιαυτοῦ νηστεύειν νενομοθετήμεθα· κανὼν γάρ ἐστιν ἀριδήλως τ. νηστεύειν νομοθετῶν· αἱ δὲ τοῦ ἐνιαυτοῦ δεκάδες οὐ τεσσαράκοντα Jo.D.*jej.*3(M. 95.68C); cf. οὐ δεῖ νηστεύειν ἑβδομάδας ὀκτὼ ἐν τῇ μεγάλῃ τ. ὡς οἱ Ἀρειανοὶ ὑπερβαίνοντες τὸν παρὰ τοῦ κυρίου δεδομένον ἡμῖν ἀριθμὸν τῶν μ′ ἡμερῶν ἐν τῷ προστιθέναι ἑβδομάδα μίαν Anast.S.*qu.et resp.*64 (M.89.661C); **4.** ascetic practice; observance enforced on penalty of deprivation for clerics and excommunication for laity, *Can.App.* 69; but fasting a matter of γνώμη rather than compulsion, Vict. *Mc.*6:21(p.292.1); practices of monks Ταβεννησιῶται διὰ πάσης τῆς τ. ἐσθίουσιν ἄπυρον Pall.*h.Laus.*18(p.48.3; M.34.1051A); ἐλέγετο [sc. Macarius] καθέζεσθαι τῇ τ. ἐν σκοτίᾳ *ib.*(p.51.13; 1059C); ἐν...τῇ τ. ἤσθιε [sc. Adolius] διὰ πέντε *ib.*43(p.130.8; 1210C); τὰς...τῆς ἁγίας τ. ἡμέρας ἀνεχώρει [sc. Euthymius] εἰς ὄρος ἔρημον Cyr.S.*v.Euthym.* 5(p.13.20); strict fasting interrupted on Saturdays (except Holy Saturday) and Sundays, Epiph.*exp.fid.*22(p.523.16; M.42.828B); Jo.D.*jej.*3(M.95.69B); *Const.Stud.*30(M.99.1716B); but τινες...τῶν Εὐσταθιανῶν νηστεύουσι τ. ἐν σαββάτῳ καὶ κυριακῇ κατὰ τὸ δόγμα τῶν λεγομένων...Μαρκιωνιστῶν...καὶ Μεσσαλιανῶν Anast.S.*qu.et resp.* 64(M.89.664A); observance forbidden by Aërius, Epiph.*anac.*75 (p.231.15; M.42.337A); **5.** liturg. οὐ δεῖ τῇ τ. ἄρτον προσφέρειν εἰ μὴ ἐν σαββάτῳ καὶ κυριακῇ μόνον CLaod.*can.*49; ἐν πάσαις τῆς ἁγίας τ. τῶν νηστείων ἡμέραις παρεκτὸς σαββάτου καὶ κυριακῆς καὶ τῆς...τοῦ εὐαγγελισμοῦ ἡμέρας γινέσθω ἡ τῶν προηγιασμένων ἱερὰ λειτουργία CTrull. *can.*52; no feasts of martyrs celebrated, CLaod.*can.*51; except that of forty martyrs of Sebaste, Gr.Nyss.*mart.*2(M.46.785C); οὐ δεῖ ἐν τ. γάμους ἢ γενέθλια ἐπιτελεῖν CLaod.*can.*52; τῇ ἁγίᾳ καὶ μεγάλῃ τ. ψάλλομεν καθίσματα δ′ καὶ τριῴδιον *Const.Stud.*12(M.99.1709B).

B. *Advent* (called fast of S. Philip as beginning on day after Feast of S. Philip), and *Fast of the Apostles* (from Sunday after Pentecost to June 29), hence of three fasts of the year περὶ τῶν ἁγίων τριῶν τ. Anast.Ant.*serm.*4(M.89.1389B); τὰς...δύο τ., τὴν τοῦ ἁγίου Φιλίππου καὶ τῶν ιβ′ ἀποστόλων κρέατος...μὴ μετέχειν τοὺς κοσμικοὺς ὁρίζομεν, τοὺς δὲ μοναχοὺς τυροῦ καὶ ᾠοῦ †Jo.Jej.*poenit.* (M.88.1916A); cf. περὶ...τῆς τ. τῆς τοῦ Χριστοῦ γεννήσεως γέγραπται ἐν τῇ περιόδῳ τοῦ ἁγίου Φιλίππου Anast.Ant.*serm.*4(1396A); Lent therefore dist. as ἡ μεγάλη τ., Anast.S.*qu.et resp.*64(M.89.661C); *Const.Stud.*12(M.99.1709B); *ib.*30(1716B).

C. *fortieth day* after Easter, *Ascension Day*, cf. CNic.(325)*can.* 5 cit. s. A.1 supra; cf. CElvir(306)*can.*43; Liberatus *breviarium* 10 (M.*PL.*68.992C).

τεσσαρανθήμερος, v. τεσσαρακονθήμερος.

τέσσαρες, *four*; of gospels τὸ ἀληθῶς διὰ τεσσάρων ἕν ἐστιν εὐαγγέλιον Or.*Jo.*5.7(p.104.31; M.14.193D); *ib.*10.3(2; p.173.21; 312B); of Tatian's *Diatessaron* (harmony of gospels), Iren.ap.Eus.*h.e.*4.29.6 (M.20.401A); τὸ διὰ τ. καλούμενον...εὐαγγέλιον Thdt.*haer.*1.20(4. 312); of passions of Sophia (Gnost.) ὁ...καρπὸς...εὑρὼν αὐτὴν ἐν πάθεσι τοῖς πρώτοις τ. ... φόβῳ καὶ λύπῃ καὶ ἀπορίᾳ καὶ δεήσει, διωρθώσατο τὰ πάθη αὐτῆς Hipp.*haer.*6.32(p.160.22; M.16.3243A); Or.*sel.in Jer.*51:21(M.13.601D); *Hom.Clem.*2.52; ἐκ τεσσάρων *from four corners*, *M.Eleuth.*4(p.152.8).

***Τεσσαρεσκαιδεκατῖται**, οἱ, *Quartodecimans*, celebrating Easter on 14th day of paschal moon without reference to day of the week, i.e. on same day as Passover, Epiph.*anac.*50(p.211.21; M.41. 848A); id.*haer.*50.1(p.244.15; M.41.884A); claiming to follow tradition of S. John, Socr.*h.e.*5.22.28(M.67.632A); Soz.*h.e.*7.18.10(M.67. 1472A); excommunicated by Pope Victor, Socr.*h.e.*5.22.15(628C); received into Church with chrismation only, CLaod.*can.*7; required to anathematize their heresy, CEph.(431)*act.*6(*ACO* 1.1.7 p.100.24; H.1.1517E); Tim.CP *haer.*(M.86.33C); Jo.D.*haer.*50(M.94. 709A); cf. *Tessarescaedecatitae dicti, quia XIV luna pascha cum Judaeis observandum contendunt*, Isid.H.*etym.*8.5.61.

***τεστάτωρ**, ὁ, (Lat.) *testator*, Ath.Scholast.*coll.*2.3(p.35).

τέταρτος, *fourth* ὁ τ. ἀριθμός· ὑλικός τις καὶ σωματικὸς ὤν, κακωτικός ἐστιν· ἐπεὶ τὰ γενικὰ σώματα τέσσαρά ἐστιν Or.*fr.79 in Jo.*(p.546. 24); ἡ τ. ἡμέρα, also ἡ τ., *Wednesday*, Eus.*qu.Marin.*2.2(M.22.941C); Ath.*h.Ar.*55(p.214.17; M.25.760B); τῇ τ. τοῦ τυροφάγου Thdr.Stud. *catech.parv.*51(*NPB* 9 p.122); τῇ ἁγίᾳ καὶ μεγάλῃ τ. [i.e. in Holy Week] *ib.*72 index (M.99.28C); neut. as adv., *four times* τ. καθ' ἑκάστην ἑβδομάδα κοινωνοῦμεν Bas.*ep.*93(3.186D; M.32.484B); γίνεται πάσχα...τρίτον τῆς ἑβδομάδος· ἔστι δ' ὅτε καὶ τ. μᾶλλον δὲ γίνεται ὁσάκις ἂν βουλώμεθα Chrys.*Jud.*3.4(1.611B).

***τετελειωμένως**, *perfectly, completely*, Epiph.*haer.*69.61(p.210.11; M.42.301A).

***τετεχνασμένως**, *shiftily, by a subterfuge*, Eust.*engast.*24(p.52.32; M.18.661B).

τετηρημένως, *attentively, scrupulously, precisely*, Gr.Naz.*or.*34.15 (M.36.253D); Max.*qu.Thal.*51(M.90.484A).

***τετράβηλον**, τό, *square veil*, Thphn.*chron.*p.419(M.108.993A).

τετραγενής, *of four kinds*, *Hom.Clem.*6.4; *ib.*20.8.

***τετράγιος**, *four times holy*, Jo.D.*trisag.*2(M.95.25D).

τετραγράμματος, *of four letters*; of Adam as signifying four quarters of the world, *Orac.Sib.*3.24; neut. as subst., the *four-lettered* ineffable *name* of God (Ex.3:14) ἔστι δέ τι τ. ἀνεκφώνητον παρ' αὐτοῖς, ὅπερ ἐπὶ τοῦ πετάλου...τοῦ ἀρχιερέως ἀναγέγραπται καὶ λέγεται μὲν τῇ Ἀδωναῒ προσηγορίᾳ, οὐχὶ τούτου γεγραμμένου ἐν τῷ τ.· παρὰ δὲ Ἕλλησι τῇ κύριος ἐκφωνεῖται Or.*sel.in Ps.*2:1–2(M.12.1104B); id.*hom.14.1 in Num.*(p.121.7; M.12.677B); τὸ τ. τούτοις γραφόμενον τοῖς στοιχείοις Ἰώθ, Ἦπ, Οὐαί, Ἱήπ, Πίπι ὁ θεός Evagr. Pont.*schol.*(p.206); cf. τινὲς δὲ ὀνομάσαι τὸ σαφηνίσαι φασὶ τὸ τ. παρ' Ἑβραίοις ὄνομα Proc.G.*Lev.*24:16(M.87.781B); ἐπὶ τῶν τριῶν κειμένον τὸ ἄφθεγκτον ὄνομα τὸ ἐπὶ μόνου γραφόμενον τοῦ θεοῦ, τ. ὄν id.*Gen.* 18:1–3(M.87.364B); Isid.H.*etym.*7.1.16; transliterated by Ἰεύω, cf. Porphyry ap.Eus.*p.e.*1.9(31A; M.21.72A).

τετράγραμμος, = foreg. τὸ τ. ὄνομα, ὃ περιέκειντο οἷς μόνοις τὸ ἄδυτον βάσιμον ἦν· λέγεται δὲ Ἰάουε, ὃ μεθερμηνεύεται ὁ ὢν καὶ ὁ ἐσόμενος Clem.*str.*5.6(p.348.17; M.9.57C); 'κύριε' διὰ τοῦ τ. ὀνόματος ἐν τῷ Ἑβραϊκῷ φέρεται, ὅπερ...ἐπὶ μόνου τοῦ θεοῦ παραλαμβάνειν εἰώθασιν, ἡμεῖς δὲ καὶ ἐπὶ τῆς τοῦ λόγου θεότητος ἐν πλείσταις κείμενον γραφαῖς προαπεδείξαμεν Eus.*d.e.*9.7(p.420.28; M.22.677C); χωρὶς τῶν τεσσάρων στοιχείων τῶν παρ' Ἑβραίοις ἀνεκφωνήτων, ὧν διὰ τῆς συνθέσεως τὸ σημαινόμενον ὄνομα ἄρρητον ὑπάρχον...οὐδέπω ποτὲ ἐπὶ ἀγγελικῆς παρείληπται δυνάμεως, ὡς ἐπιστήσεις καθ' ὅλης τῆς...γραφῆς, ἔνθα ὁ θεὸς ἢ ὁ διὰ τοῦ τ. δηλούμενος κύριος ἀναγέγραπται κεχρηκέναι τισί· πότερον ἐπὶ τὴν ἀγέννητον...θεοῦ φύσιν ἀνεκτέον τὰ δηλούμενα ἢ ἐπὶ τὸν τούτου λόγον ὄν...ἐκ τοῦ παρ' Ἑβραίοις ἀρρήτου ὀνόματος προσαγορεύειν εἴωθεν ἡ...γραφή id.*ecl.*1(M.22.1025C); cf. *nomen* τ. *quod* ἀνεκφώνητον, *id est, ineffabile putaverunt, quod his litteris scribitur, JOD, HE, VAU, HE*, Hier.*ep.*25(M.*PL.*22.429); Thdt.*qu.60 in Ex.*(1.166); ἄφραστον ὄνομα...γράφεται...διὰ τῶν τεσσάρων στοιχείων, διὸ τ. αὐτὸ λέγουσι...καλοῦσι δὲ αὐτὸ Σαμαρεῖται μὲν Ἰαβέ, Ἰουδαῖοι δὲ Ἀϊά *ib.*15(133); Cosm.Ind.*top.*5(M.88.213C).

τετραγωνιαῖος, *square-shaped*; met., *angular* ὁ...καθήμενος μετὰ ἀδελφῶν οὐκ ὀφείλει εἶναι τ., ἀλλὰ στρόγγυλος, ἵνα πρὸς πάντας κυλίηται *Apophth.Patr.*(M.65.293C).

***τετραγώνιος**, *square*, *Asen.*2(p.42.3).

τετράδερμον, τό, *ground sheet*, *M.Petr.Al.*(p.79).

τετράδιον, τό, **1.** *guard of four soldiers, quaternion*, *A.(Pass.) Andr.*A 9(p.22.9); **2.** *four-leaved pamphlet, quaternion* of papyrus or parchment, Synes.*ep.*142(M.66.1537A); Cyr.*ep.*10(p.111.33; 5².35B); ref. acts of CNic.(325) μόλις ἐδυνήθην εὑρεῖν φανερὰ τῶν ἐκεῖσε... ἐγγραφέντων...ἐν τ. παλαιοῖς Gel.Cyz.*h.e.*1 proem.21(M.85.1197B); Anast.S.*hod.*1(M.89.41B); **3.** *one of the four quarters* of the world, Mac.Mgn.*apocr.*25(p.111.20).

***τετράδιπλος**, *fourfold*, *A.Thadd.*3(p.274n.); neut. as subst., *a kind of towel*, *ib.*(p.274.16).

***τετραδῖται, οἱ**, name given to various heretics; **1.** to τεσσαρεσκαιδεκατῖται, CCP(381)‡*can.*7; Tim.CP *haer.*(M.86.72A); **2.** to group of Palestinian Origenists as attributing divinity to soul of Christ, thus adding fourth Person to Godhead, Cyr.S.*v.Sab.* 89(p.197.16); **3.** to followers of Damian of Alexandria who found the unity of God in a ὕπαρξις prior to the three Persons and called αὐτόθεος, Tim.CP *haer.*(M.86.61B); also of followers of Severus, *ib.* (60D); **4.** to those who adopted Peter Fullo's addition of ὁ σταυρωθεὶς δι' ἡμᾶς to trisagion, thus allegedly separating crucified Christ from Son of God and hence adding fourth Person to Godhead, ‡Faust.*ep.*(p.8.18; H.2.848D).

***τετραδόφρων**, *quaternity-minded*; of Nestorius who by his alleged doctrine of two Persons in Christ added a fourth Person to Trin. Νεστορίου τοῦ διαιρέτου τῆς Χριστοῦ τοῦ θεοῦ ὑποστάσεως καὶ ἀνθρωπολάτρου, καὶ τ. Jo.D.*rect.sent.*7(M.94.1432A).

***τετραέλαστος**, *drawn by four horses*, *Apoc.Bar.*6(p.88.19).

τετραέλικτος, *four times coiled*, Nonn.*par.Jo.*4:35(M.43.780C).

τετράεντον, τό, ἐκ τ. *on all four sides*, *Chron.Pasch.*p.337(M.92. 877A); ἐν τ. *IGC As.Min.*93.

τετράζυξ, *four-yoked*, Nonn.*par.Jo.*19:15(M.43.901A).

τετραήμερος, *of four days, after four days*, of Lazarus νεκρὸν Λάζαρον τ. ἀνιστᾷ Hipp.*fr.18 in Pss.*(p.146.18; M.10.609A); τὴν τοῦ Λαζάρου τ. ἀνάστασιν Cyr.H.*catech.*18.17; Gr.Naz.*ep.*102(M.37.201A); in form τετρήμερος, ‡Caes.Naz.*dial.*30(M.38.892); hence as regular epithet of Lazarus, *four days dead*, Cyr.H.*catech.*2.5; Chrys.*anom.* 9.1(1.525A); Eulog.*palm.*2(M.86.2916B); τεθήμερος, ‡Caes.Naz.*dial.* 178(1149); as synonym of Lazarus, Eulog.*palm.*2(2916B); Geo.Pis. *res.*36(M.92.1377A).

***τετραθεΐα, ἡ**, *divine quaternity* opp. trinity; ref. implication of monothelite doctrine ascribing one hypostatic will to Christ, which should logically ascribe one also to each Person, so postulating four divine wills (one of the common nature and three of the Persons), Anast.Ap.*a.Max.*2.14(M.90.152A).

***τετράθηρος**, *with four beasts* τὸ τῶν εὐαγγελίων τ. ἅρμα ‡Chrys. *circ.*(8.88A).

***τέτραθλος**, *of four labours*, Jo.Thess.*mul.ung.*4(M.59.642).

τετράϊππος, *with four horses yoked*, *Chron.Pasch.*p.112(M.92. 293B); neut. as subst., *four horse chariot, quadriga* ἔθετο τὴν ἐκκλησίαν εἰς τὸ τ. τῶν εὐαγγελικῶν ἁρμάτων Ph.Carp.*Cant.*190(M.40.121A).

τετρακάμαρον, τό, *edifice with four arches*, Thdr.Stud.*iamb.*90(M. 99.1801C).

τετρακέρατος, *four-horned*; met., ref. four vices opp. four virtues τὴν τ. τοῦ σατανᾶ θεασάμενος δύναμιν Nil.*epp.*1.223(M.79.164D).

***τετρακιόνις, ἡ**, *shrine with four pillars*, Jo.Mal.*chron.*8 p.201(M. 97.316A).

***τετρακόρυφος**, *with four ends*; of Cross, *Hymn.*1.5.18(*KlT* p.8).

τετρακτύς, ἡ, *group of four, quaternity*; of first four Valent. aeons, Iren.*haer.*1.1.1(M.7.448A); Hipp.*haer.*6.34(p.162.10; M.16. 3246A); ref. Christ ἐκ τεσσάρων τούτων σύνθετον γεγονέναι φάσκουσιν, ἀποσῴζοντα τὸν τύπον τῆς ἀρχεγόνου καὶ πρώτης τ., ἔκ τε τοῦ πνευματικοῦ ὃ ἦν ἀπὸ τῆς Ἀχαμὼθ καὶ ἐκ τοῦ ψυχικοῦ ὃ ἦν ἀπὸ τοῦ Δημιουργοῦ Iren.*haer.*1.7.2(513B); in Marcosian system, *ib.*1.14.3 (601A); *ib.*1.14.9(612B); Μωϋσῆς...τέσσαρα...ταῦτα ὀνομάσας, θεὸν καὶ ἀρχήν, οὐρανὸν καὶ γῆν, τ. ... διετύπωσεν *ib.*1.18.1(641B); of four elements, Eus.*l.C.*6(p.207.13; M.20.1344A); ‡Paul.Sil.*therm.Pyth.*160 (M.86.2266A); τέσσαρα ζῷα ἰσάριθμα τῇ τ. τῶν ποιοτήτων, δι' ὧν τὰ στοιχειώδη σώματα ὑπέστη τοῦδε τοῦ ὑλικοῦ κόσμου Areth.*Apoc.*4:8 (M.106.573A); of four gospels, Eus.*h.e.*3.25.1(M.20.268D); Thdt.*ep.* 130(4.1217); *ib.*145(1251); of cardinal virtues, Evagr.Pont.*or.*proem. (M.79.1165C); Synes.*ep.*140(M.66.1532B); of four detractors of Origen (Meth., Eust., Apoll., Thphl. Al.), Socr.*h.e.*6.13.4(M.67.701D).

***τετραμιγής**, *constituting a mixture of four*, Meth.*res.*2.10(p.352. 15).

***τετραμόδιον, τό**, *containing four modii*, Jo.Mal.*chron.*11 p.278 (M.97.420C).

***τετραμόριον, τό**, *quarter*, Afric.*chron.*18.3(M.10.92A).

τετράμορφος, *fourfold, in fourfold form*; of gospels, Iren.*haer.* 3.11.8(M.7.885B); corresponding to four beasts of Ezech. and Apoc., *ib.*(889B); cf.‡Bas.*h.myst.*44(p.388.27); of the four beasts, Meth.*res.* 2.10(p.352.13); *Hymn.*1.4.4(*KlT* 52/53 p.6); Eustrat.*stat.anim.*11 (p.394); of seraphim σὲ ὑμνοῦσι...τὰ χερουβίμ, τετραμόρφοις ὀχούμενοι σεραφίμ Ephr.3.523B; of an image, Geo.Pis.*Pers.*1.81(M.92. 1203A); ref. Devil περὶ τῆς τ. δυνάμεως τοῦ διαβόλου Nil.*epp.*1.224(M. 79.165A).

***τετράνυμφον, τό**, *fountain with four basins*, *Chron.Pasch.*p.254 (M.92.613B).

***τετρανωμένως**, *with perfect clearness*, Leont.B.*Nest.et Eut.*2(M. 86.1356C).

τετράξ, ὁ, name given to the *year* in Ἐφέσια γράμματα of Pythagorean Androcydes, as consisting of four seasons, Clem. *str.*5.8(p.356.5, v.l. τετράς M.9.72C).

τετραόδιον, τό, *place where four roads meet*, *T.Abr.*A 1(p.77.5).

***τετραπεδικός**, *squared*; of stone, Gr.Nyss.*ep.*25(M.46.1097C).

***τετραπέρατος**, *with four quarters* or *cardinal points*; of the world, exeg. Dan.7:2 τέσσαρας δὲ ἀνέμους...τὴν τ. κτίσιν σημαίνει Hipp.*Dan.*4.2.2; τὴν τ. οἰκουμένην †Cyr.*hom.div.*11(5².379D); Alex. Sal.*Barn.*proem.7(p.438E); τ. κόσμον *Hymn.*(*KlT* p.8); neut. as subst., *the world*, exeg. Ezech.1:5 τινὲς δὲ καὶ ἐξηγήσαντο τὰ ζῷα εἰς τὸ τ. Or.*hom.1.16 in Ezech.*(M.13.681D).

***τετραπλατεία, ἡ**, *place where four ways meet*, *Chron.Pasch.*p.254 (M.92.616B).

***τετράπλοκος**, *of four strands*; hence of chariot, *four-horsed* ἡσυχία καὶ προσευχὴ καὶ ἀγάπη καὶ ἐγκράτεια τ. ἐστιν ἅρμα εἰς οὐρανοὺς ἀνάγον τὸν νοῦν Thal.*cent.*1.24(M.91.1429C).

τετραπλόος (-οῦς), **1.** *fourfold*; **2.** neut. plur. as subst., Origen's edition of four chief Greek versions of OT arranged in four columns, Or.*sel.in Gen.*17:4(M.12.141C); Eus.*h.e.*6.16.4(M.20.557A; v.l. τετρασσοῖς); τ. ... εἰσι τὰ Ἑλληνικὰ ὅταν αἱ τοῦ Ἀκύλα καὶ Συμμάχου καὶ τῶν Ἑβδομηκονταδύο καὶ Θεοδοτίωνος ἑρμηνεῖαι συντεταγμέναι ὦσι Epiph.*mens.*19(M.43.268D); **3.** fem. as subst., *fourfold payment of a tax*, Bas.*ep.*21(3.98B; M.32.288A).

***τετραποδικός**, *four feet long*, Pall.*h.Laus.*18(p.49.13; τετραπέδων M.34.1052A).

***τετραπόδιον, τό**, *four-legged table* for placing bread, corn, wine, and oil for blessing, *Euchol.*(p.4); and for placing gospel book when removed from altar, *ib.*(pp.499,707).

τετράπορος, **1.** *with four openings*, Paul.Sil.*Soph.*529(M.86.2139B); *ib.*722(2147A); **2.** *facing four ways*; of four quarters of Cross, Nonn. *par.Jo.*19:6(M.43.900A); Sophr.H.*carm.*9.18(M.87.3776C).

τετραπρόσωπος, **1.** *with four faces*, of cherubim τὰ χερουβὶμ τ. καὶ τὰ πρόσωπα αὐτῶν εἰκόνες τῆς πραγματείας τοῦ υἱοῦ τοῦ θεοῦ Iren.

*haer.*3.11.8(M.7.886A); Meth.*res.*2.10(p.351.14); in Ezekiel's vision, ‡Just.*qu.et resp.*44(M.6.1289A); *πρὸς τὴν τοῦ προκειμένου χρῆσιν τ. τὰ χερουβὶμ ἑώρα· τ. ... ἀόρατος φύσις οὐκ ἔστιν* Proc.G.*Gen.*3:24(M.87.228D); *τ. ... τὰ χερουβὶμ...καὶ ὅμως τέσσαρας αὐτῶν οὐ φαμὲν καὶ τὰς ὑποστάσεις* Leont.H.*Nest.*2.16(M.86.1572C); of idols, †Bas.*poenit.*3 (2.605C; M.31.1480B); **2.** *of four persons*; in monophysite arguments against two natures, identified with persons *μή, φησίν, ὀφθῇ τῇ μεθέξει τῶν δύο τ. ἡ τριὰς νοουμένη* Geo.Pis.*Sev.*149(M.92.1633A); *τὴν σύνοδον Χαλκηδόνος ἐλέγξωσιν...δύο πρόσωπα λέγουσαν ἐν Χριστῷ ὅπως τ. εὑρεθῇ...ἡ τριάς* Anast.S.*hod.*6(M.89.108C).

τετράπυλον, τό, *building with four doors*; in Antioch, Evagr. *h.e.*3.28(p.124.29; M.86.2653B); in Alexandria (a church, where remains of Jeremiah were believed to be interred), Sophr.H.*mir. Cyr.et Jo.*36(M.87.3560C); Jo.Mosch.*prat.*77(M.87.2929D); in CP, *Chron.Pasch.*p.382(M.92.977B); *ib.*p.318(812A).

***τετράπυργος,** *with four towers*, Cosm.Ind.*top.*11(M.88.444B).

***τετράπωλος,** *with four horses*, met. *τ. ἅρμα τῶν εὐαγγελιστῶν* ‡Chrys.*neg.*1(8.136D); Procl.CP *or.*2.1(M.65.693A) cit. s. *ἅρμα*; Geo. Pis.*hex.*338(M.92.1460A); *Chron.Pasch.*p.112(M.92.296A); Jo.Mal. *chron.*7 p.175(M.97.280C).

τετράς, ἡ, 1. the *number four* *κακωτικὴν εἶναι τὴν τ.* Or.*adnot.in Gen.*23:15(M.17.13D); Gnost. *ὁ μέντοι γε Ἡρακλέων μηδὲ ἐπιστήσας τῇ ἱστορίᾳ φησὶ τὸν Σολομῶντα τεσσαράκοντα καὶ ἓξ ἔτεσι κατασκευακέναι τὸν ναόν, εἰκόνα τυγχάνοντα τοῦ σωτῆρος, καὶ τὸν ἓξ ἀριθμὸν εἰς τὴν ὕλην, τουτέστι τὸ πλάσμα, ἀναφέρει, τὸν δὲ τῶν τεσσαράκοντα, ὅ τ. ἐστι, φησίν, ἡ ἀπρόσπλοκος, εἰς τὸ ἐμφύσημα καὶ τὸ ἐν τῷ ἐμφυσήματι σπέρμα* id.*Jo.*10.38(22; p.214.34; M.14.380B); **2.** *group of four*; **a.** in gen., of cardinal virtues, Clem.*str.*2.18(p.165.12; M.8.1037B); symbolized by incense, cassia, onyx, and myrrh, Evagr.Pont.*or.*1(M.79.1168C); of covenants with Adam, Noah, Abraham, and Moses, Clem.*str.*5.6(p.348.16; M.9.57C); of letters of tetragrammaton, *ib.* (p.348.20; 60A); of four elements, Mac.Mgn.*apocr.*3.13(p.88.21); of quarters of world *πᾶσα τοῦ κόσμου τ. ἐπὶ τὴν τῆς εὐσεβείας μετέστη πανήγυριν* *ib.*4.13(p.178.12); **b.** Valent., of group of four aeons *Οὐαλεντῖνος...ὁρισάμενος εἶναι δυάδα...ἧς τὸ μέν τι καλεῖσθαι Ἄρρητον, τὸ δὲ Σιγήν· ἔπειτα...δευτέραν δυάδα προβεβλῆσθαι, ἧς τὸ μέν τι Πατέρα ὀνομάζει, τὸ δὲ Ἀλήθειαν· ἐκ δὲ τῆς τ. ταύτης καρποφορεῖσθαι Λόγον καὶ Ζωήν, Ἄνθρωπον καὶ Ἐκκλησίαν· εἶναί τε ταύτην Ὀγδοάδα πρώτην* Iren.*haer.*1.11.1(M.7.561A); *σαφῶς...δεδήλωκεν ὁ Ἰωάννης τὴν τ. τὴν δευτέραν, Λόγον καὶ Ζωήν, Ἄνθρωπον καὶ Ἐκκλησίαν. ἀλλὰ μὴν καὶ τὴν πρώτην ἐμήνυσε τ. ... Πατέρα εἰπὼν καὶ Χάριν καὶ τὸν Μονογενῆ καὶ Ἀλήθειαν* *ib.*1.8.5(536A); Marcosian *τ. κατεληλυθέναι σχήματι γυναικείῳ πρὸς αὐτόν* *ib.*1.14.1(593A); *ib.*1.15.1(613A,B); Hipp.*haer.*6.49(p.181.11,17; M.16.3278A); *τὰ τέσσαρα στοιχεῖά φασι ...εἰκόνα προβεβλῆσθαι τῆς ἄνω πρώτης τ.* Iren.*haer.*1.17.1(637A); *ἀπὸ τ. ... προῆλθον οἱ αἰῶνες· ἦν δὲ ἐν τῇ τ. Ἄνθρωπος καὶ Ἐκκλησία, Λόγος καὶ Ζωή. ἀπὸ τούτων οὖν...δυνάμεις...ἀπορρυεῖσαι ἐγενεσιούργησαν τὸν ἐπὶ γῆς φανέντα Ἰησοῦν* *ib.*1.15.3(620A); *λέγει* [sc. Secundus] *τ. εἶναι δεξιὰν καὶ τ. ἀριστερὰν καὶ φῶς καὶ σκότος* Hipp.*haer.*6.38 (p.168.8; 3254A); cf. *ὁ τὰ πάντα περιέχων...ἀντέστησεν...τοὺς ἄρρενας· Μόνον Τρίτον Πέμπτον Ἕβδομον, καὶ τὰς θηλείας· Δυάδα Τετράδα Ἑξάδα Ὀγδοάδα. αὕτη οὖν ἡ Ὀγδοὰς* Val.Gn.ap.Epiph.*haer.*31.6 (p.393.7; M.41.484C); **c.** *a period of four months*, Or.*Jo.*13.40(p.266.6; M.14.469C); **3.** *quaternity* in Godhead, opp. Trinity; **a.** in Apollinarian and monoph. arguments *ἀντὶ μιᾶς ὑποστάσεως τοῦ...Χριστοῦ δύο ὑποστάσεις καὶ πρόσωπα καὶ ἀντὶ τῆς...τριάδος τ. παρανόμως φρονήσαντες* Apoll.*quod un.Chr.*3(p.296.9; M.28.124C); *τὸ δοξάζειν δύο φύσεις τὸν ἕνα Χριστὸν τ. τὴν...τριάδα ποιεῖ* Leont.H.*monoph.*(M.86.1873C); cf. *τίς...τὴν ἀθέμιτον...ἐπενόησεν ἀσέβειαν ὥστε...εἰπεῖν, ὅτι ὁ λέγων ἐκ Μαρίας εἶναι τὸ κυριακὸν σῶμα οὐκέτι τριάδα, ἀλλὰ τ. ἐν τῇ θεότητι φρονεῖ;* Ath.*ep.Epict.*2(p.5.5; M.26.1053A); *ἐρυθριάσουσι...οἱ ...ἐνθυμηθέντες δύνασθαι ἀντὶ τῆς τριάδος γενέσθαι τ., εἰ λέγοιτο ἐκ Μαρίας εἶναι τὸ σῶμα* *ib.*8(p.13.15; 1064B); *ἐὰν ἀνθρώπινον εἴπωμεν τὸ ἐκ Μαρίας σῶμα...τ. ἀντὶ τριάδος γίνεται διὰ τοῦ σώματος προσθήκην* *ib.*(p.14.3; 1064C); **b.** anti-Apollinarian and monophysite, against consubstantiality of Christ's body with Godhead *κἂν μὴ ἐκ Μαρίας λέγωσι τὸ σῶμα, ἀλλὰ ὁμοούσιον...τῷ λόγῳ...δειχθήσονται λέγοντες τ. ... τὸ ὁμοούσιον σῶμα τοῦ λόγου οὐκ ἔστιν αὐτὸς ὁ λόγος... ἑτέρου δὲ ὄντος κατ' αὐτούς, ἔσται ἡ αὐτῶν τριὰς τ.* Ath.*ep.Epict.*9 (p.14.7; 1064C); ‡Ath.*Apoll.*1.9(M.26.1109A); *τί ἔτι ἡμᾶς μέμφεσθε ὡς τ. ἀντὶ τριάδος λέγοντας, αὐτοὶ τ. ἀντὶ τριάδος καὶ ἄκοντες ὁμολογοῦντες, λέγοντες ὁμοουσίαν εἶναι τῇ τριάδι τὴν σάρκα;* *ib.*1.12(1113C); *ἡ ἐνανθρώπησις τοῦ μονογενοῦς τὸν τῆς τριάδος οὐκ ηὔξησεν ἀριθμὸν καὶ τ. τὴν τριάδα πεποίηκεν* Thdt.*ep.*145(4.1256); †Leont.B.*sect.*9(M.86.1260A); *εἰ...ὁμοούσιος* [sc. Logos with flesh], *πῶς οὐ γέγονε τ. ἡ τριάς;* Eulog.*duab.nat.*3(M.86.2940B); **c.** anti-Nestorian *εἰ ἄλλος ὁ Χριστὸς καὶ ἄλλος ὁ θεὸς λόγος οὐκέτι τριάς, ἀλλὰ τ.* Procl.CP *or. laud.BMV* 8(p.106.23; M.65.689A); *τριάδα, οὐ τ. προσκυνοῦμεν... ἀναθεματίζομεν δὲ τοὺς λέγοντας δύο υἱούς* Paul.Em.*hom.*1(p.10.27; M.77.1436C); *εἰ δύο ὑποστάσεις τοῦ Χριστοῦ...οὐκοῦν τ. καὶ οὐ τριάδι λατρεύομεν* Jo.D.*volunt.*9(M.95.140C); id.*haer.Nest.*1(M.95.188B); **d.** against distinction of Logos from Son (cf. Marcellus' doctrine) *οὐκ ἔτι...οὐδὲ εἰς τριάδα κατ' αὐτοὺς ἡ μονὰς πλατύνεται, ἀλλ' εἰς τ.· πατέρα καὶ λόγον καὶ υἱὸν καὶ πνεῦμα ἅγιον* ‡Ath.*Ar.*4.21(p.68.1; M.26.500B); **4.** *fourth day of the week, Wednesday*, Chrys.*stat.*13.1(2.133A); as fast day *νηστεύσατε τ. καὶ παρασκευήν* *Did.*8.1; Eus.*m.P.*1 (p.908.2; M.20.1461A); *τίνι δὲ οὐ συμπεφώνηται ἐν πᾶσι κλίμασι τῆς οἰκουμένης, ὅτι τ. καὶ προσάββατον νηστεία ἐστὶν ἐν τῇ ἐκκλησίᾳ ὡρισμένη;* Epiph.*haer.*75.6(p.338.6; M.42.512C); significance *τὴν μὲν γὰρ τ. διὰ τὸ γενόμενον συμβούλιον ὑπὸ τῶν Ἰουδαίων ἐπὶ τῇ προδοσίᾳ τοῦ κυρίου* Petr.I Al.*ep.can.*15(M.18.508B); *Const.App.*5.14.1; *νηστεύσατε...τ. ... ὅτι τῇ μὲν τ. ἡ κρίσις ἐξῆλθεν ἡ κατὰ τοῦ κυρίου* *ib.* 7.23.2; cf.Epiph.*exp.fid.*22(p.522.27; M.42.825B); as day of decision of Judas to betray Christ, Ammon.*Jo.*13:30(M.85.1484D); fasting on Wednesday (day of Hermes) and Friday (day of Aphrodite) signifying abstinence from avarice and sensuality, Clem.*str.*7.12 (p.54.5; M.9.504B); importance *τὰς καθολικὰς νηστείας...μὴ ἐξὸν λύειν ἄνευ πάσης ἀνάγκης· ἐν γὰρ τ. ὁ σωτὴρ παρεδόθη, ἐν δὲ τῇ παρασκευῇ σταυροῦται· ὁ οὖν ταύτας λύων συμπαραδίδωσι τὸν σωτῆρα καὶ συνσταυροῖ* ‡Pall.*h.mon.*8.58(p.48.22; M.34.1148B); enforced on pain of deprivation for clerics and excommunication for laity, *Can.App.*69; practice *ἡ νηστεία φυλάττεται...τ. καὶ προσαββάτῳ, ἕως ὥρας ἐνάτης δίχα μόνης τῆς πεντηκοστῆς...οὔτε ἐν τῇ ἡμέρᾳ τῶν Ἐπιφανείων...ἔξεστι νηστεῦσαι κἄν τε περιτύχῃ τ. ἢ προσάββατον* Epiph.*exp.fid.*22(p.523.5; 828B); complete abstinence from food until evening, Philost.*h.e.*10.12(M.65.592C); scriptures read and sermons delivered at Alexandria, with no celebration of eucharist, Socr.*h.e.*5.22.45(M.67.636A); unlike Lenten fast, may be relaxed for entertainment of visiting friend, Eus.Al.*serm.*1(M.86.324A); rejected by Aërius, Epiph.*haer.*75.3(p.335.15; M.42.508B); id.*anac.* 75(p.231.14; M.42.337A); **5.** *the fourth year*, Or.*Jo.*6.28(14; p.138.9; M.14.249B); **6.** *quaternion* of parchment, *quire of four leaves* folded to make sixteen pages, issued as pamphlet *ἀντίγραφον...τῆς τ. ἀποστεῖλον* Synes.*ep.*141(M.66.1533A); Cyr.*ep.*10(p.110.21; 5².33B); Bas.Sel.*v.Thecl.*2.16(M.85.593A); bound together to form a book, Epiph.*exp.fid.*25(p.526.9; M.42.832C); Pall.*h.Laus.*45(p.133.13; M.34.1218A); Nil.*spir.mal.*14(M.79.1160B).

τετρασσός, *fourfold*; neut. plur. as subst., *codices having four columns* *τρισσὰ καὶ τ. διαπεμψάντων ἡμῶν* Eus.*v.C.*4.37(p.132.10; M.20.1185C); as name of Origen's edition of four chief Greek versions of OT arranged in four columns, id.*h.e.*6.16.4(v.l. *τετραπλοῖς* M.20.557A).

τετραστιχία, ἡ, *poem of four verses, quatrain*, Gr.Naz.*carm.*1.2.33 tit.(M.37.928A).

τετράστιχος, *in four rows* or *courses*, Epiph.*gemm.*6(M.43.297C); Cyr.*ador.*11(1.382B); *in quatrain*, Gr.Naz.*carm.*1.2.33 tit.(M.37.927A).

τετράστοιχος, *consisting of the four elements*, ‡Gr.Nyss.*imag.*(M.44.1328B) = ‡Anast.S.*serm.imag.*1(M.89.1148A); Dion.Ar.*c.h.*15.6 (M.3.336A).

τετράστομος, *with four mouths*, Procl.CP *annunt.*5(M.85.444A).

***τετράστῳον, τό,** *hall with four rows of columns*, Jo.Mal.*chron.*12 p.291(M.97.441A); Thphn.*chron.*p.98(M.108.289A).

τετρασύλλαβος, *of four syllables*; *λόγος τ.* as title of sermon, ? because its theme is four-syllable word (*διάβολος*) or ? *consisting of four headings*, Ephr.1.181A.

τετράτομος, *in* or *with four divisions*, Paul.Sil.*Soph.*356(M.86.2133A).

***τετραϋπόστατος,** *consisting of four elements*; of world, *cat.Apoc.* 5:8–10(p.255.20).

***τετραφυής,** *of four natures* *ἡ τ. τῶν ὅλων κατάστασις, ἡ ἄσαρκος, νοερά τε καὶ λογική, ἡ αἰσθητὴ καὶ ἔνσαρκος...* ‡Caes.Naz.*dial.*49(M.38.921).

***τετράφυλλον, τό,** *quadrifolium, quarto*, CCP(681)*act.*14(H.3.1361C).

τέτραχα, *in four rows* or *parts*, Clem.*str.*5.6(p.352.7; M.9.64C).

τετραχῆ, *in four parts* *ἡ μὲν οὖν κατὰ Μωϋσέα φιλοσοφία τ. τέμνεται* Clem.*str.*1.28(p.108.24; M.8.921C); *on four sides*, Epiph. *haer.*30.12(p.347.25); *in four rows*, Gr.Nyss.*v.Mos.*(M.44.320C).

***τετραχθόνευτος,** *four days buried*; of Lazarus, Geo.Pis.*senar.*7 (M.92.1733A).

***τετραώροφον, τό,** *four-storied building*, Chrys.*hom.52.3 in Mt.* (7.533D).

[*]**τετρήμερος**, v. τετραήμερος.

τετυφωμένως, *arrogantly*, *ostentatiously*, Clem.*paed*.2.3(p.181.2; M.8.437C).

τεῦχος, τό, *book*, *volume*, Eus.*v.C*.4.37(p.132.9; M.20.1185C); Chrys.*hom*.*3.2 in 1Tim*.(11.442C); of gospels, Hier.*vir.ill*.(tr.Sophr. Pal.)6(p.6.13); τὸ πρῶτον Μωσέως τ. ‡Caes.Naz.*dial*.136(M.38.1041).

***τεφροποιέω**, *reduce to ashes*, ‡Caes.Naz.*dial*.109(M.38.984).

***τεχνεύω**, *fashion*; of Creation, Chrys.*serm*.*1.3 in Gen*.(4.649C, v.l. τεχνιτεύω).

τεχνήμων, **1.** *cunningly wrought*, Nonn.*par.Jo*.9:26(M.43.829A); Paul.Sil.*ambo*.117(M.86.2256B); **2.** masc. as subst., *artificer* θεῷ τ. κόσμου Nonn.*par.Jo*.1:2(749A).

***τεχνίδριον, τό**, *poor*, *mean craft* τ. μαθὼν ὅθεν τὸν ἄρτον πορίσεται Pall.*h.Laus*.14(p.38.4; M.34.1036A).

τεχνίτης, ὁ, *artificer*, *craftsman*, *artist*; **1.** in gen.; of skilled workers, including makers of perfumes, Clem.*paed*.2.8(p.196.24; M.8.472A); hairdressers, *ib*.3.2(p.245.14; 557B); cooks, *Hom.Clem*. 12.6; astrologers, *ib*.14.12; copyists of scriptures, Const.ap.Eus. *v.C*.4.36(p.131.25; M.20.1185A); surgeons, *Const.App*.2.43.3; church architect, Const.ap.Gel.Cyz.*h.e*.2.7.4(τέχνη τις M.85.1232D); **2.** of God as architect of the universe and supreme artist κόσμος... κατασκευή ἐστί τινος τ. Arist.*apol*.4.2; οὐ τοῦτον [sc. τὸν κόσμον], ἀλλὰ τὸν τ. αὐτοῦ προσκυνητέον Athenag.*leg*.16.1(M.6.920C); εἴτε... τέχνη τοῦ θεοῦ [sc. ὁ κόσμος], θαυμάζων αὐτοῦ τὸ κάλλος τῷ τ. πρόσειμι *ib*.16.2(921A); Or.*Cels*.4.54(p.327.25; M.11.1120A); ὕλην... πάσης ποιότητος ἣν ὁ τ. βούλεται δεκτικήν *ib*.6.77(p.146.21; 1413D); ὅρα τοῦ τ. τὴν σοφίαν Sever.*creat*.2(M.56.443); Melet.*nat.hom*.30(M. 64.1276B); partic. as designer of human body σῶμα...ὡς ἀνδριάντα θαυμάσας, δι' οὗ κάλλους ἐπὶ τὸν τ. καὶ τὸ ὄντως καλὸν αὐτὸς αὑτὸν παραπέμπει Clem.*str*.4.18(p.299.17; M.8.1325A); ἕκαστον μέλος τοῦ σώματος ἡμῶν ἐπί τινι ἔργῳ ὑπὸ τοῦ τ. θεοῦ γεγένηται Or.*fr.hom.39 in Jer*.(p.197.26; M.13.544B); *Const.App*.1.8.24; moulder of man πηλὸς ...ἐσμεν εἰς τὴν χεῖρα τοῦ τ. *2Clem*.8.2; ὁ κατ' εἰκόνα ἐκτελούμενος τοῦ κυρίου πρὸς αὐτοῦ τοῦ τ. ἄνθρωπος τέλειος Clem.*str*.3.10(p.227.24; M. 8.1172A); ἔχεις ἐν ἑαυτῷ τοῦ τ. τῆς σοφίας τὴν εἰκόνα Sever.*creat*.2 (M.56.443); as maker of moral and spiritual order, Or.*comm.in Ex*. 10:27(M.12.269D); **3.** ref. distn. between God as creator *ex nihilo* and τ. who employs pre-existing matter τί τ. μόνον θέλεις εἶναι τὸν θεόν; τί τὴν δωρεὰν αὐτοῦ παραιτῇ ὡς τέχνην καὶ μόνην τῇ ὕλῃ χαρισάμενον, οὐχὶ δὲ καὶ τὴν τοῦ εἶναι σύστασιν; Meth.*arbitr*.22(p.206. 7); οὐ...κατὰ τοὺς παρ' ἡμῖν τ. ὕλην προϋποκειμένην λαβὼν ταῖς χερσὶν τὸ πᾶν ἐτεκτήνατο Eus.*e.th*.1.12(p.71.2; M.24.845D); ὁ θεὸς... πῶς ἔτι ποιητὴς καὶ δημιουργὸς...ἐξ ἑτέρου τὸ ποιεῖν ἐσχηκώς;...ἔσται ...οὕτως κατ' αὐτοὺς ὁ θεὸς τ. μόνον καὶ οὐ κτίστης εἰς τὸ εἶναι, εἴ γε τὴν ὑποκειμένην ὕλην ἐργάζεται, τῆς δὲ ὕλης οὐκ ἔστιν αὐτὸς αἴτιος Ath.*inc*.2.4(M.25.100B); **4.** of Logos ὁ ποιῶν τὰ πάντα...τῷ τ. λόγῳ Gr.Naz.*or*.7.23(M.35.788B); CSard.*ep.cath*.ap.Thdt.*h.e*.2.8.41(3.845); Procl.CP *or.laud.BMV* 1(p.103.21; M.65.681B); **5.** of Father in rel. to Son (Eunomian) ἀλλότριος...κατὰ τὴν φύσιν ὁ υἱὸς τῷ πατρί, ἐπειδὴ καὶ τὸ ὄργανον τῷ τ. Bas.*Spir*.6(3.6B; M.32.77C); orthodox denial ὁ τ. δημιουργός, ἀλλ' οὐχὶ πατὴρ γένοιτ' ἂν τοῦ πρὸς αὐτοῦ δημιουργουμένου· τοῦ δ' ἐξ αὐτοῦ φύντος υἱοῦ οὐκ ἂν δημιουργὸς λεχθείη Eus.*e.th*.1.10(p.68.19; M.24.841B); πατρὶ ἔοικε τὸ γεννᾶν, τεχνίτῃ δὲ τὸ κτίζειν †Ath.*exp.fid*.4(M.25.205C); **6.** of νοῦς as architectonic principle of universe, *Hom.Clem*.6.8; *ib*.6.24.

***τεχνογραφία, ἡ**, *treatise on rhetoric*, Eust.*engast*.27(p.58.32; M. 18.669A).

τεχνολογ-έω, **1.** *deal in subtle verbiage*, *quibble*, Clem.*str*.5.13 (p.383.3; M.9.128A); ~οῦσι λοιπὸν οὐ θεολογοῦσιν οἱ ἄνθρωποι· ἡ τοῦ κόσμου σοφία τὰ πρωτεῖα φέρεται Bas.*ep*.90.2(3.182A; M.32.473B); σήμερον δογματίσωμεν, αὔριον τεχνολογήσωμεν...ταῦτα ταῖς ἐκκλησίαις, ἐκεῖνα ταῖς ἀγοραῖς Gr.Naz.*or*.41.10(M.36.444A); *ib*.29.15 (p.97.4; 93B); **2.** *deal subtly with*, *quibble about* διαφόρως ~ῶν τὸ ἀγέννητον Gr.Nyss.*Eun*.12(2 p.234.14; M.45.932B); μάτην...τὰ περὶ τῶν ὀνομάτων τετεχνολόγηται *ib*.7(1 p.172.18; 764B); τί τὸ πιστεύειν ἀφέντες, ~οῦμεν τὴν πίστιν; id.*fr*.3(M.46.1109C); τὴν Ἀρείου καὶ Εὐνομίου μανίαν, οἱ καὶ ~εῖν τὴν ἄρρητον...οὐσίαν τοῦ μονογενοῦς ἐθάρρησαν Max.*schol.d.n*.1.3(M.4.192C); **3.** ptcpl. pass., *subtle*, *quibbling* ~ουμένη σοφία Gr.Naz.*or*.25.6(M.35.1205B).

τεχνολογία, ἡ, **1.** *systematic teaching*, *doctrinal system* ἡ περὶ τὸν φόβον αὐτοῦ τ. σωτηρίας ἐστὶ πηγή Clem.*paed*.1.9(p.137.27; M.8. 348B); ἐν τῇ περὶ τοῦ υἱοῦ καὶ τοῦ ἁγίου πνεύματος τ. Gr.Nyss.*Eun*.1 (1 p.103.20; M.45.337A); **2.** *grammatical system*, *terminology*, Or.*Cels*. 3.39(p.236.8; M.11.972B); Bas.*Eun*.1.9(1.221D; M.29.532C); Gr.Naz. *or*.31.18(p.167.10; M.36.153A); **3.** *verbal subtlety*, *logic-chopping* ἐκ τῆς ἔξωθεν σοφίας ἢ περὶ τῶν συλλαβῶν τ. Bas.*Spir*.3(3.4E; M.32. 76A); Gr.Nyss.*Eun*.3(2 p.23.27; M.45.588D); esp. of dialectical methods used by Eunomius, *ib*.11(2 p.258.21; 856C); τὴν θεολογίαν τ. ἀπέφηνε Thdt.*haer*.4.3(4.356); κηρυττέτω...τὴν εὐαγγελικὴν ὁ λόγος πίστιν...μὴ διαλεκτικῶς...τεχνολογίας ἀπηλλαγμένος, θεολογίᾳ κεχρημένος id.*Trin*.1.2(M.75.1149B); Max.*Pyrr*.(M.91.300A).

τεχνολόγος, ὁ, one who uses verbal subtleties, *logic-chopper*; of Eunomians, Gr.Naz.*or*.29.21(p.107.7; M.36.104A); Gr.Nyss.*Eun*. 12(1 p.385.9; M.45.1113C); Thdt.*Trin*.1.15(M.75.1168D).

***τεχνοποιέω**, *make*, *fabricate*, Cyr.*Is*.4.3(2.621B).

***τεχνοποιΐα, ἡ**, *making by art*, *device*, Eust.*engast*.12(p.36.5; M. 18.640B).

***τεχνορράφος, ὁ**, *contriver*, ‡Chrys.*hom*.9(13.237A).

***τεχνουργέω**, *fashion*, Eus.*Hierocl*.18(523D; M.22.825A); Cyr.*Is*. 4.2(2.609A); *ib*.4.3(621B); id.*Am*.5(3.310C).

τεχνούργημα, τό, *work of art*, of the universe μηδ' ἀναιτίου φύσεως ἔργον τυγχάνειν τὸ μέγα τοῦτο καὶ περικαλλὲς τ. Eus.*p.e*.7.10 (314D; M.21.532D); of idols, Cyr.*Is*.4.3(2.629A).

τεχνουργία, ἡ, **1.** *handiwork*; of sculpture opp. painting, Or. *adnot.in Ex*.20:4(M.17.16C); plur., *kinds of handiwork*, Isid.Pel. *epp*.1.403(M.78.408B); **2.** *creation*, *plan of creation*, Epiph.*haer*.23. 3(p.251.27; M.41.301C); *ib*.23.4(p.252.21; 304A).

τεχνουργός, ὁ, *artificer*, Eus.*Hierocl*.18(523D; M.22.824D); Cyr. *Os*.6(3.101D); id.*ador*.11(1.378E); of God, Melet.*nat.hom*.proem.(M. 64.1176A).

τεχνύδριον, τό, = τεχνίδριον, *petty device*, Clem.*str*.1.3(p.14.24; M.8.712B); *ib*.1.8(p.27.11; 737A); Gr.Naz.*or*.27.2(p.3.12; M.36.13B).

τζαγγάριος, ὁ, = σαγγάριος, *cobbler*, Gr.Mag.*dial*.(tr.Zach.)4.38 (M.*PL*.77.387B); τζάγκαρος, *Nomoc*.475; σαγγάριος, *ib*.102.

τζάγγη (*τζαγγίς), **ἡ**, *sandal*, Ephr.1.42C; τζαγγίς id.3.152D.

***τζαγγίον, τό**, *boot*, Jo.Mal.*chron*.17 p.413(M.97.612B); Thphn. *chron*.p 144(M.108.393B).

***τζαγγίς, ἡ**, v. τζάγγη.

[*]**τζάγκαρος, ὁ**, v. τζαγγάριος.

***τζανδάνα, ἡ**, *sandalwood*, Cosm.Ind.*top*.11(M.88.445D).

***τζούκζω**, s.v.l., *smoke*, †Gregent.*leg.Hom*.36(M.86.601B).

τηγανίζω, *fry on a τήγανον*; **1.** as torture, *Ep.Lugd*.ap.Eus.*h.e*. 5.1.38(M.20.424A); in hell, *Apoc.Petr*.B 34(p.87.21); usu. ref. rich man of Lc.16:24, Ephr.2.93B; Chrys.*hom.27.3 in Jo*.(8.158B); id. *hom.12.4 in Ac*.(9.101D); id.*hom.10.3 in 2Cor*.(10.510D); Isid.Pel. *epp*.1.340(M.78.377B); Max.*ep*.1(M.91.388A); **2.** *roast* in heat of sun, *Apophth.Patr*.(M.65.177B).

τήγανον, τό, *frying pan*, ‡Caes.Naz.*dial*.73(M.38.941); as instrument of torture, *Ep.Lugd*.ap.Eus.*h.e*.5.1.56(M.20.429B); *M.Eleuth*. 5(p.153.10); Ephr.3.249E; Chrys.*hom.38.4 in Mt*.(7.430B); *ib.89.1* (833A); id.*Jud*.5.2(1.630C); ‡Caes.Naz.*dial*.109(980).

***τηκεδανός**, *wasting*; of disease, sorrow, *Orac.Sib*.14.104; Gr. Naz.*carm*.1.2.9.27(M.37.669A).

***τηλαυγότης, ἡ**, *brightness*, *Anaph.Pil*.B 7(p.446).

τηλίκος, *so great*, Nonn.*par.Jo*.9:33(M.43.829C); of a murder, *so terrible*, *ib*.18:29(896A); of an event, *so strange*, *ib*.9:32(829C).

***τημελοῦχος**, *tutelary*, *guardian*, of angels τὰ βρέφη ἐξαμβλωθέντα ...ἀγγέλῳ τ. παραδίδοσθαι *Apoc.Petr*.ap.Clem.*ecl*.48(p.150.9; M.9. 720C); τὰ βρέφη τὰ ἐκτεθέντα τ. παραδίδοσθαι ἀγγέλῳ ὑφ' οὗ παιδεύεσθαί τε καὶ αὔξειν Clem.*ecl*.41(p.149.1; 717C); τ. ἀγγέλοις, κἂν ἐκ μοιχείας ὦσι, τὰ ἀποτικτόμενα παραδίδοσθαι παρειλήφαμεν Meth. *symp*.2.6(p.23.13; M.18.57A).

***τηξίφρων**, *soul-wasting*, Meth.*symp*.11.2(p.136.11; M.18.212D).

τηρ-έω, **1.** *guard*, *keep*, *preserve*, ref. baptism τῶν...μὴ ~ησάντων...τὴν σφραγῖδα *2Clem*.7.6; ~ήσατε τὴν σάρκα ἁγνὴν καὶ τὴν σφραγῖδα ἄσπιλον, ἵνα τὴν ζωὴν ἀπολάβωμεν *ib*.8.6; ἐὰν μὴ ~ήσωμεν τὸ βάπτισμα ἁγνὸν καὶ ἀμίαντον, ποίᾳ πεποιθήσει εἰσελευσόμεθα εἰς τὸ βασίλειον τοῦ θεοῦ; *ib*.6.9; οἱ...εἰληφότες τὴν σφραγῖδα...καὶ μὴ τηρήσαντες ὑγιῆ Herm.*sim*.8.6.3; in gen. ~ήσατε τὴν σάρκα, ἵνα τοῦ πνεύματος μεταλάβητε *2Clem*.14.3; ~ει τὴν ἁγνείαν καὶ τὴν σεμνότητα καὶ ζήσῃ τῷ θεῷ Herm.*mand*.4.4.4; of chastity, Clem.*str*.3.7(p.224. 7; M.8.1164B); id.*ecl*.29(p.146.8; M.9.713C); τὸ ἀειθαλὲς ἄνθος...τῆς παρθενίας ~ῆσαι Meth.*symp*.2.7(p.25.21; M.18.60B); ~εῖν τὴν ἑαυτοῦ σάρκα παρθένον *ib*.3.14(p.44.14; 85A); ἡ πρὸς θεὸν ἀγάπη, ἣν...ὁ Ἰησοῦς...ἄρρηκτον...μέχρι τέλους ~ῆσαι παράσχοι *ib*.4.6(p.52.9; 96B); οὐ μόνον ἄφθορα τὰ σώματα ~εῖσθαι δεῖ, ἀλλὰ τὰς ψυχάς *ib*.1.1 (p.8.9; 37B); δεῖ τὴν παρθένον πρὸ τοῦ σώματος μάλιστα ~εῖν τὴν ψυχήν †Bas.Anc.*virg*.13(M.30.693D); of work of Logos in sustaining creation μὴ...πάθῃ [sc. ἡ κτίσις] ὅπερ ἂν ἔπαθεν, εἰ μὴ ὁ λόγος αὐτὴν ἐτήρει, λέγω δὴ τὸ μὴ εἶναι Ath.*gent*.41(M.25.84B); ref. catechetical instruction τὰ λεγόμενα μάνθανε καὶ ~ει εἰς τὸν αἰῶνα Cyr.H. *procatech*.11; ~ει τοὺς λογισμοὺς καὶ φεῦγε ἀπὸ κακίας, ἵνα μὴ σκοτισθεὶς ὁ νοῦς ἄλλα ἀντ' ἄλλων βλέπῃ Thal.*cent*.1.86(M.91.1436B); ~εῖτε ἀεὶ μηδένα λογισμὸν ἐν τῇ καρδίᾳ, μὴ ἄλογον μὴ εὔλογον, ἵνα οὕτως ῥᾳδίως ἐπιγινώσκῃς τοὺς ἀλλοφύλους Hesych.S.*temp*.1.49(M.93.1496D); τὰς...αἰσθήσεις...ἀσφαλῶς ~εῖ *ib*.1.1(1481B); πέφυκεν...ἡ καρδία ἀδιαλείπτως ~ουμένη...λογισμοὺς φεγγοειδεῖς...κυΐσκειν *ib*.2.3 (1512C); ἀκριβῶς τὸν νοῦν ~ήσωμεν καὶ ἐν πύλῃ καρδίας ἡμῶν στῶμεν *ib*.1.100(1512B); ὁ ἐνοικῶν τῇ καρδίᾳ θεὸς...εἴπερ εὑρίσκει τὸν ἀέρα τῆς διανοίας...ὑπὸ φυλακῆς νοὸς ~ούμενον ἀνάπτει τὸ διανοητικὸν ἡμῶν πρὸς θεωρίαν, ὡς φλὸξ κηρόν *ib*.2.3(1512D); ὁ...πάσῃ σπουδῇ ~ῶν ἀεὶ τὴν καθαρότητα τῆς καρδίας, ἕξει διδάσκαλον τὸν...Χριστόν *ib*.2.84 (1540B); **2.** *watch, give heed to*, *Barn*.10.11; Clem.*str*.2.4(p.120.3; M.8.945A); Meth.*res*.1.2(p.221.20); c. εἰς, Clem.*str*.1.1(p.12.16; 705C); **3.** *watch for, lie in wait for*, *ib*.1.24(p.101.28; 909A); ~εῖ μὲν μῦν ἡ τούτου θηρεύτρια· μῦν δὲ νοητὸν ἡσυχαστοῦ ἔννοια Jo.Clim.*scal*.27 (M.88.1097B); ὁ...τὴν κεφαλὴν ~ῶν τὴν τοῦ ὄφεως καὶ δι' ἀντιρρήσεως...ῥήματι χρώμενος...ἀπεκρούσατο τὸν πολέμιον Hesych.S.*temp*.2.76(M.93.1537A); **4.** *notice, observe*, Or.*Cels*.1.59(p.110.3; M.11.768C); id.*comm.in Mt*.10.22(p.30.5; M.13.896A); Gr.Naz.*or*.29.5 (p.80.4; M.36.80C); **5.** *keep, observe* a law or engagement, *T.Dan* 5.1; *2Clem*.8.5; Clem.*str*.3.11(p.228.9; M.8.1172C); Or.*Cels*.5.26(p.26.25; M.11.1220B); festivals, Just.*dial*.10.3(M.6.496C); οὗτοι πάντες ἐτήρησαν τὴν ἡμέραν τῆς τεσσαρεσκαιδεκάτης τοῦ πάσχα Polycr.ap. Eus.*h.e*.5.24.6(M.20.496A); οἱ προστάντες τῆς ἐκκλησίας...αὐτοὶ μὴ ~οῦντες εἰρήνευον τοῖς ἀπὸ τῶν παροικιῶν ἐν αἷς ἐτηρεῖτο Iren.*ep. Vict*.ap.Eus.*h.e*.5.24.14(505A); **6.** *keep* a secret, in initiation oath administered by Justin the Gnostic ὀμνύω τὸν ἐπάνω πάντων, τὸν ἀγαθόν, ~ῆσαι τὰ μυστήρια ταῦτα καὶ ἐξειπεῖν μηδενί Hipp.*haer*.5.27 (p.133.2; M.16.3203A); **7.** *have regard for, reverence* τοῦ αὐτοῦ θεοῦ [i.e. of OT and NT] πρὸς ἡμῶν ~ουμένου Clem.*str*.3.12(p.234.16; M.8.1184C); ἕνα...~οῦντες θεόν Or.*hom.18.9 in Jer*.(p.163.15; M.13.481B); **8.** *retain*, Or.*Jo*.6.2(1; p.108.2; M.14.200C); ἄλλους ἐν τοῖς καλοῖς ~εῖσθαι...ἄλλους τε αὖ...τοῖς κακοῖς παραμένειν id.*princ*.3.1.23 (p.242.3; M.11.300B); of retaining literal sense of scripture, id.*Jo*.13.21(p.245.20; 436A); **9.** *reserve* ἀμετανόητος ~εῖται εἰς αἰώνιον κόλασιν *T.Gad* 7.5; τὰ ~ούμενα τοῖς ὑπομείνασιν ἀγαθά *M.Polyc*.2.3; τὸ τῆς...αἰωνίου κολάσεως τοῖς ἀσεβέσιν ~ούμενον πῦρ *ib*.11.2; τῶν ἐν οὐρανοῖς ἀπολαύσεις ἀποκεκρυμμένων, τῶν ἐμοὶ τετηρημένων Clem.*prot*.12(p.83.29; M.8.240B); ὁ κύριος...παρατίθεται τῷ πατρὶ τὸν πεπιστευκότα αἰῶσι ~ούμενον *ib*.(p.84.26; 241A); id.*paed*.1.6(p.107.13; M.8.285A); κρυπτόντων [sc. τὰ ἀπόρρητα] τῶν ἄλλων ἀγγέλων, μᾶλλον δὲ ~ούντων εἰς τὴν τοῦ κυρίου παρουσίαν id.*str*.5.1(p.332.20; M.9.24B); τὸ δὲ ἀκραιφνὲς τῆς τοῦ πατρὸς θεωρίας εἰλικρινῶς υἱῷ σὺν ἁγίῳ πνεύματι τετήρηται Cyr.H.*catech*.7.11.

***τηρήμων**, *keeping, guarding*, *Orac.Sib*.5.400.

τήρησις, ἡ, 1. *guarding, defence, preservation* ἡ σωτηρία τ. οὖσα τοῦ εὖ ἔχοντος Clem.*str*.2.18(p.155.1; M.8.1020A); of defence of tradition, *ib*.1.1(p.9.10; 700B); τὸν ζῶντα ἄρτον ἀναλαμβάνοντα εἰς τὴν τ. ἑαυτοῦ Or.*Cels*.6.44(p.114.21; M.11.1365B); δεῖ...ἀεὶ τῇ προσευχῇ σχολάζειν ἐν τῇ τ. τοῦ νοῦ, κἂν ἔξω που αὐλίζοιτο τῶν εὐκτηρίων δόμων Diad.*perf*.97(p.144.9); νοῦ τ. οὐδ' ὅλως προβήσεται χωρὶς νήψεως σὺν ταπεινώσει καὶ εὐχῇ Ἰησοῦ Χριστοῦ Hesych.S.*temp*.2.66(M.93.1533A); ὅταν τῶν...μυστηρίων Χριστοῦ...ἀξιωθῶμεν...τότε μᾶλλον τὴν νῆψιν καὶ τὴν τ. τοῦ νοὸς...ἐπιδειξώμεθα *ib*.1.100 (1512A); ἡ καθαρότης τῆς καρδίας ἤγουν ἡ τοῦ νοῦ τ. καὶ φυλακή *ib*.2.11 (1516A); νοὸς τ. ... ἥ ἐστι καὶ λέγεται πρακτικὴ φιλοσοφία νοός *ib*.2.55 (1529C); ἀκολούθει μοι πρὸς τὴν συνάφειαν τῆς μακαρίας τοῦ νοῦ τ. ... καὶ διδάξω σε...πολιτείαν νοερῶν δυνάμεων *ib*.2.97(1544A); **2.** *observation* ἡ φρόνησις...τηρήσει τῶν ὁμοίων καὶ μεταβάσει...ἐμπειρία προσαγορεύεται Clem.*str*.6.17(p.512.2; M.9.388A); Or.*Cels*.4.96(p.369.6; M.11.1173D); †Bas.*Chr.generat*.5(2.600C; M.31.1469A); **3.** *observance* φυλακὴ...τῶν ἐντολῶν τ. οὖσα αὐτῶν ἀβλαβής Clem.*str*.2.18 (p.154.24; M.8.1017B); *ib*.2.9(p.135.8; 977A); περὶ τῆς ἐν τοῖς εὐαγγελίοις τ. πάντων τῶν γεγραμμένων Or.*Cels*.3.21(p.217.19; M.11.944B); ὅτε...τις καμὼν ἐν τῇ προσευχῇ καὶ τ. τοῦ λόγου...οὐκέτι αὐτὸν τετήρηκεν, τότε τὸν θάνατον ἐθεώρησεν id.*Jo*.20.39(31; p.382.21; M.14.668C); ἐὰν...ἄρξηται προβαίνειν ὁ ἄνθρωπος τῇ τ. τῶν ἐντολῶν καὶ ἀπαύστως ἐπικαλοῖτο τὸν κύριον Ἰησοῦν, τότε καὶ ἐπὶ τὰ ἐξωτερικὰ αἰσθητήρια τῆς καρδίας τὸ πῦρ...ἐπινέμεται χάριτος Diad.*perf*.85(p.116.2); δεῖ...ἀεὶ εἰς τὴν τῶν...ἐντολῶν τ. ἀποσχολεῖσθαι τὸν νοῦν *ib*.96 (p.142.21); τ. ἐντολῶν θεοῦ τίκτει ἀπάθειαν Thal.*cent*.2.25(M.91.1440C).

***τηρητέος**, *to be observed, kept* οὐδεμία νομοθεσία κατὰ ῥητὸν τ., ἐπεί τις...ἄλογος τυγχάνει ἢ ἀδύνατος Or.*princ*.4.3(p.329.3; M.11.384A); τίς οὐκ ἂν εἴποι...ἐντολὴν 'τίμα τὸν πατέρα'...χωρὶς πάσης ἀναγωγῆς τ.; *ib*.(p.330.2; 384B); *ib*.(p.330.6; M.l.c.).

τηρητής, ὁ, 1. *watcher*, *Ascens.Is*.3.14(p.92); **2.** *overseer, taskmaster*, *Apophth.Patr*.(M.65.273C); **3.** *policeman*, *ib*.(388B).

[*]**τήρων, ὁ,** v. τίρων.

τιάρα, ἡ, 1. *military head-dress* of Persian origin; worn by Eusebius of Samosata in soldier's disguise, Thdt.*h.e*.4.13.4(3.969); **2.** *cowl, hood*; esp. of a monk, Soz.*h.e*.3.14.7(M.67.1069C).

[*]**τιαρηφόρος (τιαροφ-),** *wearing a* τιάρα, Pall.*h.Laus*.3(p.107.11; τιαροφ- M.34.1179D).

[*]**τιάφιον, τό,** v. τεάφιον.

τιθηνία, ἡ, *nursing at the breast*, ‡Nil.*narr*.6(M.79.657C).

***τιθηνίζομαι,** *nurse, rear*, Ephr.2.291A.

***τιθηνοκόμος,** *nursing, suckling* τὴν τ. καὶ κουροτρόφον τοῦ θεοῦ ἐκκλησίαν Pall.*v.Chrys*.20(p.141.14; M.47.79).

τίκτ-ω, *bear* or *beget, bring forth*; **1.** of Son's generation θεὸν ἑαυτοῦ τὸν πατέρα φησίν, καίτοι φύσει θεὸς ὑπάρχων...καὶ κατ' οὐδένα τρόπον τῆς τοῦ τεκόντος ὑπεροχῆς ἡττώμενος Cyr.*apol.Thdt*.6(p.129.17; 6[1].223D); ἐκ θεοῦ πατρὸς γεννηθέντα κατὰ φύσιν καὶ τὴν αὐτοῦ τοῦ τεκόντος ἔχοντα δόξαν id.*Is*.5.2(2.777E); αὐτός ἐστιν ἡ τοῦ τεκόντος δεξιὰ πανσθενής *ib*.(778D); **2.** of Christ's birth τὸ μὲν σῶμα ὡς σῶμα ἐτίκτετο...αὐτὸς δὲ ὁ συνὼν τῷ σώματι θεὸς λόγος...δι' ὧν εἰργάζετο ἐν τῷ σώματι, οὐκ ἄνθρωπον ἑαυτὸν ἀλλὰ θεὸν λόγον ἐγνώριζεν Ath.*inc*.18.1(M.25.128A); πρότερον μὲν τὸν δεσπότην ἡμῶν διὰ τῆς παρθένου τετέχθαι, ὕστερον δὲ τὸν ἀστέρα φανῆναι Marcell.*fr*.26 ap.Eus.*Marcell*.2.3(p.50.15; M.24.808C); ὁ λόγος τοῦ ἀοράτου θεοῦ διὰ παρθένου τεχθήσεσθαι ἔμελλεν Marcell.*fr*.98 *ib*.(p.51.15; 809B); πρὸ τοῦ ...διὰ τῆς παρθένου τεχθῆναι λόγος ἦν μόνον Marcell.*fr*.42 *ib*.(p.35.2; 784A); τέξεται ἡ δάμαλις καὶ ἐροῦσιν οὐ τέτοκεν· ἐπειδὴ...τινες λέγουσιν αὐτὸν μὴ τετέχθαι, διὰ τοῦτο τὸ τέξεται, καὶ...οὐ τέτοκεν, ἐπειδὴ οὐ τέτοκεν Μαρία ἐκ σπέρματος ἀνδρός Epiph.*haer*.30.30(p.374.16; M.41.457C); θεὸς ἦν καὶ ἔστι, γέγονε καὶ ἄνθρωπος δι' οἰκονομίαν,...τεχθεὶς ἐκ παρθένου δι' οἰκείαν φιλανθρωπίαν Gel.Cyz.*h.e*.2.19.27(M.85.1281A); οὔτε...συλλαμβανόμενος, οὔτε ὅλως ~όμενος ὁ βασιλεὺς τῆς δόξης τὰς θύρας τῆς σῆς μήτρας ἠνέῳξεν Hesych.H.*serm*.5(M.93.1464B); εἰ ἐγίνωσκες ἄνδρα, οὐκ ἂν ἔτεκες θεόν *ib*.(1465D); παρθένον ἔχεις ~ουσαν κεκλεισμένων τῶν ὀργάνων τῆς φύσεως *ib*.8(1480B); ἡ ἄφθορος τῆς παρθένου μήτρα καὶ μετὰ τὸ τεκεῖν ἄλυτος ἔμεινεν ‡Chrys.*BMV* 2.2 (8.240A); ἡ παρθένος σήμερον τὸν ὑπερούσιον ~ει Rom.Mel.(*BZ* 24 p.3); δι' ἐμοῦ τῆς σε τεκούσης παιδίον νέον id.(*BZ* 24 p.9); ὥσπερ... συλληφθεὶς παρθένον τὴν συλλαβοῦσαν ἐτήρησεν, οὕτω καὶ τεχθεὶς τὴν αὐτῆς παρθενίαν ἐφύλαξεν ἄτρωτον Jo.D.*f.o*.4.14(M.94.1161A); δι' ἀκοῆς...ἡ σύλληψις, ἡ δὲ γέννησις διὰ τῆς συνήθους τῶν ~ομένων ἐξόδου, εἰ καί τινες μυθολογοῦσι διὰ τῆς πλευρᾶς αὐτὸν τεχθῆναι τῆς θεομήτορος *ib*.; **3.** of generation of all things acc. Basilides, Hipp.*haer*.7.24(p.202.15; M.16.3311C); **4.** of birth of BMV ἡ στεῖρα ~ει τὴν θεοτόκον Rom.Mel.(*AS* 1 p.198); ~εται...ἐν τῷ τῆς προβατικῆς τοῦ Ἰωακεὶμ οἴκῳ καὶ τῷ ἱερῷ προσάγεται Jo.D.*f.o*.4.14(M.94.1157B); **5.** of spiritual birth, Nonn.*par.Jo*.3:3(M.43.765B); ἡ ἐκκλησία... τέκνα ἐν λύπαις ~ει...~ει δὲ αὐτὰ διὰ λουτροῦ παλιγγενεσίας Proc.G.*Gen*.3:16(M.87.213A); **6.** met., *produce, generate* ἡ διάνοια...~ει... φθόνον *T.Benj*.7.2; Clem.*paed*.2.10(p.221.19; M.8.525A); λογισμοῦ ἁμαρτήματος...τεχθέντος ἐκ πλάνης τοῦ ἐχθροῦ Const.ap.Gel.Cyz.*h.e*.2.7.35(M.85.1240D); ἡ ἀπιστία βίον ~ει πονηρόν Chrys.*hom.6.2 in Heb*.(12.63D); ~ουσιν [sc. dangers] ἡμῖν τὴν αἰώνιον ζωήν id.*hom.1.1 in 2Tim*.(11.658C); dep. τέξομαι, id.*stat*.2.3(2.24D); of diseases, *breed*, ref. spiritual diseases οὐδὲ ἁπλῶς ~εται τοῦτο τὸ νόσημα [sc. vainglory], ἀλλ' ὅταν πολλὰ κατορθώσωμεν τῶν ἐπιταττομένων id.*hom.19.1 in Mt*.(7.244C); id.*hom.3.4 in Eph*.(11.22A); id.*hom.15.3 in Heb*.(12.153C); of persons ἀπὸ τῆς τρυφῆς...νόσους τεκόντες id.*hom.2.4 in Eph*.(15A); id.*comm.in Gal*.1:7(10.669B); id.*hom.29.4 in Heb*.(12.276D).

***τιμιολκός, ὁ,** v. *τιμιουλκός.

τίμιος, 1. of persons, *held in honour, worthy of honour*, of God ὁ γνωστικὸς τίμιον, σεμνὸν...εἶναι τὸν μόνον θεὸν πεπεισμένος Clem.*str*.7.4(p.16.12; M.9.428B); τὸν πάντων...τιμιώτερον Or.*Jo*.10.6(4; p.176.25; M.14.316C); τὴν τοῦ μόνου τιμιωτάτου τιμήν *Hom.Clem*.11.6; ὁ δημιουργὸς τῶν ἑαυτοῦ δημιουργημάτων φύσει τε καὶ ἀξίᾳ τιμιώτερος *Const.App*.7.23.4; of Christ ὦ παιδίον τ. *A.Mt*.3(p.219.9n.); of H. Ghost ὡς...ἀληθὲς προσιέμεθα τὸ πάντων διὰ τοῦ λόγου γενομένων τὸ ἅγιον πνεῦμα πάντων εἶναι τιμιώτερον Or.*Jo*.2.10(6; p.65.20; 128B); of BMV, Mac.Mgn.*apocr*.4.28(p.216.26); τὴν τιμιωτέραν τῶν Χερουβὶμ καὶ ἐνδοξοτέραν ἀσυγκρίτως τῶν Σεραφεὶμ...τὴν ὄντως θεοτόκον σὲ μεγαλύνομεν Cosm.Mel.*hymn*.7(12.43, p.195; M.98.485A); of saints, Or.*Jo*.6.7(4; p.115.29; 213A); πρώτου κατειλεγμένου τοῦ Πέτρου εἰς τὸν ἀριθμὸν τῶν δώδεκα, τάχα ὡς τῶν λοιπῶν τιμιωτέροι *ib*.32.6(5; p.435.20; 756C); Andr.Cr.*idiomel*.(M.97.1436C); of man in creation, Clem.*prot*.1(p.9.2; M.8.64C); Mac.Mgn.*apocr*.4.28(p.217.1); of the virtuous man, Bas.*leg.lib.gent*.4(2.177C; M.31.572C); of virgins πολλῶν...οὐσῶν...τῆς ἐκκλησίας τῶν θυγατέρων μία μόνη ἐκλεκτὴ κα τιμιωτάτη ἐν ὀφθαλμοῖς αὐτῆς...τὸ τάγμα τῶν παρθένων Meth.*symp*.7.3(p.75.1; M.18.129B); of the 'gnostic' ὁ τ. τῷ θεῷ ἐν ᾧ ὁ θεὸς ἐνίδρυται Clem.*str*.7.5(p.21.29; 440A); **2.** as complimentary form of address, *honourable* (usu. superl.) to bishops, Const.ap.Gel.Cyz.*h.e.* 2.7.9(M.85.1233C); Eus.*e.th.inscr*.(p.60.1; M.24.824C); Ath.*apol.sec.* 77(M.25.385D); Bas.*ep*.90.1(3.181B; M.32.472C); to priests, Epiph. *exp.fid*.25(p.526.9; M.42.832C); id.*rescr*.1(p.155.4; M.41.157C); Chrys. *ep*.22(3.607E); to a deacon, Epiph.*exp.fid*.25(p.526.8; 832C); to civil dignitaries, Hegem.*Arch*.5(p.8.2; M.10.1436B); Const.ap.Eus. *h.e*.10.5.15(M.20.885B); **3.** of things, *precious, valuable, prized*, in gen. τὸ τιμιώτατον πάντων τῶν ἐν ἀνθρώποις κτημάτων...τὸν λόγον Clem.*paed*.2.5(p.185.15; M.8.448A); τὸν λόγον, δι' ὃν ἡ σὰρξ τιμία ὕδατι ἀναγεννωμένη *ib*.2.12(p.228.7; 540C); πολλά ἐστιν ἀνθρώπου τιμιώτερα Or.*Cels*.4.29(p.298.4; M.11.1069B); ψυχὴν γὰρ παντὸς σώματος...φαμεν εἶναι πρᾶγμα τιμιώτερον *ib*.8.49(p.265.3; 1589B); εἰ τιμιώτερον σῶμα ἀνθρώπου τῶν ἄλλων ζῴων, ὅτι χερσί τε θεοῦ λέγεται πεπλάσθαι καὶ ὅτι τιμιώτερον τῆς ψυχῆς τετύχηκε σχῆμα Meth.*res*.2.22 (p.376.9); of value of flesh, formed by God, in rel. to resurrection, †Just.*fr.res*.(p.44; M.6.1584C); of name of God, Clem.*prot*.11(p.81.26; M.8.236A); *Hom.Clem*.9.22; *Const.App*.5.6.2; of name Sabaoth in Manich. usage, Hegem.*Arch*.11(p.19.9; M.10.1445B); esp. of Christ's body and blood, *1Clem*.7.4 cit. s. αἷμα; *Const.App*.1 *inscr*.; *ib*.2.57.20; Rom.Mel.(*AS* 1 p.53); in eucharist, *A.Thom*.A 49(p.166.3, some MSS only); *Const.App*.2.57.21; *ib*.5.14.7; *Lit.Bas*.(p.318.27); *ib*.(p.330.4); *Lit.Marc*.(Brightman p.140.18); of the Cross, Cyr. *Lc*.9:30f.(*TU* 34 p.80.3; M. om.); Andr.Cr.*or*.10(M.97.1017C); *ib*. (1020D); of blood of martyrs ὥσπερ τ. αἵματι...τοῦ Ἰησοῦ ἠγοράσθημεν,...οὕτως τῷ τ. αἵματι τῶν μαρτύρων ἀγορασθήσονταί τινες Or. *mart*.50(p.46.26; M.11.636A); of saint's relics, *M.Polyc*.18.1; *A.Andr*. B 11(p.64.6); of icons, Jo.D.*imag*.3.10(M.94.1333A); *ib*.3.1(1317C); **4.** neut. as subst., *honour, dignity*, Const.ap.Eus.*v.C*.2.71(p.70.5; M.20.1044C); *ib*.(p.70.22; 1045B); **5.** *conferring honour, honourable*; of priesthood, *T.Lev*.17.3; of marriage, *Const.App*.6.11.6; **6.** *worth* so much, = ἄξιος, Clem.*paed*.3.6(p.256.6; M.8.604B).

τιμιότης, ἡ, *honour, distinction* τ. καὶ ἀξίωμα ἡ ταπεινοφροσύνη Mac.Aeg.*cust.cor*.14(M.34.840D); as complimentary style of address to bishops, Const.ap.Ath.*apol.Const*.23(M.25.624B); Acac.et Paul.*ep*.(p.154.20; M.41.157A); Gr.Naz.*ep*.6(M.37.32A); Pall.*v.Chrys*. 14(p.88.18; M.47.50); to abbots, Epiph.*haer*.proem.2(p.170.25; M.41.176C); id.*exp.fid*.25(p.526.4; M.42.832C); to monks, Jo.VI H.*v.Jo.D*. 10(M.94.445A); to prefects, Gr.Naz.*ep*.208(345A); to counts, Bas. *ep*.15(3.94D; M.32.277D).

τιμιουλκ-έω, *raise the price of* ὁ ~ῶν σῖτον, δημοκατάρατος Bas. *hom*.6.3(2.46B; M.31.268B); Chrys.*kal*.6(1.706C); Areth.*Apoc*.6:6(M.106.592A); to be read in place of ταμι-, Andr.Cr.*or*.9(M.97.1009B).

***τιμιουλκός, ὁ,** *one who raises prices* περὶ...τῶν προσφορῶν...ἐὰν ...λάβῃ (ὁ ἱερεὺς) παρὰ...τοκογλύφου ἢ τιμιουλκοῦ ἐπὶ σίτου...χωλῶν καὶ τυφλῶν προσφέρει...τῷ θεῷ ‡Ath.*syntag*.8.8(p.154; τιμιολκοῦ M. 28.845A).

τιμωρητής, ὁ, *avenger, agent of punishment*; of angels, Herm. *sim*.7.6; cf.*ib*.7.1; Meth.*symp*.9.1(p.115.20; M.18.180B).

***τιμωρητός,** *punishable, deserving of punishment*, Dion.Ar.*d.n*.4.35(M.3.736A).

τιμωρία, ἡ, A. *punishment, retribution*; **1.** in gen. ὁ ἄγγελος τῆς τ. Herm.*sim*.6.3.2; γέγονεν...ἡ τῶν Σοδομιτῶν δικαία τ. τῆς...σωτηρίας εἰκών Clem.*paed*.3.8(p.262.16; M.8.616B); εἰ οἱ πονηροὶ πονηροὶ κατὰ γένεσιν πεφύκασι προνοίας ταγαῖς, οὐκ εἰσὶ...ἄξιοι τιμωρίας τῆς ἐκ τῶν νόμων Meth.*symp*.8.16(p.110.5; M.18.172D); cf.id.*res*.1.31(p.265.20; M.41.1141C); Bas.*ep*.53.1(3.147B; M.32.397A); ἂν μετὰ καθαριότητος προσέλθῃς [sc. to Communion], εἰς σωτηρίαν προσῆλθες· ἂν δὲ μετὰ πονηροῦ συνειδότος, εἰς κόλασιν καὶ τ. Chrys.*hom*.46.4 *in Jo*.(8.274C); ref. death πειθόμεθα...μὴ μισθὸν τιμωρίας εἶναι τὸν θάνατον, ἐξ ὧν αὐτὸν καὶ ἅγιοι ὑπέστησαν ἢ καὶ αὐτὸς...ὁ Χριστός *Const.App*.5.7.9; ref. Atonement ἡμῖν...κεχρεώστητο τ. σταυροῦ Gel.Cyz.*h.e*.2.24.25 (M.85.1304C); ὁ...σωτὴρ...τὰς ἡμῖν...χρεωστουμένας τ. εἰς τὴν...αὐτοῦ ὑπεδέξατο σάρκα *ib*.2.24.26(M.l.c.); **2.** ref. Origenist view of Fall τὰ λογικά, τὰ τῆς θείας ἀγάπης ἀποψυγέντα καὶ ἐντεῦθεν ψυχὰς ὀνομασθέντα, τιμωρίας χάριν σώμασι παχυτέροις...ἐνδυθῆναι καὶ ἀνθρώπους ὀνομασθῆναι Or.*princ*.2.8.3(p.160.2); ἐκ τῶν προγενεστέρων ἁμαρτημάτων λόγῳ κολάσεως ἤτοι τιμωρίας ἐδέξατο τὸ σῶμα ἡ ψυχή...καὶ πάλιν ἐκ δευτέρου καὶ...πλεονάκις ἐμβάλλονται σώμασι πρὸς τιμωρίαν *ib*.(p.160.21); denied μὴ ἐγχωρεῖν αὐτὸ [sc. τὸ σῶμα] νομίζεσθαι διὰ τὴν παράβασιν δεσμὸν ἐπὶ τιμωρίᾳ γεγονότα Meth.*res*.1.54(p.312.1; M.41.1145C); **3.** ref. eternal punishment ὁδός...ἐστιν θανάτου αἰωνίου μετὰ τιμωρίας *Barn*.20.1; ὑπομνησθεῖσα διὰ τῆς προσκαίρου τ. τὴν αἰώνιον ἐν γεέννῃ κόλασιν *Ep.Lugd*.ap.Eus.*h.e*.5.1.26(M.20.417B); Clem. *prot*.10(p.66.31; M.8.204A); τὴν διὰ πυρὸς τ. ἀπὸ τῆς βαρβάρου φιλοσοφίας...ἡ Ἑλληνικὴ φιλοσοφία ὀφείλετο id.*str*.5.14(p.385.24; M.9.133A); αἰωνίαν δίκην ὑπ' ἐμπύροις θεοῦ τιμωρίαις παθεῖν Meth.*symp*. 11(p.135.13; M.18.212B); εἰ...τις ἀμύητος κρύψας ἑαυτὸν μεταλάβοι, κρίμα αἰώνιον φάγεται...εἰς τ. ἑαυτοῦ *Const.App*.7.25.6; μετὰ τὴν ἐντεῦθεν ἀποδημίαν κόλασις ἀφόρητος, τ. ἀθάνατοι Chrys.*stat*.5.2(2.62D); εἰ...ὁ...νόμων φόβος...ἔχει τὴν ἰσχὺν ὥστε ἀπάγειν...τῶν πονηρῶν πράξεων, πολλῷ μᾶλλον...ἡ τ. ἡ ἀθάνατος id.*hom.2.3 in 2Thess*.(11.519A); **4.** in sense of *vengeance*; of which God is incapable, Clem.*paed*.1.8(p.131.8; M.8.333C); θεὸς...οὐ τιμωρεῖται (ἔστι γὰρ ἡ τ. κακοῦ ἀνταπόδοσις), κολάζει μέντοι πρὸς τὸ χρήσιμον id.*str*.7.16(p.72.20; M.9.541B); *ib*.4.23(p.315.24; M.8.1361A); **5.** of corrective punishment θεραπεύεται...πολλὰ τῶν παθῶν τιμωρίᾳ Clem.*paed*.1.8(p.128.4; M.8.328B); ἀπολυθέντων ἡμῶν κολάσεως καὶ τ. ἁπάσης, ἃς ἐκ τῶν ἁμαρτημάτων εἰς παιδείαν ὑπομένομεν σωτήριον id.*str*.7.10(p.41.18; M.9.480B); βουλῇ θεοῦ...τοῖς σεβομένοις αὐτὸν παραπτωμάτων χάριν ἡ τ. ἕπεται...ἵνα...καθαροὺς ἐν τῇ τῶν ὅλων παραστήσῃ κρίσει *Hom.Clem*.11.16; διὰ τὸ ποσῶς φιλόθεον προσκαίροις τ. αἰωνίων σωθῶσι κολάσεων *ib*.15.9; **6.** ref. eccl. penalties πρεσβύτερος...ἀφορίζει...τοὺς ὑποβεβηκότας, ἐὰν ὦσιν ὑπεύθυνοι τῇ τοιαύτῃ τ. *Const.App*.8.28.3; τοῦτο τὸ τοὺς αἰτίους τιμωρεῖσθαι οἰκοδομεῖν ἐκκλησίας ἐστίν, ἀσφαλέστερον τῶν λοιπῶν καὶ δοκιμωτέρων διὰ τῆς τ. γινομένων *cat.2Cor*.13:10(p.443.13); **7.** τ. διδόναι *pay the penalty*, Chrys.*sac*.3.17(p.90.5; 1.398E); id.*hom.16.7 in Mt*.(7.214C); id.*hom. 2.3 in 2Thess*.(11.518C).

B. *suffering, torment* μετὰ πολλὰς...τ. ἐν ἰδίῳ...χωρίῳ τελευτήσαντος [sc. Judas] Papias *fr*.3.2; *Const.App*.5.6.5; τοῦ εὐαγγελίου... χάριν...τὰς παντοδαπὰς τ. ὑπέμενον [sc. apostles] Thdt.*2Tim*.1:9(3.678); *ib*.1:12(679).

***τιμωρικός,** *punishing*; of angels, Dor.*doct*.12.3(M.88.1752C).

τίναγμα, τό, *shaking*; of stroke of lightning, Gr.Naz.*carm*.1.2.14.81(M.37.761A); *ib*.2.1.11.134(1039A).

τίννυμι, *pay* penalty, *Const.App*.2.46.4; Chrys.*hom.10.3 in 1Tim*.(11.603F); id.*hom.28.1 in Jo*.(8.159A); Χριστοῦ...δεδωκότος ἑαυτὸν τῷ πατρὶ ὑπὲρ τῆς ἡμῶν σωτηρίας...καὶ τὰς ὑπὲρ ἡμῶν μονονουχὶ δίκας τιννύντος, ἐλυτρώθημεν τῶν τῆς ἁμαρτίας ἐγκλημάτων Cyr.*Jo*.8(4.707D).

τίρων ([*]τήρ-, [*]τύρ-), **ὁ,** (Lat. *tiro*) *recruit*, Mac.Aeg.*hom*.43.8 (M.34.777A); id.*cust.cor*.11(M.34.832B); *Cod.Afr*.90; τήρων, *V.Pach*. Φ 4(p.3.14); τύρων, *M.Eust*.(p.29).

τιρωνᾶτος, ὁ, (Lat. *tironatus*) *body of recruits, Cod.Afr*.90.

***τιρωνικόν, τό,** (cf. Lat. *tiro*) *tax to provide recruits' pay*, Synes. *ep*.79(M.66.1445A).

τιτθίς, ἡ, *nurse*, Chrys.*hom.11.4 in Heb*.(12.118C); Synes.*ep*.3(M.66.1325A).

***τιτθισμός, ὁ,** *pressure of the mother's breast by the sucking infant*, †Chrys.*salt.Herodiad*.2(8.42B).

***τιτθυρίζω,** *chatter*, Anast.S.*hod*.9(M.89.148A).

***τίτλον, τό,** *mark* on an object to denote its confiscation, Ath. Scholast.*coll*.4.10(p.56).

τίτλος, ὁ, (Lat. *titulus*) *inscription, notice*; **1.** wooden board whitened with chalk on which letters were written in ink or burnt in; of inscription on Cross (cf. Jo.19:19), Mel.*pass*.95 p.16.8; ὁ τ. ἀντὶ τοῦ χάρτου ἐπὶ τῷ σταυρῷ προετίθετο Ast.Soph.*hom.1 in Ps.5* (M.40.392B); Nonn.*par.Jo*.19:19(M.43.901B); of public notices *M.Glyc*.1(p.12*C); **2.** *tombstone, MAMA* 1.163; *ib*.167; *ib*.173; **3.** *accord*, Mac.Mgn.*apocr*.2.7(p.5.13); **4.** *written notice, letter* ὁ τῆς Ῥωμαίων ἐπίσκοπος...ἀπέστειλεν...τ. ἰδιόχειρον...διὰ δύο ἐπισκόπων Leont.Abb.*v.Gr.Agr*.35(M.98.608A); **5.** *heading*; hence *section, chapter*; in conciliar documents, *Cod.Afr*.133; in imperial legislation, Evagr.*h.e*.1.12(p.20.22; M.86.2453A); of divisions of gospels for lectionary use παρὰ τῷ Ματθαίῳ τ. ἑκατοστῷ ἐννάτῳ Oecum. *Apoc*.7:12(p.108); *ib*.9:14(p.117); **6.** *title, warrant, M.Ariadn*.4 (p.125.21).

τιτλόω, put a mark on an object to denote its confiscation, *confiscate*, Jo.Mal.*chron*.10 p.245(M.97.376A).

***τίτλωμα, τό,** *inscription, mark, Apoc.Dan*.B(p.39).

τιτρώσκ-ω, *wound, hurt*; **1.** lit., ref. Christ πλευρᾶς ἀχράντου λόγχῃ τρωθείσης Cosm.Mel.*hymn*.12(12.41, p.162; M.98.504C); **2.** lit. and met. at the same time, with a play on the word; of Christ τρωθῆναι θέλω καὶ τρῶσαι θέλω *A.Jo*.95(p.197.24); of Church as wounded for love of Christ, in her martyrs ὅτι τετρωμένη ἀγάπης ἐγώ. διὰ τῶν ἁγίων μαρτύρων, δι' ὧν, ἀγαπήσασα τὸν Χριστόν, ἐτρώθην, τὸν ὑπὲρ αὐτοῦ δεξαμένη θάνατον Ph.Carp.*Cant*.44(M.40.64A); τέτρωται ᾄδης, ἐν τῇ καρδίᾳ δεξάμενος τὸν τρωθέντα λόγχῃ τὴν πλευράν Cosm.Mel. *hymn*.8(*AHS* 2 p.171; M.98.488A); **3.** met.; **a.** of souls wounded by sin or Devil Ἰησοῦς...τὸ αἷμα τῆς ἀμπέλου τῆς Δαβίδ, ἐκχέας ἡμῶν ἐπὶ τὰς τετρωμένας ψυχάς Clem.*q.d.s.*29(p.179.11; M.9.636A); οἱ ὑπὸ τοῦ διαβόλου εἰς τὴν καρδίαν τετρωμένοι Or.*Jo.*32.2(p.428.35; M.14.745B); ‡Caes.Naz.*dial.*195(M.38.1184); faith preventing other virtues from being injured, Chrys.*hom.24.2 in Eph.*(11.182D); **b.** in good sense, by prick of conscience τὴν ἀπηλγηκυῖαν ψυχὴν καιρός ἐστι τρῶσαι, οὐ θανασίμως, ἀλλὰ σωτηρίως Clem.*paed.*1.8(p.133.15; M.8.340A); ὁ δὲ Δαβίδ,...αὐτὴν δὲ τὴν ψυχὴν καιρίαν τρωθεὶς †Bas.*hom.in Ps.*37(1.364B; M.30.88A); **4.** myst. (v. ἀγάπη, ἔρως); of souls being wounded by love of God, Or.*Jo.*1.32(36; p.41.3; M.14.85B); Mac.Aeg.*hom.*5.6(M.34.500B); *ib.*(500C); οὔπω ἐτρώθημεν [sc. those who are not yet perfect] τῷ θείῳ ἔρωτι *ib.*25.5(669D); id.*ep.*2(M.34.416C); δίδαξον ἡμᾶς, δι' ὧν εὑρίσκεται σημείων ὁ ἀόρατος, ὡς μηνῦσαι αὐτῷ περὶ τοῦ βέλους τῆς ἀγάπης, ᾧ μέσῳ τέτρωσαι τὴν καρδίαν Gr.Nyss.*hom.13 in Cant.*(M.44.1045B); τέτρωμαι γὰρ αὐτοῦ τῇ ἀγάπῃ, καὶ γὰρ βέλος ἐκλεκτὸν ὑπάρχει, καὶ ~ει τὰς βαλλομένας ψυχάς Thdt.*Cant.*2:5(3.57); of Church τρωθεῖσα τῷ ἀσωμάτῳ...βέλει τοῦ ἔρωτος Gr.Nyss.*hom.13 in Cant.*(1048C); Chrys.*stat.*5.3(2.63C); οὐδὲ τὸν τρωθέντα ἠρεμεῖν λοιπὸν τῆς μακαρίας μανίας ἐᾷ Jo.Clim.*scal.*30(M.88.1156A); πρὸς τὸν θεοῦ πόθον τρωθέντες οἱ ἅγιοι διὰ τῶν ἐνουσῶν αὐτοῖς πρὸς τὰ θεῖα φυσικῶν ἐμφάσεων Max.*ambig.*(M.91.1113C).

τληπαθ-έω, *suffer, endure, be patient* ~εῖν...φιλεῖν ὑπὲρ...τοῦ ἀγαθοῦ Cyr.*ador.*3(1.83A); *ib.*4(108D); τὸ ὑπομένειν τῷ κυρίῳ οὐδὲν ἕτερον εἶναί φαμεν πλὴν ὅτι τὸ ἑλέσθαι ~εῖν ὑπὲρ...τῆς εἰς αὐτὸν ἀγάπης id.*Ps.*32:20(M.69.881C); τρυφὴν ἀληθῶς ἡγούμενοι τὸ ὑπὲρ...τοῦ ἀγαθοῦ ~εῖν id.*ep.*1(p.10.8; 5^{2}.1B); for reward in future life, id.*Is.*3.1(2.391C); ~οῦσι...ἵνα τῶν παρὰ θεοῦ χαρισμάτων ἀναπιμπλάμενοι θυμηδίας ἁπάσης γένωνται μεστοί *ib.*5.6(913A); for faith, Gr.Agr.*Eccl.*3.12(M.98.865B); Thdr.Stud.*epp.*2.143(M.99.1449D).

τληπαθής, **1.** *enduring, patient*, Gr.Nyss.*res.*3(M.46.672C); Cyr.*ador.*4(1.120E); ὁ τληπαθέστατος Ἰώβ id.*Nest.*5.5(p.102.14; 6^{1}.136D); id.*Mich.*43(3.432A); neut. as subst., *endurance*, id.*Ag.*10(3.637D); id.*Os.*45(3.76C); id.*ador.*4(1.109B); **2.** *miserable*, id.*Os.*18(3.40D).

***τληπαθῶς**, *patiently*, Cyr.*Jo.*5.2(4.490B); id.*Joel.*10(3.209A).

***τλησικαρδίως**, *patiently*, ‡Gr.Naz.*Chr.pat.*1069(M.38.222A).

τμῆμα, τό, *part cut off*; **1.** *segment*, Hipp.*haer.*4.8(p.41.4; M.16.3071A); Gr.Nyss.*fat.*(M.45.149C); **2.** *section*, Meth.*symp.*8.11(p.24.21; M.18.156B); **3.** of time, *division*, Clem.*str.*5.4(p.340.2; M.9.41A); Eus.*l.C.*6(p.207.4; M.20.1341B); ἐν τρισὶ τ. τὸ χρονικὸν μετρεῖται διάστημα, τῷ παρῳχηκότι, τῷ ἐνεστῶτι καὶ τῷ μέλλοντι Gr.Nyss.*or.dom.*1(p.10.5; M.44.1124D); of a month τοῦτο δὲ τὸ τ. πρῶτον δωδεκατημόριον...καὶ μηνῶν ἀρχὴν...καλεῖν εἰώθασιν· τὸ δὲ πρὸ τούτου μηνῶν ἔσχατον καὶ τ. δωδέκατον Anat.Laod.*can.pasch.*ap.Eus.*h.e.*7.32.15(M.10.212A); of a minute, Gr.Nyss.*fat.*(M.45.156B); **4.** geographical *part*, Eus.*v.C.*1.49(p.30.19; M.20.964B); τὰ τῆς οἰκουμένης τ. Gr.Naz.*ep.*135(M.37.232A); Thdt.*h.e.*5.7.1(3.1024); **5.** *group*; **a.** of sex ἑκατέρῳ τ. τὸ κατάλληλον τῆς ἀρετῆς ὑπόδειγμα...ἐδείχθη Gr.Nyss.*v.Mos.*12(M.44.301D); **b.** of a group of heresies, Clem.*str.*3.5(p.214.14; M.8.1144B); of parties in Church, Evagr.*h.e.*3.30(p.126.23; χρήματα M.86.2657B); **6.** *portion*, Manich. τὰ νοητὰ μέρη, ἅτε τῆς θείας οὐσίας τ. ὑπάρχοντα, εἰς σύνθεσιν τῶν ἐναντίων οὐδαμῶς ἔρχεται *Disp.Phot.*2(M.88.541A); ref. portion of divine substance held by the evil principle, *ib.*1(536D); οὐ διαίρεσιν ἢ τομὴν γεγονέναι λέγω τῆς θείας οὐσίας, ἀλλὰ προσβολὴν ὁμοούσιον τῷ προβαλλομένῳ· καὶ πρὸς τοῦτο διαμάχεσθαι Χριστιανοὺς...οὐκ οἶμαι, [οἱ] τὸν υἱὸν τοῦ θεοῦ...οὐ τ. τῆς τούτου πατρὸς οὐσίας φατὲ καὶ ὁμοούσιον τῷ πατρί Jo.D.*Man.*2(M.96.1321B).

***τμῆξις, ἡ**, *section, division*, Gr.Naz.*carm.*1.1.2.27(M.37.403A).

τμῆσις, ἡ, **1.** *section* λόγου...οὐ τ. τῆς ἀπαθοῦς φύσεως, οὔτε προβολήν, ἀλλ' υἱὸν αὐτοτελῆ †Ath.*exp.fid.*1(M.25.201A); **2.** *beheading* of SS. Peter and Paul σταυρῷ καὶ τ. τὸν βίον ἐζημιώσαντο Mac.Mgn.*apocr.*4.14(p.181.15); **3.** *separation* of the parts of a word by intervening word(s), cf. *tmesis est sectio unius nominis per interpositionem verborum*, Isid.H.*etym.*1.37.19.

***τόγα, ἡ**, (Lat.) *toga*, Jo.Mal.*chron.*2 p.33(M.97.104A); *Chron.Pasch.*p.310(M.92.792A).

τοι, in phrase ἢ τάν, ἢ ἐπὶ τάν, by crasis for τοι ἄν, *whether this way or that*, Cyr.*ador.*6(1.198D).

***τοιουτοδύναμος**, *so powerful*, Tim.Ant.*Sym.*(M.86.244C).

***τοιουτοειδής**, *of such a kind*, Cyr.*glaph.Ex.*2(1.285A).

***τοιουτόχρως**, *of such a colour*, of hyacinth-coloured vestments of high priest symbolizing Christ γινώσκεται...ἐν ὑακίνθῳ...ἀεροφανεῖ. τ. γὰρ ὑάκινθος διὰ τὸ ἄνωθεν καὶ ἐξ οὐρανοῦ Cyr.*ador.*11(1.379C); *ib.*13(457D).

[*]**τοιχάριον, τό**, (dim. of τοῖχος) = τειχάριον, *small wall*, Nil.*epp.*2.96(M.79.244B).

τοίχαρχος, ὁ, *overseer of the rowers on each side of the ship, boatswain* παρεικάσθω ὁ μὲν κυβερνήτης Χριστῷ, ὁ πρωρεὺς ἐπισκόπῳ, οἱ ναῦται πρεσβυτέροις, οἱ τ. διακόνοις *Clem.ep.*14(M.2.49A); οἱ διάκονοι...ἐοίκασι...ναύταις καὶ τ. *Const.App.*2.57.4.

[*]**τοιχικός**, = τειχικός, *of the wall* τοιχικῇ γραφῇ CSyr.*act.*(p.94.19; H.2.1368D).

τοιχίον, τό, *small fort*, Ath.*ep.encycl.*4(M.25.229C; Τυχαίῳ p.173.6).

***τοιχοβατέω**, *climb a wall*, Marc.Diac.*v.Porph.*96; Cyr.S.*v.Euthym.*8(p.15.16).

***τοιχογραφέω**, *paint on a wall*, Thdr.Stud.*ref.*6(M.99.449A).

***τοιχογράφος, ὁ**, *wall-painter*, Adam.*dial.*5.16(p.204.10; M.11.1853C).

[*]**τοιχοδόμος, ὁ**, *builder of walls*, Dion.Al.ap.Eus.*p.e.*14.24(774A; M.21.1273A).

[*]**τοιχομαχία, ἡ**, = τειχομαχία, *attack on a fortress*, Leont.B.*mesopent.*(M.86.1992B).

τοιχοπυργίσκος, ὁ, *cupboard in a wall, armarium*, Max.*schol.d.n.*9.1(M.4.369A).

***τοιχωρύκτης, ὁ**, *burglar*, Chrys.*hom.11.4 in 1Cor.*(10.91E).

τοιῶσδε, *in such a way, so, in such wise* οὐδὲν...καθ' ἑαυτὸ τῶν πραγμάτων ἡγητέον εἶναι κακόν, ἀλλὰ παρὰ τὴν πρᾶξιν τῶν χρωμένων τ. γίνεσθαι Meth.*symp.*2.5(M.18.56A; τοιοῦτο p.22.1); Eus.*d.e.*5.1(p.214.3; M.22.556A); ἐπειδὴ γὰρ ἡ κτίσις τ., ὁ γενεσιουργὸς ἐναντίως Didym.*Trin.*1.15(M.39.312B); Cyr.*Is.*2.1(2.203A).

***τοκετικός**, *belonging to childbirth*, Epiph.*haer.*77.35(p.447.29; M.42.693C); *ib.*77.28(p.440.3; 681C).

τοκετός, ὁ, **1.** *childbearing* ἔλαθεν τὸν ἄρχοντα τοῦ αἰῶνος τούτου ἡ παρθενία Μαρίας καὶ ὁ τ. αὐτῆς Ign.*Eph.*19.1; ref. pangs of childbirth as consequence of Fall, Thphl.Ant.*Autol.*2.23(M.6.1089A); μελέτα τοὺς...νόμους, μηθὲν παρατηρουμένη, μὴ κάθαρσιν φυσικήν...μὴ τ. *Const.App.*6.27.7; **2.** *birth*; of Christ, Sophr.H.*nativ.*(p.502.13); *ib.*(p.503.28); ref. resurrection ὁ τ. μοι ἐπίκειται...ἐκεῖ παραγενόμενος ἄνθρωπος ἔσομαι Ign.*Rom.*6.1.

τοκεύς, ὁ, **1.** *father*; of God, Nonn.*par.Jo.*1:13(M.43.752B); *ib.*1:34(756B); *ib.*5:18(788B); **2.** *ancestor*, *ib.*4:20(777A); *ib.*6:31(800A).

***τοκεύω**, *bring forth*, Thdr.Stud.*ref.*(M.99.437D).

τοκίστρια, ἡ, *usurer* (fem.); met., of penitence αὕτη λαμβάνει ἃ οὐκ ἔδωκεν, ἡ εὐσεβὴς τ. Ephr.3.160D.

***τοκοληψία, ἡ**, *usury*; condemned by Church, Epiph.*exp.fid.*24(p.525.12; M.42.832A).

τόκος, ὁ, **A. 1.** *childbirth, parturition*, of BMV οὐδὲ ἁπλῶς ναὸς πλάττεται, ἀλλὰ καὶ κύησις γίνεται...καὶ ὠδῖνες καὶ τ. Chrys.*hom.8.3 in Mt.*(7.124A); ἀλόχευτον τὸν ἐκ τῆς παρθένου...τ. CTrull.*can.*79; μείνασα παρθένος μετὰ τόκον ‡Rom.Mel.(*AS* 1 p.241); ἀσπόρου συλλήψεως ὁ τ. ἀνερμήνευτος Andr.Cr.*can.mag.*282(p.155; M.97.1380C); σὺ τὴν φύσιν ἐκαίνισας τῷ τ. σου, Μαρία id.*can.Laz.*3(M.97.1389C); παρθενεύει γὰρ τ. καὶ ζωὴν προμνηστεύεται θάνατος Cosm.Mel.*can.dorm.*155(p.183); ἰλλιγιᾷ δὲ νοῦς ἅπας σου τὸν τ. νοεῖν Jo.D.*carm.pent.*124(p.217; M.96.840A); ὁ τ. τῆς θεοτόκου...τὴν οἰκουμένην ἅπασαν ἐγείρει ψάλλουσαν id.*hymn.dorm.BMV* 115(p.231; M.96.1365C); **2.** *birth*; of Christ, Chrys.*hom.4.5 in Mt.*(7.55C); ὁ ἄγγελος δεικνὺς θαυμαστὸν ὄντα τὸν τ. *ib.*4.7(58B); of spiritual birth, regeneration, Meth.*symp.*3.8(p.37.13; M.18.76A); κατὰ τὸν τ. τὸν πνευματικόν Chrys.*serm.9.1 in Gen.*(4.688E); **3.** *production*; of a poem, Synes.*ep.*141(M.66.1533A); *origin* of inanimate things, Gr.Nyss.*fat.*(M.45.165C); **4.** *offspring* εἰ γὰρ μὴ σὸς [i.e. of Joseph] ὁ τ., ἀλλὰ τὰ τοῦ πατρὸς ἐπιδείξῃ περὶ αὐτόν Chrys.*hom.4.6 in Mt.*(7.58A); τ. ...σπαργανούμενος ἐν φάτνῃ ‡Rom.Mel.(*AS* 1 p.226); τέρπου, θεοτόκε, ἐν τῇ ἐγέρσει τοῦ τ. σου Jo.D.*carm.pasch.*116(p.221; M.96.844B).

B. *interest*, Bas.*hom.in Ps.*14(1.110B; M.29.272B); *ib.*(111B; M.273C); Cyr.*fr.Jac.*4:13(p.446; M.74.1012A); *usury*; condemned in case of clerical usurers, *Can.App.*44; CNic.(325)*can.*17; CLaod.*can.*4; Bas.*ep.*188 *can.*14(3.275C; M.32.681C); Thdt.*h.e.*4.10.4(3.964); ref. practice by widows, *Const.App.*3.7.3; met. ὁ μεταδοτικὸς καὶ τόκους ἀξιολόγους λαμβάνει...ἡμερότητα...εὔκλειαν Clem.*str.*2.18(p.157.21; M.8.1024A).

τολμήεις, **1.** *bold, daring*, Nonn.*par.Jo.*9:17(M.43.828A); **2.** *presumptuous, reckless*, *ib.*3:18(769A); *ib.*13:2(860B).

***τολμηρία, ἡ**, *insolence*, Ephr.3.244C.

***τολμικόν, τό**, *violence*, Anast.S.*qu.et resp.*96(M.89.748C).

τομή, ἡ, a *cutting*;

A. *division, dissection*, metaphysical *separation*, as theol. term, used by orthodox to emphasize materialism of heret. conceptions of God; **1.** Trin. Μαρκίωνος...δίδαγμα εἰς τρεῖς ἀρχὰς τῆς μοναρχίας τ. καὶ διαίρεσις, παίδευμα ὂν διαβολικόν Dion.R.ap.Ath.*decr.*26(p.22.13; M.25.464A); οὐ γάρ ἐστιν ἐπινοῆσαι τ. ἢ διαίρεσιν κατ' οὐδένα τρόπον· ὡς ἢ υἱὸν χωρὶς πατρὸς νοηθῆναι, ἢ τὸ πνεῦμα τοῦ υἱοῦ διαζευχθῆναι Gr.Nyss.*diff.ess*.4(M.32.332D); of Son γεννηθέντα οὐκ ἐκ τοῦ μὴ ὄντος, ἀλλ' ἐκ τοῦ ὄντος πατρός, οὐ κατὰ τὰς τῶν σωμάτων ὁμοιότητας, ταῖς τ. ἢ ταῖς ἐκ διαιρέσεων ἀπορροίαις, ὥσπερ Σαβελλίῳ καὶ Βαλεντίνῳ δοκεῖ, ἀλλ' ἀρρήτως καὶ ἀνεκδιηγήτως Alex.Al.*ep. Alex*.12(p.27.6; M.18.565B); Eus.*d.e*.4.3(p.154.18; M.22.257B) cit. s. διάστασις; οἱ θεομάχοι...ἵνα μὴ τὸν υἱὸν εἰκόνα τοῦ πατρὸς ὁμολογήσωσι, σωματικὰ καὶ γήϊνα περὶ αὐτοῦ τοῦ πατρὸς φρονοῦσι, τ. καὶ ἀπορροίας...κατηγοροῦντες κατ' αὐτοῦ Ath.*Ar*.1.21(M.26.56B); Ἄρειος ...πάθος καὶ τ. καὶ ῥεῦσιν προεξεῦρεν ‡Ath.*Apoll*.1.21(M.26.1129B); γέννησιν ἀκούει θεοῦ καὶ κτίσιν καὶ θεὸν ἐξ οὐκ ὄντων καὶ τ. καὶ διαίρεσιν καὶ ἀνάλυσιν, ὁ πικρὸς τῶν λεγομένων ἀκροατής [i.e. in Eunomian doctrine] Gr.Naz.*or*.27.6(p.10.2; M.36.17C); κατάβαλέ σου τὰς ῥεύσεις καὶ τὰς διαιρέσεις καὶ τὰς τ. καὶ τὸ ὡς περὶ σώματος διανοεῖσθαι τῆς ἀσωμάτου φύσεως *ib*.29.8(p.84.12; 84C); λέγω...ταῦτα, οὐκ ἐπὶ τὴν θεότητα φέρων τὴν πλάσιν ἢ τὴν τ. ἤ τι τῶν ὅσα σώματος *ib*.31.11(p.158. 13; 145A); **2.** Christol. Χριστὸν ἕνα καὶ κύριον ὁμολογήσομεν, οὐχ ὡς ἄνθρωπον συμπροσκυνοῦντες τῷ λόγῳ, ἵνα μὴ τομῆς φαντασία παρεισκρίνηται διὰ τὸ λέγειν τὸ σύν Cyr.*ep*.4(p.28.3; 5².24B); διαίρεσιν μὲν τὴν ἀνὰ μέρος ἢ τ. οὐκ ἐπιφέρομεν τῇ μιᾷ αὐτοῦ συνθέτῳ ὑποστάσει Just.Imp.*edict*.ap.Evagr.*h.e*.5.4(p.200.1; M.86.2797B); δύο...ἐνεργείας ἔχων χωρὶς τομῆς τῶν ἐξ ὧν ὑπῆρχε...οὐ γὰρ ὑπομένει τ. ἢ σύγχυσιν, ὁ μηδέποτε τροπαῖς ὑποκείμενος Max.*opusc*.(M.91.36D).

B. *surgery*; partic. of circumcision, Nonn.*par.Jo*.7:22(M.43. 808C); *ib*.7:23(M.l.c.); met. ἔστι δὲ οἱονεὶ χειρουργία τῶν τῆς ψυχῆς παθῶν ὁ ἔλεγχος, ἀπόστασις δὲ τὰ πάθη τῆς ἀληθείας, ἃ χρὴ διελέγχειν διαιροῦντα τῇ τ. Clem.*paed*.1.8(p.128.8; M.8.328C).

C. *division, part, segment*, ref. threefold division of Peratic cosmos, Hipp.*haer*.5.12(p.104.18; M.16.3162A); ἡ πρώτη τ. καὶ προσεχεστέρα...ἐστι τριὰς καὶ καλεῖται ἀγαθὸν τέλειον *ib*.; ἀπὸ τῆς ἀγεννησίας καὶ ⟨τῆς⟩ πρώτης τοῦ κόσμου τ. ... κατεληλυθέναι... τριφυῆ τινα...ἄνθρωπον καλούμενον Χριστόν *ib*.(p.105.1; 3162B); of logical division or classification ἡ τοῦ γένους εἰς εἴδη τ. Clem.*str*.8.6 (p.92.7; M.9.585A); of division of a book into sections, Euthal. Diac.*Ac*.proem.(M.85.629B).

D. *decision*, *Cod.Afr*.59(Lat. *decisio* MS, *decisum* ed.).

E. *incisiveness*, †Jo.D.*B.J*.36(M.96.1209A).

τόμος, ὁ, 1. *roll, section* of papyrus, *A.Pil*.A 15.2(p.266); *Hom. Clem*.1.20; Ath.*exp.Ps*.39:8(M.27.192D); **2.** *book, division* of a work, Or.*Jo*.6.2(1; p.108.17; M.14.201B); *ib*.10.1(p.171.6; 308A); *document*, of a synodical letter or decree δείξουσι...ἢ διὰ τ. συνοδικοῦ ἢ δι' ἐπιστολῶν κοινωνικῶν Gr.Naz.*ep*.101(M.37.177A); συνοδικὸς τ. Δαμάσου...κατὰ τῶν δυτικῶν ἐπισκόπων Thdt.*h.e*.2.22.2n.(3.881); Philost.*h.e*.7.2(M.65.537B); *register* γράφωμεν αὐτὸν [sc. Christ] εἰς τὴν γραφὴν τοῦ τ. υἱὸν τοῦ θεοῦ Jo.Eub.*concept.BMV* 18(M.96. 1489C); *ib*.(1492A); *pamphlet, treatise*, Alex.Al.*ep.Alex*.14(p.29.15; M.18.569C); ὁ πρὸς τοὺς Ἀντιοχεῖς τ. Ath.*tom*.(M.26.796A); Thdt. *eran*.2(4.138); Philost.*h.e*.4.11(M.65.524C); Jo.D.*haer*.83(M.94.741A); **3.** met., of BMV; as book of new covenant, Procl.CP *or*.6.17(M.65. 756A); χαῖρε τ. καινοῦ μυστηρίου...ἐν ᾗ ὁ ἀνείδεος λόγος γραφίδι ἀνθρωπικῆς ἰδέας ἐζωγράφηται Thdr.Stud.*nativ.BMV* 7(M.96.692B).

τονθορύζ-ω, 1. *murmur*, of Arians ∼οντες λέγουσιν ὀνόματα μόνον εἶναι τοῦ υἱοῦ λόγος καὶ σοφία Ath.*decr*.16(p.13.19; M.25.441C); οἱ περὶ Εὐσέβιον...κατελήφθησαν...πρὸς ἑαυτοὺς ∼οντες καὶ διανεύοντες τοῖς ὀφθαλμοῖς, ὅτι καὶ τὸ ὅμοιον καὶ τὸ ἀεὶ...κοινὰ πάλιν ἐστὶ πρὸς ἡμᾶς καὶ τὸν υἱόν *ib*.20(p.16.32; 449D); id.*Ar*.3.50(M.26.429A); **2.** *grumble, complain*, Meth.*arbitr*.2(p.148.16; M.18.244A); Cyr. *glaph.Gen*.5(1.151D); Thdt.*Phil*.2:14(3.457).

τονθορυσμός, ὁ, *murmuring*, Cyr.*glaph.Gen*.5(M.69.248A; τὰ θορυσμῶν 1.153D).

***τοξοβολία, ἡ,** *bowshot*, *Chron.Pasch*.p.166(M.92.409A).

***τοξοβολίστρα, ἡ,** *engine for shooting darts*, Thphn.*chron*.p.322 (M.108.777C).

***τοπάριον, τό,** *small place* or *building*, Epiph.*haer*.80.2(p.486.3; M.42.757B).

τοπάρχης, ὁ, 1. *governor of a district*, Clem.*fr*.73(p.230.24)ap.Jo. Mal.*chron*.10 p.231(M.97.356D); Αὔγαρος τ. πόλεως Ἐδέσσης *Ep. Abg*.1(p.279.3); Eus.*p.e*.1.4(10B; M.21.37A); ὕπαρχοι καὶ τ. οὐκ ἀπολαύουσι τοσαύτης τιμῆς ὅσης ὁ τῆς ἐκκλησίας ἄρχων Chrys.*hom.3.5 in Ac*.(9.31A); Cyr.*Abac*.1(3.526D); **2.** astrol., *ascendant, lord of the ascendant*, Hipp.*haer*.5.13(p.108.5; M.16.3166C).

τοπαρχία, ἡ, 1. *district*, Eus.*l.C*.16(p.248.29; M.20.1421B); Mac. Mgn.*apocr*.4.11(p.170.19); Thdt.*Ps*.71:7(1.1105); **2.** *local government*, Eus.*d.e*.8 proem.(p.349.21; M.22.568C); id.*Ps*.45:9(M.23.412B); υἱὸν ἀνθρώπου λέγει [sc. Daniel]...συντρίβοντα πολυαρχίαν τοπαρχιῶν ...κηρύσσοντα δὲ τὸν ἕνα θεὸν καὶ χειροτονοῦντα τὴν Ῥωμαίων μοναρχίαν *Const.App*.5.20.11; **3.** astrol., *house of the ascendant*, Hipp.*haer*.5.14(p.109.11; M.16.3167C).

τοπικός, 1. *concerned with, in respect of place*, ref. God αἱ... τοιαῦται φωναί, καὶ περὶ θεοῦ πατρὸς πολλάκις ἀναγραφεῖσαι, οὐ τ. σημαίνουσι διαστάσεις Or.*fr.37 in Jo*.(p.513.9); τὰς τῆς...τριάδος ὑποστάσεις οὐ διεζευγμένας, οὐδὲ τ., ἀλλὰ...μίαν θεότητα νοεῖσθαι... τῆς...ὁμοουσίου τριάδος Gel.Cyz.*h.e*.2.22.5(M.85.1292A); Leont.H. *Nest*.2.17(M.86.1576A); ref. Creation κινεῖσθαι...αὐτὸν...νοητέον οὐ κατὰ φορὰν...ἢ τ. κίνησιν...ἀλλὰ τὸ εἰς οὐσίαν ἄγειν τὸν θεὸν καὶ συνέχειν τὰ πάντα Dion.Ar.*d.n*.9.9(M.3.916C); ref. Inc. οὕπερ τὴν ἐξ οὐρανῶν καταφοίτησιν ἀκούων, μὴ τ. μετάστασιν τῆς...αὐτοῦ ὑποπτεύσῃς θεότητος, οἰκονομίαν δὲ νόει...τὸ μέγα...τῆς εὐσεβείας μυστήριον Gel.Cyz.*h.e*.2.24.9(1300D); ἐπειδὴ...εἶπαν κατελθόντα τὸν μονογενῆ...ἵνα μὴ τ. νοήσῃς μετάβασιν...ἑρμηνεύουσι τὸ κατελθόντα..., σαρκωθέντα Thdot.Anc.*exp.symb*.16(M.77.1377A); συγκατάβασις γὰρ θεϊκή, οὐ μετάβασις δὲ τ. γέγονε ‡Serg.*acath*.178(p.144; M.92.1344A); εἰ ταῦτα μὴ κατὰ τ. περιγραφὴν τῆς ὑποστάσεώς ἐστι τοῦ λόγου, τί κωλύει μείναντα αὐτὸν θεὸν λόγον...σαρκικοὺς...ἐπικτήσασθαι διορισμοὺς κατὰ μίαν τὴν ὑπόστασιν αὐτοῦ; Leont.H.*Nest*.2.17(1576B); ref. God's indwelling, Or.*or*.23.2(p.350.17; M.11.488B); μακρύνονταί τινες ἀπὸ τοῦ κυρίου οὐ τ. διαστήμασιν, ἀλλ' ὡς...γνώσει καὶ τρόποις Cyr.*Ps*.72:27(M.69.1185B); πλησίον...οἱ τοιοίδε θεοῦ· καὶ οὐ σχέσεσι τ. ...παραστήματι δὲ διανοίας id.*Zach*.64(3.744B); ref. Second Advent οὐ δεῖ τ. ... ἐκδέχεσθαι τὴν παρουσίαν Bas.*moral*.68.2(2.286D; M.31. 808A); ref. fall of Satan οὐ τ. ῥήγματι, ἀλλὰ ἀπὸ τιμῆς εἰς ἀτιμίαν *Lit*.ap.*Const.App*.8.7.5; **2.** *localized, local* οὐκ ᾔδεσαν οἱ Σαμαρεῖται ὃ προσεκύνουν· ὅτι τ. καὶ μερικὸν θεὸν ἐνόμιζον εἶναι Chrys.*hom.33.1 in Jo*.(8.190C); τὴν τ. λατρείαν...μετεποίησεν...ἀντὶ δὲ τ. λατρείας ἀπὸ ἀνατολῶν ἡλίου μέχρι δυσμῶν...προσέταξεν δοξάζεσθαι αὐτόν *Const. App*.6.23.5; Thdt.*Is*.66:1(p.257.23; 2.398); of local churches as part of one Church, id.*Cant*.6:1(2.122); of local councils, Anast.S. *hod*.5(M.89.101B); of paschal controversy as νόσος τ. Socr.*h.e*.1.8.2 (M.67.60D); of local persecution, *ib*.1.3.2(40A).

τοπικῶς, *in respect of place, locally* θεὸς...οὐ τ., ἀλλὰ προνοητικῶς συγκαταβαίνει τοῖς ἀνθρώποις Or.*Cels*.5.12(p.13.1; M.11.1197C); ταπεινὴν περὶ θεοῦ ὑπόληψιν τῶν νομιζόντων αὐτὸν εἶναι τ. ἐν οὐρανοῖς id.*or*.23.3(p.351.3; M.11.488C); ὁ ἐπὶ πάντων θεὸς...πῶς...λέγεται...τ. ἐπιβαίνειν μέρει τινὶ τῆς γῆς; Eus.*d.e*.6.20(p.285.25; τροπικῶς M.22. 469B); Epiph.*haer*.69.53(p.200.27; M.42.285B); of Logos ἐξ ἐκείνου ἔχων τὴν ἀναφοράν, εἰς ἐκεῖνον ἑνοῦται πάλιν, ἐκείνῳ τῆς διαστάσεως συγκρίσεώς τε οὐ τ., ἀλλὰ νοερῶς γινομένης Const.*or.s.c*.3(p.156.12; M.20.1240A); ref. Inc. τοῦ θεοῦ λόγου οὐ τ. μεταβάσεις ποιουμένου, τροπικῶς δὲ τὰς...οἰκονομίας αὐτοῦ...τῆς γραφῆς ἀποκαλούσης Eus. *d.e*.6.9(p.259.16; M.22.425D); ὅρα, εἰ μὴ μυστικώτερον καὶ οὐ τ. περὶ τῆς Ἰησοῦ ψυχῆς ἀκούσει τὸ 'ἀναβὰς ὑπεράνω πάντων τῶν οὐρανῶν' Or.*Jo*.19.22(5; p.323.27; M.14.568B); ref. union with God ὅπου ἐστὶν ὁ λόγος καὶ αὐτὸς ἐστιν. οὐ...τ. τὴν ἐπαγγελίαν νοητέον id.*fr.87 in Jo*.(p.552.1); *ib*.*37*(p.513.6); ζητεῖται...παρ' ἡμῶν ὁ θεὸς οὐχὶ...τ., ἀλλ'...πραγματικῶς, διὰ γνώσεως Cyr.*Soph*.4(3.583A); id.*Os*.121(3. 152C); Dion.Ar.*ep*.8.2(M.3.1092B); of divine activity αἱ δυνάμεις τοῦ σωτῆρος, ἐξερχόμεναι ἐξ αὐτοῦ, μεταδίδονται ἑτέροις οὐ μὴν τ. ἢ σωματικῶς...ἀσώματοι δὲ οὖσαι...οὐκ ἐξίστανται αὐτοῦ Vict.*Mc*. 5:25(p.320.18).

τόπιον, τό, *field, farm*, Gr.Mag.*dial*.(tr.Zach.)3.9(M.*PL*.77.235A); *ib*.3.10(235B); *ib*.(238A).

τοποθεσία, ἡ, 1. *situation, place*, Petr.I Al.*fr*.(M.18.513D); ‡Nil. *fr.pasch*.2(M.79.1496D); Cyr.S.*v.Sab*.39(p.130.23); id.*v.Euthym*.43 (p.64.22); **2.** *disposition, arrangement*, Ign.*Trall*.5.2 cit. s. ἀρχοντικός; of heavenly bodies in regions acc. Basilides, Epiph.*haer*. 24.7(p.264.4; M.41.316B); ὑποθέσεις Χριστιανικαὶ περὶ σχημάτων καὶ τοποθεσίας παντὸς τοῦ κόσμου Cosm.Ind.*top*.1(M.88.72C).

τοποκρατέω, *become master of a place*, Cosm.Ind.*top*.2(M.88. 113C).

***τοποκρατία, ἡ,** *local sovereignty*, Eus.*Ps*.45:9f.(M.23.412B).

***τοποποιέω,** *take someone's place*, Jo.Mosch.*prat*.106(M.87.2965A).

***τοποποιός, ὁ,** *deputy*; of an abbot, Jo.Clim.*scal*.4(M.88.704B); of a bishop, Anast.S.*hod*.13(M.89.209B).

τόπος, ὁ, A. *place*; **1.** in gen. οὔτε ὡρισμένον τ., οὔτε ἐξαίρετον ἱερόν,...ἀλλὰ τὸν πάντα βίον ὁ γνωστικὸς ἐν παντὶ τ. ... τιμᾷ τὸν θεόν Clem.*str*.7.7(p.27.14; M.9.449C); τῶν δ' αἱρέσεων, αἱ μὲν ἀπὸ ὀνόματος προσαγορεύονται, ὡς ἡ ἀπὸ Οὐαλεντίνου...αἱ δὲ ἀπὸ τ., ὡς οἱ Περατικοί *ib*.7.17(p.76.24; 552C); τῷ τοῦ τ. δαιμονίῳ Or.*Cels*.8.36(p.251.23; M. 11.1572C); πᾶς τ. χρήζει Ἰησοῦ Χριστοῦ id.*engast*.7(p.290.15; M.12. 1021D); τ. γενέσεως id.*Jo*.2.34(28; p.92.5; M.14.173C); τ. κολάσεως *ib*.19.19(p.320.9; 561B); ἐπειδὴ τοῦ φαινομένου σκότους τ. αἱ δυσμαί... τούτου χάριν...πρὸς δυσμὰς ἀποβλέποντες ἀποτάσσεσθε τῷ σκοτεινῷ ἐκείνῳ...ἄρχοντι Cyr.H.*catech*.19.4; in phrase *ἐν τόποις τόποις in various places*, Philox.*ep*.35(p.183); of local churches *αἱ πανταχοῦ κατὰ τόπον ἐκκλησίαι* Ath.*ep.Jov*.2(M.26.816A); **2.** of heaven *τ. τῆς δόξης 1Clem*.5.4; *εἰς τὸν ἅγιον τ. ib*.5.7; *ἵνα...ἡ σάρξ αὕτη...σχῇ τ. τινὰ κατασκηνώσεως* Herm.*sim*.5.6.7; *τ. τῆς ἀναπαύσεως A.Jo*.99(p.200.23); *τ. ... καθαροὶ καὶ λειμῶνες* Clem.*ecl*.34(p.147.14; M.9.716C); *ψυχὴ...δεομένη κρείττονος ἐνδύματος εἰς τοὺς καθαρωτέρους καὶ αἰθερίους καὶ οὐρανίους τ.* Or.*Cels*.7.32(p.183.5; M.11.1465C); *τὰς γνωστικὰς ψυχὰς...εἰς ἀμείνους ἀμεινόνων τόπων τόπους ἀφικομένας* Clem.*str*.7.3(p.10.10; M.9.416C); *τὸν οὐράνιον διψῶσαι καὶ σύμφυτον τ.* Meth.*symp*.4.5(p.51.2; M.18.93B); *οἱ θειότεροι τ.* [sc. *πεπληρωμένοι*] ...*τῶν σεραφὶμ* id.*res*.1.49(p.303.11; M.41.1124A); *ἐν τ. οὗ ἀπέδρα ὀδύνη καὶ λύπη καὶ στεναγμός* Dion.Ar.*e.h*.7.3.4(M.3.560B); of heavenly Jerusalem, Or.*princ*.4.3.8(p.335.3; M.11.389B); *ib*.4.3.13(p.344.9; 398C); **3.** of hell *δεξιοὶ τ. A.Jo*.114(p.214.7); *τοὺς τ. τοὺς κολαστηρίους A.Thom*.A 57(p.174.11); *ἐν τῷ κάτω τ. ὤν* Or.*engast*.8(p.292.6; M.12.1025A); *εἰς τὸν τ. τοῦ πυρός Hom.Clem*.1.7; cf. *οὗτος ὁ τ. δεσμωτήριον ἀγγέλων Apoc.En*.21.10; **4.** of the holy places, Or.*Jo*.13.12(p.236.32; M.14.417A); *δυσσέβημα παμμέγεθος τοὺς ἁγίους τ. ὑπὸ τῶν ἀνοσίων χραίνεσθαι μιασμάτων* Const.ap.Eus.*v.C*.3.52(p.99.28; M.20.1113A); *τὰ γνωρίσματα τῆς...τοῦ δεσπότου...φιλανθρωπίας, τὰ ἐν τοῖς τ. δεικνύμενα* Gr.Nyss.*ep*.3(M.46.1016B); *τοὺς ἐν Ἱεροσολύμοις τ. ἰδεῖν, ἐν οἷς τὰ σύμβολα τῆς διὰ σαρκὸς ἐπιδημίας τοῦ κυρίου ὁρᾶται ib*.2(1009B); *ἐκ τῶν ἁγίων τ. ἐπὶ τὴν Κωνσταντινούπολιν* Marc.Er.*opusc*.5.6(M.65.1037C); *προσφέρομέν σοι, δέσποτα, καὶ ὑπὲρ τῶν ἁγίων σου τ., οὓς ἐδόξασας τῇ θεοφανείᾳ τοῦ Χριστοῦ σου Lit.Jac*.(p.206.25); *τοὺς ἀπὸ τῶν ἔξω χωρῶν ἐρχομένους εἰς προσκύνησιν τῶν ἁγίων τ.* Ant.Mon.*ep.Eust*.(M.89.1428B); **5.** of a church *εἰ μὴ δυνατὸν ἐν ἐκκλησίᾳ προϊέναι διὰ τοὺς ἀπίστους, κατ' οἶκον συνάξεις...οὐχ ὁ τ. γὰρ τὸν ἄνθρωπον ἁγιάζει, ἀλλ' ὁ ἄνθρωπος τὸν τ.· ἐὰν δὲ ἀσεβεῖς κατέχωσιν τὸν τ., φευκτέος σοι ἔστω Const.App*.8.34.8; *μετασχηματισάμενος...τὸ ἱερὸν τοῦτο εἰς τ. τοῦ ἁγίου Στεφάνου CIG* 8647 (saec. vi); *ἁγίασον τὸν τ. ἐκεῖνον Dorm.BMV* 42(p.109); **6.** of a place in church, ‡Pion.*v.Polyc*.21; *εἰ...τις εὑρεθῇ παρὰ τόπον καθεζόμενος, ἐπιπλησσέσθω ὑπὸ τοῦ διακόνου...καὶ εἰς τὸν καθήκοντα αὐτῷ τ. μεταγέσθω Const.App*.2.57.11; *εἰ δὲ πτωχὸς...ἢ ξένος ἐπέλθοι...καὶ τ. οὐχ ὑπάρχει, καὶ τούτοις τ. ποιήσει ἐξ ὅλης τῆς καρδίας ὁ διάκονος ib*.2.58.6; *ἐνθρονιζέσθω εἰς τὸν αὐτῷ διαφέροντα τ. παρὰ τῶν...ἐπισκόπων Lit.ib*.8.5.10; of sanctuary *ἀπὸ τοῦ θειοτέρου τ.* Dion.Ar.*e.h*.4.3.3(M.3.476D); **7.** of a burial place, *A.Petr.et Paul*.87(p.221.5); ‡Epiph.*v.proph.Jer*.13(p.22; M.43.400D); **8.** of a place on the body, Iren.*haer*.1.18.1(M.7.644B); Melet.*nat.hom*.23(M.64.1233B); **9.** *locality*, ref. circumscription of the deity; **a.** ref. pagan gods *ἑνὶ τ. ἐγκαθιδρυμένος Ἑλληνικὸς θεός* Or.*Cels*.1.70(p.124.19; M.11.789C); *ib*.5.2(p.3.16; 1184B); **b.** ref. God *θεοῦ...ἐστι μὴ...ἐν τ. χωρεῖσθαι· εἰ δὲ μήγε, μείζων ὁ χωρῶν τ. αὐτοῦ εὑρεθήσεται* Thphl.Ant.*Autol*.2.3(M.6.1049C); *οὐ γὰρ ἐν γνόφῳ ἢ τ. ὁ θεός, ἀλλ' ὑπεράνω καὶ τ. καὶ χρόνου καὶ τῆς τῶν γεγονότων ἰδιότητος* Clem.*str*.2.2(p.116.3; M.8.937A); *οὔκουν ἐν τ. τὸ πρῶτον αἴτιον, ἀλλ' ὑπεράνω καὶ τ. καὶ χρόνου καὶ ὀνόματος καὶ νοήσεως ib*.5.11(p.374.18; M.9.109B); *οὐδ' ὡς ἐν τ. ὄντος τοῦ θεοῦ ...ἐροῦμεν· πῶς ἴωμεν πρὸς αὐτόν; κρείττων γὰρ ὁ θεὸς παντὸς τ.* Or.*Cels*.7.34(p.184.14; M.11.1468C); *θεὸς...ἐν σχήματι ὢν...πῶς οὐ περιοριστός ἐστιν; περιόριστος δὲ ὤν, ἐν τ. ἐστίν. ἐν τ. δὲ ὤν, ἥττων ἐστὶ τοῦ περιέχοντος αὐτὸν τ. Hom.Clem*.17.3; *θεοῦ τ. ἐστὶ τὸ μὴ ὄν, θεὸς δὲ τὸ ὄν· τὸ δὲ μὴ ὂν τῷ ὄντι οὐ συγκρίνεται. πῶς γὰρ τ. ὤν, εἶναι δύναται; ib*.17.8; matter not the *τ.* of God, Meth.*arbitr*.6(p.159.9; M.18.252A); *οἱ...φιλόθεοι οὐκ ἐν τ. ζητοῦσι τὸν ἐπὶ πάντων θεόν* Thdt.*Dan*.1:8(2.1071); *αὕτη* [sc. Trin.] *γὰρ οὔτε ἐν τ. ἐστίν, ἵνα καὶ ἀπῇ τινος ἢ ἐξ ἑτέρων εἰς ἕτερα μεταβῇ* Dion.Ar.*d.n*.3.1(M.3.680B); ref. the ignorant *μικρῷ καὶ βραχεῖ τ. ἐμπεριλαμβανόντων τὸν ἐπὶ πάντων θεόν* Or.*or*.23.3(p.351.14; M.11.489A); ref. Son *οὐ γὰρ ἐξίσταταί ποτε τῆς αὐτοῦ περιωπῆς ὁ υἱὸς τοῦ θεοῦ, οὐ μεριζόμενος...οὐ μεταβαίνων ἐκ τ. εἰς τ.* Clem.*str*.7.2(p.5.27; 408C); cf. *καὶ ἄνω φῶς ἦν...καὶ τὸ ἐνταῦθα ὀφθὲν οὐχ ὕστερον τοῦ ἄνω, οὐδὲ...μετέστη δεῦρο, τ. ἐκ τόπου ἀμεῖβον* id.*exc.Thdot*.4(p.106.19; M.9.656A); **10.** of the place or abode of God, esp. ref. Ex.33:21, 24:10 *τίς ὁ τ. ἐκεῖνος, ὁ παρὰ τῷ θεῷ νοούμενος...τ. ... εἰπὼν οὐ περιείργει τῷ ποσῷ τὸ δεικνύμενον, ἀλλὰ...ἐπὶ τὸ ἄπειρον...χειραγωγεῖ τὸν ἀκούοντα...τοσοῦτός ἐστιν ὁ παρ' ἐμοὶ τ., ὥστε τὸν ἐν αὐτῷ διαθέοντα μηδέποτε δυνηθῆναι λῆξαι τοῦ δρόμου* Gr.Nyss.*v.Mos*.(M.44.405A); *ὁ οὖν ὑποδείξας τῷ Μωϋσεῖ τὸν τ., παρορμᾷ πρὸς τὸν δρόμον ib*.(405D); *ὅταν ὁ νοῦς τὸν παλαιὸν ἄνθρωπον ἀποδυσάμενος, τὸν ἐκ χάριτος ἐπενδύσηται, τότε καὶ τὴν ἑαυτοῦ κατάστασιν ὄψεται κατὰ τὸν καιρὸν τῆς προσευχῆς, σαπφείρῳ ἢ οὐρανίῳ χρώματι παρεμφερῆ, ἥντινα καὶ τ. θεοῦ ἡ γραφὴ ὀνομάζει* Evagr.Pont.*cap.pract*.A 70(M.40.1244A); *οὐκ ἂν ἴδῃ ὁ νοῦς τὸν τοῦ θεοῦ τ. ἐν ἑαυτῷ, μὴ πάντων τῶν ἐν τοῖς πράγμασιν ὑψηλότερος γεγονώς...ἐπιφανέντος αὐτῷ τοῦ φωτὸς ἐκείνου τοῦ κατὰ τὸν καιρὸν τῆς προσευχῆς ἐκτυποῦντος τὸν τ. τοῦ θεοῦ ib*.71(1244A,B); *κἂν ὑπὲρ τὴν θεωρίαν τῆς σωματικῆς φύσεως ὁ νοῦς γένηται, οὔπω τέλειον τὸν τοῦ θεοῦ τ. ἐθεάσατο· δύναται γὰρ ἐν τῇ τῶν νοητῶν εἶναι γνώσει καὶ ποικίλλεσθαι πρὸς αὐτήν* id.*or*.57(M.79.1180A); *θεωρεῖ δὲ οὐκ αὐτὸν (ἀθέατος γάρ), ἀλλὰ τὸν τ. οὗ ἔστι. τοῦτο δέ, οἶμαι, σημαίνει τὸ τὰ θειότατα καὶ ἀκρότατα τῶν ὁρωμένων καὶ νοουμένων ὑποθετικούς τινας εἶναι λόγους τῶν ὑποβεβλημένων τῷ πάντα ὑπερέχοντι, δι' ὧν ἡ ὑπὲρ πᾶσαν ἐπίνοιαν αὐτοῦ παρουσία δείκνυται, ταῖς νοηταῖς ἀκρότησι τῶν ἁγιωτάτων αὐτοῦ ἐπιβατεύουσα* Dion.Ar.*myst*.1.3(M.3.1000D); *λέγεται τ. θεοῦ ἔνθα ἔκδηλος ἡ ἐνέργεια αὐτοῦ γίνεται* Jo.D.*f.o*.1.13(M.94.852A); *λέγεται...θεοῦ τ., ὁ πλέον μετέχων τῆς ἐνεργείας καὶ τῆς χάριτος αὐτοῦ ib*.(852B); **11.** (Eunomian) of H. Ghost *τὸ μὲν γὰρ 'ἐξ οὗ' τὸν δημιουργὸν σημαίνειν βούλονται, τὸ δὲ 'δι' οὗ' τὸν ὑπουργὸν ἢ τὸ ὄργανον, τὸ δὲ 'ἐν ᾧ' τὸν χρόνον δηλοῦν ἢ τὸν τ., ἵνα μηδὲν μὲν ὀργάνου σεμνότερος ὁ δημιουργὸς τῶν ὅλων νοῆται, μηδὲν δὲ τῆς ἀπὸ τ. ἢ χρόνου συνεισφορᾶς εἰς τὰ ὄντα πλεῖον φαίνηται τὸ πνεῦμα τὸ ἅγιον παρεχόμενον* Bas.*Spir*.4(3.4D; M.32.73C); *τῷ μὲν υἱῷ...τὴν τοῦ ὀργάνου προσηγορίαν ἐπέθηκαν, τῷ δὲ πνεύματι τὴν τοῦ τ. ib*.6(6B; M.77B); **12.** ref. Inc., of Christ's body *τ. ἔνθεον ἑαυτῷ καθιέρωσεν ἐπὶ γῆς* Clem.*fr*.36(p.219.6); **13.** ref. divine indwelling; of soul as place of H. Ghost, Herm.*mand*.5.1.3; *ὁ...γινώσκων ἑαυτόν, τ. ἐστὶ καὶ θρόνος τοῦ κυρίου* Clem.*fr*.31(p.217.25); id.*str*.2.13(p.143.19; M.8.993B); of angelic powers *οὗτοι...εἰσιν ὡς θεοειδεῖς οἱ θεῖοι τ. τῆς θεαρχικῆς καταπαύσεως* Dion.Ar.*c.h*.7.4(M.3.212C); id.*myst*.3(M.3.1033B); of Church as place of God, Jo.D.*f.o*.1.13(M.94.852B); **14.** of God as embracing the universe *θεὸς...οὐ χωρεῖται, ἀλλὰ αὐτός ἐστι τ. τῶν ὅλων* Thphl.Ant.*Autol*.2.3(M.6.1049D); *αὐτὸς ἑαυτοῦ τ. ὢν ib*.2.10(1064B); Bas.*Spir*.62(3.52C; M.32.181C); **15.** of place of man's worship of God, spiritually interpreted *τ. ζητοῦμεν τοῦ ᾄδειν τὴν ᾠδὴν κυρίου ἐπὶ γῆς ἀλλοτρίας, τ. τοῦ προσκυνεῖν...τὸν θεόν...τίς ὁ τ.; ...ἦλθεν ἐπὶ ταύτην φορέσας σῶμα...ἵν' ἐν τούτῳ τῷ τ. ... δυνηθῶ προσκυνῆσαι τὸν θεόν* Or.*hom.7.3 in Jer*.(p.54.24; M.13.333C); *ἡ θυσία τῆς αἰνέσεως· ἐν ποίῳ...τ. ταύτην προσφέρομεν ἢ ἐν τῷ πνεύματι τῷ ἁγίῳ...; τοῦτον τὸν τ. ἰδὼν ὁ Ἰακὼβ ἔφη, ὅτι κύριος ἐν τῷ τ. τούτῳ· ὥστε τὸ πνεῦμα τ. ἀληθῶς τῶν ἁγίων, καὶ ὁ ἅγιος τ. οἰκεῖος τῷ πνεύματι...ναὸς αὐτοῦ χρηματίζων* Bas.*Spir*.62(3.52D; M.32.184A); **16.** ref. arithmetical order *τὸ ἦτα στοιχεῖον σὺν τῷ ἐπισήμῳ ὀγδοάδα εἶναι, ἀπὸ τοῦ ἄλφα ὀγδόῳ κείμενον τ.* Hipp.*haer*.6.52(p.185.14; M.16.3283B); cf.Iren.*haer*.1.16.2(M.7.632A).

B. *region, sphere*; **1.** *ὁ περίγειος τ.* the region of and around the earth *πολλάκις ἔστιν εὑρεῖν κόσμον τὸν περίγειον ὀνομαζόμενον τ.* Or.*Cels*.6.59(p.129.24; M.11.1389A); haunted by spirits, acc. pagan theory, Clem.*str*.6.3(p.446.25; M.9.249A); opp. paradise *τὸν περίγειον τ., ἐφ' ὃν ἐκβληθεὶς τοῦ παραδείσου...ἐλήλυθεν ὁ Ἀδὰμ* Or.*Cels*.7.50(p.201.14; 1493C); ref. Inc. *τῶν ἐπιδημησάντων τῷ περιγείῳ τ. ἀγγέλων διὰ τὴν Ἰησοῦ γένεσιν ib*.1.60(p.111.6; 769C); *καταλείπει* [sc. Christ]...*τὴν ἄνω Ἱερουσαλὴμ καὶ ἔρχεται εἰς τὸν περίγειον τ.* id.*hom.10.7 in Jer*.(p.77.14; M.13.365C); ref. Origen's doctrine of Fall *ὥσπερ οἱ ἐντεῦθεν...ἀποθνήσκοντες...οἰκονομοῦνται...τ. διαφόρων τυγχάνειν κατὰ τὴν ἀναλογίαν τῶν ἁμαρτημάτων, οὕτως οἱ ἐκεῖθεν, ἵν' οὕτως εἴπω, ἀποθνήσκοντες εἰς τὸν ᾅδην τοῦτον καταβαίνουσι, κρινόμενοι ἄξιοι τῶν τοῦ παντὸς περιγείου τ. διαφόρων οἰκητηρίων βελτιόνων ἢ χειρόνων* id.*princ*.4.3.10(p.337.6; M.11.393A); **2.** *ὁ σωματικὸς τ.* the *material world, bodily sphere* *τῇ ἑαυτῆς φύσει ἀσώματος ψυχὴ ἐν παντὶ σωματικῷ τ. τυγχάνουσα δέεται σώματος οἰκείου τῇ φύσει τῷ τ. ἐκείνῳ* Or.*Cels*.7.32(p.182.32; M.11.1465B); *μὴ ἐάν τινα ἐν σωματικῷ τ. εἶναι τὸν θεόν* id.*or*.23.3(p.351.4; M.11.488C); *οὗτοι...ἐν σωματικῷ τ. δώσουσιν τὸν πατέρα καὶ τὸν υἱόν, τ. ἐκ τ. ἀμείψαντα, σωματικῶς ἐπιδεδημηκέναι τῷ βίῳ καὶ οὐχὶ κατάστασιν ἐκ καταστάσεως* id.*Jo*.20.18(16; p.351.12; M.14.613D); plur. *ἀναγκαῖον...τὴν ψυχὴν ἐν τ. σωματικοῖς ὑπάρχουσαν κεχρῆσθαι σώμασι καταλλήλοις τοῖς τ.* Meth.*res*.1.22(p.246.4; M.41.1092B); **3.** of spiritual sphere *τὴν* ⟨*εἰς*⟩ *Ἱεροσόλυμα ἄνοδον σημαίνων τὴν ἀπὸ τῶν ὑλικῶν εἰς τὸν ψυχικὸν τ. ... ἀνάβασιν τοῦ κυρίου* Heracleon ap.Or.*Jo*.10.33(19; p.206.27; M.14.365C); *ἐπαγγελία ἐστὶν μὴ γεύσεσθαι θανάτου τινὰ τῶν ἑστώτων ἐν τῷ δεικνυμένῳ ὑπὸ τοῦ Ἰησοῦ νοητῷ τ.* Or.*Jo*.20.43(33; p.387.7; 676C); **4.** of the divine (Valent.) *εὐώνυμοι δυνάμεις...ὑπὸ τῆς τοῦ φωτὸς παρουσίας οὐ μορφοῦνται, κατελείφθησαν δὲ αἱ ἀριστεραὶ ὑπὸ τοῦ Τ. μορφωθῆναι* Clem.*exc.Thdot*.34(p.118.6; M.9.676C); *τῆς μητρὸς...μετὰ τοῦ υἱοῦ...εἰσελθούσης εἰς τὸ πλήρωμα, τότε ὁ Τ. τὴν ἐξουσίαν τῆς μητρὸς...ἀπολήψεται ib*.(p.118.8; M.l.c.); *οἱ μὲν δίκαιοι...παρὰ τῷ Τ. κατείχοντο κατὰ τοὺς Οὐαλεντινιανοὺς ib*.37(p.118.26; 677A); *ποταμὸς ἐκπορεύεται πυρὸς ὑποκάτω τοῦ θρόνου τοῦ τ. ... καὶ αὐτὸς δὲ ὁ τ. πύρινός ἐστι ib*.38(p.118.29; 677B); *ib*.(p.119.4; M.l.c.) cit. s. *παρακαλέω*; *ἔστι δὲ πυρώδης, φησίν* [sc. Valentinus], *ἡ ψυχικὴ οὐσία, καλεῖται δὲ* καὶ τ. ... καὶ παλαιὸς τῶν ἡμερῶν Hipp.*haer*.6.32(p.161.6; M.16.3243B); **5.** *sphere, department* of knowledge, philosophy, etc., Clem.*str*.6.7 (p.460.7; M.9.277C); ἄλλαι ἀρεταί, αἱ παρὰ Μωϋσῇ ἀναγεγραμμέναι, ἀρχὴν Ἕλλησι παντὸς τοῦ ἠθικοῦ τ. παρασχόμεναι *ib*.2.18(p.153.29; M. 8.1016B); ὁ θεὸς...ᾗ μὲν οὖν ἐστιν οὐσία, ἀρχὴ τοῦ φυσικοῦ τ.· καθ' ὅσον ἐστὶν τἀγαθόν, τοῦ ἠθικοῦ· ᾗ δ' αὖ ἐστι νοῦς, τοῦ λογικοῦ καὶ κριτικοῦ τ. *ib*.4.25(p.320.17; 1372B); τοῦ ἠθικοῦ τ. ὡς ἐν κεφαλαίῳ ὑπογραφέντος *ib*.7.18(p.78.19; M.9.556C); Or.*comm.in Gen*.ap.*philoc*. 14.2(p.69.1; M.12.89A); id.*hom.11.4 in Jer*.(p.81.23; M.13.372B); τὸν ἠθικὸν τ. οἴεται [sc. Celsus] διαβαλεῖν id.*Cels*.1.4(p.58.5; M.11.661A); **6.** of heaven; as sphere of divine presence, Clem.*prot*.4(p.44.11; M.8.153B); ἐπὶ τὸν ὑπερουράνιον ἐπὶ τῇ θέᾳ τῶν καλῶν μετατιθέντος [sc. S. Paul] τόπον Or.*Cels*.6.59(p.130.6; M.11.1389B); **7.** *region, country*; of whole of Palestine, Or.*princ*.4.3.6(p.332.2; M.11.385C); of district of Jerusalem, *Ep.Abg*.1(p.279.4n.); pleonastic τῇ...ἐκκλησίᾳ...ἥτις προκάθηται ἐν τόπῳ χωρίου Ῥωμαίων Ign.*Rom*.proem.; Or.*Jo*.10.12(10; p.183.23; M.14.325D).

C. *place, passage* in a book, *1Clem*.8.4; μυστικὸς...τ. Or.*Jo*.6.35 (18; p.144.5; M.14.260A); Eus.*d.e*.1.1(p.6.21; M.22.21A).

D. *subject, topic* περὶ...πίστεως καὶ μετανοίας...πάντα τ. ἐψηλαφήσαμεν *1Clem*.62.2; ἑώρα...μείζονος ἐπιστήμης ἑαυτὸν δεόμενον εἰς τὸν περὶ τῆς εὐχῆς τ. Or.*or*.2.4(p.302.24; M.11.421C); Μελίτων...φησὶν αὐτὸν [sc. Absalom] εἶναι τύπον τοῦ διαβόλου ἐπαναστάντος τῇ Χριστοῦ βασιλείᾳ, καὶ τούτου μόνου μνησθείς, οὐκ ἐπεξηργάσατο τὸν τ. id.*sel.in Ps*.3:1(M.12.1120A); *commonplace*, id.*Cels*.4.45(p.318.9; M. 11.1101C).

E. *occasion, opportunity, opening* θελήσετε ἀγαθοποιεῖν καὶ οὐχ ἕξετε τ. Herm.*vis*.3.9.5; τ. ... τῇ εὐποιΐᾳ Clem.*fr*.47(p.224.7); ἔσχεν ὁ πονηρὸς τ., ὅπως ὑμᾶς πειράσῃ *A.Paul*.1(p.106.7); τ. ἀπολογίας Or. *Jo*.2.15(9; p.72.12; M.14.141A); μὴ δῷ τ. τῷ ἀλλοτρίῳ κατ' αὐτῶν *Lit*.ap.*Const.App*.8.6.6.

F. ἐν τόπῳ *immediately, on the spot*, Jo.Mal.*chron*.15 p.382(M.97. 568A).

G. *position, standing* ἐν τῇ ἑνότητι ὑμῶν οὐχ ἕξουσιν [sc. λύκοι] τ. Ign.*Philad*.2.2; οὐκέτι ἔχουσιν τ., ἀλλ' ἔσονται ἔκβολοι Herm.*vis*.3.5.5; *Const.App*.4.1.1; *role, part* οἱ τὸν τ. πληροῦντες λέοντος Evagr.*h.e*. 2.18(p.67.26; M.86.2548B); *Chron.Pasch*.p.336(M.92.876A); *function* τὸν τῆς ὑπακοῆς τ. ἀναπληρῶσαι *1Clem*.63.1; *official position, office* τοῖς ἱερεῦσιν ἴδιος ὁ τ. προστέτακται *ib*.40.5; ἐκδίκει σου τὸν τ. ἐν πάσῃ ἐπιμελείᾳ Ign.*Polyc*.1.2; τ. μηδένα φυσιούτω id.*Smyrn*.6.1; τὸ... ὠφελοῦν οὐκ αὐτὸ τὸ καθέζεσθαι ἐν πρεσβυτερίῳ ἐστίν, ἀλλὰ τὸ βιοῦν ἀξίως τοῦ τ. Or.*hom.11.3 in Jer*.(p.81.3; M.13.369D); δεῖ τινα ὁρίσαι ἀντ' ἐμοῦ [sc. S. Peter] τὸν ἐμὸν ἀναπληροῦντα τ. ... ἵνα ἐπὶ τῆς Χριστοῦ καθέδρας καθεσθεὶς τὴν...ἐκκλησίαν οἰκονομῇ *Hom.Clem*.3. 40; ὁ προκαθεζόμενος Χριστοῦ τ. πεπίστευται *ib*.3.66; ἀποστόλων, ὧν καὶ τὸν τ. φυλάσσουσιν [sc. presbyters] ὡς σύμβουλοι τοῦ ἐπισκόπου *Const.App*.2.28.4; of deacons, *ib*.3.19.2.

τοποτηρέω, *act for, represent*; of papal legates, Cael.*ep.Nest*. (p.83.12; M.*PL*.50.484C); Leo Mag.*ep*.106(p.57.17; M.*PL*.54.1006A); *ib*.114(p.62.5; 1030A); of other deputies, Ath.Scholast.*coll*.4.24 (p.66); *Chron.Pasch*.p.336(M.92.876B).

τοποτηρησία, ἡ, 1. *representation, office of delegate*, *Cod.Afr*.14; Martin.*ep*.5(M.*PL*.87.153D); **2.** *delegation, embassy*, *Cod.Afr*.56.

τοποτηρητής, ὁ, 1. *legate, delegate*; of pope, *Cod.Afr*.proem.(H. 1.861A); CEph.(431)*act*.5(*ACO* 1.1.3 p.21.13; H.1.1493D); CChalc. *act*.17(*ACO* 2.1.3 p.94.33; H.2.636E); μὴ κεχωρισμένης ὑμῶν τῆς ἐμῆς παρουσίας, ὅστις διὰ τῶν τ. ὑμῖν πάρειμι Leo Mag.*ep*.93(p.31.22; M.*PL*.54.938B); Thphn.*chron*.p.86(M.108.261A); of other patriarchs, Max.*Pyrr*.(M.91.352D); τ. τοῦ ἀποστολικοῦ θρόνου Ἀντιοχείας CNic. (787)*act*.1(H.4.49B); of bishops, *Cod.Afr*.56; legate of province, Thdt.*ep*.40(4.1099); Phot.*nomoc*.11.1(M.104.1152B); **2.** *garrison commander*, Thphn.*chron*.p.329(M.108.796A); **3.** in gen., *substitute, deputy*, Ath.Scholast.*coll*.4.24(p.66); *ib*.3.1(p.44).

***τοποχωρέω**, *dwell, have a place in*, Areth.*Apoc*.11:1(M.106. 648A).

***τορκίμ, ὁ**, *king* (? Persian), Jo.Mal.*chron*.11 p.270(M.97.409A).

***τόρνα**, *turn* (imperative; Lat. dialect) τὸν δεσπότην τοῦ ζῴου προσφωνεῖ...τῇ πατρῴᾳ φωνῇ· τ., τ., φράτερ Thphn.*chron*.p.218(M. 108.556C).

τόρνευσις, ἡ, *turning* by means of a lathe, Clem.*paed*.2.9(p.205. 22; M.8.492C).

τορνευτής, ὁ, *turner*, *M.Apollon*.14; *shaper, maker*, Leont.B. *mesopent*.(M.86.1984B).

***τόρνη, ἡ**, *twist*, ‡Caes.Naz.*dial*.140(M.38.1053).

***τοσαυταπλασιόνως**, *so many times more*, Or.*Jo*.20.34(27; p.372. 14; M.14.652A).

***τοσαυταπλειόνως**, *by so many times the more*, Or.*Jo*.20.34(27; p.372.23; M.14.652B).

***τοτηνικαῦτα**, *at that very time, then*, Or.*sel.in Ps*.129:8(M.12. 1648D); Mac.Aeg.*hom*.47.13(M.34.805A).

***τούβικας**, = τοὺ βίγκας, (Lat. *tu vincas*) *be victorious*, Thphn. *chron*.p.154(*divisim* M.108.420A).

***τουβίον, τό**, *wick*, Thdr.Stud.*poen*.1.74(M.99.1741D); *Euchol*. p.348.

***τοῦλδον, τό**, (? Lat. *tultum, toltum* (*tollo*)) *baggage of an army*, Thphn.*chron*.p.212(M.108.544A); *ib*.p.265(660A).

***τουρμάρχης, ὁ**, *commander of a turma* (squadron), Thphn.*chron*. p.266(M.108.660B); *ib*.p.391(932C).

***τουρμάρχισσα, ἡ**, *wife of a* τουρμάρχης, Thdr.Stud.*epp*.2.145 (M.99.1453C).

***τοῦφα, ἡ**, (Lat. *tufa*) *tuft* taken from the wild bull's tail; an ornament for horses and standards, Cosm.Ind.*top*.11(M.88.444A).

***τραγικολογία, ἡ**, *bombast, rodomontade*, Meth.*res*.1.55(p.314.10, v.l. τερατολογία; M.41.1148D).

τραγῳδ-έω, 1. *make a show of, exhibit publicly* οὐκ αἰσχύνονται ταῦτα ἐπὶ κατηχουμένων, καὶ τό γε χείριστον, ἐπὶ Ἑλλήνων ~οῦντες τὰ μυστήρια CAlex.*ep*.(p.96.8; M.25.268A); οὐ χρὴ...τὰ μυστήρια ἀμυήτοις ~εῖν *ib*.(p.96.11; M.l.c.); *flaunt* μὴ ~εῖν τὴν εὐποιΐαν *Const.App*.3.14.4; **2.** *talk in tragic style, declaim*, *V.Mac.Aeg*.7(M. 34.224A); *declaim, inveigh against* Eus.*Marcell*.1.4(p.28.3; M.24. 769A); Thdt.*Mich*.proem.(2.1477); τὴν τῆς ἀσεβείας ὑπερβολὴν ~ῶν id.*Dan*.5:23(2.1169); Proc.G.*ep*.62(M.87.2720B); **3.** *utter pompously and absurdly*, ref. rationalistic explanations of myths given by philosophers τὰς τετραγῳδημένας ἐν φυσικαῖς ἀποδόσεσι κομψείας Eus.*p.e*.15.1(788D; M.21.1293C); in gen., *A.Thom*.B 60(p.42.31); **4.** ptcpl. pass., *tragic, calamitous*, Thdt.*h.e*.1.30.2(3.819); ‡Meth. *Sym.et Ann*.9(M.18.369C).

τραγῴδημα, τό, 1. *play*, †Ph.Carp.*ep*.(p.397.28; M.32.356C); **2.** *event in a tragedy*, Gr.Nyss.*paup*.2(M.46.477C); **3.** met., *piece of play-acting*, Epiph.*haer*.66.55(p.91.24; M.42.112B).

τραγῳδία, ἡ, 1. *tragedy* ἡ τ. ἀπὸ τῶν εἰδώλων ἀποσπῶσα εἰς τὸν οὐρανὸν ἀναβλέπειν διδάσκει Clem.*str*.5.14(p.402.15; M.9.169B); **2.** *grandeur, pomp*, Iren.*haer*.1.4.3(M.7.484A); Gr.Nyss.*or.dom*.4 (p.84.22; M.44.1172D); **3.** *calamity, disaster*, Clem.*paed*.3.3(p.249. 10; M.8.585A); Eus.*h.e*.3.6.1(M.20.224C); Gr.Nyss.*ep*.1(M.46.1004B); **4.** *plot*, Thdt.*h.e*.1.22.3(3.804); *ib*.1.25.15(813).

τραγῳδοποιός, *tragic*, Marc.Diac.*v.Porph*.2.

***τραδιτεύω**, (Lat. *trado*) *transmit*, Ath.Scholast.*coll*.8.5(p.94).

τρακταΐζω, *deal with, manage*, *A.Petr.et Paul*.3(p.179.7); *Cod. Afr*.proem.(H.1.864E); *ib*.50; CChalc.*act*.5(*ACO* 2.1.2 p.126.1; H.2. 452B); Jo.Mal.*chron*.12 p.305(M.97.460C); *Chron.Pasch*.p.339(M.92. 885A).

***τρακταϊστέος**, *to be dealt with*, *Cod.Afr*.proem.(H.1.861C).

***τρακταϊστής, ὁ**, *one skilled in management of business, man of affairs*, Jo.Mal.*chron*.12 p.314(M.97.472C).

***τρακτᾶτον, τό (τρακτᾶτος, ὁ)**, (Lat. *tractatus*) **1.** *treatment, examination* of a matter περὶ τῆς πίστεως...τοῦ ἐν Νικαίᾳ τρακτάτου *Cod.Afr*.47; Eutych.*ep.Vigil*.(M.86.2405A); **2.** *device, contrivance* τρακτάτῳ φυγῆς χρησάμενοι Ῥωμαῖοι, ἐδόκουν φεύγειν Jo.Mal.*chron*. 18 p.468(M.97.681D); **3.** *rule, procedure* εἴ τις τοῦ χειροτονουμένου κληρικοῦ κατηγορεῖν βούλεται, ὁ περὶ τῶν ἐπισκόπων καὶ ἐν αὐτῷ κρατείτω τ. Ath.Scholast.*coll*.1.2(p.8).

τρακτευτής, ὁ, *treasury official, tax clerk*; one of those who do official business for the Prefects, Bas.*ep*.144 tit.(3.236A; M.32. 593B); Eustrat.*v.Eutych*.68(M.86.2352A); Cyr.S.*v.Sab*.54(p.145.22).

τρακτεύω, 1. *deal with, examine*; of self-examination by monks, *Apophth.Patr*.(M.65.308C); of transaction of conciliar business, Leo I Imp.*ep*.ap.Evagr.*h.e*.2.9(p.60.29; M.86.2529A); **2.** *devise, contrive* γνόντος...τὸ τρακτευθὲν κατ' αὐτοῦ Jo.Mal.*chron*.7 p.181(M.97. 289B).

***τρανόλαλος**, *speaking clearly, intelligible*; of apostles at Pentecost, Rom.Mel.(*AS* 1 p.163); of readers in church, *ib*.(p.49).

τραν-όω, 1. *make clear, explain* ἓν τῶν ἀδυνάτων...~ῶσαι τὸν περὶ τῆς εὐχῆς ἀκριβῶς...πάντα λόγον Or.*or*.2.1(p.298.4; M.11.417A); οὐδὲ...~οῦν δύνανται [sc. Gnostics] ἑαυτῶν τὸν λόγον id.*Jo*.13.20 (p.244.15; M.14.432C); πρὶν ~ῶσαι περὶ...Χριστοῦ, τῷ εἰπεῖν ὅτι πατήρ, ἤδη ἐδηλώσαμεν ὅτι υἱοῦ ἐστι πατήρ Cyr.H.*catech*.8.1; τοῦ πνεύματος τὴν θεότητα ~ουμένην Gr.Naz.*or*.31.27(p.180.12; M.36. 164C); θεὸν ὁρῶν...ὃν καὶ νῦν ~οῦσθαι ἡμῖν εὐχόμεθα, ὅσον ἐφικτὸν *ib*. 38.18(333A); ἐτράνωσαν τὰ περὶ τῆς θεότητος τοῦ ἁγίου πνεύματος Justn.*conf*.(p.90.6; M.86.1013B); σύμβολον...~ωθὲν ὑπὸ τῶν ρν' ἁγίων πατέρων *ib*.(p.90.13; 1013C); of interpretation of scripture, Or.*Jo*.

10.11(9; p.182.5; 325B); id.*comm.in Mt.*10.9(p.11.10; M.13.857A); Eust.*engast.*1(p.16.22; M.18.613B); Mac.Mgn.*apocr.*3.23(p.105.19); **2.** pass., *be clear, distinct* οὐσίαν μὲν μίαν ἐπὶ τῆς θεότητος ὁμολογοῦμεν...ὑπόστασιν δὲ ἰδιάζουσαν, ἵν' ἀσύγχυτος ἡμῖν καὶ τετρανωμένη ἡ περὶ πατρὸς καὶ υἱοῦ καὶ ἁγίου πνεύματος ἔννοια ἐνυπάρχῃ Bas.*ep.*236.6(3.364A; M.32.884A); ἵνα...~ωθῇ σοι τῶν προσώπων ἡ ἰδιότης id.*hom.*24.3(2.191E; M.31.605B); ἐπὶ τῆς παρουσίας ἐναργὴς καὶ τετρανωμένη ἐστὶν ἡ ἀλήθεια †Gr.Nyss.*or.2 in Gen.1*:26(M.44.288D); of understanding of scripture, Chrys.*hom.2.1 in Ac.*(9.14E); of eccl. decisions, id.*comm.in Gal.*2:17(10.690C); ὅτι...τῆς θείας ἐστὶ τὸ πνεῦμα τὸ ἅγιον οὐσίας, τοῦτο σὺ ᾔτησας γραφικῶς ~ωθῆναι Isid.Pel.*epp.*1.60(M.78.221B); ὁ λόγος...γραφικαῖς μαρτυρίαις ~ωθείς Gel.Cyz.*h.e.*1.10.5(M.85.1212D); **3.** *understand clearly*, ref. scriptures, Or.*Jo.*2.13(7; p.68.19; M.14.133C); of spiritual interpretation, *ib.*10.5(4; p.175.11; 313B); id.*or.*27.6(p.366.21; M.11.509B); **4.** *instruct, enlighten*, med. γνώσεώς τε φωτιζούσης καὶ σοφίας ἐν ταῖς ψυχαῖς ἡμῶν ~ουμένης ‡Hipp.*fr.12 in Pss.*(p.142.4; M.10.717C); pass. προφῆται...λαλείτωσαν...καὶ εἰς διερμηνευέτω· ἄλλου δὲ ~ωθέντος, ὁ πρῶτος ὑποχωρείτω Gr.Naz.*or.*32.12(M.36.188C); *ib.*28.4(p.27.11; 32A); **5.** *portray clearly*, ref. prophecies τὰ μὲν ἐσκιογράφει, τὰ δὲ διὰ χρωμάτων ἐτράνου Isid.Pel.*epp.*2.63(M.78.508A); **6.** *utter clearly* ὥσπερ ἄλλη διάλεκτος παιδίων καὶ ἄλλη τετρανωμένων τὴν φωνήν, οὕτως πᾶσα ἐν ἀνθρώποις διάλεκτος οἱονεὶ παιδίων ἐστὶ διάλεκτος· ἡ δὲ ἀγγελικὴ οἱονεὶ ἀνδρῶν ἐστι τελείων καὶ τετρανωμένων Or.*comm.in 1Cor.*13:16(*JTS* 10 p.33); ref. restored speech, Ath.*inc.*38.4(M.25.161C); **7.** *make clear, distinct* οὐ τῆς διανοίας αὐτῶν [sc. children at Christ's entry to Jerusalem] τὸ λεγόμενον ἦν, ἀλλὰ τῆς αὐτοῦ δυνάμεως, ~ούσης τὸ τῆς γλώσσης ἐκείνων ἄωρον Chrys.*hom.67.1 in Mt.*(7.661E).

***τράνωσις**, ἡ, **1.** *clarification, explanation*, Or.*comm.in Eph.*1:13 (p.243); Bas.*ep.*113(3.206D; M.32.528A); **2.** *clear expression*, Gr.Nyss.*Eun.*12(1 p.227.18; M.45.924A); **3.** *illumination, instruction* of the baptized, Meth.*symp.*8.8(p.90.18; M.18.149C); *ib.*8.10(p.92.9; 153A).

τρανωτικός, *able to clarify*; of H. Ghost, Gr.Naz.*or.*31.29(p.185.1; M.36.168A).

τράπεζα, ἡ, **A.** *table*; **1.** in gen., ref. Last Supper σκηνὴ ἐπουράνιος ἐδείχθη τὸ ἀνώγεων...ἡ τ. ... τῶν ἐκεῖ τελεσθέντων μυστηρίων νοητὸν θυσιαστήριον Andr.Cr.*triod.*(M.97.1420A); monastic ἐν τῇ τ. ... συγκαθημένῳ μοι τῷ μεγάλῳ ἐπιστάτῃ Jo.Clim.*scal.*4(M.88.685C); χρὴ γινώσκειν ὅτι ἡνίκα κλάσει ἀδελφὸς σκεῦος...τῷ καιρῷ τοῦ ἀρίστου...παρίσταται πλησίον τῆς τ. *Const.Stud.*35(M.99.1717B); ὁ ἐπὶ τραπέζης officer in charge of imperial table, Anast.Ap.*a.Max.*1.6(M.90.120B); **2.** of table of shewbread, *1Clem.*43.2; γῆς...εἰκόνα ἡ τ. δηλοῖ τέσσαρσιν ἐπερειδομένη ποσί, θέρει, μετοπώρῳ, ἔαρι, χειμῶνι Clem.*str.*6.11(p.475.22; M.9.309A); *V.Pach.Φ* 34(p.21.16); Thdt.*qu.60 in Ex.*(1.164); **3.** of manger at Bethlehem ἐπὶ φάτνης, τῆς τῶν ἀλόγων τ. Thdt.*provid.*10(4.663); **4.** of Christian altar; **a.** in gen. ἡτοιμάσατο τὴν ἑαυτῆς [sc. σοφίας] τ. ... τὸ τίμιον...σῶμα καὶ αἷμα, ἅπερ ἐν τῇ μυστικῇ καὶ θείᾳ τ. καθ' ἑκάστην ἐπιτελοῦνται, θυόμενα εἰς ἀνάμνησιν τῆς πρώτης ἐκείνης τ. τοῦ μυστικοῦ θείου δείπνου ‡Hipp.*fr.54 in Pr.*(p.176.2f.; M.10.628B); βαπτισθέντων δὲ καὶ ἐνδυσαμένων, ἄρτον καταθεὶς ἐπὶ τὴν τ., ηὐλόγησεν *A.Thom.*A 133(p.240.6); τραπέζῃ παραστάντα καὶ χεῖρας εἰς ὑποδοχὴν τῆς ἁγίας τροφῆς προτείναντα Dion.Al.ap.Eus.*h.e.*7.9.4(M.20.656A); ὁ δὲ...πέφρικε...τῇ τ. προσιέναι Dion.Al.*ib.*7.9.5(656B); τούτου...τοῦ θύματος τὴν μνήμην ἐπὶ τραπέζης ἐκτελεῖν διὰ συμβόλων τοῦ τε σώματος αὐτοῦ καὶ τοῦ σωτηρίου αἵματος Eus.*d.e.*1.10 (p.47.33; M.22.89D); ref. schismatics τὰ νῶτα δοῦναι τῇ τοῦ κυρίου τ. Pall.*v.Chrys.*18(p.114.14; M.47.63); μετὰ...τὰς φοβερὰς...ἐπικλήσεις καὶ τὴν ἐπιφοίτησιν τοῦ...ζωοποιοῦ...πνεύματος οὐκ ἔτι ψιλὸν ἄρτον καὶ κοινὸν οἶνον, τὰ ἐπιτεθειμένα τῇ ἁγίᾳ τ., ἀλλὰ σῶμα καὶ αἷμα τίμιον...Χριστοῦ Nil.*epp.*1.44(M.79.104B); ὄψει τοὺς λευΐτας...ἄρτους καὶ ποτήριον...τιθέντας ἐπὶ τὴν τ. ... ἐπὰν δὲ ἐπιτελεσθῶσιν αἱ μεγάλαι εὐχαί, τότε γίνεται ὁ ἄρτος σῶμα καὶ τὸ ποτήριον αἷμα τοῦ κυρίου "Ath".ap.Eutych.*pasch.*8(M.86.2401A); ἥκιστα...θεότητος...φύσις ἐστὶ τὸ προκείμενον ἐν ἁγίαις τραπέζαις ἐκκλησιῶν, πλὴν ἴδιον σῶμα τοῦ ἐκ θεοῦ πατρὸς φύντος λόγου Cyr.*Nest.*4.6(p.89.6; 6[1].116A); ἐπὶ τῆς θείας τ. ... μὴ τῷ προκειμένῳ ἄρτῳ καὶ τῷ ποτηρίῳ...προσέχωμεν, ἀλλ'...πίστει νοήσωμεν κεῖσθαι ἐπὶ τῆς ἱερᾶς ἐκείνης τ. τὸν ἀμνὸν τοῦ θεοῦ Gel.Cyz.*h.e.*2.31.6(M.85.1317A); ἔδει...αὐτὸν...συνανακιρνᾶσθαι...τοῖς ἡμετέροις σώμασιν διὰ τῆς...αὐτοῦ σαρκὸς καὶ...αἵματος· ὃ καὶ ἐσχήκαμεν... ὡς ἐν ἄρτῳ καὶ οἴνῳ, ἵνα μὴ ἀποναρκήσωμεν σάρκα τε καὶ αἷμα προκείμενα βλέποντες ἐν ἁγίαις τραπέζαις Petr.Laod.*fr.in Mc.*14:22(M.86.3328B); παναχράντοιο τραπέζης Paul.Sil.*Soph.*720(M.86.2147A); τὴν ἱερὰν ἀσπασάμενος τ. Dion.Ar.*e.h.*2.2.4(M.3.393C); οὐκ εἰμὶ ἄξιος ἀντοφθαλμῆσαι τῇ ἱερᾷ ταύτῃ καὶ πνευματικῇ τ. ἐφ' ᾗ ὁ μονογενής σου υἱὸς...πρόκειται εἰς θυσίαν *Lit.Jac.*(p.160.14); ἱκάνωσόν με...παραστῆναι τῇ ἁγίᾳ σου ταύτῃ τ. καὶ ἱερουργῆσαι τὸ ἅγιόν σου σῶμα καὶ τὸ τίμιόν σου αἷμα *ib.*(p.180.6); θαμβούμεθα τὸ πρόσωπον τῇ λαμπρᾷ σου τ. προσερχόμενοι *ib.*(p.178.6); δεόμεθα...κύριε...ἐπίφανον τὸ πρόσωπόν σου ἐπὶ τὸν ἄρτον τοῦτον καὶ ἐπὶ τὰ ποτήρια ταῦτα, ἃ ἡ παναγία τ. ὑποδέχεται *Lit.Marc.*(Brightman p.124.28); εὐχὴ...μετὰ τὸ ἀποτεθῆναι τὰ ἅγια δῶρα ἐν τῇ ἁγίᾳ τ. *Lit.Chrys.*(p.319.4); ὁρῶμεν τὸν ἅγιον...ἄρτον...κατὰ τὸν καιρὸν τῆς μυστικῆς τελετῆς ἐπὶ τῆς ἀχράντου προτιθέμενον τ. ‡Caes.Naz.*dial.*169(M.38.1132); ἐκκλησία ἐστὶν οἶκος θεϊκός, ἔνθα...ἡ τ. ἡ ψυχοτρόφος καὶ ζωοποιός ‡Germ.CP *contempl.*(M.98.385A); relics placed beneath it, *A.Andr.*B 11(p.64.9); *Chron.Pasch.*p.293(M.92.733A); vessels laid upon it, Gr.Naz.*or.*43.52(M.36.564A); vestments, id.*carm.*2.1.11.1884(M.37.1161A); cross, Chosroes ap.Evagr.*h.e.*6.21 (p.238.2; M.86.2876C); surrounded by curtain, Evagr.*ib.*5.21(p.216.20; 2836A); circular in form, Bas.Sel.*v.Thecl.*1(M.85.560A); bishops consecrated at altar, Thdt.*h.e.*4.15.10(3.973); altar surrounded by priests, as throne of God by seraphim, *Pers.capt.*(M.86.3241C); oaths taken by altar despite eccl. censure of practice, Chrys.*stat.*15.5(2.158E); *ib.*(159A); Pall.*v.Chrys.*6(p.35.16; M.47.22); ref. destruction and desecration of altars practised by or alleged against heathen, heretics, and parties to eccl. disputes, Ath.*ep.encycl.*3 (p.172.13; M.25.229A); Ischyras *ep.*ap.eund.*apol.sec.*64(p.143.22; M.25.364D); ἁρπάσαντες τὰ συμψέλια καὶ τὸν θρόνον καὶ τὴν τ. (ξυλίνη γὰρ ἦν) Ath.*h.Ar.*56(p.214.36; M.25.760D); Bas.*ep.*226.2(3.347B; M.32.845B); *ib.*251.3(387B; M.936B); Synes.*ep.*67(M.66.1420C); Thdt.*h.e.*3.12.3(3.926); *Chron.Pasch.*p.391(M.92.1001A); as place of refuge or sanctuary, Synes.*ep.*58(1400C); **b.** of other furniture used as altar ἐκέλευσεν...παραθεῖναι τ., παρέθηκαν δὲ συμψέλλιον ὃ εὗρον ἐκεῖ καὶ ἁπλώσας σινδόνα ἐπ' αὐτό, ἐπέθηκεν ἄρτον τῆς εὐλογίας *A.Thom.*A 49 (p.165.19); **c.** symbolical interpretations; the manger, Chrys.*Philogon.*3(1.498A); ‡Bas.*h.myst.*33(p.265.22); Christ's tomb, *ib.*3 (p.258.8); *ib.*50(p.391.14); ‡Sophr.H.*liturg.*2(M.87.3984A); ‡Germ.CP *contempl.*(M.98.388C); *ib.*(420C); throne of God, *ib.*(385A); place of Christ's death, burial, resurrection, and ascension, *ib.*(421A); table of Last Supper, *ib.*(421C); *ib.*(388D); womb of BMV, ‡Jo.D.*corp.*4 (M.95.409B); **d.** prefigured in OT by νομικῇ τ., ἔνθα ἦν τὸ μάννα, ὅ ἐστι Χριστός ‡Germ.CP *contempl.*(388D); **5.** of monastic refectory or common table, *V.Pach.Φ* 52(p.34.12); Nil.*Eulog.*26(M.79.1128B); εἴ τις ἐν τ. ἐσθίων φλυαρεῖ, ἐγειρέσθω εἰς προσευχήν ‡Bas.*poen.mon.*28(2.528D; M.31.1309B); εἴ τις ἀπολιμπάνεται τῶν τ., μὴ εἰρηκὼς τὴν αἰτίαν, μενέτω ἄσιτος *ib.*34(529A; M.1309D); εἴ τις ἐγείρεται τῆς τ. παρὰ λυχνικοῦ *ib.*41(529C; M.1312B); ὅστις κατὰ ἀμέλειαν οὐ καθίσει μετὰ τῶν ἀδελφῶν εἰς τὴν τ., νηστευέτω λοιπὸν ἕως ὀψέ Thdr.Stud.*poen.*2.35(M.99.1753B); εἴ τις ἔξω τῆς τ. ἐσθίει, τῆς τοῦ ἡγουμένου χωρὶς εὐλογίας ἢ ἀρρωστίας δίχα, ξηροφαγείτω ἡμέρας τρεῖς *ib.*2.27(1752D); ὁ ὑστερούμενος τοῦ ἑξαψάλμου, παρεστηκέτω ἐν τῇ τ. *ib.*1.2(1733C); μοναχός, φαγὼν...πρὸ τῆς ἀπολύσεως τῆς συνάξεως, ποιείτω ἐν τῇ τ. μετανοίας ν' *ib.*2.55(1756C); talking forbidden, *ib.*1.31(1737A); and laughing, *ib.*2.29(1753A); οὐδὲ ἐπ' αὐτῆς τῆς τ. τῆς νοερᾶς ἐργασίας [i.e. mental prayer] ἐπαύοντο Jo.Clim.*scal.*4(M.88.685C); **6.** met., of BMV χαῖρε τ. βαστάζουσα εὐθηνίαν ἱλασμῶν ‡Serg.*acath.*65(p.141; M.92.1340A); ‡Epiph.*hom.*5(M.43.496A); ἦν ἡ ἁγία παρθένος ἡ τ. ἔχουσα τὴν ὕλην τοῦ σώματος ‡Jo.D.*corp.*4(M.95.409B); γέγονεν ἡ κοιλία σου ἁγία τ., ἔχουσα τὸν οὐράνιον ἄρτον Andr.Cr.*can.mesopent.*5(M.97.1425C).

B. what is set on a table, *meal, food*; **1.** in gen. πῶς ἤρκεσεν ἡ τῆς παιδικῆς σαρκὸς φύσις [sc. of Jo. Bapt.]...τ. οὕτως ἐξηλλαγμένῃ Chrys.*hom.10.4 in Mt.*(7.144C); τί...τῆς τοῦ μάννα τ. ἥδιον id.*hom.14.4 in 1Cor.*(10.122B); τραπέζης ἀρχόμενοι καὶ μέλλοντες ἄρτον διακλᾶν, θεῷ προσάγειν ὀφείλομεν Cyr.*Lc.*9:12(M.72.645A); ref. future punishment τροφὴν ἀποίσομεν τῷ πυρὶ καὶ πολλὴν τῷ σκώληκι τ. Chrys.*hom.22.3 in 2Cor.*(10.594D); **2.** ref. greed, extravagance, selfishness τῶν...ἀμφὶ τὰς φλεγμαινούσας κυπταζόντων τ. ... δαίμων καθηγεῖται λιχνότατος Clem.*paed.*2.1(p.165.8; M.8.404A); ὁ γογγυσμὸς τραπέζαις ἥδεται καὶ ἐν νηστείαις βδελύσσεται Ephr.1.12C; περὶ γαστριμαργίας ἦν ὁ λόγος καὶ τῆς τ. Chrys.*hom.30.4 in Mt.*(7.353B); ἡ τ. καὶ ἡ τροφὴ διαχέειν εἴωθε καὶ βαρύνειν *ib.*55.5(561B); **3.** monastic πολλῷ αἰσχρότερον διὰ τοὺς τρυφῶντας τὴν τ. ἡμῶν μετασκευάζεσθαι· μονότροπός ἐστιν ὁ τοῦ Χριστιανοῦ βίος Bas.*reg.fus.*20.2(2.364E; M.31.973A); ἐκεῖνοι...τραπέζης ἀπολαύσαντες, μᾶλλον δὲ νηστείας (καὶ γὰρ ἡ τ. αὐτῶν νηστεία), τοῦ φοβεροῦ δικαστηρίου...ἀναμιμνήσκουσιν Chrys.*hom.55.5 in Mt.*(7.561C); *V.Pach.Φ* 24(p.15.9); Pall.*h.Laus.*22(p.72.3; M.34.1081D); **4.** of pagan feasts, *Asen.*11(p.54.3); θεῷ θέμις οὐκ ἦν αἵματα δέχεσθαι τοιαῦτα, ἀλλὰ ἀλαστόρων δαιμόνων ἡ τοιαύτη τ. Chrys.*hom.3.6 in 2Cor.*(10.451E); id.*hom.24.3 in 1Cor.*(10.215B); Pall.*v.Chrys.*16(p.98.3; M.47.55); **5.** of Jewish sacrifices, *T.Lev.*8.16;

*T.Jud.*21.5; Chrys.*hom.79.4 in Mt.*(7.764A); **6.** (prob.) of Christian *agape* πᾶς προφήτης, ὁρίζων τ. ἐν πνεύματι οὐ φάγεται ἀπ' αὐτῆς· εἰ δὲ μήγε, ψευδοπροφήτης ἐστί *Did.*11.9; τ. κοινὴν παρατίθενται [sc. Christians], ἀλλ' οὐ κοίτην [MS κοινήν] *Diogn.*5.7; **7.** of eucharist; **a.** pre-figured by bread and wine of Melchizedek, Jo.D. *f.o.*4.13(M.94.1149C); **b.** partic. ref. Last Supper Ἰούδας...μετεῖχε τῆς ἱερᾶς τ. Chrys.*prod.Jud.*1.5(2.383E); ὁ τραπέζης κοινωνήσας μυστικῆς, ὁ δείπνου μετασχὼν φρικωδεστάτου id.*scand.*14(3.500E); μυσταγωγοῦσα φίλους ἑαυτῆς τὴν ψυχοτρόφον ἑτοιμάζει τ. ... ἡ ὄντως σοφία θεοῦ Cosm.Mel.*hymn.*6(11.14,p.190; M.98.477A); ξενίας δεσποτικῆς καὶ ἀθανάτου τ. ἐν ὑπερῴῳ τόπῳ ὑψηλαῖς φρεσί, πιστοί, δεῦτε ἀπολαύσωμεν *ib.*(11.159,p.193; 481A); **c.** in gen., ‡Hipp.*fr. 54 in Pr.*(cf.p.176.2f.; M.10.628B); μὴ κοινώνει...τῇ χρυσῇ [prob. for Χριστοῦ] τ. *A.Petr.c.Sim.*1(p.80.9); πνευματικῆς...τ. οὐδεὶς μεταλήψεται, μὴ παρ' αὐτοῦ κεκλημένος καὶ σοφίας ἀκούσας· ἐλθὲ καὶ φάγε †Dion.Al.*fr.Eccl.*2:25(p.224.7; M.10.1585D); δῴη σοι ὁ θεὸς...βαπτισθέντα τῆς αὐτῆς μοι μεταλαβεῖν τ. *Hom.Clem.*1.22; Gr.Naz.*or.*17.12 (M.35.980B); τὸ βάπτισμα καὶ ἡ τ. Chrys.*hom.23.3 in 1Cor.*(10. 204C); βάπτισμα ἐδωρήσατο· ἔδωκέ σοι τ. ἱεράν id.*hom.65.5 in Mt.* (7.660A); cf. μία ὑποδέχεται κολυμβήθρα...μία πᾶσι μυστικὴ προτίθεται τ. ‡Chrys.*ascens.Ac.*11(3.768A); αὕτη...ἡ τ. τῆς ψυχῆς ἡμῶν τὰ νεῦρα..., τὸ φῶς, ἡ ζωή Chrys.*hom.24.5 in 1Cor.*(218D); ὃ...ἦν αὐτῷ τιμιώτερον ἁπάντων, ὁ μονογενὴς παῖς, τοῦτον ἔδωκεν ὑπὲρ ἡμῶν...καὶ οὐκ ἔδωκε μόνον, ἀλλὰ καὶ μετὰ τὸ δοῦναι τράπεζαν ἡμῖν αὐτὸν παρέθηκε id.*hom.25.4 in Mt.*(311D); τὸ κεφάλαιον...τῶν ἑορτῶν αὐτῶν καταλύει, ἐφ' ἑτέραν αὐτοὺς μετατιθεὶς τ. φρικωδεστάτην *ib. 82.1*(782C); καθαρᾷ καρδίᾳ καὶ καθαροῖς χείλεσι μεταλαμβάνοντες τ. μυστικῆς τοιαύτης id.*hom.1.3 in Eph.*(11.6D); μέλλοντες προσιέναι τῇ φρικτῇ καὶ θείᾳ ταύτῃ τ., μετὰ φόβου...τοῦτο ποιεῖτε, μετὰ καθαροῦ συνειδότος, μετὰ νηστείας καὶ προσευχῆς id.*nativ.*1.7(2.364E); οὐ δέχεται ἀπεχθῶς πρὸς ἀλλήλους ἔχοντας αὕτη ἡ τ. id.*hom.16.9 in Mt.* (7.217A); festival not to be made pretext for partaking without due spiritual preparation, id.*bapt.Chr.*4(2.373D); ὥσπερ τοίνυν τῶν ἀμυήτων οὐδένα χρὴ παρεῖναι, οὕτως οὐδὲ τῶν μεμυημένων καὶ ῥυπαρῶν...πῶς ἔμεινας καὶ οὐ μετέχεις τῆς τ.; ἀνάξιός εἰμι, φησίν· οὐκοῦν καὶ τῆς κοινωνίας ἐκείνης τῆς ἐν ταῖς εὐχαῖς id.*hom.3.5 in Eph.* (23E); εὐχαριστηρίους ᾠδὰς οὐκ ἐπιφέροντες τῷ τέλει τῆς τ. id.*bapt. Chr.*4(374E); spiritual effects, id.*hom.19.9 in Mt.*(258D); οὐ γὰρ ἄν... καθάπερ ἄρτου κοινοῦ καὶ οἴνου πρὸς πλησμονὴν τῆς γαστρὸς τῆς φρικώδους ἐκείνης...τ. μετέχομεν...βραχέος δὲ μέρους τινὸς μεταδίδοται ἡμῖν ὑπὸ τῶν τῷ θεῷ λειτουργούντων Nil.*epp.*2.144(M.79.265D); τῇ μυστικῇ τ. σχολάσωμεν, δι' ἧς κόσμος ἐστήρικται καὶ οἰκουμένη συνέστηκεν Tim.Ant.*Sym.*(M.86.252A); θεὸς...καταξιώσας ἡμᾶς μετασχεῖν ταύτης τῆς ἐπουρανίου σου τ. *Lit.Jac.*(p.238.10); **8.** of spiritual food in gen. βαπτίσματος ἀξιωθέντες ἐπεὶ...τῶν ἐντελεστέρων δεῖ μαθημάτων παρατιθέναι τράπεζαν Cyr.H.*catech.*19.1; Chrys.*hom. div.*7.1(12.357B); of explanation of scriptures, id.*proph.obscurit.*1.1 (6.169D); ἄρχοντες καὶ ἀρχόμενοι...μίαν ἔχουσι τ., τὴν διδασκαλίαν τοῦ πνεύματος Thdt.*Is.*65:25(p.257.4; 2.398); ἐγενήθη τ. δικαιοσύνης καὶ ἤμην αὐλιζόμενος μετὰ τῶν ἀγγέλων *V.Zos.*18(p.107.6); of repentance as food of God μεγάλη ἡ μετάνοια...αὕτη ἐστὶν ἡ τοῦ θεοῦ τ., δι' αὐτῆς γὰρ ἐσθίει τῶν ἀνθρώπων τὴν σωτηρίαν Ephr.3.168E; *diet* πολλοὶ ...ἐν τῷ νοσοκομείῳ τοῦ παρόντος αἰῶνος τυγχάνουσιν ἄρρωστοι,...καὶ οὐ πᾶσιν ἡ αὐτὴ συμβάλλεται τ. Nil.*epp.*3.33(M.79.397B).

C. *hospitable board*; hence *hospitality*, Gr.Thaum.*pan.Or.*16(p.36. 22; M.10.1097B); ‡Bas.*const.*6.4(2.552E; M.31.1365A); Chrys.*hom.48. 6 in Mt.*(7.501D); Nonn.*par.Jo.*13:18(M.43.864A).

D. *money-changer's table, bank*; met., of the heart, Clem.*str.*1.18 (p.58.11; M.8.805B); *ib.*6.10(p.472.8; M.9.301B); πίστις μὲν γάρ ἐστι τὸ βαλεῖν τὸ ἀργύριον ἐπὶ τῇ τ. ... θεὸς δὲ παρ' ὑμῶν ἀπαιτεῖ τῆς παρακαταθήκης τοὺς λόγους Cyr.H.*catech.*5.13; Bas.*reg.br.*254(2. 500E; M.31.1252C).

***τραπεζάριον, τό,** *refectory*, *Const.Stud.*20(M.99.1712A).

τραπέζιον, τό, *meal*, Cyr.S.*v.Sab.*48(p.138.16).

τραπεζίτης, ὁ, *money-changer, banker*; met., in saying γίνεσθε δόκιμοι τραπεζῖται (i.e. capable of testing and distinguishing between good and bad in religion and morals); **1.** cited in full without ascription, Cyr.H.*catech.*6.37; *Const.App.*2.36.9; **2.** referred to as scripture (ἡ γραφή), Clem.*str.*1.28(p.109.13; M.8.924B); Or.*comm.in Mt.*17.31(p.674.1; M.13.1573A); **3.** ascribed to Christ τηρούντων τὴν ἐντολὴν Ἰησοῦ λέγουσαν· γίνεσθε δόκιμοι τ. id.*Jo.* 19.7(2; p.307.5; M.14.540A); *Hom.Clem.*2.51; *ib.*3.50; *ib.*18.20; ‡Ath. *v.Syncl.*100(M.28.1549B); Chrys.*hom.4.2 in Ac.princ.*(3.82E); **4.** described by Apelles as a saying 'in the gospel' and applied to task of discerning in scripture sayings of true God and those of demiurge, Epiph.*haer.*44.2(p.192.17; M.41.824C); **5.** ascribed to S. Paul (cf. 1Thess.5:21), Cyr.*Jo.*4.5(4.407A); id.*Is.*1.2(2.56E); id.*Nest.*1(p.13. 28; τρόφιμοι τ. 6¹.2C); described as ἀποστολικὴ φωνή, Dion.Al.ap. Eus.*h.e.*7.7.3(M.20.648C); **6.** clearly alluded to without exact quotation, Clem.*str.*6.10(p.472.9; M.9.301B); *ib.*7.15(p.64.17; 525B); Or.*Jo.* 20.32(26; p.369.33; M.14.648A); *ib.*32.17(10; p.454.31; 788C); id.*comm. in Eph.*4:25(p.419); Ath.*Dion.*9(p.52.19; M.25.493A); id.*ep.Serap.*1. 21(M.26.581A); ‡Ath.*hom. in Lc.19:36*(M.28.1036D); Bas.*hom.*19.6 (2.103B; M.31.400B); †Bas.*Is.*172(1.503C; M.30.405A); Cyr.*ador.*16 (1.568C); id.*Jo.*4.3(4.374C); Leont.H.*monoph.*(M.86.1812A); more doubtfully, Or.*hom.20.9 in Jer.*(p.193.22; M.13.524D).

***τραπεζογίγας, ὁ,** *table-giant, valiant trencherman*, Pall.*v.Chrys.* 12(p.77.29; M.47.44); *Max.invect.*(M.90.204B).

τραπεζοποιός, ὁ, *one who prepares the table, waiter*; met., of Salome τ. γιγνομένην ἑστιάσεως διαβολικῆς Chrys.*hom.28.3 in 2Cor.* (10.638C); of Moses ὁ τοῦ μάννα τ. ‡Chrys.*concept.Jo.Bapt.*(2. 793A).

***τραπεζοφορ-έω,** *bear like a table* ὦ παρθένε...~οῦσα τὸν οὐράνιον ἄρτον Χριστόν ‡Epiph.*hom.*5(M.43.497A).

τραπέζωσις, ἡ, *furnishing of a table* ὁρῶμεν...Ἰησοῦν...τὰ θεουργὰ μυστήρια παραδιδόντα διὰ τυπικῆς τ. Dion.Ar.*ep.*9.1(M.3.1108A); τ. φησι τὰ ἐν τῇ θείᾳ τραπέζῃ διὰ τοῦ ἁγίου ἄρτου καὶ τοῦ ποτηρίου τῆς εὐλογίας τελούμενα μυστήρια Max.*schol.epp.Dion.Ar.*9.1(M.4.565A).

τραυλίζω, *lisp, mispronounce a letter*; hence *twitter*, *Orac.Sib.fr.* 3.9.

τραῦμα, τό, *wound*; **1.** lit., of wounds of Christ ἦν οὖν ὁ Ἰησοῦς μετὰ θάνατον, ὡς μὲν ὁ Κέλσος οἴεται, φαντασίαν ἐξαποστέλλων τῶν ἐπὶ τῷ σταυρῷ τ. καὶ οὐκ ἀληθῶς τοιοῦτος ὢν τραυματίας Or.*Cels.*2.61 (p.183.18; M.11.892B); exeg. Jo.20:24f. ὑπὲρ μιᾶς ψυχῆς [sc. S. Thomas] δείκνυσιν ἑαυτὸν τραύματα ἔχοντα Chrys.*hom.87.1 in Jo.* (8.519C); ref. Second Advent ἐρχόμενος ἥξει μετὰ τῶν τ. αὐτοῦ καὶ ἀποδώσει ἑκάστῳ κατὰ τὰ ἔργα αὐτοῦ Hipp.*Dan.*4.10.4 [perh. for στρατευμάτων]; cf. *corpus quidem suscitavit, vulnera autem ejus servavit, ut in die judicii proficerent ad testimonium passionis contra Judaeos, et omnes, qui denegantes filium dei crucifixum in corpore, judaïzant*, ‡Chrys.*opus imperfectum in Matthaeum* (6.953B); exeg. Mt.24:30 τότε φανήσεται τὸ σημεῖον τοῦ υἱοῦ τοῦ ἀνθρώπου...καὶ τί θαυμάζεις, εἰ τὸν σταυρὸν φέρων ἔρχεται; αὐτὰ τὰ τ. μεθ' ἑαυτοῦ φέρων ἔρχεται. πόθεν δῆλον, ὅτι αὐτὰ τὰ τ. φέρει μεθ' ἑαυτοῦ; ἄκουε τοῦ προφήτου λέγοντος· ὄψονται εἰς ὃν ἐξεκέντησαν Chrys.*cruc.*2.4(2.418E); ὁ αὐτὸς τὰ τ. τῆς πλευρᾶς καὶ τὰς διατρήσεις τῶν ἥλων...ἐπεδείκνυ Leo Mag.*ep.*28.5(p.17.8; M.*PL.*54.774B); as imprinted in soul φήσομεν ἐν τῇ ψυχῇ γινόμενον μετὰ τὸν λόγον τῶν τ. τύπον, τοῦτον εἶναι τὸν ἐν ἑκάστῳ Χριστὸν ἀπὸ Χριστοῦ λόγου Or.*Cels.*6.9(p.79.22; M.11.1304B); **2.** met.; **a.** of harm caused by false teaching τραυμάτων, τῶν ἀπὸ λόγων νομιζομένων φιλοσόφων *ib.*3.75(p.267.1; 1017C); 'ἔπαθεν ὁ λόγος' ἔγνωσαν ἀπαράδεκτον ἀκοαῖς εὐσεβέσι, φάρμακον προσθεῖναι τὸ τῇ σαρκὶ τοῖς ῥημάτων τραύμασι ἐδικαίωσαν Euther.*confut.*10(M.28. 1365D); **b.** of wounds of soul; caused by sin, Clem.*paed.*2.2(p.168.23; M.8.412B); id.*q.d.s.*29(p.179.6; M.9.633D); Or.*princ.*3.1.17(p.226.9; M.11.284A); id.*Cels.*4.15(p.285.13; M.11.1048A); Chrys.*hom.63.4 in Mt.*(7.633A); Jo.Clim.*past.*10(M.88.1185B); exeg. parable of Good Samaritan, Or.*hom.34 in Lc.*(p.202.1); **c.** of healing wounds inflicted by God's love through prohibition of the forbidden fruit καλὰ...τῆς ἀγάπης τὰ τ. ... τίς δὲ φίλος, οὗ τὰ τ. τῶν φιλημάτων τοῦ ἐχθροῦ προτιμότερα [ref. Pr.27:6]; παντὶ δῆλόν ἐστι, τῷ μὴ ἀγνοοῦντι τὰ τῆς σωτηρίας μυστήρια...τραῦμα τοῖς πρωτοπλάστοις ἐδόκει ἡ διὰ τῆς ἐντολῆς γενομένη τοῦ κακοῦ ἀπαγόρευσις, τ. γὰρ ἐνομίσθη ἡ τοῦ ἡδέος ἀλλοτρίωσις Gr.Nyss.*hom.12 in Cant.*(M.44.1044B,C); **d.** ref. Church, wounded by love for Christ ὁ πρὸς τὴν ἐκκλησίαν βλέπων, πρὸς τὸν Χριστὸν ἄντικρυς βλέπει, τὸν ἑαυτὸν διὰ τῆς προσθήκης τῶν σωζομένων οἰκοδομοῦντα...ἡ τοίνυν ἀποθεμένη τῶν ὀμμάτων τὸ θέριστρον, καθαρῷ τῷ ὀφθαλμῷ τὸ ἄφραστον ὁρᾷ τοῦ νυμφίου κάλλος· καὶ διὰ τοῦτο τρωθεῖσα τῷ ἀσωμάτῳ...βέλει τοῦ ἔρωτος· ἐπιτεταμένη γὰρ ἀγάπη ἔρως λέγεται· ᾧ οὐδεὶς ἐπαισχύνεται, ὅταν μὴ κατὰ σαρκὸς γένηται παρ' αὐτοῦ ἡ τοξεία· ἀλλ' ἐπικαυχᾶται μᾶλλον τῷ τ. *ib. 13*(M.44.1048C); also of the soul wounded by this love, *ib.*4(852B); whose wound is caused by being stripped of whatever may prevent mystical union εἰ τοίνυν ἀγαθὸν ἡ τοῦ καλύμματος περιαίρεσις, ἀγαθὸν ἂν εἴη πάντως ἡ πληγή, καὶ τὸ τ., δι' ὧν κατορθοῦται ἡ περιαίρεσις...εἰ δὲ καὶ ἐν τραύματι γεγενῆσθαι λέγει, τὴν ἐν βάθει γενομένην αὐτῇ διὰ τῆς θείας ῥάβδου τύπον τῷ λόγῳ παρίστησιν,... ἐπίσημος διὰ τοῦ τ. δείκνυται ἡ πληγή, ᾗ ἐγκαυχᾶται ἡ νύμφη...οὕτω γὰρ καὶ Παῦλος ὁ τῶν τοιούτων πληγῶν στιγματίας τοῖς τ. τούτοις ἐπαγαλλόμενος ἔλεγεν· ὅτι τὰ στίγματα τοῦ Χριστοῦ ἐν τῷ σώματί μου περιφέρω,...καλὸν οὖν καὶ τὸ τ. ... δι' οὗ γέγονεν αὐτῇ [sc. νύμφῃ] τοῦ θερίστρου ἡ περιαίρεσις *ib.12*(1029D–33D).

***τραυματία, ἡ,** *injury,* Thphn.*chron*.p.294(M.108.720B).

***τραυματι-άω,** *to be wounded* μὴ θαμβηθῇς ὁρῶν αὐτὸν συγχωροῦντα τῇ ἰδίᾳ σαρκὶ ἀγωνιᾶν τὸν θάνατον· τῆς γὰρ ἀγωνίας πτωχίστερόν ἐστι τὸ μετὰ τὴν ἀνάστασιν αὐτοῦ ∼ᾶν τὰς χεῖρας καὶ τὴν πλευράν Procl.CP ap.Anast.S.*monoph*.(M.89.1188D–1189A).

τραυματικός, *wounded,* Call.*v.Hyp*.112(p.75.8); in soul, Nil.*epp*.3.33(M.79.397B).

τραυμάτιον, τό, (dim. of τραῦμα) *slight wound,* Isid.Pel.*epp*.1.391 (M.78.404A).

τραυματισμός, ὁ, *wounding,* met., of sin ὁ μόσχος ἀμώμητος...εἰς τύπον Χριστοῦ...τὸν ἐκ τῆς ἁμαρτίας τ. οὐκ ἀνασχομένου παθεῖν Cyr.*ador*.10(1.350A).

***τραυματιστής, ὁ,** *one who inflicts wounds,* of S. Barnabas ὁ...τοῦ διαβόλου τ. Alex.Sal.*Barn*.7(p.438E).

***τραυματ-όω,** *hurt, chafe,* Epiph.*haer*.66.22(p.50.13; M.42.68B); *wound,* in spiritual sense ∼οῦσι...καλὰ τραύματα οἱ...προφῆται τὴν νύμφην καὶ οἱ ἀπόστολοι Ph.Carp.*Cant*.139(M.40.105B).

***τραχεινός,** *rough,* Thphn.*chron*.p.266(M.108.661A).

***τραχηλιαστής, ὁ,** as adj., *haughty, insolent,* of Nestorius ὡς δοῦλος τ. ... ἀρνούμενος τὸν ἑαυτοῦ κύριον καὶ ἀτιμάζων τὴν δέσποιναν ἑαυτοῦ Thdr.Raith.*praep*.(p.189.17; M.91.1489A).

τραχηλιάω, *arch the neck proudly* like a horse or bull, Gr.Naz.*carm*.1.1.6.90(M.37.437A); met., *exalt oneself, Apoc.Bar.rel*.6.21; of fallen angels αἱ ἀποστατικαὶ δυνάμεις, αἱ διὰ τὸ τραχηλιάσαι κατὰ θεοῦ...ἀφηνιάζουσαι τῆς δουλείας Bas.*Spir*.51(3.43C; M.32.161C); of Satan, Cyr.*Jo*.6(4.561A); Eus.Al.*serm*.21.4(M.86.428B); Gr.Agr.*Eccl*.3.19(M.98.880B); τὸν σατανᾶν τ. κατὰ τοῦ θεοῦ *cat.Apoc*.12:7ff.(p.359.22); of heretics, Cyr.*ep*.63(p.15.22; M.77.328C).

τραχηλίζ-ω, 1. *seize by the neck, throw*; met., Eus.*p.e*.5.29 (224D; M.21.385B); id.*d.e*.3.3(p.110.1; M.22.189A); pass., *be overpowered* ὑπὸ τῆς...ἀνάγκης ∼όμενοι Nil.*exerc*.8(M.79.728C); **2.** pass., *be thrown* or *laid open*; ref. Last Judgement ὅταν γένηται πάντα γυμνὰ καὶ τετραχηλισμένα †Bas.*Is*.63(1.425B; M.30.228C); Chrys.*hom*.7.1 *in Heb*.(12.72B); τετραχηλισμένα...ἐκ μεταφορᾶς τέθεικε τῶν θυομένων ζῴων, ἃ...ἄφωνα κεῖται...οὕτω...καὶ ἡμεῖς κρινόμενοι...σιγῶντες...τὴν τῆς τιμωρίας δεχόμεθα ψῆφον Thdt.*Heb*.4:13(3.569); τὴν...ἡμέραν τῆς κρίσεως ἐν ᾗ γυμνοὶ καὶ τετραχηλισμένοι παραστησόμεθα τῷ κριτῇ Ant.Mon.*hom*.48(M.89.1584A); Anast.S.*synax*.(M.89.845B); id.*Ps*.6(M.89.1080B); Jo.D.*imag*.1.3(M.94.1233C).

***τραχηλι-όω,** *exalt oneself, be haughty* θεομάχοι Ἑβραίων παῖδες, οἱ ἀεὶ...∼οῦντες κατὰ τοῦ κυρίου καὶ κατὰ τοῦ Χριστοῦ αὐτοῦ φρυαττόμενοι ‡Jo.D.*ep.Thphl*.9(M.95.356C).

***τραχηλιώτης, ὁ,** as adj., *bull-necked,* Hipp.*haer*.4.19(p.51.12; M.16.3086B).

τράχηλος, ὁ, *neck* πάντα...ἐν τάξει ἐποίησεν ὁ θεὸς καλά...τὸν τ. συνάξας τῇ κεφαλῇ *T.Neph*.2.8; fig., exeg. Cant.4:4 τὸν τοῦ ἐκκλησιαστικοῦ σώματος τ. ... εἴ τις τὴν ἀληθινὴν...κεφαλὴν βαστάζοι,... ἥτις ἐστὶν ὁ Χριστὸς...εἰ τοῦ πνεύματός ἐστι δεκτικὸς...καὶ εἰ διὰ τῆς εὐήχου φωνῆς ὑπηρετεῖ τῷ λόγῳ...ἐχέτω δὲ οὗτος ὁ τ. καὶ τὴν θρεπτικὴν ἐνέργειαν τὴν διδασκαλίαν...τοιοῦτος τ. ὁ Παῦλος ἦν Gr.Nyss.*hom*.7 *in Cant*.(M.44.933A); ὁρμίσκον τὸν τ. αὐτῆς ὀνομάζει, τῷ μετρίῳ κεκαμμένην φρονήματι Nil.ap.Proc.G.*Cant*.4:4(M.87.1649A); met., of bending the neck in submission θεμιτὸν...ἐστὶν...ὑποθεῖναι τὸν τ. καὶ τὸν τῆς ὑπακοῆς τύπον ἀναπληρῶσαι *1Clem*.63.1; of pride, ref. Adam βλέπεις ὑπερηφάνειαν; βλέπεις τ.; Dor.*doct*.1.7(M.88.1625B).

τραχύς, *rough* ἡ στρεβλὴ ὁδὸς...τ. ἐστι καὶ ἀκανθώδης Herm.*mand*.6.1.3; ἡ...τῶν σωζομένων [sc. ὁδὸς] στενὴ μὲν καὶ τ., σώζουσα δὲ πρὸς τῷ τέλει τοὺς διαπορευθέντας ἐπιπόνως *Hom.Clem*.7.7.

***τραχυτόπος, ὁ,** *rough skin, eczema,* Ephr.3.211B.

τραχώδης, *rough,* Mac.Aeg.*hom*.26.4(M.34.676D).

τρεῖς, *three*;

A. in gen., of mysteries of Inc. ἡ παρθενία Μαρίας καὶ ὁ τοκετὸς αὐτῆς, ὁμοίως καὶ ὁ θάνατος τοῦ κυρίου· τ. μυστήρια κραυγῆς, ἅτινα ἐν ἡσυχίᾳ θεοῦ ἐπράχθη Ign.*Eph*.19.1; of concepts of deity τ. αἱ ἀνωτάτω δόξαι περὶ θεοῦ, ἀναρχία καὶ πολυαρχία καὶ μοναρχία Gr.Naz.*or*.29.2(p.74.12; M.36.76A); of angelic hierarchy πάσας ἡ θεολογία τὰς οὐρανίας οὐσίας ἐννέα κέκληκεν...ταύτας...εἰς τ. ἀφορίζει τριαδικὰς διακοσμήσεις Dion.Ar.*c.h*.6.2(M.3.200D); εἰς τρία διῄρηνται...πάντες θεῖοι νόες, εἰς οὐσίαν καὶ δύναμιν καὶ ἐνέργειαν *ib*.11.2(284D); of three orders of eccl. ministry, id.*e.h*.5.1.2(M.3.501D); αἱ τ. τῶν ἱεροτελεστῶν διακοσμήσεις διὰ τῶν τ. ... τελετῶν...ἐφεστᾶσι ταῖς τρισὶ τῶν τελουμένων τάξεσι *ib*.5.3.8(516A); of three immersions at baptism signifying three days of Christ's entombment, *ib*.2.3.7 (404B); and symbolizing Trinity, *ib*.2.2.7(396D); of threefold pouring of oil into baptismal water, *ib*.(396C); of three kinds of law (of nature, of Moses, and of grace), Thdt.*Ps*.18:1(1.716); Max.*qu.Thal*.64(M.90.728A); of three dominical precepts τ. ... δόγματα...τοῦ κυρίου· ζωῆς ἐλπὶς...δικαιοσύνη...καὶ...ἀγάπη *Barn*.1.6; of the three types of life ἡ φυτική, ἡ αἰσθητική, ἡ νοερά Max.*Pyrr*.(M.91.301A); esp. ref. threefold classifications used by writers on morals and ascetical theology ἐν τοῖς τ. τούτοις ὁ Χριστιανὸς φιλοσοφεῖ· ἐν ταῖς ἐντολαῖς, ἐν τοῖς δόγμασι καὶ ἐν τῇ πίστει id.*carit*.4.47(M.90.1057C); τ. εἰσιν ἠθικαὶ καταστάσεις γενικώτεραι ἐν τοῖς μοναχοῖς...τὸ μηδὲν ἁμαρτάνειν κατ' ἐνέργειαν...τὸ μὴ ἐγχρονίζειν ἐν τῇ ψυχῇ τοὺς ἐμπαθεῖς λογισμοὺς...τὸ τὰς μορφὰς...ἀπαθῶς θεωρεῖν κατὰ διάνοιαν *ib*.2.87 (1013A); τ. εἰσὶ τὰ κινοῦντα ἡμᾶς ἐπὶ τὰ καλά· τὰ φυσικὰ σπέρματα, αἱ ἅγιαι δυνάμεις καὶ ἡ ἀγαθὴ προαίρεσις *ib*.2.32(993D); τ. ... τὰ κινοῦντα ...ἐπὶ τὰ κακά· τὰ πάθη, οἱ δαίμονες καὶ ἡ κακὴ προαίρεσις *ib*.2.33 (996A); τὰ τ. ταῦτα τὴν κρᾶσιν κατὰ τὸ χεῖρον...ἀλλοιοῦσιν· ἡ τῆς διαίτης ἀταξία, ἡ τῶν ἀέρων μεταβολὴ καὶ ἡ τῶν δαιμόνων ἐπαφή Thal.*cent*.3.36(M.91.1452B); τ. ὑπάρχουσι πράγματα, δι' ὧν λαμβάνεις λογισμούς· ἡ αἴσθησις καὶ ἡ μνήμη καὶ ἡ κρᾶσις τοῦ σώματος *ib*.1.46 (1432C); οἱ τ. γενικώτατοι τῆς ἐπιθυμίας λογισμοὶ ἐκ τοῦ πάθους τῆς φιλαυτίας τὴν γέννησιν ἔχουσιν *ib*.3.87(1456D); ἀκολουθοῦσι...τοῖς τ. οἵ τε τῆς λύπης καὶ τῆς ὀργῆς καὶ τῆς μνησικακίας *ib*.3.90(1456D); τριχῶς τέμνεται ὁ χρόνος καὶ ἡ...πίστις τρισὶ συμπαρατείνεται τμήμασι Max.*carit*.3.100(1048A); of three general virtues of fasting, prayer, and silence, ‡Max.*cap.al*.124(M.90.1429A).

B. three as a 'male' number and its symbolism, Clem.*str*.6.16 (p.502.27; M.9.365A).

C. οἱ τ.; **1.** of Synoptists τῷ παρὰ τοῖς τ. εἰρημένῳ Or.*mart*.29 (p.25.25; M.11.600A); **2.** of Aquila, Symmachus, and Theodotion, opp. LXX καὶ τοῦτο...οἱ τ. ἡρμήνευσαν Thdt.*Ps*.18:6(1.720); id.*Is*.53:9(p.212.29; 2.360); οἱ τ. ἑρμηνευταί *ib*.61:10(p.242.32); **3.** of the three disciples of Manes, Hegem.*Arch*.13(p.22.3; M.10.1449A).

D. Trin.; **1.** ref. pre-Nicene anti-monarchian teaching οὔτ' οὖν καταμερίζειν χρὴ εἰς τ. θεότητας τὴν...θείαν μονάδα Dion.R.ap.Ath.*decr*.26(p.23.11; M.25.465A); τ. θεοὺς...κηρύττουσιν, εἰς τ. ὑποστάσεις ξένας ἀλλήλων παντάπασι κεχωρισμένας διαιροῦντες τὴν ἁγίαν μονάδα Dion.R.*ib*.(p.22.7; 464A); διαιροῦντες καὶ κατατέμνοντες...τὴν μοναρχίαν εἰς τ. δυνάμεις καὶ μεμερισμένας ὑποστάσεις καὶ θεότητας τ. *ib*.(p.22.3; 461D); Μαρκίωνος...δίδαγμα εἰς τ. ἀρχὰς τῆς μοναρχίας τομὴ καὶ διαίρεσις Dion.R.*ib*.(p.22.12; 464A); οὐδὲ...τ. ἀρχὰς ἢ τ. πατέρας εἰσάγομεν, ὡς οἱ περὶ Μαρκίωνα καὶ Μανιχαῖον Ath.*Ar*.3.15(M.26.352C); **2.** ref. Sabellian (and Marcellan) teaching οὐκ ἔτι οὖν πλατύνεσθαι ἔδει λέγειν, ἀλλ' ἡ μονὰς τριῶν ποιητική, ὥστε εἶναι μονάδα, εἶτα καὶ πατέρα καὶ υἱὸν καὶ πνεῦμα ‡Ath.*Ar*.4.13(p.57.15; M.26.485A); **3.** in Arian attack on orthodox doctrine εἰ θεὸς...καὶ θεὸς καὶ θεός, πῶς οὐχὶ τ. θεοί; Gr.Naz.*or*.31.13(p.161.9; M.36.148B); cf. τ. θεοὺς πρεσβεύεσθαι παρ' ἡμῶν αἰτιῶνται Gr.Nyss.*Trin*.2(p.72.20; M.32.685C); partic. ref. *homoousion* ὁ λέγων ὁμοούσιον τρία λέγει, οὐσίαν τινὰ προϋποκειμένην καὶ τοὺς ἐκ ταύτης γεννωμένους ὁμοουσίους εἶναι Ath.*syn*.51(p.275.1; M.26.784B); cf. objection alleged to have been brought by Paul of Samosata against use of *homoousios* εἰ μὴ ἐξ ἀνθρώπων γέγονεν ὁ Χριστὸς θεός, οὐκοῦν ὁμοούσιός ἐστι τῷ πατρὶ καὶ ἀνάγκη τ. οὐσίας εἶναι, μίαν μὲν προηγουμένην, τὰς δὲ δύο ἐξ ἐκείνης *ib*.45(p.270.2; 772C); **4.** in Arian doctrine τ. εἰσιν ὑποστάσεις καὶ ὁ μὲν θεὸς...ἔστιν ἄναρχος μονώτατος, ὁ δὲ υἱὸς...οὐκ ἦν πρὸ τοῦ γεννηθῆναι Ar.*ep.Alex*.ap.Ath.*syn*.16(p.244.8; M.26.709B); **5.** in teaching of 'Eusebian' party τῶν ὀνομάτων [sc. of Father, Son, H. Ghost] οὐχ ἁπλῶς...κειμένων, ἀλλὰ σημαινόντων...τὴν...ἑκάστου...ὑπόστασιν ...ὡς εἶναι τῇ μὲν ὑποστάσει τρία, τῇ δὲ συμφωνίᾳ ἕν *Symb.Ant*.(341)2 ap.Ath.*syn*.23(p.249.33; M.26.724B); τοὺς λέγοντας τ. εἶναι θεοὺς... ἀναθεματίζει ἡ...ἐκκλησία *Symb.Ant*.(345)*ib*.26(p.252.6; 728C); οὔτε ...τ. ὁμολογοῦντες πράγματα καὶ τ. πρόσωπα τοῦ πατρὸς καὶ τοῦ υἱοῦ καὶ τοῦ ἁγίου πνεύματος...τ. θεοὺς ποιοῦμεν *ib*.(p.252.22; 729B); εἴ τις τὸν πατέρα καὶ τὸν υἱὸν καὶ τὸ ἅγιον πνεῦμα τ. λέγοι θεούς, ἀ. ἔ. *Symb.Sirm*.1 *anath*.23; **6.** in orthodox statements, †Ath.*exp.fid*.2 (M.25.204A) cit. s. σωματοφυῶς; οὐκέτι χρὴ ζητεῖν τ. οὐσίας id.*syn*.51 (p.275.10; M.26.784D); ἐμέμφοντό τινες ὡς τ. λέγοντας ὑποστάσεις διὰ τὸ ἀγράφους...εἶναι τὰς λέξεις...ἀνεκρίναμεν...μή...ὡς ἄλλοι αἱρετικοὶ τ. ἀρχὰς καὶ τ. θεοὺς λέγουσιν, οὕτω καὶ οὗτοι φρονοῦντες τ. ὑποστάσεις λέγωσι; id.*tom*.5(M.26.801A); μήτε...εἰρηκέναι τ. θεοὺς ἢ τ. ἀρχὰς... ἀλλ' εἰδέναι ἁγίαν...τριάδα, μίαν θεότητα καὶ μίαν ἀρχήν *ib*.(801B); ἀποδέχομαι τὴν...ἑρμηνείαν περὶ τῶν τ. ὑποστάσεων καὶ τῆς μιᾶς ὑποστάσεως ἤτοι οὐσίας Paulin.T.*symb*.(p.435.1; M.42.672B); of one God or one οὐσία of Godhead in three hypostases αἰωνίῳ θεῷ, πατρὶ καὶ υἱῷ καὶ ἁγίῳ πνεύματι, ἐν τ. μὲν ὀνόμασι καὶ ὑποστάσεσιν, ἐν μιᾷ δὲ οὐσίᾳ *M.Das*.8; μία ἡ θεότης καὶ εἷς θεὸς ἐν τ. ὑποστάσεσι Ath.*inc.et c.Ar*.10(M.26.1000B); μηδεὶς οἰέσθω με...τ. εἶναι λέγειν ἀρχικὰς ὑποστάσεις...ἀρχὴ γὰρ τῶν ὄντων μία, δι' υἱοῦ δημιουργοῦσα καὶ τελειοῦσα ἐν πνεύματι Bas.*Spir*.38(3.31E; M.32.136B); τρία τοίνυν νοεῖς, τὸν προστάσσοντα κύριον, τὸν δημιουργοῦντα λόγον, τὸ στερεοῦν τὸ πνεῦμα *ib.*(32B; M.136C); οὐ...κατὰ σύνθεσιν ἀριθμοῦμεν...ἓν καὶ δύο καὶ τ. λέγοντες, οὐδὲ πρῶτον καὶ δεύτερον καὶ τρίτον...θεὸν γὰρ ἐκ θεοῦ προσκυνοῦντες, καὶ τὸ ἰδιάζον τῶν ὑποστάσεων ὁμολογοῦμεν καὶ μένομεν ἐπὶ τῆς μοναρχίας *ib.*45(38A; M.149B); id.*ep.*210.4(3.315E; M. 32.773B); τῆς μιᾶς ἐν τοῖς τ. θεότητος Gr.Naz.*or.*28.31(p.71.17; M.36. 72C); πρὸς ἓν τὸ ἐξ αὐτοῦ ἀναφορὰν ἔχει, κἂν τρία πιστεύηται *ib.*31. 14(p.162.14; 149A); τ. ἰδιότητας, θεότητα μίαν *ib.*31.28(p.181.5; 164C); εἰ...καὶ ἰδία μὲν ὑπόστασις πατρός, ἰδία δὲ υἱοῦ καὶ ἰδία πνεύματος ἁγίου, ἀλλ' οὐχὶ καὶ τ. θεοί, ὅτι μία καὶ ἡ αὐτὴ ἐν τοῖς τ. νοουμένη οὐσιώδης θεότης ‡Bas.*struct.hom.*1.3(1.325E; M.30.13C); cf.Gr.Nyss. *Trin.*2(p.72.25; M.32.685C); εἴ τις οὐχ ὁμολογεῖ...μίαν θεότητα ἐν τ. ὑποστάσεσιν ἤγουν προσώποις προσκυνουμένην...ἀνάθεμα ἔστω CCP (553)*anath.*1(Hahn p.168); πιστεύομεν...τριάδα μὲν ταῖς τ. ὑποστάσεσι, μονάδα δὲ τῷ μοναδικῷ τῆς θεότητος Sophr.H.*ep.syn.*(M.87.3152D); διὰ τῶν τ. ὑποστάσεων, πατρότης, υἱότης, ἐκπόρευσις· καὶ κοινὰ τῶν αὐτῶν πάλιν ἐστὶν ἡ οὐσία, ἡ φύσις, ἡ θεότης Thal.*cent.*2.99(M.91. 1448A); ὥσπερ...μίαν θεότητα τῆς...τριάδος λέγουσιν, οὕτως καὶ τ. τὰς ὑποστάσεις τῆς μιᾶς θεότητος δοξάζουσιν *ib.*4.85(1468A); ἀσυγχύτους τὰς ὑποστάσεις τῆς μιᾶς θεότητος διατηροῦσι *ib.*4.95(1469A); καὶ ἅγια τρία καὶ ἓν ἅγιον ὑμνεῖται θεός, ἡ τριάς Andr.Cr.*can.mag.*237(p.154; M. 97.1373A); τ. ἅγια δοξάζω, τ. ἅγια ὑμνῶ, τ. συναΐδια ἐν οὐσιότητι μιᾷ κηρύττω· εἷς γὰρ ἐν πατρὶ καὶ υἱῷ καὶ πνεύματι δοξολογεῖται θεός id. *triod.*(M.97.1400C); τριὰς...ἡ τ. οὖσα καὶ ἓν *ib.*(1405C); οὐ τοῦ πατρὸς ἐκστάντος εἰς υἱότητα, οὐδὲ υἱοῦ τραπέντος εἰς ἐκπόρευσιν, ἀλλ' ἰδίᾳ καὶ ἄμφω φῶς· θεὸν τὰ τρία δοξάζω *ib.*(1408B); ἓν τὰ τρία τῇ φύσει καὶ τρία τοῖς προσώποις *ib.*(1413D); ἕνα θεὸν κατ' οὐσίαν σέβομαι, τ. ὑποστάσεις ὑμνῶ διοριστικῶς...θεότης μία, ἐν τρισὶ τὸ κράτος *ib.*(1417B); τρισὶν ἑνιζομένη ἐν ὑποστάσεσι φύσις Jo.D.*carm.pasch.*109 (p.221; M.96.844A); **7.** symbolized ἐὰν μὴ τὰς τ. πηγὰς τῶν ὑδάτων διψήσωμεν, οὐδὲ μίαν πηγὴν εὑρήσομεν Or.*hom.18.9 in Jer.*(p.163. 8; M.13.481B); ref. Is.6:3 τὸ...τρίτον τὰ...ζῷα...προσφέρειν τὴν δοξολογίαν...τὰς τ. ὑποστάσεις τελείας δεικνύντα ἐστίν, ὡς καὶ ἐν τῷ λέγειν τὸ 'κύριος' τὴν μίαν οὐσίαν δηλοῦσιν Ath.*hom. in Mt.11*:27 (M.25.220A); μηδὲ τριῶν ἡλίων ὑπεθέμεθα τὴν εἰκόνα, ἀλλὰ ἥλιον καὶ ἀπαύγασμα καὶ τὸ ἓν τὸ ἐξ ἡλίου ἐν τῷ ἀπαυγάσματι φῶς id.*Ar.*3.15 (M.26.352C); ἀμέριστος ἐν μεμερισμένοις...ἡ θεότης καὶ οἷον ἐν ἡλίοις τρισίν, ἐχομένοις ἀλλήλων, μία τοῦ φωτὸς σύγκρασις Gr.Naz.*or.*31.14 (p.163.3; M.36.149A); ref. Pentecost τρίτη μὲν εὐμοίρησεν ὡρῶν τὴν χάριν, ὅπως ὑπεμφήνειε τ. ὑποστάσεις Jo.D.*carm.pent.*97(p.216; M.96. 837A).

E. Christol.; in polemics between orthodox and monothelites, ref. problem whether ἐνέργεια is proper to nature or person; **1.** monothelite accusation that orthodox teach three ἐνέργειαι in Christ εἰ διὰ τὸ διάφορον τῶν δύο ἐν Χριστῷ φύσεων δύο λέγετε ἐνεργείας, καὶ οὐ διὰ τὸ μοναδικὸν τοῦ προσώπου μίαν, δύο εὑρεθήσονται καὶ τοῦ ἀνθρώπου ἐνέργειαι διὰ τὸ...διάφορον...ψυχῆς...καὶ...σώματος. εἰ δὲ τοῦτο, τ. ἔσονται τοῦ Χριστοῦ ἐνέργειαι καὶ οὐ δύο Max.*Pyrr.*(M. 91.336A); **2.** orthodox reply εἰ διὰ τὸ διάφορον τῶν ἐν Χριστῷ φύσεων δύο φύσεις...λέγετε, καὶ οὐ διὰ τὸ μοναδικὸν τοῦ προσώπου μίαν, δύο εὑρεθήσονται...τοῦ ἀνθρώπου φύσεις...καὶ εἰ τοῦτο, τ. ἔσονται τοῦ Χριστοῦ φύσεις. εἰ δὲ διὰ τὸ διάφορον τῶν φύσεων...τ. οὐ λέγετε ἐπὶ Χριστοῦ φύσεις, πῶς ἡμῖν...αἱ τ. συναχθήσονται ἐνέργειαι; *ib.*(336B); εἰ ...οὐ ταὐτὸν τὸ κατ' εἶδος τοῦ ἀνθρώπου ἓν καὶ τὸ κατ' οὐσίαν ψυχῆς καὶ σώματος ἕν, οὐκ ἄρα ἀνάγκη ἡμῖν τὴν κατ' εἶδος μίαν λέγοντας ἐνέργειαν...λέγειν...τ. ἐνεργείας διὰ τὸ πρὸς φύσιν ὁρᾶν τὴν ἐνέργειαν *ib.* (336C); εἰ...ταῖς ἐνεργείαις πρόσωπα...συνεισάγεται καὶ τοῖς προσώποις ἀκολούθως αἱ ἐνέργειαι συναχθήσονται. καὶ βιασθήσεσθε...ἢ διὰ τὴν μίαν ἐνέργειαν τῆς...θεότητος καὶ ἓν λέγειν αὐτῆς πρόσωπον ἢ διὰ τὰς τ. ... ὑποστάσεις, τ. καὶ ἐνεργείας *ib.*(337A); εὑρεθήσεται...τῆς ὑπερουσίου...θεότητος...διὰ...τὰ τ. πρόσωπα, τ. καὶ τὰ θελήματα καὶ διὰ τοῦτο τ. φύσεις *ib.*(289D).

F. as indefinite number indicating a few only, '*three or four*'; of pagans who refuse to embrace Christianity, Thdt.*Ps.*65:7(1.1047).

τρεπτικός, *changeable*, of created nature ἐπὶ τῆς τ. φύσεως...τό τε ἀγαθὸν...καὶ τὸ κακὸν ταῖς διαδοχαῖς ἀλλήλων ἐναπολήγει Gr.Nyss. *hom.5 in Cant.*(M.44.873D).

τρεπτικῶς, *by twisting and tricky methods*, †Gregent.*disp.*2(M.86. 668D).

τρεπτός, *liable to change, mutable*;

A. metaphysical; **1.** characteristic of matter τ. καὶ γενητὴν οἶδεν τὴν τῶν στοιχείων φύσιν Clem.*str.*1.11(p.34.11; M.8.749C); τὴν φύσει τ. καὶ ἀλλοιωτὴν καὶ εἰς πάντα ἃ βούλεται ὁ δημιουργὸς ὕλην μεταβλητήν Or.*Cels.*6.77(p.146.19; M.11.1413D); παθητὴν [sc. ὕλην]...καὶ τ. Dion.Al.ap.Eus.*p.e.*7.19(333D; M.21.564A); *ib.*(334B; M.564B); of sub-rational relationships between persons τριττὰ δὲ εἴδη φιλίας... τὸ...τρίτον...τὸ καθ' ἡδονὴν τ. καὶ μεταβλητόν Clem.*str.*2.19(p.168.23; M.8.1045B); and of the corporeal τ. εἶναι τὴν σωματικὴν φύσιν Meth.*res.*1.20(p.243.2; M.41.1088C); therefore of God acc. Stoics εἰ δὲ πᾶν σῶμα ὑλικὸν ἔχει φύσιν...τ. ... καὶ ἀλλοιωτὴν καὶ δι' ὅλων μεταβλητήν...ἀνάγκη καὶ τὸν θεὸν ὑλικὸν ὄντα τ. εἶναι καὶ ἀλλοιωτὸν καὶ μεταβλητόν Or.*Jo.*13.21(p.245.6ff.; M.14.433A); οὐκ αἰδουμένοις λέγειν αὐτὸν τ. καὶ δι' ὅλων ἀλλοιωτὸν καὶ μεταβλητὸν καὶ...δυνάμενον φθαρῆναι, εἰ ἔχει τὸν φθείροντα id.*Cels.*1.21(p.72.16; 697A); Στοϊκῶν θεὸν φθαρτὸν εἰσαγόντων καὶ τὴν οὐσίαν αὐτοῦ λεγόντων σῶμα τ. δι' ὅλων καὶ ἀλλοιωτὸν καὶ μεταβλητόν *ib.*3.75(p.267.4; 1017C); **2.** by Christians asserted to be mark of creatures opp. God, Meth.*creat.* 3(p.496.12; M.18.336B); Ath.*Ar.*1.36(M.26.85C); Gr.Nyss.*or.catech.* 39(p.156.9; M.45.100B); Thdt.*eran.*1(4.10); id.*Rom.*8:20(3.88); εἰ μὲν ...κτιστά, πάντως καὶ τ. ‡Cyr.*Trin.*2(6³.2E; M.77.1121C); of κόσμος, Or.*Cels.*4.69(p.339.10); Meth.*creat.*3(p.495.24; 336A); mark of this world opp. next, cf. *in duos status divisit deus creaturam, praesentem et futurum; in illo quidem ad immortalitatem et immutabilitatem omnia ducturus, in praesenti vero creatura in mortem et mutabilitatem interim nos dimittens*, Thdr.Mops.*fr.Gen.*(M.66. 633A); irreconcilable with ἀθάνατος: εἰ ⟨δὲ θελήσ⟩ειέ τις καὶ αὐτὸν τ. λέγειν, οὐκ οἶδα, πῶς καὶ ἀθάνατον εἰπεῖν δύναιτ' αὐτόν *Hom. Clem.*20.5; of what is originate opp. the unoriginate, Clem.*str.*1.11 (p.34.11; M.8.749C); Dion.Al.ap.Eus.*p.e.*7.19(334B; M.21.564B); τὸ δὲ ἀγένητον αὐτοτελὲς καὶ ἄτρεπτον φανθέν...καὶ...οὐκέτι ὁ κόσμος τ. καθ' ὑμᾶς [i.e. who held matter to be unoriginate] Meth.*creat.*7 (p.498.21; M.18.340C); τρεπτῆς...φύσεώς ἐστι γενητὸς καὶ κτιστὸς ὑπάρχων Alex.Al.*ep.encycl.*3(p.8.9; M.18.573C); Ath.*Ar.*1.51(M.26. 117B) cit. sub B.3; εἰ δὲ τρεπτῆς [sc. τῆς φύσεως], δῆλον ὅτι καὶ γενητῆς ἧς ἴδιον ἡ τροπή Cyr.*thes.*20(5¹.199C); τἆλλα δὲ [i.e. other than God] γενητὰ καὶ τ. Zach.Mit.*opif.*(M.85.1112B); Proc.G.*Gen.* 1:26(M.87.109A); **3.** application to God so unthinkable that, set forth as logical conclusion of their tenets, it was made basis of an argument against Arians ἀεὶ πατήρ, καὶ οὐκ ἐπιγέγονε τῷ θεῷ τὸ πατήρ, ἵνα μὴ καὶ τ. εἶναι νομισθῇ Ath.*Ar.*1.28(M.26.72A); οὐ γὰρ ἦν ὅπερ οὐκ ἔστι νῦν...ἀλλ' ἔστιν ὥσπερ ἦν ἀεὶ...ἐπεὶ ἀτελὴς καὶ τ. φανήσεται ‡Ath. *Ar.*4.12(p.55.25; M.26.481D); and formed, in turn, an Arian accusation against orth. (ref. Rom.11:36 et al.) ὡς μέρος αὐτοῦ ὁμοουσίου καὶ ὡς προβολὴ ὑπό τινων νοεῖται, σύνθετος ἔσται ὁ πατὴρ καὶ διαιρετὸς καὶ τ. ... κατ' αὐτοὺς...ὁ...θεὸς Ar.*ep.Alex.*5(p.13.19; M.26.712A).

B. moral; of rational beings, *mutable*, i.e. *liable to moral lapse*; **1.** of angels ὅταν οἱ ἄγγελοι μὴ ὦσιν ἄμεμπτοι, τρεπτῆς γὰρ φύσεως καὶ αὐτοί Olymp.*Job* 4:17f.(M.93.77B); τ. ... ὄντες καὶ αὐτοί, κάμνουσιν ἀεὶ τῇ τροπῇ, ἀναλογιζόμενοι καὶ ἐλπίζοντες τὴν ἐλευθερίαν Cosm.Ind.*top.*2(M.88.125C); τίς οὖν οὐ συνθήσεται, πάντα τὰ ὄντα τ., ὅσα ὑπὸ τὴν ἡμετέραν αἴσθησιν· ἀλλὰ μὴν καὶ ἀγγέλους τρέπεσθαι, καὶ ἀλλοιοῦσθαι...; τὰ μὲν νοητά, ἀγγέλους φημὶ καὶ δαίμονας, καὶ ψυχάς, κατὰ προαίρεσιν τήν τε ἐν τῷ καλῷ προκοπήν, καὶ τὴν ἐκ τοῦ καλοῦ ἀποφοίτησιν ἐπιτεινομένην τε καὶ ὑφιεμένην...τ. τοίνυν ὄντα, πάντως καὶ κτιστά ‡Cyr.*Trin.*2(6³.2E–3A; M.77.1121C–D); κτιστοὶ...οἱ ἄγγελοι καὶ τ. ‡Caes.Naz.*dial.*44(M.38.912); **2.** of man εἰ...καὶ ἠκολούθουν [sc. οἱ μαθηταί] ἐκ προαιρέσεως, ἀλλ' εἶχον τὸ τ. τοῦ ἀνθρώπου Or.*fr.141 in Mt.*(p.72; M.17.292C); cf. *renatus alter factus es pro altero, non jam pars Adam mutabilis et peccatis circumfusi, sed Christi*, Thdr.Mops.*fr.catech.*(Swete 2,p.325.10; M.66.1013C); his nature τ. ἐστιν ἡ ἀνθρωπίνη φύσις Or.*fr.*77 *in Jo.*11:1(p.544.23); Gr. Naz.*ep.*32(M.37.69D); τὴν ἡμετέραν...σάρκα τὴν διὰ τὸ τ. τῆς φύσεως εἰς ἁμαρτίαν πεσοῦσαν Gr.Nyss.*Apoll.*40(M.45.1216B); id.*v.Mos.*(M. 44.325C); id.*hom.8 in Cant.*(M.44.945C); id.*or.catech.*21(p.81.7; M. 45.57D); Cyr.*inc.unigen.*(5¹.683E); Cosm.Ind.*top.*5(M.88.221C); his will τ. ἐστιν ἡ προαίρεσις τῶν ἔτι προσκοπτόντων καὶ ἐπιδεχομένη τὸ ἐναντία θέλειν οἷς πρότερον προέθετο Or.*Jo.*32.19(12; p.459.27; M.14. 796C); **3.** whence the need for redemption ἐπειδὴ...τῶν γενητῶν ἡ φύσις ἐστὶ τ. ... διὰ τοῦτο πάλιν ἀτρέπτου χρεία ἦν Ath.*Ar.*1.51(M.26. 117B); βούλεται ἡμᾶς ὁ λόγος τρεπτοὺς ὄντας κατὰ τὴν φύσιν, μὴ πρὸς τὸ κακὸν διὰ τῆς τροπῆς ἀπορρέειν· ἀλλὰ...συνεργὸν τὴν τροπὴν πρὸς τὴν ὑψηλοτέρων ἄνοδον ἔχειν, ὥστε κατορθωθῆναι διὰ τοῦ τ. τῆς φύσεως ἡμῶν τὸ πρὸς τὸ κακὸν ἀναλλοίωτον Gr.Nyss.*hom.8 in Cant.* (M.44.945C); ὁ ἄτρεπτος ἐν τῷ τ. γίνεται, ἵνα...μεταβαλὼν ἐκ τοῦ χείρονος τὴν ἐμμιχθεῖσαν τῇ τ. διαθέσει κακίαν ἐξαφανίσῃ ἀπὸ τῆς φύσεως id.*Eun.*5(2 p.119.25; M.45.700D); id.*Apoll.*2(M.45.1128A).

C. theol. (cf. A.2); **1.** no more applicable to Logos than to Father πῶς δὲ τ. καὶ ἀλλοιωτὸς ὁ λόγων [Jo.14:10 al.] Alex.Al.*ep.encycl.*14 (p.9.7; M.18.576B); τοὺς δὲ λέγοντας 'ἦν ποτε ὅτε οὐκ ἦν'...ἢ κτιστὸν ἢ τ. ἢ ἀλλοιωτὸν τὸν υἱὸν τοῦ θεοῦ...ἀναθεματίζει ἡ καθολικὴ καὶ ἀποστολικὴ ἐκκλησία *Symb.Nic.*(325)(p.52.4; M.20.1540C); cf. εἶναί ποτε ὅτε οὐκ ἦν, καὶ αὐτεξουσιότητι κακίας καὶ ἀρετῆς δεκτικὸν τὸν υἱὸν *τοῦ θεοῦ λέγοντος* CNic.(325)*ep*.(p.48.3)ap.Socr.*h.e*.1.9.3(M.67.77C); *ἀναθεματίζουσι καὶ τοὺς λέγοντας, ἢ τ. ἢ ἀλλοιωτὸν τὸν υἱὸν τοῦ θεοῦ* Thdot.Anc.*exp.symb*.23(M.77.1345C); *οὐ…θέμις εἰπεῖν ἐκ τῆς οὐσίας τοῦ ἀτρέπτου τ. γεννᾶσθαι λόγον, καὶ ἀλλοιουμένην σοφίαν* Thdt. ap.*cat.Heb*.1:12 suppl.(p.373.9); **2.** heret.; **a.** Bardesanes denied Inc. as implying change *τ. εὑρεθήσεται ὁ λόγος εἰ κατὰ σὲ γέγονε σάρξ* Adam.*dial*.4.16(p.174.16; M.11.1832B); **b.** asserted of Son by Arians *οὐκ ἔστιν ἄτρεπτος, ὡς ὁ πατήρ, ἀλλὰ τ. ἐστι φύσει, ὡς τὰ κτίσματα* Ar.ap.Ath.*Ar*.1.9(M.26.29B); *τὰς μὲν παρὰ τῶν Ἀρειανῶν ἐφευρεθείσας…λέξεις…τὸ λέγειν…ὅτι τ. ἐστι φύσεως* Ath.*ep.Afr*.5 (M.26.1037B); *τ. ὢν φύσεως ἢ ὡς λίθος καὶ ξύλον οὐκ ἔχει τὴν προαίρεσιν ἐλευθέραν* id.*Ar*.1.35(M.26.84B); *εἰ οὖν τὸ θέλημα* [sc. *τοῦ υἱοῦ*] *παραιτητέον, τ. … ἡ φύσις* Aëtius ap.Anast.S.*monoph*.(M.89.1181B); as being a creature *συναναλαμβάνοντες τῇ…κτίσει καὶ τὸν υἱὸν τοῦ θεοῦ. οἷς ἀκολούθως καί φασιν αὐτὸν τρεπτῆς εἶναι φύσεως, ἀρετῆς τε καὶ κακίας ἐπιδεκτικόν* Alex.Al.*ep.Alex*.11(p.21.12; M.18.552B); *εἷς… τῶν ποιημάτων…ἐστι…διὸ καὶ τ. ἐστι καὶ ἀλλοιωτὸς τὴν φύσιν ὡς τὰ πάντα τὰ λογικά…εἰ δύναται ὁ τοῦ θεοῦ λόγος τραπῆναι ὡς ὁ διάβολος ἐτράπη* id.*ep.encycl*.7ff.(p.8.2; M.18.573B); idea includes moral progress as well as moral decline, id.*ep.Alex*.11(p.21.12; 552B) cit. supra; *ὡς ὁ Χριστὸς τ. μὲν τῇ γε φύσει τῇ οἰκείᾳ, ἐπιμελείᾳ δὲ τῶν ἀρετῶν ἀνυπερβλήτῳ εἰς τὸ ἄτρεπτον ἀνυψωθῆναι* Philost.*h.e*.8.3(M.65. 557B); *εἰ τ. ὢν φύσεως ὁ υἱὸς…ἐφέσει τῇ περὶ τὸ ἀγαθὸν εἰς τοῦτο γέγονε καταστάσεως, ὡς μηδεμίαν ἔχειν πρὸς τὸν πατέρα διαφοράν* Cyr. *thes*.13(5^1.126A); Christ, in fact, avoiding moral lapse through exercise of will *αὐτὸν τ. τυγχάνοντα φύσεως διὰ τρόπων ἐπιμέλειαν καὶ ἄσκησιν μὴ τρεπόμενον ἐπὶ τὸ χεῖρον, ἐξελέξατο* Alex.Al.*ep.Alex*.13 (p.21.21; 552C); *καὶ αὐτεξούσιός ἐστι καὶ ἰδίᾳ προαιρέσει οὐ τρέπεται, τ. ὢν φύσεως;* Ath.*Ar*.1.22(57C); *ib*.1.35(84B); *αὐτὸς ὁ λόγος ἐστὶ τ. … ὅτε…θέλει δύναται τρέπεσθαι καὶ αὐτὸς ὥσπερ καὶ ἡμεῖς* *ib*.1.5 (21C); *τῇ μὲν φύσει τ. ἐστι, τῷ δὲ ἰδίῳ αὐτεξουσίῳ, ὡς βούλεται, μένει καλός· ὅτε μέντοι θέλει, δύναται τρέπεσθαι καὶ αὐτὸς ὥσπερ καὶ τὰ πάντα* id.*ep.Aeg.Lib*.12(M.25.564C); *Ἄρειος καὶ οἱ σὺν αὐτῷ…λέγοντες '…τ. …ἐστι, δυνάμενος, ὅτε βούλεται, τραπῆναι' ἐξεβλήθησαν τῆς ἐκκλησίας* id.*syn*.14(M.26.705C); **c.** ref. Apollinarian Christology *οὐδὲ τοῦτο συνιδεῖν ἠδυνήθησαν…ὅτι ὁ μὲν θεῖος νοῦς αὐτοκίνητός ἐστι καὶ ταυτοκίνητος, ἄτρεπτος γάρ, ὁ δὲ ἀνθρώπινος αὐτοκίνητος μέν, οὐ ταυτοκίνητος δέ, τ. γάρ, καὶ ὅτιπερ ἀτρέπτῳ νῷ τ. οὐ μίγνυται νοῦς εἰς ἑνὸς ὑποκειμένου σύστασιν* Apoll.*fr*.151(p.248.2)ap.*Doct.Patr*.41.18(p.307.14); *οὐχ ἡγεῖται* [sc. Apoll.] *πρέπειν ἀνθρώπινον νοῦν περὶ τὸν μονογενῆ θεὸν ἐννοεῖν, καὶ τὴν αἰτίαν λέγει, ὅτι τ. ὁ νοῦς ὁ ἀνθρώπινος* Gr.Nyss.*Apoll*. 40(M.45.1213B); reply of Gr. Nyss. *εἰ οὖν ὁ νοῦς διὰ τὸ τ. ἀναβάλλεται, διὰ τὴν αὐτὴν αἰτίαν, μηδὲ ἡ σὰρξ ὑπ' αὐτοῦ συγχωρείσθω* *ib*.

τρεπτότης, ἡ, 1. *liability to change* *τὸν ἐν τ. ὄντα καὶ μετατεθῆναι δυνάμενον ἐκ τοῦ κακοῦ εἰς ἀγαθόν* Flav.Ant.*anath*.4(M.48.950); **2.** *changeableness* of this life, ‡Nil.*tract*.2(M.79.1284A).

τρέπ-ω, *turn*;

I. in gen.; **A.** *divert* the attention, Gr.Nyss.*or.catech*.26(p.97.5; M.45.68B).

B. moral; pass. intrans., *turn, turn aside* *τραπομένου πρὸς ἀπόστασιν τοῦ Ἰσραήλ, καὶ εἰδώλοις λελατρευκότος* Cyr.*Nah*.31(3.508D); CCP(543)*anath*.2 cit. s. *ἑνάς*.

II. theol.; **A.** act. trans., *move, cause to turn* against *μή πως ἀναξίως τῶν δώρων ἀψάμενοι τρέψωμεν καθ' ἑαυτῶν τὸ θεῖον εἰς ἐκδίκησιν* *Lit.Jac*.(p.178.11).

B. med. and pass. intrans., *change, undergo change*; **1.** universally acknowledged as alien to God *οὐδὲ…ὡς ἐν θυμῷ τραπήσεται θεός, μένοντος αὐτοῦ ἀτρέπτου φύσει τε καὶ γνώμῃ* Thdr.Heracl. *Is*.28:21(M.18.1320A); *ὅτι…ἄτρεπτος* [sc. *ὁ θεός*]*…οὔτε πρὸς τὸ χεῖρον, οὔτε πρὸς τὸ βέλτιον τραπῆναι δυνάμενος* Gr.Nyss.*ep*.3(M.46. 1020B); *εἰ μετὰ ταῦτα ἔσχεν υἱόν…ἐτράπη ἐκ τοῦ μὴ εἶναι πατὴρ εἰς τὸ γενέσθαι πατήρ* ‡Cyr.*Trin*.7(6^3.9C; M.77.1133A); not involved in act of Creation *οὐ τραπεὶς ἀπὸ ἕξεως εἰς ἕξιν θεὸς καὶ τῇ φύσει καὶ τῇ οὐσίᾳ ἀλλοιωθεὶς…εἶχε γὰρ ἐν ἑαυτῷ τὸ ἀεὶ δημιουργικόν* Epiph.*haer*.76.38(p.391.20; M.42.597D); accusation made against pagan notions of deity *εἰ μὲν ἀήρ* [sc. *Ζεύς*]*…ἀλλοιοῦται, εἰ δὲ καιρός, ~εται* Athenag.*leg*.22.5(M.6.940); **2.** rejected as equally inapplicable to Son *ἐχάρη μὴ τραπεὶς διὰ τὸ ἐν χαρᾷ γεγονέναι τὸν μετανενοηκότα* Clem.*str*.2.16(p.151.26; M.8.1012B); cf. *unigenitus filius ejus, quoniam in omnibus inconvertibilis est et incommutabilis, et substantiale in eo omne bonum est, quod utique mutari aut converti nunquam potest, idcirco pura ejus ac sincera gloria praedicatur*, Or. *princ*.1.2.10(p.44.20; M.11.142B); *οὐκ ἐπειδὴ γέγονεν ἄνθρωπος… ἐτράπη* Ath.*Ar*.1.48(M.26.112C); *πῶς…ἡ ἀπερίληπτος θεότης εἰς μικροῦ σώματος ὄγκον περιεγράφη, εἴπερ ἐτράπη πᾶσα ἡ τοῦ μονογενοῦς φύσις;* Bas.*ep*.261.2(3.404C; M.32.973C); *τοὺς δὲ λέγοντας ψιλὸν ἄνθρωπον τὸν Χριστὸν…ἢ εἰς σάρκα τραπέντα…τούτους ἀναθεματίζει ἡ καθολικὴ…ἐκκλησία* Ambr.*fr*.ap.Jo.D.*Jacob*.(M.94. 1496A); *τέλειος θεὸς ὤν, γέγονε τέλειος ἄνθρωπος, μὴ τραπείς, μὴ ἀλλοιωθεὶς τὴν…οὐσίαν τῆς αὐτοῦ θεότητος* ‡Ath.*symb*.4(M.28.1589D); *εἷς ἐστιν ὁ Χριστός· εἷς δὲ οὐ τραπεῖσα ἡ σάρξ, ἀλλὰ ἀναληφθεῖσα εἰς τὸν θεόν* *ib*.(1592A); *οὔτε τὴν σάρκα φαμὲν εἰς θεότητος τραπῆναι φύσιν* Cyr.*ep*.17(p.35.21; 5^2.70A); id.*Chr.un*.(5^1.735E); *διὰ μὲν γὰρ τοῦ 'ἐγένετο'* [Jo.1:14] *τὸ ἀδιαίρετον τῆς ἄκρας ἑνώσεως ὁ εὐαγγελιστὴς ὑπαινίττεται…τὸ δὲ 'ἔλαβε'* [Phil.2:7] *βοᾷ τὸ ἄτρεπτον τῆς φύσεως… οὔτε γὰρ ἐξ οὐκ ὄντων παρήχθη ὁ ἀεὶ ἄναρχος, οὔτε ἐξ οὐκ ὄντων ἐτράπη ὁ ἀναλλοίωτος λόγος* Procl.CP *Arm*.6(p.190.12; M.65.861B); *εἰ …ἀδύνατον τραπῆναι τὸ ἄτρεπτον οὐκ ἐγένετο σὰρξ ὁ θεὸς λόγος τραπείς, ἀλλὰ ἀνέλαβε σάρκα καὶ ἐσκήνωσεν ἐν ἡμῖν* Thdt.ap.Cyr.*apol. Thdt*.1(p.109.5f.; 5^1.204B); *τοῦτο τὸ 'γέγονεν' εἰ μὴ σαφὲς γένοιτο, τροπὴν αἰνίττεται καὶ ἀλλοίωσιν. εἰ μὴ γὰρ σάρκα λαβὼν ἐγένετο σάρξ, τραπεὶς ἐγένετο σάρξ…ὁ δὲ τὸν θεὸν λόγον εἰς σάρκα τετράφθαι λέγων, οὐδὲ ἕνα λέγει υἱόν. σὰρξ γὰρ αὐτὴ καθ' αὑτὴν οὐχ υἱός* Thdt.*eran*.1(4. 12,14); *οὔτε…ὁ λόγος ἢ εἰς σῶμα ἢ εἰς ψυχὴν κατά τι μέρος οἰκεῖον ἐτράπη* Leo Mag.*ep*.35.2(p.41.22; M.*PL*.54.808A); *οὐ γὰρ ἐτράπη τὴν θείαν φύσιν* Max.*schol.c.h*.4.4(M.4.57D); most heretics concurred, at least verbally (Apoll.) *ἄτρεπτον ὁμολογεῖ τὸν θεὸν λόγον, καὶ οὐκ εἰς σάρκα τετράφθαι φησίν* Thdt.*eran*.1(4.71); fear of suggesting contact of deity with mutability being ground of his heresy *αὐτὸν τὸν λόγον σάρκα γεγενῆσθαι μὴ ἀνειληφότα νοῦν ἀνθρώπινον, νοῦν ~όμενον καὶ αἰχμαλωτιζόμενον λογισμοῖς ῥυπαροῖς* Apoll.*ep.Diocaes*.2(p.256.6) ap.Leont.B.*Apoll*.(M.86.1969D); yet flesh of Christ was changed acc. Apollinarian theory *τετράφθαι φασὶν οὐκ οἶδ' ὅπως εἰς ὁμοουσιότητα τὴν πρὸς θεὸν λόγον σάρκα αὐτοῦ* Cyr.*synous*.3(p.480.15; cf.M.76. 1429D); Cyr. himself accused by Easterns of same heresy *πάντες οἱ ἐκ τῆς Ἀνατολῆς νομίζουσιν ἡμᾶς τοὺς ὀρθοδόξους ταῖς Ἀπολιναρίου δόξαις ἀκολουθεῖν…(τοιαύταις γὰρ καὶ αὐτοὶ κέχρηνται φωναῖς, ὡς τοῦ θεοῦ λόγου μεταβεβληκότος εἰς φύσιν σαρκὸς καὶ τῆς σαρκὸς τραπείσης εἰς φύσιν θεότητος)* id.*ep*.44(p.35.21; 5^2.133C); (Nest.) *αὐτόν τε τὸν θεὸν λόγον εἰς σάρκα ἐάν τις εἴποι τετράφθαι ἣν ἔλαβεν… ἀ. ἔ.* Nest.*fr*.B 4(p.212.12); *τί ἐστι 'σαρκωθέντα'; οὐ τραπέντα ἀπὸ θεότητος εἰς σάρκα* id.*fr*.C 14(p.287.4); (Eutyches) *ἔφη* [sc. Eutyches] *τὸν θεὸν λόγον ἀνθρώπειον ἐκ τῆς παρθένου λαβεῖν, ἀλλ' αὐτὸν ἀτρέπτως τραπέντα καὶ σάρκα γενόμενον· τοῖς γὰρ καταγελάστοις αὐτοῦ κέχρημαι λόγοις* Thdt.*haer*.4.13(4.373); (Sev. Ant.) *τὰ ἐξ ὧν ὁ Ἐμμανουὴλ ὑφεστήκει, καὶ μετὰ τὴν ἕνωσιν οὐ τέτραπται* Sev.Ant.ap.Leont.H. *monoph*.(M.86.1845D); (Arian) Son naturally liable to change, but by an act of will avoided change (i.e. in moral sense) *εἰ δύναται ὁ τοῦ θεοῦ λόγος τραπῆναι ὡς ὁ διάβολος ἐτράπη* Alex.Al.*ep.encycl*.10 (p.8.8; M.18.573B); id.*ep.Alex*.13(p.21.21; M.18.552C); Ath.*Ar*.1.5 (M.26.21C), *ib*.1.22(57C) citt. s. *τρεπτός*.

τριαγμοί, οἱ, *of the triads*; title of work by Ion of Chios, Clem *str*.1.21(p.81.10; *τριγράμμοις* M.8.864A).

τριάδελφοι, αἱ, *The Three Sisters* [i.e. Fates], *Orac.Sib*.5.215.

τριαδικός, 1. *threefold*; **a.** of Trin. *ἕνα θεὸν τὸ τ. ὁμολογοῦντες κράτος* †Gregent.*disp*.(M.86.628C); *παράγοντος Σαβελλίου τὸ 'ἐγὼ καὶ ὁ πατὴρ ἕν ἐσμεν' καὶ ἀναιροῦντος τὴν τ. ὑπόστασιν* Leont.H. *monoph*.(M.86.1812B); *ἔλεγε…ἐν πνεύματι θεοῦ ἐκβάλλειν τὰ δαιμόνια, ἵνα δείξῃ πρόσωπον τοῦ…συμπληροῦντος τὴν τ. … καθέδραν αὐτῷ καὶ τῷ πατρί* *cat.Ac*.2:22(p.42.15); *τῆς ἁπλῆς καὶ μοναδικῆς αὐτοαληθείας καὶ κυριότητος καὶ θεότητος τῷ λόγῳ τῆς φύσεως καὶ τριαδικῆς καθ' ὑπόστασιν* ‡Gr.Nyss.*hom.5.60 in Jo*.(p.193.4); *τὴν τ. ἑνάδα…τὴν ὁμόθεον καὶ ὁμοάγαθον* Dion.Ar.*d.n*.1.5(M.3.593B); *ὑμνήσαμεν πῶς ἡ θεία καὶ ἀγαθὴ φύσις ἑνικὴ λέγεται, πῶς τριαδική* id.*myst*.3(M.3. 1033A); id.*d.n*.13.3(981A) cit. s. *ὑπερώνυμος*; *τῷ τ. καὶ ἑνιαίῳ φωτὶ τῆς μιᾶς θεότητος* *Lit.Jac*.(p.46.28); *θεολογῶ σε τὴν τ. μίαν θεότητα* Andr.Cr.*can.mag*.143(p.151; M.97.1353A); **b.** of angelic orders *ἡ θεολογία τὰς οὐρανίους οὐσίας ἐννέα κέκληκεν…ταύτας ὁ θεῖος ἡμῶν ἱεροτελεστὴς εἰς τρεῖς ἀφορίζει τ. διακοσμήσεις* Dion.Ar.*c.h*. 6.2(M.3.200D); *ib*.(201A); **c.** ref. 3Reg.18:34 *ἐκκαίων ὕδατι τ. τὰ διχοτομήματα* Sophr.H.*v.Anast*.(M.92.1688A); **2.** *consisting of three, ternary* *ἡ τοῦ Ἀβραὰμ ἀντωνομασία κατείληπται σημαίνουσα τὸν τ. ἀριθμὸν τῶν θεαρχικῶν ὑποστάσεων* Cyr.*syn.def*.(M.76.1421A); **3.** *pertaining to the Trinity, Trinitarian* *ἐξ εἰδωλολατρείας εἰς τ. θεογνωσίαν μετάστασιν* Amph.*fr*.(M.39.105A); *ἐν τῷ τ. μυστηρίῳ* ‡Gr.Nyss. *imag*.(M.44.1340D); *τ. … ἡ μυστικὴ θεολογία διὰ τὰς ὁμοουσίους ἁγίας τρεῖς ὑποστάσεις τῆς παναγίου μονάδος* Max.*ambig*.(M.91.1397C); *ἡ παράδοσις τῆς καθολικῆς ἐκκλησίας οὐ συστοιχεῖ…τοῖς Ἑλλήνων φιλοσοφικοῖς εἰς ἅπαν ὅροις· καὶ μάλιστα ἐν τῷ κατὰ Χριστὸν μυστηρίῳ καὶ τῷ τ. λόγῳ* Anast.S.*hod*.1(M.89.49B); *ὁ ἱερεὺς τὸν λαὸν διδάσκει τὴν…τ. θεογνωσίαν* ‡Bas.*h.myst*.58(p.393.2); *ταῦτα τῆς Ἰουδαϊκῆς ἀπειθείας πρὸς τὴν τ. δοξολογίαν ἐναντιώτατα τὰ ἔπαθλα* ‡Meth.*Sym*.

*et Ann.*12(M.18.377B); **4.** neut. as subst., *threefold character* ὁ λόγος ἓν πρόσωπον ὅλον ὑπάρχων, μία τε ὑπόστασις τῆς ἁγίας τριάδος· ἐξ ὑποστάσεων γάρ, οὐ φύσεων τὸ τ. συνείλεκται Leont.H.*Nest.*7.4(M.86.1768aA); ἀσεβὲς...παρ' ὀρθοδόξοις ἑκάτερον...τό τε μοναδικὸν καθ' ὑπόστασιν, τό τε τ. ἐν ταῖς φύσεσι Sophr.H.*ep.syn.*(M.87.3153C); εἰ ὑπόστασιν τὸ τῆς θεότητος καὶ τὸ τῆς ἀνθρωπότητος σημαίνουσιν ὀνόματα, ὥρα σοι λέγειν καὶ τρεῖς θεότητας διὰ τὸ τ. τῶν ὑποστάσεων καὶ ἀπείρους τὰς ἀνθρωπότητας διὰ τὸ τῶν ὑποστάσεων ἄπειρον Jo.D.*Jacob.*14(M.94.1444C); id.*trisag.*3(M.95.29B).

***τριαδικῶς**, **1.** *in a triad*, Areth.*Apoc.*4:4(M.106.569B); **2.** *by the Trinity* (i.e. not by one Person alone) τὸ τ. διακεκοσμῆσθαι τὴν κτίσιν Didym.*Trin.*2.1(M.39.452A); **3.** *in a threefold manner, as three* τριάδα...ὁμολογοῦμεν...μοναδικῶς μὲν ἐν μιᾷ οὐσίᾳ καὶ θεότητι, τ. δὲ ἐν τρισὶν ὑποστάσεσιν Nil.*epp.*1.255(M.79.177A); μία θεότης οὖσά τε μοναδικῶς καὶ ὑφεσταμένη τ. Max.*ambig.*(M.91.1036C); τὴν ...θείαν...οὐσίαν...τ. ὑμνουμένην διὰ τὴν τρισυπόστατον ὕπαρξιν *ib.*(1400D); ἡ...θεότης, ἤτοι οὐσία, τ. ἐξαπλοῦται, ἀδιαιρέτως ἐν τρισὶ γνωριζομένη ὑποστάσεσι Jo.D.*trisag.*2(M.95.25C).

***τριάδιν, τό**, *merel, nine men's morris*, a game probably identical with the modern Greek τὸ τριόδι, †Gregent.*leg.Hom.*37(M.86.601B).

***τριαδόμαχος**, *warring against* or *hostile to the Trinity* τοὺς τ. ἐχθροὺς τοῦ θεοῦ, Ἄρειον καὶ Σαβέλλιον καὶ Εὐνόμιον Dam.*troph.*suppl.(p.283.2).

***τριάδοξος**, *holding the doctrine of the Trinity*, opp. monophysites who by adding 'crucified for us' to Trisagion, were substituting quaternity in place of Trinity, ‡Faust.*ep.*(p.8.18; H.2.848D).

τριάζ-ω, *make into a trinity*, Gr.Naz.*carm.*2.1.11.658(M.37.1074A); †Gregent.*disp.*1(M.86.628B); Χριστιανοὶ ~οντες τὴν θεότητα *ib.*(628C).

τριακάς, ἡ, *group of thirty*; of Valent. aeons, Epiph.*haer.*31.6(p.392.19; M.41.484B); *ib.*(p.393.4; 484C); *ib.*(p.393.12; 484D).

***τριακονταγράμματος**, *of thirty letters*, ref. Marcosian pleroma of thirty aeons ὁ γὰρ ἐπίσημος ἀριθμὸς συγκραθεὶς τοῖς κδ' στοιχείοις, τὸ τ. ὄνομα ἀπετέλεσε Iren.*haer.*1.14.6(M.7.608B); cf.Hipp.*haer.*6.47(p.179.17; M.16.3274A).

***τριακονταετηρικός**, *of thirty years*, (sc. *in honour of*) *thirty years of rule*, Eus.*v.C.*1.1(p.7.5; M.20.912A); τ. ἑορτάς id.*l.C.*6(p.211.11; M.20.1349A); as title of a speech εἰς Κωνσταντῖνον τὸν βασιλέα τ. *ib.*(p.193; 1316B).

τριακονταετηρίς, ἡ, the *thirtieth year*, Eus.*v.C.*4.47 tit.(p.116.21; M.20.1197B); ἡ τῆς ἀφιερώσεως ἑορτὴ ἐν αὐτῇ τῇ βασιλέως τ. ... ἐπετελεῖτο *ib.*4.45(p.136.27; 1196C); *Chron.Pasch.*p.286(M.92.713A).

τριακοντάς, ἡ, **1.** the *number thirty*; of the thirty disciples of Jo. Bapt., *Hom.Clem.*2.23; in gen., Eus.*l.C.*6(p.211.3; M.20.1349A); **2.** *group of thirty*, of Valent. aeons γίνονται τριάκοντα αἰῶνες μετὰ τοῦ Χριστοῦ καὶ τοῦ ἁγίου πνεύματος· τινὲς μὲν οὖν αὐτῶν ταύτην εἶναι θέλουσιν τὴν τ. τῶν αἰώνων, τινὲς δὲ συνυπάρχειν τῷ πατρὶ Σιγὴν καὶ σὺν αὐτοῖς καταριθμεῖσθαι τοὺς αἰῶνας θέλουσιν Hipp.*haer.*6.31(p.158.28; M.16.3239D); ὁ μονογενὴς...γενόμενος ἐν τ. αἰώνων, εἰσῆλθεν εἰς τόνδε τὸν κόσμον *ib.*8.10(p.230.10; 3355A); depicted in man τὸν ἄνθρωπον...τὴν εἰκόνα τῆς τ. οὕτως ἔχειν...· ἐν μὲν ταῖς χερσὶ διὰ τῶν δακτύλων τὴν δεκάδα βαστάζειν· ἐν ὅλῳ δὲ τῷ σώματι... τὴν δωδεκάδα...τήν τε οὖν ὀγδοάδα...ἀόρατον οὖσαν, ἐν τοῖς σπλάγχνοις κρυβομένην νοεῖσθαι Iren.*haer.*1.18.1(M.7.644B); in division of time τὴν ὥραν..., τὸ δωδέκατον τῆς ἡμέρας, ἐκ τριάκοντα μοιρῶν κεκοσμῆσθαι διὰ τὴν εἰκόνα τῆς τ. *ib.*1.17.1(640A); ref. comparison of Valent. cosmogony with Hesiod's καὶ οὗτος μὲν ὁ ἀριθμὸς κατὰ ἀκολουθίαν ἀρρενοθηλείας οὕτως ἔχει τὴν τ. Epiph.*haer.*31.3(p.387.8; M.41.477C); *ib.*31.4(p.389.8; 480C); **3.** *thirtieth part*, Epiph.*haer.*15.1(p.211.3; M.41.249A).

***τριακοντώνυμος**, *named from thirty* (*aeons*), of Sophia τὴν τριακοντώνυμον μητέρα Iren.*haer.*1.17.1(M.7.640A) but cf. Lat. ad loc.: *trigesimam nominis...matrem*; cf.Hipp.*haer.*6.53(p.188.2; M.16.3290A).

***τριακοσιομέδιμνος, ὁ**, *one possessing land producing 300 medimni yearly*, Synes.*insomn.*12(p.168.9; M.66.1301D).

***τριακοστοετής**, *of thirty years*, of Christ καὶ ἕως τριακοστοετοῦς χρόνου διανύσας [sc. Christ], ἵνα πᾶσαν ἡλικίαν εὐλογήσῃ, τότε ἐπὶ τὸ βάπτισμα ἔρχεται Gel.Cyz.*h.e.*2.24.23(M.85.1304B).

***τριακοστοτέταρτος**, *thirty-fourth*, *Chron.Pasch.*p.209(M.92.512D).

***τρίαρχος**, **A.** as subst. *ruler of a third part* (cf. τετράρχης), Thphl.Ant.*Autol.*2.31(M.6.1104C).

B. as adj.; **1.** *of triple origin*, ref. Trin. ὥσπερ...ἐκ πηγῆς ἀεννάου τρίαρχος θάλασσα Dam.*troph.*suppl.(p.281.16); **2.** *with three points*; of antlers, *Phys.Gr.*B 4(p.170.3; M.43.521C).

τριάς, ἡ, **I.** the *number three*; as masculine (uneven) number (Gnost.), Hipp.*haer.*4.51(p.75.11; M.16.3119B); Eus.*l.C.*6(p.209.27; M.20.1348A).

II. *group of three, triad*;

A. in gen., ref. Mt.18:20 αἰνίσσεται ἡ...τ. ... ἀνήρ, γυνή, τέκνον... θυμός, ἐπιθυμία, λογισμός...σάρξ, ψυχή, πνεῦμα Clem.*str.*3.10(p.227.12; M.8.1169C); ἡ ἁγία τ., πίστις, ἐλπίς, ἀγάπη *ib.*4.7(p.273.6; 1265B); of stages of spiritual progress τὴν μακαρίαν τῶν ἁγίων τ. μονῶν *ib.*7.7(p.31.2; M.9.457A); (Valent.) of 'triad of corruption' (prob. κόσμος, θάνατος, φθορά) from which believer is delivered through baptism διὰ γὰρ πατρὸς καὶ υἱοῦ καὶ ἁγίου πνεύματος σφραγισθεὶς ἀνεπίληπτός ἐστι πάσῃ τῇ ἄλλῃ δυνάμει, καὶ διὰ τριῶν ὀνομάτων πάσης τῆς ἐν φθορᾷ τ. ἀπηλλάγη id.*exc.Thdot.*80(p.131.29; M.9.696B); (Peratic) λέγουσιν ἕνα εἶναι κόσμον τινά...τριχῇ διῃρημένον...ἡ δὲ πρώτη τομὴ καὶ προσεχεστέρα...ἐστιν ἡ τ. καὶ καλεῖται ἀγαθὸν τέλειον, μέγεθος πατρικόν· τὸ δὲ δεύτερον μέρος τῆς τ. οἱονεὶ δυνάμεων...πλῆθος· τρίτον ἰδικόν Hipp.*haer.*10.10(p.269.4; 3419C); cf.*ib.*5.12(p.104.19; 3162A); ref. bodily triad of ἐπιθυμία, ὀργή, λύπη and spiritual triad of λογισμός, γνῶσις, φόβος, *Hom.Clem.*20.2; ref. sons of Const. τριάδος λόγῳ τριττὴν γονὴν παίδων θεοφιλῆ Eus.*v.C.*4.40(p.133.9; M.20.1188D); ref. days of Creation τὸ φῶς, ὅπερ...ἔφη Μωσῆς...ὁρίσαι τὴν πρώτην τῶν ...ἡμερῶν τ. Dion.Ar.*d.n.*4.5(M.3.700A); of a triad of angelic orders, id.*e.h.*5.1.1(M.3.500D); *ib.*6.1.1(529D).

B. Trin.; **1.** in gen., *triad* of the divine Persons αἱ τρεῖς ἡμέραι... τύποι εἰσὶν τῆς τ. τοῦ θεοῦ καὶ τοῦ λόγου αὐτοῦ καὶ τῆς σοφίας αὐτοῦ Thphl.Ant.*Autol.*2.15(M.6.1077B); cf. implied use of term in Valent. baptismal invocation, Clem.*exc.Thdot.*80(p.131.29; M.9.696B) cit. s. A supra; διὰ γὰρ τῆς τ. ταύτης [ref. baptismal formula] πατὴρ δοξάζεται. πατὴρ γὰρ ἠθέλησεν, υἱὸς ἐποίησεν, πνεῦμα ἐφανέρωσεν Hipp.*Noët.*14(p.257.17; M.10.821B); τ. ἐστι δόξαις οὐχ ὁμοίαις· ἀνεπίμικτοι ἑαυταῖς εἰσιν αἱ ὑποστάσεις αὐτῶν Ar.*Thal.fr.*2 ap.Ath.*syn.*15(p.242.25; M.26.708A); θεότης δὲ μία ἐν Μωϋσῇ...καταγγέλλεται, δυὰς δὲ ἐν προφήταις σφόδρα κηρύττεται, τ. δὲ ἐν εὐαγγελίοις φανεροῦται Epiph.*anc.*73(p.92.7; M.43.153B); **2.** theol.; *trinity* or *'triunity'*; **a.** in gen., Hipp.*Noët.*14(p.257.17; M.10.821B) cit. s. B.1; cf. *illa vero substantia trinitatis quae principium est et causa omnium*, Or.*princ.*4.3.15(p.347.19; M.11.404A); cf. *una et incorporea natura...trinitatis*, *ib.*4.4.5(p.356.10; 407A); cf. *idem namque ipse qui ibi trinitas propter distinctionem personarum, hic unus deus intelligitur pro unitate substantiae*, id.*Cant.*3(M.13.177C); ἡνῶσθαι γὰρ ἀνάγκη τῷ θεῷ τῶν ὅλων τὸν θεῖον λόγον, ἐμφιλοχωρεῖν δὲ τῷ θεῷ καὶ ἐνδιαιτᾶσθαι δεῖ τὸ ἅγιον πνεῦμα· ἤδη καὶ τὴν θείαν τ. εἰς ἕνα, ὥσπερ εἰς κορυφήν τινα, τὸν θεὸν τῶν ὅλων τὸν παντοκράτορα λέγω, συγκεφαλαιοῦσθαί τε καὶ συνάγεσθαι πᾶσα ἀνάγκη Dion.R.ap.Ath.*decr.*26(p.22.10; M.25.464A); εἰς...τὴν τ. τὴν μονάδα πλατύνομεν ἀδιαίρετον καὶ τὴν τ. πάλιν ἀμείωτον εἰς τὴν μονάδα συγκεφαλαιούμεθα Dion.Al.ap.eund.*Dion.*17(p.58.24; M.25.505A); τ. τελεία, δόξῃ καὶ ἀιδιότητι καὶ βασιλείᾳ μὴ μεριζομένη μηδὲ ἀπαλλοτριουμένη Gr.Thaum.*symb.*(p.3.10; M.10.985A); ὁ πατὴρ διὰ τοῦ λόγου τὰ πάντα ποιεῖ καὶ οὕτως ἡ ἑνότης τῆς ἁγίας τ. σῴζεται· καὶ οὕτως εἷς θεὸς ἐν τῇ ἐκκλησίᾳ κηρύττεται Ath.*ep.Serap.*1.28(M.26.596A); μία τῆς τ. ἡ θεότης ἐξ ἑνὸς τοῦ πατρὸς γινωσκομένη *ib.*3.6(636B); μία θεότης ἐστὶν ἐν τ. id.*Ar.*1.18(M.26.48C); ἕνα διὰ τῆς τ. ὁμολογοῦμεν εἶναι τὸν θεὸν...μίαν ἐν τ. θεότητα φρονοῦμεν *ib.*3.15(353B); ὁ υἱὸς τοῦ πατρὸς υἱὸς καὶ πνεῦμα τοῦ πατρὸς πνεῦμα εἴρηται· καὶ οὕτως τῆς ἁγίας τ. μία ἡ θεότης καὶ πίστις ἐστίν id.*ep.Serap.*1.16(569B); τ. ... ἐστιν οὐχ ἕως ὀνόματος μόνον καὶ φαντασίας λέξεως, ἀλλὰ ἀληθείᾳ καὶ ὑπάρξει τ. *ib.*1.28(596A,B); εἰς ἁγίαν τ. πιστεύειν, οὐκ ὀνόματι τ. μόνον, ἀλλ' ἀληθῶς οὖσαν καὶ ὑφεστῶσαν id.*tom.*5(M.26.801B); εὐσεβὲς...ἐστι φρονεῖν καὶ ὁμολογεῖν τὴν τ. ἐν μιᾷ θεότητι Paulin.T.*symb.*(p.435.3; M.42.672C); τ., ὡς ἀληθῶς ἡ τ. ... τ. δὲ οὐ πραγμάτων ἀνίσων ἀπαρίθμησις ἤ τί κωλύει καὶ δεκάδα...ὀνομάζειν...; ἀλλ' ἴσων καὶ ὁμοτίμων σύλληψις, ἑνούσης τῆς προσηγορίας τὰ ἡνωμένα ἐκ φύσεως Gr.Naz.*or.*23.10(M.35.1161B); μονάδα ἐν τ. καὶ τ. ἐν μονάδι προσκυνουμένην, παράδοξον ἔχουσαν καὶ τὴν διαίρεσιν καὶ τὴν ἕνωσιν *ib.*25.17(1221C); πῶς ἡ αὐτὴ καὶ μονὰς νοῇ καὶ τ. εὑρίσκῃ...μία φύσις, τρεῖς ἰδιότητες *ib.*26.19(1252C); μονὰς ἐν τ. προσκυνουμένη καὶ τ. ἐν μονάδι ἀνακεφαλαιουμένη *ib.*6.22(749C); μονὰς ἐξ ἀρχῆς εἰς δυάδα κινηθεῖσα, μέχρι τ. ἔστη· καὶ τοῦτό ἐστιν ἡμῖν ὁ πατὴρ καὶ ὁ υἱὸς καὶ τὸ ἅγιον πνεῦμα *ib.*29.2(p.75.8; M.36.76B); ἐκ φωτὸς τοῦ πατρὸς φῶς καταλαμβάνοντες τὸν υἱὸν ἐν φωτὶ τῷ πνεύματι, σύντομον καὶ ἀπέριττον τῆς τ. θεολογίαν *ib.*31.3(p.148.11; 136C); λόγισαι...τὰς μὲν ὑποστατικὰς ἰδιότητας...ἐπαστράπτειν ἑκάστῳ τῶν ἐν τῇ ἁγίᾳ τ. πιστευομένων· τῆς δὲ κατὰ τὴν φύσιν ἰδιότητος μηδεμίαν ἑτέρου πρὸς τὸ ἕτερον ἐπινοεῖσθαι διαφοράν Gr.Nyss.*diff.ess.*5(M.32.336A); ἐπεὶ οὖν τὸ μέν τι κοινὸν ἐν τῇ ἁγίᾳ τ., τὸ δὲ ἰδιάζον ὁ λόγος ἐνεθεώρησεν, ὁ μὲν τῆς κοινότητος λόγος εἰς τὴν οὐσίαν ἀνάγεται, ἡ δὲ ὑπόστασις τὸ ἰδιάζον ἑκάστου σημαίνει *ib.*(336C); χρὴ διὰ τῶν ἰδιαζόντων σημείων ἀσύγχυτον ἐπὶ τῆς τ. τὴν διάκρισιν ἔχειν *ib.*(329A); εἷς ἡμῖν ὁμολογητέος θεὸς...κἂν ἡ φωνὴ τῆς θεότητος διήκει διὰ τῆς ἁγίας τ. id.*tres dii*(M.45.120D); εἰ...τὸ θεώμενον θεὸς λέγεται, οὐκέτι ἂν εὐλόγως ἀποκριθείη τι τῶν ἐν τῇ τ. προσώπων τῆς τοιαύτης προσηγορίας *ib.*(124A); οὐδὲν μᾶλλον...τρεῖς σωτῆρες...ὀνομάζονται, εἰ καὶ ὁμολογεῖται παρὰ τῆς ἁγίας τ. ἡ σωτηρία· οὕτως οὐδὲ τρεῖς θεοὶ κατὰ τὴν...τῆς θεότητος σημασίαν, κἂν ἐφαρμόζει ἡ τοιαύτη κλῆσις τῇ ἁγίᾳ τ. *ib.*(129C); εἰ...θεὸς ὄνομα οὐσίας σημαντικόν ἐστι, μίαν οὐσίαν ὁμολογοῦντες τῆς ἁγίας τ., ἕνα θεὸν εἰκότως δοξάζομεν id.*comm.not.*(M.45.176A); δυναμένης μὲν ἑκάστης θείας ὑποστάσεως ἀπροσδεῶς πάντα ποιῆσαι τελείως, ἵνα δὲ δειχθῇ τὸ συμπρακτικὸν καὶ ἀπαράλλακτον τῆς τε οὐσίας αὐτῶν...καὶ δόξης..., διὰ τοῦτο κοινῇ παρὰ τῆς ἁγίας τ. τῆς κτίσεως πληρωθείσης Didym.*Trin.*2.1(M.39.452A); ὠνόμασας υἱόν, συμπεριείληφας τῇ διανοίᾳ τὴν τ.· ἔσχες πνεῦμα ἅγιον, κατηξίωσαι τῆς δυνάμεως τῆς πατρῴας καὶ τοῦ υἱοῦ τοῦ θεοῦ· ἐδόξασας τὸν πατέρα, ἐσήμανας τὸν υἱὸν καὶ τὸ ἅγιον πνεῦμα Epiph.*anc.*10(p.18.13; M.43.36A); ὦ τ. ἁγία ἀριθμουμένη, τ. ἐν ἑνὶ ὀνόματι ἀριθμουμένη· οὐ γὰρ λέγεται ἑνὰς καὶ δυάς, οὐδὲ μονὰς καὶ μονάς, ἀλλὰ μονὰς ἐν τ. καὶ τ. ἐν μονάδι, μονοειδῶς μονωνύμως εἷς θεός, πατὴρ ἐν υἱῷ, υἱὸς ἐν πατρὶ σὺν ἁγίῳ πνεύματι *ib.*22(p.31.20; 57D); πατέρα...καὶ υἱὸν καὶ πνεῦμα ἅγιον λέγων, οὐκ ἀφ' ὧν ἐστιν ἀδιακρίτως ἡ πᾶσα τῆς θεότητος φύσις ποιεῖται τὴν δήλωσιν, ἀλλ' ἐξ ὧν τὸ τῆς ἁγίας τ. διαγινώσκεται ταυτὸν εἰς οὐσίαν ἐν ὑποστάσεσιν ἰδικαῖς Cyr.*dial.Trin.*2(5^1.422D); μίαν τὴν τῆς τ. οὐσίαν ὁμολογῶν καὶ τρεῖς ὑποστάσεις διαρρήδην κηρύσσει Thdt.*h.e.*5.3.10(3.1018); πατὴρ καὶ υἱὸς καὶ ἅγιον πνεῦμα... τ. ἐν μονάδι γινωσκομένη, καὶ μονὰς ἐν τ. προσκυνουμένη Procl.CP *annunt.*2(M.85.432A); τὴν θεαρχίαν ὁρῶμεν ἱερῶς ὑμνουμένην, ὡς μονάδα μὲν...διὰ τὴν ἁπλότητα...ὡς τ. δέ, διὰ τὴν τρισυπόστατον τῆς ὑπερουσίου γονιμότητος ἔκφανσιν, ἐξ ἧς πᾶσα πατριὰ ἐν οὐρανῷ καὶ ἐπὶ γῆς ἐστι καὶ ὀνομάζεται Dion.Ar.*d.n.*1.4(M.3.592A); εἷς θεὸς ὅτι μία θεότης· μονὰς ἄναρχος καὶ ἁπλῆ...ἡ αὐτὴ μονὰς καὶ τ.· ὅλη μονὰς ἡ αὐτὴ καὶ ὅλη τ. ἡ αὐτή· μονὰς ὅλη κατὰ τὴν οὐσίαν ἡ αὐτὴ καὶ τ. ὅλη κατὰ τὰς ὑποστάσεις ἡ αὐτή Max.*cap.theol.*2.1(M.90.1125A); μονὰς ἀσύγχυτος καὶ τ. ἀδιαίρετος id.*cap.*1.4(M.90.1180A); ταὐτόν...ἐστιν ὑπερβαθῆναι δυάδα καὶ μὴ στῆναι μέχρι δυάδος καὶ πάλιν ὁρισθῆναι τ. καὶ μέχρι τριάδος στῆναι τῆς μονάδος τὴν κίνησιν id.*ambig.*(M.91.1036A); μονὰς...ἀληθῶς ἡ μονάς· οὐ γάρ ἐστιν ἀρχὴ τῶν μετ' αὐτὴν κατὰ διαστολῆς συστολήν...ἀλλ' ἐνυπόστατος ὀντότης ὁμοουσίου τ. καὶ τ. ἀληθῶς ἡ τ., οὐκ ἀριθμῷ λυομένῳ...ἀλλ' ἐνούσιος ὕπαρξις τρισυποστάτου μονάδος· μονὰς γὰρ ἀληθῶς ἡ τ. ὅτι οὕτως ἐστί. καὶ τ. ἀληθῶς ἡ μονὰς ὅτι οὕτως ὑφέστηκεν· ἐπειδὴ καὶ μία θεότης, οὖσά τε μοναδικῶς καὶ ὑφισταμένη τριαδικῶς *ib.*(1036B,C); τ. ἐστιν ἡ μονὰς ὡς ἐν τελείοις οὖσα τελεία ταῖς ὑποστάσεσιν ἤγουν τῷ τῆς ὑπάρξεως τρόπῳ· καὶ μονάς ἐστιν ἡ τ. ἀληθῶς τῷ τῆς οὐσίας...λόγῳ *ib.*(1400D); μονὰς κατ' οὐσίαν ἐστὶν ἡ πάνσεπτος καὶ προσκυνητὴ καὶ πανεύφημος τ. τῶν ὑποστάσεων. μονὰς γὰρ ἐν τ. καὶ ἐν μονάδι τ. ἐστιν ὁ θεὸς ἡμῶν id.*qu.Thal.*28(M.90.361D); ἡ μονὰς μέχρι τ. ... κινουμένη μένει μονὰς καὶ ἡ τ. μέχρι μονάδος συναγομένη μένει τ.· ὃ καὶ παράδοξον Thal.*cent.*4.93(M.91.1468D); ὥσπερ δὲ μίαν θεότητα τῆς ἁγίας τ. λέγουσιν, οὕτως καὶ τρεῖς τὰς ὑποστάσεις τῆς μιᾶς θεότητος δοξάζουσιν *ib.*4.85(1468A); τρισυπόστατον τὴν μίαν τῆς θεότητος οὐσίαν προσκυνοῦμεν καὶ ὁμοούσιον τὴν ἁγίαν τ. θεολογοῦμεν *ib.*2.98(1448A); τ. ἀχώριστον ἐν μονάδι φύσεως Andr.Cr.*can.Laz.*1(M.97.1388B); ὦ μονὰς ἁγία τ., ἡ μία θεότης· καὶ τ. μονάς, ὁ θεός, τρισυπόστατε φύσις, ἡ ὁμότιμος καὶ ἀμέριστος δόξα id.*triod.*2.9(M.97.1409A); ὡρισμένον...ἀριθμὸν οὐκ ἔστιν εἰπεῖν ἐπὶ τῆς ἀορίστου θεότητος, εἰ μὴ μονάδα μὲν οὐσίας, τ. δὲ ὑποστάσεων Jo.D.*trisag.*5(M.95.32C); ὥσπερ...τὴν τ. ἀδύνατον λέγειν μίαν ὑπόστασιν, οὕτως οὐδεμίαν τῶν ὑποστάσεων τ. λέγειν ὅσιον *ib.*6(37A); λέγεται...ὁ θεὸς νοῦς καὶ λόγος καὶ πνεῦμα...καὶ ταῦτα κοινῶς ἐπὶ πάσης λέγεται τῆς θεότητος...καὶ ἐφ' ἑκάστης τῶν τῆς ἁγίας τ. ὑποστάσεων ὁμοίως καὶ ὡσαύτως καὶ ἀπαραλείπτως id.*f.o.*1.12(M.94.848C); ἑνὶ θεῷ προσκυνῶ...ἀλλὰ καὶ τριάδι λατρεύω ὑποστάσεων, θεῷ πατρὶ καὶ θεῷ υἱῷ σεσαρκωμένῳ καὶ θεῷ ἁγίῳ πνεύματι, ἑνὶ θεῷ id. *imag.*1.4(M.94.1236B); ἐπὶ...τῆς ἁγίας καὶ ὑπερυμνήτου τ. μίαν οὐσίαν καὶ φύσιν θεότητος, τρεῖς δὲ τελείας τὰς ὑποστάσεις σέβομεν id.*Jacob.*78(M.94.1473D); ἐπὶ...τῆς ἁγίας καὶ ὑπερουσίου θεότητος ἤτοι τῆς μοναρχικῆς καὶ ὁμοουσίου τ. *ib.*2(1437A); **b.** partic. ref. essential unity τίς οὕτω τολμηρὸς ὡς εἰπεῖν ἀνόμοιον καὶ ἑτεροφυῆ τὴν τ. πρὸς ἑαυτήν; Ath.*ep.Serap.*1.20(M.26.577A); τὸ ἀδιαίρετον καὶ ὁμοφυὲς... τῆς ἁγίας τ. *ib.*1.17(572B); id.*hom.in Mt.*11:27(M.25.220A); id.*ep. Serap.*4.12(652C), v. ἀδιαίρετος; τοιαύτης...συστοιχίας καὶ ἑνότητος τῆς ἐν τῇ ἁγίᾳ τ. οὔσης, τίς ἂν διέλοι ἢ τὸν υἱὸν ἀπὸ τοῦ πατρὸς ἢ τὸ πνεῦμα ἀπὸ τοῦ υἱοῦ; *ib.*1.20(576D); ἡ...τ. ἡνωμένη πρὸς ἑαυτήν ἐστι *ib.*1.14(565A); ἐπὶ τῆς τ. ... ἄλλος καὶ ἄλλος, ἵνα μὴ τὰς ὑποστάσεις συγχέωμεν· οὐκ ἄλλο δὲ καὶ ἄλλο· ἓν γὰρ τὰ τρία καὶ ταυτὸν τῇ θεότητι Gr.Naz.*ep.*101(M.37.180B); οὔτε τὰς ὑποστάσεις συγχέουσιν, οὔτε ἐξ ἑτερογενῶν καὶ ἀνομοίων τὴν ἁγίαν τ. συντίθενται Gr.Nyss.*ep.*5(M.46.1032D); εἰ...παρήλλακτο...ἐπὶ τῆς ἁγίας τ. ἡ φύσις, ἀκολούθως εἰς πλῆθος θεῶν ὁ ἀριθμὸς ἐπλατύνετο id.*tres dii*(M.45.133A); οὐκ ἠλλοτριωμένη ἡ τ. τῆς ἑνότητος καὶ τῆς ταυτότητος· τιμᾶται δὲ ὁ πατὴρ καθὸ πατήρ ἐστι, τιμᾶται ὁ υἱὸς καθὸ υἱός ἐστι· τιμᾶται τὸ πνεῦμα τὸ ἅγιον καθὸ πνεῦμα...θεοῦ Epiph.*anc.*10(p.18.17; M.43.36B); οὐδεμία στάσις ἢ διχονοία χωρήσει ποτὲ ἐν τῇ μιᾷ καὶ ἀχράντῳ τ. Cyr.*thes.*8(5^1.63E); τὴν...τῆς ἁγίας τ. ἑνότητα καὶ συνήθη στάσιν ἀπαράλλακτον *ib.*29(255C); ἐπὶ τῆς ἑνώσεως τῆς θείας, ἤτοι τῆς ὑπερουσιότητος, ἡνωμένον μὲν ἐστι τῇ ἐναρχικῇ τ. καὶ κοινὸν ἡ ὑπερούσιος ὕπαρξις, ἡ ὑπέρθεος θεότης, ἡ ὑπεράγαθος ἀγαθότης, ἁπάντων ἐπέκεινα τῆς ἐπέκεινα πάντων ὅλης ἰδιότητος ταυτότης Dion.Ar.*d.n.*2.4(M.3.641A); μοναρχίαν πρεσβεύομεν...ἣν ὁμότιμος φύσει τ., πατὴρ καὶ υἱὸς καὶ πνεῦμα συνίστησιν ἅγιον, ὧν πλοῦτος ἡ συμφυΐα καὶ τὸ ἓν ἔξαλμα τῆς λαμπρότητος Max.*ambig.*(M.91.1036A); ἀδιαίρετον...τὴν μίαν θεότητα τῆς τ. φυλάττουσι καὶ ἀσυγχύτους τὰς τρεῖς ὑποστάσεις τῆς μιᾶς θεότητος διατηροῦσι Thal.*cent.*4.95(M.91.1469A); μονάδα ἐν τ. καὶ τ. ἐν μονάδι ὁμολογοῦμεν, ὡς διαιρουμένην ἀδιαιρέτως καὶ συναπτομένην διῃρημένως *ib.*4.98(1469B); against materialistic and other false conceptions ὅταν...συνάψωμεν τὴν τ., μὴ ὡς ἑνὸς πράγματος ἀδιαιρέτου μέρη φαντάζου τὰ τρία...ἀλλὰ τριῶν ἀσωμάτων τελείων ἀχώριστον δέχου τὴν συνουσίαν Bas.*hom.*24.5(2.193E; M.31.609C); εἰ μερικὰς φύσεις ἐπὶ τῆς ἁγίας τ. ὁμολογεῖτε, ἑτερούσιον ταύτην δοξάζετε...εἰ δὲ ἑκάστῃ τῶν τῆς ἁγίας τ. θεαρχικῶν ὑποστάσεων ἰδιάζουσαν δῶτε οὐσίαν, ὁμοουσίους δὲ ταύτας κατὰ τὴν κοινὴν οὐσίαν ὁμολογήσετε· ταὐτὸν δὲ οὐσία καὶ ὑπόστασις, ἔσται...τετρὰς ὑποστάσεων Jo.D.*Jacob.*10(M.94.1440A); **c.** as simple, Max.*cap.theol.*2.1(M.90.1125A) cit. s. 2.a supra; id.*ambig.*(M.91.1196B); Andr.Cr.*can.mag.*(M.97.1345A); *ib.*195(p.153; 1361A); σέ, τ., δοξάζομεν...ἁπλῆ οὐσία *ib.*174(p.152; 1357B); τ. ἁπλῆ, ἀδιαίρετε *ib.*236(p.154; 1373A); **d.** ref. Godhead as transcending unity and trinity μονὰς ὑμνουμένη καὶ τ., ἡ...θεότης, οὐκ ἔστιν οὐδὲ μονάς, οὐδὲ τ., ἡ πρὸς ἡμῶν ἢ ἄλλου τινὸς τῶν ὄντων διεγνωσμένη, ἀλλ' ἵνα καὶ τὸ ὑπερηνωμένον αὐτῆς καὶ τὸ θεογόνον ἀληθῶς ὑμνήσωμεν, τῇ τριαδικῇ καὶ ἑνιαίᾳ θεωνυμίᾳ τὴν ὑπερώνυμον [sc. θεαρχίαν] ὀνομάζομεν...οὐδεμία δὲ μονὰς ἢ τ., οὐδὲ ἀριθμὸς...ἐξάγει τὴν ὑπὲρ πάντα νοῦν...κρυφιότητα τῆς...ὑπερθεότητος Dion.Ar.*d.n.*13.3(980D); **e.** as super-essential, *ib.*5.8(821C); id.*myst.*1.1(M.3.997A); beyond beginning, Andr.Cr.*can.mag.*(M.97.1345D); **f.** uncreated ἡ ἁγία τ. ... οὐδὲν ἔχει ἐν ἑαυτῇ τῶν γενητῶν Ath.*ep.Serap.*1.30(M.26.600A); οὐκ ἔστι γενητὴ ἡ τ. id.*Ar.*1.18(M.26.48C); *ib.*1.58(133B); ἄκτιστος...πέφηνε μόνη ἡ ἁγία τ. τῆς θεότητος ‡Ath.*Apoll.*1.3(M.26.1097A); οὐδὲν...ὅλως τῆς θείας...τ. κτιστόν Bas.*ep.*140.2(3.233E; M.32.589A); Gr.Naz.*or.*40.42(M.36.420A); τῆς μὲν ἀκτίστου φύσεως τὴν ἁγίαν τ. εἶναι διωρισάμεθα, τῆς δὲ κτιστῆς πάντα, ὅσα μετ' ἐκείνην λέγεταί τε καὶ ἔστι Gr.Nyss.*Eun.*1(1 p.108.4; M.45.341C); id.*ep.*5(M.46.1032C); οὐδὲν ἐν τῇ τ. κτιστὸν καὶ ὑπὸ αἰτίαν ἐμπῖπτον ἐστίν· οὐ γὰρ ἐξ οὐκ ὄντων τί ἐστιν ἐν τῇ τ. ... διὸ ἀναιτία οὖσα τῆς τοιαύτης αἰτίας ἡ τ., μόνην ἑαυτὴν...ἐδίδαξε προσκυνεῖσθαι Epiph.*haer.*76.44(p.398.14; M.42.609D); αἰτία...ἐστιν ἡ τ. τῶν ἁπάντων,...μηδὲν ἐν αὐτῇ κτιστὸν ...γινώσκουσα *ib.*(p.398.32; 612B); Evagr.Pont.*sent.mon.*134(p.164); οὐδὲν ἐν τῇ τ. κτιστὸν καὶ πρότερον οὐχ ὑπάρχον,...ἀλλ' ἅμα καὶ συνάμα μονὰς καὶ τ. καὶ ἦν καὶ ἔσται εἰς τοὺς αἰῶνας Eulog.*fr.Trin.*2.1(p.364); Andr.Cr.*can.BMV* 7(M.97.1325D); **g.** as perfect, Ath.*Ar.*1.18(M.26.49B); id.*ep.Serap.*1.28(M.26.596A); Gr.Naz.*or.*23.8(M.35.1160C) cit. s. δυάς; *ib.*26.19(1252C); Max.*ambig.*(M.91.1261A); **h.** as unchangeable, Ath.*Ar.*1.18(M.26.49B); ἡ ἁγία τ. ἀναλλοίωτος διαμένει ἐν μιᾷ θεότητι γινωσκομένη id.*ep.Serap.*4.6(M.26.648A); Gr.Nyss.*comm.not.*(M.45.180A); cf.Oecum.*Apoc.*11:17(p.133); **i.** ref. principle of causation in Godhead τὴν τοιαύτην διαφορὰν ἐπὶ τῆς ἁγίας τ. λέγοντες, ὡς τὸ μὲν αἴτιον, τὸ δὲ ἐξ αἰτίου εἶναι πιστεύειν, οὐκέτ' ἂν ἐν τῷ κοινῷ τῆς φύσεως τὸν τῶν ὑποστάσεων λόγον συντίκτειν αἰτιαθείημεν Gr.Nyss.*tres dii*(M.45.133D); τὰς ὑποστάσεις τῆς ἁγίας τ. ὁ τοῦ αἰτίου διακρίνει λόγος, τὸ μὲν ἀναιτίως εἶναι, τὸ δὲ ἐκ τοῦ αἰτίου πρεσβεύων *ib.*(136A); τὰ τοῦ ἀνθρώπου πρόσωπα πάντα οὐκ ἀπὸ τοῦ αὐτοῦ προσώπου κατὰ τὸ προσεχὲς ἔχει τὸ εἶναι...ἐπὶ δὲ τῆς ἁγίας τ. οὐχ οὕτως. ἓν γὰρ καὶ τὸ αὐτὸ πρόσωπον τοῦ πατρός, ἐξ οὗ ὁ υἱὸς γεννᾶται καὶ τὸ πνεῦμα τὸ ἅγιον ἐκπορεύεται. διὸ καὶ κυρίως τὸν ἕνα αἴτιον ὄντα τῶν αὐτοῦ αἰτιατῶν, ἕνα θεόν φαμεν id.*comm.not.*(M.45.180C); ἕνα...θεόν, τὴν ἁγίαν τ., εἰς ἓν αἴτιον υἱοῦ καὶ πνεύματος ἀναφερομένων Jo.D.*f.o.*1.8(M.94.829A); **j.** ref. attributes and external operation, in gen. μιᾶς οὔσης τῆς ὑπὲρ νοῦν καὶ λόγον... θεότητος τῆς ἁγίας τ., τὰ περὶ αὐτὴν θεωρούμενα τὰ προειρημένα εἶναι [sc. ἀγαθότητα, τὸ ἄναρχον, κτλ.] Thal.*cent.*4.84(M.91.1468A); ref. single glory of Trin., Ath.*Ar.*1.18(M.26.48C); Gr.Nyss.*diff.ess.*4(M.32.332B); operation μία...ἡ τῆς τ. ἐνέργεια Ath.*ep.Serap.*1.31(M.26.600C); Gr.Nyss.*tres dii*(M.45.124A); Max.*ambig.*(M.91.1396A);

Euchol.(p.368); grace *ὡς μία τῆς τ. ἡ χάρις, οὕτως ἀδιαίρετος ἡ τ.* Ath.*ep.Serap.*3.6(633B); *ib.*1.30(600C); Gr.Naz.*or.*28.31(p.71.17; M. 36.72C); life, Gr.Nyss.*ep.*5(M.46.1032C); providence, id.*tres dii*(M. 45.128D); ‡Gr.Nyss.*imag.*(M.44.1336C); Dion.Ar.*d.n.*3.1(M.3.689B); Max.*qu.Thal.*28(M.90.364B); of Trin. as *θεὸς παντοκράτωρ* *Lit.Jac.* (p.162.1); **k.** ref. Son's generation *πρώτη παρθένος ἐστὶν ἁγνὴ τ.* Gr. Naz.*carm.*1.2.1.20(M.37.523A); **l.** summary of theol. epithets of Trin., Eulog.*fr.Trin.*2.1(p.364); **3.** ref. heret. teaching; **a.** Sabellian *πταίσαντες...περὶ τὴν ὀρθόδοξον θρησκείαν...περὶ ἕνα τῶν ἀριθμῶν τῆς τ. διεσφαλμένοι, ὅτε μὲν τὸν τοῦ πατρός...ὅτε δὲ τὸν τοῦ υἱοῦ...ὅτε δὲ περὶ τὸν τοῦ πνεύματος* Meth.*symp.*8.10(p.93.2; M.18.153B); *εἰ...ἡ μονὰς πλατυνθεῖσα γέγονε τ., ἡ δὲ μονάς ἐστιν ὁ πατήρ, τ. δὲ πατήρ, υἱὸς καὶ ἅγιον πνεῦμα, πρῶτον μὲν...πάθος ὑπέμεινε,...ἔπειτα εἰ...ἡ μονὰς ἐπλατύνθη εἰς τ., τ. δέ ἐστι πατὴρ καὶ υἱὸς καὶ ἅγιον πνεῦμα, ὁ αὐτὸς ἄρα πατὴρ γέγονε καὶ υἱὸς καὶ πνεῦμα κατὰ Σαβέλλιον* ‡Ath. *Ar.*4.13(p.57.8; M.26.485A); *τ. μὲν πλατυνθεῖσα οὐκ ἔτι μονάς ἐστι· μονὰς δὲ οὖσα οὔπω ἦν τ.* *ib.*(p.57.18; M.l.c.); *εἰ ὁ πατὴρ ἐπλατύνθη εἰς τ., ἡ τ. πάλιν ἐστὶν ὁ πατὴρ μόνος* *ib.*4.14(p.58.6; 485B); *ἀλλότριοι ...οἱ τὴν τ. μὴ κατὰ ἀλήθειαν ὁμολογοῦντες, ἀλλ' ἐν μονάδι τὸ τριπλοῦν...κατὰ σύνθεσιν φανταζόμενοι* Apoll.*fid.sec.pt.*1(p.167.18; M.10.1105B); *ib.*13(p.171.21; 1109C); *θεὸν ἕνα φαμὲν τὴν τ., ἀλλ' οὐχ ὡς ἐκ συνθέσεως τριῶν ἕνα εἰδότες...ἀλλ' ὡς ὅπερ ἐστὶν ὁ πατὴρ ἀρχικῶς...τοῦτο ὄντα τὸν υἱόν* *ib.*18(p.173.13; 1112B); *οὗτος* [sc. Sabellius]*...πρόσωπον ἐν τῇ τ. φησὶ τριώνυμον* *Hymn.*(*KlT* 52/53 p.27); Marcellan *εἰ...διὰ τὴν ἐνανθρώπησιν ἐπλατύνθη καὶ γέγονε τότε τ., ἄρα πρὸ τῆς ἐνανθρωπήσεως οὔπω ἦν τ.* ‡Ath.*Ar.*4.14(p.59.1; M. 26.488A); **b.** Arian, cf.Ar.*Thal.fr.*2 ap.Ath.*syn.*15(p.242.25; M.26. 708A) cit. s. B.1 supra; *οἱ τὰ Ἀρείου φρονοῦντες...οὐ δύνανται νοεῖν, οὐδὲ πιστεύειν περὶ τῆς ἀδιαιρέτου καὶ ἁγίας τ.* Ath.*ep.Serap.*1.17(M. 26.572A); *μὴ δυνάμενοι νοεῖν, πῶς ἀδιαίρετός ἐστιν ἡ ἁγία τ., ποιοῦσι ...ἓν τὸν υἱὸν μετὰ τῆς κτίσεως* *ib.*(572B); *εἰ...οὐκ ἀϊδίως σύνεστιν ὁ λόγος τῷ πατρί, οὐκ ἔστιν ἡ τ. ἀΐδιος· ἀλλὰ μονὰς μὲν ἦν πρότερον, ἐκ προσθήκης δὲ γέγονεν ὕστερον τ.* id.*Ar.*1.17(M.26.48A); *εἰ...ὁ υἱὸς... ἐξ οὐκ ὄντων γέγονεν, ἐξ οὐκ ὄντων συνίσταται τ. καὶ ἦν ποτε ὅτε οὐκ ἦν τ., ἀλλὰ μονάς· καὶ ποτὲ μὲν ἐλλειπὴς τ., ποτὲ δὲ πλήρης...ἀνόμοιος ἑαυτῆς ἡ τ. εὑρίσκεται...τοῦτο δὲ οὐδὲν ἕτερόν ἐστιν εἰπεῖν ἢ γενητὴν τὴν τῆς τ. σύστασιν* *ib.*(48B); *οὐκ αἰδεῖσθαι τὰ δοῦλα συνεξισάζοντες τῇ εὐγενείᾳ τῆς τ.* *ib.*1.18(49A); *Ἑλλήνων...ἴδια ταῦτα, ὥστε γενητὴν εἰσάγειν τ.* *ib.*(49B); *ἢ...ἐν φυσικῇ δοξῇ...τὴν ὅλην τ. νοητέον ἢ μονάδα καὶ οὐκέτι τ. λέγειν ἀναγκασθησόμεθα* Apoll.*fid.sec.pt.*9(p.170.11; M. 10.1108C); *δεῖ...ὥσπερ μίαν τὴν δόξαν ὁμολογοῦμεν, οὕτως καὶ μίαν τὴν οὐσίαν ἤτοι θεότητα καὶ μίαν τὴν ἀϊδιότητα τῆς τ. ὁμολογεῖν* *ib.*10 (p.170.28; 1109A); *τοὺς κοινωνοῦντας τοῖς ἐκβάλλουσι τὸ ὁμοούσιον... καί τι ἐκ τῆς τ. κτιστὸν λέγουσι...ἀλλοτρίους ἡγούμεθα* *ib.*34(p.180. 22; 1117C); Gr.Naz.*or.*31.10(p.157.3; M.36.144B); Gr.Nyss.*Eun.*10(2 p.234.29; M.45.836D); Cyr.*dial.Trin.*(5^1.422C); Justn.*conf.anath.*1; **c.** denial by Tropici and Pneumatomachoi of divinity of H. Ghost *τὸ πνεῦμα κατάγοντες εἰς τοὺς ἀγγέλους, εἰς τὴν τ. συντάσσοντες. εἰ γὰρ μετὰ πατέρα καὶ υἱὸν...οἱ ἄγγελοι, δηλονότι τῆς τ. εἰσὶν οἱ ἄγγελοι* Ath.*ep.Serap.*1.10(M.26.557A); *διαιροῦντες ἀπὸ τοῦ λόγου τὸ πνεῦμα οὐκέτι μίαν ἐν τ. θεότητα σώζουσι, σχίζοντες αὐτήν* *ib.*1.2(533A); *οὐκέτι ἓν δείκνυσι τὴν τ., ἀλλὰ ἐκ δύο καὶ διαφόρων φύσεων συγκειμένην αὐτήν, διὰ τὸ ἑτεροούσιον τοῦ πνεύματος* *ib.*; *εἰ τ. ἐστιν...πῶς τοῖς μετὰ τὴν τ. κτίσμασι συντάττουσι τὸ τῆς τ. πνεῦμα; τοῦτο γάρ ἐστι... διαιρεῖν καὶ διαλύειν τὴν τ.* *ib.*(533B); *ib.*1.21(580C); *κτίσμα...εἰ ἦν τὸ πνεῦμα, οὐκ ἂν συνέταξεν αὐτὸ τῷ πατρί, ἵνα μὴ ᾖ ἀνόμοιος ἑαυτῇ ἡ τ.* *ib.*3.6(636A); *ib.*1.29(596C) cit. s. δυάς; *ἔδει...καθ' ὑμᾶς ἅπαξ ἀγγέλου καὶ κτίσματος ὄντος τοῦ πνεύματος καὶ συντασσομένου εἰς τ., μὴ ἕνα, ἀλλὰ πάντας τοὺς κτισθέντας ἀγγέλους συντάσσεσθαι ταύτῃ· καὶ μηκέτι τ., ἀλλὰ πληθύν τινα θεότητος ἀναρίθμητον εἶναι* *ib.*(597B); *μὴ διαιρείτωσαν τὴν τ., ἵνα μὴ διαιρεθῶσιν ἀπὸ τῆς ζωῆς, μηδὲ τοῖς κτίσμασι συναριθμείτωσαν τὸ πνεῦμα τὸ ἅγιον* *ib.*1.33(608B); *ἐκ μεταβολῆς καὶ προκοπῆς λέγουσι συνίστασθαι τὴν τ. καὶ δυάδα μὲν εἶναι, ἐκδέχεσθαι δὲ κτίσματος γένεσιν ἵνα μετὰ πατρὸς καὶ υἱοῦ συνταχθῇ καὶ γένηται ἡ τ.* *ib.*3.7(636B); *ἀρνεῖται...τὴν τῆς ἁγιωσύνης πηγήν, τὸ πνεῦμα τὸ ἅγιον, ὁ ἀφαιρῶν αὐτοῦ τὸ ἁγιάζειν...καὶ τὸ ἅγιον βάπτισμα ἀθετεῖ καὶ οὐκέτι τ. ὁμολογήσει τὴν ἁγίαν καὶ σεβάσμιον* Apoll.*fid.sec.pt.*8(p.170.10; M.10.1108C); *τὸ ἅγιον πνεῦμα...δι' ἑνὸς υἱοῦ τῷ ἑνὶ πατρὶ συναπτόμενον καὶ δι' ἑαυτοῦ συμπληροῦν τὴν πολυύμνητον καὶ μακαρίαν τ.* Bas.*Spir.*45(3.38C; M.32.152A); *οὔτε...ἡ τ. μένει τ. ἀφαιρουμένου τοῦ πνεύματος* id.*hom.*24.5(2.194B; M.31.612A); Gr.Naz.*or.*31.3(p.147.14; M.36.136B); Cyr.*thes.*34(5^1.358B); id.*dial.Trin.*3(5^1. 465D); **d.** ref. Christol. heresies *Οὐαλεντῖνος...κοινὸν τῆς τ. τὸ πάθος λέγει, τῆς θεότητος μέρος τὴν σάρκα φανταζόμενος* ‡Ath.*Apoll.*2.3(M. 26.1136C); *ἐρυθριάσουσι δὲ μεγάλως οἱ ὅλως ἐνθυμηθέντες δύνασθαι ἀντὶ τῆς τ. γενέσθαι τετράδα, εἰ λέγοιτο ἐκ Μαρίας εἶναι τὸ σῶμα. ὁμοούσιον γὰρ ἐὰν εἴπωμεν, φασί, τὸ σῶμα τῷ λόγῳ, μένει ἡ τ. τ., οὐδὲν ξένον εἰς αὐτὴν ἐπιφερομένου τοῦ λόγου· ἐὰν δὲ ἀνθρώπινον εἴπωμεν τὸ ἐκ Μαρίας σῶμα, ἀνάγκη, ξένου ὄντος κατ' οὐσίαν τοῦ σώματος, καὶ ὄντος ἐν αὐτῷ τοῦ λόγου, τετρὰς ἀντὶ τ. γίνεται διὰ τὴν τοῦ σώματος προσθήκην* Ath.*ep.Epict.*8(p.13.15; M.26.1064B); cf.*ib.*2(p.5.5; 1053A,B); Inc. involves no addition to Trin., v. *προσθήκη*; *τί ἔτι ἡμᾶς μέμφεσθε, ὡς τετράδα ἀντὶ τ. λέγοντας, αὐτοὶ τετράδα ἀντὶ τ. ... ὁμολογοῦντες, λέγοντες ὁμοούσιον εἶναι τῇ τ. τὴν σάρκα;* ‡Ath.*Apoll.* 1.12(1113C); three natures not introduced by Inc. (against monophysites) *δείξατε ἡμῖν τινα τῶν ἁγίων πατέρων τρεῖς φύσεις ἢ οὐσίας ἐπὶ τῆς ἁγίας τ. εἰπόντα καὶ ἡμεῖς σιγήσομεν* Jo.D.*Jacob.*76(M.94. 1472D); *κηρύττομεν...θεὸν...σαρκωθέντα...ἕνα Χριστόν, ἕνα υἱὸν...μίαν ὑπόστασιν, τὸν αὐτὸν θεὸν καὶ ἄνθρωπον, οὐχ ἕτερον ἐν τῇ τ. παρεισάγοντα πρόσωπον* *ib.*84(1484B); ref. monophysite addition to Trisagion *ἢ...τῇ τ. τὸ τῆς σταυρώσεως προσάγει πάθος ἢ τέταρτον τῇ τ. παρεισάγει πρόσωπον* id.*rect.sent.*5(M.94.1429D); v. *τρισάγιος*; **4.** ref. Inc. *εἴτε οὖν Χριστὸν εἴποι τις, εἴτε μυστήριον τοῦ Χριστοῦ, τούτου τὴν πρόγνωσιν μόνη κατ' οὐσίαν ἔχει ἡ ἁγία τ., πατὴρ καὶ υἱὸς καὶ ἅγιον πνεῦμα* Max.*qu.Thal.*60(M.90.624C); Christ as one of Trin. *εἴ τις... οὐχ ὁμολογεῖ τὴν ἕνωσιν τοῦ...λόγου πρὸς σάρκα...γεγενῆσθαι...καὶ διὰ τοῦτο μίαν αὐτοῦ τὴν ὑπόστασιν, ὅ ἐστιν ὁ κύριος Ἰησοῦς Χριστός, εἷς τῆς ἁγίας τ. ... ἀ. ἔ.* CCP(553)*anath.*4; *εἴ τις οὐχ ὁμολογεῖ τὸν ἐσταυρωμένον σαρκὶ κύριον ἡμῶν...εἶναι...ἕνα τῆς ἁγίας τ. ... ἀ. ἔ.* *ib.* 10; Max.*ambig.*(M.91.1268C); id.*qu.Thal.*60(M.90.624C); Thal.*cent.* 4.73(M.91.1465B); *ὡς τριάδος ἕνα σε, Χριστέ, δοξάζομεν* Andr.Cr.*can. Ann.*7(M.97.1313D); id.*can.Laz.*3(M.97.1389C); *Lit.Marc.*(Brightman p.117.1); *τὸν ἕνα τῆς ἁγίας τ., τὸν μονογενῆ υἱὸν τοῦ θεοῦ καὶ μετὰ σάρκωσιν ἕνα Χριστὸν...ὀρθοδόξως κηρύξατε* Jo.D.*Jacob.*88(M.94. 1485C); id.*trisag.*17(M.95.49B); **5.** ref. BMV *ἐν σοὶ τὸ τῆς τ. μυστήριον ὑμνεῖται...πατὴρ γὰρ ηὐδόκησε καὶ ὁ λόγος ἐσκήνωσεν ἐν ἡμῖν καὶ θεῖον πνεῦμα ἐπεσκίασεν* Andr.Cr.*can.BMV* 6(M.97.1324C); *ib.*9 (1329A); id.*can.mag.*237(p.154; M.97.1373A); **6.** ref. angels *ἄγγελοι καὶ πᾶσα φύσις, ἡ ἄνω μετὰ τὴν τ. ... πρὸς τὸ καλὸν παγιώτεροι τῇ πρὸς τὸ ἄκρον καλὸν ἐγγύτητι* Gr.Naz.*or.*31.15(p.164.7; M.36.149B); *τὸ εἰρηναῖον καὶ ἀστασίαστον, τὸ ἓν εἶναι λαβόντες παρὰ τῆς ἐπαινετῆς καὶ ἁγίας τ., παρ' ἧς καὶ τὴν ἔλλαμψιν* *ib.*6.13(M.35.740A); *αἱ πανάγιαι καὶ πρεσβύταται δυνάμεις ὄντως οὖσαι καὶ οἷον ἐν προθύροις τῆς ὑπερουσίου τ. ἱδρυμέναι, πρὸς αὐτῆς καὶ ἐν αὐτῇ καὶ τὸ εἶναι καὶ τὸ θεοειδῶς εἶναι ἔχουσι* Dion.Ar.*d.n.*5.8(M.3.821C); *ὦ τ. ὑπερούσιε...σε ὑμνεῖ...πληθὺς ἀγγέλων* Andr.Cr.*can.BMV* 8(M.97.1328B); **7.** ref. spiritual life of Christians; **a.** knowledge of Trin.; as object of hope, Or.*Ps.*70:14 (p.91); *κρείσσων γνῶσις τ. ὑπὲρ γνῶσιν ἀσωμάτων καὶ θεωρία αὐτῆς ὑπὲρ λόγους πάντων τῶν αἰώνων* Evagr.Pont.*sent.mon.*110(p.162); *γνῶσις ἀσωμάτων ἐπαίρει τὸν νοῦν καὶ τῇ ἁγίᾳ τ. παρίστησιν αὐτόν* *ib.* 136(p.165); *φυσικὴν θεωρίαν αἰνίττεται, ἐν ᾗ καὶ ὁ περὶ τῆς ἁγίας τ. ἐγκέκραται λόγος, εἴπερ ἐκ καλλονῆς κτισμάτων ἀναλόγως ὁ γενεσιουργὸς θεωρεῖται* id.*ep.*12(M.32.265B); *λόγον ἐπέχει...ἐπισκόπου...ὁ τῷ ἁγίῳ μύρῳ τελειῶν τῆς γνώσεως τῆς...ἁγίας τ.* Max.*carit.*2.21(M.90. 992A); *μετὰ τοῦ θεοῦ ἐστιν ὁ τὴν ἁγίαν γινώσκων τ.* *ib.*2.98(1016D); *τῆς μὲν τῶν σωμάτων καὶ ἀσωμάτων γνώσεως δεκτικὴ κατὰ φύσιν ἐστὶν ἡ τοῦ νοῦ δύναμις· τῆς δὲ τῆς ἁγίας τ. κατὰ μόνην τὴν χάριν δέχεται τὰς ἐμφάσεις* id.*cap.*2.42(M.90.1236B); *ἁγιασμὸς καὶ θέωσις ἀγγέλων καὶ ἀνθρώπων ἡ γνῶσις τῆς ἁγίας καὶ ὁμοουσίου τ.* Thal.*cent.*1.100(M.91. 1437A); **b.** faith in Trin. *ἐν τοῖς τρισὶ τούτοις ὁ προκόπτων φιλοσοφεῖ, ἐν ταῖς ἐντολαῖς, ἐν τοῖς δόγμασι καὶ ἐν τῇ πίστει τῆς τ.* *ib.*3.28(1449D); as gift of grace indwelling soul, Max.*carit.*4.77(M.90.1068A); credal; v. 9 infra; **c.** indwelling of Trin. *κατοικητήριον* [sc. the soul] *τῆς ὁμοουσίου τ.* Alex.Sal.*Barn.*proem.7(438E); *ὁ...τοῦ...πατρὸς...λόγος ἑκάστῃ μυστικῶς ἐνυπάρχει τῶν οἰκείων ἐντολῶν· ὁ δὲ πατὴρ ὅλος ἐστὶν ἀχώριστος ἐν...τῷ...λόγῳ· ὁ τοίνυν δεχόμενος ἐντολὴν...τὸν ἐν αὐτῇ δέχεται λόγον. ὁ δὲ τὸν λόγον...δεξάμενος δι' αὐτοῦ τὸν ἐν αὐτῷ...ὄντα συνεδέξατο πατέρα καὶ τὸ ἐν αὐτῷ...πνεῦμα ἅγιον...ὁ γοῦν ἐντολὴν δεξάμενος καὶ ποιήσας αὐτὴν λαβὼν ἔχει μυστικῶς τὴν ἁγίαν τ.* Max. *cap.theol.*2.71(M.90.1157A); *μακάριος ὄντως ἐστὶ τῆς ἀληθοῦς...τυχὼν οὐ μόνον ἑνώσεως τῆς πρὸς τὴν ἁγίαν τ., ἀλλὰ καὶ ἑνότητος τῆς ἐν τῇ ἁγίᾳ τ. νοουμένης, ὡς ἁπλοῦς καὶ...μονοειδὴς κατὰ τὴν δύναμιν πρὸς τὴν ἁπλῆν...κατὰ τὴν οὐσίαν γεγενημένος* id.*ambig.*(M.91.1196B); cf. *ὑπὲρ τὴν ὑλικὴν δυάδα γενέσθαι διὰ τὴν ἐν τῇ τ. νοουμένην ἑνότητα* Gr.Naz.*or.*21.2(M.35.1084B); *πάσης τῆς αἰσθητικῆς οὐσίας πρὸς τὴν αἰσθητὴν ἀποθεμένους φυσικὴν οἰκειότητα, τῆς δὲ θείας μόνης γνησίως ἐπιλαβομένους ἐφέσεως διὰ τὴν...νοουμένην ἐν τῇ τ. ἑνότητα* Max. *ambig.*(1193D); *ib.*(1196A); **d.** vision of Trin.; equated with kingdom of heaven, Gr.Naz.*or.*16.9(M.35.945C); as blessing of future life, *ib.*43.82(M.36.605A); **8.** ref. baptism *τὸ διὰ τοῦ ὕδατος λουτρόν... τῷ ἐμπαρέχοντι ἑαυτὸν τῇ θειότητι τῆς δυνάμεως τῶν τῆς προσκυνητῆς τ. ἐπικλήσεών ἐστιν ἡ χαρισμάτων θείων ἀρχὴ καὶ πηγή* Or.*Jo.*6.33(17;

p.142.30; M.14.257A); βαπτίζοντα πολλοὺς εἰς τὸ τῆς ζωαρχικῆς τ. ὄνομα *A.Xanthipp*.21(p.73.6); ἐν αὐτῇ τῇ τ. ἕν ἐστι τὸ βάπτισμα καὶ μία ἡ πίστις Ath.*ep.Serap*.4.3(M.26.641B); ὁ ὑπεξαιρούμενός τι τῆς τ. καὶ ἐν μόνῳ τῷ τοῦ πατρὸς ὀνόματι βαπτιζόμενος...ἢ χωρίς γε πνεύματος ἐν πατρὶ καὶ υἱῷ, οὐδὲν λαμβάνει *ib*.1.30(597C); οὐδὲ τῇ τ. συναριθμεῖταί τι τῶν ποιημάτων, ἀλλ' ἐπ' ὀνόματι τῆς ἁγίας τ. τὸ βάπτισμα καὶ ἡ ἐπίκλησις καὶ ἡ λατρεία Apoll.*fid.sec.pt*.9(p.170.15; M.10.1108D); σύμφωνον τῷ σωτηρίῳ βαπτίσματι τὴν δοξολογίαν ἀποπληροῦσθαι τῇ μακαρίᾳ τ. Bas.*ep*.91(3.183C; M.32.476D); ἡ ζωοποιὸς δύναμις ἐπὶ τῶν...ἀναγεννωμένων διὰ τῆς ἁγίας τ. παραγίνεται...καὶ ὁμοίως ἀτελὴς ἡ χάρις ἑνός τινος οἵου δήποτε τῶν ἐκ τῆς ἁγίας τ. ὀνομάτων παραλειφθέντος ἐν τῷ...βαπτίσματι Gr.Nyss.*ep*.5(M.46.1032A); ἡμῖν ἐξόδιον τὸ θεῖον...τῆς παλιγγενεσίας λουτήριον ἔσται, ἔνθεν καὶ τῆς τ. ὀψόμεθα φῶς τὸ ἄδυτον Cosm.Mel.*hymn*.2(M.98.472A); v. βάπτισμα; ref. pre-baptismal profession of faith εἰ μὴ πρῶτον ὁμολογήσειέν τις τὴν τῆς ἁγίας τ. ὁμολογίαν...οὐ βαπτίζεται Cosm.Ind.*top*.5(M.88.221B); **9.** ref. credal profession οἶκον θεοῦ τὴν ἐκκλησίαν καλεῖ...τούτου τοῦ οἴκου ἀγαθὰ τὰ τοῦ πνεύματος χαρίσματα, τά τε περὶ τῆς τ. καὶ τὰ λοιπὰ δόγματα Or.*Ps*.64:5(p.74); cf. *funis enim triplex non rumpitur, quae est trinitatis fides, ex qua dependet et per quam sustinetur omnis ecclesia*, id.*hom.9.3 in Ex*.(p.239.23; M.12.365B); αὕτη τῆς καθολικῆς ἐκκλησίας ἡ πίστις· ἐν τ. γὰρ αὐτὴν ἐθεμελίωσε...ὁ κύριος Ath.*ep.Serap*.3.6(M.26.633C); *ib*.1.32(605A); id.*Ar*.1.18(M.26.49A) cit. s. ἀεί; ἔστιν ἡμῶν ἡ πίστις...εἰς...ἕνα θεόν, τὸν ἐν τῇ ἁγίᾳ καὶ τελείᾳ τ. γινωσκόμενον id.*ep.Afr*.11(M.26.1048B); *Symb.Ant*.(345)9 ap.Ath.*syn*.26(p.253.40; M.26.733B); *Symb. Sirm.2 ib*.28(p.257.23; 744A); Gr.Naz.*or*.21.31(M.35.1120A); Cyr.*dial. Trin*.3(5[1].465E); **10.** Trin. as object of adoration, Evagr.Pont.*ep*.12(M.32.265B); Apoll. *fid.sec.pt*.37(p.181.22; M.10.1120B); *ib*.38(p.181.26; M.l.c.); Gr.Naz.*or*.42.15(M.36.476A); Cyr.*dial.Trin*.3(5[1].466A); *Lit.Jac*.(p.226.16); *Lit.Chrys*.(p.384.21); Andr.Cr.*can.mag*.29(p.148; M.97.1336B); of glorification, Gr.Naz.*or*.23.15(M.35.1165A); Marc. Diac.*v.Porph*.89; *Lit.Jac*.(p.160.7); *ib*.(p.240.2); Andr.Cr.*can.mag*.(1385C); id.*can.BMV* 4(M.97.1321C); of invocation and supplication, Ath.*ep.Serap*.3.6(M.26.633B); Gr.Naz.*or*.29.21(p.107.13; M.36.104B); *ib*.42.27(492C); †Sophr.H.*orat*.(M.87.4001C); Andr.Cr.*can.mag*.29(p.148; M.97.1336B); *ib*.(1341B); *ib*.277(p.155; 1377D); of thanksgiving, Oecum.*Apoc*.11:17(p.134); **11.** doctrine of Trin. and scripture τ. μὲν κηρυττομένην ὑπὸ τῆς θείας γραφῆς σαφῶς ἐπίστανται, τρεῖς δὲ θεοὺς οὔτε παλαιάν, οὔτε καινὴν διαθήκην κηρύττουσαν Dion.R. ap.Ath.*decr*.26(p.22.15; M.25.464A); περὶ...τριάδος...ἡμεῖς...μηδὲν σοφιζόμενοι...ἐκ θείων γραφῶν...μαρτυρίας...συνηγάγομεν Epiph.*anc*.74(p.93.8; M.43.156A); ψαλμὸς...νομοθετεῖ τὴν τ. Procl.CP *or*.2.1(M.65.693A); ὁπόταν...ἡ ἁγία γραφὴ τῷ πληθυντικῷ περὶ θεοῦ κέχρηται λόγῳ, τὴν δήλωσιν ποιεῖται τῶν...τριῶν ὑποστάσεων, μυστικῶς τὸν τῆς ὑπάρξεως σημαίνουσα τρόπον τῆς...τ. Max.*qu.Thal*.28(M.90.361D); ποῦ ε˜ ες ἐν τῇ παλαιᾷ ἢ ἐν τῷ εὐαγγελίῳ ὄνομα τ. ... αὐτολεξεί; Jo.D. *imag*.3.11(M.94.1333B); progressively revealed θεότης...μία ἐν Μωϋσῇ ...καταγγέλλεται, δυὰς δὲ ἐν προφήταις...κηρύττεται, τ. δὲ ἐν εὐαγγελίοις φανεροῦται Epiph.*anc*.73(p.92.7; M.43.153B); cf.Gr.Naz.*or*.31.26(p.179.1; M.36.161D); κατὰ πρόβασιν ἡ ἡμετέρα φύσις τὸ τῆς τ. ἐπέγνω μυστήριον ‡Gr.Nyss.*imag*.(M.44.1337C); manifested at Christ's baptism, Cosm.Mel.*hymn*.2(3.186,p.172; M.98.469C); at Pentecost, *ib*.9(14.20,p.202; 489B); *ib*.(14.65,p.203; 492A); Jo.D.*carm.pent*.84(p.216; M.96.837A); **12.** doctrine of Trin. a greater mystery than redemption, Ath.*ep.Serap*.1.20(M.26.577B); its difficulty, Cyr.*thes*. proem.(5[1].1B); essence of Trin. being unknown, Thal.*cent*.4.90(M.91.1468C); known only to Trin. itself, Gr.Naz.*or*.28.3(p.25.3; M.36.29A); Max.*ambig*.(M.91.1168B); and nature of Trin. therefore not investigated without impiety, Cyr.*dial.Trin*.3(5[1].466A); **13.** types and images of Trin., ref. 318 servants of Abraham ὁ τριακόσιος ἀριθμὸς τ. ἐστιν ἐν ἑκατοντάδι Clem.*str*.6.11(p.473.30; M.9.305A); typified by first three days of Creation, Thphl.Ant.*Autol*.2.15(M.6.1077B); prefigured by threefold *sanctus* of seraphic hymn, cf.Or. *hom.4.1 in Is*.(p.259.1; M.13.231D); by appearance of three men to Abraham, Max.*qu.Thal*.28(M.90.360D); by the Three Children, Cosm.Mel.*hymn*.12(1.137,p.164; M.98.508A); by Adam, Eve, and Seth, ‡Gr.Nyss.*imag*.(M.44.1329C); symbolized by the numbers one and three, Eus.*l.C*.6(p.210.9; M.20.1348B); by numbers three and seven, Max.*ambig*.(M.91.1393C); by man as image of God, ‡Gr. Nyss.*imag*.(M.44.1340C); *ib*.(1329B); Eulog.*fr.Trin*.2.5(p.365); with ψυχή, λόγος, and νοῦς, ‡Gr.Nyss.*imag*.(1333B); *ib*.(1336B); cf.*ib*.(1340C); *ib*.(1341A); *ib*.(1344C); Eulog.*fr.Trin*.2.6(p.365); *ib*.2.8(p.365); other images of Trin. in Nature, Jo.D.*imag*.3.21(M.94.1341B); prefigured by Plato in *Timaeus*, Clem.*str*.5.14(p.395.15; M.9.156B).

***τριαυγής**, *triply-bright* οἱ τρεῖς ἐν ὑπάρχουσιν φῶς...τριλαμπές, τ. ἰσολαμπές ‡Caes.Naz.*dial*.3(M.38.860).

τριβακός, *habitual* ὦ ἀπὸ τῆς ἁμαρτίας τῆς τ., ὅτι πρὸς τὴν ψυχὴν καὶ τὰς συνωνὰς πεποίηκεν Ephr.3.446A; τῇ πλατείᾳ...ὁδῷ τῆς τ. κακίας †Cyr.*hom.div*.14(5[2].412C); Jo.Carp.*cap*.5(M.85.1839).

***τριβακόω**, *wear away*, Didym.*Ps*.17:46(M.39.1265A).

***τριβοβατέω**, *tread a path*; hence *be versed in*, ‡Ath.*qu.script*.86(M.28.749A).

***τριβόλαιος**, *striking in three ways* πνεῦμα τ. εἰμὶ ἐν τρισὶ πράξεσι κατεργαζόμενον *T.Sal*.12.2(p.41* n.10; M.122.1333B).

***τριβόλιν, τό**, *game involving three throws of the dice*, †Gregent. *leg.Hom*.37(M.86.601B).

***τριβολώδης**, *full of briers*, Herm.*sim*.6.2.6; cf.‡Ath.*doct.Ant*.19(M.28.584A).

***τριβουνάλιον (τριβουνάριον), τό**, (Lat. *tribunal*) **1.** *tribunal*, Sergia *Olymp*.1.5(p.413.29); **2.** *dais* from which general or emperor addressed troops, *Chron.Pasch*.p.291(M.92.728B); **3.** name of public place in CP where emperors were proclaimed, Philost.*h.e*.11.3(M.65.597A); *Chron.Pasch*.p.304(M.92.772A); Thphn.*chron*.p.213(M.108.545A); and eccl. processions held with litanies, *Euchol*.(p.640); **4.** *chancel*; part of church reserved for clergy, Leont.Abb.*v.Gr. Agr*.72(M.98.677A).

***τριβουνᾶτος, ὁ**, (Lat. *tribunatus*) *military tribuneship*, Andr.Cr. *or*.17(M.97.1177B).

***τριβοῦνος, ὁ**, (Lat. *tribunus*) **1.** *military tribune*, Pall.*h.Laus*.41(p.128.16; M.34.1233D); Jo.Ant.*ep.Xyst.et Cyr*.(p.33.23; M.77.164D); Marc.Diac.*v.Porph*.70; ὁ ἀπὸ τριβούνων *ex-tribune*, Chrys. *ep*.14.3(3.598D); *Chron.Pasch*.p.319(M.92.812B); **2.** τ. νοτάριος, *imperial clerk*, CChalc.*act*.1(*ACO* 2.1.1 p.72.31; H.3.77B); **3.** met., *V.Max*.12(M.90.125C) cit. s. θυμέλη.

τρίβω, *put off*, Malchus *exc.Rom*.8(p.167.8; M.113.776A); *delay*, Men.*exc.Rom*.18(p.213.35; M.113.916B).

τριβωνοφόρος, *wearing a threadbare cloak*, Pall.*h.Laus*.37(p.111.4; M.34.1185D) cit. s. βιρροφόρος.

***τριγαμ-έω**, *marry three times* ἀναγνώστης δευτερογαμῶν, μη προσκοπτέτω εἰς βαθμὸν ἱερωσύνης· ∼ῶν δέ, πεπαυέσθω τοῦ κλήρου Ath.Scholast.*coll*.1.1(p.3); Thdr.Stud.*epp*.1.50(M.99.1093D).

***τριγάμημα, τό**, *third marriage*, Thdr.Stud.*epp*.1.50(M.99.1092A).

***τριγαμία, ἡ**, *third marriage* τριγαμίας νόμος οὐκ ἔστιν· ὥστε νόμῳ γάμος τρίτος οὐκ ἄγεται Bas.*ep*.199 *can*.50(3.297C; M.32.732C); τ. ... ἀκρασίας σημεῖον, τὸ δὲ ὑπὲρ τὴν τ. προφανὴς πορνεία καὶ ἀσέλγεια ἀναμφίβολος *Const.App*.3.2.2.

τρίγαμος, *thrice-married* ἐπὶ τούτου [sc. Callistus] ἤρξαντο ἐπίσκοποι καὶ πρεσβύτεροι καὶ διάκονοι δίγαμοι καὶ τ. καθίστασθαι εἰς κλήρους Hipp.*haer*.9.12(p.249.24; M.16.3386B); περὶ τ. καὶ πολυγάμων τὸν αὐτὸν ὥρισαν κανόνα...τοὺς...τ. ἐν τρισὶ καὶ τετράσι... ἔτεσιν ἀφορίζουσιν...συνήθειαν...κατελάβομεν ἐπὶ τῶν τ. πενταετίας ἀφορισμόν Bas.*ep*.188 *can*.4(3.271D,E; M.32.673A).

τριγενής, *of three kinds, threefold*; of soul, Clem.*paed*.3.1(p.236.4; M.8.556A); ἐκ τ. *of a threefold generation*; of Monogenes, born, acc. Docetae, of three aeons and BMV γέγονε...μόνος τοῖς ἀπείροις αἰῶσιν ἐκ τ.· τρεῖς γὰρ αὐτὸν ἐγέννησαν...αἰῶνες Hipp.*haer*.8.9(p.228.5; M.16.3351B).

***τριγενικός**, *threefold*, Clem.*str*.2.21(p.184.3; προγονικήν M.8.1076B).

***τρίγοργος**, ? *thrice-terrible*, *Pers*.(p.23.9).

τριδέσποτος, *being three Lords* οἱ τρεῖς ἐν ὑπάρχουσιν φῶς... τριπρόσωπον...τ. ‡Caes.Naz.*dial*.3(M.38.860).

***τρίδομος**, *of three floors, with three stories* καλὸς τ. καὶ τρίστυλος θεμέλιος, ἀκακία, νηστεία, σωφροσύνη Jo.Clim.*scal*.1(M.88.636D).

τριδύναμος, *with triple powers* or *faculties*, Peratic ἄνωθεν... κατεληλυθέναι...τριφυῆ τινα καὶ τρισώματον καὶ τ. ἄνθρωπον καλούμενον Χριστόν Hipp.*haer*.5.12(p.105.3; M.16.3162B); cf.Thdt.*haer*.1.17(4.310).

***τρίεκτα, τά**, *three sixes*, at dice, Leont.N.*v.Sym*.57(M.93.1740C,D).

***τριετηρῖτις, ἡ**, *woman dancer at* Egyptian *triennial festival* (i.e. in alternate years), Epiph.*exp.fid*.12(p.512.1; M.42.804A).

τριετία, ἡ, *period of three years*; of Christ's ministry, Mel.*fr*.6(M.5.1221A).

τριετίζ-ω, *be three years old*; of sacrificial animals in OT, ‡Just. *qu.et resp*.83(M.6.1324D); Anast.S.*qu.et resp*.27(M.89.553B); of BMV when presented to Temple ∼ουσα πρόεισι τῷ νομικῷ ναῷ ἀνατεθησομένη Germ.CP *or*.3(M.98.293A); Taras.*praesent.BMV* 1(M.98.1481B); *ib*.8(1488D); εἰ γὰρ ὁ θεὸς τῷ Ἀβραὰμ ἐνεγκεῖν προσέταξε δάμαλιν ∼ουσαν...πρὸς καθαρισμὸν τῶν ψυχῶν, πῶς ἡ παρθένος...οὐχὶ ...καθαρὰ...καθέστηκε; *ib*.13(1496D).

*τριημερεύ-ω (*τριση-), spend three days; of Jonah in belly of fish, Thdt.ap.cat.Mt.16:4(p.129.12); of Christ under the earth ἵνα ὁλόκληρον ἐξαναστήσῃ τὸ ζῷον, ψυχὴν καὶ πνεῦμα καὶ σῶμα, διὰ τοῦτο καὶ ~ει ‡Chrys.pasch.6.5(p.187.7; 8.273C); τριση-, ‡Gr.Naz. Chr.pat.1401(M.38.248A).

*τριημερίζω, spend three days, T.Jos.3.5.

*τριημερινός, of the day before yesterday, v. τριθημερινός.

*τριημερόνυκτος, of three days and nights; of Christ's burial, Leont.B.Nest.et Eut.2(M.86.1336B); imitated in baptism, Dion.Ar. e.h.2.3.7(M.3.404B) citt. s. ταφή.

τριήμερος, 1. after three days τ. ὑπὸ τοῦ πατρὸς ἀνίσταται Hipp.fr. 18 in Pss.(p.146.11; M.10.609A); τὴν τ. ἀνάστασιν id.Jud.3(p.19.26; M.10.789A); ὁ...ἐκ Μαρίας μόνος τ. ἀνέστη Ath.ep.Epict.11(p.17.8; M.26.1068B); τὴν τ. τῆς ἀναστάσεως χάριν Gr.Nyss.or.catech.35(p.133. 5; M.45.88D); Cyr.Is.3.1(2.354C); τ. ἐγέρσει τὸν κόσμον φωτίσαντος Cosm.Mel.hymn.12(1.83,p.163; M.98.505B); 2. during, for three days; of Christ in tomb, Nonn.par.Jo.19:42(M.43.908A); 3. lasting for three days τ. ... χρόνος Eus.theoph.3(p.14*.19; M.24.620B); τοῦ τ. πάθους Amph.Seleuc.279(M.37.1595A); τ. νέκρωσιν Gr.Nyss.or.catech. 35(p.132.10; M.45.88C); of Egyptian darkness, Cyr.Os.5(3.23D); of S. Paul's blindness, Isid.Pel.epp.1.346(M.78.381A); of repentance of Ninevites, Bas.Sel.or.5.2(M.85.77C); 4. as subst. fem., space of three days τίς ἡ τριήμερος, ἣν ὑπὸ γῆν ἔμεινε ‡Chrys.pasch.6.2(p.133. 16; 8.266D); also neut., Iren.fr.29(M.7.1245A); Epiph.haer.42.11 (p.154.2; M.41.772B); τοῦ σώματος...ἀψύχου μείναντος τὸ τ. id.exp. fid.17(p.517.27; M.42.813C); 5. neut. as subst., the third day ἀναστὰς τὸ τ. id.haer.77.29(p.441.24; M.42.684B); ib.77.35(p.448.10; 696A); ἐν τ. ἀναστάς Thphl.Al.ep.pasch.proem.4(M.65.52B).

*τριημέρως, 1. in three days, Iren.ap.cat.Lc.13:19(p.108.22); 2. after three days, of Isaac τ. βαδίσας ἐπὶ τὸ θανεῖν Cosm.Ind.top.5 (M.88.241B).

*τριθεΐα, ἡ, tritheism; 1. charged against orthodox by Macedonians in respect of belief in divinity of H. Ghost οἷς γὰρ ἂν ὑμεῖς [sc. Macedonians] τὴν διθεΐαν [i.e. charge brought against Macedonians by Eunomians] ἀποκρούσησθε λόγοις, οὗτοι καὶ ἡμῖν κατὰ τῆς τ. ἀρκέσουσι Gr.Naz.or.31.13(p.162.9; M.36.148C); ib.40.43 (420C); ib.25.18(M.35.1224B); cf.‡Caes.Naz.dial.11(M.38.868); ib.12 (869); 2. charged against Eunomians and Macedonians by orthodox τὴν ἀδιαίρετον...προσκυνουμένην θεότητα εἰς τ. παραλαμβάνουσι Thdt.Ps.57:6(1.986); 3. charged against Nestorians εἰ...αἱ ὑποστάσεις οὐδὲν ἕτερον, ἀλλ' ἢ ἰδικαὶ οὐσίαι εἰσί, τρεῖς λέγοντες τὰς ὑποστάσεις τῆς...τριάδος, δηλονότι τρεῖς καὶ οὐσίας φατέ· καὶ ἰδοὺ τὴν τ. ... ὑπεδύσασθε Leont.H.Nest.2.6(M.86.1549B); 4. ref. doctrine of John Philoponus and his followers who asserted three φύσεις, οὐσίαι, or ὑποστάσεις in Godhead ἀριθμεῖται...ἡ...τριὰς οὐκ οὐσίαις καὶ φύσεσι ...ὡς οἱ Ἀρειανοὶ μαίνονται καὶ οἱ τῆς νέας τ. λυττῶσιν ἡγούμενοι, οὐσίας τρεῖς...καὶ τρεῖς ὁμοίως κενολογοῦντες θεότητας Sophr.H.ep. syn.(M.87.3156C); Ἰωάννης...Κόνων τε καὶ Εὐγένιος, οἱ τρεῖς τῆς τ. τρισκατάρατοι πρόμαχοι ib.(3192C); ib.(3193A); 5. ref. consequences of identification of φύσις with ὑπόστασις by Severus εἰς τὸ Ἀρειανὸν τῆς τ. βάραθρον ἐξεκυλίσθη Anast.S.hod.23(M.89.304C).

*τριθεΐτης, ὁ, tritheist; 1. of Arius, Jo.D.rect.sent.7(M.94.1432A); 2. ref. Macedonian charge against orthodox believers in divinity of H. Ghost τί φατε τοῖς τ. ἡμῖν, οἱ τὸν υἱὸν σέβοντες, εἰ καὶ τοῦ πνεύματος ἀφεστήκατε; ὑμεῖς δὲ οὐ διθεῗται; Gr.Naz.or.31.13(p.161.14; M.36. 148C); 3. of followers of John Philoponus who asserted three φύσεις, ὑποστάσεις, or οὐσίαι in the Godhead τὸ δόγμα τῶν τ., οὗ αἱρεσίαρχος γέγονεν ὁ Φιλόπονος †Leont.B.sect.5.6(M.86.1232D); τ., οἱ δεχόμενοι...τὸν...Φιλόπονον...καὶ οὐσίας καὶ φύσεις ἐπὶ τῆς...τριάδος ...βλασφημοῦντες Tim.CP haer.(M.86.44A); Sophr.H.ep.syn.(M.87. 3193C); Jo.D.haer.83(M.94.744A); cf. ἄλλοι τ., οἵτινες τὰ μὲν ἄλλα πάντα συμφωνοῦσι τοῖς ἄλλοις τ., τὸν δὲ κατὰ τῆς ἀναστάσεως...λόγον ...τοῦ Φιλοπόνου...ἀποστρέφονται Tim.CP haer.(44B).

*τρίθεος, neut. as subst., belief in three gods πρὸς...τοὺς ἐπηρεάζοντας ἡμῖν τὸ τ., ἐκεῖνο λεγέσθω, ὅτιπερ ἡμεῖς ἕνα θεὸν οὐ τῷ ἀριθμῷ, ἀλλὰ τῇ φύσει ὁμολογοῦμεν Evagr.Pont.ep.2(M.32.248C).

τριθημερινός, of the day before yesterday, Or.hom.5.10 in Jer. (p.39.20; conj. for τριημερινάς M.13.309A).

*τρίθρονος, thrice-throned φῶς...ὁ πατήρ, φῶς ὁ υἱός, φῶς τὸ θεῖον πνεῦμα· ἀλλ' οἱ τρεῖς ἓν ὑπάρχουσιν φῶς...τ. ‡Caes.Naz.dial.3(M.38. 860).

τρίθυρον, τό, triple door, Mac.Aeg.hom.27.19(M.34.708A).

*τρικάμαρον, τό, house with three arches or three vaulted chambers, Chron.Pasch.p.254(M.92.613B).

*τρικάτοικος, with three habitations; of world as consisting of water, air, and earth, Pers.(p.12.20; M.10.101A).

*τρικέραυνος, with triple thunderbolt, of three heresies condemned by CCP(381) τὴν τ. Μακεδονίου, Ἀπολιναρίου καὶ Μάγνου σβεννύει δυσσέβειαν Sophr.H.ep.syn.(M.87.3185A).

*τρικλήματος, with three branches, ‡Ath.disp.36(M.28.488A).

τρίκογχος, with three apses, CIG 8623; neut. as subst., church or building with three apses, Chron.Pasch.p.317(M.92.808A).

*τρικόνδυλος, with three joints, Melet.nat.hom.26(M.64.1252A).

*τρικόρυμνος (*τρικόρυμβος), with three heads μονὰς ἄρρητα χυθεῖσα τ. ἔσχεν ἀλκάν Synes.hymn.1.66(p.60; τρικόρυμβον M.66.1589).

*τρίκρουσμα, τό, triple striking of the sounding-board πᾶς ὁ ἀκούων τοῦ τ. ... καὶ μὴ συνερχόμενος μετὰ σπουδῆς, ἀνὰ κ' μετανοίας βαλλέτω Thdr.Stud.poen.1.16(M.99.1736B).

*τριλαμπής, shining with triple brightness φῶς ἦν...ὁ θεὸς... ἀειλαμπές, τ., ὀλίγοις θεωρούμενον Gr.Naz.or.44.3(M.36.609B); γνῶσις θεοῦ μεγίστου, φάους ἑνὸς τ. id.carm.2.1.88.174(M.37.1442A); ὕμνοις ...μέλπεις οὐρανίοιο τριλαμπέα πνεύματος αἴγλην ib.2.2(poem.)3.284 (1500A); ‡Caes.Naz.dial.3(M.38.860); πιστεύομεν εἰς...μίαν θεότητα ...τ. Jo.D.haer.(M.94.777C).

*τριλέξιον, τό, a kind of song, Philox.ep.39(p.186).

*τρίλιθος, made out of three stones, Chron.Pasch.p.303(M.92.764A).

*τρίλιτρον, τό, three pounds weight, Pall.h.Laus.17(p.47.16; M. 34.1049D).

*τρίλογχος, with three points, Jo.VI H.v.Jo.D.3(M.94.433B).

τριμερής, tripartite, of principle of υἱότης in system of Basilides ἦν...ἐν αὐτῷ τῷ σπέρματι υἱότης τ., κατὰ πάντα τῷ οὐκ ὄντι θεῷ ὁμοούσιος, γεννητὴ ἐξ οὐκ ὄντων Hipp.haer.7.22(p.198.25; M.16. 3306C); cf.ib.10.14(p.274.24; 3427D); ref. tripartite division of man (body, soul, mind) κατὰ τὴν τ. τοῦ Ἀπολιναρίου τῶν ἀνθρώπων τομήν Gr.Nyss.Apoll.8(M.45.1140A); ἡ τ. ... τοῦ ἀνθρώπου τομή, ἧς τὸ μὲν δίμοιρον ἄνθρωπος, θεὸς δὲ τὸ τριτημόριον ib.35(1201B); τὸ τριφυὲς ἢ τ. ἢ ὅπως ἂν ἐθέλῃ τις ὀνομάζειν τὸ ἀνθρώπινον σύγκριμα ib.9(1140C); of the soul as made up of λογισμός, θυμός, and ἐπιθυμία, Clem. str.5.12(p.379.25; M.9.120B); Hipp.haer.5.7(p.81.6; 3130B); Or.Cels. 5.47(p.51.20; M.11.1256A); Ephr.3.430C = Jo.D.virt.(M.95.96A); Christol. σῶμα...ἀνελάβετο...ψυχῇ τ. ζωοποιούμενον ‡Cyr.Trin.14 (6^3.20E; M.77.1152B).

τριμηναῖος, v. τριμηνιαῖος.

*τριμηνήτης, after three months; of antichrist as a devil, to be born prematurely from a virgin at end of world ἐξ αὐτῆς τεχθεὶς τ. καὶ στήσεις τὸν θρόνον σου ἐπὶ τῆς γῆς Contrad.2(p.10).

τριμηνιαῖος (τριμηναῖος), three months old, of God in Nestorius' Christol. saying ἐγὼ διμηνιαῖον ἢ τ. θεὸν οὐ λέγω Cyr.ep.23(p.66.28; τριμηναῖον 5^2.84E); cf.Socr.h.e.7.34.5(M.67.813C); Thphn.chron.p.77 (M.108.240A).

τριμίσσιον (τριμίσι(ο)ν, τριμήσιον), τό, (Lat. tremissis) a coin worth ⅓ of the aureus, Cyr.S.v.Sab.81(p.187.3); Sophr.H.mir.Cyr. et Jo.49(M.87.3605A); Leont.N.v.Jo.Eleem.1(p.6.15).

*τριμόδιον, τό, vessel containing three modii, Jo.Mal.chron.11 p.278(M.97.420C).

*τριμοιρόω, reduce by a third, †Gregent.leg.Hom.57(M.86.612B).

*τρινομ-έω, have three coins (highest sum which a monk not living in monastery was permitted to possess) εἰ μὲν ~εῖτε...οὐκ ἀπόβλητοι ἐν μοναχοῖς...· εἰ δὲ ἐπάνω δεκανομοῦντες...γινώσκετε ἔκπτωτοι εἶναι τῆς μοναχικῆς καταστάσεως Thdr.Stud.epp.2.180(M.99.1557C).

τριοδία, ἡ, place where three roads meet, Soz.h.e.5.21.6(M.67.1281A).

*τριομβυρατορία (*τριουμβιρατορία), ἡ, triumvirate, Jo.Mal. chron.9 p.218(M.97.337B); ib.p.214(333A) = Chron.Pasch.p.186 (τριουμβιρ-, M.92.457B).

*τριομβυράτωρ (*τριουμβιράτωρ), ὁ, triumvir, Jo.Mal.chron. 9 p.214(M.97.333A) = Chron.Pasch.p.186(τριουμβιρ-, M.92.457A); Jo. Mal.chron.9 p.218(337B) = Chron.Pasch.p.189(τριουμβιρ-, 465C).

*τριόροφος (= τριώροφος), of three stories, ‡Ath.proph.1(M.28. 1064A).

*τριπάσσαλον, τό, third peg; in a rack for torture, A.(Pass.) Andr.10(p.23.19).

[*]τριπήχυιος, = τρίπηχυς, three cubits high, Procl.CP or.15.4 (M.65.804A).

τριπλασιάζω, triple, Hipp.haer.8.9(p.228.14; M.16.3351B); ὁ... τρίτος αἰών, ὁ ἑαυτὸν τριπλασιάσας ib.10.16(p.278.1; 3434B).

τριπλασιασμός, ὁ, tripling, triplication, of triple repetition of word 'God' in Ps.66:7 symbolizing Trin. τῷ τ. τὸ 'θεὸς' ἐπαγαγὼν ἑνικῶς τὸ 'φοβηθήτωσαν αὐτόν' καὶ τὸ τῆς...τριάδος παρεγύμνωσε μυστήριον καὶ τὸ ἑνιαῖον τῆς θεότητος Cyr.Ps.66:8(M.69.1144B); of angelic hymn (Lc.2:14) symbolizing Trin. in its three parts τῷ τ. τῆς ᾠδῆς τὸν τ. τῆς ἁγιότητος εἰσαγαγόντες ‡Meth.Sym.et Ann.5(M. 18.357C).

***τριπλοκίνδυνος**, *of triple danger*, Geo.Pis.*Heracl.*2.97(M.92.1324A).

τρίπλοκος, *threefold*, Didym.(‡Bas.)*Eun.*5(1.317D; M.29.761A); ‡Chrys.*virt.fid.*(9.854B); *τ. πίστις...ἐν τῷ κρυπτῷ τῆς καρδίας φυλαττομένη ib.*(855B); symbolic meanings, Olymp.*Eccl.*4:12(M.93.533A).

τρίπλωσις, ἡ, *tripling*, ref. argument that orthodox Christology involves three Christs (Logos and two natures) *οὕτως ἔσται ὑμῖν εἰς οὐδὲν ἀναλυομένη τῶν διπλώσεων ἐπὶ τὰς τ. ἡ ψηφολογία* Leont.H.*Nest.*7.4(M.86.1768ᵃA).

τριπόθητος ([*]τρισπ-), **1.** *thrice* (i.e. greatly) *longed for, desired*, Cyr.*Juln.*10(6².355A); Proc.G.*Dt.*32:9(M.87.960B); ‡Jo.D.*Artem.*40(M.96.1288D); **2.** *eagerly expected τοῦ ἁγίου καὶ τ. πάσχα τοῦ Χριστοῦ* Didym.*Trin.*2.16(M.39.721A); *ib.*3.21(905C); *τὴν...ἑορτὴν τῆς σκηνοπηγίας τὸν τ. ἡμῖν τῆς ἀναστάσεως κατασημαίνειν καιρόν* Cyr.*Jo.*5.1(4.468C); **3.** *greatly to be desired, most desirable οὕτω...ἐπέραστόν τι τὸ τῆς παρθενίας ἐστὶν...καὶ τ. κλέος* Meth.*symp.*7.9(p.80.4; *περιπόθητον* M.18.136C); *ib.*9.4(p.119.14; 188A); *διὰ...τῆς θείας ἐντολῆς παράβασιν τῆς τ. στερηθῆναι ζωῆς* Eus.*p.e.*7.10(316B; M.21.533D); *τῶν ἀποστολικῶν κηρυγμάτων τὴν τ. χάριν* Cyr.*Os.*62(3.96C); *τῶν δεινῶν αἱ ὑπερβολαὶ...τὸν θάνατον τ. ἔσθ' ὅτε δεικνύουσι ib.*117(148B); of resurrection, id.*Jo.*1.9(4.81C); **4.** *greatly regretted*, of the dead *τὸ τ. ... ὄνομα Παμφίλου* Eus.*m.P.*11(p.931.12; M.20.1497B); *τρισπ-*, Alex.Sal.*Barn.*proem.8(p.438E).

***τριποθήτως**, **1.** *as has been greatly desired τ. αὐτοῖς ἐμφαίνεται ὁ Χριστός* Cyr.*Jo.*3.4(4.291B); **2.** *very eagerly*, id.*Is.*2.5(2.340C).

τριπρόσωπος, **1.** *of three aspects*; Trin., Sabellian and Marcellan *Μάρκελλος...μίαν...ὑπόστασιν τ. ὥσπερ καὶ τριώνυμον εἰσάγει* Eus.*e.th.*3.6(p.164.26; M.24.1016A); *μὴ ἓν οἷόν τε σύνθετον ἀναπλάσσει καὶ τ. ἢ ἀνθρωπόμορφον ὅλως* Gr.Naz.*or.*42.16(M.36.477A); *πῶς δύνανται τρεῖς ὑποστάσεις καὶ τρία ὀνομάζεσθαι πρόσωπα, καὶ οὐχὶ μᾶλλον μία ὑπόστασις τριώνυμος ἢ τ.;* ‡Just.*qu.et resp.*17(M.6.1264C); *τὴν τριάδα μίαν τινὰ τ. ὑπόστασιν ἐξελήρησεν* [sc. Sabellius], *ὅπερ ἐστὶ τῶν τριῶν μᾶλλον ἀναίρεσις* Isid.Pel.*epp.*1.24(M.78.333A); **2.** *of three Persons οἱ τρεῖς ἐν ὑπάρχουσιν φῶς...τ., τρισυπόστατον* ‡Caes.Naz.*dial.*3(M.38.860); *of three entities ὥσπερ ὁ ἥλιός ἐστι τ., οὕτω καὶ εἷς θεὸς τρισυπόστατος. ... ἐπὶ τοῦ ἡλίου δίσκος, ἀκτὶς καὶ φῶς...ὁμοίως καὶ ἐπὶ θεοῦ, πατήρ, υἱὸς καὶ ἅγιον πνεῦμα* ‡Ath.*qu.al.*4(M.28.776C); ref. Inc. *οὐ τρισυποστάτου τριάδος ὁλικὴν τ. σάρκωσιν* Anast.S.*hod.*8(M.89.133D).

***τρισαγιολογ-έω**, *celebrate in Trisagion ἐθέλει ὁ...πατὴρ τὸ πνεῦμα αὐτοῦ συντάττεσθαι αὐτῷ ὡς τὸν μονογενῆ λόγον...διὸ καὶ ~εῖται* Didym.*Trin.*2.4(M.39.481A).

***τρισάγιος**, *thrice-holy*; used, as adj. or as subst. (*ὁ τρισάγιος* (*ὕμνος*) or *τὸ τρισάγιον*), both of threefold *Sanctus* of Is.6:3, and of hymn *ἅγιος ὁ θεός*; in some cases it cannot be said with certainty to which of the two the term refers.

A. ref. Is.6:3 *τοῦ θεϊκοῦ πνεύματος...συνδοξαζομένου...ἅμα τῷ πατρί, καὶ τῷ υἱῷ, διὰ τοῦ τ. αἴνου* Didym.*Trin.*2.7(M.39.588C); *ἡ δὲ τοῦ τ. ἄπαυστος τῶν ἁγίων ἀγγέλων ἁγιαστικὴ δοξολογία* Max.*myst.*24(M.91.709B); Jo.Eub.*concept.BMV* 2(M.96.1461C); *ἀποκεκαλύφθαι τῷ Ἡσαΐᾳ ἐκ θεοῦ...διὰ τοῦ τ. ὕμνου τὴν μίαν τρισυπόστατον θεότητα* Jo.D.*trisag.*2(M.95.25A); hence as epithet of God *τρισάγιε κύριε M.Scill.*17(p.26.23; not in Lat. original); Cosm.Ind.*top.*6(M.88.332C); sometimes used of *Tersanctus* sung after Preface in liturgy *ἄνω τὰ σεραφὶμ τὸν τ. ὕμνον ἀναβοᾷ· κάτω τὸν αὐτὸν ἡ τῶν ἀνθρώπων ἀναπέμπει πληθύς* Chrys.*hom.1.1 in Is.*(6.95D); id.*hom.in Rom.12:20*(3.164B); Eus.Al.*serm.*16.3(M.86.417B); *οὐχ ἅπαξ τῷ πατρί, καὶ οὐχ ἅπαξ τῷ υἱῷ, καὶ οὐχ ἅπαξ τῷ ἁγίῳ πνεύματι τὸν τ. ὕμνον προσάγομεν, ἀλλὰ κοινῶς τῇ ἁγίᾳ τριάδι τρὶς τὸν τ. ὕμνον προσφέρομεν* Jo.D.*trisag.*28(M.95.57D); *πλήρης γέγονεν ὁ μέγιστος οἶκος τῆς ἐκκλησίας διὰ τοῦ τ. κηρύγματος* ‡Meth.*Sym.et Ann.*12(M.18.377B); apptly. also used as a private devotion *ἰατρὸς...πᾶσαν τὴν ἡμέραν τὸ τ. ψάλλων μετὰ τῶν ἀγγέλων Apophth.Patr.*(M.65.84B).

B. used of hymn *ἅγιος ὁ θεός· ἅγιος ἰσχυρός· ἅγιος ἀθάνατος· ἐλέησον ἡμᾶς*; **1.** origin: introduced into liturgy by Procl. CP in 438; acc. legend words were revealed to a child during some public calamity, ‡Acac.CP *ep.*(p.18.8,22ff.; H.2.844B); ‡Felix III Papa *ep.Petr.*1(p.22.19; H.2.821E); Jo.D.*trisag.*6(M.95.37C); sung by fathers of Chalcedon, CChalc.*act.*1(*ACO* 2.1.1,p.195.30; H.2.272E); Jo.D.*f.o.*3.10(M.94.1021A–C); **2.** contents and interpretation; *ὁ τ. ὕμνος οὕτως ἐστίν· ἐκεῖ μὲν οἱ ἄγγελοι εἶπον δόξα ἐν ὑψίστοις...ἐνταῦθα δὲ* ⟨*ἡμεῖς*⟩*...τῶν ἀσωμάτων τὸ ᾆσμα βοῶντες πιστῶς Ἅγιος ὁ θεός, ἤτοι ὁ πατήρ· ἅγιος ἰσχυρός, ὁ υἱὸς καὶ λόγος...ἅγιος ἀθάνατος, τὸ πνεῦμα τὸ ἅγιον τὸ ζωοποιοῦν* ‡Bas.*h.myst.*34(p.265.29); *ib.*35(p.266.9); *ὁ τ. ὕμνος ᾄδεται, τῆς θεότητος τοῦ υἱοῦ δηλῶν τὴν ὑπόστασιν, καὶ μὴν καὶ αὐτοῦ τοῦ πατρὸς καὶ τοῦ ζωοποιοῦ πνεύματος* ‡Sophr.H.*liturg.*15(M.87.3996B); **3.** liturg.; sung after Little Entrance, *Lit.Jac.*(p.168.12); *Lit.Bas.*(p.313.28); **4.** used as a private devotion; by confessor and his penitent before confession, ‡Jo.Jej.*poenit.*(M.88.1889A); by people in time of earthquake, *Chron.Pasch.*p.284(M.92.984B); **5.** theopaschite addition *ὁ σταυρωθεὶς δι' ἡμᾶς*, made by Peter Fullo, became subject of an important controversy, being rejected by orthodox cf. *ποία γραφή σε ἐδίδαξε τὸ ἅγιον πνεῦμα λέγειν ἐσταυρῶσθαι, ἢ δύο υἱοὺς δογματίζειν, ἢ νοθεύειν τὴν τ. ὑμνολογίαν;...ἐν γὰρ τῷ λέγειν σε, ἅγιος ἰσχυρός· καὶ πάλιν κατωτέρω ἐπάγειν, ὁ σταυρωθεὶς δι' ἡμᾶς· δύο υἱοὺς σημαίνεις...ὅταν δὲ πάλιν εἴπῃς· ἅγιος ἀθάνατος, ὁ σταυρωθεὶς δι' ἡμᾶς· εὑρίσκῃ τῷ ἁγίῳ πνεύματι τὸν σταυρὸν ἐπιφέρων* ‡Acac.CP *ep.*(p.18.8; H.2.844A); ‡Felix III Papa *ep.Petr.*1(p.20.11; H.2.820A); *τὸν λαὸν εἰς διαίρεσιν ἤγαγε, καὶ ἐν τῷ τ. Πέτρος, τό, ὁ σταυρωθεὶς δι' ἡμᾶς, προσέθηκεν* Thdr.Lect.*h.e.*1.20(M.86.176B); Evagr.*h.e.*3.44.1(p.146.4; M.86.2697A); cf. *εἴ τις τὴν τρισαγίαν λέγει δι' ἡμᾶς σταυρωθεῖσαν θεότητα καὶ οὐχὶ τὸν κύριον...Χριστόν, καθαιρείσθω. εἴ τις κατὰ τὴν τ. φωνὴν Χριστὸν λέγει σταυρωθέντα, καὶ οὐχὶ μᾶλλον τὸν ἕνα υἱόν, τὸν ἐν μέσῳ τῆς τρισαγίας φωνῆς ἀνυμνούμενον, καθαιρείσθω* Quint.*ep.*12(p.17.5; M.85.1740A); Anast.S.*hod.*13(M.89.205B); CTrull.*can.*81; insertion of *Χριστὲ βασιλεῦ* between the text and this addition, to save the orthodoxy of the formula, ascribed to patriarch Calendion, Thdr.Lect.*h.e.*2.47(208A).

***τρισαγιότης, ἡ**, *proclamation of the threefold holiness*, ref. Is.6:3 *τὴν θείαν...φύσιν τῇ τρισαγιότητι δοξάζοντα* Ath.*hom.in Mt.11:27*(M.25.217D).

***τρισαέναος**, *thrice ever-flowing οὔτε ἡ μία οὐσία...συναιρεῖται τὴν τρίστομον καὶ τ. κρήνην τῆς θεότητος* ‡Caes.Naz.*dial.*3(M.38.860).

***τρισαθλίως**, *thrice-unhappily*, Gr.Naz.*carm.*2.1.11.767(M.37.1082A).

***τρισάκτινος**, *with triple beam*; of Trin., Eulog.*fr.Trin.*2.1(p.364).

***τρισάνασσα**, *thrice a queen ὦ πανολβία τ. θεογεννήτρια* Andr.Cr.*or.*14(M.97.1108A).

τρισάριθμος, **1.** *three in number ἡ μονὰς ἐν θεότητι, τὰ δ' ὧν θεότης τ.* Gr.Naz.*carm.*1.1.3.74(M.37.414A); **2.** *expressed in terms of three μονάδα...φρονεῖν μιᾷ καὶ ἑνιαίᾳ θεότητι...τριάδα δέ...τῷ διαφόρῳ τῆς τ. προσωπικῆς ἑτερότητος* Sophr.H.*ep.syn.*(M.87.3153D); ‡Anast.S.*Jud.disp.*1(M.89.1208A).

***τρισάρνητος**, *thrice-denying, who has thrice denied εὑρίσκονται οἱ εἰκονομάχοι οὐκ ἀρνησίχριστοι μόνον, ἀλλὰ γὰρ καὶ τ.* Thdr.Stud.*epp.*2.84(M.99.1328C).

***τρισαυγής**, *with triple splendour πιστεύομεν εἰς τὴν ἁγίαν τριάδα, ἥτις...μία οὐσία...τ.* Eulog.*fr.Trin.*2.1(p.364); Jo.D.*haer.*(M.94.777C).

***τρισαύγουστος**, *thrice-august*, CLater.*act.*3(H.3.804C); Thphn.*chron.*p.155(M.108.420A); *ib.*p.241(607A).

***τρισέβαστος**, *thrice-august*; title of emperor, Paul.Sil.*Soph.*952(M.86.2155B).

***τρίσειρος** (*-συρος), *with three strands*; of vain glory, pride, and jealousy, †Nil.*vit.*4(*τρίσυρος* M.79.1144C) cit. s. *τριφάρμακος*; of mourning, penitence, and humility *ἡ πανόσιος αὕτη τ. ἅλυσις* Jo.Clim.*scal.*25(M.88.989D).

***τρισείς**, *three-in-one, triune τρισένα ὑψιμέδοντα* ‡Ath.*templ.*(p.109.6; v.l. *τρισένη* M.28.1429A).

***τρισεννέα**, *thrice nine*, Gr.Nyss.*ep.can.*5(M.45.232A).

***τρισήλιος**, *of three suns ἐπὶ τοῦ τ. τῆς ἁγίας τριάδος φωτός* ‡Ath.*comm.essent.*49(M.28.76B); *τῇ αἴγλῃ τῆς τ. θεότητος* Eus.Al.*serm.*21.3(M.86.428A); *τῆς ἑνιαίας καὶ μιᾶς καὶ τ. θεότητος* ‡Gr.Nyss.*hom.1 in Jo.*(p.110.4); *πιστεύομεν εἰς...μίαν θεότητα...τ.* Jo.D.*haer.*(M.94.777C); as subst., *triple sun ἐξ ἧς ἐλήφθη ὁ ἥλιος, εἷς ὢν τοῦ τ. τῆς...τριάδος* Mod.*dorm.*3(M.86.3285B).

***τρίσηλος**, v. **τρίσυλος*.

***τρισημερεύω**, v. **τριημερεύω*.

***τρισθανής**, *thrice guilty of death*, Gr.Naz.*carm.*2.2(epigr.)47(M.38.107A).

***τρισκαιδεκάς, ἡ**, *thirteenth part*, Chrys.*hom.9.4 in Phil.*(11.269D).

***τρισκαιδέκατος**, *thirteenth*, Chrys.*hom.26.4 in 2Cor.*(10.624A).

τρισκατάρατος, *thrice-accursed*; superl., of antichrist, *Apoc.Dan.*C(p.119).

***τρισκύταλος**, *with three joints*; of fingers, Melet.*nat.hom.*26(M.64.1252A).

τρισμακάριος, *thrice-blessed μακάριοι οἱ ἰδόντες με καὶ πιστεύσαντες· τ. δὲ οἱ μὴ ἑωρακότες με καὶ πιστεύσαντες Ep.Abg.*2(p.281.2); *ἀπολουσάμενοι ἐπὶ τῇ τ. ἐπονομασίᾳ...τὰ...πνεύματα ἀπελάσαι δυνήσεσθε Hom.Clem.*9.19; *τ. ἐπονομασίᾳ εἰς ἄφεσιν ἁμαρτιῶν βαπτισάμενοι ib.*9.23; *τὴν...τ. τιμῶντες τριάδα* Eus.*ep.Flac.*(p.60.14;

M.24.825A); τὸ πνεῦμα τὸ ἅγιον...συμπαρείληπται τῇ...τ. τριάδι id. *e.th.*3.5(p.162.31; M.24.1012B); τῆς τ. ἐλπίδος...ἐν τούτῳ καταστησαμένης τῷ τέλει, ἐν ᾧ ὁ θεὸς ἔσται πάντα ἐν πᾶσιν *ib.*3.16(p.174.23; 1033A); τὸ τ. τέλος, καθ' ὃ...ὁ ἐπὶ πάντων θεὸς...αὐτὸς ἑαυτὸν τοῖς ὑπὸ τῷ υἱῷ βασιλευομένοις δωρήσεται *ib.*3.18(p.179.9; 1041A); τὸ...μὴ παραμελεῖν...τὰ τῆς θείας ἐπιγνώσεως...τοῦτ' ἂν εἴη τὸ πάντων τ. τέλος id.*p.e.*7.8(307D; M.21.521B); of Israel, Cyr.*Am.*25(3.275B); τ. ... ὁ κατὰ θεὸν πλουτῶν id.*Lc.*12:20(M.72.737B); of saints, Eus.*p.e.*7.8 (312B; M.528C); ὁ τ. ἀπόστολος *PLond.*1927; Thdt.*1Cor.*12:1(3.241); id.*Soph.*proem.(2.1560); of Constantine, Eus.*Marcell.*2.4(p.58.5; M. 24.821C); his soul, id.*v.C.*1.2(p.7.25; M.20.912C); his remains, *ib.*4. 71(p.147.12; 1225B); of Helena, *ib.*3.46(p.97.8; 1105D); as title of bishops, id.*Marcell.*1.4(p.18.2; 752A); Photinus et al.*ep.*ap.Epiph. *haer.*72.11(p.265.23; M.42.397B); superl., Thdt.*h.e.*4.8.1(3.956).

τρισμακάριστος, *thrice-blessed*, of heaven ἐν...ταῖς τ. αὐλαῖς Didym.*Trin.*1.26(M.39.385C); τῆς μνήμης τῶν τ. μαρτύρων Nil.*epp.*4. 62(M.79.581B); τῷ...ἐν ἁγίοις τ. πάπᾳ ἡμῶν Ἰωάννῃ Leont.N.*v.Jo. Eleem.*1(p.6.1); *ib.*7(p.13.13); Ἀνδρέα...πάτερ τ., ποιμὴν τῆς Κρήτης Andr.Cr.*can.mag.*(M.97.1385B); ὦ τ. ξύλον ἐν ᾧ ἐτάθη Χριστός Cosm.Mel.*hymn.*12(1.60,p.162; M.98.504D); τὸ τοῦ σταυροῦ ξύλον, τὸ ...τ. Jo.D.*imag.*1.16(M.94.1245B); τὸν τ. ... πατριάρχην τῆς ἁγίας... πόλεως id.*trisag.*1(M.95.24C); τ. ὁ οἶκος τοῦ Δαβὶδ ἐν ᾧ ἐβλάστησας [sc. BMV] ‡Meth.*Sym.et Ann.*9(M.18.369A).

***τρισόσιος**, *thrice-holy*, Dan.Raith.*v.Jo.Clim.*(M.88.600A).

***τρισπόθητος**, v. τριπόθητος.

τρισσάκις, *thrice*, Bas.*ep.*236.5(3.363E; M.32.884A).

τρισσεύ-ω, **1.** *repeat twice, do for the third time* οὐδαμοῦ τις... ἀπήγγειλεν ἡμῖν, ὅτι ἐν μὲν τῷ ἅπαξ εἰπεῖν τὸ 'ἅγιος' μεγάλῃ τῇ φωνῇ, ἐν δὲ τῷ δευτερῶσαι ἧσσον, ἐν δὲ τῷ ~σαι ὑποβεβηκότως Ath.*hom. in Mt.11*:27(M.25.217D); **2.** *make, treat as threefold*, Gr.Nyss.*laud. Bas.*(M.46.805C); ~ομεν τὴν θεότητα †Gregent.*disp.*1(M.86.629D).

τρισσός, *threefold*; neut. plur., *codices having three columns*, Eus.*v.C.*4.37(p.132.10; M.20.1185C).

***τρισσοφαής**, *of threefold light*, Or.*exp.in Pr.*16:22(M.17.196B) cit. s. αὐτοζωία; Gr.Naz.*carm.*1.1.4.65(M.37.421A); τ. θεότητος *ib.*2.1. 13.214(1244A); Max.*qu.Thal.*8(M.90.285A); id.*myst.*23(M.91.701B).

***τρισσοφεγγής**, *shining with triple light* λατρευταὶ τ. οὐσίας Jo.D. *carm.pent.*47(p.215; M.96.836A); ὁ τ. τῆς θεαρχίας τύπος *ib.*102(p.216; 837B).

***τρισσοφεγγόφωτος**, *shining with threefold splendour* φύσις ἡ τ. Jo.D.*carm.pent.*95(p.216; M.96.837A).

***τρισσόφωτος**, *of threefold splendour* τὴν τ. φαῦσιν ‡Paul.Sil. *therm.Pyth.*187(M.86.2268); τῇ ἀστραπῇ τῆς τ. θεότητος Jo.D.*hom.*12. 9(M.96.793B).

τρισσόω, *triple, do thrice*, Sophr.H.*or.*2.1(M.87.3217A); Max. *ambig.*(M.91.1393B).

***τρισταλαίπωρος**, *thrice-miserable*, Nil.*epp.*2.164(M.79.277D).

τριστάτης, ὁ, 1. *one who comes third, stands in the third place*, Bas. *ep.*190(3.283D; M.32.701A); of a centurion, *third in rank*, Hesych.H. *Abd.*(M.93.1353A); **2.** *one who comes next to the sovereign and his queen, vizier*, *Chron.Pasch.*p.107(M.92.285A); met., Thdr.Stud.*or.*11. 17(M.99.820B); **3.** *captain*, Or.*sel.in Ex.*14:7(M.12.288C); ‡Gr.Nyss. *occurs.*(M.46.1168D); Germ.CP *or.*2(M.98.284A).

***τρίστυλος**, *with three columns*, Jo.Clim.*scal.*1(M.88.636D).

***τρίστωον, τό**, *building with three colonnades*, Proc.G.*3Reg.*7:28 (M.87.1157D).

***τρίσυλος**, *with three nails*, ‡Gr.Naz.*Chr.pat.*1488(v.l. τρισήλῳ M.38.255A).

***τρισυπόστατος**, *of three Persons*; **1.** of deity acc. Hermetic doctrine θεὸν...φράσαι...ἀδύνατον· ἔστι γὰρ τ., ἀνερμήνευτος οὐσία καὶ φύσις ‡Jo.D.*Artem.*28(p.160.18; M.96.1277A); **2.** of Godhead ὦ πάτερ καὶ λόγε καὶ πνεῦμα, ἡ τ. οὐσία καὶ δύναμις ‡Chrys.*hom.*11(13.247C); τὴν ἁγίαν...καὶ τ. τριάδα Chrysipp.*enc.in Jo.Bapt.*15(p.47.13); Dion. Ar.*c.h.*7.4(M.3.212C) cit. s. ἑνάς; id.*d.n.*1.4(M.3.592A) cit. s. ἔκφανσις; τῆς μιᾶς τ. καὶ προσκυνητῆς θεότητος Cosm.Ind.*top.*proem.(M.88. 52A); Max.*ambig.*(M.91.1036C) cit. s. ἐνούσιος; τ. τὴν μίαν τῆς θεότητος οὐσίαν προσκυνοῦμεν Thal.*cent.*2.98(M.91.1448A); μονάδα μὲν διὰ τὴν φυσικὴν ἑνότητα καὶ κυριότητα, τριάδα δὲ διὰ τὴν τ. τελειότητα CCP(681)*act.*18(H.3.1448E); ὁ θεός, τ. φύσις Andr.Cr.*triod.*2.9(M.97. 1409A); σὲ τὴν τ. μονάδα...ἕνα θεὸν ὁμοούσιον ὑμνῶ id.*can.mag.*(M. 97.1380C); μίαν θεότητα τ., ἐν μιᾷ τῶν αὐτῆς ὑποστάσεων ὁλικῶς ἡμῖν κοινωνήσασαν Jo.D.*hom.*11.3(M.96.765A); πιστεύω εἰς πατέρα, υἱὸν καὶ πνεῦμα, τριάδα ὁμοούσιον καὶ μονάδα τ. id.*rect.sent.*1(M.94.1421B); μιᾷ προσκυνήσει λατρεύομεν μίαν τ. θεότητα ‡Meth.*palm.*5(M.18. 393A); ‡Meth.*Sym.et Ann.*2(M.18.352C) cit. s. ἑνάς; ref. seraphic hymn τρισὶν ἁγιασμοῖς ὑμνεῖν τε καὶ ἁγιάζειν τὴν τ. μίαν θεότητα Max. *myst.*19(M.91.696C); τρισάγιον ᾠδήν, ὡς τῆς τ. θεότητος ἐμφαντικήν Jo.D.*f.o.*3.10(M.94.1021B); φημὶ...ἀποκεκαλύφθαι...διὰ τοῦ τρισαγίου ὕμνου τὴν μίαν τ. θεότητα καὶ κυριότητα id.*trisag.*2(M.95.25A); cf. Andr.Caes.*Apoc.*10(M.106.257C); Areth.*Apoc.*4:8(M.106.573C); as symbolized, ‡Ath.*qu.al.*4(M.28.776C) cit. s. τριπρόσωπος; ὥσπερ ἡ ψυχὴ...μία ἐστίν, ἀλλὰ καὶ τ., ψυχή, λόγος καὶ πνοή· οὕτω καὶ ὁ θεὸς εἷς ἐστιν, ἀλλ' ἔστι καὶ τ., πατήρ, λόγος καὶ πνεῦμα ἅγιον *ib.*(780B); οὐ γὰρ μίαν τινὰ εἰκόνα καὶ ὁμοίωσιν θεοῦ ὁ ἄνθρωπος κέκτηται...ἐξεικονίζων...τῆς τ. θεότητος τὸ μυστήριον ‡Gr.Nyss.*imag.*(M.44.1329B).

***τρίσυρος**, v. *τρίσειρος.

***τρισύστατος**, *composed of three parts*; of vault of heaven, *Pers.* (p.12.19; M.10.101A).

τρισώματος, *with body composed of three parts*; of Christ acc. Peratic doctrine, Hipp.*haer.*5.12(p.105.3; M.16.3162B).

***τρισώνυμος**, *with triple repetition of the name* ἐμβλέψατε...εἰς τὸν ...τοῦ σταυροῦ τύπον καὶ εἰς τὴν τοῦ Χριστοῦ ἐν αὐτῷ τ. ἐπιγραφήν Anast.S.*hod.*12(M.89.201C).

***τριτάκιον, τό**, *parchment*, *Euchol.*(p.493); *ib.*(p.655).

τριτάλας, *thrice-wretched*, *Orac.Sib.*5.52; *ib.*5.137.

τρίτειχος, *with triple wall*, Nil.*Eulog.*10(M.79.1108A).

***τριτενναται, αἱ**, [sc. μνῆμαι] *memorials of the dead on the third and ninth day*, ‡Jo.D.*fid.dorm.*24(M.95.269D).

***τρίτευχος, ἡ**, the *three volumes*, i.e. Joshua, Judges, Ruth, Ath. *ep.Marcell.*2(M.27.12B).

τριτημόριος, 1. *tripartite*; of Christ as composed of Logos, irrational soul, and body (Apollinarian) πῶς εἰκὸς τὸν τ. ἐκεῖνον τοῦ Ἀπολιναρίου θεὸν τὸν σαρκώδη θάνατον ὑπομεῖναι; Gr.Nyss.*Apoll.*29 (M.45.1189C); **2.** neut. as subst., *third part*, Thdt.*h.e.*1.11.3(3.774); of divine element (Logos) in Christ (Apollinarian), Gr.Nyss.*Apoll.* 35(M.45.1201B).

***τριτοεκτοεννάται**, [sc. ὧραι] *terce, sext, and none*, Jo.D.*jej.*5(M. 95.69D).

τρίτος, A. *third*; **1.** of third heaven εἶδον τ. οὐρανὸν πολὺ φωτεινότερον...παρὰ τοὺς δύο *T.Lev.*2.8; ἐν τῷ τ. εἰσὶν αἱ δυνάμεις τῶν παρεμβολῶν, οἱ ταχθέντες...ποιῆσαι ἐκδίκησιν τοῖς πνεύμασι τῆς πλάνης *ib.*3.3; δυνάμει ἀνθρωπείᾳ ἄφθεγκτον εἶναι τὸ θεῖον μηνύων, εἴ γε ὑπὲρ οὐρανὸν τὸν τ. ἄρχεται λαλεῖσθαι Clem.*str.*5.12(p.378.19; M.9. 117A); **2.** Trin.; of H. Ghost; **a.** in early writers Ἰησοῦν Χριστὸν... υἱὸν...τοῦ ὄντως θεοῦ...ἐν δευτέρᾳ ἔχοντες, πνεῦμά τε προφητικὸν ἐν τ. τάξει...μετὰ λόγου τιμῶμεν Just.*1apol.*13.3(M.6.348A); δύο μὲν οὐκ ἐρῶ θεούς, ἀλλ' ἢ ἕνα, πρόσωπα δὲ δύο οἰκονομίᾳ, τήν τε τ. τὴν χάριν τοῦ ἁγίου πνεύματος. πατὴρ μὲν γὰρ εἷς, πρόσωπα δὲ δύο, ὅτι καὶ ὁ υἱός, τὸ δὲ τ. τὸ ἅγιον πνεῦμα Hipp.*Noët.*14(p.257.1; οἰκονομίαν δὲ τρίτην, τὴν χάριν τοῦ ἁγίου πνεύματος M.10.821); ἐξακούω...τὴν ἁγίαν τριάδα μηνύεσθαι. τ. μὲν γὰρ εἶναι τὸ ἅγιον πνεῦμα, τὸν υἱὸν δὲ δεύτερον Clem. *str.*5.14(p.395.15; M.9.156B); **b.** Eunomian τὴν...τῶν ἁγίων...φυλάσσοντες διδασκαλίαν, παρ' ὧν τ. αὐτὸ ἀξιώματι καὶ τάξει μαθόντες, τ. εἶναι καὶ τῇ φύσει πεπιστεύκαμεν Eun.*apol.*25(M.30.861B); τ. ὂν τὸ ἅγιον τὴν τάξιν, οὐκ ἂν πρῶτον εἴη τὴν φύσιν, ὅπερ ἐστὶν ὁ θεὸς καὶ πατήρ *ib.*; τ. καὶ φύσει καὶ τάξει προστάγματι τοῦ πατρός, ἐνεργείᾳ δὲ τοῦ υἱοῦ γενόμενον, τ. χώρᾳ τιμώμενον, ὡς πρῶτον καὶ μεῖζον πάντων καὶ μόνον τοιοῦτο τοῦ μονογενοῦς ποίημα *ib.*(861C,D); **c.** in orthodox post-Nicene writers, ref. seraphic hymn οὐδαμοῦ τις...ἀπήγγειλεν... ὅτι τὸν πρῶτον ἁγιασμὸν κυριολογοῦντα, τὸν δὲ δεύτερον ὑποτάσσοντα καὶ τὸν τ. κατώτερον τιθέντα Ath.*hom.in Mt.11*:27(M.25.220A); τίς...ἀνάγκη, εἰ τῷ ἀξιώματι καὶ τῇ τάξει τ. ὑπάρχει τὸ πνεῦμα, τ. εἶναι αὐτὸ καὶ τῇ φύσει; Bas.*Eun.*3.1(1.272B; M.29.653B); οὐ πάντως, εἴ τι τῇ τάξει καὶ τῷ ἀξιώματι δεύτερόν ἐστι καὶ τ., τοῦτο καὶ τὴν φύσιν ἑτέραν ἔχει *ib.*3.2(273C; M.657B); εἰ οὖν φύσις αὐτῷ ὁ ἁγιασμός ἐστιν, ὥσπερ πατρὶ καὶ υἱῷ, πῶς τρίτης ἐστὶ καὶ ἀλλοτρίας φύσεως; *ib.*3.3 (274D; M.660D); πατέρα καὶ υἱὸν καὶ ἅγιον πνεῦμα παραδιδοὺς ὁ κύριος, οὐ μετὰ τοῦ ἀριθμοῦ συνεξέδωκεν· οὐ γὰρ εἶπεν, ὅτι εἰς πρῶτον καὶ δεύτερον καὶ τ. ... ἀλλὰ δι' ὀνομάτων ἁγίων τὴν γνῶσιν...ἐχαρίσατο id.*Spir.*44(3.37D; M.32.148D); οὐ γὰρ κατὰ σύνθεσιν ἀριθμοῦμεν, ἀφ' ἑνὸς εἰς πλῆθος ποιούμενοι τὴν παραύξησιν, ἓν καὶ δύο καὶ τρία λέγοντες, οὐδὲ πρῶτον καὶ δεύτερον καὶ τ. *ib.*45(38A; M.149B); οἱ...τὴν ὑπαρίθμησιν ἐν τῷ πρῶτον καὶ δεύτερον καὶ τ. λέγειν τιθέμενοι, γνωριζέσθωσαν τὸ πολύθεον...τῇ ἀχράντῳ θεολογίᾳ...ἐπεισάγοντες. εἰς οὐδὲν γὰρ ἕτερον φέρει τῆς ὑπαριθμήσεως τὸ κακούργημα ἢ ὥστε πρῶτον καὶ δεύτερον θεὸν καὶ τ. ὁμολογεῖν *ib.*47(39E; M.153C); **3.** of third order in angelic hierarchy γραφήσεται [sc. a virgin] ἐν τῇ βίβλῳ τῆς ζωῆς καὶ ἐν τῷ τ. τάγματι τῶν ἀγγέλων εὑρεθήσεται Ath.*virg.*10(p.43.23; M.28. 261C); of third triad τρίτην ἐπ' ἐσχάτων τῶν οὐρανίων ἱεραρχιῶν, τὴν τῶν ἀγγέλων τε καὶ ἀρχαγγέλων καὶ ἀρχῶν διακόσμησιν Dion.Ar.*c.h.* 6.2(M.3.201A); *ib.*10.1(273A); **4.** name of Valent. aeon ὁ τὰ πάντα περιέχων...δογματίσας...κληθῆναι ἑτέραν ὀγδοάδα...ἀντέστησε ἀντὶ τῶν ἀρρένων τοὺς ἄρρενας· Μόνον, Τ., Πέμπτον, Ἕβδομον Epiph.*haer.*31.6(p.393.6; M.41.484C).

B. neut. plur. as subst., *memorial prayers for dead on third day after death* ἐπιτελείσθω δὲ τ. τῶν κεκοιμημένων ἐν ψαλμοῖς καὶ ἀναγνώσμασιν καὶ προσευχαῖς διὰ τὸν διὰ τριῶν ἡμερῶν ἐγερθέντα *Const.App.*8.42.1; Pall.*h.Laus.*21(p.68.15; M.34.1076A); μνήμην ποιεῖσθαι τῶν προλαβόντων καὶ πάλιν τ. καὶ ἔννατα καὶ τεσσαράκοντα ‡Jo.D.*fid.dorm.*15(M.95.261B).

C. fem. sing. as subst.; **1.** *third hour* of the day, *A.Jo.*113(p.212.11); **2.** *terce*, office said at third hour εἰ δέ τινες καὶ ὥρας τακτὰς ἀπονέμουσιν εὐχῇ, ὡς τ. φέρε καὶ ἕκτην καὶ ἐνάτην, ἀλλ' οὖν γε ὁ γνωστικὸς παρὰ ὅλον εὔχεται τὸν βίον Clem.*str.*7.7(p.30.29; M.9.456C); μετὰ τ. ὥραν συνάξεις ἐπιτέλει, ὅτι ταύτῃ τῇ ὥρᾳ ἐπάγη τὸ ξύλον τοῦ σταυροῦ Ath.*virg.*12(p.46.9; M.28.265A); τ., ἕκτην, ἐνάτην καὶ τὰς ἑσπερινὰς εὐχὰς ἐπιτελοῦσι Chrys.*hom.14.4 in 1Tim.*(11.631A); ἔψαλλον τὴν τ. Jo.Mosch.*prat.*136(M.87.3000B); **3.** *third day* of the week, *Tuesday*, Eus.*qu.Marin.*2.2(M.22.941C); *Const.App.*5.14.1; of Tuesday in Holy Week τῇ ἁγίᾳ καὶ μεγάλῃ τ. Andr.Cr.*triod.*(M.97.1409B); Cosm.Mel.*hymn.*4 tit.(9,p.188; M.98.473A); *Const.Stud.*30(M.99.1716C).

D. neut. as adv., *thrice*, ref. sign of cross ὅταν καθεσθῇς ἐπὶ τῆς τραπέζης καὶ ἔρχῃ κλᾶσαι τὸν ἄρτον, σφραγίσασα αὐτὸν τ. Ath.*virg.*13(p.47.2; M.28.265C); ref. reception of Communion μεταλαμβάνειν... τ. τῆς ἑβδομάδος Jo.Mosch.*prat.*17(M.87.2865A).

***τριτότοκος**, *third-born* ὁ μονογενὴς δὲ πάντως καὶ πρωτότοκος εὑρίσκεται οὐκ ἔχων δευτερότοκον ἢ τ. Didym.*Trin.*3.4(M.39.836C).

τριττύς, ἡ, 1. *triplicity*, ref. Trin. ἡ τῶν ὀνομάτων τ. †Gr.Thaum.*ep.Philagr.*26(M.46.1101C); Jo.D.*trisag.*12(M.95.45B); **2.** *triad*, Synes.*regn.*7(p.16.15; M.66.1064C).

***τρίτυπος**, *of three forms, threefold*, Eudoc.*Cypr.*2.123(M.85.849C).

***τριτώνυμος**, *bearing three names*, ‡Ath.*Trin.*1.20(M.28.1148A).

***τρίτωσις, ἡ**, *second repetition*, i.e. *third time*, Gr.Nyss.*comm.not.*(M.45.176C).

***τριφαής**, *of triple light* μία παγὰ μία ῥίζα τ. ἔλαμψε μορφά Synes.*hymn.*2.26(p.44; M.66.1592).

***τριφάλαγγος**, *with three bones between the joints*, Melet.*nat.hom.*26(M.64.1252A).

***τριφανής**, *with threefold splendour* τῆς τοῦ...ἀρχικοῦ κάλλους...τ. θεωρίας Dion.Ar.*c.h.*7.2(M.3.208C).

***τριφάρμακος**, *containing threefold poison*, of vainglory, pride, and jealousy ἡ τρίσειρος ἅλυσις τῶν κακῶν, τὸ τ. κέρασμα τῶν παθῶν, ἡ τριττὴ γλῶττα τῶν αἱρετικῶν †Nil.*vit.*4(M.79.1144C).

***τριφεγγής**, *of triple light*; Trin., Geo.Pis.*hex.*182(M.92.1447A); of baptism, ‡Jo.D.*hom.*5(M.96.656D).

***τρίφεγγος**, = foreg., Jo.D.*carm.pent.*135(p.217; M.96.840A).

τριφυής, 1. *of threefold nature* (Peratic) κατεληλυθέναι...ἐν τοῖς Ἡρώδου χρόνοις τ. τινα...καὶ τριδύναμον ἄνθρωπον καλούμενον Χριστόν, ἀπὸ τῶν τριῶν ἔχοντα τοῦ κόσμου μερῶν ἐν ἑαυτῷ πάντα τὰ συγκρίματα καὶ τὰς δυνάμεις Hipp.*haer.*5.12(p.105.3; M.16.3162B); **2.** neut. as subst., *threefold nature*, ref. Apollinarian tripartite division of man, Gr.Nyss.*Apoll.*9(M.45.1140C).

***τρίφωτος**, *thrice-brilliant*, ‡Epiph.*hom.*5(M.43.496B).

***τριχεύομαι**, *be turned into hair*, ‡Caes.Naz.*dial.*140(M.38.1053).

***τριχῆς**, *three-fold* ὅσον μὲν κατὰ τὴν δύναμιν εἷς ἐστιν θεός, ὅσον δὲ κατὰ τὴν οἰκονομίαν τ. ἡ ἐπίδειξις Hipp.*Noët.*8(p.249.22 conj. τριχῇ ἐστι τάξις; M.10.816B).

***τριχοβάπτης, ὁ**, *one who dyes his hair*, Synes.*calv.*23(p.230.16; M.66.1204D).

τριχοκόμος, *with dressed hair*, Procl.CP *or.*9.2(M.65.773C).

***τριχοκουρία, ἡ**, *cutting of* an infant's *hair* on seventh day after baptism, *Euchol.*(p.306).

***τριχομαχία, ἡ**, *battle of the hair*, Synes.*calv.*16(p.219.18; M.66.1196A).

***τριχοπλάστης, ὁ**, *one who dresses his hair elaborately*, Synes.*calv.*21(p.229.1; M.66.1204A).

***τριχοποιός**, *producing hair*, Gr.Nyss.*hom.opif.*30.27(M.44.253A).

τρίχορδον, τό, (*lyre*) *with three strings*, Clem.*str.*1.16(p.49.18; M.8.789A).

***τριχοσθενής**, *whose strength lay in his hair*; of Samson, Leont.H.*Nest.*4.37(M.86.1708A).

***τριχοφόρος**, *wearing garments of hair*; of Jo. Bapt., Isid.Pel.*epp.*1.376(M.78.396A).

***τριψεργία, ἡ**, *tergiversation, prevarication* *Cod.Afr.*138(H.1.948D).

***τριῴδιον, τό, 1.** part of ὄρθρος consisting in a *hymn of three odes* each divided into several troparia, composed (esp. by Andr. Cr., Cosm. Mel., and Thdr. Stud.) for use in Lent and days preceding Christmas and Epiphany, cf.Michael *vita Theodori Studitae* 113(M.99.216B); **2.** liturg. book containing office for use during ten weeks before Easter and eight weeks between Easter and Sunday of All Saints (following Pentecost); so called because of its inclusion of many hymns of three odes instead of nine-ode canons of rest of year; composition and introduction of book due to monastery of Studium τῇ ἁγίᾳ καὶ μεγάλῃ μ' ψάλλομεν...τὸ τ. *Const.Stud.*14(M.99.1709B).

τριώνυμος, *having three names*; **1.** of God νύμφη [sc. BMV] τριωνύμου μονοθεΐας οὖσα *Pers.*(p.13.17; M.10.101C); esp. ref. Sabellian doctrine which denied hypostatic distinction of Persons in Trin., Eus.*e.th.*3.6(p.164.27; M.24.1016A); ἐνετείλατο...βαπτίζειν... οὔτε εἰς ἕνα τ., οὔτε εἰς τρεῖς ἐνανθρωπήσαντας, ἀλλ' εἰς τρεῖς ὁμοτίμους ‡Ign.*Phil.*2; ‡Just.*qu.et resp.*17(M.6.1264C); εἷς θεὸς οὐχ ὡς τ. ‡Ath.*Maced.dial.*1.18(M.28.1320D); ὃν γὰρ Σαβέλλιος λέγει τ., τοῦτον Εὐνόμιος ὀνομάζει ἀγέννητον Gr.Nyss.*Eun.*10(2 p.234.27; M.45.836D); Thdt.*Trin.*28(M.75.1188C) cit. s. συναίρεσις; Σαβέλλιον, ἓν πρόσωπον τ. λέγοντα τὴν τριάδα Justn.*conf.*(p.72.24; M.86.995B); ὁ...Σαβέλλιος...τ. πρᾶγμα ἔλεγε τὸν θεόν †Leont.B.*sect.*3.3(M.86.1216A); **2.** of apostle variously called by evangelists Thaddaeus, Lebbaeus, or Judas of James, Hesych.H.*qu.ev.*14(M.93.1405B).

***τριωρία, ἡ**, *period of three hours*, Vict.*Mc.*6:48(p.380.7); *cat.Mt.*14:28(p.118.16); Thdr.Mops.*Mt.*14:25(M.66.709B).

***τρίωρος**, *in three hours*, *A.Jo.*86(p.193.21); *of three hours*, Jo.Clim.*scal.*13(M.88.860B).

τριώροφον, τό, *third story* of building, Or.*hom.2.1 Gen.*(p.25.25; M.12.161C); Gr.Naz.*carm.*2.1.11.1332(M.37.1120A); Chrys.*hom.52.3 in Mt.*(7.333D).

***τρόζημα, τό**, a kind of vegetable, Jo.Mosch.*prat.*184(M.87.3057B).

τρομάζω, *tremble* (*at*), *Asen.*26(p.81.1); ὃν αὐτὸς ὁ ᾅδης ἐτρόμασε *Symb.Nic.*(359)ap.Thdt.*h.e.*2.21.4(3.880); Mac.Mgn.*apocr.*2.17(p.30.6); τὰ μνημεῖα πρὸς μεθοδείαν σωμάτων ἐτρόμαζον Isid.Pel.*epp.*1.253(M.78.336B).

***τρομάσσ-ω**, *tremble with fear* δι' ὃν [sc. Christ] ἐτρόμαξεν οὐρανὸς καὶ ἡ γῆ Mel.*pass.*94 p.16.11; διὰ τί οὕτως, ὦ Ἰσραήλ, ἐπὶ τοῦ κυρίου οὐκ ἐτρόμαξας; *ib.*99 p.16.32; *A.Thom.*B 24(p.33.20); ἐμνήσθην τὴν ὥραν ἐκείνην καὶ ἐτρόμαξα Ephr.3.144D; ὁπόταν...τὸ ὄνομα τοῦ σωτῆρος...ὀνομάζηται...∼οντες φεύγουσιν ἀφ' ἡμῶν οἱ...δαίμονες Nil.*epp.*3.278(M.79.521C).

***τρομικῶς**, *in a state of trembling*, Cyr.H.*catech.*16.15.

τρόπαιον, τό, A. *trophy, memorial* or *sign of victory*; **1.** of Cross and Christ's death, Just.*1apol.*55.3(M.6.412B); τ. κατὰ πάσης ἀντικειμένης δυνάμεως τὸν σταυρὸν στήσαντος Or.*Jo.*20.36(29; p.376.17; M.14.657C); σταυρός, τ. κατὰ τῆς ἀδικίας Meth.*Porph.*1(p.504.12; M.18.400B); τῷ τ. τοῦ σταυροῦ εὔξασθαι μᾶλλον ὤφελον ἤπερ δεδιέναι *A.*(*Pass.*)*Andr.*9(p.22.24; M.2.1236A); οὐδὲ...κατ' αὐτὸ τοῦ σταυροῦ τὸ τ. ... βίαιον ὑπέμεινεν τελευτήν, ἀλλ' ἑκὼν παρεδίδου τοῖς ἐπιβουλεύουσι τὸ σῶμα...ἐλεύθερος αὐτὸς ἀφ' ἑαυτοῦ τὴν ἐκ τοῦ σώματος ἀναχώρησιν ἐποιεῖτο Eus.*d.e.*3.4(p.114.27; M.22.196D); cf.id.*theoph.*3(p.4*.15; M.24.612A); τὸ τῆς κατάρας τ. id.*d.e.*1.10(p.47.13; 89B); τῷ τοῦ πάθους σεμνυνόμενος τροπαίῳ id.*v.C.*3.1(p.76.12; M.20.1053A); τοῦ...σωτῆρος τὰ κατὰ τοῦ θανάτου τ. id.*l.C.*9(p.221.19; M.20.1369C); cf.*ib.*15(p.247.8; 1417B); τίς θεὸς ἢ ἥρως, οὕτω πολεμηθείς, ὡς ὁ...σωτήρ, τ. νικητήρια κατὰ τῶν ἐχθρῶν ἤγειρεν; *ib.*17(p.258.21; 1437B); ἐν τῷ θανάτῳ, μᾶλλον δὲ ἐν τῷ κατὰ τοῦ θανάτου τ., λέγω δὴ τῷ σταυρῷ, πᾶσα ἡ κτίσις ὡμολόγει τὸν...θεοῦ υἱὸν καὶ σωτῆρα πάντων Ath.*inc.*19.3(M.25.129B); ὃν...ἐνόμιζον ἄτιμον ἐπιφέρειν θάνατον, οὗτος ἦν τ. κατ' αὐτοῦ τοῦ θανάτου *ib.*24.4(137C); τὸν κατὰ τοῦ θανάτου τρόπαια καὶ νίκας ἐπιδειξάμενον *ib.*29.1(145B); καταργῆσθαι τὸν θάνατον καὶ τ. εἶναι κατ' αὐτοῦ τὸν...σταυρόν *ib.*30.1(148A); γευσάμενος θανάτου...σταυροῦ, ὅπως δι' αὐτοῦ τ. κατὰ τοῦ θανάτου ἡ ἀνθρωπότης λάβοι Epiph.*haer.*69.62(p.211.15; M.42.304A); ἔλαβε τὸ τ. τοῦ σταυροῦ κατὰ τοῦ διαβόλου *ib.*66.73(p.114.20; 145A); ἔνθα ὁ θάνατος ἐβασίλευσεν, ἐκεῖ καὶ τὸ τ. στῆσαι Chrys.*hom.85.1 in Jo.*(8.504B); τ. ἐξῄει βαστάζων, τὸν σταυρόν, κατὰ τῆς τοῦ θανάτου τυραννίδος *ib.*; hence **2.** of sign of the cross οἱ...Χριστιανοὶ...τὸ τ. κατὰ τοῦ θανάτου ἐπὶ μετώπῳ βαστάζοντες Hipp.*Dan.*4.9.3; τὸ τ. τοῦ σταυροῦ κατὰ τοῦ μετώπου τῇ χειρὶ ποιησάμενος *Lit.*ap.*Const.App.*8.12.4; ἠνάγκασε τοῦτον τὸ δέος ἐπιθεῖναι τῷ μετώπῳ τοῦ σταυροῦ τὸ σημεῖον. οἱ δέ [sc. demons], τοῦ δεσποτικοῦ τ. τὸν τύπον ἰδόντες, φροῦδοι...ἐγένοντο Thdt.*h.e.*3.3.3(3.913); of Constantine's vision of cross ἰδεῖν ἔφη ἐν αὐτῷ οὐρανῷ ὑπερκείμενον τοῦ ἡλίου σταυροῦ τ. ἐκ φωτὸς συνιστάμενον Eus.*v.C.*1.28

(p.21.16; M.20.944B); of labarum ἐπ' αὐτῶν τῶν ὅπλων τὸ τοῦ σωτηρίου τ. σύμβολον κατασημαίνεσθαι ἐποίει, τοῦ τε ἐνόπλου στρατοῦ προπομπεύειν...μόνον...τὸ σωτήριον τ. ib.4.21(p.125.16; 1168C); νικητικὸν τ., δαιμόνων ἀποτρόπαιον...ἀντιπαρατάξας, τὰς κατὰ πάντων ...πολεμίων...καὶ αὐτῶν δαιμόνων...ἤρατο νίκας id.l.C.6(p.212.6; M.20.1352A); **3.** ref. Inc. τίς...πώποτε...πρὶν ἰσχῦσαι καλεῖν πατέρα ἢ μητέρα ἐβασίλευσεν καὶ τρόπαια κατὰ τῶν ἐχθρῶν εἴληφεν; Ath.inc.36.1(M.25.157B); ὁ...πρὶν τῆς σωματικῆς ἐπιφανείας λαβὼν κατὰ τῶν ἀντικειμένων δυνάμεων νίκην, κατὰ τῆς εἰδωλολατρείας τρόπαια ib.37.5(160D); **4.** ref. Christ's exorcisms ὁ...μετὰ τὰ πρῶτα κατὰ δαιμόνων τ. ἤδη καὶ κατὰ θανάτου παρετάττετο Eus.theoph.3(p.8*.17; M.24.613B); **5.** ref. Christ's Resurrection, Clem.q.d.s.42(p.190.19; M.9.649D); τ. δὲ ἀθανασίας κατὰ τοῦ θανάτου τοῖς πᾶσι παρέχων ὁρᾶν Eus.l.C.15(p.247.22; M.20.1420A); θνητῷ...ὅπλῳ κεχρημένος...τ. ἀθανασίας κατὰ τοῦ θανάτου...ἔστησεν id.theoph.3(p.13*.20; M.24.617C); τὸ σῶμα ἀναστῆναι καὶ τοῦτο δειχθῆναι κατ' αὐτοῦ [sc. death] τ. Ath.inc.30.2(M.25.148B); τοῦτο γὰρ ἦν κατὰ τοῦ θανάτου τ., ταύτην [sc. Resurrection] ἐπιδείξασθαι πᾶσι ib.22.4(136A); τὸ ἴδιον ἐγείρας σῶμα καὶ τ. αὐτὸ κατὰ τοῦ θανάτου...ἐπιδειξάμενος τῷ σημείῳ τοῦ σταυροῦ ib.32.6(152C); ἀνέστησε, τρόπαια καὶ νίκας κατὰ τοῦ θανάτου φέρων, τὴν ἐν τῷ σώματι γενομένην ἀφθαρσίαν καὶ ἀπάθειαν ib.26.1(141A); **6.** of fruits of Christ's victory over death displayed in conduct of Christians, ib.29.3(145C); **7.** of martyrdom as trophy of victory, Bas.hom.19.8(2.156C; M.31.525A); **8.** of CNic.(325) τ. οὖσαν πάσης μὲν αἱρέσεως, ἐξαιρέτως δὲ τῆς Ἀρειανῆς Ath.ep.Epict.1(p.3.13; M.26.1052B); **9.** synon. with *victory, triumph* ἦν [δὲ και]νὸν τ. ἰδεῖν ἐπὶ τῶν πρωτο[τόκων νε]κρῶν ἐν μιᾷ ῥοπῇ Mel.pass.21 p.4.2; of saving acts of God, Chrys.hom.19.19 in Mt.(7.257E).

B. *memorial, monument* ἐγὼ δὲ τὰ τ. τῶν ἀποστόλων ἔχω δεῖξαι. ἐὰν γὰρ θελήσῃς ἀπελθεῖν εἰς τὸν Βατικανὸν ἢ ἐπὶ τὴν ὁδὸν τὴν Ὠστίαν, εὑρήσεις τὰ τ. τῶν ταύτην ἱδρυσαμένων τὴν ἐκκλησίαν Caius R.ap.Eus.h.e.2.25.7(M.20.209A); of memorial to healing of the woman with the issue of blood, Eus.h.e.7.18.1(680B); of church of Resurrection οἶκον εὐκτήριον, τ. τῆς κατὰ τοῦ θανάτου νίκης αὐτοῦ...ἀνέδειξεν id.l.C.18(p.259.24; M.20.1440B).

τροπαιοφορέω, *triumph*, Orac.Sib.11.299; Olymp.Job 36:7(M.93.373C).

τροπαιοφόρος, *bearing trophies, victorious*; in gen., Orac.Sib.14.343; Gr.Nyss.Eun.12(1 p.217.22; M.45.912A); Jo.D.hom.4.25(M.96.625A); of risen Christ νικηφόρος καὶ τ. Or.Jo.6.56(37; p.164.30; M.14.297B); of martyrs, Bas.hom.19.8(2.155C; M.31.521C); Nil.epp.3.118(M.79.437B); Jo.Mon.hymn.Geo.9(M.96.1400D); of truth victorious over falsehood, Gr.Nyss.Steph.1(M.46.705D).

τροπάρι(ο)ν, τό, 1. *troparion*; in gen., any metrical composition sung in church services μετὰ τὸ...ἀποτεθῆναι πάντα εἰς τὴν ἁγίαν τράπεζαν, καὶ ψαλθῆναι τὸν τελευταῖον στίχον τοῦ κοινωνικοῦ, λέγεσθαι [v.l. λέγεται] τοῦτο τὸ τροπάριν Chron.Pasch.p.390(M.92.1001C) = Lit.Bas.(p.342.5); προσθήσομεν δὲ τέρψεως χάριν καὶ ὀλιγοστὰ τ. λιγυρώτατα Cosm.Mel.schol.(M.38.531); οἱ τῶν τ. ποιηταί Thdr.Lect.h.e.1.19(M.86.173C); cf.Thphn.chron.p.98(M.108.289B); †Jo.Jej.poenit.(M.88.1889A); ὥσπερ οὖν ῥητὸν λέγοντες, ψαλμοῦ τυχὸν ἢ ᾠδῆς, ἐπιλέγομεν πολλάκις τ. ἢ μελῴδημα, μὴ τῆς τοῦ ῥητοῦ διανοίας ἐχόμενον· οὕτως ὅταν ἐν ῥητοῦ τάξει, εἰς τὸ δόξα πατρί, καὶ υἱῷ, καὶ ἁγίῳ πνεύματι λέγομεν, ἐπιλέγομεν τ. ἁρμόζον τῷ υἱῷ μόνῳ Jo.D.trisag.(M.95.36A,B); Lit.Chrys.(p.368.21,28; p.378.20); **2.** τὸ τῆς ἡμέρας τ. = ἀπολυτίκιον q.v., Lit.Praesanct.(p.345.3); **3.** by analogy, of chants of Roman liturgy οἱ Ῥωμαῖοι ἑορτάζουσι τὴν Γέννησιν...μετὰ ἀναγνωσμάτων τελείων, καὶ πολλῶν τ. καὶ στοιχαρίων Jo.Nic.nativ.(M.96.1445C); ib.(1449B).

***τροπεύομαι**, *deal craftily*, Thphn.chron.p.328(M.108.792C).

τροπή, ἡ, *turn; turning*; **1.** plur.; **a.** *the seasons* ἥλιος φαίνει καὶ τὸν ἀέρα εἰς τέσσαρας τ. τρέπει Hom.Clem.3.36; ἐκ τεσσάρων...συνεστῶτες μερῶν κατὰ τὰς διαφόρους τ. διαφόρως τρέπονται [sc. οἱ ἄνθρωποι] τὰ σώματα ib.20.5; rarely sing. τὴν μίαν τοῦ ἐνιαυτοῦ ὥραν, ἤγουν τ., δηλαδὴ τρίμηνον Andr.Caes.Apoc.54(M.106.384B); cf. καλῶς εἶπε 'πάντα πλουσίως', τὰς ἐτησίους τ. αἰνιττόμενος, τὸν ἀέρα, τὸ φῶς, τὸ ὕδωρ, τὰ ἄλλα πάντα Chrys.hom.18.1 in 1Tim.(11.655A); **b.** of the sun from month to month μὴν δὲ τροπαῖς δώδεκα ἡλίου περίοδον ἐπλήρου Eus.l.C.6(p.207.17; M.20.1344A); **2.** *turn, change* (pass., i.e. change undergone); **a.** in gen., a form of motion opp. local motion τῆς γὰρ κινήσεως οὐ μόνον κατὰ τὴν τοπικὴν μετάστασιν νοουμένης, ἀλλὰ καὶ ἐν τ. καὶ ἀλλοιώσει θεωρουμένης Gr.Nyss.hom.opif.1.4(M.44.129C); one of two chief principles blended by God in universe ἐναλλάξασα τὰς ἰδιότητας ἡ τοῦ θεοῦ σοφία, τῷ μὲν ἀεικινήτῳ τὸ ἄτρεπτον, τῷ δὲ ἀκινήτῳ τὴν τ. ἐνεποίησε...ἡ μὲν γῆ στάσιμός ἐστι, καὶ οὐκ ἄτρεπτος· ὁ δὲ οὐρανὸς τοῦ ἐναντίου τὸ τρεπτὸν οὐκ ἔχων, οὐδὲ στάσιμον ἔχει, ἵνα τῇ μὲν φύσει ἑστώσῃ τὴν τ., τῇ δὲ μὴ τρεπομένῃ τὴν κίνησιν ἡ θεία συμπλέξασα δύναμις ib.(129D); a mark of this world εἰ οὐρανοὺς καινοὺς...προσδοκῶμεν, ἐν οἷς δικαιοσύνη ἄτρεπτος πολιτεύεσθαι...πῶς αὐτὸς διδάσκεις πάλιν φόβον ἀνθρώπων...ὑπάρχειν ἐκεῖσε, καὶ τ.; Nil.epp.2.247(M.79.328C); Dion.Ar.e.h.7.1.1(M.3.553A); and of man and created things ὁ μὲν γὰρ [sc. ὁ σωτήρ] ἀτρέπτου φύσεως τυγχάνει, τέλειος ὢν...οἱ δὲ εἰς ἑκάτερα τροπῇ ὑποκείμενοι Alex.Al.ep.Alex.7(p.24.12; M.18.557D); ὅσα...ἐκ τοῦ μὴ ὄντος ὑπέστη, εὐθὺς ἀπὸ τ. τοῦ εἶναι ἀρξάμενα, πάντοτε δι' ἀλλοιώσεως πρόεισιν Gr.Nyss.or.catech.8(p.51.5; M.45.40A); τῆς τ. ἀναγκαίως ἐν τῷ ἀνθρώπῳ θεωρουμένης ib.21(p.81.12; 57D); θεοδίδακτος ὤν, τῇ μὲν φύσει τῶν γενητῶν προσέρριψε τὴν τ. ... τετήρηκε δὲ τὸ ἄτρεπτον τῷ ἐπὶ πάντας θεῷ Cyr.synous.2(p.478.26; cf.M.76.1428C); τὰ...τῆς κτίσεως ἐν ἀλλοιώσει καὶ τροπαῖς...ἡμεῖς δὲ τὴν φύσιν...εὐπαράφορον ...πρὸς ἀλλοίωσιν ἔχοντες καὶ τροπήν id.inc.unigen.(5^1.683D,E); ὧν...τὸ εἶναι ἀπὸ τ. ἤρξατο, ταῦτα τῇ τ. ὑποκείσεται πάντως, ἢ φθειρόμενα, ἢ κατὰ προαίρεσιν ἀλλοιούμενα ‡Cyr.Trin.2(6^3.2E; M.77.1121C); **b.** in physical universe χρὴ...τῶν ἄλλων πάντων ὑπεραναβαίνοντας ἐπὶ τὸν νοῦν ἵστασθαι, ὥσπερ...κἂν τῷ κόσμῳ τὰς ἐννέα μοίρας ὑπερπηδήσαντες, πρώτην μὲν διὰ τῶν τεσσάρων στοιχείων ἐν μιᾷ χώρᾳ τιθεμένων διὰ τὴν ἴσην τ. Clem.str.2.11(p.140.5; M.8.988A); ἔτι...τροπῆς εὐλάβεια καὶ τῆς ἑβδομῆς ἅπτεται περιφορᾶς ib.4.25(p.319.3; 1368B); ἐπιπορευόμενος τήν τε τῶν ὅλων καὶ τὴν ἐπὶ μέρους ἑκάστου φύσιν τ. τε τὴν πολυειδῆ καὶ μεταβολὴν τῶν ἐν τῷ κόσμῳ Gr.Thaum.pan.Or.8(p.22.10; M.10.1077B); τῆς τοῦ παντὸς τ. τε καὶ ἀλλοιώσεως Eus.p.e.11.7(522C; M.21.865C); chemical κατὰ μεταβολὴν καὶ τ. ὁ ἀὴρ ὕδωρ τὰ πρῶτα γεγονὼς εἰς πῦρ ἔληξε διὰ τῶν τροπῶν Hom.Clem.20.6; biological, in plants, animals, and men οἱ πλεῖστοι...τὰς αὐξήσεις καὶ τὰς τ. τοῖς ἄστροις κατὰ τὸ προηγούμενον ἀνατιθέασιν Clem.str.6.16(p.507.31; M.9.377C); πυροῦσθαι τὸ ἐπιθυμεῖν τῆς μεταβλητῆς γενέσεως ὀνομάζεται. ἓν δὲ ὂν τὸ πῦρ τροπὰς στρέφεται δύο. στρέφεται γάρ, φησίν, ἐν τῷ ἀνδρὶ τὸ αἷμα...εἰς σπέρμα, ἐν δὲ τῇ γυναικὶ τὸ αὐτὸ τοῦτο αἷμα εἰς γάλα. καὶ γίνεται ἡ τοῦ ἄρρενος τ. γένεσις, ἡ δὲ τῆς θηλείας τ. τροφὴ τῷ γεννωμένῳ Hipp.haer.6.17(p.143.16ff.; M.16.3219B); τῶν τῇδε προσκαίρων ποικιλμάτων, ἃ φύλλων δίκην πρὸς ὥραν θάλλοντα, συναφαυαίνονται τοῦ σώματος ταῖς τ. Meth.symp.7.2(p.73.13; M.18.128B); φερομένη ἡ ὕλη...ὥσπερ ᾠόν...καὶ τὸ...ἔμψυχον ᾠόν, ἐκ τῆς ὑποκειμένης καὶ ἀεὶ ῥεούσης ὕλης κινούμενον, παντοδαπὰς ἐκφαίνει τ. Hom.Clem.6.5; **c.** of mortal to immortal body ἀναγκαῖον χρῆσθαι σώμασι πνευματικοῖς [sc. in heaven], οὐχὶ τοῦ εἴδους τοῦ προτέρου ἀφανιζομένου, κἂν ἐπὶ τὸ ἐνδοξότερον γένηται αὐτοῦ ἡ τ., ὥσπερ ἦν τὸ Ἰησοῦ εἶδος καὶ Μωϋσέως καὶ Ἡλίου, οὐχ ἕτερον ἐν τῇ μεταμορφώσει παρ' ὃ ἦν Meth.res.1.22(p.246.10; M.41.1092B); **d.** in human life ἐν τῷ τρεπομένῳ τὸ ἄτρεπτον ἀδύνατον λαβεῖν πῆξιν...ἐν τ. δὲ τῇ συνεχεῖ, καὶ διὰ τοῦτο ἀστάτου τοῦ ἡγεμονικοῦ γινομένου, ἡ ἑκτικὴ δύναμις οὐ σῴζεται Clem.str.6.9(p.470.16; M.9.297B); ταῖς ἀχθηδόσι καὶ τ. καὶ θλίψεσι τοῦ βίου Meth.symp.8.12(p.96.20; M.18.157C); τῷ μὴ μακαρίζειν ἄνδρα πρὸ τελευτῆς διὰ τὸ τῆς τοῦ βίου τ. ἄδηλον παρηγγέλθαι Eus.v.C.1.11(p.13.4; M.20.925A); **e.** moral τὴν τ. καὶ τὴν ἐπὶ τὸ κρεῖττον μεταβολὴν Or.princ.3.1.5(M.11.253C; v.l. for προτροπὴν p.200.8); usu. signifying moral *decline*, cf. ἀλλοίωσις; ἡ πρὸς κακίαν τ. τῶν ἀνθρώπων Gr.Nyss.Eun.4(2 p.51.12; M.45.621A); id.or.catech.16(p.66.12; M.45.49B); βούλεται ἡμᾶς ὁ λόγος τρεπτοὺς ὄντας κατὰ τὴν φύσιν, μὴ πρὸς τὸ κακὸν διὰ τῆς τ. ἀπορρέειν· ἀλλὰ...σύνεργον τὴν τ. πρὸς τὴν ὑψηλοτέρων ἄνοδον ἔχειν id.hom.8 in Cant.(M.44.945C); τὸ θεῖον...ἐν τῇ τρεπτῇ...γίνεται φύσει, ἵνα τῷ ἰδίῳ ἀτρέπτῳ τὴν ἡμετέραν πρὸς τὸ κακὸν τ. ἐξιάσηται id.Apoll.2(M.45.1128A); τὸ...προαιρέσει καὶ οὐ φύσει περί τι κρατούμενον, δύναιτ' ἂν ἐφ' ἕτερα μεταβάλλεσθαι...τ. δὲ τοῦτο καὶ πάθος Cyr.thes.13(5^1.125A); ἔδει τὸν ἄτρεπτον τοῦ θεοῦ λόγον ἑαυτὸν ὑπὲρ ἡμῶν ἀντιθεῖναι τῷ πονηρῷ, ἵν' ὥσπερ διὰ τῆς ἐκείνου τ. ἐνικήθημεν, οὕτω διὰ τῆς ἀτρεψίας τοῦ λόγου κρατήσωμεν ib.20(198D); ἐπὶ τὰ χείρω τροπήν Dion.Ar.e.h.7.2(M.3.553D); οὐ...φύσει τὸ κακόν, ἀλλὰ τροπῇ Olymp.fr.Lam.3:1(M.93.744A); οὐ γὰρ ἁμαρτίαν ὁ θεὸς ἐνομοθέτησεν ἀλλὰ προαιρετικῶς τὴν τ. ὑπεμείναμεν ib.3:33(748A); **3.** *change, alteration* (act., i.e. change deliberately effected); **a.** by God, Hom.Clem.20.7; ib.20.8; ὑπομενούσης τῆς οὐσίας, τ. τινα τῶν ποιοτήτων αὐτῆς πεποιηκέναι Meth.arbitr.10(p.171.14; M.18.257C); **b.** by magic, Hom.Clem.2.26; **4.** theol., *change*; **a.** alien to divine nature ἐπευχέσθω λέγων· ὁ θεὸς...ὁ τροπῆς ἀνεπίδεκτος Lit.ap.Const.App.8.15.7; ἡ ἄκτιστος φύσις τῆς κινήσεως τῆς κατὰ τ. καὶ μεταβολὴν καὶ ἀλλοίωσίν ἐστιν ἀνεπίδεκτος Gr.Nyss.or.catech.6(p.34.1; M.45.28C); ὁ ἐν πάσῃ τῇ ἀγαθοῦ τελειότητι θεωρούμενος κατὰ πᾶν εἶδος τροπῆς τὸ ἀναλλοίωτον ἔχει id.ep.3(M.46.1020A); ἄτρεπτός...ἐστιν ὁ θεός...τ. δ' εἰς τὸ ποιεῖν τὰ μὴ πρέποντα αὐτῷ οὐ δέχεταί ποτε ‡Just.qu.et resp.36(M.6.1284A); τ. ἁπάσης καὶ ἀλλοιώσεως τῆς κατὰ τὸν τῆς οὐσίας λόγον ἡ θεία φύσις ἀνεπίδεκτος εἶναι πιστεύεται Cyr.Jo.1.4(4.36D); ὁ...φύσει μακάριος οὐδεμίαν τ. ἐπιδέχεται Thdt.*1Tim.*6:15(3.672); κινεῖσθαι...αὐτὸν... οἰητέον, οὐ κατὰ...τ., ἢ τοπικὴν κίνησιν Dion.Ar.*d.n.*9.9(M.3.916C); hence **b.** alien to divine generation οὐ τοίνυν ὡς ἕτερον ἐν ἑτέρῳ ἐξ ἀπείρων...αἰώνων ἦν ὁ υἱὸς ἀγένητος ἐν τῷ πατρί, μέρος ὢν αὐτοῦ ὃ μεταβληθὲν ὕστερον...ἐκτὸς αὐτοῦ γέγονεν· τροπῆς γὰρ...τοῦτο οἰκεῖον, καὶ δύο γ' ἂν οὕτως ἀγένητα εἶεν, τὸ προβεβληκὸς καὶ τὸ προβεβλημένον Eus.*d.e.*5.1(p.212.14; M.22.352D); χρὴ νοεῖν καὶ τῆς τῶν σαρκῶν γενέσεως ἀπηλλοτριῶσθαι τὸν τρόπον, καθ' ὃν ὁ πατὴρ ἐγέννα τὸν υἱόν...οὐδὲ γὰρ σῶμα ἦν, ὡς ἀπόρροιαν...ἢ τ. ... ἐπ' αὐτῷ λογίσασθαι id.*e.th.*1.12(p.72.18; M.24.849A); μονὰς δὲ ὢν ἀδιαίρετος ὁ θεὸς τὸν μονογενῆ αὐτοῦ υἱὸν ἐξ ἑαυτοῦ ἐγέννα, οὐ διαιρούμενος οὐδ' ἀλλοίωσιν ἢ τ. ἢ ῥοὴν ἤ τι πάθος ὑπομένων *ib.*2.6(p.103.24; 908A); Cyr.*thes.*10(5^{1}.78D); **c.** nor applicable to H. Ghost οὐ...δυνατὸν πνεῦμα ἀκούσαντα περιγεγραμμένην φύσιν ἐντυπῶσαι τῇ διανοίᾳ ἢ τροπαῖς καὶ ἀλλοιώσεσιν ὑποκειμένην ἢ ὅλως ὁμοίαν τῇ κτίσει Bas.*Spir.*22(3.19B; M.32.108B); **5.** Christol.; Inc. free from all implication of τροπή, i.e. **a.** *conversion* of Godhead into flesh ἄνθρωπος τέλειος προελθών· οὐ...κατὰ φαντασίαν ἢ τ., ἀλλὰ ἀληθῶς γενόμενος ἄνθρωπος Hipp.*Noët.*17(p.263.10; M.10.828A); ἐν σαρκὶ ἡ θεότης ὡς τὸ πῦρ ἐν σιδήρῳ...οὔτε ἐκινήθη ἐξ ἑαυτοῦ...οὔτε τ. ὑπέμεινε †Bas.*Chr.generat.*2(2.596E; M.31.1460C); ref. Phil.2:6f. διὰ τοῦ μὲν 'λαβόντος' τὸ πρόσφατον δηλοῦντος, διὰ δὲ τοῦ 'ἐν μορφῇ θεοῦ ὑπάρχοντος' εἰς τ. μὴ παρερχομένου Epiph.*haer.*76.34 (p.383.27; M.42.585B); id.*anc.*117(p.145.5; M.43.229B) cit. s. ἄνθρωπος; τὸ γενέσθαι σάρκα αὐτόν, οὐ κατὰ τ. ἢ μετάστασιν· ἄτρεπτος γὰρ ἡ θεία φύσις Cyr.*Heb.*2:14(p.464.4; M.74.965A); εἰ καὶ γέγονε καθ' ἡμᾶς τέλειος ἄνθρωπος ὁ...λόγος, οὐ τροπήν, οὐκ ἀλλοίωσιν...μεμενηκὼς δὲ μᾶλλον καὶ ἐν τῇ...ἀνθρωπότητι τοῦθ' ὅπερ ἦν id.*ep.*31(p.72.13; 5^{2}.95D); *ib.*55(p.54.26; 181D); id.*expl.xii cap.*1(p.17.12; 6^{1}.147D); ἕτερον μέν τι καὶ ἕτερον θεότης τε καὶ ἀνθρωπότης...ἀλλ' ἦν ἐν Χριστῷ ξένως τε καὶ ὑπὲρ νοῦν εἰς ἑνότητα συνδεδραμηκότα, συγχύσεως δίχα καὶ τ. id.*Chr. un.*(5^{1}.736A); ἵνα...μὴ κατὰ τροπὴν θεότητος ἄνθρωπον τὸν μονογενῆ γεγονέναι νοήσωμεν, ἀναθεματίζουσι καὶ τοὺς λέγοντας ἢ τρεπτὸν ἢ ἀλλοιωτὸν τὸν υἱὸν τοῦ θεοῦ Thdot.Anc.*exp.symb.*23(M.77.1345C); εἰ μὴ σάρκα λαβὼν λέγεται γεγενῆσθαι σάρξ, δυοῖν θάτερον ἀνάγκη λέγειν, ἢ τὴν εἰς σάρκα τ. αὐτὸν ὑπομεμενηκέναι, ἢ δοκήσει τοιοῦτον ὀφθῆναι, κατὰ τὸν ἀληθῆ λόγον ἄσαρκον εἶναι θεόν Thdt.*eran.*1(4.10); εἷς ἐστι Χριστός...οὐ τροπῇ θεότητος εἰς σάρκα, ἀλλὰ προσλήψει ἀνθρωπότητος εἰς θεότητα ‡Ath.*symb.*1(M.28.1584B); *ib.*3(1588B); γενόμενος ἄνθρωπος...ὁ...λόγος...καὶ φυσικῆς σαρκὸς περιγραφῆς ἀνασχόμενος δι' ἡμᾶς, τ. οὐχ ὑπέμεινεν ‡Hipp.*Ber.Hel.*1(p.321.26; M.10.832A); so of the two natures οὐ γὰρ ἔγνωσαν ἀδύνατον εἶναι, θείας ἐνεργείας φύσεως ἑτεροφυοῦς οὐσίας ἰδίωμα γενέσθαι δίχα τροπῆς *ib.*8(p.325.20; 837D); Max.*opusc.*(M.91.36D); δύο δὲ φύσεις λέγοντες οὐ διαιροῦμεν τὴν ἕνωσιν, τὴν δὲ τ. καὶ τὴν σύγχυσιν φεύγομεν Jo.D.*Jacob.*81(M.94. 1477C); in def. of CSirm.(357) εἴ τις...τὸν λόγον εἰς σάρκα μεταβεβλῆσθαι νομίζοι ἢ τροπὴν ὑπομεμενηκότα ἀνειληφέναι τὴν σάρκα λέγοι, ἀ. ἔ. *Symb.Sirm.1 anath.*12f.; **b.** *mutability* in the moral sphere; τροπή in this sense is frequently ass. with and not always dist. from the foregoing οὐκοῦν ὁ αὐτὸς λόγος μηδὲ τὴν σάρκα τῷ θεῷ συγχωρείτω· τὸ γὰρ τρεπτὴν αὐτὴν εἶναι οὐδὲ...ἀντείποι...ἀλλ' ὥσπερ ἐν σαρκὶ γενόμενος οὐκ ἐμολύνθη, οὕτως οὐδὲ τὸν νοῦν παραδεξάμενος, εἰς τ. ἠλλοιώθη Gr.Nyss.*Apoll.*40(M.45.1213C); μὴ χρανθέντος τοῦ νοῦ τροπῇ, ἀλλὰ τὰ ὅλα μὲν ἀνθρώπου λαβὼν...τῆς θεότητος συνευδοκούσης εἰς τὰ εὔλογα καὶ τὰ ἐκτὸς ἁμαρτίας καὶ τροπῆς ἀπηγορευμένης ὑπάρχοντα Epiph.*inc.*3 ap.*haer.*20(p.230.14,23; M.41.277Af.); ἐπειδὴ ...οἶδεν ὑπομένειν οὐκ εἰδότα τ. τὸν γεννήσαντα, οἶδε δηλονότι καὶ ἑαυτὸν ἄτρεπτον ἐξ ἀτρέπτου πατρός· τὸ δὲ τ. οὐκ εἰδός, πῶς ἂν λέγοιτό τι καὶ ἁμαρτάνειν; Cyr.*Jo.*1.4(4.33B); ὁ τῶν ὅλων δημιουργὸς ...δίχα τροπῆς...γέγονεν ἄνθρωπος φύσει κακίας ἀλλότριος ‡Hipp.*Ber. Hel.*8(p.325.33; M.10.840A); including change for the better as well as for the worse εἰ...κέχρισται...θεὸς ὢν ὁ λόγος, ἐπιδεᾶ πάντως ἁγιασμοῦ...ὑπομεμένηκεν οὖν ἄρα καὶ τ. τὴν εἰς τὰ ἀμείνω τυχὸν ὁ λόγος Cyr.*ep.*1(p.17.11; 5^{2}.11B); **c.** but alleged in objections against orthodox doctrine of Inc. τὴν...λεγομένην κατάβασιν θεοῦ πρὸς τὰ ἀνθρώπινα εἰς ἣν οὐ μεταβολῆς αὐτῷ δεῖ ὡς Κέλσος οἴεται ἡμᾶς λέγειν, οὔτε τροπῆς Or.*Cels.*4.14(p.284.15; M.11.1045A); εἰ...τῷ ἐν νῷ γενέσθαι κατηγορεῖ τὴν τ., καὶ ἡ πρὸς τὴν σάρκα οἰκείωσις οὐκ ἐκφεύγει πάντως τὴν κατηγορίαν τῆς ἀλλοιώσεως Gr.Nyss.*Apoll.*56(M.45.1261C); **d.** one of the errors of heretics τὸ...εἰς σάρκα μεταβεβλῆσθαι αὐτοῦ τοῦ λόγου τροπὴν φαντάζεσθε Ath.*ep.Epict.*4(p.8.6; M.26.1057A); ἄρα ὡς τοῦ λόγου τροπὴν ὑπομείναντος εἰς σαρκὸς μεταποίησιν, ἢ ψυχῆς ὁμοίωσιν· ἢ ὡς φανταστικὴν τὴν δεῖξιν ποιησαμένου τῆς ἀνθρωπίνης μορφῆς ‡Ath.*Apoll.*2.1(M.26.1133A); τ. τοῦ λόγου τὴν σάρκωσιν τὴν θείαν ὑπολαμβάνοντες [sc. Arians] ‡Ath.*Ar.*4.31(p.81.4; M.26.517A); Isid.Pel.*epp.*1.496(M.78.452C) cit. s. ἀνάκρασις; τ. τοῦ λόγου φαντάζωνται...εἰς αἷμά τε καὶ σάρκα Cyr.*synous.*1(p.476.8; cf.M.76.1427A); οὐχ ἅπας οὔτε μὴν δι' ὅλου μετέβαλεν, ἤτοι τ. ὑπέμεινε *ib.*2(p.477.29; cf.1428A); τὴν τοῦ λόγου φύσιν εἰς τὸ σαθρὸν...μετεστοιχειῶσθαι σῶμα, καὶ τ. φαντάζονται, τοῦ τ. οὐκ εἰδότος...θεὸς ὁ παντὸς ἐπέκεινα νοῦ γενέσεως καὶ φθορᾶς τὴν ὕπαρξιν ἔχων ἐξῃρημένην, ἀμείνων ἔσται καὶ τροπῆς id.ap.*cat.Heb.*2.:16 suppl.(p.419.21ff.); λέγοντες τὴν μὲν προσληφθεῖσαν τῷ λόγῳ σάρκα γενέσθαι ταυτουργὸν τῇ θεότητι διὰ τὴν πρόσληψιν...τροπὴν ὁμοῦ...καὶ σύγχυσιν...δογματίζοντες ‡Hipp.*Ber. Hel.*5(p.324.15; M.10.836D); how avoided by Nestorius τὸν ἐνανθρωπήσαντα τοῦτον λέγοντες τὸν σαρκωθέντα, οὐ τ. τῆς θείας φύσεως ὑπομεινάσης εἰς τὴν σάρκα, ἀλλὰ τὴν ἐνοίκησιν τὴν εἰς ἄνθρωπον Nest.*fr.*C 17(p.296.8); the danger of the heresy εἴπερ ἐστὶ ζωὴ κατὰ φύσιν...ὁ...λόγος, εἰσεδέξατο δὲ κατὰ τ. εἰς ὁμοουσιότητα...τὸ ἐξ ἀνθρωπίνου φυράματος, πολὺ δὲ τὸ δέος, μὴ ἄρα τις εἴποι καθαρῶς οὐκ εἶναι ζωὴν αὐτόν· οὐ γάρ ἐστιν ἀμιγὴς τοῦ φθείρεσθαι πεφυκότος Cyr.*synous.*2(p.479.12; cf.1429B); **6.** *metaphor*; *simile*; *figurative language* ἐπέμεινε τῇ τ., ἵνα πλείονα ποιήσῃ τὴν ἔμφασιν Chrys.*hom. 21.2 in 2Cor.*(10.585B); ἐπιμένει...τῇ τ. ... καὶ ὡς ἀπό γε τοῦ συμβαίνειν εἰωθότος, τὴν τοῦ μυστηρίου ποιεῖται δήλωσιν Cyr.*Os.*156(3. 189B); Thdt.*Ps.*106:27(1.1373).

***τροπίδιον, τό,** dim. of τρόπις *keel*, Clem.*paed.*1.1(p.90.4; M.8. 249A).

***τροπική, ἡ,** *circuit* (part of building), Thphn.*chron.*p.373(M.108. 896A).

τροπικός, 1. *figurative* πατὴρ λέγεται ὁ θεός...δῶμεν...εἶναι τ. καὶ ἐκ μεταφορᾶς λέγεσθαι...τὴν φωνὴν ταύτην Bas.*Eun.*2.24(1.260B; M. 29.625B); **2.** *allegorical*; of interpretation of pagan mythology, Or.*Cels.*3.43(p.238.26; M.11.976A); Eus.*p.e.*5.3(183A; M.21.317A); esp. ref. spiritual sense of scripture τ. λαμβάνοντες ἐντολήν, τὴν φάσκουσαν· πίνε ὕδατα ἀπὸ σῶν ἀγγείων Or.*Cels.*4.44(p.316.22; M.11. 1100B); ἡ...λέξις ἐμβαθύνουσα ταῖς τ. σημασίαις δυσκατανόητον ποιεῖ τὸ διὰ τῶν αἰνιγμάτων δηλούμενον Gr.Nyss.*hom.3 in Cant.*(M.44. 817C); τὴν ἐναντίαν ἐνέργειαν, ἣν ἡ τ. σημασία ὄρη καὶ βουνοὺς κατωνόμασε *ib.*5(861C); εἰ...πρὸς τὴν τροπικωτέραν μεταληφθείη θεωρίαν τὸ καθ' ἱστορίαν γεγενημένον, οὐδὲν ἡμῖν ἄχρηστον πρὸς τὸν ἡμέτερον εὑρεθείη σκοπόν id.*v.Mos.*(M.44.357C); μετατιθέναι τὴν ἱστορίαν εἰς τ. θεωρίαν id.*Eun.*3(2 p.10.5; M.45.573B); τ. ὁ λόγος Oecum.*Apoc.*2:7(p.50.2); **3.** neut. as subst.; **a.** *hypothetical proposition* διὰ δύο τροπικῶν θεωρήματα Or.*Cels.*7.15(p.166.20; M.11. 1441B); **b.** *spiritual interpretation* of scripture εἰ δέ τις πρὸς ταῦτα λέγῃ ὅτι κἂν ἀλληγορῆται, οὐδὲν ἧττον γέγονε...ἀκουστέον μετὰ τοῦ τροπικοῦ καὶ τῆς φασκούσης λέξεως id.*Jo.*32.12(7; p.445.10; M.14. 772C); **4.** masc. plur. as subst.; *Tropici*, heretics who, while substantially orthodox in their doctrine of the Son, maintained that H. Ghost is a creature; so named from their distortion of the plain sense of scripture to support their doctrine οἱ τῷ ὄντι τ., συνθέμενοι τοῖς Ἀρειανοῖς καὶ μερισάμενοι μετ' αὐτῶν τὴν εἰς τὴν θεότητα βλασφημίαν, ἵνα ἐκεῖνοι μὲν τὸν υἱόν, οὗτοι δὲ τὸ πνεῦμα κτίσμα λέγωσιν. ἐτόλμησαν, ὡς αὐτοί φασι, τρόπους...ἑαυτοῖς ἐφευρεῖν καὶ παρεξηγεῖσθαι...τὸ τοῦ ἀποστόλου ῥητὸν Ath.*ep.Serap.*1. 10(M.26.556B); μὴ δυνάμενοι νοεῖν, πῶς ἀδιαίρετός ἐστιν ἡ...τριάς, ποιοῦσιν οἱ μὲν Ἀρειανοὶ ἓν τὸν υἱὸν μετὰ τῆς κτίσεως, οἱ δὲ τ. τὸ πνεῦμα καὶ αὐτοὶ τοῖς κτίσμασι συναριθμοῦσιν *ib.*1.17(572B); τῶν μὲν... ῥητῶν...ὧν τὴν διάνοιαν παραποιοῦντες, ἠπάτησαν ἑαυτούς, ἀρκεῖ διὰ τούτων διελέγξαι τὴν ἐκ τῆς ἀμαθίας τῶν τ. δυσφημίαν *ib.*1.21(580D); εἰ δὲ κατὰ τὴν ὑμῶν τῶν τ. ἐπεξεύρεσιν οὐχ οὕτως ἐστίν, ἀλλ' ἐνυπνιάσθητε κτίσμα λέγειν τὸ πνεῦμα τὸ ἅγιον, οὐκέτι μία πίστις ἐστὶν ὑμῶν, οὐδὲ ἓν βάπτισμα, ἀλλὰ δύο *ib.*1.30(600A); τῶν τ. ἡ ἀλόγιστος μυθοπλαστία διαφωνεῖ μὲν πρὸς τὰς γραφάς, συμφωνεῖ δὲ τῇ τῶν Ἀρειομανιτῶν ἀλογίᾳ *ib.*1.32(605A); τοὺς πνευματομάχους, τοὺς τ., τοὺς λέγοντας τὸ πνεῦμα εἶναι κτιστὸν ‡Ath.*haer.*5(M.28.509D).

τροπικῶς, 1. *figuratively* εἰ μὴ τὴν ὁμοφροσύνην τῶν εἰς κακίαν ὑποσεσυρμένων 'σῶμα θανάτου' τ. λέγει Clem.*str.*3.3(p.204.7; M.8. 1121B); μέλι τ. τὴν θείαν λέγει διδασκαλίαν Hipp.*fr.7 in Pr.*(p.159.5; M.10.617B); παρασιωπῶμεν τὰ βαθύτερα, ἐπὰν ἁπλουστέρους θεωρῶμεν ...καὶ δεομένους λόγων τ. ὀνομαζομένων γάλα Or.*Cels.*3.52(p.248.23; M.11.989B); τὴν κακίαν καὶ τὰ ὑπ' αὐτῆς πραττόμενα καὶ τ. λεγόμενα ξύλα *ib.*4.13(p.283.6; 1044A); τ. μὲν λεγομένου προσώπου, γυμνότερον δὲ...νοῦ *ib.*5.60(p.64.2; 1276D); ὕπνου θεοῦ τ. λεγομένου ἢ ὀργῆς *ib.* 6.64(p.134.23; 1396B); 'ἀπὸ γαστρὸς τοῦ θεοῦ' καὶ 'πρὸ ἑωσφόρου' ἐλέγετο γεγεννῆσθαι, τ. ἀκουόντων ἡμῶν τὰ τοιαῦτα Eus.*d.e.*4.15 (p.181.26; M.22.304A); ἐν...τῷ τόπῳ, ὃν ὁ...Μωϋσῆς τ. παράδεισον ὠνόμασεν Ath.*gent.*2(M.25.8B); λαβύρινθον δέ φημι τ. τὴν ἀδιέξοδον τοῦ θανάτου φρουράν Gr.Nyss.*or.catech.*35(p.132.7; M.45.88B); δεῖ ὁμολογεῖν...τὸ κτίσμα, ἐπειδὴ εἶπεν ἡ γραφὴ τροπικώτερον λεγόμενον τὸ κτίσμα καὶ τ. τὸ γέννημα Epiph.*haer.*69.34(p.183.4; M.42.256B); τροπικώτερον ταῦτα τέθεικε. καὶ γὰρ ἦν προφητεία τὸ λεγόμενον

Chrys.*hom.10.3 in Mt.*(7.143A); **2.** *allegorically, according to the spiritual meaning* of scripture τοὺς ὑπὸ ἀνθρώπων γεγενημένους λόγους, τ. ... καλουμένους 'υἱοὺς ἀνθρώπων' Or.*Cels.*6.77(p.147.10; M. 11.1416B); προσχήματος ἕνεκεν τὸ ὄνομα τῆς Ἀναθὼθ...λαμβάνεται· ὅλον δὲ τὸ Ἰουδαϊκὸν μυστήριον τ. ἐν αὐτῇ εἴρηται· ἑρμηνεύεται γὰρ Ἀναθὼθ ἐπακουσμός id.*hom.10.4 in Jer.*(p.74.7; M.13.361B); ἐὰν... θεὸς...ἐν τῷ παραδείσῳ περιπατεῖν λέγηται καὶ ὁ Ἀδὰμ ὑπὸ τὸ ξύλον κρύπτεσθαι, οὐκ οἶμαι διστάζειν τινὰ περὶ τοῦ αὐτὰ τ. διὰ δοκούσης ἱστορίας καὶ οὐ σωματικῶς γεγενημένης μηνύειν τινὰ μυστήρια id. *princ.*4.3.1(p.324.3; M.11.377A); of the soul ἡ τροπικώτερον καλουμένη Ἱερουσαλήμ id. *fr.25 in Lam.*(p.246.23; M.13.621A); ref. Passover ἀρκτέον...ἐν τῷ ἐσθίειν ἀπὸ τῆς κεφαλῆς, τουτέστιν τῶν...ἀρχικῶν δογμάτων...καὶ καταληκτέον ἐπὶ τοὺς πόδας, τὰ ἔσχατα τῶν μαθημάτων...ὁ γὰρ περὶ αὐτῶν λόγος...δύναται τροπικώτερον...πόδες ὠνομάσθαι τοῦ ἀμνοῦ id.*Jo.*10.18(13; p.189.8; M.14.337B); περὶ τῶν ἐν Γενέσει γεγραμμένων τριῶν ἀνδρῶν...παρὰ τῷ Ἀβραὰμ...μεταλαβόντων ...σεμιδάλεως...μή ποτε γυμνῶς τ. ταῦτα εἴρηται id.*or.*27.11(p.370.14; M.11.513C); Meth.*symp.*7.8(p.78.20; M.18.136A); Eus.*d.e.*6.9(p.259.17; M.22.425D); ταῦτα κατὰ διάνοιαν τ. ἀποδέχεσθαι προσήκει *ib.* 7.1(p.307.29; 504A); ref. prophecies ταῦτα καὶ πρὸς λέξιν καὶ τ. ἐξειληφότες, πεπληρῶσθαι αὐτὰ δείκνυμεν ἐπὶ τῆς τοῦ σωτῆρος... γενέσεως, παριστῶντες τοτὲ μὲν ῥητῶς...τοτὲ δὲ τ. δεῖν ἐπιβάλλειν ταῖς προφητείαις *ib.*(p.319.35; 521D); ἀβύσσους...καὶ ὅσα ἄλλα...ἐπωνόμασται...τροπικώτερον ἐκληπτέον, ταῦτα μεταφέροντα τὰ σημαινόμενα ἐπὶ νοητὰς οὐσίας *ib.*5.1(p.215.9; 357A); cf.Gr.Nyss.*Eun.*3(p.20.20; M.45.585A); in Antiochene exegesis, Thdr.Mops.*Os.*4:1(M.66.148B); Thdt.*Dan.*11:41(2.1292); **3.** *symbolically, as a symbol*, cf. *ab una... specie daemonis ventriloqui* τροπικῶς *omnia daemonia nuncupavit*, Or.*hom.7.2 in Is.*(p.281.26; M.13.248B); id.*Jo.*6.13(7; p.122.23; M. 14.224C); **4.** *in a manner, in some fashion* ὁ κατὰ τὸν Ἰησοῦν τ. νοούμενος ἄνθρωπος *ib.*20.12(p.341.24; 597D).

τρόπις, ἡ, *keel*, Dion.Al.ap.Eus.*p.e.*14.24(774B; M.21.1273B); met., *foundation, groundwork*, Chrys.*hom.20.3 in Eph.*(11.147A).

τροπολογ-έω, 1. *interpret figuratively, treat as figurative* ὁ ἐχῖνος... ἐστι παρὰ τῇ γραφῇ τάχα ~ούμενος ἐπί τινας ἀνθρώπους, ὡς οἱ ὄφεις ἐπὶ τοὺς Σαδδουκαίους...καὶ ὁ ἀλώπηξ ἐπὶ τὸν Ἡρώδην †Bas.*Is.*283(1. 594D; M.30.616B); οὐ τόποις ἀψύχοις...τὴν εὐφροσύνην εὐαγγελίζεται, ἀλλὰ ~εῖ διὰ τῆς ἐρήμου τὴν αὐχμώδη ψυχὴν καὶ ἀκόσμητον Gr.Nyss. *bapt.Chr.*(M.46.593C); **2.** *interpret allegorically, interpret according to the spiritual*, opp. literal, *sense* of scripture; **a.** ref. interpretation of pagan myths as allegories of nature, Or.*Cels.*5.38(p.42.20; M.11. 1240C); **b.** ref. Philo's allegorical exegesis, *ib.*5.55(p.58.26; 1268B); **c.** ref. Valent. exegesis προφήτας ἀναγινώσκοντες...καὶ ὅσα εἰς ὁμοίωσιν δύναται ~εῖσθαι τῆς αὐτῶν αἱρέσεως, δεχόμενοι Epiph. *anac.*31(p.236.25; M.41.284D); cf.Jo.D.*haer.*31(M.96.697A); **d.** in neo-Pythagoreanism Νουμήνιος...οὐκ ὀκνήσας...χρήσασθαι...λόγοις προφητικοῖς καὶ τροπολογῆσαι αὐτούς Or.*Cels.*1.15(p.67.23; M.11. 684A); **e.** ref. pagan criticism of Christian allegorizing of scripture, *ib.*1.17(p.69.7; 692A) cit. s. ἀλληγορέω; **f.** Christian usage; allegorical interpretation corresponds to intentions of biblical writers ἐπεὶ δ' αὐτοὶ οἱ πατέρες τῶν δογμάτων καὶ συγγραφεῖς τὰ τοιαῦτα ~οῦσι, τί ἐστιν ἄλλο ὑπονοῆσαι ἢ ὅτι οὕτως ἐγράφη, ὥστε ~εῖσθαι αὐτὰ κατὰ τὸν προηγούμενον νοῦν; *ib.*4.49(p.322.7; 1108C); ὁ εὐγνωμόνως ἐντυγχάνων ταῖς ἱστορίαις...κρινεῖ, τίσι μὲν συγκαταθήσεται, τίνα δὲ τροπολογήσει, τὸ βούλημα ἐρευνῶν τῶν ἀναπλασμένων τὰ τοιαῦτα καὶ τίσιν ἀπιστήσει *ib.*1.42(p.92.24; 737C); examples of the method θεὸν...καταβαίνοντα ἐὰν λέγωσιν αἱ προφητικαὶ φωναί... ~οῦμεν. καταβαίνει γὰρ...ἀπὸ τοῦ ἰδίου μεγέθους...ὅτε τὰ τῶν ἀνθρώπων...οἰκονομεῖ *ib.*4.12(p.282.20; 1041C); εἰ δὲ τῆς Σιὼν χεῖρες ~οῦνται, πόσῳ μᾶλλον τὰ κατὰ τὴν γραφὴν μέλη τοῦ θεοῦ; id.*fr.37 in Lam.*(p.252.29; M.13.629A); ~ούντων ἡμῶν χεῖρας καὶ μέλη τοῦ θεοῦ id.*Cels.*6.61(p.132.6; 1392C); ref. stories of Eden and Fall πάντα ταῦτα οὐκ ἀσέμνως ~εῖται *ib.*4.39(p.311.13; 1089C); ἴδωμεν ~οῦντες, τίνα δυνάμεθα εἰπεῖν τὸν σεληνιαζόμενον εἶναι...καὶ τί τὸ πίπτειν...καὶ τί τὸ μὴ δεδυνῆσθαι αὐτὸν ὑπὸ τῶν μαθητῶν θεραπευθῆναι, ἀλλ' ὑπ' αὐτοῦ τοῦ Ἰησοῦ id.*comm.in Mt.*13.4(p.187.21; M.13.1101A); ὅπου ποτ' ἂν ζύμη ὀνομασθῇ, εἰς διδαχὴν ~εῖται *ib.*12.6(p.77.28; 989B); ref. *pedilavium*, id.*Jo.*32.13(8; p.446.8; M.14.773B); ἀλληγοροῦντο δ' ἂν ταῦτα σαφῶς οὕτως, ⟨ὥς τις⟩ καὶ τὴν δηλουμένην διὰ τῆς προφητείας ῥίζαν Ἰεσσαί, καὶ τὴν ῥάβδον καὶ τὸ ἄνθος ~ῶν ἑρμηνεύσειεν Eus.*d.e.* 7.3(p.343.24; M.22.560C); *ib.*7.1(p.311.12; 509A).

***τροπολογητέον,** *one must interpret figuratively*, Or.*comm.in Mt.* 12.8(p.79.13; M.13.992D); *ib.*13.5(p.191.9; 1105A).

τροπολογία, ἡ, 1. *figurative expression, figure of speech*, Eus.*p.e.* 2 proem.(44B; M.21.92C); ὅσα...περὶ οὐσίας θεοῦ ἀναγεγράφθαι δοκεῖ, τ. τισὶν ἢ καὶ ἀλληγορίαις, πρὸς ἑτέρας ἐννοίας οἱ λόγοι φέρουσιν Bas. *Eun.*1.14(1.226D; M.29.544C); Χριστὸς...θεοῦ δύναμις καὶ θεοῦ σοφία, ἥτις ἐστὶ χεὶρ δημιουργικὴ κατὰ τὸν τῆς τ. λόγον Didym.(‡Bas.)*Eun.*5 (1.297D; M.29.713C); ὁ κύριος εἷς ὢν κατ' οὐσίαν, πολυώνυμος γέγονε κατὰ τροπολογίαν ἕνεκεν τῆς οἰκονομίας σωτηρίας...πῇ μὲν πέτρα ὀνομασθεὶς καὶ θύρα, πῇ δὲ ἀξίνη Mac.Aeg.*ep.*(M.34.417A); τί ἐστιν τ. καὶ κυριολογία;...κυριολογία μέν ἐστιν βεβαία ἀπόδειξις πράγματος, τ. δέ ἐστιν ἀβέβαιος ἀπόδειξις Jo.D.*disp.*(M.96.1344B); frequency in scripture, Bas.*hom.in Ps.*44(1.161B; M.29.393B); **2.** *allegorical*, or *spiritual*, opp. literal, *interpretation*; **a.** of mythology, Or.*Cels.*3.43 (p.239.3; M.11.976B); **b.** of scripture οὐδὲ ἐνταῦθα ἀπορήσαιμεν ἂν περὶ οὐδενός, εἰ τροπολογίας ἔμπειροι κἂν μικρὸν ὑπάρχωμεν Just.*dial.* 57.2(M.6.605C); νύμφας τε καὶ θεραπαινίδας ἀνάγεσθαι ἐπὶ τροπολογίαν οὐχ ἡμεῖς διδάσκομεν, ἀλλ' ἄνωθεν ἀπὸ σοφῶν παρειλήφαμεν, ὧν εἷς τις [sc. S. Paul, ref. Gal.4:24] ἔφασκε διεγείρων...ἐπὶ τροπολογίας Or. *Cels.*4.44(p.317.7; M.11.1100C); ref. Mt.22:3f. οἱονεὶ γὰρ σιτιστὸν παρατίθησι λόγον ἢ διῃρημένον καὶ ἐν τ. λεγόμενον τεθυμένον ὁ τὴν περὶ τοῦ...προβλήματος ἀπόδειξιν πολλὴν φέρων καὶ πλήρη id.*hom.17.22 in Mt.*(p.645.3; M.13.1541C); θύσις ἡ διαίρεσις καὶ τ. τῶν προβλημάτων id. *fr.433 in Mt.*(p.181); ταῦτα κατὰ μίαν τ., ἵνα μὴ νῦν περιεργάζωμαι τὰ ὑπὲρ ἐμαυτόν id.*hom.7.3 in Jer.*(p.54.4; M.13.333B); οὐ πάντως ταῖς αὐταῖς λέξεσιν ἐπὶ τῶν αὐτῶν πραγμάτων χρῶνται αἱ γραφαί· τοῦτο δὲ ποιοῦσιν, ὅτε μὲν παρὰ τὴν ὁμωνυμίαν, ὅτε δὲ παρὰ τὴν τ., καὶ ἔσθ' ὅτε παρὰ τὴν σύμφρασιν id.*comm.in Rom.*7:7(*JTS* 14 p.12); ταῦτα οὐδ' ἄλλως ἢ μετὰ θεωρίας τῆς κατὰ μόνην τ. τὴν διάνοιαν σώζει Eus.*d.e.*7.1(p.320.16; M.22.524B); προφητεύεται...σκοτεινότερά τινα καὶ δι' αἰνιγμάτων, μακροτέρας καὶ βαθυτέρας τῆς κατὰ τροπολογίαν δεόμενα ἑρμηνείας *ib.*6.20(p.289.14; 476A); εἰ δὲ προσκόπτοι τις ταῖς τοιαῖσδε τ., ὥρα τοῦτον μηδὲ τὰς...μυίας ἢ μελίσσας...κατὰ διάνοιαν θεωρεῖν, εἰς ἀτόπους δὲ...ἐκπίπτειν μυθολογίας *ib.*2.3(p.78.3; 140C); to be employed when necessary for exegesis, Gr.Nyss.*hom.in Cant.* proem.(M.44.757A) cit. s. ἀναγωγή; καί με μηδεὶς ὑπενοείτω διὰ τῆς τ. σύγχυσιν ἐπάγειν τῇ θεωρίᾳ τῆς λέξεως, ὡς ταῖς ὑπονοίαις τῶν πρὸ ἡμῶν...τεθεωρηκότων συμφέρεσθαι id.*hex.*21(M.44.81D); Antiochene def. τ. ... ἐστιν ὡς ὅταν, πρᾶγμα διηγούμενος ὁ προφήτης, τὰς φανερὰς τῶν λέξεων τρέπῃ εἰς αὔξησιν τοῦ λεγομένου, σαφιζομένης τῆς τ. ἐκ τῆς ἀκολουθίας τῶν λεγομένων Diod.*proem.Ps.*118(p.92.10); tropological method corresponding to soul in tripartite division of man, Andr. Caes.*Apoc.*proem.(M.106.217C) cit. s. ἀναγωγή; instances of the method μέμνημαι τῶν...εἰρημένων περὶ...τῶν κατοικούντων ἐν Ἱερουσαλὴμ τ.· κατοικοῦμεν γὰρ ἡμεῖς, ἐὰν ὁ θεὸς διδῷ, ἐν τῇ Ἱερουσαλὴμ Or.*hom.5.13 in Jer.*(p.41.26; M.13.312C); οἶδα κατὰ τ. πολλοὺς ποταμοὺς Αἰγύπτου ἐναντίους Χριστῷ τῷ ἀληθινῷ ποταμῷ, οὗ τὰ ὁρμήματα τὴν ἐκκλησίαν εὐφραίνει id.*exc.in Ps.*77:14(M.17.147D); ref. creation of Eve μετὰ τροπολογίας εἴρηται id.*Cels.*4.38(p.308.25; M.11.1088A); 'πρόσωπον πρὸς πρόσωπον'...οὐ πρόσωπον αἰσθητὸν ἐν τοῖς τοιούτοις παραλαμβάνομεν, ἀλλὰ κατὰ τ. νοούμενον, ὡς καὶ ὀφθαλμοὺς καὶ ὦτα *ib.*7.38(p.188.21; 1473C); **3.** *hymn* τῶν ἐνθεαστικῶν ἐκείνων ὑμνῳδιῶν, λέγω δὴ τῆς ἐφυπνίου τ. Andr.Cr.*or.*14(M.97.1092B).

***τροπολογικός,** *allegorical*, of pagan mythologies, Nil.*epp.*4.1 (M.79.544D).

***τροπολογικῶς,** *allegorically, mystically*, Or.*hom.5.14 in Jer.*(p.43.26; M.13.317A); Max.*ambig.*(M.91.1365B); Jo.D.*disp.*(M.96.1344B).

τρόπος, ὁ, A. *tendency, direction* θεοδιδάκτου...μου γενομένης τῆς ψυχῆς συνῆκα, ὅτι τὰ μὲν καταδίκης ἔχει τ., τὰ δὲ ὅτι λύει τὴν ἐν κόσμῳ δουλείαν Tat.*orat.*29.2(M.6.868A).

B. *way, manner, fashion* πολύτροπον...οὖν τὴν σοφίαν ἡ 'ποσάκις' ἔνδεικται λέξις καὶ καθ' ἕνα ἕκαστον τ. ποιότητός τε καὶ ποσότητος πάντως σώζει τινὰς ἔν τε τῷ χρόνῳ, ἔν τε τῷ αἰῶνι Clem.*str.*1.5(p.18.23; M.8.720B); τίς...ὁ τ. ... τῆς ὑπ' αὐτοῦ κατασπαρείσης τῷ βίῳ πολιτείας; Eus.*d.e.*3.3(p.109.8; M.22.188C); ὑπενόησεν [sc. Constantius] ἀλλοιῶσαι νόμον...τὰ...τῆς ἐκκλησίας ἀλλάττων ἔθη καὶ καινὸν... ἐπινοῶν τ. τῶν καταστάσεων· ἐξ ἄλλων γὰρ τόπων...ἐπισκόπους ἀποστέλλει πρὸς τοὺς μὴ θέλοντας λαούς Ath.*h.Ar.*74(p.224.20; M.25. 784B); in various adverbial usages τρόπον τινά, τρόπῳ τινί, *in a certain way* τ. τινὶ ὕλην γενητήν, ὑπὸ τοῦ θεοῦ γεγονυῖαν Thphl.Ant. *Autol.*2.10(M.6.1065B); οἱ...τρεῖς θεοὺς τ. τινὰ κηρύττουσιν, εἰς τρεῖς ὑποστάσεις ξένας ἀλλήλων παντάπασι κεχωρισμένας διαιροῦντες τὴν ἁγίαν μονάδα Dion.R.ap.Ath.*decr.*26(p.22.7; M.25.464A); βλάσφημον ...οὐ τὸ τυχόν, μέγιστον μὲν οὖν, χειροποίητον τ. τινὰ λέγειν τὸν κύριον Dion.R.*ib.*(p.22.20; 464B); with play on sense of *trope* πρὸς δὲ τοὺς περὶ τοῦ πνεύματος ἀπατηθέντας [i.e. Tropici], τ. τινί, ὡς ἂν αὐτοὶ φαῖεν προσήκει διερευνῶντας εἰπεῖν Ath.*ep.Serap.*1.2(M.26.532C); *in a measure* τὸν καθιστάμενον ἐπίσκοπον...δεῖ ὑπάρχειν...οὐκ ἔλαττον ἐτῶν πεντήκοντα, ὅτι τ. τινὶ τὰς νεωτέρας ἀταξίας...ἐκπεφευγὼς ὑπάρχει *Const.App.*2.1.1; ἑτέρῳ τ., *in another way* μετὰ θείας τῶν ὑπ' αὐτοῦ μετεχομένων ἱερῶν γνώσεως ἑτέρῳ τ. παρὰ τὸν ἱερὸν λαὸν ἐπὶ τὴν μετάληψιν ἥξει τῆς θεαρχικῆς κοινωνίας Dion.Ar.*e.h.*6.3.5(M.3.536C); τ. παντί, κατὰ πάντα τ., *in all ways* δεῖ...τοὺς διακόνους...κατὰ πάντα τ. πᾶσιν ἀρέσκειν Ign.*Trall.*2.3; πολλὰ τῶν πρὸ τῆς μέσης τάξεως...ἐνεργουμένων ἀπείρηται τ. παντὶ τοῖς ἑνιαίοις μοναχοῖς, ὡς πρὸς τὸ ἓν αὐτῶν ὀφειλόντων ἑνοποιεῖσθαι καὶ πρὸς τὴν ἱερὰν μονάδα συνάγεσθαι Dion.Ar.*e.h.*6.3.2(M.3.533D); τὸ...κατὰ πάντα τ. τοῦ ἀγαθοῦ ἐστερημένον οὐδαμῇ οὐδαμῶς οὔτε ἦν, οὔτε ἐστίν id.*d.n.*4.20(M.3.720B); ὃν τ., *in the same way as* ἐν τῇ...νηδύϊ ὁ λόγος ἑαυτῷ τὸν οἶκον διεπλάσατο, ὃν τ. ἐξ ἀρχῆς τὸν Ἀδὰμ ἐκ τῆς γῆς ‡Ath.*Ar.*4.34(p.83.1; M.26.520B); ποίοις τ.; *in what way?* ἤθελον...γνῶναι ποίοις τ. με δεῖ δουλεῦσαι τῇ ἐπιθυμίᾳ τῇ ἀγαθῇ Herm.*mand.*12.3.1; τρόπον c. genit., *by way of* ἀλεξιφαρμάκου τρόπον...παρελήφθη ὁ θάνατος Meth.*res.*1.42(p.288.13; M.41.1112B); κατὰ τρόπον, *rightly, properly* παντὸς...τοῦ κατὰ τ. Χριστιανίζοντος ὁ τῆς ψυχῆς ἐγήγερται ὀφθαλμὸς καὶ ὁ τῆς αἰσθήσεως μέμυκε Or.*Cels.*7.39(p.190.12; M.11.1477A).

C. *kind, sort* οἱ μὲν...κολασταὶ ἐτάζουσι...σώματα, κύριος δὲ μόνος καινὸν ἔχει τ. ἐτασμῶν, ἐτάζων γάρ ἐστι καρδίας Or.*hom.*20.9 *in Jer.*(p.193.32; M.13.525A).

D. *mode*; **1.** of existence (Trin.) ἀσεβὲς...τὸ τὸν κτίστην τοῖς δημιουργήμασι παραβάλλειν καὶ τὸν αὐτὸν τῆς γενέσεως τοῖς ἄλλοις τ. ἔχειν καὶ αὐτὸν νομίζειν *Symb.Ant.*(345)8 ap.Ath.*syn.*26(p.253.32; M.26.733A); οὐδὲ πρέπει ζητεῖν πῶς ἐκ θεοῦ ἐστιν ὁ λόγος...ἢ πῶς γεννᾷ ὁ θεὸς καὶ τίς ὁ τ. τῆς τοῦ θεοῦ γεννήσεως Ath.*Ar.*2.36(M.26.224A); τὸν δημιουργὸν λόγον φάσκομεν οὐχ ἕτερόν τινα τ. ἔχειν θεότητος ἢ τὴν τοῦ μόνου θεοῦ διὰ τὸ ἐξ αὐτοῦ πεφυκέναι *ib.*3.15(353A); cf.id.*syn.*52(p.275.28; M.26.785B); ὡς γὰρ ἀπὸ πυρὸς φῶς, οὕτως ἐκ θεοῦ λόγος καὶ σοφία ἐκ σοφοῦ καὶ ἐκ πατρὸς υἱός. ταύτῃ...ὁ...υἱὸς λόγος οὐκ ἀνούσιος, οὐδὲ οὐχ ὑφεστώς, ἀλλ' οὐσιώδης ἀληθῶς. ἐπεὶ εἰ μὴ τοῦτον ἔχει τὸν τ., εἴη ἂν πάντα, ἃ λέγεται, κατ' ἐπίνοιαν...λεγόμενα ‡Ath.*Ar.*4.2(p.46.1; M.26.469C); οὐ γὰρ...οἱ δεκτικοὶ τῆς ἰδιότητος αὐτοῦ [sc. God] τρόποι τὸν τῆς ἁπλότητος λόγον παραλυπήσουσιν ἢ οὕτω γε πάντα, ὅσα περὶ θεοῦ λέγεται, σύνθετον τὸν θεὸν ἡμῖν ἀναδείξει Bas.*Eun.*2.29(1.266B; M.29.640B); ref. Eunomian teaching ἵνα...τὸ ὑφειμένον καὶ τὸ κατὰ τὴν φυσικὴν ἀξίαν ἠλαττωμένον τοῦ υἱοῦ καὶ τοῦ πνεύματος ἐπιδείξῃ, ἕτερον ἐξ ἑτέρου γενόμενον λέγει· ὡς δὲ μήποτε εἰς οἰκειότητος ἔννοιαν ἐκ τοῦ τοιούτου τ. τῆς ὑπάρξεως ἔλθοιεν οἱ τὴν ἐξ ἀλλήλων γένεσιν μεμαθηκότες Gr.Nyss.*Eun.*1(1 p.84.17; M.45.316C); τὸ ἀγέννητον καὶ γεννητὸν καὶ ἐκπορευτὸν οὐκ οὐσίας ὀνόματα, ἀλλὰ τρόπου ὑπάρξεως· ὁ δὲ τ. τῆς ὑπάρξεως τοῖς ὀνόμασι χαρακτηρίζεται τούτοις· ἡ δὲ τῆς οὐσίας δήλωσις τῇ θεοῦ ὀνομασίᾳ σημαίνεται Thdt.*rect.conf.*3(M.6.1209B); εἰ δέ τις τῆς ὑπάρξεως τοῦ υἱοῦ καὶ τοῦ ἁγίου πνεύματος ἐπιζητεῖ τὸν τ. μαθεῖν, εἰπάτω δὴ πρότερος τὸν τ. τῆς τοῦ ἀγεννήτου ὑπάρξεως, πῶς ἐστιν οὐκ ἔχων τὸν αἴτιον id.*affect.*2(p.64.15; 4.756); τὸ πνεῦμα τὸ ἅγιον ἐκ τοῦ...πατρὸς ἔχειν τὴν ὕπαρξιν μεμαθήκαμεν· ὁ δὲ τῆς ὑπάρξεως τ. οὔτε τῇ κτίσει προσέοικεν..., οὔτε τῷ...υἱῷ id.*haer.*3(4.388); εἷς ἐστιν ὁ θεὸς τῇ συνυπάρξει τῶν τριῶν...ὑποστάσεων, τῶν διαφερουσῶν ἀλλήλων οὐ τῇ οὐσίᾳ, ἀλλὰ τοῖς ὑπάρξεως τ., ἡ διαφορὰ...τῶν τῆς ὑπάρξεως τ. οὐ διαιρεῖ τὸ ἓν τῇ οὐσίᾳ ‡Just.*qu.et resp.*139(M.6.1392C); ἐν διαφόροις τῆς ὑπάρξεως τ. μένει ὁ τῆς οὐσίας λόγος εἷς ἀδιαίρετός τε καὶ ἀπαράλλακτος *ib.*(1393A); χρὴ...ἡμᾶς τὸν παντελῆ τῆς θείας ἑνώσεώς τε καὶ διακρίσεως ἐκθέσθαι τ. Dion.Ar.*d.n.*2.4(M.3.640D); πάντα κοινὰ τοῦ πατρὸς καὶ τοῦ υἱοῦ καὶ τοῦ ἁγίου πνεύματος πλὴν τοῦ τ. τῆς ὑπάρξεως Jo.D.*Jacob.*52(M.94.1461B); **2.** ref. Inc. ξένον ἐκ παρθένου τρόπον αὐτοῦ τῆς ἀποτέξεως Eus.*d.e.*1.1(p.3.19; M.22.16D); οὐκ ἄν ποτε ἀνόμοιον τῷ πατρὶ τὸν υἱὸν ἐτόλμησαν εἰπεῖν, εἴπερ ἔγνωσαν τίς ὁ τ. τῆς πτωχείας αὐτοῦ καὶ τίς ἡ δύναμις τοῦ σταυροῦ αὐτοῦ Ath.*inc.et c.Ar.*1(M.26.985A); ὅτ' ἂν μὲν σώζεσθαι δεικνύναι βουλώμεθα τῶν συνελθόντων τὴν διαφορὰν...δύο...τὰς φύσεις λέγομεν· ὅτ' ἂν δὲ τὸν ἄρρητον τοῦ μυστηρίου διακριβῶμεν τῆς ἑνώσεως τ., μίαν τοῦ...λόγου φύσιν σεσαρκωμένην φαμέν Max.*ep.*12(M.91.477B); ὁμολογοῦντες τὴν ἕνωσιν καὶ τὸν αὐτῆς...διαρθροῦντες τ. *ib.*(477C); τὸ συγκαταβῆναι...κατὰ τὸν τῆς ἐνανθρωπήσεως αὐτοῦ τ. διαληπτέον Gel.Cyz.*h.e.*2.24.21(M.85.1304A); ἐπὶ...τῆς τοῦ λόγου σαρκώσεως οὐ φύσεως ἔργον ἡ σάρκωσις, ἀλλὰ τ. οἰκονομικῆς συγκαταβάσεως...καὶ ἡ σάρκωσις δὲ τ. δευτέρας ὑπάρξεως πέφυκε μόνῳ τῷ...λόγῳ Jo.D.*Jacob.*52(M.94.1464A); δύο...φύσεις λέγοντες, οὐ διαιροῦμεν τὴν ἕνωσιν, τὴν δὲ τροπὴν καὶ τὴν σύγχυσιν φεύγομεν, λόγῳ γὰρ καὶ τ. τῆς διαφορᾶς ταύτας ἀριθμεῖσθαι γινώσκομεν *ib.*81(1477C); ἕτερον...καὶ ἕτερον λόγῳ καὶ τ. τῆς διαφορᾶς, κοινὰ δὲ ἑκατέρῳ ἑκάτερα τῷ τ. τῆς ἀντιδόσεως διὰ τὴν εἰς ἄλληλα τῶν μερῶν περιχώρησιν καὶ τὴν καθ' ὑπόστασιν ἕνωσιν *ib.*(1480B); **3.** ref. manifestation of the divine διττός ἐστι τῆς ἱερᾶς ἐκφαντορίας ὁ τ. ὁ μὲν...διὰ τῶν ὁμοίων προϊὼν ἱεροτύπων εἰκόνων· ὁ δὲ διὰ τῶν ἀνομοίων μορφοποιῶν εἰς τὸ παντελῶς ἀπεοικὸς καὶ ἀπεμφαῖνον πλαττόμενος Dion.Ar.*c.h.*2.2(M.3.140B); **4.** *mode, way*, of life τὴν...Ἰουδαίων κατηγορίαν...ὅτι...ταῖς αὐτῶν γραφαῖς καταχρώμενοι, οὐ τὸν ὅμοιον αὐτοῖς μέτιμεν τοῦ βίου τ. Eus.*d.e.*1.1(p.7.2; M.22.21B); abs. τέλος εὐσεβοῦς καὶ φιλοθέου τ. id.*v.C.*1.22(p.19.5; M.20.937C); ἓν...εἰσιν ἀνὴρ καὶ γυνὴ τῇ φύσει...τῇ ἑνώσει...τῷ βίῳ, τῷ τ. *Const.App.*7.2.9; **5.** *character, temper* ἐξετάζεται διὰ τῆς εὐχῆς ὁ τ. Clem.*str.*7.7(p.32.22; M.9.460B); ἔστιν...ἡ γνῶσις τελείωσίς τις ἀνθρώπου...διὰ τῆς τῶν θείων ἐπιστήμης συμπληρωμένη κατά τε τὸν τ. καὶ τὸν βίον καὶ τὸν λόγον *ib.*7.10(p.40.23; 477C); ὁ Ματθαῖος...τὸ φιλάληθες ὑποφαίνων τοῦ ἰδίου τ. καὶ τελώνην ἑαυτὸν ἀπεκάλει Eus.*d.e.*3.5(p.126.15; M.22.216A); ἆρα ἐπινοῆσαι δυνατόν, ἄνδρα διδάσκαλον σεμνῆς πολιτείας...γόητα τὸν τ. γεγονέναι; *ib.*3.6(p.131.30; 224A); ἀμετάβλητον αὐτοῦ τὸ ἦθος καὶ τὸν τ. διαφύλαξον Serap.*euch.*21; plur., *manners*, hence *character* οὐ πᾶς...ὁ λαλῶν ἐν πνεύματι προφήτης ἐστίν, ἀλλ' ἐὰν ἔχῃ τοὺς τ. κυρίου. ἀπὸ οὖν τῶν τ. γνωσθήσεται ὁ ψευδοπροφήτης καὶ ὁ προφήτης *Did.*11.8; ἐξεταζέσθωσαν...αὐτῶν [sc. catechumens] καὶ οἱ τ. καὶ ὁ βίος *Const.App.*8.32.2; ref. system of morals διδάσκαλος τοῦ περὶ τοῦ θεοῦ...λόγου καὶ τῆς εἰς αὐτὸν θρησκείας καὶ παντὸς ἠθικοῦ τ. Or.*Cels.*1.30(p.81.27; M.11.717A).

E. *manner* of speaking or writing, *style*; **1.** ref. use of metaphor μυρία δ' ἄν τις εὕροι...τῷ κατὰ μεταφορὰν τ. δι' ὅλης τῆς...γραφῆς εἰρημένα Eus.*e.th.*3.2(p.141.23; M.24.976B); *ib.*(p.141.5; 976A); Chrys.*hom.*34.2 *in Jo.*(8.197A); **2.** *turn of speech* προϊούσης...τῆς γραφῆς τοὺς προειρημένους ὑπὸ τοῦ προφήτου τρόπους καθ' ἑκάστην περικοπὴν σημειωσάμενοι παραστήσομεν Clem.*str.*6.15(p.497.34; M.9.356A); ἀβιάστως δ' ἂν εἴποι τις τὸν υἱὸν τοῦ θεοῦ καὶ δίχα παντὸς ἀλληγορικοῦ τ. ταῦτα ἐπαληθεύειν Eus.*e.th.*3.3(p.151.21; M.24.992C); χρὴ...τοῖς...λογίοις...συνεπομένους αἰώνια μὲν καὶ ἔγχρονα κατὰ τοὺς συνεγνωσμένους αὐτοῖς προσυπακούειν τ. Dion.Ar.*d.n.*10.3(M.3.940A); ζῆν εἴ τις φαίη τὴν αὐτοζωὴν ἢ φωτίζεσθαι τὸ αὐτόφως, οὐκ ὀρθῶς ἐρεῖ..., εἰ μή που καθ' ἕτερον ταῦτα εἴποι τ., ὅτι περισσῶς καὶ οὐσιωδῶς προένεστι τὰ τῶν αἰτιατῶν τοῖς αἰτίοις *ib.*2.8(645D); τὰ ἐν τῇ βασιλείᾳ τοῦ θεοῦ τῶν ὁσίων συμπόσια κατὰ τὸν αὐτὸν ἐκληψόμεθα τ. id.*ep.*9.5(M.3.1112D); **3.** *trope, figure* ἔστι...ὁ τ. λέξις παραγεγραμμένη ἀπὸ τοῦ κυρίου ἐπὶ τὸ μὴ κύριον κατασκευῆς ἕνεκα καὶ φράσεως τῆς ἐν τῷ λόγῳ εὐχρηστίας χάριν Clem.*str.*6.15(p.497.13; M.9.353A); παρ' ἀμφιβολίαν...ὁ κύριος τὸν διάβολον κατὰ τὸν τοῦ πειρασμοῦ σοφίζεται χρόνον, καὶ οὐκέτι ἔγωγε ἐνταῦθα συνορῶ, ὅπως ποτὲ ὁ...τῆς διαλεκτικῆς εὑρετής...παράγεται τῷ κατ' ἀμφιβολίαν ἀπατώμενος τ. *ib.*1.9(p.29.31; M.8.741B); τ. Ἑβραϊκῷ τινι λέγεται περὶ τοῦ θεοῦ...ὅτι ἔθετο σκότος ἀποκρυφὴν...ἵνα δηλωθῇ ὅτι ἀφανῆ καὶ ἄγνωστά ἐστι τὰ...περὶ τοῦ θεοῦ, ἀποκρύψαντος ἑαυτὸν...τοῖς μὴ φέρουσι τὰς τῆς γνώσεως αὐτοῦ μαρμαρυγάς Or.*Cels.*6.17(p.88.1; M.11.1316B); Chrys.*hom.*21.3 *in 2Cor.*(10.585E); ref. miraculous births in OT οὐ ταύτην μόνον τὴν γέννησιν, ἀλλὰ καὶ τὴν ἐκ παρθένου προανεφώνουν οὗτοι οἱ τ. id.*hom.*26.2 *in Jo.*(8.151C); ἄλλος γίνεται τ. νέος...ὁ τῶν στειρῶν, προοδοποιῶν τῇ πίστει τῆς παρθενικῆς ὠδῖνος *ib.*(151D); ref. Tropici ἐτολμήσατε τρόπους ἑαυτοῖς ἐπινοεῖν καὶ εἰπεῖν τὸ λεγόμενον κτίζεσθαι πνεῦμα [ref. Am.4:13] αὐτὸ εἶναι τὸ πνεῦμα τὸ ἅγιον Ath.*ep.Serap.*1.7(M.26.548B); οἱ τῷ ὄντι τροπικοὶ...ἐτόλμησαν...τρόπους...ἑαυτοῖς ἐφευρεῖν καὶ παρεξηγεῖσθαι...τὸ τοῦ ἀποστόλου ῥητόν *ib.*1.10(556B); *form of words, expression*, Eus.*e.th.*3.5(p.160.26; M.24.1008C).

F. *method* τοῦ τ. τῆς εἰς αὐτὸν εὐσεβείας Or.*Cels.*8.76(p.293.5; M.11.1632B); ref. spiritual warfare τοῦτον οὖν τὸν τ. μὴ καταπίπτωμεν τῇ διανοίᾳ, μηδὲ λογιζώμεθα ἐν τῇ ψυχῇ δειλίας Ath.*v.Anton.*42(M.26.904B); Marc.Er.*opusc.*5.12(M.65.1048C).

G. *form* of faith or piety τῆς πίστεως ὁ τ. [i.e. Nicene creed] Eust.*fr.in Pr.8:22* ap.Thdt.*h.e.*1.8.1(M.18.676C); τῆς ἐκκλησίας ἀφοριζομένης τοῦ ἰουδαϊκοῦ τ. Eus.*Marcell.*1.1(p.4.3; M.24.717A); φησιν ἐκ τῶν θείων γραφῶν μεμαθηκέναι τοῦτον τὸν τῆς θεοσεβείας τ. ... κοινὸς...οὗτος ἁπάντων ἡμῶν τῆς θεοσεβείας ὁ τ., πιστεύειν εἰς πατέρα καὶ υἱὸν καὶ ἅγιον πνεῦμα Marcell.*fr.*65 *ib.*1.4(p.18.20; 753A); τὸν νέον τῆς εὐσεβείας τ., τὸν πρὸς αὐτοῦ [sc. Christ] πᾶσιν ἀνθρώποις κατηγγελμένον Eus.*d.e.*1.1(p.3.31; M.22.17A); *ib.*(p.5.6; 20A).

τροπόω, **1.** *rout, put to flight*; **a.** in gen., Clem.*str.*1.24(p.101.22; M.8.909A); Eus.*v.C.*2.17(p.48.5; M.20.996A); Nect.*Thdr.*5(M.39.1828A); **b.** ref. Christ's defeat of powers of evil, Eus.*d.e.*4.10(p.167.4; M.22.277C); Ath.*v.Anton.*42(M.26.905A); ἄνθρωπος...γενόμενος...τροπώσας τε καὶ καταργήσας τὸν καθ' ἡμῶν θάνατον id.*ep.Serap.*2.7(M.26.620C); Chrys.*hom.*78.4 *in Mt.*(7.756B); **c.** ref. spiritual warfare, Gr.Nyss.*hom.*8 *in Eccl.*(M.44.748A); εἰ...βούλει...τὴν φάλαγγα τῶν νοητῶν ἀλλοφύλων εὐχερῶς τροπώσασθαι, ἀνίχνευσον τοὺς τρεῖς...τοῦ διαβόλου γίγαντας, λήθην...ῥαθυμίαν καὶ ἄγνοιαν Marc.Er.*opusc.*5.13(M.67.1049B); θρηνεῖσθαι...θέμις οὐ τὸν τροπωσάμενον τὴν ἁμαρτίαν...ἀλλὰ τοὺς ὑπὸ τούτων ἁπάντων ἁλόντας Isid.Pel.*epp.*2.285(M.78.717A); of a martyr ἀνδρείᾳ ψυχῆς τὸν Διοκλητιανὸν ἐτροπώσατο Pamph.Mon.*Soter.*3(p.118.5); ref. warfare against heretics, Max.*opusc.*(M.91.88C); of defeat of Christol. error by orthodox formulations, id.*ep.*12(M.91.480B); **2.** *turn back* the course of battle, *turn* war into victory ὁ...ποιητὴς...τὸν πόλεμον τοῦτον ἐτροπώσατο Chrys.*hom.35.6 in Gen.*(4.358C); id.*hom.27.3 in Heb.*(12.250B).

τροῦλλος, ὁ, *dome, domed building,* Jo.Mal.*chron.*18 p.489(M.97. 708B); Steph.Diac.*v.Steph.*(M.100.1144D).

τροφεύς, ὁ, *one who rears, brings up; foster-father;* of Christ, *Diogn.*9.6; τοῦ θεοῦ τοῦ τ. καὶ πατρὸς τῶν γεννωμένων καὶ ἀναγεννωμένων Clem.*paed.*1.6(p.114.28; M.8.300A); ὁ λόγος τὰ πάντα τῷ νηπίῳ, καὶ πατὴρ καὶ μήτηρ καὶ παιδαγωγὸς καὶ τ. *ib.*(p.115.21; 301A); ὁ...τ. ἡμῶν λόγος τὸ αὐτοῦ ὑπὲρ ἡμῶν ἐξέχεεν αἷμα *ib.*(p.116.5; 301B); ἐγώ σου τ., ἄρτον ἐμαυτὸν διδούς id.*q.d.s.*23(p.175.11; M.9.628D); *one who provides food* for the poor ὁμολογεῖ [sc. Christ] τὸν τ. καὶ ξενοδόχον Chrys.*hom.79.2 in Mt.*(7.761A); of Manich. 'hearers' who supplied food to the 'elect', Epiph.*haer.*66.53(p.90.5; M.42.109A).

τροφή, ἡ, *food, nourishment;* **1.** in gen. γῆ...κατὰ τὸ θέλημα αὐτοῦ ...τὴν πανπληθῆ...ἀνατέλλει τ. *1Clem.*20.4; οὐχ ἥδομαι τροφῇ φθορᾶς ...ἄρτον θεοῦ θέλω, ὅ ἐστιν σὰρξ Ἰησοῦ Χριστοῦ Ign.*Rom.*7.3; ἀντὶ τραπέζης τῆς πατρικῆς...ἀμειψάμενος...τὰς χοιρείους τ. Gr.Thaum. *pan.Or.*16(p.36.24; M.10.1097B); τροφῆς καὶ ποτοῦ...μεταλαβών [sc. Christ], ὁ τρέφων πάντας τοὺς χρήζοντας τροφῆς *Lit.*ap.*Const.App.*8. 12.32; **2.** in rel. to spiritual life; vegetarian diet of Greek philosophers, Clem.*str.*7.6(p.25.1; M.9.445A); of Christian diet σεμναὶ διαπρέπουσιν πορεία καὶ κατάκλισις καὶ τ. καὶ ὕπνος...καὶ ἡ λοιπὴ παιδεία id.*paed.*1.12(p.149.27; M.8.369B); ἄθετος...ἡ τοιαύτη τ. [sc. meat] πρὸς σύνεσιν ἀκριβῆ id.*str.*7.6(p.26.7; 448B); to be simple, *ib.* 1.10(p.32.6; M.8.745B); not excessively varied, id.*paed.*2.10(p.218. 16; 520A); cereals recommended, *ib.*2.1(p.154.18; 380A); πᾶν... ἀμβλὺ καὶ νόθον τῆς ψυχῆς ἢ πεφυκυίας οὕτως ἢ καὶ ὑπὸ τ. περιττῶν τοῦ σώματος παχυνομένης Gr.Thaum.*pan.Or.*7(p.20.16; M.10.1076B); ἦν αὐτῷ [sc. Antony] ἡ τ. ἄρτος καὶ ἅλας καὶ τὸ ποτὸν ὕδωρ μόνον Ath.*v.Anton.*7(M.26.853A); **3.** ref. thanksgiving for food ὁ ἐσθίων... κυρίῳ ἐσθίει καὶ εὐχαριστεῖ τῷ θεῷ...ὡς εἶναι τὴν δικαίαν τροφὴν εὐχαριστίαν Clem.*paed.*2.1(p.161.2; M.8.393C); εὐλογήσας...ἐπὶ τῆς τ. καὶ εὐχαριστήσας μετὰ τὸ κορεσθῆναι *Hom.Clem.*1.22; εὐχαριστοῦμέν σοι...ὅτι κατηξίωσας ἡμᾶς μεταλαβεῖν...τῶν σαρκικῶν τ. ... δεόμεθα... ἵνα καὶ τὰς ἐπουρανίους τ. ἡμῖν δωρήσῃ Ath.*virg.*14(p.49.12; M.28. 269A); **4.** ref. idolatry; offering of food to idols forbidden, Clem. *paed.*2.1(p.159.17; M.8.392B); incense and odours of sacrifice as food of demons, id.*str.*7.6(p.24.4; M.9.444B); Or.*mart.*45(p.41.19; M. 11.621A); **5.** ref. distribution of food in Church to widows, CAlex. *ep.*(p.101.2; M.25.277C); supervised by bishops, *Const.App.*2.25.8; alms of the wicked not to be used for supply of food but for wood for burning, *ib.*4.10.1; **6.** *support, sustenance* εἰς δημιουργίαν καὶ τ. τῆς σαρκός Clem.*str.*7.12(p.56.34; M.9.509C); plur., *livelihood, ib.* (p.52.7; 500C); **7.** met., in gen. ἡ ἁμαρτία...ἡ τοῦ θανάτου συνεργός... ἡτοίμαζεν αὐτῷ τροφάς Mel.*pass.*54 p.9.10; γεύεται δὲ θανάτου, καὶ οὐ γεύεται μόνον ἀλλὰ καὶ ἐμφορεῖται ὡς τροφῆς τοῦ θανάτου, ὁ προφερόμενος τὰ ἐναντία τοῖς ῥήμασι τῆς...ζωῆς Or.*Jo.*20.43(33; p.387.4; M. 14.676C); οἱ...τοιοῦτοι...τ. τοῖς ἀλόγοις γίνονται ἐνταῦθα πάθεσιν... καὶ ἐκεῖ πάλιν ὕλη καὶ τ. τῷ πυρί Chrys.*hom.11.6 in Mt.*(7.156E); **8.** of food of the mind τ. ... ἢ διὰ σιτίων ἢ διὰ λόγων λαμβάνεται Clem.*str.*1.1(p.6.16; M.8.693A); εἰσὶ γὰρ καὶ ψυχαὶ ἰδίας ἔχουσαι τροφάς, αἱ μὲν κατ' ἐπίγνωσιν καὶ ἐπιστήμην αὔξουσαι, αἱ δὲ τὴν Ἑλληνικὴν νεμόμεναι φιλοσοφίαν, ἧς καθάπερ καὶ τῶν καρύων οὐ τὸ πᾶν ἐδώδιμον *ib.*(p.6.21; 693B); τῆς τῶν λογικῶν ζῴων λογικῆς τ. Or. *Cels.*7.60(p.209.17; M.11.1505C); **9.** of spiritual food in gen. μόνῃ τῇ Χριστιανῇ τ. χρῆσθε, ἀλλοτρίας δὲ βοτάνης ἀπέχεσθε, ἥτις ἐστὶν αἵρεσις Ign.*Trall.*6.1; ἡ πνευματικὴ τ., γλυκεῖα μὲν διὰ τὴν χάριν ὑπάρχουσα, τρόφιμος δὲ ὡς ζωή, λευκὴ δὲ ὡς ἡμέρα Χριστοῦ Clem. *paed.*1.6(p.114.18; M.8.297C); κατήχησα ὑμᾶς ἐν Χριστῷ ἁπλῇ καὶ ἀληθεῖ...τ. τῇ πνευματικῇ *ib.*(p.111.6; 292C); τῆς ἄνω τ. ἐξέχεσθαι τῆς θείας καὶ τῆς τοῦ ὄντως ὄντος ἀπληρώτου ἐμπίπλασθαι θέας *ib.*2.1 (p.160.5; 393A); ἀγάπη...τῷ ὄντι ἐπουράνιός ἐστι τ., ἑστίασις λογική *ib.*(p.157.8; 385B); γάλα μὲν ἡ κατήχησις, οἱονεὶ πρώτη ψυχῆς τ. νοηθήσεται, βρῶμα δὲ ἡ ἐποπτικὴ θεωρία id.*str.*5.10(p.370.15; M.9. 101A); cf.*ib.*5.8(p.359.18; 77B); εἰ...ἡμῖν βρῶμα ἡ γνῶσις εἶναι συμπεφώνηται, μακάριοι τῷ ὄντι...οἱ πεινῶντες καὶ διψῶντες τὴν ἀλήθειαν, ὅτι πλησθήσονται τροφῆς ἀιδίου *ib.*5.11(p.373.3; 105C); τῶν κοσμικῶν νηστεύειν χρή, ἵνα τῷ κόσμῳ ἀποθάνωμεν καὶ μετὰ τοῦτο τ. θείας μεταλαβόντες θεῷ ζήσωμεν id.*ecl.*14(p.140.27; M.9.705A); ἐὰν σιωπήσωμεν μὴ ἀντιπαρατιθέντες... [i.e. over against heresy] τὰ ἀληθῆ... δόγματα, ἐπικρατήσουσι τῶν...ψυχῶν, ἀπορίᾳ τροφῆς σωτηρίου ἐπὶ τὰ ἀπηγορευμένα σπευδουσῶν καὶ...ἀκάθαρτα...βρώματα Or.*Jo.*5.8 (p.105.8; M.14.196A); ref. less advanced doctrine ἡ μέν τίς ἐστιν τῶν ἀλογωτέρων ψυχῶν πνευματικὴ ποώδης τ. *ib.*13.33(p.258.25; 457A); ref. spiritual senses ἄλλη μέν τις ἂν εἴη ἡ ὁρατικὴ τῆς ψυχῆς δύναμις καὶ θεωρητική, ἄλλη δὲ ἡ γευστικὴ καὶ ἀντιληπτικὴ τῆς ποιότητος τῶν νοητῶν τ. *ib.*20.43(33; p.386.27; 676B); πολλάκις...μετὰ πολλῶν ἄλλων μοναχῶν μέλλων ἐσθίειν, ἀναμνησθεὶς τῆς πνευματικῆς τ., παρῃτήσατο Ath.*v.Anton.*45(M.26.909A); ἡ στερεωτέρα τ., τουτέστιν ὁ περὶ τῶν ἀνωτάτων λόγος Cyr.*ador.*1(1.29B); τίς ἡ στερεὰ τ. καὶ τίς ἡ ὑγρά; ταύτας γὰρ ἡ...σοφία δωρεῖσθαι...ὑμνεῖται· τὴν μὲν οὖν στερεὰν τ. σύνθημα φέρειν οἴομαι τῆς νοερᾶς καὶ μονίμου τελειότητος καὶ ταυτότητος, καθ' ἣν τὰ θεῖα κατὰ...ἑνιαίαν...γνῶσιν μετέχεται...τὴν δὲ ὑγρὰν τῆς διαχυτικῆς...ἐπιρροῆς καὶ ἔτι διὰ ποικίλων...ἐπὶ τὴν ἁπλῆν ...θεογνωσίαν...χειραγωγούσης Dion.Ar.*ep.*9.4(M.3.1109D); cf.*ib.*9.3 (1109B); ἱερᾶς πληροῦσθαι καὶ θειοτάτης τ. id.*e.h.*4.3.4(M.3.480A); **10.** ref. Jo.4:34 τὸ θέλημα τοῦ πατρός, τοῦτο γὰρ αὐτοῦ τ. καὶ ἀνάπαυσις καὶ δύναμις ἦν Heracleon ap.Or.*Jo.*13.38(p.263.18; M.14. 465B); οὐκ ἄτοπόν γε λέγειν μὴ μόνον ἀνθρώπους καὶ ἀγγέλους ἐνδεεῖς εἶναι τῶν νοητῶν τ., ἀλλὰ καὶ τὸν Χριστὸν τοῦ θεοῦ· καὶ αὐτὸς γάρ... ἐπισκευάζεται ἀεὶ ἀπὸ τοῦ πατρός, τοῦ μόνου ἀνενδεοῦς Or.*Jo.*13.34 (p.259.19; 457D); **11.** of Christ, as Logos, as food of believers ὁ κύριος, ἡ τ. τῶν νηπίων...ἡ τ., τουτέστιν ⟨ὁ⟩ κύριος Ἰησοῦς, τουτέστιν ὁ λόγος τοῦ θεοῦ, πνεῦμα σαρκούμενον, ἁγιαζομένη σὰρξ οὐράνιος. ἡ τ. τὸ γάλα τοῦ πατρός, ᾧ μόνῳ τιτθευόμεθα οἱ νήπιοι Clem.*paed.*1.6 (p.116.1; M.8.301B); πίνεται γὰρ ὁ λόγος, ἡ τ. τῆς ἀληθείας...δυνατὸν δὲ τὸ αὐτὸ καὶ βρῶμα εἶναί πως ἔχον καὶ ποτόν, πρὸς ἄλλο καὶ ἄλλο νοούμενον *ib.*(p.117.7; 304B); εἰ...ἀνεγεννήθημεν εἰς Χριστόν, ὁ ἀναγεννήσας ἡμᾶς ἐκτρέφει τῷ ἰδίῳ γάλακτι, τῷ λόγῳ. πᾶν γὰρ τὸ γεννῆσαν ἔοικεν εὐθὺς παρέχειν τῷ γεννωμένῳ τ. καθάπερ δὲ ἡ ἀναγέννησις, ἀναλόγως οὕτως καὶ ἡ τ. γέγονεν τῷ ἀνθρώπῳ πνευματική *ib.* (p.119.20; 308C); τοῦ...πατρὸς ἐπομβρήσαντος τὸν λόγον, αὐτὸς ἤδη τ. γέγονεν πνευματικὴ τοῖς σώφροσιν *ib.*(p.115.9; 300B); πόσοις...ἤρκει τὸ σῶμα πρὸς βρῶσιν, ἵνα καὶ τοῦ κόσμου παντὸς τοῦτο τ. γένηται; Ath.*ep.Serap.*4.19(M.26.665D); ὁ θεὸς...ὁ τὸν οὐράνιον ἄρτον...τὴν τ. παντὸς τοῦ κόσμου, τὸν κύριον...Χριστόν, ἐξαποστείλας *Lit.Jac.*(p.180. 15); cf.*Lit.Bas.*(p.309.9); **12.** of eucharist, cf. σύ, δέσποτα...τ. τε καὶ ποτὸν ἔδωκας τοῖς ἀνθρώποις εἰς ἀπόλαυσιν, ἵνα σοι εὐχαριστήσωμεν, ἡμῖν δὲ ἐχαρίσω πνευματικὴν τ. καὶ ποτὸν καὶ ζωὴν αἰώνιον διὰ τοῦ παιδός σου *Did.*10.3; παρέθηκε τ. παντὶ ἰχθὺν ἀπὸ πηγῆς παμμεγέθη καθαρόν, ὃν ἐδράξατο παρθένος ἁγνὴ καὶ τοῦτον ἐπέδωκε φίλοις ἐσθίειν διὰ παντός Aberc.*epitaph.*13ff.; φάγεσθέ μου, φησί, τὴν σάρκα καὶ πίεσθέ μου τὸ αἷμα. ταύτας ἡμῖν οἰκείας τ. ὁ κύριος χορηγεῖ καὶ σάρκα ὀρέγει καὶ αἷμα ἐκχεῖ Clem.*paed.*1.6(p.115.23; M.8.301A); διὰ τῆς ἐνύλου καὶ τὴν ἁγίαν μνηστευόμενοι τ. *ib.*(p.117.2; 304A); ref. relationship of eucharist to baptism συγγένειάν τινα πρὸς τὸ ὕδωρ...ἔχει τὸ γάλα, καθάπερ...πρὸς τὴν πνευματικὴν τ. τὸ λουτρὸν τὸ πνευματικόν *ib.* (p.120.12; 309B); βουλόμενος παραστῆσαι ἀθλητικὴν τελειοτέροις ἁρμόζουσαν τ. φησιν· ὁ ἄρτος δέ, ὃν ἐγὼ δώσω, σάρξ μού ἐστιν Or.*or.*27.4 (p.365.13; M.11.508B); cf.id.*Cels.*3.60(p.254.23; M.11.1000B); φάγωμεν αὐτοῦ τῆς σαρκός, τῆς ἀληθινῆς τ. id.*Jo.*19.6(1; p.305.31; M.14. 536D); δοκεῖ μοι σημαίνειν τὸ 'χαροποιοὶ οἱ ὀφθαλμοὶ αὐτοῦ ἀπὸ οἴνου', καὶ τὸ 'λευκοὶ οἱ ὀδόντες αὐτοῦ ἢ γάλα' τὸ λαμπρὸν καὶ καθαρὸν τῆς μυστηριώδους τ. Eus.*d.e.*8.1(p.366.21; M.22.596A); σὰρξ...καὶ τὸ ταύτης αἷμα παρ' ἐμοῦ πνευματικῶς δοθήσεται τ. Ath.*ep.Serap.*4.19 (M.26.668A); τὴν...σάρκα βρῶσιν...οὐράνιον καὶ...πνευματικὴν τ. παρ' αὐτοῦ διδομένην *ib.*; ἀπαντήσωμεν ἐρχομένῳ καὶ συνεισελθόντες αὐτῷ τῆς ἀθανάτου μεταλάβωμεν τ. id.*ep.fest.*20(p.296.17; M.26.1433D); θυσίας ἀναφορὰ καὶ τ. ἱερᾶς δωρεά *Const.App.*2.59.4; τύπον ἔχει...τὸ... μάννα τῆς θείας τ. ... ὥσπερ γὰρ ἐκεῖνοι μετὰ τὸ διαβῆναι τὴν...θάλασσαν, καὶ τῆς ξένης τ. καὶ τοῦ παραδόξου ἀπήλαυσαν νάματος, οὕτως ἡμεῖς μετὰ τὸ...βάπτισμα τῶν θείων μεταλαμβάνομεν μυστηρίων Thdt. *qu.27 in Ex.*(1.144); **13.** of scripture and scriptural teaching αἱ δυνάμεις, αἱ συνεργοῦσαι τῇ ψυχῇ καὶ τῷ νῷ...τρέφονται λογικῇ τῇ ἀπὸ τῶν ἱερῶν γραμμάτων...τ. καὶ τρεφόμεναι δυνατώτεραι γίνονται Or. *hom.20.1 in Jos.*(p.418.25); λαοὶ προσδοκῶσι φέροντά σε τ. αὐτοῖς, τὴν ἐκ τῶν γραφῶν διδασκαλίαν Ath.*ep.Drac.*2(M.25.525B); ψυχῆς τ. θείων λόγων ἑστίασις Bas.Sel.*or.*16.1(M.85.204B); τῶν ἱερῶν ἡ... ἐπιστήμη πρῶτα μὲν αὐτοὺς τῇ τῶν μορφωτικῶν καὶ ζωοποιῶν λογίων εἰσαγωγικῇ τ. μαιεύεται Dion.Ar.*e.h.*3.3.6(M.3.433A); **14.** of food of angels ἡ ἀγγελικὴ καὶ μὴ ἀνθρωπίνη τ. [sc. manna] Or.*Jo.*10.18(13; p.189.21; M.14.337C); κοινὴν ἁγίων ἀνθρώπων καὶ ἀγγέλων τ. id.*or.*27. 11(p.370.11; M.11.513C); δυναμένων τῶν ἁγίων μεταδοῦναί ποτε τ. νοητῆς καὶ λογικῆς οὐ μόνον ἀνθρώποις, ἀλλὰ καὶ θειοτέραις δυνάμεσιν *ib.*(p.370.15; M.l.c.); αὕτη...ἐστιν...ἡ πρώτη τῶν οὐρανίων οὐσιῶν διακόσμησις...ἁπλᾶς...καὶ ἀμέσους μαρμαρυγὰς ἐλλαμπομένη καὶ θείας τ. ἀποπληρουμένη Dion.Ar.*c.h.*7.4(M.3.212A); οἱ νόες εὐπαθῶς ἡδόμενοι...τ. νοητῇ χρῶνται id.*e.h.*4.3.4(M.3.480A).

τρόφιον, τό, *bait* μικρῷ τ. αἱρεθείς, ἠγκιστρεύετο [sc. Judas] ὑπὸ τῆς ἐπιθυμίας Serap.*Man.*22(p.39; M.40.917D).

***τροφοδότης, ὁ,** *giver of food,* Thdr.Stud.*nativ.BMV* 4(M.96. 685A).

τροφοφορ-έω, *suckle* *ἡ μήτηρ ἀπέρχεται πρὸς αὐτὸ* [sc. *τὸ παιδίον*] ...*καὶ ἀναλαμβάνει καὶ...~εῖ ἐν πολλῇ στοργῇ* Mac.Aeg.*hom*.46.3(M.34.793C).

τροχαλῶς, *hurriedly*, Clem.*paed*.2.7(p.192.21; M.8.461C); Nil.*Eulog*.21(M.79.1120D).

τροχαντήρ, ὁ, a kind of *rack*, Gr.Naz.*or*.15.4(M.35.917A).

τροχιά, ἡ, 1. *wheel-track*; hence *path, way*; met., Or.*fr.68 in Lc.* 14:12(p.267); Cyr.*Am*.8(3.334A); id.*inc.unigen*.(5^1.680C); **2.** *footstep*; met., Cyr.*ador*.12(1.415A).

***τρυγητέον,** *one must gather*, Clem.*str*.1.9(p.29.3; M.8.740B) cit. s. *ἄμπελος*.

***τρυγιός, ὁ,** *dregs*, ‡Ath.*haer*.7(M.28.513A); *ib*.(516A).

τρυμαλιά, 1. *hole, aperture*, Hipp.*haer*.4.29(p.57.7; M.16.3094B); Ath.*v.Anton*.13(M.26.861C); Nil.*epp*.3.34(M.79.401C); in the ground, Proc.G.*Is*.51:1(M.87.2197A); met. *ὥσπερ ἐκεῖνος* [sc. Moses] *ἔχει ὀπὴν δι' ἧς κατανοεῖται τὰ ὀπίσω τοῦ θεοῦ, τὸν αὐτὸν τρόπον ἕκαστος ὁδὸν διδοὺς τοῦ νοεῖσθαι θεὸν διὰ τῶν λεγομένων ὑπ' αὐτοῦ, ποιεῖ ἐν αὐτῷ ὀπήν, εἰ δὲ βούλει ὀνομάσαι, τ., ἀφ' ἧς ὀπῆς ἢ τ. ὄψει* Or.*hom.16.3 in Jer*.(p.135.3; M.13.441B); *πᾶσα ἠνοίγη τῆς ψυχῆς ἡ πύλη, ἵνα εἰσέλθῃ ὁ βασιλεὺς τῆς δόξης· ἀλλ' ἡ τῆς πύλης εὐρυχωρία μικρά τις ἀπεδείχθη τ. στενὴ καὶ βραχεία, δι' ἧς οὐκ αὐτὸς ὁ νυμφίος, ἀλλ' ἡ χεὶρ αὐτοῦ μόγις ἐχώρησεν* Gr.Nyss.*hom.11 in Cant*.(M.44.1009A); **2.** *eye* of a needle (cf. Mc.10:25), *A.Petr.et Andr*.16(p.124.16); *ib*.17(p.124.25).

***τρυπάνισκος, ὁ,** *auger, gimlet* (for torture), *M.Eleuth*.8.

τρυφ-άω, 1. *live luxuriously, fare sumptuously* *τὸ...'πάρεστί μοι... διὰ τί μὴ τρυφήσω;' οὐκ ἀνθρώπινον οὐδὲ κοινωνικόν, ἐκεῖνο δὲ μᾶλλον ἀγαπητικόν· 'πάρεστί μοι, διὰ τί μὴ μεταδῶ τοῖς δεομένοις;'* Clem.*paed*.2.12(p.229.13; M.8.541C); *ἄτοπον...ἕνα ~ᾶν πενομένων πλειόνων* *ib*.(p.229.21; 544A); ref. observance of Holy Week fast *οὐχ ὅπως οὐχ ὑπερτιθέμενοι, ἀλλὰ μηδὲ νηστεύσαντες, ἀλλὰ καὶ τρυφήσαντες τὰς προαγούσας τέσσαρας* [i.e. first four days of week] Dion.Al.*ep.can*.(p.102.7; M.10.1277A); *καταισχύνων τοὺς τὸ ~ᾶν τοῦτο...ζῆν εἶναι νομίζοντας, οἳ θεὸν ἡγοῦνται τὴν κοιλίαν* Meth.*res*.1.60(p.325.1); *οἱ ἐλόμενοι τὰ παρόντα ἐξουσίαν ἔχουσιν πλουτεῖν, ~ᾶν, ἥδεσθαι...τῶν γὰρ ἐσομένων ἀγαθῶν οὐδὲν ἕξουσιν* *Hom.Clem*.15.7; *οὐ γὰρ ἄν, εἰ μὴ τοῦτο* [sc. resurrection and judgement] *ἦν, τῶν μὲν πονηρῶν εἴασε πολλοὺς ~ᾶν κατὰ τὸν παρόντα βίον, τῶν δὲ δικαίων πολλοὺς ἐν μυρίοις ἠφίει κακοῖς, ἀλλ' ἐπειδὴ παρεσκεύασται αἰὼν ἕτερος, ἐν ᾧ κατ' ἀξίαν ἑκάστῳ...ἀποδιδόναι μέλλει, διὰ τοῦτο ἀνέχεται τὸν μὲν κακούμενον, τὸν δὲ ~ῶντα ὁρῶν* Chrys.*stat*.1.9(2.13E); **2.** *run riot, wax wanton* *πᾶς...ἄνθρωπος, ὁ ~ῶν καὶ ἀπατώμενος, οὕτω βασανίζεται, ὅτι ἔχοντες ζωὴν εἰς θάνατον ἑαυτοὺς παραδεδώκασι* Herm.*sim*.6.5.4; *~ῶντες εἰκῇ καὶ μάτην* Chrys.*hom.43.2 in Jo*.(8.258A); *ib.60.4*(356C); **3.** *revel* (in), *exult* (in); **a.** in bad sense, Herm.*sim*.6.5.5; *ὁ ἐν τῇ πορφύρᾳ καὶ βυσσῷ ~ῶν* Clem.*paed*.3.6(p.256.19; M.8.604C); *τί τολμᾷς ἐν τοῖς τοῦ κυρίου ~ῶν ἀγνοεῖν τὸν δεσπότην;* id.*prot*.10(p.74.16; M.8.220A); *ὁ δικαστὴς καθέζεται δικάζων καὶ ~ῶν ἐν τῷ δικαστηρίῳ, ὁ Χριστιανὸς ἐν ᾧ ἐστι Χριστὸς δικαζόμενος, πικρίας ἐνεπλήσθη* Or.*hom.14.17 in Jer*.(p.124.2; M.13.428A); **b.** in good sense, Herm.*sim*.6.5.7 cit. s. *τρυφή*; *ἡ παρὰ τὴν ὄψιν ἀπόλαυσις αὐτοῖν* [sc. *ἄνθος* and *κάλλος*] *ὕβρις ἐστίν, οὐ τρυφή· ~ᾶν δὲ ἡμῖν, ὡς ἐν παραδείσῳ, προσῆκεν σωφρόνως...παρεπομένοις τῇ γραφῇ* Clem.*paed*.2.8(p.200.14; M.8.480B); *τὰ μὲν ἠθικὰ μαθήματα...ἄρτος ἐστὶ τῆς ζωῆς..., τὰ δὲ εὐφραίνοντα καὶ ἐνθουσιᾶν ποιοῦντα ἀπόρρητα καὶ μυστικὰ θεωρήματα, τοῖς κατατρυφῶσι τοῦ κυρίου ἐγγινόμενα καὶ οὐ μόνον τρέφεσθαι, ἀλλὰ καὶ ~ᾶν ποθοῦσιν, ἔστιν ἀπὸ τῆς ἀληθινῆς ἀμπέλου ἐρχόμενα 'οἶνος' καλούμενα* Or.*Jo*.1.30(33; p.37.31; M.14.80B); *τὰ...ψυχῆς μόνον αὔξειν πλεονεκτήματα...εὐφραινομένους καὶ ~ῶντας* Gr.Thaum.*pan.Or*.15(p.35.9; M.10.1096B); *ἐλώμεθα ἀρετήν. οὕτω γὰρ καὶ ἐνταῦθα τρυφήσωμεν καὶ τῶν μελλόντων ἐπιτευξόμεθα ἀγαθῶν* Chrys.*hom.67.5 in Mt*.(7.668D); *ἐκεῖνοι* [sc. martyrs]...*μυρίους μώλωπας ἔχοντες... τῶν ἐν παραδείσῳ μᾶλλον ἐτρύφων* *ib.33.5*(385A); *ἔχαιρον αἰκιζόμενοι καὶ ~ῶντες τῶν συνεδρίων ἐξῄεσαν* Cyr.*Mich*.34(3.420E); **4.** *rejoice in* *διάβολος...~ῶν τὴν φθορὰν τῆς φύσεως* Max.*cap*.1.11(M.90.1184A); in good sense ref. hesychast *ἄλλος τις 'Ἰσραὴλ καὶ αὐτὸς θεωρούμενος καὶ τρυφὴν ~ῶν εἰρηνικὴν καὶ οὐράνιον* Sophr.H.*ep.syn*.(M.87.3149B).

***τρυφεραγωγία, ἡ,** *luxurious treatment*, Chrys.*hom.29.3 in Heb*. 12.275B).

τρυφερία, ἡ, 1. *delicacy, delicate nurture*, ‡Just.*ep.Zen.et Ser*.17(M.6.1201B); **2.** *softness*, Melet.*nat.hom*.28–29(M.64.1260C).

***τρυφερόνοος,** *tender, feeble in spirit*, of soul before baptism *ἡ τοῦ ἀνθρώπου ψυχή, ἄρτι τῆς ἐκ παθῶν δουλείας ἐκτρέχουσα καὶ πρὸς τὰ ἀμείνω μεθορμιζομένη...τ. τέ ἐστι καὶ εὐαφεστέρα* Cyr.*ador*.3(1.87B).

τρυφερός, 1. of things, *delightful, pleasant* *ἐν...ἀληθινῷ σαββάτῳ, ἁγίῳ καὶ τ.* Didym.*Ps*.6:1(M.39.1176A); *τὰς...κυριακὰς ἁπάσας τ. ἡγεῖται ἡ...ἐκκλησία καὶ...οὐ νηστεύει* Epiph.*exp.fid*.22(p.523.14; M.42.828B); comp. *τρυφηρότερον*, Bas.Sel.*or*.18.2(M.85.233A); **2.** of persons, *tender, delicate, sensitive*, *T.Gad* 1.4; Herm.*sim*.9.2.5; *Ep. Lugd*.ap.Eus.*h.e*.5.1.21(M.20.416C); **3.** *gentle, tender* *ἐὰν...ὀξυχολία τις ἐπέλθῃ, εὐθὺς τὸ πνεῦμα τὸ ἅγιον, τ. ὄν, στενοχωρεῖται* Herm.*mand*. 5.1.3; *ib*.5.2.6; *ὁ...τῆς δικαιοσύνης ἄγγελος τ. ἐστι* *ib*.6.2.3; *ἡ μὲν... γενεὰ ἡ παλαιὰ...σκληροκάρδιος, χορὸς δὲ νηπίων, ὁ καινὸς ἡμεῖς λαός, τ. ὡς παῖς* Clem.*paed*.1.5(p.101.20; M.8.272B); *σκληροκάρδιοι μὲν...οἱ ...'Ἰουδαῖοι, τ. δὲ...εἰς ὑπακοὴν...οἱ ἐξ ἐθνῶν* Cyr.*Jo*.6.1(4.603B); *ἔστω ...ἐφ' ἡμῖν...ὁ νοῦς τ.* id.*hom.pasch*.27.4(5^2.322B); **4.** of horses, *obedient to the rein*, met. *τίνες δ' ἂν εἶεν οἱ ἵπποι; οἱ...ἀπόστολοι...οἱ τ. καὶ εὐήνιοι...οἱ Χριστὸν...ἡνίοχον ἔχοντες* Cyr.*Abac*.50(3.564B); id. *Soph*.34(3.612A); id.*ador*.1(1.16B); id.*Is*.5.4(2.826D).

τρυφή, ἡ, 1. *luxury, luxurious living* *πᾶσα...τ. μικρά ἐστι καὶ κενὴ τοῖς δούλοις τοῦ θεοῦ* Herm.*mand*.12.2.1; *ποταπαί...εἰσιν αἱ πονηρίαι ἀφ' ὧν δεῖ ἐγκρατεύεσθαι;...ἀπὸ τ. πονηρᾶς, ἀπὸ ἐδεσμάτων πολλῶν* *ib*. 8.3; *δίαιταν...τὴν...καθαρὰν ἑκατέρας κακίας, τρυφῆς τε καὶ φειδωλίας* Clem.*paed*.3.10(p.266.14; M.8.625A); *οἱ δὲ σκωλήκων δίκην περὶ... βορβόρους...κυλινδούμενοι...ἀνονήτους καὶ ἀνοήτους ἐκβόσκονται τρυφάς* id.*prot*.10(p.68.9; M.8.205B); *ταύτας ἡγοῦνται οἱ πολλοὶ τρυφάς, τὰς ἑαυτῶν ἁμαρτίας* id.*paed*.2.10(p.216.14; 516A); *μετεώρους ἀπὸ τῆς ἀληθείας ἀλαζονεία καὶ τ. ποιεῖ καὶ εἰς τὰ περιττὰ ἀπασχόλησις* *ib*.(p.219.8; 520C); *τὸ καλὸν καὶ σωτήριον ἔργον τοῦ λόγου, τὴν ἀγάπην τὴν ἡγιασμένην...ποτῷ τε καὶ τ. βλασφημοῦντες* *ib*.2.1(p.156.15; 385A); *ἀπὸ...τρυφῆς λαμπρὸς βούλει γενέσθαι; ἀλλ' οὐκ ἂν δύναιο* Chrys.*hom.29.3 in Heb*.(12.274C); *ἡμεῖς δὲ αὐτοῖς παραχωροῦμεν καὶ θρόνων καὶ ἀξιωμάτων καὶ τῆς προσκαίρου τ.* Thdt.*ep*.147(4.1278); **2.** *rioting, wantonness* *αὗται πᾶσαι αἱ τ. βλαβεραί εἰσι τοῖς δούλοις τοῦ θεοῦ* Herm.*sim*.6.5.6; *κεφαλὴ τοῦ δράκοντός ἐστιν ἡ ἀκρασία καὶ ἡ τ. ... ὁ ταύτην θλάσας ἀναδεῖται τὸν στέφανον τῆς σωφροσύνης* Meth. *symp*.8.13(p.97.22; M.18.160B); **3.** *self-indulgence*, Herm.*sim*.6.5.4; *οὔκουν ὑπὸ τρυφῆς ῥάθυμος, ὁ δι' ἡμᾶς τὴν παθητὴν ἀναλαβὼν σάρκα* Clem.*str*.7.2(p.6.22; M.9.409B); **4.** in good sense, *joy, delight*; **a.** in gen. *εἰσὶν...τρυφαὶ σῴζουσαι τοὺς ἀνθρώπους· πολλοὶ γὰρ ἀγαθὰ ἐργαζόμενοι τρυφῶσι...αὕτη οὖν ἡ τ. σύμφορός ἐστι τοῖς δούλοις τοῦ θεοῦ καὶ ζωὴν περιποιεῖται τῷ ἀνθρώπῳ* Herm.*sim*.6.5.7; *αὕτη...ἡ ἀληθὴς τ., ἡ θησαυριζομένη πολυτέλεια* Clem.*paed*.2.12(p.229.17; M.8.544A); *ἐὰν προσέχωμεν...ἡ πενία προσθήκη γίνεται καὶ τρυφῆς καὶ ἀναπαύσεως ἡμῖν* Chrys.*hom.77.4 in Jo*.(8.456E); *μὴ δὴ τὰς θύρας ἀποκλείσῃς τῷ φωτὶ τούτῳ καὶ πολλῆς ἀπολαύσῃ τῆς τ.* *ib.5.4*(40B); *ἀλλὰ τρυφῆς ἐρᾷς;...παῦσαι μεθύων. καὶ γὰρ ἐγώ σε βούλομαι τρυφᾶν, ἀλλὰ τὴν ὄντως τ., τὴν οὐδέποτε μαραινομένην* id.*hom.27.5 in 1Cor*.(10.249C); *τρυφῆς...τρόπος πνευματικὸς ἡ τελεία περὶ θεοῦ γνῶσις καὶ τῶν ἐπὶ Χριστῷ μυστηρίων ἡ ἀκριβὴς ἀποκάλυψις,...ὅλη καθαρῶς ἐν ἡμῖν...λάμπουσα καὶ τελειοτάτην ἐμποιοῦσα τὴν εἴδησιν* Cyr.*Jo*.10(4.827C); *εἰρηνεύσαντες...πρὸς θεὸν καὶ καταλύσαντες τὴν ἔχθραν ἐν πόλεσιν ἐσμὲν ἀναπαύσεως καὶ τῆς εἰς αἰῶνας τ.* id.*Is*.3.3(2.450A); *πηγὴ* [sc. Christ]...*ἐστὶ ζωῆς καὶ χειμάρρους τρυφῆς* *ib*.(472D); *ἐν ἀπολαύσει...ἡ νύμφη τοῦ νυμφίου γενομένη καὶ πείρᾳ μαθοῦσα τὴν ἄρρητον ἐκείνην τ.* Thdt.*Cant*.2:7(2.60); Sophr.H.*ep.syn*.(M.87.3149B) cit. s. *τρυφάω*; *τὸν...Ἀδὰμ τῇ παραβάσει παραζηλώσας, ἔγνων ἐμαυτὸν γυμνωθέντα θεοῦ καὶ τῆς ἀϊδίου βασιλείας καὶ τ.* Andr.Cr.*can. mag*.15(p.148; M.97.1332A); ref. eucharist *ἐνεπλήσθημεν τῆς ἀκενώτου σου τ., ... ἧς καὶ ἐν τῷ μέλλοντι πάντας ἡμᾶς τυχεῖν καταξίωσον* *Lit. Bas*.(p.344.27); **b.** of Eden and man's state before Fall, esp. ref. *παράδεισος* (q.v.) *τῆς τ.*: *ἑρμηνεύεται...ἡ...'Ἐδὲμ τ. πίστις δὲ καὶ γνῶσις καὶ εἰρήνη ἡ τ., ἧς ὁ παρακούσας ἐκβάλλεται* Clem.*str*.2.11(p.140.15; M.8.988B); *εἰς τὸν παράδεισον τῆς τ. τίθεται τὸν ἄνθρωπον ὁ θεός, νόμους...διδούς* Or.*Jo*.13.34(M.14.460B; *τροφῆς* p.260.1); *ἡ...συκῆ διὰ τὴν γλυκασίαν...τὴν τ. τὴν πρὸ τῆς παραβάσεως ἐν παραδείσῳ τοῦ ἀνθρώπου παρίστησι γεγενημένην* Meth.*symp*.10.2(p.124.5; M.18.196B); *ὁ πρῶτος ἄνθρωπος...καταπέπτωκε καὶ τὴν ἐπάρατον ταύτην γῆν τῆς πάλαι ἐνθέου τ. ἀντικατηλλάξατο* Eus.*h.e*.1.2.18(M.20.61C); *ὁ τῶν ὅλων κύριος...οὐκ ἀπέρριψεν τὸ τῶν ἀνθρώπων γένος, ἀλλὰ τῷ Ἀδὰμ...ἐν παραδείσῳ...τρυφῆς λόγῳ τὸν παράδεισον οἰκητήριον δούς* *Const.App*.7.43.4; *οὐκ ἐκτίσθη ὁ ἄνθρωπος ἐν πάσῃ τ., ἐν πάσῃ χαρᾷ, ἐν πάσῃ ἀναπαύσει, ἐν πάσῃ δόξῃ; οὐκ ἦν ἐν τῷ παραδείσῳ;* Dor.*doct*.1.7(M.88.1625A); *εἶχον τὰ θηρία ὑποταγὴν πρὸς τὸν Ἀδὰμ πρὸ τοῦ αὐτὸν παρακοῦσαι τῆς ἐντολῆς καὶ τῆς ἐν παραδείσῳ τρυφῆς ἐκπεσεῖν* Jo. Mosch.*prat*.107(M.87.2969B); met. *εἴσεσθε, ὅσα παρέχει ὁ θεὸς τοῖς ἀγαπῶσιν ὀρθῶς, οἱ γενόμενοι παράδεισος τρυφῆς, πάγκαρπον ξύλον... ποικίλοις καρποῖς κεκοσμημένοι* ‡*Diogn*.12.1; ref. life of study under Origen *οὗτος παράδεισος ἀληθῶς τρυφῆς, αὕτη ἀληθὴς εὐφροσύνη καὶ τ., ἣν ἐτρυφήσαμεν ἐν τῷ διηνυσμένῳ τῷδε χρόνῳ* Gr.Thaum.*pan.Or*.16(p.35.11; M.10.1096B); of baptism *ὄχημα πρὸς οὐρανόν, παραδείσου τ.* Cyr.H.*procatech*.16; **c.** of future bliss *ἀγνοοῦσιν...οἵαν τ. ἔχει ἡ* μέλλουσα ἐπαγγελία 2*Clem*.10.4; οὐ τὴν παραυτίκα ἡδονὴν ὁ κύριος, ἀλλὰ τὴν μέλλουσαν ἐσκόπησε τ. Clem.*paed*.1.9(p.134.11; M.8.340C); καταλείψατε...τὸ ἀηδὲς τοῦ κόσμου τούτου...ἵνα αἰωνίας τ. ἀπολαύσητε *A.Phil*.35(p.17.25); τελειωθήσῃ...ἐνδόξως καὶ...ἐλεύσῃ...ἕως τοῦ παραδείσου τῆς τ. *ib*.137(p.69.5); τί ὧδε ἐλήλυθας [sc. Christ], καταλιπὼν τοὺς ψάλλοντας ἐν τῷ παραδείσῳ καὶ τὴν ἐκεῖ τ.; *A.Mt*.1(p.218.4); σπεύσαντες τῶν πολὺ κρειττόνων ἔτυχον [sc. martyrs], ἐν αὐτοῖς οὐρανοῖς καὶ παραδείσῳ τῆς ἐνθέου τ. ἀναρπασθέντες Eus.*h.e*.10.1.5(M.20.844B); *Const.App*.7.33.3; ἡ τ. ἐπὶ τοῖς οὐρανοῖς...μένει...διηνεκής, ἀεὶ ἀκίνητος οὖσα καὶ ἀθάνατος Chrys.*hom.44.2 in Jo*.(8.261A); ζωὴν εἶναι λέγων οὐχὶ πάντως τὸ ἀναστῆναι μόνον, ἀλλ' ἐκείνην...τὴν ἐν ἀναπαύσει καὶ δόξῃ καὶ τρυφαῖς, πνευματικαῖς δὲ δηλονότι καὶ οὐχ ἑτέραις Cyr.*Jo*.10(4.827B); πόρρω...γενήσονται [sc. unbelieving Jews]...τῆς τοῖς δικαίοις ἀποδοθησομένης τ. id.*Ps*.68:28(M.69.1173C); τὴν μέλλουσαν τ. τῶν πρώτων δικαίων Diad.*perf*.90(p.128.22); ἔστι...τελευτήσαντα...ἔχειν...τ. ἐμπρέπουσαν ψυχῇ καθαρᾷ Aen.*dial*.(M.85.920C); οἱ πρὸ τῆς ἀναστάσεως ἀξιούμενοι τοῦ παραδείσου τῆς τ. ἀργοὶ μένειν οὐ δυνήσονται Eustrat.*stat.anim*.20(p.500); μνήσθητι, κύριε...καὶ...ἀνάπαυσον...ἐν τῇ τ. τοῦ παραδείσου *Lit.Jac*.(p.220.11); οὔπω...ἔκρινεν ...τοὺς δὲ τρυφῇ ἀλήκτῳ ἀποκρίνας ‡Caes.Naz.*dial*.21(M.38.880).

τρυφηλός, of things, *exquisite, graceful*, Bas.*hom*.20.1(2.157B; M.31.525C); neut. as subst., Thdt.*Jer*.46:20(2.589); of persons, *luxurious, voluptuous*, Eus.*v.C*.4.69(p.146.16; M.20.1224C); id.*l.C*.17 (p.254.19; M.20.1429B); of a manner of life, opp. ascetic, id.*v.C*. 2.14(p.47.4; 992D); Pall.*h.Laus*.38(p.120.10; M.34.1194A).

[*]**τρυφηρός**, *dainty*, v. τρυφερός.

***τρυφητιάω**, *hanker after luxuries*, Clem.*str*.2.20(p.170.22; M.8.1049A); met., of hankering after spiritual food, *ib*.1.1(p.12.2; 705A).

τρυφητικός, *luxurious, sumptuous*; of things, Clem.*paed*.2.10 (p.223.22; M.8.529B); *ib*.3.11(p.269.15; 632B); of persons, *ib*.3.4 (p.252.7; 593B); *ib*.3.11(p.276.25; 649B); *ib*.(p.268.29; 629C).

***Τρωαδήσιος**, *of the Troad*, *Chron.Pasch*.p.318(M.92.812A); *ib*. p.319(813A).

***τρωγλωτός**, *full of holes* ἐφαίνετο [sc. Satan]...ὡς στιχάριον φορῶν λινοῦν τ. *Apophth.Patr*.(M.65.261A).

***τρωτήριον**, τό, *that which can wound, wounding instrument*, of cup of Christ (Mt.26:39) ὦ ποτήριον διαβόλου τ., δαιμόνων φυγαδευτήριον ‡Caes.Naz.*dial*.135(M.38.1040).

τρωτός, *wounded*, Gr.Naz.*carm*.1.1.11.10(M.37.471).

***τυβί**, fifth Coptic month, corresponding to January, ref. Christ's baptism οἱ...ἀπὸ Βασιλείδου...τὴν ἡμέραν...ἑορτάζουσι... φασὶ δὲ εἶναι...τὴν πεντεκαιδεκάτην τοῦ τ. μηνός, τινὲς δὲ αὖ τὴν ἑνδεκάτην τοῦ αὐτοῦ μηνός Clem.*str*.1.21(p.90.24; M.8.888A); ἐβαπτίσθη τ. ια', ὥρᾳ ι' τῆς ἡμέρας [al. νυκτός] *Chron.Pasch*.p.224(M.92.545C); and birth γεννηθέντος αὐτοῦ...πρὸ ὀκτὼ εἰδῶν Ἰανουαρίου, ἥτις ἐστὶ ...τ. ἑνδεκάτη Epiph.*haer*.51.24(p.293.2; M.41.932B).

***τυλοτάπης**, *with a nap on both sides*; of rugs, Eus.*Ps*.4:9(M.23.113A).

***τυμβολέτης**, ὁ, *violator of tombs*, Gr.Naz.*carm*.2.2(epigr.)57.2, 70.4,71.4(M.38.112A,118A).

***τυμβονόμος**, *haunting graves*, Synes.*hymn*.4.47(p.28; M.66.1604).

***τυμβοφόντης**, ὁ, *violator of tombs*, Gr.Naz.*carm*.2.2(epigr.)32.1 (M.38.100A).

τυμβοχόος, ὁ, *thrower up, digger of graves*, Gr.Naz.*carm*.2.2 (epigr.)71.3(M.38.118A).

τυμβωρυχία, ἡ, *robbing of graves*, Clem.*str*.2.15(p.146.21; M.8.1000C); Gr.Nyss.*ep.can*.6(M.45.233A); Chrys.*hom.11.5 in Rom*.(9.538C).

τυμπανικός, *of a drum*, ‡Caes.Naz.*dial*.103(M.38.969).

τυμπανισμός, ὁ, *beheading* τ. γὰρ ὁ ἀποκεφαλισμὸς λέγεται ‡Ath. *qu.script*.128(M.28.772B).

τυμπανόω, *distend*, ‡Ath.*haer*.6(M.28.512D).

τυπικόν, τό, **1.** liturg., *directory* καὶ ἐν τοῖς τ. εἰσὶ γεγραμμένα *Euchol*.(p.8); cf. N. Nilles *Kalendarium Manuale* (Innsbruck, 1897, I, p.li); **2.** plur., *select verses from Psalms* μετὰ τὸ ψάλαι τὰ τ. *Const.Stud*.27(M.99.1713B); *Euchol*.(p.53); cf.*ib*.(p.158 n.).

τυπικός, *expressive of an intrinsic reality, symbolical* οὐκ ἀνίσταται δι[ὰ τὸ] μέλλον ⟨ὃ⟩ διὰ τῆς τ. εἰκόνος ὁρᾷς; Mel.*pass*.36 p.6.4; Ptol.*ep*.ap.Epiph.*haer*.33.5(p.455.1; M.41.564C); ἡ δὲ οἰκονομία αὕτη καὶ προφητικὴ καὶ τ. Clem.*str*.2.19(p.167.13; M.8.1044A); πάντα γε τὰ συμβολικὰ καὶ τ. συγκρίσει τῶν ἀληθινῶν καὶ νοητῶν μικρά ἐστι καὶ ἐπίγεια Or.*or*.14(p.330.10; M.11.460B); τοῦ τ. καὶ συμβολικοῦ σώματος [i.e. in eucharist] Or.*comm.in Mt*.11.14(p.58.8; M.13.952A); ref. high priest σκιώδη τινὰ καὶ τ. Χριστὸν ἐπιφερόμενος Eus.*d.e*.7.2(p.336.16; M.22.548D); ἐκεῖνοι μὲν γὰρ ἦσαν Χριστοὶ τυπικοί· οὗτος δὲ Χριστὸς ἀληθής Cyr.H.*catech*.11.1; φῶς δὲ τ. ... ὁ γραπτὸς νόμος, σκιαγραφῶν τὴν ἀλήθειαν καὶ τὸ τοῦ μεγάλου φωτὸς μυστήριον Gr.Naz.*or*.40.6(M.36.364D); οὐδὲν τ. δηλοῖ πάλιν, οὐδὲ σωματικόν Chrys.*hom.82.1 in Jo*.(8.484A); καὶ καθ' ἕκαστον εἶδος εὑρήσεις ἀναγωγικὴν τῶν τ. εἰκόνων ἀνακάθαρσιν Dion.Ar.*c.h*.15.7(M.3.336C); id.*ep*.9.1(M.3.1108A) cit. s. τραπέζωσις; τοὺς λόγους μόνον ὁρῶσι τῶν γεγραμμένων γυμνοὺς τῶν ἐπ' αὐτοῖς τ. συνθημάτων Max.*qu.Thal*.55(M.90.536C); Μαρίας, ἐν ᾗ συνελήφθη ὁ ἀμνὸς τοῦ θεοῦ κατὰ τὴν τοῦ τ. ἀμνοῦ σύλληψιν *Chron.Pasch*.p.196(M.92.484B); οὐ κατὰ τὴν ιδ' ἐπετέλεσεν τὸ πάσχα, ἀλλὰ πρὸ τούτου τὸ τ. ἐτέλεσεν δεῖπνον *ib*.p.218(532B).

τυπικῶς, *typically, symbolically* ὁ σωτὴρ τοὺς ἀποστόλους ἐδίδασκεν τὰ μὲν πρῶτα τ. καὶ μυστικῶς, τὰ δὲ ὕστερα παραβολικῶς καὶ ᾐνιγμένως, τὰ δὲ τρίτα σαφῶς καὶ γυμνῶς κατὰ μόνας Clem.*exc.Thdot*.66 (p.128.24; M.9.689C); ἐδίδαξαν δὲ ἡμῶν τὰς γυναῖκας τυπικώτατα κοσμίων ἀποσχέσθαι id.*paed*.2.12(p.232.29; M.8.549C); τ. μὲν παρ' ἐκείνοις τελούμενα μυστικῶς δὲ ἡμῖν ἀποκαθιστάμενα Gr.Naz.*or*.41.4 (M.36.436A); ἐκεῖνα μὲν ἐπράττετο τ., ἐγράφη δὲ πρὸς νουθεσίαν ἡμῶν Cyr.*glaph.Ex*.1(1.261B); τ. εἴ τις ἐκείνῳ προσαρμόσει ταῦτα Thdt.*Jer*. 23:6(2.516); opp. ἱστορικῶς, id.*Abac*.3:18f.(2.1559); πρὸς ἕκαστον πνευματικῶς ἐκ τῶν περὶ αὐτοῦ καθ' ἱστορίαν τ. γεγραμμένων μορφούμενος Max.*ambig*.(M.91.1149D); τρεῖς...κεφαλαὶ [sc. Adam, his son, and Eve]...πάσης τῆς ἀνθρωπότητος ὁμοούσιοι ὑποστάσεις, κατ' εἰκόνα τινά, ὡς καὶ Μεθοδίῳ δοκεῖ, τ. γεγόνασι τῆς ἁγίας καὶ ὁμοουσίου τριάδος· τοῦ μὲν ἀναιτίου καὶ ἀγεννήτου Ἀδὰμ τύπον καὶ εἰκόνα ἔχοντος τοῦ ἀναιτίου...πατρός ‡Gr.Nyss.*imag*.(M.44.1329C).

***τυποειδής (τυπώδης)**, **1.** *in the form of a likeness* ζωογραφίας τ. τιμῶσιν *Orac.Sib*.3.589; **2.** *symbolic* διά τινος...τυπώδους ἀλληγορίας Cels.ap.Or.*Cels*.6.29(p.99.9; M.11.1337B).

***τυποειδῶς**, *illustratively* (i.e. with concrete illustrations) περὶ ὧν τ. λεκτέον, ὡς ἂν ἐφικτὰ γένοιτο τοῖς ἀγνοοῦσιν αὐτά Melet.*nat. hom*.30(M.64.1285B).

***τυποπλαστία**, ἡ, *imagery, symbolism* ὅλως ἄνω καὶ κάτω τὴν ἐμπύριον τιμᾷ ἐκκρίτως τυποπλαστίαν [sc. scriptures] Dion.Ar.*c.h*.15. 2(M.3.329A).

τύπος, ὁ, **A.** *impression, mark*; **1.** lit., of a blow, wound, etc. τῶν τραυμάτων τ. Or.*Cels*.6.9(p.79.22; M.11.1304B); Serap.*Man*.53 (p.75; M.18.1253C); of a seal, Or.*Jo*.20.24(p.358.33; M.14.628B); of a tool, Eus.*v.C*.1.40(p.26.18; M.20.956A); of letters, Philost.*h.e*.9.15(M.65.580B); fig. πάντες ἀναγινώσκουσιν ἐν τῷ στήθει μου καὶ ἐν τῇ καρδίᾳ μου τοὺς τ. μου τῶν ἁμαρτημάτων Or.*hom.16.10 in Jer*.(p.142.17; M.13.452C); καρδία ἐστὶ καθαρά, ἡ...ἀνείδεον τῷ θεῷ καὶ ἀδιαμόρφωτον παραστήσασα τὴν μνήμην, καὶ μόνοις τοῖς αὐτοῦ ἑτοίμη ἐνσημανθῆναι τ. †Marc.Er.*temp*.24(M.65.1064B); **2.** met., *mental impression* ὑποφαίνειν τοὺς χαρακτῆρας τῶν τῆς ψυχῆς τ. ... πειρώμενοι Gr.Thaum. *pan.Or*.2(p.3.20; M.10.1053B); ὁ ἀπὸ τῶν πραγμάτων τ. ἐγγίνεται τῇ νοήσει Bas.*hex*.3.2(1.23A; M.29.53D); ὅταν δέ τις αἰσθήσεως βραχείας δέξηται τ. Proc.G.*Gen*.3:7(M.87.193C); **3.** *original, mould* πολλοῖς γὰρ καὶ διαφόροις τ. ἐοικυῖαι πρόκεινται [sc. αἱ γραφαί]. ἕκαστος οὖν ...περιβλεψάμενος αὐτάς...τὴν...κηρῷ ἐοικυῖαν προαίρεσιν ἐπιβαλὼν ἀπομάσσεται *Hom.Clem*.16.10; τῷ τῆς δυνάμεως ἀποσκιάσματι οἱονεὶ τύπῳ σφραγῖδος ἔνδοθεν καταμορφωθέντος Gr.Nyss.*res*.1(M.46.616B); ὁ κηρὸς παραδιδόμενος τῷ τ. τῆς γλυφῆς μορφοῦται †Bas.*bapt*.1.2.7 (2.634C; M.31.1537B).

B. *representation, image*; **1.** *representation in relief*, Athenag. *leg*.17.2(M.6.924A); on coins, Eus.*v.C*.4.73(p.147.29; M.20.1228B); hence **2.** *image* of any kind λαβεῖν τὸν Μωϋσέα χαλκὸν καὶ ποιῆσαι τ. σταυροῦ Just.1*apol*.60.3(M.6.417A); Marc.Diac.*v.Porph*.61; *CIG* 8812; **3.** *exact replica, likeness* τ. τοῦ πατρὸς τῶν ὅλων Clem.*exc. Thdot*.33(p.117.27; M.9.676B); Ἑρμοῦ λογίου τ. Synes.*ep*.101(M.66.1472B); **4.** *image*, in sense of *representation* of a heavenly reality ὑπέδειξεν ἡμῖν ὁ Ἰησοῦς τὸν τ. τοῦ οὐρανοῦ ἵνα γνῶμεν ὅτι ἀληθῆ ἐστιν ἢ οὔ *A.Andr.et Mt*.(p.79.8).

C. *shape, form*; **1.** in gen., Herm.*sim*.9.10.1; hence, fig., *shape* or *sign* of the cross, Eus.*h.e*.8.7.4(M.20.757A); τῷ τ. τοῦ σταυροῦ...κατασημαίνεσθαι Bas.*Spir*.66(3.54E; M.32.188B); *A.Pil*.B 17.3(p.324); Bas.Sel.*v.Thecl*.1(M.85.513B); ἡ δὲ τοῦ σταυροειδοῦ τ. σφραγὶς... δηλοῖ τὴν πασῶν ὁμοῦ τῶν σαρκικῶν ὀρέξεων ἀνενεργησίαν Dion.Ar. *e.h*.6.3.3(M.3.536A); plur., *features* τοὺς τ. ... τοὺς τὴν ποιότητα...τὴν σωματικὴν παριστάνοντας Meth.*res*.1.22(p.245.6; M.41.1089D–92); Ἰουδὴθ...κάλλεος τύποις θέλξασα τοῦτον id.*symp*.11(p.134.26; M.18.212A); Eus.*e.th*.3.21(p.181.18; M.24.1045B); *qualities* γενόμενοι τοίνυν ἡμεῖς κατ' εἰκόνα, τὸν υἱὸν πρωτότυπον ὡς ἀλήθειαν ἔχομεν τῶν ἐν ἡμῖν καλῶν τ. Or.*princ*.1.2.6(p.36.11); **2.** human *figure, form* Ἰησοῦ, ὁ τ. λαβὼν καὶ γενόμενος ὡς ἄνθρωπος *A.Thom*.72(p.188.2); τὸν δὲ τ. αὐτοῦ τὸν οὐράνιον ἐν τῷ ὄρει ἰδεῖν οὐκ ἠδυνήθημεν *ib*.143(p.250.9); Const.ap. Gel.Cyz.*h.e*.2.7(p.52.1; M.85.1240B); esp. in phrase τύπος σώματος: ὅταν ἴδῃς ὥσπερ σώματος τύπῳ γυναῖκας φαινομένας Chrys.*hom.5.4 in*

1 Thess.(11.465A); **3.** *phantasmal* or *image-body* (received by Christ at baptism, acc. Docetists) τ. καὶ σφράγισμα λαβὼν ἐν τῷ ὕδατι τοῦ γεγεννημένου σώματος ἀπὸ τῆς παρθένου Hipp.*haer*.8.10(p.230.17; M.16.3355A); **4.** *outward form* ἐν τῇ ὁράσει τῷ Ἑρμᾷ ἡ δύναμις ἐν τῷ τ. τῆς ἐκκλησίας φανεῖσα Clem.*str*.6.15(p.498.3; M.9.356A); οἱ τούτων [sc. τῶν οὐρανῶν] αἰσθητοὶ τ. τὰ παρ' ἡμῖν φωνηέντα στοιχεῖα *ib*.6.16 (p.503.31; 369B); perh. cf. τοῦ τε οὐρανοῦ οἱ τ. *Pap.Chr.*(*PO* 18.447); τὰ...ἐν ἡμῖν ἀποτεθέντα μαθήματά τε καὶ χαρίσματα...οὐρανίου...πολιτείας τύπος Ath.*ep.Aeg.Lib*.1(M.25.540A); esp. of a sacramental *sign* τὸ σῶμα αὐτοῦ κατὰ τὸ εὐαγγέλιον τ. ἔφερεν ἄρτου Cyr.H.*catech*.13.19; ἐν τ. γὰρ ἄρτου δίδοταί σοι τὸ σῶμα, καὶ ἐν τ. οἴνου δίδοταί σοι τὸ αἷμα *ib*.22.3; τὴν τοῦ βαπτίσματος ἡμῖν ἔθετο διαθήκην, θανάτου τ. καὶ ζωῆς περιέχουσαν· τὴν μὲν τοῦ θανάτου εἰκόνα τοῦ ὕδατος ἐκπληροῦντος, τὸν δὲ τῆς ζωῆς ἀρραβῶνα παρεχομένου τοῦ πνεύματος Bas.*Spir*.35(3.29B; M.32.129C); τοὺς τ. τῆς ἐμῆς σωτηρίας...τὴν ἱερὰν...μυσταγωγίαν Gr.Naz.*or*.17.12(M.35.980B); τ. δέ τινα καὶ σύμβολα πληροῦμεν ἐκείνων ἐπὶ τοῦ βαπτίσματος Thdr.Mops.*Rom*.6:17(p.123.17; M.66.804C); cf. *quod baptisma formam habet mortis et resurrectionis Christi*, id.*Gal*.2:15,16(p.30.13); ὡς ἐν τ. τῷ μύρῳ τὴν ἀόρατον τοῦ παναγίου πνεύματος χάριν ὑποδεχόμενοι Thdt.*Cant*.1:2(2.30); cf.id.*eran*.1(4.26); some writers opposed this usage, fearing confusion with sense D infra οὐ γὰρ τ. σώματος οὐδὲ τ. αἵματος...ἀλλὰ κατὰ ἀλήθειαν σῶμα καὶ αἷμα Χριστοῦ Mac.Mgn.*apocr*.3.23 (p.106.2); Petr.Laod.*fr.in Mt*.26:26(M.86.3325A); οὐκ ἔστι τ. ὁ ἄρτος καὶ ὁ οἶνος τοῦ σώματος καὶ αἵματος τοῦ Χριστοῦ...ἀλλ' αὐτὸ τὸ σῶμα τοῦ κυρίου τεθεωμένον Jo.D.*f.o*.4.13(M.94.1148A); **5.** *emblem, insignia* σύμβολα καὶ τ. ἀρχιερωσύνης Eus.*h.e*.1.3.11(M.20.72C); *ib*.1.3.7(72B); αἴρει ἐπὶ τοῦ ὤμου τὸν τ. τοῦ πεπλανημένου προβάτου [viz. woollen pallium] Eustrat.*v.Eutych*.3(M.86.2304A); cf. περὶ τάξεως ἐπισκόπου καὶ τίνος τύπον φέρει Isid.Pel.*epp*.1.136 tit.(M.78.272C); perh. *insignia*, or *sign* σταυρὲ παντοδύναμε, ὁ τ. τοῦ Χριστοῦ *Dial.Christ.et Jud*.13(p.75.1); *sign, indication* ἵνα κατὰ τὴν ἑξῆς τύπος δοθῇ τίνι ἐξ αὐτῶν χρὴ δοθῆναι τὸ Παλλάδιον Jo.Mal.*chron*.5 p.113(M.97.205C).

D. *type, representation, figure* (cf. Rom.5:14; 1Cor.10:6), understood as cognate either with *pattern, outline* (cf.Mel.*pass*.37f. p.6.12ff.) or with *image* (cf.Cyr.*Am*.58(3.315B)); **1.** of things to come ὁ τ. ὁ γενόμενος ἐπὶ Ἰσαάκ *Barn*.7.3; *ib*.7.7; ὅσα εἶπον καὶ ἐποίησαν οἱ προφῆται...παραβολαῖς καὶ τ. ἀπεκάλυψαν Just.*dial*.90.2(M.6.689B); Ἰακώβ,...τ. ὧν καὶ αὐτὸς τοῦ Χριστοῦ *ib*.140.1(796C); διὰ τύπων καὶ παραβολῶν ἐσημαίνετο [sc. ὁ Χριστος] Iren.*haer*.4.26.1(M.7.1052B); αὖθίς ἐστιν ὁ Ἰσαάκ...τ. ... τοῦ κυρίου Clem.*paed*.1.5(p.103.25; M.8.277A); τ. γὰρ ὁ δίκαιος ὁ παλαιὸς [sc. ὁ Ἄβελ] τοῦ νέου δικαίου [i.e. τοῦ Χριστοῦ] *ib*.1.6(p.118.20; 305C); τὸν οἶνον καὶ τὸν ἄρτον...διδοὺς [sc. Melchizedek]...εἰς τ. εὐχαριστίας id.*str*.4.25(p.320.1; M.8.1369B); ὁ τύπος νόμου καὶ προφητῶν μέχρι Ἰωάννου *ib*.5.8(p.363.13; M.9.85B); Hipp.*Dan*.1.14.6(M.10.689C); τὸ σάββατον τ. ἐστὶν καὶ εἰκὼν τῆς μελλούσης βασιλείας τῶν ἁγίων *ib*.4.23.5(645A); δύναιντο δὲ καὶ εἰς Χριστὸν οἱ δύο Θρῆνοι λαμβάνεσθαι οὗ τύπος ἦν Ἱερεμίας τοσαῦτα παρὰ Ἰουδαίων πεπονθότος καὶ τέλος τάφῳ παραδοθέντος Or.*fr*.69 *in Lam*.(p.263.15; M.13.644A); τότε ἱερὸν καὶ τὸ σῶμα τοῦ Ἰησοῦ κατὰ μίαν τῶν ἐκδοχῶν τύπος μοι εἶναι φαίνεται τῆς ἐκκλησίας id.*Jo*.10.35(20; p.209.17; M.14.369D); τ. γὰρ ὡς ἔφην ἐστὶν ὁ μὲν Ἀαρὼν τοῦ Χριστοῦ, ὁ δὲ υἱὸς Ἀαρὼν τοῦ ἐπισκόπου Meth.*lepr*.7(p.459.24); ὁ [sc. νόμος]...τῆς εἰκόνος ἐστὶ τ. καὶ σκιά, τουτέστι τοῦ εὐαγγελίου, ἡ δὲ εἰκών, τὸ εὐαγγέλιον αὐτῆς τῆς ἀληθείας id.*symp*.9.2(p.115.27; M.18.180C); Χριστός...οὐκέτι τύπους οὐδὲ εἰκόνας ἀλλ' αὐτὰς γυμνὰς ἀρετὰς...παραδοὺς Eus.*h.e*.1.3.2(M.20.69A); τύπον ἔφερε [sc. Jonah] τοῦ Χριστοῦ τοῦ καταβάντος εἰς τὴν καρδίαν τῆς γῆς Cyr.H.*catech*.14.20; τὸ γὰρ νομικὸν πάσχα...τύπου τύπος ἦν ἀμυδρότερος Gr.Naz.*or*.45.23 (M.36.656A); τ. ἐστὶν Ἰησοῦ Χριστοῦ ὁ Ἀδάμ Chrys.*hom*.10.1 *in Rom*.(9.520C); of Passover blood ἀνθρώπους ἔσωσεν· οὐκ ἐπειδὴ αἷμα ἦν, ἀλλ' ἐπειδὴ τοῦ αἵματος τούτου [sc. Χριστοῦ] τ. ἦν id.ap.Jo.D.*parall*.(M.96.17A); Νέρωνα ἐνταῦθά φησιν, ὡσανεὶ τ. ὄντα τοῦ ἀντιχρίστου id.*hom*.4.1 *in 2Thess*.(11.529F); μονονουχὶ παρεδώκαμεν τῷ τ. τῶν μελλόντων διὰ τοῦ βαπτίσματος Thdr.Mops.*Rom*.6:17(M.66.804D); τῷ βασιλεῖ Βαβυλῶνος ὃς ἦν ἐν τ. τοῦ σατανᾶ Cyr.*ador*.1(1.19E); τῶν ζεόντων τῷ πνεύματι τ. ἂν γένοιτο καὶ μάλα σαφὴς ὁ Χάμ ὃς νοεῖται θερμασία id.*glaph.Gen*.2(1.39A); οὐκοῦν μεσιτεύει μὲν ὁ Μωϋσῆς εἰς τ. Χριστοῦ, βραδυστομεῖ δὲ οὐκ ἔτι δεικνύων τὸν τ. ἐν ἑαυτῷ id.*Jon*.proem.(3.366B); τ. ἦν ἡ παλαιὰ τῆς καινῆς [sc. διαθήκης] Thdt.*qu.in Jos*.proem.(1.299); τ. γὰρ τὰ πρότερα, ἡ τεριτομὴ κτλ. Ammon.*Jo*.4:24(M.85.1424B); Bas.Sel.*or*.10.1(M.85.137B) cit. s. εἰκών; ὁ υἱὸς καὶ γέλως Ἰσαὰκ ὡς τ. σοῦ τὰ πάντα χαροποιήσαντος Χριστοῦ Anast.S.*hex*.12(M.89.1053B); ‡Gr.Nyss.*imag*.(M.44.1329D) cit. s. τυπικῶς; ἔμψυχον κλίμακα ἧς ἡ βάσις ἐπὶ γῆς ἐστήρικται, ἡ δὲ κεφαλὴ πρὸς αὐτὸν τὸν οὐρανὸν ἐφ' ἧς θεὸς ἀναπαύεται, ἧς τὸν τύπον Ἰακὼβ ἐθεάσατο ‡Jo.D.*hom*.6.3(M.96.665A); **2.** of heavenly things προκαθημένου τοῦ ἐπισκόπου εἰς τ. θεοῦ Ign.*Magn*.6.1; *Barn*.19.7; cf. ὑποταγήσεσθε κυρίοις ὡς τ. θεοῦ *Did*.4.11; cf. *sed terrena quidem, quae sunt erga nos disposita, congruit typos esse eorum quae sunt celestia ab eodem tamen deo facta*, Iren.*haer*.4.19.1(M.7.1030A); ἐν τύπῳ παρακλήτου ὁ Παῦλος ἀναστάσεως ἀπόστολος γέγονεν Clem.*exc.Thdot*.23(p.114.21; M.9.669B); γνωρίσας Μωϋσῆς τύπους οὐρανίων καὶ σύμβολα μυστηριώδεις τε εἰκόνας Eus.*h.e*.1.3.2(M.20.69A); πόλιν γὰρ ὥσπερ πεποιήμεθα τὴν ἐκκλησίαν Χριστοῦ τῆς ἄνω τὸν τ. Cyr.*Is*.3.3(2.463B); τὸ καταπέτασμα διατείνας ἐν τ. τοῦ στερεώματος Thdt.*qu*.60 *in Ex*.(1.162); ἑορτάζει τὰ ἅγια Φῶτα, ἤγουν Ἐπιφάνια...ἡ καθολικὴ καὶ ἀποστολικὴ ἐκκλησία ἐν τύπῳ αὐτοῦ [sc. Χριστοῦ] τε καὶ τῶν ιβ' μαθητῶν αὐτοῦ *Chron.Pasch*.p.209(M.92.512C); **3.** esp. in contrast to ἡ ἀλήθεια, τὰ πνευματικά, etc. τὰ φυόμενα ἐν τύπῳ προκύπτει τῶν ἀληθῶν Clem.*str*.1.7(p.24.13; M.8.732B); οὐ γὰρ νομιστέον τὰ ἱστορικὰ ἱστορικῶν εἶναι τύπους καὶ τὰ σωματικὰ σωματικῶν, ἀλλὰ τὰ σωματικὰ πνευματικῶν καὶ τὰ ἱστορικὰ νοητῶν Or.*Jo*.10.18(13; p.189.28; M.14.337D); ἵνα τοὺς τῷ τ. δεδουλωμένους οἰκονομικώτατα ἐλευθερώσας τῶν τ. προσαγάγῃ τῇ ἀληθείᾳ *ib*.13.18(p.242.26; 429B); καὶ βούλεται ὁ τ., ἵνα ὑφεστήκῃ, ἐμποδίζειν τῇ φανερώσει τῆς ἀληθείας *ib*.28.12(11; p.404.3; 705B); οἱ δὲ νοητοὶ Ἰσραηλῖται, ὧν τ. ἦσαν οἱ σωματικοὶ id.*princ*.4.3.7(p.333.16; M.11.388A); ὁ γὰρ τ. τῆς ἀληθείας οὐκ ἐναντίον, ἀλλὰ συγγενές Chrys.*hom*.2.5 *in 2Cor*.4:13 (3.274B); τ. γάρ ἐστιν...πᾶσα παρ' ἡμῶν νῦν εἶναι νομιζομένη ἀλήθεια Max.*ambig*.(M.91.1296C); **4.** of the figurative nature of baptism τὸ γὰρ πάθος τὸ ὑπὲρ Χριστοῦ ἔσται αὐτῷ [sc. τῷ μάρτυρι] γνησιώτερον βάπτισμα, ὅτι αὐτὸς μὲν πείρᾳ συναποθνήσκει τῷ κυρίῳ, οἱ δὲ λοιποὶ τύπῳ *Const.App*.5.6.8; ὅρα τοίνυν τ. μυστικόν· ὅπως εὐθὺς ἐξ ἀρχῆς δι' ὕδατος ζῶντος τῷ ἀπολλυμένῳ ἡ σωτηρία Gr.Nyss.*bapt.Chr*.(M.46.588C); κατὰ τ. διὰ τοῦ βαπτίσματος ἐν ἐκείνοις γινόμεθα Thdr.Mops.*Gal*.3:29(p.58.16; M.66.905C); **5.** in exegesis, not necessarily with any connotation of time, *symbol* τ. μὲν οὖν ἡ κώμη τοῦ βίου τοῦ παρόντος Eulog.*palm*.3(M.86.2917C); cf. ἐπέχουσι δὲ τοῦ πανδόχου τύπον οἱ ἀπόστολοι *cat.Lc*.10:35(p.89.4); Dion.Ar.*c.h*.15.2(M.3.328C); τύποις οὐκ εὐδιάκριτον ἔχουσι τὴν ἐγκεκαλυμμένην αὐτοῖς θεωρίαν ἀνάλογον φῶς id.*e.h*.5.1.2(M.3.501B); hence *symbolism* ἔχεις τὸν τ. τῆς πρώτης ὁράσεως Herm.*vis*.3.11.4; **6.** *antitype* τ. τῆς σιαγόνος τὸ σῶμα τοῦ Χριστοῦ Iren.*fr*.40(M.7.1260A).

E. *form* χρὴ γὰρ ἐν τῷ ἰδίῳ τῆς ἕξεως αὐτοῦ τ. τῶν γενητῶν ἕκαστον μένειν Meth.*res*.1.49(p.303.9; M.41.1124A); γράμματα...διατάγματος ἔχοντα τ. Ath.*ep.encycl*.2(p.170.28; M.25.225B); χάλαζαν...εἰς τ. λίθων *Chron.Pasch*.p.301(M.92.756C); *general character, type*; hence *kind, species* ἐπεὶ οὖν ἐκαίνισεν ἡμᾶς ἐν τῇ ἀφέσει τῶν ἁμαρτιῶν ἐποίησεν ἡμᾶς ἄλλον τ. ὡς παιδίων ἔχειν τὴν ψυχήν, ὡς ἂν δὴ ἀναπλάσσοντος αὐτοῦ ἡμᾶς *Barn*.6.11; *manner* βασιλεὺς ἐκ σοῦ Ἰούδα ἀναστήσεται καὶ ποιήσει ἱερατείαν νέαν, κατὰ τὸν τ. τῶν ἐθνῶν εἰς πάντα τὰ ἔθνη *T.Lev*.8.14; προσεκύνησαν τῷ Ἰωσὴφ κατὰ τὸν τ. βασιλέως Φαραὼ *T.Zab*.3.6; ἐκείνῳ τῷ τ. χρίσεις τὴν κεφαλὴν τῶν βαπτιζομένων *Const.App*.3.16.4.

F. *plan, pattern, model, example* (cf. Ex.25:39, Rom.6:17) κατὰ τοὺς ἀρχιτεκτονικοὺς τ. οἰκοδομεῖται...οἰκία Or.*Jo*.1.19(22; p.24.3; M.14.56C); κατὰ τὸν δειχθέντα αὐτῷ τ. Eus.*d.e*.4.16(p.194.4; M.22.324A); ἄλλοις τύπον σκανδάλου ὑπολειπόμενος id.*h.e*.5.3.2(M.20.437A); ὁ σωτὴρ εἰς ἡμέτερον τ. τοῦ λουτροῦ μετασχεῖν μνημονεύεται id.*v.C*.4.62(p.143.10; M.20.1216A); cf. (ref. Christ's baptism as example to faithful) λουσάμενος ἐνὶ τύποις *PAmh*.(1 p.25.11); ἵνα καὶ ἡμεῖς τ. τινὰ λαβόντες καὶ εἰς ἐκεῖνον βλέποντες, γενώμεθα ἓν Ath.*Ar*.3.20(M.26.364C); μὴ νεκρώσας ἀσελγούσας πόρνας [sc. ὁ θεός], ἵνα μὴ τῆς μετανοίας οἱ τ. ἀργήσωσιν Isid.Pel.*epp*.1.195(M.78.308B); προσευχῆς δὲ τ. τοῖς μαθηταῖς δεδωκὼς Thdt.*haer*.5.28(4.478); Leont.N.*v.Jo.Eleem*.35(p.69.4).

G. *outline* τὸν γὰρ τ. αὐτοῦ δεῖξαι μόνον...προῄρημαι νῦν Meth.*res*.2.5(p.339.1); τῶν αὐτῶν πραγμάτων τοὺς τ. ἐνσημαίνεται μὲν ὁ πατήρ, ἐπιτελεῖ δὲ ὁ λόγος Gr.Naz.*or*.30.11(p.124.14; M.36.117A); esp. in phrase ὡς τύπῳ περιλαβεῖν, *in outline, in sum*, Hipp.*haer*.7.19(p.194.19; M.16.3299C).

H. plur., *minutes, notes* ἀναγινωσκέσθωσαν οἱ δεδόμενοι τ. ἐν ταῖς προλαβούσαις ἀκροάσεσιν CChalc.*act*.3(*ACO* 2.1.2 p.92.10; H.2.384C).

I. *prescribed form* (cf. Ac.23:25); **1.** *principle, formula, standard* κατὰ τὸν ἐνθάδε τ. Gr.Thaum.*ep.can*.5(M.10.1037C); τοῦτον ἐγὼ τὸν κανόνα καὶ τὸν τ. ... παρέλαβον Dion.Al.ap.Eus.*h.e*.7.7.4(M.20.648C); καὶ περὶ τῶν διακονισσῶν...ὁ αὐτὸς τ. παραφυλαχθήσεται CNic.(325) *can*.19; ἄλλος τ. ἐστὶν οὗτος καὶ καινὸν τὸ ἐπιτήδευμα Jul.Papa *ep.Dian*.ap.Ath.*apol.sec*.35(p.113.10; M.25.308B); ὁ δυνατὸς...τύπους ἐκθέσθαι πίστεως Παῦλος Didym.*Trin*.2.6.6(M.39.524C); τοῖς πολιτικοῖς καὶ δημοσίοις τ. CChalc.*can*.17; **2.** *form* of a document, *text* τῆς ἀντιγραφῆς τῆς ἐμῆς τῷ τ. Gallienus Imp.ap.Eus.*h.e*.7.13(M.20.

673D); Meth.*symp*.3.1(p.27.6; M.18.61A); Const.ap.Ath.*apol.sec*.56 (p.136.13; M.25.349C); φωνῆς ἢ ὀνόματος ἢ τύπον ῥημάτων Gr.Nyss. *or.catech*.32(p.120.8; M.45.81B); καθὼς καὶ τῆς σῆς ἐπιστολῆς ὁ τ. σημαίνει Leo Mag.*ep*.106(p.56.13; M.*PL*.54.1002B); **3.** *written decision, decree, edict* κανόνες καὶ τ. ταῖς ἐκκλησίαις ἐδόθησαν Ath. *ep.encycl*.1(p.170.13; M.25.225A); Bas.*ep*.188.3(3.271C; M.32.672C); Socr.*h.e*.1.37.5(M.67.176A); Thdr.Lect.*h.e*.1.30(M.86.180B); hence τ. θεῖος *imperial rescript*, Jo.Mal.*chron*.13 p.332(M.97.481B); and ὁ Τύπος *the Type* of Constans II κακῶς γέγονεν ὁ τ. καὶ ἐπὶ βλάβῃ πολλῶν Anast.Ap.*a.Max*.2.9(M.90.144B); *judicial decision, judgement*, Gr.Naz.*ep*.149(M.37.256A); **4.** *rite* οὐκοῦν οὐ πρᾶξίν τινα, οὐ λόγον, οὐ τ. τινὰ μυστικόν, παρ' ὃν ἐκεῖνος κατέλιπε τῇ ἐκκλησίᾳ προσέθηκαν Bas.*Spir*.74(3.63A; M.32.208A).

τυπ-όω, A. *impress*; **1.** lit., *stamp, model* ἡ τῶν ὅλων ἀρχὴ... τετύπωκεν τὰ μεθ' ἑαυτὴν ἅπαντα γενόμενα Clem.*str*.5.6(p.353.2; M.9.65A); ἀπὸ τῆς αὐτῆς σφραγῖδος ὁμοίως ~ωθῆναι τὴν ἀνόμοιον οὐσίαν χρυσοῦ καὶ ἀργύρου Or.*Jo*.20.24(20; p.358.24; M.14.628B); ξόανα...εἰς πᾶσαν θνητῶν ζῴων ἰδέαν τετυπωμένα Eus.*p.e*.10.4(469C; M.21.781B); βόρβορον...κατὰ τοῦ μετώπου ~οῦσι τοῦ παιδίου [i.e. against evil eye] Chrys.*hom.12.7 in 1Cor*.(10.107C); ὁ δὲ ὀβολὸς...ἐν ἀργυρίοις ἐτετύπωτο Proc.G.*Ex*.29:35(M.87.660A); fig. ὅτε τὸ ἡγεμονικὸν αὐτοῦ...τῇ τῆς θεολογίας σφραγῖδι τετύπωται Or.*schol.in Cant*.4:12(M.17.273A); οὐ...ἀέρα διὰ γλώσσης ~ούμενον τὸν θεῖον λόγον νοοῦμεν Bas.*hex*.2.7 (1.19C; M.29.45B); φωνῇ...ἔνδοθεν ἐνηχουμένῃ, καὶ ἐν αὐτῷ ~ουμένῃ Thdt.*Zach*.1:13(2.1600); **2.** met.; **a.** *mould, form* αὐτίκα οὐ πολλοῖς ἀπεκάλυψεν ἃ μὴ πολλῶν ἦν, ὀλίγοις δὲ...τοῖς οἵοις τε ἐκδέξασθαι καὶ ~ωθῆναι πρὸς αὐτά Clem.*str*.1.1(p.10.2; M.8.701B); τί ἄτοπον τὸ ~οῦν τὸ ἡγεμονικὸν ἐν ὀνείρῳ δύνασθαι αὐτὸ ~οῦν καὶ ὕπαρ πρὸς τὸ χρήσιμον τῷ ἐν ᾧ ~οῦται; Or.*Cels*.1.48(p.97.28; M.11.748C); ἀπ' ἐκείνης δὲ τῆς δικαιοσύνης ἡ ἐν ἑκάστῳ δικαιοσύνη ~οῦται id.*Jo*.6.6(3; p.115.4; M.14.212B); λόγος ὁ ἀνθρώπων,...ὀξὺς εἰσδραμὼν εἰς τὰς ἀκοὰς ~ῶσαί τε τὸν νοῦν Gr.Thaum.*pan.Or*.13(p.31.28; M.10.1088C); ὁ νοῦς ἀεί σοι καμνέτω ~ούμενος θείοις νοήμασι Gr.Naz.*carm*.1.2.33.57(M.37.932A); ἡ τῆς παρ' ἡμῖν ἱεραρχίας εὐταξία...τὴν ἀγγελικὴν εὐπρέπειαν ὡς ἐν εἰκόσιν ἕξει, ~ουμένη δι' αὐτῆς Dion.Ar.*c.h*.8.2(M.3.241C); ἥτις ἐπιμείνασα καὶ ~ώσασα τὴν ψυχὴν πρὸς τὸ νοούμενον, ἐνθύμησις προσαγορεύεται Max.*opusc*.(M.91.21A); **b.** in bad sense, *mould* the mind by material images μὴ σχηματίζῃς τὸ θεῖον ἐν ἑαυτῷ προσευχόμενος, μηδὲ πρὸς μορφήν τινα συγχωρήσῃς ~ωθῆναί σου τὸν νοῦν Evagr. Pont.*or*.66(M.79.1181A); τῶν νοημάτων τὰ μὲν ~οῖ τὸ ἡγεμονικὸν ἡμῶν καὶ σχηματίζει, τὰ δὲ γνῶσιν μόνον παρέχει μὴ ~οῦντα τὸν νοῦν μηδὲ σχηματίζοντα...τὸ μὲν 'λαβὼν ἄρτον' σχηματίζει τὸν νοῦν, τὸ δὲ 'κλάσαι' πάλιν ~οῖ τὸν νοῦν †Nil.*mal.cog*.24(M.79.1228C); τὸ τοίνυν νόημα τοῦ θεοῦ οὐκ ἐν τοῖς ~οῦσι τὸν νοῦν ἀλλὰ τοῖς νοήμασι τοῖς μὴ ~οῦσι τὸν νοῦν *ib*.(1228D); **c.** *impress*, on the mind or senses ἑκάστη δὲ ἀπάτη, συνεχῶς ἐναπερειδομένη τῇ ψυχῇ τὴν φαντασίαν ἐν αὐτῇ ~οῦται Clem.*str*.2.20(p.174.3; M.8.1056B); αὗται δὲ αἱ παράνομοι ἐνέργειαι ἐν τῷ ἡγεμονικῷ ~ούμεναι Or.*or*.28.5(p.378.9; M.11.525B); εἰ...τοὺς χαρακτῆρας ἐναργῶς ἐν ἑαυτῷ ~ώσειεν Gr.Nyss.*or.dom*.2 (p.40.21; M.44.1145B); **d.** *discipline, educate* λόγῳ γὰρ ~οῦται εἰς τὸ ἡμερῶσθαι ἐκ τοῦ θηριώδους βίου Clem.*str*.6.6(p.457.14; M.9.273A); εἰ δέ ἐστί τις τῶν νεοφωτίστων...ἐκεῖνος προβληθήτω· ~ώσεις δὲ αὐτὸν πρὸς τὸ δέον Bas.*ep*.217(3.325B; M.32.796A); ~ώσας ὁ γέρων τὸν ἀδελφόν *Apophth.Patr*.(M.65.264B).

B. *typify, figure, express in outward form* σωτὴρ...ὃν Μωσῆς ἐτύπωσε προτείνας ὠλένας ἁγνάς, νικῶν τὸν Ἀμαλὴκ πίστει *Orac.Sib*.8. 251; τίς γὰρ ἢ γεννηθῆναι κάτω τὴν ἀρχήν, ἢ ἐπὶ τὸν σταυρὸν ἀνελθεῖν ἠνάγκασεν; ἐν ἑαυτῷ δέ, ὅπερ εἶπον, ~οῖ τὸ ἡμέτερον Gr.Naz.*or*.30.5 (p.115.6; M.36.109B); οἱ προφῆται τὰ εἰς Χριστὸν τετυπωμένα προανεφώνησαν Epiph.*haer*.41.3(p.93.3; M.41.693C); οἱ προφῆται...οὐκ ἔγραφον δὲ μόνον ἀλλὰ καὶ διὰ πραγμάτων ἐτύπουν Chrys.*hom.1.2 in Rom*.(9.431D); Dion.Ar.*c.h*.10.4(M.3.261B); τοῦ ~οῦντος τὴν ὅρασιν ἀγγέλου κατὰ δύναμιν τῷ θεολόγῳ μεταδιδόντος τῆς οἰκείας ἱερογνωσίας *ib*.13.4(305A); τῶν ~ούντων αὐτοὺς [sc. τοὺς λόγους...γυμνοὺς τῶν ἐπ' αὐτοῖς τυπικῶν συνθημάτων] συμβόλων Max.*qu.Thal*.55(M.90.536C); med., *express in oneself* ἡ ὕλη ἄποιος οὖσα καὶ ἀσχημάτιστος ἐκτυποῦται τὰς ἰδέας ἀπὸ τοῦ υἱοῦ ἃς ὁ υἱὸς ἀπὸ τοῦ πατρὸς ἐτυπώσατο Hipp. *haer*.5.17(p.114.23; M.16.3175C).

C. *dispose, frame, place in a certain attitude* ἱερέως χεῖρες ἐπὶ τοῦ ὄρους αἰρόμεναι καὶ εἰς εὐχὴν ~ούμεναι Gr.Naz.*or*.13.2(M.35.853B); σταυροειδῶς τὰς παλάμας ~ώσαντες Jo.D.*f.o*.4.13(M.94.1149A); hence esp. of making sign of the cross πρὶν ἢ τελείως αὐτὸ ~ωθῆναι †Jo.D. *B.J*.31(M.96.1153C).

D. *specify, prescribe, define* ἐξελθὼν καὶ τυπώσας τοῖς ἀγοραίοις τὰ τῇ ἡμέρᾳ καὶ τῷ καιρῷ ἁρμόδια *A.Xanthipp*.17(p.69.27); ἐστὶ καὶ ἕτερα βιβλία τούτων ἔξωθεν, οὐ κανονιζόμενα μέν, τετυπωμένα δὲ παρὰ τῶν πατέρων ἀναγινώσκεσθαι Ath.*ep.fest*.39.11(p.88; M.26.1438C); ᾔτησε τὸν βασιλέα Ἰοβιανὸν ~ῶσαι εὐθέως καὶ παραχρῆμα εἰρήνης πάκτα *Chron.Pasch*.p.299(M.92.749C).

E. of persons, *appoint*, Gr.Naz.*carm*.1.1.1.36(M.37.401A); ὁ θεὸς γὰρ οὕτω βούλεται ἵνα ὁ ἄρχων ὁ παρ' αὐτοῦ ~ωθεὶς τὴν οἰκείαν ἰσχὺν ἔχῃ Chrys.*hom.23.3 in Rom*.(9.689E); Pall.*v.Chrys*.14(p.87.17; M. 47.49).

F. *draw up* ἐπιστολὰς τ. Bas.*ep*.68(3.161C; M.32.429A); hence *formulate, determine, decree* ὡς ἂν τοῦτο ἐπὶ τῆς Ἀντιοχέων ἐκκλησίας ~ωθείη Const.ap.Eus.*v.C*.3.61(p.109.23; M.20.1136B); Bas.*ep*.188 *can*.1(3.270D; M.32.669C); τῆς τετυπωμένης ὥρας id.*reg.br*.136(2.461D; M.31.1172D); κλῆσιν συνοδικὴν ἐτύπωσαν Gr.Naz.*ep*.50(M.37.104A); ἐτύπωσαν ἡμέρας τεσσαράκοντα νηστείας Chrys.*Jud*.3.4(1.611C); τετύπωκε συνοδικὸν κριτήριον Leo Mag.*ep*.29(p.45.10; M.*PL*.54.784A).

τυπώδης, v. *τυποειδής.

τύπωμα, τό, 1. *image* ἅπαν εἴδωλον καὶ πᾶν τ. ἀνθρώπου Chrys.*Jud*. 5.10(1.645A); met., *mental image, concept* λόγος δ' ἔρευνα τῶν νοὸς τ. Gr.Naz.*carm*.1.2.34.29(M.37.947A); **2.** (= Lat. *forma*) *rescript*, Phot.*nomoc*.10.1(M.104.1144D).

τύπωσις, ἡ, 1. lit., *impression, configuration* διὰ τῆς τοῦ ἀέρος τ. κατὰ τὴν ἔναρθρον τῆς φωνῆς κίνησιν Bas.*hex*.3.2(1.23A; M.29.56A); ἵνα...διὰ τῆς ποιᾶς τῶν φθόγγων τ. ἑρμηνεύσῃ [sc. ὁ νοῦς] τὴν ἔνδοθεν κίνησιν Gr.Nyss.*hom.opif*.9.1(M.44.149C); **2.** *sense impression* τὴν αὐτὴν ἀπὸ τῶν ὑποκειμένων ἅπασιν ἐγγίνεσθαι τ. Clem.*str*.8.8 (p.94.10; M.9.589A); *ib*.4.23(p.315.5; M.8.1360B); cf. τυποῦσθαί ⟨τε⟩ δύναται...ἀπὸ τῶν ὄντων καὶ ὑπαρχόντων διὰ τῶν αἰσθητηρίων, καὶ παραδέχεσθαι τὰς τυπώσεις Arius Didymus ap.Eus.*p.e*.15.20(822A; M.21.1349B); **3.** *pattern, example* ἡ τ. τῆς εὐχῆς Gr.Naz.*ep*.77(M.37. 145A); id.*carm*.1.2.25.237(M.37.830A).

τυπωτικός, *materially figurative* συνθήματα...τυπωτικὰ καὶ πολύμορφα τῶν ἀμορφώτων καὶ ἀτυπώτων Dion.Ar.*ep*.9.1(M.3.1105C); τ. συμβόλοις id.*c.h*.1.2(M.3.121B).

τυρανν-έω, 1. *be, act as a despot* τὴν δουλείαν τὴν πικρὰν τῶν ~ούντων δαιμόνων Clem.*prot*.1(p.5.4; M.8.56B); ὁ θεὸς οὐ ~εῖ, ἀλλὰ βασιλεύει Or.*hom.20.2 in Jer*.(p.178.14; M.13.501C); ἐπεδήμησεν ὁ υἱὸς τοῦ θεοῦ...τῇ ὁρατῇ κτίσει, ἵνα...τὰ κράτη τῶν ~ούντων ἀνατρέψας δαιμόνων, ἐξέληται τῆς πικρᾶς τὰς ψυχὰς δουλείας Meth.*Porph*.1 (p.503.3; M.18.397C); **2.** *behave arbitrarily* οὐ ~εῖ κρίνων ὁ θεός, ἀλλὰ πείθει τὸν κρινόμενον καὶ ποιεῖ αὐτὸν θελῆσαι παραδέξασθαι τὴν ἀπόφασιν αὐτοῦ Meth.*fr.1 in Job*(p.511.3); **3.** *tyrannize over, rule despotically*; pass., *be subjected to tyranny*; **a.** in gen. ἥρμοζε...μὴ δι' ἑτέρου νικηθῆναι τὸν πονηρόν, ἀλλὰ δι' ἐκείνου, ὃν δὴ καὶ ἐκόμπαζεν ἀπατήσας αὐτὸν τετυραννηκέναι Meth.*symp*.3.6(p.33.10; M.18.69B); ἀντὶ τοῦ ~εῖσθαι τὸ βασιλεύειν μεταλαβών [sc. Christ] ‡Dion.Al.*fr.in Lc.22:42*(p.240.10); ἐρεῖ γὰρ [sc. the soul] ὡς πρὸς ἐχθράν, τὴν ~ήσασαν ἁμαρτίαν· 'μὴ ἐπίχαιρέ μοι' Cyr.*Mich*.68(3.464C); πάλιν μὲν ἐβασίλευσε [sc. ἡ ἁμαρτία], νῦν δὲ ~εῖ Thdt.*Rom*.6:23(3.67); **b.** ref. generation of Son by Father's will: Eunomian argument βουληθεὶς ...γεγέννηκε τὸν υἱὸν ἢ μὴ βουλόμενος;...εἰ μὲν γὰρ οὐ θέλων, τετυράννηται· καὶ τίς ὁ ~ήσας; καὶ πῶς ὁ ~ηθεὶς θεός; Gr.Naz.*or*.29.6(p.80. 9; M.36.80C); orthodox reply: same argument could be applied to Creation θέλων ὑπέστησε τὰ πάντα ἢ βιασθείς; εἰ μὲν βιασθείς, κἀνταῦθα ἡ τυραννὶς καὶ ὁ ~ήσας *ib*.(p.81.11; 81B); or to human generation θέλοντος ὑπέστης τοῦ σοῦ πατρὸς ἢ μὴ θέλοντος; εἰ μὲν γὰρ ἐξ οὐ θέλοντος, τετυράννηται...καὶ τίς ὁ ~ήσας αὐτόν; *ib*.(p.81.4; 81A); **c.** ref. Creation; against doctrine of pre-existence of souls and creation of body as consequence of, and punishment for, Fall ἢ κατὰ πρόθεσιν θέλων πεποίηκεν ὁ θεὸς τὰ...σώματα...ἢ κατὰ πρόθεσιν οὐ πεποίηκε καὶ μὴ θέλων ἐτυραννήθη, κατὰ βίαν ἀγόμενος πρὸς γένεσιν, ὧν τοὺς λόγους ἔχων οὐ πέφανται· καὶ εἰ μὲν ~ηθείς...ἦλθε ποιῆσαι... τὰ σώματα, λόγος καὶ σοφία τῆς τούτων γενέσεως οὐδαμῶς καθηγήσατο Max.*ambig*.(M.91.1329D); τίς...ὁ ~ήσας τὸν θεόν, εἴπερ τετυράννηται ...; καὶ πῶς ὁ ~ηθείς ἐστι θεός, πρὸς ἀνάγκης ὑφιστῶν παρὰ πρόθεσιν ...γένεσιν πραγμάτων; *ib*.(1332A); **4.** *do violence* to μὴ ~ήσῃς, ἄνθρωπε, τοῦ κάλλους, μηδὲ ἐνυβρίσῃς ἀνθοῦντι τῷ νέῳ Clem.*prot*.4 (p.38.13; M.8.140C); **5.** pass., *be overcome* by persuasion, etc. τετυραννήμεθα, ὦ φίλοι..., τετυραννήμεθα γήρᾳ πατρὸς καὶ φίλου...χρηστότητι Gr.Naz.*or*.12.4(M.35.845D); **6.** *act violently, use violence* ~ήσας [sc. a demon] ἐπεχείρησεν εἰσελθεῖν *Apophth.Patr*.(M.65.193C); **7.** *suppress, keep under* οἶδα ~εῖν θυμὸν ἐξοιδαίνοντα Thphyl.*exc. Rom*.5(M.113.933A); **8.** *be a usurper, reign as usurper*, Philost.*h.e*.3. 22(M.65.512A); Socr.*h.e*.2.34.1(M.67.296B); Soz.*h.e*.8.1.2(M.67.1509A); **9.** *rebel, make insurrection* against lawful ruler, Ammon.*Jo*.11:48 (M.85.1469C); Thdt.*qu.26 in Jud*.(1.343); Evagr.*h.e*.3.43(p.145.1; M.86.2696A); of nations against empire, Thphn.*chron*.p.177(M.108. 465C); ref. denial of subordinationist doctrine of Son οὔτε γὰρ...

ὡς ∼ῶν ὁ υἱὸς οὐχ ὑποτέτακται τῷ πατρί, οὔτε ὑποτέτακται ὡς δοῦλος καὶ ἐξουσίαν μὴ ἔχων Epiph.*haer*.69.77(p.225.30; M.42.328C); of man against God τοῦ...δεσπότου καταφρονεῖς...ἀλλὰ σκιρτᾷς καὶ ∼εῖς καὶ φεύγεις τὸν ζυγόν Thdt.*provid*.5(4.555); κατὰ τοῦ πεποιηκότος... ∼ήσας [sc. Juln. Imp.] θεοῦ id.*h.rel*.2(3.1130); ποτὲ οἱ ∼οῦντες καὶ βουλόμενοι ἄνθρωποι εἰς τὸν οὐρανὸν ἀνελθεῖν, ἄπρακτοι μεμενήκασιν Cosm.Ind.*top*.3(M.88.137B); of animals against man after Fall ∼εῖ δὲ...τινὰ τούτων καὶ στασιάζει...ἐπειδὴ...καὶ οἱ τούτων ἄρχοντες... τοῦτο δρῶσι...κατὰ τοῦ πεποιηκότος Thdt.*affect*.4(p.116.11; 4.810); ∼ούμενος ὑπὸ τούτων [sc. animals] μανθάνεις οὐ ∼εῖν, ἀλλὰ τὸν δεσπότην γνωρίζειν id.*provid*.5(4.559); of servants ἐκεῖνοι [sc. masters]... ∼οῦντας τοὺς οἰκέτας ὁρῶντες, τὴν εὐαγγελικὴν ἐβλασφήμουν διδασκαλίαν id.*1Tim*.6:1(3.668); **10.** *act overbearingly* μοναχὸς ἦν...∼ήσας δὲ κατὰ πρεσβυτέρου αὐτοῦ Max.*schol.epp.Dion.Ar*.8.1(M.4.544C).

τυραννίζω, *tyrannize over*; pass., *be under the tyranny of*, Alex. Sal.*cruc*.(M.87.4025B).

τυραννίς, ἡ, 1. *tyranny, arbitrary rule* unlimited by law and constitution; **a.** in gen. ἆρά γε...ἐπὶ τυραννίδι καὶ φόβῳ καὶ καταπλήξει; οὐ μὲν οὖν, ἀλλ'...ὡς βασιλεὺς πέμπων υἱὸν αὐτοῦ [ref. Inc.] *Diogn*.7.3; οἵ τε δοκοῦντες ἡμῶν ποιμένες...τὸ πρὸς ἀλλήλους...μῖσος ἐπαύξοντες, οἷά τε τυραννίδας τὰς φιλαρχίας...διεκδικοῦντες Eus.*h.e.* 8.1.8(M.20.741C); ref. persecution τὴν ἔννομον ἀρχὴν εἰς τ. μεταβαλών, μοιχοὺς καὶ ἀνδροφόνους ἀνευθύνους ἐᾷς...καὶ ἐπάγεις τοῖς εὐσεβέσι τοῖς ἐκείνοις ὀφειλομένην τιμωρίαν *M.Thdot*.3(p.134.18); ὁ θάνατος τοῦ ἁγίου Θεοδότου κατήργησεν τὴν εἰδωλολατρείαν καὶ κατέλυσεν αὐτῆς τὴν τ. *ib*.(p.131.19); πολλὴ τοῦ μαμωνᾶ ἡ τ. Chrys.*hom.76.3 in Jo*.(8.449D); **b.** of Devil's tyranny ἐὰν μὲν αὐτὸς ᾖ ὁ υἱός, τέλος ἕξει ἡ διαβολικὴ τ., ἐὰν δὲ κτίσμα ᾖ...οὐδεμία φροντὶς ἦν αὐτῷ Ath. *Ar*.2.73(M.26.301C); κατεμίχθη [sc. Christ] πρὸς τὸ ἡμέτερον, ἵνα τὸ ἡμέτερον τῇ πρὸς τὸ θεῖον ἐπιμιξίᾳ γένηται θεῖον, ἐξαιρεθὲν τοῦ θανάτου καὶ τοῦ ἀντικειμένου τυραννίδος ἔξω γενόμενον Gr.Nyss.*or. catech*.25(p.96.7; M.45.65D); Χριστέ,...δὸς εἰρηνεύειν τὴν ἐκκλησίαν σου, ῥυσάμενος αὐτὴν ἐκ τῆς τοῦ διαβόλου τ. *M.Thdot*.1 31(p.80.28); οὐ μόνον αὐτὸς ὁ διάβολος, ἀλλὰ καὶ οἱ τῆς τ. αὐτῷ κοινωνήσαντες δαίμονες τὴν πανωλεθρίαν ὑπέμειναν Thdt.*Ezech*.31:14(2.941); id.*Ps.* 23:10(1.755); of hell, Chrys.*hom.1.7 in Mt*.(7.16A; v.l. Gaume); of antichrist ἐν τοῖς προοιμίοις τῆς βασιλείας αὐτοῦ, μᾶλλον δὲ τ., ὑποκρίνεται ἁγιοσύνην Jo.D.*f.o*.4.26(M.94.1217B); **c.** met. οὐ βίᾳ οὐδὲ τ., ἀλλὰ πειθοῖ προσάγεται [ref. Christ's preaching] Chrys.*hom.4.1 in Eph*.(11.26C); με οὐκ εἴασε φοβηθῆναι τοῦ θανάτου τὴν τ. id. *hom.4.1 in Phil*.(11.212F); τὴν πεπλανημένην τ. τῆς εἱμαρμένης id. *comm.in Gal*.1:7(10.669C); ποῦ...εἰσὶν οἱ τῆς γενέσεως τὴν τ. ἐπιτειχίζοντες καὶ τῶν καιρῶν τὴν περιφορὰν τοῖς τῆς ἐκκλησίας δόγμασι; id.*hom.75.4 in Mt*.(7.728C); ἀκρίβειαν...πολιτείας ἀπαιτῶ...οὐ μὴν ἀπάθειαν· οὐδὲ γὰρ ἐπιτρέπει τῆς φύσεως ἡ τ. *ib.19.5*(251E); μεγάλη ...ἐν τοῖς ἀγαθοῖς καὶ ἐν τοῖς κακοῖς τῆς συνηθείας ἡ τ. id.*hom.6.4 in 2Tim*.(11.698A); τῆς τῶν παθῶν τ. ἀνώτερον εἶναι id.*hom.18.2 in 1Tim*.(11.656A); τῆς ἀθυμίας ἡ τ. id.*hom.78.4 in Mt*.(756E); of riches, *ib.59.6*(602D); *ib.58.5*(593B); id.*hom.7.3 in 1Tim*.(587D); of conjugal love, id.*hom.20.5 in Eph*.(149C); τὴν γλυκεῖαν τοῦ ὕπνου τ. κατέλυσαν Thdt.*h.rel*.proem.(3.1104); τῆς ἡδίστης περιγίνονται τ. καὶ παννύχιοι διατελοῦσι, τὸν δεσπότην ὑμνοῦντες id.*carit*.(3.1300); **2.** *high-handed conduct, insolence*, *A.Thom*.A 84(p.200.13); *A.Phil*.119(p.48. 6); Thdt.*h.e*.1.28.3(3.815); **3.** *usurpation* by a false claimant to power, Chrys.*hom.56.4 in Mt*.(7.572B); *ib.10.5*(145D); ref. apostles, in Jewish accusations, *ib.86.1*(810E); Philost.*h.e*.12.1(M.65.605A); *Chron.Pasch*.p.323(M.92.825B); met., ref. imitation of Christ's miracles by Symeon Stylites μηδεὶς τυραννίδα καλείτω τὴν μίμησιν· αὐτοῦ γὰρ ἐστι φωνή [Jo.14:12] Thdt.*h.rel*.26(3.1276); **4.** *rebellion, sedition*, id.*qu.21 in Num*.(1.235); id.*qu.in 1Par*.(1.556); id.*h.e*.5.23. 5(3.1061); Jo.Mal.*chron*.10 p.247(M.97.377A).

***τυραννογνόφος, ὁ,** *lord of darkness*, *A.Phil*.119(p.48.17); *ib*.120 (p.49.19); *ib*.121(p.50.20).

τύραννος, ὁ, 1. *despot, arbitrary ruler*; **a.** in gen. οὐ γὰρ πτωχὸς ἐκεῖ [sc. in future life], οὐ πλούσιος, οὐδὲ τ. ... κοινῇ δ' ἅμα πάντες *Orac.Sib*.2.322; of impious rulers δυσσεβέστατος καὶ...θεομισέστατος τ. [sc. Maximinus Daia] Eus.*h.e*.9.11.2(M.20.837B); esp. opp. βασιλεύς, Bas.*hom*.12.2(2.99B; M.31.389B); οὔτε...βασιλεὺς δυσσεβὴς ἔτι βασιλεὺς ὑπάρχει, ἀλλὰ τ. *Const.App*.8.2.4; opp. Christ as king βασιλεύοντος Ἰουλιανοῦ τοῦ τ. καὶ...παραβάτου, καθ' ἡμᾶς δὲ βασιλεύοντος τοῦ κυρίου...Χριστοῦ *M.Artem*.(p.175.8); **b.** of Devil ὁ... γοῦν πονηρὸς οὗτοσ τ. κα δράκων Clem.*prot*.1(p.8.6; M.8.64A); ἄτοπον...θεραπεύειν ἀντὶ μὲν τοῦ βασιλέως τὸν τ., ἀντὶ δὲ τοῦ ἀγαθοῦ τὸν πονηρόν *ib*.10(p.67.35; 205A); ὑπὸ τοῦ τ. καὶ ἄρχοντος τῆς ἀδικίας Meth.*res*.2.4(p.337.18); ἡ τοῦ δούλου μορφὴ...τὸν τῆς αἰχμαλωσίας τ. αἰχμαλωτεύσασα ‡Ath.*Apoll*.2.9(M.26.1148A); τὸν τ. τῶν ἡμετέρων ψυχῶν ‡Proc.G.*Pr*.14:28(M.87.1368A); ref. baptismal renunciation ἀποτάσσομαι...σοὶ τῷ πονηρῷ καὶ ὠμοτάτῳ τ. Cyr.H.*catech*.19.4; οἱ τελούμενοι μετὰ τὴν ἄρνησιν τοῦ τ. καὶ τὴν τοῦ βασιλέως ὁμολογίαν οἱονεὶ σφραγῖδα τινὰ βασιλικὴν δέχονται Thdt.*Cant*.1:2(2.30); **c.** of antichrist, ‡Hipp.*consumm*.30(p.301.35; M.10.933C); *ib*.24(p.299.1; 928A); Ephr.2.222F; σκευάζει ὁ τ., ἵνα πάντες τὴν σφραγῖδα τοῦ θηρίου βαστάζωσιν id.224F; δήμαρχοι...ἀπότομοι σταθήσονται κατὰ τόπον· κἂν τις φέρει...τὴν σφραγῖδα τοῦ τ. ἀγοράζει βραχὺ βρῶμα id.3. 140C; his judgement ἄγεται ὁ τ. ... ἐνώπιον τοῦ βήματος...καὶ δίδωσιν ὁ βασιλεὺς...τὴν ἀπόφασιν τὴν αἰώνιον κολάσεως ἐν τῷ πυρί id.143E; **d.** of death ὁ κύριος...τὸν τ. ἐδουλώσατο, τὸν θάνατον Clem.*prot*.11 (p.79.2; M.8.228C); **e.** of sin as tyrant opp. righteousness as king, Chrys.*hom.5.1 in 1Tim*.(11.575B); **f.** of pagan gods, Tat.*orat*.29 (p.30.14; M.6.868A); οὐκ ἦσαν θεοί, ἀλλὰ τυράννων αἰνίγματα *Hom. Clem*.5.23; **g.** ref. moral abuse βασιλεὺς τοῦ κάλλους γενοῦ, μὴ τ. Clem.*prot*.4(p.38.15; M.8.141A); **2.** *usurper, rebel*, Pall.*h.Laus*.35 (p.100.17); Δαβὶδ ὡς τ. ὑπὸ τοῦ Σαοὺλ ἐλαυνόμενον Thdt.*ep*.83(p.48. 27; 4.1145); Jo.Mal.*chron*.12 p.293(M.97.444B); of a bishop ὡς...τ. ἐξελαθῆναι παρασκευάζουσι [sc. Arians] τὸν τῆς εὐσεβείας...ἀγωνιστήν [sc. Eustathius] Thdt.*h.e*.1.21.9(3.803); of schismatic priest εἴ τις πρεσβύτερος, καταφρονήσας τοῦ ἰδίου ἐπισκόπου, χωρὶς συναγάγῃ καὶ θυσιαστήριον ἕτερον πήξῃ...καθαιρείσθω ὡς φίλαρχος, τ. γάρ ἐστιν *Can. App*.31; ref. accusation against Christ ἵνα παραδῶσιν αὐτὸν τῷ ἡγεμόνι ὡς τ. Chrys.*hom.70.1 in Mt*.(7.687B); ἵνα ὡς στασιαστὴν καὶ τ. κολάσωσιν *ib*.(687D); ἵνα ὡς παράνομος, ὡς τ., ὡς στασιώδης ἀνῃρῆσθαι δόξῃ *ib.84.3*(801D); id.*hom.5.5 in 1Cor*.(10.41B); Thdt. *Ps*.2 proem.(1.617); **3.** *one who behaves tyrannically*, though in fact the lawful ruler, *Const.App*.4.9.2; *M.Artem*.(p.175.8); Thdt.*h.e*.3. 17.4(3.933); **4.** *lawless person*; of contemporaries of Noah, *Orac. Sib*.1.176; **5.** neut. as subst., tyranny τῆς ἔχθρας ἐλύθη τὸ τ. ... διὰ τοῦ πάθους σου...Χριστέ Rom.Mel.(*AS* 1 p.116).

***τυραννόφρων,** *tyrant-minded*, of Satan τὸν τ. λέοντα ‡Chrys. *indict*.1(8.94B).

***τυραννόω,** pass., *be under the sway of tyrants*, *Orac.Sib*.8.189.

***τυραννώδης,** *tyrannous*, Steph.Diac.*v.Steph*.(M.100.1169B).

***τυροαπόθεσις, ἡ,** *beginning of abstinence from cheese*, i.e. of strict Lenten fast, *Catech.Stud*.8(M.99.1700A).

τυροφάγος, ὁ, week preceding Quinquagesima, in which cheese might still be eaten, i.e. before strict Lenten fast, Thdr.Stud. *catech.parv*.51(*NPB* 9 p.122).

[*]τύρων, ὁ, v. τίρων.

***τυφλομαχία, ἡ,** *blind fight, battle of the blind* ὥσπερ ἔν τινι νυκτομαχίᾳ, μᾶλλον δὲ τ., οἱ πολλοὶ τῶν αἱρετικῶν...τὰ περὶ Χριστοῦ δογματίζειν ἐδοκίμαζον Anast.S.*hod*.1(M.89.49A).

***τυφλόνους,** *mentally blind*, Thdr.Stud.*ref*.(M.99.457A); ὁ τ. πῶς αἰνέσω σέ, τὸν νοῦν τὸν ἑωσφόρον *Hymn*.(*AS* 1 p.615).

***τυφλώνω,** = τυφλόω, *blind*, Thphn.*chron*.p.372(M.108.892C).

***τυφλωτικός,** *capable of blinding*, Cyr.H.*catech*.6.29.

τῦφος, ὁ, 1. *conceit, vanity, pride* ταπεινοφρονήσωμεν...ἀποθέμενοι πᾶσαν ἀλαζονείαν καὶ τ. *1Clem*.13.1; οὐ γάρ ποτε ἡ ἀλήθεια οἴησις, ἀλλ' ἡ μὲν ὑπόληψις τῆς γνώσεως φυσιοῖ καὶ τύφου ἐμπίπλησιν, οἰκοδομεῖ δὲ ἡ ἀγάπη Clem.*str*.1.11(p.35.12; M.8.752C); ἡ σοφία...ἐνεφυσίωσεν τὰ ἑαυτῆς τέκνα, οὐ...τ. ἐνεποίησεν ὁ κύριος τοῖς μειρακίοις κατὰ τὴν διδασκαλίαν, ἀλλὰ τὸ ἐπὶ τῇ ἀληθείᾳ πεποιθέναι *ib*.7.16(p.74.6; M.9. 545A); καθάπερ...τὴν φιλοσοφίαν ὁ τ. καὶ ἡ οἴησις διαβέβληκεν, οὕτως καὶ τὴν γνῶσιν ἡ ψευδὴς γνῶσις *ib*.2.11(p.141.14; M.8.989A); τὸν ἄθεον τῆς πλάνης τ. id.*prot*.7(p.57.24; M.8.184C); φαρμακείᾳ...ἔοικεν ὁ ὀνειδισμὸς...τὰς ὑπερσαρκώσεις τοῦ τ. ἐξομαλίζων id.*paed*.1.8(p.128. 10; M.8.328C); εἰς τοῦτο τὸ τ. [? l. τοῦ τύφου] κατεληλύθασιν, ὥστε τοὺς μὲν ὁμοίους αὐτῷ εἶναι λέγουσι τῷ Ἰησοῦ, τοὺς δὲ καὶ ἔτι ⟨κατά τι⟩ δυνατωτέρους Hipp.*haer*.7.32(p.218.15; M.16.3338B); τῷ τὸ μὲν ἔξωθεν τοῦ πίνακος καθαίρειν..., τὴν σάρκα..., τὴν δὲ καρδίαν τύφῳ σίνεσθαι καὶ φιλοκρατίᾳ Meth.*symp*.11(p.130.2; M.18.205B); καλῶς ἡγητέον νόσον καὶ λέπραν τὸν τ. καὶ τὴν οἴησιν...εἶναι ψυχῆς id.*lepr*.12 (p.466.12); ἔοικεν ὁ τ. πάντων εἶναι τῶν ἐν ἀνθρώποις παθῶν χαλεπώτατον Bas.*Eun*.1.15(1.225D; M.29.541B); πόσος ὁ τ. τῶν ἐπαγγελλομένων εἰδέναι τοῦ θεοῦ τὴν οὐσίαν *ib*.1.12(224E; M.540C); τῇ μετριότητι ὁ τ. καταφονεύεται Gr.Nyss.*v.Mos*.(M.44.332A); δικαιοσύνη καὶ ἀδικία, τ. καὶ μετριότης καὶ πάντα τὰ ἐξ ἀντιθέτου νοούμενα *ib*.; of Satan's pride leading him to try to seize Christ as man's ransom-price, id.*or.catech*.23(p.86.11; M.45.61B); πρὸς τὸν ῥαπίσαντα ὑπηρέτην εἶπε [sc. Christ] τὰ πάντα καθελεῖν δυνάμενα τ. Chrys.*hom.84.1 in Jo*. (8.498B); καταλῦσαι τ. καὶ ἀπόνοιαν id.*compunct*.1.10(1.139D); of Novatianist refusal to afford reconciliation for sinners after baptism, Thdt.*haer*.5.28(4.476); of human pride contrasted with God's attitude to man, Ath.*decr*.7(p.7.3; M.25.'436'(428)C); id.*Ar.*

2.25(M.26.200B); and conduct of Christ ἀπετάξατο ἀνέσει, τρυφῇ... τύφῳ *Const.App.*5.5.3; ref. eccl. relations μηδένα τῶν...ἐπισκόπων ἐπαρχίαν ἑτέραν οὐκ οὖσαν ἄνωθεν...ὑπὸ τὴν αὐτοῦ...χεῖρα καταλαμβάνειν, ἀλλ' εἰ καί τις κατέλαβεν...τοῦτον ἀποδιδόναι, ἵνα μὴ ἱερουργίας προσχήματι ἐξουσίας τ. κοσμικῆς παρεισδύηται CEph.(431)*act.*7(*ACO* 1.1.7 p.122.15; H.1.1620E); **2.** plur., *pomps, vanities* ἀποφυγὼν θορύβους πολιτικούς..., ἀρχοντικοὺς τ. Bas.*hom.*18.3(2.144C; M.31.496C).

τυφόω, pass.; **1.** *be puffed up, arrogant, conceited* οἰήματι διδασκάλου ἐπαρθεὶς καὶ τυφωθεὶς [sc. Tatian] ὡς διαφέρων τῶν λοιπῶν Iren.*haer.*1.28.1(M.7.690C); Clem.*paed.*3.12(p.286.21; M.8.672A); ἡ παρθένος...μὴ τυφωθεῖσα ἐκ τῶν λόγων τοῦ ἀγγέλου...προλαμβάνει ἐν τῷ ἀσπασμῷ τὴν Ἐλισάβετ Or.*hom.7 in Lc.*(p.44.22); ref. exorcisms μὴ χρὴ ἐπὶ τούτῳ τυφωθέντας ἑαυτῶν ἀμελεῖν *Hom.Clem.*9.22; ref. pride of Devil in thinking himself God, Cosm.Ind.*top.*3(M.88.148D); dist. from ἀλάζων, Thdr.Mops.*2 Tim.*3:3(p.215.18; M.66.945C); **2.** *be deluded* οἱ σοφοὺς σφᾶς ἡγούμενοι τετύφωνται Clem.*paed.*1.6(p.109.10; M.8.288C); ὁ...μὴ πειθόμενος τῇ ἀληθείᾳ, διδασκαλίᾳ δὲ ἀνθρωπίνῃ τετυφωμένος id.*str.*5.14(p.419.5; M.9.201B); Hipp.*haer.*5.23(p.125.16; M.16.3191B); **3.** perf. ptcpl., of things, *ostentatious, proud,* Clem.*paed.*2.2(p.174.20; M.8.425A); *ib.*2.3(p.180.6; 437A).

τυφώδης, *puffed up, vain,* Geo.Pis.*hex.*1274(M.92.1532A).

τυφωνικός, *tempestuous* (Peratic) θυγάτηρ τ. πιστὴ φύλαξ ὑδάτων παντοίων, ὄνομα αὐτῇ Χορζάρ Hipp.*haer.*5.14(p.109.4; M.16.3167B); of heresies, Jo.Mon.*hymn.Bas.*9(M.96.1377B); of persecutions, id. *hymn.Geo.*4(1396C).

τύχη, ἡ, 1. *fortune*; **a.** in gen., ref. Plato *rep.*2.36E οὔκουν ἐπὶ τῇ τ. τὸ τέλος ἕξει ποτὲ ὁ γνωστικὸς κείμενον, ἀλλ' ἐπ' αὐτῷ τὸ εὐδαιμονεῖν ἂν εἴη Clem.*str.*4.7(p.272.13; v.l. ψυχῇ M.8.1264B); τοῦ θεοῦ τὴν τ. νέμοντος id.*q.d.s.*26(p.177.12; v.l. ψυχὴν M.9.632B); ὁ δὲ τὴν τ. θεὸν λέγων καὶ τὴν πρᾶξιν λεγέτω θεόν id.*prot.*10(p.74.2; M.8.217B); οἱ μέλλουσαν τ. ἀνθρώπῳ ἢ πόλει προλέγοντες...δαίμονές εἰσι Cels.ap.Or.*Cels.*8.62(p.277.29; M.11.1609B); **b.** of personified fortune of emperor (*genius Caesaris*) λέγοντος [sc. τοῦ ἀνθυπάτου] ὄμοσον τὴν Καίσαρος τ., ἀπεκρίνατο· εἰ κενοδοξεῖς, ἵνα ὀμόσω τὴν Καίσαρος τ. ... μετὰ παρρησίας ἄκουε· Χριστιανός εἰμι *M.Polyc.*10.1; *ib.*9.2; πηλίκον βδέλυγμα νομιστέον εἶναι τὸν πονηρὸν κατὰ τύχης ἀνθρώπων, πράγματος ἀνυποστάτου, ὅρκον; Or.*mart.*7(p.8.14; M.11.572B); εἰ δέ τις...ἀρνήσαιτο μὲν τὸ εἶναι ἕνα θεόν...ὁμολογήσαι δὲ δαιμόνια ἢ τύχας, ἴστω ὁ τοιοῦτος ἑτοιμάζων τῷ δαιμονίῳ τράπεζαν καὶ πληρῶν τῇ τ. κέρασμα *ib.*40(p.37.17; 616B); τύχην μέντοι βασιλέως οὐκ ὄμνυμεν ὡς οὐδ' ἄλλον νομιζόμενον θεόν· εἴτε γάρ...ἐκφορὰ μόνον ἐστὶν ἡ τ. ... οὐκ ὄμνυμεν τὸ μηδαμῶς ὂν ὡς θεόν...εἴτε καὶ (ὥς τισιν ἔδοξεν εἰποῦσι· τοῦ Ῥωμαίων βασιλέως τὸν δαίμονα ὀμνῦσιν οἱ τὴν τ. αὐτοῦ ὀμνύοντες) δαίμων ἐστὶν ἡ ὀνομαζομένη τ. τοῦ βασιλέως, καὶ οὕτως ἀποθανητέον ἐστὶ μᾶλλον ἡμῖν ὑπὲρ τοῦ μὴ ὀμόσαι μοχθηρὸν δαίμονα id.*Cels.*8.65(p.281.19; M.11.1613D); προείπομεν...μὴ δεῖν ὀμνύναι τὸν ἐν ἀνθρώποις βασιλέα ἢ τὴν ὀνομαζομένην τ. αὐτοῦ *ib.*8.67 (p.283.26; 1617B); **2.** *chance,* **a.** in gen.; plur. of accidents of life, ref. Aristotelian view that to live according to virtue does not necessarily bring happiness τύχαις ἀβουλήτοις περιπίπτοντα τὸν σοφόν...μὴ εἶναι μήτε μακάριον μήτ' εὐδαίμονα Clem.*str.*2.21(p.182.22; M.8.1073A); **b.** ref. philosophical speculations τῶν γινομένων πάντων ἢ θεόν φασιν αἴτιον εἶναι, ἢ ἀνάγκην, ἢ εἱμαρμένην, ἢ φύσιν, ἢ τ., ἢ τὸ αὐτόματον...τῆς δὲ τύχης [sc. ἔργον] τὰ σπάνια καὶ ἀπροσδόκητα· ὁρίζονται γὰρ τὴν τ. σύμπτωσιν καὶ συνδρομὴν δύο αἰτίων ἀπὸ προαιρέσεως τὴν ἀρχὴν ἐχόντων, καὶ ἄλλο τι παρ'. ὃ πέφυκεν ἀποτελούντων Nemes.*nat.hom.*39(M.40.761B) = Jo.D.*f.o.*2.25(M.94.957A); καὶ τὴν τ. ... οἱ μὲν θεὸν ὑπέλαβον, καὶ ὡς θεὸν ἐσεβάσθησαν. ὁ δὲ Πλάτων αἰτίαν εἶναι κατά τι συμβεβηκὸς γιγνομένην, καὶ πάλιν σύμπτωμα φύσεως ἢ προαιρέσεως κέκληκε...Φιλήμων δέ, ὁ κωμικός, ...ἄντικρυς κατηγορεῖ τῶν θεὸν τὴν τ. ὑπειληφότων Thdt.*affect.*6 (p.154.2; 4.851); **c.** ref. Epicurean denial of providence διὰ τοῦτό τινες, ὧν δόξαι οὐ μικραί, ἐνόμισαν οὐ τάξει τινὶ τὸ πᾶν τοῦτο συνεστάναι, ἀλλ' ἀλόγῳ τύχῃ ἄγεσθαι καὶ φέρεσθαι Athenag.*leg.*25.3(M.6.949C); ἐκ τοῦ θεοῦ τὰ πάντα...εἴρηται τὰ...κτίσματα, διὰ τὸ μὴ...κατὰ τύχην ἔχειν τὴν γένεσιν, κατὰ τοὺς λέγοντας ἐξ ἀτόμων συμπλοκῆς Ath.*decr.*19(p.16.10; M.25.449A); χρόνον οὐ τὸν κατὰ τ., ὥς τινες τῶν Ἑλλήνων νομίζοντες μυθολογοῦσιν, ἀλλ' ὃν αὐτὸς δημιουργὸς ὢν... ὥρισεν ἑκάστῳ id.*apol.fug.*14(p.78.3; M.25.661B); τῶν Ἑλλήνων οἱ μὲν νομίζουσι κατὰ τ. καὶ ἐξ ἀτόμων συμπλοκῆς...συνεστάναι τὴν κτίσιν id.*syn.*35(p.262.24; M.26.756A).

***τύχησις, ἡ,** *chance* ἢ σύμμετρον εὗρεν [sc. God] τὴν ὕλην τῷ τοῦ κόσμου μεγέθει..., τ. πρὸ θεοῦ τὸ μέτρον αὐτῷ καὶ πρὸς χρείαν τοῦ κόσμου καὶ πρὸς τὴν ἰδίαν παρεσκεύασε δύναμιν Proc.G.*Gen.*proem. (M.87.32C).

***τυχιμαῖος,** *accidental,* Eus.*Ps.*18:3(M.23.189B).

[*]τυχόρυγος, ὁ, for τοιχώρυχος, Ephr.3.475F.

***τωθεία, ἡ,** *scoffing,* Dion.Al.ap.Eus.*p.e.*14.27(782C; M.21.1288A).

***τώρα,** [τῇ ὥρᾳ (ταύτῃ)] *now,* Barth.Edess.*Agar.*(M.104.1436D); *ib.*(1440D).

Υ

ὑάκινθος, ὁ, ἡ, 1. *precious stone* of a blue colour; described, Epiph.*gemm.*7(M.43.300A); ref. blue curtain of Tabernacle τὸ δὲ [sc. ὕφασμα] ὑ. προσεοικός...ὁ μὲν γὰρ ὑ. τῷ ἀέρι προσέοικε Thdt.*qu.* *60 in Ex.*(1.165); hence **2.** *blue material, Asen.*2(p.41.21); *ib.*3(p.43.4); ἔοικε δὲ ὑ. [i.e. the stone] τῇ ἐρέᾳ ἢ ὑποπορφυρίζων (v.l. ὑποπορφυρίζει) ποσῶς. διὸ καὶ ἡ θεία γραφὴ ἐξ ὑ. καὶ πορφύρας τὰ ἱερατικὰ ἐνδύματα κεκοσμῆσθαί φησι Epiph.*gemm.*7(M.43.300A); met., of BMV χαῖρε, ὑ., τὸ φλογοφανὲς τῆς παρθενίας ἔριον Thdr.Stud.*nativ.* *BMV* 7(M.96.693D); cf. τοιουτόχρως.

ὑαλοψός (ὑελεψός), ὁ, *glass-blower,* Jo.Mosch.*prat.*77(M.87.2932A); ὑελ-, Leont.N.*v.Sym.*54(M.93.1736D).

ὑβρίζ-ω, 1. *insult, outrage* ὁ τοῦτον [sc. Christ] ~ων...καὶ τὸν πέμψαντα δῆλον ὅτι...~ει Just.*dial.*136.3(M.6.789D); of style ὕβρις σπουδαζομένη καὶ σπουδὴ πάλιν ~ομένη Gr.Nyss.*Eun.*1(1 p.25.2; M.45.252D); **2.** *upbraid,* Chrys.*hom.35.4 in Mt.*(7.404C); *ib.43.1*(458E); id.*hom.5.3 in Phil.*(11.232A).

ὕβρις, ἡ, 1. *insolence,* Gr.Nyss.*Eun.*1(1 p.25.2; M.45.252D) cit. s. ὑβρίζω; **2.** *upbraiding language, rebuke,* Chrys.*hom.23.4 in Heb.*(12.216D); id.*hom.43.1 in Mt.*(7.458C); id.*comm.in Gal.*2:21(10.694D).

ὕβρισμα, τό, *object of outrage,* Clem.*q.d.s.*32(p.181.12; M.9.637C).

***ὑβριστέον,** *one ought to do an injury,* Clem.*prot.*10(p.70.9; M.8.209A).

ὑβριστικῶς, *reprovingly, severely,* Chrys.*hom.43.1 in Mt.*(7.458C).

ὑβρίστρια, ἡ, fem. of ὑβριστήρ; *one who is insolent,* Cyr.*ador.*6(1.175D); id.*glaph.Gen.*2(1.54C); id.*Mich.*67(3.461D).

ὑγεία (ὑγίεια), ἡ, *health, soundness* of body; also of soul, Clem. *paed.*1.11(p.147.13; M.8.365A); †Bas.*jej.*1.1(2.2A; M.31.164B); of orthodoxy, Thdt.*h.e.*2.7.2(3.831); exeg. Is.9:7 interpreted of resurrection of Christ, Proc.G.*Is.*9:7(M.87.2008D) cit. s. ἀναβίωσις.

ὑγειής, = ὑγιής, *healthy, sound,* Thdt.*provid.*10(4.666).

ὑγιαίνω, *be sound, healthy; become healthy* παρὰ τῷ τῆς Χριστοκτονίας ὑγιάναμεν ξύλῳ Procl.CP *hom.*1.1(M.65.833B).

***ὑγιοποιός,** *health-giving,* Anast.S.*qu.et resp.*114(M.89.768A); κρᾶσιν τῶν ξηροποιῶν καὶ ὑ. ἀέρων *ib.*(765D, l. ὑγροποιῶν); v. ὑγροποιός.

ὑγιότης, ἡ, *health,* Mac.Aeg.*hom.*4.25(M.34.492C).

***ὑγροβάτραχος, ὁ,** kind of *frog,* dist. from ξηροβάτραχος, ‡Epiph. *phys.*22(M.43.532C); cf. ὑγρὸς βάτραχος *Phys.*B 26(p.253.10).

ὑγρόβιος, *living on* or *by the water,* as a fisherman, Nonn.*par.Jo.* 21:5(M.43.916A).

***ὑγροκόμος,** *rich in water, Orac.Sib.*14.144.

ὑγροποιός, *making moist,* Anast.S.*qu.et resp.*127(M.89.780C, l. ὑγιοποιός); v. ὑγιοποιός.

***ὑγροχαίτης,** *abundant in water,* Sophr.H.*carm.*23(M.87.3836A).

***ὑγρόχερσος,** *amphibious,* Geo.Pis.*hex.*965(M.92.1568A).

ὑγρόχυτος, *pouring forth liquid,* Nonn.*par.Jo.*2:9(M.43.761B).

***ὑδαρεύομαι,** *be lax, easy-going,* Epiph.*haer.*61.5(p.385.6; M.41.1045B); *ib.*61.7(p.387.15; 1049A).

ὑδαρής, *watery*; of Adam, Meth.*symp.*3.5(p.31.15; M.18.68B) cit. s. ἀφθαρσία; of colour τῇ τοῦ μέλανος ὑδαρεστέρᾳ χροᾷ ‡Nil.*narr.*3(M.79.616B); met., *watered down* ὑδαρεστέρα γὰρ περὶ αὐτοῦ [sc. Χριστοῦ] διάληψις, τὸ μὴ θεὸν οἴεσθαι κατὰ φύσιν ὑπάρχειν αὐτόν Cyr.*glaph.Ex.*2 (1.272C); *soft, lax,* of Babylonians δίαιταν...ὑδαρεστέραν, καὶ ἀνειμένην id.*Is.*4.3(2.637D).

***ὑδαροειδής,** *like water*; neut. as subst., Cyr.*ador.*7(1.219E).

***ὑδαρόπιστος,** *of feeble faith,* Ph.Carp.*Cant.*66(M.40.73C).

***ὑδαρότης, ἡ,** *wateriness*; fig., Pall.*v.Chrys.*12(p.72.14; M.47.41); met., of people, *weakness* τὴν τῶν ὀλισθηρῶς τὰ πολλὰ ὑπολαμβανόντων ὑ. Clem.*paed.*2.1(p.159.21; M.8.392B); moral *laxity,* Epiph.*haer.*76.5(p.345.31; M.42.524C).

***ὑδαρῶς,** *in a watery manner,* hence *feebly,* Or.*Jo.*10.19(14; p.191.2; M.14.341A); *laxly,* Epiph.*haer.*76.5(p.345.22; M.42.524B); comp., *more leniently* ὑδαρέστερον τὰ περὶ τοὺς γάμους...οἰκονομήσαντες Proc.G.*Dt.*12:31(M.87.909A).

ὑδάτιον, τό, *rivulet,* Synes.*ep.*114(M.66.1496B).

***ὑδατόστρωτος,** *laid in water,* Jo.D.*carm.theoph.*4(p.209; M.96.825B).

ὑδατόχροος, *of the colour of water* ἡ τοῦ σπάσματος ὅλη δύναμις ὑ. ἀεικίνητος Hipp.*haer*.5.14(p.108.17; M.16.3167A); *ib*.5.16(p.111.15; 3171A).

***ὑδερία**, ἡ, = ὕδερος, *dropsy*, *M.Ner.et Ach*.19(p.19.5).

ὕδρα, ἡ, *hydra*; met., of envy μακρὰν χεῖται δίκην πυρὸς ἢ ὕ. πολυκεφάλου καὶ ἐπιβόσκεται τὴν ψυχὴν Meth.*lepr*.6(p.458.1); in comparison of Heracles with ὁ γνήσιος καὶ φιλόσοφος...νοῦς: ἐκπερινοστεῖ τὸν κόσμον...σωφρονίζων τοὺς ἐντυγχάνοντας, λέγω...ἀνθρώπους ἐοικότας λέουσι...ἢ...ὕ. πολυτρόποις *Hom.Clem*.6.16; in proverbial phrase ἐκτέμνειν ὕδραν, of completing a complicated task, Meth.*res*.1.62 (p.329.4; M.41.1161C).

ὑδραγώγιον, τό, *conduit, aqueduct*, *A.Barn*.21(p.300.8); Thdt. *h.rel*.10(3.1198); Proc.G.*2Reg*.7:2(M.87.1132C).

ὑδραγωγός, *bringing water*; masc. as subst., *aqueduct, conduit*, Ath.*gent*.43(M.25.85C); Bas.*hom.in Ps*.28(1.184C; M.29.448C); *irrigation channel*, Cyr.*Os*.143(3.176D).

ὕδραυλις, ἡ, *hydraulic organ* φωναὶ αὐλητῶν καὶ ὑδραύλεων *A.Thom*.A 4(p.104.6, v.l. ὑδραύλων).

ὑδρεῖον, τό, *pitcher*, carried in Egyptian religious processions ὁ προφήτης ἔξεισι, προφανὲς τὸ ὑ. ἐγκεκολπισμένος Clem.*str*.6.4(p.449.21; M.9.253C).

***ὑδρημερία**, ***ὑδριμερία**, **ὑδριμερισία**, ἡ, v. *ὑδρομερισία.

ὑδρία, ἡ, *water-pot*, ref. Jo.2:6, water-pots kept filled by Jews to obviate need of travelling to few rivers of Palestine for legal purificatory rites, Chrys.*hom.22.2 in Jo*.(8.127D); symbolism ἓξ δὲ ὑ. ... εἰσὶ τοῖς ἐν κόσμῳ καθαριζομένοις, γεγενημένῳ ἐν ἓξ ἡμέραις Or. *princ*.4.2.5(p.315.2; M.11.368A).

ὑδρίσκη, ἡ, *water-pot, pitcher*, used for conveyance of Baptist's head to his disciples, *A.Jo.Bapt*.(p.539.12).

ὑδροβαφής, *dipped in water*; met., *not durable, insubstantial* ποιεῖ...τὴν ὑ. ἐκείνην...ἕνωσιν, μᾶλλον δὲ κένωσιν μίαν Anast.S.*serm. imag*.3(M.89.1153D); Thphn.*chron*.p.274(M.108.680B); τὴν οὕτω καλουμένην ὑ. ἕνωσιν· οἶμαι δὲ τοῦτο σημαίνειν, τὴν ἐξίτηλον καὶ ὑδαρώδη βαφήν, καὶ οἷον πεφυρμένην καὶ ἀδιάγνωστον, καὶ μηδ' ὁποτέραν τῶν χροιῶν καθαρῶς διασώζουσαν *V.Max*.9(M.90.77C).

***ὑδρόβιος**, *living in water*, Proc.G.*Gen*.9:3(M.87.257C).

ὑδροδόκος, *holding water*, Nonn.*par.Jo*.2:7(M.43.761A).

***ὑδροδοσία**, ἡ, *giving of water*; from rock in wilderness, Mel.*pass*. 88 p.14.32.

***ὑδροκωμήτης**, ὁ, (?) *official in charge of water-supply*, Synes.*ep*. 121(M.66.1500B, v.l. ὑδρομίκτης).

ὑδρολόγιον, τό, *water-clock*; fitted with alarm, and used to waken ἀφυπνιστής who roused monks for early service, *Const.Stud*.2 (M.99.1704C).

***ὑδρομερία**, ἡ, *assignment of water, water-rights*, Nil.*Magn*.35(M. 79.1012A); v. ὑδρομερισία.

***ὑδρομερισία**, ἡ, *assignment of water, water-rights*, Pall.*h.Laus*. 31(p.86.14, vv.ll. ὑδριμερισίας, ὑδριμερίας, ὑδρομερίας; ὑδρημερίας M. 34.1098D).

***ὑδρομίκτης**, ὁ, *mixer of water* (i.e. with wine, cf. Is.1:22); hence *defrauder*, Synes.*ep*.121(v.l. ὑδροκωμήτῃ M.66.1500B); †Jo. Jej.*serm*.1(M.88.1924B).

***ὑδροπαραστάται**, οἱ, *Hydroparastatae*, sect also called Apotactici (Epiph.*haer*.61.1(p.380.12; M.41.1040C)) using water instead of wine at eucharist, Bas.*ep*.188 *can*.1(3.270A; M.32.668B); Thdt. *haer*.1.20(4.312); CTrull.*can*.32.

***ὑδροπιάω**, *be swollen with dropsy*, Pall.*h.Laus*.12(p.35.6; M.34. 1034D).

ὑδροποσία, ἡ, *drinking of water only*, Daniel's practice (Dan. 1:16) a proof of high moral character of Hebrew prophets, Or.*Cels*. 7.7(p.159.23; M.11.1432A); recommended as part of discipline of fasting, Bas.*hom*.1.10(2.9D; M.31.181C); esp. as remedy for drunkenness, Chrys.*hom.10.6 in Mt*.(7.147A); ἀσθενοῦντι στομάχῳ...ἐπιδίδοσθαι οἶνον...ἐδίδαξε Παῦλος, μὴ δι' ὑπερβολὴν ἑτέρας δεηθείη ἡ ἀμετρία ὑδροποσίας Isid.Pel.*epp*.1.385(M.78.400B); ἄμεινον...ἡ μετὰ λόγου οἰνοποσία τῆς μετὰ τύφου ὑ. Pall.*h.Laus*.proem.(p.12.19; M.34.1003).

ὑδροποτ-έω, *drink water only*, Clem.*paed*.2.2(p.167.16; M.8.409A); recommended as part of discipline of fasting, Chrys.*hom.10.6 in Mt*.(7.147A); ~οῦντες [sc. Encratites] καὶ γαμεῖν κωλύοντες...μᾶλλον Κυνικοὶ ἢ Χριστιανοί Hipp.*haer*.8.20(p.238.29; M.16.3367B); ~ησε ...Πυθαγόρας καὶ Διογένης καὶ Πλάτων, ἐν οἷς καὶ Μανιχαῖοι καὶ τὸ λοιπὸν σύνταγμα τῶν ἐθελοφιλοσόφων Pall.*h.Laus*.proem.(p.12.24; M.34.1004).

ὑδροπότης, ὁ, *water-drinker*, Clem.*paed*.2.7(p.191.30; M.8.461A).

***ὑδρόπυρος**, *made of fire and water* ὡσανεὶ ὑδρόπυρον [sc. φύσιν] σὺν Σεουήρῳ συγχυτικῶς πρεσβεύοντες Thdr.Stud.*probl*.9(M.99.481C).

ὑδροσκόπιον, τό, instrument for measuring specific gravity of liquids, Synes.*ep*.15(M.66.1352A).

ὑδροσκόπος, ὁ, *water-seeker*, Thdt.*ep*.37(4.1097).

ὑδροστάτης, ὁ, *water-engine*, i.e. *fire-engine*, Steph.Diac.*v.Steph*. (M.100.1176C).

***ὑδροτόκος**, *water-producing*, †Apoll.*met.Ps*.17:16(M.33.1332C).

***ὑδροφοβέω**, *suffer from hydrophobia*, Or.*Ps*.70:1(p.89).

***ὑδροφόβης**, ὁ, *one who has hydrophobia, madman*, cf. *lymphaticus...quem Graeci ὑ. dicunt*, Isid.H.*etym*.10.161.

ὑδροφοβία, ἡ, *fear of water, hydrophobia*, Isid.H.*etym*.4.6.15.

ὑδροφορέω, *carry water*; pass., *be carried away by water*, ‡Caes. Naz.*dial*.113(M.38.996).

ὑδροχοεῖον, τό, *water-tank, cistern*, *Hom.Clem*.10.1; *ib*.10.26.

ὑδροχόη, ἡ, *vessel for holding water*, ‡Caes.Naz.*dial*.37(M.38.901).

***ὑδροχόης**, *watery* οἱ...δαίμονες...τοὺς ὑ. τόπους συνεχῶς ἐπιβαίνουσιν ‡Pall.*h.mon*.27.2(p.86.13; M.65.448C).

ὑδροχόος, *water-pouring, watery*; of vein infected septically, ‡Caes.Naz.*dial*.113(M.38.997A).

ὕδρωψ, ὁ, an amphibious reptile δίκην ὕδρωπος τοῦ ἑρπετοῦ καλουμένου ἐξ ὑδάτων εἰς γῆν ἀνελθόντος Epiph.*haer*.25.7(p.274.22; M.41. 329C); but cf. ἔστι...ὁ ὕ. μεγέθει ζῷον παρὰ πάντα τὰ ζῷα, δύο κέρατα ἔχον ἐν ἑαυτῷ πρίονος μορφὴν ἔχοντα τοῦ διαφθεῖραι πάντα τὰ εἰσερχόμενα πρὸς αὐτὸ ζῷα *Phys*.B 2(p.153.2).

ὕδωρ, τό, *water*;

I. in gen.; **A.** as one of four elements ὕ. ... ἄλλο τι τῶν στοιχείων *Diogn*.8.2; Athenag.*leg*.22.1(M.6.936C); Hegem.*Arch*.7(p.10.7; M. 10.1437B); Eus.*e.th*.3.2(p.143.31; M.24.980B); def. ἓν τῶν στοιχείων τῶν τεσσάρων...ποίημα θεοῦ κάλλιστον...στοιχεῖον ὑγρόν τε καὶ ψυχρόν, βαρύ τε καὶ κατωφερὲς εὐδιάχυτον Jo.D.*f.o*.2.9(M.94.901A); first principle, acc. Thales, cf.Iren.*haer*.2.14.2(M.7.750B); in Stoic definition of the sun ἄναμμα νοερὸν ἐκ θαλαττίων ὑδάτων Clem.*str*.8.2 (p.82.6; M.9.564A); like earth, has angel assigned to it; hence apparent personification of water in Ps.76:17, Or.*hom.10.6 in Jer*. (p.77.4; M.13.365B).

B. ref. ordinary use; **1.** water-drinking commended ἄγαμαι... τοὺς αὐστηρὸν ἐπανῃρημένους βίον καὶ τῆς σωφροσύνης τὸ φάρμακον ἐπιποθοῦντας τὸ ὕ. Clem.*paed*.2.2(p.168.12; M.8.412A); ὕ., ποτὸν φέριστον, εὐκρατοῖ φρένας Gr.Naz.*carm*.1.2.32.31(M.37.918A); water-drinking should be accompanied by thought of thirst of hell, Jo.Clim.*scal*.7(M.88.805B); Manicheans drink infusion of straw and water when pretending to fast, Cyr.H.*catech*.6.31; **2.** use of water for washing avoided by a Marcionite, on ground that water is work of evil demiurge, Thdt.*haer*.1.24(4.317); and by Manicheans, Hegem.*Arch*.10(p.16.10; M.10.1444A).

C. met., in proverbial sayings; **1.** of combining contradictory opinions τὴν ἅλμην τῷ ποτίμῳ ὕδατι συνεκέρασεν Gr.Naz.*or*.43.54 (M.36.565A); **2.** of fruitless labour ἐοίκασι τοῖς καθ' ὕδατος ταφρεύουσιν [v.l. γράφουσιν] Thdt.*affect*.4(p.107.6; 4.799); Jo.VI H.*v.Jo.D*. 25(M.94.465B).

II. in rel. to religious thought; **A.** worshipped by pagans as a god, *Diogn*.8.2; Clem.*prot*.10(p.74.1; M.8.217B); *ib*.5(p.49.24; 168B); esp. in Egypt πάντων μάλιστα Αἰγύπτιοι τὸ ὕ. προτετιμήκασι Ath. *gent*.24(M.25.48C); ‡Chrys.*puer*.3(6.617B); under name of Osiris, Hipp.*haer*.5.7(p.84.5; M.16.3134B); and by Sampsean sect τετίμηται δὲ αὐτοῖς τὸ ὕ. καὶ τοῦτο ὡς θεὸν ἡγοῦνται, σχεδὸν φάσκοντες εἶναι τὴν ζωὴν ἐκ τούτου Epiph.*haer*.53.1(p.315.24; M.41.960C).

B. vehicle of oracular inspiration among pagan prophetesses, Tat.*orat*.19(p.21.19; M.6.849B).

C. of primal waters of Creation; **1.** in pagan thought, as source of gods' existence Ὀρφέως...τὴν πρώτην γένεσιν αὐτῶν ἐξ ὕδατος συνισταντος Athenag.*leg*.18.3(M.6.928A); **2.** in Christian thought; **a.** of the 'deep' of Gen.1:2 γῆν τε διεχώρισεν ἀπὸ τοῦ περιέχοντος αὐτὴν ὕ. *1Clem*.33.3; θεμελιώσας τὴν γῆν ἐπὶ ὑδάτων Herm.*vis*.1.3.4; Just.*1apol*.60.6(M.6.420A); οὐκέτι δὲ ὁμοίως καὶ ἐπὶ τοῦ ὕ. καὶ τῆς ἀβύσσου μνησθέντος ὡς ἄρα εἴη καὶ ταῦτα γενητά, ἀλλ' ἁπλῶς εἰρηκότος, καὶ σκότος ἐπάνω τῆς ἀβύσσου, καὶ πνεῦμα...ἐπεφέρετο ἐπάνω τοῦ ὕδατος, ἀναγκαίως...διδάσκει καὶ περὶ αὐτῶν ὁ υἱός...ὅτι τε γενητὰ εἴη καὶ ὡς αὐτὸς πρὸ πάντων εἴη Eus.*e.th*.3.2(p.143.33; M.24. 980B); Thdt.*qu.6 in Gen*.(1.9); interpreted as symbolizing matter, Clem.*ecl*.2(p.137.20; M.9.700B); and as typifying baptism, Cyr.H. *catech*.3.5; related to pagan mythology εἰς μίμησιν...τοῦ...ἐπιφερομένου τῷ ὕ. πνεύματος θεοῦ, τὴν Κόρην θυγατέρα τοῦ Διὸς ἔφασαν Just.*1apol*.64.4(M.6.425C); **b.** of waters above and below firmament (Gen.1:7); purpose of former is to prevent destruction of firmament by heat of sun, Jo.D.*f.o*.2.9(M.94.901B); Origen's interpretation, that they represent good and evil spiritual powers respectively, rejected by Bas.*hex*.3.9(1.31B; M.29.73C) and Gr. Nyss., who himself distinguishes waters above firmament from material element, *hex.* (M.44.81B), and noted by Proc.G.*Gen*.1:2(M.87.48B); **c.** Gen.1:9 (*συναχθήτω τὸ ὕδωρ*) the cause of water's propensity to run downhill, Bas.*hex*.5.2(1.34D; M.29.81B,C); **d.** question discussed how earth can rest upon water (Ps.23:2), *ib*.1.9(1.9C; M.24A); **e.** water of Creation as interpreted by Sethians *τὸ δὲ σκότος ὕ. ἐστὶ φοβερόν, εἰς ὃ κατέσπασται καὶ μετενήνεκται εἰς τὴν τοιαύτην φύσιν μετὰ τοῦ πνεύματος τὸ φῶς...τούτων ἔστιν ἰδεῖν τῆς φύσεως εἰκόνα κατὰ πρόσωπον ἀνθρώπου, κόρην ὀφθαλμοῦ, σκοτεινὴν ἐκ τῶν ὑποκειμένων ὑδάτων* Hipp.*haer*.5.19(p.117.11; M.16.3179C); *ib*.5.20(p.122.11; 3187A); by Ophites, cf. *virtutem...quam et sinistram et Prunicon et Sophiam... vocant, et descendentem in aquas...movisse quoque eas*, Iren.*haer*.1. 30.3(M.7.695C); *ὄφις,...ὁ ἄνεμος τοῦ σκότους, ὁ πρωτόγονος τῶν ὕ.* Hipp.*haer*.5.19(p.120.14; 3183C); **f.** origin of water from tears of Achamoth (Valent.), Iren.*haer*.1.4.3(M.7.484B); Nil.*epp*.1.234(M.79. 169A).

D. of baptism; **1.** foreshadowed in OT; **a.** by use of water in all covenants, Cyr.H.*catech*.3.5; **b.** by Levitical lustrations, Cyr.*Lc.* 11:37(M.72.712B); **c.** by many types, e.g. water and Spirit of Gen. 1:2, Clem.*ecl*.8(p.138.33; M.9.701B); Proc.G.*Gen*.1:2(M.87.48B); water, faith, and wood (i.e. flood, Noah's faith, and ark), Just.*dial.* 138.2(M.6.793B); Elisha's wood in water signifying cross and baptism, *ib*.86.6(681B); *ὕ. πιστόν* (Is.33:16) v. infra N.5.i; v. *βάπτισμα*; **2.** sanctified by Christ's baptism *ἐβαπτίσθη ἵνα τῷ πάθει τὸ ὕ. καθαρίσῃ* Ign.*Eph*.18.2; Clem.*ecl*.7(p.138.28; M.9.701B); Gr.Naz.*or.* 29.20(p.104.8; M.36.100C); Chrys.*bapt*.2(2.369D); Procl.CP *or*.7.3(M. 65.760D); cf. *καταβάντων αὐτῶν ἐπὶ τὸ ὕ., ἀνεκόχλασαν τὰ ὕ. Chron. Pasch*.p.225(M.92.548A); **3.** not used by Christ for baptizing *Χριστὸς οὖν ἐν ὕ. οὐ βαπτίζει...ἑαυτῷ δὲ τηρεῖ τὸ ἁγίῳ πνεύματι βαπτίζειν καὶ πυρί* Or.*Jo*.6.23(13; p.133.33; M.14.241C); **4.** of water of Christian baptism; **a.** in gen., *Barn*.11.1; Herm.*vis*.3.3.5; id. *sim*.9.16.2; Clem.*paed*.2.1(p.163.21; M.8.400A); *Hom.Clem*.11.26; Thdt.*qu.26 in Gen*.(1.41); *βαπτιζόμεθα...καταδύνοντες ἐν τῷ ἁγίῳ ὕ.* Cosm.Ind.*top*.7(M.88.352A); **b.** of the nature of the water so used; **i.** 'living water' to be used if possible *βαπτίσατε...ἐν ὕ. ζῶντι. ἐὰν δὲ μὴ ἔχῃς ὕ. ζῶν, εἰς ἄλλο ὕ. ... εἰ δ' οὐ δύνασαι ἐν ψυχρῷ, ἐν θερμῷ Did*.7.1f.; *ἀγαγόντα αὐτὸν ἐπὶ ποταμὸν ἢ πηγήν, ὅπερ ἐστὶ ζῶν ὕ., ἔνθα ἡ τῶν δικαίων γίνεται ἀναγέννησις Clem.contest*.1(M.2.29A); cf.Hipp. *trad.ap*.21.2; ‡Hipp.*can*.112; *Hom.Clem*.9.19; **ii.** but *πᾶν ὕ. ἐπιτήδειον εἰς τὴν τοῦ βαπτίσματος χρείαν* Gr.Nyss.*bapt*.(M.46.421D); *ἀδιακρίτως παντὶ ὕ., καὶ ἐν θαλάττῃ...ἀνάγκης καταλαβούσης βάπτισμα γίνεται* Didym.*Trin*.2.14(M.39.693A); cf. Thecla's baptism in seals' pond, *A.Paul.et Thecl*.34(p.260.6); case of a baptism with sand, repeated, after much discussion, with water, Jo.Mosch.*prat*.176(M. 87.3045Bff.); Thdr.Stud.*epp*.2.157(M.99.1492A); **c.** consecration of water, *Const.App*.7.43.5; cf.Clem.*exc.Thdot*.82(p.132.13; M.9.696C); Gr.Nyss.*bapt.diff*.(M.46.421D); id.*bapt.Chr*.(M.46.581B); by *ἐπίκλησις* of Trin. v.s.v.; threefold sprinkling of chrism, Dion.Ar.*e.h*.2. 2.7(M.3.396C); Jo.D.*Eph*.5:26(M.95.849B); id.*f.o*.4.9(M.94.1121A); blessing of water being carried out in accordance with ancient, but non-scriptural, tradition, Bas.*Spir*.66(3.55A; M.32.188B); work of blessing ascribed to Logos rather than Spirit, Serap.*euch*.19; v. *εὐλογέω*; at Epiphany baptismal water solemnly blessed and reserved at home by faithful *μεσονυκτίῳ κατὰ τὴν ἑορτὴν ταύτην ἅπαντες ὑδρευσάμενοι οἴκαδε τὰ νάματα ἀποτίθενται, καὶ εἰς ἐνιαυτὸν ὁλόκληρον φυλάττουσιν, ἅτε δὴ σήμερον ἁγιασθέντων τῶν ὑδάτων· καὶ ...οὐ διαφθειρομένης τῆς τῶν ὑδάτων ἐκείνων φύσεως τῷ μήκει τοῦ χρόνου, ἀλλ' εἰς ἐνιαυτὸν ὁλόκληρον καὶ δύο καὶ τρία πολλάκις ἔτη τοῦ σήμερον ἀντληθέντος ἀκεραίου...μένοντος* Chrys.*bapt*.2(2.369D); *τὸν ἁλόντα πρεσβύτερον τῇ κοινωνίᾳ τῶν αἱρετικῶν...μὴ ἐξεῖναι ἱερουργεῖν ...ἢ μόνον...ἁγιάζειν τῶν θεοφανίων τὸ ὕ.* Thdr.Stud.*epp*.2.203(M.99. 1617C); *ib*.2.215 *qu*.11(1652B); blessing of water in evening (? opp. midnight) instituted by Peter Fullo, Thdr.Lect.*fr.h.e*.2.48(M.86. 209A); **d.** relation of water to H. Ghost in baptism (Gen.1:2; Jo. 3:5); **i.** H. Ghost sacramentally present in water, Clem.*ecl*.8(p.138. 33; M.9.701B); *τὸ ὕ. τὸ πνεύματι κοινωνοῦν* †Hipp.*theoph*.8(p.262.17; M.10.860B); *ὕδατος προσενεχθέντος εἶπεν· ἔλθετε τὰ ὕδατα ἀπὸ τῶν ὑδάτων τῶν ζώντων...ἡ δύναμις τῆς σωτηρίας ἡ ἀπὸ τῆς δυνάμεως ἐκείνης ἐρχομένη...ἔλθε καὶ σκήνωσον ἐν τοῖς ὕ. τούτοις, ἵνα τὸ χάρισμα τοῦ ἁγίου πνεύματος...ἐν αὐτοῖς τελειωθῇ A.Thom*.A 52(p.168.14); *πρόσεχε...τῇ μετὰ τοῦ ὕ. δεδομένῃ πνευματικῇ χάριτι* Cyr.H.*catech*.3.3; *τῷ πνεύματι τὸ ὕ. συμπαρελήφθη* Bas.*Spir*.35(3.29C; M.32.129C); *δι' ἐντεύξεως καὶ ἐπικλήσεως, τῷ ὕ. ἐπιφοιτῶντος τοῦ ἁγίου πνεύματος* Jo.D.*f.o*.4.9(M.94.1121A); baptism's double nature (*ἐξ ὕδατος καὶ πνεύματος*) illustrates general sacramental principle, id.*imag*.3.12 (M.94.1336B); †Jo.D.*B.J*.8(M.96.920A); *ὁρᾷ ἐκεῖνος ὕ. μόνον ἐπὶ τῆς κολυμβήθρας, σὺ δὲ ὁ πιστὸς καθορᾷς τὸ ὕδωρ φῶς* [v.l. *πῦρ*] *καὶ πνεῦμα* ‡Jo.D.*Const*.10(M.95.325D); **ii.** water as instrument of cleansing which precedes gift of H. Ghost, Or.*Jo*.6.33(17; p.143.15; M.14. 257B); cf.*ib*.6.48(29; p.157.21; 285A); cf.id.*princ*.1.3.7(p.58.20; M.11. 153A); **e.** waters of baptism being *Χριστοφόρα*, Cyr.H.*procatech*.15; **f.** reasons for use of water in baptism adduced from scripture, Cyr.H.*catech*.3.5; from symbolism of immersion, Chrys.*hom.25.2 in Jo*.(8.146B,C); from fact that *ἀρχὴ...τοῦ κόσμου τὸ ὕ.· καὶ ἀρχὴ τῶν εὐαγγελίων ὁ Ἰορδάνης* connected with primal waters at Creation, Cyr.H.*catech*.3.5 = Proc.G.*Gen*.1:2(M.87.48B); and that *τὸ ὕ. ἐστὶ μυστικῶς ἐμφαῖνον ἡμῖν τὸ μυστικὸν λουτρὸν τοῦ ὕ. καὶ τοῦ πυρὸς τοῦ ἁγίου πνεύματος* ‡Germ.CP *contempl*.(M.98.385D); **g.** method of its use *βαπτίσατε...ἐν ὕ. ... ἔκχεον εἰς τὴν κεφαλὴν τρὶς ὕ. Did*.7.1–2; cf.Hipp.*trad.ap*.21; Bas.*Spir*.66(3.55A; M.32.188C); Dion.Ar.*e.h*.2.2. 7(M.3.396D); Gnost. practice of anointing with water and oil, Iren. *haer*.1.21.4(M.7.664B); **h.** effects of baptismal water; **i.** cleansing, for remission of sins, *Barn*.11.11; *A.Xanthipp*.21(p.73.8); Gr.Naz. *or*.40.11(M.36.372B); Thdt.*Is*.32:20(p.131.7; 2.311); **ii.** regeneration *δεικνύντος τοῦ θεοῦ ὅτι τοιούτους ἡμᾶς εἶναι βούλεται, οἵους καὶ γεγέννηκεν ἐκ μήτρας ὕ.* Clem.*str*.4.25(p.319.12; M.8.1369A); *ἐξ ὕ. ἀναγεννηθεὶς θεῷ Hom.Clem*.11.26; *τὸ τῆς παλιγγενεσίας ὕ. ... ἐν ᾧ βαπτιζόμενος...ἀποδύεται μὲν τὸ γῆρας τῆς ἁμαρτίας, νέος δὲ ἀντὶ γεγηρακότος ἀποτελεῖται* Thdt.*Ps*.22:2(1.748); **iii.** conferment of life, Herm.*sim*.9.16.2; *γνωρίζομεν...τὸ βάπτισμα...τουτό ἐστι τὸ ὕ. τῆς ζωῆς* Just.*dial*.14.1(M.6.504C); *τὸ ὕ. τοῦ βαπτίσματος, διὰ τοῦ βαπτισθέντος* [i.e. Christ], *τοὺς θανόντας ἐζωοποίησεν* Procl.CP *or*.7.3 (M.65.760C); Thdt.*qu.26 in Gen*.(1.41); **iv.** giving of seal (v. *βάπτισμα, σφραγίς*) *ἡ σφραγὶς οὖν τὸ ὕ. ἐστίν* Herm.*sim*.9.16.4; *δός μοι τὴν ἐν Χριστῷ σφραγῖδα...καὶ εἶπεν Παῦλος, Θέκλα μακροθύμησον, καὶ λήψῃ τὸ ὕ. A.Paul.et Thecl*.25(p.253.9); **v.** symbolical burial and resurrection, Cyr.H.*catech*.20.4; Dion.Ar.*e.h*.2.3.7(M.3.404B); cf. *συνθαπτομένης τῷ ὕδατι τῆς ἁμαρτίας* Gr.Naz.*or*.40.4(M.36.364A); *θεῖα τελεῖται ἐν αὐτῷ* [sc. *ὕ.*] *σύμβολα, τάφος καὶ νέκρωσις καὶ ἀνάστασις...τρίτον δὲ τοῦτο γίνεται ἵνα μάθῃς ὅτι δύναμις πατρὸς καὶ υἱοῦ καὶ πνεύματος...ἅπαντα ταῦτα πληροῖ* Chrys.*hom.25.2 in Jo*.(8. 146C); and re-creation of soul *πλάττεται ἐν τῷ ὕ.* [sc. *ἡ ψυχή*] id.*hom. 6.4 in Col*.(11.370A); **vi.** sanctification *ἐπὶ τὸ ὕδωρ ἐλθεῖν τοῦ ἁγνισμοῦ* Meth.*res*.1.41(p.287.2; M.41.1109C); Ammon.*Jo*.3:5(M.85.1408D) cit. s. *ἀναστοιχειόω*; **vii.** tyranny of Devil (like that of Pharaoh) is overthrown in water, Cyr.H.*catech*.19.3; Bas.*hom*.13.2(2.115C; M. 31.428B); effects of baptismal water for good and ill resembling those of Red Sea, Gr.Nyss.*v.Mos*.(M.44.361C); v. *δράκων*; **viii.** extinguishing hell fire, *Hom.Clem*.11.26; **i.** relation of faith to water *ἵνα τῆς ψυχῆς διὰ τῆς πίστεως ἀναγεννηθείσης, μεταλάβῃ καὶ τὸ σῶμα, διὰ τοῦ ὕ. τῆς χάριτος* Cyr.H.*catech*.3.4; **j.** Gnost. distn. bet. baptism in water and baptism through Spirit, Clem.*exc.Thdot*.81(p.132.3; M.9.696B) cit. s. *διπλόος*; **k.** of heret. baptism *οὐκ οἰκεῖον καὶ γνήσιον ὕ.* id.*str*.1.19(p.62.3; M.8.813A); *ἀλυσιτελὲς ἔχουσι καὶ τὸ παρ' αὐτῶν διδόμενον ὕ.* Ath.*Ar*.2.43(M.26.237B); **l.** water unnecessary for martyr who is baptized in blood, Cyr.H.*catech*.3.10 cit. s. *βάπτισμα*.

E. in connexion with eucharist; **1.** use of water instead of wine *τοῦτο δὲ μόνον, κρᾶσιν ὕδατος καὶ ἕνα ἄρτον...κόμισον. ... ἄρτον κλάσας καὶ λαβὼν ποτήριον ὕδατος κοινωνὸν ἐποίησεν αὐτὴν τῷ τοῦ Χριστοῦ σώματι καὶ ποτηρίῳ τοῦ υἱοῦ τοῦ θεοῦ A.Thom*.A 120,121(pp.230. 19,231.10); *εἰσὶ γὰρ οἳ καὶ ὕ. ψιλὸν εὐχαριστοῦσιν* Clem.*str*.1.19(p.61. 31; M.8.813A); by Ebionites, Epiph.*haer*.30.16(p.353.12; M.41.432A); by Marcion, *ib*.42.3(p.98.2; 700A); by Tatian, *ib*.46.2(p.205.10; 840C); by Encratites, *ib*.47.1(p.216.11; 852B); by Apotactici (Hydroparastatae), cf.*ib*.61.1(p.380.15; 1040C); Thdt.*haer*.1.20(4.312); *οἱ τὸ ὕ. μόνον παριστῶντες τῷ ἐπὶ τοῦ θυσιαστηρίου κανῷ, ἀντὶ τοῦ κερασθέντος μετὰ τοῦ γεννήματος τῆς ἀμπέλου* Eutych.*pasch*.6(M. 86.2397D); CTrull.*can*.32; hence water, oil, bread, regarded by pagans as instruments of an apostle's magic, *A.Thom*.A 152(p.261. 18); **2.** use of water in mixed chalice *ποτήριον ὕδατος καὶ κράματος* Just.*1apol*.65.3(M.6.428A); *ἄρτος προφέρεται καὶ οἶνος καὶ ὕ. ib*.67.5 (429B); *τὸ κεκραμένον ποτήριον* Iren.*haer*.5.2.3(M.7.1125B); ‡Bas.*h. myst*.31(p.264.27); use prescribed, *Cod.Afr*.37; *Lit.Chrys*.(p.357.22); interpreted as symbolizing union of H. Ghost with man, Clem. *paed*.2.2(p.168.3; M.8.409B); **3.** for ablutions before celebration of eucharist, Dion.Ar.*e.h*.3.2(M.3.425D); and before consecration, *ib.* 3.3.10(437D).

F. in connexion with pagan rites; **1.** cup of water used sacramentally in Mithraic ritual, in diabolical imitation of eucharist, Just.*1apol*.66.4(M.6.429A); **2.** water and wine used in pagan libations, *A.Thom*.A 77(p.192.10).

G. of holy water; **1.** used by pagans to sprinkle worshippers at entrance to temples, cf.Soz.*h.e.*6.6.5(M.66.1308C); **2.** in Christian use; form of episcopal or presbyteral blessing of water *κύριε...ὁ δοὺς τὸ ὕ. πρὸς πόσιν καὶ κάθαρσιν...ἁγίασον τὸ ὕ. τοῦτο...καὶ δὸς δύναμιν ὑγείας ἐμποιητικήν, νόσων ἀπελαστικήν, δαιμόνων φυγαδευτικήν* *Const.App.*8.29.3; used in cure of demoniac, Epiph.*haer.*30.10 (p.345.18; M.41.421C); for countering magical spells, *ib.*30.12(p.348. 20; 428A); Pall.*h.Laus.*17(p.46.2; M.34.1044D); by Marcellus of Apamea in destruction of heathen temples, Thdt.*h.e.*5.21.13(3. 1057); water blessed at Epiphany and reserved at home by faithful, Chrys.*bapt.*2(2.369D); cf. *ἁγίασμα τῶν φώτων* ‡Jo.Jej.*poenit.*(M.88. 1913A); mixed with salt and reserved by priest for use at festivals, *Nomoc.*127; rite of blessing of water at Epiphany, *Euchol.*(p.366); water in stoup at church door *λουτῆρες ὕδατος πεπληρωμένοι εἰσὶ πρὸ τῶν θυρῶν τῆς ἐκκλησίας, ἵνα νίψῃ τὰς χεῖρας* Chrys.*poenit.*3.2(2.296E); cf.Synes.*ep.*121(M.66.1501A)—whether ref. Christian or pagan practice is doubtful.

H. *ὕδωρ ζῶν, ὕδωρ τῆς ζωῆς* (Jo.4:10; Apoc.21:6, etc.); interpreted of spiritual feeding on Christ, typified by water from rock (cf. 1Cor.10:4), Just.*dial.*114.4(M.6.740C); Or.*Jo.*20.41(33; p.384.7; M.14.672A); cf. *Ἰησοῦν καλοῦμεν...καὶ ἄρτον καὶ ὕ. καὶ ζωήν* *V.Aberc.* 16; of belief in Christ, Chrys.*hom.32.2 in Jo.*(8.186A); of life-giving Word of God, Cyr.*ador.*14(1.496B); of teaching of Christ *ὕ. ζωῆς γνωστικῆς* Clem.*str.*7.16(p.73.29; M.9.544C); of knowledge of God, Just.*dial.*69.6(M.6.637C); of H. Ghost, Didym.*Trin.*2.22(M. 39.553C); Cyr.*Ps.*22:2(M.69.841A); id.*Zach.*6(3.801E); of grace of H. Ghost, Cyr.H.*catech.*16.12; spiritual water flows from triple fountain of Trin., Or.*hom.18.9 in Jer.*(p.163.9; M.13.481A); 'living water' interpreted as prophetic inspiration *ὕ. ... ζῶν καὶ λαλοῦν ἐν ἐμοί, ἔσωθέν μοι λέγον· δεῦρο πρὸς τὸν πατέρα* Ign.*Rom.*7.2; *ὕδωρ ζῶν* of Christ, freq.; hence BMV as its fountain, Sophr.H.*nativ.*(p.514. 4,15); interpreted of baptism, Just.*dial.*14.1(504C); ref. Jo.3:5 cited in form *ἐὰν μὴ ἀναγεννηθῆτε ὕδατι ζῶντι, εἰς ὄνομα πατρός, υἱοῦ, ἁγίου πνεύματος, οὐ μὴ εἰσέλθητε κτλ.* *Hom.Clem.*11.26; Cyr. *Joel.*32(3.224E); Thdt.*qu.*41 *in Gen.*(1.41); cf. *ὕ. ἀληθινὸν πίεται ἀνὴρ πραΰς· ὕ. δὲ ψεύδους δοθήσεται ἀνδρὶ ὀργίλῳ* Evagr.Pont.*fr.*57(p.56).

I. *ὕδωρ λογικόν* of spiritual cleansing from heathen impurities, Clem.*prot.*10(p.72.7; M.8.213B); of spiritual grace, Proc.G.*Is.*42:10–25(M.87.2377A); cf. comparison of *σωφροσύνη* with *πηγὴ τοῦ καθαρσίου ὕ.*, Gr.Nyss.*hom.13 in Cant.*(M.44.1060A).

J. mixture of water and milk interpreted as symbolizing union of baptism with Word, Clem.*paed.*1.6(p.120.13; M.8.309B).

K. (Gnost.) of 'waters of fire' which soul must pass through on its upward ascent *μὴ καλυψάτω με ὁ σκοτεινὸς...ἀήρ, ὅπως διαπεράσω τὰ τοῦ πυρὸς ὕδατα καὶ πᾶσαν τὴν ἄβυσσον* *A.Phil.*144(p.86.3).

L. of water from side of Christ *ὁ ἐκχέας ἐκ τῆς πλευρᾶς αὐτοῦ τὰ δύο πάλιν καθάρσια, ὕ. καὶ αἷμα, λόγον καὶ πνεῦμα* Claud.*fr.pasch.*(M. 5.1300A); v. *αἷμα*; of baptism, esp. of water-baptism contrasted with baptism of blood, Cyr.H.*catech.*3.10; *ib.*13.21; Gr.Naz.*carm.* 1.2.34.217(M.37.961A); Chrys.*hom.85.3 in Jo.*(8.507E); *ὕδατι δὲ τῷ ἀπὸ σαρκῶν αὐτοῦ βαπτιζομένη αὐτῷ, πνεύματι δὲ τῷ ἀπὸ θεότητος αὐτοῦ συγκρινομένη αὐτῷ* Ph.Carp.*Cant.*26(M.40.56A); Cyr.*Jo.*12(4. 1074C); *Chron.Pasch.*p.220(M.92.536D); Thdr.Abuc.*opusc.*17(M.97. 1541C); as typified by water mixed with wine in chalice, ‡Bas. *h.myst.*31(p.264.27).

M. *ὕ. τῆς ἀθανασίας* in paradise, Thdr.Stud.*or.*1(M.99.689B).

N. various symbolical interpretations; water signifies; **1.** Word of God, Cyr.*glaph.Ex.*2(1.283A); id.*Is.*3.3(2.451A); Proc.G.*Is.*32:9–20(M.87.2288C); **2.** Christian doctrine, *ib.*15:1–9(2101A); Dion.Ar. *ep.*9.4(M.3.1112A); and spiritual advice, Jo.Clim.*scal.*27(M.88. 1113A); **3.** life, Cyr.*Zach.*59(3.738E); **4.** (plur.) multitudes, id.*Os.*67 (3.101D); cf.id.*Nah.*11(3.488B); Thdt.*Ps.*28:1(1.779); **5.** exeg. partic. texts; **a.** turning of water into blood (Ex.4:9) interpreted of pollution of doctrine by heresies, Gr.Nyss.*v.Mos.*(M.44.345A); as type of Christ's death, Cyr.*glaph.Ex.*2(1.303ff.); contrasted with saving grace afforded through baptismal water, Proc.G.*Is.*12:1–6(M.87. 2061C); **b.** water of Red Sea symbolizes corruption, acc. Peratae, who hold that *ἔστι...ἡ φθορὰ...τὸ ὕ., οὐδὲ ἄλλῳ τινὶ...ἐφθάρη τάχιον ὁ κόσμος ἢ ὕδατι* Hipp.*haer.*5.16(p.111.12,30; M.16.3171A,C); **c.** water from rock (Ex.17:6) typifies power of Word, Bas.*Spir.*31(3.26A; M. 32.121C); or Christ (cf. 1Cor.10:4), Cyr.*glaph.Ex.*3(1.314D); typifies blood of Christ, Thdt.*qu.27 in Ex.*(1.144); is proof that benefits may be expected to flow from martyrs' relics, Jo.D.*f.o.*4.15(M.94. 1165A); **d.** waters of Marah (Ex.15:23) typify bitterness of Law, sweetened by Cross, Cyr.*glaph.Ex.*2(1.283E); id.*Am.*81(3.347B); **e.** water of well of Bethlehem (2Reg.23:15) as type of Christ, Sophr.H.*nativ.*(p.514.3); **f.** in Is.1:22 (*οἱ κάπηλοί σου μίσγουσι τὸν οἶνον ὕδατι*) interpreted of false doctrine of synagogue, Cyr.*glaph. Gen.*7(1.213A); **g.** waters of Siloam (Is.8:5) typify Christ, Proc.G. *Is.*8:5(M.87.1980B); **h.** *τὸ ὕδωρ τῆς Νεμηρεὶμ ἔρημον ἔσται* (Is.15:6) as symbol of heret. doctrine, Nil.*epp.*2.123(M.79.253A); **i.** *τὸ ὕδωρ αὐτοῦ πιστόν* (Is.33:16) of baptism, Cyr.*Is.*3.3(2.460B); Proc.G. *Is.*33:16(M.87.2300C); **j.** *πορεύεσθε ἐφ' ὕδωρ* (Is.55:1) of gospel preaching, *ib.*55:1(M.87.2552A); **k.** *προσελάβετό με ἐξ ὑδάτων πολλῶν* (Ps.17:17) of troubles of life, Bas.*hom.*12.15(2.111A); **l.** in Ps.22:2 *ὥσπερ τὸ πρόβατον τρέφεται...ὕδατι, οὕτω καὶ ὁ ἄνθρωπος ζωοποιεῖται...γνώσει* Or.*sel.in Ps.*22:1(M.12.1260C); *ὕδατος τῆς ἀναπαύσεως, τουτέστι...βαπτίσματος* Cyr.*Ps.*22:2(M.69.841A); **m.** water turned into wine at Cana (Jo.2:9) signifies Christ's *ποτὸν σωτήριον*, Proc.G.*Is.*9:1–7(M.87.2000B); adduced in anti-Manichean argument, Chrys.*hom.22.2 in Jo.*(8.128A); and to prove that Christ is Logos of Creation, Ath.*inc.*18.6(M.25.128D); **n.** *ὕδατα πολλά* (Apoc. 1:15) signifies H. Ghost, cf.Iren.*haer.*4.14.2(M.7.1011B).

ὑελεψός, ὁ, v. *ὑαλοψός.*

ὑετία, ἡ, *rain-storm*, ‡Caes.Naz.*dial.*113(M.38.996).

ὑετίζω, *send rain*; of God, Cyr.*Os.*96(3.128D).

ὑετός, ὁ, *rain*, fig. *τὸν ὕ. ⟨τὸν⟩ σωτήριον* Clem.*prot.*10(p.68.7; M.8. 205A); *διὰ τῆς εὐχῆς λαμβάνοντι τὸν ὕ. τῆς ψυχῆς* Or.*or.*13.5(p.330.4; M.11.459A); *ib.*24.3(p.354.28; 493A).

ὕζ-ω, s.v.l., *prick*, of conscience *ἐὰν ὁ λογισμός σου* ~*ει σε, ὅτι ἔχει τις κατὰ σοῦ* ‡Ath.*renunt.*5(M.28.1413D), ? f.l. for *νύσσει.*

***ὑθλομαν-έω,** as pun on *ὑλομανέω*, *'run to foolishness', abound in foolishness* *τοὺς ἐξ ἀπάτης καὶ ἀνοίας ὑλομανοῦντας καὶ* ~*οῦντας* Max. *opusc.*(M.91.69C).

***ὑθλώδης,** *nonsensical*, Cyr.*Jo.*10.1(4.846E).

***υἱαρχία, ἡ,** *ultimate sonship, original sonship* *πᾶσα θεία πατριὰ καὶ υἱότης ἐκ τῆς πάντων ἐξῃρημένης πατριαρχίας καὶ υἱ. δεδώρηται* Dion.Ar.*d.n.*2.8(M.3.645C).

***υἱικός,** *of the Son* *ὑπόστασις ὢν μία τῆς θεαρχίας υἱ.* ‡Gr.Nyss. *hom.5.31 in Jo.*(p.183.28); *τῆς θεογόνου θεότητος, ἢ τῆς υἱ.* Dion.Ar. *d.n.*2.1(M.3.637B); *ὅλης τῆς υἱ. ἰδιότητος τοὺς χαρακτῆρας* Leont.B. *Nest.et Eut.*2(M.86.1353A); *διαφέρειν δὲ* [sc. *τὸν υἱὸν πρὸς τὸν πατέρα*] *μόνῳ τῷ υἱ. ἰδιώματι* Thdr.Stud.*antirr.*3.7(M.99.424A).

***υἱικῶς,** *in the manner of a son* *τὸν πατέρα πατρικῶς υἱὸν εἶναι, τὸν δὲ υἱόν, υἱ. πατέρα. καὶ ὡσαύτως ἐπὶ τοῦ πνεύματος* †Apoll.ap.Bas.*ep.* 129.1(3.220D; M.32.557C); *ὁ υἱὸς λόγος τοῦ θεοῦ υἱ. γεννητικός* Didym. *Trin.*2.2(M.39.464C); *τὸ πνεῦμα προϊὸν μὲν ἐκ τοῦ πατρός· οὐχ υἱ. δέ, ἀλλ' ἐκπορευτῶς* Jo.D.*f.o.*1.8(M.94.829C) = ‡Cyr.*Trin.*10(6^{3}.16D; M.77.829C).

υἱοθεσία, ἡ, I. *adoption as a son*; hence also position as a son; **A.** of men in rel. to God; **1.** as restored to former status through Inc. *ὁ δεσπότης ἐβαπτίσθη καὶ τὸν παλαιὸν ἄνθρωπον ἀνεκαίνισεν καὶ τὰ σκῆπτρα τῆς υἱ. αὐτῷ πάλιν ἐπίστευσεν* †Hipp.*theoph.*6(p.260.24; M. 10.857B); *ὥστε τὸν σωζόμενον ἄνθρωπον διὰ μιμήσεως Χριστοῦ τὴν ἀρχαίαν ἐκείνην υἱ. ἀπολαβεῖν* Bas.*Spir.*35(3.28D; M.32.128D); †Jo.D. *B.J.*1(M.96.861C); **2.** as given new status; **a.** through Christ, Apoll.*Rom.*1:3f.(p.57.7); Cyr.*Heb.*1:1(p.365.24) cit. s. *υἱοποιέω*; id. *Arcad.*(p.117.22; 5^{2}.125C); Proc.G.*Is.*54:1ff.(M.87.2537D); cf. exeg. Eph.1:5 *δηλοῖ δὲ τὸ ὄνομα τῆς υἱ. τὸ μὴ φύσει εἶναι υἱοὺς τοῦ θεοῦ τοὺς προορισθέντας ὑπ' αὐτοῦ· οὐκ ἂν γοῦν ταχθείη τὸ ὄνομα τῆς υἱ. ἐπὶ τοῦ σωτῆρος, ἀλλ' ἐπὶ τούτων οἱ...λαμβάνουσι τὸ πνεῦμα τῆς υἱ. ὅτε δέ τις τὸν υἱὸν λαμβάνει οὐ πρότερον ἐσχηκὼς αὐτόν, τότε καὶ τὸ πνεῦμα κεχώρηκε τῆς υἱ. οὕτως γὰρ διὰ Χριστοῦ ἡ υἱ. ἡμῖν ἐπεισέρχεται* Or. *comm.in Eph.*1:5(p.237.17); of martyrs *συμμορφωθῆναι τῷ θανάτῳ τοῦ Χριστοῦ εἰς υἱ.* *Const.App.*5.1.2; **b.** through H. Ghost *οὗ* [sc. *τοῦ νοῦ*] *δεξαμένου τὴν κοινωνίαν τοῦ πνεύματος παραγίνεται τοῖς δεξαμένοις τὸ τῆς υἱ. ἀξίωμα* Gr.Nyss.*Eun.*7(2 p.152.12; M.45.740C); *τὸ δὲ πνεῦμα ἐλευθερίαν ὀρέγει καὶ υἱ.· τὸ γὰρ πνεῦμα κράζει ἐν ταῖς καρδίαις ἡμῶν, ἀββᾶ ὁ πατήρ* Didym.(‡Bas.)*Eun.*5(1.297A; M.29.713A); Thdt. *Trin.*21(M.75.1177A); Proc.G.*Is.*54:1ff.(M.87.2616B); cf. *πολλὰ τῶν κτισμάτων οὐδὲ τὸ τῆς υἱ. πνεῦμα φύσιν ἔχει δέχεσθαι, ὡς τὰ ἄλογα καὶ τὰ ἄψυχα* Didym.(‡Bas.)*Eun.*4(287D; M.692A); **c.** esp. in baptism *ὁ πατὴρ τοὺς εἰς αὐτὸν καταπεφευγότας...ἀναγεννήσας πνεύματι εἰς υἱ.* Clem.*paed.*1.5(p.102.20; M.8.276A); †Hipp.*theoph.*10(p.263.16; M. 10.861A); Bas.*Spir.*36(3.30A; M.32.132B); id.*hom.*13.1(2.114B; M.31. 425A); *βάπτισμα...υἱοθεσίας χάρισμα* Cyr.H.*procatech.*16; id.*catech.* 3.14; *μηδεὶς...νομιζέτω τὸ βάπτισμα ἀφέσεως ἁμαρτιῶν μόνον, ἀλλὰ καὶ υἱοθεσίας χάριν τυγχάνειν* *ib.*20.6; *συναναστῆναι εἰς υἱ. τὴν ἐν αὐτῷ* [sc. *Χριστῷ*] *Const.App.*7.43.5; *ὅπου γὰρ ἁμαρτημάτων ἄφεσις, ἐκεῖ υἱ. ... οὐ πρότερον δυνάμεθα καλέσαι πατέρα, ἕως ἐν τῇ κολυμβήθρᾳ... ἀπονιψώμεθα τὰ ἁμαρτήματα* Chrys.*paralyt.*6(3.42E); Isid.Pel.*epp.*3. 195(M.78.880C); Cyr.*Os.*8(3.29A); *τὸ βάπτισμα τῆς υἱ. ἡ ῥίζα* Job.

Mon.*inc*.2(M.86.3316B); τὴν μητέρα [sc. the font] τῆς υἱ. Dion.Ar. *e.h*.2.2.7(M.3.396C); hence as synonym for baptism οἱ τῆς υἱ. ἠξιωμένοι Thdt.*Ps*.57:6(1.985); **d.** in gen. τὸν ἑκόντα μετὰ ἀσκήσεως καὶ διδασκαλίας τὴν γνῶσιν τῆς ἀληθείας ἐπανῃρημένον εἰς υἱ. καλεῖ, τὴν μεγίστην πασῶν προκοπήν Clem.*str*.2.16(p.152.25; M.8.1013B); Mac. Aeg.*ep*.(M.34.413A); οἱ γὰρ πνευματικῶς πολιτευόμενοι, τοῦ τῆς υἱ. μεταλαγχάνουσιν ἀξιώματος Thdt.*Rom*.8:14(3.85); μήποτε...ἐκπέσωμεν τῆς τοιαύτης υἱ. ὁ δὲ ταύτης ἐκπίπτων, ὅμοιος γίνεται Ἰούδᾳ Ant. Mon.*hom*.129(M.89.1840C); **e.** implying immortality τὴν υἱ. τὴν ἀθανασίαν καλῶν, ἐπειδὴ υἱῶν εἶναι νομίζει θεοῦ ἀθανάτους εἶναι Thdr. Mops.*Rom*.8:19(p.138.33; M.66.825D); Gennad.*fr.Rom*.1:7(p.352.22); cf. ἠγέρθη Χριστὸς ἐκ νεκρῶν εἰς υἱ. *ib*.6:3f.(p.365.28; M.85.1673C); to be completed in the future, ref. Rom.8:23 νῦν μὲν ὡς ἐν ἀπαρχῇ λαμβάνουσα [sc. Church] τῆς υἱ. τὸν ἀρραβῶνα, καὶ τὴν τῆς ἀναστάσεως ἐλπίδα Or.*schol.in Cant*.7:1(M.17.280D); Diod.*Rom*.8:23 (p.95.9); εἶπεν ὅτι ἐλάβομεν πνεῦμα υἱοθεσίας· ἀλλ' ὅμως διδάσκει σαφέστερον, ὅτι τὸ μὲν ὄνομα νῦν ἐλάβομεν, τοῦ δέ γε πράγματος τότε μεθέξομεν, ὅταν ἡμῶν ἀπαλλαγῇ τὰ σώματα τῆς φθορᾶς Thdt.*Rom*. 8:23(3.89); ref. 1Cor.15:28 υἱοὶ δὲ θεοῦ ἔσονται [sc. οἱ ἅγιοι] τῷ τῆς υἱ. πνεύματι κοσμηθέντες Eus.*e.th*.3.15(p.173.6; M.24.1029C).

B. not applicable to Son τῶν γὰρ ἑτεροδόξων οἱ μὲν...ἄνθρωπον εἶναι αὐτὸν...ὑποθέμενοι ἐξ ἀνθρώπου, υἱοθεσίᾳ τετιμῆσθαι αὐτὸν ἔφασαν Eus.*Marcell*.2.1(p.33.13; M.24.780B); οὐκ ἐκ δουλείας εἰς προκοπὴν υἱοθεσίας ἐλθόντα, ἀλλὰ υἱὸν ἀεὶ γεννηθέντα Cyr.H.*catech*.11. 4; αὐτὸς ἄλλου υἱοῦ τοῦ χαριζομένου αὐτῷ τὴν υἱ. οὐκ ἐπιδέεται, ἀλλ' ὅπερ ἐστὶ κατὰ φύσιν, καὶ ὀνομάζεται Gr.Nyss.*Eun*.3(2 p.41.20; M.45.609A); Didym.(‡Bas.)*Eun*.4(1.287D; M.29.692A).

II. *sonship*, of Son ὑπὲρ δὲ τῆς αὐτοῦ καταρτισθείσης υἱοθεσίας, υἱοπρεπῶς μὲν διὰ τὴν φύσιν,...προσάγων εὐχαριστήρια τῷ πατρί †Diad.*Ar*.7(M.65.1161C).

υἱοθετ-έω, *adopt as a son*; **1.** men by God; **a.** through Christ ἡ υἱότης αὐτοῦ διαφέρει τῶν δι' αὐτοῦ θέσει ~ηθέντων Alex.Al.*ep. Alex*.7(p.24.11; M.18.557C); **b.** through H. Ghost in baptism, Bas. *ep*.105(3.200B; M.32.513B) cit. s. ἀπαθανατίζω; Gr.Nyss.*bapt*.(M.46. 425B); διὰ τοῦ λουτροῦ παλιγγενεσίας καὶ ἀνακαινώσεως πνεύματος ἁγίου ~ούμεθα θεῷ Didym.(‡Bas.)*Eun*.5(1.303A; M.29.728A); Jo.D. *f.o*.4.8(M.94.1117A); **c.** in gen., Or.*exp.in Pr*.17:20(M.17.201A); of Israel θέσει...καὶ χαρακτῆρί τινι...~ούμενοι ἀπὸ τοῦ ἀληθινοῦ θεοῦ Didym.(‡Bas.)*Eun*.5(1.313B; M.752A); Max.*ep*.19(M.91.592A); **2.** pass., of Church, opp. Israel ~εῖται...δι' ἀγάπης ἁγιαζομένη Didym.(‡Bas.)*Eun*.5(1.309B; M.29.741B); **3.** met., soul by wisdom, Proc.G.*Cant*.6:8(M.87.1756B).

υἱόθετος, *adopted as a son*; of Christ into Gnost. Pleroma, Clem. *exc.Thdot*.33(p.117.19; M.9.676B).

***υἱοπατερία, ἡ,** v. *υἱοπατορία.

***υἱοπατήρ, ὁ,** v. *υἱοπάτωρ.

***υἱοπατορία (*-τερία), ἡ,** *doctrine of the identity of Son and Father*, as taught by Sabellians μήτε ἀπαλλοτριώσῃς τοῦ πατρὸς τὸν υἱόν, μήτε συναλοιφὴν ἐργασάμενος υἱ. πιστεύσῃς Cyr.H.*catech*.4.8; *ib*.15.9; Ammon.*Jo*.1:1(M.85.1392C); CCP(381)‡*can*.7; ‡Acac.CP *ep. Petr*.(p.19.20; -τερία H.2.845A); ‡Caes.Naz.*dial*.3(M.38.861).

***υἱοπάτωρ (*-πατήρ), ὁ, 1.** divine Person who is both *Father and Son* οὐδ' ὡς Σαβέλλιος τὴν μονάδα διαιρῶν υἱ. εἶπεν Ar.*ep.Alex*.(p.12. 12; M.26.709A); υἱ. τὸν θεὸν κατὰ τὸν Σαβέλλιον, εἰ καὶ μὴ γυμνῷ τῷ λόγῳ, τῇ γοῦν ἀληθείᾳ εἰσάγων [sc. Marcellus] Eus.*e.th*.1.1(p.62.33; M.24.829C); οὔτε γὰρ υἱ. φρονοῦμεν, ὡς οἱ Σαβέλλιοι λέγοντες μονοούσιον καὶ οὐχ ὁμοούσιον †Ath.*exp.fid*.2(M.25.204A); εἴ τις τὸ ἄχρονον τῆς τοῦ μονογενοῦς Χριστοῦ ἐκ πατρὸς ὑποστάσεως ἐπὶ τὴν ἀγέννητον τοῦ θεοῦ οὐσίαν ἀναφέρει, ὡς υἱ. λέγων, ἀνάθεμα ἔστω CAnc.(358) *anath*.17; Μοντανιστὰς...τὸν αὐτὸν υἱοπατέρα ὁμοῦ καὶ παράκλητον νοοῦντας Didym.*Trin*.3.18(M.39.881B); Νόητος...υἱ. τὸν Χριστὸν ἐδίδαξε, τὸν αὐτὸν εἶναι ⟨λέγων⟩ πατέρα καὶ υἱὸν καὶ ἅγιον πνεῦμα Epiph. *anac*.57(p.213.4; M.41.848D); αὐτὸν δὲ τὸν πατέρα ἕνα ὄντα δυοῖν ὀνόμασι γεραίροντα οἰόμενοι, υἱ. προσαγορεύουσιν [sc. Sabellians] ‡Gr.Nyss.*Ar.et Sab*.1(M.45.1281A); **2.** one who holds such a doctrine, *Filiopatrian* τὴν τῶν υἱοπατόρων λεγομένων ἀπάτην Gr.Nyss. *Eun*.12(1 p.227.16; M.45.924A).

υἱοποι-έω, A. *adopt as a son*, Adam.*dial*.2.19(p.104.26); met., of Christ βασιλέας ~οῦντές τινες, οὐχ ἡγοῦνται διδόναι μᾶλλον ἢ λαμβάνειν. ~ησαι σὺ τὸν Χριστόν, καὶ ἕξεις πολλὴν ἀσφάλειαν Chrys. *hom.1.4 in Phil*.(11.200F); ‡Chrys.*caec.Zacch*.4(8.126C).

B. *make into a son* of God; **1.** men, ref. Ps.81:6 σχέσει γὰρ τῇ πρὸς θεὸν υἱοποιηθέντες παρ' αὐτοῦ θεοποιούμεθα Cyr.*thes*.4(5^1.25A); through Christ υἱοποίησεν ἡμᾶς τῷ πατρί Ath.*Ar*.1.38(M.26.92B); συγκαταβάντος τοῦ λόγου, ~εῖται καὶ αὐτὴ ἡ κτίσις δι' αὐτοῦ *ib*.2.64 (284B); τοῦ υἱοῦ μετέχοντες ~ούμεθα δι' αὐτοῦ Cyr.*thes*.13(5^1.131A); id.*Ps*.83:6(M.69.1209A); through H. Ghost τοῦ Χριστοῦ ὄντος ἀληθινοῦ υἱοῦ, ἡμεῖς τὸ πνεῦμα λαμβάνοντες, ~ούμεθα Ath.*ep.Serap*.1.19 (M.26.576A); Cyr.*Nest*.2.4(p.40.39; 6^1.42E); in baptism βαπτιζόμενοι φωτιζόμεθα, φωτιζόμενοι ~ούμεθα, ~ούμενοι τελειούμεθα Clem.*paed*. 1.6(p.105.20; M.8.281A); ~ούμεθα καὶ ἡμεῖς ἀληθῶς Ath.*decr*.31(p.27. 25; M.25.473C); ἐκ ποιημάτων ὄντες, ~ούμεθα λοιπόν id.*Ar*.1.34(M.26. 84A); *Const.App*.2.33.1 cit. s. δεξιός; **2.** of Christ (heret.) τὸν φύσει υἱὸν θεοῦ, θέσει καὶ χάριτι υἱοποιηθέντα λέγουσι Didym.(‡Bas.)*Eun*.5 (1.314A; M.29.753A); Cyr.*Arcad*.(p.66.13; 5^2.49A); εἰ οὖν οὕτως καὶ ὁ λόγος καὶ ὁ Χριστὸς μεταλήψει κοινοῦ τινος ἑτέρου...~οῦνται θεῷ Leont.H.*Nest*.4.12(M.86.1648B); orthodox ἵν' ὡς ἄνθρωπος ~ηθείς, καίτοι κατὰ φύσιν ὑπάρχων θεός, ὁδοποιήσῃ δι' ἑαυτοῦ τῇ ἀνθρώπου φύσει τῆς υἱοθεσίας τὴν μέθεξιν Cyr.*Heb*.1:1(p.365.23).

***υἱοποίησις, ἡ,** *making into sons*, ref. Heb.1:6 τῆς δὲ κτίσεως πρωτότοκον διὰ τὴν τῶν πάντων υἱ. Ath.*Ar*.2.64(M.26.284C); *ib*.3.9 (340C); τὸ πνεῦμα, ἐπείπερ ἐστὶ τοῦ υἱοῦ, ἐνεργήσει...τὴν υἱ. Cyr.*dial. Trin*.3(5^1.492C).

υἱοποίητος, *adopted as a son*, Chrys.*hom.5.2 in Eph*.(11.34B); ‡Chrys.*caec.Zacch*.4(8.126C).

υἱοποιΐα, ἡ, *making into a son*, ref. Ps.2:7 τῷ ἔργῳ τῆς πρὸς αὐτὸν [sc. θεόν] υἱοποιΐας αὐτοῦ [sc. τοῦ κατὰ Χριστὸν ἀνθρώπου] Leont.H. *Nest*.3.5(M.86.1616A).

***υἱοποιός,** *son-making*, Leont.B.*Nest.et Eut*.1(M.86.1301A) cit. s. θεοποιός; γεννήσεως υἱ. Leont.H.*Nest*.4.19(M.86.1684D).

***υἱοπρεπής,** *filial, befitting a son* υἱ. ἰδιώματα [sc. τῆς τοῦ λόγου θείας φύσεως] Leont.H.*Nest*.2.21(M.86.1584A).

***υἱοπρεπῶς,** *as befits a son*, †Diad.*Ar*.7(M.65.1161C) cit. s. ἀρχιερατικῶς.

υἱός, ὁ, *son* [voc. υἱός, *T.Sal*.20.1(p.60.6); plur. υἱεῖς, Athenag. *leg*.20.2(M.6.932A); *Disp.Phot*.(M.88.565D); poet. acc. υἱέα, Gr.Naz. *carm*.1.1.2.1(M.37.401A); υἱῆα, Nonn.*par.Jo*.13:22(M.43.865A)];

A. in Hebraisms τοῖς υἱ. τῶν ἀνθρώπων *1Clem*.61.2; υἱοὶ τῆς ἀνομίας Herm.*vis*.3.6.1; τοῦ μέλλοντος αἰῶνος ὄντες υἱ. *Hom.Clem*.2. 15; γενόμενοι διὰ τὸν Ἰησοῦν υἱ. τῆς εἰρήνης Or.*Cels*.5.33(p.35.28; M. 11.1232B); ἀπειθείας υἱοὺς ὀνομάζει τοὺς ἀπειθεῖς, οἱονεὶ τῆς κατὰ τὴν ἀπείθειαν κακίας μητρὸς γινομένης καὶ γεννώσης αὐτοὺς ἔχοντας τὸν τῆς μητρὸς χαρακτῆρα id.*comm.in Eph*.5:6(p.561).

B. of a spiritual son, *Barn*.1.1; Clem.*str*.1.1(p.3.23; M.8.689A); Thdt.*haer*.proem.(4.280A); etc.

C. υἱὸς θεοῦ; **1.** of Israel, Eus.*Ps*.81:6–7(M.23.988B); υἱοὺς ἔλεγε τοὺς πάλαι λαοὺς ὁ θεός Ath.*Ar*.1.39(M.26.92C); Juln.Imp.ap.Cyr. *Juln*.9(6^2.290D); **2.** of Christian believers ὡς πρέπει υἱοῖς θεοῦ ἀντιστῶμεν *Barn*.4.9; υἱοὶ ὑψίστου πάντες δύνασθαι γενέσθαι κατηξίωνται Just.*dial*.124.4(M.6.765B); τίς δὲ υἱ. εἶναι δυνάμενος τοῦ θεοῦ δουλεύειν ἥδεται; Clem.*prot*.10(p.68.3; M.8.205A); οἱ τῆς ἀνομίας υἱ. ποτε διὰ τὴν φιλανθρωπίαν τοῦ λόγου νῦν υἱ. γεγόναμεν τοῦ θεοῦ *ib*.2 (p.20.14; 97B); υἱ. θεοῦ καὶ μαθητὴς θεοῦ ὁμοῦ καὶ φίλος καὶ συγγενής id.*str*.7.16(p.66.17; M.9.529B); διὰ τὴν ὁμοιότητα υἱοὶ ἐκείνου εἶναι λογισθέντες πάντων δεσπόται ἀποκατασταθῆναι δυνήσεσθε *Hom.Clem*.10. 6; οὐ μόνον υἱ. θεοῦ ἀλλὰ καὶ θεοὶ θνητοὶ τὴν φύσιν ἄνδρες ἐκλήθησαν [i.e. in scripture] Eus.*e.th*.1.20(p.84.23; M.24.872B); υἱ. δὲ θεοῦ ἔσονται τῷ τῆς υἱοθεσίας πνεύματι κοσμηθέντες *ib*.3.15(p.173.5; 1029C); υἱοὶ θεοῦ κατὰ μετοχὴν τῆς τοῦ μονογενοῦς αὐτοῦ κοινωνίας ἀποτελεσθέντες μετουσίᾳ τῶν τῆς θεότητος αὐτοῦ μαρμαρυγῶν *ib*.3.18(p.179. 34; 1041C); οὐκ ἄρα μισθὸν ἔσχε τὸ λέγεσθαι υἱὸς καὶ θεός, ἀλλὰ μᾶλλον αὐτὸς υἱοποίησεν ἡμᾶς τῷ πατρί, καὶ ἐθεοποίησε τοὺς ἀνθρώπους γενόμενος αὐτὸς ἄνθρωπος Ath.*Ar*.1.38(M.26.92B); γινόμεθα καὶ ἡμεῖς υἱ., οὐχ ὡς ἐκεῖνος φύσει καὶ ἀληθείᾳ, ἀλλὰ κατὰ χάριν τοῦ καλέσαντος *ib*. 3.19(361C); ἄνθρωπος...υἱ. θεοῦ γίνεται διὰ τῆς πνευματικῆς γεννήσεως Χριστῷ συναπτόμενος· ὁ δὲ τὸν ἄνθρωπον δι' ἑαυτοῦ θεοῦ υἱὸν ποιῶν αὐτὸς ἄλλου υἱοῦ τοῦ χαριζομένου αὐτῷ τὴν υἱοθεσίαν οὐκ ἐπιδέεται Gr. Nyss.*Eun*.3(2 p.41.17; M.45.609A); ἡμεῖς ὡς ἐν αὐτῷ τε καὶ δι' αὐτοῦ υἱ. θεοῦ φυσικῶς τε καὶ κατὰ χάριν, φυσικῶς μὲν ὡς ἐν αὐτῷ τε καὶ μόνῳ, μεθεκτῶς δὲ καὶ κατὰ χάριν ἡμεῖς δι' αὐτοῦ ἐν πνεύματι Cyr. *Thds*.30(p.61.31; 5^2.27A); αὐτὸς οὖν κατὰ φύσιν υἱ. ἐστιν τοῦ θεοῦ, ἡμεῖς δὲ κατὰ χάριν Justn.*conf*.(p.76.23; M.86.999B); ref. Rom.8:19–21 κτίσιν καλῶν ἐνταῦθα τοὺς ἀγγέλους, υἱ. δὲ θεοῦ τοὺς ἀνθρώπους Cosm.Ind.*top*.2(M.88.120B); *ib*.(125B); υἱοὶ δέ, οἱ μήτε φόβῳ τῶν ἠπειλημένων, μήτε πόθῳ τῶν ἐπηγγελμένων, ἀλλὰ τρόπῳ καὶ ἕξει τῆς πρὸς τὸ καλὸν...τῆς ψυχῆς ῥοπῆς...μηδέποτε τοῦ θεοῦ χωριζόμενοι Max.*myst*.(M.91.712A); Χριστιανὸς ὀρθόδοξος καὶ υἱ. τοῦ θεοῦ χάριτι *Lit.Jac*.proem.(*NBP* 10^2 p.39); Gnost., of followers of Prodicus υἱοὺς μὲν φύσει τοῦ πρώτου θεοῦ λέγοντες αὐτούς Clem.*str*.3.4(p.209.31; M.8.1136A); Basilidean υἱ. δέ, φησίν, ἐσμὲν ἡμεῖς οἱ πνευματικοί Hipp. *haer*.7.25(p.202.26; M.16.3311D); αὐτοὺς εἶναι υἱ. φασιν, οἳ τούτου χάριν εἰσὶν ἐν κόσμῳ, ἵνα...ἅμα τῇ υἱότητι ἀνέλθωσι πρὸς τὸν ἄνω πατέρα, οὗ ἡ πρώτη ἐχώρησεν υἱότης ib.10.14(p.276.4; 343OD); οἱ τὴν περὶ διαφόρων φύσεων εἰσάγοντες μυθοποιΐαν καὶ λέγοντες εἶναι φύσει καὶ ἐκ πρώτης κατασκευῆς υἱοὺς θεοῦ, μόνον διὰ τὸ πρὸς θεὸν συγγενὲς δεκτικοὺς τῶν τοῦ θεοῦ ῥημάτων Or.*Jo*.20.33(27; p.370.6; M.14.648B); Manich., *Disp.Phot*.40(M.88.565D); **3.** of heavenly beings: of antichrist appearing ὡς υἱ. θεοῦ *Did*.16.4; of pagan gods υἱ. θεοῦ καλεῖ τοὺς θεούς, ὡς υἱ. ἀνθρώπων τοὺς ἀνθρώπους. καλεῖ δὲ θεούς, οὐχ ὡς ὄντας, ἀλλ' ὡς παρὰ τοῖς ἀπίστοις νομιζομένους Thdt.*Ps*.88:7(1.1232); **4.** ref. Gen.6:2 (reading υἱοὶ θεοῦ instead of ἄγγελοι θεοῦ); interpreted of men, ‡Ath.*Ar*.4.22(p.69.2; M.26.501A); ἔξωθέν γε...αὐτὸς [sc. Julian] προσγεγράφθαι διϊσχυρίσατο, οἱ ἄγγελοι τοῦ θεοῦ, καίτοι τῆς...ἀληθεστέρας γραφῆς ἐχούσης, οἱ υἱ. τοῦ θεοῦ, ἰστέον δὲ ὅτι μετά γε τὴν τῶν ἑβδομήκοντα τῆς ἑρμηνείας ἀπόδοσιν, αὐτὸ δὴ τοῦτο διερμηνεύοντες οἱ ἕτεροι, φασὶν ἀντὶ τοῦ, υἱ. τοῦ θεοῦ, οἱ υἱ. τῶν δυναστευόντων ...οἱ υἱ. τοῦ θεοῦ, τουτ' ἔστιν οἱ ἐξ αἵματος τοῦ Ἐνώς Cyr.*Juln*.9(6^2. 296C); contrast Juln.*ib*.(290D); some maintain allusion is to angels, but angels are never designated sons of God, Chrys.*hom.22.2 in Gen*.(4.195C); interpreted of heavenly beings, †Bas.Anc.*virg*.35(M. 30.740C); v. ἄγγελος; **5.** of second Person of Trin.; **a.** in rel. to Godhead in gen. οὗτος δὲ ὁ υἱ. τοῦ θεοῦ...ὁμολογεῖται ἐν πνεύματι ἁγίῳ ἀπ' οὐρανοῦ καταβάς Arist.*apol*.15.1; δόξαν τῷ πατρὶ τῶν ὅλων διὰ τοῦ ὀνόματος τοῦ υἱ. καὶ τοῦ πνεύματος τοῦ ἁγίου Just.*1apol*.65.3(M. 6.428A); cf. *per manus ejus...hoc est per filium et spiritum sanctum*, Iren.*haer*.4 proem.4(M.7.975B); υἱ. ἐν πατρί, καὶ πατὴρ ἐν υἱῷ Clem.*paed*.1.5(p.104.14; M.8.277C); υἱὲ καὶ πατήρ, ἓν ἄμφω, κύριε *ib*.3.12 (p.291.1; 680B); οὐ μὴν οὐδὲ ὁ πατὴρ ἄνευ υἱ. ἅμα γὰρ τῷ πατὴρ υἱοῦ πατήρ, υἱὸς δὲ περὶ πατρὸς ἀληθὴς διδάσκαλος. καὶ ἵνα τις πιστεύσῃ τῷ υἱ., γνῶναι δεῖ τὸν πατέρα πρὸς ὃν καὶ ὁ υἱ. αὖθίς τε ἵνα τὸν πατέρα ἐπιγνῶμεν, πιστεῦσαι δεῖ τῷ υἱ., ὅτι ὁ τοῦ θεοῦ υἱ. διδάσκει· ἐκ πίστεως γὰρ εἰς γνῶσιν, διὰ υἱοῦ πατήρ· γνῶσις δὲ υἱοῦ καὶ πατρὸς ἡ...διάληψίς ἐστιν ἀληθείας διὰ τῆς ἀληθείας id.*str*.5.1(p.326.10; M.9.9A); τρίτον μὲν γὰρ εἶναι τὸ ἅγιον πνεῦμα, τὸν υἱ. δὲ δεύτερον *ib*.5.14(p.395.16; 156B); *ib*.7.2(p.7.22; M.9.412B) cit. s. ἐνέργεια; πρόσωπον δὲ πατρὸς ὁ υἱ., δι' οὗ γνωρίζεται ὁ πατήρ id.*exc.Thdot*.10(p.110.5; M.9.661A); Sabellian οὐκ ἄλλο εἶναι πατέρα, ἄλλο δὲ υἱ., ἓν δὲ καὶ τὸ αὐτὸ ὑπάρχειν Hipp.*haer*.9.12(p.248.27; M.16.3383C); ἐλαττόνως δὲ παρὰ τὸν πατέρα ὁ υἱ. φθάνων ἐπὶ μόνα τὰ λογικά (δεύτερος γάρ ἐστι τοῦ πατρός)...ὥστε κατὰ τοῦτο μείζων ἡ δύναμις τοῦ πατρὸς παρὰ τὸν υἱ. καὶ τὸ πνεῦμα τὸ ἅγιον, πλείων δὲ ἡ τοῦ υἱ. παρὰ τὸ πνεῦμα Or.*princ*.1.3.5(p.56.3; M.11. 150B); οὗτος δὴ ὁ υἱ. ἐκ θελήματος τοῦ πατρὸς ἐγενήθη...κτίσμα, σοφία *ib*.4.4.1(p.349.11); ὁ μὲν δημιουργὸς τοῦδε τοῦ παντὸς υἱ. ἐστι τοῦ θεοῦ, ὁ δὲ πρῶτος καὶ ἐπὶ πᾶσι θεὸς πατήρ ἐστιν αὐτοῦ id.*Cels*.6.47(p.119.2; M.11.1372C); φαμὲν τὸν υἱ. οὐκ ἰσχυρότερον τοῦ πατρὸς ἀλλ' ὑποδεέστερον *ib*.8.15(p.233.7; 1537D); Sabellian doctrine τὸν υἱ. εἶναι τὸν πατέρα Dion.R.ap.Ath.*decr*.26(p.22.7; M.25.464A); ἀεὶ ὁ θεὸς πατὴρ ἦν καὶ ὁ υἱ. οὐχ ἁπλῶς ἀΐδιός ἐστιν, ἀλλὰ τοῦ πατρὸς ἀϊδίου ὄντος, ἀΐδιος ἂν εἴη καὶ ὁ υἱ. Dion.Al.ap.Ath.*Dion*.16(p.58.4; M.25.504B); πατέρα εἶπον, καὶ πρὶν εἰσάγω τὸν υἱ. ἐσήμανα καὶ τοῦτον ἐν τῷ πατρί Dion. Al.*ib*.17(p.58.16; 504C); ὁ δὲ ἄγγελος τοῦ πατρὸς ὁ υἱ. ἐστιν, αὐτὸς κύριος καὶ θεὸς ὤν Hymen.*ep*.5(p.326.24); ἔστι δὲ ὁ υἱ., ἡ παντοδύναμος καὶ κραταιὰ χεὶρ τοῦ πατρός Meth.*creat*.9(p.498.28; M.18.341A); ἄλλο μέν τι...τὸν υἱ. εἶναι, ἄλλο δὲ τὴν εἰκόνα αὐτοῦ· ὁ μὲν γὰρ υἱ., τὰ θεῖα τῆς πατρῴας ἀρετῆς γνωρίσματα φέρων, εἰκών ἐστι τοῦ πατρός, ἐπειδὴ καὶ ὅμοιοι ἐξ ὁμοίων γεννώμενοι, εἰκόνες οἱ τικτόμενοι φαίνονται τῶν γεννητόρων ἀληθεῖς. ὁ δὲ ἄνθρωπος, ὃν ἐφόρησεν, εἰκών ἐστι τοῦ υἱ. Eust.*fr.in Pr.8:22*(M.18.677D); ἡ πρὸ τῶν γενητῶν θεία καὶ πανάρετος οὐσία, ἡ νοερὰ καὶ πρωτότοκος τῆς ἀγενήτου φύσεως εἰκών, ὁ γνήσιος καὶ μονογενὴς τοῦ τῶν ὅλων θεοῦ υἱ. Eus.*d.e*.5.1(p.210.32; M. 22.349C); in Marcellus' theology πρὸ τοῦ αἰῶνος ἐθεμελίωσέν με, δηλονότι τὴν σάρκα, διὰ τὴν πρὸς τὸν ἀληθῶς υἱ. αὐτοῦ τὸν λόγον κοινωνίαν Marcell.*fr*.17 ap.Eus.*Marcell*.2.3(p.47.3; M.24.804A); εἰ τοίνυν τὸν πατέρα χωρίζοντα ἑαυτὸν τοῦ υἱ. πρὸς τὸν Μωσέα ταῦτ' εἰρηκέναι φήσει, οὐκ εἶναι τὸν υἱ. θεὸν ὁμολογήσει. πῶς γὰρ ἐγχωρεῖ τὸν λέγοντα, ἐγώ εἰμι ὁ ὤν, μὴ συνομολογεῖν ὅτι κατὰ ἀντιδιαστολὴν τοῦ μὴ ὄντος ὁ ὢν ἑαυτὸν εἶναί φησιν; εἰ δὲ τὸν υἱ. ὑποστάσει διῃρημένον τοῦτο φάσκοι λέγειν τό, ἐγώ εἰμι ὁ ὤν, ταὐτὸν αὖθις περὶ τοῦ πατρὸς λέγειν νομισθήσεται *ib*.58 ap.eund.*e.th*.2.19(p.123.14; M.24.944A); εἷς θεὸς καὶ ὁ τούτου μονογενὴς υἱ. λόγος, ὁ ἀεὶ συνυπάρχων τῷ πατρί...οὗτος υἱ., οὗτος δύναμις, οὗτος σοφία...ἀδιαίρετον εἶναι τὴν θεότητα τοῦ πατρὸς καὶ τοῦ υἱ. παρὰ τῶν θείων μεμαθήκαμεν γραφῶν. εἰ γάρ τις χωρίζει τὸν υἱ., τουτέστι τὸν λόγον, τοῦ παντοκράτορος θεοῦ, ἀνάγκη αὐτὸν ἢ δύο θεοὺς εἶναι νομίζειν...ἢ τὸν λόγον μὴ εἶναι θεὸν ὁμολογεῖν...ἐγὼ δὲ ...μεμάθηκα ὅτι ἀδιαίρετος καὶ ἀχώριστός ἐστιν, ἧ δύναμις, τοῦ πατρὸς ὁ υἱ. Marcell.*ep*.ap.Epiph.*haer*.72.2–3(p.257.21ff.; M.42.385Bff.); Sabellian view ascribed by Eus. to Marcell. τὴν ὑπόστασιν ἀναιρεῖν τοῦ υἱ., ἕνα δὲ θεὸν ὁρίζεσθαι, καὶ τοῦτον ἑαυτοῦ πατέρα καὶ αὖ πάλιν υἱ. ἀποκαλεῖν ἑαυτοῦ...τόν τε λόγον υἱ. εἶναι αὐτοῦ, οὐκ ἀληθῶς ὄντα υἱ. ἐν οὐσίας ὑποστάσει, κυρίως δὲ...ὄντα λόγον Eus.*e.th*.1.1(p.63.1; 829C); τὸν αὐτὸν εἶναι πατέρα καὶ υἱ. *ib*.1.3(p.64.1; 832D); Σαβέλλιος...τὸν πατέρα...υἱ. λέγειν ἐτόλμα *ib*.1.14(p.74.23; 853B); in Eusebius' view θεὸν πατέρα εἰδέναι μονογενοῦς υἱ. ... ἀληθῶς υἱ. ὄντος καὶ ζῶντος καὶ ὑφεστῶτος id.*Marcell*.1.1(p.4.7; 717B); τί οὖν ἐκώλυεν καὶ πρὸ τῆς τοῦ κόσμου συστάσεως υἱ. θεοῦ ζῶντα αὐτὸν ὁμολογεῖν; *ib*.2.4(p.57.11; 821A); εἷς δὲ καὶ μονογενὴς τοῦ θεοῦ υἱ., εἰκὼν τῆς πατρικῆς θεότητος, καὶ διὰ τοῦτο θεὸς id.*e.th*.1.2(p.63.29; 832C); ἐξ αὐτῆς τῆς προσηγορίας ὁ υἱ. τὴν πρὸς τὸν πατέρα φυσικὴν σχέσιν παρίστησιν *ib*.1.10(p.68.31; 841C); ὁ δὲ μονογενὴς υἱ. ὁρατὸς γενόμενος...ἕτερος ὢν δηλαδὴ παρὰ τὸν ἀόρατον θεὸν *ib*.1.20(p.83.25; 869C); υἱόν, ὡς ἂν εἰκόνα τοῦ πατρὸς ἐξ αὐτοῦ φύντα πάντη τε καὶ κατὰ πάντα ὁμοιότατον ὄντα τῷ γεγεννηκότι *ib*.2.14(p.115.20; 928D); ὁ υἱ. ἐκ τοῦ πατρὸς ἐκπορεύεσθαι λέγεται καὶ τὸ ἅγιον πνεῦμα ὁμοίως *ib*.3.4(p.159.4; 1005A); ἕν εἰσιν ὁ πατὴρ καὶ ὁ υἱ. κατὰ τὴν κοινωνίαν τῆς δόξης *ib*.3.19(p.180.30; 1044C); in Arian doctrine ξένος τοῦ υἱ. κατ' οὐσίαν ὁ πατήρ, ὅτι ἄναρχος ὑπάρχει... αὐτίκα γοῦν υἱ. μὴ ὄντος ὁ πατὴρ θεός ἐστι Ar.*Thal.fr*.2 ap.Ath.*syn*.15 (p.242.27; M.26.708A); οὐκ ἀεὶ ὁ θεὸς πατὴρ ἦν, ἀλλ' ὕστερον γέγονεν· οὐκ ἀεὶ ἦν ὁ υἱ., οὐ γὰρ ἦν πρὶν γεννηθῇ...οὐκ οἶδε τὸν πατέρα ἀκριβῶς ὁ υἱ. ... χάριτι λέγεται υἱ. καὶ δύναμις id.*fr*.3 ap.Ath.*Ar*.1.9(M.26. 29B); ἦν ποτε ὅτε οὐκ ἦν ὁ υἱ. καὶ...ἐκ τοῦ μὴ ὄντος ὁ υἱ. ἐστι id.ap. Ursac.et Valent.ap.Ath.*apol.sec*.58(p.138.15; M.25.353C); οὐκ ἦν ὁ υἱ. πρὶν γεννηθῆναι id.ap.Ath.*decr*.3(p.3.19; M.25.'429'(421)A); id.*ib*. 15(p.13.13; '449'(441)C); ἄλλην εἶναι τὴν τοῦ λόγου οὐσίαν, καὶ ἄλλο τὸ ἐκ τοῦ πατρὸς ἐν αὐτῷ φῶς, ἵν' ᾖ τὸ μὲν ἐν τῷ υἱ. φῶς ἓν πρὸς τὸν πατέρα, αὐτὸς δὲ ξένος κατ' οὐσίαν ὡς κτίσμα id.*ib*.24(p.20.19; 460A); ἐκ μέρους καὶ οὐ πλήρης γινώσκει ὁ υἱ. τὸν πατέρα id.ap.eund.*ep.Aeg. Lib*.16(M.25.576B); ἀμέτοχον κατὰ πάντα τοῦ πατρὸς τὸν υἱ. id.ap. eund.*Ar*.1.6(24B); τί μέμφεσθε Ἀλεξάνδρῳ...λέγοντι ἐκ τοῦ πατρὸς τὸν υἱ.;...λεχθείη ἂν καὶ ὁ υἱ. ἐκ τοῦ θεοῦ, οὕτως ὥσπερ καὶ τὰ πάντα λέγεται ἐκ τοῦ θεοῦ Geo.Laod.ap.Ath.*syn*.17(p.245.10; M.26.712C); κἂν πατέρα μόνον ὀνομάζωμεν, ἔχομεν τῷ ὀνόματι τοῦ πατρὸς συνυπακουομένην τὴν ἔννοιαν τοῦ υἱ. (πατὴρ γὰρ υἱοῦ λέγεται), κἄν τε υἱ. μόνον ὀνομάσωμεν, ἔχομεν τὴν ἔννοιαν τοῦ πατρός, ὅτι υἱ. πατρὸς λέγεται id.*ep. dogm*.ap.Epiph.*haer*.73.19(p.292.7; M.42.437C); in teaching of Ath. τὸν λόγον...ἀθάνατον ὄντα καὶ τοῦ πατρὸς υἱ. Ath.*inc*.9.1(M.25.112A); μήτε κτίσμα, ἢ ποίημα, μήτε τῶν γενητῶν ἐστιν ὁ...υἱ., ἀλλὰ γέννημα ἐκ τῆς οὐσίας τοῦ πατρός id.*decr*.3(p.3.11; '428'(420)D); εἰ τοίνυν υἱ., οὐ κτίσμα, εἰ δὲ κτίσμα, οὐχ υἱ. ... καὶ οὐκ ἂν εἴη αὐτὸς υἱ. καὶ κτίσμα, ἵνα μὴ καὶ ἐκ τοῦ θεοῦ καὶ ἔξωθεν τοῦ θεοῦ ἡ οὐσία αὐτοῦ νομίζηται *ib*.13(p.12.1; '448'(440)A); ἐκ τοῦ θεοῦ τὰ πάντα...ἀλλ' ἄλλως ἢ ὡς ἔστιν ὁ υἱ. *ib*.19(p.16.9; 449A); κτίσματα...οὐχ ὡς ὁ υἱ. εἰσιν ἐκ τοῦ θεοῦ· οὐ γὰρ γεννήματα, ἀλλὰ ποιήματά εἰσι τὴν φύσιν id.*syn*.35(p.262. 20; M.26.756A); ἐκ τῆς οὐσίας τὸν υἱ. ἐκ μὲν γὰρ τούτου τὸ γνήσιον ἀληθῶς υἱοῦ πρὸς τὸν πατέρα γνωρίζεται *ib*.36(p.263.3; 756C); τοῦ υἱοῦ μετέχει τὰ πάντα κατὰ τὴν...χάριν· καὶ φανερὸν...γίνεται, ὅτι αὐτὸς μὲν ὁ υἱ. οὐδενὸς μετέχει, τὸ δὲ ἐκ τοῦ πατρὸς μετεχόμενον, τοῦτό ἐστιν ὁ υἱ. id.*Ar*.1.16(M.26.45A); ἀπαθῶς καὶ ἀμερίστως τοῦ υἱοῦ πατήρ ἐστι *ib*.1.28(69A); οὐδὲν γὰρ πλέον ἡμῖν κέρδος...ἦν, εἰ μήτε ἀληθινὸς καὶ φύσει υἱ. τοῦ θεοῦ ὁ λόγος, μήτε ἀληθινὴ σάρξ ἦν, ἣν προσελάβετο *ib*.2.70(296C); ὁ μὲν υἱ. ἐν τῷ πατρί ἐστιν, ὡς λόγος ἴδιος καὶ ἀπαύγασμα αὐτοῦ *ib*.3.24(373B); ὁ...υἱ. ... προκόπτειν οὐκ εἶχε, τέλειος ὢν ἐν τῷ πατρί *ib*.3.52(432C); ἐπεὶ φύσει καὶ μὴ ἐκ βουλήσεώς ἐστιν ὁ υἱ., ἤδη καὶ ἀθέλητός ἐστι τῷ πατρί, καὶ μὴ βουλομένου τοῦ πατρὸς ἐστιν ὁ υἱ.; οὐμενοῦν· ἀλλὰ καὶ θελόμενός ἐστιν ὁ υἱ. παρὰ τοῦ πατρὸς *ib*.3.66(461C); τὸ πατὴρ ἀεὶ πατήρ, καὶ τὸ υἱὸς ἀεὶ υἱός id.*ep.Serap*.1.16(M.26.569B); μὴ κτίστην εἶναι τὴν οὐσίαν τοῦ υἱ., ἀλλ' ὁμοούσιον τῷ πατρί *ib*.2.5(616C); μένων οὖν ἐν τῷ εἶναι υἱ., πάντα ἐστὶν ὅσα ἐστὶν ὁ πατήρ. ... ἐκ τῆς κατὰ φύσιν κοινωνίας ἔχοντος τοῦ υἱ. τῆς πατρικῆς θεότητος τὸ ἀξίωμα...ἐξ αὐτῆς τοίνυν τῆς υἱοῦ προσηγορίας διδασκόμεθα, ὅτι τῆς φύσεώς ἐστι κοινωνὸς...ἐκ τῆς οὐσίας ἐκλάμψας ἀδιαστάτως Bas.*hom*.15.2(2.132A; M.31.468A); ἀληθῶς εἶναι τὸν μονογενῆ υἱ., οὐ κατὰ θέσιν εἰσποιηθέντα ψευδωνύμῳ πατρί, ἀλλὰ κατὰ φύσιν γεννητῶς ἐκ τοῦ ὄντος ὄντα Gr.Nyss.*Eun*.4(2 p.79.14; M. 45.653B); οὐκ ἄν τις...μίαν ἐνέργειαν...διδαχθεὶς τοῦ υἱοῦ καὶ τοῦ πνεύματος διαφοράν τινα φύσεως ὑπονοεῖ id.*or.dom*.3(p.62.11; M.44. 1160A); κύριος...τῶν ὅλων ἐστὶ κατὰ φύσιν ὁ υἱ.· καὶ συγκατάρχει παντὸς γενητοῦ τῷ...πατρί Cyr.*Is*.1.5(2.145A); υἱ. καλεῖ τοῦ πατρὸς μονογενῆ, τὸ ὁμοούσιον τῇ δόξῃ παραστῆσαι θελήσασα [sc. ἡ γραφή]... βουλόμενος ὁ λόγος μίαν οὐσίαν δεῖξαι πατρὸς καὶ υἱ., λέγει υἱ. τοῦ πατρὸς τὸν ἐξ αὐτοῦ γεννηθέντα μονογενῆ· εἶτα ἐπειδὴ γέννησις καὶ υἱὸς ἐφ' ἡμῖν ἔμφασιν παρέχει τοῦ...πάθους, τοῦτον τὸν υἱ. προσαγορεύει καὶ λόγον, τὸ ἀπαθὲς τῆς γεννήσεως...δηλῶν Thdot.Anc.*hom*.2.6(p.76. 32; M.77.1376C); υἱ. δὲ κυρίως εἴρηται, ὡς ἂν εἴποις οἷος. οἷος γὰρ ὁ πατὴρ τὴν οὐσίαν, τοιοῦτος ὁ μονογενὴς Anast.S.*hod*.2(M.89.56A);

μετὰ σὲ οὐκ ἔσται ἄλλος υἱ. τῷ πατρὶ ὁμοούσιος καὶ ὁμότιμος ‡Meth. *Sym.et Ann.*6(M.18.361B); **b.** title applied in virtue of eternal sonship, not of Inc. τῷ υἱ. ἀνθρώπου καὶ υἱ. θεοῦ Ign.*Eph.*20.2; οὐχὶ υἱ. ἀνθρώπου ἀλλὰ υἱ. τοῦ θεοῦ, τύπῳ δὲ ἐν σαρκὶ φανερωθεὶς *Barn.*12.10; ὡς βασιλεὺς πέμπων υἱὸν βασιλέα ἔπεμψεν *Diogn.*7.4; ὁ...κυρίως υἱ., ὁ λόγος πρὸ τῶν ποιημάτων...γεννώμενος,...Χριστὸς μὲν κατὰ τὸ κεχρῖσθαι Just.*2apol.*6.3(M.6.453A); υἱ. γεννητόν, μονογενῆ υἱ. ... σοφίαν καὶ λόγον καὶ δύναμιν θεοῦ, πρὸ αἰώνων ὄντα οὐ προγνώσει ἀλλ' οὐσίᾳ καὶ ὑποστάσει θεόν, θεοῦ υἱόν Hymen.*ep.*2(p.324.21); ἦν οὐχ ὡς ψιλὸς θεοῦ λόγος, ἀνυπόστατος...ἀλλ' ἦν καὶ προῆν ὡς μονογενὴς υἱ. Eus.*Marcell.*1.1(p.7.34; M.24.728A); ὁ δὲ μονογενὴς υἱ. ... προϋπάρχων ἦν οὐκ ἐν τῇ διανοίᾳ τοῦ πατρός...ἀλλ' ἐν τοῖς κόλποις αὐτοῦ id. *e.th.*1.20(p.83.25; M.24.869C); *ib.*(p.84.19; 872B); εἰ, ὅτε γέγονεν ἄνθρωπος, τότε υἱ. ... ἐλέχθη, πρὸ δὲ τοῦ γένηται ἄνθρωπος, υἱοὺς ἔλεγε τοὺς πάλαι λαοὺς ὁ θεός...δῆλόν ἐστιν, ὡς μετ' αὐτοὺς καὶ υἱ. ... ἐλέχθη. πῶς οὖν πάντα δι' αὐτοῦ; Ath.*Ar.*1.39(M.26.92C); ‡Ath.*Ar.* 4.23(p.69.20ff.; M.26.501C); ὁ ἄνω υἱ., κάτω παιδίον Acac.Mel.*hom.* (p.91.8; M.77.1469B); but ἦν αὐτὸς ὁ λόγος, ἐκ πνεύματος ἁγίου καὶ παρθένου ἕνα ⟨τέλειον⟩ υἱ. θεοῦ ἀπεργασάμενος...ὁ ἐκ πνεύματος καὶ παρθένου τέλειος υἱ. θεοῦ ἀποδεδειγμένος Hipp.*Noët.*4(p.241.27ff.; M. 10.809A); Sabellian doctrine ascribed to Callistus τὸν λόγον, ὃν υἱ. προσηγόρευε διὰ τὸ μέλλειν ἄνθρωπον γενέσθαι· καὶ τὸ καινὸν [MS κοινὸν] ὄνομα τῆς εἰς ἀνθρώπους φιλοστοργίας ἀνελάμβανεν υἱ. καλούμενος· οὔτε γὰρ ἄσαρκος καὶ καθ' ἑαυτὸν ὁ λόγος τέλειος ἦν υἱ., καίτοι τέλειος ⟨λόγος⟩ ὢν μονογενής, οὔθ' ἡ σὰρξ καθ' ἑαυτὴν δίχα τοῦ λόγου ὑποστῆναι ἠδύνατο...οὕτως εἷς υἱ. τέλειος θεοῦ ἐφανερώθη *ib.*15(p.259. 16; 824B); τὸ μὲν γὰρ βλεπόμενον, ὅπερ ἐστὶν ἄνθρωπος, τοῦτο εἶναι τὸν υἱ., τὸ δὲ ἐν τῷ υἱ. χωρηθὲν πνεῦμα τοῦτο εἶναι τὸν πατέρα id.*haer.*9. 12(p.249.3; M.16.3383C); in teaching of Paul. Sam.: τὸν μὲν υἱ. εἶναι Χριστόν, τὸν δὲ λόγον ἄλλον εἶναι Paul.Sam.*fr.*E 1(p.338.10); φησὶν μὴ δύο ὑφίστασθαι υἱ.· εἰ δὲ υἱ. ὁ...Χριστὸς τοῦ θεοῦ, υἱ. δὲ καὶ ἡ σοφία, καὶ ἄλλο μὲν ἡ σοφία, ἄλλο δὲ...Χριστός, δύο ὑφίστανται υἱ. id.*fr.*B 10 (p.333.1ff.); οὐ δίδως οὐσιῶσθαι ἐν τῷ ὅλῳ σωτῆρι τὸν υἱ. τὸν μονογενῆ, τὸν...ἀϊδίως ὑπάρχοντα Malch.*fr.*(p.337.10); ὁ Σαμοσατεὺς ἐφρόνει μὴ εἶναι πρὸ Μαρίας τὸν υἱ. Ath.*syn.*45(p.270.20; M.26.773B); in Marcellus' teaching οὐκ ἄν τις εἴποι υἱ. εἶναι τὸν σημαντικὸν καὶ ἐνεργητικὸν λόγον...τὸν μὴ ὑφεστῶτα λόγον τὴν σάρκα ἀνειληφέναι... φησιν καὶ τότε...γενέσθαι...υἱ. δεδοξασμένον...μὴ ὄντα πρότερον Eus. *Marcell.*2.1(p.32.3; M.24.777A); τὸ γὰρ μὴ λόγον εἶναι φῆσαι τὸν ἐξ αὐτοῦ προελθόντα καὶ τοῦτον εἶναι τὸν τῆς γεννήσεως ἀληθῆ τρόπον, ἀλλ' ἁπλῶς υἱ. μόνον, ἔμφασίν τινα τοῖς ἀκούουσιν ἀνθρωπίνης ὄψεως παρέχειν εἴωθεν Marcell.*fr.*31 *ib.*2.2(p.36.7; 785A); οὕτω δὴ τὸν υἱ. τοῦ θεοῦ ἀρνούμενος, τὸν ἐν τῷ θεῷ λόγον ποτὲ μὲν ἔνδον εἶναι ἐν τῷ θεῷ ἔφασκεν, ποτὲ δὲ προϊέναι τοῦ θεοῦ, καὶ ἄλλοτε πάλιν ἀναδραμεῖσθαι εἰς τὸν θεὸν καὶ ἔσεσθαι ἐν αὐτῷ Eus.*ib.*(p.107.8; 913C); **c.** inapplicable to H. Ghost, sonship being a peculiar relationship, not generic, hence Pneumatomachan argument refuted εἰ...ἐκ τοῦ πατρὸς ἐκπορεύεται, οὐκοῦν υἱ. ἐστι καὶ αὐτό, καὶ δύο ἀδελφοί εἰσιν αὐτό τε καὶ ὁ λόγος· καὶ εἰ ἀδελφός ἐστι, πῶς μονογενὴς ὁ λόγος; Ath.*ep. Serap.*1.15(M.26.568A); μανία...λέγειν ἐπὶ μὲν υἱοῦ ἀδελφόν, ἐπὶ δὲ πατρὸς τὸ πάππου ὄνομα *ib.*1.16(569B); *ib.*1.25(588C); *ib.*4.3(641A); ὡς γὰρ οὐκ ἔξεστιν ἄλλως εἰπεῖν περὶ αὐτοῦ, ἢ ὅτι πατήρ, οὕτως ἀσεβὲς ἐρωτᾶν, εἰ υἱ. ἐστι τὸ πνεῦμα, ἢ τὸ πνεῦμα υἱ. διὰ τοῦτο Σαβέλλιος ἀλλότριος τῆς ἐκκλησίας ἐκρίθη, τολμήσας εἰπεῖν ἐπὶ τοῦ πατρὸς τὸ υἱός, καὶ ἐπὶ τοῦ υἱοῦ τὸ τοῦ πατρὸς ὄνομα *ib.*4.5(647C); μήτε υἱὸν τὸ πνεῦμα, εἷς γὰρ ὁ μονογενής...κοινὸν γὰρ πατρὶ μὲν υἱ. καὶ ἁγίῳ πνεύματι, τὸ μὴ γεγονέναι, καὶ ἡ θεότης· υἱ. δὲ καὶ ἁγίῳ πνεύματι, τὸ ἐκ τοῦ πατρός. ἴδιον δὲ πατρὸς μέν, ἀγεννησία· υἱοῦ δέ, ἡ γέννησις· πνεύματος δέ, ἡ ἔκπεμψις Gr.Naz.*or.*25.16(M.35.1221B); Didym.(‡Bas.) *Eun.*5(1.305B; M.29.732C).

D. υἱὸς ἀνθρώπου; **1.** in Gnost. usage, v. ἄνθρωπος; **2.** of Christ; **a.** as Son of Man coming in judgement (cf. Dan.7:12ff., etc.) ὡς υἱ. γὰρ ἀνθρώπου ἐπάνω νεφελῶν ἐλεύσεται Just.*dial.*31.1(M.6.540B); υἱ. ἀνθρώπου καλεῖται, οὐχ ὡς ἕκαστος ἡμῶν ἐκ γῆς τὴν γέννησιν ἐσχηκώς, ἀλλ' ἐρχόμενος ἐπὶ τῶν νεφελῶν κρῖναι ζῶντας καὶ νεκρούς Cyr.H. *catech.*10.4; **b.** usu. of Christ as man or Christ's humanity; **i.** in gen. Χριστῷ...τῷ υἱ. ἀνθρώπου καὶ υἱ. θεοῦ Ign.*Eph.*20.2; *Barn.*12.10; τὸ γὰρ ὡς υἱὸν ἀνθρώπου εἰπεῖν, φαινόμενον μὲν καὶ γενόμενον ἄνθρωπον μηνύει, οὐκ ἐξ ἀνθρωπίνου δὲ σπέρματος ὑπάρχοντα δηλοῖ Just.*dial.*76.1(M.6.652C); cf. *propterhoc et dominus semetipsum filium hominis confitetur, principalem hominem illum, ex quo ea quae secundum mulierem est plasmatio facta est, in semetipsum recapitulans,* Iren.*haer.*5.21.1(M.7.1179B); λόγος γὰρ ἦν, πνεῦμα ἦν, δύναμις ἦν· ὃς τὸ καινὸν ὄνομα καὶ παρὰ ἀνθρώποις χωρητὸν ἀνελάμβανεν εἰς ἑαυτόν ,οὕτω καλούμενος ἀπ' ἀρχῆς υἱ. ἀνθρώπου διὰ τὸ μέλλον καίτοι μήπω ὢν ἄνθρωπος Hipp.*Noët.*4(p.243.10; M.10.809B); λόγον... υἱ. ἀνθρώπου διὰ τὴν ὑστάτην ἐνανθρώπησιν Eus.*h.e.*1.2.26(M.20. 68A); ref. Marcellan doctrine of end of Christ's kingdom τῆς δὲ σαρκὸς...ἐρήμου καταλειφθησομένης ὑπὸ τοῦ λόγου, ὡς μήτε τὸν υἱ. τοῦ θεοῦ τότε ὑφεστάναι, μήτε τὸν υἱ. τοῦ ἀνθρώπου ὃν ἀνείληφεν id. *Marcell.*2.1(p.32.14; M.24.777B); οὐ τὴν οὐσίαν τῶν ἀνθρώπων δηλοῖ τὸ υἱός, ἀλλὰ τὴν ἐξ ἀνθρώπων γέννησιν Adam.*dial.*5.4(p.182.10; M.11. 1837B); λέγω, υἱ. ἀνθρώπου, τὸ κατὰ σάρκα καὶ ἀνθρώπινον αὐτοῦ δεἰκνυσιν Ath.*ep.Serap.*4.20(M.26.669A); ἡ δὲ κένωσις οὐκ ἄνθρωπον, ἀλλὰ υἱ. ἀνθρώπου τὸν κενώσαντα ἑαυτὸν ἀπέφηνε κατὰ τὴν περιβολήν, οὐ κατὰ μεταβολήν Apoll.*fr.*124(p.237.31) ap.Thdt.*eran.*1(4.70); υἱ. δὲ ἀνθρώπου, καὶ διὰ τὸν Ἀδάμ, καὶ διὰ τὴν παρθένον, ἐξ ὧν ἐγένετο Gr.Naz.*or.*30.21(p.142.10; M.36.132B); υἱ. δὲ ἀνθρώπου ἐνταῦθα οὐ τὴν σάρκα ἐκάλεσεν, ἀλλ' ἀπὸ τῆς ἐλάττονος οὐσίας ὅλον ἑαυτὸν...ὠνόμασε Chrys.*hom.27.1 in Jo.*(8.154D); **ii.** υἱ. ἀνθρώπου or ἄνθρωπος said to be 'son by grace' (v. ἄνθρωπος), cf. οὐχ υἱὸν θεοῦ ἑαυτὸν ὀνομάζει, ἀλλὰ πανταχοῦ υἱ. ἀνθρώπου ἑαυτὸν λέγει, ἵνα διὰ τῆς τοιαύτης ὁμολογίας θέσει τὸν ἄνθρωπον διὰ τὴν πρὸς αὐτὸν κοινωνίαν υἱὸν θεοῦ γενέσθαι παρασκευάσῃ καὶ μετὰ τὸ τέλος τῆς πράξεως αὖθις, ὡς λόγος, ἑνωθῇ τῷ θεῷ Marcell.*fr.*34 ap.Eus.*Marcell.*2.2(p.42.33; M.24.796B); ταύτην [sc. τὴν σάρκα] γὰρ δούλου μορφὴν καὶ υἱ. ἀνθρώπου καλεῖν δεδίδακται Eus.*e.th.*1.2(p.63.19; M.24.832B); εἷς θεὸς ὁ πατήρ,...καὶ εἷς κύριος... Χριστός,...ὁ προὼν τοῦ θεοῦ μονογενὴς υἱ., καὶ τρίτος ὁ κατὰ σάρκα υἱ. ἀνθρώπου, ὃν δι' ἡμᾶς ἀνείληφεν ὁ υἱ. τοῦ θεοῦ *ib.*1.6(p.65.6; 836A); χάριτι υἱ. ὁ ἐκ Μαρίας ἄνθρωπος, φύσει δὲ ὁ θεὸς λόγος· τὸ μὲν χάριτι καὶ οὐ φύσει, τὸ δὲ φύσει καὶ οὐ χάριτι· ἀρκέσει τῷ ἐξ ἡμῶν σώματι, τὸ τῆς κατὰ χάριν υἱότητος...οὐδὲ αὐτὸς ὁ θεὸς λόγος βούλεται ἑαυτὸν τοῦ Δαβὶδ εἶναι υἱ., ἀλλὰ κύριον· τὸ δὲ σῶμα καλεῖσθαι τοῦ Δαβὶδ υἱ. ... οὐκ ἐφθόνησεν Diod.*synous.*1(M.33.1560C); cf.Thdr.Mops. *fr.inc.*12.1 (p.303.3; M.66.984D); *ib.*12.2(p.303.17; 985B); *ib.*12.8(p.306.2; 988A); ὁ μὲν γὰρ μονογενὴς...καθ' ἑαυτὸν υἱ. τοῦ θεοῦ ἐστι...ὃν δὲ ἔλαβεν ἄνθρωπον, οὐ φύσει θεὸς ὢν διὰ τὸν ἀναλαβόντα αὐτὸν ἀληθῶς θεοῦ υἱ. ὁμωνύμως αὐτῷ χρηματίζει Nest.*fr.*B 5(p.217.21)ap.Cyr.*Thds.*6(p.46. 4; 5^2.5D); cf.id.*fr.*C 10(p.269.17); *ib.*(p.275.6); doctrine attacked οὔτε γὰρ οἷόν τε ἦν τὸ ὅλον υἱ. ἀνθρώπου καλεῖσθαι καταβεβηκότα ἐξ οὐρανοῦ καὶ υἱ. θεοῦ γεννηθέντα ἐκ γυναικός, εἰ δύο φύσεων διαίρεσιν ἐπιδέχεται· ἀλλὰ τὸ μὲν καταβεβηκὸς...ἐκαλεῖτο ἂν υἱ. θεοῦ καὶ οὐχ υἱ. ἀνθρώπου, τὸ δὲ γεννηθὲν ἐκ γυναικὸς ἐκαλεῖτο ἂν υἱ. ἀνθρώπου καὶ οὐχ υἱ. θεοῦ· καὶ τοῦτο ἕπεται τῇ Παυλιανικῇ διαιρέσει Apoll.*ep.Dion.*4 (p.258.5; M.*PL.*8.929C); οὐδὲ δύο υἱ., ἄλλον μὲν υἱ. θεοῦ ἀληθινὸν καὶ προσκυνούμενον, ἄλλον δὲ ἐκ Μαρίας ἄνθρωπον μὴ προσκυνούμενον, κατὰ χάριν υἱ. θεοῦ γενόμενον,...ἀλλὰ τὸν ἐκ θεοῦ...ἕνα υἱὸν θεοῦ, καὶ τὸν αὐτὸν καὶ οὐκ ἄλλον καὶ ἐκ Μαρίας γεγεννῆσθαι κατὰ σάρκα id.*ep. Jov.*1(p.251.3; M.28.28A); Cyr.*ep.*4.6(p.28.6; 5^2.24C); *ib.*17.4(p.35.27; 5^2.70C); ὡς ἑνὶ Χριστῷ καὶ υἱ. τὰς ὑπὲρ ἀνθρώπου φύσιν προσνεμοῦμεν φωνάς· οἱ δὲ διϊστάντες εἰς δύο πρόσωπα δύο που πάντως ἐπινοοῦσιν υἱούς id.*expl.xii cap.*14(p.20.7; 6^1.150E); συκοφαντεῖς τοῦ λόγου τὴν κατὰ σάρκα γέννησιν, δύο πρεσβεύων υἱ. id.*Nest.*1.1(p.18.22; 6^1.10A); *ib.*2.8(p.46.27; 51C); id.*ep.*39.5(p.17.14; 5^2.106B); cf. *Symb.Chalc.* (p.129.16; H.2.456B); cf.Justn.*conf.anath.*3; but charge of teaching two sons rejected by Antiochenes οὐκ ἤδη δύο φαμὲν τοὺς υἱ., εἷς δὲ υἱ. ὁμολογεῖται δικαίως· ἐπείπερ ἡ τῶν φύσεων διαίρεσις ἀναγκαίως ὀφείλει διαμένειν, καὶ ἡ τοῦ προσώπου ἕνωσις ἀδιασπάστως φυλάττεσθαι Thdr.Mops.*fr.inc.*12.2(p.304.1; M.66.985B); Nest.*fr.*C 10(p.275.5)ap. Cyr.*Nest.*2.7(p.44.11; 6^1.47E); ὑπείληφα δυσσεβεῖς...τοὺς τὸν...υἱ. τοῦ θεοῦ...τὸν ἐνανθρωπήσαντα θεὸν λόγον, εἰς δύο μερίζειν ἐπιχειροῦντας υἱ. εἴπερ ἄρα τινές εἰσιν· ἐγὼ γὰρ οὐκ οἴομαι· ἀλλὰ ταύτην ἀεὶ τὴν συκοφαντίαν...οἱ τῆς Ἀρείου καὶ Εὐνομίου, καὶ μέντοι καὶ Ἀπολιναρίου συμμορίας ἀναίδην ἐξύφηναν Thdt.*ep.*143(4.1238).

E. υἱ. μονογενής as Valent. aeon, Iren.*haer.*1.8.5(M.7.532B).

F. (Manich.) of son of ἀγαθός (or ζῶν) πατήρ: τὸν υἱ. αὐτοῦ ἀπέστειλεν...ἐκ τῶν κόλπων εἰς τὴν καρδίαν τῆς γῆς Hegem.*Arch.*8 (p.11.12; M.10.1437C); ἔπεμψε τὸν υἱ. αὐτοῦ τὸν ἠγαπημένον εἰς σωτηρίαν τῆς ψυχῆς *ib.*(p.12.9; 1440A).

***υἱότης, ἡ,** *sonship*; **1.** of Son τὴν υἱ. τοῦ σωτῆρος ἡμῶν, οὐδεμίαν ἔχουσαν κοινωνίαν πρὸς τὴν τῶν λοιπῶν υἱ. Alex.Al.*ep.Alex.*7(p.24.7; M.18.557C); φωνὴ πατρικὴ...ἐμαρτύρει...τὴν υἱ. Eus.*fr.Lc.*9:34(M.24. 549C); id.*e.th.*1.10(p.69.3; M.24.841D); κοινὴ μὲν ἡ θεότης· ἰδιώματα δέ τινα πατρότης καὶ υἱ. Bas.*Eun.*2.28(1.265C; M.29.637B); ἵνα καὶ τοῦτο θεϊκὸν ἔχωσι, τὸ μοναδικόν, ὁ μὲν [sc. υἱός] τῆς υἱ., τὸ δὲ [sc. πνεῦμα] τῆς προόδου, καὶ οὐχ υἱότητος Gr.Naz.*or.*25.16(M.35.1221A); ὅταν οὖν ὅπερ ὡμολόγηται εἶναι θεοῦ, τοῦτο υἱοῦ φαίνεται ὄν, κοινωνία τῆς φύσεως δείκνυται, καὶ ἀληθὴς υἱ. Apoll.*Rom.*2:1(p.60.11); τεσσάρων δὲ ὄντων τῶν τῆς θεότητος ἡγεμονικῶν ὀνομάτων...κυριότητος καὶ θεότητος, υἱ. καὶ βασιλείας αἰωνίου ‡Chrys.*pasch.*6.4(p.167.18; 8. 270D); as Son in both natures ἵνα ἐν ἑνὶ καὶ τῷ αὐτῷ προσώπῳ ἀμφοῖν τῶν φύσεων συνελθουσῶν, ὧν εἰσιν αἱ υἱότητες, μὴ ἔχοι τις *θατέραν τελείαν υἱ., ἄνευ τῆς συνθεωρίας τῆς ἑτέρας φύσεως εἰδέναι· ὡς καὶ δύο υἱοὺς ἐκ τοῦδε ὁρᾶν ὑποκειμένους, ἀλλ' ἕνα τὸν ἐν δύο φύσεσι καὶ υἱ. Χριστόν· τοῦτο γὰρ τὸ τῆς ἑνώσεως...δώρημα πραγματωδῶς ἐστιν* Leont.H.*Nest.*3.1(M.86.1604B); *εἰ οὖν ὁ υἱὸς τῆς παρθένου ἐγένετο υἱὸς τοῦ θεοῦ χάριτι, δύο υἱ., ἄλλη τοῦ φύσει καὶ ἄλλη τοῦ χάριτι, καὶ οὐχ εἷς υἱός, ἀλλὰ δύο* Jo.D.*fid.Nest.*11(p.564); *ib.*53 (p.583); **2.** as relationship of men to God *εἰκὼν οὖν εἰκόνος οἱ ἅγιοι τυγχάνοντες, τῆς εἰκόνος οὔσης υἱοῦ, ἀπομάττονται υἱότητα* Or.*or.*22.4 (p.348.24; M.11.485B); through Christ *ὅμοιοι...τῇ υἱ., ἧς μεταλαμβάνομεν παρ' αὐτοῦ* Ath.*syn.*53(p.276.33; M.26.788C); by baptism, Chrys.*hom.2.7 in 2Cor.*(10.439B); in gen. *εἰς υἱ. κεκλημένους διὰ τῆς χάριτος* Cyr.*Os.*10(3.31C); **3.** as human relationship, ‡Just.*qu.et resp.*133(M.6.1385B); Jo.D.*inst.el.*3(M.95.101C); **4.** name given by Basilides to a cosmic principle *ἦν...ἐν αὐτῷ τῷ σπέρματι υἱ. τριμερής, κατὰ πάντα τῷ οὐκ ὄντι θεῷ ὁμοούσιος, γεννητὴ ἐξ οὐκ ὄντων. ταύτης τῆς υἱ. τῆς τριχῇ διῃρημένης τὸ μέν τι ἦν λεπτομερές, τὸ δὲ ⟨παχυμερές, τὸ δὲ⟩ ἀποκαθάρσεως δεόμενον. τὸ μὲν οὖν λεπτομερὲς εὐθέως...τὴν πρώτην καταβολὴν ὑπὸ τοῦ ⟨οὐκ⟩ ὄντος διέσφυξε καὶ ἀνῆλθε...ἡ δὲ παχυμερεστέρα ἔτι μένουσα ἐν τῷ σπέρματι, μιμητική τις οὖσα, ἀναδραμεῖν μὲν οὐκ ἠδυνήθη· πολὺ γὰρ ἐνδεεστέρα τῆς λεπτομερείας, ἧς εἶχεν ἡ δι' αὐτῆς υἱ. ἀναδραμοῦσα, ἀπελείπετο. ἐπτέρωσεν οὖν αὐτὴν ἡ υἱ. ἡ παχυμερεστέρα τοιούτῳ τινὶ πτερῷ, ὁποίῳ διδάσκαλος ὢν Πλάτων Ἀριστοτέλους ἐν Φαίδρῳ τὴν ψυχὴν πτεροῖ, καὶ καλεῖ τὸ τοιοῦτο Βασιλείδης οὐ πτερόν, ἀλλὰ πνεῦμα ἅγιον, ὃ εὐεργετεῖ ἡ υἱ. ἐνδυσαμένη καὶ εὐεργετεῖται. εὐεργετεῖ μὲν...ἀναφερομένη γὰρ ὑπὸ τοῦ πνεύματος ἡ υἱ. ὡς ὑπὸ πτεροῦ ἀναφέρει τὸ πτερόν, τουτέστι τὸ πνεῦμα κτλ.* Hipp.*haer.*7.22(p.198.25ff.; M.16.3306C); *μέχρις οὗ πᾶσα ἡ υἱ. ἡ καταλελειμμένη εἰς τὸ εὐεργετεῖν τὰς ψυχὰς ἐν ἀμορφίᾳ καὶ εὐεργετεῖσθαι διαμορφουμένη κατακολουθήσῃ τῷ Ἰησοῦ καὶ...ἀποκαθαρισθεῖσα* *ib.*7.26(p.205.21; 3318A); *ib.*10.14(p.274.24; 3430A).

***υἱοτικός**, *belonging to the Son*, Cyr.*resp.*(6^2.385E); *ib.*(387A).

υἱόω, *make into a son*, Leont.H.*monoph.*testimonia(M.86.1876C).

υἵωσις, ἡ, *making into a son*, Leont.H.*monoph.*testimonia(M.86.1876C).

ὑλάκτης, ὁ, *barker*, Gr.Nar.*carm.*2.1.11.1031(M.37.1100A).

ὑλακτικός, *disposed to bark, barking*, met. *οἱ γὰρ ὑ., οἱ κυνώδεις* Or.*dial.*12(p.148.7).

***ὑλάρχιος**, *controlling matter*; of Zeus, Synes.*insomn.*8(p.161.5; M.66.1296D).

***ὑλεῖται**, prob. for *ὀλεῖται* (*ὄλλυμι*) *destroy*, Gr.Naz.*carm.*2.2 (epigr.)62.4(M.38.115A).

ὕλη, ἡ, A. *material*; **1.** in gen.; lit., Clem.*paed.*2.12(p.228.14; M.8.541A); Gr.Nyss.*hom.opif.*2.1(M.44.133A); *τῇ...πρώτῃ ἡμέρᾳ ἐποίησεν ὁ θεὸς τὰς ὕ. τῶν κτισμάτων· ταῖς δὲ ἄλλαις ἡμέραις τὴν μόρφωσιν ...τῶν κτισμάτων* Sever.*creat.*1.4(M.56.433); Thdt.*qu.24 in 3Reg.*(1.470); met. *Παῦλος εἶχε τὴν ὕ. τοῦ ἐπαίρεσθαι αὐτὸν διὰ τὰς ὀπτασίας, διὰ τὰ ὁράματα* Or.*hom.12.8 in Jer.*(p.95.8; M.13.389C); *καθάπερ ὕ. τινά, καὶ ἀφορμὴν βλασφημίας* Gr.Nyss.*Eun.*1(1 p.97.24; M.45.329D); *ὕ. οἴκου, σκεύη καὶ βρώματα· ὕ. δὲ νοός, κενοδοξία καὶ ἡδονή* Marc. Er.*opusc.*2.106(M.65.945B); *ὕ. παθῶν φιλαργυρία* Thal.*cent.*1.34(M.91.1432A); **2.** of human body, *1Clem.*38.3; *νόσοι καὶ στάσεις τῆς ἐν ἡμῖν ὕ.* Tat.*orat.*16(p.18.7; M.6.841B); *ib.*6(p.6.31; 820A); ref. creation of primal man (Valent.) *οὐκ ἀπὸ ταύτης δὲ τῆς ξηρᾶς γῆς, ἀλλ' ἀπὸ τῆς ἀοράτου οὐσίας, ἀπὸ τοῦ κεχυμένου καὶ ῥευστοῦ τῆς ὕλης* Iren.*haer.*1.5.5(M.7.500A); *τὴν μὲν ψυχὴν ἀπὸ τοῦ δημιουργοῦ, τὸ δὲ σῶμα ἀπὸ τοῦ χοός, καὶ τὸ σαρκικὸν ἀπὸ τῆς ὕ., τὸ πνευματικὸν ἄνθρωπον ἀπὸ τῆς μητρὸς τῆς Ἀχαμώθ* *ib.*1.5.6(501B); *πρότερον μὲν ἐκτίσθη ὁ κατ' εἰκόνα, οὗ ὕλη οὐχ εὑρίσκεται· οὐδὲ γὰρ ἐξ ὕλης ὁ κατ' εἰκόνα* Or.*dial.*15(p.154.10); *μηδὲ τοῦ Ἀδάμ, ὡς θεοπλάστου, καὶ ἡμῶν, ὡς ἀνθρωπογεννήτων, ἓν ὑπέρκειται γένος...μήτε ὕ. κοινὴ αὐτοῦ τε καὶ ἡμῶν* †Apoll.*ep.Bas.*1(M.32.1104A); *παρὰ μὲν τῆς ὕ. λαβὼν τὸ σῶμα ἤδη προϋποστάσης, παρ' ἑαυτοῦ δὲ πνοὴν ἐνθεὶς* Gr.Naz.*or.*38.11(M.36.321C); of Christ's body (Valent.) *ὑλικὸν δὲ οὐδ' ὁτιοῦν εἰληφέναι αὐτόν· μὴ γὰρ εἶναι τὴν ὕ. δεκτικὴν σωτηρίας* Iren.*haer.*1.6.1(505A); *τὸ...γεγεννημένον ἀπὸ τῆς παρθένου σῶμα ἦν ἀπὸ τῆς ἀνθρωπίνης ὕ. συνεστηκός, δεκτικὸν τῶν ἀνθρωπίνων τραυμάτων* Or.*Cels.*3.25(p.222.5; M.11.952A); *ἡ...παρθενία...τὴν...τῆς σαρκὸς ἐχορήγησεν ὕ.* Leo Mag.*ep.*28.4(p.14.20; M.*PL.*54.768A); **3.** ref. eucharistic elements *οὐχ ἡ ὕ. τοῦ ἄρτου ἀλλ' ὁ ἐπ' αὐτῷ εἰρημένος λόγος ἐστὶν ὁ ὠφελῶν τὸν μὴ ἀναξίως τοῦ κυρίου ἐσθίοντα αὐτόν* Or.*comm.in Mt.*10.14(p.58.6; M.13.952A); Jo.D.*imag.*2.14(M.94.1300C); **4.** of material of an image *τὴν εἰκόνα τῆς Χριστοῦ σταυρώσεως ἰδόντες...προσκυνοῦμεν οὐ τῇ ὕλῃ ἀλλὰ τῷ εἰκονιζομένῳ* Jo.D.*f.o.*4.16(M.94.1172B); *σεβῶ τὴν ὕ. ... καὶ προσκυνῶ, δι' ἧς ἡ σωτηρία μου γέγονε. σεβῶ δέ, οὐχ ὡς θεόν, ἀλλ' ὡς θείας ἐνεργείας καὶ χάριτος ἔμπλεων. ἢ οὐχ ὕ. τὸ τοῦ σταυροῦ ξύλον;* id. *imag.*2.14(M.94.1300B); *αἱ ὕ. ... καθ' ἑαυτὰς ἀπροσκύνητοι, ἂν δὲ χάριτος εἴη πλήρης ὁ εἰκονιζόμενος, μέτοχοι χάριτος γίνονται* *Schol.* in Bas.*Spir.*18 ap.eund.*imag.*1(1264B); *οὐδὲ γὰρ ἡ ὕ. ἐστὶν ἡ προσκυνουμένη, ἀλλὰ τὸ πρωτότυπον* Thdr.Stud.*antirr.*3.1(M.99.421A).

B. *the material sphere, world of matter*; **1.** in gen. *τὸν τοῦ θεοῦ θέλοντα εἶναι κόσμῳ μὴ χαρίσησθε, μηδὲ ὕλῃ κολακεύσητε* Ign.*Rom.*6.2; opp. spiritual things, Tat.*orat.*13(p.14.22; M.6.833B); Athenag. *leg.*25.3(M.6.949C); *πᾶσαν τὴν περισπῶσαν αὐτὸν* [sc. the 'gnostic'] *ὕ. ὑπερηφανήσας τέμνει διὰ τῆς ἐπιστήμης τὸν οὐρανόν* Clem.*str.*7.13(p.59.2; M.9.516A); *αἱ ἐκείνου* [sc. *διαβόλου*] *ἐπιθυμίαι φρόνημα ὕλης εἰσὶ καὶ φθορᾶς* Or.*Jo.*22.22(20; p.354.9; M.14.620B); *χρὴ...τοὺς τῇ ἀσκητικῇ προσερχομένους ζωῇ πάσης ὕ. βιωτικῆς γυμνωθέντας ἐντὸς τοῦ κατὰ φιλοσοφίαν γενέσθαι βίου* Bas.*ascet.*2.1(2.323E; M.31.881B); *τῆς κοσμικῆς ὕ. τι πνέων* Gr.Naz.*or.*43.3(M.36.541A); *ἡ περὶ τὴν ὕ. φιλοτιμία τὰς σωτηρίας ἐνίκησε παραινέσεις* Nil.*exerc.*6(M.79.725A); *γίνεται ἔρημος ἡ ψυχὴ διὰ τὸ...ἀγαπῆσαι τὴν ὕ.* Esaias *or.*7.1(p.47); ref. material possessions *διαθήκην ὕλης οὐ γράφει, ζῶν καὶ φρονῶν αὐτὴν κατεπάλαισεν* Pall.*v.Chrys.*20(p.138.13; M.47.77); **2.** as realm of Devil and demons *ἐναντίον ἐστὶ* [sc. *τῷ ἀγαθῷ*] *τὸ περὶ τὴν ὕ. ἔχον πνεῦμα...γενόμενον...ὑπὸ τοῦ θεοῦ...καὶ τὴν ἐπὶ τῇ ὕ. καὶ τοῖς τῆς ὕ. εἴδεσι πεπιστευμένον διοίκησιν* Athenag.*leg.*24.3(M.6.945cf.); *ὁ...τῆς ὕ. ἄρχων* *ib.*25.1(949A); cf.Tat.*orat.*4(p.5.10; M.6.813B); *ἡ τῶν δαιμόνων ὑπόστασις οὐκ ἔχει μετανοίας τόπον, τῆς γὰρ ὕ. καὶ πονηρίας εἰσὶν ἀπαυγάσματα, ὕ. δὲ τῆς ψυχῆς κατεξουσιάζειν ἠθέλησεν* *ib.*15(p.17.2; 840A); *ἀποπεσὼν* [sc. Satan] *τῆς καθαρᾶς ζωῆς, πρὸ πάντων ἐνδεθῆναι ὕλῃ καὶ σώματι* Or.*Jo.*1.17(p.21.15; M.14.52B); *δαίμων ὕλας* Synes.*hymn.*3.90(p.9; M.66.1595).

C. *matter*; **1.** ref. Creation; **a.** theories of eternity of matter (Platonist) *ἄλλοι δέ, ἐν οἷς ἐστὶ καὶ ὁ...Πλάτων, ἐκ προϋποκειμένης καὶ ἀγενήτου ὕ. πεποιηκέναι τὸν θεὸν τὰ ὅλα διηγοῦνται· μὴ ἂν γὰρ δύνασθαί τι ποιῆσαι τὸν θεὸν εἰ μὴ προϋπέκειτο ἡ ὕ.* Ath.*inc.*2.3(M.25.100A); *ἀρχὴν ἁπάντων τὸν θεὸν καὶ τὴν ὕ. εἶναι βούλεται* [sc. Plato]... *ἀγέννητον τὴν ὕ. ἔφησεν εἶναι, ἵνα μὴ δόξῃ τὸν θεὸν τοῦ κακοῦ ποιητὴν εἶναι λέγειν* ‡Just.*coh.Gr.*20(M.6.276C); Marcionite *οἱ μὲν ἀπὸ Μαρκίωνος φύσιν κακὴν ἔκ τε ὕ. κακῆς καὶ ἐκ δικαίου γενομένην δημιουργοῦ* Clem.*str.*3.3(p.200.31; M.8.1113B); *τρεῖς τὰς τοῦ παντὸς ἀρχάς, ἀγαθόν, δίκαιον, ὕ.* Hipp.*haer.*10.19(p.280.1; M.16.3435C); Gnost. *ἐκ τοῦ φοβηθῆναι τῶν κακῶν ποιητὴν εἰπεῖν τὸν θεὸν σύγχρονον αὐτῷ δοῦναι τὴν ὕ. ἔδοξαν* Meth.*arbitr.*4(p.155.12; M.18.248C); Manich. *ἀρχὰς ἐτίθετο, θεὸν καὶ ὕ., εἶναι δὲ τὸν μὲν θεὸν ἀγαθόν, τὴν δὲ ὕ. κακόν* Alex.Lyc.*Man.*2(p.5.1; M.18.413B); **b.** orthodox reply *οὔτε γὰρ ἄναρχος ἡ ὕ. καθάπερ καὶ ὁ θεός, οὔτε διὰ τὸ ἄναρχον* [*καὶ αὐτή*] *ἰσοδύναμος τῷ θεῷ, γενητὴ δὲ καὶ οὐχ ὑπὸ ἄλλου γεγονυῖα, μόνον δὲ ὑπὸ τοῦ πάντων δημιουργοῦ προβεβλημένη* Tat.*orat.*5(p.6.12; M.6.817A); *πᾶσαν ἔστιν ἰδεῖν τοῦ κόσμου τὴν κατασκευὴν σύμπασάν τε τὴν ποίησιν γεγονυῖαν ἐξ ὕ. καὶ τὴν ὕ. δὲ αὐτὴν ὑπὸ τοῦ θεοῦ προβεβλημένην* *ib.*12(p.12.23; 829C); *τὸ μὲν...θεῖον ἀγένητον εἶναι καὶ ἀΐδιον, νῷ μόνῳ...θεωρούμενον, τὴν δὲ ὕ. γενητήν* Athenag.*leg.*4.2(M.6.897B); *ib.*15.2(920B); Thphl.Ant.*Autol.*2.4(M.6.1032B); Dion.Al.ap.Eus. *p.e.*7.19(333C; M.21.564A); *εἰ γὰρ οὐκ ἔστι τῆς ὕ. αὐτὸς αἴτιος, ἀλλ' ὅλως ἐξ ὑποκειμένης ὕ. ποιεῖ τὰ ὄντα, ἀσθενὴς εὑρίσκεται, μὴ δυνάμενος ἄνευ τῆς ὕ. ἐργάσασθαί τι τῶν γενομένων...καὶ πῶς ἔτι ποιητὴς καὶ δημιουργὸς ἂν λεχθείη ἐξ ἑτέρου τὸ ποιεῖν ἐσχηκώς, λέγω δὴ ἐκ τῆς ὕ.;* Ath.*inc.*2.4(M.25.100B); *εἰς νοῦν βαλόμενος καὶ ὁρμήσας ἀγαγεῖν εἰς γένεσιν τὰ μὴ ὄντα, ὁμοῦ τε ἐνόησεν ὁποῖόν τινα χρὴ τὸν κόσμον εἶναι, καὶ τῷ εἴδει αὐτοῦ τὴν ἁρμόζουσαν ὕ. συναπεγέννησε* Bas.*hex.*2.2(1.14B; M.29.33A); Gr.Naz.*or.*29.9(p.85.5; M.36.85A); *τὰ ὄντα πάντα οὐκ ἔκ τινος ὑποκειμένης ὕ. πρὸς τὸ φαινόμενον μετεσκευάσθη, ἀλλὰ τὸ θεῖον θέλημα ὕλη καὶ οὐσία τῶν δημιουργημάτων ἐγένετο* Gr.Nyss.*hom. in 1Cor.15:28*(M.44.1312A); *οὐκ ἀλλαχόθεν τὴν ὕ. λαβών, ἀλλ' ἅμα τοῖς εἴδεσι καὶ τὴν ὑποκειμένην ὕ. εἰς τὸ εἶναι παρήγαγεν* Proc.G.*Gen.* 1:1(M.87.37B); *τὰ μὲν οὐκ ἐκ προϋποκειμένης ὕ.· οἷον οὐρανόν, γῆν, ἀέρα, πῦρ, ὕδωρ· τὰ δέ, ἐκ τούτων τῶν ὑπ' αὐτοῦ γεγονότων· οἷον ζῷα, φυτά, σπέρματα* Jo.D.*f.o.*2.5(M.94.880A); Manich. argument refuted, id.*Man.*1.2(M.94.1508C); **c.** ref. days of Creation *πρώτῃ... ἡμέρᾳ, ἐν ᾗ ὁ θεὸς τὸ σκότος καὶ τὴν ὕ. τρέψας κόσμον ἐποίησε* Just. *1apol.*67.7(M.6.432A); **2.** ref. resurrection *διέλυσεν* [sc. *θεὸς τὸν ἄνθρωπον*] *εἰς ὕ. πάλιν ἵνα διὰ τῆς ἀναπλάσεως ἐκτακῶσι καὶ ἐξαφανισθῶσι πάντα τὰ ἐν αὐτῷ μωμήματα...τὸ δὲ ἐκεῖ ἀναμορφοποιηθῆναι τὴν ὕ. ἢ ἀνακοσμηθῆναι, τοῦτο ἐνταῦθα τὸ ἀναστῆναι* Meth.*res.*1.43(p.291.6; M.41.1113B); *οὔτε γὰρ εἰς ὕ. ἀργὴν καὶ τοιαύτην ἔτι κατάστασιν, οἷα καὶ πρὸ τῆς διακοσμήσεως ἦν, διαλυθὲν ἀναστοιχειωθήσεται τὸ πᾶν* *ib.*1.47(p.300.2; M.41.1120C); *εἴ τις λέγει ὅτι...οὐδὲν ἐν τῷ μέλλοντι τῶν τῆς ὕ. ὑπάρξει ἀλλὰ γυμνὸς ὁ νοῦς, ἀνάθεμα ἔστω* CCP(543)*anath.* 11; **3.** evil character of matter denied *τὸ δὲ τὴν ὕ. τοῖς θνητοῖς ἐμπολιτευομένην αἰτίαν εἶναι τῶν κακῶν καθ' ἡμᾶς οὐκ ἀληθές* Or.*Cels.*4.66(p.336.27; M.11.1133D); Meth.*arbitr.*11(p.174.6; M.18.260B);

Dion.Ar.*d.n.*4.28(M.3.729B); θεοῦ ποίημα τὴν ὕ. καὶ καλὴν ταύτην ὁμολογῶ Jo.D.*imag.*2.13(M.94.1297C); **4.** opp. form, ref. Christ's body θεὸν μὲν κατὰ τὸ εἶδος· ἄνθρωπον δὲ κατὰ τὴν ὕ. ‡Ath.*dial.Trin.* 4.9(M.28.1264C); **5.** ref. qualities τὰ πάντα δι' ὧν ἡ ὕ. συνίσταται...τὸ κοῦφον, τὸ βαρύ, τὸ ναστόν, τὸ ἀραιόν...τὴν περιγραφήν, τὸ διάστημα· ἃ πάντα μὲν καθ' ἑαυτὰ ἔννοιαί εἰσι ψιλαί...· οὐ γάρ τι τούτων ἐφ' ἑαυτοῦ ὕ. ἐστίν, ἀλλὰ συνδραμόντα πρὸς ἄλληλα, ὕ. γίνεται Gr.Nyss. *hex.*7(M.44.69C); **6.** met., *matter, substance*, ref. 1Cor.12:4–6 οἶμαι δὲ τὸ ἅγιον πνεῦμα τήν, ἵν' οὕτως εἴπω, ὕ. τῶν ἀπὸ θεοῦ χαρισμάτων παρέχειν τοῖς δι' αὐτοῦ καὶ τὴν μετοχὴν αὐτοῦ χρηματίζουσιν ἁγίοις, τῆς εἰρημένης ὕ. τῶν χαρισμάτων ἐνεργουμένης μὲν ἀπὸ τοῦ θεοῦ, διακονουμένης δὲ ὑπὸ τοῦ Χριστοῦ, ὑφεστώσης δὲ κατὰ τὸ ἅγιον πνεῦμα Or.*Jo.* 2.10(6; p.65.27; M.14.129A).

***ὑληγενής**, *born of the material world, worldly*, Synes.*hymn.*3.4 (p.7; M.66.1593).

ὑλικός, *of* or *pertaining to matter, material*;

A. in gen.; **1.** lit. οὐ δέεσθαι τῆς παρὰ ἀνθρώπων ὕ. προσφορᾶς...τὸν θεόν Just.*1apol.*10.1(M.6.340C); id.*dial.*134.5(M.6.788B); of disease, Tat.*orat.*18(p.19.29; M.6.845A); τὰς τοῦ σώματος ἡδονάς, καὶ τούτων γε τὰς ὑλικωτάτας, ὅσας ἁφή τε καὶ γεῦσις πορίζουσι Synes.*regn.*14 (p.30.4; M.66.1077A); ref. eucharist τὸ ἁγιαζόμενον βρῶμα...κατ' αὐτὸ μὲν τὸ ὕ. 'εἰς τὴν κοιλίαν χωρεῖ καὶ εἰς ἀφεδρῶνα ἐκβάλλεται' Or. *comm.in Mt.*10.14(p.58.3; M.13.952A); **2.** fig. ὁ τέταρτος ἀριθμὸς ὕ. τις καὶ σωματικὸς ὢν κακωτικός ἐστιν, ἐπεὶ τὰ γενικὰ σώματα τέσσαρά ἐστιν id.*fr.79 in Jo.*(p.546.24); **3.** of persons; **a.** *materially minded*, ‡Ath.*inst.mon.*2(M.28.848B); Gr.Naz.*or.*29.11(p.90.5; M.36. 89A); Gr.Nyss.*Eun.*8(2 p.191.7; M.45.785C); **b.** Gnost. (cf. ψυχικός), of the lowest of the three divisions of men, which is incapable of salvation τριῶν οὖν ὄντων, τὸ μὲν ὕ., ὃ καὶ ἀριστερὸν καλοῦσι...τὸ δὲ ψυχικόν, ὃ καὶ δεξιὸν προσαγορεύουσιν...τὸ δὲ πνευματικόν Iren.*haer.* 1.5.6(M.7.504A); κατ' εἰκόνα μὲν τὸν ὕ. ὑπάρχειν παραπλήσιον μέν, ἀλλ' οὐχ ὁμοούσιον τῷ θεῷ, καθ' ὁμοίωσιν δὲ τὸν ψυχικόν *ib.*1.5.5(500B); πολλοὶ μὲν οὖν οἱ ὕ., οὐ πολλοὶ δὲ οἱ ψυχικοί, σπάνιοι δὲ οἱ πνευματικοί. τὸ μὲν οὖν πνευματικὸν φύσει σῳζόμενον, τὸ δὲ ψυχικὸν αὐτεξούσιον ὂν...τὸ δὲ ὕ. φύσει ἀπόλλυται Clem.*exc.Thdot.*56(p.125.17f.; M.9. 685C); ἐκ τῆς ὕ. οὐσίας οὖν καὶ διαβολικῆς ἐποίησεν ὁ δημιουργὸς ταῖς ψυχαῖς τὰ σώματα...ὁ ἔσω ἄνθρωπος, ὁ ψυχικός, ἐν τῷ σώματι κατοικῶν τῷ ὕ., ὅ ἐστιν ὕ., φθαρτός, τέλειος ἐκ τῆς διαβολικῆς οὐσίας πεπλασμένος Hipp.*haer.*6.34(p.163.7,12; M.16.3246C); τοὺς δὲ ὕ. ... παντάπασιν ἀπόλλυσθαι καὶ μηδ' ὅλως σῴζεσθαι Epiph.*haer.*31.7 (p.397.4; M.41.488B); therefore Christ had no material body ἀπὸ μὲν τῆς Ἀχαμὼθ τὸ πνευματικόν, ἀπὸ δὲ τοῦ Δημιουργοῦ ἐνδεδύσθαι τὸν ψυχικὸν Χριστόν...καὶ ὑλικὸν δὲ οὐδ' ὁτιοῦν εἰληφέναι λέγουσιν αὐτόν· μὴ γὰρ εἶναι τὴν ὕλην δεκτικὴν σωτηρίας Iren.*haer.*1.6.1(505A); **4.** of spirits ὁ κόσμος...τὰ μέν τινα φαιδρότερα, τὰ δὲ [τινα] τούτοις ἀνόμοια κεκτημένος θελήματι τοῦ δημιουργήσαντος πνεύματος μετείληφεν ὑλικοῦ Tat.*orat.*12(p.13.11; M.6.832B); πνεῦμα ὁ θεός, οὐ διήκων διὰ τῆς ὕλης, πνευμάτων δὲ ὕ. καὶ τῶν ἐν αὐτῇ σχημάτων κατασκευαστής *ib.*4(p.5.3; 813A); ψυχὴ...τοῦ ὕ. προσλαβοῦσα καὶ ἐπισυγκραθεῖσα πνεύματος Athenag.*leg.*27.1(M.6.952D); Or.*Jo.*10.18(13; p.189.5; M. 14.337B); δισσὰ μὲν ἐν ἡμῖν λογισμῶν γένη, τὸ μὲν ἀπὸ τῆς ἐπιθυμίας τῆς ἐνθωπευούσης ἐν τῷ σώματι συνιστάμενον, ἥτις ἐξ ἐπιπνοίας... ἐγενήθη τοῦ ὕ. πνεύματος, τὸ δὲ ἀπὸ τοῦ νόμου τοῦ κατὰ τὴν ἐντολήν Meth.*res.*2.7(p.340.7; M.18.304C); θεοῦ κάθοδος ἐπ' ἄνθρωπον, τρόπαιον κατὰ τῶν ὕ. πνευμάτων id.*Porph.*1(p.504.22; M.18.400C).

B. theol.; **1.** opp. immaterial; **a.** denied of God δόγματα ἀσεβέστατα, τὸ διαιρετὸν καὶ ὕ. καὶ φθαρτὸν αὐτὸν εἶναι ὑπολαμβάνειν· πᾶν γὰρ σῶμα διαιρετόν ἐστι καὶ ὕ. καὶ φθαρτόν Or.*or.*23.3(p.351.6,7; M.11. 488D); id.*Jo.*13.21(p.245.8; M.14.433A); ref. Inc. πῶς τὸ τῆς θεότητος πῦρ σαρκὶ συνεπλάκη ὕ.; Eulog.*fr.Trin.*4.1(p.369); **b.** affirmed of this world ἐπεὶ δὲ τὰ πρῶτα καλῶς εἶχεν αὐτῷ, δεύτερον ἐννοεῖ κόσμον ὕ. καὶ ὁρώμενον Gr.Naz.*or.*38.10(M.36.321A); συντελέσας γὰρ ὁ κτιστὴς τὸν ἁπλοῦν καὶ νοερώτατον τῶν ἀοράτων δυνάμεων κόσμον, μεθ' ὃν τὸν ὕ. τοῦτον καὶ ὁρώμενον, τὸν ἐκ τεσσάρων στοιχείων συγκείμενον... ποιεῖ ζῷον...ἐξ ἀσωμάτου καὶ ἀθανάτου καὶ ἀφθαρτοῦ ψυχῆς, καὶ ἐξ ὕ. καὶ ὁρωμένου τετραστοίχου σώματος συγκείμενον ‡Gr.Nyss.*or.2 in Gen.1:26*(M.44.1328B); **c.** of material desires after Fall κενωθέντες [sc. men] τοῦ ἐμφυσήματος τοῦ θεοῦ, πληρωθέντες δὲ ἐπιθυμίας ὕ., ἣν ὁ πολύπλοκος ἐνέπνευσεν εἰς ἡμᾶς ὄφις Meth.*res.*2.6(p.339.16; M.18. 304B); **2.** opp. spiritual; **a.** ref. baptism θειοτέρου πυρὸς πᾶν ὕ. ἀφανίζοντος Or.*Jo.*6.32(17; p.141.29; M.14.256A); ἐξῆλθεν ἀπὸ σοῦ τὸ ἀκάθαρτον καὶ ὕ. πνεῦμα διωχθὲν τῷ βαπτίσματι Gr.Naz.*or.*40.35(M. 36.409A); **b.** man's concern to rise above material world in search of God γυμνὴν τῆς ὕ. δορᾶς γενομένην τὴν γνωστικὴν ψυχὴν ἄνευ τῆς σωματικῆς φλυαρίας καὶ τῶν παθῶν πάντων Clem.*str.*5.10(p.371.7; M. 9.104A); *ib.*5.3(p.338.26; 37B); Or.*Cant.*2(p.128.28; M.13.113A); Meth. *res.*2.2(p.333.3; M.18.300B); πολὺν παρέχει περισπασμὸν τῇ ψυχῇ ἡ τῶν ὕ. πραγμάτων φροντίς τε καὶ ἐπιμέλεια Bas.*ascet.*2.1(2.324A; M. 31.881C); οὐ...οἷόν τε ἄλλως ἐν περινοίᾳ θεοῦ γενέσθαι σώματος ὕ. καὶ δεσμίου νοῦ πάχος μὴ βοηθούμενον Gr.Naz.*or.*45.11(M.36.637B); *ib.*20. 10(M.35.1077A); ἐκβὰς ἕκαστος αὐτὸς ἑαυτοῦ καὶ ἔξω τοῦ ὕ. κόσμου γενόμενος, καὶ ἐπανελθὼν τρόπον τινὰ δι' ἀπαθείας εἰς τὸν παράδεισον, καὶ διὰ καθαρότητος ὁμοιωθεὶς τῷ θεῷ Gr.Nyss.*hom.1 in Cant.*(M. 44.772D); τίς...με...τῷ βαράθρῳ τῆς ὕ. ζωῆς συγκαλυφθέντα, ἐπὶ τὴν πρώτην ἕλκει μακαριότητα; id.*or.dom.*1(p.10.36; M.44.1125C); id. *v.Mos.*(M.44.341D); **c.** neut. plur. as subst., *material things* ὁ κεκαθαρμένος καὶ ὑπεραναβὰς πάντα ὕ. νοῦς, ἵνα ἀκριβώσῃ τὴν θεωρίαν τοῦ θεοῦ, ἐν οἷς θεωρεῖ θεοποιεῖται Or.*Jo.*32.27(17; p.472.29; M.14. 817A); ἐπαιρόμενοι...οἱ ὀφθαλμοὶ τοῦ διανοητικοῦ ἀπὸ τοῦ προσδιατρίβειν τοῖς γηΐνοις καὶ πληροῦσθαι φαντασίας τῆς ἀπὸ τῶν ὑλικωτέρων id.*or.*9.2(p.318.28; M.11.444C); διὰ ψευδοδοξίας καὶ τῆς πολλῆς περὶ τὰ ὕ. προσπαθείας οὐδὲν ἔτι τῶν μεγάλων θεωρεῖν ἠνέσχοντο †Bas.*Is.* 174(1.505C; M.30.409B); εἴσω γενόμενος ἀπὸ τῆς ὕλης καὶ τῶν ὕ. καὶ εἰς ἐμαυτὸν ὡς οἷόν τε συστραφεὶς Gr.Naz.*or.*28.3(p.24.11; M.36.29A); ἑαυτὴν οὖν ἡ θεία σοφία γινώσκουσα, γνώσεται πάντα, ἀΰλως τὰ ὕ., καὶ ἀμερίστως τὰ μεριστά Dion.Ar.*d.n.*7.2(M.3.869B); τὴν πολλὴν περὶ τὰ ὕ. σπουδήν Max.*ambig.*(M.91.1172D).

ὑλικῶς, *in a material way*, Gr.Naz.*or.*27.6(p.10.9; M.36.20A); Max.*ambig.*(M.91.1113D); ἢ τὴν κτίσιν ἢ τὴν ἁγίαν γραφὴν ὕ. τε καὶ χαμερπῶς ἐθεώρουν *ib.*(1160B).

ὗλις, ἡ, *mud*, plur., *clay*; in an oracle about Inc. ἔνδον ὕλεων οἰκεῖ, νηδύϊ κόρης δέμας ἑαυτῷ ἀναπλάττων *Pers.*(p.9.2).

ὕλλος, ὁ, *ichneumon*, Geo.Pis.*hex.*965(M.92.1568A).

***ὑλογεώδης**, *material and earthy* ὕ. ἄψυχοι οἱ θεοὶ χρηματίζοντες Jo.Mon.*hymn.Blas.*8(M.96.1405A).

***ὑλογραφ-έω**, *depict* διαφόρως αὐτὴν [sc. τὴν οἰκείαν Χριστοῦ εἰκόνα] ~ουμένην ὁρῶμεν Thdr.Stud.*antirr.*3.10(M.99.433A).

***ὑλογραφία**, ἡ, *encaustic painting*, Thphn.*chron.*p.373(M.108. 896A); *representation* in art φυγεῖν τὸ χαμερπὲς τῆς ὑλογραφίας Thdr. Stud.*antirr.*1.13(M.99.344C); ἄλλη...φύσις ὑλογραφίας, καὶ ἑτέρα τοῦ Χριστοῦ id.*ep.imag.*(M.99.501B).

***ὑλοδίαιτος**, *of material existence* ζωᾶς ὑλοδιαίτου Synes.*hymn.*3. 383(p.18; M.66.1599); *ib.*3.732(p.26; 1604).

ὑλοκοπέω, *cut wood*, Chrys.*hom.20.6 in 1Cor.*(10.177E).

ὑλομαν-έω, **1.** *be well wooded*, Clem.*str.*1.1(p.7.19; M.8.696A); **2.** *run to wood, grow rank, run riot* ~ούσαις ἀκάνθαις ‡Nil.*perist.*2.6 (M.79.816D); fig. νόμος, ~ούσης ψυχῆς...ἐκκόπτων τὰ ἀόρατα κακὰ μοσχεύματα ‡Chrys.*pasch.*6(p.137.12; 8.267B); ἀκάνθαις ~οῦσα [sc. ἡ καρδία] Gr.Nyss.*hom.2 in Cant.*(M.44.793A); δεῖ...ἠμᾶς ~εῖν, τουτέστι μὴ ἐπιδεικτικῶς πολιτεύεσθαι,...ἀλλ' ἔγκαρπον εἶναι τῷ ἀληθινῷ γεωργῷ τὴν ἐπίδειξιν τῶν ἔργων ταμιευόμενον Bas.*hex.*5.6(1.46B; M. 29.109A); γεωργεῖν ἐκείνους, ὅσοι ἔτι ἐν τοῖς τῆς κακίας ~οῦσιν ἔργοις Nil.*exerc.*31(M.79.760C); met., of power of evil, Gr.Nyss.*nativ.*(M.46. 1132C); of men, Pall.*h.Laus.*proem.(p.9.5; M.34.1002); Max.*opusc.* (M.91.69C).

ὑλομανής, *running to wood, rank* ὑλομανοῦς βοτάνης Eus.*Is.*9:18 (M.24.156D); of land, *overgrown with wood*, Cyr.*Is.*1.3(2.80C).

***ὑλομανία**, ἡ, *running to wood*; hence *rankness*, fig. τῆς ἐξ αὐτοῦ τοῦ Ἀρείου φυείσης ὕ. Epiph.*haer.*73.1(p.267.27; M.42.400D); met. ὦ ὕλη [sc. Devil] ὑλομανίας σύνοικε καὶ ἀπιστίας γεῖτον *A.Jo.*84(p.192. 21); φιλαυτίας καὶ ὑλομανίας καὶ φθόνου Ephr.2.101E.

***ὑλομενής**, sens. dub. perh. for ὑλομανής q.v., or ὑλογενής *born in the forest* ὄφρα δαείην ὑλομενῆ, πολύμορφον ἄγαν φύσιν Eudoc. *Cypr.*2.60(M.85.848B).

ὑλότομος, *hewn out of wood*, *Orac.Sib.*3.825.

ὑλώδης, **1.** *of matter, material* ὕ. καὶ παχεῖ σώματι *A.Jo.*93(p.196. 20); Gr.Nyss.*hom.4 in Cant.*(M.44.848D); *solid*, ‡Caes.Naz.*dial.*92 (M.38.956); neut. as subst., Gr.Nyss.*anim.et res.*(M.46.33C); **2.** *connected with matter, unspiritual*, Gr.Naz.*or.*45.16(M.36.645A); ὕ. τινὰς καὶ σωματικὰς ὑπολήψεις Gr.Nyss.*Eun.*10(2 p.244.14; M.45.848B); διὰ τῶν ὑλωδεστέρων ῥημάτων τὴν ψυχὴν παγιδεύσαντες Nil.*epp.*3.121 (M.79.440C).

ὑμεδαπός, *of your country, your*, Clem.*prot.*2(p.31.6; M.8.124B); *ib.*3(p.33.6; 128C).

ὑμένινος, *of skin* or *membrane*; neut. plur. as subst., of material of garments, Clem.*paed.*2.10(p.222.19; M.8.528A).

ὑμήν, ὁ, *thin skin, membrane*; esp. *virginal membrane, hymen*, Isid.H.*etym.*9.7.22; silk ὑφάνται, τοὺς σηρῶν ὑμένας ἐξεργαζόμενοι Isid.Pel.*epp.*1.403(M.78.408B); *parchment* ἐξ ὕ. λεπτῶν ῥιπίδιον *Lit.* ap.*Const.App.*8.12.3.

ὑμνέω, **A.** *sing in praise of*, or simply *praise*; **1.** God; of Christ, ref. Ps.21:23 μετ' αὐτῶν [sc. τῶν ἀποστόλων] διάγων ὕ. τὸν θεόν Just.

dial.106.1(M.6.724A); of seraphim, Thdt.*Is*.6:3(p.31.28; 2.208); of men, *T.Jos*.8.5; ref. Rom.8:26 οὐδὲ γὰρ δύναται ἡμῶν ὁ νοῦς... συμφώνως ὑ. τὸν πατέρα ἐν Χριστῷ, ἐὰν μὴ τὸ πνεῦμα...πρότερον αἰνέσῃ καὶ ὑ. τοῦτον Or.*or*.2.4(p.302.3; M.14.421B); ὑμνήσαντες τὸν ἁγιώτατον ὕμνον πρὸς τὸν θεὸν ἠγαλλιῶμεν *M.Tar*.11(p.476); *Const.App*. 7.47.2; Thdt.*Eph*.5:19(3.432); in the eucharist, Serap.*euch*.13.1 cit. s. δοξολογέω; τὰς ἱερὰς θεουργίας ὁ ἱεράρχης ὑμνήσας, ἱερουργεῖ τὰ θειότατα, καὶ ὑπ' ὄψιν ἄγει τὰ ὑμνημένα διὰ τῶν ἱερῶς προκειμένων συμβόλων Dion.Ar.*e.h*.3.2(M.3.425D); *Lit.Jac*.(p.198.21); in future, Iren.*haer*.5.13.3(M.7.1159A); τρισὶν ἁγιασμοῖς ὑ. τε καὶ ἁγιάζειν τὸν τρισυπόστατον μίαν θεότητα διδαχθήσεται τῶν ἀνθρώπων ἡ φύσις Max. *myst*.19(M.91.696C); of sun, moon, and stars, Or.*Cels*.8.67(p.283.22; M.11.1617C); **2.** Christ ψαλμοὶ δὲ ὅσοι καὶ ᾠδαὶ ἀδελφῶν ἀπ' ἀρχῆς ὑπὸ πιστῶν γραφεῖσαι τὸν λόγον τοῦ θεοῦ τὸν Χριστὸν ὑ. θεολογοῦντες †Hipp.*Artem*.ap.Eus.*h.e*.5.28.5(M.20.513A); ‡Cyr.H.*occurs*.1(M.33. 1189A); *M.Ign.Rom*.11; **3.** BMV, Mod.*dorm*.10(M.86.3304B); **4.** the dead ὃν πάτρη ὑμενεῖ ἐπευφη[μ]ῖ δὲ ἑ δῆμος *MAMA* 1 p.xxvi.

B. abs.; **1.** *sing a song of praise*, *A.Pil*.A 15.4(p.269); **2.** *sing a hymn* αἱ γὰρ ἄνω δυνάμεις ὑ., οὐ ψάλλουσιν Chrys.*hom.9.2 in Col*.(11. 392E); ref. hymn-singing by orthodox at CP in opposition to Arians who expressed by similar singing their resistance to attempts to deprive them of their churches οἱ δὲ ἀπὸ τῆς καθολικῆς, ἐξ αἰτίας τοιᾶσδε...ὑ. ἀρξάμενοι, καὶ εἰσέτι νῦν οὕτω διέμειναν Soz.*h.e*. 8.8.5(M.67.1537B).

***ὑμνηγορία, ἡ,** *hymnody*, Epiph.*haer*.80.9(p.493.28; M.42.769A).

***ὑμνηγόρος,** *hymning*, Epiph.*haer*.80.4(p.489.15; M.42.761D).

***ὕμνημα, τό,** *theme of hymn*, Gr.Naz.*carm*.1.1.3.5(M.37.408A).

ὕμνησις, ἡ, *lauding, praising*, Gel.Cyz.*h.e*.2.6.2(M.85.1232B).

***ὑμνήτειρα, ἡ,** fem. of ὑμνητήρ, Gr.Naz.*carm*.2.2(epitaph.)78.3(M. 38.51A).

ὑμνητήρ, ὁ, *one who hymns, singer of praises*, Gr.Naz.*carm*.1.1.8. 69(M.37.452A); *ib*.1.1.34.4(515A); *ib*.1.2.1.255(541A).

***ὑμνητικῶς,** *in praising*, Dion.Ar.*d.n*.1.4(M.3.589D).

ὑμνητός, *to be praised*; of God, *Const.App*.8.40.4.

ὑμνογράφος, *composing hymns* γλῶσσαν ὑ. Jo.Mon.*hymn.Geo*.9 (M.96.1400D); as subst., *composer of hymns, psalmist*; of David, ‡Gr.Nyss.*hom.6.45 in Jo*.(p.217.10); Sever.*appar*.6(M.65.20B); Nil. *epp*.4.40(M.79.569B).

[*]**ὑμνοδία, ἡ,** for ὑμνῳδία, Alex.Sal.*Barn*.4(p.450F).

ὑμνολογ-έω, 1. *sing songs of praise*; of heavenly beings, *T.Job* 51 p.136.7); at Nativity, Or.*hom.13 in Lc*.(p.92.25); *sing in praise*; of angels, ‡Felix III Papa *ep.Petr.1*(p.22.20; H.2.821E); of men, in Church ἀδιάκριτος ἡ παράστασις τῶν ∼εῖν εἰωθότων καὶ εἰς τοῦτο συνδεδραμηκότων Cyr.*ador*.12(1.445A); of deacons προστάττουσι διακεκραγότες ἐν ἐκκλησίαις, τότε μὲν ∼εῖν ὅτι προσήκει λαοῖς *ib*.13 (454B); in heaven, id.*Ps*.41:5(M.69.1004D); **2.** *praise in song*, or simply *praise*; of heavenly beings, *A.Thom*.A 6(p.109.9); ∼εῖται [sc. ὁ υἱός] μετὰ πατρός Cyr.*thes*.32(5^1.290C); of men, Nil.*epp*.4.39(M. 79.568C); ‡Proc.G.*Pr*.22:18(M.87.1445B); ‡Jo.D.*hom*.5(M.96.649D).

ὑμνολογία, ἡ, 1. *singing of praise*; of songs of angels, *T.Job* 48 (p.135.14); combined with those of men, *V.Zos*.15(p.105.36); of men, in gen. μίαν εὐχὴν καὶ μίαν ὑ. ἀναπέμπεσθαι τῷ θεῷ ἐν ταῖς ἐκκλησίαις συμβαίνει Or.*sel.in Pss*.proem.(M.12.1060D); ἐν ὀρθριναῖς ὑ. καὶ πρῶτος καὶ μέσος καὶ τελευταῖος ὁ Δαυίδ ‡Chrys.*hom*.1(13. 202D); to be used by monks to defeat Devil, Nil.*epp*.3.197(M.79. 476A); ref. specific forms: *psalm-singing* in eucharist, Dion.Ar.*e.h*. 3.5(M.3.432A); prob. creed προομολογηθείσης ὑπὸ παντὸς τοῦ τῆς ἐκκλησίας πληρώματος τῆς καθολικῆς ὑ. *ib*.3.2(425C); Trisagion, ‡Acac. CP *ep.Petr*.(p.18.8; H.2.844A); ‡Felix III Papa *ep.Petr*.1(p.20.11; H.2.821E); Tersanctus, Oecum.*Apoc*.19:6ff.(p.200); Max.*myst*.19 (M.91.696B); *hymn-singing*, Socr.*h.e*.6.8.4(M.67.689B); at translation of relics, *Chron.Pasch*.p.293(M.92.733B); **2.** *rendering of praise* by any means, *praise*, Eus.*Ps*.150 proem.(M.24.73C); Epiph.*haer*.76.30 (p.379.19; M.42.577B); to pagan gods, Cyr.*Is*.3.3(2.444D).

***ὑμνολογικός,** *hymn-singing*; of angels, ‡Ath.*comm.essent*.51(M. 28.77B); neut. as subst., ‡Ath.*def*.3(M.28.541B) ∞ Anast.S.*hod*.2(M. 89.64B); plur., *hymns* ἀπ' οὐρανοῦ τῶν ἀγγέλων εὐφημούντων τὰ ὑ. Germ.CP *or*.1(M.98.228A).

ὑμνολόγος, *hymn-singing*; of angels, Leont.H.*Nest*.1.19(M.86. 1480C); as subst., *singer of hymns of praise*, Dion.Ar.*d.n*.3.2(M.3. 684A); Jo.D.*hymn.dorm.BMV* 3(M.96.1364A); of David, *psalmist*, Didym.*Trin*.2.11(M.39.661A).

ὑμνοποιός, *composing hymns*; as subst., of David, *psalmist*, Thdt.*eran*.2(4.77); id.*affect*.2(p.59.12; 4.751).

ὑμνοπολεύω (ὑμνοπολέω), *sing* or *compose hymns of praise* ὑμνοπολεύσω Synes.*hymn*.8.50(M.66.1613); *sing* or *compose hymns in praise of* οὔνομα...ὑμνοπολεύσω Apoll.*met.Ps*.9:3(M.33.1321B) al.; ὑμνοπόλει Χριστοῖο θεουδέες Paul.Sil.*ambo*.30(M.86.2253A).

ὑμνοπόλος, *singing hymns*; as subst., *singer* or *composer of hymns*; of angels, Gr.Naz.*carm*.1.1.8.63(M.37.451A); *ib*.1.2.1.85 (528A); of man, Synes.*hymn*.6.25(p.41; M.66.1609).

ὕμνος, ὁ, A. *song of praise*; **1.** def. and descriptions οἱ μὲν ὕ. δύναμιν καὶ θειότητα καταγγέλλουσι τοῦ θεοῦ, καὶ εἴη ἂν ὁ ἐπιστήμων τοῦ θεολογεῖν ἐν ὕ. πνευματικοῖς Or.*comm.in Eph*.5:19(p.565); ὁ δ' ὕ., αἶνος ἐμμελὴς Gr.Naz.*carm*.1.2.34.144(M.37.956A); cf. αἶνός ἐστιν ὕ. εἰς θεὸν ἐπὶ τῇ θεωρίᾳ τῶν γεγονότων Or.*sel.in Ps*.148:1(M.12.1677D); dist. from ψαλμός, ᾠδή, προσευχή, and αἴνεσις: ὕ. δέ, ἡ ἐπὶ τοῖς ὑπάρχουσιν ἡμῖν ἀγαθοῖς ἀνατιθεμένη τῷ θεῷ εὐφημία Gr.Nyss.*Pss. titt*.B 3(M.44.493B); **2.** uses of term; **a.** in gen. (where form is unspecified), *T.Gad* 7.2; ἐκείνῳ δὲ εὐχαρίστους ὄντας διὰ λόγου πομπὰς καὶ ὕ. πέμπειν Just.*1apol*.13.2(M.6.345B); τῶν εὐχαριστιῶν ἢ ὕ. καὶ αἴνων Gr.Thaum.*pan.Or*.3(p.7.21; M.10.1060A); **b.** of psalms φησὶν ἐν ὕ. ὁ προφήτης [Ps.98:6f.] Or.*engast*.2(p.284.16; M.12.1016A); *A.Mt*.25(p.253.9); ψάλλε τοὺς ὕ. Meth.*symp*.4.2(p.47.15; M.18.89A); *Const.App*.1.5.2; of certain partic. psalms ὕ. καλεῖ καὶ τοῦτον τὸν ψαλμὸν ἡ ἐπιγραφή Thdt.*Ps*.111:1(1.1403); τοῖς ὕ. ὁ ψαλμὸς ἐγκατείλεκται, σκιαγραφίαν τινὰ ἔχων τῶν δεσποτικῶν παθημάτων *ib*. 54:1(958); **c.** of other types of song or rhythmic recitation ψαλμοὶ δὲ καὶ ὕ. παρὰ τὴν ἑστίασιν πρό τε τῆς κοίτης Clem.*str*.7.7(p.37.5; M.9. 469B); ἀναλάβωμεν ὕ. ἀντὶ τυμπάνων, ψαλμῳδίαν ἀντὶ τῶν αἰσχρῶν λυγισμάτων Gr.Naz.*or*.5.35(M.35.709B); οἱ ψαλμοὶ πάντα ἔχουσιν, οἱ δὲ ὕ. πάλιν οὐδὲν ἀνθρώπινον· ὅταν ἐν τοῖς ψαλμοῖς μάθῃ, τότε καὶ ὕμνους εἴσεται, ἅτε θειότερον πρᾶγμα Chrys.*hom.9.2 in Col*.(11.392E); for examples cf. *A.Jo*.94(p.197.17); Meth.*symp*.11.2(p.131.12; M.18. 208B); τὸν ὕ. Ἀθηνογένους Bas.*Spir*.73(3.62B; M.32.205A) ref. *Hymn.vesp*.(Routh *RS* 3 p.299); composed and sung in opposition to those of Arians during dispute at CP λαμπρότεροι οἱ τοῦ ὁμοουσίου ὕ. ἐν ταῖς νυκτεριναῖς ὑμνολογίαις ἐδείκνυντο Socr.*h.e*.6.8.6(M.67. 689B); Soz.*h.e*.8.8.4(M.67.1537A); v. ἀντίφωνος, ἐπινίκιος, τρισάγιος, χερουβικός; **d.** of other words of praise, Thdt.*Dan*.2:19ff.(2.1084); ὕμνοις τὸν εὐεργέτην ἠμείψατο, βοῶν [1Tim.1:12] id.*1Tim*.1:11(3. 642); **e.** of praise of God by heavenly beings τί δὲ ἔργον τῶν ἐπουρανίων δυνάμεων ὑπάρχει; ὕ. ἄληκτος ‡Ath.*comm.essent*.52(M. 28.77B); τίς ὁ ὕ. τῶν ἄνω, τί λέγει τὰ χερουβίμ, ἴσασιν οἱ πιστοί Chrys. *hom.9.2 in Col*.(11.393D); of seraphim, Thdt.*Is*.6:3(p.31.24; 2.207); of angels at Nativity, Euther.*confut*.11(M.28.1373A); **f.** met. καλὸς ὕ. τοῦ θεοῦ ἀθάνατος ἄνθρωπος, δικαιοσύνῃ οἰκοδομούμενος, ἐν ᾧ τὰ λόγια τῆς ἀληθείας ἐγκεχάρακται Clem.*prot*.10(p.76.23; M.8.224A); **3.** in gen.; effect of hymns, ref. Ac.16:25, Chrys.*hom.in Rom.8:28* (3.153Dff.); ὕ. δὲ ἱερὸν τίκτει μὲν εὐλάβεια ψυχῆς, τρέφει δὲ συνειδὸς ἀγαθόν, δέχεται δὲ εἰς τὰ ταμιεῖα τῶν οὐρανῶν ὁ θεός id.*ordin*.1.1(1. 438A); attacked by Devil τὸν ὕ. καὶ τὴν δοξολογίαν εἰς βλασφημίαν μεθίστησιν Nil.*epp*.3.197(M.79.476A); to cease at coming of antichrist, Rom.Mel.3.268(*SBBAW* 1898^2 p.173); occasions: at eucharist, Eus.*d.e*.1.10(p.49.9; M.22.92D); at services for the dead ἧς ἐκυρὸς...ὕμνους σεμνοὺς ἀναπέμπει W. M. Ramsay, *Studies in the history and art of the eastern provinces of the Roman Empire* (London, 1906), 22.11(p.225); ἡ γὰρ τιμὴ τῷ τετελευτηκότι, οὐ θρῆνοι, ...ἀλλ' ὕ. καὶ ψαλμῳδίαι Chrys.*hom.62.5 in Jo*.(8.374E); υἱ]ὸς ὄχ' ἄριστος ἐν ὕμνοις...τεῖσεν ἀπὸ σφετ[έρης τέχνης *JRS* 14 p.55; at daybreak and during work, Bas.*ep*.2.2(3.72B; M.32.225C); at offices ἑωθινοί τε ὕ. ἐν αὐτῇ τῇ ἁγίᾳ ἐκκλησίᾳ διηνεκεῖς γίνονται καὶ προσευχαὶ ἑωθιναί Epiph.*exp.fid*.23(p.524.9; M.42.829A); Niceph.Ur.*v.Sym*.110 (M.86.3089D); ἑσπερινοὺς ὕ. *ib*.127(3104C); as grace of monks after meals, Chrys.*hom.55.5 in Mt*.(7.560E); in honour of BMV, ‡Meth. *Sym.et Ann*.10(M.18.373B); *ib*.14(381B); mystical significance ὕ. δὲ ἢ αἶνος τῇ ᾠδῇ συμμιγνύμενος παράγγελμα γίνεται, μὴ πρότερον ἡμᾶς κατατολμᾶν τῶν περὶ θεοῦ νοημάτων, πρὶν ἂν τὸν βίον ἡμῶν τῆς τοιαύτης παρρησίας ποιήσωμεν ἄξιον Gr.Nyss.*Pss.titt*.B 3(M.44.496B).

B. *praise* σοῦ γάρ ἐστιν δόξα αἰώνιος, ὕμνος *Hom.Clem*.3.72; ὁ γὰρ θεός, κἂν μηδεὶς ὑμνεῖν ἐθέλει, αἰώνιον ἔχει τὸν ὕ. καὶ διαρκῆ Thdt.*Ps*. 110:10(1.1402); οὐκ ὄντος υἱοῦ τοῦ πατρός, οὐδὲ πατρὸς τοῦ υἱοῦ, φυλαττόντων δὲ τὰ οἰκεῖα τῶν ὕ. εὐαγῶς ἑκάστῃ τῶν ἐναρχικῶν ὑποστάσεων Dion.Ar.*d.n*.2.5(M.3.641D).

ὑμνῳδέω, *sing a song of praise*; to God, Gr.Nyss.*Apoll*.47(M.45. 1237C).

ὑμνῳδία, ἡ, 1. *singing of praise, hymning* πανηγύρεις,...ὑ. νυκτεριναί Bas.*ep*.243.2(3.374A; M.32.905B); Gr.Naz.*carm*.1.2.10.650 (M.37.727A); *singing* ἐν τῇ τῶν ψαλμῶν ὑ. Nil.*Eulog*.30(M.79.1133B); ἵνα καὶ τὴν ἑσπερινὴν καὶ τὴν ἑωθινὴν ὑ. κοινῇ προσφέρωσι τῷ θεῷ Thdt.*h.rel*.5(3.1164); taught by H. Ghost to Jews and gentiles, id. *Ps*.117 proem.(1.1428); hence *praising, praise*, id.*1Tim*.1:16(3.644);

2. *song of praise, psalm*, Ath.*Ar*.1.36(M.26.85C); Thdt.*haer*.5.1(4.379); of *Benedicite*, Gr.Nyss.*Apoll*.46(M.45.1233C); of Tersanctus, Chrys.*hom.in Mt*.7:14(3.29D); of Trisagion, ‡Felix III Papa *ep.Petr*.1(p.22.27; H.2.824A); in gen.: at funerals ὑ. καὶ εὐχαὶ καὶ ψαλμοί Chrys.*pan.Bern*.3(2.638E); in heaven, Cyr.*Ps*.41:5(M.69.1004D).

ὑμνῳδός, 1. *singing songs of praise*, Gr.Naz.*carm*.1.1.32.35(M.37.513A); ἀγγέλων στάσιν...θείας ὑ. ἀξίας *ib*.1.2.10.925(747A); **2.** as subst.; **a.** *composer of* non-Christian *hymns, poet*, Gr.Thaum.*pan.Or*.13(p.29.6; M.10.1088A); **b.** *singer* or *composer of songs of praise* to God, *ib*.16(p.37.16; 1100A); of David, *psalmist*, Or.*Cels*.8.32(p.247.16; M.11.1564B); Ath.*Ar*.1.46(M.26.105C); Didym.*Trin*.3.3(M.39.824A); **c.** *giver of praise, praiser*; denied of Son and H. Ghost, Gr.Naz.*or*.34.10(M.36.249C); of human reason τὸν δὲ λόγον ἑρμηνευτὴν τῶν νοηθέντων...καὶ ὑ. Max.*ambig*.(M.91.1116D).

***ὕννη, ἡ,** *plough*, Chrys.*hom*.52.4 *in Mt*.(7.534C).

***ὕννυς, ὁ,** = foreg., Ephr.1.64E.

***ὑπαβουλεύω,** s.v.l. † *refrain from scheming*; prob. for ὑπὸ βούλησιν ἦν: λύκος μετὰ προβάτων εἰρήνευε· καὶ ὄφις ὑπηβούλευσεν Bas.Sel.*or*.2.1(M.85.41B).

ὑπαγόρευσις, ἡ, 1. *dictation*; hence *composing, writing* ὑ. τῆς ἐπιστολῆς Or.*ep*.1.16(M.11.85C); ὑ. τῶν εἰς τὸ εὐαγγέλιον id.*Jo*.32.1(p.425.7; M.14.740B); ταχύγραφοι μὴ παρόντες τοῦ ἔχεσθαι τῶν ὑ. ἐκώλυον *ib*.6.2(1; p.108.6; 201A); *edition*, Socr.*h.e*.2.1.5(M.67.185B); **2.** *injunction, bidding* ὑ. ... τῶν πρακτέων Clem.*paed*.1.3(p.95.3; M.8.260A).

ὑπαγορεύ-ω, 1. *dictate*; of oral tradition τὸ δὲ κατὰ Λουκᾶν εὐαγγέλιον ὑπηγορεύθη μὲν ὑπὸ Παύλου...συνεγράφη δὲ καὶ ἐξεδόθη ὑπὸ Λουκᾶ ‡Ath.*synops*.76(M.28.433A); hence *compose, compile*, Or.*Jo*.6.2(1; p.108.10; M.14.201A); *ib*.20.1(p.327.1; 572D); Socr.*h.e*.2.1.4(M.67.185B); *publish*, Eus.*ep.Caes*.5(p.45.5; M.20.1540C); **2.** *state* τῆς εὐσεβοῦς διδασκαλίας ~ούσης ἐκ τοῦ πατρὸς εἶναι τὸν υἱόν *ib*.(p.45.11; 1541A); **3.** *suggest*; more definitely, *enjoin*, Just.*1apol*.2.1(M.6.329A); of doctors, *prescribe*, Chrys.*hom*.11.5 *in 1Cor*.(10.93D); **4.** *communicate, explain* τὸ θεῖον εὐαγγέλιον ~ων αὐτῷ †Jo.D.*B.J*.19(M.96.1025D).

ὑπαγορία, ἡ, 1. *composition, compilation* ἐμὴ μέν ἐστιν ἡ ὑ. ἡ δὲ ὑ. ἴση ἐστὶν τῶν ἁγίων πατέρων Eut.ap.CCP(448)(*ACO* 2.1.1 p.141.12, v.l. ἡ ἔκθεσις, ἡ δὲ ὑ. H.2.164B); Anast.S.*hod*.10(M.89.188C); **2.** *style*, Justn.*monoph*.(M.86.1128C); **3.** *annotation, commentary, explanation*, Eust.*engast*.1(p.16.22; M.18.613B).

***ὑπαγροικίζω,** *show some rusticity of speech*, Gr.Nyss.*Eun*.12(2 p.295.3; M.45.908D).

ὑπάγω, 1. *lead* or *bring under*; hence, *lean on* a stick, Dor.*doct*.1.14(M.88.1636B); **2.** *suspect* cf. Ἐμπεδοκλέα μέν, καὶ Πυθαγόραν... μάγοις ὡμιληκότας οὔπω ὑπῆχθαι τέχνῃ Philostratus ap.Eus.*Hierocl*.44(540D; M.22.860A); **3.** *apply* remedies, Euther.*confut*.2(M.28.1314B); **4.** intrans., *go*, *T.Lev*.13.3(vv.ll. εἰσέρχεται, ἀπέρχεται); Herm.*vis*.4.2.5; Or.*Jo*.32.3(p.430.25; M.14.748D).

ὑπαγωγή, ἡ, 1. *leading into captivity*; of Jews, †Gregent.*disp*.(M.86.632C); *subjection*, Max.*ambig*.(M.91.1305D); **2.** *leading astray*; ref. Fall, ‡Caes.Naz.*dial*.166(M.38.1128); **3.** *depression*; of land, Philost.*h.e*.3.9(p.38.27; M.65.493A).

ὑπαίθριος, *under the sky, in the open air*; neut. as subst., *open enclosure, court*, Evagr.*h.e*.1.14(p.24.15; M.86.2461A).

ὕπαιθρος, *under the sky, in the open air*; neut. as subst. ἐν ὑ., *in the open air*; τὸ ὑ. *open enclosure, court*; of a church, Marc.Diac.*v.Porph*.84; of the Temple, Thdt.*qu. in 2Par*.(1.588).

ὑπαινίττομαι, 1. *allude to* in met. or obscure language οὕσπερ [sc. Jews]...ὑ. λέγων [Mt.19:14] Or.*fr*.114 *in Lam*.(p.275.25; M.13.657B); *indicate*, exeg. Mt.6:7 ὑ. ... ἀπαγορεύων τὴν βαττολογίαν... μὴ χρῆναι...αἰτεῖν τὰ ῥέοντα Chrys.*hom.in Mt*.7:14(3.26E); ὅτι... ἡγουμένων δίχα...διατελέσουσι καιροὺς...ὑ., τοῖς τῶν ζῴων ἀβασιλεύτοις παρεικάζων αὐτούς Cyr.*Os*.37(3.68D); *figure, symbolize* λαμπρότης [sc. of the lily] τὴν τῆς σωφροσύνης μαρμαρυγὴν ὑ. Gr.Nyss.*hom*.4 *in Cant*.(M.44.840C); **2.** *glance at, give consideration* to νεανίας... ὑπηνίττετό πως εἰς τὸ χρῆναι λοιπὸν τὴν ὑπὸ θεῷ δουλείαν εἰσέρχεσθαι Cyr.*Jo*.3.5(4.307E).

ὑπαίρω, v.l. for ὑπεραίρω, Gr Nyss.*Eun*.10(2 p.232.3; ὑπάρας M.45.833A).

ὑπακοή, ἡ, *obedience*;

A. def. and characteristics; **1.** in gen. ἡ ὑ. δὲ οὐ τὸ σωματικὸν κάλλος συνίστησιν, ἀλλὰ τὸ ψυχικόν Chrys.*exp.in Ps*.44:12(5.179A); ἡ ὑ. πρῶτον ἐν πάσαις ταῖς εἰσαγώγοις ἀρεταῖς ὑπάρχειν ἔγνωσται καλόν Diad.*perf*.41(p.46.21); ἡ ὑ. τοῦ ὄντος θελήματός ἐστιν ὑ.· οὐ τοῦ μὴ ὄντος ὑποταγή· οὐ γὰρ τὸ ἄλογον ὑπήκοον ἢ παρήκοον λέξομεν *Schol*.3 in Jo.Clim.*scal*.4(M.88.729B); ἐντολῆς ὑ., νεκρῶν ἐστιν ἀνάστασις Thal.*cent*.4.48(M.91.1464A); **2.** esp. ref. monasticism ἡ...τελεία ὑ. τῶν ὑποχειρίων πρὸς τὸν καθηγούμενον ἐν τούτῳ δείκνυται, ἐν τῷ μὴ μόνον τῶν ἀτόπων κατὰ τὴν συμβουλὴν τοῦ προεστῶτος ἀπέχεσθαι, ἀλλὰ μηδὲ αὐτὰ τὰ ἐπαινετὰ χωρὶς τῆς ἐκείνου γνώμης ποιεῖν Bas.*ascet*.2.2(2.324E; M.31.884B); for women ἡ ἀδελφότης τὰ παραγγέλματα τῆς προκαθηγουμένης ἀδιακρίτως δεχέσθω, πᾶν τὸ συμβουλευόμενον ἐπιτελοῦσα, μὴ ἐκ λύπης ἢ ἐξ ἀνάγκης, ἵνα γένηται αὐτῇ ἔμμισθος ἡ ὑ. *ib*.(326E; M.888C); ὑ. οὖν ἐστιν ἀδιάκριτος πειθώ· ἵνα τις τὸ προσταχθὲν ἀλύπως ἐπιτελέσῃ. ὑ. ἐστι παντελὴς ὑποταγὴ τοῦ ἰδίου θελήματος ἐστερημένη, καὶ μόνῳ τῷ τοῦ ἐπιστατοῦντος νεύματι ἀταράχως πρὸς πρᾶξιν κινουμένη ἐν πάσαις ἐντολαῖς Ant.Mon.*hom*.39(M.89.1556A); ὑ. ἐστιν ἄρνησις ψυχῆς οἰκείας παντελὴς διὰ σώματος ἐπιδεικνυμένη...ἢ τάχα τὸ ἔμπαλιν, ὑ. ἐστὶ νέκρωσις μελῶν ἐν ζώσῃ διανοίᾳ. ὑ. ἐστιν ἀνεξέταστος κίνησις, ἑκούσιος θάνατος, ἀπερίεργος ζωή,...ὑ. ἐστι μνῆμα θελήσεως, καὶ ἔγερσις ταπεινώσεως...ὑ. ἐστιν ἀπόθεσις διακρίσεως ἐν πλούτῳ διακρίσεως Jo.Clim.*scal*.4(M.88.680A); *ib*.(680C); *ib*.(717D); **3.** scope, ref. Phil.2:8 μέχρι πόσου ὑπακούειν δεῖ ἐν τῷ κανόνι τῆς πρὸς θεὸν εὐαρεστήσεως. ὁ ἀπόστολος ἔδειξε, προθεὶς ἡμῖν τὴν τοῦ κυρίου ὑ. Bas.*reg.br*.116(2.455D; M.31.1161B); *ib*.119(456C; M.1161D–1164A).

B. obedience to God; **1.** in OT; Abraham its prototype as having left his country, *1Clem*.10.2; and sacrificing his son, *ib*.10.7; Ephr.1.4C; ‡Bas.*const*.22.2,3(2.571A,572A; M.31.1404C,1405C); ‡Chrys.*Abr*.1(2.742C); also Enoch, *1Clem*.9.3; **2.** Christian; Christ's obedience to Father, ref. 1Cor.15:28, Eus.*e.th*.3.15(p.172.22; M.24.1029A); ὑπακούει, οὐκ ἀναγκαστὴν ὑ. ἔχων, ἀλλ' αὐτοπροαίρετον εὐπείθειαν Cyr.H.*catech*.15.30; μετὰ τὴν ἐνανθρώπησιν, διὰ τὴν ὑ., τὸ ὑπὲρ πᾶν ὄνομα τῷ υἱῷ...ὁ πατὴρ ἐχαρίσατο Didym.(‡Bas.)*Eun*.4(1.289A; M.29.693B); not, as says Eun., in his divine nature but as man, Gr.Nyss.*Eun*.2(2 p.350.25; M.45.528C); opp. man's, esp. Adam's, disobedience, cf.Clem.*paed*.1.2(p.93.6; M.8.256A); τὴν παρακοὴν τῶν ἀνθρώπων διὰ τῆς ἰδίας ὑ. ἐξιώμενος Gr.Nyss.*Eun*.2(2 p.351.8; 528D); ὁ κύριος...ὑπήκουσε...ἵνα τὸ τῆς ἀνθρωπείας παρακοῆς ἔγκλημα διὰ τῆς αὐτοῦ ἐκλύσας ὑ. εἰς τὴν μακαρίαν...τοὺς ἐν ὑ. ζήσαντας ἐπαναγάγοι ζωήν Diad.*perf*.41(p.48.5f.); Max.*ascet*.1(M.90.912B); analogous to rel. of BMV to Eve, Epiph.*haer*.78.18(p.469.16; M.42.729A); as model of Christian obedience αὐτὸν [sc. Christ] ὑποτάσσεσθαι τῷ πατρὶ λέγει, τὴν πάντων ἀνθρώπων ὑ. διὰ τῆς τοῦ υἱοῦ τοῦ μετεσχηκότος τῆς ἀνθρωπότητος πρὸς τὸν πατέρα ὑποταγῆς αἰνισσόμενος Gr.Nyss.*Eun*.1(1 p.78.16; 309B); τὴν πρὸς ἀλλήλους ὑ. ἐξ ἐκείνου μαθόντες, ὃς 'ὑπήκοος μέχρι θανάτου γέγονε...' τὸ μέτρον τῆς ὑ. ἕως τοῦδε τοῦ κινδύνου νομοθετῶν Nil.*praest*.66(M.79.1060A); which is also contrasted with Adam's sin ὥσπερ γὰρ διὰ βρώματος καὶ παρακοῆς ἐξεβλήθη ὁ Ἀδὰμ ἐκ τοῦ παραδείσου, οὕτως πάλιν διὰ νηστείας καὶ ὑ. ὁ θέλων εἰσέρχεται εἰς τὸν παράδεισον Ath.*virg*.6(p.40.4; M.28.257B); cf.Dor.*doct*.1.7(M.88.1625B); Ant.Mon.*hom*.38(M.89.1552B).

C. in rel. to other virtues; **1.** connected with πίστις: ἡ τοῦ λόγου ὑ., ἣν τὴν πίστιν φαμέν Clem.*paed*.1.13(p.150.26; M.8.372B); cf.*ib*.1.9(p.140.10; 352C); id.*str*.1.10(p.31.3; M.8.744B); τὴν ψυχὴν...εὑρήσει κατὰ τὴν ὑ. τὴν ἀναζήσασαν μὲν τῇ πίστει *ib*.4.6(p.260.14; 1240B); Marc.Er.*opusc*.2.5(M.65.932A); as title of book by Melito περὶ ὑπακοῆς πίστεως Eus.*h.e*.4.26.2(M.20.392A); **2.** and with humility ἐν οὖν τῇ ὑ. καὶ τῇ μιμήσει τὸ ταπεινὸν ἐπιδεικνύσθω...ἡ γὰρ ἀντιλογία τὸ αὐτοκρατορικὸν...δείκνυσι. φυσιώσεως οὖν μᾶλλον καὶ καταφρονήσεως ἀπόδειξιν ἔχει, ἀλλ' οὐχὶ ταπεινότητος καὶ τῆς ἐν πᾶσιν ὑ. Bas.*reg.fus*.31(2.374E; M.31.993C); ἡ ταπεινοφροσύνη γεννᾷ τὴν ὑ. Dor.*doct*.1.6(M.88.1625A); obedience produces humility, Jo.Clim.*scal*.4(M.88.705D); leading to ἀπάθεια: ἐξ ὑ. ταπείνωσις, ἐκ ταπεινώσεως ἀπάθεια ...οὐκ οὐδὲν τὸ κωλῦον εἰπεῖν, ὅτι ἐξ ὑ. ἀπάθεια *ib*.(709D).

D. effects: salvation (life, grace, etc.) ὑ., δι' ἧς ἡ σωτηρία Clem.*str*.6.12(p.481.20; M.9.320C); δι' ὑ. ἐδικαιοῦτο *ib*.4.23(p.315.9; M.8.1360B); ἡ ὑ. τῆς θείας προστάξεως ζωὴν...χαρίζεσθαι πέφυκεν Nil.*epp*.1.241(M.79.172A); Jo.Clim.*scal*.4(M.88.720D); indwelling of Christ 'ζῇ δὲ ἐν ἐμοὶ Χριστὸς' διὰ τῆς τῶν ἐντολῶν ὑ. Clem.*str*.3.18(p.245.18; M.8.1209B); ψυχή, ἐν ᾗ διὰ τῆς τῶν παραγγελμάτων ὑ. τεμενίζεται... λόγος αἰώνιος *ib*.7.3(p.12.6; M.9.421A); illumination, *ib*.3.5(p.216.20; M.8.1148B); Thdr.Stud.*or*.11.10(M.99.812D); various virtues ἡ ὑ. πρῶτον ἐν πάσαις ταῖς εἰσαγωγικαῖς ἀρεταῖς ἔγνωσται ὑπάρχειν καλόν· καὶ τὴν μὲν οἴησιν ἀθετεῖ, τὴν δὲ ταπεινοφροσύνην τίκτει. ἀρχὴ γὰρ γίνεται τῆς εἰς Χριστὸν ἀγάπης Ant.Mon.*hom*.39(M.89.1556B); *Schol*.63 in Jo.Clim.*scal*.4(M.88.752A); power over demons, Nil.*epp*.1.307(193C); answer to prayer ἡ ὑ. ἀντὶ ὑπακοῆς ἐστιν. εἴ τις ὑπακούει τῷ θεῷ, ὁ θεὸς ὑπακούει αὐτόν *Apophth.Patr*.(M.65.301B); discernment γέγονε διακριτικὸς...ἐκ τῆς ἄκρας αὐτοῦ ὑ. Jo.Clim.*scal*.4(721D).

E. obedience to superiors as fundamental virtue of religious life, which itself is called τῆς ὑ. δρόμος Jo.Clim.*scal*.4(M.88.717C); **1.** modelled on obedience due to God ὥσπερ γὰρ ὁ θεός, πατὴρ ἁπάντων...ἀκριβεστάτην παρὰ τῶν αὐτοῦ θεραπόντων ἀπαιτεῖ τὴν εὐπείθειαν, οὕτω καὶ ὁ πνευματικὸς ἐν ἀνθρώποις πατὴρ πρὸς τοὺς τοῦ θεοῦ νόμους τὰς ἑαυτοῦ διατάξεις ἁρμόζων, ἀναμφίλεκτον τὴν ὑ. ἀπαιτεῖ ‡Bas.*const.*19(2.563D; M.31.1388B); scriptural basis for this being Mt.10:40, Lc.10:16, *ib.*22.2(2.570E–571A; M.1404B); **2.** superior to ascetic practices ὁ τῆς ὑ. μισθὸς μείζων τοῦ κατὰ τὴν ἐγκράτειάν ἐστι κατορθώματος Bas.*ascet.*2.2(2.325A; M.31.884C); ἐπειδὴ γὰρ εἴωθεν ὁ πονηρὸς ἐνοχλεῖν τοῖς ἐν ὑ., καὶ ἐξουθενεῖν τὸν κόπον αὐτῶν, ὡς μήτε νηστείαν μήτε ἄσκησιν ἐχόντων ἀκριβῆ...λέγει πατήρ, ὅτι οὐδέν εἰσι ταῦτα πρὸς τὴν ὑ. *Schol.*9 in Jo.Clim.*scal.*4(M.88.732A); *Schol.*97 *ib.*(761A); **3.** perfect ὑ. exercised also in absence of superior, Jo.Clim.*scal.*4(705D); **4.** not dangerous εἰ δὲ λέγοι βλάπτεσθαι ταῖς προόδοις...ταῖς διὰ τὰς ἀναγκαίας χρείας τοῦ κοινοῦ γενομέναις ὁ ἀσκητής, καὶ διὰ τοῦτο παραιτοῖτο τὴν πρόοδον, οὔπω τῆς ὑ. τὴν ἀκρίβειαν κατενόησεν...βλεπέτω τοίνυν τὰ ὑποδείγματα τῶν ἁγίων, πῶς τὴν ὑ. ἐτελείωσαν, πρὸς οὐδὲν τῶν οὕτω δυσηνύτων ἐπιταγμάτων οὐδὲ κατὰ μικρὸν ἀντειπόντες...καὶ παιδευέσθω τὸ τῆς ὑ. τέλειον...καὶ ἐπὶ πᾶσιν ...οἷς ἂν ὁ νοῦς ὀκλάσῃ περὶ τὴν τελείαν ὑ., ἢ σατανᾶς ἐμποδίζῃ...τὸν θεὸν ἱκετεύωμεν, καὶ αἰτώμεθα δοθῆναι ἡμῖν τῶν κατορθωμάτων εὐμάρειαν ‡Bas.*const.*26.1(2.576A–C; M.31.1416A–C); unless anything unlawful be commanded δεῖ...τὸν μὲν προεστῶτα τοῦ κοινοῦ...μετὰ πολλῆς δοκιμασίας ἐγχειρισθῆναι τὴν φροντίδα ταύτην...τοὺς δὲ ὑπηκόους, τῆς εὐταξίας φυλαττομένης, καὶ τῆς ὑ. τὸ ἴδιον μέτρον γνωριζούσης, μεμνῆσθαι τοῦ κυρίου λέγοντος· 'τὰ πρόβατα τὰ ἐμὰ τῆς φωνῆς μου ἀκούει' καὶ προειπόντος, 'ἀλλοτρίῳ δὲ οὐ μὴ ἀκολουθήσουσιν'...ὥστε εἰ μέν τί ἐστι κατ' ἐντολὴν τοῦ κυρίου κατευθυνόμενον, κἂν θανάτου ἀπειλὴν ἔχῃ, ὑπακούειν χρή· εἰ δέ τι παρ' ἐντολήν ἐστιν...κἂν ἄγγελος...ἐπιτάσσῃ...οὐδαμῶς ἀνέχεσθαι χρή Bas.*reg.br.*303(2.522E; M.31.1297B); **5.** effects: producing grace, Esaias *cap.spir.*6(M.40.1208A); having power to deliver from danger of (physical) death, Dor.*doct.*1.15(M.88.1637A); purifying soul, Thal.*cent.*4.55(M.91.1464C); **6.** obedience to brethren conditional ὅπου δοκεῖ καλὸν εἶναι τὸ πρᾶγμα, ἐκεῖ δεῖξον τὴν ὑ. τοῖς ἀδελφοῖς Bars.*resp.*6(M.88.1817D); **7.** temptations against it provoked by demons, *Schol.*17 in Jo.Clim.*scal.*4(M.88.733B).

F. ref. human free will ἀπείθεια ἐφ' ἡμῖν, ὥσπερ καὶ ἡ ὑ. ἐφ' ἡμῖν Clem.*str.*2.13(p.145.7; M.8.997B); *ib.*2.15(p.146.26; 1000C); *ib.*7.2(p.8.8; M.9.412C).

G. in rel. to scripture τὰς γραφὰς ἐπιγνόντες πολιτευσώμεθα καθ' ὑπακοήν Clem.*str.*1.10(p.30.21; M.8.744A).

H. interprn. of Bethany as οἶκος ὑπακοῆς, Or.*Jo.*6.40(24; p.149.25; M.14.269B); id.*fr.80 in Jo.*(p.547.19); id.*hom.37 in Lc.*(p.217.14).

I. liturg., *response*; cf. early non-liturg. use, ref. φωνῆς ἐκ τῶν οὐρανῶν...ὑ. ἠκούετο ἀπὸ τοῦ σταυροῦ ὅτι ναί *Ev.Petr.*9(Vaganay p.302), though possibly influenced by liturg. use; semi-liturg., in psalm of virgins ὑ. opp. ψαλμός, Meth.*symp.*11(p.131.16; M.18.208C); liturg., words or verses from Psalms repeated by congregation θέλεις ψάλλειν ὑ. ἔχοντας τὸ Ἀλληλούϊα Ath.*ep.Marcell.*25(ἐπακοήν M.27.37B); Chrys.*exp.in Ps.*41:2(5.131B); later of parts of liturgy sung after Little Entrance, corresponding to Graduale of the Roman Mass, still called 'responsorium' e.g. in Dominican rite, so *Lit.Chrys.*(p.369.1).

ὑπακουστέον, *one must obey*, Clem.*paed.*2.10(p.208.9; M.8.497B).

***ὑπακουστικός**, *obedient*, Anast.S.*serm.imag.*3(M.89.1180A).

ὑπακού-ω, **A.** *obey*; **1.** of obeying God; **a.** in gen., *1Clem.*9.1; *ib.*58.1; *2Clem.*19.3; Clem.*paed.*1.9(p.142.6; M.8.255B); Gr.Thaum.*pan.Or.*19(p.39.21; M.10.1104A); Ath.*inc.*30.4(M.25.148C); id.*v.Anton.*7(M.26.853B); **b.** as cause of salvation ὁ Χριστὸς...ἔμελλε τοῖς ∼ουσιν αὐτῷ αἴτιος σωτηρίας αἰωνίου γίνεσθαι Or.*fr.88 in Jo.*(p.552.19); Dor.*doct.*1.6(M.88.1624D); **c.** motives ὁ δὲ ψιλῇ κλήσει καθὸ κέκληται ὑ. οὔτε διὰ φόβον οὔτε διὰ ἡδονὰς ἐπὶ τὴν γνῶσιν ἵεται Clem.*str.*4.22(p.312.22; M.8.1356A); **d.** effects ψυχὴ...ἡ ταῖς ἐντολαῖς ὑπακηκουῖα, μάρτυς ἐστὶ καὶ βίῳ καὶ λόγῳ *ib.*4.4(p.255.15; ἐπ- 1228C); ἐὰν ὑ., τὸ φῶς, ἐὰν παρακούσῃς, τὸ πῦρ id.*prot.*1(p.9.1; M.8.64C); *ib.*11(p.82.1f.; 236B); **e.** only possible with free will τὸν θεὸν οὐ δοκεῖ προτρέποντα τὸν ἄνθρωπον πείθεσθαι τοῖς προστάγμασιν ἀφαιρεῖν αὐτοῦ τὴν ἐξουσίαν τῆς προαιρέσεως, τοῦ δύνασθαι καὶ μὴ ὑ. τοῖς προστάγμασιν...ὥστε οὐχ ἵνα τὴν ἐξουσίαν ἣν ἔδωκεν ἀφέλῃ προστάττειν βούλεται, ἀλλ' ἵνα κρεῖττον δωρήσηται ὡς ἀξίῳ μειζόνων τυχεῖν, ἀνθ' ὧν ὑπήκουσεν τῷ θεῷ καὶ τὴν τοῦ μὴ ὑ. ἐξουσίαν ἔχων...αὐτεξούσιον...οὐχ ὡς προϋποκειμένου τινὸς ἤδη κακοῦ, οὗ τὴν ἐξουσίαν εἰ βούλοιτο τοῦ ἑλέσθαι, ὁ ἄνθρωπος ἐλάμβανεν, ἀλλὰ τὴν τοῦ ὑ. τῷ θεῷ καὶ μὴ ὑ. αἰτίαν μόνην Meth.*arbitr.*16(p.188.16ff.; M.18.265A); **f.** Christ's obedience to Father not implying subordination of Son ὑπήκοος γέγονεν, οὐκ ἴσος ἦν τῷ ὑπήκουσεν. οὐδὲν τοῦτο αὐτὸν ἐλαττοῖ...ἐπεὶ καὶ φίλοις ∼ομεν ἡμεῖς, καὶ οὐδὲν τοῦτο ποιεῖ. ὡς υἱὸς πατρὶ ὑπήκουσεν, οὐκ εἰς δουλικὸν ἀξίωμα καταπεσών, ἀλλὰ τούτῳ...φυλάττων τῆς γνησιότητος τὸ θαῦμα, τῇ πολλῇ περὶ τὸν πατέρα τιμῇ Chrys.*hom.*7.3 *in Phil.*(11.248E); **g.** ref. inanimate things ὁ θεὸς δημιουργός, ∼ουσα δὲ αὐτῷ ἡ ὕλη πρὸς τὴν τέχνην Athenag.*leg.*15.2(M.6.920B); στοιχεῖα...δεσπότῃ ὑ. Ath.*gent.*37(M.25.73A); id.*ep.Serap.*2.3(M.26.612C); **2.** of obeying sinful desires and demons τὸ παρακοῦσαι μὲν τοῦ πνευματικοῦ νόμου ...ὑ. δὲ τοῦ ὑλικοῦ Meth.*res.*2.2(p.333.2, v.l. ἐπακοῦσαι M.18.300B); μήτε ∼ωμεν αὐτῶν [sc. δαιμόνων] Ath.*v.Anton.*27(M.26.884B); *ib.*35(893B); **3.** of laity obeying clergy εἰς τὸ ὑ. ὑμᾶς τῷ ἐπισκόπῳ καὶ τῷ πρεσβυτερίῳ Ign.*Eph.*20.2; *Can.App.*74; αἱ χῆραι...κατὰ τὴν διάταξιν τοῦ ἐπισκόπου ποιείτωσαν ὡς θεῷ ὑ. *Const.App.*3.8.3; **4.** monastic; **a.** def. ἀπόθεσις διακρίσεώς ἐστι τὸ ∼ειν, ὡς καλοῖς τοῖς φαινομένοις ὡς κακοῖς *Schol.*6 in Jo.Clim.*scal.*4(M.88.729D); **b.** scope ἐν πᾶσιν ὀφείλεις ὑ. ὁ γὰρ ἐπιτάσσων ἀββᾶς σου, βαστάζει σου τὸ κρίμα, ὡς ἀπαιτούμενος λόγον ὑπὲρ σοῦ Bars.*resp.*6(M.88.1817C); **c.** true and false obedience εἰ μὲν διὰ κύριον τελείως ὑπακούσει, εἰ καὶ μὴ δόξει τελείως, τὸ ἑαυτοῦ κρίμα ἐξεδύσατο. εἰ δὲ τὸ ἑαυτοῦ ἔν τισιν ἐκπληροῖ θέλημα, ἢ καὶ δόξει ὑ. αὐτὸς τὸ φορτίον ἐπιφέρεται Jo.Clim.*scal.*4(M.88.681B).

B. (*hear and*) *answer* prayer, (Lat. *exaudio*) προσευχόμενος ὑ. ὡς φίλος θεοῦ *Const.App.*2.53.9; ὑ. [sc. θεός] ῥᾳδίως τοῖς εἰλικρινῶς ἀντιβολοῦσιν Thdt.*provid.*7(4.603).

C. liturg., *make response*; **1.** early semi-liturg. τὸ ἀμὴν ∼ετέ μοι... ∼ομεν αὐτῷ τὸ ἀμήν *A.Jo.*94(p.197.16,18, conj. for ἐπακ-); τῆς Ἀρετῆς...ψάλλειν, τὰς δὲ λοιπὰς ἐν κύκλῳ καθάπερ ἐν χοροῦ σχήματι συστάσας ὑ. αὐτῇ Meth.*symp.*11(p.131.15; M.18.208C); τοῦ δὲ Πέτρου ἀρξαμένου τῆς ὑμνῳδίας πᾶσαι αἱ δυνάμεις τῶν οὐρανῶν ὑ. τὸ ἀλληλούϊα *Dorm.BMV* 44(p.109); **2.** liturg. τὸν μὲν διάκονον ἀναγινώσκειν ψαλμόν, τοὺς δὲ λαοὺς ὑ. Ath.*fug.*24(p.84.17; M.25.676A); id.*apol.Const.*16(cj. for ἐπακοῦσαι M.25.613C); ὁ λαὸς ∼έτω· εἷς ἅγιος *Lit.*ap.*Const.App.*8.13.13; Jo.Mosch.*prat.*176(M.87.3045A).

D. οἱ ὑπακούοντες, *hearers* (grade of catechumenate) ἐν τοῖς πιστοῖς, ἐν τοῖς ∼ουσιν, ἐν τοῖς κατηχουμένοις Chrys.*hom.*22.4 *in Eph.*(11.171D).

ὑπακτέον, *one must win over*, Clem.*paed.*3.11(p.269.12; M.8.632B).

ὑπαλείφω, *anoint*; fig., Clem.*paed.*2.12(p.234.8; M.8.553A); met., esp. of anointing for a contest, so *prepare* or *encourage*, Ign.*Eph.*3.1; ‡Caes.Naz.*dial.*178(M.38.1148); Jo.VI H.*v.Jo.D.*34(M.94.477A).

***ὑπαλληλαίτιοι**, *mutually caused*, Jo.D.*f.o.*3.15(M.94.1061A).

ὑπαμείβω, *change*, Gr.Nyss.*anim.et res.*(M.46.136C); id.*Eun.*5(2 p.118.5; M.45.700A); *pervert*, id.*virg.*18(p.319.25; M.46.392C).

***ὑπαμελέω**, *be secretly neglectful of*, Nil.*Eulog.*30(M.79.1133B).

***ὑπαναβλύζω**, *gush up from below*, Thdt.*Dan.*3:87(2.1127, v.l. ἀναβλυζούσας).

ὑπαναγιγνώσκω, **1.** *read aloud*; of scripture in church, †Hipp.*Laz.*(p.216.10); Gr.Naz.*ep.*11(M.37.41B); ὁ Λουκᾶς ἡμῖν παραβολὴν ἀναπλάσας ὑπανέγνω ἀρτίως Ast.Am.*hom.*2(M.40.181A); **2.** *read from below, read*; letters in the sky, ‡Jo.D.*Artem.*45(p.7.21; M.96.1293B).

***ὑπαναγνώστης, ὁ**, *reader, lector* ὁ τῶν θείων ὑ. ποτὲ λογίων Gr.Naz.*or.*4.97(M.35.632B).

***ὑπαναγνωστικός**, neut. as subst., *that which is to be read aloud, documentary statement* ἀπέστειλεν ἡμᾶς...ἐπιφερομένους ὑ. διὰ σημείων CCP(681)*act.*12(H.3.1308D); ὑ. καθαιρέσεως καὶ ἀναθεματίσεως ἡμῶν Thdr.Stud.*epp.*1.48(M.99.1073A).

***ὑπαναθεματίζω**, *lay under anathema, anathematize*, Sev.Ant.ap.Leont.H.*monoph.*testimonia(M.86.1848C).

ὑπανάκειμαι, for ἀνάκειμαι, *be reserved*, Alex.Al.*ep.Alex.*9(M.18.561B, v.l. ἀνακείσθω p.25.17).

***ὑπαναλέγομαι**, *acquire gradually*, Eust.ap.Leont.et Jo.*sacr.*(M.86.2040C).

ὑπαναμιμνήσκω, *recall to mind*, ‡Ath.*annunt.*1(M.28.917B); Anast.S.*hex.*12(M.89.1057A).

***ὑπαναπνέω**, *breathe again*, fig. καθαροῦ...ὑ. ἀέρος Eus.*m.P.*9(p.928.4; M.20.1492A); *breathe again after, revive after, recover from* τυρα⟨ν⟩ίδος ὑ. id.*d.e.*6.13(p.265.20; M.22.436D); Pall.*v.Chrys.*9(p.51.21; M.47.30).

ὑπανάπτω, *kindle underneath* τῶν ἡμετέρων ἁμαρτιῶν ἡ φλὸξ τὸ ὑλικὸν πῦρ ὑ. ταῖς πόλεσιν Sophr.H.*v.Anast.*(M.92.1684D); met. τῇ ψυχῇ φθόνον ὑ. Niceph.Ur.*v.Sym.*14(M.86.3000B); *kindle secretly, kindle*, fig. ζηλοτυπίας ὑ. φλόγας Chrys.*hom.*30.6 *in Mt.*(7.356C); ὑ. ... τὸν σατανικὸν ἔρωτα ‡Proc.G.*Pr.*6:27ff.(M.87.1277C).

ὑπανατέλλω, *spring forth from below*; med., of a blush, *rise*, Gr.Naz.*carm.*1.2.2.304(M.37.602A).

***ὑπαναφέρω**, *refer*, Socr.*h.e.*1.19.12(M.67.128C).

***ὑπαναχαιτίζω**, *hold back by the hair*; met., *keep back, restrain*, Nil.*Eulog.*2(M.79.1096C).

ὑπαναχωρέω, *withdraw into retirement*, ‡Pion.*v.Polyc*.7; *retire slowly, withdraw* from; met. τῆς ἁμαρτίας *cat.Mt*.21:28(p.173.22).

***ὑπανδρύνομαι**, *grow a little older*, Gr.Nyss.*or.dom*.1(p.24.8; M. 44.1133C).

ὑπανοίγ-ω, *open secretly*; ? hence *open a little*, Thdt.*ep*.156(4. 1323); met., pass., *be opened, be available* εὐπέτεια τῆς εὑρέσεως ~εται ‡Chrys.*pasch*.7(8.284C).

***ὑπαντάνω**, = ὑπαντάω, Meth.*symp*.11(p.131.18; M.18.208C).

ὑπαντάω, *come* or *go to meet, meet*; **1.** lit. μετὰ τῶν ἁγίων...ὑ. Χριστῷ [sc. after death] Thdt.*1Thess*.3:13(3.515); esp. ref. ὑπαπαντή: Συμεὼν...ὑ. τῷ σωτῆρι ‡Meth.*palm*.5(M.18.392B); οἱ τῶν ἐθνῶν λαοὶ φωτοφοροῦντες ὑπαντήσωμεν ‡Cyr.H.*occurs*.3(M.33.1189B); *oppose*, Eus.*v.C*.4.41(p.133.17; M.20.1189A); abs., *attend a meeting*, *Pers*.(p.2.1); **2.** met., *come up, occur* χειραγωγῶν...εἴ που ὑ. τι σκολιόν Gr.Thaum.*pan.Or*.14(p.33.6; M.10.1093A); Dor.*doct*.14.2(M. 88.1773D); *fall in* with τὴν μὲν ἐπὶ τὴν Περσίδα πορείαν διανύσαι αὐτὸν τότε κατὰ γνώμην αὐτῷ οὐχ ὑπήντησε,...προθυμουμένῳ εἰρήνης Gel. Cyz.*h.e*.3.10.27; *ib*.3.16.25.

ὑπαντή, ἡ, *meeting* ἐν ταῖς ὑ. ὄψεων τῶν ἐξόχων Thdr.Stud.*iamb*. (M.99.1784C); partic. = ὑπαπαντή, Cyr.*hom.div*.12 tit.(5^2.385D); τῇ ...δεσπότου ὑ. φαιδροὶ...ὑπαντήσωμεν ‡Cyr.H.*occurs*.15(M.33.1201B); προκαθαιρόμεθα εἰς ὑ. καὶ προσκύνησιν τοῦ ἐκ τῆς...ἀειπαρθένου... γεννηθέντος Anast.Ant.*serm*.4(M.89.1397B).

ὑπάντησις, ἡ, *coming to meet, meeting*; in gen., *A.Thom*.B 30(p.34. 35); *A.Mt*.13(p.232.2); Gr.Nyss.*v.Macr*.(M.46.976D); ref. Christ at entry into Jerusalem, *A.Pil*.B 1.3(p.289); ‡Meth.*palm*.1(p.389.7; M. 18.384A); partic. = ὑπαπαντή: εἰς θεοῦ ὑ. ἐξέλθωμεν ‡Cyr.H.*occurs*. 15(M.33.1201C); ‡Meth.*Sym.et Ann*.tit.(M.18.348).

ὑπαντιάζω, *come* or *go to meet, encounter*; in argument, *counter* πρὸς...τοιαῦτα θερμότερον...ὑ. Cyr.*Jo*.1.9(4.87E).

***ὑπαπαίρω**, *retire*, Gr.Thaum.*Eccl*.1(M.10.989A).

ὑπαπαντάω, *meet*, Clem.*exc.Thdot*.71(p.129.26; M.9.692B); met., *counter* in argument, Socr.*h.e*.1.5.2(M.67.41B).

ὑπαπαντή, ἡ, feast of the *meeting* between Christ and Simeon, *feast of the Purification* τῷ αὐτῷ χρόνῳ [sc. 542] ἡ ὑ. τοῦ κυρίου ἔλαβεν ἀρχὴν ἐπιτελεῖσθαι ἐν τῷ Βυζαντίῳ τῇ β′ τοῦ Φεβρουαρίου μηνός Thphn.*chron*.p.188(M.108.488B); its proper observance, Anast.Ant.*fr*.(M.89.1286D); *Catech.Stud*.5(M.99.1696C); in title of treatises, ‡Cyr.H.*occurs*.(M.33.1187); ‡Chrys.*occurs*.(2.812); Hesych.H.*serm*.6(M.93.1468B); Mod.*occurs*.(M.86.3276B).

ὑπαπάντησις, ἡ, = foreg., Cyr.S.*v.Thds*.(p.236.24).

***ὑπαποδύομαι**, *put off* from oneself; met., *give up* a profession, Gr.Nyss.*Eun*.1(1 p.35.4; M.45.261C).

ὕπαρ, τό, *real appearance seen in a state of waking, waking vision*, Thdt.*h.rel*.21(3.1244); acc. abs. as adv., *in a waking state*, of visions sent in order to convert to Christianity, Or.*Cels*.1.46(p.96.12; M.11. 745A); *ib*.1.48(p.97.28; 748C); of vision of God granted to men before Flood, Meth.*symp*.7.5(p.76.21; M.18.132B); θείας ἀποκαλύψεις ἑώρα, οὐκ ὄναρ μόνον, ἀλλὰ καὶ ὕ. Thdt.*Dan*.1:17(2.1074).

***ὑπαριθμ-έω**, **A.** abs. *enumerate below*, exeg. Col.1:16 περιγράφει τοῖς ὑπαριθμηθεῖσι τῶν πάντων τὴν ἔννοιαν Gr.Nyss.*Eun*.1(1 p.111.5, v.l. ἀριθμηθεῖσι M.45.345A); Gel.Cyz.*h.e*.2.17.33; *mention below*, exeg. 2Thess.3:5 τίνα κύριον ὀνομαζόμενον; τὸν...πατέρα, ἢ τὸ πνεῦμα τὸ ἅγιον; τὸν μὲν γὰρ Χριστὸν ὑπηρίθμησεν ‡Ath.*disp*.43(M. 28.497A).

B. c. dat., *place after in numerical order, number after*; **1.** ref. Persons of Trin.; **a.** used by Anomoeans as implying subordination οὐδὲ μὴν ταὐτὸν [sc. τὸ πνεῦμα] τῷ μονογενεῖ. οὐ γὰρ ἂν ὑπηριθμήθη τούτῳ ὡς ἰδίαν ἔχων ὑπόστασιν Eun.*apol*.25(1.628A; M.30. 861C); *ib*.(628C; M.861D); οὔτε μὴν 'σὺν τῷ πατρί', φασί, 'καὶ τῷ υἱῷ' τὸ πνεῦμα τακτέον, ἀλλ' 'ὑπὸ τὸν υἱὸν καὶ τὸν πατέρα'...οὐδὲ 'συναριθμούμενον', ἀλλ' ~ούμενον Bas.*Spir*.13(3.10D; M.32.88B); cf. οὐχ ὑβρίζων τὴν ἀμέριστον φύσιν καὶ ἀξίαν, ὡς οἱ μὴ συναριθμοῦντες, ἀλλ' ~οῦντες τῷ πατρὶ τὸν υἱὸν καὶ τὸ ἅγιον πνεῦμα Didym.*Trin*.2.8(M.39.604B); **b.** this implication refuted, ref. 1Cor.15:47 εἰ τοίνυν τῷ πρώτῳ ~εῖται τὸ δεύτερον, τὸ δὲ ~ούμενον ἀτιμότερόν ἐστι τοῦ πρὸς ὃ ἔχει τὴν ὑπαρίθμησιν· ἀτιμότερος καθ' ὑμᾶς...τοῦ χοϊκοῦ ὁ ἐπουράνιος ‡Ath. *comm.essent*.20(M.28.52A); ‡Ath.*disp*.22(M.28.464D); τί κωλύει... ἐπειδὴ τὰ αὐτὰ καὶ προαριθμεῖται καὶ ~εῖται παρὰ τῇ γραφῇ διὰ τὴν ἰσοτιμίαν τῆς φύσεως, αὐτὰ ἑαυτῶν εἶναι τιμιώτερά τε καὶ ἀτιμότερα; Gr.Naz.*or*.31.20(p.170.4; M.36.156B); *ib*.34.15(256A); for full discussion v. Bas.*Spir*.41ff.(3.35Bff.; M.32.144Bff.); **2.** met., *put* as a close *second* in order of merit εἰ καὶ μὴ συναριθμηθείη, ἀλλά γε ~ηθείη Isid.Pel.*epp*.3.225(M.78.908D).

***ὑπαρίθμησις, ἡ**, *placing after in numerical order*; ref. Persons of Trin., as implying subordination, acc. Anomoeans, λέγουσιν οἱ αἱρετικοὶ κατὰ τάξιν καὶ ὑ. ἑστάναι τὴν θεότητα ‡Ath.*comm.essent*.20 (M.28.52A); ἡμεῖς [sc. Anomoeans] τοῖς μὲν ὁμοτιμίοις φαμὲν τὴν συναρίθμησιν πρέπειν· τοῖς δὲ πρὸς τὸ χεῖρον παρηλλαγμένοις τὴν ὑ. Bas.*Spir*.42(3.36A; M.32.145A); for discussion and refutation v. ὑπαριθμέω; γελῶ σου καὶ τὰς προαριθμήσεις καὶ τὰς ὑ.,...ὥσπερ ἐν τῇ τάξει τῶν ὀνομάτων κειμένων τῶν πραγμάτων Gr.Naz.*or*.31.20(p.169. 17; M.36.156B).

ὑπαρκτικός, **1.** gram., *substantival* τὸ ὑ. ῥῆμα Areth.*Apoc*.9:8(M. 106.644A); **2.** *essential* ἡ ἀρχὴ ὑ., τῆς ἑκάστου γενέσεως Jo.D.*Man*.1.17 (M.94.1521D).

***ὑπαρκτικῶς**, *substantially, really*, Max.*ambig*.(M.91.1089B); πάντων τῶν κατ' οὐσίαν ὑ. ὄντων...ἐν τῷ θεῷ προϋπάρχουσι παγίως ὄντες οἱ λόγοι *ib*.(1329A).

ὑπαρκτός, *subsisting, existent, real*, Or.*Cels*.4.90(p.362.19; M.11. 1168B); *Hom.Clem*.19.20; τρία ἅγια τρία συνάγια, τρία ὑ. τρία συνύπαρκτα Epiph.*anc*.67(p.82.2; M.43.137C om., cf.M.42.481A).

ὕπαρξις, ἡ, **1.** *coming into existence, emergence*; **a.** in gen. ἡ δὲ ὕ. τῆς ζωῆς ἐκ τῆς τοῦ θεοῦ περιγίνεται μετοχῆς Iren.*haer*.4.20.5(M.7. 1036A); ὅτι μὲν τῆς τῶν γενητῶν ὑ. τὴν διδασκαλίαν ποιεῖται, ἀθρόως τὰ πάντα μαρτυρεῖ δι' αὐτοῦ γεγονέναι Eus.*e.th*.1.9(p.67.11; M.24.840A); οὕτω [sc. with a doxology] διαιροῦσι καὶ τὰς ὑ. τὰς τέσσαρας [sc. of the subsequent books of psalms] Ath.*exp.Ps*.40:14(M.27.200D); ἐξ ἐκείνου [sc. Χριστοῦ] ἐσμὲν κατὰ τὴν δευτέραν ὑ. καθ' ἣν ἀνάστασιν ὁμοίως αὐτῷ πάντες ἐσόμεθα ἄφθαρτοι Thdr.Mops.*1Cor*.11:3(M.66. 888C); of an individual life, id.*Gal*.1:15(p.13.22; M.66.901C); ἡ πατρὸς καὶ μητρὸς ὑπουργία πρὸς ὕπαρξιν Cyr.*ador*.7(1.235D); ὁ κόσμος πρεσβύτερα τῆς ὑ. αὐτοῦ στοιχεῖα ἔχων ἐνυπόστατα CCP(543)*anath*.6; **b.** ref. Inc. σαρκοῦται γοῦν ὁ λόγος καὶ θεὸς τὸ ἡμέτερον οὐ προπλασθείσῃ σαρκὶ συναπτόμενος ἢ προμορφωθέντι...σώματι, ἢ προϋποστάσῃ ψυχῇ συντιθέμενος, ἀλλὰ τότε τούτοις παραγενομένοις πρὸς ὕπαρξιν, ὅτε αὐτοῖς ὁ λόγος...συνετίθετο φυσικῶς σύγχρονον ἔχοντα τῇ ὑ. τὴν ἕνωσιν, καὶ...σύνδρομον ἔχοντα τῇ φυσικῇ τοῦ λόγου συμβάσει τὴν ὑ., καὶ οὐκ ἐκείνης οὐδὲ ὡς ἐν ὀφθαλμοῦ ῥιπῇ ταύτην προτερεύουσαν ἔχοντα...ἅμα σὰρξ ἔμψυχος λογική, ἅμα θεοῦ λόγου σὰρξ ἔμψυχος λογική· ἐν αὐτῷ γὰρ καὶ οὐ καθ' ἑαυτὴν ἔσχε τὴν ὕ. Sophr.H.*ep.syn*.(M.87.3161B); **2.** *existence*; **a.** in gen. ἡ [sc. τοῦ σώματος] πολυχρόνιος ὕ. μετὰ τὴν ἀνάστασιν ἔσται Meth.*res*.2.22(p.376.12); ἡ...κτίσις κατὰ μετοχὴν τὴν ἀγαθότητα ἔχει...καὶ ἔστιν ὕ. τοῦ ἐν αὐτῇ ἀγαθοῦ, τὸ μετέχειν τῆς τοῦ θεοῦ, προσκολλωμένην αὐτῷ τῇ ὑπακοῇ καὶ τῷ ἔρωτι Didym.*Trin*.1. 18(M.39.352B); πάντων ὄντων, γενομένων, μελλόντων, ἐπεὶ καὶ τοῦτο τρόπος ὑπάρξεως Synes.*insomn*.10(p.177.9; M.66.1309B); εἴδωλα ἐξ ἀνθρωπίνων γινόμενα χειρῶν, ἃ πότε ἂν εἰκότως νομισθεῖεν θεοί, τοιαύτην ἔχοντα τῆς ὑ. τὴν αἰτίαν; Thdr.Mops.*Os*.8:4–6(M.66.172D); κακῆς γὰρ ὑπάρξεως ἀνυπαρξία αἱρετώτερον Vict.*Mc*.14:21(p.422.2); ἡ ψυχὴ...παρὰ τὴν τοῦ σώματος κρᾶσιν ᾧ συνδέδεται...περιγέγραπται μὲν τῷ λόγῳ τῆς ὑ. Leont.B.*Nest.et Eut*.1(M.86.1285A); **b.** of Father, Ath.*Ar*.1.14(M.26.41B); οὐ μὴν παρατάσει τινὶ διαστηματικῇ τῆς τοῦ πατρὸς ὑ. τὸν μονογενῆ διορίζεσθαι, ἀλλ' ἀεὶ τῷ αἰτίῳ τὸ ἐξ αὐτοῦ συνυπολαμβάνειν Gr.Nyss.*diff.ess*.7(M.32.337B); id.*Eun*.8(2 p.183.14; M.45.776D); ἀντιπαραθέσει τῆς σῆς ὑ. τοῦ ἀεὶ ὄντος, γνωσθήσεταί τί ὑστερῶ ἐγώ Cyr.*Ps*.38:5(M.69.973A); θεός, ὁ χρόνου ἀνωτέραν ἔχων τήν τε φύσιν καὶ τὴν ὕ. Jo.D.*f.o*.1.8(M.94.816A); **c.** of Son ἦν μὲν κυριώτερον ἐπὶ τοῦ...λόγου τό, ἔστιν, εἰπεῖν. ἀλλ' ἐπεὶ πρὸς διαφορὰν τῆς ἐνανθρωπήσεως γενομένης ἔν τινι καιρῷ ἐδήλου τὴν ὕ. τοῦ λόγου, ἀντὶ τοῦ 'ἔστιν' τῷ 'ἦν' ὁ εὐαγγελιστὴς κέχρηται Or.*fr.1 in Jo*.1:1 (p.483.18); τὴν ὕ. προτέραν εἶναι τοῦ γεγονέναι αὐτόν *ib.9 in Jo*.1:14 (p.490.23); οὐκ ἐξαπτέον τὴν ὕ. τοῦ σωτῆρος τῆς θελήσεως τοῦ πατρός· οὐ γὰρ κτίσμα τυγχάνει id.*Apoc*.26(p.32); τὸ δὲ ἦν τὴν ἄχρονον αὐτοῦ καὶ προαιώνιον ὕ. [sc. σημαίνει] Bas.*Eun*.2.17(1.252D; M.29. 608A); τὸ συναφές τε καὶ ἀΐδιον τῆς ἐκ τοῦ πατρὸς ὑ. τοῦ μονογενοῦς παραδιδοὺς ὁ ἀπόστολος ἀπαύγασμα δόξης τὸν υἱὸν κατωνόμασε Gr.Nyss.*Eun*.8(2 p.180.21; M.45.773B); ἅμα τε θεὸς νοεῖται ὁ πατὴρ καὶ συνεισβέβηκεν εὐθὺς ἡ ὕ. τοῦ δι' ὃν ἐστι πατήρ Cyr.*Abac*.35 (3.549E); ὁ υἱὸς τὴν ἐκ πατρὸς ὕ. οὐσιώδη καὶ φυσικὴν κατασημήνειεν ἂν id.*Pulch*.(p.29.30; 5^2.133C); acc. heretics τὸν συναΐδιον τῷ θεῷ ...λόγον τῇ τῆς σαρκὸς γενέσει συμπαρομαρτοῦσαν ἔχειν τῆς ὑ. τὴν ἀρχήν id.*Thds*.12(p.49.32; 5^2.11A); **d.** of H. Ghost οὔτε υἱὸν νομίζοντες οὔτε δι' υἱοῦ τὴν ὕ. εἰληφός Thdr.Mops.*symb*.(p.98.9; M.66. 1017A); τὸ πνεῦμα...ἐξ αὐτῆς τοῦ πατρὸς τῆς οὐσίας ἔχει τὴν ὕ. id. *Jo*.15:26(p.398.15; M.66.780B); **e.** τρόπος ὑπάρξεως, *mode of being* γνωστόν τι ἔστι τὸ μὲν κατὰ ἀριθμόν, τὸ δὲ κατὰ μέγεθος, τὸ δὲ κατὰ δύναμιν, τὸ δὲ κατὰ τὸν τρόπον τῆς ὑ.,...τὸ δὲ κατ' οὐσίαν Bas.*ep*. 235.2(3.359B; M.32.872C); esp. of Persons of Trin.; [ref. assertion that H. Ghost proceeds from God ὡς πνεῦμα στόματος αὐτοῦ] τὸ πνεῦμα οὐσία ζῶσα, ἁγιασμοῦ κυρία· τῆς μὲν οἰκειότητος δηλουμένης ἐντεῦθεν, τοῦ δὲ τρόπου τῆς ὑ. ἀρρήτου φυλασσομένου id.*Spir*.46(3.38E;

M.32.152B); Gr.Nyss.*Eun.*1(1 p.84.17; M.45.316C); τὸ γάρ, πατήρ, υἱὸς καὶ πνεῦμα τὸ ἅγιον τρόπου ὑ. ἤγουν σχέσεως ὀνόματα, ἀλλ' οὐκ οὐσίας ἁπλῶς Amph.*fr.*(M.39.112D); ὑπάρξεως οὖν τρόπος τὸ ἀγέννητος καὶ οὐκ οὐσίας ὄνομα. εἰ τὰ διάφορον τὴν ὕ. τοῦ εἶναι ἔχοντα, διάφορον ἔχει καὶ τὴν οὐσίαν, οὐδὲ οἱ ἄνθρωποι ὁμοούσιοι. ἄλλη γὰρ ὕ. Ἀδὰμ ἐκ γῆς πλασθέντος, ἄλλη δὲ Εὐὰς ἐκ πλευρᾶς γενομένης Didym.(‡Bas.)*Eun.*4 (1.283B; M.29.681A); ἡ διαφορὰ δὲ τῶν τῆς ὑ. τρόπων οὐ διαιρεῖ τὸ ἓν τῆς οὐσίας ‡Just.*qu.et resp.*139(M.6.1392C); τὸ μὲν ἀγέννητον καὶ γεννητὸν καὶ ἐκπορευτὸν οὐκ οὐσίας ὀνόματα ἀλλὰ τρόποι ὑπάρξεως Thdt. *rect.conf.*3(M.6.1209B); ὑπόστασις χαρακτηρίζεται...ἐπὶ...τῆς θείας οὐσίας ἀπὸ τρόπου ὑ., καθ' ὃν ἡ μὲν γεννητικῶς, ἡ δὲ γεγεννημένως, ἡ δὲ ἐκπορευτικῶς Leont.H.*Nest.*2.4(M.86.1537C); τριάς ἐστι ταῖς ὑποστάσεσι καὶ τῷ τρόπῳ τῆς ὑ. ἡ ἁγία μονάς Max.*myst.*(M.91.701A); πάντα κοινὰ τοῦ πατρὸς καὶ τοῦ υἱοῦ καὶ τοῦ ἁγίου πνεύματος πλὴν τοῦ τρόπου τῆς ὑ. Jo.D.*Jacob.*52(M.94.1461B); **f.** of Christ's human nature οἱ μὲν προσαιώνιον τὴν ὕ., οἱ δὲ ἀπὸ Μαρίας τὴν ἀρχὴν ἐσχηκέναι Bas.*ep.*260.8(3.400D; M.32.965B); οὔτε γὰρ ἡ ἀνθρωπίνη φύσις τοῦ Χριστοῦ ἁπλῶς ποτε λέγεται, ἀλλ' οὔτε ἰδίαν ὑπόστασιν, ἤτοι πρόσωπον ἔσχεν, ἀλλ' ἐν τῇ ὑποστάσει τοῦ λόγου τὴν ἀρχὴν τῆς ὑ. ἔλαβεν Justn.*conf.*(p.88.12; M.86.1011B); ποῦ δὲ καὶ ἡ θατέρου ὕ. πρὸ τῆς ἑνώσεως, τῆς ἀνθρωπότητος φημί; Leont.B.*arg.Sev.*(M.86.1933C); περὶ τῆς προσάλληλα τούτων [sc. θεότητος καὶ ἀνθρωπότητος Χριστοῦ] σχέσεως καὶ τοῦ τρόπου τῆς ὑ. πολυπραγμονεῖν id.*Nest.et Eut.*proem. (M.86.1269C); **3.** with partic. emphasis on independent existence ἡ γὰρ ὑπόστασις καὶ ἡ οὐσία ὕπαρξίς ἐστιν· ἔστι γὰρ καὶ ὑπάρχει Ath.*ep. Afr.*4(M.26.1036B); τὰ πράγματα ἰδιάζουσαν καὶ αὐτοτελῆ τὴν ὕ. ἔχειν Bas.*ep.*210.4(3.316A; M.32.733B); οὐδὲ ἐνυπόστατον ἢ ἐνούσιον ἔστιν νοῆσαι δίχα οὐσίας ἢ ὑποστάσεως. οὐ γὰρ καθ' ἑαυτὰ τὴν ὕ. ἔχουσιν, ἀλλ' ἀεὶ περὶ τὴν ὑπόστασιν θεωροῦνται Max.*opusc.*(M.91.261C); theol. οὐ γὰρ ὥς τινες οἴονται, ἐνέργειά ἐστι θεοῦ [sc. τὸ πνεῦμα] οὐκ ἔχον κατ' αὐτοὺς ὑπάρξεως ἰδιότητα Or.*fr.27 in Jo.*3:8(p.513.13); θεὸν ὁμολογεῖν τὸν ἐκ τῆς παρθένου, πρὸ αἰώνων μὲν προορισθέντα, ἐκ δὲ Μαρίας τὴν ἀρχὴν τῆς ὑ. ἐσχηκότα Paul.Sam.*fr.*D 2(p.338.3); Μαρκέλλῳ τῷ κατὰ διάμετρον [sc. Ἀρείῳ] τὴν ἀσέβειαν ἐπιδειξαμένῳ, καὶ εἰς αὐτὴν τὴν ὕ. τῆς τοῦ μονογενοῦς θεότητος ἀσεβήσαντι Bas.*ep.*69.2(162E; M.432B); ἡ ὑπόστασις τὸ ἰδιάζον τῆς ἑκάστου ὑ. σημεῖόν ἐστι, τοῦ δὲ πατρὸς ἴδιον τὸ ἀγεννήτως εἶναι ὁμολογεῖται Gr.Nyss.*diff.ess.*6(M.32.337A); ὁρᾷς δύο προσώπων ὑπόστασιν, οὐχὶ ὀνόματα ψιλὰ χωρὶς πραγμάτων λεγόμενα; ἤκουσας τὴν προαιώνιον ὕ. τοῦ μονογενοῦς; Chrys. *hom.6.2 in Phil.*(11.235A); διῃρημένως...διὰ τὸ ἐν ὑ. νοεῖσθαι τῇ καθ' ἑαυτόν...υἱὸς γάρ ἐστιν καὶ οὐχὶ πατήρ· συμφυῶς δὲ πάλιν ὅτι τῇ τοῦ τεκόντος ὑ. συμπαρομαρτήσει Cyr.*Jo.*11.5(4.952E); τὸ πνεῦμα...τῆς ἀνωτάτω πασῶν ἐξέρπον οὐσίας ἐν ἰδίᾳ τε ὑ. καὶ ἐκ πατρὸς νοούμενον id. *thes.*34(5[1].353E); hence **4.** *that which exists independently, object* ἔστιν δὲ πάλιν ὁ υἱὸς οὐκ ἀρχομένη οὐδὲ παυομένη ὕπαρξις τῆς θελήσεως ἢ μὴ θελήσεως Didym.*Trin.*1.9(M.39.284A); σῶμα ἀντὶ σώματος καὶ ψυχὴν ἀντὶ ψυχῆς δέδωκε, καὶ τελείαν ὕ. ὑπὲρ ὅλου ἀνθρώπου ‡Ath. *Apoll.*1.17(M.26.1125A); *ib.*1.16(1124A); μήτε τῶν ὑποστατικῶν ὑ. συγχεομένων καὶ συναναφυρομένων ἀλλήλαις καὶ πρὸς ἓν συντρεχουσῶν ὑποκείμενον μήτε τῆς οὐσιώδους ἑνώσεως καὶ συναφείας...διαιρουμένης τὸ σύνολον ‡Gr.Nyss.*hom.1.1 in Jo.*(p.93.10); εἴπερ ταὐτὸν ἐστιν ἡ ἰδικὴ τῶν καθέκαστα οὐσία τῇ ὑποστάσει...καὶ...οὐκ ἐξ οὐσιωδῶν ἡ ὑπόστασις συνέστηκεν, ἀλλ'...ἀπὸ τρόπου ὑπάρξεως ἔσται ὑφεστῶσα ἡ ἰδικὴ ὕ. εἴτουν οὐσία, ἔσται οὖν ἐξ ἀνουσίων ἡ οὐσία καὶ ἐξ ἀνυπάρκτων ἡ ὕ. Leont.H.*Nest.*2.6(M.86.1549C); Κύριλλός φησιν ὅτι καθ' ὑπόστασιν γέγονεν ἡ ἕνωσις, τοῦτ' ἔστι καθ' ὕ., καὶ αὐτῶν πραγμάτων, οὐ...κατὰ σχέσιν †Leont.B.*sect.*8(M.86[1].1252C); τριάς ἐστι, κατὰ μὲν τὴν φυσικὴν ἀκολουθίαν, μονάδων σύνθεσις· κατὰ δὲ τὴν θεϊκὴν οὐσίαν ὑπεράριθμος ὕ. Anast.S.*hod.*2(M.89.56B); **5.** *actuality* τὰ σημεῖα...δείκνυσι τὴν τοῦ ἀποτελέσαντος ὕ., οἷον καπνὸς μὲν πῦρ Clem.*paed.*3.11(p.268.4; M.8. 628C); αἱ φωναὶ [sc. ἀγαθὸν καὶ δίκαιον]...θέσιν καὶ ὕ. τῶν οἰκείων τῷ θεῷ...ἀποσημαίνουσιν Bas.*Eun.*1.10(1.223D; M.29.536B); Παῦλος ὁ Σαμοσατεὺς...λόγον...ὁμολογεῖ τῷ μὲν προορισμῷ πρὸ αἰώνων ὄντα, τῇ δὲ ὑ. ἐκ Ναζαρὲτ ἀναδειχθέντα ‡Ath.*Apoll.*2.3(M.26.1136B); μένων ὃ ἦν, ἔλαβε τὴν τοῦ δούλου μορφήν, οὐ λειπομένην ὑπάρξεως τῆς ἐν ἐπιδείξει φανερουμένης διά τε πάθους καὶ ἀναστάσεως καὶ πάσης τῆς οἰκονομίας *ib.*(1136B); τῆς κατ' αὐτὸν ἀνθρωπότητος...καὶ αὐτῆς τῆς τοῦ λόγου θεότητος τὴν ὕ. Leont.B.*cap.Sev.*28(M.86.1912C); **6.** *constitution, condition, nature*, in gen. γενώμεθα ὡς ὁ διδάσκαλος, οὐ κατ' οὐσίαν, ἀδύνατον γὰρ ἴσον εἶναι πρὸς τὴν ὕ. τὸ θέσει τῷ φύσει Clem.*str.*2.17 (p.153.18; M.8.1016A); μακαρία ἡμῶν ἡ ὕ. *A.Andr.fr.*1(p.38.6); τὴν μὲν τῶν ἀγγέλων ὕ. δικαίαν ὑπάρχουσαν Mac.Mgn.*apocr.*4.18(p.194.8); εἰ γὰρ οὐσίαν ἁπλῶς ὁριζόμενοι, εἴποιμεν τὴν τινος ὕ. δηλοῦν Leont.B. *arg.Sev.*(M.86.1921C); περικόψωμεν τῆς πολυΰλου ἡμῶν ὑ. τὸν ὄγκον Eulog.*palm.*13(M.86.2937A); theol. οὐ θεμιτὸν νομίζειν αἰσθητῶς ὁρᾶσθαι τὸ πνεῦμα, νοητὴν ὕ. ἔχον Or.*fr.20 in Jo.*1:31(p.500.6); πῶς ...λέγετε ὅτι εἰ μὴ ἐξ ἑαυτοῦ ἀνὴρ ὤφθη, ἀλλὰ λαβὼν ἀνθρωπίνην ὕ. ἐγένετο ἄνθρωπος; ‡Ath.*Apoll.*2.9(M.26.1145B); ὁ χριστὸς ἦν μὲν ἀπάτωρ γεννήσει τῆς ἀνθρωπείας φύσεως, ἀμήτωρ δὲ τῇ γεννήσει τῆς θείας ὑ. Thdr.Mops.*Heb.*7:3(p.207.30; M.66.961D); ἐπεὶ γάρ τοι τῆς ἀνωτάτω πασῶν οὐσίας ἀπαθὴς μὲν ἡ γέννησις καὶ μὴν καὶ οὐσιώδης ἡ τοῦ γεννήματος ὕ. καὶ διατομῆς ἐλευθέρα Cyr.*dial.Trin.*2(5[1].453D); **7.** = τὰ ὑπάρχοντα *substance, property*; **a.** properly *stock, supply* βίον οὐ...περιουσίας ὕπαρξιν παραδεχόμενον...μόνῃ δὲ τῇ τοῦ θεοῦ θεραπείᾳ προσωκειωμένον Eus.*d.e.*1.8(p.39.14; M.22.76C); μηδὲ μέχρι δευτέρου χιτῶνος αὔξειν τὴν ὕ. ... Πέτρος...ὁμολογεῖ πάσης ὑ. χρυσίου καὶ ἀργυρίου καθαρεύειν, φήσας, ἀργύριον καὶ χρυσίον οὐχ ὑπάρχει μοι *ib.*3.5(p.124.27; 212D); live *stock* (cf. Jer.9:10) εὔχεται...σκεύη... ἀναθεῖναί τις, ἕτερος ἀναθεῖναι τὴν δεκάτην τῶν καρπῶν, ἄλλος τῆς οὐσίας· ἕτερος τὰ κράτιστα τῶν ποιμνίων, ἄλλος τὴν ὕ. καθιεροῖ Meth. *symp.*5.1(p.53.17; M.18.98B); **b.** sing. or plur., *goods, possessions* generally ἀγροὺς καὶ οἰκήσεις καὶ ἑτέρας ὑ. πολλάς Herm.*sim.*1.4; τῶν ἀγρῶν σου καὶ τῆς λοιπῆς ὑ. *ib.*1.5; πόθεν μοι ὕ. εἰ μὴ ὁ κύριος παρέσχεν; Eus.Al.*serm.*4(M.86.340D); Jo.Mosch.*prat.*207(M.87.3100C); fig. ὑμεῖς ἐστε τὸ πλοῦτος τὸ καλὸν καὶ ἡ ὕ. τῆς ἄνω πόλεως *A.Phil.* 109(p.42.5).

ὑπαρτάω, 1. *hang on underneath*; pass., *be hung* οὐ πεπήγασιν [sc. τὰ ἄστρα], ἀλλ' ὑπήρτηνται τοῦ στερεώματος ‡Caes.Naz.*dial.*105(M. 38.972); **2.** *bind on*, hence *inflict* ὑ. σοι...πλημμελοῦντι τὰς δίκας Cyr. *Ps.*49:16(M.69.1084B).

***ὑπαρχικός**, s.v.l., *of a prefect* ὑ. ἀξιωμάτων Eus.*v.C.*4.1(p.118.11, v.l. ὑπατικῶν; M.20.1149C), conj. ἐπαρχικῶν.

ὕπαρχος, ὁ, *subordinate ruler*, of Logos οἷά τις μεγάλου βασιλέως ὕ. Eus.*l.C.*3(p.202.2; M.20.1332B); of prophet in rel. to God, Thdt.*qu.14 in 1Reg.*(1.368); of Const. in rel. to Christ in war against demons, Eus.*l.C.*7(p.215.31; 1357B); of wife in rel. to husband as king, Chrys.*hom.34.3 in 1Cor.*(10.314B); *prefect*, id.*hom.82. 6 in Mt.*(7.789C); Philost.*h.e.*11.6(p.136.23; M.65.601A); Evagr.*h.e.* 1.19(p.28.19; M.86.2473A); as adj., *of a prefect* (s.v.l.) ὕπαρχον... ἀρχὴν ‡Jo.D.*Artem.*67(p.175.4–5n.; M.96.1316B).

ὑπάρχ-ω, 1. *exist in the beginning* θεὸς...μόνος ἄναρχος ὢν καὶ αὐτὸς ὑ. τῶν ὅλων ἀρχή Tat.*orat.*4(p.5.1; M.6.813A); καθ' ἑτέραν μὲν αὐτοῦ [sc. τοῦ λόγου] γέννησιν ἀΐδιόν τε ~ειν καὶ ἁπλοῦν ἀληθῶς, καθ' ἑτέραν δὲ ἀρχόμενον τοῦ συνθέτως εἶναι Leont.H.*Nest.*4.3(M.86. 1657B); τῆς θεότητος τῆς ἐν τριάδι μοναδικῶς ὑπαρχούσης *Lit.Jac.* (p.162.1); **2.** *exist independently* ἐπεὶ οὖν μέλλει ἐρεῖν ὀργὴν θεοῦ μεγάλην, οὐ τὸ συμβεβηκὸς πάθος ὀνομάζεται, θεοῦ ὀργὴ καλούμενον, ἔξω ὑπάρχον αὐτοῦ Or.*Apoc.*30(p.5, v.l. ὑπάρχων); **3.** *have reality, have a basis in fact* πότερον ὑ. ἡ δι' ὀρνίθων...μαντικὴ ἢ μὴ id.*Cels.* 4.90(p.362.11; M.11.1168A); **4.** *live* in sin, Just.*dial.*116.1(M.6.744B); id.*2apol.*12.1(M.6.464A); **5.** *come from, belong to*, *A.Barn.*16(p.298. 6); c. genit., *be connected with, belong to* τὴν γυναῖκα...ἀριστερᾶς δυνάμεως...ὑ. Epiph.*anac.*45(p.4.1; M.41.581A); ἑτέρας ὑ. συμμορίας Thdt. *h.e.*5.32.6(3.1072); Jo.Mosch.*prat.*29(M.87.2876C); **6.** c. genit., *belong to, be the function of* τοῦ βασιλεύοντος ἡ κρίσις ὑ. Philost.*h.e.*8.8 (p.109.12; M.65.564A); **7.** *be* ὕπαρχος *or subordinate colleague* ἄρξαι ποτέ...ἢ ὑ. τὴν μεγίστην ἀρχὴν Syn.*ep.*103(M.66.1476A); c. dat., Philost.*h.e.*11.3(p.134.14; M.65.596C); **8.** *be chief* τῶν δὲ τὸ ἑτεροούσιον, αἴτιος μὲν καὶ Εὐνόμιος ὑ. *ib.*4.12(p.64.8; 525A); f.l. for ἐπῆρχεν, *ib.*12.11(620B).

ὑπασπιστής, ὁ, 1. lit.; **a.** *shield-bearer, armour-bearer*; emperor's *guard*, Synes.*ep.*75(M.66.1441A); *defender* σκέπτεται τῶν συγγενῶν τινα λαβεῖν σύγκληρον καὶ τῆς βασιλείας ὑ. ‡Jo.D.*Artem.*12(M.96. 1261C); **b.** plur., *guards, body-guard*, Eus.*v.C.*2.5(p.42.21; M.20. 984A); Philost.*h.e.*11.1(p.133.2; M.65.593B); Cyr.*Mich.*70(3.469B); **2.** met., *champion, supporter*, ‡Hipp.*consumm.*30(p.301.37; M.10. 933C); Didym.*Trin.*2.8(M.39.613C); τῶν διεστραμμένων δογμάτων ὑπασπισταί Cyr.*Is.*3.3(2.445D).

ὑπαστράπτω, *illuminate only a little, reveal only partially* λόγος ...πνεύματος αἰγλήεντος ὑπέστραψεν [sc. before Pentecost] θεότητα Gr.Naz.*carm.*1.1.3.28(M.37.410A).

***ὑπατακτέω,** *get somewhat out of control*; of an argument, Gr.Nyss. *Eun.*12(2 p.291.15; M.45.904D).

***ὑπατάρια, τά,** *consular calendar*, Epiph.*haer.*51.22(p.284.7; M. om.); *Chron.Pasch.*p.381(M.92.977A).

ὑπατεία (ὑπατία), ἡ, 1. *consulate*, Ast.Am.*hom.*4(M.40.225A); esp. as method of dating, Eus.*h.e.*1.9.4(M.20.108B); γράψαντες...προέταξαν τὴν ὑ., καὶ τὸν μῆνα Ath.*syn.*3(p.232.27; M.26.685A); met. ὑ. πνευματικὴν ἐκαλέσαμεν τὴν ἀποστολὴν Chrys.*hom.3.4 in Ac.princ.* (3.77B); **2.** *consular show*, games held at the consuls' expense τὰς συνήθεις ὑ. ἐπετέλεσε Socr.*h.e.*2.29.4(M.67.277A); of money, *consular largess*, Jo.Mal.*chron.*18 p.426(M.97.629A); ἔδωκεν ὑ. η' [i.e. *was* *consul eight times*] Chron.*Pasch*.p.277(M.92.689C); ἐποίησε δὲ ὑ. καὶ ἔρριψε χρήματα πολλά Thphn.*chron*.p.204(M.108.525C).

ὑπατεύω, *throw like consular largess* τὸν Πέρσην ἀπέτεμεν· εἶτα τὴν κεφαλὴν ὑπατεύσας Ῥωμαίους θάρσους ἐνέπλησεν Thphn.*chron*.p.219 (M.108.557C).

ὑπατικός, *consular*; ἡ ὑ. [sc. τάξις] *consular rank*, Marc.Diac. *v.Porph*.27.

***ὑπάτισσα, ἡ,** *wife of a consul* or *man of consular rank*, *Chron. Pasch*.p.264(M.92.645A); *cat.Mt*.15:30(p.125.4); *CIG* 9008.

ὕπατος, ὁ, *consul*; holder of title which became purely honorary after Justn., Pall.*v.Chrys*.12(p.71.32; M.47.40); Philost.*h.e*.11.4(M. 65.597C); Thphn.*chron*.p.326(M.108.788C).

***ὑπαττικίζω,** *affect Attic usage*, Gr.Nyss.*Eun*.1(1 p.41.12; M.45. 269A).

***ὑπαυχενέω,** *be haughty*, Gr.Agr.*Eccl*.6.19(M.98.1013A) perh. for ὑπεραυχενέω.

ὕπειμι, (*ibo*) v. ὑπέρχομαι.

***ὑπείργω,** *restrain*, Geo.Pis.*hex*.449(M.92.1470A).

ὑπεισδύνω, *get in secretly*; met., Epiph.*haer*.76.49(p.404.20; M.42. 621B).

ὑπεισέρχομαι, 1. *enter by stealth*; of demons into men's bodies, Clem.*str*.1.21(p.88.21; M.8.880A); ὑ. τὴν ἱερωσύνην Gel.Cyz.*h.e*.3. 15.16; *come upon unawares*, Clem.*str*.1.11(p.33.5; 748C); *attack stealthily*, Or.*hom.5.17 in Jer*.(p.47.17; M.13.321D); **2.** *come into one's mind*; of shame, Clem.*prot*.3(p.35.7; M.8.133A); *occur* to one, Eus.*v.C*.1.16(p.15.24; M.20.932A); Ath.*h.Ar*.65(p.218.32; M.25. 769C); **3.** *enter in one's turn, succeed* τὸν πατρῷον ζῆλον ὑ. Synes.*ep*. 150(M.66.1552A); εἰς τὸν αὐτοῦ τόπον ὑ. Hier.*vir.ill*.(tr.Sophr.Pal.)19 (p.21.11; M.*PL*.23.638B); ὑ. τῇ κληρονομίᾳ Jo.Mal.*chron*.18 p.440(M. 97.649A); **4.** *take upon oneself, assume* δούλειον ὑ. ζυγόν Clem.*prot*. 2(p.26.14; M.8.112C); Cael.*ep.syn*.(p.55.30; M.*PL*.50.506B); *undertake* παῖδας ἐκκλησιαστικῷ κανόνι παίγνιον ὑπεισελθόντας Gel.Cyz. *h.e*.3.15.10; **5.** *influence, persuade* ὑ. αὐτῷ, εἴτε διὰ χρημάτων εἴτε διὰ τῆς ἀθέου αὐτῶν θρησκείας, κακῶσαι τοὺς Χριστιανούς Marc.Diac. *v.Porph*.21; Thphn.*chron*.p.85(M.108.257B).

***ὑπειστρέχω,** *run in upon*, *Hom.Clem*.20.11.

***ὑπεισφέρω,** *introduce secretly*, Epiph.*haer*.66.61(p.98.8; M.42. 121B).

***ὑπέκβασις, ἡ,** *coming out, escape* τὸν γνωστικὸν τὴν ὑπέκβασιν παντὸς τοῦ κόσμου...ποιούμενον Clem.*str*.7.7(p.30.26, conj. for ὑπέρβασιν M.9.456B).

***ὑπεκδίδωμι,** *give out, come to an end* διωγμοῦ ὑπεκδόντος Tim.CP *haer*.(M.86.36A).

ὑπεκδύομαι, *strip oneself of, put off*, Eus.*v.C*.1.58(p.35.11; M.20. 973A).

***ὑπεκκακότης, ἡ,** s.v.l., *stealthy evil* ὥς κεν ὑπεκκακότητα χοὸς καὶ δέσμα φύγωσιν Gr.Naz.*carm*.1.2.2.525(M.37.620A).

ὑπέκκαυμα, τό, *fuel*; fig. ἁμαρτία, ὑ. οὖσα τοῦ ἀσβέστου πυρός Germ.CP *or*.1(M.98.237A); met., *incentive*, abs., *lust, desire* τὰ λυμαντήρια τῆς ψυχῆς...πάθη καὶ ὑ. Meth.*symp*.5.3(p.56.15; M.18. 101B); τῶν ὑ. τῆς σαρκός Nil.*epp*.1.222(M.79.164D); Isid.Pel.*epp*.1. 477(M.78.441D).

ὑπέκκαυσις, ἡ, *burning desire, lust*, Meth.*symp*.3.11(p.39.12; M. 18.77B).

ὑπεκκλέπτω, *carry off secretly*; c. reflex., *remove oneself quietly* ὑ. ἑαυτοὺς τῆς ὄψεως Or.*Cels*.2.56(p.179.32; M.11.885C); met. αὖθις ὑπεκκλέψας ἐπ' ἄλλην ἀνεπήδησεν ἔννοιαν Eust.*engast*.17(p.43.27; M. 18.649A); τῷ ἐμπεσόντι θορύβῳ...τήν τε δίκην ὑπεκκλέψαι καὶ τὴν κρίσιν ἐκφυγεῖν διανοούμενον Philost.*h.e*.2.11(p.23.19; ὑποκλέψαι M. 65.473B); *beguile from* νοῦν ὁδοῦ μὲν τῆς πρὸς ἀλήθειαν ὑ. Cyr.*Jo*.6.1 (4.646D).

***ὑπεκκλησίων, ὁ,** title of Homeritan official, equated with Roman πατρίκιος and κανικλείων, †Gregent.*disp*.(M.86.781A).

ὑπεκκρίνω, *discharge, emit*, Sophr.H.*mir.Cyr.et Jo*.23(M.87.3489B).

***ὑπεκκρούω,** *beat back insidiously*; met., *frustrate secretly*, Just. *1apol*.58.3(M.6.416B).

***ὑπεκνεύω,** abs., *withdraw covertly*, Cyr.*Jo*.3.4(4.271A); c. genit., *keep away from, shun* ὑ. τοῦ κακοῦ id.*Is*.4.3(2.648D); trans., *avoid* ὑ. ὀργήν id.*Jo*.6.1(627A); *ib*.11.9(982C).

ὑπεκρ-έω, *flow up and out*, Meth.*res*.1.25(p.251.18; M.41.1129B); *flow away imperceptibly* ῥευστῆς οὐσίας ὃν τὸ σῶμα ∼εῖ Adam.*dial*. 5.16(p.204.16; M.11.1853C).

***ὑπεκτανύω,** *stretch out*, Paul.Sil.*ambo*.83(M.86.2255A).

***ὑπεκτικός,** sens. dub., perh. for ὑπακτικός ? *suffering from diarrhoea*, or for ὑφεκτικός, *consumptive*, *T.Sal*.18.31(M.122.1345B).

ὑπεκφαίνω, *bring to light*, Aen.*dial*.(M.85.945A).

ὑπελίττω, *turn upwards*, ‡Nil.*narr*.4(M.79.628B).

***ὑπεμβαίνω,** *assail*; verbally, Gr.Nyss.*Eun*.1(2 p.30.8; M.45.257C).

***ὑπεμβολαία, ἡ,** ? *chiselling out, gouging* ὑπεμβολαίᾳ τὸ πλάτος ἐκοιλάναμεν Synes.*astrolab*.5(p.140.9; M.66.1585A).

ὑπεμφαίνω, *hint at, indicate* τῆς θυσίας τὸ τέλειον ὑ. ἂν ἡμῖν ὁ μοσχός Cyr.*glaph.Lev*.(1.372D); ‡Proc.G.*Pr*.30:29f.(M.87.1533A).

***ὑπέμφασις, ἡ,** *hint, indication*, ‡Ath.*annunt*.6(M.28.925A).

***ὑπεναλλάττομαι,** *be brought under by exchange, be subjected* ὑπενηλλαγμένη...τοῖς τοῦ διαβόλου θελήμασι Cyr.*glaph.Dt*.(1.418A).

ὑπεναντίος, *set against, opposing*; οἱ ὑ. *the enemy* ὑπὸ θεοῦ γενόμενοι [sc. οἱ ἅγιοι] τοῖς ὑ. φοβεροί Jo.D.*imag*.3.33(M.94.1352C); ὁ ὑ. of Devil, Pall.*h.Laus*.58(p.152.20; M.34.1204B).

ὑπενδίδωμι, *give way, give in*; c. acc., *yield* ἐκ τῶν περὶ τὴν οὐσίαν μόνον ὅτι ἔστι,...εὐσεβῶς θεωρουμένων, τοῖς ὁρῶσιν ὁ θεὸς ἑαυτὸν ὑ. Max.*ambig*.(M.91.1288B).

***ὑπένδοσις, ἡ,** *yielding, affording*, Athenag.*res*.5(p.53.8; M.6. 984A).

***ὑπένδυσις, ἡ,** *clothing*; *covering* of altar, Thdr.Stud.*poen*.1.107 (M.99.1748B).

***ὑπεννεσία, ἡ,** *secret counsel* ὑπεννεσίησι θεοῖο Gr.Naz.*carm*.2.2 (poem.)3.259(M.37.1498A) perh. for ὑπ' ἐννεσίησι.

ὑπεξάγ-ω, *withdraw*; met., *except*, Chrys.*hom.47.2 in Jo*.(8.278D); *exclude* οὐχ ∼ων ἑαυτὸν τῆς θεότητος ὁ Χριστὸς τοιάδε φησίν ‡Caes. Naz.*dial*.4(M.38.864).

ὑπεξαίρω, *subtract, remove* τέλος ἐμαυτὸν ὑ. τοῦ βίου *A.Thom*.A 128(p.236.18); oneself from material cares, Evagr.Pont.*rer.mon*.3 (M.40.1253C); *except, exclude* τὸν υἱὸν ὑ. τούτων [sc. τῶν γενητῶν] Ath.*Ar*.1.36(M.26.85C).

ὑπεξαναβαίνω, *win one's way up, ascend* spiritually or mentally ἡ ἀληθὴς διαλεκτική...ὑ. ἐπὶ τὴν πάντων κρατίστην οὐσίαν Clem.*str*.1.28 (p.109.7; M.8.924B); abs., *ib*.6.7(p.461.5; M.9.280B); c. genit., *transcend*, *ib*.4.25(p.317.16; M.8.1364C).

***ὑπεξαναχωρέω,** *withdraw covertly, steal away*, Gel.Cyz.*h.e*.3.10. 14; met., *act with reserve*, ‡Pion.*v.Polyc*.10.

***ὑπεξεγείρω,** *excite secretly*, Anon.ap.Eus.*h.e*.5.16.9(M.20.468B).

ὑπεξέλευσις, ἡ, *secret escape*, *A.Xanthipp*.14(p.67.14); Thphn. *chron*.p.411(p.486.10; ἐπεξέλευσις M.108.976C).

ὑπεξούσιος, *subject to the power of* another, *under authority* or *control* (opp. αὐτεξούσιος); of Jo. Bapt. opp. Christ, †Hipp.*theoph*.3 (p.259.1; M.10.853D); of elements in rel. to man, Gr.Nyss.*hom.3 in Cant*.(M.44.808A); of created things in rel. to Father, id.*Eun*.2 (2 p.313.16; M.45.485C); of servants, †Cyr.*coll.VT*(6[4].39A; M.77. 1233A); not applicable to Son in rel. to Father εἰ τὸ αὐτεξούσιον τοῦ ὑ. βέλτιον, ὁ δὲ ἄνθρωπος αὐτεξούσιος, ὁ δὲ υἱὸς τοῦ θεοῦ ὑ., ὁ ἄνθρωπος τοῦ υἱοῦ βελτίων· ὅπερ ἄτοπον Didym.(‡Bas.)*Eun*.4(1.290E; M.29. 697C); Gel.Cyz.*h.e*.2.16.18(M.85.1264C); cf. εἰ τοίνυν οὐδὲ ἐν τῷ καιρῷ τοῦ πάθους τῆς ἐξουσίας χωρίζεται, ποῦ ποτε βλέπει ἡ αἵρεσις τοῦ βασιλέως τῆς δόξης τὸ ὑ.; Gr.Nyss.*Eun*.2(2 p.354.17; 532D); ἓν θέλημα λέγοντες...εἰ δὲ ἀνθρώπινον [sc. θέλημα λέξουσι], ψιλὸν ἄνθρωπον καὶ ὑ. αὐτὸν ἔδειξαν Max.*Pyrr*.(M.91.313A); ref. Macedonian doctrine of H. Ghost εἰ γάρ, φησίν, ἀμείνων ὁ αὐτεξούσιος ὑπεξουσίου, ἤδη καὶ ὁ ἄνθρωπος αὐτεξούσιος ὤν, κρείττων παρ' ὑμῖν ἀποφανθείη τοῦ ἁγίου πνεύματος Didym.*Trin*.2.8(M.39.604C).

***ὑπεξουσι-όω,** prob. for ἐπαξιόω, *think right* τοῖς κατὰ πίστιν ∼οῦσιν εὐχὰς...γίνεσθαι...ὑπὲρ τῶν ἐν φυλακῇ κατατιμωρηθέντων... ἄξιόν ἐστιν ἐπινεῦσαι Petr.I Al.*ep.can*.11(M.18.496B).

***ὑπεξωθέω,** *extrude secretly*, Meth.*res*.1.25(p.252.6; M.41.1129C).

ὑπεράγαθος, *supremely good*, of God τῇ θείᾳ...ὑ. φύσει Leont.H. *Nest*.1.38(M.86.1500B); ἀγαθός, καὶ πανάγαθος, καὶ ὑ. θεός, ὁ ὅλος ὢν ἀγαθότης Jo.D.*f.o*.4.13(M.94.1136B); of Trin., Eulog.*fr.Trin*. 2.1(p.364); of God's providence, Thal.*cent*.1.61(M.91.1433A); ὑ. φιλανθρωπίας Jo.D.*spir.neq*.(M.95.97B); esp. as term in Dionysian theology, *who is beyond goodness, more than good*, of Trin., Dion.Ar. *myst*.1.1(M.3.997A); of Father, ‡Cyr.*Trin*.7(6[3].8C; M.77.1132B); τὸν ...ὑπερούσιον καὶ ὑ. λόγον Max.*ambig*.(M.91.1137B); neut. as subst., *goodness which is beyond goodness* τὰ μὲν οὖν ἡνωμένα τῆς ὅλης θεότητός ἐστιν...τὸ ὑ., τὸ ὑπέρθεον...καὶ ὅσα τῆς ὑπεροχικῆς ἐστιν ἀφαιρέσεως Dion.Ar.*d.n*.2.3(M.3.640B); of Son, Hier.H.*Trin*.(M.40.849A); of Christ as Saviour, †Jo.Jej.*poenit*.(M.88.1889C); ‡Sophr.H.*triod*. (M.87.3881B); of BMV, *ib*.(3881B).

***ὑπεραγαθότης, ἡ,** *goodness that is beyond goodness*, of God ἡ τῆς ὑ. ὑπερύπαρξις Dion.Ar.*d.n*.1.5(M.3.593C); *exceeding goodness* of God τῆς ἀφάτου εὐσπλαγχνίας καὶ ὑ. Mod.*dorm*.7(M.86.3293C).

***ὑπεραγάλλομαι,** *rejoice exceedingly*, Ign.*Philad*.5.1.

***ὑπεράγιος,** *supremely holy*; of Trin., Eus.Al.*serm*.16(M.86.416B); of BMV, Jo.D.*haer*.epilog.(M.94.780C).

***ὑπεραγιότης**, ἡ, *supreme holiness*, ‡Gr.Nyss.*occurs*.(M.46.1153A).

***ὑπεραγλαής**, *supremely glorious*, superl., Mod.*dorm*.10(M.86.3305A).

ὑπέραγνος, *more than pure*, Dion.Ar.*c.h*.10.3(M.3.273C); *of surpassing purity*; of BMV, Ephr.3.538E; Jo.Mon.*hymn.Nic.Myr*.3(M.96.1384D).

***ὑπεράγνωστος**, *utterly unknowable*; of God, *transcending knowledge*, Dion.Ar.*d.n*.2.4(M.3.640D) cit. s. ὑπερίδρυσις; θεότης...ὑ. καὶ πάσης ἀπειρίας ἀπειράκις ἐξῃρημένη Max.*ambig*.(M.91.1168A); τὴν τῶν μυστικῶν λογίων ὑ. ... κορυφήν Dion.Ar.*myst*.1.1(M.3.997A); ἄκρα δὲ γνῶσις τῷ ὑ. παρίστησιν Thal.*cent*.1.73(M.91.1433D); of Father, ‡Caes.Naz.*dial*.3(M.38.862); neut. as subst. τὸ ὑ.... τῆς ἀρρήτου... φύσεως Germ.CP *ep.dogm*.4(M.98.169B).

***ὑπεραγνώστως**, *so as to transcend knowledge*, Max.*carit*.3.99 (M.90.1048A).

ὑπεράγω, *surpass*, hence *precede* in time ἔτεσιν ὑ. Eus.*p.e*.10.9 (485D; M.21.808C).

ὑπεραγωνίζ-ομαι, *fight for*; truth, Eus.*h.e*.4.7.5(M.20.316C); τῶν ἀποστολικῶν ~όμενοι δογμάτων Thdt.*h.e*.5.3.1(3.1016).

***ὑπεραγωνιστής**, ὁ, *champion*; of H. Ghost as fighting on behalf of men against demons, Cyr.H.*catech*.16.19.

***ὑπεραγωνίστρια**, fem. of foreg., of prayer τοῦ...ἀγωνιστοῦ ὑ. [sc. in war against demons] Nil.*epp*.3.155(M.79.457C).

***ὑπεραθλ-έω**, *strive on behalf of*, c. genit.; of men for the faith, ‡Eus.*ant.mart.coll*.2(M.20.1524A); of God for men, Apoll.*met.Ps*. 17:31(M.33.1333B); Cyr.*Is*.1.3(2.65C); abs. καταλυπήσαντες τὸν ἀεὶ προεστηκότα καὶ ~οῦντα θεόν id.*Nah*.proem.(3.475A).

ὑπεραινετός, *to be praised exceedingly*; c. genit., *to be praised beyond* πάντων [sc. ὕμνων] ὑ. ... ἐστιν ὁ θεός †Dion.Al.*fr.2 in Job* (p.205.3).

***ὑπεραίρεσις**, ἡ, f.l. for ὑπεξαίρεσις, *removal*, Gr.Nyss.*Eun*.9(M.45.824A; ὑπεξαίρεσις 2 p.223.13).

ὑπεραιώνιος, *above all ages, eternal*, Didym.*Trin*.2.6(M.39.513B); Thal.*cent*.4.71(M.91.1465B).

***ὑπεραιωνίως**, *to all eternity*, Didym.*Trin*.2.6(M.39.516A).

ὑπερακμάζω, **1.** *be past the prime*; of virgins, ref. 1Cor.7:36, Epiph.*haer*.61.5(p.385.24; M.41.1045D); **2.** *abound* παντοίοις ὑ. κακοῖς Thphn.*chron*.p.378(M.108.905A).

ὑπέρακμος, *past the prime*; of virgins, ref. 1Cor.7:36, Epiph.*haer*.61.5(p.385.10; M.41.1045B); neut. as subst. τὸ τῆς ἡλικίας ὑ. Sophr.H.*or*.7(M.87.3329A).

ὑπερακοντίζω, **1.** *overshoot*, met., *outdo*; of Christ, Cosm.Ind.*top*.5(M.88.288C) cit. s. ἀντίπαλος; **2.** *shoot, hurl*, fig. ὑ. τὴν αὐτὴν διάνοιαν ἐπὶ τὰ ὄρη τῶν ἀρωμάτων Ph.Carp.*Cant*.249(M.40.153A); **3.** *pierce* τὸ ἄρρεν γένος τῶν Ἰουδαίων ξίφει ὑ. *Ep.Tib*.(p.80.3).

***ὑπεραληθής**, *more than true*, Max.*myst*.5(M.91.680D); *supremely true* τῆς ὑ. πατρικῆς ἀληθείας Anast.S.*hod*.3(M.89.89A).

***ὑπεραληθῶς**, *with truth that is more than truth*, Dion.Ar.*ep*.1(M.3.1065A).

ὑπεράλλομαι, *spring* or *leap over* or *beyond*; met., *rise superior to, overcome* ὑ. θανάτου Or.*exc.in Ps*.77:31(M.17.144B); ὑ. σκάνδαλα Nil.*Magn*.43(M.79.1021C); *outstrip, surpass*; of Christ in rel. to Jo. Bapt., Cyr.*thes*.11(5[1].95E); *ib*.28(249C).

***ὑπεραμέτρως**, *absolutely immeasurably*, Cyr.*Zach*.4(3.657E).

***ὑπεράμωμος**, *supremely pure*; of Son, Hier.H.*Trin*.(M.40.849A); of BMV, Andr.Cr.*or*.13(M.97.1073A); Jo.Mon.*hymn.Bas*.2 (M.96.1372B).

ὑπεραναβαίνω, *pass over, cross*, Niceph.Ur.*v.Sym*.239(M.86.3205B); ‡Jo.D.*Artem*.24(p.83.18; M.96.1273A); *go beyond* κανόνα... ὑ. Or.*Jo*.13.16(p.240.13; M.14.424A); *transcend*, Ath.*Ar*.3.53(M.26.436A); *surpass*, Cyr.*Jo*.1.9(4.98D); perf. ptcpl., *superior*, Isid.Pel.*epp*.2.179(M.78.632C); neut. as subst., *pre-eminence*, CChalc.*act*.13 (*ACO* 2.1.3 p.61.4; H.2.568E).

***ὑπερανάβασις**, ἡ, *pre-eminency, superiority* ⟨τῆς⟩ τῶν ἀγγέλων ἀξίας ⟨τὸ⟩ μέγεθος καὶ τὴν ὑ. τοῦ τὰ πρεσβεῖα κἀκείνου ἔχοντος Chrysipp.*enc.in Mich*.(p.90.11).

***ὑπεραναβεβηκότως**, *in a higher sense* ὑ. εἰπεῖν Proc.G.*Gen*.11:7 (M.87.328A).

***ὑπερανάγω**, *raise above* ἑαυτὸν τῆς συνηθείας ὑ. Chrys.*hom.22.1 in Heb*.(11.201C).

ὑπεραναπέτομαι** (ὑπερανίπταμαι**), *fly up* over an obstacle; fig., Ephr.3.199D; *fly over*; met., *surmount*, Cyr.*Jo*.1.1(4.11A); *surpass*, *ib*.4.5(412C).

***ὑπεραναπληρόω**, *more than make good, supply* ὑ. τὴν ἔλλειψιν Jo.Clim.*scal*.4(M.88.712C).

***ὑπεράναρχος**, neut. as subst., *complete absence of beginning*; exeg.Jo.1:1, Didym.*Trin*.1.15(M.39.324A).

ὑπερανέχω, *rise up over*; met., *surpass, excel, overcome* τιτρωσκόντων τὴν ψυχὴν ξιφῶν ὑ. Isid.Pel.*epp*.1.75(M.78.236A); med., Or. *schol.in Cant*.2:17(M.17.268B).

ὑπερανθέω, *bloom exceedingly*; met., of human beauty, Gr.Nyss. *v.Gr.Thaum*.(M.46.936D); id.*v.Macr*.(p.372.9; M.46.961A); Ast.Am. *hom*.14(M.40.385A).

***ὑπερανθρώπινος**, *superhuman*, Andr.Caes.ap.*cat.Apoc*.9:16 (p.322.1) for ὑπερουράνιος (M.106.301A).

ὑπεράνθρωπος, *more than human* ὑ. σοφίαν Or.*sel.in Ps*.1 ap.eund. *philoc*.2.4(p.39.21; ὑπὲρ ἄνθρωπον M.12.108B); τὸ δὲ ἀναμάρτητον, ὑ. ἐστι Didym.*Trin*.3.10(M.39.860A); λέγοντες...ἀνάξιον εἶναι θεοῦ γενέσθαι...ἄνθρωπον ὡς ἕκαστον ἄνθρωπον, κἂν ὑ. γέγονε Gr.Agr. *Eccl*.4.5(M.98.936D).

ὑπερανίσταμαι, aor. 2, perf. act., and pass., *stand up* or *project over*; met., *transcend* ὑψηλὰ...φρονήματα...ὑπερανεστηκότα τῶν γηΐνων †Bas.*Is*.66(1.427D; M.30.233B); *be superior* to τὸ ἀπρόσιτον...ἐπ' ἴσης πάντων τῶν ὄντων ὑ. Gr.Nyss.*or.catech*.27(p.104.8; M.45.72C); *excel*, of Christ πάντων...ὑ. Didym.*Trin*.1.15(M.39.305A); Μωσῆ...ὑ. Cyr. *ador*.2(1.79D); *surpass*, c. acc., *ib*.11(377C); *be pre-eminent* τοῖς τῆς ἡγεμονίας αὐχήμασιν ὑ. id.*Zach*.75(3.755C).

ὑπεραντλέομαι, *be water-logged*, Chrys.*hom.3.6 in 1Thess*.(11.450A; περι- Gaume).

ὑπεράνωθεν, *from above*, Gr.Nyss.*Eun*.2(2 p.315.10; M.45.488C); Niceph.Ur.*v.Sym*.95(M.86.3076C); *above*; c. genit., *ib*.104(3084B).

***ὑπεράξιος**, *exceedingly* or *more than worthy*, Jo.Clim.*scal*.4(M.88.689B); †Jo.D.*B.J*.21(M.96.1049A).

***ὑπεράπειρος**, *more than infinite* τὴν ὑ. αὐτοῦ τῆς δυναμοποιοῦ δυνάμεως...ποίησιν Dion.Ar.*d.n*.8.2(M.3.892A); Max.*schol.d.n*.9.2 (M.4.369D); *supremely infinite*; of God, †Jo.D.*B.J*.17(M.96.1009A); of Son, †Gregent.*disp*.(M.86.757D); of Christ's goodness, Jo.D. *hom*.9.7(M.96.732D); of eminence of BMV τὸ τοιοῦτον ὑ. ὕψος· τὸ ἀνῳκισμένον ὑπερέκεινα πασῶν τῶν οὐρανίων δυνάμεων Mod.*dorm*.1(M.86.3280A).

ὑπεραπλόω, **1.** *spread out...above*; sails, ‡Caes.Naz.*dial*.92(M.38.956); pass., *be spread out above, extend above, spread over*, †Bas.*Is*.138(1.476B; M.30.344B); Dion.Ar.*d.n*.4.4(M.3.697C); *ib*.13.1(977B); **2.** *transcend in simplicity* τὸ θεῖον...πάσης ὑπερηπλωμένον ἁπλότητος Max.*opusc*.(M.91.128A).

ὑπεραποδέχομαι, *receive most readily*, Or.*Cels*.3.40(p.236.24; M.11.972C); τοῦτο ἀποδεχόμενοι καὶ ὑ. Thdr.Stud.*epp*.2.107(M.99.1628A).

ὑπεραποθνήσκω, *die for*; of Christ for men, Clem.*paed*.1.9(p.140.5; M.8.352B); Cyr.H.*catech*.13.33 cit. s. δικαιοσύνη; Didym.*Trin*.1.27 (M.39.401A); of men πνεύματός τινος τρέψαντος αὐτῶν τὸ ἡγεμονικὸν ...ἀπὸ τοῦ μισεῖν τὸν λόγον ἐπὶ τὸ ὑ. αὐτοῦ Or.*Cels*.1.46(p.96.11; M.11 745A); of S. Paul for Christ, Cyr.H.*catech*.14.26.

***ὑπεραπόρρητος**, *supremely ineffable*; of mysteries of God, Or. *enarr.in Job* 28:18(M.17.89D).

ὑπεράριθμος, *that transcends numbers*, of Trin. κατὰ δὲ τὴν θεϊκὴν οὐσίαν ὑ. ὕπαρξις Anast.S.*hod*.2(M.89.56B).

***ὑπεράρρην**, *transcending the male principle*, Valent. τὸν... πατέρα ποτὲ μὲν μετὰ συζυγίας τῆς Σιγῆς, ποτὲ δὲ καὶ ὑ. καὶ ὑπέρθηλυ εἶναι θέλουσι Iren.*haer*.1.2.4(ὑπὲρ ἄρρεν M.7.457A).

***ὑπεράρρητος**, *more than ineffable*, of God ὑ. καὶ ὑπεραγνώστου μονιμότητος Dion.Ar.*d.n*.2.4(M.3.640D); ὑ. οἰκονομίας Max.*ambig*.(M.91.1145D); θεότης...ὑ. *ib*.(1168A); ὑ. δόξης ‡Bas.*h.myst*.62(p.397.16).

***ὑπεραρρήτως**, *in a manner that is more than ineffable*, Dion.Ar. *c.h*.13.4(M.3.304C); id.*d.n*.1.4(M.3.592D).

ὑπεράρχιος, *beyond all beginning* ἡ ἀρχίθεος καὶ ὑ. τοῦ υἱοῦ τοῦ θεοῦ ὑπόστασις ‡Ath.*annunt*.9(M.28.929D); τὴν ἀρχικὴν καὶ ὑ. τοῦ θεαρχικοῦ πατρὸς φωτοδοσίαν Dion.Ar.*c.h*.1.2(M.3.121A); πάσης οὐσίας ὑ. ἀρχὴ καὶ αἰτία *ib*.7.4(212C); ὑπέρθεος θεότης, ὑ. ἀρχή Jo.D. *f.o*.1.12(M.94.848B); id.*imag*.1.11(M.94.1241C).

ὑπερασμενίζω, *welcome gladly*, Bas.Sel.*v.Thecl*.1(M.85.537A).

ὑπερασπίζ-ω, **1.** *cover with a shield*, met., *protect, defend, champion* τὸν δὲ αἱρετικὸν Ἄρειον καὶ τοὺς ~οντας αὐτοῦ Ath.*apol.sec*. 58(p.138.15; M.25.353C); ἀποστολικῶν δόξας ~ειν δογμάτων Thdt.*h.e*. 5.3.2(3.1016); c. dat., Thphn.*chron*.p.291(M.108.713A); dep., *ib*.p.397 (948B); of heavenly protection: by God, Clem.*str*.4.7(p.269.27; M.8.1260A); by his power, *A.Xanthipp*.18(p.71.12); by angels, Or.*or*.31. 7(p.400.12; M.11.556C); **2.** *hold above as protection* θεὸς ὑπερασπιεῖ τὴν χεῖρα τὴν αὐτοῦ Chrys.*hom.7.4 in 2Tim*.(11.705B).

***ὑπεράσπισις**, ἡ, *protection*; of man by God, Hesych.S.*temp*.2.84 (M.93.1540B).

ὑπερασπισμός, ὁ, *protection, championship*; of Christ by God, ref. Ps.26:1ff. τὸν ὑ., ὃν ὑπερήσπιζεν αὐτοῦ ὁ θεός Or.*mart.*29(p.25.16; M.11.597C); of man by God, ref. Job 5:17ff., *1Clem.*56.16; against demons, Nil.*epp.*1.227(M.79.165C); by heavenly powers, †Bas.*Is.*20 (1.393B; M.30.153B).

ὑπερασπιστής, ὁ, *protector, champion*; of God in rel. to men, *Pss. Sal.*7.6; *1Clem.*45.7; of Christ, Cyr.*Ps.*17:3(M.69.821A); H. Ghost, Cyr.H.*catech.*16.19; of men ἐκκλησιαστικῆς ἐπιστήμης ὑ. Corn.ap. Eus.*h.e.*6.43.8(M.20.620A); Epiph.*haer.*69.9(p.159.24; M.42.217A); of S. Paul ὑ. τοῦ κηρύγματος Euthal.Diac.*epp.Paul.*proem.(M.85.697B).

ὑπερασπίστρια, ἡ, *protectress*, of prayer τοῦ...ἀγωνιστοῦ [sc. in spiritual warfare]...ὑ. Nil.*epp.*3.155(M.79.457C).

ὑπεραστράπτ-ω, 1. *shine exceedingly*; fig. and met., of glory of divine nature, Bas.*hom.*15.1(2.131E; M.31.465C); of BMV ∼ουσαν ταῖς μαρμαρυγαῖς...πνεύματος Mod.*dorm.*4(M.86.3289A); ὑ. ἐν... κατορθώμασιν Leont.N.*v.Sym.*64(M.93.1748A); **2.** *outshine*, Philost. *h.e.*3.26(p.51.6; M.65.512D); ‡Jo.D.*Artem.*11(p.51.14; M.96.1261B); met. τὴν εὐγένειαν ἰδὼν τοῦ μονογενοῦς...κάλλει τῶν ἀσωμάτων ∼ουσαν λειτουργῶν Mac.Mgn.*apocr.*3.27(p.116.19).

***ὑπερασώματος,** *which is above the incorporeal, being supremely incorporeal*, Didym.*Trin.*1.16(M.39.332C); of Father, *ib.*2.20(740A); τῶν ἀσωμάτων, μᾶλλον δὲ καὶ ὑ. καὶ ὑπὲρ πᾶσαν οὐσίαν Max.*schol.d.n.* 1.1(M.4.185B).

***ὑπεράτρεπτος,** *transcendently immutable, supremely changeless*, of God ὑ. ταυτότητος Dion.Ar.*d.n.*9.5(M.3.913B).

ὑπεραυγάζ-ω, 1. *outshine*, Bas.*hex.*6.3(1.53A; M.29.125A); Procl. CP *annunt.*5(M.85.441C); **2.** *shine exceedingly*, Hipp.*Dan.*2.32.5; **3.** med., *discern clearly* τὸν θεὸν...καθαρᾷ διανοίᾳ ἐν τοῖς ἀνωτάτω τυγχάνειν ∼ομαι Const.ap.Eus.*v.C.*4.9(p.121.26; M.20.1157C); **4.** pass., *be illuminated* βοηθείας χρήζει ἡ ἀσθενοῦσα...ψυχή, ἵνα ταῖς θείαις ἐντολαῖς ∼ηται Isid.Pel.*epp.*1.8(M.78.185A).

ὑπεραυγέω, *shine exceedingly*, ‡Chrys.*pasch.*6.1(8.264D; αὐγάζουσι p.117.1).

***ὑπεράφραστος,** *supremely inexpressible*, Thdot.Anc.*hom.BMV et Sym.*9(M.77.1404B).

***ὑπεράχραντος,** *supremely pure*, Ephr.3.537F.

***ὑπεράχρονος,** *supremely timeless*, Didym.*Trin.*1.15(M.39.300A).

***ὑπερβαθμίως,** *to an excessive degree*, Areth.*Apoc.*68(M.106.780A).

ὑπερβασία, ἡ, *Passover* τὴν Ἑβραΐδα γλῶσσαν εἰς τὴν Ἑλληνίδα φωνὴν μεταβάλλοντες διαβατήρια καὶ ὑπερβασία τὴν ἑορτὴν ταύτην ἐκάλουν *Chron.Pasch.*p.227(M.92.552C).

ὑπέρβασις, ἡ, 1. *passing over*, met. εἰδωλοποιῶν...τι τῶν μὴ ὄντων εἰς ὑ., μᾶλλον δὲ ἔκβασιν γνώσεως Clem.*str.*6.16(p.507.12; M.9.377B); *omission* of a parenthesis, Max.*schol.c.h.*7.2(M.4.68B); **2.** *Passover* ὑ. μὲν γάρ ἐστι...τὸ πάσχα, ὅτι ὑπερέβη τοὺς Ἑβραίων οἴκους ὁ τὰ πρωτότοκα παίδων ὀλοθρευτής ‡Chrys.*pasch.*1(8.251B); *ib.*(258E); τὸ δὲ πάσχα...ὁ δὲ Ἰώσηπος ὑ. [sc. ἑρμήνευσε] Thdt.*qu.24 in Ex.*(1.139C); *Chron.Pasch.*p.226(M.92.549B).

ὑπερβεβλημένως, *beyond all measure*, *Ep.Lugd.*ap.Eus.*h.e.*5.1.17, 20(M.20.416A,B).

Ὑπερβερεταῖος (*-τίω), ὁ, name of month corresponding to October, Chrys.*nativ.*1.5(2.362B,C); τῇ πρὸ πέντε εἰδῶν ὀκτωβρίων, ἥτις ἐστὶν ὑπερβερετίω, τουτέστιν ὀκτωβρίω ια' *M.Tar.*11 suppl. (p.476).

ὑπερβιβάζω, *let pass by*; time, Mac.Aeg.*pat.*17(M.34.877D).

ὑπέρβλυσις, ἡ, a *gushing over, overflow*; met., Dion.Ar.*d.n.*6.2 (M.3.856D).

ὑπερβράζω, *surge up*; of fire, Geo.Pis.*Heracl.*1.24(M.92.1300A).

***ὑπέρβρασις, ἡ,** *fever*, *Ep.Abg.*2(p.281.11).

***ὑπερβρέχω,** Chrys.*ecl.*39(12.726D) f.l. for πῦρ ἔβρεξε, id.*hom.4.5 in Phil.*(11.226A).

ὑπεργάζομαι, *work under*; met., *undermine, subvert*, Bas.Sel.*or.* 3.3(M.85.56A).

***ὑπεργείως,** *above the earth*, Sophr.H.*mir.Cyr.et Jo.*8(M.87. 3441C).

***ὑπεργενής,** being *above that which belongs to created things* τὴν γενητὴν...κτίσιν εἰς δόξαν ὑ. φληνάφως ἀνακομίζοντες *cat.Heb.*suppl. 7:1(p.529.11).

***ὑπεργηθέω,** *rejoice exceedingly*, Eus.*d.e.*6.12(p.262.4; M.22. 429D).

ὑπεργίγνομαι, *be over and above, be in excess*, Epiph.*mens.*21(M. 43.276A).

ὑπέργομος, *overfull*, Epiph.*mens.*21(M.43.276A).

***ὑπερδαπάνη, ἡ,** *extra consumption*, Eustrat.*v.Eutych.*62(M.86. 2345B).

***ὑπερδέ-ομαι,** *intercede for* Epiph.*haer.*69.9(p.159.24; M.42. 217A); ἀγγέλων...ἐλεούντων ἔθνη καὶ ∼ομένων αὐτῶν ἀγαθοῦ Dion. Ar.*ep.*8.1(M.3.1085C).

ὑπερδισκεύω, *throw the discus further than* another; met., *outdistance*, Clem.*str.*7.2(p.9.20; M.9.416A).

***ὑπερδόκιμος,** *supremely trustworthy*, Hipp.*haer.*6.41(p.173.5; M. 16.3259C).

***ὑπερδοξάζ-ω, 1.** *give supreme praise*, Ign.*Polyc.*1.1; *praise exceedingly*; pass., of virginity praised by Church, Epiph.*haer.*61.3 (p.383.17; M.41.1044A); **2.** *praise excessively*, ref. Mc.10:18 μετ' ἐπιτιμήσεως πρὸς τὸν βουλόμενον ∼ειν τὸν υἱόν Or.*Jo.*13.25(p.249.18; M. 14.411B).

***ὑπερδοξάσμιος,** *supremely glorious*, Thdr.Stud.*antirr.*1.7(M.99. 337A).

***ὑπερδύναμαι,** *have power beyond all power*; of God, Dion.Ar. *d.n.*8.2(M.3.889D).

ὑπερδύναμος, *supremely powerful* ὑ. πρὸς θαυματουργίαν ἰσχύς Leont.H.*Nest.*2.21(M.86.1581D).

***ὑπερέζομαι,** *sit upon*; c. genit., †Apoll.*met.Ps.*9:5(M.33.1321B).

ὑπερεθίζω ([*]-ετίζω), *provoke, excite* πρὸς ὀργὴν ὑ. Thphyl.*exc. Rom.*3(p.223.12; M.113.929C); ὑπερετίζει γὰρ ταῦτα [sc. ὁρώμενα]... καὶ παρακαλεῖ τὴν ψυχὴν προσπάσχειν αὐτοῖς Mac.Aeg.*carit.*20(M.34. 925B).

ὑπέρειμι (*sum*), *transcend*, of God ζωὴν...ὑπὲρ πᾶσαν σοφίαν καὶ σύνεσιν ὑπεροῦσαν Dion.Ar.*d.n.*7.1(M.3.865B); *ib.*11.6(953C); *ib.*13.3 (981A).

***ὑπερεισέρχομαι,** *come from above into*, Leont.N.*v.Sym.*41(M.93. 1721A).

ὑπερειστικός, *for supporting*, Gr.Naz.*or.*45.19(M.36.649C).

***ὑπερεκβαίνω,** *go out beyond, transcend*, Ath.*gent.*33(M.25.65D).

ὑπερεκβλύζω, *bubble* or *boil over*; v.l. for ὑπερκλύζω, *overflow*, Thdt.*h.e.*2.30.5(3.905).

***ὑπερεκδίκησις, ἡ,** s.v.l., *extreme vengeance* ἐφάνη...Χριστὸς...ὑ. ζητῶν Evagr.*h.e.*5.21(M.86.2836B; ὕπαρ ἐκδίκησιν p.216.25).

ὑπερέκεινα, *beyond, above* ἀγγέλων καταλήψεως ὑ. Alex.Al.*ep. Alex.*19(p.22.23; M.18.553C); θεὸς ὁ ὑ. πάσης οὐσίας...ὑπάρχων Ath. *gent.*2(M.25.5C); Gr.Nyss.*Eun.*1(1 p.85.1; M.45.316D).

***ὑπερέκκαυμα, τό,** *material for feeding a fire*, Jo.D.*haer.*102(M.94. 777A; ? l. ὑπέκκαυμα).

***ὑπερέκκρουσις, ἡ,** *complete derangement* τὸ ἀκάθαρτον πνεῦμα... χαυνῶσαν αὐτῶν τὴν γνώμην, ὡς δυναμένων τὰ ὑπὲρ τὸν θεὸν ἐννοεῖν, καὶ ἐπιτήδειον εἰς ὑ. κατασκευάσαν Iren.*haer.*1.16.3(M.7.636B).

***ὑπερεκκύπτω,** *look out from and over*, met. *rise above* ὑ. πολύθεον πλάνην Eus.*d.e.*3.6(p.135.34; M.22.229B).

***ὑπερέκλαμπρος,** *supremely radiant* or *splendid*, Hesych.H.*Ps. tit.*17.68(M.27.708C).

ὑπερεκλάμπω, 1. *outshine*; of BMV in rel. to martyrs, Procl.CP *annunt.*5(M.85.441C); **2.** *be supremely radiant*, Mod.*dorm.*8(M.86. 3297B).

***ὑπερεκνικάω,** *vanquish*; v.l. for ἐκνικάω, Eus.*h.e.*8.14.15(M.20. 785B).

***ὑπερεκπαίω,** *exceed*, Clem.*paed.*2.10(p.226.6; M.8.536A).

ὑπερεκπερισσοῦ, *superabundantly*, *T.Jos.*17.5(v.l. ἐκ περισσοῦ).

ὑπερεκπερισσῶς, = foreg., *1Clem.*20.11.

ὑπερεκπίπτ-ω, *transcend* ∼ουσαν πάσης ἀρχῆς...τὴν ζωὴν τοῦ θεοῦ Bas.*Eun.*1.7(1.219A; M.29.525C); Gr.Nyss.*Eun.*1(1 p.129.11; M.45. 365C); c. acc., Leont.H.*Nest.*1.1(M.86.1412A).

***ὑπερεκπληκτέον,** *one must marvel at*, Eus.*l.C.*11(p.227.6; M.20. 1381A).

ὑπερεκτείν-ω, 1. trans., *extend*; boundaries, †Bas.*Is.*151(1.486B; M.30.365C); **2.** intrans., *stretch out beyond*, met. εὐδρομέοντα...ἤδη καὶ τῆς μεσάτης ἀρετῆς ∼οντα Gr.Naz.*carm.*1.2.9.57(M.37.671A); med. or pass., *transcend* μέγα τὸ...παντὸς μεγέθους...∼όμενον Dion. Ar.*d.n.*9.2(M.3.909C); of Son ὑπὲρ τὰ πάντα ὑ. Jo.V H.*icon.*6(M.96. 1353C); *extend* oneself ∼ομένη [sc. ζωή]...καὶ εἰς τὴν δαιμονίαν ζωήν Dion.Ar.*d.n.*6.2(856C).

***ὑπερεκτρέχω,** *outrun*; met., *exceed*, Cyr.*Jo.*1.9(4.99A).

ὑπερέκχυσις, ἡ, *superfluity*; *excess* in drinking, Or.*fr.117 in Lam.*4:21(p.277.29; M.13.661A).

ὑπερελαύνω, *go further than, exceed*, Jo.Mon.*hymn.Nic.Myr.*6(M. 96.1385C).

ὑπερένδοξος, *supremely glorious*, Epiph.*haer.*76.43(p.397.32; M. 42.609B); ὑ. θεότητος Dion.Ar.*c.h.*8.2(M.3.241B); of name of God, *Pap.Chr.*(p.419); of BMV, *Lit.Jac.*(p.174.19).

ὑπερενόομαι, *be supremely united* or *be united in a way that transcends all unity*; of Godhead, Dion.Ar.*d.n.*2.1(M.3.637A); *ib.*2.4 (641A); *ib.*11.1(949A).

***ὑπερέντευξις**, ἡ, *intercession*; of H. Ghost for men, Gr.Naz.*or.*31.30(p.186.4; M.36.168C).

ὑπερεντυγχάν-ω, *intercede in place of*, ref. Gen.4:10 τύπος ὁ δίκαιος ὁ παλαιὸς τοῦ νέου δικαίου καὶ τὸ αἷμα τὸ ἐντυγχάνον τὸ παλαιὸν ~ει τοῦ αἵματος τοῦ νέου Clem.*paed.*1.6(p.118.21; M.8.305C); *address* ὑμῖν ~ομεν κατ' ἐκείνων, ἵνα ἀπελθόντες διορθώσητε αὐτούς Chrys.*Anna* 4.1(4.730B).

***ὑπερεξάγω**, **1.** *expel, exclude*, Eus.*h.e.*10.8.11(M.20.897B, v.l. ὑπεξάγω); **2.** *surpass*, *ib.*8.12.7(772B).

ὑπερεξαίρω, *excel*, c. genit., Mod.*dorm.*6(M.86.3292B).

***ὑπερεξαπλόομαι**, *be spread out beyond*; met., of God, *transcend* παντὸς τόπου καὶ χρόνου ὑ. Leont.H.*Nest.*1.1(M.86.1412A).

***ὑπερεξαστράπτω**, *surpass in brilliance*, of Church ὑ. ὑπὲρ τὴν λαμπρότητα...ἡλίου Ephr.3.310C.

***ὑπερεξεπαίρω**, pass., *be raised above, exalted*, Didym.*Trin.*1.15(M.39.312A).

***ὑπερεξέρχομαι**, *surpass, transcend*, Ath.*decr.*12(p.10.27; M.25.'444'(436)C).

***ὑπερέξεστι**, *it is possible*, Euther.*confut.*7(M.28.1360A).

***ὑπερεόρτιος**, *supreme among festivals*; of Easter, ‡Epiph.*hom.*3(M.43.468A).

ὑπερεπαίρομαι, *be exalted too much*, Or.*sel.in Ps.*46:10(M.12.1437C); met., *be puffed up, made unduly proud*, c. ἐπί, *ib.*4:6(1161A); ref.2Cor.12:7 ὑ. τῇ ὑπερβολῇ τῶν...ἀποκαλύψεων id.*or.*6.5(p.315.25; M.11.440B).

***ὑπερεπέκεινα**, *beyond, above* ἀγγέλων καταλήψεως ὑ. Alex.Al.*ep. Alex.*ap.Thdt.*h.e.*1.4.19(3.734; v.l. for ὑπερέκεινα (Opitz p.22.23)).

[*]**ὑπερετίζω**, v. ὑπερεθίζω.

***ὑπερευλαβής**, *exceedingly reverent*, Germ.CP *or.*8(M.98.369B).

***ὑπερευλογέω**, perf. ptcpl. pass., *blessed above all*; of BMV, Ephr.3.524E,534B; v.l. for εὐλογημένης, *Lit.Jac.*(p.214.10n.); *Lit.Bas.*(p.330.32).

***ὑπερευρύς**, *exceedingly broad*, Dion.Ar.*d.n.*9.5(M.3.913A).

***ὑπερεύσπλαγχνος**, *supremely compassionate* ὑ. καὶ ἐλεήμων θεός *Lit.Jac.*(p.196.9).

***ὑπερευφημέω**, *speak very highly of*; pass., Nil.*epp.*1.74(M.79.113D).

***ὑπερεύφημος**, *worthy of supreme praise* or *beyond praise* ὑ. καὶ πανεύφημον θεαρχίαν Dion.Ar.*c.h.*7.4(M.3.212C); Max.*comput.*1(M.19.1217C).

ὑπερευχαριστέω, *give abundant thanks*, *Barn.*5.3; Arist.*apol.*11 (*JTS* p.76); Eus.*m.P.*11.26(p.945.1; M.20.1509B).

ὑπερεύχομαι, *pray on behalf of, pray for*; to God for people, c. genit., Clem.*str.*7.11(p.45.3; M.9.485D); Bas.*ep.*46.2(3.136D; M.32.373A); ὑ. σωτηρίας Eus.*v.C.*2.14(p.47.9; M.20.993A); ὑ. σου τῆς ἁμαρτίας Synes.*ep.*72(M.66.1436B); c. acc., Eus.Al.*serm.*21.8(M.86.433B); c. dat., Thphn.*chron.*p.3(M.108.61C); abs., *make intercession*, Chrys.*hom.6.2 in 1Tim.*(11.581B).

ὑπερέχ-ω, of God, *transcend*, ref. Jo.14:28 πάντων...γενητῶν ~ειν...ὑπερβαλλούσῃ ὑπεροχῇ φαμὲν τὸν σωτῆρα καὶ τὸ πνεῦμα τὸ ἅγιον, ~όμενον τοσοῦτον ἢ καὶ πλέον ὑπὸ τοῦ πατρός, ὅσῳ ~ει αὐτὸς καὶ τὸ ἅγιον πνεῦμα τῶν λοιπῶν Or.*Jo.*13.25(p.249.19; M.14.441B).

ὑπέρζεσις, ἡ, *boiling over*; met., of the passions, Geo.Pis.*hex.*798(M.92.1495A); *inflammation* δυσκαθέκτους τῶν ποδῶν ὑ. *ib.*1557(1555A).

ὑπερζέω, *boil over*, lit. and met.; of the sun, *burn above* κεφαλῆς ὑ. Gr.Nyss.*hom.4 in Cant.*(M.44.844D).

***ὑπερζυγέω**, *take precedence*, Gr.Naz.*carm.*2.1.11.401(M.37.1057A).

ὑπέρζωος, *beyond all life, transcending life* θεότητος τὸ ὑ. Dion.Ar.*d.n.*2.3(M.3.640B); ὑ. καὶ ζωαρχικὴ ζωή *ib.*6.3(865A).

ὑπερηγορέω, *speak for, champion*, Synes.*provid.*1.18(p.107.11; M.66.1256B).

ὑπερήδω, *please exceedingly*, Bas.*hom.*6.4(2.46C; M.31.268C).

***ὑπέρημαι**, *sit upon*, c. genit., Apoll.*met.Ps.*131:12(M.33.1513C).

***ὑπερημερήσιος**, *deferred for more than a day*, Thdr.Stud.*or.*11.3.15(M.99.817C).

ὑπερήμερος, *over the day for payment*; hence *after the proper day, late*; of people delayed on a voyage, Synes.*ep.*4(M.66.1337D); *overdue* ὑ. τῆς κυρίας γενομένης, ἐν ᾗ κρίνειν ἔδει Soz.*h.e.*3.11.6(M.67.1061A); *taking more than a day* ἥλιος...μηκύνων τοῦ χρόνου τὰ μέτρα, ἵνα μὴ ὑ. νίκη λυπήσῃ τοὺς κάμνοντας Bas.Sel.*or.*31.1(M.85.341A).

[*]**ὑπερηνορίη**, ἡ, *exceedingly great courage*, tr. Vergil *ecl.*4.27 ap. Const.*or.s.c.*(p.184.21; M.20.1296B).

***ὑπερηνωμένως**, *with supreme unification* or *in a way which transcends all unification* τῆς ἑνώσεως τῆς θείας ὑ. ἑαυτὴν ἀγαθότητι πληθυούσης Dion.Ar.*d.n.*2.5(M.3.644A).

ὑπερηφανεύ-ω, **1.** med., *behave arrogantly, be arrogant* ἀρχὴν πρὸς τὸ ~εσθαι τὴν ὑπεροψίαν λαμβάνων. τοῦτο γάρ ἐστι τὸ ὑ., τὸ ὑπερφαίνεσθαι τῶν πολλῶν ἐπιχειρεῖν †Bas.*Is.*88(1.440C; M.30.261C); **2.** c. infin. *disdain*, ‡Just.*ep.Zen.et Ser.*3(M.6.1185C, v.l. ὑπερφανέω); **3.** pass., *be treated arrogantly*, Ephr.1.20D.

ὑπερηφανία, ἡ, *arrogance*; as a sin which destroys soul, *Barn.*20.1; coupled with ὕβρις as first sin, †Bas.*Is.*88(1.440A; M.30.261B); ἡ ὑ. κακὸν ἔκγονόν ἐστι τῆς ὕβρεως *ib.*(440D; M.264A); τὸ τοῦ σφόδρα δοκοῦντος ἐν ἁμαρτίαις εἶναι κατεπαρθῆναι, ὑ. δεινή, ἣν ἔπαθεν ὁ Φαρισαῖος κατὰ τοῦ τελώνου *ib.*(441A; M.264B); τοῦ γὰρ ὑπὲρ τοὺς ἄλλους θέλειν εἶναι, τὸ χαλεπὸν τοῦτο πάθος, ἡ ὑ., ὃ δὴ μάλιστα σπέρμα...πάσης τῆς κατὰ τὴν ἁμαρτίαν ἀκάνθης,...τοῦτο μάλιστα ἐκ τῆς αἰτίας τοῦ γάμου τὴν ἀρχὴν ἔχει Gr.Nyss.*virg.*4(p.268.21; M.46.337D); crushed by Christ's victory over temptation, Isid.Pel.*epp.*1.75(M.78.233D); further descriptions, Nil.*spir.mal.*17(M.79.1161Cff.); ‡Nil.*vit.cog.*(M.79.1461Cff.).

ὑπερήφανος, *arrogant*, descriptions ὁ ἐπὶ τοῖς προσοῦσιν αὐτῷ κομπάζων, καὶ ὑπὲρ ὅ ἐστι, φαίνεσθαι ἐπιτηδεύων Bas.*reg.br.*56(2.434B; M.31.1120D); τὸν πράττοντα μέν, σεμνυνόμενον δέ, καὶ τοὺς ἄλλους ὀνειδίζοντα Isid.Pel.*epp.*3.382(M.79.1025C); τοὺς ἐφ' οἷς ἔχουσι πλεονεκτήμασι μεγάλα φρονοῦντας Thdt.*Rom.*1:30(3.28); τοὺς κατὰ τῶν οὐκ ἐχόντων ἐφ' οἷς ἔχουσιν φυσωμένους Gennad.*fr.Rom.*1:29ff.(p.360.9; M.85.1669B).

ὑπερηχ-έω, *sound more loudly than, drown with noise*, ref. talkers in church τῷ ἰδίῳ θορύβῳ ~ῶν τὴν διδασκαλίαν τοῦ πνεύματος Bas.*hom.in Ps.*28(1.123B; M.29.304A); Gr.Naz.*ep.*4(M.37.25C); met. Ἰωάννης ὁ τῇ μεγαλοφωνίᾳ τῶν κατ' αὐτὸν δογμάτων ~ήσας τὰ προλαβόντα κηρύγματα Gr.Nyss.*Eun.*12(1 p.249.22; M.45.949C); c. reflex., *become louder and louder* ὑ. ἑαυτὴν ἡ σάλπιγξ id.*v.Mos.*45(M.44.316D).

ὑπερθαυμάζω, *admire more* ἔδει Μωϋσέα μὲν θαυμάζειν,...ὑ. δὲ τὸν Ἐμμανουήλ Cyr.*Lc.*5:14(M.72.557B).

***ὑπερθεάρεστος**, *exceedingly pleasing to God*, Ephr.2.19A.

***ὑπερθειάζω**, *over-deify*; hence *praise extravagantly*, Philost.*h.e.*2.3(M.65.468A); *ib.*10.6(p.128.11; 588A).

ὑπερθεματίζω, *overbid, outbid*, Ephr.2.274F.

ὑπέρθεος, **1.** *more than divine*; of God, Dion.Ar.*d.n.*2.3(M.3.646B); meaning explained, id.*ep.*2(M.3.1068A); ‡Cyr.*Trin.*7(6^3.8C; M.77.1132B); ὑ. θεότης Jo.D.*f.o.*1.12(M.94.848B); of Trin., Dion.Ar.*myst.*1.1(M.3.997A); ἡ τριὰς οὐ τελεία μόνον τῇ τῆς μιᾶς θεότητος τελειότητι, ἀλλὰ καὶ ὑπερτελὴς καὶ ὑ. δόξῃ καὶ ἀιδιότητι, καὶ βασιλείᾳ, μὴ μεριζομένη Sophr.H.*ep.syn.*(M.87.3160A); **2.** *supremely divine*; of Trin., ‡Ath.*annunt.*1(M.28.917A); Eulog.*fr.Trin.*2.1(p.364); Areth.*Apoc.*4:4(M.106.569A); of Christ, Mod.*dorm.*10(M.86.3305B); Jo.D.*trisag.*26(M.95.57C).

***ὑπερθεότης**, ἡ, *divinity which is more than divinity*, Dion.Ar.*d.n.*13.3(M.3.981A).

***ὑπερθέσιμος**, sc. νηστεία, term for fast continued beyond accustomed hour until cockcrow of following day, so *prolonged fast* τὰς καλουμένας ὑπερθεσίμους πράττουσι διήμεροι καὶ τριήμεροι τὰς νηστείας ἐκτελοῦντες Evagr.*h.e.*1.21(p.30.6; M.86.2477B); ὑ. ... ποιεῖν Jo.Clim.*scal.*14(M.88.865C).

ὑπέρθεσις, ἡ, **1.** *superior position*, Gr.Naz.*or.*32.27(M.36.205B); **2.** *extension* of a fast, Dion.Al.*ep.can.*(p.102.3; M.10.1277A).

ὑπερθετικός, *superlative*; prob. c. genit., *having the characteristic of exceeding* τὸν ὀκτὼ ἀριθμόν, ὡς τῆς κατὰ χρόνον ἑβδομαδικῆς ὑπερθετικῆς [? for ὑπερθετικὸν] ἰδιότητος Max.*ambig.*(M.91.1397D).

***ὑπέρθηλυς**, *transcending the female principle*, (Valent.) of Father ποτὲ δὲ καὶ ὑπέραρρεν καὶ ὑ. εἶναι θέλουσι Iren.*haer.*1.2.4 (ὑπὲρ θῆλυ M.7.460A).

***ὑπερθρηνέω**, *raise a lament*, *1 Apoc.Jo.*(p.94n.).

***ὑπέρθρονος**, *highly enthroned*, Gr.Naz.*carm.*2.1.16.6(M.37.1255A); *supremely enthroned*; of Trin., Eulog.*fr.Trin.*2.1(p.364).

ὑπερθρῴσκω, *leap over*; met., of God, ref. Mich.7:18 ὑ. ἁμαρτίας Cyr.*Mich.*72(3.472E); *pass beyond the bounds of* ὑ. ... τὸ φιλάλληλον, id.*ador.*8(1.267D).

***ὑπερί**, *for* (form prob. due to confusion of ὑπέρ and περί) ὑ. εὐχῆς τῶν χωρίων καὶ τοῦ λαοῦ *IGC As.Min.*2.15; spelt ὑπερεί *ib.*40.

ὑπεριδρύομαι, *be established above, be superior* to, Dion.Ar.*c.h.*7.2(M.3.208B); of God, *transcend* παντὸς λόγου, καὶ νοῦ, καὶ σοφίας ὑ. id.*d.n.*7.1(M.3.865B); ‡Cyr.*Trin.*7(6^3.8C; M.77.1132B); τὰ πάντα ἐν ἀκαταληψίᾳ ὑ. ‡Meth.*Sym.et Ann.*5(M.18.360A).

***ὑπερίδρυσις**, ἡ, *being that is established transcendentally*, i.e. *ultimate reality* καλοῦσι...τὰς μὲν ἑνώσεις τὰς θείας, τὰς τῆς... ὑπεραγνώστου μονιμότητος κρυφίας καὶ ἀνεκφοιτήτους ὑ. Dion.Ar.*d.n.*2.4(M.3.640D).

***ὑπεριλάσκομαι**, *make propitiation*, with a view to, c. genit., of Christ as high priest τῆς πάντων ὑ. σωτηρίας Eus.*l.C.*1(p.198.25; M.20.1324B).

***ὑπεριμείρομαι**, *desire exceedingly*, Iren.*haer.*1.13.2(M.7.580A).

***ὑπερισσεία, ἡ**, s.v.l., *excess, superfluity*, Isid.Pel.*epp.*4.22(M. 78.1072B; v.l. ὑπηρεσία).

***ὑπερκαθαρός**, *exceedingly pure*, of BMV ὑπερκαθαρωτέρα ἡλιακῶν μαρμαρυγῶν Ephr.3.545E.

ὑπέρκαιρος, *beyond the due time, unduly postponed*, Cyr.*glaph. Ex.*2(1.273B).

ὑπέρκαλος, *supremely beautiful*; of God, Ath.*gent.*2(M.25.5C); *ib.*41(81D); ὑ. τῆς σωφροσύνης κάλλος Isid.Pel.*epp.*2.7(M.78.464C); *more than beautiful*; of divine beauty, Dion.Ar.*d.n.*4.7(M.3.701D).

***ὑπερκαταπλήττω**, *terrify exceedingly*, Ephr.3.373A.

ὑπέρκειμαι, 1. *lie above*; met., *be placed above, excel*; *transcend*, of God πᾶσαν νόησιν...ὑ. Jo.D.*f.o.*1.8(M.94.816A); of Christ πάσης ὑ. γενητῆς οὐσίας Cyr.*Jo.*1.9(4.99C); abs., *be transcendent, supreme*; of God, Gr.Nyss.*or.catech.*1(p.8.11; M.45.13B); of God's sovereignty, Dion.Ar.*d.n.*12.3(M.3.969C); **2.** *be delayed, postponed* τὰ νῦν ὑπερκείσθω λέγειν Clem.*str.*5.6(p.350.19; M.9.61B).

***ὑπερκειμένως**, *in a superior position*, Dion.Ar.*c.h.*5(M.3.196B); *in a superior manner*, *ib.*7.4(212A); *ib.*15.1(328C).

***ὑπερκεφαλέω**, *overtop, be superior to*; c. acc., Ath.*exp.Ps.*68:16f. (M.27.309B).

***ὑπερκινδυνεύω**, *face danger on behalf of*, Chrys.*hom.7.3 in 2Tim.* (11.703C); Pall.*h.Laus.*71(p.167.10; M.34.1258A); Thphn.*chron.*p.343 (M.108.825B).

***ὑπερκλεής**, *beyond praise*, of Trin. ἰσοκλεής, ἰσομεγέθης, μᾶλλον δὲ ὑ. ‡Caes.Naz.*dial.*3(M.38.861).

***ὑπερκλονέω**, *dash against and over*; of the sea, *Orac.Sib.*4.129.

***ὑπερκόπτω**, *come out, emerge*, Nil.ap.Proc.G.*Cant.*2:9(M.87. 1600D) cit. s. ἀπόκρυψις.

***ὑπερκοσμικῶς**, s.v.l., = ὑπερκοσμίως, Ephr.3.711F.

ὑπερκόσμιος, *above the world, transcendent*; or *supernatural, celestial*; of God, Cyr.*hom.pasch.*5.6(5[2].55C); ἐγκόσμιον, περικόσμιον, ὑ. Dion.Ar.*d.n.*1.6(M.3.596C); of Son βασιλεὺς...ὑ. Afric.*ep.Arist.*1 (p.54.6; M.11.53A); ὑπέρσοφον, ὑ., ὑπεράγαθον Hier.H.*Trin.*(M.40. 849A); ref. Jo.17:5 τῆς πρὸ κόσμου καὶ τῆς ὑ. δόξης ἑαυτοῦ μνημονεύων Ath.*Ar.*1.38(M.26.92A); ref. Mt.1:20 εἰ τοίνυν τὸ ὑ. σῶμα Χριστοῦ ἐκ πνεύματός ἐστιν ἁγίου Didym.(‡Bas.)*Eun.*5(1.298B; M.29.716B); χαῖρε, δι' ἧς ἡμῖν ὁ ὑ. ἐπέφανεν ‡Jo.D.*hom.*5(M.96.652C); of his glory, Cyr.*inc.unigen.*(5[1].697A); and divinity, Proc.G.*Is.*42:10ff.(M. 87.2372C); of heavenly beings, Eus.*l.C.*1(p.196.24; M.20.1320A); Dion.Ar.*c.h.*2.4(M.3.144B); Jo.D.*f.o.*1.1(M.94.789A); of heavenly mysteries, Ath.*gent.*9(M.25.20A); Dion.Ar.*c.h.*4.2(M.3.180B); Mod. *dorm.*8(M.86.3300A); of anything *heavenly* opp. earthly; of eternal life, Clem.*q.d.s.*23(p.175.5); ἡ δὲ σωτήριος χάρις, ὑ. τινα καὶ ἀγγελικὴν ἡμῖν παρέχουσα γνῶσιν Eus.*Marcell.*1.1(p.3.19; M.24.716C); ἡ κτίσις πᾶσα...ἥ τε ὑ., ἥ τε περίγειος Bas.*hom.in Ps.*28(1.122E; M.29.301C); neut. as subst., *heaven* ἐμοῦ ὁ θρόνος ἐν τῷ ὑ. ἐστίν *T.Job* 33(p.124. 15); of the righteous ὁ δίκαιος...αἰνεῖ τὸν θεὸν ἑπτάκις ὑ. γεγονώς, τοῦ ἄνω κεχωρηκέναι τοῦ ἐν ἓξ ἡμέραις γενομένου κόσμου Ath.*exp.Ps.* 118:164(M.27.508A); ὑ. τῇ διανοίᾳ γεγενημένους ‡Bas.*const.*20.3(2. 566B; M.31.1393B); as pun on meaning '*exceedingly well ordered*', of 'gnostic' γενόμενος κόσμιος καὶ ὑ., ἐν κόσμῳ καὶ τάξει ⟨πάντα⟩ πράσσων Clem.*str.*7.3(p.13.25; M.9.424A); of the elect acc. Basilides ξένην τὴν ἐκλογὴν τοῦ κόσμου...εἴληφε λέγειν, ὡς ἂν ὑπερκόσμιον φύσει οὖσαν *ib.*4.26(p.321.30; M.8.1376A); neut. as subst. 'Ηλίου περιενόουν τὸν Κάρμηλον, καὶ 'Ιωάννου τὴν ἔρημον καὶ τῶν οὕτω φιλοσοφούντων τὸ ὑ. Gr.Naz.*or.*10.1(M.35.828A).

***ὑπερκοσμίως**, *in a manner above that of this world, in a heavenly manner* ἑορτάζωμεν...μὴ κοσμικῶς, ἀλλ' ὑ. Gr.Naz.*or.*38.4(M.36. 316B); Ephr.2.211E; ὅσα...ταῖς οὐρανίαις μὲν οὐσίαις ὑ., ἡμῖν δὲ συμβολικῶς παραδέδοται Dion.Ar.*c.h.*1.3(M.3.124A); of God ταῖς ἀνομοίοις ἐκφαντορίαις...ὑ. ὑμνεῖται *ib.*2.3(140D).

ὑπερκρατέω, intrans., *prevail*, Bas.*ep.*17(3.95E; M.32.281B).

ὑπερκρεμάννυμι, pass., *be hung up on behalf of*, ‡Gr.Naz.*Chr.pat.* 166(M.38.150A).

***ὑπέρκτησις, ἡ**, *excess*, *Orac.Sib.*4.148.

***ὑπερκτυπέω**, *out-thunder*, Gr.Naz.*carm.*2.1.11.168(M.37.1041A).

ὑπερκύδας, *exceedingly renowned* or *glorious*, Paul.Sil.*Soph.*142 (M.86.2125A); of Christ, *ib.*303(2131B).

ὑπερκύπτω, 1. *raise one's eyes above, look beyond*, fig. ὑ. τὸ καταπέτασμα Mac.Mgn.*apocr.*2.8(p.9.7); met. ὑ. τὰ γεννητά Or.*or.*9.2 (p.318.29; M.11.444C); Eus.*d.e.*1.5(p.20.32; M.22.45A); τὴν φυσικὴν ὑπερκύψαντες θεωρίαν εἰς τὴν ἄυλον παρακύπτουσι γνῶσιν Max.*ambig.* (M.91.1356B); **2.** *rise above*; met., Or.*Cels.*1.3(p.58.3; M.11.661A); ὑ. τὰ ἐμποδίζοντα *ib.*1.29(p.80.9; 716A); Procl.CP *annunt.*2(M.85. 428D); **3.** *emerge, rise up* ἐκ δὲ βυθοῦ...νῆσοι ὑ. θαλάσσης [sc. in an earthquake] *Orac.Sib.*4.60; of fallen angels οὐκέτι εἰς τὰ ὑπερουράνια ὑπερκύψαι δυνάμενοι Athenag.*leg.*25.1(M.6.948C); met., of those who deify the elements ἀποπίπτοντες τοῦ μεγέθους τοῦ θεοῦ, καὶ ὑπερκύψαι τῷ λόγῳ...οὐ δυνάμενοι *ib.*22.7(940B); Gr.Nyss.*Eun.*10(2 p.231. 28; M.45.833A); *attain to* ἀγαθοεργίᾳ...εἰς...κληρονομίαν ὑ. Clem.*str.* 6.14(p.486.8; M.9.329B); *arrive at*, Bas.*Eun.*2.14(1.249C; M.29.600A).

ὑπέρλαμπρος, 1. *exceedingly bright*, Dion.Ar.*d.n.*8.2(M.3.892A); Jo.D.*hom.*1.4(M.96.552D); hence λεπρῶν ἡ ὑ. κάθαρσις Sophr.H.*ep. syn.*(M.87.3176B); **2.** *very splendid* or *distinguished*, Clem.*q.d.s.*8 (p.165.4; M.9.612D); Isid.Pel.*epp.*3.251(M.78.929C); of works of Christ, Const.ap.Gel.Cyz.*h.e.*2.7.20(M.85.1236C); as title of honour ὑ. ὑπάρχους Thdt.*ep.*47(4.1106).

ὑπερλευκαίνω, *be very white*, Gr.Nyss.*hom.7 in Cant.*(M.44.849B).

***ὑπερλόγως**, *in a manner which is beyond understanding* ἀμφοτέροις [sc. ψυχῇ καὶ σώματι]...ὁ λόγος ὑ. ἥνωται ‡Caes.Naz.*dial.*25(M. 38.885).

ὑπέρλοφος, *with high crest*; met., *lofty, sublime*, Cyr.*ador.*1(1.29C).

ὑπερμαζάω, *have over-large breasts*, Synes.*ep.*4(M.66.1340C).

ὑπερμαχέω, *fight for* or *on behalf of*, Clem.*paed.*1.5(p.102.21; M. 8.276A); Eustrat.*v.Eutych.*89(M.86.2376A); c. dat., Thphn.*chron.* p.331(M.108.797A).

***ὑπερμαχία, ἡ**, *defence*, Anast.S.*hod.*24(M.89.309B).

ὑπέρμαχος, ὁ, *champion, defender*; esp. of God on behalf of men, *1Clem.*45.7; Meth.*res.*1.56(p.316.10; M.41.1149D); Eus.*v.C.*2.2(p.41. 13; M.20.980D).

ὑπερμεγέθης, of God, *supremely great*, *Orac.Sib.fr.*1.7; Eus.*l.C.*1 (p.196.19; M.20.1320A); *beyond greatness*, of Trin. ἰσομεγέθης, μᾶλλον δὲ...ὑ. ‡Caes.Naz.*dial.*3(M.38.861).

***ὑπερμεθύσκω**, *be excessively drunk*; met., Jo.Eub.*innoc.*(M.96. 1504C).

***ὑπερμένω**, *undergo, suffer*, Ant.Mon.*ep.Eust.*(M.89.1421B).

***ὑπερμογέω**, *be in great distress*, Gr.Naz.*carm.*2.1.50.113(M.37. 1393A).

***ὑπερνεφέω**, *soar above the clouds*; met., of the proud, Gr.Naz.*or.* 43.64(M.36.581A); id.*carm.*1.2.2.6(M.37.578A); *ib.*2.1.11.413(1057A).

ὑπερνεφής, *above the clouds*; fig., Gr.Nyss.*v.Mos.*(M.44.425B); met., *highly exalted, sublime*; of Church, Clem.*paed.*1.9(p.139.22; M.8.352A); ὑπερνεφὲς...τῆς παρθενίας...τὸ κατόρθωμα Mac.Mgn.*apocr.* 3.43(p.150.10).

***ὑπερνήχ-ομαι**, *swim over*, Chrys.*hom.25.1 in 2Cor.*(10.613C; v.l. for νηχόμενος Gaume); fig. ψυχὴ...τοῦ κλύδωνος ὑ. Thdt.*Ps.*5:2f. (1.635); hence *pass safely over* ὑ. [sc. in Church as in the ark]... θανάτου τὸ δεῖμα Cyr.*glaph.Gen.*2(1.38A); met., *rise superior to* τοῦ περὶ τῆς οὐσίας λόγου ὡς...μηδαμῶς ἁλωσίμου, ἀλλὰ πᾶσαν βάσανον ~ομένου Isid.Pel.*epp.*2.299(M.78.728A); *go beyond, transcend*, *ib.*3.58 (769B); *surpass, excel*, Cyr.*Is.*5.1(2.730C); *overstep the bounds of* τὸ... σίδηρον τοῖς τοῦ πέλας ὑπενεγκεῖν, ~εται πως...τὸ φιλάλληλον id.*ador.* 8(1.267D).

ὑπερνικάω, *prevail completely* (*over*); *be more than conqueror*; as contrasted with νικάω, Or.*comm.in Rom.*8:37(*JTS* 14 p.20); *surpass, transcend* θνητὴν διάνοιαν ὑ. Eus.*l.C.*11(p.229.11; M.20.1385A); Sophr.H.*ep.syn.*(M.87.3176C).

***ὑπέρνοια, ἡ**, *intellectual pride* τῆς ἀντιπάλου τῇ τε ἀνοίᾳ καὶ τῇ ὑ. ἕξεως, ἥ ἐστι φρόνησις· ἀντίκειται γὰρ αὕτη...τῇ...ὑ. ἐν τῷ ἐμποιεῖν αὖθις ἡμῖν τῆς οἰκείας ἀσθενείας ἐπίγνωσιν ‡Proc.G.*Pr.*3:13(M.87. 1245B); Max.*opusc.*(M.91.21A).

***ὑπέρξενος**, *exceedingly wonderful*, of feast of Annunciation ἡ τῆς βασιλίδος βασιλικὴ καὶ ὑπέρξενος ἑορτή τε καὶ πανήγυρις ‡Jo.D.*hom.* 5(M.96.648B).

ὑπέρογκος, 1. *inflated, proud, boastful* ὑ. ῥῆμα Hipp.*Dan.*3.7.1; *A.*(*Pass.*)*Andr.*3(p.5.14); Cyr.*Am.*17(3.267B); **2.** *above the normal, sublime*; of Christ's commandments, Chrys.*hom.18.1 in Mt.*(7. 234C); Sophr.H.*ep.syn.*(M.87.3176C); *difficult*, Chrys.*hom.18.6 in Mt.*(7.242D).

ὑπεροιδαίν-ω, 1. *swell over* ἄβυσσοι τῶν ἰδίων ὅρων ~ουσαι Gr. Nyss.*res.*1(M.46.609B); **2.** *swell overmuch*, met., of the heart ζήλῳ τῆς πίστεως κατὰ τῶν βλασφημούντων ὑ. id.*Eun.*4(1 p.98.11; M.45.676B).

***ὑπεροικτείρω**, *pity exceedingly*, Clem.*prot.*8(p.61.26; M.8.192B).

***ὑπερόμοιος**, *more than like* τοῦ δὲ υἱοῦ ὁμοίου ὄντος τῷ πατρὶ καὶ ὑ., διὰ τὸ ταὐτὸν εἶναι πρὸς τὸν πατέρα καὶ ἴσον πατρί Epiph.*haer.*76.2 (p.342.23; M.42.520A).

***ὑπεροξύπορος**, neut. as subst., *supreme swiftness*, exeg. Heb. 4:12 τὸ ὑ. τῆς τοῦ θεοῦ καὶ ἐπὶ τὰ ἀσώματα χωρήσεως ἐντεῦθεν δηλοῦται Max.*schol.d.n.*9.3(ὑπεροξύτερον (in error) M.4.372B).

***ὑπεροπευτής**, ὁ, *cheat, deceiver*; ? f.l. for ἠπεροπευτής, Cyr.*hom. pasch*.9.5(5^2.117C).

ὑπέροπτος, *disdainful, proud*, Or.*sel.in Ps*.65:7(M.12.1500C); Cyr.*Ps*.14:3(M.69.805C); *contemptuous of*, c. genit., Nil.*epp*.1.138 (M.79.140D).

***ὑπερορέω**, s.v.l., *go across the boundary*; hence *withdraw* οὐδὲ ἀφανῆ ἑαυτὸν παντελῶς καθιστῶν [sc. Christ], ἀλλ' ὑπερώρει χρησίμως Thdr.Heracl.ap.*cat.Jo*.12:38(p.332.9).

***ὑπέρορθρον**, *very early in the morning*, Sophr.H.*mir.Cyr.et Jo*.18 (M.87.3477A).

ὑπερορίζ-ω, *cross the border-line, go beyond* ὀρέξεσι μηδὲν ~ούσαις τῶν κατὰ φύσιν ἐπὶ τὸ μᾶλλον Clem.*str*.2.20(p.172.21; M.8.1053A).

ὑπερόριος, **1.** *over the boundaries, extraneous*, esp. ref. bounds of an eccl. province μὴ δεῖν ὑ. ἕλκεσθαι τὰς δίκας Chrys.*ep.Innoc*.1.1(3.516D); διαγογγύζοντάς τινας, ὡς εἴη ὑ. [sc. Gr. Naz. at CP] Socr.*h.e*. 5.7.2(M.67.573B); *widespread* ὑ. φήμη Mac.Mgn.*apocr*.3.28(p.119.7); **2.** *banished*, CAlex.*ep*.(p.100.17; M.25.277A); Ath.*ep.Aeg.Lib*.5(M. 25.548C); Philost.*h.e*.4.1(p.57.5; M.65.517A); **3.** *extraordinary, excessive* αἰσχροῖς καὶ ὑ. πταίσμασι Isid.Pel.*epp*.2.127(M.78.569B); of excessively prolonged sleep, Nil.*Eulog*.28(M.79.1129D); ὑπερόρια εἰπών Men.*exc.gent*.20(p.462.4; M.113.824C).

ὑπερορισμός, ὁ, *banishment*, Epiph.*haer*.76.3(p.344.14; M.42. 521C).

***ὑπερορμάω**, pass., *rush over*, †Apoll.*met.Ps*.82:15(M.33.1436D).

ὑπερουράνιος, **1.** *above the celestial*, of God ὑπερκόσμιον, ὑ. Dion.Ar.*d.n*.1.6(M.3.596C); **2.** *celestial*, of Logos τὸν ὑ. λόγον, τὸν ὑπεράνω πάσης ἀρχῆς καὶ ἐξουσίας †Bas.*Is*.198(1.527D; M.30.460C); of Christ ὑ. δόξης...Χριστοῦ ἀποκαλυφθείσης Στεφάνῳ Euthal.Diac.*Ac*. 8:3(M.85.653D); of Christ's body acc. Apoll. ὑ. τι καὶ θεῖον σῶμα Apoll.*fr*.77(p.223.9)ap.Gr.Nyss.*Apoll*.40(M.45.1216B); of heavenly beings, *A.Jo*.112(p.212.1); Eus.*e.th*.2.20(p.127.32; M.24.952A); of heaven ὑ. ... τόπον Clem.*prot*.4(p.44.11; M.8.153B); †Bas.*Is*.198(1. 527D; M.30.460D); τὰ ὑ. *heaven*, Just.*dial*.56.1(M.6.596D); Gnost. οἰκεῖν δὲ τὴν Μητέρα αὐτῶν εἰς τὸν ὑ. τόπον, τουτέστιν ἐν τῇ μεσότητι Iren.*haer*.1.5.4(M.7.497B); of anything *celestial* opp. earthly ἀεὶ ζώσης ὑ. ἀμπέλου Clem.*q.d.s*.37(p.184.19; M.9.644A); ἀναληφθήτω δὴ [sc. θυμίαμα]...εἰς τὸ ἅγιον καὶ ὑ. σου θυσιαστήριον *Lit.Jac*.(p.168.26); **3.** as intensification of preceding οὐράνιος, *supra-celestial* δυνάμεως ἡμᾶς οὐρανίου ἢ καὶ ὑ. πληττούσης ἐπὶ τὸ σέβειν τὸν κτίσαντα ἡμᾶς μόνον Or.*princ*.4.1.7(p.304.12; M.11.356A); τὴν...ἄνωθεν γέννησιν...εἰ...ὡς οὐράνιόν τινα...ἴστε,...πάσης ἑτέρας γεννήσεως μᾶλλον ἡ τοῦ λόγου ἐκ πατρὸς ὑπερουράνιός ἐστι γέννησις Leont.H.*Nest*.4.32(M.86.1697A).

***ὑπερουργέω**, *work on behalf of, serve*, Nil.*Magn*.44(M.79.1024C).

ὑπερούσιος, *above* οὐσία, *beyond all being, supra-essential*; of God; **1.** with meaning elaborated εἰ τὸ κυριώτατον καὶ πρῶτον οὐσία λέλεκται, διὰ τὸ πᾶσι τοῖς συμβεβηκόσιν αὐτὸ ὑποκεῖσθαι· οὐκ ἔστι δὲ συμβεβηκός, ᾧ καθυπόκειται θεός· οὐδὲ οὐσία ἄρα κυρίως λέγεται ἐπὶ θεοῦ. ἔστι γὰρ ὑ. Cyr.*thes*.3(5^1.19A); ὑ. ὢν καὶ πάντων ἐπέκεινα θεός id.*dial.Trin*.2(5^1.434C); ἐν οὐδεμιᾷ φύσει, εἴτε αἰσθητῇ, εἴτε νοητῇ, κατ' οὐσίαν ὁρᾶται, ὑ. ὤν Thdt.*Cant*.3:3f.(2.79); δύναμιν ...πάσης οὐσίας ἐξῃρημένην, ὡς ὑ. καὶ ὑπὲρ τὰ ὄντα οὖσαν ‡Cyr.*Trin*. 7(6^3.8C; M.77.1132B); **2.** as epithet of θεότης, Dion.Ar.*d.n*.1.1(M.3. 588A); Max.*Pyrr*.(M.91.289D); Jo.D.*Jacob*.2(M.94.1437A); of τριάς, ‡Gr.Nyss.*hom.5.9 in Jo*.(p.177.8); Dion.Ar.*myst*.1.1(M.3.997A); Leont.H.*Nest*.4.25(M.86.1689B); Ant.Mon.*hom*.1(M.89.1433D); Jo. Mon.*hymn.Bas*.10(M.96.1377A); **3.** paradoxically of οὐσία, Dion.Ar. *d.n*.1.1(M.3.588B) cit. s. εἰμί; Zach.Mit.*opif*.(M.85.1137B); Const. Diac.*laud*.16(M.88.497B); ‡Caes.Naz.*dial*.3(M.38.860); **4.** with other words applied to God ὑπέρκειται τῶν οὐσιῶν ἡ ὑ. ἀοριστία Dion. Ar.*d.n*.1.1(M.3.588B); πάσης αἰτίας αἰτία τις ὑ. Anast.S.*hod*.2(M.89. 53B); or connected with God μονὰς...ἁπλότητας ἀκροτήτων ἐνίσασα καὶ τεκοῦσα ὑ. λοχείαις Synes.*hymn*.1.62(M.66.1589); τὴν θεαρχίαν ...ὑμνουμένην ὡς τριάδα...διὰ τὴν τρισυποστάτην τῆς ὑ. γονιμότητος ἔκφανσιν Dion.Ar.*d.n*.1.4(M.3.592A); ὑ. ἐπιστήμην *ib*.1.1(588A); **5.** of Logos, Mod.*dorm*.8(M.86.3297B); Max.*opusc*.(M.91.128C); esp. paradoxically, ref. Inc., Mac.Aeg.*elev*.6(M.34.893C); οὐσιοῦται τὸ καθ' ἡμᾶς ὁ ὑ. τοῦ θεοῦ λόγος ‡Gr.Nyss.*hom.3.8 in Jo*.(p.137.22); Dion.Ar. *ep*.4(M.3.1072B); id.*myst*.3(M.3.1033A); λέγοντες, ἀνάξιον εἶναι θεοῦ... μορφὴν δούλου λαβεῖν τὸν ὑ. Gr.Agr.*Eccl*.4.5(M.98.936D).

***ὑπερουσιότης**, ἡ, *supra-essentiality*, of God τῆς γὰρ ὑπὲρ λόγον καὶ νοῦν καὶ οὐσίαν αὐτῆς ὑ. ἀγνωσία Dion.Ar.*d.n*.1.1(M.3.588A); τὴν ...ὑ. τὴν θεαρχικήν, ὅ τί ποτέ ἐστιν ἡ τῆς ὑπεραγαθότητος ὑπερύπαρξις *ib*.1.5(593C); ὑ. πάσης ἀπείρως ὑπερανεστηκὼς Thdt.*pental*.(5.131); τί τούτου [sc. Inc.] πρὸς ἀπόδειξιν θείας ὑ. γένοιτ' ἂν ἀποδεικτικώτερον, ἐκφάνσει τὸ κρύφιον καὶ λόγῳ τὴν ἀφασίαν καὶ νῷ δηλούσης τὴν καθ' ὑπεροχὴν ἀγνωσίαν; Max.*ambig*.(M.91.1049A); of Christ, ref. Inc. ἔστι δὲ οὐδὲν ἧττον ὑπερουσιότητος ὑπερπλήρης ὁ ἀεὶ ὑπερούσιος, ἀμέλει τῇ ταύτης περιουσίᾳ Dion.Ar.*ep*.4(M.3.1072B).

ὑπερουσίως, *in a supra-essential manner*, of God οὐσίας... ἐξῄρηται, καὶ ἔστιν ὑ. Dion.Ar.*d.n*.4.20(M.3.720B); πρόνοιαν ἁπάσων ...δυνάμεων ὑ. ὑπεριδρυμένην id.*c.h*.9.4(M.3.261D); ὑ. ἁγνῆς...θεωρίας *ib*.2.4(144A); id.*myst*.2(M.3.1025A) cit. s. ἀφαίρεσις; ref. Inc. ὑπερούσιος ὢν...ὑ. οὐσιώθη Thdt.*pental*.(5.131); τὸ μυστήριον...τῆς ἐνανθρωπήσεως ὡς πάσης φύσεως...πᾶσαν ὑ. ἐκβεβηκὸς τάξιν Max. *ambig*.(M.91.1409D); Jo.D.*hom*.8.1(M.96.700B); Areth.*Apoc*.1:8(M. 106.512C).

***ὑπεροφρυβλέφαρος**, *supercilious*, Jo.D.*hom*.11.13(M.96.776A).

ὑπέροφρυς, *supercilious, proud*, Gr.Naz.*carm*.2.1.16.7(M.37. 1255A); of Devil, Cyr.*glaph.Gen*.5(1.164B); exeg. Lc.18:11, id.*Is*.4.1 (2.577A); τὸν...ὑ. ἐν τοῖς ὅτι μάλιστα πολεμιωτάτοις ποιεῖται θεός id. *hom.pasch*.14.2(5^2.189E); Jo.D.*hom*.8.2(M.96.701B).

ὑπεροχή, ἡ, *excess*; hence *pre-eminence, superiority*; **1.** in gen.; in Church ἐν ἐκκλησιαστικῇ δοκοῦντας εἶναι ὑ. ἐπισκόπους καὶ πρεσβυτέρους Or.*Jo*.32.12(p.444.32; M.14.772A); of emperors ἐν ὑ. βασιλείας ἐσμέν Just.Imp.*edict*.ap.Evagr.*h.e*.5.4(p.201.1; M.86.2800B); in spiritual life, *rank* μετὰ γοῦν τὴν ἐν σαρκὶ τελευταίαν ὑ. ἀεὶ... ἐπὶ τὸ κρεῖττον μεταβάλλων Clem.*str*.7.10(p.42.12; M.9.481B); **2.** of God, *supremacy* or *majesty* ἐκ τῆς ἐκείνου ὑ., οὐκ ἐκ τῆς ἡμετέρας φύσεως, τὴν εἰς ἀεὶ παραμονὴν ἔχομεν Iren.*haer*.5.2.3(M.7.1127C); Clem.*str*.7.5(p.20.23; M.9.437A); ἐν τοῖς ἄλλοις αὐτὸς ἀπαραβλήτως τὴν ὑ. ἔχει *Hom.Clem*.10.19; τῆς θείας ὑ. ἀνοσίως κατεθρασύνετο Cyr. *Ps*.34:5(M.69.897B); Hesych.H.*Ps.tit*.71.42(M.27.944C); of Son as higher than men or angels αὕτη ἡ μεγίστη ὑ., ἣ τὰ πάντα διατάσσεται κατὰ τὸ θέλημα τοῦ πατρός Clem.*str*.7.2(p.5.23; M.9.408B); of Son and H. Ghost πάντων μὲν τῶν γενητῶν ὑπερέχειν οὐ συγκρίσει ἀλλ' ὑπερβαλλούσῃ ὑ. Or.*Jo*.13.25(p.249.19; M.14.411B); of Father in rel. to Son and H. Ghost, acc. Eunomius, Eun.*apol*.27(M.30.865A); **3.** of Christ in rel. to men, in respect of divine nature, Alex.Al. *ep.Alex*.7(p.24.8; M.18.557C); Or.*Jo*.6.30(15; p.140.16; M.14.253A); οὔτε ἡ ὑ. τὴν ὁμοίωσιν...ἐλυμήνατο, οὔτε ἡ πρὸς ἡμᾶς συγγένεια τὴν ὑ. ἠμαύρωσεν Chrys.*hom.49.2 in Gen*.(4.494A); μεμενηκὼς...ἐν ταῖς ἰδίαις ὑ. Cyr.*Ps*.44:7(M.69.1037B); μεμένηκεν...καὶ ἐν ὑ. θεότητος ὢν ἄνθρωπος οὐδὲν ἧττον Just.Imp.*edict*.(p.199.31; M.86.2797B); **4.** of divine things, ref. 1Petr.1:12 τὴν ὑ. τῶν τοῖς τελείοις ἀποκειμένων Or.*schol.in Cant*.3:1ff.(M.17.269B); τὴν εἰς ὑπερβολὴν ὑ. ... τῆς ζωῆς τοῦ θεοῦ id.*Jo*.2.17(11; p.74.32; M.14.145A); ‡Caes.Naz.*dial*.1(M.38. 852); **5.** as title, *Excellency*, Justn.*nov*.19(p.140.24); *ib*.25.5(p.200.21).

ὑπεροχικός, **1.** *supreme, pre-eminent* ὑ. θείας...δυνάμεις Areth. *Apoc*.4:6(M.106.581B); **2.** *transcendent*, Dion.Ar.*d.n*.2.3(M.3.640B) cit. s. ἀφαίρεσις; *ib*.4.3(697A); εἰσὶ δὲ καί τινα καταφατικῶς ἐπὶ θεοῦ λεγόμενα, δύναμιν ὑ. ἀποφάσεως ἔχοντα· οἷον σκότος...ὅτι οὐκ ἔστι φῶς, ἀλλ' ὑπὲρ τὸ φῶς ‡Cyr.*Trin*.3(6^3.4E; M.77.1125B); Max.*ambig*. (M.91.1105C).

ὑπεροχικῶς, **1.** *transcendentally* τὴν...ὑπερουσιότητα τὴν θεαρχικὴν ...ἁπάντων ὅσα ὄντα ἐστὶν ὑ. ἀφῃρημένην Dion.Ar.*d.n*.1.5(M.3.593C); θεὸς...ὑπὲρ πάντα ὑ. ἔχει Leont.H.*Nest*.1.10(M.86.1140A); πάντων ὑ. τῶν ὄντων ἐξῄρηται Jo.D.*f.o*.1.12(M.94.845D); **2.** *pre-eminently, supremely*, †Marc.Er.*temp*.8(M.65.1057A); Jo.D.*hom*.12.6(M.96.788D).

***ὑπεροχυρόω**, *make exceedingly firm*, Clem.*str*.1.5(p.18.7; M.8. 720A).

ὑπεροψία, ἡ, **1.** *contempt, disregard*, in good sense ἐγκράτεια τοίνυν σώματος ὑ. κατὰ τὴν πρὸς θεὸν ὁμολογίαν Clem.*str*.3.1(p.197.3; M.8.1104B); of Christ τήν τε τῆς τροφῆς ὑ. ἐφ' ὅσον βούλοιτο Gr.Nyss. *or.catech*.23(p.88.5; M.45.61C); ref. Mt.19:29 τῆς τῶν παρόντων ἁπάντων ὑ. Chrys.*hom.2.6 in Ac.princ*.(3.70A); as a virtue τῶν ἐν τῷ παρόντι βίῳ πραγμάτων ὑ. id.*virg*.63(1.320D); **2.** *contempt of others, disdain* ἀρχὴν πρὸς τὸ ὑπερηφανεύεσθαι τὴν ὑ. λαμβάνων †Bas. *Is*.88(1.440C; M.30.261C); arising from habit of judging others, Cyr. *Lc*.6:37(M.72.600A); *ib*.16:15(817C); of Israel, exeg. Os.5:5, id.*Os*.54 (3.84C); ἥστινος [sc. ἀληθοῦς ἐγκρατείας] πρῶτός ἐστιν ὄλεθρος ἡ ὑ., ἀρχὴ τῆς μεταβάσεως καὶ ἀρχαιογονία τῶν ἁμαρτημάτων Leo Mag.*ep*. 106.1(p.56.28; M.*PL*.54.1104A).

ὑπερπαθής, *suffering on behalf of* another ἡμεῖς ἐσμεν οἱ τὴν εἰκόνα τοῦ θεοῦ περιφέροντες ἐν τῷ ζῶντι...τούτῳ ἀγάλματι...συμπαθῆ, ὑ. Clem.*prot*.4(p.46.18; M.8.157C).

***ὑπερπαμφαής**, *supremely radiant*; of H. Ghost, Didym.*Trin*.2.4 (M.39.484A).

***ὑπερπανάγαθος**, *exceedingly and wholly good*; of BMV, Ephr. 3.545D.

ὑπερπάσχ-ω, **1.** *endure greater suffering*; of Pilate's wife, exeg. Mt.27:19 μακαρία δὲ ἡ τοιαῦτα ἀπέχουσα ἐν ὀνείροις τὸ παθεῖν, ἵνα μὴ ὑπερπάθῃ Or.*schol.in Mt*.17:11ff.(M.17.308C); **2.** s.v.l., *suffer on* behalf of; be very distressed for Ἀθανασίου...τῆς ἐκκλησίας ~οντος Epiph.haer.69.11(M.42.220C; conj. ὑπερασπίζοντος p.161.19).

*ὑπερπέμπω, overshoot the mark, Gr.Naz.ep.51(M.37.105A); fig. ὑ. Χριστοῦ...ἐφετμῆς id.carm.1.2.9.122(M.37.677A).

*ὑπερπερώτης, f.l. for ἡ περπερότης Ephr.3.401F.

ὑπερπηδ-άω, leap over; met., surpass, transcend ἡ γὰρ σὰρξ τοῦ λόγου ~ᾷ πάντα νοῦν καὶ λόγον Petr.Laod.fr.in Lc.22:19(M.86.3329C).

ὑπερπιαίνω, fatten overmuch, †Bas.Is.32(1.406A; M.30.184B).

ὑπερπίπτ-ω, 1. exceed, be in excess of ὑ. τὴν συμμετρίαν Bas.Spir.70(3.59D; M.32.200A); c. genit., Gr.Nyss.fid.(M.45.141A); 2. pass beyond, in thought ἀεὶ δὲ ἦν [sc. ὁ πατήρ], οὐχ ~ει γὰρ εἰς τὸ μὴ εἶναί ποτε ὁ νοῦς Gr.Naz.or.20.10(M.35.1077A).

ὑπερπλεονάζω, be overfull, overflow; of a vessel, Herm.mand.5.2.5; met., abound beyond measure in wealth ἐὰν ὑ. ὁ ἄνθρωπος, ἐξαμαρτάνει Pss.Sal.5.19; abound exceedingly; of grace, ref. 1Tim.1:14, Clem.prot.9(p.64.8; M.8.197A); abound more in resources, ‡Gr.Nyss.occurs.(M.46.1165B).

*ὑπερπλευρίζω, push past, Chrys.ecl.5(12.468A).

*ὑπερπληθύνω, be exceedingly multiplied, Mac.Aeg.hom.4.20(M.34.488C).

ὑπερπλήρης, more than full, beyond fullness τοῦ Ἰησοῦ θεότης... πλήρης ἐν τοῖς ἐνδεέσιν· ὑ. ἐν τοῖς πλήρεσιν Dion.Ar.d.n.2.10(M.3.648C); of divine light, id.c.h.10.3(M.3.273C); of God, ‡Cyr.Trin.7(6^3.8C; M.77.1132B); supremely full, of divine nature in Christ τελείαν καὶ ἀνελλιπῆ καὶ ὑ. Eulog.fr.dogm.(M.86.2948C); of God τοῦ ὑ. τῇ ἀγαθότητι cat.Apoc.19:5ff.(p.452.25); neut. as subst., divine fullness which is beyond fullness, Dion.Ar.d.n.9.2(909C).

*ὑπερπληρότης, ἡ, plenitude which is beyond plenitude; of gifts of God, Dion.Ar.d.n.9.2(M.3.909C).

ὑπερπληρόω, fill and more than fill, Dion.Ar.myst.1.1(M.3.997B).

*ὑπερπόθητος, exceedingly desirable, Ephr.3.531F.

*ὑπέρπτωσις, ἡ, passing beyond, excess, Gr.Nyss.hom.9 in Cant.(M.44.972A); id.v.Mos.(M.44.420A).

ὑπερσάρκωσις, ἡ, excessive growth of flesh; fig., Clem.paed.1.8(p.128.10; M.8.328C) cit. s. τῦφος.

ὑπερσέβ-ω, worship above another, ref. equality of Persons of Trin. μηδὲν ~οντες, μηδὲ ὑποσέβοντες Gr.Naz.or.22.12(M.35.1144C).

*ὑπερσεληναῖος, beyond the moon, Hipp.haer.4.1(p.33.1; M.16.3059A); cf.ib.5.13(p.107.20; 3166B).

*ὑπερσκοπέω, consider, take thought on behalf of another, exeg. Rom.8:26 τὸ οὖν πνεῦμα, φησί, τοῦ θεοῦ ὑ. τὰ ὑπὲρ ἡμῶν Didym.Trin.3.35(M.39.964B).

ὑπέρσοφος, 1. more than wise or supremely wise; of God's wisdom, Dion.Ar.d.n.7.2(M.3.868C); of Christ ὑ. γνῶσις Leont.H.Nest.2.21(M.86.1581D); of God σοφὸς ὢν καὶ ὑ. Max.ambig.(M.91.1192A); neut. as subst., divine wisdom which is beyond wisdom, Dion.Ar.d.n.2.3(640B); 2. exceedingly clever, Isid.Pel.epp.4.67(M.78.1124B).

*ὑπερσόφως, exceedingly wisely, Anast.S.hex.7(M.89.942B).

*ὑπερσταχύω, bear abundance of corn, Orac.Sib.1.298.

*ὑπερσυντελικῶς, in a manner which exceeds what is perfect, immoderately, exeg. Col.3:14f. μὴ ὑ. [sc. ἐνδύσασθε τὴν ἀγάπην], ἀλλ' ὡς ἐποίησεν εἰρήνην πρὸς ὑμᾶς ὁ θεός, οὕτω καὶ ὑμεῖς ποιεῖτε Chrys.hom.8.3 in Col.(11.383C, v.l. ὑπερσυντέλικος or -τελικός; Gaume omits).

*ὑπερταλαντίζω, outweigh; met., surpass; pass., Epiph.haer.76.53(p.408.8; M.42.628C).

*ὑπερτανύω, stretch out above, Cyr.hom.pasch.5.2(5^2.46B).

ὑπερτέλειος, 1. supremely perfect; of God, Leont.H.Nest.1.1(M.86.1408B); of Trin., Const.Pogon.edict.(H.3.1449B); neut. as subst., of each Person of Trin., ‡Caes.Naz.dial.3(M.38.861); 2. more than perfect; of numbers, such as twelve, the sum of whose factors (including unity) is greater than themselves (opp. ὑποτέλειοι), Meth.symp.8.11(p.95.7; M.18.156C).

*ὑπερτελειότης, ἡ, perfection which is above perfection; of God, Epiph.haer.72.7(p.262.1; M.42.392B).

ὑπερτελής, more than perfect or final, beyond perfection or supremely perfect, of God πάντων ἀρχὴ καὶ πέρας ὑπεράρχιον καὶ ὑ. Dion.Ar.d.n.4.10(M.3.708A); τὸ ἄλογον ἀνατίθεμεν τῷ ὑπὲρ λόγον, καὶ τὴν ἀτέλειαν τῷ ὑ. καὶ προτελείῳ ib.7.2(869A); τέλειον μὲν οὖν ἐστιν οὐ μόνον ὡς αὐτοτελὲς...ἀλλὰ καὶ ὡς ὑ. κατὰ τὸ πάντων ὑπερέχον ib.13.1(977B); ὑ. εἶ· καὶ γὰρ ἀρχὴν οὐκ ἔχεις· τελοῦς ἀπέστης, καὶ διέστης τοῦ μέσου, ἐκτὸς βεβηκὼς τῶν τριῶν Geo.Pis.hex.1645(M.92.1563A); ‡Cyr.Trin.4(6^3.5E; M.77.1128B); ἐν τρισὶ τελείαις ὑποστάσεσι μίαν οὐσίαν ἁπλῆν, ὑ. καὶ παντέλειον ib.9(14B; M.77.1141A); Jo.D.hom.1.8(M.96.560B); id.Jacob.78(M.94.1476B); of the Word, Max.ambig.(M.91.1068B); μεγάλη καὶ ὑ. ἡ ἀρετὴ τοῦ Χριστοῦ ὡς καὶ αὐτοὺς καλύψαι τοὺς οὐρανούς Cyr.Abac.39(3.555B, v.l. ὑπερτενής).

*ὑπερτέμνομαι, cut to pieces; met., destroy the force of ὑπερετέμνετο τὸν λόγον τὸ τῆς σαρκὸς εὐτελές Bas.Sel.or.25.3(M.85.293C).

ὑπερτενής, stretching above, high above another; met., of conquerors οἱ ὀφρῦν ἀνασπῶντες τὴν ὑ. κατὰ πάντων Cyr.Am.31(3.283D); hence lofty, sublime ὑ. ... τὴν θεωρίαν id.ador.1(1.8D); ref. 1Cor.2:8 τό γε εἶναι...τῆς δόξης κύριον, πῶς οὐ λίαν ὑ.; id.inc.unigen.(5^1.697C); neut. as subst., sublimity; of God's wisdom, id.Is.3.4(2.510C); power and glory, ib.3.5(512D); τῆς ἐξαιρέτου πολιτείας τὸ ὑ. id.ador.1(28B).

ὑπερτερ-έω, be above τῷ ~οῦντι πιεσμῷ τοῦ στερεώματος ‡Caes.Naz.dial.99(M.38.964); met., be superior, surpass, ‡Gr.Nyss.occurs.(M.46.1165B); Cyr.ador.2(1.54B); ib.(66C).

ὑπερτίθημι, 1. med., surpass, Clem.str.2.23(p.190.21; M.8.1089B); 2. med.; a. put away ὑ. ... κακὴν ζύμην Ign.Magn.10.2; b. put off, defer μὴ ὑ. μηδὲ διστάζετε πιστεῦσαι...ἐμοί Just.dial.28.2(M.6.536A); ὑ. ... βοήθειαν Or.princ.3.1.17(p.226.3; M.11.284A); ὑ. ... τοῦ ἐλθεῖν Cyr.ep.23(p.67.7; 5^2.85B); abs., delay, Ath.decr.2(p.2.20; M.25.'428'(420)A); c. pass over, omit πρὸς τὴν ζήτησιν μίαν...ὑ. ἡμέραν Hom.Clem.2.40; Isid.Pel.epp.1.114(M.78.260B); disregard μυθολογοῦσιν Ἰουδαῖοι, καὶ παρόντα τὸν νῦν καιρὸν ὑπερτίθενται Ath.inc.40.1(M.25.165A); 3. exceed or delay, of continuing a fast until cockcrow on following day οἱ μὲν καὶ πάσας [sc. τὰς ἓξ τῶν νηστειῶν ἡμέρας] ὑπερτιθέασιν ἄσιτοι διατελοῦντες, οἱ δὲ δύο Dion.Al.ep.can.(p.102.1; M.10.1277A); med. τινες, οὐχ ὅπως οὐχ ὑπερτιθέμενοι ἀλλὰ μηδὲ νηστεύσαντες ib.(p.102.6; 1277A).

*ὑπέρτιμος, 1. supremely honourable, of BMV ἡ ὑ. τῶν ὁσίων τιμή Ephr.3.551C; ὑ. πατρικίου Max.Pyrr.tit.(M.91.288A); neut. as subst., οἱ...μαθηταὶ διὰ τὸ ὑ. ... τὴν δειλίαν πρὸς τὴν ἁφὴν τοῦ σώματος αὐτῆς [sc. BMV] ἐνεδείκνυντο Germ.CP or.8(M.98.369A); 2. more or exceedingly precious ὑ. ... τῆς τοῦ θεοῦ μητρὸς ἡ μετάστασις Jo.D.hom.9.3(M.96.728D); Thphn.chron.p.236(M.108.596B).

*ὑπερτίμως, with the utmost honour, Germ.CP or.8(M.98.369B).

*ὑπερτοιχέω, rise above the sides of a ship, Gr.Naz.carm.2.1.11.138(M.37.1039A; ὑπερτειχοῦντος Combefis).

ὑπέρτονος, strained to the utmost or unduly; lit.; neut. plur. as adv., with bow-string stretched too tautly ὑ. τοξεύοντες Iren.haer.1.16.3(M.7.636B); Gr.Naz.carm.1.2.9.125(M.37.677A); at too high a pitch ὑ. ᾄδειν Clem.str.2.20(p.180.3; M.8.1068B); met., overstrained, over-intense οὐ γὰρ ὑ. ἡ ἀγωγὴ τοῦ λόγου, ἀλλ' εὔτονος id.paed.1.12(p.149.28; M.8.369B); neut. as subst. τὸ αὐστηρὸν τῆς σπουδῆς ἡμῶν καὶ τὸ ὑ. χαλῶντας ib.2.5(p.185.27; 448B); neut. as adv., solemnly, ref. 1Cor.6:18 ὁ ἀπόστολος ὑ. φθέγγεται id.str.3.12(p.237.5; 1189B).

*ὑπερτραφής, grown in excess, Philost.h.e.1.4(M.65.461C).

ὑπερτρέχ-ω, run beyond, pass beyond; fig., of Jews τὸν νόμον ἀναγινώσκοντες, οὐχ ὑ. τὴν σκιάν Cyr.Is.4.4(2.690D); met. τὸν ἐνανθρωπήσαντα...λόγον, τὸ τῆς ἀνθρωπότητος ~οντα μέτρον id.Lc.9:1(M.72.640C).

ὑπερτρυφάω, luxuriate excessively in; c. dat., Bas.Sel.or.11.1(M.85.148C).

ὑπερυθραίνω, pass., become red, blush, Meth.symp.8.17(p.112.4; M.18.173D).

ὑπερυθριάω, = foreg.; hence c. infin., be ashamed, hesitate to do something, Cyr.Jo.7(4.681D).

ὑπερύμνητος, worthy of supreme praise; of God's name, Ephr.3.126C; of God, Jo.D.carm.dorm.BMV 97(p.230; M.96.1365B); of Trin., id.Jacob.78(M.94.1473D); of BMV, id.f.o.4.14(M.94.1153C).

*ὑπερύπαρξις, ἡ, existence which is beyond existence, of God ἡ τῆς ὑπεραγαθότητος ὑ. Dion.Ar.d.n.1.5(M.3.593C).

ὑπερυψ-όω, 1. raise on high; fig., of prophets likened to a cloud, †Bas.Is.148(1.483E; M.30.361A); met., exalt exceedingly, with honour or praise; a. of God: Christ, ref. Phil.2:9 τοῦτον [sc. τὸν υἱὸν τοῦ ἀνθρώπου]...ὁ θεὸς ὑπερύψωσεν,...ὁ γὰρ λόγος ἐν ἀρχῇ πρὸς τὸν θεὸν... οὐκ ἐπεδέχετο τὸ ὑπερυψωθῆναι Or.Jo.32.25(17; p.470.16; M.14.813A); Eus.e.th.1.11(p.70.6; M.24.845A); ἄνθρωπος δι' ἡμᾶς καὶ ὑπὲρ ἡμῶν λέγεται ~οῦσθαι, ἵν' ὥσπερ τῷ θανάτῳ αὐτοῦ πάντες ἡμεῖς ἀπεθάνομεν ἐν Χριστῷ, οὕτω ἐν αὐτῷ τῷ Χριστῷ πάλιν ἡμεῖς ὑπερυψωθῶμεν Ath.Ar.1.41(M.26.97A); Gr.Nyss.Eun.5(2 p.122.10; M.45.704B); men ταπεινωθέντα τῇ ἁμαρτίᾳ τῇ ἰδίᾳ δόξῃ ὑπερύψωσεν †Bas.Is.253(1.573B; M.30.565C); Church ἐπλήρωσεν...πνευματικῆς χάριτος...καὶ ὑπερύψωσεν αὐτὴν ὡς οἶκον ἐπ' ὄρους Const.App.6.5.3; scriptures ὑπερφυῆ ...καὶ ~ούμενα εἰς αἰῶνας αἰῶνος Nil.epp.2.141(M.79.264D); b. of men: God εἴη τὸ ὄνομα τῆς δόξης αὐτοῦ...~ούμενον †Jo.D.B.J.17(M.96.1013C); Christ ~οῦντες...οὐκ ἀπολήγομεν Gr.Nyss.Eun.5(2 p.114.15; M.45.693D); themselves ἑαυτοὺς δὲ ~οῦσι, τελείους ἀποκαλοῦντες Iren.haer.1.6.4(M.7.509A); μείζων ἐβουλήθη γενέσθαι ἐκ τοῦ εἰπεῖν τι χαλεπώτερον. σὺ δὲ δεξάμενος πάλιν, ὑπερυψώθης· καὶ γέγονε κακῶν φιλονεικία ‡Bas.*Lac.*3(2.590B; M.31.1445A); ὑπερύψωσε τὸν ὑψηλόν, καὶ τὸν ταπεινὸν ἐταπείνωσεν Synes.*ep.*79(M.66.1445B); **2.** c. genit., *exalt beyond* ὧν πάντων [sc. ὕμνων] ὑπεραινετὸς καὶ ∼ούμενός ἐστιν [sc. God] ‡Dion.Al.*fr.2 in Job*(p.205.3).

***ὑπερύψωμα, τό,** *supreme exaltation,* Leont.H.*Nest.*3.8(M.86.1636C).

***ὑπερύψωσις, ἡ,** *high exaltation*; met., of Christ, ref. Phil.2:9f. ἡ δὲ ὑ. τοῦ υἱοῦ τοῦ ἀνθρώπου...αὕτη ἦν, τὸ μηκέτι ἕτερον αὐτὸν εἶναι τοῦ λόγου ἀλλὰ τὸν αὐτὸν αὐτῷ Or.*Jo.*32.25(17; p.470.18; M.14.813A); τῆς τοῦ παθόντος ὑ. Gr.Nyss.*Eun.*5(2 p.122.18; M.45.704C); of his flesh through hypostatic union θέωσιν τῆς σαρκός, καὶ λόγωσιν καὶ ὑ. λέγομεν ‡Cyr.*Trin.*24(6^3.30B; M.77.1165B) = Jo.D.*f.o.*4.18(M.94.1184B); of men through Christ ἡμῶν ἐστιν αὕτη ἡ χάρις καὶ ὑ., ὅτι τε καὶ ἄνθρωπος γενόμενος, προσκυνεῖται ὁ τοῦ θεοῦ υἱός Ath.*Ar.*1.42(M.26.100B); of a saint by God, Leont.N.*v.Jo.Eleem.*45(p.95.8).

***ὑπερύψωτος,** *highly exalted* ὁ πατήρ μου ὁ Χριστός...ὁ νοῦς ὁ ὑ. ἐν τῇ αὐτοῦ δόξῃ *A.Phil.*132(p.63.17).

***ὑπερφαής,** *bright beyond brightness* or *transcendently radiant,* of God τὴν ὑ. καὶ ὑπερώνυμον ἀγαθότητα Dion.Ar.*d.n.*1.8(M.3.597A); *ib.*7.3(872B); id.*myst.*1.1(M.3.997A).

ὑπερφανής, = foreg., Dion.Ar.*d.n.*1.4(M.3.592C); *ib.*1.5(593B); superl., id.*myst.*1.1(M.3.997B).

ὑπερφερής, *prominent*; of a hill, *Const.App.*6.5.3; met., of anything *great* or *outstanding* beyond others μείζονά τε καὶ ὑ. κατορθοῦν Cyr.*ador.*1(1.39B); τὰ μεγάλα καὶ ὑ. τῶν πλημμελημάτων id.*Soph.*38(3.615A); id.*Jo.*6.1(4.603D); comp., Epiph.*haer.*27.2(p.303.3; M.41.365C); superl., Jo.D.*hom.*1.6(M.96.553D); neut. as subst., *outstanding degree* or *quality, greatness* τῆς ἑνούσης ἀλαζονείας αὐτοῖς τὸ ὑ. Cyr.*Is.*2.5(2.330C); τῆς τοῦ θεοῦ γαληνότητος τὸ ὑ. id.*Ps.*35:7(M.69.920A); of S. John's gospel τὸ τῶν θεωρημάτων...ὑ. id.*Jo.*1 proem.(4.8A); *that which is best, goodness,* Max.*cap.theol.*3.79(M.90.1296A).

ὑπερφέρω, 1. *carry over*; hence, pass. τῆς θαλάσσης ὑπερενεχθείσης τοῦ σκάφους *overwhelm,* Chrys.*hom.*74.3 *in Mt.*(7.719C); **2.** intrans., *pass above,* Philost.*h.e.*12.8(p.146.6; M.65.616B).

***ὑπερφερῶς,** *pre-eminently,* Cyr.*ador.*16(1.569A).

ὑπερφλέγω, pass., *burn fiercely with passion,* Bas.Sel.*v.Thecl.*1(M.85.521C).

***ὑπερφορτόω,** *overload,* Ant.Mon.*hom.*4(M.89.1444A).

ὑπερφρον-έω, 1. *think unworthy, exclude through contempt* θεοῦ λόγος...οὐδὲ τὸ οἰκετικὸν γένος ∼ῶν τῆς κλήσεως Eus.*p.e.*1.1(3A; M.21.25A); **2.** *be superior, surpass* συνέσει πάντας ὑ. Athenag.*leg.*31.2(M.6.961B).

ὑπερφυής, 1. *enormous, lofty,* met. ἐπὶ τὸ ἀμωμήτως ἔχον, ἤγουν εἰς ὑ. καὶ ὑπέρλοφον πολιτείαν Cyr.*ador.*1(1.29C); **2.** *extraordinary, marvellous*; *transcending nature* because divine, *supernatural,* of God ὑ. ... ἁπλότητα Dion.Ar.*d.n.*1.4(M.3.592B); δοτῆρος ἀφθόνου καὶ ὑ., ὑπερφυᾶ κεκτημένου μεγαλοπρέπειαν Jo.D.*hom.*1.3(M.96.552A); of Christ τῷ ὑ. τόκῳ πάντα ὑ. ἠκολούθησαν Isid.Pel.*epp.*1.377(M.78.396B); σωτήρια καὶ ὑ. παθήματα Zach.Mit.*opif.*(M.85.1141C); τὸ εἰς τὴν ἡμῶν φύσιν ὑ. ἡμῖν χάρισμα ἑαυτὸν δωρήσασθαι Leont.H.*Nest.*1.38(M.86.1500B); ἐν τοῖς φυσικοῖς ἡμῶν ὑ. ἦν Dion.Ar.*d.n.*2.10(M.3.649A); πνευματικὴν καὶ ὑ. οἰκονομίαν τῆς...σαρκώσεως ‡Jo.D.*corp.*(M.95.408C); neut. as subst., of Christ τὸ ὑ. τοῦ περὶ αὐτὸν θεοπρεποῦς ἀξιώματος Eus.*e.th.*1.20(p.81.2; M.24.865A); *above* the level of *ordinary* or *unaided human nature, superhuman*; of ascetic life τὸν μὲν [sc. βίου τρόπον] ὑ. καὶ τῆς κοινῆς καὶ ἀνθρωπίνης πολιτείας ἐπέκεινα Eus.*d.e.*1.8(p.39.12; M.22.76B); of Christian life τοὺς τὸν ὑ. βίον ἠγαπηκότας Thdt.*affect.*12(p.308.21; 4.1022); οὐκ ἰδίᾳ σπουδῇ... ἀπαλλαγήσεται μάστιγος [sc. of lust]. ὑ. γάρ ἐστι τὸ πρᾶγμα ‡Nil.*vit.cog.*(M.79.1445A); as honorific title ὑ. συγκλήτου CChalc.*act.*1(*ACO* 2.1.1 p.64.37; ὑπερφυεστάτης H.2.65D); ὑ. γερουσίας Evagr.*h.e.*2.18(p.67.25; M.85.2548B); ὑ. ἀρχόντων *ib.*(p.85.4; 2576A).

ὑπερφυσ-άομαι, *be inflated excessively, swell, bubble up* τῆς κοίλης νοτίδος τῆς ∼ωμένης ἐν τοῖς κρουνοῖς Bas.*hex.*3.3(1.24B; M.29.57B); met., *be over-elated, puffed up* ∼ηθεὶς τὴν διάνοιαν †Bas.*Is.*240(1.561D; M.30.540B); *ib.*301(607D; M.645B).

***ὑπερφυσικός,** *supernatural,* Diad.*perf.*95(p.140.7) cit. s. ταπεινοφροσύνη.

***ὑπερφύσιος,** *supernatural,* superl., *A.Thadd.*3(p.274.14n.).

ὑπερφυῶς, 1. *marvellously, exceedingly*; as expression of agreement in dialogue, *exceedingly so, most certainly,* Meth.*creat.*3(p.496.9; cf.M.18.336B); **2.** *in a manner which transcends nature, supernaturally* ὑ. ὁ λόγος σὰρξ...ἐγένετο ‡Jo.D.*hom.*6.3(M.96.665B); πρέπει τὰς τοῦ ὑ. θεοῦ δυνάμεις ὑ. εἶναι ὑποστάσεις Jo.D.*Man.*1.8(M.94.1513A).

ὑπερφων-έω, 1. *overstrain oneself in speaking* or *shouting* φωναῖς, αἳ τῷ ∼εῖσθαι παντελῶς διαπίπτουσιν Gr.Naz.*or.*20.10(M.35.1077B); οὐκ ἐφικνοῦμαι τοῦ πάθους, κἂν ὑπερφωνήσω τῷ λόγῳ Gr.Nyss.*Melet.*(M.46.853C); **2.** *outbawl*; met., *surpass* Ἰωάννης...ὑπερεφώνησε τὰ προλαβόντα κηρύγματα τῇ μεγαλοφυΐᾳ τῆς γνώσεως Bas.*Eun.*2.15(1.250C; M.29.601B).

***ὑπέρφωτος, 1.** *beyond light*; of divine light, Dion.Ar.*d.n.*4.6(M.3.701B); id.*myst.*1.1(M.3.997A) cit. s. σιγή; *ib.*2(1025A), Andr.Cr.*or.*7(M.97.949C) citt. s. γνόφος; **2.** *supremely radiant* or *splendid* ἀνάψων ἡμῶν τὰς λαμπάδας τῆς πίστεως τῆς σῆς ὑ. ἐλλάμψεως *Lit.Jac.*(*NBP* 10^2 p.107); ref. Lc.1:30 χάριν παρὰ τῷ θεῷ τὴν ὑ. Sophr.H.*or.*2.25(M.87.3245B); of Christ's baptism, Max.*comput.*32(M.19.1249B).

ὑπέρχομαι, (fut. ὕπειμι) **1.** *go* or *come under,* hence *come under the rule of* τὸν αὐτὸν θεὸν ὑπιών Proc.G.*Lev.*19:32(M.87.764A); **2.** *take upon oneself*; **a.** *put on, adopt* ἐν θεάτρῳ ἀλλότριον πρόσωπον ὑ. Bas.*hom.*1.2(2.2D; M.31.165B); ἀνθρωπίνην ὑ. μορφήν Gr.Nyss.*v.Macr.*(p.396.2; M.46.981D); of Christ ὑ. τὴν πρὸς ἡμᾶς ὁμοίωσιν Cyr.*Lc.*4:1(M.72.528A); **b.** *experience* or *submit to,* of Christ δι' ὀργάνου θνητοῦ τὰς πρὸς τοὺς θνήτους ὁμιλίας τε καὶ διατριβὰς ὑ. Eus.*l.C.*13(p.241.14; M.20.1408B); χρησίμην ὑ. τὴν οἰκονομίαν *ib.*15(p.246.11; 1416C); πτωχείαν...ὑ. Niceph.Ur.*v.Sym.*32(M.86.3016B); **c.** *assume* or *succeed to* a position ὑ. ἑτέρου διαδοχήν Synes.*ep.*67(M.66.1417A); πρεσβείαν ὑ. Philost.*h.e.*3.4(p.33.21; M.65.484A); ὑ. θρόνον *ib.*4.12(p.64.12; 525A); ὑ. τῇ στρατηγίᾳ Men.*exc.Rom.*3(p.185.14; M.113.873A); **3.** *proceed, continue* ὑπελθὼν καὶ δὴ ἐπήγαγεν Clem.*str.*5.14(p.401.15; ἐπελθὼν M.9.168C).

***ὑπέρχρειος,** *superfluous,* Isid.Pel.*epp.*1.361(M.78.388B).

ὑπερχρόνιος, = ὑπέρχρονος, of eternal generation of Son, Gr.Ant.*bapt.*2(M.88.1873B).

ὑπέρχρονος, 1. *above time, transcending time*; of God, Eulog.*fr Trin.*2.4(p.364); of Trin., Gr.Naz.*or.*6.22(M.35.749C); of Son, Thdt.*eran.*3(4.213); exeg. Jo.1:1 ὑ. θεόν...τὸν λόγον δεικνύς ‡Caes.Naz.*dial.*20(M.38.876); Jo.Mon.*hymn.Bas.*10(M.96.1377B); in gen. ἤ τις πρεσβυτέρα τῆς τοῦ κόσμου γενέσεως κατάστασις...ἡ ὑ. Bas.*hex.*1.5(1.5C; M.29.13A); **2.** *superior in time, prior* οὔτε χρόνῳ ὑποπίπτει [sc. τὸ θεῖον] ἵνα ὑ. ὁ πατὴρ γένηται τοῦ υἱοῦ Epiph.*anc.*17(p.26.11; M.43.49A) ∞ ‡Caes.Naz.*dial.*18(M.38.873).

***ὑπερωμίας,** *head and shoulders taller* than others, Thphn.*chron.*p.120(M.108.336C).

***ὑπερώνυμος, 1.** *above every name*; of God, Dion.Ar.*d.n.*1.5(M.3.593B); ἡ ὑπερώνυμος ἀγαθότης *ib.*1.7(596D); τῇ τριαδικῇ καὶ ἑνιαίᾳ θεωνυμίᾳ, τὴν ὑ. [sc. θεαρχίαν] ὀνομάζομεν *ib.*13.3(981A); **2.** *pre-eminent in name, famous,* Jo.D.*hom.*1.6(M.96.553B).

ὑπερῷος, *upper*; as subst.; **1.** neut., *upper chambers* or *story*; exeg. Jer.20:2, 3Reg.17:19, 4Reg.1:2, 4:10, etc. ὑ. δὲ τὸν νοῦν τὸν ὑψηλὸν καὶ ἐπηρμένον δείξω ἐκ τῆς γραφῆς Or.*hom.19.13 in Jer.*(p.168.31; M.13.488D); ἐν...τῷ ὑ. ἐποίησεν ὁ κύριος τὸ πάσχα Alex.Sal.*Barn.*1.13(p.440E); fig., of Christ ἐκάθισεν ἐν δεξιᾷ τῆς μεγαλωσύνης ἐν ὑψηλῷ ὑ. τῆς οἰκείας ἀνατολῆς Thdt.*Ps.*67:35(1.1074); **2.** fem., *palate,* Gr.Nyss.*or.dom.*4(p.80.21; M.44.1169C); Nemes.*nat.hom.*9(M.40.656B); Leont.H.*Nest.*1.14(M.86.1457C).

ὑπεσθίω, *eat away* or *secretly,* ‡Caes.Naz.*dial.*36(M.38.901).

ὑπεσταλμένως, *restrainedly, modestly, A.Thom.*A 138(p.245.10); Chrys.*hom.18.6 in Mt.*(7.242C); Cyr.*glaph.Gen.*3(1.67B); *guardedly,* id.*Ps.*61:7(M.69.1117B); *in a veiled manner,* id.*Abac.*54(3.570A).

ὑπεύθυνος, 1. *liable to give account for* one's *administration* of an office, *responsible* ὑ. ἐστι [sc. the superior] τῇ ἀδελφότητι ἀγρυπνεῖν ὑπὲρ τῶν ψυχῶν αὐτῶν, καὶ μεριμνᾶν τὰ πρὸς σωτηρίαν ἑκάστου, ὡς λόγον ἀποδώσων Bas.*reg.fus.*25.2(2.370E; M.31.985B); ὑ. ἐστιν ὁδηγεῖν εἰς πάντα τὴν ἀδελφότητα *ib.*27(371C; M.988A); met., *concerned, responsible,* ref. prayer ὑπὲρ τῶν ἡμετέρων παρ' ἡμῶν βούλεται [sc. ὁ Χριστός] μᾶλλον τῶν ὑ. ἀξιοῦσθαι, ἢ παρ' ἑτέρων ὑπὲρ ἡμῶν Chrys.*hom.52.3 in Mt.*(7.532E); **2.** c. genit. or dat.; **a.** *under liability for,* Isid.Pel.*epp.*2.146(M.78.600A); *liable* to, Ath.*h.Ar.*44(p.208.22; M.25.745D); ὑ. ... τῷ κρίματι τῆς ἀπειθείας Bas.*jud.*4(2.217B; M.31.661A); παραδειγματισμοῦ...ὑ. Chrys.*hom.4.4 in Mt.*(7.52B); **b.** met., *subject* to; of men to death, Ath.*ep.Maxim.*3(M.26.1088C); φροντίδων...ὑ. ... πλειόνων Chrys.*hom.2.4 in Phil.*(11.208B); ἀνεῖλε [sc. Devil] τὸν πρῶτον ἄνθρωπον ὑπεύθυνον λαβὼν τῇ ἁμαρτίᾳ id.*hom.67.2 in Jo.*(8.402E); κολακείας...ὑ., ἢ εὐχερείας διάκονος Isid.Pel.*epp.*1.324(M.78.369C); neut. as subst., Ath.*inc.*8.2(M.25.109B); *subject* to people ὑ. ... τοῖς δούλοις Chrys.*stat.*11.4(2.121D); hence οἱ ὑ. *subjects, dependants,* id.*hom.43.4 in Mt.*(7.463E); **3.** *guilty*; **a.** before men, Ath.*apol.sec.*23(p.104.41; M.25.288B); Chrys.*stat.*3.6(2.46A); Thdt.*Ezech.*21:8ff.(2.840); **b.** before God, hence, *sinful* μετὰ τῶν ὑ. ὁ ἀνεύθυνος [sc. ὁ Χριστός] ‡Epiph.*hom.*2(M.43.440D); πάντες, ὡς ὑ., τοῦ λυτρουμένου δέονται Euthal.Diac.*epp.Paul.*(M.85.748C); Thdt.*Rom.*3:23(3.43); Jo.Clim.*past.*10(M.88.1185B); of abstracts κακῆς καὶ ὑ. συνειδήσεως CSard.*ep.Alex.*(p.117.11; M.25.313D); ὑ. καὶ σωματικὰς ἡδονάς Philost.*h.e.*10.3(M.65.585B).

ὑπευλαβέομαι, *be cautious, show caution*, Meth.*symp.*3.13(p.42.18, vv.ll. ἐπ-, ἀπ-; M.18.81C).

***ὑπευτρεπίζω**, *prepare secretly*, Gr.Nyss.*Eun.*12(1 p.308.17; M.45.1021A).

***ὕπεχμα, τό**, *prop, support*, Gr.Naz.*carm.*2.1.1.532(M.37.1009A).

ὑπέχω, **1.** *hold under*; *bow beneath* ὑ. τῇ εὐλογίᾳ τὴν κεφαλήν Gr.Nyss.*v.Macr.*(p.388.14; M.46.976C); **2.** *undergo, suffer*; abs. [sc. δίκην] *pay the penalty*, Bas.*mor.*7.4(3.507E; M.32.1201D); **3.** *keep safely*, exeg. Mt.11:27 ὁ δὲ υἱὸς ἐλάμβανεν, καὶ οἷα πιστὸς παραθηκοφύλαξ τὴν δόσιν ὑπεῖχεν Eus.*e.th.*1.20(p.86.7; M.24.873C).

***ὑπηγορία, ἡ**, = ὑπαγορία, *composition, compilation*, Gr.Nyss.*homm.in Cant.*proem.(M.44.764B); Pall.*v.Chrys.*8(p.47.22, v.l. ὑπαγορίαν; M.47.28).

ὑπήκοος, **1.** s.v.l., = ἐπήκοος, *hearkening* to prayer; of God, Cyr.*Ps.*19:4(M.69.836A); **2.** *obeying, subject*; **a.** in gen., of people *subject* to nations or rulers; of *subordinate* attendants at a law court οἱ μὲν τῶν ὑ. ἑστᾶσιν φοβερώτερον δεικνύντες τὸ δικαστήριον Thdt.*Dan.*7:16(2.1202); of *domestic* animals, id.*provid.*4(4.537); met. ἐλεύθερον θανάτου...δοῦλον δὲ καὶ ὑ. ἀθανασίας Meth.*res.*2.18(p.371.10; M.18.285A); **b.** *obedient*, of Abraham ὑ. τοῖς ῥήμασιν τοῦ θεοῦ *1Clem.*10.1; τοὺς πονηροὺς ὑ. αὐτοῦ [sc. Χριστοῦ] γενομένους ὑπηρετῆσαι τῇ κελεύσει Just.*dial.*42.3(M.6.565B); Clem.*str.*7.3(p.14.6; M.9.424B); τῷ ὑ. τοῦ θεοῦ Const.*or.s.c.*15(p.175.26; M.20.1277C); τῆς θεοπνεύστου γραφῆς λεγούσης, ὅτι δὴ πᾶς ἀνήκοος ἐν ἀπωλείᾳ ἐστίν, ὁ δὲ ὑ. ἔσται ταύτης ἐκτός Alex.Sal.*Barn.*proem.3(p.437A); οὐ γὰρ τὸ ἄλογον ὑ. ἢ παρήκοον λέξομεν *Schol.*3 in Jo.Clim.*scal.*4(M.88.729B); also implying simply recognition of another's authority, hence *following* ἵν' ὅπερ ἂν ἐκεῖνοι παραγγέλλωσι, τοῦτο...ὑπὸ τῶν ὑ. παραφυλάσσηται Const.*or.s.c.*12(p.171.7, v.l. οἰκείων M.20.1272A); δοκιμάσας [sc. ὁ Χριστός] τὴν πίστιν τῶν ὑ. δήμων *ib.*15(p.175.12; 1277A); **c.** of monks, *under obedience*, v. ὑπακοή; **d.** of Christ, ref. Phil.2:8, v. ὑπακοή, ὑπακούω; **e.** of Son as subordinate and *obedient* to Father acc. Eunomius, Eun.*apol.*27(M.30.864C) cit. s. γέννημα; **3.** εἰς ὑπήκοον *within the hearing* οὐκ εἰς ὑ. τινων, ἀλλ' ἐν τῇ ἑαυτῶν καρδίᾳ λέγει Didym.*Ps.*13:1(M.39.1217C).

ὑπηρεσία, ἡ, **1.** *service*; **a.** in gen. διὰ τῆς ὑ. αὐτοῦ [sc. Moses] ἔκρινεν ὁ θεὸς Αἴγυπτον *1Clem.*17.5; of men to demons, Just.*dial.*131.2(M.6.780C); Tat.*orat.*17(p.19.7; M.6.844B); τῆς τῶν ἀγγέλων προνοίας, ὑπηρεσίᾳ τοῦ θείου βουλήματος, ἐπισκοποῦντος τὴν ἐκκλησίαν Or.*or.*31.6(p.399.21; M.11.556B); ταῖς μυστικαῖς ὑ. τὰς χεῖρας ἑαυτῆς ἔχρισε Gr.Nyss.*v.Macr.*(p.376.10; M.46.965A); **b.** as duty of deacons and deaconesses, *Const.App.*3.16.1; τὰ πρὸς ἀγγελίαν, ἐκδημίαν, ὑ., δουλείαν *ib.*3.19.2; **c.** liturgical *service* διὰ εἰκοσιτεσσάρων ὑ. τὸν δρόμον τῆς ἡμέρας καὶ τῆς νυκτὸς διατελέσωμεν *V.Alex.Acoem.*30(p.680.14); *ib.*(p.681.4); **2.** *body of people who serve* or *minister*; hence **a.** *retinue*, Eus.*v.C.*4.43(p.135.30; M.20.1193B); **b.** *ministry* of Church, connoting either ministers or their office διάκονοι...μετὰ ταῦτα γαμήσαντες ἔστωσαν ἐν τῇ ὑ. CAnc.(314)*can.*10; φόβῳ τῆς στρατολογίας εἰσποιούντων ἑαυτοὺς τῇ ὑ. Bas.*ep.*54(3.148E; M.32.401A); *ib.*188 *can.*12(275C; M.681B) cit. s. δίγαμος; μνήσθητι κύριε...διακονίας· λοιπῆς πάσης ὑ.· παντὸς ἐκκλησιαστικοῦ τάγματος *Lit.Jac.*(p.208.9); **c.** *subdiaconate* ὑπὲρ πάσης τῆς ἐν Χριστῷ διακονίας καὶ ὑ. δεηθῶμεν, ὅπως ὁ κύριος ἄμεμπτον αὐτοῖς τὴν διακονίαν παράσχηται *Lit.*ap.*Const.App.*8.10.9; *ib.*8.13.4.

ὑπηρετ-έω, **1.** *be a servant*; hence *minister to, serve*; act. or med., esp. as duty of Christians χήραις ὑ. Herm.*mand.*8.10; of Logos in rel. to Father ἔχει πάντα προσονομάζεσθαι ἐκ τοῦ ~εῖν τῷ πατρικῷ βουλήματι Just.*dial.*61.1(M.6.613C); Or.*hom.20.1 in Jer.*(p.177.2; M.13.500D); λόγον ~ούμενον τῷ θεῷ αὐτοῦ καὶ πατρὶ εἰς τὴν τῶν ὅλων δημιουργίαν *Const.App.*5.20.13; *Lit.*ap.*Const.App*8.12.30; of Son as subordinate to Father, Eun.*apol.*27(M.30.864C) cit. s. γέννημα; of angels serving God, Clem.*str.*7.1(p.4.21; M.9.405A); of men serving God γνώμῃ θεοῦ ὑ. Just.*dial.*95.2(M.6.701C); Or.*hom.20.3 in Jer.*(p.182.11; 508B); *Hom.Clem.*7.11; of men serving Church **Εὐτύχιον** ὑποδιάκονον, ἄνδρα καλῶς ~οῦντα τῇ ἐκκλησίᾳ Ath.*h.Ar.*60(p.216.24; M.25.765A); ref. minor orders τοὺς ~οῦντας τῇ ἐκκλησίᾳ ἡ πάλαι...συνήθεια μετὰ πάσης ἀκριβείας δοκιμάζουσα παρεδέχετο Bas.*ep.*54(3.148B; M.32.400B); hence οἱ ~οῦντες *ministers*, *ib.*(148E; M.401A); cf. of deacons οἱ μὲν τῇ προσφορᾷ τῆς εὐχαριστίας σχολαζέτωσαν ~ούμενοι τῷ τοῦ κυρίου σώματι μετὰ φόβου *Const.App.*2.57.15; ἵνα καὶ τοῖς ἀδυνάτοις ~εῖσθαι δύνωνται *ib.*3.19.1; **2.** pass., *be served* ἰδοὺ...ἐν ὁποίοις σκεύεσιν ~εῖται ὁ Μαρίας υἱός Thdt.*h.e.*3.12.4(3.926); διὰ τὸ μὴ θέλειν αὐτὸν ~εῖσθαι *V.Pach.A* 30(p.157.5); ~οῦμαι ἀπὸ [v.l. ὑπὸ] τοιούτων ἁγίων ἀνδρῶν *ib.*3(p.126.8); **3.** *administer* διδάσκαλος ἐθνῶν, τὰ παραδοθέντα...~ῶν...ἀληθείας μαθηταῖς ‡*Diogn.*11.1.

ὑπηρέτημα, τό, *that which assists, aid*, *Hom.Clem.*20.3.

ὑπηρέτης, ὁ, *underling, servant, minister*;

A. in gen.; met. γέγονεν ἥλιος καὶ σελήνη δι' ἡμᾶς· εἶτα πῶς τοὺς ἐμοὺς ὑ. προσκυνήσω; Tat.*orat.*4(p.5.9; M.6.813B); ἀδίκως τις αὐτῷ [sc. wealth] χρῆται· πάλιν ὑ. ἀδικίας εὑρίσκεται Clem.*q.d.s.*14(p.168.30; M.9.617C).

B. as applied to divine Persons; **1.** of the Word as minister ὑ. ὢν τοῦ ποιητοῦ τῶν ὅλων θεοῦ Just.*dial.*57.3(M.6.605C); **2.** of Son in rel. to Father: Arian υἱὸς μὲν πατρὸς θελήσει γεγέννηται μόνου...ἵνα διάκονος γένηται καὶ ὑ. τῶν βουλημάτων τοῦ πατρός Philost.*h.e.*9.14(M.65.636C); Eunomian τοῦ πατρὸς δοῦλον καὶ ὑ. *ib.*6.2(533B); **3.** of H. Ghost in rel. to Son: Eunomian ὑπηρέτῃ χρώμενον τῷ παρακλήτῳ πρὸς ἁγιασμόν, πρὸς διδασκαλίαν, πρὸς βεβαίωσιν τῶν πιστῶν Eun.*apol.*27(1.629A; M.30.864C); Macedonian λέγομεν ὅτι ὁ πατήρ ἐστι βασιλεὺς καὶ ὁ υἱός· τὸ δὲ πνεῦμα ὑ. ‡Ath.*Maced.dial.*1.17(M.28.1320A); τὸ δὲ ἅγιον πνεῦμα...διάκονον καὶ ὑ. καλῶν [sc. Macedonius], καὶ ὅσα περὶ τῶν θείων ἀγγέλων λέγων τις οὐκ ἂν ἁμάρτοι Soz.*h.e.*4.27.1(M.67.1200B).

C. of supernatural beings; angels συμμαχοῦντες ἡμῖν, ὡς ἂν ὑ. θεοῦ Clem.*exc.Thdot.*72(p.130.5; M.9.692C); devils Βελίαρ καὶ τοὺς ὑ. αὐτοῦ *T.Benj.*4.8; Just.*dial.*116.2(M.6.744C); cf. μάγοι...ἀσεβείας τῆς σφῶν αὐτῶν ὑπηρέτας δαίμονας αὐχοῦσιν Clem.*prot.*4(p.45.31; M.8.157B).

D. of men, in rel. to God, Ign.*Polyc.*6.1; Sophr.H.*mir.Cyr.et Jo.*37(M.87.3561A); or to evil δαίμονες...ἀγωνίζονται ἔχειν ὑμᾶς δούλους καὶ ὑ. Just.*1apol.*14.1(M.6.348B); of Simon Magus κακίας ὑ. *Hom.Clem.*7.11; of those through whom anything is administered Μωσέα διάκονον καὶ ὑ. ... τῆς εἰς ἀνθρώπους ἐκδόσεως [sc. of Law] Eus.*e.th.*2.14(p.116.6; M.24.929B); τῆς Χριστοῦ βασιλείας τὸ εὐαγγέλιον κηρύττουσι προφῆται ἑρμηνεύουσι δὲ οἱ τῆς νέας χάριτος ὑ. ‡Chrys.*leg.*1(6.403A).

E. eccl. **1.** of deacons ἐκκλησίας θεοῦ ὑ. Ign.*Trall.*2.3; ἐμμενέτωσαν ...τοῖς ἰδίοις μέτροις, εἰδότες ὅτι τοῦ μὲν ἐπισκόπου ὑ. εἰσί CNic.(325)*can.*18; διὰ τῶν ὑ. ἃ βούλονται σημαινέτωσαν, τοῦτ' ἔστι τῶν διακόνων *Const.App.*2.28.6, cf.CAnc.(314)*can.*10; **2.** of members of minor orders οὕτως [i.e. after selection and testing] ἐνηρίθμουν τὸν ὑ. τῷ τάγματι τῶν ἱερατικῶν Bas.*ep.*54(3.148C; M.32.400C); πολλοὶ μὲν ὑ. ἀριθμοῦνται καθ' ἑκάστην κώμην, ἄξιος δὲ λειτουργίας τοῦ θυσιαστηρίου οὐδὲ εἷς *ib.*(148D; M.401A); subdeacons, lectors, cantors, and deaconesses ὑ. εἰσὶν διακόνων *Const.App.*8.28.8; τοὺς λύχνους τῆς ἐκκλησίας παρασκευάζοντα, οἷά γε ὑ. ἔσχατον Soz.*h.e.*6.31.7(M.67.1389A); **3.** *subdeacon* διάκονος, ἐὰν ἐν τῷ αὐτῷ ἁμαρτήματι περιπέσῃ, τὴν τοῦ ὑ. τάξιν ἐχέτω CNeocaes.*can.*10; διάκονοι δ' αὐτῷ καὶ ὑ. θεῷ καθιερωμένοι...φύλακες τοῦ παντὸς οἴκου καθίσταντο Eus.*v.C.*4.18(p.124.7; M.20.1165A); οὐ δεῖ ὑ. ἔχειν χώραν ἐν τῷ διακονικῷ καὶ ἅπτεσθαι δεσποτικῶν σκευῶν CLaod.*can.*21; *ib.*20,22,25,43; Bas.*ep.*217 *can.*69(3.327D; M.32.801A); τὸν ὑ. εἰς διακονίαν τούτων [sc. bishops, priests, deacons] εἶναι προσήκει Gel.Cyz.*h.e.*2.30.3(M.85.1316C); not permitted to baptize, *Const.App.*3.11.1; to be ordained by bishops alone, *ib.*3.11.3; marriage regulations, *ib.*6.17.2.

ὑπηρετικός, **1.** *of* or *for service*; *doing service*; *serviceable*; in Church, *ministrative*, Clem.*str.*7.1(p.4.20; M.9.405A) cit. s. πρεσβύτερος; neut. as subst., *ministration, service*, exeg. Jo.1:3, 1:10 λέγων δὲ δι' αὐτοῦ γεγενῆσθαι ποτὲ μὲν τὸν κόσμον ποτὲ δὲ τὰ πάντα τὸ ὑ. τοῦ θεοῦ παρίστησιν Eus.*e.th.*1.19(p.81.17; M.24.865C); ἡ διὰ πρόθεσις τὸ ὑ. σημαίνει *ib.*2.14(p.116.2; 929B); **2.** *menial* οὐ γὰρ ὑ. γέ ἐστιν ἡ εἰς ἡμᾶς θεόθεν ἥκουσα, οἷον ἐκ χειρόνων εἰς κρείττονας προϊοῦσα, ἡ πρόνοια Clem.*str.*7.7(p.32.8; M.9.460A); **3.** *subordinate* ἡ διὰ πρόθεσις τὸ ὑ. ἐμφαίνει. ... ἄτοπον ἂν ἦν εἰ ἐγέγραπτο Παῦλος ἀπόστολος...διὰ θεοῦ· εἰ δὲ τὸ θέλημα τοῦ θεοῦ ὑ. ἐστιν, ἡγουμένου ὄντος αὐτοῦ τοῦ χρωμένου αὐτῷ, οὐκ ἂν εἴη τοῦτο ἄλογον Or.*comm.in Eph.*1:1(p.234.2ff.); **4.** of people, *given to ministering*, Just.*1apol.*16.1(M.6.352C); of ideal bishop, *Const.App.*2.4.1.

***ὑπηρετικῶς**, *in the capacity of servant* τῷ πνεύματι μὲν ἔδοξε δεσποτικῶς τὰ τῇ ἐκκλησίᾳ δοθέντα νόμιμα, τοῖς δὲ ἀποστόλοις ὑ. τὰ δι' αὐτῶν ἐκφωνηθέντα προστάγματα Didym.(‡Bas.)*Eun.*5(1.309A; M.29.741A).

ὑπηρέτις, ἡ, (fem. of ὑπηρέτης), *maidservant*; met., *hand-maiden* κράτος ἐδέξατο παρὰ θεοῦ ἡ τῶν Ῥωμαίων βασιλεία, ὡς ὑ. οὖτα τῶν τοῦ Χριστοῦ οἰκονομιῶν Cosm.Ind.*top.*2(M.88.113A).

***ὑπηρέτρια, ἡ**, = foreg., *A.Thom.A* 159(p.270.13).

ὑπηχ-έω, **1.** *prompt, suggest*; of an inner voice, Clem.*paed.*2.1(p.161.24; M.8.396B); νόμους ἔθετο [sc. Moses]...ὡς τὸ θεῖον αὐτῷ ὑπήχησε Or.*Cels.*3.5(p.207.9; M.11.928A); θεὸν διδάσκαλον ~οῦντα ἐν τῷ ἀδύτῳ τῆς ψυχῆς ἡμῶν παρεῖναι εὐχόμενοι id.*Jo.*6.2(1; p.108.11; M.14.201A); *ib.*28.20(15; p.414.22; 724A); ὁ θεὸς...τὸν ἴδιον παῖδα τοῖς προφήταις ἐκέλευσεν ὑ. τὴν ἐσομένην ἑαυτοῦ παρουσίαν Meth.*symp.*7.6 (p.77.10; M.18.133); in ordinary speech ἀκοαῖς...σαρκὸς τὰς διὰ γλώττης...~ῶν διδασκαλίας Eus.*l.C.*14(p.243.2; M.20.1409D); *suggest quietly, imply*; c. ὅτι, Olymp.*Job* 6:19f.(M.93.96A); **2.** *respond*, in psalm-singing ἐπιτρέψαντες ἑνὶ κατάρχειν τοῦ μέλους, οἱ λοιποὶ ὑ. Bas.*ep.*207.3(3.311C; M.32.764B); δύο ψαλμοὺς...ὑπηχήσαντες Chrys. *hom.11.7 in Mt.*(7.158C); ὁ ψάλλων ψάλλει μόνος· κἂν πάντες ὑ., ὡς ἐξ ἑνὸς στόματος ἡ φωνὴ φέρεται id.*hom.36.6 in 1Cor.*(10.342D).

***ὑπήχησις, ἡ,** *prompting*, ‡Gr.Nyss.*occurs.*(M.46.1172D).

***ὕπικμος,** *moist*, Pall.*h.Laus.*18(p.49.15; M.34.1052A).

ὑπίχνιος, *under the foot* ὑ. ... γῆν Max.*ambig.*(M.91.1117A, v.l. ὑπίσχνιον); met., *subjected*, Gr.Nyss.*hom.5 in Cant.*(M.44.861D).

***ὑπνηλία, ἡ,** *somnolence*, Nil.*epp.*1.26(M.79.92D).

ὑπνηλός, *sleepy*; met., *indolent*; esp. spiritually, Chrys.*hom.1.2 in Jo.*(8.4B); τί τὸ ὄφελος βίου εἶναι ἀλήπτου, νωθρὸν ὄντα καὶ ὑ.; id. *hom.6.3 in Eph.*(11.43A); Thdt.*ep.*50(4.1108).

***ὑπνηλῶς,** *drowsily*, Philost.*h.e.*11.3(p.135.2; M.65.597B).

***ὕπνιον, τό,** v. *πρωτοΰπνιον.

ὕπνος, ὁ, *sleep*; **1.** lit.; **a.** description; physiological, Gr.Nyss. *hom.opif.*13(M.44.165Aff.); ὕ. λέγεται παρὰ τὸ τὰς φρένας ὑπονοστεῖν, ἤγουν ὑποχωρεῖν Melet.*nat.hom.*synops.(M.64.1133Aff.); as gift of God, Bas.*hom.*5.3(2.36B; M.31.244C); often likened to death ἑκάτερος γὰρ δηλοῖ τὴν ἀπόστασιν τῆς ψυχῆς, ὁ μὲν μᾶλλον, ὁ δὲ ἧττον Clem.*str.* 4.22(p.310.18; M.8.1349C); ὕ. ... εἰκών ἐστι θανάτου, εἰκών ἐστι συντελείας Chrys.*hom.26.3 in Ac.*(9.213A); **b.** use by Christians, Clem. *paed.*2.9(p.204.15ff.; M.8.489Bff.); id.*str.*2.23(p.192.26; M.8.1096A); night should be divided between sleep and prayer ἀλλὰ καὶ οἱ ὕ. αὐτοὶ μελετήματα ἔστωσαν τῆς εὐσεβείας Bas.*hom.*5.4(2.36B; M.31. 244D); heavy sleep should be avoided, id.*ep.*2.6(3.75A; M.32.233A); **c.** of Adam, exeg. Gen.2:21, v. Ἀδάμ, ἔκστασις; **2.** fig. and met.; **a.** of God τὴν τοῦ θεοῦ μακροθυμίαν ὕ. ἡ θεία προσαγορεύει γραφή Thdt.*Is.*37:17(p.147.2; 2.321); id.*Ps.*43:23(1.885); θεοῦ ὕ. εἶναι τὸ ἐξῃρημένον τοῦ θεοῦ καὶ ἀκοινώνητον ἀπὸ τῶν προνοουμένων Dion.Ar. *ep.*9.6(M.3.1113B); **b.** of death, in pagan sense τὸν θάνατον βαθὺν ὕ. καὶ λήθην τιθέμενοι Athenag.*leg.*12.2(M.6.913B); in Christian sense, Mac.Aeg.*hom.*15.39(M.34.601D); ἐπειδὴ...ὁ Χριστὸς...ὑπὲρ ζωῆς τοῦ κόσμου ἀπέθανεν,...καλεῖται λοιπὸν ὁ θάνατος...ὕ. καὶ κοίμησις Chrys. *coemet.*1(2.398B); id.*hom.41.5 in 1Cor.*(10.393D); ὕ. ὄντως παρὰ θεῷ... ὁ πρόσκαιρος ἡμῶν τοῦ σώματος θάνατος, ψιλῷ καὶ μόνῳ καταργούμενος νεύματι τῆς κατὰ φύσιν ζωῆς, τουτέστι Χριστοῦ Cyr.*Jo.*7(4.679C); **c.** of sloth, etc., exeg. Mt.13:25 διὰ τοῦ ὕ. ἡ ἀπώλεια γίνεται. ... τὸν μὲν οὖν φυσικὸν ὕ., οὐ δυνατὸν [sc. καθεύδειν]· τὸν δὲ διὰ τῆς προαιρέσεως, δυνατόν Chrys.*hom.46.1 in Mt.*(7.481C); exeg. Rom.13:11 ἐγγὺς ἡ ἀνάστασις...δεῖ λοιπὸν ἡμᾶς ἀπαλλαγῆναι τῆς ῥαθυμίας id.*hom. 24.1 in Rom.*(9.694C); πᾶσαν τὴν σπουδὴν εἰς τὴν τῶν πνευματικῶν ἀνάλισκε ἐπιμέλειαν. οὕτω γὰρ καὶ ἀναστῆναι ἐκ τοῦ ὕ. τούτου δυνήσῃ ...καὶ γὰρ ὕ. ὁ παρὼν βίος *ib.*24.2(697A); ref. 1Petr.3:15 διδάσκονται μὴ τῷ τῆς ἀμαθείας ἐκδιδόναι ἑαυτοὺς ὕπνῳ Isid.Pel.*epp.*4.218(M.78. 1312C); ref. Mt.25:5ff. μηδεὶς ὑμᾶς ὕ. ἡδυπαθείας ἀνακλίνῃ *ib.*1.87 (244A).

[*]ὑπνοτικός, *appearing in sleep* or *in a dream*, *T.Sal.*2.3(v.l. ὑπνωτικός).

ὑπν-όω, intrans., *fall asleep, sleep*; met.; **1.** of God, ref. Ps.43:23 ἡμῶν...νωθρῶς ἐνεργούντων, ~οῦν λέγεται ὁ θεός, ἀναξίους ἡμᾶς κρίνων τῆς ἐπισκοπούσης ἡμᾶς ἐγρηγόρσεως αὐτοῦ Bas.*hom.in Ps.*29 (1.125B; M.29.308C); τὸ ἠρεμεῖν αὐτὸν ἀφ' ἡμῶν, καὶ οἷον ἀμελεῖν, δι' ἃς αὐτὸς οἶδεν αἰτίας, ~οῦν [sc. ὠνομάσαμεν] Gr.Naz.*or.*31.22(p.172. 10; M.36.157B); ὁ μὲν γὰρ λέγων αὐτὸν ὑ. τὴν ἐπίτασιν τῆς μακροθυμίας ἐνδείκνυται, ὁ δὲ λέγων μὴ ὑ., τὸ ἀκήρατον τῆς φύσεως ἡμῖν ἐμφαίνει Chrys.*anom.*8.1(1.515A); Jo.D.*Man.*1.80(M.94.1580B); **2.** of Christ as second Adam, ref. Gen.2:21f., Meth.*symp.*3.8(p.35.13; M.18. 73A) cit. s. ἐκκλησία; ἐσήμανε [sc. Adam's sleep] τὸν δεύτερον Ἀδὰμ ...μέλλειν ~οῦν τὸν ἀνθρώπινον θάνατον ἐν τῷ σταυρῷ Nil.*epp.*1.26(M. 79.92C).

***ὑπνωτήριος,** *inducing sleep*; neut. plur. [sc. φάρμακα] *sleeping-draughts*, Jo.Clim.*past.*2(M.88.1168D).

ὑποβάθρα, ἡ, *foundation, base, support*, Gr.Nyss.*res.*3(M.46. 669B); Chrys.*hom.17.2 in 1Cor.*(10.148A); Cyr.*Is.*4.2(2.599E); fig., of Christ in rel. to Church, *ib.*(612C); ὑ., ὥσπερ τινὰ προκαταθεὶς [sc. ὁ Χριστός] ἐν ἡμῖν διὰ νόμου παιδαγωγίαν *ib.*1.1(20B); met., of body of Christ, ‡Chrys.*pasch.*2(8.257C) cit. s. ἀσύντριπτος; ref. Mt.22:40 ὑ. πάντων τῶν ἀγαθῶν...ἡ φιλία Chrys.*hom.7.3 in 2Tim.*(11.703A); ἵνα ταύτῃ [sc. monastic life] χρήσηται ὑ. τοῦ ὕψους τῆς ταπεινώσεως Isid. Pel.*epp.*1.92(M.78.245C).

***ὑπόβαθρος,** *raised on a base, elevated* τὸ κιβούριόν ἐστιν ἀντὶ τοῦ τόπου ἔνθα ἐσταυρώθη ὁ Χριστός· ἐγγὺς γὰρ ἦν ὁ τόπος καὶ ὑ. ὅπου ἐτάφη ‡Bas.*h.myst.*4(p.258.19); βῆμά ἐστιν ὑ. τόπος καὶ θρόνος ἐν ᾧ ὁ Χριστὸς προκάθηται *ib.*6(p.259.14); τὸ βῆμά ἐστι τόπος ὑ.· ὑποδεικνύει δὲ τὴν δευτέραν παρουσίαν ‡Sophr.H.*liturg.*3(M.87.3984D).

ὑποβαίνω, 1. *descend*; of Christ τῆς θεότητος ὑ. Eus.*d.e.*6.9(p.259. 9; M.22.425C); ref. Mt.8:7 πρὸς τὸ ταπεινὸν ὑ. Sev.Ant.ap.*cat.Mt.* 8:8(p.59.5); **2.** *fall short* of, *be below*, of H. Ghost in rel. to Christ ὑπερέχον...πάσης τῆς νοερᾶς καὶ λογικῆς τυγχάνον οὐσίας,...ὑποβεβηκός γε μὴν [εἶναι] αὐτοῦ Eus.*e.th.*3.5(p.162.31; M.24.1012B); τὰ ὑπ' αὐτοῦ [sc. Χριστοῦ] γεγονότα, ὑποβεβηκότα δὲ τὴν αὐτοῦ...θεότητα Epiph.*haer.*76.35(p.384.30; M.42.588B); ἀγγέλων...ὑπὸ τοῦ πατρὸς... ὑποβεβηκότων *ib.*26.2(p.301.8; M.41.364C); perf. ptcpl. abs., *inferior*, Or.*Jo.*13.59(58; p.290.13; M.14.512A).

ὑποβάλλω, 1. *put forward*; a person, *M.Polyc.*17.2; *thrust in*; words into a conversation, Clem.*fr.*5(p.222.5); reflex., of an interrupter ὑποβαλὼν ἑαυτόν, φησί Chrys.*hom.4.4 in 1Thess.*(11.456C); **2.** *put upon* ξυλοπέδας...τοῖς Ῥωμαίοις ὑ. Thphn.*chron.*p.215(M.108. 552A).

ὑποβαρβαρίζω, *speak somewhat barbarously*, Synes.*ep.*67(M.66. 1428C); *mutter gibberish*; in a spell, id.*calv.*10(p.208.18; M.66. 1185A).

***ὑποβασιλεύ-ω,** *reign under, rule in subordination* to; of position of Caesar in rel. to Augustus ~ων τε τῷ πατρί *V.Const.*(p.565.10; *GCS* p.14.20).

ὑπόβασις, ἡ, 1. *going down, retiring*; of sun, Gr.Nyss.*Eun.*12(1 p.237.4; M.45.933D); of a star, id.*fat.*(M.45.149C); καθ' ὑπόβασιν *downwards in a series*, Iren.*haer.*1.12.3(M.7.573A); *in succession*, Clem.*str.*6.16(p.508.19; M.9.380B); **2.** *declension, deterioration*, Max. *schol.c.h.*7.2(M.4.68C); **3.** *subordinate status, inferiority*; **a.** in gen. μηδὲ τὰς οὐσίας τῶν κρειττόνων συνεξισοῦσθαι ταῖς καθ' ὑπόβασιν διαφερούσαις Athenag.*res.*16(p.67.16; M.6.1005B); δυνάμεων οὐρανίων ὑ. καὶ ὑπερθέσεις Gr.Naz.*or.*32.27(M.36.205B); Epiph.*haer.*76.54 (p.410.4; M.42.632A); *grade* τὰς ὑ. τῶν ἐν τῇ δημιουργίᾳ Max.*schol. d.n.*4.32(M.4.305C); **b.** theol., *subordination*: acc. Arius ὑ. τινα διανοούμενον ἐν τῇ τριάδι ἢ ἀλλοίωσιν ἢ παραλλαγήν Epiph.*haer.*62.4 (p.393.10; M.41.1056B); of Son in rel. to Father (Arian), Gr.Nyss. *Eun.*12(2 p.294.6; M.45.908B); Epiph.*haer.*69.77(p.226.2; M.42.328C); Tim.CP *haer.*(M.86.37B); taught by Origen, Antip.Bostr.*fr.*(M.85. 1793C); †Leont.B.*sect.*10.4(M.86.1264C); of Son and H. Ghost to Father; taught by Apollinarius, acc. the Gregories, *ib.*4.2(1220C); of Christ, ref. Heb.7:25, Nil.*epp.*1.114(M.79.132D); **4.** ?*feeling of inferiority* ὁ δαίμων...ὑποβάλλει αὐτῷ καὶ λογισμοὺς μετὰ ὑποβάσεως, καὶ ὡς εἰ μὴ μεταστήσῃ ἑαυτὸν πρὸς τόπους ἑτέρους, ὁ χρόνος...μάταιος αὐτῷ γενήσεται Ant.Mon.*hom.*26(M.89.1516B); **5.** *support, seat* τὴν θείαν ἕδραν, καὶ τὴν ἀσκανδάλιστον ὑ. τῆς ἀληθείας Meth.*symp.*8.10 (p.92.12; M.18.153A); **6.** prob. for ὑποβιβάζει, *cat.Apoc.*12:7ff.(p.359. 25).

ὑποβεβηκότως, *in a subordinate way*; hence *least loudly, softly* μεγάλῃ τῇ φωνῇ,...ἧσσον,...ὑ. Ath.*hom.in Mt.*11:27(M.25.217D); *in an inferior position*, ref. Mt.28:19 προσέθηκε 'τοῦ ἁγίου'. ὥστε μονονουχὶ ὑ. αὐτοῦ [sc. τοῦ πνεύματος] οὐκ ἐμνήσθη, ἀλλὰ καὶ ἀναβεβηκότως Didym.*Trin.*2.6(M.39.525B).

ὑποβιβάζ-ω, 1. pass., *pass out* of the body, Or.*Jo.*13.3(p.228.10; M.14.401D); **2.** *lower*, met. ~ει ὁ νόμος καὶ εἰς τὸ λίαν εὐπόριστον τῆς θυσίας τὸν τρόπον Cyr.*ador.*15(1.533A); τὸν...λόγον...~ουσι τῆς ἰσότητος τῆς πρὸς τὸν πατέρα id.*Chr.un.*(5[1].715C); ~ουσι τὰς Ἰσραηλιτικὰς φυλὰς αἱ παρανόμιαι...εἰς Χριστόν ‡Proc.G.*Pr.*14:34(M.87. 1369B); med., *be inferior to* τῆς ἀρρήτου φύσεως οὐχ ~όμενον [sc. τὸ πνεῦμα] Didym.*Trin.*2.8(M.39.616A).

ὑποβιβασμός, ὁ, *inferior position*, ref. Inc. ἀφῖκται...εἰς ὑ. καὶ ταπείνωσιν Cyr.*dial.Trin.*6(5[1].590C).

ὑποβλαστάνω, *grow a little, begin to grow*, Bas.Sel.*v.Thecl.*1(M.85. 501D).

ὑποβλέπ-ω, med.; **1.** *eye suspiciously*, c. dat., Thphn.*chron.*p.347 (M.108.836B); **2.** *regard with godly fear* ὑ. τὴν θείαν ὀργήν Cyr.*ador.*5 (1.170A); exeg. Soph.1:7 ~εσθαι κελεύων· τοῦτο γὰρ οἶμαι τὸ εὐλαβεῖσθαί ἐστι τὸν τῶν ὅλων θεόν id.*Soph.*5(3.583C).

ὑποβολεύς, ὁ, *one who suggests, prompter*; of Devil, Cyr.H. *catech.*2.3; of a demon, Pall.*h.Laus.*19(M.34.1066B; p.59.19n.); as member of minor order in Church, *monitor*; prob. connoting *cantor* (cf. ψαλτής) ἐν...Ἀλεξανδρείᾳ ἀναγνῶσται καὶ ὑ. ἀδιάφορον, εἴτε κατηχούμενοί εἰσιν εἴτε πιστοί· τῶν πανταχοῦ ἐκκλησιῶν πιστοὺς εἰς τὸ τάγμα τοῦτο προβαλλομένων Socr.*h.e.*5.22.49(M.67.636B); CCP(536) *act.*5(p.62.4; H.2.1320E).

ὑποβολή, ἡ, 1. *suggestion*; esp. of Devil, Ath.*ep.Adelph.*1(M.26.

1072A); ὁ Χριστὸς διὰ τῆς ὑ. ἐθεώρει [sc. πάσας τὰς βασιλείας τῆς γῆς] Ephr.3.177C; **2.** *deceit, stratagem,* Hipp.*haer*.9.12(p.247.24; M.16.3382C); **3.** *meaning* κατὰ τρίτην ὑ. ὑπόθεσις λέγεται ἡ ἀρχὴ τῆς ἀποδείξεως Anat.Laod.*arith*.(M.10.236A).

*__ὑπόβολον, τό,__ *bridegroom's present* to bride εἴ τι γὰρ ἡ γυνὴ ἐδίδου χάριν προικός, τοσοῦτον καὶ ὁ ἀνὴρ ὑποβάλλειν ποσὸν εἰς τὴν κοινὴν περιουσίαν ἠναγκάζετο, ὅθεν καὶ ὑ. ὠνοματίσθη. τοῦτο δὲ ἀνῃρέθη. καὶ σήμερον τοιοῦτον ὑ. ὁ ἀνὴρ οὐ δίδωσιν, ἀλλ' ἀπὸ συμφώνου δίδωσί τι μέρος ὅσον συμφωνήσῃ ἐκ προτελευτῆς τῇ γυναικί Phot.*nomoc*.13.4 (M.104.1192B); fig., Chrys.*Eutrop*.2(3.398C).

*__ὑποβράσσω,__ *boil underneath,* Geo.Pis.*hex*.273(M.92.1455A).

__ὑποβρύχιος,__ *under water*; met., *below the surface, overwhelmed* ὑ. ὑπὸ τοῦ πάθους Chrys.*ecl*.16(12.542B); hence ἐφησυχάζουσιν, οἷον ὑποβρύχια στένοντες Gr.Naz.*ep*.141(M.37.241B); ψαμμαίοις...ὑποβρύχιον Sophr.H.*v.Cyr.et Jo*.29(M.87.3416C).

*__ὑπογαργαλίζω,__ *titillate,* Jo.Disc.*v.Epiph*.64(M.41.108D); Dion.Ar.*ep*.8.6(M.3.1100B).

__ὑπογάστριος,__ *sexual,* ‡Nil.*narr*.3(M.79.621B).

__ὑπογενειάζ-ω,__ *chuck under the chin* ~ουσα τὰ παιδάρια Synes.*provid*.1.15(p.98.10; M.66.1248A).

*__ὑπογνωμικός,__ *in imagination only,* Sev.Ant.ap.Eust.Mon.*ep*.(M.86.925C).

__ὑπογογγύζω,__ *murmur, mutter,* ‡Ath.*ep.Cast*.1.6(M.28.857A); Gr.Nyss.*usur*.(M.46.452B); Gel.Cyz.*h.e*.2.12.8.

*__ὑπογονάτιον, τό,__ *ceremonial garter* of bishop, *Lit.Chrys*.(p.355.36; M.63.903).

__ὑπογραμμός, ὁ,__ **1.** *sketch, outline, model* of a child's *copy-head*; examples of such, Clem.*str*.5.8(p.360.3; M.9.80A); in gen. φησὶν... διὰ Ἰεζεκιὴλ πρὸς τοὺς πρεσβυτέρους ἀποταθεὶς καί τινα αὐτοῖς σωτήριον παρατιθέμενος εὐλόγου φροντίδος ὑ. id.*paed*.1.9(p.139.16; M.8.349C); of Ath.'s defence against Arians ὑ. καὶ τύπος τοῖς μετὰ ταῦτα γιγνομένοις Ath.*apol.sec*.90(p.168.7; M.25.409C); **2.** *example, model* λαβέτω τύπον καὶ ὑ. τῆς ἐν τρυφαῖς αὐταρκείας Bas.*reg.fus*.20.2(2.364C; M.31.972C); of one Christian to another, ref. 1Cor.8:10, Nil.*Magn*.38(M.79.1016B); of a monk to his fellows, Jo.Mosch.*prat*.143 (M.87.3005B); *V.Pach.A*(p.125.14); of a saint, *M.Ner.et Ach*.2(p.1.16); *V.Marth*.73(p.431B); of S. Paul, *1Clem*.5.7; ref. pictures of martyrs εἰσιν...ἀνδρείας ὑ. Germ.CP *ep.dogm*.4(M.98.172C); of scriptures as an example to martyrs, Phil.Thm.*ep*.ap.Eus.*h.e*.8.10.2(M.20.764A); οὐκ ἔδει τὸ πνεῦμα αὐτοσύστατον γίνεσθαι ἑαυτοῦ. ἀεὶ γὰρ φυλάττεται ἡ θεία γραφὴ ὑ. ἡμῖν γίνεσθαι Epiph.*haer*.55.9(p.335.25; M.41.988B); *ib*.57.5(p.350.30; 1004B); εἰ βούλεται πρῖσαι, πρίσῃ μετὰ τὸν Ἡσαΐαν ἔχω ὑ. Chrys.*ep*.125(3.668C); of OT saints, Cyr.*hom.pasch*.12(5^{2}.3D); of God's actions recorded in OT, ‡Nil.*narr*.7(M.79.688A); of Christ: his humility, Mac.Aeg.*hom*.19.2(M.34.644B); id.*cust.cor*.13(M.34.837A); in becoming man, *1Clem*.16.17; in making request of Father, Epiph.*haer*.69.29(p.178.21; M.42.248D); in serving man, Bas.*reg.fus*.43.2(2.390A; M.31.1028C); of his virtue γέγονεν ἄνθρωπος ἵνα γένηται ἡμῖν πάσης ὑ. ἀρετῆς Cyr.*Jo*.7(4.661D); πρῶτον μὲν ἐκεῖνο διδάσκων, ὡς ἐν ὑπογραμμῷ τῷ πράγματι, ὅτι τῶν ἀγαθῶν τὴν ζήτησιν, οὐκ εἰς ὑπερθέσεις ἀναρριπτεῖσθαι καλόν *ib*.2.1(130A); of his obedience to Father, Jo.D.*f.o*.3.1(M.94.984C); ὑπέταξε τὸ ἀνθρώπινον τῷ θεῷ καὶ πατρί, τύπον ἡμῖν ἑαυτὸν ἄριστον καὶ ὑ. διδοὺς *ib*.3.18 (1076B); his baptism and fasting, *Const.App.epit*.7.22.5; his fasting, Chrys.*hom.1.3 in Gen*.(4.5B); his suffering (cf. 1Petr.2:21), Polyc.*ep*.8.2; Jo.D.*hom*.3.24(M.96.624A); of unity between Father and Son ἡμεῖς...ἀλλήλων ὄντες...ὁμογενεῖς, ἓν πρὸς ἀλλήλους τῇ διαθέσει γινόμεθα, ἔχοντες ὑ. τὴν τοῦ υἱοῦ πρὸς τὸν πατέρα φυσικὴν ἑνότητα Ath.*Ar*.3.20(M.26.365A); of God in creation ὁ κύριος ἔργοις ἑαυτὸν κοσμήσας ἐχάρη. ἔχοντες οὖν τοῦτον τὸν ὑ. ... ἐξ ὅλης ἰσχύος ἡμῶν ἐργασώμεθα ἔργον δικαιοσύνης *1Clem*.33.8; ref. Trin. as being above all illustrations πλὴν ὑπὲρ ὑπόδειγμα καὶ πᾶσαν εἰκόνα καὶ ὑ. ὁ θεός, ἀνόμοια γάρ ἐστι πάντα τὰ κτίσματα ἀκτίστου τριάδος Eulog.*fr.Trin*.2.8(p.365); **3.** *type* τὰ περὶ τῆς τῶν βρωμάτων ἀδιαφορίας καὶ τὰ περὶ ἑορτῶν καὶ σαββάτου νενομοθετημένα, ὡς ἂν σκιώδη ὄντα, ὑ. ἑτέρων ἀληθῶν καὶ μυστικῶν πραγμάτων ἔσωζεν Eus.*d.e*.4.16(p.194.18; M.22.324B); τύπον καὶ ὑ. τινα [sc. Melchizedek] τοῦ δεσπότου Didym.*Trin*.1.15(M.39.321A); τὸ...ἀπεικονισμένον καὶ ἐν πύλαις ἡμῖν εἰργμένον καὶ ἀποθήκῃ ἠσφαλισμένον πίστεώς ἐστιν ὑπόδειγμα καὶ ὑ. Epiph.*haer*.59.10(p.375.16; M.41.1033A); εἰκὸς γὰρ ἦν αὐτοὺς περὶ τοῦ νόμου φθέγγεσθαι, καὶ πολλὰ περὶ καθαρσίων καὶ τῶν ἄλλων τῶν σωματικῶν λέγειν· εἶτα ἀφεὶς ἐκεῖνα ἐλέγξαι, ὡς οὐδὲν ὄντα ἢ σκιὰς τῶν πνευματικῶν καὶ ὑ. Chrys.*hom.2.1 in 1Tim*.(11.556C); **4.** *edification, lesson* τί οὖν; οὐκ ἠδύνατο ὁ θεὸς πατάξαι τὸν βασιλέα Ἀντίοχον καὶ ῥύσασθαι τοὺς ἑπτὰ ἀδελφούς; ἠδύνατο· ἀλλ' ἵνα ἡμέτερος οὗτος γένηται ὑ. Hipp.*Dan*.2.35.8; ὑ. ἡμῖν καὶ διὰ τούτων [sc. Ps.16:4] δίδωσιν ὁ σωτήρ, μὴ φρονεῖν ἐφ' ἑαυτοῖς δεομένοις τῆς παρὰ θεοῦ βοηθείας Or.*exc.in Ps*.16:4(M.17.109B); ὁ πατὴρ...δοξάζει τὸν υἱὸν καὶ ὁ υἱὸς δοξάζει τὸν πατέρα, καὶ τούτου ἕνεκα εἰς ἡμῶν ὑ. ... ἵνα ἡμᾶς διδάξῃ τὴν αὐτοῦ τιμὴν τοῦ πατρὸς εἶναι Epiph.*haer*.69.53(p.200.10; M.42.284D).

*__ὑπογραπτέον,__ *one must describe, give a brief account of,* Clem.*paed*.2.1(p.153.20; M.8.377B); Or.*or*.33(p.401.11; M.11.557A).

__ὑπογραφή, ἡ,__ **1.** *signature,* Chrys.*hom.40.2 in 1Cor*.(10.380D); ref. orthodox or heretical documents οὕτω πιστεύω ὡς προγέγραπται καὶ δι' ὑπογραφῆς ὁμολογῶ CAnc.(358)*ep.syn*.(p.284.9; M.42.425A); τῇ ἰδίᾳ φωνῇ καὶ ὑ. Leo Mag.*ep*.30(p.46.33; M.*PL*.54.790A); *signed statement* ἀνεγνώσθη ἡ ὑ. καὶ ἐδόθη Οὐάλεντι Geo.Laod.*ep.dogm*.ap.Epiph.*haer*.73.22(p.295.30; M.42.444C); ἐπὶ τῇ ὑ. τῆς πίστεως τῆς ὑπὸ τὴν περὶ Γεώργιον ἀπὸ τῆς Κωνσταντινουπόλεως κομισθείσης Bas.*ep*.51.2(3.144B; M.32.389C); Jo.VI CP *ep*.(M.96.1428C); met., *assent* ὡς τῷ πνεύματι παρόντες τῇ συνόδῳ ἡμῶν, συνεπιψηφίσασθαι δι' ὑ. ὑμετέρας CSard.*ep.cath*.(p.123.22; M.25.336C); βλέπε τὸ γραμματεῖον τῆς φύσεως...τῷ σταυρῷ προσηλωμένον...βλέπε αὐτὸ πονηρίας ὑπογραφὴν οὐ δεδεγμένον Thdt.*provid*.10(4.671); **2.** *sketch, description* διὰ τῆς θεολογίας οἷον ὑ. τινα ἐναργῆ τῆς φύσεως τοῦ μονογενοῦς ἐντυπώσας Bas.*Eun*.2.15(1.250D; M.29.601C); Gr.Nyss.*hom.2 in Cant*.(M.44.788D); Max.*qu.Thal*.59(M.90.609A); opp. definition ἡ ὑπόστασις... οὐδὲν ἐν τῷ ὅρῳ τῆς οὐσίας αὐτῆς λαμβάνεται ἀλλ' ἐν τῇ ὑ., ἐπειδὴ ἐπουσιώδη τυγχάνουσιν, οὐκ οὐσιώδη Eulog.*fr.dogm*.(M.86.2948A); ἡ δὲ ὑ. ἐκ τῶν ἐπουσιωδῶν σύγκειται Jo.D.*dialect*.8(M.94.553B); **3.** *example,* in gen. ἐφ' ἑτέραν πάλιν ἴωμεν ὑ. Chrys.*sac*.6.12(p.167.1; 1.433B); of Christ's baptism γέγονεν ὑ. ὁ κύριος Clem.*paed*.5.26 (p.150.19; M.8.280D); **4.** *pattern, type,* of tabernacle τύπος ἦν καὶ ὑ. παντὸς τοῦ κόσμου Cosm.Ind.*top*.2(M.88.73A).

__ὑπογραφικός,__ *descriptive,* opp. definitive τοὺς οἱονεὶ ὑ. ὁρισμοὺς Χριστοῦ ὑπὸ τῶν πατέρων εἰρημένους (followed by list of quotations) Leont.H.*monoph*.(M.86.1817B); ὑποθετικοὺς λόγους φησί, τοὺς ὑ., ἢ ὡς θεωρητικοὺς τῶν ὄντων Max.*schol.myst*.1.3(M.4.420D); ὁ δὲ ὑ. ὁρισμὸς μικτός ἐστιν ἐξ οὐσιωδῶν καὶ ἐπουσιωδῶν Jo.D.*dialect*.8(M.94.553B).

__ὑπογράφ-ω,__ **1.** *subjoin, make additions* μετεμελήθησαν τῷ παρ' ἡμῶν ἐπιδοθέντι αὐτοῖς βιβλίῳ ~οντες Bas.*ep*.224.3(3.343E; M.32.837C); **2.** *sign, subscribe*; abs., of subscribing to documents, *Ep.Aeg*.(p.157.20; M.25.389A); Bas.*ep*.244.2(3.377D; M.32.913C); Philost.*h.e*.1.10(M.65.465A); in lists of signatories: Κύριλλος ἐπίσκοπος Ἀλεξανδρείας ὑπέγραψα CEph.(431)*act*.1(*ACO* 1.1.7 p.111.32ff.; H.1.1424ff.); CChalc.*act*.1(*ACO* 2.1.1 p.145.20ff.; H.2.168Eff.); οἱ ὑπογράψαντες the *signatories* to a council, CAnc.(358)*ep.syn*.ap.Epiph.*haer*.73.11(p.284.6; M.42.425A); c. dat., CSel.*ep*.(p.299.26; M.42.452C); Philost.*h.e*.2.1(M.65.465C); **3.** *make a signed statement* of belief Βασίλειος...ὑπέγραψεν οὕτως· Βασίλειος ἐπίσκοπος Ἀγκύρας· ⟨οὕτως⟩ συνευδοκῶ τοῖς προγεγραμμένοις, ὅμοιον ὁμολογῶν τὸν υἱὸν τῷ πατρὶ κατὰ πάντα Geo.Laod.*ep.dogm*.ap.Epiph.*haer*.73.22(p.295.19; M.42.444B); **4.** met., *acknowledge* ὑπογράψαντες μὲν ἀνάστασιν σωμάτων νεκρῶν, οὐ λαμβάνοντες δὲ Chrys.*hom.40.2 in 1Cor*.(10.380D); abs., *grant permission* μηδ' ὅλως βουληθέντος Φήλικος ὑπογράψαι Just.*1apol*.29.3(M.6.573A); *approve,* id.*2apol*.14.1(M.6.467A); Or.*dial*.4 (p.128.9,10); Bas.Sel.*or*.7.2(M.85.109C); *assure* ἐκεῖσε [i.e. at font] τοῦ παραδείσου αἱ δωρεαὶ ~ονται Didym.*Trin*.2.13(M.39.692A); εὖ πράξασι δὲ καὶ ζωὴν αἰώνιον ~ει [sc. the creator] *Hom.Clem*.18.2; ἡ ἀθανασία τοῖς ἀνθρώποις ὑπογέγραπται Gr.Ant.*mul.ung*.11(M.88.1864A); *authenticate* τὴν ~εῖσαν ὑπὸ τοῦ κυρίου προσευχὴν Or.*or*.18.1(p.340.7; M.11.473B); **5.** *write from dictation,* Chrys.*ep*.103 (3.649A); Evagr.*h.e*.6.23(p.239.26; M.86.2880C); **6.** *write down,* Gr.Nyss.*hom.1 in Cant*.(M.44.769D) cit. s. ᾆσμα; **7.** *underlie* εἰς συμπλήρωσιν τῆς τὸ πᾶν μεγαλοφυῶς ~ούσης ὁλότητος γινώσκεται πεποιημένη [sc. πᾶσα σύνθετος φύσις] Max.*ep*.13(M.91.517A); **8.** *represent typify* ἡ τοῦ μύρου συμβολικὴ σύνθεσις...αὐτὸν ~ει τὸν Ἰησοῦν πηγαῖον ὄντα τῶν θείων εὐωδῶν ἀντιλήψεων ὄλβον Dion.Ar.*e.h*.4.3.4(M.3.480A); οἱ δύο λῃσταὶ τοὺς δύο ὑπέγραφον λαοὺς Isid.Pel.*epp*.1.255(M.78.336C); *be typical of* τἆλλα ὅσα τὸν τέλειον ~ει τῆς φιλοσοφίας τρόφιμον Thdt.*ep*.143(4.1238A); **9.** *imagine, visualize, call up a mental picture of* ὑπόγραψόν μοι τὸν Ἠλίαν τοῖς ὀφθαλμοῖς, καὶ τὸν ἄπειρον ὄχλον περιεστῶτα Chrys.*sac*.3.4(p.53.4; 1.382E); *ib*.6.3(p.145.5; 1.423B); id.*hom.45.4 in Jo*.(8.267A,B).

*__ὑπογρυλίζω,__ *reprove gently,* *A.Thom.A* 64(p.180.16).

__ὑπόγυιος,__ neut. as adv., *recently,* Meth.*symp*.8.15(p.103.1; M.18.165C); Nil.*epp*.3.219(M.79.484B); CCP(382)*ep*.ap.Thdt.*h.e*.5.9.15(3.1032).

*__ὑπογύναιος,__ *married,* Bas.*renunt*.2(2.203C; M.31.629A).

__ὑποδάκνομαι,__ *be somewhat jealous,* Cyr.*Lc*.7:17(M.72.61[illegible]B).

ὑποδακρύω, *weep secretly*, Gr.Nyss.*usur.*(M.46.441A); Synes.*ep.* 104(M.66.1477C); Ast.Am.*hom.*3(M.40.201D).

ὑποδεής, **1.** as subst. masc., *servant*, Leont.H.*Nest.*1.12(M.86.1448D); neut., *submissiveness*, *1Clem.*19.1; Bas.*hom.in Ps.*61(1.193D; M.29.469C); **2.** comp. ὑποδεέστερος, *inferior*; of baptism of John to that of Christ, Or.*Jo.*6.32(17; p.143.8; M.14.257B; of Elisabeth to BMV, *ib.*6.49(30; p.159.17; 288C); of H. Ghost to Christ εἰ πάντα δι' αὐτοῦ ἐγένετο, καὶ τὸ πνεῦμα διὰ τοῦ λόγου ἐγένετο, ἓν τῶν πάντων τυγχάνον ὑποδεέστερον τοῦ δι' οὗ ἐγένετο νοούμενον *ib.*2.11(6; p.67.17; ὑποδεεστέρων 132C); of Son to Father φαμὲν τὸν υἱὸν οὐκ ἰσχυρότερον τοῦ πατρὸς ἀλλὰ ὑποδεέστερον...αὐτῷ πειθόμενοι εἰπόντι τό· 'ὁ πατὴρ ὁ πέμψας με μείζων μού ἐστι' id.*Cels.*8.15(p.233.8; M.11.1357D); of inferior angels οὗτός [sc. Christ] ἐστιν ὁ διδοὺς καὶ τοῖς Ἕλλησι τὴν φιλοσοφίαν διὰ τῶν ὑποδεεστέρων ἀγγέλων Clem.*str.*7.2(p.6.17; M.9.409B); ἡ ἅπαξ τρυφήσασα γυνὴ ἤτοι ψυχή...μετὰ τιμωρίας ὑπό τινα ὑποδεέστερον γίνεται παρὰ τὸν Μιχαήλ· ὑποδεέστερος γὰρ ἐκείνου ὁ τῆς μετανοίας [ref. Herm.*sim.*8.3] Or.*comm.in Mt.* 14.21(p.336.5,6; M.13.1210D); of second Christ, acc. Valentinians, Hipp.*haer.*6.36(p.166.13; M.16.3250D); of demiurge to saviour, acc. Heracleon, Or.*Jo.*20.38(31; p.380.20; M.14.665A).

ὑπόδειγμα, τό, **1.** *model, pattern* τὸ δὲ 'καθ' ὅ' τὸ ἐνθύμιον δηλοῦν ἢ τὸ ἐκκείμενον ὑ. τῷ τεχνίτῃ Bas.*Spir.*5(3.5B; M.32.76B); met., *precedent* ἄνευ τινὸς ὑ. παρὰ τοὺς κανόνας ἐπίσκοπον χειροτονῆσαι Leo Mag.*ep.*104.5(p.60.30; M.*PL.*54.998A); *ib.*104.2(p.59.33; 994C); **2.** *precept* πονηρός, πῶς λέγεις; εἰ μὲν πίστεως ἕνεκεν, φεῦγε αὐτὸν καὶ παραιτῆσαι...εἰ δὲ βίου ἕνεκεν, μὴ περιεργάζου. καὶ τοῦτο οὐκ οἴκοθεν λέγω τὸ ὑ., ἀλλ' ἀπὸ τῆς θείας γραφῆς Chrys.*hom.34.1 in Heb.*(12.311D); **3.** ?*fixed period* εἰ ἡμέρας ἀριθμεῖ καὶ χρόνον σημαίνει καὶ υἱὸν ἀνθρώπου λέγει ἑαυτόν, ἄρα καὶ μέτρον ἡλικίας ὑπέδειξε καὶ ἡμερῶν τοῦ κηρύγματος ὑ. Epiph.*haer.*42.11(p.144.9, conj. ὅρον; M.41.756B); **4.** *copy*, ref. Heb.8:5, 9:35 ἐν ἀληθείᾳ σέβειν αὐτὸν καὶ μηκέτι τύποις μηδὲ σκιαῖς καὶ ὑ., ὥσπερ οὐδὲ οἱ ἄγγελοι ὑ. καὶ σκιᾷ τῶν ἐπουρανίων λατρεύουσιν τῷ θεῷ, ἀλλὰ τοῖς νοητοῖς καὶ ἐπουρανίοις Or.*Jo.*10.24(p.248.23,24; M.14.440C); καὶ πῶς ἐστιν ὑ. τῶν ἐν τοῖς οὐρανοῖς; τίνα δὲ καλεῖ τὰ ἐν τοῖς οὐρανοῖς νῦν;...τὰ ἡμέτερα Chrys.*hom.16.2 in Heb.*(12.160C); ὑ. γὰρ τὰ τῆς παλαιᾶς, ὡς τύποι ὄντα τῆς νέας †Oecum.*Heb.*9:23(M.119.380D); ἐλάτρευον ἐν ὑ., ὡς τὸ πρόβατον προσφέροντες εἰς τύπον Χριστοῦ Jo.D.*Heb.*8:5(M.95.965D); **5.** *illustration, figure* οὐ δέδοικεν εἰπεῖν ὅτι 'καὶ ἐκ νεκρῶν ἐγείρειν δυνατὸς ὁ θεός· ὅθεν αὐτὸν καὶ ἐν παραβολῇ ἐκομίσατο' τουτέστιν ἐν ὑ. ἐν τῷ κριῷ, φησί Chrys.*hom.25.1 in Heb.*(12.229A); Παῦλον ἀσθενοῦντα, καὶ μὴ πρὸς ἀκρίβειαν τὰ ὑ. λέγοντα...'ὃς ὢν ἀπαύγασμα τῆς δόξης καὶ χαρακτὴρ τῆς ὑποστάσεως αὐτοῦ'...εἰσί τινες ἄτοπά τινα ἐκ τοῦ ὑ. ἐκλαμβάνοντες. τὸ γὰρ ἀπαύγασμα, φασίν, ἐνυπόστατον οὐκ ἔστιν, ἀλλ' ἐν ἑτέρῳ ἔχει τὸ εἶναι *ib.*2.1(13D,14A); *analogy, illustration*, esp. of analogies to Trin. or Christ's person, Gel.Cyz.*h.e.*2.21.31(M.85.1289B); *ib.*2.22.11(1292D); τὸ τοῦ φωτὸς ἡμῖν ὑ. Eus.*d.e.*4.13(p.172.30; M.22.288B); πλὴν ὑπὲρ ὑ. ... ὁ θεός Eulog.*fr.Trin.*2.8(p.365).

ὑποδείκτης, ὁ, *one who points out*, *Chron.Pasch.*p.201(M.92.493C).

ὑποδειλιάω, *dread*, Thdr.Stud.*catech.parv.*63(p.149).

ὑπόδειξις, ἡ, *teaching* ἡ δὲ ὑ. τοῦδε τοῦ λόγου [i.e. 1Reg.28:11f.] ἐστὶ τοιαύτη *M.Pion.*14.7; *argument* ταῖς ἰδίαις ὑποδείξεσι προσέχειν, ὡς ἐξέδωκε Σύμμαχος Apoll.ap.*cat.Ps.*77(2.632); προσέχειν τῷ οἰκείῳ νόμῳ ἢ ταῖς οἰκείαις ὑποδείξεσιν κατὰ Σύμμαχον Thdt.*Ps.*77:1(1.1148n.).

ὑποδέκτης, ὁ, *treasury official*, Ath.*h.Ar.*75(p.225.1; M.25.784C); Chrys.*hom.85.4 in Mt.*(7.809C).

***ὑποδέννυμι**, med., *wear shoes*, Epiph.*exp.fid.*23(p.524.25; M.42.829B).

***ὑποδερματίς, ἡ**, *prepuce*, Epiph.*mens.*16(M.43.264C) cit. s. ὑποσπαθίζομαι.

ὑπόδεσμος, ὁ, *prisoner*, *A.Thom.*A 21(p.133.1).

ὑποδέχ-ομαι, **1.** *receive*; abs., Chrys.*hom.15.18 in Mt.*(7.199B); of a woman receiving seed at conception, Hipp.*haer.*1.26(p.30.5; M.16.3053B); Meth.*symp.*8.6(p.88.12; M.18.148B); met., of Church ὑ. δὲ καὶ μορφοῖ δίκην γυναικὸς ἡ ἐκκλησία εἰς τὸ γεννᾶν ἀρετὴν καὶ ἐκτρέφειν *ib.*3.8(p.35.17; 73A); *ib.*(p.37.8; 73D); ὅσοι ὑπεδέξαντο τὸν σπόρον τῆς θεότητος Mac.Aeg.*hom.*43.5(M.34.776A); οὓς ὑπεδέξατο...ἀνθρώπους ὁ παρὼν βίος Chrys.*Thdr.*1.13(1.20A); of receiving fellow Christians, Ign.*Smyrn.*10.1; Herm.*sim.*8.10.3; *A.Phil.*108(p.41.12); after baptism τὸν μὲν ἄνδρα ~έσθω ὁ διάκονος, τὴν δὲ γυναῖκα ἡ διάκονος *Const. App.*3.16.4; of ordination τὴν...χειροτονίαν τοῦ διακόνου ὑ. Philost.*h.e.*4.8(M.65.521C); of receiving Communion κοιλάνας τὴν παλάμην, ὡς μέλλων βασιλέα ὑ., μετὰ πολλοῦ φόβου τὸ σῶμα τοῦ Χριστοῦ ὑ. Chrys.*ecl.*47(12.771C); cf.Cyr.H.*catech.*23.21; ὁ υἱὸς τοῦ θεοῦ ~εται †Cyr.*hom.div.*10(5^2.372A); ὑπόδεξαι τὸν καθαρτήριον ἄνθρακα Anast.S.*synax.*(M.89.841C); σταυροειδῶς τὰς παλάμας τυπώσαντες τοῦ ἐσταυρωμένου τὸ σῶμα ὑποδεξώμεθα Jo.D.*f.o.*4.13(M.94.1149A); of Christ τὰς ἡμῶν χρεωστουμένας τιμωρίας εἰς τὴν...ἀναμάρτητον αὐτοῦ ὑπεδέξατο σάρκα Gel.Cyz.*h.e.*2.24.26(M.85.1304C); τὸ κῦρος ὁμοῦ καὶ τὸ κράτος αὐτῇ θεότητι καὶ δυνάμει καὶ τιμῇ παρὰ τοῦ πατρὸς ὑποδεδεγμένον Eus.*h.e.*1.2.3(M.20.56A); Christol. ref. teaching of Paul. Sam. and Antiochenes οὐχὶ καταβεβηκὼς ἐξ οὐρανοῦ υἱὸς ἀνθρώπου ἀλλ' ἐκ γῆς ἀναστὰς ὑπεδέξατο τὸν ἐξ οὐρανοῦ θεόν Apoll.*inc.*2(p.305.7; M.28.92D); **2.** impers., *it is acceptable* οὐ...~εται...τι θῆλυ ἐν τῇ θεότητι διανοεῖσθαι Epiph.*haer.*66.45(p.82.29; M.42.97B).

ὑπόδημα, τό, *shoe, sandal*; **1.** lit.; exeg. Jer.17:21 (rabbinic) 'βάσταγμα' μὲν εἶναι τὸ τοιόνδε ὑ., οὐ μὴν καὶ τὸ τοιόνδε, καὶ τὸ ἥλους ἔχον σανδάλιον, οὐ μὴν καὶ τὸ ἀνήλωτον Or.*princ.*4.3.2(p.327.3; M.11.381A); to be worn by virgins when praying, Ath.*virg.*11(p.45.8; M.28.264C); **2.** fig.; **a.** ref. Cant.5:3; identified with skins representing fallen human nature which is cast off at baptism οὐδὲ γὰρ Μωϋσῆς τῷ θείῳ προστάγματι τῆς νεκρᾶς τῶν δερμάτων περιβολῆς ἐλευθερώσας τοὺς πόδας, ὅτε τῆς ἁγίας τε καὶ πεφωτισμένης ἐπέβαινε γῆς, πάλιν ἱστορεῖται διαλαβὼν τοὺς πόδας τοῖς ὑ. ... χρὴ γὰρ τὸν ἱερέα πάντως ἐπὶ τῆς ἁγίας βεβηκέναι γῆς, ἧς μετὰ νεκρῶν δερμάτων ἐπιβατεύειν οὐ θέμις. διὰ τοῦτο καὶ τοῖς μαθηταῖς ὁ κύριος ἀπαγορεύει τὰ ὑ., ἐπειδὴ κελεύει αὐτοὺς εἰς ἐθνῶν ὁδὸν μὴ πορεύεσθαι, ἀλλὰ διὰ τῆς ἁγίας ὁδοῦ προϊέναι...ἡ ἅπαξ διὰ τοῦ βαπτίσματος ὑπολυσαμένη [sc. νύμφη] τὰ ὑ.· ἴδιον γὰρ τοῦ βαπτίζοντος ἔργον τὸ λύειν τοὺς ἱμάντας τῶν ὑ., καθὼς Ἰωάννης διεμαρτύρατο, μὴ δύνασθαι τοῦτο ἐπὶ μόνου τοῦ κυρίου ποιῆσαι· πῶς γὰρ ἂν ἔλυσε τῷ μηδὲ τὴν ἀρχὴν τῷ ἱμάντι τῆς ἁμαρτίας ἐνδεδεμένῳ; αὐτὴ τοὺς πόδας ἐνίψατο, πάντα γήινον ῥύπον συναποβαλοῦσα τοῖς ὑ. Gr.Nyss.*hom.11 in Cant.*(M.44.1005C–1008A); identified with filth, Thdt.*Cant.*5:3(2.110f.); identification with skins rejected, ref. Ex.3:5, id.*qu.7 in Ex.*(1.122f.); ref. Lc.10:4, no ὑ. needed for treading the living way which is Christ, Or.*Jo.*32.7(6; p.437.16; M.14.760C); μὴ ὑποζύγια καὶ οἰκέτας πολυπραγμονεῖτε, οἵτινες ὑποδήματα τῆς πορείας τῶν πλουσίων ἀχθοφοροῦντες ἀλληγορικῶς εἴρηνται Clem.*paed.*3.7(p.259.3; M.8.609A); to be rejected by Christians λογισμῶν ἀνθρωπίνων ὡς νεκρῶν ὑ. παντελῶς ἐλεύθερον Max.*ambig.*(M.91.1148D); **b.** ref. Mt.3:11, Mc.1:7, Lc.3:16, Christ's ὑποδήματα represent his incarnation and descent into hell οἶμαι τοίνυν τὴν μὲν ἀνθρώπησιν...τὸ ἕτερον εἶναι τῶν ὑ., τὴν δὲ εἰς ᾅδου κατάβασιν...καὶ τὴν εἰς φυλακὴν μετὰ τοῦ πνεύματος πορείαν τὸ λοιπόν Or.*Jo.*6.25(18; p.144.5; M.14.260B); *ib.*6.24(18; p.143.31ff.; 260Aff.); ref. Jo.1:27 where sing. because Jo. Bapt. doubted the descent into hell ἀληθεύει...λέγων καὶ τὸν ἱμάντα τοῦ ὑ., ἐπεὶ...ἔτι διαπορεῖ τοῦ πότερον αὐτός ἐστιν ἐρχόμενος ἢ ἕτερος, ὁ κἀκεῖ προσδοκητέος *ib.*6.27(21; p.146.8; 264B); ταῦτά τις λύσας τὸν χωρὶς τῶν ὑ. ἴδῃ λόγον γυμνὸν τῶν ὑποδεεστέρων καθ' αὐτόν, υἱὸν τοῦ θεοῦ *ib.*6.25(19; p.144.33; 261B); ref. Mt.3:11 and Ps.59:10 ἐνταῦθα ὑποδήματα τὰ τῆς οἰκονομίας μυστήρια λέγει ‡Chrys.*theoph.*1(2.809C); ὑ. δὲ τῆς θεότητος ἡ σὰρξ ἡ θεοφόρος δι' ἧς ἐπέβη τοῖς ἀνθρώποις Bas.*hom.in Ps.*59(1.192B; M.29.468B); ὑ. signifies τοὺς ἀποστόλους, ἢ τοὺς ἔτι δεῦρο τῷ περὶ αὐτοῦ κηρύγματι διακονουμένους Eus.*Ps.*59:11(M.23.569A); variously interpreted Ἰδουμαία 'αἱματώδης πηλὸς' ἑρμηνεύεται· δύναται δὲ ληφθῆναι καὶ εἰς τὴν σάρκα τοῦ κυρίου· δι' ἧς ἐπέβη ὡς δι' ὑποδήματος τοῖς ἀνθρώποις· ἄλλως χωρῆσαι τὸν ποιητὴν μὴ δυναμένης τῆς κτίσεως· ἄπειρόν τε καὶ ἀχώρητον κατὰ φύσιν τυγχάνοντα. δύναται δὲ πάλιν νοηθῆναι καὶ εἰς τὴν ἑκάστου ἡμῶν σάρκα· ἐφ' ἧς ἐκτείνομεν τὸ ὑ.· τουτέστιν τὴν φρουροῦσαν τὴν ψυχὴν ἀπὸ τῶν πονηρῶν τοῦ διαβόλου τριβόλων τε καὶ ἀκανθῶν ἄσκησιν τε καὶ ἐγκρατείαν...δύναται δὲ πάλιν νοηθῆναι ὑ. ψυχῆς καὶ ἡ διὰ λόγου καὶ θεωρίας νεκρωθεῖσα αἴσθησις· δι' ἧς ἐπιβαίνουσα ἡ ψυχὴ τοῖς αἰσθητοῖς, τὸν αἰῶνα τοῦτον ἀβλαβῶς διαπορεύεται Max.*exp.Ps.59:11*(M.90.868Af.); **c.** of shoes put on the prodigal son, *Const.App.*2.41.1; ὑ. εἰς τοὺς πόδας, ἵνα καταπατήσῃς τοὺς ὄφεις καὶ τοὺς σκορπίους· καὶ ὑποδήσεται τοὺς πόδας ἐν ἑτοιμασίᾳ τοῦ εὐαγγελίου τῆς εἰρήνης Tit.Bost.*fr.Lc.*15:22(p.223).

ὑποδηματοποιός, ὁ, *shoemaker*, Chrys.*hom.49.4 in Mt.*(7.510A).

ὑποδηματορράφος, ὁ, *cobbler*, Chrys.*Anna* 5.3(4.744A); Synes.*provid.*2(p.111.8; M.66.1260C).

ὑποδιαβάλλω, *discredit*, *Hom.Clem.*2.24.

ὑποδιαίρεσις, ἡ, **1.** *subdivision* οὐκ ἂν πιστεύσαιμι εἰς τοσοῦτον αὐτοὺς παραπληξίας ἐλαύνειν, ὥστε φάναι τὸν θεὸν τῶν ὅλων ὥσπερ κοινότητά τινα, λόγῳ μόνῳ θεωρητήν, ἐν οὐδεμιᾷ δὲ ὑποστάσει τὸ εἶναι ἔχουσαν, εἰς τὰ ὑποκείμενα διαιρεῖσθαι· εἶτα τὴν ὑ. ταύτην καὶ ὑπαρίθμησιν λέγεσθαι Bas.*Spir.*41(3.35D; M.32.144C); μέρη μὲν γὰρ Χριστοῦ ἀσύγχυτα, θεότης καὶ ἀνθρωπότης. ψυχὴ δὲ καὶ σῶμα, οὐ μέρη Χριστοῦ, ἀλλὰ μέρη τοῦ μέρους· ὧν δηλωθέντων διὰ τῆς τελείας σημασίας τῆς...ἀνθρωπότητος, περιττὴ ἡ εἰς φύσεις τῶν μερῶν ὑ. Leont.B.*Nest.et Eut.*1(M.86.1297B); Euthal.Diac.*Ac.*(M.85.652B); **2.** *sect*, Gr.Naz.*or.*22.12(M.35.1145A).

ὑποδιαιρέω, *subdivide*, Bas.*Spir.*41(3.35E; M.32.144D); Gr.Naz. *or.*31.7(p.153.4; M.36.140C); of Gnost. divisions of pleroma into groups of aeons, Hipp.*haer.*6.34(p.162.21; M.16.3246B).

ὑποδιακονικόν, τό, *subdeacons' place* in church, *solea* where subdeacons and lectors were allowed to sit, CSyr.*act.*(p.98.29; H.2. 1376A).

ὑποδιάκονος, ὁ, *subdeacon* (cf. *ὑπηρέτης*); **1.** in gen., as member of order next below that of deacons, *Lit.*ap.*Const.App.*8.12.43; *λειτουργούς φησι τοὺς διακόνους καὶ τοὺς νῦν ὑ. λεγομένους* Max. *schol.e.h.*3.2(M.4.136C); ranked with bishops, priests, and deacons, as having been instituted by apostles, *Const.App.*8.46.13; but reckoned among minor orders, Serap.*euch.*11.4; *Const.App.*8.28.7,8; *ib.*8.31.2; *Can.App.*43; **2.** method of ordination, *Const.App.*8.21. 1ff.; **3.** marriage regulations; must abstain, as must bishops, priests, and deacons, from intercourse with his wife, Epiph.*haer.*59. 4(p.367.19; M.41.1024A); *τοὺς ὑ. τοὺς τὰ ἱερὰ μυστήρια ψηλαφῶντας... ἐκ τῶν συμβίων ἐγκρατεύεσθαι, ἵνα ὡς μὴ ἔχοντες ὦσιν* *Cod.Afr.*25; marriage forbidden, Justn.*cod.*1.3.44(45)1(p.30); **4.** duties *οἱ δὲ διάκονοι ἱστάσθωσαν εἰς τὰς τῶν ἀνδρῶν θύρας καὶ οἱ ὑ. εἰς τὰς τῶν γυναικῶν, ὅπως μή τις ἐξέλθοι μήτε ἀνοιχθείη ἡ θύρα...κατὰ τὸν καιρὸν τῆς ἀναφορᾶς. εἰς δὲ ὑ. διδότω ἀπόρρυψιν χειρῶν τοῖς ἱερεῦσιν* *Lit.*ap. *Const.App.*8.11.11f.; *διάκονοι τότε τὰς θύρας εἶχον· νῦν δὲ οἱ ὑ.* Max. *schol.e.h.*5.6(M.4.165A); id.*schol.c.h.*8.2(M.4.81D); **5.** numbers *ἕνα ἐπίσκοπον δεῖν εἶναι ἐν καθολικῇ ἐκκλησίᾳ,...διακόνους ἑπτά, ὑ. ἑπτά* Cornelius ap.Eus.*h.e.*6.43.11(M.20.621A); ninety at Constantinople, Justn.*nov.*3.1(p.21.7); seventy, Heracl.*nov.*22(p.36); **6.** references to individuals, Eus.*m.P.*3(p.910.19; M.20.1469C); Ath.*h.Ar.*60(p.216. 23; M.25.765A); Bas.*ep.*219.2(3.332E; M.32.813A), etc.

ὑποδιάκων, ὁ, = *ὑποδιάκονος*, cf. *hypodiacones Graece, quos nos subdiaconos dicimus, qui ideo sic appellantur, quia subjacent praeceptis et officiis levitarum. oblationes enim in templo dei a fidelibus ipsi suscipiunt, et levitis superponendas altaribus deferunt*, Isid.H. *etym.*7.12.23; *MAMA* 1.179.

***ὑποδιαλλάσσω,** *distinguish*, Athenag.*leg.*20.4(M.6.932C).

***ὑποδιασκεδάννυμι,** *scatter in profusion*, Zach.Mit.*opif.*(M.85 1037B).

***ὑποδιαστέλλω,** *make a distinction* *ἀλλ' ἵνα μὴ νομίσῃς, ὅτι ὁμοίως τοῦ υἱοῦ καὶ τῶν κτισμάτων ἐστὶ πατήρ, ὑποδιέστειλεν ἐν τοῖς ἑξῆς* Cyr.H.*catech.*11.19.

ὑποδιαστολή, ἡ, **1.** *slight pause* in reading, Or.*sel.in Gen.*1:11 (M.12.92C); **2.** *comma*, Epiph.*mens.*2(M.43.237B); **3.** *subdivision*, Gr. Nyss.*diff.ess.*2(M.32.325B).

ὑποδιδράσκω, *run away surreptitiously*, *A.Jo.*20(p.162.7).

***ὑποδιηγέομαι,** *explain implicitly*, Or.*Cels.*7.65(p.215.10; M.11. 1513B).

ὑπόδικος, **1.** *liable*, Bas.*hom.*12.9(2.106C; M.31.405D); id.*hom.in Ps.*61(1.195E; M.29.476B); *ὑ. ἐστι πρὸς τιμωρίας ἔκτισιν τὸ ἀνθρώπινον τῷ θεῷ* Gr.Nyss.*or.dom.*5(p.98.32; M.44.1181C); **2.** abs., *subject, dependent*; of wives, depending for luxuries on their husbands, Chrys.*hom.28.6 in Heb.*(12.265C).

ὑποδίπλωσις, ἡ, *folding*, SM ap.Olymp.*Job* 41:4(M.93.440B).

***ὑποδούλιος, ὁ,** *slave*, Thdr.Stud.*epp.*1.34(M.99.1025D).

***ὑπόδουλος,** *subject*, Herm.*mand.*12.5.4; Thphl.Ant.*Autol.*2.18 (M.6.1081B); Thdr.Stud.*catech.parv.*113(p.264).

ὑποδοχεύς, ὁ, **1.** *host*, Eus.*Lc.*10:6(M.24.552A); Chrys.*hom.1.1 in 1Thess.*(11.427A); **2.** *supplier, provider* *δημιουργὸν καὶ ὑ. τῶν κακῶν* Adam.*dial.*4.5(p.146.13; M.11.1812C); of George of Cappadocia as contractor for supply of pork to army, Gr.Naz.*or.*21.16(M.35. 1100A).

ὑποδοχή, ἡ, **1.** *reception*; **a.** of seed, at conception, Clem.*paed.* 3.16(p.247.19; M.8.581B); by the earth, *ib.*2.10(p.208.12; 497B); Chrys.*hom.5.3 in Rom.*(9.458C); met. *πρὸς ὑποδοχὴν τοῦ νοητοῦ καὶ μακαρίου σπέρματος* Meth.*symp.*3.8(p.35.15; M.18.73A); **b.** of Communion *χεῖρας εἰς ὑ. τῆς ἁγίας τροφῆς* Dion.Al.ap.Eus.*h.e.*7.9.4(M.20. 656A); *παρασκεύαζε τὴν διάνοιαν πρὸς τὴν τούτων ὑ. τῶν μυστηρίων* Chrys.*hom.24.5 in 1Cor.*(10.219A); *ἀξίους ἡμᾶς ποίησον τῆς ὑ. τοῦ μονογενοῦς σου υἱοῦ καὶ θεοῦ ἡμῶν* *Lit.Praesanct.*(p.348.8); **c.** by senses, i.e. *hearing* *πρὸς ὑποδοχὴν τῆς θείας βροντῆς* Didym.*2Reg.* 22:14(M.39.1117D); **d.** myst. *δι' ὧν* [sc. Cant.1:1–8] *ἀφαγνισθεῖσα ἡ ψυχὴ πρὸς τὴν ὑ. τῶν θείων παρασκευάζεται* Gr.Nyss.*hom.3 in Cant.* (M.44.808D); **2.** *hospitality*; as a Christian virtue, *M.Ner.et Ach.*6 (p.5.4); cf. *διὰ τῆς λεγομένης παρ' αὐτοῖς ἀγάπης καὶ ὑ. καὶ διακονίας τραπεζῶν* Juln.Imp.*ep.*63(p.174.4).

ὑπόδοχον, τό, *receptacle*, Epiph.*haer.*34.22(p.39.4; M.41.625D).

ὑποδράσσομαι, *seize upon*, c. genit., Philost.*h.e.*4.12(M.65.528A).

ὑποδρήσσω, **1.** *obey*, Gr.Naz.*carm.*1.1.27.25(M.37.500A); †Apoll. *met.Ps.*77:10(M.33.1424C); Nonn.*par.Jo.*12:26(M.43.853C); **2.** *serve*, †Apoll.*met.Ps.*80:7(1433B).

***ὑποδρήστειρα, ἡ,** *handmaid*, Gr.Naz.*carm.*1.1.4.79(M.37.422A).

ὑποδρηστήρ, ὁ, **1.** *minister, deacon*, Gr.Naz.*carm.*2.1.16.11(M.37. 1255A) cit. s. *διάκονος*; *ib.*2.2(epigr.)3.3(M.38.84A); **2.** *servant*, Nonn. *par.Jo.*2:7(M.43.761A); *ib.*7:46(812C); *ib.*19:23(901C); **3.** as adj., *of a servant*, *ib.*13:12(861B).

ὑποδρομή, ἡ, **1.** *running down*, of light in evening, *waning* *τῇ ὑ. τοῦ πυρὸς τὸ ὑπερκείμενον ἀπεσκιάσθη* Gr.Nyss.*hex.*15(M.44.77B); of fire, *abating* *καπνῷ διὰ τῆς τοῦ πυρὸς ὑποδρομῆς ἅπαν τὸ φαινόμενον ὑποτύφεσθαι* id.*v.Mos.*45(M.44.316B); **2.** *cove, inlet*, Bas.*hex.*7.4(1. 67B; M.29.157B).

ὑποδύτης, ὁ, *shirt*, Gr.Nyss.*v.Mos.*(M.44.320C); *ὑ. δὲ καλεῖ τὸν ἐνδότερον χιτωνίσκον* Thdt.*qu.60 in Ex.*(1.165).

ὑποδύ-ω, act. and med.; **1.** *slip in under*; **a.** *slip into*, met. *οἱ... τὴν ἐκκλησίαν λοιμώδους καὶ φωραλέας νόσου δίκην ~όμενοι* Eus.*h.e.* 2.1.12(M.20.137C); **b.** *slip away*, Nonn.*par.Jo.*10:13(M.43.833B); **c.** *come to*, Clem.*prot.*2(p.20.15; M.8.97B); **d.** *enter (into)* *εἰ μὲν φαίνοιτο* [sc. *τὸ ζητούμενον*] *ὑφ' ἕν τι ὑποδεδυκὸς τῶν στοιχείων ἢ καὶ πλείω, ἀποφανούμεθα αὐτὸ εἶναι* id.*str.*8.7(p.94.19; M.9.589B); c. acc., Nonn.*par.Jo.*10:9(M.43.833A); c. dat., Thphn.*chron.*p.7(M.108.72B); **e.** *go under* *τὸ ὕδωρ ἐπιχεάμενος καὶ ὑποδὺς τὸ στοιχεῖον ἐν τρισὶ περιόδοις* Gr.Nyss.*or.catech.*35(p.133.4; M.45.88D); **2.** *put on, assume* *φύσιν ἀνθρωπείαν ὑπεδύετο* Eus.*l.C.*11(p.225.22; M.20.1380A); *εἴ τις διαπεπλάσθαι τὸν ἄνθρωπον, εἴθ' ὑποδεδυκέναι λέγοι θεόν, κατάκριτος* Gr.Naz.*ep.*101(M.37.177C); *τὴν πρὸς ἡμᾶς ὁμοίωσιν ὑποδὺς* Cyr.*hom. pasch.*4(5^2.42C); *τὴν ὑμετέραν μορφήν τε καὶ φύσιν ὑποδὺς* id.*Jo.*11.2(4. 939E); *εἴπερ μὴ προδιαπεπλάσθαι τὸν ἄνθρωπον, εἴθ' ὑποδεδυκέναι θεὸν λέγειν τολμᾷς* Leont.B.*arg.Sev.*(M.86.1933A); of demons *βουλόμενοι ἀπάγειν τοῦ ἀληθινοῦ θεοῦ τὸ τῶν ἀνθρώπων γένος, ~ονται τῶν ζῴων τὰ ἁρπακτικώτερα* Or.*Cels.*4.92(p.365.15; M.11.1169D); Chrys.*hom.13.4, 5 in Mt.*(7.174A,B); *put on clothes, dress*, of a tight-rope walker *ἄνω περιπατοῦντα ~εσθαι καὶ ἀποδύεσθαι* id.*hom.9.4 in Heb.*(12.162D); **3.** *bear* *~εται τὸν ψόγον* Clem.*paed.*1.8(p.128.32; M.8.329B); **4.** *submit*, abs.; of Christ, Gr.Naz.*or.*29.18(p.101.3; M.36.97B); *submit to* *~σομαι τὴν ἀνάγκην* Synes.*ep.*105(M.66.1488C).

***ὑποδωρίζω,** *use Doric dialect*, Synes.*ep.*143(M.66.1536B).

ὑποεικτός, *readily yielding*, Gr.Naz.*carm.*2.2.5.55(M.37.1525A); Eudoc.*Cypr.*1.138(M.85.837B).

***ὑποεξουσία, ἡ,** ? *inferior power*, *Exorc.*22(p.340).

ὑποζέω, *boil up from below*, *Hom.Clem.*6.6.

***ὑπόζοφος, ὁ,** *deep darkness*, †Dion.Al.*fr.Cant.*1:5(p.229.2).

ὑποζύγιος, *under the yoke*, ref. spiritual interpretation of the *ὑ. πῶλος* at Christ's entry into Jerusalem, Clem.*prot.*12(p.85.19; M.8. 244A); ref. Jer.5:8 *ὑ. ἵπποι* id.*paed.*1.5(p.98.28; M.8.266D); *ὑ. ταῦρος* Gr.Nyss.*fat.*(M.45.161B); met. *ᾅδης καὶ θάνατος* ‡Chrys.*circ.*(8.88B).

[*]ὑπόζυγος, *of a spouse, consort*, of the Church *εἰ ὑπόζυγόν ἐστί τι Χριστῷ...οὐ γάρ ἐστιν ὑπόζυγον μέρος* Or.*Ps.*44:14(p.44).

ὑποζωγραφέω, *represent in figure*, Cosm.Mel.*hymn.*12(1.84,p.163; M.98.505B).

ὑπόζωμα, τό, *rib of ship*; plur., Gr.Nyss.*fat.*(M.45.165C); Chrys. *hom.8.2 in Col.*(11.383A).

***ὑποζωματίας,** *joined underneath*; of one of the brain membranes, Jo.D.*ep.*(M.95.244C).

ὑπόζωσμα, τό, plur., *drawers, pants*, *M.Perp.*20(p.91.14).

***ὑποθερίζ-ω,** *reap*; met., *secure, obtain* *τὸν ἐγκύκλιον πλοῦτον παρὰ Ῥωμαίων ~οντος* Thphyl.*exc.Rom.*26(p.54.14; M.113.929C).

ὑποθερμαίνω, pass., *grow somewhat hot, become warm*, *Hom.Clem.* 6.6.

ὑπόθεσις, ἡ, **1.** *that which underlies*; **a.** *material presupposed* *ποίας γὰρ προβολῆς χρεία ἢ ποίας ὕλης ὑ. ἵνα κόσμον θεὸς ἐργάσηται;* Hipp.*haer.*7.22(p.198.5; M.16.3306A); *ib.*7.29(p.211.9; 3326A); **b.** *foundation, groundwork, basis* *τὰ μικρὰ μυστήρια διδασκαλίας τινὰ ὑ. ἔχοντα καὶ προπαρασκευῆς τῶν μελλόντων* Clem.*str.*5.11(p.374. 1; M.9.108B); *ἐν ἀνάγκαις γενόμενον εἰδέναι ὅτι ἡ ὑ. τῶν ἀναγκαίων ὁ Χριστός ἐστιν* Or.*hom.14.4 in Jer.*(p.120.18; M.13.424A); of cross *ὑ. ἀνόδου πρὸς ἀληθινὴν ἡμέραν* Meth.*Porph.*1.7(p.504.23; M.18.400C); *μηδὲ τοῦ Ἀδάμ, ὡς θεοπλάστου, καὶ ἡμῶν, ὡς ἀνθρωπογεννήτων, ἐν ὑπέρκειται γένος· ἀλλ' αὐτὸς ἀνθρώπων ἀρχή· μήτε ὕλη κοινὴ αὐτοῦ τε καὶ ἡμῶν, ἀλλ' αὐτὸς ἡ πάντων ἀνθρώπων ὑπόθεσις...ἡ τοῦ Δαβὶδ ἰδιότης ἀπὸ τοῦ Δαβὶδ ἄρχεται, κἂν ἡ ὑ. τῶν ἐξ αὐτοῦ πάντων, αὐτός* †Apoll.*ep.Bas.*1(M.32.1104B); *ἡ ἀπάθεια τῆς κατ' ἀρετὴν ζωῆς ἀρχὴ καὶ ὑ. γίνεται* Gr.Nyss.*or.catech.*6(p.35.7; M.45.29A); of humility *ἀρετῆς πάσης ὑπόθεσις* Chrys.*hom.90.2 in Eph.*(11.70F); *ἡ...ὑ. τῆς* σωτηρίας ἡμῶν τῶν ἀγαθῶν διὰ τούτου [sc. οἴνου] τελεῖται. ἴσασιν οἱ μεμυημένοι τὸ λεγόμενον id.*hom.29.3 in Gen.*(4.284B); αὕτη...ἡ τράπεζα...τῆς παρρησίας ἡ ὑ. id.*hom.24.5 in 1Cor.*(10.218D); id.*stat.*6.4 (2.78C); βεβαίαν...ὑ., τοῦ μηκέτι καθ' ἡμῶν ἰσχῦσαι τὸν θάνατον Cyr. *glaph.Gen.*2(1.41C); Synes.*regn.*15(p.48.5; M.66.1096A); Jo.Clim. *past.*10(M.88.1185B); **c.** *ground, cause, reason* ὑ. δὲ αὐτοῖς [sc. angels] τῆς ἀποστασίας οἱ ἄνθρωποι γίνονται Tat.*orat.*8(p.8.4; M.6. 821A); πολλὰς ὑ. ὑπάρχειν τῷ θεῷ, καθ' ἃς δημιουργεῖν αὐτὸν ἔδει Meth.*arbitr.*22.3(p.203.1); τῆς γὰρ ἐκείνου ἐνσωματώσεως ἡμεῖς γεγόναμεν ὑ. Ath.*inc.*4.3(M.25.104A); Epiph.*haer.*42.8(p.104.12; M.41. 708A); Cyr.*Jo.*2.1(4.114C); Bas.Sel.*or.*20.1(M.85.245B); **d.** *occasion, opportunity* ὑ. τρυφῆς ἀσελγοῦς ποιοῦνται τὴν αἴτησιν Bas.*hom.in Ps.*14(1.357B; M.29.264A); τῷ τὸν μονήρη στέργοντι βίον οὐδεμία γυμνασίας ὑ. πρόκειται Chrys.*sac.*6.7(p.154.13; 1.427C); id.*hom.18.6 in Mt.*(7.243B); **2.** *subject*; **a.** in gen. τίς οὐκ ἂν...νομίσειεν οὕτως αὐτὰ Ὅμηρον ἐπὶ ταύτης τῆς ὑ. πεποιηκέναι; Iren.*haer.*1.9.4(M. 7.545A); Eus.*d.e.*5 proem.(p.206.25; M.22.314A); χὸρ δὲ λέγεται ἀπὸ τοῦ βουνοῦ ὑποθέσεως· χαρία γὰρ καλεῖται βουνός Epiph.*mens.*21(M. 43.272C); ἐννόει πᾶσαν τοῦ σταυροῦ τὴν ὑ. Chrys.*hom.54.4 in Mt.*(7. 551C); **b.** of a book, Or.*fr.3 in Lam.*(p.236.20; M.13.608B); τά τε Κανδίδου εἰς τὴν ἑξαήμερον, καὶ Ἀπίωνος εἰς τὴν αὐτὴν ὑ. Eus.*h.e.* 5.2(M.20.509C); Gr.Nyss.*v.Macr.*(p.370.4, v.l. σύνθεσις M.46.960A); Ἐζεκίου, περὶ οὗ καὶ τὴν ὑ. εἴληφεν τοῦ ψαλμοῦ Didym.*Ps.*19:7(M. 39.1273A); of a psalm, Thdr.Mops.*Ps.*40:1(p.254.4); *ib.*53(p.348. 2,3); Cyr.*Ps.*40:1(M.69.992C) = Thdt.*Ps.*40:1(1.864); Cosm.Ind.*top.* proem.(M.88.56A); Leont.N.*v.Jo.Eleem.*proem.(p.3.16); hence *argument*, i.e. *brief summary of contents* κακὰς ὑ. ἔργων καλῶν προεβάλλοντο *Hom.Clem.*6.18; *point* ἐφ' ἑτέραν τῆς κατ' αὐτὸν οἰκονομίας ὑ. μεταβησόμεθα, αὐτὸν δὴ τοῦτον θεὸν εἰς ἀνθρώπους ἐλεύσεσθαι δεῖν Eus.*d.e.*5.30(p.249.7; M.22.409D); *pericope* σήμερον τῆς αὐτῆς πάλιν ἀψώμεθα ὑποθέσεως Chrys.*Laz.*3(1.736C); *ib.*(737A); **c.** *book, written work* ἐν δευτέρῳ τῆς αὐτῆς ὑ. Eus.*h.e.*5.7.1(M.20.445C); Gr.Nyss. *Eun.*1(1 p.40.5; M.45.268B); hence **d.** *history* τὴν τῶν διαδοχῶν περιγράψαντες ὑ. Eus.*h.e.*7.32.32(M.20.736B); Epiph.*mens.*21(M.43. 272A); **3.** *that which is put forward, proposed*; **a.** *hypothesis, theory*; esp. of heret. theories, Iren.*haer.*1.8.1(M.7.520B); Hipp.*haer.*4.51 (p.75.32; M.16.3122A); τῷ Βασιλείδῃ ἡ ὑ. προαμαρτήσασάν φησι τὴν ψυχὴν ἐν ἑτέρῳ βίῳ τὴν κόλασιν ὑπομένειν ἐνταῦθα Clem.*str.*4.11(p.285. 4; M.8.1292C); *ib.*7.16(p.76.27; M.9.553A); ἐξ οἵων ὁ οὐρανὸς κεκόσμηται σχημάτων κατὰ τὰς Χαλδαϊκὰς ὑ. Meth.*symp.*8.14(p.100.2; M.18. 161C); of scientific theories βασανίσαι τὰς Ἑλληνικὰς ὑ. Cosm.Ind. *top.*1(M.88.56A); ἐξηγούμενος τὰς Χριστιανικὰς ὑ. ἐκ τῆς θείας γραφῆς *ib.*(56B); **b.** *religious theory* or *teaching*; hence *religion, way of life* ἡ ὑ. ἡ διὰ τοῦ προφήτου παραδοθεῖσα ἡμῖν *Hom.Clem.*1.20; τὴν τοῦ εὐαγγελίου ὑ., ὅτι δόσις ἐστὶν αἰωνίου ζωῆς Clem.*q.d.s.*6(p.164.5; M.9. 612A); τῶν δυοῖν ὑποθέσεων, Ἰουδαϊσμοῦ λέγω καὶ Χριστιανισμοῦ Eus. *d.e.*1.7(p.37.17; M.22.73A); τίς ὁ καθ' ἡμᾶς τῆς εὐαγγελικῆς ὑποθέσεως λόγος καὶ τίς ἂν κυρίως λεχθείη ὁ Χριστιανισμός, οὔτε Ἑλληνισμὸς ὢν οὔτε Ἰουδαϊσμός, ἀλλά τις καινὴ καὶ ἀληθὴς θεοσοφία id.*p.e.*1.5(16D; M.21.45D); **c.** *purpose* Ἰωάννην...ὑ. οὐκ ἄλλην τῆς εἰς τὸν βίον ἐπιδημίας ἔχοντα ἢ τὴν περὶ τοῦ φωτὸς μαρτυρίαν Or.*Jo.*2.30(24; p.86. 32; M.14.165B); Eus.*d.e.*4.15(p.173.25; M.22.289B); Gr.Nyss.*Eun.*1(1 p.39.18; M.45.268A); **d.** *pretext, excuse* προϋποκειμένης παλαιοτέρας ὑποθέσεως χάριν διεστασίαζον Eus.*v.C.*2.62(p.66.19; M.20.1036C); εὐπρόσωπον...ὑ. ἔχον Chrys.*Is.interp.*1.8(6.15B); **4.** *matter, situation, affair*; **a.** in gen. ἐν ἑκάστῳ γενέσθαι ἐχθρὸν ἢ φίλον διὰ τῶν ὑ. ὁ θεὸς ἐμηχανήσατο *Hom.Clem.*11.8; Eus.*d.e.*10.8(p.475.15; M.22.764D); Παῦλον ἐν τῷ θεσμοθετεῖν ταῖς ἐκκλησίαις σαφῶς τὰς ὑ. οἰκονομήσαντα Attic.*ep.Cyr.*(p.23.11; M.77.349A); ἀρκεῖ γὰρ ἡμῖν ἀντὶ πάντων ἡ τῶν πόνων ὑ. καὶ τὸ πεπεῖσθαι σαφῶς ὅτι διὰ τὸν θεὸν ὑπομένομεν ταῦτα πάντα Chrys.*hom.16.11 in Mt.*(7.22D); *condition* τὴν ἀνόμοιον τῆς σωματικῆς συνθήκης ὑ. Mac.Mgn.*apocr.*3.12(p.81.22); **b.** *station in life* τοὺς ἐν ὁποιαποτοῦν ὑ. τῆς βίου...εἴτε ἐν ἐκκλησιαστικῇ δοκοῦντας εἶναι ὑπεροχῇ ἐπισκόπους καὶ πρεσβυτέρους, εἴτε καὶ ἐν ἄλλοις κοσμικοῖς τισιν ἀξιώμασιν Or.*Jo.*32.12(7; p.444.30; M.14.772A); **c.** *case at law* αἰτία δ' αὐτῷ τῆς μεταναστάσεως ὑπῆρξεν ἡ κατὰ τὸν Παῦλον [sc. of Samosata] ὑ. Eus.*h.e.*7.32.5(M.20.724A); δίττος μοι φόβος...ἐκ τῆς περὶ σὲ ὑ. Bas.*ep.*45(3.133A; M.32.365A); Synes.*ep.*14(M.66.1349D).

ὑποθετικός, *hortatory*, Clem.*paed.*1.1(p.90.8,16; M.8.249A,B); of a letter, Eus.*h.e.*4.23.2(M.20.384A).

ὑποθήγω, *urge on*, Sophr.H.*v.Anast.*(M.92.1700B).

ὑποθήκη, ἡ, 1. *precept*, esp. of Christ, Clem.*paed.*1.12(p.151.28; M.8.376A); Or.*Jo.*13.49(47; p.276.10; M.14.488A); in scriptures, Gr. Nyss.*Eun.*1(1 p.126.21; M.45.361D); id.*tres dii*(M.45.121A); Thdt. *Gal.*5:16(3.390); id.*Cant.*7:13(2.151); **2.** *opinion* κατὰ τὴν αὐτῶν ὑποθήκην πλανώμενοι Cosm.Ind.*top.*2(M.88.128C).

ὑποθημοσύνη, ἡ, *precept, command*, Just.*1apol.*14.3(M.6.348C); νόμον ὑπολαμβάνοντες τὸν λόγον, τὰς ἐντολὰς καὶ τὰς ὑ. αὐτοῦ ὡς συντόμους ὁδοὺς καὶ συντόνους εἰς ἀιδιότητα γνωρίσωμεν Clem.*paed.* 1.3(p.95.22; M.8.260B); τὰς καθηκούσας πρὸς τὴν ὀρθὴν πολιτείαν ὑ. *ib.*1.12(p.150.10; 369C); Areth.*Apoc.*17:16(M.106.724C).

***ὑποθήμων, ὁ,** *one who suggests*, Eudoc.*Cypr.*1.17(M.85.833A).

***ὑποθητεύω**, *be a slave to*, Cyr.*Is.*4.4(2.669D).

ὑποθραύω, *break in part*, Bas.*hex.*6.8(1.58B; M.29.137A).

***ὑποθρόνιος**, *under the throne* ἦσαν δὲ εἰς τὸν πέμπτον οὐρανὸν καὶ ὑ. ζῷα *Ascens.Is.*B 2.20(p.345).

ὑποθυμιάω, 1. *make fragrant, impart scent to*, Clem.*paed.*2.8(p.196. 20; M.8.472A); Bas.*hom.in Ps.*28(1.122A; M.29.300C); **2.** *cense*, *Lit. Chrys.*(p.550.37).

ὑποκαθέζομαι, *lie in ambush*, Mac.Aeg.*cust.cor.*9(M.34.829A).

ὑποκάθημαι, 1. *lie in wait*, Bas.*hom.*21.1(2.164B; M.31.541C); **2.** *yield to*, Didym.*Trin.*2.20(M.39.740B); **3.** *be inferior*, Cyr.*ador.*17 (1.628B); theol. ὁ γὰρ τῷ πατρὶ τὴν ἄνω χώραν εἰς προεδρίαν ἀποδιδούς, τὸν δὲ μονογενῆ υἱὸν ὑποκαθῆσθαι λέγων Bas.*Spir.*15(3.12D; M.32.92C).

ὑποκαθίημι, *slope down*, Gr.Nyss.*v.Mos.*(M.44.401A); Max.*schol. d.n.*8.2(M.4.356C).

ὑποκαθίστημι, *substitute* εἰς τόπους [sc. of those bishops who had been banished] τῶν ἔτι περιόντων ὑποκαταστάντας ἑτέρους Leo Mag.*ep.*93(p.32.6; M.*PL.*54.940A).

ὑποκαθιστής, ὁ, *underminer* τῆς ἐκκλησίας ὑ. μᾶλλον ἤπερ καθηγητάς Leo II Papa *ep.*(H.3.1476B; M.*PL.*96.410A).

***ὑποκαλύπτ-ω**, *make concealment* τί ὑποκρινόμενοι ~ετε καὶ οὐ φανερῶς λέγετε...ὅτι ὤφθη ὡς ἄνθρωπος; ‡Ath.*Apoll.*2.4(M.26.1137B).

[*]**ὑποκάμισον** ([*]**ὑποκάμησον**), **τό,** *under-garment*, Jo.Mosch. *prat.*186(M.87.3064B); Leont.N.*v.Jo.Eleem.*21(p.40.8); *Const.Stud.*38 (-ησον M.99.1720E).

ὑποκάπηλος, ὁ, *petty huckster*, Eus.*Hierocl.*33(532C; M.22.844A).

ὑποκαπνίζ-ω, *smoke from below*, as a torture σχοίνοις τε τούτους κρεμνῶν καὶ ἀχύροις ~ων Thphn.*chron.*p.307(M.108.748A); pass., Mac.Aeg.*hom.*27.15(M.34.704C).

ὑποκάρδιος, *in the heart*, Nonn.*par.Jo.*6:15(M.43.796B); *ib.*15:7 (873B).

ὑποκάρφω, *waste away, dry gradually*, †Apoll.*met.Ps.*101:5(M.33. 1461A).

ὑποκαταβαίν-ω, 1. *descend lower* into heresy, Ath.*ep.Adelph.*1(M. 26.1673A); *descend*, of Christ acc. Eun. ~ει πρὸς τὰ ἡμέτερα τῆς γνώσεως μέτρα Gr.Nyss.*Eun.*9(2 p.208.22; M.45.805C); *descend to*, of Christ ~ων τὴν ἀσθένειαν τῆς ἀνθρωπότητος Epiph.*haer.*65.4(p.6.20; M.42.17A); **2.** *decline* from ~ει τῆς σφοδροτέρας τε καὶ δριμυτέρας ἐνεργείας ἡ κόλασις Gr.Nyss.*anim.et res.*(M.46.100C); **3.** ὑποκαταβάς *lower down* in the text, Eus.*h.e.*5.18.3(M.20.476C); **4.** *fall* τότε [sc. at end of world] εἰς τὸ μὴ ὂν ἔσται ἀνάλυσις τῆς τῶν σωμάτων φύσεως, ὑποστησομένης δεύτερον, ἐὰν πάλιν λογικὰ ὑποκαταβῇ Or.*princ.*2.3.3 (p.118.7).

ὑποκαταβάλλω, *make subject to*, Ath.Scholast.*coll.*1.1(p.3).

***ὑποκατάγνωσις, ἡ,** *condemnation*, Ephr.1.203F.

ὑποκατακλίν-ω, *lay* oneself *down under*; met., of being defeated by sin ὅταν...τοῖς...πάθεσι σαυτὸν ~ῃς Chrys.*hom.19.5 in 1Cor.*(10. 165E); similarly used in pass. οἱ...ὑποκατακλιθέντες αὐτῇ [sc. κενοδοξίᾳ] Ἰουδαῖοι id.*hom.29.5 in 2Cor.*(10.647B); ~ομένῳ τῷ σχίσματι Eus.*h.e.*6.44.1(M.20.629B); Bas.*hom.in Ps.*33(1.148B; M.29. 364A); τοῖς δαίμοσιν ~όμενοι Isid.Pel.*epp.*3.104(M.78.809B).

ὑποκατάκλισις, ἡ, *senility*, Max.*schol.c.h.*8.2(M.4.77D).

ὑποκαταλείπω, pass., *remain to be done*, *Hom.Clem.*11.27.

ὑποκατασκευάζ-ω, *prepare beforehand* or *secretly* παιδαγωγικώτατα ~ει παῖδα πιστόν Clem.*paed.*1.7(p.123.19; M.8.317B); Or.*Cels.*1. 5(p.58.22; M.11.664B); Bas.*Eun.*2.1(1.238C; M.29.573A).

ὑποκατασκευή, ἡ, *mysterious arrangement*, Or.*Cels.*4.85(p.356.9; M.11.1160B).

ὑποκατάστασις, ἡ, *substitution* σβέννυται πᾶσα ὑ. ἢ ἀποκατάστασις ὑπὸ αἵρεσιν γάμου καὶ παιδοποιείας γενομένη Ath.Scholast.*coll.*1.2 (p.13).

ὑποκατάστατος, *substituted*, CChalc.*act.*14(*ACO* 2.1.3 p.83.16; H. 2.597D).

ὑποκατέρχομαι, *be inferior*, Didym.*Trin.*1.30(M.39.416C).

***ὑποκατηχέω**, pass., *receive instruction*, Euthal.Diac.*epp.cath.* (M.85.681C).

ὑπόκειμαι, 1. *be liable to* ὑποκείμεθα κινδύνῳ *1Clem.*41.4; Eus.*d.e.* 4.6(p.158.23; M.22.264C); Jo.D.*f.o.*1.1(M.94.792A); **2.** τὸ ὑποκείμενον as equivalent of ὑπόστασις: ἓν οὐ μόνον οὐσίᾳ ἀλλὰ καὶ ὑποκειμένῳ τυγχάνοντας ἀμφοτέρους Or.*Jo.*10.37(21; p.212.15; M.14.376B); εἰ ἕτερος...κατ' οὐσίαν καὶ ὑ. ἐστιν ὁ υἱὸς τοῦ πατρός id.*or.*15.1(p.334.5; M.11.465A); Bas.*ep.*9.2(3.90D; M.32.269A); *ib.*210.5(317A; M.776C); Apoll.*fr.*150(p.247.25); ‡Gr.Nyss.*hom.1.8 in Jo.*(p.95.24).

ὑποκεν-όω, *evacuate, subtract from,* ref. sins of omission τὰς ἐντολὰς...~οῦντες Or.*sel.in Dt.*12:32(M.12.812A).

ὑποκλέπτ-ω, **1.** *steal, take away,* Eus.*l.C.*15.2(p.244.21; M.20.1413B); Epiph.*haer.*69.3(p.154.14; M.42.205C); Chrys.*hom.14.2 in 2Cor.*(10.539A); τὴν τῆς θεότητος δόξαν ~οντες οἱ χειρόκμητοι θεοί Cyr.*Nah.*26(3.504C); pass., id.*ador.*17(1.247C); reflex. ὑ. ἐμαυτὸν τῶν λαῶν Ath.*ep.encycl.*5.2(p.174.1; M.25.232C); **2.** *plagiarize,* Eus.*p.e.* 10.1(461C; M.21.768C); Epiph.*haer.*66.60(p.98.3; M.42.121A); Hier. *vir.ill.*(tr.Sophr.Pal.)10(p.14.3; M.*PL.*23.626B); **3.** *plunder,* Phot. *nomoc.*2.2(p.500; M.104.581C); **4.** *win over to one's side, Chron.Pasch.* p.339(M.92.885A); **5.** *lead astray, deceive,* Ath.*gent.*15(M.25.32B); Mac.Aeg.*cust.cor.*11,12(M.34.832A,833A); Nonn.*par.Jo.*10:24(M.43.836B); ὑποκλαπέντα εἰς τὴν αἵρεσιν Thphn.*chron.*p.35(M.108.144B); of Devil, Ath.*ep.Aeg.Lib.*2(M.25.541A); Chrys.*hom.13.2 in Mt.*(7.170A); **6.** *elude, dodge,* Eus.*m.P.*4.8(p.914.16; M.20.1476B); **7.** *steal into* ~ουσαι...λαθραίως τὴν εἴσοδον Gr.Ant.*mul.ung.*6(M.88.1856A); **8.** *conceal,* Nonn.*par.Jo.*6:61(M.43.801B); τὸ ὁμοιούσιον ἐν τῇ τοῦ ὁμοουσίου φωνῇ ὑποκλέψαντες Philost.*h.e.*1.9(M.65.465A).

ὑποκλινής, *submissive, M.Niceph.*9(p.251).

ὑποκλίνω, **1.** *bow* the head or neck, *A.Andr.et Mt.*16(p.84.4); Thdt.*h.e.*4.6.7(3.954); ὁ τῷ προδρόμῳ Ἰωάννῃ ὑποκλίνας τὴν ἄχραντον κορυφήν *Rit.Epiph.*(p.415); liturg. σοὶ...οἱ σοὶ δοῦλοι ὑπέκλιναν τὰς κεφαλάς *Euchol.*(p.32); τὰς κεφαλὰς ἡμῶν τῷ κυρίῳ κλίνωμεν. τοὺς ὑποκεκλικότας σοι τὰς ἑαυτῶν κεφαλὰς εὐλόγησον *Lit.Bas.*(p.340.15); σοὶ γὰρ τὰς ἑαυτῶν ὑπεκλίναμεν κεφαλὰς ἀπεκδεχόμενοι τὸ παρὰ σοῦ... ἔλεος *Lit.Praesanct.*(p.350); in prayer at dismissal of catechumens κατηχουμένους τοὺς ὑποκεκλικότας σοι τὸν ἑαυτῶν αὐχένα *Lit.Chrys.*(p.315); **2.** med. and pass., *bow down, submit,* Chrys.*hom.21.2 in Mt.*(7.270B); ὑποκλιθήσεταί σοι...πᾶσα ἡ γῆ Cyr.*Ps.*65:4(M.69.1133D); Sophr.H.*ep.syn.*(M.87.3152A).

***ὑπόκλισις**, ἡ, *act of bowing,* liturg. μεταλαμβάνει...ὁ ἱερεὺς τρία ῥοφήματα ἐν μιᾷ ὑ. *Lit.Chrys.*(M.63.920).

ὑπόκλοπος, *guileful,* Ephr.2.347B.

ὑποκνίζω, *offend, anger,* Chrys.*ep.*14.3(3.598D); Socr.*h.e.*7.8.5(M.67.752B); *ib.*7.29.11(805A).

ὑποκόλοβος, *somewhat stunted,* Pall.*h.Laus.*18(p.58.5; M.34.1065A).

ὑποκομίζω, *place under,* Cyr.*Nah.*10(3.487C).

ὑποκοριστικός, *cajoling, coaxing,* Anon.ap.Eus.*h.e.*5.16.8(M.20.468A).

ὑποκοριστικῶς, *coaxingly,* Epiph.*haer.*69.60(p.208.21, conj. for ὑποκριτικῶς M.42.297D).

***ὑποκρατέω**, *suppress,* Gr.Naz.*or.*40.10(M.36.372A).

ὑποκρατήριον, τό, *small bowl,* Marcell.*fr.*112 ap.Eus.*Marcell.*1.3(p.15.15; M.24.745C).

***ὑποκρατύνω**, *support,* ‡Epiph.*epit.haer.*33(p.363.5).

ὑποκρίν-ω, **A.** *separate, divide* τῇ...χέρσῳ τὰ ὕδατα ὑποκρίνας ‡Caes.Naz.*dial.*92(M.38.956).

B. med.; **1.** *profess* Ἄρειος...αὐτὸς ὤμοσε πιστεύειν ὀρθῶς καὶ ἔγγραφον ἐπιδέδωκε πίστεως, κρύψας μὲν ἐφ' οἷς ἐξεβλήθη τῆς ἐκκλησίας ...~όμενος δὲ τὰς ἀπὸ τῶν γραφῶν λέξεις Ath.*ep.mort.Ar.*2(p.179.5; M.25.688A); τὸν τοῦ Πυθαγόρου θεράποντα...τὴν τοῦ δεσπότου φιλοσοφίαν ~όμενον Aen.*dial.*(M.85.940D); **2.** *play a part;* **a.** *pretend to be* οἱ ψευδοπροφῆται...τοὺς ἀληθεῖς προφήτας ~όμενοι Or.*fr.19 in Jer.*(p.207.10; M.13.573A); Φαρισαῖος...προσελθὼν τῷ δεσπότῃ τὸν μαθητὴν ~εται Bas.Sel.*or.*28.2(M.85.321A); **b.** *feign* ἱδρῶτες ἐπιρρέουσι...ἵνα μὴ τοῦτο εἴπωσιν οἱ αἱρετικοί, ὅτι ~εται [sc. Christ] τὴν ἀγωνίαν Chrys.*hom.83.1 in Mt.*(7.791B); διὰ τί καὶ δειλίαν ~εται θεὸς ὤν; ‡Caes.Naz.*dial.*134(M.38.1037); **c.** *dissemble, deceive;* abs. διὰ...τὴν ἐπιθυμίαν τοῦ λήμματος ὑπεκρίθησαν Herm.*sim.*9.19.3; in Eleusinian formula τὸ πῦρ οὐχ ~εται Clem.*prot.*2(p.17.17; M.8.89A); ref. cleansing of Temple εἰ γὰρ ~όμενος ταῦτα ἐποίει, παραινέσαι ἐχρῆν μόνον·...οὐχ ~ομένου ἦν, ἀλλὰ πάντα αἱρουμένου πάθη Chrys. *hom.23.2 in Jo.*(8.134A); trans. ψυχὰς ἀκάκων παραλογισμῷ ὑπεκρίνοντο *Pss.Sal.*4.25; τὴν ἐκκλησίαν ~εται Eus.*e.th.*2.16(p.120.4; M.24.937A); τὸ Ἐμπεδοκλέους...δόγμα διὰ τοῦ Μανιχαίου Χριστιανισμὸν ὑπεκρίνατο Socr.*h.e.*1.22.2(M.67.136B); **d.** *counterfeit* ~εται...τὴν πίστιν ἡ εἰκασία Clem.*str.*2.4(p.120.28; M.8.948A); esp. of counterfeiting the truth, *ib.*3.4(p.212.1; 1104A); Gr.Thaum.*pan.Or.*7(p.21.7; M.10.1076C); Meth.*res.*1.29(p.259.19; M.41.1137A); without implying deceit ὧν ἡ γεῦσις τὴν τοῦ μέλιτος ἡδονὴν ὑπεκρίνετο Gr. Nyss.*v.Mos.*39(M.44.312D); Mac.Mgn.*apocr.*4.11(p.171.14); οἰκονομίας ἕνεκεν τῶν ὠφελουμένων ἑκατέρας τὰς φύσεις τὸ θεῖον ~εται *ib.*4.27(p.215.6); **3.** *imitate* at baptism τὴν σωτήριον ταφὴν καὶ ἀνάστασιν... ~όμεθα Gr.Nyss.*or.catech.*35(p.135.11; ἀποκ- M.45.89C); ἡ δὲ τὸ τῆς ἀληθοῦς ἑνότητος ~εται σχῆμα Cyr.*Jo.*11.11(4.996C).

ὑπόκρισις, ἡ, **A.** *answer,* Thdt.*Ps.*126:5(1.1497); id.*Heb.*3:16(3.565).

B. *acting,* Gr.Naz.*ep.*101(M.37.188A); Chrys.*hom.79.3 in Mt.*(7.762C); of S. Paul διὰ...τὴν τῶν πολλῶν ὠφέλειαν τοῖς τῆς ὑ. προσωπείοις ἐχρήσατο Thdt.*ep.*3(4.1062); hence **1.** *simulation;* **a.** in gen., Or.*or.*21.1(p.345.10; M.11.480D); *Hom.Clem.*11.14; Proc.G.*Is.*1:20(M.87.1849C); **b.** ref. Christ ἐκτενῶς εὔχεται, ἵνα μὴ δόξῃ ὑ. εἶναι τὸ πρᾶγμα Chrys.*hom.83.1 in Mt.*(7.791B); οἱ λέγοντες ὅτι φαντασία τις ἦν καὶ ὑ. καὶ ὑπόνοια τὰ τῆς οἰκονομίας ἅπαντα id.*hom.11.2 in Jo.*(8.64A); *ib.37.1*(212C); τὰ κατ' οἰκονομίαν τινὰ λεγόμενα ἢ πραττόμενα οὐ χρὴ ψεῦδος λέγεσθαι ἢ ὑ. Germ.CP *vit.term.*12(M.98.112A); **2.** *deceit, hypocrisy;* in gen. ἐξάραι ὁ θεὸς τοὺς ἐν ὑ. ζῶντας μετὰ ὁσίων *Pss.Sal.*4.7; μισήσεις πᾶσαν ὑ. *Barn.*19.2; ἀπεχόμενοι τῶν ἐν ὑ. φερόντων τὸ ὄνομα τοῦ κυρίου Polyc.*ep.*6.3; ἐπίστευσαν...ἐν ὑ. Herm.*vis.*3.6.1; Clem.*prot.*10(p.72.3; M.8.213A); of Pharisees, Or.*Jo.*6.28(14; p.138.19; M.14.249B); of Devil ἀεὶ μιμεῖται τῆς ἀρετῆς καὶ δικαιοσύνης τὰ σχήματα...πρὸς ἀπάτην καὶ ὑ. Meth.*symp.*10.5(p.127.2; M.18.200C); ἡ ὑ. καρπός ἐστι τοῦ φθόνου Bas.*hom.*11.6(2.97B; M.31.385B); in lists of sins τῦφος...καὶ ἀπιστία καὶ θυμὸς καὶ ὑ. ψυχῆς ἁμαρτήματα Meth.*res.*1.61(p.326.6; M.41.1160A); plur., Pall.*v.Chrys.*20(p.133.22; M.47.74); Jo.D.*spir.neq.*(M.95.88B) = Ephr.3.426C.

C. *delivery* in reading παρὰ στιγμὴν μόνην καὶ παρὰ ὑπόκρισιν μόνον ἀναγνώσεως, πολλὰ πολλάκις ἄτοπα ἐτέχθη νοήματα Chrys.*hom.34.5 in 1Cor.*(10.318B).

ὑποκριτής, ὁ, *actor, hypocrite;* met., meaning *hypocrite* explained ὥσπερ δὲ ἐν τοῖς θεάτροις δραμάτων τινῶν ὑποκριταὶ οὐχ ὅπερ λέγουσίν εἰσιν, οὐδ' ὅπερ βλέπονται καθ' ὃ περίκεινται πρόσωπον τοῦτο τυγχάνουσιν· οὕτως καὶ πάντες οἱ ἐπιμορφάζοντες τῷ δοκεῖν τὴν τοῦ καλοῦ φαντασίαν οὐ δίκαιοι ἀλλ' ὑ. εἰσι δικαιοσύνης, καὶ αὐτοὶ ἐν ἰδίῳ θεάτρῳ ὑποκρινόμενοι 'ταῖς συναγωγαῖς καὶ ταῖς γωνίαις τῶν πλατειῶν' Or. *or.*20.2(p.344.12,15; M.11.480A,B); ὑ. ἐστιν ὁ ἐν θεάτρῳ ἀλλότριον πρόσωπον ὑπελθών...οὕτω καὶ ἐν τῷ βίῳ τούτῳ, ὥσπερ ἐπὶ ὀρχήστρας, τῆς ἑαυτῶν ζωῆς, οἱ πολλοὶ θεατρίζουσιν, ἄλλα μὲν ἐν τῇ καρδίᾳ φέροντες, ἄλλα δὲ ἐν τῇ ἐπιφανείᾳ τοῖς ἀνθρώποις δεικνύντες Bas.*hom.*1.2(2.2D; M.31.165B); of Judas γέγονεν...ὑ. καὶ φίλημα δεδολωμένον ἔχων, ἄλλον παλαιὸν μιμούμενος ὑ. Clem.*paed.*2.8(p.195.6,7; M.8.468B); τοὺς τῆς Ἀρείου μανίας ὑποκριτάς Ath.*Ar.*2.1(M.26.145D); of Pharisees τούτους ὑ. καλεῖ, καὶ μάλα εἰκότως· ὅτι θεῷ προσποιούμενοι προσεύχεσθαι, ἀνθρώπους περισκοποῦσιν Chrys.*hom.19.2 in Mt.*(7.247A); of Satan ὄφεως ὑ. γεγονώς Bas.Sel.*or.*3.3(M.85.53D); in gen. οὐκ ἔσῃ...ὑ. *Did.*2.6; Herm.*sim.*9.18.3; Or.*or.*22.3(p.347.26; M.11.484C); ἴσως ἐστί τις ἐν ὑμῖν ὑ., ἀνθρωπάρεσκος, καὶ τὸ μὲν εὐλαβὲς ὑποκρινόμενος, μὴ ἀπὸ καρδίας δὲ πιστεύων, Σίμωνος ἔχων τοῦ Μάγου τὴν ὑπόκρισιν Cyr.H.*catech.*3.7; Cyr.*Lc.*6:42(M.72.604D); οἱ δὲ τῇ καρδίᾳ ὑ. ... οἱ σχῆμα μόνον εὐσεβείας περικείμενοι Olymp.*Job* 36:13(M.93.376B).

ὑποκριτικός, *pretended,* Epiph.*haer.*63.1(p.399.11; M.41.1064B).

***ὑπόκριτος**, *fictitious, Hom.Clem.*5.27.

ὑπόκρουσις, ἡ, *objection,* Max.*schol.d.n.*4.19(M.4.276A); *ib.*4.22(288B).

ὑποκρύπτω, *hide, T.Jud.*6.5; Gr.Nyss.*hex.*10(M.44.72D).

ὑποκρύφιος, *secret,* Nonn.*par.Jo.*18:20(M.43.893A); Men.*exc. Rom.*15(p.209.27; M.113.909A).

***ὑπόκρυψις**, ἡ, *concealment,* Gr.Nyss.*homm.in Cant.*proem.(M.44.756B).

***ὑποκυανίζω**, *be dark blue,* Epiph.*gemm.*8(M.43.300B).

ὑποκύπτ-ω, **1.** *bow down before* βασιλικὴν πρόοδον ὑποκύψαντες Mac.Mgn.*apocr.*4.25(p.208.4); **2.** *bow down, submit,* abs. πάντας ~οντας ἰδεῖν ποθῶν Thdt.*Rom.*9:3(3.99); πάντα ἐκεῖνα ~οντα ἔχει Isid.Pel.*epp.*3.351(M.78.1005C); c. dat. ~ειν τοῦ θεοῦ ταῖς ἐντολαῖς Clem.*q.d.s.*26.2(p.177.5; M.9.632A); Cosm.Ind.*top.*10(M.88.433A); τί ἀπρεπὲς τὸν σχήματι καὶ μορφῇ ὑποκύψαντα φιλανθρώπως δι' ἡμᾶς, εἰκονίζειν ἀναλόγως ἡμῖν αὐτοῖς; *Schol.* in Dion.Ar.*e.h.*1.2 ap.Jo.D. *imag.*1(M.94.1261A); **3.** *bow down to, obey* οὐδενὶ...~ουσα πάθει Isid.Pel.*epp.*1.129(M.78.268D); μὴ ~ειν τοῖς φόβοις καὶ τοῖς κινδύνοις *ib.*2.241(681C); τοῖς αὐτοῦ θελήμασιν ~οντες Cyr.*Os.*128(3.161A).

***ὑπολαγχάνω**, s.v.l., ? *possess in a slight degree* ὑπολαχὼν τῆς τυραννίδος καὶ ἐκνευριζόμενος, ἐπινοεῖ [sc. Devil] τὸν τέταρτον τρόπον Anast.S.*haer.*(p.258).

ὑπολαλέω, *whisper,* Gr.Nyss.*virg.*3(p.262.19; M.46.332C).

ὑπολαμπάς, ἡ, *torch* αἱ...τρίχες τῆς κεφαλῆς αὐτοῦ ὡς φλὸξ πυρὸς ὑπολαμπάδος καιομένης *Asen.*14(p.59.17).

ὑπολανθάνω, *forget*, Hom.Clem.20.13.

ὑπολεπτύνομαι, *be softened*, Paul.Sil.*ambo*.101(M.86.2255B).

***ὑπολευκαίνω**, *be pale white*, Gr.Nyss.*v.Macr*.(p.411.2; M.46.996D).

ὑπολήγω, *find rest*, Marc.Er.*opusc*.3.13(M.65.984C).

ὑπολήνιον, τό, *wine-vat*, Didym.*Zach*.5.114; Chrys.*hom.4.12 in Col*.(11.418E); Proc.G.*Is*.16:10(M.87.2117D).

ὑπόληψις, ἡ, 1. *assumption, notion, opinion*; in gen., Clem.*str*.2.4(p.119.25; M.8.944C) cit. s. αἴσθησις; οὐ...ἔστιν ὑ. ἡ ἑκούσιος πρὸ ἀποδείξεως συγκατάθεσις, ἀλλὰ συγκατάθεσις ἰσχυρῷ τινι...ἡ δὲ ἀπιστία ὑ. τοῦ ἀντικειμένου ἀσθενὴς ἀποφατική...καὶ ἡ μὲν πίστις ὑ. ἑκούσιος *ib*.2.6(p.127.29f.; 964A); πᾶσα...δόξα καὶ κρίσις καὶ ὑ. καὶ μάθησις...συγκατάθεσίς ἐστιν *ib*.2.12(p.142.27; 992C); connected with πάθη: γυμνὴν τῆς ὑλικῆς δορᾶς γενομένην τὴν γνωστικὴν ψυχὴν ἄνευ τῆς σωματικῆς φλυαρίας καὶ τῶν παθῶν, ὅσα περιποιοῦσιν αἱ κεναὶ καὶ ψευδεῖς ὑ. *ib*.5.10(p.371.9; M.9.104A); dist. from fact ἐκεῖνο μὲν γὰρ ἦν φύσει, τοῦτο δὲ λοιπὸν γέγονεν ἀπὸ τῆς ἡμετέρας ὑ. Chrys.*hom.11.1 in Phil*.(11.284A); about God ἡ μὴ πρέπουσα περὶ τοῦ θεοῦ ὑ. Clem.*str*.7.38(p.29.18; M.9.453B); τὰς ἡμετέρας περὶ τῆς θεότητος ὑ. Gr.Naz.*or*.29.1(p.73.9; M.35.73A); **2.** *attribute*; of God οὐ δὲ τὸ τέλειον ἐν ταῖς θειοτέραις τῶν ὑπολήψεων ἄπεστι, πῶς ἄν τις τοῦτο ταῖς τοῦ ἀληθινοῦ θεοῦ τιμαῖς εὐλόγως ἀποσεμνύνειεν; Gr.Nyss.*Eun*.12(1 p.231.10; M.45.928B); of Christ ὁ πρὸς τὴν οἰκονομίαν ὁρῶν, καὶ φυλάσσων τῇ τε περὶ τὸ θεῖον καὶ τῇ περὶ τὸ ἀνθρώπινον ὑ. τὸ πρόσφορον *ib*.3(2 p.20.2; 584D); υἱὸν ὀνομάζει θεοῦ καὶ πάσης ἐμπαθοῦς ὑ. ἐκκαθαίρει τὸ κήρυγμα *ib*.4(2 p.53.2; 624A); of H. Ghost ταῖς θεϊκαῖς ὑ. τοῦ ἀεὶ ὡσαύτως ἔχοντος πρὸς τὸν θεὸν πατέρα ἁγίου πνεύματος Didym.*Trin*.2.11(M.39.661D); of either nature of Christ, ‡Gr.Nyss.*hom.10.33 in Jo*.(p.305.17) cit. s. ἀντιδίδωμι; **3.** *reputation, character*; **a.** in gen.; of persons οὐχ ὅρκος ἀξιόπιστον ποιεῖ, ἀλλὰ βίου μαρτυρία καὶ πολιτείας ἀκρίβεια καὶ ὑ. ἀγαθή Chrys.*stat*.7.5(2.91A); οἱ...ψευδοπροφῆται...ἦσαν...ἐν δόξῃ καὶ ὑ. χρηστῇ Cyr.*Zach*.98(3.790E); τὰ διαβάλλοντα ψευδῶς τὴν ὑ. Nil.*Magn*.11(M.79.984C); τοῖς οὖσιν ἐν ὑ. μόνοις...προσώποις CChalc.*can*.11; of priests χραίνειν τὰς τῶν ἱερέων ὑ. CCP(381)*can*.6; of a bishop, Socr.*h.e*.7.35.4(M.67.817B); Hier.*vir.ill*.(tr.Sophr.Pal.)82(p.49.3; ἀπολήψεως M.*PL*.23.690B); of Jo. Bapt., Chrys.*hom.10.2 in Mt*.(7.141E); of Christ, Cyr.*Jo*.1.9(4.99B); **b.** of things, of the cross οὐ μόνον οὐ δοκεῖ σοφίας ἐπίδειξις εἶναι, ἀλλὰ καὶ μωρίας ὑ. Chrys.*hom.4.3 in 1Cor*.(10.27B); of circumcision τῶν ἄλλων ἐντολῶν πρεσβύτερον ἦν, καὶ πλείονα εἶχε τὴν ὑ. id.*hom.51.3 in Mt*.(7.523B); id.*hom.7.2 in Rom*.(9.474C); of churches, Cyr.*ep*.79(5^2.211D); **4.** *will* (Lat. *arbitrium*) οἵτινες τῇ ὑ. τοῦ προλεχθέντος ἐπισκόπου ἀσέβεσιν ἁλόντες ὑπογραφαῖς ἐνεβασανίσθησαν Leo Mag.*ep*.43(p.3.23; M.*PL*.54.822B).

***ὑπολικμάω**, pass., *be consumed*, †Ath.*fr.Mt*.6:25(M.27.1376B); ‡Ath.*corp*.(M.28.1433B).

***ὑπολιμνίσκος, ὁ**, a critical mark, Epiph.*mens*.8(M.43.248B).

ὑπολιμπάνω, *leave out*, Thdt.*rect.conf*.4(M.6.1213B).

ὑπολισθ-άνω, *lapse* (in ptcpl.), met., Gr.Thaum.*pan.Or*.7(p.20.22; M.10.1076B); τοῦ ποιμένος...θεραπείας ~ούσης ἐπὶ τὰ χείρω Const.ap.Eus.*v.C*.3.60(p.108.12; M.20.1132B); ἀνίστησι...τοὺς...πρὸς ἁμαρτίας ~ήσαντας Bas.*Spir*.19(3.16D; M.32.101A); Gr.Nyss.*Eun*.4(2 p.53.7; M.45.624A); Cyr.*ador*.1(1.13A).

***ὑπολιχνεύω**, *encourage*, Areth.*Apoc*.14:13(M.106.692C).

ὑπόλοξος, *oblique*, *T.Sal*.24.5(M.122.1355B).

ὑπολοξόω, *turn somewhat obliquely*, †Bas.*Is*.123(1.465A; M.30.317C).

***ὑπολόξωσις, ἡ**, *side-glance*, Germ.CP *or*.1(M.98.233C).

ὑπολυπέομαι, *grieve slightly*, Pall.*h.Laus*.2(p.17.19; M.34.1011C); *ib*.30(p.78.9; 1089D).

***ὑπολυχνιαία, ἡ**, *light*, *cat.Apoc*.11:3(p.340.33).

ὑπολωφάω, *abate gradually*, Epiph.*exp.fid*.1(p.496.27; M.42.776A); Cyr.*glaph.Gen*.2(1.2.40D); Pall.*h.Laus*.19(47.13; M.34.1049C); ἄνθρωπος...γέγονεν ὁ δημιουργὸς...ὅπως...ὑπολωφήσῃ τῆς ἐν ἡμῖν ἁμαρτίας ἡ εἴσδυσις ‡Meth.*Sym.et Ann*.13(M.18.380C).

ὑπομάζιος, *at the breast*, *Orac.Sib*.2.299; Eus.*h.e*.1.8.1(M.20.101A); Gr.Nyss.*bapt.Chr*.(M.46.588C).

***ὑπομάνικον, τό**, = ἐπιμανίκιον, *Euchol*.(p.235).

ὑπομάσχαλον, τό, *wallet slung under the arm*, *Mir.Cosm.Dam*.13(p.133).

ὑπομειόω, *diminish, reduce*, Thphn.*chron*.p.222(M.108.565A).

***ὑπομέλπω**, *sing*, ‡Jo.D.*hom*.5(M.96.652A).

***ὑπομερίζω**, *subdivide*, Iren.*haer*.1.7.5(M.7.520A).

ὑπομερισμός, ὁ, *subdivision*; a figure in rhetoric, Gr.Nyss.*bapt.diff*.(M.46.428A).

***ὑπομετρέω**, *subdivide*, Bas.*Spir*.43(3.37B; M.32.148B).

***ὑπομέτριος**, *on a lower level*, Or.*comm.in Mt*.12.15(p.103.20; M.13.1017A).

ὑπόμνημα, τό, 1. *memorial, reminder* πρὸς ἐπανόρθωσιν ὑ. καὶ νῆψιν Meth.*symp*.11.1(p.129.16; M.18.205A); of sign of cross at baptism ἔπραξαν οὐδὲν ὧν εἰώθασιν οἱ δυσσεβεῖς ἐκεῖνοι πράττειν, ἐπὶ τοῦ μετώπου τοῦ δυσσεβοῦς τὸ ὑ. σκιογραφοῦντες Juln.*ep*.79(p.94.1); ὑ. ... ἐστιν ἡ εἰκών Jo.D.*imag*.1.17(M.94.1248C); of festivals τῶν γενεθλίων καὶ τῶν θεοφανίων ὑπομνήματα τελοῦντες Thdr.Stud.*antirr*.1.10(M.99.340C); **2.** *record*; **a.** *minutes*; of a trial, Eus.*p.e*.4.2(135D; M.21.237C); Pall.*v.Chrys*.1(p.10.26; M.47.10); of a synod, *ib*.14(p.87.12; M.47.49); of Christ's trial ὑπὸ ἐξουσίᾳ...Πιλάτου τινὸς ἡγεμόνος ἀνηρτῆσθαι σταυρῷ, οὗ καὶ ὑπομνήματα κατάκειται *M.Tar*.9(p.471); ταῦτα εὗρον τὰ ὑ. ἐν ἑβραϊκοῖς γράμμασιν *A.Pil*.A proem.(p.210); ref. Last Judgement τότε οὐχ ὑπομνημάτων δεήσει, οὐκ ἐλέγχων, οὐ μαρτύρων Chrys.*hom.56.4 in Mt*.(7.572A); **b.** *account*, of an apocryphal gospel τῶν περὶ Ἰησοῦ ἐν γράμμασιν ὑπομνημάτων Or.*Cels*.2.13(p.143.18; M.11.824B); *Dial.Tim.et Aquil*.80 r°(p.68); of Acts of Pilate τὸ πλάσμα τῶν κατὰ τοῦ σωτῆρος...ὑπομνήματα...διαδεδωκότων Eus.*h.e*.1.9.3(M.20.108B); **c.** *copy* τὰ τῆς ἀσεβοῦς ἐπιστολῆς φερόμενα ὑ. ἐν τισι μὲν βιβλίοις, ὡς εἴρηται, ἐντέτακται, ἐν δὲ τοῖς αὐθεντικοῖς...οὐδαμῶς ὤρηται Justn.*conf*.(p.100.4; M.86.1023C); **d.** *petition* ἠρώτησαν ὅπως γράψω αὐτοῖς ὑπομνήματα ἐρωτήσεως *Apoc.En*.13.4(p.36.9); *ib*.(p.36.10); ἀνεγίνωσκον τὸ ὑ. τῶν δεήσεων αὐτῶν *ib*.13.7(p.36.17); **3.** *commentary* ἱερὰς γραφὰς ἐξηγητικοῖς ὑ. ... διερμηνεύσασι Eus.*p.e*.1.3(7A; M.21.32B); Ἰωάννην [sc. Chrys.], ἐν τῷ λδ´ λόγῳ τοῦ εἰς τὸ κατὰ Ἰωάννην εὐαγγέλιον ὑ. Sev.Ant.ap.*cat.1Jo*.2:18(p.118.17); ὁ ἐν ἁγίοις Βασίλειος ἐν τῷ τρίτῳ λόγῳ τοῦ ὑ. τῆς Ἑξαημέρου Justn.*Or*.(p.203.17; M.86.971B); **4.** *division, section*, 'book' of treatise ἐν ἑνὶ προθεμένοις τελειώσειν ὑπομνήματι Clem.*str*.4.1(p.248.14; M.8.1216A).

ὑπομνηματίζω, 1. *commit to writing*, Eus.*h.e*.6.6(M.20.536A); *record*, ‡Dion.Al.*fr.in Lc*.22:43(p.237.13; M.10.1592A); fig., Iren.*ep.Flor*.ap.Eus.*h.e*.5.20.7(485B); pass., Dion.Al.*ib*.7.11.6(664B); Maur.*ep*.(M.*PL*.87.103B); **2.** *comment upon*, Eus.*h.e*.4.8.2(M.20.321B); *write a commentary on* τὸν ἀπόστολον ὑπεμνηματίσεν Hier.*vir.ill*.(tr.Sophr.Pal.)46(p.33.19; M.*PL*.23.662A); *ib*.54(p.36.6; 666B); *ib*.61(p.40.1; 674A).

ὑπομνηματικός, *serving as a commentary, exegetical* ὑ. γράμμασιν Or.*Jo*.20.1(p.327.7; M.14.573A); Epiph.*haer*.42.11(p.124.22; M.41.728A).

ὑπομνηματιστής, ὁ, 1. *one who publicly demonstrates* (on the stage), Tat.*orat*.22(p.24.29; M.6.856B); **2.** *commentator* πᾶν σύγγραμμα τῶν ἀρχαίων ὑ. διελθοῦσα Pall.*h.Laus*.143(p.149.13; M.34.1244C).

ὑπομνηματογραφέω, *write an exposé of*, Max.*cap*.2.72(M.90.1248B).

ὑπομνηματογράφος, ὁ, *stenographer*, *A.Phil*.38(p.18.22); Gr.Nyss.*hom.opif*.10.3(M.44.152C); Proc.G.*Is*.proem.(M.87.1824A); the fifth of the second pentad of officials of church of S. Sophia, *Euchol*.(p.227); *ib*.(p.229); *ib*.(pp.222,224).

***ὑπομνημονεύω**, *comment*, Vict.*Mc*.1:7(p.269.25).

***ὑπομνημοσύνη, ἡ**, *reminder*, Cyr.*Is*.4.1(2.568A).

***ὑπομνησίζω**, v.l. for ὑπομιμνήσκω, Cyr.*apol.orient*.12(p.61.9; 6^1.195A).

ὑπόμνησις, ἡ, 1. *remembering, recollection*; **a.** in gen., Clem.*paed*.1.6(p.108.31; M.8.288B); τὴν ἐκ τῆς ὑ. λύπην *Hom.Clem*.13.1; τὴν ὑ. τῆς πολιτείας τῆς ἐν τῇ πατρίδι Chrys.*prod.Jud*.1.5(2.383C); of God in prayer θεοῦ...ὑ. μετὰ τῆς πρὸς αὐτὸν εὐχῆς Or.*or*.8.2(p.317.25; M.11.441D); ref. hindrances to prayer αἱ τοιαίδε φαντασίαι καὶ ὑ. τῶνδέ τινων περὶ τά, ὧν γεγόνασι αἱ ὑ. μολύνουσι τοὺς λογισμοὺς *ib*.(p.317.10; 441C); τὴν γυναῖκα...ὅτε εὔχεται...πᾶσαν...γυναικείαν ὑ. ἐξορίσασαν ἀπὸ τοῦ ἡγεμονικοῦ *ib*.9.1(p.318.10; 444A); **b.** *commemoration* (v. ἀνάμνησις); liturg., of eucharist τὴν τούτου μνήμην τοῦ τε σώματος αὐτοῦ καὶ τοῦ αἵματος τὴν ὑ. ὁσημέραι ἐπιτελοῦντες Eus.*d.e*.1.10(p.46.14; M.22.88C); 'ὁσάκις...τοῦτο ποιεῖτε, τὸν θάνατον τοῦ κυρίου καταγγέλλετε.' τουτέστιν ὑ. ποιεῖτε τῆς σωτηρίας τῆς ὑπὲρ ἡμῶν Chrys.*hom.3.4 in Eph*.(11.22C); of commemoration of the living and dead, *Const.App*.8.42.2; ἦν ἡ ἑορτὴ [sc. Easter]...ὑ. σωτηρίας διηνεκής Chrys.*prod.Jud*.1.4(2.382D); εἰς εὐεργεσίας ὑ. Proc.G.*Num*.9:10(M.88.816A); **2.** *reminding, reminder*, of icons ἐν ᾗ παρεδείχθη μορφῇ καὶ τοῖς ἀνθρώποις συναναστράφη, τοῖς πίναξιν ἐπιγράφομεν, ὑ. τῆς δι' αὐτοῦ σωτηρίας τὸν θεῖον τύπον ποιούμενοι Const.Diac.*laud*.16(M.88.500A); τὰς εἰκόνας...πρὸς ὑ. μόνην ἀγαθήν *Dial.Christ.et Jud*.1(p.52.2); εἰκόνες γὰρ ἦσαν πρὸς ὑ. κείμεναι, οὐχ ὡς θεοί, ἀλλ' ὡς θείας ἐνεργείας ὑ. ἄγουσαι Jo.D.*imag*.1.17(M.94.1248D); ἐν εἰκόσι ταῦτα γράφεσθαι, εἰς ὑ. σύντομον...τὴν εἰκόνα τοῦ Χριστοῦ σταυρώσεως ἰδόντες, τοῦ σωτηρίου πάθους εἰς ὑ. ἐλθόντες id.*f.o*.4.16(M.94.1172A);

3. *reminder, warning*, Cyr.*thes*.proem.(5[1].2B); μὴ παραλογίζου τὴν ἐκ τοῦ συνειδότος ὑ. id.ap.*cat.1Jo*.3:21(p.129.7); εἰ ἀποχρήσοιντο τῇ ὑγιεινῇ ὑ., ἀνάγκη ἡμᾶς βεβαιῶσαι κατ' αὐτῶν τὴν τῆς καταδίκης ἀπόφασιν Cael.*ep.Nest*.(p.82.23; M.*PL*.50.484A); *ib*.(p.83.8; 484C); id.*ep.Cyr*.1(p.77.2; M.77.93B); 4. *suggestion* ἡ ἁπλῶς γινομένη ὑπὸ τοῦ ἐχθροῦ ὑ., οἷον, ποίησον τόδε ἢ τόδε Ephr.3.429C = Jo.D.*virt*.(M.95.93A); 5. = ὑπόμνημα *testimony* παρ' αὐτοῦ λαβὼν τὴν χειροτονίαν χωρὶς ἡμετέρας ὑ. ἐπανῆκε Bas.*ep*.121(3.212E; M.32.541A); 6. *summons* (legal) λιτιγιόσα νοοῦνται πάντα τὰ πράγματα ὅσα περὶ δεσποτίας ἔχει ἀμφισβήτησιν δι' ἀρχικῆς ὑ. ἢ διαθέσεως βασιλεῖ προσενεχθεισῶν Ath.Scholast.*coll*.5.2(p.71).

ὑπομνηστέον, 1. *one must remind*, Or.*Jo*.1.38(42; p.49.28; M.14.100C); Eus.*p.e*.6.6(247A; M.21.420C); 2. *one must (make) mention* περὶ τῶν εἰδωλοθύτων Clem.*paed*.2.1(p.159.12; M.8.392A); ταῦτα id. *str*.6.16(p.502.12; M.9.364C).

ὑπομνηστικός, 1. *reminding*, Clem.*str*.6.1(p.422.9; M.9.208A); λάβε κρίσεως ἔννοιαν ὑ. σωτηρίας Cyr.H.*procatech*.16; †Bas.*hom.in Ps*.37(1.364E; M.30.88D); 2. *admonitory* Τιμόθεος δι' ἐγγράφου ὑ. ... προσέταξε τὸ τρισάγιον ἐν ταῖς λιταῖς μετὰ τῆς προσθήκης εἰπεῖν Thphn.*chron*.p.136(M.108.372C); 3. *mindful* παρὰ σοὶ τῷ Ἰώβ, παρὰ παντὶ ὑπομνηστικῷ Or.*enarr.in Job* 40:10(M.17.100C); 4. neut. as subst.; a. *memorandum*; i. in gen. πρὸς...τὰ ἐπερωτήματα γεγόνασί τινες ἐν τῷ ὑ. ἀποκρίσεις, οἵας ἐμοὶ δύνατον ἦν, καὶ ὡς ὁ καιρὸς ἐδίδου Bas.*ep*.232(3.355D; M.32.864B); *ib*.68(161C; M.429A); ὑ. ποιήσας παρ' ἐμαυτῷ, ὡς ᾠόμην, τῶν παρ' ἐκείνου ῥηθέντων CChalc.*act*.1(*ACO* 2.1.1 p.160.11; H.2.185E); Cyr.*ep*.10(p.110.4; 5[2].32C); Heracl.*ep*.(M.92.1021A,B); Thphn.*chron*.p.132(M.108.364B); ii. at a council ὑ. τῆς συνόδου πάσης δύσεως Pall.*v.Chrys*.4(p.22.14; M.47.15); θεῖον ὑ. δοθὲν Ἐλπιδίῳ τῷ περιβλέπτῳ κόμητι τοῦ θείου συνεδρίου CEph.(449)ap. CChalc.*act*.1(*ACO* 2.1.1 p.72.3; H.2.76D); Geo.Al.*v.Chrys*.66(p.244.13); iii. of a written work σεμνὸν καὶ ψυχωφελὲς ὑ. ἔχων, ἀδιάληπτόν τε φάρμακον λήθης Pall.*h.Laus*.proem.(p.10.9; M.34.1001); τούτῳ τῷ ὑ. ἐντυγχάνειν μὴ κατοκνείτω Epiph.*mens*.1(M.43.237A); b. *mandate, order*, Thdt.*ep*.80(4.1137); *ib*.79(1134); μετὰ θείων ὑ. τοῦ ποιῆσαι μετὰ Περσῶν πάκτα εἰρήνης Jo.Mal.*chron*.18 p.477(M.97.692D).

***ὑπομνίζω**, *bring to remembrance, issue a reminder of*, *Euchol*.(p.230) cit. s. κατηγοριάρης.

ὑπομονή, ἡ, *patient endurance*, *1Clem*.5.5; Ign.*Smyrn*.12.2; Clem.*str*.2.18(p.154.20; M.8.1017B); of Christ's suffering, Cyr.H.*catech*.4.7; *ib*.4.13; c. genit., Bas.*reg.fus*.11(2.354A; M.31.948B); *perseverance*, Just.*1apol*.16.3(M.6.352C); *patient waiting for*; c. genit., Ign.*Rom*.10.3.

ὑπομονητικός, 1. *patiently enduring*, *M.Polyc*.2.2; Clem.*str*.4.21(p.305.20; M.8.1340B); Bas.*ep*.42.2(3.127A; M.32.352A); 2. *endurable*, Or.*schol.in Lc*.1:14(M.17.317A); *A.(Pass.)Andr*.7(p.17.16).

ὑπομονητικῶς, *patiently*, Mac.Aeg.*hom*.6.1(M.34.517C); Ephr.2.10F.

***ὑπομορφόω**, *decorate*, ‡Caes.Naz.*dial*.193(M.38.1176).

***ὑπόμοσχος**, *with suckling calf*, Mel.*pass*.27 p.5.4.

***ὑπονόησις, ἡ**, *suspicion*, Or.*comm.in Mt*.15.14(p.385.31; M.13.1292A).

ὑπονοθεύω, 1. *seduce*, Epiph.*haer*.37.1(p.51.8; M.41.641C); Thdot.Anc.*hom.BMV et Sym*.(M.77.1405A); *suborn*, Martin.*ep*.12(M.*PL*.87.186C); 2. *falsify* scriptures, *Hom.Clem*.8.10; Anast.S.*hod*.1(M.89.40C); 3. *procure by corruption*, Cyr.S.*v.Sab*.33(p.118.26); Jo.Mal.*chron*.5 p.95(M.97.181A).

ὑπόνοια, ἡ, 1. *opinion, estimation*, Clem.*str*.7.7(p.29.19; M.9.453B); Ath.*gent*.15(M.25.32B); τοῦτο ἐπιλέγουσιν, οἷον, ὁ Χριστιανός· οὐκ ἂν εἰπόντες εἰ μὴ μεγάλην περὶ τοῦ δόγματος ἔσχον ὑ. Chrys.*hom*.15.8 *in Mt*.(7.198D); εἰσιν οἱ λέγοντες ὅτι φαντασία τις ἦν καὶ ὑπόκρισις καὶ ὑ. τὰ τῆς οἰκονομίας ἅπαντα id.*hom*.11.2 *in Jo*.(8.64A); 2. *expectation* ἐδοξάζετο δὲ μεγάλως ὁ Χριστὸς ἐπὶ τοῖς πρότερον ἀρνησαμένοις, τότε παρὰ τὴν τῶν ἐθνῶν ὑ. ὁμολογοῦσιν *Ep.Lugd*.ap. Eus.*h.e*.5.1.48(M.20.425C); 3. *underlying meaning, deeper sense*, in exegesis 'ἔσονται οἱ πρῶτοι ἔσχατοι καὶ οἱ ἔσχατοι πρῶτοι.' τοῦτο πολύχουν μέν ἐστι κατὰ τὴν ὑ. καὶ τὸν σαφηνισμόν Clem.*q.d.s*.26(p.176.28; M.9.632A); πᾶσαν οὖν τροπικὴν καὶ δι' ὑπονοίας ἐξήγησιν ἔν γε τῷ παρόντι κατασιγάσαντες, τοῦ σκότους τὴν ἔννοιαν ἁπλῶς καὶ ἀπεριεργάστως, ἑπόμενοι τῷ βουλήματι τῆς γραφῆς, ἐκδεξώμεθα Bas.*hex*.2.5(1.17B; M.29.40B); hence *allegory* οἱ παρὰ τούτων τῶν προφητῶν τὴν θεολογίαν δεδιδαγμένοι ποιηταὶ δι' ὑπονοίας πολλὰ φιλοσοφοῦσι, τὸν Ὀρφέα λέγω, τὸν Λίνον Clem.*str*.5.4(p.340.26; M.9.44A); of Greek myths, Gr.Naz.*or*.31.16(p.165.5; M.36.152A).

ὑπονοστ-έω, 1. *go home* τὸν Ἰσραὴλ...οἴκαδε...ἰόντα...καὶ ~οῦντα πάλιν εἰς τὴν ἁγίαν πόλιν Cyr.*Soph*.38(3.616B); met., of human nature at redemption, Germ.CP *or*.2(M.98.248D); 2. *go back, relapse*; met., Cyr.*ador*.6(1.205A); τὴν Μαγδαληνὴν Μαρίαν πρὸς ἀπιστίαν ὑπονοστήσασαν Sev.Ant.*res*.(p.812.10); 3. med., *infiltrate* δι' ὧν [sc. λήθη, ῥᾳθυμία, ἄγνοια] πᾶσα ἡ στρατιὰ τῶν πνευμάτων τῆς πονηρίας ~εῖται καὶ ὑποστηρίζεται Marc.Er.*opusc*.5.12(M.65.1049A); *ib*.5.13(1049B); 4. *go back* or *down, return*; lit., of persons, Cyr.*Lc*.10:17(p.104.2); of water πᾶσα ὑπόνομός ἐστιν ἡ γῆ, διὰ πόρων ἀφανῶν ἐκ τῶν ἀρχῶν τῆς θαλάσσης ~οῦντος τοῦ ὕδατος Bas.*hex*.46(1.39A; M.29.92D); Cyr.*ador*.6(1.209D); of blood τοῦ αἵματος ~ήσαντος εἰς τὸ βάθος καὶ ὤχραν τοῦ προσώπου τὴν ἐπιφάνειαν καταλελοιπότος Isid.Pel.*epp*.3.293(M.78.968A); medic. ~εῖ πρὸς ὑγιὲς ἡ ἐπανελθοῦσα σάρξ Cyr.*ador*.15(1.537E); met. ὥστε τὸ οἴδημα τῆς ὀργῆς ὑπονοστῆσαι Chrys.*prod.Jud*.2.1(2.387E).

ὑπονοτίζω, *moisten a little*, Or.*exc.in Ps*.77:31(M.17.141B) = Gr.Nyss.*v.Mos*.32(M.44.309C); Gr.Nyss.*hom.opif*.30.6(M.44.241C); *ib*.30.27(252B).

***ὑπονυγμός, ὁ**, *incitement*, ref. pictures of martyrs εἰσι...τοῦ δοξάζειν θεὸν ὑπονυγμὸς καὶ διέγερσις Germ.CP *ep.dogm*.4(M.98.172C).

ὑπονύσσω, lit., *spur*, Ph.Carp.*Cant*.proem.(M.40.28A); *poke, prod* τῷ ποδὶ τὸν κείμενον...ὑ. Chrys.*hom*.14.4 *in 1Tim*.(11.630A); met., *spur on, goad*, ref. Is.58:3, Cyr.*Is*.5.4(2.818A); id.*Joel*.11(3.209E; ὑπονύπτω Aubert in error); *stimulate, encourage*; pass., Epiph.*anc*.1(p.6.1; M.43.17B); *ib*.23(p.32.14; 60C).

ὑποξενίζω, *speak in a curious way*, Gr.Nyss.*beat*.2(M.44.1208D).

ὑποξίζω, *be bitter* οἱ Χριστιανοὶ ὑπέξιζον τοῖς Ἕλλησι Jo.Mal.*chron*.11 p.177(M.97.417C, cj. ὑπώξιζον Stauffenberg).

ὑποπαραιτέομαι, 1. *beg for delay*, Eus.*v.C*.1.34(p.23.17; M.20.949B); id.*h.e*.8.12.4(M.20.772A); *ib*.8.14.7(785C); 2. *prevaricate*, Soz.*h.e*.9.2.10(M.67.1600B).

ὑποπαραίτησις, ἡ, *prayer to be let off*, of Christ ἔχει...λόγον ἡ δοκοῦσα ὑ. εἶναι τοῦ καλουμένου ποτηρίου Or.*Cels*.7.55(p.205.16; M.11.1500D).

***ὑπόπεδος**, f.l. for ἰσόπεδος, Gr.Nyss.*Eun*.4(M.45.665B; ἰσόπεδον p.89.13).

ὑποπέζιος, *earthly*, Dion.Ar.*c.h*.8.1(M.3.237C).

ὑποπείθω, *persuade gradually*, Thphyl.*exc.Rom*.1(p.222.11; M.113.929A).

ὑποπεράτωσις, ἡ, *end, completion*, Max.*schol.d.n*.4.4(M.4.244D).

ὑποπιάζ-ω, = ὑπωπιάζω, 1. *bruise*, *T.Sal*.D 2.4(p.90*.17); 2. *mortify* the body, Or.*comm.in Rom*.1:1(*JTS* 13 p.212); Ath.*v.Anton*.7(M.26.852B); ἐν ἑαυτῷ ἔχει τὸν θεὸν...ὁ ὑποπιάσας τὸ σῶμα ‡Ath.*dial.Trin*.1.12(M.28.1136A); σῶμα ~όμενον...ἐκφεύγει σὺν τῇ ψυχῇ τὰς αἰωνίους βασάνους Eustrat.*v.Eutych*.90(M.86.2376C); 3. *distress, trouble*, Pall.*h.Laus*.22(p.71.4; M.34.1081B); Max.*ep*.30(M.91.624C).

***ὑποπιαίνομαι**, *grow fat* ἀπὸ γηίνης ἰκμάδος ὑ. Gr.Nyss.*v.Mos*.(M.44.417D); τῇ φυσικῇ ἰκμάδι ὑ. id.*anim.et res*.(M.46.137C).

***ὑποπιασμός, ὁ**, = ὑπωπιασμός, *bruising*; *mortification* of the body, Gr.Naz.*or*.14.3(M.35.861B, v.l. ὑπωπ-); *Apophth.Mac.Aeg*.6(M.34.236A); Nil.ap.Proc.G.*Cant*.3:6(M.87.1624B).

ὑποπιέζ-ω, *oppress, crush*; hence 1. *mortify* the body σῶμα νηστείαις ~ομεν Gr.Naz.*or*.27.7(p.12.5, v.l. ὑπωπιάζομεν; M.36.20B); Gr.Nyss.*v.Mos*.(M.44.388A); Chrys.*hom*.42.3 *in 1Cor*.(10.398C, v.l. ὑπωπιάζοντας Gaume); Jo.Mon.*hymn.Geo*.8(M.96.1400B); 2. *distress, trouble*, *Const.App*.2.17.5, v.l. ὑποπιάζειν; ἐλεγχόμενοι ὑπό τινων ~ωνται Epiph.*haer*.76.54(cj. p.413.25, v.l. ὑποπιάζ-; ὑπωπιάζ- M.42.637A).

ὑποπίπτ-ω, 1. *fall down*; in worship, *adore* ~όντων...τῷ Χριστῷ ⟨πάντων καὶ⟩ γόνυ καμπτόντων ἐν τῷ ὀνόματι Ἰησοῦ Or.*Jo*.19.21(5; p.323.14; M.14.565D); of penitents, id.*hom*.6.3 *in Jer*.(p.50.14; M.13.328A); ὑπέπιπτεν κυρίῳ καὶ ὡμολόγει τὴν ἀσέβειαν αὐτοῦ *Chron.Pasch*.p.160(M.92.396A); 2. *lapse* τοὺς ὑποπεπτωκότας τῷ κατὰ τὸν διωγμὸν πειρασμῷ Eus.*h.e*.4.15.47(M.20.361A); γράφει [sc. Διονύσιος] ...ἐπιστολὴν περὶ μετανοίας, ἐν ᾗ τὰ δόξαντα αὐτῷ περὶ τῶν ὑποπεπτωκότων παρατεθεῖται, τάξεις παραπτωμάτων διαγράψας *ib*.6.46.1(633C); Cyr.*Ps*.24:7(M.69.848D); 3. *prostrate oneself*; of third grade of penitents, Gr.Thaum.*ep.can*.8(p.565; M.10.1041D); *ib*.9(p.565; 1044D); CAnc.(314)*can*.4 cit. s. ἀκροάομαι; *ib*.5,6,22; ὑποπιπτέτωσαν μετὰ τὸν τῆς τριετοῦς ἀκροάσεως χρόνον CNic.(325)*can*.12; δύο μὲν ἔτη προσκλαύσει, τρία δὲ ἔτη ἐν ἀκροωμένοις διατελέσει, τέσσαρσιν ~ων καὶ ἐνιαυτῷ συσταθήσεται μόνον Bas.*ep*.217 *can*.57(3.326C; M.32.797B) cf. ἐν τέτρασιν ἐν ὑποπίπτουσιν †CCP (381)*can*.2; Gr.Nyss.*ep.can*.4(M.45.229A); *ib*.5(232A); CTrull.*can*.87.

ὑποπλάσσ-ω, 1. *feign, pretend*; act., Cyr.*Lc*.22:66(M.72.929B); med., id.*Nest*.1.2(p.19.6; 6[1].10E); id.*apol.Thdt*.2(p.116.6; 6[1].209E); 2. med., *lay claim to*, Dion.Al.*fr*.2 *in Jac*.(p.253.1); Cyr.*Soph*.1(3.578A); 3. med., *imitate* θείοις μὲν γὰρ νεύμασι καὶ αὐτοδιδάκτῳ τέχνῃ ζωοπλαστεῖ τὸ τικτόμενον ἡ φύσις ἐν ἑαυτῇ· δημιουργικὴν δὲ ὥσπερ ∼εται δόξαν id.*ador.*7(1.235D); **4.** c. acc., *be figured by* ∼εται...τὴν πυρὸς φύσιν ἀεὶ τὸ θεῖον *ib.*11(404A).

***ὑποπνευματέω,** *blow beneath,* ‡Caes.Naz.*dial.*106(M.38.972).

***ὑποπνίγω,** *choke, Exorc.*23(p.320).

***ὑπόποδος,** *having feet*; of certain marine animals, Bas.*hex.*7.1 (1.63B; M.29.148D); Proc.G.*Gen.*1:20(M.87.100C).

***ὑποποιμαίνω,** *act as under-shepherd,* Thdt.*h.rel.*8(3.1180).

***ὑποποίμην, ὁ,** *under-shepherd*; of Flavian and Diodore acting pastorally for Meletius of Antioch during his exile, Thdt.*h.e.*4.25.3 (v.l. ποιμένων 3.1002).

***ὑποπροίκιος,** *married,* of Zeus εἴθε κατὰ τοὺς νόμους ὑ. τις ἐγένετο καὶ μὴ κλεψίγαμος πάντοτε καὶ κακεργάτης Epiph.*anc.*105 (p.127.14; M.43.208C).

ὑποπτάω, *scorch,* Mac.Mgn.*apocr.*4.11(p.171.11)

***ὑποπτερ-όομαι,** *use as wings* βομβυλιὸς...χαύνοις καὶ πλατέσι πετάλοις ∼οῦται Bas.*hex.*8.8(1.79A; M.29.184D).

***ὑποπτευτέος,** *that must be guessed* or *supposed,* Leont.H.*Nest.*1. 26(M.86.1493A) cit. s. ἀνομοφυΐα.

***ὑποπτίων, ὁ,** *subordinate officer,* Jo.Mal.*chron.*18 p.494(M.97. 713C); perh. = κουράτωρ, cf.Thphn.*chron.*p.201(M.108.520A).

ὑπόπτωσις, ἡ, 1. *falling,* Bas.Sel.*or.*8.3(M.85.125B); **2.** *genuflexion, kneeling* ἡ μὲν οὖν ἐπὶ τὸ θεῖον θυσιαστήριον προσαγωγὴ καὶ ὑ. αἰνίσσεται πᾶσι τοῖς ἱερατικῶς τελουμένοις, ὑποτιθέναι καθόλου τελετάρχῃ θεῷ τὴν οἰκείαν ζωήν Dion.Ar.*e.h.*5.7(M.3.509D); *ib.* (509C); Areth.*Apoc.*5:14(M.106.585B); **3.** *kneeling,* ref. third grade of penitence ἡ δὲ ὑ., ἵνα ἔσωθεν τῆς πύλης τοῦ ναοῦ ἱστάμενος, μετὰ τῶν κατηχουμένων ἐξέρχηται Gr.Thaum.*ep.can.*11(p.566; M.10. 1048B); Eust.*fr.in Pr.8:22* ap.Thdt.*h.e.*1.8.4(M.18.676D); εἰ ἐπλήρωσαν τὸν τῆς ὑ. τριετῆ χρόνον, χωρὶς προσφορᾶς δεχθήτωσαν CAnc. (314)*can.*5; Bas.*ep.*217 *cann.*56,61(3.326B,327A; M.32.797A,800A) = †CCP(381)*cann.*1,6; simply *penitence,* Thdr.Stud.*epp.*2.68(M.99. 1296C); **4.** *submission,* Or.*or.*29.8(p.385.12; M.11.536B); id.*Cels.*6.57 (p.127.34; M.11.1385C); Max.*qu.Theop.*(M.90.1400B); ἡ προσκύνησις ὑ. καὶ τιμῆς ἐστι σύμβολον Jo.D.*imag.*1.14(M.94.1244A).

***ὑποπτωτικῶς,** *submissively, cat.Apoc.*14:11(p.392.12).

ὑπορθόω, 1. *prop up, support,* Gr.Nyss.*mart.*1.1(M.46.752C); *A.Thom.*A 37(p.155.10); **2.** *raise up* αὐτὸν...ὑ. εἰς τὰ ἀγαθά Mac.Aeg. *hom.*16.6(M.34.617B).

ὑπόρθωμα, τό, *prop,* Cyr.*hom.pasch.*9.3(5^2.112B).

[*]ὑπορόφιος, = ὑπωρ-, *staying indoors,* ‡Nil.*perist.*12.2(M.79. 941D).

[*]ὑπόροφος, = ὑπωρ-, ? *roofed with beams* ἐμβόλους δύο...ἔχοντας διαστήματα μιλίων δ', ὑποροφους καὶ πανευπρεπεῖς Jo.Mal.*chron.*10 p.232(M.97.360A).

***ὑποροφωσις, ἡ,** *fretted ceiling,* Jo.Mal.*chron.*13 p.339(M.97.505B).

***ὑπορραΐζω,** *be better in health,* Philost.*h.e.*7.10(M.65.548C).

ὑπορράπτω, *repair* τὸν θεμέλιον ὑ. Chrys.*hom.14.3 in Heb.*(12.144B).

ὑπορρέω, *slip away, glide down* πότε τοὺς ὑπὲρ σωφροσύνης ἱδρῶτας ἐνεγκεῖν ἀνέξῃ, κατὰ μικρὸν ὑπορρέων ἀπὸ τοῦ γέλωτος καὶ τῶν ᾀσμάτων καὶ τῶν αἰσχρῶν ῥημάτων τούτων; Chrys.*hom.37.5 in Mt.* (7.422A); τοῦ κόσμου κατὰ μικρὸν ὑπορρέοντος Thdt.*haer.*4.12(4.369); Chrys.*hom.31.2 in Mt.*(7.359C) v. περιρρέω.

ὑπορρήγνυμι, in pass., *be split, cracked, below the surface,* of a crystal μήτε τὸ βάθος ὑ. ταῖς διαφύσεσι Bas.*hex.*3.4(1.26A; M.29. 61B); *be split in the lower parts* αἱ...τῶν ὄρων κοιλότητες φάραγξι βαθείαις ὑ. *ib.*4.4(35E; M.85A); *be split apart, divided,* of the Red Sea ὑπορραγέντος τῇ ῥάβδῳ Gr.Nyss.*v.Mos.*33(M.44.312A).

***ὑπορριζόομαι,** *take root under,* ‡Chrys.*pasch.*6(p.177.9; 8.272A).

***ὑπόρροια, ἡ,** *flow,* Iren.*haer.*1.17.1(M.7.640B).

***ὑπορρώννυμι,** *overcome,* Eus.*h.e.*4.15.5(M.20.344A); cf.*M.Polyc.* 3.1 ἐπιρρώννυμι.

ὑπόρχησις, ἡ, *dancing in accompaniment to song*; introduced by Pindar, Clem.*str.*1.16(p.51.7; M.8.792B).

***ὑποσαγής,** *with a pack-saddle* ὡς γὰρ τῶν ἀπὸ τῶν ἐθνῶν σύμβολον ἦν ὁ ἀσαγὴς πῶλος, οὕτως καὶ τῶν ἀπὸ τοῦ ὑμετέρου λαοῦ ἡ ὑ. ὄνος Just.*dial.*53.4(M.6.593B).

ὑπόσαθρος, *somewhat rotten,* Amph.*hom.*4.11(M.39.83B).

ὑποσαίν-ω, 1. *fawn upon,* met. τοιούτοις λόγοις ∼ων καὶ δελεάζων τὸν ἄθλιον Bas.*hom.2 in Ps.*14(1.108A; M.29.268A); Paul.Sil.*Soph.* 1022(M.86.2158A); ὁ ὄφις ὑπέσαινε τὸν ἄνθρωπον †Jo.D.*creat.*6(p.133); †Jo.D.*B.J.*30(M.96.1148D); **2.** *revere* μόνοις δὲ ἀγγέλοις τὸν σοφὸν ποιητὴν καὶ δεσπότην θωπεύειν καὶ ὑ. ‡Caes.Naz.*dial.*29(M.38.88B); Paul.Sil.*Soph.*927(M.86.2154B).

ὑποσαλεύ-ω, *agitate and urge on gradually,* Eus.*h.e.*10.4.14(M.20. 853C); pass., *ib.*9.9.10(824A); ref. Ps.93:18 ὁ...τῆς ἁγνείας ἐραστής... ∼εται πολλάκις καταστρέφοντος τοῦ σατανᾶ πρὸς ἐκτόπους ἡδονάς Cyr. *Ps.*93:18(M.69.1237B).

***ὑποσαλπίζω,** *proclaim* φωνὴν λεπτὴν [ref. 3Reg.19:12] τρανῶς ὑπεσάλπισε τοῦ ἀγγέλου Γαβριὴλ τὸ ῥῆμα, ὃ εὐηγγελίσατο τὴν παρθένον Μαριάμ Mac.Mgn.*apocr.*3.13(p.89.23).

***ὑποσέβω,** *revere less,* Gr.Naz.*or.*22.12(M.35.1144C) cit. s. ὑπερσέβω.

ὑποσημαίν-ω, 1. *indicate, symbolize,* ref. liturg. gospel reading γενικῶς...τὴν τοῦ κόσμου τούτου συντέλειαν ∼ουσαν Max.*myst.*14(M. 91.692D); **2.** *sign, subscribe to,* CAnc.(358)*ep.syn.*(p.270.24; M.42. 405D); ὑποσημήνασθαι χειρὶ οἰκείᾳ Philost.*h.e.*4.12(p.65.24; M.65. 528A); τῷ ὁμοουσίῳ ὑπεσημήναντο *ib.*2.1(465B); τὴν ἐν Ἀριμίνῳ πίστιν ὑπεσημήναντο *ib.*5.1(528C).

ὑποσημει-όομαι, 1. *indicate,* Or.*Cels.*proem.6(p.55.2; M.11.649B); *ib.*7.32(p.182.29; 1465B); id.*comm.in Mt.*11.2(p.36.12; M.13.905C); **2.** *sign, give one's signature, Pap.Chr.*(p.362); Eus.*h.e.*5.19.3(M.20. 481B); *ib.*7.30.21(M.20.720A); **3.** ? *make a sign* μετὰ δὲ τὸ παύσασθαι τὰς τρεῖς ὑμνολογούσας...ἤκουσα ἐγὼ τὰ μεγαλεῖα, μιᾶς ∼ουμένης τῇ μιᾷ καὶ ἀνεγραψάμην τὸ βιβλίον ὅλον πλείστων σημειώσεων τῶν ὕμνων *T.Job* 51(p.136.11; v.l. ὑποσιωπωμένης).

ὑποσημείωσις, ἡ, 1. *summary,* of Christian tradition ἀγαλλιάσονται...οὐχὶ τῇ ἐκφράσει...μόνῃ δὲ τῇ κατὰ τὴν ὑ. τηρήσει Clem *str.*1.1 (p.9.10; M.8.700B); of contents of book τῶν κεφαλαίων ὑ. Cyr. *Jo.*proem.(4.5D); **2.** *explanation,* Clem.*str.*2.1(p.113.12; M.8.932A); **3.** *mark* καθ' ἕκαστον ἀριθμὸν ὑ. διὰ κινναβάρεως πρόκειται, δηλοῦσα ἐν ποίῳ τῶν δέκα κανόνων κείμενος ὁ ἀριθμὸς τυγχάνει Eus.*ep.Carp.*(M. 22.1277A); *signature,* id.*h.e.*5.19.3(M.20.481B); id.*v.C.*2.23(p.50.29; M.20.1001A); Leont.N.*serm.*1(M.93.1576B).

ὑποσιωπ-άω, 1. *pass over in silence,* Bas.*reg.fus.*43(2.390B; M.31. 1028D); **2.** *keep silent* ὦτα ∼ᾷ τοῖς κρούμασι †Bas.*Is.*158(1.491A; M. 30.377A); **3.** *silence* τὰ...χείλη ∼ήσασα Thdr.Stud.*or.*5.2(M.99.721B).

***ὑποσκεδάννυμι,** *distribute* blood *under* the skin; of causing to blush, Gr.Naz.*carm.*1.2.29.204(M.37.899A).

ὑποσκελίζ-ω, *trip up, overthrow*; with personal object, in argument Σωκρατικῶς ∼ων τῷ λόγῳ Gr.Thaum.*pan.Or.*7(p.19.28; M.10. 1076A); morally σπουδάζει ὁ ἐχθρὸς ∼ειν πάντας τοὺς ἐπικαλουμένους τὸν κύριον *T.Dan* 6.3; τῆς κενοδοξίας ἡ νόσος...μυρίους ∼ουσα Chrys. *hom.17.5 in Rom.*(9.628B); id.*poen.*4.1(2.302D); διάβολος...∼ει...δι' ἀπάτης τὸν ἄνθρωπον Jo.D.*hom.*4.8(M.96.609B); with impersonal object χαλεπὸν ἡ συνήθεια καὶ δεινὸν ὑ. Chrys.*catech.*1.5(2.233C); οἱ ∼οντες τὴν ἐκεῖσε φέρουσαν...ὁδόν id.*hom.23.6 in Mt.*(7.292E); Bas. Sel.*or.*17.2(M.85.217C).

ὑποσκέλισμα, τό, *overthrow,* Nil.*Magn.*78(M.79.1045D).

ὑποσκελισμός, ὁ, met., *occasion of stumbling,* †Jo.D.*B.J.*(M.96. 1144A).

ὑποσκευή, ἡ, *scaffolding,* met. ὡς γὰρ ὑ. ἀψῖδος, οὕτως αἱ αἱρέσεις, αἵ τε παρ' Ἕλλησι καὶ αἱ παρὰ τοῖς Χριστιανοῖς, τῷ διαβόλῳ· ὥσπερ δὲ ἀψῖδος σφιγγείσης καὶ λαβούσης τὴν οἰκείαν κατασκευήν, ἡ ὑ. αἴρεται, μένει δὲ μόνη ἡ ἀψὶς [i.e. worship of Devil] στερρά Thdr.Mops.ap *cat.2Thess.*2:3(p.387.10ff.) cf.Thdr.Mops.*2Thess.*2:4(p.51.11n.).

ὑποσκηνόω, *take shelter under,* ‡Chrys.*pasch.*6.5(p.177.11; 8. 272A).

ὑποσκι-άω, *represent in outline* διέσχε, σταυρὸν ∼άων, Μωσῆς χέρας Gr.Naz.*carm.*1.1.36.8(M.37.518A); hence *sketch* ἀνὴρ εἴδωλα χαράσσων...εἶδος ∼άει πειρώμενος *ib.*1.2.1.191(537A).

ὑποσκιρτ-άω, *dance* κἀμὲ τὸν γέροντα ∼ᾶν παρεκίνησας ‡Gr.Nyss. *ep.*26(p.82.8; M.32.1093A); met. πάντα δ' ὑπεσκίρτησεν ἐν ἄστεϊ βάθρα θεμείλων Paul.Sil.*Soph.*189(M.86.2127A).

***ὑποσκοπέω,** f.l. for ἐπισκοπέω, Or.*sel.in Lam.*1:7(M.13.617B).

***ὑπόσκοπος, ὁ,** '*underseer*' (pun on ἐπίσκοπος) Θεοδόσιον τὸν ὑ. ἀλλ' οὐκ ἐπίσκοπος *Max.invect.*(M.90.204A).

ὑποσμήχω, med., *trouble,* Mac.Mgn.*apocr.*4.18(p.197.30).

ὕποσμος, ? *guided by smell,* Mac.Mgn.*apocr.*3.11(p.78.18).

ὑποσμύχ-ω, met.; **1.** *make to smoulder* τὰς θλίψεις καὶ τὰς ἀλγηδόνας...αἳ ∼ουσι τὰς ψυχὰς τῶν τότε ἀνθρώπων διὰ τὰς τῶν πολέμων ἀκοάς Oecum.*Apoc.*16:2(p.174); **2.** *smoulder secretly* πυρετοῦ...∼οντος Bas.*hom.*13.7(2.121C; M.31.441C); θυμὸς...ἔνδοθεν ∼ων Gr.Naz.*or.*18.25(M.35.1013D); τὴν ὑπερηφανείαν ∼ουσαν... φανερὰν γενέσθαι Gr.Nyss.*nativ.*(M.46.1132B); νόσον κρυπτῶς ∼ουσαν Geo.Pis.*Pers.*2.193(M.92.1223A); med., Gr.Naz.*or.*5.3(M.35.668A); Isid.Pel.*epp.*2.49(M.78.492A).

ὑποσπαθίζομαι, *operate on with a spatula ?* ἀπὸ περιτομῆς ἀκρόβυστοι γίνονται, τέχνῃ τινὶ ἰατρικῇ διὰ τοῦ καλουμένου σπουθιστῆρος τὴν τῶν μελῶν ὑποδερματίδα ὑποσπαθισθέντες Epiph.*mens.*16(M.43. 264C).

ὑποσπανίζω, *be lacking,* Didym.*Trin.*2.10(M.39.633C).

***ὑποσπάς, ἡ,** v.l. for ἀποσπάς, *branch, twig*, Gr.Nyss.*hex*.2(M.44.64B).

ὑποσπείρ-ω, *sow secretly, implant*, of evil sown by Devil, Thphl.Ant.*Autol*.2.28(M.6.1096B); ὁ θεὸς σπείρει τὸ ἀγαθὸν ἐν τοῖς ἀνθρώποις καὶ...ὁ διάβολος ~ει τὰ πονηρὰ ἔργα ἐν τοῖς ἀνθρώποις Epiph.*haer*.66.65(p.105.26; M.42.132C); ὁ διάβολός τινα οὐ βιάζεται, ἀλλὰ μόνον ~ει Anast.S.*qu.et resp*.98(M.89.752A); good things ἀληθεῖς ~ει λόγους Meth.*symp*.7.4(p.75.14; M.18.129C); πολλὴν ἠρέμα ~ει τὴν φιλοσοφίαν Chrys.*hom.18.1 in Mt*.(7.234D); ἐλπίδας χρηστὰς ἐμαυτῷ περὶ σοῦ ὑ. Nil.*epp*.2.189(M.79.297D); of teaching ἵνα νῦν κεφαλαιωδῶς ὑποσπείραντες μὴ ἐπιλαθώμεθα... Cyr.H.*catech*.4.3.

***ὑποσπορά, ἡ,** *secret sowing*; met., *evil suggestion*, of Devil ἡ ὑ. τῆς πλάνης Epiph.*haer*.21.6(p.245.7; M.41.293C); *ib*.25.4(p.271.19; 325B); Andr.Caes.*Apoc*.4(M.106.236C); ‡Caes.Naz.*dial*.44(M.38.913).

ὑπόστασις, ἡ, etymology τὸ...ὑ. κατ' ἐτυμολογίαν διερμηνεύεται ὑπό-στασις ‡Ath.*annunt*.4(M.28.921D); its meanings, Socr.*h.e*.3.7.16ff.(M.67.396Af.); Leont.H.*Nest*.2.1(M.86.1528D–32A).

I. gen. uses; **A.** from trans. tenses of ὑφίστημι; **1.** *origination* τῶν...ἀριθμῶν ἀρχὴ γέγονε καθ' ὑπόστασιν ἡ πρώτη μονάς Hipp.*haer*.1.2(p.5.23; M.16.3024B) = *ib*.4.51(p.75.8; 3119B); esp. **a.** of Creation πόθεν...τὸ μετρεῖν τῆς ὑποκειμένης οὐσίας τὸ τοσόνδε, ὡς διαρκέσαι τῇ τηλικούτου κόσμου ὑ.; Or.*comm.in Gen*.ap.Eus.*p.e*.7.20(335B; M.12.48B); πρὸ πάσης τῆς τῶν ὁρατῶν ὑ. Eus.*l.C*.1(p.198.20; M.20.1324A); περὶ τῆς σωματικῆς ἡμῶν ὑ. καὶ τῆς πλάσεως †Bas.*struct.hom*.2.1(1.338A; M.30.41A); Gr.Nyss.*Eun*.4(2 p.58.1; M.45.628D); εἰς ὑ. καὶ μόρφωσιν κτίσεως...ἀρχὴ...τῆς ἁπάντων ὑ. ὁ λόγος Didym.(‡Bas.) *Eun*.5(1.307B; M.29.736D); v. B.4: the two usages not always clearly distinguishable; **b.** of conception of Christ οὐ χωρὶς τοῦ λόγου πνεῦμα παραγεγονὸς εἰς τὴν τοῦ βρέφους ὑ. ὑποληψόμεθα; *ib*.(1.311B; M.745C); **2.** *support, sustenance* 'πᾶν στήριγμα ἄρτου'...τουτέστιν, πᾶσαν ὑ. τροφῆς...ἕτερος ἑρμηνευτής φησι βακτηρίαν Hesych.H.*fr.Ps*.104:16 (M.93.1293C); ἀγαθότητος ὕπαρξις...ἡ τῶν ὅλων παραγωγὴ καὶ ὑ. Dion.Ar.*d.n*.1.5(M.3.593D); met., *courage, resolution*; of a martyr, *Ep.Lugd*.ap.Eus.*h.e*.5.1.20(M.20.416C); *hope, ground of confidence* πίστεως ὑ. πνεύματος πτωχεία καὶ ἡ πρὸς θεὸν ἄμετρος ἀγάπη Gr.Nyss.*instit*.(p.66.12; M.34.421C); οὐκ ἔστιν μοι ἄλλη ἐλπὶς ἢ ὑ., ἢ μόνον τὸ νήπιον τοῦτο Jo.Eub.*innoc*.2(M.96.1504B); ἡ ὑ. μου ὁ Χριστός *M.Glycer*.7(p.13*E); **3.** *giving substance to, actualization* εὐχῆς...καὶ δεήσεως ὑ. ἡ διὰ τῶν ἀρετῶν...ἐκπλήρωσις Max.*qu.Thal*.57(M.90.589D); in the mind, *treating as concrete, objectification* σέβειν...τῶν στοιχείων τὴν ὑ. ... οὔτε..."Ηραν οὔτε Ἀθηνᾶν...τοῦτ' εἶναί φησιν ὅπερ οἱ...τεμένη καθιδρύσαντες νομίζουσιν, φύσεως δὲ ὑποστάσεις Tat.*orat*.21(p.24.4ff.; M.6.853B); **4.** exeg. Heb.11:1 τὰ ἐν ἐλπίδι ἀνυπόστατα εἶναι δοκεῖ, ἡ πίστις ὑπόστασιν αὐτοῖς χαρίζεται, μᾶλλον...αὐτή ἐστιν οὐσία αὐτῶν· οἷον ἡ ἀνάστασις οὐ παραγέγονεν, οὐδέ ἐστιν ἐν ὑ., ἀλλ' ἡ ἐλπὶς ὑφίστησιν αὐτὴν ἐν τῇ ἡμετέρᾳ ψυχῇ Chrys.*hom.21.2 in Heb*.(12.197B); ἔστι γὰρ ἡ πίστις...τῶν κρειττόνων ὑ. ἐν ἐλπίδι τῆς ὑπομονῆς Nil.*Eulog*.11(M.79.1108B); λέγεται...ἡ πίστις ὑ. οἷα δή τινος καταλήψεως οὖσα ἐπιστήμη τε καὶ ἐπίστασις Leont.H.*Nest*.2.1(M.86.1529A); cf.†Bas.*hom.in Ps*.115(1.372B; M.30.105B); Thdt.*Heb*.11:1 (3.613); **5.** *plan, purpose* προϊόντων τῶν χρόνων ἡ ὑ. τῆς δυνάμεως τῶν θείων ⟨λόγων⟩ ἀποκαλύπτεται Epiph.*haer*.66.71(p.112.26; M.42.141C).

B. from intrans. tenses of ὑφίστημι; **1.** *settling*; hence *halt, stage* τῷ...τετάρτῳ ἔτει...ἡ τετρὰς τῶν ἀρετῶν καθιεροῦται τῷ θεῷ, τῆς τρίτης ἤδη μονῆς συναπτούσης ἐπὶ τὴν τοῦ κυρίου τετάρτην ὑ. Clem.*str*.2.18(p.165.14; M.8.1037B); *span of existence, life* ἡ...ἐμὴ ὑ. ὀλίγη...καὶ συνεσταλμένη Cyr.*Ps*.38:6(M.69.976A); **2.** *source, ground* ὁ δεσπότης...αὐτὸς ὑπάρχων τοῦ παντὸς ἡ ὑ. Tat.*orat*.5(p.5.18; M.6.813C); ἀρχέγονον ὀγδοάδα, ῥίζαν καὶ ὑ. τῶν πάντων Iren.*haer*.1.1.1 (M.7.448A); ἥτις [sc. the true Life] γενομένη ἐν ἡμῖν καὶ φωτὸς γνώσεως ὑπόστασις γίνεται Or.*Jo*.2.24(19; p.91.18; M.14.157A); **3.** ? *statement, argument* ὃ μηδ' εἰπεῖν εὐαγές, εἰ μὴ ὑποθέσεων καὶ ὑ. μοχθηρῶν [i.e. to be put up as a skittle] Didym.*Trin*.2.8(M.39.613A); **4.** *substance, stuff, material*, with οὐσία: οὐδὲ ἐπὶ τῶν ζώντων σωμάτων... οἷς ἡ ὑ. ἐκ τῆς τῶν στοιχείων ἐστὶ συγκράσεως, κοινωνία τις κατὰ τὸν τῆς οὐσίας λόγον ἐστὶ τῷ ἁπλῷ τε καὶ ἀειδεῖ τῆς ψυχῆς πρὸς τὴν σωματικὴν παχυμερίαν Gr.Nyss.*anim.et res*.(M.46.44B); τὸ μέγεθος τῆς αὐτοῦ [sc. τοῦ οὐρανοῦ] ὑ. καὶ τὸ ἄφθαρτον τῆς οὐσίας αὐτοῦ ‡Just.*qu.Chr*.5.2(M.6.1457A); of the ultimate stuff of the universe πέντε διαιρέσεσι διειλῆφθαι τὴν πάντων τῶν γεγονότων ὑ. Max.*ambig*.(M.91.1304D); **a.** incorporeal [sc. τὴν οὐσίαν] προηγουμένην τὴν τῶν ἀσωμάτων ὑ. εἶναι φάσκουσι Or.*or*.27(p.367.14; M.11.512A); of angels οὐκ ἴσμεν...εἰς πῦρ ἀναλυομένην τὴν ἀνθρώπου ψυχὴν ἢ τὴν ἀγγέλων...ὑ. id.*Cels*.6.71(p.141.28; M.11.1408A); of demons ἐπὶ τῆς παρουσίας τοῦ...Χριστοῦ...ἀφανεῖς δαιμόνων ὑ. πυρὶ παραδίδονται *M.Agap*.1.1; of the soul οὕτως τὴν ψυχήν, καὶ ὅλην τὴν ὑ. αὐτῆς ἐνέδυσε τὴν ἁμαρτίαν ὁ ἄρχων ὁ πονηρός Mac.Aeg.*hom*.2.1(M.34.464B); *ib*.2.4(465C); **b.** corporeal ἴδε...τίνος ὑ. ἢ τίνος εἴδους τυγχάνουσιν οὓς...νομίζετε θεούς *Diogn*.2.1; ἐκ τούτων [sc. eucharist] αὔξει καὶ συνίσταται ἡ τῆς σαρκὸς ἡμῶν ὑ. Iren.*haer*.5.2.3(M.7.1126A); οὐ γὰρ ἄλλο τὸ ἀποθνῆσκον, καὶ ἄλλο τὸ ζωοποιούμενον...τί...ἦν τὸ ἀποθνῆσκον; πάντως ἡ τῆς σαρκὸς ὑ. *ib*.5.12.3(1153C); τοὺς...ποταμοὺς καὶ ἀπὸ τῶν ὄμβρων λαμβάνειν τὴν ὑ. καὶ ἐξ ὑδάτων τῶν ἐν τῇ γῇ Hipp.*haer*.1.8(p.13.23; M.16.3033A); τὸν...σχῆμα καὶ μέγεθος ἔχοντα καὶ ὑ. Meth.*res*.2.20 (p.374.10; M.18.285B); πυθέσθαι...εἰ...σάρκα αὐτὸς ἀνείληφεν ἐκ τῆς ἡμετέρας ὑ. ...ἐξ ἐκείνης τῆς ὑ. τῆς τοῦ πρωτοπλάστου Ἀδάμ, ἐξ ἧς καὶ ἡμεῖς Adam.*dial*.4.13(p.168.20,170.7; M.11.1828Df.); τὸν ἐκ ῥευστῆς φύσεως τῶν ὑδάτων ἄπτωτον ὑ. οὐρανοῦ ποιήσαντα Cyr.H.*catech*.9.5; of the flesh of fruit, *ib*.6.5(545A); παντὸς σώματος ἡ ὑ. ἐκ τῆς τροφῆς γίνεται Gr.Nyss.*or.catech*.37(p.147.7; M.45.96C); τούτου τοῦ κάλλους ὑ. οὐδὲν ἕτερόν ἐστιν ἢ φλέγμα καὶ αἷμα κτλ. Chrys.*Thdr*.1.14(1.22A); id.*hom.in Mt.7:14*(3.27A); ἀδιαίρετος ἡ τῆς Σιναΐτιδος βάτου ὑ. πάντοθεν ἀβλαβῶς περιειλημμένη τῷ πυρί Ephr.Ant.*fr*.(M.86.2108A); **c.** Gnost. τὴν ὑλικὴν οὐσίαν ἐκ τριῶν παθῶν συστῆναι λέγουσι...ἐκ... τοῦ φόβου τὴν...ψυχικὴν ὑ., ὡς ψυχὰς ἀλόγων ζῴων...καὶ ἀνθρώπων... ἐκ δὲ τῆς λύπης τὰ πνευματικά...ὅθεν τὸν διάβολον...καὶ...τοὺς ἀγγέλους, καὶ πᾶσαν τὴν πνευματικὴν τῆς πονηρίας ὑ. Iren.*haer*.1.5.4(M.7.497Af.); *ib*.1.6.2(508A); *ib*.1.11.1(561B); *ib*.1.15.5(625B); **d.** *basic element* ἄδολος...ἰθὺς τὴν γνώμην καὶ ὀρθός· τὸ δέ ἐστιν ἁπλότητος καὶ ἀληθείας ὑ. Clem.*paed*.1.5(p.101.13; M.8.272A); τὴν ὑ. καὶ...ὕλην, ἧς ἔχειν πρὸς τὸν θεὸν ἀγάπης, τὴν τήρησιν τῶν θείων ἐντολῶν εἶναί φησιν Didym.*1 Jo*.5:3ff.(M.39.1802C); **5.** *original existence* σύγχρονον αὐτῷ [sc. Creator] ὑ. δοῦναι [i.e. to matter] πεφοβημένοι Meth.*arbitr*.4(p.155.10; M.18.248C); οὔτ' ἔστιν...ἔννοια πρεσβυτέρα τῆς τοῦ μονογενοῦς ὑ. Bas.*Eun*.2.13(1.248B; M.29.596C); τὰ...γεννητὰ...κοινὴν ἔχει τὴν ἐκ μὴ ὄντων ὑ. *ib*.2.19(1.255B; M.613B); εἰς τὴν γέννησιν τοῦ υἱοῦ ...εἰς τὴν ὑ. τοῦ ἁγίου πνεύματος *ib*.2.32(1.269C; M.648B); τῆς ἐκ τοῦ πατρὸς ὑ. τοῦ υἱοῦ Gr.Nyss.*Eun*.8(2 p.191.2; M.45.785C); τῆς φύσεως ἡμῶν...ἡ πρώτη γένεσίς τε καὶ ὑ. παρ' αὐτοῦ τὴν ἀρχὴν ἔσχε id.*or.catech*.16(p.68.12; M.45.49C); τῶν μὲν τὰς οὐσίας αὐτὸς ἐδημιούργησεν, οἱ δ' ὑποστάσεως ἀρχὴν οὐ κατέλαβον ἐν αὐτῷ Mac.Mgn.*apocr*.4.26 (p.211.23); **6.** *being, substance, reality*; explicitly equated with οὐσία: ἡ δὲ ὑ. οὐσία ἐστί, καὶ οὐδὲν ἄλλο σημαινόμενον ἔχει ἢ αὐτὸ τὸ ὄν...ἡ γὰρ ὑ. καὶ ἡ οὐσία ὕπαρξίς ἐστιν Ath.*ep.Afr*.4(M.26.1036B); ὑ. λέγομεν, ἡγούμενοι ταὐτὸν εἶναι εἰπεῖν ὑ. καὶ οὐσίαν id.*tom*.6(M.26.801C); οὐκ ἴσασι...ὅτι καὶ ὑ. καὶ οὐσία ταὐτόν ἐστι τῷ λόγῳ. ἔστι γὰρ κύριος ἐν τῇ ὑ. αὐτοῦ, καὶ τὸ [Heb.1:3]. οὐσία οὖν ἐστιν· οὐχὶ περιουσία Epiph.*haer*.69.72(p.220.11ff.; M.42.317D); οἱ νεώτεροι τῶν φιλοσόφων συνεχῶς ἀντὶ τῆς οὐσίας, τῇ λέξει τῆς ὑ. ἀπεχρήσαντο Socr.*h.e*.3.7.20(M.67.396B); v. definitions under 7; //οὐσία and/or φύσις: Βασιλείδης...οὐσίαν, ἀλλ' οὐκ ἐξουσίαν, καὶ φύσιν καὶ ὑ. ... λέγει τὴν πίστιν Clem.*str*.5.1(p.327.23; M.9.12B); Cyr.H.*catech*.9.9f. cit. s. ἐνέργεια; Mac.Mgn.*apocr*.4.16(p.186.32); so understood in West περὶ δὲ τοῦ, ὅτι ὑ. καὶ οὐσία οὐ ταὐτόν ἐστι, καὶ αὐτοὶ...ὑπεσημήναντο οἱ ἀπὸ τῆς δύσεως ἀδελφοί, ἐν οἷς τὸ στενὸν τῆς ἑαυτῶν γλώττης ὑφορώμενοι, τὸ τῆς οὐσίας ὄνομα τῇ Ἑλλάδι φωνῇ παραδεδώκασιν Bas.*ep*.214.4(3.322D; M.32.789A); Gr.Naz.*or*.21.35(M.35.1124Df.); cf. *tota saecularium litterarum schola nihil aliud hypostasim nisi usian novit. et quisquam, rogo,...tres substantias praedicabit? una est dei et sola natura quae vere est*, Hier.*ep*.15.4(M.*PL*.22.357); opp. δόκησις q.v.; opp. σχῆμα: οὐ γὰρ ἡ ὑ., οὐδὲ ἡ οὐσία τῆς κτίσεως ἐξαφανίζεται...ἀλλὰ τὸ σχῆμα παράγει τοῦ κόσμου τούτου Iren.*haer*.5.36.1(M.7.1221B); ὁ μαργαρίτης ἐν ὑ. τίκτεται...οὐ σχῆμα ὁ λεχθεὶς λίθος ἔχει μόνον, ἀλλὰ τὴν ὕπαρξιν· οὕτω...ὁ υἱὸς τοῦ θεοῦ ἐν ὑ. ἐτέχθη, καὶ οὐκ ἐν σχήματι Ephr.2.263E; σχῆμα μόνον ἐστίν, οὐ πράγματος ἀλήθεια, ἐπίδειξις καὶ προσωπεῖον, οὐχ ὑ. μένουσα Chrys.*hom.20.2 in Rom*.(9.658E); opp. ὄνομα: ὁρᾷς δύο προσώπων ὑπόστασιν οὐχὶ ὀνόματα ψιλὰ χωρὶς πραγμάτων id.*hom.6.2 in Phil*.(11.235A); opp. ἐπίνοια, Clem.*str*.7.17(p.76.10; M.9.552A) cit. s. ἐκκλησία; ἐπινοίας μόνης ἀλλ' οὐχ ὑποστάσεως Or.*fr.36 in Jo*. (p.511.21); ἐχθροί...ἤτοι τῇ ἐπινοίᾳ ἢ καὶ τῇ ὑ. id.*sel.in Lam*.1:5 (p.241.25; M.13.613C); πῶς...ἀνθρωπίνης ἐπινοίας εἶναί φατε τὰ ὀνόματα;...πραγμάτων ἐστὶ δημιουργὸς ἐν ὑ. θεωρουμένων, οὐκ ὀνομάτων ἀνυποστάτων Gr.Nyss.*Eun*.12(1 p.292.19; M.45.1001D); opp. ἐνέργεια and ἐπίνοια: λέγεται...χωρίζεσθαί τι ἀπό τινος ἢ ἐνεργείᾳ καὶ ὑ., ἢ ἐπινοίᾳ, ἢ ἐνεργείᾳ μέν, οὐ μὴν καὶ ὑ. ⟨ἐνεργείᾳ μὲν καὶ ὑ.⟩, ὡς εἰ πυρούς τις καὶ κριθὰς μεμιγμένα χωρίσειεν ἀπ' ἀλλήλων· ἃ μὲν κατὰ κίνησιν χωρίζεται, ἐνεργείᾳ λέγεται, ἃ δὲ χωρισθέντα ὑφέστηκεν, ὑποστάσει λέγεται κεχωρίσθαι. ἐπινοίᾳ δέ, ὅταν τὴν ὕλην ἀπὸ τῶν ποιοτήτων χωρίζωμεν...ἐνεργείᾳ δέ, οὐ μὴν καὶ ὑ., ὅταν χωρισθέν τι ἀπό τινος μηκέτι ὑπάρχοι, ὑπόστασιν οὐσίας οὐκ ἔχον Meth.*res*.3.6(p.397.7ff.; M.18.321B); **a.** *substantive existence, subsistence* μὴ καθ' αὑτό τινος ὑ. λαβόμενον [sc. τὸ σαρκίον] Clem.*exc.Thdot.* 52(p.124.14; M.9.684C); γνῶσιν εἶπεν ἁμαρτίας διὰ νόμου πεφανερῶσθαι, οὐχὶ ὑ. εἰληφέναι id.*str.*2.7(p.131.13; M.8.969B); δεικνύτω...ὑ. καὶ οὐσίαν Μνημοσύνης...ἢ τὰς χάριτας...παραστησάτω δύνασθαι κατ' οὐσίαν ὑφεστηκέναι Or.*Cels.*1.23(p.73.14; M.11.700B); ζῆν...εἰπὼν τὴν ἀλήθειαν, καὶ νικᾶν καὶ κρατεῖν, ἐμφαντικώτατα παρέστησεν αὐτῆς τὴν ὑ. Eus.*e.th.*1.20(p.94.17; M.24.889A); εἰ πρᾶγμα κατ' ἰδίαν ὑ. θεωρούμενον τὴν γέννησιν οἴεται [sc. Eunomius] Gr.Nyss.*Eun.*10(2 p.237.29; M.45.840C); τὸ εἴδωλον οὐδεμίαν ὑ. ἔχει Thdt.*qu.38 in Ex.*20:3(1.149); ref. problem of evil κακοῦ δὲ φύσιν οὔτε ὑπὸ θεοῦ γενέσθαι οὔτε καθ' αὑτὴν ὑ. ἔχειν, ἀλλὰ κατ' ἐναντίωσιν καὶ παρακολούθησιν τοῦ ἀγαθοῦ γενέσθαι Hipp.*haer.*1.19(p.23.20; M.16.3045C); κατ' αὐτοὺς ἡ κακία ὑ. ἔχει καθ' ἑαυτὴν καὶ οὐσίαν Ath.*gent.*6(M.25.13A); μήτε θεὸν αἴτιον ἡγοῦ τῆς ὑπάρξεως τοῦ κακοῦ μήτε ἰδίαν ὑ. τοῦ κακοῦ εἶναι φαντάζου· οὐ γάρ ἐστιν ὑφεστὼς ὥσπερ τι ζῷον ἡ πονηρία Bas.*hom.*9.5(2.78A; M.31.341B); οὔτε ὑ. ἔχει τὸ κακὸν ἀλλὰ παρυπόστασιν Dion. Ar.*d.n.*4.31(M.3.732C); **b.** *reality, actuality, fact* τὸ...ἀεὶ νοεῖν, οὐσία τοῦ γινώσκοντος...γενομένη...ζῶσα ὑ. μένει Clem.*str.*4.22(p.308.27; M.8.1345C); *ib.*7.12(p.54.29; M.9.505A); μηδ' ὅλως νομίζειν ἐν πᾶσι τοῖς εἰρημένοις ὑπ' αὐτοῦ πραγμάτων εἶναί τινα ἢ νοημάτων ὑ. Gr. Nyss.*Eun.*1(1 p.26.17; M.45.253D); Didym.*2Cor.*12:1ff.(p.41.29; M.39.1728A); ἐξ οὐκ ὄντων τὰς οὐσίας καὶ τὰς ὑ. ὑφιστᾶν Epiph.*haer.*76.51(p.406.4; M.42.624C); τῶν...κτίσεων ὁρωμένων καὶ τοῦ πλείστου μέρους τῆς οὔσης ὑ. φαινομένης *ib.*76.29(p.378.15; 576B); οὐκ εἰρωνείᾳ ἀλλ' ἀληθείᾳ...ἵνα δείξῃ σαρκὸς ὑ. ἀληθινήν *ib.*69.61(p.209.26; 300C); τὰ κίβδηλα...δηνάρια τῷ χρυσῷ βαπτόμενα τὴν μὲν ἐπιφάνειαν λαμπρὰν ἔχει...τὴν δὲ ὑ. ἄτιμον ὕλην Mac.Mgn.*apocr.*3.43(p.151.3); ἀφομοίωσις...καὶ ὑ. ταὐτὸν οὐκ ἔστι· τὸ μὲν γὰρ τύπος, τὸ δὲ ἀλήθεια τυγχάνει Marc.Er.*opusc.*10.3(M.65.1120D); τὸ ἐξ οὐκ ὄντων εἰς ὑ. ἐνεχθέν Cyr.*thes.*6(5[1].46C); τῆς προαιρέσεως...ἔχοντες τὴν ὑ., ἐστερημένοι δὲ τῆς πράξεως Ephr.Ant.*fr.*(M.86.2109C); ref. 1Jo.3:2 μήπω φανερωθείσης τῆς αὐθυπάρκτου κατὰ τὸ εἶδος τῶν μελλόντων ἀγαθῶν ὑποστάσεως [2Cor.5:7] Max.*qu.Thal.*9(M.90.285B); of an ultimate principle εἰ...κεχώρισται [sc. ἀγένητα δύο]...ἀνάγκη εἶναί τι ἀνὰ μέσον ἀμφοτέρων, ὅπερ καὶ τὸν χωρισμὸν αὐτῶν δείκνυσιν this is later referred to as τὴν...τοῦ χωρίζοντος ὑ. Meth.*arbitr.*5(pp.158.5–159.4; ἀπόστασιν M.18.249Df.); ὦ...Μανιχαῖοι, λέγετε δύο ὑ. εἶναι, ἀγαθοῦ τε καὶ πονηροῦ ‡Ath.*haer.*7(M.28.513A); λοιπὸν ὁ θεὸς καὶ οἱ ἄγγελοι αὐτοῦ τὸν ἄνθρωπον τοῦτον βούλονται οἰκειώσασθαι μεθ' ἑαυτῶν εἰς τὴν βασιλείαν· ὁμοίως ὁ διάβολος καὶ οἱ ἄγγελοι αὐτοῦ...μέση οὖν ἐστι ἡ ψυχὴ τῶν δύο ὑ. Mac.Aeg.*hom.*26.24(M.34.692A); **c.** *genuineness* τοῦτον ἐλέγχοντες, δι' αὐτοῦ καὶ τὴν ὑ. ἐξελέγχομεν τοῦ προφήτου Apollon.ap.Eus.*h.e.*5.8.10(M.20.480A); δηλῶν τὴν ὑ. τῆς οἰκείας θεότητός φησιν [Jo.10:30] Mac.Mgn.*apocr.*2.9(p.12.6); **d.** καθ' ὑπόστασιν, ἐν ὑ. *in actual fact, literally* μὴ...ζωὴν αἰώνιον περιποιεῖ ἡ ἐντολὴ τοῦ θεοῦ, ἀλλ'...αὐτή ἐστι καθ' ὑ. ἡ αἰώνιος ζωή Or.*fr.95 in Jo.*(p.558.22); id.*hom.18.4 in Jer.*(p.154.21; M.13.469A); τὸ μὲν καθ' ὑ. ὂν πρᾶγμα τῆς τοῦ πεποιηκότος δυνάμεως ἔργον εἶναι, τὰς δὲ γνωριστικὰς τῶν ὄντων φωνάς...τῆς λογικῆς δυνάμεως ἔργα τε καὶ εὑρήματα, αὐτὴν δὲ ταύτην τὴν λογικὴν...φύσιν ἔργον θεοῦ Gr.Nyss.*Eun.*12(1 p.285.13; M.45.993B); μὴ ὄντας ἐν ὑ. ἀλλὰ διὰ τῆς τινῶν ὑπολήψεως Epiph.*haer.*25.6(p.273.18; M.41.328D); Proc.G.*Gen.*3:24(M.87.228C); cf. ἄβυσσος...τὸ ἀπεράτωτον κατὰ τὴν ἰδίαν ὑ., περαιούμενον δὲ τῇ δυνάμει τοῦ θεοῦ Clem.*ecl.*2(p.137.17; M.9.700B); **e.** generic *essence, nature*, Tat.*orat.*15(p.17.1; M.6.840A) cit. s. δαίμων; ἡμῶν δὲ ἡ προηγουμένη ὑ. ἐστιν ἐν τῷ κατ' εἰκόνα τοῦ κτίσαντος· ἡ δὲ ἐξ αἰτίας ἐν τῷ ληφθέντι ἀπὸ τοῦ χοῦ τῆς γῆς πλάσματι Or.*Jo.*20.22(p.355.9; M.14.621B); τῶν ἀνθρώπων ἐκ δύο τὴν ὑ. ἐχόντων Ath.*fr.*(*AP* p.5.6); οὐκ ἔστι τάγμα ψυχῶν κατὰ φύσιν ἁμαρτανουσῶν, καὶ τάγμα ψυχῶν κατὰ φύσιν δικαιοπραγουσῶν, ἀλλ' ἐκ προαιρέσεως ἀμφότερα, μονοειδοῦς καὶ ὁμοίας οὔσης...τῆς τῶν ψυχῶν ὑ. Cyr.H.*catech.*4.20; ἀσώματον λέγοντες εἶναι τῶν ἀγγέλων τὴν φύσιν, περιγεγράφθαι φαμὲν αὐτῶν τὴν ὑ. ... περιγεγραμμένην ἔχουσιν οἱ ἄγγελοι τὴν οὐσίαν Thdt.*qu.3 in Gen.*(1.6); τοὺς...τριμερῆ τὴν ὑ. ἐσχηκότας, ψυχῆς, σώματος, καὶ πνεύματος Areth.*Apoc.*proem.(M.106.493A); **f.** *nature, constitution* ὥσπερ...τὰ δηλητήρια συνθέσεις εἰσὶν ὑλικαί, τὸν αὐτὸν τρόπον καὶ τὰ ἰώμενα τῆς αὐτῆς ὑ. ἐστιν Tat.*orat.*18(p.19.30; M.6.845A); ἄφθαρτος γίνεται, οὐκ ἐξ ἰδίας ὑ. ἀλλὰ κατὰ τὴν τοῦ κυρίου ἐνέργειαν Iren.*haer.*5.13.3(M.7.1158C); ψεῦδος εἶναί τινα, ⟨οὐ⟩ τῇ ὑ. ἐκ κατασκευῆς, ἀλλὰ ἐκ μεταβολῆς καὶ ἰδίας προαιρέσεως τοιοῦτον Or.*Jo.*20.21(19; p.353.23; M.14.617D); τὰ δὲ...περὶ τὸ σῶμα καὶ τὰ ἐκτὸς...τῆς ἰδίας τοῦ λογικοῦ ζῴου φύσεως ἀλλοτρίαν τὴν ὑ. ἔχει Eus.*Hierocl.*47(544C; M.22.865C); ὁ κρύσταλλος ὑδατώδης...ἡ ὑ., καὶ λιθώδης ἡ ἐνέργεια Cyr.H.*catech.*9.9; αὐτὸς ἐφ' ἑαυτοῦ κατ' ἰδίαν ὑ. μεστός τε ὁ ἀὴρ καὶ πλήρης ἐστί Gr.Nyss.*anim.et res.*(M.46.36C); ἐν ὑ. ... σῶμα παχύ ἐστιν Mac.Aeg.*hom.*4.9(M.34.480A); τὴν τριμερῆ ὑ., σώματος λέγω καὶ πνεύματος, καὶ ψυχῆς Marc.Er.*opusc.*3.1(M.65.965C); in Cyr. a concrete instance of a nature or constitution realized in an individual ἑτεροφυὲς...ὡς πρός γε ψυχὴν τὸ σῶμά ἐστιν, ἀλλ' ἴδιον αὐτῆς καὶ συναποτελεστικὸν τῆς ὑ. τοῦ ἑνὸς ἀνθρώπου Cyr.*ep.*50(p.92.19; 5[2].160E); of angels οἱ δὲ [sc. the fallen] ἐνύβρισαν καὶ τῇ τῆς οὐσίας ὑ. καὶ τῇ ἀρχῇ Athenag.*leg.*24.4(M.6.948B); δι' ὅλης τῆς ἑαυτῶν ὑ. κεχωρηκότα...τὸν ἁγιασμὸν ἔχουσι Bas.*Eun.*3.2(1.274B; M.29.660B); οὐ μία τίς ἐστιν ὑ. ἀγγελική, ἀλλὰ καὶ δυσαρίθμητος. τὸ δὲ...πνεῦμα ...ἀμόρφου προῆλθεν...πατρικῆς ὑ. Didym.*Trin.*2.4(M.39.484A); ἄγγελον ἕνα ἀριθμῷ ἐροῦμεν, ἀλλ' οὐχ ἕνα τῇ φύσει...οὐσίαν γὰρ μεθ' ἁγιασμοῦ τὴν τοῦ ἀγγέλου ὑ. ἐννοοῦμεν Evagr.Pont.*ep.*2(M.32.249A); **g.** in gen., *state of being, condition*, Tat.*orat.*6(p.6.27; M.6.817C); Ἠλίας ὡς ἦν ἐν τῇ τοῦ πλάσματος ὑ. ἀνελήφθη, τὴν ἀνάληψιν τῶν πνευματικῶν προφητεύων Iren.*haer.*5.5.1(M.7.1134B); **7.** *particular, concrete entity; individual*; **a.** defined and explained τοῦτο...ἐστιν ἡ ὑ., οὐχ ἡ ἀόριστος τῆς οὐσίας ἔννοια...ἀλλ' ἡ τὸ κοινόν τε καὶ ἀπερίγραπτον ἐν τῷ τινὶ πράγματι διὰ τῶν ἐπιφαινομένων ἰδιωμάτων παριστῶσα Gr.Nyss.*diff.ess.*3(M.32.328B); ὑ. ... εἶναι τὴν συνδρομὴν τῶν περὶ ἕκαστον ἰδιωμάτων...ἡ ὑ. τὸ ἰδιάζον τῆς ἑκάστου ὑπάρξεως σημεῖόν ἐστι *ib.*6(336Cff.); ὑποστάσεως...ὅρος· ἢ τὰ κατὰ τὴν φύσιν μὲν ταὐτά, ἀριθμῷ δὲ διαφέροντα· ἢ τὰ ἐκ διαφόρων φύσεων συνεστῶτα, τὴν δὲ τοῦ εἶναι κοινωνίαν ἅμα τε καὶ ἐν ἀλλήλοις κεκτημένα...οὐχ ὡς συμπληρωτικὰ τῆς ἀλλήλων οὐσίας Leont.B.*Nest.et Eut.*1(M.86.1280A); ἡ ὑ. κατὰ δύο σημαινομένων φέρεται. σημαίνει γὰρ καὶ τὸ ἁπλῶς ἐν ὑπάρξει ὄν, ὅτε μάλιστα τῶν χαρακτηριστικῶν ἰδιωμάτων ἐστέρηται· σημαίνει καὶ τὸ πρόσωπον τὸ καθ' ἑαυτὸ ὑφεστὼς †Leont.B.*fr.*(M.86.2012C) ∞ †Leont.B.*sect.*7(M.86.1240C); δύο σημαίνειν τὸ ὄνομα τῆς ὑ. οἱ πατέρες εἰρήκασι· καὶ καθ' ἕνα μὲν τρόπον δηλοῦσθαι τὴν χαρακτηριστικὴν ὑ., ἥτις κυρίως καὶ ὑ. λέγεται...καθ' ἕτερον δὲ τρόπον τὴν οὐσίαν σημαίνειν τὸ τῆς ὑ. ὄνομα Pamph.H.*panopl.*16.4(p.644f.); καλεῖται...ἡ ὑ. ὑπό τινων καὶ ἄτομον, καὶ πρόσωπον· ἄτομον μὲν διότι οὐ πέφυκεν εἰς ἕτερόν τι ὑποδιαιρεῖσθαι...πρόσωπον δὲ ὡς χαρακτηριστικὸν καὶ τοῦ τινὸς ὂν δηλωτικόν *ib.*1.1(p.597f.); ὑ. καὶ πρόσωπόν ἐστιν οὐσία ἡ τίς, μερική, ἄτομος, ἡ μήτε καθ' ὑποκειμένου τινὸς λεγομένη μήτε ἐν ὑποκειμένῳ τινὶ οὖσα Thdr.Raith.*praep.*(p.211.23); ἄτομα μέν, διὰ τὸ μηδὲν αὐτῶν τομὴν...ὑποδέχεσθαι...ὑποστάσεις δέ, ὡς ὑπὸ τὴν φύσιν ἑστῶτα καὶ μένοντα...πρόσωπα δέ, διότι ἕκαστον αὐτῶν οἰκεῖον ἔχει χαρακτῆρα τοῖς λοιποῖς ἀκοινώνητον ‡Cyr.*Trin.*13(6[3].19D; M.77.1149B); ἡ...ὑ., ποτὲ μὲν τὴν ἁπλῶς ὕπαρξιν δηλοῖ...ποτὲ δὲ τὸ ἄτομον, ἤτοι τὸ πρόσωπον· ἥτις καθ' αὑτὸ λέγεται ὑ. Jo.D.*nat.*6(M.95.120C); id.*haer.*7(M.94.745B); καθ' ὑπόστασιν...ἐστι, τὸ ἐκ διαφόρων φύσεων ὑφεστὸς πρᾶγμα id.*dialect.*65(M.94.664A); πενταχῶς... ἡ ὑ. ὑ. καὶ πρόσωπον καὶ χαρακτὴρ καὶ ἴδιον καὶ ἄτομον ‡Jo.D.*Trin.*5(M.95.17A); defined as essence and individual qualities, i.e. specific differences ἡ...ὑ. πρόσωπον ἀφορίζει τοῖς χαρακτηριστικοῖς ἰδιώμασι Leont.B.*Nest.et Eut.*1(M.86.1277D) = id.*fr.*(M.86.2004C); id.*arg.Sev.*(M.86.1928C); συσσημαίνει...τῷ τε προσώπῳ καὶ τῇ φύσει ἡ ὑ. τὸ ὑποκείμενον πρᾶγμα ἑκατέρῳ τῶν διαφόρων ὀνομάτων Leont.H.*Nest.*2.1(M.86.1532B); Pamph.H.*panopl.*1.1(p.597); *ib.*1.3(p.601); Anast.Ant.*fid.*(M.89.1401B); Thdr.Raith.*praep.*(p.205.15); Eulog.*fr.dogm.*(M.86.2948A); ἡ μὲν γὰρ ὑ., ἤτοι τὸ ἄτομον τῆς φύσεως, φύσις, ἀλλ' οὐ μόνον φύσις, ἀλλὰ μετὰ ἰδιώματος· ἡ δὲ φύσις, οὐχ ὑ., ἤτοι ἄτομον Jo.D.*Jacob.*52(M.94.1461A); id.*dialect.*30(M.94.593A); opp. οὐσία in generic sense, Bas.*ep.*236.6(3.363E; M.32.884A) cit. s. II.B.1; Gr.Nyss.*diff.ess.*1,3(M.32.325A,328C); id.*comm.not.*(M.45.185A); ὅταν...κοινῶς ἐπὶ πολλῶν ταῦτα θεωρῆται, οὐσία προσαγορεύεται· ὅταν δὲ καὶ ἐπὶ ἕνα ἰδίως συνάγεται, ὑ. ἐπονομάζεται ‡Ath.*annunt.*4(M.28.921B); τῆς οὐσίας ἡ δήλωσις, κατὰ κοινοῦ τινος ἔοικεν ἰέναι πράγματος· τὸ δὲ τῆς ὑ. ἑκάστου τυχὸν ὄνομα Cyr.*dial.Trin.*1(5[1].408E); κατὰ μὲν τὴν θύραθεν σοφίαν...ἥ τε γὰρ οὐσία τὸ ὂν σημαίνει, καὶ τὸ ὑφεστὸς ἡ ὑ. κατὰ δέ γε τὴν τῶν πατέρων διδασκαλίαν, ἣν ἔχει διαφορὰν τὸ κοινὸν ὑπὲρ τὸ ἴδιον, ἢ τὸ γένος ὑπὲρ τὸ εἶδος ἢ τὸ ἄτομον, ταύτην ἡ οὐσία πρὸς τὴν ὑ. ἔχει Thdt.*eran.*1(4.7); v. citt. from Thdt. s. III.A.2 and 3.c; τὴν μὲν φύσιν ἤτοι οὐσίαν καὶ μορφὴν τὸ κοινὸν σημαίνειν, τὴν δὲ ὑ. ἤτοι πρόσωπον τὸ ἰδικόν Justn.*conf.*(p.86.21; M.86.1009C); τὴν μὲν οὐσίαν, τὴν ὕπαρξιν ἑκάστου πράγματος σημαίνειν· τὴν δὲ ὑ., τὴν πληθὺν τῶν χαρακτηριστικῶν ἰδιωμάτων...ἡ οὖν οὐσία, τὸ κοινὸν σημαίνει· ἡ δὲ ὑ., τὸ ἰδικόν Pamph.H.*panopl.*11.1(p.639); οὐσία μὲν γὰρ αὐτὸ τὸ εἶναι μόνον δηλοῖ. ὑ. δὲ οὐ μόνον τὸ εἶναι δηλοῖ, ἀλλὰ καὶ τὸ πῶς ἔχειν καὶ τὸ ὁποῖόν τι εἶναι παρίστησι...ὥστε ἡ μὲν οὐσία κοινόν τι εἶναι σημαίνει, ἡ δὲ ὑ. ἰδικόν Thdr.Raith.*praep.*(p.204.10,16); further on the relation of the two words, *ib.*(pp.212–16); οὐσία μὲν αὐτὸ τὸ εἶδος καὶ τὴν φύσιν, ὅπερ ἐστὶ καθ' ἑαυτήν, δηλοῖ, ὑ. δέ, τόν τινα τῆς οὐσίας ἐμφαίνει Max.*opusc.*(M.91.260Df.); τὸ πῦρ μία οὐσία ἐστίν, τέμνεται δὲ εἰς ὑποστάσεις, ἤγουν λύχνους καὶ κηροὺς καὶ λαμπάδας καὶ κλιβάνους καὶ καμίνους...ὑ. γὰρ τὸ κεχωρισμένον πρόσωπον λέγεται

Anast.S.*hod*.2(M.89.61A); ἡ μὲν οὐσία, τὸ κοινὸν καὶ περιεκτικὸν εἶδος τῶν ὁμοειδῶν ὑ. σημαίνει...ἡ δὲ ὑ., ἄτομον δηλοῖ Jo.D.*f.o*.3.4(M.94.997A); τὸ κοινὸν μετὰ τοῦ ἰδιάζοντος ἔχει ἡ ὑ., καὶ τὸ καθ' ἑαυτὴν ὑπάρξαι· ἡ οὐσία δέ, καθ' ἑαυτὴν οὐχ ὑφίσταται, ἀλλ' ἐν ταῖς ὑποστάσεσι θεωρεῖται *ib*.3.6(1001Df.); opp. φύσις: explicitly τὰ μὲν ἐπὶ πλειόνων καὶ τῷ ἀριθμῷ διαφερόντων λεγόμενα πραγμάτων καθολικωτέραν τινὰ τὴν σημασίαν ἔχει, οἷον ἄνθρωπος. ὁ γὰρ τοῦτο εἰπὼν τὴν κοινὴν φύσιν ...δείξας...τὰ δὲ ἰδικωτέραν ἔχει τὴν ἔνδειξιν...πράγματός τινος περιγραφή...τὸ ἰδίως λεγόμενον τῷ τῆς ὑ. δηλοῦσθαι ῥήματι Gr.Nyss.*diff. ess*.2f.(M.32.325Bff.); ὁ μὲν τῶν ὑ. λόγος διὰ τὰς ἐνθεωρουμένας ἰδιότητας ἑκάστῳ τὸν διαμερισμὸν ἐπιδέχεται, καὶ κατὰ σύνθεσιν ἐν ἀριθμῷ θεωρεῖται. ἡ δὲ φύσις μία ἐστίν, αὐτὴ πρὸς ἑαυτὴν ἡνωμένη, καὶ ἀδιάτμητος ἀκριβῶς μονάς οὐκ αὐξανομένη...οὐ μειουμένη id.*tres dii*(M.45.120B); Leont.B.*Nest.et Eut*.1(M.86.1280A) = id.*fr*.(M.86.2005A) ∾ Max.*opusc*.(M.91.264A); Leont.B.*arg.Sev*.(M.86.1920Af.,1928Bff.); φύσις...ἔστι κατὰ τοὺς ἁγίους εἰπεῖν πατέρας, τὸ κοινὸν καὶ ἀόριστον... ὑ. δὲ τὸ μερικόν, καὶ καθ' ἑαυτὸ ὑφεστός, οὐσία τις μετὰ συμβεβηκότων, τὴν καθ' αὐτὸ ὕπαρξιν, ἰδιαιρέτως καὶ ἀποτετμημένως τῶν λοιπῶν ὑ., ἐνεργείᾳ καὶ πράγματι, κληρωσαμένη Jo.D.*volunt*.4(M.95.132D); by implication τὸ...ὁμοούσιον...πρὸς τὸ ὁμοούσιον ἕνωσιν καθ' ὑ. οὐκ ἐπιδεχόμενόν ἐστιν, ἀλλὰ κατὰ φύσιν· καθ' ὑ. δὲ τὴν ἰδίαν τελειότητα ἐκδεικνύμενον ‡Ath.*Apoll*.1.12(M.26.1113B); ref. Mc.5:2, Mt.8:28 ὁ μὲν...τὴν οὐσίαν ἐμήνυσεν, ὡς ἀνθρώπεια φύσις ἦν ἡ τυραννουμένη· ὁ δέ τὴν ὑ., ὡς οὐχ εἷς, ἀλλὰ δύο τὸν ἀριθμὸν ἐτύγχανον Mac.Mgn.*apocr*.3.11 (p.76.21f.); οὔτε γὰρ βύβλος ἢ σπόγγος ὕδατι ἐμβαφεὶς...εἰς φύσιν ἥκει μίαν σὺν τῷ ὕδατι, ἀλλ' εἰς ὑ. μίαν Leont.H.*monoph*.(1816A); ἡ ὑ. οὐδὲ τὸ τί ἐστι δηλοῖ, οὐδὲ ὁποῖόν τι ἐστιν, ἀλλὰ τίς ἐστιν...τὰ φύσει διαφέροντα ἄλλο καὶ ἄλλο λέγονται...τῷ δὲ ἀριθμῷ διαφέροντα, ἤγουν ὑ. ἄλλος καὶ ἄλλος λέγονται Jo.D.*dialect*.17(M.94.581Cff.); παντὸς εἰκονιζομένου, οὐχ ἡ φύσις, ἀλλ' ἡ ὑ. εἰκονίζεται· πῶς γὰρ ἂν καὶ εἰκονισθείη φύσις μὴ ἐν ὑ. τεθεωρημένη; Thdr.Stud.*antirr*.3.34(M.99.405A); **b.** in gen. κοινότητά τινα, λόγῳ μόνῳ θεωρητήν, ἐν οὐδεμιᾷ δὲ ὑ. τὸ εἶναι ἔχουσαν Bas.*Spir*.41(3.35D; M.32.144C); ἀπόδυσαι, φησι, τῆς πρώτης ἁμαρτικῆς ζωῆς τὴν ὑ. Cyr.H.*catech*.3.7; ἐποίησεν ἐκ τῶν μὴ ὄντων ὑ. παχείας καὶ σκληράς, οἷον γῆν λέγω Mac.Aeg.*hom*.4.10(M.34.480C); αἰὼν δέ ἐστιν οὐ φύσις ἐν ὑ. γνωριζομένη ἀλλὰ διάστημα Thdr. Mops.*Gal*.1:3ff.(p.5.18; M.66.897D); ἡ ψυχὴ...τὴν ὑ. τῷ σώματι περιγράφεται Gennad.*fr*.(*AP* p.77.7)ap.Leont.et Jo.*sacr*.(M.86.2044C); ὧν...αὐτὸς φύσεων ὑ. ἦν, τούτων καὶ τοὺς οὐσιώδεις φυσικῶς ἐπεδέχετο λόγους Max.*opusc*.(M.91.36B); ὑπόστασιν...σοφίας τὴν ἀρετήν, οὐσίαν δέ φασιν ἀρετῆς εἶναι τὴν σοφίαν *Schol.ib*.(37C); παντὸς... εἴδους ζῴων ἡ πρώτη ὑ. ἀγέννητός ἐστιν ἀλλ' οὐκ ἀγένητος Jo.D.*f.o*.1.8(M.94.817B); **c.** of rational creatures, *being, person* μιᾶς φύσεως πάσης ψυχῆς ὑποκειμένης τῷ θεῷ καὶ...ἑνὸς φυράματος ὄντος τῶν λογικῶν ὑ. Or.*princ*.3.1.22(p.239.7; M.11.297C); θεέ...ἀκατανόητε πάσῃ γεννητῇ ὑ. Serap.*euch*.13.2; οὐκ οὐσίαι δὲ ἐξ οὐσίας, ἀλλ' ὑ. ἐξ ἀγαθότητος τοῦ δημιουργοῦ πεποιημένοι [sc. οἱ ἀπόστολοι] id.*Man*.27 (p.42; M.18.1121C); τὸν νοῦν τὸν ἡμέτερον οὐχ ὑ. ἡγοῦμαι...ἀλλ' ἐνέργειάν τινα...τὸν δὲ Χριστὸν ὑ. λέγω Epiph.*haer*.77.34(p.446.33f.; M.42.692D); σατανᾶς...ἐστιν αὐτὴ ἡ τοῦ διαβόλου ὑ., ἡ καὶ τὸν κύριον πειράζειν ἐπιχειρήσασα Marc.Er.*opusc*.4(M.65.1016A); εἴ τις λέγει, ὅτι πάντων τῶν λογικῶν ἑνὰς μία ἔσται, τῶν ὑ. καὶ τῶν ἀριθμῶν συναιρουμένων τοῖς σώμασι· καὶ ὅτι...ταυτότης ἔσται τῆς γνώσεως, καθάπερ καὶ τῶν ὑ. ... ἀ. ἔ. CCP(543)*anath*.14(Hahn p.229; H.3.285Ef.); **d.** *individuality, identity*, ref. the mustard seed διὰ τὸ μὴ διακόπτεσθαι ἀλλὰ τὴν ἀδιαίρετον σώζειν ὑ. Isid.Pel.*epp*.1.199(M.78.309C); ἄλλη μὲν γὰρ φύσις ὑλογραφίας, καὶ ἑτέρα τοῦ Χριστοῦ· οὐκ ἄλλη δὲ ὑ., ἀλλὰ μία καὶ ἡ αὐτὴ τοῦ Χριστοῦ καὶ τῇ εἰκόνι γεγραμμένη Thdr.Stud.*ep. imag*.(M.99.501B); **e.** καθ' ὑπόστασιν *in one's person, in one's individual existence* ἐφ' ἑαυτοῦ νοεῖσθαί τινα καθ' ὑ. ἰδίαν ὁρώμενον Gr. Nyss.*Eun*.4(2 p.69.21; M.45.641C); *ib*.11(2 p.257.30; 865A); **8.** *substance, property*, Or.*fr.incert.in Jer*.(p.195.8) cit. s. δώρημα; τὸν... ὑποστάσεως καὶ ἐνθήκης ὄντα Epiph.*haer*.61.4(p.384.21; M.41.1045A); Mac.Aeg.*hom*.16.11(M.34.621A); *M.Ariadn*.(p.125.15); Nil.*epp*.2.246 (M.79.328C); Cyr.S.*v.Sab*.73(p.177.7); plur., *possessions, goods*, ‡Ath. *ep.Cast*.2.3(M.28.888A) = Cassian.*inst*.7.17(M.*PL*.49.310B); *Chron. Pasch*.p.394(M.92.1009B); †Gregent.*leg.Hom*.42(M.86.604B); **9.** *value* οὐσίᾳ μὲν ὑπέθετο τὴν ἀρετὴν ὁ ἀπόστολος...χρῆσιν δὲ αὐτῆς οὐκ εἰς δέον, τῷ τἀναντία διαπραττομένους ἀφανίζειν αὐτῆς τὴν ὑ. Thdr.Mops. *Gal*.4:1ff.(p.61.26; M.66.905D); **10.** *financial standing* ἐν ποίᾳ ὑ. ἦσαν οἱ γονεῖς αὐτῆς; Jo.Mosch.*prat*.207(M.87.3097D).

II. Trin.; **A.** *substantive existence, subsistence* οὗ [sc. τοῦ μονογενοῦς] χρήζειν ἔοικε τὸ ἅγιον πνεῦμα διακονοῦντος αὐτοῦ τῇ ὑ., οὐ μόνον εἰς τὸ εἶναι, ἀλλὰ καὶ σοφὸν εἶναι Or.*Jo*.2.10(6; p.65.24; M.14.129A); τῷ υἱῷ δέδωκεν [sc. Origen] ὑπόστασιν Eus.*Marcell*.1.4(p.22.5; M.24.760A); λόγον οὐ προφορικὸν ἀλλὰ λόγον ἐνυπόστατον...ἐκ πατρὸς...ἐν ὑ. γεννηθέντα Cyr.H.*catech*.11.10; τὴν...φύσιν τοῦ πατρὸς ἀνενέργητον ὡς πρὸς τὴν ὑ. τοῦ υἱοῦ μεῖναι; Gr.Nyss.*Eun*.4(2 p.78.12; M.45.652C); τοῖς ἐν ὑ. τριῶν προσώπων...μίαν καὶ τὴν αὐτὴν ὁμολογοῦσι θεότητα Soz.*h.e*.7.9.5(M.67.1437A); Χριστὸν...οὐδὲ ἄλλοθέν ποθεν ἢ ἐκ τοῦ πατρὸς τὴν ὑ. ἔχοντα Sophr.H.*ep.syn*.(M.87.3152C).

B. *one having substantive existence, subsistent entity*, in Trin. contexts freq. approx. *Person*, though in the Cappadocians it denotes rather *individual*; **1.** in gen. θρησκεύομεν...τὸν πατέρα τῆς ἀληθείας καὶ τὸν υἱὸν τὴν ἀλήθειαν, ὄντα δύο τῇ ὑ. πράγματα, ἓν δὲ τῇ ὁμονοίᾳ...καὶ τῇ ταυτότητι τοῦ βουλήματος Or.*Cels*.8.12(p.229.32; M. 11.1533C); περὶ τοῦ θελήματος τοῦ θεοῦ εἰ δύναται τάσσεσθαι ἐπὶ Χριστοῦ· ἵν' ὥσπερ ἐστὶ θεοῦ δύναμις...οὕτως ᾖ καὶ θέλημα αὐτοῦ, θεοῦ ὑ. ἔχον αὐτό id.*comm.in Eph*.1:1(p.235); cf.id.*hom.13.4 in Lev*. (p.474.11; M.12.549B); *est ergo haec trium distinctio personarum in patre et filio et spiritu sancto...sed...unus est fons; una enim substantia est et natura trinitatis*, id.*hom.12.1 in Num*.(p.95.13; M.12.657B); ὁ τοῦ θεοῦ [sc. λόγος]...ἔχων...καθ' ἑαυτὸν οἰκείαν ὑ. ... ἰδίως μὲν ὑφεστῶσαν Eus.*d.e*.5.5(p.228.30; M.22.377B); τὴν ὑ. αὐτοῦ συνίστησιν ὁ...εὐαγγελιστής id.*e.th*.1.20(p.82.32; M.24.869A); δύο πάλιν ὑ. αὐτός [sc. ὁ λόγος ἐν τῇ σαρκί] τε καὶ ὁ πατὴρ ὑπῆρχον *ib*.(p.87.27; 877A); φοβῇ...μὴ δύο ὑ. ὁμολογήσας δύο ἀρχὰς εἰσαγάγοις;... ἀλλὰ...γίνωσκε, ὡς ὁ δύο δοὺς ὑ. πατρὸς καὶ υἱοῦ...οὐ δύο θεοὺς ἀνάγκη δοῦναι τὸν τὰς δύο ὑ. τιθέντα *ib*.2.7(p.104.3; 908C); ὑποστάσεις οἱ ἀνατολικοὶ λέγουσιν, ἵνα τὰς ἰδιότητας τῶν προσώπων ὑφεστώσας καὶ ὑπαρχούσας γνωρίσωσιν Geo.Laod.*ep.dogm*.ap.Epiph.*haer*.73.16 (p.288.21; M.42.432D); οὔτε τρεῖς ὑ. μεμερισμένας καθ' ἑαυτάς, ὥσπερ σωματοφυῶς ἐπ' ἀνθρώπων Ath.*exp.fid*.2(M.25.204A); εἷς θεὸς ἐν τρισὶν ὑ. id.*inc.et c.Ar*.10(M.26.1000B); λέγοντα [sc. the trisagion] τὰς τρεῖς ὑ. τελείας δεικνύντα...ὡς ἐν τῷ λέγειν τὸ 'κύριος', τὴν μίαν οὐσίαν id.*hom.in Mt.11:27*(M.25.220A); τρεῖς ὑ., μία θεότης id.*virg*.1(p.35.10; M.28.252A); ἅπαξ...γεννηθεὶς...ὑ. ἐστί, στάσιν ἀδιάλυτον ἔχων, ὑφ' ὧν καὶ εἶναι πέφυκε ‡Ath.*annunt*.4(M.28.921C); μήτε συγχέοντες τὰς ὑ., μήτε τὴν οὐσίαν διαιροῦντες. ἄλλη γὰρ ὑ. τοῦ πατρός, ἄλλη τοῦ υἱοῦ ἄλλη τοῦ ἁγίου πνεύματος. ἀλλὰ...μία ἐστὶν ἡ θεότης ‡Ath.*symb*.4 (M.28.1588Df.); θεότητος καὶ δυνάμεως καὶ οὐσίας μιᾶς τοῦ πατρὸς καὶ τοῦ υἱοῦ καὶ τοῦ ἁγίου πνεύματος πιστευομένης...ἐν τρισὶ τελειοτάταις ὑ., ἤγουν...προσώποις CCP(381)*ep*.ap.Thdt.*h.e*.5.9.11(3.1031); τὰς ὑ. μὴ ἀθετεῖτε· τὸ ὄνομα τοῦ Χριστοῦ μὴ ἀρνεῖσθε Bas.*ep*.207.4(3.312C; M.32.765C); ref. *Symb.Nic*.(325)*anath*. οὐ...ταυτὸν εἶπον ἐκεῖ οὐσίαν καὶ ὑ. ... δῆλον, ὅτι, ὡς τῶν μὲν ἀρνουμένων ἐκ τῆς οὐσίας εἶναι τοῦ πατρός, τῶν δὲ λεγόντων, οὔτε ἐκ τῆς οὐσίας ἀλλ' ἐξ ἄλλης τινὸς ὑ., οὕτως ἀμφότερα...ἀπηγόρευσαν *ib*.125.1(215Cf.; M.548A); οὐσία...καὶ ὑ. ταύτην ἔχει τὴν διαφοράν, ἣν ἔχει τὸ κοινὸν πρὸς τὸ καθ' ἕκαστον... διὰ τοῦτο οὐσίαν μὲν μίαν ἐπὶ τῆς θεότητος ὁμολογοῦμεν...ὑ. δὲ ἰδιάζουσαν *ib*.236.6(363Ef.; M.884A); οὐ γὰρ ἀνυπόστατα ἢ κατὰ μιᾶς ὑ., ὡς εἶναι τὸν πλοῦτον ἡμῖν ἐν ὀνόμασιν, ἀλλ' οὐ πράγμασι Gr.Naz.*or*. 6.22(M.35.749C); χρὴ τὸν ἕνα θεὸν τηρεῖν, καὶ τὰς τρεῖς ὑ. ὁμολογεῖν, εἴτ' οὖν τρία πρόσωπα, καὶ ἑκάστην μετὰ τῆς ἰδιότητος *ib*.20.6(1072C); τρισὶ μέν, κατὰ τὰς ἰδιότητας, εἴτουν ὑ. ... εἴτε πρόσωπα...ἑνὶ δέ, κατὰ τὸν τῆς οὐσίας λόγον *ib*.39.11(M.36.345C); δεξιὰν τοῦ πατρὸς τὴν τοῦ θεοῦ λέγομεν δύναμιν...ἥτις ἐστὶν ὁ κύριος, οὐχ ὡς μέρος ἐξηρτημένη τοῦ ὅλου, ἀλλ' ὡς ἐξ ἐκείνου μὲν οὖσα, ἐφ' ἑαυτῆς δὲ κατ' ἰδίαν ὑ. θεωρουμένη Gr.Nyss.*Eun*.6(2 p.135.29; M.45.720D); *ib*.2(2 p.301.22; 472D), cf.*ib*.7(2 p.168.3; 757C) citt. s. διαφορά; ἵνα...τὸ τῆς φύσεως [sc. τοῦ πνεύματος] ὑπερέχον ἐνδείξηται, καὶ τὸ τῆς ὑ. ἰδιάζον μὴ συγχέῃ τῷ λόγῳ *ib*.(2 p.155.15; 744B); πνεῦμα...δύναμιν οὐσιώδη αὐτὴν ἐφ' ἑαυτῆς ἐν ἰδιαζούσῃ ὑ. θεωρουμένην...καθ' ὁμοιότητα τοῦ θεοῦ λόγου καθ' ὑπόστασιν οὖσαν, προαιρετικήν, αὐτοκίνητον, ἐνεργὸν id.*or.catech*. 2(p.15.3ff.; M.45.17C); λόγον ἐν οὐσίᾳ καὶ πνεῦμα ἐν ὑ. λέγειν ὑφηγούμενον [sc. τὸ τῆς ἀληθείας μυστήριον] *ib*.4(p.19.14; 20C); μήτ' οὖν ἀριθμῷ συγχέῃς ὑ. ... ὁ μὲν προσώπων συγχέων ὑπόστασιν, ὁ δ' αὖ μερίζων δυσσεβῶς τὴν οὐσίαν Amph.*Seleuc*.196,206(M.37.1599A); αἱ γραφαὶ διὰ τὸ ταὐτὸν τῆς θεότητος ποτὲ μὲν μίαν τῶν θείων ὑ., ποτὲ δὲ τὰς τρεῖς ὀνομάζουσιν· καὶ ἑκάστῃ αὐτῶν ὁμοίως τὸ ἀγαθὸν ἀπονέμουσιν Didym.*Trin*.1.18(M.39.341C); ἐν...εἶναι τῇ θεότητι τὰς ὑ. καὶ ἐν ἑνάδι οὐσίας διέσταλκε δίχα τὰ πρόσωπα *ib*.3.2(789D); ‡Just.*qu.et resp*. 139(M.6.1392C) cit. s. διαφέρω; *ib*.129(1380D); σὺν τῷ ἰδίῳ πληρώματι τῆς αὐτοῦ θεότητος καὶ τῇ ἰδίᾳ ὑ. τοῦ θεοῦ λόγου καὶ ἐνυποστάτου, συμπεριλαβὼν τὸ εἶναι ἄνθρωπος Epiph.*anc*.75(p.95.6; M.43.157C); ἰδοὺ τὸ πνεῦμα τὸ ἅγιον ἐν εἴδει περιστερᾶς...καθ' ἑαυτὸ ὑ. ὂν...καὶ πάλιν περὶ τοῦ πνεύματος...ἐδίδασκεν [Jo.16:7f.]...ἵνα δείξῃ ὑπόστασιν καὶ ὑπόστασιν *ib*.81(p.102.10,20; 169C,172A); id.*haer*.25.6(p.273.25; M.41.328D) cit. s. δοξολογία; θεὸς εἷς ἐν τρισὶν ὑ. ἐστι καὶ ὀνομάζεται Mac.Mgn.*apocr*.4.25(p.209.21); ὁ λόγος οὐσία τίς ἐστιν ἐνυπόστατος...ἀεὶ θεὸς πρὸς θεὸν ἦν, ἐν ὑ. μέντοι ἰδίᾳ Chrys.*hom.4.1 in Jo*.(8.27E); διαιρῶν τὰς ὑ. φησὶν [Jo.14:9] *ib*.74.1(435B); id.

incomprehens.5.2(1.482Bff.); ἐν τῷ πνεύματι ὁ πατὴρ καὶ υἱός ἐστιν, οὐ συγχύσει τριῶν ὑ., ἀλλὰ τῇ ἑνώσει τῆς...θεότητος Marc.Er.*opusc*. 4(M.65.1009A); τρεῖς ἀρχικὰς ὑ. ὑποτιθέμενοι...καὶ μέχρι τριῶν ὑ. τὴν οὐσίαν τοῦ θεοῦ προσήκειν ἰσχυρισάμενοι...ταῖς Χριστιανῶν συμφέρονται δόξαις Cyr.*Juln*.8(6².270Bf.); δέδωκεν ἑαυτὸν τῷ υἱῷ· οὐχ ὡς σῶμα χωρήσας ἐν σώματι, οὐδ' ὡς τῷ υἱῷ παραχωρήσας τὴν ἰδίαν ὑ. καὶ ἐν αὐτῷ λοιπὸν τὸ εἶναι ἔχων id.*thes*.14(5¹.145C); πῶς οὖν ἄρα δέδωκεν [sc. ὁ θεὸς τῷ υἱῷ] ὡς οὐκ ὄντι ἑτέρῳ κατά γε τὸν τῆς ὁμοουσιότητος λόγον, κἂν εἰς ὑ. ἰδικὴν ἑκάτερος ἀπετέμνετο; μία γὰρ ἡ τῆς ἀνωτάτω θεότητος φύσις ἐν τρισὶν ὑ. ἰδικαῖς νοουμένη id.*Is*.3.5(2.540A); γεγεννῆσθαι φαμὲν ἀληθῶς ἐκ τῆς τοῦ πατρὸς οὐσίας τὸν υἱὸν... καὶ ἐν ἰδίᾳ μὲν ὑ. νοεῖσθαι, τῇ δὲ ταυτότητι τῆς οὐσίας ἐνοῦσθαι τῷ γεγεννηκότι id.*ep*.1(p.13.26; 5².6B); ἀνύπαρκτόν τε καὶ ἰδικῶς οὐχ ὑφεστηκότα φαντάζονται τὸν μονογενῆ, καὶ οὐκ εἶναι μὲν ἐν ὑ. τῇ καθ' ἑαυτόν, ῥῆμα δὲ ἁπλῶς id.*Thds*.(p.50.27; 5².12B) = *inc.unigen*.(5¹.686A); ἐν τῇ φυσικῇ ταυτότητι ἕν ἐστιν ὁ ἐκ θεοῦ λόγος πρὸς τὸν... πατέρα, εἰ καὶ νοεῖται καθ' ὑπόστασιν ἑκάτερος ἰδικήν id.*Arcad*.(p.91.15; 5².86A); οὐκ ἐν οὐσίᾳ μᾶλλον ἑτέρᾳ παρὰ τὴν ὡς θεοῦ, ἀλλ' ἐν ὑ. τῇ ὡς υἱοῦ id.*dial.Trin*.1(5¹.408D); cf. Κύριλλος, ὅτε τὸ ὄντως σημαινόμενον τῆς οὐσίας καὶ τῆς ὑ. δηλῶσαι ἠβουλήθη, διαρρήδην τὸ πρὸς ἄλληλα διάφορον αὐτῶν ἐκήρυξεν Eub.*fr*.ap.*Doct.Patr*.22(p.148.8); 'ἡμετέραν' εἰρηκώς, τὸν τῶν ὑ. δεδήλωκεν ἀριθμόν Thdt.*qu.19 in Gen*.(1.23); τριάδα ὁμοούσιον, μίαν θεότητα ἐν τρισὶν ὑ., ἤγουν προσώποις CCP(553)*can*.1; in this sense also rendered by *substantia* in the West: cf. *dictum est a nostris Graecis una essentia, tres substantiae: a Latinis autem, una essentia vel substantia, tres personae; quia...non aliter in sermone nostro...essentia quam substantia solet intelligi*, Aug.*Trin*.7.4.7(M.*PL*.42.939); *ib*.7.4.9(M.942); *ib*.7.5.10(M.942); *est igitur et hominis quidem essentia, i.e.* οὐσία, *et subsistentia, i.e.* οὐσίωσις, *et* ὑπόστασις, *i.e. substantia, et* πρόσωπον *i.e. persona:* οὐσία *quidem atque essentia, quoniam est;*...ὑ. *vero atque substantia, quoniam subest ceteris, quae subsistentiae non sunt, i.e.* οὐσιώσεις...*dicimus unam esse* οὐσίαν *vel* οὐσίωσιν, *i.e. essentiam vel subsistentiam deitatis; sed tres* ὑ., *i.e. tres substantias*, Boethius *Eut.et Nest*.(M.*PL*.64.1345Af.); *fides apud Graecos de trinitate hoc modo est: una* οὐσία, *ac si dicat una natura aut una essentia: tres* ὑποστάσεις, *quod resonat in Latinum vel tres personas vel tres substantias. nam Latinitas proprie non dicit de deo nisi essentiam; substantiam vero non proprie dicit, sed abusive; quoniam vere substantia apud Graecos persona intelligitur, non natura*, Isid.H.*etym*. 7.4.11f.; other writers rendered by *subsistentia*, opp. substantia as equivalent of οὐσία: cf. (ref. CAlex.(362)*ep*.) *de differentia substantiarum et subsistentiarum sermo ejus per scripturam motus est. Graeci* οὐσίας *et* ὑ. *vocant. quidam etenim dicebant substantiam et subsistentiam unum videri; et quia tres subsistentias non dicimus in deo. alii vero...dicebant quia substantia ipsam rei alicujus naturam rationemque, qua constat, designat: subsistentia autem uniusquisque personae, hoc ipsum quod exstat et subsistit, ostendat*, Rufin.*h.e*.1.29 (M.*PL*.21.499Cf.); *deus...in subsistentia triplex est, quia sibi quisque subsistit, ita in substantia simplex*, Faustus *ep*.7(M.*PL*.58.858A); *tria nunc in una deitate doceamus, tria nomina non tria regna...tres hypostases vel subsistentias, sed non tres substantias*, Paschasius Diac.*de Spiritu sancto* 1.4(M.*PL*.62.13A); ‡Ambr.*symb*.2(M.*PL*.17.511B); **2.** in various Trin. controversies; **a.** ref. Montanists (acc. Didym.) Μοντανιστῶν ἡ πλάνη...ὅτι ἀπομαντεύονται ἓν πρόσωπον εἶναι τῶν τριῶν θείων ὑ. Didym.*Trin*.3.41(M.39.984B); **b.** ref. Monarchians οἱ συγχέοντες πατρὸς καὶ υἱοῦ ἔννοιαν καὶ τῇ ὑ. ἕνα διδόντες εἶναι τὸν πατέρα καὶ τὸν υἱόν Or.*comm.in Mt*.17.14(p.624.13; M.13.1520B); οἰόμενοι προφορὰν πατρικὴν...εἶναι τὸν υἱὸν τοῦ θεοῦ, καὶ κατὰ τοῦτο ὑπόστασιν αὐτῷ...οὐ διδόασιν id.*Jo*.1.24(23; p.29.24; M.14.65B); δογματίζων μηδὲ οὐσίαν τινὰ ἰδίαν ὑφεστάναι τοῦ ἁγίου πνεύματος ἑτέραν παρὰ τὸν πατέρα καὶ τὸν υἱόν...ἡμεῖς μέντοι γε τρεῖς ὑ. πειθόμενοι τυγχάνειν *ib*.2.10(6; p.65.16; 128A); *ib*.10.37(21; p.212.16; 376B) cit. s. διαφέρω; οὐ γὰρ ἐν ψιλαῖς φαντασίαις τοῦ θεοῦ...τὴν ὑ. ἔχει ἡ σοφία αὐτοῦ κατὰ τὰ ἀνὰ λόγον τοῖς ἀνθρωπίνοις ἐννοήμασι, φαντάσματα. εἰ δέ τις οἷός τέ ἐστιν ἀσώματον ὑ. ... ζῶσαν καὶ οἱονεὶ ἔμψυχον ἐπινοεῖν, εἴσεται τὴν ...σοφίαν τοῦ θεοῦ *ib*.1.34(39; p.43.18; 89B); esp. Sabellius εἰ τῷ τρεῖς εἶναι τὰς ὑ. μεμερισμένας εἶναι λέγουσι, τρεῖς εἰσι, κἂν μὴ θέλωσιν, ἢ τὴν θείαν τριάδα παντελῶς ἀνελέτωσαν Dion.Al.*fr*. ap.Bas.*Spir*.72(3.61A; M.32.201C); ὀνόμασιν μὲν διαφόροις πατρὸς καὶ υἱοῦ χρηματίζοντα οὐσίᾳ δὲ καὶ ὑ. ἓν ὄντα...τὸν Σαβέλλιον ὑποδυόμενος Eus.*Marcell*.1.1(p.4.26; M.24.720A); μαίνεται...Σαβέλλιος λέγων...τὸν υἱὸν εἶναι πατέρα, ὑ. μὲν ἕν, ὀνόματι δὲ δύο ‡Ath.*Ar*.4.25(p.72.22; M.26.505C); ὁ...ἓν πρᾶγμα πολυπρόσωπον λέγων [sc. ὁ Σαβελλισμός] πατέρα καὶ υἱὸν καὶ ἅγιον πνεῦμα, καὶ μίαν τῶν τριῶν τὴν ὑ. ἐκτιθέμενος Bas.*ep*.210.3(3.315A; M.32.772B); πατέρα καὶ υἱὸν ἐπινοίᾳ μὲν εἶναι δύο, ὑ. δὲ ἓν *ib*.210.5(316D; M.776A) reported as words of Gr. Thaum. but v. not. ad loc.; ὥσπερ ὁ τὸ κοινὸν τῆς οὐσίας μὴ ὁμολογῶν, εἰς πολυθεΐαν ἐκπίπτει· οὕτως ὁ τὸ ἰδιάζον τῶν ὑ. μὴ διδούς, εἰς τὸν Ἰουδαϊσμὸν ὑποφέρεται...οὐ γὰρ ἐξαρκεῖ διαφορὰς προσώπων ἀπαριθμήσασθαι, ἀλλὰ χρὴ ἕκαστον πρόσωπον ἐν ὑ. ἀληθινῇ ὑπάρχον ὁμολογεῖν *ib*.(316Ef.; M.776Bf.); Σαβελλίου...λέγοντος· ἕνα μὲν εἶναι τῇ ὑ. τὸν θεόν, προσωποποιεῖσθαι δὲ ὑπὸ τῆς γραφῆς διαφόρως, κατὰ τὸ ἰδίωμα τῆς ὑποκειμένης ἑκάστοτε χρείας *ib*.214.3(322C; M.788C); ὃν Σαβέλλιος λέγει 'τριώνυμον', τοῦτον Εὐνόμιος ὀνομάζει 'ἀγέννητον'· οὐδέτερος δὲ τούτων ἐν τῇ τριάδι τῶν ὑ. θεωρεῖ τὴν θεότητα Gr.Nyss. *Eun*.10(2 p.234.29; M.45.836D); τὴν Σαβελλίου πλάνην φαντάζεται, ὡς οὐκ ὄντος τοῦ υἱοῦ καθ' ἑαυτόν, τῇ δὲ τοῦ πατρὸς ὑ. προσαλιφέντος *ib*.(2 p.249.19; 853B); δογματίζει...τὸν αὐτὸν εἶναι πατέρα...υἱόν... ἅγιον πνεῦμα· ὡς εἶναι ἐν μιᾷ ὑ. τρεῖς ὀνομασίας...ὡς ἐὰν ᾖ ἐν ἡλίῳ ὄντι μὲν ἐν μιᾷ ὑ., τρεῖς δὲ ἔχοντι τὰς ἐνεργείας Epiph.*haer*.62.1(p.689.13ff.; M.41.1052B); **c.** ref. Paul. Sam. ἠναγκάσθησαν οἱ πατέρες, οἱ κρίναντες Παῦλον τὸν Σαμοσατέα...ἵνα δείξωσιν ὅτι ὁ υἱὸς ὑ. ἔχει Geo. Laod.*ep.dogm*.ap.Epiph.*haer*.73.12(p.285.5; M.42.428B); οὗτος [sc. Paul. Sam.]...ἀναιρεῖ...τὴν τοῦ υἱοῦ θεότητα καὶ ὑ. καὶ τοῦ ἁγίου πνεύματος Epiph.*haer*.65.3(p.5.12; 16A); ἔστι γὰρ ταὐτὸν τῇ θεότητι καὶ τῇ οὐσίᾳ ὁ υἱὸς πρὸς τὸν πατέρα...οὐδὲ ἀπὸ ἄλλης ὑ. ἀλλὰ ὡς ἀληθῶς υἱὸς πατρὸς τῇ τε οὐσίᾳ καὶ τῇ ὑ. καὶ τῇ ἀληθείᾳ *ib*.65.8(p.11.13; 25B); **d.** ref. Marcellus, Eus.*Marcell*.2.4(p.57.12; M.24.821A) cit. s. ἐνέργεια; id.*e.th*.1.1(p.63.5; M.24.829C) cit. s. υἱός; ἀχώριστον αὐτὸν τῇ ὑ. ἓν καὶ ταὐτὸν εἶναι τῷ πατρὶ παρίστησιν *ib*.1.17(p.77.23; 860A); Μάρκελλος...πάντα φύρας, ποτὲ μὲν εἰς αὐτὸν ὅλον τὸν Σαβελλίου βυθὸν χωρεῖ, ποτὲ δὲ Παύλου τοῦ Σαμοσατέως ἀνανεοῦσθαι πειρᾶται τὴν αἵρεσιν, ποτὲ δὲ Ἰουδαῖος ὢν ἄντικρυς ἀπελέγχεται· μίαν γὰρ ὑ. τριπρόσωπον ὥσπερ καὶ τριώνυμον εἰσάγει *ib*.3.6(p.164.26; 1016A); Μάρκελλος ἐτόλμησεν ἀσεβῶν εἰς τὴν ὑ. τοῦ...Χριστοῦ, καὶ ψιλὸν αὐτὸν ἐξηγούμενος λόγον Bas.*ep*.125.1(3.215B; M.32.545C); οὔτε τὰς τρεῖς ὑ. ὁμολογεῖν ἤθελον Epiph.*haer*.72.1(p.255.20; M.42.384A); Μάρκελλος ...ἠρνήθη τῶν ὑ. τὴν τριάδα Thdt.*haer*.2.10(4.336); **e.** ref. Arians ὁ κύριος...οὐ πατέρα ἑαυτὸν ἀναγορεύων οὐδὲ τὰς τῇ ὑ. δύο φύσεις μίαν εἶναι σαφηνίζων Alex.Al.*ep.Alex*.9(p.25.23; M.18.561B); *ib*.4(p.22.10; 553A) cit. s. ἰδιότροπος; ἡ θεότης οὐχ ἓν πρόσωπόν ἐστι κατὰ τὴν Ἰουδαίων ὑπόληψιν, ἀλλὰ τρία πρόσωπα καθ' ὑ. ἀληθινήν, οὐκ ὀνόματι ψιλῷ Hosius ap.Gel.Cyz.*h.e*.2.12.2(M.85.1249B); εἰ...'ἦν ὅτε οὐκ ἦν' τὸ ἀπαύγασμα· ποῦ ἡ ἀπαυγάζουσα αὐτὸ ὑ. τοῦ φωτός; Didym. *Trin*.1.15(M.39.308B); accusation by Arians λέγοντες, τὸν υἱὸν κατὰ τὴν ὑ. ὁμοούσιον λέγεσθαι παρ' ἡμῶν Bas.*ep*.214.3(3.322A; M.32.788B); ref. Sabellius and Arius ἐκεῖνοι...διὰ τῶν ἐναντίων, εἰς τὸ ἴσον κακὸν ἐμπεπτώκασιν· ὁ μὲν διὰ τὴν οὐσίαν εἰς μίαν ὑ. συγχέων τὰς ὑ., ὁ δὲ διὰ τὰς ὑ. συνδιαιρῶν ταύταις καὶ τὴν οὐσίαν Leont.B.*Nest.et Eut*.1 (M.86.1276C); its use as equivalent to οὐσία (v. infra II.D.4) forbidden by Arianizing councils τὸ...ὄνομα τῆς οὐσίας...περιαιρεθῆναι ...μήτε μὴν δεῖν ἐπὶ προσώπου πατρὸς καὶ υἱοῦ καὶ ἁγίου πνεύματος μίαν ὑ. ὀνομάζεσθαι *Symb.Nic*.(359)ap.Thdt.*h.e*.2.21.7(3.881); cf. οὐδὲ ὀφείλει ὑ. περὶ πατρὸς καὶ υἱοῦ καὶ ἁγίου πνεύματος ὀνομάζεσθαι *ib*. ap.Ath.*syn*.30(p.259.16; M.26.748C); Ἄρειον...μήτε...οὐσίαν αὐτὸν [sc. θεόν] εἶναι δογματίζειν μήτε ὑ. μήτε ἄλλο μηδὲν ὧν ὀνομάζεται Philost.*h.e*.10.2(M.65.584C); Socr.*h.e*.3.7.13f.(M.67.393A).

C. exeg. Heb.1:3 variously interpreted: cf. *figura expressa substantiae vel subsistentiae ejus*, Or.*princ*.1.2.8(p.38.2ff.; M.11.136B); early writers gen. treat as *substance, reality* πότε δὲ ἡ τῆς...ὑ. τοῦ πατρὸς εἰκών, ὁ χαρακτήρ,...οὐκ ἦν; *ib*.4.4.1(p.349.21); τὸν υἱὸν...τὸν ...χαρακτῆρα τῆς ὑ. ἀεὶ ὄντα...ὡς τὸν ἰδόντα τοῦτον, ὁρᾶν ἐν αὐτῷ καὶ τὴν ὑ., ἧς καὶ χαρακτήρ ἐστιν Ath.*Ar*.2.33(M.26.217B); τίς τολμᾷ λέγειν ἀλλότριον εἶναι τὸν χαρακτῆρα τῆς ὑ. *ib*.2.32(216B); εἰ... ὑπάρχοντος φωτός, ἔστιν εἰκὼν αὐτοῦ τὸ ἀπαύγασμα· καὶ οὔσης ὑ. ἔστι ταύτης ὁ χαρακτὴρ ὁλόκληρος *ib*.1.20(53B); ὅταν...ὁ...χαρακτὴρ πάσῃ τῇ ὑ. τοῦ πατρὸς ἐπιθεωρούμενος τὸ ἀνελλιπὲς τοῦ ἰδίου μεγέθους διασημαίνῃ, καὶ ἡ μορφὴ τοῦ θεοῦ τὴν διὰ πάντων καταμηνύῃ ταυτότητα Gr. Nyss.*Eun*.8(2 p.192.3; M.45.788A); τὸν ἄνθρωπον εἶναι τῆς τοῦ θεοῦ δόξης ἀπαύγασμα, καὶ ἐν τῷ σαρκίνῳ θεῷ...τὴν τοῦ θεοῦ ὑ. χαρακτηρίζεσθαι id.*Apoll*.19(M.45.1160C); ἄλλο δέ ἐστιν ἄνθρωπον εἰκόνα εἶναι θεοῦ...καὶ ἄλλο ἐστίν, κατὰ τὸ σύμμορφον...ἀπαύγασμα εἶναι δόξης, καὶ χαρακτῆρα ὑποστάσεως ἐνυπόστατον Didym.*Trin*.1.16(M.39.337B); but clarification of terminology which associated ὑ. with Person in Trin. set a problem in exegesis, Gr.Nyss.*diff.ess*.6(M.32.336Cf.); οὕτως οἴεται δεῖν ὁ ἀπόστολος...τὸ προσεχὲς...τοῦ μονογενοῦς πρὸς τὸν πατέρα...παρίστησιν, οὐχ ὡς οὐκ ὄντος ἐν ὑ. καὶ τοῦ μονογενοῦς· ἀλλ' ὡς οὐ παραδεχομένου μεσότητά τινα τῆς ἑαυτοῦ πρὸς τὸν πατέρα ἑνώσεως· ὥστε τὸν τῷ χαρακτῆρι τοῦ μονογενοῦς...ἐνατενίσαντα καὶ τῆς τοῦ πατρὸς ὑ. ἐν περινοίᾳ γενέσθαι *ib*.7(337Df.); ὁ τοῦ υἱοῦ τὴν οἱονεὶ μορφὴν τῇ διανοίᾳ λαβών, τῆς πατρικῆς ὑ. τὸν χαρακτῆρα ἀνετυπώσατο, βλέπων διὰ τούτου ἐκεῖνον, οὐ τὴν ἀγεννησίαν τοῦ πατρὸς ...ἀλλὰ τὸ ἀγέννητον κάλλος ἐν τῷ γεννητῷ κατοπτεύσας...ὥστε ἡ τοῦ υἱοῦ ὑ. οἱονεὶ μορφὴ καὶ πρόσωπον γίνεται τοῦ πατρὸς ἐπιγνώσεως· καὶ ἡ τοῦ πατρὸς ὑ. ἐν τῇ τοῦ υἱοῦ μορφῇ ἐπιγινώσκεται, μενούσης αὐτοῖς τῆς ἐπιθεωρουμένης ἰδιότητος εἰς διάκρισιν ἐναργῆ τῶν ὑ. *ib.*8(340Bf.); other interpretations in terms of subsistence δηλῶν...ὅτι ὥσπερ ἐστὶν ὁ πατὴρ ἐνυπόστατος, καὶ πρὸς ὑπόστασιν οὐδενὸς δεόμενος· οὕτω καὶ ὁ υἱός Chrys.*hom.2.1 in Heb.*(12.14B); οὐσίαν μίαν ἔλαβε καὶ ὑ. εἰς δύο ὑποστάσεων παράστασιν...ἑνός τινος ἐπελάβετο εἰς τὴν τῶν δύο ὑ. *ib.2.2*(12.16Cf.); τὸ μὲν πρῶτον [sc. ἀπαύγασμα τῆς δόξης]...εἰς ἀπόδειξιν τοῦ ἐκ τῆς οὐσίας ἀμερῶς εἶναι, τὸ δὲ δεύτερον, ὅτι οὐκ ἀνυπόστατον Sever.*Heb.*1:3(p.346.26); Isid.Pel.*epp.*3.18(M.78.744D); original line of exegesis persisted ἀκριβῆ...φησί, σώζει τὸν χαρακτῆρα τῆς φύσεως ὥστε ὅπερ ἂν ἐκείνην νοήσῃς τὴν ὑ., τοῦτο νόει καὶ ταύτην εἶναι Thdr.Mops.*Heb.*1:2f.(p.201.34); ταῖς ἡμετέραις ἐμπρέπει ψυχαῖς ὁ χαρακτὴρ τῆς ὑ. τοῦ θεοῦ καὶ πατρός, ἀναμορφοῦντος ἡμᾶς τοῦ ἁγίου πνεύματος, δι' ἁγιασμοῦ, πρὸς αὐτόν Cyr.*Is.*4.2(2.591B); χαρακτὴρ τῆς ὑ. τῆς τοῦ πατρὸς οὐσίας ὁ υἱός id.*thes.*12(5[1].110B); id.*dial.Trin.*5(5[1].558B); Leont.H.*Nest.*2.1(M.86.1525C,1532A).

D. as equivalent of οὐσία, *substance*; influence of Heb.1:3 together with use of *substantia* as its Latin counterpart account for many, though not all, of instances where ὑ. denotes divine essence; where it parallels οὐσία the emphasis lies on the *actual existence*, the *reality* of substance; cf. *ne forte ipsa ὑ. (id est substantia) ejus corporeum aliquid habeat...quis unquam...magnitudinem in sapientia requisivit?* Or.*princ.*1.2.2(p.28.20; M.11.130C); ‡Ath.*dial.Trin.*1.19(M.28.1148A) cit. s. στόμα; *ib.*1.4(1121C) cit. s. ἐντολή; ref. Son οὐ χρῄζειν ἔοικε τὸ ἅγιον πνεῦμα διακονοῦντος αὐτοῦ τῇ ὑ., οὐ μόνον εἰς τὸ εἶναι, ἀλλὰ καὶ σοφὸν εἶναι Or.*Jo.*2.10(6; p.65.24; M.14.129A); **1.** in Monarchian controversy, Dion.R.ap.Ath.*decr.*26 (p.22.3; M.25.461D) cit. s. δύναμις; **2.** agst. Paul. Sam. τὸν υἱόν... σοφίαν καὶ λόγον καὶ δύναμιν θεοῦ, πρὸ αἰώνων ὄντα οὐ προγνώσει ἀλλ' οὐσίᾳ καὶ ὑποστάσει, θεὸν...ὁμολογοῦμεν Hymen.*ep.*(p.324.24); ταύτην...τὴν ὑ. οὐσίαν ἐκάλεσαν οἱ πατέρες [i.e. CAnt.(269)] Geo.Laod. *ep.dogm.*ap.Epiph.*haer.*73.12(p.285.28; M.42.428D); **3.** Marcellus εἰς τὴν ἀνθρωπίνην ἣν ὁ τοῦ θεοῦ λόγος ἀνείληφεν σάρκα ἀφορῶν [sc. Ἀστέριος] καὶ δι' αὐτὴν οὕτω [sc. 'δύο ὑποστάσεις'] φανταζόμενος Marcell.*fr.*57 ap.Eus.*e.th.*2.19(p.123.8; M.24.944A); τὸν υἱὸν ὑποστάσει διῃρημένον...φάσκοι Marcell.*fr.*58 *ib.*(p.123.18; 944B); Marcell. *fr.*60 *ib.*3.4(p.158.33; 1005A); ὁμολογοῦμεν πατέρα ἀΐδιον, υἱοῦ ἀιδίου ὄντος καὶ ὑφεστῶτος· καὶ πνεῦμα ἅγιον ἀιδίως ὂν καὶ ὑφεστός. οὐ γὰρ ἀνυπόστατον τὴν τριάδα λέγομεν· ἀλλ' ἐν ὑ. αὐτὴν γινώσκομεν Eugen.*exp.fid.*2(M.18.1304B); **4.** in Arian controversy ἴδιον οὐδὲν ἔχει τοῦ θεοῦ καθ' ὑπόστασιν ἰδιότητος Ar.*Thal.fr.*2.8 ap.Ath.*syn.*15 (p.242.16; M.26.705D); τρεῖς εἰσιν ὑ. καὶ ὁ μὲν θεὸς...ἔστιν ἄναρχος ...ὁ δὲ υἱὸς...πρὸ αἰώνων κτισθεὶς id.*ep.Alex.ib.*16(p.244.8; 709B); τοὺς δὲ λέγοντας...ἐξ ἑτέρας ὑ. ἢ οὐσίας...ἀναθεματίζει ἡ...ἐκκλησία *Symb.Nic.*(325)(p.52)ap.Eus.*ep.Caes.*4(M.20.1540C); repeated in *Symb.Ant.*(341)4 ap.Ath.*syn.*25(p.251.15; M.26.728A); *Symb.Ant.* (345)*ib.*26(p.252.4; 728C); οὔτε μὴν ἐξ ἑτέρας τινὸς ὑ. παρὰ τὸν πατέρα προϋποκειμένης ἀλλ' ἐκ μόνου τοῦ θεοῦ *Symb.Ant.*(345) 3 *ib.*(p.252.11; 727A) and *Symb.Sirm.*1 *anath.*1; ‡Ath.*interpr.*(p.66. 30; M.26.1232C); τῶν ὀνομάτων...σημαινόντων...τὴν οἰκείαν ἑκάστου τῶν ὀνομαζομένων ὑ. καὶ τάξιν καὶ δόξαν· ὡς εἶναι τῇ μὲν ὑ. τρία, τῇ δὲ συμφωνίᾳ ἕν *Symb.Ant.*(341)2 ap.Ath.*syn.*23(p.249.32; 724B); πιστεύω...εἰς τὸν υἱόν...ὄντα πρὸς τὸν θεὸν ἐν ὑ. *Symb.Ant.*(341)3 *ib.*24(p.250.12; 724C); μίαν εἶναι ὑ., ἣν αὐτοὶ οἱ αἱρετικοὶ οὐσίαν προσαγορεύουσι, τοῦ πατρὸς καὶ τοῦ υἱοῦ καὶ τοῦ ἁγίου πνεύματος CSard. *ep.cath.*ap.Thdt.*h.e.*2.8.39(3.844); Οὐάλης καὶ Οὐρσάκιος...λέγοντες ...διαφόρους εἶναι τὰς ὑ. τοῦ πατρὸς καὶ τοῦ υἱοῦ καὶ τοῦ ἁγίου πνεύματος καὶ εἶναι κεχωρισμένας *ib.*2.8.38(3.844); τὴν μίαν ὑ., ἥτις ἐστὶ τοῦ πατρὸς καὶ τοῦ υἱοῦ *ib.*2.8.43(846); ἡ ἱερὰ φωνὴ ἐλάλησεν [Jo.10:30] καὶ διὰ τὴν τῆς ὑ. ἑνότητα, ἥτις ἐστὶ μία τοῦ πατρὸς καὶ μία τοῦ υἱοῦ *ib.*2.8.47(847); different usages set forth and explained: expression τρεῖς ὑ. allowed with proper safeguards οὓς... ἐμέμφοντό τινες ὡς τρεῖς λέγοντας ὑ. ... μὴ ἄρ' ὡς Ἀρειομανῖται λέγουσιν...ἑκάστην καθ' ἑαυτὴν ὑ. διῃρημένην...ἢ ὡς ἄλλοι αἱρετικοὶ τρεῖς ἀρχὰς...λέγουσιν...οὕτω...τρεῖς ὑ. λέγουσι· διεβεβαιώσαντο...εἰς ἁγίαν τριάδα πιστεύειν, οὐκ ὀνόματι τριάδα μόνον, ἀλλ' ἀληθῶς οὖσαν καὶ ὑφεστῶσαν...μήτε...τρεῖς ἀρχὰς...ἀλλ'...υἱὸν...ὁμοούσιον...πνεῦμα... ἴδιον...τῆς οὐσίας τοῦ...πατρός...οἱ δὲ [sc. λέγοντες μίαν οὐσίαν]... διεβεβαιώσαντο...ὑ. μὲν λέγομεν ἡγούμενοι ταὐτὸν εἶναι εἰπεῖν ὑ. καὶ οὐσίαν· μίαν δὲ φρονοῦμεν, διὰ τὸ ἐκ τῆς οὐσίας τοῦ πατρὸς εἶναι τὸν υἱόν, καὶ διὰ τὴν ταυτότητα τῆς φύσεως...ἀμέλει κἀκεῖ οἱ αἰτιαθέντες ὡς εἰρηκότες τρεῖς ὑ. συνετίθεντο τούτοις· καὶ αὐτοὶ δὲ οἱ εἰρηκότες μίαν οὐσίαν τὰ ἐκείνων ὥσπερ ἑρμήνευσαν καὶ ὡμολόγουν Ath.*tom.*5f.(M.26. 801Bf.); ref. Mt.3:17 ἐκβοήσαντος τὴν πατρικὴν ὑ. περὶ αὐτοῦ ‡Ath. *Ar.*4.33(p.82.19; M.26.520A); εἰ παντὶ γεννητῷ αἰτία συγκεκλήρωται ἀναίτιος δὲ ἡ ἀγέννητος φύσις, οὐκ αἰτίαν δηλοῖ τὸ ἀγέννητον ἀλλ' ὑ. σημαίνει Aët.*synt.*ap.Epiph.*haer.*76.44(p.398.5; M.42.609C); Aët.*synt. ib.*76.54(p.409.16; 629C); ὑποστάσει δὲ γεννᾷ [sc. ὁ θεός], καὶ ἐντολῇ κτίζει ‡Ath.*dial.Trin.*1.8(M.28.1128C); τὸν μὲν γὰρ υἱόν...μόνον τῇ ἑαυτοῦ δυνάμει καὶ ἐνεργείᾳ ἐγέννησέ τε καὶ ἔκτισε...οὐδὲν τῆς ἑαυτοῦ ὑ. μεταδοὺς τῷ γεννηθέντι...ὁ δ' ἄφθαρτος τῆς ἑαυτοῦ οὐσίας οὐ μεταδίδωσιν...οὔτε κατὰ τὴν ἑαυτοῦ οὐσίαν, ἀλλ' οἷον ἐβουλήθη, ἐγέννησε Eun.*apol.*28(M.30.868A); ref. H. Ghost οὐ γὰρ ἂν ὑπηριθμήθη τούτῳ [sc. τῷ μονογενεῖ] ὡς ἰδίαν ἔχων ὑ. *ib.*25(861C); τὸν πατέρα καὶ τὸν υἱὸν μιᾶς οὐσίας...πιστεύεσθαι χρῆναι, καὶ τῆς αὐτῆς ὑ. καὶ τὸ πνεῦμα τὸ ἅγιον Dam.Papa *ep.Illyr.*ap.Thdt.*h.e.*2.22.7(3.883); τί γὰρ ὄντι αὐτῷ κατὰ τὴν φύσιν καὶ τὴν ὑ. ὑπάρχει τὸ μὴ ἀρχὴν ἔχειν; Gr.Naz. *or.*28.9(p.35.8; M.36.37A); τῆς τοῦ πατρὸς ὑ. συνυφεστὸς τὸ ἀπαύγασμα Didym.*Trin.*1.9(M.39.284A); οὐδ' ὁ θεὸς ἐπεκτήσατο ἔξωθεν τὸν υἱόν, ἀλλ' ἐξ ὅλης τῆς ὑ. ἐγέννησεν ἀδιαστάτως, ἅτε ἀσώματος *ib.* 1.10(292B); εἰ γάρ, φησίν...ἐγέννησε ἐξ αὐτοῦ ὁ θεὸς ⟨υἱόν⟩, ὡς εἰπεῖν, ἐξ ἰδίας ὑ. φύσει ἢ ἐξ ἰδίας οὐσίας, οὐκοῦν ὠγκώθη ἢ τομὴν ἐδέξατο Epiph.*haer.*69.15(p.164.22; M.42.225A); **5.** in positive statements ἀκατάληπτος...ἡ ὑ. ἡ θεία Cyr.H.*catech.*6.5; αὔταρκες ἡμῖν εἰδέναι ταῦτα...φύσιν δὲ ἢ ὑ. μὴ πολυπραγμόνει *ib.*16.24; ἡ...γῆ τοῦ οἰκείου κεραμέως...τὴν ὑ. λέγειν οὐ δύναται *ib.*11.11; αὐτοὶ [sc. angels]... ἐκτίσθησαν, οὐ μέντοι ἐξεπορεύθησαν ἐκ τῆς ὑ. τοῦ θεοῦ καὶ πατρός Didym.*Trin.*2.4(M.39.481C); τὸ...ἅγιον πνεῦμα, συμφυῶς καὶ ἑνοειδῶς ἀπὸ τῆς...πατρικῆς ὑ. *ib.*(484A); ἐτέχθη...ἐκ μὲν τῆς ὑ. τοῦ πατρός, ἀνάρχως...ἐκ δὲ τῆς ἀμιάντου παρθένου *ib.*3.3(817B); τριὰς αὕτη...μία θεότης τῆς αὐτῆς οὐσίας...τῆς αὐτῆς ὑ. Epiph.*anc.*67(p.82.6; M.43. 137C); ὅπου γὰρ ὁμοούσιον, μιᾶς ὑ. ἐστι δηλωτικόν· ἀλλὰ καὶ ἐνυπόστατον σημαίνει τὸν πατέρα καὶ ἐνυπόστατον τὸν υἱὸν καὶ ἐνυπόστατον τὸ πνεῦμα *ib.*6(p.12.18; 25B); Παυλῖνος...ὃς παρῃτεῖτο τρεῖς ὑ. λέγειν ῥητῶς, δυνάμει καὶ ἀληθῶς ταῦτα φρονῶν...ἠκολούθησε δὲ τοῖς Δυτικοῖς...ἐπισκόποις τῷ ἐστενῶσθαι τὴν Ῥωμαϊκὴν φωνὴν καὶ μὴ δύνασθαι πρὸς τὴν ἡμετέραν τῶν Γραικῶν φράσιν τρεῖς ὑ. λέγειν Acac.B.*ep. Cyr.*(p.99.25ff.; M.77.100D); on Western terminology v. I.B.6; τὸν λόγον οὐσιωδῶς τέτοκεν, ἵνα τὴν ὑ., καὶ τοῦ πατρὸς δύναμιν διηγήσηται αὐτὸς λόγος ὢν Aen.Gaz.*dial.*(M.85.960A).

III. Christol; **A.** ante CChalc.(451); **1.** *state of being, constitution*, reflecting origin μαρτυρία τοῦ...βαπτιστοῦ περὶ Χριστοῦ ἐστι, τὴν προηγουμένην αὐτοῦ ὑ. ... διδάσκουσα Or.*Jo.*2.35(29; p.94.13; M.14. 177C); περὶ ποίου γεννήματος...τοῦ κατὰ σάρκα...ἢ τοῦ κατὰ τὸν μονογενῆ θεόν. διπλῆς γὰρ οὔσης τῆς θεωρίας, ἐπί τε τῆς θείας...ζωῆς καὶ ἐπὶ τῆς ὑλικῆς...ὑ. Gr.Nyss.*Eun.*4(2 p.49.12; M.45.617C); εἰ τὸ 'ἐποίησεν' [sc. in other places in scripture]...εἰς τὸ προαιώνιον ἀναπέμπει νόημα, καλῶς ἂν ἔχοι καὶ τὴν ἐνταῦθα φωνὴν [sc. 2Cor.5:21] ...εἰς τὴν πρώτην τῆς οὐσίας ἀνάγειν ὑπόστασιν *ib.*6(2 p.130.28; 713D); τὴν πρώτην τοῦ μονογενοῦς ὑ. *ib.*(2 p.133.15; 717B); οὕτως ἄυλός τις... ἡ τοῦ ὑψίστου δύναμις, τὴν δουλικὴν μορφὴν τὴν διὰ τῆς παρθένου ὑ. διαλαβοῦσα, πρὸς τὸ ἴδιον ὕψος ἀνήγαγεν id.*Apoll.*25(M.45.1177C); ἡ ἀνθρωπίνη φύσις ἐκ νοερᾶς ψυχῆς, σώματι συνδραμούσης, τὴν ὑ. ἔχει... ὥσπερ οὖν ἐφ' ἡμῶν ζωοποιός τις δύναμις ἐνθεωρεῖται τῇ ὕλῃ, ἀφ' ἧς ὁ ἐκ ψυχῆς τε καὶ σώματος συνεστὼς ἄνθρωπος διαπλάσσεται· οὕτως ἐπὶ τῆς παρθενίας ἡ τοῦ ὑψίστου δύναμις...τὴν ἐκ τοῦ παρθενικοῦ σώματος πρὸς τὸ πλασσόμενον συνεισφορὰν παρεδέξατο, καὶ οὕτως ἐκτίσθη ὁ καινὸς ὡς ἀληθῶς ἄνθρωπος, ὁ πρῶτος καὶ μόνος τὸν τοιοῦτον τρόπον τῆς ὑ. ἐφ' ἑαυτοῦ καταδείξας *ib.*54(1256Af.); ὁ σωτὴρ δηλῶν τὴν ὑ. τῆς οἰκείας θεότητος Mac.Mgn.*apocr.*2.9(p.12.6); **2.** *nature* πῶς... εἰς μίαν ὑ. συνάγει συγχέων τὰς φύσεις, φυσικὴν τὴν θείαν ἕνωσιν ἀποκαλῶν; Andr.Sam.*fr.*ap.Cyr.*apol.orient.*3(p.38.6; 6[1].164B); but v. 5.c infra; τὰς ὑ. διαιρεῖν εἴτ' οὖν φύσεις...τελεία μὲν ἡ τοῦ θεοῦ λόγου ὑ. ... τελεία δέ...ἡ τοῦ δούλου μορφή, δι' ὃ καὶ ὑποστάσεις εἴπεν, ἀλλ' οὐχ ὑπόστασιν...ἓν μὲν πρόσωπον...ὁμολογεῖν εὐσεβές, δύο δὲ τὰς ἑνωθείσας ὑ. εἴτ' οὖν φύσεις Thdt.ap.Cyr.*apol.Thdt.*3(p.117.12ff.; 6[1]. 210Ef.); cf. *ipsa substantia quae est divina, remansit an humana? nam nos unum Christum...confitemur, non naturarum confusione neque temperamento, sed manentibus utrisque naturis in sua proprietate inconfusis ita unitum accepimus*, Synodus Orientalium *decreta* 2(*ACO* 1.5.2 p.289.25); *si post unionem non sunt naturarum substantiae, divina scilicet et humana, in sua proprietate, omnis fidei corruisse videtur professio*, *ib.*3(p.290.7); **3.** concrete *instance* of an abstract essence, nature realized in an *individual*; **a.** in Thdr. Mops. and Nest. ὅταν μὲν γὰρ τὰς φύσεις διακρίνωμεν, τελείαν τὴν φύσιν τοῦ θεοῦ λόγου φαμέν, καὶ τέλειον τὸ πρόσωπον· οὐδὲ γὰρ ἀπρόσωπον ἔστιν ὑ. εἰπεῖν· τελείαν δὲ καὶ τὴν τοῦ ἀνθρώπου φύσιν, καὶ τὸ πρόσωπον ὁμοίως· ὅταν μέντοι ἐπὶ τὴν συνάφειαν ἀπίδωμεν, ἓν πρόσωπον τότε φαμέν Thdr.Mops. *fr.inc.*8(p.299.21ff.; M.66.981B); in this sense

Nestorius maintains two in Christ: cf. *conjunctionis...confiteamur dignitatem ⟨unam⟩, naturarum autem substantias duplices*, Nest.*fr.* C 27(p.340.18); cf. *je sépare les propriétés de l'union à chacune des natures, de sorte que chacune de celles-ci subsiste dans son hypostase. je ne dis pas qu'elles remontent à Dieu le Verbe, comme s'il était les deux par essence; ou que les propriétés de la chair soient prises sans (leur) hypostase par Dieu...il n'a un corps que de nom, sans hypostase et sans opération, c'est pourquoi tu l'appelles homme comme chose superflue, par le nom et en paroles seulement, puisque tu n'acceptes pas de reconnaître l'essence et l'opération de l'homme, et l'existence de deux natures dans leurs propriétés, dans l'hypostase et dans l'essence de chacune d'elles*, Nest.*Heracl.*2.1.291(pp.184f.); *on ne doit pas concevoir une essence sans hypostase, comme si l'union* (*des essences*) *avait eu lieu en une essence et qu'il y eût un prosôpon d'une seule essence. mais les natures subsistent, dans leurs prosôpons et dans leurs natures et dans le prosôpon d'union. quant au prosôpon naturel de l'une, l'autre se sert du même en vertu de l'union, ainsi il n'y a qu'un prosôpon pour les deux natures, ib.*2.1.305(pp.193f.); opp. *πρόσωπον*: *veux-tu donc que nous regardions le prosôpon comme une hypostase, comme nous disons une essence de la divinité et trois hypostases, et que, par hypostases nous entendions les prosôpons? ib.* 1.3.229(p.138); *de quel côté vous rangez-vous?...de ceux qui rapportent l'union à l'hypostase ou de ceux qui la rapportent au prosôpon? ib.*1.3.265(p.160); *un et le même (est le) prosôpon, mais (il n'en est pas de même pour) l'essence. car l'essence de la forme de Dieu et l'essence de la forme du serviteur demeurent dans leurs hypostases, ib.*1.3.252(p.152); **b.** in Cyr. *ὁ ἅγιος Κύριλλος, ποτὲ μὲν ἐπὶ τοῦ ἁπλῶς ὄντος τῷ ὀνόματι τῆς ὑ. χρησάμενος...ποτὲ δὲ...ἐπὶ τοῦ καθ' ἑαυτὸ ἰδιοσυστάτως ὑφεστῶτος προσώπου* Leont.B.*fr.*(M.86.2012D); **i.** in analysis: two before the union *διδασκέτω...εἰ δίχα τῶν ὑ. μόναι καὶ καθ' ἑαυτὰς αἱ μορφαὶ συνῆλθον ἀλλήλαις...οὐ γὰρ ὁμοιότητες ἁπλῶς ἀνυπόστατοι καὶ μορφαὶ συνέβησαν ἀλλήλαις καθ' ἕνωσιν οἰκονομικήν, ἀλλὰ πραγμάτων αὐτῶν ἢ γοῦν ὑποστάσεων γέγονεν σύνοδος* Cyr.*apol. Thdt.*1(p.112.13ff.; 6[1].206B); cf.id.*apol.orient.*3(p.40.27; 6[1].167C); united *εἴ τις...διαιρεῖ τὰς ὑ. μετὰ τὴν ἕνωσιν* id.*apol.Thdt.anath.*3(p.116. 10; 6[1].210A); *διϊστάντας* [sc. Nestorians] *εἰς δύο τὰς ὑ., ἀποφοιτώσας μὲν ἀλλήλων εἰς τὸ ἰδίᾳ τε εἶναι καὶ ἀνὰ μέρος* id.*apol.orient.*3(p.40.18; 167A); without confusion *κατ' αὐτὸ δὴ τουτὶ καὶ μόνον νοηθείη ἂν ἡ τῶν φύσεων ἢ γοῦν ὑ. διαφορά· οὐ γάρτοι ταυτὸν ὡς ἐν ποιότητι φυσικῇ θεότης τε καὶ ἀνθρωπότης* id.*ep.*40(p.26.26; 5[2].116C); *εἰ μή τις γένοιτο τῶν ὑ. εἰς ἀλλήλας ἀνάχυσις ἢ γοῦν σύγκρασις· καίτοι τῶν τῆς ἐκκλησίας διδασκάλων οὐ τοῦτον ἡμᾶς μυσταγωγούντων τὸν τρόπον* id.*Nest.*2.1 (p.34.34; 6[1].33E); *ἀσύγχυτον παντελῶς τῶν ὑ. σύνοδον* id.*apol.Thdt.*3 (p.119.19; 213B); *ἀσύγχυτοι μεμενήκασιν αἱ φύσεις ἤγουν ὑ.* id.*schol. inc.*11(M.75.1381B); **ii.** in synthesis where Cyr. is concerned to present Christ as one Person, *ὑ.* (or *πρόσωπον* with which it is often associated) denotes Person of Word (cf. II.B.1) who has taken human nature, become incarnate *ἑνὶ προσώπῳ τὰς ἐν τοῖς εὐαγγελίοις πάσας ἀναθετέον φωνάς, ὑποστάσει μιᾷ τῇ τοῦ λόγου σεσαρκωμένῃ. κύριος γὰρ εἷς...κατὰ τὰς γραφάς* Cyr.*ep.*17(p.38.22; 5[2].73D); *τὰς ἐν τοῖς εὐαγγελίοις τοῦ σωτῆρος ἡμῶν φωνὰς οὔτε ὑ. δυσὶν οὔτε μὴν προσώποις καταμερίζομεν. οὐ γάρ ἐστι διπλοῦς ὁ εἷς...Χριστός, κἂν ἐκ δύο νοῆται καὶ διαφόρων πραγμάτων εἰς ἑνότητα...συνενηνεγμένος καθάπερ ἀμέλει καὶ ἄνθρωπος...εἷς ib.*(p.38.4; 5[2].73A); *εἰ μὲν ἕνα φῂς υἱὸν καὶ μίαν ὑ. τὴν τοῦ λόγου σεσαρκωμένην, οὐκ αὐτὸς ἔσται θεότητος ὄργανον, κεχρήσεται δὲ μᾶλλον...τῷ ἰδίῳ σώματι καθάπερ ἀμέλει καὶ ἡ τοῦ ἀνθρώπου ψυχή* id.*Nest.*2.8(p.46.29; 6[1].51C); *δεδυσσέβηκεν... διϊστὰς εἰς δύο πρόσωπά τε καὶ ὑ. ... ἀλλήλων διῃρημένας ἑκατέρᾳ τε λόγους τοὺς αὐτῇ πρέποντας ἀνατιθεὶς ἰδικῶς ib.*2.1(p.34.38; 34A); *εἴ τις προσώποις δυσὶν ἢ γοῦν ὑ. ... διανέμει* [sc. what has been said of Christ] *ἀ. ἔ.* id.*apol.Thdt.anath.*4(p.120.24; 6[1].214C); *οὐκ ἐφιεὶς εἰς δύο μερίζεσθαι πρόσωπά τε καὶ ὑ. τὸν ἕνα...Χριστόν* id.*apol.orient.*4(p.42. 31; 6[1].170C); *ἐκ τελείας ὑ. τοῦ θεοῦ λόγου καὶ μὴν καὶ ἐξ ἀνθρωπότητος τελείως ἐχούσης κατὰ τὸν ἴδιον λόγον εἷς ὁ Χριστός, ὁ αὐτὸς ὑπάρχων ἐν ταυτῷ θεός τε ὁμοῦ καὶ ἄνθρωπος* id.*schol.inc.*8(p.221.9; M.75.1377C); **c.** in later writings of Thdt. (but v. 2) *ὁ...'Ισαάκ, καὶ ὁ κριός* [sc. as type of Christ], *κατὰ μὲν τὸ διάφορον τῶν φύσεων, τῇ εἰκόνι συμβαίνουσι, κατὰ δὲ τὸ διῃρημένον κεχωρισμένων τῶν ὑ., οὐκ ἔτι. θεότητος γὰρ ἡμεῖς καὶ ἀνθρωπότητος τοιαύτην κηρύττομεν ἕνωσιν ὡς ...ἓν πρόσωπον* Thdt.*eran.*3(4.203); *ἕτερος...κατὰ τὴν ὑ. ὁ ἐν μορφῇ θεοῦ ὑπάρχων, καὶ ἕτερος ἐκεῖνος οὐ ἐν μορφῇ ὑπάρχει* id.*inc.*10(M.75. 1429D); **d.** foreshadowing the terminology of Sev. Ant., v. infra B.2; *συμφέρομαι...ἀναθεματίζων τοὺς διαιροῦντας μετὰ τὴν ἕνωσιν εἰς δύο φύσεις ἢ ὑ. ἢ πρόσωπα τὸν ἕνα κύριον...μεμφόμενος...τῆς φωνῆς τῆς ἐμαυτοῦ, ἣν περὶ τῶν δύο φύσεων κατεθέμην...καὶ προσκυνῶ τὴν μίαν φύσιν τοῦ μονογενοῦς...σεσαρκωμένου* Bas.Sel.ap.CEph.(449)*act.* (*ACO* 2.1.1 p.179.18; H.2.213C); *μέμφομαι τῇ φωνῇ μου ἣν εἶπον ...δεῖν ἐν δύο φύσεσι τὸν κύριον...μετὰ τὴν ἕνωσιν, ἀναθεματίζων τοὺς εἰς δύο φύσεις ἢ δύο ὑ. ἢ δύο πρόσωπα μετὰ τὴν ἕνωσιν διαιροῦντας τὸν κύριον* Seleucus Amasenus *ib.*(p.181.10; H.2.216D); **4.** *substantive existence, concrete reality* *εἰ τὴν μὲν θεότητά τις αὐτοῦ παραδέχοιτο, τῇ δὲ ἀνθρωπότητι προσκόπτων μηδὲν ἀνθρώπινον... πιστεύοι γεγονέναι, ἢ ὑ. εἰληφέναι...ἢ εἰ ἀνάπαλιν τὰ μὲν περὶ αὐτὸν ἀνθρώπινα προσίοιτο, τὴν δὲ ὑ. τοῦ μονογενοῦς...ἀθετοῖ* Or.*Jo.*32.16(9; p.452.9ff.; M.14.784B); occasionally in Nestorius: cf. *pour ne pas faire, à l'imitation de Sabellius, les prosôpons sans hypostase et sans essence. celui qui empêche de dire que le Fils est adoré avec le Père, empêche aussi que le Fils soit en hypostase...celui qui empêche de dire deux essences et 'qui est adoré avec lui' empêche que l'humanité et la divinité ne soient en essence et en hypostase, comme nous l'avons dit de la Trinité*, Nest.*Heracl.*2.1.316f.(p.202); cf.Leont.H.*Nest.*1.39 (M.86.1500C) cit. s. *ἄνθρωπος*; **5.** *Person*; **a.** Apollinarian *μίαν ὑ. καὶ ἓν πρόσωπον, καὶ μίαν τὴν προσκύνησιν τοῦ λόγου καὶ τῆς σαρκός* Apoll.*fid.sec.pt.*28 ap.Leont.B.*Apoll.*(M.86.1972D; p.177.7 om. *μίαν ὑ. καὶ*); *οὐ διαιροῦμεν αὐτὸν ἀπὸ τῆς αὐτοῦ σαρκός, ἀλλ' ἔστιν ἓν πρόσωπον, μία ὑ., ὅλος ἄνθρωπος, ὅλος θεός* id.*fid.inc.*3(p.194.23; M.*PL.*8. 876C); *μία φύσις, μία ὑ., μία ἐνέργεια, ἓν πρόσωπον ib.*6(p.199.16; 877C); *ἐρεῖ τις...μέρος οὖν τοῦ λόγου τὸ σῶμα, συμπληρωτικὸν τῆς τοῦ υἱοῦ ὑ. ... ἐπεὶ πάλιν, εἰ μία ὑ. τοῦ λόγου καὶ τῆς σαρκός, πῶς δὲ υἱὸς αὕτη τοῦ θεοῦ;...ὁ λόγος...τέλειος...καὶ ἰδίαν καθ' ἑαυτὸν ἔχων ὑ. ἀεὶ καὶ μηδενὸς προσδεόμενος* id.*quod un.Chr.*7(p.299.5ff.; M.28.128B); orthodox accused of proclaiming two in Christ *οἱ ταῦτα κατηγοροῦντες τὴν ἑαυτῶν γνώμην φανερὰν καθιστῶσιν, ὅτι δύο ὑ. τοῦ κυρίου ἡμῶν...λέγουσιν, ἄλλην ὑ. εἰσάγοντες...τοῦ ἀναληφθέντος ἀνθρώπου, ὡς αὐτοί φασι, καὶ ἄλλην τοῦ ἀναλαβόντος θεοῦ, ἄλλο πρόσωπον τοῦ υἱοῦ τοῦ θεοῦ, καὶ ἄλλο πρόσωπον τοῦ υἱοῦ τοῦ ἀνθρώπου...ἡμεῖς δὲ... ἕνα θεὸν ὁμολογοῦμεν τὸ συναμφότερον, μίαν ὑ. καὶ ἓν πρόσωπον, οὐχ ἵνα συμπληρωτικὸν τῆς ὑ. τὸ σῶμα γένηται...ἀλλ' ὁ ἀληθῶς τέλειος καὶ τὸ ἀτελὲς ἐτελείωσεν ib.*8f.(pp.299.15–300.21; 128C–129A); *ὑ. μίαν σύνθετον καὶ πρόσωπον ἓν ἀδιαίρετον* Job.Ep.*symb.*(p.286.22)ap. Leont.B.*Apoll.*(M.86.1952C); *μίαν ὑ. καὶ ἓν πρόσωπον τοῦ θεοῦ λόγου καὶ τῆς ἐκ Μαρίας σαρκός* ‡Jul.Papa *ep.encycl.*(p.292.19); conviction that *νοῦς* necessarily entailed a *ὑ.* was reason why assumption of manhood complete and entire was rejected, Epiph.*anc.*77(p.96. 23, M.43.161B); id.*haer.*77.24(p.437.1; M.42.676A); **b.** against Paul. Sam. *δύο ὑποστάσεις λέγοντός σου καὶ δύο πρόσωπα τοῦ ἑνός... Χριστοῦ* ‡Dion.Al.*ep.Paul.Sam.*(p.3); *ἓν πρόσωπον ὢν...καὶ μία ὑ. προσώπου ib.*(p.5); cf. *καί τοι φησὶν μὴ δύο ὑφίστασθαι υἱούς· εἰ δὲ υἱὸς ὁ 'Ιησοῦς...υἱὸς δὲ καὶ ἡ σοφία, καὶ ἄλλο μὲν ἡ σοφία, ἄλλο δὲ 'Ιησοῦς Χριστός, δύο ὑφίστανται υἱοί* Paul.Sam.*fr.*B.10(p.331.1ff.) ap.Leont.B.*Nest.et Eut.*3(M.86.1393B); **c.** against Nest. *ἡ σὰρξ τοῦ κυρίου...μετέχουσα καθ' ὑπόστασιν τοῦ θεοῦ λόγου* Marc.Er. *Nest.*8(p.94.28); *ib.*15(p.100.27); *ὡς...προσώποις δυσὶν ἢ ὑ. δυσὶν ἢ υἱοῖς δυσίν, διαιροῦντας τὴν ἕνωσιν ἢ γοῦν τὸν ἕνα υἱόν, τὰς φωνὰς ἐφαρμόζειν οὐ δεῖ* Andr.Sam.ap.Cyr.*apol.orient.*4(p.41.8ff.; 6[1].168Af.); **d.** leading up to *Symb.Chalc.* *ἐγὼ...ἕνα εἰδώς τε καὶ διδαχθεὶς... υἱόν, μίαν ὁμολογῶ· τὴν τοῦ σαρκωθέντος λόγου ὑ.* Procl.CP *Arm.* (p.191.21; M.65.864D); *ἔστιν εἷς υἱός, οὐ τῶν φύσεων εἰς δύο ὑ. διαιρουμένων, ἀλλὰ τῆς φρικτῆς οἰκονομίας τὰς δύο φύσεις εἰς μίαν ὑ. ἑνωσάσης* id.*fr.*ap.*Doct.Patr.*7(p.49.3f.); *ἐκ δύο φύσεων ὁμολογοῦμεν τὸν Χριστὸν εἶναι μετὰ τὴν ἐνανθρώπησιν, ἐν μιᾷ ὑ. καὶ ἑνὶ προσώπῳ* Flav.CP ap.CCP(448)*act.*ap.CChalc.(*ACO* 2.1.1 p.114.9; H.2.128E); id.*ep.Thds.*(p.35.19; cf.M.65.892B); id.*ep.Leon.*1(p.37.10; M.*PL.*54. 726A); *τῆς ἰδιότητος ἑκατέρας φύσεως...εἰς ἓν πρόσωπον καὶ μίαν ὑ. συντρεχούσης* *Symb.Chalc.*(p.129.33; H.2.456C).

B. post CChalc.; **1.** rarely in sense A.1, *state of being, constitution* as derived from origin *ὁ λόγος εἰς τὸ εἶναι...θεός, τελείως εἶχεν ἀεί... ἀλλὰ χρεία...πρὸς συμπλήρωσιν τῆς κατ' εὐδοκίαν θεοῦ πρὸς ἀνθρώπους ἑνώσεως ἑκατέρᾳ φύσει τῆς ἑτέρας εἰς ἀποτέλεσμα τοῦ εἶναι ἐκ τῶν πεφυκότων διακεκριμένως ἐν διαφόροις ὑ. ὁρᾶσθαι φύσεων καὶ υἱοτήτων τελείων καθ' ἓν τὸ αὐτοῦ πρόσωπον γίνεσθαι συνέλευσιν* Leont.H.*Nest.* 3.1(M.86.1605B); *ib.*1.34(1497C) cit. s. *ἔνσαρκος*; *ib.*2.28(1588C) cit. s. *διαιρέω*; **2.** monophysite: equated with *φύσις* and with *πρόσωπον*; **a.** Sev.Ant.*fr.*ap.Eust.Mon.*ep.*(M.86.908A) cit. s. *ἐπίνοια*; *ἐπὶ τοῦ τριαδικοῦ λόγου οὐ ταὐτὸν φύσις καὶ ὑ.· ἐπὶ δὲ τῆς σαρκώσεως τοῦ Χριστοῦ, ταὐτὸν ἡ φύσις ἐστί, καὶ τὸ πρόσωπον, ἤγουν ἡ ὑ.* id.ap. Anast.S.*hod.*9(M.89.148C); *ἓν πρόσωπον καὶ ὑ. μία ἡ αὐτοῦ τοῦ λόγου σεσαρκωμένη* id.ap.*cat.1Petr.*4:1(p.71.28); opp. *οὐσία*: *οὐκ ἂν τὸ ἓν τῇ φύσει καὶ τῇ ὑ. ταυτὸν τῇ οὐσίᾳ* id.*fr.*ap.*Doct.Patr.*6(p.43.20); *οὐκ οὐσίας νοοῦμεν τὰς φύσεις, τὰς τῆς κοινότητος δηλωτικάς, καὶ πολλῶν ὑ. περιεκτικάς* id.ap.Eust.Mon.*ep.*(M.86.920D); *οὐκ ἄν τις...εἴποι τὴν τοῦ θεοῦ λόγου...σάρκα τὴν ἑνωθεῖσαν αὐτῷ καθ' ὑ., γεγενῆσθαι μιᾶς* οὐσίας καὶ ποιότητος id.*fr.*ap.Leont.H.*monoph.*(M.86.1848C); one in Christ though composite ἐν συνθέσει δὲ ὑφισταμέναις ταῖς φύσεσιν ἐξ ὧν ὁ εἷς Χριστός, καὶ μίαν ἀποτελούσαις ὑ. καὶ φύσιν τὴν τοῦ μονογενοῦς λόγου σεσαρκωμένου...συναπολήγει καὶ ἡ φαντασθεῖσα τῇ ἐπινοίᾳ τῶν ὑ. καὶ προσώπων δυάς, εἰς ἕν τι συνδραμοῦσα τὴν ἐξ ἀμφοῖν μίαν ὑ. id.ap.Eust.Mon.*ep.*(908Af.); τὴν μίαν ὑ. τοῦ λόγου καὶ τὴν μίαν σάρκα τὴν ἐψυχωμένην νοερῶς, ἐξ ὧν ἀτρέπτως συνενήνεκται εἰς ἓν καὶ συντέθειται. καὶ ἔστι μία φύσις τε καὶ ὑ. ἡ τοῦ λόγου σεσαρκωμένη *ib.*(920Df.); εἴ τις τὰ ἐξ ὧν ἔστι σκοπῆσαι ζητήσειεν, νοῦ μόνῃ φαντασίᾳ...θεωρεῖ δύο φύσεων, ἤγουν ὑ., σύνοδον·...συνεισιοῦσα δὲ τῇ διανοίᾳ καὶ ἡ τῆς ἑνώσεως δύναμις, καὶ τὴν ἐξ ἀμφοῖν δείξασα μίαν ὑ. *ib.*(921Af.); τὰ δύο τὰ ἐξ ὧν ἡ ἕνωσις, ἐν τῷ συντεθεῖσθαι τῷ νῷ μόνον ἀπ' ἀλλήλων συνθέτως διακρινόμενα· μεταβέβληται γὰρ οὐδαμῶς μὴ εἶναι δύο καὶ ταῖς ὑ. *ib.*(936D); entailing one ἐνέργεια: ἀκόλουθον οὖν ἐστι συνθέτου νοουμένης ἡμῖν καὶ μιᾶς τῆς θεανδρικῆς ἐνεργείας, τοιαύτην εἶναί τε καὶ λέγεσθαι καὶ τὴν τοῦ ταύτην προφέροντος φύσιν τε καὶ ὑ., ὡς ἂν μηδὲν ἔχοι κατὰ τὴν ἐνέργειαν πρὸς τὴν ἑαυτοῦ φύσιν ἀπεοικός id.*fr.*ap.*Doct.Patr.*41(p.310.11); μιᾶς ὑ. ὁμολογουμένης τοῦ Ἐμμανουήλ, ἀκόλουθον μίαν φύσιν ὁμολογεῖν τοῦ θεοῦ λόγου σεσαρκωμένην, καὶ αὐτὴν ἐνεργοῦσαν τὰ θεοπρεπῆ καὶ ἀνθρώπινα· καὶ οὐ κατὰ τὸν Λέοντος τόμον ἐνεργούσας δύο φύσεις id.ap.CCP(681)*act.*10(H.3.1244A); cf.Sev.Ant.*ib.*(H.3.1241D); **b.** Jo. Philoponus' attempt to systematize the terminology cf. ἑκάστη φύσις...λέγεται...διχῶς· καθ' ἕνα μὲν τρόπον, ὅταν τὸν κοινὸν ἑκάστης φύσεως λόγον αὐτὸν ἐφ' ἑαυτοῦ θεωρῶμεν...καθ' ἕτερον δέ, ὅταν αὐτὴν δὴ ταύτην τὴν κοινὴν φύσιν ἐν τοῖς ἀτόμοις γινομένην κατίδωμεν Jo.Philop.*arb.*ap.*Doct.Patr.* 36(p.275.26ff.) also ap.Jo.D.*haer.*83(M.94.748A); ὅτι δὲ καὶ ἰδικώτερον πάλιν τὸ τῆς φύσεως γινώσκομεν ὄνομα, τὸν κοινὸν λόγον τῆς φύσεως ἐφ' ἑκάστου τῶν ἀτόμων ἤγουν τῶν ὑ. ἑκάστης ἴδιον γενόμενον θεωροῦντες *ib.*(p.277.8; M.94.748C); οὐ γὰρ δὴ τὴν κοινὴν [sc. φύσιν] ἐπὶ τῆς ἁγίας τριάδος νοουμένην τῆς θεότητος σεσαρκῶσθαί φαμεν...οὐδὲ τὸν κοινὸν τῆς ἀνθρωπίνης φύσεως λόγον ἡνῶσθαι τῷ θεῷ λόγῳ...φύσιν θεότητος ἐνταῦθά φαμεν τὴν ἐν τῇ ὑ. τοῦ λόγου τῆς κοινῆς θεότητος ἐξιδιασθεῖσαν φύσιν...καὶ φύσιν πάλιν ἀνθρωπότητος λέγομεν ἡνῶσθαι τῷ λόγῳ τὴν μερικωτάτην ἐκείνην ὕπαρξιν ἣν μόνην ἐκ πασῶν ὁ λόγος προσείληφεν. ὥστε σχεδὸν κατὰ τοῦτο τῆς φύσεως τὸ σημαινόμενον ταυτὸν ἂν εἴη φύσις καὶ ὑ., πλὴν ὅτι τῆς ὑ. ὄνομα συνεπινοουμένας ἔχει καὶ τὰς ἐπιγινομένας παρὰ τὴν κοινὴν φύσιν ἑκάστῳ τῶν ἀτόμων ἰδιότητας...ἔνθεν τῶν ἡμετέρων πολλοὺς διαφόρως εὑρεῖν ἔστι λέγοντας φύσεων ἤγουν ὑ. ἕνωσιν γεγονέναι. ἡ γὰρ ὑ., ὡς ἐδείξαμεν, τὴν ἰδικὴν ἑκάστου καὶ ἄτομον σημαίνει ὕπαρξιν *ib.*(pp.277.19–278.23; 748C–749A); οὐκοῦν ὡς ἐπὶ τῆς θεότητος τοῦ Χριστοῦ καὶ φύσιν αὐτῆς καὶ ὑ. ὁμολογοῦμεν, οὕτω δήπου καὶ ἐπὶ τῆς ἀνθρωπότητος αὐτοῦ, ὥσπερ φύσιν, οὕτω καὶ τὴν ἰδικὴν ταύτην ὑ. ὁμολογεῖν ἀνάγκη, ἵνα μὴ ἀνυπόστατον...τὴν φύσιν ἐκείνην λέγειν ἀναγκαζώμεθα *ib.*(p.281.3ff.; 752B); ἀλλ' εἰ προϋπέστη ἡ ἑνωθεῖσα τῷ λόγῳ μερικὴ φύσις, ἀνάγκη πᾶσα προϋποστῆναι καὶ τὴν αὐτῆς ὑ. τούτων γὰρ οὐκ ἐνδέχεται θάτερον εἶναι τοῦ λοιποῦ μὴ ὄντος, τὴν μερικὴν λέγω φύσιν ἄνευ τῆς ἰδίας αὐτῆς ὑ. ἢ τὴν μερικὴν ὑ. ἄνευ τῆς ἰδίας αὐτῆς φύσεως. ἓν γάρ ἐστιν ἄμφω τῷ ὑποκειμένῳ καὶ εἰς ταυτὸν πολλάκις συντρέχουσι παρὰ τοῖς χρησαμένοις...εἰ τοίνυν ὥσπερ ἡ ὑ., οὕτω καὶ ἡ φύσις ἡ τῷ λόγῳ ἑνωθεῖσα οὐ προϋπέστη τῆς πρὸς αὐτὸν ἑνώσεως, διόπερ ἄρα μίαν τὴν τοῦ Χριστοῦ ἀξιοῦσιν ὑ., διὰ τοῦτο καὶ φύσιν αὐτοῦ μίαν ἀξιούτωσαν εἶναι *ib.*(p.283.5; 753C); human element in Christ is neither a φύσις nor an ὑ. in full sense of word but τὸ ἀνθρώπινον, *ib.*(p.282.15; 752A); ἡ μερικὴ φύσις or ἡ μερικὴ ὑ., *ib.*(p.283.8f.) (since for practical purposes he identified the two); **c.** other monophysites μίαν αὐτοῦ τὴν ὑ. σύνθετον καταγγέλλω, μηδετέρας τραπείσης διὰ τὴν ἕνωσιν φύσεως...ἡ γὰρ κατὰ σύνθεσιν ἤτοι καθ' ὑ. ἕνωσις τὴν σύγχυσιν ἀποβάλλεται *Ep.*ap.CCP(681)*act.*10(H.3.1249E); cf.Leont.B.*arg.Sev.*(M.86.1929D) cit. s. ἐπίνοια; **3.** orthodox; **a.** ref. Nestorians εἰ ἐκ φύσεων ὑ. σύνθετόν φατε, συμφήσομεν· εἰ δὲ τὴν ὡς ἐξ ὑποστάσεων, μὴ γένοιτο Leont.H.*Nest.*2.24(M.86.1585C); οὐ μὴν πραγματικῶς ἀνὰ μέρος τὴν τῶν φύσεων ποιοῦνται διαίρεσιν εἰς δύο ὑ. ἤτοι πρόσωπα Justn.*conf.*(p.84.17; M.86.1007B); κ]ατὰ [Νε]στορίου τοῦ διελόντος τὸν Χριστὸν εἰς δύο ὑ. *CIG* 8961.5; and Eutychians ὁ μὲν τέμνει τὰς φύσεις εἰς ὑ., ὁ δὲ φύρει τὰς φύσεις εἰς φύσιν Leont.B.*Nest.et Eut.*1(M.86.1276C); **b.** ref. Sev. Ant. and Jo. Philop. παρὰ τίνος σοι τὸ ἐξ ὑποστάσεων τὸν Χριστὸν συντιθέναι...; πότε γὰρ διῃρημένας τὰς φύσεις, καὶ καθ' ἑαυτὰς ὑποστάσας ἔγνως, ἵνα ταύτας συνάψας ἐξ ὑποστάσεων αὐτὸν εἶναι δογματίσῃς; Leont.B.*arg.Sev.*(M.86.1933A); cf. φύσεως καὶ προσώπου οὐκ οἶδεν διαφοράν Eust.Mon.*ep.*(M.86.932C); εἰ μὲν ταυτόν ἐστι φύσις καὶ ὑ., ἀνάγκη ἡμᾶς ὁμολογῆσαι τὸ ἄτομον. εἰ δὲ ἄλλο ἐστὶ φύσις, καὶ ἄλλο ὑ., τίς ἡ ἀποκλήρωσις, λέγοντας ἡμᾶς δύο φύσεις, ὁμολογῆσαι πάντως καὶ δύο ὑ.; †Leont.B.*sect.*5.6(M.86.1233A); Max.*opusc.*(M.91.40A) cit. s. διαίρεσις; tritheistic conclusions to which this identification with φύσις leads, *ib.*; Cyr.S.*v.Sab.*56(p.149.23); Tim.CP *haer.*(M.86.61B); **c.** on terminology: of Cyril λέγεται γὰρ καὶ ὑ. παρὰ τὸ ὑφεστηκέναι ἡ φύσις Leont.H.*monoph.*(M.86.1825A); Eulog.*fr.dogm.*(M.86.2953Bf.); ὑποστάσεων ἕνωσιν λέγει ὁ...Κύριλλος καὶ διαφορὰν καὶ ἰδιότητα, ἀντὶ οὐσιῶν κέχρηται τῇ φωνῇ, τὸ ὑφεστὸς τῶν πραγμάτων ...δεικνύς, σαφῶς διδάσκων, ὡς οὐχ ὁμοιοτήτων τινῶν ἢ μορφῶν ἀνυποστάτων γέγονεν ἕνωσις, ἀλλ' αὐτῶν τῶν πραγμάτων Eub.*fr.*ap.*Doct.Patr.*22(p.142.4); of monophysites λεγέτω τις τὸν λόγον, καθ' ὃν ὑ. μὲν καὶ οὐσία, ἤγουν φύσις καὶ πρόσωπον· ἐπὶ τῆς θεολογίας τὸ κοινὸν ἢ τὸ ἴδιον ὁρίζουσι...οὐχ οὕτω δὲ καὶ ἐπὶ τῆς οἰκονομίας Leont. B.*arg.Sev.*(M.86.1924A); cf.Sev.Ant.ap.Anast.S.*hod.*9(M.89.148C); ἐν καταχρήσει ἔστι πολλάκις μεταγενόμενα εὑρεῖν καὶ τὰ τῆς φύσεως καὶ οὐσίας καὶ ὑ. καὶ προσώπου ὀνόματα ἐπὶ τῆς οἰκονομίας Leont.H. *monoph.*(1852B); οὐδὲ καθ' ὃ μίαν ὑ. λέγομεν τῆς θεότητος καὶ τῆς ἀνθρωπότητος τοῦ Χριστοῦ, οὕτω δυνατὸν καὶ μίαν φύσιν λέγειν Χριστοῦ, ἐπειδὴ μὴ ταὐτὸν φύσις τε καὶ ὑ. Justn.*conf.*(p.86.17f.; M.86.1009C); Σευῆρος κακούργως ταυτὸν εἶναι λέγει τῇ φύσει τὴν ὑ., ἵνα τὴν σύγχυσιν διὰ τῆς μιᾶς κυρώσῃ φύσεως...καὶ πάλιν τὴν διαίρεσιν εἰσηγήσηται τὴν ἐξ ὑ. πρεσβεύων ἕνωσιν καὶ ὅτι καθάπερ Νεστόριος ψιλὴν λέγων τὴν ἕνωσιν, πραγματικὴν εἰσῆγε διαίρεσιν· οὕτω καὶ Σευῆρος ψιλὴν λέγων φύσεων διαφοράν, πραγματικὴν ποιεῖται τὴν σύγχυσιν Max.*opusc.*(M.91.40A); **d.** doctrine εἰ οὐκ ἔστι φύσις ἀνυπόστατος ἐκ δύο δὲ φύσεων ὁμολογεῖτε τὸν κύριον, ἐκ δύο ἄρα ἔσται καὶ ὑ. ... οὐ ταυτὸν...ὑ. καὶ ἐνυπόστατον. ὥσπερ ἕτερον οὐσία καὶ ἐνούσιον· ἡ μὲν γὰρ ὑ. τόν τινα δηλοῖ, τὸ δὲ ἐνυπόστατον τὴν οὐσίαν· καὶ ἡ μὲν ὑ., πρόσωπον ἀφορίζει τοῖς χαρακτηριστικοῖς ἰδιώμασι· τὸ δὲ ἐνυπόστατον, τὸ μὴ εἶναι αὐτὸ συμβεβηκὸς δηλοῖ, ὃ ἐν ἑτέρῳ ἔχει τὸ εἶναι...ὁ τοίνυν λέγων, οὐκ ἔστι φύσις ἀνυπόστατος, ἀληθὲς μὲν λέγει· οὐ μὴ ὀρθῶς συμπεραίνει, τὸ μὴ ἀνυπόστατον συνάγων εἰς τὸ ὑ. εἶναι Leont.B.*Nest.et Eut.*1(M.86.1277Cf.); τῇ...ἰδίᾳ ὑ. αὐτὴν [sc. τὴν σάρκα] ἀνειληφὼς ἐπροσωποποίησεν Leont.H.*Nest.*5.25(M.86.1748A); οὐδεὶς εὐσεβῶν δύο ὑ. ἔχειν αὐτόν φησι ὄντως τὸν λόγον· ἀλλὰ τὴν μίαν αὐτοῦ ὑ., πάλαι μὲν ἐξ ἀποιήτων...γνωρίζεσθαι ἰδιωμάτων...νῦν δὲ καὶ ἐκ ποιητῶν ἔχειν λόγων καὶ πραγμάτων ἐκ περιουσίας τὰς ὑποστατικὰς ἑαυτῆς ὑπογραφάς *ib.*2.39(1596C); *ib.*2.7,22(1549D,1584B); δύο...κατὰ φύσιν τὰ ἑνούμενα, ὡς ἑνούμενα· ἓν δὲ τὴν ὑ. ὡς ἡνωμένα id.*monoph.*3 (M.86.1772A); τὸ δὲ ἀριθμῷ ἓν λεγόμενον, τὸ τῇ ὑ. ἓν ὄν φαμεν, καὶ οὐ τὸ τῇ φύσει ἓν *ib.*61(1804B); ἕνωσις μὲν ὑποστάσεων ἐν μιᾷ φύσει ἐπὶ τῆς...τριάδος, ἕνωσις δὲ τῶν φύσεων ἐν μιᾷ ὑ. ἐπὶ τῆς...σαρκώσεως τοῦ λόγου *ib.*18(1780D); διπλοῦς κατὰ τὴν οὐσίαν...οὐ διπλοῦς τῇ χαρακτηριστικῇ ὑ. Ephr.Ant.*fr.*(M.86.2108D); εἴ τις τὴν μίαν ὑ. τοῦ... Χριστοῦ οὕτως ἐκλαμβάνει, ὡς ἐπιδεχομένην πολλῶν ὑ. σημασίαν, καὶ διὰ τούτου εἰσάγειν ἐπιχειρεῖ...δύο ὑ., ἤτοι δύο πρόσωπα...ἀλλὰ μὴ ὁμολογεῖ τὸν...λόγον σαρκὶ καθ' ὑπόστασιν ἑνωθῆναι καὶ διὰ τοῦτο μίαν αὐτοῦ τὴν ὑ. ἤτοι ἓν πρόσωπον...ἀ. ἔ. CCP(553)*anath.*5; πεπρᾶχθαί φαμεν τὴν ἕνωσιν καθ' ὑ. ... ὁ θεὸς λόγος, τουτέστιν ἡ μία ὑ. ἐκ τῶν τριῶν τῆς θεότητος ὑ. ... ἐδημιούργησεν ἑαυτῷ...ἐν τῇ ἰδίᾳ ὑ. σάρκα ἐψυχωμένην ψυχῇ λογικῇ καὶ νοερᾷ ὅπερ ἐστὶ φύσις ἀνθρωπίνη...διὰ γὰρ τοῦ εἰπεῖν 'ὃς ἐν μορφῇ θεοῦ ὑπάρχων' τὴν τοῦ λόγου ὑ. ὑπάρχουσαν ἔδειξεν ἐν οὐσίᾳ θεοῦ, διὰ δὲ τοῦ εἰπεῖν 'μορφὴν δούλου ἔλαβεν' οὐσίᾳ ἀνθρώπου καὶ οὐχ ὑ. ἤτοι προσώπῳ ἑνωθῆναι τὸν λόγον ἐσήμανεν Justn.*conf.*(p.74.24ff.; M.86.997B); μίαν ὑ. τοῦ θεοῦ λόγου σύνθετον ...ἐπειδὴ ὅτε καθ' ἑαυτὴν ἁπλῶς φύσις λέγεται μὴ προσκειμένου ταύτῃ ἰδικοῦ τινος προσώπου, ἀόριστόν τι καὶ ἀνυπόστατον δηλοῖ *ib.*(p.86.36; 1011A); μίαν ὑ. σύνθετον, ἐκ δύο συντεθειμένην φύσεων... ἀλλήλαις ἡνωμένων κατ' αὐτὴν τὴν τοῦ λόγου ὑ. ... οὐ γὰρ ὑπέστη καθ' αὑτὸ κἂν ἀκαριαίως τὸ τοῦ Χριστοῦ ἀνθρώπινον ὡς ἂν ὑ. τοῦτο λέγοιτο ‡Cyr.*Trin.*18(6³.24Bf.; M.77.1157A); κενωθεὶς μὲν σπορὰ γέγονε τῆς οἰκείας σαρκός, ἀρρήτῳ δὲ συλλήψει συντιθεὶς αὐτῆς ὑ. γέγονε τῆς προσληφθείσης σαρκὸς Max.*ambig.*(M.91.1037A); ἐκ τούτων δὲ θείας φύσεως καὶ ἀνθρωπίνης φύσεως λέγω, καὶ ἐν ταύταις, καὶ τούτων ὑ. ἐστι...ὁ εἷς καὶ μόνος Χριστὸς καὶ υἱὸς id.*opusc.*(M.91.96A); ‡Gr.Nyss.*hom.9.50 in Jo.*(p.296.5); ἕνα...Χριστὸν...ἐκ δύο καὶ ἐν δύο οὐσίαις...ὑποστῆναι γινώσκομεν...σωζομένης τῆς ἰδιότητος ἑκατέρας φύσεως καὶ εἰς ἓν πρόσωπον καὶ μίαν ὑ. συντρεχούσης Agath.Papa *ep.syn.*(M.*PL.*87.1222C); ἡ θεότης...καὶ ἡ ἀνθρωπότης τοῦ Χριστοῦ...ἔχει...ἑκατέρα κοινὴν τὴν μίαν σύνθετον αὐτοῦ ὑ.· ἡ μὲν θεότης προαιωνίως...ἡ δὲ...σὰρξ...ἐπ' ἐσχάτων τῶν χρόνων ὑπ' αὐτῆς προσληφθεῖσα καὶ ἐν αὐτῇ ὑπάρξασα, καὶ αὐτὴν ἐσχηκυῖα ὑ. Jo.D.*nat.*6(M.95.120D); ἡ αὐτὴ...τοῦ λόγου ὑ., ἀμφοτέρων τῶν φύσεων ὑ. χρηματίσασα, οὔτε ἀνυπόστατον αὐτῶν μίαν εἶναι συγχωρεῖ, οὔτε μὴν ἑτεροϋποστάτους ἀλλήλων εἶναι παραχωρεῖ...ἀεὶ ἀμφοτέρων ἀδιαιρέτως, καὶ ἀχωρίστως ὑπάρχει ὑ. id.*f.o.*3.9(M.94.1017Af.); so two ἐνέργειαι of one Person καθ' ἑκάτερον ὧν ὑπῆρχεν ὑ. φυσικῶς ἐνήργει μὴ διαιρούμενος Max.*opusc.*(M.91.36C); ὁ αὐτὸς θεὸς τέλειός ἐστιν ὁμοῦ καὶ ἄνθρωπος τέλειος, ἐκ δύο φύσεων...καὶ ἐν δύο φύσεσι...θελητικαῖς τε καὶ ἐνεργητικαῖς...μιᾷ δὲ συνθέτῳ ὑ. Jo.D.*f.o.*1.2(M.94.793A); ἐπειδὴ μὲν οὖν δύο φύσεις τοῦ Χριστοῦ, δύο αὐτοῦ καὶ τὰ φυσικὰ θελήματα, καὶ τὰς φυσικὰς ἐνεργείας φαμέν. ἐπειδὴ δὲ μία τῶν δύο φύσεων αὐτοῦ ἡ ὑ., ἕνα καὶ τὸν αὐτόν φαμεν θέλοντά τε καὶ ἐνεργοῦντα φυσικῶς *ib.*3.14(1033A).

ὑποστατικός, **A.** *substantive*; **1.** *being of the substance of, belonging to* τὸ δὲ ἑξῆς, ἑτέρας ὂν διανοίας ὑ., συνάψωμεν τοῖς ἐπιλεγομένοις Eus.*qu.Marin.*1.2(M.22.940B); **2.** *giving substance to, causing the existence of* εἰς συνηγορίαν προβάλλεται τῶν ἰδίων ῥημάτων τὴν ὑ. τῆς κτίσεως ἐν τῷ θείῳ θελήματι κίνησιν Gr.Nyss.*Eun.*12(2 p.291.7; M.45.1000D); τὴν ἀγαθὴν καὶ αἰωνίαν ζωήν, καὶ ὡς σοφήν, καὶ ὡς αὐτοσοφίαν ὑμνῶμεν, μᾶλλον δὲ ὡς πάσης σοφίας ὑ. Dion.Ar.*d.n.*7.1(M.3.865B); τὸν θεὸν τοῦ κόσμου τοῦ καθ' ἡμᾶς αὐτῷ συναϊδίου ποιητικήν τε καὶ ὑ. αἰτίαν καταφάσκειν Zach.Mit.*opif.*(M.85.1113A); **3.** *essential* αὐτὴν ὑ. ὁρῶντες τὴν τοῦ θεοῦ δικαιοσύνην Eus.*fr.Lc.*6:20(M.24.536B); τὸ οὖν θέλημα τοῦ ἀνθρώπου ὡς παράστασις ὑ.· μὴ παρόντος δὲ θελήματος, οὐδ' αὐτὸς ὁ θεός τι ποιεῖ, καίπερ δυνάμενος, διὰ τὸ αὐτεξούσιον Mac.Aeg.*hom.*37.10(M.34.757A); ref. 2Cor.3:7 ὑ. φωτὸς ἐν ταῖς ψυχαῖς βεβαία καὶ διηνεκὴς ἔλλαμψις id.*libert.ment.*22(M.34.956D); **4.** *actual* (opp. potential) τὰ μὲν ὑ. τοῦ νοὸς εἴδωλα πονηρότερά ἐστι καὶ ἐπικρατέστερα, τὰ δὲ λογιστικά, τούτων αἴτια καὶ προηγητικά Marc.Er.*opusc.*1.183(M.65.928B).

B. theol., *of* or *pertaining to a person, personal, hypostatic*; **1.** of Father and Son ὁ λόγος θεός, ζῶσα σοφία, ὑ., λόγος ἐνεργὴς καὶ υἱός, αὐτὴ οὐσιωμένη Acac.Caes.*fr.Marcell.*ap.Epiph.*haer.*72.7(p.262.16; M.42.392D); εἰ μὲν γὰρ οὐσιώδη καὶ ὑ. εἶναι δώσετε ταύτην [sc. τὴν βούλησιν τοῦ πατρός], πῶς ἔτι μονογενὴς ὁ υἱός, τρίτος ὢν ἐκ πατρός; Cyr.*thes.*8(5^1.61B); μήτε τῶν ὑ. ὑπάρξεων συγχεομένων ‡Gr.Nyss.*hom.1.15 in Jo.*(p.98.10); of Trin. πᾶσαν ὑ. πληθὺν ἐκτρεπομένων Sophr.H.*ep. syn.*(M.87.3153D); τῆς ἀγεννησίας, καὶ τῆς γεννήσεως, καὶ τῆς ἐκπορεύσεως· ἐν ταύταις γὰρ μόναις ταῖς ὑ. ἰδιότησι διαφέρουσιν ἀλλήλων αἱ ἅγιαι τρεῖς ὑποστάσεις ‡Cyr.*Trin.*9(6^3.14B; M.77.1140D) = Jo.D.*f.o.*1.8(M.94.824B); διαιρετὴν μὲν ταῖς ὑποστάσεσι καὶ ταῖς ὑ. ἰδιότησιν, ἡνωμένην δὲ τῇ οὐσίᾳ †Jo.D.*B.J.*19(M.96.1028A); **2.** Christol.; **a.** in gen. τὴν αὐτὴν [sc. ὑπόστασιν] ἔχει, μετὰ μέν τοι προσθήκην τῶν τε ὑ. ἰδιωμάτων σαρκός Leont.H.*Nest.*1.28(M.86.1493D); οὔτε μὴν ὑ. δυὰς κατὰ Νεστόριον Max.*ep.*13(M.91.525B); διὰ τὴν ὑ. ταυτότητα, ἤγουν τὴν μίαν ὑπόστασιν *ib.*(516C); **b.** opp. προφορικός: ἀποστελλόμενον, κατὰ καιρὸν εὐδοκίας τοῦ πατρικοῦ θελήματος, οὐχ ὡς προφορικὸν κατὰ καιρὸν χρόνου πρὸς χρείαν ἀπογεννώμενον, ἀλλ' ὡς ὑ. ‡Ath.*annunt.*4(M.28.921C); **c.** opp. φυσικός: τῆς φυσικῆς δυάδος τὴν ἕνωσιν, καὶ τὴν ὑ. μονάδα Leont.H.*monoph.*(M.86.1809B); κατὰ τὸ φυσικὸν ὄνομα, ὁμοιότης τινὸς πρὸς τινά ἐστιν πότε· κατὰ δὲ ὑ., ἑτερότης μόνον id.*Nest.*2.18(M.86.1577B); εἰ μὲν ὑ. αὐτὸ [sc. θέλημα] φήσουσιν, ἑτερόβουλος οὕτω γε ἔσται ὁ υἱὸς τῷ πατρί. μόνης γὰρ ὑποστάσεως χαρακτηριστικὸν τὸ ὑ. Max.*Pyrr.*(M.91.313C); τίς γὰρ ὁ λέγων ὑ., ὑπάρχειν ἐνέργειαν; καὶ οὕτως ἀλλότριον τοῦ πατρὸς κατ' ἐνέργειαν αὐτὸν ὁ τοιοῦτος ἀποφαίνει λόγος, εἴπερ ὑ., καὶ οὐ φυσικὴν ἔχει παρὰ τὸν πατέρα ἐνέργειαν. τοῖς γὰρ ὑ. ἰδιώμασιν, τὴν πρὸς αὐτὸν κέκτηται διαφορὰν προδήλως ὁ λόγος id.*opusc.*(M.91.85B); ἰδιώματα τῆς θείας φύσεως...φυσικὰ καὶ οὐχ ὑ. ‡Cyr.*Trin.*13(6^3.19B; M.77.1149A); φυσικὰ γάρ, καὶ οὐχ ὑ. φαμεν τὰ θελήματα καὶ τὰς ἐνεργείας...εἰ γὰρ ὑ. δῶμεν αὐτά, ἑτεροθελεῖς καὶ ἑτεροενεργεῖς τὰς τρεῖς ὑποστάσεις τῆς ἁγίας τριάδος εἰπεῖν ἀναγκασθησόμεθα Jo.D.*f.o.*3.14(M.94.1036A); τὸ πρωτότυπον καὶ ἡ εἰκών, ἕν μέν ἐστι τῇ ὑ. ὁμοιώσει δύο δὲ τῇ φύσει Thdr.Stud.*antirr.*3.3.1(M.99.428C); **d.** ref. hypostatic union ἐν τῇ κατ' οὐσίαν ὑ. ἑνώσει Leont.B.*Nest.et Eut.*proem.1(M.86.1308C); λέγεται [sc. ἕνωσις]...φυσική, ἡ ὡς κατὰ λόγον φύσεως οὖσα τῷδέ τινι...λέγεται φυσικὴ καὶ ἡ ὡς φύσεών τινων ἁπλῶς ἢ φύσεως οὖσα καὶ οὐ συμβεβηκότων...ὡσαύτως δὲ καὶ ὑ. ἡ μέν τις λέγεται μερῶν κατὰ λόγον ὑποστάσεως, ἡ δὲ ὡς ὑποστάσεων· φυσικὴν μὲν οὖν φαμεν ἡμεῖς τὴν ἕνωσιν ἐπὶ Χριστοῦ, ὡς φύσεων ἡνωμένων κατ' αὐτόν...καὶ ὑ. δέ φαμεν τὴν ἕνωσιν ἐπὶ Χριστοῦ· ἀνάπαλιν μέντοι τῷ σημαινομένῳ ἡμῖν κατὰ τὴν φυσικήν· οὐ γὰρ ὡς ὑποστάσεων, ἀλλ' ὡς τοῦ λόγου οὖσαν τῆς ὑποστάσεως αὐτοῦ Leont.H.*Nest.*1.50(M.86.1512Cff.); *ib.*3.5(1617A); ὑ. οὖν ἕνωσίς ἐστιν, ἡ τὰς διαφόρους οὐσίας ἤγουν φύσεις εἰς ἓν πρόσωπον, καὶ μίαν καὶ τὴν αὐτὴν ὑπόστασιν συνάγουσά τε καὶ συνδέουσα· ὑ. δὲ διαφορὰ τυγχάνει λόγος, καθ' ὃν ἡ κατὰ τὸ ἄθροισμα τῶν ἐνθεωρουμένων ἰδιωμάτων τῷ κοινῷ τῆς οὐσίας ἑτερότης, τέμνουσα κατ' ἀριθμὸν ἄλλον ἐπ' ἄλλου, τὴν τῶν ἀτόμων ποιεῖται πληθὺν Max.*opusc.*(M.91.152B); *ib.*(61C); αὕτη [sc. ἕνωσις] δὲ πρὸς ἑαυτὴν οὐδεμίαν ὑ. ἔχει διαφορὰν Jo.D.*dialect.*66(M.94.665B); **e.** ref. θέλημα of Christ ποτὲ δὲ ὑ. αὐτὸ λέγων, τῇ διαφορᾷ τῶν ὑποστάσεων συνεισῆγε καὶ τὸ διάφορον τῶν θελημάτων ἐπὶ τῶν ὁμοουσίων Max.*Pyrr.*(M.91.329C); and properties τὴν μίαν αὐτοῦ ὑπόστασιν, πάλαι μὲν ἐξ ἀποιήτων τὸ ὅλον γνωρίζεσθαι ἰδιωμάτων ἐντελῶς, νῦν δὲ καὶ ἐκ ποιητῶν ἔχειν λόγων καὶ πραγμάτων ἐκ περιουσίας τὰς ὑ. ἑαυτῆς ὑπογραφάς Leont.H.*Nest.*2.39(M.86.1596C); τοῖς ὑ. ἰδιώμασιν Thdr.Stud.*antirr.*3.1.34(M.99.405C).

ὑποστατικῶς, **1.** *fundamentally* ὅταν ἴδῃς τὰ ἐγκείμενα ὑ. κινούμενα καὶ εἰς πάθος προκαλούμενα τὸν νοῦν ἡσυχάζοντα Marc.Er.*opusc.*1.180(M.65.928A); **2.** *in person* πῶς...τὸ πανάγιον πνεῦμα κατελθὸν ἐν τῇ Ἰορδάνῃ καὶ μεῖναν ἐν Χριστῷ; κατ' οὐσίαν καὶ κατ' ἀλήθειαν ὑ. Anast.S.*hod.*22(M.89.272C); **3.** Christol., *hypostatically*; *in virtue of* or *in terms of the Person, as one Person* ὅσα...ὑ. ἥνωται, κἂν ἐκ δύο νοεῖται, ὅμως τὸ τῇ τοῦ δυνατωτέρου φύσει συνενωθέν, ἐκεῖνο καὶ νοεῖται καὶ ὀνομάζεται Marc.Er.*opusc.*10.5(M.65.1124B); τὴν μὲν [sc. διαφορὰν] ἐν τῷ φυσικῷ λόγῳ...τελείως συντηρουμένην, τὴν δὲ [sc. ἕνωσιν]...ἐν τῷ οἰκονομικῷ τρόπῳ...ὑ. σωζομένην Max.*opusc.*(M.91.84B); εἰς ὁ προαιώνιος λόγος τοῦ θεοῦ καὶ μετὰ τὴν πρόληψιν τῆς σαρκὸς ὑ. καὶ οὐ φυσικῶς Jo.D.*disp.*(M.96.1345B).

ὑπόστατις, ἡ, fem. of ὑποστάτης, *one who gives substance* or *reality*; of God as πάντων αἰτία, Dion.Ar.*d.n.*1.7(M.3.596C).

ὑποστατός (ὑπόστατος), *substantially existing* καθ' ἑαυτὴν...οὐκ ἔστιν ὑ. [sc. ὕλη] Alex.Lyc.*Man.*6(p.10.25; M.18.420C); ὡς ἐκ θεοῦ θεός ἐστι...οὕτως ἐξ ὑποστάσεως ὑ. ‡Ath.*Ar.*4.1(p.45.4; M.26.469A); of Logos, Didym.*Trin.*3.4(M.39.789A); as subst. οὔτε ἡ ψυχὴ μόνη γίνεται ὑπόστασις οὔτε τὸ σῶμα, ἀλλ' ἐν ὑ. Melet.*nat.hom.*31(M.64.1309B).

ὑποστέγω, *hold out, resist* an attack, Geo.Pis.*carm.*1.34.

ὑποστεναχίζω, *groan under*, Paul.Sil.*Soph.*190(M.86.2127A).

***ὑποστερηνέω**, ? *strengthen* πῶς γὰρ οἰκέτης δεσπότην ἐνισχύσειεν, ἢ πνεῦμα πέτραν ὑποστερηνήσειεν ‡Caes.Naz.*dial.*29(M.38.888).

ὑπόστημα, τό, **1.** *garrison* [Hebr. נְצִיב], ref. 1Reg.13:3 ὑ. ... ἐκάλεσε τὴν φρουράν Thdt.*qu.27 in 1Reg.*(1.373); *position*, Sophr.H.*nativ.*(p.513.12); **2.** = ὑπόστασις in sense of *substance*, ref. Jer.23:8 οὔτε τις ἄλλος...ἔστη ἐν ὑ. καὶ οὐσίᾳ κυρίου Gr.Naz.*or.*28.19(p.51.8; M.36.52B); ἔωλον μὲν τῶν ἡμερῶν διαστήμασι, ζῷον δὲ τῷ ἐκ τῆς θεότητος ὑ. Germ.CP *or.*2(M.98.261A).

ὑποστήριγμα, τό, *prop, support* τὰ ὀστᾶ ταῦτα τὰ τῆς σαρκὸς ὑ. Bas.*hom.in Ps.*33(1.156C; M.29.381C); ἐπὶ οἰκίας σαθρῶς διακειμένης, οὐδεὶς ὑ. τίθησιν...ἀλλὰ καταλύσας...ἀνακαινίζει Chrys.*hom.5.3 in Tit.*(11.761B); ἔπηξε τὴν γῆν, ἀναδείξας τὰ ὑ. αὐτῆς Cyr.*Jo.*12.1(4.1094B); fig. ὑπὸ...ῥαθυμίας λήθης τε καὶ ἀγνοίας τὰ τῶν λοιπῶν παθῶν ὑποστηρίγματα κραταιοῦνται καὶ μεγαλύνονται Marc.Er.*opusc.*5.12(M.65.1049A); τὸ ὑ. τῶν νοητῶν ἀλλοφύλων *ib.*5.13(1049B).

***ὑποστηριγμός**, ὁ, = foreg. ἔστω [sc. bishop] αὐτοῖς ὑπό σε βακτηρία καὶ ὑ. *Euchol.*(p.256).

ὑποστηρίζ-ω, *underprop, sustain*, met. ὅση δ' αὐτοῦ τῇ ψυχῇ πίστεως ἐνθέου ὑπεστήρικτο δύναμις Eus.*v.C.*4.15(p.123.18; M.20.1164A); ἐλπίδι δὲ καὶ ὑπομονῇ ἀντὶ βακτηρίας...~εσθαι Gr.Nyss.*virg.*18(p.318.20; M.46.392A); τοὺς τὸ ὁμοούσιον δοξάζοντας ὀρθοδόξους ὑπεστήριζε Thphn.*chron.*p.53(M.108.188C).

***ὑποστήριξις**, ἡ, *support*, Geo.Pis.*hex.*263(M.92.1455A).

ὑποστιγμή, ἡ, **1.** *comma*, ref. exegesis ἀναγνωσόμεθα...οὐ πάντως προστακτικῶς ἀλλ' ὡς ἐν συνέσει μᾶλλον καὶ ὑ. Cyr.*Jo.*3.2(4.260C); ὑμεῖς δὲ σοφιστικῶς τελείᾳ στίζοντες, καὶ οὐχ ὑποστιγμῇ καθ' ἡμᾶς 'τὸν ἕνα υἱόν' Leont.H.*monoph.*(M.86.1864B); Anast.S.*hod.*proem.(M.89.36B); **2.** *pause, punctuation mark*, used in conjunction with ἐρώτησις: ὡς ἐν ὑ. τε καὶ ἐρωτήσει λέγων τὰ ἑξῆς Cyr.*Rom.*5:14(p.184.12; M.74.785B); ἀγαγνωσόμεθα...τὸν πρῶτον στίχον κατ' ἐπερώτησιν καὶ ὑ. id.*Os.*155(3.188A); id.*Jo.*5.4(4.511A); *ib.*6.1(593B).

ὑποστίζω, *put a comma*, Eus.*qu.Marin.*1.2(M.22.940A); Chrys.*hom.15.2 in 1Cor.*(10.127A); Sev.Ant.*res.*(p.842.1; M.46.645A).

ὑποστικτέον, *one must punctuate* or *put a comma*, Didym.*Pr.*1:7(M.39.1624B); Thdt.*Rom.*11:7(3.119); id.*Ps.*4:5(1.631).

***ὑποστιρίτης**, ὁ, *base*, *IGC As.Min.*10 (saec. iv–v).

ὑποστολή, ἡ, *shrinking back*; **1.** *humility* τῷ δὲ λέγειν κλίνειν αὐτὸν οὐρανὸν καὶ κατεληλυθέναι σημαίνει τὴν ὑ. τῆς ἐνθέου δόξης Eus.*d.e.*6.1(p.252.8; M.22.413C); **2.** *retirement* τοῦ δὲ κατ' αὐτοὺς τρόπου ἐν ὑ. γενόμενος [sc. of Zerah, Gen.38:28–30] id.*qu.Steph.*7.5(M.22.909B); **3.** *reserve* of language περιγράψας δὲ ἐνταῦθα τὴν κατ' αὐτῶν πρόρρησιν, ὑ. χρῆται id.*d.e.*2.3(p.72.24; M.22.132B); οὐδεμιᾶς ὑ. κατὰ τὸ ὑψηλὸν τῆς ἐννοίας ἔν τινι τῶν ὀνομάτων ἐπ' αὐτοῦ [sc. θεοῦ] γινομένης Gr.Nyss.*Eun.*7(2 p.162.28; M.45.752C); Chrys.*hom.3.1 in 1Tim.*(11.563B); **4.** *caution*, Proc.G.*Is.*48:18(M.87.2457D); **5.** *timidity* τί οὖν βούλεται ἡ ὑ. τῆς ψυχῆς καὶ ἡ μεγαλοψυχία ἐπὶ μὲν τοῦ πατρὸς φιλοτιμουμένων καὶ τῷ υἱῷ τυχεῖν τὰ ἴσα χαριζομένων, ἐπὶ δὲ τοῦ πνεύματος σμικρολογούντων τὴν χάριν; Gr.Nyss.*Maced.*11(M.45.1313C); of preaching gospel χωρὶς ὑ. τινος, καὶ μετὰ ἐλευθερίας ἁπάσης Chrys.*hom.34.2 in Mt.*(7.390D); id.*hom.73.2 in Jo.*(8.431B);

Cyr.*Am.*9(3.261C); Thdt.*ep.*122(4.1205); **6.** *reluctance*, Areth.*Apoc.* 9:4(M.106.624C).

ὑποστόρνυμι (ὑποστρώννυμι), 1. *spread out*, of God *νύκτα δ' ὑποστρώσας μελαντέρῳ χρώματι* Eus.*l.C.*6(p.207.30; M.20.1344B); *τὴν θάλασσαν ὑπεστόρεσεν* Chrys.*hom.23.3 in 1Cor.*(10.204A); medic. *ὑπεστορῆσθαι τὸν πλεύμονα τῇ καρδίᾳ* id.*hom.5.5 in Heb.*(12.60C); with personal object *κήρυκας...ὑποστρωννύμενοι M.Polyc.*2.4; reflex. *ὑποστρώσασα ἑαυτὴν εἰς προσευχήν M.Ner.et Ach.*22(p.21.21); **2.** *scatter*, Eust.*engast.*30(p.62.17; M.18.673C); **3.** met., act., *make subject*, Eus.*d.e.*10.8(p.489.14; M.22.785C); *ὡς ὀλετῆρα...τοῦ ἰδίου καρποῦ, ταῖς ἰσορρόποις ὑπέστρωσε δίκαις* Cyr.*ador.*7(1.242A); *τὰς τῶν ζῴων ἀγέλας τοῖς ποσὶν ὑπεστόρεσε* [sc. *τοῦ Ἀδάμ*] Bas.Sel.*or.* 29.1(M.85.328A); of an adulteress *ἑτέροις αὑτὴν ὑποστρώσασα* Vict. *Mc.*8:38(p.351.4); *μὴ βάϊα καταστρωννύντες αὐτοῦ τῇ ὁδῷ, ἀλλ' ἡμᾶς αὐτοὺς ὑποστρωννύντες ὡς ἐφικτὸν ψυχῆς ταπεινότητι καὶ γνώμης ὀρθότητι* Andr.Cr.*or.*9(M.97.992D).

ὑποστρέφ-ω, *turn back, return*, of penitents *ἡ ψυχὴ...τῇ κακίᾳ προσκλινομένη...εἰ μὴ ~οι, ὑπὸ τῆς ἀνοίας ἀποκτηνοῦται* Or.*princ.*1.8.4 (p.104.9; M.11.180B); *ἐν τῇ τῶν ~όντων τάξει ὑποπίπτειν* Gr.Thaum. *ep.can.*8(M.10.1041D); *Euchol.*(p.538).

ὑποστροφή, ἡ, *return*; **1.** *recurrence*, astron. *τὴν στροφήν, μᾶλλον δὲ ὑ. τοῦ σεληνιαίου κύκλου* Mac.Mgn.*apocr.*2.10(p.15.16); medic. *ὁ ὑ. πρὸς ἴασιν πάλιν οὐκ ἔχει Hom.Clem.*14.5; in gen. *τὴν ὑ. τῶν δαιμόνων* Tit.Bost.*fr.Lc.*8:38(p.179); to former way of life *εἰς ἀπώλειαν* Chrys.*serm.8.5 in Gen.*(4.682C); id.*hom.42.2 in 1Cor.*(10.397B); *δύο κατὰ ταυτὸν αἰτεῖ, ἀπόλυσιν μὲν τῆς συμβάσης ἀποστροφῆς, τοῦ γε ἁγίου πνεύματος ὑποστροφὴν εἰς ἡμᾶς* Cyr.*Ps.*50:13(M.69.1100B); ref. Lot's wife *ἔχουσα τῆς πονηρᾶς προαιρέσεως καὶ ὑ. τὴν μνήμην* Cyr.H. *catech.*19.8; **2.** in phrase *ἐξ ὑποστροφῆς turning sharply round*, met. *ὥσπερ ἐξ ὑ. νῦν τὰ περὶ αὐτῶν διδάσκεται* Oecum.*Apoc.*11:3-6(p.128); *πρὸς τὸν σατανᾶν ἐξ ὑ. αὐτομολῆσαι ib.*12:1(p.135).

ὑπόστρωμα, τό, *bed*, met. *ἡ τῶν ἐθνῶν πληθύς...ὑ. δὲ καὶ καθέδρα δαιμονίων τυγχάνουσα* Job.Mon.*inc.*1(M.86.3316A).

ὑποστρώννυμι, v. *ὑποστόρνυμι.*

ὑπόστρωσις, ἡ, *spreading, scattering*, Nil.*epp.*3.243(M.79.497C).

***ὑποστυγνάζω,** *make dimmer*, Thdr.Stud.*poen.*1.73(M.99.1741D).

***ὑποσυγκεχυμένως,** *somewhat confusedly*, Or.*comm.min.in Cant.* (p.51.9; *συγκεχυμένως* M.13.36B).

ὑποσυλ-άω, *steal away secretly* *~ᾷ τὰ τῆς ἀληθείας Hom.Clem.*2.22; *ὑπεσύλα καὶ τὸν νοῦν ἔκλεπτεν* Eust.*engast.*12(p.36.16; M.18.640B); *ἵν' ἐκείνων τῶν προσδοκωμένων ~ήσω τὸν ὄγκον* Thdt.*h.rel.*28(3.1287); *τοὺς ἁπλουστέρους...~ᾶν* Zach.Mit.*opif.*(M.85.1036A).

***ὑποσύλησις, ἡ,** *suborning*, Leont.H.*monoph.*(M.86.1884C).

ὑποσύμβολον, τό, plur., *veiled language τὰ σκοτεινῶς ὑπὸ τοῦ Πυθαγόρου λεγόμενα πρὸς τοὺς μαθητὰς δι' ὑποσυμβόλων* Hipp.*haer.* 6.27(p.153.16; M.16.3234A).

***ὑποσυνᾴδω,** *chime in with*; met. *agree with*, Areth.*Apoc.*1:4(M. 106.504D).

***ὑποσφύζω,** *throb underneath*, ‡Nil.*narr.*2(M.79.600A); fig., Jo.VI CP *ep.*(M.96.1429B).

***ὑποσχεδιάζω,** *do* something *off-hand*; hence *make without difficulty*, of God *κτίσιν ὑποσχεδιάσας* Cyr.*Juln.*1(6^2.24E).

ὑποσῴζω, s.v.l., *preserve*, Cyr.*hom.div.*21.5(M.77.1113C; *ἀποσῴζων* p.539.23).

***ὑποταγάδην,** *in subjection, like subjects*, Thphn.*chron.*p.313(M. 108.760C).

ὑποταγή, ἡ, A. *subjection, submission*; *obedience*; **1.** of creatures to God *πάντα ἐν ὑ. μένει τοῦ θεοῦ· ὑ. δὲ θεοῦ, ἀφθαρσία* Iren.*haer.*4.38. 3(M.7.1108A); Eus.*l.C.*1(p.197.20; M.20.1321A); ref. Ps.102:19 and Is.66:1 *θρόνοι δηλοῦσιν τὴν ὑ. πάσης κτίσεως* ‡Ath.*serm.fid.*29(p.26; M.26.1284B); of angels to Logos *ἡ δὲ τῶν ἀγγέλων ὑ. τὴν θεότητα τοῦ λόγου δείκνυσιν* Ath.*Ar.*3.40(M.26.409B); of the world to Christ, id. *inc.et c.Ar.*(M.26.1020A); **2.** of Christ on earth to God, Cyr.*ador.*11 (1.396C); for discussion of subjection of Son, esp. ref. 1Cor.15:28, v. *ὑποτάσσω*; **3.** of things to men, ref. Ps.8:6, Thphl.Ant.*Autol.* 1.6(M.6.1033A); Thdr.Mops.*fr.Apoll.*(p.320.30; M.66.1001A); **4.** of members of body and of body to spirit *τὰ δὲ ἐλάχιστα μέλη τοῦ σώματος ἡμῶν ἀναγκαῖα...πάντα...ὑ. μιᾷ χρῆται εἰς τὸ σῴζεσθαι ὅλον τὸ σῶμα 1Clem.*37.5; *ζητητέον πῶς χωρὶς ὑ. οὐδεὶς ὄψεται τὸν θεόν; τί γάρ; ἡ Αἰγυπτία Μαρία, καὶ ἄλλοι τινὲς μὴ ὑποταγέντες τινί, οὐκ ὄψονται τὸν κύριον; λέγομεν οὖν, ὅτι οὐ λέγει περὶ τῆς σωματικῆς μόνης ὑ., ἀλλὰ καὶ περὶ τῆς ψυχικῆς. οὐδένα οὖν εὕρομεν τῶν ἁγίων, ὃς οὐχ ὑπέταξε τὸ σῶμα τῷ πνεύματι Schol.*14 in Jo.Clim.*scal.*4(M.88.732D); **5.** of laity to bishop, *A.Phil.*91(p.35.25); **6.** monastic; in gen., Bas. *renunt.*9(2.211B; M.31.648A); Marc.Er.*opusc.*2.166(M.65.956D); *ib.*2. 169(956D); Esaias *or.*5.3(p.37); illustrated met. *τύπος...ἀρίστης ὑ. ὁ ...ὑδρώδης ἄργυρος ἔστω· ὑποκάτω γὰρ κυλινδούμενος πάντων, παντὸς ῥυπουμένου μένει ἀνεπίμικτος* Jo.Clim.*scal.*4(M.88.716C); in description of *ὑπακοή*, Ant.Mon.*hom.*39(M.89.1556B); its necessity, Jo.Clim. *scal.*4(M.88.725C); *μετὰ δὲ τὴν ἐν τῷ σταδίῳ λοιπὸν τῆς...ὑ. εἴσοδον, μηκέτι τὸν καλὸν ἡμῶν ἀγωνοθέτην ἔν τινι τὸ σύνολον ἀνακρίνωμεν... εἰ δὲ μή, οὐδὲν ἐκ τῆς ὑ. οἱ ἀνακρίνοντες ὠφελούμεθα ib.*(680D); conditions *ἐν ὑ. δὲ ὤν, μηδέποτε πιστεύσῃς τῇ καρδίᾳ σου· τυφλώττει γὰρ ἀπὸ τῶν παλαιῶν προσπαθειῶν* Dor.*doct.*17.3(M.88.1804A); *ὁ θέλων ἐν ὑ. γενέσθαι, ἀποτασσέσθω τὰ ἴδια θελήματα...ὁ θέλων οὖν ἐν ὑ. εἶναι, καταλείψῃ τὰ νεκρὰ αὐτοῦ θελήματα...νεκρωσάτω ἑαυτὸν ἀπὸ τῆς προσκαίρου ζωῆς* Ant.Mon.*hom.*113(M.89.1785B); perfect renunciation of world, Thdr.Stud.*or.*11.9(M.99.812C); temptation to combine with selfish desire, Marc.Er.ap.*Schol.*38 in Jo.Clim.*scal.*4 (741C); *μηδέποτε ὑποδέχου τὸν ἐν ὑ. σου· παράσχου μοι, λέγοντά σοι, ἐξουσίαν χρόνον πρὸς ἀρετήν...ὁ γὰρ δὴ οὕτως λέγων, δῆλον ὅτι τὸ ἴδιον ἀποτελεῖ θέλημα καὶ τῆς...ὑ. τὰς συνθήκας ἀθετεῖ* Jo.Carp. *cap.*32(M.85.1844); *ἀπάτη...τοῦ πονηροῦ πρὸς τὸ ἐμποδίσαι τῇ...ὑ., καὶ τῇ κατ' αὐτὴν ἀσφαλεῖ σωτηρίᾳ* Dor.*doct.*17.3(M.88.1804A); Jo.Clim. *scal.*4(708B); *ib.*(725B); effects *ὁ ἐν ὑ. ὢν παρὰ πολλῶν ὑβριζόμενος... καθαίρεται, καὶ γίνεται ὡς τὸ πυρούμενον ἀργύριον ἐναποστίλβον* Ant. Mon.*hom.*113(M.89.1785C); cf. *ἡ ὑ. μετὰ ἐγκρατείας ὑποτάσσει θηρία Apophth.Patr.*(M.65.88B); freeing from fear of death, Jo.Clim.*scal.* 4(705A); defeating arrogance, *ib.*(708A).

B. *appendix* or *footnote μηδὲν ἕτερον διδούς, εἰ μὴ τὰ τῇ ὑ. τῆς διατάξεως περιεχόμενα* Ath.Scholast.*coll.*4.4(p.54).

***ὑποτακτήτης, ὁ,** v. **ὑποτακτίτης.*

ὑποτακτικός, 1. *submissive, subordinate, Const.App.*4.11.3; Marc. Er.*opusc.*2.24(M.65.933C); of wife's status, Chrys.*hom.20.1 in Eph.* (11.144A); esp. ref. monastic obedience, Isid.Pel.*epp.*1.278(M.78. 345C); Nil.*epp.*1.46(M.79.104B); Marc.Er.*opusc.*2.170(956D); *V.Alex. Acoem.*43(p.692.10); in Arian theology, of Son in rel. to Father, ‡Chrys.*Trin.*2(1.835A); **2.** *befitting a subordinate*, ref. Ps.15:10, †Gregent.*disp.*(M.86.645D).

ὑποτακτικῶς, *in the subjunctive mood*, ‡Hipp.*fr.26 in Pss.*(p.150. 13; M.10.721C).

***ὑποτακτίτης (-τήτης), ὁ,** *one under obedience* or *under a rule*; of a monk, Thdr.Stud.*catech.parv.*125(p.295); id.*or.*11.44(*ὑποτακτήτης* M.99.848C).

***ὑποτάκτρια, ἡ,** fem. of foreg., Steph.Diac.*v.Steph.*(M.100.1130A).

***ὑποταξία, ἡ,** *obedience, submission*; of monks, Nil.*epp.*2.101 (M.79.245B).

***ὑποταπεινόω,** *humble ἑαυτοὺς ὑ. τοῖς ὑποδεεστέροις* Bas.*hom.in Ps.*33(1.155E; M.29.381A); med., Thdr.Stud.*epp.*2.105(M.99.1624A).

ὑποτάσσ-ω, *subject, subdue, make subordinate*;

A. act.; **1.** of God subjecting all things to Christ, ref. 1Cor.15:27, Clem.*str.*1.24(p.100.25; M.8.908B); **2.** his subjection of creation to man, ref. Ps.8:6, *Diogn.*10.2; Just.*2apol.*5.2(M.6.452B); **3.** of Christ, ref. Ps.2:8 *τὴν ὑπὸ τοῦ πατρὸς δεδομένην αὐτῷ κληρονομίαν ὑπέταξε τοῖς ἀποστόλοις αὐτοῦ καὶ προφήταις, τῷ τοὺς εἰς αὐτὸν πεπιστευκότας τοῖς τούτων ὑποτετάχθαι λόγοις* Eus.*d.e.*6.2(p.253.20; M.22.416D); **4.** of man *ὑ. αὐτοῦ τὸ σῶμα εἰς ἁγνείαν* Meth.*res.*1.59 (p.323.17; M.41.1156D); of a monk *ἑαυτὸν ὑποτάξας τῇ τῶν συνασκουμένων ὑπηρεσίᾳ* Nil.*epp.*2.101(M.79.245A).

B. pass.; **1.** *be submissive, obedient*, or *made subject*, of creation to God, *1Clem.*20.1; Athenag.*leg.*18.2(M.6.925B); Meth.*res.*2.27(p.384. 8; M.41.1157B); of all things to Christ, Polyc.*ep.*2.1; of demons to his name, Just.*dial.*30.3(M.6.540B); of Christ to his parents, ref. Lc.2:51, ‡Ath.*Maced.dial.*1.19(M.28.1324A); to Law, ref. Phil.2:7, Procl.CP *hom.*2.3(M.65.840B); of man to God's commandments, Herm.*mand.*12.5.1; exeg. Ps.36:7 *οὐ δεῖ πρότερον περὶ ἁμαρτίας ἱκετεύειν, ἢ ὑποταγέντα τῷ κυρίῳ, τουτέστιν ἐκστάντα τῆς ἁμαρτίας* Or.*exc.in Ps.*36:7(M.17.124B); of his mind to Father, Esaias *or.*4.12 (p.31); of Christians to one another *μηδὲν ἀλαζονευόμενοι, ~όμενοι μᾶλλον ἢ ~οντες 1Clem.*2.1; *ib.*38.1; to bishops and presbyters, Ign. *Eph.*2.2; to presbyters and deacons, Polyc.*ep.*5.3; deacon to bishop, Ign.*Magn.*2; slaves to masters, *Did.*4.11; of woman to man (v. *γυνή*), Chrys.*hom.26.2 in 1Cor.*(10.229E); of the passions *εἰ τῷ νῷ τῶν ἁγίων ὑπετάγησαν αἱ ἀντιστρατευόμεναι τῷ νῷ κινήσεις, πῶς οὐχὶ τῷ θεῷ λόγῳ ὑποταγήσονται, ἑνωθέντι ψυχῇ νοερᾷ μετὰ σαρκός;* ‡Ath.*dial.Trin.*5.50(M.28.1285B); **2.** *be subordinate*; **a.** Trin.; of Son in rel. to Father *οἴδαμεν γὰρ καὶ αὐτόν, εἰ καὶ ὑποτέτακται τῷ πατρὶ καὶ τῷ θεῷ, ἀλλ' ὅμως πρὸ αἰώνων γεννηθέντα ἐκ τοῦ θεοῦ θεὸν κατὰ φύσιν τέλειον εἶναι καὶ ἀληθῆ καὶ μὴ ἐξ ἀνθρώπων μετὰ ταῦτα θεόν Symb.Ant.*(345)(p.252.30; M.26.729C); *οὐ γὰρ συντάσσομεν υἱὸν τῷ πατρί, ἀλλ' ὑποτεταγμένον τῷ πατρί Symb.Sirm.* 1 *anath.*18(p.255.31; M.26.737D); *καὶ τοῦτο δὲ καθολικὸν εἶναι οὐδεὶς* *ἀγνοεῖ δύο πρόσωπα εἶναι πατρὸς καὶ υἱοῦ, καὶ τὸν μὲν πατέρα μείζονα, τὸν δὲ υἱὸν ὑποτεταγμένον τῷ πατρὶ μετὰ πάντων, ὧν αὐτῷ ὁ πατὴρ ὑπέταξε* Symb.*Sirm.*2(p.251.15; M.26.741C); *ὑποτεταγμένον οὐσίᾳ καὶ γνώμῃ* Eun.*apol.*26(M.30.864B); of H. Ghost in rel. to Son and Son to Father, *ib.*27(865A); of H. Ghost *τρίτης γε* [sc. *οὐσίας*] *τῆς μηδεμιᾷ μὲν τούτων συνταττομένης, ἀλλὰ τῇ μὲν διὰ τὴν αἰτίαν, τῇ δὲ διὰ τὴν ἐνέργειαν καθ' ἣν γέγονεν ∼ομένης* id.ap.Gr.Nyss.*Eun.*1(1 p.67.28; M.45.297A); doctrine refuted, Gr.Nyss.*Eun.*1(1 p.77.27ff.; 308Dff.); **b.** perf. ptcpl. pass., *subordinate*; of monks, Bas.*reg.fus.*26 (2.371B; M.31.985C); Mac.Aeg.*perf.*9(M.34.848B); **c.** exeg.; **i.** scriptural senses discussed, ref. Pss.8:6, 46:4ff., 1Cor.15:24, Gr.Nyss. *Eun.*1(1 p.77.27ff.; M.45.308Dff.); and 1Petr.2:18, concluding *ἡμεῖς ἀλλήλοις ∼όμενοι διὰ τὴν ἀγάπην, οὐχ ὡς τὰ κτήνη φυσικῶς, οὐθ' ὡς τὰ ἔθνη τῇ πίστει, οὐθ' ὡς δοῦλοι τῷ νόμῳ* ‡Ath.*Maced.dial.*1.18 (M.28.1321C); **ii.** Rom.8:7, Meth.*res.*1.59ff.(p.322.15; M.41.1156A); **iii.** 1Cor.15:28, acc. Marcellus *τὴν δ' ὑποταγὴν τοῦ υἱοῦ ἕνωσιν ἑρμηνεύει τοῦ λόγου, ἓν καὶ ταυτὸν γενησομένου τῷ πατρὶ καθ' ἃ καὶ πρότερον ἦν, ὡς αὐτὸς ἔφη* Eus.*e.th.*3.15(p.172.6; M.24.1028C); cf. *τοῦτο δηλοῖ καὶ τὸν υἱὸν ἀναλύεσθαι εἰς πατέρα* Cyr.H.*catech.*15.30; ref. Marcellus' exegesis *ὥσπερ οὐχ ἕνωσιν ὁ ἀπόστολος ἐδήλου λέγων ὑποταγήσεσθαι τῷ υἱῷ τὰ πάντα, ἀλλὰ τὴν ἐξ αὐθεκουσίου προαιρέσεως ὑπακοήν...ἣν ἀποδώσει αὐτῷ τὰ πάντα οἷα...βασιλεῖ τῶν ὅλων, τὸν αὐτὸν τρόπον καὶ τὸ αὐτὸν ὑποταγήσεσθαι τῷ πατρὶ οὐδὲν ἕτερον σημαίνοι ἂν ἢ τὴν δόξαν...τήν τε αὐθεκούσιον ὑπακοήν, ἣν καὶ αὐτὸς ἀποδώσει τῷ θεῷ καὶ πατρί, ἐπειδὰν τοὺς πάντας ἀξίους τῆς πατρικῆς θεότητος εἶναι παρασκευάσῃ* Eus.*e.th.*3.15(p.172.17ff.; M.24.1029Aff.); *ὁ υἱὸς...ὑποταγήσεται, οὐχ ὅτι τότε ἄρχεται πειθαρχεῖν τῷ πατρὶ... ἀλλ' ὅτι καὶ τότε ὑπακούει* Cyr.H.*catech.*15.30; *ὅταν φησὶν ὑποταγῶμεν οἱ πάντες τῷ υἱῷ, εὑρεθῶμεν αὐτοῦ μέλη, καὶ γενώμεθα αὐτῷ εἰς υἱοὺς θεοῦ...τότε δὲ αὐτὸς ὑποταγήσεται ἀνθ' ἡμῶν τῷ πατρί, ὡς κεφαλὴ ὑπὲρ τῶν ἰδίων μελῶν* Ath.*inc.et c.Ar.*20(M.26.1020C); *τὴν ὑποταγὴν τῆς δουλικῆς μορφῆς ἀνειληφώς, ὑπὲρ ἡμῶν ∼εται τῷ ἑαυτοῦ πατρί, οὐ φύσει θεότητος, ἀλλ' ἑνώσει μορφῆς δουλικῆς, ἧς ἔλαβε* ‡Ath.*Maced. dial.*1.18(M.28.1321D); Gr.Naz.*or.*30.4,5(p.113.15ff.; M.36.108Bff.); Gr.Nyss.*Eun.*1(1 p.78.15; M.45.309B); full discussion, id.*hom.in 1Cor.15:28*(M.44.1304ff.); Cyr.*thes.*29(5^{1}.253Cff.); Max.*ambig.*(M. 91.1076A); ‡Caes.Naz.*dial.*127(M.38.1024); cf. exeg. Ps.109:1 *ἐν τῷ παρόντι βίῳ καὶ ὁ πατὴρ ∼ει τῷ υἱῷ, καὶ ὁ υἱὸς ∼ει τῷ πατρὶ τὴν ἀνθρωπότητα* Hesych.H.*fr.Ps.*109:1(M.93.1324A); **d.** Eph.1:22 *οὐχ ἁπλῶς ἀνώτερον ἐποίησεν, ὡς προτιμᾶσθαι αὐτῶν, οὐδὲ κατὰ σύγκρισιν, ἀλλ' ὡς δούλων προκαθῆσθαι* Chrys.*hom.3.2 in Eph.*(11.19C); **e.** Eph.5:22, *ib.20.2*(143D).

ὑποτέλειος, *less than complete*; *ὑ. ἀριθμοί* numbers *which exceed the sum of their factors*, Meth.*symp.*8.11(p.95.11; M.18.156C).

ὑποτελέω, *pay, discharge* an oath, Ath.Scholast.*coll.*4.1(p.51); *ib.*9.4(p.101).

***ὑποτεταγμένως**, *submissively*, *1Clem.*37.2.

***ὑποτετρακάνθηλος**, ? *supported on four pack-saddles ἐπενοήθη διὰ ζῴων σαγματουμένων ὑ. σανίδας ἐπιτίθειν, καὶ οὕτως ἐκφέρειν τοὺς νεκρούς* Thphn.*chron.*p.355(M.108.853B).

ὑποτεχνάομαι, *construct below*, ‡Caes.Naz.*dial.*92(M.38.956).

ὑποτηρέω, *hold in store*, Gr.Naz.*or.*16.4(M.35.940A).

ὑποτίμησις, ἡ, *toning-down, modification*, Or.*Cels.*2.25(p.155.5; M.11.845B); Proc.G.*Jos.*13:1(M.87.1024C).

***ὑποτινάσσω**, *shake from below*, Pall.*v.Chrys.*1(p.5.15; M.47.6); met., Nil.*epp.*1.26(M.79.92D).

ὑποτίτθιος, *at the breast*, Clem.*paed.*1.6(p.117.12; M.8.304C); Chrys.*hom.12.4 in 1Cor.*(10.102E); ‡Meth.*Sym.et Ann.*3(M.18.353A).

ὑπότιτθος, = foreg., Cyr.*Joel.*29(3.220C); Thdt.*h.e.*1.21.6(3.802); *τὰ ὑ. children at the breast*, ‡Caes.Naz.*dial.*109(M.38.984).

***ὑπότιτλος, ὁ**, *sub-section*, Ath.Scholast.*coll.*9(p.111).

***ὑποτίτλωσις, ἡ**, *entering under sub-sections*, Jo.Scholast.*nomoc.* (p.9.3).

ὑποτοπητέον, *one must surmise, suppose*, Clem.*paed.*2.10(p.219. 24; M.8.521B); id.*str.*3.12(p.232.19; M.8.1181A); Cyr.*Is.*4.1(2.570A).

ὑποτραυλίζω, med., *lisp somewhat*, Gr.Nyss.*res.*3(M.46.672C).

ὑποτραχύνομαι, met., *become somewhat exasperated*, Gr.Nyss.*ep.* 29(M.45.237C).

ὑποτρίβω, *rub a little*, met. *ὑ. τὸ μέτωπον harden* the forehead; hence *be shameless*, Epiph.*haer.*57.1(p.344.14; M.41.996B).

***ὑποτροφέω**, s.v.l., *nourish, rear*, Clem.*paed.*1.6(M.8.300C; *ὑποτροφ⟨ὴν⟩ οὖσαν* p.115.18).

ὑποτρύζω, *murmur*, Nonn.*par.Jo.*7:12(M.43.805C); *ib.*7:32(809B).

ὑποτυπ-όω, **1.** *form, represent*; **a.** lit. *ῥῖνας στέρνα τε καὶ ὤμους ∼ωσάμενος τέχνῃ τῇ πλαστικῇ* Eus.*d.e.*4.5(p.157.1; M.22.261B); **b.** met. *ἀλληγοροῦντες τὴν διαταγὴν τῶν ἀστρολόγων τὸ μὲν κέντρον οἱονεὶ θεὸν καὶ μονάδα καὶ κύριον τῆς πάσης γενέσεως ∼οῦσι* Hipp.*haer.*5. 15(p.110.31; M.16.3170D); *ἱστορίας τῶν πάλαι θεοφιλῶν Ἑβραίων, ὥσπερ τινὰς ἀρετῶν εἰκόνας ∼ωσάμενος* Eus.*d.e.*5 proem.(p.206.13; 341C); Nil.*epp.*2.9(M.79.205A); **2.** ? *form* an idea, so *imagine τοῦτο ταῖς ἑαυτοῦ παροινίαις καθ' αὑτὸν* (sic) *∼ωσάμενος, ἔγνω στρατεύειν ἐπ' αὐτόν* [sc. *τὸν Χριστόν*] *V.Const.*11(p.553.17); **3.** *represent in words*; hence *draft, compose, outline παρατηρητέον ὅτι ὁ Ματθαῖος καὶ ὁ Λουκᾶς δόξαιεν ἂν τοῖς πολλοῖς τὴν αὐτὴν ἀναγεγραφέναι ὑποτετυπωμένην πρὸς τὸ δεῖν οὕτως προσεύχεσθαι προσευχήν* Or.*or.*18 (p.340.11; M.11.473B); Hipp.*haer.*6.37(p.166.16; M.16.3251A); *ὡς ἀσθενὴς ὢν ὁ λόγος, περιυβρίζων μᾶλλον, ἤπερ ἐξομοιούμενος σοῖς ἔργοις τῇ δυνάμει, ∼ώσεται* Gr.Thaum.*pan.Or.*2(p.5.4; M.10.1056B); Eus.*h.e.*4.23.1(M.20.384B); **4.** *symbolize, exemplify τὸ δειλὸν τῶν τρυγόνων τὴν πρὸς τὰς ἁμαρτίας εὐλάβειαν ∼οῦται* Clem.*paed.*1.5 (p.98.16; M.8.265B); *τούτων ἤδη προδιηνυσμένων ἑπόμενον ἂν εἴη τὸν παιδαγωγὸν ἡμῶν Ἰησοῦν τὸν βίον ἡμῖν τὸν ἀληθινὸν ∼ώσασθαι καὶ τὸν ἐν Χριστῷ παιδαγωγῆσαι ἄνθρωπον* ib.1.12(p.148.14; 368A); *ὁ δὲ μακάριος Ἰωάννης...τὰς τῶν καμήλων εἵλατο τρίχας καὶ ταύτας ἠμπίσχετο, τὸ εὐτελὲς καὶ ἄδολον τοῦ βίου ∼ούμενος* ib.2.10(p.224.14; 532B); **5.** *typify, figure τοῦτό τοι πάλιν καὶ νόμος ἡμῖν ἱερὸς αἰνιγματωδῶς ὑπετύπου* Cyr.*ador.*14(1.480D); Euthal.Diac.*epp.Paul.*(M.85. 761B); Dion.Ar.*e.h.*4.11(M.3.484C); *οἱ δὲ ἑπτὰ τῶν τετρακισχιλίων ἄρτοι τὴν νομικήν, ὡς οἶμαι, μυσταγωγίαν ὑποτυποῦσιν* Max.*ambig.*(M. 91.1401D).

ὑποτύπωσις, ἡ, **1.** *outline, sketch*, Clem.*str.*4.1(p.248.10; M.8. 1216A); *ἁπλῶς δὲ καὶ ὡς ἐν ὑ., ἐν κεφαλαίῳ εἰπεῖν* Chrys.*hom.5.3 in Phil.*(11.232E); *οὐ γάρ ἐστιν ὅρος ἡ ὑ., ἀλλὰ διαζωγράφησίς τις τῆς τῶν πραγμάτων φύσεως cat.2Tim.*1:13(p.61.3); **2.** *form, shape, pattern ἔστι δὲ ἡ κατὰ τὸν θεὸν παιδαγωγία κατευθυσμὸς ἀληθείας εἰς ἐποπτείαν θεοῦ καὶ πράξεων ἁγίων ὑποτύπωσις ἐν αἰωνίῳ διαμονῇ* Clem.*paed.*1.7(p.122.10; M.8.313B); [Ezech.18:4–9] *ταῦτα ὑποτύπωσιν Χριστιανῶν περιέχει πολιτείας* ib.1.10(p.146.27; 364C); *ὅθεν τὸ ἀσθενὲς τῆς μνήμης τῆς ἐμῆς ἐπικουφίζων, κεφαλαίων συστηματικὴν ἔκθεσιν μνήμης ὑπόμνημα σωτήριον πορίζων ἐμαυτῷ, ἀναγκαίως κέχρημαι τῇδε τῇ ὑ.* id.*str.*1.1(p.10.27; M.8.704A); *ib.* (p.11.29; 705A); *ib.*1.12(p.36.4; 753B); *πληρωθείσης ὡς ἔνι μάλιστα κατὰ τὰ προκείμενα ἡμῖν ὑποτυπώσεως* ib.4.1(p.248.16; 1216A); *ἡ τῶν Στρωματέων ἡμῖν ὑ. λειμῶνος δίκην πεποίκιλται* ib.6.1 (p.423.5; M.9.209A); Ant.Mon.*hom* 66(M.89.1628A); **3.** plur., *marks, characteristics αὗται γὰρ αἱ πρὸς αὐτὴν ὑ. οὐκ ἐῶσι σκώληκι παραβάλλεσθαι τοὺς δυνάμει ἔχοντας τὴν ἀρετήν* Or.*Cels.*4.25(p.294.17; M.11.1064A); *αἱ τῶν εὐαγγελικῶν πολιτευμάτων ὑ.* Bas.*Spir.*35 (3.28D; M.32.128D); *μάλιστα δὲ οὗτος* [sc. Melchizedek], *ὡς τῶν ἄλλων ἁπάντων πλείους ἐν ἑαυτῷ φέρων τοῦ Χριστοῦ τὰς ὑ.* Max. *ambig.*(M.91.1141C); *ib.*(1361C); **4.** *example, model, pattern εἰς τὴν τῶν λοιπῶν ὑ. ὑποδεικνύων ὅτι μηδὲν φοβερὸν ὅπου πατρὸς ἀγάπη* *Ep.Lugd.*ap.Eus.*h.e.*5.1.23(M.20.417A); Chrys.*hom.4.2 in 1Tim.*(11. 569E); *γένοιτο δ' ἂν τοῖς ἐθέλουσι εὐσεβεῖν ὑ. ἀγαθή* Cyr.*glaph.Gen.*5 (1.157C); id.*Is.*4.4(2.669B); *ὡς καὶ ἑτέροις ὑ. εἶναι πολιτείας ἀγγελικῆς* id.*Lc.*12:41(M.72.752D); Antip.Bost.*fr.*(M.85.1796C); Max.*ambig.* (M.91.133C); id.*ep.*14(M.91.544A); '*πλυνεῖ ἐν οἴνῳ τὴν στολὴν αὐτοῦ*', *τὸ σῶμα τοῦ αὐτοῦ κυρίου λέγων, ὃ ἐν τῷ ἀχράντῳ αὐτοῦ πάθει εἰς ὑ. ἡμῶν ἐκαθάρθη* Areth.*Apoc.*3:4(M.106.552B); **5.** perh. *maxim ποθούσης γὰρ οἶμαι ψυχῆς τὴν μακαρίαν παράδοσιν ἀδιάδραστον φυλάττειν ἡ τοιάδε ὑ.* '*ἀνδρὸς δὲ φιλοῦντος σοφίαν εὐφρανθήσεται πατήρ*' Clem. *str.*1.1(p.9.11; M.8.700B); **6.** *image, representation πνευματικῶς οὖν τῶν νοητῶν ὑποτύπωσιν ποιούμενοι τὰ σωματικά* Or.*adnot.in Dt.*23:14 (M.17.33A); *ἔστι δὲ τὸ περὶ τοῦ Λαζάρου καὶ τοῦ πλουσίου διήγημα ὑποτύπωσις λόγου διδασκαλίαν ἔχοντος τοῦ μὴ δύνασθαι μετὰ τὴν ἐκ τοῦ σώματος ἔξοδον τῆς ψυχῆς* ‡Just.*qu.et resp.*60(M.6.1304A); *κατὰ τὴν ὑ. τῆς παραβολῆς* ib.140(1393C); **7.** *representation, symbol ποθεῖ δὲ ὁ πιστὸς καὶ τὴν ὅλην ὑ. κατανοῆσαι, πῶς ἔχει πρὸς τὴν ἀλήθειαν* ‡Chrys.*pasch.*1(8.251C); Cyr.*ador.*13(1.455B); *ὑ. δὲ τὸ δρώμενον ἦν τοῦ κατὰ καιροὺς ὑπάρξειν μέλλοντος τῇ μεμοιχευμένῃ τῶν Ἰουδαίων συναγωγῇ* id.*Os.*34(3.61D); *παρελήφθη πάλιν ὁ μακάριος Ἀαρὼν εἰς ὑ. τοῦ Ἐμμανουὴλ* id.*Jon.*1(3.366B); *ἐξεικονισμὸς δὲ ἄρα καὶ ὑ. τὸ δρώμενον ἦν τῶν διὰ Χριστοῦ κατωρθωμένων* id.*Abac.*33(3.548A); of Mosaic law *ὅπως ἂν ἡμᾶς ἀληθῶς μυήσαιτο, θείας αὐτὴν εἶναι καὶ ἱερᾶς* [sc. *θεσμοθεσίας*] *ὑποτύπωσιν* Dion.Ar.*c.h.*4.3(M.3.180D); of pictures of martyrs *οὐδὲν ἕτερόν εἰσι, ἢ ἀνδρείας ὑπογραμμός, πολιτείας τε εὐαγοῦς καὶ ἀρετῶν ὑ.* Germ.CP *ep.dogm.*4(M.98.172C); **8.** plur. as title of a theological treatise; perhaps *outlines, characteristics*, or *patterns*, Clem.*fr.*(p.195 et sq.); *Θεόγνωστος...ἐν τῷ δευτέρῳ τῶν Ὑ.* Ath.*decr.*25(p.20.35; M.25.460C); '*αἱ θεολογικαὶ ὑ.*' Dion.Ar.*d.n.*1.1 (M.3.585B); **9.** figure of speech, prob. misunderstood by Isid. H. from Quintilian *inst.*9.2.40; cf. *nona species definitionis est, quam*

Graeci κατὰ ὑποτύπωσιν, *Latini per quandam imaginationem dicunt, ut: 'Aeneas est Veneris et Anchisae filius'*, Isid.H.*etym*.2.29.10; but cf. *quot modis in divina lege allegoria cognoscitur?...aut secundum translationem vel metaphoram, ut est: 'iratus est Dominus et descendit'* [Ex.4:14]...*aut secundum imaginationem vel hypotyposin, ut est in Evangelio: 'homo quidam descendebat ab Jerusalem in Jericho': et rursus parabola vineae atque agricolarum*, Junilius. *inst.reg*.1.5(M.*PL*.68.18D).

***ὑποτυπωτέον**, *one must outline*, Or.*princ*.4.2.7(14; p.318.8; M.11. 372A).

ὑποτυφόομαι, *become infuriated*, Pall.*v.Chrys*.6(p.34.1; M.47.21).

ὑπότυφος, *conceited*, Synes.*Dion* 3(p.241.4; M.66.1120D).

***ὑπουλέω**, pass., ? *become a spy* τοῦτον [sc. Moses] ὑπουληθῆναι τοῖς Αἰγυπτίοις [ref. education of Moses in Egyptian learning] ὁ θεὸς ᾠκονόμησεν Proc.G.*Ex*.2:11(M.87.517A), or ? f.l. for ὑπαυληθῆναι *be lodged with*.

***ὑπουλία, ἡ**, *deceit*, Gel.Cyz.*h.e*.2.27.13(M.85.1309B).

ὑπουλότης, ἡ, **1.** *deceitfulness*; of actors, †Cyr.*hom.div*.14(5^{2}. 411E); of Devil, Jo.Clim.*scal*.24(M.88.981D); in a list of πάθη, Jo.D. *virt*.(M.95.88B) = Ephr.3.426D ὑπουλώτης; **2.** *corruption*; met., ref. heresy, CNic.(787)*act*.1(H.4.64C).

ὑπούλως, *deceitfully*, Hipp.*Dan*.4.47.5(M.10.664B); Chrys.*hom. 13.2 in Mt*.(7.170A); of Nestorians λέγουσι...τὸ ἀδιαίρετον καὶ τὴν ἕνωσιν...ὑ. Leont.H.*monoph*.testimonia(M.86.1809D).

***ὑπουρανός**, *beneath the sky*; neut. as adv. κέντρον τῆς ὑπουρανόν Didym.*Trin*.1.15(M.39.324B); ὁ μέλλων κρίνειν πᾶσαν τὴν ὑπουρανόν *Mir.Geo*.6(p.72.12).

ὑπουργ-έω, **1.** *render service* or *help, assist* τὸν μὲν πατέρα καὶ ποιητὴν εἰσάγων ὡς ἂν πανηγεμόνα βασιλικῷ νεύματι προστάττοντα, τὸν δὲ τούτῳ δευτερεύοντα θεῖον λόγον...ταῖς πατρικαῖς ἐπιτάξεσιν ~οῦντα Eus.*h.e*.1.2.5(M.20.56A); εἴ τις λέγων θεὸν τὸν Χριστὸν πρὸ αἰώνων υἱὸν τοῦ θεοῦ ~ηκότα τῷ πατρὶ εἰς τὴν τῶν ὅλων δημιουργίαν μὴ ὁμολογοίη, ἀνάθεμα ἔστω *Symb.Sirm*.1 *anath*.3; πνεῦμα...οὐδὲ ~εῖ ἀλλὰ συνεργεῖ καὶ δεσποτικῶς ἐνεργεῖ Thdt.*haer*.5.3(4.390); id.*Trin*. 26(M.75.1184D); **2.** c. dat. rei, *promote* ~ῆσαι τῷ πράγματι Phot. *nomoc*.2.1(p.491; M.104.572B).

***ὑπούργησις, ἡ**, *service* βελτίονος ἄξιον τὸ δῶμα ὑπουργήσεως ποιήσει [sc. God] Mac.Mgn.*apocr*.4.16(p.187.28); εἰς ὑ. τῶν ἁγίων αὐτοῦ ἐντολῶν Mac.Aeg.*hom*.27.11(M.34.757D).

ὑπουργία, ἡ, **1.** *aid, help* οὔτε γὰρ ἐνέργεια οὔτε διάθεσις οὐδὲ μὴν μέρος τι ἡμέτερον ἡ ἡδονή, ἀλλ' ὑ. ἕνεκα παρῆλθεν εἰς τὸν βίον, ὥσπερ τοὺς ἅλας φασὶ τῆς παραπέψεως τῆς τροφῆς χάριν Clem.*str*.2.20(p.177. 19; M.8.1064A); τίνος...ἂν...ὑ. δέοιτο ὁ θελήματι μόνῳ δημιουργῶν; Bas.*Eun*.2.21(1.257B; M.29.617C); **2.** *service* ἐπλήθυνεν τὰς τρίχας... εἰς σήν, ἄνθρωπε, ὑ., κεῖραι διδάξας τοὺς πόκους Clem.*paed*.3.3(p.25. 19; M.8.589A); δεύτερον...φῶς ἄγγελος, τοῦ πρώτου φωτὸς ἀπορροή τις, ἢ μετουσία, τῇ πρὸς αὐτὸ νεύσει καὶ ὑ. τὸν φωτισμὸν ἔχουσα Gr. Naz.*or*.40.5(M.36.364B); τὴν παρθένον, παραληφθεῖσαν εἰς ὑ. τοῦ γεννῆσαι σαρκικῶς τὸν ἑνωθέντα σαρκί Cyr.*hom.pasch*.17(5^{2}.228C); εἰς τύπον...τοῦ πάντων δημιουργοῦ, ἡ πατρὸς καὶ μητρὸς ὑ. πρὸς ὕπαρξιν id.*ador*.7(1.235D); **3.** *use*, Clem.*paed*.3.4(p.253.14; M.8.596C); κατάρχουσαι τῶν ἀνδρῶν τῶν οἰκείων, εἰς ὑ. ἀπρεπῶν ἐχρῶντο πραγμάτων Thdr.Mops.*Am*.4:1-3(M.66.265B).

ὑπουργικός, *rendering service, ministering* καταδεξάμενος δὲ ἅπαξ ἐγκαταλεγῆναι τῷ σώματι τῆς ἀδελφότητος, ἐὰν κριθῇ σκεῦος γενέσθαι ὑ. Bas.*reg.fus*.28.2(2.372D; M.31.989B); πῶς οὐκ εἰσὶ τῶν φθορίμων πραγμάτων τὰ ἄφθαρτα ὑ.; ‡Just.*qu.Chr*.9(M.6.1476B); of angels, Cyr. *Zach*.105(3.799C); ὑ. ὥσπερ τινὰ τὴν διακονίαν ἀποπληρῶν [sc. Christ] id.*dial.Trin*.3(5^{1}.478E); *servile, subordinate* γένος ὑπηρετικὸν καὶ ὑ. τοῖς κρείττοσιν Juln.Imp.ap.eund.*Juln*.4(6^{2}.143B); denied of Son, Cyr.*Jo*.11.6(4.957A); and of H. Ghost, Thdt.*Trin*.22(M.75.1177C).

***ὑπουργικῶς**, *subordinately*, ref. Christ ὡσπεροῦν ἐν ὁμοιώματι κινήσεως ὁ υἱὸς ὑ. καὶ οὐ ταυτὸν ὡς ὁ πατὴρ αὐθεντικῶς Geo.Laod.*ep. dogm*.ap.Epiph.*haer*.73.18(p.291.5; M.42.436D); 'καταβέβηκα', ἔφη· αὐθαιρετικῶς, φησίν, οὐχ ὑ. Didym.*Trin*.3.12(M.39.860C); οὐχ ὑ. κτίζοντος αὐτὸν [sc. ἄνθρωπον] τοῦ υἱοῦ, θεϊκῶς δὲ μᾶλλον, ὡς φύσει δημιουργοῦ Cyr.*Arcad*.(p.76.21; 5^{2}.63E); ref. H. Ghost οὔτε ἀλλότριον τοῖς βαπτιζομένοις ἐνιέντα πνεῦμα δουλοπρεπῶς καὶ ὑ., ἀλλ' ὡς θεὸν κατὰ φύσιν μετ' ἐξουσίας τῆς ἀνωτάτω id.*inc.unigen*.(5^{1}.706A); id.*Nest*.4.2(p.79.34; 6^{1}.101D); id.*dial.Trin*.3(5^{1}.469A).

ὑπουργός, *rendering service*; as subst., *minister, assistant, servant*, of parents (cf. ὑπουργία) ὑπὲρ ὃν [sc. θεόν] οὐ δεῖ ἀγαπᾶν πατέρα ἢ μητέρα· οἱ μὲν γάρ, ὑ. πρὸς τὴν γένεσιν· ὁ δέ, κτίζων θεός Proc.G.*Ex*.2:11(M.87.517A); of Moses ἔδει Μωϋσέα μὲν θαυμάζειν ὡς νόμου διάκονον καὶ χάριτος ὑ. ... ὑπερθαυμάζειν δὲ τὸν Ἐμμανουήλ... ὡς υἱὸν ἀληθινὸν τοῦ θεοῦ Cyr.*Lc*.5:13(M.72.557B); τῶν θείων θεσπισμάτων μεσίτης καὶ ὑ. id.*ador*.7(1.224B); τῶν τύπων τὸν ὑ. *ib*.10 (339D); of Jo. Bapt., ‡Bas.*h.myst*.40(p.387); of Christ λόγον ὄντα θεοῦ δημιουργικὸν καὶ τῷ πατρὶ συνεῖναι...ὑ. τε καὶ συνεργὸν τῷ πατρὶ τῆς τῶν ὅλων οὐσιώσεώς τε καὶ διακοσμήσεως γεγενημένον Eus.*d.e*. 5.1(p.212.32; M.22.353B); ἕτερος ὢν τοῦ πατρὸς ὑ. ἦν αὐτοῦ, ὥστε ἐπικελευομένου τοῦ μείζονος αὐτὸν δημιουργεῖν *ib*.5.5(p.227.18; 376B); τοῦ πατρὸς ὑ., ναὶ μὴν καὶ κύριον τῶν ὅλων *ib*.6 proem.(p.251.7; 412C); τὸν τῆς ἀρρήτου γνώμης τοῦ πατρὸς ὑ., τὸν τῶν ἁπάντων σὺν τῷ πατρὶ δημιουργόν id.*h.e*.1.2.3(v.l. τελειοτήν M.20.56A); τελειότατος γέγονεν ὑ. πρὸς πᾶσαν δημιουργίαν καὶ γνώμην τοῦ πατρός Eun.*apol*.15(M.30. 852D); *ib*.27(864C) cit. s. γέννημα; ὑ. αὐτῷ ἐχρήσατο εἰς τὴν τῶν λοιπῶν δημιουργίαν ὁ θεός Geo.Laod.*ep.dogm*.ap.Epiph.*haer*.73.13 (p.286.11; M.42.429B); ὑ. αὐτὸν ὀνομάζουσι [sc. Arius and Eunomius] Thdt.*1Cor*.3:9(3.181); Gel.Cyz.*h.e*.2.16.2(M.85.1260C); orthodox refusal of term to Son τίς ἄρα ταύτην ὑμῖν τὴν μωρὰν καὶ καινὴν ἐπίνοιαν ὑπέβαλεν, ἵνα εἴπητε τὸν μὲν υἱὸν μόνον μόνος ὁ πατὴρ αὐτούργησε, τὰ δ' ἄλλα πάντα διὰ τοῦ υἱοῦ γέγονεν ὡς δι' ὑ.; Ath.*decr*.7 (p.6.28; M.25.'436'(428)B); *ib*.8(p.7.19; '437'(429)A); ἀσθένειαν περὶ τὸν θεὸν εἰσάγουσι οἱ ἄφρονες...ὅτι μὴ μόνος ἠδυνήθη ποιῆσαι, συνεργοῦ δὲ ἢ ὑ. χρείαν ἔσχε id.*Ar*.2.29(M.26.208B); εἰ...οὐκ ἐν τῷ θεὸς εἶναι τέλειος τὸ τῆς δόξαν κέκτηται, ἀλλ' ἐν τῷ ὑ. ἀκριβής, τί διοίσει τῶν λειτουργικῶν πνευμάτων, ἀμέμπτως τὸ ἔργον τῆς διακονίας ἐπιτελούντων; Bas.*Eun*.2.21(1.257C; M.29.620A); τὸν Χριστὸν αἴτιον πάντων γενόμενον, καὶ οὐδαμοῦ τὸ τοῦ ὑ. ὄνομα, οὐδὲ τὸ τοῦ διακόνου Chrys.*hom. 2.1 in Eph*.(11.10D); ὅτι κατὰ φύσιν δημιουργὸς ὁ υἱὸς μετὰ πατρός, ὡς ἐκ τῆς οὐσίας ὑπάρχων αὐτοῦ, καὶ οὐχ ὥσπερ ὑ. παραλαμβανόμενος Cyr.*Jo*.1.5 tit.(4.43C); 'διὰ Ἰησοῦ Χριστοῦ'. καὶ ἵνα μή τις ὑπολάβῃ ὑ. εἶναι τοῦ πατρὸς τὸν υἱόν, εὑρὼν προσκείμενον τὸ διά, ἐπήγαγε 'τοῦ θεοῦ πατρὸς τοῦ ἐγείραντος αὐτὸν ἐκ νεκρῶν' Thdt.*Gal*.1:1(3.360); and to H. Ghost ἵνα μή τις αὐτὸ ὑ. ὑπολάβῃ, ἀναγκαίως προστέθεικεν ὅτι κύριος τὸ πνεῦμα id.*2Cor*.3:17(3.306); id.*Ps*.57:6(1.986); τοῖς ὑ. λέγουσι τοῦ πατρὸς τὸ πνεῦμα τὸ ἅγιον, ἐνταῦθα πάλιν ὁ Παῦλος καιρίαν δίδωσι τὴν πληγήν *cat.Ac*.28:25(p.417.31).

***ὑπόφανσις, ἡ**, *suggestion* ψευδὴς ἡ...ὑ. τῆς πρώτης...προτάσεως Leont.H.*Nest*.1.1(M.86.1401D).

***ὑποφαντικός**, *significant*, Epiph.*anc*.36(p.46.5; M.43.81C).

ὑποφαρμάττω, *drug, doctor*; met., Gr.Nyss.*Eun*.1(1 p.26.4; M.45. 253C).

ὑπόφασις, ἡ, a *being half seen*; plur., ref. objects which are lower in the field of vision ἐντεῦθεν [sc. in a perspective drawing] ἐπιφάσεις καὶ ὑ. καὶ φάσεις σώζονται, καὶ τὰ μὲν δοκεῖ προὔχειν, τὰ δὲ εἰσέχειν, τὰ δ' ἄλλως πως φαντάζεσθαι ἐν τῷ ὁμαλῷ καὶ λείῳ Clem.*str*.6.7(p.460.10; ὑποθέσεις M.9.277C).

ὑποφέρω, *bring down, bring*, of Devil ἀνθρώπους εἰς θάνατον ὑ. Clem.*prot*.1(p.8.12; M.8.64A); pass., *slip* εἰς...προδήλους ἐναντιότητας ὑ. Bas.*Eun*.1.5(1.213D; M.29.513C); φιλεγκλήμονες...ἐπιτωθάζουσι τοῖς ἄλλοις, εἰ δήπου συμβαίνοι παρολισθεῖν καὶ ὑ. Cyr.*Ps*.37:8(M.69. 960D); *bring under, subject*, c. dat., id.*Is*.1.4(2.96C); pass., id.*Ps*. 34:8(900B); id.*ador*.1(1.11D).

***ὑπόφημι**, s.v.l., *express* ὁ κάλαμος τὸ βασίλειον σκῆπτρον...ὑπέφησεν ‡Dion.Al.*fr.in Lc*.22:42(p.240.14, v.l. ὑπέφηνεν M.10.1592B).

ὑποφητεύ-ω, *be an interpreter, act as mouthpiece*, of Balaam ὑ. τῷ θείῳ θελήματι Gr.Nyss.*v.Mos*.(M.44.325C); ἀληθῶς ἐστι προφήτης,... ~ων τῷ πνεύματι id.*Apoll*.1(M.45.1125A); *interpret*, Gr.Thaum.*pan. Or*.15(p.33.17; M.10.1093B).

ὑποφήτης, ὁ, *interpreter, expounder* τοῦ προσκυνήτου νόμου ὑ. Const.ap.Ath.*apol.sec*.87(p.166.14; M.25.405B); Eus.*h.e*.10.4.23(M.20. 857C); γνήσιον ὑ. τοῦ πνεύματος Gr.Nyss.*laud.Bas*.(M.46.789C); ὑ. τοῦ ψεύδους Thdt.*1Tim*.4:2(3.659); ὑ. ... δαιμόνων Bas.Sel.*v.Thecl*. proem.(M.85.561B).

***ὑποφητικός**, *interpreting, communicating*, ref. order of archangels τοῖς δέ [sc. ἀγγέλοις κοινωνεῖ], ὅτι καὶ τῆς ὑ. ἐστι τάξεως Dion. Ar.*c.h*.9.2(M.3.257C); *ib*.12.2(293A); τῶν ἐσομένων τὰς ὑ. προαναρρήσεις id.*e.h*.3.3.4(M.3.429C); Mod.*dorm*.4(M.86.3289A).

***ὑποφητικῶς**, *so as to interpret*, Dion.Ar.*c.h*.4.2(M.3.180B); Mod. *dorm*.9(M.86.3301A).

ὑποφθέγγομαι, *speak quietly, suggest*; of Father speaking to men through Son, Eus.*e.th*.2.22(p.132.13; M.24.957D); of H. Ghost, Cyr.H.*catech*.16.20; *mutter*, Philost.*h.e*.3.11(p.41.26; M.65.497B).

ὑποφθείρω, *corrupt gradually* or *secretly*, Or.*schol.in Cant*.8:6(M. 17.285C); ὑ. ἀπὸ τῆς ὀρθῆς πίστεως Epiph.*haer*.69.3(p.155.7; M.42. 208B); pass., *be disordered*; of the stomach, Gr.Nyss.*hom.opif*.13.15 (M.44.173A).

ὑποφλεγμαίνω, *be somewhat inflamed*, met. ὁ τοῦ βασιλέως θυμὸς ὑπεφλέγμαινεν Thphyl.*exc.Rom*.3(p.223.19; M.113.929D).

ὑποφορά, ἡ, a *bringing down*, Cyr.*ador*.7(1.244D).

ὑπόφορος, *subject to tribute, subject*, *T.Jud.*7.8(v.l. ὑποσπόνδους); Eus.*h.e.*1.6.6(M.20.88B); of Christ ὁ κριτὴς τοῦ παντὸς ὑ. τοῖς δυναστεύουσι γίνεται Gr.Nyss.*beat.*1(M.44.1201B); fig. γαστρίμαργος μοναχός, κοιλίας ὑ. Nil.*spir.mal.*2(M.79.1145C).

***ὑποφραστήρ, ὁ,** *expounder*, Gr.Naz.*carm.*2.2(poem.)7.131(M.37.1561A).

***ὑπόφρουρος,** *under garrison*, Proc.G.*2Reg.*7:14(M.87.1132D).

***ὑποφύωσις, ἡ,** *gradual growth*, Or.*schol.in Lc.*17:12f.(M.17.365C).

ὑποφων-έω, 1. *sing in answer, respond*, *T.Job* 31(p.122.25); *ib.*33(p.124.10); ὑ. τὸ ἀμὴν ὁ λαϊκός Chrys.*hom.35.3 in 1Cor.*(10.325E); ∼ουμένης εὐχῆς Thdr.Stud.*epp.*2.115(M.99.1648C); **2.** *cheer on* a contestant, c. acc., Gr.Nyss.*v.Mos.*1(M.44.300A); c. dat., id.*Eun.*2(2 p.387.21; M.45.569B); pass., ‡Caes.Naz.*dial.*29(M.38.889); **3.** *say quietly, hint, suggest* αἰνιγματωδῶς ἡμῖν ∼οῦντος τοῦ πράγματος, ὡς... Cyr.*ador.*2(1.78E); *ib.*7(220A); *ib.*14(511D).

***ὑποφώνημα, τό,** *shout of encouragement*, Bas.*ep.*222(3.335A; M.32.817C).

ὑποφώνησις, ἡ, *shouting of encouragement*, Bas.*hom.*12.14(2.110D; M.31.417A); Gr.Naz.*ep.*18(M.37.52C); Gr.Nyss.*Eun.*2(2 p.387.26; M.45.569B); *exhortation*, *M.Thdot.1* 9(p.671.1); τῆς τοῦ νόμου ὑ. *Const.App.*7.33.3; *cry* (liturg.) ἐφ' ἑκάστῳ ἀναγνώσματι τῆς εἰρήνης ὑ. Max.*myst.*12(M.91.689D).

***ὑποφωνητής, ὁ,** *one who sings in response*; met., *humble follower*, ‡Ign.*Philad.*5.

ὑποχάλασις, ἡ, *letting down, lowering*, ‡Just.*qu.et resp.*29(M.6.1277B).

ὑποχαλ-άω, 1. *slacken a little, lower, relax* χεῖρας...ὑ. [i.e. after prayer] Evagr.Pont.*or.*106(M.79.1189D); ὑ. τῆς ὀργῆς *cat.Jo.*7:35(p.268.20); pass., ‡Ath.*syntag.*5.9(p.125; M.28.841C); *be slack, lax, abandoned*, Epiph.*haer.*75.1(p.333.15; M.42.504B); **2.** *yield* βαρβάρῳ φρονήματι ἥκιστα ∼ῶν Men.*exc.Rom.*5(p.189.22; M.113.880B).

ὑποχαράσσω, *carve out underneath*, Gr.Nyss.*ordin.*(M.46.545A); *trace for a pattern* τὰ πρῶτα στοιχεῖα...παιδίοις ὑ. id.*Eun.*1(1 p.36.20; M.45.264C).

***ὑποχαρίζομαι,** perf. ptcpl. as adj., *attractive*, *Chron.Pasch.*p.312(M.92.793D).

ὑποχάσκω, *gape below*, Nil.*Magn.*9(M.79.981B).

ὑποχαυνόω, *relax, slacken*, Bas.*ep.*45(3.133E; M.32.365C); Gr.Nyss.*v.Gr.Thaum.*(M.46.908B); Cyr.*Jo.*3.4(4.289D).

***ὑποχειμάζω,** pass., *be tempest-tossed*; met., Cyr.*Jo.*11.9(4.983C).

ὑποχείριος, *under* one's *hand* or *control, under command, subject*, of men δαίμοσιν ὑ. γεγόνατε *Hom.Clem.*10.25; of demons to God, Gr.Nyss.*v.Gr.Thaum.*(M.46.917A); c. genit., Epiph.*haer.*28.6(p.318.21; M.41.384D); neut. as subst., *body of men under* one's *command*, Gr.Nyss.*v.Gr.Thaum.*(913D); of Son (Eunomian) ὡς μέρος τῆς...ὑ. φύσεως καὶ τὸν υἱὸν ποιῆσαι id.*Eun.*2(2 p.359.20; M.45.537C); of H. Ghost, id.*Maced.*16(M.45.1320D).

***ὑποχειριότης, ἡ,** *subordination*; of clergy to bishop, Procl.CP *ep.*13(p.67.32; M.65.881B).

***ὑποχερσόω,** *make solid ground beneath*, Gr.Nyss.*or.catech.*23(p.88.3; M.45.61C).

***ὑποχλωρίζω,** *be pale*, Or.*comm.in Mt.*10.7(p.8.18; M.13.852A).

ὑποχορηγέω, *supply*, Gr.Nyss.*Eun.*1(1 p.34.18; M.45.261C).

ὑποχρεμετίζω, *neigh in response*, Cyr.*Am.*3(3.317A,B).

ὑπόχρεως, *indebted*; hence *dependent* upon ὥσπερ ὑ. υἱὸς πατρί, οὕτω καὶ πᾶς διάκονος ἐπισκόπῳ *Const.App.*2.30.2.

***ὑποχρόνιος,** *subject to time, within time* ἀρχὴν ὑ. δεικνυσιν ἡ κατὰ σάρκα γέννησις [sc. Χριστοῦ] Thdot.Anc.*hom.BMV et Sym.*4(M.77.1393D).

ὑπόχρονος, = foreg., Leont.H.*Nest.*4.4(M.86.1660B); of incarnate Christ, *ib.*2.23(1584Dff.); Jo.D.*haer.Nest.*17(M.95.196D).

***ὑποχρόνως,** *in subjection to time*, of Christ's human nature κατὰ τὸ εἶναι ὑ. Leont.H.*Nest.*4.3(M.86.1657C).

***ὑποχρυσίζω,** *have a golden tinge* ὑ.... κατὰ τὴν κόμην Gr.Nyss.*Eun.*2(2 p.360.2; M.45.537D).

***ὑποχώννυμι,** *cover with a heap of earth*, Gr.Nyss.*v.Mos.*(M.44.429A).

ὑποχωρητικός, *inclined to withdraw, retiring*, Gr.Naz.*or.*36.3(M.36.268C).

ὑποψάλλω, 1. *sing in response*, of congregational singing of refrain between verses of psalms ὑ. ... τὸ ἀλληλούια *A.Mt.*B 25(p.254.9); τοὺς τοῦ Δαυὶδ ψαλλέτω ὕμνους, καὶ ὁ λαὸς τὰ ἀκροστίχια ὑ. *Const.App.*2.57.6; Chrys.*exp.in Ps.*144:1(5.466E); id.*hom.36.5 in 1Cor.*(10.340B); **2.** *sing* καλὸν ἐπιτάφιον αὐτῷ ὁ Δαυὶδ ὑ. id.*exp.in Ps.*3:1(5.5C); Thdt.*h.rel.*3(3.1137).

***ὑπόψαλμα, τό,** *chanted response*; of words of a psalm sung as refrain between verses, Gr.Nyss.*ordin.*(M.46.552B).

ὑποψελ(λ)ίζω, *lisp* or *stammer a little*, *Libell.*ap.CSyr.*act.*(p.108.13; H.2.1392A); met., ὑποψελίζων [sc. Law] ἡμῖν τὸ τῷ θεῷ δοκοῦν Cyr.*Ps.*48:1(M.69.1068C).

ὑποψεύδω, pass., *be devised falsely*, Bas.Sel.*or.*6.3(M.85.97A).

***ὑποψηφίζομαι,** *be a candidate for election*, Gr.Nyss.*v.Gr.Thaum.*(M.46.933D).

***ὑποψήφιος,** = sq.; Soz.*h.e.*2.20.1(M.67.984C); of a bishop-elect, *Euchol.*(p.252).

***ὑπόψηφος, 1.** *liable for election* τοὺς ὑ. τῇ βασιλείᾳ Synes.*provid.*1.6(p.74.4; M.66.1221A); as bishop, Socr.*h.e.*4.29.2(M.67.541B); *ib.*5.5.6(572A); Soz.*h.e.*6.23.1(M.67.1348B); **2.** *under trial*, ‡Chrys.*prov.*4(2.765B).

***ὑποψιάομαι,** *fear*, Ephr.3.162D.

ὑποψιθυρίζω, *whisper softly*, Gr.Naz.*ep.*11(M.37.41B); Synes.*ep.*79(M.66.1445C); Isid.Pel.*epp.*1.275(M.78.345A).

***ὕποψιν,** for ὑπ' ὄψιν, Thdr.Heracl.*Is.*63:11(M.18.1369B).

***ὑποψυχία, ἡ,** *coldness*; of the affections, Dor.*doct.*20(M.88.1812B).

***ὑποψυχραίνω,** pass., *be somewhat cold*, met. οἱ πρὸς τὸν ἅγιον ὑποψυχρανθέντες Niceph.Ur.*v.Sym.*139(M.86.3116B).

ὑπόψυχρος, *rather cold, lukewarm*, ‡Ath.*occurs.*18(M.28.996D); †Leont.B.*sect.*9(M.86.1257C).

ὑποψύχω, pass., *become somewhat cold, cool off*, ref. Origenist theory of soul ψυχὰς...ὑποψυγείσας μὲν τῆς τοῦ θεοῦ ἀγάπης, ἐντεῦθεν δὲ ψυχὰς ὀνομασθείσας Thdr.Scyth.*libell.*1(M.86.233B).

ὑπτιάζω, *behave arrogantly*, †Bas.*Is.*123(1.465B; M.30.320A).

ὑπτιόω, 1. *make supine, sluggish*; met., Tit.Bost.*Man.*2.15(M.18.1164A); Isid.Pel.*epp.*1.345(M.78.378C); pass., *be sluggish*, Cyr.*Is.*2.5(2.321B); Jo.Carp.*cap.*43(M.85.1845); ‡Meth.*Sym.et Ann.*11(M.18.376C); **2.** pass., *be elated, puffed up*, Jo.Mal.*chron.*6 p.153(M.97.253B); *ib.*7 p.190(301A); *ib.*9 p.224(349A).

ὑπτίως, 1. *backwards*, Geo.Pis.*hex.*396(M.92.1464A); **2.** *supinely*; met., *sluggishly*; comp., Chrys.*hom.21.2 in Heb.*(12.195D).

ὑπτίωσις, ἡ, *supineness*, moral *sluggishness*, Cyr.*Is.*4.2(2.590D).

***ὑπτιωτέον,** *one must be supine, sluggish*; met., Cyr.*Jo.*6(4.572B).

ὑπωπιάζω, (often confused with ὑποπιάζω and ὑποπιέζω), *strike under the eye*; met., *bruise, mortify*, ref. 1Cor.9:27, Epiph.*haer.*64.71(p.519.8; M.41.1196C); Chrys.*hom.33.4 in Heb.*(12.309B, vv.ll. ὑποπιάζω, ὑποπιέζω); Thdt.*h.rel.*proem.(3.1103); ὑ. τὰ μέλη ἡμῶν ἀπὸ παντὸς πράγματος νεκροῦ Esaias *or.*25.18(p.171; cf.M.40.1186C); cf. οὐκ ἀνέχομαι, ἀλλὰ καταστέλλω καὶ ὑποτάττω μετὰ πολλῶν τῶν ἱδρώτων αὐτήν [sc. ἐπιθυμίαν]. ... οὐκ εἶπεν, ἀναιρῶ οὐδὲ κολάζω· οὐδὲ γὰρ ἐχθρὰ ἡ σάρξ· ἀλλ' ὑ., ὃ δεσπότου ἐστίν, οὐ πολεμίου Chrys.*hom.23.2 in 1Cor.*(10.202C); ἡ φιλοπονία καὶ ἡ ἐγκράτεια ἐμὲ μὲν ῥώννυσι, τὸν δὲ ἀνταγωνιστὴν καταβάλλει Thdt.*1Cor.*9:27(3.225); οὐκ ἀφίημι, φησί, τῇ γαστρὶ καὶ τῷ σώματι τὰς ἡνίας, ἀλλὰ περισφίγγω αὐτὸ καὶ ὑποτάσσω *cat.1Cor.*9:27(p.183.29); ref. acceptance of a reprimand, Nil.*Magn.*40(M.79.1017C).

ὑπωπιασμός, ὁ, *mortification*, of the body, ref. 1Cor.9:27 μετὰ... σεμνότητος ἐσθίουσι...διὰ τοῦ ὑ. τῆς σαρκός Ephr.2.128C; ὁ ὑ. τοῦ σώματος...ὑπὸ τῆς ἐγκρατείας Bas.*reg.fus.*16.1(2.358B; M.31.957B); *ib.*37.1(382A; M.1009C); ἀποχὴν τῶν βρωμάτων...διὰ τοῦ ὑ. τῆς σαρκὸς τὸν ἁγιασμὸν κατορθοῦσαν †Bas.*Is.*31(1.404D; M.30.180C); Gr.Naz.*or.*32.19(M.36.196C).

ὑπώπιον, τό, 1. *bruise*, met. ὑ. τῶν κακῶν Mac.Mgn.*apocr.*2.51(p.44.4); *ib.*3.9(p.70.20); **2.** *disgrace*, *ib.*2.19(p.35.7); *ib.*3.12(p.83.15); **3.** neut. plur., ? as adv., *before the eyes* τὴν παρ' αὐτοῖς μαθήτειαν λαβόντες ὑ. Nil.*Magn.*64(M.79.1056C).

ὕσσωπος, ἡ (-πον, τό), *hyssop*; in gen., symbol of healing ἐντέταλται...περιτιθέναι τὸ ἔριον τὸ κόκκινον ἐπὶ ξύλον...καὶ τὸ ὕ., καὶ οὕτως ῥαντίζειν τὰ παιδία καθ' ἕνα τὸν λαόν...διατί δὲ ἅμα τὸ ἔριον καὶ τὸ ὕ.; ὅτι ἐν τῇ βασιλείᾳ αὐτοῦ [sc. Χριστοῦ] ἡμέραι ἔσονται πονηραὶ καὶ ῥυπαραί, ἐν αἷς ἡμεῖς σωθησόμεθα· ὅτι ὁ ἀλγῶν σάρκα διὰ τοῦ ῥύπου τοῦ ὑ. ἰᾶται *Barn.*8.1ff.; of baptismal cleansing τοὺς μέλλοντας ὑσσώπῳ ῥαντίζεσθαι, καὶ καθαρίζεσθαι ὑ. τῷ νοητῷ, καὶ τῇ δυνάμει τοῦ κατὰ τὸ πάθος ὑ. καὶ καλάμῳ ποτισθέντος Cyr.H.*catech.*3.1; exeg. Ps.50:9, connected with Ex.12:22 as type of Passion, Thdt.*Ps.*50:9(1.939); ὑ. τὴν τοῦ ἁγίου πνεύματος ἐνέργειαν ἀφομοιοῖ Cyr.*Ps.*50:9(M.69.1096C,D); exeg. Jo.19:29 οὕτως αὐτὸν ἐπότιζον, ὡς τοῖς καταδίκοις αὐτὸ προσφέρονται, ἐπεὶ καὶ τὸ ὕ. διὰ τοῦτο πρόσκειται Chrys.*hom.85.2 in Jo.*(8.507B); ref. harmonization with parallel passages οἱ μὲν καλάμῳ περιθέντες τὸν σπόγγον, οἱ δὲ τῷ ξύλῳ τῆς καλουμένης ὑ., βοτάνης δὲ εἶδος ἡ ὕ. Cyr.*Jo.*12(4.1067E); symbol of healing through Resurrection, ‡Dion.Al.*fr.in Lc.22:42*(p.240.14; M.10.1592B); exeg. Heb.9:19 διὰ τί τῷ ὑ.; πυκνόν ἐστι καὶ κρατητικόν Chrys.*hom.16.2* in *Heb.*(12.159B); *τύπος ἦν...τῆς τοῦ θείου πνεύματος χάριτος, ἡ τοῦ ὑ. θερμότης* Thdt.*Heb.*9:18ff.(3.602).

ὑστέρα, ἡ, *womb*; name given by Cainites to maker of Universe, Epiph.*haer.*38.1(p.63.15; M.41.656B); cf.Iren.*haer.*1.31.2(M.7.705A).

***ὑστερεύω,** *be later* than, c. genit., Didym.*Trin.*1.15(M.39.328B).

ὑστερ-έω, 1. *be behind, occur later; delay εἴ τις ∼ησεν εἰς τὴν ἐννάτην* ‡Chrys.*pasch.*1(8.250A); **2.** *fall short, be wanting,* Clem.*str.*4.13(p.287.26; M.8.1297B); med., Just.*dial.*82.1(M.6.669B); *fall short of μηδεὶς ∼είτω τῆς κλήσεως* ‡Meth.*palm.*1(M.18.384B); **3.** *be in need, Did.*11.12; med., *Barn.*10.3; Herm.*vis.*3.9.2; *be in need of, lack*; c. genit., Clem.*ecl.*12(p.139.29; M.9.704B); cf. *∼ηθεὶς τοῖς ὀψωνίοις* Hipp.*Dan.*4.46.4; **4.** *make to fail of οὐχ ∼ησάς με ἐκ τῆς ἐπιθυμίας μου* Gr.Nyss.*v.Macr.*(M.46.977A, v.l. *ἐστέρησας* p.389.12); *take away τούτῳ τῷ Ἔβερ θεὸς οὐχ ∼ησε τὴν ἀρχαίαν φωνήν* Jo.Mal.*chron.*1 p.12(M.97.76B).

ὑστέρημα, τό, *deficiency, lack*; **1.** in gen., *T.Benj.*11.5; *1Clem.*38.2; *shortcoming,* Herm.*vis.*3.2.2; **2.** Gnost., ref. abortive passion of Sophia, Iren.*haer.*1.14.1(M.7.593A); *τὸν...μόνον θεὸν παντοκράτορα... ἐξ ὑ., καὶ αὐτοῦ ἐξ ἄλλου ὑ. γεγονότος, προβεβλῆσθαι λέγοντες· ὥστε ...εἶναι αὐτὸν προβολὴν τρίτου ὑ.* ib.1.16.3(636A); *τὴν δυοδεκάδα περὶ ἣν καὶ τὸ μυστήριον τοῦ πάθους τοῦ ὑ. γεγονέναι, ἐξ οὗ πάθους τὰ βλεπόμενα κατεσκευάσθαι θέλουσιν* ib.1.18.4(648B); of region outside Pleroma, Clem.*exc.Thdot.*22(p.114.14; M.9.669B); *καλεῖται Ὅρος μὲν οὗτος, ὅτι ἀφορίζει ἀπὸ τοῦ πληρώματος ἔξω τὸ ὑ.* Hipp.*haer.*6.31(p.159.13; M.16.3242A); *τῷ Δημιουργῷ ἄνω τῷ ἐν ὑ. γεγονότι* Epiph.*haer.*36.2(p.46.10; M.41.636A); as name of aeon, ib.31.4(p.388.1; 480A); **3.** exeg. Col.1:24 *ἀνταναπληρῶ, φησί, τὰ ὑ. τῶν θλίψεων τοῦ Χριστοῦ...δοκεῖ μὲν μέγα εἶναι ὅπερ ἐφθέγξατο, ἀλλ' οὐκ ἔστιν ἀπονοίας...ἀλλὰ καὶ πολλῆς φιλοστοργίας τῆς περὶ τὸν Χριστόν· οὐ γὰρ βούλεται αὐτοῦ εἶναι, ἀλλ' ἐκείνου τὰ πάθη, τούτους οἰκειῶσαι αὐτῷ βουλόμενος. καὶ ἃ ἐγὼ πάσχω, δι' ἐκεῖνον πάσχω, φησίν· ὥστε μὴ ἐμοὶ χάριν ὁμολογεῖτε, ἀλλ' ἐκείνῳ· αὐτὸς γὰρ πάσχει ταῦτα* Chrys.*hom.4.2 in Col.*(11.352C); cf. *τί δὲ ἦν τὸ προσλεῖπον; τὸ μαθόντας ὑμᾶς τίνα ἐστὶν τὰ ὑπὲρ ὑμῶν κατορθωθέντα παρ' αὐτοῦ, δέξασθαι τὴν περὶ αὐτῶν ἐπαγγελίαν. τοῦτο δὲ ἄνευ...θλίψεων γενέσθαι οὐδαμῶς οἷόν τε ἦν· ὑπὲρ δὴ τούτων πάσχω, περιϊὼν καὶ κηρύττων...ὥστε ὑμᾶς...τὴν πρὸς αὐτὸν οἰκείωσιν δέξασθαι* Thdr.Mops.*Col.*1:24(p.279.24; M.66.929A); *Χριστὸς τὸν ὑπὲρ τῆς ἐκκλησίας κατεδέξατο θάνατον...καὶ ὁ...ἀπόστολος ὡσαύτως ὑπὲρ αὐτῆς ὑπέστη τὰ...παθήματα...ἀνταναπληροῦν δὲ ἔφη τὰ ὑ. ... ὡς τὸ λειπόμενον πληρῶν. ... ἐλείπετο δὲ τὸ κηρῦξαι τοῖς ἔθνεσιν* Thdt.*Col.*1:24(3.481).

ὑστέρησις, ἡ, *deficiency, want,* Herm.*sim.*6.3.4; Serg.*Olymp.*1.12(p.418.20); *defect, failure,* Bas.*renunt.*10(2.211B; M.31.648A).

***ὑστερινός,** *last-born, youngest,* Barth.Edess.*Agar.*(M.104.1421D).

***ὑστεροβουλέω,** *deliberate after the event,* Cyr.*Jo.*5.3(4.499B); ib.6.1(594C); id.*Juln.*8(6^2.286A).

ὑστεροβουλία, ἡ, *deliberation after the event, second thoughts, change of mind,* Gr.Naz.*or.*40.24(M.36.392C); Gr.Nyss.*virg.*3(p.256.24; M.46.325B); Cyr.*Juln.*9(6^2.309C).

ὑστερογενής, *later in origin τὴν ψυχὴν οὐκ ἀξιώσω ποτὲ σώματος ὑστερογενῆ νομίζειν* Synes.*ep.*105(M.66.1485B); of Christ in rel. to Moses *πρεσβύτερος μὲν...κατὰ τὴν θεότητα· ὑστερογενέστερος δὲ κατὰ τὴν ἀνθρωπότητα* †Cyr.*coll.VT*(6^4.8D; M.77.1188A).

***ὑστεροδόμιον, τό,** *top part of a house, gable,* Cyr.*ador.*8(1.284E); met., of belief in Christ as God, ref. Jo.3:16 *κορωνίδα...καὶ ὑ. τῶν ἰδίων ἡμῖν ἐποιήσατο συγγραμμάτων* id.*dial.Trin.*4(5^1.507A; M.75.864D).

***ὑστερομέσως,** *with the natural order reversed,* so that what should come last in a sentence or paragraph comes in the middle, Didym.*Trin.*3.31(M.39.953B).

***ὑστερόμητις,** *wise after the event,* Nonn.*par.Jo.*20:28(M.43.913B).

***ὑστερόπρωτος,** *in inverted order,* Hipp.*Dan.*1.5.3(M.10.689A).

***ὑστεροπρώτως,** *with the natural order reversed,* so that words which should come second in a sentence come first, Didym.*Trin.*1.32(M.39.428C).

***ὑστεροστάτης, ὁ,** *member of the lowest grade* in a monastery, Thdr.Stud.*iamb.*13(M.99.1785A).

***ὑστεροτόκια, τά,** *rights of the younger son,* opp. *πρωτοτόκια,* Leont.H.*Nest.*3.9(M.86.1641B).

***ὑστεροφεγγής,** *shining later,* Synes.*hymn.*4.215(p.32; M.66.1607).

ὑστερόφωνος, *sounding afterwards,* Gr.Naz.*carm.*1.2.29.153(M.37.895A); ib.2.2(poem.)3.209(1495A); neut. as subst., *after-sound,* Germ.CP *or.*2(M.98.281C).

***ὑστεροχρονέω,** *be subsequent in time,* Clem.*str.*8.9(p.99.9; M.9.597A).

***ὑφαδρύνομαι,** *become mature,* Nil.*exerc.*52(M.79.784B).

ὑφαίρεσις, ἡ, 1. *purloining, pilfering,* met. *παρὰ...τῆς ἁμαρτίας εἴσοδον, ἐνωτίου τις ὑ. ἦν ἡ τοῦ παρακοῦσαι τῆς ἐντολῆς συμβουλή* Gr.Nyss.*v.Mos.*(M.44.396D); **2.** *withdrawal, subtraction σοφῶς ὑπαλλάττων ἡμᾶς ταῖς κατὰ μικρὸν ὑ., καὶ μετάγων ἐπὶ τὸ εὐαγγέλιον* Gr.Naz.*or.*45.12(M.36.640B); *παραδοθείσης τῆς πίστεως οὔτε ὑ. ... οὔτε προσθήκην ποιούμεθα* Gr.Nyss.*Eun.*2(2 p.297.20; M.45.468C); *μηδὲ μιᾶς γενομένης προσθήκης τῇ...τριάδι, ἢ ὑ., ἐκ τῆς τοῦ λόγου σαρκώσεως* Max.*ep.*12(M.91.468D).

ὑφαιρ-έω, 1. *subtract,* Hipp.*haer.*6.52(p.186.8; M.16.3286A); ‡Ath.*dial.Trin.*3.11(M.28.1220B); **2.** med., *refuse διαδέχεσθαι πενίας... ∼οῦνται πάντες* Just.*1apol.*12.8(M.6.544B).

***ὑφάλλομαι,** *escape from ὑ. θάνατον* Cyr.*glaph.Ex.*2(1.290C).

ὕφαλος, *clandestine,* Sophr.H.*carm.*1.102(M.87.3737B); *abstruse,* Thdt.*affect.*8(p.195.4; 4.898).

***ὑφανσία, ἡ,** *weaving,* Thdr.Stud.*poen.*1.110(M.99.1748C).

ὑφάπτω, *give light from underneath*; of candles in church compared with stars in heavens, ‡Sophr.H.*liturg.*3(M.87.3984C).

***ὑφαρπαγή, ἡ,** *leading astray, deception*; esp. in argument or doctrine, Ath.*Ar.*3.59(M.26.448A); *τοῦ καθ' ὑφαρπαγὴν αὐτῷ προληφθέντος λόγου* Bas.*Eun.*1.5(1.216D; M.29.520B); Gr.Nyss.*ep.*16(M.46.1056C); Max.*opusc.*(M.91.181A).

ὑφαρπάζω, *lead astray, mislead,* Alex.Al.*ep.Alex.*1(p.19; M.18.548B); Const.ap.Thdt.*h.e.*1.20.7(3.799); Ath.*ep.Aeg.Lib.*8(M.25.556A).

ὑφεδρία, ἡ, *lower seat,* Gr.Naz.*or.*4.111(M.35.648B); met., *subordinate ministry,* ib.43.27(M.36.533B).

***ὑφεδριάομαι,** *be seated below,* Gr.Naz.*carm.*2.1.16.9(M.37.1255A).

***ὑφεί,** v. **ὑφή.*

***ὑφειλμός, ὁ,** *subtraction,* †Gregent.*leg.Hom.*57(M.86.612C).

***ὑφερμηνευτής, ὁ,** *interpreter,* Eus.*v.C.*4.32(p.129.33; M.20.1181A); met., id.*l.C.*11(p.225.16; M.20.1377C).

***ὑφερμηνεύω,** *interpret,* Eus.*v.C.*3.13(p.83.13; M.20.1069B); id.*Hierocl.*21(M.22.828B); id.*p.e.*11.10(M.21.873C, v.l. *ἐφ-* 527C); abs., ref. a dream, id.*h.e.*4.15.10(M.20.345C).

ὕφεσις, ἡ, *letting down, slackening*; **1.** met., *falling short, defect τὸ ἀγέννητον οὐχὶ ἐπίτασίς ἐστι τοῦ γεννητοῦ· οὐδὲ μὴν τὸ γεννητὸν ὕ. τίς ἐστι τοῦ ἀγεννήτου* Bas.*Eun.*2.28(1.264E; M.29.637A); Gr.Nyss.*Eun.*12(2 p.294.14; M.45.908B); *ὑ. καὶ ἐπιτάσεως...τὸ μέσον ἀπολαβὼν τὴν ἀρετὴν ἐκ τῆς κακίας διέκρινε* id.*virg.*8(p.283.1; M.46.353B); *υἱόν... ὡς ἐν ὑ. τυχὸν* [l. *τυχόντα*] *τῆς πρὸς τὸν πατέρα ἰσότητος, καθὸ πέφυκεν ἄνθρωπος* Cyr.*ador.*10(1.334E); **2.** *inferiority* within Trin.; denied, Gr.Naz.*or.*31.9(p.156.1; M.36.141D); Didym.*Trin.*2.2(M.39.460C); as taught by Eun. *οὐσίας...πηλικότητι καὶ ἀξιωμάτων ὑφέσει διαφερούσας* Gr.Nyss.*Eun.*1(1 p.87.1; 317D); *ἐν ὁμοειδεῖ μέν, ὑφειμένῳ δὲ φωτὶ νοεῖν τὸν υἱόν, μὴ τὴν οὐσίαν ἐξαλλάττοντας, ἀλλὰ τὸ αὐτὸ ὑπερβεβληκὸς καὶ ἐν ὑ. θεωροῦντας* †Apoll.*ep.Bas.*2(M.32.1104C); **3.** *low estate*; of man contrasted with heavenly powers, Nil.*epp.*2.188(M.79.297C); Dion.Ar.*c.h.*7.1(M.3.205D); assumed by Christ, Cyr.*Pulch.*10(p.33.20; 5^2.139A); id.*ador.*9(1.306E); *lowliness* of Christ on earth, id.*Is.*3.5(2.536E); **4.** *moderation* in behaviour, *modesty,* Gr.Naz.*ep.*53(M.37.109B); *restraint* in speech, Chrys.*hom.23.4 in 1Cor.*(10.600C); **5.** of numbers, *lowering,* Cyr.*ador.*17(1.627C).

***ὑφεστώτως,** *in actual existence, in actual fact τὰ ἐν αὐτῷ* [sc. *Χριστῷ*] *ὑ. ὄντα ὁμολογεῖν, οὐκ ἔστι πρὸ αὐτοῦ, ἀλλ' ἐν αὐτῷ* Leont.H.*monoph.*58(M.86.1801B).

***ὑφεύρεμα, τό,** f.l. for *ἐφεύρημα,* Epiph.*haer.*proem.2(M.41.176A).

***ὑφή (ὑφεί, ὕφη, ὕφι),** = *οἰφεί, ephah,* a Hebr. measure, Epiph.*mens.*24(M.43.281A); *ὕφη* ib.21(272B); *ὕφι* Gr.Nyss.*Eun.*12(1 p.283.18; M.45.992B); *ὑφεί* Thdt.*qu.*59 *in 1Reg.*(1.394).

ὑφή, ἡ, *web*; met., *course*; of a letter, Chrys.*hom.in Philm.*proem.(11.774B); *ὑ. τῶν νοημάτων* Sever.*Gal.*4:23f.(p.302.19); Euthal.Diac.*epp.Paul.*(M.85.701A).

ὑφήγησις, ἡ, 1. *leading, guidance τοῖς μὴ κατὰ τὴν ἐπιθυμίαν τῆς σαρκὸς περιπατοῦσιν, ἀλλὰ κατὰ τὴν ἐπιθυμίαν τοῦ πνεύματος καὶ τὴν ὑ.* Meth.*res.*2.8(p.345.2; M.41.1176C); of God *ταῖς σαῖς ὑ. ἐνεστησάμην σωτηριώδη πράγματα* Eus.*v.C.*2.55(p.63.28; M.20.1029C); *ἐπιστολὰς ...Παῦλος...ἐπέστειλε καθ' ὑφήγησιν τοῦ ἁγίου πνεύματος* *Const.App.*2.57.7; **2.** *teaching, Hom.Clem.*11.20; *ἀρετῆς τὴν ὑ.* Gr.Nyss.*v.Mos.*(M.44.340D); *κατὰ τὴν ὑ. τοῦ διδασκάλου* Isid.Pel.*epp.*2.251(M.78.688D); **3.** *exposition,* Eus.*h.e.*2.18.1(M.20.184C); Gr.Nyss.*hom.2 in Cant.*(M.44.788C); **4.** *interpretation, explanation,* Or.*Jo.*20.10(p.337.29; M.14.592C); Thdt.*Ps.*51:1(1.946); **5.** *narration,* Eus.*p.e.*11.4(512C; M.21.849C); Epiph.*haer.*30.9(p.344.22; M.41.420D); of a play, *plot οὐκ ὢν βασιλεύς, ἀλλὰ σχῆμα ἔχων διὰ τῆς ὑ.* Chrys.*Laz.*6.5(1.780C).

ὑφήλιος, *under the sun*; *ἡ ὑ. the world,* Ath.*inc.*14.3(M.25.121A); Mac.Mgn.*apocr.*3.4(p.57.8); Cyr.*Ps.*67:18(M.69.1152B).

***ὑφήμερος,** *over-polite, obsequious,* Cosm.Mel.*schol.*(M.38.531) in Gr.Naz.*carm.*2.1.44.36.

***ὑφήνιος,** *under control, subject,* Max.*ep.*11(M.91.457D); Jo.D. *hom.*11.6(M.96.768D).

***ὕφι,** v. *ὑφή.

ὑφιζάν-ω, 1. *sink*; of the skin in starvation, *sag,* Chrys.*Thdr.*1.14(1.22B); met., of Christ, ref. Jo.5:19 ὡς ἠρέμα μὲν ~ει τὸ τῷ μονογενεῖ πρέπον ἀξίωμα, ἀναβαίνει δὲ τὴν ἀνθρώπου φύσιν Cyr.*Jo.*2.6(4.215A); **2.** *be lower* than, *inferior* to, of angels ὑ. τοῦ ἀκτίστου πνεύματος Didym.*Trin.*2.4(M.39.481B); of Christ ~ων τι βραχὺ τοῦ ἐν δόξῃ θεοπρεποῦς, ὡς ἄνθρωπος Cyr.*inc.unigen.*(5^{1}.698C).

ὑφίζησις, ἡ, 1. *sinking,* Cyr.*glaph.Gen.*2(1.40B); **2.** *inferiority* ἐν ὑπεροχῇ τριάδος...ὁ...θεὸς λόγος· ἐν ὑ. δὲ τὸ ἀνθρώπινον *ib.*6(187A).

ὑφίζω, = ὑφιζάνω; τὰ ὑφιζηκότα *inferior things,* Cyr.*Juln.*2(6^{2}.68E).

ὑφιστάω, = sq.; participial form ὑφιστῶσα (? for ὑφιστᾶσα, but cf. vv.ll.): τῆς μὲν νοητῆς φύσεως τὰς νοητὰς ὑφιστώσης δυνάμεις Gr. Nyss.*hom.opif.*24.2(M.44.213B; v.l. ὑφεστώσης); ἐπακολουθοῦσαν πρὸς τὴν τῶν ὄντων ὑπόστασιν τὴν ὑφιστῶσαν τὰ πάντα δύναμιν id. *Eun.*1(1 p.135.24, v.l. ὑφεστῶσαν; M.45.373C).

ὑφίστημι, A. trans.; **1.** *place* or *set under*; *lay as a foundation* τῶν ὄντων ἁπάντων πρῶτον ὑφίστησι αὐτοῦ γέννημα τὴν πρωτότοκον σοφίαν Eus.*d.e.*4.1(p.15.31; M.22.253A); **2.** *support, uphold* θεὸς...ἐν ἀρχῇ ...κατὰ μὲν τὴν μηδέπω γεγενημένην ποίησιν μόνος ἦν· καθὸ δὲ πᾶσα δύναμις ὁρατῶν τε καὶ ἀοράτων [αὐτὸς ὑπόστασις] ἦν σὺν αὐτῷ, τὰ πάντα σὺν αὐτῷ διὰ λογικῆς δυνάμεως αὐτὸς [καὶ ὁ λόγος, ὃς ἦν ἐν αὐτῷ] ὑπέστησεν Tat.*orat.*5(p.5.21; M.6.813C); Christ ὑποστήσαντα ἰδίῳ θελήματι ἄτρεπτον καὶ ἀναλλοίωτον κτίσμα τοῦ θεοῦ τέλειον, ἀλλ' οὐχ ὡς ἓν τῶν κτισμάτων Ar.*ep.Alex.*ap.Ath.*syn.*16(p.243.33; M.26.709A); **3.** *take up,* of Christ ὅλον τὸ Ἀδαμιαῖον φύραμα ἐν ἑαυτῷ ὑποστήσαντι Germ.CP *or.*2(M.98.261C); **4.** *institute, set up, introduce* ὁ θεὸς...φῶς δεύτερον κατὰ πάντα ἑαυτῷ ἀφωμοιωμένον ὑπεστήσατο Eus.*d.e.*4.3(p.153.16; M.22.256B); πρὸς ἡδονὴν σαρκὸς κατέσεισεν ὁ διάβολος, δι' ἧς ὑποστήσας τὸν θάνατον Thdt.*pental.*(5.131); **5.** ? *prick up* τὸ οὖς ὑποστήσαντες Cyr.*ador.*6(1.209D); **6.** *give substance to, cause to subsist* or *exist, make*; in gen. οὐδὲ γὰρ ὑπέστησέν τις ἐν αὐτῷ πατὴρ τὴν πονηρίαν, ἀλλ' ἡ ἀπὸ θεοῦ ἐκτροπὴ γεγέννηκεν αὐτήν Or.*Jo.*20.22(20; p.355.26; M.14.621C); τότε εἰς τὸ μὴ ὂν ἔσται ἀνάλυσις τῆς τῶν σωμάτων φύσεως, ὑποστησομένης δεύτερον, ἐὰν πάλιν λογικὰ ὑποκαταβῇ id.*princ.*2.3(p.118.7); ἀκρογωνιαῖος...λίθος μίαν ἐκ δυεῖν οἰκοδομῶν ὑποστησάμενος Eus.*d.e.*1.7(p.37.22; M.22.73A); Chrys.*hom.*13.5 *in Rom.*(9.550B); met. ἡ ἐλπὶς ὑφίστησιν αὐτὴν [sc. ἀνάστασιν] ἐν ἡμετέρᾳ ψυχῇ· τοῦτό ἐστιν 'ὑπόστασις πραγμάτων' id.*hom.*21.2 *in Heb.*(12.197B); of God at Creation εἰ θελήσας ὑποστῆσαι ὅ τι βούλεται ὁ θεός Or.*comm.in Gen.*ap.Eus.*p.e.*7.20(334D; M.12.48A); ἐργάζεται ...οὐκ ἐξ αὐτοῦ προάγων τὰ δημιουργήματα, ἀλλ' ἐνεργητικῶς ὑφιστάς Didym.(‡Bas.)*Eun.*5(M.29.736B); (Arian) of God making Son οὐκοῦν ὁμοιότητα διασώζει, οὐ κατὰ τὴν οὐσίαν, ἀλλὰ κατὰ τὸν τῆς θελήσεως λόγον, οἷον ἠθέλησεν ὑπεστήσατο *Symb.*ap.Geo.Laod.*ep.dogm.*ap. Epiph.*haer.*73.21(p.294.2; M.42.441A); Aët.*synt.*3 *ib.*76.11(p.353.7; 536C); βουλήσει, φασίν, ὁ πατὴρ τὸν υἱὸν ὑποστήσας, οὕτως αὐτὸν ἐποίησε καὶ δημιουργόν Cyr.*thes.*21(5^{1}.211E); of God as creator ἀγαθότητι πάσας ἡ...θεαρχία τὰς τῶν ὄντων οὐσίας ὑποστήσασα, πρὸς τὸ εἶναι παρήγαγεν Dion.Ar.*c.h.*4.1(M.3.177C); τὴν μὲν οὐσίαν ἡμῶν καὶ ζωὴν...ὑποστήσασα, καὶ ἀρχετύποις κάλλεσι τὸ θεοειδὲς ἡμῶν μορφώσασα id.*e.h.*3.3.7(M.3.436C); of Christ's flesh σάρκα ἐμψυχωμένην ψυχῇ λογικῇ τε καὶ νοερᾷ ὑπεστήσατο Jo.D.*f.o.*3.2(M.94.985C); cf.id.*fid.Nest.*23(p.569); **7.** *treat as subsisting* μὴ τὸν πατέρα μὲν οὐσιώσωμεν, τἄλλα δὲ οὐχ ὑποστήσωμεν Gr.Naz.*or.*31.32(p.188.2; M.36.169B).

B. intrans.; **1.** *exist,* of Christ πότερον οὖν ἐφ' ἑαυτοῦ ὑπέστη, καὶ ὑποστὰς προσκεκόλληται τῷ πατρί; ‡Ath.*Ar.*4.3(p.46.13; M.26.472A); ἐξ αὐτῆς δὲ τῆς ἀρχῆς ἐστι φύσει...οὐχ ὡς ἀρχῇ ἑτέρα καθ' ἑαυτὸν ὑφεστὼς οὐδ' ἔξωθεν ταύτης γεγονὼς *ib.*4.1(p.44.7; 468B); εἰ δύναται καὶ πρὸ τοῦ ὑποστῆναι τὸν υἱὸν ὁ θεὸς καλεῖσθαι πατήρ; Socr.*h.e.*5.23.2(M.67.645B); εἰ...οὐκ ἐκ τῆς οὐσίας τοῦ πατρὸς προῆλθεν ὁ υἱός, ὑπέστη δὲ ἐξουσιαστικῶς; Cyr.*thes.*10(5^{1}.81B); of dead persons δεῖ τοίνυν ὑφεστάναι καὶ Ἀβραὰμ καὶ Ἰσαὰκ καὶ Ἰακώβ, ἵνα τῶν ὄντων θεὸς ᾖ ὁ θεός Cyr.H.*catech.*18.11; **2.** *subsist, exist as a substance* or *entity,* of Trin. οὐκ ὀνόματι τριάδα μόνον, ἀλλ' ἀληθῶς ὄντα καὶ ὑφεστῶτα, πατέρα τε ἀληθῶς ὄντα καὶ ὑφεστῶτα, καὶ υἱὸν ἀληθῶς ἐνούσιον ὄντα καὶ ὑφεστῶτα, καὶ πνεῦμα ἅγιον ὑφεστὸς καὶ ὑπάρχον οἴδαμεν Ath.*tom.*5(M.26.801B); of Father and Son τὸ τελείως μὲν ὑφεστάναι πατέρα καθ' ἑαυτόν, τελείως καὶ τὸν υἱὸν καθ' ἑαυτὸν ὑφεστάναι ‡Ath.*Sabell.*9(M.28.112B); of Son and H. Ghost πατέρα ἀΐδιον, υἱοῦ ἀιδίου ὄντος καὶ ὑφεστῶτος καὶ πνεῦμα ἅγιον ἀιδίως ὂν καὶ ὑφεστὸς Eugen.*exp.fid.*2(M.18.1304B); of Son τοῦ λόγου, δι' οὗ τὰ πάντα γέγονεν, ὑφεστηκότος οὐσιωδῶς κατὰ τὸ ὑποκείμενον, τοῦ αὐτοῦ ὄντος τῇ σοφίᾳ Or.*Jo.*6.38(22; p.146.14; M.14.264C); πατὴρ λόγου ζῶντος, σοφίας ὑφεστώσης καὶ δυνάμεως καὶ χαρακτῆρος ἀιδίου Gr. Thaum.*symb.*(p.3.2; M.10.984); ὁ τοῦ θεοῦ λόγος, τῷ μὲν ὑφεστάναι καθ' ἑαυτόν, διῄρηται πρὸς ἐκεῖνον παρ' οὗ τὴν ὑπόστασιν ἔχει Jo.D. *f.o.*1.6(M.94.804B); of heavenly powers τἀγαθὸν...πᾶσι τοῖς οὖσιν... ἐφίησι τὰς τῆς...ἀγαθότητος ἀκτῖνας. διὰ ταύτας ὑπέστησαν αἱ νοηταὶ καὶ νοεραὶ...οὐσίαι καὶ δυνάμεις καὶ ἐνέργειαι Dion.Ar.*d.n.*4.1(M.3.693B); ref. existence of creatures by virtue of participation in essential divine goodness, *ib.*4.20(720B); *ib.*4.23(725A); cf.*ib.*5.4(817D); of grace, ref. 1Cor.12:4–6 τῆς εἰρημένης ὕλης τῶν χαρισμάτων ἐνεργουμένης μὲν ἀπὸ τοῦ θεοῦ, διακονουμένης δὲ ὑπὸ τοῦ Χριστοῦ, ὑφεστώσης δὲ κατὰ τὸ ἅγιον πνεῦμα Or.*Jo.*2.10(6; p.65.30; 129A); **3.** *be eclipsed* ἡ δὲ σελήνη ὑπέστη Thphn.*chron.*p.255(M.108.637B).

***ὑφομολογέω,** *admit covertly,* Gr.Nyss.*Eun.*9(2 p.208.24; M.45.805D).

ὑφοράομαι, 1. *view with suspicion, distrust; fear,* Just.*dial.*131.5(M.6.781B); Clem.*str.*7.11(p.48.8; M.9.493A); Bas.*hom.*21.8(2.169E; M.31.556B); *suspect,* Or.*Cels.*1.68(p.121.29; M.11.788A); c. ὅτι, *ib.*1.69(p.123.21; 789B); ὑπιδόμενος τὴν...ἀπολογίαν *ib.*3.42(p.238.7; ὑπειδόμενος 973C); **2.** *respect, pay attention to,* Chrys.*hom.18.2 in Rom.*(9.632E); id.*hom.17.1 in Jo.*(8.96C).

***ὑφορμάω,** v.l. for -έω, Chrys.*hom.37.1 in Mt.*(7.415B).

ὑφορμέω, *beset, arise to trouble*; abs., *be troublesome,* Chrys.*hom.*79.2 *in Jo.*(8.467C); *ib.*5.2(37A); Synes.*ep.*4(M.66.1336A); neut. ptcpl. as subst., *problem, difficulty arising,* Bas.*ep.*156.2(3.246B; M.32.616C); Chrys.*hom.55.1 in Ac.*(9.411D); Thdt.*Rom.*6:14(3.65).

ὕφος, τό, *web*; *woven material* or *structure*; met., of words τὸ τῆς ὑποθέσεως ὑ. Pall.*v.Chrys.*1(p.3.33; M.47.5); *text,* M.*Ner.et Ach.*11(p.10.15); *complete text*; of a connected passage opp. isolated phrases, Clem.*str.*7.16(p.68.9; M.9.533B); Or.*Cels.*6.55(p.126.18; M.11.1384B); *arrangement in a series, ordered succession,* Eus.*qu. Steph.suppl.*3(M.22.961A); id.*ep.Carp.*(M.22.1276C).

***ὑψάντυξ,** *high-arched,* Nonn.*par.Jo.*5:2(M.43.784C).

ὑψαυχενία, ἡ, = ὑψηλαυχενία, *haughtiness, pride,* *A.Thom.*A 99(p.211.15); Didym.*Ps.*91:10(M.39.1501A); Epiph.*haer.*65.1(p.2.15; M.42.12C).

ὑψαυχενίζω, med., *behave arrogantly,* Thphyl.*exc.Rom.*5(p.224.16; M.113.932B).

***ὑψαυχένιος,** *haughty,* †Cyr.*hom div.*10(5^{2}.370E).

***ὑψαύχενος,** = foreg., *Orac.Sib.*8.37; *ib.*12.230.

***ὑψηγόρως,** *in lofty language,* Clem.*str.*6.15(p.494.28; M.9.348C).

ὑψηλαυχενία, ἡ, *pride,* Thdr.Heracl.*Is.*38:1f.(M.18.1329A).

***ὑψηλαυχέω,** *behave proudly,* Nil.*epp.*3.99(M.79.432B).

***ὑψηλοβατέω,** *ascend on high*; of Elijah, ‡Chrys.*Petr.et El.*2(2.732E).

ὑψηλογνώμων, *high-minded,* Bas.Sel.*v.Thecl.*1(M.85.504D).

***ὑψηλοκαρδία, ἡ,** *pride,* Esaias *or.*5.6(p.41).

ὑψηλοκάρδιος, *proud in heart, arrogant* οὐδὲ μοναχὸς ὑ. sc. ὑποκλίνει] ὑπακοὴν κτήσασθαι. ἀνὴρ ὑ. τοῦ ἄρχειν ὀρέγεται...ἀκάθαρτος παρὰ κυρίῳ πᾶς ὑ. Jo.Clim.*scal.*23(M.88.965D); Hesych.S.*temp.*1.63(M.93.1501A).

***ὑψηλοπετέω,** v. *ὑψιπετέω.

ὑψηλοπέτης, *flying high,* Eus.*Lc.*12:22(M.24.557A); †Gr.II Papa *ep.Leon.*1(Hard.4.5B).

ὑψηλός, *high*; **1.** lit. τὰ ὑ. *high places* devoted to idol worship, Eus.*l.C.*9(p.218.24; M.20.1364B); exeg. 4Reg.23:9 ὅτι δὲ ὑψηλὰ οὐ μόνον οἱ τῶν εἰδώλων ἐκαλοῦντο βωμοί, ἀλλὰ καὶ τὰ ἐν τοῖς ὑ. χωρίοις δομηθέντα τῷ θεῷ θυσιαστήρια Thdt.*qu.55 in 4Reg.*(1.551); of persons, *tall,* Herm.*sim.*8.1.2; *ib.*9.3.1; of flesh, *rounded,* Chrys.*hom.1.3 in 1Cor.*(10.7C); **2.** met.; in gen., *high, lofty*; of persons, *of high degree,* *Barn.*19.6; of God, *sublime,* Chrys.*exp.in Ps.*143:3(5.462A); Thdt.*Ps.*98:5(1.1308); *lofty in mind, spiritual in outlook,* Chrys. *hom.64.1 in Mt.*(7.636A); ὑ. λοιπὸν καὶ πρόθυμοι πρὸς ἐλεημοσύνην *ib.80.2*(767C); τὸ πνεῦμα τὸ δυνάμενον ὑ. αὐτοὺς ποιῆσαι *ib.90.2*(841B); esp. paradoxically ref. humility ἐπεὶ μέγαν ἔχεις δεσπότην, γενοῦ καὶ σὺ ὑ. ... ὑ. δὲ ὁ ταπεινὸς τὴν διάνοιαν καὶ τὰς φαντασίας τοῦ παρόντος βίου οὐδὲν εἶναι νομίζων id.*exp.in Ps.*144:3(5.468D); id. *hom.1.3 in 1Cor.*(10.7A); ref. heights of contemplation or virtue, Or.*Jo.*20.10(p.338.23; M.14.593B); Gr.Nyss.*hom.6 in Cant.*(M.44.889C); id.*v.Mos.*(M.44.372C) cit. s. ἀκόλουθος; *profound* σημαινέτω τι καὶ ὑψηλότερον ἡ κάμηλος Clem.*q.d.s.*26(p.177.24; M.8.632C); Or. *princ.*4.2.6(12; p.315.13; M.11.368B); as epithet of scriptural writers, Gr.Nyss.*v.Mos.*(M.44.377A); ‡Caes.Naz.*dial.*107(M.38.973); *ib.*108(977); *serious* ὑ. αἱμομιξιῶν †Jo.Jej.*poenit.*(M.88.1904D).

***ὑψηλοφανῶς,** *with sublime appearance, in sublime form,* Thdr. Stud.*antirr.*2.28(M.99.372A).

***ὑψηλοφερής,** *raising on high,* †Cyr.*hom.div.*10(5^{2}.377E).

***ὑψηλόφθαλμος**, *with uplifted eyes*, prob. implying immodest curiosity, *Did*.3.3.

ὑψηλοφρον-έω, *be proud*, Hipp.*Dan*.3.10.4; †Bas.*Is*.127(1.468A; M.30.325A); ref. 1Tim.6:17, Chrys.*stat*.2.5(2.27C); *ἀσφαλίζου τὴν αὐθάδειαν, μὴ ἐπιπλήξεις τινί, ἵνα μὴ κατακριθῇς ὡς ~ήσας* Nil. *paraen*.135(M.79.1261B); *μετανοοῦντι ~εῖν ἀλλότριον* Marc.Er.*opusc*. 2.102(M.65.945A).

***ὑψηλοφροσύνη, ἡ**, *haughtiness*; as a sin, Herm.*mand*.8.3; Meth.*symp*.11(p.129.27; M.18.205A); Ephr.3.305F; *ὑστέρησις καὶ ἀτιμία ἐξ ὑ. τίκτεται* Bas.*renunt*.10(2.211B; M.31.648B); induced by Devil, Mac.Aeg.*pat*.13(M.34.876C); Isid.Pel.*epp*.1.15(M.78.189B); *ὅταν λογισμὸς ὑ. ... ὑπεισέλθοι σε, ἐρεύνα σοῦ τὸ συνειδός Apophth. Patr*.(M.65.389B); Max.*ambig*.(M.91.1352D); esp. as sin of Adam, ref. Gen.3:5, Mac.Aeg.*cust.cor*.12(M.34.832C); id.*hom*.27.5(M.34. 696D); Dor.*doct*.1.7(M.88.1625C).

ὑψηλόφρων, *haughty, conceited*, Herm.*sim*.8.9.1; †Bas.*Is*.92(1. 443E; M.30.269C); *οὐκ ἔστιν ὑ. εἶναι μὴ ὄντα μωρόν* Chrys.*hom.8.5 in Phil*.(11.252E).

ὑψηλόφωνος, *shrill-sounding*, ‡Caes.Naz.*dial*.20(M.38.877).

ὑψηλῶς, *loftily*; met., Clem.*str*.1.12(p.35.32; M.8.753B); *ib*.7.13 p.59.30; M.9.516C); comp., *in a higher* or *more subtle sense εἰ ...ὑ. ἀκοῦσαι βούλει τοῦ* [Jer.12:11] Or.*hom.11.2 in Jer*.(p.79.12; M. 13.368D); id.*fr.57 in Lam*.2:11(p.258.17; M.13.636D); *in a more spiritual manner*, Chrys.*hom.50.2 in Mt*.(7.516D); in form *ὑψηλοτέρως*, Epiph.*haer*.31.4(p.387.25; M.41.480A).

ὑψήνωρ, *exalting men*, Nonn.*par.Jo*.3:36(M.43.773A); *ib*.7:18 (808B).

ὕψι, *above*; c. genit., Nonn.*par.Jo*.3:31(M.43.772B).

***ὑψιβιβάς**, *walking proudly*, Gr.Naz.*carm*.2.1.32.18(M.37.1302A).

ὑψιβρεμέτης, *high-thundering*; of God, *Orac.Sib*.3.1.

***ὑψιγένεθλος**, *of high birth*, Nonn.*par.Jo*.1:1(M.43.749A).

***ὑψίδμητος**, *high-built*, *Orac.Sib*.14.217.

ὑψιθέμεθλος, *high-founded, high-set ὑ. Ἰουδαίων πέδον* Nonn.*par. Jo*.4:3(M.43.773B).

***ὑψιθέω**, *move swiftly on high*, Gr.Naz.*carm*.1.1.4.40(M.37.418A).

***ὑψιθόωκος**, *seated on high*, Gr.Naz.*carm*.1.1.3.6(M.37.408A); *ib*. 1.2.9.148(679A).

ὑψίθρονος, *high-throned*; of God, Gr.Naz.*carm*.1.2.2.452(M.37. 614A); Nonn.*par.Jo*.12:26(M.43.853C); of Christ, Gr.Naz.*carm*.2.1. 38.10(1326A).

***ὑψίθωκος**, *throned on high*, Synes.*hymn*.1.54(p.59; M.66.1589).

ὑψικάρηνος, *with head held high*, Gr.Naz.*carm*.1.2.1.216(M.37. 539A); met., of virginity, *ib*.1.2.1.529(562A).

ὑψικέλευθος, *on a lofty path*; of man as *tending heavenwards*, Gr. Naz.*carm*.2.2(poem.)7.53(M.37.1555A).

***ὑψικέραυνος**, *thundering on high*; of God, *Orac.Sib*.1.323; *ib*.2. 239; *ib*.5.302.

ὑψίκομος, *with plumage* soaring *aloft*; of phoenix, *cat.Apoc*.7:9 (p.292.4).

***ὑψιλόγος**, *talking loftily σοφιστῶν...ὑ.* Gr.Naz.*carm*.2.2(epitaph.) 5.6(M.38.13A).

ὑψιμέδων, *ruling on high*; of God, *Orac.Sib*.2.309; Gr.Naz.*carm*. 1.2.1.6(M.37.522C); *CIG* 8608.

ὑψινεφής, *dwelling high in the clouds*, Nonn.*par.Jo*.8:50(M.43. 821A); *ib*.15:9(873B).

***ὑψιπετέω**, *fly high*, Meth.*Porph*.1(p.504.32); fig., *soar ἡ ἱερωσύνη εὐπαρρησιάστως ὑ. ἀπὸ γῆς εἰς οὐρανόν* Ephr.3.2E = ‡Chrys.*sac*.7 (*ὑψηλοπετεῖ* 1.805D); of humility, Ant.Mon.*hom*.70(M.89.1637A).

ὑψιπετής, *lofty*; neut. as subst., met., of Church, Eus.*d.e*.7.1 (p.313.32; M.22.513A).

***Ὑψιστάριοι (*Ὑψιστιανοί), οἱ**, *worshippers of the Most High*, name of a Judaistic sect *τὰ εἴδωλα καὶ τὰς θυσίας ἀποπεμπόμενοι, τιμῶσι τὸ πῦρ καὶ τὰ λύχνα·...τὸ σάββατον αἰδούμενοι καὶ τὴν περὶ τὰ βρώματα ἔστιν ἃ μικρολογίαν, τὴν περιτομὴν ἀτιμάζουσιν. ὑ. τοῖς ταπεινοῖς ὄνομα, καὶ ὁ παντοκράτωρ δὴ μόνος αὐτοῖς σεβάσμιος* Gr. Naz.*or*.18.5(M.35.992A); *τοῖς λεγομένοις ὑψιστιανοῖς, ὧν αὕτη ἐστὶν ἡ πρὸς τοὺς Χριστιανοὺς διαφορά, τὸ θεὸν μὲν αὐτοὺς ὁμολογεῖν εἶναί τινα, ὃν ὀνομάζουσιν ὕψιστον ἢ παντοκράτορα, πατέρα δὲ αὐτὸν εἶναι μὴ παραδέχεσθαι* Gr.Nyss.*Eun*.2(2 p.310.28; M.45.484A).

ὕψιστος, *most high*; of God *Most High ἡ ἀνδρεία ἀπὸ ὑ. δίδοται τοῖς ἀνθρώποις T.Sym*.2.5; *εὐλογήσω τὸν ὕ. ib*.6.7; *1Clem*.45.7; *Orac. Sib*.2.245; Arist.*apol*.15.1; Just.*dial*.32.3(M.6.514C); *ὕ. δὲ διὰ τὸ εἶναι αὐτὸν ἀνώτερον τῶν πάντων* Thphl.Ant.*Autol*.1.4(M.6.1029B); *ὕ. αὐτὸν καλῶν, οὐ τόπῳ αὐτὸν περιορίζω· ἀλλὰ καὶ τὸ ὑψηλὸν καὶ μεγαλεῖον αὐτοῦ τῆς φύσεως δηλῶ* Chrys.*exp.in Ps*.143:3(5.462A); of Father, Clem.*paed*.3.12(p.291.18; M.8.681B); *Hom.Clem*.18.4; perh. as Patripassian interpolation *τοῦ ᾅδου σκυλευομένου* [*ἐπὶ τῷ πάθει τοῦ ὑ.*] *T.Lev*.4.1; used by Callistus, Hipp.*haer*.9.15(p.253.15; M.16.3391A); of Son before Creation, Ath.*Ar*.1.38(M.26.92B); *ὕ. ἄρα υἱός, ἐπειδήπερ καὶ κύριος* Thdt.*haer*.5.2(4.384); exeg. Lc.1:35 (Valent.) *ὕ. ἐστιν ὁ δημιουργός...οἱ κατὰ τὸν Ἀδὰμ κτισθέντες ἀπὸ μόνου ἐκτίσθησαν τοῦ ὑ., τουτέστι...τοῦ δημιουργοῦ· ὁ δὲ Ἰησοῦς...ἀπὸ πνεύματος ἁγίου* ⟨*καὶ τοῦ ὑ.*⟩ Hipp.*haer*.6.35(p.164.20; 3246C); *ib*.6.51(p.253.15; 3391A).

***ὑψίτμητος**, f.l. for *ὑψίδμητος*, *Orac.Sib*.14.217.

ὑψιφανής, *exhibited on high*; of Christ crucified, Nonn.*par.Jo*. 19:23(M.43.901C).

ὑψιφόρητος, *borne from on high*, Synes.*hymn*.4.36(p.42; M.66.1612).

***ὑψίφορος**, neut. as subst., *flight heavenwards*, Dion.Ar.*c.h*.15.8 (M.3.337A).

ὑψίφρων, *high-minded*, Gr.Naz.*carm*.2.2(poem.)6.104(M.37.1550A).

ὑψόθι, c. genit., *above*, Nonn.*par.Jo*.19:18(M.43.901B); *upon*, *ib*. 2:14(764A); *ib*.6:10(793C).

***ὑψοποιός**, *exalting*; of humility, Hesych.S.*temp*.1.63(M.93. 1500C); neut. as subst., of temperance, *ib*.1.2(1481B).

ὕψος, τό, *height*; **1.** lit., for *εἰς ὕ.*, ref. carrying on a shield in triumph *ἀναγαγόντες αὐτὸν ὕψος Chron.Pasch*.p.338(M.92.881B); of heaven *τὰ ὕ. τῶν οὐρανῶν 1Clem*.36.2; *ἀνέρχομαι εἰς ὕψος A.Phil*.140 (p.75.9); Cosm.Ind.*top*.2(M.88.128C); **2.** met., *sublimity τὸ ὕ. εἰς ὃ ἀνάγει ἡ ἀγάπη ἀνεκδιήγητόν ἐστι 1Clem*.49.4; Clem.*str*.7.7(p.35.5; M.9.465C); Gr.Nyss.*Pss.titt*.B 16(M.44.597B) cit. s. *ἀνάβασις*; consisting in humility, Chrys.*hom.65.5 in Mt*.(7.650C); ref. Abraham, Gen.18:27 *ἀπὸ πολλοῦ διανοίας ὕ. ἐφθέγγετο τὸ ῥῆμα,...ἀπὸ ὕ., οὐκ ἀπὸ ἀπονοίας* id.*hom.1.3 in 1Cor*.(10.7C); *ἡ πρόσπτωσις αὕτη* [i.e. before love of Christ] *ὕψους ἐστὶν ὑπόθεσις καὶ ῥίζα* Cyr.*Ps*.44:6 (M.69.1038A); *ὄρος Σιών, τοὺς τὸ ὕ. τῆς θεολογίας πεπιστευμένους ἐκάλεσε* Thdt.*Ps*.47:12(1.911); in bad sense *ὅπως ἐξ ὕ. κατενεχθῇ εἰς γέλωτα Const.App*.6.9.4; of God, Gr.Nyss.*Eun*.5(2 p.117.7; M.45. 697B) cit. s. *δεξιός*; *δείκνυται...σοῦ τὸ ὕ. διὰ τῆς ἀρρήτου δυνάμεως* Thdt.*Ps*.20:14(1.732); also as synonym for God, *Pss.Sal*.17.7; *οὐκ ἐσμέν τινες χαμαιρριφεῖς, ὑπὸ τοιούτου ὕ. γνωρισθέντες A.Andr.fr*.1 (p.38.7); *τίς ἐλάλησε τοσαύτην ἀδικίαν εἰς τὸ ὕ. ποτέ;* Bas.*Eun*.1.16(1. 229A; M.29.549C); *ib*.2.19(254C; M.612A); **3.** *arrogance θρασύτης, ὕ., ἀλαζονεία Did*.5.1; cf.*Barn*.20.1.

ὑψόω, A. *lift high, raise up*; **1.** of levitation *ὁρᾷ αὐτὴν ὑψωθεῖσαν ὡς ἕνα πῆχυν ἀπὸ τῆς γῆς...καὶ οὕτω προσευχεσθαι* ‡Sophr.H.*v.Mar. Aeg*.15(M.87.3708D); **2.** ref. buildings, *erect*, Eus.*v.C*.2.45(p.60.10; M.20.1021B); id.*l.C*.9(p.220.14; M.20.1368B); **3.** Christ, ref. Jo.3:14 *ὁ ὑψωθεὶς ἐπὶ κεράτων μονοκέρωτος* Claud.*fr.pasch*.(M.5.1297A); Clem. *paed*.2.8(p.202.19; M.8.485B); Eus.*d.e*.10.6(p.468.17; M.22.753C); *τὸ ὑψωθῆναι δηλοῖ τὸ ἐμφανῆναι καὶ ἐπίσημον γενέσθαι* Ammon.*Jo*.3:14 (M.85.1409D); *οὐκ εἶπε, κρεμασθῆναι δεῖ, ἀλλ', ὑψωθῆναι. ὅπερ γὰρ εὐφημότερον εἶναι ἐδόκει διὰ τὸν ἀκροώμενον, καὶ ἐγγὺς τὸν τύπον, τοῦτο τέθεικεν* Chrys.*hom.27.2 in Jo*.(8.155E); *εἴη δὲ καὶ ἡμᾶς διαφυγεῖν τὰ τῶν ὄφεων δήγματα· εἰ δὲ καὶ δηχθείημεν, εἰς τὸν ὑψωθέντα ὑπὲρ ἡμῶν ἀπιδεῖν, καὶ τὴν θεραπείαν ἑλκύσαι* Thdt.*Cant*. 8:14(2.164); exeg. Jo.12:32 *εὐφήμως δὲ λίαν, ἀντὶ τοῦ σταυρωθῆναι τὸ ὑ. φησι* Cyr.*Jo*.8(4.707E); contrast exeg. Jo.8:28 *τοῦτ' ἔστιν ὅταν τῆς ἐπ' ἐμοὶ μικρᾶς τε καὶ χαμαιπετοῦς ἀποπαύσησθε διαλήψεως, ὅταν ὑψηλόν τε καὶ ὑπέργειον φρονήσητε περὶ ἐμοῦ, καὶ θεὸν ἐκ θεοῦ πεφηνότα πιστεύσητε ib*.5.4(516A); **4.** liturg., *elevate*, Max.*schol.e.h*.3.2(M.4. 137A); *Lit.Jac*.(p.226.20); Thdr.Stud.*praesanct*.(M.99.1689A); *Lit. Bas*.(p.341.14); *τὸ δὲ ὑ. τὸν θεῖον ἄρτον μόνον, τοῦτό ἐστιν, ἐπεὶ αὐτὸς ἐστιν ὁ βασιλεὺς κύριος καὶ αὐτός ἐστιν ἡ κεφαλή,...τὰ δὲ ἄλλα τίμια δῶρα, μέλη Χριστοῦ, καὶ σῶμα* ‡Germ.CP *contempl*.(M.98.448D); *ὑψοῦται ἐν ταῖς χερσὶ τοῦ ἱερέως ὡς ἐπὶ σταυροῦ* ‡Jo.D.*corp*.5(M.95.409C).

B. *elevate, exalt*; **1.** God *εἰ δὲ θεὸς γενετὴς ὑψούμενός ἐστι δι' αὐτοῦ* [sc. Christ], *καὶ...ὑψώσειε...υἱῆα* Nonn.*par.Jo*.13:32(M.43.865A); ref. Jo.21:19 *δοξάσωμεν οὖν καὶ ἡμεῖς ὑψώσαντες τῷ ἑαυτῶν θανάτῳ τὸν θεόν* Or.*mart*.50(p.47.3; M.11.636A); *οὐ ταπεινὸς ὢν ὁ θεὸς ὑψοῦται οὐδὲ ὃ μὴ ἔχει προσλαμβάνει· ἀλλ' ὅπερ ἔχει δείκνυσιν...δείκνυται γὰρ σοῦ τὸ ὕψος διὰ τῆς ἀρρήτου δυνάμεως* Thdt.*Ps*.20:14(1.732); *τὸ δὲ ὑψοῦτε, ἀντὶ τοῦ τὸ ὑψηλὸν αὐτοῦ κηρύττετε ib*.98:5(1308); Christ, ref. Phil.2:9 *ὡς ἄνθρωπος ὑψοῦται* Ath.*inc.et c.Ar*.11(M.26.1004B); *πρῶτον οὖν τὸ ἴδιον σῶμα ἤγειρεν ὁ κύριος ἐκ νεκρῶν, καὶ ὕψωσεν ἐν ἑαυτῷ· μετὰ ταῦτα ἐγερεῖ καὶ τὰ μέλη...αὐτὸς οὖν...ἑαυτὸν ὑψοῖ ib*.12 (1004B); Ath.*Ar*.1.45(M.26.104C) cit. s. *ἄνθρωπος*; *οὐχ ἵνα αὐτὸς ὑψωθῇ· ὕψιστος γάρ ἐστιν· ἀλλ' ἵνα αὐτὸς μὲν ὑπὲρ ἡμῶν δικαιοσύνη γένηται, ἡμεῖς δὲ ὑψωθῶμεν ἐν αὐτῷ ib*.1.41(97B); ref. God's exaltation of men: martyrs, *Ep.Lugd*.ap.Eus.*h.e*.5.2.5(M.20.436A); *πλέον ὑψουμένων παρ' ὃ ὑψώθησαν ἂν δίκαιοι μὲν γενόμενοι μὴ μαρτυρήσαντες δέ* Or.*mart*.50(p.46.27; M.11.636A); *πάντων αὐτὸν* [sc. S. Peter] *προὔθηκεν, ὑψώσας ταῖς ἄνωθεν δωρεαῖς* Ast.Am.*hom*.8(M.40.273D);

ὅσον τις ἑαυτὸν ταπεινοῖ, πολλαπλασίως ὑψοῖ αὐτὸν ὁ θεός Ant.Mon. *hom.*70(M.89.1637A); as between men ὑψῶν τὸ διανοητικὸν ἡμῶν ὁ ἀπόστολος Or.*princ.*4.3.6(p.332.7; M.11.388A); in honour, Eus.*v.C.* 3.59(p.105.23; M.20.1125B); τὸ τῆς ἐκκλησίας ἦθος [γρ. ἔθος], οἷον ὑ. μὲν ταπεινόν, ταπεινῶσαι δὲ ὑψηλόν Synes.*ep.*90(M.66.1456D); **2.** of pride and self-exaltation, *T.Jos.*17.8; οὐχ ὑψώσεις σεαυτόν, ἔσῃ δὲ ταπεινόφρων *Barn.*19.3; Herm.*sim.*9.22.3; of antichrist ἄρχεται ἑαυτὸν ὑ. καὶ δοξάζειν ὡς θεόν Hipp.*antichr.*47(p.30.16; M.10.765B); med., *be exalted, proud* ἐν πλεονεξίᾳ ὑ. *T.Jud.*21.8; Clem.*q.d.s.*1 (p.160.3; M.9.605A); Chrys.*exp.in Ps.*3:1(5.5A); **3.** pres. ptcpl. act. as adj. ἡ ὑ. ὁδός *the higher interpretation*, ‡Chrys.*pasch.*4(8.260B).

ὕψωμα, τό, 1. lit.; **a.** *height*; of buildings, Const.*or.s.c.*17(p.178. 1; M.20.1284A); of high places used in pagan worship, Cyr.*ador.*6 (1.178E); id.*Os.*3(3.76B); esp. of heaven, *A.Jo.*23(p.163.27); ὁ θεὸς τῶν ὑ. *Protev.*6.2(p.13); λέγουσί τινα εἶναι ἐν ἀοράτοις...ὑ. τέλειον Αἰῶνα πρόοντα Iren.*haer.*1.1.1(M.7.445A); ἐξ ἁγίων ὑ. καὶ κατοικητηρίων σου καταβάς Niceph.Ur.*v.Sym.*146(M.86.3124A); **b.** *lifting up* χειρὸς ὑ. Const.*or.s.c.*17(p.178.34; M.20.1285A); Gr.Naz.*carm.*1.2. 8.147(M.37.659A); **c.** *being lifted up, elevation*, Hipp.*haer.*7.23(p.201. 2; M.16.3310B); **2.** met.; **a.** *height* τὸ ὑ. τῶν διδασκομένων Cyr.H. *procatech.*12; τὰ πονηρὰ τῆς τῶν δαιμόνων κακίας ὑ. Gr.Nyss.*hom.5 in Cant.*(M.44.861B); ἐν ἀπορρήτοις νοημάτων ὑ. Proc.G.*Is.*6:1ff.(M. 87.1933A); **b.** of God's sublimity ἡ θεία...φύσις, οὐκ ἔν γε τοῖς καθ' ἡμᾶς, ἀλλ' ἐν ἰδίοις, καὶ ταῖς αὐτῇ πρέπουσιν ὑ. Cyr.*Is.*1.4(2.123A); id.*Pulch.*13(p.36.4; 5².142D); id.*Ps.*44:2(M.69.1029B); **c.** *exaltation* πρὸς τῷ κλήρῳ τὰ ταπεινώματα καὶ ὑ. ἀνθρώποις γίνεται *Hom.Clem.* 19.23; **d.** of pride, *T.Job* 41(p.130.17); ὁ ὄφις...ὑπέσπειρε τῷ Ἀδὰμ ὑ., ὅτι ὡς θεὸς γίνῃ Mac.Aeg.*cust.cor.*12(M.34.832C); ἐν τῷ ὑ. τῆς ὑπερηφανίας Gr.Nyss.*v.Mos.*(M.44.417B).

***ὑψώνω**, s.v.l., *exalt, make proud*, ‡Chrys.*hom.*10(13.245A).

ὕψωσις, ἡ, *raising high*; **1.** lit., of Ascension, exeg. Ac.5:31 οὐχ ἁπλῶς τὴν ἀνάστασιν τοῦτο μόνην, ἀλλὰ καὶ τὴν ὕ., τουτέστιν, τὴν ἀνάληψιν, δηλοῖ Chrys.*hom.13.1 in Ac.*(9.104B); **2.** *exaltation*; met., of Christ as man, Ath.*Ar.*1.45(M.26.105A) cit. s. ἄνθρωπος; τὸ... ὑπερύψωσεν, οὐ τὴν οὐσίαν τοῦ λόγου ὑψουμένην σημαίνει...ἀλλὰ τῆς ἀνθρωπότητός ἐστιν ἡ ὕ. *ib.*1.41(96C); and of men in him τὴν δὲ τοιαύτην εἰς ἡμᾶς γενομένην ὕ. προανεφώνει τὸ πνεῦμα [Ps.88:17] *ib.*(97C); *ib.*1.45(105A); ‡Ath.*Apoll.*2.9(M.26.1148B); of martyrs λόγον...ἔχει τὸ ἴδιως τὸν ἐν μαρτυρίῳ θάνατον ὕ. καλεῖσθαι, ὡς δῆλον ἐκ τοῦ [Jo.12:32] Or.*mart.*50(p.47.1; M.11.636A); in gen., of men ὕ. ἡ προέρχεται...κατόρθωσις Or.*fr.20 in Lam.*1:7(p.243.26; M.13.617B); ἐκ ταπεινώσεως...σωτηρία καὶ ὕ. Jo.D.*hom.*4.39(M.96.641D); of pride ποῦ ἐστιν...ἡ δόξα σου καὶ ἡ ὕ. σου; *A.Andr.et Mt.*26(p.104.11); **3.** liturg.; **a.** *elevation* τάχα τὸν κουφισμὸν καὶ τὴν ὕ. τῆς μιᾶς εὐλογίας τοῦ θείου ἄρτου φησίν, ὃν ὑψοῖ ὁ ἱερεύς, λέγων, τὰ ἅγια τοῖς ἁγίοις Max.*schol.e.h.*3.2(M.4.137A); Jo.D.*trisag.*27(M.95.57D); ἡ δὲ ὕ. τοῦ τιμίου σώματος, εἰκονίζει τὴν ἐπὶ τοῦ σταυροῦ ὕ., καὶ τὸν ἐν αὐτῷ θάνατον, καὶ αὐτὴν τὴν ἀνάστασιν ‡Germ.CP *contempl.*(M.98.448B); Thdr.Stud.*praesanct.*(M.99.1689A); **b.** *Exaltation* of Cross, feast celebrated on 14th Sept. ἐν τῇ ὕ. τοῦ τιμίου καὶ ζωοποιοῦ σταυροῦ... τῇ ἁγίᾳ καὶ πανυμνήτῳ ἑορτῇ Leont.N.*v.Sym.*5(M.93.1673C); ἐν τῇ τρίτῃ ὕ. ἀποδεθεὶς τῷ ζωοποιῷ σταυρῷ ὁ τίμιος σπόγγος καὶ αὐτὸς συνυψοῦται αὐτῷ ἐν τῇ ἁγιωτάτῃ μεγάλῃ ἐκκλησίᾳ *Chron.Pasch.*p.385 (M.92.988B); Sophr.H.*v.Anast.*(M.92.1713A); ‡Sophr.H.*v.Mar.Aeg.* 22(M.87.3712D); Thphn.*chron.*p.135(M.108.372A); Eustrat.*v.Eutych.* 70(M.86.2353C).

ὑώδης, *swinish*; of men, Clem.*prot.*10(p.68.9; M.8.205B); id. *paed.*3.11(p.278.4; M.8.652B); id.*str.*1.12(p.35.25; M.8.753A).

Φ

***φαβρικήσιος (φαβρικίσιος), ὁ,** (cf. Lat. *faber*) *armourer*, Justn. *nov.*85.3(p.415.27); -ίσιος, Ath.Scholast.*coll.*20.4(p.176).

***φαβρικόν, τό,** *arsenal*, Jo.Mal.*chron.*12 p.307(M.97.464B).

***φαβρίξ, ἡ,** = foreg., Ath.*h.Ar.*18(M.25.713B); Jo.Mal.*chron.*12 p.307(M.97.464B); *ib.*13 p.343(512A).

φαγᾶς, ὁ, *glutton*, †Gregent.*leg.Hom.*45(M.86.605B).

***φαγίον, τό,** *food*, *Apophth.Patr.*(M.65.408B); Cyr.S.*v.Sab.*40 (p.131.10); *V.Dan.*(p.69.24).

***φαγόγηρος, ὁ,** *old glutton*, Pall.*h.Laus.*22(M.34.1083C; v.l. for κακόγηρε p.73.23); v.l. for πολιόφαγε *ib.*18(p.57.2; 1065D).

φαγολοίδορος, *swallowing insults*, Hier.*Ezech.*proem.(M.*PL.*28. 940A).

***φαγοπόλιος, ὁ,** *hoary old glutton*, Zos.*alloquia* 9(M.78.1693B); Anast.Ap.*a.Max.*2.27(M.90.164C).

***φαιδράζω,** *appear bright*, Leont.H.*monoph.*(M.86.1892C).

***φαιδρόκοσμος,** *brightly arrayed*, Meth.*symp.*11.2(p.133.12; M.18. 209B).

***φαιδροποιός,** *making to shine*, Eus.*d.e.*4.15(p.175.20; M.22.292D).

***φαιδροπρεπῶς,** *joyously*, ‡Ath.*occurs.*13(M.28.989B).

φαιδρός, *bright, beaming, cheerful*; fem. as subst., *festival*, *Cod. Afr.*61; cf.Meth.*res.*2.21(p.376.4; M.18.316A).

φαιδρότης, ἡ, 1. *brightness, brilliance*, met. τὴν ἔσω καὶ εἰς νοῦν πνευματικὴν φ. Cyr.*Ps.*23:4(M.69.845B); id.*Lc.*12:35(M.72.744D); Isid.Pel.*epp.*2.210(M.78.649C); **2.** *splendour*, Eus.*v.C.*3.53(p.100.19; M. om.); Chrys.*scand.*17(3.504D); Gel.Cyz.*h.e.*2.7.30(M.85.1240A).

***φαιδρόψυχος,** *bright-souled*, Thdr.Stud.*cant.*2.7(p.340).

φαιδρυντικός, *illuminatory*, Bas.*hom.in Ps.*33(1.147A; M.31.360C).

***φαίδρυσμα, τό,** *radiancy*, Clem.*paed.*3.11(p.272.5; M.8.640A).

***φαινακίζω,** = φενακίζω, *deceive*, Max.*opusc.*(M.91.76D).

***φαῖναξ, ἡ,** *moon*, ‡Caes.Naz.*dial.*95(M.38.960); *ib.*130(1032).

***φαινής,** *renowned*, Anast.S.*defunct.*(M.89.1200C).

[*]**φαινόλιον, τό,** = φελόνιον, ‡Germ.CP *contempl.*(M.98.393D).

***φαινότης, ἡ,** *splendour*, Nil.*epp.*1.12(M.79.88A).

φαίν-ω, *bring to light, cause to appear, show*; perf. act. and pass.; **1.** *appear, come into being, be made manifest*, esp. of Christ κύριος ὁ θεὸς ἡμῶν φανήσεται ἐπὶ γῆς *T.Sym.*6.5; *T.Benj.*10.7; οὗτος ὁ ἀπ' ἀρχῆς, ὁ καινὸς φανεὶς καὶ παλαιὸς εὑρεθεὶς καὶ πάντοτε νέος ἐν ἁγίων καρδίαις γεννώμενος ‡*Diogn.*11.4; τὸ γὰρ ὡς υἱὸν ἀνθρώπου εἰπεῖν, ~όμενον μὲν καὶ γενόμενον ἄνθρωπον μηνύει Just.*dial.*76.1(M.6.625C); τὸν θεὸν λόγον, ὅστις ποτ' ἦν ὁ διὰ τοῦ ~ομένου ἀνδρὸς τὰς θαυματουργίας ἐκτελῶν, ἐποπτεῦσαι Eus.*d.e.*3.7(p.147.15; M.22.248B); τὸν ἐκ θεοῦ πεφηνότα θεὸν ἀληθινὸν Cyr.*Jo.*6(4.564E); θεὸς γὰρ ἦν φύσει, πεφηνὼς καθ' ἡμᾶς, εἷς τε καὶ μόνος υἱὸς καὶ ὅτε γέγονε σάρξ id.*expl.xii cap.* 5(p.21.13; 6¹.152B); τὸν χρόνῳ ~όμενον [sc. Χριστόν] καὶ ἀεὶ ὄντα *V.Aberc.*16(p.14.7); Manich. ἐλθὼν ὁ υἱὸς μετεσχημάτισεν ἑαυτὸν εἰς ἀνθρώπου εἶδος· καὶ ἐφαίνετο τοῖς ἀνθρώποις ὡς ἄνθρωπος, μὴ ὢν ἄνθρωπος, καὶ οἱ ἄνθρωποι ὑπελάμβανον αὐτὸν γεγεννῆσθαι Hegem. *Arch.*8.4(p.12.11; M.10.1440B); **2.** abs., of what *appears* to the senses; hence *be visible*; **a.** in gen. ἐὰν γὰρ εὑρεθῶ [sc. Χριστιανός] καὶ λέγεσθαι δύναμαι, καὶ τότε πιστὸς εἶναι, ὅταν κόσμῳ μὴ ~ωμαι. οὐδὲν ~όμενον καλόν· ὁ γὰρ θεὸς ἡμῶν Ἰησοῦς Χριστός, ἐν πατρὶ ὤν, μᾶλλον ~εται Ign.*Rom.*3.2–3; id.*Polyc.*2.2; τὸ νοερόν, ὃ δὴ λογιστικὸν καλεῖται, ὁ ἄνθρωπός ἐστιν ὁ ἔνδον, ὁ τοῦ ~ομένου τοῦδε ἄρχων ἀνθρώπου Clem.*paed.*3.1(p.236.5; M.8.556A); ὁ...~όμενος κόσμος Mac.Aeg.*hom.*15.49(M.34.609B); Chrys.*hom.29.1 in Mt.*(7.343B); neut. ptcpl. sing. and plur., *the visible world*, Arist.*apol.*1.5; Clem. *str.*7.2(p.8.19; M.9.413A); ἐν τοῖς ~ομένοις γὰρ πάντα τὰ τοῦ νυμφίου τῆς νύμφης εἰσί Mac.Aeg.*hom.*16.13(624A); of the heavenly bodies τὰ δὲ ἐν οὐρανῷ ~όμενα Clem.*prot.*4(p.48.21; M.8.164B); cf.Athenag. *leg.*5.2(M.6.900B); **b.** theol.; **i.** distinguishing outward form from spiritual reality ὁ ἄρτος καὶ τὸ ἔλαιον ἁγιάζεται τῇ δυνάμει τοῦ ὀνόματος θεοῦ, τὰ αὐτὰ ὄντα κατὰ τὸ ~όμενον οἷα ἐλήφθη· ἀλλὰ δυνάμει εἰς δύναμιν πνευματικὴν μεταβέβληται Clem.*exc.Thdot.*82(p.132.11; M. 9.696C); ὁ ~όμενος ἄρτος οὐκ ἄρτος ἐστίν, εἰ καὶ τῇ γεύσει αἰσθητός, ἀλλὰ σῶμα Χριστοῦ Cyr.H.*catech.*22.9; **ii.** distinguishing the literal from the spiritual sense of scripture τὸ γὰρ ~όμενον αὐτοῖς μόνοις Ἰουδαίοις ἁρμόττει· τὸ δὲ μυστικόν τε καὶ κεκρυμμένον, πᾶσιν ἀνθρώποις Thdt.*Ezech.*34:12(2.966); **iii.** expressing implications of docetic heresies with regard to Christ's body ἐξεκέντησαν δὲ τὸ ~όμενον, ὃ ἦν σὰρξ τοῦ ψυχικοῦ Clem.*exc.Thdot.*62(p.128.4; 689A); **3.** *be obvious, apparent*, Or.*princ.*4.1.1(p.292.10; M.11.341B); μακραῖς, καὶ ταύταις οὐ ~ομέναις, ἐπαγγελίαις πεπιστευκότες Thdt.*affect.*9 (p.240.14; 4.947); ἡ παιδεία ἀνιαρὰ μὲν ἔχει καὶ ἀλγεινὰ τὰ ~όμενα ὀνησιφόρα δὲ τὰ μετὰ ταῦτα id.*Jer.*1:12(2.408); **4.** impers, *it seems good*; cf.Aristeas ap.Eus.*p.e.*8.3(351C; M.21.589C); hence τὰ φανέντα, *my opinions*, Eus.*d.e.*6.11(p.260.25; M.22.428D).

***φαιοτρίβων,** *black-cloaked*, Gr.Nyss.*Eun.*1(1 p.30.13; φακοτρίβων M.45.257C).

[*]**φακεόλιον,** [*]**φακεώλιον,** v. φακιόλιον.

[*]**φακή, ἡ,** *pulse, lentil*; as part of monastic diet, Anton.Hag. *v.Sym.Styl.*(p.34.22).

φακιάλιον, v. φακιόλιον.

φακιόλιον, τό, (variant spellings) *cloth* for head or face, *towel, kerchief*, worn by Christ at Passion (= καθάπλωμα) ὁ κούρσωρ...τὸ φακεώλιον αὐτοῦ ἥπλωσε χαμαὶ καὶ...αὐτὸν περιπατῆσαι πεποίηκεν *A.Pil.*A 1.2(p.217, v.l. φακεόλ-); *ib.*1.6(p.222, v.l. φακεολ-); by which he was bound τὸ ἐπιτραχήλιόν ἐστι τὸ φ. μεθ' οὗ ἐπεφέρετο ὑπὸ τοῦ ἀρχιερέως δεδεμένος ἐπὶ τῷ τραχήλῳ ὁ Χριστός ‡Bas.*h.myst.*

19(p.262.10) ∞ ‡Germ.CP *contempl.*(φακεώλιον M.98.393C); worn by desert fathers οὐκ ὀθόνην ἐφόρεσεν ἐκτὸς φ. Pall.*h.Laus.*1(p.15.15; φακιαλίου M.34.1009B); ὁ μὲν τὴν προσκομίδην ἔλεγεν, οἱ δὲ φακιολίοις ἐρρίπιζον Jo.Mosch.*prat.*196(M.87.3081A); ἐλίξαντα τὰς χεῖρας ...φακεολίῳ ἢ ἄλλῳ τινὶ ῥάκει *Schol.*28 in Jo.Clim.*scal.*15(M.88.913B); used as *towel* or *handkerchief* τὰς ὄψεις...εἴς τι φ. ἐκμαξάμενος Sophr.H.*mir.Cyr.et Jo.*2(M.87.3429B); Anast.S.*Ps.*6(M.89.1113A); as *head covering* for a woman (= ὠράριον), *A.Petr.et Paul.*80b(p.214. 3,6,10, v.l. φακεολ-); *headband, turban* ἐν...τῇ κεφαλῇ αὐτοῦ λινόχρυσον φακιόλιν ἐσφενδονισμένον Jo.Mal.*chron.*18 p.457(M.97.669B); ἀποδύεται τὸ ἱμάτιον αὐτοῦ καὶ ἐπετέθη αὐτὸ εἰς τὴν κεφαλὴν αὐτοῦ, δήσας αὐτὸ εἰς αὐτὴν ὡς φακιόλιν Leont.N.*v.Sym.*35(M.93.1713B).

φακός, ὁ, *vessel, casket* shaped like a lentil, ‡Just.*coh.Gr.*37(M.6. 309A); hence *oil-flask*, Epiph.*haer.*79.2(p.477.16; M.42.741D); *water-flask*, Chrys.*hom.in Rom.12*:20(3.170A).

***φακοτρίβων,** v. *φαιοτρίβων.

***φακτιωνάριος, ὁ,** (Lat. *factio*) *principal charioteer*; of a circus faction, Jo.Mal.*chron.*16 p.395(M.97.585B).

***φάκτον, τό,** (Lat. *factum*) *action*, Leo Mag.*ep.*23.1(p.46.32; M. *PL.*54.734A).

φαλάκρα, ἡ, *baldness*, Synes.*calv.*tit.(p.190.2; M.66.1168); *ib.*8 (p.206.8; 1181B).

φάλκη, ἡ, *bat*, *Orac.Sib.*14.160.

φαλλαγώγια, τά, festival on which phallic procession took place, Evagr.*h.e.*1.11(p.20.13; M.86.2452C).

φαλλαγωγία, ἡ, = foreg., Thdt.*affect.*3(p.92.10; 4.783); *ib.*7(p.183. 20; 885).

***φαλλαρίζω,** *practise obscenity*, Epiph.*exp.fid.*10(p.510.19; φαλα- M.42.800B).

***φάλσευμα, τό,** (cf. Lat. *falsum*) *falsification*, Steph.Diac. *v.Steph.*(M.100.1141B).

***φαλσεύω,** (Lat. *falso*) *falsify*, CCP(681)*act.*3(H.3.1068E); *ib.*12 (1312B); Anast.S.*hod.*10(M.89.184D).

***φαλσόγραφος,** *spurious*, Leont.H.*monoph.*(M.86.1852A).

***φάλσος,** (Lat. *falsus*) *spurious*, Adam.*dial.*1.5(p.8.25; M.11. 1721B); *ib.*(p.10.19; 1724A); CCP(681)*act.*12(H.3.1312A).

***φαμενώθ,** Coptic month, Petr.I Al.*fr.*(M.18.516A); *PLond.*1913. 1; roughly corresponding to April, Epiph.*haer.*51.27(p.298.24; M. 41.936C).

φαμιλία, ἡ, (Lat. *familia*) *household*, †Gregent.*leg.Hom.*64(M.86. 616B); Rom.Mel.2.163(*SBBAW* 1901 p.742); *Chron.Pasch.*p.394(M. 92.1009B).

***φάμουσον (φάμοσον), τό,** (cf. Lat. *famosus*) plur., *slanderous, libellous information*, Leont.N.*v.Jo.Eleem.*36(p.72.5); *ib.*(p.72.11); φάμοσα Phot.*nomoc.*9.36(p.574; M.104.795D).

φανδόν, s.v.l., *openly*, Eust.*engast.*22(M.18.660A; cj. ἀναφανδὸν p.51.1).

***φάνεια, ἡ,** *appearing, manifestation*, Eus.*qu.Steph.suppl.*(M.22. 972B).

***φανεροβλαβής,** *openly pernicious*, *Proem.*in Dor.*doct.*(M.88. 1612B).

***φανερολογία, ἡ,** *clear statement, demonstration*, Marc.Er.*opusc.*4 (M.65.1024C).

φανεροποιέω, *make manifest, evident*, *1Clem.*60.1; Or.*fr.59 in Jo.* (p.532.3); Marc.Er.*opusc.*4(M.65.1009C).

φανερός, 1. = τις, *certain, some*; **a.** of persons, Pall.*h.Laus.*46 (p.134.9; M.34.1225A); Soz.*h.e.*1.4.3(M.67.868B); Jo.Mal.*chron.*5 p.108 (M.97.200B); **b.** of times ἐν ἡμέρᾳ τινὶ φανερᾷ τοῦ ἔτους Epiph.*haer.* 79.1(p.476.17; M.42.741A); Marc.Diac.*v.Porph.*11; of things, CChalc. *act.*4(*ACO* 2.1.3 p.104.23; H.2.437A); **2.** *definite* φανερὸς γὰρ ἑκάστῳ εἰς τὸ βασιλεύειν ὡρίσθη καιρός Thdt.*Dan.*7:12(2.1200); id.*Os.*4:8(2. 1328); Socr.*h.e.*3.19.10(M.67.428C).

φανερότης, ἡ, *clarity*, Leo Mag.*ep.*44.1(p.25.18; M.*PL.*44.828B).

φανερ-όω, *reveal, make manifest*; **1.** in gen. χάρις...\~οῦσα μυστήρια ‡*Diogn.*11.5; τὸ αἷμα τοῦ λόγου πεφανέρωται ὡς γάλα Clem.*paed.*1.6 (p.114.20; M.8.297C); φωτισμὸς ἡ μαθητεία κέκληται ἡ τὰ κεκρυμμένα \~ώσασα id.*str.*5.10(p.369.12; M.9.97B); δι' αὐτοῦ [sc. τοῦ σταυροῦ] τὰ τῆς θεογνωσίας ἔργα πᾶσι πεφανέρωται Ath.*gent.*1(M.25.4B); of revelations in prayer or visions, *M.Polyc.*12.3; Ath.*v.Anton.*59 (M.26.928B); impers., *Barn.*14.5; *ib.*16.5; ἐπεὶ...τελείως πεφανέρωτο ὅτι... *Diogn.*9.2; **2.** of God ὁ πατὴρ πάντα \~οῖ περὶ τοῦ υἱοῦ Ἰησοῦ *Barn.*12.8; εἰ οὖν ἐν τοσαύταις μορφαῖς οἴδαμεν πεφανερῶσθαι τὸν θεόν Just.*dial.*75.4(M.6.652B); Clem.*exc.Thdot.*48(p.122.10; M.9.681B); Pall.*v.Chrys.*8(p.51.7; M.47.30); of God's revelation through Christ εἷς θεός ἐστιν· ὁ \~ώσας ἑαυτὸν διὰ Ἰησοῦ Χριστοῦ Ign.*Magn.*8.2; δι' οὗ καὶ ἐφανέρωσεν ἡμῖν τὴν ἀλήθειαν *2Clem.*20.5; διὰ τοῦ ἀγαπητοῦ παιδὸς...ἐφανέρωσε τὰ ἐξ ἀρχῆς ἡτοιμασμένα *Diogn.* 8.11; διὰ...Χριστοῦ, κατὰ τὸ ἐφικτὸν ἡμῖν τὴν ἑαυτοῦ ἐφανέρωσε γνῶσιν Jo.D.*f.o.*1.1(M.94.792A); **3.** of Christ in Inc. θεοῦ ἀνθρωπίνως \~ουμένου Ign.*Eph.*19.3; *Barn.*5.6; ὅτε δὲ τοὺς ἰδίους ἀποστόλους... ἐξελέξατο...τότε ἐφανέρωσεν ἑαυτὸν εἶναι υἱὸν θεοῦ *ib.*5.9; ἐν σαρκὶ... αὐτοῦ μέλλοντος \~οῦσθαι *ib.*6.7; σάρξ, δι' ἧς πεφανέρωται Clem.*paed.* 1.5(p.103.24; M.8.277A); τοῦ θεοῦ καὶ τοῦ μονογενοῦς αὐτοῦ, ἐν Ἰησοῦ ἡμῖν \~ουμένου Or.*Cels.*8.34(p.249.18; M.11.1565D); at Resurrection ἀνέστη ἐκ νεκρῶν καὶ \~ωθεὶς ἀνέβη εἰς οὐρανούς *Barn.*15.9; in OT types, *ib.*7.7; *ib.*12.10; docetist δοκήσει τινὲς αὐτὸν πεφανερῶσθαι ὑπέλαβον Clem.*str.*6.9(p.467.13; M.9.292C); Gnost. αὐτὸς ἑαυτὸν ἀπὸ ἑαυτοῦ προαγαγὼν ἐφανέρωσεν ἑαυτῷ τὴν ἰδίαν ἐπίνοιαν Hipp.*haer.*6. 18(p.144.26; M.16.3222B); **4.** of Spirit, containing power of all the aeons, which descended at Christ's baptism (Marcosian) τὸ πνεῦμα ...τὸ ὁμολογῆσαν ἑαυτὸ υἱὸν ἀνθρώπου καὶ \~ῶσαν τὸν πατέρα *ib.*6.51 (p.184.2; 3282A); **5.** of Church ἦν γὰρ πνευματική, ὡς καὶ ὁ Ἰησοῦς ἡμῶν, ἐφανερώθη δὲ ἐπ' ἐσχάτων τῶν ἡμερῶν ἵνα ἡμᾶς σώσῃ· ἡ ἐκκλησία δὲ πνευματικὴ οὖσα ἐφανερώθη ἐν τῇ σαρκὶ Χριστοῦ *2Clem.* 14.2; of its members ἐν ἀρχῇ τοίνυν συνελογίσθημεν, φασί, καὶ ἐφανερώθημεν Clem.*exc.Thdot.*41(p.119.24; M.9.677D); eschatol. \~ωθήσονται ἐν τῇ ἐπισκοπῇ τῆς βασιλείας τοῦ θεοῦ *1Clem.*50.3; ὅταν οὖν ἐπιλάμψῃ τὸ ἔλεος τοῦ κυρίου, τότε \~ωθήσονται οἱ δουλεύοντες τῷ θεῷ, καὶ πάντες \~ωθήσονται Herm.*sim.*4.2.2.

φανέρωσις, ἡ, 1. *disclosure*, Or.*fr.15 in Mt.*1:19(p.22.32); φ. τοῦ ἁγίου...μνήματος Eus.*v.C.*3.28 tit.(p.73.20; M.20.1088D); **2.** *revealing* βούλεται ὁ τύπος, ἵνα ὑφεστήκῃ, ἐμποδίζειν τῇ φ. τῆς ἀληθείας Or.*Jo.* 28.12(11; p.404.4; M.14.705B); id.*fr.42 in Jo.*(p.517.6); Max.*myst.*5 (M.91.680B); ἐνέργεια, καὶ ἡ διὰ τῆς προφορᾶς τοῦ λόγου φ. καὶ ἐξάπλωσις τῶν νενοημένων Jo.D.*f.o.*3.15(M.94.1048C); **3.** *revelation* ἡ τῶν κεκρυμμένων φ. Gr.Nyss.*Eun.*3(2 p.10.6; M.45.573B); ‡Proc.G. *Pr.*12:1(M.87.1336A); †Jo.D.*B.J.*8(M.96.917B); *prophetic revelation*, Hipp.*haer.*7.38(p.224.9; M.16.3346A); *ib.*10.20(p.280.23; 3438B); **4.** *manifestation* τῆς οἰκονομίας τὴν φ. Didym.(‡Bas.)*Eun.*4(1.292B; M.29.701A); of Inc., Just.*1apol.*32.2(M.6.377B); id.*dial.*49.3(M.6. 584B); περὶ φανερώσεως τῆς θεότητος καὶ ἀνθρωπότητος αὐτοῦ Or.*fr. 53 in Jo.*(p.527.21); Ath.*inc.*1.3(M.25.97B); of Transfiguration εἰς τὸ ὑψηλὸν τῆς φ. αὐτοῦ ὄρος Or.*schol.in Lc.*9:27(M.17.340D); of Resurrection τὴν τοῖς αὐτοῦ μαθηταῖς φ. Eus.*d.e.*1.1(p.4.9; M.22.17B); Gnost. εἷς δέ ἐστιν ἀγαθός, οὗ παρρησία ἡ διὰ τοῦ υἱοῦ φ. Val.Gn.ap. Clem.*str.*2.20(p.175.2; M.8.1057B); Hipp.*haer.*5.8(p.93.7; M.16.3146B).

Φάνης, ὁ, a divinity in the Orphic system, representing first principle of life, Athenag.*leg.*20.3(M.6.932B); *Hom.Clem.*6.5; Gr. Naz.*or.*31.16(p.164.16; M.36.152A).

***φανητία, ἡ,** *ostentation*, Jo.Mosch.*prat.*187(M.87.3065A); ‡Max. *cap.al.*185(M.90.1444D).

***φανητίας, ὁ,** *ostentatious person*, Gr.Naz.*carm.*1.2.34.84(M.37. 951A).

φανητιασμός, ὁ, *love of show and ostentation*, Jo.Clim.*scal.*2(M.88. 656C); Hesych.S.*temp.*2.73(M.93.1536C); Jo.D.*imag.*2(M.94.1284B).

***φανητιάω,** *love ostentation, swagger*, Afric.ap.Eus.*h.e.*1.7.11(M.20. 93C); Mac.Mgn.*apocr.*2.9(p.12.15); Marc.Er.*opusc.*2.181(M.65.957D).

***φανητικῶς,** *ostentatiously*, Eus.*qu.Steph.*14(M.22.928B).

***φανίζω,** s.v.l., *publish*, Cyr.*ep.*40(5².110C; ἐνεφανίσθη p.21.17).

***φανταζομένως,** *imaginatively*, Meth.*symp.*8.17(M.18.173D; φανταζομένη p.112.3).

φαντάζ-ω, A. act.; **1.** *delude*, *T.Sim.*4.9; ἵνα τὸν ἄνθρωπον \~ειν ἀεὶ πρὸς ἀδικίαν ἔχῃ Meth.*res.*1.38(p.281.11; M.41.1105B); ἀσέμνως καὶ ἄχρι αὐτῆς μυσαρᾶς πράξεως \~ει ἡμᾶς ὁ δράκων Ephr.1.209B; τῶν δαιμόνων, τῶν φαντασάντων τὰς ὄψεις τῶν ὁρώντων ‡Just.*qu.et resp.* 26(M.6.1273B); abs., *create an illusion* \~ων καὶ μαγεύων Epiph.*haer.* 34.1(p.5.13; M.41.581D); ἆρα \~ων, καὶ οὐκ ἐργαζόμενος τὰ σημεῖα Chrys.*hom.49.1 in Jo.*(8.288C); c. cogn. acc. μέλλομεν...ἐλέγχεσθαι ὡς ψευδεῖς. ἃ ἐφαντάσαμεν, ἐφαντάσαμεν *Pers.*(p.15.1; M.10.104B); esp. ref. docetic views of Christ ὁρώμενος καὶ ὑπὸ ἁφὴν τοῖς μαθηταῖς εὑρισκόμενος καὶ μὴ \~ων Epiph.*haer.*42.11(p.150.28; 765D); *ib.* (p.157.2; 768A); *create an illusory appearance of* οὐ γὰρ ψιλὴν μόνην ἐφάντασεν ἡμῖν ἐν ἑαυτῷ τὴν ἐν εἴδει σαρκὸς διαμόρφωσιν Max.*ambig.* (M.91.1048C); οὐ φαντάσας σαρκὸς εἴδει καὶ σχήματι τὴν οἰκονομίαν *ib.*(1320C); id.*opusc.*(M.91.93C); **2.** *astonish* φαντάσω...τούτους τῷ σῷ ἀργυρίῳ †Polyb.*v.Epiph.*44(M.41.80D); \~ειν ἅπαντας τοὺς ἐπὶ τῆς γῆς τῷ μεγέθει τῶν γιγνομένων Thdr.Mops.*Zach.*10:1(M.66. 564C); **3.** = med., *imagine* ὁ ὑπὲρ ἐκείνους ἑαυτὸν \~ων Nil.*exerc.*34 (M.79.764A).

B. med. and aor. pass.; **1.** *form a conception of, picture to oneself, imagine* γέγονεν...ἀπὸ τοῦ τελείου ἀνθρώπου ὁ υἱὸς τοῦ ἀνθρώπου, ὃν ἔγνωκεν οὐδείς, \~εται δέ...ὡς γέννημα θηλείας ἡ κτίσις πᾶσα τὸν υἱὸν ἀγνοοῦσα Hipp.*haer*.8.13(p.233.8; M.16.3359A); οὐχὶ κακῶς ὁρῶν ὀφθαλμός, ἔργον ἐστὶ τοῦ κυρίου, ἀλλ' ὁ ὁρῶν καὶ ~όμενος τὰ θεῖα Or. *exp.in Pr*.20:12(M.17.212C); μὴ νοήσαντες, μόνον δὲ τὸ ἀπαθὲς... φαντασθέντες id.*Jo*.10.6(4; p.176.19; M.14.316B); δόγματα ἀνθρώπων μηδ' ὄναρ φύσιν ἀόρατον καὶ ἀσώματον πεφαντασμένων, οὖσαν κυρίως οὐσίαν *ib*.20.18(16; p.351.11; 613D); ὑπερθαυμάσαντες τῆς τοσαύτης αὐτὸν σοφίας τε καὶ δυνάμεως, ἣν ἐκ τῶν ἔργων ἐφαντάσθησαν Eus.*p.e.* 1.6(17C; M.21.48B); ἐν ὕλῃ...τὸ θεῖον εἶναι ~ομένοις id.*l.C*.14(p.241. 27; M.20.1409A); εἰκότως ~ονται τοιούτου υἱοῦ ἀεὶ μὴ εἶναι τὸν θεὸν πατέρα Ath.*decr*.10(p.9.16; M.25.433A); ~ου τὸ φρικῶδες ἐκεῖνο κρῖμα Ammonas *fr*.2(p.486.11); ἔνεστι γὰρ καὶ ἐπὶ γῆς ὄντα ἑστάναι ἐν οὐρανῷ, καὶ τὰ ἐκεῖ ~εσθαι Chrys.*hom.2.5 in Jo*.(8.14C); ὁ παράκλητος...ἔτι μένοντας ἐν σαρκὶ τὴν τῶν ἀγγέλων ἔπεισε ~εσθαι διακονίαν id.*sac*.3.4(p.51.6; 1.382C); ὅταν μὲν οὖν πρὸς τὴν θεότητα βλέψωμεν...ἐν ἡμῖν τὸ ~όμενον ‡Cyr.*Trin*.10(6^3.16C; M.77.1144C); ὃν καὶ φαντασίαν καλοῦσι τοῦ ζῴου...περὶ ἣν συνίστασθαι τὴν αἴσθησίν φασιν οἱ σοφοὶ τὰ τοιαῦτα, ὄργανον αὐτῆς οὖσαν ἀντιληπτικὸν τῶν αὐτῇ φαντασθέντων Max.*ambig*.(M.91.1116A); μονοφυσῖται ταυτοβουλίαν καὶ ταυτοπραξίαν ἐφαντάσθησαν Anast.S.*hod*.1(M.89.48B); **2.** μεγάλα ~εσθαι περί τινος *think great things of, have high opinion of*, Chrys. *hom.26.2 in Mt*.(7.315C); id.*hom.33.4 in Heb*.(12.309A); *ib.5.1*(51D); **3.** *perceive, contemplate* ὁ ὠφελούμενος εὐλαβεῖται ἐμβλέψαι εἰς τὸ πρόσωπον τοῦ θεοῦ διὸ ~όμενος τὸν θεὸν πίπτει ἐπὶ πρόσωπον Or. *comm.in 1Cor*.14:24(*JTS* 10 p.39); καθαροῖς διανοίας ὄμμασι φαντασθέντες Eus.*h.e*.1.2.6(M.20.57A); τὸν θεὸν ἀεὶ ~ονται [sc. οἱ ἄγγελοι] Chrys.*hom.15.2 in Jo*.(8.86B); τὴν θείαν ~όμενος θεωρίαν id.*h.rel.* 12(3.1202); **4.** *pretend to* Κολλούθου τοῦ πρεσβυτέρου φαντασθέντος ἐπισκοπήν Ath.*apol.sec*.76(p.156.6; M.25.385B); ἐπὶ τιμῇ ~εται, ὡς ἄτε δὴ ἐγχειρισθείς Ephr.1.16F.

C. pass.; **1.** *be deluded*, Bas.*mor*.15.3(3.556A; M.32.1312B); **2.** *appear, become visible* μή σε τὰ πολλὰ καὶ ἐπιτερπῆ ~όμενα ἀφέληται σοφίας Clem.*prot*.10(p.78.6; M.8.225C); οὕτω καὶ ἡ φιλοσοφία ἐκ τῆς θείας γραφῆς τὸ ἐμπύρευμα λαβοῦσα ἐν ὀλίγοις ~εται id.*str*.6.17(p.508. 28; M.9.380C); ἐν μόνῃ γὰρ τῇ τοῦ προφορικοῦ λόγου τὸ τῆς σοφίας ὄνομα ~εται *ib*.7.10(p.40.33; 477D); **3.** *pose as, appear as* σεμνός τις τοῖς πολλοῖς ἐφαντάζετο Eus.*d.e*.3.4(p.119.34; M.22.204C).

φαντασία, ἡ, 1. *unreal appearance, illusion*; esp. ref. docetic Christologies τῶν κατὰ φαντασίαν λεγόντων τὰ διὰ τοῦ σωτῆρος γεγενῆσθαι Or.*schol.in Lc*.1:6(M.17.312C); οὐ δοκήσει καὶ φ. τῆς ἐνανθρωπήσεως γενομένης, ἀλλὰ τῇ ἀληθείᾳ Cyr.H.*catech*.4.9; μίσησον τοὺς λέγοντας, ὅτι κατὰ φ. ἐσταυρώθη. εἰ γὰρ κατὰ φαντασίαν ἐσταυρώθη, ἐκ σταυροῦ δὲ ἡ σωτηρία, καὶ ἡ σωτηρία φ. εἰ φ. ὁ σταυρός, φ. καὶ ἡ ἀνάστασις *ib*.13.37; Bas.*ep*.260.8(3.400D; M.32.965B); Bas. Sel.*or*.10.1(M.85.140C); ἄνθρωπος γέγονε...οὐδὲ κατὰ δόκησιν ἢ φ. ὡς Εὐτυχιανισταὶ λέγουσιν Oecum.*Apoc*.3:7(p.60); ‡Cyr.*Trin*.17(6^3.23E; M.77.1156C); CCP(681)*act*.11(H.3.1276D); in Jewish argument, ref. virgin birth λοιπὸν ἐν φ. καὶ δοκήσει ἐξ αὐτῆς ἐγεννήθη, καὶ οὐκ ἀληθείᾳ· ἀδύνατον γὰρ τοῦτο †Gregent.*disp*.(M.86.657B); **2.** *delusion*, Chrys.*hom.43.3 in Mt*.(7.462C); **3.** *vision in a dream*, Juln.Imp.ap. Cyr.*Juln*.9(6^2.314D); Diad.*perf*.37(p.42.16); *ib*.38(p.44.8); **4.** *fantasy* εἰς φ. μοναρχίας Or.*dial*.4(p.126.17); ‡Just.*coh.Gr*.21(M.6.280B); Evagr.*h.e*.3.5(p.106.1; M.86.2608A).

φαντασιάζω, 1. *delude*, Epiph.*anc*.63(p.76.7; M.43.129B); id.*haer*. 19.4(p.221.12; M.41.265B); *ib*.55.1(p.325.10; 972C); **2.** pass., *be vainly imagined*, *ib*.55.6(p.332.14; 984A); *ib*.64.63(p.502.8; 1180A); **3.** s.v.l., *give form to*, Iren.*haer*.1.13.6(M.7.589A).

***φαντασιανισταί, οἱ,** name given to *Eutychians*, Eust.Mon.*ep*. (M.86.904D,909B).

φαντασιασταί, οἱ, name given to *Manicheans*, Tim.CP *haer*.(M. 86.57B); Geo.Pis.*Pers*.1.149(M.92.1208A).

φαντασιαστικός, *visible*, Clem.*paed*.3.1(p.237.22; M.8.557C).

φαντασιοκοπέω, 1. *conceive vain fancies*, Malch.*ep*.ap.Eus.*h.e*.7. 30.9(M.20.712C); Eust.*engast*.4(p.21.24; M.18.621A); Bas.Sel.*v.Thecl.* 1(M.85.504B); **2.** *delude by mere appearances*, Ath.*inc*.55.4(M.25. 193C); Chrys.*hom.7.3 in Phil*.(11.248B); Nil.*Eulog*.29(M.79.1132B).

***φαντασιοκοπία, ἡ,** *vain fancy*, Eust.*engast*.9(p.29.3; M.18.629D); *ib*.25(p.56.13; 665C).

φαντασιοκόπος, 1. *conceiving vain fancies*, Eus.*d.e*.3.6(p.133.4; M.22.224D); masc. as subst., Cosm.Ind.*top*.1(M.88.57D), v.l. φαντασιοσκόπους; **2.** *deluding by appearances*, Chrys.*hom.37.1 in Jo*.(8. 212E); **3.** neut. as subst., *illusion, trick* of a conjuror, Hesych.S. *temp*.1.43(M.93.1493D).

***φαντασιολογία, ἡ,** *strange, fanciful language*, Epiph.*haer*.25.4 (p.271.26; M.41.325B).

***φαντασιομάχος,** *champion of fancy*; of Manes, Eulog.*palm*.8(M. 86.2928B) cit. s. ἀνθρωπολάτρης.

***φαντασιοποιός, ὁ,** *illusionist, conjuror*, Hesych.S.*temp*.1.43(M. 93.1493D).

***φαντασιοσκοπέω,** *show as an illusion*, Cyr.H.*catech*.15.10; *ib*. 15.14 (vv.ll. φαντασιοκοπῶν, φαντασιοκοπεῖ); ? f.l. for φαντασιοκοπέω, Eustrat.*stat.anim*.16(p.458).

***φαντασιοσκόπος, ὁ,** *illusionist, conjuror*, Hesych.S.*temp*.2.4(M. 93.1513A); v.l. for φαντασιοκόπος, Cosm.Ind.*top*.1(M.88.57D).

φαντασι-όω, 1. act.; **a.** *bring images before* the mind of, *inform by images* ἤτοι ψιλὸν ἄνθρωπον...ἤτοι τὸν θεὸν ὁμολογοῦντες, ἀναίνονται πάλιν τὸν ἄνθρωπον, πεφαντασιωκέναι διδάσκοντες τὰς ὄψεις αὐτῶν τῶν θεωμένων Hipp.*fr.in Mt.25:24*(p.209.7; M.10.868A); εἴτ' ἀγγέλου εἴθ' οὑτινοσοῦν ~οῦντος τὴν ψυχήν Or.*Cels*.1.66(p.120.8; M.11.784C) ἄλλα μυρία δαιμονίων ~ούντων ἡμᾶς id.*Jo*.20.36(29; p.376.6; M.14. 657B); *Hom.Clem*.17.2; **b.** *imagine* τὸ μὲν γὰρ μεταξὺ πατρὸς καὶ υἱοῦ οὐδὲν δείκνυσιν εἶναι διάστημα, οὐδ' ἄχρι τινὸς ἐννοίας τοῦτο φαντασιῶσαι τῆς ψυχῆς δυναμένης Alex.Al.*ep.Alex*.4(p.22.17; M.18. 553B); **2.** med. and pass., *imagine, form a mental picture*, Meth. *symp*.8.2(p.83.15; M.18.141A); πολλάκις μὲν ~οῦται [sc. ὁ νοῦς] περὶ τῶν οὐκ ὄντων ὡς ὄντων Bas.*ep*.233.1(3.355E; M.32.865A); Chrys. *hom.5.4 in 1Thess*.(11.465B); ἵνα τῷ νῷ φαντασιωθῶμεν τοῦ κτιστοῦ τὸ μέγεθος Mac.Mgn.*apocr*.4.16(p.189.3); **3.** pass.; **a.** of the mind, *be informed by images*, Or.*Cels*.1.48(p.97.24; M.11.748B); *ib*.4.3(p.276.6; 1032C); †Bas.*Is*.184(1.515A; M.30.432B); **b.** *be deluded* τὴν διάνοιαν πεπονηρευμένην ἀπὸ τῆς...πλάνης καὶ πεφαντασιωμένην Epiph.*haer*.21. 2(p.239.13; M.41.288A); **c.** *be imagined* οὕτω δυνατὸν ἀπὸ τῶν αὐτῶν φαντασιῶν τοὺς παραπλησίους ἐγγενέσθαι τύπους τοῖς ἐν διαφόροις οὐσίαις τυγχάνουσι καὶ ~ουμένοις Or.*Jo*.20.24(20; p.358.27; M.14.628B).

φαντασιώδης, 1. *fantastic*, Hipp.*haer*.1.2(p.8.23; M.16.3028A); Epiph.*exp.fid*.11(p.511.16; M.42.801B); Chrys.*hom.14.4 in 1Tim*.(11. 630A); **2.** *unreal, imaginary*, Cyr.H.*catech*.13.4; Thdt.*eran*.2(4.93).

φαντασιωδῶς, 1. *in appearance*, Iren.*haer*.2.32.4(M.7.828C); Eustrat.*stat.anim*.10(p.384); **2.** *in imagination*, *ib*.16(p.457).

φάντασμα, τό, 1. *apparition, phantom*, ref. Christ's Resurrection πείθοντα ὅτι αὐτὸς εἴη καὶ οὐ φ., ἀλλὰ ἔνσαρκος ἦν Hipp.*haer*.7.38 (p.224.17; M.16.3346B); Or.*fr.106 in Jo*.(p.561.14); Chrys.*hom.75.3 in Jo*.(8.442C); **2.** *image*; met., applied to Devil σὺ τοῦ κόσμου φ. εἶ, ἐγὼ δὲ διὰ τοῦτο ἀπὸ γυναικὸς ἐγεννήθην *Contrad*.1(p.5); *ib*.2(p.9).

φανταστικός, 1. *imaginative* ἡ δὲ σοφιστικὴ τέχνη...δύναμίς ἐστι φ. Clem.*str*.1.8(p.25.30; M.8.736A); Or.*Jo*.20.24(20; p.358.7; M.14.625C); φύσεως φ. τεταγμένως κινούσης τὴν ὁρμήν id.*princ*.3.1.2(p.197.3; M.11.249C); τὰ δὲ αἰσθήσεως ὁρμῆς τε φ. μεμοιραμένα, οἷα ζῴων τὰ ἄλογα Eus.*p.e*.7.4(302D; M.21.513B); Synes.*ep*.154(M.66.1556D); ἡ δὲ ὄρεξις φ. μόνης ἐστὶ τῆς διανοητικῆς δυνάμεως ἄνευ τοῦ βουλευτικοῦ λόγου τῶν ἐφ' ἡμῖν Max.*opusc*.(M.91.13B); neut. as subst., *the imaginative faculty* ἐπιδημοῦντος ἡμῶν τῷ φ. πνεύματος θεοῦ καὶ φαντάζοντος ἡμᾶς τὰ τοῦ θεοῦ Or.*Cels*.4.95(p.368.20; M.11.1173C); Melet.*nat.hom*.synops.(M.64.1108A); **2.** *imaginary* οὐδὲν ἦν σωματικὸν ἢ φ. Chrys.*hom.8.1 in Heb*.(12.81B); ἢ ὡς φ. τὴν δεῖξιν ποιησαμένου τῆς ἀνθρωπίνης μορφῆς ‡Ath.*Apoll*.2.1(M.26.1133A).

φανταστός, 1. *acting upon the imagination* διὰ τοῦτο δεῖν ἐπὶ τῶν θείων τὸ φ. οἴεσθαι μὴ παρεῖναι νομίζω πρόσφορον Max.*ambig*.(M.91. 1236B); **2.** *imagined* ὥσπερ γὰρ θεὸς οὐ κτιστός, οὕτως ὁ αὐτὸς καὶ ἄνθρωπος οὐ φ. Procl.CP *Arm*.12(p.193.8; M.65.868C).

***φαραγγίζω,** *make into valleys*, ref. Lc.3:5 ἐγέννησεν ἡ Ἐλισάβετ τὸν φαραγγίσαντα τὸν ἔρημον Chrysipp.*enc.in Jo.Bapt*.(p.33.4).

***φαράγγωσις, ἡ,** met., *plunge*, ‡Justic.*ep*.(p.12.28; H.2.841A).

***Φαραώ, ὁ,** (Hebr. פַּרְעֹה) *Pharaoh*; **1.** etym.; cf. *nec enim poterat cum exterminatore—hoc enim interpretatur in lingua nostra Pharao —virtus habitare*, Or.*hom.6.2 in Gen*.(p.67.17; M.12.196A); τὸ δέ γε Φ. τῆς βασιλείας δηλωτικόν Thdt.*Jer*.44:29(2.583); cf.Proc.G.*Is*.30:1 (M.87.2260B); **2.** esp. exeg. Ex.7:3; against Marcionites, Iren.*haer*. 4.29.2(M.7.1064B); ὁ θεός φησιν· 'ἐγὼ δὲ σκληρυνῶ τὴν καρδίαν Φ.', πλεονάκις. εἰ γὰρ ὑπὸ θεοῦ σκληρύνεται καὶ διὰ τὸ σκληρύνεσθαι ἁμαρτάνει, οὐκ αὐτὸς ἑαυτῷ τῆς ἁμαρτίας αἴτιος· εἰ δὲ τοῦτο, οὐδὲ αὐτεξούσιος ὁ Φ. Or.*princ*.3.1.7(p.204.15; M.11.260A); cf.Thdt.*qu. 12 in Ex*.(1.125); **3.** Pharaoh's daughter as figure of Church, cf.Or. *hom.2.4 in Ex*.(p.159.29; M.12.308D); *sed et nos etiam si Pharaonem habuimus patrem, etiam si nos in operibus malis genuit princeps hujus mundi cum venimus ad aquas, assumamus ad nos legem dei*, *ib*.(p.161.3; 309D); Cyr.*glaph.Ex*.1(1.252B); **4.** as manifestation or figure of Devil, cf. *Pharaonem, id est diabolum*, Or.*hom.6.1 in Ex*. (p.192.26; M.12.332C); cf.id.*hom.22.3 in Jos*.(p.435.6; M.12.932B); τὸν Φ. φασὶ τύπον ἀπενέγκασθαι [τὸν] κατὰ τὴν Αἴγυπτον τοῦ διαβόλου Meth.*symp*.4.2(p.47.19; M.18.89A); Cyr.H.*catech*.19.2–3; Cyr. *hom.pasch*.28(5^2.328A); **5.** cf. Φαραώ[θ]; one of the angels in system of Justinus, Hipp.*haer*.5.26(p.127.15; M.16.3195A).

***Φαραωνίζομαι**, *behave like Pharaoh*, Isid.Pel.*epp*.1.419(M.78.416C).

***Φαραώνιος**, *of Pharaoh*, Tim.Ant.*cruc*.(M.86.261D).

***Φαραωνίτης**, ὁ, *Pharaonian*, ‡Jo.D.*hom*.5(M.96.653A).

***Φαραωνιτικός**, *Pharaonic*, ‡Jo.D.*ep.Thphl*.23(M.95.373D).

φαρετροφόρος, *quiver-bearing*, *Orac.Sib*.11.174; *ib*.14.68.

***Φαρισαΐζω**, *play the Pharisee*, Sophr.H.*v.Cyr.et Jo*.3(M.87.3384B).

***Φαρισαϊκός**, *of the Pharisees, Pharisaical*, Cyr.*Ps*.16:1(M.69.813C); Nil.*exerc*.8(M.79.728B); Tim.Ant.*caec*.9(M.28.1013D).

***Φαρισαϊκῶς**, *Pharisaically*, Or.*Jo*.6.22(13; p.132.16; M.14.240B); Evagr.Pont.*or*.102(M.79.1189C).

***Φαρισαῖος**, ὁ, *Pharisee*, member of Jewish sect; **1.** in gen., derivation of name ἐλέγοντο δὲ Φ. διὰ τὸ ἀφωρισμένους εἶναι αὐτοὺς ἀπὸ τῶν ἄλλων διὰ τὴν ἐθελοπερισσοθρησκείαν τὴν παρ' αὐτοῖς νενομισμένην. Φάρες γὰρ κατὰ τὴν Ἑβραΐδα ἑρμηνεύεται ἀφορισμός Epiph.*haer*.16.1(p.211.8; M.41.249A); coupled with Scribes ἡ τῶν Φ. αἵρεσις ἄλλη τις· οἵτινες τὰ αὐτὰ τούτοις [sc. τοῖς Γραμματεῦσι] ἐφρόνουν *ib*.(p.210.9; 248B); rigorous self-discipline, *ib*.(p.210.12ff.; 248B,C); apparel τῷ δὲ προειρημένῳ σχήματι τῶν Γραμματέων προήρχοντο διά τοι τῆς ἀμπεχόνης...καὶ γυναικικῶν ἱματίων ἐν πλατείαις ταῖς κρηπῖσιν καὶ γλώτταις τῶν ὑποδημάτων προϊόντες *ib*.(p.211.4ff.; 249A); beliefs ὡμολόγουν δὲ οὗτοι ἀνάστασιν νεκρῶν, ἐπίστευόν τε ἀγγέλους εἶναι καὶ πνεῦμα. ἠγνόησαν δὲ υἱὸν θεοῦ ὡς οἱ ἄλλοι. ἀλλὰ καὶ εἱμαρμένῃ καὶ ἀστρονομίᾳ παρ' αὐτοῖς σφόδρα ἐχρημάτιζεν *ib*.16.2(p.211.11ff.; 249B); belief in fate inconsistent with belief in Judgement, *ib*.16.3(p.212.17ff.; 253A); said to give half possessions as alms, Chrys.*hom*.*44.4 in Mt*.(7.641A); blasphemy against H. Ghost in rejection of Jo. Bapt., Ath.*ep.Serap*.4.12(M.26.653A,B); pride and delight in power, Amph.*hom*.4(M.39.69C); Chrys.*hom*.*62.4 in Mt*.(7.625B); innocent of death of Jo. Bapt. but guilty through a previous generation of that of Zacharias, Or.*comm.ser*.*26 in Mt*.(p.44.17; M.13.1632B); their blasphemy against Christ οἱ τότε Φ. τῷ βεελζεβοὺλ τὰ τοῦ πνεύματος ἀνετίθεσαν Ath.*ep.Serap*.1.33(M.26.608B); τίνος γοῦν ἕνεκεν οἱ Φ. τὸν Χριστὸν ἔλεγον δαιμονᾶν; οὐκ ἐπειδὴ τῆς παρὰ τῶν πολλῶν ἐπεθύμουν δόξης; Chrys.*hom*.*40.4 in Mt*.(7.443B); and its punishment τοιαῦτα καὶ νῦν τολμῶντες οἱ Φ. τοιαύτην ἐσχήκασι παρὰ τοῦ σωτῆρος τὴν ἀπόφασιν οἵαν καὶ ὁ...βεελζεβοὺλ ἔσχεν ἤδη καὶ ἔχει· ὥστε αὐτοὺς εἰς τὸ ἡτοιμασμένον πῦρ ἐκείνῳ αἰωνίως συγκατεσθίεσθαι μετ' αὐτοῦ Ath.*ep.Serap*.4.17(M.26.661B); their position as interpreters of the Law οἱ γραμματεῖς καὶ οἱ Φ. εἶχον τὰς κλεῖς τῶν θυρῶν τῆς βασιλείας τοῦ θεοῦ, τουτέστι τὰς θείας γραφάς Or.*fr.in Mt*.23:13(p.187); ὡς τὴν κλεῖδα τῆς βασιλείας πεπιστευμένων [sc. τῶν Φ.] ἥτις ἐστὶ γνῶσις, ἣ μόνη τὴν πύλην τῆς ζωῆς ἀνοῖξαι δύναται...ἀλλὰ ναί, φησίν [sc. ὁ Χριστός], κρατοῦσι μὲν τὴν κλεῖν τοῖς δὲ βουλομένοις εἰσελθεῖν οὐ παρέχουσιν *Hom.Clem*.3.18; denial of Christ's Resurrection ἐπ' ὄψει πάντων γενομένων τοῦ τε θανάτου καὶ τῆς ἀναστάσεως, οὐκ ἠθέλησαν οἱ τότε Φ. πιστεύειν ἀλλὰ καὶ τοὺς ἑωρακότας τὴν ἀνάστασιν ἠνάγκασαν ἀρνήσασθαι ταύτην Ath.*inc*.23.3(M.25.137A); **2.** ref. Lc.18:9ff. ἐπειδὴ αὐτὸν [sc. τὸν τελώνην] ἐκάκισεν ὁ Φ. ἀπῆλθεν ἅπαντα ἀπολέσας Chrys.*stat*.3.5(2.42D); Pharisee's allegations serve only to bring forgiveness to publican, id.*David* 3.4(4.775D); ἐπεὶ καὶ ὁ Φ. ἐδόκει πληθύνειν τὴν δέησιν...'σταθεὶς δὲ ὁ Φ. ταῦτα πρὸς ἑαυτὸν προσηύχετο', οὐχὶ πρὸς τὸν θεόν, ἐπανήρχετο γὰρ πρὸς ἑαυτὸν ἐπείπερ ἐν ἁμαρτίᾳ τῆς ὑπερηφανίας ἐγίνετο †Bas.*Is*.36(1.408E; M.30.189C); πάλιν ἕτερος ηὔξατο καὶ προσέκρουσε τῷ θεῷ· τοσοῦτόν ἐστι τὸ μὴ ποιεῖν τι διὰ τὸν θεόν· ὁ Φ. λέγω...οὐ παρὰ τὴν εὐχὴν ἀλλὰ παρὰ τὴν γνώμην, μεθ' ἧς ηὔξατο κατέπεσε προσκρούσας Chrys.*kal*.6(1.706B).

***φαρμάζω**, *poison*, Sophr.H.*mir.Cyr.et Jo*.59(M.87.3633A).

φαρμακεύω, **1.** *practise sorcery*, *Did*.2.2; Eus.*d.e*.3.6(p.133.15; M.22.225A); **2.** *purge*, Bas.Sel.*or*.35.2(M.85.377A); **3.** act. and med., *poison*, Meth.*symp*.8.16(p.108.1; M.18.169D); ‡Epiph.*phys*.16(M.43.529A); **4.** *season*, in cookery, Chrys.*Anna* 5.3(4.744D).

φαρμακοθήκη, ἡ, *medicine-chest*, Procl.CP *or*.18.1(M.65.820A).

***φαρμακολύτρια**, ἡ, *one who cures* wounds, etc.; epithet of S. Anastasia, *Exorc*.(p.345).

φαρμακόμαντις, ὁ, *one who is at once* φαρμακός *and* μάντις, *Apophth.Mac.Aeg*.(M.34.212C); Jo.Sync.*narr*.(H.4.320D).

φάρμακον, τό, **1.** *remedy*, of death of Christ τῷ θανάτῳ [sc. τοῦ Χριστοῦ]...ἀναδιδομένῳ τρόπον φαρμάκου ἐπὶ τὰς ἀντικειμένας ἐνεργείας Or.*Jo*.1.32(37; p.41.28; M.14.85D); of baptism ἀφιεμένων τῶν πλημμελημάτων ἑνὶ παιωνίῳ φ., λογικῷ βαπτίσματι Clem.*paed*.1.6(p.108.2; M.8.285C); Gr.Naz.*or*.40.12(M.36.373B); φ. ... πρὸς τὴν τῶν ἁμαρτιῶν ἀναίρεσιν Chrys.*proph.obscurit*.2.9(6.196A); of Lent, id. *hom*.*1.1 in Gen*.(4.1B); of good works as prescribed by Church, *ib*.(4.2C) cit. s. ἐκκλησία; of name of Jesus in visitation of sick, Serap.*euch*.8.2; of eucharist τῷ παρ' ἑαυτῆς φ. τούτῳ τὸ σῶμα πᾶν ἐπαλείφουσα Gr.Naz.*or*.8.18(M.35.809C); of penance τὸν δὲ ὀλίγα ἡμαρτηκότα, δι' ὑπερηφανίαν μὴ προελθεῖν τῷ φ. τῆς ἐξομολογήσεως *cat.Lc*.7:43(p.62.20); **2.** *medicine* as a means, of eucharist φ. ἀθανασίας Ign.*Eph*.20.2; φ. ζωῆς Serap.*euch*.13.15; of Christian life φ. ἀθανασίας Clem.*prot*.10(p.76.3; M.8.221B); φ. σωτηρίας id.*str*.7.11(p.44.30; M.9.485C); of action φ. ὁλοκληρίας Serap.*euch*.17.2; *ib*.29.1; of baptism φ. σωτηρίας Thdt.*Is*.10:23(p.57.23; 2.247).

φαρμακός, ὁ, *wizard, witch*, *Orac.Sib*.3.283; Arist.*apol*.8.2; Or.*Cels*.5.38(p.43.2; M.11.1241A); *M.Glyc*.1.4(p.13*.4B).

***φαρμουθί**, Coptic month, Petr.I Al.*fr*.(M.18.516B); *Chron.Pasch*.p.252(M.92.609A).

φασήλιον, τό, kind of bean, *calavance*, Epiph.*haer*.66.28(p.64.2; M.42.76C); *ib*.66.34(p.73.22, v.l. φασίλεος 81D).

φάσις, ἡ, *appearance*, plur., of objects in the middle distance, opp. ἐπιφάσεις and ὑποφάσεις, Clem.*str*.6.7(p.460.11; M.9.277C).

***φασκιάριος**, ὁ, ? *potter* (Lat. *vascularius*), Ephr.2.176C.

***φασκίδιον**, τό, (cf. Lat. *fascia*) *strap, thong*, *V.Dan*.(pp.52.25, 55.22).

φασκιόω, (Lat. *fascio*) *bandage, tie up, swathe*, Anton.Hag.*v.Sym.Styl*.5(p.24.16); v. φουσκιάζω.

φάσμα, τό, **1.** *apparition, phantom* φ. μὲν νενομικέναι τὸν Ἰησοῦν, μετὰ τὴν ἐκ νεκρῶν ἀνάστασιν Or.*Cels*.7.35(p.185.30; M.11.1469C); **2.** *appearance* ὁ ἀπιστῶν τῷ περὶ τοῦ εἴδους τῆς περιστερᾶς φάσματι τοῦ ἁγίου πνεύματος *ib*.1.43(p.93.10; 737C); Cyr.ap.*cat.Heb*.suppl.7:1(p.525.2); *outward appearance, form* τοὺς αὐτῶν θεοὺς...ἀπογυμνοῦντες τοῦ φ. καὶ τὴν εἴσω τῆς ἐπικεχρωσμένης μορφῆς ἀμορφίαν τοῖς πάντων ὀφθαλμοῖς ἐνδεικνύμενοι Eus.*v.C*.3.54(p.102.15; M.20.1120A); id.*l.C*.8(p.217.17; M.20.1361A).

φασματώδης, **1.** *phantasmal*, Meth.*symp*.8.3(p.83.22; M.18.141B); Jo.D.*hom*.12.21(M.96.809C); ref. Inc. ὡς ἄνθρωπον οὐ φορέσαντα ἄνθρωπον, ἀλλὰ δόκησίν τινα φ. Hipp.*fr.in Mt*.*25:24*(p.209.9; M.10.868A); **2.** *monstrous, fantastic*, Thphn.*chron*.p.128(M.108.353A).

***φατνιάω**, *be stabled*, Geo.Pis.*Heracl*.2.53(M.92.1321A).

φάτνωσις, ἡ, *panelling*; of ceiling, Eus.*v.C*.3.49(p.98.18; M.20.1109B); Gr.Nyss.*hom*.*4 in Cant*.(M.44.837A).

φατρία, ἡ, **1.** *family, tribe, nation*, Epiph.*exp.fid*.10(p.509.26; M.42.797C); gentiles regarded as a φατρία, Mac.Mgn.*apocr*.3.29(p.122.21); **2.** *league, association* τὴν τῶν δαιμόνων καὶ φιλοσόφων...φ. Chrys.*hom*.*32.4 in Rom*.(9.759E); Sever.*Eph*.3:15(p.310.26); Eustrat.*v.Eutych*.38(M.86.2320A); **3.** *conspiracy*, CChalc.*can*.18; Rom.Mel.(*SBBAW* 1901 p.745); **4.** *faction*, Bas.*ascet*.2.2(2.325B; M.31.885A); Socr.*h.e*.6.4.4(M.67.672A); Thdr.Lect.*h.e*.1.19(M.86.173C).

φατριάζω, *conspire*, CChalc.*can*.18; †Pach.*poen*.(p.63).

***φατριάρχης**, ὁ, *chief conspirator* (play on πατριάρχης), term of abuse for iconoclast patriarchs, ‡Jo.D.*Const*.15(M.95.332B); ὁ ἀνάξιος τοῦ πῖ, καὶ μᾶλλον ἐπάξιος τοῦ φῖ· φ. γὰρ ἤπερ πατριάρχης τῇ ἐκκλησίᾳ ἐξέφανεν Steph.Diac.*v.Steph*.(M.100.1112C).

***φατριαστής**, ὁ, *conspirator*, Thphn.*chron*.p.341(v.l. for φρατρ- M.108.821D).

***φατριόω**, *conspire against*, *Hymn*.(*AS* 1 p.609).

***φαυλεπιθυμία**, ἡ, *evil desire*, Gr.Agr.*Eccl*.1.21(M.98.801B).

φαυλισμός, ὁ, *contempt, disparagement*, Or.*enarr.in Job* 2:11(M.17.64C); Bas.*reg.fus*.8.2(2.349B; M.31.937A); Gr.Nyss.*Eun*.3(2 p.35.26; M.45.601D).

φαῦλος, **1.** *bad* οἱ φ. δαίμονες Just.*1apol*.57.1(M.6.413C); τὸ θέλειν τὰ καλὰ καλόν ἐστιν ἢ φ. Or.*princ*.3.1.18(p.229.19; M.11.288A); τῇ φύσει οὐδὲν φ. ... τῷ δὲ τῆς χρήσεως τρόπῳ κακόν Meth.*arbitr*.15(p.183.7; κακόν M.18.264A); Ath.*inc*.3.4(M.25.101C); **2.** of health, *injured, damaged*, Marc.Diac.*v.Porph*.81; **3.** phrase παρὰ φαῦλον τίθεσθαι *despise*, *V.Const*.19(p.555.34).

***φαυλοτριβής**, *occupied with mean things*, Isid.Pel.*epp*.1.439(M.78.424C).

φαῦσις, ἡ, *illumination*, Cyr.*hom.pasch*.14(5^2.195B); ‡Paul.Sil.*therm.Pyth*.(M.86.2267); †Jo.D.*B.J*.7(M.96.909A).

***Φεβρουάριος** (*Φευρ-), *February*, Φευρ-, Ath.*h.Ar*.81(p.230.20; M.25.795B v.l.); Epiph.*haer*.51.25(p.295.16; Φευρ- M.41.933C); Φευρ- *Chron.Pasch*.p.11(M.92.89A); Thphn.*chron*.p.72(M.108.229A).

***φεγγάριον**, τό, *moon*, †Andr.Cr.*cycl*.(M.19.1333A).

φεγγίτης, as adj., *light-giving*, ‡Chrys.*hom.in Jo*.*17:11*(8.43C).

φεγγοβολέω, *shed rays of light*, Hesych.S.*temp*.1.35(M.93.1492D); Anast.S.*qu.et resp*.40(M.89.585B).

***φεγγοβόλος**, *shedding rays of light, radiant*, Eust.*engast*.6(p.24.9; M.18.624C); Bas.Sel.*or*.41.7(M.85.468C).

***φεγγοειδής**, *shining, radiant*, met., Hesych.S.*temp*.1.35(M.93.1492D); *ib*.2.3(1512C).

***φεγγοτόκος**, *radiant*, Sophr.H.*carm*.9.85(M.87.3780A).

***φεγγώδης,** = φεγγοειδής, *A.Thom.*A 34(p.151.16); †Gr.Thaum. *ep.Philagr.*(M.46.1105C).

***φειδεκόμμισσον, τό,** v. *φιδεκόμμισσον.

φείδ-ομαι, 1. *spare* μηδὲν βδελυσσομένου ὧν ἐποίησεν καὶ ~ομένου πάντων Or.*Jo.*20.17(15; p.349.29; M.14.621C); ἵνα τί ἐπὶ τοσοῦτον ἐφείσω ἡμῶν, οὐκ ἐπισκεπτόμενος ἡμᾶς ἐπὶ ταῖς ἁμαρτίαις; id.*princ.* 3.1.12(p.215.3; M.11.269B); Ath.*inc.*13.6(M.25.120A); **2.** *have consideration, care for,* Eus.*h.e.*8.6.5(M.20.753A); Hegem.*Arch.*5(p.6.5; M.10.1433B); *ib.*(p.7.15; 1436B); διὰ τί μὴ ~ονται τῆς σωτηρίας τῆς αὐτῶν [sc. εἰδώλων]; Chrys.*hom.8.5 in 2Tim.*(11.713B); Thdot.Anc. *hom.*3.1(p.71.26; M.77.1385B); neg. *pay no heed to* μηδὲ φείσασθαι τῷ πατρί μου Ἰακώβ *T.Sym.*2.7.

φειδώ, ἡ, 1. *mercy,* Diod.*Gen.*49:4(M.33.1578C); Evagr.Pont.*or.* 26(M.79.1172D); Geo.Pis.*Pers.*2.237(M.92.1226A); of God, Clem.*fr.* 56(p.226.15); Or.*hom.7.1 in Jer.*(p.52.1; M.13.329B); Cyr.*Is.*1.1(2. 3C); **2.** *care, consideration,* Clem.*str.*3.12(p.231.20; M.8.1177C); ἵνα... πολλῇ τῇ φ. καὶ προνοίᾳ τειχίζῃ [sc. τὸ πνεῦμα] πάντοθεν τὸ νεοπαγὲς τῆς πίστεως φυτόν Chrys.*hom.1.5 in 2Cor.4:13*(3.264D); Cyr.*Jo.*11 (4.978D); φειδοῖ, *with regard for* τὸν ὄφιν, φειδοῖ τῆς σαρκὸς τὴν βρῶσιν ὑποτιθέμενον Bas.*hom.*1.4(2.3C; M.31.168B); Evagr.*h.e.*1.11 (p.18.29; M.86.2449B); **3.** *caution,* Thdt.*Rom.*7:6(3.70).

***φειδωλεῖον, τό,** *parsimony,* †Nil.*vit.*3(M.79.1141D).

φειδωλῶς, *sparingly,* Phot.*nomoc.*9.1(p.533; M.104.709A).

φελλάτας, ὁ, a kind of *stone,* of which statues were made, Clem. *prot.*4(p.36.24; M.8.137A).

[*]**φελόνιον (φελώνιον), τό,** (Lat. *paenula*) *chasuble,* φελόνιον Gr.Mag.*dial.*(tr.Zach.)1.9(M.*PL.*77.195A); φελώνιον ‡Sophr.H.*liturg.* (M.87.3988B); *Euchol.*(p.48).

***φεράλληλος,** *mutually linked*; of Persons of Trin., ‡Gr.Nyss. *imag.*(M.44.1341D); *ib.*(1344A).

***φεραλλήλως,** *in being mutually linked,* Anast.S.*hod.*16(M.89. 261C).

***φερέδειπνος,** *which summons to a meal,* Nonn.*par.Jo.*6:8(M.43. 793B).

φερέζωος, *life-bringing,* †Apoll.*met.Ps.*4:8(M.33.1317A); *ib.*19:6 (1337A); Nonn.*par.Jo.*16:27(M.43.881C).

φερέοικος, ὁ, *snail,* Gr.Naz.*carm.*1.2.1.535(M.37.562A).

φερεπόνως, *patiently, laboriously,* Anast.S.*haer.*(p.257).

***φέρι,** exclamation of anger, Ath.*ep.Jov.*(M.26.821A).

***φερνοφόρος,** *dowry-bearing,* title of Ptolemy Philadelphus, Hier.*Dan.*11:6(φορνοφόρος M.*PL.*25.560B).

φέρ-ω, [ἔφερα = ἤνεγκον, Jo.Mosch.*prat.*140(M.87.3004A)]; **1.** *bear, carry,* met. τὸ ὄνομα τοῦ τὴν αἵρεσιν ἐφευρόντος ~ουσιν Ath.*Ar.* 1.3(M.26.17B); of Son τὴν ἡμετέραν σάρκα ~ων *ib.*1.66(285A); τὰς ἁμαρτίας ἡμῶν αὐτὸς ~ει...καὶ σῶμα τὸ ἐν αὐτῷ ~ον αὐτὰς αὐτοῦ ἴδιόν ἐστι *ib.*3.31(389B); τὸ δὲ ἅγιον πνεῦμα...ἀεί ἐστιν ἐν ταῖς χερσὶ τοῦ πέμποντος πατρὸς καὶ τοῦ ~οντος υἱοῦ id.*exp.fid.*4(M.25.208A); τρόπαια καὶ νίκας κατὰ τοῦ θανάτου ~ων τὴν ἐν τῷ σώματι γενομένην ἀφθαρσίαν καὶ ἀπάθειαν id.*inc.*26.1(M.25.141A); πᾶσαν ἐν αὐτῷ ~οντος τὴν θεότητα Thdt.*Col.*2:9(3.486); **2.** *bear a character* φόνος δικαιοσύνην ἤνεγκε Chrys.*Thdr.*2.3(1.38C); **3.** med., *bear oneself, be* τὸ ~εσθαι ἐξ ἐναντίας πᾶσι τοῖς ἔθνεσιν Eus.*d.e.*3.5(p.121.8; M.22. 205C); **4.** pass., *be carried away,* met. οὐκοῦν ἔδει τοὺς ἀνθρώπους μὴ ἀφιέναι ~εσθαι τῇ φθορᾷ Ath.*inc.*6.10(M.25.107B); τὸ τῶν ἀνθρώπων γένος ἄμοιρον τῆς τοῦ θεοῦ γνώσεως ~εσθαι id.*gent.*46(M.25.92A); **5.** *produce, bear*; met. ἡ μὲν γὰρ ἤνεγκεν αὐτόν [sc. Christ], ἡ Βεθλεέμ Chrys.*hom.29.1 in Mt.*(7.342C); pass., *arise from* τὸ πρᾶγμα ἀφ' οὗ ~εται τὸ φωνεῖν Clem.*str.*7.11(p.44.26; M.9.485C); **6.** *provide, bring* βάπτισμα τὸ ~ον ἄφεσιν ἁμαρτιῶν *Barn.*11.1; τοῦτο γὰρ ὑμῖν ~ει μεγίστην κατάγνωσιν Ath.*apol.sec.*36(p.114.14; M.25.309B); βομβύκια ἅτινα ~ει [sc. ὁ διάβολος]...οὐδὲν τῷ βίῳ χρήσιμον id.*ep.Amun.*(M.26. 1172A); οὐκ ἔστι ταῦτα λέγοντας ἐνεγκεῖν δόξαν...τῷ κυρίῳ id.*Ar.*1.18 (M.26.49A); οὐ γὰρ ἀδοξίαν ἤνεγκεν ἡ σὰρξ τῷ λόγῳ id.*ep.Adelph.*4 (M.26.1077A); **7.** *bring forward, summon,* persons as witnesses, Jul.Papa *ep.Dian.*(p.108.26; M.25.296D); for judgement, Thdt.*eran.* 3(4.262); *Chron.Pasch.*p.327(M.92.844A); **8.** *bring, lead* into a certain condition ὅρος ἀνθρώπου εἰς τελειότητα ~ων Ath.*fug.*11(p.76. 16; M.25.660A); ~ει γὰρ αὐτοὺς ἡ ἀκολουθία τοιαῦτα...ὑπονοεῖν id. *Ar.*1.63(M.26.144A); ταῦτα ποιοῦσιν...ἵνα τοὺς ἀκεραίους εἰς ἀπόγνωσιν ἐνέγκωσιν id.*v.Anton.*25(M.26.881B); ref. Logos τὰ κτίσματα ...εἰς οὐσίαν ἤνεγκε id.*Ar.*2.64(284B); τὸ φθαρτὸν εἰς ἀφθαρσίαν ἐνεγκεῖν id.*inc.*7.5(M.25.109A); Arian ἀρχὴν τὸν υἱὸν ἔθηκε τῶν γεννητῶν ὁ ἄναρχος καὶ ἤνεγκεν εἰς υἱὸν ἑαυτῷ τόνδε τεκνοποιήσας Ar. *thal.*2 ap.eund.*syn.*15(p.242.15; M.26.705D); pass., *be swayed, influenced* τοὺς ὑπ' ἐκείνου [sc. τοῦ εὐαγγελίου] ~ομένους Chrys.*hom.* *3.1 in 1Tim.*(11.561E); κατὰ συκφαντίαν...κατά τινων ~εσθαι Epiph. *haer.*16.3(p.212.15; M.41.252B); met., *be permeated, inspired* τὸ πνεῦμα ᾠκείωται τῇ ὑπ' αὐτοῦ ~ομένῃ ψυχῇ Clem.*paed.*2.2(p.168.10; M.8. 412A); **9.** *assert, hold* οἱ ἀσεβεῖς...ταῦτα ~οντες δυσφημοῦσι μὲν τὸν κύριον Ath.*Ar.*3.7(M.26.333C); *ib.*3.11(344A); pass., be *recorded, written* τὰ ἐν τοῖς εὐαγγελίοις αὐτοῦ ~όμενα Eus.*d.e.*1.3(p.17.22; M. 22.40A); *Symb.Sel.*3 ap.Ath.*syn.*29(p.252.11; M.26.729A); Thdt.*Os.* 8:4(2.1347); **10.** *place, attribute* μετὰ τὸ ἑκατοστὸν ἔτος τῆς Ἰλίου ἁλώσεως τὴν Ὁμήρου ἡλικίαν ~ει Clem.*str.*1.21(p.74.14,21; M.8. 845A); κατὰ τὴν Ἰωνικὴν ἀποικίαν...~εσθαι αὐτόν *ib.*(p.74.1; 844A); **11.** pass., *be in circulation, be extant*; of literary works, Chrys. *hom.7.3 in 1Cor.*(10.54A); Max.*schol.c.h.*15.6(M.4.112A); of heresies, *survive* τῶν...αἱρέσεων...ἐξ ὧν οὐκέτι ~ονται [ἀλλ'] ἢ τρεῖς μόναι τῶν Σαμαρειτῶν Epiph.*haer.*20.3(p.227.2; v.l. ἐμφέρονται M.41.273B); hence *exist* τῷ μηδὲ ~εσθαι θείαν βίβλον ἐξ ἐκείνου καὶ μέχρι τῶν τοῦ σωτῆρος χρόνων Eus.*d.e.*8.1(p.354.25; M.22.577A); *be in circulation as the work of, be attributed to* τὴν ~ομένην Ἰωάννου...ἐπιστολήν id.*h.e.*3.25(p.250.23; M.20.268D); Dion.Al.*ib.*7.25(p.694.14; 700A); **12.** *refer, apply* to τοῦτο...ἀλληγοροῦντες ~ουσιν ἐπὶ τὸν σωτῆρα Hipp.*ben.Jac.*(p.27.10); of a word or term σῶμα γὰρ ἔμψυχον λέγεται ἐφ' ᾧ ἐνυποστάτως τὸ τῆς ψυχῆς ~εται ὄνομα ‡Ath.*Apoll.*1.20(M.26. 1128B); **13.** *come within the sphere of* καὶ τὰ λοιπὰ πάντα ὅσα ὑπομνημάτων χρῄζουσι, πλὴν εἰ μὴ εἰς ἀρχικὴν ~ουσι δικαιοδοσίαν Ath. Scholast.*coll.*4.19(p.66); **14.** *turn*; as nautical term, *bear* τὸ δεξιὸν ~οντα, νῦν δὲ τὸ εὐώνυμον μεταφέροντα Thdt.*provid.*2(4.500); met., *turn, adapt* to a purpose τὰ τῆς φύσεως ἁμαρτήματα ταῦτα ~ουσιν εἰς τέρψιν Chrys.*hom.3.3 in 1Tim.*(11.565E); **15.** imperative used parenthetically, *for instance* ἐξ ἐκκλησίας, φέρε, ἢ ἀγορᾶς Clem. *paed.*2.10(p.215.8; M.8.512B); id.*str.*7.7(p.30.29; M.9.456C); Eus.*p.e.* 3.13(120A; M.21.216A); **16.** neut. ptcpl., *advantage* πῶς...τῷ ~οντι ἤδη τὸ δοκοῦν ἀποφθέγγεσθε; Leont.H.*Nest.*4.12(M.86.1673B).

φευκταῖος, *to be avoided,* ‡Ath.*v.Syncl.*87(M.28.1540D).

***Φευρουάριος,** v. *Φεβρουάριος.

***φημάριον, τό,** *reputation,* †Ath.*fr.Mt.*(M.27.1381A); †Ath.*fr.* (M.26.1253C).

φθάζ-ω, *arrive at, attend* ~ουσιν ἐν τῇ Τύρῳ τῶν θαυμαστῶν ἐπισκόπων τὴν σύνοδον Gel.Cyz.*h.e.*3.18.4; pass., *be overtaken, caught* πρὸς τὸ μὴ καταδιωχθέντα αὐτὸν φθασθῆναι Jo.Mal.*chron.*13 p.331(M.97.493B).

φθάν-ω, *anticipate*; **1.** ptcpl., expressing previous action (= *already*) καθὼς φθάσαντες εἴπομεν Gr.Nyss.*hex.*14(M.44.77A); Didym.*Trin.*1.26(M.39.384C); Cyr.*Is.*2.3(2.260E); **2.** *arise* from ἀπὸ δὴ τούτων τὰ κακὰ...ἔφθασεν Ath.*gent.*25(M.25.49C); **3.** *reach, arrive at,* places [Ps.131:7] οὗ ἔφθασαν οἱ πόδες αὐτοῦ [sc. τοῦ θεοῦ] οἱ ἀπόστολοι Clem.*paed.*2.8(p.194.19; M.8.465C); φθάσαντες τὴν Κωνσταντινούπολιν Gel.Cyz.*h.e.*3.13.7; Dor.*doct.*1.15(M.88.1637B); words in prayer ὡς ἔφθασαν εἰς τὸν λόγον τοῦ 'ἄφες ἡμῖν τὰ ὀφειλήματα' Leont.N.*v.Jo.Eleem.*39(p.78.1); death τοὺς ἐφθακότας εἰς τοῦτον [sc. τὸν θάνατον] Eus.*d.e.*6.7(p.257.21; M.22.424A); ref. Inc. ὥστε καὶ εἰς ἡμᾶς φθάσαι καὶ φανῆναι τὸν κύριον ἐν ἀνθρώποις Ath.*inc.* 4.2(M.25.104A); of abstracts οὐχὶ καὶ αἱ προαιρέσεις ~ουσι πρὸς τὸν θεόν Clem.*str.*7.7(p.29.8; M.9.453A); ἄχρι τούτων ἔφθασεν αὐτῶν ἡ ματαιοπονία Epiph.*haer.*66.6(p.27.10; M.42.40B); *ib.*78.2(p.453. 8; 701B); Dor.*doct.*1.9(M.88.1628B); of news, reports, Or.*Cels.*7.42 (p.193.5; M.11.1481B); ἔφθασεν εἰς πάντας ἀνθρώπους ἡ φήμη Eus.*d.e.* 3.6(p.137.14; M.22.232C); τὸ γενόμενον...ἄχρι τῆς βασιλίδος ἔφθασεν Gel.Cyz.*h.e.*3.10.5; *extend* to, Epiph.*haer.*30.17(p.357.6; M.41.433D); *have recourse* to ~ουσι γὰρ καὶ ἕως μαγειῶν καὶ φαρμακειῶν †Jo.Jej. *poenit.*(M.88.1904B); met., *come within the sphere of* τῶν...εἰς τὴν ἡμετέραν πρόνοιαν ~όντων Gr.Nyss.*tres dii*(M.45.125C); **4.** *approach, draw near* ἐπ' αὐτὴν γὰρ οὔπω δυνάμεθα φθάσαι τὴν κεφαλὴν [sc. τοῦ Ἰησοῦ] Or.*schol.in Lc.*7:48(M.17.337B); πρὸς θεὸν ἔφθασε Cyr.H. *catech.*6.3; καταφευγέτω Χριστόν, ὅπου ὁ πολέμιος τῆς ζωῆς ἡμῶν οὐ δύναται καταδιώκων φθάσαι Nil.*epp.*3.100(M.79.432D); ref. Creation ὁ μὲν θεὸς καὶ πατὴρ συνέχων τὰ πάντα ~ει εἰς ἕκαστον τῶν ὄντων, μεταδιδοὺς ἑκάστῳ ἀπὸ τοῦ ἰδίου τὸ εἶναι Or.*princ.*1.3.5(p.56.1; M.11. 150B); **5.** *arrive* ἔφθασεν ὁμοῦ αὐτὸς εἰσερχόμενος εἰς τὸν πυλῶνα Leont.N.*v.Jo.Eleem.*22(p.41.11); *come to pass* ἔφθασεν γάρ σου τὸ τέλος τῆς ἀπωλείας *A.Thom.*A 33(p.150.1); πρᾶξίς τις ἔγγραφος ἔφθασε καθ' ἡμῶν *Pers.*(p.14.19; M.10.104B); *occur, fall on a date* ἐὰν ἐν κυριακῇ φθάσῃ ἡ ιδ' τῆς σελήνης *Chron.Pasch.*p.226(M.92.549A); met., *come upon* ἔφθασε δὲ αὐτοὺς ἡ ὀργὴ τοῦ θεοῦ εἰς τέλος *T.Lev.*6. 11; ἀπὸ δὴ τούτων τὰ κακὰ τοῖς ἀνθρώποις εἰς πλῆθος ἔφθασεν Ath. *gent.*25(M.25.49C); τοῦ Ἀδὰμ παραβάντος, εἰς πάντας ἀνθρώπους ἔφθασεν ἡ ἁμαρτία id.*Ar.*1.51(M.26.117C); of disease τῆς φθασάσης αὐτὴν...νόσου Gel.Cyz.*h.e.*3.10.5; exeg. Mt.12:28, Lc.11:20 ἐπειδὴ... ταῦτα...πληροῦται...οὐχ ἑτέρως ἀλλ' ἢ τῇ δυνάμει τοῦ πνεύματος... οὐδὲν ἕτερόν ἐστιν εἰπεῖν ἢ τὸ ἠγγικέναι τὴν βασιλείαν, ἧς εὐαγγελιστὴς ὑμῖν καὶ πρόξενος ἐγώ, ὑπισχνούμενος ὑμῖν τὴν μετάδοσιν τοῦ πνεύματος, ὑφ' οὗ καὶ γίνεται πάντα τὰ πρὸς συμπλήρωσιν τῆς βασιλείας... γενήσεσθαι ὀφείλοντα Or.*fr.264 in Mt.*(p.120); ἐὰν πιστεύητε, ἔφθασεν ἐφ' ὑμᾶς ἡ βασιλεία τοῦ θεοῦ· εἰ δὲ οὔκ, ἀπωλείᾳ παραδοθήσεσθε *ib.*266 (p.121); τεκμήρια δὲ ταῦτα...τῆς τοῦ θεοῦ βασιλείας καθαιρούσης... πᾶσαν ἀρχὴν...καὶ πᾶσαν...τυραννίδα...διό φησι...'ἔφθασεν ἐφ' ὑμᾶς ἡ βασιλεία' Eus.*Lc.*11:21(M.24.553C,D); ἔφθασεν...ἐφ' ὑμᾶς· ὡσανεὶ ἔλεγεν, ὑμῖν ἥκει τὰ ἀγαθά· διατί οὖν πρὸς τὰ οἰκεῖα καλὰ ἀηδῶς διάκεισθε;...οὗτος ἐκεῖνος ὁ καιρός, ὃν πάλαι προὔλεγον οἱ προφῆται Chrys.*hom.41.2 in Mt.*(7.447A); πεπλούτηκεν ἡ ἀνθρώπου φύσις ἐν ἐμοὶ καὶ πρώτῳ τὴν θεοπρεπῆ βασιλείαν. ... τοῦτό ἐστι τὸ ἔφθασεν κτλ. Cyr.*Lc.*11:20(M.72.704C); **6.** *attain, achieve* τὸν ἀναγνώστην καὶ διάκονον φθάσας Pall.*v.Chrys.*16(p.95.12; M.47.54); ref. abstracts οἱ δὲ μήπω τὴν τελειότητα φθάσαντες Thdt.*Cant.*1:3(2.35); ὅπως τὴν τῆς *Δομετίλλας* ~ει σύνεσιν *M.Ner.et Ach.*19(p.18.12); *attain to, equal* μηδεμία εἰκὼν ~ει πρὸς τὴν ἀλήθειαν Gr.Naz.*or.*23.11(M.35.1164A); [Gen.13:10] αὕτη [sc. ἡ περίχωρος]...ἡ ~ουσα τῇ εὐθηνίᾳ τὸν παράδεισον τοῦ θεοῦ Chrys.*hom.8.3 in 1Thess.*(11.481B); Trin. ἵνα ὁ μὲν υἱὸς προκόψας μὴ φθάσῃ τὴν τοῦ πατρὸς μεγαλειότητα Epiph.*haer.*69. 53(p.200.19; M.42.285A); **7.** *succeed in, be able to* οὕτως δὴ ~ειν ἐπιχειροῦντα τῇ ἐπιβουλῇ Clem.*str.*1.21(p.88.28; M.8.880B); οὐ ~ει πρὸς *Πέτρον* ἐλθεῖν...οὐδὲ γενέσθαι αὐτῶν ἐγγύς Chrys.*oppugn.*3.19(1. 111A); †Jo.D.*B.J.*9(M.96.932A); **8.** *refer, apply to* τὸ γὰρ 'ποιήσωμεν ἄνθρωπον κατ' εἰκόνα καὶ καθ' ὁμοίωσιν ἡμετέραν' ~ει ἐπὶ πάντας ἀνθρώπους Or.*hom.2.1 in Jer.*(p.17.10; M.13.277C); οὐκ εἰς τὸν *Δαβὶδ* ~ει τὰ τοιαῦτα ῥητά Ath.*Ar.*2.16(M.26.180A,B); Epiph.*haer.*5. 35(p.310.21; M.41.953B).

φθάρμα, τό, *destructive creature* τῆς ἀποθήκης τὰ φ., τουτέστι καὶ σκώληκας καὶ σῆτας Epiph.*haer.*59.10(p.375.13; M.41.1033A).

***φθαρτολάτραι, οἱ,** *worshippers of the corruptible*, name given to one of the branches of the *Γαϊανῖται*: φ. καὶ κτιστολάτρας ὀνομάζουσι Tim.CP *haer.*(M.86.57B).

***φθαρτοποιός,** *rendering corruptible*, Amph.*hom.*2.4(M.39.40D).

φθαρτός, *subject to decay, corruption*; **1.** in gen.; of matter etc., Arist.*apol.*4.1; Just.*1apol.*9.3(M.6.340B); Athenag.*leg.*4.2(M.6.897B); of things of this world οὐχ ὁρᾷ [sc. ὁ ἀγαθός] ἐμπαθῶς τὰ φ. *T.Benj.* 6.2; εἰ γὰρ ἐν τῷ ἀφθάρτῳ κοινωνοί ἐστε, πόσῳ μᾶλλον ἐν τοῖς φ.; *Barn.*19.8; Χριστιανοὶ παροικοῦσιν ἐν φθαρτοῖς τὴν δὲ ἐν οὐρανοῖς ἀφθαρσίαν προσδεχόμενοι *Diogn.*6.8; as created, v. γενητός; **2.** partic.; **a.** of human flesh, Herm.*sim.*5.7.2; ἐν φ. καὶ παθητῷ κατοικοῦσα σώματι μηδὲν ἠδίκηται [sc. ἡ ψυχή] Athenag.*res.*10(p.59. 3; M.6.992C); not created φθαρτός but made so because of transgression, Meth.*symp.*9.2(p.116.15; M.18.181A); ἡ σάρξ...ἐκρατήθη δὲ διὰ τὴν ἡδονὴν ὑπὸ τῆς φθορᾶς...γεγένηται φ. id.*res.*2.18(p.368.16; M. 18.264A); εἰ δὲ φ. [sc. ὁ *Ἀδάμ*] τί πλέον ἀπὸ τῆς ἀποφάσεως λεγούσης 'ᾗ δ' ἂν ἡμέρᾳ φάγητε ἀπ' αὐτοῦ, θανάτῳ ἀποθανεῖσθε' Proc.G.*Gen.*3:18 (M.87.216C); contrast οἱ δὲ ἄνθρωποι...κατὰ φύσιν φ., χάριτι δὲ τῆς τοῦ λόγου μετουσίας τοῦ κατὰ φύσιν ἐκφυγόντες εἰ μεμενήκεισαν καλοί Ath.*inc.*5.1(M.25.105A); no longer φθαρτός after resurrection οὐκ ὄντος τοῦ σώματος τοῦ αὐτοῦ, εἰς τὸ ἐνδοξότερον τὸ εἶδος αὐξηθὲν οὐκέτι ἐν φ. ἀλλ' ἐν ἀπαθεῖ καὶ πνευματικῷ δειχθήσεται σώματι Meth. *res.*1.25(p.252.21); redeemed by Inc. and death of Christ, *Diogn.* 9.2; μίξας τὸ φ. τῷ ἀφθάρτῳ...σώσῃ τὸν ἀπολλύμενον ἄνθρωπον Hipp. *antichr.*4(p.6.23; M.10.732B); αὐτοῦ [sc. τοῦ θεοῦ λόγου] γὰρ ἦν πάλιν καὶ τὸ φ. εἰς ἀφθαρσίαν ἐνεγκεῖν Ath.*inc.*7.5(109A); id.*ep.Serap.*2.1(M. 26.609A); **b.** of soul (pagan) τὴν ψυχήν...σύνθετον καὶ γενητὴν καὶ φ. Hipp.*haer.*1.19(p.21.9; M.16.3044A); in controversy with Heracleon οὐ ταὐτὸν δέ ἐστιν ⟨τὸ⟩ τὴν φ. φύσιν ἐνδύεσθαι ἀφθαρσίαν καὶ τὸ τὴν φ. φύσιν μεταβάλλειν εἰς ἀφθαρσίαν Or.*Jo.*13.61(59; p.293.21; M.14. 516C); **c.** ref. body of Christ ὁ *Κέλσος* παραβάλλων τὰς ἀνθρωπίνας τοῦ 'Ἰησοῦ σάρκας χρυσῷ καὶ ἀργύρῳ...ὅτι αὗται ἐκείνων φθαρτότεραι id. *Cels.*3.42(p.237.23; M.11.973B); οὕτω μετὰ τὴν ἀνάστασιν αὐτὸν ὁρῶντες τοὺς τύπους ἔχοντα οὐκ ἐροῦμεν αὐτὸν φ. εἶναι λοιπόν Chrys. *hom.87.1 in Jo.*(8.520D); ὡς δῆλον, πρὸ μὲν τῆς ἀναστάσεως φ. εἶναι τὸ σῶμα, μετὰ δὲ τὴν ἀνάστασιν, ἄφθαρτον †Leont.B.*sect.*10.2(M.86. 1261B); περὶ φ. καὶ ἀφθάρτου μόνον διαφερόμενοι [sc. οἱ *Θεοδοσιανοί*] Tim.CP *haer.*(M.86.41B); *Γαϊανῖται*...λέγουσι τὸ σῶμα τοῦ κυρίου δυνάμει μὲν φ. μηδόλως δὲ φθαρῆναι τῇ ἐγκρατείᾳ τοῦ λόγου *ib.*(44B); **d.** ref. materialist conception of nature of God οὐκ αἰδοῦνται λέγειν ὅτι καὶ φθαρτός ἐστιν [sc. ὁ θεός] σῶμα ὤν, φ. δὲ ὄντα μὴ φθείρεσθαι τῷ μὴ εἶναι τὸν φθείροντα αὐτὸν λέγουσιν Or.*Jo.*13.21(p.245.10ff.; M.14.433A,B); **3.** of what is transient and typical, opp. real οὕτως ἐστὶν...φ. καὶ ἄφθαρτον, θνητὸν καὶ ἀθάνατον τὸ τοῦ πάσχα μυστήριον ...φ. κατὰ τὴν τοῦ προβάτου σφαγήν Mel.*pass.*2 p.1.6; *ib.*3 p.1.11; **4.** *poor, contemptible, worthless* ἦν ἡμῶν τὸ κατοικητήριον τῆς καρδίας φ. καὶ ἀσθενές *Barn.*16.7; εἰς τοὺς φ. ἀγῶνας καταπλέουσιν πολλοί *2Clem.*7.1; τῶν μὲν οὖν *Ἀρειανῶν* θνητὸν καὶ φ. τὸ τοιοῦτον φρόνημα Ath.*ep.Serap.*2.2(M.26.609B).

φθείρ-ω, 1. *defile*, met. ἐάν τις ἡμῶν τηρήσῃ αὐτὴν [sc. τὴν ἐκκλησίαν] ἐν τῇ σαρκὶ καὶ μὴ ~ῃ, ἀπολήψεται αὐτὴν ἐν τῷ πνεύματι τῷ ἁγίῳ· ἡ γὰρ σὰρξ αὕτη ἀντίτυπός ἐστιν τοῦ πνεύματος· οὐδεὶς οὖν τὸ ἀντίτυπον φθείρας τὸ αὐθεντικὸν μεταλήψεται *2Clem.*14.3; ὁ τὸν φθαρτὸν ἀγῶνα ἀγωνιζόμενος, ἐὰν εὑρεθῇ ~ων...ἔξω βάλλεται τοῦ σταδίου...ὁ τὸν τῆς ἀφθαρσίας ἀγῶνα ~ας τί παθεῖται; *ib.*7.4f.; **2.** *ravish, violate* one's virginity, Or.*Cels.*8.66(p.283.1; M.11.1617A); of BMV οὐκ ἐφθάρη παρὰ τοῦ 'Ἰωσήφ †Gregent.*disp.*(M.86.656C); **3.** *hold to be subject to decay* or *dissolution* κατὰ τοὺς ~οντας τὸν κόσμον Or.*Cels.* 4.60(p.332.4,6; M.11.1128B); σωματικὰς λέγοντας [sc. τοὺς *Στωϊκούς*] εἶναι τὰς ἀρχὰς καὶ διὰ τοῦτο πάντα ~οντας κινδυνεύοντας δὲ καὶ αὐτὸν φθεῖραι τὸν ἐπὶ πᾶσι θεόν *ib.*6.71(p.141.16,17; 1405C); **4.** pass.; **a.** *perish, be subject to decay* ὁ θεὸς...ἄφθαρτος ὅτι μὴ ~εται Didym. (‡Bas.)*Eun.*4(1.284D; M.29.684C); of Christ as life αἰώνιος γὰρ ἡ ζωὴ αὐτοῦ καὶ μηδέποτε ~ομένη...ἀναφαίρετος γὰρ ἡ χάρις καὶ ἡ δωρεὰ τοῦ σωτῆρος ἡμῶν καὶ μὴ ἀναλισκομένη μηδὲ ~ομένη ἐν τῷ μετέχοντι αὐτῆς Or.*Jo.*13.10(p.234.22,25; M.14.413B); **b.** *go, betake oneself* εἰς τὴν *Ἀλεξάνδρειαν* αὖθις ~εται Gr.Naz.*carm.*2.1.11.1013(M.37.1099A).

***φθινοπωρεία, ἡ,** *produce*, ‡Caes.Naz.*dial.*147(M.38.1096).

***φθονητός,** *envied*, Clem.*str.*7.2(p.7.5; M.9.409C).

φθόνος, ὁ, *envy, ill-will*, **1.** in gen.; as cause of disorder in Church, *1Clem.*3.2; resulting in murder of Abel ζῆλος καὶ φ. ἀδελφοκτονίαν κατειργάσατο *ib.*4.7; καταλήγει γάρ πως ἐν τούτοις ὁ φ. ἀεί Cyr.*glaph.Gen.*6.2(1.181E); responsible for martyrdom of SS. Peter and Paul, *1Clem.*5.2; τὸν δὲ σὸν φ. δύνασαι στῆσαι, ἐὰν ἐν οἷς χαίρει ὁ ὑπὸ σοῦ φθονούμενος συγχαίρῃς Max.*carit.*3.91(M.90. 1045A); **2.** ref. Phil.1:15 τινὲς μὲν διὰ φθόνον [sc. τὸν Χριστὸν κηρύσσουσι]...ἐπειδὴ κατεσχέθη ὁ *Παῦλος*, τὸν πόλεμον ἐγεῖραι βουλόμενοι...τὸν παρὰ τοῦ βασιλέως πολλοὶ τῶν ἀπίστων, καὶ αὐτοὶ τὸν *Χριστὸν* ἐκήρυττον· ὥστε μείζονα γενέσθαι τῷ βασιλεῖ τὴν ὀργήν,... καὶ εἰς τὴν τοῦ *Παύλου* κεφαλὴν τὸ πᾶν ἐλθεῖν τοῦ θυμοῦ Chrys.*hom. 2.2 in Phil.*(11.205A); cf.Thdr.Mops.*Phil.*1:15(p.207.24ff.); Thdt. *Phil.*1:15(3.448); **3.** denied of God; ref. Creation ἀγαθῷ γὰρ περὶ οὐδενὸς ἂν γένοιτο φ.· ὅθεν οὐδὲ τὸ εἶναί τινι φθονεῖ Ath.*gent.*41(M. 25.81D); id.*inc.*3.3(M.25.101B); ref. will to save οὔτ' οὖν φθονοίη ποτ' ἄν τισιν ὁ πάντας μὲν ἐπ' ἴσης κεκληκώς, ἐξαιρέτους δὲ τοῖς ἐξαιρέτως πεπιστευκόσιν ἀπονείμας τιμάς...ἀλλ' οὐδὲ ἅπτεται τοῦ κυρίου ἀπαθοῦς ἀνάρχως γενομένου φθόνος Clem.*str.*7.2(p.7.4; M.9. 409C); ref. revelation through allegories etc. οὐ φθόνῳ (οὐ γὰρ θέμις ἐμπαθῆ νοεῖν τὸν θεόν), ἀλλ', ὅπως εἰς τὴν τῶν αἰνιγμάτων ἔννοιαν ἡ ζήτησις παρεισδύουσα ἐπὶ τὴν εὕρεσιν τῆς ἀληθείας ἀναδράμῃ *ib.*5.4(p.341.2; 44A); ref. participation in pagan cults θεὸς ἅπασι κοινός...καὶ ἔξω φ.· τί οὖν κωλύει τοὺς...καθωσιωμένους αὐτῷ καὶ τῶν δημοτελῶν ἑορτῶν μεταλαμβάνειν; Cels.ap.Or.*Cels.*8.21(p.238.17; M. 11.1549A); **4.** ref. Devil οὗ τῷ φ. θάνατος εἰσῆλθεν εἰς τὸν κόσμον Or.*Jo.* 32.2(p.428.23; M.14.745A); ὁ θεὸς...ηὐδόκησε...καθαίρεσιν...ποιήσασθαι τοῦ διὰ φθόνον ἀπατήσαντος ἐχθροῦ ‡Ath.*Apoll.*2.9(M.26.1148B).

φθορά, ἡ, 1. *destruction*; of gen. destruction of world at Flood, Or.*Cels.*4.21(p.291.10; M.11.1056A); Stoic τῇ φ. τῶν πάντων ἀνθρώπων *ib.*4.45(p.318.24; 1101D); of world in future, *ib.*4.57(p.330.14; 1124B); *ib.*4.61(p.333.3; 1128C); in gen. λέγεται γὰρ φ. ἡ παντελὴς διάλυσις τοῦ σώματος εἰς τὰ στοιχεῖα...καὶ λέγεται φ. τὰ ἀνθρώπινα ταῦτα πάθη, τοῦτ' ἔστι τὸ πεινῆν καὶ διψῆν...ὅταν οὖν εἴπῃ τις τῶν πατέρων ὅτι οὐχ ὑπέμεινε φ. τὸ σῶμα τοῦ Χριστοῦ, τοῦτο λέγει, ὅτι οὐ διαμπὰξ ἐλύθη †Leont.B.*sect.*10.2(M.86.1261C); **2.** *defilement*, i.e. *sin*, esp. of the flesh οὗτος ὁ αἰὼν...λέγει μοιχείαν καὶ φ. καὶ φιλαργυρίαν *2Clem.*6.4; **3.** *corruption*, of corruptible state of present life πρὶν ἐκδύσασθαι τὴν φ. Clem.*ecl.*12(p.140.10; M.9.704B); id.*str.*3.9 (p.225.12; M.8.1165C) cit. s. γένεσις; ὁ δὲ ἄνθρωπος...τῆς ἀφθαρσίας ἐν μέσῳ βεβηκὼς καὶ τῆς φ., εἰς ὁποτέραν ⟨ἂν⟩ αὐτῶν νεύσας προσκλιθῇ... ἐκκλίνας μὲν γὰρ εἰς τὴν φ. φθαρτὸς γίνεται καὶ θνητός Meth.*symp.*3.7 (p.34.6; M.18.72A); τὸ ἡμέτερον σῶμα οὐ φ. ἢ ἀφθαρσία τυγχάνον δέχεται κατὰ διαφόρους χρόνους τὰς ἐγκειμένας οὐσιώδεις ποιότητας Didym.*1Cor.*15:42f.(p.10.2); ref. Fall ἀθάνατον δὴ τὸν ἄνθρωπον γεγονέναι φαίνεται, φθορᾶς τε ἁπάσης καὶ νόσων ἐκτός Meth.*res.*1.34 (p.272.10; M.41.1097D); ἡ σὰρξ οὐκ οὖσα οὔτε φ. οὔτε ἀφθαρσία, ἐκρατήθη δὲ διὰ τὴν ἡδονὴν ὑπὸ τῆς φ., ποίημα τῆς ἀφθαρσίας καὶ κτῆμα ὑπάρχουσα *ib.*2.18(p.368.14; M.18.284A); *ib.*2.21(p.375.2; 285C); μετὰ τὸ μετοικισθῆναι τὸν ἄνθρωπον ἐκβληθέντα διὰ τὴν παράβασιν, τὸ ῥεῦμα τῆς φ. ἐπὶ πολὺ προσεχύθη id.*symp.*4.2(p.46.7; 88C); contrast εἰ...παραβαῖεν...γιγνώσκοιεν ἑαυτοὺς τὴν ἐν θανάτῳ κατὰ φύσιν φ. ὑπομένειν καὶ μηκέτι μὲν ἐν παραδείσῳ ζῆν, ἔξω δὲ τούτου λοιπὸν ἀποθνήσκοντας μένειν ἐν τῷ θανάτῳ καὶ ἐν τῇ φ. Ath.*inc.*3.4(M.25. 101C); man's state discussed; ref. Adam's sin, Proc.G.*Gen.*3:18(M.

87.216C,D); of salvation from corruption by Inc. and Resurrection οἱ δὲ ἄνθρωποι...συμβουλίᾳ τοῦ διαβόλου εἰς τὰ τῆς φ. ἐπιστραφέντες ἑαυτοῖς αἴτιοι τῆς ἐν τῷ θανάτῳ φ. γεγόνασιν...διὰ γὰρ τὸν συνόντα τούτοις λόγον καὶ ἡ κατὰ φύσιν φ. τούτων οὐκ ἤγγιζε Ath.*inc*.5.1(M.25.104D); τὴν παρ' αὐτοῦ γενομένην τῆς φ. ἀπάλειψιν *ib*.22.4(136B); ἀπεσόβησε μὲν αὐτῆς [sc. τῆς σαρκός] τὴν φ. Cyr.*Lc*.22:19(M.72.909A); Thdt.*Eph*.1:10(3.405); Max.*ambig*.(M.91.1044D) cit. s. θεουργέω; ref. baptism ἵνα θάνατος θανάτῳ λυθῇ, ἀναστάσει δὲ ἡ φ.· διὰ γὰρ πατρὸς καὶ υἱοῦ καὶ ἁγίου πνεύματος σφραγισθεὶς ἀνεπίληπτός ἐστι πάσῃ τῇ ἄλλῃ δυνάμει καὶ διὰ τριῶν ὀνομάτων πάσης τῆς ἐν φ. τριάδος ἀπηλλάγη Clem.*exc.Thdot*.80(p.131.27; M.9.696B); τῶν ἀποκαθαιρομένων τὴν φ. τῷ λουτρῷ Meth.*symp*.8.6(p.88.6; 148A); διὰ τῆς παλιγγενέσεως τοῦ παναγίου βαπτίσματος, τῆς μὲν προτέρας ἐλευθεροῦντα φ. Thdt.*Ps*.18:15(1.724); ref. birth of Christ τὴν παρθενικὴν καὶ καθαρὰν γέννησιν καὶ ἀπὸ μηδεμιᾶς φ. τοῦ...σώματος Or.*Cels*.6.73(p.142.24; M.11.1408C); ref. Christ's human nature μὴ τοῖς τῆς φ. ἔξωθεν ἐνικλυσθεὶς ῥεύμασιν Meth.*symp*.3.5(p.31.22; 68C); Christ's body not committed to φθορά and ἀπώλεια, Eus.*l.C*.15.2(p.244.23; M.20.1413C); αὐτὸ δὲ τὸ σῶμα φύσιν ἔχον θνητὴν ὑπὲρ τὴν αὐτοῦ φύσιν ἀνέστη διὰ τὸν ἐν αὐτῷ λόγον, καὶ πέπαυται μὲν τῆς κατὰ φύσιν φ. ἐνδυσάμενον δὲ τὸν ὑπὲρ ἄνθρωπον λόγον, γέγονεν ἄφθαρτον Thdt.*eran*.3(4.239); Christol. εἴ τις...τὴν θεότητα αὐτοῦ φθορὰν...ὑπομεμενηκέναι λέγοι, ἀνάθεμα ἔστω *Symb.Sirm*.1 *anath*.13; of Devil φ. καὶ λύμη ὑπάρχων Ath.*ep.Amun*.(M.26.1172A).

***φθορεργάτης, ὁ,** *worker of corruption*, Thdr.Stud.*epp*.2.156(M.99.1489B).

***φθοριμαῖος,** *corrupt*, *pernicious*, *destructive*, of words, doctrines, etc. ξένην τε καὶ φθοριμαίαν ψευδοδοξίαν Eus.*h.e*.4.28.1(M.20.400A); ἔχοντες φ. ὑπόνοιαν Epiph.*ep.Arab*.78.22(p.472.4; M.42.733B); φ. δὲ γνῶσιν <σχηματί>ζονται id.*haer*.38.3(p.66.19; M.41.657D); of persons τὸ ἄθροισμα οἱ φ. ... μαγγανείας ἕνεκα ἐποιοῦντο *ib*.30.8(p.343.20; 420A); of demons, Thdt.*h.e*.4.8.4(3.957).

***φθοροκτόνος,** *ending* or *saving from destruction*, ref. Resurrection ἡ φ. φύσις Geo.Pis.*carm*.75.2(14 p.61).

***φθοροποιΐα, ἡ,** *poisoning*, Leont.H.*Nest*.5.20(M.86.1741D).

φθοροποιός, 1. *deadly*, *bringing destruction* τοῦ ἀντικειμένου φ. διαβόλου Ptol.*ep*.ap.Epiph.*haer*.33.3(p.451.3; M.41.557B); οὐ φ. θεοῦ ἀλλὰ δικαίου καὶ μισοπονήρου *ib*.(p.451.17; 557C); φ. δαίμων Eus.*h.e*.10.4.58(M.20.872C); of fruit of tree of knowledge, Gr.Nyss.*hom.12 in Cant*.(M.44.1021C); met., *pernicious*, of doctrine, etc. τὴν φ. ... διδασκαλίαν Alex.Al.*ep.Alex*.2(p.21.1; M.18.552A); τῆς...φ. ὑπονοίας Epiph.*haer*.66.55(p.91.27; M.42.112B); φ. ψευδοδοξίαν *Chron.Pasch*.p.260(M.92.633C); **2.** *subject to corruption* ὁ σαρκικὸς...οὑτοσὶ καὶ φ. ... βίος Clem.*paed*.2.1(p.156.11; M.8.384B); ταῦτα γεώδη καὶ θνητὰ καὶ μέρη τῆς κάτω φ. καὶ γεώδους φύσεως Eus.*d.e*.4.3(p.154.11; M.22.257A).

φίβλα, ἡ, (Lat. *fibula*) *brooch*; used with chlamys at emperor's coronation, *Euchol*.(p.726).

φιβλίον, τό, *clasp*, for f.l. βιβλίον, Cosm.Mel.*schol*.(M.38.450) in Gr.Naz.*carm*.2.1.34.193ff.

***φιβλ-όω,** *pierce*, *transfix* τοὺς αὐτοῦ πόδας ∼οῖ ἐπὶ τὰ σφυρά Jo.Mal.*chron*.5 p.111(M.97.204A); ∼ωθεὶς ὁ Ἀχελῷος *ib*.6 p.165(268C).

***φιδεκόμμισσον (*φειδεκόμμισσον), τό,** (Lat. *fideicommissum*) *legacy in trust*, Gr.Naz.*test*.(M.37.389C); φειδ-, Phot.*nomoc*.2.1(p.489; M.104.569C).

***φικόλα, ἡ,** ? *jar*, *water-pot* (cf. Mod. Gr. βίκα, βικοῦλλα) ἔοικε δὲ εἶναι κατὰ τὸν Σηθιανῶν λόγον...τὸ σκοτεινὸν ὕδωρ...ἡ φ. Hipp.*haer*.5.20(p.122.11; M.16.3187A), v. περεηφικόλα.

φιλαγαθία, ἡ, *love of goodness*, Clem.*paed*.1.8(p.130.29; M.8.333B); Maximinus Daia ap.Eus.*h.e*.9.7.14(M.20.813C); Chrys.*hom.21.4 in Heb*.(12.200A).

φιλάγαθος, *loving goodness*; of God, Isid.Pel.*epp*.3.153(M.78.845A); Cyr.*Mich*.53(3.444D); Dion.Ar.*e.h*.7.3.7(M.3.564B).

***φιλαγαθοσύνη, ἡ,** *love of goodness*, Chrys.*hom.27.7 in Gen*.(4.267A).

φιλαγάθως, *benignantly*, Clem.*str*.4.23(p.314.11; M.8.1357C); κρίνει ὁ θεὸς ἢ φ. ἢ δικαίως Cyr.*Ps*.18:11(M.69.833A); id.*Os*.71(3.107A).

***φιλάγγελος,** *loving angels*, Dion.Ar.*c.h*.13.4(M.3.320C).

***φιλαγέννητος,** *fond of term 'unbegotten'*, Gr.Naz.*or*.23.7(M.35.1160A); *ib*.29.11(p.89.8; M.36.88C).

***φίλαγνος,** *chaste*, Jo.Clim.*scal*.1(M.88.636B); Jo.D.*hom*.9.19(M.96.752B); ‡Gr.Naz.*Chr.pat*.2590(M.38.337A).

φιλάγρυπνος, *watchful*, Cyr.*Jo*.4.6(4.427E).

***φιλαγρύπνως,** *watchfully*, Cyr.*Jo*.12.1(4.1122B).

φιλάγων, *fond of contests*, Steph.Diac.*v.Steph*.(M.100.1120A).

φιλαδελφέω, *show brotherly love*, Gr.Naz.*ep*.215(M.37.352A).

φιλαδελφία, ἡ, 1. *brotherly love*, between Christians φ. ἡ φιλανθρωπία τοῖς τοῦ αὐτοῦ πνεύματος κεκοινωνηκόσιν Clem.*str*.2.9(p.135.7; M.8.977A); ἐπὶ τῆς ψυχῆς ἀρετῇ, πίστει καὶ...ἀγάπῃ καὶ φ. id.*q.d.s*.18(p.171.9; M.9.621C); Pall.*v.Chrys*.3(p.17.1; M.47.12); φ. ἐνταῦθα τὴν τῶν χρημάτων φιλοτιμίαν ἐκάλεσε Thdt.*1Thess*.4:10(3.517); as complimentary style of address, Pall.*v.Chrys*.19(p.120.3; M.47.67); **2.** in concrete sense, *brotherhood*, *1Clem*.47.5.

φιλαδέλφως, *affectionately*, *in a brotherly manner*, Clem.*q.d.s*.3(p.161.10; M.9.605D).

***φιλάζω,** *pretend friendship*, †Cyr.*coll.VT*(6^{4}.51A; M.77.1252A).

***φιλαίθριος,** *loving fresh air*, Gr.Naz.*carm*.2.1.11.1356(M.37.1122A).

***φιλαινίδειος,** *following the doctrines of Philaenis* of Leucadia, Just.*2apol*.15.3(M.6.468C).

***φιλαιρετικός,** *fond of heretics*, Bas.*ep*.237.2(3.365D; M.32.888A).

***φιλακροάμων, ὁ,** *one who listens attentively*, *eagerly*, Cyr.*Os*.proem.(3.2A); Zach.Mit.*opif*.(M.85.1037A); Mod.*dorm*.1(M.86.3280B).

φιλαλήθης, *loving truth*, Clem.*prot*.1(p.8.21; M.8.64B); Or.*Cels*.2.15(p.144.15; M.11.825B); αἱ φ. γραφαί *ib*.6.16(p.86.23; 1313C); φ. λογισμῷ *Hom.Clem*.1.18; ἡ σὴ εὐσέβεια φ. οὖσα Ath.*apol.Const*.1(p.279.15; M.25.597A); in complimentary address φ. βασιλεῦ *ib*.9(605B); *ib*.26(628A); superl., Pall.*v.Chrys*.4(p.25.29; M.47.17); *ib*.13(p.79.14; M.47.45); neut. as subst.; **1.** *love of truth* or *fact*, Or.*Cels*.4.44(p.317.22; 1101A); *ib*.1.63(p.115.19; 777B); ὁ Ματθαῖος δι' ὑπερβολὴν ἐπιεικείας τὸ φ. ὑποφαίνων τοῦ ἰδίου τρόπου Eus.*d.e*.3.5(p.126.14; M.22.216A); σκόπει...τὸ φ. τῶν ἀποστόλων, πῶς τὰ ἐλαττώματα οὐ κρύπτουσιν Chrys.*hom.87.1 in Jo*.(8.519E); **2.** title of a work by Hierocles against Christianity, Eus.*Hierocl*.1(511A; M.22.796A); title of a polemical work by Severus of Antioch, directed against John of Caesarea (saec. vi), Eust.Mon.*ep*.(M.86.920A); Anast.S.*hod*.6(M.89.105C).

φιλαλληλία, ἡ, *love of one another*, Or.*adnot.in Dt*.(M.17.28A); τί ...ἀγαπᾷ τὸ θεῖον πνεῦμα ἢ τὴν...ὁμόνοιαν καὶ τὴν φ. τῶν ἀδελφῶν; Nil.*epp*.1.146(M.79.144A); τὸ δὲ ἀγαπᾶν ἔλεος, τῆς φ. ἔχει τὰ αὐχήματα Cyr.*Mich*.56(3.448E); id.*Zach*.36(3.712D); Μωσέα τὸν...τῆς φ. εἰσηγητὴν καὶ διδάσκαλον Sophr.H.*mir.Cyr.et Jo*.27(M.87.3497D); in bad sense ἐπιζήμιον δὲ κομιδῇ τὸ μὴ ἐν καιρῷ μαλακίζεσθαι πρὸς ἀνάνδρους φ. Cyr.*ador*.6(1.180E).

φιλαλλήλως, *with love towards one another*, Cyr.*Ps*.37:12(M.69.964B); id.*Chr.un*.(5^{1}.734E).

***φιλαλλογενής,** *loving the alien*, Cyr.*glaph.Num*.(1.381C).

φιλαμαρτήμων, *prone to sin*; of persons, Or.*exc.in Ps*.36:1(M.17.120A); Tit.Bost.*Man*.2.12(M.18.1157A); Cyr.*Abac*.49(3.563B); of the flesh, Ath.*exp.Ps*.21:31(M.27.137D); τὴν φ. γνώμην Nil.*epp*.2.168(M.79.285A); Isid.Pel.*epp*.1.11(M.78.188A); Max.*ambig*.(M.91.1045B).

***φιλαμάρτητος,** *loving sin*, Gr.Nyss.*bapt.diff*.(M.46.428A); Cyr.*ador*.1(1.46E).

***φιλάμαρτος,** = foreg., Nil.*epp*.3.4(M.79.365B); Ant.Mon.*hom*.18(M.89.1485A).

***φιλάναρχος,** *upholding doctrine of* one as ἄναρχος: προσερήσομαί σε...φιλαγέννητε σὺ καὶ φ., πότερος θεὸς ἀτιμάζει μᾶλλον Gr.Naz.*or*.23.7(M.35.1160A); ref. Creation, id.*carm*.1.1.4.18(M.37.417A).

φιλανθρώπευμα, τό, *act of mercy* οὐ καθέλκεται...τὸ ἅγιον πνεῦμα ἐκ τῶν...περὶ ἡμᾶς αὐτοῦ φ. Didym.*Trin*.2.8(M.39.620A).

φιλανθρωπεύ-ω, *show kindness*, *love to men* ∼σαι τὸν ἀδελφόν, τοῦτο πρέπει Χριστιανοῖς Chrys.*hom.14.3 in 2Cor*.(10.541C); usu. med.; in gen., c. acc., Ath.*apol.Const*.35(M.25.641C); Eus.*h.e*.10.8.11(M.20.897B); Chrys.*hom.3.2 in Philm*.(11.788D); c. dat., Gr.Nyss.*v.Gr.Thaum*.(M.46.924A); abs. τὴν ἐλεημοσύνην διαφερόντως ἀγαπῶν, τὸ λαθεῖν ∼όμενος ἐθηρᾶτο...οἱ γὰρ μετ' ἐπιδείξεως ταύτην διαπραττόμενοι οὔ μοι δοκοῦσι ∼εσθαι Isid.Pel.*epp*.2.151(M.78.605C); impers. pass. τῶν δὲ ὄχλων κραζόντων φιλανθρωπευθῆναι αὐτοῖς, συνεχώρησεν ὁ Φωκᾶς Thphn.*chron*.p.247(M.108.620B); *show mercy* towards penitent, CAnc.(314)*can*.5; ref. divine love; of God, Ath.*Ar*.3.67(M.26.465C); ὁ γὰρ κύριος πολὺ ∼εται σπλαγχνιζόμενος Mac.Aeg.*hom*.4.16(M.34.484D); τὸν θεὸν θαυμάζομεν...ὅταν θαύματα ἐργάζεται, πολλῷ δὲ πλέον ὅταν ∼ηται Chrys.*hom.3.6 in Heb*.(12.37B); *Chron.Pasch*.p.324(M.92.829A); ref. Inc. πάντας εἶναι βούλεται, ἵνα καὶ ∼εσθαι δύναται Ath.*gent*.41(M.25.84A); of Christ διὰ τὴν ἡμῶν σωτηρίαν ἐφιλανθρωπεύσατο καὶ ἐν ἀνθρωπίνῳ γενέσθαι καὶ φανῆναι σώματι id.*inc*.4.3(M.25.104A); id.*Ar*.2.51(M.26.233C); Ἰουδαίοις ὁ Χριστὸς ∼εται Hesych.H.*Os*.16(M.93.1348A).

φιλανθρωπία, ἡ, *love towards men*;

A. in gen.; **1.** characteristics ἥ τε φ. ... φιλικὴ χρῆσις ἀνθρώπων ὑπάρχουσα...εἰ δ' ὁ τῷ ὄντι ἄνθρωπος ὁ ἐν ἡμῖν ἐστιν ὁ πνευματικός, φιλαδελφία ἡ φ. τοῖς τοῦ αὐτοῦ πνεύματος κεκοινωνηκόσιν Clem.*str*.2.9(p.135.3ff.; M.8.977A); τὸ ὄνομα τοῦ Ἰησοῦ...ἐμποιεῖ...φ. καὶ χρηστότητα...ἐν τοῖς...παραδεξαμένοις...τὸν περὶ θεοῦ καὶ Χριστοῦ...

λόγον Or.*Cels*.1.67(p.121.25; M.11.785C); ἡ φ. μέγιστον ἀγαθόν *Clem. ep*.8(M.2.44A); ἀγνοεῖν τί ποτ' ἐστὶ φιλανθρωπίας μέγεθος, ἥτις ἐστὶν ἡ ἄνευ τοῦ φυσικῶς πείθοντος ἡ πρὸς οἷον δήποτε στοργὴ καθὸ ἄνθρωπός ἐστιν *Hom.Clem*.12.25; φ. ἐστὶν ἀρρενόθηλυς, ἧς τὸ θῆλυ μέρος ἐλεημοσύνη λέγεται, τὸ δὲ ἄρρεν αὐτῆς ἀγάπη πρὸς τὸν πλησίον ὠνόμασται...χρὴ οὖν τὸν ἀσκοῦντα μιμητὴν εἶναι τοῦ θεοῦ, εὐεργετοῦντα δικαίους καὶ ἀδίκους...εἰ δὲ θέλεις ἀγαθοὺς μὲν εὐεργετεῖν, κακοὺς δὲ μηκέτι...οὐ τὸ τῆς φ. σπουδάζεις ἔχειν *ib*.12.26; cf.*ib*.12.32; πολλὴ δὲ διαφορὰ μεταξὺ φιλίας καὶ φ. ὅτι ἡ μὲν φιλία ἐξ ἀμοιβῆς γίνεται *ib*.12. 25; ἀθανασίας γὰρ αἰτία οὖσα ἡ φ. πολλοῦ δίδοται...ταύτην...λαβεῖν ἔστιν ἐὰν πληροφορηθῇ τις ὅτι οἱ ἐχθροὶ πρὸς καιρὸν κακουχοῦντες οὓς μισοῦσιν, αἰωνίου κολάσεως ἀπαλλαγῆς αὐτοῖς αἴτιοι γίνονται· προσέτι δὲ αὐτοὺς ὡς εὐεργέτας σφόδρα ἀγαπήσουσιν. ἡ δὲ ὁδὸς τοῦ ταύτην λαβεῖν...ἐστὶ φόβος θεοῦ *ib*.12.33; as an attribute of Christians, *ib*. 9.23; ὁ δὲ διδάσκαλος...ἐλεεῖν συνεβούλευσεν ὡς φ. ἀσκοῦσιν...ἀδικουμένους καὶ ἀπολύειν τῆς καταδίκης τοὺς ἀδικοῦντας *ib*.12.30; of Christian doctrine ὁ *Κέλσος*...τὴν τοῦ λόγου φ. καὶ φθάνουσαν ἐπὶ πᾶσαν ψυχὴν...οἴεται εἶναι ἰδιωτικήν Or.*Cels*.1.27(p.79.8; 712C); **2.** in objective sense πλὴν ὅσων ἀπολαύομεν ἀγαθῶν, τῷ αὐτοῦ ἐλέῳ εἰς τὴν ἡμετέραν φ. βιάζεται τὴν κτίσιν *Hom.Clem*.11.10; **3.** in bad sense στερηθέντες γὰρ τῆς Ἰησοῦ βοηθείας δι' ὑπερηφανίας ἢ φ. ἢ κενοδοξίας Hesych.S.*temp*.1.52(M.93.1497B).

B. of divine love towards humanity (cf. ἀγάπη); **1.** of God, in gen. ὁ γὰρ θεὸς ἐκ πολλῆς τῆς φ. ἀντέχεται τοῦ ἀνθρώπου Clem.*prot*.10 (p.67.20; M.8.204B); id.*q.d.s*.3(p.161.30; M.9.608B); διὰ δὲ τὴν ἐκείνου φ., καὶ ἡμῖν τοῖς ἀνθρώποις τὰ τῆς αἰωνίου ζωῆς ἀψευδῶς ἐπήγγελται Cyr.H.*catech*.18.29; Euthal.Diac.*epp.cath*.(M.85.618A) cit. s. ἀνεξικακία; ἐξιστάμενοι τῆς φ. τὸν κύριον ὅτι μὴ ἄρδην τὸ ὅλον συνέστειλεν Petr.II Al.*encycl*.ap.Thdt.*h.e*.4.22.6(3.988); φιλανθρωπίας δὲ γενομένης παρὰ θεοῦ ἐπὶ τὸ χεῖρον πάλιν γεγόνασιν [sc. οἱ ἄνθρωποι] Thphn.*chron*.p.196(M.108.508B); extended also towards animals, Thdt.*Ps*.35:8(1.831); as a divine attribute σωφροσύνην καὶ...φ. καὶ ὅσα οἰκεῖα θεῷ ἐστι Just.*1apol*.10.1(M.6.340C); ἐστὶ θεὸς...εὐεργέτης, φ. νομιστεύων *Hom.Clem*.2.45; compared with human beneficence ὅσον σταγὼν πρὸς πέλαγος ἄπειρον, τοσοῦτον ἡμῶν ἡ ἀγαθότης πρὸς τὴν ἄφατον αὐτοῦ φ. Chrys.*hom.in Mt.18:23*(3.5B); shown in making man in divine image, *Hom.Clem*.16.19; ref. Mosaic law ὅτι ὁ νόμος ἀπαγορεύει ἀδελφῷ δανίζειν...ἆρ' οὐ δοκεῖ σοι φιλανθρωπίας εἶναι τὸ παράγγελμα τοῦτο; Clem.*str*.2.18(p.157.24; M.8.1024A); shown in admonishing wrongdoers, id.*prot*.9(p.62.11; M.8.193A); id.*paed*.1.8 (p.133.12; M.8.340A); and even in afflictions, *Hom.Clem*.15.9; shown towards penitents ἡ γὰρ χρηστότης καὶ ἡ φ. τοῦ θεοῦ...τὸν μετανοοῦντα ἀπὸ τῶν ἁμαρτημάτων...ὡς δίκαιον καὶ ἀναμάρτητον ἔχει Just. *dial*.47.5(M.6.577C); εὖ ποιεῖ δὲ ἐπὶ μετανοίᾳ ἡ φ. Clem.*prot*.10(p.75. 7; 220C); contrast false conception τῇ τοῦ θεοῦ φ. ταῦτα φθέγγονται ...πάντα ὁ θεὸς ἀφίησιν ἡμῖν τὰ ἁμαρτήματα Chrys.*hom.28.1 in Jo*. (8.158C); expressed in Christ's Inc. and death; by pre-existent Word, Clem.*paed*.1.8(p.126.26; M.8.325A); id.*str*.7.2(p.7.23; M.9. 412B) cit. s. εὐπάθεια; Or.*Cels*.4.15(p.284.30; M.11.1045B); ἡ ἡμῶν παράβασις τοῦ λόγου τὴν φ. ἐξεκαλέσατο Ath.*inc*.4.2(M.25.104A); by Father, *Diogn*.9.2; κατὰ τὴν τοῦ πατρὸς φ. καὶ τὴν σφαγὴν ἀνεδέξατο Or.*Jo*.6.53(35; p.162.7; M.14.292D); κατὰ φ. καὶ ἀγαθότητα τοῦ ἑαυτοῦ πατρός,...ἐν ἀνθρωπίνῳ σώματι ἡμῖν πεφανέρωται Ath.*inc*.1.3(97C); **2.** of Logos μιγνύμενος γὰρ ὁ λόγος φιλανθρωπίᾳ ἰᾶταί τε ἅμα τὰ πάθη καὶ ἀνακαθαίρει τὰς ἁμαρτίας Clem.*paed*.1.6(p.120.21; M.8.309C); **3.** of Christ τῆς φ. αὐτοῦ ἔργον ἐστὶ καταλιπεῖν τὴν οἰκίαν καὶ ἀπιέναι πρὸς τοὺς μὴ δυναμένους ἥκειν πρὸς αὐτόν Or.*comm.in Mt*.10.1(p.1. 5; M.13.836A); id.*Jo*.6.57(37; p.165.34; M.14.300B) cit. s. ἁρπαγμός; μάθε καὶ τοῦ σταυρωθέντος τὴν φ. ... λέγει '*Πάτερ ἄφες αὐτοῖς*' Chrys. *hom.4.9 in Ac.princ*.(3.95A); ref. future reward '*εἴσελθε εἰς τὴν χαρὰν τοῦ κυρίου σου*' ἧς γένοιτο πάντας ἡμᾶς ἐπιτυχεῖν χάριτι καὶ φ. τοῦ κυρίου...Ἰησοῦ Χριστοῦ ‡Hipp.*consumm*.49(p.309.22; M.10.952A); Chrys.*hom.3.6 in Heb*.(12.37C); ‡Nil.*tract*.4(M.79.1285B); **4.** of H. Ghost (ref. Rom.8:26) τοὺς ἡμετέρους διὰ τὴν πολλὴν φ. ... ἀναδεχόμενον στεναγμοὺς Or.*or*.2.3(p.301.14; M.11.420C); **5.** *clemency, providence* εὔξασθε ὑπὲρ ἐμοῦ ἵνα ἀποθῶμαι τὸ ἐν τῇ γαστρὶ μετὰ φ. Marc.Diac.*v.Porph*.39; *Chron.Pasch*.p.335(M.92.872A).

C. *clemency, mercy* in interpreting law, towards those committing impieties τῶν ἁγίων πατέρων φ. ἐπ' αὐτῶν χρησαμένων Gr.Nyss.*ep. can*.(M.45.225D); *ib*.(228A); towards penitents, CAnc.(314)*can*.5; towards those abandoning schism, Jul.Papa *ep.Dian*.ap.Ath.*apol. sec*.28(p.108.21; M.25.296C); towards those who profess virginity and subsequently marry, CChalc.*can*.16; of emperor ἡ δὲ τοῦ θεοῦ χάρις...τὴν εὐσέβειαν τοῦ βασιλέως εἰς φιλανθρωπίαν κεκίνηκε Ath. *apol.sec*.9(p.95.19; 265A); CSard.*ep.Alex.ib*.39(p.117.26; 316B); as complimentary title in address to emperor παρὰ τῇ σῇ φ. Ath. *apol.Const*.2(p.280.1; M.25.597A); *ib*.10(608A); id.*syn*.55(p.278.12; M.26.792B).

φιλάνθρωπος, **A.** *loving mankind, benevolent*; **1.** of divine love, *Diogn*.8.7; τοσούτῳ τινές εἰσιν ἀθεώτεροι ὅσῳ φιλανθρωπότερος ὁ θεός Clem.*prot*.9(p.62.32; M.8.193B); καταστήσας δὲ εἰς δέος τὴν ἐπὶ τὰς ἁμαρτίας ἀνέκοψεν φορὰν καὶ τὸ φ. αὐτοῦ ἐνδείκνυται id.*paed*.1.8(p.129. 34; M.8.332B); ἐνδείκνυταί τε παρὰ τὴν οἰκονομίαν τῆς ἀπειλῆς ἡσυχῇ τὸ φ. τὸ ἑαυτοῦ *ib*.(p.130.30; 333B); *ib*.(p.133.24; 340B) cit. s. ἐμπαθής; ἆρά γε καὶ ὁ θεὸς μέλλων ποτὲ κρίνειν...οὐ φ. ἐστιν;... τοὐναντίον λέγεις. ἐπεὶ γὰρ κρίνει διὰ τοῦτο φ. ἐστιν *Hom.Clem*.12.27; ὁ θεὸς ἡμῶν ὡς φ. χαρίσεται ἡμῖν τὸν φόβον αὐτοῦ Dor.*doct*.4.11(M.88. 1673D); towards penitents, Just.*dial*.107.2(M.6.725A); Clem.*paed*.1. 9(p.134.26; 341A); of Logos, *ib*.1.1(p.91.17; 252B); *ib*.1.7(p.124.22; 320B); ὅρα δὲ εἰ μὴ φιλανθρωπότερον ὁ θεῖος λόγος εἰσάγει τὸν 'ἐν ἀρχῇ πρὸς τὸν θεόν', θεὸν λόγον γινόμενον σάρκα Or.*Cels*.7.42(p.193.5; M. 11.1481B); Ath.*inc*.15.2(M.25.121C); as παιδαγωγός, Clem.*paed*.1.3 (p.94.5; 257A); *ib*.3.8(p.261.21; 613B); of Christ τὸ φ. αὐτοῦ μὴ ὑπερορῶντος...οὐδὲ κώμην τινὰ τῆς Ἰουδαίας ἵνα πανταχοῦ ἀπαγγείλῃ τὴν βασιλείαν τοῦ θεοῦ Or.*Cels*.2.38(p.163.19; 860B); διὰ τὸ πρὸς ἐκείνους φ. θέλων μὴ παθεῖν τὸν λαὸν ἃ ἔμελλε πάσχειν φησὶ τὸ 'πάτερ εἰ δυνατόν ἐστι παρελθέτω ἀπ' ἐμοῦ τὸ ποτήριον τοῦτο' *ib*.2.25(p.155.9; 845B); **2.** of abstracts, met. ὀλιγωρεῖται...τὸ ἀγαθὸν χρηστευόμενον ἀεί, θεραπεύεται δὲ ὑπομιμνῆσκον τῷ φ. τῆς δικαιοσύνης φόβῳ Clem. *paed*.1.9(p.140.28; M.8.353B); κοινωνικὸν δὲ ἡ σοφία καὶ φ. id.*str*.1.1 (p.3.16; M.8.689A); of Mosaic law, *ib*.2.18(p.161.21; 1032A); of Christian law, Or.*Cels*.3.8(p.209.5; M.11.929C); **3.** of emperor, Ath. *ep.Aeg.Lib*.23(M.25.592A); id.*apol.sec*.3(p.89.13; M.25.252C); id.*apol. Const*.3(M.25.600A).

B. *lenient, merciful* μέχρις ἂν τῷ κοινῷ τῶν ἐπισκόπων δόξῃ τὴν φιλανθρωποτέραν...ἐκθέσθαι ψῆφον CNic.(325)*can*.5; *ib*.12.

φιλανθρώπως, *lovingly towards mankind* τὸν θεὸν...λογικῶς καὶ φ. κατηχοῦντα Clem.*prot*.10(p.75.1; M.8.220C); ref. Inc. εἰ μὴ τῇ φύσει τῶν ἀνθρώπων ἡνώθη φ. Isid.Pel.*epp*.1.124(M.78.265A); *ib*.1.310 (361C); comp., Clem.*paed*.1.7(p.124.29; M.8.321A); superl., Or.*Cels*. 3.75(p.267.9; M.11.1017C).

***φιλαπατέων**, *loving to deceive*, Diad.*perf*.56(p.62.20).

***φιλαπερίγραπτος**, *following the doctrine that Christ is ἀπερίγραπτος*, Thdr.Stud.*antirr*.1.4(M.99.332D).

***φιλαπόστολος**, *loving the apostles*, ‡Dion.Al.*ep.Paul.Sam*.2.9 (p.36); φιλοπροφήτης...ὁ σωτὴρ καὶ φ. Cyr.*Jo*.2.5(4.200D).

φιλάρπαξ, *ravening*, Geo.Pis.*Heracl*.2.95(M.92.1323B).

φιλαυτέω, *love oneself, be self-centred*, Or.*Jo*.28.23(18; p.418.6; M. 14.729A); Cyr.*Jo*.6.1(4.646B).

φιλαυτία, ἡ, *love of self* ἀρχὴ κακῶν τῇ ψυχῇ ἡ φ. γέγονεν· φ. δέ ἐστιν ἡ τοῦ σώματος φ. Thal.*cent*.2.4(M.91.1437B); ἐκ γὰρ τῆς περὶ θεοῦ ἀγνοίας ἡ φ. Max.*ep*.2(M.91.397A); alleged of Christ 'ὁ μὴ πιστεύων ἤδη κέκριται'...τὸν μὲν γὰρ Χριστὸν ἐνόμισαν ἂν φ. ἕνεκεν ταῦτα... φθέγγεσθαι καὶ κομπάζειν Chrys.*hom.31.1 in Jo*.(8.176A).

***φιλείδωλος**, *prone to idol-worship*, ‡Ath.*qu.Ant*.4(M.28.601B); Sophr.H.*mir.Cyr.et Jo*.31(M.87.3521C).

***φιλειρηνικός**, *peace-loving*; of Constantine, Jo.Nic.*nativ*.(M.96. 1440C).

***φιλείρηνος**, = foreg., Heracl.*ep*.(M.92.993C).

φιλεκδημητής, *inclined to travel about* μὴ ἔσο φ. περιάγων τὰς κώμας †Ph.Carp.*ep*.(p.396.9; v.l. φιλενδείκτης M.32.352B).

***φιλεκκλήσιος**, *loving the Church*, Max.*ep*.44(M.91.645D); *ib*.45 (649A).

***φιλέλεος**, *merciful*, Cyr.*Joel*.26(Aubert; πολυέλ- 3.219D).

φιλέμπορος, *fond of trading*, Ast.Am.*hom*.13(M.40.368B); Nonn. *par.Jo*.2:14(M.43.764A); fig. οἱ τοῦ λόγου φ. Amph.*mesopent*.(M.39. 124A).

***φιλενδείκτης, ὁ**, *ostentatious person* ἀποκαλεῖ τὸν σπουδαῖον ἐν ψαλμῳδίᾳ φ. Ephr.1.13E; †Ph.Carp.*ep*.(M.32.352B; φιλεκδημητής p.396.9); κενόδοξός ἐστι πᾶς φ. Jo.Clim.*scal*.22(M.88.949C).

***φιλενδειξία, ἡ**, *ostentation*, Max.*cap.theol*.21(M.90.1092A).

***φιλέννυχος**, *shining through the darkness* φέγγος ἔλαμπε φ. Paul. Sil.*Soph*.827(M.86.2150B).

φιλέντολος, ὁ, *lover of* God's *commandments*, Pall.*h.Laus*.52 (p.145.6–8not.; M.34.1217B).

φιλέορτος, *loving festivals*, Gr.Naz.*or*.5.35(M.35.709C); Gr.Nyss. *res*.3(M.46.652D); τὴν φ. τοῦ θεοῦ ἐκκλησίαν ‡Meth.*palm*.1(M.18. 384A).

***φιλεπίσκοπος**, *loving guidance*, Jo.Clim.*scal*.1(M.88.636B).

φιλεπίστροφος, *recrudescent*, ‡Nil.*vit.cog*.(M.79.1448B); Jo.Clim. *scal*.3(M.88.664D).

φιλεπιτιμητής, ὁ, *censorious person*, *Const.App*.2.21.1.

***φιλεργασία**, ἡ, *congenial task*, Or.*adnot.in Dt.*20:5(M.17.28D).

***φιλεργάτης**, ὁ, *hard worker*, Thdr.Stud.*cant.*2.4(p.339).

***φιλεργάτις**, ἡ, fem. of foreg. τὴν μέλισσαν τὴν φ. Geo.Pis.*hex.* 1328(M.92.1537A).

***φιλεργής**, *welcoming work*, Cyr.*Os.*4(3.23A).

***φιλερημέω**, *love solitude*, Pall.*v.Chrys.*19(p.123.11; M.47.69).

φιλεριστ-έω, *strive, argue*, Just.*dial.*118.1(M.6.749A); *ib.*123.7 (764B); περὶ τούτου τοῦ κεφαλαίου μὴ ~ήσαντες πρὸς ἑαυτούς Iren. ap.Eus.*h.e.*5.24.16(M.20.505B); ἐπιδεικνύναι ~οῦσιν Iren.*haer.*1.18.4 (M.7.649B).

***φιλεριστικῶς**, *contentiously*, Iren.*haer.*5.13.2(M.7.1157B).

φιλέριστος, *contentious*, Just.*dial.*64.2(M.6.621C); *ib.*67.11(632C).

***φιλερίστως**, *contentiously, for the sake of argument*, Adam.*dial.* 3.1(p.116.1; M.11.1792C).

***φιλευγενής**, *loving nobility*, Thphyl.*exc.gent.*5(p.482.9; M.113. 941C).

φιλεύδιος, *loving calm weather*, Geo.Pis.*bell.Avar.*128(M.92.1273A).

***φιλευλαβής**, *loving piety*, Cyr.*Jo.*2.5(4.201E).

***φιλεύνοος**, *benignant*, ‡Caes.Naz.*dial.*192(M.38.1169).

φιλευποιΐα, ἡ, *kindliness, love of good deeds*, Ephr.1.72C.

***φιλευπρόσωπος**, *under cloak of respectability*, ‡Pion.*v.Polyc.*14; ἡ γὰρ πολυγαμία...φιλευπρόσωπος πορνεία †Bas.*contub.*10(M.30.825B).

***φιλευσεβέω**, *love piety*, Sophr.H.*carm.*5.58(M.87.3757B).

***φιλευσεβής**, *reverent* φ. λογισμὸς ἐσοφίσατο τὸ ἀδύνατον Ast.Am. *hom.*9(M.40.312A); τῆς Ῥωμαίων ἡγεμονίας ἄνδρες φ. *ib.*(313A); Jo. Eleem.*v.Tych.*2(p.112).

***φιλεύσπλαγχνος**, *showing pity, compassionate*, of God ὡς κηδεμών, ὡς φ. ‡Chrys.*Bass.*1(2.725C); *Apophth.Patr.*(M.65.397D); of BMV, Ephr.3.526A; Jo.VI H.*v.Jo.D.*18(M.94.457A).

***φιλευσπλάγχνως**, *kindly*, †Jo.Jej.*poenit.*(M.88.1901D).

***φιλεχθρία**, ἡ, *pleasure in strife*, †Bas.*Is.*19(1.391E; M.30.149D).

φίλεχθρος, *discordant, hostile* συμπέφυκε...τῇ ἀσεβείᾳ τὸ φ. τε καὶ πολεμοχαρές Leont.B.*Nest.et Eut.*2(M.86.1317B); of fire and water τὴν φ. μίξιν ‡Paul.Sil.*therm.Pyth.*159(M.86.2266).

φιλέχθρως, *in a hostile manner*, Tat.*orat.*1(p.1; M.6.804A); Or. *Cels.*3.36(p.232.7; M.11.965B); Cyr.*Ps.*36:12(M.69.932B).

φιλ-έω, **1.** *love, regard with affection*; **a.** dist. from ἀγαπάω v.s.v.; **b.** used interchangeably; v. ἀγαπάω; **c.** contrasted with love of creator through his creatures οὐδὲ ἄρα ~εῖ τινα τὴν κοινὴν ταύτην φιλίαν, ἀλλ' ἀγαπᾷ τὸν κτίστην διὰ τῶν κτισμάτων Clem.*str.*6.9(p.467. 30; M.9.293A); **d.** characterized τὸν ~οῦντά με οὐχ ὅταν ἐπαινῇ με μόνον ἀλλὰ καὶ ὅταν ἐγκαλῇ καὶ διορθῶται, τότε φαίην ἂν ἔγωγε ~εῖν Chrys.*hom.3.1 in Ac.*9:1(3.115E); ὁ ~ῶν οὐκ ἐπιτάττειν βούλεται οὐδὲ ἄρχειν ἀλλὰ χάριν ἔχει μᾶλλον ἀρχόμενος καὶ ἐπιταττόμενος· χαρίζεσθαι βούλεται μᾶλλον ἢ χάριν λαμβάνειν· ~εῖ γάρ, καὶ ὡς οὐκ ἐμπλήσας αὐτοῦ τὴν ἐπιθυμίαν, οὕτω διάκειται id.*hom.2.4 in 1Thess.* (11.438E); **e.** of Christian love towards one's neighbour τοὺς πλησίον ~οῦσι [sc. οἱ Χριστιανοί] Arist.*apol.*15.4; ~ῶμεν οὖν ἀλλήλους ὡς καὶ ταύτῃ τὸν ~οῦντα ἡμᾶς ἀγαπήσοντες θεόν Chrys.*hom.23.4 in Rom.*(9.690C); ἡ ἀγάπη...εἰ οὐκ ἔστιν ἀνθρωπίνη, ἀλλὰ διὰ τὸν θεὸν ~εῖς, πάντας ~εῖ· ὁ γὰρ θεὸς οὕτως ἐπέταξε καὶ τοὺς ἐχθροὺς ~εῖν id.*hom.2.2 in 2Thess.*(11.516D); ὅταν δὲ τοὺς ἐχθροὺς ~ήσωμεν, τοῦ θεοῦ κατὰ δύναμιν ἀνθρωπίνην ὅμοιοι γεγόναμεν id.*cruc.*1.5(2.411A); ὁ μὲν γὰρ ὅτι ~εῖται ~εῖ· ὁ δὲ ὅτι ἐτιμήθη...διὰ δὲ τὸν Χριστὸν δύσκολόν ἐστιν εὑρεῖν τινα γνησίως καὶ ὡς ἐχρῆν ~εῖν τὸν πλησίον ~οῦντα...ἀλλ' οὐχ ὁ Παῦλος οὕτως ἐφίλει, ἀλλὰ διὰ τὸν Χριστόν· διὸ καὶ μὴ ~ούμενος οὕτως ὥσπερ ἐφίλει, οὐ κατέλυσε τὴν ἀγάπην, ἐπειδὴ ῥίζαν ἰσχυρὰν κατεβάλετο τοῦ φίλτρου id.*hom.61.3 in Mt.*(7.609Cff.); **f.** of man's love for God καὶ τοῦτο δόξα δεσπότου, τὸ οὕτω ~εῖν αὐτὸν τοὺς δούλους id.*hom.2.4 in Philm.*(11.785C); **g.** of God's love for man οὐ παύεται...~ῶν Clem.*prot.*10(p.68.29; M.8.208A); ~εῖται ἄρα πρὸς τοῦ θεοῦ ὁ ἄνθρωπος. πῶς γὰρ οὐ ~εῖται δι' ὃν ὁ μονογενὴς ἐκ κόλπων πατρὸς καταπέμπεται λόγος τῆς πίστεως; id.*paed.*1.3(p.94. 29; M.8.257C); Chrys.*hom.2.4 in Philm.*(11.785D); **2.** *kiss* (v. also ἀσπάζομαι); ref. custom of kissing doors of church ναός ἐσμεν τοῦ Χριστοῦ· τὰ τοίνυν πρόθυρα ~οῦμεν τοῦ ναοῦ καὶ τὴν εἴσοδον, ἀλλήλους ~οῦντες. ἢ οὐχ ὁρᾶτε ὅσοι καὶ τὰ πρόθυρα τοῦ ναοῦ τούτου ~οῦσιν... καὶ διὰ τούτων τῶν πυλῶν καὶ τῶν θυρῶν καὶ εἰσῆλθε καὶ εἰσέρχεται πρὸς ἡμᾶς ὁ Χριστός, ἡνίκα ἂν κοινῶμεν...διὰ τοῦτο...~οῦμεν Chrys. *hom.30.2 in 2Cor.*(10.650D); in gen. between Christians οὕτως ἀλλήλους ~ῶμεν ὡς ἀδελφοὺς ἀδελφοί,...καὶ ἐξ ἀποδημίας ἐπανιόντες ἀλλήλους ~οῦμεν, τῶν ψυχῶν ἐπιγινομένων εἰς τὴν πρὸς ἀλλήλους συνουσίαν *ib.30.1*(650C); at ordination πάντων αὐτὸν [sc. τὸν ἐπίσκοπον] φιλησάντων τῷ ἐν κυρίῳ φιλήματι *Lit.*ap.*Const.App.*8.5.10; **3.** med., c. dat., *be content with* τῇ χρείᾳ ~ούμενοι Serap.*ep.mon.*3 (M.40.929A).

***φιληδον-έω**, **1.** *take pleasure in, delight in*, Or.*Cels.*7.5(p.157.9; M.11.1428A); **2.** abs., *pursue pleasure* τὰ νοήματα...ἐφθάρη ~ούντων ἡμῶν Clem.*str.*3.14(p.239.16; M.8.1193C); *ib.*3.17(p.244.31; 1209A); Marc.Er.*opusc.*4(M.65.997A); Cyr.*Jo.*10.2(4.895E).

***φιληδόνως**, *in pleasure-seeking* ζῶσιν ὡς βούλονται· βούλονται δὲ φ. Clem.*str.*3.4(p.209.33; M.8.1136A); *Hom.Clem.*11.15.

φιληκοΐα, ἡ, **1.** *attentiveness, love of hearing*, Chrys.*hom.*5.4 *in 2Tim.*(11.691D); Bas.Sel.*or.*31.1(M.85.337D); in complimentary address πρὸς τὴν ὑμετέραν φιληκοΐαν βοῶ Chrys.*pan.Rom.*2.2(2. 619D); **2.** met., *observance* διὰ τὴν τοῦ νόμου φ. Vict.*Mc.*1:21(p.274. 28).

φιλήκοος, *fond of hearing* discourses, *eager to listen* εἰδὼς...σὲ δὲ τῶν αὐτοῦ [sc. τοῦ Παύλου] ῥημάτων φ. Ath.*apol.Const.*1(p.279. 5; M.25.596A); αἱ φ. τε καὶ εὐμαθεῖς...ψυχαί Cyr.*Jo.*2.1(4.131A); of S. Peter, Nonn.*par.Jo.*13:36(M.43.865B); of Joseph of Arimathea Χριστοῖο φ. ... μαθητής *ib.*19:38(905C).

φίλημα, τό, *kiss*, **1.** myst., exeg. Cant.1:2; cf. *cum enim nullo hominis vel angeli ministerio divinis sensibus et intellectibus mens repletur, tunc 'oscula' ipsius verbi dei suscepisse se credat. ... dum enim incapax fuit, ut ipsius verbi dei caperet meram solidamque doctrinam, necessaria suscepit oscula, id est sensus ab ore doctorum. ...ideo autem et pluraliter oscula posuit, ut intelligamus uniuscujusque obscuri sensus illuminationem osculum esse verbi dei ad animam perfectam delatum...os autem sponsi intelligamus virtutem dici, qua illuminat mentem et...incognita quaeque sibi et obscura manifestat et hoc est verius propiusque, et sanctius osculum, quod ab sponso dei verbo porrigi dicitur sponsae, purae scilicet animae et perfectae. cujus rei imago est illud osculum, quod in ecclesia sub tempore mysteriorum nobis invicem damus*, Or.*Cant.*1(p.91.16ff.; M. 13.85Cff.); ὁ διὰ τῆς κατὰ στόμα γινομένης αὐτῷ παρὰ τοῦ θεοῦ ὁμιλίας ...ἐν ἐπιθυμίᾳ μείζονι τῶν τοιούτων φ. ἐγένετο Gr.Nyss.*hom.1 in Cant.*(M.44.777C); ὁ κύριος...οὐδένα βούλεται τῶν σωζομένων τοῦ τοιούτου φ. εἶναι ἀμέτοχον· καθάρσιον γάρ ἐστι ῥύπου παντὸς τοῦτο τὸ φ. *ib.*(780A); φ. γὰρ πνευματικὸν φ. σαρκικοῦ πολὺ καὶ ἀσυγκρίτως διενήνοχε, καθάπερ ἡ ἡμέρα τῆς νυκτὸς φωτὶ ἐπερίσσευσεν Ph.Carp. *Cant.*1:1(M.40.33A); φ. δὲ νοοῦμεν οὐ στομάτων συνάφειαν ἀλλ' εὐσεβοῦς ψυχῆς καὶ θείου λόγου κοινωνίαν Thdt.*Cant.*1(2.28); **2.** *kiss of peace* (cf. ἀσπασμός); **a.** in greeting between Christians, *A.Andr. et Mt.*19(p.90.8); φ. ... ἅγιον καὶ σεμνὸν καὶ γνησίας ἀγάπης γέμον Chrys.*exp.in Ps.*140:3(5.436C); ἀσπάσασθε ἀλλήλους ἐν φ. ἁγίῳ. τί ἐστιν ἁγίῳ; μὴ ὑπούλῳ, μὴ δολερῷ, καθάπερ ὁ Ἰούδας τὸν Χριστὸν ἐφίλησε. διὰ γὰρ τοῦτο τὸ φ. δέδοται, ἵνα ἐμπύρευμα τῆς ἀγάπης γένηται, ἵνα ἀνακαίῃ τὴν διάθεσιν, ἵνα οὕτως ἀλλήλους φιλῶμεν, ὡς ἀδελφοὺς ἀδελφοί, ὡς παῖδες πατέρας...οὕτως αἱ ψυχαὶ ἀλλήλαις συνδέονται id. *hom.30.1 in 2Cor.*(10.650C); abused, Athenag.*leg.*32.3(M.6.964C); **b.** at eucharist ἀλλήλους φιλήματι ἀσπαζόμεθα παυσάμενοι τῶν εὐχῶν Just.*1apol.*65.2(M.6.428A); μὴ ὑπολάβῃς τὸ φ. ἐκεῖνο σύνηθες εἶναι τοῖς ἐπ' ἀγορᾶς γινομένοις ὑπὸ τῶν κοινῶν φίλων. οὐκ ἔστι τοίνυν τοιοῦτον τὸ φ. ἀνακίρνησι τὰς ψυχὰς ἀλλήλαις καὶ πᾶσαν ἀμνησικακίαν αὐταῖς μνηστεύεται. σημεῖον τοίνυν ἐστὶ τὸ φ. τοῦ ἀνακραθῆναι τὰς ψυχὰς καὶ πᾶσαν ἐξορίζειν μνησικακίαν...οὐκοῦν τὸ φ. διαλλαγή ἐστι, καὶ διὰ τοῦτο ἅγιον Cyr.H.*catech.*23.3; ἀσπαζέσθωσαν ἀλλήλους οἱ ἄνδρες καὶ ἀλλήλας αἱ γυναῖκες τὸ ἐν κυρίῳ φ. *Const.App.*2.57.17; *Lit.ib.*8.11.9; μνημονεύωμεν...τῶν ἁγίων φ. καὶ τοῦ φρικωδεστάτου ἀσπασμοῦ τοῦ πρὸς ἀλλήλους Chrys.*prod.Jud.*1.6(2.385D); ἀσπαζόμενοι μὲν ἀλλήλους μέλλοντος τοῦ δώρου προσφέρεσθαι...; ὁ δὲ κύριος...βούλεται...τὸ ἀπὸ τῆς ψυχῆς φ. καὶ τὸν ἀπὸ τῆς καρδίας ἀσπασμὸν διδόναι τῷ πλησίον ἡμᾶς id.*compunct.*1.3(1.127B); cf.*Lit.Marc.*(Brightman p.123.15,23); *Lit.Chrys.*(p.382.18); its abuse ἀγάπη δὲ οὐκ ἐν φ. ἀλλ' ἐν εὐνοίᾳ κρίνεται. οἱ δὲ οὐδὲν ἀλλ' ἢ φ. καταψοφοῦσι τὰς ἐκκλησίας, τὸ φιλοῦν ἔνδον οὐκ ἔχοντες αὐτό, καὶ...τοῦτο ἐκπέπληκεν ὑπονοίας αἰσχρᾶς καὶ βλασφημίας τὸ ἀνέδην χρῆσθαι τῷ φ. ὅπερ ἐχρῆν εἶναι μυστικόν ('ἅγιον αὐτὸ κέκληκεν ὁ ἀπόστολος)...ἔστι δὲ καὶ ἄλλο ἄναγνον φ. πλῆρες ἰοῦ ἁγιωσύνην ὑποκρινόμενον Clem.*paed.*3.11(p.281.5ff.; M.8.661A); **c.** at baptism, Chrys.*hom.3.6 in Ac.princ.*(3.81B) cit. s. εἰρήνη; **d.** at ordination, *Lit.*ap.*Const.App.*8.5.10; **3.** of Judas φ. δεδολωμένον ἔχων Clem.*paed.*2.8(p.195.6; M.8.468B); ὢ φιλήματος αἵματος πεπληρωμένου. ὢ πολέμου κεχρωσμένου φιλήματι. ὢ φίλημα δῆγμα θανάτου γενόμενον. ὢ φ. ἀσπίδων ἰὸν ἐρευγόμενον Bas.Sel.*prod.Jud.* 5(M.28.1052C); Chrys.*exp.in Ps.*140:3(5.436C).

φιλήσυχος, *loving quiet, solitude*, Nil.*Eulog.*12(M.79.1109B); Cyr. S.*v.Sab.*6(p.90.24); Thdr.Stud.*or.*12.26(M.99.880D).

φιλητής, ὁ, **1.** *lover*, Hipp.*haer.*4.23(p.52.23; M.16.3087B); *ib.*4. 24(p.53.4; 3087C); πράγματος μουσικοῦ φιληταί *ib.*(p.53.3; 3087C); **2.** *follower* γενοῦ αὐτοῦ φ. καὶ σπουδαστής Chrys.*hom.11.3 in Col.*(11. 409A); Pall.*v.Chrys.*20(p.129.1; M.47.72).

***φιλητικῶς**, *affectionately* ἡ φιλοσοφία...φ. διατεθεῖσα πρὸς τὴν σοφίαν Clem.*str*.6.7(p.459.21; M.9.277A).

φιλία, ἡ, *affectionate regard, friendship*; **1.** in gen. τριττὰ δὲ εἴδη φιλίας διδασκόμεθα...τὸ μὲν πρῶτον καὶ ἄριστον τὸ κατ' ἀρετήν...τὸ δὲ δεύτερον καὶ μέσον ⟨τὸ⟩ κατ' ἀμοιβήν...κοινὴ γὰρ ἡ ἐκ χάριτος φ.· τὸ δὲ ὕστατον...ἡμεῖς μὲν τὸ ἐκ συνηθείας φαμέν, οἱ δὲ τὸ καθ' ἡδονὴν τρεπτὸν καὶ μεταβλητόν...ἣ μὲν φιλοσόφου φ., ἣ δὲ ἀνθρώπου, ἣ δὲ ζῴου Clem.*str*.2.19(p.168.18ff.; M.8.1045B); **2.** in Christian life, characterized πάντα γὰρ κοινὰ ποιούμεθα...καὶ λύπας καὶ εὐφροσύνας· τοιοῦτον γὰρ ἡ φ. Gr.Naz.*ep*.15(M.37.48C); τοῦτό ἐστι φ., ἵνα μὴ τὰ αὐτοῦ ἑαυτοῦ τις νομίζῃ ἀλλὰ τὰ τοῦ πλησίον, τὰ δὲ αὐτοῦ ἀλλότρια Chrys.*hom.2.4 in 1Thess*.(11.438A); τεῖχος ὄντως ἀρραγὲς ἡ φ. καὶ οὐδὲ τῷ διαβόλῳ ἁλώσιμον μήτι γε ἀνθρώποις id.*hom.40.4 in Ac*.(9.307B); διὰ τοῦτο καὶ τὰς φ. ἐποίησεν ὁ θεὸς οὐκ ἐπὶ κακῷ...ἀλλ' ἐπ' ἀγαθῷ καὶ χρησίμῳ id.*hom.49.7 in Mt*.(7.503C); οὐδὲν ἡμῖν ἐστι χρηστὸν φιλίας χωρίς id.*hom.40.3 in Ac*.(9.305E); ἡ γὰρ ὑποβάθρα πάντων τῶν ἀγαθῶν...ἐστι...φ. id.*hom.7.3 in 2Tim*.(11.703A); contrasted with spiritual love τῆς μὲν σωματικῆς φ. ὀφθαλμοὶ πρόξενοι γίνονται...τὴν δὲ ἀληθινὴν ἀγάπην ἡ τοῦ πνεύματος δωρεὰ συνίστησι Bas.*ep*.133(3.225B; M.32.569B); *ib*.154(243B; M.609C); its causes ἔχομεν γὰρ φήμην πρόξενον τῆς φ., μεγαλοφώνως τὰ σὰ πᾶσιν ἀνθρώποις συμβοῶσαν *ib*.63(156E; M.420A); ὁμοτροπία...ὃ μάλιστα πήγνυσι τὰς φ. Gr.Naz.*ep*.230(M.37.373A); καὶ θλῖψις ποιεῖ φιλίας καὶ συνάγει Chrys.*hom.40.3 in Ac*.(306A); πολλαὶ προφάσεις εἰσὶν αἱ φ. ποιοῦσαι ...βιωτικαὶ μὲν οὖν εἰσιν αὗται· οἷον εὖ ἔπαθέ τις, ἀπὸ προγόνων ἐκτήσατο φίλον, ἐκοινώνησε τραπέζης ἢ ἀποδημίας...αἱ δὲ φυσικαὶ οἷον πατρὸς πρὸς υἱόν...μητρὸς πρὸς τέκνα...καὶ τὴν τῆς γυναικὸς πρὸς ἄνδρα id.*hom.1.3 in Col*.(11.325E); καὶ πάντοθεν μᾶλλόν ἐσμεν φίλοι ἢ ἀπὸ εὐσεβείας, δέον ἐκ ταύτης μόνης συνάπτεσθαι τὰς φ. id.*hom.59.5 in Mt*.(7.602A); ὃ γὰρ λέγει [sc. ὁ Χριστός] τοιοῦτόν ἐστιν· εἴ τις ἐμὲ τῆς πρὸς τὸν πλησίον φ. ὑπόθεσιν προηγουμένην ἔχει, μετ' αὐτοῦ ἔσομαι ...νῦν δὲ τοὺς πλείονας ὁρῶμεν ἑτέρας ἔχοντας φ. ἀφορμάς *ib*.61.3(609B); enjoined by Christ ὁ Χριστὸς...εἰς φ. ... καλῶν Just.*dial*.139.4(M.6.796B); causes of its dissolution ἡ κολακεία τὴν φ. ὑποδυομένη λύμη ἐστὶ τῆς φ. Bas.*ep*.272(3.418C; M.1005C); οὐδὲν γὰρ οὕτω φ. διαλύειν εἴωθεν ὡς δειλία καὶ προδοσίας φήμη Chrys.*hom.1.2 in 2Tim*.(11.661E); friendship with heretics harmful to soul, Ath.*v.Anton*.68(M.26.940B); **3.** between God and mankind (usu. ἀγάπη) ἡ τῆς εὐδαιμονίας ἐλπὶς...[sc. καί] ἡ πρὸς τὸν θεὸν ἀγάπη...τῆς θείας ἀπαρτωμένη φ. ἀδούλωτος ἄνω περιπολεῖ Clem.*str*.4.8(p.274.19; M.8.1269B); καθ' ὁμοίωσιν οὖν τοῦ θεοῦ ὁ εἰς υἱοθεσίαν καὶ φ. τοῦ θεοῦ καταταγείς ...γίνεται *ib*.6.14(p.489.21; M.9.337C); of God towards Abraham φ. ... ἐπιστατικῆς ἐστι κοινωνία id.*paed*.1.7(p.123.21; M.8.317B); δοκεῖ καὶ Πυθαγόρας σοφὸν μὲν εἶναι τὸν θεὸν λέγειν μόνον...ἑαυτὸν δὲ διὰ φ. τὴν πρὸς τὸν θεὸν φιλόσοφον id.*str*.4.3(p.252.6; 1221A); βίον ὃν Ἰησοῦς ἐδίδαξεν ἀνάγοντα ἐπὶ τὴν πρὸς θεὸν φ. Or.*Cels*.3.28(p.226.17; M.11.956D); ἡ κατὰ τοῦτον ζωῆς ἔξαψις, ᾗ καὶ ἡ πρὸς αὐτὸν [sc. τὸν θεόν] ἐγγίνεται φ. ... τῷ δὴ οὖν τὴν πρὸς αὐτὸν στειλαμένῳ φ. τί ἂν ἔτι λείποιτο; Eus.*p.e*.1.1(2B; M.21.24B); **4.** towards Christ ἀλλὰ ἀνάγκη καὶ τὴν φ. τὴν πρὸς τὸν Χριστὸν ἔχθραν ποιῆσαι πρὸς τὸν ὄφιν, καὶ τὴν φ. τὴν πρὸς τὸν ὄφιν ἔχθραν γεννῆσαι τὴν πρὸς τὸν Χριστόν Or.*hom.20.7 in Jer*.(p.188.20; M.13.517A); ὁ τὸ στάσιμον ἔχων καὶ ἀμετακίνητον τῆς εἰς Χριστὸν φ., οὗτος ἄξιος τῆς αὐτοῦ φ. Bas.*hom.in Ps*.44(1.160D; M.29.392C); τοῖς ἁγίοις ἀποστόλοις ἢ καὶ τοῖς ἄλλοις ἅπασι τυχὸν διὰ πίστεως εἰς φ. ἀναβαίνουσι τὴν πρὸς τὸν...Χριστόν Cyr.*Jo*.10.2(4.889C); **5.** of Devil σατανᾶ...ἀποτάσσομαί σοι ἐπιβούλῳ ὄντι καὶ προσποιήσει φιλίας πράξαντι πᾶσαν παρανομίαν Cyr.H.*catech*.19.4; **6.** fig., *harmony* διὰ τὸ καλὸν αἱ πάντων ἐφαρμογαὶ καὶ φ. καὶ κοινωνίαι Dion.Ar.*d.n*.4.8(M.3.704A); τἀγαθὸν...ὡς ἀπὸ μιᾶς ἀρχῆς καὶ ἑνὸς ἔκγονον αἰτίου, κοινωνίᾳ καὶ...φ. χαίρει *ib*.4.19(717A); ὁ ἀκόλαστος... μετέχει δὲ ὅμως τἀγαθοῦ κατ' αὐτὸ τὸ τῆς ἑνώσεως καὶ φ. ἀμυδρὸν ἀπήχημα *ib*.4.20(720C).

φιλιάζ-ω, *be friendly, show friendship*, Ephr.3.322F; τὸ ἑαυτῶν θέλημα ἐπιδιδόντες τῇ κακίᾳ καὶ συνηδόμενοι καὶ ∼οντες Mac.Aeg.*hom*.27.2(M.34.693D); Chrys.*exp.in Ps*.3:1(5.3E); met., of opposing elements φύσει μὲν ὄντα ἐναντία, τῇ δὲ τοῦ κυβερνῶντος βουλήσει ∼οντα Ath.*gent*.37(M.25.73B).

***φιλικά, τά**, *banquets* of kinsfolk, Jo.Mal.*chron*.7 p.180(M.97.288B).

φίλιος, *friendly*; met., of wind, *favourable*, Thdt.*provid*.4(4.538).

φιλι-όω, pass., *become friends*, of Christ τῷ λῃστῇ σταυρούμενος ἐφιλιώθη †Epiph.*num.myst*.4(M.43.513B); towards God ἵν' ἡ ψυχὴ ...φιλιωθῇ τῷ θεῷ Or.*Jo*.1.32(36; p.41.1; M.14.85B); with Devil, Martin.*ep*.13(M.*PL*.87.194B); met. οὔτε ἄσπλαγχνος...λογισμὸς τῇ ἀγαθοθελείᾳ ∼οῦσθαι ἀνέχεται Nil.*epp*.1.298(M.79.192B).

***φιλιππότης, ὁ**, *keen horseman*, Geo.Pis.*res*.79(M.92.1380B).

φιλιστορ-έω, *love research* φιλεῖ γὰρ ἐν τοῖς τοιούτοις ∼εῖν ἡ ψυχή Gr.Naz.*or*.43.7(M.36.501C).

φιλόβιβλος, *fond of the Bible*, ‡Chrys.*pseud*.1(8.73A).

***φιλόβιος**, *loving the things of this life*, Anast.S.*qu.et resp*.95(M.89.733A).

***φιλοβλαβής**, *pernicious*, Geo.Pis.*Pers*.2.198(M.92.1223B).

***φιλοβόρβορος**, *fond of the dirt*, met. ὁ μὴ τηρήσας τὴν ἐντολὴν ἀκάθαρτος...καὶ φ. Cyr.*Jo*.10(4.833E); ὁ...γήινος καὶ φ. [sc. νοῦς] id.*hom.pasch*.10(5².137B).

***φιλόβρομος**, *loving noise*, Jo.Clim.*scal*.1(M.88.636B).

***φιλογαστορίδης, ὁ**, *glutton*, Gr.Naz.*carm*.2.2(epigr.)29.6(M.38.99A).

***φιλόγλωσσος**, *talkative*, Gr.Naz.*carm*.2.1.11.1232(M.37.1113A).

***φιλογνήσιος**, *loving legitimacy* φ. φύσις Cyr.*glaph.Gen*.3(1.74D).

***φιλογράμματος, ὁ**, *book-lover*, *Pers*.(p.21.6).

***φιλογρηγόριος**, *loving the works of Gr. Naz.*; as subst., Cosm. Mel.*schol*.proem.(M.38.346).

***φιλογρήγορος**, *vigilant*, Cyr.*ep*.41(p.42.23; 5².124B).

***φιλοδαίμων**, *loving demons*, Gr.Naz.*or*.4.88(M.35.617A); id.*carm*.2.2(poem.)7.73(M.37.1556A); οἱ φ. Ἰουδαῖοι Leont.B.*mesopent*.(M.86.1980B).

[*]**φιλοδάκρυος (φιλόδακρυς)**, **1.** *prone to weeping, tearful*, Cyr.*Jo*.12(4.1064B); Μαγδαληνὴ Μαρίη φ. Nonn.*par.Jo*.19:25(M.43.904B); *ib*.20:1(908B); Sophr.H.*carm*.13.87(p.45; M.87.3800A); **2.** *woeful* τὸν φιλόδακρυν ἀποσείσασθαι πόλεμον Thphyl.*exc.gent*.(p.479.36; -δάκρυον M.113.940A).

φιλόδενδρος, *fond of trees* ἔχις...δρυΐνας καλεῖται, ἀπὸ τοῦ φ. εἶναι Epiph.*haer*.65.9(p.13.8; M.42.28D).

***φιλοδεσποτικός**, *loving one's master*, ‡Chrys.*neg*.2(8.138A).

φιλοδέσποτος, = foreg., *Const.App*.4.12.3; Chrys.*stat*.12.2(2.148A); ref. God, *M.Polyc*.2.2; Ephr.3.423D.

***φιλόδηρις**, *quarrelsome*, Gr.Naz.*carm*.1.1.7.78(M.37.444A).

***φιλοδιδάσκαλος**, *loving one's teacher*, Pall.*v.Chrys*.9(p.58.9; M.47.34).

***φιλοδοκήτης, ὁ**, *follower of docetist teaching*, Eust.Mon.*ep*.(M.86.916D).

***φιλόδολος**, *crafty, cunning*, *A.Thom*.A 159(p.271.16, cj. φειδωλός).

***φιλοέταιρος**, *companionable*, Jo.Mosch.*prat*.172(M.87.3040C).

***φιλοζηλία, ἡ**, *diligence*, Thdr.Stud.*or*.11.5(M.99.808B).

***φιλοζητητής, ὁ**, **1.** *one fond of inquiry*, Cyr.*Ps*.48:2(M.69.1068D); id.*Jo*.1.9(4.102A); id.*Is*.3.5(2.529E); **2.** *inquisitive person*, id.*hom.pasch*.24.3(5².289C).

φιλοζωέω, *love life*, Clem.*paed*.3.11(p.279.15; M.8.656B); in bad sense, id.*str*.4.4(p.256.6; M.8.1229B); Or.*Cels*.8.54(p.271.12; M.11.1600A); Chrys.*hom.9.2 in 1Thess*.(11.487B).

***φιλοθεέω**, *be a lover of God*, Cyr.*ador*.14(1.517B); id.*Jo*.5.4(4.513C; ἢ φιλοθέους, ὡς Aubert).

φιλοθεΐα, ἡ, *love of God, piety*, Pall.*h.Laus*.11(p.32.17; M.34.1033D); ‡Ammon.*Mt*.26:54(M.85.1388D); ἡ πρακτικὴ καὶ ἡ φυσικὴ καὶ ἡ θεολογικὴ...φιλοσοφία ταὐτὸν δέ ἐστιν εἰπεῖν φ. Max.*ambig*.(M.91.1296B); in complimentary address τῆς σῆς φ. Jo.Ant.*ep.Nest*.5(p.96.11; M.77.1456D); Thdt.*ep*.12(4.1070); *ib*.16(1077); *ib*.28(1090).

***φιλοθεόδωρος**, *admirer of Theodore* φ. ἦν ὁ Χριστόδωρος Sophr.H.*mir.Cyr.et Jo*.8(M.87.3441A).

φιλόθεος, *loving God, devout*, Just.*dial*.118.3(M.6.749C); τὸν ἄνθρωπον...φ. ζῷον Clem.*paed*.1.8(p.127.9; M.8.325B); Or.*Jo*.2.2(p.54.23; M.14.108C); of Abraham ἀντὶ φυσιολόγου σοφὸς καὶ φ. γενόμενος Clem.*str*.5.1(p.331.9; M.9.20A); of the soul, Cyr.*Os*.20(3.43C); Diad.*perf*.71(p.88.15); cf.Eus.*v.C*.3.29(p.91.16); of abstracts ταῖς φ. ὑπὲρ ἡμῶν ἱερουργίαις id.*p.e*.1.1(1A; M.21.24A); χρὴ οὖν τὴν ἐκκλησίαν...φ. ἔχειν τάξιν *Hom.Clem*.3.67; φ. ἱστορία Thdt.*h.rel*.tit.(3.1099); comp., Dion.Al.ap.Eus.*h.e*.7.23.4(M.20.692C); superl., Or.*Jo*.13.1(p.226.1; M.14.400A); Cyr.*Am*.31(3.281B).

φιλοθεότης, ἡ, *love towards God*, ‡Chrys.*pasch*.5(8.263E); Euthal. Diac.*epp.Paul*.(M.85.760A).

φιλοθέως, *devoutly, reverently*, Cyr.*Os*.170(3.195D); Dion.Ar.*c.h*.7.2(M.3.208B).

φιλοθηρ-έω, **1.** *seek, pursue zealously*, met. χρῆναι...τὸ ὠφελοῦν... ∼εῖν Cyr.*ador*.5(1.152C); ∼εῖν...τὴν ἀλήθειαν id.*glaph.Ex*.2(1.287B); ∼εῖν...τὴν τῶν δογμάτων ἀκριβείαν id.*Jo*.11.3(4.947A); οὐδὲ δόξαν ἐροῦμεν ∼εῖν τὴν διάκενον *ib*.5.2(489A); **2.** *influence, impel* τὰς τῶν οὕτω πεπιστευκότων ψυχὰς ∼εῖν εἰς εὐσέβειαν *ib*.10.2(893B).

φιλοθρέμμων, *that delights in nourishing*, *Orac.Sib*.5.395.

φιλόθρηνος, *oft-lamented*, Nonn.*par.Jo*.11:13(M.43.841A).

***φιλοϊερεύς**, *showing goodwill to priests*, ‡Jo.D.*ep.Thphl*.27(M.95.380B).

***φιλοικειότης, ἡ,** *goodwill towards one's neighbour,* Cyr.*ador.*8(1.269E).

***φιλοιν-έω,** ? *entertain* τοὺς κεκλημένους ὁ βασιλεὺς ~εῖ Eulog.*fr. Novat.*(M.104.349B).

φιλοΐστωρ, *fond of literary research,* Epiph.*mens.*14(M.43.260C); Πυθαγόρας καὶ Πλάτων...φιλομαθέστατοι καὶ φ. Cyr.*Juln.*1(6^2.29E); *Dial.Tim.et Aquil.*115 v°(p.90).

***φιλοκαθεδρέω,** *be ambitious of high authority, Clem.ep.*3(M.2.37A).

***φιλοκαθεδρία, ἡ,** *desire for episcopal office* φ. καὶ πρωτοκαθεδρίας πάθει, δι' ὧν εἰργάσαντο τὸ σχίσμα Pall.*v.Chrys.*20(p.145.11; M.47.81); Ἀρείου...φ. λοιμικῆς τὸ ἐπιθύμημα Cyr.*hom.div.*4(p.103.15; 5^2.356E); Socr.*h.e.*5.21.13(M.67.624A).

***φιλοκακοῦργος,** *delighting to do evil* τὰ φ. τῶν δαιμόνων στίφη Cyr.*Ps.*31:7(M.69.868B); id.*Is.*2.1(2.190D); of Devil δεινός ἐστι καὶ φ. *ib.*3.1(371E); τὴν τοῦ διαβόλου φ. γνώμην id.*Jo.*12.1(4.1110D).

***φιλοκακούργως,** *with delight in contriving evil,* Cyr.*Ps.*63:4(M.69.1125C); id.*ador.*6(1.205D); id.*hom.pasch.*23(5^2.279E).

φιλοκαλ-έω, 1. *value highly, cherish,* Gr.Naz.*ep.*33(M.37.73A); Nil.*epp.*3.52(M.79.416D); *be enthusiastic about* ~εῖν...τὴν τούτων ἐκμάθησιν Proc.G.*Is.*3:1(M.87.1893C); in bad sense τὰ συμπόσια φιλοκαλήσωμεν Pall.*v.Chrys.*12(p.75.5; M.47.42); **2.** *look after, tend,* Mac.Mgn.*apocr.*3.11(p.77.23); Nil.*epp.*1.101(M.79.125B); *ib.*2.213 (312B); **3.** *put in good order, prepare,* Epiph.*haer.*16.1(p.210.17; M.41.248C); *Apophth.Patr.*(M.65.120D); Cyr.S.*v.Sab.*66(p.167.12); met., Nil.*epp.*3.25(M.79.381D); Dor.*doct.*12.5(M.88.1756C).

φιλοκαλία, ἡ, 1. *love for what is beautiful* or *good,* Clem.*paed.*3.7 (p.258.5; M.8.608B); Melet.*nat.hom.*synops.(M.64.1113B); **2.** *care, attention,* Cyr.S.*v.Sab.*82(p.187.11); Dor.*doct.*12.4(M.88.1756A); in criticism or research, *scholarship,* Epiph.*haer.*8.8(p.195.2; M.41.220B); *ib.*42.11(p.124.15; 725D); *ib.*76.13(p.360.11; M.42.545B); **3.** *work of scholarship* Βήρυλλος σὺν ἐπιστολαῖς καὶ συγγραμμάτων διαφόρους φ. καταλέλοιπεν Eus.*h.e.*6.20.2(M.20.572B); **4.** *adornment,* id.*v.C.*3.47(p.97.30; M.20.1108B); τὰς...πόλεις ταῖς τῶν εὐκτηρίων φ. ἐκπρέπειν ἐποίει *ib.*3.50(p.98.27; 1109C); Jo.Schol.*coll.cap.*27(p.387).

***φιλοκαλλιπρόσωπος,** *loving beauty of face,* Jo.Clim.*scal.*8(M.88.832B).

φιλόκαλος, *loving what is beautiful* or *good*; of those devoted to ascetic life, Ath.*v.Anton.*4(M.26.845B); *interested in learning, scholarly* ἐπιστολὰς ἐγκυκλίους αἵτινες παρὰ φιλοκάλοις ἔτι σώζονται Epiph.*haer.*69.4(p.155.27; M.42.209A); *ib.*69.9(p.159.28; 217A).

***φιλοκαλοῦργος,** Cyr.*Is.*2.1(2.200E) for φιλοκακοῦργος.

***φιλοκαρτερία, ἡ,** *perseverance* φ. ... ἐν εὐχαῖς Chrys.*hom.36.5 in 1Cor.*(10.340A).

φιλόκενος, *loving empty words,* Const.Diac.*laud.*21(M.88.504B).

***φιλοκοιρανίη, ἡ,** *desire for* or *love of power, Orac.Sib.*14.4.

***φιλόκολπος,** *fond of the* κόλπος: καταλέγειν τὰ περὶ...Ἀθηνᾶς τῆς φιλοκόλπου Thphl.Ant.*Autol.*3.3(M.6.1125A).

φιλόκομος, *proud of one's hair,* Synes.*calv.*3(p.193.9; M.66.1169D); *ib.*4(p.196.7; 1173A); *ib.*24(p.232.1; 1205C).

***φιλοκομπαστής, ὁ,** *boastful person,* Cyr.*Jo.*2.5(4.202D).

***φιλοκομπέω,** *delight in pompous words,* Cyr.*apol.Thdt.*2(p.116.2; 6^1.209D).

***φιλοκομπία, ἡ,** *ostentation, display,* Cyr.*fr.Ac.*2:3(M.74.760A); id.*Is.*2.5(2.322D); id.*Juln.*10(6^2.353B).

***φιλόκομπος,** *boastful, ostentatious,* Just.*2apol.*3.1(M.6.448A); Cyr.*Abac.*8(3.523E).

***φιλοκόμπως,** *boastfully,* Cyr.*Jo.*3.4(4.294C).

***φιλοκοσμέω,** *love ornaments,* Apollon.ap.Eus.*h.e.*5.18.11(M.20.480B); Clem.*paed.*2.10(p.223.6; M.8.529A).

φιλοκοσμία, ἡ, 1. *love of ornament,* Clem.*paed.*2.8(p.194.21; M.8.465C); ἀνέτρεψε τὴν Ἑλλάδα ἡ βάρβαρος φ. ... αἱ βάρβαροι φ. ἑταίραν ἤλεγξαν τὴν Διὸς θυγατέρα *ib.*3.2(p.244.1; M.8.573B); μέγα μὲν καὶ καθ' ἑαυτὸ κακὸν ἡ φ. Chrys.*hom.10.5 in Col.*(11.403D); Isid.Pel.*epp.*1.461(M.78.436B); **2.** *love of worldly things,* Diad.*perf.*27(p.30.6).

φιλόκοσμος, *loving worldly things* ἀμαθεῖς δὲ καὶ φ. Bas.*hom.in Ps.*1(1,92C; M.29.216B); Gr.Naz.*carm.*2.1.44.11(M.37.1350A); Cyr.*Is.*1.3(2.69D).

***φιλοκρατία, ἡ,** *love of power,* Meth.*symp.*11(p.130.2; M.18.205B).

φιλοκριν-έω, variant for φυλοκρινέω, *distinguish, Hom.Clem.*19.12; *ib.*20.8; ~εῖ τοὺς μέλλοντας ὁ θεός, τοὺς μὲν παράγων ὡς ἀγαθοὺς ἐσομένους, τοὺς δὲ κωλύων Proc.G.*Gen.*1:26(M.87.109D).

***φιλοκρινητέον,** v. *φυλοκρινητέον.

φιλόκροτος, *noisy,* Nonn.*par.Jo.*2:23(M.43.765A).

φιλοκτέανος, *greedy for gain,* Nonn.*par.Jo.*2:16(M.43.764B); *ib.*13:2(860B); *ib.*13:26(864C).

φιλοκτημοσύνη, ἡ, *love of possessions,* ‡Chrys.*hom.*10(13.242D) = Ephr.3.227B.

φιλοκτήμων, *loving possessions,* Clem.*str.*4.6(p.261.27; M.8.1241C); Or.*adnot.in Dt.*20:5(M.17.28D) = Cyr.*ador.*5(1.149C); Gr.Nyss.*Eun.*11(2 p.253.23; M.45.860C).

***φιλόκτιστος,** *devoted to building,* fig. τεσσαράκοντα φ. ἐνιαυτῶν Nonn.*par.Jo.*2:20(M.43.764C).

***φιλοκτονία, ἡ,** *love of murder,* Nil.*epp.*3.105(M.79.433B).

φιλολαλία, ἡ, *talkativeness,* Gr.Naz.*or.*32.32(M.36.212A).

φιλόλιθος, *fond of precious stones,* Clem.*paed.*3.2(p.242.2; M.8.569B).

***φιλολογεύς, ὁ,** *learned scholar,* Or.*fr.59 in Jo.*(p.531.22).

***φιλολόγημα, τό,** *argument, contention,* Thdr.Stud.*antirr.*1.3(M.99.332B).

***φιλολογητέον,** *one must study,* Clem.*paed.*2.9(p.207.12; M.8.496B).

***φιλολογιστικός,** *fond of reasoning,* Epiph.*haer.*76.26(p.373.23; M.42.568B).

φιλόλυπος, *grieving, nursing one's grief,* Bas.*hom.*4.5(2.29C; M.31.228C).

φιλομαθῶς, *with zeal for knowledge, learnedly,* Or.*Cels.*2.55(p.179.12; M.11.885A); Ath.*decr.*2(p.2.33; M.25.420B); Isid.Pel.*epp.*1.449 (M.78.429B).

***φιλομάκελλος,** (cf. Lat. *macellum*) *loving the shambles* τὸν φ. κύνα Jo.Clim.*scal.*1(M.88.636B); φ. κύων Ἰσμαὴλ ‡Jo.D.*hom.*5(M.96.657B).

***φιλόμαρτυς,** *fond of martyrs, reverencing martyrs,* Bas.*hom.*19.1 (2.149B; M.31.508B); Nil.*epp.*4.62(M.79.581B); Eus.Al.*serm.*8(M.86.357C).

***φιλομετρία, ἡ,** *love of versification,* Synes.*Dion* 18(p.278.14; M.66.1161D).

***φιλομονάζω,** v. φιλομόναχος.

φιλομόναχος, *befriending monks,* Pall.*h.Laus.*52(p.145.2, v.l. φιλομονάζων M.34.1217A); Nil.*epp.*2.60(M.79.225D); Jo.Mosch.*prat.*196(M.87.3080D).

***φιλομυθής,** *full of fables, devoted to fables* βίβλον τὴν λεγομένην φιλαλήθη, μᾶλλον δὲ φ. Anast.S.*hod.*6(M.89.105A).

***φιλομύστης, ὁ,** *fellow devotee,* Jo.Clim.*scal.*8(M.88.832B).

φιλονεικ-έω, 1. *strive contentiously, strive to surpass,* usu. in bad sense; fig. μὴ ~είτω ἡ τέχνη πρὸς τὴν φύσιν Clem.*paed.*2.12(p.233.14; M.8.552B); *quarrel,* c. dat., *T.Gad* 6.4; Meth.*fr.17 in Job*(p.516.8); *Hom.Clem.*15.6; *rival, challenge comparison with* Ἀβραὰμ καὶ Σάρρα...ἀρχὴ καὶ ῥίζα πληθύος ἀνθρώπων ~ούσης τοῖς ἄστροις Cyr.*Is.*4.5(2.700D); fig. ὡς δικαιοσύνην ἔχων, ἥτις ~εῖ τοῖς λίαν ἡρμένοις τῶν ὀρῶν id.*Ps.*35:6(M.69.917C); **2.** *endeavour, strive* κἂν μυριάκις φιλονεικήσωμεν Chrys.*hom.3.5 in Mt.*(7 43A); id.*hom.32.3 in Jo.*(8.189A); id.*hom.12.8 in Rom.*(9.554C); c. infin. κἂν εἰς ὕψος ἀρθῆναι φιλονεικήσῃ ποτὲ ἡ φλόξ id.*virg.*34(1.292E); Isid.Pel.*epp.*2.94(M.78.540A); Thdt.*Mal.*1:3(2.1672); **3.** *tend* to, *be wont* to ὁ χρόνος... τοιαῦτα ἀμείβειν ~ῶν Thdt.*h.rel.*5(3.1164); **4.** *assert, argue contentiously, contend* τὸ πάσχα τῇ τεσσαρεσκαιδεκάτῃ ἐπιτελεῖν ~οῦντες Hipp.*haer.*8.5(p.225.17; M.16.3347E); Meth.*symp.*8.10(p.93.6; M.18.153C); ~οῦσι ποίημα εἶναι τὸν τοῦ θεοῦ υἱόν Ath.*fr.Job*(M.27.1344B); Chrys.*hom.35.4 in Mt.*(7.404A); **5.** *dispute, question* ~εῖν τὴν ἀκατάληπτον καὶ ἄρρητον τοῦ θεοῦ πρόνοιαν id.*scand.*2(3.467A).

φιλονεικητέον, *one must strive, contend,* Isid.Pel.*epp.*2.146(M.78.592C).

φιλονικέω, *strive to surpass,* Meth.*res.*1.27(p.256.4; v.l. φιλονεικεῖν).

[*]**φιλόνυμφος,** *loving one's bride,* Jo.D.*hom.*11.19(M.96.781A).

***φιλοξενιτεύω,** *act hospitably,* Eus.Al.*serm.*1(M.86.324C).

***φιλοπάθεια, ἡ,** *sensuality,* Isid.Pel.*epp.*1.220(M.78.321A).

φιλοπαθής, *sensual, devoted to one's passions,* Esaias *or.*23.7 (cf. M.40.1174A); *ib.*25.18(cf.1186C).

***φιλοπαιδευτήριος,** *fond of teaching* (or perh. as subst.) κατὰ φύσιν δὲ ἡ πατρὶς φ. ἐστιν ἐν τῇ παιδεύσει τῶν γραμμάτων Call.*v.Hyp.*(p.7).

φιλοπαιδία, ἡ, 1. *love of children,* Cyr.*ador.*6(1.179D); id.*Mich.*15(Pusey p.624.10; Aubert om.); **2.** *childishness,* ‡Caes.Naz.*dial.*35 (M.38.897).

***φιλοπατορία, ἡ,** *love of parents,* ‡Caes.Naz.*dial.*130(M.38.1032).

φιλοπάτωρ, *loving one's father,* of one's spiritual father ὅσοι τέλειοι φ. τοῦ...θεοφόρου ἀνδρός [sc. S. Paul]...καὶ γνήσιοι παῖδες τυγχάνετε Eustrat.*v.Eutych.*101(M.86.2389A); of God, ref. Sabellians δέον μήτε οὕτως εἶναί τινας φ. ὡς καὶ τὸ εἶναι πατέρα περιαιρεῖν Gr.Naz.*or.*2.38(M.35.445B) = *ib.*20.6(1072C).

***φιλοπείσμων,** s.v.l., *persuasive*; of persons, Meth.*symp.*proem. (M.18.29C, v.l. φιλόπευστον; φιλοπευστῶν p.4.16).

***φιλοπενής**, *friend to the poor*, ‡Chrys.*eleem*.1(9.832B,C).

***φιλόπιστος**, *faith-loving* ὁ πιστὸς...μὴ ἐξηγητικὸς ἀλλὰ φ. †Ph. Carp.*ep*.(M.32.352A); Alex.Sal.*Barn*.37(448F).

***φιλοπλατύνω**, *be arrogant*, *Apophth.Patr*.(M.65.184A); *Schol*.12 in Jo.Clim.*scal*.15(M.88.908A).

φιλοπλούσιος, *loving riches* ἔστω δὲ ὁ ἐπίσκοπος...μὴ φ. *Const. App*.2.6.1.

***φιλοποίμην**, *loving one's shepherd* λίαν φ. γεγόναμεν, καὶ οὐκ ἔχομεν εὑρεῖν ἀγαθῶν δύο [sc. Meletius and Paulinus] τὸ αἱρετώτερον Gr.Naz.*or*.23.4(M.35.1156A).

φιλοπόλεμος, *fond of war* ὁ...σωτὴρ...τὸν...φ. διάβολον ἐξ ὑμῶν ἀπελάσειεν Gr.Ant.*bapt*.2.10(M.88.1884A); neut. as subst., Thphyl. *exc.gent*.4(p.481.7; M.113.940D).

φιλοπολίτης, *fond of cities*, †Ph.Carp.*ep*.3(3.127D; M.32.353A).

***φιλοπονεῖον, τό**, *infirmary*, Sophr.H.*mir.Cyr.et Jo*.5(M.87. 3432C).

φιλοπονηρία, ἡ, *love of wickedness, depravity*, Areth.*Apoc*.6:23 (M.106.544C).

***φιλοπονητέον**, *one must strive, toil*, Or.*comm.in Eph*.4:31(p.558).

***φιλοπονικός**, *industrious*; superl., Cosm.Ind.*top*.7(M.88.340A).

φιλόπονος, **1.** adj.; **a.** *industrious*; hence *painstaking, conscientious*, of those fasting until fourth watch before Easter τοὺς... μέχρι τετάρτης φυλακῆς διεγκαρτεροῦντας...ὡς γενναίους καὶ φ. ἀποδεχόμεθα Dion.Al.*ep.can*.(p.101; M.10.1277A); of writers of lives of saints ὁ μὲν σκοπὸς εἷς ἐστιν ἡμῶν τε καὶ τῶν πρὸ ἡμῶν φ. καὶ ὁσίων ἀνδρῶν ὁ ἐπὶ τῇ παρούσῃ τοῦ ἀοιδίμου ἀνδρὸς τοῦ βίου διηγήσει Leont. N.*v.Jo.Eleem*.proem.(p.1.5); Geo.Al.*v.Chrys*.1(p.158.15); **b.** painstaking in mental tasks, *learned*, Clem.*str*.7.18(p.79.6; M.9.557A); τοῦ φ. Ὠριγένους Ath.*decr*.27.1(p.23.19; M.25.465B); Bas.Sel.*or*. 1.1(M.85.28B); **2.** subst.; member of a lay group which undertook certain duties in church, Leont.N.*v.Jo.Eleem*.19(p.37.6); ἦν δὲ καὶ πλῆθος σχολαστικῶν καὶ ταχυγράφων καὶ φ. ἐκλαμβανόντων τὰ λεγόμενα ὑπ' αὐτοῦ [sc. Chrys.] Geo.Al.*v.Chrys*.41(p.217.25); acting as nurses to sick, Sophr.H.*mir.Cyr.et Jo*.5(M.87.3432C); τοὺς φιλοπόνους (ἐξ αὐτῶν δέ εἰσι ἀσθενῶν οἱ δυνάμενοι) *ib*.35(3544C).

φιλοπόνως, *learnedly*, Didym.(‡Bas.)*Eun*.5(1.318C; M.29.764A); τοῦ Ὠριγένους φ. περὶ τὸ βιβλίον τοῦτο σπουδάσαντος Gr.Nyss.*hom.in Cant*.proem.(M.44.764A); *Proem*.in Dor.*doct*.(M.88.613B).

***φιλόπορνος**, *lecherous*, Ephr.3.400F; Nil.*epp*.2.142(M.79.265A); id.*sent*.84(M.79.1248C).

***φιλοπόρφυρος**, *loving purple*, *Orac.Sib*.13.21; Clem.*paed*.3.2 (p.242.2; M.8.569B).

φιλοπραγματίας, ὁ, *meddlesome person, busybody*, Cyr.*Is*.5.4(2. 831E).

φιλοπραγμονέω, *busy oneself about, investigate*, Pall.*h.Laus*.32 (p.90.6; M.34.1100A); *ib*.37(p.110.10; 1185D); abs., *be busy*, Isid.Pel. *epp*.2.240(M.78.680B).

φιλοπρόβατος, *loving one's sheep* τοῦ σωτῆρος...τοῦ φ. ποιμένος Pall.*v.Chrys*.5(p.33.15; M.47.21).

***φιλοπροεδρία, ἡ**, *ambition*, Soz.*h.e*.7.2.5(M.67.1420C).

***φιλοπροτιμία, ἡ**, *ambition*, Bas.Sel.*or*.28.1(M.85.320A).

***φιλοπροφήτης**, *loving prophets*; of Christ, Cyr.*Jo*.2.5(4.200D).

φιλοπρωτεύω, *be ambitious*, Nil.*epp*.3.241(M.79.496B).

φιλοπτωχία (φιλοπτώχεια), ἡ, *love of the poor* ἦν γὰρ τοῖς Ἰουδαίοις...τὸ τῆς φ. ἐξαίρετον †Or.*schol.in Lc*.3:11(M.17.328D); Ath. *v.Anton*.17(M.26.869B); Gr.Naz.*or*.14.1(M.35.860A); τῆς χήρας... δεῖγμα...τὰ τῆς φιλοξενίας, τὰ τῆς φ. Chrys.*hom.36.5 in 1Cor*.(10. 340A); δεῖ τὸν θησαυρὸν πρὸ ὀφθαλμῶν ἔχειν τὸν τῆς ἀληθείας...τὸν τῆς φ. ‡Chrys.*hom.in Ps.95:1*(5.631E); Cyr.*ador*.8(1.268D); of Judas ὢ φιλαργυρίας φ. ἐνδυομένης προσωπεῖον...κάπηλος φ. Ἰούδας καὶ αὐτὸ τῆς φ. τὸ σχῆμα πραγματευόμενος Bas.Sel.*prod.Jud*.2(M.28.1049B).

***φιλόπτωχος**, *loving the poor*, ‡Hipp.*consumm*.42(p.306.20; M.10. 944C); τῶν ἀσκητῶν τὴν νηστείαν...τὸ φ. Ath.*v.Anton*.30(M.26.889A); ὁ Ἀβραὰμ...ἦ...φ. Isid.Pel.*epp*.1.172(M.78.296A).

φιλόργιος, *abounding in worship*, Nonn.*par.Jo*.6:4(M.43.793A).

***φιλορύπαρος**, *loving what is foul* or *sordid* φ. δαίμων Nil.*epp*. 2.167(M.79.284B); *ib*.4.12(556A).

***φιλόρυπος (φιλόρρυπος)**, = foreg., Nil.*epp*.1.327(M.79.201A); *ib*.3.143(449C).

***φιλόρφανος**, *loving orphans*, *Didasc.patr*.8(p.17.11).

φίλος, A. adj., *beloved, dear*; **1.** *dear* to God εἰκότως ἄρα φ. ὁ ἄνθρωπος τῷ θεῷ ἐπεὶ καὶ πλάσμα αὐτοῦ ἐστιν Clem.*paed*.1.3(p.94.8; M.8.257A); of prophets, Gr.Thaum.*pan.Or*.15(p.34.3; M.10.1093C); in complimentary address τῷ θεοφιλεστάτῳ καὶ φ. τοῦ θεοῦ Ἀθανασίῳ Ath.*ep.Jov*.(M.26.813A); **2.** *pleasing* to God, *according to* God's *will* οὐδὲν ὑγιὲς δρῶσιν οὐδὲ θεῷ φ. Just.*dial*.3.3(M.6.480B); ὃ φ. τῷ θεῷ, τοῦτο γενέσθω id.*1apol*.68.2(M.6.432A); ταῦτα μὲν ὅπῃ τῷ θεῷ φίλον ταύτῃ ἐχέτω Dion.Ar.*d.n*.13.4(M.3.984A); τὰ τῷ θεῷ φ. ἀναζητεῖ ποιεῖν *Const.App*.1.4.1; τὰ θειωδῶς ἐπηγγελμένα καὶ φ. θεῷ Dion.Ar. *e.h*.7.3.7(M.3.564B); of abstracts ὢ ἐγκράτεια φ. θεοῦ καὶ παρὰ ἁγίοις ἐγκωμιαζομένη Ath.*virg*.24(p.59.15; M.28.280D); **3.** *friendly, kind*, met. τὸ διάδημα τοῦτο [sc. crown of thorns] τοῖς ἐπιβουλεύουσι πολέμιον ἐκώλυσεν αὐτούς, τοῖς συνεκκλησιάζουσιν φίλον ἐθρίγκωσεν αὐτοὺς Clem.*paed*.2.8(p.203.3; M.8.485C); = *harmonious*, of elements ὡς φ. καὶ ἀδελφά Ath.*gent*.42(M.25.84C); διὸ καὶ φ. τἀγαθὰ καὶ ἐναρμόνια πάντα Dion.Ar.*d.n*.4.21(M.3.724A); **4.** *delighting* in, fig. τίνα δ' ἂν φωνὴν ἄλλην, εἰ φωνὴν λάβοιεν Αἰγυπτίων θεοί,... προσήσονται ἢ τὴν Ὁμηρικήν τε καὶ ποιητικήν, τῆς κνίσης τε καὶ ὀψαρτυτικῆς φ. Clem.*prot*.2(p.31.12; M.8.124C).

B. as subst., *friend*; **1.** characterized ὁ δὲ εἰς δύναμιν ἀμειβόμενος δι' ἀγάπης τὴν εὐποιίαν ἤδη φ. Clem.*str*.7.3(p.15.17; M.9.425B); φ. μὲν γάρ ἐστιν ἀληθινός τε καὶ βέβαιος ὁ καὶ ἐχθροὺς γενομένους ἡμᾶς τοῦ ἀγαπᾶν μὴ παυσάμενος Gr.Nyss.*hom.13 in Cant*.(M.44.1044B); ποιῶμεν φ. τοὺς δυναμένους ἡμῶν ἀεὶ ῥυθμίσαι τὴν ψυχήν, συμβουλεῦσαι τὰ δέοντα...καὶ εὐχαῖς βοηθοῦντας προσάγειν τῷ θεῷ Chrys.*kal*.4(1. 703C); οἶδα ἐγώ τινα ὃς ὑπὲρ φίλου τοὺς ἁγίους ἄνδρας παρακαλῶν, παρεκάλει εὔχεσθαι πρότερον ὑπὲρ αὐτοῦ, καὶ τότε ὑπὲρ ἑαυτοῦ id.*hom. 2.3 in 1Thess*.(11.437E); φ. ἐκεῖνός ἐστι γνήσιος ὁ τὰς ἐκ περιστάσεως θλίψεις καὶ ἀνάγκας καὶ συμφορὰς ἐν καιρῷ πειρασμοῦ συνυποφέρων τῷ πλησίον ὡς ἰδίας ἀθορύβως καὶ ἀταράχως Max.*carit*.3.79(M.90. 1041B); excellence and desirability of friends εἴ τις ἐρωτήσειέ με τί τῶν ἐν τῷ βίῳ κάλλιστον; εἴποιμι ἂν ὅτι φίλοι Gr.Naz.*ep*.103(M.37. 201C); φ. πιστὸς θησαυρὸς ἔμψυχος...ὑπὲρ χρυσίον καὶ λίθον τίμιον πολύν...κῆπος κεκλεισμένος, πηγὴ ἐσφραγισμένη, κατὰ καιρὸν· ἀνοιγόμενά τε καὶ μεταλαμβανόμενα...λιμὴν ἀναψύξεως...εἰ δὲ καὶ υἱὸς φωτὸς...τοῦτο μὲν ἤδη δῶρον θεοῦ καὶ φανερῶς ὑπὲρ τὴν ἀξίαν τὴν ἡμετέραν id.*or*.11.1(M.35.832B); ὄντως φ. πιστὸς φάρμακον ζωῆς... πιστὸς σκέπη κραταία...κἂν μυρίους θησαυροὺς εἴπῃς οὐδὲν ἀντάξιον γνησίου φ. Chrys.*hom.2.3 in 1Thess*.(11.437C); καὶ τοῦ φωτὸς αὐτοῦ ποθεινότερος φ.· τὸν γνήσιον λέγω...βέλτιον γὰρ ἡμῖν σβεσθῆναι τὸν ἥλιον ἢ φίλων ἀποστερηθῆναι· βέλτιον ἐν σκότῳ διάγειν ἢ φίλων εἶναι χωρίς...πολλοὶ τὸν ἥλιον ὁρῶντες ἐν σκότῳ εἰσί, φίλων δὲ εὐποροῦντες οὐδ' ἂν ἐν θλίψει γένοιντο· περὶ φίλων λέγω τῶν πνευματικῶν, τῶν οὐδὲν προτιμώντων φιλίας...πατέρας καὶ υἱοὺς ὑπερβαίνουσι φ., φ. οἱ κατὰ Χριστὸν...καὶ τῆς παρούσης ζωῆς ὁ φ. ἡδύτερος· πολλοὶ γοῦν μετὰ τὴν τῶν φ. τελευτὴν οὐκ ηὔξαντο ζῆσαι λοιπόν, μετὰ φίλου καὶ ὑπερορίαν τις ἡδέως ἂν ἐνέγκοι, χωρὶς δὲ φίλου οὐδὲ τὴν αὐτοῦ οἰκῆσαι ἕλοιτο ἄν· μετὰ φίλου καὶ πενία φορητόν, τούτου δὲ ἄνευ καὶ ὑγεία καὶ πλοῦτος ἀφόρητον *ib*.2.4(438B–439D); dist. from flatterers, etc. φ. κόλακος διενήνοχε τῷ τὸν μὲν πρὸς ἡδονὴν ὁμιλεῖν, τὸν δὲ μηδὲ τῶν λυπούντων ἀπέχεσθαι Bas.*ep*.20(3.98A; M.32.285C); τὸ δὲ ἐπαινεῖν μὲν ἄν τι τῶν δεόντων γίνηται, ἐγκαλεῖν δὲ ἄν τι διαμαρτάνηται, τοῦτο φ. καὶ κηδεμόνος...τὸ ἁπλῶς πάντα ἐπαινεῖν...οὐκ ἔστι φ. ἀλλὰ πλανῶντος Chrys.*hom.3.1 in Ac*.9:1(3.115E); enemies more beneficial than friends (ref. Lc.6:22) οὐκ ὠφελοῦσι φ. ἐπαινοῦντες καὶ χαριζόμενοι, τοσαῦτα ὠφελοῦσιν ἐχθροὶ κακῶς λέγοντες...οἱ μὲν γὰρ φ. ... κολακεύουσιν· οἱ δ' ἐχθροὶ τὰ ἁμαρτήματα εἰς μέσον ἄγουσιν id.*David* 3.4(4. 774E); exeg. Mt.5:29 ὁ Χριστὸς ἐκέλευσεν...τοὺς φ. ἐκείνους, τοὺς ἐν ὀφθαλμῶν τάξει ποθεινοὺς ὄντας...ἀποκόπτειν καὶ βάλλειν ἂν παραβλάπτωσιν εἰς τὴν τῆς ψυχῆς σωτηρίαν ἡμᾶς id.*kal*.4(1.703D); id. *exp.in Ps*.4:10(5.27C,E); cf.id.*incomprehens*.1(1.451A); **2.** partic. of friends of God κἂν Σκύθης ᾖ τις ἢ Πέρσης, ἔχει δὲ τὴν τοῦ θεοῦ γνῶσιν ...περιτέτμηται τὴν καλὴν καὶ ὠφέλιμον περιτομὴν καὶ φ. ἐστὶ τῷ θεῷ Just.*dial*.28.4(M.6.536C); ὁ ἄρα γνωστικὸς...τέλειος ὄντως ἀνὴρ καὶ φ. τοῦ θεοῦ, ἐν υἱοῦ καταλεγεὶς τάξει Clem.*str*.7.11(p.49.13; M.9.496A); οὐ ...πρέπον ἔτι τὸν φ. τοῦ θεοῦ...ἡδοναῖς ἢ φόβοις περιπίπτειν καὶ περὶ τὴν καταστολὴν ἀποσχολεῖσθαι τῶν παθῶν *ib*.6.9(p.469.25; 296C); εἰ δὲ 'κοινὰ τὰ τῶν φίλων', θεοφιλὴς δὲ ὁ ἄνθρωπος (καὶ γὰρ οὖν φ. τῷ θεῷ μεσιτεύοντος τοῦ λόγου) γίνεται δὴ οὖν τὰ πάντα τοῦ ἀνθρώπου, ὅτι τὰ πάντα τοῦ θεοῦ, καὶ κοινὰ ἀμφοῖν τοῖν φ. τὰ πάντα, τοῦ θεοῦ καὶ ἀνθρώπου id.*prot*.12(p.86.10; M.8.244C); δίκαιοι ἄνδρες γεγένηνται φ. θεοῦ Hipp.*haer*.10.33(p.290.26; M.16.3450C); ὁ δὲ βαπτιζόμενος ὑπαρχέτω...φ. θεοῦ *Const.App*.3.18.1; ἐπειδὴ γὰρ πρὸ τοῦ φωτίσματος ἐχθρὸς ἦν, μετὰ δὲ τὸ φώτισμα γέγονε φ. τοῦ κοινοῦ πάντων ἡμῶν δεσπότου Chrys.*hom.3.6 in Ac.princ*.(3.81B); of Abraham, *1Clem*. 17.2; Clem.*paed*.3.8(p.261.14; M.8.613B); *Hom.Clem*.18.12; ref. Jo. 15:12–15 τῷ ὄντι μόνοι φ. θεοῦ καὶ ἀλλήλοις οἱ ἅγιοι· οὐδεὶς δὲ τῶν πονηρῶν καὶ ἀμαθῶν φ. Bas.*hom.in Ps*.44(1.160D; M.29.392C); δεῖ... ὑπὲρ δὲ τῶν φ. τὴν ψυχὴν τιθέναι ὅταν χρεία καλῇ. τοιαύτην ἔχοντα ἀγάπην οἵαν ἔσχε πρὸς ἡμᾶς ὁ θεὸς καὶ ὁ Χριστὸς αὐτοῦ id.*moral*.5(2. 238C; M.31.708B); of Christ τῶν προφητῶν καὶ τῶν ἀνδρῶν ἐκείνων οἳ εἰσι Χριστοῦ φ. Just.*dial*.8.1(M.6.492C); εἰ δὲ καὶ οἷός τέ ἐστιν...

ῥύσασθαι αὐτοὺς ἐκ τοῦ δεσμωτηρίου, μακάριος ἔσται καὶ φ. τοῦ Χριστοῦ *Const.App.*5.1.3; Μωσῆς...καὶ Ἠλίας...ὡς φ. Χριστοῦ καὶ οἰκεῖοι *ib.*6.19.4; τίς ἂν οἰηθείη τι μεῖζον, τί δὲ εἶναι λαμπρότερον ἐρεῖ τοῦ φ. εἶναι καὶ λέγεσθαι Χριστοῦ; Cyr.*Jo.*10.2(4.889A); οἱ μὲν τοῦ Χριστοῦ φ. πάντας ἀγαπῶσι γνησίως. οὐχ ὑπὸ πάντων δὲ ἀγαπῶνται. οἱ δὲ τοῦ κόσμου φ., οὐδὲ πάντας ἀγαπῶσι οὐδὲ ὑπὸ πάντων ἀγαπῶνται. καὶ οἱ μὲν τοῦ Χριστοῦ μέχρι τέλους τὴν συνέχειαν τῆς ἀγάπης διατηροῦσιν· οἱ δὲ τοῦ κόσμου μέχρις οὗ ἀλλήλοις διὰ τὰ κόσμου προσκρούσωσι Max.*carit.*4.98(M.90.1072D); of God as friend of the humble, *Const. App.*8.39.3; **3.** of friends (ministers) of emperor βασιλεὺς...διὰ φίλων αὐτοῖς [sc. countries under his rule] ἐπιστέλλει Ath.*inc.*13.5 (M.25.120A); **4.** *supporter, adherent*: of persons φ. τοῦ μακαρίου Δανιήλ Ath.*apol.Const.*17(M.25.617B); φίλους τῶν ἐπισκόπων id.*h.Ar.* 31(p.200.18; M.25.729A); Παῦλος ἀπόστολος εἶχε φ. τοὺς τῆς τοῦ καίσαρος οἰκίας *ib.*52(p.213.11; 756C); id.*apol.sec.*59(p.139.20; M.25. 357A); οἱ τοιοῦτοι [sc. Arians]...Χριστιανῶν μὲν ἀλλότριοι, διαβόλου δὲ καὶ δαιμόνων φ. id.*ep.Aeg.Lib.*5(M.25.549A); id.*v.Anton.*28(M.26. 885A); of abstracts φ. τῶν ἀρετῶν καὶ προήγορος Gr.Thaum.*pan.Or.* 12(p.28.9; M.10.1085B); τῆς ἀληθείας...φ. Ath.*gent.*31(M.25.61C); id. *ep.Aeg.Lib.*4(M.25.548B).

***φιλοσαρκέω,** *love the flesh*, Cyr.*Jo.*2.5(4.191D); *ib.*12(1065D).

φιλοσαρκία, ἡ, *love of the flesh, sensuality*, Or.*adnot.in Dt.*20:8 (M.17.29B); Cyr.*ador.*1(1.7A); id.*glaph.Ex.*2(1.287C).

***φιλόσαρκος, 1.** *loving human flesh* τῶν ἑπτὰ Μακκαβαίων ἡ μήτηρ, διὰ τὸ ψυχὴν ἔχειν φιλόθεον μᾶλλον ἢ φ. Gr.Nyss.*mart.*2(M.46.785C); μὴ λέγε, ὁ φιλάνθρωπος τοῦ θεοῦ λόγος, ἀλλὰ μᾶλλον εἰπέ, ὁ φ.· εἰ γὰρ οὐ κατηξίωσεν ἑνωθῆναι ἀνθρώπῳ, πῶς φιλάνθρωπος; ‡Ath.*dial.Trin.* 4.9(M.28.1264B); **2.** *sensual*; of persons, Pall.*v.Chrys.*5(p.32.20; M. 47.20); of demons, Nil.*epp.*3.33(M.79.392B); of abstracts τοῖς φ. ἐνηδυπαθοῦντες λογισμοῖς Chrys.*hom.in Mt.*7:14(3.26D); τὴν φιλήδονον καὶ φ. ... ζωήν Cyr.*Jon.*5(3.371E); τῶν φ. παθῶν κατεκράτησε Rom.Mel.(*AS* 1 p.69).

***φιλοσεβής,** *reverent, pious*, ‡Jo.D.*hom.*5(M.96.653D).

***φιλοσκιρτητής,** *fond of dancing*, Ast.Am.*hom.*10(M.40.324C).

φιλοσοφ-έω, A. *be a philosopher, practise philosophy*; **1.** pagan; ref. Plato's doctrine of the philosopher-king, Just.*1apol.*3.3(M.6. 332A); ref. schools of philosophy ἕκαστος τῶν ~εῖν νομιζόντων,... ἀπὸ τοῦ πατρὸς τοῦ λόγου τὸ ὄνομα ἧς ~εῖ φιλοσοφίας ἡγεῖται φέρειν id.*dial.*35.6(M.6.552B); ref. inability of philosopher to attain the wise men's goal of divine knowledge, Clem.*str.*6.7(p.462.25; M.9. 284A); ref. possession by philosophers of σωφροσύνη θνητή, opp. γνῶσις θεία, *ib.*6.15(p.495.10; 349A); opp. δεισιδαιμονεῖν, Or.*Cels.*5. 35(p.38.14; M.11.1236A); opp. μυθοποιεῖν, *ib.*5.57(p.60.7; 1272A); ref. inferiority of philosophy to Judaism οἱ μὲν ~οῦντες μετὰ τοὺς σεμνοὺς ἐν φιλοσοφίᾳ λόγους καταπίπτουσιν ἐπὶ τὰ εἴδωλα καὶ τοὺς δαίμονας *ib.*5.43(p.47.1; 1248D); ref. philosophers' perception of God καὶ κατ' ἔμφασιν δὲ καὶ διάφασιν οἱ ἀκριβῶς παρ' Ἕλλησι ~ήσαντες διορῶσι τὸν θεόν· τοιαῦται γὰρ αἱ κατ' ἀδυναμίαν φαντασίαι ἀληθείας, ὡς φαντασία καθορᾷ τὰ ἐν τοῖς ὕδασιν ὁρώμενα Clem.*str.*1.19(p.61.2; M.8.812A); ref. philosophy learnt by poets from Hebrew sources ποιηταὶ δι' ὑπονοίας πολλὰ ~οῦσι, τὸν Ὀρφέα λέγω,...τὸν Ὅμηρον *ib.* 5.4(p.340.26; M.9.44A); οἱ ~οῦντες opp. οἱ πολλοί, *Hom.Clem.*4.9; poverty of many philosophers rebuts Celsus' reproach of Christ's poverty, Or.*Cels.*2.41(p.164.31; 861C); **2.** ref. Jewish lawgivers and prophets, Tat.*orat.*40(p.41.6; M.6.884B); συμβολικῶς ~ούντων Clem.*str.*5.9(p.364.6; M.9.88A); **3.** ref. following of Christian doctrine πάντες οἱ βουλόμενοι ~εῖν παρ' ἡμῖν Tat.*orat.*32(p.33.27; M.6. 873A); ἔξεστι γὰρ τῷ καθ' ἡμᾶς πολιτευομένῳ καὶ ἄνευ γραμμάτων ~εῖν, κἂν βάρβαρος ᾖ κἂν Ἕλλην...κἂν παιδίον κἂν γυνή Clem.*str.*4. 8(p.275.5; M.8.1272A); hence, *practise Christianity* ~ήσει ὅ τε οἰκέτης ἥ τε γυνή *ib.*(p.278.25; 1277C); πῶς δὲ ἔτι ἀγαπᾷς τὸν θεὸν καὶ τὸν πλησίον σου, μὴ ~ῶν; id.*paed.*3.11(p.279.14; M.8.656B); teach Christianity πλήθη ~οῦντος ἀκουσόμενα βασιλέως [sc. Constantine] Eus.*v.C.*4.29(p.128.22; M.20.1177B).

B. *live like a philosopher*, (i.e. rationally and virtuously, and esp. in accordance with Christian morality); **1.** in gen. οἱ πανταχοῦ κατὰ λόγον τὸν ὀρθὸν νομοθετήσαντες καὶ φ. ἄνθρωποι Just.*2apol.* 7.7(M.6.456C); ἀναγκαῖον γοῦν τὸ πολιτεύεσθαι ὀρθῶς, ἄριστον δὲ τὸ φ. Clem.*str.*1.25(p.104.3; M.8.913A); **2.** of Jews under Law βουληθῆναι γνησίως ~εῖν *ib.*2.20(p.180.22; 1069A); ἔθνος ὅλον ~οῦν Or. *Cels.*4.31(p.302.3; M.11.1076C); **3.** Christian; **a.** in gen. οὐ πάντες, φησί, ~οῦμεν. μή τι οὖν οὐδὲ πάντες τὴν ζωὴν μετερχόμεθα;...καὶ ταύτῃ ~ούντων οἱ ἀγοραῖοι καὶ οἱ κάπηλοι· 'οὐ γὰρ λήψῃ τὸ ὄνομα κυρίου ἐπὶ ματαίῳ...' Clem.*paed.*3.11(p.279.12,27; M.8.656B–657A); ὁ ...τῶν ἄλλων γάμος ἐφ' ἡδυπαθείᾳ ὁμονοεῖ, ὁ δὲ τῶν ~ουντων ἐπὶ τὴν κατὰ λόγον ὁμόνοιαν ἄγει id.*str.*2.23(p.192.3; M.8.1093B); *A.(Pass.) Andr.*12(p.29.11); Gr.Thaum.*pan.Or.*6(p.15.27; M.10.1069B); τοιαῦτα μανθάνειν ~εῖν μὴ μόνον ἄνδρας ἀλλὰ καὶ γυναῖκας Eus.*d.e.*1.6(p.34. 27; M.22.68B); ~οῦντες ἐν οὐ ~οῦσιν Gr.Naz.*or.*25.6(M.35.1205B); οἱ ὑπὲρ τῶν οὐρανῶν ~οῦντες Chrys.*hom.51.3 in Jo.*(8.303B); **b.** ref. special virtues; implying esp. poverty, Clem.*str.*2.5(p.124.15; 953C); τίνες γὰρ ἐν ἀνέσει, οἱ τῷ παρόντι παραχρησάμενοι βίῳ, ἢ οἱ ~ήσαντες; Chrys.*hom.9.3 in 2Cor.*(10.501D); ἐὰν γὰρ ~ῇς, καὶ μυρίων ἀγαθῶν ἔσται [πενία] σοι πηγή id.*hom.90.3 in Mt.*(7.843C); fasting τοῖς γε ~εῖν ἐθέλουσι καὶ σφόδρα ἡδὺ τὸ πρᾶγμα *ib.30.3*(352C); ἐνήστευσεν Ἠλίας...~ῶν Thdt.*Os.*1:4(2.1315); patience and forbearance τί γάρ σε καὶ τοιοῦτον ἐλύπησεν ὁ λελυπηκώς...; ἂν...~ῇς, εἰς τὴν ἐκείνου κεφαλὴν περιστήσεται τὸ δεινόν Chrys.*hom.61.5 in Mt.*(617C); ὁ ~ήσας, καὶ τρόπαιον λαμπρὸν...ἔστησε κατὰ τῆς ὀργῆς *ib.84.3*(802B); ὁ γὰρ ~ῶν...φέρων ὕβρεις Isid.Pel.*epp.*4.196(M.78.1284C); Thdt. *Rom.*12:19f.(3.135); ἐὰν διαβληθεῖσα ~ήσῃς †Jo.Jej.*serm.*(M.88. 1945D); humility, Chrys.*hom.52.2 in Mt.*(531D); ὁ Ματθαῖος ~εῖ, οὐκ ἀποκρυπτόμενος τοὺς ἑαυτοῦ προτιμηθέντας *ib.56.1*(565D); ref. publican (Lc.18:11ff.), id.*poenit.*4.4(2.307D); **c.** effects τέλος τῷ ~οῦντι ἡ πρὸς θεὸν ὁμοίωσις †Just.*fr.*122(p.53; M.6.1600C); ἡ ~οῦσα ψυχὴ εὐτονωτέρα Chrys.*hom.27.3 in Ac.*(9.220A); κἂν πένης ᾖς, δύνασαι μετὰ εὐθυμίας ζῆν ~ῶν id.*hom.29.6 in 1Cor.*(10.268A); hence **4.** *practise, exercise, oneself in*, virtue ἵνα ~ήσῃ τὸ ταπεινὸν εἰς κάθαρσιν Gr.Naz.*or.*24.12(M.35.1184B); παρὼν ἐφιλοσόφει τῷ βίῳ *ib.* 24.19(1193A); πάμπολλα ὑπὲρ προσευχῆς ~ει Evagr.Pont.*or.*18(M.79. 1172A); **5.** *live as an ascetic*, Gr.Nyss.*v.Macr.*(p.379.18; M.46.968C); τῶν ἐν τῷ τόπῳ ~ούντων *ib.*(p.411.4; 996D); τῶν ~ούντων ὁ βίος, καὶ τῶν τὴν μονήρη δίαιταν ᾑρημένων Chrys.*comp.*1(1.116C); ἴσα τοῖς ἀγγέλοις ~οῦντες Hesych.H.*fr.Ps.*49:8(M.93.1197B); παρὰ τοῖς ἐν Σκήτει ~οῦσιν Soz.*h.e.*8.12.1(M.67.1545B); Thdt.*affect.*12(p.307.19; 4.1021).

C. *behave like a philosopher*; intrans., *remain indifferent, show indifference* φ. ἐν ἀλλοτρίοις παθήμασιν Bas.*ep.*289(3.428A; M.32. 1028A); ἐν ταῖς ἀλλοτρίαις φ. συμφοραῖς Chrys.*sac.*4.9(p.126.16; 1. 414E); id.*oppugn.*2.8(1.70A); trans., *bear with indifference* οὐ συγχωρεῖται ~ῆσαι τὴν ἑαυτοῦ κλοπήν Gr.Naz.*or.*24.17(M.35.1189C); νόσος ~εῖται *ib.*43.63(M.36.577C).

D. *treat, investigate philosophically* δεήσει μὲν τὸν ~οῦντα τὰ τοῦ λόγου κατασκευάζειν μετὰ παντοδαπῶν ἀποδείξεων Or.*Cels.*4.9(p.280. 21; M.11.1040A); *ib.*3.79(p.270.15; 1024B); *ib.*4.40(p.313.17; 1093A); *treat, discuss spiritually* περὶ τούτου χρίσματος φ. Cyr.H.*catech.* 21.7; περί τε τῆς ψυχῆς ἡμῖν ~οῦσα Gr.Nyss.*v.Macr.*(M.46.977C); Chrys.*hom.46.3 in Jo.*(8.273B); περὶ ἀθανασίας, καὶ περὶ ἀναστάσεως ~οῦσι †Chrys.*Jud.et gent.*1(1.559C); *meditate* περὶ ἀναστάσεως φ. Chrys.*stat.*1.6(2.9A); *interpret allegorically* περὶ τῶν τοῦ Δαυὶδ καὶ τοῦ Γολιὰθ ὅπλων ἐφιλοσοφοῦμεν...εἰ γὰρ τῷ Παύλῳ ~εῖν ἔξεστι περὶ τῆς κατὰ τὴν ἔρημον πέτρας, πάντως οὐδὲ ἡμῖν νεμεσήσει τις τὸν λίθον τοῦτον [i.e. David's weapon] κατὰ τὸν αὐτὸν ἐκλαμβάνουσι τρόπον id. *anom.*11.1(1.541D,E).

***φιλοσόφησις, ἡ,** *study of philosophy*, Gr.Thaum.*pan.Or.*14(p.31. 4; M.10.1089B).

φιλοσοφία, ἡ, I. *philosophy*;

A. pagan; **1.** gen. descriptions φ. ... ἐπιστήμη ἐστὶ τοῦ ὄντος καὶ τοῦ ἀληθοῦς ἐπίγνωσις, εὐδαιμονία δὲ ταύτης τῆς...σοφίας γέρας Just.*dial.*3.4(M.6.481A); φ. ... πολυχρόνιός ἐστι συμβουλή, σοφίας ἀΐδιον μνηστευομένη ἔρωτα Clem.*prot.*11(p.79.25; M.8.229B); φ. οὔσης ὀρέξεως τοῦ ὄντως ὄντος καὶ τῶν εἰς τοῦτο συντεινόντων μαθημάτων id.*str.*2.9(p.137.7; M.8.981A); τοῦτο δὴ τὸ ἄριστον φ. ἔργον, ὃ δὴ καὶ δαιμόνων τῷ μαντικωτάτῳ ἀνατίθεται ὡς πάνσοφον πρόσταγμα, τὸ 'γνῶθι σαυτόν' Gr.Thaum.*pan.Or.*11(p.27.8; M.10. 1084B); φ., τὴν ὄντως ὑψηλήν τε καὶ ἄνω βαίνουσαν, ὅση τε πρακτικὴ καὶ θεωρητική, ὅση τε περὶ τὰς λογικὰς ἀποδείξεις καὶ ἀντιθέσεις ἔχει καὶ τὰ παλαίσματα, ἣν δὴ διαλεκτικὴν ὀνομάζουσιν Gr.Naz.*or.*43. 23(M.36.528A); τῶν θείων καὶ ἀνθρωπίνων πραγμάτων γνῶσις ἡ φ. Chrys.*hom.9.1 in Col.*(11.391B); definitions by various Gr. philosophers, Isid.Pel.*epp.*5.558(M.78.1637A); **2.** systems; discussion why these are so many, Just.*dial.*2.1,2(M.6.476B); cf.id.*1apol.*7.3(M.6. 337A); φ. δὲ οὐ τὴν Στωϊκὴν λέγω οὐδὲ τὴν Πλατωνικὴν ἢ τὴν Ἐπικούρειόν τε καὶ Ἀριστοτελικήν, ἀλλ' ὅσα εἴρηται παρ' ἑκάστῃ τῶν αἱρέσεων τούτων καλῶς,...τοῦτο σύμπαν τὸ ἐκλεκτικὸν φ. φημί Clem. *str.*1.7(pp.24.30–25.2; M.8.732C,D); discussion of various schools of Gr. philosophy, *ib.*1.14,15 passim(pp.37.16–47.19; 757B–784A); **3.** derived from OT revelation; Plato admits having learned what is best in his philosophy from 'barbarians', Clem.*str.*1.15(p.42.3; M. 8.768B); *ib.*5.14(p.388.23; M.9.140B); ἐκ τῆς βαρβάρου φ. μαθὼν [sc. Heraclitus] τὴν διὰ πυρὸς κάθαρσιν *ib.*5.1(p.332.1; 21A); τὴν Περιπατητικὴν φ. ἔκ τε τοῦ κατὰ Μωϋσέα νόμου καὶ τῶν ἄλλων ἠρτῆσθαι προφητῶν *ib.*5.14(p.390.17; 145A); connexion with Pythagoreans, *ib.* 5.5(p.342.20; 45C); φ. ... πολυωφελές τι χρῆμα πάλαι μὲν ἤκμασε παρὰ βαρβάροις κατὰ τὰ ἔθνη διαλάμψασα, ὕστερον δὲ καὶ εἰς Ἕλληνας κατῆλθεν *ib.*1.15(p.45.19; M.8.777A); ἐκ τῆς βαρβάρου φ. πᾶσαν φερομένην τὴν παρ' Ἕλλησιν ἐνδεικνύμενοι σοφίαν *ib.*5.14(p.420.22; M.9.205A); **4.** favourably regarded by Christians: God as source and giver of Gr. philosophy πάντων...αἴτιος τῶν καλῶν ὁ θεός, ἀλλὰ τῶν μὲν κατὰ προηγούμενον ὡς τῆς τε διαθήκης τῆς παλαιᾶς καὶ τῆς νέας, τῶν δὲ κατ' ἐπακολούθημα ὡς τῆς φ. Clem.*str.*1.5(p.18.1; M.8.717D); *ib.*6.5(p.452.22; M.9.261B); κἂν λέγῃ τις κατὰ σύνεσιν ἀνθρώπων φ. ηὑρῆσθαι πρὸς Ἑλλήνων, ἀλλὰ τὰς γραφὰς εὑρίσκω τὴν σύνεσιν θεόπεμπτον εἶναι λεγούσας *ib.*6.8(p.463.15; 284C); κινδυνεύουσι...οἱ φάσκοντες μὴ θεόθεν φ. δεῦρο ἥκειν ἀδύνατον εἶναι λέγειν πάντα τὰ ἐπὶ μέρους γινώσκειν τὸν θεὸν μηδὲ μὴν πάντων εἶναι τῶν καλῶν αἴτιον...οὐκ ἂν δὲ τὴν ἀρχὴν ὑπέστη τι τῶν ὄντων ἀβουλήτως ἔχοντος τοῦ θεοῦ, εἰ δὲ βουλομένου, θεόθεν ἡ φ., τοιαύτην εἶναι βουληθέντος αὐτήν, οἷα ἐστίν *ib.*6.17(p.512.12ff.; 388B); communicated through inferior angels, *ib.*7.2(p.6.17; 409B); hence leading to worship of God ἔργον ἐστὶ φ., ἐξετάζειν περὶ τοῦ θείου Just.*dial.*1.3(M.6.473B); Clem.*str.*1.5(p.19.18; M.8.724A); φιλοσοφίαν ἐκ τῆς θείας προνοίας δεδόσθαι προπαιδεύουσαν εἰς τὴν διὰ Χριστοῦ τελείωσιν, ἣν μὴ ἐπαισχύνηται γνώσει βαρβάρῳ μαθητεύουσα [φ.] προκόπτειν εἰς ἀλήθειαν *ib.*6.17(p.510.22ff.; M.9.384C); as preparation for Christian faith, *ib.*1.2(p.14.1; M.8.709B); *ib.*1.5(p.17.33; 717C); therefore necessary for the Greeks, *ib.*; its place in Christian life: leading to piety, *ib.*1.4(p.17.24ff.; 717B,C); assisting truth agst. sophistic arguments, *ib.*1.20(p.63.31; 817A); in life of the 'gnostic' εἰ δέ που σχολὴ...ἀντὶ τῆς ἄλλης ῥᾳθυμίας καὶ τῆς Ἑλληνικῆς ἐφάπτεται φ. *ib.*6.18(p.515.19; M.9.396A); ἡ ἠθικὴ τε καὶ φυσικὴ φ. γένοιτο ἄν ποτε τῷ ὑψηλοτέρῳ βίῳ σύζυγος...μόνον εἰ τὰ ἐκ ταύτης κυήματα μηδὲν ἐπάγοιτο τοῦ ἀλλοφύλου μιάσματος Gr.Nyss.*v.Mos.*(M.44.337A); defence; this the purpose of *Stromateis*, Clem.*str.*1.1(p.13.9ff.; M.8.708B); μήτε...τὴν φ. λυμαίνεσθαι τὸν βίον,...φαύλων ἔργων δημιουργὸν ὑπάρχουσαν, ᾗ τινες διαβεβλήκασιν ἀληθείας οὖσαν εἰκόνα ἐναργῆ, θείαν δωρεὰν Ἕλλησι δεδομένην, μήτε ἡμᾶς ἀποσπᾶσθαι τῆς πίστεως...ἀλλ' ὡς ἔπος εἰπεῖν, περιβολῇ πλείονι χρωμένους, ἀμῇ γέ πῃ συγγυμνασίαν τινὰ πίστεως ἀποδεικτικὴν ἐκπορίζεσθαι *ib.*1.2(p.13.28; 709B); cf.*ib.*2.11(p.141.14; 989A); ἡ...Ἑλληνικὴ φ., ὡς μέν τινες, κατὰ περίπτωσιν ἐπήβολος τῆς ἀληθείας ἀμῇ γέ πῃ, ἀμυδρῶς δὲ καὶ οὐ πάσης, γίνεται· ὡς δὲ ἄλλοι βούλονται, ἐκ τοῦ διαβόλου τὴν κίνησιν ἴσχει. ἔνιοι δὲ δυνάμεις τινὰς ὑποβεβηκυίας ἐμπνεῦσαι τὴν πᾶσαν φ. ὑπειλήφασιν. ἀλλ' εἰ καὶ μὴ καταλαμβάνει ἡ Ἑλληνικὴ φ. τὸ μέγεθος τῆς ἀληθείας, ἔτι δὲ ἐξασθενεῖ πράττειν τὰς κυριακὰς ἐντολάς, ἀλλ' οὖν γε προκατασκευάζει τὴν ὁδὸν τῇ βασιλικωτάτῃ διδασκαλίᾳ, ἀμῇ γέ πῃ σωφρονίζουσα καὶ τὸ ἦθος προτυποῦσα καὶ προστύφουσα εἰς παραδοχὴν τῆς ἀληθείας ⟨τὸν⟩ τὴν πρόνοιαν δοξάζοντα *ib.*1.16(p.52.15ff.; 796A); *ib.*1.17(p.55.31; 801B); *ib.*6.8(p.465.3ff.; M.9.288Bff.); **5.** its inferiority; **a.** to Judaism τὴν δὲ ἀνὰ τὸν κλύδωνα τὸν ἐθνικὸν γεννωμένην...φ. Ἑλληνικὴν οἱ ἰχθύες ἐμήνυον, εἰς διατροφὴν ἐκτενῆ τοῖς ἔτι χαμαὶ κειμένοις δεδομένοι· αὐξήσαντες μὲν οὐκέτι Clem.*str.*6.11(p.479.7; M.9.316A); ὅτι μὴ ἄνευ λόγου σώφρονος δεύτερα θέμενοι τὰ τῆς Ἑλλήνων φ. τὴν παρ' Ἑβραίοις θεολογίαν προτετιμήκαμεν, γνοίης ἄν, μαθὼν ὡς καὶ αὐτῶν Ἑλλήνων οἱ δὴ μάλιστα ὀρθότερον φιλοσοφίας ἁψάμενοι,...οὐδ' ἕτερα τῶν παρὰ τοῖς Ἑβραίοις προκεκυρωμένων ἐφεῦρον ἀληθῆ δόγματα Eus.*p.e.*10.4(468D; M.21.780C) cf. supra 3; **b.** to Christianity ἀληθῆ σοφίαν...ἣν φιλοσοφίας ἄκροι μόνον ᾐνίξαντο, οἱ δὲ τοῦ Χριστοῦ μαθηταὶ...ἀνεκήρυξαν Clem.*prot.*11(p.79.15; M.8.229A); ἡ μὲν Ἑλληνικὴ φ. τῇ ἐκ τῆς θρυαλλίδος ἔοικεν λαμπηδόνι, ἣν ἀνάπτουσιν ἄνθρωποι...κηρυχθέντος δὲ τοῦ λόγου πᾶν ἐκεῖνο τὸ ἅγιον ἐξέλαμψεν φῶς id.*str.*5.5(p.345.4; M.9.52B); δεῖ...διὰ Χριστοῦ τὴν ἀλήθειαν μεμαθηκότας σώζεσθαι, κἂν φιλοσοφήσαντες τὴν Ἑλληνικὴν φ. τύχωσιν *ib.*5.13(p.383.19; 128C); ὁ...τοῦ διδασκάλου τοῦ ἡμετέρου λόγος οὐκ ἔμεινεν ἐν Ἰουδαίᾳ μόνῃ, καθάπερ ἐν Ἑλλάδι ἡ φ. ... καὶ τὴν μὲν φ. τὴν Ἑλληνικὴν ἐὰν ὁ τυχὼν ἄρχων κωλύσῃ, οἴχεται παραχρῆμα, τὴν δὲ ἡμετέραν διδασκαλίαν...κωλύουσιν ὁμοῦ βασιλεῖς καὶ τύραννοι...ἣ δὲ καὶ μᾶλλον ἀνθεῖ *ib.*6.18(p.518.5ff.; 400B); cf. *philosophia enim neque in omnibus legi dei contraria est neque in omnibus consona. multi enim philosophorum unum esse deum, qui cuncta creavit, scribunt. in hoc consentiunt legi dei...moralis vero et physica, quae dicitur philosophia, paene omnis, quae nostra sunt, sentit. dissidet vero a nobis, cum deo dicit esse materiam coaeternam*, Or.*hom.14.3 in Gen.*(pp.123.30–124.5; M.12.237D–238A); πολλὴ διαφορὰ...μεταξὺ τῶν τῆς θεοσεβείας λόγων καὶ τῶν τῆς φ. ὁ γὰρ τῆς ἀληθείας λόγος ἀπόδειξιν ἔχει τὴν ἐκ προφητείας, ὁ δὲ τῆς φ. καλλιλογίας παρέχων ἐκ στοχασμῶν δοκεῖ παριστάνειν τὰς ἀποδείξεις *Hom.Clem.*15.5; **c.** defects ψυχαὶ...Ἑλληνικὴν νεμόμεναι φ., ἧς καθάπερ καὶ τῶν καρύων οὐ τὸ πᾶν ἐδώδιμον Clem.*str.*1.1(p.6.23; M.8.693B); *ib.*6.8(p.465.34; M.9.289B); ποτέραν δεῖ τῶν φ. ἑλέσθαι μᾶλλον, τὴν ἔξω καὶ παίζουσαν τὰς τῆς ἀληθείας σκιὰς ἐν τῷ τῆς φ. σχήματι...ἢ τὴν ἡμετέραν Gr.Naz.*or.*25.4(M.35.1204A); τὰ καλὰ τῶν δογμάτων παρὰ τῇ ἔξω φ. ταῖς ἀτόποις προσθήκαις καταμολύνεται Gr.Nyss.*v.Mos.*(M.44.337B); its useless fruits, such as κατηγορίαι τινές, καὶ ἀναλύσεις, καὶ μίξεις κτλ. Gr.Naz.*or.*25.6(1205B); οἱ δὲ ἐξ ἐθνῶν...ἀεὶ τοῖς τῶν παραπαιόντων ἐνστρεφόμενοι μύθοις (τοῦτο γὰρ ἡ τῶν ἔξωθεν φ.) Chrys.*hom.9.1 in Jo.*(8.53C); μέγα ἀγαθὸν φ.· φ. δὲ λέγω τὴν παρ' ἡμῖν. τὰ γὰρ τῶν ἔξωθεν, ῥήματα καὶ μῦθοι μόνον εἰσί· καὶ οὐδὲ αὐτοὶ οἱ μῦθοι φιλόσοφόν τι ἔχοντες *ib.43.1*(375E); Ἕλληνες ἄνδρες τριωβολιμαῖοί τινες καὶ κύνες, φ. τοιαύτην ἀναδεξάμενοι τριωβολιμαῖον· τοιαύτη γὰρ ἡ Ἑλληνική· μᾶλλον δὲ οὐδὲ αὐτήν, ἀλλ' ὄνομα αὐτῆς καὶ τρίβωνα περιθέμενοι...πολλοὺς δυσωποῦσι id.*hom.21.3 in Eph.*(11.162C); **6.** S. Paul's attitude Παῦλος...οὐ φ. διαβάλλων φαίνεται, τὸν δὲ τοῦ γνωστικοῦ μεταλαμβάνοντα ὕψους οὐκέτι παλινδρομεῖν ἀξιοῖ ἐπὶ τὴν Ἑλληνικὴν φ., στοιχεῖα τοῦ κόσμου ταύτην ἀλληγορῶν Clem.*str.*6.8(p.463.2ff.; M.9.284B); Παῦλος συνιδὼν ὅτι ἔστιν ἐν φ. Ἑλληνικῇ οὐκ εὐκαταφρόνητα τοῖς πολλοῖς πιθανά Or.*Cels.* proem.5(p.54.9; M.11.648B); **7.** Origen as teacher of philosophy, Gr.Thaum.*pan.Or.*11(p.25.24; M.10.1081C); **8.** relations between φ. and σοφία, v. σοφία.

B. Christian (and Jewish); **1.** gen. description ἔστι...φ. μέγιστον κτῆμα καὶ τιμιώτατον θεῷ, ᾧ τε προσάγει καὶ συνίστησιν ἡμᾶς μόνη, καὶ ὅσιοι ὡς ἀληθῶς οὗτοί εἰσιν οἱ φιλοσοφίᾳ τὸν νοῦν προσεσχηκότες Just.*dial.*2.1(M.6.476B); φ. γάρ ἐστιν ἠθῶν κατόρθωσις μετὰ δόξης τῆς περὶ τοῦ ὄντος γνώσεως ἀληθοῦς Nil.*exerc.*3(M.79.721B); **2.** of Jewish religion ἡ...κατὰ Μωϋσέα φ. τετραχῇ τέμνεται, εἴς τε τὸ ἱστορικὸν καὶ τὸ κυρίως λεγόμενον νομοθετικόν...τὸ τρίτον δὲ εἰς τὸ ἱερουργικόν...καὶ τέταρτον ἐπὶ πᾶσι τὸ θεολογικὸν εἶδος Clem.*str.*1.28(p.108.24; M.8.921C); Meth.*symp.*7.4(p.75.15; M.18.129C); ἡ τῶν Ἑβραίων φ. Thdt.*affect.*2(p.59.11; 4.751); **3.** of Christianity; **a.** in gen. Χριστιανοὶ καλοῦνται...ὄνομα τῆς φ. κοινὸν ἔχουσιν Just.*1apol.*26.6(M.6.369A); ἡ ἡμετέρα φ. Tat.*orat.*31(p.31.5; M.6.868C); Χριστιανῶν φ. Eus.*h.e.*2.13.6(M.20.169A); Evagr.Pont.*ep.*1(M.32.248A); τοῦτο οἰκετῶν εὐγνωμόνων, τὸ κακῶς πάσχοντας μένειν τὸν δεσπότην θεραπεύοντας· ταῦτα φιλοσοφίας διδάγματα Chrys.*exp.in Ps.*43:21f.(5.157A); id.*hom.4.4 in Col.*(11.357B); ἡ καθ' ἡμᾶς φ. Dion.Ar.*d.n.*2.2(M.3.640A); †Jo.D.*B.J.*23(M.96.1069A); **b.** as ἡ βάρβαρος φ.: χαίρειν εἰπὼν καὶ τῇ Ῥωμαίων μεγαλαυχίᾳ καὶ τῇ Ἀθηναίων ψυχρολογίᾳ...τῆς καθ' ἡμᾶς βαρβάρου φ. ἀντεποιησάμην Tat.*orat.*35(p.37.7; M.6.877C); cf.Athenag.*leg.*2.4(M.6.896B); ἡ γὰρ καθ' ἡμᾶς φ. πρότερον μὲν ἐν βαρβάροις ἤκμασεν Mel.*fr.*ap.Eus.*h.e.*4.26.7(M.20.393B); ἡ...βάρβαρος φ., ἣν μεθέπομεν ἡμεῖς, τελεία τῷ ὄντι καὶ ἀληθής Clem.*str.*2.2(p.115.10; M.8.933C); contrasted with wranglings of contemporary Gr. philosophers, *ib.*8.1(p.80.5ff.; M.9.557C–560A); hence ὁρᾷς φ. βάρβαρον ἔργα ἐπαγγελλομένην, οὐ λόγους *ib.*1.16(p.50.20; M.8.792A); Chrys.*hom.6.3 in 1Cor.*(10.47A); **c.** its superiority as the true philosophy διαλογιζόμενός τε πρὸς ἐμαυτὸν τοὺς λόγους αὐτοῦ [sc. Χριστοῦ] ταύτην μόνην εὕρισκον φ. ἀσφαλῆ Just.*dial.*8.1(M.6.492D); πάσης μὲν φ. ἀνθρωπείου ὑπέρτερα id.*2apol.*15.3(M.6.468C); τὴν ἀληθῆ φ. δι' υἱοῦ παραδιδομένην Clem.*str.*1.18(p.58.2; M.8.805A); ὁ Χριστιανισμός, οὔτε Ἑλληνισμός τις ὢν οὔτε Ἰουδαϊσμός, ἀλλὰ τὸ μεταξὺ τούτων...ἀρχαιοτάτη μέν τις φ. πλὴν ἀλλὰ νεωστὶ πᾶσιν ἀνθρώποις...νενομοθετημένη Eus.*d.e.*1.2(p.8.35; M.22.25A); ἀνωτάτω φ. *ib.*1.6(p.31.32; 61D); ἱερὰ φ. Gr.Nyss.*res.*3(M.46.677D); ref. Magi οὐδὲ γὰρ πρόβατα καὶ μόσχους ἔθυσαν, τῆς δὲ ἐκκλησιαστικῆς ἐγγὺς ὄντα φ.· ἐπίγνωσιν γὰρ καὶ ὑπακοὴν καὶ ἀγάπην αὐτῷ προσῆγον Chrys.*hom.8.1 in Mt.*(7.119B); φ. ἀληθῆ id.*hom.2.4 in Jo.*(8.13C); φιλοσοφεῖν ἐπετήδευσαν...Ἑλλήνων πολλοί, καὶ Ἰουδαίων δὲ οὐκ ὀλίγοι· μόνοι δὲ τὴν ἀληθῆ φ. ἐζήλωσαν οἱ τοῦ Χριστοῦ μαθηταί Nil.*exerc.*1(M.79.720A); *ib.*3(721C); **4.** in rel. to virtue; **a.** ἀρετή and φ. freq. coupled or equated, Meth.*symp.*proem.(p.4.22; M.18.32A); Eus.*h.e.*1.2.19(M.20.61C); Chrys.*hom.29.6 in 1Cor.*(10.268B); Thdt.*Dan.*proem.(2.1062); id.*Cant.*6:7f.(2.126); id.*provid.*9(4.642); ἀρετὴν μὲν ὁριζόμεθα, φρόνησιν, σωφροσύνην, ἀνδρίαν, δικαιοσύνην, καὶ τὰ ἀπὸ τούτων γεννώμενα...τῆς φ. μόρια *ib.*6(566); τοὺς μὲν ἀκτημοσύνην ἀσκοῦντας, καὶ τῇ ἄλλῃ φ. διαλάμποντας Isid.Pel.*epp.*3.17(M.78.744B); **b.** practice involving self-control, temperance, moderation οὐδεὶς κακῷ κακὸν ἰᾶται, ἀλλ' ἀγαθῷ τὸ κακόν. ταῦτα παρ' Ἕλλησί τινες φιλοσοφοῦσιν. αἰσχυνθῶμεν τοίνυν, εἰ παρ' Ἕλλησι τοῖς ἀνοήτοις τοσαύτης οὔσης τῆς φ., ἡμεῖς ἐλάττους φαινόμεθα. πολλοὶ ἠδικήθησαν, καὶ ἤνεγκαν· πολλοὶ ἐσυκοφαντήθησαν, καὶ οὐκ ἠμύναντο Chrys.*hom.51.3 in Jo.*(8.303A); οὐ δοκεῖ σοι φιλοσοφίας εἶναι μεγάλης, ὅταν κύων δακνόμενος ὑπὸ τοῦ λιμοῦ, ὅταν τὸ λαβεῖν καὶ θηρεῦσαι, παρούσης ἀπέχηται τῆς τροφῆς; id.*hom.34.5 in Ac.*(9.266D); γυναῖκες, ὅσαι πᾶσαν μὲν ἐπεδείξαντο φ., ταύτην δὲ τὴν δυσκληρίαν [sc. childlessness] οὐκ ἤνεγκαν id.*Anna* 2.1(4.712C); *ib.*2.3(4.715B); id.*hom.87.3 in Mt.*(7.821B); ref. David's moderation towards

Saul, id.*David* 3.3(4.772E–773A); Thdt.*qu.56 in 1Reg.*(1.391); also patience *παλαιῶν ἀνδρῶν ἐν...πλήθει τῶν ἀνιόντων ἀκατάσειστον...φ.* Dion.Ar.*e.h.*3.3.4(M.3.429C); magnanimity, Chrys.*hom.15.10 in Mt.*(7.202C); humility and meekness, *ib.57.4*(580E); id.*hom.32.2 in Jo.*(8.186C); **5.** denoting spiritual life; **a.** in gen., Gr.Nyss.*instit.* (p.83.3; M.34.436B); Chrys.*hom.14.1 in Gen.*(4.107C); Thdt.*h.rel.*2 (3.1121); id.*affect.*12(p.299.1; 4.1012); **b.** ref. asceticism *ἄπαιδες γεγόνασιν...γυναικείας δ' ἀποστροφῇ μίξεως, ἣν...φιλοσοφίας ἔρωτι προείλοντο* Eus.*v.C.*4.26(p.127.8; M.20.1173C); *χρὴ...σώματος ἐπιμέλειαν ποιεῖσθαι, οὐ διὰ τὸ σῶμα, ἀλλ' ὑπηρεσίαν...φιλοσοφίᾳ κτωμένους. ἀδύνατον γὰρ τὴν ὑπηρεσίαν τοῦ σώματος εὐήνιον πρὸς φιλοσοφίαν μὴ ἔχοντας, ἢ ἀναγνώσμασι φιλοσόφοις ἀρκέσαι, ἢ τὸν νοῦν...πρὸς εὐχὴν δεόντως συντεῖναι, ἢ συνόλως τι τῶν φιλοσοφίᾳ ἐπιβαλλόντων...ἐργάσασθαι* †Bas.Anc.*virg.*11(M.30.692B); *καλὴ ἡ φ. ... ὅτι οὐδὲ ἰατρεύεσθαι πολυτελῶς τοῖς τροφίμοις αὐτῆς ἐπιτρέπει· ἀλλὰ τὸ αὐτὸ καὶ ὄψον ἐστὶ παρ' αὐτῇ, καὶ πρὸς ὑγιείαν ἀρκεῖ* Bas.*ep.*186(3.267C; M.32.661D); *οὐδὲν ὁ μετέχων τῆς τροφῆς, τοῦ μὴ μετέχοντος δεύτερος εἰς φ. φανεῖται* ‡Bas.*const.*4.4(2.547A; M.31.1352C); *ὅσοι τῆς φ. τρόφιμοι...τὴν ἁγίαν τεσσαρακοστὴν χαίροντες ὑποδέξασθε* Ast.Am.*hom.*14(M.40.372B); possible and necessary also for those living in the world, Chrys. *hom.55.6 in Mt.*(7.564C); id.*oppugn.*3.9(1.91A); Thdt.*h.rel.*2(3.1123); **c.** sources of φ. and means of attaining it: *ἐνῆγεν* [sc. Christ] *εἰς φ.* Chrys.*hom.19.1 in Mt.*(7.244B); *ταύτην παρὰ τοῦ διδασκάλου τὴν φ. ἐμάνθανε* id.*stat.*1.3(2.5C); *ἡ δὲ τοῦ πνεύματος χάρις...πᾶσι τοῖς προσέχουσι φ. ἐντίθησι ib.*1.1(3A); *ἀρκεῖ δὲ ἕκαστος στίχος* [sc. of Pss.] *πολλὴν ἡμῖν ἐνθεῖναι φ.* id.*exp.in Ps.*41:3(5.141D); poverty, Bas.*ep.*4 (3.76C; M.32.236C); humility *τὸ μετὰ τῶν ἐσχάτων ἑαυτὸν ἀριθμεῖν. τοῦτο φ. πάσης ἀρχή* Chrys.*hom.3.5 in Mt.*(7.42C); solitude, id.*hom. 42.1 in Jo.*(8.248D); prayer, id.*exp.in Ps.*4:2(5.8A); simplicity, id. *hom.7.3 in Ac.*(9.59E); purity of mind, Max.*cap.*5.94(M.90.1388D); **d.** highest degree *οὗτος γὰρ φιλοσοφίας ὅρος, μετὰ συνέσεως ἄπλαστον εἶναι· τοῦτο βίος ἀγγελικός* Chrys.*hom.62.4 in Mt.*(7.624E); *ὅσοι τῆς φ. εἰς ἄκρον ἐληλύθασι, καὶ σφᾶς ἄγειν δύνανται καὶ μόνοι διατρίβειν* Soz.*h.e.*6.31.4(M.67.1388C); **6.** of spiritual doctrine *οὓς ἀμφὶ τὰ Ἑλλήνων...μαθήματα δεινῶς ἐπτοημένους, φιλοσοφίας αὐτοῖς ἐνεὶς* [sc. Or.] *ἔρωτα* Eus.*h.e.*6.30(M.20.589B); *πόθος...τῶν θείων δογμάτων, καὶ τῆς περὶ ἐκεῖνα φ. ... πρὸς τὴν ἀνωτάτω φ. παιδαγωγῶν* Evagr.*ep.*1 (M.32.248A); *αὐτὰ δὲ εἰρημένα Παύλῳ φιλοσοφίας ἔγεμε* Chrys.*hom. 49.3 in Ac.*(9.368A); Thdt.*ep.*7(4.1066); ref. apostolic teaching *μεστὴ ...πάσης φ.* Cyr.*Lc.*6:27(M.72.596A); *ἐπιστολὴν...πολλῆς γέμουσαν φ.* †Jo.D.*B.J.*36(M.96.1201A); **7.** of religious life *ἠξίου* [sc. Constantine] *τιμῆς πλείονος τοὺς τὸν σφῶν βίον τῇ κατὰ θεὸν ἀναθέντας φ.* Eus.*v.C.*4.28(p.128.13; M.20.1177A); id.*h.e.*6.10(M.20.541B); *πάσης ὕλης βιωτικῆς γυμνωθέντας ἐντὸς τοῦ κατὰ φιλοσοφίαν γενέσθαι βίου* Bas.*ascet.*2.1(2.323E; M.31.881B); *τὴν τῶν μοναχῶν φ. ... λάμπουσαν* Chrys.*hom.6.3 in 1Cor.*(10.48A); *φ. ἀποστρέφεται θόρυβον, καὶ γυμνασία μοναχικὴ ἔξω κατορθοῦται συγχύσεως* Isid.Pel.*epp.*1.92(M.78. 245B); Thdt.*h.e.*4.28.1(3.1007); *οἱ δὲ τῆς εὐαγγελικῆς ἐρασθέντες φ. πόρρωθεν τῶν πολιτικῶν θορύβων γεγένηνται* id.*affect.*12(p.306.1; 4. 1019); *τῶν μοναχῶν φιλοσοφίαν, ἐν ἐπιστήμῃ τῶν ἑνοποιῶν ἐντολῶν ἐνεργουμένην* Dion.Ar.*e.h.*6.3.2(M.3.533D); †Jo.D.*B.J.*18(M.96. 1017D); **8.** virtually equated with sanctity *τὴν Ἰωάννου εὐχάριστον φ.* Pall.*v.Chrys.*11(p.66.14; M.47.37); *οὐκ ἤνεγκεν ὁ φθόνος τὰς τῆς ἐκείνου φ. μαρμαρυγάς* Thdt.*h.e.*5.34.1(3.1073); id.*h.rel.*21(3.1240); **9.** of love of God *ἀρετὴ δὲ καὶ φ., μόνη μένει ἀγαθῶν...ἀδύνατον γὰρ κατορθῶσαι φ. τὸν μὴ θερμὸν τοῦ θεοῦ γενόμενον ἐραστήν· μᾶλλον δὲ αὐτὸ τοῦτο φ. καλεῖται. σοφία γὰρ ὁ θεὸς καὶ ἔστι, καὶ καλεῖται* Thdt. *carit.*(3.1311); id.*h.rel.*3(3.1145).

II. *discipline, adherence to* medic. *regime οἱ νοσοῦντες, ἂν μὴ διαπαντὸς εὐτακτῶσιν, οὐδὲν αὐτοῖς ὄφελος τῆς μέχρι τριῶν καὶ τεσσάρων ἡμερῶν φ.* Chrys.*stat.*3.7(2.46D).

***φιλοσοφικῶς**, *with the austerity becoming to a philosopher*, Eus. *Hierocl.*18(523D; M.22.824D); Epiph.*haer.*77.18(p.432.5; M.42.665D).

φιλόσοφος, ὁ, A. *philosopher*; **1.** gen. characteristics *ἀγαπᾷ τὴν ἀλήθειαν ὁ φ., ἐκ τοῦ θεράπων εἶναι γνήσιος δι' ἀγάπην ἤδη φίλος νομισθείς* Clem.*str.*2.9(p.136.30; M.8.980C); fleeing licentiousness and luxury, *ib.*2.20(p.181.16; 1069C); *τριῶν...ἀντέχεται ὁ ἡμεδαπὸς φ., πρῶτον μὲν τῆς θεωρίας, δεύτερον δὲ τῆς τῶν ἐντολῶν ἐπιτελέσεως, τρίτον ἀνδρῶν ἀγαθῶν κατασκευῆς ib.*2.10(p.137.14; 981B); *φ. δὲ λέγονται παρ' ἡμῖν μὲν οἱ σοφίας ἐρῶντες τῆς τοῦ πάντων δημιουργοῦ... υἱοῦ τοῦ θεοῦ, παρ' Ἕλλησι δὲ οἱ τῶν περὶ ἀρετῆς λόγων ἀντιλαμβανόμενοι ib.*6.7(p.459.22; M.9.277B); *δύο...δυσκράτητα, θεὸς καὶ ἄγγελος· καὶ τὸ τρίτον φ., ἄυλος ἐν ὕλῃ, ἐν σώματι ἀπερίγραπτος, ἐπὶ γῆς οὐράνιος...νικῶν τῷ νικᾶσθαι τοὺς κρατεῖν νομίζοντας* Gr.Naz.*or.*26.13 (M.35.1245B); *φ. ... καλῶ τοὺς οὐδὲν περιττὸν ἐπιζητοῦντας* Chrys. *hom.34.5 in 1Cor.*(10.317D); id.*hom.21.4 in Eph.*(11.164A); traits unworthy of a philosopher: calumny, Just.*2apol.*3.2(M.6.448A); avarice, id.*dial.*2.3(M.6.477A); **2.** pagan *οἱ φ. περὶ θεοῦ τὸν ἅπαντα ποιοῦνται λόγον...καὶ περὶ μοναρχίας αὐτοῖς καὶ προνοίας αἱ ζητήσεις γίνονται ἑκάστοτε* Just.*dial.*1.3(M.6.473B); Athenag.*leg.*5.1(M.6. 900A); moral teaching, Clem.*paed.*1.10(p.145.17; M.8.361A); *ib.*1.13 (p.150.22; 372B); *ἡ...ἀνθρωπίνη ἐγκράτεια, ἡ κατὰ τοὺς φ. λέγω τοὺς Ἑλλήνων* id.*str.*3.7(p.222.14; M.8.1161A); Gr.Thaum.*pan.Or.*11(p.26. 24; M.10.1084B); *πρὸς τὸν αἴτιον καὶ αὐτῶν τῶν ὄντων καὶ τῆς γνώσεως αὐτῶν ἐχρῆν ἀνάγεσθαι τοὺς ἀληθεῖς φ.* Dion.Ar.*ep.*7.2(M.3.1080B); errors *φιλοσόφων παρατρέπεται χορὸς πρὸς μὲν τὴν οὐρανοῦ θέαν παγκάλως γεγονέναι τὸν ἄνθρωπον ὁμολογούντων, τὰ δὲ ἐν οὐρανῷ φαινόμενα...προσκυνούντων* Clem.*prot.*4(p.48.19; M.8.164B); condemnation of Christians, id.*str.*7.1(p.3.4; M.9.401B); *Hom.Clem.*1.10; *ἐνηδρεύθησαν...οἱ τῶν Ἑλλήνων φ. ib.*2.7; derided by Christians *τίς ...τοὺς ληρώδεις ἐκείνων λόγους ἀποδέχῃ τῶν...φ.; Diogn.*8.2; Tat. *orat.*19(p.20.27; M.6.848B); *ὁ φ. ... μετὰ τῆς μακρηγορίας, καὶ ἀσαφείας πολλῆς τὰ εἰρημένα ἐνέπλησεν* Chrys.*hom.1.5 in Mt.*(7.11A); *ποῦ νῦν εἰσιν οἱ τῶν Ἑλλήνων φ. ... ; ib.10.4*(144C); in rel. to Christianity *νήπιοι...οἱ φ., ἐὰν μὴ ὑπὸ τοῦ Χριστοῦ ἀπανδρωθῶσιν* Clem.*str.*1.11(p.34.22; M.8.752A); cf.*ib.*5.4(p.341.20; M.9.44B); Chrys. *hom.5.1 in 1Cor.*(10.34B); teaching borrowed from revelation *οἱ... φ. ἔκλεψαν ἐκ τῶν ἁγίων γραφῶν* Thphl.Ant.*Autol.*1.14(M.6.1045A); Clem.*str.*6.4(p.448.20; M.9.253A); cf.*ib.*1.21(p.64.18; M.8.820A); *κλέπτας λέγεσθαι τοὺς τῶν Ἑλλήνων φ., παρὰ Μωϋσέως καὶ τῶν προφητῶν τὰ κυριώτατα τῶν δογμάτων οὐκ εὐχαρίστως εἰληφότας ib.*5.1 (p.332.15; M.9.24A); Christians retain what is true in pagan teaching, Gr.Thaum.*pan.Or.*14(p.33.11; M.10.1093A); **3.** Christian; **a.** of Christians in gen., as true philosophers, Just.*dial.*8.2(M.6.492D); Gr.Naz.*or.*25.6(M.35.1205A); **b.** of ascetics *βίῳ φ. ἀληθῆ...Πάμφιλον* Eus.*h.e.*7.32.25(M.20.732B); *οὗτοι γάρ εἰσιν...φ. θεοῦ, οἱ ὁδηγούμενοι ...κατὰ τὸν ἔσω ἄνθρωπον ὑπὸ τῆς θεϊκῆς δυνάμεως* Mac.Aeg.*hom.*17. 10(M.34.629D).

B. *ascetic, monk ὁ γὰρ ἀκριβὴς φ. φροντιστήριον ἔχων τὸ σῶμα, καὶ καταγωγὴν τῆς ψυχῆς ἀσφαλῆ, κἂν ἐπ' ἀγορᾶς ὢν τύχῃ, κἂν ἐν πανηγύρει, κἂν ἐν ὄρει...ἐν τῷ φυσικῷ μοναστηρίῳ καθίδρυται, ἔνδον συνάγων τὸν νοῦν* ‡Bas.*const.*5(2.550C; M.31.1360B); Thdt.*affect.*12 (p.305.12; 4.1019); *πρὸ πάντων ἐλεύθερον εἶναι δεῖ τὸν φ., καὶ μᾶλλον φεύγειν τὸ δοῦλον εἶναι παθῶν, ἢ ἀργυρώνητον* Nil.*exerc.*1(M.79.720B).

C. as adj.; **1.** *loving wisdom*, opp. *φιλόδοξος*, Just.*2apol.*3.6(M.6. 449B); opp. *μικρόψυχος*, Chrys.*hom.38.7 in 1Cor.*(10.361B); **2.** *wise*; of a chaste woman, *Hom.Clem.*5.8; of Magi, Chrys.*hom.7.5 in Mt.* (7.113A); *μετὰ τῆς χάριτος, καὶ ἡ γνώμη τῶν γυναικῶν φ. ἦν* id.*hom. 62.3 in Jo.*(8.373A); *δόξης καταφρονῶν καὶ φ. ἐστιν· οἶδε γὰρ τὰ ἀνθρώπινα πράγματα* id.*hom.9.1 in Col.*(11.391B); **3.** *Christian φ. βίος* Eus.*l.C.*17(p.255.14; M.20.1432C); *φ. δόγματα ib.*(p.258.2; 1436D); id.*h.e.*4.7.14(M.20.321A); id.*d.e.*3.5(p.124.14; M.22.212C); hence **4.** *virtuous ψυχὴ φιλοσοφωτέρα τοσαύταις ἐντρεφομένη μελέταις* [sc. prayer and thanksgiving] Chrys.*hom.2.4 in Mt.*(7.28A); free from passions, *ib.*4.4(52B); showing forbearance, *ib.*48.5(500B); *ib.* 73.4(713B); *φιλοσοφωτέρας δεῖται ψυχῆς, τὸ χαίρειν μετὰ χαιρόντων, μᾶλλον ἢ τὸ κλαίειν μετὰ κλαιόντων* id.*hom.22.1 in Rom.*(9.680D); ref. ascetical life of early Christians *ἄσκησις φιλοσοφωτάτη* Eus.*h.e.*2.16. 2(M.20.173A); *φ. βίος ib.*6.9.6(540B); of Jo. Bapt., Chrys.*hom.37.3 in Mt.*(7.418E); *φ. ὁ ἀνήρ, καὶ τῷ σκληρῷ βίῳ συντεθραμμένος* Thdt.*h.rel.* 3(3.1144); **5.** *contemplative φ. γνώμης καὶ ὑψηλῆς διανοίας* Chrys.*hom. 8.1 in Rom.*(9.498B); *ib.17.2*(623D); *ὁ τέλειος καὶ φ. βίος* Thdt.*qu.1 in Lev.*(1.180); **6.** *τὸ φ. solitary, contemplative life μήτε τὸ φ. ἀκοινώνητον ᾖ, μήτε τὸ πρακτικὸν ἀφιλόσοφον* Gr.Naz.*or.*43.62(M.36.577B); *humility*, Chrys.*hom.53.1 in Mt.*(7.539B); *ib.58.2*(586C); **7.** *monastic μετασχεῖν τῆς φ. τραπέζης* Gr.Nyss.*v.Macr.*(p.411.12; M.46.997A).

***φιλοσοφροσύνη, ἡ,** v. **φιλοσωφροσύνη*.

φιλοσόφως, *philosophically*; hence **1.** *uncomplainingly, patiently*, Chrys.*David* 3.5(4.775E); id.*hom.84.4 in Mt.*(7.802C); **2.** *ascetically*, Gr.Nyss.*instit.*(p.66.14; M.34.421C).

***φιλοσπεύδω**, v. **φιλοσπουδέω*.

***φιλοσπουδέω**, *be eager to learn*, *Apoc.En.*21.5(p.50.12) v.l. *φιλοσπεύδεις*.

***φιλόσταυρος**, *loving the Cross*, Leont.N.*v.Sym.*5(M.93.1673C).

φιλοστοργία, ἡ, *tender love, affection*, esp. of family *affection*; **1.** in gen. *ἥ τε φ. φιλοτεχνία τις οὖσα περὶ στέρξιν φίλων ἢ οἰκείων* Clem.*str.*2.9(p.135.5; M.8.977A); *ib.*2.16(p.152.20; 1013A); of Christians *τὴν φ. ἔχουσι πρὸς ἀλλήλους Diogn.*1; *παραχωρείτω δὲ ἕκαστος τῶν πρωτείων τῷ πέλας. τοῦτο γὰρ τῆς...φ. τεκμήριον* Thdt.*Rom.* 12:10(3.133); of S. Paul for his converts, Chrys.*comm.in Gal.*4:13 (10.707A); Thdt.*1Thess.*2:11(3.509); enjoined on BMV and S. John by Christ on the Cross, Cyr.H.*catech.*7.9; *ὅνπερ γὰρ τρόπον ἡ Μαρία* μήτηρ Ἰωάννου διὰ τὴν φ. οὐ διὰ τὸ γεννῆσαι *ib.*; **2.** of God's love for humanity, Chrys.*Is.1 interp.*(6.13D); id.*Eutrop.*1.3(3.383C); τὴν τοῦ πλάστου πρὸς ἡμᾶς κηδεμονικὴν φ. Areth.*Apoc.*11:1(M.106.648A); **3.** of Christ's love for Father (ref. Sonship) οὐ γὰρ δοῦλός ἐστιν, ἵνα ἀνάγκῃ ὑποταγῇ· ἀλλὰ υἱός ἐστιν· ἵνα προαιρέσει καὶ φ. πεισθῇ Cyr.H.*catech.*15.30.

φιλόστοργος, *loving tenderly, affectionate*; of Father, Clem.*prot.* 10(p.68.28; M.8.205C); ὁ δὲ θεὸς...μητέρων φιλοστοργότερος Chrys. *hom.4.9 in Ac.princ.*(3.95B); Nonn.*par.Jo.*15:15(M.43.876A); of Christ, *ib.*13:23(864B); φιλοξείνους δὲ γυναῖκας Ἰησοῦς ἀγάπαζε φ. τινὶ θεσμῷ *ib.*11:5(840B); met. ἡ τοῦ γάλακτος ζωοτρόφος οὐσία φιλοστόργοις πηγάζουσα μαστοῖς Clem.*paed.*1.6(p.111.7; M.8.292C); φ. τραπέζης Nonn.*par.Jo.*13:2(860B); of devout use of scripture φιλοσυνήθης τε γάρ ἐστιν αὕτη καὶ φ. Euthal.Diac.*Ac.*(M.85.633A).

φιλοστόργως, *lovingly, tenderly*, ref. God, towards the dead τὸν προσλαβόμενον αὐτὸν φ. δεσπότην Nil.*epp.*2.170(M.79.285D); ref. Creation τοῦ δημιουργήσαντος...πανσόφως ἅμα καὶ φ. τεκτηναμένου τὸ δαίδαλμα Bas.Sel.*or.*2.1(M.85.37B).

***φιλοσυγγένεια, ἡ,** *love of relatives*, Pall.*h.Laus.*6(p.22.13; M.34.1018B).

***φιλοσύγχυτος,** *leading to confusion*, Sophr.H.*ep.syn.*(M.87.3172D).

***φιλοσυμπαθής,** *compassionate*, Jo.Mosch.*prat.*37(M.87.2885D); *ib.*184(3056D); Thdr.Stud.*epp.*1.49(M.99.1084D).

***φιλοσχισματικός,** *schismatic*; of persons, Esaias *or.*5.2(p.36; cf. M.40.1122A).

φιλοσώματος, *loving the body*, i.e. *loving earthly life*, Chrys.*hom.34.4 in Mt.*(7.394C); μέλλων ἀπιέναι θρηνεῖς, καὶ ἐμφιλοχωρεῖς τοῖς ἐνταῦθα φ. ὤν; id.*hom.2.4 in Col.*(11.338C); Max.*ambig.*(M.91.1101D).

***φιλοσωφροσύνη, ἡ,** *courtesy, respect*, Geo.Al.*v.Chrys.*(p.238.10, v.l. φιλοσοφρ-); Anast.S.*qu.et resp.*146(M.89.800D).

φιλοσώφρων, *loving virtue* or *chastity*, Gr.Naz.*or.*24.10(M.35.1180A).

φιλοτάραχος, *loving tumult, confusion*, Eust.Mon.*ep.*(M.86.932C); of Devil, Gr.Ant.*bapt.*2.10(M.88.1884A).

φιλοτερπής, *fond of pleasure*, ‡Chrys.*meretr.*3(10.783E).

φιλοτεχνέω, 1. *make, produce, skilfully*, Thdt.*provid.*5(4.547); Bas.*hom.*7.4(3.56A; M.31.289A); Const.Diac.*laud.*28(M.88.572B); of God ὑπ' αὐτοῦ τοῦ θεοῦ φιλοτεχνηθέντα παντοῖα γένη τῶν φυτῶν †Bas.*parad.*3.1(1.347F; M.30.64A); Gr.Nyss.*anim.et res.*(M.46.153C); ref. creation of man, ‡Gr.Nyss.*or.2 in Gen.1:26*(M.44.280C); **2.** *invent* Ὄλυμπος ὁ Μυσὸς τὴν Λύδιον ἁρμονίαν ἐφιλοτέχνησεν Clem.*str.*1.16(p.49.16; M.8.788B).

φιλοτέχνημα, τό, *work of art*, ref. creation of man by God, ‡Gr.Nyss.*or.1 in Gen.1:26*(M.44.260C); Nil.*epp.*4.42(M.79.569C).

***φιλοτεχνήμων, ὁ,** *artificer*; of God, Cyr.*thes.*32(5[1].329E).

***φιλοτέχνησις, ἡ,** *artistic skill*; of God, ‡Gr.Nyss.*or.2 in Gen.1:26*(M.44.281A).

φιλοτιμ-έω, A. act., *honour* with gifts σοὶ τὰ σά. ~οῦμέν σε, οὐρανοδύναμε *Pers.*(p.18.7; M.10.108B).

B. usu. med.; **1.** *be generous, indulgent, behave generously* δαψιλέστερον πρός με ~ούμενος *Hom.Clem.*5.3; ὁ δὲ ~ούμενος ἥδεται Thdt.*2Cor.*9:5(3.334); ref. Mt.18:21 νομίσαντος αὐτοῦ μεγάλα ~εῖσθαι, καὶ δαψιλεύεσθαι Chrys.*hom.in Mt.18:23*(3.5B); id.*hom.61.1 in Mt.*(7.610D); **2.** *endow, present, bestow* τὴν Ῥωμαίων ὤνησε πόλιν...καὶ γὰρ πολλὰ ἐφιλοτιμήσατο Socr.*h.e.*5.18.1(M.67.609B); πάντας ἐφιλοτιμεῖτο δώροις †Jo.D.*B.J.*3(M.96.877C); Thphn.*chron.* p.183(M.108.477A); of God μετὰ τὸν κατακλυσμὸν πλείονι τοῦτον [sc. τὸν ἄνθρωπον] ~εῖται τρυφῇ Thdt.*qu.55 in Gen.*(1.67); τῷ γένει τῶν ἀνθρώπων ἐφιλοτιμήσατο τῆς βασιλείας τὴν πρόνοιαν Heracl.*ep.*(M.92.992B); μέλλοντος κατὰ χάριν ~εῖσθαι τοῖς οὖσι τὴν ἑαυτῶν, καὶ ἄλλων, ὅ τί ποτε κατ' οὐσίαν ὑπάρχουσι γνῶσιν Max.*cap.*4.32(M.90.1317B); pass. ὡς πειραθησόμενοι...μετουσίας...τῆς τῶν ~ουμένων ὑπὲρ τοῦ εὖ ἀγαθῶν παρὰ τοῦ θεοῦ Didym.*Trin.*2.8(M.39.589C); μὴ οὖν...τῷ τοῦ αὐτεξουσίου δώρῳ ~ούμενοι πρὸς ἀλογίαν ἐκπίπτωμεν Const.Diac.*laud.*14(M.88.496C); **3.** *seek to contrive, design* ~ουμένου τοῦ σατανᾶ καὶ δι' ἐκείνων [sc. τῶν ἁγίων μαρτύρων] ῥηθῆναί τι τῶν βλασφήμων Eus.*h.e.*5.1.16(M.20.413C); παντοδαποὶ γάρ, τῶν τοιούτων τρόπων παρὰ Πέρσαις εἰς ὠμότητα ~ουμένων Soz.*h.e.*2.14.4(M.67.969A).

***φιλοτίμησις, ἡ, 1.** *ambition, aspiration*, Epiph.*haer.*63.1(p.399.12; M.41.1064B); **2.** *generosity, benefaction* τὰς εἰς τοὺς πτωχοὺς φ. †Bas.*miser.*(2 p.1069C; M.31.1709D).

φιλοτιμητέον, *one must strive*, Clem.*str.*2.21(p.184.4; M.8.1076B); Or.*Jo.*13.63(60; p.296.3; M.14.520D); †Bas.*Is.*63(1.425C; M.30.229A).

φιλοτιμία, ἡ, A. *ambition, desire*; **1.** ref. God ἀγνοούμενος ὁ θεὸς ἐν ἀνθρώποις, καὶ παρὰ τοῦτ' ἔλαττον ἔχειν δοκῶν, ἐθέλοι ἂν γνωρισθῆναι ...πολλήν τινα καὶ πάνυ θνητὴν φ. τοῦ θεοῦ καταμαρτυροῦσι Cels.ap. Or.*Cels.*4.6(p.278.21; M.11.1036B); οὐδεμίαν οὖν θνητὴν φ. ὁ Χριστιανῶν λόγος καταμαρτυρεῖ τοῦ θεοῦ *ib.*(p.279.3; 1036D); ἐνεργετικῇ φ. ἐκτίσθη ὁ υἱός Ast.Soph.*fr.*5 ap.Ath.*syn.*19(p.246.29; M.26.716B); **2.** in concrete sense, *object of ambition* οὐ τετυχηκότα τῆς φ. Cyr. *Lc.*9:42(M.72.657B); **3.** *position of honour, office* οἱ μετασχόντες στρατείας ἢ ἀξίας ἢ συνηγορίας ἢ δημοσίας φ. ... παρὰ μόνων ὀρθοδόξων κληρονομοῦνται Phot.*nomoc.*10.8(M.104.832C); **4.** *distinction, distinguishing mark* εἰ μὴ ἐφόρει χλαμύδα ἔχουσαν φ. βασιλικῆς ἐσθῆτος Jo.Mal.*chron.*2 p.34(M.97.103A); **5.** *ambitious display, ostentation* Jul.Papa *ep.Dian.*ap.Ath.*apol.sec.*21(p.103.10; M.25.284B); **6.** *contention* in argument διὰ τὴν πρὸς ἡμᾶς φ. Clem.*str.*1.19(p.60.14; M.8.809B).

B. *zeal, care* τὴν μεγίστην φ. εἰς τοῦτο προσενεγκαμένου Clem.*str.*1.22(p.92.9; M.8.892A); Or.*fr.incert.in Jer.*(p.195.11; M.14.1309C).

C. *lavish outlay*; **1.** *munificence* σὺν οἷᾳ πάντων ὑμῶν φ. Eus.*h.e.*10.4.26(M.20.860B); ἀφθόνῳ φ. τῶν ἀναλωμάτων χρώμενος *ib.*10.4.42(865B); plur., *munificent works*; **a.** of buildings τὰς...πόλεις ταῖς τῶν εὐκτηρίων φ. ἐκπρέπειν ἐποίει Eus.*v.C.*3.50(p.98.27; M.20.1109B); **b.** of public entertainments, shows, *M.Perp.*10(p.79.4); Eus.*m.P.*6.2(p.920.16; M.20.1481A); *M.Ign.Ant.*5(M.5.984C); **2.** *generosity, liberality* οὐ γὰρ οἶμαι τῷ ποσῷ τῆς διδομένης ὕλης...ταῖς δὲ προσφερούσαις γνώμαις μᾶλλον καὶ προαιρέσεσι τὴν φ. καὶ τὴν μεγαλοπρέπειαν, ὁ ἱερὸς λόγος ἐσταθμήσατο Gr.Thaum.*pan.Or.*3(p.7.4; M.10.1057D); οὐ...μόνον ἃ βούλεται λαβεῖν κελεύει δοῦναι ἀλλὰ καὶ πλείονα ἐπιδείξασθαι φ. Chrys.*hom.18.2 in Mt.*(7.236C); καὶ γὰρ ὁ θεὸς διὰ τοῦτο ἡμᾶς βούλεται ἄρχεσθαι τῆς τοιαύτης φ., ἵνα ἀφορμὴν λάβῃ τοῦ πλείονα ἡμῖν ἀντιδοῦναι *ib.15.10*(202B); φιλαδελφίαν ἐνταῦθα τὴν τῶν χρημάτων φ. ἐκάλεσε, περὶ ἧς ἔφη μὴ χρῄζειν αὐτοὺς παραινέσεως ἐκ θείας γὰρ αὐτοῖς προσγεγενῆσθαι χάριτος τὸ κατόρθωμα Thdt. *1Thess.*4:10(3.517); shown in extending forgiveness, *generosity* of mind *benevolence, kindliness*, id.*2Cor.*2:10(3.298); of God τὰ μὲν λοιπὰ τῶν ἀγαθῶν ἔδωκεν ἐκ φ. τῇ ἀνθρωπίνῃ φύσει Gr.Nyss.*hom.opif.*9.1(M.44.149B); τὴν ἀνεκδιήγητον φ. Chrys.*hom.15.8 in Mt.*(7.199A); λοιπὸν ἀναγκαίως εἰσφέρεται τῆς διὰ Χριστοῦ φ. ἡ χάρις, δικαιοῦσα τὸν ἀσεβῆ καὶ ἀπαλλάττουσα τῶν πλημμελημάτων τοὺς ἐνισχομένους αὐτοῖς Cyr. *Is.*3.5(2.518D); Thdt.*qu.18 in Num.*(1.231); κἂν γὰρ μυριάκις ὑπόσχηται ἀγαθά, ἀναξίους δὲ ἡμᾶς αὐτοὺς τῆς δωρεᾶς καταστήσωμεν, ἐμπόδιον γινόμεθα τῇ θείᾳ φ. id.*Dan.*9:3(2.1229); in bad sense, *lavishness, prodigality* πολλὴν ἐν τοῖς βιωτικοῖς φ. ἐπιδείκνυσθαι Chrys.*hom.45.3 in Mt.*(480A); id.*hom.6.2 in Gal.*(10.725E); **3.** *generous bestowal* ὡραιότης δὲ τοῦ οἴκου, [sc. κατὰ τὸν ἀπόστολον] ἡ χάρις τοῦ ἁγίου πνεύματος, ἡ τοῦτον ὡραΐζουσά τε καὶ λαμπρύνουσα τῇ παντοδαπῇ φ. τῶν δωρεῶν Thdt.*Ps.*67:13(1.1062).

D. *abundance* βούλεται...δεῖξαι τὴν ὑπερβολὴν...ἀπὸ...τῆς φ. τοῦ καλλωπισμοῦ τῆς δοθείσης τοῖς κρίνοις Chrys.*hom.22.1 in Mt.*(7.274D); οὐκ ἔχοντες ἁπλῶς ὅπως χρήσωνται τῇ φ. τοῦ ὕδατος Nil.*narr.*5(M.79.648C).

φιλότιμος, 1. *generous, liberal, lavish*; of God, Chrys.*hom.15.5 in Gen.*(4.121D); Mac.Mgn.*apocr.*4.25(p.207.12); χαρίζεται γὰρ τῇ φ. δεξιᾷ τὰ ἀναγκαῖα πρὸς τὸ ζῆν Cyr.*Ps.*5:8(M.69.740D); of entertainments or hospitality, Eus.*m.P.*6(p.920.16; M.20.1480C); ἡ...φ. τράπεζα †Cosm.Mel.*schol.*(M.38.546) in Gr.Naz.*carm.*2.2(epitaph.) 50; of praise etc., Gr.Thaum.*pan.Or.*3(p.6.16; M.10.1057B); ὅσοι δὲ φιλοτιμώτερον τὸ σέβας ἐνδείκνυνται Jo.VI H.*v.Jo.D.*1(M.94.429A); in bad sense, *prodigal*, Chrys.*hom.66.3 in Mt.*(7.657C); **2.** *abundant*, met. ὅπως...πληρώσῃ τὴν χρείαν φ. Nil.*Magn.*16(M.79.989D).

φιλοτίμως, 1. *liberally, generously*, Chrys.*hom.50.4 in Mt.*(7.519E); Isid.Pel.*epp.*1.217(M.78.320B); Thdt.*Rom.*12:7(3.132); **2.** *with care, zeal*, Clem.*fr.*22(p.201.20)ap.Eus.*h.e.*6.14.2(M.20.549B).

***φιλότμητος,** *appointed for circumcision*, Nonn.*par.Jo.*14:5(M.43.868A).

***φιλότοπος,** *loving one's country*, ‡Chrys.*Abr.*1(2.742A).

***φιλοτρυφητής, ὁ,** *one fond of luxurious living*, Jo.Sync.*narr.*(H.4.320E).

***φιλοϋλία, ἡ,** *love of worldly things*, ‡Proc.G.*Pr.*21:6(M.87.1432A); as a ψυχικὸν πάθος, Ephr.3.426C = Jo.D.*virt.*(M.95.88B).

***φιλόϋλος,** *loving material things, unspiritual* οὐκ ἔστιν ἐν ἐμοὶ πῦρ φ. Ign.*Rom.*7.2; τὴν...φ. ... ζωὴν ‡Proc.G.*Pr.*10:3(M.87.1309D); ὁ ταραχώδης καὶ φ. λογισμὸς ὑπὲρ τοῦ εἰσοικίσασθαί τι τῶν αἰσθητῶν Max.*ambig.*(M.91.1120B); of persons, id.*qu.Thal.*19(M.90.532B).

***φιλοφλύαρος,** *foolish, trifling*, Jo.Carp.*cap.*59(M.85.1849).

***φιλόφονος,** *murderous*; neut. as subst., Thphn.*chron.*p.222(M.108.565C).

φιλοφρον-έω, 1. *treat kindly*, usu. med.; act., Thphn.*chron.*p.91(M.108.272B); pass., *be treated kindly*, *ib.*p.335(M.108.808C); *be treated* *with honour* ἡ τῆς θείας εἰρήνης ~εῖται παρουσία Max.*ep*.43(M.91.641C); **2.** med.; *be disposed to* φ. διαφέρεσθαι πρὸς ταῦτα Meth.*creat*.12(p.499.20; M.18.344A).

φιλοφρόνημα, τό, *act* or *proof of kindness*, ‡Gr.Naz.*Chr.pat*.1381(M.38.246A).

***φιλόφρονος,** *kindly*, Eus.*v.C*.4.44(p.136.5; M.20.1193C).

φιλόχηρος, *kind to widows*, *Const.App*.2.4.1; *ib*.2.50.1; Euthal. Diac.*Ac*.14:1(M.85.656A).

φιλόχρηστος, *aspiring, ambitious* πάθος...τὴν ψυχὴν λυμαινόμενον οἷον...τὸ φ. Gr.Nyss.*hom.12 in Cant*.(M.44.1017B).

φιλόχριστος, *loving Christ, devout*; of persons, Ath.*apol.Const*.3(M.25.600A); Cyr.H.*catech*.6.12; Cyr.*ep*.55(p.60.11; 5[2].189D); of cities, *Lit.Marc*.(p.120.7); Leont.N.*v.Jo.Eleem*.2(p.7.19); of abstracts φ. εὐσέβεια Ath.*syn*.39(p.265.25; M.26.761C); Bas.*ep*.70(3.163D; M.32.433B); Chrys.*hom.3.2 in 1Cor*.(10.17B).

***φιλόχρονος,** *taking account of time*, ref. Eunomian view of generation of Son ἵνα σου ῥᾳδίως φύγωμεν τὰς περιέργους ἐνστάσεις καὶ φ. Gr.Naz.*or*.29.5(p.79.8; M.36.80B).

***φιλοχρυσέω,** *love wealth*, Thdr.Stud.*epp*.2.180(M.99.1557D).

φιλοχρυσία, ἡ, *love of gold*, Chrys.*Is.1 interp*.(6.15B).

φιλόχρυσος, *greedy for gold*, Clem.*paed*.3.2(p.242.1; M.8.569B); φ. μᾶλλον ἢ φιλοχρίστους Gr.Naz.*or*.21.21(M.35.1105A); met. παλάμῃσι φ. id.*carm*.2.2(epigr.)62.4(M.38.115A).

φιλόχωρος, *fond of a place* μὴ φ. μὴ φιλοπολίτης ἀλλὰ φιλέρημος †Ph.Carp.*ep*.3(3.127D; M.32.353A); of creatures, *with fixed habitat*, Gr.Naz.*or*.28.23(p.57.17; M.36.57C).

φιλοψία, ἡ, *fondness for dainties*, Clem.*paed*.2.10(p.213.18; M.8.508B); *ib*.3.2(p.241.28; 569B).

***φιλοψογέω,** *delight in being censorious*, Cyr.*glaph.Ex*.1:7(1.255E); id.*Am*.37(3.291C); id.*Is*.3.2(2.418A).

***φιλοψογία, ἡ,** *censoriousness*, Cyr.*glaph.Gen*.6(1.180D); id.*Zach*.17(3.674A); id.*Jo*.4.4(4.385E).

***φιλόψοφος,** *loving noise*, opp. φιλόσοφος, Just.*2apol*.3.1(M.6.448A); Tat.*orat*.3(p.4.12; M.6.812A).

φιλόψυχος, *loving souls*; of God, Or.*Jo*.20.17(15; p.349.29; M.14.612C); οὐ γὰρ βούλεται τῶν πλημμελούντων τὴν ἀπώλειαν φ. ὤν Pall. *v.Chrys*.1(p.6.12; M.47.7); ‡Jo.D.*fid.dorm*.16(M.95.261D).

φιλόω, pass., *become friends* (variant of φιλιόω q.v.), Eus.*h.e*.1.6.3(M.20.88A); *Hom.Clem*.5.3; *Chron.Pasch*.p.177(M.92.433D); towards God, Max.*ep*.24(M.91.609A); met., of human nature τὴν ὑλικὴν τῶν ἀνθρώπων φύσιν...τῷ θεῷ καὶ πατρὶ προσαγαγὼν [sc. ὁ λόγος] σωθεῖσαν, φιλωθεῖσάν τε καὶ θεωθεῖσαν *ib*.12(468C); of elements στοιχεῖα... φιλωθέντα ἀλλήλοις Epiph.*exp.fid*.9(p.506.28; M.42.792C).

φίλτρον, τό, *love charm, that which arouses love*; hence *love, affection*; **1.** ref. human love ἐνέθηκε γὰρ ὁ θεὸς φ. τῇ φύσει τῇ ἡμετέρᾳ, ὥστε ἀλλήλους ἀγαπᾶν Chrys.*hom.2.3 in Eph*.(11.12E); of disciples towards Christ, Nonn.*par.Jo*.15:10(M.43.881C); Chrys.*hom.70.2 in Jo*.(8.415A); τὸ περὶ τὸν διδάσκαλον φ. Thdt.*1Cor*.15:5(3.266); towards God ἵν' ἴδωμεν, ὅσον δύναται κατὰ τῶν τραχυτάτων πόνων... εὐσέβεια καὶ τὸ πρὸς θεὸν φ., παντὸς φ. καθ' ὑπερβολὴν πλεῖον δυνάμενον Or.*mart*.27(p.23.27; M.11.596C); ἡ λογικὴ ψυχὴ...φ....ἀναλαμβάνει φυσικὸν τὸ πρὸς τὸν κτίσαντα, καὶ διὰ τὸ πρὸς ἐκεῖνον φ. ὑπεραποδέχεται καὶ τὸν ταῦτα πρῶτον πᾶσι τοῖς ἔθνεσι παραστήσαντα id. *Cels*.3.40(p.236.22; M.11.972C); Gr.Naz.*or*.6.5(M.35.728B); τῷ θείῳ πυρπολούμενοι φ. Thdt.*Ps*.118:165(1.1479); διήγειρας ἡμᾶς πρὸς ἔρωτά σου, καὶ φ. σου id.*Cant*.4(2.100); met., of abstracts τῷ φ. τῆς ὁμονοίας Gel.Cyz.*h.e*.3.19.39(M.85.1353D); φ. τῆς ἀληθείας *Cod.Afr*.57; within soul ἀγαθὸς ὢν ἀγαθὸν ἠγάπησεν, καὶ τὸ φ. ἔνδον ἐστὶν ἐν τῷ ἀνθρώπῳ, τοῦθ' ὅπερ ἐμφύσημα εἴρηται θεοῦ Clem.*paed*.1.3(p.94.15; M.8.257B); **2.** of passion οἰστροῦνται τῷ φ. Hegem.*Arch*.9(8; p.14.5; M.10.1441A); Chrys.*hom.33.5 in 1Cor*.(10.306B); τῷ φ. καιόμενον id.*sac*.6.12(p.166.14; 1.433A); **3.** met., *desire* φ. κλαπέντος εἰς ξένον ποθούμενον καλοῦσι δ' αὐτὴν ζηλοτυπίαν οἱ πάλαι Gr.Naz.*carm*.1.2.34.80(M.37.951A); **4.** of divine *love* for man; of Christ πάντα ἐμοὶ μικρὰ...πρὸς τὸ φ. ἐκεῖνο Chrys.*hom.15.5 in Rom*.(9.600D); Nonn. *par.Jo*.15:10(M.43.873C); of God, Mac.Aeg.*libert.ment*.20(M.34.953D); Chrys.*scand*.6(3.474A); Thdt.*Jer*.2:33(2.420); ὁ...θεὸς τοῦ περὶ ἡμᾶς φ. δηλοῖ τὴν ὑπερβολήν, τοῦ Χριστοῦ τὸν θάνατον, οὐχ ὑπὲρ δικαίων ἀλλ' ὑπὲρ ἁμαρτωλῶν γεγενῆσθαι Thdt.*Rom*.5:9(3.54).

φιλτροποιός, *making love-charms*, Thdr.Stud.*epp*.1.55(M.99.1108C).

***φίλυλος,** *loving material things, unspiritual* φ. διαθέσει κατὰ φύσιν Max.*ambig*.(M.91.1033B); of persons, *ib*.(1101D).

Φιλωνίζω, *imitate Philo*, Isid.Pel.*epp*.3.81(M.78.788C).

[*]**φίμετρον, τό,** variant of φίμωτρον; met., *means of checking* ἀκηδίας...φ. Dan.Raith.*v.Jo.Clim*.(M.88.601A).

φιμόω, 1. *silence*, met. τὰ στόματα φιμώσαντες Anon.ap.Eus.*h.e*.5.16.17(M.20.472A); ἔγραψε καὶ...Σαβέλλιον ἐφίμωσεν Ath.*Dion*.27(p.66.15; M.25.520C); φιμωθέντες τῇ ἀληθείᾳ ‡Meth.*palm*.7(M.18.396D); φιμοῦσθε τοῦ λέγειν ‡Anast.S.*Jud.disp*.3(M.89.1241D); of Christ ἐφίμωσε τοὺς δαίμονας Ath.*ep.Aeg.Lib*.3(M.25.544A); ὁ...διάβολος...ἐφιμώθη δὲ παρὰ τοῦ σωτῆρος *ib*.8(556B); id.*syn*.39(p.265.18; M.26.761B); of God ὁ θεὸς...'Ιουδαίων ἐφίμωσε στόματα Procl.CP *or*.5.4(M.65.721A); **2.** *bridle, subdue*, met. φιμώσωμεν τῆς ἑαυτῶν σαρκὸς τὸ φρόνημα Marc.Er.*opusc*.9(M.65.1116A); ὁ διάβολος φιμωθήτω *A.Jo*.114(p.214.8); ref. Inc. ἵνα λοιπὸν ὁ θάνατος φιμωθῇ Cyr.H.*catech*.3.11; of God ὁ τὴν ἀπόκρυφον νόσον τῆς ψυχῆς μου φιμώσας *A.Jo*.113(p.213.7); ἐφίμωσέν τε ὁ θεὸς καὶ πᾶν ἔθνος ἀπὸ τοῦ περικύκλου αὐτοῦ †Gregent.*leg.Hom*.(M.86.580C).

φιμώτης, ὁ, *subduer*, †Gregent.*disp*.(M.86.756A).

φίμωτρον, τό, *muzzle*; met., †Nil.*vit*.2(M.79.1141B); ‡Anast.Ant. *serm*.4(M.89.1392C).

***φισκίνα, ἡ,** (Lat. *piscina*) *fountain* εἰς τὸ χεῖλος τῆς φ. ὅπου ἐβαπτίσατέ με †Anast.S.*relat*.51(*OC* 3 p.74).

***φισκόομαι,** (cf. Lat. *fiscus*) *be confiscated, appropriated to the public treasury*, Phot.*nomoc*.3.14(p.505; M.104.609B).

φίσκος, ὁ, (Lat. *fiscus*) *imperial treasury*, Maximinus Daia ap. Eus.*h.e*.9.10.11(M.20.836A); Nil.*epp*.2.178(M.79.292B); Phot.*nomoc*.9.27(p.561; M.104.1121B).

***φλαγελλόω,** (Lat. *flagello*) *scourge*, ‡Chrys.*poenit*.5(9.771D).

***φλαμία, ἡ,** *spear*, *A.Thom*.A 165(p.278.8).

***φλάμουλον, τό,** (Lat. *flammula*) *banner*, Thphn.*chron*.p.305(M.108.744A).

φλασκίον, τό, *wine-flask*, Jo.Mosch.*prat*.143(M.87.3029D).

***φλεβοσυλία, ἡ,** *drawing from the veins*, Tim.Ant.*descr.BMV* 9(M.28.957C).

φλεβοτομέω, *open a vein, bleed*; pass., Adam.*dial*.5.17(p.210.2; M.11.1856C).

φλεγμαίνω, 1. *be heated, inflamed*; met., of language, *be grandiose*, Synes.*ep*.4(M.66.1332C); **2.** *inflame*; met., Clem.*paed*.2.1(p.165.8; M.8.404A); ἡ...διάθεσις...τὸν λογισμὸν...πιέζει καὶ φλεγμαίνει ταῖς συντρόφοις ἐπιθυμίαις id.*q.d.s*.15.2(p.169.19; M.9.620B).

φλεγμονή, ἡ, *stiffness, numbness, phlegma autem dixerunt quod sit frigida. Graeci enim rigorem* (v.l. *frigorem*) φ. *appellant*, Isid.H. *etym*.4.5.7.

***φλεκτικός,** *burning*, Geo.Pis.*hex*.1563(M.92.1556A).

***φληναφέω,** *babble*, Gr.Nyss.*Eun*.1(1 p.116.9; M.45.352A); Cyr. *ep.Calos*.(6[2].364C; φλυαροῦντες Pusey, p.604.22); Sophr.H.*ep.syn*.(M.87.3192C).

φληνάφημα, τό, *idle talk, nonsense*; of heresy, Jo.D.*dialect*. proem.(M.94.524C).

φληναφία (-εια), ἡ, *babbling, nonsense* τὴν Ἀρειανικὴν λέγων φ. εἶναι Germ.CP *syn.haer*.11(M.98.49B); Jo.D.*hom*.4.6(M.96.608C); *cat.Apoc*.9:3(p.313.32).

***φληνάφως,** *foolishly, thoughtlessly*, Cyr.*ador*.6(1.175A); id.*glaph. Gen*.2(1.57C); id.*hom.pasch*.11(5[2].146E).

φλιά, ἡ, *lintel* of a door, ref. Passover anointing (v. χρίω), as moral allegory and esp. as type of baptismal sealing (v. σφραγίζω, σφραγίς) καθίξετε τῆς φ., καὶ ἐπ' ἀμφοτέρων τῶν σταθμῶν, ἀπὸ τοῦ αἵματος ὅ ἐστι παρὰ τὴν θύραν, φλιᾶς μέν, ὡς ἀποδέδωκέ τις τῶν πρὸ ἡμῶν, τοῦ λογικοῦ· ἀμφοτέρων δὲ σταθμῶν, θυμικοῦ καὶ ἐπιθυμητικοῦ Or.*sel.in Ex*.12:22(M.12.285A); ἀνάμνησιν τῆς κατ' Αἴγυπτον τῶν πατέρων αὐτῶν γεγενημένης σωτηρίας ἡγούμενοι [sc. οἱ 'Ιουδαῖοι] μόνην εἶναι τὸ μυστήριον τοῦ προβάτου, ὅποτε...διεσώθησαν, τὰς φ. τῶν σφετέρων οἴκων φοινίξαντες τῷ αἵματι· οὐκέτι δὲ καὶ τῆς σφαγῆς τύπον ἡγήσαντο τοῦτο προδηλωτικὸν γεγονέναι Χριστοῦ, οὗ αἱ κατησφαλισμέναι τῷ αἵματι καὶ σφραγισθεῖσαι ψυχαὶ...περισωθήσονται τῆς ὀργῆς Meth.*symp*.9.1(p.115.15; M.18.180B); ref. Easter χθὲς ὁ ἀμνὸς ἐσφάζετο καὶ ἐχρίοντο αἱ φ., καὶ ἐθρήνησεν Αἴγυπτος τὰ πρωτότοκα, καὶ ἡμᾶς παρῆλθεν ὁ ὀλοθρεύων, καὶ ἡ σφραγὶς φοβερὰ καὶ αἰδέσιμος, καὶ τῷ τιμίῳ αἵματι ἐτειχίσθημεν Gr.Naz.*or*.1.3(M.35.397A); ὡς γὰρ ὄλεθρον 'Εβραίων ποτὲ παῖδες ὑπέκφυγον αἵματι Χριστῷ, τὸ φλιὰς ἐκάθηρεν, ὅτ' ὤλετο πρωτογένεθλος Αἰγύπτου γενεὴ νυκτὶ μιῇ, ὡς καὶ ἔμοιγε σφρηγὶς ἀλεξικάκοιο θεοῦ τόδε [sc. baptism] id.*carm*.1.1.9.89(M.37.463A); διπλῆ δέ τίς ἐστιν ἡ εἴσοδος τῷ θανάτῳ, καὶ διὰ τοῦτο διπλῆ γίνεται τοῦ αἵματος ἡ σφραγίς· ἐπὶ τῶν δύο, φησί, σταθμῶν καὶ ἐπὶ τῆς φ. εἰσέρχεται μὲν γὰρ δι' ἁμαρτίας ὁ θάνατος...ἁμαρτία δέ, ἡ μὲν κατὰ τὸ πάθος τὸ ἐν ἡμῖν (διττὸν δὲ τοῦτο, ἢ μαλακτικὸν τῆς ψυχῆς εἰς ἁπαλότητα, ἢ σκληροποιὸν εἰς τραχύτητα)· ἡ δὲ κατὰ τὸν λογισμόν. ...καὶ ἔστιν ὁ μὲν λογισμός, οἱονεὶ φλιά, τουτέστιν ὑπέρθυρον... ἡγεμονικὸς γὰρ καὶ ἀνώτερος τῇ φύσει, τὸ δὲ πάθος ἀνάλογον ἔχει τοῖς σταθμοῖς, ὑποκείμενον τῷ λογισμῷ ‡Chrys.*pasch*.2(8.254E–255A);

Χριστὸς γὰρ τὸ ἀληθινὸν...ἀρνίον ἐσφάγη, καὶ τὸ αἷμα αὐτοῦ ἐχρίσθη ἐπὶ τῶν φ. τῆς καρδίας, ὅπως γένηται τὸ...αἷμα τοῦ Χριστοῦ τῇ μὲν ψυχῇ εἰς...ἀπολύτρωσιν, τοῖς δὲ...δαίμοσιν εἰς...θάνατον Mac.Aeg. *hom.*47.8(M.34.801A); πάντων τὸ τέλος ἤγγικεν· εἴ τις οὐκ ἐνεσημάνθη τῇ σφραγῖδι τοῦ πνεύματος, σημειωθήτω φωτὶ τοῦ βαπτίσματος, καὶ τῷ ἀχράντῳ αἵματι τὰς νοερὰς ἐπιχρίσει φλιάς, καὶ τοὺς σταθμοὺς τῶν αἰσθήσεων. οὐ γὰρ ἄλλως τὸν ὀλοθρευτὴν διαφεύξεται Const.Diac. *laud.*37(M.88.521C).

***φλιοβατέω**, *cross the threshold*, Geo.Al.*v.Chrys.*18(p.180.10).

***φλογής**, *blazing*; of fire, *T.Abr.*A 17(p.99.18).

***φλογιέω**, s.v.l., *burn up, consume with fire*, Gr.Naz.*or.*40.36(M. 36.412A).

φλογίζ-ω, *burn*, fig. πόθῳ πατρικῷ ~όμενοι Sophr.H.*ep.syn.*(M.87. 3197A).

φλόγινος, *flaming, fiery*, Hipp.*haer.*6.17(p.143.25; M.16.3219C); *A.Phil.*B 27(p.332.3); Cyr.*Jo.*5.1(4.466A).

φλογισμός, ὁ, *burning*, Nect.*Thdr.*6(M.39.1828B).

***φλογιφόρος**, *blazing*, Anast.S.*hex.*12(M.89.1076A).

φλογμός, ὁ, *flame, blaze*; fig., *fiery heat*, of desire ὁ τῶν σωμάτων φ. ... ἐξάπτει τὴν ψυχήν Chrys.*hom.3.5 in 1Thess.*(11.447C); of temptation, Gr.Nyss.*hom.2 in Cant.*(M.44.795A); *ib.4*(844D).

***φλογοειδῶς**, *passionately*, *Mir.Geo.*4(p.32.3).

***φλογοείκελος**, *flame-like* αἱ φ. τῶν ἀγγέλων ἀξίαι τῶν ἀνθρώπων ἀεὶ μακρῷ καλλίους εἰσίν Eust.*engast.*10(p.31.4; M.18 om.).

***φλογοτρόφος**, *blazing*; of a furnace, Gr.Nyss.*Thdr.*(M.46.737D).

***φλογοφανής**, *fire-coloured*, Thdr.Stud.*nativ.BMV* 7(M.96.693D).

***φλογοφόρος**, *flaming*, Ephr.3.530C; of BMV ἡ φ. βάτος ἣν εἶδε ...Μωϋσῆς ‡Jo.D.*hom.*5(M.96.649B).

φλογόω, *blaze, burn with fire*; met., *be inflamed* with passion, Meth.*symp.*11(p.134.14; M.18.209D).

***φλοισβόπορος**, *noisy, turbulent*, fig. φ. βιότοιο Geo.Pis.*carm. vit.*29.

φλόξ, ἡ, **1.** *flame* ὁ σωτὴρ...τῷ πυρὶ δεδίττεται τοὺς ἀνθρώπους, ἀνάπτων ἐκ κίονος τὴν φ., δεῖγμα ὁμοῦ χάριτος καὶ φόβου Clem.*prot.*1 (p.8.32; M.8.64C); met. σὺ δέ, Αὐρηλιανέ, φ. πάντων ἀδικημάτων Const.*or.s.c.*24(p.190.16; M.20.1309A); δεινοτέραν ἢ οἱ πρόσθεν τὴν τῆς δυσσεβείας ἐξάπτων φ. Eus.*v.C.*2.1(p.40.6; M.20.980A); ἀνάλωσον ἡμῶν τὰς εὐθύνας· τῇ καθαρτικῇ φ. τῆς θεότητός σου *Lit.Jac.*(*NBP* 10² p.107); **2.** *fever*, Chrys.*sac.*1(p.22.7; 1.370A); id.*laud.Paul.*7(2.512E); **3.** *blade* of a sword φ. δὲ τὸ σιδήριον τῆς μαχαίρας ὠνόμασε Thdt.*qu.9 in Jud.*(1.329).

***φλυκτιδόομαι**, *become blistered*, *Pers.*(p.24.15).

φλυκτίς, ἡ, **1.** *boil*, Gr.Nyss.*v.Mos.*28(M.44.309A); **2.** *blister*, *Pers.* (p.24.17).

φοβερίζω, *terrify*, *M.Tar.*7(p.465); *ib.*8(p.469); Hipp.*Dan.*3.1.

φοβερισμός, ὁ, *that which terrifies, terror* οἱ δὲ τοῦ πατρὸς φ. μόνον αὐτὸν ἐξετάραξαν Didym.*Ps.*87:17(M.39.1485B); Epiph.*haer.*69.34 (p.182.22; M.42.256A); CCP(681)*act.*4(H.3.1124D).

φοβεροειδής, *of terrifying appearance*, *M.Ariadn.*(p.133).

φοβερός, **1.** *fearful, awful*; of death, Clem.*str.*7.11(p.44.28; M.9. 485C); πάλαι μὲν...φ. ἦν καὶ αὐτοῖς τοῖς ἁγίοις ὁ θάνατος...ἄρτι δὲ τοῦ σωτῆρος ἀναστήσαντος τὸ σῶμα, οὐκέτι μὲν ὁ θάνατός ἐστι φ. Ath.*inc.* 27.2(M.25.141D); ὁ θεὸς τότε [sc. in the time of the prophets] ἐβούλετο φ. εἶναι τὸν θάνατον, ἵνα δειχθῇ μετὰ ταῦτα τῆς χάριτος τὸ μέγεθος Chrys.*pan.Bern.*3(2.637E); τὸν θάνατον δεδοίκαμεν, οὐκ ἐπειδὴ φ. ἐστιν ἐκεῖνος, ἀλλ' ἐπειδὴ οὔθ' ὁ τῆς βασιλείας ἡμᾶς ἔρως ἀνῆψεν, οὔτε ὁ τῆς γεέννης φόβος κατέσχεν, καὶ...ὅτι τὸ συνειδὸς οὐκ ἔχομεν ἀγαθόν id.*stat.*6.3(2.77B); of God's judgement-seat, id.*hom.34.4 in Mt.* (7.394A); id.*cruc.*2.4(2.418C); id.*hom.3.2 in 2Tim.*(11.675A); of heavenly powers, *Lit.Jac.*(p.198.28); of angels, †Bas.*hom.in Ps.*33 (1.151D; M.30.372A); of God, Max.*qu.Thal.*10(M.90.289A); *Lit.Jac.* (pp.194.4,196.9); of sanctuary of a church, *ib.*(p.178.6); of eucharist, *ib.*(p.190.22); **2.** *formidable* ἔστι δὲ ὁ χαρακτηρισμὸς οὐ φ. ἄγαν αὐτοῦ [sc. τοῦ παιδαγωγοῦ] Clem.*paed.*1.12(p.148.16; M.8. 368A); **3.** *wonderful, impressive*, of objects ἐκαύθη...ἡ μεγάλη ἐκκλησία πᾶσα σὺν τοῖς φ. ... κίοσι *Chron.Pasch.*p.337(M.92.877A); Thphn.*chron.*p.198(M.108.513A); of persons ἀνὴρ φ. ἐν σοφίᾳ Jo.Mal. *chron.*2 p.26(M.97.92B); of abstracts φ. φιλοτιμία *ib.*16 p.398(589A).

***φοβεροχάριτος**, *full of terror and grace*; of the Cross, ‡Chrys. *ador.*2(11.824B).

φοβερωπός, *terrible of aspect*, *Orac.Sib.*13.78.

φοβ-έω, *fear*;

A. act. οὐ φ. οὖν τὴν ἀνομίαν τῆς πτέρνης Or.*Ps.*48:6(p.49).

B. usu. med.; **1.** in gen., ref. Christ εἰ μὲν ἄνθρωπος ψιλός ἐστιν ὁ λαλῶν, κλαιέτω καὶ ~είσθω τὸν θάνατον, ὡς ἄνθρωπος· εἰ δὲ λόγος ἐν σαρκὶ...τίνα θεὸς ὢν εἶχε ~εῖσθαι; ἢ διὰ τί τὸν θάνατον ἐφοβεῖτο ζωὴ ὢν αὐτὸς καὶ ἄλλους ἐκ τοῦ θανάτου ῥυόμενος; ἢ πῶς λέγων 'μὴ φοβεῖσθε τὸν ἀποκτείνοντα τὸ σῶμα', αὐτὸς ἐφοβεῖτο; Ath.*Ar.*3.54 (M.26.436C); death ἐκεῖνοι μὲν γὰρ καλῶς ~οῦνται τὸν θάνατον, ἀναστάσεως γὰρ ἐλπίδα οὐκ ἔχουσι Chrys.*stat.*5.2(2.62B); καὶ πρὸς τούτοις πάλιν οὐ ~ούμεθα γέενναν, διὰ τοῦτο ~ούμεθα θάνατον *ib.*5.3 (63D); in other contexts οὔτε γὰρ τὴν φωνὴν τοῦ πατρὸς ἐφοβήθησαν, οὔτε τοῦ σωτῆρος ἠδέσθησαν τὰ ῥήματα Ath.*Ar.*2.32(M.26.216A); cf. id.*ep.Serap.*1.3(M.26.536A); πάνυ ~οῦνται [sc. οἱ δαίμονες] τὸ σημεῖον τοῦ κυριακοῦ σταυροῦ id.*v.Anton.*35(M.26.893B); **2.** ref. fear of God ὁ...πατὴρ ἔχει σπλάγχνα ἐπὶ τοὺς ~ουμένους αὐτόν *1Clem.*23.1; ~ούμενος γὰρ τὸν κύριον πάντα καλῶς ἐργάσῃ· οὗτος δέ ἐστιν ὁ φόβος, ὃν δεῖ σε φοβηθῆναι καὶ σωθήσῃ Herm.*mand.*7.1; τοῖς ~ουμένοις γὰρ τὸν θεὸν αἱ ἐντολαὶ τοῦ θεοῦ οὐκ εἰσὶ βαρεῖαι Ath.*virg.*23(p.58.20; M. 28.280B); Chrys.*exp.in Ps.*111:1(5.277E); ὁ τὸν θεὸν ~ούμενος...τῶν κυμάτων ἀπηλλαγμένος, ἐν γαλήνῃ κάθηται καὶ λιμένι, τὴν ὄντως δρεπόμενος μακαριότητα *ib.*127:1(359A); ref. fear of God excluding fear of demons, etc. τὸν δὲ διάβολον μὴ φοβηθῇς· ~ούμενος γὰρ τὸν κύριον κατακυριεύσεις τοῦ διαβόλου, ὅτι δύναμις ἐν αὐτῷ οὐκ ἔστιν Herm. *mand.*7.2; τὸν θεὸν ἄρα μόνον ~εῖσθαι δεῖ...καὶ μηδ' ὅλως αὐτοὺς [sc. τοὺς δαίμονας] δεδιέναι Ath.*v.Anton.*30(M.26.888C); explanations ἐπὰν οὖν ἀκούσωμεν '...πλὴν δὲ αὐτοῦ μὴ φοβοῦ ἄλλον', τὸ ~εῖσθαι ἁμαρτάνειν...ἐκδεχόμεθα...~εῖται γάρ τις οὐ τὸν θεὸν ἀλλὰ τὸ ἀποπεσεῖν τοῦ θεοῦ· ὁ δὲ τοῦτο δεδιὼς τὸ τοῖς κακοῖς περιπεσεῖν ~εῖται καὶ δέδιεν τὰ κακά Clem.*str.*2.8(p.134.5; M.8.976A); οὐχ ὡς ~οῦμαι τὸ θηρίον καὶ μισῶ (διττοῦ τυγχάνοντος τοῦ φόβου), ὡς δὲ καὶ τὸν πατέρα δέδια, ὃν ~οῦμαι ἅμα καὶ ἀγαπῶ· πάλιν, ~ούμενος μὴ κολασθῶ, ἐμαυτὸν ἀγαπῶ, αἱρούμενος τὸν φόβον· ὁ ⟨δὲ⟩ ~ούμενος προσκόψαι τῷ πατρὶ ἀγαπᾷ αὐτόν *ib.*2.12(p.142.7f.; 992A); Dor.*doct.*4.1(M.88.1657D); ref. its attainment λέγει γὰρ ὅτι ἠρώτησεν ἀδελφός τινα τῶν γερόντων, τί ποιήσω, πάτερ, ἵνα ~οῦμαι τὸν θεόν; καὶ λέγει αὐτῷ ὁ γέρων, ὕπαγε, κολλήθητι ἀνθρώπῳ ~ουμένῳ τὸν θεὸν καὶ ἐκ τοῦ ~εῖσθαι αὐτὸν τὸν θεὸν διδάσκει καὶ σὲ ~εῖσθαι τὸν θεόν *ib.*4.5(1664D); **3.** *honour, revere* οὕτως ἐστὶ πᾶσα παρθένος μὴ ἔχουσα ὃν ~εῖται Ath.*virg.*14 (p.48.24; M.28.268C).

φοβητέον, *one must fear* φ. ἄρα οὐχὶ νόσον τὴν ἔξωθεν, ἀλλὰ ἁμαρτήματα, δι' ἃ νόσος, καὶ νόσον ψυχῆς, οὐ σώματος Clem.*ecl.*11(p.139. 24; M.9.704A); God τὸν μὲν γὰρ ἄνθρωπον ἀνθρωπίνως τιμητέον, φ. δὲ μόνον τὸν θεόν Tat.*orat.*4(p.4.25; M.6.813A).

φόβητρον, τό, *that which terrifies, terror* δαίμονες φαῦλοι...φόβητρα ἀνθρώποις ἔδειξαν Just.*1apol.*5.2(M.6.336A); id.*2apol.*9.1(M.6.460A); Eus.*d.e.*3.5(p.120.29; M.22.205B); id.*theoph.*3(p.12.4; M.24.617B); of sign of the cross, id.*v.C.*2.16(p.47.32; M.20.993C); fig. γαστριμαργία ...στοχασμοῦ φ. †Nil.*vit.*2(M.79.1141B).

φόβος, ὁ, **A.** *fear*; **1.** in gen., placed among φυσικὰ καὶ ἀδιάβλητα πάθη assumed by Christ at Inc., Jo.D.*f.o.*3.20(M.94.1081B); ref. Apollinarian Christology σῶμα δὲ πάλιν ἄψυχόν τε καὶ ἄνουν...οὐδ' ἂν ἐννοήσειέ τι τῶν σκυθρωπῶν ἢ τὸν ἐκ τῶν ἔσεσθαι προσδοκωμένων προαναθρήσει φ. Cyr.*Pulch.*39(p.58.28; 5².176B); arising from lack of faith οὐ πᾶς φ. ἀγαθόν ἐστι καὶ σωτήριον, ἀλλ' ἔστι τις καὶ ἐχθρὸς φ., ὃν ἀπεύχεται ὁ προφήτης ἐγγενέσθαι αὐτοῦ τῇ ψυχῇ...ἐχθρὸς γὰρ φ. ὁ θανάτου ἡμῖν δειλίαν ἐμποιῶν...καὶ ὁ ὑπὸ δαιμόνων εὐπτόητος τὸν ἐχθρὸν ἔχει φ. ἐν αὐτῷ. καὶ ὅλως ὁ τοιοῦτος φ. ἀπιστίας ἔοικεν ἔγγονον εἶναι πάθος Bas.*hom.in Ps.*33(1.151B; M.29.369C); from anticipation of evil φ. δὲ ἐλπιζομένων κακῶν ἐπίτασις, ἐπὶ κατεγνωσμένῳ συνιστάμενος συνειδότι Chrys.*hom.1.2 in Is.6*:1(6.98C); ref. fear of hell οὐδὲν τοῦ ταύτης χρησιμώτερον φ.· ὁ γὰρ τῆς γεέννης φ. τὸν τῆς βασιλείας ἡμῖν κομίζει στέφανον. ἔνθα φ. ἐστίν...ἐπιθυμία κατέσταλται πονηρά, ἅπαν ἀλόγιστον ἐξώρισται πάθος...καὶ πᾶσαν εἰσάγει μετὰ πολλῆς εὐκολίας τὴν ἀρετήν...διὰ τοῦτο τὸν μὴ συζῶντα φόβῳ, ἀδύνατον κατορθοῦσθαι· ὥσπερ οὖν τὸν ἐν φ. ζῶντα ἀδύνατον διαμαρτεῖν id.*stat.* 15.1(2.152Bff.); εἰ ὁ τῆς γεέννης φ. κατεῖχεν ἡμῶν τὰς ψυχάς, οὐκ ἂν ὁ τοῦ θανάτου φ. κατέσχεν *ib.*5.3(64A); of all creation at Crucifixion τὴν κτίσιν πᾶσαν...μαρτυροῦσαν τῷ φ. τὴν τοῦ δεσπότου παρουσίαν Ath. *inc.*9.3(M.25.129B); at baptism, Clem.*exc.Thdot.*83(p.132.18; M.9. 696D); v. χαρά; **2.** Valentinian, as a source of material substance, Iren.*haer.*1.5.3(M.7.497A); τὸν μὲν φ. ἐποίησεν οὐσίαν Hipp.*haer.*6.32 (p.160.28; M.16.3243A); ποιεῖ [sc. ὁ δημιουργός]...ἐκ τοῦ φ. τὰ θηρία Val.Gn.ap.Clem.*exc.Thdot.*47(p.122.15; M.9.681C); **3.** *fear* of God; **a.** in gen. Δαβὶδ δὲ καὶ τὸν φ. τὸν θεῖον ἐν τοῖς διδακτοῖς τίθεται †Bas. *Is.*40(1.411C; M.30.196C); ἐὰν μὴ φ. παιδεύῃ ἡμῶν τὴν ζωήν, ἀμήχανον κατορθωθῆναι τὸν ἁγιασμὸν ἐν τῷ σώματι id.*hom.in Ps.*33(1.149C; M. 29.365B); its goodness, Clem.*str.*2.8(p.134.1; M.8.976A); ὁ τοῦ ἀπαθοῦς θεοῦ φ. ἀπαθής· φοβεῖται γάρ τις οὐ τὸν θεὸν ἀλλὰ τὸ ἀποπεσεῖν τοῦ θεοῦ...ἀνάγει γοῦν ὁ τοιοῦτος φ. ἐπὶ τὴν μετάνοιαν ἐπί τε τὴν ἐλπίδα *ib.* (p.134.10; M.l.c.); its value ἔχεις τοῦ θεοῦ τὸν φ., πάντων χρημάτων εὐπορώτερον θησαυρόν Chrys.*kal.*3(1.700E); must not be superficial only ὁ γὰρ μόνοις τοῖς ἤθεσι τὸν τοῦ θεοῦ φ. ὑποκρινόμενος, οὐδὲν τοῦ πιθήκου τὸ σύνολον διενήνοχεν, ἀνθρώπων ἤθη μιμουμένου...ὥσπερ καὶ ὁ τὰ μὲν ἤθη τῶν ἀληθῶς φοβουμένων τὸν κύριον πρὸς τὴν τῶν ὁρώντων ἀπάτην μιμούμενος, τὴν δὲ τῆς γνώμης διάθεσιν οὐκ ἔχων κατὰ τὸ ἴσον ἐκείνοις τῷ θείῳ φ. πεποιωμένην, Σαδδουκαῖός τις ἕτερος ἢ γραμματεὺς καὶ ὢν καὶ καλούμενος Max.*ep*.20(M.91.600D); contrasted with fear of punishment διττός ἐστιν ὁ τοῦ θεοῦ φ.· ὁ μὲν ἐκ τῶν ἀπειλῶν τῆς κολάσεως ἡμῖν ἐντικτόμενος...ὁ δέ, αὐτῇ τῇ ἀγάπῃ συνέζευκται, εὐλάβειαν τῇ ψυχῇ ἀεὶ ἐμποιῶν, ἵνα μὴ διὰ τὴν τῆς ἀγάπης παρρησίαν, εἰς καταφρόνησιν θεοῦ ἔλθῃ id.*carit*.1.81(M.90.977C); id.*cap*.1.69,70(M.90.1208A,B); id.*qu.Thal*.10(M.90.289A–C); exeg. 1 Jo.4:18 δεῖξαι ἡμῖν θέλει ὁ ἅγιος ὅτι δύο εἰσὶ φ., εἷς εἰσαγωγικὸς καὶ εἷς τέλειος· καὶ ὅτι ὁ μὲν εἷς τῶν ἀρχομένων ἐστίν, ὡς ἂν εἴποι τις τοῦ θεοσεβοῦς· ὁ δὲ ἄλλος τῶν ἁγίων τῶν τελειωθέντων ἐστὶ τῶν φθασάντων εἰς τὸ μέτρον τῆς ἀγάπης. οὗτος οὐ ποιεῖ ἀκμὴν δι' αὐτὸ καλόν, ἀλλὰ διὰ τὸν φ. τῶν πληγῶν. ἄλλος δὲ ποιεῖ τὸ θέλημα τοῦ θεοῦ, ἀγαπῶν αὐτὸν τὸν θεόν...οὗτός ἐστι ὁ ἔχων τὴν ἀληθινὴν ἀγάπην, ἣν λέγει ὁ ἅγιος τελείαν, καὶ αὕτη ἡ ἀγάπη φέρει αὐτὸν εἰς τὸν τέλειον φ. οὗτος οὖν ὁ τέλειος φ. ὁ ἐκ τῆς ἀγάπης ταύτης γινόμενος, ἔξω βάλλει τὸν εἰσαγωγικὸν φ. ... ἀδύνατον δέ ἐστιν ἐλθεῖν τὸν τέλειον φ. εἰ μὴ διὰ τοῦ εἰσαγωγικοῦ Dor.*doct*.4.1(M.88.1657C,D); **b.** exeg. Pr.1:7(Ps.110:10) τὴν σοφίας λέγει ποίησιν, ἥ ἐστι φ. θεοῦ ὁδοποιῶν εἰς σοφίαν Clem.*str*.2.7(p.130.21; M.8.968C); 'ἀρχὴ σοφίας φ.' εἴρηται 'κυρίου', παρὰ κυρίου διὰ Μωϋσέως δοθεὶς τοῖς ἀπειθοῦσι καὶ σκληροκαρδίοις· οὓς γὰρ οὐχ αἱρεῖ λόγος, τιθασεύει τούτους φ. *ib*.2.8(p.132.20f.; M.8.972C); τί τοῦτο λέγων ἀρχὴν σοφίας; τὸν φ. οὐ γὰρ ἀπὸ θεωρίας ἀρξαμένους εἰς φ. χρὴ καταλήγειν...ἀλλὰ φ. στοιχειουμένους...εἰς ὕψος αἵρεσθαι, οὗ γὰρ φ., ἐντολῶν τήρησις Gr.Naz.*or*.39.8(M.36.344A); οὕτω δὴ...εἰπὼν τὸν φ., οὐκ ἐκεῖνον μόνον λέγει τὸν ἀπὸ τῆς γνώσεως, ὃν καὶ δαίμονες ἔχουσιν· ἀλλὰ καὶ τοῦτο προστίθησιν λέγων ἐν ταῖς ἐντολαῖς αὐτοῦ θελήσει σφόδρα Chrys.*exp.in Ps*.111:1(5.277B); ἀρχὴν λέγει τὸν εἰσαγωγικὸν φ., μεθ' ὅν ἐστιν ὁ τέλειος ὁ τῶν ἁγίων. ὁ οὖν εἰσαγωγικὸς φ. τῆς καταστάσεως ἡμῶν ἐστιν· οὗτος φυλάττει τὴν ψυχήν, ὥσπερ ἡ γάνωσις ἀπὸ τῆς κακίας...ἐὰν οὖν ἐκκλίνῃ πᾶς ἀπὸ κακοῦ διὰ τὸν φ. τῆς κολάσεως... ἔρχεται κατὰ μέρος καὶ εἰς τὸ ποιῆσαι τὸ ἀγαθόν Dor.*doct*.4.3(M.88.1660D); Gnost. οἱ ἀμφὶ τὸν Βασιλείδην τοῦτο ἐξηγούμενοι τὸ ῥητὸν αὐτόν φασιν Ἄρχοντα ἐπακούσαντα τὴν φάσιν τοῦ διακονουμένου πνεύματος ἐκπλαγῆναι τῷ τε ἀκούσματι καὶ τῷ θεάματι παρ' ἐλπίδας εὐηγγελισμένον, καὶ τὴν ἔκπληξιν αὐτοῦ φ. κληθῆναι ἀρχὴν γενόμενον σοφίας φυλοκρινητῆς...καὶ τελεωτικῆς καὶ ἀποστατικῆς Clem.*str*.2.8(p.132.3; M.8.972A); Val.Gn.*ib*.(p.132.8f.; 972B); criticized, Clem.*ib*.(p.133.3f.; 973A,B); **c.** in rel. to Law ὁ νόμος φόβου ἐμποιητικός *ib*.2.7(p.130.22; 968C); εἰ τοίνυν κακῶν ἀποχὴν ἀφοβίαν εἴρηκεν ἣν ὁ τοῦ κυρίου φ. ἐργάζεται, ἀγαθὸν ὁ φ., καὶ ὁ ἐκ τοῦ νόμου φ. οὐ μόνον δίκαιος, ἀλλὰ καὶ ἀγαθὸς κακίαν ἀναιρῶν· φόβῳ δὲ ἀφοβίαν εἰσάγων οὐ πάθει ἀπάθειαν, παιδείᾳ δὲ μετριοπάθειαν ἐμποιεῖ *ib*.2.8(p.134.1f.; 976A); οἱ τοίνυν ἐμπαθοῦς φ. περιποιητικὸν τὸν νόμον ὑπολαβόντες οὔτε ἀγαθοὶ συνιέναι οὔτε ἐνενόησαν τῷ ὄντι τὸν νόμον. 'φ. γὰρ κυρίου ζωὴν ποιεῖ' *ib*.2.18(p.157.6; 1021C); ὃν ἐγέννησε φ. ὁ νόμος, ἐλεήμων οὗτος εἰς σωτηρίαν *ib*.1.27(p.108.13; 921B); old and new covenants contrasted ἡ δὲ παλαιὰ διαθήκη...μετὰ φ. καὶ τρόμου διετάγη τοῖς πατράσιν ὑμῶν ...ἑτέραν διαθήκην ἔσεσθαι ὁ θεὸς ὑπέσχετο...ἄνευ φ. καὶ τρόμου Just.*dial*.67.9(M.6.632B); τῷ πρεσβυτέρῳ λαῷ πρεσβυτέρα διαθήκη ἦν καὶ νόμος ἐπαιδαγώγει τὸν λαὸν μετὰ φ. καὶ λόγος ἄγγελος ἦν, καινῷ δὲ καὶ νέῳ λαῷ καινὴ καὶ νέα διαθήκη δεδώρηται καὶ ὁ λόγος ⟨σάρξ⟩ γεγένηται καὶ ὁ φ. εἰς ἀγάπην μετατέτραπται Clem.*paed*.1.7(p.124.31f.; M.8.321A); Christian fear of God contrasted with that of Hebrews διττὸν δὲ τὸ εἶδος τοῦ φ., ὧν τὸ μὲν ἕτερον γίνεται μετὰ αἰδοῦς, ᾧ χρῶνται πολῖται μὲν πρὸς ἡγεμόνας ἀγαθοὺς καὶ ἡμεῖς πρὸς τὸν θεόν, καθάπερ οἱ παῖδες οἱ σώφρονες πρὸς τοὺς πατέρας...τὸ δὲ ἕτερον εἶδος τοῦ φ. μετὰ μίσους γίνεται, ᾧ δοῦλοι πρὸς δεσπότας κέχρηνται χαλεποὺς καὶ Ἑβραῖοι δεσπότην ποιήσαντες, οὐ πατέρα τὸν θεόν *ib*.1.9(p.140.29; 353B); teaching of Christ as παιδαγωγός being free from fear, *ib*.1.3(p.95.24; 260B); καὶ γὰρ ὁ νόμος αὐτοῦ τὸν φ. ὑπεκλύειν βούλεται τὸ ἑκούσιον ἐλευθερώσας εἰς πίστιν *ib*.3.12(p.284.5; 665B); **d.** in rel. to πίστις: τῆς οὖν πίστεως ἡμῶν εἰσιν βοηθοὶ φ. καὶ ὑπομονή *Barn*.2.2; τοὺς ἐκ φ. εἰς πίστιν ἐπιστραφέντας καὶ δικαιοσύνην εἰς αἰῶνα παραμένειν λέγει Clem.*ecl*.60(p.154.24; M.9.728B); ὡς οὖν αἱ ἡμέραι μόριον βίου τοῦ κατ' ἐπανάβασιν, οὕτω καὶ ὁ φ. τῆς ἀγάπης ἀρχή, κατὰ παραύξησιν πίστις γινόμενος, εἶτα ἀγάπη id.*str*.2.12(p.142.6; M.8.992A); ref. pagan opinion that faith is founded in fear, *ib*.2.6(p.129.6; 965A); **e.** as σωτήριος: ἱστᾶσιν γοῦν τῶν ἁμαρτιῶν τὰς νομὰς αἱ πικραὶ τοῦ φ. ῥίζαι· διὸ καὶ σωτήριος, εἰ καὶ πικρός, ὁ φ. id.*paed*.1.9(p.139.2; M.8.349B); id.*ecl*.20(p.142.17; M.9.708B); *Lit*.ap.*Const.App*.8.6.5; ἀρχὴ σωτηρίας ἀνθρώπων ὁ τοῦ θεοῦ φ. Sever.ap.†Max.*loc.comm*.24(M.91.864A); ὁδὸς δὲ πρὸς σωτηρίαν...ὁ τοῦ θεοῦ φ. Cyr.*Is*.3.2(2.418E); **f.** as preventative of sin φ. ... αἴτιος τοῦ μὴ ἁμαρτάνειν τοῖς πολλοῖς Clem.*str*.6.12(p.481.19; M.9.320B); τὸ ἁμαρτάνειν ἡμῖν κατὰ ἀπουσίαν τοῦ φ. τοῦ θεοῦ γίνεται Bas.*ep*.174(3.262B; M.32.652A); οὐδὲν γάρ ἐστι κακὸν ὃ μὴ σβέννυσιν ὁ τοῦ θεοῦ φ. ... καὶ τοὺς ὑπ' αὐτοῦ βαφέντας οὐδενὶ τῶν ἀνθρωπίνων ἀφίησιν ὑποσκελίζεσθαι Chrys.*exp.in Ps*.127:1(5.359E); φ. κατέχοντος ψυχὰς οὐδὲν τῶν ἀνελευθέρων παθῶν ἐπεισέρχεται ῥᾳδίως ἡμῖν id.ap.†Max.*loc.comm*.24(M.91.864A); double effect δισσοὶ οὖν εἰσιν οἱ φ.· ἐὰν γὰρ θέλῃς τὸ πονηρὸν ἐργάσασθαι, φοβοῦ τὸν κύριον καὶ οὐκ ἐργάσῃ αὐτό· ἐὰν δὲ θέλῃς πάλιν τὸ ἀγαθὸν ἐργάσασθαι, φοβοῦ τὸν κύριον καὶ ἐργάσῃ αὐτό. ὥστε ὁ φ. τοῦ κυρίου ἰσχυρός ἐστι καὶ μέγας καὶ ἔνδοξος Herm.*mand*.7.4; **g.** exeg. Gen.31:53 φ. τοῦ Ἰσαὰκ τὴν εὐσέβειαν ἐκάλεσε, τουτέστι τὸν θεόν, οὗ τὸν φ. ἐν τῇ ψυχῇ περιέφερεν Thdt.*qu.91 in Gen*.(1.99); **4.** of Christ μαθέτωσαν ἄπιστοι πάντες ὅτι ὁ τοῦ Χριστοῦ φ. πᾶσαν ἐξουσίαν δύναται χαλινοῦν Chrys.*stat*.6.3(2.77A); **5.** *fear, reverence*, towards God's ministers πάσῃ βασιλείᾳ καὶ ἀρχῇ ὑποτάγητε ἐν οἷς ἀρέσκει θεῷ... πάντα φ. τὸν ὀφειλόμενον αὐτοῖς ἀποπληρώσατε *Const.App*.4.13.1; of deacons at eucharist οἱ μὲν τῇ προσφορᾷ τῆς εὐχαριστίας σχολαζέτωσαν ὑπηρετούμενοι τῷ τοῦ κυρίου σώματι μετὰ φόβου *ib*.2.57.15; of widows and orphans παραινοῦμεν οὖν ταῖς χήραις καὶ τοῖς ὀρφανοῖς μετὰ παντὸς φ. ... μεταλαμβάνειν τῶν αὐτοῖς χορηγουμένων *ib*.4.5.1; cf. *Can.App*.41; **6.** *respect, honour*, towards masters or magistrates, *Did*.4.11; ὀφειλήματα...καὶ τὸν φ. καὶ τὴν τιμὴν ὀνομάζει Thdt.*Rom*.13:7(3.137).

B. *that which causes fear* or *terror* εἰ γὰρ 'οἱ ἄρχοντες οὐκ εἰσὶ φ. τῷ ἀγαθῷ ἔργῳ', πῶς ὁ φύσει ἀγαθὸς θεὸς φ. ἔσται τῷ μὴ ἁμαρτάνοντι; Clem.*paed*.1.9(p.138.16; M.8.349A); ὁ διάβολος μόνον φ. ἔχει, ὁ δὲ φ. αὐτοῦ τόνον οὐκ ἔχει Herm.*mand*.12.4.7.

C. *that which causes fear* or *reverence* δίκαιον γὰρ καὶ φόβου μεστὸν τὸ θεοῦ κριτήριον Thdt.*Ps*.6:11(1.644).

φοιβάω, *prophesy*, Cyr.*Os*.99(3.131D).

***φοιδερατικός**, (cf. Lat. *foederatus*) *pertaining to confederates* τὰς στρατιωτικὰς καὶ φ. δισcussίονας (sic) Ath.Scholast.*coll*.20.5(p.178).

***φοιδερᾶτος**, (Lat. *foederatus*) *allied*, Nil.*epp*.1.284 tit.(M.79.185C); plur. as subst. οὓς δὴ καὶ φοιδεράτους οἱ Ῥωμαῖοι καλοῦσιν Malchus *exc.gent*.4(p.571.28; M.113.785B); Jo.Mal.*chron*.14 p.364(M.97.541B); *ib*.18 p.493(713B).

***φοινικεῖον, τό,** *red dye*, †Cyr.*hom.div*.14(5^2.413D).

φοινικίζω, *stain red*, Proc.G.*Is*.1:20(M.87.1852D).

φοινίκιον, τό, *date*, Pall.*h.Laus*.87(p.107.6; M.34.1179D); Dor.*doct*.11.8(M.88.1745A).

***φοινικός**, *dark red*, Thdt.*haer*.5.28(4.475).

***φοινικόχρως**, *dark red*, Sophr.H.*mir.Cyr.et Jo*.25(M.87.3493B).

φοῖνιξ, ὁ (A), the fabulous bird *phoenix*; its legend interpreted as an image of the resurrection μέγα καὶ θαυμαστὸν οὖν νομίζομεν εἶναι, εἰ ὁ δημιουργὸς τῶν ἁπάντων ἀνάστασιν ποιήσεται...ὅπου καὶ δι' ὀρνέου [sc. τοῦ φοίνικος] δείκνυσιν ἡμῖν τὸ μεγαλεῖον τῆς ἐπαγγελίας αὐτοῦ *1Clem*.26.1; Cyr.H.*catech*.18.8; *Const.App*.5.7.15; coupled with misinterpretation of Ps.91:13 (where φοῖνιξ = *palm-tree*) πῶς ...οἱ Ἰουδαῖοι ἠπίστησαν τὴν τριήμερον ἀνάστασιν τοῦ κυρίου ἡμῶν Ἰησοῦ Χριστοῦ, ἐπείπερ τὸ ὄρνεον διὰ τριῶν ἡμερῶν ἐζωοποιήθη, καὶ ὁ κύριος ἡμῶν...τῷ τρόπῳ οὐκ ἐδύνατο ἐγεῖραι αὐτὸν ἐκ νεκρῶν; διὰ τοῦτο ἔλεγεν ὁ προφήτης· δίκαιος ὡς φοῖνιξ ἀνθήσει †Epiph.*phys*.11(M.43.528A); cf.Tert.*de resurrectione carnis* 13(M.*PL*.2.811B); Thdt.*Cant*.5:1(2.117) cit. s. ἐλάτη; another legend, *Apoc.Bar*.6(pp.88f.).

φοῖνιξ, ὁ (B), name of a wind φ., ὁ καλούμενος εὐρόνοτος Jo.D.*f.o*.2.8(M.94.900D).

φοίνιξις, ἡ, a *becoming red, reddening*, Max.*ambig*.(M.91.1344B).

φοιτάω, *spring up, pullulate*, of doctrines τὰς ἐν Αἰγύπτῳ φοιτησάσας τῶν ἀκεφάλων αἱρέσεις Anast.S.*haer*.(p.265).

φοίτησις, ἡ, *coming*; of Christ's second coming, ‡Caes.Naz.*dial*.21(M.38.881A).

φοιτητής, ὁ, *pupil, disciple*; in OT, Eus.*d.e*.1.1(p.5.24; M.22.20B); Max.*ambig*.(M.91.1124C); of disciples of Christ, Eus.*d.e*.1.7(p.38.32; 76A); διὰ τῆς τῶν φ. ... διδασκαλίας καὶ παραδοξοποιΐας id.*h.e*.2.3.2(M.20.144A); Isid.Pel.*epp*.2.88(M.78.532A); of disciples of apostles, Clem.*str*.3.18(p.246.32; M.8.1212C); Μάρκος γνώριμος καὶ φ. [sc. τοῦ Πέτρου] Eus.*d.e*.3.5(p.127.5; 216C); ref. Clement of Rome, id.*h.e*.5.11.1(M.20.456C); in gen., *ib*.6.3.8(528C); *ib*.6.4.2(532A); *ib*.6.6(536A); fig. τῆς ἀρετῆς...φ. Thdt.*eran*.3(4.181); Max.*ambig*.(1209B).

***φολερόν, τό,** = φολλερόν q.v., Jo.Mosch.*prat*.61(M.87.2913C); Leont.N.*v.Sym*.32(M.93.1709B); *ib*.47(1728B).

[*]**φόλης, ὁ**, v. φόλλις.

φολιδόομαι, *be covered with scales*, Or.*Cels*.4.76(p.346.25; M.11.1148C).

[*]**φόλις, ὁ**, v. φόλλις.

φολίς, ἡ, *horny scale* of reptiles; of scales upon eyes, Bas.Sel. *v.Thecl.*2.7(M.85.576C); plur., of scale-armour, *Orac.Sib.*14.326; fig. ὁ...ὁλκὸς τοῦ θηρίου τῷ ἀνθρωπίνῳ βίῳ συνεσπαρμένος...τῇ φ. τῆς ἁμαρτίας ἀεὶ περιτραχύνει τὸν βίον Cyr.*resp.*25(6^2.396C).

φόλις ([*]**φόλης**), **ὁ,** (Lat. *follis*) *a small coin,* $\frac{1}{288}$ of a *solidus* φόλης ὃ καὶ ταλάντιον καλεῖται· διπλοῦν δέ ἐστιν, ὑπὸ δύο ἀργύρων συγκείμενον, οἳ γίνονται σῃ' δηνάρια· καὶ φ., δύο λεπτοὶ κατὰ τὸν δηναρισμὸν ἀλλ' οὐ κατὰ τὸν ἀργυρισμόν Epiph.*mens.*24(M.43.292A); πέντε φόλεις Jo.Mosch.*prat.*111(M.87.2976A).

***φολ(λ)ερόν (*φαλερόν), τό,** a small coin = Lat. *follis,* Jo.Mal. *chron.*p.400(M.97.593A); cf. *nummis quos Romani Terentianos* [forte *Teruntios*]...*vocant, Graeci follares, Anastasius princeps suo nomine figuratis placabilem plebi commutationem distraxit,* Marcellinus *chron.*(M.*PL.*51.935B); Jo.Mosch.*prat.*61(M.87.2913C); *ib.*111(2976A); given as alms, φαλερόν, *ib.*85(2941C).

***φονειωδής,** *murderous,* Ephr.2.307C.

***φόνευσις, ἡ,** *murder, A.Andr.et Mt.*31(p.113.6).

***φονευτήριον, τό,** *place of execution,* Steph.Diac.*v.Steph.*(M.100. 1169C).

φονευτής, ὁ, *slayer, Protev.*22.1(p.42); v. αὐτοφονευτής.

φονεύτρια, ἡ, *murderess*; fig., Geo.Pis.*carm.*3.58; λάβωμεν πίστιν τῶν φόνων φ. Thphn.*chron.*p.257(M.108.641B); as adj. γενεᾶς τῶν Ἰουδαίων τῆς ἀπίστου καὶ φ. Cyr.*Ps.*11:8(M.69.797D).

φονοκτονέω, 1. *defile with blood,* ref. Num.35:33, Ps.106:38 ἐφονοκτόνουν τὴν γῆν θύοντες τὰ τέκνα Chrys.*fr.in Jer.*3:9(M.64. 784B); pass., met., *be defiled* τῇ ἁμαρτίᾳ πεφονοκτόνητο ἡ γῆ ‡Ath. *pass.*16(M.28.213A); **2.** *murder,* Gr.Nyss.*v.Mos.*(M.44.396D); Leont.B. *mesopent.*(M.86.1992A).

φονοκτονία, ἡ, *murder,* Epiph.*haer.*26.2(p.277.5; M.41.333B); Nil. *epp.*1.245(M.79.172D); fig. ἐβασίλευεν ὁ ζόφος τῆς φ. ‡Bas.Sel.*or.*41 (M.85.465B).

φονοκτόνος, ὁ, *murderer,* Geo.Pis.*carm.*48.10.

φονώδης, *murderous,* Epiph.*haer.*26.3(p.280.3; M.41.337A).

φοράδιον, τό, dim. of sq., Gr.Naz.*test.*(M.37.392A).

φοράς, ἡ, *mare, T.Jud.*2.3 margin; Bas.*ep.*303(3.440A; M.32. 1052D); Pall.*h.Laus.*17(p.45.3; M.34.1044B).

[*]**φοράω,** *detect,* Diod.*Ps.*63:7(M.33.1598B).

φορβαία, ἡ, *halter,* Ath.*v.Anton.*24(M.26.880B); *Apophth.Patr.* (M.65.181A).

***φόρβειος, ὁ,** *pupil of the eye,* ‡Ath.*qu.al.*19(M.28.792A).

***φορβιάζω,** *put a halter on,* Pall.*h.Laus.*17(p.45.12, v.l. φορτιάσας M.34.1044C).

φόρεμα, τό, *apparel, dress,* Hipp.*haer.*9.15(p.254.5; M.16.3391B); Mac.Aeg.*hom.*2.4(M.34.465D); Nil.*epp.*1.285(M.79.185C).

***φορεσία, ἡ,** *apparel, dress, costume, M.Areth.*(p.46); *Chron. Pasch.*p.44(M.92.164A); *ib.*p.47(169B); Phot.*nomoc.*3.10(p.504; M. 104.1052C).

φορ-έω, A. *bear, carry*; in chains or bonds, *1Clem.*5.6; Ath.*apol. sec.*43(p.120.20; M.25.328B); met., of bearing sign of the cross; of Christians id.*inc.*29.4(M.25.145D); id.*ep.Aeg.Lib.*2(M.25.541B); τὴν σάρκα...ἣν ἡμεῖς ~οῦμεν καὶ τὰ λοιπὰ ζῷα id.*virg.*19(p.54.19; M.28. 276A); εἰκόνα αὐτοῦ [sc. of God] ~οῦντες [sc. οἱ ἄνθρωποι] *ib.*15(p.50. 9; 269B); of bearing name of Christ ἐὰν [οὖν] τὸ ὄνομα ~ῇς, τὴν δὲ δύναμιν μὴ ~ῇς αὐτοῦ, εἰς μάτην ἔσῃ τὸ ὄνομα αὐτοῦ ~ῶν...ὃς ἂν τὸ ὄνομα τοῦ υἱοῦ τοῦ θεοῦ ~ῇ, καὶ τούτων [sc. τῶν παρθένων] ὀφείλει ~εῖν τὰ ὀνόματα· καὶ γὰρ αὐτὸς ὁ υἱὸς τὰ ὀνόματα τῶν παρθένων τούτων ~εῖ...τῶν τοιούτων δὲ ~ούντων τὰ ὀνόματα τῶν παρθένων ἐστὶν ἡ κατοικία εἰς τὸν πύργον Herm.*sim.*9.13.2–5; βλέπεις οὖν ποίους βαστάζει; τοὺς ἐξ ὅλης καρδίας ~οῦντας τὸ ὄνομα αὐτοῦ *ib.*9.14.6; *ib.*9.15.2,3; πρὶν γάρ, φησί, ~έσαι τὸν ἄνθρωπον τὸ ὄνομα [τοῦ υἱοῦ] τοῦ θεοῦ, νεκρός ἐστιν *ib.*9.16.3; ref. indwelling of H. Ghost ὅσοι γὰρ πνεῦμα θεοῦ ~οῦσι, φῶς ~οῦσι· καὶ οἱ ~οῦντες φῶς Χριστὸν εἰσιν ἐνδεδυμένοι...οἱ γὰρ ~οῦντες τὸ πνεῦμα τοῦ θεοῦ ἀφθαρσίαν ~οῦσιν Ath.*inc.et c.Ar.*15(M.26.1009C).

B. *wear*; **1.** Christol.; **a.** exeg. Jo.1:14 οὐκ εἰς σάρκα ἀναλυθεὶς ἀλλὰ σάρκα ~έσας ‡Ath.*serm.fid.*1(p.5; M.26.1265A); 'ὁ λόγος σὰρξ ἐγένετο'...οὐκ εἶπεν δὲ σῶμα, ἵνα μὴ εἴπωσί τινες, τὸ οὐράνιον σῶμα ἐφόρεσεν Ammon.*Jo.*1:14(M.85.1397C); **b.** in gen. μὴ νομίσῃς, ὅτι φύσεως ἀκολουθίᾳ σῶμα πεφόρηκεν ὁ σωτήρ Ath.*inc.*1.3(M.25.97C); τοῦ ἐκ Μαρίας δι' ἡμᾶς ἐφόρεσε σώματος ‡Ath.*serm.fid.*24(p.20; 1277A); οὐ κενωθεὶς τὸ εἶναι λόγος διὰ τὸ σάρκα ~έσαι *ib.*25(p.22; 1280B); *ib.*35(p.29; 1288D); **c.** ref. human attributes and sensations of incarnate Word ὡς σῶμα ~ῶν ὁ Ἰησοῦς ἤσθιεν Or.*Cels.*7.13(p.165. 3; M.11.1440A); ὡς δὲ σῶμα ~ῶν, ἐδίψα καὶ ἐκοπία καὶ ἔπασχεν· οὐ γὰρ ἦν ἴδια ταῦτα τῆς θεότητος Ath.*ep.Serap.*4.14(M.26.656C); ἐκ τῶν τῆς σαρκὸς παθῶν ἐδείκνυσεν ὅτι ἀληθὲς ἐφόρει σῶμα id.*Ar.*3.41(M.26. 412A); θεότης δὲ οὔτε σῶμα οὔτε αἷμα ἔχει, ἀλλ' ὃν ἐφόρεσεν ἐκ τῆς Μαρίας ἄνθρωπον, αἴτιος τούτων γέγονε ‡Ath.*serm.fid.*29(p.26; M. 26.1284C); **d.** ref. purpose and effects of Inc. εἰ γὰρ μὴ διὰ τὸ ἐλευθερῶσαι τὴν σάρκα καὶ ἀναστῆσαι σάρκα ἐφόρεσε, τί καὶ περισσῶς σάρκα ἐφόρει; Meth.*res.*2.18(p.370.4; M.18.284C); ὁ ἀληθινὸς καὶ φύσει υἱὸς τοῦ θεοῦ τοὺς πάντας ἡμᾶς ~εῖ, ἵνα οἱ πάντες τὸν ἕνα φορέσωμεν θεόν Ath.*inc.et c.Ar.*8(M.26.997A); ref. Jo.16:64 ἴσον τῷ εἰπεῖν...ὑπὲρ τῆς τοῦ κόσμου σωτηρίας ἐστὶν ἡ σὰρξ ἣν ἐγὼ ~ῶ id.*ep.Serap.*4.19 (M.26.668A); εἰ γὰρ μὴ ἤμην ἐλθὼν καὶ ~έσας τὸ τούτων σῶμα, οὐδεὶς ἂν αὐτῶν ἐτελειώθη, ἀλλ' ἔμενον οἱ πάντες φθαρτοί...καὶ ὥσπερ δέδωκάς μοι τοῦτο ~έσαι, δὸς αὐτοῖς τὸ πνεῦμά σου id.*Ar.*3.23(M.26.372B); ὡς ἂν πάντες ~εσθέντες παρ' ἐμοῦ, πάντες ὦσιν ἓν σῶμα καὶ ἓν πνεῦμα, καὶ εἰς ἄνδρα τέλειον καταντήσωσιν *ib.*3.22(369A); cf. εἰκότως ἄρα ~ῶν τοὺς δύο [sc. Jews and gentiles] ἐν αὐτῷ *ib.*2.55(265A); ref. baptism of Christ ἡ εἰς αὐτὸν ἐν τῷ Ἰορδάνῃ τοῦ πνεύματος γενομένη κάθοδος, εἰς ἡμᾶς ἦν γινομένη, διὰ τὸ ~εῖν αὐτὸν τὸ ἡμέτερον σῶμα *ib.*1.47 (108C); at Ascension ἀναφέρων εἰς τὸν οὐρανὸν ἣν ἐφόρει σάρκα *ib.*3.48 (425B); fig. καὶ ἡ ζωὴ τὸ νεκρὸν ἐφόρεσεν ἔνδυμα, ἵνα εἰς τὴν ἰδίαν ἀφθαρσίαν μεταβάλῃ τὴν νέκρωσιν Bas.Sel.*or.*10.1(M.85.140D); Gnost. διδάσκοντες...ὡς ἄνθρωπον οὐ ~έσαντα ἄνθρωπον, ἀλλὰ δόκησίν τινα Hipp.*fr.in Mt.25:24*(p.209.8; M.10.868A); Sabellian τὸν ἄνθρωπον, ὃν ἐφόρεσεν ὁ λόγος, αὐτὸν εἶναι λέγουσι τὸν υἱὸν τοῦ θεοῦ τὸν μονογενῆ, καὶ μὴ τὸν λόγον υἱόν ‡Ath.*Ar.*4.20(p.66.1; M.26.497A); καί φασι μὴ τὸν ἄνθρωπον καθ' ἑαυτόν, ὃν ἐφόρησεν ὁ κύριος, ἀλλὰ τὸ συναμφότερον, τόν τε λόγον καὶ τὸν ἄνθρωπον, εἶναι υἱόν *ib.*4.21(p.68.4; 500B); ref. denial of real humanity of Christ's flesh τίς δὲ ἤκουσεν ἐν ἐκκλησίᾳ ἢ ὅλως παρὰ Χριστιανῶν, ὅτι θέσει καὶ οὐ φύσει σῶμα πεφόρηκεν ὁ κύριος; Ath.*ep.Epict.*2(p.4.14; M.26.1053A); **2.** fig. στεφάνους δόξης φ. *T.Benj.*4.1; **3.** *be dressed* καλῶς φ. Dor.*doct.*2.5(M.88.1645B); ἐν σχήματι ἐπισκόπου ~οῦντα *ib.*5.5(1681D).

φόρησις, ἡ, *carrying*; of restless *movement* in sickness βοαί, φορήσεις, ὠχρότητες...τῶν εὐπορούντων [sc. εἰσί]· τῶν κόρων οὗτοι τόκοι Gr.Naz.*carm.*1.2.8.128(M.37.658A).

***φορητέον,** *one must wear,* Clem.*paed.*3.11(p.270.3; M.8.633A).

***φορητῶς,** *tolerably,* Cyr.*Os.*49(3.80A); id.*Nah.*25(3.504B); id. *Zach.*102(3.795C).

φόριμος, *fruitful,* Clem.*str.*6.15(p.491.16; M.9.341C).

φόρμιγξ, ἡ, *lyre*; fig., of the tongue, Geo.Pis.*carm.*47.

***φορνοφόρος,** v. *φερνοφόρος.

***φορογράφος, ὁ,** *clerk employed on the tribute,* Gr.Naz.*carm.*2.1. 12.154(M.37.1177A).

***φοροθετέω,** *make a charge for* τίς...τῶν ἐπισκόπων τοὺς λόγους ἐφοροθέτησε Gr.Nyss.*ep.*27(M.32.1092C; v.l. for ἐφορολόγησε p.82.3).

φόρον, τό, (Lat. *forum*), Gr.Naz.*carm.*2.1.11.1212(M.37.1112A); Jo.Mal.*chron.*7 p.171(M.97.276A); *Chron.Pasch.*p.305(M.92.776B).

φόρος, ὁ, *payment, tribute,* met. ἄλλον τινὰ φ. παντὶ προσφέρει τῷ ζῴῳ Thdt.*provid.*6(4.573); τῆς ὑποσχέσεως ἀπαιτηταὶ φοροὶ [l. φόρου] καθεστήκατε Bas.Sel.*or.*3.1(M.85.49B).

***φοροστάσιον, τό,** ? *platform* ἄλλα τινὰ νεώτερα γέγονεν ἔν τε δομήσεσι καὶ...περιβόλοις καὶ λοετροῖς καὶ φ. καὶ πράγμασι διαφόροις Cosm.Mel.*schol.*(M.38.547) in Gr.Naz.*carm.*2.2(epigr.)50.1f.

φορτηγέω, *carry loads* or *burdens,* Bas.Sel.*v.Thecl.*2.7(M.85.576C).

***φορτιάζω,** *load a beast of burden,* Pall.*h.Laus.*17(M.34.1044C; v.l. φορβιάσας p. 45.12).

φορτικός, 1. *burdensome, hard to bear* φ. καὶ βάναυσα Just.*dial.*3.3 (M.6.481A); τὸ γὰρ σεμνὸν κατάστημα οὐ προσθήκῃ τοῦ φ. ... περιγίγνεται Clem.*paed.*3.11(p.269.14; M.8.632B); Chrys.*hom.35.1 in Mt.*(7.397B); of life, *ib.53.4*(543D); ref. Inc. τὸ τῆς οἰκονομίας φ. οὐκ ἐσόμενον ἔξω θαύματος Cyr.*Is.*4.4(2.664A); of persons, Clem. *paed.*2.8(p.194.13; 465C); ἀλαζόνα καὶ φ. Hipp.*haer.*6.8(p.135.27; M.16.3207B); οὐκ ἂν αὐτοὺς ἐνομίσαμεν εἶναι φ. [sc. τοὺς πένητας] Chrys.*hom.35.5 in Mt.*(405A); **2.** *difficult* τῇ Ῥωμαίων φωνῇ...φ. ...ἐμοί Gr.Thaum.*pan.Or.*1(p.3.4; M.10.1053A); Cyr.*ador.*2(1.58C); **3.** *severe*; of laws, Cyr.*Is.*3.4(2.504A); id.*ador.*13(1.460A); of punishments, etc., id.*Am.*31(3.282E); id.*Mich.*17(3.406B); φορτικώτερον τῶν διδασκόντων τὸ κρίμα id.*Lc.*12:41ff.(M.72.752C); of any judgement οὐδὲ γὰρ εἶπε λύουσιν, ἀλλὰ τὸ φορτικώτερον, βεβηλοῦσι [sc. the Sabbath] Chrys.*hom.39.2 in Mt.*(7.433E); of persons φ. ὧν καὶ λυπῶν ὑμᾶς διὰ τῶν ῥημάτων *ib.43.5*(465B); *ib.45.1*(476E); id.*hom. 65.2 in Jo.*(8.392A); Cyr.*Jo.*5.1(4.462E).

***φορτισμός, ὁ,** *carrying burdens* ὁ θεὸς...ἔδησεν αὐτοὺς δεσμοῖς ἀλύτοις στιβώσει φορτισμοῦ *Const.App.*6.20.6.

φορτοφορέω, *be pregnant, Orac.Sib.*2.190.

φορτ-όω, 1. *load, burden,* †Gregent.*leg.Hom.*26(M.86.596B); Thphn.*chron.*p.286(M.108.704A); Manich. πλοῖα γὰρ θέλει λέγειν ἥλιον καὶ σελήνην· καὶ τὸ μὲν μικρὸν πλοῖον ~οῦσθαι ἕως ἡμερῶν δεκαπέντε Epiph.*haer*.66.9(p.30.18; M.42.44B); met. ἐφόρτωσεν ἡμῶν τὰς ἀκοὰς Ἰωάννης καταπληκτικοῖς λόγοις ‡Chrys.*theoph*.1(2.810C); βουνοῖς καὶ λόφοις πεφορτωμένην χέρσον Mac.Mgn.*apocr*.4.17(p.191.8); **2.** *oppress, afflict* οὔτε κρύος αὐτοὺς [sc. Ἀδὰμ καὶ Εὔαν] ἐφόρτου Epiph.*haer*.52.2(p.313.16; M.41.957A); **3.** *take a burden on oneself* σὺ μὲν ἐφόρτους τὴν ἀποσκευὴν Ast.Am.*hom*.2(M.40.181C).

***φορτώνω**, *lay a load upon* ὥσπερ τοῖς ζῴοις...τούτοις φορτώνειν *A.Thom*.A 83(p.198.22).

[*]**φόρυβος, ὁ,** for θόρυβος, *noise, tumult, Exorc*.21(p.339).

φορυτός, ὁ, *what is blown about by the wind, rubbish*; met., *heap, burden,* of evil τὴν δὲ ψυχὴν φ. τοσούτων κακῶν ἐπισυρομένην περιορᾷς; Chrys.*hom.42.4 in Mt*.(7.457A); id.*hom.24.4 in Rom*.(9.699D); πολὺν δὲ ἁμαρτημάτων φ. ἐπιφέρεσθαι Thdt.*h.rel*.9(3.1190).

φοσσατεύω** (φουσατεύω**, ***φωσατεύω**), (cf. Lat. *fosso*) **1.** *encamp,* Jo.Mal.*chron*.12 p.293(M.97.444A); φωσα-, Thphn. *chron*.p.163(v.l. ἐφοσάτευσεν M.108.440A); **2.** *campaign* κατὰ τῶν Σκυθῶν...ἐφουσάτευσεν Steph.Diac.*v.Steph*.(M.100.1125C, v.l. ἐφοσσάτευσεν); **3.** *enroll an army,* φουσ-, Barth.Edess.*Agar*.(M.104.1436B).

φοσσάτον ([*]**φουσάτον (-ᾶ-)**, [*]**φοσάτον**), **τό,** (Lat. *fossatum*) **1.** *trench,* Jo.Mal.*chron*.18 p.461(M.97.676A); φοσάτον *ib*.p.309(465A); **2.** *entrenched camp,* Anast.Ap.*a.Max*.1.31(M.90.168B,C); **3.** *army* τὸ φοσάτον ὅλον τοῦτο διελάλει *ib*.1.1(112B); φουσ-, Barth.Edess.*Agar*.(M.104.1389A; 1440A); v. φώσατον.

***φοσσεύω**, (cf. Lat. *fosso*) *besiege,* Jo.Mal.*chron*.12 p.304(M.97.460A); *ib*.15 p.389(577A); *ib*.18 p.465(680B).

***φουκά,** (= Heb. פּוּךְ, cf.Is.54:11) a dark stone, *Apoc.En*.18.8 (p.46.19).

***φουλκίζω**, variant for φουρκίζω, Jo.Mal.*chron*.18 p.431(M.97.636B).

***φοῦλκον, τό,** *wedge, body of troops drawn up in the form of a wedge,* Thphn.*chron*.p.265(M.108.660A; de Boor om.).

***φουμίζ-ω**, (cf. Lat. *fumus, fumosus*) *vaunt* περὶ κομπαζόντων καὶ ∼όντων Leont.et Jo.*sacr*.10.15 tit.(M.86.2024D).

***φούρκα, ἡ,** (Lat. *furca*) *gibbet,* Leont.N.*v.Sym*.50(M.93.1732C); Thphn.*chron*.p.156(M.108.424B); τὸν τίμιον καὶ ζωοποιὸν σταυρὸν φ. ὀνομάσει *Vaticin*.2(p.53).

***φουρκίζω**, (cf. Lat. *furca*) *gibbet,* Ephr.3.xxixC; Jo.Mal.*chron*.18 p.431(M.97.636B); Leont.N.*v.Sym*.50(M.93.1732B); εἰς ἄνθρωπον πεφουρκισμένον καὶ κατάδικον ἐλπίζετε ‡Anast.S.*Jud.disp*.3(M.89.1241A); v. φουσκιάζω.

***φούρναξ, ὁ,** (Lat. *fornax*) *kiln,* Epiph.*haer*.30.12(p.347.29; M.41.425B); *ib*.(p.348.21; 428A).

φοῦρνος, ὁ, (Lat. *furnus*) *oven,* ‡Rom.Mel.(*OC* 2 p.59); Cyr.S. *v.Sab*.5(p.89.17); Jo.Mosch.*prat*.92(M.87.2949B); τοῦ σκευοφυλακίου τοῦ φουρίου (v.l. φούρνου, ? f.l. for φρουρίου) *Chron.Pasch*.p.337(M.92.880A).

***φουσατεύω**, v. *φοσσατεύω.

[*]**φουσάτον (-ᾶ-), τό,** v. φοσσάτον.

***φουσκάριον, τό,** (cf. Lat. *posca*) *wine-shop,* Leont.N.*v.Sym*.41 (M.93.1721A); *ib*.42(1721B); *ib*.56(1740B).

***φουσκάριος, ὁ,** (cf. Lat. *posca*) *seller of wine,* Leont.N.*v.Sym*.31(M.93.1709A).

***φουσκιάζω**, prob. for φουρκίζω: κεφαλὰς...φουσκιάσας τῷ βασιλεῖ ...ἀπέστειλεν Thphn.*chron*.p.334(φασκιώσας M.108.805A, vv.ll. φουσκίσας, φουρκίσας).

***φραγγελλόω**, v. φραγελλόω.

***φραγγελόω**, = foreg.

φραγέλλιον, τό, (Lat. *flagellum*) *scourge, M.Con*.6.2(p.66.24); *Chron.Pasch*.p.391(M.92.1000C); ref. Jo.2:15, †Bas.*Is*.131(1.470C; M.30.329C); interpreted by Heracleon τὸ φ. δὲ πεποιῆσθαι ἐκ σχοινίων ὑπὸ τοῦ Ἰησοῦ, οὐχὶ παρ' ἄλλου λαβόντος ἰδιοτρόπως ἀπαγγέλλει, λέγων τὸ φ. εἰκόνα τυγχάνειν τῆς δυνάμεως καὶ ἐνεργείας τοῦ ἁγίου πνεύματος ἐκφυσῶντος τοὺς χείρονας, καί φησι τὸ φ. καὶ τὸ λίνον καὶ τὴν σινδόνα, καὶ ὅσα τοιαῦτα, εἰκόνα τῆς δυνάμεως καὶ τῆς ἐνεργείας εἶναι τοῦ ἁγίου πνεύματος. [ἔπειτα ἑαυτῷ προσείληφεν τὸ μὴ γεγραμμένον, ὡς ἄρα] εἰς ξύλον ἐδέδετο τὸ φ.· ὅπερ ξύλον τύπον ἐκλαβὼν εἶναι τοῦ σταυροῦ [φησι] τούτῳ τῷ ξύλῳ ἀνηλῶσθαι καὶ ἠφανίσθαι τοὺς κυβευτὰς ἐμπόρους καὶ πᾶσαν τὴν κακίαν. [καὶ οὐκ οἶδ' ὅπως φλυαρῶν φησιν] ἐκ δύο τούτων πραγμάτων φ. κατασκευάζεσθαι. ... οὐ γὰρ ἐκ δέρματος...νεκροῦ ἐποίησεν αὐτό, ἵνα τὴν ἐκκλησίαν κατασκευάσῃ οὐκέτι λῃστῶν καὶ ἐμπόρων σπήλαιον, ἀλλὰ οἶκον τοῦ πατρὸς αὐτοῦ Heracleon ap.Or.*Jo*.10.33(19; p.207.5f.; M.14.365Df.); ref. Mt.21:12, use denied, Max.*ambig*.(M.91.1208B).

***φραγελλίτης, ὁ,** *lictor,* Jo.Mosch.*prat*.49(M.87.2904C).

φραγελλόω ([*]**φραγγελλόω**, [*]**φραγγελόω**), (Lat. *flagello*) *scourge,* φραγγελλ-, *T.Benj*.2.3; *A.Paul.et Thecl*.21(p.249.10); Gr.Naz.*or*.38.18(M.36.332C); ref. Christ, φραγγελ-, Hesych.H.*Ps.tit*.21.35(M.27.725B); φραγγελ-, ‡Ath.*doct.Ant*.9(M.28.693D); Ast.Am. *hom*.8(M.40.288C); Nil.*epp*.1.85(M.79.120C).

***φραγέλλωσις, ἡ,** *scourging,* ‡Epiph.*hom*.2(M.43.461C).

φραγμός, ὁ, *fence,* met. φ. ἐστιν ἀπάθεια ψυχῆς λογικῆς Or.*exp.in Pr*.30:30(M.17.232A); Christ breaking the φ. in Hades, *Ep.Chr. suppl*.ap.Eus.*h.e*.1.13.20(M.20.128C); ‡Nil.*perist*.12.11(M.79.961C); of Law, Jo.D.*hom*.2.4(M.96.584B); ref. Eph.2:14 ἡ ἔχθρα τὸ μεσότοιχον ἦν τοῦ φ. κωλῦον τοῦ ἑνοῦσθαι τὴν ἀνθρώπων φύσιν, τῇ μακαριότητι τῶν κρειττόνων. τοῦτο οὖν τὸ μεσότοιχον τοῦ φ. ... ἐλύθη διὰ τοῦ ἐνηνθρωπηκέναι τὸν σωτῆρα Or.*comm.in Eph*.2:14(p.406); φ. ὁ νόμος ἦν, ἀλλ' οὗτος ἐγένετο μὲν ἀσφαλείας ἕνεκεν· διὸ καὶ φ. ὠνόμαστο, ἵνα περιφράττῃ...γέγονε δὲ μεσότοιχον, οὐκέτι αὐτοὺς ἐν ἀσφαλείᾳ καθιστῶν, ἀλλὰ χωρίζον αὐτοὺς ἀπὸ τοῦ θεοῦ Chrys.*hom.5.2 in Eph*.(11.34D); v. μεσότοιχος.

***φραγμόω**, *fence,* Geo.Pis.*hex*.146(M.92.1443A).

φράσσ-ω, 1. *fortify,* met. τοῖς ὅπλοις τοῦ κυρίου πεφραγμένος Clem. *str*.7.11(p.47.15; M.9.492A); ὁ...λόγος τοῦ θεοῦ δικαιοσύνης φράξας τὸν ἄνθρωπον ὅπλοις Meth.*Porph*.1(p.504.17; M.18.400B); τῇ τοῦ... βαπτίσματος πανοπλίᾳ φραξάμενον Thdt.*h.e*.4.12.2(3.968); Gel.Cyz. *h.e*.1.10.10(M.85.1214C); **2.** *guard, shield* τὰ ὦτα φ. ἀπὸ δυσφημίας Meth.*symp*.5.4(p.57.21; M.18.104A); **3.** *restrict, confine* ἐν ἑαυτῇ ∼ουσαν τὴν ὀργήν id.*arbitr*.2(p.149.18; M.18.244A).

φρατρία, ἡ, 1. *association, company* ref. Eph.3:15 (v.l.) τινὲς πατριὰν ἀνέγνωσαν, οὐ συνιέντες τὸ κείμενον· ἔστι δὲ φρατρία· πατριὰ μὲν γὰρ ἡ συγγένεια λέγεται, φρατρία δὲ τὸ σύστημα Thdr.Mops. *Eph*.3:15(M.66.917A); **2.** *faction,* Gr.Naz.*ep*.41(M.37.85C); Ast.Am. *hom*.2(M.40.188D); Thdt.*haer*.2.5(4.331) s.v.l.; v. φατρία.

φρατριάζω, *conspire,* Jo.Mal.*chron*.18 p.480(M.97.696D); Jo.Eub. *innoc*.1(M.96.1501B); Thdr.Stud.*poen*.1.30(M.99.1737A); v. φατριάζω.

φρατριαστής, ὁ, v. φατριαστής.

***φρατριαστικός,** *of a faction,* Leont.H.*monoph*.(M.86.1845B).

***φρατριόω**, *communicate,* Or.*exp.in Pr*.30:24(M.17.232A).

φρέαρ, τό, *well*; **1.** ref. lit. and spiritual exegesis of scripture (cf. πηγή), Or.*hom.18.4 in Jer*.(p.154.16; M.13.468A); **2.** exeg. Cant.4:15 πηγὴ δὲ κήπων, ὁ τοὺς ἀσθενεστέρους ποτίζων λόγος· καὶ φ. ὕδατος ζῶντος, ὁ τὰ βαθύτερα τοῖς πολλοῖς ἀσύνοπτα παραδιδοὺς μυστήρια· ῥοιζοῦσαν δὲ αὐτὴν ἀπὸ τοῦ Λιβάνου εἶπεν τὴν πηγὴν ἢ τὸ φ., διὰ τὸ τοὺς διδασκάλους τῆς ἐκκλησίας ἀπὸ τοῦ Ἰουδαϊκοῦ ὁρμᾶσθαι γένους Nil.ap.Proc.G.*Cant*.4:15(M.87.1668A); οὐ γὰρ μόνον τὴν εὐαγγελικὴν ἔχει διδασκαλίαν προφανῶς ῥέουσαν, ἀλλὰ καὶ τοῦ νόμου τὸ φ. Thdt. *Cant*.4:15(2.105); **3.** of BMV χαῖρε, τὸ φ. τοῦ ἀεὶ ζῶντος ὕδατος Chrysipp.*enc.in BMV* 1(p.337.8); **4.** of depth of hell, *Apoc.Paul* 41 (pp.61,62); *1 Apoc.Jo*.24(p.90).

φρεναπατάω, *deceive,* Hipp.*haer*.4.7(p.39.20; M.16.3070A); Ammon.*Ac*.17:32(M.85.1568C); *ib*.26:5(1596C).

***φρεναπατέω**, *deceive,* Iren.*haer*.1.9.1(M.7.537A); Ammon.*Ac*. 16:23(M.85.1560B); Marc.Er.*opusc*.5.3(M.65.1033D).

φρεναπάτης, ὁ, *deceiver,* †Bas.*Is*.102(1.450A; M.30.284B); Pall.*v. Chrys*.9(p.56.23; M.47.33); Eust.Mon.*ep*.(M.86.941B).

***φρενερημία, ἡ,** *senseless idea,* Didym.*Trin*.3.42(M.39.992A).

***φρενητεία, ἡ,** *madness,* ‡Caes.Naz.*dial*.140(M.38.1069).

φρενῖτις ([*]**φρενῆτις**), **ἡ,** *brain-fever*; met., *distraction, madness,* Cyr.*Ps*.9:21(M.69.777A); τῇ φ. τῆς ἑαυτῶν προλήψεως ὑποσυρόμενοι Flav.Ant.*anath*.1(M.48.945); φρενῆτις, ‡Caes.Naz.*dial*.102(M.38.968).

***φρενοβάρβαρος,** *with the mind of a barbarian,* Sophr.H.*ep.syn*. (M.87.3192B).

φρενοβλαβέω, *be frantic,* Pall.*h.Laus*.25(p.80.9; M.34.1090D).

φρενοβλαβία, ἡ, = φρενοβλάβεια, *madness, folly* πρὸς ἔλεγχον δὲ τῆς Ἰουδαϊκῆς σκληροκαρδίας καὶ φ. *Dial.Christ.et Jud*.18(p.82.33).

***φρενοβλάβος,** *mad, Orac.Sib*.8.115.

***φρενοβλαβῶς,** *madly,* Eust.*engast*.20(p.47.22; M.18.653C).

***φρενοδινής,** *making the mind giddy,* Nonn.*par.Jo*.12:27(M.43.856A).

***φρενοκηδής,** *grieving,* Synes.*hymn*.2.85(p.47; M.66.1593).

***φρενοκρατής,** *mastering the mind* φ. ἔρως Geo.Pis.*carm*.4.36.

φρενόληπτος, *demented,* CCP(536)*act*.1(H.2.1209D); Jo.D.*hom*.12.13(M.96.797D).

***φρενόλυσσος,** *frenzied,* ‡Caes.Naz.*dial*.145(M.38.1096).

φρενοπλήξ, *demented,* Gr.Naz.*carm*.1.1.6.99(M.37.437A); *ib*.2.2 (poem.)5.83(1527A).

***φρενόσπορος,** *wise,* Geo.Pis.*bell.Avar*.12(M.92.1264A).

***φρενοφθόρος,** *destroying the mind,* Geo.Pis.*van*.123(M.92.1590A).

φρένωσις, ἡ, *admonition* φ. δέ ἐστι, ψόγος φρενῶν ἐμποιητικός Clem.*paed*.1.9(p.136.13; M.8.344C).

φρεωρυχία, ἡ, *digging, sinking, of wells*; *well-shaft* τῶν ἐπὶ τοῦ χείλους τῆς φ. ἑστώτων Philost.*h.e*.3.9(M.65.492C).

φρεωρύχος, ὁ, *well-digger*, Bas.*hex*.1.7(1.8C; M.29.20B); Gr.Nyss. *Eun*.1(1 p.135.2; M.45.373A); id.*hex*.58(M.44.109D).

[*]**φριγάω,** = σφριγάω, *be at full growth* μονονουχὶ φριγώσης νυκτός, καὶ ἐν ἀκμαῖς ὄντος τοῦ σκότους Cyr.*Is*.2.2(2.233).

***φριγμός, ὁ,** *heat*, Gr.Nyss.*hom.9 in Cant*.(M.44.972D).

φρίκη, ἡ, *shivering fear, religious awe* τοῦ πνεύματος ἡμῖν διαλεγομένου...μετὰ πολλῆς δὲ τῆς φ. ἀκούειν ἡμᾶς δεῖν Chrys.*hom.47.1 in Jo*.(8.275B); ὅσαπέρ ἐστι φρίκης μεστά id.*hom.30.2 in 2Cor*.(10.651A); *ib.4.5*(218C).

φρικιάω, *shiver*, from ague, *Ep.Abg*.2(p.281.10); Jo.Mosch.*prat*.1 (M.87.2853A); from fear, *Pers*.(p.13.7; M.10.101B); Pall.*v.Chrys*.20 (p.139.20; M.47.78); ‡Felix III Papa *ep.Petr*.2(H.2.824E); from horror and indignation, Pall.*v.Chrys*.12(p.70.12; M.47.39).

φρικτός, *causing to shudder*; **1.** *shocking, abominable* φρικτὰ πεποιήκασι, τὸν κύριον...ἀποκτείναντες Or.*hom.18.8 in Jer*.(p.162.17; M.13.479D); συνίετε τὸ τῆς ἀσεβείας φ. Bas.*Eun*.2.25(1.262C; M.29. 629D); Chrys.*hom.21.1 in Mt*.(7.269D); **2.** *terrible, frightening* τοῦ πολεμιωτάτου ἀνθρώποις ὄφεως καὶ φρικτοτάτου Or.*Cels*.6.28(p.98.30; M.11.1537A); φ. τε καὶ πρὸς ὠμότητα οἱ τῆς θρησκείας...νόμοι Const. *or.s.c*.17(p.178.1; M.20.1284A); Eus.*v.C*.2.2(p.41.6; M.20.980C); φ. ἐγκλήμασιν Cyr.*Am*.36(3.290A); **3.** *inspiring fear and awe*; **a.** in gen. φ. ... ὅρκοις Hipp.*haer*.5.23(p.125.16; M.16.3191B); μύθῳ φ. Χριστὸς ἔμελλεν ἐπὶ τρίτον ἦμαρ ἐγείρειν Nonn.*par.Jo*.2:21(M.43.764C); of words of warning, etc., Chrys.*hom.48.4 in Mt*.(7.498C); id.*hom.3.2 in 2Tim*.(11.675A); †Jo.D.*B.J*.8(M.96.928B); **b.** of God φ. καὶ φοβερὸς τοῖς ἀγγέλοις Epiph.*haer*.69.38(p.186.20; M.42.261A); **c.** of BMV ὦ παρθένε, φρικτὸν τῆς ἐκκλησίας κειμήλιον ‡Epiph.*hom*.5(M. 43.497A); ὁ φ. τῆς οἰκονομίας ἱστὸς ἐν ᾧ...ὑφάνθη ὁ τῆς ἑνώσεως χιτών Procl.CP *or.laud.BMV* 1(p.103.18; M.65.681B); **d.** of death and judgement τοῦ βήματος τοῦ φ. Chrys.*hom.12.3 in Jo*.(8.71B); φ. ὁ θάνατος *ib.83.1*(489A); τῇ ἡμέρᾳ τῇ φοβερᾷ καὶ φ. id.*hom.3.2 in 2Tim*.(11.674D); τοῦ ἀδεκάστου καὶ φ. κριτηρίου Isid.Pel.*epp*.1.30(M. 78.201A); **e.** of mysteries, Hipp.*antichr*.36(p.23.9; M.10.756A); of sacrament of penance, ‡Jo.D.*conf*.9(M.95.293B); of eucharist τὴν φ. τῶν μυστηρίων κοινωνίαν Chrys.*hom.10.3 in Jo*.(8.61B); id.*hom.18.3 in 2Cor*.(10.568B); id.*hom.3.4 in Phil*.(11.217E); id.*exp.in Ps*.140:3 (5.433D); τὴν φ. θυσίαν Philost.*h.e*.2.13(M.65.476C); καθαρᾶς...καὶ φ. σαρκός ‡Jo.D.*hom*.5(M.96.656D); **f.** in other contexts σημεῖον... δέδορκα φ. ἅδην πάντεσσιν Eudoc.*Cypr*.1.138(M.85.837B); τὸ φ. ... τοῦ θεογράφου τύπου...ἀπεικόνισμα Geo.Pis.*Pers*.2.86(M.92.1218A); of Ascension, Hipp.Th. *fr*.4.3(p.19.14).

***φρικτοτελής,** *filling with awe* τῇ φ. τραπέζῃ προσεγγίζειν τολμῶντες ‡Jo.D.*hom*.5(M.96.656D).

φρικτῶς, *in an awe-inspiring manner*, Chrys.*hom.16.1 in 1Tim*. (11.642B).

φρικώδης, 1. *that causes shuddering* or *horror*, of dissent within Church τὸ φ., αὐτοὺς τοὺς προεστῶτας...ἐν τοσαύτῃ...τῇ πρὸς ἀλλήλους διαφορᾷ γνώμης τε καὶ δόξης καθεστῶτας Bas.*jud*.1(2.214A; M.31. 653B); of sight of gold and the desire arising from it, Chrys.*hom.9.6 in Mt*.(7.139A); *ib.21.1*(269D); **2.** *inspiring awe, awful*; of Jewish religious objects, id.*sac*.3.4(p.51.9; 1.382C); of ornaments of church τί γὰρ οὐχὶ ἐνταῦθα μέγα καὶ φ. id.*hom.32.6 in Mt*.(7.373C); of eucharist κατ' ἐκείνην τὴν φρικωδεστάτην ὥραν δεῖ ἄνω ἔχειν τὴν καρδίαν Cyr.H.*catech*.23.4; τῆς φρικωδεστάτης...θυσίας *ib*.23.9; Chrys. *laed*.11(3.457B); τῆς φρικωδεστάτης...τραπέζης id.*ep*.2.2(3.536B); τὸ ποτήριον τὸ φ. id.*hom.7.6 in Mt*.(7.114A); τὰ φ. μυστήρια *ib.25.3* (310D); τὴν γλῶσσαν τὴν φοινισσομένην αἵματι φρικωδεστάτῳ *ib.82.5* (788B); τῆς φ. ἐκείνης καὶ ποθεινῆς τραπέζης Nil.*epp*.2.144(M.79.265D); of kiss of peace τοῦ φρικωδεστάτου ἀσπασμοῦ τοῦ πρὸς ἀλλήλους Chrys.*prod.Jud*.1.6(2.385D); of Last Judgement τὸ φ. ... καὶ ἀδέκαστον δικαστήριον Chrys.*hom.20.6 in Mt*.(7.267E); πανταχόθεν φ. ἡ ἡμέρα ἐκείνη τότε *ib.79.1*(758C); in gen. ἀναπέμψαι τὴν φρικωδεστάτην φωνήν id.*hom.6.3 in Is*.6:1(6.141C); ὃ...ἦν φρικωδέστερον, τὸ γενέσθαι ὁμοίους τῷ θεῷ id.*hom.18.4 in Mt*.(7.239A); of admission to God's presence in prayer εἰς βασίλεια εἰσιών, οὐ τὰ ἐν τῇ γῇ, ἀλλὰ τὰ πολλῷ φρικωδέστερα τούτων, τὰ ἐν τοῖς οὐρανοῖς *ib.19.3*(248C); of baptismal renunciation id.*hom.2.7 in 2Cor*.(10.438D); of priest's mouth instructing candidate for baptism, *ib.30.2*(561A); τῇ φοβερᾷ καὶ φ. ἡμέρᾳ, ὅταν ἔλθῃ τὴν δόξαν ἐνδεικνύμενος τὴν ἑαυτοῦ id.*scand*. 17(3.504C); of subjects of Christ's teaching ἀπορρήτων πραγμάτων καὶ μυστηρίων φρικωδεστάτων id.*hom.43.3 in Mt*.(461D); εἴ τις ἐν γῇ ...ἀπείρῳ πολλοὺς ἔτεινεν οὐρανούς, καινὸν καὶ φ. ἂν ἔδειξε τὸ θέατρον *ib.69.3*(684B); οἱ τὰ πολλῷ τούτων ἀπορρητότερα καὶ φρικωδέστερα περιεργαζόμενοι, τουτέστι, πῶς ἐγέννησε τὸν υἱὸν κτλ. id.*hom.2.6 in Rom*.(9.447C).

***φρῖξις, ἡ,** *horror*, Epiph.*haer*.26.4(p.281.1; M.41.337C).

φρίσσω, 1. *shiver, shudder*, with fear and awe; *be terrified* πέφρικέ τε τῇ τραπέζῃ προσιέναι Dion.Al.ap.Eus.*h.e*.7.9.5(M.20.656B); of heavenly powers, at Creation ὅτε ἐγένετο τὰ ἄστρα...ἔφριξαν καὶ ἐθαύμασαν Chrys.*hom.76.3 in Mt*.(7.736A); at Second Advent πῶς οὐ φρίξουσι καὶ σαλευθήσονται [sc. αἱ δυνάμεις τῶν οὐρανῶν]; *ib*.(736B); **2.** *make to shudder, terrify* τὸ μὲν εὐκαταφρόνητον φρίττει προσωπεῖον id.*stat*.5.3(2.64C).

***φρονεύω,** *take thought* καλῶς ἐφρονεύσατε Eus.Al.*serm*.21.13(M. 86.440B).

φρόνημα, τό, 1. *thought, purpose, will* τὸ φ. τῆς σαρκός, opp. φ. πνεύματος or φ. ψυχῆς: δουλεύοντα τῷ φ. τῆς σαρκός Bas.*hom.in Ps*.33 (1.148B; M.29.364A); τὰ πάθη...ἐκ τοῦ φ. τῆς σαρκὸς ἐκφυόμενα †Bas. *Is*.230(1.553D; M.30.521A); μηκέτι τοῦ φ. τῆς σαρκὸς πρὸς τὴν ψυχὴν στασιάζοντος [sc. after resurrection]...ἀλλά...ἓν δι' ἀμφοτέρων ἔσται τὸ φ., τῆς σαρκός φημι καὶ τοῦ πνεύματος Gr.Nyss.*hom.1 in Cant*.(M. 44.777A); exeg. Rom.8:6–7 οὐ γὰρ τὴν σάρκα αὐτὴν ἀλλὰ τὸ φ. τῆς σαρκὸς ὑποτάσσεσθαι μὴ δύνασθαι τῷ νόμῳ τοῦ θεοῦ ὑπέθετο, ἕτερον παρὰ τὴν σάρκα ὑπάρχον Meth.*res*.1.59(p.322.14; M.41.1156A); φ. γὰρ σαρκὸς ἐνταῦθά φησι τὸν γεώδη λογισμόν, τὸν παχύν, τὸν πρὸς τὰ βιωτικὰ καὶ τὰς πονηρὰς πράξεις ἐπτοημένον Chrys.*hom.13.6 in Rom*. (9.566D); φ. τῆς σαρκός, τρυφή, σπατάλη· φ. τῆς σαρκός, πλεονεξία καὶ πᾶσα ἁμαρτία. διὰ τί φ. σαρκὸς εἴρηται; καίτοι γε οὐδὲν ἄνευ ψυχῆς εἰργάσατο ἄν. ... τί οὖν ἐστι σαρκικὰ φ.; αἱ ἁμαρτίαι. ... ἀρετὴ γὰρ σαρκὸς τὸ ὑποτετάχθαι τῇ ψυχῇ, κακία δὲ τὸ ἄρχειν ψυχῆς...τίνος οὖν ἕνεκεν φ. αὐτὸ σαρκὸς καλεῖ; ὅτι τῆς σαρκὸς ὅλον γίνεται id.*hom. 5.4 in Eph*.(11.36C–37C); τὸ φ. τῆς σαρκός, τουτέστι, τὰ τῶν παθημάτων σκιρτήματα Thdt.*Rom*.8:6(3.82); Gennad.*Rom*.8:5–6(p.376.3; M.85.1689C); **2.** *modesty*, Thdt.*1Cor*.15:10(3.267); id.*2Cor*.11:16(344); *ib*.12:11(350); **3.** *presumption, arrogance*; ref. Devil τῷ φ. πεσών [sc. ἐκ τῶν οὐρανῶν] Ath.*ep.Aeg.Lib*.8(M.25.556B); **4.** *faith, doctrine, tenet* ὀρθὸν τὸ φ. *ib*.20(585A); ἀποστολικὸν...τὸ φ. id.*syn*.5(p.234.12; M.26. 688D); τοῦ περὶ ἑνὸς θεοῦ φ. Didym.(‡Bas.)*Eun*.5(1.301C; M.29.724A); τὸ ἐν τοῖς ἠθικοῖς τῆς ἐκκλησίας φ. Thdt.*haer*.5.23(4.460); of Arian beliefs, Ath.*hom.in Mt.11:27*(M.25.209C); id.*ep.Aeg.Lib*.19(584B); τῶν νῦν Ἰουδαίων τὸ φ. id.*Ar*.1.38(M.26.92A); οὐκ ἔστι μὲν τὸ τοιοῦτον ὑμῶν φ. εἰς ἕνα θεόν id.*ep.Serap*.1.29(M.26.596C); Thdt.*h.e*.2.29.2,4(3. 902,903); ref. interpretation of scripture πόθεν...τὸ καινὸν φ. τοῦτο; Ath.*Ar*.2.47(248B); fig. τὸ ὑδαρὲς τοῦ φ. ἐζωοποίησεν, [sc. ὁ Χριστός] τοῦ νόμου τὴν ἐργάτιν ἐξ Ἀδάμ, τὸν κόσμον ὅλον αἵματι πληρώσας ἀμπέλου Clem.*paed*.2.2(p.174.1; M.8.424B).

***φρονηματιάω,** *be self-confident*, Chrys.*hom.28.6 in Heb*.(12. 265C).

φρόνησις, ἡ, 1. *intellect, understanding* ἴδε μὴ μόνον τοῖς ὀφθαλμοῖς ἀλλὰ καὶ τῇ φ. *Diogn*.2.1; Clem.*str*.2.4(p.119.25; M.8.944C); τὸν διορατικὸν τῆς φ. ὀφθαλμὸν δείκνυσιν Meth.*symp*.7.2(p.72.21; M.18. 128A); defined φησὶν ἡ γραφὴ 'πνεῦμα αἰσθήσεως' δεδόσθαι τοῖς τεχνίταις ἐκ τοῦ θεοῦ, τὸ δὲ οὐδὲν ἀλλ' ἢ φ. ἐστι, δύναμις ψυχῆς θεωρητικὴ τῶν ὄντων καὶ τοῦ ἀκολούθου ὁμοίου τε καὶ ἀνομοίου διακριτικὴ τε αὖ καὶ συνθετικὴ καὶ προστατικὴ καὶ ἀπαγορευτικὴ τῶν τε μελλόντων καταστοχαστική· διατείνει δὲ οὐκ ἐπὶ τὰς τέχνας μόνον, ἀλλὰ καὶ ἐπὶ τὴν φιλοσοφίαν αὐτήν...πολυμερὴς δὲ οὖσα ἡ φ., δι' ὅλου τεταμένη τοῦ κόσμου διά τε τῶν ἀνθρωπίνων ἁπάντων, καθ' ἕκαστον αὐτῶν μεταβάλλει τὴν προσηγορίαν [sc. νόησις, γνῶσίς τε καὶ σοφία καὶ ἐπιστήμη, πίστις, δόξα ὀρθή, τέχνη, ἐμπειρία] Clem.*str*.6.17(p.511.16; M.9.385B); in pagan philosophy ἐπεὶ καὶ Ξενοκράτης ἐν τῷ Περὶ φ. τὴν σοφίαν ἐπιστήμην τῶν πρώτων αἰτίων καὶ τῆς νοητῆς οὐσίας εἶναί φησι, τὴν φ. ἡγούμενος διττήν, τὴν μὲν πρακτικήν, τὴν δὲ θεωρητικήν, ἣν δὴ σοφίαν ὑπάρχειν ἀνθρωπίνην. διόπερ ἡ μὲν σοφία φ., οὐ μὴν πᾶσα φ. σοφία *ib*.2.5(p.125.20; M.8.957B); as image of Logos in man, id. *prot*.10(p.71.29; M.8.213A); v. εἰκών; fig. ἔσται ἡ ἐκκλησία τοῦ θεοῦ ἓν σῶμα, μία φ., εἷς νοῦς Herm.*sim*.9.18.4; **2.** *wisdom, prudence*, in moral philosophy and Christian teaching; **a.** in gen. ἡ μὲν φ. πάσης τῆς ἐν Χριστῷ εἰς δόξαν θεοῦ ἀρετῆς θησαυρὸς ἀγαθός ἐστιν· ἡ δὲ φ. τῆς κακίας τῶν ἀπαγορευμένων ὑπὸ τοῦ κυρίου θησαυρὸς πονηρός ἐστιν Bas. *reg.br*.239(2.495E; M.31.1241C); πηγὴ γὰρ ὄντως καὶ ῥίζα φρονήσεως ἐστιν ἡ ἀρετὴ ὥσπερ οὖν καὶ πᾶσα πονηρία ἐξ ἀνοίας ἔχει τὴν ἀρχήν. καὶ γὰρ ὁ ἀλαζὼν καὶ ὁ ὀργίλος ἐξ ἐνδείας φ. ὑπὸ τῶν παθῶν ἁλίσκεται Chrys.*hom.41.3 in Jo*.(8.246E); ἡ φ. τῇ ἁπλότητι κιρνωμένη θεῖόν τι χρῆμα, φημὶ δὲ ἐντελεστάτην ἀρετήν, ἀποτελεῖ Isid.Pel.*epp*.2.175(M. 78.625C); φ. δὲ μὴ κοσμουμένη τῇ θείᾳ σοφίᾳ ἀνό[ν]ητος, ἅτε δὴ μὴ ἀνθηνιοχουμένη *ib*.5.271(1496A); its sphere ἐπὶ δὲ τῇ ἐπιθυμίᾳ τάττεται καὶ ἡ σωφροσύνη καὶ ἡ σωτήριος φ. Clem.*str*.4.23(p.315.16; M.

8.1360C); ὡς γὰρ τὸ τεχνικῶς τι ποιεῖν ἐν τοῖς τῆς τέχνης θεωρήμασι περιέχεται, οὕτω τὸ φρονίμως ὑπὸ τὴν φ. τέτακται· ἀρετὴ δὲ ἡ φ.· καὶ ἴδιον αὐτῆς γνωρίζειν τά τε ἄλλα καὶ πολὺ πρότερον τὰ καθ' ἑαυτήν *ib.*6.17(p.514.15; M.9.392C); opp. σωφροσύνη: γνώσει μὲν οὖν ἕπεται φ., σωφροσύνη δὲ τῇ φ.· εἰρήσθω γὰρ τὴν μὲν φ. ὑπάρχειν γνῶσιν θείαν καὶ ἐν τοῖς θεοποιουμένοις, τὴν δὲ σωφροσύνην θνητὴν καὶ ἐν ἀνθρώποις εἶναι φιλοσοφοῦσιν, οὐδέπω σοφοῖς...ἡ σωφροσύνη δὲ οἷον ἀτελὴς φ., ἐφιεμένη μὲν φρονήσεως, ἐργατικὴ δὲ ἐπιπόνως καὶ οὐ θεωρητική *ib.*6.15(p.495.7; 349A); opp. σοφία: δύο γὰρ αὗται μερίδες φιλοσοφίας, θεωρία καὶ πρᾶξις· καὶ δῆτα δύο δυνάμεις ἑκατέρα παρ' ἑκατέραν μερίδα, σοφία, καὶ φ.· αὕτη μὲν δεομένη τύχης· σοφία δὲ αὐτάρκης Synes.*ep.*103(M.66.1476D); from which man has fallen, Gr.Nyss.*or.catech.*8(p.51.18; M.45.40B); attributed to serpent, ref. Mt.10:16, Chrys.*hom.33.2 in Mt.*(7.379C); οὐ γάρ ἐστιν ἐν τοῖς ἀλόγοις ζώοις φ. μετὰ ἁπλότητος, ἀλλὰ τὰ μὲν τὴν πονηρίαν, τὰ δὲ τὴν ἁπλότητα μεταδιώκει Isid.Pel.*epp.*2.175(M.78.625C); **b.** as a virtue κεκοσμημένη ψυχὴ ἁγίῳ πνεύματι καὶ τοῖς ἐκ τούτου ἐμπνεομένη φαιδρύμασιν, δικαιοσύνῃ, φ. κτλ. Clem.*paed.*3.11(p.272.5; M.8.640A); Or.*Cels.*5.28(p.29.11; M.11.1224A); ἐκεῖνα κτώμεθα, ἃ καὶ μεθ' ἑαυτῶν ἆραι δυνάμεθα, ἅτινά ἐστι φ., δικαιοσύνη, σωφροσύνη, ἀνδρεία Ath.*v. Anton.*17(M.26.869B); defined ἐπιστήμη ἀγαθῶν καὶ κακῶν ἡ ποιητέων καὶ οὐ ποιητέων ἡ φ. Gr.Thaum.*pan.Or.*9(p.24.8; M.10.1080C); τὴν φ. τοίνυν ἐπιστάμεθα οὖσαν μίαν τῶν γενικῶν ἀρετῶν, καθ' ἣν ἐπιστήμονες γινόμεθα ἀγαθῶν καὶ κακῶν καὶ οὐδετέρων οἱ ἄνθρωποι...ἢ δῆλον, ὅτι διπλοῦν ἐστι τὸ τῆς φ. ὄνομα; ἡ μὲν γάρ τις ἐστὶ φυλακὴ τοῦ οἰκείου συμφέροντος μετὰ τῆς τοῦ πλησίον ἐπιβουλῆς, οἵα ἡ τοῦ ὄφεως, τὴν κεφαλὴν ἑαυτοῦ συντηροῦντος...ἡ δὲ ἀληθὴς φ. διάγνωσίς ἐστι τῶν ποιητέων καὶ οὐ ποιητέων· ᾗ ὁ κατακολουθῶν, οὐδέποτε δὲ τῷ ὀλέθρῳ τῆς κακίας περιπαρήσεται Bas.*hom.*12.6(2.102D; M.31.397C); φ. μέν ἐστι τοῦ ἐν ἡμῖν λογικοῦ ἡ ἐγρήγορσις Thdt.*provid.*6(4.566); its function οὕτω γὰρ ἂν ποτε παραγενέσθαι ψυχῇ τὰς θείας ἀρετάς, φ. τε τὴν αὐτὰ ταῦτα τῆς ψυχῆς τὰ κινήματα κρίνειν πρῶτον δυναμένην, ἐξ αὐτῶν καὶ τῆς περὶ τὰ ἔξω ἡμῶν, εἴ τινά ἐστιν, ἀγαθῶν καὶ κακῶν ἐπιστήμης γενομένης Gr.Thaum.*pan.Or.*9(p.23.28; 1080B); φρονεῖν δὲ πάλιν οὐχ ἧττον τῷ πρὸς ἑαυτὴν εἶναι καὶ ἑαυτοὺς γινώσκειν ἐθέλειν τε καὶ πειρᾶσθαι· τὸ δὲ εἶναι ὄντως ἔργον φρονήσεως, καὶ ταύτην εἶναι τὴν θείαν φ. καλῶς τοῖς παλαιοῖς λέγεται· τὴν αὐτὴν ὄντως οὖσαν θεοῦ καὶ ἀνθρώπου ἀρετήν, αὐτῆς τῆς ψυχῆς ἑαυτὴν ὥσπερ ἐν κατόπτρῳ ὁρᾶν μελετώσης καὶ τὸν θεῖον νοῦν,...ἐν αὐ⟨τῇ⟩ κατοπτριζομένης ὁδόν τε ἀπόρρητόν τινα ταύτης ἀποθεώσεως ἐξιχνευομένης *ib.*11(p.27.6; 1084C); τοῦτο δὴ τὸ κενὸν καὶ ἀνωφελὲς μάθημα, εἰ ὁ λόγος εἴη τῶν ἔργων δίχα, καὶ φ. οὐχὶ ποιοῦσα τὰ ποιητὰ καὶ ἀποτρέπουσα τῶν οὐ ποιητῶν, γινώσκειν δὲ ταῦτα παρεχομένη τοῖς ἔχουσιν αὐτήν *ib.*9(p.24.9; 1080C); ὅπερ γάρ ἐστι, ὥς φασιν, ὁ αἰθὴρ ἤγουν τὸ πύρινον στοιχεῖον ἐν τῷ κατ' αἴσθησιν κόσμῳ, τοῦτο ἐν τῷ κόσμῳ τῆς διανοίας ἐστὶν ἡ φ., ὡς ἕξις φωτιστικὴ καὶ τῶν ἐφ' ἑκάστου τῶν ὄντων ἰδίως πνευματικῶν λόγων ἀποδεικτική Max.*ambig.*(M.91.1245B); μυστικῶς λόγον ἐπέχει... αἰθέρος δὲ καὶ φ. τὸ κατὰ Ἰωάννην [sc. εὐαγγέλιον], ὡς πάντων ἀνώτατον, καὶ ἁπλῆν μυστικῶς τὴν περὶ θεοῦ πίστιν εἰσάγον, καὶ ἔννοιαν *ib.*(1245D); **c.** as angelic virtue οἱ δαίμονες...ἐκπεσόντες δὲ ἀπὸ τῆς οὐρανίου φ. Ath.*v.Anton.*22(M.26.876A); **d.** of God, exeg. Jer.10:12 τρεῖς οἱονεὶ ἀρετὰς παραλαβὼν ὁ προφήτης τοῦ θεοῦ, ⟨τὴν⟩ ἰσχὺν αὐτοῦ καὶ τὴν σοφίαν αὐτοῦ καὶ τὴν φ. αὐτοῦ, ἑκάστῃ αὐτῶν οἰκεῖόν τι ἔργον ⟨ἀπονέμει⟩...τῇ δὲ φ. τὸν οὐρανόν Or.*hom.8.1 in Jer.*(p.55.5,7; M.13.336A,B); οὐ συντυχικῶς τὴν φ. παρέλαβεν ἐπὶ τοῦ οὐρανοῦ· εὑρήσεις γὰρ ἐν ταῖς Παροιμίαις λεχθέν· 'ὁ θεὸς...ἡτοίμασεν δὲ οὐρανοὺς ἐν φ.' ἔστιν οὖν τις φ. θεοῦ, ἣν μὴ ζήτει ⟨εἰ μὴ⟩ ἐν Χριστῷ Ἰησοῦ. πάντα γὰρ ὅσα τοῦ θεοῦ τοιαῦτά ἐστιν, ὁ Χριστός ἐστιν·... οὕτως φ. αὐτός ἐστιν θεοῦ...οὕτως οὖν καὶ φ. αὐτὸν νοήσεις, ὅτε ἐπιστήμη ἐστὶν ἀγαθῶν καὶ κακῶν καὶ οὐθετέρων *ib.8.2*(p.57.2; 337B); [ref. Pr.8:14] ὡς γὰρ αὐτὸς [sc. ὁ λόγος] ὢν ἡ φ., ἐν ᾗ τοὺς οὐρανοὺς ἡτοίμασε, καὶ...ἰσχὺς καὶ δύναμις Ath.*Ar.*3.63(M.26.457A); *ib.*3.65 (460C); ὁ ἄρα τοῦ θεοῦ υἱός, αὐτός ἐστιν ὁ λόγος καὶ ἡ σοφία, αὐτὸς ἡ φ. καὶ ἡ ζῶσα βουλή *ib.*(461A); ἔδει δὲ αὐτοὺς [sc. Arians] λέγοντας βουλήσει τὸν υἱόν, εἰπεῖν, ὅτι καὶ φ. [sc. τοῦ πατρός] γέγονε· ταὐτὸν γὰρ ἡγοῦμαι φ. καὶ βούλησιν εἶναι...περὶ δὲ τὸν θεὸν φ. καὶ βουλὴν καὶ σοφίαν ὡς ἕξιν συμβαίνουσαν καὶ ἀποβαίνουσαν ἀνθρωπίνως γίνεσθαι μυθολογοῦσι *ib.*(460B); **e.** of Christ χορός σε παρθένων προσεννέπει, τέλειον ἄνθος,...φ., σοφία Meth.*symp.*11(p.133.8; M.18.209A); **3.** as style of address, Const.ap.Ath.*apol.sec.*70(p.148.14; M.25.373A); ἡ ὑμετέρα φ. δυνήσεται κρίνειν Constantius ap.eund.*apol.Const.*23 (M.25.624B); Bas.*ep.*68(3.161C; M.32.429A); Isid.Pel.*epp.*5.276(M.78. 1497B); **4.** *opinion, faith* τῆς ἐν Χριστῷ πίστεως τὴν ὀρθήν μου φ. Dion.Al.ap.Ath.*Dion.*(p.55.2; M.25.497B); ὅσον εὐσεβοῦς φ. ἡ Ἀρειανὴ αἵρεσις ἐστέρηται Ath.*decr.*2(p.2.21; M.25.420A); id.*Ar.*2.34(M.26. 220B); ref. adoptionism ἐπὶ ταύτῃ τῇ φ., μᾶλλον δὲ ἀφροσύνῃ, ἀφορισθέντος τῆς κοινωνίας †Hipp.*Artem.*ap.Eus.*h.e.*5.28.9(M.20. 513B); [ref. Arianism] τὴν ἀσεβῆ φ. Ath.*Ar.*2.5(M.26.157A); ἡ φ. αὐτῶν οὐκ ἔστι κατὰ θεὸν ἀλλ' ἀνθρωπίνη id.*h.Ar.*33(p.201.27; M.25. 732B); ref. Apollinarianism, ‡Ath.*Apoll.*2.4(M.26.1127C).

φρονητικός, *exercising the understanding*, Max.*opusc.*(M.91. 21B).

φρόνιμος, *intelligent*; of the serpent, Clem.*str.*6.17(p.511.21; M.9. 385C); Thdt.*qu.31 in Gen.*(1.44,45); Eus.Al.*serm.*4(M.86.337C); of air φρονιμώτατός ἐστι διὰ τὴν καθαρότητα *Hom.Clem.*6.7; of fire ἀγαθὴ γὰρ δύναμις τὸ πῦρ...φθαρτικὴ τῶν χειρόνων καὶ σωστικὴ τῶν ἀμεινόνων διὸ καὶ φ. λέγεται παρὰ τοῖς προφήταις Clem.*ecl.*25(p.144.8; M. 9.709C); id.*paed.*3.8(p.262.13; M.8.616B); id.*str.*7.6(p.27.7; M.9.449B); denied of God οὔτε μὴν φ. [sc. ὁ θεός]...ἀνθρώπων γὰρ τὰ τοιαῦτα *Hom.Clem.*19.10; acc. Basileides ἐποίησεν υἱὸν [sc. ὁ δημιουργός] φρονιμώτερον καὶ σοφώτερον Hipp.*haer.*10.14(p.275.28; M.16.3430C).

φρονιμότης, ἡ, *wisdom, cleverness*, ‡Ath.*pat.*7(M.26.1305C); τὴν τοῦ ὄφεως φ. Eus.Al.*serm.*4(M.86.337B); in bad sense, *self-assurance*, *M.Tar.*5(p.459); of Eve ἐπὶ τῇ ἰδίᾳ φ. ἀντελάβετο τῆς ἀσθενείας Or.*or.* 29(p.392.13; M.11.545A).

φροντίζ-ω, 1. *take thought for* ἤτοι γὰρ οὐ ~ει πάντων ἀνθρώπων ὁ κύριος; Clem.*str.*7.2(p.6.19; M.9.409B); Meth.*symp.*8.16(p.109.9; M.18.172C); id.*res.*2.10(p.349.12); **2.** *be in charge of* τῶν γηδίων φ. Pall.*v.Chrys.*14(p.86.20; M.47.49); φ. τῶν ἐκκλησιαστικῶν πραγμάτων Cyr.*ep.*10(p.110.19; 5².33A).

φροντίς, ἡ, 1. *care, attention, solicitude*, ref. pagan deities πῶς οὖν τῶν ἀνθρώπων φ. ποιήσεται; Arist.*apol.*11.4(p.107.8); of God, Athenag.*res.*12(p.61.3; M.6.996B); ὁ θεὸς προνοεῖς...τῆς ψυχῆς φροντίδι νόμων *Lit.*ap.*Const.App.*8.16.3; Cyr.*ador.*4(1.112B); of Logos as παιδαγωγός: σωτήριον...εὐλόγου φροντίδος ὑπογραμμόν Clem.*paed.*1.9 (p.139.16; M.8.349C); **2.** *charge, oversight, cure* τὴν κοινὴν φ. τῆς ἐκκλησίας τοῦ θεοῦ...ἀναδέξασθαι Or.*Cels.*8.75(p.292.7; M.11.1629B); Eus.*v.C.*3.62(p.110.12; M.20.1137A); τοῦ ἐπισκόπου...ᾧ ἡ φ. ἀνῆκε προηγουμένως τῆς ἐκκλησίας Bas.*ep.*156.2(3.245E; M.32.616B); τῶν ἱερῶν τῆς Ἀντιοχείας φροντίδων Philost.*h.e.*3.18(M.65.509B); **3.** a marginal mark, ⳩ *phi et ro, id est* φροντίς. *haec, ubi aliquid obscuritatis est, ob sollicitudinem ponitur*, Isid.H.*etym.*1.21.23.

φρόντισμα, τό, 1. *care, anxiety* ἵνα...κοινωνήσωσιν ὑμῖν τῶν φ. Const.ap.Eus.*v.C.*4.42(p.134.27; M.20.1192B); Firminus *ep.Bas.*(3. 209B; M.32.533B); **2.** *office, charge*, Nil.*epp.*3.241(M.79.496B); τῆς ἀξίας ἢ τοῦ φ. CChalc.*can.*2.

φροντιστήριον, τό, *place for meditation*, esp. *monastery* τῶν ἀσκητῶν φ. Pall.*v.Chrys.*11(p.65.11; M.47.37); Thdt.*h.e.*3.24.2(3. 941); *V.Max.*5(M.90.72D); established on Christian model by Julian πήξασθαι...παρθενῶνας καὶ φ. Gr.Naz.*or.*4.111(M.35.648C); *monastic cell* τοιαῦτα γὰρ ὑπ' αὐτῶν πεπονθέναι ἐν τοῖς αὐτόθι φ. ἑκάστοις ὑμῶν γεγράφηκε Nil.*epp.*3.98(M.79.429C); *house of refuge* εἰς φ. ἀσθενῶν καταφεύγει Gr.Presb.*v.Gr.Naz.*(M.35.269B); φ. ταῦτα καλέσας πτωχῶν *ib.*(273C); fig. τὸ τῶν φρονούντων συνέδριον τῆς ἀληθείας φ. ἦν Gr.Nyss.*Steph.*1(M.46.713A); τὴν Ῥωμαίων ἐκκλησίαν. ...ὡς ἀποστόλων φ. καὶ εὐσεβείας μητρόπολιν Soz.*h.e.*3.8.5(M.67. 1053A).

φροντιστής, ὁ, 1. *one who bears responsibility* τοὺς ἁπλῶς μεριμνητάς τε καὶ φ. Clem.*str.*4.6(p.263.2; M.8.1245A); καὶ τούτων ἐστὶν ἐπιστάτης ἢ φ. ἢ δημιουργὸς οὐδείς Hipp.*haer.*7.24(p.202.16; M.16. 3311C); in bad sense μούλτων καὶ στάσεων φ. Thphn.*chron.*p.400 (M.108.956A); **2.** *one in charge, guardian*, in gen. σὺ αὐτῶν [sc. τῶν χηρῶν] φ. ἔσο Ign.*Polyc.*4.1; *M.Bon.*1(p.325); *Hom.Clem.*12.10; of God φ. δὲ τῆς χρείας πάρεστιν...ὁ θεὸς ‡Nil.*perist.*11.14(M.79.924B); in Church, Cyr.*Jo.*6.1(4.623E); as regular official φήσας...οἰκονόμους τε καὶ φ. κατ' οἰκείαν αὐθεντίαν ἐπιστῆναι τῇ ἐκκλησίᾳ Procl.CP *ep.* (p.67.36; M.65.881C); τῆς ἐκκλησίας τῶν ἐν Ἱππῶν φ. *Cod.Afr.*78; *ib.*93; **3.** *champion, upholder* ἀρετῆς φ. Thdt.*h.e.*3.7.8(3.920); *ib.*4. 29.4(1009); id.*haer.*5(4.425).

φροῦδος, neut. as adv., *utterly to ruin* εἰ μὴ ἡ τοῦ...θεοῦ φιλανθρωπία...φ. αὐτῶν τὰς βουλὰς ἀπετέλεσεν *Mir.Geo.*4(p.21.3).

***φρούδως**, *vainly, to no purpose*, Epiph.*haer.*64.63(p.501.10; M.41. 1177C σφοδρῶς).

φρουμεντάριος, ὁ, (Lat. *frumentarius*) *soldier employed on special duty* as member of a corps of investigators and messengers, Dion. Al.*fr.*ap.Eus.*h.e.*6.40.2(M.20.601B).

***φρούξ, ὁ,** *custodian*, of harbour-master φ. λιμένος *Chron.Pasch.* p.382(M.92.980A).

φρουρά, ἡ, 1. *prison*; to which earthly life is compared, *Diogn.* 6.7; **2.** *protection, guardianship*; of God, Athenag.*leg.*6.1(M.6. 901A); Clem.*str.*7.12(p.56.7; M.9.508C); Or.*Cels.*4.32(p.303.12; M.11. 1077C).

φρουράρχης, ὁ, *commander of the watch*, Thphyl.*exc.Gent.*5(p.481. 22; M.113.941A).

[*]**φρουρεῖον, τό,** *prison* πρὸς τὸ φ. ἑλκέσθω Sophr.H.*v.Anast.*(M. 92.1701C); fig. πῶς τὰς τούτων [sc. martyrs] ἱκεσίας μὴ κτησώμεθα φρουρεῖον; ‡Jo.D.*Const.*22(M.95.340C).

***φρουριστής, ὁ,** *jailer*, Thdr.Stud.*epp.*2.218(M.99.1657C).

***φρουρόπωρος,** *keeping fruit* παραδείσου φυτοκόμου καὶ φ. ‡Caes. Naz.*dial.*3.144(M.38.1093).

***φρουροφυλακή, ἡ,** *guard*, *M.Ign.Rom.*1(p.494 v.l. for φρουρῶν φυλακῆς).

φρύαγμα, τό, 1. *pride* ἐλαθόμην...μητρός τε καὶ γένους φ. Meth. *symp.*11.12(p.133.1; M.18.209A); γράφεται [sc. τὰ τέρατα] Χριστιανικοῦ χάριν φ. Sophr.H.*mir.Cyr.et Jo.*(M.87.3437B); in bad sense, *insolence, arrogance* ἴδωμεν εἰ τὸ φ. τῶν λόγων σοῦ δι' ἔργων βεβαιοῦνται †Gregent.*disp.*(M.86.773D); **2.** *raging, fierceness* ἡ πόλις δὲ τὸ φ. μὲν κάτω βεβλήκει Gr.Naz.*carm.*2.1.11.1402(M.37.1126A); κατάβαλε τὸ φ. τῶν ἐθνῶν *Lit.Jac.*(p.210.24).

φρυγανίζω, *gather firewood*, Bas.*hex.*9.6(1.86E; M.29.204A); Gr. Nyss.*hom.7 in Eccl.*(M.44.713C).

φρυγανώδης, *like twigs* τὰ φ. μου πάθη, καὶ τὸν νοῦν καθαρὸν ὑλομανήσαντα Jo.Mon.*hymn.Blas.*3(M.96.1401C).

Φρύγες, οἱ, *Phrygians*, a name for Montanists, Anon.ap.Eus.*h.e.* 5.16.22(M.20.472C); τῶν δ' αἱρέσεων αἱ μὲν ἀπὸ ὀνόματος προσαγορεύονται...αἱ δὲ ἀπὸ τόπου...αἱ δὲ ἀπὸ ἔθνους, ὡς ἡ τῶν Φ. Clem.*str.*7. 17(p.76.25; M.9.552C); *ib.*4.13(p.289.13; M.8.1300C); Eus.*h.e.*4.27(M. 20.397B); Ath.*Ar.*1.3(M.26.17A); Cyr.H.*catech.*16.8(l. Κατάφρυγας); their baptism invalid, Didym.*Trin.*2.15(M.39.720A) cit. s. ἀναβαπτίζω; Epiph.*haer.*48.1(p.219.7; M.41.856A); id.*anac.*2.3(p.211.7; M.41.845D Καταφρυγαστῶν); Soz.*h.e.*7.18.12(M.67.1472B); Thdt.*haer.* 2(4.341).

φρυγία, ἡ, *burning heat*, ‡Caes.Naz.*dial.*1.41(M.38.908).

φρύγιον, τό, *dry stick, firewood* τί ἐστι φ., ὁ Σύμμαχος ἐδήλωσεν· ἐκδέδωκε γάρ, ἀπόκαυμα Hesych.H.*fr.Ps.*101:4(M.93.1273A).

φρυκτωρ-έω, 1. *make signals by beacons*, fig. ἅπασι ∼εῖ [sc. ὁ Παῦλος] τὴν εὐσεβῆ πίστιν ὀρθόδοξον Thdr.Stud.*cant.*1.4(p.337); **2.** *illuminate, shed light on* ἥλιος ∼εῖ πάσῃ τῇ οἰκουμένῃ Gr.Naz.*or.*29 (p.67.15; M.36.68C); ἥλιον...πάντα ∼οῦντα τοῖς ἀγλαοῖς ἀμαρύγμασι Jo.D.*hom.*4.5(M.96.608B); fig. ἐγκάρδιος οὐρανὸς ἀπὸ τῆς θείας μόνης ∼ούμενος χάριτος Nil.*epp.*3.148(M.79.452D); **3.** pass., *be kindled*, as a beacon τὸ παρὰ τοὺς λιμένας ∼ούμενον πῦρ...ἐπιδείκνυσι τοῦ λιμένος τὸ στόμα Thdt.*ep.*10(4.1069).

φρυκτωρία, ἡ, *firebrand, torch*, of H. Ghost τῇ φ. λαμπομένῃ τοῦ πνεύματος Jo.D.*hom.*9.6(M.96.732C).

φυγαδευτήριον, τό, 1. *refuge, retreat*, of church of Resurrection at Jerusalem τὸ καταφύγιον καὶ φ. πάντων τῶν ἀδικουμένων ἐκ παντὸς τοῦ κόσμου Cyr.S.*v.Sab.*57(p.153.27); fig. ὦ παθῶν δεινῶν φ. ‡Just.*or. Gr.*5(M.6.237B); *city of refuge*, Eus.*onomast.*(p.6.11); Ath.*fug.*11 (p.76.6;M.25.657C); Cyr.*Ag.*3(3.629A); **2.** *that which will banish* or *put to flight*, fig. Χριστοῦ τὸ αἷμα δαιμόνων καθέστηκε φ. Cyr.H. *catech.*19.3; Mac.Aeg.*hom.*25.10(M.34.673D); Jo.Clim.*scal.*22(M.88. 940D).

***φυγαδευτής, ὁ,** *one who banishes* ὁ Βαρνάβας...ὁ τῶν δαιμόνων φ. Alex.Sal.*Barn.*proem.7(438E); Gr.Mag.*dial.*(tr.Zach.)1.10(M.*PL.* 77.199); παθῶν φ.... καὶ ἐλατῆρα Philost.*h.e.*2.8(M.65.472A).

φυγαδευτικός, *banishing, able to banish*; fig., Clem.*paed.*2.5(p.186. 22; M.8.449B); χρὴ νοεῖν τὸ πνεῦμα...φῶς καὶ ἡμέραν, ἧς ἡ πνοὴ φ. τῶν σκιῶν τῆς ματαιότητος γίνεται Gr.Nyss.*hom.7 in Cant.*(M.44.937A); δὸς δύναμιν...δαιμόνων φ. *Const.App.*8.29.3.

φυγαδεύ-ω, 1. *put to flight, drive away* Ναυατιανῷ...τό τε πνεῦμα τὸ ἅγιον...∼οντι Dion.Al.*fr.*ap.Eus.*h.e.*7.8(M.20.653A); ἐπαοιδὸς... ∼ει...ἑρπετόν ‡Just.*or.Gr.*5(M.6.237C); Bas.*hom.in Ps.*33(1.148C; M. 29.364B); Thphn.*chron.*p.121(M.108.340A); of Christ πάντα δαίμονα φ. *Hom.Clem.*1.6; Isid.Pel.*epp.*2.212(M.78.652C); of abstracts ἡ γὰρ ...ἀληθὴς μετάνοια...∼ει τὸ σκότος *T.Gad* 5.7; Mac.Aeg.*hom.*47.1(M. 34.797A); **2.** *allow to escape*, *A.Thom.*A 140(p.247.2); *ib.*151(p.261.7); Proc.G.*1Reg.*19:13(M.87.1105A).

φυγοδικέω, *shirk trial*, Ath.*apol.sec.*37(p.116.9; M.25.313A); *Can. App.*74.

***φυγοκύρις, ὁ,** *runaway*, Pall.*h.Laus.*21(p.65.8; M.34.1073D).

φυγόπατρις, ὁ, *fugitive from one's country*, Gr.Naz.*or.*26.14(M.35. 1248A); id.*ep.*32(M.37.72A).

***φυγοπόλεμος,** *shunning war, cowardly*, Cyr.*ador.*6(1.176D); id. *apol.Thds.*(p.80.16; 6¹.247B); Thphn.*chron.*p.55(M.108.193A).

***φυγοπονέω,** *shun toil*, Or.*Cels.*7.10(p.162.7; M.11.1436A).

φυκόω, *redden with rouge* τὰς παρειὰς φ. Clem.*paed.*3.2(p.239.13; M.8.561B).

***φύκωμα, τό,** *paint, rouge* πρῶτον τῆς ἀσελγείας, φυκώματα καὶ ἐπιτρίμματα Chrys.*fr.in Jer.*16:5(M.64.912B).

φυλακή, ἡ, 1. *protection, care*, ref. Ps.126:1 τὰ μὴ τυγχάνοντα τῆς ἀπὸ τούτου [sc. τοῦ θεοῦ] φ. ... ἀνηνύτως τηρεῖται Or.*princ.*3.1.18 (p.231.6; M.11.289A); fig. ὁ...ψυχῶν ἰατρός, ὃ μάλιστα ἡμῶν οἶδε πρὸς ἁμαρτίαν ὀλισθηρότερον, τοῦτο ἰσχυροτέραις προκατελάβετο φυλακαῖς Bas.*hom.*3.1(2.17B; M.31.200C); **2.** *preventive* ἀλεξητήριον τοῦ κακοῦ...ἢ φ. παρέξειν τοῖς ὑγιαίνουσιν Bas.*Eun.*1.1(1.208A; M.29. 500B); **3.** *control* τὰ...ἄστρα, τὰ εἰς διορισμὸν καὶ φ. ἀριθμῶν χρόνου γεγονότα...καὶ τροπὰς καιρῶν Meth.*symp.*8.15(p.104.2; M.18.168A); **4.** *observance, heed*, of sermons ὅπως...λάβοιτέ τινα ἀπὸ τῆς φ. ταύτης αἴσθησιν ὠφελείας πνευματικῆς Chrys.*Laz.*3(1.736D); of laws, ordinances φ. τῶν ἐντολῶν Clem.*str.*2.18(p.154.24; M.8.1017B); Thdt. *qu.3 in Jos.*(1.306); of Mosaic Law ὁ Χριστὸς...τοῖς Ἰουδαίοις... περιτιθεὶς...μήτε...φ. τινος ὅλως ἄξιοῦν τὸν ἄνωθεν αὐτοῖς διορισθέντα νόμον Cyr.*Jo.*6(4.582D); ἐπέδειξε [sc. ὁ Μωσῆς] τῆς τῶν νόμων φ. τὴν εὐκολίαν Thdt.*qu.38 in Dt.*(1.287); τὴν εἰρήνην διὰ τῆς τῶν ἐντολῶν προσκτώμενοι φ. id.*Ps.*118:165(1.1479); of sabbath, Eus.*e.th.*2.20 (p.127.13; M.24.949C); τῆς τοῦ σαββάτου φ. οὐχ ἡ φύσις διδάσκαλος ἀλλ' ἡ θέσις τοῦ νόμου Thdt.*Ezech.*20:13(2.826); **5.** *watch* of night, fig. ἑσπερινὴ γὰρ φ. ὁ καιρός ἐστι τῆς ἀκμῆς τοῦ ἀνθρώπου καὶ ἡ νεότης Meth.*symp.*5.2(M.18.100C); **6.** *prison*, of hell ἀνυπέρβατον τὸ τεῖχος τῆς φ. †Cyr.*hom.div.*14(5².411C); fig. τὸ σῶμα...δεσμὸν...καὶ φ. καὶ σῆμα...εἶναι ἔφης Meth.*res.*1.30.4(p.263.8; M.41.1140C); *ib.*1. 32.6(p.269.7; 1144D); **7.** *prisoner* εἰς διατροφὴν...τῶν πτωχῶν καὶ ὀρφανῶν καὶ φυλακῶν σιτομέτριον προσέθηκεν *Chron.Pasch.*p.294(M. 92.737B).

φυλακίζ-ω, *imprison*, *1Clem.*45.4; Ἰησοῦ Χριστέ...ὁ δι' ἡμᾶς... ∼όμενος ἐν δεσμωτηρίῳ *A.Thom.*A 48(p.164.19); Petr.I Al.*ep.can.*1 (M.18.468A).

φυλακίτης, ὁ, *prisoner*, *Const.App.*4.2.1; Jo.Mosch.*prat.*189(M. 87.3068B); fig. ὁ χειμὼν...φ. ἡμᾶς...πεποίηκε Mac.Mgn.*apocr.*4.11 (p.172.12).

***φυλακταῖος,** *to be guarded* παραδιδότω ἀμφοτέρους φ. τοῖς κληρικοῖς τοῦ τόπου Ath.Scholast.*coll.*10.9(p.130).

[*]**φυλακτάρεον, τό,** v. φυλακτήριον.

φυλακτήριον (-άρεον), τό, 1. *protection, safeguard*, of baptism τὸ τέλειον...φ. ... τὴν σφραγῖδα τοῦ κυρίου Clem.*q.d.s.*42(p.188.17; M.9. 648C); of eucharist γίνεσθαι πᾶσι φ. εἰς ἀνάστασιν ζωῆς αἰωνίου Ath. *ep.Serap.*4.19(M.26.668A); τὰ μυστικὰ σύμβολα φ. ... τῶν περὶ τὴν ψυχὴν ἀγαθῶν Gr.Nyss.*Eun.*11(2 p.271.17; M.45.880D); τῶν ἀχράντων τοῦ Χριστοῦ μυστηρίων...μεταλαβεῖν, ἀσφαλὲς φ. Niceph.Ur.*v.Sym.* 106(M.86.3085C); **2.** *amulet* ἐγὼ...λαβὼν περιεζωσάμην, καὶ εὐθέως ἀφανεῖς ἐγένοντο...οἱ σκώληκες...διότι φ. ἐστιν τοῦ πατρός...περιζώσασθε αὐτὰς πρὶν τελευτήσω *T.Job* 47(p.135.6); γυνὴ μάντις, καὶ φυλακτάρεα (sic) καὶ ἐπαοιδίας ποιοῦσα Leont.N.*v.Sym.*8.53(M.93. 1736C); in eccl. legislation οὐ δεῖ ἱερατικοὺς...ποιεῖν τὰ λεγόμενα φ. ἅτινά ἐστι δεσμωτήρια τῶν ψυχῶν αὐτῶν· τοὺς δὲ φοροῦντας ῥίπτεσθαι ἐκ τῆς ἐκκλησίας ἐκελεύσαμεν CLaod.*can.*36; μὴ ἀπέρχεσθαι πρὸς ἐπαοιδόν, μήτε φ. ἑαυτῷ περιτιθέναι ‡Ath.*syntag.*2.5(p.122; M.28. 837B); περὶ ὑδρομίκτων...περὶ τῶν φορούντων φ. †Jo.Jej.*serm.*(M.88. 1924C); **3.** *phylactery* as worn by Jews φ. ἐν ὑμέσι λεπτοτάτοις γεγραμμένων χαρακτήρων τινῶν...περικεῖσθαι ὑμᾶς ἐκέλευσε [sc. ὁ θεός] Just. *dial.*46.5(M.6.576B); καὶ τίνα ταῦτά ἐστι τὰ φ. καὶ κράσπεδα;...ἐκέλευσεν [sc. ὁ θεός] ἐγγραφῆναι βιβλίοις μικροῖς τὰ θαύματα αὐτοῦ, καὶ ἐξηρτῆσθαι αὐτὰ τῶν χειρῶν αὐτῶν...ἃ φ. ἐκάλουν. ὡς πολλαὶ νῦν τῶν γυναικῶν εὐαγγέλια τῶν τραχήλων ἐξαρτῶσαι ἔχουσι Chrys.*hom.72.2 in Mt.*(7.703B); φ. ... δελτία ἦν μικρά, ἴσω [l. ἔσω] τὸν νόμον ὠδίνοντα, ἅπερ ἐφόρουν οἱ τῶν Ἰουδαίων καθηγηταί, ὥσπερ νῦν [αἱ γυναῖκες τὰ] εὐαγγέλια [τὰ] μικρὰ Isid.Pel.*epp.*2.150(M.78.604B); cf. εἰώθόν τινες τὰ περίαπτα φ. ὀνομάζειν...τὰ δὲ σήματα τῆς πορφύρας φ. εἴωθον οἱ ἠκριβωμένοι μετονομάζειν Epiph.*haer.*15(p.209.18; M.41.245A); **4.** of things used by Christians as protective charms τὸ σῶμα κ(αὶ) τὸ δέμα (l. αἷμα) τοῦ χῦ φεῖσαι τοῦ δούλου σοῦ τὸν φοροῦντα (l. τοῦ -τος) τὸ φ. *PBerol.*9096.22(*PO* 18.412); of a metal cross worn round neck τὸ τοῦ σταυροῦ φ. Gr.Nyss.*v.Macr.*(p.404.12; M.46.989C); of a relic ἐδέοντο...καί τι παρ' αὐτοῦ κομίζεσθαι φ. Sophr.H.*v.Anast.*(M.92. 1720C).

φυλακτήριος, ὁ, *purveyor of amulets*, CTrull.*can.*61.

***φυλακτόν, τό,** *amulet* ποιήσω σοι...φ. ἵνα μηδέποτε λάβῃς ἀπὸ ὀφθαλμοῦ Leont.N.*v.Sym.*53(M.93.1736C); ἐν τῷ τραχήλῳ φυλακτά Thphn.*chron.*p.318(M.108.769B).

φύλαξ, ὁ, 1. *guardian, protector*; **a.** ref. pagan gods and images ἀθέμιτον...ἀνθρώπους θεῶν εἶναι φ. Just.*1apol.*9.5(M.6.340B); φ. ἀποκαλοῦνται τῆς τῶν σφῶν σωτηρίας...οὐκ ἐξαρκοῦντες ἑαυτοὺς φυλάσσειν...πῶς ἄλλοις γένοιντο φ. καὶ σωτῆρες; †Jo.D.*B.J.*10(M.96.

944B); **b.** of God ἀγαθῶν γάρ ἐστι καὶ δοτὴρ καὶ φ. Clem.*paed*.3.12 (p.283.28; M.8.665A); **c.** of Christ ὁ...λόγος...ὁ τῆς ἀνθρωπότητος φ. *ib*.3.4(p.262.9; 616A); ὁ σωτὴρ πάντων...ὁ ἄγρυπνος φ. Gr.Thaum. *pan.Or*.17(p.38.18; M.10.1101A); ref. Mt.11:27, Lc.10:22 οἷα φ. ἀγαθὸς...τὴν παραθήκην...παραδώσει τῷ θεῷ Eus.*e.th*.3.16(p.175.10; M.24.1033C); τῶν τε κατ' οὐρανὸν καὶ τῶν ἐπὶ γῆς...κηδεμόνα καὶ φ. ... ἀνέδειξε πατήρ *ib*.1.13(p.73.11; 852A); **d.** of guardian angels θεῖος δέ τις συνοδοιπόρος καὶ πομπὸς ἀγαθὸς καὶ φ. ... ὁ θεῖος ἄγγελος Gr. Thaum.*pan.Or*.5(p.14.16; M.10.1068C); καθηδυνόμενος ἢ κατανυσσόμενος ἐν λόγῳ προσευχῆς, μένε ἐν αὐτῷ· ὁ γὰρ φ. ἡμῶν τότε ὑπάρχει ὁ συμπροσευχόμενος ἡμῖν Jo.Clim.*scal*.28(M.88.1132B); v. ἄγγελος; **e.** of patron saints πόλεις καὶ κῶμαι ταῦτα [sc. bodies of martyrs] διανειμάμεναι σωτῆρας καὶ ψυχῶν καὶ σωμάτων καὶ ἰατροὺς ὀνομάζουσι καὶ ὡς πολιούχους τιμῶσι καὶ φ. Thdt.*affect*.8(p.199.9; 4.902); **f.** of clergy τοὺς τοῦ θεοῦ ἱερέας ἐπήγετο...ὥσπερ τινὰς ψυχῆς ἀγαθοὺς φ. Eus.*v.C*.2.4(p.42.3; M.20.981C); **g.** met. ἀφάνισον πάντα οἶκον πλεονεξίας φ. Bas.*hom*.7.6(2.48D; M.31.273B); φ. αὐτός τέ εἰμι καί σε παρακαλῶ τῶν φιλοσοφίας ὀργίων εἶναι Synes.*ep*.142(M.66.1536D); τύμβον...ἀρηρότα λαϊνέσσιν φ. σώματος ἄχρι σάλπιξ ἠχηνέσσα *MAMA* 1.226; **2.** *one who shows care, attention* ἔσο...τῶν παρόντων φ., προνοητικὸς τοῦ μέλλοντος Bas.*hom*.3.5(2.20C; M.31.208B); **3.** *deputy* Μοδέστῳ...φ. ... τοῦ ἀποστολικοῦ θρόνου Sophr.H.*v.Anast*.(M.92. 1688A); cf.Leo Mag.*ep*.89(p.47; M.*PL*.54.930B); **4.** *one who observes* commands, etc. φ. τῶν παραδεδομένων ὑπ' αὐτοῦ [sc. τοῦ Χριστοῦ] διδαγμάτων Just.*dial*.69.7(M.6.640A); φ. τῶν ἐντεταλμένων id.*1apol*. 65.1(M.6.428A); *ib*.2.2(329A); καὶ ταύτην εἶναι, σωτειράν τινα καὶ φ. δογμάτων οὖσαν, τὴν ἀρετὴν ταύτην Gr.Thaum.*pan.Or*.11(p.27.24; cf. M.10.1085A).

φυλάσσ-ω, **1.** *guard, defend, protect* φυλάξεις δὲ ἃ παρέλαβες, μήτε προστιθεὶς μήτε ἀφαιρῶν *Did*.4.13; δεῖ οὖν ἡμᾶς ὡς ναὸν θεοῦ ~ειν τὴν σάρκα *2Clem*.9.3; οὐχ ὁ ἔχων καὶ ~ων ἀλλ' ὁ μεταδιδοὺς πλούσιος Clem.*paed*.3.6(p.257.16; M.8.605B); of God ὁ δὲ θεὸς τῶν πατέρων μου ἐφύλαξέν με *T.Jos*.1.4; of angels κατ' ἔθνος καὶ κατὰ βασιλείαν ἀρχάγγελοι διοικοῦσιν ~οντες· οὐ μόνον δὲ ἀλλὰ καὶ καθ' ἕνα ἄνθρωπον ἄγγελος ἕπεται ~ων Cosm.Ind.*top*.2(M.88.132C); met. τὴν ἀλήθειαν ἀγαπᾶτε καὶ αὕτη φυλάξει ὑμᾶς *T.Reub*.3.9; τῷ μὴ ἁμαρτεῖν τὸ μὴ παθεῖν πεφυλαγμένοι Clem.*paed*.3.8(p.262.19; M.8.616B); αὕτη φραγμὸς ἡ ἀρετὴ...ἀσύλητα ~ουσα τῆς ψυχῆς τὰ κειμήλια ‡Nil.*perist*.12.11 (M.79.961C); ὁ...~ων τὴν ἀλήθειαν, δύναται ἑαυτῷ ζωὴν περιποιήσασθαι· ~εται γὰρ ὑπὸ τῆς ἀληθείας Ant.Mon.*hom*.66(M.89.1629C); **2.** *keep watch over* προσευχόμενος, τὴν μνήμην σου...~ε Evagr.Pont. *or*.44(M.79.1176C); **3.** met., *keep unchanged, retain, preserve* τὸν σίδηρον ἡ χρῆσις καθαρώτερον ~ει Clem.*str*.1.1(p.9.14; M.8.701A); αὕτη γὰρ ἡ κατὰ δύναμιν ἐξομοίωσις πρὸς θεόν, τὸ ~ειν τὸν νοῦν ἐν τῇ κατὰ τὰ αὐτὰ σχέσει *ib*.4.22(p.310.8; 1349B); λόγον περὶ Ἰωάννου... παραδεδομένον καὶ μνήμῃ πεφυλαγμένον id.*q.d.s*.42.1(p.188.2; M.9. 648B); Thdt.*h.e*.5.9.2(3.1028); ἴσον τῶν ψαλμῶν ~ουσιν ἀριθμόν id.*Ps*. 115(1.1421); πῶς δὲ καὶ πολλοῖς οὖσι [sc. θεοῖς] τὸ ἀπερίγραπτον φυλαχθήσεται Jo.D.*f.o*.1.15(M.94.801B); ref. order of Persons in baptismal formula ἀκίνητον...~ειν προσήκει τὴν ἀκολουθίαν ἣν... παρελάβομεν Bas.*ep*.125.3(3.217A; M.32.549D); of infinite power of God τὸ ἀνέκλειπτον τῆς τοιαύτης δυνάμεως...δυναμοῖ καὶ τὰς ἀθανάτους ζωὰς τῶν ἀγγελικῶν ἑνάδων...εἰς τὸ ~εσθαι ἀδιαλωβήτους. ~ει καὶ τὰς οὐρανίας τάξεις ἀναλλοιώτους Dion.Ar.*d.n*.8.5(M.3.904A); Christol. ~ει γὰρ ἑκατέρα [sc. ἡ τοῦ Χριστοῦ φύσις] τὴν ἑαυτῆς φυσικὴν ἰδιότητα ἀμετάβλητον Jo.D.*f.o*.3.5(1001A); **4.** *set aside* for a purpose, *reserve* ὅταν τὸν ὄντως θάνατον φοβηθῇς ὃς ~εται τοῖς κατακριθησομένοις εἰς τὸ πῦρ τὸ αἰώνιον *Diogn*.10.7; [sc. οἱ Ἀκέφαλοι] ἀρύονται ὕδατα καὶ ταῦτα ~οντες ἐν αὐτοῖς βαπτίζουσιν· [sc. ἔχουσι] κοινωνίαν πεφυλαγμένην ἐκ τῶν παλαιότερων χρόνων Tim.CP *haer*.2(M.86.57A); **5.** *maintain, uphold* τὴν περὶ τῶν μεγίστων ὁμολογίαν ἡμεῖς μὲν ~ομεν οἱ δὲ παραβαίνουσι Clem.*str*.7.15(p.64.7; M.9.525A); ~έ μοι ταύτας τὰς ἰδιότητας [sc. τοῦ πατρὸς καὶ τοῦ υἱοῦ] Bas.*hom*.15.2(2. 132A; M.31.468A); **6.** *observe, keep* φυλάξατε...τὴν ἐντολὴν τοῦ κυρίου *T.Dan* 5.1; *2Clem*.8.4; Meth.*res*.1.38.4(p.281.4; M.18.265D); Thdt. *Ezech*.20:12(2.824); of bond of marriage τὴν διαλυθεῖσαν θανάτῳ συζυγίαν ἄχραντον ~ων Clem.*str*.3.12(p.234.2; M.8.1184B); **7.** of festivals, Just.*dial*.26.1(M.6.532A); Hipp.*haer*.8.18(p.237.17,19; M. 16.3366B); Eus.*v.C*.3.18(p.85.8; M.20.1073D); Epiph.*exp.fid*.22(p.523. 4; M.42.828A); ~ομεν τὴν ἡμέραν τῆς κυριακῆς ἵνα...τῇ εὐχῇ σχολάσωμεν Eus.Al.*serm*.16.3(M.86.417A); of sabbath, Just.*dial*.8.4(M.6. 493B); **8.** *pay heed to, study, observe* μάγους ~οντας τὰ μετέωρα τῶν... ...νεφῶν Clem.*str*.6.3(p.446.11; M.9.248B); παλμῶν ἑρμηνεύς, ~όμενος ἐν συναντήσει λώβας ὄψεως ἢ ποδῶν *Const.App*.8.32.11; **9.** *take care* ~εσθε πάντα εἰς ὑπακοὴν θεοῦ πράσσειν *ib*.1.1.1; **10.** *guard against, beware of, avoid* φ. τοῦ σχίσαι τὰ ἱμάτιά σου *Apoc.Bar.rel*.2.5; ~ου δὲ καὶ τῆς ὑπερηφανίας τὰ σύμβολα Clem.*fr*.(p.221.26); τὴν ἀκολουθίαν τῆς ἁμαρτίας φυλαξάμενος id.*paed*.3.8(p.261.32; M.8. 616A); εἰσὶν ἀστέρες πονηροὶ τῆς ἀσεβείας...~εσθε ἀπὸ τῆς ἐξουσίας τῶν ἡμερῶν ἀρχῆς αὐτῶν Hipp.*haer*.9.16(p.254.23; M.16.3391D); ref. Pr.10:3 ἀπὸ...τῆς ἐν τῷ κρυπτῷ νηστείας φυλαξώμεθα Bas.*hom*.2.8(2. 15E; M.31.197A); of persons ~εσθε τοὺς τοιούτους Ign.*Trall*.7.1; id.*Eph*.7.1.

φυλλοβόλος, *shedding its leaves*, Bas.*hex*.5.9(1.49A; M.29.116B); †Bas.*parad*.5(M.30.65C).

φύλλον, τό, **1.** *leaf*; *leaf, page* of book, ‡Nil.*vit.cog*.(M.79.1457C); *Chron.Pasch*.p.320(M.92.856B); **2.** *plant* φ. Ἰνδικόν *clove*, Thphyl. *exc.Gent*.15(p.488.23; M.113.952B); Thphn.*chron*.p.324(M.108.589C).

***φυλλοροή, ἡ**, *shedding of leaves*, ‡Caes.Naz.*dial*.3.147(M.38. 1096).

***φυλοκρίνησις, ἡ**, *distinction, discrimination*, Gnost. τὴν φ. τῆς τε ἐκλογῆς τῶν τε κοσμικῶν Clem.*str*.2.8(p.133.12; M.8.973B); cf. Hipp.*haer*.7.27(p.207.12; M.16.3319B).

***φυλοκρινητέον**, *one must choose, select*, Synes.*regn*.27(p.57.18; v.l. φιλοκ- M.66.1104C).

***φυλοκρινητικός**, *able to distinguish*, Clem.*str*.2.8(p.132.4; M.8. 972A).

φῦλον, τό, *tribe*, of Christian *community* πᾶν τὸ Χριστιανικὸν φ. Thdr.Stud.*epp*.1.7(M.99.932A).

φύραμα, τό, **1.** *mixture, paste* φυράμασί τισι καταπλαττόμεναι ψύχουσι μὲν τὸν χρῶτα Clem.*paed*.3.2(p.239.16; M.8.561C); **2.** *mass, bulk*, of any uncoordinated material, esp. potter's clay, or dough intended for baking; **a.** in gen., Hipp.*haer*.5.21(p.123.11; M.16. 3187C); Or.*hom.18.1 in Jer*.(p.151.3; M.13.464A); Synes.*insomn*.17 (11; p.180.20; M.66.1313A); **b.** fig. ἑαυτοὺς ἐκκαθάρωμεν τῆς παλαιᾶς ζύμης, καὶ νέον γενώμεθα φ. (ref. 1Cor.5:7) Jo.D.*hom*.4.3(M.96. 604B); ref. Rom. 9:21 πηλὸς ἀφ' οὗ φ. γίνεται εἰς τιμὴν καὶ εἰς ἀτιμίαν σκεύη...οὕτως...ἑνὸς φ. ὄντος τῶν λογικῶν ὑποστασέων Or.*princ*.3.1. 22(p.239.4,6; M.11.297B); **c.** met., of human substance ὡς εἶναι τὸν ἄνθρωπον ἐκ φ. δύο, θηλείας τε καὶ ἄρρενος *Hom.Clem*.20.2; [sc. ἡμεῖς γυναῖκες] ἐκ τοῦ αὐτοῦ φ....τοῖς ἀνδράσιν ἐσμέν Bas.*hom*.5.2(2.34D; M. 31.241A); Chrys.*hom.1.3 in Mt*.(7.8A); ref. BMV καίπερ οὕτω τῇ καθαρότητι ὑπερανέχουσα τοῦ αὐτοῦ ἡμῖν μέτειχεν φ. *Cat.Apoc*.12:2 (p.351.24); assumed in Inc. τοῦτον ἄνθρωπον ἴσμεν ⟨ἐκ⟩ τοῦ καθ' ἡμᾶς φ. γεγονέναι Hipp.*haer*.10.33(p.291.26; M.16.3451C); [sc. τὴν ἐννοίαν] ἣν ἔχειν τινὲς ἡμῖν καταγγέλλονται, ὡς αὐτοῦ τοῦ θεοῦ εἰς σάρκα τραπέντος καὶ οὐχὶ προσλαβόντος, διὰ τῆς ἁγίας Μαρίας, τὸ τοῦ Ἀδὰμ φ. Bas.*ep*.262.1(3.404A; M.32.973B); Χριστοῦ...τοῦ ταπεινώσαντος ἑαυτὸν μέχρι τοῦ ἡμετέρου φ. Gr.Naz.*or*.14.15(M.35.876C); ἀνέλαβε τὸ φ. ὅλης τῆς ἀνθρωπίνης φύσεως ‡Sophr.H.*liturg*.10(M.87. 3989D); in rel. to ἀπαρχή q.v., ἀναλαβὼν μὲν τὸ φ. ὅλον τῆς ἀνθρωπίνης φύσεως...προσενεχθεὶς ὡς ἀπαρχὴ...τῷ θεῷ καὶ πατρί ‡Bas.*h.myst*.28 (p.263.25); cf.Gr.Nyss.*hom.in 1Cor.15:28*(M.44.1313B); ἦλθε μιμήσασθαι τὴν φύσιν ἵνα ἁγιάσῃ τὸ φ. διὰ τῆς ἀπαρχῆς Chrys.*hom.in Lc. 2:1*(2.804D); σήμερον τὴν ἀπαρχὴν τοῦ ἡμετέρου φ., τουτέστι, τὴν σάρκα ἐν οὐρανοῖς Χριστὸς ἀνήγαγεν ‡Chrys.*ascens*.4(3.784B); Leont.H. *Nest*.1.18(M.86.1468B) cit. s. ἀνθρώπινος; Jo.D.*f.o*.3.2(M.94.985B,C); σάρκα λαβὼν...ἀπαρχὴν τοῦ ἡμετέρου φ. οὐ σπερματικῶς ἀλλὰ δημιουργικῶς διὰ τοῦ ἁγίου πνεύματος CNic.(787)*act*.3(H.4.144D); ref. effects of Inc. τὸ νέον φ. τῆς ἱερᾶς αὐτοῦ [sc. Χριστοῦ] συγκράσεως ἀπειλήφαμεν, ὅλοι δυνάμει κρείττονι ἀναζυμωθέντες καὶ ἀναφυραθέντες αὐτοῦ τῷ πνεύματι ‡Chrys.*pasch*.6.3(8.269E); exeg. Jo.6:35 τὴν ζύμην τοῦ ἀνθρωπείου φ. ἑνώσας καὶ καθάρας Isid.Pel.*epp*.1.360(M.78.388A); ἀνεζύμωσε καὶ τὸ ὅλον φ. Leont.B.*Nest.et Eut*.2(M.86.1344A); ὃς καὶ πρῶτον συγκατέβη τῷ ἡμετέρῳ φ. ὥστε ἀνελκύσαι τοῦτο πρὸς τὸ ὑπερουράνιον αὐτοῦ ὕψος Proc.G.*Pr*.30:4(M.87.1524A); **d.** *common mass, multitude of people*, Chrys.*pan.Eust.Ant*.4(2.610A); ἔχει δὲ καί τινα ὁμοίωσιν ὁ Νῶε πρὸς τὸν δεσπότην Χριστὸν κατὰ σάρκα. ὥσπερ γὰρ ἐκ τοῦ φ. τῶν πρώτων ἀνθρώπων διεφυλάχθη Cosm.Ind.*top*.5(M. 88.236C).

***φυρασία, ἡ**, *interest* on investments οἱ μὴ ψηφίζοντες τὴν φ. τῆς ἐνθήκης, καὶ τὰ κεφαλαῖα ζημιοῦνται †Cyr.*hom.div*.14(5^2.414C).

φυρατής, ὁ, *deceiver*, Cyr.*ep*.10(p.111.22; 5^2.34D).

φυρμός, ὁ, *confusion*, in gen. ἐμίαινον ἑαυτὰς ἐν φ. ἀναμίξεως *Pss. Sal*.2.15; φ. ἔσται πραγμάτων Cyr.*Is*.2.5(2.336D); πάντα...ἕστηκεν ἀσύγχυτα καὶ παντὸς ἐλεύθερα φ. Max.*ambig*.(M.91.1176C); Christol. ὡς ἰδίαν ἔχων αὐτὴν [sc. τὴν σάρκα] οὐ κατὰ σύγχυσιν ἢ φ. Cyr.*dogm*. (6.392D); σύγκρασις ἤτοι σύγχυσις ἢ φ. γέγονε τοῦ λόγου πρὸς τὸ σῶμα id.*ep*.45(p.152.27; 5^2.136E); *ib*.39(p.19.2; 107E); σύγχυσιν ἤτοι...φ. εἰσάγοντας τῇ ἐνανθρωπήσει Justn.ap.*Chron.Pasch*.p.343(M.92.896A); οὔτε γὰρ ἐν τῇ ἑνώσει τροπή τις ἢ φ. ἐμεσίτευσεν Sophr.H.*ep.syn*.(M. 87.3164B).

φύρσις, ἡ, **1.** *confusion* φ. πολλὴ καὶ κάματος Epiph.*haer*.70.9 (p.242.12; M.42.356A); πολλὴν φ. εἰργάσατο *ib*.73.23(p.296.19; 445); πολλὴ δὲ φ. καὶ φόβος...τοῖς ναυμαχοῦσι...συνήρχετο Geo.Pis.*bell. Avar*.464(M.92.1290B); **2.** *mixing, mingling*; Christol., Leont.H. *monoph*.(M.86.1813B); εἰ δὲ μήτε κατὰ φ. μήτε κατὰ τροπὴν, πῶς ἔσται μία φύσις; *ib*.(M.1833C); τροπὴν ὁμοῦ καὶ φ. καὶ σύγχυσιν...δογματίζοντες ‡Hipp.*Ber.Hel*.5(p.324.15; M.10.836D).

***φύρτης**, ὁ, *one who mingles, mixes*, of monophysites ὁ φ. πάντα συγχέει, τοῖς Δοκήταις δῆθεν ἀντιλέγων Eust.Mon.*ep*.(M.86.932C).

***φυρτόω**, *load with cargo*, ‡Nil.*perist*.12.11(M.79.961D).

***φύσα**, ἡ, *crop* of birds, Proc.G.*Lev*.1:16(M.87.701A).

[*]**φυσαλίς**, ἡ, (= φυσαλλίς) *bubble*, fig. τοιαῦται τοῦ λογογράφου νοημάτων αἱ φ. Gr.Nyss.*Eun*.7(2 p.159.19; M.45.748D).

φύσησις, ἡ, *blowing upon* or *up* τὰς δὲ φ. τε καὶ ἀντιφυσήσεις, ἃς... ἀντεπεδείκνυτο, τὸ ἐπιβώμιον πῦρ ἀνάπτων Gr.Naz.*or*.5.22(M.35.689C).

***φυσιθεσίτης**, ὁ, term applied to those tainted with Nestorian heresy, advocates of double sonship in Christ—by nature and by adoption, *Schol.1 in Max.qu.Thal*.62(M.90.661A).

φυσικός, **1.** *belonging to one's nature, essential* ὁ θεὸς...οὐδεμίαν ἔχει πρὸς ἡμᾶς φ. σχέσιν...εἰ μή τις μέρος αὐτοῦ καὶ ὁμοουσίους... τολμήσει λέγειν Clem.*str*.2.16(p.152.6; M.8.1012C); θέλησίς ἐστι φ. δύναμις...φ. ὄρεξις...φ. αὐτοκράτορος νοῦ αὐτεξούσιος κίνησις id.*fr*.40 (p.220.13ff.; M.9.752A); οὐ προαιρέσει διδοὺς τὴν μάχην ἀλλὰ φ. διαστάσει, μηδέποτε ἐλθεῖν εἰς εἰρηνικὴν σύμβασιν δυναμένη Bas.*hom*.24. 4(2.192C; M.31.605D); φ. τινι...ἀξίᾳ τῆς ἀλόγου ζωῆς ἡ ἀνθρωπίνη κεχώρισται Gr.Nyss.*Eun*.1(1 p.153.28; M.45.393D); ὁ καιόμενος λύχνος οὐκ οὐσιῶδες καὶ φ. ἔχει τὸ φῶς ἀλλ' ἐπίβλητον ‡Gr.Nyss.*hom.1.44 in Jo*.(p.108.25); ἐνύπαρκτον δέ ἐστι τὸ οὐσιῶδους καὶ φ. μετέχον ὑπάρξεως...ἐνδύναμον δέ ἐστι τὸ οὐσιώδη καὶ φ. ἔχον τὴν δύναμιν Max. *opusc*.(M.91.205B); λέγεται καὶ ἀρχὴ κατὰ τὸ αἴτιον...ἢ γὰρ φ., ὡς ἀρχὴ υἱοῦ, πατήρ· ἢ ποιητικὸν...ἢ μιμητικόν Jo.D.*Man*.1.3(M.94. 1509B); **2.** *natural, produced* or *caused by nature, innate* ἡ φ. κατασκευή opp. ἡ προαίρεσις, Or.*Jo*.13.10(p.235.5; M.14.413D); opp. γνωμικός q.v., Thdt.*Cant*.(2.10); ἡ φ. ἔχουσα δίαρμα ψυχή Or.*Jo*.10. 23(16; p.195.3; 348A); τὴν ἐν τῇ κοιλίᾳ γινομένην φ. σῆψιν τῶν εἰσφερομένων βρωμάτων Meth.*res*.2(p.382.13; M.18.329C); φ. τις ἔκκρισις ἀβουλήτως γίνεται...τῇ τῆς φύσεως ἀνάγκῃ Ath.*ep.Amun*.(M.26. 1172B); [sc. σάρξ] ᾗ φ. μὲν τὸ ἡγεμονεύεσθαι Apoll.*fr*.76(p.222.22) ap.Gr.Nyss.*Apoll*.40(M.45.1213C); τί...φ. εἶναι τὴν ἁμαρτίαν λέγοντες, κατὰ τὸν...Μανιχαῖον; ‡Ath.*Apoll*.1.14(M.26.1120B); τὰ μὲν φ. καὶ ἀναγκαῖα τῷ ζῴῳ, τὰ δὲ ἐκ προαιρέσεως Bas.*ep*.261.3(3.402E; M.32. 972A); θυμοῦ λέγω καὶ ἐπιθυμίας (ταῦτα γάρ ἐστι μάλιστα τὰ τυραννοῦντα ἐν ἡμῖν καὶ τῶν ἄλλων ὄντα φυσικώτερα) Chrys.*hom.17.1 in Mt*.(7.222E); ἔχον χάριτι θεοῦ φ. σύνεσιν Marc.Er.*opusc*.5.3(M.65. 1032C); ταύτην...τὴν γλῶτταν [i.e. Hebrew] διδακτὴν οὖσαν οὐ φ. Thdt.*qu.61 in Gen*.(1.73); οὐκ ἔσται φιλανθρωπίας συγκατάβασις [sc. on assumption of Sev. Ant.], ἀλλὰ φ. τοῦ ὑψηλοῦ πρὸς τὸ ταπεινὸν ἡ συνάφεια Leont.B.*arg.Sev*.(M.86.1940A); οὐ φ. ὄντος τοῦ τόκου [sc. of Christ] Leont.H.*Nest*.4.17(M.86.1684B); ref. birth of Christ τότε τοίνυν τὴν θείαν μορφήν, μορφῇ δούλου μεταμορφωθείς, περιεκάλυψε· νῦν δὲ [sc. at Transfiguration] τὴν μορφὴν τοῦ δούλου πρὸς τὴν φ. ἀποκαθίστησιν· οὐκ ἀποθέμενος μὲν τὴν οὐσίαν τὴν δουλικήν· φαιδρύνας δὲ αὐτὴν τοῖς θεϊκοῖς ἰδιώμασι Anast.Ant.*serm*.1.4(M.89.1368B); of physical necessity φ. ... ἀνάγκῃ θείας οἰκονομίας γενέσει θάνατος ἕπεται Clem.*str*.3.9(p.225.24; M.8.1168A); *ib*.2.3(p.118.26; 941C); οὐ ...βιασθεὶς ὁ πατὴρ ὑπὸ ἀνάγκης φ. *Symb.Sirm.1 anath*.25(p.256.12; M.26.740B); *Disp.Phot*.(M.88.565D); φ. ἀκολουθία *order of nature* τὴν τῶν σωμάτων διάλυσιν...φ. τινι ἀκολουθίᾳ καὶ τάξει τῶν στοιχείων μεταβολῇ ᾠκονόμησε γίνεσθαι Clem.*fr*.42(p.221.1; M.9.768B); τὴν ἑαυτοῦ [sc. θεοῦ] μεγαλειότητα παρὰ τὰ εἰωθότα φ. ἔχειν τὴν ἀκολουθίαν id.*str*.6.3(p.448.9; M.9.252C); Marc.Er.*opusc*.2.56(M.65.937D); also φ. λόγος: φ. λόγῳ πρὸς τὴν ἀρετὴν τῆς κακίας ἀντικειμένης Athenag.*leg*. 3.1(p.4.25; M.6.896C); νόμος...φ. τοῖς γεννῶσιν ἀγαπᾶν τὰ γεννώμενα ...φ. ... διάθεσις...πρὸς τὰ τέκνα Or.*fr.50 in Jo*.3:35(p.525.3f.); φ. ἔννοιαι *innate ideas* ὑπὸ...νόμων πονηρῶν διαφθαρέντες τὰς φ. ἐννοίας ἀπώλεσαν Just.*dial*.93.1(M.6.697A); Clem.*str*.1.19(p.60.15; M.8.809B); τὴν φ. τοῦ θεοῦ ἔννοιαν Or.*Cels*.4.14(p.284.26; M.11.1045A); Eus. *h.e*.1.4.4(M.20.77B); of natural law τῶν...δικαιωθέντων ἐν τῷ φ. νόμῳ ‡Ath.*Apoll*.2.9(M.26.1148B); ἅπερ τοῖς παλαιοῖς νενομοθέτητο τοῖς πρὸ τοῦ νόμου φ. *Const.App*.6.12.13; v. νόμος; of principles of reason λόγου ὄντος φ. τὸ ἓν καὶ τέλειον τῶν διαφόρων κρεῖττον εἶναι Ath.*gent*.39(M.25.77D); in animals ἐν ζῴοις ἀλόγοις...μὴ φθείρεσθαι τὴν φύσιν οὐ κακόν, φθορὰ δὲ φύσεως...καὶ ἔλλειψις τῶν φ. ἕξεων Dion. Ar.*d.n*.4.25(M.3.728B); οἱ πάντες φ. λόγοι παρὰ τῆς καθόλου φύσεως *ib*.4.26(728C); opp. rational, *instinctive*, Or.*Cels*.4.87(p.358.7; M.11. 1161C); **3.** *of* or *concerning the order of external nature*; **a.** *natural, physical* ἴσως...φ. ... τις ἐπ' αὐτοῖς...λόγος...Ζεὺς μὲν τὸ πῦρ, Ἥρα δὲ ἡ γῆ Athenag.*leg*.22.1(p.26.9; M.6.936C); τὰ περὶ θεῶν αὐτοῖς μυθολογούμενα ἐπὶ τὰ φ. τοῦ κόσμου μέρη μεταφέρειν Eus.*p.e*.3.13 (119A; M.21.213B); οὐδ' αὖ διὰ τοῦ κτίσματος ἡ φ. μορφὴ τοῦ κτίσαντος κατανοεῖσθαι Didym.*Trin*.1.16(M.39.337A); φ. λέγει τὰ αἰσθητὰ καὶ ὁρατά Max.*schol.c.h*.13.3(M.4.97A); **b.** *concerned with the physical sciences*; abs. *natural philosopher*; superl. iron., *super-scientist*, Leont.H.*Nest*.4.17(M.86.1684B); **c.** *pertaining to the body*; **i.** *physical, material* πέμπτη τις...οὐσία, φ. ἀπηλλαγμένη στοιχείων πάντων... οἱονεί...τις ὑπερκόσμιος Hipp.*haer*.7.19(p.194.9; M.16.3299B); μὴ ἐγκαλεῖσθαι ὑπὸ θεοῦ κατὰ ἀνάγκην φ. διαδοχῆς παραβαίνοντας Marc.Er. *opusc*.4(M.65.1017C); τῇ δι' ὕδατος φ. καθάρσει Dion.Ar.*e.h*.2.3.1(M.3. 397B); τὸν ἔρωτα, εἴτε θεῖον, εἴτε ἀγγελικόν, εἴτε νοερόν, εἴτε ψυχικόν, εἴτε φ. id.*d.n*.4.15(M.3.713A); κινεῖσθαι...αὐτὸν [sc. τὸν θεόν]... οἰητέον, οὐ κατὰ φορὰν...ἢ ἀλλοίωσιν...ἢ τοπικὴν κίνησιν...οὐ τὴν νοητήν, οὐ τὴν ψυχικήν, οὐ τὴν φ. *ib*.9.9(916C); *ib*.9.10(917A); of Mosaic Law, Oecum.*Rom*.5:13f.(p.424.23); **ii.** ref. fallen nature with its disordered passions ὁ ταῦτα κατὰ τῶν φ. τοῦ σώματος ἐνεργῶν [i.e. ἡ ψυχή] Ath.*gent*.32(M.25.65A); θέλημα σαρκός, ἔστιν ἡ φ. τοῦ σώματος κίνησις μετὰ τῆς ἑπομένης χωρὶς λογισμοῦ πυρώσεως Marc.Er.*opusc*.7.21(M.65.1101D); **iii.** *natural, illegitimate* παλλακὴν ἢ φ. παῖδας μὴ ἐχέτωσαν [sc. οἱ κληρικοί] Ath.Scholast.*coll*.1.2(p.8); **4.** *essential, real* ὁ δέ γε 'υἱὸς' τὴν ἐκ πατρὸς ὕπαρξιν οὐσιώδη τε καὶ φ. κατασημήνειεν ἄν Cyr.*Pulch*.(p.29.30; 5².133C); μηδεμίαν τούτων [sc. Godhead and manhood in Christ] ἔρημον ἐπιστάμεθα φ. ὑπάρξεως Max.*opusc*.(M.91.96A); ‡Gr.Nyss.*hom.3.2 in Jo*.(p.135.19); *having actually taken place, actual, historical* εἰ μὲν γὰρ μυθικαὶ αἱ περὶ αὐτῶν ἱστορίαι, οὐδέν εἰσιν εἰ μὴ μόνον λόγοι· εἰ δὲ φ., οὐκ ἔτι θεοὶ εἰσιν οἱ ταῦτα ποιήσαντες καὶ παθόντες Arist.*apol*.13.7; of birth of Christ φ. καὶ ἀληθεστάτην τὴν γέννησιν ‡Ath.*Apoll*.1.7(M.26.1105B); ἐκ παρθένου...φ. γεννήσει *ib*.1.6(1104A); ἡ μορφὴ τοῦ δούλου, ἣν...ὁ λόγος ἰδιοποιήσατο φ. γεννήσει *ib*.1.12(1113A); *ib*.2.2(1133C); *ib*.2.5(1140A,B); **5.** Trin.; **a.** *belonging to one's nature, essential*; **i.** of Son, Eus.*d.e*.5.4 (p.225.25; M.22.372D) cit. s. ἐπίκτητος; ἐξ αὐτῆς τῆς προσηγορίας [i.e. μονογενής] ὁ υἱὸς τὴν πρὸς τὸν πατέρα φ. σχέσιν παρίστησιν id.*e.th*.1.10 (p.69.1; M.24.841C); cf.Clem.*str*.2.16(p.152.6; M.8.1012C) cit. s. 1; τὴν ἐκ τοῦ πατρὸς φ. γέννησιν Ath.*Ar*.2.7(M.26.161A); ὁ Χριστὸς ἡ φ. καὶ ἀληθινὴ δύναμις τοῦ θεοῦ id.*ep.Aeg.Lib*.12(M.25.565B); εἰκὼν θεοῦ φ. ὁ υἱός Didym.(‡Bas.)*Eun*.5(1.314C; M.29.753B); φ. υἱός, οὐ θετός Epiph.*anc*.6(p.12.13; M.43.25B); ἐν...τῇ φ. ταυτότητι ἕν ἐστιν ὁ ἐκ θεοῦ λόγος πρὸς τὸν...πατέρα εἰ καὶ νοεῖται καθ' ὑπόστασιν ἑκάτερος ἰδικήν Cyr.*Arcad*.(p.91.14; 5².86A); μένων υἱὸς δείκνυσι τὸν ἐξ οὗ, καθάπερ εἰκὼν αὐτοῦ φ. ‡Cyr.*Trin*.13(6³.20A; M.77.1149C); **ii.** of H. Ghost τὸ πνεῦμα φ. ἔχει τὴν ἁγιότητα, οὐ κατὰ χάριν λαβὸν Bas. *ep*.159.2(3.248C; M.32.621B); τὸ πνεῦμα...οὐκ ἀλλότριον ἄρα τῆς θείας οὐσίας ἐστίν, ἀλλ' ὡς ἐνέργεια φ. τε καὶ οὐσιώδης καὶ ἐνυπόστατος ἐξ αὐτῆς προιοῦσα καὶ ἐν αὐτῇ μένουσα πάντα ἐργάζεται τὰ τοῦ θεοῦ Cyr. *thes*.34(5¹.341C); **iii.** of Trin. τοῖς...τι ἐκ τῆς τριάδος κτιστὸν λέγουσι καὶ χωρίζουσι τῆς μιᾶς φ. θεότητος Apoll.*fid.sec.pt*.34(p.180.23; M. 10.1117C); opp. ψιλῷ λόγῳ: ἡμῶν...ὁμολογούντων φ. εἶναι πατέρα καὶ φ. εἶναι υἱὸν καὶ φ. εἶναι ἅγιον πνεῦμα Epiph.*haer*.76.33(p.382.16; M. 42.584A); **iv.** of ἰδιώματα etc. ἢ...ἐν φ. δόξῃ καὶ ἀληθινῇ τὴν ὅλην τριάδα νοητέον, ἢ μονάδα καὶ οὐκέτι τριάδα λέγειν ἀναγκασθησόμεθα Apoll.*fid.sec.pt*.9(p.170.11; M.10.1108C); τὰ προσόντα τῷ θεῷ...φ. τε καὶ οὐσιώδη...ἰδιώματα Cyr.*thes*.14(5¹.145C); *ib*.32(297D); καὶ ἐν σαρκὶ γεγονότα τὸν ἴδιον υἱόν, οὐκ ἔξω τίθησιν ὁ πατὴρ τῶν ἐνόντων αὐτῷ φ. ἀξιωμάτων id.*hom.pasch*.17.2(5².226A); ἐξ οἰκείας...καὶ φ. ἀγαθότητος Dion.Ar.*e.h*.2.2.1(M.3.393A); **b.** *in terms of nature, relating to nature* τὴν πρὸς τὸν πατέρα τοῦ υἱοῦ φ. ὁμοιότητα καὶ ἰδιότητα Ath.*Ar*.3.36(M.26.401A); τοῦ υἱοῦ πρὸς τὸν πατέρα φ. ἑνότητα *ib*.3.20(365A); τὴν...τοιαύτην ἑνότητα καὶ φ. ἰδιότητα πῶς ἂν... ὀρθῶς καλέσειεν ἢ ὁμοούσιον γέννημα; id.*decr*.24(p.20.11; M.25.457C); ὁ ἐν αὐτῷ τε καὶ ἐξ αὐτοῦ κατὰ φύσιν υἱός, διῃρημένως τε ἅμα καὶ συμφυῶς καθ' ἑνότητα φ. Cyr.*Jo*.11.5(4.952E); Ammon.*Jo*.14:23(M. 85.1492C) cit. s. ἕνωσις; μίαν οὖν ἀρχὴν ὁμολογῶ, ὡς αἴτιον φ., τὸν πατέρα λόγου καὶ πνεύματος Jo.D.*Man*.1.4(M.94.1512A); **6.** Christol.; **a.** *proper to one's nature, essential*; **i.** ref. sonship of Christ (opp. χάριτι), exeg. Heb.2:10 ἐν τῷ τῆς υἱότητος λόγῳ καὶ συγκατατάττων ὁ ἀπόστολος φαίνεται τὸν ἀναληφθέντα ἄνθρωπον τοῖς πολλοῖς, οὐ καθ' ὁμοίωσιν ἐκείνοις τῆς υἱότητος μετέχων, ἀλλὰ καθ' ὁμοίωσιν καθ' ὃ χάριτι προσείληφεν τὴν υἱότητα, τῆς θεότητος μόνης τὴν φ. υἱότητα κεκτημένης Thdr.Mops.*fr.inc*.12(p.303.18; M.66.985B); ὡς ὁ μὲν θεὸς λόγος κατὰ τὴν φ. γέννησιν υἱὸς εἶναι λέγεται· ὁ δὲ ἄνθρωπος...τῆς ἀξίας ἀπολαύειν, διὰ τὴν πρὸς ἐκεῖνον συνάφειαν *ib*.(p.306.16; 988B); πεφόρηκε τὴν τοῦ δούλου μορφήν, καὶ...μεμένηκεν ἐν...κυριότητι τῇ φ. Cyr.*ep*.45(p.153.7; 5².137A); in rel. to mankind ἐν τοῖς φ. ἡμῶν ὑπερφυὴς ἣν ἐν τοῖς κατ' οὐσίαν ὑπερούσιος Dion.Ar.*d.n.*2.10(M.3.649A); **ii.** of ἰδιώματα etc., *inherent in, proper to the nature*, ref. either nature of Christ οὐ...ταὐτὸν ὡς ἐν ποιότητι φ. θεότης τε καὶ ἀνθρωπότης Cyr.*ep.*40(pp.26.26,27.14; 5².116C,117A); τὸ μὲν δύο σκοπεῖν, τῇ φαντασίᾳ τοῦ νοῦ μόνον ἐφίεται, διακρίνοντος τὴν διαφοράν, τὴν ὡς ἐν ποιότητι φ. Sev.Ant.ap.Eust.Mon.*ep.*(M.86.908A); ἑκατέραν φύσιν τῷ ἑνὶ...Χριστῷ ζωὴν συνεισάγειν φησίν· ἀλλὰ τὴν μέν, τὴν φ. ἀνθρώπῳ· τὴν δέ, τὴν φ. θεῷ ζωήν Leont.H.*monoph.*(M.86.1856D); δύο φ. θελήσεις...ἐν αὐτῷ καὶ δύο φ. ἐνεργείας...δύο μὲν φ. θελήματα οὐχ ὑπεναντία *Symb.CP*(681)(H.3.1400C); Max.*Pyrr.*(M.91.293D) cit. s. φυσικῶς; opp. what characterizes the individual ἓν μὲν κατὰ τὴν ὑπόστασίν τε καὶ πρόσωπον, δύο δὲ κατὰ τὰς φύσεις αὐτάς, καὶ τὰς φ. αὐτῶν ἰδιότητας Sophr.H.*ep.syn.*(M.87.3168A); τῆς θείας φύσεως ἰδιώματα...τῆς θείας μὲν φύσεως, ὅτι φ., καὶ οὐχ ὑποστατικά, ταῖς τρισὶν...προσόντα τῆς θεότητος ὑποστάσεσιν ‡Cyr.*Trin.*13(6³.19B; M.77.1148D); φ. εἶναι θέλημα διωθούμενοι, ἢ ὑποστατικὸν αὐτό, ἢ παρὰ φύσιν λέξουσιν; Max.*Pyrr.*(M.91.313C); Anast.S.*hod.*17(M.89.264C); **b.** *in terms of nature, relating to nature* Χριστὸν σάρκα γενόμενον λόγον ...μείναντα τῆς φ. αὐτοῦ μονάδος ἐντός Apoll.*fr.*152(p.248.11); τῆσδε τῆς φ. δυάδος τὴν ἕνωσιν, καὶ τὴν ὑποστατικὴν μονάδα Leont.H.*monoph.*(M.86.1809B); οὔτε ἁπλῶς σῶμα, οὔτε μόνος ψυχὴ ὁ ἄνθρωπος λέγοιτο, φ. εἴδους λόγῳ...οὔτε θεός, οὔτε ἄνθρωπος, οὔτε θεὸς καὶ ἄνθρωπος ἅμα, ἀλλ' ἕτερόν τι εἶδος φ. ὁ Χριστός *ib.*4(1772Af.); of terms, *denoting nature* opp. προσωπικός and ὑποστατικός: τὸ... 'Χριστὸς' προσωπικόν, καὶ οὐ φ. ... ὄνομα Leont.H.*Nest.*4.37(M.86.1709A); τὸ 'θεὸς' πρῶτον μὲν φ. ὄνομά ἐστιν, οὐσίαν πρώτως καὶ οὐ πρόσωπον σημαῖνον· ὥσπερ καὶ τὸ 'ἄνθρωπος', οὐ τὴν ὑπόστασιν Παύλου, ἀλλὰ τὴν φύσιν λέγει...κατὰ τὸ φ. ὄνομα, ὁμοιότης τινὸς πρός τινά ἐστί ποτε· κατὰ δὲ τὸ ὑποστατικὸν ἑτερότης μόνον *ib.*2.18(1577B); **c.** of hypostatic union, *real*, cf. 4; Cyr.*ep.*1(p.15.32; 5².9B) cit. s. ἀνακίρνημι; Leont.H.*Nest.*1.14(M.86.1457B) cit. s. ἄνθρωπος; τὴν ἀσύγχυτον ὁμοῦ καὶ ἀμέριστον...ἕνωσιν, ἣν μόνην γνωρίζειν ἐπίσταται ἡ φ. καθ' ὑπόστασιν σύνοδος Sophr.H.*ep.syn.*(M.87.3165B); v. ἕνωσις; **7.** eucharistic; of benefits of sacrament not being within physical sphere, Sever.*creat.*6.4(M.56.488)ap.Cosm.Ind.*top.*10(M.88.425A) cit. s. δῶρον; of eucharistic union οὐ κατὰ σχέσιν τινὰ μόνην...ἐν ἡμῖν ἔσεσθαι...ὁ Χριστός, ἀλλὰ καὶ κατὰ μέθεξιν ἤτοι φ. Cyr.*Jo.*10.2(4.863A).

φυσικῶς, **A.** *by nature*; **1.** *in virtue of one's nature* or *essence* δύναμιν συνεστηριγμένην φ. τῷ φωτὶ τῷ λάμψαντι Hipp.*haer.*7.26(p.205.25; M.16.3318A); ἐκ τῆς αὐτοῦ φύσεως ἴδιον ἔχων τὸ ψεῦδος, φ. μὴ δυνάμενός ποτε ἀλήθειαν εἰπεῖν Heracleon ap.Or.*Jo.*20.28(22; p.365.12; M.14.637D); Bas.*hom.*9.7(2.79E; M.31.345B) cit. s. ἀνόρμητος; τὸ ἔκ τινος τοίνυν, ἢ δημιουργικῶς, ἢ γεννητικῶς, ἢ φ. ἐστιν ἐξ αὐτοῦ, ὡς ἡ ἐνέργεια ἡμῶν ἐξ ἡμῶν, ἢ ὡς τὸ ἀπαύγασμα τοῦ ἡλίου ἐξ αὐτοῦ Didym.(‡Bas.)*Eun.*5(1.298B; M.29.716B); οὐ πάντως ἴδιόν ἐστι σαρκὸς τὸ δι' αὐτῆς μὲν ἐκφαινόμενον, οὐκ αὐτῆς δὲ φ. ἐκφυόμενον...ἐγὼ γὰρ γλώσσῃ λαλῶν...τῆς...ψυχῆς ἐκφαίνω διάνοιαν, ἐνέργειαν αὐτῆς ὑπάρχουσαν φυσικήν, μηδενὶ λόγῳ δείξας αὐτὴν γλώσσης...φ. ἐκφυομένην ‡Hipp.*Ber.Hel.*8(p.325.22ff.; M.10.837Df.); οὐδεὶς...λόγος...τὴν ψυχὴν τῶν προσόντων αὐτῇ φ. ... ἀλλοτριῶσαι δυνάμενος Max.*ep.*7(M.91.437A); **2.** *naturally*; opp. affectedly λαλεῖν φυσικώτερον Tat.*orat.*26(p.28.17; M.6.864A); ἡ...φιλανθρωπία ἄνευ τοῦ φ. πείθοντος πάντα ἄνθρωπον, καθὸ ἄνθρωπός ἐστι, φιλοῦσα εὐεργετεῖ *Hom.Clem.*12.25; φ. αἱ ἁμαρτίαι ἀναιροῦσι τὸν ἁμαρτάνοντα, κἂν ἀγνοῶν πράσσῃ ἃ μὴ δεῖ *ib.*10.12; φ. ἐψυχώθην opp. θείᾳ ἐμψυχίᾳ, ‡Ath.*dial.Trin.*4.1(M.28.1252A); [sc. the different members of the body] φ. ... οὕτω τέτακται i.e. to work in harmony, Chrys.*hom.10.1 in Eph.*(11.76A); opp. ἐπινοητικῶς Marc.Er.*opusc.*8.3(M.65.1105D); φ. διψῶμεν, φ. καθεύδομεν, φ. ἀναπνέομεν τὸν ἀέρα Thdt.ap.Cyr.*apol.Thdt.*3(p.117.1f.; 6.210C); οὐδὲ τῆς ἀνθρωπίνης ψυχῆς τὴν πρὸς τὸ ἑαυτῆς σῶμα συνάφειαν φ. πάσχειν, ἄνευ τῆς θείας δυνάμεως Leont.B.*arg.Sev.*(M.86².1940B); τὰς φ. ἐνεσπαρμένας αὐτῇ [sc. τῇ τῶν νοερῶν...αὐτεξουσιότητι] πρὸς τὸ φωτίζεσθαι δυνάμεις Dion.Ar.*e.h.*2.3.3(M.3.400A); Jo.D.*f.o.*1.1(M.94.789B) cit. s. γνῶσις; *ib.*1.3(793C); **3.** of second nature, *naturally, as a matter of course* ὥσπερ ἐσθίομεν...οὕτω καὶ μετανοεῖν φ. κεχρεωστήκαμεν Marc.Er.*opusc.*3.11(M.65.981C).

B. *physically, outwardly* τῷ σώματι καθαιρομένῳ φ. δι' ὕδατος Dion.Ar.*e.h.*2.3.1(M.3.397B); *by means of physical images* σωματοπρεπῶς...ἢ φ. id.*ep.*9.1(M.3.1105A).

C. *in fact, truly* τούτων οὕτως φ. εἰρημένων καὶ μὴ ἐχόντων ἀντίρρησιν Pall.*v.Chrys.*13(p.82.12; M.47.47); superl., Eus.*Ps.*13:1(*AS* 3 p.408) int. opp. Thdt.(1.682).

D. Trin.; *by nature, essentially*; **1.** esp. of relation between Persons, of Son υἱὸς...οὐχ ἁρπάσας τοῦ κυριεύειν, ἀλλὰ παρ' αὐτοπροαιρέτου λαβὼν φ. Cyr.H.*catech.*10.9; υἱὸν...φ. τὴν πατρικὴν θεότητα ἔχοντα Apoll.*fid.sec.pt.*27(p.176.20; M.10.1116B); ἡ τοῦ θεοῦ εἰκὼν...ἐπὶ μὲν τοῦ ἀνθρώπου μιμητικῶς εἰκών, ἐπὶ δὲ τοῦ θεοῦ φ. *Dial.Ath.et Zacch.*19(p.15); γεννητῶς ὑπάρχων ἐκ τοῦ πατρὸς ὁ υἱός, καὶ φ. ἐκτυπῶν ἐν ἑαυτῷ τὸν πατέρα Bas.*hom.*24.4(2.192C; M.31.608A); ὁ...θεὸς λόγος πατρικὴν θεότητα φ. καὶ ἀνάρχως ἐξεικονίζει Didym.*Trin.*1.16(M.39.336C); ἐκ πατρὸς φ. γεγεννημένος [sc. ὁ λόγος] ὥσπερ...τὸ φῶς ἐξ ἡλίου προελθὸν...τὰ αὐτῷ προσόντα φορεῖν φ. Cyr.*thes.*14(5¹.139Ef.); ἔχει...ὁ υἱὸς ἐν ἑαυτῷ τὸν γεννήτορα, μιᾶς πρὸς αὐτὸν ὑπάρχων οὐσίας, ἔστι δὲ καὶ αὐτὸς ἐν πατρὶ φ. id.*Jo.*10(4.831C); *ib.*12(1039C) cit. s. ἀλήθεια; **2.** of H. Ghost τὸ πνεῦμα ὁμοίως καλεῖται τοῦ θεοῦ, καὶ τοῦτο φ. κατ' αὐτὴν τὴν οὐσίαν, οὐ κατὰ μετουσίαν θεοῦ Apoll.*fid.sec.pt.*25(p.176.8; M.10.1116A); οὐ γὰρ ἀλλότριον τῆς οὐσίας τοῦ μονογενοῦς τὸ ἅγιον νοεῖται πνεῦμα, πρόεισι δὲ φ. ἐξ αὐτῆς, οὐδὲν ἕτερον παρ' αὐτὸν ὑπάρχον, ὅσον εἰς ταυτότητα φύσεως, εἰ καὶ νοοῖτο τυχὸν ἰδιοσυστάτως Cyr.*Jo.*10.2(4.925C); οἱ ἐκ μετοχῆς τῆς τοῦ...πατρὸς εἶναι, καὶ οὐ φ. †Cyr.*Spir.*(M.75.1141A); **3.** of Trin. ἡ θεότης μία φ. ἐν τριάδι μαρτυρουμένη Apoll.*fid.sec.pt.*14(p.172.5; M.10.1109C); **4.** of modes of being, attributes, etc. φ. ἀγεννήτου...ὄντος τοῦ πατρός *ib.*33(p.180.15; 1117C); τὰ τῇ θεαρχίᾳ φ. καὶ ὑπερφυῶς ἐνόντα Dion.Ar.*c.h.*3.3(M.3.168A); of mutual knowledge of Father and Son, Cyr.*Jo.*2.6(4.223A) cit. s. διδακτῶς.

E. Christol., *by nature, essentially*; **1.** Logos not so united to human nature, Leont.H.*Nest.*1.41(M.86.1501A) cit. s. γνωμικῶς; **2.** Christ as man not so related to Father τοῖς λοιποῖς τοῖς μετεσχηκόσιν τῆς υἱότητος ἐλέγχεται, ἐπείπερ χάριτι καὶ αὐτὸς μετέσχηκεν τῆς υἱότητος, οὐ φ. ἐκ τοῦ πατρὸς γεγεννημένος Thdr.Mops.*fr.inc.*12(p.306.3; M.66.988A); though Christ is one his flesh cannot be so related to divinity εἷς...Χριστὸς καὶ εἷς υἱός, καὶ ὅτε γέγονεν ἄνθρωπος. ταύτῃ τοι λαβεῖν νοεῖται τὴν ἕνωσιν, παραδεχθεὶς εἰς τοῦτο καὶ μετὰ σαρκὸς... σχετικῶς δῆλον ὅτι καὶ οὐ φ. Cyr.*Jo.*11.12(4.1001D); **3.** of Christ's possession and operation of both divinity and humanity Χριστὸς... τὰς ἑκατέρας φ. οὐσίας εἰργάζετο κατὰ τὴν ἑκατέρᾳ προσοῦσαν οὐσιώδη ποιότητα ἢ καὶ φυσικὴν ἰδιότητα Sophr.H.*ep.syn.*(M.87.3168B); εἰ...ὁ φυσικὰ ἐπὶ Χριστοῦ λέγων τὰ θελήματα, πᾶσαν, κατὰ σέ, ἑκούσιον ἐπ' αὐτοῦ ἀναιρεῖ κίνησιν, ἀνάγκη τὰ μὲν φ. θέλοντα, ἀκούσιον ἔχειν κίνησιν· τὰ δὲ φ. μὴ θέλοντα, ἑκούσιον Max.*Pyrr.*(M.91.293D); τά τε θεῖα καὶ ἀνθρώπινα φ. ἔχων id.*opusc.*(M.91.96A); *ib.*(36B); **4.** *in terms of nature*; **a.** opp. οἰκονομικῶς: μὴ φ. ἐκλάμβανε τὰ λεγόμενα, ἀλλ' οἰκονομικῶς...διὸ καὶ ὁ κύριος τῇ φιλανθρωπίᾳ τῆς συγκαταβάσεως οὐκ ἔλαθε τὴν τῶν ὑδάτων φύσιν, ὅπερ ἐποίησεν †Hipp.*theoph.*2(p.258.10; M.10.853A); **b.** opp. ὑποστατικῶς: εἰς ὁ προαιώνιος λόγος τοῦ θεοῦ καὶ μετὰ τὴν πρόληψιν τῆς σαρκὸς ὑποστατικῶς καὶ οὐ φ. Jo.D.*disp.*(M.96.1345B).

***φυσιογεν-έω**, *analyse* something *in respect of its nature* ὅτε δὲ ∼εῖται ὁ ἄνθρωπος, δύο ἐπ' αὐτοῦ φύσεις θεωρηθήσονται, ψυχῆς λέγω καὶ σώματος Jo.D.*Jacob.*57(M.94.1465D).

φυσιολογ-έω, **1.** *inquire into the nature of, seek to explain*, ref. inquiry into nature of God ∼είτω τὴν πάντα νοῦν ὑπερέχουσαν δύναμιν Gr.Nyss.*Eun.*10(2 p.227.26; M.45.828C); ὡς ἂν μὴ διὰ τοῦ ∼εῖσθαι τὴν ἀνέφικτόν τε καὶ ἀνεκφώνητον φύσιν ὕλην λάβοι κατὰ τῆς ἀληθείας ἡ αἵρεσις id.*hom.11 in Cant.*(M.44.1013C); παρακαλῶ τὸν θέλοντα ∼εῖν τὸν θεὸν φορῆσαι ἡμῖν, πρὸ τοῦ θεοῦ, τὴν τοῦ βραχυτάτου ψύλλου κατασκευήν Hier.H.*Trin.*(M.40.856D); ref. Son τὸ ἐν τῷ παρὰ Πλάτωνι Τιμαίῳ ∼ούμενον περὶ τοῦ υἱοῦ τοῦ θεοῦ Just.*1apol.*60.1(M.6.417A); Gr.Naz.*or.*31.8(p.155.5; M.36.141B); Eut.ap.CCP(448)*act.*7(p.142.9; H.2.164D); **2.** *explain in materialistic terms*, Eus.*p.e.*3.15(125B; M.21.224A); ταῦτα περὶ ψυχῆς ἡμῖν ∼οῦντος δι' αἰνιγμάτων τοῦ λόγου Gr.Nyss.*v.Mos.*(M.44.353C); ∼εῖ δὲ καὶ Κορινθίοις ἐπιστέλλων ἀπὸ σάλπιγγος ‡Caes.Naz.*dial.*1.15(M.38.872); **3.** *refer, relate, to natural phenomena* Ζεὺς ἡ ζέουσα οὐσία...Ἥρα ὁ ἀὴρ...ἄλλοι δὲ ἄλλως ∼οῦσιν Athenag.*leg.*22.2(M.6.937A); *Hom.Clem.*4.24; *ib.*6.20; **4.** *assert, declare*, in physiology οἱ ἰατροὶ ψυχρὸν εἶναι ∼οῦντες τὸν ἐγκέφαλον, μύρῳ χρίεσθαι ἀξιοῦσι τὰ στήθη Clem.*paed.*2.8(p.199.24; M.8.477B).

φυσιολογία, ἡ, **1.** *study of natural phenomena*, often in vague sense, of any scientific or physiological studies; of examples taken from natural science κεχρῆσθαι πέφυκεν ἡ θεία γραφὴ καὶ φυσιολογίαις ‡Caes.Naz.*dial.*1.15(M.38.872); **2.** *nature*; of animals, ‡Petr.I Al.*phys.*31; τίς ἑκάστου δύναται διασκέψασθαι τὴν φ.; Cyr.H.*catech.*9.13; ἀγνοοῦμεν...καὶ τὰ ἄλλα ὅσα τῆς ὑπερφυοῦς ἐστιν Ἰησοῦ φ. Dion.Ar.*d.n.*2.9(M.3.648A); τὸ μέγα τῆς ὑπερφυοῦς Ἰησοῦ φ. ποιησαμένη μυστήριον Max.*ambig.*(M.91.1052B); **3.** *rationalization*, of myths by relating or referring to natural phenomena ἡ θαυμαστὴ καὶ ἀπόρρητος φ. τῆς Ἑλληνικῆς θεολογίας θεῖον μὲν οὐδὲν...ἐπήγετο Eus.*p.e.*3.2(87A; M.21.161B); *ib.*3.15(125C; M.224B); τῶν τε μύθων τὰς ἀλληγορουμένας φ. *ib.*10.1(460D; M.768A).

***φυσιολογικῶς**, 1. *naturally*, Max.*schol.c.h.*1.2(M.4.32A); 2. *physiologically, from a physiological point of view*, Epiph.*mens.* 8(M.43.248C); Thdt.*eran.*3(4.178).

***φυσιουργέω**, *create*, ‡Caes.Naz.*dial.*1.3(M.38.861).

φυσι-όω A (ῡ), *puff up*; met., *fill with conceit* τόπος μηδένα ~ούτω Ign.*Smyrn.*6.1; exeg. 1Cor.8:1 ἡ δοκοῦσα γνῶσις ~οῦν λέγεται Clem. *str.*7.16(p.73.30; M.9.544C); ταύτην ὁδὸν βελτίονα οἶδεν εἰς γνῶσιν τῆς ~ούσης οἰήσεως Gr.Naz.*or.*32.12(M.36.188C); pass. met., *be puffed up with conceit* φυσιωθήσεσθε ἐπὶ τῇ ἱερωσύνῃ ὑμῶν *T.Lev.*14.7; οἶδα ὅτι οὐ ~οῦσθε· Ἰησοῦν γὰρ ἔχετε ἐν ἑαυτοῖς Ign.*Magn.*12.1; Hipp. *haer.*8.20(p.238.28; M.16.3367B); ἐπίνοιαν πεφυσιωμένης καρδίας *ib.* 9.13(p.252.10; 3390A).

φυσι-όω B (ῠ), 1. *become natural, become second nature*, pass.; also act., Or.*Cels.*3.69 (v. infra) τῷ ἄρα ἀναπόβλητον τὴν ἀρετὴν ἀσκήσει γνωστικῇ πεποιημένῳ ~οῦται ἡ ἕξις Clem.*str.*7.7(p.35.10; M.9.468A); φυσιωθῆναι ἔν τισι τὴν κακίαν, πειθόμεθα ὅτι...ἀμεῖψαι κακίαν φυσιώσασάν ἐστιν...οὐκ ἀδύνατον Or.*Cels.*3.69(p.261.16,17; M.11.1009D); 2. pass.; *be conditioned, endowed with a nature* παραμυθήσει καὶ τὸ περὶ τοῦ ψεῦδος εἶναί τινα ⟨οὐ⟩ τῇ ὑποστάσει ἐκ κατασκευῆς, ἀλλὰ ἐκ μεταβολῆς καὶ ἰδίας προαιρέσεως τοιοῦτον γεγενημένον, καὶ οὕτως, ἵνα καινῶς ὀνομάσω, πεφυσιωμένον Or.*Jo.*20.21(19; p.353.25; M.14.617D).

φύσις, ἡ, *nature*;

I. etymology, definitions, and relations to other terms;

A. etymology, Thdr.Raith.*praep.*(p.202.18) cit. s. C.1; φ. λέγεται, παρὰ τὸ πεφυκέναι Max.*opusc.*(M.91.265D); Anast.S.*hod.*2(M.89.56D); ref. Trin. καλεῖται...φ. ... ὡς φύουσα τὰς ὑποστάσεις ‡Cyr.*Trin.*13(6[3]. 19B; M.77.1149A).

B. definitions, Clem.*fr.*37(p.219.19; M.9.752A) cit. s. C.2; φ. ἐστιν ἡ ἑκάστου κατ' οὐσίαν καὶ ποιὰ τῷ παντὶ ὕπαρξις Pamph.H. *panopl.*2.6(p.605) ∞ Max.*opusc.*(M.91.265D); τρία...σημαίνειν ὁ Ἀριστοτέλης λέγει τὸ τῆς φ. ὄνομα, τὴν ὕλην τὴν κοινῶς πᾶσιν ὑποκειμένην· τὸ εἶδος ἑκάστου τὸ ταύτην εἰδοποιοῦν· τὴν λεγομένην ἔκφυσιν, τουτέστι τὴν ἀπό του δυνάμει ἐπὶ τῇ ἐνεργείᾳ πρόοδον Pamph.H. *panopl.*2.6(p.606); φ. ... ἐστιν ἀρχὴ τῆς ἑκάστου τῶν ἀπηριθμημένων τούτων κινήσεώς τε καὶ ἠρεμίας, ἐν οἷς πρώτοις τούτοις αὐτοῖς ὑπάρχει, καὶ οὐ κατὰ συμβεβηκός Thdr.Raith.*praep.*(p.202.10); φ. ἐστὶ κατὰ τοὺς ἔξω, ἀρχὴ κινήσεως καὶ ἠρεμίας Max.*opusc.*(265D); φ. ἐστί, τὸ ἐξ ἴσου πᾶσι τοῖς ὑπὸ τὸ αὐτὸ εἶδος ἀναγορευομένοις ἐνθεωρούμενον *ib.*(265C); φ. μέν ἐστι κατὰ τὸ φρόνημα τῆς ἐκκλησίας, ἀληθὴς πράγματος ὕπαρξις...κατὰ τὸν...Ἀπόστολον, πᾶν τὸ ἐν ἀληθείᾳ ὄν, ἀλλ' οὐκ ἐν φαντασίᾳ λεγόμενον Anast.S.*hod.*2(M.89.56D); ἡ φ. ἢ ψιλῇ θεωρίᾳ κατανοεῖται· καθ' ἑαυτὴν γὰρ οὐχ ὑφέστηκεν· ἢ κοινῶς ἐν πᾶσι τοῖς ὁμοειδέσιν ὑποστάσεσι. ταύτας συνάπτουσα...ἢ ὁλικῶς ἡ αὐτὴ ἐν προσλήψει συμβεβηκότων, ἐν μιᾷ ὑποστάσει Jo.D.*f.o.*3.11(M.94. 1021Df.); φ. ... εἶναι οἴεται, τὸν κοινὸν τοῦ εἶναι λόγον τῶν τῆς αὐτῆς μετεχόντων οὐσίας id.*haer.*7(M.94.745B).

C. φ. and οὐσία; 1. explicitly equated φ. ... καὶ οὐσία ταὐτόν ἐστιν ...καὶ πάντες...οἱ τῆς ἀληθινῆς πίστεως ὁμολογηταὶ τοῦτο γινώσκουσιν Val.Apoll.*apol.*7(p.290.19)ap.Leont.B.*Apoll.*(M.86.1957A); ἰστέον... ὅτι οὐσία καὶ φ. ταυτόν ἐστι παρ' αὐτοῖς [sc. τοῖς πατράσιν] ὅπερ οἱ φιλόσοφοι λέγουσιν εἶδος †Leont.B.*sect.*1.1(M.86.1193A); τὴν μὲν φ. ἤτοι οὐσίαν καὶ μορφὴν τὸ κοινὸν σημαίνειν, τὴν δὲ ὑπόστασιν ἤτοι πρόσωπον τὸ ἰδικόν Justn.*conf.*(p.86.20; M.86.1009C); παρῆκται... αὐτὸ τὸ ὄνομα τῆς φ. παρὰ τὸ πεφυκέναι, τουτέστιν ὑπάρχειν. ὥστε τὸ αὐτὸ σημαίνει τὸ ὄνομα τῆς οὐσίας καὶ τῆς φ. ... ἀμφότερα γὰρ δηλοῦσιν τὴν ὕπαρξιν Thdr.Raith.*praep.*(p.202.18ff.); περὶ τῆς φ. δεῖ γινώσκειν, ὅτι ἄλλο τι παρὰ τὴν οὐσίαν οἱ ἔξω σοφοὶ παραδεδώκασι ταύτην...τοὺς δὲ...πατέρας...τοῖς τοιούτοις ὀνόμασι κέχρηνται, τὴν αὐτὴν οὐσίαν καὶ φ. ἀποκαλοῦντες Pamph.H.*panopl.*2.5(p.604); κοινὸν...καὶ καθολικόν, ἤγουν γενικόν, κατὰ τοὺς πατέρας, ἡ οὐσία καὶ ἡ φ.· ταὐτὸν γὰρ ἀλλήλαις ταύτας ὑπάρχειν φασίν. ἴδιον δὲ καὶ μερικόν, ἡ ὑπόστασις καὶ τὸ πρόσωπον Max.*ep.*15(M.91.545A); οὐσία καὶ φ., ταὐτό· ἄμφω γὰρ κοινὸν καὶ καθόλου. ὡς κατὰ πολλῶν καὶ διαφερόντων τῷ ἀριθμῷ κατηγορούμενα id.*opusc.*(M.91.149B); Anast.S.*hod.*2(M.89.57A); treated as synonymous or parallel τὰ προηγούμενα τῶν...εἰδῶν... τὴν οὐσίαν καὶ φ. διασημαίνει τοῦ πράγματος Clem.*str.*8.6(p.93.9; M.9. 585D); ἐπιούσιος...ἄρτος ὁ τῇ φ. τῇ λογικῇ καταλληλότατος καὶ τῇ οὐσίᾳ αὐτῇ συγγενής Or.*or.*27(p.369.19; M.11.513A); εἰς δύο τὸ πᾶν διαιρούντων εἴς τε νοητὸν καὶ αἰσθητόν, καὶ τὸ μὲν νοητὸν ἀσώματον καὶ λογικὸν τὴν φ. ... ὁριζομένων τὸ δ' αἰσθητὸν ἐν ῥύσει καὶ φθορᾷ μεταβολῇ τε καὶ τροπῇ τῆς οὐσίας ὑπάρχειν Eus.*p.e.*11.9(524A; M.21. 868D); τίς οὖν τῆς γῆς ἡ οὐσία;...οὐδὲ τῆς γῆς...τὴν φ., ἥτις ἐστίν, ἐπιστάμενοι Bas.*Eun.*1.12f.(1.225A,E; M.29.540C,541C); Gr.Nyss. *Eun.*8(2 p.202.29; M.45.800B); τὸ...τῆς θεότητος καὶ τῆς ἀνθρωπότητος ὄνομα τῶν οὐσιῶν ἤτοι τῶν φ. ἐστὶ παραστατικόν Jo.D.*f.o.*3.4(M. 94 997A); Trin., v. III.A.1; 2. dist. οὐσία ἐστὶν τὸ δι' ὅλου ὑφεστός. φ. ἐστὶν ἡ τῶν πραγμάτων ἀλήθεια ἢ τούτων τὸ ἐνούσιον, κατὰ δὲ τοὺς ἄλλους ἡ τῶν εἰς τὸ εἶναι παραγενομένων γένεσις, καθ' ἑτέρους δὲ ἡ τοῦ θεοῦ πρόνοια ἐμποιοῦσα τοῖς γενομένοις τὸ εἶναι καὶ τὸ πῶς εἶναι Clem. *fr.*37(p.219.19; M.9.752A); οὐκ ἂν ἐγένετο εἰ φ. ἦν ταῦτα, καὶ εἰς τὸν λόγον τῆς οὐσίας ἀνήγετο. οὐ γάρ ἐστι δυνατὸν τὸν ἔξω γεγονότα τῆς φ. ἐν τῷ εἶναι μένειν...ἀληθῶς φ. τοῦτό ἐστιν, ἐν ᾧ τὸ εἶναι τῆς οὐσίας καταλαμβάνεται Gr.Nyss.*anim.et res.*(M.46.53C); τὴν μὲν ἁπλῶς ὕπαρξιν, ἐπὶ τῆς οὐσίας οἱ πατέρες ἔλαβον· τὴν δὲ ποιάν, ἐπὶ τῆς φ. τὸ προσὸν μᾶλλον καὶ πεφυκὸς ταῖς οὐσίαις ἰδίως, εἴτε κατ' ἐνέργειαν εἴτε κατὰ δύναμιν φ. ἀποκαλέσαντες Pamph.H.*panopl.*2.6(p.606); τούτοις [sc. τοῖς πατράσι] ἑπόμενοι...ἐν τοῖς τοῦ θεοῦ καὶ σωτῆρος ἡμῶν... δόγμασι τὴν αὐτὴν οὐσίαν καὶ φ. ὀνομάζοντες. καθ' ἑτέραν δὲ ἐπίνοιαν ἀκριβέστερον τὸν περὶ τούτων γυμνάζοντες λόγον, καὶ διαφορὰν τούτων εἰπεῖν δυνάμεθα. τὸ μὲν γὰρ τῆς φ. ὄνομα φερόμενον εὑρίσκομεν, καταχρηστικῶς κατὰ ἀνυποστάτων, καὶ κατὰ τῶν ἐν οὐσίᾳ καὶ ὑποστάσει ἰδίᾳ θεωρουμένων· τὸ δὲ τῆς οὐσίας ὄνομα, κατὰ ἐνυποστάτων μόνον· οὐσίαν γὰρ οὐκ ἂν εἴπομεν ἀνυπόστατον· φύσεις δὲ πολλὰς εὑρίσκομεν ἀνυποστάτους καθ' ἑαυτὰς δίχα οὐσίας μηδέ ποτε ὑφεστώσας, ὡς θυμοῦ, καὶ ἀγάπης, καὶ χρόνου, καὶ ψεύδους *ib.*2.5(p.604f.); οὐσίαν...καλοῦσι τὴν ἁπλῶς τῶν ὄντων ὕπαρξιν, φ. δὲ τὴν ἁπλῶς τῶν ὄντων κίνησιν Anast.S.*qu.et resp.*154(M.89.824B); οἱ μὲν ἔξω φιλόσοφοι...διαφορὰν εἶπον οὐσίας καὶ φ., οὐσίαν μὲν εἰπόντες τὸ ἁπλῶς εἶναι· φ. δὲ οὐσίαν εἰδοποιηθεῖσαν ὑπὸ τῶν οὐσιωδῶν διαφορῶν, καὶ μετὰ τὸ ἁπλῶς εἶναι, καὶ τὸ τοιῶσδε εἶναι ἔχουσαν...ταύτην ἐκάλεσαν 'φ.' ἤγουν τὰ εἰδικώτατα εἴδη...ὡς καθολικώτερα καὶ περιεκτικὰ τῶν ὑποστάσεων, καὶ ἐν ἑκάστῃ τῶν...ὑποστάσεων ὁμοίως καὶ ἀπαραλείπτως ὑπάρχοντα Jo.D.*dialect.*30(M.94.589C).

D. φ. and ὑπόστασις; 1. opposed: v. ὑπόστασις; theol.: Gr.Nyss. *diff.ess.*4(M.32.333A); id.*Eun.*2(2 p.301.22; M.45.472D); *ib.*7(2 p.155. 15; 744B); *ib.*(2 p.168.3; 757C); Cyr.*Is.*3 5(2.540A) cit. s. ὑπόστασις; Christol. v. ὑπόστασις; 2. // ὑπόστασις: αὔταρκες ἡμῖν εἰδέναι ταῦτα ...φ. δὲ ἢ ὑπόστασιν μὴ πολυπραγμόνει Cyr.H.*catech.*16.24; τί γὰρ ὄντι αὐτῷ [sc. θεῷ] κατὰ τὴν φ. καὶ τὴν ὑπόστασιν ὑπάρχει τὸ μὴ ἀρχὴν ἔχειν; Gr.Naz.*or.*28.9(p.35.8; M.36.37A); Christol. v. ὑπόστασις.

II. in gen. contexts;

A. *nature*; *essence* of a person or thing *with the attributes proper to it*; *essence* considered from the point of view of activity or function; 1. divine *nature* τὴν ἀγένητον τοῦ θεοῦ φ. Or.*Cels.*4.38(p.311.2; M.11.1089B); κατὰ διττὸν...τρόπον τὰ οὐσιωδῶς προσόντα τῇ θείᾳ φ. πλεονεκτήματα δηλοῦν εἰθίσμεθα. ἢ γὰρ ἀφ' ὧν ἐστιν, ἢ ἀφ' ὧν οὐκ ἔστιν Cyr.*dial.Trin.*1(5[1].415B); of God in himself ὁ δὲ θεὸς...ἐν πᾶσι μέν ἐστι κατὰ τὴν ἑαυτοῦ ἀγαθότητα καὶ δύναμιν, ἔξω δὲ τῶν πάντων πάλιν ἐστὶ κατὰ τὴν ἰδίαν φ. Ath.*decr.*11(p.10.4; M.25.'441'(433)D); τίς δέ ἐστι [sc. God] τὴν φ., οὐκ ἀπεκάλυψεν ‡Ath.*dial.Trin.*2.27(M.28. 1197D); τὸ τῆς θείας φ. ἀθεώρητον Gr.Nyss.*v.Mos.*(M.44.376D); id. *deit.*(M.46.573D); ὅτι μὲν γὰρ ὑφέστηκε καὶ ἔστι θεός, πιστεύομεν· τί δὲ κατὰ φ. ἐστίν, ἀπηχὲς ἐρευνᾶν...νοῦ γὰρ ἐπέκεινα παντὸς ἡ θεοῦ φ. Cyr.*dial.Trin.*4(5[1].511C,D); and of God manifesting himself *ad extra* τὸ ἀγαθοποιεῖν, φ. ... αὕτη τοῦ θεοῦ ὡς τοῦ πυρὸς τὸ θερμαίνειν Clem. *str.*1.17(p.55.26; M.8.801A); ‡Gr.Nyss.*hom.*4.47 *in Jo.*(p.171.21); and because God is his φ., of God himself τίς δ' ἂν εἴποι τὸ Μωυσέως ἔργον, δάκτυλον εἶναι τῆς τοῦ θεοῦ φ. Diod.*Gen.*6:6(M.33.1571A); προσβαίνει τῷ ὄρει...τῇ θείᾳ φ. προσηγγισεν Gr.Nyss.*v.Mos.*(M.44. 425D); ὑπὸ πόδας...ἔχει τὴν κτίσιν ἡ ἀνωτάτω φ. Cyr.*Jul.*3(6[2].100E); CNic.(787)*act.*7(H.4.456B); 2. of incorporeal creation τῶν ἀσωμάτων καὶ ὧν ἡ φ. τὸ ἔκ τινος ὕλης εἶναι διαπέφυγε Cyr.*thes.*12(5[1].107B); of angels γεννητοῦ παντὸς ἥδε ἡ φ., κακίας καὶ ἀρετῆς δεκτικὸν εἶναι Just. *2apol.*7.6(M.6.456C); ἄγγελοι...καὶ τὴν φ. καὶ τὴν τάξιν ἀνώτεροι [sc. than other creatures] Ath.*hom.in Mt.11:27*(M.25.217C); ἄλλον [sc. τὸν υἱόν] εἶναι τῆς τῶν ἀγγέλων φ. id.*Ar.*1.57(M.26.132B); of demons, id.*v.Anton.*21(M.26.876A); φιλοσόφει...περὶ λογικῶν φ. βελτιόνων τε καὶ χειρόνων Gr.Naz.*or.*27.10(p.20.6; M.36.25A); of heathen deities εἰ ...μία φ. τῶν θεῶν ὑπῆρχεν Arist.*apol.*13.5; 3. human *nature* τὸ ἀδύνατον τῆς ἡμετέρας φ. εἰς τὸ τυχεῖν ζωῆς *Diogn.*9.6; ἐκ τῆς ἐκείνου [sc. τοῦ θεοῦ] ὑπεροχῆς, οὐκ ἐκ τῆς ἡμετέρας φ., τὴν εἰς ἀεὶ παραμονὴν ἔχομεν Iren.*haer.*5.2.3(M.7.1127C); ἀπὸ τοῦ εἶναι ἄγγελοι ἐπὶ τὴν ἀνθρωπίνην καταβεβήκασι φ. Or.*Jo.*2.31(25; p.88.23; M.14.168D); ὅπερ...ἐπὶ τοῦ κοινοῦ ἀνθρώπου ἐκ δύο μερῶν ἀτελῶν γίνεται, φ. μίαν πληρούντων καὶ ἑνὶ ὀνόματι δηλουμένων Apoll.*corp.et div.*5(p.187.11)ap.Leont.H. *monoph.*(M.86.1865B); πρὸ τούτου ἡ ἀνθρωπίνη φ. εὐκατάλλακτος ἦν, οἷον ἐπὶ τῶν ἁγίων καὶ πρὸ τοῦ νόμου Chrys.*hom.*5.3 *in Eph.*(11. 36A); ἡμεῖς...καὶ ὁ Ἀδὰμ μιᾶς φ. ἔσμεν Marc.Er.*opusc.*4(M.65.1013C); ἵνα τὸ κοινωνὸν τῆς φ. ἐπιγινώσκουσι, κατὰ τὸ δυνατὸν κοινωνοῦντες τοῖς δικαίοι κοινωνίας οὐχ ἔχουσι πλὴν τοῦ κατὰ φ. ὅτι ἄνθρωποι Proc.G.*Lev.*19:9(M.87.757A); ἡ φ. τῶν ἀνθρώπων κοινωνική ἐστι τῶν πνευμάτων τῆς πονηρίας [Messalian] Jo.D.*haer.*80(M.94.729A); as never free from sin since Fal]v. ἀναμάρτητος; of ψυχή in partic. τὸ 'θεὸς' οὐκ ὄνομά ἐστιν, ἀλλὰ πράγματος δυσεξηγήτου ἔμφυτος τῇ φ. τῶν ἀνθρώπων δόξα Just.2apol.6.3(M.6.453B); ἔχουσι μέν τι οἰκεῖον φύσεως ἰδίωμα οἱ σοφοί Clem.str.1.4(p.17.4; M.8.716C); τὸ... προαιρεῖσθαι...λογικῆς φ. ἐστι...πάθος Ath.Ar.3.62(M.26.453C); of Christ ὁ μὲν Παῦλος τῆς νοερᾶς φ. τὴν μαρτυρίαν ποιεῖται, ὁ δὲ Ἰωάννης τῆς ὀργανικῆς τοῦ σώματος ἐπιδείξεως ‡Ath.Apoll.2.1(M.26.1133A); ἐδάκρυσε...ἀληθῶς τὴν φ. τὴν ἡμετέραν περιεβάλετο Chrys.hom.63.2 in Jo.(8.377C); of body in partic. ἡ ὅρασις φύσεώς ἐστιν ἐνέργεια Gr.Nyss.or.catech.5(p.27.11; M.45.24D); ἡ τῶν παίδων... ἀνθρωπίνη φ. ... τῇ σώματος...περιεπάτει ἐνεργείᾳ, καὶ...τέλειος ἦν Ἀζαρίας ἐν πυρότητι καὶ ἐν ἀνθρωπότητι Ephr.Ant.fr.(M.86.2108B); ‡Jo.D.Artem.61(M.96.1309A); of Christ τῇ...τοῦ λόγου εἰς αὐτὸ ἐπιβάσει, οὐκέτι κατὰ τὴν ἰδίαν φ. ἐφθείρετο [sc. τὸ σῶμα] Ath.inc.20.4 (M.25.132B); **4.** *nature, substance* of created things in gen. τὴν λογικὴν ψυχὴν...κρείττονα πάσης σωματικῆς φ. Or.Cels.6.71(p.141.21; M.11.1405C); τὸ βάπτισμα...ὅπερ ἐστὶ θεότητος ἔργον καὶ οὐ κτιστῆς φ. Apoll.fid.inc.7(p.199.23; M.PL.8.877D); Gr.Nyss.hex.31(M.44.91C); Thdr.Mops.Gal.1:4f.(p.5.18; M.66.897D); **5.** of a particular substance πυρὸς φ. χρυσὸν μὲν καθαίρει, μόλιβδον δὲ τήκει κτλ. Eus.d.e.4.5(p.157.15; M.22.261D); ἥνωται τῇ φ. τοῦ ἡλίου τὸ ἐξ αὐτοῦ φῶς Ath.hom.in Mt.11:27(M.25.216A); id.ep.Aeg.Lib.13(M.25.568C); Cyr.H.catech.9.9 cit. s. ἐνέργεια; πάσης...τῆς τῶν ὑδάτων φ. κατὰ τὴν Αἴγυπτον...εἰς αἷμα τραπείσης Gr.Nyss.v.Mos.26(M.44.308C); μετασκευάσαντος εἰς οἶνον τὴν τοῦ ὕδατος φ. Cyr.Jo.3.4(4.278A); of eucharistic elements τῇ τῆς εὐλογίας δυνάμει πρὸς ἐκεῖνο [sc. τὸ ἀθάνατον] μεταστοιχειώσας τῶν φαινομένων τὴν φ. Gr.Nyss.or.catech.37(p.152.8; M.45.97B); also of parts of man not existing in themselves οὐ γὰρ ἄλλη θεοῦ μὲν δυνάμει κεφαλῆς ὑπέστη φ., ἄλλη δὲ ὀφθαλμῶν Eus.d.e.4.5(p.155.23; M.22.260B); ref. soul and body ἑκατέρᾳ τῇ φ. Chrys.hom.15.1 in Mt.(7.185A); **6.** collectively, that which is characterized by φ.; **a.** *kind, sort, species* ἐπὶ τῶν κρειττόνων δυνάμεων τὰ ὀνόματα οὐχὶ φύσεων ζῴων ἐστὶν ὀνόματα ἀλλὰ τάξεων Or.Jo.2.23(17; p.79.17; M.14.153A); οὐκ ἀνθρώπους μόνον, ἀλλὰ καὶ πᾶσαν λογικὴν φ. Bas.Eun.1.14(1.226B; M.29.544A); τὴν νηκτὴν φ. Gr.Naz.or.28.4(p.58.4; M.36.57D); Mac.Mgn.apocr.3.11(p.76.14); esp. of men ἐπὶ τῷ βοηθεῖν τῇ τῶν ἀνθρώπων φ. Or.hom.13.1 in Jer.(p.102.12; M.13.400B); id.mart.10(p.10.15; M.11.576C); ἡ ἀνθρωπίνη φ. ... καὶ τὸ ἀγγελικὸν τάγμα Apoll.corp.et div.11(p.190.3; M.PL.8.874D); Didym.Trin.3.21(M.39.904D); **b.** abs. the *race of men, mankind* καθάπερ ἑνός τινος ὄντος ζῴου πάσης τῆς φ. ἡ τοῦ μέρους ἀνάστασις ἐπὶ τὸ πᾶν διεξέρχεται κατὰ τὸ συνεχὲς...τῆς φ. ἐκ τοῦ μέρους ἐπὶ τὸ ὅλον συνεκδιδομένη Gr.Nyss.or.catech.32(p.117.4; M.45.80B); οὐκ εἶπεν, ὁ Ἰουδαῖος, ἀλλὰ πᾶσα ἡ φ. Chrys.hom.7.1 in Rom.(9.483D); Thdt.qu.53 in Gen.(1.66); Bas.Sel.or.34.1(M.85.368A); **c.** in wider sense, *creation, world* οὐδὲ αἱ νοηταὶ φ. ... ἀδικηθεῖεν ἂν...οὐδὲ τῶν ἀλόγων ἡ φ. Athenag.res.10(p.58.14,17; M.6.992B); Or.Cels.7.46(p.198.15; M.11.1490A); τῆς ὑποστάσεως αὐτοῦ [sc. Son] πάσῃ τῇ γενητῇ φ. ἀπεριεργάστου τυγχανούσης Alex.Al.ep.Alex.12(p.27.8; M.18.565B); Eus.ep.Caes.6(p.45.20; M.20.1541B); [sc. τὸν υἱόν] τῆς...τῶν γενητῶν ἀποδιορίζοντες φ. τε καὶ ὁμοειδίας...θεὸν ἐκ θεοῦ κατὰ φ. ὁμολογήσομεν Cyr.Jo.1.5(4.45A); Didym.Trin.1.34(M.39.436A); **7.** *character*; **a.** of men οὐδὲ τῆς αὐτῆς φ. κατόρθωμα τὸ συντακτικὸν καὶ διδασκαλικὸν εἶδος εἶναι Clem.ecl.27.2(p.144.29; M.9.712B); Hipp.haer.4.22(p.52.16; M.16.3087A); φ. εἰμὶ τοιαύτης καὶ οὐ δύναμαι μὴ ὀργίζεσθαι ‡Just.ep.Zen.et Ser.2(M.6.1184C); φύσιν στοργῆς πρὸς τοὺς γεννήσαντας οὐκ ἔχοντες Hom.Clem.5.24; Chrys.hom.21.4 in Ac.(9.168A); **b.** *second nature* [ref. τοὺς ἁμαρτάνειν πεφυκότας τε καὶ εἰθισμένους] φ. γὰρ ἀμεῖψαι τελέως παγχάλεπον Cels.ap.Or.Cels.3.65 (p.259.11; M.11.1005C); εἰ...ἡ χλιαρότης καὶ ἡ νωθρεία φ. ἀπέστησαν, πολλῷ μᾶλλον ἡ σπουδὴ καὶ νῆψις φ. πάλιν γενέσθαι δυνήσεται Nil.epp.3.318(M.79.537B); ἕξις μὲν ἀπὸ συνηθείας, ἀπὸ δὲ ἕξεως φ. ἐγγίνεσθαι εἴωθεν ib.2.239(321C); **c.** *character, nature, constitution* of things, qualities, activities, Iren.haer.1.2.5(M.7.461A); τὸ τῆς νεότητος ὅσον ἐπὶ τῇ φ. ἄστατον Or.princ.3.1.5(p.201.2; M.11.256A); κρύπτει...ὑπὸ τὸ μέλι τὴν τοῦ πικροῦ φ. id.hom.20.3 in Jer.(p.180.16; M.13.505A); ἐν τῇ φ. τῶν ὄντων μία ἡ περὶ ἑκάστου ἀλήθεια id.Jo.2.4(p.58.23; M.14.116C); εἰκὸς...εἶναι ἐν τῇ φ. τῶν πραγμάτων...φ. τοιαύτην, ὡς ἕνα δίκαιον ὑπὲρ τοῦ κοινοῦ ἀποθανόντα ἑκουσίως id.Cels.1.31(p.82.26; M.11.720A); πᾶσαν ἀνθρώπινον λογισμοῦ χωρητικὴν φ. ἡ τοῦ θαύματος τούτου πίστις ὑπερβαίνει Const.ap.Eus.v.C.3.30(p.91.31; M.20.1089C); τὴν φ. τῆς σωματικῆς οὐσίας...ἄλογον...καὶ...ἄψυχον Eus.p.e.7.3 (301C; M.21.512B); οὐ τῶν πολλῶν εἷς ἦν οὗτος· οὐδὲ γὰρ ἔχει ταύτην τὴν φ. ἀστὴρ οὐδὲ εἷς Chrys.hom.7.3 in Mt.(7.109A); *function* αὕτη...τῶν ἰδιωμάτων ἡ φ. ἐν τῇ τῆς οὐσίας ταυτότητι δεικνύναι τὴν ἑτερότητα Bas.Eun.2.28(1.265C; M.29.637C); **8.** ref. Gnost. determinism τὴν ἄφθαρτον τῆς ἐκλογῆς φ. Heracleon ap.Or.Jo.13.51(50; p.280.2; M.14.493B); ἀνθρώπων...τρία γένη ὑφίστανται [sc. Valentinians] πνευματικόν, χοϊκόν, ψυχικόν Iren.haer.1.7.5(M.7.517B); ib.1.7.3(516B); τῶν μὴ βιούντων ὀρθῶς Βασιλειδιανῶν, ὡς...σωθησομένων φύσει Clem.str.3.1(p.196.19; M.8.1104A); παρέλκουσι...αἱ ἐντολαὶ...φύσει σῳζομένου, ὡς Οὐαλεντῖνος βούλεται, τινὸς καὶ φύσει πιστοῦ καὶ ἐκλεκτοῦ ὄντος, ὡς Βασιλείδης νομίζει ib.5.1(p.327.26f.; M.9.12C); μία...ἐστι...ἡ μακαρία φ. τοῦ μακαρίου ἀνθρώπου τοῦ ἄνω, τοῦ Ἀδάμαντος· μία δὲ ἡ θνητὴ κάτω Hipp.haer.5.8(p.89.11; M.16.3139B); ᾔδει [sc. the Naassene] ἐξ ὁποίας φ. ἕκαστος τῶν μαθητῶν αὐτοῦ ἐστι, καὶ ὅτι ἕκαστον αὐτῶν εἰς τὴν ἰδίαν φ. ἐλθεῖν ἀνάγκη ib.(p.91.10f.; 3142Cf.); τοῖς οἰομένοις αὐτὸν [sc. Ἰούδα] φύσει ἀνεπίδεκτον σωτηρίας Or.Jo.32.19(12; p.459.2; 796A); ib.28.21(16; p.415.18; 724D); id.princ.3.1.8(p.207.1ff.; M.11.261Af.); orthodox reply ἡμῖν μὲν ἀναγκαῖον εἶναι τὴν ἀγαθὴν πρᾶξιν...ἄλλως γὰρ ἀδύνατον σωθῆναι, αὐτοὺς δὲ μὴ διὰ πράξεως, ἀλλὰ διὰ τὸ φύσει πνευματικοὺς εἶναι, πάντη τε καὶ πάντως σωθήσεσθαι δογματίζουσιν Iren.haer.1.6.2(M.7.505B); εἰ φύσει οἱ μὲν φαῦλοι, οἱ δὲ ἀγαθοὶ γεγόνασιν, οὐθ' οὗτοι ἐπαινετοὶ...οὔτ' ἐκεῖνοι μεμπτοί...ἀλλ' ἐπειδὴ οἱ πάντες τῆς αὐτῆς εἰσι φ., δυνάμενοί τε κατασχεῖν καὶ πρᾶξαι τὸ ἀγαθόν, καὶ δυνάμενοι...μὴ ποιῆσαι, δικαίως καὶ παρ' ἀνθρώποις ...καὶ...παρὰ θεῷ, οἱ μὲν ἐπαινοῦνται...οἱ δὲ καταιτιῶνται ib.4.37.2 (1100B); παριστάντες τῷ λόγῳ φ. εἶναι ὑποκειμένας διαφόρους τῶν ὑπὸ τὴν σαγήνην ἐληλυθότων πονηρῶν καὶ δικαίων...οὐ φ. ἐν ἡμῖν αἰτία τῆς πονηρίας, ἀλλὰ προαίρεσις Or.comm.in Mt.10.11(p.12.9,24; M.13.860A,C); **9.** φύσει as adv., *essentially, intrinsically, by nature* τὰ καθόλου καὶ φ. καὶ αἰώνια καλὰ ἐποίουν Just.dial.45.4(M.6.572C); οὐ φ. ὄντων, ἀλλὰ γενομένων Athenag.leg.19.2(p.22.2; M.6.929B); φ. μὲν γεγόναμεν πρὸς ἀρετήν, οὐ μὴν ὥστε ἔχειν αὐτὴν ἐκ γενετῆς, ἀλλὰ πρὸς τὸ κτήσασθαι ἐπιτήδειοι Clem.str.6.11(p.480.3; M.9.317A); cf. οὐκ ἔστι τῇ φ. πονηρὸν ἢ ἀγαθόν, ἀλλὰ νόμῳ διαφέρει καὶ ἔθει Hom.Clem.19.19; οὐ διδακτόν, ἀλλὰ φ. τὸ εἰδέναι θεὸν τοῖς ἀνθρώποις ὑπάρχει Juln.Imp.ap.Cyr.Juln.2(6².52B); opp. θέσει: κατὰ...τὴν αὐτοῦ [sc. Simon Magus'] χάριν σῴζεσθαι αὐτοὺς φάσκουσι· μηδὲν γὰρ εἶναι αἴτιον δίκης εἰ πράξει τις κακῶς, οὐ γάρ ἐστι φ. κακός, ἀλλὰ θέσει Iren.haer.1.23.3(cf.M.7.672B); πότερον...θέσει εἰσὶ τὰ ὀνόματα ἢ...φ., μιμουμένων τῶν πρώτων φωνῶν τὰ πράγματα Or.Cels.1.24(p.10.13; M.11.704A); also κατὰ φύσιν: ἄνθρωπος κατὰ φ. οὔτε ψυχὴ χωρὶς σώματος οὔτ' αὖ πάλιν σῶμα χωρὶς ψυχῆς Meth.res.1.34(p.272.7; M.18.292B); ὁ...ἀνδριάς...ἡ τεχνητὴ...εἰκὼν...οὐδὲ κατὰ φ. ... ἐκφαίνουσι τὸν πρωτότυπον Didym.Trin.1.16(M.39.336C); Cyr.Jo.2.1(4.128A); **10.** κατὰ φύσιν *according to one's nature* ὁπόταν ὁ ἄνθρωπος ἀναδράμῃ εἰς τὸ κατὰ φ., μηκέτι κακοποιῶν Thphl.Ant.Autol.2.17(M.6.1081A); Ath.v.Anton.14(M.26.865A).

B. *nature* as manifest in physical world; **1.** *nature* as an originating power, *order of nature, law of nature* φύσεως κρείττων ὁ θεός, καὶ παρ' αὐτῷ τὸ θέλειν Iren.haer.2.29.2(M.7.813B); ἐν τῷ τῆς φ. ἐργαστηρίῳ διαπλαττομένου τοῦ σπέρματος εἰς ἔμβρυον Clem.str.3.12(p.234.13; M.8.1184C); ib.4.23(p.315.3; 1360B); Or.Cels.6.60(p.131.1; M.11.1389C); πῶς...ἡ φ. τῷ προστάγματι μάχοιτο τοῦ θεοῦ; Juln.Imp.ap.Cyr.Juln.4(6².143C); οὐκ ἔστιν αὕτη [sc. servitude of one man to another] φύσεως ἡ δουλεία, ἀλλ' αἰτίας ἐστὶ καὶ περιστάσεως Chrys.hom.16.2 in 1Tim.(11.646C); freq. with νόμος (q.v.): παρὰ τὸν τῆς φ. νόμον...πόρους ἡδονῆς...ποιεῖσθαι Just.2apol.2.4(M.6.444B); τὰ θηρία τῶν ὁμογενῶν οὐχ ἅπτεται καὶ νόμῳ φ. καὶ πρὸς ἕνα καιρὸν τὸν τῆς τεκνοποιΐας...μίγνυνται Athenag.leg.3.1(p.4.20; M.6.896C); Eus.h.e.8.13.12(M.20.780A); Bas.Eun.2.30(1.267Aff.; M.29.641Bff.); or ἀνάγκη: κατὰ ἀπαραίτητον φύσεως ἀνάγκην Arist.apol.4.2; πάσχει [sc. Christ] ...οὐκ ἀνάγκῃ φ. ἀβουλήτου καθάπερ ἄνθρωπος, ἀλλ' ἀκολουθίᾳ φύσεως Apoll.fr.102(p.231.10f.) cited and commented ἐν τίνι διαφέρειν βλέπει τὴν ἀνάγκην τῆς φ. καὶ τὴν ἀκολουθίαν τῆς φ.; Gr.Nyss.Apoll.58(M.45.1265D); ἡ...φ. ἀναγκαστικόν τί ἐστι καὶ ἀβούλητον χρῆμα Thdt.ap.Cyr.apol.Thdt.3(p.116.19; 6.210C); cf. μεγάλη...ἡ τῆς φ. τυραννὶς καὶ ἄμαχος ἡ τῶν ὠδίνων ἀνάγκη Chrys.stat.17.2(2.172E); *natural position* εἰς τὴν ἑαυτῶν ἠφίεσαν τοὺς κλάδους φέρεσθαι φ. Eus.h.e.8.9.2(M.20.760B); opp. συνήθεια: τῆς συνηθείας οὐ πολὺ ἔλαττον πρὸς τὴν φ. δυναμένης Hom.Clem.4.18; **2.** *the natural world, creation*, Tat.orat.21 (p.24.9; M.6.853B); ὁ διὰ πάσης φ. ἑαυτὸν γνωρίσας A.Jo.112(p.211.5); συνέχων ἐν τῷ εἶναι τὴν φ. Gr.Nyss.or.catech.25(p.96.4; M.45.65D); of universe πᾶσαν τὴν σωματικὴν φ. CCP(543)anath.6(p.228; H.3.285A); οὐδὲ ἐν τῇ ὅλῃ φ. τὸ κακόν...φύσεως δὲ κακία τὸ παρὰ φύσιν, ἡ στέρησις τῶν τῆς φ. Dion.Ar.d.n.4.26(M.3.728C); **3.** of persons; *creature, being* πᾶσα γενητὴ φ. τὰς ἐπιθυμίας τοῦ ἰδίου πατρὸς θέλει ποιεῖν Or.Jo.20.22(20; p.355.22; M.14.621C); ὥσπερ...κατὰ κεφαλῆς δίδωσίν σοι τὴν τιμωρίαν, οὕτως κἀγὼ...εἰς τὴν ἐμαυτοῦ φ. ἀποστέλλομαι A.Thom.A 76(p.191.4); cf. ὁ τὴν φ. ἡμῶν διαγελῶν καὶ τὴν γενεάν ib.75(p.190.12); αἱ διάφοροι φ. καὶ τὰ διάφορα πρόσωπα ἕνα καὶ μόνον ἑνώσεως τρόπον τὴν κατὰ θέλησιν σύμβασιν Paul.Sam.*fr.*F 5(p.339.8) ap.*Doct.Patr.*(p.303.26); ὥσπερ τὸ γάλα ἀμελχθὲν τυρὸς γίνεται, οὕτω καὶ τὸ σπέρμα ἀποστάξαν καὶ συστραφὲν φ. γίνεται Chrys.*fr.Job* 10:10 (M.64.605D); τῇ φ. *in person* βούλομαί σε...τῇ φ., ἐν τῷ πυλῶνι...παρίστασθαι Jo.Clim.*scal.*4(M.88.689A); in derogatory sense, *creature*, addressed to a soul ὦ φ. μὴ καταβαλλομένη πρὸς τὸ κρεῖττον...ὦ οὐσία φθορᾶς σκότους πλήρης *A.Jo.*84(p.192.17); to persons ὦ ἀσθενὴς φ., ἥτις ἐπαίρει μὲν ἑαυτὴν ἐφ' ἡμᾶς *A.Phil.*18(p.10.1); ὦ τῶν κακῶν πορισμωτάτη φ. Leont.B.*Nest.et Eut.*3.28(M.86.1372B); **4.** *elementary substance* τῶν ὑλικῶν συμπάντων ἀποίου φ. ... δίκην Athenag.*leg.*10.2(p.11.11; M.6.909A); φ. αἰῶνος ἐξ ἧς πάντες ἔφυσαν *ib.*22.6(p.28.2; 940A); πέμπτην...φ. σωμάτων παρὰ τὰ στοιχεῖα Or.*Jo.*13.21(p.245.4; M.14.433A); *A.Thom.*A 37(p.155.10); Cyr.H.*catech.*9.5; Gr.Naz.*or.*28.4(p.58.5; M.36.57D); ἀπὸ ποίων φ. ἐτμήθη τὰ ὄρη; Epiph.*haer.*64.66(p.508.15; M.41.1185A); *M.Thdot.1* 25(p.77.2); other *substance, stuff* πῶς ἀπὸ γῆς γέγονε σαρκὸς φ.; Chrys.*serm.1.2 in Gen.*(4.648B); προσκυνοῦντες τὸν σταυρόν, οὐ τὴν φ. τοῦ ξύλου...ἀλλὰ τὸν σταυρωθέντα ἐν αὐτῷ *Dial.Christ.et Jud.*1(p.51.15); κἀγὼ τὴν εἰκόνα τοῦ θεοῦ προσκυνῶν, οὐ τὴν φ. τῶν ξύλων καὶ χρωμάτων προσκυνῶ...ἀλλὰ τὸν ἄψυχον χαρακτῆρα Χριστοῦ κρατῶν, δι' αὐτοῦ Χριστὸν κρατεῖν δοκῶ καὶ προσκυνεῖν Leont.N.*serm.*3(M.93.1600C); eucharistic, v. οὐσία; **5.** *physical constitution, body* τοῖς μὲν διάφορα σχήματα φύσεως δίδονται καὶ μορφαί Meth.*res.*1.35(p.274.2; M.18.292C); Bas.*hom.*5.9(2.43B; M.31.260C); of Christ εἰ...τὴν φ. ἐξ ἀνθρώπων ἔσχεν, ἀλλὰ τὴν ζωὴν ἐκ θεοῦ Apoll.*fr.*6(p.205.25)ap.Thdt.*eran.*2(4.174); **6.** φύσιν ἔχω; **a.** *be natural to* [*one*] τοῦ ἀγαθοῦ φ. ἔχοντος τὰ ὅμοια ἑαυτῷ καὶ ὁμοούσια γεννᾶν τε καὶ προφέρειν Ptol.*ep.*ap.Epiph.*haer.*33.7(p.457.12; M.41.568B); **b.** *be possible for one* ἐλπίδι τοῦ γενέσθαι ὃ μὴ ἔχει φ. *Hom.Clem.*3.24; οὐκ ἔχει φ. μὴ εἶναι [sc. Christ], οὐ δυνατόν Chrys.*hom.*5.2 *in 2Tim.*(11.686F); φ. οὐκ εἶχεν εἰς ᾅδου καταλιμπάνεσθαι Leont.B.*Nest.et Eut.*2(M.86.1341B); Max.*opusc.*(M.91.208C); **c.** impers., *it is possible* θνητοῖς ὄμμασι...οὐκ ἔχει φ. τὰ θεῖα καταλαμβάνεσθαι Eus.*l.C.*10(p.223.21; M.20.1373D); οὐκ ἔχει φ. τὸ αὐτὸ καὶ τέλειον καὶ...ἀτελὲς ὀνομάζειν Gr.Nyss.*ep.*24(M.46.1093A); Leont.B.*arg.Sev.*(M.86.1924B); **7.** phrases; **a.** φύσει as adv. and κατὰ φύσιν *naturally* ἄμωμον διάνοιαν...ὑμᾶς ἔχοντας, οὐ κατὰ χρῆσιν ἀλλὰ κατὰ φ. Ign.*Trall.*1.1; τὸ πολυαγάπητον ὄνομα ὃ κέκτησθε φ. id.*Eph.*1.1; ἡ...γνῶσις κατὰ φ. προηγεῖται τῆς πίστεως Marc.Er.*opusc.*1.112(M.65.920A); opp. θέσει: τίς δὲ ἤκουσεν...ὅτι θέσει καὶ οὐ φ. σῶμα πεφόρηκεν ὁ κύριος; Ath.*ep.Epict.*2(p.4.14; M.26.1053A); opp. προθέσει, προνοίᾳ, κατὰ προαίρεσιν etc., Hipp.*haer.*7.19(p.194.14; M.16.3299C); τὰ πολλὰ οὐ κατὰ προαίρεσιν ἁμαρτάνει ἄνθρωπος ἀλλὰ κατὰ φ. εἰ γὰρ μὴ εἶχεν φύσεως ποιεῖν τὰ φαῦλα, οὐκ ἄν ποτε αὐτὰ ἐποίει προαιρέσει [view controverted] *V.Aberc.*38(p.29.11); ἵνα ἐκ τῶν κατὰ φ. ἐκείνων [sc. παραδειγμάτων] τὰ ἐκ προαιρέσεως φαίνηται τῶν ἀνθρώπων κινήματα Ath.*Ar.*3.18(M.26.361A); ἀναιροῦντες...τὸ κατὰ φ., πῶς τὸ κατὰ βούλησιν προηγεῖσθαι θέλοντες; *ib.*2.2(149C); οἰκίαν μὲν οὖν τις βουλευόμενος κατασκευάζει, υἱὸν δὲ γεννᾷ κατὰ φ. *ib.*3.62(453B); Cyr.H.*catech.*2.5; in a comparison of action of eucharistic grace with that of tree of knowledge ἆρα αὐτὸ τὸ δῶρον φυσικὴν ἔχει σωτηρίαν;...εἰ ταῦτα φύσει σώζει, καὶ οὐ τῇ χάριτι, κἀκεῖνο τῇ φ. ἀνεῖλεν, καὶ οὐ τῇ προθέσει, εἰ τοῦτο τὸ βρῶμα φύσει σώζει, καὶ οὐ τῇ χάριτι, κἀκεῖνο φύσει ἀναιρεῖ, καὶ οὐ παραβάσει Sever.*creat.*6(M.56.488); cf. οὐδεὶς ἐκ φ. τὸν νόμον τοῦ θεοῦ ποιεῖ, ἀλλ' ἐκ προαιρέσεως *Schol.in* Anast.S.*hod.*8(M.89.125B); **b.** παρὰ φύσιν *contrary to nature, unnatural* τὰς παρὰ φ. ἡδονὰς μετιέναι Eus.*p.e.*1.4(11C; M.21.40A); ἀνάγκη...ἕτερον εἶναι τὸ τὰ ἐναντία καὶ παρὰ τὴν φ. τοῦ σώματος λογιζόμενον Ath.*gent.*32(M.25.64C); of conception of Isaac τῷ παρὰ φ. θαύματι Gr.Nyss.*deit.*(M.46.565D); Marc.Er.*opusc.*8.1(M.65.1104A); ‡Gr.Nyss.*hom.3.67 in Jo.*(p.152.16,18); τὸ παρὰ φ. of a *forced meaning* λέξεις καὶ ὀνόματα...μεταφέρουσι...ἐκ τοῦ κατὰ φ. εἰς τὸ παρὰ φ. Iren.*haer.*1.9.4(M.7.544B); **c.** ὑπὲρ φύσιν *above nature, supernatural* καὶ ὁ μὲν [? Devil] παρὰ φ. κατῆλθεν, ὁ δὲ [sc. Christ] ὑπὲρ φ. ἀνῆλθεν ‡Ath.*diab.*7(p.8.6f.); οὐκ ἀνθρωπίνῃ ἰσχύι ταῦτα ἐγίνετο. οὐ γὰρ ἔχει φ. τὰ γινόμενα, ἀλλὰ ὑπὲρ φ. ἦν τὰ κατορθούμενα Chrys.*hom.3.4 in 1Cor.*(10.21A); τρεῖς εἰσι νοητοὶ τόποι, εἰς οὓς ὁ νοῦς ἐκ μεταβολῆς εἰσέρχεται· κατὰ φ., παρὰ φ., ὑπὲρ φ. Marc.Er.*opusc.*2.83(M.65.941C); id.*opusc.*4(1013A); σχέσει τῇ πρὸς τὸ θεῖον τὸ ὑπὲρ τὴν φ. ἀποκερδαίνων ἀγαθόν Cyr.*Jo.*1.9(4.95A); ποτοῦ...δίχα καὶ τῆς...τροφῆς ὡς ἐν δυνάμει πνεύματος ὑπὲρ φ. τὴν καθ' ἡμᾶς διεκαρτέρει [sc. Christ] id.*Pulch.*(p.46.9; 5^{2}.157D).

C. *origin*; **1.** of a first principle, Rhodo ap.Eus.*h.e.*5.13.4(M.20.460C); **2.** of persons, *birth*; φύσει or κατὰ φύσιν of blood relationship of a *natural* son Καίσαρος φύσει υἱῷ Just.*1apol.*1.1(M.6.328A); **3.** in gen. *relationship, kinship*, Thdt.*provid.*8(4.620A); concrete, *kin*, Bas.Sel.*or.*8.1(M.85.116D); esp. *child*, or collectively *offspring*, Eus. *l.C.*13.6(p.238.11; M.20.1401A); Gr.Nyss.*deit.*(M.46.569B).

D. *fact, reality* ὅταν ἄλλως μὲν φύσεως ἔχῃ τὰ πράγματα, ἄλλως δὲ οἱ λόγοι περὶ αὐτῶν ἀναπείθωσι Bas.*hom.*12.7(2.103D; M.31.401A); τῆς θείας οὐσίας τὴν φ. ἀρνησάμενος Mac.Mgn.*apocr.*3.26(p.114.4); 'Ηλίας ἐν ἵπποις εἰς οὐρανοὺς ἡρπάγη ἀγγέλοις οὖσι τὴν φ. τοῦ πράγματος *ib.*4.12(p.176.8); ἀνθρωποτόκος ἢ θεοτόκος ἡ Μαρία...τὸ μὲν γὰρ τῇ φ. τοῦ πράγματος, τὸ δὲ τῇ ἀναφορᾷ Thdr.Mops.*fr.inc.*15(p.310.13; M.66.992B); Jo.D.*1Cor.*2:14(M.95.588C); φύσει as adv. and κατὰ φύσιν; **1.** *in fact, literally, actually* τριχῶς δεῖ ἀκούειν τῆς κατὰ τέκνα ὀνομασίας, πρῶτον φ., δεύτερον γνώμῃ, τρίτον ἀξίᾳ Heracleon ap.Or.*Jo.*20.24(20; p.359.20; M.14.629A); τῷ σαββάτῳ φ., τῷ μετὰ τὴν ἡμέραν τῶν ἀζύμων εἰς σάββατον λελογισμένην Epiph.*haer.*30.32(p.378.10; M.41.468A); τὰ μὲν...φ. αὐτοψίᾳ...ἔγνωμεν, τὰ δὲ ἐκ συγγραμμάτων *ib.*39.1(p.72.6; 668A); τὰ ἀλληγορικῶς...περὶ τοῦ θεοῦ λεχθέντα κατ' ἀναφορὰν ἐλέχθη ἐκ τῶν φ. εἰς τὸ οὐ φ. οἷον ὡς τὸ [Gen.8:21]· ἐπὶ μὲν τῶν ἀνθρώπων 'ὠσφράνθη' κατὰ φ., ἐπὶ δὲ τοῦ θεοῦ καταχρηστικῶς καὶ οὐ φ. ‡Just.*qu.et resp.*10(M.6.1260B); οὐ φ. ταῦτα γεγενῆσθαι, ἀλλὰ τῇ τῶν ἀνιωμένων διαθέσει Thdt.*Ezech.*32:7f.(2.946); freq. with ἀληθείᾳ, ἀληθῶς, †Ath.*Apoll.*2.9(M.26.1148B); ἓν πνεῦμα ἅγιον φ. καὶ ἀληθείᾳ τῶν πάντων ἁγιαστικὸν καὶ θεοποιόν Apoll.*fid.sec.pt.*27(p.176.22; M.10.1116B); ref. Eph.2:3 προσκείμενον...τὸ 'φ.', οὐ τὸ κατὰ φ. σημαίνει, ἀλλὰ τὸ ἀληθείᾳ Didym.*Man.*3(M.39.1089C); [sc. τὸ πνεῦμα] φ. καὶ ἀληθείᾳ θεός ἐστιν id.*Trin.*2.7(M.39.561B); Cyr.*apol.orient.*3(p.40.25; 6.167C); id.*expl.xii cap.*3(p.19.4; 6.149D); id.*ador.*10(1.344E); ἑνώσεως...τῆς κατὰ φ. καὶ ἀληθοῦς id.*Arcad.*(p.69.23; 5^{2}.53E); Anast.S*hod.*2(M.89.57C); τί ἐστι, φ.; τοῦτ' ἔστιν, ἐν ἀληθείᾳ. φύσις γάρ ἐστιν... ἡ τῶν πραγμάτων ἀλήθεια *ib.*8(124C); **2.** φύσει *positively, actually*, expressing surprise φ. τολμῶσι λέγειν Epiph.*anc.*77.4(p.96.24; M.43.161B); οὐ δέχονται φ. τὰ βιβλία τὰ ἀπὸ τοῦ ἁγίου 'Ιωάννου κεκηρυγμένα id.*haer.*51.3(p.251.1; M.41.892B); *ib.*61.1(p.380.15; 1040C); *ib.*64.4(p.409.21; 1076C); **3.** as interjection, *really! indeed!* φ. ἐὰν κάθηταί τις ἐν ἡσυχίᾳ *Apophth.Patr.*(M.65.96A); *ib.*(124C); φ. οὐκ ἀκούετέ μου *V.Dan.*(p.380.10); φ., ἀδελφέ, οὐδένα ἔχω ἵνα ἀποστείλω Jo.Mosch.*prat.*157(M.87.3025B); Gr.Mag.*dial.*(tr.Zach.)2.22(M.*PL*.66.175B).

III. Trin.;

A. divine *nature*, possessed in common by; **1.** Father and Son ἐκ τούτων δείκνυται τὸ ταὐτὸν τῆς φ. ‡Ath.*dial.Trin.*3.28(M.28.1248C); υἱός...διὰ...τὸ πρὸς τὸν πατέρα τῆς φ. ἀπαράλλακτον Didym.*Trin.*1.16(M.39.340A); ἐν ἐλευθέρᾳ τῇ πατρικῇ φ. ἦν *ib.*1.26(389A); πάντα...προσέστι τῷ κυρίῳ τὰ τοῦ πατρὸς ἴδια [sc. ἀξιώματα φυσικὰ ἃ μόνον πρέπει τῇ θείᾳ φ.] καὶ ἡ τῆς θεότητος φ. ἐν αὐτῷ διαγράφεται Cyr.*thes.*32(5^{1}.297E); freq. // οὐσία: μίαν...φρονοῦμεν διὰ τὸ ἐκ τῆς οὐσίας τοῦ πατρὸς εἶναι τὸν υἱόν, καὶ διὰ τὴν ταυτότητα τῆς φ. Ath.*tom.*6(M.26.801C); τῆς κατὰ τὴν φ. ὁμοουσιότητος τοῦ λόγου τὴν πρὸς τὸν πατέρα Apoll.*fid.inc.*4(p.195.19; M.*PL*.8.876D); τῆς οὐσίας ἢ τῆς φ. ἢ τῆς θεότητος τεμνομένης καὶ τῇ...ὁμοουσίῳ...τριάδι μεταγενεστέρας τινὸς...ἢ ἑτεροουσίου φ. ἐπαγομένης CCP(382)*ep.*ap.Thdt. *h.e.*5.9.11(3.1032); Cyr.*Jo.*5.5(4.525D); τὴν αὐτὴν ἔχει τῷ πατρὶ φ. Thdt.*Is.*42:8(p.166.35; 2.334); as Son φύσει or κατὰ φύσιν: ἀληθινὸν καὶ φύσει λόγον τοῦ θεοῦ opp. κατ' ἐπίνοιαν, Ath.*Dion.*24(p.64.15; M.25.516B); υἱὸς ἀληθινὸς καὶ φ. γνήσιος *ib.*25(p.65.8; 517B); id.*ep. Epict.*2(p.5.12; M.26.1053B); id.*Ar.*1.28(M.26.69B); *ib.*3.62(453B) cit. s. γεννάω; θεός...ὁ υἱός, εἰκὼν τῆς...θεότητος ὢν ἀληθὴς κατὰ γέννησιν καὶ φ., ἣν ἐκ τοῦ πατρὸς ἔχει Apoll.*fid.sec.pt.*35(p.180.27; M.10.1117D); ἄνθρωπον γεγενῆσθαι...ἵνα...θεοποιηθῶμεν πρὸς ὁμοιότητα τοῦ κατὰ φ. ἀληθινοῦ υἱοῦ τοῦ θεοῦ *ib.*31(p.179.9; 1117B); Cyr.*Jo.*2.1(4.127D); id.*Chr.un.*(5^{1}.717B) cit. s. γεννάω; opp. θέσει: cf. *non enim per adoptionem spiritus filius fit extrinsecus, sed natura filius est*, Or. *princ.*1.2.4(p.33.3; M.11.133C); υἱός...φ. καὶ οὐ θέσει Cyr.H.*catech.*11.7; τῶν μὲν ἀνθρώπων...καταχρηστικῶς...Χριστοῦ δὲ μόνου κατὰ φ. ἐστὶ πατὴρ ὁ θεὸς οὐ κατὰ θέσιν *ib.*7.10; ἀνάγκη...τὸν κατὰ φ. [sc. υἱόν] ἕτερον εἶναι παρ' αὐτοὺς [sc. τοὺς κατὰ θέσιν] καὶ κατὰ τὴν οὐσίαν ἐξηλλαγμένον Cyr.*thes.*15(5^{1}.168D); opp. χάριτι: v. χάρις; of Son's generation, opp. βουλήσει or κατὰ βούλησιν, v. βούλησις; **2.** also by H. Ghost μαίνοιτ' ἄν τις λέγων τὸ πνεῦμα τῆς κτιστῆς φ. ... εἰ δὲ θεοποιεῖ...ἡ τούτου φ. θεοῦ ἐστι Ath.*ep.Serap.*1.24(M.26.585C,588A); λέγουσι...ἀκοινώνητον...εἶναι πρὸς πατέρα καὶ υἱὸν τὴν τοῦ πνεύματος φ. Gr.Nyss.*Trin.*6(p.77.12; M.32.692C); κατὰ φ. εἶναι ἀληθινὸν πνεῦμα τοῦ θεοῦ Didym.*Trin.*2.2(M.39.464B); ref. Gal.4:6 τὴν πρὸς αὐτὸν κοινωνίαν τῆς φ. ἐδήλωσε *ib.*(460A); ἐξ ἰδίας φ. τετοκὼς...τὸν...υἱόν // τὴν ἐκ τῆς οὐσίας πρόοδον [sc. of H. Ghost] Cyr.*Is.*5.3(2.809E); dist. from οὐσία: οὐχ ἁπλῶς θείας εἶναι φ. [sc. τὸ πνεῦμα], ἀλλὰ τῆς οὐσίας ‡Ath.*dial.Trin.*1.7(M.28.1128A); **3.** one φ. of Trin. ἡ...θεότης μία φυσικῶς ἐν τριάδι μαρτυρουμένη τὴν ἑνότητα τῆς φ. βεβαιοῖ Apoll. *fid.sec.pt.*14(p.172.6; M.10.1109C); κενώσας...ἑαυτὸν...ἀναλλοίωτος...

οὐδεμία ἀλλοίωσις περὶ τὴν θείαν φ. id.*corp.et div.*6(p.188.3; M.*PL*.8. 874A); οὐδὲ ἡ τῆς θεότητος ἤλλακται φ. ἐν τῇ κοινωνίᾳ τοῦ ἀνθρωπείου σώματος *ib.*8(p.188.16); οὔτε τοῦ ἀνάρχου τὸ ἄναρχον φ., ἢ τὸ ἀγέννητον· οὐδεμία γὰρ φ. ὅ τι μὴ τόδε ἐστίν, ἀλλ' ὅ τι τόδε...ὄνομα δέ, τῷ μὲν ἀνάρχῳ, πατήρ· τῇ δὲ ἀρχῇ, υἱός· τῷ δὲ μετὰ τῆς ἀρχῆς, πνεῦμα ἅγιον. φύσις δὲ τοῖς τρισὶ μία, θεός Gr.Naz.*or.*42.15(M.36.476B); *ib.*38.4 (332A); Gr.Nyss.*Trin.*6(p.78.8; M.32.693A) cit. s. ἐνέργεια; μία τίς ἐστιν ἡ θεία φ. ... κἂν ἐν τριάδι κηρύσσεται id.*Eun.*5(2 p.104.21; M.45. 684B); id.*or.dom.*3(p.62.26; M.44.1160C); id.*ep.*3(M.46.1017C); περὶ τοῦ πατρὸς...ὡσαύτως περί τε τοῦ υἱοῦ καὶ τοῦ...πνεύματος φρονεῖν ὀφείλομεν· ἐπὶ γὰρ τῆς πάντων ἐπικρατούσης μιᾶς φ., εἰς ἣν αὗται αἱ πάντιμοι ὑποστάσεις Didym.*Trin.*1.15(M.39.312C); τρεῖς μὲν ὑποστάσεις...μίαν δὲ τούτων φ. καὶ οὐσίαν καταγγέλλομεν Leont.B.*arg. Sev.*(M.86.1920D); πατρὸς καὶ υἱοῦ καὶ ἁγίου πνεύματος μίαν φ. ἤτοι οὐσίαν...ἐν τρισὶν ὑποστάσεσιν ἤγουν προσώποις CCP(553)*anath.*1 (p.168; H.3.193D); ἐπὶ τῆς θεότητος μίαν οὐσίαν, μίαν φ., μίαν μορφὴν δογματίζομεν ‡Cyr.*Trin.*13(6^3.19E; M.77.1149A); **4.** the φ. of each Person (cf. B infra) ὁ σωτὴρ ὅτε μὲν περὶ ἑαυτοῦ ὡς περὶ ἀνθρώπου διαλέγεται, ὅτε δὲ ὡς περὶ θειοτέρας φ. καὶ ἡνωμένης τῇ ἀγενήτῳ τοῦ πατρὸς φ. Or.*Jo.*19.2(1; p.299.16; M.14.525C); τὸ ἀπαθὲς τῆς τοῦ λόγου φ. καὶ τὰς διὰ τὴν σάρκα λεγομένας ἀσθενείας αὐτοῦ Ath.*Ar.*3.34(M. 26.396A); φ. ὅλη τοῦ λόγου ἐν ἐπιδείξει μορφῆς τῆς ἀνθρωπίνης...οὐκ ἐν διαιρέσει προσώπων ἀλλ' ἐν ὑπάρξει θεότητος καὶ ἀνθρωπότητος ‡Ath. *Apoll.*2.10(M.26.1148C); Didym.*Trin.*1.27(M.39.404A); id.(‡Bas.) *Eun.*5(1.303E; M.29.728D); Isid.Pel.*epp.*2.157(M.78.612B).

B. = ὑπόστασις, of Persons of Trin. (cf. A.4); ref. Jo.10:20 οὐ πατέρα ἑαυτὸν ἀναγορεύων, οὐδὲ τὰς τῇ ὑποστάσει δύο φ. μίαν εἶναι σαφηνίζων Alex.Al.*ep.Alex.*9(p.25.23; M.18.561B); ὧν μεσιτεύουσα φ. μονογενής *ib.*11(p.26.27; 564C); [sc. Χριστοῦ] τὴν πρὸς τὸν γεγεννηκότα αὐτὸν ὁμοτιμίαν· τῆς ἀξίας τὴν κοινωνίαν, τῆς φ. τὴν ἐξ ἀϊδίου ὕπαρξιν †Bas.*Is.*247(1.568B; M.30.553C); cf. περὶ μὲν πατρὸς καὶ υἱοῦ εὐσεβῶς πρεσβεύει [sc. Pierius], πλὴν ὅτι οὐσίας δύο καὶ φ. δύο λέγει τῷ τῆς οὐσίας καὶ φ. ὀνόματι, ὡς...ἀντὶ τῆς ὑποστάσεως Phot.*cod.* 119(M.103.400B); this use deemed responsible for many heresies τοῦτό ἐστι τὸ ποιοῦν τοῖς αἱρετικοῖς τὴν πλάνην, τὸ ταὐτὸ λέγειν τὴν φ. καὶ τὴν ὑπόστασιν...ἀδύνατον...μιᾶς φ. λέγειν τὴν ψυχὴν καὶ τὸ σῶμα πρὸς ἄλληλα συγκρινόμενα. ἀλλ' ἐπειδὴ πλεῖσται ὑποστάσεις τῶν ἀνθρώπων εἰσί, πάντες δὲ τὸν αὐτὸν ἐπιδέχονται λόγον τῆς φ. ... τῶν πλείστων καὶ διαφόρων ὑποστάσεων μίαν φ. φαμέν· ἑκάστης δηλαδὴ ὑποστάσεως δύο φ. ἐχούσης, καὶ ἐν δυσὶ τελούσης ταῖς φ., ψυχῆς λέγω καὶ σώματος Jo.D.*f.o.*3.3(M.94.992B).

IV. Christol.; orthodox writers before Nestorius, in so far as they think in terms of number, speak of two natures, as was admitted by Sev.Ant.ap.Anast.S.*hod.*7(M.89.113Df.);

A. of natures of Christ; **1.** as two; **a.** explicitly τῶν Γαλιλαίων δύο ὀνομαζόντων φ. ἔχειν τὸν Χριστὸν...ὡς οὐκ εἰδότων ὅτι ἡ οὐσία τοῦ φωτὸς ἑτέρᾳ οὐ μίγνυται ὕλῃ Man.*ep.Add.*ap.Eust.Mon.*ep.*(M.86. 904A); λέγουσι γὰρ καὶ αὐτοὶ ὡς ἀκούω δύο φ. Apoll.*ep.Dion.*1.2 (p.257.10; M.*PL*.8.929B); cf. οὐ δύο πρόσωπα οὐδὲ δύο φ. id.*fid.sec. pt.*31(p.179.3)ap.Leont.H.*monoph.*(M.86.1873C); θεὸς...ἀμφότερα, τὸ δὲ προσλαβόν, καὶ τὸ προσληφθέν· δύο φ. εἰς ἓν συνδραμουσαι, οὐχ υἱοὶ δύο Gr.Naz.*or.*37.2(M.36.285A); αἱ φ. διΐστανται...εἰ...καὶ τὸ συναμφότερον ἕν, ἀλλ' οὐ τῇ φ., τῇ δὲ συνόδῳ τούτων *ib.*30.8(p.120.6; 113B); φύσεις...δύο θεὸς καὶ ἄνθρωπος, ἐπεὶ καὶ ψυχὴ καὶ σῶμα· υἱοὶ δὲ οὐ δύο, οὐδὲ θεοί id.*ep.*101(M.37.180A); κατηγοροῦσιν ἡμῶν [sc. Apollinarians], ὡς δύο φ. εἰσαγόντων ἀπηρτημένας, ἢ μαχομένας *ib.* 102(201A); Gr.Nyss.*Apoll.*40(M.45.1246A); ὁ Χριστὸς δύο ὑπάρχων φ. id.*fr.*5(M.46.1112C); ὁ Χριστός, ὁ υἱὸς τοῦ θεοῦ, ὁ δύο τελείων φ. εἷς υἱός Amph.*fr.*(p.55); ἕνα...υἱὸν τὸν Χριστὸν δύο φύσεών φημι ἀσυγχύτως ἀτρέπτως ἀδιαιρέτως, οὐκ ἀρνούμενος τὴν θείαν οὐδὲ τὴν ἀνθρωπείαν...ἡ ληφθεῖσα πάσχει φ., ἡ δὲ λαβοῦσα ἀπαθὴς μένει ...εἰς ἓν πρόσωπον συντελοῦσιν αἱ διτταὶ φ. *ib.*(p.55; M.39.113Af.); δύο...φ. τελείων ἕνωσις γεγένηται ἀφράστως Ambr.*fr.symb.*ap.Thdt. *eran.*2(4.139); ἐν αὐτῷ ἑκατέρα φ. ἐστίν...ὡς θεὸς λαλεῖ τὰ θεῖα...ὡς ἄνθρωπος λαλεῖ τὰ τοῦ ἀνθρώπου id.*fr.*ap.*Doct.Patr.*2(p.15.6); εἰ γὰρ θεὸς τέλειος ὁ αὐτός, δύο φ. ἄρα ὁ αὐτός, καθάπερ ἡ τῶν Καππαδοκῶν εἰσηγεῖται καινοτομία Διοδώρου τε καὶ Ἀθανασίου ἡ οἴησις καὶ τῶν ἐν Ἰταλίᾳ ὁ τῦφος...κηρύττουσι δὲ καθάπερ οἱ Γρηγόριοι τὴν τῶν φ. δυάδα Polem.*fr.*174(p.274.20)ap.Leont.H.*monoph.*(M.86.1864C); οὕτω...τῆς θείας ἐνιδρυμένης τῷ σώματι φ. ... ἐν πρόσωπον τὰ συναμφότερα ἀπετέλεσεν...οὐκ ἐν μιᾷ μόνῃ φ., ἀλλ' ἐν δυσὶ τελείαις ‡Chrys. *ep.Caes.*(3.744C); cf. also later pre-Chalcedonian writers δύο φ. κηρύττοντα (ref. Jo.1:14), καὶ ἕνα υἱόν Paul.Em.*hom.*2(p.13.12; M. 77.1441A); (two-natures formula in Isid.Pel.*epp.*1.23,303,323,405 (M.78.197A,360A,369B,409A) is of doubtful authenticity): καί ἐστιν εἷς υἱός, οὐ τῶν φ. εἰς δύο ὑποστάσεις διαιρουμένων, ἀλλὰ τῆς φρικτῆς οἰκονομίας τὰς δύο φ. εἰς μίαν ὑπόστασιν ἑνωσάσης Procl.CP *fr.* (p.49.2ff.; M.65.885C); **b.** implicitly ὥσπερ...ἡ κιβωτὸς κεχρυσωμένη ...οὕτω καὶ τὸ τοῦ Χριστοῦ σῶμα...ἔσωθεν μὲν τῷ λόγῳ κοσμούμενον, ἔξωθεν δὲ τῷ πνεύματι φρουρούμενον· ἵνα ἐξ ἀμφοτέρων τὸ περιφανὲς τῶν φ. παραδειχθῇ Iren.*fr.*8(M.7.1233A)ap.Leont.B.*Nest.et Eut.*1(M.86.1312A); ἀπ' ἐκείνου [sc. Ἰησοῦ] ἤρξατο θεία καὶ ἀνθρωπίνη συνυφαίνεσθαι φ. Or.*Cels.*3.28(p.226.14; M.11.956D); id.*Jo.*32:16 (9; p.451.28ff.; M.14.784A); cf.id.*princ.*1.2.1(p.27.22; M.11.130A); *ib.*2.2.6(p.141.8ff.; 210Df.); ἵνα...τὰ περὶ τῆς θειοτέρας αὐτοῦ φ. ... διαλάβωμεν...παριστῶντες ὡς οὐκ ἀνθρωπείας ἄρα ἦν φ. ἡ περὶ αὐτὸν δύναμις Eus.*d.e.*3.2(p.108.19ff.; M.22.185Df.); cf.Hilarius *Ps.* 54.2(M.*PL*.9.348A); id.*Trin.*9.14(M.*PL*.10.292B); *ib.*9.11(291A); *ib.*9. 3(283A); *ib.*11.40(425A); εἰ μὲν οὖν ἀνθρώπου γενόμενος υἱὸς ἀμέτοχος ἦν τῆς ἀνθρωπίνης φ., ἀκόλουθον ἂν ἦν θεοῦ υἱὸν ὄντα αὐτὸν μηδὲ κοινωνεῖν τῆς θείας οὐσίας λέγειν Gr.Nyss.*Eun.*3(2 p.32.7; M.45. 597C); οὐ δύο λέγομεν, θεὸν ἰδίᾳ, καὶ ἄνθρωπον ἰδίᾳ (εἷς γὰρ ἦν), ἀλλὰ κατ' ἐπίνοιαν τὴν ἑκάστου φ. λογιζόμενοι Didym.(‡Bas.)*Eun.*4(1. 293D; M.29.704C); μὴ συγχύσῃς τὰς φ., καὶ οὐ ναρκήσῃς περὶ τὴν οἰκονομίαν Ant.Ptol.ap.Anast.S.*hod.*10(M.89.160B); **c.** denoting at one time the divinity, at another the manhood of Christ τὸ ἀληθὲς...τῆς ψυχῆς αὐτοῦ, καὶ τοῦ σώματος τῆς καθ' ἡμᾶς ἀνθρωπίνης φ. ... θεὸς γὰρ ὢν ὁμοῦ τε καὶ ἄνθρωπος ‡Mel.*fr.*7(M.5.1221A)ap. Anast.S.*hod.*13(M.89.229A); τὸν Μαρκίωνα...ἀθετοῦντα αὐτοῦ τὴν ἐκ Μαρίας γένεσιν κατὰ τὴν θείαν αὐτοῦ φ. ἀποφήνασθαι ὡς ἄρα ἐγεννήθη ἐκ Μαρίας Or.*Jo.*10.6(4; p.176.10; M.14.316B); *ib.*19.2(1; p.299. 16; 525C) cit. s. III.A.4; τὸ διαλλάττον τῆς φ. τοῦ υἱοῦ πρὸς τὰ γενητά Ath.*Ar.*1.55(M.26.128A); ref. Lc.2:52 ὡς εἶναι τῆς ἀνθρωπίνης φ. τὴν προκοπήν *ib.*3.53(436A); ἵνα μή τις αὐτὸν κοινὸν ἄνθρωπον ἐκ τοῦ πάθους ὑπολάβῃ...τὸ πρὸς ἡμᾶς ἀνόμοιον τῆς φ. διηγεῖται ἡ γραφή id.*inc.*34.3(M.25.156A); οὐχ ἁπλῶς ἄνθρωπος, ἀλλὰ ζωὴ πάντων ...κἂν ὅμοιος κατὰ τὴν φ. τοῖς ἀνθρώποις ἐτύγχανε *ib.*37.2(160B); τὴν κυριευτικὴν φ. Apoll.*corp.et div.*4(p.186.19; M.*PL*.8.873A); Gr. Nyss.*Apoll.*42(M.45.1224A,B); ἐδάκρυσε...ἀληθῶς τὴν φ. τὴν ἡμετέραν περιεβάλετο Chrys.*hom.63.2 in Jo.*(8.377C); id.*pent.*1.2(2.461A); **2.** though Christ has a human φ. he is not man φύσει in same way as he is divine ὡς ἄνθρωπος ταφείς, ἀνέστη...ὡς θεός, φύσει θεὸς ὢν καὶ ἄνθρωπος Mel.*pass.*8 p.2.16; καθεύδει ὁ ἄυπνον ἔχων τὴν φ. ὡς θεός Hipp.*Noet.*18(p.263.13; M.10.828B); φύσει μὲν αὐτοῦ ἀρχὴ ἡ θεότης, πρὸς ἡμᾶς δέ, μὴ ἀπὸ τοῦ μεγέθους αὐτοῦ δυναμένους ἄρξασθαι τῆς περὶ αὐτοῦ ἀληθείας, ἡ ἀνθρωπότης αὐτοῦ, καθ' ὃ τοῖς νηπίοις καταγγέλλεται Ἰησοῦς Χριστός, καὶ οὗτος ἐσταυρωμένος Or.*Jo.*1.18 (20; p.22.32; M.14.53D); ἔργῳ μὲν ἔνδοθεν...καὶ πράξει θεὸν καὶ φύσει θεοῦ γνήσιον υἱόν, ἄνθρωπον δὲ καθαρόν...ἐξωτάτω περικείμενον...καὶ ναοῦ χρῆμα περικαλλές Eust.*engast.*10(p.31.12; M.18.633B); θεὸν ἐν ἀνθρώπου γεγονέναι σώματι καὶ οὐδὲν ἄλλο τὴν φ. εἶναι ἢ θεοῦ λόγον Eus.*d.e.*3.7(p.143.25; M.22.241B); τῶν...ἀτόπων ἐστὶν υἱὸν θεοῦ... κατὰ φ. ὄντα θεὸν...ὅτε παρὰ φ. μὲν ἑαυτοῦ ἐκ Μαρίας γέγονεν ἄνθρωπος, ὅμοιον αὐτὸν γενέσθαι τοῖς κατὰ φ. ἀνθρώποις ἐν τῷ ἑαυτοῦ παρὰ φ. (παρὰ φ. γὰρ ἦν αὐτῷ θεῷ ὄντι γενέσθαι ἄνθρωπον), ἐν τῷ κατὰ φ. δὲ ἑαυτοῦ μὴ εἶναι αὐτὸν ὅμοιον τῷ πατρὶ τῷ γεννήσαντι Geo.Laod. *ep.dogm.*ap.Epiph.*haer.*73.18(p.291.10ff.; M.42.437A); τοῦ σωτῆρος... φύσει λόγου ὄντος Ath.*Ar.*2.4(M.26.153B); ref. Pr.8:22 οὐ πάντως τὸ λεγόμενον κτίζεσθαι ἤδη καὶ τῇ φ. καὶ τῇ οὐσίᾳ κτίσμα ἐστί *ib.*2.45 (244A); συνεχώρησεν παθεῖν τὸν τῇ φ. ἀπαθῆ, τὸν υἱόν *Const.App.*2.24. 3; Gr.Nyss.*Eun.*5(2 p.117.8; M.45.697B); τὴν τοῦ δούλου μορφὴν... 'πεποιῆσθαι' φησιν, ὅπερ ὁ ἀναλαβὼν κατὰ τὴν ἑαυτοῦ φ. ἦν *ib.*6(2 p.133.9; 717A); **3.** of the divine nature in partic. τὴν γραφὴν...τοῖς τῆς φ. χαρακτηριστικοῖς κεχρημένην...υἱὸν ἀληθινὸν...σοφίαν, καὶ λόγον Bas.*Spir.*17(3.14C; M.32.96C); τὴν μὲν φ. νόει θεοπρεπῶς, τὰ δὲ ταπεινότερα τῶν ῥημάτων δέχου οἰκονομικῶς Bas.*hom.*15.2(2.132D; M.31.468C); λόγος ὤν, διὰ τὸ ἀπαθὲς σὰρξ ἐγένετο, ἀμεταβλήτου μενούσης τῆς φ. Chrys.*nativ.*2.1(6.392C); καταβέβηκεν μὲν τῇ εἰς τὸν ἄνθρωπον ἐνοικήσει· ἔστιν δὲ ἐν οὐρανῷ τῷ ἀπεριγράφῳ τῆς φ. πᾶσιν παρών Thdr.Mops.*fr.inc.*10(p.301.26; M.66.984C); ὁ βροτὸς γενόμενος, μένων θεός, μὴ τραπεὶς τὴν φ. ... ὁ λόγος σὰρξ γενόμενος, κἀκεῖνο μείνας, οὐκ εἰς τοῦτο μεταπεσὼν τῇ φ. ‡Caes.Naz.*dial.*1.20 (M.38.876); opp. οἰκονομία: θεὸς αὐτοῦ [sc. of Christ] γέγονε κατ' οἰκονομίαν, διότι ἄνθρωπος, ἡμῶν δὲ κατὰ φ. δεσπότης ἐστὶ καὶ θεός Ath.*inc.et c.Ar.*8(M.26.996C); ἵνα...γινώσκῃς, τίς μὲν φύσεως λόγος, τίς δὲ λόγος οἰκονομίας Gr.Naz.*or.*29.18(p.102.5; M.36.97C); μορφὴ... θεοῦ καὶ μορφὴ δούλου, τὰ μὲν κατὰ τὴν ὑπάρχουσαν φ. ὤν, τὰ δὲ κατὰ τὴν φιλάνθρωπον οἰκονομίαν γενόμενος Gr.Nyss.*Eun.*4(2 p.66.5; M.45. 637C); συνάπτει ἀεὶ τῷ περὶ τῆς ἀκτίστου φ. καὶ τὸν τῆς οἰκονομίας λόγον Chrys.*hom.3.2 in Heb.*(12.26B); cf.Hilarius *Trin.*10.22(M.*PL*. 10.360A); *ib.*10.66(394B); Leont.B.*arg.Sev.*(M.86.1937A); cf. δέῳ εἰπεῖν ἐν τῷ ὅρῳ τῆς φ. τὸν θεὸν λόγον ἔχειν τὴν πρὸς τὸ ἡμέτερον ἕνωσιν *ib.*

(1940B); carried to length of denying substantial existence to σάρξ: οὐ γὰρ οὐσία τοῦ Χριστοῦ, οὐδὲ φ. ἡ σὰρξ αὐτοῦ, ἀλλὰ νόμος οἰκονομίας Tim.II Al. *fr.*ap.Eust.Mon.*ep.*(M.86.904B); cf. οὐ γὰρ φύσεως ἔχει λόγον ἡ τοῦ θεοῦ λόγου σάρκωσις, ἀλλ' οἰκονομίας ὑπὲρ φ. πραττομένης ὑπὸ θεοῦ ἐκ μὲν τῆς κοινῆς...ἡμῶν φ. ἤτοι οὐσίας id.*fr.*2(M.86.273D).

B. pre-Chalcedonian views later regarded as heterodox: problem complicated by conviction of many that to be anything more than a mental abstraction a φ. must be realized in a concrete, independent entity, a hypostasis; hence (1) two φύσεις meant two hypostases, but there are two φύσεις in Christ, therefore union cannot be φυσική or καθ' ὑπόστασιν and must be explained in some other way: thus Antiochenes, esp. Nestorius; (2) two φύσεις meant two hypostases, but Christ is one hypostasis, therefore can only have one φύσις: so forerunners of monophysites; φασὶ γάρ [sc. Eutychians]· εἰ δύο φ. ἐπὶ τοῦ ἑνὸς Χριστοῦ φατε, οὐκ ἔστι δὲ φ. ἀνυπόστατος, δύο ἄρα ἂν εἶεν καὶ αἱ ὑποστάσεις· εἷς δέ ἐστιν ἀμφοτέροις...ἀγών, κἂν ὁ σκόπος ᾖ διάφορος. οἱ μὲν γὰρ ἵνα ταῖς φ. συνεισάγωσι τὰς ὑποστάσεις, οἱ δὲ ἵνα διὰ τῶν ὑποστάσεων καὶ τὰς φ. ἀνέλωσι, τῷ αὐτῷ κέχρηνται προβλήματι Leont.B.*Nest.et Eut.*1(M.86.1276D); **1.** Diodorus, *synous.*(M.33.1560B) cit. s. λόγος; *ib.*(1560C) cit. s. χάρις; Thdr.Mops. *fr.inc.*8(p.299.19ff.; M.66.981A,B) cit. s. ἀπρόσωπος; *ib.*(p.300; 981C); cf.*ib.*13(p.308.2; 989B); *ib.*5(p.292; 969cf.); τήν τε διαίρεσιν τῶν φ. ποιεῖται, καὶ...τὴν διαφορὰν τῆς τε τοῦ λαβόντος φ. καὶ τῆς τοῦ ληφθέντος ἡμῖν ὑποδείκνυσιν ἡ...γραφή id. *fr.Apoll.*4(p.321.13); [ref. Jo.5:19] ἐγὼ μέν, ὡς ὁρᾶτε, δύναμαι μὲν ποιεῖν οὐδὲν κατὰ τὴν οἰκείαν φ., ἅτε ἄνθρωπος ὤν· ἐργάζομαι δέ, ἐπειδὴ ἐν ἐμοὶ μένων ὁ πατὴρ ἅπαντα ποιεῖ *ib.*3(p.317.2; M.66.1000B); ὁ...λόγος...εἴληφεν...ἄνθρωπον τέλειον τὴν φ. ἐκ ψυχῆς τε νοερᾶς καὶ σαρκὸς συνεστῶτα ἀνθρωπίνης· ὃν ἄνθρωπον ὄντα καθ' ἡμᾶς τὴν φ. id.*symb.*(p.98.17f.; M.66.1017B); Nest.: cf. toute nature complète n'a pas besoin d'une autre nature pour être et pour vivre...comment donc, des deux natures complètes, dis-tu une seule nature, puisque l'humanité est complète et n'a pas besoin de l'union de la divinité pour être homme? Nest. *Heraclid.*2.1(p.268); toute union...qui aboutit par une composition de natures à compléter une nature, a lieu à l'aide de natures incomplètes. celle qui a lieu à l'aide de natures complètes, se fait en un prosôpon et c'est en cela qu'elle subsiste...je ne sépare pas les natures, par translation et par isolement...je ne parle pas non plus d'une liaison qui a lieu par amour et par rapprochement... je n'ai pas dit non plus que l'union a eu lieu par égalité d'honneur et puissance, mais (que c'est une union) de natures, et de natures complètes, *ib.*(p.276); τῶν δύο φ. μία ἐστὶν αὐθεντία...καὶ ἓν πρόσωπον κατὰ μίαν ἀξίαν καὶ τὴν αὐτὴν τιμήν id. *fr.*A 11(p.196.16)ap. Justn.*conf.*(p.98.2; M.86.1021B); *ib.*C 12(p.281.9)ap.Cyr.*Nest.*2.6 (p.42.6; 6[1].44E) cit. s. διπλόος; cf. *oportet manere naturas in suis proprietatibus et sic per mirabilem...unitatem unam intelligi gloriam et unum confiteri filium...non duas personas unam personam facimus, sed una appellatione Christi duas naturas simul significamus*, *ib.*A 11 (p.196.22); *ib.*B 9(p.224.5)ap.CLater.*act.*5(H.3.896C) cit. s. συνάπτω; *ib.*C 9(p.262.6)ap.Cyr.*apol.orient.*3(p.39.12; 6[1].165C) cit. s. προσκυνητός; id.*ep.Cyr.*2(p.30.18; M.77.52C) cit. s. λόγος; cf. tu prends pour point de départ de ton histoire le créateur des natures et non le prosôpon d'union. ou bien évite de dire deux natures unies sans confusion, on bien confesse et dis-le, et il ne te paraîtra pas impossible de dire dans l'union un autre et un autre en ce qui concerne l'essence et non en ce qui concerne l'unité du prosôpon, id. *Heraclid.*1.3(p.136); l'union des prosôpons a eu lieu en prosôpon, et non en essence ni en nature...les natures subsistent dans leurs prosôpons et dans leurs natures et dans le prosôpon d'union. quant au prosôpon naturel de l'une, l'autre sert du même en vertu de l'union; ainsi il n'y a qu'un prosôpon pour les deux natures, *ib.*2.1(p.193f.); c'est au Christ qu'appartiennent les deux natures, et non à Dieu le Verbe, *ib.*1.3(p.150); il en est du nom de Dieu comme du nom de Fils, l'un indique les natures et l'autre le prosôpon pour les deux natures et non pour une essence, *ib.*2.1 (p.191); τὸ 'Χριστὸς' καὶ τὸ 'υἱὸς' καὶ τὸ 'κύριος', ἐπὶ τοῦ μονογενοῦς...λαμβανόμενον, τῶν φ. ἐστὶ τῶν δύο σημαντικὸν καὶ ποτὲ μὲν δηλοῦν τὴν θεότητα, ποτὲ δὲ τὴν ἀνθρωπότητα, ποτὲ δὲ ἀμφότερα id.*fr.*C.10(p.269.18); cf. parce que j'ai dit que Dieu le Verbe n'est pas mort...mais la chair, c'est pour cela que je suis accusé, id. *Heraclid.*2.1(p.229); **2.** in view ascribed to Montanus μίαν ὁ Χριστὸς ἔχει τὴν φ. ... καὶ πρὸ τῆς σαρκὸς καὶ μετὰ τῆς σαρκός, ἵνα μὴ διάφορος γένηται, ἀνόμοια...πράττων ‡Mont.*fr.*ap.*Doct.Patr.*41 (p.306.8); Arian πιστεύομεν...τὸν υἱόν...σαρκωθέντα, οὐκ ἐνανθρωπήσαντα, οὔτε γὰρ ψυχὴν ἀνθρωπίνην ἀνείληφεν...οὐ δύο φ., ἐπεὶ μὴ τέλειος ἦν ἄνθρωπος, ἀλλ' ἀντ ψυχῆς θεὸς ἦν ἐν σαρκί, μία τὸ ὅλον κατὰ σύνθεσιν φ. Eudox.*fr.*ap.*Doct.Patr.*9(p.65.7f.); Χριστὸς...ἓν πρόσωπον, μία σύνθετος φ., καθάπερ τὸν ἐκ ψυχῆς καὶ σώματος ἄνθρωπον γνωρίζομεν· εἰ δὲ καὶ ψυχὴν εἶχεν...μάχεται τὰ κινήματα θεοῦ καὶ ψυχῆς Luc.Al.*fr.pasch.*(p.65.20); ref. Jo.14:10 τὸ ἓν εἶναι πάντως οὐ κατὰ φ. λέγει [sc. ὁ Ἄρειος], ἀλλὰ κατὰ ὁμόνοιαν...καὶ ἀρνοῦνται ψυχὴν αὐτὸν ἀνθρωπείαν εἰληφέναι Epiph.*haer.*69.19(p.169.3; M.42.232B); Thdt.*haer.*4(4.350); Manich. ὁ δὲ τοῦ ἀϊδίου φωτὸς υἱὸς τὴν ἰδίαν οὐσίαν ἐν τῷ ὄρει ἐφανέρωσεν, οὐ δύο ἔχων φ., ἀλλὰ μίαν ἐν τῷ ὁρατῷ καὶ ἀοράτῳ Man.*ep.Scyth.*(p.406)ap.Eust.Mon.*ep.*(M.86.904B); μία τοῦ φωτός ἐστιν...ἡ φ. καὶ μία αὐτοῦ ἡ ἐνέργεια...οὐ γὰρ οὐσίας ἥψατο σαρκός, ἀλλ' ὁμοιώματι...σαρκὸς ἐσκιάσθη id.*ep.Zeb.* ap.*Doct.Patr.*41(p.306.12); cf.Isid.Pel.*epp.*1.102(M.78.252cf.); Apollinarian ἐστὶ θεὸς ἀληθινὸς ὁ ἄσαρκος ἐν σαρκὶ φανερωθείς...οὐ δύο πρόσωπα οὐδὲ δύο φ. Apoll.*fid.sec.pt.*31(p.179.3)ap.Leont.H. *monoph.*(M.86.1873C); Apoll.*fid.inc.*6(p.199.16; M.*PL.*8.877C) cit. s. ἐνέργεια; μία φ. ἐστίν, ἐπειδὴ πρόσωπον ἓν οὐκ ἔχον εἰς δύο διαίρεσιν ...ἀλλ' ὥσπερ ἄνθρωπος μία φ. id.*ep.Dion.*1.2(p.257.15ff.; M.*PL.*8.929B); *ib.*1.6(p.258.19; 931A); εἷς μὲν φύσει υἱὸς θεοῦ εἷς δὲ θετός id.*fr.*81(p.224.15)ap.Gr.Nyss.*Apoll.*42(M.45.1220C); ἀδύνατον...τὸν αὐτὸν εἶναι θεόν τε καὶ ἄνθρωπον ἐξ ὁλοκλήρου, ἀλλ' ἐν μονότητι συγκράτου φ. θεϊκῆς σεσαρκωμένης *ib.*9(p.206.28)ap.Leont.B.*Apoll.*(M.86.1973B); οὐκ αἰσχύνεται [sc. ὁ Διόδωρος] φ. μὲν τὴν αὐτὴν λέγων, γένεσιν δὲ διάφορον...περιττὸν τὴν ἐκ παρθένου γέννησιν εἰσάγεσθαι, εἰ μὴ καὶ τὸ γεννώμενον ἐπάξιον εἴη τῆς γεννήσεως *ib.*142(p.241.19)ap. *eund.*(1965D); *ib.*10(p.207.13)ap.Justn.*monoph.*(p.17.13; M.86.1124B); *ib.*107(p.232.21)ap.*eund.*(p.17.8; 1124A); ἄνθρωπος εἷς ὁ Χριστὸς ὡς εἷς θεὸς ὁ πατήρ, ὅ ἐστι φύσεως· ὥστε καὶ τοῦτο φύσεως συνθέτου μεταξὺ οὔσης θεοῦ καὶ ἀνθρώπων *ib.*111(p.233.28)ap.*eund.*(p.16.39; 1121D); φύσει μὲν θεὸν καὶ φύσει ἄνθρωπον τὸν κύριον λέγομεν· μιᾷ δὲ συγκράτῳ φ. σαρκικῇ τε καὶ θεϊκῇ *ib.*149(p.247.14f.)ap.*eund.*(p.17.14f.; 1124B); προϋπάρχει ὁ ἄνθρωπος Χριστὸς...ὡς τοῦ κυρίου ἐν τῇ τοῦ θεοῦ ἀνθρώπου φύσει θείου πνεύματος ὄντος *ib.*32(p.211.27)ap. Gr.Nyss.*Apoll.*12(M.45.1145D); ὁμολογεῖται...ἐν αὐτῷ τὸ μὲν εἶναι κτιστὸν ἐν ἑνότητι τοῦ ἀκτίστου, τὸ δὲ ἄκτιστον ἐν συγκράσει τοῦ κτιστοῦ, φ. μιᾶς ἐξ ἑκατέρου μέρους συνισταμένης, μερικὴν ἐνέργειαν καὶ τοῦ λόγου συντελέσαντος εἰς τὸ ὅλον μετὰ τῆς θεϊκῆς τελειότητος, ὅπερ ⟨καὶ⟩ ἐπὶ τοῦ κοινοῦ ἀνθρώπου ἐκ δύο μερῶν ἀτελῶν γίνεται, φ. μίαν πληρούντων καὶ ἑνὶ ὀνόματι δηλουμένων id.*corp.et div.*5(p.187.7ff.; M.*PL.*8.873C); id. *fr.*108(p.232.31)ap.Max.*opusc.*(M.91.169C) cit. s. ἐνέργεια; *ib.*151f.(p.248.6,9ff.).

C. formula μία φ. τοῦ θεοῦ λόγου σεσαρκωμένη; **1.** origin, Apoll. *ep.Jov.*1(p.250.7f.; M.28.28A) cit. s. προσκύνησις; cf.id.*fr.*9(p.206.28) cit. supra; εἷς...ἦν ἐξ ἀμφοῖν θεότητός τε καὶ ἀνθρωπότητος, τελείως ἐχουσῶν κατὰ τὸν ἴδιον λόγον τῶν φ. ... ὁ Ἐμμανουὴλ ἐκ δύο φ. εἷς ὢν καὶ μία ὑπόστασις καὶ μία φ. αὐτοῦ τοῦ λόγου σεσαρκωμένη Sever.*1Tim.*2:5f.(p.337.3); for long ascribed to Ath., Cyr.*Arcad.*(p.65.27; 5[2].48B); id.*apol.orient.*8(p.48.30; 6[1].178B); Justn.*monoph.*(p.18.30f.; M.86.1125B) where *ep.Jov.* is preserved; cf. τινὲς...τὴν ἰδίαν αἵρεσιν κρατῦναι βουλόμενοι, τινὰς τῶν Ἀπολιναρίου λόγων ὡς Γρηγορίου τοῦ Θαυματουργοῦ, ἢ Ἀθανασίου, ἢ Ἰουλίου ἐπέγραψαν Leont.B.*Apoll.*(M.86.1948A); ascribed to Arius as well as to Apoll. Ἄρειος μίαν φ. τοῦ θεοῦ λόγου σεσαρκωμένην φησὶ...καὶ Ἀπολινάριος τὴν αὐτὴν λέγει ἀπαραλλάκτως φωνήν Leont.H.*monoph.*(M.86.1809C); **2.** as expounded by Cyr. in rel. to Nestorian controversy ὡς ἐξ ἑνὸς προσώπου τὰ πάντα λελέξεται; μία γὰρ ἤδη νοεῖται φ. μετὰ τὴν ἕνωσιν ἡ αὐτοῦ τοῦ λόγου σεσαρκωμένη...ἄνθρωπος γὰρ εἷς ἀληθῶς συγκείμενος ἐξ ἀνομοίων πραγμάτων, ψυχῆς δὴ λέγω καὶ σώματος...τὸ ἑνωθὲν τῷ θεῷ λόγῳ σῶμα φαμὲν ἐψυχῶσθαι ψυχῇ λογικῇ Cyr.*Nest.*2 proem.(p.33.7; 6[1].31C); συνῆλθον ἀλλήλαις καθ' ἕνωσιν ἀδιάσπαστον ἀσυγχύτως καὶ ἀτρέπτως· ἡ γὰρ σὰρξ σάρξ ἐστιν καὶ οὐ θεότης, εἰ καὶ γέγονεν θεοῦ σάρξ· ὁμοίως δὲ καὶ ὁ λόγος θεός ἐστι καὶ οὐ σάρξ, εἰ καὶ ἰδίαν ἐποιήσατο τὴν σάρκα οἰκονομικῶς...μετὰ μὲν τὴν ἕνωσιν οὐ διαιροῦμεν τὰς φ. ἀπ' ἀλλήλων ...ἀλλ' ἕνα φαμὲν υἱὸν καὶ ὡς οἱ πατέρες εἰρήκασιν, μίαν φ. τοῦ λόγου σεσαρκωμένην id.*ep.*45(p.153.17ff.; 5[2].137Cff.); μεμένηκε...ὅπερ ἦν, τουτέστι φύσει θεός, προσλαβὼν δὲ καὶ τὸ εἶναι ἄνθρωπος...εἷς μεμένηκεν υἱός, πλὴν οὐκ ἄσαρκος...ἀμφιεσάμενος δὲ ὥσπερ καὶ τὴν ἡμετέραν φ. ἕνα γε μὴν ὁμολογοῦμεν υἱὸν καὶ Χριστὸν καὶ κύριον ὡς γεγονότος σαρκὸς τοῦ λόγου· τὸ δὲ σαρκὸς ὅταν εἴπωμεν, ἀνθρώπου φαμέν. ποία τοίνυν ἀνάγκη παθεῖν αὐτὸν εἰς ἰδίαν φ., εἰ λέγοιτο μετὰ τὴν ἕνωσιν μία φ. υἱοῦ σεσαρκωμένη;...ἐν τῷ σεσαρκωμένην εἰπεῖν σύμπας ὁ λόγος τῆς μετὰ σαρκὸς οἰκονομίας εἰσφέρεται (ἐσαρκώθη γὰρ οὐχ ἑτέρως, ἀλλὰ σπέρματος Ἀβραὰμ ἐπιλαβόμενος καὶ ὁμοιωθεὶς κατὰ πάντα τοῖς ἀδελφοῖς)...κατὰ ἀλήθειάν ἐστι μία φ. τοῦ λόγου σεσαρκωμένη. εἰ γὰρ εἷς ἐστιν υἱὸς ὁ φύσει καὶ ἀληθῶς ἐκ θεοῦ πατρὸς λόγος...εἶτα κατὰ πρόσληψιν σαρκὸς... ἐψυχωμένης νοερῶς προῆλθεν ἄνθρωπος ἐκ γυναικός, οὐκ εἰς δύο μερισθήσεται διὰ τοῦτο πρόσωπα καὶ υἱούς, ἀλλὰ μεμένηκεν εἷς πλὴν οὐκ ἄσαρκος, οὐδὲ ἔξω σώματος, ἀλλ' ἴδιον ἔχων αὐτὸ καθ' ἕνωσιν ἀδιάσπαστον *ib.*46(p.158.18ff.; 5^{2}.142Bf.); εἰ γὰρ καὶ εἷς λέγοιτο πρὸς ἡμῶν ὁ μονογενὴς υἱὸς τοῦ θεοῦ σεσαρκωμένος καὶ ἐνανθρωπήσας, οὐ πέφυρται διὰ τοῦτο...οὔτε μὴν εἰς τὴν τῆς σαρκὸς φ. μεταπεφοίτηκεν ἡ τοῦ λόγου φ. ἀλλ'...ἐν ἰδιότητι τῇ κατὰ φ. ἑκατέρου μένοντός τε καὶ νοουμένου...ἀφράστως ἑνωθεὶς μίαν ἡμῖν ἔδειξεν υἱοῦ φύσιν, πλήν, ὡς ἔφην, σεσαρκωμένην...οὔτε γὰρ μεμείωται [sc. ἡ ἀνθρώπου φ.] οὔτε καθά φησιν ὑποκλέπτεται· ἀρκεῖ γὰρ πρὸς δήλωσιν τὴν τελειοτάτην τοῦ ὅτι γέγονεν ἄνθρωπος, τὸ λέγειν ὅτι σεσάρκωται *ib.*(p.159.19ff.; 5^{2}.143Bff.); cf.id.*Nest.*2.8(p.46.29; 6^{1}.51D); id.*ep.*17(p.38.22; 5^{2}.73D); περιττοεπὴς ὁ λέγων φυρμὸν γενέσθαι καὶ σύγκρασιν, εἰ δὴ μία πρὸς ἡμῶν ὡμολόγητο φ. υἱοῦ σεσαρκωμένου τε καὶ ἐνανθρωπηκότος id.*Chr. un.*(5^{1}.737A); δύο μὲν φ. ἡνῶσθαί φαμεν μετὰ δέ γε τὴν ἕνωσιν...μίαν εἶναι πιστεύομεν τὴν τοῦ υἱοῦ φ., ὡς ἑνός, πλὴν ἐνανθρωπήσαντος καὶ σεσαρκωμένου id.*ep.*40(p.26.9; 5^{2}.115E); μίαν τὴν τοῦ υἱοῦ φ., ὁποῖόν ἐστιν καὶ ἐπὶ τοῦ κοινοῦ εἰπεῖν ἀνθρώπου· ἐστὶν μὲν γὰρ ἐκ διαφόρων φ., ἀπό τε σώματος φημὶ καὶ ψυχῆς, καὶ ὁ μὲν λόγος καὶ ἡ θεωρία οἶδεν τὴν διαφοράν, ἑνώσαντες δέ, τότε μίαν ποιοῦμεν ἀνθρώπου φ. ... οὐκέτι διίστανται ἀλλήλων τὰ ἑνωθέντα, ἀλλ' εἷς λοιπὸν υἱός, μία φύσις αὐτοῦ, ὡς σαρκωθέντος τοῦ λόγου *ib.*44(p.35.14ff.,36.12; 5^{2}.133B, 134A); **3.** monophysite use of formula and of Cyrilline terms used to explain it ἐγὼ ἀνέγνων τοῦ μακαρίου Κυρίλλου καὶ τῶν ἁγίων πατέρων καὶ τοῦ ἁγίου Ἀθανασίου ὅτι ἐκ δύο μὲν φ. εἶπον πρὸ τῆς ἑνώσεως, μετὰ δὲ τὴν ἕνωσιν...οὐκέτι δύο φ. εἶπον, ἀλλὰ μίαν Eut.ap. CCP(448)(*ACO* 2.1.1 p.144.19f.; H.2.168A); Eut.*ib.*(p.143.10f.; H. 165B); ὁ Εὐτυχὴς...φάσκων πρὸ μὲν τῆς ἐνανθρωπήσεως...δύο φ. εἶναι θεότητος καὶ ἀνθρωπότητος, μετὰ δὲ τὴν ἕνωσιν μίαν φ. γεγονέναι Flav. CP *ep.Leon.*1(p.38.24; H.2.5A); Leont.B.*Nest.et Eut.*1(M.86.1277A); διὰ τοῦτο καθῄρηται Φλαβιανός, ὅτι μετὰ τὴν ἕνωσιν δύο φ. εἶπεν. ἐγὼ δὲ χρήσεις ἔχω τῶν ἁγίων πατέρων Ἀθανασίου Γρηγορίου Κυρίλλου ἐν πολλοῖς τόποις ὅτι οὐ δεῖ λέγειν μετὰ τὴν ἕνωσιν δύο φ., ἀλλὰ μίαν σεσαρκωμένην τοῦ λόγου φ. Dioscorus cit.ap.CChalc.*act.*1(*ACO* 2.1.1 p.117.6ff.; H.2.132D); cf. τὸ ἐκ δύο δέχομαι· τὸ δύο οὐ δέχομαι *ib.*(p.120.14; H.136C); φ. Χριστοῦ μόνη θεότης εἰ καὶ σεσάρκωται Tim.II Al.*fr.*2(M.86.273C); Sev.Ant.ap.Eust.Mon.*ep.*(M.86.921A) cit. s. ἕνωσις; μιᾶς...ὑποστάσεως ὁμολογουμένης τοῦ Ἐμμανουήλ, ἀκόλουθον μίαν φ. ὁμολογεῖν τοῦ θεοῦ λόγου σεσαρκωμένην, καὶ αὐτὴν ἐνεργοῦσαν τὰ θεοπρεπῆ καὶ ἀνθρώπινα· καὶ οὐ κατὰ τὸν Λέοντος τόμον ἐνεργούσας δύο φ. καὶ μορφὰς ὑποτίθεσθαι, κοινωνούσας ἀλλήλαις κατὰ συνάφειαν σχετικήν Sev.Ant.*ep.Paul.*ap.CCP(681)*act.*10(H.3.1244A); εἰ...μετεστοιχείωσεν ὁ λόγος ἣν ἥνωσεν ἑαυτῷ καθ' ὑπόστασιν ἀνθρωπότητα, οὐκ εἰς τὴν ἑαυτοῦ φ., ἔμεινε γὰρ τοῦτο ὅπερ ἦν, ἀλλ' εἰς τὴν ἑαυτοῦ δόξαν τε καὶ ἐνέργειαν· καὶ τὰ τῆς σαρκὸς ἴδια, γέγονεν ἴδια τοῦ λόγου· πῶς ἑκατέραν μορφὴν ἐνεργεῖν τὰ ἴδια δώσομεν;...τῶν μὲν γὰρ ἐνεργουμένων καὶ πραττομένων παρὰ τοῦ ἑνὸς Χριστοῦ πολὺ τὸ διάφορον. τὰ μὲν γάρ ἐστι θεοπρεπῆ, τὰ δὲ ἀνθρώπινα...ἀλλ' εἷς ὁ σαρκωθεὶς λόγος τοῦτό τε κἀκεῖνο ἐνήργηκε, καὶ οὐ τὸ μὲν τῇσδε, τὸ δὲ τῇσδε τῆς φ. οὐδὲ ἐπειδὴ διάφορα τὰ ἐνεργηθέντα, διὰ τοῦτο δύο τὰς ἐνεργούσας φ. ἤτοι μορφὰς δικαίως ὁριούμεθα Sev.Ant.*ep.Oecum.ib.*(H.1241D); with φ. replaced by ὑπόστασις, id.ap.*cat.1Pet.*4:1(p.71.28); τὴν μίαν σεσαρκωμένην τοῦ...λόγου φ. Oecum.*Phil.*3:20f.(p.453.23); τοῦ Χριστοῦ τοῦ ἐν μιᾷ φ. προσκυνουμένου id.*Heb.*1:4(p.462.4); ἐκ δύο φ. ἕνα Χριστὸν ὁμολογοῦμεν...μίαν ὑπόστασιν σύνθετον, καὶ μίαν τοῦ θεοῦ λόγου, σεσαρκωμένην σαρκί, ἐψυχωμένην νοερῶς, καθὰ Κύριλλος...ἐδίδαξε· καὶ ἐν δύο φ. τὸν αὐτὸν εἶναι δοξάζοντες, ὡς ἐν θεότητι καὶ ἀνθρωπότητι τὸν ἕνα Χριστόν, τὸν ἀληθινὸν θεὸν γνωρίζεσθαι ὁμολογοῦμεν Serg.*ep.*1(H.3.793E); **4.** later use of formula τὸ γὰρ μὴ λέγειν...τέλειον ἐν ἀνθρωπότητι...ἀλλὰ μίαν φ. τοῦ θεοῦ λόγου σεσαρκωμένην, ἄψυχόν τε καὶ ἄνουν τὸ τοῦ κυρίου σῶμα, τὴν Ἀπολιναρίου αἵρεσιν κρατύνει ‡Felix III Papa *ep.Petr.*1(H.2.820B); in Cyril's sense phrase had received orthodox recognition μίαν μὲν τοῦ θεοῦ λόγου φ. σεσαρκωμένην μέντοι καὶ ἐνανθρωπήσασαν, λέγειν οὐκ ἀρνούμεθα, διὰ τὸ ἐξ ἀμφοῖν ἕνα καὶ τὸν αὐτὸν εἶναι τὸν κύριον Flav.CP *ep.Thds.*(p.35.20; M.65.892B); πρὸς τοῦτο λέγομεν ὅτι πρῶτον μὲν οὐδὲν ἡμῖν ἐναντιοῦται...ἀλλὰ δοξάζομεν μίαν φ. τοῦ θεοῦ λόγου σεσαρκωμένην. ἔπειτα δὲ οὐδ' ἔστι τοῦ ἁγίου Ἀθανασίου †Leont.B.*sect.* 8.4(M.86.1256C); interpretations discussed ἡ μία φ. τοῦ θεοῦ λόγου σεσαρκωμένη τριπλῆν ἔχει τὴν ἔννοιαν· ἢ γὰρ κατὰ ἀντιστροφὴν λέγοιτο ...ἢ κατὰ τροπὴν οὐσίας...ἢ ὅτι μία οὖσα ἡ τοῦ λόγου φ. οὐ μόνον καθ' ἑαυτὴν ἀλλὰ μετὰ σαρκὸς οὖσα θεωρεῖται...εἰ δὲ κατὰ τὸ τελευταῖον σημαινόμενον, πῶς ἡ μετὰ σαρκὸς τοῦ λόγου φ. ... μία τῇ φ. ἐστίν, ἢ πῶς μὴ οὖσα μία τῇ φ., μία φ. λεχθήσεται; Leont.B.*cap.Sev.*17(M.86. 1905C); Leont.H.*monoph.*(M.86.1805B) cit. s. δυάς; dist. from μία φ. τοῦ λόγου σεσαρκωμένου: εἰ μίαν φ. τοῦ θεοῦ λόγου σεσαρκωμένου καὶ οὐ σεσαρκωμένην εἴποιτε, πῶς οὐ φανερῶς τὴν πατρικὴν διδασκαλίαν παραχαράξετε; εἰ δὲ σεσαρκωμένην ὁμολογεῖτε καὶ οὐ σεσαρκωμένου τοῦ λόγου μίαν φατέ, διὰ τόδε αὐτὸ δύο φ. ἔσται ὁ ἐκ λόγου καὶ σαρκὸς Χριστὸς...ἆρά γε φύσει σαρκὸς τὴν φ. τοῦ λόγου σεσαρκωμένην ὁμολογεῖτε, ἢ οὐχί; εἰ μὲν οὖν οὐχὶ ἢ λόγῳ μόνον, ἢ φαντασίᾳ, ἢ τροπῇ τοῦ λόγου, τὴν σάρκωσιν εἰδέναι ὑμᾶς ἀπολείπεται· εἰ δὲ φύσει σαρκὸς τὴν φ. σεσαρκῶσθαι τοῦ λόγου φατέ, ἄλλην τὴν σαρκοῦσαν καὶ ἄλλην τὴν σαρκουμένην ἐν τῷ ἑνὶ συνθέτῳ προσώπῳ Χριστοῦ γινωσκόντες, πῶς ἀριθμεῖν ἄνευ δυάδος ταύτας δυνήσεσθε; *ib.* 42(M.86.1796A); formally defined: εἴ τις...μίαν φ. τοῦ θεοῦ λόγου σεσαρκωμένην λέγων, μὴ οὕτως αὐτὰ λαμβάνῃ...ὅτι ἐκ τῆς θείας φ. καὶ τῆς ἀνθρωπίνης, τῆς ἑνώσεως καθ' ὑπόστασιν γενομένης, εἷς Χριστὸς ἀπετελέσθη· ἀλλ' ἐκ τῶν τοιούτων φωνῶν μίαν φ., ἤτοι οὐσίαν, θεότητος καὶ σαρκὸς τοῦ Χριστοῦ εἰσάγειν ἐπιχειρεῖ...ἀ. ἔ. CCP(553)*anath.*8(Hahn p.170); μίαν φ. ἁπλῶς ἐπὶ Χριστοῦ λέγειν οὐ παραδέχεται, ἀλλὰ μίαν φ. τοῦ θεοῦ λόγου σεσαρκωμένην· διὰ τῆς προσθήκης τοῦ 'σεσαρκωμένην' δηλοῦσιν τὴν φ. τῆς ἀνθρωπότητος, ἣν ἡ φ. τοῦ θεοῦ λόγου προσλαμβανομένη ἅμα τε καὶ σὺν ταύτῃ εἷς...Χριστὸς γέγονεν Thdr.Raith.*praep.*(p.190.18ff.; M.91.1489D); διὰ τοῦ σεσαρκωμένην εἰπεῖν τῆς καθ' ἡμᾶς φ. εἰσκεκομισμένην νοοῦντες τὴν οὐσίαν Max.*ep.*13(M.91.525A); only ground for exclusion εἰ τὰ συνοδικῶς καὶ μόνον εἰρημένα χρὴ ὁμολογεῖν, οὔτε τὴν μίαν τοῦ θεοῦ λόγου φ. σεσαρκωμένην, περιεκτικὴν πάσης τῆς τοῦ μυστηρίου οὖσαν εὐσεβείας, χρὴ λέγειν, συνοδικῶς οὐ πεφωνημένην. πλὴν ὅτι καὶ οὕτω ταῖς φ. καὶ τοῖς αὐτῶν ἰδιώμασι καὶ τὰ θελήματα συνομολογεῖν βιασθήσεσθε id. *Pyrr.*(M.91.300C); εἴ τις οὐχ ὁμολογεῖ...μίαν φ. τοῦ θεοῦ λόγου σεσαρκωμένην, διὰ τοῦ σεσαρκωμένην εἰπεῖν, τῆς καθ' ἡμᾶς οὐσίας ἐντελῶς ἐν αὐτῷ Χριστῷ τῷ θεῷ, καὶ ἀπαραλείπτως, μόνης δίχα τῆς ἁμαρτίας, σημαίνειν, εἴη κατάκριτος CLater.*can.*5.

D. in Cyril; **1.** doctrine; **a.** Cyr.'s interpretation of formula μία φ. τοῦ θεοῦ λόγου σεσαρκωμένη v. C.2. supra; **b.** Cyr.'s rejection of φυρμός, σύγχυσις, and σύγκρασις v.s.vv.; **c.** monophysitism of Cyr. verbal only φύσει τῇ καθ' ἡμᾶς τὸν ἐκ θεοῦ φύντα λόγον συνδοῦντες εἰς ἕνωσιν, καὶ εἰς ἕν τι τὸ ἐξ ἀμφοῖν ἀναπλέκοντες...εἰ καὶ νοοῖτο τῶν εἰς ἑνότητα συνδεδραμηκότων ἡ φ. διάφορος, εἰς υἱὸν ἕνα παραδεχθεὶς Cyr.*hom.pasch.*17.2(5^{2}.226D,E); φαμὲν...ὅτι σάρκα ἐψυχωμένην ψυχῇ λογικῇ ἑνώσας ὁ λόγος ἑαυτῷ καθ' ὑπόστασιν...καὶ ὅτι διάφοροι μὲν αἱ πρὸς ἑνότητα τὴν ἀληθινὴν συνενεχθεῖσαι φ. ... οὐχ ὡς τῆς τῶν φ. διαφορᾶς ἀνῃρημένης διὰ τὴν ἕνωσιν, ἀποτελεσασῶν δὲ μᾶλλον ἡμῖν τὸν ἕνα...Χριστόν...θεότητός τε καὶ ἀνθρωπότητος διὰ τῆς...συνδρομῆς id. *ep.*4(p.27.2; 5^{2}.23B,C); ὁ...τῷ φύσαντι συναΐδιος...υἱὸς ἐπειδὴ καταβέβηκεν εἰς τὴν ἀνθρώπου φ., οὐκ ἀπολισθήσας τοῦ εἶναι θεὸς id.*Thds.* (p.58.28; 5^{2}.23A) = *inc.unigen.*(5^{1}.696B); τεθναίη...ἂν οὐδαμῶς τό γε ἧκον εἰς ἰδίαν φ. θεὸς ὢν ὁ λόγος οὐδ' ἂν νοοῖτο τῶν ὅλων δημιουργὸς καθ' ἡμᾶς ὢν ἄνθρωπος, εἰ μὴ δεδημιούργηκε μὲν ὡς θεός, καὶ εἰ μὴ δίχα σαρκὸς νοοῖτο μετὰ τὴν ἕνωσιν, πρωτότοκος δὲ καὶ ἐκ νεκρῶν καθὸ πέφηνεν ἄνθρωπος, οὐκ ἀποβαλὼν τὸ εἶναι θεὸς διὰ τὴν ἐνανθρώπησιν... μεσίτης γάρ ἐστι θεοῦ καὶ ἀνθρώπων...φύσει μὲν ὑπάρχων θεὸς καὶ οὐ δίχα σαρκός, ἄνθρωπος δὲ ἀληθῶς καὶ οὐ ψιλὸς καθ' ἡμᾶς, ἀλλ' ὢν ὅπερ ἦν, καὶ εἰ γέγονε σάρξ *ib.*(p.69.7,23; 5^{2}.37A,D); cf.*inc.unigen.*(5^{1}.709B,E); ἐν τῇ τῆς θεότητος φ. πρὸς τὸν πατέρα, οὕτω καὶ πρὸς ἡμᾶς ἐν γένηται σχέσει τῇ κατὰ ἀνθρωπότητα id.*Arcad.*(p.91.9; 5^{2}.86B); ἔστι...μεσίτης θεοῦ, διὰ τὸ τῆς αὐτῆς οὐσίας ὑπάρχειν τῷ πατρί, ἔστι δὲ πάλιν καὶ ἀνθρώπων μεσίτης διὰ τὸ καὶ τῆς ἀνθρωπείας μετεσχηκέναι φ. τελείως χωρὶς ἁμαρτίας id.*deip.BMV* 12(p.24.16; M.76.269B); τὸν μεθ' ἡμῶν ὑπὸ νόμον ὡς ἄνθρωπον καὶ ὑπὲρ ἡμᾶς ὑπὲρ νόμον ὡς θεὸν... υἱὸν εἶναι τοῦ θεοῦ κατὰ ἀλήθειαν πιστεύομεν· οὔτε ψιλοῦντες θεότητος τὸ ἀνθρώπινον οὔτε μὴν ἀνθρωπότητος ἀπαμφιεννύντες τὸν λόγον μετὰ τὴν ἄφραστον...ἕνωσιν· ἀλλ' ἕνα καὶ τὸν αὐτὸν ὁμολογοῦντες υἱόν, ἐκ δυοῖν πραγμάτοιν, εἰς ἕν τι τὸ ἐξ ἀμφοῖν...ἐκπεφηνότα, καθ' ἕνωσιν... τὴν ἀνωτάτω, καὶ οὐ φύσεως παρατροπὴν id.*Thds.*(p.72.23; 5^{2}.41D) = *inc.unigen.*(5^{1}.713D); ἕνα καὶ τὸν αὐτὸν εἶναι πιστεύοντες ὡς ἐν θεότητι καὶ ἀνθρωπότητι, τουτέστι θεόν τε ὁμοῦ καὶ ἄνθρωπον. ὁ δέ γε τῆς νεωτάτης ἡμῖν ἀσεβείας εὑρέτης, καίτοι Χριστὸν ἕνα λέγειν προσποιούμενος, διαιρεῖ μὲν πανταχοῦ τὰς φ. id.*Nest.*2 proem.(p.32.36ff.; 6^{1}.30E–31A); προῆλθεν ἄνθρωπος ἐκ γυναικός, οὐχ ὅπερ ἦν, ἀποβεβληκώς, ἀλλ' ...μεμενηκὼς ὅπερ ἦν, θεὸς δηλονότι φύσει τε καὶ ἀληθείᾳ id.*ep.*17(p.35.20; 5^{2}.70A); cf. δύο...φύσεων ἕνωσις γέγονε...τὰς δὲ εὐαγγελικὰς καὶ ἀποστολικὰς περὶ τοῦ κυρίου φωνὰς...τὰς μὲν κοινοποιοῦντας ὡς ἐφ' ἑνὸς προσώπου, τὰς δὲ διαιροῦντας ὡς ἐπὶ δύο φ. Jo.Ant.*ep.Xyst.*(p.159.26,31) quoted and approved by Cyr.*ep.*39(p.17.14,19; 5^{2}.106B,C); εἷς γὰρ...Χριστός, κἂν ἡ τῶν φ. μὴ ἀγνοῆται διαφορά, ἐξ ὧν...τὴν ἕνωσιν πεπρᾶχθαί φαμεν *ib.*(p.18.26; 5^{2}.107E); *ib.*40(p.26.7,22ff.; 5^{2}.115D,116B,C); *ib.*44(p.36.10ff.; 5^{2}.133E); οὐ μεταβολῇ φύσεως καθ' ἡμᾶς γεγονώς ,ἀλλ' εὐδοκίᾳ μᾶλλον οἰκονομικῇ. ἠθέλησε γὰρ ἄνθρωπος γενέσθαι τὸ εἶναι θεὸς κατὰ φ. οὐκ ἀποβαλών *ib*.45(p.153.3ff.; 5².137A); *ib*.(p.155.25; 139C) cit. s. ἀφθαρσία; οὐκ αὐτὸν τὸν μονογενῆ... υἱὸν...παθεῖν εἰς ἰδίαν φ. ... παθεῖν δὲ μᾶλλον τῇ χοϊκῇ φ. *ib*.46(p.161.6; 5².144C); ref. Ac.2:32f., Jo.2:19 σύνες οὖν ὅπως αὐτὸς ἐγείρειν τὸν ἑαυτοῦ ναὸν ἐπαγγέλλεται, καίτοι τοῦ...πατρὸς ἀναστῆσαι λεγομένου... ἐνεργεῖν ὁ πατὴρ λέγεται...δι' υἱοῦ...οὐκοῦν [i.e. in Christ] παρεχώρει μὲν τὸ σῶμα τοῖς τῆς ἰδίας φ. νόμοις καὶ τὴν τοῦ θανάτου γεῦσιν ἐδέχετο ...θείᾳ γε μὴν ἐζωοποιεῖτο δυνάμει τῇ τοῦ ἑνωθέντος αὐτῷ καθ' ὑπόστασιν λόγου id.*Nest*.5.6(p.103.38; 6¹.139A); ἕνα...υἱὸν καὶ μίαν αὐτοῦ φ. εἶναί φαμεν κἂν εἰ ἐν προσλήψει νοοῖτο γενέσθαι σαρκὸς ψυχὴν ἐχούσης τὴν νοεράν. αὐτοῦ γὰρ...γέγονε τὸ ἀνθρώπινον id.*Chr. un*.(5¹.735E); **2.** terminology; **a.** φ. and ὑπόστασις equated: ἀμέλει τοι καὶ αὐτὸς ὁ πατήρ, ὁσάκις μίαν φ. εἶπεν τοῦ θεοῦ λόγου σεσαρκωμένην, ἐπὶ τούτου τῷ τῆς φ. ὀνόματι ἀνθ' ὑποστάσεως ἐχρήσατο Justn. *conf*.(p.78.9; M.86.1001A); **b.** φ. as equivalent of οὐσία; Cyr. recognized difference between οὐσία or φ. and ὑπόστασις in Trinitarian doctrine, cf.Cyr.*dial.Trin*.1(5¹.408C,D); id.*Is*.3.5(2.540A); id.*Jo*.1.2 (4.16B); id.*Arcad*.(p.91.14; 5².86A); he repeats with approval statement of Jo. Ant. where φ. is opp. πρόσωπον, Jo.Ant.*ep.Xyst*.(p.159. 26,31) and Cyr.*ep*.39(p.17.14,19; 5².106B,C); for Cyr.'s approximation of ὑπόστασις and πρόσωπον v. ὑπόστασις; at other times φ. is equated with ὑπόστασις in sense of οὐσία: ἡ τῶν φ., ἢ γοῦν ὑποστάσεων διαφορά Cyr.*ep*.40(p.26.25; 5².116C); ἀσύγχυτοι μεμενήκασιν αἱ φ., ἤγουν ὑποστάσεις id.*schol.inc*.11(5¹.785B); **c.** as approximating to πρόσωπον: ἐφ' ἑνὸς προσώπου καὶ φ. ἢ γοῦν ὑποστάσεως μιᾶς id. *apol.orient*.8(p.50.6; 6¹.180A); τὴν καθ' ὑπόστασιν ἕνωσιν γενέσθαι φαμέν...οὐδὲν ἕτερον ὑποφαίνοντος πλὴν ὅτι μόνον ἡ τοῦ λόγου φ. ἤγουν ὑπόστασις, ὅ ἐστιν αὐτὸς ὁ λόγος...εἷς νοεῖται...ὁ αὐτὸς θεὸς καὶ ἄνθρωπος id.*apol.Thdt*.2(p.115.13,15; 6¹.209B); ὑπόστασις replaces φ. in the formula μία φ. σεσαρκωμένη, id.*ep*.17(p.38.22; 5².73D); id. *Nest*.2.8(p.46.29; 6¹.51D); **d.** comments of later writers: cf.Leont.B. *arg.Sev*.(M.86.1924Dff.); ref. Cyr.*schol.inc*.11(5¹.785B) λέγεται γὰρ καὶ ὑπόστασις παρὰ τὸ ὑφεστηκέναι ἡ φ. Leont.H.*monoph*.(M.86.1825A); πῇ μὲν τὴν ὑπόστασιν ἀντὶ οὐσίας καὶ φ. ... πῇ δὲ τὴν φ. ἀντὶ ὑποστάσεως ἐκφωνοῦντες ἐπὶ τῆς θείας ἐνανθρωπήσεως...τὰ τοίνυν καταχρηστικῶς λεγόμενα οὐκ εἰσὶ κυρίως, ἃ λέγονται...οὔτε δὲ νοοῦνται, ὡς ὀνομάζονται. ἡνίκα τοιγαροῦν ὑποστάσεων ἕνωσιν λέγει ὁ ἐν ἁγίοις Κύριλλος...ἀντὶ οὐσιῶν κέχρηται τῇ φωνῇ, τὸ ὑφεστὸς τῶν πραγμάτων ...διὰ τοῦ ὀνόματος τῆς ὑποστάσεως δεικνύς Eub.*fr*.1 ap.*Doct.Patr*.22 (p.141.22ff.); ref. those who assert φ. and ὑπόστασις to be identical τί ἐστι τὸ ἐκ τῶν ὀνομάτων τούτων φ. τε καὶ ὑποστάσεως ἐπὶ Χριστοῦ σημαινόμενον καθ' ὑμᾶς ταὐτόν; οὐσία ἢ τὸ κοινὸν...σημαίνουσα καὶ κατὰ πολλῶν ὑποστάσεων ἤγουν ἀτόμων κατηγορουμένη, ἢ καταχρηστικὸν πρόσωπον; id.*fr*.2 *ib*.(p.145.2ff.); *ib*.(p.147.9ff.); ὁ Ἀθανάσιός τε καὶ Κύριλλος...καταχρηστικῶς, καὶ οὐ κυρίως, τῷ τῆς φ. ὀνόματι τὴν ὑπόστασιν ἐδήλωσαν Jo.D.*Jacob*.52(M.94.1461D); it is pointed out that μία φ. σεσαρκωμένη refers to Logos, not to Christ, †Leont.B.*sect*.8(M.86.1253A); by this term Son is shewn to be truly and essentially Son opp. son by grace, Leont.H.*monoph*.(M.86. 1876B); word φ. has been deliberately chosen in contradistinction to other terms ὥστε τὸ εἰπεῖν, φ. τοῦ λόγου, οὔτε τὴν ὑπόστασιν μόνην σημαίνει, οὔτε τὸ κοινὸν τῶν ὑποστάσεων, ἀλλὰ τὴν κοινὴν φ. ἐν τῇ τοῦ λόγου ὑποστάσει ὁλικῶς θεωρουμένην Jo.D.*f.o*.3.11(M.94.1025B).

E. in subsequent Christology; **1.** formulations leading up to Chalcedonian definition ἐκ δύο φ. τὸν Χριστὸν μετὰ τὴν σάρκωσιν ...ἐν μιᾷ ὑποστάσει καὶ ἐν ἑνὶ προσώπῳ ἕνα Χριστὸν...ὁμολογοῦμεν Flav.CP *ep.Thds*.(p.35.17; M.65.892B); ἐκ δύο φ. ὁμολογοῦμεν τὸν Χριστὸν εἶναι μετὰ τὴν ἐνανθρώπησιν ἐν μιᾷ ὑποστάσει CCP(448)*act*. (p.114.9; H.2.128E); προσκυνοῦμεν τὸν ἕνα κύριον...ἐν δύο φύσεσι γνωριζόμενον τὴν μὲν...εἶχεν ἐν ἑαυτῷ προαιώνιον...τὴν δὲ ὡς ἐκ μητρὸς...γεννηθεὶς λαβὼν...ἥνωσεν ἑαυτῷ καθ' ὑπόστασιν Bas.Sel. *ib*.(p.117.22; 132E); πιστεύομεν...εἰς τὸν ἕνα κύριον...ἐν δύο φ. μετὰ τὴν ἐνανθρώπησιν Seleucus of Amasea *ib*.(p.118.2; 133A); but cf. retractations of two last ap.CEph.(449)*act*.(pp.179.18,181.10; H.2.213C,216D); σωζομένης...τῆς ἰδιότητος ἑκατέρας **φ.** καὶ εἰς ἓν πρόσωπον συνιούσης...φυλάττει γὰρ ἑκατέρα φ. τὴν ἑαυτῆς ἰδιότητα Leo Mag.*ep*.28.3(p.13.11,27; M.*PL*.54.764A,766A); οὐ τῆς αὐτῆς ἐστι φ. τὸ λέγειν [Jo.10:30; 14:28]. εἰ καὶ...ἐν τῷ...Χριστῷ τοῦ θεοῦ καὶ **τοῦ** ἀνθρώπου ἕν ἐστιν πρόσωπον, ὅμως ἕτερόν ἐστιν ἐκεῖνο ἐξ οὗ...κοινόν ἐστιν τὸ τῆς ὕβρεως, καὶ ἕτερον ἐξ οὗ κοινὸν τὸ τῆς δόξης καθέστηκεν *ib*.28.4(p.16.3; 772A); Διόσκορος ἔλεγεν· τὸ ἐκ δύο φ. δέχομαι, τὸ δὲ δύο οὐ δέχομαι· ὁ δὲ Λέων δύο φ. λέγει εἶναι ἐν τῷ Χριστῷ ἡνωμένας ἀσυγχύτως...τίνα τοίνυν ἀκολουθεῖτε;...προστίθετε οὖν τῷ ὅρῳ...δύο φ. εἶναι ἡνωμένας ἀτρέπτως καὶ ἀμερίστως καὶ ἀσυγχύτως ἐν τῷ Χριστῷ CChalc.*act*.5(*ACO* 2.1.2 p.125.17ff.; H.2.449E); **2.** *Symb.Chalc*. τοὺς δύο μὲν πρὸ τῆς ἑνώσεως φύσεις...μίαν δὲ μετὰ τὴν ἕνωσιν ἀναπλάττοντας ἀναθεματίζει (p.129.21; H.2.456B); ἐν δύο φ. ἀσυγχύτως ἀτρέπτως ἀδιαιρέτως ἀχωρίστως γνωριζόμενον, οὐδαμοῦ τῆς τῶν φ. διαφορᾶς ἀνῃρημένης διὰ τὴν ἕνωσιν, σῳζομένης δὲ μᾶλλον τῆς ἰδιότητος ἑκατέρας φ. καὶ εἰς ἓν πρόσωπον καὶ μίαν ὑπόστασιν συντρεχούσης *ib*.(p.129.30ff.; 456C); though ἐν δύο φύσεσι was correct form of *Symb.Chalc*., †Leont.B.*sect*.4.7(M.86.1228A); Sev.Ant.ap.Leont.H.*monoph*.(M.86.1849A); cf.id.ap.Eust.Mon.*ep*. (M.86.903D) cit. s. ἕνωσις; CCP(536)*act*.1(*ACO* 3 p.6.13; H.2.1200B); *Symb.Chalc*.ap.Evagr.*h.e*.2.4(p.49.30; M.86.2508C); repeated in *Symb.CP* (681)(H.3.1400C); ἐκ δύο φ. was current at same time ἔστιν ὅτε ἐκ δύο οὖν φ. λέγοντες τὸν Χριστόν, καὶ δύο φ., καὶ ἐν δυσὶ φ. λέγομεν εἶναι αὐτόν, τὸν τοῦ ἀσυγχύτου...φυλάττοντες λόγον Sev.Ant. *fr*.ap.Eust.Mon.*ep*.(M.86.912A); ἡμεῖς δὲ...ἐκ δύο μὲν φ. λέγομεν τὸν Χριστόν, ὥσπερ καὶ ἐκ πολλῶν μελῶν...τὸ ἓν σῶμα Eust.Mon.*ep*. (912A); τὴν φ. τῆς σαρκὸς...δι' ἣν καὶ τὸ ἐκ δύο φ. λέγεται δύο φ. *ib*. (916B); *ib*.(917D); καὶ ἐκ δύο φ. τὸν Χριστὸν ὀνομάζοντες...καὶ διπλοῦν κατὰ τὰς φ. ... διὸ καὶ ἐν δυσὶν αὐτὸν δογματίζομεν φ. Sophr.H.*ep.syn*. (M.87.3165C); ‡Cyr.*Trin*.18(6³.24D; M.77.1157B) cit. s. ἀσυγχύτως; τὰς αὐτοῦ φ., ἐξ ὧν, καὶ ἐν αἷς ὑπάρχει Max.*Pyrr*.(M.91.289B); ἐκ τούτων δέ, θείας φ. καὶ ἀνθρωπίνης φ. λέγω, καὶ ἐν ταύταις, καὶ τούτων ὑπόστασίς ἐστι...ὁ εἷς καὶ μόνος Χριστὸς καὶ υἱός id.*opusc*.(M.91. 96A); τέλειός ἐστιν...ἐκ δύο φ. ... καὶ ἐν δύο φ. Jo.D.*f.o*.1.2(M.94. 793A); **3.** monophysite statements (pre-Chalcedonian v. C.3) τὸ λέγειν δύο φ. ἐπὶ Χριστοῦ, πάσης κατηγορίας ἐπίμεστον, εἰ καὶ ὑπὸ πλειόνων...πατέρων εἴρηται...μὴ...εἴπῃς ὡς τῇ λέξει τῇ τῶν δύο φ. τινὲς τῶν πατέρων ἐχρήσαντο. ἐχρήσαντο γὰρ ἀδιαβλήτως Sev.Ant. *fr*.ap.*Doct.Patr*.2(p.24.17ff.); ἀναθεματίζομεν...τοὺς δύο λέγοντας...φ. μετὰ τὴν...ἕνωσιν τὸν ἕνα κύριον id.*fr*.ap.Eust.Mon.*ep*.(M.86.909C); ἡμεῖς [i.e. Acephaloi] εὐλαβούμενοι ἐκ φ. μὲν δύο, οὐ μὴν ἐν δυσὶ φ. ὑπάρχειν τὸν Χριστὸν ὁριζόμεθα Leont.B.*arg.Sev*.(M.86.1929A); ἐσαρκώθη μίαν λοιπὸν μετὰ τῆς ἰδίας σαρκὸς φ. ἔχων, κἂν ἐκ δύο συνέστη τῶν ἐναντίων Oecum.*Col*.2:9(p.455.5); ἐκ θεότητος καὶ ἀνθρωπότητος εἰς μίαν ὑπάρχει φ. id.*Eph*.4:13(p.450.1); and monothelite confessions μίαν ὑπόστασιν σύνθετον ἐν δύο καὶ μετὰ τὴν ἕνωσιν κηρύττοντες φ., τὴν διαφορὰν ἑκατέρας γνωρίζοντες φ. κατὰ τὴν αὐτῶν ἰδιότητα...ἓν θέλημα Paul.CP *ep.Thdr*.(M.*PL*.87.95A); εἴ τις οὐχ ὁμολογεῖ ἐκ δύο φ. ... ἕνα Χριστόν...ἀ. ἔ. Cyrus Al.*cap*.6(H.3. 1341B); εἴ τις τὸν ἕνα...Χριστὸν ἐν δυσὶ θεωρεῖσθαι λέγων ταῖς φ., οὐχ ἕνα τῆς...τριάδος τὸν αὐτὸν ὁμολογεῖ...ἀ. ἔ. *ib*.7(1341C); v. supra C.3 and ὑπόστασις; **4.** though μία φ. τοῦ...λόγου σεσαρκωμένη (rightly interpreted) was never condemned (v. supra C.4), δύο φ. came to be generally accepted by orthodox ὁ υἱός, εἷς ὢν καὶ δύο φ. Thdt. *rect.conf*.11(M.6.1225C); *ib*.12(1232A); οἱ τὸν Χριστιανισμὸν σχηματιζόμενοι, οἱ ἐπ' ἀναιρέσει τῶν δύο φ. τοῦ Χριστοῦ...ζητοῦντες *ib*.15 (1233B); εἰ...ἐκ δύο φ. λέγουσιν...πῶς ἐν θεότητι καὶ ἀνθρωπότητι λέγοντες μετὰ τὴν ἕνωσιν, οὐκ ἐν δύο φ. λέγειν...ἀναγκασθήσονται; Leont.B.*cap.Sev*.3(M.86.1901C); δῆλον πῶς δύο μὲν φ. λέγομεν ἐπὶ Χριστοῦ, μίαν δὲ ὑπόστασιν· ὅτι τῇ ἀφοριστικῇ ἰδιότητι τῇ ἀπὸ τοῦ πατρὸς συνάπτεται πρὸς τὴν σάρκα· ὥσπερ ἀμέλει τῇ συναπτούσῃ αὐτὸν φυσικῇ ἰδιότητι τῷ πατρί, τὸ διάφορον ἔχει πρὸς τὴν σάρκα· καὶ ὥσπερ πρὸς τὸν πατέρα μία φ. ἐστὶ διὰ τὴν τῆς φ. ταυτότητα, οὕτως οὐ μία φ. πρὸς τὴν σάρκα διὰ τὴν ταύτης καὶ ἐν τῇ πρὸς τὸν λόγον ἑνώσει ἄτρεπτον ἰδιότητα *ib*.25(1909C); Leont.H.*monoph*.18(M.86.1780D) cit. s. ἕνωσις; τῇ μὲν φωνῇ τῶν δύο φ. ἐχρήσαντο ἅγιοι πρὸ τῶν αἱρετικῶν, τῇ δὲ μιᾶς φ. πρὸ τῶν χρησαμένων αὐτῇ πατέρων, εὕρεται γεγόνασιν αἱρετικοὶ Eust.Mon.*ep*.(M.86.905C); ὁμολογοῦμεν δύο φ. μετὰ τὴν ἕνωσιν ἐν μιᾷ ὑποστάσει...καὶ οὐχ ὥσπερ οἱ...Εὐτυχιανισταὶ...πρὸ τῆς ἑνώσεως δύο λέγομεν φ., μίαν δὲ μετὰ τὴν ἕνωσιν *Libell*.ap.CCP(536)*act*.5(*ACO* 3 p.31.8; H.2.1272D); εἴ τις ἐκ δύο φ. ... ὁμολογῶν τὴν ἕνωσιν γεγενῆσθαι ἢ μίαν φ. τοῦ θεοῦ λόγου σεσαρκωμένην λέγων...ἐκ τῶν τοιούτων φωνῶν μίαν φ., ἤτοι οὐσίαν...τοῦ Χριστοῦ εἰσάγειν ἐπιχειρεῖ· ὁ τοιοῦτος ἀ. ἔ. CCP(553)*anath*.8(p.170; H.3.197B); εἴ τις οὐχ ὁμολογεῖ...κυρίως καὶ ἀληθῶς ἐκ δύο φ. ... καὶ ἐν δύο φ. ... καθ' ὑπόστασιν ἡνωμέναις...τὸν αὐτὸν καὶ ἕνα κύριον ἡμῶν...ὑπάρχειν, εἴη κατάκριτος CLater *can*.6; *ib*.7; Max.*ep*.15(M.91.556B) cit. s. διαφορά; διπλοῦν τὴν φ., ἤτοι τὴν οὐσίαν *ib*.11(468C); *ib*.12(484A) cit. s. ἕνωσις; θεὸς ὢν ὁ αὐτὸς φύσει, καὶ ἄνθρωπος φύσει Pamph.H.*panopl*.7.3(p.625); Anast.S.*hod*.8(M. 89.137B); εἰ δὲ ἐν ἀληθείᾳ ἄνθρωπος γέγονε, φύσει ἄνθρωπός ἐστι καὶ μετὰ τὴν ἕνωσιν ὁ Χριστός, καὶ φύσει θεός *ib*.(137C); τὸ δέ, Χριστός, ὄνομα τῆς ὑποστάσεως λέγομεν, οὐ μονοτρόπως λεγόμενον, ἀλλὰ τῶν δύο φ. ὑπάρχον σημαντικόν. αὐτὸς γὰρ ἑαυτὸν ἔχρισε...ὡς θεὸς...ὡς ἄνθρωπος· αὐτὸς γάρ ἐστι τοῦτο κἀκεῖνο Jo.D.*f.o*.3.3(M.94.989A); ἡ ἁγία σύνοδος ἡ ἐν Χαλκηδόνι...κατὰ Εὐτύχους καὶ Διοσκόρου τῶν ἀρνησαμένων εἶνε [εἶναι] δύο φ. ἐν τῷ Χριστῷ *CIG* 8962.

V. of divine nature in rel. to man;

A. divine nature bestowed on man; **1.** in Inc. τὴν καταβᾶσαν εἰς τὴν ἀνθρωπίνην φ. ... δύναμιν...συμβαλλομένην εἰς σωτηρίαν τοῖς πιστεύουσιν, ὁρῶσιν ὅτι ἀπ' ἐκείνου ἤρξατο θεία καὶ ἀνθρωπίνη συνυφαίνεσθαι φ., ἵν' ἡ ἀνθρωπίνη τῇ πρὸς τὸ θειότερον κοινωνίᾳ γένηται θεία...ἐν...πᾶσι τοῖς μετὰ τοῦ πιστεύειν ἀναλαμβάνουσι βίον, ὃν Ἰησοῦς ἐδίδαξεν Or.*Cels*.3.28(p.226.10ff.; M.11.956cf.); ἀνείληφε σῶμα ἀνθρώπινον, ἵνα...ποιήσῃ τοὺς ἀνθρώπους κοινωνῆσαι θείας καὶ νοερᾶς φ. Ath.*v.Anton*.74(M.26.945c); id.*ep.Adelph*.4(M.26.1077b); ἀνθρωπίνως εἰληφέναι...ἵνα δι' αὐτὸν οἱ ἄνθρωποι, ἐπὶ μὲν τῆς γῆς ὡς κοινωνοὶ γενόμενοι θείας φ., λοιπὸν ἐξουσίαν ἔχωσι κατὰ δαιμόνων, ἐν δὲ τοῖς οὐρανοῖς, ὡς ἐλευθερωθέντες ἀπὸ τῆς φθορᾶς, αἰωνίως βασιλεύσωσι id.*Ar*.3.40(M.26.409a); εἰ δὲ καὶ θεοί τινες ἐκλήθησαν ἀλλ' οὐ τῇ φ., ἀλλὰ τῇ μετουσίᾳ τοῦ υἱοῦ id.*ep.Serap*.2.4(M.26.613c); Cyr. *apol.Thdt*.3(p.120.3; 6[1].213d); id.*Chr.un*.(5[1].756e); συνάψας [sc. Christ] τοῖς ἐπουρανίοις τὰ ἐπίγεια, τὴν...τῶν ἀνθρώπων φ. ... τῷ θεῷ ...προσαγαγὼν σωθεῖσαν...καὶ θεωθεῖσαν οὐκ οὐσίας ταυτότητι, ἀλλὰ δυνάμει...τῆς ἐνανθρωπήσεως· θείας κοινωνοὺς φ., διὰ τῆς ἐξ ἡμῶν ἁγίας αὐτοῦ σαρκός, ὡς ἀπαρχῆς καὶ ἡμᾶς ἀπεργάσηται Max.*ep*.11 (M.91.468c); *ib*.43(640b); μυρία λαβόντες ἀγαθὰ διὰ τῆς ἐπιφανείας Χριστοῦ, δι' ὧν δυνάμεθα καὶ θείας φ. γενέσθαι κοινωνοί, καὶ πρὸς ζωὴν καὶ εὐσέβειαν γενέσθαι *cat.2Pet*.1:3f.(p.85.32); **2.** through H. Ghost τῇ τοῦ πνεύματος μετουσίᾳ γινόμεθα κοινωνοὶ θείας φ. Ath.*ep.Serap*.1. 4(M.26.585c); *ib*.(585b); id.*Ar*.3.25(M.26.376b); ‡Ath.*dial.Trin*.1.7 (M.28.1125d).

B. its likeness bestowed on the contemplative, Bas.*hom.in Ps*. 29(1.129b; M.29.317b).

φυσίωμα, τό, *being puffed up*; met., *pride, elation* ἔπαρμα καρδίας καὶ φ. πνεύματος Hipp.*Noet*.1(p.235.6; M.10.804a); *ib*.(p.237.3; 806a).

φυσίωσις, ἡ, *puffing up*; fig., *pride* τοὺς παραφυσῶντας εἰς φ.... τῶν αἱρέσεων ἀνέμους Clem.*paed*.1.5(p.101.1; M.8.269c); Eus.*h.e*. 6.43.1(M.20.616b); Chrys.*hom.12.1 in 1Cor*.(10.97c).

φυτεία, ἡ, *that which is planted, plantation*, Clem.*str*.6.1(p.422.25; M.9.209a); *ib*.7.18(p.78.28; 557a); Gr.Nyss.*hom.in Cant*.proem.(M. 44.761a); fig. ὁ παράδεισος ὁ πνευματικὸς αὐτὸς ἡμῶν ὁ σωτὴρ ὑπάρχει, εἰς ὃν καταφυτευόμεθα μετατεθέντες...ἡ μεταβολὴ δὲ τῆς φ. εἰς εὐκαρπίαν συμβάλλεται Clem.*str*.6.1(p.423.15; 209b); of men ἡ φ. αὐτῶν [sc. τῶν ὁσίων] ἐρριζωμένη εἰς τὸν αἰῶνα *Pss.Sal*.14.3; οὗτοι γὰρ οὐκ εἰσιν φ. πατρός Ign.*Trall*.11.1; id.*Philad*.3.1; of Church τὴν φυτ⟨ε⟩ίαν ἣν φυτεύσουσιν οἱ δώδεκα ἀπόστολοι *Ascens.Is*.4.3; τὴν ἀπὸ Πέτρου καὶ Παύλου φ. γενηθεῖσαν Ῥωμαίων τε καὶ Κορινθίων συνεκεράσατε Dion.Cor.ap.Eus.*h.e*.2.25.8(M.20.209a); θεοῦ φ. ἡ καθολικὴ ἐκκλησία *Const.App*.1 proem.; Epiph.*haer*.45.4(p.202.5; M.41. 836b); of tree of life τῆς ἀνθρωπίνης οὐσίας ὁ ἀρχηγὸς τὴν διαβολὴν ...ἀσμενίσας...ἔξω βάλλεται τοῦ θείου περιβόλου...καὶ τῶν θεσπεσίων ἀλλοτριοῦται μονῶν ἀλλότριος τῆς πανολβίου φ. γενόμενος Mac.Mgn. *apocr*.2.21(p.43.21).

φυτεύ-ω, 1. *plant, sow*, fig. ἡ γὰρ φυτευθεῖσα ὑπὸ τοῦ θεοῦ ἄμπελος καὶ σωτῆρος Χριστοῦ ὁ λαὸς αὐτοῦ ἐστι Just.*dial*.110.4(M.6.729c); θεὸς μὲν καλὴν ἄμπελον ἐφύτευσε τὴν τοῦ ἀνθρώπου ψυχήν Or.*hom.2.1 in Jer*.(p.17.21; M.13.277c); φ. ... ὑμᾶς [sc. ὁ θεός] εἰς τὴν ἐκκλησίαν Cyr.H.*procatech*.17; ἐπιθυμίαι ἀποτυχοῦσαι ~ουσι λύπας Nil.*Eulog*.7 (M.77.1104a); **2.** *found* μοναστήριά τε φ. Mart.Ant.*pan*.2(M.47.xliii); **3.** med., *kindle* τὸ πῦρ ἐφυτεύσαντο ‡Caes.Naz.*dial*.1.60(M.38.928).

φυτηκόμος, *tending* or *cultivating plants*, Gr.Nyss.*hom.4 in Cant*. (M.44.829b); Nonn.*par.Jo*.20:15(M.43.909c); Thdt.*eran*.3(4.255).

***φυτοεργείη, ἡ,** *cultivation*, Gr.Naz.*carm*.1.2.1.257(M.37.542a).

φυτοκομία, ἡ, *grafting*; of plants, Gr.Nyss.*hex*.2(M.44.64b, v.l. φυτηκομία).

***φυτοκομίζω,** *cultivate, nurture* a plant, fig. ὁ τῶν ἀνθρώπων σπόρος, ὁ...εὐσεβείᾳ φυτοκομισθεὶς Areth.*apoc*.43(M.106.693b).

***φυτοκόμος,** *tending* or *nurturing plants* or *trees*; **1.** as subst., *gardener*, Bas.*hex*.5.6(1.45c; M.29.108a); Mac.Mgn.*apocr*.2.21(p.43. 11); Thdt.*h.e*.4.15.1(3.971); fig. ῥιζοτόμος ἀλλ' οὐ φ. πάσης κακίας πέφηνας Jo.Mon.*hymn.Nic*.6(M.96.1385c); of God τὸν καρπὸν...ὁ θεὸς εὐφρανθήσεται, ὡς ἀγαθὸς φ. τοῖς ἰδίοις ἔργοις ἐπαγαλλόμενος Gr.Nyss.*bapt.Chr*.(M.46.596a); id.*hom.in Cant*.proem.(M.44.761b); **2.** met., *that bears trees* or *plants* γαίης ἀπὸ φ. Eudoc.*Cypr*.2.212(M. 85.853b); ‡Caes.Naz.*dial*.3.144(M.38.1093).

φυτοσκαφία, ἡ, *digging*, Gr.Naz.*carm*.1.2.1.436(M.37.555a).

φυτουργ-έω, 1. *tend, cultivate*, Thdt.*eran*.1(4.69); **2.** *plant* παραδείσου τε πολιοῦχον πεποίηκεν ὃν κατ' ἀνατολὰς πεφυτούργηκεν Jo.D.*hom*.4.7(M.96.609a); fig. ὁ ἔμψυχον σπείρων ἄρουραν...διὰ τὸν θεὸν ~εῖ Clem.*paed*.2.10(p.208.9; M.8.497a); πῶς ~εῖ [sc. τὸ τοῦ σπόρου σύστημα] τὴν πυρώδη καρδίαν Geo.Pis.*hex*.647(M.92.1486a).

φυτούργημα, τό, *that which is planted, plant*, fig. βουλόμενοι... παγιῶσαι τὰ ζιζανιώδη φ. Eust.*fr.in Pr.8*:22(M.18.676d).

φυτουργία, ἡ, 1. *cultivation of plants*, Clem.*str*.1.7(p.24.24; M.8. 732c); **2.** *that which is planted, plantation*, fig. αὔξοι δὲ τὴν σὴν εὐσεβῆ φ. Geo.Pis.*bell.Avar*.531(M.92.1294a).

φυτουργός, *tending* or *caring for plants*; as subst., *one who plants, sower*; fig., *sower, originator* τῷ φ. τῆς μάχης Geo.Pis.*Sev*.167(M.92. 1633b); τῷ φ. τῶν φρενοσπόρων λόγων id.*bell.Avar*.12(M.92.1264a); of God σὺ εἶ ὁ φ. τοῦ ἀγαθοῦ δένδρου *A.Thom*.A 10(p.114.13); ὁ κοινὸς ἁπάντων φ. δι' ὃν ἡ τῶν ὅλων οὐσία φύει καὶ θάλλει Eus.*l.C*.12(p.231. 23; M.20.1389b); of Christ μάθε παρὰ τοῦ καλοῦ φ. ... τὴν ἄμπελον τὴν πνευματικὴν θεραπεύοντος Chrys.*hom.11.5 in Rom*.(9.538b); ὅταν εἰς τὸν τῆς ἐκκλησίας ἀποβλέψω λειμῶνα, τὸν τοῦ παραδείσου τούτου φ., τὸν δεσπότην λέγω Χριστόν, ὑπερεκπλήττομαι Bas.Sel.*or*.34.1(M.85. 365d); αὐτὴ γὰρ τὸν φ. τῆς κτίσεως καὶ τοῦ παραδείσου...ἐκυοφόρησεν Jo.Eub.*concept.BMV* 12(M.96.1480a); of H. Ghost ἐν ᾧ ὁ θεὸς καὶ πατὴρ...γέγονε γεωργός, καὶ φ. τὸ πανάγιον πνεῦμα Mod.*dorm*.2(M. 86.3284b).

φυτώριον, τό, *nursery-garden*, Clem.*str*.1.7(p.24.24; M.8.732c).

φύω, 1. *beget* ὁ κύριος ἡμῶν Ἰησοῦς Χριστὸς ἰσοσθενῆ καὶ ἰσοκλεᾶ τῷ φύσαντι καταδεικνὺς ἑαυτόν Cyr.*Is*.3.1(2.366b); **2.** *be begotten* τὸν ἐκ θεοῦ φύντα λόγον id.*inc.unigen*.(5[1].682d).

[*]φωλίς, ἡ, (= φολίς) *horny scale* of reptiles, Gr.Naz.*carm*.1.2. 28.101(M.37.864a); Gr.Nyss.*hom.opif*.7.3(M.44.141d).

***φωνάζω,** *shout*, Barth.Edess.*Agar*.(M.104.1428b).

φωνή, ἡ, 1. *voice*; **a.** in prayer ἔξεστιν οὖν μηδὲ φωνῇ τὴν εὐχὴν παραπέμπειν, συντείνοντα μόνον δ' ἔνδοθεν τὸ πνευματικὸν πᾶν εἰς φ. τὴν νοητὴν κατὰ τὴν ἀπερίσπαστον πρὸς τὸν θεὸν ἐπιστροφήν Clem.*str*. 7.7(p.32.30ff.; M.9.461a); **b.** of God, *Barn*.8.7; Or.*Cels*.2.72(p.194. 12ff.; M.11.909a); ἔστιν οὖν φ. πληγὴ ἀέρος...ἡ δὲ τοῦ κυρίου φ. ἑτερογενής τίς ἐστι, φαντασιοῦντος τοῦ θεοῦ οἷς ἀκούειν βούλεται τῆς φ. αὐτοῦ· ὥστε ἀναλογίαν ἔχειν τὴν φαντασίαν ταύτην πρὸς τὴν ἐν τοῖς ὀνείροις γινομένην...οὐχὶ τοῦ ἔξωθεν ἀέρος πληγέντος εἰσέπεσε διὰ τῆς ἀκοῆς τῶν λεγομένων ἡ αἴσθησις, ἀλλ' αὐτοῦ τοῦ ἡγεμονικοῦ παραδεξαμένου τὰ νοήματα, τῇ μνήμῃ τῶν θεασαμένων πέφυκε παραμένειν †Bas.*hom.in Ps*.28(1.358eff.; M.30.73c); ref. generation of Logos καὶ πῶς ἄρα προήει [sc. ὁ λόγος] πάντως που κατὰ προφορὰν φωνῆς ἐνάρθρου; φθεγγομένου δηλαδὴ καὶ λαλοῦντος τοῦ θεοῦ ὁμοίως ἀνθρώποις Eus.*e.th*.2.9(p.109.10; M.24.917b); **c.** φ. ἐξ οὐρανοῦ; of divine voice φ. ἐξ οὐρανοῦ ἐγένετο...καὶ τὸν μὲν εἰπόντα οὐδεὶς εἶδεν, τὴν δὲ φ. τῶν ἡμετέρων οἱ παρόντες ἤκουσαν *M.Polyc*.9.1; *A.Jo*.18(p.161.3); φ. ἄνωθεν καταπληκτικῶς ἐπιρρηγνυμένης ἐφ' ἅπαν τὸ ὑποκείμενον... ἡ δὲ φ. αὕτη ἔναρθρος ἦν, θείᾳ δυνάμει, δίχα τῶν φωνητικῶν ὀργάνων, τοῦ ἀέρος διαρθροῦντος τὸν λόγον Gr.Nyss.*v.Mos*.45(M.44.316c); at Transfiguration, Or.*Cels*.2.72(p.194.2; M.11.908c); *Hom.Clem*.3.53; Eus.*e.th*.1.12(p.71.28; M.24.848b); **d.** of prophets and others speaking with voice of God, Ign.*Philad*.7.1; [sc. ὁ ἐπίσκοπος] δι' οὗ κύριος ἐν τῷ φωτισμῷ ὑμῶν...ἐφ' ἑκατέρων ὑμῶν τὴν ἱερὰν ἐξέτεινεν φ. λέγων 'υἱός μου εἶ σύ' *Const.App*.2.32.3; Ἀγγαῖος ὁμοίως ἀπὸ θεϊκῆς φ. Didym.*Trin*.2.2(M.39.453c); **e.** ἀπὸ φωνῆς (edited) *by the hand of*, Philost.*h.e*.tit.(M.65.460a); †Leont.B.*sect*.tit.(M.86.1193); **f.** met., of voice of the heavens, declaring glory of God, Thdt.*Ps.18*:4(1. 719); **g.** fig.; of Jo. Bapt. ὁ Ἰωάννης...τὸ πᾶν γίνεται φ. προτρεπτική ...φ. δὲ ὁμολογήσει ἐν ἐρήμῳ βοῶσα Clem.*prot*.1(p.9.14; M.8.65a); φ. κυρίου ὁ Ἰωάννης, ἄγγελος ἀπὸ θεοῦ ἀπεσταλμένος πρὸ προσώπου κυρίου τοῦ ἑτοιμάσαι κυρίῳ λαὸν κατεσκευασμένον. αὕτη οὖν ἡ φ. ἐπὶ τῶν ὑδάτων ἦν, ἐπὶ τῷ Ἰορδάνῃ, ἐν ᾧ ἐβάπτισε...οὐκοῦν φ. κυρίου ἐπὶ τῶν ὑδάτων ὁ Ἰωάννης ἐστὶν ἐπὶ τοῦ βαπτίσματος †Bas.*hom.in Ps*.28 (1.359c; M.30.76b); Thdt.*h.rel*.21(3.1245); of Christ ὁ λόγος ὁ θεοῦ, ὁ πρωτόγονος πατρὸς παῖς, ἡ πρὸ ἑωσφόρου φωσφόρος φ. Hipp.*haer*. 10.33(p.290.25; M.16.3450c); Ἰησοῦ ὕψιστε, φ. ἀνατείλασα ἀπὸ τῶν σπλάγχνων τῶν τελείων, πάντων σωτήρ *A.Thom*.A 48(p.164.11); Ἰ[η]σοῦς ἡ φ. ἡ [π]αραφήσασα τῶν ἁμαρτιῶν *Pap.Chr.*(*PO* 18.406); **2.** *utterance of words, speech, statement* ἄλογον φ. καὶ τολμηράν Just.*1apol*.3.1(M.6.329b); Chrys.*hom.18.3 in 1Cor*.(10.568d); παρεπέμφθη...τῷ ἄρχοντι...ὅστις καὶ τὰς φ. αὐτοῦ ἔλαβεν Jo.Mal.*chron*.14 p.370(M.97.552a); **3.** *saying, precept*, of Trin. εἰσὶ φ. ἴδιαι τοῦ πατρὸς καὶ εἰσὶ φ. ἴδιαι τοῦ υἱοῦ καὶ εἰσὶ φ. ἴδιαι τοῦ πνεύματος· καὶ εἰσὶ κοιναὶ πατρός, υἱοῦ καὶ ἁγίου πνεύματος ‡Ath.*Trin*.3.22(M.28.1236d); of God ὁ πιστεύσας τοίνυν ταῖς γραφαῖς ταῖς θείαις...ἀπόδειξιν ἀναντίρρητον τὴν τοῦ τὰς γραφὰς δεδωρημένου φωνὴν λαμβάνει θεοῦ Clem.*str*.2.2 (p.118.6; M.8.941a); of Christ ἡ σωτήριος φ. *ib*.1.3(p.15.13; 713a); ὥστε εὐλόγως ἂν χρησμοὺς νομίσαι τὰς φ. αὐτοῦ [sc. τοῦ Ἰησοῦ] Or. *princ*.4.1.2(p.295.9; M.11.345a); [sc. τὴν πίστιν] ἣν ἑκασταχοῦ μόνον οὐχὶ φ. ἀφιεὶς ὁ σωτὴρ...ἀπαιτεῖ μάλιστα παρ' ὑμῶν Eus.*v.C*.4.42(p.134. 23; M.20.1192b); of prophets, apostles, etc. τῶν δώδεκα ἀποστόλων... δι' ὧν τῆς φ. ἡ πᾶσα γῆ τῆς δόξης καὶ χάριτος τοῦ θεοῦ...ἐπληρώθη Just.*dial*.42.1(M.6.565a); εἰς τοὺς ὀψιγόνους οὕτως διὰ τῆς συντάξεως παραπεμπομένης τῆς φ. Clem.*ecl*.27(p.145.2; M.9.712c); Meth.*symp*.

3.12(p.40.22; M.18.80A); αἱ παρατεθεῖσαι τοῦ Κλήμεντος φ. δεδηλώκασιν Eus.h.e.2.23.3(M.20.196D); Bas.Spir.74(3.62C; M.32.205B); of passages of scripture ἐξιχνεύειν ἀπὸ τῶν ὁμοίων φ. τὸν πανταχοῦ διεσπαρμένον τῆς γραφῆς νοῦν Or.princ.4.3.5(19; p.331.6; M.11.385A); τὰς τῶν προφητῶν πολυσήμους φ. Clem.ep.Petr.1(M.2.25B); αἰνιγματώδες...οἷα πολλὰ ἐν ταῖς ἱεραῖς ἐστι φ. Gr.Thaum.pan.Or.15(p.33.18; M.10.1093B); Meth.symp.1.3(p.11.20; M.18.44A); **4.** *word*; opp. ἔργον: μέχρι φωνῆς ἀρνεῖσθαι τὸν Χριστόν Just.dial.131.2(M.6.780C); οὐκ ἐν φωναῖς καὶ λεξιδίοις ζητῶ τὸ διδόναι κυρίῳ...δόξαν, ἀλλ' ἐν πράξεσιν Or.hom.12.11 in Jer.(p.97.14; M.13.393A); τὸ τοῦ υἱοῦ ὄνομα μέχρι φωνῆς συγχωροῦσι Bas.hom.24.2(2.190C; M.31.601B); Gr.Nyss.Eun.3(2 p.37.11; M.45.604C); **5.** *term, expression*, in gen. τῆς 'θανατος' φ. Or.Jo.13.61(59; p.293.10; M.14.516B); Bas.hex.3.4(1.25D; M.29.61A); ref. Christ οὐδὲ γὰρ ἀνέχῃ προσώποις δυσίν, ἤγουν ὑποστάσεσι, τὰς φ. διανέμειν...φωνῶν δὲ διαφορὰς κατ' οὐδένα τρόπον ἀνῃρήκαμεν Cyr.ep.40(p.26.15,19; 5^{2}.116A); διαιρεῖσθαι δὲ μόνας διατείνονται τὰς ἐπὶ τῷ κυρίῳ φ. πρέπειν τε φασὶν αὐτὰς...τὰς μὲν τῇ θεότητι αὐτοῦ, τὰς δὲ πάλιν τῇ ἀνθρωπότητι αὐτοῦ. αἱ μὲν γάρ εἰσι τῶν φ. ὅτι μάλιστα θεοπρεπεῖς, αἱ δὲ οὕτω πάλιν ἀνθρωποπρεπεῖς, αἱ δὲ...μέσην τινὰ τάξιν ἐπέχουσιν, ἐμφανίζουσαι τὸν υἱὸν θεὸν ὄντα καὶ ἄνθρωπον ib.(p.27.22ff.; 117Aff.); μὴ τοίνυν διέλῃς ἐν τούτοις τὰς ἐπὶ τῷ κυρίῳ φ. ... ἕτερον τοίνυν ἐστὶ τὸ διαιρεῖν τὰς φύσεις...ἕτερον τὸ φωνῶν εἰδέναι διαφοράν ib.(p.28.18ff.; 118Bff.); ref. theol. language, Bas.Eun.2.22(1.258B; M.29.620D); ἡ δὲ οἰκειότης ἐν τοῖς πράγμασιν οὐκ ἐν ψιλαῖς θεωρεῖται ταῖς τῶν ὀνομάτων φ. Gr.Nyss.Eun.3(2 p.32.17; M.45.597D); πᾶσα σχεδὸν φ. δογματικὴ κακουργεῖσθαι δύναται παρὰ τῶν αἱρετικῶν Eust.Mon.ep.(M.86.905A); πολλαὶ φ. παρὰ τοῖς πατράσιν ἀδιαβλήτως λεγόμεναι, ὕστερον οὐκ ἀσφαλεῖς ὤφθησαν μετὰ Νεστόριον Sev.Ant.fr.ap.eund.(905C); **6.** *language, speech* Χριστιανοὶ γὰρ οὔτε γῇ οὔτε φ. οὔτε ἔθεσι διακεκριμένοι τῶν λοιπῶν εἰσιν ἀνθρώπων Diogn.5.1; οἶμαι αὐτὴν [sc. τὴν Ἑβραΐαν] ἱερὰν εἶναι φ. Thdt.qu.61 in Gen.(1.73).

φώνησις, ἡ, *utterance*, Iren.haer.1.15.4(M.7.621B).

***φωνητέον,** *one must summon*, Or.Jo.13.11(p.235.29; M.14.416B).

***φωνοκτυπέω,** pass., *be struck with amazement*, ‡Jo.D.hom.5(M.96.652A).

φωρατός, *that can be detected* φ. ἔσται ἡ τοιαύτη αἵρεσις, μῦθός τις οὖσα Epiph.haer.24.10(p.267.5; M.41.320C); ib.25.5(p.273.8; 328C); ib.26.1(p.275.4; 332A).

***φωρολαμβάνω,** *detect, suprise*, in pass. ἐπ' αὐτὸ φωροληφθέντες Proc.G.Gen.3:7(M.87.196C).

φῶς, τό, *light*;

I. physical;

A. in gen.; its creation does not imply temporal priority of physical darkness, Bas.hex.2.5(1.17B; M.29.40C); Thdt.qu.6 in Gen.(1.10); created light as symbol of God who is only light of heavenly sphere, Gr.Naz.or.44.3(M.36.609C); and as image of divine light τῆς ἀΰλου φωτοδοσίας εἰκόνα, τὰ ὑλικὰ φ. Dion.Ar.c.h.1.2(M.3.121D); distribution of created light among heavenly bodies necessitated by limited capacity of human eyesight, Thdt.qu.16 in Gen.(1.19); of light of star heralding Christ's birth τὸ φ. αὐτοῦ ἀνεκλάλητον ἦν, καὶ ξενισμὸν παρεῖχεν ἡ καινότης αὐτοῦ... αὐτὸς δὲ ἦν ὑπερβάλλων τὸ φ. αὐτοῦ ὑπὲρ πάντα Ign.Eph.19.2.

B. liturg.; **1.** in funeral ceremonies τὸ σκῆνος...βάθρον ἐφ' ὑψηλὸν κατετίθεντο, φῶτά τ' ἐξάψαντες κύκλῳ ἐπὶ σκευῶν χρυσῶν θαυμαστὸν θέαμα...παρεῖχον Eus.v.C.4.66(p.145.4; M.20.1221A); cf.Gr.Nyss.v.Macr.(p.408.8; M.46.993C); **2.** in church services, cf.T.Dom.1.19; Thdr.Mops.1Tim.3:13–15(p.133.7; M.66.941C); θυμίαμα γὰρ καὶ λυχνιαῖον φ. προσφέρομεν τῷ θεῷ Thdt.qu.60 in Ex.(1.164); at feast of Purification, ‡Cyr.H.occurs.15(M.33.1201B); **3.** at baptism; candidates' torches signifying divine light, Gr.Naz.or.45.2(M.36.624C); **4.** Epiphany as feast of lights commemorating Christ's baptism; a season for administering 'illumination' of baptism, Gr.Naz.or.40.1(M.36.360B); cf.id.or.39 tit.(336A); γενέθλιον ἑορτάζομεν... φῶτα πανήγυριν ἄγομεν Ast.Am.hom.4(M.40.217C); †Jo.Jej.poenit.(M.88.1913A); Chron.Pasch.p.209(M.92.512C).

C. of lighting of lamps at evening, accompanied by singing of hymn τοῦ ἑσπερινοῦ φ. Bas.Spir.73(3.62B; M.32.205A).

II. spiritual;

A. of God, cf. ἄδυτος; **1.** of God as light (cf. 1Jo.1:5) and dwelling in light (cf. 1Tim.6:16) τοῦ δὲ πατρὸς τῶν ὅλων...ἡ οὐσία ἐστὶν...φ. αὐτοόν Ptol.ep.ap.Epiph.haer.33.7(p.457.6; M.41.568B); τὸ ἄτρεπτον αὐτοῦ φ. καὶ ἀσχημάτιστον Clem.str.1.24(p.102.17; M.8.909C); εἰ δή τις νοεῖ θεόν...ὡς δυνατόν ἐστι, νοείτω μέγα καὶ ἀπερινόητον καὶ κάλλιστον φ. ἀπρόσιτον, πᾶσαν δύναμιν ἀγαθήν, πᾶσαν ἀστείαν ἀρετὴν συγκεκληρωμένον id.ecl.21(p.142.22; M.9.708B); πρὸς τὸ ἀΐδιον ἀνατρέχομεν φ., οἱ παῖδες πρὸς τὸν πατέρα id.paed.1.6(p.109.5; M.8.288C); τὸν ὅλων δημιουργόν, ὅς ἐστι φ. Or.Cels.6.66(p.136.22; M.11.1400A); εἷς ἐστι...φ. ἀΐδιον ἀνελλιπῶς ἀστράπτον Cyr.H.catech.6.9; σὺ εἶ...ἡ πηγὴ τοῦ φ. Serap.euch.13.5; φ. ἦν ἀπρόσιτον, καὶ ἀδιάδοχον, ὁ θεός, οὔτε ἀρξάμενον...ὀλίγοις ὅσον ἐστὶ θεωρούμενον, οἶμαι δέ, οὐδὲ ὀλίγοις Gr.Naz.or.44.3(M.36.609B); ὁ φ. οἰκῶν ἀπρόσιτον, ὁ τῇ φύσει ἀόρατος Lit.ap.Const.App.8.15.7; ἄλλο τὸ φ. αὐτός, καὶ ἄλλο ὃ οἰκεῖ; οὐκοῦν καὶ τόπῳ ἐμπεριείληπται; ἄπαγε. ... ἵνα τὸ ἀκατάληπτον τῆς θείας φύσεως παραστήσῃ, φ. οἰκεῖν αὐτὸν εἶπεν ἀπρόσιτον Chrys.hom.18.1 in 1Tim.(11.654C); φ.,... φησίν, οἰκῶν ἀπρόσιτον, ἀλλ' οὐδὲ τοῦτο ἁρμόδιον θεῷ· ἀπερίγραφον γὰρ ἔχει τὴν φύσιν...ἀλλ' ὡς δύναται ὑμνεῖ...εἰ δὲ τὸ περὶ αὐτὸν φ. ἀπρόσιτον, πῶς οἷόν τε αὐτὸν κατιδεῖν; Thdt.1Tim.6:16(3.672); φ. ἀχώρητον καὶ ἀκατάληπτον predicated not of one Person but of whole Trin., Gel.Cyz.h.e.2.22.9(M.85.1292C); θεὸς...ὡς φωτὸς οὐσία, καὶ αὐτοῦ τοῦ εἶναι καὶ ὁρᾶν αἴτιος Dion.Ar.c.h.13.3(M.3.301D); φῶς as one of many names given by man to God who is nameless, id.d.n.1.6(M.3.596A); ἀόρατόν φησι τὰ λόγια τὸ παμφαὲς φῶς ib.7.1(865B); deity cannot be truly characterized as light, id.c.h.1.3(140C); but only analogously, ib.1.5(144D); οὔτε δύναμις...οὔτε φ. ... οὐδὲ σκότος ἐστίν, οὐδὲ φ. id.myst.5(M.3.1048A); in Brahmin thought, Hipp.haer.1.24(p.28.6; M.16.3052A); Persian, ib.4.43(p.65.10; 3106B); **2.** Trin.; **a.** ref. relation of Father to Son ἄτμητον δὲ καὶ ἀχώριστον τοῦ πατρὸς ταύτην τὴν δύναμιν ὑπάρχειν, ὅνπερ τρόπον τὸ τοῦ ἡλίου φασὶ φ. ἐπὶ γῆς εἶναι ἄτμητον καὶ ἀχώριστον ὄντος τοῦ ἡλίου ἐν τῷ οὐρανῷ· καὶ ὅταν δύσῃ, συναποφέρεται τὸ φ.· οὕτως ὁ πατὴρ ὅταν βούληται...δύναμιν αὐτοῦ προπηδᾶν ποιεῖ· καὶ ὅταν βούληται, πάλιν ἀναστέλλει εἰς ἑαυτόν Just.dial.128.3(M.6.776A); ὥσπερ γὰρ ἀπὸ μιᾶς δᾳδὸς ἀνάπτεται...πυρὰ πολλά, τῆς δὲ πρώτης δᾳδὸς...οὐκ ἐλαττοῦται τὸ φ. οὕτως ὁ λόγος προελθὼν...οὐκ ἄλογον πεποίηκε τὸν γεγεννηκότα Tat.orat.5(p.6.2; M.6.817A); Clem.exc.Thdot.4(p.106.17; M.9.656A) cit. s. ἄνω; ὁ...υἱὸς...ἀπρόσιτον φ. καὶ δύναμις θεοῦ ib.12(p.110.30; 664A); υἱὸς τοῦ νοῦ γνήσιος ὁ θεῖος λόγος, φωτὸς ἀρχέτυπον φῶς id.prot.10(p.71.26; M.8.212C); ὁ υἱὸς...ὅλος φ. πατρῷον id.str.7.2(p.6.1; M.9.408C); Or.hom.9.4 in Jer.(p.70.19; M.13.357A) cit. s. ἀπαύγασμα; εἰκὼν γάρ ἐστιν τῆς ἀγαθότητος αὐτοῦ καὶ ἀπαύγασμα οὐ τοῦ θεοῦ ἀλλὰ τῆς δόξης αὐτοῦ καὶ τοῦ ἀϊδίου φ. αὐτοῦ id.Jo.13.25(p.249.30; M.14.444A); οὐ λόγον μόνον, ὡς ἐδόκει Μαρκέλλῳ, ἀλλὰ καὶ θεὸν καὶ φ. αὐτὸν ὠνόμασεν Eus.e.th.1.20(p.81.11; M.24.865B); τὸν...υἱὸν ἀπαύγασμα τοῦ πατρικοῦ φ. ὁρισάμενος, ὥστε εἶναι τὸ ἀπαύγασμα γέννημα τοῦ πρώτου φ., οὐ κατὰ τὴν τῶν...ζῴων ὑποστὰν γένεσιν, κατὰ δὲ τὸ ῥηθὲν παράδειγμα ib.(p.92.24; 885B); ib.2.11(p.112.15; 924A); (Arian) τὸ φ. ἦν ποτε χωρὶς αὐγῆς Ath.Ar.1.14(M.26.41C); τὸ ἀπαύγασμα...μὴ μειοῦν τὴν οὐσίαν τοῦ φ. ἀλλ' ὡς γέννημα ἀληθινὸν ἐξ αὐτοῦ ib.2.33(217B); τὸ ἀπαύγασμα φ. ἐστιν, οὐ δεύτερον τοῦ ἡλίου οὐδὲ ἕτερον φ., οὐδὲ κατὰ μετουσίαν αὐτοῦ, ἀλλ' ὅλον ἴδιον αὐτοῦ γέννημα ib.3.4(329A); ἔνθα γὰρ τὸ φ., ἐκεῖ καὶ τὸ ἀπαύγασμα id.ep.Serap.1.30(M.26.600B); φ. ... ἀληθινὸν πρὸς φ. ἀληθινόν, κατ αὐτὴν τοῦ φ. τὴν ἔννοιαν, οὐδεμίαν ἕξει παραλλαγήν Bas.ep.52.2(3.145D; M.32.393B); (Eunomian) συλλογισαμένου διὰ τῆς τῶν τεθέντων ἀκολουθίας, ὅτι ἀναλόγως τῇ ἀγεννησίᾳ καὶ τῇ γεννήσει, τοῦ πατρικοῦ φ. πρὸς τὸ τοῦ υἱοῦ παραλλάσσοντος, ἀνάγκη πᾶσα μὴ ἐλάττωσιν φωτὸς ἐπὶ τοῦ υἱοῦ νοηθῆναι, ἀλλὰ παντελῆ ἀλλοτρίωσιν Gr.Nyss.Eun.12(p.281.7; M.45.892D); φ. ἀπρόσιτον ἄρα ὁ υἱός, ἐν ᾧ οἰκεῖ ὁ πατήρ ib.(p.384.6; 896C); acc. Eunomius, divine light non-existent before creation of Son, ib.9(p.223.5; 821D); Gel.Cyz.h.e.2.22.14(M.85.1293A); Dion.Ar.d.n.2.4(M.3.641A,B); in phrase φῶς ἐκ φωτός applied to Son ἕτερον δὲ λέγων οὐ δύο θεοὺς λέγω, ἀλλ' ὡς φ. ἐκ φ. Hipp.Noët.11(p.253.10; M.10.817C); Eus.e.th.1.8(p.66.20; M.24.837B); Ath.Ar.1.9(M.26.29A); Cyr.H.catech.11.4; Bas.ep.52.2(3.145D; M.32.393B); ib.125.1(215D; M.548B); Epiph.haer.76.35(p.385.18; M.42.588D); Cosm.Ind.top.5(M.88.280B); credal, Symb.Caes.(p.43.10; M.20.1537B); Symb.Nic.(325)(p.44.13; M.20.1540B); Symb.Ant.(341)4(p.251.4; M.26.725B); cf.Symb.Sard.Orient.(p.190); Symb.Ant.(345)(p.251.25; M.26.728B); Symb.Sirm.1(p.254.20; M.26.736A); Symb.Sirm.2(p.257.17; M.26.741C); Symb.ap.Epiph.anc.118,119(pp.147.2,148.7; M.43.232C,233B); Symb.Nic.–CP(p.80.5; H.2.288B); τὸ φῶς τὸ ἐκ τοῦ φωτός Cyr.ep.4(p.26.21; 5^{2}.23A); Char.libell.(p.97.18; H.1.1516A); Sophr.H.ep.syn.(M.87.3152C); **b.** ref. relation of H. Ghost to Godhead ἀπόρροια, ὡς φ. ἀπὸ πυρός, τὸ πνεῦμα Athenag.leg.24.2(M.6.945B); ἐσημειώθη ἐφ' ἡμᾶς τὸ φ. τοῦ προσώπου σου, κύριε. τί γὰρ ἂν εἴη ἄλλο τὸ πνεῦμα, ὃ παρὰ τοῦ πατρός, ἢ ἐκ τοῦ φ. ἐκπορεύεται; Didym.Trin.2.3(M.39.473B).

B. of Christ ὁ λόγος μὲν ἔστι τὸ τοῦ θεοῦ φ. Tat.orat.13(p.14.20; M.6.833B); λόγος ἀέναος, αἰὼν ἄπλετος, φ. ἀΐδιον Clem.paed.3.12(p.292.36; M.8.684A); Ἰησοῦ...ἡ δεξιὰ τοῦ φ. ἡ καταστρέφουσα τὸν πονηρόν A.Thom.A 48(p.164.13); ἴδε τὸ μακάριον φ., Ἰησοῦν A.Andr.

A 16(p.56.15); ὁ...σωτήρ, φ. ὢν τοῦ κόσμου, φωτίζει...τὸν ἀσώματον νοῦν Or.*Jo.*1.25(24; p.31.17; M.14.68C); Is.9:2 applied to ὁ θεὸς Ἰησοῦς, id.*Cels.*6.66(p.136.28; M.11.1400A); Χριστέ, ὁ μέτοχος τοῦ φ. καὶ τῶν κρυπτῶν γνώστης *A.Xanthipp.*28(p.78.17); ὁ κύριος, ἡ ἀλήθεια, τὸ φ. Meth.*symp.*1.5(p.13.12; M.18.45B); Eus.*e.th.*1.20(p.84.35; M.24.872C); Chrys.*hom.14.1 in Mt.*(7.178D); ἀρκέσει γὰρ ὁ Χριστὸς εἰς φ. ἡμῖν αἰώνιον Cyr.*Zach.*105(3.800C); φ. τὸ ἀΐδιον, φ. τὸ ἄχρονον καὶ χρόνῳ παραδειχθέν, φ. τὸ σαρκὶ φανερούμενον καὶ φύσει κρυπτόμενον Andr.Cr.*or.*9(M.97.1001C); φ. τὸ ἀΐδιον, φ. τὸ ἀένναον, φ. τὸ ὑπέρτατον, φ. τὸ ἄϋλον,...φ. τὸ φωτίσαν τοὺς αἰῶνας...Χριστὸς ἀληθινὸς ἡμῶν θεός ‡Meth.*Sym.et Ann.*13(M.18.380A); credal, *Symb. Ant.*(341)2(p.249.16; M.26.721C); *Symb.Sel.*(p.258.9; M.26.745A); in phrase φῶς ἐκ φωτός v. supra; of Christ as life and light v. ζωή; exeg. Jo.1:4; of Christ as τὸ φ. τὸ ἀληθινόν (Jo.1:9), *A.Phil.*124 (p.53.6); Or.*Jo.*1.26(24; p.31.29; M.14.69A); Jo.1:9 capable of two interpretations: τὸ φ. ἐρχόμενον εἰς τὸν κόσμον ἐπὶ τῷ φωτίσαι τὸν ἄνθρωπον, or τὸ φ. τὸ ἀληθινὸν φωτίζει πάντα τὸν ἐρχόμενον εἰς τὸν κόσμον ἄνθρωπον id.*fr.6 in Jo.*(p.488.27); ἐν τῷ φωτισμῷ τοῦ πνεύματος [sc. ὀψόμεθα] φ. τὸ ἀληθινόν Bas.*Spir.*47(3.39D; M.32.153B); *Const.App.*5.16.6; εἴπερ ἐστὶ τὸ φ. τὸ ἀληθινὸν ὁ μονογενής, φ. δὲ ὁμοίως ἀληθινὸν εἶναι δύναται καὶ ἡ κτίσις Cyr.*Jo.*1.8(4.68C); of Christ as means whereby light of God illuminates universe, id. *glaph.Ex.*3(1.320E), and is made accessible to man, Clem.*prot.*9 (p.64.6; M.8.196C); Dion.Ar.*c.h.*1.2(M.3.121A); as βασιλεὺς φωτός, *A.Phil.*144(p.84.10); as eternal beauty, dwelling as light ἐν ἀφράστοις καὶ ἀπροσίτοις, Meth.*symp.*6.1(p.64.16; M.18.113B); as being himself φ. ἀπρόσιτον (1Tim.6:16), Clem.*exc.Thdot.*12(p.110.30; M.9.664A); Gr.Nyss.*Eun.*12(p.384.6; M.45.896C); as light of νοητὸς κόσμος, compared with sun as light of sensible world, Or.*Jo.*1.25(24; p.31.2; M.14.68B); Dion.Ar.*d.n.*4.4(M.3.697D); illuminating saints and angels, id.*e.h.*1.1(M.3.372B); illuminating soul, Or.*Jo.*1.25(24; p.31.17; 68C); id.*Cels.*7.17(p.168.22; M.11.1445A); φ. ἦν ἀληθῶς καθ' ὃ τὸ νοερὸν καὶ λογικὸν ταῖς κατ' εἰκόνα τὴν αὐτοῦ πεποιημέναις ψυχαῖς ἐναυγάζει φέγγος Eus.*e.th.*2.14(p.118.10; M.24.933B); ἐνδύσασθαι τὸ ἱμάτιον...τὸν κύριον...τὸ ἄρρητον φ., ὃν φορέσασαι ψυχαὶ οὐκ ἀποδυθήσονται εἰς τὸν αἰῶνα Mac.Aeg.*hom.*20.3(M.34.652B); hence BMV as πηγὴ τοῦ φ., ‡Gr.Thaum.*annunt.*1(M.10.1152B); ‡Meth.*Sym.et Ann.*14(M.18.381B).

C. of H. Ghost; as light by which alone men may see light of God, Clem.*paed.*1.6(p.106.26; M.8.284A); πληρώσας ἡμᾶς πνεύματος ἁγίου ἀπὸ τοῦ φ. αὐτοῦ ἐποίησεν ἡμᾶς γνωρίζειν αὐτὸν τίς ἐστιν *A.Phil.* 9(p.5.16); πνεῦμα σκιᾶς ποιητικὸν οὐκ ἄν ποτε γένοιτο. πνεῦμα δὲ ὅτι αὐτὸς ὁ θεὸς ὁ σωτὴρ ἔφη...ὅτι δὲ ὁ θεὸς φ. ἐστιν αὐτὸς διδάσκει Marcell.*fr.*57 ap.Eus.*e.th.*2.1(p.100.6; M.24.900D); ὅσοι γὰρ πνεῦμα θεοῦ φοροῦσι, φ. φοροῦσι, καὶ οἱ φοροῦντες φ. Χριστὸν εἰσιν ἐνδεδυμένοι, καὶ οἱ ἐνδεδυμένοι Χριστὸν πατέρα ἐνδέδυνται Ath.*inc.et Ar.*15(M.26.1009C); τὸ θεϊκὸν φ. τοῦ πνεύματος Mac.Aeg.*hom.*30.6(M.34.725A); τοῦ πνεύματος ἔλλαμψις, οὐχ οἷον...φωτισμὸς χάριτος...ἀλλ' ὑποστατικοῦ φ. ἐν ταῖς ψυχαῖς βεβαία καὶ διηνεκὴς ἔλλαμψις id.*libert. ment.*22(M.34.956D); φ. ... τὸ ἀληθινὸν καὶ αἴτιον τοῦ αἰσθητοῦ φ. ... ἐστι τὸ πνεῦμα τὸ σεπτόν Didym.*Trin.*2.12(M.39.681B); φ. τοῦ θεϊκοῦ προσώπου τὸ πνεῦμα *ib.*2.15(720A); ἓν πνεῦμα ἅγιον τὸ ἐκ θεοῦ πατρὸς ἐκπορευόμενον, τὸ φ. καὶ θεόν Sophr.H.*ep.syn.*(M.87.3152C); ἡμεῖς, ἐκ φ. τοῦ πατρὸς φ. περιλαμφθέντες τὸν υἱὸν ἐν φ. τῷ ἁγίῳ πνεύματι †Jo.D.*B.J.*10(M.96.945B).

D. of angels; **1.** as νοερὸν πῦρ καὶ πνεύματα νοερά contrasted with φ. νοερόν and ἀπρόσιτον φ. (which is Son), Clem.*exc.Thdot.*12(p.110.27; M.9.664A); **2.** as heavenly lights ὁ διάβολος...ἦν μετὰ τῶν ἀγγέλων ἀνατέλλων τοῦ φ. Meth.*res.*1.37(p.279.3); φῶτά τε πάντα καὶ φώτων ἀσωμάτων θεῖα καὶ νοερὰ γένη τὸν...χῶρον οὐρανοῦ λαχόντα Eus.*l.C.*1(p.196.28; M.20.1320B); φῶτα δεύτερα, τοῦ πρώτου φ. ἀπαυγάσματα, αἱ περὶ αὐτὸν δυνάμεις καὶ τὰ λειτουργικὰ πνεύματα Gr. Naz.*or.*44.3(M.36.609B); *ib.*40.5(367B); exeg. Jac.1:17 ἢ τὰς λογικὰς δυνάμεις φῶτα καλεῖ, ἢ τοὺς πεφωτισμένους διὰ πνεύματος ἁγίου *cat. Jac.*1:17(p.6.23); **3.** as revealing and reflecting divine light νεφέλης αὐτοῖς ἰδέαν ἡ θεολογία περιπλάττει, σημαίνουσα...τοὺς ἱεροὺς νόας τοῦ μὲν κρυφίου φ. ὑπερκοσμίως ἀποπληρουμένους, τὴν...πρωτοφάνειαν... εἰσδεχομένους, καὶ ταύτην...εἰς τὰ δεύτερα δευτεροφανῶς καὶ ἀναλόγως διαπορθμεύοντας Dion.Ar.*c.h.*15.6(M.3.336A); εἶναι ἀγγέλους...οἷον φ. φανὰ τοῦ ἐν ἀδύτοις ὄντος ἑρμηνευτικά id.*d.n.*4.2(M.3.696B); ὁ ἄγγελος, φανέρωσις τοῦ ἀφανοῦς φ. *ib.*4.22(724B); **4.** as dwelling in light, Bas.*hex.*2.5(1.17C; M.29.41A).

E. of kingdom of God as βασιλεία φωτός; **1.** as future abode of redeemed, Meth.*res.*1.32(p.269.14; M.41.1145A); **2.** as present possession of soul ὅσους ἂν ἐξέδυσεν ὁ Ἰησοῦς τὰ ἐνδύματα τῆς βασιλείας τοῦ σκότους, ἐνεδύσαντο τὸν...ἐπουράνιον ἄνθρωπον Ἰησοῦν...καὶ ἐνέδυσεν αὐτοὺς ὁ κύριος ἐνδύματα βασιλείας φ. ἀρρήτου Mac.Aeg.*hom.* 2.4,5(M.34.465D); ἡ βασιλεία τοῦ φ....μυστικῶς νῦν τὴν ψυχὴν φωτίζει *ib.*2.5(468A); **3.** (Manich.) [sc. Μάνης] δύο σέβει θεούς...τὸν μὲν ἀγαθόν, τὸν δὲ πονηρὸν...φ. τῷ ἑνὶ ὄνομα θέμενος καὶ τῷ ἑτέρῳ σκότος· καὶ τοῦ μὲν φ. εἶναι μέρος τὴν ἐν ἀνθρώποις ψυχήν, τοῦ δὲ σκότους τὸ σῶμα Hegem.*Arch.*7(p.9.14; M.10.1437A); Jo.D.*Man.*22(M.94.1525C).

F. divine light manifested in theophanies, and angelic appearances; **1.** in burning bush ἐπεὶ...ὁ...κύριος...τῷ Μωσεῖ καταφανὴ ἐβούλετο γενέσθαι τὴν αὐτοῦ δύναμιν, ὄψις αὐτῷ δείκνυται θεοειδὴς φ. μεμορφωμένου ἐπὶ...βάτῳ Clem.*paed.*2.8(p.203.16; M.8.488A); ὁ...διὰ τοῦ φ. ἑαυτὸν τῷ Μωϋσῇ δείξας Gr.Nyss.*Eun.*8(2 p.176.29; M.45.769B); interpreted of Inc. τοῦ φ. ... ὃ μέχρι τῆς ἀνθρωπίνης κάτεισι φύσεως, οὐκ ἀπό τινος τῶν περὶ τὰ ἄστρα φωστήρων λαμπόμενον...ἀλλ' ἀπὸ γηΐνης θάμνου...δι' οὗ διδασκόμεθα...τὸ κατὰ τὴν παρθένον μυστήριον, ἀφ' ἧς τὸ τῆς θεότητος φ. ἐπιλάμψαν τῷ ἀνθρωπίνῳ βίῳ διὰ γεννήσεως, ἀδιάφθορον ἐφύλαξε τὴν...θάμνον id.*v.Mos.* (M.44.332D); and of mystical contemplation of divine light, *ib.* (333A); Max.*ambig.*(M.91.1200C); **2.** in fiery pillar οἷς...στῦλος φωτὸς ἔλαμπεν, ἵνα καὶ παρὰ τὸν πάντα ἄλλον λαόν, ἰδίῳ καὶ ἀνελλιπεῖ ...φωτὶ χρῆσθαι ἔχητε Just.*dial.*131.3(M.6.780D); Clem.*str.*1.24(p.102.19; M.8.909C); **3.** in cloudy pillar regarded as νεφέλη τοῦ φωτός, Or.*Cels.*2.74(p.195.18; M.11.909D); **4.** in Christ at his baptism ἐξελθόντα...ἐκ τοῦ ὕδατος, φ. περιαστράπτει καὶ δόξα Gr.Naz.*or.*18.13 (M.35.1001A); at Transfiguration, *A.Jo.*90(p.195.10); καίτοι οὐδὲ σαρκικοῖς ὀφθαλμοῖς τὸ φ. ἑωράκεισαν (οὐδὲν γὰρ συγγενὲς...ἐκείνῳ τῷ φ. καὶ τῇδε τῇ σαρκί) ἀλλ' ὡς ἡ δύναμις...τοῦ σωτῆρος ἐνεδυνάμωσεν τὴν σάρκα εἰς τὸ θεάσασθαι Clem.*exc.Thdot.*5(p.107.6; M.9.656C); *ib.*12(p.111.2; 664A); ὁ κύριος...φωτὶ περιλάμπεται πνευματικῷ, τὴν δύναμιν...παραγυμνώσας εἰς ὅσον οἷόν τε ἦν ἰδεῖν...θεὸς ἐν σαρκίῳ τὴν δύναμιν ἐνδεικνύμενος id.*str.*6.16(p.503.11; M.9.368A); compared with 'shining forth' of the just at Parousia (Mt.13:43), Chrys.*hom.56.4 in Mt.*(7.571D,E); in 'cloud of light' at Ascension ἀναλαμβανόμενον ἐν νεφέλῃ φωτὸς εἰς τοὺς οὐρανοὺς ἐθεάσαντο ἐν τῷ αὐτῷ σώματι οἷον πρὸ παραβάσεως ἔπλασε τὸν Ἀδάμ ‡Pion.*v.Polyc.*13; **5.** in other theophanies and miraculous appearances ὁ ὕψιστος...κελεύει Μιχαὴλ καὶ λέγει, λάβε νεφέλην φωτὸς...καὶ...λάβε...Ἀβραὰμ ἐπὶ ἅρματος χερουβικοῦ *T.Abr.*A 9(p.87.12); ἦλθέν μοι μεγάλη φωνὴ ἐν μείζονι φ. ... καὶ ἀποκριθεὶς ἐμοὶ εἶπεν τὸ φ. *T.Job* 3,4(p.105.9,21); ἦλθον πρὸς...Φίλιππον, καὶ εἶδον αὐτὸν ὡς μέγα τι φ. *A.Phil.*60(p.25.16); εὐχομένη ξενοφωνεῖται φωτὶ καταλαμπομένη καὶ ἀναστενάζουσα λέγει, ἦλθέν μοι τὸ ἀληθινὸν φ. Ἰησοῦς *ib.*124(p.53.4); ὁ σωτὴρ ἀνέτεινεν τὴν ...χεῖρα καὶ ἐχάραξεν σταυρὸν ἐν τῷ ἀέρι καταβαίνοντα...ἕως τῆς ἀβύσσου, καὶ ἐπλήσθη ἡ ἄβυσσος φωτὸς *ib.*138(p.70.5); προσευχομένου τοῦ Ματθεία...ἔλαμψεν φ., καὶ ἐξῆλθεν ἐκ τοῦ φ. φωνὴ *A.Andr.et Mt.*3 (p.67.7); *A.Thom.*A 156(p.264.15); δόξα φωτὸς οὐρανίου περιήστραψε πάντας, καὶ...οἱ μὲν εἶδεν περὶ τὴν κεφαλὴν Πολυκάρπου περιστερὰν περὶ ἣν κύκλος ἦν φωτὸς...φῶς τῷ προσώπῳ αὐτοῦ περιλάμπον ‡Pion. *v.Polyc.*21; as bestowed on martyrs ὁρῶν τὸ φ. περὶ αὐτούς, ἀτενίσας εἰς τὸν οὐρανὸν ἰδεῖν πόθεν τὸ φ., εἶδεν στεφάνους κατερχομένους *M.Seb.*9.

G. divine light as revealed to, or attained by, man in moral, intellectual, and spiritual illumination; **1.** universally diffused by Logos (cf. Jo.1:9) φ. ἐστι κοινόν, ἐπιλάμπει πᾶσιν ἀνθρώποις· οὐδεὶς Κιμμέριος ἐν λόγῳ Clem.*prot.*9(p.65.26; M.8.200B); ὅς ἐστι λογικὸς μετέχει τοῦ ἀληθινοῦ φ., λογικὸς δέ ἐστι πᾶς ἄνθρωπος Or.*hom.14.10 in Jer.*(p.114.21; M.13.416A); id.*fr.6 in Jo.*(p.488.28); freely available, to be apprehended in proportion to man's capacity, Dion.Ar. *c.h.*9.3(M.3.260C–261A); rejected only by man's deliberate inclination to evil, id.*e.h.*2.3.3(M.3.397D); as means by which God is apprehended, Athenag.*leg.*10.1(M.6.908B); **2.** communicated in scriptural revelation; **a.** in OT, Eus.*d.e.*5 proem.(p.206.15; M.22.341C); which afforded light proportionate to man's capacity, Dion. Ar.*e.h.*5.1.2(M.3.501C); but after Christ's advent Law hindered man's participation in light, †Bas.*Is.*76(1.433A; M.30.245C); Gr. Nyss.*hom.15 in Cant.*(M.44.1089B); **b.** in gospel, *A.Phil.*25(p.14.4); Clem.*str.*5.5(p.345.7; M.9.52B); Eus.*l.C.*proem.(p.196.7; M.20.1317C); Cyr.*Is.*1.2(2.40A); and in NT, Or.*Jo.*1.6(8; p.11.23; M.14.36B); contrasted with Plato's teaching and likened to wise virgins' lamps, id.*Cels.*6.5(p.75.23; M.11.1297A); **3.** in Christ's advent and spread of Christianity, *1Clem.*59.2; *2Clem.*1.4; Just. *dial.*7.3(M.6.492C); Clem.*str.*1.1(p.9.25; M.8.701B); ἡμᾶς ὁ κύριος φωτίζει, εἰς τὸ φ. ἄγων τὸ ἄσκιον καὶ οὐκέτι ὑλικόν id.*ecl.*5(p.138.18; M.9.701A); ὁ σωτὴρ...φ. ὀρέγων ἄσκιον, ἄπαυστον id.*q.d.s.*42(p.190.21; M.9.652A); διὰ τοῦ σοῦ υἱοῦ...καθαρὸν φ. ἀνασχὼν Const.ap.Eus. *v.C.*2.56(p.64.20; M.20.1032C); κύριε...ὁ ὁδηγὸς τοῦ φ. Anton.Hag. *v.Sym.Styl.*14(p.38.20); by Cross δόξα...κυρίου...ὁ θεῖος σταυρὸς...

ἔνθα δὲ μνήμη φωτός, καὶ φ. ἀδύτου, καὶ τοὺς ἐν νυκτὶ τῆς ἀκηδίας φωτίζοντος Germ.CP *or*.1(M.98.221D); by 'Christian law' ἡ τοῦ φ. δύναμις καὶ ὁ τῆς ἱερᾶς θρησκείας νόμος...ἅπασαν ὁμοῦ τὴν οἰκουμένην κατήστραψεν Const.ap.Eus.*v.C*.2.67(p.67.26; 1040A); contrasted with darkness of paganism, Or.*Cels*.6.67(p.137.11; 1400C); Chrys. *hom.14.1 in Mt.*(7.178C); also of Judaism, Or.*fr.83 in Lc.*(p.273); id.*fr.94 in Jo.*(p.558.2); and heresy, *Const.App*.8.34.12; hence, apostles as lights of the world, Or.*Jo*.1.25(24; p.31.17; M.14.68C); and Christians as 'sons of light', Clem.*paed*.2.9(p.206.24; M.8.493C); *Const.App*.1.2.4; *ib*.2.32.3; **4.** communicated in sacraments; **a.** baptism ὦ τῶν ἁγίων ὡς ἀληθῶς μυστηρίων, ὦ φ. ἀκηράτου. δᾳδουχοῦμαι τοὺς οὐρανοὺς καὶ τὸν θεὸν ἐποπτεῦσαι Clem.*prot*.12 (p.84.23; M.8.241A); καλεῖται...φώτισμα...καὶ λουτρόν·...φώτισμα δὲ δι' οὗ τὸ ἅγιον ἐκεῖνο φ. τὸ σωτήριον ἐποπτεύεται id.*paed*.1.6(p.105.26; M.8.281A); conferred by H. Ghost in baptism, *ib*.(p.106.26; 284A); associated with baptismal seal, Eus.*v.C*.4.62(p.143.21; M.20.1217A); *Const.App*.2.32.3; cf.Bas.*hom*.13.4(2.117B; M.31.432C); hence baptism is πρῶτον φῶς, Dion.Ar.*e.h*.3.1.1(M.3.425A); baptismal light esp. associated with renunciation of devil and turning towards light ἐπὶ τοῖς ἡμαρτημένοις μετανενοηκότες, ἀποταξάμενοι τοῖς ἐλαττώμασιν αὐτῶν, διυλιζόμενοι βαπτίσματι, πρὸς τὸ ἀΐδιον ἀνατρέχομεν φ., οἱ παῖδες πρὸς τὸν πατέρα Clem.*paed*.1.6(p.109.5; M.8.288C); τὴν...προτέραν ζωὴν ἀπεκδύσασα...γυμνὸν καὶ ἀνυπόδετον ἵστησι πρὸς δυσμὰς ἀφορῶντα καὶ...τὰς τῆς ἀλαμποῦς κακίας ἀναινόμενον κοινωνίας...οὕτω...πρὸς ἕω μετάγει, τὴν ἐν τῷ θείῳ φ. στάσιν τε καὶ ἀνάνευσιν ἔσεσθαι...διαγγέλλουσα Dion.Ar.*e.h*.2.3.5 (401B); **b.** in eucharist and other sacramental rites, *ib*.3.1.1(425A); **5.** by moral illumination; **a.** in gen., by passage of believer from darkness of sin into light, *A.Phil*.140(p.75.13); Gr.Nyss.*hom.opif*.21.3(M.44.204A); αὐτὸς...ἐξήγαγεν αὐτὴν [sc. τὴν ψυχήν] ἐκ σκοτίας, ἰδίῳ φ. δοξάσας αὐτήν Mac.Aeg.*hom*.20.6(M.34.653B); **b.** by purification from sin and demonic powers, which is initial stage of illumination, Clem.*str*.2.20(p.175.12; M.8.1057C); Gr.Naz.*or*.39.1(M.36.336A); Dion.Ar.*c.h*.10.3(M.3.273C); divine light destroys power of demons, Or.*Cels*.1.60(p.110.28; M.11.769B); **c.** by practice of virtue; **i.** in gen. ἐκλέξασθε ἑαυτοῖς ἢ τὸ φ. ἢ τὸ σκότος, ἢ τὸν νόμον κυρίου, ἢ τὰ ἔργα τοῦ βελίαρ *T.Lev*.19.1; ὁδοὶ δύο εἰσὶν διδαχῆς καὶ ἐξουσίας, ἥ τε τοῦ φ. καὶ ἡ τοῦ σκότους...ἡ οὖν ὁδὸς τοῦ φ. ἐστιν αὕτη· ἐάν τις θέλων ὁδὸν ὁδεύειν ἐπὶ τὸν ὡρισμένον τόπον σπεύσῃ τοῖς ἔργοις αὐτοῦ *Barn*.18.1; 19.1; cf.*Did*.1.1; ἐργασίαν τῶν τοῦ φ. ἔργων *Const.App*.8.34.7; **ii.** esp. moral discernment, Diad.Phot.*perf*.6 (p.8.11); purity, Meth.*symp*.5.8(p.63.7; M.18.112B); τὸ φ. ἄσβεστον ἀνακαίεσθαι τῆς ἁγνείας *ib*.6.2(p.65.19; 116A); righteousness, *ib*.5.5 (p.60.1; 108A); **d.** by light of conscience ἐγκαθειρκτέον τῇ ψυχῇ τὸ αἰδῆμον οἱονεὶ φ. τοῦ λογισμοῦ Clem.*paed*.2.10(p.215.14; M.8.512C); **6.** by intellectual illumination; **a.** divine light as φῶς νοητόν, φῶς νοερόν Clem.*paed*.2.10(p.216.28; M.8.516B); in Greek philosophy and Christian doctrine, id.*str*.5.14(p.388.2; M.9.137B); obscured by desires and pleasures, *ib*.2.20(p.175.27; M.8.1060B); εἰκονικὸν φ. τὸ αἰσθητόν...ἀληθινὸν δὲ φ. τὸ νοητόν· μᾶλλον δὲ τὸ τῶν νοητῶν φωτιστικόν Or.*fr.6 in Jo.*(p.488.16); id.*Jo*.13.22(p.246.3; M.14.436B); id.*Cels*.5.10(p.11.9; M.11.1196B); Mac.Aeg.*libert.ment*.27(M.34.960C); described fully, Dion.Ar.*d.n*.4.6–7(M.3.701Aff.); **b.** as source of truth, which illuminates the mind, *T.Aser* 5.3; ἵνα τῆς ἀληθείας τὸ φ., ὁ λόγος, τῶν προφητικῶν αἰνιγμάτων τὴν μυστικὴν ἀπολύσηται σιωπήν Clem.*prot*.1(p.10.7; M.8.65C); id.*str*.5.5(p.343.21; M.9.49A); τὸ...φ. τῆς ἀληθείας φ. ἀληθές, ἄσκιον, ἀμερῶς μεριζόμενον πνεῦμα κυρίου εἰς τοὺς διὰ πίστεως ἡγιασμένους, λαμπτῆρος ἐπέχον τάξιν εἰς τὴν τῶν ὄντων ἐπίγνωσιν *ib*.6.16(p.502.4; 364B); Or.*Cels*.4.29(p.299.1; M.11.1072A); τοῦ νοῦ, ἐν ᾧ ἐστι τὸ κατὰ τὸν ἔσω ἄνθρωπον πρόσωπον, πληρούμενον φωτὸς καὶ δόξης ἀπὸ τῆς περὶ τῶν κατὰ τοὺς νόμους ἀληθείας *ib*.5.60(p.64.5; 1276D); τῷ τῆς ἀληθείας φ. ὁδηγούμενος τὴν θείαν πίστιν ἐπιγινώσκω Const.ap.Eus.*v.C*.4.9(p.121.12; M.20.1157B); id.ap.Gel.Cyz.*h.e*.2.7.7(M.85.1233B); full apprehension of light of truth necessitates removal of 'skins' in which soul was clothed after Fall παρ' ἐκείνου τοῦ φ. διδασκόμεθα τί ποιήσαντες ἐντὸς τῶν ἀκτίνων τῆς ἀληθείας στησόμεθα ὅτι οὐκ ἔστι δεδεμένοις ποσὶν ἀναδραμεῖν πρὸς τὸ ὕψος ἐκεῖνο, ἐν ᾧ τὸ φ. τῆς ἀληθείας ὁρᾶται, εἰ μὴ περιλυθείη τῶν τῆς ψυχῆς βάσεων ἡ νεκρά τε καὶ γηΐνη τῶν δερμάτων περιβολὴ ἡ περιτεθεῖσα κατ' ἀρχὰς τῇ φύσει Gr.Nyss.*v.Mos*.(M.44.332D); **c.** as consisting in, or apprehended by, knowledge of God φῶς γνώσεως φωτιεῖς ἐν τῷ Ἰακώβ *T.Lev*.4.3; τὴν μὲν ἀπάτην ἀπεικάζουσα τῷ σκότει, τὴν δὲ γνῶσιν ἡλίῳ καὶ φ. τοῦ θεοῦ Clem.*prot*.8(p.59.27; M.8.188B); *ib*.11(p.81.22; 236A); id.*str*.7.10(p.41.28; M.9.480C); id.*ecl*.32(p.147.6; M.9.716B); ἐν φ. τῷ ἀληθινῷ καὶ ἀλήκτῳ τῆς γνώσεως τὸν νοῦν καταλαμπόμενοι Or.*mart*.47(p.43.16; M.11.632A); νοητὸν γνώσεως φ. id.*Cels*.5.10(p.11.9; M.11.1196B); mediated through NT, id.*Jo*.1.6(8; p.11.23; M.14.36B); and through traditional rites of baptism, Bas.*Spir*.26(3.22B; M.32.113B); *Const.App*.2.5.7; ἀγνοίας ζόφον, ἀλλ' οὐ θεογνωσίας ἔχουσι φ. Thdt.*1Tim*.6:21 (3.673); ‡Meth.*Sym.et Ann*.8(M.18.368A); **d.** intellectual apprehension of light rendered possible through Christ, *1Clem*.36.2; **7.** by spiritual illumination (not clearly distinguishable from φῶς γνώσεως); **a.** perfectly enjoyed by soul in primal paradise, Max. *hymn*.1(M.91.1418C); divine light contemplated by men in east, the sphere of light, before their removal from east to plain of Shinar, Or.*Cels*.5.30(p.31.20; M.11.1225C); cf. parable of soul's return to paradise ηὔθυνον δὲ αὐτὸ καὶ τὴν ὁδὸν πρὸς τὸ φ. τῆς κατὰ ἀνατολὴν πατρίδος *Hymn*.ap.*A.Thom*.A 111(p.222.18); **b.** bestowed on soul, in varying degrees, in course of its progress towards perfection, Clem.*paed*.1.6(p.106.31; M.8.284B); *ib*.2.9(p.206.24; 493C); μηδαμῶς τοίνυν ἐπικαλυπτώμεθα τὸ σκότος, τὸ γὰρ φ. ἔνοικον ἡμῖν· καὶ ἡ σκοτία...αὐτὸ οὐ καταλαμβάνει *ib*.2.10(p.217.1; 516C); πάντη εἰς τὸ βάθος τῆς ψυχῆς ἁπάσης τὸ φ. τῆς δυνάμεως ἐκλάμπει id.*str*.7.7 (p.29.12; M.9.453B); φωτὸς ἔμπλεοι, φῶτες Ἰσραηλῖται τῷ ὄντι γινόμεθα id.*ecl*.33(p.147.11; M.9.716B); Plato's φῶς ἐν τῇ ψυχῇ (*ep*.7 341D) compared with Christian φῶς, Or.*Cels*.6.5(p.74.23; M.11.1296B); as inward illumination by H. Ghost, Ath.*inc.et c.Ar*.15 (M.26.1009C); Mac.Aeg.*libert.ment*.22(M.34.956D); *ib*.26(960A); τὴν δόξαν τοῦ φ. ἐν ταῖς ψυχαῖς δέχονται οἱ Χριστιανοί id.*hom*.47.1(M.34.797A); τὸ...θεοπρεπὲς κάλλος...μεταδοτικὸν...κατ' ἀξίαν ἑκάστῳ τοῦ οἰκείου φ. Dion.Ar.*c.h*.3.1(M.3.164D); *cat.1Jo*.1:5(p.109.4); necessary for ἡ τῶν πραγμάτων θεωρία, Clem.*str*.7.12(p.52.13; M.9.500D); and for θεωρία πνευματική, Max.*cap*.4.17(M.90.1309C); may be stage towards fuller illumination ἔστι δ' ὅτε καὶ αὐτὸ τὸ φ. τὸ φαῖνον ἐν καρδίᾳ, τῷ ἐνδοτέρῳ δήπου καὶ βαθυτέρῳ διανοίγει φ., ὥστε ὅλον τὸν ἄνθρωπον τῇ γλυκύτητι ἐκείνῃ καὶ θεωρίᾳ καταποθέντα μηκέτι ἐν ἑαυτῷ εἶναι Mac.Aeg.*carit*.9(M.34.916C); bestowal of divine light restores divine image in soul ὁ...ζωγράφος Χριστὸς τοῖς πιστεύουσιν αὐτῷ...ζωγραφεῖ κατὰ τὴν εἰκόνα αὐτοῦ ἐπουράνιον ἄνθρωπον...ἐκ τῆς ὑποστάσεως αὐτοῦ τοῦ φ. τοῦ ἀνεκλαλήτου, γράφει εἰκόνα οὐράνιον id. *hom*.30.4(M.34.724B); θεὸς ὡς φ. ἐν φ. ἐστιν ἐν ἡμῖν· ὁ γὰρ φύσει φῶς ὁ θεὸς ἐν τῇ μιμήσει γίνεται φ., ὡς ἐν εἰκόνι ἀρχέτυπον *cat.Jo*.1:5 (p.109.5); **c.** φῶς equated with ζωή (cf. Jo.1:4), Iren.*haer*.1.9.3(M.7.544A); Clem.*prot*.11(p.80.18; M.8.232B); (Egyptian) προσῳκείωται ...τῇ μονάδι τὸ φ., τῇ δὲ δυάδι τὸ σκότος, καὶ τῷ μὲν φ. κατὰ φύσιν ἡ ζωή, τῇ δὲ δυάδι ὁ θάνατος Hipp.*haer*.4.43(p.66.27; M.16.3107B); τοὺς μεταβεβηκότας ἀπὸ σκοτεινῆς τῆς τοῦ θανάτου...οἰκίας, ἐπὶ τὰ πεπληρωμένα οἰκοδομήματα ἐκ λίθων ζώντων φωτὸς ζωῆς Or.*mart*.41 (p.38.26; M.11.617A); id.*Jo*.2.18(12; p.76.2; M.14.148A); id.*fr.2 in Jo.*(p.486.23); ζωὴν τῇ ψυχῇ τὸ θεϊκὸν φ. τοῦ πνεύματος Mac.Aeg.*hom*.30.6(M.34.725A); **d.** believers themselves becoming light (cf. Eph. 5:8) through spiritual illumination καταμαθὼν ἄνθρωπε ἐν ἑαυτῷ, ὅτι ἄϋλος ὑπάρχεις, ὅτι ἅγιος, ὅτι φ. *A.Andr.fr*.6(p.40.32); ἦτε γάρ ποτε σκότος, νῦν δὲ φ. ἐν κυρίῳ. ἐντεῦθεν τὸν ἄνθρωπον ὑπὸ τῶν παλαιῶν ἡγοῦμαι κεκλῆσθαι φῶτα Clem.*paed*.1.6(p.106.29; M.8.284B); cf.id. *ecl*.33(p.147.11; M.9.716B); soul as mirror of divine light, Gr.Nyss. *hom.2 in Cant.*(M.44.805D); βλέπει...πρὸς τὸ ἀρχέτυπον κάλλος· περιστερὰ δὲ τὸ κάλλος. διὰ τοῦτο τῷ φωτὶ προσεγγίσασα, φ. γίνεται. τῷ δὲ φ. τὸ καλὸν τῆς περιστερᾶς εἶδος ἐνεικονίζεται...ἧς τὸ εἶδος τὴν τοῦ...πνεύματος παρουσίαν ἐγνώρισεν *ib*.5(869A); *ib*.(876B); καλὴ γίνεται, τῷ φ. τῆς ἀληθείας περιλαμφθεῖσα *ib*.*11*(1001B); ψυχὴ...ἡ καταξιωθεῖσα κοινωνῆσαι τῷ πνεύματι τοῦ φ. αὐτοῦ...ὅλη φῶς γίνεται Mac. Aeg.*hom*.1.2(M.34.452A); Dion.Ar.*e.h*.3.3.14(M.3.445A); **e.** participation in, or union with, divine light as summit of mystical ascent (considered positively) ἀναψάμενοι τοίνυν τῆς ἀρχῆς τοῦ φ. ἐκείνου ἐκ τοῦ πόθου τοῦ περὶ αὐτὸ ⟨αὐτῷ⟩ ὡς ἔνι μάλιστα ἐξομοιοῦσθαι πειρώμενοι Clem.*ecl*.33(p.147.9; M.9.716B); Dion.Ar.*e.h*.5.1.3(M.3.504B); κατὰ πάσης νοερᾶς ἐνεργείας ἀπόπαυσιν ἡ τοιάδε γίγνεται τῶν ἐκθεουμένων νοῶν πρὸς τὸ ὑπέρθεον φ. ἕνωσις id.*d.n*.1.5(M.3.593C); ἡ τοῦ νοητοῦ φ. παρουσία...ἐπιστρεπτικὴ πρὸς τὸ ὄντως ὂν...ἑνὸς καὶ ἑνωτικοῦ φ. ἐμπιπλῶσα *ib*.4.6(701B); ὅταν ἡ ψυχὴ θεοειδὴς γινομένη δι' ἑνώσεως ἀγνώστου ταῖς τοῦ ἀπροσίτου φ. ἀκτῖσιν ἐπιβάλλῃ *ib*.4.11 (708D); Anast.S.*defunct*.(M.89.1192A); divine light illuminating soul in prayer reveals the 'place' of God (cf. Ex.24:10), Evagr. Pont.*cap.pract*.A 71(M.40.1244B); (negatively) transcendence of God implies that mystical experience is passage from light into γνόφος (q.v.) wherein God dwells (cf.Ex.20:21) ἐναντίον γὰρ δοκεῖ πως εἶναι τῇ πρώτῃ θεοφανείᾳ τὸ νῦν ἱστορούμενον· τότε μὲν γὰρ ἐν φ., νῦν δὲ ἐν γνόφῳ τὸ θεῖον. ... ἡ γνῶσις τῆς εὐσεβείας φ. γίνεται παρὰ τὴν πρώτην οἷς ἂν ἐγγίνηται...προϊὼν δὲ ὁ νοῦς...ὅσῳ προσεγγίζει μᾶλλον τῇ θεωρίᾳ, τοσούτῳ πλέον ὁρᾷ τὸ τῆς θείας φύσεως ἀθεώρητον Gr.Nyss.

v.Mos.(M.44.376D); διὰ φωτὸς ἤρξατο ἡ τοῦ θεοῦ ἐπιφάνεια, μετὰ ταῦτα διὰ νεφέλης αὐτῷ διαλέγεται id.*hom.11 in Cant.*(M.44.1000C); ἀνατίθεμεν...τὸν...ἀόρατον γνόφον τῷ φ. τῷ ἀπροσίτῳ, καθ' ὑπεροχὴν τοῦ ἀοράτου φ. Dion.Ar.*d.n.*7.2(M.3.869A); cf.id.*myst.*1.3(M.3.1000C,D); τὸν ὑπερούσιον ἐκεῖνον ἴδωμεν γνόφον, τὸν ὑπὸ παντὸς τοῦ ἐν τοῖς οὖσι φ. ἀποκρυπτόμενον *ib.*2(1025B); ὁ θεῖος γνόφος ἐστὶ τὸ ἀπρόσιτον φ. id.*ep.*5(M.3.1073A); cf.Max.*ambig.*(M.91.1168A); **f.** such participation mediated to soul by love φ. ἡνωμένον ψυχῇ δι' ἀγάπης ἀδιαστάτου Clem.*str.*6.12(p.484.18; M.9.325B); τὸ τῆς ἀγάπης ἀξίωμα ἐκλάμπει ἐκ φ. εἰς φ. *ib.*7.9(p.41.6; 480A); Dion.Ar.*d.n.*4.5(M.3.701A); cf. διὰ τοῦ μυστικοῦ ἐκείνου φιλήματος τῇ πηγῇ τοῦ φ. προσαγαγεῖν τὸ στόμα ἐπόθησε Gr.Nyss.*hom.11 in Cant.*(M.44.1001B); and associated with spiritual ecstasy, Mac.Aeg.*carit.*9(M.34.916C); **g.** divine light as possession of blessed in future life ἄφετέ με καθαρὸν φ. λαβεῖν Ign.*Rom.*6.2; δέχονται αὐτοὺς τόποι φωτὸς καὶ ἀνέσεως καὶ αἰωνίας ἀπολαύσεως *A.Thom.*A 12(p.118.14); ἐὰν ὑπακούσῃς, τὸ φ., ἐὰν παρακούσῃς, τὸ πῦρ Clem.*prot.*1(p.9.1; M.8.64C); ἐσόμενος, ὡς εἰπεῖν, φ. ἑστὸς καὶ μένον ἀϊδίως id.*str.*7.10(p.42.15; M.9.481B); Meth.*symp.*4.5(p.51.21; M.18.96A); οἱ...τυφλοὶ ταῖς ψυχαῖς... μήτε ἐν τῷ θνητῷ βίῳ τῷ φ. ... φωτισθέντες, μήτε ἐν τῷ μέλλοντι τοῦ αἰωνίου φ. ἀξιωθησόμενοι Ath.*exp.in Is.*48:19(M.27.229A); οἱ τὰ τῆς ἀποδοχῆς ἄξια εἰργασμένοι, ἐν τῷ ὑπερκοσμίῳ φ. τὴν ἀνάπαυσιν ἔχουσιν Bas.*hex.*2.5(1.17D; M.29.41A); Chrys.*hom.56.4 in Mt.*(7.571D,E); enjoyed by soul in this life, by body hereafter, Mac.Aeg.*hom.*20.3(M.34.652B); id.*pat.*29(M.34.889B); ἡ...εὐχὴ...δεῖται,...κατατάξαι... αὐτὸν ἐν φ. καὶ χώρᾳ ζώντων Dion.Ar.*e.h.*7.3.4(M.3.560B); id.*ep.*9.5(M.3.1113A).

H. exeg.: Ps.17:29 ἐπειδὴ σκότος πολλάκις τὰς θλίψεις ἐκάλεσεν, εἰκότως φ. ὀνομάζει τὴν τούτων ἀπαλλαγήν Thdt.ad loc.(1.709); Ezech.43:16 τὸ δὲ ἀριὴλ σημαίνει...φ. θεοῦ id.ad loc.(2.1031); Mt. 5:16 οὐ γάρ φησιν, λαμψάτω τὸ φ. ὑμῶν ἔμπροσθεν τοῦ θεοῦ· τοῦτο γὰρ εἰ ἐνετέλλετο, ἀδύνατον ἂν ἐδίδου ἐντολήν Or.*Jo.*2.17(11; p.74.18; M.14.144D).

I. Gnost.; **1.** simile of 'light from light' applied to emanation of aeons, Iren.*haer.*2.17.4(M.7.762C); **2.** first principles, light and darkness, Hipp.*haer.*5.19(p.116.26; M.16.3179A); *ib.*6.38(p.168.9; 3254A); (Nicolaitan) προεβλήθησάν τινες τέσσαρες αἰῶνες, ἐκ δὲ τῶν τεσσάρων αἰώνων ἄλλοι δεκατέσσαρες, καὶ γέγονε δεξιά τε καὶ ἀριστερά, φ. καὶ σκότος Epiph.*haer.*25.5(p.273.4; M.41.328B); angels of light in opposition to ἀρχοντικοί, Or.*Cels.*6.27(p.97.9; M.11.1333A); **3.** wisdom as ἡ κόρη τοῦ φωτὸς θυγάτηρ *Hymn.*ap.*A.Thom.*A 6(p.109.1).

J. Manich.; **1.** first principles, light and darkness, Hegem. *Arch.*5(p.6.12; M.10.1433C); cf. E.3 supra; **2.** warfare between them, *ib.*7(p.10.4; 1437A); supported by interpretation of Jo.1:5, Epiph.*haer.*66.64(p.103.18; M.42.128D); **3.** part of light formed into human soul, Hegem.*Arch.*7(p.9.15; 1437A); at creation of man, *ib.*12(p.20.2; 1448A); **4.** 'pillar of glory', filled by purified souls, becomes 'pillar of light', *ib.*8(p.13.12; 1440C); **5.** παρθένος τοῦ φωτός (cf. I.3 supra), *ib.*13(p.21.11; 1449A); Thdt.*eran.*2(4.114).

K. Pythagorean δύο εἶναι ἀπ' ἀρχῆς τοῖς οὖσιν αἴτια, πατέρα καὶ μητέρα· καὶ πατέρα μὲν φ., μητέρα δὲ σκότος...ἐκ δὲ τούτων πάντα τὸν κόσμον συνεστάναι Hipp.*haer.*1.2(p.7.5; M.16.3025B).

L. of light of fire of divine retribution ἓν μόνον φ. φεύγωμεν, τὸ τοῦ πικροῦ πυρὸς ἔκγονον. μὴ πορευθῶμεν τῷ φ. τοῦ πυρὸς ἡμῶν, καὶ τῇ φλογὶ ᾗ ἐξεκαύσαμεν Gr.Naz.*or.*40.36(M.36.409D).

M. (pagan) of a provincial governor φ. τὸ ἡμέτερον *M.Ariad.*(p.126.28).

III. (= φωτικόν) *porch*, Thdt.*Ezech.*42:12–14(2.1025) cit. s. φωτικόν.

φώς, ὁ, *man* ῥηγνῦντες πελέκει καὶ τέκτονος ἐντεῖ φωτός †Apoll. *met.Ps.*73:6(M.33.1417B); derived from φῶς, *light* ἦτε γάρ ποτε σκότος, νῦν δὲ φῶς ἐν κυρίῳ. ἐντεῦθεν τὸν ἄνθρωπον ὑπὸ τῶν παλαιῶν ἡγοῦμαι κεκλῆσθαι φῶτα Clem.*paed.*1.6(p.106.30; M.8.284B); φωτὸς ἔμπλεοι, φῶτες Ἰσραηλῖται id.*ecl.*33(p.147.11; M.9.716B).

***φωσατεύω,** v. *φοσσατεύω.

***φωσατικῶς,** *with an army, in force* φ. ἠπλήκευσεν Thphn.*chron.* p.309(M.108.752C).

[*]**φώσατον (φωσᾶτον, φώσσατον), τό,** (Lat. *fossatum*) *entrenched camp*, *M.Pers.*7(p.453.3); Proc.G.*1Reg.*20:20(M.87.1108A); φωσᾶτον *Chron.Pasch.*p.396(M.92.1016A); fig. ὁ παρὼν βίος ὁδός τίς ἐστι καὶ στρατεία, καὶ ὡς ἂν εἴποι τις τὸ λεγόμενον...φώσσατον Chrys.*hom.23.3 in Eph.*(11.178F); cf. φοσσάτον.

φωστήρ, ὁ, *luminary*;

A. lit.; **1.** of heavenly bodies in gen. ἡλίου τε καὶ σελήνης καὶ τῶν λοιπῶν στοιχείων ἢ φ. Arist.*apol.*3.2; ἔστιν οὖν πνεῦμα ἐν φωστῆρσιν, πνεῦμα ἐν ἀγγέλοις, πνεῦμα ἐν φυτοῖς Tat.*orat.*12(p.13.28; M.6.832C); τὸ στερέωμα ⟨σὺν⟩ τοῖς φ. Hipp.*Dan.*2.29.7; to which angelic hosts are likened, Eus.*d.e.*4.6(p.158.16; M.22.264C); **2.** esp. of sun and moon τοὺς δύο φ. τοὺς μεγάλους *A.Petr.et Paul.*5(p.181.5); ἑωσφόρον...προσημαίνοντα ἔρχεσθαι τὸν τέλειον φ. Thphl.Ant.*Autol.* 1.6(M.6.1033B); Eus.*l.C.*6(p.211.4; M.20.1349A); Gr.Nyss.*v.Mos.*(M.44.348C); as objects of worship; by early man before rise of idolatry, Eus.*d.e.*9(p.164.2; M.22.273B); ὁ δὲ Πλάτων θεὸν καὶ θεοὺς παρὰ τὸ θέειν...τοὺς ἐν οὐρανῷ φ. ἐπικεκλῆσθαί φησι id.*p.e.*11.6(517D; M.21.857D); Cyr.*Os.*148(3.182A); (Stoic) τὸν...θεὸν νοῦν ὁρίζουσι... σῶμα δὲ αὐτοῦ τὸ πᾶν...καὶ ὀφθαλμοὺς τοὺς φ. Jo.D.*haer.*7(M.94.684B); Manich.: creation of luminaries by 'living spirit', Hegem. *Arch.*8(p.11.7; M.10.1437C); illumination of other worlds by sun and moon after they have set in this world's sky, *ib.*10(p.17.8; 1444C); souls are taken from the 'wheel' by sun's rays and transferred to moon, *ib.*8(p.13.1; 1440B); hence πλοῖα...ἤτοι πορθμεῖα εἶναι...τοὺς δύο φ. *ib.*(p.13.4; 1440B).

B. met.; **1.** of men; patriarchs ὡς γάρ ἐστιν ὁ ἥλιος...ἐπὶ τὴν γῆν, οὕτω καὶ ὑμεῖς ἐστε, οἱ φ. τοῦ Ἰσραὴλ παρὰ πάντα τὰ ἔθνη *T.Lev.*14.3; apostles, *A.Petr.et Paul.*18(p.187.4); Παῦλος, ὁ...φ. τῆς οἰκουμένης *A.Xanthipp.*7(p.62.11); Cyr.*Ps.*67:28(M.69.1156C); bishops and theologians, Thdt.*h.e.*4.27.1(3.1006); id.*h.rel.*14(3.1216); Nil.*epp.*3.279(M.79.521C); *Chron.Pasch.*p.9(M.92.85A); Eustrat.*v.Eutych.*2(M.86.2276D); φ. τοῦ ἐκκλησιαστικοῦ στερεώματος Jo.VI H.*v.Jo.D.*2(M.94.432B); Constantine, Eus.*v.C.*2.2(p.41.14; M.20.980D); a martyr, *M.Thdot.1* 21(p.74.16); all 'pillars' of Church, Gr.Nyss.*v.Mos.*(M.44.385B); the blessed in kingdom of God φωστῆρες τοῦ νέου αἰῶνος Eus. *e.th.*3.15(p.173.4; M.24.1029C); churches collectively αἱ...Χριστῷ μαθητευθεῖσαι ἐκκλησίαι, συνεξεταζόμεναι ταῖς ὧν παροικοῦσι δήμων ἐκκλησίαις, ὡς φ. εἰσιν ἐν κόσμῳ Or.*Cels.*3.29(p.227.9; M.11.957B); **2.** of Christ τὸν φ. τῆς ζωῆς Ἰησοῦν *A.Phil.*21(p.11.18); φ. τὸν θεὸν λόγον Eus.*l.C.*6(p.211.24; M.20.1349C); **3.** of God (Pythagorean) θεὸς εἷς...φ. καὶ πάντων πατήρ Clem.*prot.*6(p.55.12; M.8.180A); **4.** of divine revelation, in mysteries of Eleusis, Hipp.*haer.*5.8(p.96.14; M.16.3150C); of moral law of God, Eus.*p.e.*6.6(250A; M.21.425A).

***φωστηρικός,** *of* or *belonging to the heavenly bodies* διαφυλάττει... τὰς οὐρανίας καὶ φ. καὶ ἀστρῴους οὐσίας Dion.Ar.*d.n.*8.5(M.3.892D); τὸ ἀστρῷον καὶ φ. ὑπερνικῶν κάλλος Andr.Caes.*Apoc.*55(M.106.385C).

φωσφόρος, *light-bearing* ὁ λόγος ὁ θεοῦ...ἡ πρὸ ἑωσφόρου φ. φωνή Hipp.*haer.*10.33(p.290.25; M.16.3450C); Geo.Pis.*Pers.*1.3(M.92.1197A); of face of Moses, Nil.*epp.*1.113(M.79.132C).

φωταγωγ-έω, A. *guide by light, illuminate the way for*; **1.** lit. εἶδον...τὸν ἥλιον...τὰς ἀκτῖνας αὐτοῦ κυκλοῦντα καὶ ~οῦντά με *T.Abr.*A 7(p.84.1); Mac.Aeg.*hom.*47.11(M.34.804B); **2.** met. ἐπεὶ δέ με ~εῖς, κύριε, καὶ τὸν θεὸν εὑρίσκω διὰ σοῦ Clem.*prot.*11(p.80.10; M.8.232A); in language of mysteries ἱεροφαντεῖ δὲ ὁ κύριος καὶ τὸν μύστην σφραγίζεται ~ῶν *ib.*12(p.84.25; 241A); Cyr.*Jo.*1.4(4.29D); ἵνα καὶ ταῖς ἀσβέστοις τοῦ σωτῆρος ~ούμενοι λαμπάσιν εἰς τὴν ἄνω καταντήσωμεν Ἱερουσαλήμ id.*hom.pasch.*1.1(5^2.1B); ἡ σάρκωσις τοῦ μονογενοῦς ~εῖ τοὺς ἀνθρώπους πρὸς τὴν ἀληθῆ θεογνωσίαν Ammon. *Jo.*1:4(M.85.1393C); πρὸς αὐτῶν ~ούμεθα πρὸς τοὺς θεαρχικοὺς ὕμνους Dion.Ar.*d.n.*1.3(M.3.589B).

B. *illuminate*; **1.** lit. στῦλος πυρὸς ἐφωταγώγει τὴν νύκτα Bas.Sel. *or.*31.1(M.85.340C); **2.** met., *enlighten*; by Christian conversion, Or. *Cels.*2.71(p.193.25; M.11.908C); Ναθαναὴλ φωταγωγηθεὶς παρὰ τοῦ Φιλίππου Gr.Nyss.*hom.15 in Cant.*(M.44.1089C); ὁ Ἀπελλῆς...τῇ χάριτι θεοῦ φωταγωγηθεὶς Ammon.*Ac.*18:25(M.85.1572C); Sophr.H. *v.Anast.*(M.92.1680A); by instruction, through H. Ghost, Cyr.H. *catech.*16.22; Cyr.*Arcad.*19(p.69.7; 5^2.53B); by inward spiritual illumination, ref. Moses at bush τὴν...ἀκοὴν τοῖς ἀκηράτοις δόγμασιν ἐφωταγώγει Gr.Nyss.*v.Mos.*1(M.44.305D); Χριστὸς...διὰ τοῦ ἰδίου... πνεύματος εἰς ἕκαστα τῶν δεόντων ~ῶν, καὶ ἀρρήτοις τισὶ δᾳδουχίαις... ἑαυτὸν ἐκκαλύπτων Cyr.*Jo.*10(4.828B); Thal.*cent.*3.45(M.91.1452D).

C. *enable to see*; **1.** lit. εἶδον αὐτὸν τυφλοὺς ~οῦντα *A.Petr.et Paul.* 41(p.196.13); ‡Meth.*palm.*3(M.18.388C); **2.** met., Clem.*prot.*4(p.41.8; M.8.148A); id.*paed.*1.9(p.139.4; M.8.349B); ὁ...τοῦ σταυροῦ στέφανος, ἐφωταγώγησε μὲν τοὺς ἐν ἀγνωσίᾳ τυφλοὺς Cyr.H.*catech.*13.1.

D. *cause to shine* ἐγὼ τὸν νόμον παράπτω, αὐτὸς δὲ τὴν χάριν ~εῖ †Hipp.*theoph.*3(p.259.3; M.10.853D).

***φωταγωγής,** *illuminating* τὰς φ. ἐννοίας ‡Gr.Nyss.*hom.4.37 in Jo.*(p.168.29).

φωταγωγία, ἡ, A. lit.; **1.** *leading by light* ἡ τοῦ ἀστέρος φ. Isid. Pel.*epp.*1.18(M.78.193B); **2.** *procession of lights*, at Easter baptismal ceremonies, Gr.Naz.*or.*45.2(M.36.624C); at funeral of martyrs, Cyr.S. *v.Euthym.*44(p.66.12); **3.** *entry of light, illumination* (by windows, etc.) τὴν εἴσοδον πλατεῖαν καὶ τὴν φ. ἱκανῶς εἰσδεχομένην ἐκ τῆς ἡλιακῆς ἀκτῖνος id.*v.Sab.*18(p.102.5); τὴν τριάδα διὰ τῆς τῶν θυρίδων τριπλῆς φ. ἐξεικονίσασα Jo.D.*hom.*12.19(M.96.808B).

B. met., of spiritual illumination; **1.** effected by H. Ghost, Didym.*Trin.*2.14(M.39.705B); Cyr.*Os.*24(3.48B); id.*Jo.*1 proem.(4.10A); *ib.*10.2(923A); esp. in baptism, Epiph.*fid.*15(p.516.23; M.42.812C); Dion.Ar.*e.h.*2.3.3(M.3.400B); πασῶν ἀρχὴ [sc. baptism] τῶν θείων φ. *ib.*3.1(425A); by presence of H. Ghost in soul, Thdt.*2Tim.*1:14(3.680); in decisions of CNic.(325), Cyr.*Nest.*1.5(p.25.36; 6.20D); **2.** conferred by special revelation ποίας ἐδεήθη φ. ἄνωθεν, ἵνα μάθῃ τὸ...μυστήριον; Cyr.*Arcad.*106(p.88.31; 5^2.82B); **3.** by the gospel εὐαγγελικῆς φ. τῆς ἐν κόσμῳ δι' αὐτοῦ καὶ τῶν μαθητῶν αὐτοῦ γεγενημένης Epiph.*haer.*20.4(p.233.3; M.41.280B); τὴν...εὐαγγελικὴν παίδευσιν καὶ φ. Cyr.*Zach.*84(3.769A); by scriptural truth, Epiph.*haer.*69.37(p.185.24; M.42.260C); **4.** consisting in conversion καύχημα ...διδασκάλων,...οἱ διὰ τῆς αὐτῶν σεσωσμένοι φ. Cyr.*Is.*5.5(2.865B); in inward illumination in gen., *ib.*4.1(568A); in mystical illumination θεὸς δέ ἐστιν ἡ ἀλήθεια, ἡ ἐμφανισθεῖσα τότε διὰ τῆς ἀρρήτου ἐκείνης φ. τῷ Μωσῇ Gr.Nyss.*v.Mos.*(M.44.332C); πρὸς τὸ μεῖζον τῶν τῆς ψυχῆς κατορθωμάτων, διά τε τῆς μακρᾶς ἐπιμελείας, καὶ διὰ τῆς ἐν τῷ ὕψει γενομένης φ. ἐπαρθέντι *ib.*(337C); as goal of spiritual progress, Gr.Naz.*or.*39.20(M.36.360A).

***φωταγωγικός**, *guiding by light, illuminating* ἡ...τῶν ἱερέων φ. τάξις ἐπὶ τὰς θείας τῶν τελετῶν ἐποψίας χειραγωγεῖ τοὺς τελουμένους Dion.Ar.*e.h.*5.3.6(M.3.505D).

φωταγωγός, *giving light, illuminating*;

A. as adj.; **1.** lit., of sun, *Anaph.Pil.*A 9(p.440); **2.** met., of God τὸν κύριον τῶν πνευμάτων...τὸν ἡλίου φ. θεὸν ἐπιζητῶ Clem.*prot.*6(p.51.25; M.8.172C); of Christ ὁ ζωοποιὸς ὁ φ. Eus.*h.e.*10.4.12(M.20.853A); of angels ὁδοὶ δύο...ἥ τε τοῦ φωτὸς καὶ ἡ τοῦ σκότους...ἐφ' ἧς μὲν γάρ εἰσιν τεταγμένοι φ. ἄγγελοι τοῦ θεοῦ, ἐφ' ἧς δὲ ἄγγελοι τοῦ σατανᾶ *Barn.*18.1; τοὺς μὲν ἁγίους φ. φυλάττουσιν ἄγγελοι, τοὺς δὲ φαύλους σκοτεινοί Didym.ap.Jo.D.*parall.*7(M.95.1097C); φ. ... πρὸς τὴν ἱερὰν ταύτην τελείωσιν ἡγεμόνας, τὰς περὶ θεὸν πρωτίστας οὐσίας Dion.Ar.*e.h.*5.1.2(M.3.501A); of resurrection τῇ φ. τῶν νεκρῶν ἀναστάσει Geo.Pis.*hex.*1342(M.92.1538A); of scriptures αἱ δὲ φ. διαθῆκαι στηρίζουσι τὸ φρόνημα Ph.Carp.*Cant.*7(M.40.44D); of councils τὰς ἱερὰς συνόδους...ἃς ὡς φωταγωγοὺς ταῖς...ψυχαῖς περιέπομεν Sophr.H.*ep.syn.*(M.87.3184C); myst., of ἡσυχία as διανοίας φ., ‡Chrys.*pat.et consumm.*(12.819D).

B. as subst. ἡ φ. [sc. θυρίς], *window*, Gr.Nyss.*hom.5 in Cant.*(M.44.864D); Thdt.*qu.49 in 1Reg.*(1.385); id.*Ps.*27:2(1.775).

φωταύγεια, ἡ, *resplendent light* τὰ...σεραφὶμ...καθαρᾶς αὐτοῦ φωταυγείας μετέχοντα Sophr.H.*or.*2.3(M.87.3220C); Jo.Clim.*past.*15(M.88.1204A); of divine illumination in soul τὴν ἐν τῷ ἡγεμονικῷ σου φ. Jo.Carp.*cap.*82(M.85.1853); of revelation of God in creation, Cosm.Mel.*ind.*(M.38.346).

***φωταυγ-έω**, *shine brightly* ἄστρον ~οῦν Rom.Mel.1.13(*AS* 1 p.6).

***φωταυγής**, *brilliant, shining*; of bright cloud at Transfiguration, Jo.D.*carm.transfig.*17(M.96.572C); of BMV σοῦ...ὡς φ. ἡμέρας ἐπιφανείσης τῷ κόσμῳ καὶ τὸν τῆς δικαιοσύνης ἥλιον προαγαγούσης ‡Meth.*Sym.et Ann.*5(M.18.360A); met. ταῖς φ. ἐντολαῖς Nil.*epp.*4.19(M.79.560B); ἀγάπη ταῖς φ. πράξεσιν ἁπάσῃ προσχαίρει ψυχῇ id.*Eulog.*32(M.79.1136D).

***φώταυγος**, *brilliant, shining*, Jo.D.*carm.theoph.*69(p.211; M.96.828C).

***Φωτεινιανός**, ὁ, *follower of Photinus*, Epiph.*haer.*71.1(p.249.10; M.42.373C); linked doctrinally with Ebionites, Theodotians, and Artemonites, Thdt.*haer.*5.11(4.420); Tim.CP *haer.*10(M.86.61B).

φωτεινός, **I.** *shining, brilliant*;

A. lit.; of star (Num.24:17) which typifies Christ, Just.*1apol.*32.13(M.6.380C); in comparison of blood of Christ with milk given to catechumens τὸ αἷμα ἐπὶ τὸ φωτεινότατον καὶ λευκότατον ὑπὸ τοῦ πνεύματος τρέπεσθαι Clem.*paed.*1.6(p.114.14; M.8.297C).

B. met., of divine and spiritual radiance; **1.** of divine glory; **a.** of God οἱ...Πέρσαι ἔφασαν τὸν θεὸν εἶναι φ. Hipp.*haer.*4.43(p.65.10; M.16.3106B); ὁ...τὸν ἥλιον κατασκευάσας...ὀφείλει πολλῷ μᾶλλον ...εἶναι...φωτεινότερος Cyr.H.*catech.*4.5; **b.** of Logos, Just.*dial.*121.2(M.6.757A); **c.** of H. Ghost illuminating soul ὅσῳ τις...γνωστικώτερος γίνεται, προσεχέστερον τούτῳ τὸ πνεῦμα τὸ φ. Clem.*str.*4.17(p.295.23; M.8.1316A); **d.** (Basilidean) of great Archon emanating from Deity, Hipp.*haer.*7.23(p.201.5; M.16.3310C); **e.** as revealed in theophanies; in pillar of cloud, typifying Christ ὁ στῦλος τῆς φ. νεφέλης Ἰησοῦ Or.*Jo.*32.1(p.425.5; M.14.740B); in Elijah's cloud κατ' ἴχνος ἐκείνης τῆς φ. ἀεροβατοῦντα νεφέλης Clem.*prot.*10(p.68.6; M.8.205A); in countenance of Christ transfigured, id.*exc.Thdot.*5(p.106.26; M.9.656B); in φωτεινὴ νεφέλη of Transfiguration, contrasted with dark cloud of Sinai, Chrys.*hom.56.3 in Mt.*(7.569D); in other theophanies, *A.Phil*124(p.53.10); **f.** in 'bright cloud' of glory in which saints are transported from place to place, *A.Petr.et Andr.*1(p.117.3); in fire which embraces martyr and conveys soul to heaven, Bas.*hom.*4.2(2.34E; M.31.241A); **g.** in heavenly spheres, *T.Lev.*2.8; and heavenly mansions, *A.Phil.*148(p.89.18); **h.** in Cross as ladder by which souls escape from Hades, *ib.*133(p.65.5); *ib.*138(p.70.17); **i.** in divine glory bestowed on priesthood, Dion.Ar.*ep.*8.2(M.3.1092B); **2.** of angelic glory εἰ...ὡς ἄγγελος φωτὸς προφητεύει, ἀληθῆ ἄρα ἐρεῖ. εἰ ἀγγελικὰ καὶ φ., προφητεύσει καὶ ὠφέλιμα Clem.*str.*6.8(p.465.7; M.9.288B); ἀγγέλους...ἐκ τῆς ψυχικῆς καὶ φ. οὐσίας id.*exc.Thdot.*47(p.122.1; M.9.681A); ἐν...ἀγγέλοις τῇ πρώτῃ φ. φύσει μετὰ τὴν πρώτην Gr.Naz.*or.*45.2(M.36.624C); *Rit.Bapt.*(p.394); ὄρη φωτεινά (Jer.13:12) interpreted as οἱ ἅγιοι ἄγγελοι τοῦ θεοῦ, οἱ προφῆται, Μωσῆς ὁ θεράπων, οἱ ἀπόστολοι Ἰησοῦ Χριστοῦ Or.*hom.12.12 in Jer.*(p.98.11; M.13.393C); **3.** Gnost., (Docetae) of the earthly copies of eternal ideas οὐκ εἴασεν ἐπὶ πολὺ τοὺς φ. χαρακτῆρας ἄνωθεν ὑπὸ τοῦ σκότους κάτω κατασπασθῆναι Hipp.*haer.*8.9(p.228.18; M.16.3351C); (Saturninus) of archetypal image after which man was created, *ib.*7.28(p.208.14; 3322A); **4.** ref. that which illuminates soul; of revealed truth, Clem.*str.*6.3(p.448.16; M.9.252C); τὰ καθαρὰ τῶν λογίων φ. τε Gr.Thaum.*pan.Or.*15(p.34.1; M.10.1093C); of Christian instruction τὸν φωτεινότερον καὶ εὐωδέστερον λειμῶνα τοῦδε τοῦ παραδείσου Cyr.H.*catech.*19.1; of γνῶσις, Or.*Jo.*2.5(4; p.60.7; M.14.117D); hence γνωστικός is himself φωτεινός, Clem.*str.*6.17(p.510.14; 384B); *ib.*6.13(p.485.1; 328A); *ib.*7.12(p.56.29; 509B); of Christian way of life, *ib.*3.7(p.223.3; M.8.1161B); of ministry in Church, *ib.*6.3(p.448.17; M.9.252C); **5.** of baptism ἔνδυσόν με τὴν ἔνδοξόν σου στολήν, τὴν φ. σου σφραγῖδα τὴν πάντοτε λάμπουσαν, ἕως ἂν παρέλθω πάντας τοὺς κοσμοκράτορας *A.Phil.*144(p.86.6); ἔνδυμα φ. Cyr.H.*procatech.*16; Bas.*hom.*13.5(2.117D; M.31.433A); hence of φωτεινὰ ἱμάτια of Christ assumed by those who are συμμορφωθέντες αὐτῷ πρὸς τὸ ἀπαθές τε καὶ θειότερον Gr.Nyss.*hom.1 in Cant.*(M.44.764D); of indwelling H. Ghost providing soul with a φωτεινὸς χαρακτήρ, Clem.*str.*4.18(p.299.18; M.8.1325A); cf. Jo.D.*transfig.*4(M.96.552D); **6.** of sign of cross worn on forehead βλέπετε ἐπὶ τοῦ μετώπου μου γραφεῖσαν φ. λάμπαδα; *M.Glyc.*(p.13*A).

II. *clear, clear-sighted*, of the eye, Clem.*paed.*1.6(p.106.24; M.8.284A).

***φωτεμβολ-έω**, *throw light upon, illuminate* ἔχει...αἴνιγμα ἡ λυχνία...τοῦ σημείου τοῦ Χριστοῦ, οὐ τῷ σχήματι μόνῳ, ἀλλὰ καὶ τῷ ~εῖν...τοὺς εἰς αὐτὸν πιστεύοντας Clem.*str.*5.6(p.349.10; M.9.60B).

φωτίζ-ω, *illuminate, enlighten*;

I. lit., of physical illumination;

A. *shine, shine upon, make bright* οὐκ ἔστι φῶς ὃ μὴ ~ει Clem.*paed.*1.3(p.95.17; M.8.260B) = Dion.Ar.*d.n.*4.24(M.3.728A); ὁ ἥλιος ...τὸν ὅλον κόσμον ~ει Clem.*str.*7.3(p.15.29; M.9.428A); *Hom.Clem.*17.8; Ath.*gent.*16(M.25.33C); Bas.*hom.*5.3(2.36A; M.31.244B); of shining of sun's rays compared with illumination by H. Ghost, Didym.(‡Bas.)*Eun.*5.1(1.321A; M.29.769B); ἡ τῆς ἡλιακῆς ἀκτῖνος διάδοσις...προσβάλλουσα...ταῖς ὕλαις, ἀμυδροτέραν ἔχει τὴν διαδοτικὴν ἐπιφάνειαν ἐκ τῆς τῶν ~ομένων ὑλῶν πρὸς φωτοδοσίαν διαπορθμευτικὴν ἕξιν ἀνεπιτηδειότητος Dion.Ar.*c.h.*13.3(M.3.301B); ref. prayer to be said at dawn ὅτι ἐφώτισεν ὑμῖν ὁ κύριος *Const.App.*8.34.2; ὁ πεφωτισμένος στῦλος symbolizing τὸ ἑστὸς καὶ μόνιμον τοῦ θεοῦ καὶ τὸ ἄτρεπτον αὐτοῦ φῶς Clem.*str.*1.24(p.102.17; M.8.909C); of deity πῦρ ἀβλαβῶς ~ον Dion.Ar.*c.h.*2.5(144D).

B. *enlighten, make to see* τοῦτον ἐν τῷ τοῦ θεοῦ σου ὀνόματι ἐὰν φωτίσῃς *M.Ner.et Ach.*22(p.21.15).

C. *bring to light, make manifest* ὁ ~ων τὰ ἐπικεκρυμμένα λόγος... δι' οὗ εἰς φῶς καὶ γένεσιν ἕκαστον τῶν κτισμάτων παρῆλθεν Clem.*str.*6.16(p.506.24; M.9.376C); ἐδόθη...ἡ ζωή, θανάτῳ δὲ ἐζοφώθη, πάλιν τῇ ἀναστάσει...ἡ ζωὴ ~εται Sever.ap.*cat.2Tim.*1:12(p.60.17).

II. met.; **A.** of enlightenment of the mind, *illustrate, explain* ~ει τοῖς πλανωμένοις τὴν ἀλήθειαν Clem.*paed.*1.10(p.145.10; M.8.360C); ἀπὸ τοῦ βάθους...τῶν γραφῶν ~ων τὸν νόμον τοῦ πνεύματος Meth.*symp.*5.4(p.57.11; M.18.101D); Max.*ambig.*(M.91.1136C).

B. of spiritual enlightenment; **1.** *reveal, make manifest*; **a.** of God's self-revelation πρόσωπον...τοῦ θεοῦ ὁ λόγος, ᾧ ~εται ὁ θεὸς καὶ γνωρίζεται Clem.*paed.*1.7(p.124.4; M.8.320A); **b.** of God's revelation of hidden truths and mysteries Γαβριὴλ...θαρρεῖται τοὺς ἀρρήτους τῆς τοῦ θεοῦ σοφίας θησαυροὺς καὶ τὸ βάθος τῶν ἀνεξιχνιάστων αὐτοῦ κριμάτων ~εται Anast.Ant.*serm.*3.1(M.89.1385D); τοῦ τὰ ἐσκοτισμένα ~οντος θεοῦ Max.*myst.*(M.91.661D); **2.** *enlighten, enable to see* ἡ...κατὰ θεὸν ἀληθὴς μετάνοια...~ει τοὺς ὀφθαλμοὺς *T.Gad* 4.7; φωτί...θείῳ, ~οντι ψυχῆς ὀφθαλμοὺς εἰς κατανόησιν τῶν...θείων θεωρημάτων †Bas.*Is.*76(1.432E; M.30.245B); Ast.Am.*hom.*8(M.40.288C); τὸ τῆς διανοίας ὄμμα πεφωτισμένον ἔχων Cyr.*Jo.*1.2(4.15B); **3.** *illuminate, make bright*; **a.** of divine goodness illuminating all things, Dion.Ar.*d.n.*4.4(M.3.697C); **b.** of Logos illuminating heavenly sphere τῶν...ἐν οὐρανῷ καὶ πρότερον ὑπὸ τοῦ λόγου πεφωτισμένων Or.*or.*26(p.361.12; M.11.501B); and world of men, id.*Cels.*6.79(p.150.15; M.11.1417B); **4.** of inward illumination and enlightenment of soul; **a.** in gen. τοῖς ἐκλεκτοῖς ἔσται φῶς καὶ χάρις...καὶ ἔσται ἐν ἀνθρώπῳ πεφωτισμένῳ φῶς καὶ ἀνθρώπῳ ἐπιστήμονι νόημα *Apoc.En.*5.8(p.22.22); οὐαὶ τῷ ἀσεβεῖ, ὅτι, ὅταν πάντες ~ωνται, τότε ἐκεῖνος σκοτίζεται Nil.*sent.*78(M.79.1248B); Bars.*resp.*(M.86.900B); of celestial hierarchy καθαίρεται καὶ ~εται καὶ τελεσιουργεῖται Dion.Ar.*c.h.*7.3(M.3.209C); *ib.*8.1(240B); ref. functions of earthly hierarchy ἡ...δύναμις ἡ πρώτη...ἐστιν ἡ καθαιρομένη· μέση δὲ μετὰ τὴν κάθαρσιν ἡ ~ομένη...τελευταία δὲ...ἐλλαμπομένη τὴν τελειωτικὴν ἐπιστήμην id.*e.h.*5.1.3(M.3.504B); **b.** its source; **i.** God τοῦ ~οντος πατρὸς καὶ...τοῦ...λόγου διδάσκοντος τοῦ τε πνεύματος ἐνεργοῦντος εἰς τὸ νοεῖν, Or.*or.*2(p.303.18; M.11.424A); **ii.** Christ ἡμᾶς...τοὺς διὰ Ἰησοῦ πεφωτισμένους Just.*dial.*122.1(M.6.760A); ἡμᾶς ὁ κύριος ~ει, εἰς τὸ φῶς ἄγων τὸ ἄσκιον καὶ οὐκέτι ὑλικόν Clem.*ecl.*5(p.138.18; M.9.701A); ὁ μὲν Ἰωάννης πολλοὺς...ἐπέστρεψε πρὸς κύριον,...ὁ δὲ Ἰησοῦς...πάντας ἐφώτισεν εἰς τὴν ἐπίγνωσιν τῆς ἀληθείας Or.*hom.4 in Lc.*(p.28.10); id.*Jo.*13.48(46; p.275.28; M.14.485C); ἀνέτειλέν σοι ὁ ἥλιος τῆς δικαιοσύνης Χριστὸς ἵνα σε φωτίσῃ *A.Phil.*115(p.46.13); ‡Gr.Thaum.*annunt.*1(M.10.1452B); ὁ ἐρχόμενος φωτίσαι τὰ κρυπτὰ τοῦ σκότους Bas.*jud.*8(2.222D; M.31.673B); Gr.Naz.*carm.*1.1.32.13(M.37.512A); φωτισθήσῃ μυστήρια βαθέα παρὰ Χριστοῦ Hesych.S.*temp.*1.29(M.93.1489A); or divinity of Logos, Or.*Cels.*7.2(p.173.13; M.11.1452C); exeg. Jo.1:9, 8:12 ὁ δὲ σωτὴρ...~ει οὐ σώματα ἀλλὰ ἀσωμάτῳ δυνάμει τὸν ἀσώματον νοῦν, ἵνα ὡς ὑπὸ ἡλίου ἕκαστος ἡμῶν φωτιζόμενος καὶ τὰ ἄλλα δυνηθῇ βλέπειν νοητά...ἔστι δὲ ὁ Χριστὸς...φῶς ἀληθινὸν πρὸς ἀντιδιαστολὴν αἰσθητοῦ, οὐδενὸς αἰσθητοῦ ὄντος ἀληθινοῦ id.*Jo.*1.25(23; p.31.17; 68C); Ἰησοῦν ἐπικαλεσάμενοι, τὸ πατρικὸν φῶς, τὸ ὂν τὸ ἀληθινόν, ὃ ~ει πάντα ἄνθρωπον...δι' οὗ τὴν πρὸς τὸν ἀρχίφωτον πατέρα προσαγωγὴν ἐσχήκαμεν Dion.Ar.*c.h.*1.2(M.3.121A); exeg. Mt.5:14 τοῖς μαθηταῖς φησιν, ὑμεῖς ἐστε τὸ φῶς τοῦ κόσμου,...τὸ δ' ἀνάλογον σελήνῃ καὶ ἄστροις ὑπολαμβάνομεν εἶναι περὶ τὴν νύμφην ἐκκλησίαν καὶ τοὺς μαθητάς, ἔχοντας οἰκεῖον φῶς ἢ ἀπὸ τοῦ ἀληθινοῦ ἡλίου ἐπίκτητον, ἵνα φωτίσωσι μὴ δεδυνημένους πηγὴν ἐν αὐτοῖς κατασκευάσαι φωτός Or.*Jo.*1.25(23; p.31.9; 68C); **iii.** H. Ghost, Or.*princ.*4.7(14; p.318.9; M.11.374A); Eus.*d.e.*1.10(p.44.11; M.22.84D); in rel. to prophetic inspiration φωτισθεὶς διὰ τοῦ πνεύματος τὰ περὶ τῆς παρουσίας τοῦ μονογενοῦς ὁ μακάριος Δαυὶδ Ath.*exp.in Ps.*85:1(M.27.375C); †Bas.*Is.*254(1.573E; M.30.568A); ἵνα φωτίσῃ τῇ διὰ πνεύματος δᾳδουχίᾳ τοὺς ἐσκοτισμένους Cyr.*Os.*3(3.65A); ψυχικός ἐστιν ὁ κατὰ σάρκα ζῶν καὶ μήπω τὸν νοῦν φωτισθεὶς διὰ τοῦ πνεύματος, ἀλλὰ μόνην τὴν ἔμφυτον καὶ ἀνθρωπίνην σύνεσιν ἔχων, ἣν ταῖς ἁπάντων ψυχαῖς ἐμβάλλει ὁ δημιουργός id.*1Cor.*2:14(M.74.865C); ὑπὸ...τοῦ παναγίου πνεύματος ~όμενοι τὰς τοῦ μονογενοῦς σου θεωροῦμεν ἀκτῖνας Thdt.*Ps.*35:10(1.832); **c.** ref. means by which men are enlightened; **i.** OT dispensation, Mosaic Law illuminating Jews only, ‡Chrys.ap.Phot.*cod.*277(M.104.273A); cf. εἰ νόμος εἶχε τὸ ~ειν τὰ ἔθνη καὶ τοὺς ἔχοντας αὐτόν, τίς χρεία καινῆς διαθήκης; Just.*dial.*122.5(M.6.760C); **ii.** by divine grace ἐκκλησίᾳ ἠγαπημένῃ καὶ πεφωτισμένῃ ἐν θελήματι τοῦ θελήσαντος τὰ πάντα ἃ ἔστιν, κατὰ πίστιν καὶ ἀγάπην Ἰησοῦ Χριστοῦ Ign.*Rom.*proem.; Cyr.*Jo.*proem.(4.1A); Diad.*perf.*88(p.122.26); **iii.** by conversion περὶ τῶν ἐθνῶν τῶν πεφωτισμένων εἴρηται Just.*dial.*122.3(M.6.760C); and Christian teaching, Or.*Jo.*13.53(52; p.282.2; M.14.497A); of S. Peter illuminating West by his preaching, *Clem.ep.*1(M.2.33B); *Hom.Clem.*3.27; Pall.*v.Chrys.*5(p.29.15; M.47.19) cit. s. ἀλίζω; Proc.G.*Cant.*6:8(M.87.1756A); by study of scripture, Bas.*struct.hom.*1.1(1.324A; M.30.12A); ref. Roman church, opp. heretics Πέτρου καὶ Παύλου τὰς θήκας, τῶν πιστῶν τὰς ψυχὰς ~ούσας Thdt.*ep.*113(4.1188); hence pass., *be a catechumen*, Cyr.H.*procatech.*1; CLaod.*can.*46; CTrull.*can.*78; **iv.** by the truth, Clem.*paed.*2.9(p.206.26; M.8.496A); Eus.*p.e.*11.5(513B; M.21.852B); **v.** by faith, Procl.CP *Arm.*5(p.188.13; M.65.857B); **vi.** by conscience ὅτε ἐποίησεν ὁ θεὸς τὸν ἄνθρωπον, ἐνέσπειρεν αὐτῷ τί ποτε θεῖον, ὥσπερ λογισμόν τινα θερμότερον καὶ φωτεινὸν σπινθῆρος λόγον ἐπέχοντα· ~οντα τὸν νοῦν Dor.*doct.*3.1(M.88.1652D); **vii.** by knowledge φῶς γνώσεως φωτιεῖς ἐν τῷ Ἰακώβ *T.Lev.*4.3; ἀνατελεῖ ἄστρον αὐτοῦ ἐν οὐρανῷ ὡς βασιλέως ~ον φῶς γνώσεως ἐν ἡλίῳ ἡμέραν *ib.*18.3; ἐφωτίσθημεν γάρ· τὸ δὲ ἔστιν ἐπιγνῶναι τὸν θεόν Clem.*paed.*1.6(p.105.1; M.8.280B); ἡ γνῶσις ...ἡ τῷ ὄντι θεία σοφία εἴη ἄν, τὸ φῶς τὸ εἰλικρινές, τὸ...~ον τοὺς καθαροὺς id.*ecl.*32(p.147.6; M.9.716B); οἱ ἐν οὐρανῷ ἀστέρες ζῷά εἰσι λογικὰ καὶ σπουδαῖα καὶ ἐφωτίσθησαν τῷ φωτὶ τῆς γνώσεως ὑπὸ τῆς σοφίας Or.*Cels.*5.10(p.11.14; M.11.1196C); φωτισθέντος γὰρ τοῦ νοῦ τῇ γνώσει, ὁ μαθὼν δύναται ἀγαθὸς εἶναι *Hom.Clem.*11.29; cf. φρόνιμοι ψυχαί, καθαραὶ ὡς παρθένοι, συνεῖσαι σφᾶς αὐτὰς ἐν ἀγνοίᾳ καθεστώσας κοσμικῇ, τὸ φῶς ἀνάπτουσι καὶ τὸν νοῦν ἐγείρουσι καὶ ~ουσι τὸ σκότος Clem.*str.*5.3(p.337.8; M.9.36A); ἐὰν δὲ φωτισθῇ σοι τὰ πράγματα...κτησάμενος ἰσχὺν ἐν γνώσει ποίει δύναμιν *ib.*2.18(p.165.16; M.8.1040A); **viii.** by baptism; through instruction received before the rite καλεῖται...τὸ λουτρὸν φωτισμός, ὡς ~ομένων τὴν διάνοιαν τῶν ταῦτα μανθανόντων Just.*1apol.*61.12(M.6.421B); through efficacy of Christ's name οἳ καὶ λαμβάνουσι δόματα ἕκαστος ὡς ἄξιοί εἰσι, ~όμενοι διὰ τοῦ ὀνόματος τοῦ Χριστοῦ τούτου id.*dial.*39.2(M.6.560B); through rite as a whole ~όμενοι φωτιζόμεθα Clem.*paed.*1.6(p.105.20; M.8.281A); διὰ τοῦ λουτροῦ πεφωτισμένον Eus.*d.e.*2.3(p.77.27; M.22.140B); ὁ δὲ μὴ βαπτισθεὶς οὐ πεφώτισται Bas.*hom.*13.1(2.113E; M.31.424C); ἐβάπτιζον γὰρ...οἱ ἐπίσκοποι πάντας τοὺς προσερχομένους αὐτοῖς...καὶ ἐφωτίζοντο ὁ λαός †Gregent.*leg.Hom.*(M.86.573D); τῷ λουτρῷ τῆς παλιγγενεσίας φωτισθέντας Evagr.*h.e.*4.36(p.186.8; M.86.2769C); hence as synonym for βαπτίζω, *baptize*; ref. baptism of Christ, CNeocaes.*can.*11; ref. Christian baptism ὕδασι ~ων κλητοὺς ἐν δώδεκα πηγαῖς *Orac.Sib.*8.247; τὸν νεανίσκον ἔτρεφε, συνεῖχεν, ἔθαλπε, τὸ τελευταῖον ἐφώτισε Clem.*q.d.s.*42(p.188.16; M.9.648C); εἰς ἀφθαρσίαν ἀναγεννῶνται...οἱ πεφωτισμένοι Meth.*symp.*3.8(p.36.10; M.18.73C); εἰλικρινῶς τοῦ Χριστοῦ προσλαμβάνουσιν οἱ ~όμενοι *ib.*8.8(p.90.9; 149C); καινὴ κτίσις, οὐχ ὡς ἄλλης κτίσεως γενομένης, ἀλλὰ τῶν ~ομένων ἐπὶ βελτίοσιν ἔργοις κατασκευαζομένων Didym.(‡Bas.)*Eun.*4(1.293B; M.29.704B); *Const.App.*3.16.2; τῆς θεότητος...ἐν μιᾷ σφραγῖδι ὀνομάτων πατρὸς καὶ υἱοῦ καὶ ἁγίου πνεύματος τοῖς ~ομένοις κηρυττομένης Epiph.*haer.*76.20(p.367.15; M.42.557A); ‡Pall.*h.mon.*11.5(p.55.14; M.65.449C); Marc.Diac.*v.Porph.*47; ref. post-baptismal sin οὐκ ἂν ἔτι μετὰ τὸ φωτισθῆναι συνέβαινεν ἀδικεῖν, ἅτε παντάπασιν εἰλικρινῶς ἀφῃρημένης ἀφ' ἡμῶν τῆς ἁμαρτίας Meth.*res.*1.41(p.286.15; M.18.269B); ἐκεῖνοι [sc. Ναυατιανοί]...παντοίαν μετὰ τὸ φωτισθῆναι ἀρνοῦνται μετάνοιαν Nil.*epp.*3.243(M.79.497B); **ix.** by inward and spiritual effects of baptism ὁ μόνον ἀναγεννηθείς, ὥσπερ οὖν καὶ τοὔνομα ἔχει, φωτισθεὶς ἀπήλλακται...τοῦ σκότους Clem.*paed.*1.6(p.106.16; M.8.281C); ἐβαπτίσθη, ἀλλ' οὐκ ἐφωτίσθη· καὶ τὸ μὲν σῶμα ἔβαψεν ὕδατι, τὴν δὲ καρδίαν οὐκ ἐφώτισε πνεύματι Cyr.H.*procatech.*2; which are not present in heretical baptisms, ‡Chrys.*hom.in Jo.*1:1(12.418E) cit. s. φώτισμα; **x.** by fear of God, Mac.Aeg.*hom.fr.*(B 39)17(p.309).

***φωτικόν, τό,** *porch*, exeg. *Ezech.*42:12 φῶς δὲ τοῦ περιπάτου καλεῖ τὸ παρ' ἡμῖν καλούμενον φ. Thdt.*Ezech.*42:12–14(2.1025).

φώτισμα, τό, *illumination*;

A. in gen. πάσχα, καινῆς λαμπαδουχίας τὸ φ. ‡Chrys.*pasch.*6.5(8.273E).

B. of Christian baptism; **1.** of effects of baptism, dist. from outward rite μὴ ἀπατάτω σε τῶν αἱρετικῶν τὰ συστήματα· βάπτισμα γὰρ ἔχουσιν, οὐ φ.· καὶ βαπτίζονται μὲν σώματι, ψυχῇ δὲ οὐ φωτίζονται ‡Chrys.*hom.in Jo.*1:1(12.418E); **2.** as synonym for βάπτισμα: καλεῖται...τὸ ἔργον τοῦτο χάρισμα καὶ φ. καὶ τέλειον καὶ λουτρόν Clem.*paed.*1.6(p.105.23; M.8.281A); οὐ δεῖ μετὰ δύο ἑβδομάδας τῆς τεσσαρακοστῆς δέχεσθαι εἰς τὸ φ. CLaod.*can.*45; τὸ λουτρὸν...ὃ εἴτε βάπτισμα εἴτε φ. εἴτε παλιγγενεσίαν βούλοιτό τις ὀνομάζειν Gr.Nyss.*or.catech.*32(p.122.12; M.45.84A); Chrys.*hom.in Ac.princ.*1.5(3.58B); id.*hom.41.2 in Ac.*(9.311C); ἓν βάπτισμα καὶ ἀκαπήλευτον φ. Tim.Ant.*caec.*13(M.28.1021B); Thdr.Stud.*epp.*2.219(M.99.1665A); plur. τῷ καιρῷ τῶν φ. ‡Ath.*qu.Ant.*2(M.28.601A); κληρικοὺς τοὺς ἐπὶ τῶν φ. τεταγμένους Jo.Mosch.*prat.*207(M.87.3100B); ref. clinical baptism δεῖ τοὺς ἐν νόσῳ παραλαμβάνοντας τὸ φ. καὶ εἶτα ἀναστάντας, ἐκμανθάνειν τὴν πίστιν CLaod.*can.*47; ref. post-baptismal sin, Chrys.*hom.20.1 in Heb.*(12.186A); ταῦτα...πάντα ἔπραξεν οὐ πρὸ τῆς εἰς Χριστὸν μυσταγωγίας, ἀλλὰ μετὰ τὸ φ. Pall.*v.Chrys.*15(p.92.19; M.47.52); ref. baptismal creed τὴν πίστιν τὴν παραδοθεῖσαν ἐν τῇ μυσταγωγίᾳ τοῦ φ. Didym.*Trin.*1.15(M.39.304B); Zeno *henot.*(p.53.24; M.86.2624A); **3.** nature and effects of baptismal φώτισμα: described, Gr.Naz.*or.*40.3(M.36.361B); as work of H. Ghost, Ath.*exp.in Ps.*133:2(M.27.524D); πνεῦμα...τὸ ἀπελαῦνον τῷ φ. δαιμόνων στίφη Didym.*Trin.*1.2(M.39.452B); cf. φ. ... δι' οὗ ἐκεῖνο φῶς τὸ σωτήριον ἐποπτεύεται Clem.*paed.*1.6(p.105.25; M.8.281A); as beginning of γνῶσις, *ib.*(pp.107.25, 108.6; 285B,C); **4.** as necessary for salvation, Chrys.*hom.3.4 in Phil.*(11.217C); id.*hom.9.1 in 1Thess.*(11.486F); **5.** of Epiphany feast of lights, commemorative of a time of solemn administration of baptism, Job.Mon.*inc.*2(M.86.3316C); **6.** *font* κώμη...ἐν ᾗ ἐστιν φ., ἐν τοῖς ἁγίοις θεοφανίοις ἱδροῦν Jo.Mosch.*prat.*214(M.87.3105C); φ. ὅπερ...ἀφ' ἑαυτοῦ γεμίζεται ἄφνω *ib.*215(3108A).

φωτισμός, ὁ, *illumination*;

A. physical; **1.** in gen. σκότος...ἔνθα οὐδεὶς φ. *cat.Mt.*25:24(p.211.13); τὸν στῦλον πυρὸς ἐν νυκτὶ εἰς φ. *Const.App.*6.3.2; **2.** of heavenly bodies, *phase* περὶ τῶν συνόδων καὶ φ. ἡλίου καὶ σελήνης Clem.*str.*6.4(p.449.5; M.9.253B); οὗτος [sc. Anaxagoras] ἀφώρισε πρῶτος τὰ περὶ τὰς ἐκλείψεις καὶ φ. Hipp.*haer.*1.8(p.14.11; M.16.3033C); Θαλῆς... περὶ τροπῶν ἡλίου καὶ ἐκλείψεως, καὶ φωτισμῶν σελήνης...διελέχθη Eus.*p.e.*10.14(504A; M.21.837D).

B. mental and spiritual; **1.** in gen. τὸ φώτισμα [i.e. baptism]... παντὸς ἄλλου τῶν παρ' ἡμῖν φ. ὂν ἁγιώτερον Gr.Naz.*or.*40.3(M.36.361C); οὐκ ἔσχον...φ. οἱ πεπλανημένοι Epiph.*haer.*51.11(p.262.27; M.41.908C); θεοῦ χάριτι καὶ μαρτύρων φωτισμῷ καὶ προστάγματι Sophr.H.*mir.Cyr.et Jo.*36(M.87.3549A); Dor.*doct.*6.6(M.88.1692B); **2.** in Judaism, of spiritual illumination caused by light of Law, *T.Lev.*14.4; mediated to Christians through OT, Ath.*exp.in Ps.* 118:91(M.27.497A); **3.** Christian; **a.** conferred by, or consisting in: μαθητεία, Clem.*str.*5.10(p.369.11; M.9.97B); ἡ ἔνθεος διδασκαλία ‡Chrys.*Spir.*1(3.797A); Christian law, *Const.App.*2.5.7; gospel, Epiph.*haer.*76.9(p.350.25; M.42.432D); *Rit.Bapt.*(p.394); knowledge ἡ ἄγνοια δὲ τὸ σκότος...φ. ἄρα ἡ γνῶσίς ἐστιν Clem.*paed.*1.6(p.107.30; M.8.285B); ἐπειδὰν...σοὶ παραστῶ, καὶ αὐτῇ τῇ περὶ σοῦ θεωρίᾳ διὰ τοῦ νοῦ προσεγγίσω, τότε τὴν ἐποπτικὴν ἐνέργειαν διὰ τοῦ κατὰ τὴν γνῶσιν φωτισμοῦ ἀναλήψομαι †Bas.*Is.*162(1.494D; M.30.385B); φαίην ἂν οὐκ ἀπεικότως, ὅτι καὶ κάθαρσίς ἐστι, καὶ φ. ... ἡ τῆς θεαρχικῆς ἐπιστήμης μετάληψις Dion.Ar.*c.h.*7.3(M.3.209C); Max.*ambig.*(M.91.1401D); defined as knowledge of God, †Bas.*Is.*159(492C; M.30.380C); Cyr.*inc.unigen.*(5[1].702D); or of Christ, Bas.*ep.*243.3(3.374E; M.32.908B); possessed by angelic orders in varying degrees, Dion.Ar.*c.h.*8.2(M.3.240C); a gift of grace, hence contrasted with φῶς τὸ ἀληθινόν which is Christ, Ammon.ap.*cat.Jo.*1:9(p.183.24); conferred by Logos, Meth.*Porph.*1(p.504.8; M.18.400A); by H. Ghost, Or.*Jo.*6.43(26 p.152.31; M.14.276B); Bas.*Spir.*47(3.39D; M.32.153B); †Bas.*Is.*65(1.426C; M.30.232A); κέκληνται διὰ τῆς πίστεως εἰς τὸν διὰ τοῦ πνεύματος φ. Cyr.*Zach.*2(3.693E); οὐδὲ γὰρ ἂν δίχα τοῦ διὰ πνεύματος φ. πρὸς ἐπίγνωσιν τῆς ἀληθείας ἴοι τις ἂν id.*Jo.*11.9(4.985A); by divine fire in soul, Mac.Aeg.*hom.*25.10(M.34.673D); esp. through baptism, φ. being often synonymous with βάπτισμα, Just.*1apol.*61.12(M.6.421B); Clem.*prot.*10(p.69.3; M.8.208A); τοῦ ἁγίου βαπτίσματος ὁδὸν αὐτοῖς ἀνοίγοντος φ. Ath.*exp.in Ps.*41.7(M.27.201C); ὁ τοῦ βαπτίσματος φ. Gr.Naz.*or.*40.6(M.36.365B); *ib.*40.24(392A); κύριος ἐν τῷ φ. ὑμῶν, τῇ τοῦ ἐπισκόπου χειροθεσίᾳ μαρτυρῶν, ἐφ' ἑκατέρων ὑμῶν τὴν ἱερὰν ἐξέτεινεν φωνήν *Const.App.* 2.32.3; Thdt.*Ps.*33:9(1.815); Dion.Ar.*e.h.*5.1.3(M.3.504B); or through understanding of power of baptism, Gr.Naz.*or.*40.1(360C); consisting in Christian truth, Meth.*res.*1.58(p.321.22); love, Diad.*perf.*89(p.126.1); wisdom, Proc.G.*Pr.*1:7(M.87.1223A); divine blessedness, Dion.Ar.*c.h.*3.2(M.3.165C); to shine upon soul at Christ's second advent, Didym.*Trin.*1.28(M.39.409B); God as illumination, *Lit.Jac.*(p.172.17); *Lit.Praesanct.*(347.15); **b.** its effects including: prophetic insight, †Bas.*Is.*65(1.426B; M.30.232A); power of διάκρισις πνευμάτων, Ath.*exp.in Ps.*59:5(M.27.269B); power to see Christ, the image of God, Bas.*Spir.*64(3.54A; M.32.185B); cf. ἐν τῷ φωτί σου ὀψόμεθα φῶς· τουτέστιν ἐν τῷ φ. τοῦ πνεύματος, φῶς τὸ ἀληθινόν, ὃ φωτίζει πάντα ἄνθρωπον *ib.*47(39D; M.153B); attainment of divine ὁμοίωσις, Diad.*perf.*89(p.126.1); **4.** of illumination bestowed upon incarnate Christ by Father κύριος φ. μου...οὐδὲ ἄλλου τινός ἐστι ταῦτα ἐν τῷ προφήτῃ λεγόμενα τὰ ῥήματα ἢ τοῦ σωτῆρος διὰ τὸν ἀπὸ τοῦ πατρὸς φ. ... οὐδένα φοβουμένου Or.*mart.*29(p.25.15; M.11.597B); and of illumination of Christ's flesh by his divinity, †Bas.*Is.*183(1.513E; M.30.429A); of illumination brought by presence of incarnate Christ, which is a shadow of his divine glory, Clem.*exc.Thdot.* 18(p.112.26; M.9.665C); by Christ's presence in Church ἄσβεστος... ὁ παρὰ Χριστοῦ φ. ἐν ἐκκλησίαις σώζεται ταῖς τῶν ἱεράσθαι κεκληρωκότων ἐπιεικείαις Cyr.*ador.*9(1.321B); **5.** of goal of redemption αὐτὸς γὰρ τὴν πρώτην μόρφωσιν τὴν κατὰ τὴν γένεσιν αὐτοῖς παρέσχε, τὰ ὑπ' ἄλλου σπαρέντα εἰς μορφὴν καὶ εἰς φ. καὶ περιγραφὴν ἰδίαν ἀγαγών Heracleon ap.Or.*Jo.*2.21(15; p.77.29; M.14.149D).

φωτιστήριον, τό, *place of illumination*, hence *baptistery* ὡς εἰσῆλθον ἐν τῷ φ. ὅπως βαπτισθῶσιν †Polyb.*v.Epiph.*52(M.41.88C); Chrys.*p.redit.*2.2(3.428C); CSyr.(p.99.30; H.2.1377A); Jo.Mosch.*prat.* 207(M.87.3100B); Sophr.H.*mir.Cyr.et Jo.*31(M.87.3524B); used as meeting place of episcopal assemblies, Pall.*v.Chrys.*14(p.85.13; M.47.48); as place of sanctuary for fugitives, *Chron.Pasch.*p.325(M.92.836B).

φωτιστής, ὁ, *illuminator*; ref. God's self-manifestation in fire at Sinai ἔδει...φ. ὁρᾶσθαι καὶ κολαστὴν Cyr.*Jo.*3.2(4.258B).

φωτιστικός, *illuminating*;

A. lit. φ. ... τὸ πῦρ Bas.*hex.*2.3(1.15A; M.29.36A); of light at Creation ἡ φ. δύναμις Gr.Nyss.*hex.*12(M.44.73D); τῆς...φ. οὐσίας τῆς τῷ παντὶ κατεσπαρμένης *ib.*13(76C).

B. met.; **1.** of God εἰ δὲ νοῦς [v.l. νοῦ] ἐστιν φωτιστικὸς κατὰ τὸ λεγόμενον· κύριος φωτισμός μου Or.*Jo.*13.23(p.246.23; M.14.436C); id.*fr.*6 *in Jo.*1:8(p.488.18); θεὸς μέν ἐστι φῶς...πάσης φωτιστικὸν λογικῆς φύσεως Gr.Naz.*or.*40.5(M.36.364B); Jo.D.*f.o.*1.14(M.94.860A); **2.** of Son δευτερούσης δὲ μετὰ τὸν πατέρα τῆς δημιουργικῆς ὁμοῦ καὶ φ. δυνάμεως τοῦ θείου λόγου Eus.*p.e.*7.15(325B; M.21.549B); τὸν υἱὸν ...αὐτόφως...καὶ πάσης νοερᾶς καὶ λογικῆς οὐσίας φ. id.*e.th.*1.8(p.66.34; M.24.837D); αὐτὸς ὢν τὸ θεοποιὸν καὶ φ. τοῦ πατρός Ath.*syn.*51(p.274.27; M.26.784A); *Lit.Marc.*(Brightman p.142.14); exeg. Apoc. 19:12 ὡς γὰρ ἡ φλὸξ τὸ λαμπρὸν ἅμα καὶ φ. ... οὕτως οἱ...ὀφθαλμοὶ τοῦ λόγου Or.*Jo.*2.7(4; p.61.27; M.14.121B); Sabellian ὡς...ἐν ἡλίῳ, ὄντι μὲν ἐν μιᾷ ὑποστάσει, τρεῖς δὲ ἔχοντι τὰς ἐνεργείας...τὸ φ. καὶ τὸ θάλπον καὶ αὐτὸ τὸ τῆς περιφερείας σχῆμα...εἶναι τὸ θάλπον...τὸ πνεῦμα, τὸ δὲ φ. τὸν υἱόν, τὸν δὲ πατέρα αὐτὸ εἶναι τὸ εἶδος τῆς πάσης ὑποστάσεως Epiph.*haer.*62.1(p.390.1; M.41.1052B); **3.** of operation of H. Ghost μίαν εἶναι δεῖ...τὴν ἁγιαστικὴν καὶ φ. ζῶσαν ἐνέργειαν αὐτοῦ Ath.*ep.Serap.*1.20(M.26.580A); revealing image of invisible God, Bas.*Spir.*47(3.39C; M.32.153A); οἱ τούτων [sc. ἀποστόλων] τῆς...χάριτος διάδοχοι ποιμένες τε καὶ διδάσκαλοι τὴν φ. τοῦ πνεύματος χάριν δεξάμενοι ‡Cyr.*Trin.*1(M.77.1121B); ‡Jo.D.*hom.*6.6(M.96.669D); **4.** of divine goodness, Dion.Ar.*d.n.*4.4(M.3.697D); **5.** of angels τῶν θείων δυνάμεων τὸ λαμπρὸν καὶ φ. Areth.*Apoc.*55(M.106.725C); of Satan as Lucifer, ‡Caes.Naz.*dial.*1.44(M.38.913); of angelic wisdom, Dion.Ar.*c.h.*7.1(M.3.205C); **6.** of that by which men are illuminated, divine guidance in gen. ὅπως ἐκ τῶν φ. αὐγῶν φωτιζόμενος, τὴν ὁδὸν βλέπειν ἔχῃς Cyr.*Ps.*31:8(M.69.868C); divine law, Or.*Cels.*7.34(p.185.3; M.11.1469A); gospel, Sophr.H.*or.*2.10(M.87.3228C); apostles' teaching, *I.G.C.As.Min.*61; Sev.Ant.ap.*cat.Ac.*2:3(p.20.27); Christian doctrine in gen., Gr.Nyss.*Eun.*12(2 p.282.20; M.45.893C); and those who perform teaching functions in Church's ministry οἱ δὲ φ. ἐπαναβεβήκασι τῇ διδασκαλίᾳ, οἷον οἱ πρεσβύτεροι καὶ οἱ διάκονοι Max.*schol.c.h.*3.3(M.4.52B); baptism τὴν τῶν καθαρθέντων φ. μύησιν Dion.Ar.*e.h.*5.1.3(M.3.504A); faith ὀφθαλμὸς πάσης συνειδήσεως φ. ἐστιν ἡ πίστις Cyr.H.*catech.*5.4; φρόνησις as ἕξις φ., Max.*ambig.*(M.91.1245B).

φωτιστικῶς, *with brilliant light* πρὸς Μαριὰμ...μόνην...Γαβριὴλ ὁ ἀρχάγγελος φ. παρεγένετο ‡Gr.Thaum.*annunt.*1(M.10.1152D).

***φωτοβολ-έω,** *emit light, shine*, †Gregent.*disp.*(M.86.716B); met. λύχνον ~οῦντα...σε...Πέτρε τὸ ἅγιον πνεῦμα τοῖς ἐσκοτισμένοις ἀνέδειξεν ἔθνεσιν Jo.Mon.*hymn.Petr.*2(M.96.1392A).

φωτοβολία, ἡ, *ray of light*, ‡Jo.D.*Artem.*42(M.96.1289C).

***φωτογενής,** *light-begotten, produced by light*; of cloud at Transfiguration, Cosm.Mel.*hymn.*10.149(p.179; M.98.497A).

***φωτογονία, ἡ,** *emission of light*, Dion.Ar.*ep.*9.1(M.3.1105A).

***φωτογόνος,** *light-producing, shining*, Sophr.H.*carm.*5.34(M.87.3756C); φωτὸς ἀειγενέος, Παῦλε γεμίσθης, φωτογόνους δαΐδας πᾶσιν ἐρίζεις *ib.*9.100(p.44; 3780B).

***φωτοδοσία, ἡ,** *giving of light, illumination*; of divine revelation, Dion.Ar.*c.h.*1.2(M.3.121A); of mystical illumination, id.*d.n.*2.11(M.3.649D); τῆς...νοητῆς αὐτοῦ φ. ἐν ἀπαθεῖ καὶ ἀΰλῳ τῷ νῷ μετέχοντες *ib.*1.4(592C); Max.*schol.c.h.*5(M.3.61D).

φωτοδότης, *light-giving, illuminating*; **1.** lit., *Apoc.Bar.*7(p.89.14); ὁ τῶν ἐμῶν ὀφθαλμῶν φ. Tim.Ant.*caec.*11(M.28.1017A); **2.** met. σφρηγὶς ἀρίστη Χριστοῦ φωτοδόταο θεόρρυτος Gr.Naz.*carm.*1.1.9.93(M.37.464A); ὁ φ. Ἰησοῦς Ephr.1.29F; ‡Chrys.*sac.*7.1(1.805A).

***φωτοδότις,** *light-giving, illuminating* (fem. of φωτοδότης), of baptism τῆς ἀρχιφώτου καὶ φ. θεογενεσίας Dion.Ar.*e.h.*7.3.3(M.3.557C).

***φωτοδότος,** *light-giving*, Epiph.*anc.*71(p.88.15; M.43.148B).

***φωτοδόχος,** *receiving light* τὰ φωτεινὰ ἡμῶν εὐαγγέλια τοῖς φ. ὑμῖν...κηρύττεται Sophr.H.*or.*219(M.87.3228C).

φωτοειδής, 1. lit., *radiant* with physical light; of moon πάλιν ἀπολαμβάνει τὸ σῶμα τὸ φ. Cyr.H.*catech.*18.10; of Cross; as it appeared in sky during Julian's attempt to rebuild Temple, Thdt.*h.e.*3.20.7(3.937); as it will appear before Parousia (Mt.24:30) φ. σταυροῦ σημεῖον προάγει τὸν βασιλέα Cyr.H.*catech.*15.22; **2.** met., *radiant, glorious*, with spiritual illumination; of splendour of Christ at Transfiguration, Max.*ambig.*(M.91.1160C); of H. Ghost τὸ...ἔνθεον πνεῦμα, φ. μᾶλλον δὲ φῶς αὐτὸ τυγχάνον, ᾗ δ' ἂν ἐπέλθῃ ψυχῇ...φωτὸς ἡμέραν ἐν αὐτῇ κατειργάζετο Eus.*d.e.*5 proem.(p.208.6; M.22.345B); of BMV ἡ...τῶν πυρίνων Σεραφὶμ φωτοειδεστέρα ἐν πνεύματι Thdr.Stud.*nativ.BMV* 7(M.96.689D); of angelic beings, Dion.Ar.*c.h.*2.3(M.3.141B); of soul, ref. one who abstains from wine οὕτω δ' ἂν καὶ ἡ ψυχὴ...ὑπάρξαι καθαρὰ καὶ ξηρὰ καὶ φ. Clem.*paed.*2.2 (p.174.13; M.8.424C); ref. righteous at Parousia, ‡Dion.Al. *fr.Cant.* (p.228.2; *AS* 3 p.597); of those illuminated by divine revelation, Gr.Naz.*or.*28.17(p.48.6; M.36.48C); Didym.*Trin.*1.28(M.39.409A); of garment of incorruption worn by Church as bride of Christ, Or.*Ps.* 44:10(p.42); of products of mental activity τοῦ νοῦ φωτοειδὲς ἔγγονον Synes.*ep.*138(M.66.1529C); of mind's propensity towards intellectual activity, and of objects of its activity, Gr.Agr.*Eccl.*9.15 (M.98.1113A,B); of monastic habit, Synes.*ep.*147(1544A).

***φωτοειδῶς**, *brilliantly*, Gel.Cyz.*h.e.*1.5.1(M.85.1204B).

***φωτόζωος**, *giving light to all life*, Sophr.H.*or.*2.26(M.87.3249C).

***φωτόκλονος**, *with shining branches* ἐρίκινοι φ. ‡Petr.I Al.*phys.* 3(p.34).

***φωτόκοσμος**, *giving light to the world*, Geo.Pis.*hex.*18(M.92. 1428A).

***φωτοκυήτωρ, ἡ**, *conceiver of light*; of BMV, ‡Sophr.H.*triod.*(M. 87.3940C).

φωτολαμπής, *shining, glorious* met. ἕτερον φ. καὶ θαυμαστώτατον ...ἄκουσον ‡Ath.*qu.al.*19(M.28.789C).

***φωτοληψία, ἡ**, *reception of light*, Dion.Ar.*d.n.*4.4(M.3.697D).

***φωτόμαλλος**, *having a bright* or *shining fleece*, Agath.*v.Gr.Ill.* 114.

***φωτομαρμαρυγ-έω**, *shine with light* τυφλώττοντι...ἐν τοῖς ἔνδον ὄμμασιν, ἀδύνατον ὁρᾶν...~οῦντα τὸν Ἰησοῦν Hesych.S.*temp.*2.28(M. 93.1520D).

***φωτόμορφος**, *in the form of light, glorious*, met. τέκνα φ. τῆς ἐκκλησίας Jo.D.*carm.pent.*53(p.215; M.96.836A); τὴν ψυχοσωτήριον καὶ φ. κατέχομεν πίστιν ‡Jo.D.*hom.*5(M.96.656D).

***φωτοποι-έω**, *illuminate*, met. ὦ φωτὸς ἀϊδίου, ~οῦντος τοὺς ἐσκοτισμένους Cyr.H.*catech.*13.31; hence *baptize* προτρέχων ἐφωτοποίει αὐτάς *A.Thom.*(*consumm.*)1(p.289.17; v.l. ἐν φωτοποιεῖ; Tischendorf(p.236) ἐν ὁδῷ φωτοποιεῖ αὐτάς).

φωτοποιός, *illuminating, enlightening*; of God, Jo.D.*f.o.*4.20(M. 94.1196D); of Christ, Mod.*dorm.*7(M.86.3296B); of Easter Eve, on which baptisms took place τῆς λαμπρᾶς καὶ φ. νυκτός Dor.*doct.*15.1 (M.88.1788D).

***φωτοστόλιστος**, *robed in light*; of BMV, Thdt.Anc.*hom.BMV et Sym.*3(M.77.1393B).

***φωτοσωτήριος**, *giving saving light*; of Christ's birth, ‡Jo.D.*hom.* 5(M.96.656D).

***φωτοτόκος**, *light-producing* μὴ πέφυκεν ἀρετὴ ἡ τοιαύτη φ. τερπνὴ ἐργασία, εἰ μὴ τῇ πείρᾳ διδάσκεσθαι; Hesych.S.*temp.*1.88(M. 93.1508B).

***φωτότροφος**, *nourished by light*, of Christians τέκνα τοῦ φωτὸς καὶ φ. γεννήματα Sophr.H.*or.*2.10(M.87.3228C).

***φωτουργός**, *illuminating*, Dion.Ar.*c.h.*8.2(M.3.240C).

***φωτοφαής**, *shining*, Eudoc.*Cypr.*1(M.85.841C).

φωτοφάνεια (φωτοφάνια), ἡ, *illumination*;

A. lit., of glory of a theophany, *Dorm.BMV* 38(p.107); of the parousia, ‡Bas.*h.myst.*10(p.260.16).

B. met., of spiritual illumination; **1.** of divine revelation, Dion. Ar.*c.h.*4.4(M.3.181C); **2.** of divine illumination; in gen., *ib.*1.1 (120B); id.*d.n.*1.3(M.3.589B); Ant.Mon.*hom.*27(M.89.1524B); received through mystical contemplation τὰ περὶ τῆς πάντα νοῦν ὑπερεχούσης οὐσίας διασκεπτόμενος καί τινος ἐκεῖθεν φ. καταξιούμενος ‡Max.*cap. al.*102(M.90.1424A); **3.** of state of blessed in future life οἱ δίκαιοι ἐν φωτοφανείαις Cyr.*hom.div.*14(5^2.410C).

***φωτοφανής**, *shining, glorious*; of apostles, Sophr.H.*or.*8.1(M. 87.3356B).

***φωτοφορ-έω**, *carry light*, ref. celebration of feast of Purification οἱ τῶν ἐθνῶν λαοὶ ~οῦντες ὑπαντήσωμεν ‡Cyr.H.*occurs.*3(M.33.1189B); and of Annunciation χαῖρε, δι' ἣν ἡμεῖς σήμερον ~οῦντες...ἐν ἐκκλησίᾳ σε μεγαλύνομεν ‡Jo.D.*hom.*5(M.96.660D).

***φωτοφορία, ἡ**, *carrying of lights, procession of torches*; of marriage feast (Mt.25) εἰς παρθένων φ. *cat.Apoc.*19:10(p.454.29); of heavenly triumph of the blessed τῆς ἄνω φ. Isid.Pel.*epp.*1.74 (M.78.233C).

***φωτοφόρος**, *light-bringing, illuminating, brilliant*; **1.** lit. ἀπὸ φ. θύρης σεπτὴ βάλεν ὄμμα Eudoc.*Cypr.*2(M.85.680B); Sophr.H.*or.*2.9 (M.87.3228B); φ. καὶ πολυτίμους μαργαρίτας Anast.S.*hod.*3(M.89. 89A); **2.** met., of that which illuminates the soul, or which is spiritually glorious; ref. baptism of Christ ἡ φ. ἐπιφάνεια Jo.Eub. *concept.BMV*(M.96.1476A); of BMV παρθενομήτωρ, φ. Cyr.*hom.div.* 11(5^2.380C); ‡Jo.D.*hom.*5(M.96.649A); of angelic beings εἶδον ἄνδρα φ. ἐκ τοῦ οὐρανοῦ κατελθόντα *T.Abr.*A 7(p.84.4); ἄγγελος φ. *ib.*12 (p.91.5); of spiritual grace, ‡Sophr.H.*triod.*(M.87.3872C) cit. s. ἐκμειόω; μῆτερ τοῦ ζῶντος θεοῦ, καὶ τῇ φ. σου καὶ θείᾳ ἐπισκίασον χάριτι Jo.D.*carm.dorm.BMV* 158(p.232; M.96.1368A); of night of Epiphany feast (when baptism was administered) ὦ φ. καὶ θαυμαστῆς νυκτός ‡Chrys.*hom.*11(13.246D); of Hebrews at Passover τοὺς ...φ. παῖδας τῶν Ἑβραίων ἐμακάριζε *ib.*2(207A); of a bishop's chair, as place from which teaching is given, Isid.Pel.*epp.*1.32(M.78. 201C).

***φωτοχυσία, ἡ**, *shedding of light*, *1Apoc.Jo.*2(p.71); of Transfiguration, Cosm.Mel.*hymn.*10.161(p.179; M.98.497A); of spiritual illumination φῶς νοητὸν λέγεται τὸ ὑπὲρ πᾶν φῶς ἀγαθόν, ὡς...ὑπερβλύζουσα φωτοχυσία Dion.Ar.*d.n.*4.6(M.3.701A); Andr.Cr.*or.*7(M.97. 952C); ἀστέρας...καλεῖ τοὺς ἀγγέλους διὰ τὴν δαψιλῆ φ. τὴν ἐν αὐτοῖς τοῦ Χριστοῦ Areth.*Apoc.*2(M.106.521A).

***φωτοχύτος**, *shedding light*, Geo.Pis.*carm.vit.*49.

***φωτωνυμία**, *naming as light*, Dion.Ar.*d.n.*4.5(M.3.700D).

***φωτωνυμικῶς**, *by naming as light, under the title of light* φ. ὑμνεῖται τἀγαθόν Dion.Ar.*d.n.*4.4(M.3.697C).

X

χαβῶνες, οἱ, (Hebr. כַּוָּנִים) *sacrificial cakes* ἄρτους μεγάλους. τὸ γὰρ χαβῶνας ἐστὶ λέξις Ἑβραϊκή Chrys.*fr.in Jer.*7:18(M.64.837D); χαβῶνας δέ φησι πέμματά τινα Olymp.*fr.Jer.*7:18(M.93.644C).

χαίν-ω, **1.** *gape* in eager expectation; c. περί Clem.*paed.*2.10 (p.218.10; M.8.517C); Chrys.*hom.9.5 in Mt.*(7.137C); Thdt.*h.e.*4.19.5 (3.980); **2.** trans., *open wide* ὡς δόλιον ~ει στόμα δεινὸς ἀλείτης †Apoll.*met.Ps.*108:2(M.33.1481A); pass., *Hom.Clem.*6.4; εὔχεσθαι χῆναι σφίσι τὴν γῆν Thdt.*h.e.*1.30.9(3.820); **3.** *show a hiatus* δασύνουσιν Ἑβραῖοι τὰς παρ' ἡμῖν κεχηνυίας λέξεις *cat.Mt.*1:5(p.7.4).

χαιρέκακος, *rejoicing in* another's *misfortune*, Didym.*Ps.*12:4 (M.39.1217A); τὸ χ. τῶν αἱρέσεων Pall.*h.Laus.*38(M.34.1188D; *ep.ix*-p.117.13); *cat.Apoc.*18:20(p.560.11) but cf. Andr.Caes.*Apoc.*55(M. 106.393A) χαιρεσίκακοι.

***χαιρεσίκακος**, = foreg., Or.*sel.in Ps.*29:2(M.12.1292C); Cosm. Ind.*top.*3(M.88.181B); Andr.Caes.*Apoc.*55(M.106.393A).

χαιρετίζω, *hail, salute*, ‡Meth.*Sym.et Ann.*13(M.18.380A).

χαίρ-ω, 1. *rejoice*; **a.** ref. spiritual joy, ref. Phil.3:1, 4:4 οὐκ ἔστιν τὸν κατὰ κόσμον ~οντα ὁμοῦ καὶ κατὰ θεὸν χαίρειν· πᾶς γὰρ ὁ κατὰ κόσμον ~ων, ἐπὶ πλούτῳ ~ει, ἐπὶ τρυφῇ...ὁ δὲ κατὰ θεόν, ἐπὶ ἀτιμίᾳ τῇ δι' αὐτόν, ἐπὶ πενίᾳ, ἐπὶ ἀκτημοσύνῃ Chrys.*hom.16.4 in Ac.*(9.133B); id.*hom.10.1 in Phil.*(11.275A); ταῦτα γὰρ οὐδέν ἐστιν, ἢ ὅτι τοιοῦτον ἐπιδείκνυσθε βίον, ὥστε ~ειν *ib.14.1*(304D); πάσης θυμηδίας πνευματικῆς ἐμφορεῖσθε Thdt.*Phil.*3:1(3.460); in rel. to Mt.5:5 v. δάκρυον; med., *Herm.vis.*3.3.2; ‡Meth.*Sym.et Ann.*8(M.18.365B); **b.** of God ὁ θεὸς...~ει μάλιστα μὲν καθαρεύοντας ἡμᾶς ὁρῶν τῷ τῆς διανοίας κόσμῳ Clem.*paed.*3.1(p.236.2; M.8.556A); ~ει δὲ ὁ θεὸς τῇ δικαιοσύνῃ Meth.*symp.*8.16(p.105.19; M.18.169A); Thdr.Heracl.*Is.*27:16(M.18. 1316A); **2.** *delight in, favour* ἔχαιρε...ὁ βασιλεὺς εἰς τὸ πράσινον μέρος Jo.Mal.*chron.*15 p.379(M.97.564B).

χαλάδριον, τό, *mat* or *pallet*, *Apophth.Patr.*(M.65.101C,D); Cyr.S. *v.Sab.*44(p.135.2); *V.Max.*39(M.90.108B) cit. s. βέργος.

***χαλαδριός, ὁ**, name of a bird, ‡Petr.I Al.*phys.*6.

***χαλαζηφόρος**, *bringing hail*, Gr.Nyss.*usur.*(M.46.441B).

χαλαζοβολέω, *shower hail*, Clem.*str.*6.3(p.446.12; M.9.248B).

χαλαστόν, τό, *chain-pattern*, Thdr.Stud.*antirr.*3.3(M.99.421D).

χαλεπός, 1. *difficult*, c. prep. χ. εἰς πίστιν Synes.*ep.*147(M.66. 1545A); **2.** *hard to bear*; *grievous, piteous* νεκροὺς τῶν ἐν πολέμῳ... χαλεπωτέρους Chrys.*hom.8.8 in Rom.*(9.509B); Mac.Mgn.*apocr.*3.8 (p.64.4); **3.** *serious* λιμοῦ...χ. Gr.Nyss.*laud.Bas.*(M.46.805D); οὐ γὰρ χ. τὸ ἀποθανεῖν, ἀλλὰ χ. τὸ παροξῦναι τὸν δεσπότην Chrys.*Laz.*6.2 (1.775C); id.*hom.8.5 in 1Cor.*(10.71C); of sin, Or.*princ.*3.17(p.229.6; M.11.285C); Eus.*d.e.*1.3(p.15.2; M.22.33D); **4.** *evil, harmful*, = κακός (cf. 1Tim.6:10): ἀρχὴ δὲ πάντων χαλεπῶν φιλαργυρία Polyc.*ep.*4.1.

***χαλεπωδής**, s.v.l., *serious* τὰ περὶ ἡμᾶς χείρω...καὶ χαλεπωδέστερα τοῖς κτηνωδεστέροις Gr.Nyss.*or.dom.*5(M.44.1188B; v.l. χαλεπώτερα p.108.6).

χαλιναγωγ-έω, *guide with bit and bridle, curb*; met. ~οῦντες ἑαυτοὺς ἀπὸ παντὸς κακοῦ Polyc.*ep.*5.3; χαλιναγωγήσεις αὐτήν [sc. τὴν πονηρὰν ἐπιθυμίαν] Herm.*mand.*12.1.1; τὸ σῶμα...ταῖς τῆς ψυχῆς ἡνίαις ὑπεῖκον καὶ ~ούμενον Athenag.*res.*15(p.66.34; M.6.1005A); τὴν νεότητα...~ῶν τῷ φόβῳ τοῦ θεοῦ Nil.*epp.*3.43(M.79.409A); of

God τῷ φόβῳ χαλιναγωγήσας Thdr.Heracl.*Is*.27:16(M.18.1316A); of Word at Inc. ἄνωθεν ἀπὸ πατρὸς προελθὼν εὐδοκήσας ἐν σαρκὶ γενέσθαι ἐχαλιναγώγει τὸ σκεῦος Epiph.*anc*.79(p.99.9; M.43.165B); ὑποταττομένην καὶ ~ουμένην ὑπὸ τοῦ θεοῦ τὴν καθ' ὑπόστασιν ἡνωμένην αὐτῷ ψυχὴν καὶ σάρκα Anast.S.*hod*.21(M.89.281D); of H. Ghost ἡ ψυχὴ...~ουμένη ὑπὸ τοῦ πνεύματος Mac.Aeg.*hom*.24.2 (M.34.661A).

χαλιναγωγός, ὁ, *controller*, ‡Chrys.*concept.Jo.Bapt*.(2.793E).

***χαλίνωμα, τό,** *curb, bridle*, met. ὦ ἁγνεία, χ. ὀφθαλμῶν Ephr.2.132D.

***χαλινωτέον,** *one must curb*, met. χ. ... τὰς ἀλόγους τῶν ὁρμῶν Clem.*paed*.3.11(p.266.27; M.8.625C); χ. τοὺς ὀφθαλμούς Isid.Pel.*epp*.3.66(M.78.777A).

***χαλιφάτης, ὁ,** *caliph*, Barth.Edess.*Agar*.(M.104.1421B).

***χαλκαλέκτωρ, ὁ,** *brazen cock*; term of abuse for a rhetorician, Nil.*epp*.2.73(M.79.233A).

***χαλκέα, ἡ,** a kind of lizard σὴψ...ὁ οὐκ ὄφις, ἀλλ' ὥς φασι χ. πῶς ἐστι τετράπουν ἑρπετόν, ἀσκαλαβώτῃ ἐοικός Epiph.*haer*.36.6(p.50.7; M.41.640D).

***χαλκεδόνιος, ὁ,** *chalcedony*, *A.Thom*.A 108(p.220.1).

χαλκεοθώρηξ, *with brazen breastplate*, *Orac.Sib*.1.395.

χαλκευτέον, *one must forge*, Clem.*paed*.2.3(p.179.18; M.8.436A).

χαλκεύ-ω, *forge*, met. ~έσθω ἡ ψυχή Cyr.H.*procatech*.15; Chrys.*Laz*.3.2(1.738D); Cyr.*Jo*.10.2(4.920B); c. εἰς, *weld into* τῶν δὲ ἥλων τοὺς μὲν εἰς τὴν ἑαυτοῦ περικεφαλαίαν ἐχάλκευσεν [sc. Const.] Thphn.*chron*.p.21(M.108.112B).

χάλκινος, neut. as subst., *copper coin*, Epiph.*mens*.(M.43.289A).

χαλκοπλάστης, ὁ, *bronze-worker*, *Chron.Pasch*.p.48(M.92.173A).

***χαλκοπρόσωπος,** *brazen-faced* ἡμῖν ἔθος πολλάκις τοὺς ἐρυθριᾶν μὴ εἰδότας χ. καλεῖν Chrys.*Jud*.5.4(1.634D).

***χαλκόσπλαγχνος,** *steely-hearted*, *Apophth.Patr*.(M.65.320B).

***χαλκόστεγος,** *roofed with bronze*, *Chron.Pasch*.p.337(M.92.876C); Thphn.*chron*.p.157(M.108.424C).

***χαλκοτύμπανος,** *with bronze bells*, Pall.*v.Chrys*.12(p.72.2; M.47.40).

***χαλκοτύπης,** *of wrought bronze*, Eudoc.*Cypr*.1.198(M.85.840B).

χαλκουργέω, *make a bronze statue of* Πράξιλλαν...Λύσιππος ἐχαλκούργησεν Tat.*orat*.3(p.34.8; M.6.873B); Meth.*creat*.7(p.497.29; M.18.337C).

χαλκ-όω, *cover with bronze*, fig. ~οῖ τὸ νῶτον Gr.Naz.*carm*.1.2.28.213(M.37.872A).

χαμαί, 1. *on the ground*; **2.** = χαμᾶζε *to the ground*, met. ἑλιχθέντες τοῖς πάθεσι καὶ ἀποπίπτουσι χ. Clem.*str*.7.2(p.8.27; M.9.413B); Μάρκελλος χ. βαλὼν τὴν διάνοιαν Eus.*e.th*.3.2(p.144.11; M.24.980C).

χαμαιευνάς, *sleeping on the ground*; fem. adj., used of men metr. gr., Gr.Naz.*carm*.2.2.5.147(M.37.1532A).

***χαμαιζηλία, ἡ,** *earthly-mindedness, unspirituality*, Chrys.*hom*.*4.1 in Jo*.(8.27B); id.*hom.7.1 in 2Cor*.(10.480E).

χαμαίζηλος, 1. *resting upon the ground* κλίμακι ἐκείνῃ, ἣν εἶδέ ποτε ὁ μακάριος Ἰακώβ, ἧς τὰ μὲν ἦν...χ. Bas.*hom.in Ps*.1(1.93C; M.29.217C); **2.** *base, abject, unspiritual*; **a.** of persons, Chrys.*hom.4.6 in 1Cor*.(10.32D); Isid.Pel.*epp*.3.296(M.78.972B); Thdt.*h.e*.3.7.9(3.920); **b.** of abstracts τὸν χ. πλοῦτον Clem.*prot*.10(p.68.23; M.8.205C); χ. ῥημάτια [sc. of Arians] Ath.*decr*.18(p.15.31; M.25.448C); τὴν κοίλην καὶ χ. τῶν ἀνθρώπων ζωήν Gr.Nyss.*ep*.3(M.46.1016C); ὑπόληψιν μικροπρεπῆ καὶ χ. Ast.Am.*hom*.7(M.40.256D); neut. as subst., Chrys.*hom.7.3 in 2Cor*.(10.483B); τὸ χ. τῶν ἐπὶ γῆς πραγμάτων Cyr.*Ps*.10:1(M.69.789D); plur., Gr.Nyss.*or.dom*.1(p.24.32; M.44.1136A); **3.** *modest, unassuming* Χριστιανικῆς δ' οὔσης τῆς ἱστορίας, διὰ σαφήνειαν ταπεινὸς καὶ χ. πρόεισιν ὁ λόγος Socr.*h.e*.3.1.4(M.67.368A).

χαμαικοιτέω (χαμοκ-), *lie on the ground*, in supplication, *T.Jos*.4.3(χαμοκ-); ascet., Ephr.1.42D; id.3.152E(χαμοκ-); Jo.D.*spir.neq*.(M.95.84A).

χαμαικοιτία (χαμοκ-), ἡ, *lying* or *sleeping on the ground*; ascet., Ephr.1.43A; Nil.*epp*.2.159(M.79.276C); τῇ μὲν ἤρκεσεν ἡ χ. πρὸς ἄκεσιν Sophr.H.*mir.Cyr.et Jo*.(M.87.3492D); †Jo.D.*B.J*.24(M.96.1089B); χαμοκ-, Ephr.3.153E; id.2.203F; Agath.*v.Gr.Ill*.158(p.80).

χαμαιπαγής, *fixed in the ground*, Paul.Sil.*Soph*.542(M.86.2140A).

***χαμαιπάτιον, τό,** *footmark on the ground* μάθωμεν τὰ χαμαιπάτια τίνος εἰσί, πατήτια ἐν τῷ ἐπισκοπείῳ πῶς εὑρέθη; CSyr.*act*.(p.103.10; H.2.1381E).

χαμαιπετής, *falling to the ground*; met., *base, unspiritual*; of persons, Just.*2apol*.11.7(M.6.464A); Gr.Naz.*or*.29.11(p.90.4; M.36.89A); of abstracts τὰ χ. καὶ τὰ διαφθορᾶς μᾶλλον πάθη Just.*dial*.134.2 (M.6.785C); Hipp.*haer*.4.45(p.67.23; M.16.3110A); οὐδὲν...τῆς κοσμικῆς σοφίας...χαμαιπετέστερον Nil.*epp*.2.49(M.79.220A).

***χαμαιπόρος,** *moving on the ground*, ‡Caes.Naz.*dial*.3.173(M.38.1140).

χαμαιρ(ρ)επής, *inclined towards the ground* τῷ χ. τοῦ ποδός Sophr.H.*v.Anast*.(M.92.1721B); met., *base, unworthy* τῆς χ. κενοδοξίας οὐδὲν γηϊνώτερον Nil.*epp*.2.115(M.79.249D).

χαμαιρ(ρ)ιφής, 1. *thrown to the ground*, Gr.Naz.*carm*.1.2.32.141 (M.37.927A); **2.** *rejected, despised*; of persons, *A.Andr.fr*.1(p.38.7); Nil.*epp*.3.33(M.79.400D); **3.** *degraded, base*, Gr.Nyss.*Eun*.1(1 p.211.8; M.45.460A); χ. τὸ φρόνημα Cyr.*ador*.7(1.222E); χ. ἡδονῆς id.*hom. pasch*.12.1(5².162E).

***χαμαιστρωτία, ἡ,** *act of being stretched on the ground* χαμαιστρωτίᾳ ἀνεκλίθημεν ‡Gr.Naz.*Chr.pat*.1832(M.38.282A χαμαιστρωτίαι).

***χαμαίσυρτος,** *writhing along on the ground*; of the serpent, ‡Gr.Naz.*Chr.pat*.1640(M.38.267A).

***χαμαιτρόφος,** *nourishing those below* τῆς χ. διαίτης μάννα Sophr.H.*ep.syn*.(M.87.3149B).

χαμαιφερής, *near to the ground*, met. τὰ...χ. καὶ τὰ ἐπίγεια φρονοῦσι, καταβαρούμενοι ὑπὸ τῶν ἁμαρτιῶν Thphl.Ant.*Autol*.2.17 (M.6.1080B).

χαμερπής, *crawling on the ground*; met., *base, unworthy*, esp. *unspiritual* τὸ χ. δοξάριον Bas.*ep*.45.1(3.133B; M.32.365A); χ. ... νοήμασιν Gr.Nyss.*or.dom*.5(p.102.23; M.44.1184C); χ. βουλάς Nil.*epp*.4.1(M.79.544C).

***χαμερπῶς,** *meanly, unspiritually*, Just.*dial*.112.4(M.6.736A); Jo. Eleem.*v.Tych*.38(p.148); Max.*ambig*.(M.91.1160B) cit. s. ὑλικῶς.

χαμευνέω, *sleep on the ground*; of ascetics, Epiph.*exp.fid*.23 (p.524.25; M.42.829B); Chrys.*hom.77.5 in Mt*.(7.748E); Ph.Carp. *Cant*.88(M.40.85C).

χαμεύνης, *sleeping on the ground*; ascet., Gr.Naz.*or*.44.9(M.36.617B); id.*carm*.2.1.12.576(M.37.1208A).

χαμευνία, ἡ, *sleeping on the ground*; ascet., Gr.Naz.*or*.8.13(M.35.804B); Chrys.*hom.7.5 in Rom*.(9.490C); Isid.Pel.*epp*.1.69(M.78.229C).

***χαμεύρετος,** *found on the ground*; of Bellerophon, Jo.Mal.*chron*.4 p.83(M.97.165A).

χαμηλός, *humble, unpretentious*; of literary style, Leont.N.*v.Jo. Eleem*.proem.(p.3.19).

χαμοκοιτέω, v. χαμαικοιτέω.

***χαμοκοιτία, ἡ,** v. χαμαικοιτία.

***χάμος, ὁ,** *muzzle*, Petr.I Al.*ep.can*.14(H.1.233E; M.18.550A χάνον, v.l. χάμον).

χαμοσόριον, τό, *flat tomb*, *MAMA* 1.169 (saec. iv).

***χαμόω,** *muzzle, bridle*; met., *control* τὸν ὀφθαλμὸν ἐχάμωσεν Jo. Mosch.*prat*.109(M.87.2972C).

***Χαναν̂ῖτις,** *Canaanite*; fig., in derogatory sense μὴ παραλογίζου τὸν νοῦν σου ἀβουλίᾳ ῥημάτων, ἵνα μὴ κρημνησθείη ἡ Χ. σου γλῶσσα Nil.*Eulog*.21(M.79.1120D).

***χάνδαξ, ὁ,** *fortified place*, *Apoc.Dan*.C (Klostermann p.121.20).

***χαννιαῖος, ὁ,** a gem, one of the varieties of the hyacinth stone (identified by Epiph. with the lyncurium or tourmaline) (? from χάννα sea perch), Epiph.*gemm*.7(M.43.300A).

***χανότου,** sens. dub., *A.Xanthipp*.21(p.73.27 perh. for †κογκοστάτου).

***χανόω,** *swallow up* ἔχανεν ἡ γῆ...οὔτε τις κτίσις τῆς πάσης πόλεως ἔμεινεν, ἀλλὰ πάντα ἐχανώθη ‡Ath.*Melch*.(M.28.528C).

χαόω, *destroy utterly*, *Apophth.Patr*.(M.65.221B); ἵνα μὴ σκοτιζόμενος ὁ νοῦς χαώσῃ τὴν νῆψιν Hesych.S.*temp*.2.83(M.93.1540A); τὸ ἔργον αὐτοῦ...κατακαήσεται καὶ χαωθήσεται ‡Ath.*qu.script*.98(M.28.757A); Thphn.*chron*.p.183(M.108.477A).

χαρά, ἡ, *joy*; **1.** in gen. ἡ δὲ χ. οἷον σκίρτημά τί ἐστι τῆς ψυχῆς ἐπαγαλλομένης τοῖς κατὰ γνώμην Bas.*hom*.4.4(2.28B; M.31.225B); χ. γάρ ἐστι καταθυμίων πλήρωσις καὶ ἡδέων ἀπόλαυσις, καὶ ἀνιαρῶν λήθη Chrys.*hom.in Is*.6:1(6.98B); at baptism ἐπὶ τὸ βάπτισμα χαίροντας ἔρχεσθαι προσῆκεν, ἀλλ' ἐπεὶ πολλάκις συγκαταβαίνει τισὶ καὶ ἀκάθαρτα πνεύματα παρακολουθοῦντα καὶ τυχόντα μετὰ τοῦ ἀνθρώπου τῆς σφραγῖδος ἀνίατα τοῦ λοιποῦ γίνεται, ἃ τῇ χ. συμπλέκεται φόβος, ἵνα τις μόνος καθαρὸς αὐτὸς κατέλθῃ Clem.*exc.Thdot*.83(p.132.18; M.9.696D); **2.** of spiritual joy τὸ ἐπὶ τοῖς κατ' ἐντολὴν τοῦ κυρίου εἰς δόξαν θεοῦ γινομένοις χαίρειν, ἡ ἐν κυρίῳ χ. ἐστιν Bas.*reg. br*.193(2.480D; M.31.1212B); ὅπου χ., λύπη οὐ πάρεστιν· ὅπου χ. εὐφροσύνης σύμβολα Eus.Al.*serm*.18(M.61.735); μόνη γὰρ κυρίως ἂν εἴη χ. ἡ ἐκ καμάτων τε καὶ θλίψεων ζωὴν αἰώνιον πραγματευομένη· ἀλλὰ καὶ χ. τῆς ἀληθινῆς πληροῦνται οἱ δικαιοπραγοῦντες, εἰς ἔργον αὐτοῖς προχωροῦντος τοῦ σκοποῦ, καὶ ἀταράχου μενούσης τῆς ψυχῆς, καὶ γαληνιζούσης ἐν αὐτῇ Thdt.*Is*.57:18(2.370); ἡ...ὄντως ἐγγινομένη χ. τῇ ψυχῇ καὶ τῷ σώματι ὑπόμνησίς ἐστιν ἀπλανὴς τῆς ἀφθάρτου βιότητος Diad.*perf*.25(p.28.4); opp. worldly joy *αὕτη μεγίστη χ.· τοιαύτην καὶ οἱ ἀπόστολοι ἔχαιρον· χ. κέρδος φέρουσα, ἡ ἀπὸ δεσμωτηρίων, ἡ ἀπὸ μαστίγων. ... ἡ ἀπὸ τῶν λυπηρῶν πάντως ἔχουσα τὴν ἀρχὴν καὶ τὴν ῥίζαν καὶ τὴν ὑπόθεσιν· ὅθεν καὶ εἰς χρηστὸν ἀπαντᾷ τέλος. ἡ δὲ τοῦ κόσμου τοὐναντίον, ἄρχεται μὲν ἀπὸ ἡδέων, τελευτᾷ δὲ εἰς τὰ λυπηρά* Chrys.*hom.16.4 in Ac.*(9.133A); *πληρεστάτην γὰρ ὄντως καὶ τελείαν εἶναι χ. λογιζόμεθα, τὴν ἐν θεῷ καὶ διὰ θεὸν καὶ ἐπ' ἔργοις ἀγαθοῖς, διὰ τὸ πεπηγὸς καὶ ἀκλόνητον τῆς ἐλπίδος...ἀτελῆ δὲ χ. τὴν ἐν κόσμῳ φαμὲν διά τε τὸ εὐπαράφορον καὶ τὸ ἐφ' οἷς ἥκιστα χρῆν τελουμένην ὁρᾶσθαι, τουτέστι, πράγμασι κοσμικοῖς, ἃ φαντασμάτων καὶ σκιᾶς ἐξίπταται δίκην* Cyr.*Jo.*10.2(4.886C); **3.** of God *σὺ ὁ βοηθός...ἡ χ. ... σὺ ἡμῖν τὰ πάντα Hom.Clem.*4.72; of blood of Christ *ἣν ἀσπάζομαι ἐν αἵματι Ἰησοῦ Χριστοῦ, ἥτις ἐστὶν χ. αἰώνιος καὶ παράμονος* Ign.*Philad.*proem.

***χαραγή, ἡ,** *impress* on a coin, ‡Jo.D.*Const.*14(M.95.329D); Thphn.*chron.*p.305(M.108.741B).

χάραγμα, τό, any *mark engraved, printed* or *branded*; **1.** *sign, mark*; of the cross, ‡Hipp.*consumm.*28(p.300.39; M.10.932B); fig. *ἕκαστον γὰρ τῶν παθῶν ὥσπερ γράμμα καὶ χ. ἡμῖν καὶ σημεῖον* Clem. *ecl.*24.2(p.143.16; M.9.709A); opp. *γράμμα: ἐξάλειψον τὰ γράμματα μᾶλλον δὲ τὰ χ., ἅπερ ὁ διάβολος ἐνετύπωσέ σου τῇ ψυχῇ* Chrys.*hom. 11.7 in Mt.*(7.158C); **2.** *letter of the alphabet*; of tetragrammaton *τῶν ἀνεκφωνήτων χ.* Leont.H.*Nest.*5.16(M.86.1737D); of inscription on tables of Law *ἔργον θεοῦ ἐπίσης ἑκάτερα ἦν, ἥ τε ὕλη καὶ τὰ ἐπὶ ταύτῃ χ.* Gr.Nyss.*v.Mos.*(M.44.322A); *τὰ θεῖα χ. ib.*(372D); **3.** plur., *writings* (ref. 2Pet.1:4) *τὰ καθολικὰ...χ.* Didym.*Trin.*2.12(M.39. 683A); *τῶν...πρώτων ἐπιστολιμαίων χ. ib.*3.4(833A); of scripture, *A.Petr.et Paul.*60(p.205.9); *γραφικοῖσι χ.* Nonn.*par.Jo.*12:34(M.43. 856B); **4.** *stroke, line* in drawing, Chrys.*hom.17.2 in Heb.*(12.167A).

***χάραγον, τό,** *stamped coin οὐ...λαβεῖν ἀντὶ τοῦ βασιλικοῦ χαράγματος τὸ ἔξω χ.* ‡Ath.*qu.Ant.*112(M.28.665D).

χαραδρεών, ὁ, *ground broken up by gullies*, Gr.Naz.*ep.*4(M.37. 25C).

[*]**χαράδριον, τό,** variant of *χαλάδριον*, *mat* or *pallet*, ‡Ath. *v.Syncl.*53(M.28.1520B); *Apophth.Patr.*(M.65.385D).

χαραδρόομαι, *be broken into clefts, made rugged*, Gr.Nyss.*v.Gr. Thaum.*(M.46.929D); ‡Chrys.*sicc.*(10.776B).

χαραδρώδης, *like a torrent*, ‡Nil.*perist.*2.4(M.79.821A).

***χαρακοειδής,** f.l. for *ταραχοειδής*, Jo.D.*ep.*(M.95.244C).

***χαρακόπλεκτος,** *made of stakes* or *palisades τὴν στρωμνὴν ἀεὶ χ. ἐκέκτητο Hymn.*61.8(*AS* 1 p.616).

χαρακτήρ, ὁ, 1. *impress, stamp*, fig. *ὥσπερ γάρ ἐστιν νομίσματα δύο, ὃ μὲν θεοῦ, ὃ δὲ κόσμου, καὶ ἕκαστον αὐτῶν ἴδιον χ. ἐπικείμενον ἔχει, οἱ ἄπιστοι τοῦ κόσμου τούτου, οἱ δὲ πιστοὶ ἐν ἀγάπῃ χ. θεοῦ πατρὸς διὰ Ἰησοῦ Χριστοῦ* Ign.*Magn.*5.2; *ὅσοι δὲ ἐξομοιοῦσθαι σπεύδουσι τῷ ὑπ' αὐτοῦ* [sc. *τοῦ λόγου*] *δεδομένῳ χ. ἀνεπιθύμητοι ἐξ ἀσκήσεως γενέσθαι βιάζονται* Clem.*str.*7.12(p.52.1; M.9.500C); *ἡ ψυχὴ...αὐτῆς τῆς θείας μακαριότητος ἐν αὐτῇ σώζειν τὸν χ.* Gr.Nyss.*anim.et res.* (M.46.96C); Cyr.*thes.*(5^1.359B); Proc.G.*Pr.*25:4(M.87.1472D); ref. creation of man *ἄνθρωπον...ἔπλασεν τῆς ἑαυτοῦ εἰκόνος χαρακτῆρα 1Clem.*33.4; ref. Heb.1:3, of Christ; denied by Arians, Ath.*ep.Afr.* 5(M.26.1037B); *ib.*6(1040A); *χ. ἀσώματος* id.*Ar.*3.1(M.26.324A); *ὁ δὲ υἱὸς χ. ἐνυπόστατος* ‡Ath.*Trin.*1.5(M.28.1124C); *δηλῶν διὰ τῆς ἐπαγωγῆς, ὅτι ὥσπερ ἐστὶν ὁ πατὴρ ἐνυπόστατος, καὶ πρὸς ὑπόστασιν οὐδενὸς δεόμενος· οὕτω καὶ ὁ υἱός. ἐνταῦθα γὰρ τὸ ἀπαράλλακτον δεικνὺς τοῦτό φησι, καὶ πρὸς τὸν ἰδιάζοντα χ. τοῦ πρωτοτύπου παραπέμπων σε, καὶ διδάσκων ὡς ἐν ὑποστάσει ἐστὶ καθ' ἑαυτὸν* Chrys. *hom.2.1 in Heb.*(12.14B); opp. *πρωτότυπος ib.2.2*(16D); Nil.*epp.*1. 286(M.79.188A); *εἰ χ. ἐστιν ὁ υἱὸς τῆς τοῦ πατρὸς ὑποστάσεως... λεγέτωσαν οἱ ἐπ' αὐτοῦ τό, οὐκ ἦν, τολμῶντες φέρειν, πότε χάριτος χωρὶς ἦν ἡ ὑπόστασις τοῦ πατρός; ὁμοῦ γὰρ τῇ ὑποστάσει καὶ ὁ ταύτης χ. συνεισάγεται* Cyr.*thes.*(5^1.28D); id.*Jo.*3.5(4.301E); id.*resp.*(6^2. 387D); ref. Mt.3:17 *οὗτός ἐστιν ὁ τῆς ἐμῆς τελειότητος τέλειος χ.* Gr.Ant.*bapt.*2.2(M.88.1872D); of H. Ghost *τὸ πνεῦμα ἄρα οὐ κτίσις ἀλλὰ τῆς ἁγιότητος τοῦ θεοῦ χ.* Didym.(‡Bas.)*Eun.*5(1.303A; M.29. 725C); **2.** *picture, image στηθάριον ἀληθινὸν ἔχοντα* [l. *ἔχον*] *τὸν χ. τοῦ αὐτοῦ βασιλέως Ἰουστίνου* Jo.Mal.*chron.*17 p.413(M.97.612B); Jo.D.*imag.*1.17(M.94.1248C); **3.** *face, countenance*, *P.Lond.*1927. 48; *ἐκτύπωμα τοῦ προσώπου, ἤτοι χ. αὐτοῦ* Jo.Mal.*chron.*7 p.172 (M.97.276B); of a comet *ὁ δὲ χ. αὐτοῦ ἀστραπὰς ἀπέπεμπεν ib.*18 p.454(665B); **4.** plur., *features τοὺς χ. καὶ τὴν ἐκτύπωσιν...εἰλικρινῶς τοῦ Χριστοῦ προσλαμβάνουσιν οἱ φωτιζόμενοι* Meth.*symp.*8. 8(p.90.8; M.18.149B); Peratic *ὥσπερ ζωγραφῶν...ἐπὶ τὸν πίνακα μεταφέρει τὰς ἰδέας ἐγγράφων, οὕτω ὁ υἱὸς τῇ δυνάμει τῇ ἑαυτοῦ ἀπὸ τοῦ πατρὸς ἐπὶ τὴν ὕλην τοὺς πατρικοὺς μεταφέρει χαρακτῆρας... εἰ γάρ τις, φησίν, ἐξισχύσει τῶν ἐνθάδε καὶ ἐννοηθῆναι ὅτι ἐστὶ πατρικὸς χ. ἄνωθεν μετενηνεγμένος ἐνθάδε σωματοποιηθείς...ὁμοούσιον τῷ πατρὶ τῷ ἐν τοῖς οὐρανοῖς ὅλως, καὶ ἐκεῖ ἀνέρχεται...ὅταν οὖν, φησί, λέγῃ ὁ σωτήρ· ὁ πατὴρ ὑμῶν ὁ ἐν τοῖς οὐρανοῖς, ἐκεῖνον λέγει ἀφ' οὗ ὁ υἱὸς μεταλαβὼν τοὺς χ. μετενήνοχεν ἐνθάδε· ὅταν δὲ λέγῃ· ὁ ὑμέτερος πατὴρ ἀπ' ἀρχῆς ἀνθρωποκτόνος ἐστί, τὸν ἄρχοντα καὶ δημιουργὸν τῆς ὕλης λέγει, ὃς ἀναλαβὼν τοὺς διαδοθέντας ἀπὸ τοῦ υἱοῦ χ. ἐγέννησεν ἐνθάδε, ὅς ἐστιν ἀπ' ἀρχῆς ἀνθρωποκτόνος·...οὐδεὶς οὖν, φησί, δύναται σωθῆναι δίχα τοῦ υἱοῦ οὐδὲ ἀνελθεῖν· ὅς ἐστιν ὁ ὄφις. ὡς γὰρ κατήνεγκεν ἄνωθεν τοὺς πατρικοὺς χ., οὕτως πάλιν ἐντεῦθεν ἀναφέρει τοὺς ἐξυπνισμένους καὶ γεγονότας πατρικοὺς χ. ὑποστατοὺς ἐκ τοῦ ἀνυποστάτου ἐντεῦθεν ἐκεῖ μεταφέρων. τοῦτ' ἐστί, φησί, τὸ εἰρημένον· ἐγώ εἰμι ἡ θύρα* Hipp.*haer.*5.17(p.114.34; M.16.3175Dff.); **5.** *form, figure εὐειδέσταται τῷ χ.* Herm.*sim.*9.9.5; *οὐδέπω γὰρ τὸν χ. Παύλου ἑωράκει A.Paul.et Thecl.*7(p.241.5); of Christ (ref. Passion) *ἐπιτιμᾷ σοι κύριος, διάβολε, ὁ διὰ τοῦ ἐμπτύσματος τοῦ τιμίου αὐτοῦ χ. πᾶν δάκρυον ἐκ παντὸς προσώπου ἐκμάξας Lit.Chrys.*(M.63.1065B); *προσκύνει...τὸ σεβάσμιον ἐκτύπωμα τοῦ δεσποτικοῦ χ. τοῦ δι' ἡμᾶς ἐνανθρωπήσαντος θεοῦ λόγου* †Jo.D.*B.J.*19(M.96.1032B); **6.** *person ὥστε τὸν πατέρα καὶ τὸν υἱὸν μιᾶς οὐσίας...καὶ ἑνὸς χ. πιστεύεσθαι χρῆναι* Dam.Papa *ep.Illyr.*ap.Thdt.*h.e.*2.22.7(3.883); *ἐν τρισὶ χ. κατάγεται περιηχούμενος T.Sal.*11.6(M.122.1334A); **7.** *carved* or *chased figure ἀφελόμενος...τοὺς κανθάρους καὶ χ. χρυσοῦς Chron.Pasch.*p.185 (M.92.453B); **8.** *written document ἐν χ. γραφῆς Ἐνώχ T.Sym.*5.4; Epiph.*haer.*42.9(p.105.4; M.41.708B,C); plur. *τῶν ἀποστολικῶν χ.* Bas.*ep.*92.3(3.186B; M.32.484A); **9.** *mood* of a verb, Or.*or.*24.5(p.355. 23; M.11.493C).

χαρακτηρίζ-ω, 1. *characterize, designate by a characteristic mark*, fig. *εὐσεβείας...εὐσεβεῖς εἶναι ∼ούσης τοὺς τὰ κατ' αὐτὴν πράττοντας* Or.*Cels.*5.28(p.29.6; M.11.1224A); *∼εται...ὁ γεγεννημένος ἐκ τοῦ θεοῦ τῷ ἁμαρτίαν μὴ ποιεῖν* id.*Jo.*20.15(13; p.346.6; M.14.605C); *ἀγάπη τῆς τὸν Χριστιανισμὸν ∼ούσης* Chrys.*hom.6.3 in Tit.*(11.768B); Trin. *ἐν οἷς ∼εται θεὸς ὁ πατὴρ καὶ ὁ υἱὸς ἐν τῇ γραφῇ, ἐν αὐτοῖς ∼εται καὶ τὸ πνεῦμα τὸ ἅγιον* Didym.(‡Bas.)*Eun.*5(1.296A; M.29.712A); of Son *τοῦ γεννωμένου υἱοῦ πρὸς τὸν πατέρα ∼οντος τὸ γένος* Epiph. *haer.*76.3(p.343.13; M.42.520C); med., *be a characteristic ὅπερ ποτὲ ἐχαρακτηρίζετο ἐν τῇ σαρκί, τοῦτο χαρακτηρισθήσεται ἐν τῷ πνευματικῷ σώματι* Meth.*res.*1.23(p.247.5; M.41.1092D); **2.** *represent, symbolize*, Const.*or.s.c.*20(p.185.20; M.20.1297C); *ὁ μὲν Οὐρίας ἱερεὺς συμβολικῶς ∼ων τὸν διὰ Μωσέως παραδεδομένον νόμον* †Bas.*Is.* 207(1.534C; M.30.476C); *τῇ πυκνῇ τῶν φολίδων θέσει τὸ πολύτροπον τῆς κακίας ∼ων* Gr.Nyss.*ep.*3(M.46.1017A); *ὁ γὰρ πνευματικὸς...βίος τῷ τῆς περιστερᾶς εἴδει ∼εται* id.*hom.13 in Cant.*(M.44.1057D); *ὁ μόσχος, ὃς τῶν ἁγίων μαρτύρων τὰς ἱερὰς θυσίας ∼ει* Areth.*apoc.* 14(M.106.588D); **3.** *delineate, portray ὅσαι τῶν ἁγίων γραφῶν ∼ουσαι τὸν τῶν Χριστιανῶν βίον* Clem.*paed.*3.12 tit.(p.282.17; M.8.664A); *ὃν μόνον ὄντα θεὸν πατέρα ἀγαθὸν ∼ει ὁ σωτὴρ ἡμῶν καὶ θεός* id.*str.* 7.10(p.43.6; M.9.484A); *οὐ θέμις ἐστὶ* ⟨*ἀπὸ*⟩ *τῆς σωματικῆς ἀνθρωπίνης γεννήσεως τὴν τοῦ μονογενοῦς γέννησιν τὴν πρὸ τῶν αἰώνων ∼εσθαι* Melit.Ant.*hom*.ap.Epiph.*haer.*73.31(p.306.27; M.42.464A); *ἀπὸ τῆς ἀγάπης αὐτοὺς χ.* Chrys.*hom.72.3 in Jo.*(8.427A); **4.** *observe the character of ὅλως...∼οντας ἕνα καὶ τὸν αὐτὸν συνορᾶν τοῦ τε εὐαγγελίου καὶ τῆς ἐπιστολῆς χρῶτα πρόκειται* Dion.Al.ap.Eus.*h.e.*7.25.21(M. 20.701C); **5.** *imitate κατὰ τὸ ἐνὸν τῆς ἀσθενοῦς...δυνάμεως τὸν βίον αὐτῶν ∼ομεν* †Jo.D.*B.J.*12(M.96.972C); **6.** *frame, fashion*, met. *∼ει* [sc. *ὁ παιδαγωγός*] *τὰς ἐντολὰς* ⟨*ὡς ἡμᾶς*⟩ *αὐτὰς ἐκτελεῖν δύνασθαι* Clem.*paed.*1.12(p.148.17; M.8.368A); Chrys.*hom.8.2 in Jo.*(8.50C); *οὕτω χ. τὴν λέξιν ὡς συμφέρον ἦν ἀκοῦσαι* id.*comm.in Gal.*2:14(10. 688E); **7.** *define, declare τὴν ἀλήθειαν περὶ τοῦ θεοῦ διδάξαντα καὶ χαρακτηρίσαντα ὅτι θεὸς καὶ πατὴρ εἷς* Clem.*str.*7.10(p.43.2; M.9. 481C); *Πυθαγόρας καὶ οἱ Περιπατητικὴν ἐπαγγελλόμενοι ∼ουσιν ἕνα θεόν* Epiph.*haer.*7(p.186.2; M.41.205A); Melet.*nat.hom.*7(M.64.1184C); *propound, demonstrate χ. τεκμήριον μέγιστον τῶν λαλουμένων* Cyr. *hom.div.*10(5^2.371B); **8.** *designate, indicate ἴδια δὲ* [sc. *ὀνόματα*] *τὴν ἰδιότητα χ. τῶν ὑποστάσεων* Chrys.*incomprehens.*5.2(1.482D); *τὰ ἀρχαιότατα τῇ τοῦ αἰῶνος ἐπωνυμίᾳ ∼ει* Dion.Ar.*d.n.*10.2(M.3.937C); a point of time or a place *ἀκριβῶς ἡμῖν χ. τὸν χρόνον* Chrys.*hom. 6.4 in Mt.*(7.92A); *οὐκ ἤρκει οὕτω στενὸν τόπον χ. ib.6.2*(88B); of stars marking times and seasons, id.*scand.*7(3.477E); pass., *be named διὰ τῆς τούτου προσηγορίας ἅπαν τὸ ἔθνος ∼εσθαι* id.*hom.53.5 in Gen.*(4.520E); **9.** *imprint, impress*, fig. *ἀλλοτριοουσίῳ χ. τὴν τοῦ πατρὸς θεότητα* Ath.*syn.*50(p.274.14; M.26.781C); *τὰ ἄλλα ὅσα, τῷ εἶναι ὄντα, τὰ ὄντα πάντα ∼ει* Dion.Ar.*d.n.*5.7(M.3.821C); **10.** *bear an impress of*, fig. *τὸ κατ' εἰκόνα αἱ πράξεις ∼ουσι καὶ οὐχὶ ἡ τοῦ σώματος μορφή* Or.*sel.in Gen.*(M.12.96A); id.*Cels.*6.63(p.133.13; M.11.1393C); *εἰκὼν γὰρ τοῦτο ἐκείνης* [sc. *τὸ πρόσωπόν ἐστιν τῆς ψυχῆς*] *τρανῶς ∼ον αὐτῆς τὴν ἐνδομυχοῦσαν διάθεσιν* ‡Nil.*narr.*6(M.79.672B); *ἰδικῶς* *γὰρ ἡ ἀρετὴ αὕτη μιμεῖται θεόν· ~ει αὐτόν* Dor.*doct.*14.6(M.88.1784C); of Christ (ref. Mt.3:17) *οὗτός ἐστιν ὁ τὴν ἐμὴν θεότητα ~ων ἐν ἑαυτῷ* Gr.Ant.*bapt.*2.2(M.88.1872D); Naassene *ὁ Χριστὸς...κεχαρακτηρισμένος ἀπὸ τοῦ ἀχαρακτηρίστου λόγου* Hipp.*haer.*5.7(p.87.6; M.16.313A); *ib.*8(p.93.3; 3146B); ref. Heb.1:3 *τῷ μὴ εἶναι τὸν τῆς ὑποστάσεως τοῦ θεοῦ χαρακτῆρα, συναναιρεῖται κἀκεῖνος, ὁ πάντως ὑπ' αὐτοῦ ~όμενος* Alex.Al.*ep.Alex.*7(p.24.6; M.18.557C); Gr.Nyss.*Eun.* 2(2 p.313.21; M.45.485C); *ὡς γὰρ τὸ ἡλιακὸν σῶμα ὅλῳ τῷ περιέχοντι κύκλῳ ~εται...οὕτως εἶπεν ἐν τῷ μεγέθει τῆς τοῦ υἱοῦ δυνάμεως τὸ τοῦ πατρὸς μεγαλεῖον ~εσθαι* *ib.*8(2 p.181.8,12; 773A); *τοῦ πατρὸς τὴν οὐσίαν ὁ υἱὸς ἀπαραλλάκτως ~εσθαι λέγεται* Cyr.*thes.*(5^{1}.144A).

χαρακτήρισμα, τό, *characteristic,* Leont.H.*Nest.*2.7(M.86.1552D).

χαρακτηρισμός, ὁ, *characterization, description,* Clem.*paed.*1.12 (p.148.15; M.8.368A).

χαρακτηριστικός, *characteristic* *οὐδὲν γὰρ οὕτως ἴδιον καὶ χ. τῆς θείας φύσεως, ὡς τὸ ἀΐδιον* Isid.Pel.*epp.*2.18(M.78.744C); *οὐ διπλοῦς τῇ χ. ὑποστάσει* [sc. *ὁ Χριστός*] Ephr.Ant.*fr.*(M.86.2108D); *τῆς θείας φύσεώς ἐστι χ. τὸ ἄναρχον καὶ ἀγένητον* Jo.D.*Man.*2(M.96.1325B).

***χαραποιέομαι,** *rejoice* *χ. ἐπὶ τῷ τοῦ Φλορεντίου θανάτῳ* Gr.Mag. *dial.*(tr.Zach.)2.8(M.*PL.*66.150A).

χαράσσω, 1. *cut into furrows,* met. *δολιχοῖς ἐλατῆρες ὕδωρ ἐχάρασσον ἐρετμοῖς* Nonn.*par.Jo.*6:18(M.43.796C); **2.** *write,* Eus. *h.e.*3.4.6(M.20.220C); Nonn.*par.Jo.*2:17(M.43.764B); *ib.*7:41(812B); Thphyl.*exc.Gent.*14(p.488.5; M.113.949D); fig. *ἔχουσι τὰς ἐντολὰς αὐτοῦ τοῦ κυρίου...ἐν ταῖς καρδίαις κεχαραγμένας* Arist.*apol.*15.3 (p.111.2); *ἡ νέα διαθήκη παλαιῷ κεχαραγμένη γράμματι* Clem.*paed.* 1.7(p.125.8; M.8.321B); **3.** *mark out, plan* *μεγάλην αὐτὴν* [sc. *τὴν ἐκκλησίαν*] *ἐχάραξεν ὀλίγων ὄντων τῶν Χριστιανῶν ἐν τῇ πόλει* Marc. Diac.*v.Porph.*93; **4.** *strike out, delete,* fig. *ἐξήλειψεν, οὐκ ἐχάραξε μόνον* [sc. *ὁ θεὸς τὰ παραπτώματα*] Chrys.*hom.*6.2 *in Col.*(11.368A); *ἅμα...τὴν ἁμαρτίαν ὁ κείμενος ἔλεγε, ταύτην ἐκεῖνος τῷ καλάμῳ ἐχάραττεν* Jo.Clim.*scal.*4(M.88.684C); **5.** *dispel* *ἐχάραξε λιπόσκιον ὄρθρος ὁμίχλην* Nonn.*par.Jo.*6:22(M.43.797A); **6.** of torture *χαράξατε αὐτοῦ τὰς κνήμας εὐτονώτατα* *M.Tar.*(p.456).

***χαρβάσιος,** (Lat. *carbaseus*) *made of flax,* Thphn.*chron.*p.268(M. 108.665A *καρβάσια*).

***χαρζανή, ἡ,** ? *chain* *ἤλαυνον μυριάδας ψυχὰς ἀνηλεῶς τύπτοντες αὐτὰς ἐν πυρίναις χ.* *T.Abr.*A 12(p.90.17).

χαρία, ἡ, (Hebr. כְּרִי ,כָּרָה, v. Jastrow *Dict. of the Targumim*) *heap, pile;* in etym. of *χόρ*: *χὸρ δὲ λέγεται ἀπὸ τοῦ βουνοῦ ὑποθέσεως· χ. γὰρ καλεῖται βουνός* Epiph.*mens.*21(M.43.272C).

χαριεντιστέον, *one must be polite* or *charming,* Clem.*paed.*2.5 (p.185.18; M.8.448B).

χαρίζ-ω, I. act., *show favour to* *τοὺς δικαίους...χ.* *Apoc.Esd.* (p.25).

II. med.; **A.** intrans.; **1.** *grant pardon* to *μάρτυρες τοῖς μὴ μάρτυσιν ἐχαρίζοντο* *Ep.Lugd.*ap.Eus.*h.e.*5.1.45(M.20.425B); **2.** in bad sense, *ingratiate oneself, curry favour* (with) *ἵνα μὴ δόξῃ ~εσθαι* Chrys.*hom.*3.2 *in Ac.*(9.25B); *θεῷ ~εσθαι θέλοντας* Olymp.*Job* 17:8 (M.93.192B).

B. trans.; **1.** *give, bestow freely;* **a.** of abstracts *ἡ μακροθυμία σου ...παρρησίαν ἡμῖν ~εται* *Hom.Clem.*20.5; *ἡ...πρὸς τὸν θεὸν ὁμοιότης τὸ διηνεκὲς τῆς ζωῆς ἡμῖν ~εται* Bas.*ascet.*1.1(2.319A; M.31.872A); **b.** of God, *2Clem.*1.4; *τὴν σωτηρίαν ἁπάσῃ ~εται τῇ ἀνθρωπότητι* Clem.*paed.*1.11(p.147.9; M.8.365A); *κἂν ὁ υἱὸς λέγηται ~εσθαι, ὁ πατήρ ἐστιν ὁ διὰ τοῦ υἱοῦ καὶ ἐν τῷ υἱῷ παρέχων* Ath.*Ar.*3.13(M.26. 349B); pass., of what is granted in answer to prayer *τῆς...ἐκκλησίας ...αἰτησαμένης μετὰ νηστείας πολλῆς καὶ λιτανείας, ἐπέστρεψε τὸ πνεῦμα τοῦ τετελευτηκότος, καὶ ἐχαρίσθη ὁ ἄνθρωπος ταῖς εὐχαῖς τῶν ἁγίων* Iren.*haer.*2.31.2(M.7.825A); of what is granted in revelation *πατὴρ παρὰ τοῦ κυρίου ἡμῶν ἐγνώσθη καὶ κεχάρισται* Ath.*decr.*31 (p.27.17; M.25.473B); **c.** reflex., of God *λόγον ~ομαι ὑμῖν, τὴν γνῶσιν τοῦ θεοῦ, τέλειον ἐμαυτὸν ~ομαι* Clem.*prot.*12(p.85.4; M.8.241B); *αὐτὸν ~εται εἰς ἀνάπαυσιν* *Hom.Clem.*17.10; in gen., *devote oneself* to *Ἀρίστιππος μυρισθεὶς ὅλον αὐτὸν Ἀφροδίτῃ ~εται* *ib.*5.18; **d.** *deliver up, hand over* *τὸν τοῦ θεοῦ θέλοντα εἶναι κόσμῳ μὴ χαρίσησθε* Ign. *Rom.*6.2; *offer* to God, Cyr.*Os.*158(3.191B); **2.** *grant, allow,* of God *εὐλογητὸς...ὁ χαρισάμενος ὑμῖν ἀξίοις οὖσι τοιοῦτον ἐπίσκοπον κεκτῆσθαι* Ign.*Eph.*1.3; *μὴ δωρησαμένην ἰδεῖν ἃ ἑτέροις θεάσασθαι ἐχαρίσατο* Or.*princ.*3.1.17(p.228.10; M.11.285C); *τὸ κατὰ θεὸν ζῆν ἡμῖν ἐχαρίσατο τῇ τοῦ λόγου χάριτι* Ath.*inc.*5.1(M.25.104D); *ἐχαρίσατο ...εἰκόνα τῆς τῶν ἀγγέλων ἁγιότητος ἔχειν ἡμᾶς ἐπὶ γῆς τὴν παρθενίαν* id.*apol.Const.*33(M.25.640A); **3.** *forgive* *τίς...τίνι ~εται τὰ ἁμαρτήματα;* Apollon.ap.Eus.*h.e.*5.18.7(M.20.477B); *δούλων...ἦν ἀπαιτεῖν μόνον τοὺς καρπούς· υἱοῦ δὲ καὶ δεσπότου χαρίσασθαι τὰς ὀφειλάς, καὶ μεταθεῖναι τὸν ἀμπελῶνα* Ath.*Ar.*1.59(M.26.136A); cf. supra A.1; **4.** *give credit for, ascribe* *τὸν διάβολον...ἑαυτῷ χαρισάμενον ἃ εἶχε προτερήματα, ὅτε ἄμωμος ἦν* Or.*princ.*3.1.12(p.216.8; M.11.272A); Ath.*ep.fest.*39.12(p.88; M.26.1439A); **5.** perf. ptcpl. pass., *flattering,* also neut. as subst., *flattery* *ἐγκώμια ψευδῆ καὶ κ.* id.*gent.*17(M.25. 36B); *κ. οὐδὲν ὁ πατὴρ ἐρεῖ περὶ ἐμοῦ* Cyr.*Jo.*2.9(4.243C); *κεχαρισμένα πράσσω* or *ποιέω, favour* unjustly *ὡς ἂν μὴ δοκοίημεν κ. πράττειν τῷ λόγῳ* Eus.*p.e.*1.6(18D; M.21.49B); *οὐ κ. πεποιήκασιν οὐδὲ ἀναγκαζόμενοι παρά τινος* Ath.*apol.sec.*58(p.138.31; M.25.356A); *ib.*89(p.167. 17; 409A).

χάρις, ἡ, *grace;*

I. in gen.; **A.** of God as source of grace; **1.** Father *πατὴρ...τὰς χ. αὐτοῦ ἀποδιδοῖ τοῖς προσερχομένοις αὐτῷ ἁπλῇ διανοίᾳ* *1Clem.*23.1; Hipp.*haer.*1 proem.(p.3.12; M.16.3020D); *πάτερ...ἡ πηγὴ πάσης χ.* Serap.*euch.*13.5; almost as synon. with God *ἀμείψεται αὐτὸν ἡ χ. κατὰ πάντα* Ign.*Smyrn.*12.1; *εὕροιμεν...χ. ἐνώπιον τοῦ θρόνου τῆς χ.* Cosm.Ind.*top.*2(M.88.136A); **2.** Christ; **a.** as mediating grace of Father *διὰ τῆς παρὰ...'Ιησοῦ κατὰ τὸ θέλημα τοῦ πατρὸς αὐτοῦ χ.* Just.*dial.*116.1(M.6.744B); cf. *majorem donationem paternae gratiae per suum adventum effudit in humanum genus,* Iren.*haer.*4.36.4(M. 7.1094A); *παρ' αὐτοῦ* [sc. *τοῦ υἱοῦ*] *λαβόντες τὴν χ.* *ib.*2.32.4(829A); through whom it passed from Jews to Christians, Or.*Cels.*5.50(p.54. 29; M.11.1260C); *ἡ διδομένη δὲ χ. μία ἐστὶ παρὰ τοῦ πατρὸς ἐν υἱῷ διδομένη* Ath.*Ar.*2.42(M.26.236B); Gr.Nyss.*Maced.*19(M.45.1325A); **b.** as himself the giver of grace *οἱ ὑπὸ τὸν ζυγὸν τῆς χ. αὐτοῦ δι' αὐτοῦ ἐλθόντες* *1Clem.*16.17; *πιστεύω τῇ χ. 'Ιησοῦ Χριστοῦ* Ign. *Philad.*8.1; id.*Smyrn.*6.2; *ὁ κύριος...πάσης χ.* *Barn.*21.9; ‡*Diogn.* 11.5; called *χ.*, Or.*fr.*9 *in Jo.*(p.491.5); *V.Aberc.*16; *ὁ λόγος...ὁ τῆς χ. δοτήρ* Ath.*Ar.*1.40(M.26.96A); *ἡ παρ' αὐτοῦ καὶ δι' αὐτοῦ γενομένη χ.* *ib.*1.59(136A); *ἐν τῷ Χριστῷ ἦν ἀποκειμένη ἡ εἰς ἡμᾶς φθάνουσα χ.* *ib.*2.76(308C); *χ. τῆς ἐκ τοῦ πληρώματος τοῦ Χριστοῦ* Bas.*hom.in Ps.*7 (1.100B; M.29.233D); *χρίεται καὶ ἁγιάζεται δι' ἡμᾶς, ἵνα δι' αὐτοῦ τρέχῃ λοιπὸν εἰς πάντας ἡ χ. ... διὸ δὴ καί φησιν· ἐγώ εἰμι ἡ ὁδός· δι' ἧς ὥσπερ πρὸς ἡμᾶς ἡ θεία καταβέβηκε χ., ὑψοῦσα...καὶ θεοποιοῦσα τὴν φύσιν ἐν πρώτῳ Χριστῷ* Cyr.*thes.*20(5^{1}.197C,D); *πηγὴν κατὰ τὴν Βηθλεὲμ τεκεῖν· τῆς πηγῆς ἡ χ., οὐρανοπόθητον γενέσθαι καὶ χάριν χάριτος συλλαβεῖν* *Pers.*(p.15.13f.; M.10.104C); **c.** through Inc. *τὸ ἐν αὐτῇ* [sc. Christ's birth] *τὴν...χ. δεδόσθαι ἀνθρώποις* *Const.App.*8.33. 6; *τὴν τοῦ σωτῆρος ἐπιδημίαν, ἤγουν τῆς μετὰ σαρκὸς οἰκονομίας τὴν χ.* Cyr.*Is.*1.2(2.40B); **d.** through Cross *ὁ σταυρὸς ἐν τῷ ταῦ ἤμελλεν ἔχειν τὴν χ.* *Barn.*9.8; *Χριστέ, τὸν ἐπὶ τῆς σῆς χ.* [sc. Cross] *κρεμασθέντα ὁ ἀντίδικός σου μὴ λυέτω με* *A.(Pass.)Andr.*14(p.31.25); *Χριστὸς...τῇ ἁμαρτίᾳ θανόντας, διὰ τοῦ ἰδίου αἵματος ἐξηγόρασε, καὶ τοῖς οὕτω πιστεύουσι, τὴν χ. ἐδωρήσατο* Marc.Er.*opusc.*2.20(M.65. 933A); ref. gift of H. Ghost *ὁ γὰρ ἐν τρίτῃ ὥρᾳ σταυρωθεὶς...τρίτῃ ὥρᾳ νῦν κατέπεμψε τὴν χ. οὐ γὰρ ἄλλη χ. ἐκείνου, καὶ ἄλλη χ. τούτου ἀλλ' ὁ τότε σταυρωθείς, καὶ ἐπαγγειλάμενος, ἐπλήρωσεν ὃ ἐπηγγείλατο* Cyr.H.*catech.*17.19; **e.** in rel. to Christ's divinity and humanity *ἔστι παράδοξον...ἣν γὰρ δίδωσιν ὁ υἱὸς παρὰ τοῦ πατρὸς χ., ταύτην αὐτὸς ὁ υἱὸς λέγεται δέχεσθαι...ὡς μὲν λόγος, τὰ παρὰ τοῦ πατρὸς δίδωσι...ὡς δὲ υἱὸς ἀνθρώπου, αὐτὸς ἀνθρωπίνως λέγεται τὰ παρ' ἑαυτοῦ δέχεσθαι, διὰ τὸ μὴ ἑτέρου, ἀλλ' αὐτοῦ εἶναι τὸ σῶμα, τὸ φύσιν ἔχον τοῦ δέχεσθαι τὴν χ.* Ath.*Ar.*1.45(M.26.105B); *εἴληφεν ἄρα ὡς ἄνθρωπος κατὰ χ., ἅπερ εἶχεν ὡς θεὸς φυσικῶς* Cyr.*thes.*20(5^{1}.196E); *χρίεται δὲ ὡς ἄνθρωπος...δῆλον ὅτι περὶ τὴν ἀνθρωπότητα ἡ χ.* *ib.* (197D); **3.** H. Ghost; **a.** in gen. *πνεῦμα θεοῦ δόντος...χ. αὐτοῖς εὐσεβέσιν* *Orac.Sib.*4.189; *δόματα ἃ ἀπὸ τῆς χ. τῆς δυνάμεως τοῦ πνεύματος ἐκείνου τοῖς...πιστεύουσι δίδωσιν* Just.*dial.*87.5(M.6.684C); Iren.*haer.*5.8.1(M.7.1142A); Clem.*paed.*3.3(p.251.8; M.8.592A) cit. s. *αἷμα*; *πνεύματος ἁγίου χ. ἀπολαῦσαι* Cyr.H.*catech.*3.8; *ib.*16.22; *πνεῦμα θεοῦ ἐν ἐμοί, καὶ διὰ τῆς ἀπ' αὐτοῦ χ. σοφισθεὶς ἀναφέρω τὴν δόξαν* Bas.*Spir.*63(3.53D; M.32.185A); Mac.Aeg.*hom.*4.26(M.34. 492D); *ib.*10.3(541C); *μία μέν ἐστι...ἡ χ. τοῦ πνεύματος· ἐνεργεῖ δὲ ἑκάστῳ, καθὼς βούλεται* Marc.Er.*opusc.*2.108(M.65.945B); Jo.Carp. *cap.*19(M.85.1841); Jo.D.*f.o.*4.9(M.94.1121A) cit. infra C.1; **b.** almost equated with H. Ghost *ἓν πνεῦμα τῆς χ. τὸ ἐκχυθὲν ἐφ' ἡμᾶς* *1Clem.* 46.6; Hipp.*Noët.*14(p.257.1; M.10.821A); *ἡ τῆς χ. ἐπίκλησις σφραγίσασα τὴν ψυχήν* Cyr.H.*catech.*3.12; *πνεῦμα ἅγιον...χ. τελειοποιόν* Bas. *ep.*105(3.200B; M.32.513B); Gr.Nyss.*tres dii*(M.45.129B); *οἱ βλασφημήσαντες τὸ πνεῦμα τῆς χ. καὶ ἀποπτύσαντες τὴν παρ' αὐτοῦ δωρεὰν μετὰ τὴν χ.* *Const.App.*6.18.3; Didym.*Trin.*2.1(M.39.452C); *πνεύματος ἁγίου δόσις ἦν, ἀλλ' ἣν αὕτη ἡ χ. συσταλεῖσα...καὶ ἀπὸ τῆς γῆς ἀπολιποῦσα ἀπὸ τῆς ἡμέρας ἐκείνης, ἀφ' ἧς ἐρρήθη, ἀφίεται ὁ οἶκος ὑμῶν ἔρημος...ἐπειδὴ οὖν ταύτην ἔμελλον λαμβάνειν τὴν χ., οὔπω δὲ ἦν δοθεῖσα, διὰ τοῦτό φησιν, οὔπω γὰρ ἦν πνεῦμα ἅγιον* Chrys.*hom.*51.2 *in Jo.*(8.300D–301A); *ἡ παλαιὰ δὲ...πνεῦμα...ἅγιον ἐκάλει, ἤτοι πνεῦμα* θεοῦ, τὴν χ. αὐτοῦ Thdr.Mops.*Ag.*2:1–5(M.66.485A); **c.** in controversy with Macedonians τὰς δὲ περὶ τὸν ἄνθρωπον οἰκονομίας, τὰς ὑπὸ τοῦ...Χριστοῦ...γενομένας, τίς ἀντερεῖ μὴ οὐχὶ διὰ τῆς τοῦ πνεύματος χ. πεπληροῦσθαι; Bas.*Spir.*39(3.33D; M.32.140B); τίς οὖν ἄρα ἡ χ., ἢ πάντως ἡ τοῦ ἁγίου πνεύματος χύσις ἡ ἐν ταῖς καρδίαις ἡμῶν γινομένη,...πῶς οὖν ἀληθινὴ...ἡ ἐν ἡμῖν χ., εἴπερ διηκονήθη διὰ κτίσματος; Cyr.*thes.*34(5¹.352D); in alleged teaching of Paul of Samosata, who named H. Ghost χ. so as to deny him personality, †Leont.B.*sect.*3.3(M.86.1216B); **4.** whole Trin. ἐν πολλῇ...ἐκχεομένη ἀπὸ θεοῦ εἰς ἀνθρώπους χ. θεοῦ διὰ τοῦ τῆς...εἰς ἡμᾶς χ. ὑπηρέτου Ἰησοῦ Χριστοῦ καὶ τοῦ συνεργοῦ πνεύματος Or.*or.*1(p.297.4f.; M.11.416A); τοῦ υἱοῦ...τὴν τοῦ ἁγίου πνεύματος χ. ... τοῖς ἁγίοις δωρουμένου πατρικῷ βουλήματι *Symb.Ant.*(345)9(p.254.4; M.26.733C); μετοχῇ τοῦ λόγου διὰ τοῦ πνεύματος ταύτην ἔχουσι τὴν χ. παρὰ τοῦ πατρὸς Ath.*Ar.*1.9(M.26.29A); cf.*ib.*1.50(117B); μία γάρ ἐστιν ἐκ τοῦ πατρὸς χ. δι' υἱοῦ ἐν πνεύματι ἁγίῳ πληρουμένη id.*ep.Serap.*1.14(M.26.565B); *ib.*3.6 (636A).

B. as bestowed on Church; **1.** contrasted with Mosaic dispensation viewed **a.** as not having grace but Law εἰ γὰρ μέχρι νῦν κατὰ Ἰουδαϊσμὸν ζῶμεν, ὁμολογοῦμεν χ. μὴ εἰληφέναι Ign.*Magn.*8.1; in New Covenant ἐγένετο...ἡ ἐντολὴ χ. Mel.*pass.*2.11 p.89; λέγων τὴν ἀνάγνωσιν νόμου τε καὶ προφητῶν πρόδρομον τῆς χ. ‡Pion.*v.Polyc.*19; Gr.Naz.*or.*2.97(M.35.500B); οὐ γάρ ἐστι νόμος ὁ κελεύων μόνον, ἀλλὰ καὶ χ. ἡ καὶ τὰ πρότερα ἀφεῖσα, καὶ πρὸς τὰ μέλλοντα ἀσφαλιζομένη. ἐκεῖνος μὲν γὰρ μετὰ τοὺς πόνους τοὺς στεφανοὺς ἐπήγγελτο, αὕτη δὲ πρότερον ἐστεφάνωσε, καὶ τότε εἰς τοὺς ἀγῶνας εἵλκυσεν Chrys.*hom.* *11.3 in Rom.*(9.535A); ὁ μὲν γὰρ νόμος ἐπαχθής, ἡ δὲ χ. ῥᾳδία· ὁ νόμος...οὐ σώζει· ἡ χ. καὶ τὴν ἐξ ἑαυτῆς καὶ τὴν ἐκ τοῦ νόμου παρέχει δικαιοσύνην *ib.17.3*(624D); κέκληται γὰρ τῶν ἐθνῶν ἡ πληθύς, οὐ διὰ τῆς τοῦ νόμου παιδαγωγίας...ἀγείρει δὲ μᾶλλον αὐτὰ θεία χ. Cyr.*Is.*1.2 (2.36E); ὁ μὲν νόμος μόνοις ἐδόθη τοῖς ἐξ Ἰσραήλ. ἡ δὲ χ. ... τοῖς ἀνὰ πᾶσαν τὴν ὑπ' οὐρανόν *ib.*3.2(402C); **b.** as receiving (in case of OT saints and prophets) grace of H. Ghost or of Christ by anticipation οἱ λειτουργοὶ τῆς χ. τοῦ θεοῦ διὰ πνεύματος ἁγίου περὶ μετανοίας ἐλάλησαν *1Clem.*8.1; οἱ...προφῆται...ἐμπνεόμενοι ὑπὸ τῆς χ. αὐτοῦ [sc. Christ] Ign.*Magn.*8.2; οἱ προφῆται, ἀπ' αὐτοῦ ἔχοντες τὴν χ., εἰς αὐτὸν ἐπροφήτευσαν *Barn.*5.6; καλὸν ἂν εἴη ὑμᾶς...παρὰ τῶν λαβόντων χ. ἀπὸ τοῦ θεοῦ ἡμῶν τῶν Χριστιανῶν μανθάνειν,...διὸ καὶ εἰς ἡμᾶς μετετέθη ἡ χ. αὕτη Just.*dial.*78.10,11(M.6.661A); cf.*ib.*32.5(545A); Iren.*haer.*4.11.3(M.7.1002C); *ib.*4.36.4(1093B–1094A); ὁ δὲ νόμος χ. ἐστὶν παλαιὰ διὰ Μωσέως ὑπὸ τοῦ λόγου δοθεῖσα...ἡ δὲ ἀΐδιος χ. καὶ ἡ ἀλήθεια διὰ Ἰησοῦ Χριστοῦ ἐγένετο. ... ἐπὶ μὲν τοῦ νόμου ἐδόθη φησὶ μόνον, ἡ δὲ ἀλήθεια, χ. οὖσα τοῦ πατρός, ἔργον ἐστὶ τοῦ λόγου αἰώνιον Clem.*paed.*1.7(p.125.17ff.; M.8.321C); ἔφθασε...καὶ ἐπὶ τοὺς πατέρας ἡ χ., ἀλλ' ὧδε ὑπερβολικῶς. ἐκεῖ...μετέσχον ἁγίου πνεύματος, ὧδε δὲ αὐτοτελῶς ἐβαπτίσθησαν Cyr.H.*catech.*17.18; φαίνεται γὰρ προφητικῶς καὶ κατὰ νόμον, καὶ κατὰ χ., τὰς θυσίας πληρῶν. κατὰ νόμον μέν, τὰς διαφόρους· κατὰ χ. δέ, τὸν ἕνα μόσχον τὸν περὶ ἁμαρτίας Didym.*fr.* *Job* 1:5(M.39.1121A); εἰ τοίνυν οὐκ ἐξ οἰκείων κατορθωμάτων ἐξελέγησαν παρὰ θεοῦ, δῆλον ὅτι χ. ταύτης ἔτυχον τῆς τιμῆς. καὶ ἡμεῖς δὲ χ. πάντες ἐσώθημεν, ἀλλ' οὐχ ὁμοίως. οὐ γὰρ ἐπὶ τοῖς αὐτοῖς, ἀλλ' ἐπὶ πολλῷ μείζοσι...οὐ τοίνυν τοιαύτη παρ' ἡμῖν χ. οὐδὲ γὰρ δὴ μόνον ἁμαρτημάτων συγχώρησις ἡμῖν ἐδόθη...ἀλλὰ καὶ δικαιοσύνη, καὶ ἁγιασμὸς...καὶ πνεύματος χ. φαιδροτέρα...διὰ ταύτης τῆς χ. ἐγενόμεθα τῷ θεῷ ποθεινοί Chrys.*hom.14.2 in Jo.*(8.81A); πάλαι...χ. ἡμῖν δεδώρηται νομικὴν δούλοις συμβαλλομένοις, νῦν δὲ οὐχ ὡς δούλοις, ἀλλ' ὡς τέκνοις...εὐαγγελικὴν ἡμῖν ἐδωρήσατο χ. ὑψηλοτέραν τῆς πρώτης...δι' ἧς...ἐγγίζομεν τῷ θεῷ...ὡς υἱοί Nil.*epp.*2.314(M.79.353C); **c.** exeg. Jo.1:16 χ. ἀντὶ χ.· δεικνὺς ὅτι χ. Ἰουδαῖοι ἐσώζοντο Chrys.*hom.14.2 in Jo.*(8.80E–81A); χ. μὲν ἀνθρώποις καὶ ὁ νόμος ἐδίδου, καλῶν ὅλως εἰς θεογνωσίαν...ἡ δὲ διὰ τοῦ μονογενοῦς ἀλήθειά τε καὶ χ., οὐκ ἐν τύποις ἡμῖν εἰσφέρει τὸ ἀγαθὸν...ἀλλ' ἐν λαμπροῖς ...διατάγμασι Cyr.*Jo.*1.9(4.102B); cf.Marc.Er.*opusc.*2.74(M.65.941A); **2.** passing from Israel to Church, Just.*dial.*78.11(M.6.661A) cit. supra; Cyr.H.*catech.*13.7; ἐγκαταλιπὼν οὖν τὸν λαὸν...περιελὼν δὲ ἀπ' αὐτῶν καὶ τὸ πνεῦμα τὸ ἅγιον...ἐπλήρωσεν τὴν αὐτοῦ ἐκκλησίαν πνευματικῆς χ. *Const.App.*6.5.3; Apoll.*Rom.*10: 14f.(p.69.25); μεταβέβηκε γὰρ ἡ χ. ἐκ τῶν ἀπειθεῖν ἑλομένων εἰς τοὺς διὰ τῆς πίστεως κεκλημένους Cyr.*Is.*1.2(2.37E); built on rock, which is identified with εὐαγγελικὴ χ., Gr.Nyss.*hom.5 in Cant.*(M.44.877B); hence καινὴ χ. ... τῆς ἐκκλησίας Meth.*symp.*6.5(p.69.23; M.18.121A); **3.** its universality τῆς θείας χ. ὁ ὑετὸς ἐπὶ δικαίους καὶ ἀδίκους καταπέμπεται Clem.*str.* 5.3(p.338.12; M.9.37A); ἡ χ. δὲ οὐ στενή, οὐδὲ τόποις περιγραπτὸς Gr.Naz.*ep.*41(M.37.84B); ὁ γὰρ τῆς χ. ποταμὸς ῥεῖ πανταχοῦ, οὐκ ἐν τῇ Παλαιστίνῃ τὰς πηγὰς ἔχων...ἀλλὰ πᾶσαν τὴν οἰκουμένην κυκλῶν Gr.Nyss.*bapt.diff.*(M.46.420C); id.*hom.opif.*16(M.44.185C); ἡ σαγήνη τῆς χ. ἐφαπλοῦται ἐπὶ πάντας Mac.Aeg.*hom.*16.52(M.34.612B); almost = Christianity, *Const.App.*6.7.2.

C. mediated through sacraments; **1.** baptism χ. βαπτισμοῦ ‡Ath. *Ar.*4.25(M.26.508A); Gr.Nyss.*Maced.*19(M.45.1324D); id.*bapt.Chr.* (M.46.588D); Chrys.*hom.4.2 in 2Thess.*(11.532C); Cyr.*Is.*1.2(2.53C); Thdt.*h.e.*4.18.11(3.979); efficacy of baptismal grace μία χ. αὕτη τοῦ φωτίσματος τὸ μὴ τὸν αὐτὸν εἶναι τῷ πρὶν ἢ λούσασθαι τὸν τρόπον Clem.*paed.*1.6(p.108.4; M.8.285C); *ib.*1.5(p.105.32; 281A); ὁ δὲ βαπτιζόμενος...ἀνακαινίζεται δέ, ἄνωθεν γεννηθεὶς τῇ τοῦ πνεύματος χ. Ath.*ep.Serap.*4.13(M.26.656B); cf.Cyr.H.*catech.*1.2; γυμνούμεθα, τῇ χ. τοῦ πνεύματος αὐτοῦ, τῶν ἁμαρτιῶν Didym.*Trin.*2.12(M.39.680A); καὶ σὺ θείας ἀπήλαυσας χ. βαπτιζόμενος...εἰ καὶ μὴ πρὸς τὰ σημεῖα ποιεῖν, ἀλλ' ὅσον ἀρκεῖ πρὸς τὸ πολιτείαν ὀρθὴν...λαβεῖν Chrys. *compunct.*1.8(1.136D); πᾶς ὁ βαπτισθεὶς ὀρθοδόξως ἔλαβε μυστικῶς πᾶσαν τὴν χ.· πληροφορεῖται δὲ λοιπὸν κατὰ τὴν ἐργασίαν τῶν ἐντολῶν Marc.Er.*opusc.*2.85(M.65.944A); ὕδατος διὰ τῆς τοῦ πνεύματος χ. καθαίροντος τὸ σῶμα τῆς ἁμαρτίας...τὸν δὲ τῆς ζωῆς ἀρραβῶνα παρεχομένου τοῦ πνεύματος Jo.D.*f.o.*4.9(M.94.1121A); almost = baptism πρὶν γὰρ προσέλθῃς τῇ χ., ματαιότης...ἦν τὰ ποιήματά σου Cyr.H. *catech.*22.8; *ib.*3.2; ref. water ἐπίβλεψον ἐπὶ τὰ ὕδατα ταῦτα...πληρούμενα τῆς σῆς χ. Serap.*euch.*19.2; *Const.App.*7.43.5; baptismal oils as vehicles of grace, Serap.*euch.*22.2; cf.*Const.App.*7.42.2; **2.** eucharist ὅταν διδῷ τὴν χ. τὸ πνεῦμα...ὅταν ἴδῃς τὸ πρόβατον ἐσφαγιασμένον Chrys.*coemet.*3(2.401D); οὐδὲ τὸ...σῶμα μεταβληθήσεται, ἀλλ'...ἡ ζωοποιὸς χ. διηνεκὴς ἐστιν ἐν αὐτῷ Cyr.*ep.*83(5².365B); τὰ ὁρώμενα σύμβολα τῇ τοῦ σώματος καὶ αἵματος προσηγορίᾳ τετίμηκεν, οὐ τὴν φύσιν μεταβαλών, ἀλλὰ τὴν χ. τῇ φύσει προστεθεικώς Thdt.*eran.*1(4.26); as vehicle of grace and almost equated with it εὐχαριστία... χ. ἐπαινουμένη Clem.*paed.*2.2(p.168.6; M.8.412A); ὁ ἱερεὺς...καταφέρων...τὸ πνεῦμα τὸ ἅγιον...ἵνα ἡ χ. ἐπιπεσοῦσα τῇ θυσίᾳ δι' ἐκείνης ...ἀνάψῃ ψυχάς Chrys.*sac.*3.4(p.53.15; 1.383A); οἱ βεβαπτισμένοι καὶ τῆς θείας ἀπογευσάμενοι χ.·...ὁ σατανᾶς...αὐτὴν ἀποφρίττειν ἀναπείθει τὴν χ. ... ἀπορρήξαντες τοίνυν τὸν ἐκεῖνου δεσμὸν...προσίωμεν τῇ θείᾳ χ., καὶ εἰς ἁγίαν μετάληψιν ἀναβαίνωμεν τοῦ Χριστοῦ Cyr.*Jo.* 3.6(4.324E–325C); ‡Pall.*h.mon.*18(p.78.7; M.34.1179A); Dion.Ar.*e.h.* 3.3.15(M.3.443B,C); ἡ χ. ... τοῖς ἀξίοις...ἀπανουργήτως μεταδοτέον CTrull.*can.*23; contrasted with forbidden fruit ἐκεῖ βρῶμα θανατοποιόν, ὧδε βρῶμα ζωοποιόν. εἰ ταῦτα φύσει σώζει, καὶ οὐ τῇ χ., κἀκεῖνο τῇ φύσει ἀνεῖλεν, καὶ οὐ τῇ προθέσει, εἰ τοῦτο τὸ βρῶμα φύσει σώζει, καὶ οὐ τῇ χ., κἀκεῖνο φύσει ἀναιρεῖ, καὶ οὐ παραβάσει Sever. *creat.*6.4(M.56.488).

II. sanctifying grace; **A.** its necessity for Christian life and salvation δεῖ...τὴν γνώμην ὑγιῆ κεκτῆσθαι...πρὸς ὅπερ μάλιστα τῆς θείας χρῄζομεν χ. Clem.*str.*5.1(p.330.1; M.9.16C); θεὸς...τὸ κατὰ θεὸν ζῆν ἡμῖν ἐχαρίσατο τῇ τοῦ λόγου χ. Ath.*inc.*5.1(M.25.104D); οἱ καὶ ἐν τῷ ἁγιάζεσθαι δεόμενοι τῆς τοῦ πνεύματος χ. id.*Ar.*1.50(M.26.117A); χρεία...ἡμῖν χ. ... ἵνα μὴ ζιζάνιον ὡς σῖτον φαγόντες, ἐξ ἀγνοίας βλαβῶμεν Cyr.H.*catech.*4.1; προσδοκῶντες τὴν θείαν ἐπαμφιέννυσθαι δόξαν...αἰτία δὲ τῆς τοιαύτης ἀποδοθησομένης ἡμῖν δόξης ἡ παροῦσα χ. Apoll.*Rom.*5: 1–6(p.62.21); οὐ γὰρ ἐν δυνάμει ἀνθρώπου, οὐδὲ ἐν σοφίᾳ, ἀλλ' ἐν τῇ χ. τοῦ θεοῦ ἐστιν ἡ σωτηρία Bas.*hom.in Ps.*33 (1.144D; M.29.353C); πτωχοὶ γὰρ ἅπαντες, καὶ τῆς θείας χ. ἐπιδεεῖς Gr.Naz.*or.*14.1(M.35.860A); Gr.Nyss.*diff.ess.*4(M.32.329A); διὰ χ. τοῦ κυρίου πιστεύομεν σωθῆναι *Const.App.*6.12.11; οὐκ ἐν τοῖς πόνοις σου μόνον καὶ τοῖς κινδύνοις παρέστηκεν αὕτη ἡ χ., ἀλλὰ καὶ ἐν τοῖς εὐκολωτάτοις δοκοῦσιν εἶναι συμπράττει, καὶ πανταχοῦ τὴν παρ' ἑαυτῆς εἰσφέρει συμμαχίαν Chrys.*hom.14.7 in Rom.*(9.585C).

B. in rel. to human cooperation; **1.** relation to faith πιστεύσασι ...ἡ χ. ὑπερπλεονάσει Clem.*prot.*9(p.64.8; M.8.197A); υἱὸς...τῇ πίστει τὴν ἁγιάζουσαν χ. ἐπινείμας Apoll.*Rom.*5: 1–6(p.62.10); τὸ δὲ ζωοποιοῦν τοὺς βαπτιζομένους, τὸ πνεῦμά ἐστι...ζωοποιεῖ δὲ οὐκ αὐτὸ μόνον εἰς τὴν τελείωσιν τῆς χ. ταύτης διὰ τῆς πίστεως λαμβανόμενον, ἀλλὰ χρὴ τὴν εἰς τὸν κύριον προϋποκεῖσθαι πίστιν, δι' ἧς ἡ ζωτικὴ χ. τοῖς πιστεύσασι παραγίνεται...ἀλλ' ἐπειδὴ καὶ ἡ διὰ τοῦ υἱοῦ διακονουμένη χ. ἤρτηται τῆς ἀγεννήτου πηγῆς, διὰ τοῦτο προηγεῖσθαι τὴν εἰς τὸ ὄνομα τοῦ πατρὸς πίστιν ὁ λόγος διδάσκει...ὡς ἂν ἐκεῖθεν ἀφορμηθεῖσαν τὴν ζωοποιὸν χ. ... τῇ ἐνεργείᾳ τοῦ πνεύματος τελειοῦσθαι τοῖς ἀξιουμένοις Gr.Nyss.*Maced.*19(M.45.1325A); διὰ τῆς πίστεως... λαβεῖν χ. Mac.Aeg.*hom.*24.6(M.34.665C); διὰ τοῦτο εἰσῆλθεν ἡ πίστις, ...ἵνα τὴν χ. ἐπισπάσηται Chrys.*hom.51.2 in Jo.*(8.301B); διὰ τὴν σὴν ἀπιστίαν οὐκ ἐνήργηκεν ἡ χ. Cyr.*Lc.*9:37–40(p.83.8; M.72.656D); id. *Is.*2.5(2.334B); διὰ γὰρ πίστεως ἡ τῆς χ. δόσις, καὶ πρὸς τὸ μέτρον τῆς πίστεως χορηγεῖται τὰ δῶρα τῆς χ. Thdt.*Rom.*12:3(3.131); grace attracts faith, Chrys.*hom.8.4 in Rom.*(9.502D); **2.** preserved by constant human effort οὐχ ἡμέτερον ἔργον ἔσται τὸ κατ' ἀρετὴν βιοῦν, ἀλλὰ πάντη θεία χ. ταῦτα μὲν ἐρεῖ ὁ ἀπὸ τῶν ψιλῶν ῥητῶν τὸ ἐφ' ἡμῖν ἀναιρῶν Or.*princ.*3.1.15(p.222.6; M.11.280A); ἵνα εὑρεθῇ πάντων ὑμῶν ἡ ψυχὴ μὴ ἔχουσα σπῖλον...οὐ λέγω πρὸ τοῦ λαβεῖν τὴν χ. ... ἀλλ' ἵνα διδομένης τῆς χ., ἀκατάγνωστος ἡ συνείδησις εὑρεθεῖσα συνδράμῃ τῇ χ. Cyr.H.*catech.*3.2; ἀμήχανόν ἐστι χωρητικοὺς ἡμᾶς γενέσθαι τῆς θείας χ., μὴ τὰ ἀπὸ κακίας πάθη προκατασχόντα τὰς ψυχὰς ἡμῶν ἐξελάσαντας Bas.*hom.in Ps.*61(1.196D; M.29.477D); Gr.Naz.*or.*40.34(M.36.408C); id.*carm.*2.1.83.28(M.37.1430); ἡ τοῦ θεοῦ πνευματικὴ τῆς χ. ἐνέργεια ἐν ψυχῇ γιγνομένη, μετὰ πολλῆς μακροθυμίας...καὶ οἰκονομίας νοὸς μυστικῆς κατεργάζεται, καὶ μετὰ πολλῆς ὑπομονῆς...καιροῖς τοῦ ἀνθρώπου ἀγωνιζομένου Mac.Aeg.*hom.*9.1(M.34.532D); ἐκεῖνο [sc. baptism], φησί, χ. μόνης ἦν...εἰ γὰρ ἔνθα χ. ἦν μόνη, συνήργησεν· ἔνθα καὶ πόνους ἐπιδείκνυσθε, οὐ πολλῷ μᾶλλον συμπράξει; Chrys.*hom.39.4 in Mt.*(7.436B); χάριτος ἦν ἡ κλῆσις· τίνος οὖν ἕνεκεν ἀκριβολογεῖται; ὅτι τὸ μὲν κληθῆναι καὶ καθαρθῆναι χ. ἦν· τὸ δὲ κληθέντα καὶ καθαρὰ ἐνδυσάμενον, μεῖναι τοιαῦτα διατηροῦντα τῆς τῶν κληθέντων σπουδῆς *ib.69.2*(681D); ἡ χ. δὲ πῶς γίνεται μεθ' ἡμῶν; ἂν μὴ ὑβρίσωμεν εἰς τὴν εὐεργεσίαν, ἂν μὴ ῥάθυμοι γενώμεθα περὶ τὴν δωρεάν id.*hom.34.2 in Heb.*(12.316A); **3.** esp. in practice of self-denial and virtue ὀφείλουσιν...οἱ ἔχοντες τὴν χ. τοῦ θεοῦ, ταπεινοφρονεῖν καὶ ὁμολογεῖν τὴν πτωχείαν αὐτῶν Mac.Aeg.*hom.*15.27(M.34.593); charity, *ib.*26.16(685B); purification, id.*elev.*13(901A); ἡ τοῦ πνεύματος χ., παρόντων μὲν ἡμῖν ἔργων ἀγαθῶν, καὶ ἐλεημοσύνης πολλῆς ἐπιχεομένης τῇ ψυχῇ, μένει καθάπερ ἐλαίῳ κατεχομένη ἡ φλόξ· ταύτης δὲ οὐκ οὔσης, ἄπεισι Chrys.*hom. 1.6 in 2Cor.4:13*(3.265A); humility, Cyr.*Is.*1.3(2.65B); ἡ μὲν χ., τοῖς ἐν Χριστῷ βαπτισθεῖσι, μυστικῶς δεδώρηται· ἐνεργεῖ δὲ κατὰ ἀναλογίαν τῆς ἐργασίας τῶν ἐντολῶν, καὶ κρυφίως βοηθεῖν ἡμῖν ἡ χ. οὐ παύεται, ἐφ' ἡμῖν δέ ἐστι ποιεῖν ἢ μὴ ποιεῖν τὸ ἀγαθὸν κατὰ δύναμιν. πρῶτον μὲν θεοπρεπῶς διεγείρει τὴν συνείδησιν. ὅθεν καὶ κακοποιοὶ μετανοήσαντες τῷ θεῷ εὐηρέστησαν. πάλιν ἐν διδασκαλίᾳ τοῦ πλησίον ἐγκρύπτεται. ἔστι δὲ ὅτε καὶ ἐν τῇ ἀναγνώσει τῇ διανοίᾳ παρέπεται, καὶ διὰ τῆς φυσικῆς ἀκολουθίας ἐκδιδάσκει τὸν νοῦν τὴν ἑαυτῆς ἀλήθειαν. εἰ οὖν τῆς μερικῆς ταύτης ἀκολουθίας μὴ κρύψωμεν τὸ τάλαντον, εἰς τὴν χαρὰν τοῦ κυρίου ἐναρχῶς εἰσελευσόμεθα Marc.Er.*opusc.*2.56(M.65.937D); prayer, Nil.*epp.*3.271(M.79.520A); **4.** hence may be lost: **a.** indefectibility maintained by Gnostics ἡμᾶς [sc. orthodox]...ἐν χρήσει τὴν χ. λαμβάνειν λέγουσι, διὸ καὶ ἀφαιρεθήσεσθαι αὐτῆς· αὐτοὺς δὲ ἰδιόκτητον ἄνωθεν ἀπὸ τῆς ἀρρήτου...συζυγίας συγκατεληλυθυῖαν ἔχειν τὴν χ. Iren.*haer.*1.6.4(M.7.509A); ἀναφαίρετος γὰρ ἡ χ. Heracleon ap.Or.*Jo.*13.10(p.234.23; M.14.413B); *A.Barn.*8(p.295.10); **b.** lost; esp. through pride, *Const.App.*8.2.7; πῶς πίπτουσιν οἱ ἐνεργούμενοι ὑπὸ χ. θεοῦ; αὐτοὶ οἱ λογισμοὶ οἱ καθαροὶ ἐν τῇ ἰδίᾳ φύσει...πίπτουσιν. ἄρχεται γὰρ ἐπαίρεσθαι, κατακρίνειν καὶ λέγειν· σὺ ἁμαρτωλὸς εἶ, ἔχειν δ' ἑαυτὸν δίκαιον Mac.Aeg.*hom.*7.4(M.34.525C); οἱ ἔχοντες τὴν χ., ἐὰν ἐπαρθῶσι. ... αἴρει ἀπ' αὐτοῦ ὁ κύριος τὴν χ. αὐτοῦ *ib.*15.27(593C); cf.Gr.Naz.*or.*9.2(M.35.821B); through voluntary evil ὅπου γὰρ αὐτοπροαίρετος πονηρία, ἐκεῖ καὶ ἀποχὴ τῆς χ. Cyr.H.*catech.*6.28; *ib.*15.25; through negligence and instability τοῖς διὰ τὸ τῆς γνώμης ἀνίδρυτον, εὐκόλως, ἣν ἐδέξαντο χ. ἀπωθουμένοις Bas.*Spir.*61(3.51E; M.32.180D); εἰ δύναται πεσεῖν ἄνθρωπος ἔχων χ.; ἐὰν ἀμελήσῃ, πίπτει...πολλὴ γάρ σοι ζημία γίγνεται ἀμελοῦντι, εἰ καὶ ἐν αὐτῷ τῷ μυστηρίῳ τῆς χ. δοκεῖς ἐξετάζεσθαι Mac.Aeg.*hom.*15.16(M.34.585C); οὐχ ὅτι ὁ θεὸς τρεπτός ἐστι...ἀλλ' αὐτοὶ οἱ ἄνθρωποι οὐ συμφωνοῦσι τῇ χ.· διὰ τοῦτο ἐκτρέπονται *ib.*15.36(600D); ἐκπίπτουσι δὲ τῆς χ. ἀπὸ δύο πραγμάτων· ἢ ὅτι τὰς ἐπιφερομένας θλίψεις οὐχ ὑπομένουσιν· ἢ ὅτι εἰς τὰς ἡδονὰς τῆς ἁμαρτίας ἐνηδυνθεῖσαι ἀπέμειναν *ib.*42.2(769D); **c.** but restored by penitence ἡ μὲν χ. ἀμεταμέλητος διαμένει τοῖς βουλομένοις, κἂν τις ἐκπεσὼν μετανοῇ Ath.*Ar.*3.25(M.26.376B); Mac.Aeg.*hom.*15.16(M.34.585C); **5.** grace and free will: **a.** grace does not exclude free will οὐκ ἠδύναντο ἁμαρτάνειν οἱ ἀπόστολοι, εἰ ἤθελον, ἢ καὶ αὐτοῦ τοῦ θελήματος ἰσχυροτέρα ἦν ἡ χ.;...οὐ λέγομεν, ὅτι ἡ χ. ἐν αὐτοῖς ἠσθένει, ἀλλὰ λέγομεν, ὅτι παραχωρεῖ ἡ χ. καὶ τοῖς τελείοις πνευματικοῖς ἔχειν τὰ θελήματα...καὶ τρέπεσθαι ὅπου βούλονται Mac.Aeg.*hom.*27.11(M.34.700D–701A); ὁρᾷς, ὅτι μετὰ τῆς χ. τοῦ θεοῦ καὶ τὰ παρ' ἑαυτῶν εἰσέφερον; πανταχοῦ γὰρ τοῦτο χρὴ παρατηρεῖν, ὅτι μετὰ τῆς χ. τοῦ θεοῦ καὶ τὰ παρ' ἑαυτῶν ἐπιδεικνύουσι Chrys.*hom.11.1 in Ac.*(9.90B); *ib.13.2*(106A); χ. ἄνωθεν δεδομένη. οὐ μὴν ἐπειδὴ δωρεά, διὰ τοῦτο τὸ αὐτεξούσιον ἀνῄρηται id.*hom.45.1 in Mt.*(7.476); id.*hom.18.2 in Rom.*(9.633C); nor the reward due to good works, *ib. 2.3*(440A); but cf. Marc.Er.*opusc.*2.2(M.65.929C); **b.** view that grace depends on human effort οὔτε ἡ τοῦ πνεύματος χ. τὴν ἡμετέραν προφθάνει προαίρεσιν Chrys.*hom.1.5 in 2Cor.4:13*(3.264C); id.*hom. 15.3 in Ac.*(9.123D); cf.id.*hom.19.5 in Mt.*(7.251C); modified by divine foreknowledge ἡ γὰρ χ. εἰ μὴ τὰ παρ' ἡμῶν πρότερον ἐζήτει, ἀθρόως ἂν εἰς τὰς ἁπάντων ἐξεχύθη ψυχάς...ἐπειδὴ δὲ τὰ παρ' ἡμῶν ζητεῖ, διὰ τοῦτο τοῖς μὲν ἕπεται καὶ παραμένει, τῶν δὲ ἀφίπταται, εἰς δὲ τοὺς λοιποὺς οὐδὲ τὴν ἀρχὴν καθικνεῖται. ὅτι δὲ προαίρεσιν πρότερον ἐξετάσας, οὕτω τὴν χ. ἔδωκεν ὁ θεὸς πρὶν ἤ τι θαυμαστὸν ἐπιδείξασθαι τὸν μακάριον ἐκεῖνον, ἄκουσον τί περὶ αὐτοῦ φησι· σκεῦος ἐκλογῆς μοί ἐστι...ταῦτα οὔπω τῆς χ. παρούσης ἐμαρτύρησεν ὁ τὰς καρδίας ἐμβατεύων ἡμῶν id.*compunct.*1.9(1.137E–138A); **c.** but 'prevenient grace' not excluded καὶ γὰρ τὰ τοῦ νόμου καὶ αὐτὰ χάριτος ἦν, καὶ αὐτὸ τὸ γενέσθαι ἡμᾶς ἐξ οὐκ ὄντων. οὐ γὰρ κατορθωμάτων προϋπηργμένων ταύτην ἐλάβομεν τὴν ἀμοιβήν· πῶς γὰρ οἱ μηδὲ ὄντες; ἀλλὰ θεοῦ πανταχόθεν τῆς εὐεργεσίας κατάρχοντος id.*hom.14.2 in Jo.*(8.81B); id.*hom.9.1 in Gen.*(4.66A); *ib.23.5*(215A); **6.** imparted by evangelism ψυχαὶ ἐλλαμφθεῖσαι παρὰ τοῦ πνεύματος...εἰς ἑτέρους τὴν χ. ἐξαποστέλλουσιν Bas.*Spir.*23(3.20C; M.32.109B); Mac.Aeg.*hom.*17.8(M.34.629A); εἰ μὴ μεταδοίην ἑτέροις τῆς δοθείσης μοι χ., λόγον ὑφέξω ἐν ἡμέρᾳ κρίσεως Nil.*epp.*2.30(M.79.212C); Ἐφραὶμ...τῇ Σύρων κεχρημένος φωνῇ τῆς...χ. τὰς ἀκτῖνας ἠφίει Thdt.*h.e.*4.29.1(3.1008).

C. effects; **1.** purification from sin and salvation οἵτινες, ἐν... πάσῃ ῥυπαρᾷ πράξει ὑπάρχοντες, διὰ τῆς παρὰ τοῦ...Ἰησοῦ...χ. τὰ ῥυπαρὰ πάντα...κακὰ ἀπεδυσάμεθα Just.*dial.*116.1(M.6.744B); ἐκ τοῦ κατὰ χ. τὴν ἀπὸ τοῦ κυρίου...περιλειφθέντος εἰς τὴν αἰώνιον σωτηρίαν *ib.*32.2(544B); ὁ ἄνθρωπος...δεξάμενος τὴν χ. τοῦ πνεύματος...καὶ τὴν χ. μὴ ἐνυβρίζων δι' ἀμελείας...δυνήσεται τῆς αἰωνίου ζωῆς ἐπιτυχεῖν Mac.Aeg.*hom.*24.6(M.34.665C); freeing soul from devil, *ib.*17.3(625B); τί ἐστιν ἡ χ....; ἡ ἄφεσις τῶν ἁμαρτιῶν, ἡ κάθαρσις Chrys.*hom. 34.2 in Heb.*(12.316A); ἡ χ. σώζει id.*hom.45.1 in Ac.*(9.337C); οὐκ ἔστι μισθὸς ἔργων ἡ βασιλεία τῶν οὐρανῶν, ἀλλὰ χ. δεσπότου Marc.Er. *opusc.*2.2(M.65.929C); χρὴ πρῶτον ἐν τῇ καρδίᾳ ἔχειν τὴν χ. ... καὶ οὕτω κατ' ἀναλογίαν εἰσελθεῖν εἰς τὴν βασιλείαν τῶν οὐρανῶν *ib.*2.137(952A); *ib.*2.135(949D); νικᾷ γὰρ ἡ χ. δικαιοῦσα τὸν ἀσεβῆ, καὶ μώμου παντὸς ἀπαλλάττουσα τοὺς ἠλεημένους Cyr.*Is.*5.2(2.759D); ref. Rom. 7:23 δεῖξαι [sc. S. Paul] τίνες μὲν πρὸ τῆς χ. ἦμεν, τίνες δὲ μετὰ τὴν χ. γεγόναμεν· καὶ οἱόν τι προσωπεῖον τῶν πρὸ τῆς χ. ὑπὸ τῆς ἁμαρτίας πολιορκηθέντων ἀναλαβών...δείκνυσι δὲ τὸν νόμον ἐπικουρῆσαι μὴ δυνάμενον Thdt.*Rom.*7:23(3.79); **2.** sonship ὧν ἐστι ποιητής, τούτων καὶ πατὴρ κατὰ χ. ὕστερον γίνεται...ἵνα γινώσκωσιν, ὅτι ἐξ ἀρχῆς μέν εἰσι κτίσματα, ὅταν δὲ κατὰ χ. λέγωνται γεννᾶσθαι, ὡς υἱοί, ἀλλ' οὐδὲν ἧττόν εἰσι πάλιν οἱ ἄνθρωποι ποιήματα κατὰ φύσιν Ath.*Ar.*2.59(M.26.273A,C); κατὰ χ. ἔχοντες τὸ υἱοὶ εἶναι θεοῦ διὰ τὴν τοῦ πνεύματος... μετουσίαν, κατὰ χ. ἔχομεν τὸ ἡγεμονικὸν ἐν τῇ κτίσει Apoll.*Rom.* 8:20(p.66.4f.); cf.Mac.Aeg.*hom.*2.5(M.34.468A); ἀντὶ δούλων ἐλευθέρους, ἀντὶ νηπίων τελείους, ἀντὶ ἀλλοτρίων κληρονόμους ἐποίησε καὶ υἱοὺς ἡ χ. Chrys.*comm.in Gal.*4:6f.(10.705C); **3.** virtues in gen. φεύγοντες...βδελυκτὰς ἐπιθυμίας...κολληθῶμεν οὖν ἐκείνοις, οἷς ἡ χ. ἀπὸ τοῦ θεοῦ δέδοται· ἐνδυσώμεθα τὴν ὁμόνοιαν ταπεινοφρονοῦντες *1Clem.*30.3; πιστεύω γὰρ τῇ χ., ὅτι ἕτοιμοί ἐστε εἰς εὐποιΐαν θεῷ ἀνήκουσαν Ign.*Polyc.*7.3; αἰσθάνεσθαι ὀφείλει τῆς χ. ... ἐν ταῖς ἀρεταῖς Mac.Aeg.*hom.*24.6(M.34.665D); *ib.*44.9(785B); ἡ χ., ταῖς καρδίαις τῶν πιστῶν ἀτρέπτως ἐπιβάλλουσα, ἁρμοζούσας ταῖς ἀρεταῖς τὰς ἐνεργείας χαρίζεται· τῷ διὰ Χριστὸν πεινῶντι γίνεται τροφή Marc.Er.*opusc.*2.109(M.65.945B); esp. humility ἡ χ. διδάσκει αὐτὸν εἶναι πτωχὸν τῷ πνεύματι Mac.Aeg.*hom.*12.3(M.34.557D); *ib.*16.12(621B); οὐκ ἔστι συνειδήσεως κατάγνωσις ἡ ταπεινοφροσύνη, ἀλλὰ χ. θεοῦ Marc.Er.*opusc.*2.103(M.65.945A); proof of its presence, Mac.Aeg.*hom.*15.37(601A); **4.** victory over nature πολλαὶ γυναῖκες ἐνδυναμωθεῖσαι διὰ τῆς χ. τοῦ θεοῦ ἐπετελέσαντο πολλὰ ἀνδρεῖα *1Clem.*55.3; τὰ διὰ τὸ εἶναι μέγιστα καὶ ὑπὲρ ἄνθρωπον τυγχάνειν...ἀδύνατα τῷ λογικῷ καὶ θνητῷ γένει καταλαβεῖν ἐν πολλῇ...ἐκχεομένῃ ἀπὸ θεοῦ εἰς ἀνθρώπους χ. θεοῦ διὰ τοῦ τῆς...χ. ὑπηρέτου...Χριστοῦ καὶ τοῦ συνεργοῦ πνεύματος βουλήσει θεοῦ δυνατὰ γίνεται Or.*or.*1(p.297.4f.; M.11.416A); τὴν γὰρ ἀπὸ τῆς φύσεως συμπάθειαν μεσιτεύουσα ἡ χ. ἐνίκησε Chrys.*Anna* 3.2(4.724C); συμπαρῆν αὐτῷ [sc. Joseph]...χ., καὶ αὐτὴ αὐτῷ πάντα τὰ δυσχερῆ ἐξευμάριζεν id.*hom.62.3 in Gen.*(4.595A); making men invincible, *ib.4.2*(23D); strengthening martyrs, id.*pan.Macc.*1.1(2.624A); removing fear, id.*hom.1.1 in 1Cor.*(10.5C); **5.** summaries χ. ... παρέχουσα νοῦν, φανεροῦσα μυστήρια, διαγγέλλουσα καιρούς, χαίρουσα ἐπὶ πιστοῖς, ἐπιζητοῦσι δωρουμένη ‡*Diogn.*11.5; ἡ μὲν χ. ἀδιαλείπτως σύνεστι καὶ ἐρρίζωται,...καὶ ὡς φυσικὸν καὶ πηκτὸν ἐγένετο, αὐτὸ τὸ συνὸν τῷ ἀνθρώπῳ ὡς μία οὐσία· πολυτρόπως δέ, ὡς θέλει πρὸς τὸ συμφέρον, οἰκονομεῖ τὸν ἄνθρωπον...καὶ αὐτὴ ἡ λαμπὰς πάντοτε καιομένη...ὅταν φαιδρυνθῇ πλέον ἐν μέθῃ ἐξάπτεται τῆς ἀγάπης τοῦ θεοῦ Mac.Aeg.*hom.*8.2(M.34.528D); οὐ γὰρ ὅσον ἐχρῄζομεν εἰς τὴν τῆς ἁμαρτίας ἀναίρεσιν, τοσοῦτον ἐλάβομεν μόνον ἐκ τῆς χ., ἀλλὰ καὶ πολλῷ πλέον...κολάσεως ἀπηλλάγημεν, καὶ κακίαν ἀπεδυσάμεθα πᾶσαν, καὶ ἀνεγεννήθημεν ἄνωθεν, καὶ ἀπελυτρώθημεν, καὶ ἡγιάσθημεν, καὶ εἰς υἱοθεσίαν ἤχθημεν...καὶ ἐγενόμεθα ἀδελφοὶ τοῦ μονογενοῦς, καὶ εἰς τὴν σάρκα αὐτοῦ τελοῦμεν, καὶ ὥσπερ σῶμα κεφαλῇ, οὕτως ἡνώμεθα. ταῦτα οὖν ἅπαντα περισσείαν χ. ἐκάλεσεν ὁ Παῦλος Chrys.*hom.10.2 in Rom.*(9.522B); τοιαύτη γὰρ ἡ χ. ἐκείνη·

κἂν ἀθυμίαν εὕρῃ, διαλύει, κἂν ἐπιθυμίαν πονηράν, δαπανᾷ, κἂν δειλίαν, ἐκβάλλει, καὶ οὐκ ἀφίησι λοιπὸν ἄνθρωπον εἶναι τὸν μετασχόντα αὐτοῦ, ἀλλ' ὥσπερ εἰς αὐτὸν μεταστάντα τὸν οὐρανόν, πάντα τὰ ἐκεῖ φαντάζεσθαι παρασκευάζει id.*hom.75.5 in Jo.*(8.445A); id.*hom.44.1 in Gen.*(4.448A); grace as clothing of soul, Ign.*Polyc.*1.2.

D. in myst. life; **1.** bringing about myst. experience *οὐ χάριτος ἄνευ τῆς ἐξαιρέτου...ἄνω τῶν ὑπερκειμένων αἴρεται ἡ ψυχή* Clem.*str.*5.13(p.381.19; M.9.124B); *ἔκδιψος* [sc. *ψυχή*]...*εἰς τὰ τῆς χ. μυστήρια ...καὶ πόθον ἔμπυρον διὰ τῆς χ. ἀεὶ ἐν αὐτῇ πρὸς τὸν οὐράνιον νυμφίον ἀνακινοῦσα* Mac.Aeg.*hom.*10.4(M.34.544A); *κατὰ βάθος ἐνεργουμένη χ. βαστάζει τὸν νοῦν, καὶ ἀναφέρει εἰς τοὺς οὐρανούς...εἰς τὴν αἰώνιον κατάπαυσιν* *ib.*16.12(621C); *ib.*18.7(640B); knowledge of God *λείπεται δὴ θεία χ. ... τὸ ἄγνωστον νοεῖν* Clem.*str.*5.12(p.381.7; M.9.124A); Or.*Cels.*6.13(p.83.11; M.11.1309B); *ib.*7.44(p.195.1; 1484C); *ψυχῇ τῇ διὰ τῆς χ. ἐπιγινωσκούσῃ τὸν θεόν* Mac.Aeg.*hom.*15.4(577C); liberation from passions, *ib.*9.7(536C); *ib.*9.13(540D); *ἡ ψυχὴ δύναται διὰ τῆς χ. ἀξιωθῆναι τῆς ἀπαθείας* Philox.*ep.*37(p.184); spiritual consolation *ἔχουσαι παράκλησιν τῆς χ. ἐν ἀναπαύσει, καὶ πόθῳ, καὶ γλυκύτητι πνευματικῇ* Mac.Aeg.*hom.*10.3(541C); and enlightenment *τῶν ἰδίων πτερύγων* [i.e. which man had before Fall] *ἐγυμνώθημεν· διὰ τοῦτο ἐπεφάνη ἡ τοῦ θεοῦ χ. φωτίζουσα ἡμᾶς, ἵνα ἀποθέμενοι τὴν ἀσέβειαν...πάλιν δι' ὁσιότητος...πτεροφυήσωμεν* Gr.Nyss.*hom.15 in Cant.*(M.44.1101A); **2.** workings of grace in spiritual life *ἡ τοῦ θεοῦ σοφία...τὰς οἰκονομίας τῆς χ. εἰς τὸ γένος τῆς ἀνθρωπότητος ἐξεργάζεται ποικίλως, πρὸς τὴν τοῦ αὐτεξουσίου θελήματος δοκιμασίαν...οἷς μὲν γὰρ προαπαντῶσι τὰ...δωρήματα...ἄνευ καμάτων...ἔτι δίδωσι τὴν χ. ὁ θεός, οὐκ ἀργῶς...ἀλλὰ σοφίᾳ τινὶ ἀρρήτῳ...εἰς τὸ δοκιμασθῆναι τὴν προαίρεσιν...τῶν ταχέως ἐπιτυχόντων τῆς θείας χ., εἰ ἥσθοντο τῆς εὐεργεσίας...καὶ γλυκύτητος τοῦ θεοῦ, κατὰ ἀναλογίαν τῆς ἄνευ πόνων ἰδίων χ., ἧς καταξιωθέντες ὀφείλουσι...τὸν ἐκ...προαιρέσεως ἀγάπης καρπὸν ἐπιδείξασθαι...οἷς δὲ καὶ ἀναχωρήσασι τοῦ κόσμου...καὶ ἐν πολλῇ προσκαρτερήσει εὐχῆς καὶ νηστείας...τυγχάνουσιν, οὐκ εὐθὺς ὁ θεὸς δίδωσι τὴν χ. ... ἀλλὰ σοφίᾳ τινὶ ἀρρήτῳ εἰς δοκιμασίαν τοῦ αὐτεξουσίου θελήματος* Mac.Aeg.*hom.*29.1,2(M.34.716B–D); *ἡ χ. κρυπτῶς ἐργάζεται ἐν ταῖς καρδίαις τὴν ἑαυτῆς ἀγάπην, καὶ μεταβάλλει ἀπὸ πικρότητος εἰς γλυκύτητα* *ib.*16.7(617C); *ib.*15.20(589A,B); *ἔστιν ὅτε μέλλοντος τοῦ ἀνθρώπου πειρασμῷ...προλαβοῦσα ἡ χ. ... παρηγορεῖ τὴν ψυχήν...ὅταν τοίνυν ὁ ἄνθρωπος...ἐπικρατήσαντος τοῦ πολεμίου, καὶ ἀθυμήσῃ, καὶ ἀπογνῷ ἑαυτοῦ, τότε πάλιν ἡ χ. ἐφίπταται τοῦ θεοῦ, φυγαδεύουσα μὲν τὸν δαίμονα* Nil.*epp.*3.40(M.79.405D); *ἡ χ. τὴν ἀρχὴν ἐν αἰσθήσει πολλῇ τὴν ψυχὴν τῷ οἰκείῳ εἴωθε περιαυγάζειν φωτί· προϊόντων δὲ τῶν ἀγώνων ἀγνώστως τὰ πολλὰ ἐνεργεῖ τῇ θεολόγῳ ψυχῇ τὰ ἑαυτῆς μυστήρια, ἵνα τότε μὲν ἡμᾶς χαίροντας εἰς τὸ ἴχνος ἐπιβάλλοι τῶν θείων θεωρημάτων ὡς ἐξ ἀγνοίας εἰς γνῶσιν καλουμένους, ἐν δὲ τῷ μέσῳ τῶν ἀγώνων ἀκενόδοξον ἡμῶν τὴν γνῶσιν διαφυλάττοι* Diad.*perf.*69(p.84.17); different degrees, Mac.Aeg.*hom.*16.12(622C); *ib.*41.2(768D–769A); **3.** difference between operations of grace and delusions *τὰ τῆς χ. χαρὰν ἔχει, εἰρήνην ἔχει...τὰ δὲ τῆς ἁμαρτίας εἴδη ἐστὶ τεταραγμένα...ἐν...τῇ χ. ἔστιν ὅμοια ἀληθείας, καὶ ἔστιν αὐτὴ ἡ ὑπόστασις τῆς ἀληθείας...οὕτως ἐστί τινα τῆς χ., ὅτε μακρόθεν αὐτοῦ ὡς ὁράσεις τινὰς βλέπει ὁ ἄνθρωπος, καὶ χαίρει εἰς αὐτὰς τὰς ὁράσεις, καὶ ἔστιν ἄλλος, ὅτε εἰσέρχεται εἰς αὐτὸν ἡ δύναμις τοῦ θεοῦ* *ib.*7.3(525A,B); *Παῦλος...εἶπε γὰρ πάσας τὰς θεωρίας ἃς ἡ γλῶσσα ἱκανοὶ δεῖξαι αὐτὰς ἐν τῇ χώρᾳ τῶν σωμάτων, φαντασίαι εἰσὶ τῶν λογισμῶν τῆς ψυχῆς, καὶ οὐχὶ ἐνεργεία τῆς χ.* *Philox.ep.*36(p.184).

E. grace and sin *ἀκμὴν γὰρ οὐδένα εἶδον τέλειον ἄνθρωπον Χριστιανόν...ἀλλ' εἰ καὶ ἀναπαύεταί τις ἐν τῇ χ., καὶ εἰσέρχεται εἰς μυστήρια...καὶ εἰς ἡδύτητα πολλὴν τῆς χ., ὅμως καὶ ἡ ἁμαρτία σύνεστιν ἀκμὴν ἔσω· αὐτοὶ δέ, διὰ τὴν ὑπερβάλλουσαν χ. ... νομίζουσιν ἐλεύθεροι εἶναι καὶ τέλειοι, παρὰ ἀπειρίαν σφαλλόμενοι, ἐπειδὴ ἔχουσιν ἐνέργειαν τῆς χ.* Mac.Aeg.*hom.*8.5(M.34.532B); *πολλοὶ καίτοι συνούσης τῆς χ., κλεπτόμενοι ὑπὸ τῆς ἁμαρτίας οὐκ οἴδασιν* *ib.*15.28(593D); sin coexisting with grace even in case of apostles, *ib.*17.7(628D); but abundance of grace deadens sin, *ib.*16.4(616C); *θεὸς...οὐκ ἀφίησι πάντα ἄνθρωπον ἄνευ τῆς αὐτοῦ χ. οὐ γὰρ μόνον τοῖς δικαίοις δίδωσι χ., ἀλλὰ καὶ τοῖς ἁμαρτωλοῖς...οὐ παρορᾷ τὸν ἁμαρτωλόν, ἀλλὰ δίδωσι κἀκείνῳ μικρὰν χ. ... ἐὰν δὲ καὶ λαβὼν τὴν χ. ἐπιμείνῃ τοῖς αὐτοῖς κακοῖς, τότε λοιπὸν ἀρθήσεται ἀπ' αὐτοῦ καὶ ἣν ἔλαβε χ.* Eus.Al.*serm.*5(M.86.341D–344A).

F. *χ.* and *φύσις*; **1.** deification by grace, ref. Ps.81:6 *μονογενὴς ...ἔχει γὰρ πολλοὺς ἀδελφούς, οὐ φύσει, ἀλλὰ χ.* ‡Ath.*descr.BMV* 9(M.28.957C); *ἡμεῖς ἄνθρωποι κατὰ φύσιν ὑπάρχοντες χάριτι πλουτοῦμεν τὸ καλεῖσθαι θεοί* Cyr.*thes.*32(5^1.313B); Proc.G.*fr.Cant.*6:10(M.87.1757B); *οὐσίας μέν, ὡς ὅταν λέγωσιν* ⟨*ἄνθρωπος*⟩*· σχέσεως δέ, ὡς ὅταν λέγωσιν ἀγαθός...χ. δέ, ὅταν θεὸς ὁ ἄνθρωπος τοῖς λόγοις ὀνομάζηται... οὔτε κατὰ φύσιν οὔτε κατὰ σχέσιν ἔχων τὸ εἶναι ἢ καλεῖσθαι θεός, ἀλλὰ κατὰ...χ. γενόμενος...ἡ γὰρ χ. τῆς θέσεως ἄσχετός ἐστι παντάπασιν, οὐκ ἔχουσα τὴν οἱανοῦν δεκτικὴν ἑαυτῆς ἐν τῇ φύσει δύναμιν, ἐπεὶ οὐκ ἔτι χ. ἐστίν* Max.*ambig.*(M.91.1237A,B); **2.** analogy between divine *φύσις* and *χ.*: *ἑκάστη τῆς ἱεραρχικῆς διακοσμήσεως τάξις, κατὰ τὴν οἰκείαν ἀναλογίαν ἀνάγεται πρὸς τὴν θείαν συνεργείαν, ἐκεῖνα τελοῦσα χάριτι...τὰ τῇ θεαρχίᾳ φυσικῶς...ἐνόντα* Dion.Ar.*c.h.*3.3(M.3.168A); ref. creation in divine image *ἅπερ ἐστὶν ὁ θεὸς τῇ φύσει, ταῦτα κατὰ τὴν αὐτοῦ χ. ἔχειν δυνηθῇ καὶ ὁ ὑπ' αὐτοῦ κτισθεὶς ἄνθρωπος* Gel.Cyz.*h.e.*2.15.8(M.85.1260B); **3.** ref. H. Ghost *τὸ πνεῦμα φυσικὴν ἔχει τὴν ἁγιότητα, οὐ κατὰ χ. λαβών* Bas.*ep.*159.2(3.248C; M.32.621B); **4.** ref. BMV *φύσις μὲν γὰρ τὴν τεκοῦσαν οὐκ οἶδεν οὐκέτι παρθένον, ἡ δὲ χ. καὶ τίκτουσαν ἔδειξε καὶ παρθένον ἐφύλαξε* Thdt.Anc.*hom.*1.1(p.80.35; M.77.1349A); **5.** nature remaining after reception of grace *ἵνα τὸ θέλημα καὶ μετὰ τὴν χ. δοκιμασθῇ, ποῦ ῥέπει...μένει ἐν τῇ ταυτότητι ἡ φύσις, ὁ σκληρὸς ἐν τῇ σκληρότητι, καὶ ὁ κοῦφος ἐν τῇ κουφότητι* Mac.Aeg.*hom.*26.5(M.34.677A); cf.Sever.*1Cor.*6:20(p.249.8).

G. grace contrasted with: works, exeg. Rom.11:6 *δεῖξαι σπουδάζων, ἀσύμβατον ὄντα παντελῶς τὸν νόμον τῇ χ.· καὶ οὐ δυνάμενα κατὰ ταὐτὸν ἀμφότερα ταῦτα, ἀλλὰ ἀναγκαίως ἔχον θατέρῳ θάτερον ὑπεξίστασθαι. ὥστε ἐν χ. ἐκλεγόμεθα, ῥᾴδιον τὸ προσελθεῖν καὶ πιστεῦσαι Χριστῷ...κατὰ χ. γάρ, οὐ δι' ἔργα προσδέχεται, ὥστε εἰ χάριτι καλεῖ καὶ προσδέχεται, οὐκ ἔχομεν εἰς τοῦτο χρείαν ἔργων. ἐπεὶ εἰ χρείαν σχοίημεν ἔργων, οὐκέτι ἡ χ. χ. μένει. ... εἰ γὰρ ἐξ ἔργων προσιέναι δεῖν ἡμᾶς νομίσομεν, δῆλον ὡς ἀνήρηται ἡ χ.· ἐπεὶ εἰ μὴ ἀνήρηται, οὐκέτι οὐδὲ τὸ ἔργον μένει ἔργον· τῆς χ. οὐκ ἐώσης ὅλως ἔργον ὑποστῆναι· ἀλλὰ προῖκα τὴν ἐκλογὴν ἐπιδεικνυμένης. κεχώρισται μὲν γὰρ ἀπ' ἀλλήλων τῇ φύσει χ. καὶ ἔργον· καὶ τῷ μὲν ἔργῳ ἕπεται μισθὸς καὶ οὐ χ.· ἡ δὲ χ. δίδοται, οὐχ ὡς ἀντιμισθία, ἀλλὰ δῶρον* Gennad.*Rom.*11:6(M.85.1716A,B); human achievements in gen. *οὐκ ἐκ συνειδότος, ἀλλ' ἐκ χ. θεοῦ...ἵνα...θεοῦ ἐπιτύχω* Ign.*Smyrn.*11.1; *οἱ γὰρ συγγραφεῖς πάντες διὰ τῆς ἐνούσης ἐμφύτου τοῦ λόγου σπορᾶς ἀμυδρῶς ἐδύναντο ὁρᾶν τὰ ὄντα. ἕτερον γάρ ἐστι σπέρμα τινὸς καὶ μίμημα κατὰ δύναμιν δοθέν, καὶ ἕτερον αὐτὸ οὗ κατὰ χ. τὴν ἀπ' ἐκείνου ἡ μετουσία καὶ μίμησις γίνεται* Just.*2apol.*13.6(M.6.468A); *οὐ γὰρ διὰ τῆς ἔξωθεν φιλοσοφίας...οὐδὲ διὰ τῆς ἔξωθεν παιδεύσεως, ἀλλὰ διὰ τῆς χ. τοῦ θεοῦ* Chrys.*hom.2.1 in 1Cor.*(10.9C); divine judgement *ἢ γὰρ τὴν μέλλουσαν ὀργὴν φοβηθῶμεν, ἢ τὴν ἐνεστῶσαν χ. ἀγαπήσωμεν* Ign.*Eph.*11.1; *ὑπακοὴς ἡ χ. ... παρακοῆς ἡ κρίσις* Clem.*prot.*10(p.69.29; M.8.209A); *ib.*(p.75.3; 220C); *ib.*12(p.86.29; 245B); this world *ἐλθέτω χ. καὶ παρελθέτω ὁ κόσμος οὗτος* *Did.*10.6; and Devil *δεκτικὴ οὖν ἡ φύσις...ἤτοι θείας χ., ἤτοι ἐναντίας δυνάμεως* Mac.Aeg.*hom.*15.25(M.34.592D); *ἡ καρδία ποίου θησαυροῦ μεμέστωται, τῆς χ. ἢ τοῦ σατανᾶ;* *ib.*27.19(708B).

H. grace of Adam before Fall *Ἀδάμ, προλαμβάνων τὴν χ. καὶ ἅμα τῷ γενέσθαι τεθεὶς ἐν τῷ παραδείσῳ* Ath.*decr.*6(p.6.18; M.25.428A); id.*Ar.*2.68(M.26.292C); *ἐπειδὴ δὲ διὰ τὴν παράβασιν ἐκολάζετο... ἀπεγυμνώθη τῆς χ.* Cyr.*Jo.*1.9(4.95A); restored by Christ, Bas.*Spir.*39(3.34A; M.32.140D); Gr.Nyss.*Eun.*4(2 p.63.25; M.45.636A); fully recovered in myst. life *ὁ ἄνθρωπος, δι' ἀπαθείας...τὴν ἀρχέτυπον χ. ἀπομιμούμενος* id.*mort.*(M.46.521D); id.*hom.15 in Cant.*(M.44.1101B); cf.id.*hom.opif.*30(M.44.256C).

I. praise of grace *οὐδὲν τῆς χ. πλουσιώτερον* Gr.Naz.*or.*32.25(M.36.201C); *τοιαύτη γὰρ ἡ τοῦ θεοῦ χ.· οὐκ ἔχει τέλος, οὐκ οἶδε πέρας ἀλλὰ κ ι ἐπὶ μείζονα ἀεὶ πρόεισιν* Chrys.*hom.9.2 in Rom.*(9.512E); Max.*carit.*4.77(M.90.1068A,B).

III. special manifestations of grace; **A.** in eccl. offices, etc., sts. almost equated with office itself *λάβῃς τὴν τῆς ἐπισκοπῆς χ.* Ath.*ep.Drac.*2(M.25.525B); in prayer said at consecration of bishop, Serap.*euch.*28.1; *Lit.*ap.*Const.App.*8.5.3; *Κύριλλος τῆς ἐπισκοπικῆς χ. ἠξιώθη* Thdt.*h.e.*2.26.6(3.893); *ib.*2.30.3(905); cf. *ὁ...ἱεροτελεστὴς...οὐκ αὐτὸς ἰδίᾳ χ. τοὺς τελουμένους ἐπὶ τὴν ἱερατικὴν ἄγων τελείωσιν, ἀλλ' ὑπὸ θεοῦ κινούμενος* Dion.Ar.*e.h.*5.3.5(M.3.512B); priesthood *ἱερατικὴ χ.* Gr.Nyss.*ep.can.*5(M.45.232C); id.*Eun.*6(2 p.133.17; M.45.717B); lost by schism, Bas.*ep.*188 *can.*1(3.270A,B; M.32.669A); monks *τελεστικὴν αὐτοῖς ἐδωρήσατο χ., ἡ ἱερὰ θεσμοθεσία* Dion.Ar.*e.h.*6.1.3(533A).

B. prophecy *προφητῶν χ. γινώσκεται* ‡*Diogn.*11.6; *χ. προφητικὴ* Or.*Jo.*1.30(33; p.37.14; M.14.77D); Ath.*ep.Drac.*5(M.25.529A); Gr.Naz.*or.*2.109(M.35.508B); Chrys.*David* 2.1(4.761A); Cyr.*Ps.*36:25(M.69.941A).

C. miracles *οὐχ ὁμοία δύναμις ἡ τῶν ἐν Αἰγύπτῳ ἐπαοιδῶν τῇ ἐν τῷ Μωϋσεῖ παραδόξῳ χ.* Or.*Cels.*2.50(p.173.12; M.11.876C); *οὐκ ἰδίᾳ δυνάμει ποιεῖν τὰ σημεῖα, ἀλλὰ τῇ τοῦ κυρίου χ.* Ath.*Ar.*3.2(M.26.325C); *ὅ τε γὰρ βίον ἄριστον ἐπιδεικνύμενος, ἐπισπᾶται ταύτην τὴν χ.* [sc. of miracles]*· ὅ τε λαμβάνων τὴν χ., διὰ τοῦτο λαμβάνει, ἵνα τὸν ἑτέρων διορθώσηται βίον* Chrys.*hom.46.3 in Mt.*(7.485C); ‡Pall.*h.mon.*10(p.53.18; M.34.1154C); cf.*Const.App.*8.26.2.

D. teaching and preaching, ‡*Diogn.*11.7; Or.*Cels.*6.2(p.72.2; M.11.1289D); Ath.*v.Anton.*14(M.26.865A); Chrys.*hom.*5.3 *in* 1*Cor.*(10.37D); ‡Pall.*h.mon.*21(p.81.15; M.34.1172A).

E. martyrdom *παρεστὼς ὁ κύριος ὡμίλει αὐτοῖς* [sc. martyrs]. *καὶ προσέχοντες τῇ τοῦ Χριστοῦ χ. τῶν κοσμικῶν κατεφρόνουν βασάνων* *M.Polyc.*2.3; Or.*mart.*2(p.4.16; M.11.565B).

F. scriptures; **1.** as inspired *ὅσοι τοῦ θεοῦ λόγοι παρὰ τοῦ Μωϋσέως ἢ τῶν προφητῶν ἐγράφησαν, ἐνδείξεις εἰσὶ τοῦ θείου θελήματος ἄλλως καὶ ἄλλως κατὰ τὴν ἀξίαν τῶν μετεχόντων τῆς χ. τῷ...ἡγεμονικῷ τῶν ἁγίων ἐλλάμπουσαι* Gr.Nyss.*Eun.*12(1 p.289.16; M.45.997D); **2.** as understood *χ. παρὰ θεοῦ μόνη εἰς τὸ συνιέναι τὰς γραφὰς αὐτοῦ ἐδόθη μοι, ἧς χ. καὶ πάντας κοινωνοὺς...παρακαλῶ γίνεσθαι* Just.*dial.*58.1(M.6.608A); *οἴεσθε ἄν ἡμᾶς ποτε...νενοηκέναι δυνηθῆναι ἐν ταῖς γραφαῖς ταῦτα, εἰ μὴ θελήματι τοῦ θελήσαντος αὐτὰ ἐλάβομεν χ. τοῦ νοῆσαι*; *ib.*119.1(752A); Cosm.Ind.*top.*proem.1(M.88.53C).

G. other partic. manifestations of grace: *γνῶσις* opp. *ζήτησις*, Clem.*str.*5.11(p.374.23; M.9.109B); Dion.Ar.*c.h.*4.4(M.3.181B); discernment of spirits, Ath.*ep.Aeg.Lib.*1(M.25.540B); *ib.*4(548A); id. *v.Anton.*44(M.26.908A); prolonged prayer, *M.Polyc.*7.3; Mac.Aeg. *hom.*19.4(M.34.645A); faith, Clem.*str.*1.7(p.25.16; M.8.733A); cf.*ib.*2.4 (p.120.6; 945A); Ath.*ep.mon.*(M.26.1188A); id.*ep.Adelph.*1(M.26.1072A); continence and virginity *ἐγκράτεια...θεία χ.* Clem.*str.*3.1 (p.197.9; M.8.1104B); *ib.*3.7(p.223.18ff.; 1161A); Gr.Nyss.*virg.*1(p.251.16; M.46.320C); fasting, Bas.*hom.*1.1(2.1A; M.31.164A); repentance, 1*Clem.*7.4; exorcism, Ath.*v.Anton.*30(M.26.889A); *ib.*38(900A).

IV. Christol.; **A.** Arian *οὐ γάρ ἐστι τοῦ πατρὸς ἴδιον καὶ φύσει γέννημα ὁ λόγος, ἀλλὰ καὶ αὐτὸς χ. γέγονεν* Ar.*Thal.fr.*4 ap.Ath.*Ar.*1.5(M.26.21B); *κατὰ χ. λόγον καὶ υἱὸν αὐτόν* Ar.*Thal.fr.*7; *οὐδὲ θεὸς ἀληθινός ἐστιν ὁ λόγος...ἀλλὰ μετοχῇ χ., ὥσπερ καὶ οἱ ἄλλοι πάντες* Ar. *Thal.fr.*10 ap.eund.1.6(21D); orthodox rejection *οὐχ ὁ λόγος τοῦ θεοῦ κατὰ χ. ἔλαβε τὸ καλεῖσθαι θεός* Ath.*inc.et c.Ar.*3(M.26.989A); *αὐτὸς οὖν κατὰ φύσιν υἱός ἐστι τοῦ θεοῦ, ἡμεῖς δὲ κατὰ χ. καὶ πάλιν αὐτὸς κατ' οἰκονομίαν καὶ χ. ἡμετέραν υἱὸς γέγονε τοῦ Ἀδάμ, ἡμεῖς δὲ κατὰ φύσιν ἐσμὲν υἱοὶ τοῦ Ἀδάμ...πατὴρ γὰρ αὐτοῦ ἐστιν ὁ θεός...κατὰ φύσιν, ἡμῶν δὲ κατὰ χ.* *ib.*8(996B,C); id.*Ar.*1.38(M.26.89B); *ποίαν δὲ καὶ χ. ἔλαβεν ὁ τῆς χ. δοτήρ*; *ib.*1.40(96A); Gr.Naz.*or.*30.9(p.121.5; M.36.113C) cit. s. *ἐπίκτητος*.

B. Diodore's view *χάριτι υἱὸς ὁ ἐκ Μαρίας ἄνθρωπος, φύσει δὲ ὁ θεὸς λόγος· τὸ μὲν χ. καὶ οὐ φύσει, τὸ δὲ φύσει καὶ οὐ χ.· ἀρκέσει τῷ ἐξ ἡμῶν σώματι, τὸ τῆς κατὰ χ. υἱότητος...ὅτι ναὸς τοῦ θεοῦ λόγου γέγονεν* Diod.*synous.*(M.33.1560C).

C. Thdr. Mops. *τοῖς λοιποῖς τοῖς μετεσχηκόσιν τῆς υἱότητος ἐλέγχεται, ἐπείπερ χάριτι καὶ αὐτὸς μετέσχηκεν τῆς υἱότητος...ἔχων μέντοι παρὰ τοὺς λοιποὺς τὴν ὑπεροχήν, ὅτι τῇ πρὸς αὐτὸν ἑνώσει κέκτηται τὴν υἱότητα· ὃ δὴ κυριότερον αὐτῷ τοῦ πράγματος χαρίζεται τὴν μετουσίαν* Thdr.Mops.*fr.inc.*12(p.306.1; M.66.988A).

D. later statements of orthodox position opp. Arius and Nestorius *οὐ μερικὴν αὐτῷ* [sc. Christ] *τὴν χ. εἰργάζετο, καθάπερ ἐν τοῖς ἁγίοις...ἀλλ' ἦν πλήρωμα τῆς θεότητος* Cyr.*Is.*2.1(2.194B); id.*thes.*3 (5^1.25A); *μόνος...ὁ κύριος κυρίως Χριστός, ὡς ὅλος διόλου καὶ οὐ χ.* ‡Cyr.*Trin.*22(6^3.28B; M.77.1164A); Leont.H.*Nest.*3.8(M.86.1632B,C); *οὐ γάρ ἐστι καὶ χ. υἱὸς ὁ ἅπαξ τὴν τοῦ φύσει υἱοῦ φύσιν ἔχων* id. *monoph.*(M.86.1876B).

V. Gnost.; **1.** sacramental (Marcosian) *δοκεῖν τὴν ἀπὸ τῶν ὑπὲρ τὰ ὅλα χ. τὸ αἷμα τὸ ἑαυτῆς στάζειν ἐν τῷ ἐκείνῳ ποτηρίῳ...ἵνα καὶ εἰς αὐτοὺς ἐπομβρήσῃ ἡ διὰ τοῦ μάγου τούτου κληϊζομένη χ.* Iren.*haer.*1.13.2(M.7.580A); *δοκεῖν τοὺς ἀπατωμένους χ. τινὰ κατιέναι καὶ αἱματώδη δύναμιν παρέχειν τῷ πόματι* Hipp.*haer.*6.39(p.171.3; M.16.3258A); *ib.* 6.40(p.171.16; 3258C); **2.** as aeon, Iren.*haer.*1.1.1(M.7.445A).

VI. grace as supernatural beauty in face of martyr, *M.Polyc.*12.1; *ἀεὶ τὸν θεὸν ἐννοουμένη* [sc. *ψυχή*]...*ἀγγελικῇ τὸν ἄνθρωπον ἐξισάζει χ.* Clem.*paed.*2.9(p.207.28; M.8.496C); cf.id.*prot.*11(p.83.5; M.8.237B); Ath.*v.Anton.*67(M.26.940A); Chrys.*hom.*1.3 *in Eph.*(11.6D).

VII. as designation of BMV *ζωητόκος χ. ... παρθένος* Meth. *symp.*11(p.135.23; M.18.212C).

χάρισμα, τό, *favour*, *gift*, esp. spiritual gift;

A. sources; **1.** divine; **a.** God *πᾶσι γὰρ θέλει δίδοσθαι ὁ πατὴρ ἐκ τῶν ἰδίων χ.* *Did.*1.5; *οὐ δύναται ἄνθρωπος ἔχειν τι χ. θεῖον, ἐὰν μὴ ᾖ δοθὲν αὐτῷ ἐκ τοῦ οὐρανοῦ. δίδοται δὲ τὰ ἐκ θεοῦ χ. τοῖς πίστει καὶ ἀρετῇ πρὸς τὸ λαβεῖν αὐτὰ παρεσκευασμένοις* Or.*fr.*44 *in Jo.*(p.519.6ff.); *περὶ τῶν χ., ὅσαπερ ὁ θεὸς κατ' ἰδίαν βούλησιν πάρεσχεν ἀνθρώποις* *Const.App.*8.3.1; **b.** Christ *ἄμπελος...ἐκ τῶν μαθημάτων τοὺς βότρυς...ἀπαιωροῦσα τῶν χ. καταστάζοντας ἀγάπην, ὁ κύριος ἡμῶν ἐστιν Ἰησοῦς* Meth.*symp.*5.5(p.59.5; M.18.105B); Ath.*ep.Aeg.Lib.*1 (M.25.540A); **c.** H. Ghost *καὶ παρ' ἡμῖν ἔστιν ἰδεῖν καὶ θηλείας καὶ ἄρσενας, χαρίσματα ἀπὸ τοῦ πνεύματος τοῦ θεοῦ ἔχοντας* Just.*dial.*88.1(M.6.685A); *A.Thom.*A 52(p.168.20); Cyr.H.*catech.*16.22; Gr.Nyss.*Eun.*3(2 p.20.19; M.45.585A); Philox.*ep.*27(p.177); **d.** Trin., ref. 1Cor.12:4ff. *οἶμαι δὲ τὸ ἅγιον πνεῦμα τήν, ἵν' οὕτως εἴπω, ὕλην τῶν ἀπὸ θεοῦ χ. παρέχειν τοῖς δι' αὐτὸ καὶ τὴν μετοχὴν αὐτοῦ χρηματίζουσιν ἁγίοις, τῆς εἰρημένης ὕλης τῶν χ. ἐνεργουμένης μὲν ἀπὸ τοῦ θεοῦ, διακονουμένης δὲ ὑπὸ τοῦ Χριστοῦ, ὑφεστώσης δὲ κατὰ τὸ ἅγιον πνεῦμα* Or.*Jo.*2.10(6; p.65.27; M.14.129A); Ath.*ep.Serap.*1 (M.26.600B); *ib.*3(633A); Chrys.*hom.*86.3 *in Jo.*(8.517C); **e.** grace of baptism *τὸ διὰ τοῦ ὕδατος λουτρόν...καθ' αὐτὸ τῷ ἐμπαρέχοντι ἑαυτὸν τῇ θειότητι τῆς δυνάμεως τῶν τῆς...τριάδος ἐπικλήσεών ἐστιν ἡ χ. θείων ἀρχὴ καὶ πηγή* Or.*Jo.*6.33(17; p.143.1; M.14.257A); *ἐν αὐτῇ* [sc. *κολυμβήθρᾳ*]...*πάντα ὑποδεχόμεθα τῆς διαμονῆς τὰ χ.* Didym.*Trin.*2.13(M.39.692A); conferring *υἱοθεσίας χ.*, Cyr.H.*procatech.*16; *Rit. Bapt.*(p.401); **2.** human; charity *ἡ γέμουσα...τῶν χ.* Meth.*symp.*9.4 (p.118.31; *χαρίτων* M.18.185C); Ath.*ep.Amun.*(M.26.1173C); *ἀπάθεια*, ‡Pall.*h.mon.*8.15(p.37.3; M.34.1139A).

B. H. Ghost as *χ.*: *ἀνεπυρώθησαν τῷ πνεύματι...ἀνεκαίετο ἐν αὐτοῖς τὸ χ.* Chrys.*hom.*11.1 *in Ac.*(9.90B); ref. Rom.8:23 *ἐντυγχάνειν δὲ τὸ πνεῦμα τὸ χ. λέγει* Thdr.Mops.*Rom.*8:27(p.141.14; M.66.829C); ref. 1Cor.5:5 *ἵνα σωθῇ τὸ ἐν αὐτῷ πνεῦμα ὅπερ ἐστὶ τὸ χ.* Sever.1*Cor.*5:1–5(p.244.8); *πνεῦμα δὲ ἐνταῦθα οὐ τὴν ψυχὴν καλεῖ, ἀλλὰ τὸ χ.* Thdt.1*Cor.*5:4f.(3.193); ref. 1Cor.6:19–20 *δοξάσατε οὖν τὸν θεὸν μὴ μόνον ἐν τῷ χ. ἀλλὰ καὶ ἐν τῷ σώματι, ἵνα καὶ φύσις καὶ προαίρεσις καὶ χ. δοξάσῃ τὸν θεόν* Sever.1*Cor.*6:20(p.249.7f.).

C. baptism as *χ.*: *καλεῖται...τὸ ἔργον τοῦτο, χ. ... χ. δὲ ᾧ τὰ ἐπὶ τοῖς ἁμαρτήμασιν ἐπιτίμια ἀνεῖται...τί γὰρ ἔτι λείπεται τῷ θεὸν ἐγνωκότι; καὶ γὰρ ἄτοπον ὡς ἀληθῶς χ. κεκλῆσθαι θεοῦ τὸ μὴ πεπληρωμένον· τέλειος δὲ ὢν τέλεια χαριεῖται δήπουθεν* Clem.*paed.*1.6(p.105.23ff.; M.8.281A); in Gnost. baptismal invocation *ἐλθὲ τὸ χ. τὸ ὕψιστον* *A.Thom.*A 27(p.142.15); *δέξωμαι τὸ χ. τὸ τοῖς συγγενεῦσί μου δεδωρημένον* *ib.*43(p.161.10); *A.Xanthipp.*14(p.67.10); Gr.Naz.*or.*39.14(M.36.352A); *ib.*40.4(361C–364A); Gr.Nyss.*Maced.*19(M.45.1325B).

D. other sacramental usage; eucharist *τοῦτο γὰρ τὸ χ. ... προσιόντας ἰᾶται* *A.Thom.*A 51(p.167.11); chrism called *Χριστοῦ χ.*, Cyr.H. *catech.*21.3; priesthood, Epiph.*haer.*48.9(p.231.13; M.41.868D).

E. *χαρίσματα* as endowment of Church *ἐκκλησίᾳ...ἠλεημένῃ ἐν παντὶ χ. ... ἀνυστερήτῳ οὔσῃ παντὸς χ.* Ign.*Smyrn.*proem.; *οὐκ ἔστιν ἀριθμὸν εἰπεῖν τῶν χ., ὧν κατὰ παντὸς τοῦ κόσμου ἡ ἐκκλησία παρὰ θεοῦ λαβοῦσα...ἑκάστης ἡμέρας ἐπ' εὐεργεσίᾳ τῇ τῶν ἐθνῶν ἐπιτελεῖ* Iren.*haer.*3.32.4(M.7.829C); through episcopal office, cf. (ref. episcopate as guardian of Church's doctrinal tradition) *eis qui in ecclesia sunt, presbyteris obaudire oportet;...qui cum episcopatus successione charisma veritatis certum, secundum placitum Patris acceperunt,* Iren.*haer.*4.26.2(M.7.1053C); *διὰ τῆς ἐπιθέσεως τῶν χειρῶν ...εἶχον τὸ χ. τὸ πνευματικόν* Bas.*ep.*188 *can.*1(3.270A; M.32.669A); *τὸ δὲ ἀπόστολον ἢ ἐπίσκοπον ἢ ἄλλο τι οὐκ ἐφ' ἡμῖν, ἀλλ' ἐπὶ τῷ διδόντι θεῷ τὰ χ. ταῦτα...ἐπὶ τοσοῦτον εἰρήσθω διὰ τοὺς ἀξιωθέντας χ. ἢ ἀξιωμάτων* *Const.App.*8.1.21f.; opp. prophetic *χ.* of Montanists *αἱ περὶ Μοντανὸν διεδέξαντο γυναῖκες τὸ προφητικὸν χ. ... δεῖν γὰρ εἶναι τὸ προφητικὸν χ. ἐν πάσῃ τῇ ἐκκλησίᾳ μέχρι τῆς τελείας παρουσίας ὁ ἀπόστολος ἀξιοῖ* Anon.ap.Eus.*h.e.*5.17.4(M.20.473B); cf.*ib.*5.16.8 (468A); *λέγοντες ὅτι δεῖ ἡμᾶς...καὶ τὰ χ. δέχεσθαι. καὶ ἡ ἁγία... ἐκκλησία ὁμοίως τὰ χ. δέχεται, ἀλλὰ τὰ ὄντως χ. ... εἰ γὰρ δεῖ χ. δέχεσθαι καὶ δεῖ εἶναι ἐν ἐκκλησίᾳ χ., πῶς οὐκέτι μετὰ Μοντανὸν καὶ Πρίσκιλλαν...ἔχουσι προφήτας;* Epiph.*haer.*48.1,2(pp.220.6–221.12; M.41.856B–D); *ib.*48.3(p.223.4; 857D).

F. gifts of grace in gen.; **1.** Christian vocation as such *ὑποτασσέσθω ἕκαστος τῷ πλησίον αὐτοῦ, καθὼς ἐτέθη ἐν τῷ χ. αὐτοῦ* 1*Clem.*38.1; *ἀγνοοῦντες τὸ χ., ὃ πέπομφεν ἀληθῶς ὁ κύριος* Ign.*Eph.*17.2; *οὐκ ἔστιν ἄνθρωπος πιστεύσας διὰ Χριστοῦ εἰς τὸν θεόν, ὃς οὐκ εἴληφεν ⟨χ. πνευματικόν⟩. αὐτό τε γὰρ τὸ ἀπαλλαγῆναι πολυθέου ἀσεβείας καὶ πιστεῦσαι θεῷ πατρὶ διὰ Χριστοῦ χ. ἐστι θεοῦ, τό τε ἀπορρίψαι τὸ ἰουδαϊκὸν κάλυμμα...ὁ ταῦτα* [sc. doctrines of faith] *πιστεύσας...χ. εἴληφε ἐκ θεοῦ* *Const.App.*8.1.9ff.; **2.** diversity of gifts, *ib.*8.1.12; Chrys.*hom.*86.3 *in Jo.*(8.517A); **3.** including: forgiveness of sins, Clem.*paed.*1.2(p.93.24; M.8.256B); Chrys.*serm.*7.3 *in Gen.*(4.679B); chastity, Meth.*symp.*4.2(p.46.14; M.18.88C); *ib.*7.1(p.71.26; 125A); Gr.Nyss.*virg.*1(p.251.20; M.46.320C); almsgiving, Jo.Mosch.*prat.*9 (M.87.2860A); eloquence *A.Xanthipp.*14(p.68.3); **4.** perfection of God's gifts, *A.Thom.*A 25(p.141.7); *ib.*60(p.177.15); *τὸ γὰρ χ. τοῦ θεοῦ ὑπερπαίει τὴν χρείαν* Or.*Jo.*32.9(7; p.441.3; M.14.765A).

G. special gifts (cf. 1Cor.12:4ff.); for faith as a *χ.* v. *πίστις*; **1.** diversity and inequality *ἔστι διαφορὰ χαρισμάτων* Gr.Naz.*or.*41.16(M.36.449C); *προφητείας...τὰ χ. τῶν ἰαμάτων δεύτερα· διὰ τί δὲ καὶ διδασκαλίας; ὅτι οὐκ ἔστιν ἴσον, λόγον καταγγέλλειν κηρύγματος... καὶ δυνάμεις ποιεῖν* Chrys.*hom.*32.1 *in* 1*Cor.*(10.287A); **2.** prophecy *προφητικὰ χ.* Just.*dial.*82.1(M.6.669B); *ὁ Παῦλος εἰπὼν τὰ χ., ἐν οἷς ἐστιν ἡ προφητεία, φησίν· ταῦτα δὲ πάντα ἐνεργεῖ ἓν καὶ τὸ αὐτὸ πνεῦμα…λέγοις δ' ἂν πνεῦμα προσώπου Χριστόν, τὸν δωρησάμενον ἡμῖν τὸ πνεῦμα τῆς προφητείας· αὕτη γὰρ προφητῶν πρόσωπον, πνεῦμα δὲ τὸ χ., σκιὰ δὲ ὁ νόμος…τὸ οὖν χ. τὸ προφητικόν, πρὸς ὃ βλέπει πάσης τῆς προφητείας ἡ ἔκβασις…ἀπὸ Χριστοῦ* Or.*fr.116 in Lam.*(p.277.4ff.; M.13.660B,C); Meth.*symp.*10.2(p.123.23; M.18.196A); Eus.*h.e.*3.37.1(M.20.292D); ref. David, whose prophetic *χ.* was preserved by repentance, Gr.Naz.*or.*39.18(M.36.356C); Montanist, v. supra E; **3.** miracles *φησὶ πᾶσιν ἅμα περὶ τῶν ἐξ αὐτοῦ διὰ τοῦ πνεύματος διδομένων χ.· σημεῖα δὲ τοῖς πιστεύσασιν· ταῦτα παρακολουθήσει…τούτων τῶν χ. πρότερον μὲν ἡμῖν δοθέντων τοῖς ἀποστόλοις …ἔπειτα τοῖς δι' ἡμῶν πιστεύσασιν ἀναγκαίως χορηγουμένων οὐκ εἰς τὴν τῶν ἐνεργούντων ὠφέλειαν, ἀλλ' εἰς τὴν τῶν ἀπίστων συγκατάθεσιν* *Const.App.*8.1.1,2; *ib.*8.1.4; *ib.*8.26.2; **4.** ref. martyrs *Ἀλέξανδρος…ἦν …οὐκ ἄμοιρος ἀποστολικοῦ χ.* *Ep.Lugd.*ap.Eus.*h.e.*5.1.49(M.20.428A); Meth.*fr.mart.*1(p.520.5; M.18.345C); **5.** discernment of spirits, in OT *ἦν χ. διάκρισις πνευμάτων, ἀφ' οὗ χ. ἐκρίνετο ὁ ἀληθὴς προφήτης καὶ ὁ ψευδοπροφήτης* Or.*schol.in Lc.*1:1(M.17.312A); in Church *μέγα τι χ. δέδωκεν ἡμῖν ὁ λόγος, ὥστε μὴ ἐκ τῶν φαινομένων ἀπατᾶσθαι, ἀλλὰ…κἂν ταῦτα κεκαλυμμένα τυγχάνῃ, διακρίνειν* Ath.*ep.Aeg.Lib.* 1(M.25.540B); *ib.*4(548A); id.*v.Anton.*22(M.26.876B); Gr.Naz.*or.*41.16 (M.36.449C); **6.** knowledge of invisible things otherwise than by faith, Ign.*Polyc.*2.2; private revelations in gen., Ath.*v.Anton.*66(M. 26.936C); cf.*ib.*67(940A); **7.** gift of tears, Ath.*virg.*17(M.28.272C); **8.** *θεολογία*, Diad.*perf.*66(p.80.19); *ib.*67(p.80.28); **9.** discussion whether their presence is proof of orthodoxy *πῶς οὐ θεάρεστος ἡ κατ' αὐτοὺς δόξα, ἔνθα…τινες αὐτοῖς ὁμόδοξοι, καὶ τῶν προκοιμηθέντων ὤφθησαν ἰαμάτων, καὶ σημείων θεόθεν ἔχειν τὸ χ.;…πρὸς ὃ λεκτέον, ὡς οὐκ ἀρκεῖ τόδε πρὸς ἀσφαλῆ πληροφορίαν τῷ…τῶν θείων δογμάτων κριτῇ…καὶ Ἀρειανοί ποτε, καὶ μέχρι νῦν ἐν Λογγοβάρδοις, καὶ Νεστοριανοὶ παρὰ Πέρσαις ποιοῦσι τάδε θαύματα· ἀλλ' οὐκ εἰς μαρτυρίαν ἁπλῶς τῆς κατ' αὐτοὺς…αἱρέσεως, ἀλλὰ τῆς τῶν Χριστιανῶν πίστεως…ἔτι μὴν ἔστιν ὁρᾶν πολλάκις θαυμάτων χ. ἔν τισιν ὀρθοδόξοις τε καὶ ἑτεροδόξοις ὁμοίως, οὐ δι' εὐσέβειαν μόνον· ἡ γὰρ ἂν ἦν ἐν τοῖς ἐναντίοις λόγοις…ἡ ἀλήθεια, ἀλλὰ διὰ φυσικὴν ἁπλότητα, καὶ ἀτυφίαν* Leont.H.*monoph.*(M.86.1896C,D); **10.** dangers *πατὴρ… αὐτῷ* [sc. S. Paul] *ἐν χαρίσματος μοίρᾳ ἔδωκεν ἄγγελον σατάν, ἵνα αὐτὸν κολαφίζῃ, ἵνα μὴ ὑπεραίρηται* Or.*hom.12.8 in Jer.*(p.95.16; M. 13.389C); practice of saints not to glory in *χαρίσματα*, Gr.Naz.*or.*8. 15(M.35.808A); *μὴ ἐπαίρεσθαι τοὺς λαβόντας χ. τοιάδε κατὰ τῶν μὴ λαβόντων. χ. δὲ λέγομεν τὰ διὰ τῶν σημείων* *Const.App.*8.1.8,9; **11.** iron., of boils produced by magician *ἰδοὺ τοῦ σατανᾶ τὰ χ.* *Pers.* (p.24.19).

H. exeg.; **1.** 1Cor.12:4ff. *ὁ Παῦλος δ' ἐν τῷ καταλόγῳ τῶν ὑπὸ τοῦ θεοῦ διδομένων χ. πρῶτον ἔταξε τὸν λόγον τῆς σοφίας, καὶ δεύτερον, ὡς ὑποβεβηκότα παρ' ἐκεῖνον, τὸν λόγον τῆς γνώσεως, τρίτον δέ που καὶ κατωτέρω τὴν πίστιν. καὶ ἐπεὶ τὸν λόγον προετίμα τῶν τεραστίων ἐνεργειῶν, διὰ τοῦτ' ἐνεργήματα δυνάμεων καὶ χ. ἰαμάτων ἐν τῇ κατωτέρω τίθησι χώρᾳ παρὰ τὰ λογικά χ.* Or.*Cels.*3.46(p.242.22ff.; M.11.980C); cf.*ib.*6.13(p.83.29ff.; 1309C); id.*Jo.*2.24(19; p.81.22; M. 14.157A); *ib.*13.53(52; p.282.8; 497A); *ib.*20.32(26; p.369.24; 645D); **2.** 1Cor.12:31 *ὃ δὲ λέγει, τοῦτό ἐστι· μένετε ἐπιθυμοῦντες χαρισμάτων, καὶ δείκνυμι ὁδὸν χ. ὑμῖν…οὐδὲ γὰρ ἓν καὶ δύο…χ. δείκνυμι ὑμῖν, ἀλλ' ὁδὸν μίαν τὴν ἐπὶ πάντα ταῦτα φέρουσαν…ὥστε εἰ μὴ διὰ τὸ ὀφείλειν βούλει τὸν ἀδελφὸν ἀγαπᾶν, διὰ τὸ κρείττονος ἐπιλαμβάνεσθαι σημείου καὶ χ. δαψιλοῦς καταδέξαι τὴν ἀγάπην* Chrys.*hom.32.3 in 1Cor.*(10. 289A–E); id.*hom.3.6 in Heb.*(12.35D–36A).

I. as endowment of Christ's human nature, Ath.*Ar.*3.39(M.26. 408B); *τὰ παρὰ τοῦ θεοῦ εἰς ἡμᾶς ἐστι χ. δι' αὐτοῦ διδόμενα…διὰ γὰρ τὸν ἐν ἀνθρώπῳ λόγον ἐδόθη ταῦτα τὰ χ.* ‡Ath.*Ar.*4.6(M.26.476B,C).

J. title of work of Hipp., CIG 8613A; cf.Hipp.*trad.ap.*1; *Const. App.*8.3.1.

χαριστέον, *one must yield εἰ…ἐπιθυμίᾳ χ.* Clem.*str.*3.5(p.214.30; M.8.1144D).

***χαριστέω,** s.v.l., ? *show favour ὁ χαριστήσων ἐγγύς* ‡Just.*ep.Zen. et Ser.*18(M.6.1201C).

χαριστήριος, **1.** *offered in thanksgiving χ. ἀποδιδοὺς εὐχήν* Eus.*l.C.* 9(p.219.11; M.20.1365A); *θυσίαι χαριστήριοί τε καὶ σωτήριοι* Gr.Nyss. *hom.9 in Cant.*(M.44.957A); *τὸν χ. προσέφερον ὕμνον* Thdt.*h.e.*3.24.3 (3.941); neut. as subst. *ἀναφέρωμεν τῷ σωτῆρι τὰ χ.* Cyr.*hom.pasch.* 2(5^2.17E); *ᾄσωμεν χ. μετὰ Δαβίδ* Jo.D.*hom.*2.7(M.96.680D); Areth. *Apoc.*12(M.106.581D); of a religious ceremony *συνεορτάσαι τὰ χ.* Gr. Naz.*ep.*20(M.37.56B); Jewish, Gr.Nyss.*v.Mos.*(M.44.321C); **2.** Gnost. aeon, Epiph.*haer.*31.6(p.395.7; M.41.485B); ‡Epiph.*epit.haer.*31 (p.361.18).

χαριστικός, **1.** *pleasing*, Epiph.*haer.*66.50(p.88.4; M.42.105B); **2.** *bestowing* or *dispensing grace τοῦ…χαριστικωτάτου Ἰορδάνου* Or. *Jo.*6.47(28; p.155.33; M.14.281A); *τάξιν* [sc. *τῶν ἀγγέλων*] *ψυχῶν χ.* ‡Ath.*comm.essent.*52(M.28.77B).

χαριστικῶς, *through favour χ. ⟨μᾶλλον⟩ ἤτοι κατὰ ἀλήθειαν τοῦτο ᾄδεται* Epiph.*haer.*77.17(p.430.19; M.42.664C).

***χαρίστιος,** *of thanks, thankful*, Gr.Naz.*carm.*2.2.4.205(M.37. 1521A).

χαριτήσιον, τό, *spell for winning favour τέχνας…μαγικὰς… φίλτρα τε καὶ χαριτήσια* Iren.*haer.*1.25.2(cf.M.7.681B).

***χαριτοδοσία, ἡ,** *gift of grace*, Tim.Ant.*Sym.*(M.86.240C).

χαριτόω, **1.** *favour, shed grace upon*; exeg. Eph.1:6 *οὐκ εἶπεν, ἧς ἐχαρίσατο, ἀλλ' 'ἐχαρίτωσεν ἡμᾶς'. τουτέστιν οὐ μόνον ἁμαρτημάτων ἀπήλλαξεν ἀλλὰ καὶ ἐπεράστους ἐποίησε* Chrys.*hom.1.3 in Eph.*(11. 6B); Thdt.*Eph.*1:6(3.403); Jo.D.*Eph.*1:6(M.95.824B); of the number seven *πανίερος διαπέφηνεν ὁ ἑπτὰ ἀριθμὸς καὶ μᾶλλον κεχαρίτωκε τῶν ἱερῶν ἡμῖν ἀγώνων τὰς ἡμέρας* Anast.Ant.ap.Jo.D.*jej.*7(M.95.76B); pass. ptcpl. *τὸ πνεῦμα ἐκεῖνο τὸ κεχαριτωμένον οὐ κατηξιώθημεν ὑπακοῦσαι* Clem.*str.*1.1(p.10.18; M.8.704A); *τὸ δὲ* [sc. *τὸ σῶμα*] *τῷ πάθει τοῦ μαρτυρίου χαριτωθέν* Gr.Nyss.*Thdr.*(M.46.740B); of persons *κεχαριτωμένος σὺ ἐν εἰρήνῃ Χριστοῦ* *A.Phil.*48(p.21.18); *ὦ παιδίον κεχαριτωμένον* *A.Mt.*1(p.218.2); exeg. Lc.1:28 *χαῖρε κεχαριτωμένη… προεσήμανεν· ἐπειδὴ μετ' αὐτῆς ὅλος ὁ θησαυρὸς τῆς χάριτος ἐναπέκειτο* Gr.Thaum.*annunt.*1(M.10.1149D); cf. *ὅπερ δὲ ἄνω εἶπε, κεχαριτωμένη, ὥσπερ ἑρμηνεύων φησίν· εὗρες γὰρ χάριν ἐνώπιον τοῦ θεοῦ· τοῦτο γάρ ἐστι τὸ κεχαριτῶσθαι, τὸ εὑρεῖν χάριν παρὰ τῷ θεῷ, τουτέστιν, ἀρέσαι θεῷ* Theophylactus *Lc.*1:26–30(M.123.701D); **2.** c. reflex. pron., *win favour for oneself αὐτὸς διὰ τῶν τῆς ἀρετῆς ἔργων χαριτώσας ἑαυτόν* [sc. *ὁ Νῶε*] Proc.G.*Gen.*6:8(M.87.272C); **3.** *show favour to*, Dor.*doct.* 6.7(M.88.1693B); of God *ἐν φυλακῇ ἤμην καὶ ὁ σωτὴρ ἐχαρίτωσέ με* *T.Jos.*1.6; *ὁ οὖν κύριος…ἐχαρίτωσεν αὐτοὺς ἐν πάσῃ πράξει αὐτῶν* Herm.*sim.*9.24.3.

χαριτώνυμος, *named after grace*, i.e. with a name derived from Hebr. חֵן, of Jo. D. *ὁ…χ. οὗτος ἀνήρ* Jo.VI H.*v.Jo.D.*3(M.94.433A); of S. Anna, Taras.*praesent.BMV* 8(M.98.1488D).

***χάρμιος,** *joyful*; superl., Meth.*res.*2.5(M.18.301A; *χαρτός* p.338.2).

***χαρμολύπη, ἡ,** *bitter joy*, Jo.Clim.*scal.*7(M.88.804B).

χαρμονικός, *joyful χ. χείλεσι* Taras.*praesent.BMV* 8(M.98.1483D); *χ. δοξολογίαι* *ib.*(1489D).

***χαρμονικῶς,** *joyfully*, ‡Jo.D.*hom.*5(M.96.649A).

χαροποι-έω, *make joyful*, *Dial.Tim.et Aquil.*(v° 124); †Gregent. *disp.*(M.86.684B); Eustrat.*v.Eutych.*71(M.86.2356B); pass., *ib.*40 (2321A); Heracl.ap.*Chron.Pasch.*p.402(M.92.1028A); of Christ as the Vine *~οῦσαν καρδίαν ἀνθρώπου* ‡Ath.*disp.*32(M.28.480D); Anast.S. *hex.*12(M.89.1053B); of Father *ὁ κύριος…χαροποιήσει ἡμᾶς ἐν τῇ ἀτελευτήτῳ ζωῇ* Ephr.3.369B.

χαροποιός, **1.** *bringing joy, gladdening πρόσωπον ἀγγέλου ἔχοντα, χ. τοῖς ὀφθαλμοῖς* Pall.*h.Laus.*50(M.34.1132B); *τοῦ χ. πένθους* Jo. Clim.*scal.*7 tit.(M.88.801C); of the 'oil of gladness' (Ps.44:8), Mac. Aeg.*hom.*17.1(M.34.624D); **2.** *full of joy χ. τοῖς προσώποις γινόμενοι* ‡Chrys.*hom.*6(13.213E); *δάκρυον…τὸ μὲν λυπηρόν, τὸ δὲ χ.* Eustrat. *v.Eutych.*71(M.86.2356A); **3.** *bright* (? f.l. for *χαροπός*) *οἱ ὀφθαλμοὶ αὐτοῦ* [sc. *τοῦ Ἰακώβ*] *χ. καὶ ἐξαστράπτοντες* *Asen.*22(p.73.2); *χ.* … *εἶχε τοὺς ὀφθαλμούς* Ath.*v.Anton.*67(M.26.940B).

χάρτης, ὁ, **1.** *papyrus*; **2.** *official document*, Const.ap.Eus.*h.e.*10. 5.18(M.20.885C); Ath.*syn.*8(p.235.17; M.26.692B); *ib.*15(p.242.15; 705C); of an indictment *διδασκαλικὸν χ. κατὰ τοῦ Παύλου* Ammon. *Ac.*24:1(M.85.1592B); Jo.Clim.*scal.*4(M.88.684C); fig. *γράφων τε τὴν δέησιν εἰς τὸν ἐξαπλωθέντα χ. τῆς οἰκείας καρδίας* Nil.*epp.*3.129(M.79. 444C); *ὅσα ὑπέσχου ἐν τῷ τῆς ὁμολογίας χ. τῷ πάντων δεσπότῃ* [i.e. at baptism] †Jo.D.*B.J.*21(M.96.1052C).

***χάρτινος,** *made of paper*, Olymp.*fr.Jer.*36:2(M.93.696D).

χαρτίον, τό, **1.** *papyrus*; **2.** *written document*, Gr.Naz.*test.*(p.158; M.37.392A); Pall.*v.Chrys.*6(p.36.11; M.47.22); Cyr.*ep.*2(p.24.6,10,16; 5^2.20B,C).

***χαρτοθέσιον, τό,** *archive chamber*, *Cod.Afr.*86 tit.; Thphn.*chron.* p.362(M.108.868B).

***χαρτοκόκκινον, τό,** *red paper*; plur., Ephr.2.176B.

***χαρτόν, τό,** *joy*, Clem.*str.*2.15(p.151.21; M.8.1012B).

***χαρτουλαρεύω,** *hold the office of keeper of the archives*, Thdr. Stud.*epp.*2.190(M.99.1580A).

χαρτουλάριος, ὁ, *keeper of archives*, *Chron.Pasch.*p.384(M.92. 985A); ‡Jo.D.*ep.Thphl.*18(M.95.368D).

χαρτοφυλάκιον, τό, *case for storing archives*, CCP(681)act.11(H. 3.1296E).

χαρτοφύλαξ, ὁ, *keeper of archives*, Ast.Soph.*Ps*.5(M.40.396A); CCP(536)*act*.(p.59.25; H.2.1316E).

***χαρτῷος,** *of paper*, CCP(681)*act*.9(H.3.1196C).

***Χαρυβδηδόν,** *in the manner of Charybdis* οἱ νεοφανεῖς δράκοντες χ. καταπίνοντες ψυχὰς μὴ ἐστηριγμένας τῷ λόγῳ τῆς ἀληθείας Thdr.Stud. *epp*.2.190(M.99.1580A).

χάσκω, *gape at*; c. acc., Nil.*epp*.2.148(M.79.269A); *ib*.3.122(440C).

***χασματιαῖος,** *destroyed by earthquake*, Rheg.*serm*.(p.71.6; H.1. 1445B).

χασμάω, *yawn, gape*; fig., in hesitation or confusion, Bas.Sel. *v.Thecl*.2.16(M.85.593A); usu. med.; fig., Ath.*Dion*.3(p.47.19; M.25. 481C).

χάσμησις, ἡ, *yawning*; plur., Chrys.*stat*.1.5(2.7E).

χάσμος, ὁ, *yawning, gaping*, Jo.Clim.*scal*.13(M.88.860C).

χαυνότης, ἡ, *slackness, weakness* τὴν χ. τῆς διανοίας Bas.*hom*.3.5 (2.21A; M.31.209A); Mac.Aeg.*or*.7(M.34.857D); *Const.App*.5.6.5.

χαυν-όω, 1. *soften* θέρμη...~οῦσα καὶ σφίγγουσα [sc. τοὺς ὀπώρας] τῷ ξένῳ λόγῳ Geo.Pis.*hex*.326(M.92.1459A); fig. πᾶσα ἡ ὑπόστασις τῶν σπλάγχνων μου ἐχαυνοῦτο *T.Zab*.2.4; met., *soften, weaken* αὐτῆς τῆς περιουσίας καθ' αὐτὴν ἱκανῆς οὔσης χαυνῶσαι τὰς ψυχάς Clem.*q.d.s*.1(p.159.12; M.9.604A); ἐχαυνώθη τὸ κράτος αὐτοῦ *A.Xanthipp*.17(p.70.13); ἔχειν τὴν ἄσκησιν, καὶ μὴ ζητεῖν τὰ ~οῦντα τὸ σῶμα Ath.*v.Anton*.7(M.26.853A); καθάπερ γὰρ ῥεῦμα ἐπιρρέον ἡ ἄνεσις χ. τὴν ψυχήν Chrys.*hom.24.3 in Ac*.(9.196E); πολλὰ τὰ ~οῦντα τὴν ἀγάπην, χρήματα, πράγματα, κτλ. id.*hom.34.1 in 1Cor*.(10.310E); **2.** *weaken, become weak*, met. οὐ μὴ χαυνώσω ἐμαυτὴν εἰς τὴν ζωὴν τὴν πρὸς καιρὸν ταύτην, ἵνα μὴ ἀποθάνω θάνατον τὸν αἰώνιον *M.Pers*. 3.4(p.443.6); c. genit., *weaken, make to cease from* τῆς ἐγκρατείας χαυνωθέντι κολακείᾳ ἡδονῶν Nil.*Eulog*.22(M.79.1121C); τοῦτο λεχθὲν ἐχαύνωσε τοὺς μοναχοὺς τῆς ὁρμῆς Socr.*h.e*.6.7.7(M.67.684B); **3.** *soften, touch, propitiate* ἵνα μήτε ὁ ἔλεος χαυνώσῃ ἡμᾶς Nil.*epp*. 1.36(M.79.100A); **4.** *make loose* or *slack*, fig. χαυνωθέντων αὐτοῖς καὶ χαλασθέντων τῶν τόνων Meth.*symp*.8.1(p.81.18; M.18.140A); οὐδὲ γὰρ ἴσχυσεν αὐτῆς τὰς σανίδας χαυνῶσαι τῆς κακίας ὁ χειμών Chrys.*laud.Paul*.1(2.478D); ‡Chrys.*ascet.facet*.(1.810A); ταῦτα...τὸν τόνον τῶν φιλονεικεῖν αἱρουμένων ἐχαύνωσε Socr.*h.e*.3.25.5(M.67. 452B); τοῦ χαλινοῦ αὐτοῦ χαυνωθέντος Jo.Clim.*past*.4(M.88.1173A); hence *uncurb, let go* ἀμέτρως χ. [sc. τοὺς ἵππους] Ephr.1.59A; fig., id.59C.

χαύνωσις, ἡ, 1. of ripening fruit *softening*, Geo.Pis.*hex*.324 (M.92.1459A); **2.** *loosening, slackening*, fig. σύν τε τῷ φόβῳ τῆς γαστρὸς ἐκινεῖτο χ. Socr.*h.e*.1.38.7(M.67.177A); met., *indolence* Or. *hom.20.3 in Jer*.(p.181.27; M.13.508A); χ. μᾶλλον ἤπερ ὠφέλειαν εἰδότων τῶν ᾀσμάτων τοῖς ἀνθρώποις ἐνεργάζεσθαι ‡Just.*qu.et resp*. 54(M.6.1297B); ἀκηδία...ἀσκήσεως χ. [sc. ἐστιν] ‡Nil.*tract*.4(M.79. 1144B); **3.** *space* or *interval* δεῖ οὖν, τινῶν κατακλυζομένων, ἀλλαχοῦ χ. εἶναι, καὶ φανῆναι τὴν ἶριν Proc.G.*Gen*.9:13(M.87.300C).

***χειλέος, ἡ,** *chest, box*, Sophr.H.*mir.Cyr.et Jo*.35(M.87.3545B).

***χειλοστρόφιον, τό,** *instrument of torture for twisting the lips*, Synes.*ep*.58(M.66.1400C).

χειμάδιος, *of winter*, Eus.*d.e*.10.7(p.470.5; M.22.756D); *wintry* ἡμέρα...πῃ μὲν εὔδιος...καὶ πάλιν χ. Mac.Mgn.*apocr*.4.11(p.173.5).

χειμάζω, pass., *be afflicted*; of the ἐνεργούμενοι as a class in the congregation, CAnc.(314)*can*.17; *Lit*.ap.*Const.App*.8.12.47; *Const. App*.8.35.2; *ib*.38.1.

***χειμαρριαῖος,** *from a torrent*, Tim.Ant.*Sym*.(M.86.240A).

***χειμαρροειδής,** *like a torrent*, Olymp.*Job* 22:33(M.93.236A).

***χειμερία, ἡ,** *tempestuous weather*, Thphn.*chron*.p.190(M.108. 492B).

***χειμευτής, ὁ,** *alchemist*, Jo.Mal.*chron*.16 p.395(M.97.584B); cf. χυμευτής.

χειμωνικός, *wintry*, ‡Epiph.*hom*.3(M.43.465D).

χείρ, ἡ, [acc. χεῖραν *Ev.Barth*.2.17], *hand*; **1.** purpose or function of hands in man καί τις ἴδιον τῆς λογικῆς φύσεως τὴν τῶν χ. ὑπηρεσίαν εἰπὼν οὐ τοῦ παντὸς ἁμαρτήσεται Gr.Nyss.*hom.opif*.8.2(M.44.144B,C); *ib*.8.8(148C–149A); πρὸς τὸ ἔργον αἱ χ. id.*anim.et res*.(M.46.141C); χ. δὲ ἐδόθησαν ἵνα ἀνατείνῃς αὐτὰς εἰς εὐχάς Chrys.*diab*.2.3(2.264A); ἐποίησέ σοι χεῖρας; ταύτας αὐτῷ κέκτησο, μὴ τῷ διαβόλῳ, μὴ εἰς ἁρπαγὰς καὶ πλεονεξίας, ἀλλ' εἰς ἐντολὰς καὶ εὐποιίας, καὶ εἰς εὐχὰς ἐκτενεῖς ἀνατείνων αὐτάς, εἰς τὸ τοῖς πεπτωκόσιν ὀρέγειν χ. id.*hom. 10.5 in Phil*.(11.281A); in angels τοὺς ὤμους δὲ καὶ...τὰς χ., τὸ ποιητικὸν καὶ ἐνεργητικόν Dion.Ar.*c.h*.15.3(M.3.332C); **2.** fig.; made fruitful by almsgiving, Chrys.*hom.25.5 in Heb*.(12.232C); and purified ἔπλυνας τὰς χ. τὰς αἰσθητὰς τῷ ὕδατι; πλῦνον τὰς χ. τῆς ψυχῆς τῇ ἐλεημοσύνῃ id.*poenit*.3.2(2.297A); **3.** exeg.: **a.** Ex.4:6ff. ἡ χ. πράξεων πολλαχοῦ σύμβολόν ἐστιν Or.*Jo*.32.21(13; p.462.21; M.14.800D); ᾧ μοι δοκεῖ δι' αἰνίγματος τὸ διὰ σαρκὸς παραδηλοῦσθαι τοῦ κυρίου μυστήριον τῆς φανείσης τοῖς ἀνθρώποις θεότητος [cf.Ps.77:11]...καὶ γὰρ ἐκεῖ τοῦ νομοθέτου ἡ χ. προβληθεῖσα τοῦ κόλπου, πρὸς τὸ παρὰ φύσιν ἠλλοιώθη χρῶμα· καὶ πάλιν ἐν κόλποις γενομένη, πρὸς τὴν ἰδίαν αὐτῆς καὶ κατὰ φύσιν ἐπανῆλθε χάριν. καὶ ὁ μονογενὴς θεός, ὁ ὢν ἐν κόλποις τοῦ πατρὸς οὗτός ἐστιν ἡ δεξιὰ τοῦ ὑψίστου. ὅτε δὲ ἡμῖν ἐκ τῶν κόλπων ἐφάνη, καθ' ἡμᾶς ἠλλοιώθη· ἐπεὶ δὲ τὰς ἡμετέρας ἀσθενείας ἐκμάξας, πάλιν ἐπανήγαγε τὴν ἐν ἡμῖν γενομένην χ., καὶ καθ' ἡμᾶς χρωσθεῖσαν ἐπὶ τὸν ἴδιον κόλπον (κόλπος δὲ τῆς δεξιᾶς ὁ πατήρ) τότε οὐ τὸ ἀπαθὲς τῆς φύσεως εἰς πάθος ἠλλοίωσεν, ἀλλὰ τὸ τρεπτόν τε καὶ ἐμπαθὲς διὰ τῆς πρὸς τὸ ἄτρεπτον κοινωνίας εἰς ἀπάθειαν μετεστοιχείωσεν Gr.Nyss.*v.Mos*.(M.44.333Dff.); **b.** Ex.17:11–12 οὐδὲ τὸ μέχρις ἑσπέρας μεῖναι τὸν προφήτην Μωϋσῆν, ὅτε τὰς χ. αὐτοῦ ὑπεβάσταζον Ὢρ καὶ Ἀαρών, ἐπὶ τοῦ σχήματος τούτου εἰκῇ γέγονε. καὶ γὰρ ὁ κύριος σχεδὸν μέχρις ἑσπέρας ἔμεινεν ἐπὶ τοῦ ξύλου Just.*dial*.97.1(M. 6.704C); cf.*ib*.91.3(693B); *ib*.111.1(732B); cf. infra 6; **c.** Cant.5:14 χ. δὲ νοοῦμεν πάντως τὴν τὰ κοινὰ τῆς ἐκκλησίας εἰς τὰς τῶν ἐντολῶν χρείας διαχειρίζουσαν...πάντως δὲ πρόδηλα πᾶσίν ἐστιν ὅσα μὴ περιαιρεθέντα τῆς χ. τῷ κάλλει λυμαίνεται, οἷον τὸ ἀνθρωπάρεσκον, τὸ φιλόδοξον κτλ. Gr.Nyss.*hom.14 in Cant*.(M.44.1069A); **d.** Mt.5:30 ὁ γὰρ δεξιὸς ὀφθαλμὸς καὶ ἡ δεξιὰ χ., οὐδὲν ἡμῖν ἕτερον αἰνίττεται, ἢ τοὺς ἐπὶ βλάβῃ φιλοῦντας ἡμᾶς Chrys.*compunct*.1.3(1.127D); **e.** Jo.13:3 ἔδωκεν εἰς τὰς χωρούσας τὰ πάντα χ., ἵνα ᾖ τὰ πάντα αὐτῷ ὑποχείρια, ἢ πάντα ἔδωκεν αὐτῷ ὁ πατὴρ εἰς τὰς χ., τουτέστιν εἰς τὰς πράξεις αὐτοῦ καὶ τὰ ἀνδραγαθήματα Or.*Jo*.32.3(p.430.19; M.14.748C); **4.** ceremony of washing hands on entering a church ἐπειδὴ γὰρ αἱ χ. σύμβολον πράξεως...τὸ νίψασθαι τὰς χ. τοῦ ἀνυπεύθυνον εἶναι ἁμαρτήμασι σύμβολόν ἐστιν Cyr.H.*catech*.23.2; Chrys.*hom.51.4 in Mt*.(7.526B); χ. μὲν νιπτόμεθα, εἰς ἐκκλησίαν εἰσιόντες...τί γὰρ ὄφελος, ἂν τὰς ἔξωθεν μὲν χ. ἀποσμήξῃς, τὰς δὲ ἔνδον ἀκαθάρτους ἔχῃς;...τὸ μὲν οὖν ἀνίπτοις χ. εὔξασθαι, ἀδιάφορον· τὸ δὲ ἀνίπτῳ διανοίᾳ, τοῦτό ἐστι τὸ πάντων ἔσχατον τῶν κακῶν id.*hom.73.3 in Jo*.(8.433C,D); cf. πρὸ τοῦ αἰσθητοῦ τὸ νοητὸν διδάσκου. ὥσπερ γὰρ τῷ ὕδατι ἀποπλύνει τοὺς σωματικοὺς ῥύπους, οὕτω διὰ τῆς εὐχῆς τὴν ψυχὴν ἐκλαμπρύνει Nil. *epp*.1.24(M.79.89D); **5.** washing of celebrant's hands at eucharist, Dion.Ar.*e.h*.3.1.2(M.3.425D); *ib*.3.3.10(437D); ὁ μὲν ἱερὸς λουτὴρ...ἐν τῇ κατὰ νόμον ἦν ἱεραρχίᾳ· νῦν δὲ τοῦ ἱεράρχου καὶ τῶν ἱερέων ἡ τῶν χ. ἀποκάθαρσις αὐτὸν ὑπαινίσσεται *ib*.(440A); **6.** of the hands outstretched: to God in appeal ἐξετείνατε τὰς χ. ὑμῶν πρὸς τὸν παντοκράτορα θεόν *1Clem*.2.3; Ath.*apol.Const*.16(M.25.613C); id.*h.Ar*. 34(p.202.5; M.25.732C); in prayer [cf.Ps.141:2, 1Tim.2:8] τὰς χ. εἰς οὐρανὸν αἴρομεν Clem.*str*.7.7(p.30.19; M.9.456B); μετ' ἐκτάσεως τῶν χ. Or.*or*.31(p.396.11; M.11.549D); Eus.*v.C*.4.15(p.123.25; M.20. 1164B); τάχα δέ τι καὶ βαθύτερον ὁ λόγος παραδηλοῖ· ὅτι ὁ τὰ μεγάλα καὶ οὐράνια καὶ ὑψηλὰ ἐργαζόμενος, οἱονεὶ διηρμένην ἔχων τὴν πρακτικὴν δύναμιν, ἐπαίρειν τὰς χ. λέγεται· ὁ δὲ ταπεινὰ καὶ γήϊνα... εὐεργῶν, κάτω ῥεπούσας καὶ καταβεβλημένας τὰς χ. ἔχει †Bas.*Is*.35 (1.408C; M.30.189A); τὰς χ. ἑκατέρωθεν πετάσας εἰς τὸν ἀέρα, τοῦ σταυροῦ τὸ πάθος ἀκριβῶς ἐξεικονίζει Ast.Am.*phar*.(p.117.17); τί βούλεται καὶ τῶν χ. ἡ ἔκτασις ἐν τῇ εὐχῇ; ἐπειδὴ πολλαῖς πονηρίαις διακονοῦνται αὗται...δι' αὐτὸ μὲν οὖν τοῦτο κελευόμεθα αὐτὰς ἀνατείνειν, ἵνα ἡ τῆς εὐχῆς διακονία δεσμὸς αὐταῖς γένηται τῆς κακίας... ἵν' ὅταν μέλλῃς ἁρπάζειν ἢ πλεονεκτεῖν, ἢ τύπτειν ἕτερον, ἀναμνησθεὶς ὅτι ταύτας μέλλεις ἀντὶ συνηγόρων πρὸς τὸν θεὸν πέμπειν, καὶ διὰ τούτων τὴν θυσίαν ἀναπέμπειν ἐκείνην τὴν πνευματικήν, μὴ καταισχύνῃς αὐτὰς καὶ ἀπαρρησιάστους ἐργάσῃ τῇ διακονίᾳ τῆς πονηρᾶς ἐργασίας. κάθαιρε τοίνυν αὐτὰς ἐλεημοσύνῃ, φιλανθρωπίᾳ...καὶ οὕτως αὐτὰς εἰς εὐχὴν ἄγε. ... τὸ δὲ καταρρυπωθείσας αὐτὰς μυρίοις ἁμαρτήμασι προσάγειν, τοῦτο πολλὴν φέρει ὀργήν Chrys.*exp.in Ps*.140:2(5.431C,D); in blessing, cf. εὐλογέω, εὐλογία; αἱ γὰρ χ. Ἀαρὼν ἄνω ἐξαίρονται ὅτε μέλλει εὐλογεῖν τὸν λαόν. καὶ εἴπερ τις κάτω ἔχοι τὰς χ. εἰς τὰ γήϊνα, οὐκ ἂν ἀνύσοι βουλόμενος εὐλογεῖν τινα. καίπερ οὐδὲ κάτω κείμεναι αἱ Μωσέως χ. ὠφέλουν τὸν λαόν, ἀλλ' ὅτεπερ ἐπήροντο. τούτου σύμβολον ἦν καὶ ἡ ἔπαρσις τῶν χ. τοῦ σωτῆρος. ταῖς γὰρ ὑπὲρ ἀνθρώπων πράξεσιν ὕψωσεν αὐτῶν τὰς χ., καὶ ἔσωσε τοὺς πιστεύοντας Or.*fr.87 in Lc*.(p.275.6ff.); **7.** position of hands in receiving the eucharist μὴ τεταμένοις τοῖς τῶν χ. καρποῖς προσέρχου...ἀλλὰ τὴν ἀριστερὰν θρόνον ποιήσας τῇ δεξιᾷ, ὡς μελλούσῃ βασιλέα ὑποδέχεσθαι Cyr.H.*catech*.23.21; τὰς χ. σχηματίζων εἰς τύπον σταυροῦ CNic.(787) *can*.101; **8.** imposition of hands, in blessing, Clem.*paed*.3.11(p.271. 21; M.8.637B); in healing, Iren.*haer*.2.32.4(M.7.829B); αἱροῦνται μᾶλλον...νοσεῖν καὶ κινδυνεύειν ἢ χ. τῶν Ἀρειανῶν ἐλθεῖν ἐπὶ τὴν κεφαλὴν αὐτῶν Ath.*ep.encycl*.5(p.175.6; M.25.233C); upon penitents, CLaod. *can*.19; διὰ τῆς ἐπιθέσεως τῶν ἡμετέρων χ. ἐδίδοτο τὸ πνεῦμα τὸ ἅγιον τοῖς πιστεύουσιν *Const.App*.2.41.2; *ib*.6.7.3; in reconciliation of schismatics, Eus.*h.e*.7.2(M.20.641A); of imposition of hands by

SS. Peter and John (Ac.8:17) ὡς οὖν ὁ ἀπόστολος δυνατὸς ἦν διδόναι τὸ βρῶμα (ref. 1Cor.3:2), οἷς γὰρ ἂν ἐπετίθουν χεῖρας, ἐλάμβανον πνεῦμα ἅγιον, ὅ ἐστι βρῶμα ζωῆς, ἐκεῖνοι [sc. Corinthians] δὲ ἠδυνάτουν λαβεῖν αὐτό, διὰ τὸ ἀσθενῆ ἔτι καὶ ἀγύμναστα ἔχειν τὰ τῆς ψυχῆς αἰσθητήρια τῆς πρὸς θεὸν γυμνασίας Iren.*haer*.4.38.2(M.7.1106C); at baptism (Marcosian) ἐπιτιθέντες χ. τῷ τὴν ἀπολύτρωσιν λαβόντι Hipp.*haer*.6.41(p.173.3; M.16.3259C); perh. implied, Iren. *haer*.4.38.2(1106C) cit. supra; at confirmation of baptized, cf. Hipp.*trad.ap*.22.1(p.38); Ath.*ep.Serap*.1.6(M.26.544B); at ordination of priests or bishops, Eus.*h.e*.7.32.21(M.20.729C); Serap.*euch*. 27.1; symbolizing hand of God, Chrys.*hom.14.3 in Ac*.(9.114C); v. χειροτονία; conferring H. Ghost, Bas.*ep*.188.1(3.270; M.32.669A); conferring right to perform sacred offices, *Const.App*.3.10.2; hands laid also on deacons (v. διάκονος) and deaconesses, *ib*.8.19.2; and on readers, *ib*.8.22.2; κοινὰ μὲν ἔστι τοῖς ἱεράρχαις τε καὶ ἱερεῦσι καὶ λειτουργοῖς ἐν ταῖς ἱερατικαῖς αὐτῶν τελειώσεσιν...ἡ τῆς ἱεραρχικῆς χ. ἐπίθεσις Dion.Ar.*e.h*.5.3.1(M.3.509C); significance of this rite ἡ δὲ τῆς ἱεραρχικῆς χ. ἐπίθεσις ὁμοῦ μὲν ἐμφαίνει τὴν τελεταρχικὴν σκέπην, ὑφ' ἧς ὡς παῖδες ἱεροὶ περιέπονται πατρικῶς, αὐτοῖς μὲν ἕξιν καὶ δύναμιν ἱερατικὴν δωρουμένης, τὰς ἐναντίας δὲ αὐτῶν δυνάμεις ἀπορραπιζούσης· διδάσκει δὲ ἅμα καὶ πάσας τελεῖν τὰς ἱερατικὰς ἐνεργείας, ὡς ὑπὸ θεῷ πράττοντας τοὺς τελεσθέντας, καὶ τῶν οἰκείων ἐνεργειῶν αὐτὸν ἔχοντας ἐν παντὶ καθηγεμόνα *ib*.5.3.3(512A); ref. ordinations performed by Colluthus πρεσβύτερος ὢν ἐτελεύτησε, καὶ πᾶσα χ. αὐτοῦ γέγονεν ἄκυρος Ath.*apol.sec*.12(p.97.5; M.25.269A); **9.** stretching forth of hand; in succour, *Const.App*.1.8.7; *ib*.3.3.2; in token of pre-baptismal renunciation of Satan, Dion.Ar.*e.h*.2.3.5(M.3.401B); **10.** of Christ; **a.** at Crucifixion, v. ἁπλόω; διὰ τῆς θείας ἐκτάσεως τῶν χ., τοὺς δύο λαοὺς εἰς ἕνα θεὸν συνάγων. δύο μὲν γὰρ αἱ χ., ὅτι καὶ δύο λαοὶ διεσπαρμένοι εἰς τὰ πέρατα τῆς γῆς Iren.*haer*.5.17.4(M.7.1171C); ἔπρεπεν...τὰς χ. ἐκτεῖναι, ἵνα τῇ μὲν τὸν παλαιὸν λαόν, τῇ δὲ τοὺς ἀπὸ τῶν ἐθνῶν ἑλκύσῃ, καὶ ἀμφοτέρους ἐν ἑαυτῷ συνάψῃ Ath.*inc*. 25.3(M.25.140A); Cyr.H.*catech*.13.28(M.33.805B); **b.** met. ἡ ἐν τῇ χ. αὐτοῦ φυλαττομένη καρδία ὑμῶν Taras.*ep*.1(M.98.1428B); CNic.(787) *act*.7(H.4.472D); **c.** exeg. Jo.10:28ff. οὐδεὶς ἁρπάζει αὐτὰ ἐκ τῆς χ. μου, προϊὼν ἔδειξε τὴν αὐτοῦ χ. καὶ τοῦ πατρὸς μίαν οὖσαν...χ. δὲ ὅταν ἀκούσῃς, μηδὲν αἰσθητὸν νομίσῃς, ἀλλὰ τὴν δύναμιν, τὴν ἐξουσίαν Chrys.*hom.61.2 in Jo*.(8.363C,E); οὐ γὰρ δυνατὸν τοὺς ὄντας ἐν τῇ τοῦ Χριστοῦ χ. ἁρπαγῆναι εἰς τὸ κολασθῆναι, διὰ τὸ ἄγαν ἰσχύειν τὸν Χριστόν· ἡ γὰρ χ. ἐν τῇ θείᾳ γραφῇ τὴν δύναμιν δηλοῖ· ὅτι μὲν οὖν ἀνίκητος ἡ τοῦ Χριστοῦ χ. καὶ εἰς πάντα ἰσχύουσα, ἀναμφίβολον Cyr. *Jo*.7(4.666B); λέγεται δὲ ὁ πατὴρ διδόναι τῷ υἱῷ, οὐχ ὡς μὴ ἔχοντι ἀεὶ ὑπὸ χεῖρα τὴν κτίσιν, ἀλλ' ὡς ὄντι αὐτῷ φύσει ζωῇ, προσκομίζων ἡμᾶς τοὺς ἐπιδεομένους ζωῆς, ἵνα διὰ τοῦ υἱοῦ ζωοποιηθῶμεν τοῦ ὄντος φύσει ζωῆς, καὶ οἴκοθεν ἔχοντος τοῦτο *ib*.(666D); **11.** of Father; **a.** in gen. ποῦ γάρ τις ἡμῶν δύναται φυγεῖν ἀπὸ τῆς κραταιᾶς χ. αὐτοῦ; *1Clem*. 28.2; **b.** at Creation ἄνθρωπον ταῖς ἱεραῖς καὶ ἀμώμοις χ. ἔπλασεν τῆς ἑαυτοῦ εἰκόνος χαρακτῆρα *ib*.33.4; Meth.*symp*.2.2(p.17.8; M.18.49B); id.*res*.2.22(p.376.9; M.103.1137B); **c.** writing Law, *Const.App*.7.36.4; **d.** shown in Inc. χ. κυρίου διαφόρως ἐδείχθη καθ' ἑκάστην γενεὰν διὰ τῶν δυναμένων χωρῆσαι τὴν ἐνέργειαν τῶν θαυμασίων...νῦν δὲ χ. κυρίου δείκνυσθαι λέγεται κατὰ τὴν ἐπιδημίαν τοῦ σωτῆρος ἡμῶν †Bas.*Is*. 248(1.568D; M.30.556A,B); **e.** liturg., at blessing of catechumens, symbolized by hand of bishop τὴν χ. ἐκτείνομεν, δέσποτα, καὶ δεόμεθα τὴν χ. τὴν θείαν καὶ ζῶσαν ἐκταθῆναι εἰς εὐλογίαν τῷ λαῷ τούτῳ Serap.*euch*.4.1; at blessing of sick κύριε...ἔκτεινόν σου τὴν χ. καὶ χάρισαι θεραπευθῆναι τοὺς νοσοῦντας πάντας *ib*.8.1; **f.** ref. Pr.21:1 δίκαιον τὴν χ. τοῦ θεοῦ ἐν πρώτοις προσκυνεῖν, καὶ οὕτως τὸ στόμα τοῦ βασιλέως καταφιλεῖν *A.Jo*.7(p.155.12); ἐφίλησεν αὐτὸν κατὰ τοῦ στέρνου καὶ τῆς κεφαλῆς...ἐπειδὴ γέγραπται καρδία βασιλέως ἐν χ. κυρίου· καὶ πάλιν χ. κυρίου ἐπὶ κορυφὴν βασιλέως *ib*.(p.155.29); **g.** ref. indivisible nature of Trin. τὸ δὲ ἅγιον πνεῦμα, ἐκπόρευμα ὂν τοῦ πατρός, ἀεί ἐστιν ἐν ταῖς χ. τοῦ πέμποντος πατρὸς καὶ τοῦ φέροντος υἱοῦ †Ath.*exp.fid*.4(M.25.208A); Dion.Al.ap.Ath.*Dion*.17 (p.58.21; M.25.505A); **h.** explanations ὡς χ. κυρίου τὴν πνευματικὴν ὠνόμασε χάριν Thdt.*qu.12 in 4Reg*.(1.518); ref. Ps.143:7 χ. δὲ ἐνταῦθα τὴν βοήθειαν, τὴν συμμαχίαν λέγει Chrys.*exp.in Ps*.143:7(5.463C); exeg. Is.19:16 χ. δὲ κυρίου σαβαὼθ ἐν τούτοις τὸ παναλκὲς θέλημα τοῦ θεοῦ διορίζεται Cyr.*Is*.2.4(2.291D); esp. as symbol of activity of God at Creation θεοῦ χ. μὲν τὸ δημιουργικόν Or.*fr.in 1Reg*.15:9–11(p.295. 26; M.12.992A); τὴν πρακτικὴν αὐτοῦ καὶ ἐνεργητικὴν δύναμιν τῷ τοιούτῳ διασημαίνει ὀνόματι Gr.Nyss.*Eun*.8(2 p.187.7; M.45.781B); cf.Thdt.*haer*.5.1(4.380); πλεισταχοῦ μὲν τὸ γράμμα τὸ ἱερὸν χ. ὀνομάζει θεοῦ, τὰς δραστηρίους αὐτοῦ δυνάμεις, δι' ὧν εἰς τὸ εἶναι τὰ πάντα παρήνεγκεν Cyr.*Is*.4.4(2.674E); id.*glaph.Gen*.3(1.104B); Proc.G.*Is*. 26:8(M.87.2217A); οὐκ ἀληθῶς χ. ἔχειν νοεῖς τὸν θεόν...ἀλλ' ἐκ τῶν ἡμετέρων, διὰ μὲν τῆς χ., οἶδας σημαίνεσθαι τὴν ἐνέργειαν, ἐπειδὴ χ. ἡμεῖς ἐνεργοῦμεν Gennad.*fr.Gen*.1:26(M.85.1633B); (Arian), Ath. *decr*.8(p.7.18; M.25.429A) cit. s. ἄκρατος; id.*Ar*.2.24(M.26.200A); also of vengeance (ref. Jer.51:25) χ. δέ, τὴν τιμωρητικὴν δύναμιν Or.*fr. 41 in Jer*.(p.219.21; M.13.604C); χ. θεοῦ διαφόρως ἐκληπτέον, ἢ τὴν κολαστικὴν καὶ εἰς τοῦτο ὑπηρετικὴν δύναμιν, ἥτις καὶ σκεῦος ὀργῆς λέγεται [cf. Ps.43:2,3]...ἢ τὴν φρουρητικὴν καὶ σκεπαστικὴν δύναμιν [cf.Ps.138:5] Didym.*Job* 1:11(M.39.1121D); **i.** theol. of Logos or Son as hand of God ἔστι δὲ ὁ υἱὸς ἡ παντοδύναμος καὶ κραταιὰ χ. τοῦ πατρός, ἐν ᾗ μετὰ τὸ ποιῆσαι τὴν ὕλην ἐξ οὐκ ὄντων κατακοσμεῖ Meth. *creat*.9(p.498.29; M.18.341A); ἑνός ἐστι θεοῦ ὡς χ. χρωμένου τῷ ἰδίῳ λόγῳ [cf. Is.66:2] Ath.*decr*.7(p.7.9; M.25.428D); αὐτὸς γάρ ἐστιν ἡ χ. καὶ αἱ χ. τοῦ πατρός id.*inc.et c.Ar*.12(M.26.1004C); ref. Is.48:13 χ. τὴν τοῦ μονογενοῦς δύναμιν τῷ αἰνίγματι λέγων Gr.Nyss.*Eun*.7(2 p.161.12; M.45.749D); χ. ὧδε τὴν δύναμιν καλεῖ, ἣν ἔχει ὁ υἱὸς φυσικῶς καὶ οὐ μεταληπτῶς Ammon.*Jo*.3:35(M.85.1417A); cf.Cyr.*Jo*.7(4. 666C,D); χ. καλῶν τὴν ἰδίαν ἰσχύν τε καὶ δύναμιν, τὸν Χριστόν Proc.G. *Is*.49.14–26(M.87.2480C); of Son and H. Ghost as hands of God, Iren.*haer*.4.20.1(M.7.1032B); cf. *per manus enim patris, id est, per filium et spiritum, fit homo secundum similitudinem dei*, *ib*.5.6.1 (1137A); *ib*.16.1(1167B); Or.*schol.38 in Apoc*.(p.43.2); Proc.G.*Gen*. 1:27(M.87.133A); of H. Ghost exeg. Mt.6:3 οὐ βούλεται δὲ ὁ μονογενὴς εἰδέναι τοὺς σαρκικοὺς λογισμοὺς τί ποιεῖ ἡ δεξιὰ χεὶρ τοῦ ἁγίου πνεύματος †Ath.*fr.Mt*.(M.27.1372B,C); **12.** of Son, liturg., at blessing of laity ἡ ζῶσα καὶ καθαρὰ χ., ἡ χ. τοῦ μονογενοῦς, ἡ πάντα τὰ πονηρὰ καθηρηκυῖα καὶ πάντα τὰ ἅγια βεβαιώσασ⟨α⟩ καὶ ἠσφαλισμένη ἐκταθήτω ἐπὶ τὰς κεφαλὰς τοῦ λαοῦ τούτου Serap.*euch*.6.1; **13.** prepositional uses: ἐν χερσίν, met., of fame or talents *within one's grasp*, Gr.Nyss.*v.Macr*.(p.378.16; M.46.968A); *at hand* ἐν χ. ἔχεις πᾶν τὸ ἀπόθετον *ib*.(p.403.4; 989A); *by the hand of*, fig. ἐλέγχεσθαι ψυχὴν ἐν χ. σαπρίας αὐτῆς *Pss.Sal*.16.14; μετὰ χεῖρα *in the hand*; lit., Clem.*str*.6.4(p.448.30; M.9.253A); Eus.*v.C*.4.17(p.124.1; M.20.1165A); plur., Just.*dial*.86.1(M.6.680B); Socr.*h.e*.2.1.7(M.67.185C); met. τὰ μετὰ χεῖρας *the words* or *passage before us*, Eus.*d.e*.5.1(p.211.3,20; M.22.349D,352A); *ib*.5.3(p.220.18; 364B); *practically* μετὰ χεῖρας ἀναλαβόντι τὴν σπουδήν Eus.*d.e*.1.1.3(p.3.25; M.22.16D); πρὸς χεῖρα *in the service of*, *A.Phil*.40(p.19.6); ὑπὸ χεῖρα *in the hand*, Eus.*h.e*.9.9.10 (M.20.824A); plur., fig. ὑπὸ τὰς χ. γίνεται τοῦ νόμου Phot.*nomoc*.9.1 (M.104.712C); met., *readily* ἐὰν δὲ ὑπὸ χεῖρα ἁμαρτάνῃ Herm.*mand* 4.3.6; **14.** *force, vigour* ἀπλήστῳ διανοίας χ. Eus.*h.e*.10.4.26(M.20. 860B); **15.** s.v.l, *ray* of light ἀστέρων χεῖρες τρέμουσαι Bas.Sel.*or*.33. 2(M.85.364B); **16.** *measure*, ? *handful* λαβὼν τὸ παλλίον αὐτοῦ ἔδησεν ἐν αὐτῷ φοίνικας ὡσεὶ χ. δύο *A.Jo*.5(p.154.22); **17.** *part* (cf. Hebr. יָד), Thdt.*qu.37 in 2Reg*.(1.441); **18.** *written document* or *letter* χ. ὁλόγραφον αὐθεντικήν Jul.Papa ap.Ath.*apol.sec*.28(p.107.34; M.25. 296A); Ischyras ap.eund.64(p.143.26; 364D); τὰς...τῶν βασιλέων χ... ἐμιμήσαντο Ath.*apol.Const*.11(M.25.608C).

χειραγωγ-έω, *lead by the hand*; in gen., *lead, guide*; met. ἐπὶ τὴν ἀγάπην χ. [sc. ἡ ἐλπίς] Clem.*str*.2.9(p.134.19; M.8.976B); τὴν...τοῦ νόμου παίδευσιν ~οῦσαν ἡμᾶς εἰς Χριστὸν Or.*exc.in Ps*.77:31(M.17. 144D); Meth.*symp*.2.3(p.18.3; M.18.52A); πίστει ~ούμενος Jo.D.*f.o*. 4.11(M.94.1128C); of God τὸν...Κωνσταντῖνον ὑψηλῷ βραχίονι ἐπὶ τὰ τῇδε χειραγωγήσας Eus.*h.e*.10.8.19(M.20.901B) = id.*v.C*.2.2(p.41. 15; M.20.981A); τὸν βασιλέα...χ. πρὸς τὴν ἀλήθειαν Chrys.*hom.9.1 in Mt*.(7.131B); of Christ as Word σκάζοντας τὼ πόδε ἢ πλανωμένους εἰς δικαιοσύνην χειραγωγῆσαι Clem.*prot*.1(p.6.29; M.8.60B); χ. ἐπ' αὐτὸν τοὺς μαθητευομένους Or.*Jo*.19:22(5; p.324.15; M.14.568C); ὁ λόγος χ. τὴν διάνοιαν Gr.Nyss.*v.Mos*.(M.44.372C) cf.id.*hom.5 in Cant*.(M. 44.876B); of H. Ghost, id.*ep*.3(M.46.1024B); of a road, fig. ἡ ὁδὸς τῆς ἀληθείας, ἥτις τοὺς ὁδεύοντας αὐτὴν εἰς τὴν αἰώνιον ~εῖ βασιλείαν Arist.*apol*.16(p.111.22); ὁδὸν εἰς ἀρετὴν ~οῦσαν Chrys.*hom.10.2 in Heb*.(12.176B); ὁδὸν ἐφαίνετο ~ῶν [sc. star of Bethlehem] id.*hom. 6.2 in Mt*.(7.88A); *ib*.7.3(108C).

χειραγωγία, ἡ, *leading by the hand*; met.; **1.** *guidance*, esp. spiritual, Ath.*gent*.34(M.25.68B); ἡ ἀκριβὴς σεαυτοῦ κατανόησις αὐτάρκη παρέξει χ. καὶ πρὸς τὴν ἔννοιαν τοῦ θεοῦ Bas.*hom*.3.7(2.23C; M.31.213C); ὁ θεὸς καὶ τὴν ἐκ τοῦ νόμου σοι χ. προσέθηκε †Bas.*Is*. 220(1.544C; M.30.500B); ἡ παρὰ τῶν ἐντολῶν χ. Gr.Nyss.*ep*.2(M.46. 1009C); ref. Ps.44:4 φωτισμὸν τοῦ προσώπου τοῦ θεοῦ...ὀνομάζει...τὴν εἰς ἕκαστα τῶν ὄντων χ. Cyr.*Jo*.1.8(4.70C); of OT in rel. to NT εὕροι γὰρ ἄν τις...χ. τινὰ παιδευτικὴν τὴν παλαιὰν πρὸς τὴν νέαν ὑπάρχουσαν Proc.G.*Gen*.proem.(M.87.28A); **2.** *assistance* δεχέσθω τὴν κατάλληλον χ. παραμυθούμενος †Gregent.*leg.Hom*.55(M.86.609C).

χειραγωγός, ὁ, *leader, guide*, met. οἱ χ. καὶ πατέρες [sc. τοῦ λαοῦ] Cyr.Mich.23(3.411C); of S. Paul, Dion.Ar.*d.n*.2.11(M.3.649D); of God ἡ μακαριστὴ πίστις αὔξοιτο ὑπὸ χ. τῷ κρείττονι Const.ap.Eus.

v.C.2.28(p.53.13; M.20.1005C); fig. μηδενὶ χ. χρησάμενος, μηδὲ ταῖς θείαις γραφαῖς Eus.e.th.2.9(p.110.14; M.24.920A).

[*]**χειρακρατέω**, *grasp by the hand*, Anast.S.hod.13(M.89.233B).

***χειραλγία, ἡ**, *gout in the hands*; plur., Chrys.hom.22.3 in Jo.(8.130C); ‡Chrys.prov.6(2.775B); Thphn.chron.p.242(M.108.609C).

χειραλγός, *suffering from gout in the hand*, Ephr.1.214F.

***χειραπλόω**, *stretch out one's hands*, ‡Ath.occurs.11(M.28.988A).

***χειρένθεος**, s.v.l., *made by divine hands*, ‡Epiph.hom.2(M.43.456A), ? l. χειροθέοις.

***χειρεπιθεσία, ἡ**, *laying on of hands*, at ordination εἰκονικῇ τινι καὶ ματαίᾳ χ. ἐπισκοπὴν αὐτῷ δοῦναι Corn.ap.Eus.h.e.6.43.9(M.20.620B); in reconciliation of schismatics [i.e. opp. rebaptism] δῆλον ἐπάνω υἱῶν ἀλλοτρίων...διὰ μόνης χ. μὴ δύνασθαι ἅγιον πνεῦμα κατελθεῖν CCarth.(256)act.21(H.1.165D).

***χειρέργιον, τό**, *manual labour*, Bas.renunt.9(2.911B; M.31.648A).

***χείρεργον, τό**, = foreg., Jo.Mosch.prat.13(M.87.2861B).

χειρίδιον, τό, *sleeve*, A.Petr.et Paul.47(p.199.9); Ath.virg.11(p.44.25; M.28.264B); symbolically explained ref. monk's habit, Dor.doct.1.12(M.88.1632C).

χειρίζω, **1.** *handle, manipulate* χ. ἀνάγνως τὰ ἅγια Isid.Pel.epp.1.120(M.78.264A); †Gr.II Papa ep.Leon.2(H.4.16C); **2.** *hold* an office τὴν τοῦ πραίτωρος χ. ἀρχήν Socr.h.e.5.8.12(M.67.577B); τὰς ἱεραρχίας χ. Sophr.H.ep.syn.(M.87.3149D); **3.** *hold, entertain* an opinion τὸν ἐναντίον χ. λόγον Clem.str.5.1(p.329.1; M.9.16A).

***χειρικῶς**, *with the hand*, Hesych.S.temp.36(M.93.1521D).

χειριστέον, *one must handle*, met. τά τε ὁμώνυμα χ. καὶ τὰ συνώνυμα...τακτέον κατὰ τῆς σημασίας Clem.str.8.6(p.90.10; M.9.581B).

χείριστος, *worst*; neut. plur. as adv., Philost.h.e.11.8(p.139.29; M.65.605A).

χειρογραφέω, **1.** *write, record* δίκην βίβλων τῶν ὑπὸ πάντων... κεχειρογραφημένων Or.or.28.5(p.378.11; M.11.525B); **2.** *acknowledge in writing*, of recanting persons, Petr.I Al.ep.can.5(M.18.476A); *give a written bond* or *receipt for* χ. τὸ δάνεισμα Thphyl.exc.gent.8(p.485.30; M.113.948B); met., *acknowledge oneself bound by, in debt to* (ref. Col.2:14), †Bas.Is.233(1.556B; M.30.528A); διὰ τοῦ Ἀδὰμ πάντες τὴν ἁμαρτίαν ἐχειρογραφήσαμεν Procl.CP or.laud.BMV 5(p.105.3; M.65.685B); Bas.Sel.or.3.1(M.85.49B); cf. χειρόγραφον; of acknowledging the faith ἐν τῷ βαπτίσματι [sc. τὴν πίστιν] τῇ γλώττῃ ἐχειρογραφήσαμεν Procl.CP Arm.4(p.189.9; M.65.860B); τοῖς οἰκείοις αἵμασιν...τὴν ὁμολογίαν χειρογραφήσαντες [sc. οἱ μάρτυρες] Sophr.H.v.Anast.(M.92.1681C).

χειρόγραφον, τό, *written record of a debt, bond*; **1.** lit., T.Job 11(p.110.23); Epiph.mens.21(M.43.272B); χ. γάρ ἐστιν, ὅταν τις ὀφλημάτων ὑπεύθυνος κατέχεται Chrys.hom.2.4 in Col.(11.369C); **2.** fig.; **a.** given by man to God at baptism τῷ ἰδίῳ χ. ... ὃ ἐπὶ τῆς κατὰ τὴν πίστιν ὁμολογίας κατέθετο Bas.Spir.26(3.22A; M.32.113B); **b.** given by God to man δὸς καὶ ἐγὼ ἀποδώσω, βοᾷ γράψας ἐν εὐαγγελίοις, ἐν χ. δημοσίῳ τῆς οἰκουμένης, ὃ τέσσαρες ἔγραψαν εὐαγγελισταί Gr.Nyss.usur.(M.46.440A); πίστευσον χ. μὴ βλεπομένῳ μηδὲ σπαρασσομένῳ ib.(440B); χ. σοι ἐποίησεν ὁ θεός· ὁ γὰρ ἐλεῶν πτωχόν, φησί, δανείζει θεῷ [Pr.19:17]...καὶ νῦν τοῦτο δὸς τὸ χ. τοῖς παιδίοις, καὶ καταλίπε τὸν θεὸν αὐτοῖς ὀφειλέτην Chrys.hom.66.5 in Mt.(7.659E–660B); **c.** of sins ὅπως ὁ θεὸς [ἀκυρόσῃ?] τὸ χ. τῶν ἁμαρτιῶν μου διὰ τ[ῶ]ν...ὑμῶ[ν πρ]οσευχῶν P.Lond.1917; ὁ ἄγγελος ἐπὶ χεῖρας ἔχων τὸ χ. τῶν ἁμαρτημάτων σου Apoc.Paul.(p.47); of all actions διὰ τοῦ βίου οἱονεὶ χ. ἡμῶν γράφομεν, τῷ μνημονικῷ ἡμῶν τοὺς τύπους τῶν πραγμάτων ἐναποσφραγιζόμενοι †Bas.Is.233(1.556A; M.30.525Cff.); **d.** ref. Col.2:14, of χ. nailed to Cross, and wiped out by Christ's death; **i.** explanations ὁρᾷς σπουδὴν τοῦ ἀφανισθῆναι τὸ χ. ὅσην ἐποιήσατο;...ποῖον χ.; ἢ τοῦτό φησιν, ὃ ἔλεγον πρὸς τὸν Μωϋσέα, ὅτι 'πάντα ὅσα εἶπεν ὁ θεὸς ποιήσομεν καὶ ἀκουσόμεθα'· ἢ εἰ μὴ τοῦτο, ὅτι ὀφείλομεν τῷ θεῷ ὑπακοήν· ἤ...ὅτι κατεῖχεν ὁ διάβολος τὸ χ. ὃ ἐποίησε πρὸς τὸν Ἀδὰμ ὁ θεός, εἰπών· ᾗ ἂν ἡμέρᾳ φάγῃς ἀπὸ τοῦ ξύλου, ἀποθανῇ Chrys.hom.2.3 in Col.(11.368B); χ. τινες τὸν νόμον ἔφασαν... ἀλλὰ τῶν Ἰουδαίων χ. ἦν, οὐ πάντων ἀνθρώπων. ἡγοῦμαι τοίνυν καὶ τὸ σῶμα ἡμῶν καλεῖσθαι χ. διὰ τοῦτο γὰρ πᾶσαν παράνομον τολμῶμεν πρᾶξιν Thdt.Col.2:14(3.488); **ii.** in gen. ἕκαστος δὲ ἡμῶν ὀφειλέτης ἐστὶ ταῖς ἁμαρτίαις καὶ ὀφειλέτης ἐστὶν ἔχων χ. Or.hom.15.5 in Jer.(p.129.6; M.13.433C); ἐξαγοράζω οὖν τὸ σῶμα τὸ πραθέν σοι διὰ τοῦ πρώτου Ἀδάμ, παραλύω σου τὰ χ. Mac.Aeg.hom.11.10(M.34.552C); σταυρὸς τὸ χ. ἡμῶν διέρρηξε Chrys.hom.in Mt.26:39(3.19C); εἰ τὸ χ. ἡμῶν ὁ σωτὴρ...προσήλωσε τῷ σταυρῷ...τὸ σῶμα ἄρα προσήλωσεν. ἐν γὰρ τῷ σώματι πᾶς ἄνθρωπος, οἷόν τινα γράμματα, πήγνυσι τὰς τῶν ἁμαρτημάτων κηλῖδας Thdt.eran.1 suppl.(4.278); διὰ τὴν ἁμαρτίαν ἔσχε τὸ καθ' ἡμῶν χ. ὁ διάβολος Olymp.fr.Bar.4.6(M.93.769C); commemorated in liturg. anaphora, Lit.Jac.(p.204.11); v. προσηλόω.

χειροδίκης, ὁ, *one who asserts his right by hand, uses the right of might*, Gr.Thaum.Eccl.4:2(M.10.997B).

***χειρόδμητος**, *built by hand*, Gr.Nyss.or.dom.3(p.48.6; M.44.1149C).

χειροθεσία, ἡ, *imposition of the hands*; **1.** in blessing, ref. Christ and the children εἰς χ. εὐλογίας Clem.paed.1.5(p.97.2; M.8.261C); on catechumens, Eus.v.C.4.61(p.143.3; M.20.1213A); Serap.euch.4(tit.); on congregation at eucharist, A.Jo.46(p.173.22); Serap.euch.15(tit.); on sick, ib.8(tit.); **2.** in baptismal rite; Gnost., Clem.exc.Thdot.22.5(p.114.8; M.9.669A); orthodox, associated with consignation, Const.App.2.32.3; signifying royal priesthood of Christians, ib.3.16.3; its importance ἑκάστου γὰρ ἡ δύναμις τῆς χ. ἐστὶν αὕτη. ἐὰν γὰρ μὴ εἰς ἕκαστον τούτων ἐπίκλησις γένηται παρὰ τοῦ εὐσεβοῦς ἱερέως τοιαύτη τις, εἰς ὕδωρ μόνον καταβαίνει ὁ βαπτιζόμενος ὡς οἱ Ἰουδαῖοι, καὶ ἀποτίθεται μόνον τὸν ῥύπον τοῦ σώματος, οὐ τὸν ῥύπον τῆς ψυχῆς ib.7.44.3; Ammon.Ac.9:17(M.85.1536A); **3.** at ordination πρεσβείου χ. Eus.h.e.6.23.4(M.20.576C); χ. ... ἐπισκόπων εἰληφότες CAnt.(341)can.10; οἱ οὖν διάκονοι προσήγαγον πρὸς τὴν διὰ τῶν χειρῶν τῶν ἐπισκόπων...χ. ‡Pion.v.Polyc.23; τὴν ἀρχιερατικὴν χ. Philost.h.e.2.11(M.65.476A); of deaconesses, CChalc.can.15; Paulianist deaconesses apparently an exception ἐπεὶ μηδὲ χ. τινὰ ἔχουσιν, ὥστε ἐξάπαντος ἐν τοῖς λαϊκοῖς αὐτὰς ἐξετάζεσθαι CNic.(325)can.19; as means of remitting sins τὰ γὰρ λοιπὰ ἁμαρτήματα ἔφασαν οἱ πολλοὶ καὶ τὴν χ. ἀφιέναι CNeocaes.can.9; Phot.nomoc.9 tit.(M.104.1094A); at reordination of heretics τοῦ αἱρετικοῦ ἐπὶ τὴν ὀρθοδοξίαν ἐρχομένου τὸ σφάλμα διορθοῦται...τῆς χειροτονίας τῇ χ. ‡Just.qu.et resp.14(M.6.1261D); opp. χειροτονία: Ταράσιος...εἶπεν ὅτι ἐπ' εὐλογίας ἐνταῦθα ἡ χ. λέγεται, καὶ οὐκ ἐπὶ χειροτονίας Schol.in CNic.can.8(p.644); v. χειροτονία.

χειροθετ-έω, *lay the hands upon*; **1.** in blessing, etc.; as priestly prerogative, V.Max.21(M.90.92C); on catechumens καθημέραν χ. Hom.Clem.3.73; in baptismal rite after candidate's renunciation of Satan and profession of faith, Dion.Ar.e.h.2.2.7(M.3.396B); at reconciliation of penitents, Const.App.2.18.7; ib.2.41.2; in healing sick, Hom.Clem.19.25; of priest laying his hand upon eucharistic bread, †Sophr.H.orat.(M.87.4004A); **2.** at ordination, hence *ordain*, Const.App.epit.13 cit. s. καθίστημι; cf.‡Hipp.can.7.48(p.70); Μελίτιον ...μηδεμίαν ἐξουσίαν ἔχειν...μήτε ~εῖν, μήτε προχειρίζεσθαι Socr.h.e.1.9.6(M.67.80A); perhaps intentionally confusing χειροθετέω and χειροτονέω: ~εῖ, φησίν [sc. Aerius], ἐπίσκοπος, ἀλλὰ καὶ ὁ πρεσβύτερος Epiph.haer.75.3(p.334.28; M.42.505C); ref. Novatianist clergy ἔδοξε...~ουμένους αὐτοὺς μένειν οὕτως ἐν τῷ κλήρῳ CNic.(325)can.8.

***χειροκμητέω**, *manufacture*, Dion.Al.fr.ap.Eus.p.e.7.19(p.334B; M.21.564C).

***χειροκοπία, ἡ**, *cutting off of hands*, Anast.S.serm.imag.3(M.89.1156C).

χειροκρατέω, *hold by the hand*, Anast.S.hod.13(M.89.220C).

χειροπέδη, ἡ, *handcuff*, contemptuously of bracelets χαίρουσι... αἱ φιλόχρυσοι δεδεμέναι ταῖς χ., μόνον ἐὰν χρυσὸς ὁ δεσμῶν αὐτὰς ᾖ Bas.hom.7.4(2.55D; M.31.289B).

***χειροπλαστέω**, *form with the hand*; of God creating Adam, ‡Jo.D.hom.5(M.96.652D).

χειροποιέω, *make by hand*, v.l. for χεῖρον ἐποίει, Meth.res.1.47(M.41.1117D).

***χειρότευκτος**, *wrought* or *fashioned by hand*, Eust.fr.in Pr.8:22(M.18.677D); Cyr.Is.2.4(2.293D); Jo.D.imag.1.15(M.94.1244D); neut. as subst., of a surgical operation τὸ χ. ἐργάζονται τῆς τῶν μελῶν ἀφαιρέσεως Epiph.haer.58.1(p.358.24; M.41.1012B); ib.58.3(p.360.14).

χειροτεχν-έω, *be an artisan* ὁ ἀράχνης...~ῶν ἐξ ἑαυτοῦ Dion.Al.ap.Eus.p.e.14.4(774D; M.22.1273C).

χειρότμητος, *cut by hand*, Gr.Nyss.v.Mos.(M.44.380B); Thdt.Heb.9:24(3.603).

χειροτον-έω, **A.** *appoint*; **1.** in gen., ref. imperial appointment Γάλλον Καίσαρα χ. Philost.h.e.3.25(M.65.512C); Socr.h.e.1.38.13(M.67.177C); Soz.h.e.7.24.1(M.67.1489C); ref. divine appointment Χριστὸν ...συντρίβοντα πολυαρχίαν τοπαρχιῶν...καὶ ~οῦντα τὴν Ῥωμαίων μοναρχίαν Const.App.5.20.11; πᾶς ἄρχων ὑπὸ θεοῦ κεχειροτόνηται Isid.Pel.epp.2.216(M.78.657D); esp. kings, Or.adnot.in Gen.7:4(M.17.13A); id.engast.5(p.287.20; M.12.1020A); Thdt.qu.27 in 3Reg.(1.473); OT high priesthood, Const.App.2.27.5; Chrys.sac.4.1(p.101.11; 1.404A); Abraham as πατὴρ πάντων, Thdt.Rom.4:17(3.51); apostles, Chrys.hom.3.4 in Ac.princ.(3.77B); Thdt.qu.11 in Ex.(1.125); and bishops, Serap.euch.28; ref. Devil's use of an unworthy Christian κεχειροτονημένος ὑπὸ τοῦ διαβόλου σκυβαλίζειν τὴν ἐκκλησίαν Const.App.2.43.3; fig. ~εῖ ῥᾳδίως ἡμῖν πολλοὺς μὲν ἁγίους πολλοὺς δ' ἀθέους παρὰ τὸ εἰκὸς ὁ καιρός Gr.Naz.

*or.*22.6(M.35.1137B); **2.** theol. γεννηθεὶς [sc. Son] οὐ κτισθεὶς...οὐ χειροτονηθείς Gr.Ant.*bapt.*2.2(M.88.1872C); cf. μὴ χειροτονήσητε δύο μονογενεῖς τὸν ἕνα μονογενῆ *ib.*6(1877B); **3.** in Church; **a.** *appoint* to office or to a particular function χειροτονήσατε οὖν ἑαυτοῖς ἐπισκόπους καὶ διακόνους ἀξίους τοῦ κυρίου *Did.*15.1; πρέπον ἐστὶν ὑμῖν, ὡς ἐκκλησίᾳ θεοῦ, χειροτονῆσαι διάκονον εἰς τὸ πρεσβεῦσαι ἐκεῖ θεοῦ πρεσβείαν Ign.*Philad.*10.1; of appointment (election) of bishops, Philost.*h.e.*7.6(M.65.544A); Soz.*h.e.*6.8.6(M.67.1316A); of S. Paul's appointment of Titus as apostle of Crete, Thdt.*Is.*11:14 (p.63.3; 2.255); **b.** *ordain* by imposition of hands; **i.** of episcopal consecration τῶν λοιπῶν δὲ ἐπισκόπων [sc. Novatianists] διαδόχους εἰς τοὺς τόπους ἐν οἷς ἦσαν χειροτονήσαντες, ἀπεστάλκαμεν Corn.ap.Eus.*h.e.*6.43.10(M.20.621A); *Clem.ep.*2(M.2.36A); ἐπίσκοπος ...ὑπὸ ἐπισκόπων χειροτονείσθω δύο ἢ τριῶν, πρεσβύτερος ὑπὸ ἑνὸς ἐπισκόπου καὶ διάκονος καὶ οἱ λοιποὶ κληρικοί *Can.App.*1; *Const. App.*3.20.1; *ib.*8.27.2; *Cod.Afr.*13; **ii.** ref. distinction of orders which do and do not receive χειροτονία: πρεσβύτερον ~ῶν, ὦ ἐπίσκοπε, τὴν χεῖρα ἐπὶ τῆς κεφαλῆς ἐπιτίθει αὐτὸς...καὶ εὐχόμενος λέγε *Const.App.*8.16.2; cf.‡Hipp.*can.*5.38; ὑποδιάκονον ~ῶν *Const.App.*8. 21.2 (but cf. Isid.Pel.*epp.*3.75(M.78.784A)); ὁμολογητὴς οὐ ~εῖται... ἐὰν δὲ χρεία αὐτοῦ ᾖ εἰς ἐπίσκοπον ἢ πρεσβύτερον ἢ διάκονον, ~εῖται *ib.*8.23.2; παρθένος...χήρα...ἐπορκιστὴς οὐ ~εῖται *ib.*8.24.2; 8.25.2; 8.26.2; Soz.*h.e.*8.9.1(M.67.1540A); διακόνισσαν...~εῖσθαι CChalc.*can.* 15; **iii.** power to ordain restricted to bishops, *Const.App.*8.28. 2; ‡Ign.*Her.*3; πρεσβύτερος...χειροθετεῖ, οὐ ~εῖ *Const.App.*8.28.3; Epiph.*haer.*75.4(p.336.8; M.42.508D); Chrys.*hom.13.1 in 1Tim.*(11. 618B); but presbyters join with bishop in ordination of presbyters, cf.Hipp.*trad.ap.*8.1; cf.*Const.App.*8.16.2; **iv.** ref. treatment of Paulianist clergy on readmission to Church ἀναβαπτισθέντες χειροτονείσθωσαν ὑπὸ τοῦ τῆς καθολικῆς ἐκκλησίας ἐπισκόπου CNic. (325)*can.*19; cf. ~εῖσθαι τοὺς προσερχομένους Thphl.Al.*cathar.*(M.65. 44B); **v.** contrasted with election τὸ μὲν...χειροτονῆσαι [sc. the Seven]...αὐτῶν [sc. apostles] ἦν, τὸ δὲ ἑλέσθαι ἐκείνοις [sc. the people] ἐπιτρέπουσι Chrys.*hom.14.3 in Ac.*(9.114B); **vi.** in rel. to grace of H. Ghost οὔτε τοῦ ~εῖν εἶχον τὴν ἐξουσίαν, οὐκέτι δυνάμενοι χάριν πνεύματος ἁγίου ἑτέροις παρέχειν ἧς αὐτοὶ ἐκπεπτώκασι Bas.*ep.* 188.1(3.270B; M.32.669A); unseen hand of God being symbolized by outward action, Chrys.*hom.14.3 in Ac.*(9.114E); **vii.** ordinations performed outside a bishop's proper diocese declared void, CNic.(325)*can.*16 = CAnt.(341)*can.*3; **viii.** penalty of deposition enacted for ordainer and ordained in cases of simoniacal ordination, *Can.App.*29; CChalc.*can.*2; CTrull.*can.*22; CNic.(787)*can.*5; **ix.** heret. ordination, *Can.App.*68; Socr.*h.e.*1.9.5(M.67.80A); v. χειροθεσία, χειροθετέω, χειροτονία.

B. *ordain, decree* αὐτῷ μεταδίδωμι τὴν ἐξουσίαν τοῦ δεσμεύειν καὶ λύειν, ἵνα περὶ παντὸς οὗ ἂν χειροτονήσῃ ἐπὶ τῆς γῆς ἔσται δεδογματισμένον ἐν οὐρανοῖς *Clem.ep.*2(M.2.36B).

χειροτονητής, ὁ, *one who appoints* or *ordains* εἰ μέλλομεν τοὺς βίους ἐρευνᾶν τῶν ἀρχόντων, αὐτοὶ μέλλομεν εἶναι χ. τῶν διδασκάλων Chrys.*hom.2.3 in 2Tim.*(11.669B); ‡Jo.D.*ep.Thphl.*13(M.95.361C).

χειροτονία, ἡ, A. *stretching forth of the hand*, exeg. Is.58:9 χ. δὲ τάχα πού φησι τὴν δωροδοκίαν...ἢ καὶ καθ' ἕτερον τρόπον τὸ ἀνταμύνασθαι δηλοῖ, καὶ τὸ ἀνταποδιδόναι κακὸν ἀντὶ κακοῦ Cyr.*Is.*5.4(2. 820B); χ. δὲ τὴν ἄδικον τῶν χειρῶν κίνησιν, ἢ ἐπὶ πληγαῖς γινομένην, ἢ ἐπὶ γράμμασι Thdt.*Is.*58:10(p.228.25; 2.372).

B. *election*, hence *appointment* to office; **1.** in gen., of investiture of king with regal power τὸν βασιλέα φοβηθήσῃ, εἰδὼς ὅτι τοῦ κυρίου ἐστὶν ἡ χ. *Const.App.*7.16; Socr.*h.e.*5.2.2(M.67.568B); Thdt.*qu.26 in 1Reg.*(1.372); id.*qu.45 in 2Reg.*(1.449); of OT priests, id.*qu.47 in Num.*(1.253); **2.** eccl., *ordination*; including both election and ordination by imposition of hands, context sometimes indicating that emphasis is on one or other of these in partic.; **a.** in gen., *appointment* to eccl. office, Dion.Al.ap.Eus.*h.e.*7.9.2(M.20.653A); Pall.*v.Chrys.*5(p.31.9; M.47.19); *ib.*11(p.64.8; 36); Philost.*h.e.*5.3(M. 65.529B); of appointment of the Seven by prayer and imposition of hands, Eus.*h.e.*2.1.1(133B); **b.** partic., of *election* τῶν...ἀδελφῶν ἁπάντων χ. ἕνεκεν τῆς τοῦ μέλλοντος διαδέξεσθαι τὴν ἐπισκοπὴν συγκεκροτημένων *ib.*6.29.3(588C); id.*v.C.*3.62(p.110.27; M.20.1137B); Phot.*nomoc.*1.8(p.466); **c.** partic., of *ordination* to major orders by imposition of bishop's hands, Eus.*m.P.*12(p.947.1; M.20.1513A); *Const.App.*2.2.3; τοῦτο γὰρ ἡ χ. ἐστίν· ἡ χεὶρ ἐπίκειται τοῦ ἀνδρός, τὸ δὲ πᾶν ὁ θεὸς ἐργάζεται καὶ ἡ αὐτοῦ χείρ ἐστιν ἡ ἁπτομένη τῆς κεφαλῆς τοῦ χειροτονουμένου, ἐὰν ὡς δεῖ χειροτονῆται Chrys.*hom.14.3 in Ac.* (9.114C); ἐν ταῖς χ. τῶν ἱερέων τὸ εὐαγγέλιον τοῦ Χριστοῦ ἐπὶ κεφαλῆς τίθεται ‡Chrys.*leg.*4(6.410B); οὐδὲ νενόμισται αὐτοὺς [sc. subdeacons and readers] πρὸ τοῦ θυσιαστηρίου τὴν χ. δέχεσθαι, ἐπεὶ μηδὲ αὐτῷ ὑπηρετοῦνται τῷ μυστηρίῳ Thdr.Mops.*1Tim.*3:15(p.132.13; M.66. 941D); hence sometimes almost synon. with χειροθεσία, Eus.*h.e.*6. 19.16(M.20.569B); cf.*ib.*23.4(576C); πρεσβύτερος ἐὰν...ὁμολογήσῃ ὅτι ἥμαρτεν πρὸ τῆς χ., μὴ προσφερέτω...τὰ γὰρ λοιπὰ ἁμαρτήματα ἔφασαν οἱ πολλοὶ καὶ τὴν χειροθεσίαν ἀφιέναι CNeocaes.*can.*9; εἰ δὲ καὶ τολμήσειέ τις ὑφαρπάσαι τὸν τῷ ἑτέρῳ διαφέροντα, καὶ χειροτονῆσαι ἐν τῇ αὐτοῦ ἐκκλησίᾳ, μὴ συγκατατιθεμένου τοῦ ἰδίου ἐπισκόπου, οὗ ἀνεχώρησεν ὁ ἐν τῷ κανόνι ἐξεταζόμενος, ἄκυρος ἔσται ἡ χ. CNic.(325) *can.*16; ἐπίσκοπον μὴ ἐπιβαίνειν ἀλλοτρίᾳ πόλει...ἐπὶ χ. τινός...εἰ δὲ τολμήσειέν τις τοιοῦτο ἄκυρον εἶναι τὴν χειροθεσίαν CAnt.(341)*can.*22; ref. those ordained by Meletius τοὺς δὲ ὑπ' αὐτοῦ κατασταθέντας μυστικωτέρᾳ χ. βεβαιωθέντας...ἔχειν...τὴν τιμὴν καὶ λειτουργίαν CNic.*ep.*(p.49.5)ap.Socr.*h.e.*1.9.5(M.67.80A); related to χειροθεσία as whole to part, ‡Just.*qu.et resp.*14(M.6.1261D) cit. s. χειροθεσία; forbidden to presbyters, Chrys.*hom.11.1 in 1Tim.*(11.604D); cf. Arian accusation against Athanasius ὡς ὅτε παρὰ πρεσβυτέρων ἔχει τὴν χ. *Apophth.Patr.*(M.65.341B); reordination unlawful in all cases of regular ordination, *Can.App.*68; οὐ δυνατὸν εἴη δὶς τὴν αὐτὴν ἐπιτεθῆναι χ. Thdt.*h.rel.*13(3.1208); simoniacal ordination void, CChalc. *can.*2; **d.** of consecration of bishops, by all bishops of province or at least three, CNic.(325)*can.*4; cf.CAnt.(341)*can.*19; CLaod.*can.*5.

***χειροχρήστης, ὁ,** *trustee* ὁ χ., ὁ τὰ ἀλλότρια πιστευόμενος ἐπὶ τῷ διαδοῦναι τοῖς πένησιν ‡Ath.*qu.Ant.*88(M.28.652B).

χειρόω, *master, subdue*; usu. med.; **1.** fig., Gr.Nyss.*or.catech.*23 (p.89.6; M.45.64A); μέθη γάρ τίς ἐστι βαθεῖα· διὸ καὶ δυσανάγωγον τὸν χειρωθέντα ποιεῖ τοῦτο τὸ πάθος Chrys.*hom.3.5 in Jo.*(8.23B); pass., *be subjected* to ὡς γὰρ ὑμῖν πατρὶ καὶ υἱῷ πάντα κεχείρωται Athenag. *leg.*18.2(M.6.925B); **2.** *bind by affection*, Chrys.*ep.*149(3.687B); *ib.*172 (698C); id.*hom.16.1 in 2Cor.*(10.552D).

***χελάνδιον, τό,** *barge*, Thphn.*chron.*p.316(M.108.764C).

χερμάδιος, *of the shape* or *size of a slingstone*, χ. λίθος stone *for slinging*, ‡Nil.*perist.*12.9(M.79.956B).

***χερμάς,** *stone-throwing*, Nonn.*par.Jo.*10:31(M.43.837A).

χερουβείμ, τά, v. χερουβίμ.

***χερουβικός, 1.** *of the nature of the cherubim* τῶν χ. ζῴων *A.Phil.* 132(p.63.8); of celestial powers in whose company sacred ministers enter sanctuary, ‡Bas.*h.myst.*49(p.390.21); **2.** *belonging to the cherubim, of the cherubim*; **a.** of the heavenly chariot (Ecclus.49:8), *Apoc.BMV* (p.124.17); sent from heaven to fetch Abraham, *T.Abr.* A 9(p.87.14); τῶν σεραφὶμ τὴν λειτουργίαν τὴν ζέουσαν, ἢ τῶν χ. ἁρμάτων τὴν διφρείαν Mac.Mgn.*apocr.*2.20(p.39.16); τὸν [sc. infant Jesus] ἐν ναῷ καὶ ἐν ὑψίστοις· τὸν ἐπὶ θρόνου βασιλικοῦ καὶ ἐπ' ὀχήματος χερουβικοῦ ‡Meth.*Sym.et Ann.*6(M.18.360C); **b.** of throne formed by cherubim for God in heaven (Ps.79:2) τοῦ χ. ... αἰωνίου θρόνου Didym.*Trin.*2.11(M.39.656B); ref. Lc.2:28 αὐτὸν ἐν ἀγκάλαις τοῦ πρεσβύτου οἰκονομικῶς, καὶ αὐτὸν ἐν θρόνοις χ. θεοπρεπῶς ‡Cyr.H. *occurs.*5(M.33.1192B); Thdot.Anc.*hom.BMV et Sym.*10(M.77.1404D); Procl.CP *or.*6.11(M.65.741B); ὡς τῷ θρόνῳ τῷ χ. παρεστὼς [sc. Gabriel at Annunciation] οὕτως ἀτενίσαι εἰς αὐτὴν [sc. BMV]...οὐκ ἐτόλμα Abr.Eph.*annunt.*4(p.445.20); ἔπιδε ἐφ' ἡμᾶς...τοὺς τῷ ἁγίῳ τούτῳ θυσιαστηρίῳ ὡς τῷ χ. σου παρισταμένους θρόνῳ *Lit.Praesanct.*(p.349. 8); of deacon's sedilium in sanctuary conceived of as possessed and used by cherubim τὸν δὲ πρεσβύτερον, τὸν σεραφικὸν ἐπέχειν θρόνον· τὸν δὲ διάκονον, τὸν χ. Gel.Cyz.*h.e.*2.31.3(M.85.1316C); met., of BMV, Jo.Eub.*concept.BMV* 14(M.96.1481); of S. John τὸ χ. στόμα ‡Chrys.*Jo.theol.*1.1(8.130C); ref. Ezech.10:1, of sacerdotal cap as ἑδραίωμα τοῦ χ. θρόνου Sophr.H.*liturg.*8(M.87.3988C); **c.** liturg., of hymn sung at Great Entrance; various forms: cf. ἄρχονται οἱ ἀναγνῶσται τοῦ χ. [Brightman p.41.24] σιγησάτω πᾶσα σὰρξ βροτεία· κτλ. ... ἄλλο· οἱ τὰ χερουβὶμ μυστικῶς εἰκονίζοντες *Lit.Jac.*(p.176. 20); ὁ χ. ὕμνος· οἱ τὰ χερουβὶμ κτλ. *Lit.Chrys.*(p.377.8); cf. νῦν αἱ δυνάμεις τῶν οὐρανῶν σὺν ἡμῖν ἀοράτως λατρεύουσιν· ἰδοὺ γὰρ εἰσπορεύεται ὁ βασιλεὺς τῆς δόξης *Lit.Praesanct.*(p.348.21); ὁ χ. ὕμνος ἐμφαίνει...τὴν εἴσοδον τῶν ἁγίων...μετὰ τοῦ ἁγίου τῶν ἁγίων ὑπάρχοντος, συνεισπορευομένων...ἔμπροσθεν τῶν χ. δυνάμεων...καὶ δορυφορουσῶν ἔμπροσθεν...τοῦ βασιλέως Χριστοῦ προερχομένου εἰς μυστικὴν θυσίαν ‡Bas.*h.myst.*49(p.390.18); ὁ χ. ὕμνος παρακελεύεται πάντας ἐντεῦθεν καὶ μέχρι τοῦ τέλους τῆς ἱερουργίας προσεκτικώτερον ἔχειν τὸν νοῦν, πᾶσαν βιωτικὴν μέριμναν κάτω ἀφέντας, ὡς βασιλέα μέλλοντας μέγαν ὑποδέχεσθαι ‡Sophr.H.*liturg.*20(M.87.4001A); ‡Germ. CP *contempl.*(M.98.420A).

χερουβίμ (χερουβείμ, χερουβίν), τά, *cherubim*;

A. angelic beings; **1.** etym. τὸ ὄνομα τῶν χ. δηλοῦν ἐπίγνωσιν πολλήν Clem.*str.*5.6(p.350.4; M.9.61A); cf.Or.*comm.in Rom.*3.8(M. 14.948B) cit. infra B.2; πληθυσμὸς δὲ γνώσεως ἑρμηνεύεται τὰ χ. Didym.*Zach.*1.332; τί...ἐστι χ.; πεπληθυσμένη γνῶσις Chrys.

*incomprehens.*3.5(1.468C); Thdt.*Ezech.*1:18b(2.689); **2.** nature: second in first triad of celestial hierarchy, Dion.Ar.*c.h.*6.2(M.3.201A); τὰ...τρίτα σεραφίμ· τὰ δὲ δεύτερα χ.· καὶ τὰ πρῶτα θρόνοι Max.*schol.c.h.*7.1(M.4.65A); equated with thrones, ref. Col.1:16 ὁ... θρόνων μνημονεύσας ἄλλῳ ὀνόματι τὰ χ. διηγήσατο, τῇ γνωριμωτέρᾳ προσηγορίᾳ τὸ ἀσαφὲς τῆς Ἑβραΐδος ἐξελληνίσας. καθῆσθαι γὰρ τὸν θεὸν ἐπὶ τῶν χ. ἀκούσας τὰς δυνάμεις ταύτας τοῦ ἐπ' αὐτῶν καθεζομένου θρόνους ὠνόμασεν Gr.Nyss.*Eun.*1(1 p.112.27; M.45.348A); θρόνους ἡγοῦμαι τὰ χ. αὐτὸν λέγειν. τούτοις γὰρ εἶδεν τὸν θεῖον ἐπικείμενον θρόνον...Ἰεζεκιήλ Thdt.*Col.*1:16(3.478); incorporeal intelligences οὐκ ἀοράτους τινὰς δυνάμεις λέγει [Gen.3:24] τὰ χ. ... οὔτε ἡ φλογίνη ῥομφαία φύσις ἦν πυρός...οὔτε τὰ χ. ζῷα, ἀλλ' ὄψις τοιαύτη...χ. καλεῖ πᾶν τὸ δυνατόν Thdr.Mops.*Gen.*3:24(M.66.641C); cf. οἱ θρόνοι λογικόν ἐστι καὶ ἀσώματον σύστημα...τοῦτο δὲ καὶ ἡ τῶν χ. ἑρμηνεία δηλοῖ Thdt.*Ezech.*1:18b(2.689); with pre-eminent gift of knowledge (v. 1 supra) τῶν χ. τὸ γνωστικὸν...καὶ θεοπτικόν, καὶ τῆς ὑπερτάτης φωτοδοσίας δεκτικόν Dion.Ar.*c.h.*7.1(M.3.205C); hence title of BMV χαῖρε, χ., ὁ πυροειδὴς νοῦς, ἡ ὡς ὄμματα τὰ θεῖα νοήματα πλήθουσα Thdr.Stud.*nativ.BMV* 7(M.96.692A); yet creatures, Jo.D.*imag.*1.15(M.94.1244C); unable to see or comprehend God as he is in himself, *A.Xanthipp.*14(p.68.14) cit. s. ἀτενιστός; *ib.*12(p.65.31); Chrys.*incomprehens.*3.5(1.468C); *ib.*4.3(475) cit. s. σεραφίμ; ‡Caes.Naz.*dial.*140(M.38.1056); Jo.D.*f.o.*1.1(M.94.789A); cf. τοὺς ἐπάνω τῶν χ. ὀφθαλμῶν ὑψουμένους τῇ προπετείᾳ †Diad.*Ar.*1(M.65.1152A); **3.** appearance: χ. πύρινα *Apoc.En.*14.11; τὰ χ. τετραπρόσωπα· καὶ τὰ πρόσωπα αὐτῶν εἰκόνες τῆς πραγματείας τοῦ υἱοῦ τοῦ θεοῦ...καὶ τὰ εὐαγγέλια...τούτοις σύμφωνα, ἐν οἷς ἐγκαθέζεται Χριστός Iren.*haer.*3.11.8(M.7.886A) cit. ‡Bas.*h.myst.*44(p.388.26); πολυόμματα ἑξαπτέρυγα χ. τε καὶ σεραφίμ ‡Hipp.*consumm.*39(p.305.17; M.10.941B); πολυόμματα καὶ πολύπτερα τάγματα, χ. ... καὶ σεραφίμ Dion.Ar.*c.h.*6.2(M.3.201A); not to be literally understood τὰ περὶ τῶν...σεραφὶμ...καὶ τὰ περὶ τῶν...χ. ..., καὶ τῶν ὡσανεὶ σχημάτων αὐτῶν, καὶ τίνα τρόπον ὀχεῖσθαι λέγεται ἐπὶ τῶν χ. ὁ θεὸς ...κεκρυμμένως εἴρηται Or.*Cels.*6.18(p.89.13ff.; M.11.1317C); Gr.Naz.*or.*31.22(p.172.6; M.36.157A); **4.** functions: operating heavenly chariot, *Apoc.Mos.*(p.12); αὕτη [sc. παρθένος]...καὶ ὄχημα γίνεται βασιλικόν, καθάπερ τὰ χ. ... καὶ παρέστηκεν αὐτῷ καθάπερ τὰ σεραφίμ Chrys.*fem.reg.*6(1.262D); κύριε...ὁ...ἡνίοχος τῶν χ. Anton.Hag.*v.Sym.Styl.*14(p.38.21); praising God, Clem.*str.*5.6(p.350.20; M.9.61C) cit. s. δοξολόγος; *A.Petr.et Andr.*15(p.124.8); λέγεται...τοὺς ἀγγέλους ταύτῃ τῇ φωνῇ [sc. ἀλληλούϊα] αἰνεῖν τὸν θεὸν ὥσπερ τὰ χ. τό· ἅγιος, ἅγιος, ἅγιος Ath.*exp.Ps.*104 proem.(M.27.441C); τῶν χ. ἐσμεν συγχορευταί Chrys.*hom.79.3 in Jo.*(8.469B); assisting at Judgement, *T.Abr.*B 10(p.114.21); ‡Hipp.*consumm.*39(p.305.17; M.10.941B); defending Church, Anast.S.*hex.*12(M.89.1064C,1076A); regarded as occupying sanctuary during liturgy and typified by presbyters, *Const.Cap.*8; or by fans, Tim.Ant.*descr.BMV* 7(M.28.953D); or by deacons, ‡Bas.*h.myst.*59(pp.393.26,394.4); *ib.*60(p.394.12); themselves represented by sphinxes, *A.Andr.et Mt.*13(p.79.14); **5.** in magical formula χ., σεραφίμ, βοηθεῖτε *T.Sal.*18.34(p.58.4; M.122.1345C).

B. OT figures representing cherubim; **1.** affixed to gates of Antioch by Vespasian, *Chron.Pasch.*p.247(M.92.593B); brought from Jerusalem by Titus, Niceph.Ur.*v.Sym.*12(M.86.2997A); cf. *Chron.Pasch.*p.247(593C); **2.** interpretations: cf. *cujus ergo formam duo ista cherubin habere existimanda sunt? cherubin enim in nostram linguam interpretatum 'plenitudinem scientiarum' significat. ...significatur igitur...in isto propitiatorio, hoc est in anima Jesu, Verbum dei...et spiritum...sanctum semper habitare: et hoc est quod indicant duo cherubin propitiatorio superposita*, Or.*comm.in Rom.*3.8(M.14.948Bf.); ἔπηξα [i.e. Moses]...χ. ὁμοίωμα τῶν ἀοράτων, διεπέτασα εἰς τὰ ἅγια ὡς τύπον καὶ σκιὰν τῶν μελλόντων Sever.ap.Jo.D.*imag.*1(M.94.1276D); ἦν δὲ ἐκεῖ τὰ τῶν χερουβεὶμ εἰκάσματα τύπον τῶν ἀσωμάτων δυνάμεων ἔχοντα *cat.Heb.*13:17(p.276.15); cf. περί τε τῶν ποιηθέντων χ. τῷ Μωϋσεῖ...τὴν μὲν ποίησιν αὐτῶν ὁμολογεῖ [sc. Pierius] οἰκονομίας δὲ λόγῳ συγχωρηθῆναι ματαιολογεῖ, ὡς οὐδὲν ἦσαν ...οὐδὲ τύπον ἄλλον ἔφερε μορφῆς, ἀλλὰ μόνον πτερύγων κενολογεῖ φέρειν αὐτὰ σχῆμα Phot.*cod.*119(M.103.400C); as adumbrating Christian use of icons, Jo.D.*imag.*1.15(1244C); CNic.(787)*act.*4(H.4.161C).

χερσία, ἡ, *barrenness*, Cyr.*Is.*1.3(2.81E).

***χερσομανέω,** *go to waste*; of land, Gr.Naz.*or.*16.12(M.35.949B); met., of Church, *ib.*18.16(1004C); of soul, Andr.Cr.*or.*17(M.97.1176C).

χερσ-όομαι, 1. *become dry* or *barren*; met., Cyr.*Ps.*79:15(M.69.1200C); of a pagan city, Thdt.*h.e.*4.18.14(3.979); trans., *make dry*, met. Ἰωάννης...οὐκ εἶχεν ἀμπελῶνα, ἵνα μὴ ἑαυτὸν χερσοώσῃ Jo.Jej.*poenit.cont.virg.*(M.88.1972B); **2.** *become overgrown* with thistles (cf. τρίβολος χερσαῖος, *caltrop*) οἱ ἀμπελῶνες...∼οῦνται ἀπὸ τῶν ἀκανθῶν Herm.*mand.*10.1.5; Chrys.*hom.49.6 in Mt.*(7.513A); fig. πόλιν κεχερσωμένην καὶ ἀκανθῶν Ἑλληνικῶν πεπληρωμένην Thdt.*h.e.*4.18.14(3.979); Proc.G.*Is.*5:7(M.87.1912A); met., *be neglected* τὴν ἐπιφάνειαν καλλωπιζόμεναι καὶ τὰ βάθη ∼ούμεναι Clem.*paed.*3.2(p.237.29; M.8.560A).

χερσώδης, *barren*, met. τοὺς παχεῖς τὸν νοῦν καὶ χ. Μοντανιστάς Didym.*Trin.*3.18(M.39.881B).

***χερχάλ, τό,** (Hebr. כִּכָּר) *cake* τὸ δὲ χερχὰλ ἄρτου κολλυρίδα ἐν ταῖς βασιλείαις εὑρήκαμεν Thdt.*qu.1 in Par.*(1.562).

χέω, *pour*; med. and pass.; **1.** of a land, *be spread* or *extended* χθὼν δὲ ἡ γῆ εἰς μέγεθος κεχυμένη Clem.*str.*5.8(p.358.9; M.9.76B); **2.** of a robe, *fall in folds, be flowing*, Gr.Nyss.*v.Mos.*(M.44.320D); **3.** of word of God, *be spread abroad* τοῦ σωτηρίου λόγου χυθέντος Gr.Naz.*or.*4.74(M.35.600A); ἔδει χυθῆναι τὸ ἀγαθόν *ib.*38.11(M.36.320C); **4.** *be unrestrained*, of laughter γέλως κεχυμένος Chrys.*hom.1.6 in Col.*(11.331B); fig. τὸ συστέλλεσθαι μὲν ἐν τοῖς ὀλίγοις...χεῖσθαι ⟨δὲ⟩ ἐν τοῖς μεγάλοις Meth.*Porph.*2(p.505.11; M.18.401D).

χηνόπλουμα, τό, (cf. Lat. *pluma*) *mattress of goose feathers*, ‡Chrys.*salt.Herodiad.*1(8.40B); ‡Chrys.*hom.*3.6(M.64.437D).

χήρα, ἡ, A. *widow*; **1.** in gen. ἡ χ. τῷ Χριστῷ ἁρμόζεται ἐν τῇ χηρείᾳ Chrys.*hom.15.1 in 1Tim.*(11.634C); cf.*ib.13.2*(620B); ἐπειδὴ δὲ ἐκεῖνον ἔλαβε πρὸς ἑαυτὸν ὁ θεός, ἀντ' ἐκείνου σοι [sc. widow] γέγονεν αὐτός [cf.Ps.145:9] id.*vid.*1.1(1.339B); **2.** care of widows enjoined as a Christian duty, Herm.*mand.*8.10; id.*sim.*1.8; *ib.*5.3.7; certain schismatics reproached for neglect, Ign.*Smyrn.*6.2; Polyc.*ep.*6.1; offerings presented to God distributed among widows and needy, Just.*1apol.*67.6(M.6.429C); *Const.App.*8.30.2; ὅταν λέγῃ, 'χήρας τίμα', τοῦτο λέγει περὶ τῆς τῶν ἀναγκαίων τροφῆς...καὶ πάλιν, 'τίμα τὰς ὄντως χήρας'· τουτέστι, τὰς ἐν πενίᾳ· ὅσῳ γὰρ ἂν τις ἐν πενίᾳ ᾖ, τοσούτῳ μᾶλλόν ἐστι χ. Chrys.*hom.15.2 in 1Tim.*(11.635E,F); **3.** remarriage of widows ὁρᾷς ὅτι οὐ τὸ μὴ δευτέροις ὁμιλῆσαι γάμοις ἀρκεῖ δεῖξαι τὴν χήραν, ἀλλ' ἑτέρων δεῖ πολλῶν; διὰ τί γὰρ...δευτέροις οὐχ ὁμιλῆσαι γάμοις προτρέπει; ἆρα κατέγνω τοῦ πράγματος; οὐδαμῶς· τοῦτο γὰρ αἱρετικῶν· ἀλλ' ἀπησχολῆσθαι βουλόμενος λοιπὸν αὐτὴν ἐν τοῖς πνευματικοῖς, καὶ πρὸς τὴν ἀρετὴν μετατάξασθαι *ib.14.2*(626E); second marriage allowed but third forbidden, †Gregent.*leg.Hom.*49(M.86.608A); **4.** their importance βούλει μαθεῖν ὅσον ἐστὶ χ.; πῶς ἐστι τιμία τῷ θεῷ, καὶ ἐπέραστος καὶ συνήγορος μεγίστη; καὶ τοὺς καταδικασθέντας...καὶ τοὺς ἐκπεπολεμωμένους τῷ θεῷ καὶ πάσης ἐστερημένους ἀπολογίας φανεῖσα ἐξαρπάζει καὶ καταλλάττει, καὶ οὐχὶ συγγνώμην αὐτοῖς κομίζει μόνον...ἀλλὰ καὶ πολλὴν τὴν παρρησίαν καὶ τὴν λαμπρότητα...τὴν προστασίαν ἐπιδείκνυται τὴν ἑαυτῆς, οὐ παρὰ ἄρχοντι καὶ βασιλεῖ τῶν ἐπὶ τῆς γῆς, ἀλλὰ παρ' αὐτῷ τῷ τῶν οὐρανῶν βασιλεῖ Chrys.*hom.in 1Tim.*5:9(3.312Bff.); **5.** in rel. to virgins, v. παρθένος; **6.** description of true widow εἴ τις...μὴ κοσμικὸν ἐπανήρηται βίον, καὶ ἐν χηρείᾳ οὖσα, αὕτη ὄντως χ. ἐστίν, ἡ ἐπὶ τὸν θεὸν ἐλπίζουσα ὡς χρή, ἡ δεήσει προσανέχουσα, καὶ προσκαρτεροῦσα νυκτὸς καὶ ἡμέρας, αὕτη χ. ἐστίν· οὐχ ὡς καὶ τῆς τέκνα ἐχούσης, οὐχὶ χήρας οὔσης...ἀλλ' εἴ τις τέκνα μὴ ἔχει, τουτέστιν ἡ μεμονωμένη οὖσα Chrys.*hom.13.2 in 1Tim.*(11.620A,B).

B. of order of widows in Church (cf. 1Tim.5.9ff.); **1.** in gen., cf. *instituit etiam* [sc. *Petrus*] *ordinem viduarum atque omnia ecclesiae ministeria disponit*, *Clem.recogn.*6.15(M.1.1356A); χ. καθιστανέσθωσαν τρεῖς· αἱ δύο προσμένουσαι τῇ προσευχῇ περὶ πάντων ἐν πείρᾳ, καὶ πρὸς τὰς ἀποκαλύψεις περὶ οὗ ἂν δέῃ· μία δὲ παρεδρεύουσα ταῖς ἐν ταῖς νόσοις πειραζομέναις *Sent.App.*2(p.84); παραγγέλλωμεν τὰς σπαταλώσας τῶν χηρῶν ἐκτὸς εἶναι τοῦ καταλόγου τῶν χηρῶν Chrys.*hom.13.4 in 1Tim.*(11.624D); ὥσπερ...ἐπισκόπους καὶ πρεσβυτέρους καὶ διακόνους καὶ παρθένους καὶ ἐγκρατευομένους ἀριθμῷ, τὰ μέλη τῆς ἐκκλησίας καταλέγων, οὕτω καὶ χ. id.*hom.30.4 in 1Cor.*(10.274D); **2.** regulations concerning appointment; must have reached age of 60 years, *Const.App.*3.2.1; cf.Bas.*ep.*199.24(3.293D); once married, *ib.*; *Const.App.*3.3.1 cit. s. ἀληθινός; but cf. 'γεγονυῖα ἑνὸς ἀνδρὸς γυνή', ἀντὶ τοῦ, μὴ δεύτερον ἀγαγομένη, ἀλλ' ἐκείνῳ μόνῳ προσκαρτερήσασα καὶ σωφρόνως βιώσασα, εἴτε ἕνα τοῦτον εἶχεν, εἴτε καὶ δεύτερον ἠγάγετο Thdr.Mops.*1Tim.*5:9(p.160.19; M.66.944A,B); Thdt.*1Tim.*5:9(3.664); selection of suitable persons by bishop, Chrys.*sac.*3.16(p.84.23; 1.396A,B); reason for establishing qualifications οὐ περὶ τῶν εἰς διακονίαν προαχθῆναι ὀφειλουσῶν διαλέγεται, ἀλλὰ περὶ τῶν εἰς τὸ χηρικὸν ἐγκαταλεγῆναι...ἀλλ' ἐπειδὴ κατελέγοντο χῆραι διὰ τὸ τῆς ἐκκλησιαστικῆς ἐπιμελείας ἀξιοῦσθαι, οὐκ ἀρετῆς ἐπιθυμίᾳ τὴν χηρείαν μετιοῦσαι, ἀλλ' ὥστε ἀμερίμνως τὰς σωματικὰς ἐκ τῆς ἐκκλησίας πορίζεσθαι χρείας, ἐκ δὲ τούτου πλεῖστα... ἐπετελεῖτο κακά· διὰ τοῦτο ἡλικίᾳ καὶ ἀρετῇ ὡρίσατο τὴν εἰς τὸν καταλογον τῶν χ. συντελεῖν ὀφείλουσαν Thdr.Mops.*1Tim.*5:9(p.159n.; 944A); **3.** order distinct from clergy and laity, *Const.App.*3.15.5; and from deaconesses, *ib.*3.8.1; CTrull.*can.*40; not to receive ordination χήρα οὐ χειροτονεῖται...κατατασσέσθω εἰς τὸ χηρικὸν *Const.App.*8.25.2; **4.** special place assigned in church, *ib.*2.57.12; **5.** behaviour ὑπαρχέτω δὲ πᾶσα χ. πραεῖα, ἥσυχος, ἐπιεικής, ἄκακος, ἀόργητος, κτλ. *ib.*3.5.1; *ib.*7.1–8; σεμνὰς οὖν δεῖ εἶναι τὰς χ., πειθομένας τοῖς ἐπισκόποις καὶ τοῖς πρεσβυτέροις...εὐλαβουμένας, ἐντρεπομένας, φοβουμένας, μὴ κατεξουσιαζούσας μηδὲ παρὰ τὴν διαταγήν τι ποιεῖν θελούσας δίχα γνώμης τοῦ διακόνου...εἰ δὲ μὴ κελευσθεῖσα ποιήσει ἕν τι τούτων, ἐπιτιμάσθω νηστείᾳ ἢ ἀφορισμῷ ὡς προπετής *ib.*3.8.1; **6.** honoured in church τὰς χ. σωφρονούσας περὶ τὴν τοῦ κυρίου πίστιν...γινωσκούσας, ὅτι εἰσὶ θυσιαστήριον θεοῦ καὶ ὅτι πάντα μωμοσκοπεῖται Polyc.*ep.*4.3; αἵ τε χ. καὶ οἱ ὀρφανοὶ εἰς τύπον τοῦ θυσιαστηρίου λελογίσθωσαν ὑμῖν *Const.App.*2.26.8; *ib.*3.6.3; ‡Ign. *Tars.*9; likened to brazen altar in OT, Meth.*symp.*5.8(p.62.21; M. 18.112A); **7.** regular provision for widows, abolished by Julian μέχρι τε παρθένων καὶ χ., τὰς δι' ἔνδειαν ἐν τοῖς κλήροις τεταγμένας εἰσπράττεσθαι προσέταξεν ἃ πρὶν παρὰ τοῦ δημοσίου ἐκομίσαντο Soz. *h.e.*5.5.2(M.67.1228A); restored by his successor, and mentioned by Thdt. as existing in his own day, Thdt.*h.e.*1.11.2(3.774).

C. of those vowing to abstain from a second marriage ἐκεῖναι χ. λέγονται αἱ εἰς εὐτέλειαν ἐσχάτην καταπεσοῦσαι, καὶ ἐγγεγραμμέναι, καὶ ἐκ τῶν ἐκκλησιαστικῶν τρεφόμεναι χρημάτων...κἀκεῖναι, αἱ μηδενὸς μὲν δεόμεναι, ἀλλὰ εὐπορίας ἀπολαύουσαι...τὸν δὲ ἄνδρα ἀποβαλοῦσαι μόνον. ἴδωμεν οὖν περὶ ποίας χήρας ἐνταῦθά φησι [sc. 1Tim.5:9]... ἆρα περὶ τῆς δεομένης βοηθείας καὶ χρείαν ἐχούσης ἐξ ἐκκλησιαστικῶν τρέφεσθαι χρημάτων;...χηρῶν τὸ παλαιὸν ἦσαν χοροί, καὶ οὐκ ἐξῆν αὐταῖς ἁπλῶς εἰς τὰς χήρας ἐγγράφεσθαι. οὐ περὶ ἐκείνης οὖν λέγει [sc. ὁ Παῦλος] τῆς ἐν πενίᾳ ζώσης καὶ δεομένης βοηθείας, ἀλλὰ περὶ ταύτης τῆς ἑλομένης χηρείαν Chrys.*hom.in 1Tim.*5:9(3.312D–313B); ἡ χ. καὶ ἡ παρθένος...τοῦτον αἱροῦνται τὸν βίον...ἵνα τὰ τοῦ κυρίου μεριμνῶσιν, ἵνα ἐξ ὁλοκλήρου τῇ τοῦ θεοῦ θεραπείᾳ προσεδρεύωσι id.*vid.*2.3(1.354B).

***χήρανδρος**, *deprived of one's husband* ἐκκλησία...οὐκέτι χ., ἀλλὰ θέανδρος ἐξανθοῦσα ‡Epiph.*hom.*1(M.43.432B).

***χηρανεία, ἡ**, s.v.l., *widowhood*, prob. for χηρεία, Chrys.*Is.interp.* 1.6(6.12C).

χηρεύω, 1. *be without, lack* πίστεως...χ. τινες τῶν αἱρετικῶν Didym. *Trin.*3.28(M.39.944C); ἀρετῆς...χ. Isid.Pel.*epp.*1.147(M.78.281B); of Christ ἡ πότε σῶμα χηρεῦον θεότητος πράξεις ἐνήργησεν οὐσιωδῶς γνωριζομένας θεότητος; Sophr.H.*ep.syn.*(M.87.3168B); **2.** *be widowed*, met. of a church without a bishop, Philost.*h.e.*5.1(M.65.528D); CChalc.*can.*25; Gel.Cyz.*h.e.*2.1.13(M.85.1225D); in gen., *be deprived of* χηρεύσαντα [sc. τὰ ἔθνη] βασιλικῆς εὐκοσμίας Eus.*v.C.*1.22(p.19.4; M.20.937C); οὐκ ἀφῆκε χρηστῆς ἐλπίδος ὁ θεὸς τὴν φύσιν χηρεύσασαν Bas.Sel.*or.*3.4(M.85.61B); τῆς ἡμέρας ἡ κτίσις ἐχήρευε *ib.*6.1(85B).

χηρικόν, τό, *order of widows* χηρικὰ συστησάμενος [sc. ὁ Πέτρος] *Hom.Clem.*11.35; *Const.App.*3.2.1; *ib.*8.25.2; εἰς τὸ χ. ἐγκαταλεγῆναι Thdr.Mops.*1Tim.*5:9(p.159n.; M.66.944A).

***χηροτροφεῖον, τό**, *home for widows*, Soz.*h.e.*5.15.5(χηροτροφία M.67.1256).

***χθαμαλοπετής**, *flying near the ground*, Cyr.*Jo.*3(4.317A).

χθαμαλός, *low-lying, low*; **1.** met., **a.** *inferior, mean*, Gr.Nyss.*hom. 8 in Cant.*(M.44.941B); Cyr.*Ps.*42:3(M.69.1016C); id.*Os.*130(3.162C); **b.** *humble*, of persons, Nil.*epp.*4.1(M.79.544C); **2.** *small* in stature, Jo.Mal.*chron.*8 p.194(M.97.308A).

χθαμαλότης, ἡ, 1. *lowness, flatness*; **2.** *humility, lowliness*, in self-depreciation ἐκ τῆς ἡμετέρας χ. Nil.*epp.*4.1(M.79.544B); Steph.Diac. *v.Steph.*(M.100.1145D); †Jo.D.*B.J.*14(M.96.984C); **3.** *inferiority, inadequacy*; of language, Didym.*Trin.*3.4(M.39.837A).

***χθαμαλοφρονέω**, *be lowly-minded*, Gr.Naz.*carm.*1.2.9.130(M.37. 678A).

***χθαμαλοφροσύνη, ἡ**, *humility*, Gr.Naz.*carm.*1.2.17.40(M.37.784A).

***χθαμαλόφρων**, *lowly-minded*, †Apoll.*met.Ps.*17:28(M.33.1333A); *ib.*33:19(1356D).

***χθαμαλῶς**, *so as to be low-lying*, Cosm.Ind.*top.*4(M.88.185C).

χθεσινός, *of yesterday*, Chrys.*stat.*4.6(2.58A); *Cod.Afr.*90; Leont.H. *Nest.*4.30(M.86.1696C).

***χθονοβριθής**, *weighing...down to earth*, Synes.*hymn.*4.289(p.34; M.66.1608).

***χθονογηθής**, *rejoicing in earthly things*, Synes.*hymn.*1.114(p.62; M.66.1592).

***χία, ἡ**, *Syrian gum* κόψας χίας μνᾶς ἑπτά *A.Petr.c.Sim.*11 (p.100.1); Leont.H.*monoph.*(M.86.1816A) cit. s. κηρός.

χιάζω, 1. *set in the form of a* X φυσιολογούμενον περὶ τοῦ υἱοῦ τοῦ θεοῦ, ὅτε λέγει [sc. Plato (*Timaeus* 36B,C)]· ἐχίασεν αὐτὸν ἐν τῷ παντί Just.*1apol.*60.1(M.6.417A); *ib.*60.5(420A); **2.** *mark with a* X, of labarum χιαζομένου τοῦ ῥῶ κατὰ τὸ μεσαίτατον Eus.*v.C.*1.31(p.22. 3; M.20.945A).

χίασμα, τό, *form of a* X, *two lines placed crosswise*, Just.*1apol.*60. 5(M.6.420A).

***χιδάριον, τό**, prob. f.l. for σχεδάριον, Chrys.ap.Jo.D.*parall.*(M. 95.1508A).

χιλιάκις, *a thousand times*, Pall.*h.Laus.*71(p.167.11; M.34.1258A).

***χιλιακός**, *millenary*, Areth.*Apoc.*10(M.106.572A).

χιλιάς, ἡ, *period of a thousand years*; of millennial reign of Christ acc. Papias, Eus.*h.e.*3.39.12(M.20.300A).

***χιλιαστής, ὁ**, *one who believes in the millennial kingdom*, cf. *mille annos post resurrectionem in voluptate carnis futuros praedicant* [sc. *Cerinthiani*]. *unde et Graece Chiliastae, Latine Miliasti sunt appellati*, Isid.H.*etym.*8.5.8.

***χιλιετία, ἡ**, *period of a thousand years*, Areth.*Apoc.*63(M.106. 756C).

χιλιοέτης, *of a thousand years* ἡ χ. καὶ ληρώδης ἐν τῷ παραδείσῳ τρυφή Gr.Naz.*ep.*102(M.37.197C).

***χιλιονταετηρίς (χιλιονταετερίς), ἡ**, *period of a thousand years* Or.*or.*27.13(p.372.22; M.11.517B); Meth.*symp.*9.1(p.114.7,18; M.18. 177A,B); -ερίς, Dam.*troph.*3.10.4(p.259.4).

***χιλιονταετής**, *lasting a thousand years*, Just.*1apol.*8.4(M.6.337C).

***χιλιονταετία, ἡ**, *period of a thousand years*, Jo.Mal.*chron.*1 p.7 (M.97.69B); duration of earthly kingdom of Christ, acc. Cerinthus, Caius ap.Eus.*h.e.*3.28.2(M.20.273D); Tim.CP *haer.*(M.86.28C).

***χιλιοντάς, ἡ**, *a thousand years* ὅσαις...ἡμέραις ἐγένετο ὁ κόσμος, τοσαύταις χ. συντελεῖται Iren.*haer.*5.28.3(M.7.1200A); †Andr.Cr.*cycl.* (M.19.1329B).

χιλιοπλάσιος, *a thousand-fold*, Areth.*Apoc.*28(M.106.637C).

***χιλιοστία, ἡ**, *period of a thousand years*, *cat.Apoc.*11:2(p.338.6); *ib.*17:11(p.433.23).

***χιλιοστῶς**, *in a thousand years*, Areth.*Apoc.*1(M.106.501B).

***χιλιωντώτης**, *for a thousand years* μὴ μόνον τεθημέρους...ἢ αὐθημέρους...ἀλλὰ καὶ χ. νεκρούς, καὶ τοὺς ἀπ' αἰῶνος φθαρέντας ‡Caes.Naz.*dial.*177(M.38.1149).

χιόνινος, *snow-white*, Herm.*vis.*1.2.2.

χιονόομαι, *become snow-white*; fig., of soul, ‡Chrys.*hom.in Lc.* *15:11*(10.839B).

***χιονόσωμος**, *with snow-white body*; of Church, Meth.*symp.*11.2 (p.136.5; M.18.212D).

***χιονοφανής**, *snow-white*, Agath.*v.Gr.Ill.*121.

***χιονοφεγγής**, *gleaming like snow*, Jo.Mon.*hymn.Geo.*9(M.96. 1400C).

χιονόφεγγος, = foreg., ‡Chrys.*hom.in Jo.17:11*(8.43C).

χιονόχροος, *snow-white*, ‡Chrys.*hom.in Ps.75:12*(5.604C).

***χιονωπός**, = foreg., Nonn.*par.Jo.*4:46(M.43.781C).

χιτών, ὁ, *tunic, coat*; χιτὼν δερμάτινος (mostly plur. as Gen.3:21) *coat of skin* δερμάτινον χ.... τὸ αἰσθητὸν σαρκίον εἶναι λέγουσι Iren. *haer.*1.5.5(M.7.501A).

A. lit. exegesis; **1.** in gen. θεὸς...γυμνώσας αὐτοὺς [sc. Adam and Eve] τῆς δόξης...πρὸς τὸ μὴ γυμνοὺς εἶναι καὶ ἐνασχημονεῖν, χ. αὐτοῖς ἐργάζεται δερματίνους καὶ ἀμφιέννυσι Chrys.*hom.18.1 in Gen.*(4. 151C); id.*fem.reg.*7(1.263B); thought by some to refer to bark of trees ἐζήτηται, τί ἐστι χ. δερματίνους· ἀλλ' εἰ μὲν ζῴων σφαγέντων ἐξ αὐτῶν ἐγένοντο τὰ ἐνδύματα, εὔδηλον, ὅτι ἐπέλιπε τὸ γένος τῶν σφαγέντων...τοὺς μὴ ὄντας δὲ χ. ἔτι πλέον ἀπρεπὲς νομίζειν ὅτι παρήγαγεν ὁ θεός, ὃς ἐν τῇ τοῦ ἀνθρώπου ποιήσει τοῦ ποιεῖν τὸ μὴ ὂν ἀπεπαύσατο...ἀλλὰ γὰρ ἠγνόησαν, ὡς ἔοικεν, οἱ περὶ τούτων ζητοῦντες, ὅτι δέρματα οὐ μόνον τὰ ἐκ τῶν ζῴων ἀφαιρούμενα λέγεται, ἀλλὰ καὶ τὰ ἐκ τῶν δένδρων, ἃ καὶ φλοιοὺς ὀνομάζειν ἔθος τοῖς πολλοῖς Thdr.Mops. *Gen.*3:22(M.66.641A,B); **2.** combined with repudiation of allegorical exegesis τοὺς χ. τοὺς δερματίνους τί νοητέον; οἱ μὲν ἀλληγορηταὶ τὴν θνητὴν σάρκα φασὶ τὰ δέρματα· ἄλλοι δέ τινες ἀπὸ φλοιῶν δένδρων τούτους κατεσκευάσθαι εἰρήκασιν· ἐγὼ δέ γε οὐδέτερον τούτων προσίεμαι· τὸ μὲν γὰρ περίεργον, τὸ δὲ ἄγαν μυθῶδες. τῆς γὰρ θείας γραφῆς καὶ πρὸ τῆς ψυχῆς τὸ σῶμα διαπεπλάσθαι φησάσης, πῶς οὐ μυθῶδες τὸ λέγειν μετὰ τὴν παράβασιν τῆς ἐντολῆς σάρκα αὐτοὺς εἰληφέναι θνητήν; Thdt.*qu.39 in Gen.*(1.52); ‡Ath.*qu.Ant.*56(M.28.632B,C).

B. met. exegesis; **1.** as denoting the body; **a.** Docetic χ. δὲ δερματίνους ἡγεῖται ὁ Κασσιανὸς τὰ σώματα περὶ ὧν ὕστερον καὶ τοῦτον καὶ τοὺς ὁμοίως αὐτῷ δογματίζοντας πεπλανημένους ἀποδείξομεν Clem.*str.*3.14(p.239.26; M.8.1196A); Valent. δερματίνους χ. ... τὸ δὲ ὑλικὸν αὐτοῦ ἐνεργὸν εἰς σπέρμα καὶ γένεσιν id.*exc.Thdot.*55(p.125. 8; M.9.685B); **b.** Origenist τί δεῖ δὲ νοεῖν τοὺς δερματίνους χ.;... ἀνάξιον τοῦ θεοῦ, τὸ οἴεσθαι ζῴων τινῶν περιελόντα δέρματα τὸν θεὸν *ἀναιρεθέντων...πεποιηκέναι σχήματα χιτώνων, καταρράψαντα δέρματα δίκην σκυτοτόμου...λέγειν τοὺς δερματίνους χ. οὐκ ἄλλους εἶναι, ἢ τὰ σώματα, πιθανὸν μέν, καὶ εἰς συγκατάθεσιν ἐπισπάσασθαι δυνάμενον· οὐ μὴν σαφὲς ὡς ἀληθές. εἰ γὰρ οἱ δερμάτινοι χ. σάρκες καὶ ὀστέα εἰσί, πῶς πρὸ τούτων φησὶν ὁ Ἀδάμ, τοῦτο νῦν ὀστοῦν...ταύτας οὖν τὰς ἀπορίας περιϊστάμενοί τινες, δερματίνους χ., τὴν νέκρωσιν, ἣν ἀμφιέννυται ὁ Ἀδάμ...οὐδὲ αὐτοὶ εὐχερῶς δυνάμενοι παραστῆσαι, πῶς ὁ θεός, καὶ οὐχὶ ἁμαρτία, νέκρωσιν ἐμποιεῖ τῷ παραβεβηκότι. πρὸς τούτοις, ἀνάγκην ἔχουσι λέγειν σάρκα καὶ ὀστέα τῷ ἰδίῳ λόγῳ μὴ εἶναι φθαρτά... λεκτέον, ὅτι οὐ δεῖ περιέχεσθαι τοῦ γράμματος ὡς ἀληθοῦς* Or.*sel.in Gen.*3:21(M.12.101A); *τοὺς δερματίνους χ. εἶναι τὰ σώματα* Meth.*res.*1. 29(p.261.2; M.41.1137B,C); *ἐντεῦθεν φησὶ* [sc. Origen] *καὶ τοὺς χ. τοὺς δερματίνους ἐπισημάνασθαι τὴν γραφήν· ὅτι, φησίν, ⟨τὸ⟩ ἐποίησεν αὐτοῖς χ. δερματίνους καὶ ἐνέδυσεν αὐτούς, τὸ σῶμα, φησίν, ἐστί* Epiph. *haer.*64.4(p.412.12ff.; M.41.1077B); id.*anc.*62(p.74.7; M.43.128B); cf. *praetereo frivolam ejus* [sc. *Origenis*] *expositionem super tunicis pelliciis, quanto conatu quantisque egerit argumentis, ut tunicas pellicias humana esse corpora crederemus, qui inter multa ait: numquid coriarius aut scortiarius erat deus, ut conficeret pelles animalium et consueret ex eis tunicas pellicias Adam et Evae? manifestum est ergo, inquit, quod de corporibus nostris loquatur,* Hier.*ep.*51.5(*CSEL* 54 p.403.11ff.); id.*c.Jo.Hier.*7(M.*PL*.23.360B); **c.** refutation of this view *τοὺς δερματίνους χ. μὴ εἶναι τὰ σώματα... αὐτὸς πρὸ τῆς κατασκευῆς αὐτῶν ὁ πρωτόπλαστος ὁμολογεῖ καὶ ὀστᾶ ἔχειν καὶ σάρκας, ὁπότε δή, τὴν γυναῖκα αὐτῷ προσαχθεῖσαν θεασάμενος, τοῦτο νῦν ὀστοῦν, ἐφώνησεν, ἐκ τῶν ὀστῶν μου* Meth. *res.*1.39(p.282.4; M.41.1105C); cf. A.2 supra; **2.** signifying mortality, Meth.*res.*1.38(p.281.14; M.18.293B), *ib.*1.39(p.283.11; M.41. 1108A) citt. s. *νεκρότης*; *ib.*1.40(p.285.8; M.41.1109A); Ephr.3.477E cit. s. *νεκρώσιμος*; *ἔδει γὰρ αὐτὸν* [sc. Christ] *εἰσάγοντα τὸν ἄνθρωπον εἰς τὸν παράδεισον, ἀπεκδύσασθαι τοὺς χ., οὓς ἔλαβεν ὁ Ἀδὰμ ἐκβαλλόμενος ἐκ τοῦ παραδείσου. ὅτε γὰρ ἥμαρτε...ἔλαβε δερματίνους χ., ἐκ νεκρῶν ζώων γενομένους, σύμβολον ὄντας τῆς διὰ τὴν ἁμαρτίαν νεκρώσεως αὐτῷ προσγενομένης* ‡Ath.*pass.*20(M.28.221A); *ib.*12 (205D); *ἐπειδὴ οὖν ὁ Ἀδὰμ παρακούσας τοῦ θεοῦ ἐν τῷ φαγεῖν τὸ κεκωλυμένον, θάνατον ἐπεσπάσατο, διὰ τοῦτο ὁ θεὸς ἐνδιδύσκει αὐτὸν χ. δερμάτινον, ὅπως ἂν μνημονεύῃ...τὰ γὰρ νεκρὰ δέρματα δηλοῦσι νεκρότητα καὶ φθοράν* Nil.*epp.*1.241(M.79.172A); **3.** acc. Gr. Nyss., signifying whole of man's animal nature (comprising passions, mortality, etc.) which does not constitute man, but was 'super-added' to his nature after Fall *ἡμῶν ἀποδυσαμένων τὸν νεκρὸν ἐκεῖνον καὶ εἰδεχθῆ χιτῶνα, τὸν ἐκ τῶν ἀλόγων δερμάτων ἡμῖν ἐπιβληθέντα (δέρμα δὲ ἀκούων τὸ σχῆμα τῆς ἀλόγου φύσεως νοεῖν μοι δοκῶ, ᾧ πρὸς τὸ πάθος οἰκειωθέντες περιεβλήθημεν), πάντα ὅσα τοῦ ἀλόγου δέρματος περὶ ἡμᾶς ἦν ἐν τῇ ἀπεκδύσει τοῦ χ. συναποβαλλόμεθα, ἔστι δὲ ἃ προσέλαβεν ἀπὸ τοῦ ἀλόγου δέρματος, ἡ μίξις, ἡ σύλληψις, ὁ τόκος, ὁ ῥύπος, ἡ θηλή, ἡ τροφή, ἡ ἐκποίησις, ἡ κατ' ὀλίγον ἐπὶ τὸ τέλειον αὔξησις, ἡ ἀκμή, τὸ γῆρας, ἡ νόσος, ὁ θάνατος anim.et res.*(M.46.148C); id.*or.catech.*8(p.43.5; M.45.33C); *ζῶντος ἐν ἡμῖν τοῦ Ἀδὰμ πάντες...ἄνθρωποι ἕως τοὺς δερματίνους τούτους χ. περὶ τὴν ἑαυτῶν βλέπωμεν φύσιν, καὶ τὰ πρόσκαιρα φύλλα τῆς ὑλικῆς ταύτης ζωῆς, ἅπερ τῶν ἰδίων τε καὶ λαμπρῶν ἐνδυμάτων γυμνωθέντες* id.*or.dom.*5(p.100.35; M.44.1184B); *τῆς γὰρ καθαρότητος ἐκπεσοῦσα, τὸ ζοφῶδες εἶδος ἐνεδυσάμην. τοιοῦτος γὰρ τῷ εἴδει ὁ χ. δερμάτινος. νῦν δὲ διὰ τὴν ἀγαπήσασάν με πάλιν εὐθύτητα, καλή τε καὶ φωτοειδὴς γενομένη* id.*hom.2 in Cant.*(M.44.800D); *ib.11*(1004D) cit. s. *ποὺς*; after death *ἀπέθετο τοὺς δερματίνους χ.· οὐδὲ γάρ ἐστι χρεία τοῖς ἐν παραδείσῳ διάγουσι, τῶν τοιούτων χιτώνων. ἀλλ' ἐνδύματα, ἃ τῇ καθαρότητι τοῦ βίου αὐτοῦ ἐξυφήνας, ἐπεκοσμήσατο* id.*Melet.*(M.46. 861B); similarly *τοὺς δερματίνους χ., ἴσως τὴν παχυτέραν σάρκα, καὶ θνητήν, καὶ ἀντίτυπον* Gr.Naz.*or.*38.12(M.36.324C); id.*carm.*1.1.8.116 (M.37.455A) cit. s. *νεκροφόρος*.

[*]**χλαινοφόρος**, *wearing a cloak*, Gr.Naz.*ep.*86(M.37.157).

***χλευαστέον**, *one must jest, scoff*, ‡Just.*ep.Zen.et Ser.*7(M.6.1192A).

χλευαστικός, *derisory*, Gr.Nyss.*Eun.*12(1 p.325.18; M.45.1041A); Thdot.Anc.*hom.BMV et Sym.*(M.77.1405A).

χλεύη, ἡ, 1. *joke, jest*; in bad sense, *mockery, ridicule, Diogn.* 4.4; Ath.*gent.*10(M.25.21C); Eus.*v.C.*2.61(p.66.16; M.20.1036C); **2.** *object* or *cause of ridicule*, Clem.*prot.*2(p.13.13; M.8.76B); Meth.*symp.* 11(p.130.17; M.18.205C); **3.** *illusion, deceptive image*, Jo.Mal.*chron.*7 p.189(M.97.300C); Gr.Mag.*dial.*(tr.Zach.)2.10(M.*PL*.66.153).

***χλημητίζω**, *neigh*; of horses, *V.Mac.*B (p.142).

χλιαρότης, ἡ, *lukewarmness*, ‡Ath.*ep.Cast.*2.3(M.28.884C); *ἡ χ. καὶ ἡ νωθρεία* Nil.*epp.*3.318(M.79.537B).

***χλοαίνομαι**, *become green*, Gr.Nyss.*res.*3(M.46.669B); *Const.App.* 7.24.4.

χλοανός, *green*, ‡Caes.Naz.*dial.*113(M.38.996).

***χλοερῶπις**, *coloured green*, Paul.Sil.*Soph.*388(M.86.2134B); id. *ambo.*255(M.86.2261A).

χλοηρός, *green* *χλοηρότερον* Meth.*res.*14(M.18.288; *χλοερώτερον* p.378.2); ‡Gr.Naz.*Chr.pat.*676(M.38.190A).

χλοηφαγία, ἡ, *pasturage τῇ κατὰ τὰς χλοηφαγίας ἐνυπαρχούσῃ νοτίδι* ‡Eust.*hex.*(M.18.736B).

χλοηφάγος, *herbivorous*, ‡Diod.*fr.Gen.*3:8(M.33.1568C).

***χλοοποιέω**, *produce herbage*, ‡Caes.Naz.*dial.*1.43(M.38.912).

χλοοποιός, *producing herbage*; of water, which typifies H. Ghost, Cyr.H.*catech.*16.12; ‡Caes.Naz.*dial.*1.43(M.38.909).

***χλωροκοπ-έω**, *cut down* or *kill whilst young* *∼εῖσθαι τὰ βρέφη προσέταξεν* [sc. Herod] ‡Chrys.*infant.*(10.752B).

***Χοιάκ**, name of an Egyptian month, corresponding roughly to December, Epiph.*haer.*51.24(p.294.1; M.41.932C); Cosm.Ind.*top.*5 (M.88.197A); *Chron.Pasch.*p.224(M.92.545C).

χοϊκός, *earthy, earthly*; **1.** exeg. 1Cor.15:47–49 v. *εἰκών*; Mt. 22:21 *ὅτε χ. ἦμεν, Καίσαρος ἦμεν. Καῖσαρ δέ ἐστιν ὁ πρόσκαιρος ἄρχων, οὗ καὶ εἰκὼν ἡ χ. ὁ παλαιὸς ἄνθρωπος, εἰς ὃν ἐπαλινδρόμησεν. τούτῳ οὖν τὰ χ. ἀποδοτέον, ἃ 'πεφορέκαμεν ἐν τῇ εἰκόνι τοῦ χ.'* Clem. *ecl.*24(p.143.13ff.; M.9.709A); **2.** ref. man as having become *χοϊκός* through transgression, Or.*schol.in Lc.*20:19ff.(M.17.369A); id.*Jo.*13. 24(p.247.26; M.14.437C); Ath.*Ar.*2.65(M.26.285B); *καὶ γὰρ διὰ τοῦτο ἐγενόμεθα χ., ἐπειδὴ πονηρὰ ἐπράξαμεν· οὐκ ἐπειδὴ ἐξ ἀρχῆς χ. διεπλάσθημεν, ἀλλ' ἐπειδὴ ἡμάρτομεν* Chrys.*hom.42.1 in 1Cor.*(10. 395D); *ἐκ γῆς ὁ ἄνθρωπος κατὰ φύσιν, χ. δὲ κατὰ τὴν προαίρεσιν* Sever.*1Cor.*15:47(p.276.5); Max.*ambig.*(M.91.1112C); **3.** opposite view: man's body created *χοϊκός*: *μαρτυρεῖ ἡ γραφὴ δι' αὐτοῦ θείου ἐμφυσήματος δημιουργήσασα τῷ χ. ἡμῶν σώματι ψυχὴν ζωτικήν* Anast.S.*hod.*1(M.89.45B); **4.** ref. body of Christ *διοριζόμενοι...ἄλλοι χ., ἄλλοι δὲ ἐπουράνιον σῶμα* Bas.*ep.*260.8(3.400D; M.32.965B); in Apollinarian Christology v. *ἐπουράνιος*; **5.** ref. Jo.8:44 *κατ' εἰκόνα γινόμενον τοῦ πονηροῦ πατρὸς* [sc. *τοῦ διαβόλου*] *ἀφ' οὗ ἔρχονται καὶ τυποῦνται αἱ ἐκείνου τοῦ χ. εἰκόνες. πρῶτος γὰρ χ. ἐκεῖνος, ὁ πρῶτος ἀποπεπτωκὼς τῶν κρειττόνων...καὶ εἰ μὲν ὡσπερεὶ ἐπιλαθόμενοι τῆς ἐν ἡμῖν κρείττονος οὐσίας ὑποτάξομεν ἑαυτοὺς τῷ ἀπὸ τοῦ χοῦ πλάσματι, καὶ τὸ κρεῖττον τὴν εἰκόνα τοῦ χ. λήψεται* Or.*Jo.*20.22(20; p.355.4ff.; M.14.621A,B); *τοὺς φύσει τοῦ διαβόλου υἱούς, τοὺς χ.,* [opp. *τοὺς ψυχικούς*] *θέσει υἱοὺς διαβόλου γινομένους* Heracleon *ib.*20.24(20; p.359.13; 628D); **6.** Gnost. uses (cf. *ψυχικός*) ref. creation of man, Iren.*haer.*1.5.5(M.7.500A) cit. s. *ἐμφυσάω*; *ἀνθρώπων δὲ τρία γένη ὑφίστανται, πνευματικόν, χ., ψυχικόν, καθὼς ἐγένοντο Κάϊν, Ἄβελ, Σήθ· καὶ ἐκ τούτων τὰς τρεῖς φύσεις, οὐκέτι καθ' ἕν, ἀλλὰ κατὰ γένος. καὶ τὸ μὲν χ. εἰς φθορὰν χωρεῖν ib.*1.7.5(517B); Heracleon ap.Or.*Jo.*20.24(20; p.359.13; M.14.628D) cit. supra; *ὁ μὲν χ. ἐστι 'κατ' εἰκόνα', ὁ δὲ ψυχικὸς 'καθ' ὁμοίωσιν' θεοῦ, ὁ δὲ πνευματικὸς κατ' ἰδίαν...τοῖς τρισὶν ἀσωμάτοις ἐπὶ τοῦ Ἀδὰμ τέταρτον ἐνδύεται τὸν χ. τοὺς 'δερματίνους χιτῶνας'* Clem.*exc.Thdot.*54.2,55.1(p.125.1,9; M.9.685A,B); Hipp.*haer.*5.7(p.78.13; M.16.3126B); ref. Inc. *ταῦτα δὲ πάντα...τὰ νοερὰ καὶ ψυχικὰ καὶ χ. κεχώρηκε καὶ κατῆλθ⟨εν εἰ⟩ς ἕνα ἄνθρωπον ὁμοῦ, Ἰησοῦν τὸν ἐκ τῆς Μαρίας γεγενημένον· καὶ ἐλάλουν, φησίν, ὁμοῦ κατὰ τὸ αὐτὸ οἱ τρεῖς οὗτοι ἄνθρωποι ἀπὸ τῶν ἰδίων οὐσιῶν τοῖς ἰδίοις ἕκαστος· ἔστι γὰρ τῶν ὅλων τρία γένη κατ' αὐτούς, ἀγγελικόν, ψυχικόν, χ.· καὶ τρεῖς ἐκκλησίαι, ἀγγελική, ψυχική, χ. ib.*5.6 (p.78.16ff.; 3126B); met. *τούτῳ δὲ ἀκόλουθόν ἐστι πρώτην λέγειν εἶναι τὴν χ. ἡμέραν καὶ τὴν δευτέραν τὴν ψυχικήν, οὐ γεγενημένης τῆς ἐκκλησίας τῆς ἀναστάσεως ἐν αὐταῖς* Heracleon ap.Or.*Jo.*10.37(21; p.212.30; 376C).

***χοιράκανθος, ὁ,** (cf. *ἀκανθόχοιρος*) *hedgehog*, Geo.Pis.*carm.*1.83.

χοίρειος, *of a swine*; *χοίρεια* [sc. *κρέα*] *pig's flesh ὁ πάνσοφος διὰ Μωϋσέως παιδαγωγὸς χοιρείων ἀπηγόρευσεν μεταλαμβάνειν τῷ λαῷ τῷ πρεσβυτέρῳ, ἐμφαίνων μὴ δεῖν τοὺς θεὸν ἐπιβωμένους ἀκαθάρτοις ἀναμίγνυσθαι ἀνθρώποις* Clem.*paed.*3.11(p.278.5; M.8.652B).

***χοιρέλαφος, ὁ,** *hog-deer*, perh. *sus babyrussa τὸν δὲ χ. καὶ εἶδον καὶ ἔφαγον* Cosm.Ind.*top.*11(M.88.444C).

***χοιρόβιος**, *living like a hog*, ‡Jo.D.*ep.Thphl.*19(M.95.656D).

χοιρογρύλλιος, ὁ, *hyrax, cony, rock-rabbit*, ‡Caes.Naz.*dial.*148 (M.38.1100); ref. Pr.24:61, fig. *χ. εἰσὶν ἔθνη ἀκάθαρτα τὰς ἐντολὰς δεξάμενα τοῦ σωτῆρος ἡμῶν Χριστοῦ* Evagr.Pont.*cap.*18(M.40.1265D).

***χοιροκέφαλος**, *swine-headed*, Jo.Mal.*chron.*5 p.120(M.97.213B).

χοῖρος, ὁ, *swine*; met., ref. Mt.7:6 *χ. τοὺς ἐν ἀκολάστῳ βίῳ διατρίβοντας διὰ παντός, οὕσπερ ἅπαντας ἀναξίους ἔφησεν εἶναι τῆς τοιαύτης ἀκροάσεως* Chrys.*hom.23.3 in Mt.*(7.287D); id.*hom.16.2 in Gen.*(4.125E); Isid.Pel.*epp.*1.143(M.78.280A).

***χοιρότροπος**, *behaving like swine μὴ βάλωμεν...τοὺς μαργαρίτας ἡμῶν...ἔμπροσθεν τῶν χ. ἀνθρώπων* †Ath.*fr.Mt.*7:6(M.27.1380C).

χοιρώδης, *swinish*; met., of persons, Chrys.*hom.16.2 in Gen.*(4.125E); of life χ. βίον Meth.*creat.*1(p.494.14; M.18.333B); Gr.Nyss.*or.dom.*2(p.38.16; M.44.1144C); Isid.Pel.*epp.*1.143(M.78.280A).

χολαίνω, *be angry*, Gr.Nyss.*v.Ephr.*(M.46.825B).

***χολέω,** *become angry*, *A.Xanthipp.*21(p.73.23); Jo.Mal.*chron.*14 p.362(M.97.537B); *Chron.Pasch.*p.98(M.92.268D).

***χολιοδόχος,** *containing bile* μηδὲ αὐτὴν [sc. τὴν περιστεράν] ἔχειν τὸ χ. ὄργανον ‡Caes.Naz.*dial.*192(M.38.1169).

χολλαΐζω, *paint with antimony*, Jo.Mal.*chron.*5 p.101(M.97.189B).

***χοοπλαστέω,** *form out of dust* τὸν...χοοπλαστηθέντα...Ἀδάμ ‡Ath.*descr.BMV* 2(M.28.945C); ‡Ath.*caec.*4(M.28.1008B).

***χοόφρων,** *earthly-minded*, Sophr.H.*or.*2.49(M.87.3285C).

***χόρ, ὁ,** (Hebr. כֹּר) a large dry measure εἴληπται...ὁ κόρος ἐκ τῆς Ἑβραϊκῆς διαλέκτου, ὃς καλεῖται χόρ· εἰσὶ δὲ μόδιοι λ' Epiph.*mens.*21(M.43.272C); v. χαρία.

***χοράρχης, ὁ,** *chorus-leader* ὁ ἐκκλησιαστὴς ἐγὼ καὶ χ. τῆς χάριτος Germ.CP *or.*1(M.98.224A).

χοραυλέω, *accompany the chorus on a flute*, Ephr.3.52B.

***χοραυλία, ἡ,** *dancing to the flute*; a work of Devil, Ephr.2.217A; *dancing* to any instrument, ref. Ex.15:20ff., Jo.VI H.*v.Jo.D.*31(M.94.473A).

χορδή, ἡ, *girdle*, *T.Job* 46,47(p.134.5ff.).

χορεία, ἡ, 1. *choral dance*; **2.** *chorus, choir, company*; of angels, Bas.*ep.*2.2(3.72B; M.32.225C); *SEG* 7.865a(suppl.); of apostles, Serap.*Man.*15(p.35; M.40.912C); in gen. τῇ ἁγίᾳ χ. τῶν ὀρθοδόξων τοῦ θεοῦ ἱερέων Gel.Cyz.*h.e.*1 proem.11(M.85.1196A); πνευματικῆς χ. *ib.*2.19.7 (1277A).

***χορειάρχης, ὁ,** *chorus leader*, Chrys.*Anna* 3.4(4.728C).

***χορευτρία, ἡ,** fem. of χορευτής; **1.** *choral dancer*, *Const.App.* 7.5.5; **2.** *member of a choir* χ. Χριστοῦ Ath.*virg.*25(p.59.25; M.28.281A).

χορηγ-έω, *bestow, provide*, of God πᾶσιν ἡμῖν ~ῶν ὧν προσδεόμεθα *Diogn.*3.4; τοῦ ἁγίου πνεύματος...τοῦ ἐκ θεοῦ ~ουμένου Clem.*str.*5.4 (p.341.28; M.9.44C); τὴν δύναμιν τοῦ θεοῦ τὴν διὰ τοῦ Χριστοῦ ~ουμένην *ib.*7.12(p.56.28; 509B); ἃ γὰρ τὸ πνεῦμα ἑκάστῳ διαιρεῖ, ταῦτα παρὰ τοῦ πατρὸς διὰ τοῦ λόγου ~εῖται Ath.*ep.Serap.*1.30(M.26.600B); τὸ πνεῦμα ἐχορήγει λαλεῖν ἐν αὐτῷ *ib.*1.31(604B).

***χορηγητέον,** *one must provide*, Meth.*symp.*6.4(p.68.17; M.18.120A).

***χορηγητήρ, ὁ,** *one who bestows* or *provides*, *Orac.Sib.*7.90.

***χορηγητικός,** *supplying, bestowing*, Eus.*Ps.*35:10(M.23.321C).

***χορηγός,** *that furnishes* or *provides*, neut. plur. as subst. τὰ χ. τῆς ἐνσάρκου ζωῆς ἥλιον εἶναι καὶ σελήνην καὶ ἀστέρας ὑποτοπάσαντες Eus.*p.e.*7.2(299D; M.22.509A).

χορηγός, ὁ, *bestower, provider*, of Father, Clem.*str.*6.5(p.452.22; M.9.261B); πάσης ζωῆς χ. Or.*Cels.*8.19(p.236.17; M.11.1545C); χ. τῆς ἀθανασίας Serap.*euch.*13.5, etc.; of Logos ὁ ταύτης [sc. τῆς προνοίας] χ. καὶ δημιουργός Ath.*inc.*54.2(M.25.192B); of Christ τῆς ἀγαθοῦ κτήσεως διδάσκαλός τε καὶ χ. Clem.*str.*5.1(p.330.18; M.9.17B); τοῦ τε πνεύματος τοῦ ἁγίου χ. Ath.*Ar.*1.46(M.26.108A); τῆς σωτηρίας τὸν χ. Cyr.*Is.*3.2(2.409C); met., Clem.*q.d.s.*19(p.172.11; M.9.624C); χ. καὶ πρόξενός ἐστι [sc. πλοῦτος] θανάτου *ib.*26(p.177.17; 632B).

***χορίαρχος, ὁ,** *leader of the chorus*; of angel Gabriel, ‡Jo.D.*hom.*5 (M.96.649A).

χορός, ὁ, 1. *choir, chorus*, of Christians ἐν ἀγάπῃ χ. γενόμενοι Ign.*Rom.*2.2; Thdt.*h.e.*2.24.9(3.889) cit. s. ἀντίφωνος; esp. of angels or saints, Clem.*str.*7.12(p.56.8; M.9.508C); ἡ ἐκκλησία κυρίου, ὁ πνευματικὸς καὶ ἅγιος χ. *ib.*7.14(p.62.20; M.9.521B); χ. τῶν προφητῶν Thdt.*Dan.*proem.(2.1005,1057); χ. ἀγγέλων *OGIS* 610 (Zorava, Syria; A.D. 516); met. τὸ ἔσχατον τοῦ χ. τῆς ἀρετῆς...μέρος Chrys.*hom.46.3 in Mt.*(7.486B); fig., of stars in orderly arrangement, *1Clem.*20.3; Ign.*Eph.*19.2; Ath.*gent.*29(M.25.57C); met. τῆς ἀληθείας χ. μυστικοῦ Clem.*str.*7.7(p.34.5; M.9.464C); **2.** *choral chant*, Marc.Diac.*v.Porph.*20; **3.** *choir*, place where church singers stand ἱσταμένου οὖν αὐτοῦ εἰς τὸν χ. Jo.Mosch.*prat.*126(M.87.2988B).

χοροστασία, ἡ, *choir*, Gr.Nyss.*v.Macr.*(p.407.12; M.46.993A); Cyr.*Is.*3.4(2.498D); τῆς ἄνω χ. Gr.Naz.ap.Cosm.Ind.*top.*10(p.299.19; M.88.416D); ἀπόστολοί τε καὶ προφῆται τῆς πνευματικῆς χ. Gr.Nyss.*aud.Bas.*(M.46.789A); Jo.Jej.*liturg.*(p.441); χ. τῶν ἀγγέλων ‡Bas.*h.myst.*49(p.391.6).

χοροστατέω, 1. *institute a choir*, Cyr.*Is.*4.1(2.543E); **2.** *lead a chorus* or *choir*; met., ‡Ath.*occurs.*1(M.28.973A); **3.** *order* or *arrange a choir* χ. αὐτοὺς ἁρμοδίως Thdr.Stud.*poen.*1.105(M.99.1748B).

χοροστάτης, ὁ, *leader of a chorus*; met., of Christ διδάσκαλόν τε καὶ χ. Cels.ap.Or.*Cels.*5.33(p.35.3; M.11.1229C).

χορτασία, ἡ, *feeding*, *A.Mt.*2(p.218.15); Agath.*v.Gr.Ill.*19.

χόρτασμα, τό, *fodder* τὸ ἄλογον τῆς τροφῆς πλήρωμα χ., οὐ βρῶμα εἰπών Clem.*paed.*1.11(p.147.17; M.8.365B).

χορτασμός, ὁ, *satiety*, met. ὁ δὲ μακαριζόμενος χ. ἔσται ἐν τῷ ὀφθῆναι καὶ τρανωθῆναι τὴν δόξαν τοῦ θεοῦ Or.*sel.in Ps.*16:15(M.12.1224B).

***χόρτινος,** *made of grass*, Socr.*h.e.*7.37.5(M.67.824A).

[*]**χορτοβολίον, τό,** (= χορτόβολον) *hay-loft*, Agath.*v.Gr.Ill.*19.

***χορτογενής,** *born of grass* χοϊκοῦ καὶ χ. σαρκικοῦ χιτῶνα ἄφατον περιθεμένου Anast.S.*hex.*12(M.89.1064B).

χορτοφαγέω, *eat grass*, Bardesanes ap.Eus.*p.e.*6.10(273C; M.21.464B).

χορτώδης, *like grass*; met., of human life (cf. 1Pet.1:24), Gr.Nyss.*hom.5 in Cant.*(M.44.884B); τῶν ἀσθενῶν...ἀρρένων ἡ χ. οὐσία ‡Jo.D.*hom.*5(M.96.657C); *cat.Apoc.*9:6(p.315.20).

χοῦς, ὁ, *dust*, from which man was formed (Gen.2:7), Or.*hom.1.10 in Jer.*(p.9.9; M.13.268A); Hipp.*haer.*6.35(p.165.12; M.16.3250A); Ath.*ep.Serap.*2.1(M.26.609A); fig. ἐκείνων καθαρῶς ἀπολυθείς, δι' ὧν ἔτι χ. ἐστιν [sc. ὁ ἄνθρωπος] Clem.*paed.*2.1(p.154.8; M.8.377C).

χραισμήτωρ, ὁ, 1. *protector*, of Christ as Son of God χ. φωτῶν Nonn.*par.Jo.*3:16(M.43.769A); χ. κόσμου *ib.*3:34(772C); *ib.*5:38 (792B); **2.** *helper*; met., of abstracts ἐμῷ χ. μύθῳ ζωγρήσας ὅλον ἄνδρα *ib.*7:23(808C); Paul.Sil.*Soph.*301(M.86.2131A); *ib.*314(2131B).

χράω, A. *proclaim, declare*; of an oracle; **1.** of God ταῦτα διὰ ...τοῦ προφήτου ἐχρήσθη Eus.*d.e.*6.12(p.261.5; M.22.429B); Chrys.*hom.30.2 in 2Cor.*(10.650E); id.*hom.23.1 in Heb.*(12.210B v.l. κιχρᾷ); **2.** of inspired utterances of NT scriptures, Didym.*Trin.*1.11(M.39.316B); *ib.*2.2(461B); *ib.*2.3(573C).

B. med.; **1.** *use*, ref. Inc. θεότης σαρκὶ ἐμψύχῳ κεχρημένη Bas.*ep.*236.1(3.361D; M.32.877C); **2.** *submit oneself to* μὴ χ. σεαυτὸν τῷ ἀνθρωποκτόνῳ *ib.*145.2(134D; M.368C).

***χρειοκόλαξ, ὁ,** *flatterer for the sake of gain*, Cyr.*ep.*11.3(p.11.7; 5^{2}.37C).

***χρειωδῶς,** *usefully*, Bas.*renunt.*8(2.209B; M.31.641D); Cyr.*Zach.*33(3.704D); ‡Just.*confut.*56(M.6.1556C); superl., Cyr.*dial.Trin.*2(5^{1}.443E).

χρεμέθω, *neigh, whinny*, Gr.Naz.*carm.*2.1.45.307(M.37.1375A).

***χρεμετιστέον,** *one must neigh*, fig., ref. Jer.5:8 ἡ πλησίον γυνή... ἐφ' ἣν οὐ χ. ‡Just.*ep.Zen.et Ser.*16(M.6.1201A).

***χρεμετιστής,** *neighing* ἵππος δὲ χ. τῶν νέων τοὺς ἀκολάστους [sc. δηλώσῃ] Cyr.H.*catech.*9.13.

***χρέμψις, ἡ,** *coughing*, Tim.CP *haer.*(M.86.48B).

***χρεολύτης, ὁ,** *one who liquidates a debt*; met., of Christ ὁ πάντων χ. τῶν ἀνθρώπων ‡Serg.*acath.*266(= M.92.1345C).

***χρεωποιέομαι,** *need the assistance of*, *need* ὁ δεσπόζων τοῦ οἰκήματος χ. αὐτὸ εἰς ἰδίαν ἀνάπαυσιν †Gregent.*leg.Hom.*57(M.86.612C).

χρεωστ-έω, A. act.; **1.** *owe*, Pall.*h.Laus.*21(p.57.1; M.34.1065C); μύρια τάλαντα...χ. Anast.S.*Ps.6*(M.89.1081A); met. τὴν κεχρεωστημένην θρησκείαν Constantius ap.Ath.*apol.Const.*23(M.25.624B); εἰ μὴ ἔλαττω ~εῖς, οὐ μέντοι ἀπηλλαγμένος τυγχάνεις ἁμαρτημάτων Tit. Bost.*fr.Lc.*7:39ff.(p.169.10); χ. γὰρ ὡς εὐγνώμων υἱός...τὴν διὰ τῶν προσευχῶν γηροκομίαν Gr.Nyss.*ep.can.*8(M.45.236B); τῶν γὰρ ἀνθρώπων ὑπὲρ τῶν οἰκείων ἁμαρτημάτων θάνατον ~ούντων Thdr. Heracl.*Is.*63:1(M.18.1368D); τὴν ἐκείνου [sc. Adam] παράβασιν ἕκαστος ~εῖ Cyr.*dogm.*7(6^{2}.375C); cf. διὰ δὲ τοῦ μὴ ~ουμένου θανάτου καταργῶν [sc. Christ] τὸν ὀφειλόμενον Thdt.*rect.conf.*10(M.6.1225A); **2.** *owe a debt, be a debtor to*, Eus.Al.*serm.*21.3(M.86.425D); οὐ θέλω ὑμᾶς ἀγαπᾶν ἐκείνους οὓς ~εῖτε, ἀλλ' οἷς οὐκ ὀφείλετε Ammon. *Jo.*13:34(M.85.1485A); Anast.S.*qu.et resp.*106(M.89.760C); **3.** *ought* ἀρχικὸς ὑποστατικῷ ~εῖ λέγειν τὸ ὀφειλόμενον Marc.Er.*opusc.*2.120(M.65.948C); *ib.*3.12(981C); Ant.Mon.*hom.*72(M.89.1645A); Jo.D.*imag.*3.30(M.94.1349B).

B. med.; **1.** *have a debt owing to one*, ‡Caes.Naz.*dial.*4.195(M.38.1185); met., of God ἵνα ποσῶς ἡμεῖς κατὰ δύναμιν ἐκ τῶν αὐτοῦ κτισμάτων ~ούμενον αὐτὸν ἀνυμνήσωμεν Max.*qu.Thal.*51(M.90.480A); **2.** *be subject* or *liable to* ~ούμενοι θανάτῳ καὶ φθορᾷ Cyr.*Jo.*2 (4.114D); **3.** *be necessary*, logically τοῖς ὀπίσω ~ούμενον τὸν ἐφεξῆς εὐρύθμως ποιεῖται λόγον *ib.*1.9(96E).

χρεώστημα, τό, *debt*, Marc.Er.*opusc.*1.155(M.65.924D); *ib.*7.14 (1092C).

***χρεωστικός,** *of a debt*, Jo.Mosch.*prat.*193(M.87.3073B).

χρεωστικῶς, *as a debt, as a duty*, ‡Amph.*circ.*1(21A); *V.Chrys.*33 (p.315.33); Areth.*Apoc.*2(M.106.513D).

***χρεώστρια, ἡ,** *debtor* (fem.), *A.Petr.c.Sim.*1(p.80.12).

χρηματίζ-ω, 1. *utter a message*; of God to prophets, Or.*princ.*

3.1.7(p.204.14; M.11.260A); Eus.*d.e.*5.9(p.231.18; M.22.381C); Pall.*v.Chrys.*4(p.27.22; M.47.18); of H. Ghost, Didym.*Ps.*22:5(M.39.1293A); of angels, Hipp.*haer.*9.13(p.251.14; M.16.3387B); Or.*Cels.*1.61(p.112.9; M.11.772C); pass.; *receive a divine message*; of prophets, Clem.*str.*3.4(p.213.26; M.8.1141C); *χρηματισθέντες καθ' ὃν ἔδει τρόπον οἰκοδομῆσαι* *A.Phil.*88(p.34.29); Marc.Er.*opusc.*10.1(M.65.1117C); **2.** *be called* by a name or title; *λόγος θεοῦ καὶ σοφία ∼ουσα* Eus.*h.e.*1.2.14(M.20.61A); *Ἰησοῦς ὁ υἱὸς τοῦ θεοῦ ἐχρημάτισε καί ἐστι διὰ τὸν ἐν αὐτῷ κρυβέντα λόγον* ‡Ath.*serm.fid.*32(p.28; M.26.1288A); *κεχρημάτικε δοῦλος, διὰ τὸ ἀνθρώπινον* Cyr.*Zach.*33(3.678A); of an era, *be reckoned ∼ει οὖν τῆς μεγάλης Ἀντιοχείας εἰς τιμὴν αὐτῆς ἔτος α'* *Chron.Pasch.*p.187(M.92.460A); *ἔτους ∼οντος κατὰ Ἀντιόχειαν τὴν μεγάλην ζλ' καὶ φ'* *ib.*p.328(848B); *ib.*p.331(857B); **3.** *call, name*, Pamph.H.*can.*1; [*οἱ Ῥόδιοι*] *ἐχρημάτισαν ἑαυτοὺς ἔκτοτε Κολοσσαεῖς* Jo.Mal.*chron.*5 p.149(M.97.248C); **4.** *be enrolled* among, *reckoned* among *εἰς λαὸν θεοῦ χρηματίσαι* *cat.Lc.*1:56(p.16.19); *receive a charter*, of a city obtaining a grant or confirmation of its liberties on submitting to empire *∼ούσης τῆς πόλεως* [sc. Antioch] Evagr.*h.e.*2.12(p.63.15; M.86.2536A); *ib.*3.33(p.131.21; 2668A); **5.** *be, exist οὐκέτι βασιλεῖς Ἰουδαίων ἐχρημάτισαν* Or.*princ.*4.1.3(p.296.11; M.11.345C); *ἐν μέσῳ τούτων* [sc. cherubim] *τὸν θεὸν ∼ειν συνέβαινεν* Thdr.Mops.*Ex.*26:35(M.66.648B); †Gregent.*disp.*(M.86.725C); *εἱμαρμένη καὶ ἀστρονομία παρ' αὐτοῖς σφόδρα ἐχρημάτιζεν* [i.e. *were prevalent*] Epiph.*haer.*16.2(p.211.13; M.41.249B).

χρηματικῶς, *civilly, in a civil suit*; opp. *ἐγκληματικῶς*, Ath. Scholast.*coll.*1.3(p.15); *ib.*5.5(p.76).

χρηματισμός, ὁ, 1. *divine injunction* or *message*, Or.*Jo.*20.10(p.338.3; M.14.592D); *Γαβριὴλ...ἐν τῷ πρὸς τὴν παρθένον χ. φάσκων* Eus.*d.e.*7.1(p.326.26; M.22.533B); *ἐν τῇ Ἐξόδῳ τὸν χ.* †Bas.*Is.*176(1.507D; M.30.416A); **2.** *charter*, instrument recording liberties of a city, Jo.Mal.*chron.*12 p.309(M.97.465B); Evagr.*h.e.*4.9(p.159.28; M.86.2720A).

***χρηματολαῖλαψ, ὁ,** lit., *whirlwind for money, one who is very grasping*, ‡Ign.*Magn.*9; *Const.App.*2.50.1.

χρηματολήπτης, ὁ, *one who receives bribes*; *one guilty of simony οὔτε αἱρετικός, οὔτε...ἐκ χ. εἴτ' οὖν Σιμωνιανοῦ κεχειροτονημένος* Thdr.Stud.*epp.*1.53(M.99.1105B).

***χρηματολογέω,** *calculate about money*, *Const.App.*3.7.4.

***χρησείδιον, τό,** *little citation, quotation*, Anast.S.*hod.*3(M.89.92A); *ib.*12(201A); *ib.*22(292A).

***χρησιμαῖος,** *useful*, *A.Thom.*A 130(p.238.7); Gr.Nyss.*Cant.* proem.(M.44.756A).

χρησιμότης, ἡ, *usefulness, benefit*, Eus.*h.e.*9.10.7(M.20.833A); Epiph.*haer.*29.5(p.327.1; M.41.400A); *Cod.Afr.*66.

***χρησιμουργέω,** *work effectively*, Leont.H.*Nest.*1(M.86.1425C).

χρῆσις, ἡ, *saying*; of a passage from scripture, Epiph.*haer.*33.9(p.461.1; M.41.573A); Thdt.*haer.*5.1(4.378); †Leont.B.*sect.*4.1(M.86.1220A); from other writers, Cyr.*ep.*39(p.19.18; 5^{2}.108C); Dor.*doct.*7.5(M.88.1704B); Jo.Mosch.*prat.*40(M.87.2896A).

***χρησμεύω,** *utter an oracle*, *M.Carp.*17.

χρησμηγόρος, *uttering oracles*, *Orac.Sib.*4.4.

χρησμοδοσία, ἡ, *giving of oracles*, Hipp.*haer.*4.28(p.56.18; M.16.3091D).

χρησμοδοτέω, 1. *utter* a prophecy or warning, Cyr.*ador.*7(1.227B); Areth.*Apoc.*26(M.106.621B); *ib.*28(644A); of God *χρησμοδοτήσας τῷ προφήτῃ* Bas.*Eun.*5(1.301A; M.29.721C); **2.** pass., *be warned by an oracle*, *1Clem.*55.1; Jo.Mal.*chron.*2 p.50(M.97.124A).

χρησμοδότης, ὁ, *one who gives oracles, prophet, soothsayer*, Eus.*p.e.*4.2(135B; M.21.237B); id.*d.e.*5 proem.(p.205.1; M.340B).

χρησμός, ὁ, *oracular response, oracle*; of scriptural texts, Clem.*str.*2.7(p.131.5; M.8.969A); Or.*princ.*4.1.2(p.295.9; M.11.345A); Chrys.*hom.26.6 in Mt.*(7.321C).

χρησμῳδέω, *utter* an oracle, *prophesy*; of utterances of scripture, Didym.*Trin.*1.15(M.39.313A); *ib.*1.16(340A); Cyr.*Is.*3.5(2.517D).

χρησμῴδημα, τό, *divine utterance* or *revelation*, Cyr.*ador.*1(1.6E); id.*glaph.Gen.*3(1.88D); id.*Os.*71(3.107A).

χρησμῳδία, ἡ, 1. *answer of an oracle, prophecy*, Gr.Nyss.*v.Gr.Thaum.*(M.46.916A); **2.** *divine utterance*, Didym.*Trin.*1.27(M.39.408A).

χρησμῳδός, *uttering divine messages* or *revelations*; of prophets, Clem.*prot.*8(p.60.22; M.8.189A); Isid.Pel.*epp.*5.99(M.78.1384B).

***χρησμῳδοτία, ἡ,** *giving of oracles*, ‡Jo.D.*ep.Thphl.*18(M.95.369B).

***χρηστέμπορος,** v. **Χριστέμπορος*.

χρηστεύομαι, *be kind* or *merciful*; c. dat., *Pss.Sal.*9.11; *1Clem.*14 3; Meth.*lepr.*(p.467.2); c. prep. *ἐπ' ἀλόγων ζῴων χ.* Clem.*str.*2.18(p.163.2; M.8.1033A); Eus.*h.e.*5.1.46(M.20.425B); CNic.(325)*can.*11; c. acc., Mac.Aeg.*hom.*4.18(M.34.485D); c. infin., *ib.*4.22(489B); pass. impers. *ὡς χρηστεύεσθε, οὕτως χρηστευθήσεται ὑμῖν* Clem.*str.*2.18(p.162.3; M.8.1032A).

***χρηστοδότος,** *giving good things*, Cosm.Mel.*schol.*7(M.38.412).

***χρηστοέπεια, ἡ,** *kindly speech*; plur., Cyr.*Rom.*11:2(p.237.21; M.74.845A).

***χρηστοεπέω,** *use kind language, speak kindly*, Cyr.*glaph.Gen.*5(1.159D); id.*Mich.*20(3.408E); Proc.G.*Is.*4:12ff.(M.87.1908B).

***χρηστοεπής,** *speaking kindly*; neut. as subst., Cyr.*ador.*12(1.425A).

χρηστολογέω, *use kind language, speak kindly*, Chrys.*hom.78.3 in Mt.*(7.755E); Isid.Pel.*epp.*1.281(M.78.348B); Cyr.*Is.*2.1(2.195E).

χρηστολογία, ἡ, *fair speaking*, Jo.Jej.*canonar.*2(p.438); in bad sense, Or.*fr.in Pr.*5:3(M.17.157C); Cyr.H.*catech.*4.2; Cyr.*Zach.*77(3.759E).

χρηστομαθέω, *learn what is worthy* or *good*, Cyr.*ador.*10(1.348E); id.*dial.Trin.*2(5^{1}.456C); id.*Juln.*1(6^{2}.15A).

χρηστομαθής, 1. *desirous of learning what is useful* or *good*, Clem.*str.*1.9(p.29.7,9; M.8.740C); Cyr.*ador.*8(1.267E); id.*Ag.*5(3.633A); **2.** of abstracts, *worthy of study*, Euthal.Diac.*Ac.*proem.(M.85.633B); Cyr.*Jo.*3.3(4.268B); **3.** neut. as subst., *useful learning*, Eus.*h.e.*1.1.5(M.20.52B); Cyr.*Juln.*7(6^{2}.225B).

[*]**χρηστομαθία (χρηστομάθεια), ἡ,** *good* or *useful learning*, Clem.*str.*1.1(p.12.18; M.8.705C); -*εια*, Eus.*h.e.*6.13.8(M.20.549A); Epiph.*haer.*8.8(p.194.16; M.41.220A).

***χρηστοποιέομαι,** *exercise usefully*, Nil.*Eulog.*26(M.79.1128C).

χρηστότης, ἡ, *goodness, kindness*; of God, *1Clem.*9.1; Clem.*str.*5.1(p.329.21; M.9.16B); Or.*Cels.*5.12(p.13.1; M.11.1197C); as complimentary style of address *τῆς σῆς χ.* Ursacius and Valens ap. Ath.*apol.sec.*58(p.138.5; M.25.353B); Arsenius *ib.*69(p.147.22; 372C); Eust.Seb.*ep.*ap.Socr.*h.e.*4.12.11(M.67.485C).

***χρηστοφαγία, ἡ,** *dainty food*, Pall.*v.Chrys.*12(p.76.17; M.47.43).

***χρηστοφάγος,** *who eats dainty food ὁ ἐπίσκοπος...ἔστω...μὴ χ.* *Const.App.*2.5.3.

***χρηστοφανής,** *appearing good* or *gentle χ. νοημάτων* Or.*sel.in Ps.*139:6(M.12.1661C); *χ. ἐν τῇ ἐρωτήσει* Pall.*v.Chrys.*6(p.36.3; M.47.22); *παρακλήσεσι...χ.* Diad.*perf.*23(p.38.7).

***Χρηστοφόρος,** v. **Χριστοφόρος*.

***χρισιάζω,** *anoint, smear*, ref. use of cosmetics, Cyr.*thes.*proem.(5^{1}.2D).

χρῖσις, ἡ, *anointing, unction*;

A. in gen.; **1.** of use of perfumes, etc.; unbecoming to Christians, Clem.*paed.*2.8(p.197.10; M.8.473A); at pagan festivals *μύρων περίεργοι χρίσεις* ‡Just.*or.Gr.*4(M.6.236C); **2.** of Christ's anointing at Bethany (Mt.26:7), Chrys.*hom.80.1 in Mt.*(7.766C).

B. as religious rite; **1.** in OT; **a.** in gen., of unction as action of H. Ghost *τὸ γὰρ προηγούμενον ἐν τῇ χ., τὸ πνεῦμά ἐστι· διὸ καὶ τὸ ἔλαιον παραλαμβάνεται· καὶ ποῦ χριστοὺς καλεῖ τοὺς μὴ χρισθέντας ἐλαίῳ; ὅπου λέγει, μὴ ἅπτεσθε τῶν χριστῶν μου...τότε γὰρ οὐδὲ ἡ κατασκευὴ τῆς χ. ἦν τοῦ ἐλαίου* Chrys.*hom.1.1 in Rom.*(9.430B); **b.** of kings, Or.*Jo.*1.28(30; p.35.21; M.14.76B); *τίνος σύμβολόν ἐστιν ἡ χ.; οὐχὶ τῆς βασιλείας;* Gr.Nyss.*Maced.*16(M.45.1320D); Bas. Sel.*or.*16.2(M.85.205A); **c.** of priests, Or.*Jo.*1.28(30; p.35.22; 76B); v. *χρίω*; **2.** of Christ's anointing *τῆς...εἰς αὐτὸν γενομένης ἀσωμάτου καὶ ἐνθέου χ.* Eus.*h.e.*1.3.19(M.20.76A); Gr.Naz.*or.*30.2(p.111.1; M.36.105B) cit. s. *ἀνθρωπότης*; *διὰ τοῦτο γὰρ ἡ χ. ἐγένετο, οὐχ ὡς θεοῦ χρίσεως δεομένου, οὐδ' αὖ πάλιν τῆς χ. δίχα θεοῦ γενομένης, ἀλλὰ θεοῦ μὲν τὴν χ. προσαγομένου, ἐν δὲ τῷ δεκτικῷ τῆς χ. σώματι δεχομένου* ‡Ath.*Apoll.*2.3(M.26.1136A); *εἰ δὲ καὶ τὸ σῶμα καλεῖ πολλαχοῦ ἡ γραφὴ 'χριστόν'...ταὐτὸν δὲ τῇ χ. πολλαχόσε τὴν ἀνάδειξιν καὶ τὴν ἀποστολὴν εὑρίσκομεν...διαφόρως τὴν πρὸς τὸν ἐκ Μαρίας ἄνθρωπον τοῦ θεοῦ λόγου ἕνωσιν γενομένην ὀνομάζουσι ποτὲ μὲν 'χ.', ποτὲ δὲ 'ἀποστολήν', ἄλλοτε δὲ 'ἀνάδειξιν'* ‡Ath.*Ar.*4.35(p.84.9ff.; M.26.521B); *χ. δὲ νοητέον, τὴν ὅλον τοῦ χρίσματος εἰς ὅλον τὸ χρισθὲν περιχώρησιν. οὕτω γὰρ ἂν εἴη τὸ τὴν χ. δεδεγμένον ταῖς ἀληθείαις ὅλον χριστόν* ‡Cyr.*Trin.*22(6^{3}.28A; M.77.1164A); Proc.G.*Lev.*7:29(M.87.720A); unction being with H. Ghost *ἡ...τῆς χ. ἔννοια, τὸ μηδὲν εἶναι διάστημα μεταξὺ τοῦ υἱοῦ καὶ τοῦ ἁγίου πνεύματος δι' ἀπορρήτων αἰνίσσεται· ὡς γὰρ μεταξὺ τῆς τοῦ σώματος ἐπιφανείας, καὶ τῆς τοῦ ἐλαίου χ. οὐδὲν ἐπινοεῖ μέσον οὔτε ὁ λόγος, οὔτε ἡ αἴσθησις, οὕτως ἀδιάστατός ἐστι πρὸς τὸ πνεῦμα τὸ ἅγιον τῷ υἱῷ ἡ συνάφεια* Gr.Nyss.*Maced.*16(M.45.1321A); cf.Chrys.*hom.1.1 in Rom.*(9.430B); *ἡ τοῦ Χριστοῦ δὲ προσηγορία τῆς τοῦ πνεύματος ἀνέμνησε χ.* id.*comm.in Gal.*1.4(10.663A); *χρίεται γὰρ ἡ ἀνθρωπότης* τῷ θείῳ πνεύματι...χ. δέ ἐστιν οἷον ὅλη τοῦ χριοντος παρουσία Cyr. Heb.1:8(M.74.961B); ἡ χ., καθ' ἣν γεννώμενος θειότερον ἢ κατὰ ἀνθρώπους καὶ τραφεὶς θειοτέρως ἢ καθ' ἡμᾶς Χριστός Apoll.quod un.Chr.11(p.302.13; M.28.132A); of unction of pre-existent Christ with glory of H. Ghost, Gr.Nyss.Apoll.53(M.45.1252C); **3.** of anointing of Christians; **a.** in baptismal rite; **i.** before baptism (v. χρίω, χρῖσμα, βάπτισμα) τίς ἡ πρὸς ἄμυναν τοῦ τοιούτου πάθους θεράπεια; λέγει...ἐπίκλησις ὀνόματος καινοῦ, καὶ χ. ἐλαίου καὶ λοῦτρον ὕδατος A.Xanthipp.2(p.59.6); ἔρχεται καὶ εἰς τὴν τοῦ ἐλαίου χ., εὐλογεῖται δὲ τοῦτο παρὰ τοῦ ἱερέως εἰς ἄφεσιν ἁμαρτιῶν καὶ προκατασκευὴν τοῦ βαπτίσματος...ἵνα δώσῃ χάριν πνευματικὴν καὶ δύναμιν ἐνεργητικὴν...εἶτα ἔρχεται εἰς τὸ ὕδωρ Const.App.7.42; as rite of exorcism, ‡Just.qu.et resp.137(M.6.1389C); v. χρίω, χρῖσμα; **ii.** after baptism; a rite without scriptural authority but sanctioned by tradition αὐτὴν τοῦ ἐλαίου τὴν χ. τίς λόγος γεγραμμένος ἐδίδαξε;...οὐκ ἐκ τῆς...διδασκαλίας, ἣν...οἱ πατέρες ἡμῶν ἐφύλαξαν; Bas.Spir.66(3.55A; M.32.188B); bestowing gift of H. Ghost, Cyr. Is.3.1(2.353D); ἡ...τοῦ μύρου τελειωτικὴ χ. εὐώδη ποιεῖ τὸν τετελεσμένον, ἡ γὰρ ἱερὰ τῆς θεογενεσίας τελείωσις ἑνοῖ τὰ τελεσθέντα τῷ θεαρχικῷ πνεύματι Dion.Ar.e.h.2.3.8(M.3.404C); signifies 'putting on' Christ (cf. Rom.13:14), ‡Chrys.pasch.2(8.255B); **b.** in reception of heretics, cf.‡Just.qu.et resp.14(M.6.1261D); **c.** in unction of sick, Jo.D.fid.dorm.18(M.95.264D); **d.** and of dead, Dion.Ar.e.h.7.2(M.3.556D); **e.** material used εἰ δὲ μήτε ἔλαιον ᾖ μήτε μύρον, ἀρκεῖ τὸ ὕδωρ καὶ πρὸς χ. καὶ πρὸς σφραγῖδα καὶ πρὸς ὁμολογίαν τοῦ ἀποθανόντος Const.App.7.22.3.

χρῖσμα, τό, *unction, unguent, chrism*;

I. in gen. of any kind of unction τὸ χ. πᾶν εἴτε ἐλαίου, εἴτε στακτῆς, εἴτε τῶν ἄλλων τῶν τῆς συνθέσεως τοῦ μύρου χρισμάτων Just.dial.86.3(M.6.681A).

II. of scents and cosmetics χρίσματα...παρειῶν Clem.paed.3.2(p.238.16; M.8.560C); use deprecated, ib.2.8(p.196.26; 472B); v. χρίω; although moderate use may be proper cause of thanksgiving to God, id.str.7.36(p.28.19; M.9.452C).

III. religious use; **A.** of unction of OT kings, Clem.paed.3.2(p.243.4; M.8.572C); βασιλείας...σύμβολόν ἐστι τὸ χ. Gr.Nyss.Maced.16(M.45.1320D); compared with Christ's unction bestowed by Father, Just.dial.86.3(M.6.681A); of OT priests, Eus.h.e.1.6.11(M.20.89A); †Bas.Is.130(2.469E; M.30.329A); τὸ ἱερατικὸν μύρον λέγεται χ. Ph.Carp.Cant.4(M.40.37C).

B. of unction received by Christ as the 'anointed'; **1.** in gen., Just.dial.86.3(M.6.681A); Or.Cels.6.79(p.150.33; M.11.1417C); βασιλικὸν χ. ὁμόψυχον τῆς πάντων συνέσεως Const.or.s.c.11(p.169.2; M.20.1265B); ὁ διὰ τὸ χ. τὸ πατρικὸν Χριστὸς ἀνηγορευμένος Eus.e.th.1.20(p.95.21; M.24.892B); signifies Christ's kingship and 'odour' spread through world by Inc., Ph.Carp.Cant.4(M.40.37C); **2.** consisting of anointing with H. Ghost τῷ ἀληθινῷ χ. ... τῇ τοῦ ἁγίου πνεύματος ...ἐπιδημίᾳ Bas.hom.in Ps.44(1.165E; M.29.405A); Gr.Nyss.Eun.2(2 p.301.3; M.45.472B); id.Maced.16(M.45.1320); or of his humanity with Logos τὸ γὰρ χ. ἐγὼ ὁ λόγος, τὸ δὲ χρισθὲν...ὁ ἄνθρωπος ‡Ath.Ar.4.36(p.86.1; M.26.524B); **3.** consisting in Inc. ἐχρίσθη ὡς βασιλεὺς ...τῷ χ. τῆς σαρκώσεως ‡Germ.CP contempl.(M.98.385C).

C. of unction bestowed on Christians; **1.** spiritually; **a.** by participation in Christ's anointing Χριστὸς...τὴν ἀπαρχὴν εἴληφε τοῦ χ. καὶ...ὅλον τὸ χ. τοῦ τῆς ἀγαλλιάσεως ἐλαίου· οἱ δὲ μέτοχοι αὐτοῦ ...μετέσχον καὶ τοῦ χ. αὐτοῦ Or.Cels.6.79(p.150.33; M.11.1417C); cf. Hipp.haer.5.9(p.102.15; M.16.3159); **b.** by bestowal of H. Ghost; **i.** in gen., Clem.paed.2.8(p.194.14; M.8.465C); id.str.4.18(p.299.19; M.8.1325A); ἡ σωτήριος σφραγὶς [sc. τὸ πνεῦμα] καὶ τὸ θεῖον χ. Didym.Trin.2.1(M.39.452C); **ii.** in baptismal rite (v. infra), whole of which is termed χ.: οἱ...πεπιστευκότες καὶ τοῦ ἁγίου τῆς ἐν τῷ Χριστῷ παλιγγενεσίας χ. κατηξιωμένοι Eus.d.e.4.16(p.190.27; M.22.317C); **c.** and by various gifts of grace, Clem.paed.1.12(p.149.6; M.8.368B); χρισθέντα τῷ χ. τῆς ἱερωσύνης Gr.Naz.or.6.9(M.35.733A); **2.** physically; **a.** in pre-baptismal anointing with oil, Const.App.7.22.2; cf. προσάγεται βρέφος τῆς κατηχήσεως τὸ χ. λαμβάνειν Cyr.Jo.7,8(4.683E); **b.** in post-baptismal chrismation χρίεσθαι τὸν βεβαπτισμένον, ἵνα λαβὼν χ., μέτοχος γένηται Χριστοῦ Cypr.ep.2(H.1.155A); cf. *unctio chrismatis et gratia...baptismi*, Or.hom.6.5 in Lev.(p.367.11; M.12.472D); *baptizati...in aquis istis visibilibus, et in chrismate visibili*, id.comm.in Rom.5.8(M.14.1038C); τὸ χ. τὸ μυστικόν Ath.exp.Ps.22:5(M.27.140C); Cyr.H.catech.21.1; μόνον βάπτισμα ὑποδέξηται καὶ τὸ χ. ῥώσῃ Didym.Trin.2.14(M.39.712A); H. Ghost being bestowed: **i.** through pre-baptismal unction χρίσεις...πρῶτον ἐλαίῳ...ἔπειτα βαπτίσεις, καὶ τελευταῖον σφραγίσεις μύρῳ, ἵνα τὸ μὲν χ. μετοχὴ ᾖ τοῦ ἁγίου πνεύματος, τὸ δὲ ὕδωρ σύμβολον τοῦ θανάτου, τὸ δὲ μύρον σφραγὶς τῶν συνθηκῶν Const.App.7.22.2; **ii.** through post-baptismal chrismation τὸ πνευματικὸν χ. Ast.Soph.hom.5 in Ps.5(M.40.441C); cf. χριστοί..., τὸ ἁγίου πνεύματος ἀντίτυπον δεξάμενοι Cyr.H.catech.21.1; χ., τὸ ἀντίτυπον οὗ ἐχρίσθη Χριστός, τοῦτο δέ ἐστι τὸ ἅγιον πνεῦμα ib.; Gr.Naz.or.40.15(M.36.377A); σύμβολον τοῦ μεταλαχεῖν ἁγίου πνεύματος τὸ χ. ποιούμενοι Cyr.Is.3.1(2.353D); Thdt.Cant.1:2(2.30); CCP(381)‡can.7; Dion.Ar.e.h.4.3.11(M.3.484C); Jo.D.f.o.4.9(M.94.1125B); unction with chrism conferring status of 'Christian', Cyr.H.catech.21.5; and membership of Christ, Bas.hom.1.2(2.2C; M.31.165A); and of Christ's kingdom, CLaod.can.48; chrism used in post-baptismal signing with cross, v. χρίω; in consecration of font, Dion.Ar.e.h.2.2.7(M.3.396C); **c.** in Gnost. initiatory rites, Hipp.haer.5.7(p.83.7; M.16.3131C); cf.ib.5.9(p.102.15; 3159); Cels.ap.Or.Cels.6.27(p.97.5; M.11.1333A); v. χρίω; **d.** not used by Novatianists, Thdt.haer.3.5(4.346); **e.** employed in reconciliation of heretics, CLaod.can.7; Bas.ep.188 can.1(3.270D; M.32.669C); χρίονται...οἱ ἀπὸ πάσης αἱρέσεως μετερχόμενοι, ἐπειδὴ οὐκ ἔχουσι τὸ ἅγιον χ. Didym.Trin.2.15(M.39.720A); Thdt.haer.3.5(4.346); CCP(381)‡can.7; CTrull.can.95; **f.** in unction of dead, ‡Chrys.pat.1(9.808D); cf.Dion.Ar.e.h.7.2(M.3.556D); **g.** in consecration of bishops, Thdr.Stud.epp.2.87(M.99.1333A).

D. preparation and consecration of chrism used for post-baptismal unction; **1.** material used; **a.** oil, Thphl.Ant.Autol.1.12(M.6.1041C), if referring to physical unction; cf.Clem.exc.Thdot.82(p.132.10; M.9.696C); Bas.Spir.66(3.55A; M.32.188B); ‡Germ.CP contempl.(M.98.385C); Rit.Bapt.(p.402); **b.** balsam; in Gnost. ritual, Iren.haer.1.21.4(M.7.665A); v. μυρίζω; **c.** μύρον q.v., cf. Hipp.Dan.1.16(p.27.1; M.10.693A); Eus.Is.25:7(M.24.268C); Cyr.H.catech.21.3; contrasted with pre-baptismal use of oil, Const.App.3.16.4; Thdt.Cant.1:2(2.30); cf.‡Just.qu.et resp.137(M.6.1389D); cf.Dion.Ar.e.h.4.3.4(M.3.477C) (for composition of this unguent v. μύρον); **d.** water permissible in absence of unguents, Const.App.7.22.3; **2.** its consecration, cf.Hipp.trad.ap.21; cf.Clem.exc.Thdot.82(p.132.10; M.9.696C); Cyr.H.catech.21.3; Bas.Spir.66(3.55A; M.32.188B); cf.Dion.Ar.e.h.4.2(M.3.473A); Thdr.Lect.h.e.2.48(M.86.208A); prayer at consecration ἐνεργῆσαι ἐν τῷ χ. τούτῳ ἐνέργειαν θείαν καὶ οὐράνιον Serap.euch.25.1; εὐλόγησον...τὸ ἔλαιον τῇ δυνάμει...τοῦ ἁγίου σου πνεύματος, ὥστε γενέσθαι αὐτὸ χ. ἀφθαρσίας Rit.Bapt.(p.402); to be performed by bishop, cf.Hipp.trad.ap.21; ἐπίσκοπος δὲ μόνος τῇ ἄνωθεν χάριτι τελεῖ τὸ χ. Didym.Trin.2.15(M.39.721A) but here χ. may = χρίσις; χρίσματος ποίησις, καὶ κορῶν καθιέρωσις, ἀπὸ πρεσβυτέρων μὴ γένηται Cod.Afr.6; cf.Dion.Ar.e.h.4.2(M.3.473A); consecrated at Easter, Isid.H.etym.6.18.16.

***Χριστάδελφος,** *of the brotherhood of Christ* τὰ Χ. ψηλαφήσωμεν μέλη Geo.Pis.bell.Avar.518(M.92.1293A).

***Χριστεμπαίκτης, ὁ,** *mocker of Christ*, Thdr.Stud.epp.2.10(M.99.1141C).

***Χριστεμπορία, ἡ,** *making Christ a source of gain, simony* οἱ... τὴν ἐκείνου [sc. Κολλούθου] Χ. θεωροῦντες [sc. Arius and his followers] οὐκ ἔτι τῆς ἐκκλησίας ὑποχείριοι μένειν ἐκαρτέρησαν Alex.Al.ep.Alex.1(p.20.2; M.18.549A).

***Χριστέμπορος, ὁ,** *one who makes Christ a source of gain*, Did.12.5; Hipp.fr.in Ruth(p.120.21); †Ath.fr.(M.26.1253C); Bas.ep.240.3(3.370B; M.32.897A); ‡Ign.Magn.9; χρηστ-, Ant.Mon.hom.37(M.89.1548A); of heretics, Gr.Naz.or.21.31(M.35.1117C); as reproach brought by opponents against Christians, Chrys.hom.6.1 in 1 Thess.(11.467C).

***Χριστεπώνυμος,** *called by Christ's name*, †Gregent.disp.(M.86.757C); Jo.VI H.v.Jo.D.5(M.94.436B).

***Χριστιανίζ-ω,** [Χριστιανῆσαι, ‡Tim.CP haer.suppl.5(M.86.72B)]; **1.** *become a Christian, turn Christian* Σαββάτιος ἀπὸ Ἰουδαίων Χριστιανίσας Socr.h.e.5.21.6(M.67.621B); τοὺς...ἐξ Ἑβραίων Χριστιανίσαντας Soz.h.e.1.12.11(M.67.893C); Nil.epp.1.250(M.79.176A); Thdr.Lect.h.e.2.34(M.86.204A); Zach.Mit.opif.(M.85.1109D); **2.** *live as a Christian, behave as a Christian*, Or.Cels.3.80(p.270.16; M.11.1024B); ib.7.39(p.190.12; 1477A); ἐξετάζεται δὲ παρὰ τοῖς τελειότερον ~ειν ἐθέλουσι ib.7.49(p.200.8; 1492C); ἀναγκαῖον πνευματικῶς καὶ σωματικῶς ~ειν id.Jo.1.7(9; p.13.4; M.14.37B); οὐκ ἐχριστιάνιζον ῥητορεύων Gr.Naz.ep.11(M.37.41C); Cyr.ador.6(1.215B); οἱ μὴ γνησίως ~οντες id.Os.92(3.124B); Cyr.S.v.Sab.36(p.124.26).

Χριστιανικός, *Christian, pertaining to Christianity*; **1.** usu. of things; of Christian religion in gen. ἐπιστήμη τίς ἐστιν ἡ Χ. θεοσέβεια· ὅνπερ...τρόπον ἑκάστης ἐπιστήμης ἴδιοι λόγοι εἰσίν...οὕτως καὶ ἡ Χ. ἐπιστήμη ἀπὸ τῶν κατ' αὐτὴν λόγων περιγίνεται. ἴδιοι γὰρ καὶ οἱ Χ. λόγοι εἰσίν Clem.fr.68(p.229.3); ἔτι...θρησκεύουσαν Χ. τινι τάξει M.Agap.6.3; of appellation 'Christian' Φρύγες ἡμῖν πάλιν ἐπαναστάντες πολέμιοι καὶ μεταμορφούμενοι εἰς Χ. ἐπίκλησιν Epiph.haer.48.12(p.235.11; M.41.873A); τῆς Χ. προσηγορίας ‡Gr.Nyss.*hom.7.62 in Jo.*(p.253.33); ‡Jo.D.*ep.Thphl.*14(M.95.364B); of doctrine Χ. διδασκαλίας Epiph.*haer.*61.5(p.385.21; 1045C); Mac.Mgn.*apocr.*3.23(p.103.2); *ib.*4.19(p.198.7); Socr.*h.e.*5.10(M.67.585C); Cosm.Ind.*top.*2(M.88.128B); *ib.*5(221B); of a particular article of faith Ἰουδαίων οἱ ἄπιστοι...μηδὲ Χ. ἀνάστασιν ὁμολογοῦντες *Chron.Pasch.*237(M.92.573B); of scriptures ἱερῶν βιβλίων, φημὶ δὲ τῶν Χ. Epiph.*haer.*66.5(p.24.5; M.42.37A); Chrys.*hom.32.2 in Jo.*(8.188A); of priesthood, Leont.H.*Nest.*2.6(M.86.1548B); of baptism, Socr.*h.e.*7.4.2(M.67.745A); of souls (i.e. persons), ‡Chrys.*hom.*1(M.64.11); **2.** superl., of persons Δομέτιλλα Χριστιανικωτάτη *M.Ner.et Ach.*18(p.17.6); Cosm.Ind.*top.*6(M.88.321B); βασιλεύσει ἕτερος [i.e. Jovian]...Χριστιανικώτατος καὶ θεοφιλέστατος ‡Jo.D.*Artem.*66(M.96.1313C); as title of honour for emperors, CNic.(787)*act.*2(H.4.84B).

***Χριστιανικῶς,** *in a Christian manner,* ref. Abraham διὰ μόνου τοῦ κατ' ἀρετὴν βίου δείκνυται Χ., ἀλλ' οὐχὶ Ἰουδαϊκῶς βεβιωκώς Eus.*d.e.*1.6(p.24.8; M.22.49C); Χ. ἀνήγετο καὶ αὐτός Ath.*v.Anton.*1(M.26.841A); Leont.H.*Nest.*4.37(M.86.1712D); Ant.Mon.*hom.*53(M.89.1596A).

***Χριστιανισμός, ὁ,** *Christianity, the Christian system of belief and practice* κατὰ Χ. ζῆν Ign.*Magn.*10.1; *ib.*10.3; id.*Rom.*3.3; ἄμεινον γάρ ἐστι παρὰ ἀνδρὸς περιτομὴν ἔχοντος Χ. ἀκούειν ἢ παρὰ ἀκροβύστου Ἰουδαϊσμόν id.*Philad.*6.1; τὸν τοῦ Χ. μαθεῖν λόγον *M.Polyc.*10.1; Clem.*str.*7.1(p.3.15; M.9.404A); τῶν ἐν Χ. αἱρέσεων Or.*Cels.*3.12(p.211.18; M.11.933B); ὁ Χ. οὔτε Ἑλληνισμός τίς ἐστιν οὔτε Ἰουδαϊσμός, οἰκεῖον δέ τινα φέρων χαρακτῆρα θεοσεβείας Eus.*d.e.*1.2(p.7.19; M.22.24A); Ath.*Ar.*1.1(M.26.13C); Bas.*ep.*199 *can.*45(3.296C; M.32.729B); πάντες δὲ τὸν Κωνσταντῖνον...ἴσασιν ἐκθειαζόμενον ἐν Χ. Epiph.*haer.*69.1(p.153.6; M.42.204A); εἰσιν ἑβδομήκοντα πέντε καὶ τούτων αἱ μητέρες πέντε, ὥσπερ Ἑλληνισμός...καὶ Ἰουδαϊσμός...καὶ αἵρεσις Σαμαρειτική...καὶ Χ. ἀφ' οὗ ἐξεκλάσθησαν ὥσπερ κλάδοι αἱ ἀφορισθεῖσαι αἱρέσεις *ib.*80.10(p.495.11; 772B); τοῦτό ἐστι τὸ σημεῖον τοῦ Χ., αὐτὴ ἡ ταπείνωσις Mac.Aeg.*hom.*15.37(M.34.601B); Χ. ἐστι δόγμα τοῦ σωτῆρος ἡμῶν Ἰησοῦ Χριστοῦ ἐκ πρακτικῆς καὶ φυσικῆς καὶ θεολογικῆς συνεστώς Evagr.Pont.*cap.*1(M.40.1221D); ὁ Χ. καὶ τὸ τῆς τῶν δογμάτων ὀρθότητος καὶ πολιτείαν ὑγιαίνουσαν ἀπαιτεῖ Chrys.*hom.28.2 in Jo.*(8.161B).

***Χριστιανοδιώκτης, ὁ,** *persecutor of Christians*; of Antony, iconoclast metropolitan of Silaeus, ‡Jo.D.*ep.Thphl.*22(M.95.373C).

***Χριστιανοκατήγορος, ὁ,** *accuser of Christians* Τιβέριος θάνατον ἠπείλησεν τοῖς Χ. *Chron.Pasch.*229(M.92.556C); of iconoclasts, Germ.CP *ep.*4(M.98.189B); Jo.D.*haer.*101(M.94.773A); ‡Jo.D.*ep.Thphl.*22(M.95.373C).

***Χριστιανομερῖται, οἱ,** name of supposed Jewish party, who did not accept baptism though they became friendly to Christians, *Pers.*(p.44.1).

Χριστιανός, *Christian*;

A. adj., of things and abstracts μόνῃ τῇ Χ. τροφῇ χρῆσθε Ign.*Trall.*6.1; ὀνόματος δὲ Χ. προσωνυμίαν ὁμολογοῦντα Just.*2apol.*2.16(M.6.445C); αἰτήσασθε...Χ. ὑμῶν τὰ τέλη, ἵλεω...τὸν θεόν *Const.App.*8.6.8; ὑπὲρ πάσης ψυχῆς Χ. δεηθῶμεν *Lit.*ap.*Const.App.*8.10.20.

B. as subst., *a Christian person*; **1.** descriptions and definitions πρέπον...ἐστιν μὴ μόνον καλεῖσθαι Χριστιανοὺς ἀλλὰ καὶ εἶναι Ign.*Magn.*4; Χ. ἑαυτοῦ ἐξουσίαν οὐκ ἔχει ἀλλὰ θεῷ σχολάζει id.*Polyc.*7.3; προνοήσατε πῶς μὴ ἀργὸς μεθ' ὑμῶν ζήσεται Χ. εἰ δ' οὐ θέλει οὕτω ποιεῖν, Χριστέμπορός ἐστιν *Did.*12.4; ὁμολογοῦντας ἑαυτοὺς εἶναι Χ. καὶ τὸν σταυρωθέντα Ἰησοῦν ὁμολογεῖν καὶ κύριον καὶ Χριστόν Just.*dial.*35.2(M.6.549B); θυμὸς Χριστιανοῖσιν ὑπέρτερος, εὖτε διώκτης καιρὸς ἐπισπέρχῃσι θεοῦ πέρι δῆριν ἐγείρων Gr.Naz.*carm.*1.2.2.515(M.37.619A); οὐδένα οἶμαι τῶν Χ. ἀγνοεῖν ὅτι ἀγαθὸς ὅτι χρηστὸς ὅτι ἅγιος...εὐεργέτης κύριος Gr.Nyss.*Eun.*1(1 p.166.25; M.45.409A); καὶ τὸ πρᾶγμα καὶ τὸ ὄνομα ἔχειν ὀφείλεις, καὶ εἶναι καὶ καλεῖσθαι Χ. Chrys.*hom.58.4 in Jo.*(8.342D); ταῦτα πρὸς Χριστιανοὺς λέγω, τοὺς λέγοντας πείθεσθαι γραφαῖς *ib.66.3*(397D); Cyr.*inc.unigen.*(5^1.680A); Χ. ἐστιν, μίμημα Χριστοῦ...λόγοις καὶ ἔργοις καὶ ἐννοίᾳ εἰς τὴν ἁγίαν τριάδα ὀρθῶς καὶ ἀμέμπτως πιστεύων Jo.Clim.*scal.*1(M.88.633B); Χ. ἐστιν ἀληθινὸς οἶκος Χριστοῦ λογικός, δι' ἔργων ἀγαθῶν καὶ δογμάτων εὐσεβῶν συνιστάμενος Anast.S.*hod.*2(M.89.77A); to be applied only to orthodox, Eunomians being no more entitled to it than Jews or Manicheans, Gr.Nyss.*Maced.*15(M.45.1320C); **2.** as generic term opp. Jews, Greeks, etc. τοῦ θεοφιλοῦς καὶ θεοσεβοῦς γένους τῶν Χ. *M.Polyc.*3; ὅπερ ἐστὶν ἐν σώματι ψυχή, τοῦτ' εἰσὶν ἐν κόσμῳ Χριστιανοί. ἔσπαρται κατὰ πάντων τῶν τοῦ σώματος μελῶν ἡ ψυχή, καὶ Χ. κατὰ τὰς τοῦ κόσμου πόλεις...καὶ Χ. ἐν κόσμῳ οἰκοῦσιν, οὐκ εἰσὶ δὲ ἐκ τοῦ κόσμου *Diogn.*6.1–3; οἱ τῶν παρ' ὑμῖν λεγομένων θεῶν προσκυνηταὶ καὶ Ἰουδαῖοι καὶ Χ. Arist.*apol.*2.1; **3.** avowed in persecutions μετὰ παρρησίας ἄκουε, Χ. εἰμι, *M.Polyc.*10.1; Πολύκαρπος ὡμολόγησεν ἑαυτὸν Χ. εἶναι *ib.*12.1; Just.*2apol.*2.11(M.6.445A); *M.Carp.*5; **4.** used in derision by pagan opponents, Thphl.Ant.*Autol.*1.12(M.6.1041B); ὅταν μάλιστα ἡμῖν ὀνειδίσαι βούλωνται... τοῦτο ἐπιλέγουσιν, οἷον, ὁ Χ. Chrys.*hom.15.8 in Mt.*(7.198C); id.*hom.18.2 in Eph.*(11.129B); **5.** origin and derivation of name; **a.** said to have been first given to Christians by Euodius, bishop of Antioch, Jo.Mal.*chron.*p.246(M.97.377); **b.** derivations; **i.** connected with χριστός (*anointed*) i.e. Christian is one who partakes of Christ's anointing ἡμεῖς τούτου εἵνεκεν καλούμεθα Χ., ὅτι χριόμεθα ἔλαιον θεοῦ Thphl.Ant.*Autol.*1.12(M.6.1041C); Gnost., Naassene ἐσμὲν...ἡμεῖς Χ. μόνοι, ἐν τῇ τρίτῃ πύλῃ ἀπαρτίζοντες τὸ μυστήριον καὶ χριόμενοι ἐκεῖ ἀλάλῳ χρίσματι Hipp.*haer.*5.9(p.102.15; M.16.3159A); cf.Or.*Cels.*6.79(p.150.33; M.11.1417C); Cyr.*Lc.*9.18(M.72.648D); this unction represented by post-baptismal anointing τούτου τοῦ...χρίσματος καταξιωθέντες, καλεῖσθε Χ. Cyr.H.*catech.*21.5; **ii.** derived from name of Christ οἱ δὲ Χ. γενεαλογοῦνται ἀπὸ τοῦ κυρίου Ἰησοῦ Χριστοῦ Arist.*apol.*15.1; Ἰησοῦς Χριστός, ἀφ' οὗ καὶ τὸ Χ. ἐπονομάζεσθαι ἐσχήκαμεν Just.*1apol.*12.9(M.6.345A); ἀπὸ τοῦ ὀνόματος αὐτοῦ Χ. καλεῖσθαι πάντες ἐσχήκατε id.*dial.*64.1(M.6.621C); **iii.** connected with χρηστός by play on words Χ. γὰρ εἶναι κατηγορούμεθα· τὸ δὲ χρηστὸν μισεῖσθαι οὐ δίκαιον id.*1apol.*4.1(333A); περὶ δὲ τοῦ σε καταγελᾶν μου, καλοῦντά με Χ. οὐκ οἶδας ὃ λέγεις. ... τὸ Χριστὸν ἡδὺ καὶ εὔχρηστον...ἐστι Thphl.Ant.*Autol.*1.12(M.6.1041B); cf. ζῶντες ἑαυτοῖς καὶ Ἀνδρονίκῳ Χρηστιανοὶ χρηστῷ ἐποίησαν *CIG* 3857 p; **6.** in restricted sense, of those about to be admitted to first grade of catechumenate τοὺς...θέλοντας προστίθεσθαι τῇ ὀρθοδοξίᾳ, ὡς Ἕλληνας δεχόμεθα, καὶ τὴν πρώτην ἡμέραν ποιοῦμεν αὐτοὺς Χ., τὴν δὲ δευτέραν κατηχουμένους CCP(381)‡*can.*7; but usu. of those actually baptized, cf. *plurimis vero in partibus neque Christianos vocant eos qui non perceperunt baptisma,* Thdr.Mops.*1Tim.*3:6(p.112.9); Χ. γὰρ παρὰ πάντων καλοῦνται, ἅτε διὰ τοῦ παναγίου βαπτίσματος τὸν Χριστὸν ἐνδυσάμενοι Thdt.*Is.*62:2(p.243.15; 2.386); **7.** moral and spiritual characteristics of Christian τὸν...Χ. εἰπεῖν πλούσιόν τε καὶ σώφρονα καὶ εὐγενῆ καὶ ταύτῃ εἰκόνα τοῦ θεοῦ μεθ' ὁμοιώσεως, καὶ λέγειν καὶ πιστεύειν δίκαιον καὶ ὅσιον...γενόμενον ὑπὸ Χριστοῦ Ἰησοῦ καὶ εἰς τοσοῦτον ὅμοιον ἤδη καὶ θεῷ Clem.*prot.*12(p.86.14; M.8.245A); χαρακτῆρες δὲ τοῦ ὄντως Χ. πάντα κἀκεῖνά ἐστιν, ὅσα περὶ τὸν Χριστὸν ἐνοήσαμεν Gr.Nyss.*perf.*(p.178.11; M.46.256C); τρία τὰ χαρακτηριζόμενα τοῦ Χ. τὸν βίον ἐστί, πρᾶξις, λόγος, ἐνθύμιον *ib.*(p.210.5; 284A); ἐν...τῇ τοῦ νοὸς ἀνακαινίσει καὶ τῇ τῶν λογισμῶν εἰρήνῃ, καὶ τῇ τοῦ κυρίου ἀγάπῃ καὶ οὐρανίῳ ἔρωτι, ἡ καινὴ κτίσις τῶν Χ. πάντων ἀνθρώπων τοῦ κόσμου διαφέρει Mac.Aeg.*hom.*5.5(M.34.497D).

***Χριστιανόφρων,** *following the Christian faith, Christian,* Thphn.*chron.*p.8(M.108.76B).

***Χριστιανωσύνη, ἡ,** *Christianity, Mir.Geo.*suppl.4(p.26.3).

***Χριστόγονος, ὁ,** *child of Christ* χορὸς εἰρήνης οἱ Χ. Clem.*paed.*3.12(p.292; M.8.684B).

***Χριστοδίδακτος,** *taught by Christ* τάσσεσθαι τῇ Χ. δικαιοσύνῃ Meth.*symp.*2.3(p.18.11; M.18.52A).

***Χριστοδιώκτης, ὁ,** *persecutor of Christ*; of emperor Valens, ‡Jo.D.*ep.Thphl.*7(M.95.353D).

***Χριστοδόκος,** *receiving Christ* σταυρῷ Χ. Eudoc.*Cypr.*2(M.85.860D).

***Χριστοειδής,** *after Christ's likeness,* of the righteous ὅλους αὐτοὺς ἀπολήψεσθαι τὴν Χ. λῆξιν εἰδότες, ὅταν ἐπὶ τὸ πέρας ἔλθωσι τοῦ τῇδε βίου...θείας ἡδονῆς ἀποπληροῦνται Dion.Ar.*e.h.*7.1.3(M.3.553D); ὅταν...ἀθάνατοι γενώμεθα, καὶ τῆς Χ. καὶ μακαριωτάτης ἐφικώμεθα λήξεως id.*d.n.*1.4(M.3.592B); ἡ ἐν ἀνθρώποις Χ. κατάστασις Max.*ambig.*(M.91.1285A).

***Χριστοειδῶς,** *after the form of Christ, in a manner resembling Christ,* Dion.Ar.*ep.*8.2(M.3.1092C).

***Χριστόθεν,** *from Christ,* Sophr.H.*or.*4(M.87.3308B).

***Χριστοθεράπευτος,** *cured by Christ,* Jo.VI H.*v.Jo.D.*30(M.94.472A).

***Χριστοκάπηλος,** *making Christ a subject for business deals,* ref. deferment of baptism μηδὲ γενώμεθα Χ. καὶ Χριστέμποροι Gr.Naz.*or.*40.11(M.36.372C); of women who sing profane songs in church, Isid.Pel.*epp.*1.90(M.78.245A).

***Χριστοκῆρυξ, ὁ,** *herald of Christ*; of S. Paul, Mac.Mgn.*apocr.*3.24(p.108.22).

***Χριστοκίνητος,** *moved by Christ,* ref. S. Paul ἡ Χ. γλῶττα ‡Gr.Nyss.*occurs.*(M.46.1152A).

***Χριστόκλητος,** *called by Christ,* Leont.Abb.*v.Gr.Agr.*95(M.98.716A).

***Χριστοκτονέω**, *be a slayer of Christ*, Didym.*Zach*.4.186; Cyr. *hom.div*.4(5².356D).

***Χριστοκτονία, ἡ**, *slaying of Christ* ἐπὶ τὴν Χ. ἐλθόντες, ὡς τὸ ἔθνος αὐτοὶ καὶ τὴν χώραν διασώσοντες Bas.*hom*.20.2(2.158C; M.31.529A); ὁ διάβολος...ἐκεῖνον...τὸν λαὸν διὰ τῆς Χ. εἰς ἑαυτὸν ὑπηγάγετο *Const.App*.6.5.5; Chrys.*hom.85.1 in Mt*.(7.807B); διὰ τὴν Χ. ἠρήμωται πᾶσα Ἰουδαία ὑπὸ Ῥωμαίων Nil.*epp*.1.56(M.79.108C); Cyr. *Jo*.12(4.1038E).

***Χριστοκτόνος, ὁ**, *slayer of Christ*; **1.** of those who killed Christ, †Ath.*fr*.(M.26.1224B); Chrys.*hom.86.3 in Mt*.(7.815B); id.*hom.48.1 in Jo*.(8.283B); Καϊάφας προεφήτευσε Χ. ὢν id.*hom.3.4 in Col*.(11.349A); Procl.CP *or*.12.2(M.65.789A); their fate shared by impenitent sinners who receive Communion, Chrys.*hom.47.5 in Jo*.(281E); **2.** of Jews in gen. ἐγώ εἰμι Ἰεζεκιήλ, ὃν ἔπειραν οἱ Χ. *Apoc.Paul*.49(p.67); **3.** of opponents of Christianity, esp. Jews, *Const.App*.2.61.1; *ib*.6.25.1.

***Χριστολάτρης, ὁ**, *worshipper of Christ, Christian*, Germ.CP *or*.1 (M.98.233C).

***Χριστόλη(μ)πτος**, *possessed by Christ*, of author of Apocalypse ὁ Χ. ... Ἰωάννης Meth.*symp*.1.5(p.13.18; M.18.45B); τῶν φωτισθέντων τὸν Χ. νοῦν *ib*.8.10(p.92.8; 153A); ἀσπάζομαι τὰς Χριστολήμπτους παρθένους ‡Ign.*Ant*.12.

***Χριστολύται, οἱ**, *those who dissolve Christ*; members of sect which held that Christ ascended in his deity alone, Jo.D.*haer*.93 (M.94.757C).

***Χριστομαθής, ὁ**, *student of the things of Christ* ἐπαπορήσειε δ' ἂν εἰκότως ὁ Χ., τί δ' ἂν εἴη...τὸ αἴνιγμα Cyr.*ador*.16(1.581D); φιλομαθεῖς, ἤγουν Χ. Mod.*dorm*.1(M.86.3280B); neut. as subst., *subject of Christian study*, Cyr.*ador*.2(55C).

***Χριστομαθία (Χριστομάθεια), ἡ**, *Christian discipleship* μηδὲν κατ' ἐρίθειαν πράσσετε ἀλλὰ κατὰ Χ. Ign.*Philad*.8.2; ‡Ign.*Philad*.8 (v.l. χριστομάθειαν).

***Χριστομάκαρ**, *blessed in Christ*, Thdr.Stud.*cant*.10.10(p.357).

***Χριστομανία, ἡ**, *fury against Christ* ὢ τῆς ἐκείνου [sc. Leo the Armenian] Χ. Thdr.Stud.*epp*.2.77(M.99.1316C).

***Χριστομάρτυς, ὁ**, *witness* or *martyr for Christ*, Thdr.Stud.*epp*. 2.37(M.99.1228A).

***Χριστομαχ-έω**, *make war against Christ*, of Arians προθέμενοι ~εῖν Alex.Al.*ep.encycl*.16(p.9.15; M.18.576C); Eunomians, Gr.Nyss. *Eun*.10(M.45.844B; χριστομάχων 2 p.241.4); Didym.(‡Bas.)*Eun*.5.2 (1.314B; M.29.753A).

***Χριστομάχος, 1.** adj.; *contending against Christ*, of Arianism τὴν...Χ. αἵρεσιν Alex.Al.*ep.encycl*.3(p.7.8; M.18.572C); Ath.*Ar*.1.7(M.26.25B); *ib*.2.13(173B); ἡ...δυσωδία τῆς εἰς τὰ εἴδωλα θυσίας τοῦ συνηγόρου [sc. Asterius] ἔτι πλέον τὴν αἵρεσιν Χριστομάχον ἐδείκνυε id. *syn*.20(p.247.7; M.26.716D); Oecum.*Apoc*.3(p.64.7); of Valens Χ. βασιλεύς Gr.Naz.*or*.43.44(M.36.553B); **2.** as subst.; *enemy of Christ*, of Arians, Ath.*decr*.15(p.13.10; M.25.441B); *ib*.18(p.15.30; 448C); Cyr. *Jo*.2.1(4.152D); id.*thes*.22(5¹.220A); of Jews, Bas.*hex*.9.6(1.87D; M.29.205A); of persecuting emperors, Gr.Naz.*or*.7.11(M.35.768C); of Eunomians who relegate Christ to status of an angel, Gr.Nyss. *Eun*.11(2 p.260.5; M.45.868B); of Origen, Meletius, Arius, *V.Pach*. Σ 88(p.268.10); of Valens εἰ καὶ οὐκ ἀποστάτης, ἀλλά γε Χριστοδιώκτης καὶ Χ. ‡Jo.D.*ep.Thphl*.7(M.95.353D).

***Χριστομίμητος**, *imitating Christ*, ‡Jo.Jej.*serm*.1(M.88.1925D); οἱ Χ. μάρτυρες Sophr.H.*mir.Cyr.et Jo*.(M.87.3569A); ὁ διὰ Χ. πολιτείας ...εἰσιὼν εἰς τὸν βίον τῶν μοναχῶν *Schol*.16 in Jo.Clim.*scal*.25(M.88.1008B); of emperors ἡ Χ. ὑμῶν γαληνότης CCP(681)*act*.4(H.3.1077C).

***Χριστομιμήτως**, *in imitation of Christ*, Max.*opusc*.(M.91.92B); Andr.Caes.*Apoc*.59(M.106.404C); ‡Jo.D.*ep.Thphl*.26(M.95.377C).

***Χριστόμορφος**, *in Christ's likeness* τὰς Χ. ... προσκυνοῦμεν εἰκονογραφίας ‡Jo.D.*hom*.5(M.96.657A).

***Χριστόνομος**, *governed by Christ*, Ign.*Rom*.proem.

***Χριστοπάτωρ, ὁ**, *father of Christ* Ἀβραὰμ ὁ Χ. θύτης ‡Epiph. *hom*.2(M.43.452C).

***Χριστόπολις, ἡ**, *city of Christ*, Gr.Naz.*carm*.1.1.27.76(M.37.504A).

***Χριστοπρεπῶς**, *in a manner befitting Christ*, Max.*ep*.28(M.91.621B).

χριστός, ὁ, *anointed person, Messiah, Christ*;

A. of anointed persons in OT; **1.** in gen. πλεῖστοι μὲν γὰρ οἱ, ὡς ἀπό γε τοῦ κεχρῖσθαι παρὰ θεοῦ, κατὰ διαφόρους τρόπους ὠνομασμένοι χ. Cyr.*Lc*.9:18(M.72.648C); **2.** of kings, priests, prophets οἱ βασιλεῖς πάντες καὶ οἱ χ. ἀπὸ τούτου μετέσχον καὶ βασιλεῖς καλεῖσθαι καὶ χ. Just.*dial*.86.3(M.6.681A); Clem.*paed*.2.8(p.195.24; M.8.468C); Eus. *d.e*.4.10(p.168.4; M.22.280C); καὶ σύ, μάκαρ, χριστοῖσι φέρων κέρας, ἁγνὲ Σαμουήλ Gr.Naz.*carm*.1.2.1.319(M.37.546A); *Const.App*.5.20.7; Cyr.*Lc*.9:18(M.72.648C); id.*Chr.un*.(5¹.726D); χ. δὲ οἱ πατριάρχαι, οὐκ ἐλαίῳ χρισθέντες, ἀλλὰ τῇ μετουσίᾳ τοῦ πνεύματος, ἀφ' ἧς καὶ προφῆται ἐλέγοντο Hesych.H.*fr.Ps*.104:15(M.93.1293C); ref. high-priestly succession μέχρι τούτου οἱ ἀπὸ Κύρου χ. ἡγούμενοι διαρκέσαντες ἔτεσιν υπγ' *Chron.Pasch*.p.188(M.92.464C); cf. Λευὶ...ἀρχιερεὺς χ. *T.Reub*. 6.8; of patriarchs who received revelation of Christ τὰ περὶ τοῦ Χριστοῦ κοινῶς ἡμῖν τε κἀκείνοις παραδέδοται. ἔνθεν καὶ χ. αὐτοὺς δὴ ἐκείνους τοὺς πρὸ Μωσέως θεοφιλεῖς...εὕροις ἂν κεκλημένους Eus. *d.e*.1.5(p.23.1; M.22.48C).

B. esp., of Jewish Messiah πάντες ἅγιοι, καὶ βασιλεὺς αὐτῶν χ., κύριος *Pss.Sal*.17.36; ὑπὸ ῥάβδον παιδείας χ. κυρίου *ib*.18.8; cf. *T.Lev*.10.2(prob. Christian); ἡμεῖς τὸν χ. ἄνθρωπον ἐξ ἀνθρώπων προσδοκῶμεν γενήσεσθαι Just.*dial*.49(M.6.581A); οἱ δὲ πάντες ὁμοίως χ. προσδέχονται...διὰ τὸ παρόντα μὴ ἐπεγνωκέναι Hipp.*haer*.9.30 (p.263.25; M.16.3410C); Chrys.*hom.51.1 in Jo*.(8.299D); Thdt.*Ps*. 109:1(2.1391).

C. of Jesus as the Christ; significance of name, Just.*2apol*.6.3 (M.6.453B) cit. s. ἄγνωστος; anointed by Father, id.*dial*.86.3(M.6.681A); cf.Hipp.*Dan*.4.32.4(p.272.12); Or.*Cels*.6.79(p.150.33; M.11.1417C); ἀρχιερεὺς αἰώνιος καὶ δὴ Χριστὸς τοῦ πατρὸς προσαγορεύεται, οὕτω παρ' Ἑβραίοις χ. ἐπικαλουμένων πάλαι τῶν τὴν εἰκόνα τοῦ πρώτου διὰ συμβόλων ἐπιτελούντων Eus.*d.e*.4.10(p.168.3; M.22.280C); θεὸς γὰρ ἐν τούτοις χριόμενος ὑπὸ τοῦ θεοῦ τίς ἂν ἕτερος εἴη ἢ αὐτὸς ὁ διὰ τὸ χρῖσμα τὸ πατρικὸν Χ. ἀνηγορευμένος; id.*e.th*.1.20(p.95.21; M.24.892B); ἡ τοῦ Χ. προσηγορία τὴν βασιλείαν ἐνδείκνυται Gr.Nyss.*Eun*. 6(2 p.149.5; M.45.736A); ὁ αὐτὸς καὶ ὢν χ. καὶ γενόμενος id.*Apoll*.55(M.45.1257B); Cyr.*Chr.un*.(5¹.726C); τὸ δέ, Χ., ὑπόστασιν δηλοῖ σύνθετον, ἐκ θεότητός τε καὶ ἀνθρωπότητος. καὶ τὸ χρῖσαν μὲν ἡ θεότης, ἡ ἀνθρωπότης δὲ τὸ χρισθέν...μόνος τοίνυν ὁ κύριος κυρίως Χ., ὡς ὅλος διόλου καὶ οὐ χάριτι ‡Cyr.*Trin*.22(6³.27Eff.; M.77.1161D–1164A); ὁ Χ. ἐχρίσθη ὡς βασιλεὺς καὶ ἱερεὺς τῷ χρίσματι τῆς σαρκώσεως ‡Germ.CP *contempl*.(M.98.385C); Christ being anointed with H. Ghost, Bas. *hom.in Ps*.44(1.165E; M.29.405A); Gr.Nyss.*Maced*.15(M.45.1320C); εἰ χρίεται Χ., οὐκ ἐν ἐλαίῳ γηΐνῳ, ἀλλὰ πνεύματι θεοῦ *Dial.Ath.et Zacch*. 58(p.36); at hands of Elijah in person of John, Just.*dial*.49.3(M.6.584D); Jesus fulfils expectation of Messiah from Judah and from Levi, Hipp.*ben.Jac*.15(p.31.19,26).

D. heret. distinction between the Christ and Jesus; **1.** Cerinthus τὸν δὲ Ἰησοῦν ὑπέθετο...γεγονέναι...ἐξ Ἰωσὴφ καὶ Μαρίας...καὶ μετὰ τὸ βάπτισμα κατελθεῖν εἰς αὐτὸν τὸν ἀπὸ τῆς ὑπὲρ τὰ ὅλα αὐθεντίας, τὸν Χ. ἐν εἴδει περιστερᾶς...πρὸς δὲ τῷ τέλει ἀποστῆναι τὸν Χ. ἀπὸ τοῦ Ἰησοῦ, καὶ τὸν Ἰησοῦν πεπονθέναι...τὸν δὲ Χ. ἀπαθῆ διαμεμενηκέναι Iren.*haer*.1.26.1(M.7.686B); Hipp.*haer*.7.33(p.221.3; M.16.3342A) = *ib*. 10.21(p.281.12; 3438D); Christ identified with H. Ghost, Epiph.*haer*. 28.1(p.314.5; M.41.380A); Thdt.*haer*.2.3(4.329); cf. similar doctrine of Ebionites, Epiph.*haer*.30.3(p.337.7; 409B); and of Elchezaites, Hipp. *haer*.10.29(p.284.13; 3442C); **2.** Ebionite Ἰησοῦν...δεδικαιῶσθαι ποιήσαντα τὸν νόμον· διὸ καὶ Χ. αὐτὸν τοῦ θεοῦ ὠνομάσθαι καὶ Ἰησοῦν, ἐπεὶ μηδεὶς τῶν ἑτέρων ἐτέλεσε τὸν νόμον· εἰ γὰρ καὶ ἕτερός τις πεποιήκει τὰ ἐν νόμῳ προστεταγμένα, ἦν ἂν ἐκεῖνος ὁ Χ. δύνασθαι δὲ καὶ ἑαυτοὺς ὁμοίως ποιήσαντας Χ. γενέσθαι Hipp.*haer*.7.34(p.221.12; M.16.3342B); τινὲς γὰρ ἐξ αὐτῶν καὶ Ἀδὰμ τὸν Χ. εἶναι λέγουσιν, τὸν πρῶτόν τε πλασθέντα καὶ ἐμφυσηθέντα ἀπὸ τῆς τοῦ θεοῦ ἐπιπνοίας Epiph.*haer*.30.3 (p.336.5; M.41.409A); **3.** Elchezaite Χ. δὲ ἕνα οὐχ ὁμολογοῦσιν, ἀλλ' εἶναι τὸν μὲν ἄνω, αὐτὸν δὲ μεταγγιζόμενον ἐν σώμασι πολλοῖς πολλάκις καὶ νῦν ἐν τῷ Ἰησοῦ Hipp.*haer*.10.29(p.284.10; M.16.3442C); Thdt. *haer*.2.7(4.333); **4.** Theodotus of Byzantium; teaching described as like that of Cerinthus, Hipp.*haer*.7.35(p.222.9; M.16.3343A).

E. Valent. teaching; **1.** Christ and H. Ghost as aeons τὸν Μονογενῆ πάλιν ἑτέραν προβαλέσθαι συζυγίαν...Χ., καὶ πνεῦμα ἅγιον εἰς πῆξιν καὶ στηριγμὸν τοῦ πληρώματος Iren.*haer*.1.2.5(M.7.461A); ἐπιπροβληθεὶς οὖν ὁ Χ., καὶ τὸ ἅγιον πνεῦμα ὑπὸ τοῦ Νοῦ καὶ τῆς Ἀληθείας Hipp.*haer*.6.31(p.159.2; M.16.3239D); Thdt.*haer*.1.7(4.298); this being πρῶτος Χριστός, Iren.*haer*.1.3.1(468A); **2.** 'Christ' identified with Soter or Jesus or Logos, produced by all the aeons, Iren.*haer*.1.2.6(M.7.465A); Thdt.*haer*.1.7(4.298); this being δεύτερος Χριστός, Iren.*haer*.1.3.1(468A); **3.** Christ born of Mary προβαλέσθαι αὐτὸν καὶ Χ. υἱὸν ἴδιον, ἀλλὰ καὶ ψυχικόν·...εἶναι δὲ τοῦτον τὸν διὰ Μαρίας διοδεύσαντα καθάπερ ὕδωρ διὰ σωλῆνος ὁδεύει Iren.*haer*.1.7.2 (M.7.513A); Epiph.*haer*.31.22(p.419.22; M.41.517B); **4.** Christ the Σωτήρ descending upon Christ born of Mary at Baptism, Iren. *haer*.1.7.2(M.7.516A); Epiph.*haer*.31.22(p.420.7; M.41.517C); hence **5.** Lord is ἐκ τεσσάρων τούτων σύνθετον; hence also ἔπαθε...ὁ ψυχικὸς Χ., καὶ ὁ ἐκ τῆς οἰκονομίας κατεσκευασμένος μυστηριωδῶς, ἵν' ἐπιδείξῃ αὐτοῦ ἡ μήτηρ τὸν τύπον τοῦ ἄνω Χ., ἐκείνου τοῦ ἐπεκταθέντος τῷ σταυρῷ Iren.*haer*.1.7.2(M.7.513B,516A); Epiph.*haer*.31.22(pp.419.28,420.10; M.41.517B,C); cf. τὸν ἐπιφανέντα Σωτῆρα λαβεῖν φησιν, ἀπὸ *μὲν τῆς Ἀχαμὼθ τὸ πνευματικόν, ἀπὸ δὲ τοῦ Δημιουργοῦ τὸν ψυχικὸν ἐνδεδύσθαι Χ., ἀπὸ δὲ τῆς Οἰκονομίας περιθέσθαι σῶμα ψυχικὴν ἔχον οὐσίαν, ἀῤῥήτῳ δὲ σοφίᾳ πεποιημένον πρὸς τὸ ἁπτὸν καὶ ὁρατὸν γενέσθαι καὶ παθητόν* Thdt.*haer*.1.7(4.300); **6.** through mutual participation of aeons in each other's characteristics, all partake of character of *Χριστοί*, Iren.*haer*.1.2.6(M.7.464A).

F. Basilides' teaching, cf. *patrem...misisse primogenitum Nun suum (et hunc esse qui dicitur Christus) in libertatem credentium ei, a potestate eorum qui mundum fabricaverunt et...apparuisse eum in terra hominem*, Iren.*haer*.1.24.4(M.7.677A).

G. distinction between Christ and Logos; **1.** acc. Paul of Samosata *ὁ λόγος μείζων ἦν τοῦ Χριστοῦ, Χ. γὰρ διὰ σοφίας μέγας ἐγένετο... ὁ λόγος μὲν γὰρ ἄνωθεν, Ἰησοῦς δὲ Χ. ἄνθρωπος ἐντεῦθεν* Paul.Sam.*fr*.(p.331.4); cf. *ἄλλο μὲν ἡ σοφία, ἄλλο δὲ Ἰησοῦς ib*.(p.333.3); *οὗτος... Χριστοῦ μὲν ὄνομα ἐνδεδυμένος, Ἰουδαίων δὲ τὸ φρόνημα ἐπανῃρημένος, λόγον Χ. ὁμολογῶν, οὐκ ὄντα δὲ τοῦτον διανοούμενος* Epiph.*haer*.65.9(p.13.12; M.42.28D); *Παῦλος ἀνύπαρκτον Χ. ὀλίγου δεῖν διαβεβαιοῦται, λόγον προφορικὸν αὐτὸν σχηματίσας, ἀπὸ Μαρίας δὲ καὶ δεῦρο εἶναι* Jo.D.*haer*.65(M.94.717A); **2.** acc. Marcellus *τήρει ὅπως διὰ τούτων Μάρκελλος τοῦ Ἰησοῦ καὶ Χριστοῦ ὄνομα...οὐ βούλεται κεῖσθαι ἐπὶ τοῦ λόγου ἀλλ' ἐπὶ τῆς σαρκὸς ἧς ἀνείληφεν* Eus.*Marcell*.2.3(p.44.12; M.24.800A); *ὁ λόγος σὰρξ ἐγένετο. διὰ τοῦτο τοίνυν τοῦ λόγου μνημονεύων φαίνεται μόνου· εἴτε γὰρ Ἰησοῦ εἴτε Χ. ὀνόματος μνημονεύει ἡ θεία γραφή, τὸν μετὰ τῆς ἀνθρωπίνης ὄντα σαρκὸς τοῦ θεοῦ λόγον ὀνομάζειν φαίνεται* Marcell.*fr*.42 ap.Eus.*Marcell*.2.3(p.43.32; M.24.797C); Eus.*e.th*.2.2(p.100.24; M.24.901B); **3.** orthodox condemnation of such teaching, implicit *ὁ κυρίως υἱὸς θεοῦ, θεὸς λόγος, θεοῦ δύναμις καὶ θεοῦ σοφία, ὁ καλούμενος Χ.* Or.*Cels*.1.66(p.120.23; M.11.785A); explicit, cf. *πῶς εἶναι Χριστιανοὶ δύνανται οἱ λέγοντες ἄλλον εἶναι τὸν υἱὸν καὶ ἄλλον τὸν τοῦ θεοῦ λόγον;* Ath.*ep.Epict*.2(p.5.20; M.26.1053C); **4.** Nestorian separation of Christ from Logos *ἔοικε...καταμόνας τῷ ἐκ γυναικὸς καὶ ἐκ σπέρματος τοῦ Δαυείδ, τὸ Χ. ὄνομα, διὰ τοῦ κεχρίσθαι τῷ ἁγίῳ πνεύματι· δεηθείη δ' ἂν οὐδαμῶς, τό γε ἧκον εἰς ἰδίαν φύσιν, ὁ ἐκ θεοῦ λόγος τοῦ τοιοῦδε χαρίσματος. ... ἐοικέναι γε μὴν οὐχὶ δήπου μᾶλλον τῷ ἐκ θεοῦ πατρὸς φύντι λόγῳ τὸ Χ. ὄνομα βούλονται* Cyr.*Chr.un*.(5^1.726C,E); *ἢ τοίνυν λεγέτωσαν τὸν ἐκ θεοῦ πατρὸς λόγον εἰς ἰδίαν κεχρίσθαι φύσιν...ἤγουν διδασκέτωσαν πῶς ἂν νοοῖτο Χ., ὁ μὴ κεχρισμένος ib*.(743A); *ib*.(746D); *εἴ τις λέγει θεὸν ἢ δεσπότην εἶναι τοῦ Χ. τὸν ἐκ θεοῦ πατρὸς λόγον...ἀ. ἔ.* id.*ep*.17(p.41.8; 5^2.76D); *διὰ τοῦτο καὶ Χ. ὁ θεὸς λόγος ὀνομάζεται, ἐπείπερ ἔχει τὴν συνάφειαν τὴν πρὸς τὸν Χ. διηνεκῆ* id.*Nest*.2.8(p.45.41; 6^1.50C); *εἴ τις ἀντιποιεῖται Θεοδώρου τοῦ Μοψουεστίας τοῦ εἰπόντος ἄλλον εἶναι τὸν θεὸν λόγον, καὶ ἄλλον τὸν Χ.* Justn.*conf*.(p.92.27; M.86.1017A); implying doctrine of two Christs, or Christ divided into two persons *ὡς ἑνὶ Χ. καὶ υἱῷ τὰς ὑπὲρ ἀνθρώπου φύσιν προσνεμοῦμεν φωνάς. οἱ δὲ διιστάντες εἰς δύο πρόσωπα δύο που πάντως ἐπινοοῦσιν υἱούς* Cyr.*expl.xii cap*.14(p.20.6; 6^1.150E); id.*Nest*.1.1(p.18.22; 10A); *αὐτὸς ἡρμήνευσε τῆς συναφείας τὴν δύναμιν· οὐ γὰρ ἔστι, φησί, τὸν θεὸν λόγον ἄνευ τῆς ἀνθρωπότητος πρᾶξαί τι. ὁμόφρονες οὖν ἀλλήλοις καὶ ὁμογνώμονες κατὰ σέ...πῶς οὐ δύο Χ. καὶ υἱοὶ καὶ κύριοι ib*.2.8(p.46.27; 51C); *ib*.2.10(p.48.15; 54A); Thdt.*ep*.143(4.1238); Leont.H.*Nest*.2.42(M.86.1597A); *Νεστοριανοὶ καὶ τὸν θεὸν λόγον Χ. καλοῦντες, καὶ τὸν ἄνθρωπον κεχωρισμένως Χ. ὀνομάζοντες* Justn.*conf*.(p.90.32; 1015A); *εἰ δύο ὑποστάσεις, ἄλλος καὶ ἄλλος· καὶ ἔσονται δύο Χ.· ἢ ἄλλος ὁ Χ. ἢ ἄλλος ὁ θεὸς λόγος, καὶ οὐκέτι εἷς υἱός* Jo.D.*volunt*.9(M.95.140B); but *οὐ...ἔχομεν δύο Χ.* Nest.*fr*.12(p.281.5); **5.** orthodox teaching *ὁ Χ. πρὸ τῆς σαρκώσεως ἐν ταῖς θείαις γραφαῖς ὡς Χ. ὠνόμασται...εἰ δὲ Χ. καθὸ θεοῦ δύναμις καὶ θεοῦ σοφία πρὸ αἰώνων ἐστίν, οὕτω καὶ καθὸ Χ., ἓν γὰρ καὶ τὸ αὐτὸ ὢν τῇ οὐσίᾳ* Hymen.*ep*.9(pp.329.13,330.1); *τὸ ὄνομα...Χριστοῦ, ὡς ταυτησὶ τῆς προσηγορίας πᾶσαν ἐχούσης τοῦ θείου κηρύγματος τὴν δύναμιν. καὶ τοῦτο...ἐδίδαξεν ὁ μέγας Βασίλειος ...ἡ...τοῦ Χ. προσηγορία τοῦ παντός ἐστιν ὁμολογία· δηλοῖ γὰρ τὸν πατέρα τὸν χρίσαντα, τὸν υἱὸν τὸν χρισθέντα, τὸ πνεῦμα τὸ ἅγιον ᾧ ἐχρίσθη...χρὴ δὲ κἀκεῖνο προσθεῖναι...ὡς οὐ χρὴ λέγειν, μετὰ τὴν ἀνάληψιν οὐκ ἔστι Χ. ὁ δεσπότης Χ., ἀλλὰ υἱὸς μονογενής* Thdt.*ep*.146(4.1270); *ἡ...Χριστοῦ προσηγορία σημαντική ἐστι δύο φύσεων, ἤγουν οὐσιῶν ἡνωμένων κατ' οὐσίαν ἀσυγχύτως καὶ ἀτρέπτως, ἐν ἑνὶ καὶ τῷ αὐτῷ ἀτόμῳ ἤγουν προσώπῳ* Pamph.H.*panopl*.9.4(p.634).

H. refutation of idea that identification of Christ with *σοφία* makes Christ a goddess, *Dial.Ath.et Zacch*.10(p.7).

I. application of title *Χριστός* to himself by Manes, Thdt.*haer*.1.26(4.321).

J. of Christians, as those anointed in baptism (v. *χρίω*), or as partakers of Christ *οἱονεὶ γὰρ καθ' ἕκαστον ἅγιον Χριστὸς εὑρίσκεται, καὶ γίνονται διὰ τὸν ἕνα Χ. πολλοὶ χ. οἱ ἐκείνου μιμηταὶ καὶ κατ' αὐτὸν εἰκόνα ὄντα θεοῦ μεμορφωμένοι* Or.*Jo*.6(3; p.115.17; M.14.212C); *τοὺς χαρακτῆρας...τοῦ Χ. προσλαμβάνουσιν οἱ φωτιζόμενοι...ὥστε ἐν ἑκάστῳ γεννᾶσθαι τὸν Χ. νοητῶς. καὶ...ἡ ἐκκλησία...ὠδίνει, μέχριπερ ἂν ὁ Χ. ἐν ἡμῖν μορφωθῇ γεννηθείς, ὅπως ἕκαστος τῶν ἁγίων τῷ μετέχειν Χριστοῦ χριστὸς γεννηθῇ...οἱονεὶ χ. γεγονότων τῶν κατὰ μετουσίαν τοῦ πνεύματος εἰς Χ. βεβαπτισμένων* Meth.*symp*.8.8(p.90.9; M.18.149C); *εἶεν δ' ἂν...πλείους οἱ ἐξ αὐτοῦ καὶ δι' αὐτὸν Χ. χρηματίζοντες, περὶ ὧν εἴρηται, μὴ ἅψεσθε τῶν χ. μου...οἵ τε εἰς αὐτὸν πεπιστευκότες καὶ τοῦ ἁγίου τῆς ἐν τῷ Χ. παλιγγενεσίας χρίσματος κατηξιωμένοι, καὶ οἱ δυνάμενοι λέγειν...μέτοχοι τοῦ Χ. γεγόναμεν* Eus.*d.e*.4.16(p.190.24; M.22.317B); *χ. γενήσονται πνεύματι τῆς αὐτοῦ εὐωδίας χρισθέντες* id.*e.th*.3.15(p.173.3; M.24.1029C); *διὰ τοῦτο Χ. ἐπεκλήθη, ἵνα τῷ αὐτῷ ἐλαίῳ, ᾧ αὐτὸς ἐχρίσθη, καὶ ἡμεῖς χρισθέντες γενώμεθα χ., τῆς αὐτῆς, ὡς εἰπεῖν, οὐσίας καὶ ἑνὸς σώματος* Mac.Aeg.*hom*.43.1(M.34.772C); *ἡμεῖς, καὶ τῷ ἁγίῳ πνεύματι κατακεχρισμένοι, τὴν τοῦ Χ. κλῆσιν ἐσχήκαμεν* Cyr.*Lc*.9:18(M.72.648C); *χριόμεθα δὲ τῷ παλαιῷ* [conj. *ἁπλῷ*] *ἐλαίῳ, ἵνα γινώμεθα χ.* ‡Just.*qu.et resp*.137(M.6.1389D); *Χριστοὺς οἶδεν τοὺς ζῶντας κατὰ Χριστόν* Eustrat.*v.Eutych*.8.82(M.86.2368A); *χ. ὁμοίως καλεῖ, καὶ τοὺς μὴ ἔχοντας μὲν χρῖσμα, τὴν δὲ τοῦ Χ. εὐσέβειαν κεκτημένους* Proc.G.*Gen*.39:2(M.87.476A); Cosm.Ind.*top*.5(M.88.253C); Jo.D.*f.o*.4.9(M.94.1125B) cit. s. *ἔλαιον*; hence, Church described as 'Christ' *Χ. ... τὸν χρισθέντα λαὸν εἰς βασίλειον ἱεράτευμά φησιν* Ath.*exp.Ps*.27:8(M.27.152A).

***Χριστοτερπής,** *delighting in Christ*, Jo.D.*carm.theog*.127(p.209; M.96.825A).

***Χριστότης, ἡ,** *Christ-hood πάντες τὴν κυριότητα αὐτοῦ καὶ Χ. ἐπιγνόντες Χριστιανοὶ ἐπεκλήθημεν* Didym.*Trin*.3.6(M.39.848B); *πῶς ...τὴν Χριστοῦ φύσιν ὀνομάσομεν; Χριστότητα; ἀλλ' οὐδεὶς τῶν θεοπνεύστων εἴρηκε τοῦτο* Jo.D.*Jacob*.35(M.94.1453A); *εἰ μία φύσις τοῦ Χριστοῦ μετὰ τὴν ἕνωσιν, πῶς ὀνομάζεται; Χριστότης· δηλαδὴ ἡ θεανθρωπότης* id.*volunt*.8(M.95.140A).

Χριστοτόκος, *Christ-bearing, who is mother of Christ*; adj. and subst., of BMV;

A. employed by Nestorius in place of *θεοτόκος* q.v., which he rejected, cf. *sed et virginem Christotocon ausi sunt cum (modo quodam) deo tractare divinam. hanc enim theotocon vocantes non perhorrescunt*, Nest.*ep*.1(p.167.4); *πανταχοῦ τῆς θείας γραφῆς... γέννησις ἡμῖν καὶ πάθος οὐ τῆς θεότητος ἀλλὰ τῆς ἀνθρωπότητος τοῦ Χριστοῦ παραδίδοται, ὡς καλεῖσθαι κατὰ ἀκριβεστέραν προσηγορίαν τὴν ἁγίαν παρθένον Χ., οὐ θεοτόκον* id.*ep.Cyr*.2(p.31.3; M.77.53B); *ad hanc quidem vocem, quae est θεοτόκος, nisi secundum Apollinaris et Arii furorem ad confusionem naturarum proferatur, volentibus dicere non resisto; nec tamen ambigo, quin haec vox θεοτόκος illi voci cedat, quae est Χριστοτόκος, tamquam prolatae ab angelis et evangeliis*, id.*ep*.6(p.181.21); *τὸ προελθεῖν τὸν θεὸν ἐκ τῆς Χ. παρθένου παρὰ τῆς θείας ἐδιδάχθην γραφῆς* id.*serm*.11(p.277.25); *τὸ Χριστοτόκος dicere nihil aliud sit, quam communem deitatis et humanitatis rem confiteri*, id.*serm*.18(p.303.8); *υἱὸν γὰρ ἐγέννησε θεοῦ καὶ ἡ Χ. παρθένος* id.*serm*.10(p.274.14); *qui dicit θεοτόκος, si et ἀνθρωποτόκος dicat, Χριστοτόκος dicat, quod nomen sit duarum significatio naturarum*, *ib*.18(p.312.20); *οὐδαμοῦ τοίνυν ἡ θεία γραφὴ θεὸν ἐκ τῆς Χ. παρθένου λέγει γεγεννῆσθαι, ἀλλὰ Χριστὸν Ἰησοῦν* id.ap.Cyr.*ep*.40(p.24.22; 5^2.114B); *θεοτόκον μὲν οὐκ εἶναι λέγων τὴν ἁγίαν παρθένον, Χ. δὲ μᾶλλον καὶ ἀνθρωποτόκον* Cyr.*Chr.un*.(5^1.716C); Thdt.*haer*.4.12(4.371); *οὐκ ἔλεγε γὰρ ἕνωσιν τοῦ λόγου τοῦ θεοῦ πρὸς τὸν ἄνθρωπον, ἀλλὰ δύο ὑποστάσεις ἔλεγε καὶ διαίρεσιν· ὅθεν οὐδὲ...Μαρίαν ἐκάλει θεοτόκον, ἀλλὰ Χ.* †Leont.B.*sect*.4.4(M.86.1221C); Evagr.*h.e*.1.2(p.7.7; M.86.2424A).

B. this substitution rejected by Cyril and subsequent orthodox theologians, on ground that **1.** it implies rejection of Christ's divinity *εἰ λέγοιεν...ἥκιστα μὲν θεοτόκον ὀνομάζεσθαι δεῖν τὴν ἁγίαν παρθένον, Χ. δὲ μᾶλλον, δυσφημοῦσιν ἀναφανδόν, καὶ τοῦ εἶναι θεὸν καὶ υἱὸν ἀληθῶς ἀποσοβοῦσι Χριστόν. εἰ γὰρ εἶναι πιστεύουσι θεὸν ἀληθῶς αὐτόν, ὡς καθ' ἡμᾶς γεγονότος τοῦ μονογενοῦς, ἀνθ' ὅτου καταπεφρίκασι θεοτόκον εἰπεῖν τὴν τεκοῦσαν αὐτόν, κατά γε φημὶ τὴν σάρκα;* Cyr.*Chr.un*.(5^1.726A); Thdr.Abuc.*opusc*.14(M.97.1537B); Jo.D.*f.o*.3.12(M.94.1032B); **2.** title could be applied to others besides BMV *ἄτοπον γὰρ οὐδέν, κἂν εἰ ἕλοιτό τις καὶ τὴν ἑκάστου τῶν κεχρισμένων μητέρα Χ. ἀποκαλεῖν* Cyr.*ep*.1(p.14.28; 5^2.7D); *οὐκ ἂν ἁμάρτοι τἀληθοῦς, εἴ τις ἕλοιτο λέγειν ὡς αἱ μὲν τῶν ἄλλων μητέρες Χριστοτόκοι μέν, οὐ μὴν ἔτι καὶ θεοτόκοι, μόνη δὲ παρ' ἐκείνας ἡ ἁγία παρθένος Χ. τε ὁμοῦ καὶ θεοτόκος νοεῖται ib*.(p.15.1; 8A); hence, while title itself is commendable, it is inadequate without *θεοτόκος*; *ὁ μὴ ὁμολογῶν τὴν παρθένον Χ., οὐδὲ τὸν Χριστὸν ὁμολογεῖ ὅπερ ἐστί·... ἀλλ' οὐκ ἰδίως σημαντικὴ προσηγορία τῆς παρθένου ἁγίας, τὸ Χριστοτόκος· καὶ αἱ μητέρες γὰρ Δαβὶδ καὶ Σαμουὴλ καὶ τῶν ἱερέων, Χ. ὀρθῶς λέγοιντο ἂν* Leont.H.*Nest*.4.48(M.86.1720C); Jo.D.*f.o*.3.12(M.94.1032A); *Χ. γὰρ καὶ ἄλλαι τῶν τροφητῶν καὶ βασιλέων μητέρες, μόνη δὲ* θεοτόκος, ἡ ἁγία θεοτόκος Μαριάμ id.*Nest*.43(M.95.224C); **3.** doctrine of *communicatio idiomatum* forbids its use ἔργον γὰρ γέγονε τῆς... ἑνώσεως, τὸ ποιῆσαι θεὸν τὸν ληφθέντα, καὶ ἄνθρωπον κληθῆναι τὸν λαβόντα· ἐπεὶ οὖν ὁ κυριακὸς ἄνθρωπος...ἐστὶν ἐκ παρθένου, ὑπομεῖναι λέγεται γέννησιν ὁ λόγος ὡς τὰ τούτου οἰκειούμενος ἴδια· ἴδιον γὰρ σαρκὸς τὸ γεννᾶσθαι, καὶ διὰ τοῦτο κυρίως...θεοτόκος ἡ παρθένος ὑπάρχει καὶ οὐ Χ. Pamph.H.*panopl*.4.1(p.611); **4.** consequence of Nestorian view that union of natures is subsequent to Christ's human generation μετὰ τὴν ἕνωσιν αὐτὸ τὸ χρῖσμα γεγενῆσθαι πάντως ὁμολογήσουσιν· εἰ δὲ μετὰ τὴν ἕνωσιν κέχρισται, τὴν δὲ ἕνωσιν οὐ βούλονται λέγειν πρὶν ἐκ τῆς παρθένου τεχθῆναι, οὐδὲ Χ. οὐκέτι πρὸς αὐτῶν ἡ παρθένος ὁμολογηθήσεται. εἰ γὰρ Χ., πάντως ὅτι καὶ θεοτόκος· εἰ δὲ οὐ θεοτόκος, οὐδὲ Χ. Cyr.*deip.BMV* 9(p.22.38; M.76.265B); **5.** Χ. is no more scriptural than θεοτόκος, id.*ep*.10(p.111.35; 5^{2}.35B).

C. hence substitution of Χ. or ἀνθρωποτόκος for θεοτόκος anathematized, Justn.*conf*.(p.92.2; M.86.1015B); and its use turned as weapon of argument against Monophysites οἶδα δὲ τοὺς...λέγοντας τὸν Χριστόν, ᾗ Χριστός ἐστιν, μηδενὶ εἶναι ὁμοούσιον καὶ μήτε θεὸν εἶναι μήτε ἄνθρωπον. εἰ δὲ τοῦτο ἀληθές, οὔτε θεός ἐστιν ὁ Χριστός, οὔτε θεοτόκος ἡ παρθένος, ἀλλ' ὡς λέγουσι Χ. κατὰ Νεστόριον Eust.Mon.*ep*.(M.86.913A); εἰ μὴ δύο φύσεις θεοῦ καὶ ἀνθρώπου, ἀλλὰ μία, τίς ἰδίως Χριστοῦ ἐστὶ φύσις; ἄρα γε ὄντως καθ' ὑμᾶς Χ. ἡ ἁγία παρθένος καὶ οὐ θεοτόκος λέγοιτο Leont.H.*monoph*.55(M.86.1800A).

***Χριστοτύπος**, *typifying Christ*; of Isaac, ‡Epiph.*hom*.2(M.43.452C).

***Χριστόφατος**, *speaking of Christ*, Eudoc.*Cypr*.1(M.85.844B).

***Χριστοφιλής**, *Christ-loving*, ‡Gr.Nyss.*hom.7.22 in Jo*.(p.242.17).

***Χριστόφιλος**, = foreg., Cosm.Ind.*top*.proem.2(M.88.53D).

***Χριστοφονία**, ἡ, *murder of Christ*, Vict.*Mc*.3:12(p.295.18).

***Χριστοφόνος**, ὁ, *murderer of Christ*, Bas.*Spir*.25(3.21B; M.32.112B); εἰσῆλθεν εἰς τὸ συνέδριον τῶν Χ. ὁ Χριστοφόρος Gr.Nyss.*Steph*.2(M.46.724D).

***Χριστοφόντης**, *Christ-slaying*, Gr.Naz.*carm*.2.1.11.1545(M.37.1136A).

Χριστοφόρος** (Χρηστοφόρος**), *Christ-bearing*, i.e. filled or inspired by Christ; **1.** of Christians in gen. ἐστὲ οὖν...θεοφόροι καὶ ναοφόροι, Χ., ἁγιοφόροι Ign.*Eph*.9.2; Ath.*Ar*.3.45(M.26.417C); ὁ Χ. ἀνὴρ ὡς θεός ἐστιν ἐπὶ γῆς ‡Ath.*pass*.30(M.28.237A); Χ. γενόμεθα, τοῦ σώματος αὐτοῦ καὶ τοῦ αἵματος εἰς τὰ ἡμέτερα ἀναδιδομένου μέλη Cyr.H.*catech*.22.3; **2.** of especially inspired persons: apostles, Ath.*gent*.5(M.25.12C); Adam.*dial*.5.22(p.218.18; M.11.1861B); martyrs, Eus.*h.e*.8.10.3(M.20.764B); Gr.Nyss.*Steph*.2(M.46.721A); *ib*.(724A); of a consecrated virgin, Ath.*v.Anton*.60(M.26.932A); of Constantine τοῦ ἀοιδίμου καὶ Χ. τότε βασιλεύοντος *V.Pach.Σ* 76(p.251.22); **3.** as courtesy title, τῷ τιμιωτάτῳ καὶ Χρηστοφόρῳ ἄπα Παφνουτίῳ *P.Lond*.1926.1; **4.** impers. of the heart or soul, Gr.Naz.*carm*.1.2.38.8(M.37.967A); Diad.*perf*.82(p.108.22); of mouth of those who praise God, Gr.Naz.*carm*.2.2.7.313(M.37.1575A); of love, Nil.*Eulog*.25(M.79.1125C); of baptismal water, Cyr.H.*procatech*.15; met., of martyr's body Χριστοφόρου...ναοῦ Chrys.*pan.Juln*.3(2.675B); of the boat of Lc.8:22, ‡Chrys.*hom*.6(13.243B).

***Χριστόφρων**, *Christ-minded*, ‡Gr.Nyss.*hom.7.2 in Jo*.(p.236.8); *ib*.(p.242.17).

***Χρίστυβρις**, ἡ, *insult to Christ*; of Leo the Armenian, Thdr.Stud.*epp*.2.77(M.99.1316B); id.*ref*.2(M.99.444C).

***Χριστώνυμος**, *bearing Christ's name* ὁ Χ. λαός Jo.D.*imag*.3.42(M.94.1357D); οἱ ἑαυτοὺς τῆς Χ. κλήσεως ἀποξενώσαντες ‡Jo.D.*ep.Thphl*.15(M.95.365A); *cat.Apoc*.16:19(p.423.11).

χρί-ω, *anoint smear*;

A. in gen.; **1.** of caulking of ships, and painting of houses, Thphl.Ant.*Autol*.1.12(M.6.1041B); **2.** of athletes' anointing, *ib*.; **3.** ref. use of scents and unguents, unsuitable for Christians, Clem.*paed*.2.8(p.196.5; M.8.469A); σήμερον...τὰ πρῶτα μύρα ~όμενος... αὔριον ἀντὶ γελοιαστοῦ σύννους Gr.Naz.*or*.44.9(M.36.617B); στρατιώτης εἶ πνευματικός· στρατιώτης δὲ οὐ ~εται μύροις Chrys.*Laz*.1.8(1.718D); but distinction recognized between τὸ μυραλοιφεῖν and τὸ μύρῳ ~έσθαι: τὸ μὲν γὰρ θηλυδριῶδες, τὸ δὲ ~εσθαι τῷ μύρῳ καὶ λυσιτελεῖ ἔσθ' ὅτε Clem.*paed*.2.8(p.198.22; 476B).

B. with religious significance; **1.** in pagan and semi-pagan rites; **a.** of smearing children with mud as prophylactic against evil eye, Chrys.*hom.12.7 in 1Cor*.(10.107C); **b.** of magical unctions, *Hom.Clem*.20.16; **c.** in sacrificial rites, Hipp.*haer*.4.30(p.57.9; M.16.3094B); **2.** ref. unction of OT kings, Clem.*paed*.3.2(p.243.4; M.8.572C); id.*str*.1.21(p.71.16; M.8.837A); *Const.App*.3.16.3; Cyr.*Lc*.9:18(M.72.648C); contrasted with perfect anointing of Christ, ‡Cyr.*Trin*.22(6^{3}.28A; M.77.1164A); compared with Christ's anointing by Father, through which he is βασιλεὺς καὶ Χριστὸς καὶ ἱερεὺς καὶ ἄγγελος Just.*dial*.86.3(M.6.681A); ‡Germ.CP *contempl*.(M.98.385C); with 'royal anointing' of all Christians κύριε, σῶσον τὸν βασιλέα, τουτέστι τὸν εἰς βασιλείαν κεχρισμένον λαόν Clem.*ecl*.64(p.155.9; M.9.728D); οἱ γὰρ ἐκλεκτοὶ αὐτοῦ ~ονται τὸ ἁγιαστικὸν ἔλαιον, καὶ γίγνονται ἀξιωματικοὶ καὶ βασιλεῖς Mac.Aeg.*hom*.15.35(M.34.600B); with anointing of Christians with H. Ghost, Cyr.H.*catech*.21.6; and with baptismal anointing, *Const.App*.3.16.3; **3.** of OT priests, *T.Lev*.17.2; Clem.*str*.4.25(p.318.15; M.8.1368A); Chrys.*exp.in Ps*.132.1(5.380B); compared with Christians' baptismal unction which constitutes, not ordination to priesthood, but membership of βασίλειον ἱεράτευμα (1Pet.2:9), *Const.App*.3.16.3; **4.** of OT prophets, Clem.*str*.4.25(p.318.15; M.8.1368A); *ib*.5.13(p.382.8; M.9.125B); Cyr.*Lc*.9:18(M.72.648C); prophet is ἐνεργείᾳ ~όμενος, whereas Christ is anointed παρουσίᾳ...ὅλου τοῦ ~οντος Jo.D.*f.o*.4.14(M.94.1161A); **5.** of anointing of doorposts at Passover, Cyr.H.*catech*.19.2; Chrys.*hom.27.1 in Heb*.(12.245D); v. φλιά; **6.** of anointing of Christ's feet, Clem.*paed*.2.8(p.194.26; M.8.468A); **7.** of Christ as the 'anointed' (esp. exeg. Ps.44:9, Is.61:1); **a.** in gen., Just.*dial*.86.3(M.6.681A); Hipp.*Dan*.4.32.4(p.270.12); cf.Or.*Cels*.6.79(p.150.33; M.11.1417C); θεὸς γὰρ...~όμενος ὑπὸ τοῦ θεοῦ τίς ἂν ἕτερος εἴη ἢ αὐτὸς ὁ διὰ τὸ χρῖσμα τὸ πατρικὸν Χριστὸς ἀνηγορευμένος Eus.*e.th*.1.20(p.95.21; M.24.892B); ‡Germ.CP *contempl*.(M.98.385C); **b.** question discussed whether Christ fulfilled expectation of Messiah's anointing by Elijah, Just.*dial*.49.1(M.6.581B); **c.** Christ's anointing is with H. Ghost (cf. Ac.10:38), ‡Paul.Sam.*fr*.1(p.339.1); Ath.*Ar*.1.47(M.26.109A); ἐχρίσθη τῷ ἀληθινῷ χρίσματι ἡ σὰρξ τοῦ κυρίου, τῇ τοῦ ἁγίου πνεύματος εἰς αὐτὴν ἐπιδημίᾳ...ἐχρίσθη δὲ παρὰ τοὺς μετόχους αὐτοῦ· τουτέστιν ὑπὲρ πάντας...τοὺς μετέχοντας τοῦ Χριστοῦ· διότι ἐκείνοις μὲν μερική τις ἐδίδοτο πνεύματος κοινωνία, ἐπὶ δὲ τὸν υἱὸν...τὸ πνεῦμα ...ἔμεινεν ἐπ' αὐτόν Bas.*hom.in Ps*.44(1.165E; M.29.405A); τῇ φύσει βασιλεὺς ὁ υἱός, ἀξίωμα δὲ βασιλείας τὸ πνεῦμα τὸ ἅγιον, ᾧ υἱὸς ~εται Gr.Nyss.*Maced*.16(M.45.1321B); Didym.*Trin*.2.23(M.39.556C); αὐτὸς κεχρίσθαι λέγεται, οὐδαμοῦ χρισάμενος ἐλαίῳ, ἀλλὰ πνεῦμα δεξάμενος, Chrys.*hom.1.5 in Ac*.(9.9D); *Dial.Ath.et Zacch*.58(p.36.3); Cosm.Ind.*top*.5(M.88.253C) cit. s. ἀνθρωπότης; **d.** Trin. and Christol., Paul.Sam.*fr*.B 4(p.331.2) cit. s. λόγος; οὐκ ἄρα ὁ λόγος ἐστίν, ᾗ λόγος ἐστὶ καὶ σοφία, ὁ τῷ παρ' αὐτοῦ διδομένῳ πνεύματι ~όμενος, ἀλλ' ἡ προσληφθεῖσα παρ' αὐτοῦ σάρξ ἐστιν, ἡ ἐν αὐτῷ καὶ παρ' αὐτοῦ ~ομένη Ath.*Ar*.1.47(M.26.109C); id.*ep.Serap*.1.13(M.26.585A); τὸ γὰρ χρῖσμα ἐγὼ ὁ λόγος, τὸ δὲ χρισθὲν ὑπ' ἐμοῦ ὁ ἄνθρωπος ‡Ath.*Ar*.4.36(p.86.2; M.26.524B); οὐ γὰρ κέχρισται τῷ ἁγίῳ πνεύματι θεὸς ὢν ὁ λόγος Gr.Naz.ap.*cat.Heb*.1:8 suppl.(p.336.30); εἰ γὰρ κτίσμα ἦν [sc. τὸ πνεῦμα] οὐκ ἂν τῷ ἰδίῳ ἐχρίσατο ποιήματι ὁ ἄκτιστος Didym.*Trin*.2.23(M.39.556D); ἀνθρωπίνως κέχρισται μεθ' ἡμῶν, καίτοι τοῖς ἀξίοις τοῦ λαβεῖν τὸ πνεῦμα διδοὺς αὐτός Cyr.*ep*.17.4(p.36.4.5^{2}.70C); ἢ τοίνυν λεγέτωσαν τὸν ἐκ θεοῦ...λόγον εἰς ἰδίαν κεχρίσθαι φύσιν...ἤγουν διδασκέτωσαν πῶς ἂν νοοῖτο Χριστός, ὁ μὴ κεχρισμένος id.*Chr.un*.(5^{1}.743A); id.*deip.BMV* 9(p.22.37; M.76.265B); in Christ humanity is anointed with deity; Gr.Naz.*or*.30.2(p.111.1; M.36.105B) cit. s. ἀνθρωπότης; τὸ χρίσαν μὲν ἡ θεότης, ἡ ἀνθρωπότης δὲ τὸ χρισθέν ‡Cyr.*Trin*.22(6^{2}.27E; M.77.1161D); Χριστὸς...ὡς τῇ θεότητι χρίσας τὴν ἀνθρωπότητα, διὰ τὴν ἐν αὐτῷ καθ' ὑπόστασιν τῶν τοιούτων φύσεων ἕνωσιν ‡Proc.G.*Pr*.30:5(M.87.1524C); ὥσπερ...φησιν ὁ διδάσκαλος, χρίσας τὴν ἀνθρωπότητα τῇ θεότητι Max.*ambig*.(M.91.1388B); ~ων ὡς θεὸς ἑαυτὸν ὡς ἄνθρωπον Jo.D.*f.o*.4.14(M.94.1161A); **8.** of Christians as 'anointed people' (by etymology), Thphl.Ant.*Autol*.1.12(M.6.1041C) cit. s. Χριστιανός; Hipp.*haer*.5.9(p.102.15; M.16.3159A); Or.*Cels*.6.79(p.150.33; M.11.1417C); Cyr.*Lc*.9:18(M.72.648C); **9.** ref. anointing of Christians; **a.** spiritually; **i.** with H. Ghost; in gen., Eus.*e.th*.3.15(p.173.4; M.24.1029C); Bas.*hom.in Ps*.44(1.165E; M.29.405A); Gr.Naz.ap.*cat.Heb*.1:8 suppl.(p.337.27); Cyr.*Lc*.9:18(M.72.648C); **ii.** with blood of Christ, esp. as typified by anointing of doorposts at Passover τὸ μυστήριον...τοῦ προβάτου...τύπος ἦν τοῦ Χριστοῦ· οὗ τῷ αἵματι ...~ονται τοὺς οἴκους ἑαυτῶν, τουτέστιν ἑαυτοὺς οἱ πιστεύοντες Just.*dial*.40.1(M.6.561B); Mel.*pass*.67 p.11.7; cf.Hipp.*trad.ap*.37.3; ‡Chrys.*pasch*.1(8.251); διττὸν...τὸ αἷμα τοῦ κυρίου· τὸ μέν ἐστιν αὐτοῦ σαρκικόν, ᾧ τῆς φθορᾶς λελυτρώμεθα, τὸ δὲ πνευματικόν, τουτέστιν ᾧ κεχρίσμεθα Clem.*paed*.2.2(p.168.1; M.8.409B); **iii.** with grace and mercy, *Hom.Clem*.3.20; **b.** physically; **i.** in baptism; in pre-baptismal rite of exorcism, cf.Hipp.*trad.ap*.21; Cyr.H.*catech*.20.3; ‡Just.*qu.et resp*.137(M.6.1389C) cit. s. ἔλαιον; Dion.Ar.*e.h*.2.2.7(M.3.396C); in pre-baptismal unction corresponding in purpose and effect to more usual post-baptismal chrismation, perh. cf. *T.Lev*.8.4; *A.Xanthipp*.2(p.59.6); *Const.App*.3.16.4; *ib*.7.22.2; in post-baptismal unction by presbyters, followed by chrismation by bishop, cf.Hipp.*trad.ap.*22; in post-baptismal chrismation, *A.Thom.*A 27(p.142.12); *τί δὲ τὸ ἔλαιον ἀλλ' ἢ τοῦ ἁγίου πνεύματος δύναμις; αἷς* [i.e. *λόγου ἐντολαὶ καὶ δύναμις*] *μετὰ τὸ λουτρὸν ὡς μύρῳ ~ονται οἱ πιστεύοντες* Hipp.*Dan.*1.16.3(p.27.1; M.10.693A); *ἀνάγκη δέ ἐστι καὶ ~εσθαι τὸν βεβαπτισμένον, ἵνα λαβὼν χρῖσμα μέτοχος γένηται Χριστοῦ* Cypr.*ep.*2(H.1.155A); exeg. Is.25:7, Eus.*Is.*25:7(M.24.268C); *ἐνεργῆσαι ἐν τῷ χρίσματι τούτῳ ἐνέργειαν θείαν...ἵνα οἱ βαπτισθέντες καὶ ~όμενοι ἐν αὐτῷ τὸ ἐκτύπωμα τοῦ σημείου τοῦ σωτηριώδους σταυροῦ...μέτοχοι γένωνται τῆς δωρεᾶς τοῦ...πνεύματος* Serap.*euch.*25.1f.; Cyr.H.*catech.*21.3ff.; Bas.*hom.*1.2(2.2C; M.31.165A) cit. s. *ἀλείφω*; *δεῖ τοὺς φωτιζομένους μετὰ τὸ βάπτισμα ~εσθαι χρίσματι ἐπουρανίῳ, καὶ μετόχους εἶναι τῆς βασιλείας τοῦ Χριστοῦ* CLaod.*can.*48; *Const.App.*7.44.1; Thdt.*Cant.*1:2(2.30); Jo.D.*f.o.*4.13(M.94.1141B); combined with consignation, cf.Hipp.*trad.ap.*22; Serap.*euch.*25.1; *Rit.Bapt.*(p.405); v. *χρῖσμα*; baptismal unction as sacrament of bestowal of H. Ghost; given before baptism, *Const.App.*7.22.2; given in chrismation after baptism, Hipp.*Dan.*1.16.3(p.26.24; 693A); *τῷ μὲν φαινομένῳ μύρῳ τὸ σῶμα ~εται, τῷ δὲ ἁγίῳ...πνεύματι ἡ ψυχὴ ἁγιάζεται* Cyr.H.*catech.*21.3; cf.Cyr.*Is.*3.1(2.353D); Thdt.*Cant.*1:2(2.30); CCP(381)‡*can.*7; baptism and chrismation together constituting means of gift of H. Ghost, Jo.D.*f.o.*4.13(M.94.1141B); *~ει ὁ ἱερεὺς τοὺς βαπτισθέντας τὸ ἅγιον μύρον...λέγων, σφραγὶς δωρεᾶς πνεύματος ἁγίου* *Rit.Bapt.*(p.405); in Gnost. initiation, cf.Iren.*haer.*1.21.3(M.7.664B); cf.Clem.*exc.Thdot.*82(p.132.10; M.9.696C); *τὸν λουόμενον κατ' αὐτοὺς ζῶντι ὕδατι καὶ ~όμενον ἀλάλῳ χρίσματι* Hipp.*haer.*5.7(p.83.7; M.16.3131C); cf.*ib.*5.9(p.102.15; 3159); *λουτροῖς χρεισαμένη Χριστοῦ μύρον ἄφθιτον, ἁγνὸν* *CIG* 4.9595a; *τοῦ σφραγιζομένου λεγομένου νέου καὶ υἱοῦ καὶ ἀποκρινομένου· κέχρισμαι χρίσματι λευκῷ ἐκ ξύλου ζωῆς* Cels.ap.Or.*Cels.*6.27(p.97.5; M.11.1333A); cf. *A.Pil.*19(p.325); **ii.** in ordination, Gr.Naz.*or.*43.37(M.36.545C,548A) [or perh. ref. unction of sick]; *τελειοῦται διὰ τῆς αὐτοῦ χειρός τε καὶ εὐχῆς...~εται τῷ ἁγίῳ πνεύματι* Eustrat.*v.Eutych.*25(M.86.2304A); cf. *χρισθέντα τῷ χρίσματι τῆς ἱερωσύνης* Gr.Naz.*or.*6.9(M.35.733A) where prob. met. (v. *χρῖσμα*); **iii.** in penance; ref. Jac. 5:14 so interpreted, cf.Or.*hom.*2.4 *in Lev.*(p.297.1; M.12.419A); **iv.** in reception of heretics, CLaod.*can.*7; Bas.*ep.*188 *can.*1(3.270D; M.32.669C); *~ονται δὲ οἱ ἀπὸ πάσης αἱρέσεως μετερχόμενοι, ἐπειδὴ οὐκ ἔχουσι τὸ ἅγιον χρῖσμα* Didym.*Trin.*2.15(M.39.720A); cf.‡Just.*qu. et resp.*14(M.6.1261D); Thdt.*haer.*3.5(4.346); CCP(381)‡*can.*7; *πρώτη μὲν τάξις ἐστὶ τῶν δεομένων τοῦ ἁγίου βαπτίσματος. δευτέρα δὲ τῶν μὴ βαπτιζομένων, ~ομένων δὲ τῷ μύρῳ τῷ ἁγίῳ. καὶ τρίτη τῶν μήτε βαπτιζομένων, μήτε ~ομένων* Tim.CP *haer.*(M.86.13A); CTrull.*can.* 95; **v.** in anointing of sick, v. *ἔλαιον*; *ὁ περιχρίειν θέλων νοσοῦντα πρῶτον ἐκεῖνος, εἴτουν ὁ ~ων, μετέχει τῆς χρίσεως* Jo.D.*fid.dorm.*18(M.95.264D); *Euchol.*(p.335); of sick animals, Thdt.*h.rel.*8(3.1183); **vi.** of dead, (Gnost.) Iren.*haer.*1.21.5(M.7.665B); cf.‡Chrys.*pat.*1(9.808D); Dion.Ar.*e.h.*7.2(M.3.556D); *ib.*7.3.8(565A); **vii.** of holy places, Thdt.*qu.*84 *in Gen.*(1.94) cit. s. *ἔλαιον*; **viii.** of images, Eustrat. *v.Eutych.*45(M.86.2328A) cit. s. *εἰκών*.

***χροακός**, *coloured*, Cyr.S.*v.Euthym.*22(p.35.19).

***χροΐδιον, τό,** *superficial appearance*, ref. images *οὐ γὰρ χροϊδίοις, ἀλλὰ ἐν ὑπομνήσει τοῦ ἀντιτύπου γράμματος, ὁρῶντες τὸν ἀόρατον διὰ τῆς ὁρωμένης γραφῆς* Sym.Styl.J.*imag.*(M.86.3220A).

***χροιέω**, *colour*, Gr.Naz.*carm.*1.2.29.275(M.37.904A).

***χρονεύω**, *spend one's time, remain*, Eus.*Is.*26:12–13(M.24.273B).

χρονικός, *temporal, within time*; of pagan deities, Didym.*Trin.*1.34(M.39.437B); denied of origin of Son and H. Ghost, Cyr.H.*catech.*11.20(M.33.716B); Epiph.*haer.*76.22(p.370.17; M.42.561C); Sophr.H. *ep.syn.*(M.87.3161A); Thal.*cent.*4.96(M.91.1469A); as synon. with *χρονίτης* q.v. *σὺ δὲ μᾶλλον χ. ὑπάρχεις* Epiph.*haer.*76.15(p.361.19ff.; M.42.548A,B); cf.‡Ath.*dial.Trin.*2.11(M.28.1173C) cit. s. *γεννάω*.

χρονικῶς, *with reference to time*, Or.*Jo.*2.19(13; p.76.16; M.14.148C); Bas.*Eun.*2.11(1.246D; M.29.592C); Dion.Ar.*d.n.*5.10(M.3.825B).

χρόνιος, *temporal*, i.e. *transient*, Nonn.*par.Jo.*7:24(M.43.809A); *within time* *αἰωνίου φύσεως ἀρχὴ χ.* Const.*or.s.c.*11(p.168.25; M.20.1265A).

***χρονῖται, οἱ,** name applied by Anomoeans to orthodox Christians, because the latter predicated generation of the Son, which is a temporal concept acc. Arians, Aët.*synt.*(pp.351.23,352.10; M.42.533D); ‡Ath.*dial.Trin.*2.11(M.28.1173C) cit. s. *γεννάω*.

χρονογραφεῖον, τό, *chronological record, chronicle*, Thphn.*chron.* p.3(M.108.61A).

χρονογραφέω, *compile annals, chronicle*, Mac.Mgn.*apocr.*4.15(p.184.3); Cyr.*Juln.*1(6^2.8A); c. *περί*, Jo.Mal.*chron.*4 p.90(M.97.176A); c. acc., *ib.*6 p.157(260A).

***χρονογράφη, ἡ,** *chronological record*, *Didasc.Jac.*1.22(p.759.1).

χρονογραφία, ἡ, 1. *chronological record, annals*, Clem.*str.*1.21(p.71.27; M.8.837B); Eus.*h.e.*6.7(M.20.536A); Ath.*syn.*3(p.232.34; M.26.685A); **2.** *chronological scheme* or *table*, *Chron.Pasch.*p.288(M.92.720).

***χρονοποιητής, ὁ,** *creator of time*, Tim.Ant.*Sym.*(M.86.248A).

χρόνος, ὁ, 1. *time*; **a.** in gen. *χρόνον τοίνυν εἶναί φησι* [sc. Eunomius] *ποιάν τινα κίνησιν ἀστέρων...ὅσοις καθ' ἑαυτὰ κινεῖσθαι δύναμίς ἐστι* Bas.*Eun.*1.21(1.232C; M.29.557C); *χ. δέ ἐστι τὸ συμπαρεκτεινόμενον τῇ συστάσει τοῦ κόσμου διάστημα* *ib.*(233A; M.560B); *οὐκ ἄρα ἀΐδιός τε καὶ ἄναρχος ὁ χ.· διὸ οὔτε ἡ κίνησίς ἐστιν ἀΐδιός τε καὶ ἄναρχος, ἧς ὁ χ. ἐστὶν ἀριθμός* ‡Just.*confut.*31(M.6.1525D); *γενητὸς ὁ χ. καὶ οὐκ ἀΐδιος, ἠργμένος καὶ οὐκ ἄναρχος, πεπερασμένος καὶ οὐκ ἄπειρος* *ib.*32(1528B); created by God, Cyr.*thes.*21(5^1.218E); *τὸν δὲ θεὸν καὶ ὡς αἰῶνα καὶ ὡς χ. ὑμνεῖν, ὡς χ. παντὸς καὶ αἰῶνος αἴτιον, καὶ παλαιὸν ἡμερῶν, ὡς πρὸ χρόνου, καὶ ὑπὲρ χρόνον, καὶ ἀλλοιοῦντα καιροὺς καὶ χρόνους* Dion.Ar.*d.n.*10.3(M.3.940A); *καιρῶν καὶ χρόνων αὐτὸς ποιητής* Proc.G.*Gen.*9:4(M.87.292C); **b.** opp. *καιρός* (but cf. 3 infra), Mel.*pass.*38 p.6.18; *χ. μέν ἐστι τὸ διάστημα καθ' ὃ πράττεταί τι, καιρὸς δὲ ὁ ἐπιτήδειος τῆς ἐργασίας χ.* Olymp.*Eccl.*3:1(M.93.508A); Evagr.*h.e.*2.3(p.41.27; M.86.2496B); ‡Caes.Naz.*dial.*1.35(M.38.900); exeg. Ac.1:7 *χ. δὲ καὶ καιροὺς μή μοι νόει αἰσθητοὺς ἀλλὰ διαστήματά τινα γνώσεως ὑπὸ τοῦ νοητοῦ ἡλίου γινόμενα* Evagr.Pont. *ep.*7(M.32.260B); **c.** opp. *αἰών*, Clem.*paed.*1.6(p.107.5; M.8.284B); Bas.*Eun.*2.13(1.248A; M.29.596B); Gr.Naz.*or.*38.8(M.36.320A) cit. s. *αἰών*; *αἰών...ἐστιν ὁ χ., ὅταν στῇ τῆς κινήσεως, καὶ χ. ἐστὶν ὁ αἰών, ὅταν μετρῆται κινήσει φερόμενος, ὡς εἶναι τὸν μὲν αἰῶνα...χρόνον ἐστερημένον κινήσεως, τὸν δὲ χ. αἰῶνα κινήσει μετρούμενον* Max. *ambig.*(M.91.1164B,C); **d.** ref. divine timelessness *ὄντως οὗτος θεὸς ...οὐ δεόμενος ὡρῶν οὔτε ἡμερῶν οὔτε χρόνων* *A.Andr.*A 5(p.49.6); *οὐ τόπον ἔχων, οὐ χ.* Hipp.*haer.*6.29(p.156.10; M.16.3235D); **e.** ref. eternity of Son or Word *πρὸ γὰρ παντὸς χ. καὶ αἰῶνος 'ἐν ἀρχῇ ἦν ὁ λόγος'* Or.*Jo.*2.1(p.53.23; M.14.105C); *προτετάχθαι τοῦ υἱοῦ τὸν πατέρα φαμέν· κατὰ δὲ τὴν τῆς φύσεως διαφοράν, οὐκέτι, οὐδὲ κατὰ τὴν τοῦ χ. ὑπεροχήν* Bas.*Eun.*1.20(1.232C; M.29.557B); *οὐχ ὑποβάλλει χρόνοις τοῦ υἱοῦ τὴν οὐσίαν* *ib.*2.11(246C; M.592C); *οὐκ ἦν ἄρα χ. ὅτε οὐκ ἦν ὁ υἱός* Cyr.*thes.*4(5^1.21D); denied by Arians *ἦν ποτε χ. ὅτε οὐκ ἦν ὁ λόγος* Ath.*Ar.*1.11(M.26.33B); *ib.*3.9(340C); *χρόνῳ μόνον ἡμῶν διαφέρει* *ib.*3.18(360B); **f.** in Trin. teaching of Noëtus *ἓν καὶ τὸ αὐτὸ φάσκων ὑπάρχειν πατέρα καὶ υἱὸν καλούμενον...ὀνόματι μὲν πατέρα καὶ υἱὸν καλούμενον κατὰ χρόνων τροπήν* Hipp.*haer.*9.10(p.245.2; M.16.3378B); **g.** phrases, *ἀπὸ χρόνου* *within time*; of incarnate Son, opp. *ἄχρονος*, Didym.*Trin.*1.15(M.39.321A); *ἐκ πολλῶν χρόνων* *from ancient times*, *1Clem.*42.5; *ἐν χρόνῳ* *in time, after a time*, Dion.Ar. *d.n.*4.25(M.3.728B); *within time*, opp. *ἐν αἰῶνι*, *ib.*5.10(825B); *ἐπὶ χρόνους* *for a time, temporarily*, Dam.*troph.*2.4.4(p.225.3); *ἕως χρόνου* *for a time*, *T.Jos.*3.8; *κατὰ χρόνον* *for a time*; opp. *ἁπλῶς*, Dion.Ar. *d.n.*4.21(M.3.724A); *πρὸς χρόνον* *for a time*, Or.*Jo.*10.33(27; p.371.18; M.14.649B); *ὑπὸ χρόνου* *subject to time, limited by time*, ref. eternity of Son, Or.*fr.*1 *in Jo.*(p.484.6); **2.** *occasion* (= *καιρός*) *ἐν ἑτέρῳ χ. λέγει μοι* *T.Jos.*5.1; *ὁ χ. τῆς γεννήσεως* Thdt.*Mal.*1:3(2.1672); **3.** *year* *ἤμην δὲ ἐγὼ χρόνων εἴκοσι ὅτε ἐγένετο ὁ πόλεμος οὗτος* *T.Jud.* 7.10; *A.Paul.et Thecl.*45(p.270.9,11); †Jo.Jej.*serm.*(M.88.1929A); Thphn.*chron.*p.78(M.108.241A).

χρυσαΐζω, *adorn with gold*; pass., Cyr.*Os.*21(3.44C); id.*Is.*1.3(2.67E).

χρύσαμμος, ἡ, *golden sand*, i.e. sand bearing alluvial gold, Cosm.Mel.*schol.*59(M.38.472).

***χρυσάντυγος**, *with golden rails*; of a chariot, ‡Jo.D.*Artem.*42(p.162.24; M.96.1289B).

χρυσάργυρον, τό, *tribute of gold and silver*; tax levied by Constantine and abolished by Anastasius, Thdr.Lect.*h.e.*2.53(M.86.209B); Evagr.*h.e.*3.39(p.136.33; M.86.2677C); cf.Proc.G.*Anast.*13(p.10.11; M.87.2812C).

[*]**χρυσαυγάζω**, = *χρυσαυγίζω*, ‡Chrys.*phar.*(8.111C).

χρυσαυγίζω, *shine like gold*, Jo.Mon.*hymn.Chrys.*6(M.96.1381A).

***χρυσέμπαστος, 1.** *inlaid with gold*, v.l. for *χρυσόπαστος*, Chrys. *hom.*63.4 *in Mt.*(7.633C); Agath.*v.Gr.Ill.*71; Cosm.Ind.*top.*5(M.88.204B); **2.** *embroidered with gold*, v.l. ap.Chrys.*hom.*89.3 *in Mt.*(7.835C).

***χρυσεμπαστοφόρια, τά,** *objects inlaid with gold*, Agath.*v.Gr.Ill.* 71.

χρυσεοκόλλητος, *soldered with gold*, Paul.Sil.*Soph.*668(M.86.2145A).

***χρυσεολόγχης**, *bearing a golden spear*, Synes.*regn.*12(M.66.1084A).

χρυσεότευκτος, *wrought of gold*, Paul.Sil.*Soph.*386(M.86.2134B).
***χρυσεπώνυμος**, *surnamed after gold*; of Chrysostom, ‡Jo.D.*fid. dorm.*6(M.95.252C).
***χρυσήεις**, *golden*, *Orac.Sib.fr.*3.25.
χρυσίζω, med., *amass gold*, Taras.*ep.*3(M.98.1441B).
χρύσινος, masc. as subst., *a gold coin*, cf. Lat. *aureus*, v.l. ap. *T.Jos.*16.5; Gr.Nyss.*ep.*25(M.46.1097C); Synes.*ep.*129(M.66.1509C); also neut., *Apophth.Patr.*(M.65.236D); Pall.*h.Laus.*37(M.34.1186D) s.v.l.
***χρυσίων**, ὁ, *goldsmith's workshop*, Thphn.*chron.*p.395(M.108. 941B).
***χρυσοβελοθήκη**, ἡ, *golden quiver*, Cyr.*hom.div.*11(M.77.1036A).
***χρυσογέννητος**, *golden-born* χ. θεῶν Agath.*v.Gr.Ill.*140.
***χρυσογνώμων**, *one who is skilled in working gold*, Gr.Nyss.*hom. 4 in Cant.*(M.44.832B).
***χρυσογράμματος**, *inscribed with letters of gold*, ‡Chrys.*ador.*2(11. 825D).
***χρυσογραφέω**, *write* or *represent in gold*, Thdr.Stud.*ref.*(M.99. 436B).
***χρυσογράφος**, ὁ, *one who writes* or *illuminates with gold*, Melet. *nat.hom.*(M.64.1309B).
χρυσοειδής, *like gold*, *golden*; comp., Gr.Naz.*or.*44.10(M.36.617C).
χρυσόζωνος, *with girdle of gold*, ‡Chrys.*hom.3 in Gen.*(6.552A); ‡Pall.*h.mon.*30.2(p.92.15; M.34.1050C); *Apophth.Patr.*(M.65.104A).
***χρυσοκαταλλακτικός**, *pertaining to the exchange of gold*, *Mir. Artem.*38(p.62.1).
***χρυσοκλαβάριος**, ὁ, *embroiderer*, Thphn.*chron.*p.395(M.108. 941B).
χρυσόκομος, *golden-haired*; of flowers *having golden petals*, ‡Chrys.*praecurs.*2(8.5A); ‡Chrys.*poenit.*4(9.852A).
***χρυσολάμπης**, *shining with gold* or *like gold*, ‡Jo.D.*hom.*5(M.96. 657D).
***χρυσολάτρις**, *worshipping gold*, Isid.Pel.*epp.*1.152(M.78.285A).
***χρυσόλεκτος**, *of golden speech*, Geo.Pis.*carm.*36.1.
χρυσολογέω, **1.** *speak golden words*, *Hymn.*82.7(*AS* 1 p.656); **2.** *gather gold*, Gr.Naz.*carm.*2.2(epigr.)92.6(M.38.127A).
χρυσολόγος, *of golden speech*, Melet.*nat.hom.*proem.(M.64.1076B); *cat.Rom.*8: 10(p.228.10); Jo.D.*hom.*11.17(M.96.780B).
***χρυσολόγχης**, *having a spear of gold*, Thphn.*chron.*p.263(M.108. 653B).
χρυσομανής, *mad after gold*, Bas.*ep.*115(3.208B; M.32.532A); Nonn. *par.Jo.*6: 71(M.43.804C); *ib.*13: 18(864A).
***χρυσομιγής**, *bound* or *interwoven with gold*, Gr.Nyss.*virg.*3 (p.259.19; M.46.329A).
***χρυσομίμητος**, *like gold*, Geo.Pis.*Heracl.*1.141(M.92.1310A).
χρυσομόρφος, *like gold in form*, ‡Paul.Sil.*therm.Pyth.*123(M.86. 2265).
χρυσόνημα, τό, *gold wire*, or *thread*, Cosm.Ind.*top.*5(M.88.212D).
***χρυσόνημος**, *woven with golden threads*, Anast.S.*qu.et resp.*40(M. 89.585A); ‡Jo.D.*hom.*5(M.96.657C).
***χρυσόνηστος**, *woven of gold*, Jo.D.*hom.*10.2(M.96.756B).
***χρυσόνους**, *golden-minded*; of BMV, Thdr.Stud.*nativ.BMV* 7 (M.96.689C).
χρυσόπαστος, *inlaid* or *overlaid with gold* ὀρόφοις χ. Ast.Am.*hom.* 3(M.40.209B); Nil.*exerc.*70(M.79.804B); Thdt.*eran.*2(4.101).
χρυσοπέδιλος, *gold-sandalled*; fig., of a city, *Orac.Sib.*5.434; of city of Rome or perh. of Church, Aberc.*epitaph.*8 cit. s. βασίλισσα.
***χρυσόπλαστος**, *made of gold*, of BMV χαῖρε, στάμνε, τὸ χ. ἄγγος Jo.D.*hom.*2.7(M.96.689B) s.v.l.
***χρυσόπλοκος**, *wreathed with gold*, of BMV χρυσοπλοκώτατε πύργε Rom.Mel.(Maas *KlT* p.9); παστὰς χ. Jo.Mon.*hymn.Chrys.*6 (M.96.1381C).
χρυσοποίκιλτος, *gold-embroidered*, Clem.*paed.*2.9(p.204.21; M.8. 489B).
***χρυσόπορος**, s.v.l., *golden*, χ. ... μίτων Paul.Sil.*Soph.*805(M.86. 2150A), ? for χρυσοφόρων.
***χρυσόπυργος**, *having golden towers*, ‡Hesych.H.*m.Long.*6(M. 93.1549C).
***χρυσόραντος**, *sprinkled with gold*, Eus.Al.*serm.*21.17(M.86. 444C).
***χρυσόρευστος**, *affluent*, Sophr.H.*mir.Cyr.et Jo.*18(M.87.3476B).
***χρυσορρεῖθρον**, τό, *golden stream*, *Hymn.*82.5(*AS.*1 p.656).
***χρυσορρεῖθρος**, *gold-streaming*, met. τῇ χ. αἴγλῃ τῶν θείων δογμάτων σου Thdr.Stud.*cant.*11.1(p.358).
χρυσορρήμων, *of golden speech*; of Chrysostom, Ephr.(3.513C); ‡Jo.D.*fid.dorm.*6(M.95.252C).
***χρυσορρήτης**, ὁ, *golden orator*; of Chrysostom, *Hymn.*82.10 (*AS* 1 p.656).
χρυσορ(ρ)όας, *streaming with gold*; of Nile, Gr.Naz.*or.*21.29(M. 35.1116B); Epiph.*haer.*66.1(p.17.5; M.42.32A); *Apophth.Patr.*(M.65. 140A); χρυσορόας, *Chron.Pasch.*p.30(M.92.129A); fig. ποταμὸς χ. ... Ἰωάννης [sc. Chrys.] Nil.*epp.*2.183(M.79.296B); epithet of Jo. D., Thphn.*chron.*p.350(M.108.841A).
***χρυσόρροος**, *flowing with gold*, met. λόγον...χ. Jo.D.*hom.*11.1 (M.96.764A).
χρυσόρρυτος, *streaming with gold* χ. ὄρη Jo.Mal.*chron.*18 p.455(M. 97.668B); neut. as subst. τῶν χ. τῶν εὑρεθέντων...ἐπὶ Ἀναστασίου *ib.*
χρυσορύκτης, ὁ, *gold-miner*, Socr.*h.e.*7.18.4(M.67.773C).
[*]**χρυσορύχιον**, τό, = χρυσωρυχεῖον, *gold-mine*, v.l. ap.Thphn. *chron.*p.152(M.108.412B).
χρυσός, ὁ, *gold*; *a gold coin*, Gr.Nyss.*tres dii*(M.45.132A,B); Sophr.H.*mir.Cyr.et Jo.*46(M.87.3597B).
***χρυσοστιγής**, *with golden spots*; of a type of sapphire, Epiph. *gemm.*5(p.227.32; M.43.297A).
***χρυσόστικτος**, *gold-spotted*, Clem.*paed.*2.3(p.178.11; M.8.433A).
***χρυσοστόλιστος**, *gold-robed*, fig. χ. ὤφθη πᾶσα ἐκκλησία *Hymn.* 82.12(*AS* 1 p.656).
***χρυσόστολος**, *gold-robed*; fig., of city of Rome or perh. of Church, Aberc.*epitaph.*8 cit. s. βασίλισσα.
χρυσόστομος, *golden-mouthed*; of John Chrysostom, bishop of CP, Soz.*h.e.*8.10.1(M.67.1541B); Dor.*doct.*12.3(M.88.1752D); †Leont.B. *sect.*4.3(M.86.1221A).
***χρυσόστρωτος**, *inlaid with gold*, *Pers.*(p.2.14).
***χρυσοτέλεια**, ἡ, *tax* or *tribute of gold*, i.e. to be paid in gold, introduced by Anastasius I, Jo.Mal.*chron.*16 p.394(M.97.584A); Evagr.*h.e.*3.42(p.144.22; M.86.2692B).
***χρυσοτελής**, *paying tribute in gold*, Thdt.*ep.*42(4.1101).
χρυσουργέω, *fashion from gold*; fig., Gr.Nyss.*v.Ephr.*(M.46.821C).
χρυσουργός, ὁ, *goldsmith*, Cyr.*ador.*2(1.60A).
χρυσοΰφαντος, *interwoven with gold*, *Asen.*2(p.41.20); met., of BMV χαίροις...χ. λόγιον ‡Jo.D.*hom.*5(M.96.649C).
***χρυσόφθογγος**, *golden-tongued*, met. χ. διδαχῇ Thdr.Stud.*cant.* 11.2(p.359).
***χρυσόφιλος**, *gold-loving*, Gr.Naz.*carm.*2.2(epigr.)58(M.38.113A).
***χρυσοφυλακέω**, *guard gold*, Clem.*paed.*2.12(p.229.1; M.8.541B); *ib.*3.4(p.251.25; 592B).
[*]**χρυσοχαλίνωτος**, = χρυσοχάλινος, *having a golden bridle*, Chrys.*hom.1.2 in Ps.48*: 17(5.507B).
χρυσοχίτων, *gold-robed*; met., of the month ξανθικός, Paul.Sil. *Soph.*599(M.86.2142A).
[*]**χρυσυφής**, (for χρυσοϋφής) *interwoven with gold*, †Apoll.*met. Ps.*44: 10(M.33.1376A).
***χρυσώνυμος**, *golden-named*; of BMV, Thdr.Stud.*nativ.BMV* 7 (M.96.693C).
χρυσωρυχέω, *dig for gold*, Clem.*paed.*2.12(p.228.24; M.8.541B).
***χρωϊκός**, *coloured*, ‡Just.*qu.Chr.*(M.6.1461B).
***χρωματεύω**, *colour*; met., Synes.*regn.*8(p.17.14; M.66.1065B).
***χρωματογραφέω**, *paint with colours*; pass., †Bas.Anc.*virg.*1 (M.30.672A).
***χρωματουργέω**, *work in colour*, *paint*; pass., Jo.D.*imag.*1.8(M. 94.1237D); *ib.*3.8(1328C).
χρωματουργία, ἡ, *painting* of pictures, Germ.CP *ep.dogm.*1(M. 98.149D); Jo.D.*imag.*3(M.94.1420A); Taras.*ep.*1(M.98.1429B).
***χρωματουργικός**, *in colours*, Thdr.Stud.*antirr.*2.17(M.99.361B).
χρώννυμι, *colour*, Clem.*prot.*4(p.37.32; M.8.140B); met. χ. τὸ πορι-ζόμενον τῇ δικαιοσύνῃ Or.*exc.in Ps.*36: 16(M.17.129D); *defile* μετὰ κακίας...τὴν εὐωδίαν τὴν ἔξω χ. id.*fr.68 in Jer.*(p.231.5).
χρώς, ὁ, *complexion*; met., of literary style τὸν αὐτὸν χ. εὑρί-σκεσθαι...ταύτης τε τῆς ἐπιστολῆς καὶ τῶν πράξεων Clem.*fr.*22(p.201. 21; M.9.748B).
χυδαιολογία, ἡ, *nonsensical language*, Epiph.*haer.*16.3(p.212.11; M.41.252B); *ib.*55.6(p.333.11; 985A); *ib.*66.9(p.30.23; M.42.44B).
χυδαῖος, **1.** *confused* τῶν χ. ἀτόμων Dion.Al.ap.Eus.*p.e.*14.25 (776D; M.21.1277C); met. ἐν χ. φράσει Max.*ambig.*(M.91.1065A); **2.** *common*, *ordinary*, of persons; comp., Max.*Pyrr.*(M.91.304B).
χυδαιότης, ἡ, **1.** *confusion*, *lack of order* μὴ...τὸν βίον...ἐν χ. διατελῶμεν Ephr.1.114F; **2.** *coarseness*, *grossness*, Cyr.H.*catech.*4.37; τῆς παχύτητος τοῦ νοῦ καὶ τῆς χ. Didym.*Trin.*3.3(M.39.820B); Cyr. *Is.*4.3(2.629C).
χυδαιόω, *make vulgar*, *debase*, Epiph.*haer.*70.3(p.235.25; M.42. 344B).
χυδαίως, *confusedly*, *indiscriminately* χ. ὀνομασθὲν Bas.*ep.*364(3.

466C; M.32.1108A); Epiph.*haer*.76.15(p.361.21; M.42.548B); Nil.*epp*. 2.294(M.79.348A).

***χυμαίνομαι,** *become juice*; of moisture in the apple, ‡Caes.Naz. *dial*.3.140(M.38.1053).

***χυμευτής, ὁ,** *alchemist*, Thphn.*chron*.p.128(M.108.353B).

***χυμοειδής,** *like juice*, ‡Nil.*narr*.3(M.79.616B).

***χυμοποιής,** *producing juice* πάντων τῶν κακοχύμων ἀπέχεσθαι αὐτοὺς προσέταξεν, ἤγουν τοῦ σελουρίου, καὶ πάντων τῶν ἄνευ λεπίδων· χ. γὰρ ταῦτα Dam.*troph*.3.6.5(p.248.5).

χύσις, ἡ, 1. *flood, stream*, fig. ἡ ῥέουσα τοῦ βίου χ. Geo.Pis.*Pers*.1. 56(M.92.1201B); *pouring forth, effusion*, met. πλείστη...ἡ τοῦ ἁγίου πνεύματος χ. τοῖς ἁγίοις ἐκνεμηθήσεται Cyr.*Zach*.106(3.801B); *infusion* σπορὰν γὰρ ἔσχε [sc. ὁ Χριστός] τὴν χ. τοῦ πνεύματος Andr.Cr. *Agath*.86(M.97.1441C); **2.** *profusion, abundance* τοσήνδε τῆς κακίας χ. Or.*or*.29.13(p.388.3; M.11.540A); id.*Jo*.28.14(12; p.408.1; M.14.712B); cf. τῆς κατὰ τὴν κακίαν χύσεως *ib*.19.12(3; p.312.16; 548D); χ. ἁμαρτημάτων id.*Cels*.2.8(p.133.25; M.11.805B); ὀλίγοι χύσεως μακαρισμοῦ ἐπιτεύξονται id.*mart*.14(p.14.6; M.11.581B); κακίας χ. †Bas.*Is*.16(1. 338C; M.30.144A).

χυτρόγαυλος, ὁ, *a kind of pot*, Thdt.*qu.24 in 3Reg*.(1.471).

χωλαίνω, *be lame*, fig. οὐδὲ περὶ ἐπαγγελίαν ἐχώλανας ‡Chrys. *theatr*.3(M.6.561B); ἐπὶ τὴν πέτραν τῆς ἀποστολικῆς πίστεως τοὺς χωλάναντάς μου πόδας κατέπηξας *Libell*.ap.CNic.(787)(H.4.137C).

χώλανσις, ἡ, *lameness*; fig., of the Jews as descendants of Jacob, who rejected Christ τὴν ἐκ τούτου φανησομένην αὐτῶν πανολέθριον χ., ἣν Ἰωάννης παντελῶς οὐχ ὑπέμεινε Sophr.H.*or*.7.7(M.87.3333B).

χωλεύ-ω, *be lame*; met., *be imperfect* ~ει τὰ τῆς γνώσεως Clem. *str*.2.10(p.137.17; M.8.981B); ἡ δικαιοσύνη...οὐδαμῶς ~ουσα *ib*.6.12 (p.483.17; M.9.324B); of persons πρὸς τὴν πίστιν ~ειν Chrys.*scand*. 10(3.489A); περὶ τὰ δόγματα...χ. id.*hom.2.5 in Gen*.(4.13B); οὐχ ὑγιαίνουσι τῇ πίστει, ἀλλὰ ~ουσι Ammon.*Ac*.15:38(M.85.1552C); χ. ...περὶ τὴν τελειότητα ‡Nil.*perist*.12.13(M.79.968A).

χωλόω, med., *be lame*, Or.*hom.2.1 in Jer*.(p.17.6; M.13.277B).

***χωλῶς,** *lamely, haltingly*, fig. χ. ἐπιβαίνοντα σοφίας Meth.*res*.1.27 (p.256.14; M.41.1133C).

χωνεία, ἡ, *refinery* [sc. of gold or silver], Thdr.Mops.*Mal*.3:3–4 M.66.621B); fig. ὥσπερ τινὶ χ. τῶν παλαιῶν ἐκκαθήρας πλημμελημάτων *ib*.(624C); Jo.Mon.*hymn.Chrys*.4(M.96.1380B); χαῖρε, χρυσίον καθαρὸν ἡ ἐν χ. τοῦ θεοῦ δοκιμασθεῖσα τῷ πυρὶ τοῦ πνεύματος Thdr. Stud.*nativ.BMV* 7(M.96.693B).

χωνευτήριον, τό, *smelting furnace*, Gr.Nyss.*or.catech*.35(p.139. 1; M.45.92B); Chrys.*comm.in Gal*.6:4(10.724C); Dion.Ar.*ep*.9.1(M.3. 1105A); fig. ὡς εἰς χ. τῆς γῆς καθίσταται [sc. τὸ σῶμα] Iren.*fr*.12(M.7. 1236A); Chrys.*stat*.1.1(2.2E); διὰ τὸ ἐμβαλεῖν αὐτὸν ὑμᾶς ἐν τῷ χ. τῆς θεϊκῆς γνώσεως καὶ τῆς διδασκαλικῆς παιδεύσεως Agath.*v.Gr.Ill*.112; *ib*.150.

χωνευτής, ὁ, *smelter, metal-caster*, Thphl.Ant.*Autol*.2.2(M.6. 1048B); fig. ὁρᾷς τῶν ἁμαρτιῶν τὸν χ. [sc. τὸν Πρόδρομον] Chrysipp. *enc.in Jo.Bapt*.(p.37.17).

χωνευτός, *formed of cast metal*, Clem.*str*.5.5(p.344.9; M.9.49B); *A.Pil*.A 9(p.242); Proc.G.*Is*.42:10–25(M.87.2380B).

χωνεύ-ω, 1. *cast, form by casting*, Just.*1apol*.9.2(M.6.340A); Or. *fr.in 1Reg*.15:10–11(M.17.44B); *Hom.Clem*.10.8; **2.** *melt down*, Clem. *prot*.4(p.40.24,32; M.8.145A,B); Socr.*h.e*.7.21.4(M.67.784A); Justn.*nov*. 120.10(p.589.34); **3.** met., *test* as in a furnace ἀρετὴν...αἱ τῆς ζωῆς περιστάσεις ~ουσιν Bas.Sel.*or*.16.2(M.85.205C); cf.*ib*.8.3(125A).

χώνη, ἡ, 1. *crucible*, *Hom.Clem*.6.4; Cyr.H.*procatech*.9; **2.** *treasury* of a shrine, *Mir.Geo*.11(p.108.18); καρποφορίας...ἐπικομίζων...ἐν ταῖς χ. ... λαβὼν χρήματα οὐκ ὀλίγα...ἐπορεύετο εἰς τὸν ναὸν τοῦ...Μιχαὴλ ἐν ταῖς χ. *ib*.(p.108.22); *ib*.(pp.109.9,112.2).

***χωνοειδής,** *like a crucible*, *Schol.Clem.paed*.(p.327.36; M.9.788C).

χώρα, ἡ, A. *place*; **1.** of passages of scripture φωτίζων πάσας τὰς χ. τῆς γραφῆς Or.*Jo*.13.42(p.268.16; M.14.473B); met. οὐδεμίαν χ. ἀπονέμομεν ἡδονῇ Clem.*paed*.2.8(p.198.3; M.8.473C); Chrys.*hom. 86.3 in Mt*.(7.814C); **2.** χώραν ἔχω *have place, apply* ἐπὶ παντὸς ἀνθρώπου χ. ἔχει τοῦτο [sc. τὸ ἐκ γυναικὸς γενέσθαι] Or.*comm.in Rom*. 3:29(*JTS* 13 p.223.18); **3.** *place, position* Ἰησοῦν Χριστὸν...υἱὸν αὐτοῦ τοῦ ὄντως θεοῦ μαθόντες καὶ ἐν δευτέρᾳ χ. ἔχοντες Just.*1apol*.13.3(M. 6.348A); **4.** *opportunity, occasion* πῶς χ. εἶχον πυνθάνεσθαι...εἰ αὐτὸς Ἠλίας ἐστίν; Or.*Jo*.6.21(12; p.130.26; M.14.237A); δέδωκας καὶ ἡμῖν χ. ἀπολογεῖσθαι Ath.*apol.Const*.2(p.280.9; M.25.597B); χ. ἀπολογίας δὸς ἡμῖν *Pers*.(p.2.15); Philost.*h.e*.3.4(M.65.481C).

B. *country*; meton. *inhabitants* of a district συναθροίσαντες πᾶσαν τὴν ἀγροικικὴν χ. Jo.Mal.*chron*.2 p.48(M.97.121A); Anast.Ant.*sac*. (p.437.14).

χωράφιον, τό, *small farm*, Nil.*epp*.3.153(M.79.458D).

χωρεπίσκοπος, ὁ, *country-bishop* appointed to superintend churches at a distance from city where bishop resided; **1.** in gen., dist. from both bishops and presbyters, Ath.*apol.sec*.85(p.163. 22; M.25.400B); as typifying the seventy (Lc.10:1), CNeocaes.*can*. 14; **2.** powers; **a.** restricted powers of ordination χωρεπισκόποις μὴ ἐξεῖναι πρεσβυτέρους ἢ διακόνους χειροτονεῖν, ἀλλὰ μὴν μηδὲ πρεσβυτέρους πόλεως, χωρὶς τοῦ ἐπιτραπῆναι ὑπὸ τοῦ ἐπισκόπου μετὰ γραμμάτων ἐν ἑτέρᾳ παροικίᾳ CAnc.(314)*can*.13; τοὺς καλουμένους χωρεπισκόπους...καθιστᾶν δὲ ἀναγνώστας καὶ ὑποδιακόνους καὶ ἐφορκιστάς καὶ τῇ τούτων ἀρκεῖσθαι προαγωγῇ, μήτε πρεσβύτερον μήτε διάκονον χειροτονεῖν τολμᾶν δίχα τοῦ ἐν τῇ πόλει ἐπισκόπου...εἰ δὲ τολμήσειέ τις παραβῆναι τὰ ὁρισθέντα, καθαιρεῖσθαι αὐτὸν καὶ ἧς μετέχει τιμῆς CAnt.(341)*can*.10; cf.Bas.*ep*.54(3.148C; M.32.400Cff.); **b.** could grant letters of communion τοὺς δὲ ἀνεπιλήπτους χ. διδόναι εἰρηνικάς CAnt.(341)*can*.8; **c.** could officiate in city church in presence of bishop and presbyters of city (opp. ἐπιχώριοι πρεσβύτεροι) χ. ... ὡς...συλλειτουργοὶ διὰ τὴν σπουδὴν εἰς τοὺς πτωχοὺς προσφέρουσι τιμώμενοι CNeocaes.*can*.13–14; **d.** could sit and vote in councils, CEph.(431)*act*.1(p.58; H.1.1425E); **3.** replaced by περιοδευταί q.v., cf.CLaod.*can*.57; mentioned after this date τῶν κυρίων μου τῶν συμπρεσβυτέρων...Εὐλαλίου τοῦ χ. καὶ Κελευσίου Gr.Naz.*ep*.152(M. 37.257C); id.*carm*.2.1.11.447(M.37.1060A); Pall.*h.Laus*.106(p.142.16; M.34.1211B); τῶν...θεοφιλεστάτων πρεσβυτέρων Ὑπατίου καὶ Ἀβραμίου τῶν χ. Thdt.*ep*.113(4.1192); **4.** ref. treatment of Novatianist bishops εἰ δὲ τοῦ τῆς καθολικῆς ἐκκλησίας ἐπισκόπου ἢ πρεσβυτέρου ὄντος προσέρχονταί τινες, πρόδηλον, ὡς ὁ μὲν ἐπίσκοπος τῆς ἐκκλησίας ἕξει τὸ ἀξίωμα τοῦ ἐπισκόπου, ὁ δὲ ὀνομαζόμενος παρὰ τοῖς λεγομένοις Καθαροῖς ἐπίσκοπος τὴν τοῦ πρεσβυτερίου τιμὴν ἕξει· πλὴν εἰ μὴ ἄρα δοκοίη τῷ ἐπισκόπῳ, τῆς τιμῆς τοῦ ὀνόματος αὐτὸν μετέχειν· εἰ δὲ τοῦτο αὐτῷ μὴ ἀρέσκοι, ἐπινοήσει τόπον ἢ χ. ἢ πρεσβυτέρου, ὑπὲρ τοῦ ἐν τῷ κλήρῳ ὅλως δοκεῖν εἶναι, ἵνα μὴ ἐν τῇ πόλει δύο ἐπίσκοποι ὦσιν CNic.(325)*can*.8.

χωρ-έω, A. intrans., implying motion; **1.** *go forth, depart* τὸν ἑαυτοῦ λόγον...οὐκ ἔξω αὐτοῦ ~οῦντα ἀλλ' ἐν αὐτῷ ἀεὶ ὄντα Jo.D.*f.o*. 1.6(M.94.804A); **2.** *advance, proceed*, met. οὐ πιστεῦσαι ἄξιον· πόρρω γὰρ κεχώρηκε τῆς ἀνθρωπίνης φύσεως Just.*dial*.10.2(M.6.496C); ἄνθρωπον...τὸν πόρρω μὲν τῆς ἀνθρωπότητος πρὸς αὐτὸν τὸν θεὸν κεχωρηκότα Tat.*orat*.15(p.16.15; M.6.837B); ἐπὶ τοὺς τούτων χ. μαθητάς Hipp.*haer*.4.51(p.76.22; M.16.3122D); phrases ὁμόσε χωρεῖν *proceed to, approach*, Dion.Al.ap.Eus.*h.e*.7.11.2(M.664A); Eus. *h.e*.5.21.1(M.20.488A); c. διά, *engage in, proceed to* ἐχώρει δὲ δι' αἱμάτων id.*v.C*.1.7(p.10.15; M.20.920A); δι' ἔργων ἐχώρει τὰ πρὸς τοῦ νόμου διηγορευμένα *put into effect*, *ib*.2.43(p.59.22; 1020B); c. κατά *advance against, meet* κατ' ἀμφοτέρων [sc. Jews and Greeks] ὁ λόγος οὐκ ὀκνήσει χωρῆσαι Ath.*inc*.33.2(M.25.152D); *apply to* κεχώρηκε [sc. ὁ νόμος]...κατὰ μόνων τοῦ λεπροῦ καὶ γονορρυοῦς Cyr.*ador*.12 (1.421E); **3.** *continue*, Cyr.H.*catech*.19.2; c. dat., *continue in, persist in* χ. τῇ ἀρνήσει τῆς τοῦ σωτῆρος ἡμῶν εἰκόνος καὶ οὐσίας Acac.Caes. *fr.Marcell*.ap.Epiph.*haer*.72.8(p.262.26; M.42.393A); **4.** *issue, end* ἵνα καὶ ἡ ἐπιθυμία καὶ ἡ ἀγρυπνία εἰς τι ἀγαθὸν χωρήσῃ *Barn*.21.7; εἰ εἰς ἀναισθησίαν ἐχώρει [sc. ὁ κοινὸς θάνατος] ἕρμαιον ἂν ἦν τοῖς ἀδίκοις Just.*1apol*.18.1(M.6.356A); ἡ τοῦ νόμου γραφὴ εἰς Χριστὸν Ἰησοῦν κεχώρηκεν Mel.*pass*.5 p.2.7; τούτοις οὕτω χωρήσασιν ἐπιμαρτυρῶν Eus.*h.e*.4.13.8(M.20.336B); **5.** *return* Χριστὸν τὸν ἀφ' ἑνὸς πατρὸς προελθόντα καὶ εἰς ἕνα ὄντα καὶ χωρήσαντα Ign.*Magn*.7.2; οὐκ ἔστιν ἡ ψυχὴ ἔτι, ἀλλὰ...ὅθεν ἐλήφθη ἐκεῖσε ~εῖ πάλιν Just.*dial*.6.2 (M.6.492A); met. χ. ἐπὶ κεφαλὰς τῶν λεγόντων Or.*engast*.(p.284.23; M.12.1016A); **6.** *spread* αὐτὴ ἡ ἀκοὴ...εἰς ἡμᾶς ἐχώρησεν *1Clem*.47.7; τοσαύτη διὰ τῆς σαρκὸς αὐτοῦ καὶ ἐπὶ τῆς γῆς ἔκρυσις ἐχώρησεν Papias *fr*.3.3; τὴν κρύφιον κακίαν εἰς τὸ βάθος κεχωρηκυῖαν τῆς ψυχῆς Or.*comm.in Ex*.10:27(M.12.272A).

B. intrans., implying extension; **1.** *be extended*, i.e. occupy space, *subsist* τῆς ὕλης, δι' ἧς φασι [sc. Stoics] τὸ πνεῦμα ~εῖν τοῦ θεοῦ Athenag.*leg*.6.4(M.6.904A); *ib*.22.3(937B); δι' ὅλης κεχωρηκέναι [sc. τὸν θεόν] τῆς ὕλης Meth.*arbitr*.6.3(p.160.6; M.18.252B); διὰ πάντων χωρῶν πάντων τε ἐφαπτόμενος Eus.*d.e*.4.13(p.171.13; M.22.285B); αἱ ἅγιαι δυνάμεις...δι' ὅλης τῆς ἑαυτῶν ὑποστάσεως κεχωρηκότα ἤδη καὶ συμπεφυσιωμένον τὸν ἁγιασμὸν ἔχουσι Bas.*Eun*.3.2(1.274B; M.29. 660B); ἡ καθαρῶς ἀσώματος φύσις ~εῖ μὲν ἀκωλύτως διὰ πάντων, δι' αὐτῆς δὲ οὐδέν Nemes.*nat.hom*.3(M.40.608A); of Father and Son πῶς ...δύναται ὁ πατήρ, μείζων ὤν, ἐν τῷ υἱῷ ἐλάττονι ὄντι ~εῖν; Ath.Ar. 3.1(M.26.321C); ὡς χωρεῖν τὸν πατέρα ἐν αὐτῷ Nil.*epp*.2.39(M.79. 213D); πῶς ὁ μείζων ἐν ἐλάττονι κατ' ἐκείνους ὄντι τῷ υἱῷ χωρήσει καὶ ὀφθήσεται; Cyr.*Jo*.1.3(4.29B); abs. ἀλλ' ἴσως καὶ τοῦτ' ἂν εἴπῃς· εἰ ὁ πατὴρ τέλειος ὢν τὰ πάντα πληροῖ ποῖον ὑπολείπεται τῷ υἱῷ τελείῳ ὄντι εἰς τὸ χωρῆσαι; ‡Gr.Nyss.*Ar.et Sab*.12(M.45.1297B); ὁ πατὴρ καὶ ὁ *υἱὸς κατὰ τοῦ αὐτοῦ κεχωρηκότες τόπου καὶ ἀλλήλων δεκτικοὶ γεγονότες καὶ ἓν ὄντες...μόνῃ ὑποστάσει καὶ προσηγορίᾳ θάτερος θατέρου διενήνοχεν* ib.(1297D); *ἀναπιμπλάντος γὰρ ἡμῖν τὰ πάντα τοῦ...πατρὸς... ὅποιπερ ἂν ἔτι χωρήσειεν ἡ δι' υἱοῦ πλήρωσις, κατιδεῖν οὐκ ἔχω...εἰ μή ἐστιν ἐν ἀμφοῖν οὐσιωδῶς ἑκάτερος* Cyr.*dial.Trin.*3(5^1.467C); *καὶ πανταχοῦ παροῦσα* [sc. *τριάς*] *μὴ κινουμένη, καὶ μηδαμοῦ ~οῦσα καὶ ~ουμένη ὅπου δέησις ἐκ βάθους ἀνάπτεται* Geo.Pis.*Pers.*1.9(M.92.1199A); met., *apply to γενικὸς οὖν ἄρα καὶ κατὰ πάντων ὁ διπλοῦς οὑτοσὶ κεχώρηκεν ἔλεγχος* Cyr.*Jo.*10.2(4.921E); **2.** *have room enough ὁ λόγος οὐ ~εῖ ἐν τοῖς μὴ προκόψασιν ἀπὸ τοῦ εἶναι σπέρμα τοῦ Ἀβραάμ* Or.*Jo.*20.6(p.333.35; M.14.585B); *μὴ ~ούσης τῆς γλώσσης ἐν τῷ ὡρισμένῳ...τόπῳ* Pall.*v.Chrys.*17(p.104.22; M.47.59); hence *be wholly contained κεχώρηκε γὰρ ὡς ἔφην θεότης ἀνθρωπότητι* Cyr.*glaph.Ex.* 1(1.262E).

C. trans., *contain*; **1.** *hold, contain* a given measure, met. *ἀρετὴν...οὐκ ἂν χωρηθεῖσαν ἐν ὑποθέσει βίου βασιλείας ἐλάττονι* Synes.*regn.*3(p.11.12; M.66.1060C); abs., *hold out, suffice οὐ ~εῖ τὸ ἄγγος ἐκεῖνο ἀλλ' ὑπερπλεονάζει* Herm.*mand.*5.2.5; **2.** *enclose* or *contain* in a physical or quasi-physical sense, *receive, admit*; **a.** in gen. *ἵνα ὁ ἄνθρωπος τὸν λόγον χωρήσας...υἱὸς γένηται θεοῦ* Iren.*haer.* 3.19.1(M.7.939B); *ὡς ὅλῃ καρδίᾳ δυνηθῆναι χωρῆσαι τὸν θεόν* Clem. *prot.*10(p.76.12; M.8.221C); *τὸν δι' ἀμέλειαν τὰ σπέρματα τῆς ἁμαρτίας κεχωρηκότα* Or.*princ.*3.1.13(p.218.6; M.11.273A); *εἴ τις ἐστὶ 'Πέτρος', χωρήσας τὴν τῆς ἐκκλησίας ἐν ἑαυτῷ οἰκοδομὴν ἀπὸ τοῦ λόγου* id.*Cels.* 6.77(p.147.18; M.11.1416B); *δυνήσεται χωρῆσαι ὃν τέως οὐκ ἐχώρει λόγον θεοῦ* id.*Jo.*20.6(p.334.11; M.14.585C); **b.** of God *μηδὲ τὸ ἐν τόπῳ ~εῖσθαι* [sc. *τὸν θεόν*]· *εἰ δὲ μή γε, μείζων ὁ ~ῶν τόπος αὐτοῦ εὑρεθήσεται· μείζων γάρ ἐστι τὸ ~οῦν τοῦ ~ουμένου. θεὸς γὰρ οὐ ~εῖται, ἀλλὰ αὐτός ἐστι τόπος τῶν ὅλων* Thphl.Ant.*Autol.*2.3(M.6. 1049C,D); *μικρότερον αὐτὸν τῆς ὕλης λέγει, εἴ γε δὴ μέρος αὐτῆς ὅλον ἐχώρησεν τὸν θεόν* Meth.*arbitr.*6.3(p.160.5; M.18.252B); **c.** ref. Inc. *θέλων ἐχωρήθη ἐν σώματι ἐμψύχῳ* Hipp.*pasch.*3(p.269.6); *τὸ ἐκ τῆς παρθένου σῶμα χωρῆσαν πᾶν τὸ πλήρωμα τῆς θεότητος σωματικῶς* Hymen.*ep.*8(p.329.2); *τὸ ἐκλεκτὸν σκεῦος τῆς Μαρίας διὰ τὸ πυροειδὲς τῆς τοῦ σωτῆρος θεότητος χωρηθὲν ἐν τῇ παρθένῳ* Epiph.*haer.*30.30 (p.374.25; M.41.457D); *χωρήσασαν* [sc. *τὴν παρθένον*] *τὸν ἀχώρητον, ὃν οὐρανὸς καὶ γῆ ~εῖν οὐ δύνανται* ib.30.31(p.376.3,4; 460C); Marcosian *τὸν Ἰησοῦν...τεθεῖσθαι δὲ* ⟨*εἰς*⟩ *ἐξομοίωσιν καὶ μόρφωσιν τοῦ μέλλοντος εἰς αὐτὸν κατέρχεσθαι Ἀνθρώπου, ὃν χωρήσαντα ἐσχηκέναι αὐτόν* Hipp. *haer.*6.51(p.184.8; M.16.3283B); in Sabellian view attributed to Callistus *τὸ μὲν γὰρ βλεπόμενον, ὅπερ ἐστὶν ἄνθρωπος, τοῦτο εἶναι τὸν υἱόν, τὸ δὲ ἐν τῷ υἱῷ χωρηθὲν πνεῦμα, τοῦτο εἶναι τὸν πατέρα* ib.9.12 (p.249.3; 3383C); Arian *εἰ ὁ λόγος τῆς γενητῆς φύσεως...ἀδυνάτου τυγχανούσης ~εῖν τὴν τοῦ θεοῦ αὐτουργίαν* Ath.*Ar.*2.26(M.26.201B); **3.** *admit of, allow οὐ τροπολογίαν ~οῦσιν οἱ λόγοι* Just.*dial.*129.2(M. 6.777A); Or.*Jo.*32.7(p.437.11; M.14.760B); ib.32.15(p.450.5; 780C); impers. so far as *circumstances admit καθὼς ἐμὲ ἐχώρησε περὶ αὐτοῦ λέγειν* Arist.*apol.*2.1(p.100.14); **4.** of spiritual and intellectual capacity, *take in, comprehend μήποτε οὐ δυνηθέντες χωρῆσαι στραγγαλωθῆτε* Ign.*Trall.*5.1; *μὴ πάντας...κεχωρηκέναι τὸ μέγεθος τῆς γνώσεως* Clem.*str.*7.16(p.73.24; M.9.544B); *πατέρα δὲ εἶναι* [sc. *ἑαυτὸν*] *καὶ τοῖς ~οῦσιν μὴ ἀποκρύψαντα* Hipp.*haer.*9.10(p.245.6; M.16.3378B); *εἰξάμενος ὡς ἄνθρωπος (οὐ γάρ που ἐμαυτῷ δίδωμι ~εῖν τὴν προσευχήν)* Or.*or.*2.6(p.303.21; M.11.424A); pass. *ἤτω σοι καρδία γνῶσις, ζωὴ δὲ λόγος ἀληθής, ~ούμενος* ‡*Diogn.*12.7; *σωματικώτερον τοῖς βαρυτάτοις τὴν διάνοιαν ἔδει περὶ τοῦ θεοῦ τοὺς προφήτας ὁμιλεῖν, ἵνα χωρηθῇ* [sc. *ὁ θεός*] Or.*fr.in 1Reg.*15:11(p.296.7; M.12.992A); esp. ref. Inc. *ὁ ἀχώρητος καὶ ἀκατάληπτος καὶ ἀόρατος ὁρώμενον ἑαυτὸν καὶ καταλαμβανόμενον καὶ ~ούμενον τοῖς πιστοῖς πάρεσχεν, ἵνα ζωοποιήσῃ τοὺς ~οῦντας καὶ βλέποντας αὐτόν* Iren.*haer.*4.20.5(M.7.1035C); *ἀχώρητος δὲ ὅτε μὴ ~εῖσθαι θέλει, χωρητὸς δὲ ὅτε ~εῖται* Hipp.*haer.*9.10(p.244. 15; M.16.3378A); *ἑαυτὸν ἐκένωσεν ἵνα χωρηθῆναι ὑπ' ἀνθρώπων δυνηθῇ* Or.*Cels.*4.15(p.284.30; M.11.1045B); *ταῖς τῶν ἀγαθῶν ψυχαῖς οἰκιζόμενος, ἀχώρητος καὶ ~ούμενος* [sc. *ὁ θεός*] *Hom.Clem.*2.45; Gr.Naz.*or.*39.13(M.36.49A); Jo.D.*hom.*1.4(M.96.552B); cf. *χωρητός*; **5.** *have the capacity, be able τὸ ἄνθος τοῦτο γῆ βαστάζειν οὐ κεχώρηκεν* Clem.*paed.*2.8(p.202.8; M.8.485A); *ὡς μόνους ~οῦντας τὴν τότε δόξαν αὐτοῦ θεωρῆσαι* Or.*Cels.*2.64(p.186.3; M.11.896D); *ὅσα ἐχωρήσαμεν περὶ τῆς Κανᾶ, ἐν τοῖς ἀνωτέρω εἴπομεν* id.*Jo.*13.57(56; p.287.27; M. 14.505D); *τοῦτο τὸ πόμα γεννᾶν οὐκ ἐχώρησε γῆ* Meth.*symp.*1.1(p.8. 4; M.18.37B); *μὴ δυνάμενος...μηδὲ ~ῶν βασιλεύεσθαι* ib.10.3(p.125.9; 197A); *οὐ ~ῶ ἐπιτρέψαι* Thdr.Stud.*epp.*2.11(M.99.1149C); **6.** of God *pervade, permeate θεὸς ὁ...πάντα ~ῶν, μόνος δὲ ἀχώρητος ὢν* Herm. *mand.*1.1; *σπέρμα ἐνεδύσατο...χωρήσας αὐτὸ δυνάμει* Clem.*exc.Thdot.* 59.1(p.126.18; M.9.688A); *οἱ δὲ ἀλλήλους ~οῦντες* [sc. Father and Son] *ἴσοι ἂν εἶεν ἀλλήλοις τὸ μέγεθος* ‡Gr.Nyss.*Ar.et Sab.*12(M.45. 1297B); *τῷ ἰδίῳ πατρὶ κατὰ πάντων ὅμοιος...ὡς ~εῖν τὸν πατέρα ἐν αὐτῷ καὶ ~εῖσθαι ὑπὸ τοῦ πατρός* Nil.*epp.*2.39(M.79.213D).

***χωρηγέομαι**, *be inspired οἱ προφῆται...καθὼς ἐχωρηγήθησαν, οὕτως καὶ ἐλάλησαν* Dam.*troph.*3.10.2(p.258.8).

χώρημα, τό, 1. *space, room; recess*, ref. Ex.33:22 *πέτρα, καὶ τὸ ἐν ταύτῃ χ. ὅπερ ὀπὴ ὀνομάζεται, καὶ ἡ ἐκεῖ τοῦ Μωϋσέως εἴσοδος* Gr. Nyss.*v.Mos.*(M.44.400D); ib.(405A); met., *innermost corner τὸν ποθούμενον...ἑαυτῇ περιάπτει* [sc. *ἡ νύμφη*] *μεταξὺ τῶν λογικῶν μαζῶν...τῷ χ. τῆς καρδίας ἐνδυσαμένη* id.*hom.6 in Cant.*(M.44.888C); *ἠσπασάμην τῷ πνεύματι, καὶ ὅλον τῷ χ. τῆς καρδίας περιλαβὼν ἀπεθέμην* Max.*ep.*43(M.91.637B); *τὸ χ. τῆς ψυχῆς πάσης ἀγνοίας διακαθᾶραι βουλόμενος* id.*opusc.*(M.91.229B); **2.** *container*, of BMV *χαίροις, χ. ἐλάχιστον, χωρήσασα τὸν τοῖς πᾶσιν ἀχώρητον* Thdot.Anc.*hom.BMV et Sym.*3(M.77.1393C); *τὸ μεῖζον τοῦ παντὸς πάναγνον χ. τοῦ ἀχωρήτου θεοῦ* Mod.*dorm.*13(M.86.3309A); **3.** *capacity, volume*, met. *εἰ δὲ καὶ* ⟨*περὶ*⟩ *τῶν ὑπὲρ οὐρανὸν ἔσται λόγος διὰ τὸ ἐν αὐτῷ τῷ ἀποστόλῳ τῆς γνώσεως βαθύτατον χ.* Epiph.*haer.*66.45(p.83.13; M.42.97D); ref. Mt.19:11 *ἐπὶ τῷ αὐτεξουσίῳ κληθήσονται, καὶ οὐκέτι κατὰ φύσιν ἔσται τὸ χ.* ib.77(p.118.17; 149D); *χ. καρδίας, ἐλπὶς εἰς θεόν· στενοχωρία δὲ αὐτῆς, φροντὶς σωματική* Marc.Er.*opusc.*2.107(M.65.945B).

χώρησις, ἡ, *capacity μαλασσόμενοι ἀσκοὶ ἐπιδιδοῦσι τῇ χ., περιφρονούμενοι δὲ οὐ τοσοῦτον δέχονται* Jo.Clim.*scal.*14(M.88.868B); met. *ἐξομοιοῖ ἑαυτόν, σωματοποιῶν κατὰ χώρησιν, ταῖς ἁγίαις καὶ ἀξίαις πισταῖς ψυχαῖς, ἵνα ὁραθῇ αὐταῖς ὁ ἀόρατος* Mac.Aeg.*hom.*4.11(M.34. 480D).

χωρητικός, 1. *able to hold* a given measure *σώματα...τὰ μὲν πλείονος, τὰ δὲ ἐλάττονος δεῖται τροφῆς, οὐ τῶν ἴσων ὄντα χ.* Or.*Jo.*13. 33(p.258.9; M.14.456C); *ἀγγεῖον ὥσπερ μυρίων σωμάτων χ.* Mac.Mgn. *apocr.*2.20(p.39.7); *able* or *intended to hold* a certain substance *ἀνθρώπους εἶναι τροπικῶς...χ. οἴνου. καὶ ὀνομάζω αὐτοὺς κατὰ τοῦτο ἀσκούς* Or.*hom.12.2 in Jer.*(p.87.4; M.13.377D); *οἰνηρὸν καὶ ἐλαιηρὸν σκεῦος καλεῖται τὸ τούτων χ.* Meth.*res.*3.16(p.413.10; M.118.888A); **2.** *susceptible* to influence *εὑρεθήσεται δὲ καὶ δεκτικὴ ἅμα καὶ χ. ἡ σὰρξ τῆς τοῦ θεοῦ δυνάμεως* [i.e. able to be raised up at Last Day] Iren.*haer.*5.3.2(M.7.1130B); *πᾶσαν ἀνθρωπίνου λογισμοῦ χ. φύσιν* Const.ap.Eus.*v.C.*3.30(p.91.31; M.20.1089C); *νεύματι γὰρ αὐτοῦ ἐκινεῖτο καὶ Μωϋσῆς, καὶ Δαβίδ, καὶ ὅσοι τῆς θείας ἐνεργείας χ.* Max. *Pyrr.*(M.91.297A); **3.** spiritually *receptive χ. γινόμενος ὡς ἅγιος ἁγίου πνεύματος* Or.*or.*16.3(p.338.5; M.11.470C); *τὸ δημιουργηθὲν ἡγεμονικὸν ἐπὶ τῷ εἶναι θεοῦ χ.* id.*fr.27 in Lam.*(p.248.9; M.13.624A); *καθόσον ἐσμὲν χ. ... τῇ πρὸς τὸν θεὸν...ὁμοιώσει προσάγει* Bas.*Eun.*1.27(1. 238A; M.29.572A); *ὁ γὰρ ἄνθρωπός ἐστι χ. καὶ δεκτικὸς τοῦ πονηροῦ* Mac.Aeg.*hom.*11.11(M.34.552D); *ὅσον ἐστί τις χ. αὐτός τε πληροῦται τῆς ἀγαθῆς ἐπιθυμίας* Gr.Nyss.*virg.*4(p.268.7; M.46.337C); intellectually *receptive διδάσκαλος τελείαν ἔχων ἐπιστήμην, διὰ συγκαταβάσεων τοῖς εἰσαγομένοις ταῦτα φαίνεται γινώσκων, ὧν εἰσιν ἐκεῖνοι χ.* Didym. *Ps.*68.6(M.39.1453A); **4.** *fit for, worthy of*, ref. Jo.11:20 *Μαρία ἀναμένει οἴκοι αὐτὸν ὑποδέξασθαι ὡς χ. τῆς αὐτοῦ ἐπιδημίας* Or.*fr.80 in Jo.*(p.548.7); *χ. τῶν θειοτέρων κατέστητε μυστηρίων, θείου καὶ ζωοποιοῦ βαπτίσματος ἀξιωθέντες* Cyr.H.*catech.*19.1; **5.** *able to contain* or *apprehend, co-extensive with ἀλλήλων φημὶ γεγονέναι δεκτικοὺς καὶ χ.· 'ἐγὼ' γάρ φησιν 'ἐν τῷ πατρὶ καὶ ὁ πατὴρ ἐν ἐμοί ἐστιν'* ‡Gr.Nyss. *Ar.et Sab.*12(M.45.1297B); *ἐπὶ γὰρ ἀνθρώπων τοῦτο νομιστέον· οὔτε γὰρ ἑτέρων χ. τυγχάνομεν, οὐδ' αὖ χωροῦμεν εἰς ἕτερον* ib.(1297C); *ὁ υἱὸς ὁ τοῦ τελείου χ. καὶ χαρακτὴρ τοῦ μεγάλου πατρός* Cyr.*Jo.*1.3 (4.29B); hence *limiting, confining ἐκυοφορήθη ὁ ἀχώρητος ἐν χ. σκεύει* ‡Ath.*nativ.Chr.*7(M.28.969D); **6.** for *χωριτικός, rustic ἀστοὶ καὶ χ.* Thdt.*h.e.*2.2.5(3.826); id.*h.rel.*17(3.1228C); ib.20(1233); id.*affect.*9(4. 943); but cf. *ἐν ἀστοῖς καὶ ἐν χωριτικοῖς* id.*Ps.*71:7(1.1105).

***χωρητός, A.** *passable τὴν παχύτητα τοῦ φαύλου λεπτύνοντος ἢ στενότητα τῆς εἰσόδου χ. αὐτῷ ποιοῦντος* Or.*comm.in Mt.*15.20(p.407. 6; M.13.1312A).

B. 1. *contained in spatial dimensions, finite ἐὰν τόπον τοῦ θεοῦ τὴν ὕλην εἴπωμεν, ἐξ ἀνάγκης αὐτὸν καὶ χ. λέγειν δεῖ καὶ πρὸς τῆς ὕλης περιγραφόμενον* Meth.*arbitr.*6.1(p.159.10; M.18.252A); *οὐ προσήκει νοεῖν, καθάπερ σῶμα ἐν σώματι ἢ σκεῦος ἐν σκεύει, οὕτως εἶναι χ. ἐν υἱῷ τὸν πατέρα...οὗτος δὲ ἐν ἐκείνῳ...φαίνεται ὡς ἐν ταυτότητι τῆς οὐσίας ἀπαραλλάκτῳ* Cyr.*Jo.*1.3(4.28D); *ἡ οὐσία τοῦ θεοῦ...εἶναί φασι... τόποις χ. καὶ διαστήμασι περιληπτήν* id.*resp.*(6^2.385E); ref. implications of Noëtus' Trin. doctrine *ἀχώρητος δὲ ὅτε μὴ χωρεῖσθαι θέλει, χ. δὲ ὅτε χωρεῖται* Hipp.*haer.*9.10(p.244.15; M.16.3378A); Sabellian *τὸν ἀχώρητον καὶ ἀπαθῆ πατέρα χ. ἅμα καὶ παθητὸν διὰ τῆς ἐνανθρωπήσεως ὑποτίθενται* *Symb.Ant.*(345)7 ap.Ath.*syn.*26(p.253.17; M.26. 732C); of Son *πῶς οὖν ὅμοιος ἔσται τῷ πατρὶ χ. ὢν* [sc. *ὁ υἱός*] *ἐν ἡμῖν τοῖς ἐκεῖνον* [sc. *τὸν πατέρα*] *οὐ δυναμένοις χωρεῖν;* Cyr.*thes.*13(5^1. 136B); Christol. *πρότερον μὲν οὐκ ἄνθρωπον, ἀλλὰ θεὸν καὶ υἱὸν μόνον* *προαιώνιον...ἐπὶ τέλει δὲ καὶ ἄνθρωπον, προσληφθέντα ὑπὲρ τῆς σωτηρίας τῆς ἡμετέρας, παθητὸν σαρκί, ἀπαθῆ θεότητι...τὸν αὐτὸν... χ. καὶ ἀχώρητον* Gr.Naz.*ep.*101(M.37.177B); *θεὸς τῷ ἐκ παρθένου ναῷ κατηυλίζετο, καθεὶς ἑαυτὸν...καὶ οἱονεὶ περιστέλλων τὴν ἄκρατον τῆς ἰδίας φύσεως προσβολὴν ἵνα γένηται χ.* Cyr.*glaph.Ex.*1(1.262D); *Χριστὸν...χ. καὶ ἀχώρητον* CLater.*can.*4(H.3.921D); **2.** *comprehensible, capable of being discerned δεόμεθα σοφίας, χ. τυγχανούσης μόνῳ τῷ δυναμένῳ εἰπεῖν 'ἡμεῖς δὲ νοῦν Χριστοῦ ἔχομεν'* Or.*Jo.*10.41 (p.219.8; M.14.388C); *ἀλλ' ἐπειδὴ κενοῦται δι' ἡμᾶς, ἐπειδὴ κατέρχεται ...διὰ τοῦτο χ. γίνεται* Gr.Naz.*or.*37.3(M.36.285B); *ὁ γὰρ αὐτὸς λόγος ...χ. διὰ φιλανθρωπίαν τοῖς οὕτως ηὐτρεπισμένοις ib.*39.10(344D); *διὰ τῶν χ. ἡμῖν ὑποδειγμάτων* Gr.Nyss.*Eun.*7(2 p.168.16; M.45.760A); id.*or.catech.*10(p.55.12; M.45.41C); *μάλιστά γε τῇ βραχύτητι τῆς ἀνθρωπίνης οὐδενείας ἀχώρητον· χ. δὲ τῇ ἐπικήρῳ τῆς σαρκὸς φύσει τότε γενόμενον ὅτε ἐκένωσε...τὴν...τῆς θεότητος δόξαν* id.*Apoll.*20(M.45. 1164C); *τὸ κοινὸν ὄνομα καὶ παρὰ ἀνθρώποις χ. ἀνελάμβανεν εἰς ἑαυτόν, οὕτω καλούμενος υἱὸς ἀνθρώπου, υἱὸς ὢν θεοῦ* Epiph.*haer.*57.8(p.354. 16; M.41.1008B); **3.** *capable μηκέτ' ἔχοντά τι χ. ὀφθῆναι τοῖς πολλοῖς* Or.*Cels.*2.64(p.186.28; M.11.897B); *τὸ γὰρ διὰ τῆς τοῦ σώματος περιβολῆς χ. τὴν θείαν δύναμιν ἐπινοῆσαι γενέσθαι* Gr.Nyss.*or.catech.*23 (p.90.6; M.45.64A); of a person, *able οὐ γὰρ ἔην χ. ἐμοῖς παθέεσσι πελάσσαι* Gr.Naz.*carm.*1.1.9.55(M.37.461A).

χωρίζ-ω, 1. *separate, divide*; **a.** Trin., in refutation of Monarchianism *καὶ λόγον τοιοῦτον καθ' αὑτὸν ζῶντα καὶ ἤτοι οὐ κεχωρισμένον τοῦ πατρὸς καὶ κατὰ τοῦτο τῷ μὴ ὑφεστάναι οὐδὲ υἱὸν τυγχάνοντα ἢ καὶ κεχωρισμένον καὶ οὐσιωμένον ἀπαγγελλέτωσαν ἡμῖν θεὸν λόγον* Or.*Jo.* 1.24(23; p.29.28; M.14.65B); in refutation of Arian doctrine of Son or Word as entirely distinct from Father, *Symb.Ant.*(345)9 ap.Ath. *syn.*26(p.253.35; M.26.733B) cit. s. *διάστημα*; *~όντων δὲ σαφῶς τὸν μονογενῆ τοῦ θεοῦ τὸν ἀχώριστον τῇ φύσει, εἰ καὶ τοῖς λόγοις οὗτοι μεμηνότες ~ουσιν, οὐ νοοῦντες οἱ δυσσεβεῖς, ὡς οὐκ ἂν χωρισθείη ποτὲ τὸ φῶς τοῦ ἡλίου, ἀλλ' ἔστιν ἐν αὐτῷ φυσικῶς* Ath.*hom.in Mt.*11:27 (M.25.215D); *τοὺς...~οντας τὸν υἱὸν καὶ ἀπαλλοτριοῦντας τὸν λόγον ἀπὸ τοῦ πατρός* id.*apol.sec.*49(p.123.14; M.25.336B); id.*Ar.*3.14(M.26. 352B); *γινώσκοντες...οὐχ ὡς ἑτεροφυῆ, ὥσπερ ἡμεῖς ἐσμεν, ~όμενός ἐστι τοῦ πατρός* id.*syn.*45(p.270.9; M.26.773A); *~εσθαι αὐτὸν* [sc. *τὸν λόγον*] *ἀπὸ τοῦ πατρὸς τῷ ἑτεροφυεῖ χωρισμῷ ib.*48(p.272.23; 777C); *Ἀστέριος...τὸν υἱὸν τοῦ θεοῦ ~ων τοῦ πατρός, ὡς καὶ υἱὸν ἀνθρώπου χωρίσειεν ἄν τις τοῦ κατὰ φύσιν πατρός* Marcell.*fr.*63 ap.Eus. *e.th.*2.19(p.123.11; M.24.944A); *εἰ γάρ τις ~ει τὸν υἱόν, τουτέστι τὸν λόγον, τοῦ παντοκράτορος θεοῦ, ἀνάγκη αὐτὸν ἢ δύο θεοὺς εἶναι νομίζειν...ἢ τὸν λόγον μὴ εἶναι θεὸν ὁμολογεῖν ib.*129(p.215.26); denied of Father ref. generation of Son *θεὸν...οὐ τὴν οὐσίαν καθ' ἥν ἐστιν εἷς, ~όμενον ἢ μεριζόμενον εἰς πλείους* Eun.*exp.fid.*1(p.254); *ἀναθεματίζομεν...τοὺς λέγοντας τὸν λόγον τοῦ θεοῦ τῇ ἐκτάσει καὶ τῇ συστολῇ ἀπὸ τοῦ πατρὸς κεχωρίσθαι* Dam.Papa *anath.*ap.Thdt.*h.e.*5.11.5(3.1037); *ὁ υἱὸς ἐκ τοῦ πατρὸς γεννᾶται, μηδόλως αὐτοῦ ~όμενος, ἀλλ' ἀεὶ ἐν αὐτῷ ὤν* ‡Cyr.*Trin.*8(6³.11B; M.77.1136B); and of H. Ghost *μισείσθωσαν οἱ ~ειν τολμῶντες τοῦ ἁγίου πνεύματος τὴν ἐνέργειαν* [sc. from Father and Son] Cyr.H.*catech.*16.3; ref. Trin. *εἰς τρεῖς ὑποστάσεις ξένας ἀλλήλων παντάπασι κεχωρισμένας διαιροῦντες* [sc. pluralistic opponents of Sabellius, likened to Marcionites] *τὴν ἁγίαν μονάδα* Dion.R.ap.Ath.*decr.*26(p.22.8; M.25.464A); *ἡ...τριὰς...συνάπτεται...ἀσυγχύτως, ὥσπερ καὶ ἀτμήτως ἡ μονὰς ~εται* Ath.*hom.in Mt.*11:27(M.25.220A); *οὔτε ~ομεν τὴν ἁγίαν τριάδα ὥς τινες· οὔτε συναλοιφήν, ὡς Σαβέλλιος, ἐργαζόμεθα* Cyr.H.*catech.*16.4; *τοῦ νοῦ ~οντος τὰ ἀχώριστα* Evagr.*h.e.*5.4(p.198.27; M.86.2796B); **b.** Christol. *ταῦτα δέ φαμεν οὐ ~οντες τὸν υἱὸν τοῦ θεοῦ ἀπὸ τοῦ Ἰησοῦ* Or.*Cels.* 2.9(p.136.30; M.11.809D); *μὴ ~ειν ἡμᾶς τὴν Ἰησοῦ ψυχὴν τοῦ πρωτοτόκου ib.*6.48(p.119.22; 1373A); *τὸν μηδέποτε κεχωρισμένον τοῦ μονογενοῦς* id.*princ.*2.6.4(p.143.22; M.11.212C); *οὐ χρὴ ἕτερον μὲν τὸν λόγον, ἕτερον δὲ Χριστὸν νοεῖν...εἰ δὲ καὶ νοοῖτο διχῶς, ἀλλ' ὡς τοῦ λόγου κεχωρισμένου* [sc. as acc. followers of Paul. Sam.] ‡Ath.*Ar.*4.31 (p.80.11; M.26.516C); *τὸ λεγόμενον* [sc. Ac.17:31]...*οὐ τὴν ὑπόστασιν ~ον τοῦ θεοῦ λόγου ἀπὸ τοῦ ἐκ Μαρίας ἀνθρώπου ib.*35(p.84.16; 521B); *δύο ἐπὶ τοῦ Χριστοῦ ὁμολογοῦμεν φύσεις ἡνωμένας ἀρρήτῳ ἑνώσει, καὶ μηδαμῶς ἀλλήλων ~ομένας ἢ συγχεομένας* Leont.H.*monoph.*(M.86. 1837A); union between Word and human nature not resolved at death of Christ *τοῦτο ἦν τὸ ἐν μνημείῳ τεθὲν ὅτε αὐτὸς* [sc. *ὁ λόγος*] *ἐπορεύθη, μὴ χωρισθεὶς αὐτοῦ* Ath.*ep.Epict.*5(p.9n.; M.26.1060A); *μήτε τῆς θεότητος τοῦ σώματος ἐν τῷ τάφῳ ἀπολιμπανομένης, μήτε τῆς ψυχῆς ἐν τῷ ᾅδῃ ~ομένης* ‡Ath.*Apoll.*2.14(M.26.1156C); *ὥστε οὐκ ἄνθρωπος θεοῦ ἐχωρίζετο...εἰ δὲ ὁ θεὸς ἐχωρίσθη τοῦ σώματος, καὶ οὕτως ἡ νέκρωσις ἐδείκνυτο, πῶς τὸ σῶμα, χωρισθὲν τοῦ ἀφθάρτου θεοῦ, τὴν ἀφθαρσίαν ἐπεδείκνυτο; ib.*2.15(1157A); *οὔτε οὖν ὁ ἡμέτερος ἐκεῖ γέγονε θάνατος, εἰ θεοῦ χωρισθέντος ἡ νέκρωσις τοῦ σώματος γέγονε. πῶς δὲ καὶ τὸ σῶμα τοῦ ἀφθάρτου θεοῦ χωρισθὲν ἐν ἀφθαρσίᾳ διέμεινεν; ib.*2.16(1160C); in anti-Apollinarian controversy *οὐδὲ γὰρ τὸν ἄνθρωπον ~ομεν τῆς θεότητος, ἀλλ' ἕνα καὶ τὸν αὐτὸν δογματίζομεν* Gr.Naz. *ep.*101(M.37.177B); *ἐπειδὴ γὰρ οὐδὲν ἕτερόν ἐστιν ὁ θάνατος εἰ μὴ διάλυσις ψυχῆς τε καὶ σώματος, πρὸς ἀμφότερα ἑαυτὸν ἑνώσας...οὐθ' ἑτέρου χωρίζεται* [sc. *ὁ λόγος*] Gr.Nyss.*Apoll.*17(M.45.1153D); *οὐκοῦν ἦν φησιν Ἀπολινάριος σάρκα ἔμψυχον καὶ ἐμπροαίρετον, ταύτην οὐδὲ τοῦ νοῦ κεχωρίσθαι ὁμολογεῖ ib.*47(1240B); Nestorian *ἀχώριστος τοῦ φαινομένου θεός· διὰ τοῦτο τοῦ μὴ ~ομένου τὴν τιμὴν οὐ ~ω. ~ω τὰς φύσεις, ἀλλ' ἑνῶ τὴν προσκύνησιν* Nest.*fr.*C 9(p.262.5)ap.CEph.(431) *act.*1(*ACO* 1.1.2 p.48.1,2); *μετὰ τὴν ἀνάληψιν οὐ δύναται καλεῖσθαι κεχωρισμένος υἱός, ἵνα μὴ δύο υἱοὺς δογματίσωμεν* id.*fr.*C 10(p.275. 4)*ib.*(p.48.6); *τὰ τῶν φύσεων ~οντες ἴδια, τὴν τῆς ἑνώσεως ἀξίαν συνάπτωμεν* id.*fr.*C 5(p.242.14); *διαιροῦντες δὲ πάλιν εἰς ὑποστάσεις δύο κεχωρισμένας τε καὶ ἀποφοιτώσας ἀλλήλων* Cyr.*ep.*50(p.97.27; 5². 167C); *θεὸν λόγον ἀνθρώπου χωρίσουσιν* Thdot.Anc.*exp.symb.*7(M.77. 1324A); **c.** of soul's separation from body at death *τὰς κεχωρισμένας ψυχὰς τῶν ἀνθρώπων* Athenag.*leg.*23.2(M.6.941B); *μένοντος ἔτι νεκροῦ τοῦ Λαζάρου σώματος, καὶ τῆς ψυχῆς κεχωρισμένης μὲν...παρακαθεζομένης δὲ τῷ σώματι* Or.*Jo.*28.6(5; p.396.5; M.14.689D); Meth.*res.* 1.57(p.319.14; M.41.1153B); *αἱ ψυχαὶ...ἐχωρίζοντο τῶν σωμάτων κατὰ τὴν ἡμέραν τῆς τελευτῆς ib.*2.8(p.343.17; 1176A); *ἐπεὶ δὲ λέγεται ἐν τῷ θανάτῳ τὸ εἶδος ~εσθαι ἀπὸ τῆς σαρκός, φέρε τὸ χωριζόμενον ποσαχῶς λέγεται ~εσθαι ἐπισκεψώμεθα. λέγεται τοίνυν ~εσθαί τι ἀπό τινος ἢ ἐνεργείᾳ καὶ ὑποστάσει, ἢ ἐπινοίᾳ, ἢ ἐνεργείᾳ μέν, οὐ μὴν καὶ ὑποστάσει. ⟨ἐνεργείᾳ μὲν καὶ ὑποστάσει⟩, ὡς εἰ πυρούς τις καὶ κριθὰς μεμιγμένα χωρίσειεν ἀπ' ἀλλήλων· ᾗ μὲν γὰρ κατὰ κίνησιν ~εται, ἐνεργείᾳ λέγεται, ᾗ δὲ χωρισθέντα ὑφέστηκεν, ὑποστάσει λέγεται κεχωρίσθαι. ἐπινοίᾳ δέ, ὅταν τὴν ὕλην ἀπὸ τῶν ποιοτήτων ~ομεν καὶ τὰς ποιότητας ἀπὸ τῆς ὕλης. ἐνεργείᾳ δέ, οὐ μὴν καὶ ὑποστάσει, ὅταν χωρισθέν τι ἀπό τινος μηκέτι ὑπάρχοι, ὑπόστασιν οὐσίας οὐκ ἔχον ib.*3.6(p.397.4ff.; M.18. 321Aff.); **2.** pass., *be exiled*, Ath.*ep.Jov.*4(M.26.820C); *depart*, from earthly life *τὸν...τοῦδε τοῦ βίου κεχωρισμένον* Clem.*str.*3.12(p.236.21; M.8.1188C); **3.** *exclude* from church, *excommunicate κεχωρισμένον τῆς ἐκκλησίας* CGangr.*can.*proem.; *τῆς ἡμετέρας κοινωνίας χωρισθέντες* CArim.*ep.Const.*1 ap.Ath.*syn.*10(p.237.19; M.26.697A); *Const. App.*2.17.4; *Apophth.Patr.*(M.65.272A); **4.** *lead away, cut off* from the faith *χ. ἑαυτοὺς ἀπὸ τῆς ἀληθείας* Ath.*decr.*1(p.2.10; M.25.417C); **5.** *remove, delete χωρίσει* [sc. *σε ὁ θεός*] *τοῦ καταλόγου τῶν ζώντων* Thdt.*Ps.*51:7(1.948).

***χωρικία, ἡ,** *rusticity, ignorance αἱρετικοὶ...ἀπὸ χ.* Thdr.Stud. *epp.*2.219(M.99.1665C).

***χωρικοβοήθεια, ἡ,** s.v.l., *local auxiliary force ἀποστέλλει...δύο στρατηγοὺς...μετὰ στρατοῦ καὶ γεωργικοῦ λαοῦ χωρικοβοηθείας* Thphn.*chron.*p.315(M.108.764B).

χωρικός, *rustic, rural*; opp. *σχολαστικός*, Mac.Aeg.*hom.*26.17 (M.34.685C); as subst., *peasant*, *A.Jo.*48(p.175.9); Jo.Mal.*chron.*7 p.179(M.97.285B); *Chron.Pasch.*p.114(M.92.299A).

***χωρικῶς,** *in rustic fashion*, Synes.*ep.*4(M.66.1337C).

χωρίς, *without*, exeg. Heb.2:9 (ref. *χωρὶς θεοῦ*, variant for *χάριτι θεοῦ*) *εἴτε δὲ 'χωρὶς θεοῦ ὑπὲρ παντὸς ἐγεύσατο θανάτου' οὐ μόνον ὑπὲρ ἀνθρώπων ἀπέθανεν, ἀλλὰ καὶ ὑπὲρ τῶν λοιπῶν λογικῶν· εἴτε 'χάριτι θεοῦ ἐγεύσατο τοῦ ὑπὲρ παντὸς θανάτου', ὑπὲρ πάντων χωρὶς θεοῦ ἀπέθανε* Or.*Jo.*1.35(40; p.45.20ff.; M.14.93A,B); *περὶ τοῦ Χριστοῦ διαλέγεται* [sc. *ὁ Παῦλος*], *οἷός τίς ἐστι, καὶ τίνα τὴν πρὸς τοὺς ἀγγέλους ἔχων διαφοράν, ἀφ' ὧν ἐξηνέχθη εἰς τὸ εἰπεῖν κατὰ τί δὲ αὐτῶν ἠλαττῶσθαι δοκεῖ, καὶ ὅτι διὰ τὸν θάνατον. ... εἰπὼν γὰρ ὅτι 'χωρὶς θεοῦ ἐγεύσατο τοῦ θανάτου', οὐδὲν πρὸς τοῦτο παραβλαβείσης τῆς θεότητος, καὶ διὰ τοῦτο ἀπὸ τῆς οἰκείας φύσεως τὴν κατὰ βραχὺ τοῦτο ἐλάττωσιν ἐδέξατο, ὥστε φαίνεσθαι ἐντεῦθεν αὐτὸν καὶ τῆς τιμῆς μετέχοντα διὰ τὴν πρὸς ἕτερον συνάφειαν, ἐπειδήπερ ἀκόλουθον ἦν τοὺς ταῦτα ἀκούοντας περιττὴν ἐν τῷ τοῦ πάθους καιρῷ νομίζειν εἶναι τοῦ θεοῦ λόγου τὴν ἐνοίκησιν, οὐδὲν τοῖς προκειμένοις συμβαλλομένην, εἴπερ δὴ χωρὶς ἐκείνου τῆς πείρας ἐγεύσατο τοῦ θανάτου, ἐπάγει 'ἔπρεπε γὰρ αὐτῷ...τὸν ἀρχηγὸν τῆς σωτηρίας αὐτῶν διὰ παθημάτων τελειῶσαι'* Thdr.Mops.*Heb.*2:9(M.66.956D–957A); *τοῦτο γὰρ εἶπεν, ὅπως 'χωρὶς θεοῦ ὑπὲρ παντὸς γεύσηται θανάτου'. μόνη, φησίν, ἡ θεία φύσις ἀνενδεής, τἄλλα δὲ πάντα τοῦ τῆς ἐνανθρωπήσεως ἐδεῖτο φαρμάκου* Thdt.*Heb.*2:9(3.557).

χωρισμός, ὁ, *separation*; **1.** in gen. *χ. δὲ τοῦ θεοῦ, θάνατος· καὶ χ. φωτός, σκότος· καὶ χ. θεοῦ ἀποβολὴ πάντων τῶν παρ' αὐτοῦ ἀγαθῶν* Iren.*haer.*5.27.2(M.7.1196B); of soul from body at death [cf. Plato *Phaedo* 67D], Clem.*str.*4.3(p.253.30; M.8.1225A); *πεπίστευται οὐ παρὰ Χριστιανοῖς καὶ Ἰουδαίοις μόνοις ἀλλὰ καὶ παρ' ἄλλοις πολλοῖς Ἑλλήνων καὶ βαρβάρων ὅτι ζῇ καὶ ὑπάρχει μετὰ τὸν ἀπὸ τοῦ σώματος χ. ἡ ἀνθρωπίνη ψυχή* Or.*Cels.*7.5(p.156.24; M.11.1425C); *ἐμποιεῖ* θάνατον, οὐ τὸν κατὰ τὸν χ. τῆς ψυχῆς ἀπὸ τοῦ σώματος, ἀλλὰ τὸν κατὰ τὸν χ. τῆς ψυχῆς ἀπὸ τοῦ θεοῦ id.*Jo.*13.23(p.247.19,20; M.14.437C); Ath.*gent.*3(M.25.9A); ref. death of Christ οὐ χ. θεότητος δηλούσης, ἀλλὰ νέκρωσιν σώματος ‡Ath.*Apoll.*2.14(M.26.1156C); ψυχῆς ἀπὸ σώματος χ. *ib.*2.15(1157A); *ib.*2.16(1160B); πευστέον αὐτῶν, ἆρά γε ἐπὶ τῷ θανάτῳ τοῦ κυρίου ἴσασι χ. τινα τινῶν φύσεων, ἢ οὐχί; εἰ μὲν οὐχί, φαντασία τε ὁ θάνατος καὶ ψευδὴς ἡ περὶ αὐτοῦ δόξα ἐν τῷ κυρίῳ· θάνατος γὰρ χ. ἐστι ψυχῆς ἀπὸ σώματος ἀναντιρρήτως· εἰ δὲ ὄντως χ. γέγονε φυσικός, πάντως καὶ κατὰ τούσδε δύο φύσεις τὰ κεχωρισμένα τῶν Χριστοῦ. ἆρα οὖν εἰ ὁμολογοῦσι τὸν θάνατον τοῦ κυρίου, καὶ δύο φύσεις αὐτοῦ τινας εἶναί ποτε δώσουσι Leont.H.*monoph.*33(M.86.1789A,B); ref. Father and Son (Arian) χωρίζεσθαι αὐτὸν [sc. τὸν λόγον] ἀπὸ τοῦ πατρὸς τῷ ἑτεροφυεῖ χ. Ath.*syn.*48(p.272.23; M.26.777C); **2.** *excommunication*, Cyr.*ep.*79(M.77.365B); **3.** *divorce* χ. γυναικός Meth.*res.*1.39(p.282.17; M.18.268B); **4.** from pass.; *a being separated, departure*, met. χ. τῆς ἁμαρτίας Clem.*str.*4.3(p.253.18; M.8.1224C); σώματός τε καὶ τῶν τούτου παθῶν ἀμετανόητος χ. *ib.*5.11(p.370.27; M.9.101B); ὁ χ. τοῦ κακοῦ Bas.*hom.in Ps.*1(1.93D; M.29.220A); sc. from earthly life, *death* κλαιόντων...ἡμῶν καὶ ἀνιωμένων ἁπάντων ἐπὶ τῷ χ. αὐτοῦ *A.Andr.*B 10(p.63.23); v. χωρίζω.

χωριστικός, **1.** *separative* χ. μὲν δυνάμει, τὸ πνεῦμα Clem.*ecl.*25(p.143.33; M.9.709C); Geo.Pis.*hex.*1406(M.92.1542A); **2.** *expressing separation* τοῖς χ. ... ῥήμασιν Gr.Nyss.*Eun.*12(1 p.378.23; M.45.1105B).

χωροβατ-έω, *walk in, tread* οὐρανὸν χ. ‡Chrys.*palm.*2(10.767E); λῃστὴς...ἤμελλε ~εῖν τὸν παράδεισον Jo.D.*hom.*4.21(M.96.620B).

χωρογραφέω, *give a local* or *geographical description of, describe* χ. ... τὸν τόπον Hesych.H.*qu.ev.*60(M.93.1448A); Evagr.*h.e.*4.31(p.180.11; M.86.2757C).

Ψ

ψάγδας, ὁ, an Egyptian unguent, Clem.*paed.*2.8(p.196.10; M.8.469B).

*__Ψαθυριανοί, οἱ__, name of certain Arians, Socr.*h.e.*5.23.12(M.67.648B); Soz.*h.e.*7.17.11(M.67.1468A); οὗτοι δέ φασι, πατὴρ ὁ θεός, ἀεὶ δὲ καὶ ὁ υἱὸς ὑπὸ τοῦ θεοῦ ἐκτισμένος· ταὐτὸν γάρ ἐστιν ἐπὶ τοῦ θεοῦ τὸ κτίσαι καὶ τὸ γεννῆσαι. τούτους οἱ Ἀντιοχεῖς Ψαθυριανοὺς ὀνομάζουσι. τὸν γὰρ τῆς αἱρέσεως ἄρχοντα λέγουσι τοιούτων ποπάνων γεγενῆσθαι δημιουργόν Thdt.*haer.*4.4(4.358); v. ψαθυροπώλης.

ψαθύριον, τό, a kind of *friable cake*, Leont.N.*v.Sym.*8.55(M.93.1737B).

*__ψαθυροπώλης, ὁ__, *seller of friable cake* ἐκαλοῦντο...οὗτοι Ψαθυριανοί, ὅτι Θεόκτιστός τις ψ., Σύρος τὸ γένος, διαπύρως τῷ λόγῳ τῷδε συνίστατο Socr.*h.e.*5.23.7(M.67.648A); Soz.*h.e.*7.17.11(M.67.1468A).

ψακάζω, *cause rain*, Eus.*Hierocl.*30.2(43; M.22.837C).

ψαλ(λ)ίδιον, τό, *scissors*, Jo.Mosch.*prat.*118(M.87.2982C); Leont.N.*v.Sym.*2.12(M.93.1684D); ψαλλίδιον *Euchol.*(pp.385f.); *ib.*(p.411).

ψαλίς, ἡ, **1.** *scissors*, Pall.*h.Laus.*11(p.33.7; M.34.1034A); **2.** *arch* οἱ ἐπὶ τῆς ψ. λίθοι ἀλλήλοις εἰσὶν αἴτιοι τοῦ μένειν Clem.*str.*8.9(p.99.17; M.9.597B); Evagr.*h.e.*2.13(p.65.2; M.86.2540B); *ib.*4.31(p.180.12f.; 2757Cf.); **3.** = ψάλιον *curb-chain* οὐδεὶς αὐτῇ ψαλίδας περιτίθησιν οὐδὲ ποδόστροφα οὐδὲ χαλινούς Chrys.*hom.34.5 in Ac.*(9.267C); **4.** *staple*, on a door οἱ ἀγκωνίσκοι καὶ οἱ μοχλοὶ διὰ τῶν δακτυλίων, ἤτοι τῶν ψ., δικνούμενοι ἐδέσμενον ἀσφαλῶς πᾶσαν τὴν σκηνήν Cosm.Ind.*top.*5(M.88.204B).

*__ψαλίτης, ὁ__, a pest which damages crops, perh. *red spider* (cf. ψύλλα, ψύλλος, *LS*), *Euchol.*(p.555).

ψάλλ-ω, [aor. ἔψαλα, Pall.*h.Laus.*22(p.72.7; M.34.1082A); Leont.N.*v.Sym.*14(M.93.1688D); *Const.Stud.*27(M.99.1713B)]; *sing with musical accompaniment*;

A. in gen. κἂν πρὸς κιθάραν ἐθελήσῃς ἢ λύραν ᾄδειν τε καὶ ~ειν, μῶμος οὐκ ἔστιν Clem.*paed.*2.4(p.183.28; M.8.444B); ~οντες γοῦν τὸ ὑπέρτονον τῆς σεμνότητος ἐμμελῶς ἀνίεμεν id.*str.*1.1(p.12.3; M.8.705A); *ib.*6.11(p.477.1; M.9.312A).

B. esp., *sing psalms*; **1.** in gen. χρὴ...~ειν κατὰ τὴν περὶ τῶν ἠθῶν διέξοδον Or.*comm.in Eph.*5:19(p.565); οὐκ εἴ τις τῷ στόματι προφέρει τὰ τοῦ ψαλμοῦ ῥήματα, οὗτος ~ει τῷ κυρίῳ· ἀλλ' ὅσοι ἀπὸ καρδίας καθαρᾶς ἀναπέμπουσι τὰς ψαλμῳδίας καὶ ὅσοι εἰσὶν ὅσιοι... οὗτοι δύνανται ~ειν τῷ θεῷ τοῖς ῥυθμοῖς τοῖς πνευματικοῖς ἁρμοζόντως ἀκολουθοῦντες Bas.*hom.in Ps.*29(1.127A; M.29.312C); οἱ μετὰ συνέσεως ~οντες τὴν τοῦ πνεύματος καλοῦσι χάριν Chrys.*exp.in Ps.*41(5.132B); ἔξεστι κα ἰχωρὶς φωνῆς ~ειν, τῆς διανοίας ἔνδον ἠχούσης. οὐ γὰρ ἀνθρώποις ~ομεν, ἀλλὰ θεῷ *ib.*(134A); τῇ καρδίᾳ ~ει ὁ μὴ μόνον τὴν γλῶτταν κινῶν, ἀλλὰ καὶ τὸν νοῦν εἰς τὴν τῶν λεγομένων κατανόησιν διεγείρων Thdt.*Eph.*5:19(3.433); fig. ὁ σωτὴρ...~ων παρακαλεῖ [sc. τοὺς ἀνθρώπους] Clem.*prot.*1(p.8.30; M.8.64C); **2.** in church services, *Const.App.*2.57.6; by a cantor, *Lit.*ap.*Const.App.*8.14.1; confined to authorized persons, Gel.Cyz.*h.e.*2.31.4(M.85.1316D); μὴ δεῖν πλέον τῶν κανονικῶν ψαλτῶν, τῶν ἐπὶ τὸν ἄμβωνα ἀναβαινόντων καὶ ἀπὸ διφθέρας ~όντων, ἑτέρους τινὰς ~ειν ἐν ἐκκλησίᾳ CLaod.*can.*15; originally allowed to women, but later disputed, Isid.Pel.*epp.*1.90(M.78.244Dff.); at eucharist, Cyr.H.*catech.*23.20(M.33.1124B); **3.** at other times καὶ παρὰ πότον καθήκει ~ειν αὐτῷ τῶν αὐτοῦ μεταλαμβάνοντας κτισμάτων Clem.*paed.*2.4(p.184.3; M.8.444B); ἐν παντὶ καιρῷ ~ειν ἔξεστι κατὰ δύναμιν...κἂν χειροτέχνης ᾖς, ἐν ἐργαστηρίῳ καθήμενος καὶ ἐργαζόμενος, δυνήσῃ ~ειν Chrys.*exp.in Ps.*41(5.133E); **4.** c. dat. τῷ θεῷ...~ειν Just.*dial.*74.3(M.6.649B); Clem.*prot.*1(p.6.14; M.8.60A); id.*paed.*2.4(p.184.3; M.8.444C); c. acc. ~ωμεν ὁμοῦ θεὸν εἰρήνης id.*paed.hymn.*64(p.292; 684B); trans., *sing* ψ. παλινῳδίαν id.*paed.*3.11(p.280.30; 660A); ψ. καὶ ὕμνους καὶ εὐχαριστίας Eus.*h.e.*8.9.5(M.20.760D); ψαλθῆναι τὸ τρισάγιον *Chron.Pasch.*p.384(M.92.984B); *ib.*p.390(1001B,C); *Const.Stud.*36(M.99.1717D); *ib.*37(1720A); **5.** met. ~ούσῃ συνᾴδοντες προφητείᾳ Clem.*paed.*1.1(p.90.6; M.8.249A); ὃν κιθάρῃ ~ουσα θεηγόρος ἔννεπε μολπή Nonn.*par.Jo.*19:24(M.43.904A); **6.** *utter in a psalm, compose a psalm* τούτους [sc. τοὺς λόγους] Δαβὶδ μὲν ἔψαλλεν Just.*dial.*29.2(M.6.537A); ὁ Δαβίδ, τουτέστι τὸ πνεῦμα τὸ δι' αὐτοῦ, ἄμφω περιλαβὼν ἐπὶ τοῦ αὐτοῦ ~ει θεοῦ Clem.*paed.*1.9(p.141.13; M.8.353C); id.*str.*3.4(p.211.4; M.8.1137B); Ath.*decr.*9(p.8.23; M.25.432A); ref. psalms as divinely inspired 'ὁ οὐρανὸς θρόνος σου' τὸ ἅγιον πνεῦμα ἔψαλλεν Clem.*paed.*1.8(p.132.24; 337B); *ib.*2.4(p.182.19; 441A); *ib.*10(p.225.9; 533A); pres. ptcpl., *the psalmist*, of David, Ath.*Ar.*1.46(M.26.105C); id.*ep.Serap.*1.9(M.26.553A); Vict.*Mc.*4:3(p.303.2); Cyr.*hom.pasch.*10(5^2.126B).

ψάλμα, τό, *tune played on a stringed instrument*, Gr.Naz.*carm.*2.1.12.618(M.37.1211A).

*__ψαλμικός__, **1.** *in a psalm*; of a passage or verse, Chrysipp.*enc. in BMV* 2(p.338.33); Dion.Ar.*e.h.*7.3.2(M.3.556C); Jo.Mosch.*prat.*proem.(M.87.2852B); neut. as subst., Chrysipp.*enc.in Thdr.*(p.59.17); **2.** *of the nature of a psalm* ὕμνον τινὰ ψ. Eutych.*pasch.*8(M.86.2401A).

*__ψαλμικῶς__, *in the language of the Psalms*, Gr.Nyss.*Apoll.*(M.45.1141B); Thdr.Stud.*cant.*15.2(p.369).

*__ψαλμοκίνητος__, *moved by psalms*, Geo.Pis.*hex.*1878(M.92.1578).

*__ψαλμολογέω__, *compose psalms*, Gr.Naz.*ep.*101(M.37.193A).

*__ψαλμολογία, ἡ__, *psalmody*, Bas.*hom.in Ps.*29(1.127A; M.29.312C).

ψαλμός, ὁ, **A.** *song sung to the harp, psalm*; **1.** of Psalms of David; **a.** in gen. ὁ ψ. ἐμμελής ἐστιν εὐλογία καὶ σώφρων· 'ᾠδὴν πνευματικήν' ὁ ἀπόστολος εἴρηκε τὸν ψ. Clem.*paed.*2.4(p.184.4; M.8.444C); ψ. λόγος ἐστὶ μουσικός, ὅταν εὐρύθμως κατὰ τοὺς ἁρμονικοὺς λόγους πρὸς τὸ ὄργανον κρούηται Bas.*hom.in Ps.*29(1.124C; M.29.305C); opp. ᾠδή: πρᾶξιν μὲν ὁ ψ., θεωρίαν δὲ ἡ ᾠδὴ δηλοῖ Ath.*fr.Pss comm.*(M.27.576B); ψ. μὲν γάρ ἐστιν, ἡ διὰ τοῦ ὀργάνου τοῦ μουσικοῦ μελῳδία· ᾠδὴ δὲ ἡ διὰ στόματος γενομένη τοῦ μέλους μετὰ τῶν ῥημάτων ἐκφώνησις Gr.Nyss.*Pss.titt.*B 3(M.44.493B); **b.** reason for musical accompaniment τὸ ἐκ τῆς μελῳδίας τερπνὸν τοῖς δόγμασιν ἐγκατέμιξεν, ἵνα τῷ προσηνεῖ καὶ λείῳ τῆς ἀκοῆς τὸ ἐκ τῶν λόγων ὠφέλιμον λανθανόντως ὑποδεξώμεθα...διὰ τοῦτο τὰ ἐναρμόνια ταῦτα μέλη τῶν ψ. ἡμῖν ἐπινενόηται, ἵνα...τῷ μὲν δοκεῖν μελῳδῶσι, τῇ δὲ ἀληθείᾳ τὰς ψυχὰς ἐκπαιδεύωνται Bas.*hom.in Ps.*1(1.90D; M.29.212B); **c.** divine inspiration of psalms τὸ πνεῦμα τὸ ἅγιον, διὰ τῶν ψ. λέγον Ath.*Ar.*2.50(M.26.253B); *ib.*2.52(257B); *ib.*2.57(268C); **d.** their purpose ἐν τοῖς ψ. καὶ πῶς δεῖ φέρειν τὰς θλίψεις, καὶ τί θλιβόμενον δεῖ λέγειν, καὶ τί μετὰ τὰς θλίψεις, καὶ πῶς ἕκαστος δοκιμάζεται, καὶ τίνες οἱ λόγοι τῶν ἐλπιζόντων ἐπὶ κύριον, γέγραπται καὶ κεχάρακται...καὶ τί δεῖ λέγειν εὐχαριστοῦντας διδάσκουσιν οἱ ψ. id.*ep.Marcell.*10(M.27.21A); ψ. γαλήνη ψυχῶν, βραβευτὴς εἰρήνης, τὸ θορυβοῦν καὶ κυμαῖνον τῶν λογισμῶν καταστέλλων. μαλάσσει μὲν γὰρ τῆς ψυχῆς τὸ θυμούμενον, τὸ δὲ ἀκόλαστον σωφρονίζει. ψ. φιλίας συναγωγός· ἕνωσις διεστώτων· ἐχθραινόντων διαλλακτήριον. ... ψ. δαιμόνων φυγαδευτήριον· τῆς τῶν ἀγγέλων βοηθείας ἐπαγωγή· ὅπλον ἐν φόβοις νυκτερινοῖς, ἀνάπαυσις κόπων ἡμερινῶν· νηπίοις ἀσφάλεια· ἀκμάζουσιν ἐγκαλλώπισμα· πρεσβυτέροις παρηγορία· γυναιξὶ κόσμος ἁρμοδιώτατος. τὰς ἐρημίας οἰκίζει, τὰς ἀγορὰς σωφρονίζει· εἰσαγομένοις στοιχείωσις, προκοπτόντων αὔξησις, τελειουμένων στήριγμα, ἐκκλησίας φωνή. οὗτος τὰς ἑορτὰς φαιδρύνει, οὗτος τὴν κατὰ θεὸν λύπην δημιουργεῖ. ... ψ. τὸ τῶν ἀγγέλων ἔργον, τὸ οὐράνιον πολίτευμα, τὸ πνευματικὸν θυμίαμα Bas.*hom.in Ps.*1(1.90Eff.; M.29.212Cff.); ἵνα μὴ πορνικὰ ᾄσματα οἱ δαίμονες εἰσάγοντες, ἅπαντα ἀνατρέψωσι, τοὺς ψ.

ἐπετείχισεν ὁ θεὸς ὥστε ὁμοῦ καὶ ἡδονὴν τὸ πρᾶγμα καὶ ὠφέλειαν εἶναι Chrys.*exp.in Ps*.41(5.132A); καὶ γὰρ διὰ τοῦτο τοὺς ψ. ἡμῖν ᾖσεν ὁ μακάριος ἐκεῖνος, μᾶλλον δὲ ἡ τοῦ πνεύματος χάρις, οὐχ ἵνα τὰ ῥήματα λέγωμεν μόνον, ἀλλ' ἵνα καὶ δι' αὐτῶν τῶν ἔργων αὐτοὺς μελετῶμεν *ib*.(138B); μυρίων ἀγαθῶν αἴτιον ὁ ψ.· ἀφίστησι γὰρ τὴν διάνοιαν τῆς γῆς, καὶ πτεροῖ τὴν ψυχήν, κουφίζει καὶ μεταρσίους ποιεῖ *ib*.146(479C); ἡ τοῦ ψ. καὶ τῆς ᾠδῆς τῆς πνευματικῆς δύναμις...οὐ...μόνον τοὺς παρόντας ἡμᾶς, ἀλλὰ καὶ τὸν τελευτήσαντα τοῖς ζῶσιν ἀνέμιξε id.*hom.div*.5.2(12.349C); **e.** sung in church services, and at prayer by ascetics τοσούτους δὲ ψ. εἰπέ, ὅσους δύνῃ στήκουσα εἰπεῖν· ψαλμὸν εὐχῇ καὶ γονυκλισία ἐπιτελείσθω...μετὰ δὲ τρεῖς ψαλμοὺς λέγε τὸ ἀλληλούϊα Ath.*virg*.20(p.55.21–24; M.28.276C); πάντες κοινῇ ὡς ἐξ ἑνὸς στόματος...τὸν τῆς ἐξομολογήσεως ψ. ἀναφέρουσι τῷ κυρίῳ Bas.*ep*.207(3.311C; M.32.764B); τὸν ἐπιλύχνιον ψ. *Const.App*.8.35.2; only Psalms of David to be used οὐ δεῖ ἰδιωτικοὺς ψ. λέγεσθαι ἐν τῇ ἐκκλησίᾳ CLaod.*can*.59; not to be said without a lection between them, *ib*.17; at eucharist, while people are communicating ψ. δὲ λεγέσθω λγ' ἐν τῷ μεταλαμβάνειν πάντας τοὺς λοιποὺς *Lit*.ap.*Const.App*.8.13.16; cf.Chrys.*exp.in Ps*.144(5.466E); at funerals οἱ γὰρ ψ. ἐπιθυμίας σύμβολον...ἐπεὶ οὖν ἐπιθυμίας ἐσμὲν πεπληρωμένοι, διὰ τοῦτο ἐπὶ τοῖς νεκροῖς ψ. θαρρεῖν ὑπὲρ τῆς τελευτῆς παρακελευομένοις Chrys.*pan.Bern*.3(2.638E); on other occasions θυσίαι μὲν αὐτῷ [sc. τῷ γνωστικῷ] εὐχαί τε καὶ αἶνοι καὶ...ψ. δὲ καὶ ὕμνοι παρὰ τὴν ἑστίασιν πρό τε τῆς κοίτης Clem.*str*.7.7(p.37.4; M.9.469B); ἐπειδὴ γὰρ ὡς τὰ πολλὰ ἐν συμποσίοις ὁ διάβολος ἐφεδρεύει μέθην καὶ ἀδηφαγίαν ἔχων αὐτῷ συμμαχοῦσαν, καὶ γέλωτα ἄτακτον, καὶ ψυχὴν ἀνειμένην, μάλιστα τότε δεῖ καὶ πρὸ τραπέζης, καὶ μετὰ τράπεζαν, ἐπιτειχίζειν αὐτῷ τὴν ἀπὸ τῶν ψ. ἀσφάλειαν, καὶ κοινῇ μετὰ τῆς γυναικὸς καὶ τῶν παίδων ἀναστάντας ἀπὸ τοῦ συμποσίου, τοὺς ἱεροὺς ᾄδειν ὕμνους τῷ θεῷ Chrys.*hom.in Ps*.41(5.132D); **f.** plur., the *Book of Psalms*, Clem.*str*.5.4(p.341.10; M.9.44B); Or.*princ*.3.1.6(p.201.17; M.11.256B); cf.Bas.*hom.in Ps*.1(1.91C; M.29.213B); **2.** of other sacred songs or hymns, *A.Thom*.A 108(p.219.20); ψ. δὲ ὅσοι καὶ ᾠδαὶ ἀδελφῶν ἀπ' ἀρχῆς ὑπὸ πιστῶν γραφεῖσαι τὸν λόγον τοῦ θεοῦ τὸν Χριστὸν ὑμνοῦσιν θεολογοῦντες †Hipp.*Artem*.ap.Eus.*h.e*.5.28.5(M.20.512C); ψ. δὲ τοὺς μὲν εἰς τὸν κύριον ἡμῶν Ἰησοῦν Χριστὸν παύσας [sc. Paul of Samosata] ὡς δὴ νεωτέρους καὶ νεωτέρων ἀνδρῶν συγγράμματα Malch.*ep*.ap.eund.7.30.10(713A).

B. a musical instrument, s.v.l. εἶχον δὲ ἐξ ψ. καὶ δεκάχορδον κιθάραν *T.Job* 14(p.111.22).

***ψαλμῳδ-έω**, *sing psalms* ~εῖν γυναῖκας παρασκευάζων [sc. Paul of Samosata] Malch.*ep*.ap.Eus.*h.e*.7.30.10(M.20.713B); τῆς ~ουμένης γραφῆς Gr.Nyss.*v.Macr*.(p.373.22; M.46.961D); Socr.*h.e*.3.18.3(M.67.425C).

ψαλμῳδία, ἡ, 1. *singing of psalms* ἡ εἰς θεὸν δι' εὐχαριστίας καὶ ψ. γενέσθω φιλοφροσύνη Clem.*paed*.2.4(p.183.18; M.8.444B); τὸ μέγιστον τῶν ἀγαθῶν τὴν ἀγάπην ἡ ψ. παρέχεται, οἱονεὶ σύνδεσμόν τινα πρὸς τὴν ἕνωσιν τὴν συνῳδίαν ἐπινοήσασα Bas.*hom.in Ps*.96(1.90E; M.29.212D); γίνεται γὰρ καὶ ὁ ἀὴρ ἅγιος ἀπὸ ψ. Chrys.*terr.mot*.(2.718C); liturg., Eus.*h.e*.10.3.3(M.20.848B); *Const.App*.2.54.1; Epiph.*haer*.80.3(p.489.22; M.42.764A); διὰ τοῦτο μετὰ τὰς ψ. ὕμνοι, ἅτε τελειότερόν τι πρᾶγμα Chrys.*hom.9.2 in Col*.(11.393E); at funerals, id.*hom.62.5 in Jo*.(8.374E); Jo.Mosch.*prat*.88(M.87.2945C); *Chron.Pasch*.p.293(M.92.733B); **2.** *composing of psalms*; Nepos, Dion.Al.ap.Eus.*h.e*.7.24.4(M.20.693A); **3.** *psalm* ἔν τινι προοιμίῳ τῆς ψ. Gr.Nyss.*Eun*.1(1 p.121.13; M.45.356D); Cyr.*Ps*.7:15(M.69.756A).

ψαλμῳδός, ὁ, *psalmist*, Clem.*prot*.8(p.61.23; M.8.192B); Hipp.*haer*.8.17(p.237.11; M.16.3366A); Gr.Nyss.*v.Mos*.1(M.44.300C).

***ψαλταναγνώστης, ὁ,** *psalm-reader* or *-singer*, member of a minor order lower than that of sub-deacon, Gennad.*fr*.(p.83.21); *MAMA* 6.237(c. A.D. 600); v. ψάλτης.

ψαλτήριον, τό, 1. *stringed instrument, psaltery, harp*, fig. ἡ γλῶττα τὸ ψ. κυρίου Clem.*paed*.2.4(p.182.22; M.8.441B); Max.*myst*.(M.91.676A); **2.** *the Book of Psalms*, Hipp.*haer*.5.8(p.92.2; M.16.3143B); Epiph.*mens*.23(M.43.277D); πάντα τὸν προάγεσθαι μέλλοντα εἰς τὸν τῆς ἐπισκοπῆς βαθμὸν πάντως τὸ ψ. γινώσκειν CNic.(787)*can*.2; in concrete sense, *psalter* τὸ ψ. ἔτι κατέχουσαν ἐν ταῖς χερσὶ Ath.*ep.encycl*.4(p.173.18; M.25.232B); id.*virg*.12(p.46.7; M.28.265A).

ψάλτης, ὁ, *one who sings psalms in church, cantor*, duties and regulations, CLaod.*can*.15 cit. s. ψάλλω; τῶν εἰς κλῆρον παρελθόντων ἀγάμων κελεύομεν βουλομένους γαμεῖν ἀναγνώστας καὶ ψ. μόνους *Can.App*.26; εἴ τις...ψ. τὴν ἁγίαν τεσσαρακοστὴν οὐ νηστεύει ἢ τετράδα ἢ παρασκευήν, καθαιρείσθω *ib*.69; not allowed to baptize, *Const.App*.3.11.1; ἐπειδὴ ἔν τισιν ἐπαρχίαις συγκεχώρηται τοῖς ἀναγνώσταις καὶ ψ. γαμεῖν, ὥρισεν ἡ ἁγία σύνοδος μὴ ἐξεῖναί τινα αὐτῶν ἑτερόδοξον γυναῖκα λαμβάνειν CChalc.*can*.14.

ψαλτῳδός, ὁ, = foreg., *Const.App*.2.28.5; ὑπηρέτας δὲ καὶ ψ. καὶ ἀναγνώστας καὶ πυλωροὺς...μονογάμους εἶναι κελεύομεν *ib*.6.17.2; in OT, Cyr.*Is*.3.4(2.498A); Thdt.*qu.in 1Par*.(1.556); id.*Ps*.26:5(1.770).

***ψαμαθηδόν,** *like sand*, i.e. *in great numbers*, *Orac.Sib*.5.97.

ψαμμαῖος, *of sand*, Leont.H.*Nest*.1(M.86.405D); neut. plur. as subst., *sand*, Sophr.H.*v.Cyr.et Jo*.29(M.87.3416C).

***ψαφαρῶς,** *on sandy soil*, Cosm.Mel.*schol*.36 *in carm*.24.2(M.38.446).

ψεκτῶς, *culpably*, Or.*hom.4.4 in Jer*.(p.27.4; M.13.289D); id.*Jo*.20.25(21; p.360.17; M.14.629C).

***ψελιοτρύπης, ὁ,** *a ring which pierces* the nose, Hyper.*mon*.(M.79.1489A).

ψελιόω, med., *put on an armlet* ψελιούμενον...γύναιον subject of statue by Praxiteles, Tat.*orat*.34(p.36.20; σπιλούμενον M.6.877A).

ψέλλιον, τό, *ring*; securing pierced lips, Ath.*v.Anton*.24(M.26.880B); for shackling a horse ἵππῳ δυσηνίῳ ψέλλια...ἐπιτιθεὶς Chrys.*hom.36.2 in Jo*.(8.209B).

ψέλλισμα, τό, *inarticulate speech*; of a child's attempts at talking; plur., Gr.Nyss.*v.Ephr*.(M.46.849C); Olymp.*Job* 21:8(M.93.225C); Jo.D.*hom*.2.1(M.96.576C); met. ψ., λέγω δὴ Μωσαϊκὰ καὶ προφητικὰ τοῦ λόγου αἰνίγματα Gr.Nyss.*imag*.(M.44.1337D).

ψελλισμός, ὁ, 1. = ψέλλισμα Jo.Eub.*innoc*.4(M.96.1505D); of the aged, Gr.Nyss.*Pulch*.(M.46.869B); met. τὸν Ἀθηναίων ψ. Tat.*orat*.26(p.28.17; M.6.864A); **2.** *slowness of speech*, of one teaching children, Chrys.*anom*.10.2(1.531C).

***ψευδαββᾶς, ὁ,** *false monk*, Leont.N.*v.Sym*.7.46(M.93.1725D ψευδο-); Thphn.*chron*.p.277(M.108.685C); *ib*.p.319(772C).

ψευδάδελφος, ὁ, *false brother, pretended Christian*, Polyc.*ep*.6.3; *Const.App*.2.37.5.

ψευδαλέος, *false, counterfeit*, Nonn.*par.Jo*.7:3(M.43.805A).

***ψευδαληθής,** *falsely true*; epithet coined to describe Severus, Thdr.Raith.*praep*.(p.197.20; M.91.1500B).

***ψευδαπάτη, ἡ,** *lying deceit*, Ammon.*Ac*.27:31–32(M.85.1601C).

***ψευδαπάτης, ὁ,** *lying deceiver*, *Orac.Sib*.2.144,166; as adj., *ib*.2.266; *ib*.14.260.

ψευδαπόστολος, ὁ, *false apostle*, Just.*dial*.35.3(M.6.552A); ἀπὸ τῶν ἑπτὰ αἱρέσεων...ψευδόχριστοι, ψευδοπροφῆται, ψ., οἵτινες ἐμέρισαν τὴν ἕνωσιν τῆς ἐκκλησίας Heges.ap.Eus.*h.e*.4.22.6(M.20.381A); διὰ τῶν λοιπῶν ψ. ἐνήργει ὁ διάβολος *Const.App*.6.9.6.

***ψευδαποφάσκω,** *deny falsely*, Clem.*str*.5.1(p.333.20; M.9.25B).

***ψευδαρέσκεια, ἡ,** *feigned obsequiousness*, ‡Meth.*Sym.et Ann*.10(M.18.373B).

***ψευδεορταστικός,** *falsely called festal*; of a sermon or epistle, Jo.D.*jej*.tit.(M.94.77A).

***ψευδέπεια, ἡ,** *falsehood*, Cyr.*hom.pasch*.14(5^2.192C).

ψευδεπέω, *speak falsely, lie*, Cyr.*ador*.6(1.186B).

ψευδεπίγραφος, *with false superscription* or *title, not genuine* εἴ τις τὰ ψ. τῶν ἀσεβῶν βιβλία ὡς ἅγια ἐπὶ τῆς ἐκκλησίας δημοσιεύει...καθαιρείσθω *Can.App*.60; Jo.D.*disp*.2(M.96.1337A); neut. plur. as subst., Serap.Ant.ap.Eus.*h.e*.6.12.3(M.20.545A).

***ψευδεπίπλαστος,** *feigned* ἀρετήν *Schol*.7 in Jo.Clim.*scal*.6(M.88.801B).

***ψευδεπίσκοπος, ὁ,** *pretended bishop*; of Marcionites, Adam.*dial*.1.8(p.18.1; M.11.1729B); of a follower of Sev. Ant., Max.*opusc*.(M.91.49C); of an iconoclast, Thphn.*chron*.p.343(M.108.825B).

***ψευδεργία, ἡ,** *deceitful action*, Clem.*paed*.3.4(p.252.14; M.8.593B).

***ψευδερημίτης, ὁ,** *pretended hermit*, ‡Jo.D.*ep.Thphl*.17(M.95.368B); Thphn.*chron*.p.413(M.108.981A).

***ψευδευλάβεια, ἡ,** *pretended piety*, Jo.Clim.*scal*.18(M.88.933C).

ψευδευλαβής, *with pretended piety*, Ephr.3.137F.

ψευδηγορέω, *falsify*, Epiph.*haer*.39.9(p.78.17; M.41.673D); *ib*.42.3(p.99.2; 700C).

***ψευδηγόρημα, τό,** *lie, falsehood*, Cyr.*inc.unigen*.(5^1.688A); id.*Os*.112(3.144A); id.*dial.Trin*.3(5^1.462B).

ψευδηγορία, ἡ, *untruth, deceptive statement*; of Gnost. theol. statements, Iren.*haer*.1.9.5(M.7.549A); of Artemon's doctrine, Eus.*h.e*.5.28.2(M.20.512B); τὴν...τοῦ Μαρκίωνος ἐπινενοημένην ψ. Epiph.*haer*.42.10(p.106.9; M.41.709A); of Devil's statements, *A.Thom*.A 32(p.149.15); at Temptation, Eust.*engast*.10(p.31.20; M.18.633B).

ψευδηγόρος, *speaking falsely, lying*; of persons, Adam.*dial*.1.13(p.30.15; M.11.1740B); Pall.*h.Laus*.141(M.34.1242D); Cyr.*inc.unigen*.(5^1.680E); of abstracts, Eus.*h.e*.6.19.11(M.20.568B); Epiph.*haer*.42.12(p.166.10; M.41.750A); *ib*.66.63(p.103.2; M.42.128B).

***ψευδηγόρως,** *falsely, in a lying manner*, ‡Gr.Naz.*Chr.pat*.2326(M.38.318A).

ψευδήμων, *false*, Nonn.*par.Jo*.8:44(M.43.820C); *ib*.18:25(893B).

ψευδιερεύς, ὁ, *pretended priest*, *Can.App.*47; ‡Jo.D.*ep.Thphl.*14 M.95.361D).

***ψευδοβραχμᾶνες, οἱ,** *pretended Brahmins*, Epiph.*exp.fid.*10 (p.509.27; M.42.797C).

***ψευδογνωσία, ἡ,** *false knowledge*, Esaias *or.*28.1(p.194); *Schol.*in Jo.Clim.*scal.*8(M.88.836B).

***ψευδογνωστικός,** *falsely claiming knowledge*, of a Gnostic Ἰουστίνου τοῦ ψ. Hipp.*haer.*5.28(p.133.25; M.16.3203C).

ψευδογραφ-έω, 1. *depict falsely*, *Orac.Sib.*3.430; Clem.*str.*6.7(p.460.8; M.9.277C); met., ἐψευδογραφημένας δαιμόνων εἰκόνας Eus.*l.C.*5 (p.204.4; M.20.1336B); **2.** *prove falsely* οὐ τὸ τυχὸν τῶν ψευδομένων ἐν γεωμετρικοῖς θεωρήμασι ~ούμενόν τις ἂν λέγοι Or.*Cels.*proem.5 (p.54.24; M.11.648C).

ψευδογραφία, ἡ, *false statement in writing*, Pall.*v.Chrys.*18(p.113.27; M.47.63).

ψευδογράφος, ὁ, *writer of falsehoods*, *Orac.Sib.*3.419.

***ψευδοδιάκονος, ὁ,** *false deacon*, Max.*opusc.*(M.91.173B).

***ψευδοδιδακτέω,** *teach false things*; pass., Chrys.*fr.in Pr.*23:31 (M.64.732A).

***ψευδοδιδασκαλία, ἡ,** *false teaching*, Polyc.*ep.*7.2; Taras.*ep.*1(M.98.1432A).

ψευδοδιδάσκαλος, ὁ, *false teacher*, Just.*dial.*82.1(M.6.669B); Cyr.*Os.*6.139(3.172E); Hesych.H.*fr.Ps.*1:1(M.93.1180B).

ψευδόδοξος, *holding a false opinion* or *notion*, *M.Just.*2.3(p.15.28; M.6.1568A); Athenag.*leg.*27.2(M.6.953A).

***ψευδοέπεια, ἡ,** *false statement, lie*, Cyr.*ador.*6(1.183F); id.*Abac.*35 (3.549E); id.*dial.Trin.*6(5^1.617E).

ψευδοεπέω, *speak falsely, lie* ἀμήχανον...ψευδοεπῆσαι θεόν Cyr.*Is.*1.1(2.1C); Sophr.H.*v.Cyr.et Jo.*32(M.87.3420B); Thdr.Stud.*epp.*1.49 (M.99.1088D).

***ψευδοεπής,** *speaking falsely, lying*, Cyr.*ador.*6(1.187B); id.*Os.*99 (3.131D); id.*dial.Trin.*2(5^1.437E).

***ψευδόθεος, ὁ,** *false god*; of pagan deities, Ath.*gent.*15(M.25.32C); *ib.*25(49A); id.*inc.*30.5(M.25.148D).

***ψευδοϊουδαῖος, ὁ,** *false Jew*, ‡Ign.*Trall.*10.

***ψευδοκατάνυξις, ἡ,** *pretended compunction*, Anast.S.*qu.et resp.*16(M.89.476D).

ψευδοκατηγορία, ἡ, *false accusation*, Cyr.*Jo.*7(4.683A).

***ψευδοκλοπή, ἡ,** *fraud*, Ephr.2.379B.

***ψευδολατρεία (ψευδολατρία), ἡ,** *false worship*, Cyr.*ador.*10(1.354B); id.*Os.*1(3.8A); id.*Jo.*1.5(4.44C); -ιά, id.*Juln.*5(6^2.167C).

ψευδολογέω, med., *speak falsely, spread false reports*, Just.*2apol.*13.1(M.6.465B).

***ψευδομαντεία (ψευδομαντία), ἡ,** *false prophecy*, -ία, Cyr.*ador.*6(1.183A); -εία, id.*Os.*100(3.132B); *ib.*44(75E).

ψευδομαρτυρ-έω, *bear false witness*; pass., *have false witness borne against one* Χριστὸς ~ούμενος Or.*Cels.*proem.1(p.52.1,11; M.11.641A,644A); id.*hom.14.2 in Jer.*(p.107.15; M.13.405C).

***ψευδομονάζω,** *be a pretended monk*, Pall.*v.Chrys.*6(p.34.6; M.47.21) = Geo.Al.*v.Chrys.*36(p.207.10).

***ψευδομόναχος, ὁ,** *false monk*, Nil.*epp.*3.119(M.79.437C).

ψευδομοτέω, *commit perjury*, Cyr.*Juln.*6(6^2.187D).

***ψευδομυθέω,** *tell a false tale, lie*, Cyr.*ador.*1(1.42C); id.*Jo.*9.1 (4.808B); id.*hom.pasch.*9(5^2.119B).

***ψευδομυθία, ἡ,** *telling of a false tale, lying*, Cyr.*ador.*6(1.185A); id.*Is.*3.1(2.378A); id.*Nest.*2.8(p.46.6; 6^1.50D).

***ψευδομωυσῆς, ὁ,** *one pretending to be Moses*, Socr.*h.e.*7.38.11(M.67.825D).

***ψευδόπατρις,** *claiming a country not one's own*, *Orac.Sib.*3.420; *ib.*11.40.

ψευδοποιέω, 1. *misrepresent*, Or.*Cels.*1.32(p.84.1; M.11.721A); *ib.*1.22(p.73.6; 700B); c. ὅτι *ib.*4.89(p.361.9; 1165B); **2.** *deceive*, Clem.*paed.*3.4(p.252.12; M.8.593B).

ψευδοποιΐα, ἡ, *falsification*, of women's make-up τοῦ προσώπου τὴν ψ. Clem.*paed.*3.2(p.243.3; M.8.572C).

***ψευδοποιμήν, ὁ,** *false shepherd*, Pall.*v.Chrys.*4(p.24.29; M.47.16); Cyr.*Mich.*48(3.437D); of Nestorius, id.*ep.*49(5^2.158A).

***ψευδοπρεσβύτερος, ὁ,** *false priest*, Pall.*v.Chrys.*4(p.27.7; M.47.17).

***ψευδοπρεσβύτης, ὁ,** *false elder*, Didym.*Trin.*1.20(M.39.373A).

***ψευδοπροφητεία, ἡ,** *false prophecy* τῶν τῆς Μαξιμίλλης ψ. Eus.*h.e.*5.16.18(M.20.472A); Epiph.*haer.*48.3(p.223.16; M.41.860A); Cyr.*Jo.*5(4.449E); ψ. Μοντανοῦ *Chron.Pasch.*p.263(M.92.641B).

ψευδοπροφητεύω, *utter false prophecy*, *Ascens.Is.*3.1(p.88); *ib.*3.7 (p.90); Cyr.*Jo.*5(4.449E); Barth.Edess.*Agar.*(M.104.1432A).

ψευδοπροφήτης, ὁ, *false prophet*; **1.** in OT, Clem.*str.*1.21(p.73.4; M.8.841A); Or.*fr.1 in Lc.*(p.3.10; M.17.312A); Cyr.*Os.*101(3.133A); **2.** in Church, *Did.*11.5,6; Heges.ap.Eus.*h.e.*4.22.6(M.20.381A) cit. s. ψευδαπόστολος; †Bas.*bapt.*1.14(2.639E; M.31.1549C); of Montanists, Clem.*str.*1.17(p.55.13; M.8.800C); of Mohammed, Thphn.*chron.*p.276 (M.108.684B).

***ψευδοπροφητικός,** *of false prophecy*, ref. Montanist inspiration τὸ ψ. ... πνεῦμα Anon.ap.Eus.*h.e.*5.16.9(M.20.468C).

***ψευδοπροφῆτις, ἡ,** *false prophetess* τοῦ Μοντανοῦ...ταῖς ψ. Eus.*h.e.*4.27(M.20.397B).

ψευδορκέω, *swear falsely*, Clem.*str.*7.8(p.38.18; M.9.473A); ‡Chrys.*salt.Herodiad.*2(8.41E).

ψευδορκία, ἡ, *perjury*, Gr.Naz.*carm.*1.2.24.31(M.37.792A); Cyr.*ador.*6(1.196A); id.*hom.pasch.*26(5^2.305C).

***ψευδορράφος,** *fabricating lies*; masc. as subst., Eust.*engast.*75 (p.41.17; M.18.645C).

***ψευδορρημοσύνη, ἡ,** *lying*, ‡Proc.G.*Pr.*21:6(M.87.1432A).

***ψευδοσημεῖον, τό,** *false miracle*, *Apoc.Dan.*B(p.43).

ψευδοσοφία, ἡ, *false wisdom*, Eus.*Hierocl.*42(M.22.856A).

ψευδόσοφος, *pretending to be wise*, Eus.*Hierocl.*42(M.22.856A).

***ψευδόσπορος,** *of false origin*, Geo.Pis.*bell.Avar.*215(M.92.1277A).

***ψευδοσύγγραμμα, τό,** *false writing*, CNic.(787)*can.*9.

***ψευδοσύλλογος, ὁ,** *pretended synod*, CNic.(787)*act.*6(H.4.325B); Thdr.Stud.*ref.*2(M.99.444D); id.*or.*11.4.24(M.99.828A).

***ψευδοσύνοδος, ἡ,** = foreg. ἐπιστολὴ ψευδοσυνόδου Ἀγκυρίνης Epiph.*haer.*73.2 tit.(M.42.404A); τῆς ἐν Σελευκείᾳ ψ. *ib.*73.25 tit. (449A); ψ. ἐπισκόπων Thphn.*chron.*p.319(M.108.772C).

***ψευδοτεχνικός,** *falsely qualified*; of doctors, Ephr.3.391C.

ψευδοτόκος, ἡ, *lying mother*, Pall.*h.Laus.*141(M.34.1243D).

ψευδοτρόφιον, τό, *pretended nourishment*, Cyr.S.*v.Sab.*4.4 (p.135.7).

***ψευδοϋπογράφω,** *forge a signature*, †Jo.Jej.*serm.*(M.88.1924C).

***ψευδοφαντασία, ἡ,** *false appearance*, *1 Apoc.Jo.*1.7(p.75).

***ψευδοφιλόσοφος, ὁ,** *false philosopher*, Nil.*epp.*1.112(M.79.132B).

***ψευδόχρηστος,** *feigning honesty*, Thphn.*chron.*p.406(M.108.965C).

***ψευδοχρηστότης, ἡ,** *pretended goodness*, Thphn.*chron.*p.403 (M.108.960C).

***ψευδοχριστιανός, ὁ,** *pretended Christian*, Cyr.*hom.div.*10(5^2.378B); ‡Jo.D.*ep.Thphl.*(M.95.365B).

ψευδόχριστος, ὁ, *false Christ*, Just.*dial.*82.2(M.6.669B); Heges.ap.Eus.*h.e.*4.22.6(M.20.381A) cit. s. ψευδαπόστολος; Gr.Naz.*or.*11.6 (M.35.840B).

***ψευδωνυμία, ἡ,** *pseudonymity*, *Const.App.*2.31.3.

***ψεύστειρα, ἡ,** *lying woman*, *Orac.Sib.*3.816.

ψηκτρίζω, *rub down*, Thdr.Stud.*poen.*1.91(M.99.1745A).

***ψηλαφητί,** *by feeling, by groping*, ‡Nil.*narr.*2(M.79.605B).

***ψηλαφητικός,** *feeling, groping*, met. ψ. λόγῳ Max.*ambig.*(M.91.1352C).

ψηλαφητός, *that can be felt* or *touched*; of Christ's humanity opp. deity, ‡Ath.*Apoll.*1.3(M.26.1097B); Gr.Nyss.*Eun.*12(2 pp.274.22,275.11; M.45.885B,C); Jo.D.*fid.Nest.*28(p.573).

ψήν, ὁ, *fruit of the male palm*, Bas.*hex.*5.7(1.47C; M.29.112A).

ψηφάς, ὁ, *juggler*, ‡Ath.*qu.Ant.*125(M.28.677B); Leont.N.*v.Sym.*10.56(M.93.1740B).

ψηφίζ-ω, A. act.; **1.** *take into account, consider* ψ. καὶ τὸν κατ' αὐτῆς [sc. τῆς ἀρετῆς] ἐπιόντα πόλεμον Nil.*Eulog.*3(M.79.1097B); **2.** *reckon upon* θάνατος εὗρεν ἄνδρα ἁμαρτωλὸν καὶ πλούσιον, ~οντα τὰ ἔτη πολλὰ Ephr.2.296B; **3.** *give consideration to, attach importance to* ἡ ταπείνωσίς ἐστι, τὸ μὴ ~ειν ἑαυτὸν ἔν τινι πράγματι ὅλως Dor.*doct.*21.5(M.88.1817A); *ib.*21.6(1820A); Bars.*resp.*(M.86.900D).

B. med.; **1.** *vote with*, met. *agree with* οὐ τὸ ἐμὲ παθεῖν ἀπρεπές ἀλλὰ σὺ σαρκικῇ γνώμῃ τούτοις ~ῃ Chrys.*hom.54.4 in Mt.*(7.550D); τὰ ἑξῆς ἐπελθόντες ἴδωμεν τίσι ~εται ὁ Χριστός id.*hom.38.4 in Jo.*(8.222B); *ib.39.3*(230D); **2.** *pass a judgement, declare* τὸ αὐτὸ πάλιν ψ. *ib.76.1*(446B); id.*comm.in Gal.*4:26(10.710E); ψ. τὸ πικρὸν γλυκὺ εἶναι Nil.*epp.*2.21(M.79.209B).

C. pass., *be reckoned* among ὁ Ἰσκαριώτης, εἰ καὶ πρώην ἐν τοῖς δώδεκα ἐψηφίζετο Epiph.*haer.*20.4(p.232.2; M.41.277D).

ψήφινος, ? *made of marble* ψ. εἴδωλον *A.Andr.et Mt.*14(p.80.16).

ψηφίς, ἡ, 1. *pebble*; of tesserae in mosaic-work, Gr.Nyss.*Thdr.*(M.46.740A); ‡Jo.D.*ep.Thphl.*3(M.95.630C); **2.** *mosaic work*, Gr.Naz.*or.*14.16(M.35.877A); Taras.*ep.*1(M.98.1429B); **3.** *calculation, reckoning* διὰ τῆς ψ. τῶν δακτύλων ‡Bas.*h.myst.*45(p.389.15).

ψήφισμα, τό, *number*, Iren.*haer.*5.30.1(M.7.1203C).

ψηφισμός, ὁ, *reckoning*, Ephr.1.296B.

ψηφιστής, ὁ, *calculator*, Hipp.*haer.*4.17(p.51.2; M.16.3086A); Sever.*creat.*3.2(M.56.449); Soz.*h.e.*4.27.4(M.67.1200C).

***ψηφιστικός,** *making calculations*, Just.*dial.*85.4(M.6.677A).

***ψηφιστρία, ἡ,** *calculator*, met. ἀφορίας ψ. ‡Chrys.*fil.vid.*(10.849A).

ψηφιωτής, ὁ, *mosaic-worker, IGC As.Min.*226[5] (Miletus saec. vi–vii).

***ψηφόβολον, τό,** *dice-box*, Jo.Mal.*chron.*5 p.103(M.97.192B).

ψηφοθέτης, ὁ, *mosaic-worker*, ‡Just.*fr.res.*6(M.6.1584A); Bas.*hom.* 7.4(2.55E; M.31.289C).

ψηφολογέω, intrans., *be made of mosaic work*, Nil.ap.Proc.G. *Cant.*3.10(M.87.1632D).

ψηφολογία, ἡ, *calculation*, Leont.H.*Nest.*7.4(M.86.1768[a]A).

ψηφολογικός, *of calculations*, Gr.Naz.*ep.*103(M.37.200B); met., *rifling*, id.*or.*5.40(M.35.717A).

ψηφοπαίκτης, ὁ, *one who juggles*, Eust.*engast.*9(p.28.15; M.18. 629B); Eust.Mon.*ep.*(M.86.920C).

***ψηφοπαικτικός,** *juggling*, met. ψ. ... φυσιολογίαν Eust.Mon.*ep.* (M.86.920C).

ψῆφος, ἡ, 1. *number, cipher*, corresponding to a person's name (i.e. sum of numerical values of letters), *IGC As.Min.*321; **2.** *decree, sentence* ἀπαραλόγιστος γὰρ ἡ τοῦ θεοῦ ψ. εἰς τὸ δικαιότατον κρῖμα Clem.*str.*7.3(p.15.3; M.9.425A); Or.*hom.13.1 in Jer.*(p.162.15; M.13. 400B); Chrys.*David* 2.4(4.766E); **3.** *resolve*, of a vow or pledge τῆς ἑαυτοῦ πτωχείας τὴν ψ. στερεᾷ φυλακῇ ἐκράτει Gr.Mag.*dial.*(tr.Zach.) 3.14(M.*PL.*77.246B); **4.** *election*, Thphn.*chron.*p.64(M.108.212C); **5.** also masc; **a.** *calculation, reckoning, ib.*p.117(332A); **b.** *numerical symbol, cipher, ib.*p.362(868B).

ψήφωσις, ἡ, *mosaic work*, inscr. (saec. vi) at Caesarea, Palestine, (*BZ* 5 p.160).

***ψιαθίδιον, τό,** *little mat* τὰ παλαιὰ ψ., ἅπερ ἑαυτοῖς ὑπεστρώννυον Jo.Eleem.*v.Tych.*33(p.143).

ψιάθιον, τό, *rush-mat*; for sleeping on, Ath.*v.Anton.*7(M.26.853A); *Apophth.Patr.*(M.65.185C); Anast.S.*relat.*12(p.67).

ψιθυριστής, ὁ, *whisperer*, hence *slanderer*, *Contrad.*1(p.5).

ψιθυρός, *whispering*, hence *slandering, slanderous*, Clem.*str.*5.5 (p.342.23; M.9.45C); Cyr.*ador.*11(1.397A); id.*Juln.*7(6[2].227A).

***ψιλάνθρωπος,** *merely human* οὐ ψ. εἶχε τὰ ἀνθρώπινα, ἀλλὰ θεανδρικῶς...τυγχάνοντα Anast.S.*hod.*13(M.89.216C).

***ψιλέθειρον, τό,** *depilatory*, Gr.Nyss.*Eun.*12(1 p.330.28; M.45. 1048D).

[*]**ψίλοθρον, τό,** (= ψίλωθρον), *depilatory*, Leont.H.*Nest.*7.2(M. 86.1764A).

ψιλός, 1. *bare, unprotected*; of a city, *unfortified*, Cyr.*glaph.Num.* (1.388C); **2.** *mere, simple*; **a.** in gen.; of a statement, *literal* opp. spiritual or allegorical, Or.*princ.*3.1.15(p.222.7; M.11.280A); *ib.*4.2.2 (p.308.10; 360B); 'λουτροῦ παλιγγενεσίας', ὃ καὶ βάπτισμα θεῖον ὀνομάζεται, οὐκέτι μὲν ψ. ὕδωρ id.*fr.36 in Jo.*(p.512.13,21); οἱ ἐν ψ. ὀνόματι τοῦ ἁγίου πνεύματος, καὶ οὐχ ὡς ἐν ὀνόματι θεοῦ καὶ πνεύματος θεοῦ...βαπτιζόμενοι, ὡς ὕδατι ψ. λουόμενοι, ἀνόνητον ἔχουσι τὴν ἐλπίδα Didym.*Trin.*2.12(M.39.677D–680A); ὁ Χριστὸς...ἐν πνεύματι ἁγίῳ βαπτίζων, ὡς ψ. ὄντος ὕδατος τοῦ βαπτίσματος Ἰωάννου Ammon. *Jo.*1:30(M.85.1401C); of eucharistic bread and wine before consecration, 'Ath.'ap.Eutych.*pasch.*8(M.86.2401B); Cyr.H.*catech.*17.6; μὴ ὡς ψ. ἄρτῳ προσερχώμεθα τῷ ἄρτῳ τῷ μυστικῷ· σὰρξ γὰρ ὑπάρχει θεοῦ Nil.*epp.*3.39(M.79.405B); Anast.S.*hod.*23(M.89.297B) cit. s. ἀντίτυπος; of chrism μὴ ὑπονοήσῃς ἐκεῖνο τὸ μύρον ψ. εἶναι... ἀλλὰ Χριστοῦ χάρισμα Cyr.H.*catech.*21.3; of Barnabas and Paul ὧδε δὲ ψ. ἦσαν ἄνθρωποι, διὰ πνεύματος θείου τερατουργοῦντες Ammon.*Ac.*14:10,11(M.85.1545B); ref. miracles of Christ τῶν τῆς φύσεως ἀρρωστημάτων διόρθωσιν ἀπραγμάτευτόν τινα καὶ ψιλὴν Gr. Nyss.*or.catech.*23(p.87.3; M.45.61C); *ordinary, unimportant* ἐν ψ. πράγμασι opp. ἐν πολέμῳ καὶ κινδύνοις, Chrys.*hom.9.2 in Phil.*(11. 265D); μηδὲ ψ. τι πρᾶγμα εἶναι νομίσῃς, τὸ τὴν ἐξ ἡμῶν σάρκα αὐτὸν ἀναλαβεῖν id.*hom.5.1 in Heb.*(12.51B); ψ. ἄνθρωπος opp. βασιλεύς, Eus.*Lc.*14:16(M.24.576A); *common* soldier, Chrys.*hom.58.4 in Mt.* (7.589D); **b.** Christol. ψ. ἄνθρωπος: Ἰησοῦς οὐ ψ. ἄνθρωπος ὤν, ἀλλὰ θεὸς γενόμενος ἄνθρωπος Or.*fr.33 in Jo.*(p.508.24); οἱ μὲν...τὸν... ἄνθρωπον, ὃν ἀνείληφεν ἀρνησάμενοι· οἱ δὲ ψ. ἄνθρωπον ὑποθέμενοι, τὸν δ' ἐν αὐτῷ θεὸν ἀγνοήσαντες Eus.*e.th.*1.3(p.63.33; M.24.832C); Amph.*hom.*5.2(M.39.92B); *Const.App.*6.11.10; Gr.Ant.*bapt.*2.6(M. 88.1877B) cit. s. γυμνός; asserted by Jews, Ath.*exp.Ps.*88(M.27. 392C); id.*Ar.*2.15(M.26.177B); *ib.*2.16(180C); ‡Gr.Nyss.*comm.in Jo.* 7.150(p.278.10); ‡Anast.S.*Jud.disp.*(M.89.1217C); by Ebionites, Eus.*h.e.*6.17.1(M.20.560A); Epiph.*haer.*30.18(p.358.8; M.41.436B); Tim.CP *haer.*(M.86.28B); by Paul of Samosata, Eus.*h.e.*5.28.2(512B); Tim.CP *haer.*(29C); by Photinus, Thdot.Anc.*hom.*2.3(p.75.9; M.77. 1372C); by Nestorius, Thphn.*chron.*p.76(M.108.236B); **c.** Trin. ἡ θεότης οὐχ ἓν πρόσωπόν ἐστι κατὰ τὴν Ἰουδαίων ὑπόληψιν, ἀλλὰ τρία πρόσωπα καθ' ὑπόστασιν ἀληθινήν, οὐκ ὀνόματι ψ. Gel.Cyz.*h.e.*2.12.1 (M.85.1249B); **3.** of a river, *shallow*; comp., Chrys.*hom.8.4 in 2Tim.* (11.711B); **4.** *subtle* ψ. δὲ δὴ σφόδρα καὶ σὺν ἱδρωτὶ ληπτὸς τῶν τεθεσπεσμένων ὁ νοῦς Cyr.*glaph.Dt.*(1.416D); **5.** fem. as subst.; **a.** *carpet* or *tapestry* ἐν τῇ προνομῇ ψ. ποικίλην id.*ador.*5(1.146D); **b.** *cloak*, Gr.Naz.*carm.*1.2.6.63(M.37.648A); τὴν δὲ ψ. ὁ Ἀκύλας στολὴν ἡρμήνευσεν· ὁ δὲ Ἰώσηπος χλανίδα Thdt.*qu.10 in Jos.*(1.310).

ψιλότης, ἡ, *the spiritus lenis*, Or.*mart.*46(p.42.15; M.11.628A).

ψιλωτέον, *one must shave off*, Clem.*paed.*3.11(p.270.22; M.8.636A).

***ψιμυθισμός, ὁ,** *painting* the complexion *with white lead*, Clem. *paed.*2.10(p.219.23; M.8.521B).

ψίμυθος, ὁ, *white lead*, used as a pigment to whiten the face, Gr. Naz.*carm.*1.2.29.99(M.37.891A).

[*]**ψίφαρος, ὁ,** for σιφάρος, *top-sail*; plur., Hipp.*antichr.*59(p.40. 7; ψήθαροι M.10.780A).

[*]**ψιχία, ἡ,** = ψιχίον, *crumb*, *V.Dan.*(p.255.17).

ψιχίον, τό, *crumb*, ref. Mt.15:27, *Hom.Clem.*2.19; Bas.Sel.*or.*20 (M.85.253A); ref. Lc.16:21, †Jo.D.*BJ* 9(M.96.933B); βρέξας ὀλίγα ψ. ἐκ τοῦ κοινοῦ ἄρτου *Apopth.Patr.*(M.65.433C); met. ὧν ἔλαβον ψ. μεταδοῦναι τοῖς ὁμοπίστοις Thdt.*Is.*proem.(p.1.8).

ψιχολογ-έω, *pick up crumbs*; met., ref. Mt.15:27 ἡμεῖς τὰ λείψανα...λεληθότα ~οῦμεν Leont.N.*v.Jo.Eleem.*proem.suppl.(p.4).

ψογίζω, *blame*, Epiph.*haer.*66.52(p.89.13; M.42.108C).

ψοφέω, *perish, die*, Jo.Mal.*chron.*10 p.555(M.97.388B); Leont.N. *v.Sym.*10.56(M.93.1740B); *Didasc.Jac.*7(p.746.17); of an animal ἐψόφισεν Ephr.3.xxiiiB (for ἐψόφησεν).

ψόφημα, τό, *noise*, Epiph.*haer.*35.2(p.41.9; M.41.628D); Gr.Naz. *carm.*2.1.12.619(M.37.1211A).

ψοφοδέεια, ἡ, *fear at* every *noise*, Cyr.*Nah.*39(3.513E).

***ψυγέω,** s.v.l., = ψύχω (ψύγω), *grow cold* ἀγάπη...ἡ πρὸς θεὸν ψυγήσασα Hesych.H.*fr.Ps.*35:9(M.93.1189D).

ψυγμός, ὁ, *cooling*, met. ὁ ψ. τῆς ἀγάπης Chrys.*hom.9.4 in Eph.* (11.73F).

ψύδραξ, ἡ, *pimple, blister*, Epiph.*gemm.*5(M.43.297B).

***ψυλλίτης, ὁ,** a pest which damages crops, prob. = ψαλίτης (q.v.), *Euchol.*(p.555).

***ψυχαγελάρχης, ὁ,** *shepherd of souls*, *Hymn.*58.1.2(*AS* 1 p.610).

ψυχαγωγ-έω, 1. *beguile, delude* ἐψυχαγωγῆσθαι ὑπὸ τοῦ Ἰησοῦ Cels.ap.Or.*Cels.*2.1(p.126.14; M.11.793A); *ib.*(p.128.5; 798A); **2.** *encourage, console* ~ῶν τε ἅμα καὶ νουθετῶν Clem.*paed.*3.8(p.261.23; M. 8.613C); Gr.Naz.*ep.*7(M.37.33A); ψαλμὸς...~εῖ τοὺς ἐν ὀδύναις Procl. CP *or.*2.1(M.65.692C); **3.** *refresh*, Thdt.*Ps.*65:12(1.1048); Thphn. *chron.*p.257(M.108.641C).

ψυχαγωγία, ἡ, 1. *relief, refreshment*, Hipp.*haer.*5.23(p.125.11; M. 16.3191B); Gr.Naz.*or.*5.13(M.35.680B); **2.** *consolation, comfort*, ‡Gr. Nyss.*hom.5.89 in Jo.*(p.201.34); Synes.*ep.*70(M.66.1433C); Nil.*epp.* 3.33(M.79.389A); **3.** *entertainment, amusement*, Eus.*m.P.*6(p.920.14; M.20.1480C); **4.** *indulgence, pleasure* τέλος ὑπάρχειν διδάσκει Ἀπολλόδοτος ὁ Κυζικηνὸς τὴν ψ. Clem.*str.*2.21(p.184.15; M.8.1077A); **5.** *captivation, delusion*, Bas.*leg.lib.gent.*3(2.176A; M.31.569B); Chrys. *hom.14.1 in Hebr.*(12.140A).

***ψυχαγωγικῶς,** *persuasively*, Ammon.*Jo.*20:11(M.85.1516D).

ψυχαγωγός, 1. *leading departed souls to the nether world*, of Hermes, Hipp.*haer.*5.7(p.85.23; M.16.3136A); **2.** *charming, captivating*, of children οἱ ψ. μαργαρῖται τοῦ βίου Geo.Pis.*carm.*4.117; **3.** as subst., *necromancer, deceiver*, Clem.*str.*1.8(p.27.3; M.8.737A).

ψυχάζω, *cool*, ‡Paul.Sil.*therm.Pyth.*153(M.86.2266).

***ψυχανδρικῶς,** *with the soul of a man*, Anast.S.*serm.imag.*3(M. 89.1161C) cit. s. εἰκών.

***ψυχαπώλεια, ἡ,** *ruin of souls*, Jo.Carp.*cap.*5(M.85.1839).

***ψυχάρπαξ, ὁ,** *robber of souls*, Geo.Pis.*van.*129(M.92.1590).

ψυχή, ἡ, *soul*, i.e. *vital principle* in creatures;

I. philosophical and theological; **A.** problems to be discussed, cf. *animae quaedam etiam sui agnitio, per quam scire debet, quae sit ejus substantia, utrum corporea an incorporea et utrum simplex an ex duobus vel tribus an vero ex pluribus composita. sed et juxta quorundam quaestiones utrum facta an omnino a nullo sit facta; et, si facta sit, quomodo facta sit, utrum, ut putant aliqui, in semine corporali etiam ipsius substantia continetur et origo ejus pariter cum origine corporis traducitur, an perfecta extrinsecus veniens ...formato intra viscera muliebria corpore induitur. et si ita sit, utrum nuper creata veniat et tunc primum facta, cum corpus videtur esse formatum...an prius et olim facta ob aliquam causam ad corpus sumendum venire aestimetur;...sed et illud requiritur, utrum semel tantum corpore induatur et id postmodum depositum ultra non quaerat, an cum semel susceptum deposuerit, iterum assumat; et si secundo, sumptum semper habeat an aliquando iterum abiciat...et* *adhuc in cognitione sui anima requirat, si est aliquis ordo aut sunt aliqui spiritus ejusdem cum ipsa substantiae...et hoc adhuc in cognoscenda semet ipsa anima requirat, si virtus animi ejus accedere potest et decedere*, Or.*comm.in Cant.*2(pp.146.17–148.4; M.13.126B–127A).

B. definitions and properties; **1.** of its essence; Aristotle's definition reproduced *ἔστι γάρ, φησί, ψ. φυσικοῦ σώματος ὀργανικοῦ ἐντελέχεια* Hipp.*haer.*7.19(p.194.23; M.16.3299D); *ib.*7.24(p.201.21; 3311A); cf. *definitur namque anima hoc modo, quia sit substantia φανταστική et ὁρμητική*, Or.*princ.*2.8.1(p.152.20; M.11.219A); *substantia rationabiliter sensibilis et mobilis anima*, *ib.*2.8.2(p.154.15; 220B); *τὴν δὲ ψ., ἁπλῆν εἶναι φαμὲν καὶ λογικὴν καὶ ἀθάνατον, οὐ μὴν προϋπάρχειν τοῦ σώματος* Thdt.*haer.*5.9(4.412); *ψ. ἐστιν οὐσία νοερά, ἀσώματος, ἀπαθής, ἀθάνατος* ‡Ath.*qu.Ant.*16(M.28.608A); a purely natural definition as breath *ψ. μέν, ἣν καὶ πνεῦμά φαμεν, ἔτι δὲ καὶ τὸ διὰ τοῦ στόματος ἀναπνεόμενον ἀνύπαρκτον πνεῦμα, ὃ καὶ ἆσθμα καλοῦμεν, πᾶς ἄνθρωπος ἔχει* Didym.*Trin.*2.20(M.39.736A); for identification with blood v. *αἷμα*; **2.** discussion of a purely intellectual definition *ψ. ἐστιν οὐσία γεν[ν]ητή, οὐσία ζῶσα, νοερά, σώματι ὀργανικῷ καὶ αἰσθητικῷ, δύναμιν ζωτικὴν καὶ τῶν αἰσθητῶν ἀντιληπτικὴν δι' ἑαυτῆς ἐνιεῖσα, ἕως ἂν ἡ δεκτικὴ τούτων συνέστηκε φύσις* Gr. Nyss.*anim.et res.*(M.46.29B); this challenged *ἀναλαβὼν τῇ διανοίᾳ τὸν ὁρισμόν, ὃν ἐν τοῖς πρὸ τούτου λόγοις περὶ ψ. ἐποιήσατο, οὐχ ἱκανῶς ἐνδεδεῖχθαί μοι τὸν λόγον ἐκεῖνον τὰς ἐνθεωρουμένας τῇ ψ. δυνάμεις...πολλὰ μὲν γὰρ ἔστιν ἰδεῖν, ὧν τὸ ἐπιθυμητικὸν καθηγεῖται· πολλά γε πάλιν ἃ τῆς θυμοειδοῦς αἰτίας ἐκφύεται, καὶ οὐδὲν τοῦτο σῶμά ἐστι...νοερὸν δέ τι τὴν ψ. ὁ ὁρισμὸς ἀπεφήνατο, ὥστε δυοῖν ἀτόποιν τὸ ἕτερον ἐκ τῆς ἀκολουθίας ἀνακύπτειν τοῦ λόγου, ἢ καὶ τὸν θυμὸν καὶ τὴν ἐπιθυμίαν ἄλλας ἐν ἡμῖν εἶναι ψ., καὶ πλῆθος ψυχῶν ἀντὶ μιᾶς καθορᾶσθαι, ἢ μηδὲ τὸ διανοητικὸν τὸ ἐν ἡμῖν ψ. οἴεσθαι. τὸ γὰρ νοερὸν ἐπίσης πᾶσιν ἐφαρμοζόμενον, ἢ πάντα ψ. ἀποδείξει ταῦτα, ἢ ἕκαστον τούτων ἐκ τοῦ ἴσου τοῦ ἰδιώματος τῆς ψ. ἐξαιρήσει* *ib.*(48C–49A); challenge refuted *ὁμοίωμα θεοῦ τὴν ψ. εἶναι φήσας, πᾶν ὃ ἀλλότριόν ἐστι θεοῦ, ἐκτὸς εἶναι τοῦ ὅρου τῆς ψ. ἀπεφήνατο ib.*(52A); *φαμὲν γὰρ τῆς ψ. τὴν μὲν θεωρητικήν τε καὶ διακριτικὴν... δύναμιν οἰκείαν εἶναι καὶ κατὰ φύσιν αὐτήν,...διὰ τοῦτο σώζειν ἐν αὐτῇ τὴν εἰκόνα. ἐπεὶ καὶ τὸ θεῖον, ὅ τί ποτε κατὰ τὴν φύσιν ἐστίν, ἐν τούτοις ὁ λογισμὸς εἶναι στοχάζεται· ἐν τῷ...διακρίνειν τὸ καλὸν ἀπὸ τοῦ χείρονος. ὅσα δὲ τῆς ψ. ἐν μεθορίῳ κεῖται πρὸς ἑκάτερον τῶν ἐναντίων ἐπιρρεπῶς κατὰ τὴν ἰδίαν φύσιν ἔχοντα· ὧν ἡ ποία χρῆσις, ἢ πρὸς τὸ καλὸν ἢ πρὸς τὸ ἐναντίον ἄγει τὴν ἔκβασιν, οἷον τὸν θυμόν, ἢ τὸν φόβον, ἢ εἴ τι τὸ τοιοῦτον τῶν ἐν τῇ ψ. κινημάτων ἐστίν, ὧν ἄνευ οὐκ ἔστιν ἀνθρωπίνην θεωρηθῆναι φύσιν· ταῦτα ἔξωθεν ἐπιγενέσθαι αὐτῇ λογιζόμεθα, διὰ τὸ τῷ ἀρχετύπῳ κάλλει μηδένα τοιοῦτον ἐνθεωρηθῆναι χαρακτῆρα ib.*(57B,C); **3.** in definition of man, v. *ἄνθρωπος*; **4.** divisions of soul; **a.** twofold division *ἄμφω γὰρ δυνάμεις τῆς ψ., γνῶσίς τε καὶ ὁρμή* Clem.*str.*6.8(p.466.13; M.9.289C); *τὸ μὲν λογικόν ἐστι καὶ νοερὸν τῆς ψ., τὸ δέ, παθητικόν τε καὶ ἄλογον. καὶ τῷ μὲν φύσει τὸ κρατεῖν ὑπάρχει, τοῖς δέ, τὸ ὑπακούειν τῷ λόγῳ* Bas.*hom.*3.7(2.23B; M.31.213C); *διττὴν γὰρ εἶναι τῆς ψ. ἔγωγε οἶμαι τὴν δύναμιν, μιᾶς καὶ τῆς αὐτῆς ὑπαρχούσης· τὴν μέν τινα τοῦ σώματος ζωτικήν, τὴν δὲ ἑτέραν τῶν ὄντων θεωρητικήν, ἣν δὴ καὶ λογιστικὴν ὀνομάζομεν* ‡Bas.*const. mon.*2.2(2.541E; M.31.1340D); *ἴδιον τοῦ λογιστικοῦ τῆς ψ., σχολάζειν γνώσει θεοῦ· τοῦ δὲ παθητικοῦ αὐτῆς, ἀγάπη καὶ ἐγκράτεια* Thal.*cent.* 2.52(M.91.1441D); *τῆς ψ., τὸ μὲν...εἶναι θεωρητικόν...τὸ δὲ πρακτικόν· καὶ τὸ μὲν θεωρητικὸν ἐκάλει νοῦν· τὸ δὲ πρακτικόν, λόγον· ὡς πρώτας ...δυνάμεις τῆς ψ. ... διεξοδικῶς...τῆς ψ. ἔφασκεν εἶναι, κατὰ μὲν τὸ νοερόν, τὸν νοῦν, τὴν σοφίαν...τὴν ἄληστον γνῶσιν· τούτων δὲ τέλος εἶναι τὴν ἀλήθειαν· κατὰ δὲ τὸ λογικόν, τὸν λόγον, τὴν φρόνησιν...τὴν πίστιν· τούτων δὲ τέλος εἶναι τὸ ἀγαθόν* Max.*myst.*5(M.91.673C); **b.** threefold *τριγενοῦς οὖν ὑπαρχούσης τῆς ψ. τὸ νοερόν, ὃ δὴ λογιστικὸν καλεῖται, ὁ ἄνθρωπός ἐστιν ὁ ἔνδον...τὸ δὲ θυμικόν, θηριῶδες ὄν, πλησίον μανίας οἰκεῖ· πολύμορφον δὲ τὸ ἐπιθυμητικὸν καὶ τρίτον, ὑπὲρ τὸν Πρωτέα...ποικίλον* Clem.*paed.*3.1(p.236.4; M.8.556A); *τὸ τριμερὲς τῆς ψ. ... τὸν θυμὸν...τὸ ἐπιθυμητικὸν...τὸ δὲ λογιστικόν* Hesych.S. *temp.*2.24(M.93.1520A); Theodore of Edessa ap.Jo.Clim.*scal.*26 schol.14(M.88.1077D); cf.Or.*Cels.*5.47(p.51.21f.; M.11.1256A); **c.** fourfold, ref. Ezech.1:5 *τύπον δὲ ἔφερον τὰ τέσσαρα ζῶα τὰ φέροντα τὸ ἅρμα, αὐτῶν τῶν ἡγεμονικῶν λογισμῶν τῆς ψ. ὥσπερ γὰρ ὁ ἀετὸς βασιλεύει τῶν ὀρνέων, καὶ ὁ λέων τῶν ἀγρίων θηρίων, καὶ ὁ ταῦρος τῶν ἡμέρων ζώων, καὶ ὁ ἄνθρωπος τῶν κτισμάτων· οὕτως εἰσὶ καὶ οἱ βασιλικώτεροι λογισμοὶ τῆς ψ.· λέγω δέ, τὸ θέλημα, ἡ συνείδησις, ὁ νοῦς, ἡ ἀγαπητικὴ δύναμις· δι' αὐτῶν γὰρ τὸ ἅρμα τῆς ψ. κυβερνᾶται, καὶ εἰς τούτους ἐπαναπαύεται ὁ θεός* Mac.Aeg.*hom.*1.3(M.34.452C); **d.** manifold *ψ. ... ἡ τῶν ἀνθρώπων πολυμερής ἐστι καὶ οὐ μονομερής. συνθετὴ γάρ ἐστιν ὡς εἶναι φανερὰν αὐτὴν διὰ σώματος· οὔτε γὰρ ἂν αὐτὴ φανείη ποτὲ χωρὶς σώματος οὔτε ἀνίσταται ἡ σὰρξ χωρὶς ψ.* Tat.*orat.*15(p.16.6; M.6.837A); *μέλη ψ. εἰσι πολλά, νοῦς, συνείδησις, θέλημα, λογισμοὶ κατηγοροῦντες καὶ ἀπολογούμενοι, ἀλλὰ ταῦτα πάντα εἰς ἕνα λογισμόν εἰσιν ἀποδεδεμένα, καὶ μέλη ἐστὶ ψ., ὁ ἔσω ἄνθρωπος* Mac.Aeg.*hom.*7.8(M.34.528B); **5.** immortality *ὅτι μένουσιν αἱ ψ. ἀπέδειξα ὑμῖν ἐκ τοῦ καὶ τὴν Σαμουὴλ ψ. κληθῆναι ὑπὸ τῆς ἐγγαστριμύθου* Just.*dial.*105.4(M.6.721B); †Just.*fr.res.*8(M.6.1588A) cit. s. *ἐμφύσημα*; Iren.*haer.*5.7.1(M.7.1140B); Clem.*str.*5.14(p.386.8; M.9.133A); Or.*princ.*3.1.23(21; p.242.19; M.11.302A); Meth.*res.*1.51 (p.307.3; M.18.281D); hence no resurrection of souls, *ib.*1.52(p.308. 1ff.; M.41.1128A); *ἀθάνατος...ἡ ψ.* Cyr.H.*catech.*4.20; *ὁ Χριστὸς προφανῶς ἡμᾶς διδάσκει...τὸ ἀθάνατον τῆς ἡμετέρας ψ.* ‡Ath.*qu.Ant.*17 (M.28.608B); *ἡ ψ. ἁπλῆ οὖσα, καὶ μὴ ἐκ διαφόρων συγκειμένη μερῶν ...διὰ τοῦτο ἄφθαρτος καὶ ἀθάνατος ἔσται* Max.*anim.*(M.91.357C); derived from divine life, Dion.Ar.*d.n.*6.1(M.3.856B); v. *ἀθάνατος, ἀθανασία*; **6.** immateriality; **a.** view that soul consists of very subtle matter, as in Stoic theory (cf.Clem.*str.*5.14(p.384.19; M.9. 129B)); cf. *ipsae animae corporis habeant figuram*, Iren.*haer.*2.19.6 (M.7.774B); *animas...habere hominis figuram, ut etiam cognoscantur*, *ib.*2.34.1(835A); *incorporales animae, quantum ad comparationem mortalium corporum*, *ib.*5.7.1(1140A); *τὸ λεπτομερέστερον, ἡ ψ.* Clem. *str.*6.6(p.458.6; M.9.273C); *αἱ δὲ ψ. ... σώματα νοερὰ ὑπάρχουσαι* Meth. *res.*3.18(p.415.13; M.18.328A); *οἱ ὀφθαλμοὶ...οἱ φωτισθέντες βλέπουσι τὴν εἰκόνα τῆς ψ., ἀλλὰ ταύτην ὀλίγοι ὁρῶσι Χριστιανοί* Mac.Aeg. *hom.*7.6(M.34.528A); *εἰ ἔχει μορφὴν ἡ ψ.; ἔχει εἰκόνα καὶ μορφὴν ὁμοιάζουσαν τῷ ἀγγέλῳ ib.*7.7(M.l.c.); perh. in definition as *πνεῦμα λεπτομερές* Ammon.*Ac.*17:30(M.85.1568A); **b.** immateriality affirmed *τὴν ψ. ἔχων ἄϋλον* †Clem.*fr.*(p.220.1); cf. *omnes animae atque omnes rationabiles naturae...secundum propriam naturam incorporeae sunt*, Or.*princ.*1.7.1(p.86.5; M.11.171A); *si qui autem sunt qui mentem ipsam animamque corpus esse arbitrantur, velim mihi responderent, quomodo tantarum rerum, tam difficilium tamque subtilium, rationes assertionesque recipiat. unde ei virtus memoriae, unde rerum invisibilium...corpori inest? ib.*1.1.7(p.23.15; 126C); but cf. *τὸ τῇ φύσει λεπτὸν καὶ εὐκίνητον, ὅπερ ἐστὶν ἡ ψ. ib.*1.8.4(p.103.7); and conception of wings δι' *ἀρετῆς* [sc. *ψ.*] *πτεροφυήσασαι μετεωροποροῦσιν, ἐκεῖθεν δὲ διὰ κακίας τῶν πτερῶν ἐκπιπτόντων χαμαιπετεῖς πρόσγειοι γίνονται ib.*(p.103.17); id.*fr.53 in Lc.*(p.259.29); *ἀσώματον νόει τὸν θεὸν ἐκ τῆς ἐνυπαρχούσης σοι ψ. ἀσωμάτου* Bas.*hom.*3.7(2. 23D; M.31.216A); *ἡ διδάσκαλος τῶν περὶ ψ. ὑπολήψεων αὐτὴ ἡ ψ., ὅτι ἄϋλός τις καὶ ἀσώματος* Gr.Nyss.*anim.et res.*(M.46.29A); full discussion, Nemes.*nat.hom.*2(M.40.537Bff.); *πᾶν σῶμα ἤτοι ἔξωθεν κινεῖται ἢ ἔνδοθεν· ἀλλ' εἰ μὲν ἔξωθεν, ἄψυχον ἔσται· εἰ δὲ ἔνδοθεν, ἔμψυχον. εἰ δὲ σῶμα ἡ ψ., εἰ μὲν ἔξωθεν κινοῖτο, ἄψυχός ἐστιν· εἰ δὲ ἔνδοθεν, ἔμψυχος ἄτοπον δέ, καὶ τὸ ἄψυχον, καὶ τὸ ἔμψυχον, λέγειν τὴν ψ.· οὐκ ἄρα σῶμα ἡ ψ. ib.*(541A); *ἡ δὲ ψ., ἀσώματος οὖσα καὶ μὴ περιγραφομένη τόπῳ ib.*3(597B); arguments for immateriality, Chrys.*incomprehens.*5.4(1. 485B); id.*serm.7.4 in Gen.*(4.681A); id.*hom.5.3 in Col.*(11.3624A,B); summary of arguments *εἰ πάσης τῆς σωματικῆς οὐσίας, εἴς τε τὸ ἔμψυχον καὶ τὸ ἄψυχον διῃρημένης· σῶμα δὲ καὶ ἡ ψ., ἢ ἔμψυχον, ἢ ἄψυχον ἔσται πάντως. ἀλλ' εἰ μὲν ἔμψυχον, διὰ ψυχούσης...ἢ οὐσίας, ἢ δυνάμεως, ἤτοι συμβεβηκότος ψυχωθήσεται. ψ. δὲ ψυχοῦσθαι λέγειν, ὥσπερ καὶ φῶς φωτίζεσθαι...καταγέλαστον. καὶ εἰ μὲν οὐσίαν ψυχοῦν τὴν ψ. εἴπωμεν, ἢ σῶμα ἢ ἀσώματον αὐτὴν πάλιν λέξομεν. καὶ εἰ μὲν σῶμα, τὰς αὐτὰς ἀεὶ τῶν λογισμῶν ἀτόπους ἐξ ἀτόπων ἐφόδους... μέχρις οὗ ἀσώματον τὴν ψ. εἶναι συνδιομολογηθῇ. εἰ δὲ δύναμιν, ἤτοι ποιότητα ψυχοῦν τὴν ψ. εἴπωμεν, τῆς οὐσίας ζωοποιητικόν τε καὶ κινητικόν, τὸ ἀκούσιον ἔσται καὶ ἀνυπόστατον...εἴπερ σώματος ἄρχειν κατὰ φύσιν δημιουργηθεῖσα ἡ ψ., ὡς ἀσώματος οὐσία, ὡς σῶμα κατ' αὐτοὺς ὑπὸ τοῦ μὴ κατ' οὐσίαν ὄντος· τῆς κατὰ τὸ ποιὸν λέγω δυνάμεως, ἀρχθήσεται· ἡ κατ' οὐσίαν οὖσα...καὶ τὴν κοινὴν πάντων πρόληψιν. εἰ δὲ ἄψυχον αὐτὴν εἴπωμεν...ἄλογον...ἔσται. ἀλλὰ μὴν ταῦτα πάντα περὶ τὴν ψ., καὶ ἐν τῇ ψ., καὶ ἔστι καὶ ὁρᾶται· οὐκ ἄρα σῶμα ἡ ψ.* Max.*ep.*6(M.91.428A–C); *ib.*(428C–429A); **7.** self-moving *φύσις ψ., ἐξ ἑαυτῆς ὁρμῶν* Clem.*str.*6.12(p.480.13; M.9.317B); id.*ecl.*22 (p.142.26; M.9.708C); cf. *neque motus ullius corporis sine anima effici potest*, Or.*princ.*1.7.3(p.89.1; M.11.173A); *ib.*2.8.5(p.163.3; 224C); *ἡ ψ. ... καταλλήλως τῇ ἰδίᾳ φύσει ἐνεργοῦσά τε καὶ κινουμένη, καὶ διὰ τῶν σωματικῶν ὀργάνων τὰς ἰδίας κινήσεις ἐνδεικνυμένη* Gr.Nyss.*anim.et res.*(M.46.29A); *ἡ ψ. αὐτοκινητός* Max.*anim.*(M.91. 357D); **8.** endowed with free will *τὸ αὐθαίρετον τῆς ἀνθρωπίνης ψ. καὶ ἀδούλωτον πρὸς ἐκλογὴν βίου* Clem.*str.*7.3(p.11.22; M.9.420A); *ἡγοῦμαι δὴ τὸν θεὸν ἑκάστην λογικὴν οἰκονομεῖν ψ., ἀφορῶντα εἰς τὴν ἀΐδιον αὐτῆς ζωήν, ἀεὶ ἔχουσαν τὸ αὐτεξούσιον καὶ παρὰ τὴν ἰδίαν αἰτίαν ἤτοι ἐν τοῖς κρείττοσι κατ' ἐπανάβασιν ἕως τῆς ἀκρότητος τῶν ἀγαθῶν γινομένην ⟨ἢ⟩ καταβαίνουσαν διαφόρως ἐξ ἀπροσεξίας ἐπὶ τὴν...τῆς κακίας χύσιν* Or.*or.*29.13(p.387.26; M.11.540A); cf. *liberi* *namque arbitrii semper est anima, etiam cum in corpore hoc, etiam cum extra corpus est; et libertas arbitrii vel ad bona semper vel ad mala movetur, nec umquam rationabilis sensus, id est mens vel anima, sine motu aliquo esse vel bono vel malo potest*, id.*princ*.3.3.5 (p.262.9ff.; M.11.318C); αὐτεξούσιός ἐστιν ἡ ψ.· καὶ ὁ διάβολος τὸ μὲν ὑποβάλλειν δύναται, τὸ δὲ ἀναγκάσαι παρὰ προαίρεσιν, οὐκ ἔχει τὴν ἐξουσίαν Cyr.H.*catech*.4.21; ἔστιν εἰπεῖν, καὶ τῇ ψ. θεόθεν μὲν εἶναι τὴν σύστασιν, μηδεμιᾶς δὲ νοουμένης περὶ τὸ θεῖον κακίας, ἔξω τῆς κατ' αὐτὴν ἀνάγκης εἶναι· γενομένην δὲ οὕτως τῇ ἰδίᾳ γνώμῃ πρὸς τὸ δοκοῦν ἄγεσθαι, ἢ ἐκ προαιρέσεως πρὸς τὸ καλὸν ἐπιμύουσαν, ἢ ἐξ ἐπιβουλῆς τοῦ συνοικοῦντος ἡμῶν τῇ ζωῇ πολεμίου τὸν ὀφθαλμὸν βλαπτομένην Gr. Nyss.*anim.et res*.(M.46.120C); **9.** rational ἡ λογικὴ δὲ δύναμις, ἰδία οὖσα τῆς ἀνθρωπείας ψ. Clem.*str*.2.20(p.173.23; M.8.1056A); hence human souls dist. from animal, Anast.Ant.*serm*.3(M.89.1168B); ὅτι δὲ λογικὴ ἡμῶν ἡ ψ., ἐκ πολλῶν ἄν τις δείξειε· καὶ πρῶτον μὲν ἐκ τοῦ τὰς τέχνας...ταύτην αὐτὰς εὑρηκέναι...ἔπειτα ἐκ τοῦ τὰς αἰσθήσεις ἡμῶν ἱκανὰς εἶναι πρὸς τὴν τῶν πραγμάτων κατάληψιν, λογικὴ ἡμῶν ἡ ψ. ἀποδείκνυται Max.*anim*.(M.91.360B); **10.** sexless ἀποστᾶσα γὰρ τοῦδε τοῦ σχήματος, ᾧ διακρίνεται τὸ ἄρρεν καὶ τὸ θῆλυ, ψ. μετατίθεται εἰς ἕνωσιν, οὐθέτερον οὖσα Clem.*str*.3.13(p.239.5; M.8.1193B); ὅμοιαι πᾶσαι αἱ ψ. εἰσιν ἀνδρῶν τε καὶ γυναικῶν· τὰ γὰρ μέλη τοῦ σώματος διακέκρινται μόνον Cyr.H.*catech*.4.20; **11.** essence unknown to men, Cyr.H.*catech*.6.6; Chrys.*incomprehens*.5.4(1.485B); views of pagan philosophers recapitulated and criticized, Nemes.*nat.hom*.2(M.40. 536B–581A); **12.** unity, cf. *requirendum si in...hominibus, qui ex anima constamus et corpore ac spiritu vitali, est etiam aliud aliquid, quod incitamentum habeat proprium et commotionem ad malum provocantem; sicut haberi a quibusdam quaestio solet hujusmodi, utrumnam velut duae animae in nobis dicendae sunt, una quaedam divinior et caelestis et alia inferior, an vero ex hoc ipso, quod corporibus inhaeremus...trahimur...ad haec mala, quae corpori grata sunt, an vero tertium, quod quidam Graecorum opinati sunt, quia anima nostra cum una sit per substantiam, ex pluribus tamen constet, id est quod pars ejus rationabilis dicatur, pars vero inrationabilis, et ea quidem pars, quam inrationabilem dicunt, in duos rursum dividatur affectus cupiditatis et iracundiae. has ergo tres quas supra diximus de anima opiniones a nonnullis haberi invenimus. ex quibus illud interim, quod quibusdam Graecorum philosophis visum diximus, quia tripartita sit anima, non valde confirmari ex divinae scripturae auctoritate pervideo; et alia vero duo, quae reliqua sunt, inveniri possunt aliquanta, quae ex divinis litteris aptari posse videantur*, Or.*princ*.3.4.1(pp.263.21–264.14; M.11.319D–320B); discussion adducing biblical arguments, but refraining from giving decision, *ib*.3.4.2–5; **13.** Gnost. and pagan ζητοῦσιν...τίς ἐστιν ἡ ψ. καὶ πόθεν καὶ ποταπὴ τὴν φύσιν, ἵν' ἐλθοῦσα εἰς τὸν ἄνθρωπον καὶ κινήσασα καταδουλώσῃ καὶ κολάσῃ τὸ πλάσμα τοῦ τελείου ἀνθρώπου...εἶναι δέ φασι τὴν ψ. δυσεύρετον...οὐ γὰρ μένει ἐπὶ σχήματος οὐδὲ μορφῆς τῆς αὐτῆς πάντοτε Hipp.*haer*.5.7(p.80.15ff.; M.16.3130A,B); Ἀσσύριοι τὴν ψ. τριμερῆ νομίζουσιν εἶναι καὶ μίαν. ψυχῆς γάρ, φασί, πᾶσα φύσις, ἄλλη δὲ ἄλλως, ὀρέγεται. ἔστι γὰρ ψ. πάντων τῶν γινομένων αἰτία· πάντα γὰρ ὅσα τρέφεται, φασί, καὶ αὔξει, ψ. δεῖται. οὐδὲν γὰρ οὔτε τροφῆς...οὔτε αὐξήσεως...ἐπιτυχεῖν ψ. μὴ παρούσης...πᾶσα οὖν φύσις...ψ. ὀρέγεται, κτλ. *ib*.(p.81.6ff.; 3130B,C); in interprn. of Eden and Elohim Ἐδὲμ μὲν τὴν ψ., Ἐλωεὶμ δὲ τὸ πνεῦμα...ἐν τῇ Εὔᾳ τῇ εἰκόνι ψ. μὲν ἀπὸ τῆς Ἐδέμ, πνεῦμα δὲ ἀπὸ τοῦ Ἐλωείμ *ib*.5.26 (p.128.3,8; 3195B,C); *ib*.(p.130.24f.; 3199C); *ib*.10.15(p.276.27; 3431B).

C. origin; **1.** Origen's theory of pre-existence; **a.** no definite teaching on origin given by Church of his time, Or.*princ*.1 proem.5 (p.13.7; M.11.118C); **b.** theory evolved to reconcile differences among created beings with justice of God πρὸ τῶν αἰώνων νόες ἦσαν πάντες καθαροί, καὶ οἱ δαίμονες καὶ αἱ ψ. καὶ οἱ ἄγγελοι... ὑπελείποντο δὲ αἱ ψ., αἵτινες οὐδὲ τοσαῦτα ἦσαν ἁμαρτήσασαι, ἵνα δαίμονες γένωνται, οὐδὲ πάλιν οὕτω κουφοτέρως, ἵνα ἄγγελοι γένωνται. ἐποίησεν οὖν ⟨ὁ θεὸς⟩ τὸν παρόντα κόσμον, καὶ τὴν ψ. συνέδησε τῷ σώματι πρὸς κόλασιν...δῆλον ὅτι ἕκαστον πρὸς ὃ ἥμαρτε τιμωρούμενος, τὸν μὲν ἐποίησε δαίμονα, τὸν δὲ ψ., τὸν δὲ ἄγγελον. εἰ μὴ γὰρ ἦν τοῦτο, καὶ προϋπῆρχον αἱ ψ., διὰ τί τινὰς μὲν τῶν νεωστὶ τεχθέντων εὑρίσκομεν τυφλούς, μηδὲν ἁμαρτήσαντας, ἄλλους δὲ μηδὲν ἔχοντας κακὸν τικτομένους; ἀλλὰ δῆλον ὅτι προϋπῆρχόν τινες ἁμαρτίαι ταῖς ψ., ἀφ' ὧν ἑκάστη πρὸς τὴν ἀξίαν ἀπολαμβάνει...διόπερ καὶ δέμας κέκληται τὸ σῶμα διὰ τὸ δεδέσθαι τὴν ψ. ἐν τῷ σώματι *ib*.1.8.1(pp.96. 1–97.4); theory rejected πρὶν παραγένηται εἰς τόνδε τὸν κόσμον ἡ ψ., οὐδὲν ἥμαρτεν· ἀλλ' ἐλθόντες ἀναμάρτητοι, νῦν ἐκ προαιρέσεως ἁμαρτάνομεν Cyr.H.*catech*.4.19; **c.** scriptural proofs, cf. *si hominis anima, quae utique inferior est, dum hominis est anima, non cum corporibus ficta, sed proprie et extrinsecus probatur inserta, multo magis eorum animantium, quae caelestia designantur. nam quantum ad homines spectat, quomodo cum corpore simul ficta anima videbitur ejus, qui in ventre fratrem suum subplantavit, id est Jacob? aut quomodo simul cum corpore ficta est anima...ejus, qui adhuc ⟨in ventre matris suae positus, repletus est spiritu sancto⟩...? quomodo simul cum corpore ficta est...illius anima, qui antequam in utero formaretur, notus esse dicitur Deo?...ne forte non judicio neque pro meritis replere aliquos videatur Deus spiritu sancto et sanctificare non merito. et quomodo effugiemus illam vocem, qua ait: numquid injustitia est apud Deum? absit. ... hoc enim consequitur eam defensionem, quae animas subsistere simul cum corporibus adseverat*, Or.*princ*.1.7.4(p.90.5ff.; M.11.173C–174A); for case of Jo. Bapt., cf.id.*Jo*.2.30(24; p.87.8ff.; M.14.165C); εἰσίν τινες τῶν ἐνσωματουμένων ψ. πρὶν εἰς γένεσιν ἐλθεῖν μεμαθητευμέναι παρὰ τῷ πατρί *ib*. 20.7(p.335.14; 588C); exeg. Ps.118:67 τὸ γὰρ εἰπεῖν τὸν προφήτην πρὶν ἢ ταπεινωθῆναί με, ἐγὼ ἐπλημμέλησα, ἐξ αὐτῆς φησι τῆς ψ. ὁ λόγος, ὡς ἄνω ἐν οὐρανῷ ἐπλημμέλησε, πρὶν ἢ ἐν τῷ σώματι τεταπεινῶσθαι id. *princ*.2.8.3(p.158.3); **d.** etym. argument from ψυχή–ψυχρός; cf. *sicut ergo deus ignis est...ita e contrario hi, qui deciderunt a dilectione dei, sine dubio refrixisse in caritate ejus ac frigidi effecti esse dicendi sunt...requirendum est ne forte et nomen animae, quod Graece dicitur* ψ., *a refrigescendo de statu diviniore...dictum sit, ib*.(pp.156.13–157. 15; 222A–D); cf. teaching of Docetists μέχρι...τῆς τοῦ σωτῆρος φανερώσεως ὑπὸ τοῦ θεοῦ τοῦ φωτὸς τοῦ πυρώδους...πολλή τις ἦν πλάνη τῶν ψ. ψ. γὰρ αἱ ἰδέαι καλοῦνται, ὅτι ἀποψυγεῖσαι τῶν ἄνω ἐν σκότει διατελοῦσι Hipp.*haer*.8.10(p.229.13; M.16.3354B); ψ. διὰ τοῦτο κληθῆναι, διὰ τὸ ψυγὲν τὸ θερμὸν τοῦ νοῦ ‡Caes.Naz.*dial*.3.149(M.38.1100); **e.** 'fall' of souls from their own 'city' ἔθνη τινὰ τῶν ψ. ἀποτίθεται ἐν ἰδιαζούσῃ τινὶ πολιτείᾳ πρὸς τὴν ἐν σώματι ζωὴν βιοτεύοντα ἐν τῷ λεπτῷ τε καὶ εὐκινήτῳ τῆς φύσεως ἑαυτῶν τῇ τοῦ παντὸς συμπεριπολοῦντος δινήσει. προκεῖσθαι δὲ κἀκεῖ τά τε τῆς κακίας καὶ τῆς ἀρετῆς ὑποδείγματα. καὶ παραμένουσαν μὲν ἐν τῷ καλῷ τὴν ψ. τῆς πρὸς τὸ σῶμα συμπλοκῆς μένειν ἀπείρατον. ῥοπῇ δέ τινι τῇ πρὸς κακίαν πτερορρυούσας τὰς ψ. ἐν σώμασι γίνεσθαι, πρῶτον μὲν ἀνθρωπ⟨ίν⟩οις, εἶθ' οὕτως διὰ τῆς πρὸς τὰ ἄλογα τῶν παθῶν ὁμιλίας...ἀποκτηνοῦσθαι...κἀκεῖθεν μέχρι τῆς φυσικῆς ταύτης καὶ ἀναισθήτου καταπίπτειν ζωῆς Or.*princ*. 1.8.4(pp.102.12–103.3; M.46.112C); passage preserved and refuted by Gr.Nyss. τὸ δὲ τοιοῦτον δόγμα...ἐλέγχεται...εἰ γὰρ ἀπὸ τῆς οὐρανίας ζωῆς διὰ κακίας ἐπὶ τὸν ξυλώδη βίον ἡ ψ. κατασύρεται, ἀπὸ τούτου δὲ πάλιν δι' ἀρετῆς ἐπὶ τὸν οὐράνιον ἀνατρέχει, εὑρίσκεται ὁ λόγος αὐτῶν ἀπορῶν, ὅ τι προτιμότερον οἴεται, εἴτε τὴν ξυλίνην, εἴτε τὴν οὐρανίαν ζωήν. κύκλος γάρ τίς ἐστι διὰ τῶν ὁμοίων περιχωρῶν, ἀεὶ τῆς ψ., ἐν ᾧπερ ἂν ᾖ, ἀστατούσης...οὔτε γὰρ ἡ οὐρανία διαγωγὴ ἐν τῷ μακαρισμῷ διαμένει, εἴπερ κακία τῶν ἐκεῖ ζώντων καθάπτεται· οὔτε τὰ ξύλα τῆς ἀρετῆς ἀμοιρήσει, εἴπερ ἐντεῦθεν μὲν ἐπὶ τὸ ἀγαθὸν παλινδρομεῖν οἴονται τὴν ψ., ἐκεῖθεν δὲ τοῦ κατὰ κακίαν ἀνάρχεσθαι Gr.Nyss.*anim. et res*.(M.46.113B,C); also refuted on ground that hypothesis would imply that evil existed before creation, *ib*.(116C); **f.** ascent and descent of souls, cf. *quia comparavimus de isto mundo ad inferna pergentes animas his animabus, quae de superiori caelo ad nostra habitacula venientes quodammodo mortuae sunt, prudenti investigatione rimandum est, an hoc ipsum possimus etiam in nativitate dicere singularum; ut quomodo quae in ista terra nostra nascuntur animae vel de inferno rursum meliora cupientes ad superiora veniunt et humanum corpus adsumunt, vel de melioribus locis ad nos usque descendunt: sic et ea loca, quae supra sunt in firmamento, aliae animae possideant, quae de nostris sedibus ad meliora proficiant, aliae, quae de caelestibus ad firmamentum usque delapsae sunt nec tantum fecere peccati, ut ad loca inferiora, quae incolimus, truderentur*, Or.*princ*.4.3.11(p.339.7ff.; M.11.394B); ἐπὶ τῆς νοητῆς καταβάσεως τῆς ψ. διὰ τὴν κακίαν καὶ τὰ μοχθηρὰ δόγματα καὶ νοητῆς ἀναβάσεως αὐτῆς id.*Jo*.19.22(5; p.323.24; M.14.568A); **g.** hypothesis of the mutability of soul into spirit and vice versa ὥσπερ σῶσαι τὸ ἀπολωλὸς ἦλθεν ὁ σωτήρ, ὅτε μέντοι σώζεται τὸ ἀπολωλός, οὐκέτι ἐστὶν ἀπολωλός, οὕτως, εἰ σῶσαι ἦλθε ψ., ὡς σῶσαι τὸ ἀπολωλός, οὐκέτι μένει ψ. ἡ σωθεῖσα ψ. ἔτι βασανιστέον εἰ, ὥσπερ τὸ ἀπολωλὸς ἦν ὅτε οὐκ ἀπολώλει καὶ ἔσται ποτὲ ὅτε ἔσται ἀπολωλός, οὕτω καὶ ἡ ψ. ἦν ὅτε οὐκ ἦν ψ. καὶ ἔσται ὅτε οὐκ ἔσται ψ. ... *fortassis etiam hoc quod salvatur anima dicitur; cum autem jam salva facta fuerit, ex perfectioris partis suae vocabulo nuncupabitur...anima, quae perisse dicitur, videbitur fuisse quid aliquando, cum nondum perisset et propter hoc anima diceretur, quae rursum ex perditione liberata potest iterum illud esse quod fuit, antequam periret et anima diceretur*, id.*princ*.2.8.3(pp.155.14–156.12; M.11.221B–222A); cf.*ib*.(p.159. 1; 223C); but *quod diximus mentem in animam verti vel si qua alia quae in hoc videntur aspicere, discutiat apud se qui legit...a nobis* *tamen non putentur velut dogmata esse prolata, sed tractandi more ac requirendi discussa*, ib.2.8.4(p.162.7; 224A); cf.*ib*.3.1.23(21; p.242.19; 302A); of souls into angels, cf. *tertius vero creaturae rationabilis ordo est eorum spirituum, qui ad humanum genus replendum apti judicantur a deo, id est animae hominum, ex quibus per profectum etiam in illum angelorum ordinem quosdam videmus assumi*, *ib*.1.8.4 (p.101.29; 180A); cf. ἀνεστοιχειοῦτο γοῦν αὐτῇ ψ. [sc. Helena's] ἐπὶ τὴν ἄφθαρτον καὶ ἀγγελικὴν οὐσίαν Eus.*v.C*.3.46(p.97.10; M.20.1105D); Epiph.*haer*.64.4(p.411.2; M.41.11076D); **h.** traces of idea of metempsychosis εἰ γὰρ διά τινος κακίας ἀποσπασθεῖσα τῆς ὑψηλοτέρας ἡ ψ. πολιτείας, μετὰ τὸ ἅπαξ γεύσασθαι τοῦ σωματικοῦ βίου πάλιν ἄνθρωπος γίνεται, ἐμπαθέστερος...ὁ ἐν σαρκὶ βίος ὁμολογεῖται παρὰ τὸν... ἀσώματον, ἀνάγκη πᾶσα τὴν ἐν τῷ τοιούτῳ γινομένην βίῳ ἐν ᾧ πλείους αἱ πρὸς τὸ ἁμαρτάνειν εἰσὶν ἀφορμαί, ἐν πλειονί τε κακίᾳ γενέσθαι... ἀνθρωπίνης δὲ ψ. πάθος ἡ πρὸς τὸ ἄλογόν ἐστιν ὁμοίωσις. τούτῳ δὲ προσοικειωθεῖσαν αὐτήν, εἰς κτηνώδη φύσιν μεταρρυῆναι Or.*princ*.1.8.4(p.103.17ff.); ἡ ψ. ἀπορρέουσα τοῦ καλοῦ...εἰ μὴ ὑποστρέφοι, ὑπὸ τῆς ἀνοίας ἀποκτηνοῦται...καὶ αἱρεῖται πρὸς τὸ ἀλογωθῆναι καὶ τὸν ἔνυδρον, ἵν' οὕτως εἴπω, βίον· καὶ τάχα κατ' ἀξίαν τῆς ἐπὶ πλεῖον ἀποπτώσεως τῆς κακίας ἐνδύεται σῶμα ⟨τοι⟩οῦδε ἢ τοιοῦδε ἀλόγου ζῴου *ib*.(p.104.8; 180B); **2.** development of creationism; **a.** its roots in account in Gen. of different origin of man's body and soul, cf. *insufflavit enim in faciem hominis deus flatum vitae et factus est homo in animam viventem, flatus autem vitae incorporalis*, Iren.*haer*.5.7.1(M.7.1140A); πλάσμα ὑμᾶς τοὺς ἀνθρώπους [ἐπι]γεγονότας τοῦ θεοῦ καὶ παρ' αὐτοῦ τὴν ψ. εἰληφότας Clem.*prot*.10(p.67.33; M.8.205A); ἐκ γῆς μὲν τὸ σῶμα διαπλάττεσθαι λέγει ὁ Μωυσῆς...ψ. δὲ τὴν λογικὴν ἄνωθεν ἐμπνευσθῆναι ὑπὸ τοῦ θεοῦ εἰς πρόσωπον id.*str*.5.14(p.388.10; M.9.140A); soul infused before physical conception εἰσιοῦσαν γὰρ τὴν ψ. εἰς τὴν μήτραν ἀπὸ τῆς καθάρσεως ἠυτρεπισμένην εἰς σύλληψιν ...καταβληθέντος δὲ τοῦ σπέρματος ὡς εἰπεῖν ἐξοικειοῦσθαι τὸ ἐν τῷ σπέρματι πνεῦμα καὶ οὕτως συλλαμβάνεσθαι τῇ πλάσει...καὶ αἱ στεῖραι διὰ τοῦτό εἰσι στεῖραι, ὡς ἂν μὴ εἰσκρινομένης τῆς ψ. τὴν τοῦ σπέρματος καταβολὴν συναγούσης εἰς κατοχὴν συλλήψεως καὶ γεννήσεως id.*ecl*.50(pp.150.22–151.9; M.9.721A); παρὰ μὲν τῆς ὕλης λαβὼν τὸ σῶμα ἤδη προϋποστάσης, παρ' ἑαυτοῦ δὲ πνοὴν ἐνθεὶς (ὃ δὴ νοερὰν ψ. καὶ εἰκόνα θεοῦ οἶδεν ὁ λόγος) Gr.Naz.*or*.38.11(M.36.321D); ἐν...τῇ διαπλάσει τοῦ ἀνθρώπου πρότερον τὸ σῶμα παραγίνεται, καὶ τότε ἡ ψ. ἡ τιμιωτέρα...πρὸ τῆς ψ. τὸ σῶμα δημιουργεῖται, ἵνα ἐπειδὰν κατὰ τὴν ἀπόρρητον αὐτοῦ σοφίαν ἡ ψ. παραχθῇ... Chrys.*hom.13.3 in Gen*.(4.102C); Anast.Ant.*serm*.3(M.89.1165C); **b.** this, however, does not imply that soul is part of the divinity, Chrys.*hom.13.2 in Gen*.(4.101A–D); Thdt.*qu.23 in Gen*.(1.39); **c.** creationist doctrine clearly stated ἡ δὲ ἐκκλησία, τοῖς θείοις πειθομένη λόγοις...λέγει, τὴν ψ. συνδημιουργεῖσθαι τῷ σώματι, οὐκ ἐκ τῆς ὕλης τοῦ σπέρματος ἔχουσαν τῆς δημιουργίας τὰς ἀφορμάς, ἀλλὰ τῇ βουλήσει τοῦ ποιητοῦ μετὰ τὴν τοῦ σώματος συνισταμένην διάπλασιν id.*haer*.5.9(4.414); ἡ δὲ τοῦ ἀνθρώπου ψ. ἰδιάζουσαν ὑπόστασιν ἔχει· ἐνεργεῖ δὲ καὶ τὴν ζωὴν ἐν σαρκί...ὁ σπόρος ἐκ συνουσίας· ἡ δὲ πλάσις ἐκ θείου νεύματος· κτίζεται ἡ ψ. ὅτε καὶ τὸ σῶμα εἰκονίσθη, θεοῦ τὴν πλάσιν παρέχοντος Proc.G.*Gen*.2:7(M.87.153B); **3.** traducianism (cf. Tertullian); **a.** not always clearly distinguishable from creationism λείπεται οὖν μίαν καὶ τὴν αὐτὴν ψ. τε καὶ σώματος ἀρχὴν τῆς συστάσεως οἴεσθαι Gr.Nyss.*anim.et res*.(M.46.125A); ἐπὶ τῆς τοῦ ἀνδρὸς καὶ γυναικὸς συμπλοκῆς συνίσταται θεοῦ κελεύσει σῶμα καὶ ψ. ‡Ath.*qu.Ant*.16(M.28.608B); **b.** explicitly taught Ἀπολιναρίῳ δὲ δοκεῖ τὰς ψ. ἀπὸ τῶν ψ. τίκτεσθαι ὥσπερ ἀπὸ τῶν σωμάτων. προϊέναι γὰρ τὴν ψ. κατὰ διαδοχὴν τοῦ πρώτου ἀνθρώπου εἰς τοὺς ἐξ ἐκείνου πάντας τεχθέντας καθάπερ τὴν σωματικὴν διαδοχήν· μήτε γὰρ ἀποκεῖσθαι ψ. μήτε νῦν κτίζεσθαι ‡Gr.Nyss.*anim*.(M.45.205C); ὥσπερ ἐπὶ τῆς πρώτης πλάσεως τὸ μὲν σῶμα ἐκ τῆς γῆς ἔσχεν ὁ ἄνθρωπος, τὴν δὲ ψ. ἐξ αὐτοῦ τοῦ θεοῦ γεννηθεῖσαν· οὕτω καὶ νῦν τὸ μὲν σῶμα ἐκ τῆς γυναικείας γῆς καὶ αἵματος συνίσταται, ἡ δὲ ψ. διὰ τῆς σπορᾶς ὥσπερ διά τινος ἐμφυσήματος ἐκ τοῦ ἀνθρώπου ἀρρήτως μεταδίδοται...τὸ μὲν σῶμα διὰ τῶν οἰκείων... χειρῶν αὐτοῦ ἔπλασεν ὁ θεός, τὴν δὲ ψ. ὡς ἀόρατον ἐκ τῆς παναοράτου αὐτοῦ ψ. διὰ τοῦ ἐμφυσήματος προήγαγε καὶ ἐποίησε παρ' ἑαυτοῦ Anast. Ant.*serm*.3(M.89.1165B); **4.** Gnost.; **a.** origin of souls from different seed as cause of their difference from each other (Valentinian) τὰς δὲ ἐσχηκυίας τὸ σπέρμα τῆς Ἀχαμὼθ ψ. ἀμείνους λέγουσι γεγονέναι τῶν λοιπῶν· διὸ καὶ πλεῖον τῶν ἄλλων ἠγαπῆσθαι ὑπὸ τοῦ Δημιουργοῦ, μὴ εἰδότος τὴν αἰτίαν, ἀλλὰ παρ' αὐτοῦ λογιζομένου εἶναι τοιαύτας. διὸ καὶ εἰς προφήτας, φασίν, ἔτασσεν αὐτούς [l. αὐτάς], καὶ ἱερεῖς, καὶ βασιλεῖς. καὶ πολλὰ ὑπὸ τοῦ σπέρματος τούτου εἰρῆσθαι διὰ τῶν προφητῶν ἐξηγοῦνται, ἅτε ὑψηλοτέρας φύσεως ὑπαρχούσας [sc. ψυχὰς τὸ σπέρμα ἐχούσας]· πολλὰ δὲ καὶ τὴν μητέρα περὶ τῶν ἀνωτέρω εἰρηκέναι λέγουσιν, ἀλλὰ καὶ διὰ τούτου καὶ τῶν ὑπὸ τούτου γενομένων ψ. Iren.*haer*.1.7.3(M.7.516A,B); refutation, cf. *sermo arguitur falsus ...in eo quod dicant eas animas quae habuerint a Matre semen, meliores reliquis fieri: quapropter...principes, et reges, et sacerdotes ordinatas esse. si enim erat hoc verum, primus utique Caiaphas... et Annas, et reliqui summi sacerdotes...et principes populi credidissent Domino...et ante hoc etiam Herodes rex. quoniam autem nec hic, nec summi sacerdotes...accurrerunt ei; sed e contrario qui erant in viis mendici sedentes...non itaque erant meliores tales animae*, *ib*. 2.19.7(775A,B); οἱ ἀντίμιμοι τοῦ Δημιουργοῦ, οἱ τῇ ἐκ μεσότητος ψ., τῇ σφετέρᾳ εἰκόνι, ἐμφυσῶντες τὴν ζωὴν τὴν ἄνωθεν Clem.*str*.4.13(p.288.17; M.8.1300A); cf.*ib*.(p.288.2ff.; 1297B); οἱ δ' ἀπὸ Οὐαλεντίνου πλασθέντος φασὶ τοῦ ψυχικοῦ σώματος τῇ ἐκλεκτῇ ψ. οὔσῃ ἐν ὕπνῳ ἐντεθῆναι ὑπὸ τοῦ λόγου σπέρμα ἀρρενικόν id.*exc.Thdot*.2(p.105.15; M.9.653A) view rejected, Cyr.H.*catech*.4.20; **b.** soul's embodiment as a punishment (Marcion, Basilides) οἱ φιλόσοφοι...παρ' ὧν τὴν γένεσιν κακὴν εἶναι ἀσεβῶς ἐκμαθόντες οἱ ἀπὸ Μαρκίωνος...φρυάττονται, οὐ φύσει κακὴν βούλονται ταύτην εἶναι, ἀλλὰ τῇ ψ. τῇ τὸ ἀληθὲς διδούσῃ· κατάγουσι γὰρ ἐνταῦθα τὴν ψ. θείαν οὖσαν καθάπερ εἰς κολαστήριον τὸν κόσμον, ἀποκαθαίρεσθαι δὲ ταῖς ἐνσωματουμέναις ψ. προσήκει κατ' αὐτούς. κἄστιν τὸ δόγμα τοῦτο οὐ τοῖς ἀπὸ Μαρκίωνος ἔτι, τοῖς δὲ ἐνσωματοῦσθαι...τὰς ψ. ἀξιοῦσιν οἰκεῖον Clem.*str*.3.3(p.201.16ff.; M.8.1116A,B); τῷ Βασιλείδῃ ἡ ὑπόθεσις προαμαρτήσασάν φησι τὴν ψ. ἐν ἑτέρῳ βίῳ τὴν κόλασιν ὑπομένειν ἐνταῦθα *ib*.4.12(p.285.4; 1292C).

D. in rel. to body, cf. σάρξ, σῶμα, αἴσθησις; **1.** manner in which soul is in body, diffused through it, *Diogn*.6.1 cit. s. Χριστιανός; ἔστι ψ. ἐν ὅλοις τοῖς μέλεσι, καὶ ἄνω ἐν τῷ ἐγκεφάλῳ ἐνεργεῖ, καὶ κάτω τοὺς πόδας αὐτὴ κινεῖ Mac.Aeg.*hom*.40.3(M.34.764C); τὴν μὲν ζωτικὴν δύναμιν, ἐπεὶ συγκέκραται τῷ σώματι ἡ ψ., φυσικῶς διὰ τὴν σύγκρασιν, καὶ οὐκ ἐκ προαιρέσεως χορηγεῖ...ψ. ἀμήχανον μὴ ζωοποιεῖν σῶμα, ᾧ ἂν ἐγγέννηται ‡Bas.*const*.2.2(2.542A; M.31.1341A); denied τί λέγω, τί τὴν οὐσίαν ἐστὶν ἡ ψ.; ὅπως ἡμῶν ἐστιν ἐν τῷ σώματι, οὐδὲ τοῦτο ἔστιν εἰπεῖν. τί γὰρ ἔχοι τις ἂν εἰπεῖν ὅτι παρεκτείνεται τῷ τοῦ σώματος ὄγκῳ; ἀλλὰ τοῦτο ἄλογον, σωμάτων γὰρ ἴδιον τοῦτο· ὅτι δὲ ἐπὶ ψ. οὐκ ἔστι τοῦτο ἐντεῦθεν δῆλον. πολλάκις καὶ τῶν χειρῶν καὶ τῶν ποδῶν ἐκκεκομμένων, ὁλόκληρος ἐκείνη μένει...ἀλλ' οὐκ ἔστιν ἐν ὅλῳ τῷ σώματι, ἀλλ' ἐν μέρει τινὶ συνείληπται. οὐκοῦν νεκρὰ ἀνάγκη τὰ λοιπὰ εἶναι μέλη· τὸ γὰρ ἄψυχον πάντως νεκρόν. ἀλλ' οὐδὲ τοῦτο ἔστιν εἰπεῖν, ἀλλ' ὅτι μέν ἐστιν ἐν τῷ σώματι τῷ ἡμετέρῳ ἴσμεν, τὸ δὲ πῶς ἐστιν οὐκ ἴσμεν Chrys.*incomprehens*.5.4(1.485C); discussion, Nemes.*nat.hom*.3(M.40.592Aff.); Max.*anim*.(M.91.356D–357A); **2.** soul superior to body, Clem.*str*.4.26(p.321.16f.; M.8.1373C); Chrys.*hom.21.6 in Gen*.(4.190E); *ib*.12.5(97E–98A); Max.*ep*.12(M.91.488D–489A); hence honour due to body as receptacle of soul, Or.*Cels*.8.30 (pp.245.27–246.5; M.11.1561A,B); **3.** soul as guide of body τῆς ψ. οὔσης τε καὶ διαμενούσης ὁμαλῶς ἐν ᾗ γέγονεν φύσει καὶ διαπονούσης ἃ πέφυκεν (πέφυκεν δὲ ταῖς τοῦ σώματος ἐπιστατεῖν ὁρμαῖς καὶ τὸ προσπῖπτον ἀεὶ τοῖς προσήκουσι κρίνειν καὶ μετρεῖν κριτηρίοις καὶ μέτροις) Athenag.*res*.12(p.63.1; M.6.1000A); Iren.*haer*.2.33.3(M.7.832B); *ib*.2.33.4(833A); Dion.Al.*fr*.(p.227.7f.); Cyr.H.*hom*.18(M.33.1152C); ὅπερ ἐστὶ θεὸς ψυχῇ, τοῦτο ψ. σώματι γένηται παιδαγωγήσασα δι' ἑαυτῆς τὴν ὑπηρέτιν ὕλην, καὶ οἰκειώσασα θεῷ τὸ ὁμόδουλον Gr.Naz.*or*.2.17(M.35.428A); ἐὰν...ὁ ἡνίοχος τὰς ὁρμὰς τοῦ ὑποζυγίου δεόντως οἰκονομήσῃ, ἑαυτῷ τε πρὸς τὸ συμφέρον ἐχρήσατο, καὶ τοῦ σκοποῦ τοῦ προκειμένου τετύχηκε, καὶ αὐτὸς δὲ σέσωσται, καὶ τὸ ὑποζύγιον ὤφθη τὴν χρῆσιν ἄριστον,...οὕτω καὶ ἐπὶ τῆς ψ. καὶ τοῦ σώματος ὑπολάμβανε ...ἐὰν μὲν γὰρ αὐτὴ τὰς τοῦ σώματος ὁρμὰς δεόντως οἰκονομῇ, αὐτό τε περιεσώσατο, καὶ αὐτὴ ἔξω κινδύνων διατελεῖ ‡Bas.*const*.2.3(2.542D; M.31.1341C); ὅπερ γάρ ἐστιν ἡνίοχος ἅρματι, καὶ κυβερνήτης πλοίῳ, καὶ μουσικὸς ὀργάνῳ, τοῦτο εἶναι τῷ γηΐνῳ τούτῳ σκεύει τὴν ψ. ὁ πλάστης ἐνομοθέτησεν. αὕτη γὰρ κατέχει τὰς ἡνίας, καὶ κινεῖ τὰ πηδάλια, καὶ τὰς χορδὰς ἀνακρούεται Chrys.*hom.in Mt*.7:14(3.25D); **4.** gives life and movement to body ὑπὸ ψ. κινεῖται [sc. σῶμα], τῆς καὶ τὸ ζῆν αὐτῷ παρεχούσης. εἰ τοίνυν τῷ σώματι ἡμῶν ψ. δείκνυται τὸ ζῆν παρέχουσα, ἔσται καὶ καθ' ἑαυτὴν ἡ ψ. ἐκ τῶν ἐναντίων γνωριζομένη Max.*anim*.(M.91.356B); id.*ep*.6(M.91.425B); which is its instrument, Iren.*haer*.2.33.4(M.7.833A); Cyr.H.*catech*.4.23; ‡Bas.*struct.hom*.1.7(1.327D; M.30.17C); Chrys.*hom.14.5 in Gen*.(4.113C); but limits its capacities, cf. *anima...tantum autem impeditur a sua velocitate, quantum corpus participat de ejus motione; sed non amittit suam scientiam...anima participans suo corpori, modum quidem impeditur, admixta velocitate ejus in corporis tarditate*, Iren. *haer*.2.33.4(M.7.833A); Clem.*paed*.2.9(p.207.20ff.; M.8.496C); ψυχῆς οὐσία, τὴν φύσιν οὖσα νοερὰ καὶ λογική, ἐν νηπιάζοντι κατὰ φύσιν σώματι παρὰ φύσιν αὐτὴ χώραν ἀλόγου μετείληφε Eus.*p.e*.6.6(247A; M.21.720D); ὅμως...ἐξακολουθεῖ...τῷ σώματι ἡ ψ. ὁμοῦ γὰρ εἶναι δεῖ τὸ σύνθετον. ἀλλὰ προηγουμένως μέν, τοῦ σώματος ὁ τόπος, ἡ ψ. δὲ κατ' ἐπακολούθησιν περικλείεται τόπῳ, διὰ τῆς πρὸς τὸ σῶμα σχέσεως †Bas.*parad.*7(1.349F–350A; M.30.68B); cf.Jo.Clim.*scal.*26(M.88.1072C); **5.** interaction of both, cf. δεσμὸς δὲ τῆς σαρκὸς ψ., σχετικὴ δὲ τῆς ψ. ἡ σάρξ Tat.*orat.*15(p.16.21; M.6.837B); idea that both grow together, resulting from a material conception of soul ὅτι μὲν οὐκ εἰσὶν ἀγέννητοι αἱ ψ., τοῦτο δείκνυσι σαφέστερον ἡ τῶν ἀρτιγόνων ἡλικία βρεφῶν. εἰ...ἅμα τῷ τεχθῆναι τὰ παιδία, τελείας ἐξῆπτο φρονήσεως, ἐξῆν ἴσως ὑποκρίνεσθαί τινας ἄνοιαν· εἰ δὲ λείπεται νοῦ...οὐκ ἄρα καθέστηκαν ἀγέννητοι τὴν φύσιν αἱ ψ. σύμπαντες οὖν ἴσμεν ὅτι τοῖς τῶν σωμάτων ὄγκοις ἡ ψ. συνεκτέταται διαρκῶς, οὐ μεγέθει μόνον...μελῶν, ἀλλὰ καὶ ταῖς ἄλλαις τῆς γνώμης ἀναλογίαις...εἰ δὲ ταῦτα ἴδια μέν ἐστι ψυχῆς, ἐκ περιουσίας δὲ τὰς κρείττους ἐπιδέχονται προσθήκας ...δῆλον ὅτι συναυξάνει μὲν τῷ σώματι Eust.*fr.*4(Spanneut p.96.2) ap.Leont.et Jo.*sacr.*2(M.86.2040B,C); orthodox conception of a progressive revelation of its functions ἐπὶ τῆς ἀνθρωπίνης συστάσεως, πρὸς λόγον τῆς σωματικῆς ποσότητος, καὶ ἡ τῆς ψ. διαφαίνεται δύναμις· πρῶτον μὲν διὰ τοῦ θρεπτικοῦ καὶ αὐξητικοῦ τοῖς ἔνδοθεν πλασσομένοις ἐγγινομένη. μετὰ ταῦτα δὲ τὴν αἰσθητικὴν χάριν τοῖς εἰς φῶς προελθοῦσιν ἐπάγουσα, εἶθ' οὕτω...τὴν λογικὴν ἐμφαίνουσα δύναμιν Gr.Nyss.*anim.et res.*(M.46.128A); without idea of growth θαύμαζε τὸν τεχνίτην, πῶς τῆς ψ. σου τὴν δύναμιν πρὸς τὸ σῶμα συνέδησεν, ὡς μέχρι τῶν περάτων αὐτοῦ διϊκνουμένην, τὰ πλεῖστον διεστῶτα μέλη πρὸς μίαν σύμπνοιαν...ἄγειν. σκόπει τίς ἡ ἀπὸ σαρκὸς πρὸς ψ. ἐπανιοῦσα συμπάθεια· πῶς δέχεται μὲν τὴν ζωὴν ἐκ τῆς ψ. τὸ σῶμα, δέχεται δὲ ἀλγηδόνας ἀπὸ τοῦ σώματος ἡ ψ. Bas.*hom.*3.7(2.23E; M.31.216A,B); πῶς τρέφεται διὰ ψ. σῶμα, καὶ πῶς ψ. διὰ σώματος κοινωνεῖ πάθους; Gr.Naz.*or.*32.27(M.36.205A); soul reflected in face, ‡Nil.*perist.*9.2 (M.79.865B); **6.** heret. views; **a.** that soul is imprisoned in body τὴν ψ. συνέδησε [sc. ὁ θεός] τῷ σώματι πρὸς κόλασιν Or.*princ.*1.8.1 (p.96.11); ἡ ὕλη...κατεσκεύασε τὸν ἄνθρωπον τὸν κατὰ τὴν ἰδέαν τοῦ πρώτου ἀνθρώπου ἐκείνου καὶ ἔδησε τὴν ψ. ἐν αὐτῷ Hegem.*Arch.*8(7; p.12.6; M.10.1440A); rejected εἰ γὰρ πρὸ τῆς παραβάσεως...σῶμα ἐκέκτηντο αἱ ψ., πῶς ⟨ὡς⟩ εἰς παγίδα ὕστερον, μετὰ τὴν παράβασιν, εἰς ⟨τὸ⟩ σῶμα ἐμβιβάζονται, οὐκ ὄντος χρόνου, ἐν ᾧ πρὶν αὐτὰς τὸ σῶμα λαβεῖν ἐξημάρτησαν; Meth.*res.*1.54(p.310.18; M.41.1145A); ἦν ἄρα ἡ ψ. μετὰ σώματος καὶ πρὸ τῆς ἁμαρτίας *ib.*(p.311.19; 1145C); on ground that soul could not sin without body χρὴ γὰρ πρὸ τῆς ἁμαρτίας τὴν ψ. ὑπάρχειν μετὰ σώματος. ἐπεὶ εἰ ἄληπτος ἡ ψ. καθ' ἑαυτὴν τῇ ἁμαρτίᾳ, οὐκ ἂν ἥμαρτεν ὅλως πρὸ τοῦ σώματος *ib.*1.57 (p.318.18; 1152Dff.); εἰ πρὸ τοῦ ἐνδεθῆναι τὴν ψ. φὴς ἡμαρτηκέναι, περισσὸν τὸ λέγειν αἴτιον τῶν κακῶν τὸ σῶμα. εἰ γὰρ πρὸ τοῦ σώματος ἥμαρτε, καὶ ἀπαλλαγεῖσα νῦν ἐκ τοῦ σώματος αὖθις ἁμαρτήσει διὰ τὸ καὶ πρὸ τούτου ἡμαρτηκέναι, καὶ οὐκ αἴτιον τὸ σῶμα, ἀλλ' ἡ ψ. εἰ δεσμὸν ψ. τὸ σῶμα ὑπέθετο, ὁ δὲ δεσμὸς ἐπέχειν πέφυκε τὸν ἁμαρτάνοντα...τὸ σῶμα οὐ δεσμός ἐστι ψ., ἀλλὰ συνεργόν. πῶς; ὁ δεσμὸς οὐ συνεργεῖ τῷ δεδεμένῳ πρὸς ἁμαρτίαν ἀλλ' ἐπέχει...τὸ δὲ σῶμα συνεργεῖ τῇ ψ. εἰς φόνους καὶ μοιχείας. δείκνυται οὖν ὁ θεὸς οὐ δεσμὸν δοὺς τῇ ψ. τὸ σῶμα, ἀλλὰ συνεργόν Adam.*dial.*5.21(p.218.4ff.; M.11.1861A,B); οὐ γὰρ κατ' οὐρανὸν ἁμαρτοῦσαι ψ. ἐν σώματι κατεκρίθησαν τιμωρεῖσθαι, μηκέτι δυνάμεναι συμπεριπολεῖν τῇ ὑπερκοσμίῳ τελευτῇ. εἰ γὰρ πρὸς διόρθωσιν ...τοῖς σώμασι τούτοις κατεκλείσθησαν, πῶς ἐν τούτῳ βαρυτέρως ἁμαρτάνουσιν; ‡Caes.Naz.*dial.*3.149(M.38.1100); **b.** that body is cause of sin to soul οὐχὶ τὸ σῶμά ἐστι τὸ τυφλοῦν τὴν ψ., ἄπαγε...ἀλλ' ἡ τρυφή ...οὐδὲ γὰρ ψ. μόνον, ἀλλὰ καὶ αὐτῷ τῷ σώματι...πολέμιον ἡ τρυφή Chrys.*hom.39.9 in 1Cor.*(10.376B); ὅτι δὲ οὐδὲ κακίας αἴτιον τῇ ψ. τὸ σῶμα, δῆλον ἐκ τοῦ δυνατὸν εἶναι καὶ ἄνευ σώματος παρυφίστασθαι κακίαν, ὥσπερ ἐν δαίμοσι· τοῦτο γάρ ἐστι καὶ νοΐς, καὶ ψ., καὶ σώμασι κακόν, ἡ τῆς ἕξεως τῶν οἰκείων ἀγαθῶν ἀσθένεια καὶ ἀπόπτωσις Dion. Ar.*d.n.*4.27(M.3.728D); **c.** that God is cause of the soul, but not of body; discussed and refuted, Or.*Cels.*4.54–61(pp.326.24–333.3; M. 11.1117A–1128C); **7.** relation of Christians to world analogous to that of soul to body, *Diogn.*6.1–9.

E. in rel. to νοῦς and πνεῦμα qq.v.; **1.** dist. from νοῦς: ἡμεῖς... ἐσμεν ἡ ψ. καὶ ὁ νοῦς Bas.*hom.*3.3(2.18C; M.31.204A); αἱ κινήσεις αἱ τῶν νοῶν, αἱ τῶν ψ. Dion.Ar.*d.n.*4.7(M.3.704C); πόλις τροπικῶς ἡ ψ.· ἧς ὁ βασιλεὺς νοῦς Olymp.*Eccl.*10:16f.(M.93.604A); **2.** νοῦς as part of ψ.: ἐν...τοῖς μαχίμοις ζῴοις δι' ἐμψύχων τε καὶ ἀψύχων ψ. τὸ τάττον ἐστὶ καὶ νοῦς, ἐν δὲ τοῖς τῆς ψ. πάθεσιν...λογισμός ἐστι τὸ τακτικόν Clem.*str.*1.24(p.100.16f.; M.8.908A); τῆς λογικῆς ψ. αὐλὴ μὲν ἡ αἴσθησις· ναὸς δέ, ἡ διάνοια· ἀρχιερεὺς δέ, ὁ νοῦς ‡Max.*cap.al.*158(M.90. 1437B); **3.** change of νοῦς into ψ. and vice versa (Origen), cf. *mens de statu ac dignitate sua declinans, nuncupata est anima; quae si reparata fuerit et correcta, redit in hoc, ut sit mens*, Or.*princ.*2.8.3 (p.159.1; M.11.223C); νοῦς...*corruens facta est anima, et rursum anima instructa virtutibus mens fiet*, *ib.*(p.161.7; 223C); idea rejected τοὺς γὰρ βαθμοὺς τῶν ψ. καὶ τὰς ἀναβάσεις καὶ καταβάσεις, ἃς Ὠριγένης εἰσάγει, μηδὲν προσηκούσας ταῖς θείαις γραφαῖς, μηδὲ συνᾳδούσας τοῖς τῶν Χριστιανῶν δόγμασι, παραλειπτέον Nemes.*nat. hom.*3(M.40.608A); **4.** position of soul between flesh and spirit Χριστός, εἰς ὃν ἐλπίζουσιν σαρκί, ψ., πνεύματι Ign.*Philad.*11.2; ψ. ἐν σώματί ἐστιν, οὐ ζῇ δὲ ἄψυχον. σῶμα, ψ. ἀπολειπούσης, οὐκ ἔστιν. οἶκος γὰρ τὸ σῶμα ψ.· πνεύματος δὲ ψ. οἶκος. τὰ τρία ταῦτα τοῖς ἐλπίδα εἰλικρινῆ καὶ πίστιν ἀδιάκριτον ἐν τῷ θεῷ ἔχουσι σωθήσεται †Just.*fr.res.*10(M.6.1589B); cf. *sunt tria, ex quibus...perfectus homo constat, carne anima et spiritu: et altero quidem salvante et figurante, qui est spiritus; altero quod unitur et formatur, quod est caro; id vero quod inter haec est duo, quod est anima: quae aliquando quidem subsequens spiritum, elevatur ab eo; aliquando autem consentiens carni, decidit in terrenas concupiscentias*, Iren.*haer.*5.9.1(M.7.1144B); *spiritus* understood as Holy Spirit, cf. *cum autem spiritus hic commistus animae unitur plasmati, propter effusionem spiritus, spiritualis et perfectus homo factus est...si autem defuerit animae spiritus, animalis est vere, qui est talis*, *ib.*5.6.1(1137C–1138C); Or. *princ.*2.8.4(p.162.18ff.; M.11.224B); a disembodied soul called πνεῦμα τῆς ψ. Clem.*prot.*11(p.82.30; M.8.237A); ψ. equated with πνεῦμα, Serap.*euch.*30.2.

F. soul after death; **1.** its eternal life dependent on God ἡ ψ. ἤτοι ζωή ἐστιν ἢ ζωὴν ἔχει. εἰ μὲν οὖν ζωή ἐστιν, ἄλλο τι ἂν ποιήσειε ζῆν, οὐχ ἑαυτήν,...ὅτι δὲ ζῇ ψ., οὐδεὶς ἀντείποι. εἰ δὲ ζῇ, οὐ ζωὴ οὖσα ζῇ, ἀλλὰ μεταλαμβάνουσα τῆς ζωῆς· ἕτερον δέ τι τὸ μετέχον τινὸς ἐκείνου οὗ μετέχει. ζωῆς δὲ ψ. μετέχει, ἐπεὶ ζῆν αὐτὴν ὁ θεὸς βούλεται. οὕτως ἄρα καὶ οὐ μεθέξει ποτέ, ὅταν αὐτὴν μὴ θέλοι ζῆν. οὐ γὰρ ἴδιον αὐτῆς ἐστι τὸ ζῆν ὡς τοῦ θεοῦ· ἀλλὰ ὥσπερ ἄνθρωπος οὐ διὰ παντός ἐστιν οὐδὲ σύνεστιν ἀεὶ τῇ ψ. τὸ σῶμα καὶ ὁ ἄνθρωπος οὐκ ἔστιν, οὕτως καί, ὅταν δέῃ τὴν ψ. μηκέτι εἶναι, ἄπεστι ἀπ' αὐτῆς τὸ ζωτικὸν πνεῦμα καὶ οὐκ ἔστιν ἡ ψ. ἔτι, ἀλλὰ καὶ αὐτὴ ὅθεν ἐλήφθη ἐκεῖσε χωρεῖ πάλιν Just.*dial.*6.1,2(M.6.489B–492A); οὐκ ἔστιν ἀθάνατος...ἡ ψ. καθ' ἑαυτήν, θνητὴ δέ· ἀλλὰ δυνατὸς ἡ αὐτὴ καὶ μὴ ἀποθνήσκειν. θνήσκει...μετὰ τοῦ σώματος μὴ γινώσκουσα τὴν ἀλήθειαν, ἀνίσταται δὲ εἰς ὕστερον ἐπὶ συντελείᾳ τοῦ κόσμου σὺν τῷ σώματι θάνατον διὰ τιμωρίας ἐν ἀθανασίᾳ λαμβάνουσα· πάλιν τε οὐ θνήσκει, κἂν πρὸς καιρὸν λυθῇ, τὴν ἐπίγνωσιν τοῦ θεοῦ πεποιημένη. καθ' ἑαυτὴν γὰρ σκότος ἐστίν, καὶ οὐδὲν ἐν αὐτῇ φωτεινόν...ψ. γὰρ οὐκ αὐτὴ τὸ πνεῦμα ἔσωσεν, ἐσώθη δὲ ὑπ' αὐτοῦ...λόγος μέν ἐστι τὸ τοῦ θεοῦ φῶς, σκότος δὲ ἡ ἀνεπιστήμων ψ. διὰ τοῦτο μόνη μὲν διαιτωμένη πρὸς τὴν ὕλην νεύει κάτω συναποθνήσκουσα τῇ σαρκί, συζυγίαν δὲ κεκτημένη τὴν τοῦ θείου πνεύματος οὐκ ἔστιν ἀβόηθος, ἀνέρχεται δὲ πρὸς ἅπερ αὐτὴν ὁδηγεῖ χωρία τὸ πνεῦμα· τοῦ μὲν γάρ ἐστιν ἄνω τὸ οἰκητήριον, τῆς δὲ κάτωθέν ἐστιν ἡ γένεσις· γέγονεν...συνδίαιτον ἀρχῆθεν τῇ ψ. τὸ πνεῦμα· τὸ δὲ πνεῦμα ταύτην ἕπεσθαι μὴ βουλομένην αὐτῷ καταλέλοιπεν Tat.*orat.*13(p.14.10ff.; M. 6.833A,B); **2.** retaining its identity, cf.Iren.*haer.*2.34.1(M.7.834C); ἡ νοερὰ τῆς ψ. φύσις, καὶ συνδρομῇ τῶν στοιχείων ἐνθεωρεῖται, καὶ διαλυθέντων οὐκ ἀποκρίνεται, ἀλλὰ καὶ ἐν αὐτοῖς μένει καὶ ἐν τῷ χωρισμῷ αὐτῶν συμπαρεκτεινομένη οὐ διακόπτεται, οὐδὲ πρὸς τὸν ἀριθμὸν τῶν στοιχείων εἰς μερικὰ τμήματα κατακερματίζεται Gr.Nyss. *anim.et res.*(M.46.48B); which extends also to future resurrection body, *ib.*(109A); ἡ ψ. οὖν ἀεί τε οὖσα, ἀφ' οὗ γέγονεν, καὶ ὑφισταμένη διὰ τὸν οὕτως αὐτὴν δημιουργήσαντα θεόν, ἀεὶ νοεῖ καὶ λογίζεται...καὶ καθ' ἑαυτήν, καὶ μετὰ σώματος, δι' ἑαυτὴν καὶ τὴν ἑαυτῆς φύσιν. οὐδεὶς οὖν εὑρεθήσεται λόγος, ὁ τὴν ψ. τῶν προσόντων αὐτῇ φυσικῶς, καὶ οὐ διὰ τὸ σῶμα, μετὰ τὴν τούτου λύσιν ἀλλοτριῶσαι δυνάμενος Max.*ep.*7(M.91.436D–437A); which, acc. those who attribute a certain materiality to soul (v. I.B.6.a), is linked to body, cf. *animas... habere hominis figuram, ut etiam cognoscantur*, Iren.*haer.*2.34.1(835A); τότε ἡ ψ. ἐξέρχεται ἀπὸ τοῦ σώματος, καὶ ἀσπάζονται αὐτὴν οἱ ἄγγελοι· ἡμεῖς δὲ θεωροῦμεν τὸ εἶδος τῆς ψ. ὡς εἶδος φωτὸς πεπληρωμένον καθ' ὅλου τοῦ σώματος χωρὶς τοῦ ἄρσενος καὶ τῆς θηλείας *V.Zos.*14(p.105. 21ff.); cf. Methodius' view that soul has teeth to gnash ζητητέον τῶν κολαζομένων τὸν βρυγμὸν τῶν ὀδόντων τῆς ψ. δύναμιν μασητικὴν ἐχούσης, ἥτις ἐν καιρῷ τοῦ ἐλέγχου περὶ τῶν ἁμαρτημάτων κατὰ τὸν συγκρουσμὸν τῶν ὀδόντων ὧν ἐφρόνησε βρύξει τοὺς ὀδόντας *res.*1.24 (p.248.19; M.41.1093C); hence **3.** rejection of: **a.** metempsychosis ἕως ἐν τῷ σωματί ἐστιν ἡ ψ. βλέπει, ἢ ἀπαλλαγεῖσα τούτου; καὶ ἕως μέν ἐστιν ἐν ἀνθρώπου εἴδει...μάλιστα δὲ ἀπολυθεῖσα τοῦ σώματος τυγχάνει οὗ ἤρα...πάντως. ... ἢ καὶ μέμνηται τούτου πάλιν ἐν ἀνθρώπῳ γενομένη; οὔ μοι δοκεῖ, ἔφην. τί οὖν ὄφελος ταῖς ἰδούσαις...; οὐκ ἔχω εἰπεῖν...αἱ δὲ ἀνάξιαι ταύτης τῆς θέας κριθεῖσαι τί πάσχουσιν; ἔφη· εἴς τινα θηρίων ἐνδεσμεύονται σώματα, καὶ αὕτη ἐστὶ κόλασις αὐτῶν. οἴδασιν οὖν ὅτι διὰ ταύτην τὴν αἰτίαν ἐν τοιούτοις εἰσὶ σώμασι καὶ ὅτι ἐξήμαρτόν τι; οὐ νομίζω. οὐδὲ ταύταις ἄρα ὄφελός τι τῆς κολάσεως, ὡς ἔοικεν· ἀλλ' οὐδὲ κολάζεσθαι αὐτὰς λέγοιμι...οὔτε οὖν ὁρῶσι τὸν θεὸν αἱ ψ., οὔτε μεταμείβουσιν εἰς ἕτερα σώματα Just.*dial.*4.4–7(M.6.485A,B);

cf. *de corpore autem in corpus transmigrationem ipsorum subvertamus ex eo, quod nihil omnino eorum quae ante fuerint, meminerint animae,* Iren.*haer*.2.33.1(M.7.830C); *perseverare animas, et non de corpore in corpus transire, ib*.2.34.1(835A); Manich. view stated *ἐρῶ...πῶς μεταγγίζεται ἡ ψ. εἰς πέντε σώματα. πρῶτον καθαρίζεται μικρόν τι ἀπ' αὐτῆς, εἶτα μεταγγίζεται εἰς κυνὸς ἢ εἰς καμήλου ἢ εἰς ἑτέρου ζώου σῶμα. ἐὰν δὲ ᾖ πεφονευκυῖα ψ., εἰς κελεφῶν σώματα μεταφέρεται· ἐὰν δὲ θερίσασα εὑρεθῇ, εἰς μογγιλάλους. τῆς δὲ ψ. ἐστι τὰ ὀνόματα ταῦτα, νοῦς, ἔννοια, φρόνησις, ἐνθύμησις, λογισμός* Hegem.*Arch*.10(p.15.6ff.; M.10.1441C); *τινὲς...ὑβρίζουσι τῇ κοινότητι τὸ ἀνθρώπινον, τὴν αὐτὴν ἀνὰ μέρος ἀνθρώπου τε καὶ ἀλόγου ψ. διοριζόμενοι γίνεσθαι, μετενδυομένην τὰ σώματα...ἢ πτηνόν, ἢ ἔνυδρον, ἢ χερσαῖόν τι ζῶον γινομένην μετὰ τὸν ἄνθρωπον* Gr.Nyss.*anim.et res*.(M.46.108B); **b.** belief that souls can become demons, Chrys.*hom.28.2 in Mt*.(7.336B–D); **c.** that they dissolve into air, v. *ἀήρ*; **4.** soul leaving earth immediately after death *ἔγνω δὲ ἐπακουσθεὶς* [sc. Christ], *ἐπείπερ πνεύματι εἶδεν ὅτι ἀποκατέστη ἡ τοῦ Λαζάρου ψ. ἐπὶ τὸ σῶμα αὐτοῦ, ἀναπεμφθεῖσα ἀπὸ τοῦ χωρίου τῶν ψ. οὐ γὰρ νομιστέον ὅτι ἡ ψ. τοῦ Λαζάρου παρῆν τῷ σώματι μετὰ τὴν ἔξοδον, καὶ ὡς παροῦσα ταχέως ἤκουσεν κράξαντος Ἰησοῦ...ἢ εἴπερ τις τοῦτο περὶ τῆς Λαζάρου ψ. ὑπολαμβάνει καὶ προσίεται τὸ περὶ τῆς ἀπαλλαγείσης ψ. σώματος ἄτοπον, ὡς παρακαθεζομένης τῷ νεκρῷ, λεγέτω πῶς ἠκούσθη ὁ Ἰησοῦς ἀπὸ τοῦ πατρός, μένοντος ἔτι νεκροῦ τοῦ Λαζάρου σώματος, καὶ τῆς ψ. κεχωρισμένης μέν,...παρακαθεζομένης δὲ τῷ σώματι. ἵνα γὰρ τοῦτο συγχωρηθῇ, οὐκ ἂν ἠκοῦσθαι εἴποι μὲν τὸν Ἰησοῦν μέλλοντα ἀκούεσθαι ὅτε ἡ ψ. ἐνοικίζετο τῷ σώματι...ᾔτησεν γὰρ ἐπανελθεῖν τὴν ψ. καὶ ἐνοικισθῆναι πάλιν τῷ σώματι* Or.*Jo*.28.6(5; pp.395.31–396.10; M.14.689C–692A); *τοῦ σώματος αἱ ψ. ἐξελθοῦσαι, οὐκ ἔτι ἐνταῦθα διατρίβουσιν, ἀλλ' εὐθέως ἀπάγονται* Chrys.*Laz*.2.2(1.729A); *οὐδὲ γὰρ ἔνι ψ. ἀπορραγεῖσαν τοῦ σώματος ἐνταῦθα πλανᾶσθαι λοιπὸν...αἱ τῶν δικαίων, καὶ αἱ τῶν παίδων...καὶ αἱ τῶν ἁμαρτωλῶν δὲ εὐθέως ἐντεῦθεν ἀπάγονται. καὶ δῆλον ἀπὸ τοῦ Λαζάρου καὶ τοῦ πλουσίου... οὐχ οἷόν τε ψ. ἐξελθοῦσαν τοῦ σώματος ἐνταῦθα πλανᾶσθαι...πῶς ἡ τοῦ σώματος ἀπορραγεῖσα ψ. καὶ τῆς συνηθείας ἐξελθοῦσα πάσης, εἴσεται ποῦ δεῖ βαδίζειν ἄνευ τοῦ καθοδηγοῦντος αὐτήν; καὶ πολλαχόθεν δὲ ἑτέρωθεν ἄν τις κατίδοι, ὅτι οὐκ ἔνι ψ. ἐξελθοῦσαν ἐνταῦθα μεῖναι* id. *hom.28.3 in Mt*.(7.336D–337A); this doctrine discussed, ref. apparition of saints in their sanctuaries, ‡Ath.*qu.Ant*.26(M.28.613B); **5.** intermediate state of souls before gen. resurrection; assumed by some authors against those who deny resurrection of body *βλασφημεῖν τολμῶσι τὸν θεόν...οἳ καὶ λέγουσι μὴ εἶναι νεκρῶν ἀνάστασιν, ἀλλὰ ἅμα τῷ ἀποθνήσκειν τὰς ψ. αὐτῶν ἀναλαμβάνεσθαι εἰς τὸν οὐρανόν* Just.*dial*.80.4(M.6.665A); *αἱ ψ. ἀπέρχονται εἰς τὸν... τόπον τὸν ὡρισμένον αὐταῖς ἀπὸ τοῦ θεοῦ, κἀκεῖ μέχρι τῆς ἀναστάσεως φοιτῶσι, περιμένουσαι τὴν ἀνάστασιν· ἔπειτα ἀπολαβοῦσαι τὰ σώματα, καὶ ὁλοκλήρως ἀναστᾶσαι, τουτέστι σωματικῶς* Iren. *haer*.5.31.2(M.7.1209B); Hipp.*Graec*.2(M.10.800A); *δῆλον, ὅτι μετὰ τὴν ἐντεῦθεν ἀποδημίαν εἰς χώραν τινὰ ἀπάγονται αἱ ψ., οὐκ ἔτι κυρίαι οὖσαι ἐπανελθεῖν, ἀλλὰ τὴν φοβερὰν ἐκείνην ἡμέραν ἀναμένουσαι* Chrys.*hom.28.3 in Mt*.(7.337B); v. *ᾅδης*; **6.** difference in souls' eternal destiny dependent on their earthly life, opp. pagan philosophers' views *ὁ τοῦτ' αὐτό, φησί* [sc. Plato], *ὂν ἐπέκεινα πάσης οὐσίας,...ἐξαίφνης ταῖς εὖ πεφυκυίαις ψ. ἐγγινόμενον διὰ τὸ συγγενὲς καὶ ἔρωτα τοῦ ἰδέσθαι...τίς οὖν ἡμῖν, ἔλεγε* [sc. Trypho], *συγγένεια πρὸς τὸν θεόν ἐστιν; ἢ καὶ ἡ ψ. θεία καὶ ἀθάνατός ἐστι καὶ αὐτοῦ ἐκείνου τοῦ βασιλικοῦ νοῦ μέρος; ὡς δὲ ἐκεῖνος ὁρᾷ τὸ θεῖον, οὕτω καὶ ἡμῖν ἐφικτὸν τῷ ἡμετέρῳ νῷ συλλαβεῖν τὸ θεῖον;...πᾶσαι δὲ αὐτὸ διὰ πάντων αἱ ψ. χωροῦσι τῶν ζώων, ἠρώτα, ἢ ἄλλη μὲν ἀνθρώπου, ἄλλη δὲ ἵππου καὶ ὄνου; οὐκ, ἀλλ' αἱ αὐταὶ ἐν πᾶσίν εἰσιν, ἀπεκρινάμην. ὄψονται ἄρα, φησί, καὶ ἵπποι...τὸν θεόν; οὔ, ἔφην· οὐδὲ γὰρ οἱ πολλοὶ τῶν ἀνθρώπων, εἰ μή τις ἐν δίκῃ βιώσαιτο* Just.*dial*.4.1,2(M.6.484A,B); *εἰ δὲ κόσμος γεννητός, ἀνάγκη καὶ τὰς ψ. γεγονέναι...ἀλλὰ μὴν οὐδὲ ἀποθνήσκειν φημὶ πάσας τὰς ψ. ἐγώ· ἕρμαιον γὰρ ἦν ὡς ἀληθῶς τοῖς κακοῖς. ἀλλὰ τί; τὰς μὲν τῶν εὐσεβῶν ἐν κρείττονί ποι χώρῳ μένειν, τὰς δὲ ἀδίκους...ἐν χείρονι, τὸν τῆς κρίσεως ἐκδεχομένας χρόνον τότε. οὕτως αἱ μέν, ἄξιαι τοῦ θεοῦ φανεῖσαι, οὐκ ἀποθνήσκουσιν ἔτι· αἱ δὲ κολάζονται, ἔστ' ἂν αὐτὰς καὶ εἶναι καὶ κολάζεσθαι ὁ θεὸς θέλῃ ib*.5.2,3(488A); Clem.*str*.4.26(p.322.29; M.8.1377A); Or.*Cels*.6.23 (p.93.24; M.11.1325C); *ὅταν ἐξέλθῃ ἐκ τοῦ σώματος ψ. ἀνθρώπου μυστήριόν τι μέγα ἐκεῖ ἐπιτελεῖται. ἐὰν γὰρ ᾖ ὑπεύθυνος ἐν ἁμαρτίαις, ἔρχονται χοροὶ δαιμόνων...παραλαμβάνουσι τὴν ψ. ἐκείνην, καὶ κρατοῦσιν εἰς τὸ ἴδιον μέρος...ἀπὸ τοῦ μέρους τοῦ ἀγαθοῦ ὀφείλεις νοῆσαι, ὅτι οὕτως ἔχει τὰ πράγματα...ὅταν ἐξελθῶσιν ἀπὸ τοῦ σώματος, οἱ χοροὶ τῶν ἀγγέλων παραλαμβάνουσιν αὐτῶν τὰς ψ.* Mac.Aeg.*hom*. 22(M.34.660A,B); souls can be saved only if they have image of Christ impressed on them, *ib*.30.5(724C,D); *ὅταν γὰρ ἐξέλθῃ ἡ ψ. ἀπὸ τοῦ σώματος, πορεύονται μετ' αὐτῆς οἱ ἄγγελοι. καὶ τότε ἐξέρχονται εἰς συνάντησιν αὐτῆς πᾶσαι αἱ δυνάμεις τοῦ σκότους, θέλουσαι αὐτὴν κατασχεῖν, ἐξερευνῶντες εἰ ἄρα ἔχουσί τι τῶν ἑαυτῶν ἐν αὐτῇ. τότε οὐχ οἱ ἄγγελοι πολεμοῦσιν αὐτοῖς, ἀλλὰ τὰ ἔργα ἃ ἔπραξε περιτειχίζει καὶ φυλάττει αὐτὴν ἀπ' αὐτῶν, ἵνα μὴ ἅψωνται αὐτῆς* Esaias *or*.16; ‡Ath. *qu.Ant*.19(M.28.609A); **7.** necessity of purification either before or after death in order to obtain beatitude *εἰ τοίνυν εἴτε ἐκ τῆς νῦν ἐπιμελείας, εἴτε ἐκ τῆς μετὰ ταῦτα καθάρσεως ἐλευθέρα γένοιτο ἡμῖν ἡ ψ. τῆς πρὸς τὰ ἄλογα τῶν παθῶν συμφυΐας, οὐδὲν πρὸς τὴν τοῦ καλοῦ θεωρίαν ἐναποδισθήσεται...εἰ οὖν πάσης κακίας ἡ ψ. καθαρεύσειεν, ἐν τῷ καλῷ πάντως ἔσται* Gr.Nyss.*anim.et res*.(M.46.89B); *τῆς κακίας τῷ ἀκοιμήτῳ πυρὶ δαπανωμένης, ἀνάγκη πᾶσα καὶ τὴν ἐνωθεῖσαν αὐτῇ ψ. ἐν τῷ πυρὶ εἶναι, ὡς ἂν τὸ κατεσπαρμένον νόθον καὶ ὑλῶδες, καὶ κίβδηλον ἀπαναλωθῇ τῷ αἰωνίῳ πυρὶ δαπανώμενον ib*.(100A); hence souls can profit if eucharist is offered for them *οὐκ αἰσθάνονταί τινος εὐεργεσίας καὶ αἱ τῶν ἁμαρτωλῶν ψ., γινομένων ὑπὲρ αὐτῶν συνάξεων καὶ εὐποιιῶν καὶ προσφορῶν; εἰ μή τινες εὐεργεσίας μετεῖχον ἐκ τούτου, οὐκ ἂν ἐν τῇ προσκομιδῇ ἐμνημονεύοντο. ἀλλ' ὥσπερ ὅταν ἡ ἄμπελος ἀνθεῖ ἔξω ἐν τῷ ἀγρῷ, αἰσθάνεται δὲ τῆς ὀσμῆς αὐτῆς ὁ ἀποκεκλεισμένος οἶνος, καὶ συνανθεῖ καὶ αὐτός· οὕτω νόει καὶ τὰς τῶν ἁμαρτωλῶν ψ. μετέχειν εὐεργεσίας τινὸς ἐκ τῆς ὑπὲρ αὐτῶν γενομένης ἀναιμάκτου θυσίας καὶ εὐποιΐας, ὡς μόνος ἐπίσταται...θεὸς ἡμῶν* ‡Ath.*qu.Ant*. 34(M.28.617B); and they are prayed for in liturgy, Serap.*euch*.13.18; **8.** description of soul's eternal life; **a.** of beatitude, ref. 2Cor.5:3 *ἐὰν γὰρ καταλυθῇ ἡμῶν ὁ οἶκος τοῦ σώματος, οὐκ ἔχομεν ἄλλον οἶκον, εἰς ὃν καταλύσει ἡμῶν ἡ ψ. 'εἴγε', φησί, 'καὶ ἐνδυσάμενοι οὐ γυμνοὶ εὑρεθησόμεθα' τουτέστιν ἀπὸ τῆς κοινωνίας...τοῦ ἁγίου πνεύματος, εἰς ἣν μόνον ἡ πιστὴ ψ. ἀναπαύεσθαι δύναται* Mac.Aeg.*hom*.5.7(M.34. 512D); *ψ. πᾶσα καλὴ καὶ θεοφιλής, ἐπειδάν, τοῦ συνδεδεμένου λυθεῖσα σώματος, ἐνθένδε ἀπαλλαγῇ, εὐθὺς μὲν ἐν συναισθήσει καὶ θεωρίᾳ τοῦ μένοντος αὐτὴν καλοῦ γενομένη* Gr.Naz.*or*.7.21(M.35.781B); *ἡ ψ. ἐξέρχεται τοῦ σώματος καὶ προσέρχεται τοῖς ἀγγέλοις· καὶ ἰδόντες τὴν ψ. ἄσπιλον ἐξερχομένην χαίρουσιν οἱ ἄγγελοι, καὶ ἁπλώσαντες τὰς στολὰς αὐτῶν δέχονται αὐτήν· τότε μακαριοῦσιν αὐτὴν οἱ ἄγγελοι λέγοντες· μακαρία σὺ ψ., ὅτι ἐπληρώθη τὸ θέλημα τοῦ κυρίου ἐν σοί V.Zos*.13 (p.105.2ff.); **b.** of damnation *ἐμπαθὴς ψ., πάντοτε κολάζεται...ὑπὸ τῆς ἰδίας κακοεξίας, ἔχουσα ἀεὶ τὴν πικρὰν μνήμην...τῶν παθῶν...πικροτέρα πάσης γεέννης ἡ κόλασις τῆς αἰσχύνης...πάντα γὰρ μέμνηνται αἱ ψ. τῶν ἐνταῦθα...καὶ λόγων καὶ ἔργων καὶ ἐνθυμήσεων* Dor.*doct*.12.3(M.88. 1752C–1753A); **c.** of souls' partic. characteristics and activities in eternity; facilities for knowing each other, ‡Ath.*qu.Ant*.22(M.28. 612A); relations to the living *ἆρα δὲ μέμνηνται ἡμῶν αἱ ἀπελθοῦσαι ψ.;...αἱ μὲν τῶν ἁγίων πάντως, αἱ δὲ τῶν ἁμαρτωλῶν...οὐδαμῶς. τὴν γὰρ μένουσαν αὐτοῖς ἐκδεχόμενοι κόλασιν, εἰκότως περὶ ταύτης καὶ μόνον μεριμνῶσι, μηδενὸς ἑτέρου φροντίζοντες ib*.32(616C,D); their way of life *τί...τὸ ἔργον ἐκεῖ τῶν προαπελθουσῶν ψ.; ψ. σώματος ἀπηλλαγμένη οὔτε ἀγαθόν τι οὔτε πονηρὸν διαπράξασθαι δύναται... ὥσπερ γὰρ ἡ λύρα, ἐὰν μὴ ἔχει τὸν κρούοντα, ἀργὴ ὁρᾶται καὶ ἄπρακτος· οὕτω καὶ ἡ ψ. καὶ τὸ σῶμα, ἐξ ἀλλήλων χωρισθέντα, οὐδὲν ἐνεργῆσαι δύναται. αἱ γοῦν τῶν ἁγίων ψ., ὑπὸ τοῦ ἁγίου πνεύματος ἐνεργούμεναι, μετὰ ἀγγέλων ἐν χώρᾳ ζώντων θεὸν ὑμνοῦσι ib*.33(617A); **9.** soul's reunion with body, v. *ἀνάστασις*; **a.** in gen. *ἑκάστῳ σώματι ἡ ἰδία ψ. ἀποδοθήσεται* Iren.*fr*.12(M.7.1236A); exeg. Eccl.12:5 *παχύνεται ἡ ἀκρίς (ἡ πτερωτὴ ψ., τὸ σῶμα περιβαλλομένη)* Cyr.H.*catech*.15.20; *ἐν δὲ τῇ ἀναστάσει τῶν σωμάτων, ὧν προανέστησαν καὶ προεδοξάσθησαν αἱ ψ., τότε καὶ τὰ σώματα συνδοξάζονται, καὶ φωτίζονται τῇ ἀπὸ τοῦ νῦν πεφωτισμένῃ καὶ δεδοξασμένῃ ψ.* Mac.Aeg.*hom*.34.2(M.34.745A); Gr.Nyss.*or.catech*.16(p.72.9; M.45.52D) cit. s. *ἀνάστασις*; **b.** exeg. 1Thess.4:15f. *οἱ νεκροὶ ἐν Χριστῷ ἀναστήσονται πρῶτον (τουτέστι τὰ σκηνώματα. ἐνεκρώθησαν γὰρ ἀπαμφιασθέντα τῶν ψ.). ἔπειτα ἡμεῖς οἱ ζῶντες ἅμα σὺν αὐτοῖς ἁρπαγησόμεθα, τὰς ψ. λέγων· ἡμεῖς γὰρ κυρίως οἱ ζῶντές ἐσμεν αἱ ψ., αἵτινες μετὰ τῶν σωμάτων, ἀπειληφυῖαι ταῦτα, ἐν νεφέλαις ὑπαντησόμεθα* Meth.*symp*.6.4(p.69.8ff.; M.18.120B); **c.** its necessity argued on ground of justice *εἰ δὲ φθείροιτο μὲν τὸ σῶμα ...μένοι δὲ ἡ ψ. καθ' ἑαυτὴν ὡς ἄφθαρτος, οὐδ' οὕτως ἕξει χώραν ἡ κατ' αὐτῆς κρίσις, μὴ παρούσης δικαιοσύνης...κατορθωμάτων τε γὰρ τιμωμένων, ἀδικηθήσεται τὸ σῶμα σαφῶς ἐκ τοῦ κοινωνῆσαι μὲν τῇ ψ. τῶν ἐπὶ τοῖς σπουδαζομένοις πόνων, μὴ κοινωνῆσαι δὲ τῆς ἐπὶ τοῖς κατορθωθεῖσι τιμῆς καὶ συγγνώμης μὲν τυγχάνειν πολλάκις τὴν ψ. ἐπί τινων πλημμελημάτων διὰ τὴν τοῦ σώματος ἔνδειαν ...ἐκπίπτειν δὲ αὐτὸ τὸ σῶμα ἐπὶ τοῖς κατορθωθεῖσι κοινωνίας, ὑπὲρ ὧν τοὺς ἐν τῇ ζωῇ συνδιήνεγκεν πόνους. καὶ μὴν καὶ πλημμελημάτων κρινομένων οὐ σῴζεται τῇ ψ. τὸ δίκαιον, εἴ γε μόνη τίνοι δίκην ὑπὲρ ὧν ἐνοχλοῦντος τοῦ σώματος καὶ πρὸς τὰς οἰκείας ὀρέξεις...ἕλκοντος ἐπλημμέλησεν...ἢ πῶς οὐκ ἄδικον τὴν ψ. κρίνεσθαι καθ' ἑαυτὴν ὑπὲρ ὧν οὐδ' ἡντινοῦν ἔχει, κατὰ τὴν ἑαυτῆς φύσιν, οὐκ ὄρεξιν;* Athenag.*res*.

20f.(pp.73.17–74.7; M.6.1013C–1016B); Epiph.*anc.*88(p.109.26f.; M.43.180D); ἀδικεῖς τὴν ψ. συνηγορίας προσχήματι, καὶ τῇ πρὸς τὸ σῶμα μάχῃ κατ' ἐκείνης ὁπλίζῃ. τὰς γὰρ τῶν πραττομένων ἀμοιβὰς μὴ μερίζων τῇ ψ., καὶ τὴν τῆς σαρκὸς ὡς μόνῃ πλημμελούσῃ τιμωρίαν εἰσάγεις. εἰ γὰρ ψ. μόνης αἱ τῶν πόνων...ἀμοιβαί, δῆλον ὅτι καὶ ὧν ἥμαρτεν ὁ ἄνθρωπος αἱ τιμωρίαι...μὴ σώματι καὶ ψ. καθίζῃς κατ' ἀλλήλων κριτήριον. σῶμα μὲν γὰρ εἰκότως καταβοήσεται ψυχῆς, τῶν κατορθωμάτων αὐτοῦ τὰς τιμὰς ἁρπαζούσης· ψ. δ' αὖ σώματος, τὰς ὀφειλομένας πληγὰς ἐκείνῳ μόνῃ εἰσπραττομένη ‡Nil.*fr.Pasch.*1(M.79.1493B,C); αἱ...ἱεραὶ ψ. πρὸς τὴν ἐπὶ τὰ χείρω κατὰ τὸν τῇδε βίον δυνάμεναι καταπίπτειν τροπήν, ἐν τῇ παλιγγενεσίᾳ τὴν ἐπὶ τὸ ἄτρεπτον ἕξουσι...μετάταξιν. τὰ δὲ καθαρὰ τῶν ἱερῶν ψ., ὁμόζυγα...σώματα συναπογραφέντα...κατὰ τοὺς θείους αὐτῶν ἱδρῶτας, ἐν τῇ τῶν ψ. ἀτρέπτῳ...ἱδρύσει, συναπολήψεται τὴν οἰκείαν ἀνάστασιν· ἑνωθέντα γὰρ αἷς ἥνωντο κατὰ τὸν τῇδε βίον ἱεραῖς ψ. ... τὴν θεοειδῆ...ἀπολήψεται λῆξιν Dion.Ar.*e.h.*7.1.1(M.3.553A,B); heterodox opinions refuted τῶν δὲ ἀνιέρων...οἱ δὲ τὴν σωματικὴν εἰσάπαξ ἀπορρήγνυσθαι τῶν οἰκείων ψ. συζυγίαν, ὡς ἀνάρμοστον αὐταῖς, ἐν θεοειδεῖ ζωῇ καὶ μακαρίαις λήξεσιν, οὐκ ἐννοήσαντες...ἀρχθεῖσαν ἤδη τὴν καθ' ἡμᾶς ἐν Χριστῷ...ζωήν. ἄλλοι δὲ σωμάτων ἄλλων ἀπονέμουσι ταῖς ψ. συζυγίας, ἀδοκοῦντες τὸ ἐπ' αὐτοῖς...τὰ συμπονήσαντα ταῖς θείαις ψ. *ib.*7.1.2(553B,C); εἰ γὰρ ἐν ψ. καὶ σώματι τὴν θεοφιλῆ ζωὴν ὁ κεκοιμημένος ἐβίω, τίμιον ἔσται μετὰ τῆς ὁσίας ψ. καὶ τὸ συναθλῆσαν αὐτῇ σῶμα... ἔνθεν ἡ θεία δικαιοσύνη μετὰ τοῦ σφετέρου σώματος αὐτῇ δωρεῖται τὰς ἀμοιβαίας λήξεις...διὸ καὶ τῶν ἱερῶν ἡ θεία θεσμοθεσία τὰς θεαρχικὰς κοινωνίας ἀμφοῖν δωρεῖται· τῇ ψ. μὲν ἐν καθαρᾷ θεωρίᾳ...τῷ σώματι δὲ κατὰ τὸ θειότατον ὡς ἐν εἰκόνι μύρον *ib.*7.3.9(565B); **10.** Gnost.; **a.** distinction between different types of souls and their destiny τὸ μὲν χοϊκὸν εἰς φθορὰν χωρεῖν· καὶ τὸ ψυχικόν, ἐὰν τὰ βελτίονα ἕληται, ἐν τῷ τῆς μεσότητος τόπῳ ἀναπαύ[σ]εσθαι· ἐὰν δὲ τὰ χείρω, χωρήσειν καὶ αὐτὸ πρὸς τὰ ὅμοια· τὰ δὲ πνευματικά, ἃ ἂν κατασπείρῃ ἡ Ἀχαμὼθ ἔκτοτε ἕως τοῦ νῦν δικαίαις ψ., παιδευθέντα ἐνθάδε καὶ ἐκτραφέντα, διὰ τὸ νήπια ἐκπεπέμφθαι, ὕστερον τελειότητος ἀξιωθέντα, νύμφας ἀποδοθήσεσθαι τοῖς τοῦ Σωτῆρος ἀγγέλοις δογματίζουσι, τῶν ψ. αὐτῶν ἐν μεσότητι κατ' ἀνάγκην μετὰ τοῦ Δημιουργοῦ ἀναπαυσαμένων εἰς τὸ παντελές. καὶ αὐτὰς μὲν τὰς ψυχικὰς [sc. ψυχάς] πάλιν ὑπομερίζοντες λέγουσιν, ἃς μὲν φύσει ἀγαθάς, ἃς δὲ φύσει πονηράς· καὶ τὰς μὲν ἀγαθὰς ταύτας εἶναι τὰς δεκτικὰς τοῦ σπέρματος γινομένας· τὰς δὲ φύσει πονηρὰς μηδέποτε ἂν ἐπιδέξασθαι ἐκεῖνο τὸ σπέρμα Iren.*haer.*1.7.5(M.7.520A); cf.*ib.*1.7.1(512B–513A); λαβὼν χοῦν ἀπὸ τῆς γῆς...ποικίλης ὕλης μέρος, ψ. γεώδη καὶ ὑλικὴν ἐτεκτήνατο ἄλογον καὶ τῇ τῶν θηρίων ὁμοούσιον Clem.*exc.Thdot.*50(p.123.10; M.9.681D); ἡ...τῶν πνευματικῶν ἀνάπαυσις ἐν κυριακῇ, ἐν ὀγδοάδι, ἡ κυριακὴ ὀνομάζεται, παρὰ τῇ μητρί, ἐχόντων τὰς ψ., τὰ ἐνδύματα, ἄχρι συντελείας, αἱ δὲ ἄλλαι πισταὶ ψ. παρὰ τῷ δημιουργῷ, περὶ δὲ τὴν συντέλειαν ἀναχωροῦσι καὶ αὗται εἰς ὀγδοάδα *ib.*63(p.128.10ff.; 689B); exeg. Gen.2:23 ἐν τῷ παραδείσῳ... χοϊκὴ σὰρξ οὐκ ἀναβαίνει, ἀλλ' ἦν τῇ ψ. ⟨τῇ⟩ θείᾳ οἷον σὰρξ ἡ ὑλική. ταῦτα σημαίνει 'τοῦτο νῦν ὀστοῦν ἐκ τῶν ὀστῶν μου', τὴν θείαν ψ. αἰνίσσεται τὴν ἐγκεκρυμμένην τῇ σαρκί...'καὶ σὰρξ ἐκ τῆς σαρκός μου' τὴν ὑλικὴν ψ. σῶμα οὖσαν τῆς θείας ψ. *ib.*51(pp.123.20–124.3; 684A,B); **b.** salvation of souls only, not of bodies, Iren.*haer.*1.24.5(M.7.678A); refuted, *ib.*2.29.1(812C); Adam.*dial.*2.7(p.70.8ff.; M.11.1769A); scriptural argument οὔτε προφῆται οὔτε ἀπόστολοι μνήμην ἐποιήσαντο σαρκὸς ἢ αἵματος ἀλλὰ ψ. μόνης, ἣν καὶ ηὔχοντο σῶσαι *ib.*5.20(p.214.4; 1860A); refuted δέδεικται δὲ ὅτι ὅλον τὸν ἄνθρωπον ψ. ὀνομάζει ἡ γραφή *ib.*(p.214.25; 1860B); **c.** description of progressive purification of souls (Manichean), Hegem.*Arch.*8(pp.12.14–13.13; M.10.1440B–1441A); cf.Thdt.*haer.*1.26(4.320); **11.** resurrection of souls (heret.) ἐπὶ τῆς Ἀραβίας...ἐπιφύονται δόγματος ἀλλοτρίου τῆς ἀληθείας εἰσηγηταί, οἳ ἔλεγον τὴν ἀνθρωπείαν ψ. τέως μὲν κατὰ τὸν ἐνεστῶτα καιρὸν ἅμα τῇ τελευτῇ συναποθνῄσκειν τοῖς σώμασιν... αὖθις δέ ποτε κατὰ τὸν τῆς ἀναστάσεως καιρὸν σὺν αὐτοῖς ἀναβιώσεσθαι Eus.*h.e.*6.37(M.20.597B); refuted ἐὰν γὰρ ἀνάστασιν εἴπωσιν αἱ αἱρέσεις καὶ ὅλως ἀνάστασιν ἡγοῦνται, περὶ ψ. δὲ τοῦτο ὁρίζωνται, εὔηθές ἐστι τὸ τοιοῦτον. πῶς γὰρ ψ. ἀναστήσεται ἡ μὴ πεπτωκυῖα; οὐ γὰρ θάπτομεν τὰς ψ. ἐν τοῖς μνημείοις, ἀλλὰ τὰ σώματα. ψ. γὰρ οὐ πίπτουσιν, ἀλλ' αἱ σάρκες...τοίνυν εἰ ἀνάστασις παρ' αὐτοῖς ὁμολογεῖται ...δῆλόν ἐστιν ⟨ὅτι⟩ οὐ ψ., ἀλλὰ σώματος τοῦ πεπτωκότος Epiph.*anc.*86(p.106.11ff.; M.43.176C); **12.** pagan; superstitious practices as evidence of belief in immortality ψ. ἀνθρωπίνων κλήσεις...πεισάτωσαν ὑμᾶς, ὅτι καὶ μετὰ θάνατον ἐν αἰσθήσει εἰσὶν αἱ ψ. Just.*1apol.*18.3(M.6.356A); punishment after death also taught by pagans τῷ δὲ κολάζεσθαι ἐν αἰσθήσει καὶ μετὰ θάνατον οὔσας τὰς τῶν ἀδίκων ψ., τὰς δὲ τῶν σπουδαίων ἀπηλλαγμένας τῶν τιμωριῶν εὖ διάγειν *ib.*20.4(357C); who derived ideas from scripture, *ib.*44.9(396A); Or.*Cels.*7.5(p.156.25; M.11.1425C).

G. non-human souls; **1.** essential difference between human and non-human souls ψ. ... ἀόρατοι, οὐ μόνον αἱ λογικαί, ἀλλὰ καὶ αἱ τῶν ἀλόγων ζῴων Clem.*str.*6.18(p.516.11; M.9.396C); βούλεται ὁ Κέλσος (καὶ γὰρ ἐν πολλοῖς Πλατωνίζειν θέλει) ὁμοειδῆ εἶναι πᾶσαν ψ., καὶ μηδὲν διαφέρειν τὴν τοῦ ἀνθρώπου τῆς τῶν μυρμήκων καὶ τῶν μελισσῶν· ὅπερ κατάγοντός ἐστι τὴν ψ. ἀπὸ τῶν ἁψίδων τοῦ οὐρανοῦ οὐκ ἐπὶ τὸ ἀνθρώπινον σῶμα μόνον ἀλλὰ καὶ ἐπὶ τὰ λοιπά. τούτοις δ' οὐ πείσονται Χριστιανοί, προκατειληφότες τὸ ⟨κατ' εἰκόνα⟩ γεγονέναι θεοῦ τὴν ἀνθρωπίνην ψ. καὶ ὁρῶντες ὅτι ἀμήχανόν ἐστι τὴν ⟨κατ' εἰκόνα⟩ θεοῦ δεδημιουργημένην φύσιν πάντῃ ἀπαλεῖψαι τοὺς χαρακτῆρας αὐτῆς καὶ ἄλλους ἀναλαβεῖν οὐκ οἶδα κατ' εἰκόνας τίνων γεγενημένους ἐν τοῖς ἀλόγοις Or.*Cels.*4.83(p.354.12ff.; M.11.1157B); which rules out metempsychosis, Bas.*hex.*8.2(1.71C,D; M.29.168A,B); **2.** world soul; **a.** in pagan philosophy ὅ γε τῆς αἱρέσεως πατήρ [sc. Aristotle], τῶν ὅλων οὐ νοήσας τὸν πατέρα, τὸν καλούμενον ὕπατον ψ. εἶναι τοῦ παντὸς οἴεται· τουτέστι τοῦ κόσμου τὴν ψ. θεὸν ὑπολαμβάνων αὐτὸς αὑτῷ περιπείρεται Clem.*prot.*5(pp.50.29–51.1; M.8.169B); Ἑλλήνων...τινες, ψ. τοῦ κόσμου τὸν θεὸν εἶπον Cyr.H.*catech.*8.2; **b.** Ophite ἡ τῶν ὅλων ψ. καὶ ὠνομάζετο Λευϊαθάν, ὅντινα αἱ Ἰουδαίων γραφαὶ ὅ τί ποτ' οὖν αἰνισσόμεναι ἔλεγον πεπλάσθαι ὑπὸ τοῦ θεοῦ παίγνιον Or.*Cels.*6.25(p.95.5; M.11.1329A); *ib.*6.35(p.104.15; 1349B); **3.** souls of stars, cf. *de caelestibus requirendum est quod non eo tempore, quo factus est mundus, solis anima vel quodcumque eam appellari oportet, esse coeperit, sed antequam lucens illud et ardens corpus intraret. de luna et stellis similiter sentiamus, quod ex causis praecedentibus licet invitae conpulsae sint subici vanitati*, Or.*princ.*2.8.3(p.161.8ff.; M.11.223C,D); ἡ ψ. τοῦ ἡλίου ἐν σώματι καὶ πᾶσα ἡ κτίσις, περὶ ἧς ὁ ἀπόστολός φησι· πᾶσα ἡ κτίσις στενάζει id.*Jo.*1.17(p.21.21; M.14.52C); πρεσβυτέρα ἡ ψ. τοῦ ἡλίου τῆς ἐνδέσεως αὐτοῦ τῆς εἰς τὸ σῶμα id. *princ.*1.7.4(p.91.5; M.11.174A); **4.** plant and animal souls Ἀριστοτέλης δὲ τῆς φυτικῆς τε καὶ θρεπτικῆς ψ. μετέχειν οἴεται τὰ φυτά Clem.*str.*8.4(p.86.2; M.9.573A); ref. divination εἴπερ δὲ θεία ἐστὶν ἡ τῶν ὀρνίθων ψ. διὰ τὸ δι' αὐτῶν προλέγεσθαι τὰ μέλλοντα, πῶς οὐχὶ μᾶλλον ὅπου κληδόνες ἀπὸ ἀνθρώπων λαμβάνονται, θείαν εἶναι φήσομεν τὴν ψ. ἐκείνων, δι' ὧν αἱ κληδόνες ἀκούονται;...ἤδη δὲ ὅρα, εἴπερ οἱ ὄρνιθες θείαν ἔχουσι ψ. καὶ αἰσθάνονται τοῦ θεοῦ ἤ, ὡς Κέλσος ὀνομάζει, τῶν θεῶν· δηλονότι καὶ ἡμεῖς πταρνύμενοι οἱ ἄνθρωποι ἀπό τινος ἐν ἡμῖν οὔσης θειότητος καὶ μαντικῆς περὶ τὴν ψ. ἡμῶν πταρνύμεθα Or.*Cels.*4.94(p.367.3ff.; M.11.1172D–1173D); Anast.S.*serm.imag.*3(M.89.1165D).

II. spiritual life of soul; **A.** foundations; **1.** affinity between God and soul made in his image (cf. εἰκών), Or.*princ.*2.3.3(p.117.20; M.11.191B); id.*mart.*47(p.42.30; M.11.629A); τὸ συγγενὲς ἐπιγνοῦσα ἡ λογικὴ ψ. ἀπορρίπτει μὲν ἃ τέως ἐδόξαζεν εἶναι θεοὺς φίλτρον δ' ἀναλαμβάνει φυσικὸν τὸ πρὸς τὸν κτίσαντα id.*Cels.*3.40(p.236.22; M.11.972C); *ib.*7.66(p.216.9; 1516A); Meth.*symp.*6.1(p.64.18; M.18.113B); Cyr.H.*catech.*4.18; οὔτε γὰρ φύσεως τῆς θεότητός ἐστιν ἡ ψ., οὔτε φύσεως τοῦ σκότους τῆς πονηρίας, ἀλλ' ἐστὶ κτίσμα τι νοερόν, καὶ ὡραῖον...καὶ καλὸν ὁμοίωμα καὶ εἰκὼν θεοῦ Mac.Aeg.*hom.*1.7(M.34.457B); ὥσπερ βρέφος νεογενὲς εἰκόνα τοῦ τελείου διασῴζει ἀνδρός, οὕτω δὴ καὶ ψ. εἰκών τίς ἐστι τοῦ πεποιηκότος αὐτὴν θεοῦ. ὡς οὖν καὶ παιδίον κατὰ μέρος μὲν αὐξανόμενον ἐκ μέρους ἐπιγινώσκει καὶ τὸν πατέρα...οὕτω καὶ ἡ ψ. πρὸ τῆς παρακοῆς προκόπτειν ἔμελλε id. *pat.*18(M.34.877D–880A); cf. χρὴ καὶ τὴν ψ. πρὸς τὴν ἰδίαν ἀπιδεῖν εἰκόνα, καὶ ὅπερ ἂν ἴδῃ ἐν τῷ χαρακτῆρι, ᾧ ἀφωμοίωται, ὡς ἴδιον ἑαυτῆς τοῦτο θεάσασθαι...ἐπὶ...τῆς ἐν τῷ κατόπτρῳ μορφῆς, ἡ εἰκὼν πρὸς τὸ ἀρχέτυπον σχηματίζεται· ἐπὶ δὲ τοῦ τῆς ψ. χαρακτῆρος, τὸ ἔμπαλιν νενοήκαμεν· κατὰ γὰρ τὸ θεῖον κάλλος, τὸ τῆς ψ. εἶδος ἀπεικονίζεται. οὐκοῦν ὅταν πρὸς τὸ ἀρχέτυπον ἑαυτῆς βλέπῃ ἡ ψ., τότε δι' ἀκριβείας ἑαυτὴν καθορᾷ. τί τοίνυν ἐστὶ τὸ θεῖον, ᾧ ἡ ψ. προσωμοίωται; οὐ σῶμα, οὐ σχῆμα...οὐκ ἄλλο τι τοιοῦτον οὐδέν, δι' ὧν ἡ ὑλικὴ κτίσις γνωρίζεται· ἀλλὰ...νοερόν τι καὶ ἄϋλον...εἰ τοίνυν τοιοῦτος ὁ χαρακτὴρ τοῦ ἀρχετύπου καταλαμβάνεται, ἀκόλουθον πάντως κατὰ τὸ εἶδος ἐκεῖνο μεμορφωμένην τὴν ψ. διὰ τῶν αὐτῶν χαρακτήρων ἐπιγνωσθῆναι· ὥστε καὶ ταύτην ἄϋλόν τε εἶναι...καὶ ἀσώματον Gr. Nyss.*mort.*(M.46.509C,D); κατ' εἰκόνα εἶπεν, ἐπειδὴ ἄφθαρτον καὶ αὐτεξούσιον ἐποίησεν ὁ θεὸς τὴν ψ. Dor.*doct.*12.6(M.88.1757C); but dist. from image δύο πνευμάτων διαφορὰς ἴσμεν ἡμεῖς, ὧν τὸ μὲν καλεῖται ψ., τὸ δὲ μεῖζον μὲν τῆς ψ., θεοῦ δὲ εἰκὼν καὶ ὁμοίωσις· ἑκάτερα δὲ παρὰ τοῖς ἀνθρώποις τοῖς πρώτοις ὑπῆρχεν, ἵνα τὸ μέν τι ὦσιν ὑλικοί, τὸ δὲ ἀνώτεροι τῆς ὕλης Tat.*orat.*12(p.12.19; M.6.829C); hence reason for the soul's existence is to diffuse divine goodness, Gr.Nyss.*anim.et res.*(M.46.105A); **2.** dignity and beauty of soul, Clem.*paed.*3.6(p.257.18; M.8.605B); ψ. γὰρ παντὸς σώματος... πρᾶγμα τιμιώτερον, εἰ καὶ τὸ κατ' εἰκόνα τοῦ κτίσαντος ψ. μὲν χωρεῖ οὐδαμῶς δὲ τὸ σῶμα Or.*Cels.*8.49(p.265.2,4; M.11.1589B,C); μὴ ἁπλῶς τῇ νοερᾷ τῆς ψ. οὐσίᾳ πρόσχης,...τίμιόν τι σκεῦός ἐστιν ἡ ἀθάνατος ψ. Mac.Aeg.*hom.*26.1(M.34.676A); τὴν...ψ., ὡς ἐκ θειοτέρων ἔχων ἥκεν, ἄλλῳ νομίζειν ὑποκεῖσθαι προσῆκον, καὶ θεῷ ὀφείλεσθαι παρ' αὐτῆς χρέα τὰ πάντων χρεῶν πρεσβύτατα Bas.*ep.*276(3.421A; M.32.1012B); ψ. ... τὴν ἐκ θεοῦ καὶ θείαν, καὶ τῆς ἄνωθεν εὐγενείας μετέχουσαν Gr. Naz.*or.*2.17(M.35.425B); εἴ γε ἐνῆν τοῖς σωματικοῖς ὀφθαλμοῖς τὸ τῆς ψ. κάλλος ἰδεῖν, κατεγέλασας ἂν τῶν σωματικῶν ὑποδειγμάτων Chrys. *Thdr.*1.14(1.22E); not affected by time or disease, id.*anom.*12.5 (1.556E); reflected in body, id.*hom.*34.5 *in Mt.*(7.396A); consisting in virtue, id.*Eutrop.*2.17(3.403D); αἱ ψ. ἡμῶν συγγενεῖς εἰσι τῶν ἀγγέλων Sever.*creat.*1.3(M.56.434); ἐκ τοῦ κυρίου μέρους τῆς ὄψεως δεικνὺς τὸ ἀξίωμα τῆς ψ., ὅτι ἡγεῖται πάσης αὐτοῦ τῆς ὑποστάσεως Proc.G.*Gen.*2:7(M.87.153C); πᾶς ὁ κόσμος ψυχῆς οὐκ ἀντάξιος· ὁ μὲν γὰρ παροίχεται· ἡ δὲ ἄφθαρτος Jo.Clim.*past.*13(M.88.1196D); **3.** divine indwelling, cf. *deus...eas animas, quae verbi ejus ac sapientiae efficiuntur capaces, una cum filio suo inhabitans*, Or. *princ.*1.1.2(p.17.27; M.11.122A); *ib.*2.3.2(p.116.4; 189C); ἐν τῇ ἐμῇ ψ. ὀφείλω ἔχειν ἔνδον μου τὸν Χριστόν id.*hom.*5.6 *in Jer.*(p.36.21; M.13. 304D); ἐν ταῖς γραφαῖς λέγεται, τὸ εἶναι τὸν πατέρα καὶ τὸν υἱὸν καὶ τὸ ἅγιον πνεῦμα ἐν τῇ τοῦ ἀνθρώπου ψ. *ib.*8.1(p.56.2; 336C); καθαρὰν ἔχουσιν αὐτὴν τὴν ψ. καὶ ἀεὶ τὸ πνεῦμα τὸ ἅγιον ἐν αὐτῇ κατοικεῖ Meth. *symp.*11(p.138.11; M.18.216B); οἰκείωσις δὲ πνεύματος πρὸς ψ. οὐχ ὁ διὰ τόπου προσεγγισμός...ἀλλ' ὁ χωρισμὸς τῶν παθῶν, ἅπερ ἀπὸ τῆς πρὸς τὴν σάρκα φιλίας ὕστερον ἐπιγινόμενα τῇ ψ., τῆς ἀπὸ τοῦ θεοῦ οἰκειότητος ἠλλοτρίωσε Bas.*Spir.*23(3.20A; M.32.109A); τὴν περὶ θεοῦ ἔννοιαν, οἷον ἐν ναῷ τινι...τῇ σαυτοῦ ψ. ἐνιδρυμένην ἔχοντα id.*ep.* 146(3.237A; M.32.596B); πνεύματος ἁγίου...μετέλαβον...σωτηριώδους πυρός...λαμπρύνοντος δὲ τὴν ψ. τοῦτο μέλλει νῦν ἔρχεσθαι καὶ ἐφ' ὑμᾶς· καὶ τὰς μὲν ἀκανθώδεις ὑμῶν ἁμαρτίας...ἀναλίσκειν, τὸ δὲ τῆς ψ. ὑμῶν κτῆμα τὸ τίμιον ἔτι λαμπρύνειν Cyr.H.*catech.*17.15; ἐνοικεῖ...ἡ θεία τριὰς ἐν τῇ καθαρῶς ἐχούσῃ ψ. Mac.Aeg.*carit.*28(M.34.932A).

B. its disturbance through sin; **1.** sin not natural to soul, but rather a disease πάθη...ἃ δὴ ψυχῆς νόσοι Clem.*prot.*11(p.81.17; M. 8.233B); id.*paed.*1.8(p.128.12; M.8.328C); εἰσὶ...παρ' ἡμῖν αἱ ἀρεταὶ κατὰ φύσιν, πρὸς ἃς οἰκείωσις τῆς ψ. οὐκ ἐκ διδασκαλίας ἀνθρώπων, ἀλλ' ἐξ αὐτῆς τῆς φύσεως ἐνυπάρχει. ὡς γὰρ οὐδεὶς ἡμᾶς λόγος διδάσκει τὴν νόσον μισεῖν, ἀλλ' αὐτόματον ἔχομεν τὴν πρὸς τὰ λυποῦντα διαβολήν· οὕτω καὶ τῇ ψ. ἔστι τις ἀδίδακτος ἔκκλισις τοῦ κακοῦ. κακὸν δὲ πᾶν ἀρρωστία ψυχῆς Bas.*hex.*9.4(1.83D,E; M.29.196B,C); ψ. ... ἐποίησεν ὁ θεός, οὐχὶ δὲ ἁμαρτίαν· ἐκακώθη δὲ ἡ ψ., παρατραπεῖσα τοῦ κατὰ φύσιν id.*hom.*9.6(2.78E; M.31.344B); cf.*ib.*9.5(78B; M.341C); ψ. τίς εἶναι λέγει κακάς; εἰ μέν, ὅτι συγγίνονται κακοῖς προνοητικῶς...τοῦτο οὐ κακόν, ἀλλ' ἀγαθόν...εἰ δὲ τὸ κακύνεσθαι ψ. φαμεν, ἐν τίνι κακύνονται, εἰ μὴ ἐν τῇ τῶν ἀγαθῶν ἕξεων...ἐλλείψει; Dion.Ar.*d.n.*4.24(M.3.725D–728A); ἆρα ἡ ψ. τῶν κακῶν αἰτία, καθάπερ τὸ πῦρ τοῦ θερμαίνειν...ἢ ἀγαθὴ μὲν ἡ τῆς ψ. φύσις, ταῖς δὲ ἐνεργείαις, ποτὲ μὲν οὕτως ἔχει, ποτὲ οὕτως; εἰ μὲν φύσει καὶ τὸ εἶναι αὐτῆς κακόν, καὶ πόθεν αὐτῇ τὸ εἶναι; ἢ ἐκ τῆς δημιουργικῆς τῶν ὅλων ὄντων ἀγαθῆς αἰτίας; ἀλλ' εἰ ἐκ ταύτης, πῶς κατ' οὐσίαν κακόν; *ib.*4.30(732A); **2.** causes leading soul into sin κάθοδον αὐτῇ [sc. ἀκολασίᾳ] διδόντες εἰς ψ. διὰ τῶν αἰσθήσεων Clem.*paed.*2.8(p.197.19; M.8.473B); *ib.*3. 11(p.266.32; 628A); αἱ τῶν σαρκικῶν ἐπιθυμιῶν ἀναδόσεις καχεξίαν προστρίβονται ψυχῇ, κατασκεδαννύουσαι τὰ εἴδωλα τῆς ἡδονῆς ἐπίπροσθε τῆς ψ. ἐπισκοτοῦσι γοῦν τῷ φωτὶ τῷ νοερῷ ἐπισπωμένης τῆς ψ. τὰς ἐκ τῆς ἐπιθυμίας ἀναδόσεις id.*str.*2.20(p.175.26f.; M.8.1060A,B); id.*q.d.s.*20(p.172.25; M.9.624D); Or.*fr.*52 *in Lam.*(p.257.26; M.13. 636B) cit. s. αἴσθησις; δεῖξαι τῆς τρυφῆς τὴν ἀηδίαν, καὶ τὴν ζημίαν... τὰς νόσους καταλέγοντα ὅσας ἐναπομόργνυται τῇ ψ. πολλῷ πλείους καὶ χαλεπωτέρας οὔσας τῶν σωματικῶν Chrys.*virg.*71(1.325B); τὰ φαιδρά σε τῆς γῆς μὴ τερπέτω,...ἄγκιστρα γάρ ἐστι τὴν ψ. ὡς ἰχθὺν δελεάζοντα Nil.*sent.*20(M.79.1241C); διὰ τεσσάρων πραγμάτων ἡ ψ. μιαίνεται· διὰ τὸ περιπατεῖν ἐν πόλει, καὶ μὴ φυλάττειν τοὺς ὀφθαλμούς, καὶ τὸ ἔχειν φιλίαν μετὰ γυναικὸς ὅλως, καὶ τὸ ἔχειν φιλίαν μετὰ τῶν ἐνδόξων τοῦ κόσμου, καὶ τὸ ἀγαπῆσαι τοὺς κατὰ σάρκα γονεῖς ἐν ὁμιλίαις...διὰ τεσσάρων πραγμάτων σκοτίζεται ἡ ψ.· διὰ τοῦ μισῆσαι τὸν πλησίον, καὶ ἐξουδενῶσαι, καὶ ζηλῶσαι, καὶ γογγύσαι. διὰ τεσσάρων πραγμάτων γίνεται ἔρημος ἡ ψ.· διὰ τὸ περιέρχεσθαι ἀπὸ τόπου εἰς τόπον, καὶ ἀγαπῆσαι τὸν περισπασμόν, καὶ ἀγαπῆσαι τὴν ὕλην, καὶ διὰ κνιπείαν Esaias *or.*7; τὸ ἀγαπᾶν τὴν χρείαν τοῦ κόσμου ποιεῖ τὴν ψ. σκοτισθῆναι *ib.*16; ἀρχὴ κακῶν τῇ ψ. ἡ φιλαυτία γέγονεν Thal.*cent.*2.4(M.91.1437B); πονηρὸν ἔργον ψ. λογικῆς, καταλιμπάνειν τὸν κτίσαντα, καὶ λατρεύειν τῷ σώματι *ib.*2.7(1437C); view that body itself is cause of sin to soul, as Origenists maintain, Epiph.*haer.*64.21(p.433.20; M.41.1136D); *ib.* 64.52(p.482.2; 1157A); v. ἁμαρτία; τίς οὖν ἀκριβής ἐστιν ἀντίδικος;... τὸ σῶμα τῆς ψ.· οὗτος ἀντίδικός ἐστι τοῦ ἐν σοὶ πνεύματος ‡Chrys. *Herod.*2(8.290E); not generally held and expressly denied, e.g. by Chrys.*hom.*39.9 *in 1Cor.*(10.376B); cf. ποῦ γὰρ καθ' ἑαυτὴν ἡ σὰρξ ἁμαρτῆσαι δυνήσεται ἐὰν μὴ τὴν ψ. ἔχῃ προηγουμένην;...ὥσπερ γὰρ ζεῦγος βοῶν λυθέντων ἀπ' ἀλλήλων τοῦ ζυγοῦ, οὐδέτερος αὐτῶν κατ' ἰδίαν ἀροῦν δύναται· οὕτως οὐδὲ ψ. καὶ σῶμα, λυθέντα τῆς συζυγίας, καθ' ἑαυτὰ ποιῆσαί τι δύναται †Just.*fr.res.*8(M.6.1584D); τὸ σῶμα οὐχ ἁμαρτάνει καθ' ἑαυτό, ἀλλὰ διὰ τοῦ σώματος ἡ ψ. Cyr.H.*catech.*4.23; **3.** consequences of sin; **a.** separation from God and grace πτέρωσις γὰρ ἡ τῆς ψ. πνεῦμα τὸ τέλειον, ὅπερ ἀπορρίψασα διὰ τὴν ἁμαρτίαν ἔπτηξεν ὥσπερ νεοσσὸς καὶ χαμαιπετὴς ἐγένετο Tat.*orat.*20(p.22.12; M.6.852A); εἰς δὲ ἀκάθαρτον ψ. θεοῦ χάρις οὐ παραδύεται Clem.*q.d.s.*16 (p.170.1; M.9.620C); οὔτε ψ. ταῖς βιωτικαῖς προειλημμένην μερίμναις, καὶ τοῖς ἐκ τοῦ φρονήματος τῆς σαρκὸς ἐπισκοτουμένην πάθεσι, δυνατὸν ὑποδέξασθαι τοῦ ἁγίου πνεύματος τὰς ἐλλάμψεις Bas.*ep.*210.6(3.317C; M.32.777B); ψ. γὰρ ἡ ἀκμὴν ζῶσα ἐν τῷ...σκότει τῆς ἁμαρτίας... οὐκ ἔστι τοῦ σώματος τοῦ Χριστοῦ Mac.Aeg.*hom.*1.6(M.34.456D); **b.** weakening of its powers, sterility, etc. πᾶσα ψ. ἡ μὴ ἡλισμένη τῷ ἁγίῳ πνεύματι...σέσηπται, καὶ δυσωδίας πολλῆς λογισμῶν πονηρῶν ἐμπέπλησται...καὶ τῶν παθῶν τῶν ἐν τοιαύτῃ ψ. ἐνοικούντων *ib.* 1.5(456A); Chrys.*hom.*4.1 *in Ac.*9:1(3.130D); id.*hom.*2.3 *in Tit.*(11. 740E); id.*hom.*10.5 *in Rom.*(9.526D,E); **c.** hardening and death ὅρα ὅτι ἔστιν τις καὶ ψ. νεκρουμένη τὰ μέλη, ὥστε μὴ αἰσθάνεσθαι ἀπὸ τῶν μαστίγων, κἂν ἐπίπονα προσφέρηταί τινα. δεινὰ προσφέρεται, ἀλλ' οὐκ αἰσθανθήσεται ἡ δεῖνα ψ., ἄλλη δὲ αἰσθανθήσεται Or.*hom.*6.2 *in Jer.* (p.49.14ff.; M.13.325D); ref. Mt.13:5f. αὕτη ἡ πέτρα ἀνθρωπίνη ἐστὶ ψ. διὰ τὴν ἀμέλειαν σκληρυνθεῖσα id.*princ.*3.1.14(p.219.4; M.11.276A); ψ. δὲ ἡ ἁμαρτάνουσα αὐτὴ ἀποθανεῖται, καὶ ἡμεῖς ἐροῦμεν αὐτὴν θνητήν id.*Jo.*13.61(59; p.293.13; M.14.516C); ὁ Ἀδὰμ παραβὰς τὴν ἐντολὴν τοῦ θεοῦ...ἐπώλησεν ἑαυτὸν τῷ διαβόλῳ· καὶ ἐνεδύσατο τὴν ψ. ὁ πονηρός...τούτου τοίνυν ἕνεκεν σῶμα λέγεται ἡ ψ. τοῦ σκότους τῆς πονηρίας Mac.Aeg.*hom.*1.7(M.34.457A); πᾶσα γὰρ ἁμαρτία, θάνατός ἐστι ψ. Gr.Naz.*or.*37.23(M.36.308B); ὁ δὲ τῆς ψ. [sc. θάνατος]... φοβερός. οὐ γὰρ ἐὰν διαλυθῇ, καθάπερ τὸ σῶμα αὐτὴν παραπέμπει, ἀλλὰ καταδεθεῖσαν πάλιν ἀφθάρτῳ σώματι, εἰς τὸ πῦρ ἐμβιβάζει ἄσβεστον. οὗτος τοίνυν ἐστὶν ὁ ψ. θάνατος. ὥσπερ οὖν ἔστι ψ. θάνατος, οὕτω καὶ σφαγὴ ψ. τί ἐστι ψ. σφαγή; καὶ αὐτὸ νέκρωσις. τί δὲ νέκρωσις ψ.; ὥσπερ γὰρ τὸ σῶμα τότε νεκροῦται, ὅταν ἔρημον αὐτὸ καταλίπῃ τῆς οἰκείας ἐνεργείας ἡ ψ.· οὕτω καὶ ἡ ψ. τότε νεκροῦται, ὅταν ἔρημον αὐτὴν καταλίπῃ τῆς οἰκείας ἐνεργείας τὸ πνεῦμα τὸ ἅγιον Chrys.*hom.* 18.3 *in Eph.*(11.130B,C); cf.*ib.*18.2(130A); id.*hom.*19.1 *in Gen.*(4.161D); id.*exp.in Ps.*129(5.368B); Pall.*v.Chrys.*8(p.47.27; M.47.28); πεπωρωμένη ψ. μαστιζομένη οὐκ αἰσθάνεται, καὶ εἰς συναίσθησιν ἐλθεῖν τοῦ εὐεργέτου οὐκ ἀνέχεται Thal.*cent.*2.61(M.91.1444B); *ib.*2.64(1444C); heresy as death of soul, †Bas.*Is.*233(1.556A; M.30.525C); **4.** struggle of soul with evil ἐν τῇ καρδίᾳ τῶν ἀγωνιζομένων θέατρον τῶν πονηρῶν πνευμάτων παλαιόντων τῇ ψ., καὶ θεοῦ καὶ ἀγγέλων θεωρούντων τὸν ἀγῶνα· λοιπὸν καθ' ἑκάστην ὥραν κτίζονται ὑπὸ τῆς ψ. πολλοὶ λογισμοὶ νεαροί· ὁμοίως καὶ ὑπὸ τῆς κακίας ἔνδον. καὶ γὰρ ἡ ψ. πολλοὺς ἀποκρύφους ἔχει λογισμούς...καὶ αὐτὴ ἡ κακία λογισμοὺς ἔχει πολλοὺς ...καὶ καθ' ὥραν γεννᾷ λογισμοὺς νεαροὺς κατὰ τῆς ψ. καὶ γὰρ ὁ νοῦς ἡνίοχός ἐστι καὶ ζεύγνυσι τὸ ἅρμα τῆς ψ. κατέχων ἡνίας τῶν λογισμῶν· καὶ ὧδε τρέχει κατὰ τοῦ ἅρματος τοῦ σατανᾶ, ὅπου καὶ αὐτὸς ἔζευξε κατὰ τῆς ψ. Mac.Aeg.*hom.*40.5(M.34.765B); ἀδύνατον ψ. δι' ἑαυτῆς... διαπεράσαι τὴν πικρὰν θάλασσαν τῆς ἁμαρτίας...εἰ μὴ τὸ ἐλαφρὸν...τοῦ Χριστοῦ πνεῦμα δέξεται *ib.*44.6(781D); τῶν πονηρῶν πνευμάτων ἀεὶ ἀντιπραττόντων τῇ τῶν ψ. σωτηρίᾳ Pall.*v.Chrys.*12(p.72.32; M.47.41); **5.** good and bad souls contrasted τὴν μὲν τοῦ φαύλου...ἐν τῇ κακίᾳ ψ. φήσομεν καταλείπεσθαι ὑπὸ τοῦ θεοῦ, τὴν δὲ τοῦ βουλομένου ζῆν κατ' ἀρετὴν...ἀποφανούμεθα πληροῦσθαι ἢ μετέχειν θείου πνεύματος Or.*Cels.*4.5(p.278.2; M.11.1036A); οἶδα ψ. οἰκουμένην, οἶδα ψ. ἔρημον. εἰ γὰρ οὐκ ἔχει τὸν θεόν, ⟨εἰ⟩ οὐκ ἔχει τὸν Χριστὸν...εἰ οὐκ ἔχει τὸ πνεῦμα τὸ ἅγιον ψ., ἔρημός ἐστιν. οἰκουμένη δέ ἐστιν, ὅτε πεπλήρωται θεοῦ, ὅτε ἔχει τὸν Χριστόν, ὅτε πνεῦμα ἅγιόν ἐστιν ἐν αὐτῇ id.*hom.*8.1 *in Jer.*(p.55.21ff.; M.13.336C); αἱ μὲν σωμασκοῦσαι ψ. τὸν αἰσθητὸν τουτονὶ κόσμον ἀμφὶ τὸν τράχηλον τὸν ἔξω τῆς σαρκὸς περιτιθέασι πρὸς ἀπάτην τῶν θεωμένων, αἱ δὲ ἁγνεύουσαι ἔνδοθεν ἔμπαλιν τὸν κόσμον ἐξάπτονται Meth.*symp.*7.2(p.73.6; M.18.128B); ψ., ἢ κηρὸς ὡς φιλόθεος, ἢ πηλός, ὡς φιλόϋλος...πᾶσα ψ. φιλόϋλος... ἀπὸ θεοῦ νουθετουμένη, καὶ ὡς πηλὸς κατὰ γνώμην ἀντιτυποῦσα σκληρύνεται...πᾶσα δὲ φιλόθεος, ὡς κηρὸς ἀπαλύνεται, καὶ τοὺς τῶν θείων τύπους...εἰσδεχομένη, γίνεται θεοῦ κατοικητήριον ἐν πνεύματι Max.*cap.theol.*1.12(M.90.1088B).

C. soul's way to perfection; **1.** its beginning; **a.** baptismal exorcisms and faith ἄνευ ἐπορκισμῶν οὐ δύναται καθαρθῆναι ψ. ... τῶν ἐπορκιζόντων διὰ πνεύματος θείου ἐμβαλλόντων τὸν φόβον, καὶ ὥσπερ ἐν χώνῃ, τῷ σώματι, τὴν ψ. ἀναζωπυρούντων· φεύγει μὲν ὁ ἐχθρὸς δαίμων...καὶ λοιπὸν ἡ ψ. καθαρθεῖσα τῶν ἁμαρτημάτων ἔχει τὴν σωτηρίαν Cyr.H.procatech.9; ἀναγέννησιν δὲ οὐ σωμάτων λέγω, ἀλλὰ ψυχῆς τὴν πνευματικὴν ἀναγέννησιν. τὰ μὲν γὰρ σώματα διὰ τῶν φαινομένων γονέων γεννῶνται, αἱ δὲ ψ. διὰ τῆς πίστεως ἀναγεννῶνται id.catech.1.2; **b.** repentance εἴ τίς γε ἱκανός ἐστι κινῆσαι ψ. ἀκροατοῦ μάλιστα ἡμαρτηκότος, τοιούτους εὔχεται λόγους λέγειν, οἵτινες ἀπὸ δυνάμεως...ἀπαγγελλόμενοι ἱερῶν σείσουσι τὴν ψ. τοῦ ἀκούοντος καὶ κινήσουσιν ἐπὶ πένθος Or.hom.20.6 in Jer.(p.186.6ff.; M.13.513B); ὁ τὰ τοιαῦτα δάκρυα [sc. of repentance] σταλάζων, οὐδὲν ἡγεῖται τὰ ἐπὶ τῆς γῆς, ἀλλὰ πάσης πολιορκίας ἀπαλλάττει τὴν ψ., τοῦ ἡλίου λαμπροτέραν καθίστησι τὴν διάνοιαν Chrys.exp.in Ps.6(5.46C); **c.** through Passion and example of Christ τοῦ πάθους, οὗ ἔπαθεν ὑπὲρ τῶν καθαιρομένων τὰς ψ. ἀπὸ πάσης πονηρίας ἀνθρώπων Just.dial.41.1(M.6.564B); τὰς ᾅδου διαρρήξας [sc. Christ] πύλας ἐπὶ τὴν πεπλανημένην εἰσῆλθε ψ., ἑαυτὸν ὑπόδειγμα ταύτῃ θέμενος, δι' οὗ δυνατὸν αὐτῇ ἔσται πρὸς μέτρον ἡλικίας πρὸς τὴν τελειότητα τοῦ πνεύματος καταντῆσαι Mac.Aeg.pat.18(M.34.880B); τὴν ἡμετέραν ψ. προσερχομένην τῷ ἀληθινῷ ἀρχιερεῖ Χριστῷ, δεῖ τυθῆναι ὑπ' αὐτοῦ, καὶ τῷ φρονήματι ἀποθανεῖν, καὶ...τῇ ἁμαρτίᾳ id.hom.1.6(M.34.456C); **2.** instruments and means of its progress; **a.** help given by God συνεξάπτει δὲ ἡ γραφὴ τὸ ζώπυρον τῆς ψ. καὶ συντείνει τὸ οἰκεῖον ὄμμα πρὸς θεωρίαν Clem.str.1.1(p.8.11; M.8.697A); ib.2.11(p.139.7; 985A); Mac.Aeg.hom.41.2(M.34.768D–769A); ὥσπερ γὰρ ἵππος, ἕως μὲν ἂν ἐν ταῖς ὕλαις τοῖς ἀγρίοις ζώοις συννέμηται, ἀνυπότακτος ἀνθρώποις ἐστίν· ἐπὰν δὲ πρὸς τὸ ἡμερωθῆναι κρατηθῇ, προτιθέασιν αὐτῷ βαρὺν χαλινόν, ἕως οὗ μάθῃ εὐτάκτως...περιπατεῖν· εἶτα γυμνάζεται ὑπὸ ἐμπείρου καθιστοῦ, ἵνα καὶ εἰς πόλεμον εὔχρηστος γένηται... τὸν αὐτὸν τρόπον καὶ ἡ ψ. ἀπὸ τῆς παραβάσεως οὖσα ἀγρία καὶ ἀνυπότακτος, ἐν ἐρημίᾳ τοῦ κόσμου πελάζεται μετὰ θηρίων...ὅταν δὲ ἀκούσῃ λόγον θεοῦ, καὶ πιστεύσῃ, χαλιναγωγουμένη ὑπὸ τοῦ πνεύματος, ἀποτίθεται τὸν ἄγριον ἦθος...ἡνιοχουμένη ὑπὸ τοῦ ἐπιβάτου Χριστοῦ ...οὕτως ἡ ψ. ἐνδυομένη τὸν θώρακα τῆς δικαιοσύνης,...διδάσκεται πολεμεῖν τοῖς ἐχθροῖς αὐτοῖς ib.23.2(661A,B); Nil.epp.1.132(M.79.140A); λήψῃ θεὸν τὸν τῆς σῆς ψ. κατέχοντα οἴακα, καὶ ἀκινδύνως κυβερνῶντά σε Jo.Clim.scal.28(M.88.1133C); divine–human co-operation τῆς ψ. τίς ἐστιν εὐθηνία τῆς πεπληρωμένης παντοδαπῶν ἔργων· ἣν πρῶτον μὲν γεωργηθῆναι δεῖ φιλοπόνως, καὶ τότε ταῖς ἀφθόνοις τῶν οὐρανίων ὑδάτων ἐπιρροίαις πιανθῆναι, ὥστε καρποφορῆσαι Bas.hom.in Ps.29(1.128C; M.29.316B); **b.** virtue ψ. δὲ αὔξειν διὰ πίστεως καὶ γνώσεως Clem.str.3.4(p.208.9; M.8.1132A); ib.5.12(p.379.26; M.9.120B); προκοπὴ γὰρ ψ., προκοπὴ ταπεινώσεως Bas.renunt.10(2.211B; M.31.648A); ἐλεημοσύνη καὶ ἡ περὶ τοὺς πένητας δαψίλεια· τοῦτο τὸ μέγιστον τῆς ψ. περιβόλαιον Chrys.hom.21.6 in Gen.(4.191D); τέσσαρες ἀρεταί εἰσιν αἱ ἁγνίζουσαι τὴν ψ., ἡ σιωπή, καὶ τὸ φύλαξαι τὰς ἐντολάς, καὶ ἡ στενοχωρία, καὶ ἡ ταπεινοφροσύνη...τέσσαρες ἀρεταὶ περιτειχίζουσι τὴν ψ. ... ὁ ἔλεος, καὶ ἡ ἀοργησία, καὶ ἡ μακροθυμία, καὶ τὸ ἀποτινάξαι πάντα σπόρον ἐπερχόμενον τῆς ἁμαρτίας Esaias or.7; exeg. Ex.1:21 διδάσκει ἡμᾶς...ἡ γραφή, ὅτι ὁ φόβος τοῦ θεοῦ παρασκευάζει τὴν ψ. φυλάττειν τὰς ἐντολάς, καὶ διὰ τῶν ἐντολῶν οἰκοδομεῖται ὁ τῆς ψ. οἶκος...πῶς δὲ οἰκοδομεῖται ὁ οἶκος τῆς ψ., ἀπὸ τοῦ αἰσθητοῦ οἴκου δυνάμεθα μαθεῖν...χρήζει γὰρ ὁ θέλων οἰκοδομῆσαι τὸν οἶκον τοῦτον, πανταχόθεν ἀσφαλίσασθαι αὐτόν...οὕτως ἐστὶ καὶ ἐπὶ τῆς ψ. χρήζει γὰρ ὁ ἄνθρωπος μηδενὸς μέρους τῆς οἰκοδομίας αὐτοῦ ἀμελεῖν Dor.doct.14(M.88.1773A,B); ἀγάπη καὶ ἐγκράτεια ψ. καθαίρουσι Thal.cent.1.11(M.91.1429A); ἡ δὲ τῶν ἐντολῶν τήρησις, ψ. ποιεῖ τὴν κάθαρσιν ib.2.77(1445A); practice of virtue being natural to soul, Bas.hex.9.4(1.83E; M.29.196C); **c.** asceticism κενοῖ τῆς ὕλης τὴν ψ. ἡ νηστεία καὶ καθαρὰν καὶ κούφην σὺν καὶ τῷ σώματι παρίστησι τοῖς θείοις λόγοις Clem.ecl.14(p.140.28; M.9.705A); οὐκ ἀγαθὸν τῇ ψ. αἰσθητὸν βρῶμα ἢ πόμα. ἡ γὰρ σὰρξ προστρεφομένη πολεμεῖ τῇ ψ. Dion.Al.fr.(p.224.3); τὴν σεαυτοῦ ψ. ἀσφαλίζου, νηστείαις, προσευχαῖς, ἐλεημοσύναις Cyr.H.catech.4.37; κάθαρσις δὲ ψ. ... τὰς διὰ τῶν αἰσθήσεων ἡδονὰς ἀτιμάζειν Bas.leg.lib.gent.7(2.181E; M.31.581C); ἡσυχία οὖν ἀρχὴ καθάρσεως τῇ ψ., μήτε γλώττης λαλούσης τὰ τῶν ἀνθρώπων, μήτε ὀφθαλμῶν εὐχροίας σωμάτων καὶ συμμετρίας περισκοπούντων, μήτε ἀκοῆς τὸν τόνον τῆς ψ. ἐκλυούσης ἐν ἀκροάμασι μελῶν πρὸς ἡδονὴν πεποιημένων μήτε ῥήμασιν εὐτραπελῶν καὶ γελοιαστῶν ἀνθρώπων, ὃ μάλιστα λύειν τῆς ψ. τὸν τόνον πέφυκε id.ep.2.2(3.72C; M.32.228A); **d.** prayer and γνῶσις: ἡ γνῶσις ἰδίωμα ψ. τυγχάνει λογικῆς εἰς τοῦτο ἀσκουμένης, ἵνα διὰ τῆς γνώσεως εἰς ἀθανασίαν ἐπιγραφῇ Clem.str.6.8(p.466.12; M.9.289C); ib.7.7(p.29.28; 453C); ἄγονοι...ἐπὶ πολὺ γεγενημέναι ψ., ᾐσθημέναι τῆς στειρώσεως τῶν ἰδίων ἡγεμονικῶν καὶ τῆς ἀγονίας τοῦ νοῦ ἑαυτῶν, ἀπὸ τοῦ ἁγίου πνεύματος διὰ ἐπιμόνου εὐχῆς κυήσασαι σωτηρίους λόγους, θεωρημάτων ἀληθείας πεπληρωμένους, γεγεννήκασιν Or.or.13.3(p.327.7; M.11.456A); ib.13.5(p.330.4; 459A); ἡ εὐχὴ καλὴ μὲν καὶ καθ' ἑαυτήν· καλλίων δὲ...γίνεται, ὅταν μετὰ...ζεούσης ψ. ἀναφέρηται, ὅταν θυμιατήριον ἡ ψ. γένηται καὶ πῦρ ἀνάπτῃ σφοδρόν Chrys.exp.in Ps.140(5.431A); φέγγος ψυχῆς ἡ γνῶσίς ἐστιν Thal.cent.1.51(M.91.1432D); ib.2.2(1437B); τέλος γὰρ τῆς κατὰ ψυχὴν λογικῆς ἐνεργείας, ἡ ἀληθὴς γνῶσίς ἐστι Max.ep.31(M.91.625A); **e.** temptations εἰς ταῦτα δὲ τὰ μέτρα ψ. ἐλθεῖν, οὔτε ὑφ' ἕν, οὔτε ἀδοκιμάστως ἐστίν, ἀλλὰ διὰ πόνων πολλῶν καὶ ἀγώνων, καὶ χρόνων καὶ σπουδῆς, μετὰ δοκιμασίας καὶ πειρασμῶν ποικίλων τὴν πνευματικὴν αὔξησιν...λαμβάνει Mac.Aeg.hom.10.5(M.34.544C); ψ. ζέουσα...οὐχ ὑπό τινων κωλυτικῶν ἐμποδίζεται τὴν οἰκείαν ἀρετὴν ἐπιδείξασθαι, ἀλλὰ καὶ δι' αὐτῶν μάλιστα τῶν κωλυόντων ἐπὶ πλεῖον αἴρεται Chrys.hom.43.2 in Gen.(4.437C); πλεῖστα χαρίσματα θεῖα μετὰ τὴν συνοχὴν καὶ τὴν θλῖψιν εὑρίσκομεν ἐν τῇ ψ. κυϊσκόμενα Nil.epp.3.182(M.79.469C); id.Eulog.19(M.79.1117B); **f.** true doctrine as soul's food ὃ γάρ ἐστιν ἐν σώματι τροφή, τοῦτο ἐν ψ. λόγος Gr.Naz.or.17.1(M.35.965A); ib.42.8(M.36.468B); ὥσπερ γὰρ τρέφεται τὰ σώματα, οὕτω τρέφεται καὶ ἡ ψ.· ἀλλὰ τὸ μὲν σῶμα ἄρτῳ, ἡ δὲ ψ. λόγῳ Chrys.hom.4.1 in Is.6:1(6.121D); ἡ ψ. χρήζει τῆς πνευματικῆς τροφῆς id.hom.4.6 in Gen.(4.29B); καθάπερ ἐφ' ἑκάστης ἡμέρας τῷ σώματι τὴν τροφὴν χορηγεῖς...οὕτω καὶ τὴν ψ. μὴ περιορᾶν λιμῷ φθειρομένην, καὶ παρέχειν αὐτῇ τὴν κατάλληλον τροφὴν τὴν ἐκ τῆς τῶν γραφῶν ἀναγνώσεως ib.21.6(191B); ὥσπερ γὰρ τρέφεται σῶμα, οὕτω τρέφεται καὶ ψ. ... ταύτην οὖν λέγει τὴν τροφήν, τὴν διὰ τοῦ λόγου διδασκαλίαν, τὴν παίδευσιν, τὴν φιλοσοφίαν id.exp.in Ps.110(5.272B); οὐ δίκαιόν ἐστιν...τὴν τῆς ψ. βρῶσιν καταλιπόντας, τὸ σῶμα πρὸ τῆς ψ. διαναπαῦσαι Leont.N.v.Jo.Eleem.1(p.7.10f.); **3.** soul's way from the sensible to the spiritual and from discursive thought to contemplation γυμνάσιον μέν φαμεν εἶναι τῆς ψ. τὴν ἀνθρωπίνην σοφίαν, τέλος δὲ τὴν θείαν Or.Cels.6.13(p.83.17; M.11.1309B); οὐ ταὐτόν ἐστι νοσοῦντας τὴν ψ. ἐπὶ θεραπείαν καλεῖν καὶ ὑγιαίνοντας ἐπὶ τὴν τῶν θειοτέρων γνῶσιν καὶ ἐπιστήμην. καὶ ἡμεῖς δὲ ἀμφότερα ταῦτα γινώσκοντες, κατ' ἀρχὰς μὲν προκαλούμενοι ἐπὶ τὸ θεραπευθῆναι τοὺς ἀνθρώπους...ἐπὰν δὲ οἱ προκόπτοντες τῶν προτραπέντων παραστήσωσι τὸ κεκαθάρθαι ὑπὸ τοῦ λόγου καὶ ὅση δύναμις βέλτιον βεβιωκέναι, τὸ τηνικάδε καλοῦμεν αὐτοὺς ἐπὶ τὰς παρ' ἡμῖν τελετάς ib.3.59(p.254.4; 997D); ἡ γὰρ ψ. συντραφεῖσα σώματι...ἀπὸ τῶν ὁρωμένων ἐπὶ τὰ νοητὰ χειραγωγηθῆναι ἐδεῖτο. ὅθεν καὶ τοῖς προφήταις περὶ θεοῦ διαλεγομένοις ἐγένετο χρεία ἀνθρωπίνων μνησθῆναι μελῶν...ἵνα τὴν αἰσθητοῖς συντραφεῖσαν ψ. ἐκ τῶν ἀνθρωπίνων τὰ ὑπὲρ ἄνθρωπον παιδεύσωσι δόγματα Chrys.exp.in Ps.43(5.149A,B); ὅταν ἡμῶν ἡ ψ. ταῖς νοεραῖς ἐνεργείαις ἐπὶ τὰ νοητὰ κινεῖται, περιτταὶ μετὰ τῶν αἰσθητῶν αἱ αἰσθήσεις· ὥσπερ καὶ αἱ νοεραὶ δυνάμεις, ὅταν ἡ ψ. θεοειδὴς γινομένη, δι' ἑνώσεως ἀγνώστου ταῖς τοῦ ἀπροσίτου φωτὸς ἀκτῖσιν ἐπιβάλλῃ Dion.Ar.d.n.4.11(M.3.708D); commented ἡνίκα τὸν προφορικὸν λόγον κινοῦμεν, τοῦτον περί τινος τῶν αἰσθητῶν...καὶ γραφῶν δεόμεθα πρὸς δήλωσιν τοῦ λαλουμένου. εἰ δὲ ἀφ' ἑαυτῆς ἡ ψ. πρὸς τὰ νοητὰ κινεῖται διὰ τῶν ὀρθῶν ἐνεργειῶν, περιτταὶ μετὰ τῶν αἰσθητῶν αἱ αἰσθήσεις· ὑψηλὰ γὰρ φαντάζεται· ὅταν δὲ θεοειδὴς γένηται, προκόπτουσα ταῖς κατὰ μικρὸν ἀνατάσεσι, καὶ δι' ἑνώσεως ἀγνώστου πρὸς τὸ ἀπρόσιτον φῶς τὰς ἐπιβολὰς ἔχῃ, τότε καὶ αἱ νοηταὶ ἐνέργειαι περιτταί εἰσιν, ὡς καὶ αἰσθήσεις, ἐπειδὴ τὰ ὑψηλότερα τούτων ἡ ψ. διανοεῖται, λοιπὸν ἡνωμένη θεῷ Max.schol.d.n.4.11(M.4.261C,D); **4.** threefold way and threefold movement of soul, first adumbrated in a twofold 'perfection' ἡ γνωστικὴ ψ. ἁγιάζεται κατὰ τὴν ἀποχὴν τῶν γεωδῶν πυρώσεων...ὁ δὲ ἐν τῷ σώματι καθαρισμὸς τῆς ψ. πρῶτος οὗτός ἐστιν, ἡ ἀποχὴ τῶν κακῶν, ἥν τινες τελείωσιν ἡγοῦνται, καὶ ἔστιν ἁπλῶς τοῦ κοινοῦ πιστοῦ...ἡ τελείωσις αὕτη· τοῦ δὲ γνωστικοῦ μετὰ τὴν ἄλλοις νομιζομένην τελείωσιν ἡ δικαιοσύνη εἰς ἐνέργειαν εὐποιΐας προβαίνει Clem.str.6.7(p.462.6ff.; M.9.281B); fully developed ἐδιδάχθημεν γὰρ πολλαχοῦ τῆς γραφῆς καὶ παιδικὴν κατάστασιν τῆς ψ.· καὶ ἄλλην ἀκμαστικήν· καὶ ἄλλην ἤδη πρεσβύτου. οἷον, ὡς παρὰ Παύλου μεμαθήκαμεν, οἱ ἐν Κορίνθῳ νήπιοι ἦσαν· διόπερ καὶ γάλακτος ἔτι ἐδέοντο...νεανίσκος δὲ κατὰ ψ. ἐστιν ὁ πᾶσι τοῖς μέρεσι τῆς ἀρετῆς κατηρτισμένος πρὸς τὸ τέλειον, ὁ τῷ πνεύματι ζέων...πρεσβύτερος δὲ κατὰ ψ., ὁ τετελειωμένος κατὰ τὴν φρόνησιν Bas.hom.12.13(2.108E–109A; M.31.412C–413A); ψ. δὲ κίνησίς ἐστι, κυκλικὴ μὲν ἡ εἰς ἑαυτὴν εἴσοδος ἀπὸ τῶν ἔξω, καὶ τῶν νοερῶν αὐτῆς δυνάμεων ἡ ἑνοειδὴς συνέλιξις...ἑλικοειδῶς δὲ ἡ ψ. κινεῖται καθ' ὅσον οἰκείως ἑαυτῇ τὰς θείας ἐλλάμπεται γνώσεις, οὐ νοερῶς καὶ ἑνιαίως, ἀλλὰ λογικῶς καὶ διεξοδικῶς...τὴν κατ' εὐθεῖαν δέ, ὅταν οὐκ εἰς ἑαυτὴν εἰσιοῦσα καὶ ἑνικῇ νοερότητι κινουμένη...ἀλλὰ πρὸς τὰ περὶ ἑαυτὴν προϊοῦσα, καὶ ἀπὸ τῶν ἔξωθεν Dion.Ar.d.n.4.9(M.3.705A); interpreted, Max.schol.d.n.4.9(M.4.256–257D); **5.** relation between body and soul in progress to perfection βαπτίσθητε τὴν ψ. ἀπὸ ὀργῆς...καὶ ἰδοὺ τὸ σῶμα καθαρόν ἐστι Just.dial.14.2(M.6.504D); ἐπιδεκτικὸν γίνεται τῆς... ψ. τὸ οἰκητήριον τοῦτο καὶ πνεύματος ἁγίου κατὰ τὸν τῆς ψ. τε καὶ σώματος ἁγιασμὸν καταξιοῦται τῷ τοῦ σωτῆρος καταρτισμῷ τελειούμενον Clem.str.4.26(p.320.26f.; M.8.1373A); εἰ δὲ ἡ ψ. ... τοῖς θείοις ἐντραφῇ μαθήμασιν, υἱός ἐστι ἐλευθέρων ,καὶ ὁρμὰς ἔχει λογισμῶν...τά τε σώματι καθήκοντα, καὶ ὅσα τῇ ψ. κατάλληλα Olymp.*Eccl.*10:16f.(M.93.604B); διὰ γὰρ τοῦ σώματος τούτου περισπᾶται ἡ ψ. ἀπὸ τῶν παθῶν αὐτῆς Dor.*doct.*12.2(M.88.1752A); ἀρεταὶ ψ. εἰσιν αὗται· ἀγάπη, ταπείνωσις, πραΰτης, μακροθυμία...ἀρεταὶ δὲ σώματος...νηστεία, χαμευνία, ἀγρυπνία Max.*qu.dub.*1(M.90.785C); διῃρημένης γὰρ εἰς ψ. τε καὶ αἴσθησιν τῆς τε λύπης καὶ ἡδονῆς· ὁ τὴν τῆς ψ. περιποιούμενος ἡδονήν, τὴν δὲ τῆς αἰσθήσεως καταδεχόμενος λύπην, δόκιμος γίνεται καὶ τέλειος id.*qu.Thal.*58(M.90.593D); **6.** relation between soul and νοῦς: ἐπειδὴ νεκροῦται ὁ νοῦς, ὅσον ἡ ψ. μεριμνᾷ τὰ ἔξωθεν, καὶ λοιπὸν τὰ ἔνδοθεν πάθη πράττει τὰς ἐνεργείας αὐτῶν ἀδιαφόρως. ἐὰν οὖν ἡ ψ. ἀκούσῃ τοῦ λόγου τοῦ Ἰησοῦ...τότε ἐγείρεται ὁ νοῦς, καὶ ἵσταται, ἕως οὗ ἀπορρίψῃ αὐτὰ ἐκ τοῦ οἴκου αὐτοῦ, προσέχων τῇ ψ. αὐτοῦ ἀδιαλείπτως, καὶ φυλάττων αὐτὴν μὴ ὑποστρέψαι εἰς τὰ ὀπίσω ἐπὶ τοὺς ἀδικήσαντας αὐτήν. ἡ ψ. γὰρ ὁμοία ἐστὶ γυναικὶ νεάνιδι οὔσῃ μετὰ ἀνδρός, ἥτις ὅταν ἀπέλθῃ ἐπὶ ξένης ὁ ἀνὴρ αὐτῆς, ἄφοβος καὶ ἀναίσχυντος γίνεται... ἐπὰν δὲ ἔλθῃ ὁ ἀνὴρ αὐτῆς εἰς τὸν οἶκον αὐτοῦ, παραχρῆμα φοβουμένη ἀφίσταται ἀπὸ τῶν πραττομένων ὑπ' αὐτῆς, καὶ φροντίζει κατὰ τὸ θέλημα τοῦ ἀνδρός...τοιοῦτός ἐστιν ὁ νοῦς. ἐὰν ἐγερθῇ, φροντίζει τῆς ψ. καὶ φυλάττει αὐτὴν...ἕως γεννήσῃ μετ' αὐτοῦ καὶ ἐκθρέψῃ τὰ τέκνα αὐτῆς, καὶ λοιπὸν οἱ ἀμφότεροι μία καρδία γίνονται, καὶ ὑποτάσσεται ἡ ψ. τῷ νοΐ Esaias *or.*25; τὸ αἰσθητὸν γύναιον σημαίνει ψ. πρακτικήν· ᾗ ὁ νοῦς συγγενόμενος ἀποτίκτει τὰς ἀρετάς Thal.*cent.*2.27(M.91.1440C); ψ. καθαρὰ ἡ τὸν θεὸν ἀγαπῶσα, καὶ νοῦς ἐστιν καθαρὸς ὁ ἀγνοίας χωρισθεὶς *ib.*2.79(1445A); ἀνάγνωσις καὶ προσευχὴ νοῦν καθαίρουσιν· ἀγάπη δὲ καὶ ἐγκράτεια τὸ παθητικὸν τῆς ψ. *ib.*2.84(1445C).

D. the perfect soul; **1.** possessing various virtues: prudence, Clem.*str.*7.12(p.52.10,14; M.9.500C,D); obedience and purity, id.*q.d.s.*18(p.171.26; M.9.624A); Meth.*symp.*11(p.139.27; M.18.217D); Nil.*epp.*3.185(M.79.469D); humility, Mac.Aeg.*hom.*10.4(M.34.541D); simplicity, Gr.Nyss.*anim.et res.*(M.46.93C–96A); sobriety and vigilance, Chrys.*David* 1.5(4.756E); id.*hom.23.2 in Gen.*(4.207D); ψ. πραεῖα θρόνος ἁπλότητος...ψ. ἠπία χωρήσει λόγους σοφίας...ψ. εὐθὴς σύμβιος ταπεινώσεως...ψ. πραέων πλησθήσονται γνώσεως Jo.Clim.*scal.*26(M.88.981A,B); ψ. δέ ἐστι τελεία, ἡ ταῖς ἀρεταῖς ἀνακραθεῖσα Thal.*cent.*2.54(M.91.1444A); **2.** in its relation to Christ; **a.** in gen. παρόντος αὐτῷ τοῦ πατρὸς καὶ συμβασιλεύοντος τῷ πατρὶ τοῦ Χριστοῦ ἐν τῇ τετελειωμένῃ ψ. Or.*or.*25.1(p.357.7; M.11.496C); id.*mart.*49(p.45.8; M.11.633A); cf. *cum ipse utique qui est dominus et creator animae Christus Jesus indumentum sanctis esse dicatur* [cf.Rom.13:14]...*sicut ergo Christus indumentum est animae, ita...anima indumentum esse dicitur corporis,* id.*princ.*2.3.2(p.115.15ff.; M.11.189B); ἡ ψ. ἡμῶν κατ' αὐτὸν [sc. Χριστόν] μεμορφῶσθαι Bas.*ep.*159(3.247E; M.32.620B); χρὴ...ἀτενίζειν ἡμᾶς εἰς αὐτὸν [sc. κύριον] πιστεύοντας, καὶ ἀγαπῶντας αὐτὸν...ἵνα γράψας τὴν ἑαυτοῦ εἰκόνα τὴν ἐπουράνιον, ἀποστείλῃ ἐν ταῖς ψ. ἡμῶν Mac.Aeg.*hom.*30.4(M.34.724C); τὴν ψ. μεταπλασθῆναι κατὰ τὴν γνώμην πρὸς τὴν θείαν ὁμοίωσιν, καὶ γενέσθαι ...πνεύματος ἁγίου...οἰκητήριον,...ἴσα θεῷ τῆς ψ. κατὰ τὴν χάριν τῆς κλήσεως ἄσυλον φυλαττούσης ἐν ἑαυτῇ τῶν δωρηθέντων καλῶν τὴν ὑπόστασιν· καθ' ἣν ἀεὶ θέλων Χριστὸς γεννᾶται μυστικῶς, διὰ τῶν σωζομένων σαρκούμενος· καὶ μητέρα παρθένων ἀπεργαζόμενος τὴν γεννῶσαν ψ. Max.*or.dom.*(M.90.889B,C); **b.** as a bride συνεχῶς ἡ ψ. τὸν νυμφίον λόγον ἐπιζητεῖ· καὶ εὑροῦσα πάλιν ἑτέροις ἀποροῦσα ζητεῖ· κἀκεῖνα θεωρήσασα ποθεῖ τὴν ἑτέρων ἀποκάλυψιν· καὶ τυχοῦσα τούτων, ἐπ' ἄλλοις εὔχεται τὸν νυμφίον ἐπιδημεῖν Or.*schol.in Cant.*5:9(M.17.273C); *ib.*6:7f.(277C,D); φησὶ πρὸς τὴν νύμφην ψ. θεὸς εἶναι ζηλωτὴς id.*mart.*9(p.10.4; M.11.576B); ψ. ἣν ἂν μνηστεύσηται νύμφην ὁ ἐπουράνιος νυμφίος Χριστός, πρὸς τὴν ἑαυτοῦ μυστικὴν...κοινωνίαν...ἐν πολλῇ σπουδῇ γνησίως ἀρέσκειν ὀφείλει τῷ αὐτῆς μνηστῆρι Χριστῷ...καὶ τὸ πνεῦμα ἐν μηδενὶ λυπεῖν...ἰδοὺ ἡ τοιαύτη ψ. πάντων τῶν τοῦ κυρίου ἀγαθῶν δέσποινα καθίσταται, καὶ αὐτὸ τὸ ἔνδοξον τῆς θεότητος αὐτοῦ, σῶμα αὐτῆς τυγχάνει Mac.Aeg.*hom.*15.2(M.34.576C,D); v. νύμφη, νυμφίος; **3.** in its relation to H. Ghost πνεῦμα δὲ τοῦ θεοῦ...παρὰ δέ τισι τοῖς δικαίως πολιτευομένοις καταγινόμενον καὶ συμπεριπλεκόμενον τῇ ψ. διὰ προαγορεύσεων ταῖς λοιπαῖς ψ. τὸ κεκρυμμένον ἀνήγγειλε Tat.*orat.*13(p.15.2; M.6.836A); χρὴ...ἡμᾶς...ζευγνύναι τε τὴν ψ. τῷ πνεύματι τῷ ἁγίῳ καὶ τὴν κατὰ θεὸν συζυγίαν πραγματεύεσθαι *ib.*15(p.16.5; 837A); τὸ πνεῦμα ᾠκείωται τῇ ὑπ' αὐτοῦ φερομένῃ ψ. Clem.*paed.*2.2(p.168.10; M.8.412A); κεκοσμημένη ψ. ἁγίῳ πνεύματι *ib.*3.11(p.272.4; 640A); ἡ ψ. δὲ ἐπαιρομένη καὶ τῷ πνεύματι ἑπομένη τοῦ τε σώματος χωριζομένη καὶ οὐ μόνον ἑπομένη τῷ πνεύματι ἀλλὰ καὶ ἐν αὐτῷ γινομένη,...πῶς οὐχὶ ἤδη ἀποτιθεμένη τὸ εἶναι ψ. πνευματικὴ γίνεται; Or.*or.*9.2(p.319.4ff.; M.11.444D); ἄγγελοι...χαίρουσι τῇ ψ. τῇ ἐκ πνεύματος γεννηθείσῃ, καὶ γενομένῃ πνεῦμα. τοῦτο γὰρ τὸ σῶμα ὁμοίωμα τυγχάνει τῆς ψ., ἡ δὲ ψ. εἰκὼν τοῦ πνεύματος ὑπάρχει· καὶ ὥσπερ τὸ σῶμα χωρὶς τῆς ψ. νεκρόν ἐστι...οὕτως ἄνευ τῆς ἐπουρανίου ψ., χωρὶς τοῦ θεϊκοῦ πνεύματος, νεκρὰ τυγχάνει ἀπὸ τῆς βασιλείας ἡ ψ. Mac.Aeg.*hom.*30.3(M.34.724A); ὅταν ἡ ψ. σου κοινωνήσῃ τῷ πνεύματι, καὶ εἰσέλθῃ ψ. ἐπουράνιος εἰς τὴν ψ. σου, τότε εἶ τέλειος ἄνθρωπος *ib.*32.6(737C); *ib.*32.9(740B); ἐὰν ἀναμφιβόλῳ...κινήσει ἡ ψ. πρὸς τὴν ἀγάπην ἐξάπτηται τοῦ θεοῦ...εἰδέναι δεῖ τοῦ ἁγίου πνεύματος εἶναι τὴν ἐνέργειαν. ἡδυνομένη γὰρ ὅλη ὑπ' ἐκείνης...γλυκύτητος οὐδὲν ἕτερον δύναται τότε ἐννοεῖν, ἐπειδὴ ἀνενδότῳ εὐφραίνεται χαρᾷ Diad.*perf.*33(p.36.18); **4.** attaining perfect contemplation ὅταν γὰρ ψ. γενέσεως ὑπεξαναβᾶσα καθ' ἑαυτήν τε ᾖ καὶ ὁμιλῇ τοῖς εἴδεσιν...οἷον ἄγγελος ἤδη γενόμενος σὺν Χριστῷ τε ἔσται, θεωρητικὸς ὢν Clem.*str.*4.25(p.317.15; M.8.1364C); ἐκείνας φημὶ τὰς γνωστικὰς ψ., τῇ μεγαλοπρεπείᾳ τῆς θεωρίας ὑπερβαινούσας ἑκάστης ἁγίας τάξεως τὴν πολιτείαν...οὐκ ἐν κατόπτροις...ἔτι τὴν θεωρίαν ἀσπαζομένας τὴν θείαν, ἐναργῆ δὲ ὡς ἔνι μάλιστα καὶ ἀκριβῶς εἰλικρινῆ τὴν ἀκόρεστον ὑπερφυῶς ἀγαπώσαις ψ. ἑστιωμένας θέαν *ib.*7.3(p.10.7ff.; M.9.416C); πύργοι δὲ ἐκλήθησαν, οἱ τὰ ἀρεστὰ τῷ νυμφίῳ ποιοῦντες, σκοπευτήριον ἔχοντες τὴν θεωρητικὴν ψ., ἐκ μετεώρου σκοπεύουσαν ἅπαντα Or.*schol.in Cant.*7:4(M.17.281C); ψ. τὸ λογικὸν ἔχουσι διεξοδικῶς μὲν καὶ κύκλῳ περὶ τὴν τῶν ὄντων ἀλήθειαν περιπορευόμεναι, καὶ τῷ μεριστῷ καὶ τῷ παντοδάπῳ τῆς ποικιλίας ἀπολειπόμεναι τῶν ἑνιαίων νοῶν· τῇ δὲ τῶν πολλῶν εἰς τὸ ἓν συνελίξει, καὶ τῶν ἰσαγγέλων νοήσεων, ἐφ' ὅσον ψυχαῖς οἰκεῖον καὶ ἐφικτόν, ἀξιούμεναι Dion.Ar.*d.n.*7.2(M.3.868B,C); commented, Max.*schol.d.n.*7.2(M.4.345C); **5.** ref. mystical union; **a.** in gen. φθάνει δὲ ἡ θεία δύναμις, καθάπερ φῶς, ὅλην διϊδεῖν τὴν ψ. ... εἰς τὸ βάθος τῆς ψ. ἁπάσης τὸ φῶς τῆς δυνάμεως ἐκλάμπει Clem.*str.*7.7(p.29.8,12; M.9.453A,B); ἐνταῦθα ...τῆς γνωστικῆς ψ. ἡ τελείωσις, πάσης καθάρσεως τε καὶ λειτουργίας ὑπερβᾶσαν σὺν τῷ κυρίῳ γίγνεσθαι *ib.*7.10(p.42.1; 481A); ἡ γνωστικὴ ψ. ... καθαρὰ τέλεον γενομένη...πνευματικὴ γὰρ ὅλη γενομένη πρὸς τὸ συγγενὲς χωρήσασα ἐν πνευματικῇ τῇ ἐκκλησίᾳ μένει εἰς τὴν ἀνάπαυσιν τοῦ θεοῦ *ib.*7.11(p.49.16ff.; 496A); ἡ τῷ κυρίῳ προσκολληθεῖσα ψ. εἰς τὸ γενέσθαι πρὸς αὐτὸν ἓν πνεῦμα Gr.Nyss.*virg.*15(p.310.10; M.46.381C); δεῖ γὰρ τὴν ψ. τὴν ἐν ἀληθείᾳ πιστεύουσαν Χριστῷ, μετατεθῆναι ...εἰς ἑτέραν θείαν φύσιν, καὶ καινὴν αὐτὴν ἀπεργασθῆναι διὰ τῆς δυνάμεως τοῦ ἁγίου πνεύματος Mac.Aeg.*hom.*44.5(M.34.781B); ἐπαναπαύεται ὁ κύριος τῇ ἀγαθῇ τῆς ψ. προαιρέσει, θρόνον δόξης αὐτὴν ἐργαζόμενος, ἐπικαθήμενός τε καὶ ἐπαναπαυόμενος ἐπ' αὐτήν...ἐστιν ἡ ψ. ἡ βαστάζουσα τὸν θεόν, μᾶλλον δὲ βασταζομένη ὑπὸ τοῦ θεοῦ *ib.*33.2(741D); αἱ ψ., τοὺς παντοδαποὺς αὐτῶν λόγους ἑνοῦσαι, καὶ πρὸς μίαν νοερὰν συνάγουσαι καθαρότητα, προβαίνουσιν οἰκείως ἑαυταῖς, ὁδῷ καὶ τάξει διὰ τῆς ἀΰλου...νοήσεως ἐπὶ τὴν ὑπὲρ νόησιν ἕνωσιν Dion.Ar.*d.n.*11.2(M.3.949D); ἆρα τὰ θεῖα οὐ πάσχει καὶ πᾶσα ψ., ἡ τὴν θείαν καταξιωθεῖσα κομίσασθαι εἰρήνην; Max.*myst.*5(M.91.680D); cf.id.*carit.*3.98(M.90.1048A); **b.** through *via negativa* αὐτοὶ [sc. θεόλογοι] τὴν διὰ τῶν ἀποφάσεων ἄνοδον προτετιμήκασιν, ὡς ἐξιστῶσαν τὴν ψ. τῶν ἑαυτῇ συμφύλων, καὶ διὰ πασῶν τῶν θείων νοήσεων ὁδεύουσαν, ὧν ἐξῄρηται τὸ ὑπὲρ πᾶν ὄνομα...ἐπ' ἐσχάτων δὲ τῶν ὅλων αὐτῷ συνάπτουσαν Dion.Ar.*d.n.*13.3(981B); **c.** likened to union of iron with fire ἔοικε γὰρ ἡ ψ. σιδήρῳ, ὅτι ἐὰν ἀμεληθῇ ἰοῦται, ἐπειδὰν δὲ πυρωθῇ τὸ πῦρ καθαρίζει αὐτό. καὶ ὅσον ἐστὶν εἰς τὸ πῦρ, ὅμοιον τοῦ πυρός ἐστι, καὶ οὐδεὶς δύναται αὐτὸ κατέχειν, ὅτι πῦρ ἐστι. τοιαύτη ἐστὶν ἡ ψ. ὅσον μένει μετὰ τοῦ θεοῦ καὶ ἀδολεσχεῖ αὐτῷ, πῦρ γίνεται καὶ κατακαίει πάντας τοὺς ἐχθροὺς αὐτῆς...καὶ ἁγνίζει αὐτὴν ἐν καινότητι ὡς τὸ σίδηρον Esaias *or.*25; ὁπόταν ἀπὸ τῶν ἔξωθεν σχολάσασα ᾖ ἡ ψ., τότε οἷά τις φλὸξ περικυκλώσασα ταύτην, ὡς σίδηρον καθάπαξ τῷ πυρὶ πεπυρακτωμένην ὅλην καθίστησι, καὶ ἔστι ψ. μὲν ἡ αὐτή, οὐκέτι δὲ καὶ ἁπτή, ὡς οὐδὲ ὁ πυρακτωθεὶς σίδηρος, ταῖς ἔξωθεν ἐπαφαῖς ‡Max.*cap.al.*103(M.90.1424B); **d.** effects of union γυμνὴν τῆς ὑλικῆς δορᾶς γενομένην τὴν γνωστικὴν ψ. ἄνευ τῆς σωματικῆς φλυαρίας καὶ τῶν παθῶν πάντων...τῷ φωτὶ καθιερωθῆναι ἀνάγκη Clem.*str.*5.11(p.371.8; 104A); αἱ τῶν ἐναρέτων ἀνθρώπων ἐπίνοιαι κατὰ ἐπίπνοιαν θείαν γίγνονται, διατιθεμένης πως τῆς ψ. καὶ διαδιδομένου τοῦ θείου θελήματος εἰς τὰς ἀνθρωπίνας ψ. *ib.*6.17(p.513.3f.; 389A); exeg. Lam.1:1 Ἰερουσαλὴμ εὐθηνοῦσα...ἡ θεία ἐστὶ ψ. καὶ οὐ θαυμαστόν, εἰ οὐ μόνον οἰκία...ἀλλὰ πασῶν πόλεων διαφέρουσα καὶ παρὰ θεῷ τετιμημένη Ἰερουσαλὴμ χρηματίζει ἡ τελεία ψ. Or.*fr.8 in Lam.*(pp.237.29,238.3; M.13.609A,B); *ib.*19(p.242.27; 616C); ψυχῆς γὰρ μυστήριον ἐθεώρει [sc. Ezech.], τῆς μελλούσης δέχεσθαι τὸν ἑαυτῆς κύριον, καὶ θρόνος δόξης αὐτῷ γενέσθαι. ψ. γὰρ ἡ καταξιωθεῖσα κοινωνῆσαι τῷ πνεύματι τοῦ φωτὸς αὐτοῦ...ὅλη φῶς γίνεται, καὶ ὅλη πρόσωπον, καὶ ὅλη ὀφθαλμὸς Mac.Aeg.*hom.*1.2(M.34.452A); ψ. ἡ ἔχουσα τὸν δεσπότην αὐτῆς πρὸς ἑαυτὴν καὶ ἐν αὐτῇ καταμένοντα, πάσης ὡραιότητος καὶ εὐπρεπείας γέμει *ib.*33.3(744A); τὴν μεγάλην καὶ φιλόσοφον ψ. οὐδὲν τῶν ἐν τῷ παρόντι βίῳ λυπηρῶν δύναται δακεῖν, οὐκ ἔχθραι, οὐ κατηγορίαι...τοιαύτη ἦν ἡ τοῦ Παύλου ψ., πάσης ἀκρωρείας ὑψηλότερον τόπον τὸν τῆς φιλοσοφίας καταλαβοῦσα τῆς πνευματικῆς Chrys.*hom.3.1 in Phil.*(11.211D); cf.id.*hom.9.3 in 1 Thess.* 11.490B,C); ἡ γὰρ τῆς ψ. ἀνδρεία οὐκ ἐν τῇ ἡσυχίᾳ δείκνυται μόνον τοῦ στόματος, ἀλλὰ καὶ ἐν τῇ τῶν λογισμῶν ἀνδραγαθίᾳ, καὶ τῇ τῶν ὕβρεων, καὶ ἀδικιῶν εὐσταθείᾳ Nil.*Eulog*.18(M.79.1117A); ‡Nil.*perist*.3(M.79.905C); ἑνοειδῆ γενομένην ψ., καὶ πρὸς ἑαυτὴν καὶ τὸν θεὸν συναχθεῖσαν, οὐκ ἔσται ὁ εἰς πολλὰ κατ᾽ ἐπίνοιαν αὐτὴν ἔτι διαιρῶν λόγος, τῷ...ἑνὶ λόγῳ τε καὶ θεῷ κατεστεμμένην τὴν κεφαλήν· ἐν ᾧ κατὰ μίαν ἀπερινόητον ἁπλότητα πάντες οἱ τῶν ὄντων λόγοι ἑνοειδῶς...ὑφεστήκασιν Max.*myst*.5(M.91.681B).

E. senses of the soul, v. αἰσθητήριον; **1.** definitions ἡ σύνεσις ὄψις ἐστὶ ψ. Clem.*paed*.1.9(p.135.9; M.8.341C); ὀφθαλμὸν...τὸν τῆς ψ. φησι, τὸ διορατικὸν ἐκεῖνο καὶ λογικόν, ὅπερ ἡ ἔννοια τῶν οἰκείων ἁμαρτημάτων ταράττειν εἴωθεν Chrys.*exp.in Ps*.6(5.46E); **2.** in gen. ἐμβλέψωμεν τοῖς ὄμμασιν τῆς ψ. εἰς τὸ μακρόθυμον αὐτοῦ βούλημα *1Clem*.19.3; οἱ τῆς ψ. ὀφθαλμοί Just.*dial*.134.5(M.6.788B); ὑπεχέτω τὰ ὦτα τῆς ψ. Clem.*str*.7.16(p.72.36; M.9.541C); ἀνοίξαντος τοῦ λόγου τοὺς ὀφθαλμοὺς τῆς ψ. ἡμῶν Or.*Cels*.6.67(p.137.15; M.11.1400C); **3.** needing purification and enlightenment τό τε ἴδιον τοῦ ἀνθρώπου, τὸ ὄμμα τῆς ψ., ἐκκαθαίρειν Clem.*paed*.2.1(p.154.7; M.8.377C); ὁ δὲ λόγος ὁ ὑγιής, ὅς ἐστιν ἥλιος ψ., δι᾽ οὗ μόνου ἔνδον ἀνατείλαντος ἐν τῷ βάθει τοῦ νοῦ αὐτῆς καταυγάζεται τὸ ὄμμα id.*prot*.6(p.52.15; M.8.173B); τὸν ὀφθαλμὸν τῆς ψ. ἀποκαθαρθῆναι, ὥστε πᾶσαν τὴν ἀπὸ τῆς ἀγνοίας ἐπισκότησιν, οἱονεί τινα λήμην, ἀφαιρεθέντα, δύνασθαι ἐνατενίζειν τῷ κάλλει τῆς δόξης τοῦ θεοῦ, οὐ μικροῦ ἔργου κρίνω Bas.*ep*.150.1(3.239E; M.32.601B); εἴ τις ἀκριβῶς ἐθέλοι τὴν αἰτίαν σκοπεῖν τῶν...μοχθηρῶν ὑπολήψεων, οὐκ ἄν μοι δοκεῖ ἄλλην εὑρεῖν, ἢ τὸ μὴ ἀκριβῶς ἡμῶν γεγυμνάσθαι τὰ τῆς ψ. αἰσθητήρια πρὸς τὴν τοῦ καλοῦ καὶ μὴ τοιούτου διάκρισιν Gr.Nyss.*virg*.11(p.292.22; M.46.364D); **4.** apprehending the divine Χριστιανὸς...εὐχόμενος, μύσας τοὺς τῆς αἰσθήσεως ὀφθαλμοὺς καὶ ἐγείρας τοὺς τῆς ψ., ὑπεραναβαίνει τὸν ὅλον κόσμον Or.*Cels*.7.44(p.196.1; M.11.1485B); ref. Christ ἐγὼ δέ φημι ὅτι καὶ μετὰ τὴν ἐνανθρώπησιν ἀεὶ εὑρίσκεται τοῖς ἔχουσιν ὀφθαλμοὺς ψ. ὀξυδερκεστάτους θεοπρεπέστατος καὶ ἀληθῶς θεόθεν πρὸς ἡμᾶς κατελθὼν *ib*.3.14(p.213.26; 937A); ὁ δὲ κεκωφωμένος τὴν τῆς ψ. ἀκοὴν ἀναισθητεῖ λέγοντος θεοῦ *ib*.2.72(p.194.18; 909A); τὰ τῆς κεκαθαρμένης ψ. ὄμματα ὑπὸ νοεροῦ φωτὸς καταυγαζόμενα Eus.*Is*.6:1(M.24.125A); τοὺς ὀφθαλμοὺς τῆς ψ. διανοίγοντος εἰς κατανόησιν ὧν βούλεται θεαμάτων †Bas.*Is*.proem.3(1.380B; M.30.124B); αἰσθητήρια δὲ τάχα μὲν τὰ τῆς ψ. κινήματα καὶ διανοήματα, καὶ τούτων μάλιστα, ὅσα ἐκ τῆς αἰσθήσεως, οἷς ὁ δίκαιος σπαράσσεται, καὶ θερμαίνεται... καὶ οὐδὲ καθεκτός ἐστι διὰ τὴν ζέσιν τοῦ πνεύματος Gr.Naz.*or*.17.1(M.35.965A); μακάριος μὲν μοναχός, ὁ τοῖς τῆς ψ. ὄμμασιν ταῖς νοεραῖς δυνάμεσιν ἐνατενίζειν δυνάμενος Jo.Clim.*scal*.7(M.88.809A); **5.** relation between physical and spiritual senses, exeg. Gen.3:5ff. διηνοίχθησαν...αὐτῶν οἱ ὀφθαλμοὶ τῆς αἰσθήσεως, οὓς καλῶς ἦσαν μύσαντες, ἵνα μὴ περισπώμενοι ἐμποδίζωνται βλέπειν τῷ τῆς ψ. ὀφθαλμῷ· οὓς δὲ τέως εἶχον βλέποντας τῆς ψ. ὀφθαλμοὺς καὶ εὐφραινομένους ἐπὶ τῷ θεῷ...τούτους οἶμαι διὰ τὴν ἁμαρτίαν ἔμυσαν Or.*Cels*.7.39(p.190.2f.; M.11.1476C); contrasted with Jo.9:39 μὴ βλέποντας μὲν αἰνιττόμενος τοὺς τῆς ψ. ὀφθαλμούς, οὓς ὁ λόγος ποιεῖ βλέπειν, βλέποντας δὲ τοὺς τῶν αἰσθήσεων· τούτους δὲ ἐτύφλου ὁ λόγος, ἵνα ἀπερισπάστως ἡ ψ. βλέπῃ ἃ δεῖ. παντὸς οὖν τοῦ κατὰ τρόπον Χριστιανίζοντος ὁ τῆς ψ. ἐγήγερται ὀφθαλμὸς καὶ ὁ τῆς αἰσθήσεως μέμυκε· καὶ ἀνάλογον τῇ ἐγέρσει τοῦ κρείττονος ὀφθαλμοῦ καὶ τῇ μύσει τῶν ὄψεων τῆς αἰσθήσεως νοεῖται καὶ θεωρεῖται ὁ ἐπὶ πᾶσι θεὸς καὶ ὁ υἱὸς αὐτοῦ *ib*.(p.190.9ff.; 1476D–1477A); exeg. Cant.4:9ff. ἐκαρδίωσας ἡμᾶς...ἑνὶ ἀπὸ ὀφθαλμῶν σου τὸν διορατικὸν τῆς φρονήσεως ὀφθαλμὸν δεικνυσιν... δισσὴν γὰρ ὄψεως δύναμιν εἶναι παντί που καταφανές, μίαν μὲν ψ., θατέραν δὲ σώματος Meth.*symp*.7.2(p.72.24; M.18.128A).

F. types and symbols of soul; **1.** exeg.; ref. Exodus ταῦτα... μυστήριόν ἐστι ψ., τῆς ἐν τῇ παρουσίᾳ τοῦ Χριστοῦ λυτρωθείσης Mac. Aeg.*hom*.47.5(M.34.800B); *ib*.47.9(801C); ἐξάγει οὖν τὴν ψ. ἐξ Αἰγύπτου καὶ τῆς ἐν αὐτῇ δουλείας...ἀπολαμβάνει γὰρ ἐξιοῦσα τοῦ σκότους ἡ ψ. τὰ ἀργυρᾶ καὶ χρυσᾶ σκεύη, ἤγουν τοὺς ἰδίους ἀγαθοὺς λογισμοὺς *ib*.47.10(801D); ἀπαίρουσιν υἱοὶ Ἰσραὴλ τὸ πάσχα ποιήσαντες· προκόπτει ἡ ψ., λαβοῦσα ζωὴν πνεύματος ἁγίου *ib*.47.11(804A); ref. Is.1:2 εἰπὼν...οὐρανὸν τὴν τοῦ γνωστικοῦ ψ. Clem.*str*.4.26(p.319.24; M.8.1377B); Is.4:2 γῆν πολλαχοῦ τὴν ψ. ὁ λόγος λέγει τὴν ὑποδεχομένην τὰ τοῦ λόγου σπέρματα †Bas.*Is*.1.19(1.391B; M.30.149A); Is.5:1ff. ἀμπελὼν δὲ ἡ ψ., τὴν καρποφορίαν ἀξίαν τῆς ἐξ ἀρχῆς φυτείας καὶ τῆς τοῦ θεοῦ γεωργίας ἀπαιτουμένη *ib*.1.21(1.393E; M.156B); Is.6:3 Χερουβὶμ...σύμβολον δ᾽ ἐστὶ λογικῆς μὲν τὸ πρόσωπον ψ. Clem.*str*.5.6(p.351.4; M.9.61C); Jer.4:19 κοιλίαν μὲν τὴν ἑαυτοῦ ψ. ὀνομάζων, κατὰ τοὺς τῆς τροπῆς νόμους. οὕτω γὰρ εὑρίσκω πολλαχοῦ τῆς γραφῆς, εἴτε ὡς ἀπόκρυφον καὶ ἀόρατον (τὸ γὰρ αὐτὸ καὶ ψ. καὶ γαστρὸς τὸ κρύπτεσθαι) Gr.Naz.*or*.17.1(M.35.965A); Cant.6.7f. εἶναι γὰρ νύμφην μὲν τὴν ἐκκλησίαν, βασιλίσσας δὲ τὰς βασιλικὰς ἐκείνας τὰς πρὸ τοῦ κατακλυσμοῦ ψ. εὐαρέστους τῷ θεῷ γεγενημένας...παλλακὰς δὲ τὰς μετὰ τὸν κατακλυσμὸν τῶν προφητῶν, αἷς πρὸ τοῦ τὴν ἐκκλησίαν ἁρμοσθῆναι τῷ κυρίῳ παλλακίδων δίκην συγγινόμενος ἀληθεῖς ὑπέσπειρε λόγους... ἵνα γεννήσωσιν αὐτῷ συλλαβοῦσαι πίστιν...τοιαῦτα γὰρ ἀποβλαστήματα φύουσιν αἱ ψ. Meth.*symp*.7.4(p.75.11; M.18.129C); Jo.2:14 Ἰησοῦς...εἰσέρχεται εἰς τὴν Ἱεροσόλυμα καλουμένην ψ. ... τοῦ τ᾽ ἐπὶ τὴν θεραπείαν τῆς ψ. ἀνάγοντος τὰ γεγραμμένα καὶ ἐπ᾽ αὐτὴν αὐτὰ ἀλληγοροῦντος...μόνος δὲ εἰς τὴν Ἱεροσόλυμα ψ. οὐκ ἔρχεται, ἀλλ᾽ οὐδὲ μετὰ ὀλίγων τινῶν Or.*Jo*.10.28(18; p.201.23ff.; M.14.357B,C); **2.** Church as type of soul εἰκόνα...εἶναι δύνασθαι τὴν ἁγίαν ἐκκλησίαν ἐδίδασκεν...τῆς ψ. καθ᾽ ἑαυτὴν τῷ λόγῳ θεωρουμένης Max. *myst*.5(M.91.672D); κατὰ τὴν θεωρίαν εἰκαζομένη τῇ ψ. ἡ ἁγία... ἐκκλησία...καὶ πάντα συνάγουσα πρὸς τὸ τελούμενον ἐπὶ τοῦ θείου θυσιαστηρίου μυστήριον· ὅπερ διὰ τῶν κατὰ τὴν ἐκκλησίαν ἐπιτελουμένων ὁ δυνηθεὶς...σοφῶς μυηθῆναι, ἐκκλησίαν ὄντως θεοῦ, καὶ θείαν τὴν ἑαυτοῦ ψ. κατεστήσατο *ib*.(681C,D); **3.** ψ. as term for spiritual sense of scripture, v. γραφή.

III. soul of Christ; **A.** outside Christol. controversies; **1.** in gen. Χριστὸν γεγονέναι, καὶ σῶμα, καὶ λόγον, καὶ ψ. Just.*2apol*.10.1(M.6.460B); περὶ δὲ τοῦ Ἰησοῦ εἴποιμεν ἄν, ἐπεὶ συμφέρον ἦν τῷ τῶν ἀνθρώπων γένει παραδέξασθαι αὐτὸν ὡς υἱὸν θεοῦ, θεὸν ἐληλυθότα ἐν ἀνθρωπίνῃ ψ. καὶ σώματι Or.*Cels*.3.29(p.226.27; M.11.957A); εἰ... σῶμα θνητὸν καὶ ψ. ἀνθρωπίνην ἀναλαβὼν ὁ ἀθάνατος θεὸς λόγος δοκεῖ τῷ Κέλσῳ ἀλλάττεσθαι καὶ μεταπλάττεσθαι, μανθανέτω ὅτι ὁ λόγος τῇ οὐσίᾳ μένων λόγος, οὐδὲν μὲν πάσχει ὧν πάσχει τὸ σῶμα ἢ ἡ ψ. *ib*.4.15(p.285.15,18; 1048A); *ib*.6.47(p.119.5; 1372C); cf. *filius dei...suscepit non solum corpus humanum, ut quidam putant, sed et animam, nostrarum quidem animarum similem per naturam, proposito vero et virtute similem sibi et talem, qualis omnes voluntates...verbi ac sapientiae indeclinabiliter posset implere,* id.*princ*.4.4.4(31; p.353.11; M.11.405B); *illa anima, quae quasi ferrum in igne sic semper in verbo,...semper in deo, posita est, omne quod agit, quod sentit, quod intelligit, deus est,* *ib*.2.6.6(p.145.18; 214A); exeg. Ps.21:21 μονογενῆ δὲ τὴν ἰδίαν ψ. εἶπεν, ὡς μόνην ἁμαρτίαν μὴ γνοῦσαν· ἀλλὰ καὶ ὅτι μόνη διὰ παντὸς εἶχε τοῦ θεοῦ λόγου τὴν ἕνωσιν id.*Ps*.21:21(p.477); θεὸς σαρκὶ διὰ μέσης ψ. ἀνεκράθη, καὶ συνεδέθη τὰ διεστῶτα τῇ πρὸς ἄμφω τοῦ μεσιτεύοντος οἰκειότητι Gr.Naz.*or*.2.23(M.35.432B); πάντα ὑπὲρ πάντων γενόμενος...σῶμα, ψ., νοῦς *ib*.30.21(M.36.132B); σάρκα φορεῖ διὰ τὴν σάρκα, καὶ ψ. νοερᾷ διὰ τὴν ἐμὴν ψ. μίγνυται *ib*.45.9(633C); ὁ ἀχώρητος, χωρεῖται, διὰ μέσης ψ. νοερᾶς μεσιτευούσης θεότητι καὶ σαρκὸς παχύτητι *ib*.(636A); Justn.*conf*.(p.74.27; M.86.997B) cit. s. ὑπόστασις; **2.** Origen's doctrine of pre-existence applied to soul of Christ τάχα γὰρ ἡ μὲν τοῦ Ἰησοῦ ψ. ἐν τῇ ἑαυτῆς τυγχάνουσα τελειότητι ἐν θεῷ καὶ τῷ πληρώματι ἦν, καὶ ἐκεῖθεν ἐξεληλυθυῖα, τῷ ἀπεστάλθαι ἀπὸ τοῦ πατρός, ἀνέλαβεν τὸ ἐκ τῆς Μαρίας σῶμα Or.*Jo*.20.19(17; p.351.26; M.14.616A); *ib*.19.22(5; p.324.14; 568C); cf. *haec vero anima, quae in Jesu fuit, priusquam sciret malum, elegit bonum...oleo ergo laetitiae ungitur, cum verbo dei immaculata foederatione conjuncta est et per hoc sola omnium animarum peccati incapax fuit,* id.*princ*.4.4.4(31; p.354.10ff.; M.11.405C); ὥσπερ ὁ υἱὸς καὶ πατὴρ ἕν εἰσιν, οὕτω καὶ ἣν εἴληφεν ὁ υἱὸς ψ. καὶ αὐτὸς ἕν εἰσιν *ib*.4.4.4(31; p.354.16; 406A); rejected εἰκότως καταγνώσονται ἑαυτῶν πάντες οἱ νομίσαντες πρὸ τῆς Μαρίας...τινὰ ἐσχηκέναι ψ. ἀνθρωπίνην τὸν λόγον Ath.*ep.Epict*.8(p.13.9; M.26.1064B); **3.** soul as mediating between his body and his Godhead, cf. *illa anima...ab initio creaturae et deinceps inseparabiliter ei...inhaerens utpote sapientiae et verbo dei...et tota totum recipiens...facta est cum ipso principaliter unus spiritus...hac ergo substantia animae inter deum carnemque mediante (non enim possibile erat dei naturam corpori sine mediatore misceri) nascitur, ut diximus, deus-homo...sed neque rursum anima illa utpote substantia rationabilis, contra naturam habuit capere deum,* Or.*princ*.2.6.3(p.142.4ff.; M.11.211C,D); **4.** discussion whether his soul, regarded as an independent creature, is subject to change εἰ δ᾽ ἐπὶ τῆς Ἰησοῦ ψ. λαμβάνει τις τὴν μεταβολήν, αὐτῆς εἰς σῶμα ἐλθούσης, πευσόμεθα, πῶς λέγει μεταβολήν. εἰ μὲν γὰρ τῆς οὐσίας, οὐ δίδοται οὐ μόνον ἐπ᾽ ἐκείνης, ἀλλ᾽ οὐδὲ περὶ ἄλλου λογικῆς ψ.· εἰ δ᾽ ὅτι πάσχει τι ὑπὸ τοῦ σώματος ἀνακεκραμένη αὐτῷ καὶ ἀπὸ τοῦ τόπου, εἰς ὃν ἐλήλυθε, καὶ τί ἄτοπον ἀπαντᾷ τῷ λόγῳ, ἀπὸ πολλῆς φιλανθρωπίας καταβιβάζοντι σωτῆρα τῷ γένει τῶν ἀνθρώπων; id.*Cels*.4.18(p.288.1; M.11.1049D); **5.** ascent of his soul ὅρα εἰ μὴ μυστικώτερον καὶ οὐ τοπικῶς περὶ τῆς Ἰησοῦ ψ. ἀκούσει τό· Ἀναβὰς ὑπεράνω πάντων τῶν οὐρανῶν· ἡ γὰρ νοητὴ ἀνάβασις ἐκείνης τῆς ψ. ὑπερπεπήδηκεν καὶ πάντας τοὺς οὐρανοὺς καί, ὡς ἔστιν εἰπεῖν, ἤδη ἔφθασεν πρὸς αὐτὸν τὸν θεόν id.*Jo*.19.22(5; p.323.28ff.; M.14.568B); **6.** symbol of his soul: leaven in eucharist ἡ γὰρ ζύμη ἀντὶ ψ. τῷ φυράματι γίνεται ‡Jo.D.*azym*. proem.(M.95.388A); **7.** acc. Carpocrates τὸν δὲ Ἰησοῦν ἐξ Ἰωσὴφ γεγενῆσθαι...τὴν δὲ ψ. αὐτοῦ εὔτονον καὶ καθαρὰν γεγονυῖαν, διαμνημονεῦσαι τὰ ὁρατὰ μὲν αὐτῇ ἐν τῇ μετὰ τοῦ ἀγεννήτου θεοῦ περιφορᾷ...τὴν δὲ τοῦ Ἰησοῦ λέγουσι ψ. ἐννόμως ἠσκημένην ἐν Ἰουδαϊκοῖς ἔθεσι, καταφρονῆσαι αὐτῶν, καὶ διὰ τοῦτο δυνάμεις ἐπιτετελεκέναι, δι' ὧν κατήργησε τὰ ἐπὶ κολάσει πάθη προσόντα τοῖς ἀνθρώποις. τὴν οὖν ὁμοίως ἐκείνῃ τῇ τοῦ Χριστοῦ ψ. δυναμένην καταφρονῆσαι τῶν κοσμοποιῶν ἀρχόντων, ὁμοίως λαμβάνειν δύναμιν πρὸς τὸ πρᾶξαι τὰ ὅμοια Iren.*haer*.1.25.1(M.7.680A,B).

B. denials of Christ's human soul outside Apollinarian controversy; **1.** Eusebius: *Marcell*.2.4(p.57.8; M.24.821A) cit. s. σάρξ; ἐνοικῶν δ' ἐν τῇ σαρκὶ ὁ λόγος...εἰ μὲν τοῦ πατρὸς ἐκτὸς ἦν, ζῶν καὶ ὑφεστὼς καὶ τὴν σάρκα κινῶν ψυχῆς δίκην id.*e.th*.1.20(p.87.26; M.24.877A); *ib*.(p.88.5; 877B); where he speaks of Christ's ψ. he only reproduces scriptural passages, e.g.*d.e*.3.2(p.105.27ff.; M.22.181Dff.); *ib*.10.1(p.449.27ff.; 724Bff.); cf. θεὸς...ἅτε ψ. ἀψύχῳ σώματι, τῇ τῶν σωμάτων ἀλόγῳ φύσει τὸν αὐτοῦ λόγον ἐμβαλὼν *l.C*.12(p.231.30; M.20.1389C); **2.** Lucian of Antioch and Arians Λουκιανὸς γὰρ καὶ πάντες Λουκιανισταὶ ἀρνοῦνται τὸν υἱὸν τοῦ θεοῦ ψ. εἰληφέναι Epiph.*anc*.33 (p.42.20; M.43.77A); discussion of views, *ib*.35,36(p.44.26ff.; 80Dff.); teaching opposed, Eust.*fr*.56(p.91; M.18.689D) cit. s. ὁμογενής; ἡ ψ. τὴν συγγενῆ ψ. [sc. of penitent thief] ὁδηγοῦσα *ib*.(p.91; 692A); **3.** Pseudo-Ignatius ἐάν τις...νομίζῃ τὸν κύριον, οὐχὶ θεὸν μονογενῆ... ἀλλ' ἐκ ψ. καὶ σώματος αὐτὸν εἶναι νομίζῃ, ὁ τοιοῦτος ὄφις ἐστίν ‡Ign. *Philad*.6; ‡Ign.*Phil*.5; cf. τινὲς...ἀσεβοῦσι, ψιλὸν ἄνθρωπον εἶναι φανταζόμενοι τὸν κύριον, ἐκ ψ. καὶ σώματος αὐτὸν εἶναι νομίζοντες *Const. App*.6.26.2.

C. in Apollinarian controversy; **1.** Apollinarius' denial of a human soul in Christ ἔζησεν τὸ σῶμα θεότητος ἁγιασμῷ καὶ οὐκ ἀνθρωπίνης ψ. κατασκευῇ Apoll.*corp.et div*.(p.190.19; M.*PL*.8.875A); ἤρκει καὶ μόνον τὸ αὐτοῦ θέλημα διὰ τοῦ ἐν τῇ σαρκὶ σκηνώσαντος λόγου πρὸς τὸ ταύτην ζωοποιεῖν καὶ κινεῖν, ἀναπληρούσης τῆς θείας ἐνεργείας τὸν τῆς ψ. τόπον καὶ τοῦ ἀνθρωπίνου νοός id.*fr*.2 (p.204.8)ap.Anast.S.*monoph*.(M.89.1181D); εἰπὼν γὰρ ὅτι ὁ λόγος σὰρξ ἐγένετο, οὐ προσέθηκε καὶ ψ. ἀδύνατον γὰρ δύο νοερὰ καὶ θελητικὰ ἐν τῷ ἅμα κατοικεῖν...οὐκοῦν οὐ ψ. ἀνθρωπίνης ἐπελάβετο ὁ λόγος, ἀλλὰ μόνου σπέρματος Ἀβραάμ· τὸν γὰρ τοῦ σώματος Ἰησοῦ ναὸν προδιέγραψεν ὁ ἄψυχος καὶ ἄνους καὶ ἀθελὴς τοῦ Σαλομῶντος ναός *ib*. (p.204.11ff.; 1184A); v. νοῦς; **2.** orthodox refutation; **a.** salvation of whole man requires a human soul in Saviour οὐδὲ γὰρ οἷόν τε ἦν, τοῦ κυρίου δι' ἡμᾶς ἀνθρώπου γενομένου, ἀνόητον εἶναι τὸ σῶμα αὐτοῦ, οὐδὲ σώματος μόνου, ἀλλὰ καὶ ψ. ἐν αὐτῷ τῷ λόγῳ σωτηρία γέγονεν Ath.*tom*.7(M.26.804B) but cf. infra f; ὅπου κεκράτητο ἡ ψ. ἡ ἀνθρωπίνη ἐν θανάτῳ, ἐκεῖ ἐπιδείκνυται ὁ Χριστὸς τὴν ἀνθρωπίνην ψ. ἰδίαν οὖσαν, ἵνα καὶ παρῇ ὡς ἄνθρωπος ὁ ἀκράτητος ἐν θανάτῳ, ὡς θεός· ἵνα...ὅπου ἐβασίλευσεν ὁ θάνατος ἐν μορφῇ ψ. ἀνθρωπίνης, παρὼν ὁ ἀθάνατος ἐπιδείξηται τὴν ἀθανασίαν ‡Ath.*Apoll*.1.17(M.28.1124C); πῶς ἡ κράτησις τοῦ θανάτου τελείαν ἐλάμβανε τὴν λύσιν, εἰ τὸ κατὰ φρόνησιν ἁμαρτῆσαν, τὴν ψ. Χριστὸς ἀναμάρτητον οὐ συνεστήσατο ἐν ἑαυτῷ; ἔτι οὖν βασιλεύει ὁ θάνατος τοῦ ἔσωθεν ἀνθρώπου· τίνος γὰρ ἄλλου καὶ ἐβασίλευσέ ποτε, οὐχὶ ψ. τῆς ἐν φρονήσει ἁμαρτησάσης...ὑπὲρ ἧς τὴν ἰδίαν ψ. τέθεικεν ὁ Χριστὸς λύτρον ἀντιδιδούς; *ib*.1.19(1125C,D); τῷ σώματι καὶ τῇ ψ. ἑαυτὸν ἐπιμερίσας, διὰ μὲν τῆς ψ. ἀνοίγει τῷ λῃστῇ τὸν παράδεισον Gr.Nyss.*Apoll*.17(M.45.1156A); ὁ μονογενὴς θεός, αὐτὸς ἀνίστησι τὸν ἀνακραθέντα ἄνθρωπον αὐτῷ, καὶ χωρίσας τοῦ σώματος τὴν ψ., καὶ ἑνώσας πάλιν ἀμφότερα, καὶ οὕτως ἡ κοινὴ γίνεται σωτηρία τῆς φύσεως *ib*.(1156C); **b.** full humanity of Christ requires a human soul ὁ γὰρ ἐκ ψ. νοερᾶς καὶ σώματος συνεστηκώς, ἄνθρωπος λέγεται· ᾧ δὲ μὴ συνεπινοεῖται τὰ δύο, πῶς ἡ τοῦ ἀνθρώπου κλῆσις ἐφαρμοσθήσεται; *ib*.2(M.45.1128B); ὁ ἀνθρωπίνην σάρκα, καὶ ταύτην ἔμψυχον, προσοικίζων τῷ λόγῳ, οὐδὲν ἕτερον, ἢ ὅλον συνάπτει τὸν ἄνθρωπον· οὐδὲν γὰρ ἄλλο παρὰ τὴν νοερὰν φύσιν τῆς ἀνθρωπίνης ψ. ἐστιν ἰδίωμα... ὁ τοίνυν λέγων ἄνθρωπον εἶναι τὸν προσειλημμένον, ἔμψυχον δὲ τοῦτον διδούς, οὐδὲν ἕτερον ἢ καὶ νοητὴν αὐτῷ προεμαρτύρησε δύναμιν, ὅπερ ἴδιον τῆς ἀνθρωπίνης ἐστὶ ψ. *ib*.7(1137B); **c.** proof from Christ's human emotions εἰ δὲ ἐπ' ἀληθείας εἴρηται, ἀλλοτρία δὲ καθόλου ἡ ψ. τοῦ κυρίου ἐγεγόνει τῆς ἰδίας νοήσεως, θεὸν τὸν λόγον ἔχουσα νοῦν, τετράφθαι τὸ ἄτρεπτον εἰς λύπην...καὶ ταραχήν, τὸ ἐννοεῖν, ἀσεβές ἐστι...ἀλλὰ δείκνυσι τὸν νοῦν ὁ κύριος εἰρηκώς· ἡ ψ. μου τετάρακται. εἰ δὴ ψ. ἰδίας νόησιν ὁ κύριος ἐπιδείκνυται, εἰς συμπάθειαν τῆς ἡμετέρας ψ., ἵνα οὕτω καὶ αὐτοῦ νοήσωμεν εἶναι τὸ πάθος, καὶ αὐτὸν ἀπαθῆ ὁμολογῶμεν. ὥσπερ γὰρ τῷ αἵματι τῆς σαρκὸς αὐτοῦ ἐλυτρώσατο ἡμᾶς, οὕτω καὶ τῇ νοήσει τῆς ψ. αὐτοῦ τὴν νίκην ὑπὲρ ἡμῶν ἐπιδείκνυται ‡Ath.*Apoll*.1.16(M.28.1121B,C); **d.** from death and descent into Hades ὁ κύριος...παραδοὺς τὸ πνεῦμα, τὸ ἔσωθεν τοῦ ἰδίου σώματος, τουτέστι τὴν ψ. ἐσήμανε· περὶ ἧς καὶ εἴρηκεν, ὅτι τίθημι ὑπὲρ τῶν προβάτων τῶν ἐμῶν. ὥστε τὴν ἔκπνευσιν οὐκ ἄν τις εἴποι θεότητος μετάστασιν, ἀλλὰ ψ. ἀποχώρησιν. εἰ γὰρ κατὰ μετάστασιν θεότητος ὁ θάνατος γέγονε καὶ ἡ τοῦ σώματος νέκρωσις, ἴδιον ἄρα θάνατον ἀπέθανε, καὶ οὐ τὸν ἡμέτερον. καὶ πῶς εἰς ᾅδου κατῆλθεν ἀπαρακαλύπτῳ τῇ θεότητι; ποῦ οὖν ἡ ψ., ἣν ἐπηγγείλατο ὁ κύριος τιθέναι ὑπὲρ τῶν προβάτων...εἰ δὲ ψ. ἀποχώρησις γέγονε, διὰ τοῦτο εἴρηται, ὅτι τὸν ἡμέτερον ἀπεδέξατο θάνατον *ib*.1.18(1125B,C); **e.** refutation of Apollinarian idea that ψ. belongs to the 'outer man' τί οὖν περὶ τῆς ψ. ἐρεῖτε, ὅτι καὶ τὸ σῶμα καὶ ἡ ψ. ὁ ἔξωθέν ἐστιν ἄνθρωπος, ὡς ἂν εἴποι τις, τὸ αἷμα καὶ τὴν σάρκα; ἀλλ' ὥσπερ τὸ σῶμα καὶ τὸ αἷμα οὐ διαφεύγουσι τὴν ψηλάφησιν...δείξατε ἡμῖν καὶ τὴν ψ. μὴ διαφεύγουσαν ταῦτα...ἤ, εἰ μὴ δύνασθε δεῖξαι,...οὔτε ὁρᾶται ψ., οὔτε ἀποκτείνεται ὑπὸ ἀνθρώπου...οὐ μόνον ἐφ' ἡμῖν τούτων δεικνυμένων, ἀλλὰ καὶ ἐν αὐτῷ τῷ θανάτῳ τοῦ Χριστοῦ ἐδείκνυτο· τὸ μέν τοι [sc. σῶμα], μέχρι τάφου φθάσαν· ἡ δέ [sc. ψ.], μέχρι ᾅδου διαβᾶσα *ib*.1.13(1116D–1117A); **f.** rejection of thesis that Christ had only an animal, but not an intellectual, soul τὴν νοερὰν τοῦ ἀνθρώπου φύσιν, ἥτις νοεῖται ψ.,... ἄφευκτον ταύτην τῆς ἁμαρτίας διοριζόμενοι· κἂν ὅτι μάλιστα καὶ ψ. σαρκικὴν γεγράφατε, πόθεν μαθόντες οὐ συνεπίσταμαι...πῶς εἰ σαρκικὴ ἡ ψ. καθ' ὑμᾶς, οὐ συνθνήσκει τῷ σώματι *ib*.2.8(1144C,D).

D. in Monothelite controversy; **1.** in gen. ὅρα...τὸ...πεπλανημένον τῶν αἱρετικῶν· πάντα τὰ συγγενῆ ὄντα τῶν ἀλόγων ἀνελλιπῶς ὁμολογοῦσιν ἐν Χριστῷ...τὰ δὲ τῆς νοερᾶς καὶ ἀθανάτου ψ. ἰδιώματα... ταῦτα ὡς πονηρὰ ὄντα ὁμολογεῖν ἐν Χριστῷ...οὐκ ἀνέχονται Anast.S. *serm.imag*.3(M.89.1168A); **2.** comparison with soul of Adam ἐπιδημήσας οὖν ὁ τοῦ θεοῦ λόγος ἐπὶ τὸ ἀνακαινίσαι τὸν Ἀδάμ, τοιαύτην ἑαυτῷ ψ. ἐδημιούργησεν, οἵαν ἀπαρχῆς ἐξ ἑαυτοῦ διὰ τοῦ ἐμφυσήματος τῷ Ἀδὰμ μετέδωκεν *ib*.(1169D); ἡ μὲν γὰρ τοῦ Ἀδὰμ ψ. ἐκ θεοῦ τὴν ὕπαρξιν διὰ τοῦ ἐμφυσήματος ἔσχεν· ἡ δὲ τοῦ Ἐμμανουὴλ ψ. ἔνθεον, καὶ σύνθεον, καὶ ὁμόθεον τὴν οὐσίωσιν ἔσχεν *ib*.(1172A); **3.** proof of orth. position from descent into Hades τίς τὰς ἀπ' αἰῶνος δεσμίους ψ. τῶν κεκοιμημένων ἀνθρώπων ἐπεσκέψατο; πρόδηλον, ὅτι ἡ...Χριστοῦ τοῦ θεοῦ ψ. τὰς ὁμοουσίους αὐτῆς ψ. τὰς λογικὰς ἐπεσκέψατο *ib*.(1172D); αὐτὴ [sc. the soul of Christ] βοήσασα...ἐξέλθετε, ὡς τόπον ἀναπληροῦσα τελείου ἀνθρώπου τοῦ ἐκ ψ. συνισταμένου καὶ σώματος...ἡ νοερὰ τὰς νοερὰς ἐπιβλέψασα, ψ. τὰς ψ. ... πῶς γὰρ ἂν καὶ ἐδέξαντο τὸ τῆς ἁγίας ψ. κήρυγμα, εἰ μὴ διὰ τῆς νοερᾶς αὐτῶν λογικῆς θελήσεως; *ib*.(1173A); *ib*.(1173D); **4.** from Christ's obedience, *ib*.(1173C) cit. s. ἀθελής.

ψυχικός, A. *of the soul, spiritual*; **1.** in gen. ἐν νόσῳ ψ. ὑπάρχοντα Just.*dial*.30.1(M.6.537C); Clem.*str*.6.12(p.481.30; M.9.320C); *ib*.7.16 (p.67.3; 532A); Or.*fr*.25 *in Jer*.(p.210.18; M.13.592C); τῶν ψ. ... κακῶν *ib*.36(p.217.4; 600D); ὑπὸ ψ. μοιχείας καὶ θάνατος γίνεται *Hom.Clem*.3.28; Chrys.*hom*.27.2 *in Mt*.(7.327D); ἵνα...ἡμᾶς ἐλευθερώσῃ ψ. ἀρρωστημάτων Cyr.*Lc*.4:38(M.72.552C); *ib*.6:41(601D); τὰς ψ. ... ἕξεις Dion.Ar.*e.h*.2.1(M.3.392A); *ib*.3.3.5(432A); opp. σωματικός, Clem. *str*.7.7(p.28.26; M.9.453D); φυσικός, id.*paed*.3.2(p.243.11; M.8.573A); Didym.*Trin*.2.27(M.39.765A); κοσμικός, Ath.*exp.Ps*.118:170(M.27.508B); **2.** ref. senses of soul τοῖς ψ. ... ὄμμασι Or.*fr*.94 *in Jo*.(p.557.30); ὀφθαλμοί...οἱ δὲ ψ. εἰς μῆκος ἀποτείνονται Adam.*dial*.2.11(p.78.22; M.11.1777A); Sophr.H.*ep.syn*.(M.87.3197A); **3.** ὁ ψ. *the spiritual man* ἔλαιον ὁ ἐπιχεόμενος λόγος τοῦ ψ., τοῦ τὴν ἀγαθὴν πρᾶξιν ἐργαζομένου Or.*comm.ser.in Mt*.63(p.147.16; M.17.304C); **4.** ref. spiritual life ἐν ταῖς διδασκαλίαις αὐτῶν εὑρηκὼς...πολλὴν ψ. λυσιτέλειαν Thdr.Stud.*test*.(M.99.1816C); **5.** ref. spiritual sense of scripture, Or. *princ*.4.2.5(p.314.13; M.11.368A); **6.** ref. Christ's resurrection body ψ. ὂν γέγονε πνευματικόν, καὶ ἐκ γῆς γενόμενον, τὰς οὐρανίους διέβη πύλας Ath.*ep.Epict*.9(p.15.10; M.26.1065B).

B. *natural, carnal, material-minded*, opp. spiritual, **1.** in gen. οἱ ψ. opp. τοῖς πνεύματι θεοῦ φρουρουμένοις, Tat.*orat*.15(p.16.31; M.6.840A); acc. Thales, of demons, opp. God as νοῦς, Athenag.*leg*.23.2 (M.6.941B); Clem.*paed*.1.6(p.108.24; M.8.288A) cit. s. πνευματικός; cf.id.*str*.2.3(p.118.17; M.8.941B); Or.*Jo*.13.61(59; p.293.25ff.; M.14.516D); combined with ἐπίγειος and δαιμονιώδης, id.*fr*.46 *in Jo*. (p.521.19); id.*hom*.12.1 *in Jer*.(p.85.22; M.13.377A); ἐκκλησία...ἀναγεννῶσα τοὺς ψ. εἰς πνευματικούς Meth.*symp*.8.6(p.88.11; M.18.148B); Ath.*ep.Serap*.1.32(M.26.605B); ψ. πάθη id.*inc*.50.4(M.25.185C); in discussion of 'Second Adam' Christology, ‡Ath.*Apoll*.1.8(M.26.1105B) cit. s. πνευματικός; τὸ δὲ τοὺς δοκοῦντας εἶναι πιστούς, τούτους εὑρίσκεσθαι ψ., τουτό ἐστιν τὸ θρήνων ἄξιον Chrys.*hom*.63.3 *in Jo*.(8.379D); ἐγκόσμιον...καὶ δαιμονιώδη καὶ ψ. σοφίαν Cyr.*Ps*.9:23 (M.69.780A); ψ. πάθη Diad.*perf*.81(p.104.24); γνώμη [sc. self-will] ἐν τοῖς ψ. κρατεῖ Thdt.*qu*.53 *in 4 Reg*.(1.547); **2.** of the body ἡ τοῦ ψ. σώματος ἰδιότης, ἀεὶ διά τινος ῥοῆς καὶ κινήσεως ἀπὸ τοῦ ἐν ᾧ ἐστιν ἀλλοιοῦσθαι Gr.Nyss.*anim.et res*.(M.46.156B); **3.** of sin ψ. τι ἁμάρτημα CNic.(325)*can*.2; **4.** ref. state of the unbaptized ἅπερ οὐκ ἐφυλαξάμεθα ψ. ὑπάρχοντες, τὰ ὅπλα τῆς δικαιοσύνης λαβόντες ἐν τῇ δυνάμει τηρήσωμεν τοῦ θεοῦ Diad.*perf*.78(p.100.3); **5.** ref. scriptural passages alluding to natural experiences of incarnate Logos, ‡Ath.

*dial.Trin.*4.8(M.28.1261D); **6.** dist. from *σαρκικός* and *πνευματικός*: *ὁ ψ. ἄνθρωπος, οὐδέπω καλός· ὁ σαρκικὸς δέ, καὶ λίαν πάθους φιλός· ὁ πνευματικὸς δέ, οὐ μακρὰν τοῦ πνεύματος* Gr.Naz.*carm.*1.2.34. 242(M.37.963); *γνώρισμα τοῦ μὲν σαρκικοῦ, τὸ κακῶς μόνον εἰδέναι ποιεῖν. τοῦ δὲ ψ., τὸ μήτε ποιεῖν βούλεσθαί ποτε μήτε πάσχειν κακῶς. τοῦ δὲ πνευματικοῦ, τὸ ποιεῖν μόνον καλῶς βούλεσθαι, καὶ ὑπὲρ ἀρετῆς εἰ συμβαίνει πάσχειν* Max.*ep.*9(M.91.448A); cf.*cat.1Cor.*suppl.(p.461. 25); **7.** as name of derision for orthodox, used by Montanists and Gnostics, Clem.*str.*4.13(p.289.12ff.; M.8.1300C); **8.** exeg.; **a.** 1Cor. 2:14 *ἐκεῖ ψ. εἰσάγεταί τις καὶ πνευματικὸς ἄνθρωπος, ὁ μὲν πνευματικὸς τῶν σωζομένων, ὁ δὲ ψ. τῶν ἀπολλυμένων* Meth.*res.*1.58(p.321.26f.); *ψ. ἐστιν ὁ τὸ πᾶν τοῖς λογισμοῖς τοῖς ψυχροῖς διδούς, καὶ μὴ νομίζων ἄνωθέν τινος δεῖσθαι βοηθείας, ὅπερ ἐστὶν ἀνοίας* Chrys.*hom.7.4 in 1Cor.*(10.56B) ∞ Jo.D.*1Cor.*2:14(M.95.588B), cf. derivation of *ψυχή* from *ψυχρός*, v. *ψυχή*; *ψ. δὲ λέγει τὸν στοιχοῦντα τοῖς οἰκείοις λογισμοῖς ἢ τὸν νοσοῦντα τοῖς τῆς ψυχῆς λογισμοῖς καὶ μὴ ἐρρωμένον περὶ τὴν γνῶσιν τῆς ἀληθείας...ὁ ψ. οὐ δύναται δεκτικὸς εἶναι τῆς ἀληθείας, ἀλλ' οὕτως κεκάκωται τὴν ψυχὴν ὡς μωρίαν ἡγεῖσθαι τὴν οἰκονομίαν τοῦ θεοῦ...ὁ ψ. ἄνθρωπος τεχνικοὺς ἐπιζητῶν λογισμοὺς ἐπὶ τοῦ σταυροῦ ὡς μῶρον...ἀπωθεῖται τὸ κήρυγμα* Sever.*1Cor.*2:14f.(p.234.38ff.); *ψ. ἐστιν ὁ κατὰ σάρκα ζῶν καὶ μήπω τὸν νοῦν φωτισθεὶς διὰ τοῦ πνεύματος, ἀλλὰ μόνην τὴν ἔμφυτον καὶ ἀνθρωπίνην σύνεσιν ἔχων, ἣν ταῖς ἁπάντων ψυχαῖς ἐμβάλλει ὁ δημιουργός* Cyr.*1Cor.*2:14(p.257.11; M.74.865B); *ψ. καλεῖ τὸν μόνοις τοῖς οἰκείοις ἀρκούμενον λογισμοῖς, καὶ τὴν τοῦ πνεύματος διδασκαλίαν μὴ προσιέμενον, οὔτε μὴ ἐπιγνῶναι δυνάμενον* Thdt.*1Cor.*2:14(3.178); *τοῦτο μὲν εἰπὼν ψ., ὡς τῇ τῆς ψυχῆς κινούμενον παρουσίᾳ* Proc.G.*Gen.*2:7(M.87.156B); **b.** 1Cor. 15:44,46 *ἐπειδὴ δὲ ἡ τοῖς πάθεσιν ἐμμένουσα ψυχή, εἰκότως καὶ τὸ τῆς τοιαύτης ψυχῆς σῶμα ψ. καλεῖται...ἐπειδὴ προκόπτουσα ἡ ψυχὴ ἐπὶ τὸ πνευματικὸν ἀναβαίνει, πρῶτον εἶπεν εἶναι τὸ ψ. σῶμα, ἔπειτα τὸ πνευματικόν... διὸ οὐ προσέχομεν τοῖς λέγουσιν ὅτι τοιοῦτον ἀνίσταται τὸ σῶμα οἷον εἶχεν ὁ Ἀδὰμ ψ.* Didym.*1Cor.*15:44–46(p.10.21ff.); *σῶμα ψ. λέγει τὸ τῇ ἁμαρτίᾳ τῆς ψυχῆς θανατωθέν* Sever.*1Cor.*15:44(p.275.27); *ὥσπερ γὰρ εἴπερ ἕλοιτό τις τὸ ἀπὸ γῆς ἡμῶν σῶμα ψ. ἀποκαλεῖν, περιθείη ἂν τις εἰκότως οὐ τὸ ψυχῆς εἶδος αὐτῷ, περιτρέψει δὲ μᾶλλον τοῦ λόγου τὴν δύναμιν εἰς τὸ φρόνημα τὸ ψ. ἤγουν τὸ σαρκικόν, καθάπερ ἀμέλει καὶ σοφίαν νοοῦμεν ψ. καὶ ἐπίγειον τὴν καθ' ἡμᾶς...οὕτω κἂν εἰ λέγοιτο σῶμα ψ., οὐκ ἂν οἶμαι τῷ αὐτῷ τὸ ψυχῆς εἶδος περιτιθείς, τὴν ἐπὶ τῷ πεπλανῆσθαι διαφύγοι γραφήν, ἐπεὶ κατὰ τίνα τρόπον ζῶντές τε ἔτι καὶ ἐν αὐτοῖς δὴ τούτοις τοῖς ἀπὸ γῆς ὄντες σώμασι, ψ. λέγονταί τινες καὶ πνευματικοί;...ὅτι τοίνυν ὁ ψ. οὐ φύσεως ἡμῖν διαφορὰς ὑπεμφήνειεν ἄν, ζωῆς δὲ μᾶλλον ἠθῶν τε καὶ τρόπων ποιότητα, καθ' ἣν ὁ μέν τίς ἐστι τῷ γεωδεστέρῳ...φρονήματι κάτοχος, ὁ δὲ τῇ τοῦ πνεύματος ἐλευθερίᾳ περιφανής, ἀποδείκνυσι σαφῶς ἀπὸ τε Ἀδὰμ τοῦ πρώτου καὶ τοῦ δευτέρου* Cyr.*1Cor.*15:44(pp.312.16–314.5; M.74.908C–909B); *ἐπειδὴ ἔφη σπείρεσθαι μὲν εἰς γῆν τὸ σῶμα ψ., ἀποφαίνει λευκῶς ὡς ἔστιν οὐκ ἀπαράδεκτον τῇ τοῦ ἀνθρώπου φύσει τὸ ἐκ φρονήματος ψ. μεταφοιτᾶν εἰς πνευματικόν, καὶ ὅτι πρεσβύτερον τοῦ πνευματικοῦ τὸ ψ. εἴη ἂν* *ib.*15:46(p.314.19ff.; 909D); *ψ.... τὸ ὑπὸ τῆς ψυχῆς κυβερνώμενον· πνευματικὸν δέ, ὑπὸ τοῦ πνεύματος οἰκονομούμενον* Thdt.*1Cor.* 15:44(3.278); **9.** Valent., v. *ὑλικός, πνευματικός, Χριστός*; **a.** opp. *ὑλικός* and *πνευματικός*, Iren.*haer.*1.5.1(M.7.492A); *χοϊκός*, Clem.*exc. Thdot.*51(p.123.17; M.9.684A); *ἀγγελικός* and *χοϊκός*, Hipp.*haer.*5.6 (p.78.16ff.; M.16.3126B); *σαρκικός* and *πνευματικός*, *ib.*5.8(p.97.15; 3151B); *ἔσω ἄνθρωπος πνευματικὸς ἐν τῷ ψ.* *ib.*7.27(p.206.26; 3319A); *νοερός* and *χοϊκός*, *ib.*10.9(p.268.17; 3419B); *πνευματικός*, Or.*Cels.*5.61 (p.64.22; M.11.1277B); distinction of *ὁμοουσίους...διαβόλῳ...ἀνθρώπους, ψ.*, and *πνευματικούς*, Heracleon ap.Or.*Jo.*20.20(18; p.352.35; M.14.617A); *οἱ ψ. πρὸς χρόνον πιστεύοντες* *ib.*20.33(p.371.18; 649B); *ἀπὸ τῶν ὑλικῶν εἰς τὸν ψ. τόπον* *ib.*10.33(19; p.206.27; 365C); *οἱ ψ.*, being *ἔξω τοῦ πληρώματος*, compared with vendors in Temple, *ib.* (p.207.1; 365C); *οὐ πρὸς τοὺς φύσει τοῦ διαβόλου υἱούς, τοὺς χοϊκούς, ἀλλὰ πρὸς τοὺς ψ., θέσει υἱοὺς διαβόλου γινομένους* *ib.*20.24(20; p.359. 14; 628D); **b.** Christol. *ὡς εἰκὼν πατρὸς πατὴρ γίνεται καὶ προβάλλει πρῶτον τὸν ψ. Χριστὸν υἱοῦ εἰκόνα...εἶτα ἀγγέλους ἀρχαγγέλων ἐκ τῆς ψ. καὶ φωτεινῆς οὐσίας* Clem.*exc.Thdot.*47(p.121.22ff.; M.9.681A); *ib.* 59(p.126.21ff.; 688B); *τὸ δὲ πνευματικόν, ὃ ἀνείληφεν, καὶ τὸ ψ. οὕτως ἐμφαίνει· 'τὸ δὲ παιδίον ηὔξανεν καὶ προέκοπτεν ἐν σοφίᾳ.' σοφίας μὲν γὰρ τὸ πνευματικὸν δεῖται, μεγέθους δὲ τὸ ψ.* *ib.*61(p.127.6ff.; 688B,C); *κάθηται ὁ ψ. Χριστὸς ἐν δεξιᾷ τοῦ δημιουργοῦ* *ib.*62(p.128.1; 689A); cf. *ib.*3(p.105.15; 653A); *οἱ μὲν ἀπὸ τῆς Ἰταλίας, ὧν ἐστιν Ἡρακλέων καὶ Πτολεμαῖος, ψ. φασι τὸ σῶμα τοῦ Ἰησοῦ γεγονέναι, καὶ διὰ τοῦτο ἐπὶ τοῦ βαπτίσματος τὸ πνεῦμα ὡς περιστερὰ κατελήλυθε,...καὶ ἐγήγερκεν αὐτὸν ἐκ νεκρῶν τῷ ψ., καὶ ἐγήγερκεν αὐτὸν ἐκ νεκρῶν* Hipp.*haer.*6.35(p.165.6ff.; M.16. 3250A); cf.Tim.CP *haer.*(M.86.17B); *ἐνανθρωπῆσαι δὲ τὸν Ἰησοῦν... σῶμα ἐκ τῆς ψ. οὐσίας ἀνειληφότα* Thdt.*haer.*5.11(4.420); *ψ. Χριστὸς* *ib.*1.8(300); **c.** *ἡ ψ. εἰκών* in man, claimed by Valentinians to be saved, Clem.*str.*4.13(p.288.23; M.9.1300A); **d.** of demiurge *ἔστι δὲ πυρώδης, φησίν, ἡ ψ. οὐσία, καλεῖται δὲ καὶ τόπος μεσότητος ὑπ' αὐτοῦ καὶ ἑβδομὰς καὶ παλαιὸς τῶν ἡμερῶν. καὶ ὅσα τοιαῦτα λέγουσι περὶ τούτου, ταῦτα εἶναι τοῦ ψ., ὅν φησιν εἶναι τοῦ κόσμου δημιουργόν* Hipp.*haer.*6.32(p.161.6ff.; M.16.3243B).

ψυχικῶς, 1. *spiritually*, opp. *σωματικῶς*, Epiph.*haer.*42.11(p.134. 3; M.41.741A); ref. Adam *ἐν ᾗ ἡμέρᾳ ἔφαγεν ἀπὸ τοῦ ξύλου, ἐν αὐτῇ ἐθανατώθη ψ.* ‡Felix III Papa *ep.Petr.*1(p.20.24; H.2.820B); *ψ. ἐθανάτωσαν τοὺς ἐξαγγέλλοντας, ἄλλο ἀντ' ἄλλου διδάξαντες* Sophr.H.*conf.* (M.87.3368A); **2.** *carnally, materially*, ref. Nicodemus *ὁ Χριστὸς σαφέστερον ἀποκαλύπτει τῆς γεννήσεως τὸν τρόπον...τῷ ψ. ἐρωτῶντι* Chrys.*hom.25.1 in Jo.*(8.143C).

ψυχίον, τό, *butterfly* or *moth*, Meth.*symp.*9.1(p.113.24; v.l. *φύκια* M.18.177A).

***ψυχοανακάλυπτος,** *soul-revealing πορνεία...ψ.... ἁμαρτία* ‡Chrys. *ador.*2(11.824F).

***ψυχοβλαβής,** *soul-destroying*, Nil.*epp.*2.286(M.79.341D); ‡Jo.D. *hom.*6.10(M.96.676B); masc. as subst., Chrys.*hom.56.3 in Gen.*(4. 542D).

***ψυχοβλαβῶς,** *in a way which harms the soul*, Didym.*Trin.*2.8 (M.39.616D).

ψυχοβόρος, *soul-devouring*, Synes.*hymn.*3.96(p.10; M.66.1595); *ib.* 4.244(p.33; 1607).

***ψυχοδιάβατος,** *piercing the soul*, Tim.Ant.*Sym.*(M.86.248A).

***ψυχοδότης, ὁ,** *giver of the soul* or *life*; of Christ, Didym.*Trin.* 3.16(M.39.869C); Synes.*hymn.*4.186(p.31; M.66.1606).

***ψυχοκερδής,** *gaining souls*, Geo.Pis.*hex.*473(M.92.1472).

***ψυχοκλέπτης, ὁ,** *stealer of souls*, Geo.Pis.*hex.*761(M.92.1492).

ψυχοκλόνος, *confusing the soul*, Sophr.H.*carm.*21.109(M.87. 3829A).

***ψυχόκομπος,** *distending the soul*, Geo.Pis.*hex.*775(M.92.1494).

***ψυχοκράτης,** *supporting the soul*, Geo.Pis.*hex.*1416(M.92.1542).

***ψυχοκτονία, ἡ,** *slaughter of souls*, ‡Caes.Naz.*dial.*3.140(M.38. 1048).

***ψυχοκτόνος,** *slaying the soul, deadly*, Cyr.*hom.div.*19(M.77.1109A); Dor.*doct.*proem.1(M.88.1613D); *τοῦ ψ. πολεμίου τὴν δύναμιν βυθισθῆναι* *Rit.Bapt.*(p.398).

***ψυχολατρεία, ἡ,** *worship in which the soul takes part*, Eust. *engast.*2(p.18.2; M.18.616C).

***ψυχόλεθρος,** *destroying the soul, deadly*, ‡Chrys.*hom.jej.*5(9.800E); Geo.Pis.*hex.*1817(M.92.1574A); Thphn.*chron.*p.423(M.108.1000D).

***ψυχολέτειρα, ἡ,** *destroyer of the soul*, Geo.Pis.*carm.vit.*6.

ψυχομαχ-έω, *fight for one's life*, met. on one's death-bed *τινὰς μὲν δικαίους ∼οῦντας...τινὰς δὲ ἁμαρτωλοὺς εἰρηνικῶς...ἀποθνήσκοντας* ‡Ath.*qu.Ant.*105(M.28.661D); Anast.S.*qu.et resp.*96(M.89.741B).

***ψυχονοσέω,** *be sick in soul*, Jo.Clim.*past.*13(M.88.1196A).

ψυχοπομπός, ὁ, *conductor* or *guide of souls*, as adj. *ψ. γοήτων* Synes.*insomn.*14(p.176.2; M.66.1309A).

***ψυχορραγικῶς,** *at the point of death*, Leont.H.*Nest.*1.19(M.86 1484C).

ψυχοστόλος, *soul-summoning*; of Christ calling Lazarus, Nonn. *par.Jo.*12:1(M.43.849B).

***ψυχοστρόφος,** *soul-converting*, †Apoll.*met.Ps.*18:8(M.33.1336C).

***ψυχοσώστης,** *that saves life*, Steph.Diac.*v.Steph.*(M.100.1096C).

***ψυχοσωτήριος,** = foreg., ‡Jo.D.*hom.*5(M.96.656D).

***ψυχοτερπέως,** *with a rejoicing soul*, Sophr.H.*carm.*20.95(M.87. 3824A).

***ψυχότης, ἡ,** *soul-hood τίνος ἕνεκα μὴ ἐκ ψ. τὸν ἄνθρωπον καὶ σωματότητος, ὥσπερ τὸν Χριστὸν ἐκ θεότητος καὶ ἀνθρωπότητος* Jo.D. *Jacob.*56(M.94.1465B).

***ψυχοτόκος,** *soul-bearing ἡ γυνὴ τίκτει μὲν τὸ σῶμα, ψυχοῖ δὲ ὁ θεός, καὶ οὐκ ἂν λέγοιτο γυνὴ ψ.* Nest.*fr.*D 2(p.352.10)ap.Cyr.*Nest.*1.4 (p.23.34; 6[1].17E); Cyr.*ep.*1(p.15.21,30; 5[2].8E,9B).

***ψυχοτροφέω,** *sustain alive*, *Orac.Sib.fr.*3.8(p.230).

ψυχοτρόφος, *sustaining life*, Or.*exp.in Pr.*28:19(M.17.245A); of God, *Orac.Sib.*5.500; Synes.*hymn.*1.170(p.12; M.66.1596); of Heraclius, Geo.Pis.*Sev.*692(M.92.1673A); met. *ἐγεώργησας στάχυν ψ.* Jo. Mon.*hymn.Geo.*1(M.96.1393C).

ψυχοφθόρος, *soul-destroying τοῖς ἰώδεσσι καὶ ψ. δηλητηρίοις τὰς... ψυχὰς φαρμάττοντος* Eus.*h.e.*10.4.14(M.20.853B); *τοῦ Μανιχαίων ψ. δόγματος* Didym.*Trin.*3.42(M.39.989B); *τὴν φιλαργυρίαν...τὴν ψ.* Chrys. *hom.23.6 in 1Cor.*(10.211A); of demons, ‡Chrys.*serm.pasch.*88.

***ψυχοχωριστικός,** *separating the soul* from the body, of an angelic rank *τάξιν ψ.* ‡Ath.*qu.Ant.*31(M.28.616C).

ψυχόω, A. (*ψυχή*); **1.** *animate, bring to life τὸν τῶν ἑπτὰ δυνάμεων*

...ἐψύχωσε κόσμον Iren.haer.1.14.7(M.7.609A); esp. ref. creation of man ἐψύχωσε [sc. ὁ θεὸς τὸν ἄνθρωπον] διὰ τοῦ ἐμφυσήματος Gr.Nyss.hom.opif.28.1(M.44.229C); Bas.hom.5.5(2.38A; M.31.248D); Procl.CP annunt.2(M.85.429C); ref. all nature πάντα ψυχοῦται καὶ κινεῖται Ath.gent.44(M.25.88B); ref. rod of Moses, Epiph.anc.96(p.117.24; M.43.192C); ref. Lazarus raised from dead, Nonn.par.Jo.11:44(M.43.845C); ib.12:9(852B); πολλὰ σώματα τῶν τετελευτηκότων ψ. Gr.Nyss.res.3(M.46.665C); exeg. Cant.4:9, id.hom.8 in Cant.(M.44.948B) cit. s. καρδιόω; fig. τὰς λήθῃ τεθνηκυίας πράξεις ψυχῶσαι τῷ λόγῳ Evagr.h.e.proem.(p.5.21; M.86.2420B); met., *endue speech with vigour and animation* ὅταν [sc. λόγος]...ὑπὸ τοῦ καιροῦ μάλιστα ψυχωθεὶς ζωτικώτερος φαίνηται Isid.Pel.epp.5.121(M.78.1396B); **2.** *personify* μόνον οὐχὶ τὸν καιρὸν αὐτὸν ψυχώσας Chrys.hom.22.4 in Mt.(7.280B); id.hom.20.1 in Heb.(12.187B); **3.** *endow with a soul* τὸ λογιστικὸν...αἴτιον εἶναί φαμεν τῆς συστάσεως τῷ ζῴῳ, ἀλλὰ καὶ τοῦ τὸ ἄλογον μέρος ἐψυχῶσθαι Clem.str.6.16(p.500.16; M.9.360B); Thdt.affect.5(p.138.3; 4.834); Nest.fr.D 2, cit. s. ψυχοτόκος; Christol. ἥνωσεν ἑαυτῷ τὴν κτιστὴν σάρκα ἐψυχωμένην ψυχῇ λογικῇ τε καὶ νοερᾷ Didym.Heb.1:6(p.45.6); Cyr.Thds.16(p.52.15; 5^{2}.14D); ὁ λόγος...γέγονεν ἐν προσλήψει σαρκὸς ἐψυχωμένης νοερῶς id.Chr.un.(5^{1}.743E); id.inc.unigen.(5^{1}.679C); γεννηθέντος ἐξ αὐτῆς τοῦ ἁγίου σώματος ψυχωθέντος λογικῶς id.ep.4(p.28.21; 5^{2}.25A); id.apol.Thdt.(p.113.21; 6^{1}.207C); Leont.H.Nest.2.20(M.86.1581A); Max.ep.12(M.91.468A); in phrase attributed to Apollinarians Ὀρθ., καὶ πῶς ἔμψυχον τὸ μὴ ἔχον ψυχήν; Ἀπολλ., θείᾳ ἦν ἐμψυχίᾳ ψυχωθέν [opp. φυσικῶς ἐψυχώθην] ‡Ath.dial.Trin.4.1(M.28.1252A).

B. (ψῦχος), *cool* ὁ χειμὼν...κρυμοῖς ἀπλήστοις ψυχώσας τὸν ἀέρα Mac.Mgn.apocr.4.11(p.172.8).

ψυχρεύομαι, *make vain inquiries*, Or.comm.16.12 in Mt.(p.512.20; M.13.1412B).

ψυχρία, ἡ, *cold*, Epiph.haer.52.2(p.313.18; M.41.957A).

ψυχρίζω, *cool*; pass., Tit.Bost.Man.2.37(M.18.1205A).

***ψυχριστήριον, τό,** *that which cools*, met. πολυλαλία ἐστὶν... θέρμης ψ. Jo.Clim.scal.11(M.88.852B).

ψυχρολογέω, 1. *talk of vain matters*, Epiph.exp.fid.3(p.499.8; M.42.777C); **2.** *talk nonsense*, Cyr.resp.(6^{2}.387A).

ψυχρολογία, ἡ, *talk of vain matters, discussion of unimportant topics* τῇ Ἀθηναίων ψ. Tat.orat.35(p.37.6; M.6.877C); ταῖς γραμματικαῖς ψ. Gr.Nyss.Apoll.39(M.45.1212A); id.Eun.4(2 p.52.14; M.45.621C); Epiph.haer.77.16(p.429.28; M.42.664A).

***ψυχρόπορος,** *cold in its onset*, †Apoll.met.Ps.106:18(M.33.1477B).

ψυχρότης, ἡ, *coldness*; met., *sluggishness*, Chrys.hom.13.1 in Tim.(11.617E); id.hom.3.1 in Phil.(11.203B).

ψυχροφόρος, *containing unwarmed wine*, Gr.Naz.or.4.84(M.35.612A).

***ψυχρόω,** *cool*, Geo.Pis.hex.372(M.92.1462A).

ψύχωσις, ἡ, 1. *endowment with life* τὴν ἐκ παρθένου καὶ κατ' αὐτὴν τελείαν καὶ ἑνοειδῆ σάρκωσιν καὶ ψ. Didym.Trin.3.4(M.39.829C); ἐν τοῖς ζώοις ἅπασι μετὰ τὴν διάπλασιν ἡ ψ. γίνεται Jo.Philop.opif.6.25(p.280.10); ib.5.11(p.224.24); **2.** *principle of life*, in incarnate Christ ὁ...τῶν ὅλων δημιουργὸς...ποιεῖται τὴν ψ. Cyr.Nest.1.5(p.24.12; 6^{1}.18C).

ψυχωφελής, *profiting the soul*, Eus.v.C.1 index 10(p.3.16; M.20.907A); Gr.Nyss.res.1(M.46.617D); Cyr.Jo.2.5(4.210D).

***ψυχωφέλιμος,** *of benefit to the soul*, ‡Chrys.ador.(11.824B); superl., Jo.D.spir.neq.tit.(M.95.85 note c).

***ψυχωφελῶς,** *with profit to the soul*, Isid.Pel.epp.1.213(M.78.317A); ‡Proc.G.Pr.29:17(M.87.1517C); Jo.Thess.dorm.BMV 1.1(p.377.5).

ψωμίζω, *feed*, T.Lev.8.5; fig. ἵνα ψωμίσω σε τὸ μάννα τῆς γνώσεως Jo.Carp.cap.(M.85.1858D); *feed, support* πολλοὶ ἑαυτοὺς παρέδωκαν εἰς δουλείαν καὶ λαβόντες τὰς τιμὰς αὐτῶν ἑτέρους ἐψώμισαν 1Clem.55.2.

ψωμίον, τό, 1. *morsel* of bread, ref. Jo.13:26ff. λαβὼν γὰρ τὸ ψ. [sc. ὁ Ἰούδας]...ἐξῆλθεν...οὐδὲ ὁ εἰσελθὼν μετὰ τὸ ψ.... σατανᾶς ἐχώρει φέρειν τὸ εἶναι ἐν τῷ αὐτῷ τόπῳ μετὰ τοῦ Ἰησοῦ...οὐ προσκεῖται τῷ 'λαβὼν τὸ ψ.' τὸ 'καὶ φαγών'...ὅπου γὰρ βούλεται προστίθησι καὶ τὸ φαγεῖν ὁ λόγος τῷ λαβεῖν· ὥσπερ ἐπὶ τοῦ τῆς εὐλογίας ἄρτου γέγραπται...· ἆρ' οὖν λαβὼν τὸ ψ. οὐκ ἔφαγεν ὁ Ἰούδας...μετὰ τὸ ψ. οὖν, τάχα μὴ βρωθὲν ὑπὸ τοῦ Ἰούδα, προλαβόντος τοῦ εἰσελθόντος... σατανᾶ τὴν χρῆσιν τοῦ ψ., ἵνα μὴ ὄνηται ὁ Ἰούδας τῆς...δόσεως τοῦ ψ. ...τὸ ἀπὸ τοῦ Ἰησοῦ ψ. ὁμογενὲς ἦν τῷ δοθέντι καὶ τοῖς λοίποις ἀποστόλοις ἐν τῷ 'λάβετε, φάγετε', ἀλλ' ἐκείνοις μὲν εἰς σωτηρίαν, τῷ δὲ Ἰούδᾳ εἰς κρῖμα...νοείσθω δὲ ὁ ἄρτος καὶ τὸ ποτήριον τοῖς μὲν ἁπλουστέροις κατὰ τὴν κοινοτέραν περὶ τῆς εὐχαριστίας ἐκδοχήν, τοῖς δὲ βαθύτερον ἀκούειν μεμαθηκόσι κατὰ τὴν θειοτέραν καὶ περὶ τοῦ τροφίμου τῆς ἀληθείας λόγου ἐπαγγελίαν Or.Jo.32.24(16; p.467.8; M.14.808B); διὰ τοῦ ψ. ἐπλήρωσε τὴν προφητείαν ὁ κύριος τὴν λέγουσαν· ὁ ἐσθίων ἄρτους μου ἐμεγάλυνεν ἐπ' ἐμὲ πτερνισμόν Ammon.Jo.13:26(M.85.1484B); δέδωκεν αὐτῷ τὸ ψ. ἵνα ἐλέγξῃ αὐτόν, ὅτι κοινῆς μετέχων αὐτῷ τραπέζης οὔτε τὸν κοινὸν τῶν ἀνθρώπων αἰδεσθεὶς νόμον εἵλατο αὐτὸν ἐκδοῦναι εἰς θάνατον Thdr.Mops.Jo.13:21–26(p.382.19); μήτις οἰέσθω πάλιν, τοῦ δεδέχθαι τὸν σατανᾶν τὸ ψ. τῷ προδότῃ γενέσθαι παραίτιον. οὐ γὰρ εἰς τοσοῦτον ἀποπληξίας ἥξομεν μέτρον... εἰσόδου πρόφασιν δεδόσθαι τῷ πονηρῷ τὴν εὐλογίαν ὑπονοήσομεν Cyr.Jo.9(4.737D); **2.** *loaf*, PLond.1914.49,52; Apophth.Patr.(M.65.196C); Cyr.S.v.Euthym.(p.27.20).

ψωμισμός, ὁ, *morsel*, Germ.CP or.1(M.98.221C).

ψωραγριάω, *have malignant itch*; of animals, Chrys.hom.20.2 in Rom.(9.657E).

***ψωριός,** *itchy, scabby, mangy*, ‡Ath.syntag.8(M.28.844D).

ψώχω, *rub small*, Epiph.haer.30.32(p.377.26; M.41.464A).

Ω

[*]**ὤα, ἡ,** *border, edge* of garment, Olymp.Job 30:18(M.93.313D) perh. for ὠία.

***ὠᾶτος,** (Lat. *ovatus*) *egg-shaped, ovate*; neut. as subst., of *triclinium* of Great Palace at Constantinople, also called τροῦλλος, Steph.Diac.v.Steph.(M.100.1144D).

***ὠβλίας,** epithet of S. James, explained as Greek corruption of עֹפֶל עָם διὰ...τὴν ὑπερβολὴν τῆς δικαιοσύνης αὐτοῦ ἐκαλεῖτο ὁ δίκαιος καὶ ὠ., ὅ ἐστιν Ἑλληνιστὶ περιοχὴ τοῦ λαοῦ, καὶ δικαιοσύνη Heges.ap.Eus.h.e.2.23.7(M.20.197B); cf.Phot.cod.222(M.103.808D); or of עֹפֶל simply ὠ., ἑρμηνευόμενον τεῖχος Epiph.haer.78.7(p.457.19; M.42.709A).

ὠγύγιος, *immense* τὰ τῶν ἔργων ὠ. †Bas.Sel.or.41(M.85.461D).

ᾠδή, ἡ, 1. *song, lay, ode*; of song of Moses, Clem.paed.1.7(p.123.7; M.8.317A); Proc.G.Ex.32:34(M.87.669A); Leont.B.Nest.et Eut.3.37(M.86.1376B); liturg., Const.App.3.7.7; τὴν ἐπινίκιον ἐκείνην ἀνήνεγκας ᾠ. τῷ θεῷ Chrys.bapt.4(2.374C); sung at funerals αἱ δὲ τῶν θεαρχικῶν ἐπαγγελιῶν ᾠδαὶ καὶ ἀναγνώσεις ἐκφαντορικαὶ μέν εἰσι τῶν μακαριωτάτων λήξεων, εἰς ἃς οἱ θείαν ἐσχηκότες τελείωσιν αἰωνίως καταταχθήσονται· τοῦ δὲ κοιμηθέντος ἱερῶς ἀποδεκτικαί, τῶν ἔτι δὲ ζώντων προτρεπτικαὶ πρὸς τὴν ὁμοίαν τελείωσιν Dion.Ar.e.h.7.3.2(M.3.557B); **2.** of the singing of birds, Clem.paed.2.10(p.209.21; M.8.500C); Synes.ep.4(M.66.1337B); Thdt.Ps.118:147(1.1475).

ὠδίν, ἡ, usu. plur.; **1.** *pangs* or *throes of childbirth*; **a.** of BMV ἀνώδυνος δὲ ἡ ὠ. Gr.Nyss.hom.13 in Cant.(M.44.1053A); κύησις γίνεται καὶ ἐννεαμηνιαῖος χρόνος καὶ ὠ. Chrys.hom.8.3 in Mt.(7.124A); denied, cf.Ascens.Is.11.14; *neque vocem illius audivimus*, A.Petr.c.Sim.24(p.72.6); οὐδὲ ὠ. ἐπηκολούθησε Jo.D.f.o.4.14(M.94.1160C); c. adj. ἀλόχευτος, Procl.CP or.3.3(M.65.705D); τὰς ἀσπάρτους δὲ καὶ ἀλοχεύτους ἐκείνας ὠ. Γαβριὴλ προείρηκεν Thdt.qu.42 in Dt.(1.290); **b.** λύω τὰς ὠ.; of the mother *be delivered*, Chrys.hom.8.1 in Mt.(7.118B); of the child *be born*, id.hom.16.5 in Rom.(9.610E); ib.19.8(654B); id.hom.34.4 in 1Cor.(10.315B); also ref. spiritual birth τὰς αὐτὰς πάντες ἐλύσαμεν ὠ. id.hom.32.7 in Mt.(7.375A); id.hom.8.8 in Rom.(509E); ib.21.2(674D); τὰς πνευματικὰς ὠ. id.sac.3.5(p.55.22; 1.384A); τὰς ὠ. τοῦ πνεύματος Thdt.Philm.1:10(3.714); fig. τῶν νεφῶν ἔλυσε τὰς ὠ. id.qu.58 in 3Reg.(1.504); **c.** met., *anguish* ὅπου γὰρ ἐὰν βούληται ἡ γραφὴ ἀφορητόν τινα ἡμῖν ὀδύνην ἐνδείξασθαι, τῷ ὀνόματι τῆς ὠ. αὐτὴν ὑπογράφει Chrys.exp.in Ps.7(5.71C); **2.** *pangs* of death, Thdt.Ps.17:5(1.703); ib.114:3(1417); id.Col.1:18(3.479); **3.** *fruit of travail*; met., of the mind, esp. of doctrine, Chrys.hom.56.6 in Mt.(7.575A); τῶν πονηρῶν ὠ. ἀρξάμενος Thdt.h.e.4.10.1(3.963); τὴν ὠ. τῆς ἀσεβείας id.haer.4.12(4.370); in gen., id.Ps.146:8(1.1571); id.provid.2(4.505); of spiritual offspring ὠ. ἔτεκεν [sc. ἡ Παύλου ἅλυσις] ἐφ' αἷς ἄγγελοι χαίρουσι Chrys.hom.8.5 in Eph.(11.60E).

***ὠδίνησις, ἡ,** *travail*, Didym.Ps.7:15(M.39.1101D).

ὠδίν-ω, 1. *be in travail*, fig. ~ουσαν αὐτῶν τὴν ἐπιθυμίαν ἐπέχει Chrys.hom.68.2 in Mt.(7.672E); ib.70.1(686E); **2.** *be in travail of, bring forth, bear*; met.; **a.** c. acc. ἡ γὰρ ἐνταῦθα ἀδοξία, δόξαν ἀθάνατον ~ει Isid.Pel.epp.3.205(M.78.889A); ~ει δὲ τοῦτο διπλῆν... ἔννοιαν Cyr.Is.1.2(1.37B); id.Am.75(3.335D); ἔλεγχον οὖν...~ει τὸ εἰρημένον id.Jo.6.1(4.624A); Thphyl.exc.Rom.(M.113.929B); **b.** c. dat. ψυχὴ...~ουσα πολλοῖς ἔρωσι καὶ κοσμικοῖς Clem.q.d.s.16.2(p.170.2; M.9.620C); **c.** pass., Diod.Ps.89:1(M.33.1624C); ἡ γὰρ ἁμαρτία, ἕως μὲν ἂν ~ηται, ἔχει τινὰ αἰσχύνην Chrys.*hom.10.1 in Ac.*(9.80C); Socr.*h.e.*4.3.3(M.67.468B); **3.** *long for, be eager*; c. ὥστε, Chrys.*hom. 2.3 in Tit.*(11.741B); **4.** *contain*, Isid.Pel.*epp.*2.150(M.78.604B) cit. s. φυλακτήριον.

***ὤθημα, τό,** *jostling*, Geo.Pis.*hex.*112(M.92.1440A).

ὤθησις, ἡ, *thrusting, pressure*, Chrys.*hom.1.2 in Is.6:1*(6.97E).

ᾠία, ἡ, *edge, hem* of garment, Cosm.Ind.*top.*5(M.88.213B).

ὠκεανός, ὁ, *ocean*, met. πρὸς Μωϋσέα τὸν τῆς θεολογίας ὠ. μεταβαίνομεν, ἐξ οὗπερ, ποιητικῶς εἰπεῖν, πάντες ποταμοὶ καὶ πᾶσα θάλαττα Thdt.*affect.*2(p.51.3; 4.742).

***ὠκυποδέω,** *hasten, approach swiftly*, c. ἐπί, ‡Caes.Naz.*dial.*1.48 (M.38.920); c. acc., *ib.*2.99(964); met. πάλιν ἐπ' αὐτὴν [sc. τὴν γλῶσσαν] ὠ. *ib.*3.140(1069).

***ὠκυποδία, ἡ,** *swiftness, fleetness of foot*, ‡Caes.Naz.*dial.*2.112 (M.38.992).

***ὠκυπόδως,** *swiftly, expeditiously* ‡Caes.Naz.*dial.*1.1(M.38.856) cit. s. διαθέω.

***ὠλεσίθυμος,** *soul-destroying*, Paul.Sil.*Soph.*566(M.86.2141A).

ὠλεσίκαρπος, *losing its fruit*, fig. κῆπος Ἀδώνιδος ἧδε τεὴ χάρις ὠ. Gr.Naz.*carm.*1.2.29.53(M.37.888A).

***ὤλεσις, ἡ,** *destruction, death*, Geo.Al.*v.Chrys.*13(p.174.41); *ib.*67 (p.247.23).

***ὠμοβάρβαρος,** *barbarously cruel*, Geo.Al.*v.Chrys.*31(p.199.35).

***ὠμοβορία, ἡ,** *eating raw flesh*, Tat.*orat.*2(p.2.20; M.6.808A).

[*]ὠμόβροτος, = ὠμόβρωτος, *eaten raw*, Proc.G.*Gen.*9:3(M.87.289B).

ὠμόβυρσος, *of raw hide*, plur. as subst. ἐκέλευσεν ἐνεχθῆναι ἑπτὰ ζυγὰς ὠμοβύρσων *M.Pers.*10.28(p.496.14).

***ὠμόθυρος,** f.l. for ὠμόθυμος, *savage-hearted*, Pall.*v.Chrys.*20 (p.143.7; M.47.80).

***ὠμοπλατικός,** *of the shoulder blades*, Melet.*nat.hom.*(M.64.1132B).

***ὠμόπλινθος, ὁ,** *unbaked brick*, Marc.Diac.*v.Porph.*21.

***ὠμοποιέω,** *be cruel, violent*, Or.*Cels.*4.67(p.337.14; M.11.1136B).

ὦμος, ὁ, *shoulder*, Valent. τὰ σπέρματα ὁ Ἰησοῦς διὰ τοῦ σημείου ἐπὶ τῶν ὤ. βαστάσας εἰσάγει εἰς τὸ πλήρωμα. ὦμοι γὰρ τοῦ σπέρματος ὁ Ἰησοῦς λέγεται, κεφαλὴ δὲ ὁ Χριστός Clem.*exc.Thdot.*42(p.120.3,4; M.9.680A).

***ὠμόσαρκος,** *raw*, Geo.Pis.*hex.*1439(M.92.1544A).

***ὠμοτύραννος, ὁ,** *cruel tyrant*, Hipp.*antichr.*25(p.18.5; ὅμως τύραννος M.10.748B); of Devil, Meth.*symp.*10.1(p.122.13; M.18.193A).

ὠμοφαγία, ἡ, *eating of raw flesh*, Clem.*prot.*2(p.11.15; M.8.72A); Pall.*h.Laus.*12(p.34.4; M.34.1034B).

***ὠμοφορέω,** *bear on one's shoulders*, Dion.Al.ap.Eus.*h.e.*7.22.9 (M.20.689B); ‡Chrys.*eleem.*3.1(9.832D).

ὠμοφόριον, τό, 1. *cape* or *tippet*, worn by women, Pall.*h.Laus.*59 (M.34.1236B; μαφόριον p.153.18); **2.** *pallium*, long scarf worn by bishops, passing round shoulders, tied loosely on left shoulder, ends falling nearly to ground at front and back; originally perh. of linen, cf.Gr.Nyss.*v.Gr.Thaum.*(M.46.941D); but usu. of wool (or later of embroidered silk) representing lost sheep carried on shoulders of Christ represented by bishop, Isid.Pel.*epp.*1.136(M.78.272C); ‡Bas.*h.myst.*20(p.262.16); *ib.*38(p.266.30); ‡Sophr.H.*liturg.*16(M.87.3996D); put off by bishop before reading of gospel to signify that Christ is himself present, Isid.Pel.l.c.; associated with gospel-book as symbol of priesthood, Anast.Ap.*a.Max.*1.4(M.90.117B); worn on non-liturgical occasions by patriarchs, Pall.*v.Chrys.*6(p.37.25; M.47.23); taken by patriarch into exile, Eustrat.*v.Eutych.*37 (M.86.2317C); *ib.*76(2360D); cf.Jo.Mosch.*prat.*36(M.87.2885C); distinguishing mark of patriarch, *ib.*139(3004A); cf.Thdr.Lect.*h.e.*2.15 (M.86.189B); or bishop, Sophr.H.*v.Anast.*(M.92.1708C); put off by patriarch as token of resignation, Thphn.*chron.*p.342(M.108.825A); taken off at deposition, CCP(681)*act.*8(H.3.1181B); exception to this rule, Eustrat.*v.Eutych.*77(2361C,2364A); conferred by emperor on iconoclast patriarch ὑπὸ τῶν τοῦ βασιλέως χειρῶν τὴν ἱερὰν ὁ ἀνίερος ἐνδιδύσκεται διπλοΐδα καὶ τὸ ὠ. ‡Jo.D.*ep.Thphl.*13(M.95.361C); associated with stole worn by OT high priest, ‡Sophr.H.*liturg.*7(3988C); ‡Bas.*h.myst.*20(p.262.14); as symbol of Trin. τριπλοῦν τὸ ὠ. περιβέβληται διότι τὴν τριάδα ὑφίεται ‡Sophr.H.*liturg.* 6(3985D); embroidered with crosses to commemorate Christ's carrying of Cross, ‡Germ.CP *contempl.*(M.98.396A); borne by archdeacon in procession at Great Entrance, ‡Sophr.H.*liturg.*20(4001B).

Ὠμοφόρος, ὁ, *Omophorus, who carries* the earth *on his shoulders* in Manich. myth, Hegem.*Arch.*8(p.11.9; M.10.1437C); *ib.*9(p.15.4; 1441B); Epiph.*haer.*66.22(p.50.3; M.42.68A).

***ὠμυλία, ἡ,** for ὁμιλία, ref. Pr.7:21 ὁμιλίᾳ ἢ ὠμυλίᾳ ὡς ἔχει ἔνια τῶν ἀντιγράφων Didym.*Zach.*1.378.

***ὠνειακός,** *of* or *concerning purchase*, Ath.Scholast.*coll.*2.2(p.32).

ὠνέομαι, *buy*; met., *redeem* Χριστοῦ ὠνησαμένου ἡμᾶς τῷ ἰδίῳ αἵματι Or.*or.*28.3(p.377.1; M.11.524B); id.*mart.*12(p.13.5; M.11.580C); id.*Jo.*6.53(35; p.162.7; M.14.292D).

***ὠνεωκόν, τό,** *ransom-price*, Jo.Mal.*chron.*10 p.233(M.97.360C).

ὠνή, ἡ, 1. *buying, purchasing*; **2.** *deed of sale, contract, bond*, *A.Thom.*A 2(p.102.1); met. μέχρι τίνος οὐ...διαρρήγνυτε τὰς ὠ. τῆς φιλοχρηματίας; Chrys.*hom.90.3 in Mt.*(7.842D).

***ὠνήσιμος,** *that can be bought*, Jo.Clim.*scal.*27(M.88.1096C).

***ὠνησιφόρος,** *profitable*, Cyr.*Jon.*16(3.379C).

ὠνητέον, *one must buy*; met., Clem.*paed.*3.11(p.279.10; M.8.656B).

***ὠνικόν, τό,** *buying, purchasing*, ‡Chrys.*serm.jej.*4(11.837C).

***ὦος,** *venal*; superl., Cyr.*hom.pasch.*10(5^2.141A).

***ὠπηείς,** *having clear sight*, Gr.Naz.*carm.*1.2.9.102(M.37.675A).

ὥρα, ἡ, *hour*; **1.** of hours of prayer εἰ δέ τινες καὶ ὥ. τακτὰς ἀπονέμουσιν εὐχῇ, ὡς τρίτην φέρε καὶ ἕκτην καὶ ἐνάτην, ἀλλ' οὖν γε ὁ γνωστικὸς παρὰ ὅλον εὔχεται τὸν βίον...ἀλλὰ καὶ τὰς τῶν ὥ. διανομὰς τριχῇ διεσταμένας καὶ ταῖς ἴσαις εὐχαῖς τετιμημένας ἴσασιν οἱ γνωρίζοντες τὴν μακαρίαν τῶν ἁγίων τριάδα μονῶν Clem.*str.*7.7(p.30.28; M.9.456C); grounds of observance, cf. *orent autem tertia hora, quia illo tempore salvator voluntarie crucifixus est ad salvandos nos...deinde etiam hora sexta orate, quia illa hora universa creatura perturbata est propter facinus scelestum a Judaeis perpetratum. hora nona iterum orent, quia illa hora Christus oravit et tradidit spiritum in manus patris sui. etiam nona, qua sol occidit...quia est completio diei*, ‡Hipp.*can.*25.2.233–236(pp.127–8); μετὰ τρίτην ὥ. συνάξεις ἐπιτέλει, ὅτι ταύτῃ τῇ ὥ. ἐπάγη τὸ ξύλον τοῦ σταυροῦ. ἕκτῃ ὥ. ἐπιτέλει τὰς προσευχὰς μετὰ ψαλμῶν καὶ κλαυσμοῦ καὶ δεήσεως, ὅτι ἐν αὐτῇ τῇ ὥ. ἐκρεμάσθη ὁ υἱὸς...ἐπὶ σταυροῦ· ἐνάτῃ ὥ. πάλιν ἐν ὕμνοις καὶ δοξολογίαις μετὰ δακρύων ἐξομολογουμένη τὰ παραπτώματά σου, τὸν θεὸν ἱκέτευε, ὅτι ἐν αὐτῇ τῇ ὥ. ὁ κύριος...ἀπέδωκε τὸ πνεῦμα Ath. *virg.*12(p.46.9ff.; M.28.265A); τὸν μὲν ὄρθρον, ὥστε τὰ πρῶτα κινήματα τῆς ψυχῆς, καὶ τοῦ νοῦ, ἀναθήματα εἶναι θεοῦ...πάλιν δὲ κατὰ τὴν τρίτην ὥ. εἰς τὴν προσευχὴν ἀνίστασθαι...ὑπομνησθέντας τῆς τοῦ πνεύματος δωρεᾶς, τῆς κατὰ τὴν τρίτην ὥ. τοῖς ἀποστόλοις δεδομένης προσκυνῆσαι πάντας ὁμοθυμαδὸν εἰς τὸ ἀξίους γενέσθαι καὶ αὐτοὺς τῆς ὑποδοχῆς τοῦ ἁγιασμοῦ...ἐν δὲ τῇ ἕκτῃ ὥ. κατὰ μίμησιν τῶν ἁγίων ἀναγκαίαν εἶναι τὴν προσευχὴν ἐκρίναμεν...καὶ ὥστε ῥυσθῆναι ἀπὸ συμπτώματος καὶ δαιμονίου μεσημβρινοῦ, ἅμα καὶ τοῦ ψαλμοῦ τοῦ ἐνενηκοστοῦ λεγομένου...ἡ δὲ ἐννάτη ἀναγκαία εἰς προσευχὴν...ὅτι Πέτρος καὶ Ἰωάννης ἀνέβαινον εἰς τὸ ἱερὸν ἐπὶ τὴν ὥ. τῆς προσευχῆς τὴν ἐννάτην Bas.*reg.fus.*37(2.383Bff.; M.31.1013Aff.); εὐχὰς ἐπιτελεῖτε ὄρθρου καὶ τρίτῃ ὥ. καὶ ἕκτῃ καὶ ἐνάτῃ καὶ ἑσπέρᾳ καὶ ἀλεκτοροφωνίᾳ· ὄρθρου μὲν εὐχαριστοῦντες, ὅτι ἐφώτισεν ὑμῖν ὁ κύριος...τρίτῃ δέ, ὅτι ἀπόφασιν ἐν αὐτῇ ὑπὸ Πιλάτου ἔλαβεν ὁ κύριος· ἕκτῃ δέ, ὅτι ἐν αὐτῇ ἐσταυρώθη· ἐνάτῃ δέ, ὅτι πάντα κεκίνητο τοῦ δεσπότου σταυρωμένου ...ἑσπέρᾳ δὲ εὐχαριστοῦντες, ὅτι ὑμῖν ἀνάπαυσιν ἔδωκεν τῶν μεθημερινῶν κόπων τὴν νύκτα· ἀλεκτρυόνων δὲ κραυγῇ διὰ τὸ τὴν ὥ. εὐαγγελίζεσθαι τὴν παρουσίαν τῆς ἡμέρας εἰς ἐργασίαν τῶν τοῦ φωτὸς ἔργων *Const.App.*8.34.1; καὶ γὰρ εἶπον ὑμῖν πολλάκις περὶ τῆς ὥ. ταύτης [sc. τῆς ἐνάτης], ὅτι ἐν αὐτῇ παράδεισος ἀνεῴγη, καὶ ὁ λῃστὴς εἰσῆλθεν, ἐν αὐτῇ ἡ κατάρα ἀνῃρέθη, ἐν αὐτῇ ἡ θυσία τῆς οἰκουμένης προσηνέχθη, ἐν αὐτῇ τὸ σκότος ἐλύθη, ἐν αὐτῇ τὸ φῶς ἔλαμψε, καὶ τὸ αἰσθητὸν καὶ τὸ νοητὸν Chrys.*hom.2.3 in Ac.princ.*(3.67E); Anton. Hag.*v.Sym.Styl.*3(p.22.5); hence **2.** *office* οὐκ ἐᾷ με ψάλλειν τὰς ὥ. ‡Amph.*non.desp.*(p.265); **3.** *appointed hour*, exeg. Jo.8:20 τουτέστιν, ὅτι οὐδέπω καιρὸς ἦν ἐπιτήδειος καθ' ὃν ἠθέλησε σταυρωθῆναι Chrys. *hom.53.1 in Jo.*(8.310B); τουτέστιν, οὔπω παρῆν ὁ τοῦ θανάτου καιρός Cyr.*Jo.*5.3(4.497C); exeg. Mt.24:36, Mc.13:32, v. γνῶσις, ἄγνοια, οἶδα; **4.** *fitting time*; ὥρα (ἐστίν) *it is fitting* or *necessary*, Eus.*d.e.*3.6 (p.138.17; M.22.233B); ὥ. καὶ τοὺς ἀγγέλους...εἶναι...υἱούς Ath.*Ar.*3.10(M.26.341A); Cyr.*Jo.*1.4(4.42A); **5.** phrases: πρὸς ὥραν *for a time*, Ath.*fug.*5(p.71.6; M.25.649C); μετὰ ὥρας *after a time*, id.*h.Ar.*12 (p.189.12; M.25.708A); id.*v.Anton.*82(M.26.957A); κατὰ ὥραν *at intervals*, Marc.Diac.*v.Porph.*28; πολλὴν ὥραν *for a long time*, Epiph.*haer.* 30.10(p.345.23; M.41.421C); *Apophth.Patr.*(M.65.96C); **6.** met., *lifetime* ὀψὲ δέ που τῆς ὥ. Euthal.Diac.*epp.Paul.*proem.1(M.85.700A).

ὡραΐζω, 1. *beautify, adorn*, Or.*adnot.in Dt.*23:3(M.17.32A); Meth. *res.*1.28(p.256.18; M.41.1133D); Gr.Nyss.*hom.3 in Cant.*(M.44.819B); fig. ἔργοις...εὐαρέστοις τῷ θεῷ τὴν σαυτοῦ ψυχὴν ὠ. Nil.*epp.*1.83(M.97.120B); Cyr.*Os.*21(3.44B); **2.** *honour, glorify* ὠ. διὰ τῶν ἐγκωμίων τῆς σοφίας τὸ κάλλος Gr.Nyss.*hom.1 in Cant.*(M.44.768C); Sophr.H. *or.*7.7(M.87.3332C).

***ὡραιογραφέω,** *write beautifully*, Thdr.Stud.*or.*11.3(M.99.805C).

***ὡραιόθεος,** *of divine beauty*; of BMV, Thdr.Stud.*nativ.BMV* 7 (M.96.692C).

***ὡραιοκόσμητος**, *adorned with beauty*; of the Cross, ‡Chrys.*ador.* 2(11.824B).

***ὡραιόμορφος**, *fair, beautiful*, ‡Chrys.*neg.*1(8.137B).

[*]**ὡραῖον, τό**, v. *ὅριον*.

ὡραιόομαι, *be beautiful* ὡς ὡραιώθης Jo.D.*hom.*8.11(M.96.719D).

ὡραῖος, **1.** *seasonable, timely*; met., *appropriate* οὐχ ὡ., αἶνος ἐν στόματι ἁμαρτωλοῦ Cyr.*Is.*1.4(2.106B); **2.** *beautiful*; of persons, *T.Reub.*3.4; Tat.*orat.*10(p.11.9; M.6.828B); Clem.*str.*3.4(p.207.19; M.8.1129B); of virtue καθ' ἑαυτὴν ὡ. Chrys.*hom.77.4 in Jo.*(8.455E); ἐλεημοσύνη…φωτίζει ψυχήν,…καλὴν καὶ ὡ. ποιεῖ *ib.81.3*(482B); neut. as subst., Eus.*Is.*16:8(M.24.201D); **3.** *fair, specious* δι' ὀνόματος ὡ. εἰδωλολατροῦντας Clem.*paed.*2.10(p.220.17; M.8.524A); **4.** Gnost.; **a.** one of six emanations in Ophite mythology, Iren.*haer.*1.30.5(M.7.697A); Or.*Cels.*6.31(p.101.29; M.11.1345A); cf.*Hesp.*suppl.8(p.44); **b.** of Seth's wife, becoming a spiritual power acc. Sethians γυναῖκά τινα Ὡραίαν λέγουσιν εἶναι τοῦ Σήθ…εἰσὶ μὲν γὰρ ἄλλαι τινὲς αἱρέσεις, αἵτινες δύναμίν τινα εἶναι λέγουσιν, ἣν καλοῦσιν ὀνομαστικῶς Ὡραίαν, τὴν παρ' ἄλλοις τοίνυν νομιζομένην δύναμιν, Ὡραίαν τε καλουμένην, οὕτω γυναῖκα τοῦ Σὴθ λέγουσιν Epiph.*haer.*39.5(p.75.14ff.; M.41.669D).

***ὡραΐσμα, τό**, = ὡραϊσμός, *ornament, adornment*, Gr.Naz.*or.*8.3 (M.35.793A).

ὡραϊσμός, ὁ, 1. *adornment*, Clem.*paed.*3.11(p.270.27; M.8.636A); προσώπων ὡ. Bas.*ascet.*1.2(2.319E; M.31.873A); id.*moral.*73.4(2.309B; M.31.853A); τοῖς εἰς ὡ. κοσμήμασιν Cyr.*Am.*34(3.288D); fig. τῶν ἔξωθεν ὡ. ἐλευθέραν προστιθέασι τὴν ἀλήθειαν Thdr.Mops.*1Cor.*1:17–18(p.173.18; M.66.877A); τοὺς ἐξ ἁπάσης ἀρετῆς ὡ. ἑαυτῇ περιτίθησιν Cyr.*Ps.*45.6(M.69.1049A); id.*ador.*1(1.4B); of attributes of God μὴ ψιλή τις εἰκὼν…τοῖς ἔξωθεν ὡ. μεμορφωμένη νοῆται πρὸς τὸ ἀρχέτυπον id.*Jo.*11.2(4.931A); **2.** *beauty, elegance*, Meth.*symp.*10.2(p.124.5; M.18.196B); plur., Synes.*astrolab.*5(p.139.11; M.66.1584C).

***ὡράριον (ὀράριον), τό**, (Lat. *orarium*) **1.** *kerchief*; = φακιόλιον, *A.Petr.et Paul.*80(p.213.13); *M.Thdot.3*(p.142); ὁ. … οἷα πρὸς τὸ ἀπομάττεσθαι…ἱδρῶτας, πτύελον, δάκρυον, καὶ τὰ ὅμοια Ammon.*Ac.*19:12(M.85.1576B); Diod.*Gen.*38:18(M.33.1577C); **2.** *deacon's stole*, a narrow strip of embroidered silk (originally linen) worn by deacon when officiating; worn over left shoulder and passed under right arm with end thrown back over left shoulder and so hanging back and front; not to be worn by those in minor orders, CLaod.*can.22*; οὐ δεῖ ἀναγνώστας ἢ ψάλτας ὡ. φορεῖν καὶ οὕτως ἀναγινώσκειν ἢ ψάλλειν *ib.23*; symbolizing towel used by Christ in washing disciples' feet, cf.Isid.Pel.*epp.*1.136(M.78.272C); ‡Bas.*h.myst.*16(p.262); or wings of angels whom deacons represent, cf.‡Chrys.*prodig.*1.3(8.37A); ‡Bas.*h.myst.*16(p.261.1); ‡Sophr.H.*liturg.*7(M.87.3988A); ‡Germ.CP *contempl.*(M.98.393C); presented by deacon to priest for blessing before vesting, *Lit.Chrys.*(p.355.2); kissed by deacon putting it on, *Lit.Chrys.*(12.776D); and cross on it kissed by deacon during mass of the faith, *Lit.Chrys.*(p.382.32) cit. s. ἀσπάζομαι; crossed at back and front by deacon before Communion ζώννυται καὶ τὸ ὡ. αὐτοῦ σταυροειδῶς *ib.*(p.393.8); its two ends representing OT and NT, ‡Sophr.H.*liturg.*8(M.87.3988).

ὡρεῖον (ὡρεῖον), τό, v. *ὅριον*.

ὡρέω, *take care of, attend to*, *Orac.Sib.*5.396(p.123).

***Ὠριγένειος**, *pertaining to Origen*, Eust.*engast.*1(p.17.8; M.18.616A); Eus.*Marcell.*1.4(p.21.23; M.24.760A).

***Ὠριγενιανοί, οἱ**, *Origenists* Ὠ., τινὸς Ὠριγένους…ἀρρητοποιοῦντες καὶ τὰ ἑαυτῶν σώματα φθορᾷ παραδιδόντες…Ὠ. ἄλλοι, Ὠριγένους τοῦ καὶ Ἀδαμαντίου…οἱ τὴν νεκρῶν ἀνάστασιν ἀποβαλλόμενοι, Χριστὸν δὲ κτίσμα καὶ τὸ ἅγιον πνεῦμα εἰσηγούμενοι, παράδεισόν τε καὶ οὐρανοὺς…ἀλληγοροῦντες, Χριστοῦ δὲ τὴν βασιλείαν παυθήσεσθαι ληροῦντες Epiph.*anac.*3.63–64(p.213.24; M.41.849B).

***Ὠριγενιασταί, οἱ**, *Origenists*, Soz.*h.e.*8.12.12(M.67.1549A); Tim.CP *haer.*(M.86.64C).

***Ὠριγένιοι, οἱ**, = foreg., Epiph.*haer.*63.1(p.398.14; M.41.1061D).

***Ὠριγενισταί, οἱ**, = foreg., Meth.*res.*2.15(p.361.9n.; M.18.309B).

ὡριμάζω, *mature, ripen*, Call.*v.Hyp.*(p.107); fig. καρπὸς ἡμῶν ἀεὶ ἄωρος ἀνέμεινε τῷ μὴ ἔχειν πρόθεσιν, ἵνα καλῶς ὡριμάσῃ ἐν ἔργοις τοῖς ἀγαθοῖς Ephr.1.172D,F; trans. οὐκ ἔχει γὰρ δάκρυα ὁ ὑμέτερος καρπός, ἵνα αὐτὸν ὡριμάσῃ *ib.*172D.

[*]**ὡρίον, τό**, v. *ὅριον*.

***ὡροθέτης, ὁ**, *sign in the ascendant at the hour of birth*, Gr.Naz.*carm.*1.1.5.45(M.37.427).

[*]**ὡρολογεῖον, τό**, = ὡρολόγιον, *instrument for telling the time*, Jo.Mal.*chron.*18 p.479(M.97.696B).

ὡρολογ-έω, *tell the hours*, trans. τίς…ἔπεισεν ὄρνιν ~εῖν τὴν εὐφρόνην; Geo.Pis.*hex.*1102(M.92.1519A).

ὡροσκοπεῖον (ὡροσκόπιον), τό, 1. *instrument for telling the time*, Synes.*astrolab.*5(p.139.3; M.66.1584C); **2.** *horoscope*, Hipp.*haer.*4.3 (p.34.4; M.16.3062A); plur., Bas.*hex.*6.5(1.55A; M.29.129A).

ὡροσκόπος, ὁ, Egyptian official who bore the ὡρολόγιον in a procession, Clem.*str.*6.4(p.448.30; M.9.253A).

ὤρυμα, τό, *roaring*, ‡Nil.*perist.*12.4(M.79.945B).

ὡσαννά, (Hebr. הוֹשִׁיעָ־נָּה) *Hosanna* τὰ ἀντὶ τοῦ 'ὦ κύριε, σῶσον δή'…ἑβραϊκῶς ἐκκεῖσθαι ἐν τῷ 'ὡ. τῷ υἱῷ Δαυΐδ' Or.*comm.in Mt.*16.19(p.541.24; M.13.1440A); cf.Theophylactus *Mc.*11:7–10(M.123.612D); Germ.CP *or.*8(M.98.364D); wrongly explained τοῦ δὲ ὡ. μεγαλοσύνη ὑπερκειμένη ‡Just.*qu.et resp.*50(M.6.1296A).

[*]**ὡσημέραι**, = ὁσημέραι, *every day*, Pamph.Mon.*Soter.*2(p.117.10); Jo.D.*hom.*11.6(M.96.768C).

***ὦσμα, τό**, *pushing, jostling*, *M.Pion.*10.3.

ὥστε, 1. *and so, therefore*; c. subj., Bas.*reg.br.*proem.(2.414E; M.31.1081C); **2.** *because, since* ὁ νεκρὸς ὄφις τοὺς ζῶντας ἐνίκα, ὡ. τύπος ἐστὶ τοῦ σώματος τοῦ κυρίου Mac.Aeg.*hom.*11.9(M.34.549C); **3.** as final conj. *that, in order that* χρεία καὶ πολλῆς ἐρεύνης…ὡ. μηδὲν ἡμᾶς λαθεῖν Chrys.*hom.24.1 in Gen.*(4.216D); ὡ. γὰρ πηλὸν πατεῖν καὶ βόρβορον…γέγονε τὰ ὑποδήματα id.*hom.49.5 in Mt.*(7.511D).

ὠστέον, *one must thrust out*, Isid.Pel.*epp.*5.250(M.78.1484B).

***ὠτάγρα, ἡ**, *instrument* of torture *for taking hold of the ears*, Synes.*ep.*58(M.66.1399C).

***ὠτότμησις, ἡ**, *slitting* or *cropping the ears*, Evagr.Pont.*cap.*12 (M.40.1265B).

ὠτότμητος, *with ears slit* or *cropped*, Pall.*h.Laus.*11(p.33.10; M.34.1034A).

ὠχρία, ἡ, *pallor* τὸν Χριστιανὸν…ἡ ἐκ τῆς ἐγκρατείας ἐπανθοῦσα ὠ. δείκνυσιν Bas.*reg.fus.*17.2(2.361A; M.31.964C); ‡Caes.Naz.*dial.*3.140 (M.38.1077).

ADDENDA ET CORRIGENDA

I. AUTHORS AND WORKS

Note. The additional material in the following pages consists of further words found in Patristic authors but not attested, or poorly attested, in *LS*; second or third examples of words not listed in *LS*, of which only one or two examples have hitherto been given; instances, earlier than the first instances hitherto cited, of words not contained, or poorly attested, in *LS*; additional definitions and usages of words already treated in this Lexicon; words which are well attested in *LS* but have some theological or exegetical interest and which have not been included in the body of this work; and material supplementary to the existing articles, partly drawn from works which had not been published at the time when the publication of this Lexicon began.

Of the many new critical editions which have appeared since the completion of the manuscript of this Lexicon (see Preface, p. x) only those are now added to the list which have been consulted for the purpose of corrections and additions to the entries.

AMPHILOCHIUS ICONIENSIS
‡*circ.*: for '1544' read '1644'.

ANASTASIUS SINAITA
†*relat.*: for '1903' read '1913'.

APOPHTHEGMATA
Apophth. Patr.: after '345A' add 'Other *Apophthegmata* in F. Nau, *PO* 8 (1912) pp. 168–83'.

ASTERIUS SOPHISTA
fr. Ps.: after 'p. 356' add 'also M. Richard *Symbolae Osloenses* fasc. supplet. 16 (1956) p. 249'.
hom. 1–31 in Pss.   *homiliae in Psalmos*, Richard, pp. 1–245 (1. 10, 14, 24, 26, 27 are dubious).

ATHANASIUS
fr.   *fragmenta*, *AP* pp. 5–8.
‡*Maced.*   *contra Macedonianos fragmentum*, M.26.1313 (partly identical with *ep. Aeg. Lib.* 11).

BASILIUS CAESARIENSIS CAPPADOCIAE
‡*exp. fid. Nic.*: after 'Hahn p. 308' add 'M.28.1637'.

CAESARIUS NAZIANZENUS: for 'post saec. vii' read 'prob. by Severian, saec. vi (*BZ* 52 (1959) pp. 276 ff.)'.

CHRYSOSTOMOS, JOHANNES
catech.   *homiliae catecheticae*, A. Wenger *SC* 50 (1957).
†*hom. prec.* 1, 2: for 'G.3' read 'G.2'.
pan. Aeg.: for 'G.3' read 'G.2'.

CLEMENTINA
Hom. Clem. 1–20: add 'B. Rehm *GCS* (1953)'.

CONCILIA
C Arim. *ep. Const.* 1 and 2: after 'Ath. *syn.* 10' add 'also ap. Thdt. *h.e.* 2. 19'; after 'Ath. *syn.* 55. 4–7' add 'also ap. Thdt. *h.e.* 2. 20'.
CCP (381): after '*ep.*' add '(382)'.
C Eph. Orient. *ep.*: for '*ACO* 1.1.3, 5' read '*ACO* 1.1.3 pp. 36, 38–39; 1.1.5 pp. 124–35'.

CYRILLUS ALEXANDRINUS
Lc.: for 'pp. 470–4' read 'pp. 470–5'.

DIDYMUS ALEXANDRINUS
Zach.   *commentarius in Zachariam*, L. Doutreleau *SC* 83–85 (1962).

EPIPHANIUS CONSTANTIENSIS
mens.: add 'P. A. de Lagarde *Symmicta* 2 Göttingen 1880 p. 152'.

EUSEBIUS CAESARIENSIS
Ps.: for '*Pss.* 119–50, M.24.76' read '*Pss.* 119–50, M.24.9'.

EUSTATHIUS ANTIOCHENUS
exegetica
fr.: for 'pp. 65–67 etc.' read 'pp. 65–66, 70–74, 79–85; M.18. 685, 689–92; M. Spanneut *Recherches sur les écrits d'Eustathe d'Antioche* Lille 1948'.
fr. in Ps.: for 'pp. 68–72' read 'pp. 67–69'.
fr.: for 'M.18.689–96' read 'M.18.692–6'.

EUTYCHES
conf.: for '*ACO* 2.1.1 p. 40' read '*ACO* 2.1.1 p. 90'.

GEORGIUS PISIDA POETA
for '*eracl.*' read '*Heracl.*'.

HIERONYMUS STRIDONENSIS
vir. ill.: for '602' read '632'.

JOANNES IV CONSTANTINOPOLITANUS, JEJUNATOR
canonar. 1–3: for 'L. Morinus' read 'J. Morinus'.

JOANNES SCHOLASTICUS
nomoc.: for '*titularum*' read '*titulorum*'.

MACARIUS AEGYPTIUS (MAGNUS)
hom. 1–50: H. Dörries, E. Klostermann, M. Kroeger, Berlin 1964.
hom. (typus 3) 1–28   *homiliae* (typus 3), E. Klostermann, H. Berthold, *TU* 72 (1961).
hom. fr. (B 39)   *homiliae fragmentum*, H. Dörries, *TU* 80 (1962) p. 309.

MARCELLUS ANCYRANUS
ep.: for '72. 2. 3' read '72. 2–3'.

MARTYRUM ACTA
M. Thdot. 3: for 'p. 132' read 'p. 131'.

METHODIUS OLYMPIUS
res.: after '64. 12–62' add ', Oecumenium Triccensem *Rom.*7:18–22 (M.118.461C, 465D–468A); *ib.*8:5–8(473B); *ib.*9:19–21(516B); id.*1Cor.*15:42–46(888A); *ib.*15:47–50(889B); id.*2Cor.*5:5–9 (973B); id.*Phil.*3:20–21(1312CD); id.*1Thess.*4:14–17(M.119. 92B)'.

NESTORIUS CONSTANTINOPOLITANUS
ep. Cyr.: for '99' read '49'.

NILUS ANCYRANUS
for '*inst.*' read '†*inst.* (perh. by Evagrius Ponticus).
†*mal. cog.*: add 'prob. by Evagrius Ponticus'.

ORIGENES
fr. 1–140 in Jo.: for 'p. 485' read 'p. 483'.

ADDENDA ET CORRIGENDA

PHILO CARPASIANUS
ep.: for 'p. 293' read 'p. 393'.

SOZOMENUS SALAMINUS
h.e.: J. Bidez *GCS* (1960).

SYMEON STYLITES JUNIOR
ep. Thom.: for '*v. Marth.*' read '*V. Marth.*'.

THEODORUS PHARANITA
fr.: for 'H.3.1246' read 'H.3.1245'.

THEODOSIUS II IMPERATOR
cod.: for 'H.1.1717' read 'H.1.1716'.

VALENTINIANUS III IMPERATOR
ep. Thds.: for 'p. 57' read 'p. 5'.

VITAE SANCTORUM ANONYMAE
V. Chrys.: for 'p. 249' read 'p. 294'.

IV. LIST OF PERIODICALS AND WORKS CITED BY THEIR TITLE

PAmh.: for '*Amhurst*' read '*Amherst*'; for '1901–2' read '1900–1'.
PFlor.: for '1905–15' read '1906–15'.

V. GENERAL ABBREVIATIONS

Imp.	Imperator
voc.	vocative

s.v. **ἀβαθμίδοτος**: add '(for -δωτος)'.
s.v. **ἀβάπτιστος B3**: after '*ib*.115(672A)' add 'cit. infra'.
s.v. **ἀβελτηρία**: add '(f.l. for *ἀβελτερία*)'.
s.v. **ἀβιάστως 2**: for 'cit. s. *νοῦς*' read 'cit. s. *ἐπιστημοσύνη*'.
ἀγγελιῶτις, *angelic* *τῆς ἀ. τάξεως* Areth.*Apoc*.28(M.106.636D).
s.v. **ἄγγελος IIH2c**: after 'Temple veil' insert 'Mel.*pass*.98 p.16. 29'.
s.v. **ἀγένητος B2**: for *τὸ ἀγέννητον* read *τὸ ἀ.*
s.v. **ἁγιολεκτέω**: for *ἁγιόλεκτος* read *ἅγιος*.
s.v. **ἀγκτικός 2**: for '*able to raise, uplifting*' read '*subduing, overpowering*'.
s.v. **ἀγκωνίσκος**: for 'M.88.504B' read 'M.88.204B'.
s.v. **ἁγνός A2**: for *ἰχθύς* read *ἰχθῦς*.
s.v. **ἄγραφος B**: after '*scripture*' add '(v. *ἔγγραφος, παράδοσις*)'.
B1: delete 'ref. Pneumatomachoi'; after *βιαζέσθωσαν* add '[sc. Macedonians]'.
E: after *εἰκὼν ἄ.* insert '[? l. *ἄγραπτος*]'.
s.v. **ἀγριέλαιος**: add **ἡ**; for '*of a wild olive*, fem. as subst.' read '*wild olive*'; for 'M.9.341B' read 'M.9.341C'.
s.v. **ἀγρυπνία A1**: after 'individuals' insert 'ref. extreme ascetics, likened to those who refuse to render to Caesar (i.e. the body) the things of Caesar *νηστείαις καὶ ἀ. κακοῦντες τὸ σῶμα* Or. *comm.in Mt*.17.27(p.659.27; M.13.1557A)'.
s.v. **ἀγωγή 1**: add '**e.** *way of treating, treatment περὶ τῆς τοῦ Χριστοῦ ἀ. καὶ...διδασκαλίας τοῦ τὸν Σὴθ αὐτὸν νομίζειν...εἶναι* Epiph. *haer*.39.10(p.80.11; M.41.676D)'; at end of article add '**3.** *manner*, ref. discrepancy in Passion narrative between reed, sponge, and hyssop *δοκεῖ...μίαν ἔχειν τῆς γενέσεως ἀ. ὅ τε κάλαμος καὶ ὁ σπόγγος καὶ ἡ ὕσσωπος...δέον γοῦν εἰπεῖν κάλαμον, εἶπεν ὕσσωπον διὰ τὴν ὁμοίαν τῆς βλάστης καὶ τῆς τομῆς ἀ.* Mac. Mgn.*apocr*.2.17(p.29.7); **4.** *instance καθ' ἑκάστην ἀ. καὶ τρίτον καὶ τέταρτον φωνεῖν εἴωθεν ὁ ἀλεκτρυών* Chrys.*hom.85.2 in Mt*. (7.805C)'.
s.v. **Ἀδάμ A4**: after '(M.*PL*.4.992Bf.)' add 'name being composed of initial letters of *ἀνατολή, δύσις, ἄρκτος, μεσημβρία*, cf.Aug. *tract.in Jo*.9.14(M.*PL*.35.1465)'.
H2d: after 'assumed by Christ' insert 'acc. view ascribed to Or. *ἡ τοῦ σωτῆρος ψυχὴ ἡ τοῦ Ἀ. ἦν* Phot.*cod*.117(M.103.396A)'.
ἀδελφόπαις, ὁ, *nephew*, Thphn.*chron*.p.108(M.108.312B).
***ἀδελφοποιητός**, *made a brother* or *sister by adoption*, *Nomoc*.277.
s.v. **ἀδελφότης A3**: for 'p.338.6' read 'p.338.7'.
s.v. **ἀδιαφορία B**: for *εἴ τε* read *εἴ τι* and for '224' read '224.2'.
s.v. **ἀεροφανής**: for 'Cyr.*ador*.11(1.375C)' read 'Cyr.*ador*.11(1. 379C)'.
s.v. **ἀερώδης**: for 'M.18.888A' read 'M.118.888A'.
s.v. **ἄζυμος 3**: after *ἐντολῆς* insert full stop, and continue: *ὅσοι ἐν ὑμῖν (ἐγγὺς γάρ ἐστι τὸ πάσχα) ἄ. ἄγετε, κτλ.*; delete '*ib*.(p.122. 27ff.; 425B)'.
s.v. **ἀζυμοφαγία**: after '*bread*' read '*τῶν ἑπτὰ ἡμερῶν τὴν ἀ.* Gr. Nyss.*res*.1(M.46.617C); plur. *Passover season*...(M.6.505A)'.
for **ἀθωοθέω** read **ἀθῳοθέω**.
for **ἀθώως** read **ἀθῴως**.
s.v. **αἰτία A**: delete 'physical *taint*...baptism', and read '*harm, damage εὑρέθη τὰ σώματα αὐτῶν ὁλόκληρα ἐκ πάσης αἰ. Pers*. (p.25.1); *μηδεμίας εὑρεθείσης αὐτῷ ἐκ τοῦ πυρὸς αἰ.* Jo.Mosch. *prat*.36(M.87.2885C)'.
C: after '(p.27.16; 650A)' add '*affair, matter οὕτως...γέγονεν ἡ περὶ τούτου αἰ.* Epiph.*haer*.58.4(p.361.3; M.41.1093D); *ἔγνω ὁ ἅγιος τῆς γυναικὸς τὴν αἰ.* Marc.Diac.*v.Porph*.29(p.27.12)'.
s.v. **αἰώνιος B2cii**: after *καλοί τε καὶ* read *κακοί· ἀλλὰ καὶ τὸ*....
s.v. **ἀκηδία B2**: after '(M.93.1697A)' insert 'esp. of novices, Pall.*h. Laus*.21(p.63.20; M.34.1068D); cf.*Apophth.Patr*.(M.65.201C)'.
B3: after 'such as' insert 'weariness in spiritual warfare *ἡ συνεχὴς προσβολὴ τῆς ἁμαρτίας διαλύει πολλάκις τὸν τόνον τῶν λογισμῶν, καὶ...τὴν καλουμένην ἀ. ἐργάζεται* Or.*fr.in Ps*.118:28 (p.106)'; after '*v.Euthym*.19(p.30.19)' insert 'esp. of lust and anger, Evagr.Pont.*cap.pract*.A 14(M.40.1225A); Max.*carit*.1.49 (M.90.969C)'.
B4: after 'causes monks' insert 'to hate their surroundings, Evagr.Pont.*vit.cog*.7(M.40.1273C); ‡Nil.*vit.cog*.(M.79.1456D)'; after '*ib*.13(860B)' insert 'causes sleep, Or.*fr.in Ps*.118:28 (p.106); ‡Nil.*vit.cog*.(1457A); *Apophth.Patr*.103(*PO* 8 p.180.5); but may induce false zeal, †Nil.*mal.cog*.25(M.79.1229D)'.
B5: after 'remedies' insert 'staying in cell, Evagr.Pont.*sent. mon*.55(p.157); id.*cap.pract*.A 19(M.40.1225CD); †Nil.*mal.cog*. 12(M.79.1213C); Max.*carit*.1.52(M.90.969D)'; after 'prayer and work' insert 'Evagr.Pont.*rer.mon*.8(M.40.1260CD)'; after 'patience...(M.79.1144C)' insert 'and tears, Evagr.Pont.*sent. virg*.39(p.149); ‡Nil.*vit.cog*.(M.79.1457C); tears being driven away by *ἀ.*, Evagr.Pont.*sent.mon*.56(p.157); hope, id.*cap. pract*.A 18(M.40.1225C); meditation on scripture, Ath.*exp. Ps*.118:28(M.27.484D); prayer, fasting, and avoidance of attendance at choral services, *Apophth.Patr*.103(*PO* 8 p.180. 24)'.
s.v. **ἀκηδιάω 6b**: after '*ib*.16(p.40.22; 1041D)' insert '*Apophth.Mac. Aeg*.(M.34.209B); *Apophth.Patr*.(M.65.185C)'.
s.v. **ἀλαβαστροθήκη**: add 'Soz.*h.e*.9.2.16(M.67.1601B) cit. s. *λείψανον*'.
s.v. **ἀλάθητος 1**: before 'neut. as subst.' insert 'of grace, Mac.Aeg. *hom.fr*.(B39)76(p.311)'.
***ἀλείωνε**, s.v.l., ? for *ἀλεείνῳ*, *warm*, or ? from *ἀλεῖον*, *distilled ἀλείωνε...ἀποσβέσας ὕδατι Exorc*.(p.343).
ἀλλήλων, *each other, one another*, nom. *γυναῖκες...ἄλληλαι πρὸς ἀλλήλας διαφέρονται* Epiph.*exp.fid*.10(p.510.11; M.42.800A).
s.v. **ἀλλοιόω C2**: for 'Meth.*creat*.... M.18.33C)' read 'Meth.*creat*.... M.18.333C)'.
***ἀμανίκωτος**, *without sleeves*, Thphn.*chron*.p.372(M.108.389B).
s.v. **ἀμερίστως 2**: delete *ὁ* before *θεάνθρωπος*.
for **ἀμφισβητήτως** read **ἀμφισβητητῶς**.
s.v. **ἀναγνώστης 6**: for 'cit. s. *ἐξορκιστής*' read 'cit. s. *ἐπορκιστής*'.
***ἀναγυρεύω**, *see to, attend to, Euchol*.(p. 225) cit. s. *ἔξαρχος*.
s.v. **ἀνάδειξις 1b**: for *χρίσις* read *χρῖσις*.
s.v. **ἀναίρεσις**: for 'M.26.353B' read 'M.26.333B'.
s.v. **ἀναιρέω**: for *αὐτοεξούσιον* read *αὐτεξούσιον*.
s.v. **ἀνακιρνάω 2**: delete '*ib*.4.6...cit. s. *συγχέω*'; for '6.45E' read '6^2.45E'.
s.v. **ἀνάληψις IIB1**: for '*ib*.1.17' read 'id.*e.th*.1.17'.
IIB2: for 'p.222.23' read 'p.222.20'.
ἀναμένω: delete entry.
s.v. **ἀναμίγνυμι**: delete asterisk.
s.v. **ἀνανεόω 1**: for 'M.85.452B' read 'M.85.1272A'.
s.v. **ἀναπαλέω**: for 'prob. for' read 'f.l. for'.
s.v. **ἀναπτυκτέον**: delete 'adj. ... explained'.
s.v. **ἀναρτάω**: before '*hang upon*' insert '**1.**'; after '(*AS* 1 p.154)' add '**2.** *tie up* for flogging, Chrys.*hom.15.3 in Eph*.(11. 113E)'.
s.v. **ἀνάστασις IIID4a**: after 'p.413.7' add 'M.118.888A'.
IIIG2: citation from Bas.*hom*.13.1 should precede that from Gr.Nyss.*Apoll*.55.
s.v. **ἀναστράπτω**: after '*shine forth*' insert 'Cyr.*Ag*.20(3.650E)'.
s.v. **ἀνατολή A1**: add to this section 'perh. of Resurrection *σῆς... ἀντολίης θεεικὴν δόσιν* A. C. Bundy, 'Early Christian Inscriptions of Crete' 11.9(*Hesp*.32 p.242).
s.v. **ἀναφορικός**: before 'gram.' insert '**1.** *high, hilly ἐν ἀ. τόποις Phys*.B 25(p.294.11); **2.**'.
p. 129^2, column heading: for *ἀνδρε* read *ἀνδρεία*.
s.v. **ἀνδρεία 2a**: after 'cardinal virtues' insert 'Clem.*str*.2.18(p.154. 17; M.8.1017B)'.
2c: after '(p.48.19; *ἀνδρίας* M.9.493A)' insert 'cf.*ib*.6.9(p.469.20; 296C)'.
s.v. **ἀνεμοκαύσων**: add '(for *ἄνεμος καύσων*)'.
s.v. **ἀνεμπεπλόκως**: add '(for *ἀνεμπεπλοκότως*)'.
s.v. **ἀνέξοδος 2**: for 'as subst., *beggar*' read '*destitute, indigent*'.
s.v. **ἀνθοροθετέω**: for '*destroy*' read '*reverse*'.
s.v. **ἀνθρώπειος 1**: for *ἡμετέρα* read *ἡμέτερα*.
s.v. **ἀνθρωπίνως D**: after 'id.*Ps*.109:1(1.1392)' add 'comp. *ἀνθρωπινωτέρως*', and transfer 'Didym....M.29.728C)' to follow this.
s.v. **ἀνθρωπολάτρης 2a**: after 'Euthal.' insert 'Diac.'.
s.v. **ἄνθρωπος I6**: for 'cit. s. *χρίσις*' read 'cit. s. *χρῖσις*'; for 'M.45. 1212A' read 'M.45.1213C'; for 'aganst' read 'against'.
I9: for 'Eus.*d.e*.4.14(p.173.13; M.22.170D)' read 'Eus....M.22. 289A)'.
s.v. **ἀνίερος 1**: after '(p.69.12; M.25.645C)' add 'of Jewish high priests, with play on sense 2 infra, Jo.D.*hom*.2.5(M.96.585A)'.
2: for 'Tim.CP *haer*.' read '‡Jo.Nic.*fr*. and delete ref. to Jo.D. *hom*.2.5.
s.v. **ἀντίμιμος 1a**: for 'M.9.1300A' read 'M.8.1300A'.

s.v. **ἀντιφιλοτιμέομαι 1**: for 'Or.*Eph.*1:8' read 'Or.*comm.in Eph.* 1:8'.

ἀντολίη, ἡ, = ἀνατολή, *rising*, A. C. Bundy, 'Early Christian Inscriptions of Crete' 11.9(*Hesp.*32 p.242) cit. (addenda) s. ἀνατολή.

s.v. **ἀνυστάκτως**: for '*Arm.*5' read '*Arm.*11'; add 'Jo.Clim.*scal.*27 (M.88.1097A)'.

s.v. **ἀξίνη**: after '*axe*' insert 'ref. 4 Reg.6:1–7 as type of Christ, Just.*dial.*86.6(M.6.681B); *cum...ferrum excussum de securi cecidisset in Jordanem...supernatavit ferrum securis, et de superficie aquae sumserunt illud qui ante amiserant:* δι' ἔργου ἔδειξεν ὁ προφήτης, ὅτι τὸν...λόγον τοῦ θεοῦ, ὃν...ἀποβαλόντες οὐχ ηὑρίσκομεν, ἀποληψόμεθα πάλιν διὰ τῆς τοῦ ξύλου οἰκονομίας. ὅτι δὲ ἀξίνῃ ἔοικεν ὁ λόγος τοῦ θεοῦ, Ἰωάννης...φησι περὶ αὐτοῦ, ἤδη δὲ ἡ ἀ. πρὸς τὴν ῥίζαν τῶν δένδρων κεῖται Iren.*haer.*5.17.4(M.7. 1171A); Ἰησοῦς...τὴν ἀ. τὴν ἑαυτοῦ πρὸς τὰς ῥίζας τῆς κακίας προσαγαγών Clem.*q.d.s.*29(p.179.9; M.9.663D)'.

s.v. **ἄξιος**: add '**3.** c. genit., *worthy calling, worthy of the name of* θεοσημείας ἀληθῶς ἄ. πράγματα Bas.Sel.*v.Thecl.*1(M.85.544D)'.

ἀπαισίως, *in an undignified manner*, Cels.ap.Or.*Cels.*6.15(p.85.19; M.11.1312D).

***ἀπάλειψις, ἡ,** *wiping out, abolition*, Ath.*inc.*22.4(M.25.136B).

s.v. **ἀπάντησις 1**: after '(M.65.392C)' add 'ἐν ἀ. γίνεσθαι c. dat., *meet*, Gr.Mag.*dial.*(tr.Zach.)1.12(M.*PL.*77.214B)'.

s.v. **ἀπαράθραυστος**: for 'ἔχειν...473B)' read 'Dion.Ar.*e.h.*4.3.1(M.3. 473B, v.l. for ἀπαράφθαρτος)', and add 'id.*d.n.*1.4(M.3.592A, v.l. for ἀπαράφθαρτος)'.

***ἀπαραθραύστως**, *invincibly*, Dion.Ar.*e.h.*4.3.4(M.3.477D, v.l. for ἀπαραφθάρτως).

s.v. **ἀπαράλλακτος IIB1**: for '(p.16.18; M.25.449C)' read '(p.16. 28...'.

s.v. **ἀπαραλλάκτως A2**: after 'Dion.' add 'Ar.'.

s.v. **ἀπαρασαλεύτως**: add 'CTrull.*can.*55'.

s.v. **ἀπαράφθαρτος**: after '*inviolate*' read 'ἔχειν...τὰς κατ' ἀρετὴν ἐν ψυχαῖς ἀ. εἰκόνας Dion.Ar.*e.h.*4.3.1(M.3.473B, v.l. ἀπαραθραύστους)' and for 'Dion.Ar.*d.n.*' read 'id.*d.n.*'.

s.v. **ἀπασχολέω 2b**: after '(p.70.17; M.8.209B)' insert 'id.*str.*6.9 (p.469.28: M.9.297A)'.

s.v. **ἀπαύγασμα A1**: for 'M.13.337A' read 'M.13.357A'.

s.v. **ἀπειρόγαμος 2**: for 'M.22.517B' read 'M.22.493B'.

***ἀπειροδυνάμως**, *with infinite power*, Max.*ambig.*(M.91.1328C).

s.v. **ἄπειρος A2**: after 'of God' insert 'ἄπειρον, οὐ κατὰ τὸ ἀδιεξίτητον νοούμενον, ἀλλὰ κατὰ τὸ ἀδιάστατον, καὶ μὴ ἔχον πέρας Clem. *str.*5.12(p.380.23; M.9.121B)'.

s.v. **ἅπλωμα 2**: after '*T.Benj.*9.4' insert 'Ast.Soph.*hom.21.8 in Pss.*(p.163.3)'.

ἅπλωσις, ἡ, *state of being unfolded* or *spread out*; of a cloak, ‡Bas.*h.myst.*24(p.263.9); ‡Germ.CP *contempl.*(M.98.396B) cit. s. μανδύας.

s.v. **ἀπογράφομαι 2**: for περισσοπρακτίαι read περισσοπρακτίᾳ.

s.v. **ἀποδημέω 1**: after 'met.' insert 'βασανιζόμενοι τῆς σαρκὸς ἀπεδήμουν οἱ...μάρτυρες *M.Polyc.*2.2'.

s.v. **ἀποκαθίστημι B1b**: after '(p.395.31; M.14.689C)' insert 'οὐδεὶς ἀποκαθίσταται εἴς τινα τόπον μηδαμῶς ποτε γενόμενος ἐκεῖ, ἀλλ' ἡ ἀποκατάστασίς ἐστιν εἰς τὰ οἰκεῖα...λέγει οὖν...πρὸς ἡμᾶς τοὺς ἀποστρέψαντας ὅτι, ἐὰν ἐπιστρέψωμεν, ἀποκαταστήσει ἡμᾶς. καὶ γὰρ τὸ τέλος τῆς ἐπαγγελίας τοιοῦτόν ἐστιν ὡς ἐν ταῖς Πράξεσι τῶν ἀποστόλων γέγραπται [Ac.3:21] id.*hom.14.18 in Jer.*(p.124. 20; M.13.428B); ref. Origen's doctrine of ultimate salvation of wicked and Devil, †Leont.B.*sect.*10.6(M.86.1265C) cit. s. ἀποκατάστασις; ἀποκατασταθήσονται ἀσεβεῖς τε καὶ δαίμονες εἰς τὴν προτέραν αὐτῶν τάξιν Justn.*Or.*(p.205.10; M.86.975A); id.*ep.CP* (M.86.991C)'; delete ref. to Or.*princ.*2.10.8, and continue: 'cf. ἀποκατάστασις'.

s.v. **ἀποκεκληρωμένως**: after '*specifically*' insert 'Chrys.*hom.14.2 in Gen.*(4.108B)'; for 'Chrys.*hom.5.1*...' read 'id.*hom.5.1*...'.

s.v. **ἀπόκρυψις 3**: for '*disclosure*' read '*response*'.

s.v. **ἀποκτηνόω 1**: after ψυχὴ insert '...'.

s.v. **ἀπόμοτος**: add '(for ἀπώμοτος)'.

s.v. **ἀπομύρισμα**: after '*oil*' insert '‡Bas.*h.myst.*53(p.391.21)'.

s.v. **ἀπόνοια 1b**: after '(9.662A)' add 'id.*hom.17.1 in 1Tim.*(11. 647E)'.

3: after '*simplicity*' add '(? for ἀπονία)'.

4: after '*detachment*' add '(? for ἀπονία)'.

s.v. **ἀποξενόω 3b**: after ἀπεσχοινισμέναι insert ', ...'.

s.v. **ἀποτακτήτης**: entry should read only 'v. ἀποτακτίτης'.

for **ἀποτακτῖται, οἱ,** read **ἀποτακτίτης (-ήτης), ὁ,** and continue: '**1.** *one who renounces* the world, *hermit*, *M.Thdot.1* 19(p.73. 21); **2.** plur., *Apotactites*...'.

ἀποτρίχω: delete entry.

s.v. **ἀποφοιτάω 2**: for 'M.69' read 'M.72'.

ἀποχρυσόω: *turn into gold* or *money*, pass., Bas.*hom.*6.5(2.47C; M.31.269C).

s.v. **ἀπροσκύνητος**: for 'M.28.29A' read 'M.28.28A'.

s.v. **ἀπροστρόπαιος**: delete '? *guiltless*', and after '1394–5' read '(M.38.247A) f.l. for ἐσθῆτα προστρόπαιον (Teub.p.106)'.

s.v. **ἀργυρίζομαι 1**: after '*pass.*' insert '86'.

ἀρδεύω, *water*; *flood* with light, *Rit.Epiph.*(p.426).

s.v. **ἀρετή B2**: after 'cardinal virtues' insert 'Clem.*str.*2.18(p.154. 17; M.8.1017B)' and continue: '*ib.*7.3...'.

s.v. **ἀριθμός 1**: add to this section '*one of a number, member of a numerical group* περὶ ἕνα τῶν ἀ. τῆς τριάδος διεσφαλμένοι Meth.*symp.*8.10(p.93.2; M.18.153B)'.

***ἀρκτομῦς, ὁ,** '*bear-mouse*', i.e. *marmot*, wrongly used to translate Hebr. שָׁפָן *rock-badger* (*hyrax syriacus*); ref. Ps.103:18, cf. *omnes* χοιρογρυλλίοις *voces transtulerunt, exceptis LXX qui* lepores *interpretati sunt. sciendum autem animal esse...habens similitudinem muris et ursi: unde in Palaestina ἀ. dicitur.* Hier.S.*ep.*106.65(M.*PL.*22.861).

s.v. **ἅρμα 2**: add 'cf.Mac.Aeg.*hom.*15.14(M.34.584D) where perh. l. ἄρμα'.

s.v. **ἄρμα 2**: after '(929B)' add 'perh. also sing., *equipment*, Mac. Aeg.*hom.*15.14(M.34.584D), v. ἅρμα (addenda)'.

s.v. **ἁρμόνιος 1b**: after '*ib.*' insert '6.45'.

for **ἀρνησοχριστεῖα** read **ἀρνησοχριστ(ε)ία.**

s.v. **ἁρπαστής**: delete asterisk (cf. *LS* s.v. ἁρπαστός).

s.v. **ἀρρανής**: entry should read only 'error for ἀρραγής, Cyr.*Is.*3.3 (2.441E)'.

s.v. **ἀρτίας**: entry should read 'f.l. for ἀρτίως, Gr.Mag.*dial.*(tr. Zach.)1.12(M.*PL.*77.214B)'.

s.v. **ἀρτίων**: entry should read only 'error for ἀρτύων, Cyr.*Is.*2.1 (2.195E)'.

s.v. **ἀρτοθήκη**: for 'p.27.19' read 'p.27.20'.

***ἀρτοποίειον, τό,** *bakery*, *V.Pach.Σ* 79(p.256.4).

s.v. **ἀρχιμανδρίτησσα**: add '(for -τισσα)'.

***ἀρχιραββίτης, ὁ,** *chief rabbi*, *Clem.recogn.suppl.*2.2(M.1.1457D).

s.v. **ἀρχιτεκτόνημα**: for '515B; M.22.253B' read '515A; M.22.805A'.

s.v. **ἀσβέστιον**: for '*unquenched* or ? *unquenchable fire*' read '= ἄσβεστος as subst., *unslaked lime*'.

s.v. **ἀσημείωτος**: for '3.117C' read '2.117C'.

s.v. **ἀσπλαγχνία**: after '*V.Pach.A*' insert '5'.

***ἀστειόλογος**, *of elegant speech*, Taras.*ep.*1(M.98.1433C).

s.v. **ἀστενοχώρητος**: after '*unconstricted*' read '*cat.Apoc.*3:9(p.227. 20); *ib.*18:14...'.

s.v. **ἀσυγκρίτως 3**: for 'M.46.1112D' read 'M.46.1121B'.

s.v. **ἀσυστρόφημα**: for νεοκατηχητῶν read νεοκατηχήτων.

s.v. **ἀσφαλίζω 1**: after '**a.** *secure*' insert '*fasten* ἀσφαλισθῆναί με ἐν τῷ ξύλῳ Leont.Abb.*v.Gr.Agr.*59(M.98.653B)'.

2: add to this section '*secure oneself against, take precautions against* ἀμφοτέρους ὁ θεὸς ἠσφαλίσατο Chrys.*hom.21.4 in 2Cor.* (10.587C)'.

s.v. **ἄτρεπτος IA2**: for ἄ. καὶ ἀναλλοωτος read ἄ. καὶ ἀναλλοίωτος.

s.v. **ἀτυφία**: after '*humility*' insert 'Clem.*q.d.s.*18(p.171.10; M.9. 621C)'.

s.v. **Αὐγουστάλιος 1**: after '1.169a' insert '*ib.*1.216'.

s.v. **αὐτοαγαθός 2a**: for '*princ.*1.2' read '*princ.*1.2.13'.

s.v. **αὐτοαρετή**: after '*principle of virtue*' insert '*absolute virtue* ἡ παρθένος...αὐτοαρετῆς ἄγαλμα οὖσα †Bas.Anc.*virg.*22(M.30. 716A)'.

s.v. **αὐτοζωία**: for '*Pr.*16' read '*Pr.*16:22'.

αὐτοθελῶς, *of one's own free will*, Ephr.3.432F = Jo.D.*virt.*(M.95. 96D).

***αὐτοϊσότης, ἡ,** *absolute equality*, Dion.Ar.*d.n.*9.10(3.936A).

s.v. **αὐτοκίνητος 3**: for '*princ.*3.2' read '*princ.*3.2.2'.

***αὐτομέριμνος**, *anxious about oneself*, Jo.Clim.*scal.*5(M.88.764B); *Schol.*2 in loc.cit.(M.88.781C).

s.v. **αὐτοπαράκτως**: add '*ib.*5.1(1456B)'.

s.v. **ἀφίημι**: add '**8.** *discharge* τόξον...ἀφεθῆναι *A.Thom.*A 91 (p.205.16)'.

s.v. **ἀφόδευσις**: for '=' read 'cf.'.

ἀφομοι-όω, *make like*, pass. c. μετά: κεγχρῖτις...~ουμένη μετὰ τῶν ὄντων Epiph.*haer.*66.88(p.132.2; M.42.172B).

ἀφομοιωτικός, *able to assimilate*, Dion.Ar.*c.h.*7.1(M.3.205C); *ib.*15.3 (332D).

ἄφραστος, *inexpressible, ineffable*, of God φῶς ἐν ἀφράστοις καὶ ἀπροσίτοις ἀναπαυόμενον Meth.*symp.*6.1(p.64.16; M.18.113B); τῶν ἀστέρων...κίνησιν...ἀ. σοφίᾳ διέπει *ib.*8.16(p.105.10; 168D); πῶς δ' ἄν τις ὑπ' ὄψιν ἀγάγοι τὸ ἀ.; Gr.Nyss.*virg.*10(p.289.16; M.46.361A).

ἀχαριστέω, *take no delight* in, *be displeased* with ἐὰν ἀχαριστήσῃ τις ἐν τοῖς ἑαυτοῦ κληρονόμοις Ast.Soph.*hom.1 in Ps.*5(M.40.393A).

ἄχρηστος, *useless*; *unkind, cruel* ἀλλ' ἄ. γίνεται, φησί. τοῦτο σκῆψις τῆς ἰδίας μικροψυχίας· ἑτέρως ἄ. γίνεται, ἂν ἀμύνῃ. εἰ ᾔδει ὁ θεός, ὅτι διὰ τοῦ μὴ ἀμύνεσθαι ἄ. ἐγίνοντο οἱ ἄδικοι, οὐκ ἂν τοῦτο ἐπέταξεν, ἀλλ' εἶπεν ἄν, ἄμυνον σαυτῷ Chrys.*hom.31.3 in Ac.* (9.245B).

s.v. **ἀχωρίστως 2**: after '*Chalc.*' insert '(p.129.31; H.2.456C)'.

s.v. **ἄψυχος 1**: delete † before 'Gr.Thaum.'.

βαθέως, *profoundly*; ref. exegesis, *non-literally, in a spiritual sense*, Epiph.*haer.*77.36(p.449.11; M.42.696D).

βαθύτης, ἡ, *depth, profundity*, ref. spiritual sense of scripture ἐν β. σαφηνιζόμενα Epiph.*haer.*77.36(p.449.10; M.42.696D).

s.v. **βαίνω 1**: for 'id.*Ar.*' read 'Ar.*Thal.fr.*1 ap.eund.*Ar.*'.
add '**4.** *depart*, i.e. *die*, A. C. Bundy 'Early Christian Inscriptions of Crete' 6(*Hesp.*32 p.235)'.

for **βαλαντιόσκοπος** read **βαλαντιοσκόπος**; after '*covetous person*' insert '(but perh. for *βαλαντιοκόπος cut-purse*)'.

s.v. **βάλλω C5**: add 'ἔβαλεν...ὀρύσσειν Cyr.S.*v.Euthym.*38(p.57.8); ἔβαλεν προσκαλεῖσθαι τοὺς γείτονας id.*v.Sab.*41(p.131.25)'.
add '**D.** *draw* breath βάλας [aor. ptcpl.] ῥόγχον *Contrad.*2(p.9)'.

s.v. **βαραθρόω**: add 'met. β. ... τοὺς θείους νόμους Didym.*Zach.*5.66'.

for **βαρυογκωδής** read **βαρυογκώδης**.

s.v. **βασιλεία IIB1**: for 'ap.Eus.*Marcell.*3.4' read 'ap.Eus.*Marcell.* 2.4'.
IIB31: for '*haer.*29' read '*haer.*29.4'.

s.v. **βασιλιδίπολις**: for 'cf.' read 'prob. f.l. for'.

***βεβαιοτερέω**, *be more certain*, Anast.S.*hod.*23(M.89.297A).

s.v. **βέλος**: after 'exeg. Is.49:2' insert 'Didym.*Zach.*3.190 cit. (addenda) s. φαρέτρα'.

s.v. **βλέπω B**: add '**7.** reflex., *feel* πῶς ~εις σεαυτὸν ἄρτι; Anast.S. *defunct.*(M.89.1196D)'.

for **βλοσυρέω (βλοσσυρέω)** read **βλοσυρόω (βλοσσυρόω)**.

for **βορβοροκοίλιστος** read **βορβοροκύλιστος**.

βορ(ρ)έας, ὁ, *north wind*; exeg. Cant.4:16, as signifying power of evil, Or.*schol.in Cant.*4:16(M.17.273A) cit. (addenda) s. νότος; τῷ ὀνόματι τούτῳ [sc. βορρέᾳ] ἡ ἀντικειμένη διασημαίνεται δύναμις Gr.Nyss.*hom.10 in Cant.*(M.44.984B); Didym.*Zach.*5. 53, Nil.ap.Proc.G.*Cant.*4:16(M.87.1668D) citt. (addenda) s. νότος.

s.v. **βούλησις IA**: for 'Gr.Naz.*carm.*1.1.34.35' read 'Gr.Naz.*carm.* 1.2.34.35'.
IC2: for '*hex.*5' read '*hex.*7'.

***βραυκάνομαι**, *cry*; of children, Philost.*h.e.*11.6(M.65.600B).

***βραχύλεκτος**, *of few words*; of God, Dion.Ar.*myst.*1.3(M.3. 1000C) cit. s. πολύλογος.

for **βωμόσκοπος** read **βωμοσκόπος** and (s.v.) μωμοσκόπος.

for **Γαιανῖται** read **Γαϊανῖται**.

s.v. **γαστριμαργικός**: for '406A' read '405E'.

s.v. **γενέθλιος 3**: after 'v. θεοφάνεια' add ' θεοφάνια'.

s.v. **γηραλαῖος**: add '(for -λέος)'.

s.v. **γί(γ)νομαι 3**: delete 'with (ἑνὸς) μόνου' and '*one thing only*'; after '*be concerned with*' insert 'τῆς ἀσφαλείας γινόμενος Ath.*Ar.* 2.10(M.26.168B); ἑνὸς...γενόμενος, τοῦ τρέφειν τοὺς πεινῶντας Attic.*ep.*ap.Socr.*h.e.*7.25(M.67.793C)'.

***γλωσσοδεξιότμητος**, *with the tongue and the right hand cut off*, *Max.invect.*(M.90.204A).

s.v. **γνῶσις C5**: for '‡Just.' read '†Just.'; before 'M.6' insert 'p.52;'.

***γράδος, ὁ**, (Lat. *gradus*) *step*, *CIG* 3.3900; *ib.*3902 i.

s.v. **γραφή A3a**: for 'Chrys.*hom.22 in 2Cor.*' read 'Chrys.*hom.2.2 in 2Cor.*'
A5b: for 'Ath.*exp.in Ps.*' read 'Ath.*exp.Ps.*'.

s.v. **δαιμόνιον 3a**: for καταλαλία, καταλαλίαν read καταλαλιά, καταλαλιάν.

s.v. **δάκτυλος 2d**: after '*v.Mos.*' delete '2'.

s.v. **δαπάνη 1**: after '(4.267B)' add 'δ. μεγίστη ἔσται τῶν ἡμῖν ἡμαρτημένων *ib.*4.7(30C)'.

δαπάνημα, τό, *consumable object*, ‡Bas.*struct.hom.*1.7(1.327F; M.30. 20A).

s.v. **δεκακέρατος 1**: for τοὺς λεγομένους δεκακεράτων συνομοκεράτους read τοῦ λεγομένου δεκακεράτου συνομοκερώτους.

s.v. **δεκουρίων**: for '*IGCAeg.*584.6' read '*CIG* 8646 cit. s. Αὐγουστάλιος'.

δέρκω, *see* διορατικὸν γὰρ τὸ ζῷον τοῦτο [sc. δορκάς] ὡς αὐτὴ ἡ προσηγορία δηλοῖ ἀπὸ τοῦ δέρκειν εἰρημένη Didym.*Zach.*5.59; Anast.S.*hod.*2(M.89.68D).

s.v. **δερμακατούδιον**: after '(M.104.1405B)' add 'prob. f.l. for δέρμα κατουδίου'.

***δευτεροδότως**, *so as to be given secondly*, †Proc.G.*Procl.*1(M.87. 2792^{h}B).

δέω, *bind*; *clasp* or *fold* the hands μόνον δὲ τὰς αὐτοῦ χεῖρας δήσας οἴκοι καθεζέσθω Chrys.*hom.16.1 in Eph.*(11.117B); δήσαντες... τὰς χεῖρας καὶ προσκυνήσαντες...λέγουσιν *Lit.Chrys.*(M.63. 906).

s.v. **δηλόω**: after '**4.** *declare*...(M.92.716A)' insert '**5.** *ask* ἐδήλωσεν εἰ ...καταπαύουσι τὰς ζητήσεις Soz.*h.e.*7.12.7(M.67.1445A)' and for '**5**' read '**6**'.

s.v. **δημιουργία A3b**: for '*Zach.*' read '*Zacch.*'.

s.v. **διάθεσις 3**: before 'in complimentary address' insert '**4.** *affection, love*, Bas.*ep.*227(3.349E; M.32.852B); Chrys.*hom.30.1 in 2Cor.*(10.650C); Thdr.Mops.*Ag.*2:1–5(M.66.485B)'.

s.v. **διαθέω 2**: for '*dial.*1' read '*dial.*1.1'.

s.v. **διαίρεσις IA1**: for πανιώδη read μανιώδη.

διαιρέτης, ὁ, *divider, distributor*, Thdt.*Cant.*8:12(2.163); of Anomoeans who divide Trin., Chrys.*pan.Phoc.*3(2.708D).

s.v. **διακονέω IIB**: for 'Or.*Cels.*1.25(p.76.11; M.11.708A); *ib.*5.4...' read 'Or.*Cels.*5.4...'; after '(p.4.18; 1185B)' insert 'ἀγγέλων τῇ τούτου [sc. μάννα] δωρεᾷ διακεκονηκότων Thdt.*qu.29 in Ex.* (1.144)'.

s.v. **διάστημα A2aiii**: after '*Symb.Ant.*(345)9' insert 'ap.Ath. *syn.*26'.

s.v. **διαφίημι**: add '**3.** *discharge* against τούτων ὥσπερ ἀπό τινος... μηχανήματος...τῇ τῶν ἐναντίων πυργοποιΐᾳ διαφεθέντων Const. Diac.*laud.*26(M.88.526C)'.

s.v. **διαφορά**: add '**5.** *sort, kind* τρεῖς ξύλων διαφοραί Sever.*creat.*6.1 (M.56.484)'.

s.v. **διάφορος**: before 'comp.' insert '*different*; *special, particular* γέγονεν...ἅπαξ...ἐπὶ δ. προσώπων Chrys.*exp.in Ps.*113.2(5. 294C)'.

διαφόρως, *on various occasions*, Cyr.S.*v.Euthym.*27(p.44.15); Leont.N.*v.Sym.*53(M.93.1736B).

s.v. **διαψεύδω**: after '(p.537.11)' add '*disappoint, fail to come up to expectations* λέγομεν, τὰ λήϊνα διεψεύσατο, τουτέστιν οὐδὲν ἐκόμισεν ἄξιον τῆς ἐλπίδος· καί, ὁ ἐνιαυτὸς διεψεύσατο Chrys. *exp.in Ps.*115.3(5.313C)'.

s.v. **δίδωμι 3b**: after '*allow*' insert 'τῇ προαιρέσει διδούς Ath.*h.Ar.* 67(p.220.5; M.25.773A)'.

s.v. **διθελής**: after '*wills*' insert 'οὐ γέγονε...δ. σαρκωθεὶς ὁ λόγος... ἀλλὰ σύνθετος Eun.Berrh.*fr.*(p.276.25)ap.*Doct.Patr.*41(p.309. 9)'.

s.v. **δικαιοπραξία**: add '*ib.*47.2(577A)'.

s.v. **δικαιόω G2fv**: for 'Chrys.*hom.8.4 in Rom.*' read 'Chrys.*hom. 7.4 in Rom.*'.
G2fviii: for 'Chrys.*hom.16.2 in Rom.*' read 'Chrys.*hom.15.2 in Rom.*'.

s.v. **διορατικός 1**: before 'Chrys.*hom.4.3 in 1Tim.*' insert 'Didym. *Zach.*5.59'.

***διόροφος**, (= διώροφος), *of two stories*, Ath.*proph.*1(M.28.1064A).

***δίπλασις, ἡ**, *doubling, duplication*, Leont.H.*monoph.*(M.86.1813D).

***δίρρυτος**, *flowing two ways*, †Gr.Thaum.*ep.Philagr.*(M.46.1105D).

διφθέρωμα, τό, *piece of leather*; *scroll, volume*, ref. THDN Is.8:1, Eus.*Is.*8:1(M.24.140D) cit. s. κεφαλίς; προστάττει τῷ προφήτῃ λαβεῖν τόμον, ἢ τεῦχος ἢ δ. ἢ κεφαλίδα κατὰ τοὺς λοιπούς Proc.G. *Is.*8:1–4(M.87.1973C).

s.v. **διφυής A3**: after '(M.38.279A)' add 'Apollinarian denial, Eun. Berrh.*fr.*(p.276.25f.)ap.*Doct.Patr.*41(p.309.9f.) cit. s. σύνθετος'.

s.v. **δόγμα D3**: for ἀλληλῶν read ἀλλήλων.

s.v. **δοκιμάζω**: add '**4.** *attempt, try*, Leont.Abb.*v.Gr.Agr.*80(M.98. 692C); τυράννων τοῦτο δοκιμασάντων Anast.S.*Jud.disp.*1(M.89. 1224B); καταμαλακίζεσθαι ~ει τὸν ἄνθρωπον Jo.D.*hom.*12.10 (M.96.796A)'.

s.v. **δοκιμαστικός**: after *πυρὸς* insert '... .

s.v. **δορκάς**: add '**4.** etym. δ. ... ἀπὸ τοῦ δέρκειν Didym.*Zach*.5.59'.

s.v. **δοῦλος A3**: for '2:8' read '2:7ff.'.

s.v. **δροῦγγος**: after 'ὁ' insert '**1.**'; after '*drungus*' insert 'cf. Gothic *driugan*'; after '(3.596C)' add '**2.** (Phrygian) = *ῥύγχος, nose*, Epiph.*haer*.48.14(p.239.12ff.; M.41.877B) cit. s. *Τασκοδρουγῖται*'.

s.v. **δρύφακτος 3**: for 'id.*qu.60*...' read 'Didym.*Zach*.4.30; Thdt. *qu.60*...'.

***δυναμοποιός**, *acting mightily*; of God's power, Dion.Ar.*c.h*.15.8 (M.3.337A); id.*d.n*.8.2(M.3.892A).

***δύσαρχος**, *ill-disciplined*, Athenod.*fr*.ap.Leont.et Jo.*sacr*.2(M.86. 2089A) cit. s. *προτυπόω*.

s.v. **δυσπαραστάτως**: for 'Jo.4:42' read 'Jo.4:44'.

***δωδεκακέφαλος**, *twelve-headed*, *IGC As.Min*.210^3.8 (Amorgus).

s.v. **ἑβδομάς B1**: after '(1345C)' add 'typifying Christ's generation, incarnation, epiphany at Cana, raising of Lazarus, institution of eucharist, crucifixion, Ast.Soph.*hom.21.12 in Pss.* (p.165.5)'.

ἐγκαρσίως, *transversely*, Gr.Nyss.*res*.1(M.46.625A).

s.v. **ἐγκίσσημα**: after '(M.16.3175C)' insert '*ib*.(p.115.4; 3178A)'.

***ἐγκλίνιος**, *lying on a bed*, Andr.Cr.*or*.21(M.97.1284B).

for **ἐγκόλπω** read **ἐγκολπόω**.

s.v. **ἐγκυκλητής**: add '? l. *ἐκκυκλητής*, v. *ἐκκυκλέω*'.

s.v. **εἶδος**: add '**8.** *thing, object, matter*, Iren.*haer*.1.21.1(M.7.657B); Ast.Soph.*hom.4.21 in Pss*.(p.33.13); Anast.S.*Ps.6*(M.89.1101C)'.

εἴδω: delete entry.

s.v. **εἰκών IIIA2**: for '*ib*.1(1148D–1149A); cf.Anast.S.*serm.imag*.(M. 89.1161C)' read 'Anast.S.*serm.imag*.3(M.89.1161C); cf.‡Anast. S.*serm.imag*.1(M.89.1148D–1149A)'.

***εἰρηνοβράβευτος**, *winning the reward of peace*; of Cross, Thdr. Stud.*or*.2(M.99.697D).

s.v. **εἷς E**: add '**3.** *εἷς καὶ δεύτερος, one or two πάντα τὸν βίον τοιοῦτον εἶναι δεῖ..., οὐ μίαν ἡμέραν καὶ δευτέραν* Chrys.*hom.13.1 in 1Cor*.(10.109E); Jo.D.*hom*.12.16(M.96.801C); **4.** *εἷς καὶ ὁ αὐτός, one and the same ἐν ἑκατέραις ταῖς οὐσίαις εἷς καὶ ὁ αὐτὸς ὑπάρχει Χριστός* Cyr.S.*v.Euthym*.1(p.79); also *ὁ αὐτὸς καὶ εἷς*: *διὰ τὴν αὐτὴν καὶ μίαν αἰτίαν* Gr.Agr.*Eccl*.1.1(M.98.748A); **5.** *ὑφ' ἕν, at once, simultaneously*, Epiph.*haer*.64.72(p.523.9; M.41.1200A); **6.** *πρὸς ἕνα* (cf. Lat. *ad unum*), *one and all, to a man*, Synes.*insomn*.13(p.174.2; M.66.1308B)'.

s.v. **εἰσαγωγικός 1**: after *ὑπακοὴ...ἐν* insert '...'.

s.v. **εἰσαγωγός**: for *ἀρεταί* read *ἀρεταῖς*.

s.v. **ἐκ C1bi**: for *μυθολόγιαν* read *μυθολογίαν*.

ἕκαστος, *each*; *any*, ref. Inc. *διατρίβοντα...ὡς ἕ. ἄνθρωπον, κἂν οὐχ ὡς ἕ. ἄνθρωπος ἦν* Gr.Agr.*Eccl*.10.2(M.98.1140B).

s.v. **ἔκπτωσις 2b**: for '*princ*.4.14' read '*princ*.4.2.14'.

***ἐκσκορακίζω**, *treat with utter contempt*, Thdr.Stud.*epp*.1.53(M.99. 1108A).

s.v. **ἔκτασις 2**: for 'Thdt.*haer*.2.10(3.336)' read 'Thdt.*haer*.2.10 (4.336)'.

ἐκχωρέω, *cease*, *τὰς μὲν* [sc. *θυσίας*] *ἐκκεχωρηκυίας* Chrys.*hom.11.3 in Heb*.(12.115B).

s.v. **ἔμβαθμος**: add '; *ib*.(1912B)'.

s.v. **ἐμπύριος**: for *τυποπλαστία* read *τυποπλαστίαν*.

s.v. **ἐν**: add '**H.** *with, possessing*, *τῶν ἐν λεπίσι...οὐκ ὄντων* Cyr. *Juln*.9(6^2.316D).

s.v. **ἐναπόκειμαι 2**: for '*princ*.4.17' read '*princ*.4.1.7'.

s.v. **ἐνδιαιτάομαι**: for 'Dion.Al.' read 'Dion.R.'.

s.v. **ἐνδιδύσκω A1**: transfer 'fig. *ἐ. τὴν καλάμην ἀμιάντῳ* Ath.*inc*.44.7 (M.25.176B)' to **B** to follow '(M.99.1296A)'.

s.v. **ἐνέργεια B2c**: for 'p.339.27' read 'p.339.30'.

B2f: after 'Apoll.*fid.inc*.6' for '(p.199.17)' read '(p.199.17; M.*PL*. 8.877C)'.

B2gii: for '*ib*.4' read '*ib*.2.4'.

ἐνθυσιάζω: delete entry.

s.v. **ἐνόω C3b**: for 'Leont.B.*Nest.et Eut*.1(M.87.1305B)' read 'Leont.B.*Nest.et Eut*.1(M.86.1305B)'.

ἐνσφίγγω, *bind tightly*, Cyr.*Soph*.29(3.606E).

s.v. **ἐντευκτικός**: for '*v.Chrys*.2' read '*v.Chrys*.1'.

s.v. **ἕνωσις C2a**: for 'Thdt.*eran*.2(4.101A)' read 'Thdt.*eran*.2(4. 101)'.

s.v. **ἐνώτιος**: delete 'Gr.Nyss.*v.Mos*.(M.44.396C)'.

s.v. **ἔξαθλος 1**: add 'Didym.*Zach*.1.194'.

s.v. **ἐξαμαρτάνω**: add 'Didym.*Zach*.4.132'.

***ἐξαναχώρησις, ἡ**, *withdrawal*; of sinners from God, Didym.*Zach*. 1.13.

s.v. **ἐξανδραποδίζω 2**: add 'Didym.*Zach*.4.192'.

s.v. **ἐξαπτέρυγος**: for 'M.11.143C' read 'M.11.148C'.

s.v. **ἐξόδιος 1**: add '**c.** *fatal πυρετοῦ...παρεστῶτος τοῦ ἐ.* Gr.Naz.*or*. 40.12(M.36.373B)'.

2.: delete '**b.** *death*...(M.36.373B)', and for '**c**' and '**d**' read '**b**' and '**c**'.

ἐξορρόομαι: entry should read '***ἐξορρόω**, *curdle*; act., Clem.*paed*. 1.6(p.120.30; M.8.312A); pass., *ib*.(p.120.26; 312A)'.

ἐξώβλητος, *cast out*; of a wife, *repudiated*, Didym.*Zach*.2.223.

s.v. **ἐπαναπαύω 1**: for *παρθενεία* read *παρθενία*.

s.v. **ἐπεργάζομαι**: add '**4.** *gain interest* on capital, Gr.Naz.*ep*.183(M. 37.300B, v.l. *ἀπεργαζομένοις*); *ἔχουσα οὖν τὸν ἀρραβῶνα τοῦ βαπτίσματος τὸ μὲν τάλαντον τέλειον ἔχεις, μὴ ἐπεργασαμένη δὲ ἀτελὴς ἔσῃ* Mac.Aeg.*hom*.(typ.3)28.3(p.166.14); Evagr.Pont. *sent.mon*.73(p.159)'.

s.v. **ἐπερείδω 2a**: for *οἱ...καθαροὶ...ταῖς λεγομέναις κτλ.* read *οὗτοι δὲ* [sc. *οἱ Ἀποστολικοί*] *ταῖς λεγομέναις Πράξεσιν κτλ.*

s.v. **ἐπίκλησις B2**: after ref. to Thdr.Lect., for 'cit. s. *θεοφάνεια*' read 'cit. s. *θεοφάνια*'.

s.v. **ἐπιμανίκιον**: for 'v. *ὑπομανίκιον*' read 'v. *ὑπομάνικον*'.

***ἐπιπεπλεγμένως**, *in combination*, †Bas.*Is*.96(1.445E; M.30.273C).

***ἐπιστηρισμός, ὁ**, *support*, *Const.App*.6.18.11, cit. s. *μνημόσυνον*.

ἐπιχύτης, ὁ, *ewer*, *Euchol*.(p.656).

s.v. **ἑπτά 2**: add to this section 'seven days of Creation corresponding to seven ages of man, Ast.Soph.*hom.21.9f.in Pss*.(p.163. 8ff.)'.

s.v. **ἑπτάφωτος**: for *καταφλέγει* read *καταφλέγεις*.

***Ἑρμόλαος, ὁ**, *Hermolaos*, name given to antichrist '*Ε. ὁ πλάνος* *Didasc.Jac*.5.1(p.70.17), cf. אַרְמִילוֹס, perh. denoting *Romulus*, v. Jastrow *Dict. of the Targumim* s.v., Saadia Gaon *Book of Beliefs and Opinions* 8.5–6 (tr. S. Rosenblatt, New Haven, 1948, pp. 301, 304).

s.v. **ἑτερόλεκτος**: for *ταπεινῷ* read *ὑπερηφάνῳ*; for 'M.88.100C' read 'M.88.1000C'.

***ἑτοιμολάτρις**, *ready to worship ἡ ψυχὴ διὰ τοῦ φόβου* [sc. of God] *φωτισθεῖσα εἶδεν...τὴν λογικὴν αὐτῆς φύσιν ἑστῶσαν...εὔελπιν, εἰς πίστιν...μονοδέσποτον, αὐτεξούσιον, ἰδιότρεπτον, ἑτοιμολάτριν* Mac.Aeg.*hom.fr*.(B39)17(p.309).

εὖ, *well*, ref. Christian life as divine gift *αἴτιος γοῦν ὁ λόγος, ὁ Χριστός, καὶ τοῦ εἶναι πάλαι ἡμᾶς...καὶ τοῦ εὖ εἶναι* Clem.*prot*. 1(p.7.17; M.8.61B); *ἐφάνη γὰρ θεὸς...ἵν' ὁ τὸ εἶναι δοὺς καὶ τὸ εὖ εἶναι χαρίσηται· μᾶλλον δέ, ῥεύσαντας ἡμᾶς ἀπὸ τοῦ εὖ εἶναι διὰ κακίαν, πρὸς αὐτὸ πάλιν ἐπαναγάγῃ διὰ σαρκώσεως* Gr.Naz.*or*.38. 3(M.36.313C); *ἡδοναὶ αἱ...ταῖς ἀρεταῖς ἐπιγινόμεναι, ἅσπερ ἐν τοῖς...περισπουδάστοις θετέον, οὐκ εἰς τὸ εἶναι ἁπλῶς...ἀλλ' εἰς τὸ εὖ εἶναι...συντελούσας* Nemes.*nat.hom*.18(M.40.680C); *θεοῦ... τὸ εἶναι καὶ εὖ εἶναι καὶ ἀεὶ τοῖς οὖσι χαρισαμένου* Max.*carit*.3.23 (M.90.1024A); *τὸ οὖν εἶναι καλόν, τὸ δὲ εὖ εἶναι κάλλιον...ὁ οὖν θεὸς...καὶ τῷ πονηρῷ τὰ ἀγαθὰ δέδωκε, τὸ εἶναι καὶ τὸ εὖ εἶναι* Jo.D.*Man*.1.35(M.94.1541A).

s.v. **εὐθύβολος**: for 'M.87.1500D' read 'M.87.1600D'.

s.v. **εὐκταίως**: for '7.3.1' read '7.1.3'.

s.v. **εὐλογία H**: for 'p.51.14' read 'p.52.14'.

εὐνοία, ἡ, *loyalty*; of servant to master, Cyr.*Juln*.7(6^2.249D).

εὔνους, *loyal*; of servant towards master, subject towards sovereign, Chrys.*hom.in 1Cor.7:2*(3.199A); Socr.*h.e*.1.25.4(M. 67.148B).

s.v. **εὐστάθεια**: add '**3.** *endurance τῇ τῶν ὕβρεων...εὐσταθείᾳ* Nil. *Eulog*.18(M.79.1117A)'.

for **ζηλωτρία** read **ζηλώτρια**.

s.v. **ζιζανιώδης**: before 'Gr.Nyss.' insert 'Eust.*fr.in Pr.8:22*(M.18. 676D)'.

s.v. **ζοφηφορία**: add 'codd. *ξουφηρία*'.

s.v. **ζυγοστάτης**: for '3.247' read '3.242'.

s.v. **ζωηρός 2**: add '*ζ. λόγον* Mac.Aeg.*hom*.(typ.3)14.1(p.71.7)'.

s.v. **ζωητόκος**: delete 'as subst.'.

s.v. **ζωοποιός 4a**: before '*ζ. πάντων*' insert 'Ast.Soph.*hom.8.9 in Pss*.(p.67.18); *ζ. θεότης ib*.22.7(p.174.20)'.

4f: after 'eucharist' insert '*τὰ ζ. μυστήρια τοῦ ἄρτου καὶ τοῦ αἵματος* Ast.Soph.*hom.21.12 in Pss*.(p.165.25)'.

s.v. **ἡλικία 2**: add 'ref. Christians, Gr.Naz.*or*.43.36(M.36.545B)'.

***θαυμασιουργός**, *working wonders*, Eust.*engast*.15(p.40.27; *θαυματουργοῦ* M.18.645B).
s.v. **θέλημα IVA1**: for '*Pyrrh.*' read '*Pyrr.*'
***θεόβλαστος**, *made to grow by God*, of BMV *ἄνθος θ.* Andr.Cr.*can. BMV*(M.97.1328D).
s.v. **θεόγραφος 1**: after '(M.92.1208A)' add '*ib* 2.86(1218A)'.
***θεοκηρύκτως**, *by God's proclamation*, Thdr.Stud.*epp*.2.121(M.99.1397C).
***θεοκλινής**, *turning*, or *directed, towards God θ. προσευχάς* Thdr.Stud.*epp*.2.157(M.99.1493A).
***θεότεκνος**, *born of God τὴν θ. ἀειδίην θεότητα* A. C. Bundy 'Early Christian Inscriptions of Crete' 11.5(*Hesp*.32 p.242).
s.v. **θεουργέω**: add '*perform as a religious rite ~ηθείσης πορνείας* Evagr.*h.e*.1.11(p.20.5; M.86.2452C)'.
s.v. **θεοχαρίτωτος**: after 'of BMV' add 'Thdot.Anc.*hom.BMV* 11 (p.329.19)'.
for **θηρολεκτής** read **θηρολέκτης**.
θιασίτης, ὁ, = *θιασώτης*, of a member of a community [*θι*]*ασίτης ἐν μοναστηρίῳ* A. C. Bundy 'Early Christian Inscriptions of Crete' 5.6(*Hesp*.32 p.233).

s.v. **ἰδιαιρέτως**: after '(p.579)' add 'id.*volunt*.4(M.95.132D)'.
***ἰδιότρεπτος**, *self-determined*, Mac.Aeg.*hom.fr*.(B 39)17(p.309) cit. (addenda) s. *ἑτοιμολάτρις*.
s.v. **ἰδιόχειρος 2**: before 'neut.' insert '*written with one's own hand*, Bas.*ep*.224.3(3.343D; M.32.837B)'.
s.v. **ἰσελαστικός**: for 'v.l.' read 'codd.'.
s.v. **ἰχθῦς 4e**: for *ὑπερβρύχιον* read *ὑποβρύχιον*.
***Ἰωνίτης, ὁ,** *Ionian*, Jo.Mal.*chron*.2 p.37(M.97.108C).

s.v. **καθαρότης D**: after 'bishops' insert 'Const.ap.Eus.*v.C*.3.61 (p.109.20; M.20.1136B); Bas.*ep*.91(3.182D; M.32.476A)'.
s.v. **καθέδρα A2a**: for *σιδερᾶν* read *σιδηρᾶν*.
s.v. **καθικνέομαι**: add to section **2** 'act. form, ref. Ex.12:22 (*καθίξετε τῆς φλιᾶς*), Or.*sel.in Ex*.12:22(M.12.285A) cit. s. *φλιά*.
s.v. **καθισμάτιον 1**: for *κέλλια* read *κελλία*.
καινοπρεπῶς, *in a novel manner*, Eust.*engast*.17(p.45.6; M.18.652A).
for **καινοφωνῶς** read **καινοφώνως**.
s.v. **καιροσκοπέω**: before '*watch for opportunity*' insert '**1.**'; after '(p.64.9; M.47.36)' add '**2.** *be a clock-watcher οὐχ ὡς μίσθιος... ~εῖν ὀφείλει ἐπὶ τῷ καμάτῳ ὑποστελλόμενος ὁ Χριστιανός* Mac. Aeg.*hom*.(typ.3)7.6(p.34.4)'.
***κακοδόξως**, *in an unorthodox way*, Eust.*engast*.22(p.50.31; M.18.657D).
κακόμισθος, *working for an evil reward εὐνούχων γένος...κ.* Bas.*ep*.115(3.208A; M.32.532A).
***κακοπραγμονικῶς**, *so as to cause harm*, Gr.Naz.*or*.23.12(M.35.1164C).
s.v. **κακύνω**: after '(2.513E)' add 'Dion.Ar.*d.n*.4.24(M.3.728A)'.
s.v. **καλάμιον 2**: after '*corn-dole*' insert 'Jo.Mal.*chron*.12 p.289 (M.97.437A)'; for 'M.92.461B' read 'M.92.641B'.
for **καλλιελαία** read **καλλιέλαιος**.
s.v. **καλοπραγμοσύνη**: for 'Pall.*h.Laus*.proem.' read 'Pall.*ep. Laus*.'; delete all after '(p.12.5)'.
s.v. **καμίσι(ο)ν**: delete asterisk; delete '*garment*, perh.'.
κάρπιμα, τό (cf. *LS κάρπημα*), Alex.Sal.*Barn*.9(439A).
s.v. **καρτεροψυχία**: before 'Bas.' insert 'Eust.*engast*.21(p.49.2; M.18.656C)'.
s.v. **κατακιρνάω**: after '(M.46.1137C)' add 'Cyr.*Nest*.4.6(p.90.23; 6[1].118B) cit. s. *συγχέω*'.
***κατανυγή, ἡ,** *compunction*, †Jo.D.*creat*.1(p.61).
s.v. **κατάρρησις 1**: after '*charge*' insert 'Bas.*ep*.24(3.102D; M.32.297A)'.
s.v. **κατασπιλόω**: after 'pass.' insert '*ἁμαρτίαις κατεσπιλωμένος* †Ast.Soph.*hom.24.9 in Pss*.(p.185.2)'.
s.v. **κατασχηματίζω 2**: for *φαντασιοσκοπεῖ* read *φαντασιοκοπεῖ*.
s.v. **κατατρέχω**: before '*hasten*' insert '**1.**'; after '(11.727C)' add '**2.** *flee for refuge πρὸς...τὸν φιλάνθρωπον κριτὴν καταδεδράμηκεν* A. C. Bundy 'Early Christian Inscriptions of Crete' 2.3(*Hesp*. 32 p.229)'.
for **κατεξουσιάστης** read **κατεξουσιαστής**.
***κατεπινοέω**, *know something against οὐδὲ κατεπενοήθη τι τοῦ ἀνδρός* Bas.*ep*.271(3.418A; M.32.1005A).
s.v. **κάτω B2a**: for *πολιτογραφθέντας* read *πολιτογραφηθέντας*.
s.v. **κέρασμα 1**: for *τρισφάρμακον* read *τριφάρμακον*.
s.v. **κηλιδόω**: after 'morally' insert 'Clem.*paed*.1.2(p.92.13; M.8 253B)'.
s.v. **κῆνσος**: before *νομικοὶ* insert 'ref. Mt.22:15–20'; after '(M.36.288B)' add 'v. *νόμισμα, Φαρισαῖος*'.
s.v. **κιγκλίς 2**: for '2.1.13' read '2.1.11'.
s.v. **κλάδος**: for **τό** read **ὁ**.
***κληματοβολέω**, *put forth vine-shoots*, met. *ἡ ἄμπελος* [sc. Christ] *ἐκληματοβόλησε τοὺς ἀποστόλους* Ast.Soph.*hom.16.6 in Pss*.(p.119.10).
κλυτόκαρπος, *glorious with fruit*, met. *πόνος κ.* A. C. Bundy 'Early Christian Inscriptions of Crete' 11.3(*Hesp*.32 p.242).
s.v. **κογνιτίων**: before 'CCP(449)' insert 'CCP(448)act.3(*ACO* 2.1.1 p.177.4; H.2.210D).
κολλούριον, τό, *eye-salve*, Evagr.Pont.*sent*.14(M.40.1269A) cit. s. *ξένος*.
s.v. **κολλυρίς**: before '*haer*.78' insert '*ep.Arab*.ap.'.
s.v. **κολόβιον**: after '*A.Barth.*' insert '2'.
s.v. **κόλπος A3**: after '*ib*.8.41.5' insert 'cf. A. C. Bundy 'Early Christian Inscriptions of Crete' 7.5(*Hesp*.32 p.236)'.
for **κομενταρίον** read **κομεντάριον**.
s.v. **κομήτισσα**: add '(***κομίτισσα**)'; after '(313B)' add '*κομίτισσα*, Thdr.Stud.*epp*.2.157(M.99.1493A)'.
s.v. **κομίτισσα**: entry should read only 'v. **κομήτισσα*'.
s.v. **κομπολογέω**: add 'Eust.*engast*.10(p.29.28; M.18.632B)'.
s.v. **κονδός**: for '389B' read '889B'.
κονδυλιστής, ὁ, *horse which injures its hoofs in a stable*, met. of Job, *ὁ τοῦ διαβόλου κ.* †Ast.Soph.*hom.26.14 in Pss*.(p.212.12).
s.v. **κορυφόω 2a**: after '*enlarged*' insert 'Clem.*paed*.2.10(p.213.21; M.8.508C)'.
for **κοσμοπλάνης** read **κοσμοπλανής**.
***Κουράνιον, τό,** *Koran*, Barth.Edess.*Agar*.(M.104.1396B).
s.v. **κουρατορία**: before **ἡ** insert (***κουρατωρ(ε)ία**); after **ἡ** insert '**1.** *office of curator*, Phot.*nomoc*.8.13(M.104.685A) cit. s. *ἀλειτουργησία*; **2.**'.
***κραμβίτης, ὁ,** ? *vegetarian*, or ? *greengrocer*, L. Robert 'Inscriptions de Corinthe' (*Rev. des Études grecques* 79 p.765).
s.v. **κρατήρ**: add to entry 'at church door for washing of hands' Chrys.ap.Jo.D.*parall*.(M.95.1508A), cf.Chrys.*hom.3.11 in 2Cor. 4:13*(3.289D) cit. s. *κρήνη*'.
κρίνον, τό, *lily*, ref. Ps.44 tit.(AQ, THDN; Hebr. עַל־שׁשַׁנִּים; LXX *ὑπὲρ τῶν ἀλλοιωθησομένων* as though from שָׁנָה) *ὁ μέν, ὑπὲρ τῶν ἀνθῶν, ὁ δέ, ὑπὲρ τῶν κ., ἀντὶ τῆς ἀλλοιώσεως τῷ λόγῳ προσέγραψαν...ἣ δὲ τοῦ κ. ὄψις πρὸς ὅ τι χρὴ γενέσθαι τὴν ἀλλοίωσιν διερμηνεύει· ὁ γὰρ δι' ἀλλοιώσεως λαμπρὸς γενόμενος... χιονῶδες εἶδος μεταλαμβάνει* Gr.Nyss.*Pss.titt*.B 4(M.44.501D).
s.v. **κριός A1b**: for 'Mel.*fr*.' read 'Mel.*fr.Gen*.'
s.v. **κρυφιόμυστος**: for *θεολογίας κτλ.* read 'Dion.Ar.*myst*.1.1(M.3. 977B) cit. s. *σιγή*'.
s.v. **κτισματολάτρης**: delete all after '‡Eust.*alloc*.(M.18.676A)'.
s.v. **κτιστολάτρης**: after '(M.39.429C)' add 'applied to orthodox by Julianists who believed Christ's body to be both incorruptible and uncreated, Tim.CP *haer*.(M.86.58B)'.
***κυανοβαφής**, *dyed blue*, Ast.Soph.*hom.29.12 in Pss*.(p.234.6).
s.v. **κυκλάριος**: for *ψευδηρεμιτῶν* read *ψευδερημίτων*.
s.v. **κυριόδουλος**: after 'Person of Trin.' insert 'Eulog.*fr.Trin*.2.2 (p.364)'.
s.v. **κυριολεκτέω 1**: before 'Isid.Pel.' insert 'Eus.*p.e*.7.8(307B; M.21. 520D)'.
κωπεύς, ὁ, *rower*, Synes.*ep*.132(M.66.1517B).

***λαοπλανία, ἡ,** *mass-deception*, Dam.*troph*.suppl.(p.283.9).
s.v. **λέβης**: add 'Ephr.3.249E'.
s.v. **λεξιθηρέω 2**: after 'doctrine', for *~οῦντες* read *~οῦντας*.
s.v. **λεοντώνυμος**: after 'Leo III' insert 'Steph.Diac.*v.Steph*.(M. 100.1084C)'.
s.v. **λεπτομερής A2**: for 'M.18.521C' read 'M.18.321C'.
B: delete first citation and ref. to Hipp.; add '**C.** neut. as adv., *carefully ἴδωμεν λ., τί λέγει Δανιήλ* Hipp.*antichr*.19(p.14.21; v.l. *λεπτομερέστερον* M.10.741D)'.
s.v. **λευιτών**: add '*λεβιτών*, Pall.*h.Laus*.32(p.89.9; M.34.1099D)'.
λευκῶς, *plainly, clearly*, Eus.*h.e*.1.2.14(M.20.61A); Eust.*engast*.26 (p.57.28; M.18.668B); Ath.*apol.sec*.1(p.88.7; M.25.249B).
s.v. **λήμ(μ)η**: after 'met.' add 'Bas.*ep*.150.1(3.239E; M.32.601B)'.
s.v. **λῃσταρχέω**: before '*proceed*' insert '**1.** *be a brigand chief*, Chrys. *Thdr*.1.17(1.31A); **2.**'.
s.v. **λίβανος 2**: add 'exeg. Cant.5:16 etc. *τῶν τοῦ Λ. ξύλων τὸ κάλλος*,

δι' ὧν τὸ θεῖον εἶδος χαρακτηρίζεται Gr.Nyss.*hom.9 in Cant.*(M.44.976B); *δύο...Λ. ὁ λόγος νοεῖν ὑποτίθεται, ἕνα μὲν τὸν πονηρὸν καὶ ἀπόβλητον, ἕτερον δὲ ἐκλεκτὸν...οὗ τὸ κάλλος θεοπρεπές ἐστι ib.14*(1080C); *θεότητα γὰρ δηλοῖ τὸ 'Λ.'* Didym.*Zach.*3.303'.

λογογραφέω, *set down in writing λ. τὴν τοῦ ἀνδρὸς πολιτείαν* Gr.Naz.*or.*43.80(M.36.604A).

s.v. **λογομάχος 1**: add '*πάντα δι' αὐτοῦ* [sc. *τοῦ θεοῦ*] *μανθάνομεν, ἃ οὔτε οἱ νομοδιδάσκαλοι οὔτε οἱ λ. διδάσκειν δύνανται* Mac.Aeg.*hom.*(typ.3)22.3(p.113.5)'.

s.v. **λοῦδος**: for *κατεκρίθη* read *κατακριθῇ*.

λυγίζω, *vary, modulate*, a tune, Synes.*ep.*148(M.66.1548D); cf. *λύγισμα*.

λύγιος, *shrill*; neut. as adv. *λ. κωκύουσα* Evagr.*h.e.*4.36(p.185.32; M.86.2769B).

s.v. **λωρί(ο)ν**: after *τό*, insert '(cf. Lat. *lorum*)'.

s.v. **μαγαρίζω**: for '*become a Mohammedan*' read '*apostatize*'.

s.v. **μαγαρισμός 1**: for '*Mohammedanism*' read '*apostasy*'.

***μαγαρίτης, ὁ**, *apostate*, Thphn.*chron.*p.262(M.108.653A).

***μαγίως, ὁ**, *magician*, *Ep.Chr.dom.*(p.25).

s.v. **μακαριστρία**: add 'cit.ap.Thdr.Stud.*conf.*6(M.99.1724C)'.

***μακροδία, ἡ**, *distance, length of journey*, Epiph.*haer.*59.12(p.377.19; M.41.1036C).

s.v. **μακροημέρευσις**: for *οὐ μ.* read *οὐ τὴν μ.*

s.v. **μανικῶς 2**: for *ἐνθυσιώντων* read *ἐνθουσιώντων*.

s.v. **ματαιοφρονέω**: before 'Epiph.' insert 'Bas.*ep.*331(3.451D; M.32.1076B)'.

s.v. **μάχαιρα**: after '(p.243)' insert '*εἰπόντων δὲ τῶν ἀποστόλων, κύριε, ἰδοὺ μ. ὧδε δύο...αὐτός φησιν, ἱκανόν ἐστι, καίτοι γε οὐκ ἦν ἱκανόν. εἰ μὲν γὰρ ἀνθρωπίνης βοηθείας κεχρῆσθαι αὐτοὺς ἐβούλετο, οὐδὲ εἰ ἑκατὸν ἦσαν μ., ἱκαναὶ ἦσαν· εἰ δὲ μὴ τοῦτο, καὶ δύο περιτταί* Chrys.ap.*cat.Lc.*22:38(p.159.4)'.

for **μεγαλοήλιξ** read **μεγαλοῆλιξ**.

for **μεγαλόμαρτυς** read **μεγαλομάρτυς**.

s.v. **μεγαλόσχημος**: delete 'cf....581n.)'.

s.v. **μεγαλοφυΐα 3**: after 'title' insert 'Bas.*ep.*66.2(3.160B; M.32.425C)'.

μεγαλοψυχία, ἡ, *generosity*; as style of address *τῇ σῇ μ.* Bas.*ep.*59.3(3.154B; M.32.413B).

s.v. **μεθεκτῶς**: add 'Christol., Cyr.*Pulch.*19(p.37.18; 5².144D) cit. s. *σχετικῶς*'.

s.v. **μεῖξις**: for *μῖξις* read *μίξις*.

Μελιτιανοί** (Μελητιανοί**, ***Μελετιανοί**), **οἱ**, *Melitians*, followers of Melitius of Lycopolis, Egyptian schismatic sect originating during last persecution *τοὺς μοναχοὺς τῶν Μ.* *P.Lond.*1914.20; *ἐν τῇ συνόδῳ τῇ κατὰ Νίκαιαν...οἱ Μ.... ἐδέχθησαν* (v. Socr.*h.e.*1.1.9(M.67.84B)...*οἱ δὲ...πάλιν τὰς ἐκκλησίας ἐτάραττον, Εὐσέβιος ...προϊστάμενος τῆς Ἀρειανῆς αἱρέσεως...ὠνεῖται τοὺς Μ. ἐπὶ πολλαῖς ἐπαγγελίαις* Ath.*apol.sec.*59(p.139.14; M.25.356C); id.*Ar.*1.3(M.26.17A); Epiph.*haer.*68.1(p.140.19; *Μελητιανοί* M.42.184B); *ib.*68.7(p.147.19; *Μελητιανοί* M.42.196B); claiming to be church of the martyrs, cf.*ib.*68.3(p.143.22; 189A); *Μελετιανοί*, Thdt.*haer.*4.7(4.361).

s.v. **μέλος 4**: after 'Gr.Nyss.*hom.7 in Cant.*(M.44.917C)' insert '*τῶν μ. τοῦ σώματος οἱ μὲν πρακτικοὶ χεῖρες τυγχάνουσιν, πόδες οἱ τῇ σπουδῇ μὴ ὀκνηροί, ὀφθαλμοὶ οἱ κατὰ τὸν νοῦν διορατικοί, κεφαλὴ οἱ νομίμως ἐπιστατοῦντες, ἄρχοντες ὡς δεῖ* Didym.*Zach.*2.28'.

s.v. **μεμερισμένως 2**: for *ὁλοκαυμάτων* read *ὁλοκαυτωμάτων*.

s.v. **μεταίρω 2**: after '*migrate*' insert 'Eust.*engast.*14(p.39.27; M.18.644C)'.

s.v. **μετακίνησις 2**: for *νεύματι* read *πνεύματι*.

s.v. **μεταρσίως**: before 'Cosm.Ind.' insert 'Eust.*engast.*20(p.47.30; M.18.653D)'.

s.v. **μητροπάτωρ**: add 'Clem.*str.*5.14(p.411.18; M.9.185C)'.

s.v. **μισοξενία**: before '*cat.Lc.*' insert '*V.Aberc.*72(p.51.7)'.

s.v. **μονοδέσποτος**: before 'Leont.H.' insert 'Mac.Aeg.*hom.fr.*(B39)17(p.309)'.

***Μονοθελῆται, οἱ**, *Monothelites*, adherents of the doctrine of one will in Christ (v. *ἐνέργεια, θέλημα*), Jo.D.*haer.*99(M.94.761A); id.*volunt.*20(M.95.152A); CNic.(787)*act.*6(H.4.349A); Thphn.*chron.*p.276(M.108.684A).

***Μονοθέλητος**, *Monothelite M. δόγμα* Thphn.*chron.*p.274(M.108.680B).

***Μονοφυσῖται, οἱ**, *Monophysites*, adherents of the doctrine of one nature in Christ (v. *ἐνέργεια, φύσις*), usu. known by names of individua sects, Anast.S.*hod.*1(M.89.41B); Jo.D.*haer.*83(M.94.741A).

***Μοντανισταί, οἱ**, *Montanists*, followers of Montanus (v. *Φρύγες, Κατάφρυγες, Καταφρυγασταί*), Epiph.*anac.*48(p.211.7; M.41.845D); alleged to deny distinction of Persons in Trin., Didym.*Trin.*3.18(M.39.881B); to be baptized on entering Church, CCP(381)‡*can.*7.

***μονύδριον, τό**, *monastery*, *Hymn.*ap.*Mir.Geo.*(p.153.23).

***μοσχομόρφος**, *in the form of a calf*, *Vitae Propheticae Fabulosae* appendix (T. Schermann, Leipzig, 1907 p.130.9).

***μοῦλος, ὁ**, = *μῶλος*, *Didasc.Jac.*5.6(p.77.3); Thphn.*chron.*(M.108.880A codd.; *μωλ-* p.367).

for **μουσουργικός** read §**μουσουργικός**.

s.v. **μυέω 2**: before 'Jo.D.' insert '*Mir.Cosm.Dam.*34.37(p.185)'.

***μυριόζωος**, *consisting of thousands of animals ἐν ταῖς μ. ἀγέλαις* Ast.Soph.*hom.10.6 in Pss.*(p.72.6).

for **Νειλαγαθίον** read **Νειλαγάθιον**.

s.v. **νεκρικός**: delete asterisk.

for **νεκροπαθεία** read **νεκροπάθεια**.

s.v. **νεοφωτιστικός**: for '*prat.*208' read '*prat.*207(M.87.3099B)'.

s.v. **νηστεία A**: after section **8f** add '**9.** ref. encratite excesses, likened to refusal to render to Caesar (i.e. the body) the things of Caesar *ν. καὶ ἀγρυπνίαις κακοῦντες τὸ σῶμα* Or.*comm. in Mt.*17.27(p.659.27; M.13.1557A)'.

for **Νικολαΐτης** read **Νικολαΐτης**.

***Νιοβῖται, οἱ**, followers of Stephen Niobe, a monophysite sect also called *Διαφορῖται*: *οἵτινες...τὴν διαφορὰν τῆς σαρκὸς καὶ τῆς θεότητος μετὰ τὴν ἕνωσιν ἀναιροῦσιν* Tim.CP *haer.*(M.86.44A); *Θεοδοσιανοὶ οἱ καὶ Ν. ib.*(53B); *Ν. οἵτινες Σεβῆρον καὶ Θεοδόσιον δεχόμενοι, δέχονται καὶ Στέφανον τὸν σοφιστήν, τὸν ἐπίκλην Νιόβην ib.*(65A).

s.v. **νίπτω IA4b**: after 'entering church' insert 'Chrys.ap.Jo.D.*parall.*(M.95.1508A); cf.Chrys.*hom.3.11 in 2Cor.4:13*(3.289D) cit. s. *κρήνη*'.

νότος, ὁ, *south wind, south*; exeg. Cant.4:16 *ἔοικεν ἐπιτιμᾶν ἡ νύμφη τῷ βορρέᾳ, τὴν ἐξουσίαν λαβοῦσα παρὰ τοῦ ἐπιτιμήσαντος τῷ ἀνέμῳ νυμφίου. ... Χριστὸς οὖν ἐξωθουμένου τοῦ διαβόλου εἰσοικίζεται ταῖς ψυχαῖς· περὶ οὗ τό, ὁ θεὸς ἀπὸ Θαιμὰν ἥξει, τουτέστιν ἐκ νότου* Or.*schol.in Cant.*4:16(M.17.273A); *οἱ...μαθηταὶ...τῇ πνοῇ τοῦ τοιούτου ν., τὴν διὰ τῶν γλωσσῶν διδασκαλίαν ἐξήνθησαν* Gr.Nyss.*hom.10 in Cant.*(M.44.984D); *βορέας...ἡ πονηρὰ δύναμις, μᾶλλον δὲ αὐτὸς ὁ σατανᾶς, ν. δὲ ὁ σωτὴρ... προσαγορεύεται* Didym.*Zach.*5.53; *ἡ νύμφη τῶν πειρασμῶν προσκαλεῖται τὰ πνεύματα, καὶ τὸν μὲν βορρᾶν ἡττηθέντα ἀποπέμπεται, τὸν δὲ ν. ἀγωνισόμενον προσκαλεῖται* Nil.ap.Proc.G.*Cant.*4:16(M.87.1668D).

νυγμός, ὁ, *pricking* of conscience, Diad.*perf.*23(p.24.26).

s.v. **νύμφη E2**: after '(M.44.944C)' insert '*θείαν ν. τυγχάνουσαν θείαν ψυχὴν καὶ ἔνδοξον ἐκκλησίαν* Didym.*Zach.*3.303'.

s.v. **Νῶε 4**: after 'repentance' insert 'and hence prophet'; after '(M.6.1145C)' insert 'Clem.*str.*1.21(p.84.7; M.8.869C); Or.*Cels.*7.7(p.159.25; M.11.1432B)'.

***νωθροποιός**, *making sluggish*, Diad.*perf.*58(p.64.19).

s.v. **ξενηλατέω 1**: after '*T.Lev.*6.10' add 'met., Evagr.*h.e.*3.1(p.100.3; M.86.2596A); *ib.*6.1(p.223.10; 2845B)'.

s.v. **ξένος D**: for 'ap.Jo.D.*parall.*(M.96.289C)' read '*sent.*14(M.40 1269A)'.

s.v. **ξέω 5**: before 'Ath.' insert '*M.Carp.*23(p.12.15)'.

***ξουφηρία, ἡ**, *mousehole*, Gr.Naz.*ep.*4(P.Gallay, Paris 1964 p.3), v. *ζοφηφορία*.

s.v. **ξύλον B2**: before '*κρούσαντος*' insert 'Thdr.Pet.*v.Thds.*(p.82.18)'.

s.v. **ὄγδοος A1**: after 'Ast.Soph.*Ps.*6(M.40.444C)' insert '*εἰς τὸ τέλος ὑπὲρ τῆς ὀ., ὅτε τὸ τέλος τοῦ κόσμου ἀρχὴ κόσμου ἐγένετο καὶ ὡς ἐν ὀ. ὁ θάνατος περιετέμνετο...ὅτε καὶ ἐν τῇ δευτέρᾳ ὀ. Θωμᾶ ἐνεφανίζετο καὶ τὴν ἀπιστίαν αὐτοῦ πίστει περιέτεμεν* id.*hom.21.13 in Pss.*(p.166.10)'; for '*ib.*(448C)' read 'id.*Ps.6*(448C)'.

s.v. **ὀγκύλλομαι**: add 'id.*Zach.*4.26'.

s.v. **ὁδηγία**: after '*guidance*' insert 'of H. Ghost, Bas.*ep.*283(3.424E; M.32.1020B)'.

s.v. **οἰκονομέω B1h**: after '(364C; M.884C)' insert '*τοῦ πάντα ∼οῦντος ib.*2(74E; M.232D)'.

s.v. **οἰκονομικῶς 5b**: for 'id.*theoph.*' read '†Hipp.*theoph.*'.

s.v. **οἰκονόμος A1**: after 'spiritual things' insert 'of God as dispenser of grace *ὁ θεὸς...ὁ οἰ.* **τῶν** *χαρίτων καὶ τῆς ἀγαθότητος* S. Wobbermin *Catalogus Codicum Astrologorum* 9^{2}(p.167.5); of Christ, cf. *verbum dispensator paternae gratiae factum est,* Iren.*haer*.4.20.7(M.7.1037B)'.

B: after 'of God' insert '*εἷς μόνος οἰ. ἄριστος* Or.*princ*.3.1.14 (p.220.10; M.11.276C)'; after '(p.151.4; M.22.252B)' insert '*οἰ. καὶ κυβερνήτην καὶ σωτῆρα* Serap.*euch*.7.1'; after 'of Christ' insert '*σὺ δοῦλος, σὺ οἰ. A.Petr.c.Sim*.10(p.98.4); *οἰ.* [v.l. *προστάτης*] *τῶν χηρῶν A.Thom.*A 19(p.130.3)'.

for **οἰκοπαῖς** read **οἰκόπαις**.

s.v. **οἰνόπληκτος**: add 'id.*ep*.210.6(3.317C; M.32.777A)'.

***ὀλιγομβρία, ἡ,** *shortage of rain*, Cyr.S.*v.Euthym*.44(p.65.14).

s.v. **ὁλοπόλιος**: add '*entirely grey*; of the beard, Cyr.S.*v.Euthym*.40 (p.59.19)'.

s.v. **ὁμήγυρις 2**: after '*company*' insert '*τῶν πολλῶν θεῶν ἡ ὁ.* Tat. *orat*.27(p.29.1; M.6.865A); *ib*.33(p.34.26; *πανηγύρει* 876A)'.

s.v. **ὁμογάστριος**: before citation insert 'Eust.*engast*.20(p.47.7; M. 18.653B)'.

ὁμόθυμος, *agreeing, united, ὁ. σπουδῇ* Eust.*engast*.2(p.17.20; M.18. 616B).

s.v. **ὁμοούσιος IIB2ciii** (last citation: after *οὐ λέγομεν* insert '...'.

***ὀνειροκάπηλος, ὁ,** *one who trades in dreams*, Bas.*ep*.211(3.318B; M.32.780A).

***ὀνειροπώλης, ὁ,** *seller of dreams*, Bas.*ep*.211(3.318B; M.32.780A).

ὀξυποδίζω: delete entry.

s.v. **ὀξυχολία**: for *ἐὰν...ὀ. ἐπέλθῃ, εὐθὺς τὸ πνεῦμα τὸ ἅγιον στενοχωρεῖται* read *ἐὰν δὲ ὀ. τις ἐπέλθῃ, εὐθὺς τὸ πνεῦμα τὸ ἅγιον... στενοχωρεῖται.*

s.v. **ὁραματισμός**: after '*vision*' add 'Eus.*d.e*.8.2(p.372.7; M.22. 604D)'.

ὁρατῶς, *visibly, Mir.Cosm.Dam*.18.99(p.147).

for **ὀρεινοβατής** read **ὀρεινοβάτης**.

ὀρθογνώμων, *thinking rightly*, Men.*exc.gent*.7(p.452.16; M.113.809A).

s.v. **ὀρχισμός**: after '*dance*' insert '*M.Thdot.1* 14(p.70.15)'.

ὀσφραίνομαι, *make to smell* something *ὀσφρανθείη κύριος παρ' ὑμῶν ὀσμὴν εὐωδίας* Gr.Naz.*ep*.153(M.37.260B).

***Οὐαλεντινιανοί, οἱ,** *Valentinians*; Gnost. sect, followers of Valentinus, Egyptian teacher at Rome in second century, Just.*dial*.35.6(M.6.552B); Heges.ap.Eus.*h.e*.4.22.5(M.20.381A); Ath.*Ar*.1.3(M.26.17A).

***Οὐαλεντῖνοι, οἱ,** = foreg., Const.ap.Eus.*v.C*.3.64(p.111.17; M.20. 1140B); Epiph.*anac*.31(p.236.23; M.41.284C); id.*haer*.31.1(p.382. 17; M.41.473A).

s.v. **οὐρανοπολίτης**: after '(M.78.916A)' insert 'Cyr.S.*v.Euthym*.2 (p.8.20); id.*v.Thds*.(p.235.27)'.

s.v. **ὀχληδόν**: before 'Ph.Carp.' insert 'Diad.*perf*.70(p.86.15)'.

s.v. **πάθος IV**: after 'martyrs' insert '*M.Perp*.5(p.71.2); *ib*.17(p.87. 13)'.

s.v. **παλιγκάπηλος**: add 'Men.*exc.gent*.6(p.449.17; M.113.804C)'.

s.v. **παλινδωμήτωρ**: add '(metr. gr. for -δομήτωρ)'.

for **παλίνζῳος** read **παλίνζωος**.

for **παλ(λ)ίον** read ***παλ(λ)ίον**.

παμμελεί, *entirely*, Eust.*engast*.6(p.23.9; M.18.624A).

s.v. **παμψηφεί** add '(**παμψηφί**)'; after '*vote*' insert 'Bas.*ep*.251.2 (3.386D; M.32.933B)'.

s.v. **πανδέκτης 3**: for 'sens. dub.' read '*feast of all kinds of dishes*'; add '**4.** *cemetery* for burying strangers, cf.Sev.Ant.*hymn*.204 (*PO* 7 p.669)'.

s.v. **πάνδοχος 1**: before 'Gr.Naz.' insert 'Bas.*ep*.115(3.208B; M.32. 532A)'.

s.v. **πανθάνω**; before 'Thdr.' insert '*V.Nicol.Sion* 36(p.30.16)'.

s.v. **παν(ν)ίον**: add '*Mir.Cosm.Dam*.30.60(p.175)'.

πάπυρος, as adj., *of papyrus ἐν ταῖς χάρταις...παπύροις A.Phil*.143 (p.83.23).

s.v. **παραβραβεύω 2**: for *∼ωσι* read *∼σωσι*.

***παραγογγύζω,** *murmur, complain, V.Nicol.Sion* 47(p.39.2).

s.v. **παραθήκη 1**: add 'of soul as entrusted to man by God *παραδιδόναι τὴν π. V.Nicol.Sion* 77(p.53.4); *παρακαλεῖν τὸν θεὸν... δέξασθαι ἀπ' αὐτοῦ τὴν π. ib*.78(p.53.11)'.

παρακαταθήκη, ἡ, *deposit*, of soul as entrusted to man by God *δεῦρο τελεύτα,...δὸς τὴν π. Apoc.Esd*.p.31.

s.v. **παρακερδαίνω**: before 'Niceph.' insert 'Gr.Naz.*or*.43.58(M.36. 572B)'.

***παρακρινέω,** s.v.l., *condemn falsely, Nomoc*.483.

s.v. **παραλαμβάνω 1**: before '*Chron.Pasch.*' insert 'Marc.Diac.*v. Porph*.18(p.16.23)'.

for **παράληπτος** read §**παράληπτος**; after '*captive*' insert 'Rom. Mel.(*SBBAW*1898^{2} p.157)'.

παραρτύω, *season*, fig. *ὕμνοις, ὥσπερ ἅλατι, π. τὰς ἐργασίας* Bas.*ep*. 2.2(3.72B; M.32.228A).

παρασκαίρ-ω, *frisk alongside πώλους...μητράσιν...∼οντας* Gr.Naz.*or*. 43.12(M.36.509C).

s.v. **παραταράσσω**: before 'Epiph.' insert 'Bas.*ep*.258.2(3.393D; M. 32.949C)'.

s.v. **παρεισαγωγή**: after '*introduction*' insert 'Bas.*ep*.258.2(3.393E; M.32.949C)'.

παρεκφαίνομαι, *appear gradually*, Gr.Naz.*or*.43.38(M.36.548C).

s.v. **παρευθύ**: for 'M.1108D' read 'M.79.1108D'; then insert '*V.Aberc*. 70(p.50.6); Cyr.S.*v.Jo.Hes*.18(p.215.17)'.

s.v. **πάροδος 2**: for '*ib*.7.2(p.122.7; 941A)' read '*ib*.2.18(p.122.7; 941A)'; for 'Thdt.*ep*.145(4.1248B)' read 'Thdt.*ep*.145(4.1248)'.

s.v. **παροινία**: add '**4.** *madness τὴν τοῦ Σαβελλίου π.* Caes.Naz.*dial*.10 (M.38.868)'.

s.v. **πατρακούομαι**: add 's.v.l.,'; after 'M.96.837B' add 'prob. l. *πατρακουστής*'.

***πατρακουστής, ὁ,** *hearer of the Father*, Jo.D.*carm.pent*.107 (Nauck, *Bull. de l'Acad. des Sciences de Petersbourg* 36.1 p.120; *πατρακουσθεὶς AGC* p.217; M.96.837B).

s.v. **Πατροπασσιανοί**: add 'Eust.Seb.*ep*.ap.Socr.*h.e*.4.12.12(M.67. 488A)'.

παύω, med., *die*, Synes.*ep*.73(p.685; M.66.1440C); *Chron.Pasch*. p.382(M.92.977B).

s.v. **πεδόω**: after *∼ούμενος* add [sc. *ὁ λόγος*].

s.v. **περικτυπέω** before 'Cyr.' insert 'Bas.*ep*.223.3(3.339A; M.32. 828A)'.

περίοδος, adj., *travelling about ὁ π. ἱεροκήρυξ...Παῦλος* Eust. *engast*.11(p.32.16; *περιοδεύων* M.18.633D).

περιπάρειμι: delete entry.

περιπαρίημι: delete entry.

s.v. **περιτέμνω 4b**: after 'circumcision' insert '(v. *ὄγδοος*, text and addenda)'.

s.v. **περιτομή IIB**: add 'v. *ὄγδοος*'.

περιχαίρω, *rejoice exceedingly*, Gr.Naz.*or*.43.39(M.36.548C).

***περιχαραγή, ἡ,** *marking* the sign of the cross *round ἐπαρξάμενος τῇ τῶν κογχῶν π. V.Nicol.Sion* 4(p.5.13).

s.v. **περιχύτης**: add '*Mir.Cosm.Dam*.14.25(p.135)'.

s.v. **περπερότης**: after 'Ephr.3.102F' insert 'id.3.401F (for f.l. *ὑπερπερώτης*)'.

***Πετρῖται, οἱ,** *Petrites*, a monophysite sect *ἄλλοι Σεβηρῖται, ἤγουν Θεοδοσιανοί, οἱ καὶ Π.* Tim.CP *haer*.(M.86.53B); *οἱ δὲ Π.... Πέτρον...τινα ἐπίσκοπον δέχονται, ἕτερον παρὰ τὸν...Πέτρον τὸν Μογγόν ib*.(56A).

s.v. **πικρῶς**: add '**4.** comp. *πικροτέρως M.Ariadn*.16(p.132.20)'.

s.v. **πλάνος 2**: after 'Hipp.*Dan*.4.7.1' add '*συντριβομένης τῆς Ῥωμανίας καὶ...εἰς δέκα τοπαρχίας γινομένης δεῖ τὸν διάβολον ἔρχεσθαι; ναί, ὄντως Ἑρμόλαος ὁ π. μέλλει ἔρχεσθαι διαιρουμένης τῆς Ῥωμανίας Didasc.Jac*.5.1(p.70.17); v. *ἀντίχριστος*, '*Ἑρμόλαος* (addenda)'.

πλήσσω, *strike*; of a scorpion, *sting*, Pall.*h.Laus*.48(p.143.1; M.34. 1211C).

s.v. **πνευματικός D5**: for 'Pall.*h.Laus*.proem.' read 'Pall.*ep.Laus*.

D8a: for 'Ign.*Eph*.8.21' read 'Ign.*Eph*.8.2'.

s.v. **πνηγηδόν**: add '(for *πνιγηδόν*)'; delete 's.v.l.'; before '*crowd*' insert '*choking*'.

***ποδόστροφον, τό,** *leg-rope*; for a horse, Chrys.*hom.34.5 in Ac*.(9. 267C).

s.v. **ποιέω IIA3**: for 'v. infra 6' read 'v. infra 8'.

s.v. **πολίτισσα**: for '*πόλιτις*' read '*πολῖτις*'.

s.v. **πολιτογραφέω 2**: after '(M.29.421B)' insert 'Chrys.*catech*.1.20 (p.118); *ib*.4.6(p.185)'.

***πολυβουλία, ἡ,** *multiplicity of will*; ref. Nestorian separation of wills in Christ, Max.*opusc*.(M.91.192C) cit. s. *ταυτοβουλία*.

πολυκύμων, *very fruitful*, Synes.*hymn*.2.8(p.43; M.66.1592).

s.v. **πολυπροσκύνητος 1**: after 'of Cross' insert 'Andr.Cr.*or*.11 (M.97.1040A)'.

s.v. **πολύς**: add '*πολύ* c. adj., *very π. ... σπάνιον* Chrys.*comp*.4 (1.121B); *π. ἀνάξιος* Marc.Diac.*v.Porph*.26(p.24.7)'.

for **ποταμίτις** read **ποταμῖτις**.

s.v. **πραιδεύω**: after '*plunder*' insert 'Call.*v.Hyp*.(p.12); *ib*.(p.62)'.

s.v. **πραίτωρ**: after '*praetor*' add 'Socr.*h.e*.5.8.12(M.67.577B)'.

s.v. **πρεσβύτερος IIA2**: for '*veteran* soldier' read 'military *officer*'.

***πρισμή, ἡ**, *sawing*, *V.Nicol.Sion* 19(p.15.16).

προαπαίρω, *depart before, die before*, Bas.*ep*.301(3.438C; M.32.1049A).

s.v. **προαριθμέω**: entry should read '*place before in numerical order*, Gr.Naz.*or*.31.20(p.170.3; M.36.156B)'.

***προαρίθμησις, ἡ**, *placing before in numerical order*; Trin., Gr. Naz.*or*.31.20(p.169.17; M.36.156B).

s.v. **προδιαμαρτάνω**: entry should read '*sin before*, Bas.*ep*.193(3.286A; M.32.705C, v.l. *προδιαρπασθῶμεν*); in previous existence, Aen.*dial*.(M.85.926A)'.

for **προθεωρός** read **προθέωρος**.

s.v. **προθρυλλέω**: delete asterisk.

s.v. **προικῷος**: add 'ref. spiritual marriage *τίνα οὖν...τὰ π. γραμματεῖα; τί δὲ ἕτερον ἀλλ' ἢ ὑπακοὴ καὶ αἱ συνθῆκαι αἱ μέλλουσαι πρὸς τὸν νυμφίον;* Chrys.*catech*.1.16(p.116)'.

***προκαταθάπτω**, *bury before*, Gr.Naz.*or*.18.40(M.35.1040A).

***προσαγιόω**, s.v.l., *consecrate to ἑαυτὴν τῷ Χριστῷ προσηγίωχεν* Pamph.Mon.*Soter*.3(p.119.20).

s.v. **προσκομίζω 3bvii**: before 'Thdt.' insert 'Ambr.*fr*.ap.'.

s.v. **προσυπαντάω**: after '(p.113.9)' add '*Mir.Geo*.4(p.16.2)'.

s.v. **προφητεύω A2**: add 'women in OT, Clem.*str*.1.21(p.84.16; M.8.872A)'.

B: after 'of Jo. Bapt.' insert 'Clem.*str*.1.21(p.84.18; M.8.872A)'.

s.v. **προφήτης IQ**: after 'Adam' insert 'Clem.*str*.1.21(p.84.6; M.8.869C)'; after 'Meth.*symp*.7.6(p.77.15; M.18.133A)' insert 'Noah, Abraham, Isaac, Jacob, Clem.*str*.1.21(p.84.7; 869C)'; after 'Joshua' insert 'Clem.*str*.1.21(p.84.10; 872A)'; at end of section add 'total number of prophets 35, Clem.*str*.1.21(p.84.15; 872A)'.

πυρομαχέω, *contend with fire*; of smelting, *T.Sal*.18.44(p.59*n.; M.122.1348A).

***ῥυθμιστικός**, *controlling, directing*, Areth.*Apoc*.27(M.106.632C).

s.v. **σκηνή A2a**: after '(141D)' add 'cf.Ast.Soph.*hom.21.8 in Pss*.(p.162.28)'.

s.v. **σκηνοπηγία 3**: after '(p.132.9; 737D)' add 'symbolizing the cosmos σ. *σοι ἔστω ἡ φαινομένη τοῦ κόσμου σκηνή* Ast.Soph. *hom.21.8 in Pss*.(p.162.28)'.

s.v. **σκόλοψ 1**: before 'Eudoc.' insert 'Didym.*Zach*.4.253'.

s.v. **συγγενής 2**: add '*ἡ ψυχὴ* [sc. of Christ] *τὴν σ. ψυχὴν* [sc. of penitent thief] *ὁδηγοῦσα* Eust.*fr*.56(p.91; M.18.692A)'.

s.v. **συμπολίτης**: after *ὀξυποδισάτω* add [l. *-ησάτω*].

s.v. **συνάπτω IIB2c**: for 'Nest.*fr*.C 9' read 'Nest.*fr*.B 9'.

s.v. **τιτρώσκω 4**: after '(M.44.1045B)' insert 'Didym.*Zach*.3.190'.

τόξον, τό, *bow*, of Christ *ὁ αὐτὸς σωτὴρ τ. καὶ τοξότης καὶ βέλος ὑπάρχει. ... τοῦ θείου τ., ἀφ' οὗ ἐντείνεται...τὰ πλήττοντα εἰς θεῖον ἔρωτα βέλη* Didym.*Zach*.3.190–1.

τοξότης, ὁ, *archer*; of Christ, Didym.*Zach*.3.190 cit. (addenda) s. *τόξον*; id.*Ps*.44:5(M.39.1365D).

τριοδῖτις, ἡ, *street-walker, prostitute*, Didym.*Zach*.1.45.

s.v. **υἱοπάτωρ 1**: after '(M.39.881B)' insert '*οἱ υἱ. φρονοῦντες* id. *Zach*.4.87'.

φαρέτρα, ἡ, *quiver*, ref. Is.49:2 *πῶς γὰρ οὐκ ἐκλεκτὸν βέλος ὁ κατασκευάζων ἐκλεκτοὺς τοὺς τιτρωσκομένους, κρυπτόμενον ἐν τῇ φ. ᾗ ἔσχεν ἐκ τῆς Μαρίας σαρκί;* Didym.*Zach*.3.190.

s.v. **Φαρισαῖος**: add '**3.** exeg. Mt.22:15–21, Pharisees and Herodians typifying respectively extreme ascetics who withhold from Caesar (i.e. the body) the things of Caesar, and the licentious who fail to render to God the things of God, Or.*comm.in Mt*. 17.27(pp.659f.; M.13.1557)'.

s.v. **χοιρογρύλλιος**: after '*hyrax*' add '*syriacus*'; for '*cony, rock-rabbit*' read '*rock-badger* (Hebr. שָׁפָן)'; after '(M.40.1265D)' add 'ref. Ps.103:18, v. (addenda) *ἀρκτομῦς*'.

***ψαλιστής, ὁ**, *one who snips*, ? the fringes of garments for magical purposes or ? the edges of coins, cf.Hipp.*trad.ap*.16.22 (*ψελλιστής* Dix).

ψελλιστής, ὁ, *stammerer*; ? *one who speaks obscurely*, i.e. *ventriloquist, wizard*, cf.Hipp.*trad.ap*.16.22, v. (addenda) *ψαλιστής*.